2007

This Edition of ***Resources for College Libraries*** was prepared by:

ACRL & Choice:
Project Editor: Marcus Elmore
Editorial Director, Choice: Francine Graf
Editor & Publisher, Choice: Irving Rockwood

Special Thanks to Our Proofreaders:
Monika Maslowski, Jinna Anderson, Chris Sullivan, Jennifer Donahue, Judith Douville, Rebecca Bartlett, and Carolyn Wilcox

Record Entry Completed By:
Monika Maslowski, Laurie Trulock, and Sheila Laverty

R. R. Bowker LLC:
John Krafty: Product Manager, RCL
Ashley Ludwig: Managing Editor, RCL
Frank Morris: IT Director
Minh Huynh: Senior Programmer Analyst
Robert Zeisler: Senior Programmer Analyst

Editorial Staff:
Ian Singer: Vice President, Data Services
Roy Crego: Senior Managing Director, Editorial
Eleanor Schubauer: Managing Editor
Michael Olenick: Managing Editor
Beverly Palacio: Associate Editor

Production Department:
Doreen Gravesande: Senior Director, Production
Ralph Coviello, Manager, Manufacturing Services
Myriam Nunez: Project Manager, Product Development & Content Integrity
Kennard McGill: Production Consultant

Research Completed By:
Pat Diaz, Bobbie Ferraro, Kathy Griner, Becky Housel, and Diane Johnson.

Record Entry Completed By:
Jenny Marie DeJesus, Dorothy Perry-Gilchrist, Anthony Giuffra, and Steven Zaffuto

RCL
RESOURCES *for* COLLEGE LIBRARIES

2007

Volume 4: Social Sciences

Mary Ellen Davis, Executive Director, ACRL

Published by
R. R. Bowker LLC
630 Central Avenue, New Providence
New Jersey 07974

Annie Callanan, President and CEO

URL: http://www.rclweb.net
E-mail address: rclfeedback@bowker.com

Readers may send any corrections and/or updates to the information in this work to:
rclfeedback@bowker.com

International Standard Book Number:

7 Volume Set:	ISBN: 0-8352-4855-0 ISBN13: 978-0-8352-4855-6
Vol. 1: Humanities:	ISBN: 0-8352-4856-9 ISBN13: 978-0-8352-4856-3
Vol. 2: Language & Literature:	ISBN: 0-8352-4857-7 ISBN13: 978-0-8352-4857-0
Vol. 3: History:	ISBN: 0-8352-4858-5 ISBN13: 978-0-8352-4858-7
Vol. 4: Social Sciences:	ISBN: 0-8352-4859-3 ISBN13: 978-0-8352-4859-4
Vol. 5: Science and Technology:	ISBN: 0-8352-4860-7 ISBN13: 978-0-8352-4860-0
Vol. 6: Interdisciplinary & Area Studies:	ISBN: 0-8352-4861-5 ISBN13: 978-0-8352-4861-7
Vol. 7: Indexes:	ISBN: 0-8352-4862-3 ISBN13: 978-0-8352-4862-4

Printed and bound in the United States of America

Table of Contents

ANTHROPOLOGY . . . p.1
Reference Works, Dictionaries, Encyclopedias, Collections . . . p.3
History and Biography . . . p.3
Archaeology . . . p.5
General and Introductory Works . . . p.5
Theory and History of Archaeology . . . p.6
Analytic Methods . . . p.6
Field Methods . . . p.7
Archaeology by Continent . . . p.7
Historical Archaeology . . . p.13
Biological Anthropology . . . p.14
General and Introductory Works . . . p.14
Human Evolution . . . p.15
Paleoanthropology . . . p.16
Human Groups, Discussions of Race . . . p.17
Linguistic Anthropology . . . p.17
General, Introductory, and Historical Works . . . p.17
Theory and Methods . . . p.18
Origin and Evolution of Language and Language Change . . . p.19
Language and Culture . . . p.20
Language in Relation to Gender, Ethnicity, and Power . . . p.20
Anthropology of Oral and Written Language . . . p.21
Social and Cultural Anthropology . . . p.22
General and Introductory Works . . . p.22
Theory and Methodology . . . p.23
Field Methods . . . p.25
Anthropology of Art: Visual, Performing, Music, Dance . . . p.25
Cognitive Anthropology . . . p.26
Critical and Engaged Anthropology . . . p.27
Economic Anthropology . . . p.27
Educational Anthropology . . . p.29
Anthropology and Environment . . . p.29
Gender . . . p.30
Kinship, Marriage, Family, Household Systems . . . p.31
Legal Anthropology . . . p.33
Political Anthropology . . . p.34
Psychological Anthropology . . . p.35
Religion . . . p.36
Urban Anthropology . . . p.37
World Ethnography by Continent . . . p.38
Applied Anthropology . . . p.44
Electronic Resources . . . p.45
Athropology of Food Habits, Cuisine, Drink, and Nutrition . . . p.45
Medical Anthropology . . . p.46
Museum Anthropology . . . p.47

BUSINESS ADMINISTRATION . . . p.49
Business Environment . . . p.51
Social Policy . . . p.51
International Trade and Foreign Investment . . . p.57
Energy / Environment . . . p.61
Management Function . . . p.64
General Management . . . p.64
Finance . . . p.88
Accounting, Taxation, and Law . . . p.103
Operations . . . p.112
Human Resource Management . . . p.119
Marketing . . . p.134
Company and Industry Information . . . p.146
Business History . . . p.146
Company Information . . . p.148
Industries and Markets (Selected) . . . p.148
Careers, Personal Skills Development, and Vocational Guidance . . . p.166
Job-seeking . . . p.168
Business Writing and Communications . . . p.171
Business Mathematics . . . p.174
Management Education . . . p.176
Business Information Sources . . . p.179

ECONOMICS . . . p.183
General Economics . . . p.185
Dictionaries. Handbooks . . . p.186
Encyclopedias . . . p.192
Biographical . . . p.193
General Methodology . . . p.194
Econometrics. Mathematical Economics . . . p.197
General Equilibrium . . . p.205
Simultaneous Equation Models. Multiple Variables. p.206
Panel Data . . . p.206
Time-Series . . . p.206
Modeling/Forecasting . . . p.206
Game Theory . . . p.207
Systems . . . p.207
History . . . p.208
Capitalist . . . p.214
Socialist . . . p.235
Comparative . . . p.237
Macroeconomics and Monetary Economics . . . p.237
Models . . . p.239
Marxian/Sraffian/Institutional/Evolutionary . . . p.241
Business Cycles/Economic Growth/Prices . . . p.242
Consumption/Investment/Savings . . . p.245
Central Banking and Monetary Policy/Interest Rates . . . p.246
Public . . . p.247
Government Taxation and Expenditure . . . p.248
Microeconomics . . . p.248

Concepts . . . p.248
Consumption/Consumer Behavior . . . p.249
Market Structure and Pricing . . . p.251
Competition . . . p.251
Monopoly/Oligopoly . . . p.252
Employment/Unemployment . . . p.252
Labor and Demographic . . . p.253
International . . . p.255
Trade . . . p.256
Economic Development . . . p.258
Globalization . . . p.260
Relations . . . p.262
Financial Economics . . . p.262
Health/Education/Welfare/Poverty . . . p.264
Agricultural/Land/Environmental/Energy Economics . p.267
Urban and Rural Economics . . . p.268
Cultural Economics. Social Economics . . . p.268
Experimental Economics . . . p.271
Cognitive Economics . . . p.272
Feminist Economics . . . p.272

EDUCATION . . . p.275
Education and Training of Teachers and Administrators . . . p.277
Certification of Teachers . . . p.278
Professional Aspects of Teaching and School Administration . . . p.278
Teacher Training in Universities and Colleges . . p.279
School Administration and Organization . . . p.280
Administrative Personnel . . . p.281
Teaching Personnel, Work Conditions . . . p.282
Classroom Management and Discipline . . . p.283
School Facilities . . . p.288
Student Life (Including Organizations and Activities). p.288
Higher Education . . . p.289
Institutions of Higher Education . . . p.289
Teaching Personnel, Academic Freedom, Work Conditions . . . p.292
Scholarships, Grants, Student Financial Aid . . . p.293
Administration and Finance . . . p.293
Entrance Requirements. College Choice . . . p.294
Curriculum . . . p.294
Graduate and Professional Education . . . p.295
Academic Degrees . . . p.295
State and Federal policy . . . p.295
Special Forms of Education . . . p.296
Home Schooling . . . p.296
Private schools. Boarding Schools . . . p.296
Social Aspects of Education . . . p.297
Economic Aspects of Education . . . p.297
Education and the State . . . p.297
Compulsory Education. Attendance. Dropouts . . p.299
Literacy . . . p.299
Educational Sociology . . . p.300
Community and the School . . . p.303
Types of Education . . . p.303
Humanistic and Liberal Education . . . p.303
Competency Based Education . . . p.303
Basic Education (Including Basic Skills Education) . . . p.304
Career and Vocational Education . . . p.304
Moral, Religious, and Character Education . . . p.306
Multicultural Education (General) . . . p.308
Comparative and International Education . . . p.312
Education in Developing Countries . . . p.314
Rural Education. Urban Education . . . p.314
Special Education. Exceptional Children and Youth . . . p.315
Adult and Continuing Education . . . p.319
Distance Education . . . p.321
Education (General) . . . p.322
Philosophy of Education . . . p.323
History of Education . . . p.324
General Education by Period, Level, and Type (Public or private) . . . p.324
History of Higher Education . . . p.330
By Place (Non-U.S. Regions or Countries) . . . p.333
Biography . . . p.337
Theory and Practice of Education . . . p.338
Systems of Individual Educators . . . p.340
Teaching (Principles and Practice) . . . p.346
Educational Research . . . p.354
Educational Psychology. Child Study . . . p.355
Education by Level (Includes Teaching of Individual Subjects) . . . p.359
Primary Education . . . p.360
Elementary . . . p.361
Secondary Education . . . p.366
Kindergarten . . . p.368
Early Childhood Education . . . p.368
Preschool Education. Nursery Schools . . . p.370

GEOGRAPHY . . . p.371
General . . . p.373
Reference . . . p.373
Dictionaries . . . p.373
Gazetteers . . . p.374
General Works . . . p.374
Philosophy . . . p.375
Methodology . . . p.375
Geographical Education . . . p.376
Geography History . . . p.377
Ancient . . . p.377
Modern . . . p.377
Exploration . . . p.378
Atlases . . . p.379
General . . . p.379
Historic . . . p.380
Subject . . . p.381
Regions . . . p.381
United States . . . p.381
Mexico and Latin America . . . p.382
Europe . . . p.383
Africa . . . p.384

Asia . . . p.384
Oceania and Antarctica . . . p.384
Cartography . . . p.385
Geographic Information Systems . . . p.386
Remote Sensing . . . p.388
Surveying . . . p.389
Global Positioning Systems . . . p.389
Physical Geography . . . p.390
Geology . . . p.390
Topography . . . p.390
Geomorphology . . . p.390
Hydrology . . . p.391
Climatology . . . p.393
Biogeography . . . p.394
Hazards and Disasters . . . p.394
Urban Geography . . . p.395
Rural Geography . . . p.395
Human Geography . . . p.396
General . . . p.396
Regional . . . p.396
Development Studies . . . p.397
Economic Geography . . . p.398
Cultural Geography . . . p.399
Historical . . . p.399
Geopolitics . . . p.400

JOURNALISM AND COMMUNICATION . . . p.401
Journalism . . . p.403
History and Criticism . . . p.403
Law and Ethics . . . p.405
Special Topics . . . p.406
Print Journalism . . . p.409
Broadcast Journalism . . . p.412
Communication . . . p.415
Mass Media . . . p.415
Telecommunications . . . p.419
Theory . . . p.422
Advertising . . . p.426
Public Relations . . . p.428

LAW . . . p.431
Law (General) . . . p.433
Law in General . . . p.433
History of Law. Biography. Anthropology . . . p.433
Jurisprudence. Philosophy and Theory . . . p.433
Comparative Law. International Uniform Law . . . p.434
United Kingdom and Ireland . . . p.435
Canada . . . p.436
United States . . . p.436
Bibliography. Reference Works . . . p.436
Collections . . . p.437
Criminal Trials . . . p.437
Civil Trials . . . p.438
Legal Research. Legal Composition . . . p.439
Legal Education . . . p.439
Legal Profession . . . p.440
History of United States Law . . . p.440
Philosophy. General and Comprehensive Works . . . p.441
Special Branches of United States Civil Law . . . p.442
Intellectual Property. Copyright. Trademarks . . . p.445
Labor Law . . . p.446
Social Insurance . . . p.447
Human Reproduction . . . p.447
Public Health. Medical Legislation . . . p.448
Veterinary Laws. Animals . . . p.448
Food, Drugs, Tobacco, Cosmetics, Alcohol . . . p.448
Public Safety. Firearms, Hazardous Materials, Explosives . . . p.449
Control of Social Activities. Amusements, Sports, Gaming . . . p.449
Education . . . p.449
Science and the Arts . . . p.451
Constitutional Law . . . p.451
Local Government . . . p.462
Administrative Organization and Procedure . . . p.463
Public Property: General Works. Water Resources. Public Land . . . p.463
Regional and City Planning. Zoning. Building . . . p.463
Government Property. Public Records . . . p.464
Government Measures in Time of War, National Emergency, or Economic Crisis . . . p.464
Public Finance. Taxation . . . p.464
National Defense. Military Law . . . p.464
Indians . . . p.464
Courts. Procedure . . . p.465
Criminal Law. Criminal Procedure . . . p.471
States, A-W . . . p.474
Confederate States of America . . . p.474
Latin America . . . p.474
South America . . . p.474
Europe . . . p.474
Eurasia . . . p.475
Middle-East. Southwest Asia . . . p.475
South Asia. Southeast Asia. East Asia . . . p.475
Africa . . . p.475
Australia. New Zealand . . . p.476
Pacific Island Jurisdictions . . . p.476
Law of Nations . . . p.476
War Crimes Trials . . . p.477
20th Century . . . p.477
21st Century . . . p.477
United Nations . . . p.477
Law of the Sea . . . p.478
Law of War and Neutrality . . . p.478

POLITICAL SCIENCE . . . p.479
Political Science: General . . . p.481
Government Documents . . . p.481
Reference Works . . . p.482
Research Methods . . . p.483
Relations to Other Subjects . . . p.483
Political Theory . . . p.488
History of Political Thought . . . p.488
Ancient . . . p.488

Medieval . . . p.490
Modern . . . p.490
Theories of State. . . . p.493
Forms of the State . . . p.500
Purpose, Functions and Relations of the State . . p.510
American Government and Politics . . . p.516
History of American Government . . . p.516
Federal Government . . . p.522
State Government . . . p.541
Local Government . . . p.542
Public Administration . . . p.545
Citizenship . . . p.547
Campaigns and Elections . . . p.547
Mass Media and Politics . . . p.558
Public Policy . . . p.559
Foreign Policy. . . . p.560
Environmental Policy . . . p.566
Economic Policy. . . . p.566
Social Policy . . . p.567
Political Issues. . . . p.567
Comparative Government . . . p.574
Constitutional History. General . . . p.574
Organs and Functions of Government . . . p.574
Political Rights and Representation . . . p.576
Political Participation. . . . p.577
Political Parties . . . p.578
Public Administration . . . p.580
Local Government . . . p.581
Colonies and Colonization . . . p.582
Democratization . . . p.584
North America. . . . p.586
Latin America . . . p.591
Europe . . . p.594
Africa. . . . p.610
Middle East . . . p.614
Asia . . . p.616
Australia. New Zealand. Pacific Ocean Islands . . p.624
International Relations. Transnational Relations . . . p.624
Theory. Study and Teaching . . . p.625
History . . . p.627
International Organization . . . p.628
By Country, Territory, or Region . . . p.640
Diplomacy . . . p.644
War and Peace. . . . p.646
International Security. . . . p.654
Globalization . . . p.662
Migration . . . p.667
Global Health . . . p.668
Human Rights . . . p.669
Humanitarian Assistance . . . p.670

SOCIOLOGY . . . p.673
Principles. . . . p.675
Teaching/Communicating . . . p.675
Dictionaries and Encyclopedias . . . p.676
Theories . . . p.679
History of Sociology . . . p.682
Research Methods . . . p.686
Models . . . p.687
Statistical Methods. . . . p.689
Frameworks/Methodology . . . p.690
Social Psychology. . . . p.691
History . . . p.692
Theory . . . p.692
Perception. . . . p.692
Influence . . . p.695
Interaction. . . . p.697
Social History. . . . p.699
Culture . . . p.699
Things . . . p.709
Mass Phenomena . . . p.710
Organizations . . . p.716
Work . . . p.717
Military. . . . p.717
Bureaucracy. . . . p.718
Sociology of Business . . . p.718
Voluntary Organizations . . . p.719
Secret Societies . . . p.719
Sociology of Religion . . . p.719
Christianity . . . p.720
Islam . . . p.721
Other Religions . . . p.721
Stratification/Differentiation . . . p.722
Social Stratification . . . p.722
Race . . . p.728
Family Life. . . . p.731
By Country or Region . . . p.732
Socialization. . . . p.734
Childhood. . . . p.735
Youth/Adolescence. . . . p.735
Adulthood. . . . p.736
Aging. . . . p.740
Death/Dying. . . . p.742
Family Violence . . . p.742
Gender/Sexuality . . . p.743
Gender Role. . . . p.743
Sexuality . . . p.746
Social Problems. . . . p.750
Gerontology. . . . p.751
Criminology. . . . p.751
Social Welfare Programs . . . p.754
Social Work Practice . . . p.757
Social Change. . . . p.759
Economics . . . p.759
Development . . . p.759
Revolution . . . p.760
Environmental Interactions . . . p.760
Technology . . . p.760
Sociology of Education . . . p.761
Public Schools. . . . p.762
Lifetime Learning . . . p.762
Colleges and Universities. . . . p.762
Demography . . . p.763
Assimilation. . . . p.763
Immigration. . . . p.763
Political Sociology . . . p.765
War and Conflict. . . . p.766
Political Systems. . . . p.767

Policy Studies p.768
Community/Regional Studies p.770
Urban. p.770
Rural p.771
Electronic Communities p.772
Social Control. p.773
Power. p.773
Law p.773
Police. p.774
Health p.774
Mental Health p.774
Body p.775
Compulsive Behaviors p.775
Health Care p.778

SPORTS AND RECREATION p.781
Recreation and Leisure. p.783
General p.783
Administration. p.785
Outdoor Recreation p.787
Hiking p.788
Orienteering. Outward Bound p.788
Canoeing p.789
Mountaineering. Rock Climbing. p.789
Fitness and Health. p.789
Weight Lifting. p.792
Aquatics p.792
Health Clubs p.792
Yoga p.792
Pilates p.793
Exercises p.793
Physical Education and Training p.794
General p.794
Elementary and Middle School p.797
High School. p.799
College p.800
Adaptive p.800
Nutrition. Health and Hygiene p.801
Sport Studies p.801
Philosophy p.802
History p.803
Literature (Including Sports Writing). p.811
Research. Theory p.812
Sociology p.813
Education p.820
General p.823
Religion. p.824
Sport Medicine p.824
Doping. Drugs in Sport. p.826
Injuries and Rehabilitation p.827
Athletic Training. p.828
Physical Therapy p.829
Therapeutic Recreation p.829
Minorities and Specific Groups in Sport p.830
African Americans p.830
Latinos p.833
Asians p.834
Women p.834
Gays and Lesbians p.839
Youth. p.839
Seniors p.840
Native Americans p.841
Disabled p.842
Jewish p.842
International Contests and Sporting Events p.842
General p.842
Olympics p.845
World Games p.847
World Cups p.847
Senior and Master Contests. p.847
Sports A-L p.847
General. Miscellaneous Sports, A-Z p.847
Auto Racing. p.848
Baseball. p.849
Basketball. p.853
Billiards. p.855
Bodybuilding p.855
Boxing p.855
Bullfighting p.856
Cricket p.856
Cycling p.856
Extreme. p.857
Fencing p.857
Field Hockey p.857
Football (American) p.858
Diving p.860
Golf p.860
Gymnastics p.861
Ice Hockey p.862
Lacrosse p.862
Sports M-Z p.863
Martial arts p.863
Marathon p.863
Polo p.863
Professional Wrestling p.863
Racquet Sports p.863
Rodeo p.865
Rowing p.865
Rugby p.865
Running p.866
Sailing p.866
Shooting p.866
Skating (Roller, Ice) p.866
Skiing p.866
Soccer p.867
Softball p.868
Surfing p.868
Swimming p.868
Track and Field p.869
Volleyball p.869
Weight Lifting. p.869
Wrestling p.870
Science of Sport. p.870
Manufacture of Sporting Goods p.870
Physics and Mathematics of Sport. p.871
Other Scientific Factors in Sport p.871
Exercise Science p.872
General p.872

Exercise Physiology *p.874*
Sport Nutrition *p.876*
Sport Psychology *p.876*
Exercise Training *p.878*

Facilities and Structures *p.880*

Business of Sport *p.881*
Administration and Management *p.881*
Economics *p.886*
Politics and Government *p.890*
College *p.893*
Professional *p.895*
International *p.898*
Gambling. Entertainment *p.899*
Law. Legal Issues *p.900*
Media. *p.901*

Careers in Sport. *p.903*
Coaching *p.904*
Officiating. *p.905*
Law. Agents. *p.905*
Management and Administration *p.905*
Media and Journalism *p.906*

Biomechanics *p.907*

Motor Learning *p.909*

Resources for College Libraries: General Introduction

Like its predecessors, the three editions of *Books for College Libraries* (BCL) that appeared in 1988, 1975, and 1964, *Resources for College Libraries* (RCL) is a bibliography of carefully selected works spanning the college curriculum and comprising a recommended core collection for all academic libraries. In the tradition of its predecessors, which drew on the such sources as the published catalog of Harvard's Lamont Library (1954), the shelflist of the undergraduate library of the University of Michigan, and, crucially, Charles Shaw's *List of Books for College Libraries* (1931), RCL attempts to balance multiple, often contradictory demands. It seeks to provide a balanced set of recommendations that take note of the weight of the various academic disciplines within the undergraduate curriculum, the degree to which those various disciplines depend on book materials for their essential teaching and research resources, and the extensive pattern of changes that have reshaped the academic curriculum since 1988, the year in which BCL3, the most recent edition of *Books for College Libraries,* appeared.

Of necessity, RCL also embodies a paradox identified by the late Virginia Clark, editor of BCL3: it "can fully succeed only by failing. It would be disastrous should the collection it suggests serve perfectly to ratify the finished work of book selection in any library."[1] Not only will individual institutions create collections significantly larger than the roughly 65,000 titles recommended by RCL, but they will tailor those collections to reflect the size and strength of their own individual departments, majors, and programs. RCL attempts to make general recommendations, within individual subject areas, of those titles most necessary for teaching the subject to undergraduates. In many cases, this means a foundation to which the smallest institutions should aspire but which larger collections will far surpass.

We describe RCL as a successor to, rather than a new edition of, BCL for two reasons. The first is formal, and lies behind the change in nomenclature: RCL includes in its recommendations a variety of electronic resources, including Web sites, subscription databases, e-books, and other electronic materials. The second, procedural reason follows from this: unlike its predecessors, RCL will appear as both a multivolume print edition and a searchable, continuously updated electronic database. In addition, there is a third, tacit distinction which may be made between RCL and the various editions of BCL: although bibliographers compiling subject lists for RCL often took the titles listed in BCL3 as a starting point, our bibliographic work emphasized building a comprehensive, retrospective list of titles by reference to the current undergraduate curriculum, and thus much of the work on RCL was from scratch. In contrast, the relationship between the various editions of BCL was demonstrably that of revision; from one edition to the next, there was an expectation that a title would be retained unless it was actively removed (if, for instance, it had been superseded by a more recent work). Because so much more time had passed between the appearance of BCL3 and the development of RCL than between any successive editions of BCL, bibliographers faced the simultaneously daunting and liberating prospect of creating a subject list *de novo.* That this same period (1988-2006) has seen momentous sea changes in many of the academic disciplines in the humanities and the sciences, as well as the growth of interdisciplinary study across all the academic disciplines, made this an opportunity to take measure of the way subjects are taught to undergraduates, as well as the sorts of subjects which are taught, when developing our core list.

One result of this reassessment was the decision to recognize and include as separate subject divisions in RCL a number of interdisciplinary fields, e.g., Environmental Studies and Gender Studies. The decision about which fields to include was based primarily on the degree to which those subjects function as areas of formal study at undergraduate institutions in the U.S., whether as major programs, academic minors, or areas of concentration housed within another department (film studies, for instance, is often offered as a program or concentration within the departments of English, Comparative Literature, or Theater). We recognized that the lists of titles recommended for teaching interdisciplinary subjects, e.g., Asian American Studies, might overlap significantly with the corresponding title lists for related traditional fields, e.g., American Literature. At the same time, we were confident that many of the recommended interdisciplinary titles would be unique, and so it has proved. The degree of overlap between the various sections of RCL is, throughout, fortuitous and reflects actual overlap between various undergraduate curricula. Effort was made to regularize the editions selected, but the work of compiling the various subject lists proceeded on an independent basis.

1. Virginia Clark, "Introduction," *Books for College Libraries: A Core Collection of 50,000 Titles,* (3rd ed., Chicago: American Library Association, 1988), vii.

The other dramatic difference between RCL and BCL is the decision to move away from Library of Congress classification as the primary framework for the selection and classification of titles. Though this is bound to be regarded by many librarians as a controversial decision, we are confident that it will prove in retrospect to be a sound one. The rationale for doing so is the desire to have titles classified in a fashion which closely follows the contours of the undergraduate curriculum. While LC accomplishes this for some subjects (for instance, British or American Literature, which are taught by chronological periods, and within periods by major authors and by forms such as poetry or drama), other curricula fail to mesh well with LC classification: Business Administration, for example, is responsible for the largest portion of baccalaureate degrees conferred by U.S. colleges and universities,[2] yet the classification of materials in the business curriculum in LC class HB-HJ, while sufficient for cataloging purposes, offers no insight on the relationship between materials so classified and the curriculum in which they are used. It is, furthermore, an arrangement which makes perfect sense to, but only to, librarians. Not all copies of BCL resided in technical services departments, but it seems unlikely that they were much consulted by students or faculty. Our hope is that the new classification scheme will work to the advantage of all the academic library's constituencies: librarians, especially those lacking strong background in a given subject, will be able to see not only the recommended titles but also, in the subject taxonomy, a map of the undergraduate curriculum; faculty will find recommendations of essential works in a form more accessible than LC, and bearing a closer correspondence to the way their courses and departments are organized; students, searching for a place to begin research on a particular topic, will also be able to recognize in the classification scheme something corresponding to their own encounter with the subject matter in the classroom and laboratory. Finally, since each entry in RCL retains its LC classification, those who prefer to search for materials in this fashion will still be able to.

RCL is the result of the collaborative efforts of 332 contributors, almost exclusively teaching faculty or librarians at U.S. colleges and universities. There were three kinds of contributors: subject editors, bibliographers, and referees. Subject editors were selected on the basis of their subject expertise and teaching or collection development experience: eighteen hold doctorates, four are members of the teaching faculty at research universities, two are independent scholars, and the remainder are academic librarians. Many have previously contributed to or authored major bibliographies in their subject areas. They were responsible for developing the subject classification taxonomy for their respective subject areas, for recruiting bibliographers and coordinating their efforts, and for reviewing the results. The subject editors represented a change from the various editions of BCL, where the bibliographers (mainly Choice reviewers) dealt directly with the project editor. By inserting a layer of subject experts we sought to ensure that the titles selected and the taxonomies in which they were classified reflected as much as possible the realities of the contemporary undergraduate curriculum. The second class of RCL contributors, bibliographers, was responsible for the bulk of the actual selection of titles. Like the subject editors, they were faculty and librarians selected for their subject knowledge, often with particular expertise in one specific aspect of a field. Finally, a pool of sixty-four referees, senior faculty or subject-specialist librarians, provided independent assessment of the initial lists developed by the bibliographers; the subject editors used this feedback to further refine their lists prior to publication.

The development of RCL had presumed from the beginning that bibliographers would be manipulating electronic bibliographic records in some sort of online environment, but the decision of the Association of College and Research Libraries (ACRL) Board of Directors to partner with publisher R. R. Bowker to produce RCL allowed us access to Bowker's massive database of bibliographic records, as well as the extensive technical support and expertise Bowker deployed on behalf of the project. Bibliographers selected titles in Bowker's *booksinprint.com* database, in a particular edition, and then imported them to the online RCL Authoring System, where they assigned subject headings and recommended audience levels. In those instances where no bibliographic record existed for a desired title, one was created from a reliable source (preferably with book in hand, though this was not always possible). At the same time, bibliographers submitted corrections to Bowker records when they identified errors or inconsistencies. While this system allowed us to avoid much of the brute effort which was expended on the creation of bibliographic records for the various editions of BCL, it also meant that bibliographers spent thousands of person-hours in the *booksinprint.com* database, identifying the most recent and reliable edition of particular works; in some cases, editors elected to include multiple editions, especially where the differences between them are significant for undergraduate teaching (see, for instance, the decision to include multiple, equally worthwhile translations of Dante's *Divine Comedy* in the Italian literature section).

The use of an online system for the manipulation of electronic bibliographic records was in part a matter of efficiency, but more importantly, it finally addresses one longstanding issue faced by BCL, that of obsolescence.

2. http://nces.ed.gov/fastfacts/display.asp?id=37: U.S. Department of Education, National Center for Education Statistics. (2006). *Digest of Education Statistics, 2005* (NCES 2006-030), chapter 3.

When *Choice* magazine was founded in 1964, it was envisioned as, among other things, an ongoing supplement to BCL1. This approach did not prove practical, and the second and third editions of BCL were required. In contrast, RCL will be updated on an ongoing basis beginning almost immediately after its initial publication; bibliographic records will reflect changes in print status, and new titles will be introduced at regular intervals, to supplement or replace extant titles.

In addition to the tireless efforts of the contributors, on whom I cannot lavish sufficient praise, special thanks to the ACRL Board of Directors and Mary Ellen Davis, ACRL Executive Director, without whose approval and generous support this project would not have been possible. Oversight and advice were provided throughout the project by the RCL Editorial Board: Carolyn Sheehy, North Central College, Chair; and other members Joan Ellen Broome, Georgia Southern University; Barbara Burd, College Misericordia; Brian E. Coutts, Western Kentucky University; Bradford Lee Eden, University of California, Santa Barbara; Stacey Marien, American University; and Richard Shaw, Technical College of the Lowcountry.

Thanks are also due the editorial staff of *Choice*, all of whom contributed effort and advice to the production of this work in varying degrees (and all of whom exhibited tremendous kindness in their efforts, especially in the final days): Becky Bartlett, Judith Douville, Fran Graf, Lisa Mitten, and Carolyn Wilcox. Fran Graf and Irv Rockwood, the Publisher of *Choice*, deserve another helping of praise for their advice, encouragement, and oversight of the project, as well as for handling negotiations of our partnership with R. R. Bowker. Judith Douville made superhuman contributions to a number of subject areas in addition to her own responsibilities in Chemistry. Although almost every member of the *Choice* office staff contributed to this work, Sheila Laverty deserves special praise for her work on the Dance section. Finally, the work would not have been completed if it had not been for the tireless effort of a small cadre of freelance staff, namely Jennifer Donahue, Monika Maslowski, Teri Staab, and Laurie Trulock, who proofread and edited subject headings and section notes, entered titles, cataloged records, and helped maintain communication with subject editors, with extraordinary care, intelligence, and persistence.

With our partners at R. R. Bowker, we enjoyed the highest degree of collegiality and cooperation. Special thanks are due to Angela D'Agostino, Vice-President of Marketing; John Krafty, Product Manager of *Books In Print*; Ashley Ludwig, Managing Editor; Todd Rudloff, Project Manager of *Books In Print*; Frank Morris, Senior Programmer; Minh Huynh, Senior Programmer Analyst, all of whom made significant contributions to bringing this work to the light of day.

Finally, my deep thanks to my family, Colleen and Graham, for their patience and support throughout this project.

Marcus Elmore,

Editor

A Note on the RCL Subject Taxonomy

One of the distinctive features of *Resources for College Libraries* is the subject taxonomy used to organize the titles included in RCL. Developed specifically for RCL by the RCL editorial team, and in particular by the subject editors, the RCL taxonomy reflects the contours of today's undergraduate curriculum. The RCL taxonomy's major headings, therefore, generally correspond to academic majors, departments, or courses of study, e.g., anthropology, business administration, or physics. (In some cases an academic discipline has been further subdivided in order to create sections of manageable size, e.g., the subdivision of History by geographical region.) The goal is a classification scheme, which organizes materials as they would be taught by faculty and encountered in the classroom and the laboratory by undergraduate students.

In some subject areas, e.g. British and American literature, the RCL subject taxonomy closely resembles the Library of Congress classification scheme used in *Books for College Libraries,* 3rd edition. In most cases, however, the differences between LC and today's undergraduate curriculum, have been so substantial as to require the development of a new taxonomy from scratch. This has been especially true for the interdisciplinary subjects such as African American Studies, Criminal Justice, and Native American Studies, which draw upon materials from a dizzying range of LC classes. Gender Studies, for example, draws from a large array of academic disciplines, including (but not limited to) psychology, sociology, literature, philosophy, political science, medicine, and history.

The coverage of interdisciplinary subjects in RCL is another of its distinguishing features, and one deemed essential from the very inception of the project. Although there is some overlap between the interdisciplinary title lists and those of related traditional subjects, e.g., American literature and Chicano/a literature (a subsection of Latino Studies), the interdisciplinary sections inevitably include many unique titles. In addition, the inclusion of the interdisciplinary subjects makes it possible to distinguish those titles which have been selected as essential resources for a traditional subject such as American literature (e.g., Carson McCullers' *Collected Novels*), from those selected for an interdisciplinary area (e.g., Pat Mora's *Communion,* selected for Latino Studies > Humanities > Literature > Chicano/a Literature), and also from those selected for both (e.g., Mora's *Borders*).

By making the ways in which titles are actually used in the classroom the focus for our classification of titles in RCL, we hope to both dramatically increase its usefulness to students and faculty members and also to underscore the extent to which titles were selected on the basis of their importance to undergraduate study and teaching.

RCL Contributors

John Abbott, Graduate Student, GSLIS, University of Illinois, Urbana-Champaign.
Subject Editor: European History.

Randy Abbott, Head Reference Librarian, University of Evansville.
Referee.

Anthony Adam, Assistant Director, John B. Coleman Library, Prairie View A&M University.
Bibliographer: GLBT Studies.

Jan Adamczyk, Slavic Reference Service, University of Illinois.
Bibliographer: Russian Languages and Literatures.

Michael Adams, Librarian, CUNY Graduate Center.
Bibliographer: American Literature.

Paulita Aguilar, Curator, Indigenous Nations Library Program, University of New Mexico.
Bibliographer: Native American Studies.

Flavia Alaya, Professor of English, Ramapo College of New Jersey.
Referee.

Jean Alexander, Head of Reference, Hunt Library, Carnegie Mellon University.
Referee.

Duncan Alford, Head of Reference, Law Library, Georgetown University.
Bibliographer: Law.

Karen Antell, Head, Reference Department, University of Oklahoma.
Bibliographer: Technology and Engineering.

Ralph Arcari, Director Emeritus, Health Center Library, University of Connecticut.
Subject Editor: Medicine.

Susan Ariew, University Librarian, University of South Florida.
Bibliographer: Education.

Jan Armstrong, Professor of Education, University of New Mexico.
Referee.

Teresa Arrington, Associate Professor of Modern Languages, Blue Mountain College.
Bibliographer: Spanish Language and Literature.

Susan Awe, Director of Parish Memorial Library, University of New Mexico.
Referee.

David Azzolina, Reference librarian, University of Pennsylvania.
Bibliographer: General Language and Literature.

Pete Banholzer, Technical Information Specialist, NASA.
Bibliographer: Geology.

Ron Banks, Human Subjects Coordinator, Institutional Review Board, University of Illinois.
Bibliographer: Education.

David Bantz, Chief Information Architect, University of Alaska.
Referee.

Adele Barsh, Business and Economics Librarian, Carnegie Mellon University.
Bibliographer: Business Administration.

Jennifer Bartlett, Head of Research & Instructional Services, Murray State University.
Bibliographer: American Literature.

Edwin Battistella, Dean of Arts and Letters and Professor of English, University of Southern Oregon.
Bibliographer: General Language and Literature.

Frederic Baumgartner, Professor of History, Virginia Tech University.
Bibliographer: European History.

Robert Beauregard, Professor, Urban Policy Analysis and Management, New School University.
Referee.

Linda Behrend, Cataloging Librarian, University of Tennessee, Knoxville.
Bibliographer: American Literature.

Penny Beile, Head, Curriculum Materials Center, University of Central Florida.
Bibliographer: Education.

Dean Bell, Dean and Chief Academic Officer, Spertus Institute of Jewish Studies.
Bibliographer: European History.

Dennis Benamati, Director, Ryan-Matura Library, Sacred Heart University.
Referee.

Riva Berleant-Schiller, Professor emerita of Anthropology, University of Connecticut, emerita.
Subject Editor: Anthropology.

Jay Bernstein, Reader Services Librarian, Kingsborough Community College.
Referee.

John Berry, Native American Studies Librarian, University of California, Berkeley.
Subject Editor: Native American Studies.

Sharon Black, Librarian, Annenberg School for Communication, University of Pennsylvania.
Bibliographer: Journalism and Communication.

Steve Blackburn, Library Director, Hartford Seminary.
Referee.

Robert Bland, Associate University Librarian Automation and Technical Services, University of North Carolina, Asheville.
Bibliographer: Philosophy.

Richard Bleiler, Humanities Bibliographer, University of Connecticut.
Bibliographer: General Language and Literature.

Laurel Blewett, Manager of Library Services, Edward Hospital.
Referee.

Christopher Bloss, Instructional Services Librarian, University of South Dakota.
Bibliographer: American Literature.

Ellen Bosman, Head of Technical Services, New Mexico State University.
Subject Editor: GLBT Studies.

Jesús Bottaro, Instructor, CUNY / Medgar Evers College.
Bibliographer: Spanish Language and Literature.

Steven Botterill, Professor of Italian, University of California, Berkeley.
Referee.

Sally Bowdoin, Head of Serials, Brooklyn College.
Subject Editor: British Literature.

Linda Bowles-Adarkwa, Subject Specialist, Black Studies and Women Studies, San Francisco State University.
Bibliographer: African American Studies.

James Boxall, Director, GIS Centre, Dalhousie University.
Subject Editor: Geography.

James Bracken, Assistant Director for Main Library Research and Reference Services, Ohio State University.
Subject Editor: Other Literatures in English.

Laura Braunstein, Research and Reference Services, Dartmouth University.
Bibliographer: General Language and Literature.

Tony Bremholm, Life Sciences Librarian, Texas A&M University.
Referee.

Karl Bridges, Coordinator of Electronic Instruction Resources, University of Vermont.
Bibliographer: U.S. and Canadian History.

JoEllen Broome, Reference Specialist, Georgia Southern University.
Subject Editor: Environmental Studies.

Mitchell Brown, Research Librarian for Chemistry and Earth System Sciences, University of California, Irvine.
Referee.

Mary Jane Brustman, Bibliographer for Social Welfare and Criminal Justice, SUNY Albany.
Subject Editor: Criminal Justice.

Mark Bullock, Graduate Student, History Department, University of Illinois at Chicago.
Bibliographer: European History.

Merry Burlingham, Chief Bibliographer and Collections Officer, University of Texas.
Bibliographer: Asian History, Languages, and Literatures.

Angela Cannon, Reference Librarian, Library of Congress.
Bibliographer: Russian Languages and Literatures.

Karen Cary, Head, Collection Management, Virginia Commonwealth University.
Bibliographer: Sociology.

Melissa Cast, Reference Librarian and Subject Specialist for Education, University of Nebraska Omaha.
Bibliographer: Education.

Rafaela Castro, Bibliographer, University of California, Davis.
Subject Editor: Latino Studies.

Tina Ching, Reference Librarian, Arizona State University.
Referee.

Diana Chlebek, English and Modern Languages and Literature Bibliographer, University of Akron.
Bibliographer: French Language and Literature.

Michael Chromey, Humanities Librarian, Atlanta University Center.
Bibliographer: African American Studies.

Hui Hua Chua, US Documents Librarian, Michigan State University.
Bibliographer: Journalism and Communication.

Alan Church, Professor of English, University of Texas at Brownsville.
Referee.

Janet Clarke, Asian American Studies Selector, Stony Brook University.
Bibliographer: Asian American Studies.

Kim Clarke, Assistant Librarian, Selector for Women's Studies, University of Minnesota, Twin Cities.
Subject Editor: Gender Studies.

Rudolph Clay, Subject Librarian, African and African-American Studies, Washington University.
Bibliographer: African American Studies.

Ana Maria Cobos, Library Department Chair, Saddleback College.
Subject Editor: Latino Studies.

Francesca Colecchia, Professor of Spanish, Duquesne University.
Referee.

Gerardo Colmenar, Associate Librarian, Asian American Studies, University of California, Santa Barbara.
Subject Editor: Asian American Studies.

Mark Connell, Director, Center for Advancement of Technology in Education, SUNY College at Cortland.
Referee.

Paul Connors, Research Analyst, Michigan Legislative Service Bureau.
Bibliographer: U.S. and Canadian History.

Miriam Conteh-Morgan, Collection Manager for African Studies, Ohio State University.
Bibliographer: African American Studies.

Kate Corby, Education and Psychology Bibliographer, Michigan State University.
Subject Editor: Education.

Ronald Cormier, Professor of French, Longwood College.
Referee.

Alice Crosetto, Acquisitions Librarian, University of Toledo.
Bibliographer: British Literature.

Cynthia Crosser, Social Sciences and Humanities Librarian, University of Maine.
Bibliographer: Education.

Gwyneth Crowley, Coordinator of Collection Development, Social Science Libraries, Yale University.
Subject Editor: Economics.

Alice Daugherty, Reference Librarian, Louisiana State University.
Bibliographer: American Literature.

Stephanie Davis, Librarian, Spring Arbor University.
Bibliographer: Education.

Judith de Luce, Professor of Classics, Miami University of Ohio.
Referee.

Kathy Dean, Humanities Bibliographer, Ohio State University.
Bibliographer: Other Literatures in English.

Louise Deis, Science & Technology Reference Librarian, Princeton University.
Subject Editor: Environmental Sciences; General Science.

JoAnn DeVries, Associate Librarian, Reference/Bibliographer, University of Minnesota.
Bibliographer: Agriculture.

Jan Dixon, Reference Librarian, University of Arkansas.
Bibliographer: Geology.

Deborah Dolan, Social Science Librarian, Hofstra University.
Bibliographer: Psychology.

Travis Dolence, Instruction Librarian, Minnesota State University Moorhead.
Referee.

Michael Doorley, Associate Lecturer in Humanities, American College, Dublin.
Bibliographer: European History.

Judith Douville, Visual Arts, Science and Technology Editor, CHOICE.
Subject Editor: Chemistry.

Bill Drew, Associate Librarian, Systems and Reference, SUNY – Morrisville.
Referee.

Heather Dubnick, Field Bibliographer, Modern Language Assoc.
Subject Editor: Spanish Language and Literature.

Dana Dunn, Professor of Psychology, Moravian College.
Referee.

Lisa Dunn, Head of Reference, Colorado School of Mines.
Bibliographer: Geology.

Karin Durán, Teacher Curriculum Center Librarian, California State University Northridge.
Bibliographer: Latino Studies.

David Eastman, Doctoral Candidate, Department of Religious Studies, Yale University.
Bibliographer: Religion.

Mary Edsall, Professor of Library and Information Science, Catholic University of America.
Subject Editor: Dance.

Marcus Elmore, CHOICE.
Subject Editor: General Language and Literature.

Robert Elsie, Independent scholar.
Bibliographer: European History.

Kimberly Embelton, Literature and Languages Librarian, California State University Northridge.
Bibliographer: British Literature.

Michael Emery, Professor of English, Cottey College.
Bibliographer: GLBT Studies.

Mark Emmons, Head, Instruction Services, University of New Mexico.
Subject Editor: Film.

Carlene Engstrom, Director, D'Arcy McNickle Library, Salish Kootenai College.
Bibliographer: Native American Studies.

Pam Enrici, Associate Librarian, University of Maryland.
Bibliographer: Technology and Engineering.

Robert Entenmann, Professor of History, St. Olaf College.
Referee.

Isabel Espinal, Librarian for Afro American Studies, Anthropology, Native American Indian Studies, University of Massachussetts.
Bibliographer: African American Studies.

James Allan Evans, Professor Emeritus of Classical Near Eastern and Religious Studies, University of British Columbia.
Bibliographer: European History.

Angel Falcon, Harvard University, formerly.
Bibliographer: African American Studies.

David Feldman, Professor of Mathematics, University of New Hampshire.
Referee.

Robert Fernekes, Information Services Librarian, Business Specialist, Georgia Southern University.
Bibliographer: Business Administration.

Anne Fields, OSU Libraries Coordinator for Research and Reference, Ohio State University.
Bibliographer: Education.

Jenifer Flaxbart, Head Librarian, Reference and Information Services, University of Texas, Austin.
Bibliographer: Journalism and Communication.

Adonna Fleming, GIS / Maps Librarian, University of Nebraska – Lincoln.
Bibliographer: Geology.

Nicole Fluhr, Professor of English, Southern Connecticut State University.
Referee.

Michael Fosmire, Science Librarian, Purdue University.
Subject Editor: Physics.

Stephen Foster, University Librarian, Wright State University.
Referee.

Gerri Foudy, Government and Politics, Public Affairs, and Law Librarian, University of Maryland.
Bibliographer: Political Science.

Kathleen Fountain, Political Science and Social Work Librarian, California State University, Chico.
Bibliographer: Political Science.

Kristine Fowler, Mathematics Librarian, University of Minnesota, Twin Cities.
Subject Editor: Mathematics.

Stephen Fowlkes, Bibliographer for Sociology, Social Work and Reference, Tulane University.
Bibliographer: Sociology.

Ann Fox, Professor of English, Davidson College.
Referee.

Joe Fugate, Professor of German, Kalamazoo College.
Referee.

Steve Fullwood, Manuscripts Librarian, Schomburg Center for Research in Black Culture, New York Public Library.
Bibliographer: African American Studies.

Ronald Ganze, Professor of English, Valparaiso University.
Bibliographer: Medieval Studies.

Bill Gargan, Reference Librarian and Bibliographer, Brooklyn College.
Bibliographer: British Literature.

Meryle Gaston, Islamic and Middle Eastern Studies Librarian, University of California, Santa Barbara.
Subject Editor: Middle Eastern History, Languages, and Literatures.

Cameron Gearen, Lecturer in English, Yale University.
Bibliographer: General Language and Literature.

Caroline Geck, Librarian, Kean University.
Referee.

Jennifer Geddes, Research Associate Professor of Religious Studies, University of Virginia.
Bibliographer: General Language and Literature.

Mary Gilles, Business Reference Librarian, Washington State University.
Subject Editor: Law.

David Giovacchini, Arabic Librarian, Middle East Collection, Stanford University.
Referee.

Ed Goedeken, Humanities Bibliographer, Iowa State University.
Subject Editor: U.S. and Canadian History.

Melissa Goldsmith, Lecturer, Louisiana State University.
Referee.

Millie Gonzalez, Reference Librarian, Framingham State College.
Bibliographer: Business Administration.

Olympia Gonzalez, Professor of Spanish, Loyola University of Chicago.
Referee.

David Goodman, Professor of Library and Information Science, Long Island University.
Subject Editor: Biology.

Candice Goucher, Professor of History, Washington State University, Vancouver.
Referee.

Malaika Grant, Reference/Instruction Librarian, University of Minnesota, Twin Cities.
Bibliographer: Gender Studies.

Laura Graves, Professor of History, South Plains College.
Bibliographer: Native American Studies.

Chip Green, Professor of Geology, University of South Carolina Upstate.
Referee.

Susan Green, Professor of History, California State University, Chico.
Referee.

Cheryl Grossman, Electronic Services Supervisor, LearningWork Connection, Ohio State University.
Bibliographer: Education.

Anna Marie Guengerich, Librarian, College of Education, University of Iowa.
Bibliographer: Psychology.

Richard Hacken, European Studies Bibliographer, Brigham Young University.
Referee.

Michael Handis, Associate Librarian for Collection Management, CUNY Graduate Center.
Bibliographer: European History.

Shaun Hardy, Librarian, Carnegie Institution of Washington.
Bibliographer: Geology.

Sara Harrington, Art Librarian, Rutgers University.
Referee.

Jon Harrison, Social Sciences Collections Coordinator, Missouri State University.
Bibliographer: Criminal Justice.

Elizabeth Hartung, Professor of Sociology, California Sate University Channel Islands.
Bibliographer: Sociology.

Laurence Hauptman, Professor of History, SUNY New Paltz.
Bibliographer: Native American Studies.

Peter Hayes, Professor of History, Northwestern University.
Bibliographer: European History.

Charles Hayford, Research Fellow, Department of History, Northwestern University.
Subject Editor: Asian History, Languages, and Literatures.

Jeremy Hein, Professor of Sociology, University of Wisconsin – Eau Claire.
Referee.

Eileen Herring, Agriculture Librarian, University of Hawaii.
Bibliographer: Agriculture.

Martin Hewitt, Head of History Department, Trinity and All Saints College, University of Leeds.
Referee.

Terry Hill, Customer Representative for North America, OTTO HARRASSOWITZ GmbH & Co. KG.
Bibliographer: Political Science.

Baraba Hillson, Public and International Affairs and Psychology Liaison Librarian, George Mason University.
Referee.

Lee Hilyer, Mathematics Subject Librarian, University of Houston.
Bibliographer: Education.

Keith Hitchins, Professor of History, University of Illinois.
Bibliographer: European History.

Adrian Ho, Assistant Librarian, University of Houston.
Bibliographer: Journalism and Communication.

David Hogg, Astronomer, National Radio Astronomy Observatory.
Referee.

Jane Holmquist, Astrophysics Librarian, Princeton University.
Subject Editor: Astronomy.

Emily Horning, Librarian for Philosophy, Religious Studies and Anthropology, Yale University.
Subject Editor: Religion.

John Hunter, Science/Engineering Librarian, Rice University.
Bibliographer: Geology.

Carol Hutchins, Head Librarian, Courant Institute of Mathematical Sciences, New York University.
Subject Editor: Computing.

Robin Imhof, Reference Librarian, University of the Pacific.
Bibliographer: GLBT Studies.

Richard Irving, Associate Librarian, SUNY Albany.
Bibliographer: Criminal Justice.

Kristin Jacobi, Head, Catologing Department, Eastern Connecticut State University.
Bibliographer: Native American Studies.

James Jaffe, Professor of History, University of Wisconsin – Whitewater.
Bibliographer: European History.

Arif Jamal, Social Sciences Bibliographer, University of Pittsburgh.
Bibliographer: African American Studies.

Sylvia James, Sylvia James Consultancy.
Bibliographer: Business Administration.

Fred Jenkins, Head of Collection Management, University of Dayton.
Subject Editor: Ancient History; Classics.

Donald Clay Johnson, Curator, Ames Library of South Asia, University of Minnesota.
Bibliographer: Asian History, Languages, and Literatures.

Melissa Johnson, Reference and Instruction Librarian, Lynn University.
Bibliographer: European History.

Sarah Johnson, Librarian, Eastern Illinois University.
Bibliographer: General Language and Literature.

Lisa Johnston, Head of Public Services, Sweet Briar College.
Bibliographer: British Literature.

Scott Johnston, Librarian, CUNY Graduate Center.
Subject Editor: Urban Studies.

David P. Jordan, Professor of History, University of Illinois at Chicago.
Bibliographer: European History.

Jonathan Judaken, Professor of History, University of Memphis.
Bibliographer: European History.

Jeannie Kamerman, Director, Curriculum Materials Library, University of West Florida.
Bibliographer: Education.

James Kelly, Humanities Bibliographer, University of Massachussetts.
Subject Editor: American Literature.

Marcia Keyser, Instruction and Reference Librarian, Drake University.
Bibliographer: Education.

Shayee Khanaka, Librarian, Middle Eastern Collection, University of California Berkeley.
Bibliographer: Middle Eastern History, Languages, and Literatures.

Sherise Kimura, Reference Librarian, University of San Francisco.
Bibliographer: Asian American Studies.

Douglas King, Librarian, University of South Carolina.
Bibliographer: American Literature.

Laura Kinner, Coordinator, Cataloging Services, University of Toledo.
Bibliographer: British Literature.

Harold Kirkwood, Librarian, Purdue University.
Bibliographer: Business Administration.

Patricia Kirkwood, Science Librarian, University of Arkansas.
Bibliographer: Technology and Engineering.

Sheila Kirven, Education Services Librarian, New Jersey City University.
Bibliographer: Education.

Linda Klein, Reference Librarian, Eastern Kentucky University.
Bibliographer: British Literature.

Michael Knee, Science Bibliographer and Reference Librarian, University of Albany.
Bibliographer: Computing.

Norma Kobzina, Head of Information Services, Marian Koshland Bioscience and Natural Resources Library, University of California, Berkeley.
Subject Editor: Agriculture.

David Koenigstein, Librarian, Brooklyn College.
Bibliographer: British Literature.

Gayla Koerting, Special Collections Librarian, University of South Dakota.
Bibliographer: U.S. and Canadian History.

Laura Koltutsky, Information Services Librarian, University of Houston.
Bibliographer: Education.

Kwasi Konadu, Professor of History, Winston Salem State University.
Bibliographer: African History, Languages, and Literatures.

Svetlana Korolev, Science Librarian, University of Wisconsin, Madison.
Referee.

Wade Kotter, Social Sciences Librarian, Weber State University.
Bibliographer: Criminal Justice.

Joe Kraus, Science Librarian, University of Denver.
Referee.

Eiko Kuwana, Professor of History, University of the Sacred Heart, Tokyo.
Bibliographer: European History.

Sharon Ladenson, Gender Studies and Communications Bibliographer, Michigan State University.
Bibliographer: Journalism and Communication.

Carolyn Laffoon, Earth and Atmospheric Sciences Librarian, Purdue University.
Bibliographer: Geology.

Blake Landor, Bibliographer for Philosophy, Classics, and Religion, University of Florida.
Subject Editor: Philosophy.

Jeffry Larson, Librarian for Romance Languages and Literatures, Linguistics, and Classics, Yale University.
Subject Editor: French Language and Literature; Italian Language and Literature.

Jason E. Lavery, Professor of History, Oklahoma State University.
Bibliographer: European History.

Bernadette Lear, Behavioral Sciences and Education Librarian, Pennsylvania State University.
Bibliographer: Psychology.

Patrick Leary, Research Fellow, Department of History, Northwestern University.
Subject Editor: Victorian Studies.

Richard S. Levy, Professor of History, University of Illinois at Chicago.
Bibliographer: European History.

Kevin Lindstrom, Behavioral Sciences and Education Librarian, University of British Columbia.
Bibliographer: Geology.

Ken Liss, Communication Librarian, Boston College.
Bibliographer: Journalism and Communication.

Carol Loranger, Professor of English, Wright State University.
Referee.

Jack Lynch, Professor of English, Rutgers University.
Bibliographer: British Literature.

Karen MacDonald, Business Subject Specialist Librarian, Texas A&M University.
Bibliographer: Business Administration.

Peter Magierski, Librarian for the Middle East Studies, New York University.
Bibliographer: Middle Eastern History, Languages, and Literatures.

Diane Maher, University Archivist, University of San Diego.
Bibliographer: American Literature; British Literature.

Janice Mathews, Librarian for Urban Studies and Social Work, University of Connecticut.
Referee.

Rhonda McGinnis, Business and Economics Librarian, Wayne State University.
Bibliographer: Business Administration.

Glenn McGuigan, Business Reference Librarian, Penn State University.
Subject Editor: Business Administration.

Peter McKay, Business Librarian, University of Florida.
Bibliographer: Business Administration.

Paula McMillen, Social Sciences Librarian, Oregon State University.
Bibliographer: Education.

Lori Mestre, Digital Learning Librarian, University of Illinois.
Bibliographer: Education.

Sue Metcalf, Social Sciences Librarian, New Mexico State University.
Referee.

Marion Miller, Professor of History, University of Illinois at Chicago, emerita.
Bibliographer: European History.

Lisa Mitten, CHOICE.
Subject Editor: Native American Studies.

Sandy Mooney, Design Librarian, Louisiana State University.
Referee.

Fred Muratori, Bibliographer for Anglo-American and Comparative Literature and Film, Cornell University.
Bibliographer: Drama and Theater.

Paula Murphy, Library Consultant.
Referee.

Linda Musser, Head, Fletcher L. Byrom Earth and Mineral Sciences Library, Pennsylvania State University.
Bibliographer: Geology.

Theodore Natsoulas, Professor of History, University of Toledo.
Bibliographer: European History.

Sharon Naylor, Education, Psychology and TMC Division Head, Illinois State University.
Bibliographer: Education.

Antoinette Nelson, Branch Manager, Science and Engineering Library, University of Texas Arlington.
Subject Editor: Technology and Engineering.

Jan Newberry, Professor of Anthropology, University of Lethbridge.
Referee.

Shawn Nicholson, Bibliographer for Sociology, Social Work, Urban Planning, Michigan State University.
Referee.

Jim Niessen, World History Librarian, Rutgers University.
Bibliographer: European History.

Byron Nordstrom, Professor of History, Gustavus Adolphus University.
Bibliographer: European History.

Akilah Nosakhere, Manager, Reference and Research Division, Auburn Avenue Research Library of African American Culture and History.
Subject Editor: African American Studies.

Nancy O'Brien, Head, Education and Social Science Library, University of Illinois.
Subject Editor: Education.

Darby Orcutt, Collection Manager for the Humanities and Data Analysis, North Carolina State University.
Bibliographer: Journalism and Communication.

Harriet Ottenheimer, Professor of Anthropology, Kansas State University.
Bibliographer: Anthropology.

Mark Padnos, Coordinator of Public Services, Bronx Community College.
Subject Editor: Germanic Languages and Literatures.

John Page, Associate Dean, Learning Resources Division, University of the District of Columbia.
Bibliographer: African American Studies.

Tim Parrish, Professor of English, Southern Connecticut State University.
Bibliographer: General Language and Literature.

Lucy Patrick, Head of Special Collections, Florida State University.
Referee.

Christopher Peebles, Associate Vice President for Information Technology and Professor of Anthropology, Indiana University.
Bibliographer: Anthropology.

Ed Peters, Professor of History, University of Pennsylvania.
Bibliographer: European History.

Carmelita Pickett, African American Studies Librarian, Emory University.
Bibliographer: African American Studies.

Lisa Pillow, Collection Development Librarian, University of Wisconsin – River Falls.
Bibliographer: African American Studies.

Chestalene Pintozzi, Science-Engineering Librarian, University of Arizona.
Bibliographer: Geology.

Don Polzella, Professor of Psychology and Associate Dean for Faculty Development and Graduate Programs, University of Dayton.
Subject Editor: Psychology.

Diethelm Prowe, Professor of History, Carleton College.
Bibliographer: European History.

Eleanor Randall, Reference Librarian, Edinboro University of Pennsylvania.
Bibliographer: Biology.

Brenda Reed, Public Services Librarian, Education Library, Queen's University.
Bibliographer: Education.

Ira Revels, Instruction Librarian, Cornell University.
Bibliographer: African American Studies.

Leslie Reynolds, Director of Policy Sciences and Economics Library, Texas A&M University.
Bibliographer: Business Administration.

Amy Robb, Field Librarian for Women's Studies and Communication, University of Michigan.
Bibliographer: Journalism and Communication.

Gloria Roberson, Reference Librarian, Adelphi University.
Bibliographer: African American Studies.

Beth Roberts, Earth and Mineral Sciences Librarian, Pennsylvania State University.
Bibliographer: Geology.

Elizabeth Robertson, Professor of English, University of Colorado.
Bibliographer: British Literature.

Martin Roden, Professor emeritus of Engineering, UCLA.
Bibliographer: Technology and Engineering.

Raquel Rodriguez, Librarian for the African American Collection, University of Pittsburgh.
Bibliographer: African American Studies.

Lisa Romero, Communications Librarian, University of Illinois.
Subject Editor: Journalism and Communication.

Lana Kay Rosenberg, Director, Dance Theatre, Miami University of Ohio.
Referee.

Tony Rosso, Professor of English, Southern Connecticut State University.
Bibliographer: British Literature.

Dana Roth, Chemistry Librarian, Caltech.
Bibliographer: Chemistry.

Linda Salem, Education Librarian, San Diego State University.
Bibliographer: British Literature.

Mark Sanders, Student Outreach Reference Librarian, East Carolina University.
Bibliographer: Environmental Studies.

Rachel Sandoval, Historical Records Project Archivist, University of California, Irvine.
Bibliographer: Latino Studies.

Victoria Santana, Electronic Services Librarian, Oklahoma City University.
Bibliographer: Native American Studies.

Román Santillán, Reference/Instruction Librarian, CUNY / College of Staten Island.
Bibliographer: Spanish Language and Literature.

Vernon Schlotzhauer, Social Science Librarian, Pennsylvania State University.
Bibliographer: Psychology.

Geoff Schmidt, Professor of English, Illinois State University – Edwardsville.
Bibliographer: General Language and Literature.

Alan Schroeder, Business Librarian, California State University Northridge.
Bibliographer: Business Administration.

Kate Schroeder, Doctoral Candidate, History Department, Indiana University.
Subject Editor: African History, Languages, and Literatures.

Friedrich Schuler, Professor of History, Portland State University.
Subject Editor: Latin American History.

Katrin Schultheiss, Professor of History, University of Illinois at Chicago.
Bibliographer: European History.

Jason Schultz, Communications Librarian, Georgia State University.
Bibliographer: African American Studies.

Catherine Shreve, Librarian for Public Policy and Political Science, Duke University.
Subject Editor: Political Science.

Jack Shreve, Professor of English, Allegany College.
Bibliographer: GLBT Studies.

Adam Siegel, Reference Librarian, University of California, Davis.
Bibliographer: Native American Studies.

Dorothy Siles, Librarian, Taylorville Public Library.
Bibliographer: Native American Studies.

Jane Sloan, Media Librarian, Rutgers University.
Subject Editor: Film.

Becky Smith, Head, Business and Economics Library, University of Illinois.
Bibliographer: Business Administration.

Helen Smith, Life Sciences Librarian, Penn State University.
Bibliographer: Agriculture.

Michael Smith, Business Librarian, Texas A&M University.
Bibliographer: Business Administration.

Jacqueline Snider, Librarian, ACT.
Bibliographer: Education.

Doug Southard, DRA International.
Bibliographer: Business Administration.

Roland Spickermann, Professor of History, University of Texas, Permian Basin.
Bibliographer: European History.

Jill Spreitzer, Assistant Librarian, Public Services, University of Detroit Mercy.
Bibliographer: Technology and Engineering.

Jennifer Stevens, Humanities Liaison Librarian, George Mason University.
Bibliographer: Other Literatures in English.

David Stoloff, Professor of Education, Eastern Connecticut State University.
Referee.

Fred Stoss, Biological Science Librarian, SUNY Buffalo.
Subject Editor: Biology.

Stephen Stratton, Head of Collection Development, California State University, Channel Islands.
Subject Editor: Sociology.

Cindy Stretch, Professor of English, Southern Connecticut State University.
Referee.

Leanne Strum, Library Liaison to the School of Business, Regent University.
Bibliographer: Business Administration.

Mila Su, Coordinator of Reference Services, Pennsylvania State University.
Subject Editor: Sport and Recreation.

Helen Sullivan, Head, Slavic Reference Service, University of Illinois.
Subject Editor: Russian Languages and Literatures.

Sarah Sussman, Curator, French and Italian Collections, Stanford University.
Bibliographer: European History.

Marek Suszko, Professor of History, Purdue University North Central.
Bibliographer: European History.

Laura Taddeo, Reference Librarian, SUNY Buffalo.
Bibliographer: British Literature.

Kornelia Tancheva, Director of Instructional Services, Cornell University.
Subject Editor: Drama and Theater.

Wendy Tann, Librarian, Federal Reserve Bank.
Bibliographer: Business Administration.

Cornelia Akins Taylor, Special Collections Librarian, Florida A & M University.
Bibliographer: African American Studies.

Betty Taylor-Thompson, Professor of English, Texas Southern University.
Referee.

Edward Teague, Head, Architecture & Allied Arts Library, University of Oregon.
Subject Editor: Visual Arts.

Samantha Teplitzky, Earth Sciences Librarian and Bibliographer, Stanford University.
Bibliographer: Geology.

Stephen Thompson, Co-Leader, Technical Services Department, Brown University.
Bibliographer: American Literature.

Erik Thomson, Collegiate Assistant Professor, Social Sciences, University of Chicago.
Bibliographer: European History.

Charles Thurston, Reference Librarian and Bibliographer, University of Texas at San Antonio.
Bibliographer: Education.

Judie Triplehorn, Librarian, Geophysical Institute, University of Alaska.
Bibliographer: Geology.

Markel Tumlin, English and American Literature Librarian, San Diego State University.
Bibliographer: American Literature.

Andrea Twiss-Brooks, Bibliographer for Chemical and Geophysical Sciences, University of Chicago.
Subject Editor: Geology.

Kent Underwood, Music Librarian, New York University.
Subject Editor: Music.

Alan Unsworth, Reference Librarian, University of Rochester.
Referee.

David Vaccari, Professor of Engineering, Stevens Institute of Technology.
Bibliographer: Technology and Engineering.

Susan Vega Garcia, Reference & Instruction Librarian, Bibliographer, Iowa State University.
Bibliographer: Latino Studies.

Tom Volkening, Engineering Librarian, Michigan State University.
Bibliographer: Technology and Engineering.

Heather Ward, University of Oregon, formerly.
Subject Editor: Medieval Studies.

Diane Warner, Monographs and Special Formats Cataloger, Texas Tech University.
Bibliographer: American Literature.

Gary Wasdin, Library Director, New School University.
Referee.

Matthew Wayman, Instruction Coordinator, Penn State University.
Bibliographer: U.S. and Canadian History.

Jeneen Willemssen, Librarian, Conserve School.
Bibliographer: Education.

Wendy Williamson, Economics Librarian, University of Minnesota.
Referee.

Suzanne Wise, Collection Development Librarian, Appalachia State University.
Referee.

Ada Woods, Reference Librarian, Towson University.
Bibliographer.

Peng Xu, Reference Librarian, Michigan State University.
Bibliographer: Business Administration.

Lisa Yuro, Reference Librarian/Humanities and Social Sciences Coordinator, University of Alabama.
Bibliographer: Journalism and Communication.

Ann Zawistoski, Reference and Instruction Librarian, Carleton College.
Bibliographer: Geology.

Linda Zellmer, Head, Geology Library, Indiana University.
Subject Editor: Geology.

HOW TO USE
RESOURCES FOR COLLEGE LIBRARIES

Resources for College Libraries (RCL) was designed to be easily searchable by author, title, and the RCL subject taxonomy. The set consists of seven volumes, Volumes 1-6 arranged by RCL Subject, and sorted alphabetically by author. Volume 7 is a comprehensive author, title and subject index. The volumes are arranged by *Resources for College Library* Subject Headings, a full listing of which is present in the Subject Headings Index in volume 7.

Each title in *Resources for College Libraries* has been classified with a specific RCL Subject and/or subjects. Titles can and often do appear within more than one RCL Subject area. Titles have been given a specific readership level through audience code: g=general, l=lower-division undergraduate, u=upper-division undergraduate graduate, and/or f=faculty level resources. Titles previously mentioned in *Books for College Libraries, 3rd Edition*, have been noted with a specific BCL3 icon B. Non-book entries can be easily identified with the icons for Web, Ebook, or CD/DVD-ROM.

Title entries can include the following bibliographic information, when available: author, co-author, editor, co-editor, translator, co-translator, title, number of volumes, edition, series information, binding type, publisher, publisher location, date of publication, number of pages, ISBN, ISBN-13, Library of Congress Classification Number, Dewey Decimal Number, Library of Congress Control Number, Audience Code, and whether it has been reviewed in Choice Magazine.

Entries in the Author Index can include the following bibliographic information when available: author, co-author, editor, co-editor, translator, co-translator, along with page number(s) and volume number(s) of the selected works within the 6-volume set. Entries are not cross-referenced by other than primary author and/or first contributor. Entries in the Title Index include the title, page number(s) and volume number(s) of the selected works within the 6-volume set.

Titles in *Resources for College Libraries* have been alphabetized using the following rules:

- Initial articles of titles in English, French, German, Italian, and Spanish are not included for sorting purposes.
- Titles beginning with acronyms appear before those beginning with words. For example, B E A M A Directory would precede Baal, Babylon.
- As a general rule, U.S. and UN are filed in strict alphabetical order.

SAMPLE RCL ENTRY

1 DRAMA AND THEATER > Western Drama > United States

2 **Wilmeth, Don B. & Bigsby, Christopher (Editors)** **PN2221**
3 The Cambridge History of American Theater: 4 1870-1945. 5 Ed. 2
6 Don B. Wilmeth & Christopher Bigsby (Contribution by). 7 Trade Paper.
8 Cambridge University Press. 9 New York, NY. 10 2006. 11 608p.
12 Cambridge History of American Theater Ser. 13 ISBN: 0-521-67984-2, ISBN13: 978-0-521-67984-8. 14 Dewey:792/.0973.
15 LCCN: 00-000000
16 Audience: **l,u,f.** 17 *Choice, 2005* B

1. RCL Subject Heading
2. Author/First Contributor
3. Title
4. Subtitle
5. Ed. Info
6. Additional Contributors
7. Binding Type
8. Publisher
9. Publisher Location
10. Publication Date
11. Number of Pages
12. Series Title
13. ISBN, ISBN-13
14. Dewey
15. LCCN
16. Audience Code
17. Choice Review and Date

- Numeric Titles may be found near the end of the Title Index

Authors in *Resources for College Libraries* have been alphabetized using the following rules:

- Proper names beginning with "Mc" and "Mac" are filed in strict alphabetical order. For example, entries for contributors' names such as MacAdam, MacAvory, and MacCarthy are located prior to the pages with entries for names such as McAdam, McCoy, and McDermott.
- When author names are represented with initials, they are alphabetized before author first names. For example, Smith, H. C. appears before Smith, Harold A.

Any errors in bibliographic data should be E-mailed directly to: rclwebfeedback@bowker.com

ABBREVIATIONS AND CODE LIST:

BCL3	*Books for College Libraries, 3rd Edition*
Bk.(s.)	Book(s)
Ed.	Edition
F	Faculty
G	General
Inc.	Incorporated
Jr.	Junior
ISBN	International Standard Book Number
L	Lower-Division Undergraduate
LCCN	Library of Congress Control Number
p.	Pages
RCL	Resources for College Libraries
Ser.	Series
Sr.	Senior
U	Upper-Division Undergraduate

Geographical Abbreviations

AL	Alabama
AK	Alaska
AB	Alberta
AE	American Europe
AS	American Samoa
AZ	Arizona
AR	Arkansas
ACT	Australian Capital Territory
BC	British Columbia
CA	California
CM	Central Marianas
CO	Colorado
CT	Connecticut
DE	Delaware
DC	District Of Columbia
FM	Federated States Of Micronesia
FL	Florida
GA	Georgia
GU	Guam
HI	Hawaii
ID	Idaho
IL	Illinois
IN	Indiana
IA	Iowa
KS	Kansas
KY	Kentucky
LA	Louisiana
ME	Maine
MB	Manitoba
MH	Marshall Islands
MD	Maryland
MA	Massachusetts
MI	Michigan
MP	Middle Pacific
MN	Minnesota
MS	Mississippi
MO	Missouri
MT	Montana
NE	Nebraska
NV	Nevada
NB	New Brunswick
NH	New Hampshire
NJ	New Jersey
NM	New Mexico
NSW	New South Wales
NY	New York
NF	Newfoundland
NC	North Carolina
ND	North Dakota
NP	Northern Marianas
N.T.	Northern Territory (Australia)
NT	Northwest Territory
NS	Nova Scotia
NU	Nunavut
OH	Ohio
OK	Oklahoma
ON	Ontario
OR	Oregon
TT	Pacific Territories
PW	Pacific West
PA	Pennsylvania
PE	Prince Edward Island
PR	Puerto Rico
PQ	Quebec
QLD	Queensland
RI	Rhode Island
SK	Saskatchewan
SA	South Australia
SC	South Carolina
SD	South Dakota
TAS	Tasmania
TN	Tennessee
TX	Texas
UT	Utah
VT	Vermont
VIC	Victoria
VI	Virgin Islands
VA	Virginia
WA	Washington
WV	West Virginia
W.A.	Western Australia
WI	Wisconsin
WY	Wyoming
YT	Yukon Territory

ANTHROPOLOGY

An emphasis on the group aspects of human behavior defines the anthropological perspective. It is an inclusive perspective, encompassing social, cultural, biological, and ecological aspects of human groups, past and present, and is represented by what is called the "four-field" approach to anthropology. This section embodies my conviction that the unifying four-field conception of human beings in groups binds biological anthropology, linguistic anthropology, archaeology, and social-cultural anthropology into one discipline. Each of those fields is a primary taxon in the classification scheme of this section. The reader will find more than four main taxa because each anthropological subfield that combines or crosses any of the four primary fields, such as medical anthropology, is given its own heading. Basic usefulness in the undergraduate curriculum guided selection, and which in general leaned toward works of the last twenty years. Anthropology is a synthesizing discipline. That means that many titles to be found in other categories—human geography, area studies, demography, gender studies, human genetics, and primate paleontology to name a few—will also be effective parts of the anthropology collection. Topics that could have been included in this section, but that have been assigned to others instead, are the indigenous peoples of the Americas and the study of non-human primates and their evolution. A new category is Electronic Resources, selected for their quality and reliability, and also by the number and quality of links they offer. I hope that no one will use this list as a weeding tool. Many titles that appeared in previous editions still belong in a good anthropology collection, even though they are not repeated here.

— Riva Berleant-Schiller

Reference Works, Dictionaries, Encyclopedias, Collections

GN4
Anthropology Today: An Encyclopedic Inventory. Paper Text. Textbook Publishers. Temecula, CA. 2003. xv, 966p. ISBN:0-7581-2360-4, ISBN13: 978-0-7581-2360-2. Dewey:572.082.
Audience: **l,u.**

P41
Routledge Library Editions: Anthropology and Ethnology. Library Binding. Routledge. New York, NY. 2004. 2000p. Routledge Library Editions Ser., :Anthropology and Ethnography, US/Can. Edition Ser. ISBN:0-415-33762-3, ISBN13: 978-0-415-33762-5. Dewey:306.44.
Audience: **g,l,u,f.**

Barfield, Thomas (Editor) **GN307**
The Dictionary of Anthropology. Book, Other. Blackwell Publishing, Inc. Malden, MA. 1997. 640p. ISBN:1-55786-282-6, ISBN13: 978-1-55786-282-2. Dewey:306/.03. LCCN:96-037337.
Audience: **g,l,u,f.** *Choice, 1998.*

Barnard, Alan & Spencer, Jonathan (Editors) **HM17**
Encyclopedia of Social and Cultural Anthropology. Ed. 2. Trade Paper. Routledge. New York, NY. 2002. 688p. World Reference Ser. ISBN:0-415-28558-5, ISBN13: 978-0-415-28558-2. Dewey:301/.03.
Audience: **g,l,u,f.** *Choice, 1997.*

Biolsi, Thomas (Editor) **E76.6.C66 2005**
Companion to the Anthropology of American Indians. Trade Cloth. Blackwell Publishing, Inc. Malden, MA. 2004. 584p. Blackwell Companions to Anthropology Ser., Vol. 3 ISBN:0-631-22686-9, ISBN13: 978-0-631-22686-4. Dewey:970.004/97. LCCN:2004-006543.
Audience: **l,u,f.** *Choice, 2005.*

Birx, H. James (Editor) **GN11.E63 2006**
Encyclopedia of Anthropology. Trade Cloth. SAGE Publications, Inc. Thousand Oaks, CA. 2005. 2500p. ISBN:0-7619-3029-9, ISBN13: 978-0-7619-3029-7. Dewey:301/.03. LCCN:2005-013953.
Audience: **g,l,u,f.**

Boas, Franz **GN6**
A Franz Boas Reader: The Shaping of American Anthropology, 1883-1911. George W. Stocking Jr. (Editor). Trade Paper. University of Chicago Press. Chicago, IL. 1989. 368p. ISBN:0-226-06243-0, ISBN13: 978-0-226-06243-3. Dewey:301.
Audience: **g,l,u.**

British Library of Political and Economic Science Staff (Contribution by) **Z5112**
International Bibliography of Anthropology. Paper over Boards. Routledge. New York, NY. 2003. 526p. International Bibliography of the Social Sciences Ser., Vol. 48:Anthropology Ser. ISBN:0-415-32634-6, ISBN13: 978-0-415-32634-6. Dewey:016.301.
Audience: **g,l,u,f.**

Gacs, Ute D. (Editor), et al. **GN20**
Women Anthropologists: A Biographical Dictionary. Aisha Khan, Jerrie McIntyre & Ruth Weinberg (Editors). Cloth Text. Greenwood Publishing Group, Inc. Portsmouth, NH. 1988. 445p. ISBN:0-313-24414-6, ISBN13: 978-0-313-24414-8. Dewey:306/.092/2 B. LCCN:87-011983.
Audience: **g,l,u,f.** *Choice, 1988.*

Gaillard, Gerald **GN20.G3513 2003**
The Routledge Dictionary of Anthropologists. Paper over Boards. Routledge. New York, NY. 2004. 408p. ISBN:0-415-22825-5, ISBN13: 978-0-415-22825-1. Dewey:301/.092/2 B. LCCN:2003-046986.
Audience: **g,l,u,f.**

Goulbourne, Harry (Editor) **HT1503.A3R33 2001**
Race and Ethnicity, Set. Children's Board Books. Routledge. New York, NY. 2001. 1728p. Critical Concepts in Sociology Ser. ISBN:0-415-22499-3, ISBN13: 978-0-415-22499-4. Dewey:305.8. LCCN:2001-034878.
Audience: **l,u.**

Lee, Richard B. & Daly, Richard (Editors) **GN388.C35 1999**
The Cambridge Encyclopedia of Hunters and Gatherers. Trade Paper. Cambridge University Press. New York, NY. 2004. 534p. ISBN:0-521-60919-4, ISBN13: 978-0-521-60919-7. Dewey:306.3/64/03.
Audience: **g,l,u,f.** *Choice, 2000.*

Lowie, Robert H. **GN325.L66**
Selected Papers in Anthropology. Paper Text. Textbook Publishers. Temecula, CA. 2003. 509p. ISBN:0-7581-2746-4, ISBN13: 978-0-7581-2746-4. Dewey:306.
Audience: **u,f.**

Malinowski, Bronislaw **HM22.U6**
Bronislaw Malinowski: Collected Works, Set. Library Binding. Routledge. New York, NY. 2001. 3500p. ISBN:0-415-21671-0, ISBN13: 978-0-415-21671-5. Dewey:301/.092.
Audience: **u,f.**

Stocking, George W. Jr. (Editor) **GN29.A4223 2003**
American Anthropology, 1921-1945: Papers from the American Anthropologist. Paper Text. University of Nebraska Press. Lincoln, NE. 2002. 544p. ISBN:0-8032-9296-1, ISBN13: 978-0-8032-9296-3. Dewey:301. LCCN:2002-022325.
Audience: **u,f.**

Winick, Charles **GN11**
Dictionary of Anthropology. Paper Text. Textbook Publishers. Temecula, CA. 2003. vii, 578p. ISBN:0-7581-9582-6, ISBN13: 978-0-7581-9582-1. Dewey:572/.03.
Audience: **g,l,u,f.** B

History and Biography

Ackerman, Robert **GN21.F65A27 1987**
J. G. Frazer: His Life and Work. Cloth Text. Cambridge University Press. New York, NY. 1987. 358p. ISBN:0-521-34093-4, ISBN13: 978-0-521-34093-9. Dewey:301/.092/4 B. LCCN:87-009343.
Audience: **g,l,u,f.** *Choice, 1988.*

Amit-Talai, Vered (Editor) **GN20**
Biographical Dictionary of Social and Cultural Anthropology. Paper over Boards. Routledge. New York, NY. 2004. 640p. ISBN:0-415-22379-2, ISBN13: 978-0-415-22379-9. Dewey:301/.092/2. LCCN:2003-046528.
Audience: **g,l,u,f.** *Choice, 2004.*

Asad, Talal (Editor) **GN17**
Anthropology and the Colonial Encounter. Trade Cloth. Prometheus Books, Publishers. Amherst, NY. 1973. 287p. ISBN:1-57392-589-6, ISBN13: 978-1-57392-589-1. Dewey:306.
Audience: **u,f.**

Baker, Lee D. **GN17.3.U6 B35 1998**
From Savage to Negro: Anthropology and the Construction of Race, 1896-1954. Trade Cloth. University of California Press. Berkeley, CA. 1998. 313p. ISBN:0-520-21167-7, ISBN13: 978-0-520-21167-4. Dewey:305.8. LCCN:97-031602.
Audience: **u,f.** *Choice, 1999.*

Cole, Douglas **GN21.B56C65 1999**
Franz Boas: The Early Years, 1858-1906. Trade Cloth. University of Washington Press. Seattle, WA. 1999. 360p. ISBN:0-295-97903-8, ISBN13: 978-0-295-97903-8. Dewey:301/.092 B. LCCN:99-042589.
Audience: **g,l,u,f.** *Choice, 2000.*

Darnell, Regna **GN21.S27D37 1990**
Edward Sapir: Linguist, Anthropologist, Humanist. Trade Cloth. University of California Press. Berkeley, CA. 1989. 499p. ISBN:0-520-06678-2, ISBN13: 978-0-520-06678-6. Dewey:306/.092. LCCN:89-005016.
Audience: **g,u,f.** *Choice, 1991.*

Darnell, Regna **GN17.3.N7D37 2001**
Invisible Genealogies: A History of Americanist Anthropology. Cloth Text. University of Nebraska Press. Lincoln, NE. 2001. 374p. Critical Studies in the History of Anthropology, Vol. 1 ISBN:0-8032-1710-2, ISBN13: 978-0-8032-1710-2. Dewey:301/.097. LCCN:00-055956.
Audience: **u,f.** *Choice, 2001.*

Gacs, Ute D. (Editor), et al. **GN20**
Women Anthropologists: A Biographical Dictionary. Aisha Khan, Jerrie McIntyre & Ruth Weinberg (Editors). Cloth Text. Greenwood Publishing Group, Inc. Portsmouth, NH. 1988. 445p. ISBN:0-313-24414-6, ISBN13: 978-0-313-24414-8. Dewey:306/.092/2 B. LCCN:87-011983.
Audience: **g,l,u,f.** *Choice, 1988.*

Grinker, Roy Richard **GN21.T85G75 2001**
In the Arms of Africa: The Life of Colin M. Turnbull. Trade Paper. University of Chicago Press. Chicago, IL. 2001. 375p. ISBN:0-226-30904-5, ISBN13: 978-0-226-30904-0. Dewey:301/.092 B. LCCN:2001-027980.
Audience: **g,l,u,f.** *Choice, 2001.*

Hays, Terence E. (Editor) **GN17.3.P36E84 1992**
Ethnographic Presents: Pioneering Anthropologists in the Papua New Guinea Highlands. Trade Cloth. University of California Press. Berkeley, CA. 1992. 318p. Studies in Melanesian Anthropology, No. 12 ISBN:0-520-07745-8, ISBN13: 978-0-520-07745-4. Dewey:305.8009953. LCCN:91-047735.
Audience: **u,f.**

Hodgen, Margaret Trabue **GN17.H63 1971**
Early Anthropology in the Sixteenth and Seventeenth Centuries. E-Book. NetLibrary, Inc. Boulder, CO. 1971. ISBN:0-585-17264-1, ISBN13: 978-0-585-17264-4. Dewey:572.09.
Audience: **u,f.**

Kerns, Virginia **GN21.S78K47 2003**
Scenes from the High Desert: Julian Steward's Life and Theory. Trade Cloth. University of Illinois Press. Champaign, IL. 2003. 448p. ISBN:0-252-02790-6, ISBN13: 978-0-252-02790-1. Dewey:301/.092 B. LCCN:2002-008814.
Audience: **u,f.** *Choice, 2004.*

Kiste, Robert C. & Marshall, Mac (Editors) **GN669.A48 1998**
American Anthropology in Micronesia: An Assessment. Trade Cloth. University of Hawaii Press. Honolulu, HI. 1999. 648p. ISBN:0-8248-2017-7, ISBN13: 978-0-8248-2017-6. Dewey:306/.09965. LCCN:98-029104.
Audience: **u,f.**

Kuklick, Henrika **GN308.3.G7**
The Savage Within: The Social History of British Anthropology, 1885-1945. Trade Cloth. Cambridge University Press. New York, NY. 1992. 335p. ISBN:0-521-41109-2, ISBN13: 978-0-521-41109-7. Dewey:301.094109034. LCCN:91-020109.
Audience: **l,u,f.** *Choice, 1993.*

Malinowski, Bronislaw **GN671.N5M343 1989**
A Diary in the Strict Sense of the Term. Raymond Firth (Introduction by). Trade Cloth. Stanford University Press. Palo Alto, CA. 1989. 360p. ISBN:0-8047-1706-0, ISBN13: 978-0-8047-1706-9. Dewey:306/.0899912. LCCN:88-062043.
Audience: **u,f.**

Parezo, Nancy **GN20.H53 1993**
Hidden Scholars: Women Anthropologists and the Native American Southwest. Trade Cloth. University of New Mexico Press. Albuquerque, NM. 1993. 429p. ISBN:0-8263-1428-7, ISBN13: 978-0-8263-1428-4. Dewey:301/.092/2. LCCN:93-009994.
Audience: **u,f.**

Patterson, Thomas C. **GN17.3.U6**
A Social History of Anthropology in the United States. Trade Paper. Berg Publishers. Oxford, 2003. 224p. ISBN:1-85973-494-4, ISBN13: 978-1-85973-494-0. Dewey:301/.0973. LCCN:01-130235.
Audience: **l,u.** *Choice, 2002.*

Silverman, Sydel (Editor) **GN17.T69 2003**
Totems and Teachers: Perspectives on the History of Anthropology. Ed. 2. Trade Paper. AltaMira Press. Walnut Creek, CA. 2003. 304p. ISBN:0-7591-0460-3, ISBN13: 978-0-7591-0460-0. Dewey:301/.092/2. LCCN:2003-012186.
Audience: **u,f.**

Silverman, Sydel, et al. **GN17.O48 2005**
One Discipline, Four Ways: British, German, French, and American Anthropology. Fredrik Barth, Robert Parkin & Andre Gingrich (Authors). Trade Cloth. University of Chicago Press. Chicago, IL. 2005. 408p. The Halle Lectures ISBN:0-226-03828-9, ISBN13: 978-0-226-03828-5. Dewey:306. LCCN:2004-024388.
Audience: **u,f.** *Choice, 2005.*

Slotkin, James S. **GN17**
Readings in Early Anthropology. Library Binding. Routledge. New York, NY. 2004. 552p. Routledge Library Editions Ser., :Anthropology and Ethnography, US/Can. Edition Ser. ISBN:0-415-33067-X, ISBN13: 978-0-415-33067-1. Dewey:301/.09.
Audience: **l,u,f.**

Stocking, George W. Jr. **HN385.5**
After Tylor. Trade Cloth. Continuum International Publishing Group, Ltd. London, 592p. ISBN:0-485-30072-9, ISBN13: 978-0-485-30072-7. Dewey:306.0941.
Audience: **u,f.**

Stocking, George W. Jr. (Editor) **GN308.C64**
Colonial Situations: Essays on the Contextualization of Ethnographic Knowledge. Trade Paper. University of Wisconsin Press. Chicago, IL. 1993. 348p. History of Anthropology Ser., Vol. 7 ISBN:0-299-13124-6, ISBN13: 978-0-299-13124-1. Dewey:305.8.
Audience: **u,f.** *Choice, 1992.*

Stocking, George W. Jr. **GN308.S76**
The Ethnographer's Magic: And Other Essays in the History of Anthropology. Trade Paper. University of Wisconsin Press. Chicago, IL. 1994. 448p. ISBN:0-299-13414-8, ISBN13: 978-0-299-13414-3. Dewey:301.09. LCCN:92-025829.
Audience: **u,f.**

Stocking, George W. Jr. (Editor) **HN385.5**
Functionalism Historicized: Essays on British Social Anthropology. Trade Paper. University of Wisconsin Press. Chicago, IL. 1988. 250p. History of Anthropology Ser., Vol. 2 ISBN:0-299-09904-0, ISBN13: 978-0-299-09904-6. Dewey:306/.0941. LCCN:84-040160.
Audience: **u,f.** **B**

Stocking, George W. Jr. (Editor) **GN346**
Observers Observed: Essays on Ethnographic Fieldwork. Trade Paper. University of Wisconsin Press. Chicago, IL. 1985. 248p. History of Anthropology Ser., Vol. 1 ISBN:0-299-09454-5, ISBN13: 978-0-299-09454-6. Dewey:306/.072. LCCN:83-047771.
Audience: **u,f.** **B**

Stocking, George W. Jr. **GN17**
Race, Culture, and Evolution: Essays in the History of Anthropology. Trade Paper. University of Chicago Press. Chicago, IL. 1982. 408p. Phoenix Ser. ISBN:0-226-77494-5, ISBN13: 978-0-226-77494-7. Dewey:306/.09. LCCN:81-023154.
Audience: **u,f.**

Stocking, George W. Jr. (Author, Editor) **GN50.4.B66**
Bones, Bodies, Behavior: Essays in Behavioral Anthropology. Trade Paper. University of Wisconsin Press. Chicago, IL. 1990. 272p. History of Anthropology Ser., No. 5 ISBN:0-299-11254-3, ISBN13: 978-0-299-11254-7. Dewey:573/.09. LCCN:87-040377.
Audience: **u,f.**

Stocking, George W. Jr. (Author, Editor) **GN504**
Malinowski, Rivers, Benedict and Others: Essays on Culture and Personality. Trade Paper. University of Wisconsin Press. Chicago, IL. 1997. 266p. History of Anthropology Ser., No. 4 ISBN:0-299-10734-5, ISBN13: 978-0-299-10734-5. Dewey:306. LCCN:86-040061.
Audience: **u,f.**

Stocking, George W. (Author, Editor) **GN345**
Romantic Motives: Essays on Anthropological Sensibility. Trade Paper. University of Wisconsin Press. Chicago, IL. 1996. 280p. History of Anthropology Ser., Vol. 6 ISBN:0-299-12364-2, ISBN13: 978-0-299-12364-2. Dewey:306/.01. LCCN:89-040268.
Audience: **u,f.**

Vermeulen, Han & Roldan, Arturo A. (Editors) **GN17.3.E85F54 1995**
Fieldwork and Footnotes: Studies in the History of European Anthropology. Paper over Boards. Routledge. New York, NY. 1995. 280p. European Association of Social Anthropologists Ser. ISBN:0-415-10655-9, ISBN13: 978-0-415-10655-9. Dewey:306/.094. LCCN:94-011724.
Audience: **u,f.**

Wilcox, Clifford **GN21.R43W55 2004**
Robert Redfield and the Development of American Anthropology. Trade Cloth. Lexington Books. Lanham, MD. 2004. 248p. ISBN:0-7391-0728-3, ISBN13: 978-0-7391-0728-7. Dewey:301/.092 B. LCCN:2004-044182.
Audience: **u,f.**

Young, Michael W. **GN21.M25Y68 2004**
Malinowski: Odyssey of an Anthropologist, 1884-1920. Cloth over Boards. Yale University Press. Cumberland, RI. 2004. 720p. ISBN:0-300-10294-1, ISBN13: 978-0-300-10294-9. Dewey:301/.092 B. LCCN:2004-001545.
Audience: **g,l,u,f.** *Choice, 2005.*

Young, Virginia Heyer **GN21.B45Y68 2005**
Ruth Benedict: Beyond Relativity, Beyond Pattern. Trade Cloth. University of Nebraska Press. Lincoln, NE. 2005. 432p. Critical Studies in the History of Anthropology ISBN:0-8032-4919-5, ISBN13: 978-0-8032-4919-6. Dewey:301/.092 B. LCCN:2004-028319.
Audience: **u,f.** *Choice, 2006.*

Archaeology > General and Introductory Works

Bellwood, Peter **GN799.A4B45 2004**
First Farmers: The Origins of Agricultural Societies. Trade Paper. Blackwell Publishing, Inc. Malden, MA. 2004. 384p. ISBN:0-631-20566-7, ISBN13: 978-0-631-20566-1. Dewey:630/.9/01. LCCN:2004-003944.
Audience: **l,u,f.** *Choice, 2005.*

Merriman, Nick & Schadla-Hall, Tim (Editors) **CC75.7.P83 2004**
Public Archaeology. Trade Cloth. Routledge. New York, NY. 2004. 320p. ISBN:0-415-25888-X, ISBN13: 978-0-415-25888-3. Dewey:659.2/99301. LCCN:2003-019795.
Audience: **l,u,f.**

Murray, Tim (Editor) **CC100.E54 2001**
Encyclopedia of Archaeology: History and Discoveries. Ed. 2. Library Binding. ABC-CLIO, Inc. Santa Barbara, CA. 2001. 1500p. Encyclopedia of Archaeology Ser., Vol. 2 ISBN:1-57607-198-7, ISBN13: 978-1-57607-198-4. Dewey:930.1. LCCN:2001-002617.
Audience: **g,l,u,f.** *Choice, 2002.*

Renfrew, Colin & Bahn, Paul **CC165**
Archaeology: Theories, Methods and Practice. Ed. 4. Trade Paper. Thames & Hudson. New York, NY. 2004. 656p. ISBN:0-500-28441-5, ISBN13: 978-0-500-28441-4. Dewey:930.1. LCCN:2003-108923.
Audience: **l,u,f.**

Scarre, Chris **GN740**
Human Past. Trade Paper. Thames & Hudson. New York, NY. 2005. 784p. ISBN:0-500-28531-4, ISBN13: 978-0-500-28531-2. Dewey:930.1. LCCN:2004-109562.
Audience: **g,l,u,f.**

Smith, Bruce D. **GN799.A4S52 1994**
The Emergence of Agriculture. Trade Cloth. Henry Holt & Company. New York, NY. 1994. 256p. ISBN:0-7167-5055-4, ISBN13: 978-0-7167-5055-0. Dewey:630/.9. LCCN:94-022833.
Audience: **g,l,u,f.** *Choice, 1995.*

Archaeology > Theory and History of Archaeology

Beaudry, Mary C. (Editor) **E159.5.D63 1987**
Documentary Archaeology in the New World. Wendy Ashmore, Francoise Audouze, Cyprian Broodbank, Tim Murray, Colin Renfrew, Nathan Schlanger, Timothy Taylor, Norman Yoffee & Andrew Sherratt (Contribution by). Trade Paper. Cambridge University Press. New York, NY. 1993. 224p. New Directions in Archaeology Ser. ISBN:0-521-44999-5, ISBN13: 978-0-521-44999-1. Dewey:973.1.
Audience: **l,u,f.** *Choice, 1990.*

Binford, Lewis Roberts **CC165.B48 2002**
In Pursuit of the Past: Decoding the Archaeological Record: With a New Afterword. Ed. 2. Trade Paper. University of California Press. Berkeley, CA. 2002. 260p. ISBN:0-520-23339-5, ISBN13: 978-0-520-23339-3. Dewey:930.1. LCCN:2001-053963.
Audience: **g,l,u,f.** B

Hodder, Ian **CC173.H63**
Theory and Practice in Archaeology. Trade Paper. Routledge. New York, NY. 1995. 304p. ISBN:0-415-12777-7, ISBN13: 978-0-415-12777-6. Dewey:930.1.
Audience: **l,u.**

Johnson, Matthew V. **CC72.J65 1999**
Archaeological Theory: An Introduction. Book, Other. Blackwell Publishing, Inc. Malden, MA. 1999. 256p. ISBN:0-631-20295-1, ISBN13: 978-0-631-20295-0. Dewey:930.1/01. LCCN:98-056262.
Audience: **l,u.**

Jones, Andrew **CC72.J66 2002**
Archaeological Theory and Scientific Practice. Cloth Text. Cambridge University Press. New York, NY. 2001. 222p. Topics in Contemporary Archaeology Ser. ISBN:0-521-79060-3, ISBN13: 978-0-521-79060-4. Dewey:930.101. LCCN:2001-035689.
Audience: **u,f.**

Lucas, Gavin **CC75.7.L83 2005**
The Archaeology of Time. Paper over Boards. Routledge. New York, NY. 2005. 160p. Themes in Archaeology Ser. ISBN:0-415-31197-7, ISBN13: 978-0-415-31197-7. Dewey:930.1. LCCN:2004-009689.
Audience: **l,u,f.**

O'Brien, Michael J., et al. **CC75.7.O2725 2005**
Archaeology As a Process: Processualism and Its Progeny. R. Lee Lyman & Michael B. Schiffer (Authors). Trade Cloth. University of Utah Press. Salt Lake City, UT. 2005. 520p. ISBN:0-87480-817-0, ISBN13: 978-0-87480-817-9. Dewey:930.1. LCCN:2004-020485.
Audience: **u,f.** *Choice, 2006.*

Pinsky, Valerie & Wylie, Alison (Editors) **CC72.C75 1989**
Critical Traditions in Contemporary Archaeology. Trade Cloth. Cambridge University Press. New York, NY. 1990. 170p. New Directions in Archaeology Ser. ISBN:0-521-32109-3, ISBN13: 978-0-521-32109-9. Dewey:930.1. LCCN:89-009842.
Audience: **u,f.** *Choice, 1991.*

Preucel, Robert **CC173.C66 1996**
Contemporary Archaeology in Theory: A Reader. Ian Hodder (Editor). Trade Cloth. Blackwell Publishing, Inc. Malden, MA. 1996. 704p. Social Archaeology Ser. ISBN:0-631-19559-9, ISBN13: 978-0-631-19559-7. Dewey:930.1. LCCN:96-002055.
Audience: **l,u,f.**

Renfrew, Colin & Bahn, Paul G. (Editors) **CC165.A635 2005**
Archaeology: The Key Concepts. Paper over Boards. Routledge. New York, NY. 2004. IV, 308p. Routledge Key Guides Ser. ISBN:0-415-31757-6, ISBN13: 978-0-415-31757-3. Dewey:930.1/01. LCCN:2004-008902.
Audience: **g,l,u,f.**

Schiffer, Michael Brian **CC72.4.S63 2000**
Social Theory in Archaeology. Trade Paper. University of Utah Press. Salt Lake City, UT. 2000. 200p. Foundations of Archaeological Inquiry Ser. ISBN:0-87480-642-9, ISBN13: 978-0-87480-642-7. Dewey:930.1. LCCN:99-088528.
Audience: **l,u.**

Trigger, Bruce G. **CC100.T75 1989**
A History of Archaeological Thought. Trade Cloth. Cambridge University Press. New York, NY. 1990. 516p. ISBN:0-521-32878-0, ISBN13: 978-0-521-32878-4. Dewey:930.1. LCCN:88-016926.
Audience: **l,u,f.**

Ucko, Peter J. (Editor) **CC72.T485 1995**
Theory in Archaeology: A World Perspective. Paper over Boards. Routledge. New York, NY. 1995. 416p. ISBN:0-415-10677-X, ISBN13: 978-0-415-10677-1. Dewey:930.1/01. LCCN:94-027877.
Audience: **u,f.**

Yoffee, Norman (Editor, Contribution by) **CC72.A65 1993**
Archaeological Theory: Who Sets the Agenda? Andrew Sherratt (Editor), Wendy Ashmore, Francoise Audouze, Cyprian Broodbank, Tim Murray, Colin Renfrew, Nathan Schlanger & Timothy Taylor (Contribution by). Trade Paper. Cambridge University Press. New York, NY. 1993. 149p. New Directions in Archaeology Ser. ISBN:0-521-44958-8, ISBN13: 978-0-521-44958-8. Dewey:930.101. LCCN:92-025825.
Audience: **u,f.**

Archaeology > Analytic Methods

Conolly, James & Lake, Mark **CC79.G46**
Geographical Information Systems in Archaeology. Graeme Barker, Peter Bogucki & Elizabeth Slater (Contribution by). Cloth Text. Cambridge University Press. New York, NY. 2006.

358p. Cambridge Manuals in Archaeology Ser. ISBN:0-521-79330-0, ISBN13: 978-0-521-79330-8. Dewey:930.10285.
Audience: **u,f.**

Gremillion, Kristen J. (Editor) **CC79.5.P5P45 1997**
People, Plants, and Landscapes: Studies in Paleoethnobotany. Trade Paper. University of Alabama Press. Tuscaloosa, AL. 1997. 296p. ISBN:0-8173-0827-X, ISBN13: 978-0-8173-0827-8. Dewey:581.6. LCCN:96-013617.
Audience: **u,f.** *Choice, 1997.*

Hastorf, Christine A. & Popper, Virginia S. (Editors) **CC79.5.P5C87 1988**
Current Paleoethnobotany: Analytical Methods and Cultural Interpretations of Archaeological Plant Remains. Trade Cloth. University of Chicago Press. Chicago, IL. 1995. 243p. Prehistoric Archeology and Ecology Ser. ISBN:0-226-31892-3, ISBN13: 978-0-226-31892-9. Dewey:930.1. LCCN:88-020467.
Audience: **u,f.**

Lock, Gary **CC80.4.L63 2003**
Using Computers in Archaeology: Towards Virtual Pasts. Paper over Boards. Routledge. New York, NY. 2003. 320p. ISBN:0-415-16620-9, ISBN13: 978-0-415-16620-1. Dewey:930.1/028. LCCN:2002-035669.
Audience: **u,f.**

Orton, Clive **CC80.6.O78 2000**
Sampling in Archaeology. Graeme Barker & Don Brothwell (Contribution by). Cloth Text. Cambridge University Press. New York, NY. 2000. 274p. Cambridge Manuals in Archaeology Ser. ISBN:0-521-56226-0, ISBN13: 978-0-521-56226-3. Dewey:930. LCCN:99-028846.
Audience: **u,f.**

Orton, Clive, et al. **CC79.5.P6O78 1993**
Pottery in Archaeology. Paul Tyers & Alan Vince (Authors). Cloth Text. Cambridge University Press. New York, NY. 1993. 287p. Cambridge Manuals in Archaeology Ser. ISBN:0-521-25715-8, ISBN13: 978-0-521-25715-2. Dewey:930.1028. LCCN:92-025814.
Audience: **l,u,f.**

Pearsall, Deborah M. **CC79.5.P5P43 2000**
Paleoethnobotany: A Handbook of Procedures. Ed. 2. Trade Cloth. Elsevier Science & Technology Books. Saint Louis, MO. 2000. 700p. ISBN:0-12-548042-3, ISBN13: 978-0-12-548042-0. Dewey:930.1. LCCN:99-068199.
Audience: **u,f.** *Choice, 2001, 1989.*

Reitz, Elizabeth J. & Wing, Elizabeth S. **CC79.5.A5R45 1999**
Zooarchaeology. Graeme Barker & Don Brothwell (Contribution by). Cloth Text. Cambridge University Press. New York, NY. 1999. 475p. Cambridge Manuals in Archaeology Ser. ISBN:0-521-48069-8, ISBN13: 978-0-521-48069-7. Dewey:930.1. LCCN:98-007989.
Audience: **u,f.** *Choice, 1999.*

Shennan, Stephen **CC80.6.S54 1997**
Quantifying Archaeology. Ed. 2. Trade Paper. Edinburgh University Press. Edinburgh, 1996. 224p. ISBN:0-7486-0791-9, ISBN13: 978-0-7486-0791-4. Dewey:930.1/01/51. LCCN:97-060561.
Audience: **l,u,f.**

Archaeology > Field Methods

Drewett, Peter **CC75**
Field Archaeology: An Introduction. Paper over Boards. Taylor & Francis Group. Philadelphia, PA. 1999. 216p. ISBN:1-85728-737-1, ISBN13: 978-1-85728-737-0. Dewey:930.1/028.
Audience: **l,u,f.**

Gater, John & Gaffney, C. F. **CC79.G46**
Revealing the Buried Past: Geophysics for Archaeologists. Trade Cloth. Tempus Publishing, Ltd. Stroud, Gloucestershire, 2004. 176p. ISBN:0-7524-2556-0, ISBN13: 978-0-7524-2556-6. Dewey:930.1/028.
Audience: **u,f.**

Hardesty, Donald L. & Little, Barbara J. **E159.H26 2000**
Assessing Site Significance: A Guide for Archaeologists and Historians. Book, Other. AltaMira Press. Walnut Creek, CA. 2000. 200p. Heritage Resources Management Ser., Vol. 3 ISBN:0-7425-0316-X, ISBN13: 978-0-7425-0316-8. Dewey:930.1/028. LCCN:00-042004.
Audience: **u,f.** *Choice, 2001.*

Little, Barbara J. (Editor) **CC77.H5P83 2002**
Public Benefits of Archaeology. Trade Cloth. University Press of Florida. Gainesville, FL. 2002. xix, 277p. ISBN:0-8130-2455-2, ISBN13: 978-0-8130-2455-4. Dewey:973. LCCN:2001-043730.
Audience: **g,l,u,f.** *Choice, 2002.*

Orton, Clive **CC80.6.O78 2000**
Sampling in Archaeology. Graeme Barker & Don Brothwell (Contribution by). Cloth Text. Cambridge University Press. New York, NY. 2000. 274p. Cambridge Manuals in Archaeology Ser. ISBN:0-521-56226-0, ISBN13: 978-0-521-56226-3. Dewey:930. LCCN:99-028846.
Audience: **u,f.**

Roskams, Steve **CC76.R67 2001**
Excavation. Graeme Barker, Don Brothwell, Peter Bogucki & Elizabeth Slater (Contribution by). Cloth Text. Cambridge University Press. New York, NY. 2001. 328p. Cambridge Manuals in Archaeology Ser. ISBN:0-521-35534-6, ISBN13: 978-0-521-35534-6. Dewey:930.1. LCCN:00-040376.
Audience: **u,f.** *Choice, 2002.*

Archaeology > Archaeology by Continent > Africa

Connah, Graham **DT352.3.C66 2001**
African Civilizations: An Archaeological Perspective. Ed. 2. Douglas Hobbs (Illustrator). Cloth Text. Cambridge University Press. New York, NY. 2001. 356p. ISBN:0-521-59309-3, ISBN13: 978-0-521-59309-0. Dewey:967/.01. LCCN:00-033704.
Audience: **g,u,f.**

Hassan, Fekri A. (Editor) **GN861.D76 2002**
Droughts, Food, and Culture: Ecological Change and Food Security in Africa's Later Prehistory. Trade Cloth. Springer. New York, NY. 2002. 366p. ISBN:0-306-46755-0, ISBN13: 978-0-306-46755-4. Dewey:960/.1. LCCN:2002-022218.
Audience: **u,f.** *Choice, 2002.*

Kemp, Barry J. **DT61.K44 1989**
Ancient Egypt: Anatomy of a Civilization. Cloth Text. Routledge. New York, NY. 1989. 320p. ISBN:0-415-01281-3, ISBN13: 978-0-415-01281-2. Dewey:932. LCCN:88-018484.
Audience: **l,u.** *Choice, 1989.*

Mitchell, Peter J. **DT1050.M57 2002**
The Archaeology of Southern Africa. Susan Alcock, Tom Dillehay, Stephen Shennan, Carla Sinopoli & Norman Yoffee (Contribution by). Cloth Text. Cambridge University Press. New York, NY. 2002. 532p. Cambridge World Archaeology Ser. ISBN:0-521-63307-9, ISBN13: 978-0-521-63307-9. Dewey:968/.009/01. LCCN:2003-271206.
Audience: **l,u.** *Choice, 2003.*

Phillipson, David W. **GN861.P47 2004**
African Archaeology. Ed. 3. Cloth Text. Cambridge University Press. New York, NY. 2005. 404p. ISBN:0-521-83236-5, ISBN13: 978-0-521-83236-6. Dewey:960/.1. LCCN:2004-049657.
Audience: **g,l,u,f.** B *Choice, 1985.*

Shaw, Thurstan (Editor), et al. **GN861.A73 1993**
The Archaeology of Africa. Paul Sinclair, Bassey Andah & Alex Okpoko (Editors). Paper over Boards. Routledge. New York, NY. 1993. 896p. One World Archaeology Ser., Vol. 20 ISBN:0-415-08444-X, ISBN13: 978-0-415-08444-4. Dewey:960.1. LCCN:92-013921.
Audience: **l,u.** *Choice, 1994.*

Vogel, Joseph O. **DT.E53 1996**
The Encyclopedia of Precolonial Africa: Archaeology, History, Languages, Cultures and Environments. Trade Cloth. AltaMira Press. Walnut Creek, CA. 1997. 606p. ISBN:0-7619-8902-1, ISBN13: 978-0-7619-8902-8. Dewey:960/.2. LCCN:96-051227.
Audience: **g,l,u,f.** *Choice, 1998.*

Wendorf, Fred, et al. **GN776.42.E3W46 2001**
Holocene Settlement of the Egyptian Sahara. Romuald Schild & Kit Nelson (Authors). Trade Cloth. Springer. New York, NY. 2002. 120p. ISBN:0-306-46613-9, ISBN13: 978-0-306-46613-7. Dewey:932. LCCN:2001-041355.
Audience: **u,f.**

Archaeology > Archaeology by Continent > Asia

Akkermans, Peter M. & Schwartz, Glenn **DS94.5.S36 2002**
The Archaeology of Syria: From Complex Hunter-Gatherers to Early Urban Societies (C.16,000-300 BC). Norman Yoffee, Susan Alcock, Tom Dillehay, Stephen Shennan & Carla Sinopoli (Contribution by). Cloth Text. Cambridge University Press. New York, NY. 2004. 486p. Cambridge World Archaeology Ser. ISBN:0-521-79230-4, ISBN13: 978-0-521-79230-1. Dewey:939.43. LCCN:2002-031240.
Audience: **l,u,f.**

Algaze, Guillermo **DS73.1**
The Uruk World System: The Dynamics of Expansion of Early Mesopotamian Civilization. Ed. 2. Trade Paper, Perfect. University of Chicago Press. Chicago, IL. 2005. 174p. ISBN:0-226-01382-0, ISBN13: 978-0-226-01382-4. Dewey:935. LCCN:2005-002709.
Audience: **u,f.** *Choice, 1993.*

Allchin, Bridget (Editor) **CC79.E85L58 1994**
Living Traditions: Studies in the Ethnoarchaeology of South Asia. Trade Cloth. Oxbow Books, Ltd. Oxford, 1995. 391p. ISBN:81-204-0901-9, ISBN13: 978-81-204-0901-9. Dewey:930.1. LCCN:94-907183.
Audience: **u,f.**

Allchin, Bridget & Allchin, F. Raymond **DS339.A45 1997**
Origins of a Civilization: The Prehistory and Early Archaeology of South Asia. Trade Cloth. Penguin Group (USA) Inc. New York, NY. 1997. 287p. ISBN:0-670-87713-1, ISBN13: 978-0-670-87713-3. Dewey:954. LCCN:97-904966.
Audience: **l,u,f.**

Allchin, Raymond **DS338.A45 1995**
The Archaeology of Early Historic South Asia: The Emergence of Cities and States. Trade Cloth. Cambridge University Press. New York, NY. 1995. 389p. ISBN:0-521-37547-9, ISBN13: 978-0-521-37547-4. Dewey:934. LCCN:94-023181.
Audience: **l,u,f.** *Choice, 1996.*

Bagley, Robert (Editor) **DS793.S8A528 2001**
Ancient Sichuan: Treasures from a Lost Civilization. Trade Cloth. Princeton University Press. Princeton, NJ. 2001. 360p. ISBN:0-691-08851-9, ISBN13: 978-0-691-08851-8. Dewey:931. LCCN:00-068782.
Audience: **g,l,u,f.** *Choice, 2001.*

Barnes, Gina L. **DS509.3.B37 1993**
China, Korea and Japan: The Rise of Civilization in East Asia. Trade Cloth. Thames & Hudson. New York, NY. 1993. 304p. ISBN:0-500-05071-6, ISBN13: 978-0-500-05071-2. Dewey:950.1. LCCN:93-060205.
Audience: **g,u,f.**

Chakrabarti, Dilip K. **DS418**
The Oxford Companion to Indian Archaeology: The Archaeological Foundations of Ancient India. Trade Cloth. Oxford University Press, Inc. New York, NY. 2006. 700p. ISBN:0-19-567342-5, ISBN13: 978-0-19-567342-5. Dewey:934.
Audience: **l,u,f.**

Dani, A. H. **DS329.4**
History of Civilizations of Central Asia, Set. V. M. Masson, B. A. Litvinsky, M. S. Asimova & C. E. Boaworth (Editors). Trade Paper. Motilal Banarsidass Publishers (Pvt. Ltd). New Delhi, 1999. 2163p. ISBN:81-208-1409-6, ISBN13: 978-81-208-1409-7. Dewey:958.
Audience: **l,u,f.**

Higham, Charles **DS523.H54 1989**
The Archaeology of Mainland Southeast Asia: From 10,000 B. C. to the Fall of Angkor. Cloth Text. Cambridge University Press. New York, NY. 1989. 404p. World Archaeology Ser. ISBN:0-521-25523-6, ISBN13: 978-0-521-25523-3. Dewey:959/.01. LCCN:88-020303.
Audience: **l,u,f.** *Choice, 1990.*

Higham, Charles **DS523.H55 1996**
The Bronze Age of Southeast Asia. Cloth Text. Cambridge University Press. New York, NY. 1996. 400p. World Archaeology Ser. ISBN:0-521-49660-8, ISBN13: 978-0-521-49660-5. Dewey:959/.01. LCCN:95-039223.
Audience: **l,u,f.** *Choice, 1997.*

Kenoyer, Jonathan M. **DS425.K43 1998**
Ancient Cities of the Indus Valley Civilization. Paper Text. Oxford University Press, Inc. New York, NY. 1998. 264p. ISBN:0-19-577940-1, ISBN13: 978-0-19-577940-0. Dewey:934. LCCN:98-930419.
Audience: **l,u,f.**

Lewin, Ariel **DS111.L4913 2004**
The Archaeology of Ancient Judea and Palestine. Dinu Mendrea, Sandu Mendrea & Radu Mendrea (Photographers). Saddle Stitched, Cloth over Boards, Dust Jacket. Getty Conservation Institute. Los Angeles, CA. 2005. 204p. ISBN:0-89236-800-4, ISBN13: 978-0-89236-800-6. Dewey:933. LCCN:2004-017938.
Audience: **l,u,f.** *Choice, 2005.*

Loewe, Michael & Shaughnessy, Edward L. **DS741.5 .C35 1999**
The Cambridge History of Ancient China: From the Origins of Civilization to 221 BC. Cloth Text. Cambridge University Press. New York, NY. 1999. 1180p. ISBN:0-521-47030-7, ISBN13: 978-0-521-47030-8. Dewey:931. LCCN:97-033203.
Audience: **g,l,u,f.** *Choice, 1999.*

Macqueen, J. G. **DS66**
The Hittites: And Their Contemporaries in Asia Minor. Ed. 4. Trade Paper. Thames & Hudson. New York, NY. 1996. 176p. Ancient Peoples and Places Ser. ISBN:0-500-27887-3, ISBN13: 978-0-500-27887-1. Dewey:939.2. LCCN:85-051750.
Audience: **u,f.**

Mair, Victor H. **GN778.32.C45B76**
The Bronze Age and Early Iron Age Peoples of Eastern Central Asia. Trade Paper. Institute for the Study of Man, Inc. Washington, DC. 1999. 912p. Journal of Indo-European Studies Monographs, Vol. 26 ISBN:0-941694-66-6, ISBN13: 978-0-941694-66-7. Dewey:939.6.
Audience: **l,u,f.**

Nelson, Sarah Milledge **DS903.N45 1993**
The Archaeology of Korea. Norman Yoffee, Susan Alcock, Tom Dillehay, Stephen Shennan & Carla Sinopoli (Contribution by). Trade Paper. Cambridge University Press. New York, NY. 1993. 323p. World Archaeology Ser. ISBN:0-521-40783-4, ISBN13: 978-0-521-40783-0. Dewey:951.901. LCCN:91-040202.
Audience: **l,u.**

Pearson, Richard J. **DS822.P44 1992**
Ancient Japan. Trade Cloth. George Braziller Inc. New York, NY. 1992. 324p. ISBN:0-8076-1282-0, ISBN13: 978-0-8076-1282-8. Dewey:952/.01. LCCN:92-015138.
Audience: **u,f.** *Choice, 1993.*

Portal, Jane **N7360.P67 2000**
Korea: Art and Archaeology. Trade Paper. Thames & Hudson. New York, NY. 2000. 240p. ISBN:0-500-28202-1, ISBN13: 978-0-500-28202-1. Dewey:709.5/19. LCCN:99-066554.
Audience: **g,l,u,f.** *Choice, 2000.*

Rawson, Jessica (Editor) **DS715.M97 1996**
Mysteries of Ancient China: New Discoveries from the Early Dynasties. Trade Cloth. George Braziller Inc. New York, NY. 1996. 288p. ISBN:0-8076-1412-2, ISBN13: 978-0-8076-1412-9. Dewey:931. LCCN:96-015451.
Audience: **g,l,u.**

Archaeology > Archaeology by Continent > Mesoamerica

Adams, Richard E. W. **F1219.A22 2005**
Prehistoric Mesoamerica: Third Edition. Ed. 3. Trade Paper. University of Oklahoma Press. Norman, OK. 2005. 544p. ISBN:0-8061-3702-9, ISBN13: 978-0-8061-3702-5. Dewey:972/.01. LCCN:2005-043955.
Audience: **l,u,f.**

Carrasco, David (Editor) **F1218.6.O95 2001**
The Oxford Encyclopedia of Mesoamerican Cultures: The Civilizations of Mexico and Central America. Trade Cloth. Oxford University Press, Inc. New York, NY. 2000. ISBN:0-19-514257-8, ISBN13: 978-0-19-514257-0. Dewey:972/.01. LCCN:00-032624.
Audience: **g,l,u,f.** *Choice, 2001.*

Coe, Michael D. **F1435**
Maya. Ed. 7. Trade Paper. Thames & Hudson. New York, NY. 2005. 272p. ISBN:0-500-28505-5, ISBN13: 978-0-500-28505-3. Dewey:970.3.
Audience: **l,u,f.** B

Coe, Michael D. & Koontz, Rex **F1219.7.C63 2002**
Mexico: From the Olmecs to the Aztecs. Ed. 5. Trade Paper. Thames & Hudson. New York, NY. 2002. 248p. ISBN:0-500-28346-X, ISBN13: 978-0-500-28346-2. Dewey:972/.01. LCCN:2001-094767.
Audience: **l,u,f.**

Diehl, Richard A. **F1219.8.O56**
Olmecs. Trade Cloth. Thames & Hudson. New York, NY. 2004. 208p. ISBN:0-500-02119-8, ISBN13: 978-0-500-02119-4. Dewey:972/.01. LCCN:2004-101751.
Audience: **u,f.** *Choice, 2005.*

Flannery, Kent V. & Marcus, Joyce (Editors) **F1219.8.M59**
The Cloud People: The Divergent Evolution of the Zapotic and Mixte Civilizations. Trade Cloth. Elsevier Science & Technology Books. Saint Louis, MO. 1983. xxviii, 391p. ISBN:0-12-259860-1, ISBN13: 978-0-12-259860-9. Dewey:972/.01. LCCN:82-016464.
Audience: **u,f.**

Freidel, David, et al. **F1435.3.R3 F74**
Maya Cosmos. Linda Schele & Joy Parker (Authors). Trade Paper. HarperCollins Publishers. New York, NY. 1995. 544p. ISBN:0-688-14069-6, ISBN13: 978-0-688-14069-4. Dewey:299/.79281.
Audience: **u,f.**

Hendon, Julia A. & Joyce, Rosemary A. (Editors) **F1435.M557 2004**
Mesoamerican Archaeology: Theory and Practice. Trade Cloth. Blackwell Publishing, Inc. Malden, MA. 2003. 368p. Blackwell Studies in Global Archaeology ISBN:0-631-23051-3, ISBN13: 978-0-631-23051-9. LCCN:2003-001667.
Audience: **u,f.** *Choice, 2004.*

Hoopes, John W. **CB311**
The Archaeology of Central America. Norman Yoffee (Contribution by). Cloth Text. Cambridge University Press. New

York, NY. 2008. Cambridge World Archaeology Ser. ISBN:0-521-84025-2, ISBN13: 978-0-521-84025-5. Dewey:930.
Audience: **g,l,u,f.**

López Luján, Leonardo & Levin, Judy **F1219.1.M5L67 2005**
Tenochtitlán. Book, Other. Oxford University Press, Inc. New York, NY. 2006. 48p. Digging for the Past Ser. ISBN:0-19-517851-3, ISBN13: 978-0-19-517851-7. Dewey:972/.53. LCCN:2005-021703.
Audience: **u,f.**

Masson, Marilyn A. **F1219.A594 2000**
Ancient Civilizations of Mesoamerica: A Reader. Michael E. Smith (Editor). Trade Cloth. Blackwell Publishing, Inc. Malden, MA. 2000. 520p. ISBN:0-631-21115-2, ISBN13: 978-0-631-21115-0. Dewey:972/.01. LCCN:99-048855.
Audience: **g,l,u,f.**

Phillips, Charles **F1219**
Aztec and Maya World. Trade Cloth. Anness Publishing. London, 2006. 256p. ISBN:0-7548-1575-7, ISBN13: 978-0-7548-1575-4. Dewey:972.00497.
Audience: **l,u,f.**

Sharer, Robert J. **F1435.S53 2006**
The Ancient Maya. Ed. 6. Perfect, Paper over Boards. Stanford University Press. Palo Alto, CA. 2005. 931p. ISBN:0-8047-4816-0, ISBN13: 978-0-8047-4816-2. Dewey:972.81/016. LCCN:2005-003043.
Audience: **g,l,u,f.**

Archaeology > Archaeology by Continent > North America

Ames, Kenneth M. & Maschner, Herbert D. **E78.N78**
Peoples of the Northwest Coast: Their Archaeology and Prehistory. Trade Cloth. Thames & Hudson. New York, NY. 1999. 272p. ISBN:0-500-05091-0, ISBN13: 978-0-500-05091-0. Dewey:979/.00497. LCCN:98-060253.
Audience: **u,f.**

Arnold, Jeanne E. **E99.C815O75 2001**
The Origins of a Pacific Coast Chiefdom: The Chumash of the Channel Islands. Trade Cloth. University of Utah Press. Salt Lake City, UT. 2001. 336p. ISBN:0-87480-674-7, ISBN13: 978-0-87480-674-8. Dewey:979.4/91. LCCN:00-012452.
Audience: **u,f.**

Bense, Judith A. **E78.S65B45 1994**
Archaeology of the Southeastern United States: Paleoindian to World War I. Trade Cloth. Elsevier Science & Technology Books. Saint Louis, MO. 1994. 388p. ISBN:0-12-089060-7, ISBN13: 978-0-12-089060-6. Dewey:975. LCCN:93-046445.
Audience: **l,u,f.**

Bonnichsen, Robson & Turnmire, Karen L. (Editors) **E77.9**
Ice Age Peoples of North America: Environments, Origins, and Adaptations of the First Americans. Trade Cloth. Texas A&M University Press. College Station, TX. 2004. 536p. ISBN:1-58544-368-9, ISBN13: 978-1-58544-368-0. Dewey:970.01.
Audience: **g,l,u,f.**

Bourque, Bruce J. **E78**
Twelve Thousand Years: American Indians in Maine. Steven L. Cox & Ruth H. Whitehead (Contribution by). Trade Cloth. University of Nebraska Press. Lincoln, NE. 2005. 369p. ISBN:0-8032-6231-0, ISBN13: 978-0-8032-6231-7. Dewey:974.1. LCCN:00-064779.
Audience: **u,f.** *Choice, 2002.*

Chappell, Sally Anderson Kitt **E99.M6815C55 2001**
Cahokia: Mirror of the Cosmos. Trade Cloth. University of Chicago Press. Chicago, IL. 2002. 238p. ISBN:0-226-10136-3, ISBN13: 978-0-226-10136-1. Dewey:977.3/89. LCCN:2001-027511.
Audience: **g,l,u,f.** *Choice, 2003, 2002.*

Coe, Michael, et al. **E61.C66 1986**
Atlas of Ancient America. Dean Snow & Elizabeth Benson (Authors). Trade Cloth. Facts On File, Inc. New York, NY. 1986. 240p. Cultural Atlas Ser. ISBN:0-8160-1199-0, ISBN13: 978-0-8160-1199-5. Dewey:970. LCCN:84-025999.
Audience: **g,l,u,f.**

Cordell, Linda **E78.S7C66 1997**
Archaeology of the Southwest. Ed. 2. Cloth Text. Elsevier Science & Technology Books. Saint Louis, MO. 1997. 522p. ISBN:0-12-188225-X, ISBN13: 978-0-12-188225-9. Dewey:976/.01. LCCN:97-080320.
Audience: **l,u,f.**

Dumond, Don E. **E99.E7D85 1987**
The Eskimos and Aleuts. Ed. 2. Trade Paper. Thames & Hudson. New York, NY. 1987. 180p. Ancient Peoples and Places Ser. ISBN:0-500-27479-7, ISBN13: 978-0-500-27479-8. Dewey:979.8/01. LCCN:87-050399.
Audience: **l,u.**

Emerson, Thomas E. **E99.M6815C34 2000**
Cahokia and the Hinterlands: Middle Mississippian Cultures of the Midwest. Trade Paper. University of Illinois Press. Champaign, IL. 1999. 376p. ISBN:0-252-06878-5, ISBN13: 978-0-252-06878-2. Dewey:977.3/89. LCCN:00-266193.
Audience: **l,u,f.** *Choice, 1991.*

Fagan, Brian M. **E77.8.F34 2000**
Ancient North America: The Archaeology of a Continent. Ed. 3. Trade Paper. Thames & Hudson. New York, NY. 2000. 528p. ISBN:0-500-28148-3, ISBN13: 978-0-500-28148-2. Dewey:970.01/1. LCCN:99-070860.
Audience: **g,l,u,f.**

Fagan, Brian M. **E78.N65F34 2005**
Chaco Canyon: Archeologists Explore the Lives of an Ancient Society. Trade Cloth. Oxford University Press, Inc. New York, NY. 2005. 256p. ISBN:0-19-517043-1, ISBN13: 978-0-19-517043-6. Dewey:978.9/2. LCCN:2004-023630.
Audience: **g,l,u,f.** *Choice, 2006.*

Frison, George C. (Editor) **E78.G73F74 1991**
Prehistoric Hunters of the High Plains. Ed. 2. Bruce A. Bradley, Julie E. Francis, George W. Gill & James C. Miller (Contribution by). Cloth Text. Elsevier Science & Technology Books. Saint Louis, MO. 1991. 426p. New World Archaeological Record Ser. ISBN:0-12-268561-X, ISBN13: 978-0-12-268561-3. Dewey:978. LCCN:91-003393.
Audience: **g,l,u,f.** *Choice, 1992.*

Gordon, Bryan **E78.N79**
People of Sunlight and Starlight: Barrenland Archaeology in the Northwest Territories. Trade Paper. Canadian Museum of Civilization/Musee Canadien des Civilisations. Gatineau, PQ. 1996. 300p. Mercury Ser., ASC No. 154 ISBN:0-660-15963-5, ISBN13: 978-0-660-15963-8. Dewey:930.1097192.
Audience: **u,f.** *Choice, 1997.*

Haury, Emil W. **E78.S7H37 1986**
Emil W. Haury's Prehistory of the American Southwest. J. Jefferson Reid & David E. Doyel (Editors). Trade Cloth. University of Arizona Press. Tucson, AZ. 1986. 506p. ISBN:0-8165-0896-8, ISBN13: 978-0-8165-0896-9. Dewey:979/.01. LCCN:85-020900.
Audience: **u,f.** *Choice, 1986.*

Knight, Vernon J. Jr. & Steponaitis, Vin (Editors) **E78.A28**
Archaeology of the Moundville Chiefdom. Trade Cloth. University of Alabama Press. Tuscaloosa, AL. 2006. 208p. ISBN:0-8173-1529-2, ISBN13: 978-0-8173-1529-0. Dewey:976.1/43.
Audience: **u,f.**

Mason, Ronald, J. **E78.G7M37 2002**
Great Lakes Archaeology. Perfect. Blackburn Press, The. Caldwell, NJ. 2002. 426p. ISBN:1-930665-46-6, ISBN13: 978-1-930665-46-0. Dewey:977/.01. LCCN:2002-100887.
Audience: **u,f.** B

Maxwell, Moreau **E99.E7M465 1985**
Prehistory of the Eastern Arctic. Trade Cloth. Elsevier Science & Technology Books. Saint Louis, MO. 1985. xiii, 327p. New World Archaeological Record Ser. ISBN:0-12-481270-8, ISBN13: 978-0-12-481270-3. Dewey:971.901/11. LCCN:84-014488.
Audience: **u,f.** B *Choice, 1985.*

McEwan, Bonnie G. (Editor) **E78.S65I52 2000**
Indians of the Greater Southeast: Historic Archaeology and Ethnohistory. Trade Cloth. University Press of Florida. Gainesville, FL. 2000. xvi, 336p. ISBN:0-8130-1778-5, ISBN13: 978-0-8130-1778-5. Dewey:975/.00497. LCCN:99-049534.
Audience: **g,l,u,f.** *Choice, 2001.*

McGhee, Robert **E78.C2**
Ancient Canada. Trade Cloth. Canadian Museum of Civilization/Musee Canadien des Civilisations. Gatineau, PQ. 1992. 175p. ISBN:0-660-10795-3, ISBN13: 978-0-660-10795-0. Dewey:971.01/11.
Audience: **g,l,u,f.**

Potter, Stephen R. **E99.A35**
Commoners, Tribute, and Chiefs: The Development of Algonquian Culture in the Potomac Valley. Paper Text. University Press of Virginia. Charlottesville, VA. 1993. 288p. ISBN:0-8139-1540-6, ISBN13: 978-0-8139-1540-1. Dewey:975.2004973. LCCN:92-028417.
Audience: **u,f.**

Snow, Dean R. **E99.I7S63 1996**
The Iroquois. Alan Koliata (Contribution by). Trade Paper. Blackwell Publishing, Inc. Malden, MA. 1996. 288p. The Peoples of America Ser. ISBN:1-55786-938-3, ISBN13: 978-1-55786-938-8. Dewey:973/.04975. LCCN:95-049250.
Audience: **l,u,f.** *Choice, 1995.*

Archaeology > Archaeology by Continent > South America

Bird, Junius B. **F3069**
Travels and Archaeology in South Chile. John Hyslop (Editor), Margaret Bird (Commentaries by), Gordon R. Willey (Contribution by, Introduction by). Trade Paper. University of Iowa Press. Iowa City, IA. 2005. 278p. ISBN:1-58729-343-9, ISBN13: 978-1-58729-343-6. Dewey:983/.01.
Audience: **u,f.** *Choice, 1988.*

Bruhns, Karen Olsen **F2229.B78 1994**
Ancient South America. Susan Alcock, Tom Dillehay, Stephen Shennan, Carla Sinopoli & Norman Yoffee (Contribution by). Trade Cloth. Cambridge University Press. New York, NY. 1994. 448p. World Archaeology Ser. ISBN:0-521-25920-7, ISBN13: 978-0-521-25920-0. Dewey:980.01. LCCN:93-008264.
Audience: **l,u,f.** *Choice, 1995.*

Burger, Richard L. **F3429.1.C48B86 1992**
Chavin and the Origins of Andean Civilization. Trade Cloth. Thames & Hudson. New York, NY. 1993. 240p. ISBN:0-500-05069-4, ISBN13: 978-0-500-05069-9. Dewey:983.01. LCCN:92-080337.
Audience: **l,u,f.** *Choice, 1993.*

D'Altroy, Terence N. **F3429.D35 2003**
The Incas. Trade Paper. Blackwell Publishing, Inc. Malden, MA. 2003. 408p. ISBN:1-4051-1676-5, ISBN13: 978-1-4051-1676-3. Dewey:985/.019. LCCN:2001-025267.
Audience: **l,u,f.** *Choice, 2003, 2002.*

Demarest, Arthur A. & Conrad, Geoffrey W. (Editors) **E59.P45I44 1992**
Ideology and Pre-Columbian Civilizations. Trade Cloth. School of American Research Press. Santa Fe, NM. 1992. 280p. Advanced Seminar Ser. ISBN:0-933452-82-9, ISBN13: 978-0-933452-82-4. Dewey:970.01/1/01. LCCN:92-014578.
Audience: **u,f.**

Dillehay, Thomas D. **E58.D538 2000**
The Settlement of the Americas: A New Prehistory. Trade Cloth. Basic Books. New York, NY. 2000. 384p. ISBN:0-465-07668-8, ISBN13: 978-0-465-07668-0. Dewey:970.01/1. LCCN:00-027572.
Audience: **g,l,u,f.**

Dillehay, Tom D. **F3069.D55 1989**
Monte Verde: A Late Pleistocene Settlement in Chile: The Archaeological Context and Interpretation. Trade Cloth. Smithsonian Institution Press. Washington, DC. 1997. 1080p. Smithsonian Series in Archaeological Inquiry ISBN:1-56098-680-8, ISBN13: 978-1-56098-680-5. Dewey:983/.56. LCCN:88-023947.
Audience: **u,f.**

Dillehay, Tom D. **F3069.D55 1989**
Monte Verde: A Late Pleistocene Settlement in Chile: A Paleoenvironment and Site Context. Trade Cloth. Smithsonian Institution Press. Washington, DC. 1989. 336p. Series in Archaeological Inquiry ISBN:0-87474-350-8, ISBN13: 978-0-87474-350-0. Dewey:983/.56. LCCN:88-023947.
Audience: **u,f.**

Heckenberger, Michael J. **F2536**
The Ecology of Power: Culture, Place and Personhood in the Southern Amazon, AD 1000-2000. Paper over Boards.

Routledge. New York, NY. 2004. 432p. Critical Perspectives in Identity, Memory and the Built Environment Ser. ISBN:0-415-94598-4, ISBN13: 978-0-415-94598-1. Dewey:981/.72. LCCN:2004-015651.
Audience: **u,f.**

Lavallee, Daniele **F2229.L4313 2000**
The First South Americans: The Peopling of a Continent from the Earliest Evidence to High Culture. Paul G. Bahn (Translator). Trade Paper. University of Utah Press. Salt Lake City, UT. 2000. xii, 260p. ISBN:0-87480-665-8, ISBN13: 978-0-87480-665-6. Dewey:980/.012. LCCN:00-010190.
Audience: **g,l,u,f.**

McEwan, Colin (Editor), et al. **F2519.U56 2001**
Unknown Amazon: Culture in Nature in Ancient Brazil. Cristiana Barreto & Eduardo Neves (Editors). Trade Paper. British Museum Press. London, 2001. 304p. ISBN:0-7141-2558-X, ISBN13: 978-0-7141-2558-9. Dewey:981/.01. LCCN:2002-392005.
Audience: **g,l,u,f.**

Archaeology > Archaeology by Continent > Europe

Balter, Michael **GN776.32.T9B35 2005**
The Goddess and the Bull: Catalhöyük: An Archaeological Journey to the Dawn of Civilization. Trade Cloth. Simon & Schuster. New York, NY. 2004. 416p. ISBN:0-7432-4360-9, ISBN13: 978-0-7432-4360-5. Dewey:939/.2. LCCN:2004-057413.
Audience: **l,u.** *Choice, 2006.*

Bogucki, Peter I. & Crabtree, Pam J. (Editor, Translators) **D62.A52 2004**
Ancient Europe 8000 B.C.—A.D. 1000: An Encyclopedia of the Barbarian World. Trade Cloth. Thomson Gale. Farmington Hills, MI. 2003. ISBN:0-684-80670-3, ISBN13: 978-0-684-80670-9. Dewey:936. LCCN:2003-015251.
Audience: **g,l,u,f.**

Bradley, Richard **GN776.2.A1B73 1998**
Significance of Monuments: On the Shaping of Human Experience in Neolithic and Bronze Age Europe. Paper over Boards. Routledge. New York, NY. 1998. 192p. ISBN:0-415-15203-8, ISBN13: 978-0-415-15203-7. Dewey:936. LCCN:97-027536.
Audience: **l,u.**

Chapman, Robert **GN778.22.S6C47 1989**
Emerging Complexity: The Later Prehistory of South-East Spain, Iberia and the West Mediterranean. Cloth Text. Cambridge University Press. New York, NY. 1990. 318p. New Studies in Archaeology ISBN:0-521-23207-4, ISBN13: 978-0-521-23207-4. Dewey:936.6. LCCN:89-036122.
Audience: **u,f.** *Choice, 1991.*

Chippindale, Christopher **DA142**
Stonehenge Complete. Ed. 3. Trade Paper. Thames & Hudson. New York, NY. 2004. 312p. ISBN:0-500-28467-9, ISBN13: 978-0-500-28467-4. Dewey:936.2/319. LCCN:2003-110208.
Audience: **g,l,u,f.**

Collis, John **GN780.2.A1**
European Iron Age. Ed. 2. Trade Paper. Routledge. New York, NY. 1997. 192p. ISBN:0-415-15139-2, ISBN13: 978-0-415-15139-9. Dewey:936.
Audience: **l,u.**

Cornell, Tim **DG233.C67 1995**
Beginnings of Rome: Italy and Rome from the Bronze Age to the Punic Wars (c. 1000-264 B. C.). Trade Paper. Routledge. New York, NY. 1995. 528p. History of the Ancient World Ser. ISBN:0-415-01596-0, ISBN13: 978-0-415-01596-7. Dewey:937/.01. LCCN:94-043757.
Audience: **u,f.**

Cunliffe, Barry W. **D80**
Facing the Ocean: The Atlantic and Its Peoples 8000 BC-AD 1500. Trade Paper. Oxford University Press, Inc. New York, NY. 2004. 608p. ISBN:0-19-285355-4, ISBN13: 978-0-19-285355-4. Dewey:936.
Audience: **u,f.**

Cunliffe, Barry W. (Editor) **GN803.O98 2001**
The Oxford Illustrated History of Prehistoric Europe. Trade Paper. Oxford University Press, Inc. New York, NY. 2001. 544p. Oxford Illustrated Histories Ser. ISBN:0-19-285441-0, ISBN13: 978-0-19-285441-4. Dewey:936.
Audience: **g,l,u,f.**

Gregg, Susan A. **GN776.2.A1G73 1988**
Foragers and Farmers: Population Interaction and Agricultural Expansion in Prehistoric Europe. Trade Paper. University of Chicago Press. Chicago, IL. 1988. 296p. Prehistoric Archeology and Ecology Ser. ISBN:0-226-30736-0, ISBN13: 978-0-226-30736-7. Dewey:936. LCCN:88-021926.
Audience: **u,f.**

Harding, A. F. **GN778.2.A1H38 2000**
European Societies in the Bronze Age. Norman Yoffee, Susan Alcock, Tom Dillehay, Stephen Shennan & Carla Sinopoli (Contribution by). Trade Paper. Cambridge University Press. New York, NY. 2000. 570p. World Archaeology Ser. ISBN:0-521-36729-8, ISBN13: 978-0-521-36729-5. Dewey:936.
Audience: **l,u,f.** *Choice, 2001.*

Marciniak, Arkadiusz **GN776.22.C36M37 2005**
Placing Animals in the Neolithic: Social Zooarchaeology of Prehistoric Farming Communities. University of London, Institute of Archaeology Staff (Contribution by). Paper over Boards. Taylor & Francis Group. Abingdon, 2005. 304p. ISBN:1-84472-092-6, ISBN13: 978-1-84472-092-7. Dewey:338.19409012. LCCN:2006-271542.
Audience: **u,f.**

Menotti, Francesco **GN803.L64 2004**
Living on the Lake in Prehistoric Europe: 150 Years of Lake-Dwelling Research. Paper over Boards. Routledge. New York, NY. 2004. 304p. ISBN:0-415-31719-3, ISBN13: 978-0-415-31719-1. Dewey:936. LCCN:2003-026816.
Audience: **u,f.**

Osborne, Robin & Cunliffe, Barry W. (Editors) **DE86**
Mediterranean Urbanization 800-600 BC. Trade Cloth. Oxford University Press, Inc. New York, NY. 2006. 300p. Proceedings of the British Academy Ser., Vol. 126 ISBN:0-19-726325-9, ISBN13: 978-0-19-726325-9. Dewey:938.02. LCCN:2006-275050.
Audience: **u,f.**

Whitley, James **DF77.W537 2001**
The Archaeology of Ancient Greece. Norman Yoffee, Susan Alcock, Tom Dillehay, Stephen Shennan & Carla Sinopoli (Contribution by). Trade Paper. Cambridge University Press. New York, NY. 2001. 510p. World Archaeology Ser. ISBN:0-521-62733-8, ISBN13: 978-0-521-62733-7. Dewey:938. LCCN:2001-018438.
Audience: **l,u,f.** *Choice, 2003, 2002.*

Whittle, Alasdair W. R. **GN776.2.A1W45 1996**
Europe in the Neolithic: The Creation of New Worlds. Ed. 2. Norman Yoffee (Contribution by). Cloth Text. Cambridge University Press. New York, NY. 1996. 459p. World Archaeology Ser. ISBN:0-521-44476-4, ISBN13: 978-0-521-44476-7. Dewey:936. LCCN:95-012812.
Audience: **l,u,f.**

Archaeology > Archaeology by Continent > Australia and the Pacific

Bellwood, Peter S. **GN670.B36**
The Polynesians: Prehistory of an Island People. Trade Cloth. Thames & Hudson. New York, NY. 1978. 180p. ISBN:0-500-02093-0, ISBN13: 978-0-500-02093-7. Dewey:996. LCCN:78-055086.
Audience: **g,l,u,f.** B

Bellwood, Peter S. **GN855.I6B45 1997**
Prehistory of the Indo-Malaysian Archipelago. Ed. 2. Trade Cloth. University of Hawaii Press. Honolulu, HI. 1997. 400p. ISBN:0-8248-1883-0, ISBN13: 978-0-8248-1883-8. Dewey:959/.01. LCCN:96-044400.
Audience: **u,f.** *Choice, 1986.*

Flood, Josephine **GN875.A8F56 1990**
Archaeology of the Dreamtime: The Story of Prehistoric Australia and Its People. Cloth over Boards. Yale University Press. Cumberland, RI. 1990. 304p. ISBN:0-300-04924-2, ISBN13: 978-0-300-04924-4. Dewey:994.01. LCCN:90-070927.
Audience: **u,f.**

Glover, Ian & Bellwood, Peter **DS523.S65 2004**
Southeast Asia: From Prehistory to History. Paper over Boards. Taylor & Francis Group. Philadelphia, PA. 2004. 376p. ISBN:0-415-29777-X, ISBN13: 978-0-415-29777-6. Dewey:959. LCCN:2003-016628.
Audience: **l,u,f.**

Kirch, Patrick V. **GN871.K57 1997**
The Lapita Peoples: Ancestors of the Oceanic World. Book, Other. Blackwell Publishing, Inc. Malden, MA. 1996. 384p. The Peoples of Southeast Asia and the Pacific Ser. ISBN:1-55786-112-9, ISBN13: 978-1-55786-112-2. Dewey:995. LCCN:96-008287.
Audience: **l,u,f.** *Choice, 1997.*

Kirch, Patrick V. **GN871.K575 2000**
On the Road of the Winds: An Archaeological History of the Pacific Islands before European Contact. Trade Cloth. University of California Press. Berkeley, CA. 2000. 446p. ISBN:0-520-22347-0, ISBN13: 978-0-520-22347-9. Dewey:995. LCCN:99-036664.
Audience: **g,l,u,f.** *Choice, 2000.*

Lourandos, Harry **GN871.L68 1997**
Continent of Hunter-Gatherers: New Perspectives in Australian Prehistory. Trade Cloth. Cambridge University Press. New York, NY. 1997. 408p. ISBN:0-521-35106-5, ISBN13: 978-0-521-35106-5. Dewey:994/.01. LCCN:96-028528.
Audience: **u,f.**

Spriggs, Matthew **GN668.S67 1997**
The Island Melanesians. Trade Cloth. Blackwell Publishing, Inc. Malden, MA. 1997. 320p. The Peoples of Southeast Asia and the Pacific Ser. ISBN:0-631-16727-7, ISBN13: 978-0-631-16727-3. Dewey:305.8995. LCCN:96-027372.
Audience: **l,u,f.** *Choice, 1998.*

Archaeology > Historical Archaeology

Baram, Uzi & Carroll, Lynda (Editors) **DR485.H536 2000**
The Historical Archaeology of the Ottoman Empire: Breaking New Ground. Trade Cloth. Springer. New York, NY. 2000. 282p. Contributions to Global Historical Archaeology Ser. ISBN:0-306-46311-3, ISBN13: 978-0-306-46311-2. Dewey:956.1/015. LCCN:00-022108.
Audience: **u,f.** *Choice, 2001.*

Casella, E. C. & Symonds, J. (Editors) **T37**
Industrial Archaeology: Future Directions. Trade Cloth. Springer. New York, NY. 2005. 330p. Contributions to Global Historical Archaeology Ser. ISBN:0-387-22608-7, ISBN13: 978-0-387-22608-8. Dewey:609.
Audience: **u,f.**

De Cunzo, Lu Ann & Jameson, John H. **E159.5.U55 2005**
Unlocking the Past: Celebrating Historical Archaeology in North America. Society for Historical Archaeology Staff (Contribution by). Trade Cloth. University Press of Florida. Gainesville, FL. 2005. 256p. ISBN:0-8130-2796-9, ISBN13: 978-0-8130-2796-8. Dewey:973. LCCN:2004-066138.
Audience: **g,l,u,f.** *Choice, 2006.*

Deagan, Kathleen A. & Cruxent, Jose Maria **F1939.I8D42 2002**
Archaeology at La Isabela: America's First European Town. Cloth over Boards. Yale University Press. Cumberland, RI. 2002. 416p. ISBN:0-300-09041-2, ISBN13: 978-0-300-09041-3. Dewey:972.93. LCCN:2001-057515.
Audience: **u,f.** *Choice, 2003.*

Deagan, Kathleen A. & MacMahon, Darcie A. **F319.F734D43 1995**
Fort Mose: Colonial America's Black Fortress of Freedom. Trade Cloth. University Press of Florida. Gainesville, FL. 1995. 125p. ISBN:0-8130-1351-8, ISBN13: 978-0-8130-1351-0. Dewey:975.9/18. LCCN:94-042953.
Audience: **l,u,f.**

Farnsworth, Paul (Editor) **F1609.5.I83 2001**
Island Lives: Historical Archaeologies of the Caribbean. Trade Paper. University of Alabama Press. Tuscaloosa, AL. 2001. 408p. ISBN:0-8173-1093-2, ISBN13: 978-0-8173-1093-6. Dewey:972.9. LCCN:2001-001002.
Audience: **l,u,f.** *Choice, 2002.*

Handler, Jerome & Lange, Frederick **HT1105.B3H34**
Plantation Slavery in Barbados: An Archaeological and Historical Investigation. Trade Cloth. Replica Books. Bridgewater, NJ. 2000. 382p. ISBN:0-7351-0319-4, ISBN13: 978-0-7351-0319-1. Dewey:301.44/93/0972981.
Audience: **u,f.**

Hicks, Dan & Beaudry, Mary C. (Editors) **CC165**
The Cambridge Companion to Historical Archaeology. Cloth Text. Cambridge University Press. New York, NY. 2006. 420p. ISBN:0-521-85375-3, ISBN13: 978-0-521-85375-0. Dewey:930.1.
Audience: **l,u,f.**

Jamieson, Ross W. **F3791.C9J36 2000**
Domestic Architecture and Power: The Historical Archaeology of Colonial Ecuador. Trade Cloth. Springer. New York, NY. 1999. 246p. Contributions to Global Historical Archaeology Ser. ISBN:0-306-46176-5, ISBN13: 978-0-306-46176-7. Dewey:986.6/24. LCCN:99-046707.
Audience: **u,f.** *Choice, 2000.*

Noel-Hume, Ivor **F229.N84 1997**
The Virginia Adventure: Roanoke to James Towne: An Archaeological and Historical Odyssey. Trade Paper. University Press of Virginia. Charlottesville, VA. 1997. 519p. Virginia Bookshelf Ser. ISBN:0-8139-1758-1, ISBN13: 978-0-8139-1758-0. Dewey:975.5/425. LCCN:97-016651.
Audience: **g,l,u,f.**

Orser, Charles E. **CC77.H5O77 2004**
Historical Archaeology. Ed. 2. Trade Paper. Prentice Hall PTR. Upper Saddle River, NJ. 2003. 384p. ISBN:0-13-111561-8, ISBN13: 978-0-13-111561-3. Dewey:930.1/09. LCCN:2003-022461.
Audience: **l,u.**

Schmidt, Peter **DT13.S35 2006**
Historical Archaeology in Africa: Representation, Social Memory, and Oral Traditions. Trade Cloth. AltaMira Press. Walnut Creek, CA. 2006. 240p. The African Archaeology Ser. ISBN:0-7591-0964-8, ISBN13: 978-0-7591-0964-3. Dewey:960/.1. LCCN:2005-035499.
Audience: **u,f.**

Silliman, Stephen **CC77.H5H565 2006**
Historical Archaeology. Martin Hall (Editor). Trade Cloth. Blackwell Publishing, Inc. Malden, MA. 2006. 360p. Blackwell Studies in Global Archaeology, Vol. 9 ISBN:1-4051-0750-2, ISBN13: 978-1-4051-0750-1. Dewey:930.1. LCCN:2005-017584.
Audience: **l,u.**

Society for Historical Archaeology Staff **CC77.U5S67 2003**
Submerged Cultural Resource Management: Preserving and Interpreting Our Maritime Heritage: Proceedings of the Society for Historical Archaeology Conference on Historical and Underwater Archaeology (33rd: 2000: Quebec). Della A. Scott-Ireton & James D. Spirek (Editors). Trade Paper. Springer. New York, NY. 2003. 198p. The Plenum Series in Underwater Archaeology ISBN:0-306-47856-0, ISBN13: 978-0-306-47856-7. Dewey:930.1/028/04. LCCN:2003-050650.
Audience: **u,f.**

Biological Anthropology > General and Introductory Works

Delisle, Richard G. **GN282.D43 2006**
Debating Human Kind's Place in Nature; 1860-2000: The Nature of Paleoanthropology. Trade Paper. Prentice Hall PTR. Upper Saddle River, NJ. 2006. 528p. ISBN:0-13-177390-9, ISBN13: 978-0-13-177390-5. Dewey:599.93/8. LCCN:2005-054958.
Audience: **g,l,u,f.**

Fuentes, Agustin **GN51.F84 2006**
Core Concepts in Biological Anthropology. Trade Cloth. McGraw-Hill Companies, The. New York, NY. 2006. xxiii, 388p. ISBN:0-7674-2426-3, ISBN13: 978-0-7674-2426-4. Dewey:599.9. LCCN:2005-044394.
Audience: **l,u,f.**

Katzenberg, M. Anne & Saunders, Shelley R. (Editors) **GN60.H82 2000**
Biological Anthropology of the Human Skeleton. Trade Cloth. John Wiley & Sons, Inc. Hoboken, NJ. 2000. 528p. ISBN:0-471-31616-4, ISBN13: 978-0-471-31616-9. Dewey:599.9/47. LCCN:99-054718.
Audience: **l,u,f.**

Larsen, Clark Spencer **CC77.B8**
Bioarchaeology: Interpreting Behavior from the Human Skeleton. R. A. Foley, Nina Jablonski, Michael Little, C. G. Nicholas Mascie-Taylor, Karen Strier & Kenneth M. Weiss (Contribution by). Trade Paper. Cambridge University Press. New York, NY. 1999. 474p. Cambridge Studies in Biological Anthropology, Vol. 21 ISBN:0-521-65834-9, ISBN13: 978-0-521-65834-8. Dewey:599./97.
Audience: **u,f.**

Marks, Jonathan **GN280.7M37 2002**
What It Means to Be 98% Chimpanzee: Apes, People, and Their Genes. Trade Cloth. University of California Press. Berkeley, CA. 2002. 328p. ISBN:0-520-22615-1, ISBN13: 978-0-520-22615-9. Dewey:599.93/5. LCCN:2001-007085.
Audience: **g,l,u,f.** *Choice, 2002.*

Mascie-Taylor, C. G. Nicholas (Editor, Contribution by) **GN60.A67 1991**
Applications of Biological Anthropology to Human Affairs. Gabriel W. Lasker (Editor), R. A. Foley, Nina Jablonski, Michael Little, Karen Strier & Kenneth M. Weiss (Contribution by). Trade Cloth. Cambridge University Press. New York, NY. 1991. 262p. Cambridge Studies in Biological Anthropology, No. 8 ISBN:0-521-38112-6, ISBN13: 978-0-521-38112-3. Dewey:573. LCCN:90-025499.
Audience: **u,f.** *Choice, 1992.*

Montagu, Ashley **HQ1206.M65 1999**
The Natural Superiority of Women. Ed. 5. Trade Cloth. AltaMira Press. Walnut Creek, CA. 1999. 300p. ISBN:0-7619-8981-1, ISBN13: 978-0-7619-8981-3. Dewey:305.4. LCCN:98-040173.
Audience: **g,l,u,f.**

Park, Michael Alan **GN60.B54 2005**
Biological Anthropology: An Introductory Reader. Ed. 4. Paper Text. McGraw-Hill Higher Education. Burr Ridge, IL. 2004. 272p. ISBN:0-07-286889-9, ISBN13: 978-0-07-286889-0. Dewey:599.9. LCCN:2004-042673.
Audience: **g,l,u,f.**

Quigley, Christine **GN70.Q54 2001**
Skulls and Skeletons: Human Bone Collections and Accumulations. Cloth Text. McFarland & Company, Incorporated Publishers. Jefferson, NC. 2001. 271p. ISBN:0-7864-1068-X, ISBN13: 978-0-7864-1068-2. Dewey:599.9/47. LCCN:2001-030340.
Audience: **g,l,u,f.** *Choice, 2002.*

Rhine, Stanley **GN69.8.R45 1998**
Bone Voyage: A Journey in Forensic Anthropology. Trade Cloth. University of New Mexico Press. Albuquerque, NM. 1998. 268p. ISBN:0-8263-1967-X, ISBN13: 978-0-8263-1967-8. Dewey:614/.1. LCCN:98-023459.
Audience: **g,l,u,f.** *Choice, 1999.*

Strum, Shirley C. & Lindburg, Donald G. **GN60.N45 1999**
The New Physical Anthropology. David Hamburg (Editor). Cloth Text. Prentice Hall PTR. Upper Saddle River, NJ. 1998. 285p. Advances in Human Evolution Ser. ISBN:0-13-206517-7, ISBN13: 978-0-13-206517-7. Dewey:599.9. LCCN:98-037467.
Audience: **l,u,f.**

Sussman, Robert W. (Author, Editor) **GN635.9.B532 1999**
The Biological Basis of Human Behavior: A Critical Review. Ed. 2. Trade Paper. Prentice Hall PTR. Upper Saddle River, NJ. 1998. 448p. ISBN:0-13-799735-3, ISBN13: 978-0-13-799735-0. Dewey:304.5. LCCN:98-025995.
Audience: **l,u,f.**

Thompson, Jennifer L. (Editor), et al. **GN281.4.P375 2003**
Patterns of Growth and Development in the Genus Homo. Gail Krovitz & Andrew Nelson (Editors), R. A. Foley, Nina Jablonski, Michael Little, Nicholas C. G. Mascie-Taylor, Karen Strier & Kenneth M. Weiss (Contribution by). Trade Cloth. Cambridge University Press. New York, NY. 2003. 470p. Cambridge Studies in Biological and Evolutionary Anthropology Ser., Vol. 37 ISBN:0-521-82272-6, ISBN13: 978-0-521-82272-5. Dewey:599.93/8. LCCN:2003-053080.
Audience: **u,f.**

Biological Anthropology > Human Evolution

Arsuaga, Juan Luis & Martínez, Ignacio **GN282**
The Chosen Species: The Long March of Human Evolution. Rachel Gomme (Translator), Mauricio Anton (Illustrator). Trade Cloth. Blackwell Publishing, Inc. Malden, MA. 2005. 296p. ISBN:1-4051-1532-7, ISBN13: 978-1-4051-1532-2. Dewey:599.93/8. LCCN:2004-027275.
Audience: **l,u.**

Brantingham, Jeffrey P. (Editor), et al. **GN772.2.A1E37 2004**
The Early Upper Paleolithic Beyond Western Europe. Steven L. Kuhn & Kristopher W. Kerry (Editors). Trade Cloth. University of California Press. Berkeley, CA. 2004. 384p. ISBN:0-520-23851-6, ISBN13: 978-0-520-23851-0. Dewey:939/.6. LCCN:2003-010136.
Audience: **u,f.** *Choice, 2005.*

Cachel, Susan **GN281**
Primate and Human Evolution. C. G. Nicholas Mascie-Taylor, R. A. Foley, Nina Jablonski, Karen Strier, Michael Little & Kenneth M. Weiss (Contribution by). Trade Cloth. Cambridge University Press. New York, NY. 2006. 488p. Cambridge Studies in Biological and Evolutionary Anthropology Ser. ISBN:0-521-82942-9, ISBN13: 978-0-521-82942-7. Dewey:599.938. LCCN:2006-296967.
Audience: **l,u,f.**

Finlayson, Clive **GN285.F55 2004**
Neanderthals and Modern Humans: An Ecological and Evolutionary Perspective. Nina Jablonski, Michael Little, C. G. Nicholas Mascie-Taylor, Karen Strier & Kenneth M. Weiss (Contribution by). Trade Cloth. Cambridge University Press. New York, NY. 2004. 266p. Cambridge Studies in Biological and Evolutionary Anthropology Ser., Vol. 38 ISBN:0-521-82087-1, ISBN13: 978-0-521-82087-5. Dewey:569.9. LCCN:2003-055285.
Audience: **l,u,f.**

Kennedy, Kenneth A. R. **GN58.S64K46 2000**
God-Apes and Fossil Men: Paleoanthropology of South Asia. Trade Cloth. University of Michigan Press. Chicago, IL. 2000. 504p. ISBN:0-472-11013-6, ISBN13: 978-0-472-11013-1. Dewey:599.9. LCCN:00-022837.
Audience: **l,u,f.** *Choice, 2001.*

Kingdon, Jonathan **GN282.K54 2003**
Lowly Origin: Where, When, and Why Our Ancestors First Stood Up. Trade Cloth. Princeton University Press. Princeton, NJ. 2003. 408p. ISBN:0-691-05086-4, ISBN13: 978-0-691-05086-7. Dewey:599.93/8. LCCN:2002-072852.
Audience: **g,l,u,f.** *Choice, 2003.*

Klein, Richard G. **GN281.K55 1989**
The Human Career: Human Biological and Cultural Origins. Trade Cloth. University of Chicago Press. Chicago, IL. 1999. 544p. ISBN:0-226-43962-3, ISBN13: 978-0-226-43962-4. Dewey:599.93/8. LCCN:88-036259.
Audience: **u,f.** *Choice, 1990.*

Mai, Larry L., et al. **QP34.5.M24 2004**
The Cambridge Dictionary of Human Biology and Evolution. Marcus Young Owl & M. Patricia Kersting (Authors). Trade Paper, Perfect. Cambridge University Press. New York, NY. 2005. 668p. ISBN:0-521-66486-1, ISBN13: 978-0-521-66486-8. Dewey:612/.003. LCCN:2004-043553.
Audience: **g,l,u,f.** *Choice, 2006.*

Marks, Jonathan **GN280.7M37 2002**
What It Means to Be 98% Chimpanzee: Apes, People, and Their Genes. Trade Cloth. University of California Press. Berkeley, CA. 2002. 328p. ISBN:0-520-22615-1, ISBN13: 978-0-520-22615-9. Dewey:599.93/5. LCCN:2001-007085.
Audience: **g,l,u,f.** *Choice, 2002.*

Richerson, Peter J. & Boyd, Robert **GN360.R5 2006**
Not by Genes Alone: How Culture Transformed Human Evolution. Trade Paper. University of Chicago Press. Chicago, IL. 2006. 342p. ISBN:0-226-71212-5, ISBN13: 978-0-226-71212-3. Dewey:306.
Audience: **g,l,u,f.**

Richerson, Peter J. & Boyd, Robert **GN360.R5 2005**
Not by Genes Alone: How Culture Transformed Human Evolution. Trade Cloth. University of Chicago Press. Chicago,

IL. 2004. 342p. ISBN:0-226-71284-2, ISBN13: 978-0-226-71284-0. Dewey:306. LCCN:2004-006601.
Audience: **g,l,u,f.**

Rightmire, G. Philip **GN284.R54 1993**
The Evolution of Homo Erectus: Comparative Anatomical Studies of an Extinct Human Species. Trade Paper. Cambridge University Press. New York, NY. 1993. 272p. ISBN:0-521-44998-7, ISBN13: 978-0-521-44998-4. Dewey:569.9.
Audience: **u,f.**

Schwartz, Jeffrey H., et al. **GN282**
The Human Fossil Record, Set. Ian Tattersall, Douglas C. Broadfield, Ralph L. Holloway & Michael S. Yuan (Authors). Trade Cloth, Quantity Pack, In A Box. John Wiley & Sons, Inc. Hoboken, NJ. 2005. 1843p. ISBN:0-471-67864-3, ISBN13: 978-0-471-67864-9. Dewey:569.9.
Audience: **l,u,f.**

Stringer, Chris **GN281**
Complete World of Human Evolution. Trade Cloth. Thames & Hudson. New York, NY. 2005. 240p. ISBN:0-500-05132-1, ISBN13: 978-0-500-05132-0. Dewey:599.93/8. LCCN:2004-110563.
Audience: **g,l,u,f.** *Choice, 2005.*

Stringer, Christopher & McKie, Robin **GN281.S87 1997**
African Exodus: The Origins of Modern Humanity. Trade Cloth. Henry Holt & Company. New York, NY. 1997. 304p. ISBN:0-8050-2759-9, ISBN13: 978-0-8050-2759-4. Dewey:599.93/8. LCCN:96-037718.
Audience: **g,l,u,f.** *Choice, 1997.*

Tattersall, Ian **GN281.T357 1995**
The Fossil Trail: How We Know What We Think We Know about Human Evolution. Trade Cloth. Oxford University Press, Inc. New York, NY. 1995. 288p. ISBN:0-19-506101-2, ISBN13: 978-0-19-506101-7. Dewey:573.2. LCCN:94-031633.
Audience: **g,l,u,f.** *Choice, 1995.*

Tattersall, Ian **GN281**
The Monkey in the Mirror: Essays on the Science of What Makes Us Human. Trade Paper. Harcourt Trade Publishers. New York, NY. 2003. 240p. ISBN:0-15-602706-2, ISBN13: 978-0-15-602706-9. Dewey:599.93/8.
Audience: **g,l,u,f.** *Choice, 2002.*

Tattersall, Ian, et al. **GN285**
The Last Human: A Guide to 19 Species of Extinct Humans. Kenneth Mowbray & Esteban Sarmiento (Authors), Donald C. Johanson (Foreword by), Meave G. Leakey (Afterword by), G. J. Sawyer, Studio V Staff & Viktor Deak (Other Primary Creators). Cloth over Boards. Yale University Press. Cumberland, RI. 2007. 256p. ISBN:0-300-10047-7, ISBN13: 978-0-300-10047-1. Dewey:573.3.
Audience: **g,l,u,f.**

Weiner, J. S. **GN282.5**
The Piltdown Forgery. Ed. 2. Chris Stringer (Introduction by). Trade Paper. Oxford University Press, Inc. New York, NY. 2004. 232p. ISBN:0-19-860780-6, ISBN13: 978-0-19-860780-9. Dewey:573.3. LCCN:2004-268231.
Audience: **g,l,u,f.**

Wolpoff, Milford H. **GN2**
Modern Human Origins: The Other View. James K. Whittaker (Editor). Trade Cloth. Aldine Transaction. Somerset, NJ. 2004. 376p. Modern Applications of Social Work Ser. ISBN:0-202-30732-8, ISBN13: 978-0-202-30732-9. Dewey:301.
Audience: **l,u,f.**

Biological Anthropology > Paleoanthropology

Arsuaga, Juan Luis de **GN285**
The Neanderthal's Necklace: In Search of the First Thinkers. Trade Cloth. John Wiley & Sons, Inc. Hoboken, NJ. 2003. 356p. ISBN:0-470-85157-0, ISBN13: 978-0-470-85157-9. Dewey:599.9/38.
Audience: **g,l,u,f.**

Boaz, Noel T. & Ciochon, Russell L. **GN284.7.B63 2004**
Dragon Bone Hill: An Ice-Age Saga of Homo Erectus. Trade Cloth. Oxford University Press, Inc. New York, NY. 2004. 252p. ISBN:0-19-515291-3, ISBN13: 978-0-19-515291-3. Dewey:569.9. LCCN:2003-012339.
Audience: **l,u,f.**

Brantingham, Jeffrey P. (Editor), et al. **GN772.2.A1E37 2004**
The Early Upper Paleolithic Beyond Western Europe. Steven L. Kuhn & Kristopher W. Kerry (Editors). Trade Cloth. University of California Press. Berkeley, CA. 2004. 384p. ISBN:0-520-23851-6, ISBN13: 978-0-520-23851-0. Dewey:939/.6. LCCN:2003-010136.
Audience: **u,f.** *Choice, 2005.*

Clottes, Jean **GN772.2.M3C57 2003**
Chauvet Cave: The Art of Earliest Times. Paul G. Bahn (Translator). Trade Cloth. University of Utah Press. Salt Lake City, UT. 2003. 226p. ISBN:0-87480-758-1, ISBN13: 978-0-87480-758-5. Dewey:709/.0113/09449. LCCN:2002-116011.
Audience: **l,u,f.** *Choice, 2003.*

Gamble, Clive **GN772.2.A1G38 1999**
The Palaeolithic Societies of Europe. Ed. 2. Susan Alcock, Tom Dillehay, Stephen Shennan, Carla Sinopoli & Norman Yoffee (Contribution by). Trade Paper. Cambridge University Press. New York, NY. 1999. 527p. World Archaeology Ser. ISBN:0-521-65872-1, ISBN13: 978-0-521-65872-0. Dewey:936. LCCN:98-038087.
Audience: **l,u,f.** *Choice, 2000.*

Goring-Morris, A. Nigel & Belfer-Cohen, Anna (Editors) **GN772.32.N4M67 2003**
More than Meets the Eye: Studies on Upper Palaeolithic Diversity in the Near East. Trade Cloth. Oxbow Books, Ltd. Oxford, 2002. 306p. ISBN:1-84217-082-1, ISBN13: 978-1-84217-082-3. Dewey:939/.4. LCCN:2004-300766.
Audience: **u,f.**

Graslund, Bo **GN282.G73 2005**
Early Humans and Their World. Paper over Boards. Routledge. New York, NY. 2005. 192p. ISBN:0-415-35344-0, ISBN13: 978-0-415-35344-1. Dewey:599.93/8. LCCN:2004-020988.
Audience: **l,u.**

Guthrie, R. Dale **GN772G87 2005**
The Nature of Paleolithic Art. Trade Cloth. University of Chicago Press. Chicago, IL. 2006. 520p. ISBN:0-226-31126-0, ISBN13: 978-0-226-31126-5. Dewey:930.1/2. LCCN:2004-014399.
Audience: **g,l,u,f.** *Choice, 2006.*

Megarry, Tim **GN281.M444 1995**
Society in Prehistory: The Origins of Human Culture. Trade Cloth. New York University Press. New York, NY. 1995. 216p. ISBN:0-8147-5537-2, ISBN13: 978-0-8147-5537-2. Dewey:304.5. LCCN:95-037355.
Audience: **l,u,f.** *Choice, 1996.*

Mellars, Paul **GN285.M45 1996**
The Neanderthal Legacy: An Archaeological Perspective of Western Europe. Trade Cloth. Princeton University Press. Princeton, NJ. 1995. 494p. ISBN:0-691-03493-1, ISBN13: 978-0-691-03493-5. Dewey:936. LCCN:95-004300.
Audience: **l,u,f.** *Choice, 1996.*

Petraglia, M. D. & Korisettar, Ravi **GN771.E27 1998**
Early Human Behaviour in the Global Context: The Rise and Diversity of the Lower Paleolithic Period. Paper over Boards. Routledge. New York, NY. 1998. 512p. One World Archaeology Ser. ISBN:0-415-11763-1, ISBN13: 978-0-415-11763-0. Dewey:930.1/2. LCCN:97-042581.
Audience: **u,f.**

Schick, Kathy D. & Toth, Nicholas **GN799.T6.S35 1993**
Making Silent Stones Speak: Human Evolution and the Dawn of Technology. Trade Cloth. Simon & Schuster. New York, NY. 1993. 352p. ISBN:0-671-69371-9, ISBN13: 978-0-671-69371-8. Dewey:573.2. LCCN:92-035337.
Audience: **g,l,u,f.** *Choice, 1993.*

Soffer, O. & Praslov, N. D. **GN772.2.A1.F76 1993**
From Kostenki to Clovis: Upper Paleolithic-Paleo-Indian Adaptations. Trade Cloth. Basic Books. New York, NY. 1993. 354p. Interdisciplinary Contributions to Archaeology Ser. ISBN:0-306-44271-X, ISBN13: 978-0-306-44271-1. Dewey:930.12. LCCN:92-036558.
Audience: **u,f.** *Choice, 1993.*

Straus, L. G. **GN836.C33.S77 1992**
Iberia Before the Iberians: The Stone Age Prehistory of Cantabrian Spain. Trade Cloth. University of New Mexico Press. Albuquerque, NM. 1992. 344p. ISBN:0-8263-1336-1, ISBN13: 978-0-8263-1336-2. Dewey:936.6. LCCN:91-039171.
Audience: **l,u,f.** *Choice, 1992.*

Trinkaus, Erik **GN285.T73 1993**
The Neanderthals: Changing the Image of Mankind. Trade Cloth. Alfred A. Knopf Inc. New York, NY. 1993. xxii, 454p. ISBN:0-394-58900-9, ISBN13: 978-0-394-58900-8. Dewey:573.3. LCCN:91-047553.
Audience: **g,l,u,f.** *Choice, 1993.*

Wilson, Peter J. **GN360.W55 1988**
The Domestication of the Human Species. Trade Cloth. Yale University Press. Cumberland, RI. 1988. xvi, 201p. ISBN:0-300-04243-4, ISBN13: 978-0-300-04243-6. Dewey:306. LCCN:88-005516.
Audience: **l,u,f.** *Choice, 1989.*

Biological Anthropology > Human Groups, Discussions of Race

Aguirre, Adalberto Jr. & Baker, David V. **E184.A1**
Sources: Notable Selections in Race and Ethnicity. Ed. 2. Trade Paper. McGraw-Hill Higher Education. Burr Ridge, IL. 1998. 416p. ISBN:0-697-34332-4, ISBN13: 978-0-697-34332-1. Dewey:305.8/00973.
Audience: **g,l,u,f.**

Alland, Alexander **HT1521.A39 2002**
Race in Mind: Race, IQ, and Other Racisms. Cloth over Boards. Palgrave Macmillan. New York, NY. 2002. 224p. ISBN:0-312-23838-X, ISBN13: 978-0-312-23838-4. Dewey:305.8. LCCN:2002-020117.
Audience: **g,l,u,f.** *Choice, 2003.*

Corcos, Alain F. **GN269.C69 1997**
The Myth of Human Races. Trade Paper. Michigan State University Press. East Lansing, MI. 1997. 214p. ISBN:0-87013-439-6, ISBN13: 978-0-87013-439-5. Dewey:305.8. LCCN:97-017769.
Audience: **g,l,u,f.**

Firmin, Joseph-Antenor **HT1521.F513 2002**
The Equality of the Human Races: Positivist Anthropology. Trade Paper. University of Illinois Press. Champaign, IL. 2002. 536p. ISBN:0-252-07102-6, ISBN13: 978-0-252-07102-7. Dewey:305.8. LCCN:2002-025372.
Audience: **g,l,u,f.**

Graves, Joseph L. Jr. **GN269.G73 2001**
The Emperor's New Clothes: Biological Theories of Race at the Millennium. Trade Cloth. Rutgers University Press. Piscataway, NJ. 2004. 272p. ISBN:0-8135-2847-X, ISBN13: 978-0-8135-2847-2. Dewey:599.97. LCCN:00-034205.
Audience: **l,u,f.** *Choice, 2001.*

Marks, Jonathan **GN62.8.M37**
Human Biodiversity: Genes, Race and History. Trade Cloth. Walter De Gruyter Inc. Ossining, NY. 1995. xiv, 321p. ISBN:3-11-014855-2, ISBN13: 978-3-11-014855-8. Dewey:573.
Audience: **u,f.**

Mielke, James H., et al. **QH431.M525 2006**
Human Biological Variation. Lyle W. Konigsberg & John Relethford (Authors). Trade Paper. Oxford University Press, Inc. New York, NY. 2005. 432p. ISBN:0-19-518871-3, ISBN13: 978-0-19-518871-4. Dewey:599.9/4. LCCN:2005-040639.
Audience: **l,u,f.**

Molnar, Stephen **GN62.8.M64 2001**
Human Variation, Races, Types, and Ethnic Groups. Ed. 5. Trade Paper. Prentice Hall PTR. Upper Saddle River, NJ. 2001. 384p. ISBN:0-13-033668-8, ISBN13: 978-0-13-033668-2. Dewey:599.9. LCCN:2001-021521.
Audience: **l,u,f.**

Linguistic Anthropology > General, Introductory, and Historical Works

Blount, Ben G. (Editor) **P35.L33 1995**
Language, Culture, and Society: A Book of Readings. Ed. 2. Paper Text. Waveland Press, Inc. Prospect Heights, IL. 1995.

608p. ISBN:0-88133-850-8, ISBN13: 978-0-88133-850-8. Dewey:306.4/4. LCCN:96-133955.

Audience: **g,l,u,f.**

Brenneis, Donald & Macaulay, Ronald K. S. (Editors) **P35.M29 1996**
Matrix of Language: Contemporary Linguistic Anthropology. Trade Paper. Westview Press. Boulder, CO. 1996. 352p. ISBN:0-8133-2321-5, ISBN13: 978-0-8133-2321-3. Dewey:306.4/4/089. LCCN:95-043947.

Audience: **l,u,f.**

Coulmas, Florian **Z40.C67 1999**
The Blackwell Encyclopedia of Writing Systems. Trade Paper. Blackwell Publishing, Inc. Malden, MA. 1999. 640p. ISBN:0-631-21481-X, ISBN13: 978-0-631-21481-6. Dewey:411/.03.

Audience: **g,l,u,f.** *Choice, 1997.*

Daniels, Peter T. & Bright, William (Editors) **P211.W714 1996**
The World's Writing Systems. Trade Cloth. Oxford University Press, Inc. New York, NY. 1996. 966p. ISBN:0-19-507993-0, ISBN13: 978-0-19-507993-7. Dewey:411. LCCN:95-002247.

Audience: **g,l,u,f.**

Dryer, Matthew S. & Comrie, Bernard (Editors) **P143**
The World Atlas of Language Structures. Hans-Jorg Bibiko, Hagen Jung & Claudia Schmidt (As told tos). Trade Cloth, CD-ROM. Oxford University Press, Inc. New York, NY. 2005. 712p. ISBN:0-19-925591-1, ISBN13: 978-0-19-925591-7. Dewey:415.90223.

Audience: **g,l,u,f.**

Duranti, Alessandro (Editor) **P35**
A Companion to Linguistic Anthropology. Trade Cloth. Blackwell Publishing, Inc. Malden, MA. 2004. 648p. Blackwell Companions to Anthropology Ser., Vol. 1 ISBN:0-631-22352-5, ISBN13: 978-0-631-22352-8. Dewey:306.44. LCCN:2003-056026.

Audience: **l,u,f.** *Choice, 2004.*

Duranti, Alessandro (Editor) **P35.L48 2001**
Linguistic Anthropology: A Reader. Trade Cloth. Blackwell Publishing, Inc. Malden, MA. 2000. 504p. Blackwell Anthologies in Social and Cultural Anthropology Ser., Vol. 1 ISBN:0-631-22110-7, ISBN13: 978-0-631-22110-4. Dewey:306.4/4/089. LCCN:00-057919.

Audience: **g,l,u,f.**

Foley, William A. **P35.F64 1997**
Anthropological Linguistics. Trade Paper. Blackwell Publishing, Inc. Malden, MA. 1997. 520p. Language in Society Ser., No. 24 ISBN:0-631-15122-2, ISBN13: 978-0-631-15122-7. Dewey:306.4/4/089. LCCN:96-041302.

Audience: **l,u,f.**

Harris, Randy A. **P69**
The Linguistics Wars. Trade Paper. Oxford University Press, Inc. New York, NY. 1995. 368p. ISBN:0-19-509834-X, ISBN13: 978-0-19-509834-1. Dewey:410/.904.

Audience: **g,l,u.** *Choice, 1994.*

Hymes, Dell H. **P35.H95X 1983**
Essays in the History of Linguistic Anthropology. Trade Cloth. John Benjamins Publishing Company. Philadelphia, PA. 1983. 406p. Studies in the History of Linguistics Sciences Ser., Vol. 25 ISBN:90-272-4507-X, ISBN13: 978-90-272-4507-6. Dewey:401/.9. LCCN:83-672353.

Audience: **l,u,f.**

Matthews, Peter H. **P146.M36 2001**
A Short History of Structural Linguistics. Trade Paper. Cambridge University Press. New York, NY. 2001. 174p. ISBN:0-521-62568-8, ISBN13: 978-0-521-62568-5. Dewey:410/.1/8. LCCN:00-045524.

Audience: **l,u,f.** *Choice, 2001.*

Ottenheimer, Harriet Joseph **P35.O94 2006**
The Anthropology of Language: An Introduction to Linguistic Anthropology. Paper Text. Thomson Wadsworth. Belmont, CA. 2005. 336p. ISBN:0-534-59436-0, ISBN13: 978-0-534-59436-7. Dewey:306.44. LCCN:2005-920352.

Audience: **l,u,f.**

Linguistic Anthropology > Theory and Methods

Agar, Michael H. **P35.A37**
Language Shock: Understanding the Culture of Conversation. Trade Paper. HarperCollins Publishers. New York, NY. 1996. 288p. ISBN:0-688-14949-9, ISBN13: 978-0-688-14949-9. Dewey:306.4/4.

Audience: **g,l,u,f.**

Bauman, Richard & Sherzer, Joel (Editors) **P35.E95 1989**
Explorations in the Ethnography of Speaking. Ed. 2. Judith Irvine, Bambi Schieffelin, Marjorie H. Goodwin, Joel Kuipers, Don Kulick, John Lucy, Elinor Ochs & Michael Silverstein (Contribution by). Trade Paper. Cambridge University Press. New York, NY. 1989. 536p. Cambridge Studies in the Social and Cultural Foundations of Language, No. 8 ISBN:0-521-37933-4, ISBN13: 978-0-521-37933-5. Dewey:408.9. LCCN:88-029427.

Audience: **l,u,f.**

Burling, Robbins **P53**
Learning a Field Language. Trade Paper. Waveland Press, Inc. Prospect Heights, IL. 2000. 112p. ISBN:1-57766-123-0, ISBN13: 978-1-57766-123-8. Dewey:418/.007.

Audience: **g,l,u,f.**

Comrie, Bernard **P204.C6 1989**
Language Universals and Linguistic Typology: Syntax and Morphology. Ed. 2. Trade Paper. University of Chicago Press. Chicago, IL. 1989. 275p. ISBN:0-226-11433-3, ISBN13: 978-0-226-11433-0. Dewey:415. LCCN:89-040280.

Audience: **l,u,f.**

Coulmas, Florian (Editor) **P40.H3426 1998**
The Handbook of Sociolinguistics. Trade Paper. Blackwell Publishing, Inc. Malden, MA. 1998. 544p. Blackwell Handbooks in Linguistics ISBN:0-631-21193-4, ISBN13: 978-0-631-21193-8. Dewey:306.44. LCCN:98-026119.

Audience: **l,u,f.**

Headland, Thomas N. (Editor), et al. **GN0033.E48**
Emics and Etics: The Insider/Outsider Debate. Kenneth L. Pike & Marvin Harris (Editors). Trade Paper. Books on Demand. Ann Arbor, MI. 1990. 226p. Frontiers of Anthropology Ser., Vol. 7

ISBN:0-608-04312-5, ISBN13: 978-0-608-04312-8. Dewey:306/.01. LCCN:90-008741.
Audience: **l,u,f.**

Hymes, Dell **P35.H87 1995**
Ethnography, Linguistics, Narrative Inequality: Toward an Understanding of Voice. Paper over Boards. Taylor & Francis Group. Abingdon, 1996. 270p. ISBN:0-7484-0347-7, ISBN13: 978-0-7484-0347-9. Dewey:401. LCCN:95-023856.
Audience: **l,u,f.**

Hymes, Dell **P40.D49 1986**
Directions in Sociolinguistics: The Ethnography of Communication. John J. Gumperz (Editor). Trade Paper. Blackwell Publishing, Inc. Malden, MA. 1986. 608p. ISBN:0-631-14987-2, ISBN13: 978-0-631-14987-3. Dewey:401/.9. LCCN:86-001018.
Audience: **g,l,u,f.**

Moerman, Michael **P95.45.M64 1988**
Talking Culture: Ethnography and Conversation Analysis. Trade Cloth. University of Pennsylvania Press. Philadelphia, PA. 1988. xiii, 211p. University of Pennsylvania Publications in Conduct and Communication Ser. ISBN:0-8122-8072-5, ISBN13: 978-0-8122-8072-2. Dewey:401/.9. LCCN:87-014973.
Audience: **g,l,u,f.** *Choice, 1988.*

Newman, Paul & Ratliff, Martha (Editors) **P128.F53L56 2001**
Linguistic Fieldwork. Cloth Text. Cambridge University Press. New York, NY. 2001. 300p. ISBN:0-521-66049-1, ISBN13: 978-0-521-66049-5. Dewey:410/.7/2. LCCN:00-063073.
Audience: **g,l,u,f.**

Saville-Troike, Muriel **P40.S26 2003**
The Ethnography of Communication: An Introduction. Ed. 3. Trade Cloth. Blackwell Publishing, Inc. Malden, MA. 2002. 336p. Language in Society Ser. ISBN:0-631-22841-1, ISBN13: 978-0-631-22841-7. Dewey:306.44. LCCN:2002-006271.
Audience: **g,l,u,f.**

Sherzer, Joel **P304.S53 2002**
Speech Play and Verbal Art. Trade Cloth. University of Texas Press. Austin, TX. 2002. 218p. ISBN:0-292-77768-X, ISBN13: 978-0-292-77768-2. Dewey:401/.41. LCCN:2001-008474.
Audience: **l,u,f.**

Linguistic Anthropology > Origin and Evolution of Language and Language Change

Burling, Robbins **P116**
Talking Ape: How Language Evolved. Trade Cloth. Oxford University Press, Inc. New York, NY. 2005. 296p. Studies in the Evolution of Language Ser., Vol. 5 ISBN:0-19-927940-3, ISBN13: 978-0-19-927940-1. Dewey:401. LCCN:2005-018558.
Audience: **g,l,u,f.**

Crystal, David **P40.5.L33C79 2002**
Language Death. Trade Paper. Cambridge University Press. New York, NY. 2002. 208p. Canto Refresh Your Ser. ISBN:0-521-01271-6, ISBN13: 978-0-521-01271-3. Dewey:417.7.
Audience: **l,u.** *Choice, 2001.*

Crystal, David **P107.C79 2004**
The Language Revolution. Trade Cloth. Polity Press. Cambridge, 2004. 152p. Themes for the 21st Century Ser. ISBN:0-7456-3312-9, ISBN13: 978-0-7456-3312-1. Dewey:410. LCCN:2003-017872.
Audience: **u,f.**

Hinton, Leanne & Hale, Kenneth (Editors) **P40.5.L356G74 2001**
The Green Book of Language Revitalization in Practice: Toward a Sustainable World. Trade Paper. Elsevier Science & Technology Books. Saint Louis, MO. 2001. 472p. ISBN:0-12-349354-4, ISBN13: 978-0-12-349354-5. Dewey:417/.7. LCCN:00-111386.
Audience: **l,u,f.**

King, Barbara J. (Editor) **P116.O87 1999**
Origins of Language: What Nonhuman Primates Can Tell Us. Trade Paper. School of American Research Press. Santa Fe, NM. 1999. 464p. Advanced Seminar Ser. ISBN:0-933452-60-8, ISBN13: 978-0-933452-60-2. Dewey:401. LCCN:99-028268.
Audience: **g,l,u,f.**

Kulick, Don (Author, Contribution by) **GN671.N5**
Language Shift and Cultural Reproduction: Socialization, Self and Syncretism in a Papua New Guinean Village. Judith T. Irvine, Bambi B. Schieffelin, Marjorie Harness Goodwin, Joel Kuipers, John Lucy, Elinor Ochs & Michael Silverstein (Contribution by). Trade Paper. Cambridge University Press. New York, NY. 1997. 335p. Cambridge Studies in the Social and Cultural Foundations of Language, No. 14 ISBN:0-521-59926-1, ISBN13: 978-0-521-59926-9. Dewey:305.8009953.
Audience: **u,f.**

Lieberman, Philip **P132.L533 2006**
Toward an Evolutionary Biology of Language. Trade Cloth. Harvard University Press. Cambridge, MA. 2006. 448p. ISBN:0-674-02184-3, ISBN13: 978-0-674-02184-6. Dewey:401. LCCN:2005-059101.
Audience: **u,f.**

Nettle, Daniel & Romaine, Suzanne **P40.5.L33N48 2000**
Vanishing Voices: The Extinction of the World's Languages. Trade Cloth. Oxford University Press, Inc. New York, NY. 2000. 254p. ISBN:0-19-513624-1, ISBN13: 978-0-19-513624-1. Dewey:417/.7. LCCN:99-016979.
Audience: **g,l,u.** *Choice, 2001.*

Savage-Rumbaugh, Sue **P106**
Apes, Language, and the Human Mind. Trade Paper. Oxford University Press, Inc. New York, NY. 2001. 244p. ISBN:0-19-514712-X, ISBN13: 978-0-19-514712-4. Dewey:156.3/6.
Audience: **l,u,f.**

Thomason, Sarah G. **P130.5.T457 2001**
Language Contact. Trade Paper. Georgetown University Press. Washington, DC. 2001. 240p. ISBN:0-87840-854-1, ISBN13: 978-0-87840-854-2. Dewey:303.44/6. LCCN:00-068180.
Audience: **l,u,f.**

Linguistic Anthropology > Language and Culture

Enfield, N. J. (Editor) **P35.E876 2002**
Ethnosyntax: Explorations in Grammar and Culture. Trade Cloth. Oxford University Press, Inc. New York, NY. 2002. 336p. ISBN:0-19-924906-7, ISBN13: 978-0-19-924906-0. Dewey:306.44. LCCN:2003-269481.
Audience: **u,f.**

Gumperz, John J. & Levinson, Stephen C. (Editors) **P35.R465 1996**
Rethinking Linguistic Relativity. Judith Irvine, Bambi Schieffelin, Marjorie Harness Goodwin, Joel Kuipers, Don Kulick, John Lucy, Elinor Ochs & Michael Silverstein (Contribution by). Trade Paper. Cambridge University Press. New York, NY. 1996. 496p. Cambridge Studies in the Social and Cultural Foundations of Language, No. 17 ISBN:0-521-44890-5, ISBN13: 978-0-521-44890-1. Dewey:401.9. LCCN:95-038476.
Audience: **u,f.**

Lakoff, George **P37**
Women, Fire, and Dangerous Things. Trade Paper. University of Chicago Press. Chicago, IL. 1990. 632p. ISBN:0-226-46804-6, ISBN13: 978-0-226-46804-4. Dewey:401.9. LCCN:86-019136.
Audience: **u,f.**

Lakoff, George & Johnson, Mark **P106.L235 2003**
Metaphors We Live By. Ed. 2. Trade Paper. University of Chicago Press. Chicago, IL. 1981. 256p. ISBN:0-226-46801-1, ISBN13: 978-0-226-46801-3. Dewey:401. LCCN:2003-044774.
Audience: **u,f.** B

Lucy, John Arthur **P35 .L84 1992**
Language Diversity and Thought: A Reformulation of the Linguistic Relativity Hypothesis. Judith Irvine, Bambi Schieffelin, Marjorie Harness Goodwin, Joel Kuipers, Don Kulick, Elinor Ochs, Michael Silverstein & John Lucy (Contribution by). Trade Paper. Cambridge University Press. New York, NY. 1992. 340p. Cambridge Studies in the Social and Cultural Foundations of Language, No. 12 ISBN:0-521-38797-3, ISBN13: 978-0-521-38797-2. Dewey:401.9. LCCN:91-027644.
Audience: **u,f.**

Sapir, Edward **P105**
Language an Introduction to the Study of Speech. Trade Paper. Kessinger Publishing, LLC. Whitefish, MT. 2005. ISBN:0-7661-9576-7, ISBN13: 978-0-7661-9576-9. Dewey:404.
Audience: **g,l,u,f.**

Sapir, Edward **P27.S33**
Selected Writings of Edward Sapir in Language, Culture, and Personality. David G. Mandelbaum (Editor). Trade Paper. University of California Press. Berkeley, CA. 1949. 653p. ISBN:0-520-05594-2, ISBN13: 978-0-520-05594-0. Dewey:408.9.
Audience: **u,f.**

Schieffelin, Bambi B. **DU740.42.S33 2005**
The Give and Take of Everyday Life: Language Socialization of Kaluli Children. Ed. 2. Trade Paper. Wheatmark. Tucson, AZ. 2005. 292p. ISBN:1-58736-440-9, ISBN13: 978-1-58736-440-2. Dewey:305.23/089/9912. LCCN:2005-920280.
Audience: **u,f.**

Schieffelin, Bambi B. & Ochs, Elinor (Editor, Contribution by) **P118.L385 1986**
Language Socialization across Cultures. Judith T. Irvine, Marjorie Harness Goodwin, Joel Kuipers, Don Kulick, John Lucy & Michael Silverstein (Contribution by). Trade Paper. Cambridge University Press. New York, NY. 1987. 286p. Cambridge Studies in the Social and Cultural Foundations of Language, No. 3 ISBN:0-521-33919-7, ISBN13: 978-0-521-33919-3. Dewey:401/.9. LCCN:86-014798.
Audience: **l,u,f.**

Scollon, Ronald & Scollon, Suzanne Wong **P94.6.S36 2001**
Intercultural Communication: A Discourse Approach. Ed. 2. Trade Paper. Blackwell Publishing, Inc. Malden, MA. 2000. 336p. Language in Society Ser., Vol. 21 ISBN:0-631-22418-1, ISBN13: 978-0-631-22418-1. Dewey:306.4/4. LCCN:00-057907.
Audience: **l,u,f.**

Whorf, Benjamin Lee **P27.W53**
Language, Thought, and Reality: Selected Writings. Paper Text. Textbook Publishers. Temecula, CA. 2003. xi, 278p. ISBN:0-7581-3222-0, ISBN13: 978-0-7581-3222-2. Dewey:404.
Audience: **g,l,u,f.** B

Yamada, Haru **HF5718.Y363 1997**
Different Games, Different Rules: Why Americans and Japanese Misunderstand Each Other. Trade Cloth. Oxford University Press, Inc. New York, NY. 1997. 186p. ISBN:0-19-509488-3, ISBN13: 978-0-19-509488-6. Dewey:302.2/0952. LCCN:96-039554.
Audience: **g,l,u,f.**

Linguistic Anthropology > Language in Relation to Gender, Ethnicity, and Power

Basso, Keith H. **E99.A6B2295**
Portraits of the Whiteman: Linguistic Play and Cultural Symbols among the Western Apache. Trade Paper. Cambridge University Press. New York, NY. 1979. 144p. ISBN:0-521-29593-9, ISBN13: 978-0-521-29593-2. Dewey:301.2/1. LCCN:78-031535.
Audience: **u,f.** B

Bender, Margaret Clelland **PE2922.L56 2004**
Linguistic Diversity in the South: Changing Codes, Practices, and Ideology. Trade Cloth. University of Georgia Press. Athens, GA. 2004. 160p. Southern Anthropological Society Proceedings Ser., No. 37 ISBN:0-8203-2585-6, ISBN13: 978-0-8203-2585-9. Dewey:427/.975. LCCN:2004-001446.
Audience: **u,f.**

Bilaniuk, Laada **P119.32.U38B55 2005**
Contested Tongues: Language Politics and Cultural Correction in Ukraine. Trade Cloth. Cornell University Press. Ithaca, NY. 2005. 256p. Culture and Society after Socialism Ser. ISBN:0-8014-4349-0, ISBN13: 978-0-8014-4349-7. Dewey:306.44/09477. LCCN:2005-016117.
Audience: **g,l,u,f.**

Blommaert, Jan **P302.84.B585 2004**
Discourse: A Critical Introduction. Rajend Mesthrie (Contribution by). Cloth Text. Cambridge University Press. New York, NY. 2005. 314p. Key Topics in Sociolinguistics Ser. ISBN:0-521-82817-1, ISBN13: 978-0-521-82817-8. Dewey:401.41. LCCN:2004-045825.
Audience: **g,l,u,f.**

Bourdieu, Pierre **P106.B6813 1991**
Language and Symbolic Power. John B. Thompson (Editor, Introduction by), Gino Raymond & Matthew Adamson (Translators). Trade Cloth. Harvard University Press. Cambridge, MA. 1991. 320p. ISBN:0-674-51040-2, ISBN13: 978-0-674-51040-1. Dewey:400. LCCN:90-047099.
Audience: **u,f.**

Cameron, Deborah & Kulick, Don **P120.S48**
Language and Sexuality. Cloth Text. Cambridge University Press. New York, NY. 2003. 192p. ISBN:0-521-80433-7, ISBN13: 978-0-521-80433-2. Dewey:306.4/4.
Audience: **u,f.** *Choice, 2004.*

Eckert, Penelope & McConnell-Ginet, Sally **P120.S48E34 2003**
Language and Gender. Cloth Text. Cambridge University Press. New York, NY. 2003. 378p. ISBN:0-521-65283-9, ISBN13: 978-0-521-65283-4. Dewey:306.44. LCCN:2002-067619.
Audience: **u,f.**

Errington, J. Joseph **PL5161.E778 1998**
Shifting Languages: Interaction and Identity in Javanese Indonesia. Judith Irvine & Bambi Schieffelin (Contribution by). Cloth Text. Cambridge University Press. New York, NY. 1998. 240p. Cambridge Studies in the Social and Cultural Foundations of Language, No. 19 ISBN:0-521-63267-6, ISBN13: 978-0-521-63267-6. Dewey:306.4/4/09598. LCCN:98-020577.
Audience: **u,f.**

Jaffe, Alexandra **P40.45.F8J34 1999**
Ideologies in Action: Language Politics on Corsica. Trade Cloth. Walter De Gruyter Inc. Ossining, NY. 1999. 323p. Language, Power and Social Process Ser., No. 3 ISBN:3-11-016445-0, ISBN13: 978-3-11-016445-9. Dewey:306.44/0944/945. LCCN:99-032850.
Audience: **u,f.**

Keating, Elizabeth A. **GN671.C3K43 1998**
Power Sharing: Language, Rank, Gender and Social Space in Pohnpei, Micronesia. Trade Cloth. Oxford University Press, Inc. New York, NY. 1998. 224p. Studies in Anthropological Linguistics ISBN:0-19-511197-4, ISBN13: 978-0-19-511197-2. Dewey:306.44/09966. LCCN:98-036857.
Audience: **l,u,f.**

Lakoff, Robin Tolmach **HQ1206.L36 2004**
Language and Woman's Place: Text and Commentaries. Ed. 2. Mary Bucholtz (Editor). Trade Paper. Oxford University Press, Inc. New York, NY. 2004. 328p. Studies in Language and Gender, Vol. 3 ISBN:0-19-516757-0, ISBN13: 978-0-19-516757-3. Dewey:305.4. LCCN:2003-056479.
Audience: **u,f.** *Choice, 2005.*

Lippi-Green, Rosina L. **PE2808.8.L57 1997**
English with an Accent. Paper over Boards. Routledge. New York, NY. 1997. 304p. ISBN:0-415-11476-4, ISBN13: 978-0-415-11476-9. Dewey:427.9/73. LCCN:96-033234.
Audience: **g,u,f.**

Livia, Anna & Hall, Kira (Editors) **P120.S48Q44 1997**
Queerly Phrased: Language, Gender, and Sexuality. Trade Cloth. Oxford University Press, Inc. New York, NY. 1997. 480p. Oxford Studies in Sociolinguistics ISBN:0-19-510470-6, ISBN13: 978-0-19-510470-7. Dewey:408/.6/64. LCCN:97-006284.
Audience: **g,l,u,f.**

Morgan, Marcyliena **PE3102.N44M67 2002**
Language, Discourse and Power in African American Culture. Judith Irvine, Bambi Schieffelin, Marjorie Harness Goodwin, Joel Kuipers, Don Kulick, John Lucy, Elinor Ochs & Michael Silverstein (Contribution by). Cloth Text. Cambridge University Press. New York, NY. 2002. 196p. Studies in the Social and Cultural Foundations of Language, No. 20 ISBN:0-521-80671-2, ISBN13: 978-0-521-80671-8. Dewey:427/.973/08996073. LCCN:2001-043689.
Audience: **l,u,f.**

Patrick, Donna **PM55.Z9K886 2003**
Language, Politics, and Social Interaction in an Inuit Community. Trade Paper. Walter de Gruyter GmbH & Co. KG. Berlin, 2003. xii, 269p. Language, Power, and Social Process Ser., Vol. 8 ISBN:3-11-017652-1, ISBN13: 978-3-11-017652-0. Dewey:497/.1247/09714. LCCN:2003-052748.
Audience: **u,f.**

Schieffelin, Bambi B. (Editor), et al. **P35.L333 1998**
Language Ideologies: Practice and Theory. Kathryn A. Woolard & Paul V. Kroskrity (Editors). Trade Paper. Oxford University Press, Inc. New York, NY. 1998. 352p. Oxford Studies in Anthropological Linguistics, No. 16 ISBN:0-19-510562-1, ISBN13: 978-0-19-510562-9. Dewey:306.4/4. LCCN:97-023336.
Audience: **u,f.**

Tannen, Deborah **P95**
Gender and Discourse. Trade Paper. Oxford University Press, Inc. New York, NY. 1996. 240p. ISBN:0-19-510124-3, ISBN13: 978-0-19-510124-9. Dewey:302.2/242. LCCN:93-038839.
Audience: **g,l,u,f.**

Van Dijk, Teun A. **HT1521**
Communicating Racism: Ethnic Prejudice in Thought and Talk. Trade Paper. SAGE Publications, Inc. Thousand Oaks, CA. 1989. 440p. ISBN:0-8039-3627-3, ISBN13: 978-0-8039-3627-0. Dewey:305.8. LCCN:86-015514.
Audience: **g,l,u,f.** *Choice, 1988.*

Zentella, Ana C. **P115.2.Z46 1997**
Growing up Bilingual: Puerto Rican Children in New York. Trade Paper. Blackwell Publishing, Inc. Malden, MA. 1997. 336p. ISBN:1-55786-407-1, ISBN13: 978-1-55786-407-9. Dewey:420.4/261/083/097471. LCCN:96-025064.
Audience: **g,l,u,f.**

Linguistic Anthropology > Anthropology of Oral and Written Language

Besnier, Niko **P211.3.T88B47 1995**
Literacy, Emotion and Authority: Reading and Writing on a Polynesian Atoll. Marjorie Harness Goodwin, Judith Irvine, Joel Kuipers, Don Kulick, John Lucy, Elinor Ochs, Bambi Schieffelin & Michael Silverstein (Contribution by). Trade

Cloth. Cambridge University Press. New York, NY. 1995. 254p. Cambridge Studies in the Social and Cultural Foundations of Language, No. 16 ISBN:0-521-48087-6, ISBN13: 978-0-521-48087-1. Dewey:302.2/244/099682. LCCN:94-034107.
Audience: **u,f.**

Boyarin, Jonathan (Editor) **Z1003.E87 1993**
The Ethnography of Reading. Trade Cloth. University of California Press. Berkeley, CA. 1993. 285p. ISBN:0-520-07955-8, ISBN13: 978-0-520-07955-7. Dewey:028.9. LCCN:92-034690.
Audience: **g,l,u,f.** *Choice, 1994.*

Coe, Michael D. **F1435.3.W75C64 1999**
Breaking the Maya Code. Trade Paper. Thames & Hudson. New York, NY. 1999. 304p. ISBN:0-500-28133-5, ISBN13: 978-0-500-28133-8. Dewey:972. LCCN:99-070864.
Audience: **g,l,u,f.**

Coulmas, Florian **P211.C669 2003**
Writing Systems: An Introduction to Their Linguistic Analysis. S. R. Anderson, J. Bresnan, B. Comrie, W. Dressler & C. J. Ewen (Contribution by). Trade Paper, Perfect. Cambridge University Press. New York, NY. 2002. 290p. Cambridge Textbooks in Linguistics Ser. ISBN:0-521-78737-8, ISBN13: 978-0-521-78737-6. Dewey:411. LCCN:2003-268845.
Audience: **g,l,u,f.**

Kendon, Adam **P117.K46 2004**
Gesture: Visible Action as Utterance. Trade Cloth. Cambridge University Press. New York, NY. 2004. 410p. ISBN:0-521-83525-9, ISBN13: 978-0-521-83525-1. Dewey:808.5. LCCN:2004-049686.
Audience: **g,l,u,f.** *Choice, 2005.*

Monaghan, Leila Frances (Editor) **HV2395.M36 2003**
Many Ways to Be Deaf. Trade Cloth. Gallaudet University Press. Washington, DC. 2003. 320p. ISBN:1-56368-135-8, ISBN13: 978-1-56368-135-6. Dewey:305.9/08162. LCCN:2002-192872.
Audience: **g,l,u,f.** *Choice, 2003.*

Social and Cultural Anthropology > General and Introductory Works

Auge, Marc **GN345.A92513 1995**
Non-Places: Introduction to an Anthropology of Supermodernity. John Howe (Translator). Trade Cloth. Analytical Psychology Club of San Francisco, Inc. San Francisco, CA. 1995. 128p. ISBN:1-85984-956-3, ISBN13: 978-1-85984-956-9. Dewey:301/.01. LCCN:94-046299.
Audience: **l,u,f.**

Benedict, Ruth **GN506.B46 2005**
Patterns of Culture. Trade Paper. Houghton Mifflin Company Trade & Reference Division. Boston, MA. 2006. 320p. ISBN:0-618-61955-0, ISBN13: 978-0-618-61955-9. Dewey:306. LCCN:2006-273414.
Audience: **l,u.** B

Benedict, Ruth **GN6.B4 1977**
An Anthropologist at Work: Writings of Ruth Benedict. Margaret Mead (Editor). Trade Cloth. Greenwood Publishing Group, Inc. Portsmouth, NH. 1977. 583p. ISBN:0-8371-9576-4, ISBN13: 978-0-8371-9576-6. Dewey:301.2/08. LCCN:77-003017.
Audience: **u,f.**

Firth, Raymond William **GN24.F5**
Human Types, an Introduction to Social Anthropology. Paper Text. Textbook Publishers. Temecula, CA. 2003. 224p. ISBN:0-7581-3310-3, ISBN13: 978-0-7581-3310-6. Dewey:301.2.
Audience: **l,u,f.** B

Geertz, Clifford **GN315.G36**
Interpretation of Cultures. Trade Paper. Basic Books. New York, NY. 1977. 480p. Basic Books Classics ISBN:0-465-09719-7, ISBN13: 978-0-465-09719-7. Dewey:306. LCCN:73-081196.
Audience: **g,l,u,f.** B

Gingrich, Andre & Fox, Richard Gabriel (Editors) **GN345.A579 2002**
Anthropology, by Comparison. Paper over Boards. Routledge. New York, NY. 2002. 288p. ISBN:0-415-26053-1, ISBN13: 978-0-415-26053-4. Dewey:306. LCCN:2001-048452.
Audience: **l,u,f.**

Harris, Marvin **GN320.H328 1989**
Cows, Pigs, Wars, and Witches: The Riddles of Culture. Trade Paper. Knopf Publishing Group. New York, NY. 1989. 288p. ISBN:0-679-72468-0, ISBN13: 978-0-679-72468-1. Dewey:392.
Audience: **g,l,u,f.**

Harris, Marvin **GN357**
Our Kind: Who We Are, Where We Came from, Where We Are Going. Trade Paper. HarperCollins Publishers. New York, NY. 1990. 560p. ISBN:0-06-091990-6, ISBN13: 978-0-06-091990-0. Dewey:304.2. LCCN:88-045514.
Audience: **g,l,u,f.**

Harris, Marvin **GN357.H39 1999**
Theories of Culture in Postmodern Times. Trade Cloth. AltaMira Press. Walnut Creek, CA. 1998. 240p. ISBN:0-7619-9020-8, ISBN13: 978-0-7619-9020-8. Dewey:306. LCCN:98-040132.
Audience: **l,u,f.** *Choice, 1999.*

Harris, Marvin **HN59.2.H375 1987**
Why Nothing Works: The Anthropology of Daily Life. Trade Paper. Simon & Schuster. New York, NY. 1987. 224p. ISBN:0-671-63577-8, ISBN13: 978-0-671-63577-0. Dewey:973.92. LCCN:86-026100.
Audience: **g,l,u,f.**

Henry, Jules **HN65**
Culture Against Man. Trade Paper. Random House, Inc. New York, NY. 1965. ISBN:0-394-70283-2, ISBN13: 978-0-394-70283-4. Dewey:309.1/73/0924.
Audience: **g,l,u,f.** B

James, Wendy **GN25**
Ceremonial Animal: A New Portrait of Anthropology. Trade Paper. Oxford University Press, Inc. New York, NY. 2005. 408p. ISBN:0-19-926334-5, ISBN13: 978-0-19-926334-9. Dewey:301.
Audience: **l,u,f.**

Kehoe, Alice B. **GN25.K45 1998**
Humans: An Introduction to Four-Field Anthropology. UK-B Format Paperback. Routledge. New York, NY. 1998. 256p.

ISBN:0-415-91985-1, ISBN13: 978-0-415-91985-2. Dewey:301. LCCN:97-040017.
Audience: **l,u,f.**

Mead, Margaret **GN482 .M4**
Sex and Temperament: In Three Primitive Societies. Trade Cloth. Peter Smith Publisher, Inc. Magnolia, MA. 1987. ISBN:0-8446-2568-X, ISBN13: 978-0-8446-2568-3. Dewey:305.309.
Audience: **l,u,f.** B

Mead, Margaret & Lutkehaus, Nancy **GN21.M36A32 1995**
Blackberry Winter: My Earlier Years. Philip Turner (Editor). Trade Paper. Kodansha America, Inc. New York, NY. 1995. 336p. Kodansha Globe Ser. ISBN:1-56836-069-X, ISBN13: 978-1-56836-069-0. Dewey:306/.092 B. LCCN:95-013302.
Audience: **g,l,u,f.**

Metcalf, Peter **GN25.M47 2005**
Anthropology: The Basics. Perfect, Paper over Boards. Routledge. New York, NY. 2005. 215p. The Basics Ser. ISBN:0-415-33119-6, ISBN13: 978-0-415-33119-7. Dewey:301. LCCN:2005-002416.
Audience: **g,l,u,f.**

Rapport, Nigel & Overing, Joanna **GN316.R37 2000**
Social and Cultural Anthropology: The Key Concepts. Paper over Boards. Routledge. New York, NY. 2000. 480p. Key Guides ISBN:0-415-18155-0, ISBN13: 978-0-415-18155-6. Dewey:306. LCCN:00-710863.
Audience: **g,l,u,f.** *Choice, 2001.*

Social and Cultural Anthropology > Theory and Methodology

Bateson, Gregory **GN6.B3 2000**
Steps to an Ecology of Mind: Collected Essays in Anthropology, Psychiatry, Evolution, and Epistemology. Trade Paper. University of Chicago Press. Chicago, IL. 2000. 565p. ISBN:0-226-03905-6, ISBN13: 978-0-226-03905-3. Dewey:108. LCCN:99-045031.
Audience: **u,f.**

Bidney, David **GN24.B492 1996**
Theoretical Anthropology. Ed. 2. Martin Bidney (Introduction by). Trade Paper. Transaction Publishers. Somerset, NJ. 1995. 528p. ISBN:1-56000-832-6, ISBN13: 978-1-56000-832-3. Dewey:306. LCCN:95-012862.
Audience: **u,f.**

Bloch, Maurice **GN345.15.B55 2004**
Marxism and Anthropology: The History of a Relationship. Library Binding. Routledge. New York, NY. 2004. 192p. Routledge Library Editions Ser., :Anthropology and Ethnography, US/Can. Edition Ser. ISBN:0-415-33061-0, ISBN13: 978-0-415-33061-9. Dewey:301.
Audience: **g,l,u,f.**

Bourdieu, Pierre **DT298.K2B6913 1977**
Outline of a Theory of Practice. Richard Nice (Translator), Meyer Fortes, Jack Goody, Edmund Leach & Stanley Tambiah (Contribution by). Trade Paper. Cambridge University Press. New York, NY. 1977. 224p. Cambridge Studies in Social and Cultural Anthropology, No. 16 ISBN:0-521-29164-X, ISBN13: 978-0-521-29164-4. Dewey:306/.01. LCCN:76-011073.
Audience: **u,f.**

Brown, Donald E. **GN357.B76 1991**
Human Universals. Paper Text. McGraw-Hill Higher Education. Burr Ridge, IL. 1991. 160p. ISBN:0-07-008209-X, ISBN13: 978-0-07-008209-0. Dewey:306. LCCN:92-022171.
Audience: **g,l,u,f.** *Choice, 1992.*

Carneiro, Robert L. **GN360.C37 2003**
Evolutionism in Cultural Anthropology: A Critical History. Trade Paper. Westview Press. Boulder, CO. 2003. 336p. ISBN:0-8133-3766-6, ISBN13: 978-0-8133-3766-1. Dewey:303.4. LCCN:2002-015342.
Audience: **g,l,u,f.** *Choice, 2003.*

Clifford, James & Marcus, George E. (Editors) **GN307.7.W75 1986**
Writing Culture: The Poetics and Politics of Ethnography. Trade Paper. University of California Press. Berkeley, CA. 1986. 345p. ISBN:0-520-05729-5, ISBN13: 978-0-520-05729-6. Dewey:306/.08. LCCN:85-014860.
Audience: **u,f.** *Choice, 1986.*

Crehan, Kate A. F. **GN357.C74 2002**
Gramsci, Culture and Anthropology. Trade Paper. University of California Press. Berkeley, CA. 2002. 230p. ISBN:0-520-23602-5, ISBN13: 978-0-520-23602-8. Dewey:301/.01. LCCN:2002-074224.
Audience: **u,f.** *Choice, 2003.*

Erickson, Paul A. & Murphy, Liam Donat **GN33.E74 2003**
A History of Anthropological Theory. Ed. 2. Trade Paper. Broadview Press. Peterborough, ON. 2003. 283p. ISBN:1-55111-526-3, ISBN13: 978-1-55111-526-9. Dewey:301/.01. LCCN:2004-353923.
Audience: **u,f.**

Erickson, Paul A. & Murphy, Liam Donat (Editors) **GN33.R4 2001**
Readings for a History of Anthropological Theory. Trade Paper. Broadview Press. Peterborough, ON. 2001. xxii, 714p. ISBN:1-55111-411-9, ISBN13: 978-1-55111-411-8. Dewey:301/.01. LCCN:2001-273693.
Audience: **l,u,f.**

Gupta, Akhil & Ferguson, James (Editors) **GN34.3.F53A56 1997**
Anthropological Locations: Boundaries and Grounds of a Field Science. Trade Paper. University of California Press. Berkeley, CA. 1997. 284p. ISBN:0-520-20680-0, ISBN13: 978-0-520-20680-9. Dewey:301/.07/23. LCCN:96-046305.
Audience: **l,f.**

Harris, Marvin **GN308.H35 2001**
Rise of Anthropological Theory: A History of Theories of Culture. Trade Cloth. AltaMira Press. Walnut Creek, CA. 2000. 824p. ISBN:0-7591-0132-9, ISBN13: 978-0-7591-0132-6. Dewey:306/.09. LCCN:2001-037436.
Audience: **g,l,u,f.** B

Hertz, Robert **GN486.H423 2004**
Death and the Right Hand. Library Binding. Routledge. New York, NY. 2004. 184p. Routledge Library Editions Ser., :Anthropology and Ethnography, US/Can. Edition Ser. ISBN:0-415-33024-6, ISBN13: 978-0-415-33024-4. Dewey:393.
Audience: **u,f.**

Herzfeld, Michael **GN345.H47 2001**
Anthropology: Theoretical Practice in Culture and Society. Trade Paper. Blackwell Publishing, Inc. Malden, MA. 2000. 384p. ISBN:0-631-20659-0, ISBN13: 978-0-631-20659-0. Dewey:301. LCCN:00-057915.
Audience: **u,f.** *Choice, 2001.*

Hymes, Dell **GN43.A2H9 1999**
Reinventing Anthropology. Trade Paper. University of Michigan Press. Chicago, IL. 1999. 528p. Ann Arbor Paperback Ser. ISBN:0-472-08607-3, ISBN13: 978-0-472-08607-8. Dewey:301.2. LCCN:99-055250.
Audience: **u,f.**

Ingold, Tim (Editor) **GN345.K49 1996**
Key Debates in Anthropology. Paper over Boards. Routledge. New York, NY. 1996. 320p. ISBN:0-415-15019-1, ISBN13: 978-0-415-15019-4. Dewey:306. LCCN:96-007493.
Audience: **l,u.**

Johnson, Christopher **GN362.J64 2003**
Claude Levi-Strauss: The Formative Years. Trade Cloth. Cambridge University Press. New York, NY. 2003. 218p. ISBN:0-521-81641-6, ISBN13: 978-0-521-81641-0. Dewey:301. LCCN:2002-074192.
Audience: **u,f.**

Kroeber, A. L. **GN6**
The Nature of Culture. Paper Text. Textbook Publishers. Temecula, CA. 2003. 437p. ISBN:0-7581-2607-7, ISBN13: 978-0-7581-2607-8. Dewey:572.04.
Audience: **u,f.** B

Kuznar, Lawrence A. **HN29**
Reclaiming a Scientific Anthropology. Book, Other. AltaMira Press. Walnut Creek, CA. 1997. 256p. ISBN:0-7619-9113-1, ISBN13: 978-0-7619-9113-7. Dewey:301/.0723. LCCN:97-035699.
Audience: **u,f.** *Choice, 1997.*

Levi-Strauss, Claude **HM101**
Structural Anthropology. C. Arensberg (Introduction by). Trade Paper. Basic Books. New York, NY. 1974. 448p. Structural Anthropology Ser., Vol. 1 ISBN:0-465-09516-X, ISBN13: 978-0-465-09516-2. Dewey:306. LCCN:63-017344.
Audience: **u,f.**

Lewin, Ellen & Leap, William L. (Editors) **HQ75.5.O936 2002**
Out in Theory: The Emergence of Lesbian and Gay Anthropology. Trade Cloth. University of Illinois Press. Champaign, IL. 2002. 344p. ISBN:0-252-02753-1, ISBN13: 978-0-252-02753-6. Dewey:305.9/0664. LCCN:2001-007366.
Audience: **g,l,u,f.** *Choice, 2003.*

McKinnon, Susan & Silverman, Sydel (Editors) **GN27.C648 2005**
Complexities: Beyond Nature and Nurture. Trade Paper, Perfect. University of Chicago Press. Chicago, IL. 2005. 296p. ISBN:0-226-50024-1, ISBN13: 978-0-226-50024-9. Dewey:301. LCCN:2004-020978.
Audience: **u,f.** *Choice, 2005.*

Moore, Henrietta L. **GN33.A445 1999**
Anthropological Theory Today. Trade Cloth. Polity Press. Cambridge, 1999. 304p. ISBN:0-7456-2022-1, ISBN13: 978-0-7456-2022-0. Dewey:301/.01. LCCN:99-026798.
Audience: **u,f.**

Noblit, George W. & Hare, R. Dwight **GN345.N63 1988**
Meta-Ethnography: Synthesizing Qualitative Studies. Trade Cloth. SAGE Publications, Inc. Thousand Oaks, CA. 1988. 88p. Qualitative Research Methods Ser., Vol. 11 ISBN:0-8039-3022-4, ISBN13: 978-0-8039-3022-3. Dewey:306/.018. LCCN:87-022330.
Audience: **u,f.**

Radcliffe-Brown, A. R. **GN490.R33X**
Structure and Function in Primitive Society, Essays and Addresses. Paper Text. Textbook Publishers. Temecula, CA. 2003. vii, 219p. ISBN:0-7581-3181-X, ISBN13: 978-0-7581-3181-2. Dewey:572.04.
Audience: **l,u,f.**

Radin, Paul A. **GN345**
The Method and Theory of Ethnology. Arthur J. Vidich (Introduction by). Paper Text. Greenwood Publishing Group, Inc. Portsmouth, NH. 1987. 388p. ISBN:0-89789-118-X, ISBN13: 978-0-89789-118-9. Dewey:306/.01/8. LCCN:86-029921.
Audience: **u,f.**

Redfield, Robert **GN0006.R4.A2**
Papers of Robert Redfield, Vol. 1. Margaret P. Redfield (Editor). Trade Paper. Books on Demand. Ann Arbor, MI. 523p. ISBN:0-8357-6249-1, ISBN13: 978-0-8357-6249-6. Dewey:572. LCCN:62-010995.
Audience: **f.**

Roseberry, William **GN448.R48 1989**
Anthropologies and Histories: Essays in Culture, History, and Political Economy. Paper Text. Rutgers University Press. Piscataway, NJ. 1989. 256p. ISBN:0-8135-1446-0, ISBN13: 978-0-8135-1446-8. Dewey:306. LCCN:89-030378.
Audience: **l,u,f.** *Choice, 1990.*

Sahlins, Marshall David **HM101.S168 2000**
Culture in Practice: Selected Essays. Trade Cloth. Zone Books. Brooklyn, NY. 2000. 600p. ISBN:0-942299-37-X, ISBN13: 978-0-942299-37-3. Dewey:306. LCCN:99-011469.
Audience: **l,u,f.**

Sanjek, Roger (Editor) **GN346.F52 1990**
Fieldnotes: The Makings of Anthropology. Book, Other. Cornell University Press. Ithaca, NY. 1990. 432p. ISBN:0-8014-2436-4, ISBN13: 978-0-8014-2436-6. Dewey:306/.072. LCCN:89-046169.
Audience: **g,l,u,f.** *Choice, 1991.*

Shore, Bradd **GN502.S49 1996**
Culture in Mind: Cognition, Culture, and the Problem of Meaning. Ed. 319. Trade Cloth. Oxford University Press, Inc. New York, NY. 1996. 448p. ISBN:0-19-509597-9, ISBN13: 978-0-19-509597-5. Dewey:155.8. LCCN:95-011828.
Audience: **u,f.** *Choice, 1996.*

Wallace, Anthony F. **HM101**
Revitalization Movements: Some Theoretical Considerations for Their Comparative Study. Paper Text. Irvington Publishers. New York, NY. 1991. Irvington Reprint Ser. ISBN:0-8290-2605-3, ISBN13: 978-0-8290-2605-4. Dewey:306.
Audience: **u,f.**

Wolf, Eric R. **JC330**
Envisioning Power: Ideologies of Dominance and Crisis. Trade Paper. University of California Press. Berkeley, CA. 1999. 352p. ISBN:0-520-21582-6, ISBN13: 978-0-520-21582-5. Dewey:303.3. LCCN:98-023792.
Audience: **l,u,f.**

Social and Cultural Anthropology > Field Methods

Agar, Michael H. **GN346.A42 1996**
The Professional Stranger: An Informal Introduction to Ethnography. Ed. 2. Paper Text. Elsevier Science & Technology Books. Saint Louis, MO. 1996. 276p. ISBN:0-12-044470-4, ISBN13: 978-0-12-044470-0. Dewey:301/.01/8. LCCN:96-003356.
Audience: **u,f.**

Agar, Michael H. **GN345.A34 1986**
Speaking of Ethnography. Trade Paper. SAGE Publications, Inc. Thousand Oaks, CA. 1985. 80p. Qualitative Research Methods Ser., Vol. 2 ISBN:0-8039-2492-5, ISBN13: 978-0-8039-2492-5. Dewey:306. LCCN:85-050781.
Audience: **l,u,f.**

Bernard, H. Russell **GN345.B36 2005**
Research Methods in Anthropology: Qualitative and Quantitative Approaches. Ed. 4. Trade Cloth. AltaMira Press. Walnut Creek, CA. 2005. 824p. ISBN:0-7591-0868-4, ISBN13: 978-0-7591-0868-4. Dewey:301/.072. LCCN:2005-018836.
Audience: **l,u,f.** *Choice, 2002.*

Dresch, Paul, et al. **GN34.3.F53A57 2000**
Anthropologists in a Wider World: Essays on Field Research. Wendy James & David J. Parkin (Authors). Trade Cloth. Berghahn Books, Inc. New York, NY. 2000. 288p. Methodology and History in Anthropology Ser., Vol. 6 ISBN:1-57181-800-6, ISBN13: 978-1-57181-800-3. Dewey:301/.07/23. LCCN:99-087034.
Audience: **u,f.**

Hastrup, Kirsten & Hervik, Peter **GN346.S63 1994**
Social Experience and Anthropological Knowledge. Trade Paper. Routledge. New York, NY. 1994. 264p. European Association of Social Anthropologists Ser. ISBN:0-415-10658-3, ISBN13: 978-0-415-10658-0. Dewey:306/.01. LCCN:93-044330.
Audience: **u,f.**

Kemper, Robert V. & Royce, Anya Peterson (Editors) **GN33.3.F53C57 2002**
Chronicling Cultures: Long-Term Field Research in Anthropology. Book, Other. AltaMira Press. Walnut Creek, CA. 2002. 392p. ISBN:0-7591-0193-0, ISBN13: 978-0-7591-0193-7. Dewey:301/.07/2. LCCN:2001-053564.
Audience: **u,f.** *Choice, 2002.*

Lewin, Ellen & Leap, William L. (Editors) **GN34.3.F53O87 1996**
Out in the Field: Reflections of Lesbian and Gay Anthropologists. Trade Paper. University of Illinois Press. Champaign, IL. 1996. 328p. ISBN:0-252-06518-2, ISBN13: 978-0-252-06518-7. Dewey:301. LCCN:95-032456.
Audience: **g,l,u,f.** *Choice, 1996.*

Michrina, Barry P. & Richards, CherylAnne **GN34.3.F53M53 1996**
Person to Person: Fieldwork, Dialogue, and the Hermeneutic Method. Paper Text. State University of New York Press. Albany, NY. 1996. 176p. ISBN:0-7914-2834-6, ISBN13: 978-0-7914-2834-4. Dewey:301. LCCN:95-008930.
Audience: **u,f.**

Powdermaker, Hortense **E357.B88**
Stranger and Friend. Trade Paper. W. W. Norton & Company, Inc. New York, NY. 1967. ISBN:0-393-00410-4, ISBN13: 978-0-393-00410-6. Dewey:973.52.
Audience: **u,f.**

Rose, Dan **GN345.R668 1990**
Living the Ethnographic Life. Trade Paper. SAGE Publications, Inc. Thousand Oaks, CA. 1990. 64p. Qualitative Research Methods Ser., Vol. 23 ISBN:0-8039-3999-X, ISBN13: 978-0-8039-3999-8. Dewey:305.8/0072. LCCN:90-008775.
Audience: **l,u,f.**

Starr, June & Goodale, Mark (Editors) **K190.P73 2002**
Practicing Ethnography in Law: New Dialogues, Enduring Methods. Cloth over Boards. Palgrave Macmillan. New York, NY. 2002. 224p. ISBN:1-4039-6069-0, ISBN13: 978-1-4039-6069-6. Dewey:340/.115. LCCN:2002-032175.
Audience: **u,f.**

Stoller, Paul **GN345.S85 1997**
Sensuous Scholarship: Contemporary Ethnography. Trade Cloth. University of Pennsylvania Press. Philadelphia, PA. 1997. 160p. Contemporary Ethnography Ser. ISBN:0-8122-3398-0, ISBN13: 978-0-8122-3398-8. Dewey:305.8/001. LCCN:96-053514.
Audience: **u,f.**

Social and Cultural Anthropology > Anthropology of Art: Visual, Performing, Music, Dance

Amerlinck, Mari-Jose (Editor) **NA2543**
Architectural Anthropology. Trade Cloth. Greenwood Publishing Group, Inc. Portsmouth, NH. 2001. 232p. ISBN:0-89789-683-1, ISBN13: 978-0-89789-683-2. Dewey:306.4/7. LCCN:00-031201.
Audience: **u,f.** *Choice, 2001.*

Blundell, Valda **N72.A56B58 2000**
Art and Anthropology: Directions in Theory and Research. Trade Paper. Golden Dog Press. Kemptville, ON. 2004. 112p. ISBN:0-919614-88-4, ISBN13: 978-0-919614-88-8. Dewey:701/.03. LCCN:00-361389.
Audience: **u,f.**

Campbell, Shirley Faye **GN671.N5C36 2002**
The Art of Kula. Cloth over Boards. Berg Publishers. Oxford, 2002. 288p. ISBN:1-85973-513-4, ISBN13: 978-1-85973-513-8. Dewey:305.8/009954/1. LCCN:2002-008613.
Audience: **u,f.**

Garfinkel, Yosef **GN848.G37 2003**
Dancing at the Dawn of Agriculture: Dance and Display at the Beginning of Farming. Trade Cloth. University of Texas Press. Austin, TX. 2003. 346p. ISBN:0-292-72845-X, ISBN13: 978-0-292-72845-5. Dewey:709/.01/12091822. LCCN:2002-009359.
Audience: **u,f.**

Gell, Alfred **N72.A56G45 1998**
Art and Agency: An Anthropological Theory. Trade Paper. Oxford University Press, Inc. New York, NY. 1998. 296p. ISBN:0-19-828014-9, ISBN13: 978-0-19-828014-9. Dewey:701.03. LCCN:97-051845.
Audience: **u,f.**

Kaemmer, John E. **ML3798.K33 1993**
Music in Human Life: Anthropological Perspectives on Music. Cloth Text. University of Texas Press. Austin, TX. 1993. 259p. Sourcebooks in Anthropology, No. 17 ISBN:0-292-74313-0, ISBN13: 978-0-292-74313-7. Dewey:306.4/84. LCCN:92-014937.
Audience: **l,u,f.** *Choice, 1994.*

Kleinert, Sylvia & Neale, Margo (Editors) **NX590.A1O94 2000**
The Oxford Companion to Aboriginal Art and Culture. Cloth Text. Oxford University Press, Inc. New York, NY. 2001. 804p. ISBN:0-19-550649-9, ISBN13: 978-0-19-550649-5. Dewey:994.004/9915. LCCN:2001-269497.
Audience: **l,u,f.** *Choice, 2002.*

Largey, Michael **ML3565.L35 2006**
Vodou Nation: Haitian Art Music and Cultural Nationalism. Trade Cloth. University of Chicago Press. Chicago, IL. 2006. 256p. Chicago Studies in Ethnomusicology Ser. ISBN:0-226-46863-1, ISBN13: 978-0-226-46863-1. Dewey:780/.97294. LCCN:2005-023830.
Audience: **l,u,f.**

McClusky, Pamela & Thompson, Robert Farris **N7391.65.M28 2002**
Art from Africa: Long Steps Never Broke a Back. Seattle Art Museum Staff (Contribution by). Trade Cloth. Princeton University Press. Princeton, NJ. 2002. 304p. ISBN:0-691-09275-3, ISBN13: 978-0-691-09275-1. Dewey:709.6. LCCN:2001-049735.
Audience: **g,l,u,f.**

Morphy, Howard & Perkins, Morgan **N72.A56A67 2005**
Anthropology of Art: A Reader. Trade Cloth. Blackwell Publishing, Inc. Malden, MA. 2006. 576p. Blackwell Anthologies in Social and Cultural Anthropology Ser. ISBN:1-4051-0561-5, ISBN13: 978-1-4051-0561-3. Dewey:709/.01.1. LCCN:2005-013067.
Audience: **l,u,f.**

Nettl, Bruno **ML3798.N47 2005**
The Study of Ethnomusicology: Thirty-One Issues and Concepts. Ed. 2. Trade Cloth. University of Illinois Press. Champaign, IL. 2005. 528p. ISBN:0-252-03033-8, ISBN13: 978-0-252-03033-8. Dewey:780/.89. LCCN:2005-011181.
Audience: **u,f.** *Choice, 2006.*

Pitts, Victoria **GN419.15.P57 2003**
In the Flesh: The Cultural Politics of Body Modification. Trade Paper. Palgrave Macmillan. New York, NY. 2003. 256p. ISBN:0-312-29311-9, ISBN13: 978-0-312-29311-6. Dewey:391.6/5. LCCN:2002-044979.
Audience: **l,u,f.**

Post **ML3799.E79 2005**
Ethnomusicology: A Contemporary Reader. Perfect, Paper over Boards. Routledge. New York, NY. 2005. 464p. ISBN:0-415-97203-5, ISBN13: 978-0-415-97203-1. Dewey:780/.89. LCCN:2005-013598.
Audience: **g,l,u,f.**

Rovine, Victoria **DT551.45.B35R68 2001**
Bogolan: Shaping Culture Through Cloth in Contemporary Mali. Trade Cloth. Smithsonian Institution Press. Washington, DC. 2001. 184p. ISBN:1-56098-942-4, ISBN13: 978-1-56098-942-4. Dewey:391. LCCN:2001-020697.
Audience: **u,f.**

Royce, Anya Peterson **PN1590.A58R68 2004**
Anthropology of Performing Arts: Artistry, Virtuosity, and Interpretation in a Cross-Cultural Perspective. Trade Cloth. AltaMira Press. Walnut Creek, CA. 2004. 272p. ISBN:0-7591-0223-6, ISBN13: 978-0-7591-0223-1. Dewey:791/.01/03. LCCN:2003-025785.
Audience: **u,f.** *Choice, 2005.*

Schneider, Arnd & Wright, Christopher (Editors) **N72.S6**
Contemporary Art and Anthropology. Cloth over Boards. Berg Publishers. Oxford, 2006. 320p. ISBN:1-84520-102-7, ISBN13: 978-1-84520-102-9. Dewey:701/.08. LCCN:2005-028551.
Audience: **l,u,f.**

Sharma, Sanjay P. (Editor), et al. **ML3431.5.D57 1996**
Dis-Orienting Rhythms: The Politics of the New Asian Dance Music. John Hutnyk & Ashwani Sharma (Editors). Trade Cloth. Zed Books, Ltd. London, 1996. 240p. ISBN:1-85649-469-1, ISBN13: 978-1-85649-469-4. Dewey:305.8/914/041. LCCN:96-024976.
Audience: **u,f.** *Choice, 1997.*

Social and Cultural Anthropology > Cognitive Anthropology

Atran, Scott **GN468.4.A87 1990**
Cognitive Foundations of Natural History: Towards an Anthropology of Science. Cloth Text. Cambridge University Press. New York, NY. 1990. 372p. ISBN:0-521-37293-3, ISBN13: 978-0-521-37293-0. Dewey:303.45. LCCN:89-036129.
Audience: **u,f.** *Choice, 1991.*

Berlin, Brent **GN468.4.B47 1992**
Ethnobiological Classification: Principles of Categorization of Plants and Animals in Traditional Societies. Cloth Text. Princeton University Press. Princeton, NJ. 1992. 326p. ISBN:0-691-09469-1, ISBN13: 978-0-691-09469-4. Dewey:574.6/1. LCCN:91-025245.
Audience: **u,f.**

Bloch, Maurice **GN25**
Anthropology and Cognitive Science: Essays on Cultural Transmission. Cloth over Boards. Berg Publishers. Oxford, 2005. 256p. London School of Economics Monographs on

Social Anthropology Ser., Vol. 75 ISBN:1-84520-286-4, ISBN13: 978-1-84520-286-6. Dewey:155.8/2. LCCN:2005-010965.
Audience: **u,f.**

Bloch, Maurice E. **GN502.B56 1998**
How We Think They Think: Anthropological Approaches to Cognition, Memory and Literacy. Trade Paper. Westview Press. Boulder, CO. 1997. 216p. ISBN:0-8133-3373-3, ISBN13: 978-0-8133-3373-1. Dewey:153. LCCN:98-113392.
Audience: **u,f.** *Choice, 1998.*

Boyer, Pascal **GN345.6.B69 1990**
Tradition as Truth and Communication: A Cognitive Description of Traditional Discourse. Meyer Fortes, Jack Goody, Edmund Leach & Stanley Tambiah (Contribution by). Trade Cloth. Cambridge University Press. New York, NY. 1990. 153p. Cambridge Studies in Social and Cultural Anthropology, No. 68 ISBN:0-521-37417-0, ISBN13: 978-0-521-37417-0. Dewey:303.4/82. LCCN:89-007285.
Audience: **u,f.** *Choice, 1990.*

D'Andrade, Roy G. **GN502.D36 1995**
The Development of Cognitive Anthropology. Trade Paper. Cambridge University Press. New York, NY. 1995. 286p. ISBN:0-521-45976-1, ISBN13: 978-0-521-45976-1. Dewey:155.8. LCCN:94-004749.
Audience: **u,f.** *Choice, 1995.*

D'Andrade, Roy G. & Strauss, Claudia J. (Editors) **HM101.H85 1992**
Human Motives and Cultural Models. Cloth Text. Cambridge University Press. New York, NY. 1992. 252p. Publications for the Society for Psychological Anthropology ISBN:0-521-41233-1, ISBN13: 978-0-521-41233-9. Dewey:306. LCCN:91-011155.
Audience: **u,f.**

Holland, Dorothy & Quinn, Naomi (Editors) **P35.C8 1987**
Cultural Models in Language and Thought. Cloth Text. Cambridge University Press. New York, NY. 1987. 412p. ISBN:0-521-32346-0, ISBN13: 978-0-521-32346-8. Dewey:401/.9. LCCN:86-017524.
Audience: **u,f.** *Choice, 1987.*

Kay, Paul
Color Naming in Human Languages. Library Binding. C S L I Publications/Center for the Study of Language & Information. Stanford, CA. 2001. 250p. ISBN:1-57586-325-1, ISBN13: 978-1-57586-325-2.
Audience: **u,f.**

Lakoff, George & Johnson, Mark **BD418.3.L35 1999**
Philosophy in the Flesh: The Embodied Mind and Its Challenge to Western Thought. Trade Cloth. Basic Books. New York, NY. 1998. 640p. ISBN:0-465-05673-3, ISBN13: 978-0-465-05673-6. Dewey:128. LCCN:98-037113.
Audience: **u,f.** *Choice, 1999.*

Lave, Jean **BF311 .L29 1988**
Cognition in Practice: Mind, Mathematics and Culture in Everyday Life. Trade Paper. Cambridge University Press. New York, NY. 1988. 234p. ISBN:0-521-35734-9, ISBN13: 978-0-521-35734-0. Dewey:153.4. LCCN:87-023289.
Audience: **u,f.** *Choice, 1989.*

Reyna, Stephen P. **GN357.R49 2002**
Making Connections: Brain, Mind, and Culture in a Social Anthropology. Paper over Boards. Routledge. New York, NY. 2002. 240p. ISBN:0-415-27154-1, ISBN13: 978-0-415-27154-7. Dewey:306. LCCN:2001-048454.
Audience: **u.**

Social and Cultural Anthropology > Critical and Engaged Anthropology

Ahmed, Akbar & Shore, Chris (Editors) **GN345.F87 1995**
The Future of Anthropology: Its Relevance to the Contemporary World. Trade Cloth. Continuum International Publishing Group, Ltd. London, 1995. 280p. ISBN:0-485-11445-3, ISBN13: 978-0-485-11445-4. Dewey:305.8/001. LCCN:95-034567.
Audience: **u,f.** *Choice, 1996.*

Biolsi, Thomas & Zimmerman, Larry J. (Editors) **E76.6.I53 1997**
Indians and Anthropologists: Vine Deloria, Jr., and the Critique of Anthropology. Trade Cloth. University of Arizona Press. Tucson, AZ. 1997. 240p. ISBN:0-8165-1606-5, ISBN13: 978-0-8165-1606-3. Dewey:301/.01. LCCN:96-045804.
Audience: **u,f.** *Choice, 1997.*

Bodley, John H. **GN380.B63 1999**
Victims of Progress. Ed. 4. Paper Text. McGraw-Hill Higher Education. Burr Ridge, IL. 1998. xi, 276p. ISBN:0-7674-0505-6, ISBN13: 978-0-7674-0505-8. Dewey:306/.08. LCCN:98-020615.
Audience: **g,l,u,f.**

Farmer, Paul **HM821.F37 2003**
Pathologies of Power: Health, Human Rights, and the New War on the Poor. Amartya Sen (Foreword by). Trade Cloth. University of California Press. Berkeley, CA. 2003. 419p. California Series in Public Anthropology, Vol. 4 ISBN:0-520-23550-9, ISBN13: 978-0-520-23550-2. Dewey:305.5/69. LCCN:2002-013311.
Audience: **u,f.** *Choice, 2004.*

Harrison, Faye V. (Editor) **GN345.D43 1997**
Decolonizing Anthropology: Moving Further Toward an Anthropology of Liberation. Trade Cloth. American Anthropological Association. Arlington, VA. 1997. ISBN:0-913167-83-5, ISBN13: 978-0-913167-83-0. Dewey:301/.01. LCCN:97-036965.
Audience: **u,f.**

Tsing, Anna Lowenhaupt **GN345.6.T75 2005**
Friction: An Enthography of Global Connection. Trade Cloth. Princeton University Press. Princeton, NJ. 2004. 376p. ISBN:0-691-12064-1, ISBN13: 978-0-691-12064-5. Dewey:303.48/2. LCCN:2004-043422.
Audience: **u,f.**

Social and Cultural Anthropology > Economic Anthropology

Bales, Kevin **HT867.B35 2004**
Disposable People: New Slavery in the Global Economy. Ed. 2. Trade Paper, Perfect. University of California Press. Berkeley, CA. 2004. 320p. ISBN:0-520-24384-6, ISBN13: 978-0-520-24384-2. Dewey:306.3/62. LCCN:2004-008180.
Audience: **g,l,u,f.** *Choice, 1999.*

Cook, Scott **GN564.M6C66 2004**
Understanding Commodity Cultures: Explorations in Economic Anthropology with Case Studies from Mexico. Book, Other. Rowman & Littlefield Publishers, Inc. Lanham, MD. 2004. 368p. ISBN:0-7425-3490-1, ISBN13: 978-0-7425-3490-2. Dewey:306.3/0972. LCCN:2003-027874.
Audience: **u,f.** *Choice, 2005.*

Cruz-Torres, Maria Luz **F1219.1.S56C78 2004**
Lives of Dust and Water: An Anthropology of Change and Resistance in Northwestern Mexico. Trade Cloth. University of Arizona Press. Tucson, AZ. 2004. 270p. ISBN:0-8165-2388-6, ISBN13: 978-0-8165-2388-7. Dewey:305.8/9707232. LCCN:2004-008526.
Audience: **u,f.** *Choice, 2005.*

Douglas, Mary **GN449.6**
The World of Goods. Library Binding. Routledge. New York, NY. 2002. 200p. Mary Douglas, Vol. 6:Collected Works ISBN:0-415-29109-7, ISBN13: 978-0-415-29109-5. Dewey:301.5/1.
Audience: **l,u,f.**

Durrenberger, E. Paul **GN448.2.S63 2005**
Labor in Cross-Cultural Perspective. Book, Other. AltaMira Press. Walnut Creek, CA. 2005. 338p. ISBN:0-7591-0582-0, ISBN13: 978-0-7591-0582-9. Dewey:306.3. LCCN:2005-009749.
Audience: **u,f.**

Firth, Raymond William **GN448.T45 2004**
Themes in Economic Anthropology. Library Binding. Routledge. New York, NY. 2004. 312p. Routledge Library Editions Ser., :Anthropology and Ethnography, US/Can. Edition Ser. ISBN:0-415-33019-X, ISBN13: 978-0-415-33019-0. Dewey:306.3.
Audience: **u,f.**

Forman, Shepard **HN0283.5.F6**
The Raft Fishermen: Tradition and Change in the Brazilian Peasant Economy. Trade Paper. Books on Demand. Ann Arbor, MI. 174p. Indiana University Publications International Studies Ser. ISBN:0-598-06247-5, ISBN13: 978-0-598-06247-5. Dewey:309.1/81/3. LCCN:78-126208.
Audience: **l,u,f.**

Freeman, Carla C. **HD6073.D372C274 2000**
High Tech and High Heels in the Global Economy: Women, Work and Pink-Collar Identities in the Caribbean. Trade Cloth. Duke University Press. Durham, NC. 1999. 384p. ISBN:0-8223-2403-2, ISBN13: 978-0-8223-2403-4. Dewey:331.4/81004/0972981. LCCN:99-025937.
Audience: **l,u,f.** *Choice, 2000.*

Goldstein, Melvyn C. & Beall, Cynthia M. **DS798.4.G65 1994**
The Changing World of Mongolia's Nomads. Trade Paper. University of California Press. Berkeley, CA. 1994. 176p. ISBN:0-520-08551-5, ISBN13: 978-0-520-08551-0. Dewey:951.7. LCCN:93-024004.
Audience: **g,u,f.**

Haugerud, Angelique (Editor), et al. **GN492.A5925 2004**
The Anthropology of Development and Globalization: From Classical Political Economy to Contemporary Neoliberalism. Professor Angelique Haugerud & Marc Edelman (Editors). Trade Cloth. Blackwell Publishing, Inc. Malden, MA. 2004. 416p. Blackwell Anthologies in Social and Cultural Anthropology Ser., Vol. 5 ISBN:0-631-22879-9, ISBN13: 978-0-631-22879-0. Dewey:306.2. LCCN:2004-012937.
Audience: **g,l,u.** *Choice, 2005.*

Malinowski, Bronislaw **GN671.N5**
Argonauts of the Western Pacific. James George Frazer (Preface by). Paper Text. Waveland Press, Inc. Prospect Heights, IL. 1984. 527p. ISBN:0-88133-084-1, ISBN13: 978-0-88133-084-7. Dewey:572.9953.
Audience: **g,l,u,f.**

Mauss, Marcel **GT3040**
The Gift: The Form and Reason for Exchange in Archaic Societies. Ed. 2. Paper over Boards. Taylor & Francis Group. Abingdon, 2001. 224p. ISBN:0-415-26748-X, ISBN13: 978-0-415-26748-9. Dewey:305.
Audience: **u,f.**

Meillassoux, Claude **HT1321.M4513**
The Anthropology of Slavery. Alide Dasnois (Translator). Trade Cloth. Continuum International Publishing Group, Ltd. London, 421p. ISBN:0-485-11395-3, ISBN13: 978-0-485-11395-2. Dewey:306.362096.
Audience: **g,l,u,f.**

Nash, June C. & Fernandez-Kelly, Maria P. (Editors) **HD5710.7 .W65 1983**
Women, Men, and the International Division of Labor. Paper Text. State University of New York Press. Albany, NY. 1984. 463p. SUNY Series in the Anthropology of Work ISBN:0-87395-684-2, ISBN13: 978-0-87395-684-0. Dewey:306/.36. LCCN:82-010447.
Audience: **u,f.**

Orlove, Benjamin S. & Custred, Glynn (Editors) **HN253.5.L36 1980**
Land and Power in Latin America: Agrarian Economics and Social Process in the Andes. Trade Cloth. Holmes & Meier Publishers, Inc. Teaneck, NJ. 1980. 258p. ISBN:0-8419-0476-6, ISBN13: 978-0-8419-0476-7. Dewey:301.35/098. LCCN:79-026598.
Audience: **l,u,f.**

Panter-Brick, Catherine (Editor, Contribution by) **GN388.H865 2001**
Hunter-Gatherers: An Interdisciplinary Perspective. Robert H. Layton & Peter Rowley-Conwy (Editors). Trade Paper. Cambridge University Press. New York, NY. 2001. 354p. The Biosocial Society Symposium Ser., Vol. 13 ISBN:0-521-77672-4, ISBN13: 978-0-521-77672-1. Dewey:306.3/64. LCCN:00-058511.
Audience: **l,u,f.**

Rothstein, Frances A. & Blim, Michael L. **HD2329**
Anthropology and the Global Factory. Paper Text. Greenwood Publishing Group, Inc. Portsmouth, NH. 1991. 296p. Studies of the New Industrialization in the Late Twentieth Century ISBN:0-89789-233-X, ISBN13: 978-0-89789-233-9. Dewey:338. LCCN:91-018922.
Audience: **u,f.**

Sahlins, Marshall David **GN489.S24 2004**
Stone Age Economics. Trade Cloth. Routledge. New York, NY. 2005. 368p. ISBN:0-415-33007-6, ISBN13: 978-0-415-33007-7. Dewey:306.3.
Audience: **u,f.**

Wolf, Eric R. **HD111**
Peasants. Ed. 1. Trade Paper. Prentice Hall PTR. Upper Saddle River, NJ. 1997. 116p. ISBN:0-13-655456-3, ISBN13: 978-0-13-655456-1. Dewey:301.35.
Audience: **l,u,f.**

Social and Cultural Anthropology > Educational Anthropology

Hemmings, Annette B. **LC205.H46 2004**
Coming of Age in U.S. High Schools: Economic, Kinship, Religious, and Political Crosscurrents. Cloth over Boards. Lawrence Erlbaum Associates, Inc. Mahwah, NJ. 2004. 232p. Sociocultural, Political, and Historical Studies in Education ISBN:0-8058-4666-2, ISBN13: 978-0-8058-4666-9. Dewey:373.18/0973. LCCN:2003-049328.
Audience: **u,f.** *Choice, 2004.*

Hourigan, Maureen M. **LC151.H68 1994**
Literacy as Social Exchange: Intersections of Class, Gender, and Culture. Cloth Text. State University of New York Press. Albany, NY. 1994. 152p. SUNY Series in Literacy, Culture, and Learning, :Theory and Practice ISBN:0-7914-2069-8, ISBN13: 978-0-7914-2069-0. Dewey:370.19/2/0973. LCCN:93-043234.
Audience: **l,u,f.**

Reed-Danahay, Deborah **LC191.8.F8**
Education and Identity in Rural France: The Politics of Schooling. Meyer Fortes, Edmund Leach, Jack Goody & Stanley Tambiah (Contribution by). Trade Paper. Cambridge University Press. New York, NY. 2004. 254p. Cambridge Studies in Social and Cultural Anthropology Ser. ISBN:0-521-61617-4, ISBN13: 978-0-521-61617-1. Dewey:370.19094459.
Audience: **u,f.** *Choice, 1996.*

Spindler, George D. (Editor) **LB45.E237 1997**
Education and Cultural Process: Anthropological Approaches. Ed. 3. Paper Text. Waveland Press, Inc. Prospect Heights, IL. 1997. 561p. ISBN:0-88133-958-X, ISBN13: 978-0-88133-958-1. Dewey:306.43. LCCN:98-115988.
Audience: **l,u,f.**

Spindler, George D. & Hammond, Lorie (Editors) **LB45.N49 2005**
Innovations in Educational Ethnography: Theories, Methods and Results. Tessie L. Barcenal, Purita P. Bilbao & Carol Brandt (Contribution by). Cloth over Boards. Lawrence Erlbaum Associates, Inc. Mahwah, NJ. 2006. 408p. ISBN:0-8058-4530-5, ISBN13: 978-0-8058-4530-3. Dewey:306.43. LCCN:2005-040154.
Audience: **l,u,f.**

Spindler, Louise S. **LB45.S66 2000**
Fifty Years of Anthropology and Education, 1950-2000: A Spindler Anthology. George D. Spindler (Editor), Frederick Erickson, Raymond McDermott & Susan Parman (Contribution by). Cloth over Boards. Lawrence Erlbaum Associates, Inc. Mahwah, NJ. 2000. 456p. ISBN:0-8058-3495-8, ISBN13: 978-0-8058-3495-6. Dewey:306.43. LCCN:99-086789.
Audience: **l,u,f.**

Stambach, Amy **LA1844.K54S72 2000**
Lessons from Mount Kilimanjaro: Schooling, Community and Gender in East Africa. Paper over Boards. Routledge. New York, NY. 2000. 224p. ISBN:0-415-92582-7, ISBN13: 978-0-415-92582-2. Dewey:306.43/09678/26. LCCN:00-026956.
Audience: **u,f.**

Social and Cultural Anthropology > Anthropology and Environment

Bennett, John W. **GF50.B46 1996**
Human Ecology As Human Behavior: Essay in Environmental and Development Anthropology. Ed. 2. Trade Paper. Transaction Publishers. Somerset, NJ. 1995. 387p. ISBN:1-56000-849-0, ISBN13: 978-1-56000-849-1. Dewey:304.2. LCCN:95-022325.
Audience: **u,f.**

Crumley, Carole E. (Editor) **GF90.H57 1994**
Historical Ecology: Cultural Knowledge and Changing Landscapes. Trade Paper. School of American Research Press. Santa Fe, NM. 1994. 304p. ISBN:0-933452-85-3, ISBN13: 978-0-933452-85-5. Dewey:304.2. LCCN:93-006108.
Audience: **u,f.**

Crumley, Carole E. **GF50.N48 2001**
New Directions in Anthropology and Environment: Intersections. Trade Paper. AltaMira Press. Walnut Creek, CA. 2001. 324p. ISBN:0-7425-0265-1, ISBN13: 978-0-7425-0265-9. Dewey:304.2. LCCN:00-059406.
Audience: **l,u,f.**

Ellen, Roy **GN345.E44 1982**
Environment, Subsistence and System: The Ecology of Small-Scale Social Formations. John Dunn, Jack Goody & Geoffrey Hawthorn (Contribution by). Trade Paper. Cambridge University Press. New York, NY. 1982. 344p. Themes in the Social Sciences Ser. ISBN:0-521-28703-0, ISBN13: 978-0-521-28703-6. Dewey:304.2. LCCN:81-018035.
Audience: **u,f.**

Forde, Daryll **GN316**
Habitat, Economy and Society: A Geographical Introduction to Ethnology. Ed. 7. Library Binding. Routledge. New York, NY. 2005. 528p. Routledge Library Editions Ser., :Anthropology and Ethnography, US/Can. Edition Ser. ISBN:0-415-33006-8, ISBN13: 978-0-415-33006-0. Dewey:305.8.
Audience: **l,u,f.**

Geertz, Clifford **HC447.G4 1963**
Agricultural Involution: The Processes of Ecological Change in Indonesia. Trade Cloth. University of California Press. Berkeley, CA. 1963. 176p. ISBN:0-520-00459-0, ISBN13: 978-0-520-00459-7. Dewey:330.9598. LCCN:63-020356.
Audience: **u,f.**

Ingold, Tim **GN407.3.I54 1987**
The Appropriation of Nature: Essays on Human Ecology and Social Relations. Cloth Text. University of Iowa Press. Iowa City, IA. 1987. 297p. ISBN:0-87745-167-2, ISBN13: 978-0-87745-167-9. Dewey:304.2. LCCN:86-051130.
Audience: **u,f.** *Choice, 1988.*

Ingold, Tim (Editor), et al. **GN388**
Hunters and Gatherers: Property, Power and Ideology. James Woodburn & David Riches (Editors). Trade Paper. Berg

Publishers. Oxford, 1997. 330p. Explorations in Anthropology Ser., Vol. 2 ISBN:0-85496-735-4, ISBN13: 978-0-85496-735-3. Dewey:306.3/64. LCCN:87-021216.
Audience: **u,f.**

Johansen, Bruce E. **GF50**
Indigenous Peoples and Environmental Issues: An Encyclopedia. Cloth Text. Greenwood Publishing Group, Inc. Portsmouth, NH. 2003. 552p. ISBN:0-313-32398-4, ISBN13: 978-0-313-32398-0. Dewey:304.2. LCCN:2003-040582.
Audience: **g,l,u,f.** *Choice, 2004.*

Kempton, Willett M., et al. **GE180**
Environmental Values in American Culture. James S. Boster & Jennifer A. Hartley (Authors). Trade Paper. MIT Press. Cambridge, MA. 1996. 336p. ISBN:0-262-61123-6, ISBN13: 978-0-262-61123-7. Dewey:363.7/00973.
Audience: **g,l,u,f.**

McCabe, J. Terrence **DT433.545.T87M33**
Cattle Bring Us to Our Enemies: Turkana Ecology, Politics, and Raiding in a Disequilibrium System. Trade Cloth. University of Michigan Press. Chicago, IL. 2004. 320p. Human-Environment Interactions Ser. ISBN:0-472-09878-0, ISBN13: 978-0-472-09878-1. Dewey:333.74/137/0967627. LCCN:2004-008130.
Audience: **u,f.** *Choice, 2005.*

Milton, Kay **GE195.M55 1996**
Environmentalism and Cultural Theory: Exploring the Role of Anthropology in Environmental Discourse. Paper over Boards. Routledge. New York, NY. 1996. 288p. Environment and Society Ser. ISBN:0-415-11529-9, ISBN13: 978-0-415-11529-2. Dewey:304.2. LCCN:95-026822.
Audience: **u,f.**

Moran, Emilio F. (Editor) **GN33.E27 1990**
The Ecosystem Approach in Anthropology: From Concept to Practice. Ed. 2. Trade Paper. University of Michigan Press. Chicago, IL. 1991. 496p. ISBN:0-472-08102-0, ISBN13: 978-0-472-08102-8. Dewey:301. LCCN:90-011306.
Audience: **u,f.**

Moran, Emilio F. **GF51**
People and Nature: An Introduction to Human Ecological Relations. Trade Cloth. Blackwell Publishing, Inc. Malden, MA. 2006. 232p. Blackwell Primers in Anthropology Ser., Vol. 1 ISBN:1-4051-0571-2, ISBN13: 978-1-4051-0571-2. Dewey:304.2. LCCN:2005-021020.
Audience: **l,u,f.**

Rappaport, Roy A. **DU740.42.R36**
Pigs for the Ancestors: Ritual in the Ecology of a New Guinea People. Ed. 2. Paper Text. Waveland Press, Inc. Prospect Heights, IL. 2000. 501p. ISBN:1-57766-101-X, ISBN13: 978-1-57766-101-6. Dewey:306/.09953.
Audience: **u,f.** B

Salzman, Philip Carl **GN387.S24 2004**
Pastoralists: Equality, Hierarchy, and the State. Trade Paper. Westview Press. Boulder, CO. 2004. 208p. ISBN:0-8133-3814-X, ISBN13: 978-0-8133-3814-9. LCCN:2003-023824.
Audience: **l,u,f.** *Choice, 2005.*

Steward, Julian H. **HM131**
The Concept and Method of Cultural Ecology. Paper Text. Irvington Publishers. New York, NY. 1993. Reprint Series in Social Sciences ISBN:0-8290-2923-0, ISBN13: 978-0-8290-2923-9. Dewey:302.35.
Audience: **u,f.**

Sutton, Mark Q. & Anderson, E. N. **GF50.S88 2004**
An Introduction to Cultural Ecology. Trade Paper. AltaMira Press. Walnut Creek, CA. 2004. 400p. ISBN:0-7591-0531-6, ISBN13: 978-0-7591-0531-7. Dewey:304.2. LCCN:2003-022110.
Audience: **l,u.** *Choice, 2005.*

Social and Cultural Anthropology > Gender

Abu-Lughod, Lila **DT72**
Veiled Sentiments: Honor and Poetry in a Bedouin Society. Trade Paper. University of California Press. Berkeley, CA. 2000. 358p. ISBN:0-520-22473-6, ISBN13: 978-0-520-22473-5. Dewey:306/.089927. LCCN:86-006948.
Audience: **g,l,u,f.** *Choice, 1987.*

Boddy, Janice **HQ1793.5.B64 1989**
Wombs and Alien Spirits: Women, Men and the Zar Cult in Northern Sudan. Paper Text. University of Wisconsin Press. Chicago, IL. 1989. 384p. New Directions in Anthropological Writing Ser. ISBN:0-299-12314-6, ISBN13: 978-0-299-12314-7. Dewey:305.3/09625. LCCN:89-040250.
Audience: **u,f.**

Busby, Cecilia **HN690.K4**
The Performance of Gender: An Anthropology of Everyday Life in a South Indian Fishing Village. Cloth over Boards. Berg Publishers. Oxford, 2000. 256p. London School of Economics Monographs on Social Anthropology Ser. ISBN:1-84520-035-7, ISBN13: 978-1-84520-035-0. Dewey:306/.0954/83.
Audience: **u,f.**

Di Leonardo, Micaela (Introduction by) **GN33.G46 1991**
Gender at the Crossroads of Knowledge: Feminist Anthropology in the Postmodern Era. Trade Cloth. University of California Press. Berkeley, CA. 1991. 423p. ISBN:0-520-07092-5, ISBN13: 978-0-520-07092-9. Dewey:305.42. LCCN:90-011297.
Audience: **g,l,u,f.**

Goheen, Miriam **DT571.N74G64 1996**
Men Own the Fields, Women Own the Crops: Gender and Power in the Cameroon Grassfields. Trade Cloth. University of Wisconsin Press. Chicago, IL. 1996. 272p. ISBN:0-299-14670-7, ISBN13: 978-0-299-14670-2. Dewey:305.3/096711. LCCN:95-025275.
Audience: **u,f.** *Choice, 1997.*

Haraway, Donna Jeanne **QL737.P9H245 1989**
Primate Visions: Gender, Race and Nature in the World of Modern Science. Trade Cloth. Routledge. New York, NY. 1989. 544p. ISBN:0-415-90114-6, ISBN13: 978-0-415-90114-7. Dewey:599.8/072. LCCN:89-010079.
Audience: **u,f.**

Ifekwunigwe, Jayne O. **HT1523.I36 1999**
Scattered Be-Longings: Cultural Paradoxes of Race, Nation and Gender. Paper over Boards. Routledge. New York, NY. 1999. 240p. ISBN:0-415-17095-8, ISBN13: 978-0-415-17095-6. Dewey:305.8. LCCN:98-020493.
Audience: **l,u,f.**

Jolly, Margaret **GN671.N6J65 1994**
Women of the Place: Kastom, Colonialism and Gender in Vanuatu. Cloth Text. Gordon & Breach Publishing Group. New York, NY. 1994. Studies in Anthropology and History ISBN:3-7186-5453-9, ISBN13: 978-3-7186-5453-6. Dewey:305.4/099595. LCCN:93-005291.
Audience: **u,f.**

Kapchan, Deborah A. **HF3882.K37 1996**
Gender on the Market: Moroccan Women and the Revoicing of Tradition. Trade Cloth. University of Pennsylvania Press. Philadelphia, PA. 1996. 352p. Series in Contemporary Ethnography, :New Cultural Studies; Publication of AFS ISBN:0-8122-3155-4, ISBN13: 978-0-8122-3155-7. Dewey:381/.18/082. LCCN:95-051427.
Audience: **u,f.** *Choice, 1996.*

McClaurin, Irma (Editor) **GN33.8.B53 2001**
Black Feminist Anthropology: Theory, Politics, Praxis and Poetics. Johnnetta B. Cole (Foreword by). Cloth Text. Rutgers University Press. Piscataway, NJ. 2001. 272p. ISBN:0-8135-2925-5, ISBN13: 978-0-8135-2925-7. Dewey:305.42. LCCN:00-045686.
Audience: **g,l,u,f.** *Choice, 2002.*

Momsen, Janet H. (Editor) **HQ1240.5.C27.W66**
Women and Change in the Caribbean. Trade Cloth. Indiana University Press. Bloomington, IN. 1993. 320p. ISBN:0-253-33897-2, ISBN13: 978-0-253-33897-6. Dewey:305.4209729. LCCN:93-000422.
Audience: **u,f.** *Choice, 1994.*

Moore, Henrietta **GN479.7.M66 1988**
Feminism and Anthropology. Trade Paper. University of Minnesota Press. Minneapolis, MN. 1989. ix, 246p. Feminist Perspectives Ser. ISBN:0-8166-1750-3, ISBN13: 978-0-8166-1750-0. Dewey:305.4/2. LCCN:88-022032.
Audience: **g,l,u,f.** *Choice, 1989.*

Moore, Henrietta L., et al. **GN658.T46 1999**
Those Who Play with Fire: Gender, Fertility and Transformation in East and Southern Africa. Todd Sanders & Bwire Kaare (Authors). Cloth over Boards. Berg Publishers. Oxford, 1999. 320p. London School of Economics Monographs on Social Anthropology Ser., Vol. 69 ISBN:0-485-19569-0, ISBN13: 978-0-485-19569-9. Dewey:306/.09676. LCCN:99-012208.
Audience: **u,f.**

Parker, Richard G. **HQ76.2.B6P37 1999**
Beneath the Equator: Cultures of Desire, Male Homosexuality, and Emerging Gay Communities in Brazil. UK-B Format Paperback. Routledge. New York, NY. 1998. 256p. ISBN:0-415-91620-8, ISBN13: 978-0-415-91620-2. Dewey:305.9/0664/0981. LCCN:98-017428.
Audience: **u,f.** *Choice, 1999.*

Roscoe, Will **E99.Z9R78 1991**
The Zuni Man-Woman. Trade Cloth. University of New Mexico Press. Albuquerque, NM. 1991. 302p. ISBN:0-8263-1253-5, ISBN13: 978-0-8263-1253-2. Dewey:306.73/089974. LCCN:90-021397.
Audience: **u,f.** *Choice, 1992.*

White, Sarah C. **HQ1745.6.W54 1992**
Arguing with the Crocodile: Gender and Class in Bangladesh. Cloth over Boards. Zed Books, Ltd. London, 1992. 192p. ISBN:1-85649-085-8, ISBN13: 978-1-85649-085-6. Dewey:305.42095492. LCCN:92-017852.
Audience: **u,f.** *Choice, 1993.*

Wiber, Melanie G. **GN799.W66**
Erect Men/Undulating Women: The Visual Imagery of Gender, "Race" and Progress in Reconstructive Illustrations of Human Evolution. Trade Paper. Wilfrid Laurier University Press. Waterloo, ON. 1998. 290p. ISBN:0-88920-308-3, ISBN13: 978-0-88920-308-2. Dewey:301/.082.
Audience: **g,l,u,f.**

Social and Cultural Anthropology > Kinship, Marriage, Family, Household Systems

Carsten, Janet **GN487.C37 2004**
After Kinship. Cloth Text. Cambridge University Press. New York, NY. 2003. 230p. New Departures in Anthropology Ser. ISBN:0-521-66198-6, ISBN13: 978-0-521-66198-0. Dewey:306.83. LCCN:2003-053191.
Audience: **u,f.**

Carsten, Janet (Editor) **GN487.C85 2000**
Cultures of Relatedness: New Approaches to the Study of Kinship. Cloth Text. Cambridge University Press. New York, NY. 2000. 225p. ISBN:0-521-65193-X, ISBN13: 978-0-521-65193-6. Dewey:306.83. LCCN:99-015844.
Audience: **u,f.**

Carsten, Janet **GN635.M4C39 1997**
The Heat of the Hearth: The Process of Kinship in a Malay Fishing Community. Trade Paper. Oxford University Press, Inc. New York, NY. 1997. 330p. Oxford Studies in Social and Cultural Anthropology - Cultural Forms ISBN:0-19-828046-7, ISBN13: 978-0-19-828046-0. Dewey:306.8/3/09595. LCCN:96-035165.
Audience: **u,f.** *Choice, 1998.*

Edwards, Jeanette **HQ616.15.B33E38 2000**
Born and Bred: Idioms of Kinship and New Reproductive Technologies in England. Trade Cloth. Oxford University Press, Inc. New York, NY. 2000. 278p. Oxford Studies in Social and Cultural Anthropology - Cultural Forms ISBN:0-19-823394-9, ISBN13: 978-0-19-823394-7. Dewey:306.8/3/0942. LCCN:00-701420.
Audience: **u,f.**

Edwards, Jeanette **HQ761.T43 1999**
Technologies of Procreation: Kinship in the Age of Assisted Conception. Ed. 2. Library Binding. Routledge. New York, NY. 1999. 256p. ISBN:0-415-17055-9, ISBN13: 978-0-415-17055-0. Dewey:304.6/32. LCCN:98-035025.
Audience: **u,f.**

Feinberg, Richard & Ottenheimer, Martin (Editors) **GN487.C83 2001**
The Cultural Analysis of Kinship: The Legacy of David M. Schneider. Trade Cloth. University of Illinois Press. Champaign, IL. 2001. 248p. ISBN:0-252-02673-X, ISBN13: 978-0-252-02673-7. Dewey:306.83. LCCN:2001-000389.
Audience: **u,f.**

Fortes, Meyer **GN480 .F6**
Marriage in Tribal Societies. Paper Text. Textbook Publishers. Temecula, CA. 2003. vii, 157p. ISBN:0-7581-5443-7, ISBN13: 978-0-7581-5443-9. Dewey:301.42.
Audience: **l,u,f.**

Franklin, Sarah & McKinnon, Susan (Editors) **GN487.R45 2001**
Relative Values: Reconfiguring Kinship Studies. Trade Cloth. Duke University Press. Durham, NC. 2001. 496p. ISBN:0-8223-2786-4, ISBN13: 978-0-8223-2786-8. Dewey:306.83. LCCN:2001-040472.
Audience: **l,u,f.** *Choice, 2003, 2002.*

Franklin, Sarah & Ragone, Helena (Editors) **GN482.1.R46 1998**
Reproducing Reproduction: Kinship, Power, and Technological Innovation. Trade Cloth. University of Pennsylvania Press. Philadelphia, PA. 1997. 264p. ISBN:0-8122-3352-2, ISBN13: 978-0-8122-3352-0. Dewey:306.4/61. LCCN:97-036945.
Audience: **u,f.**

Goody, Esther N. **DT510.43.G65G66 2005**
Contexts of Kinship: An Essay in the Family Sociology of the Gonja of Northern Ghana. Meyer Fortes, Edmund Leach, Jack Goody & Stanley Tambiah (Contribution by). Trade Paper. Cambridge University Press. New York, NY. 2005. 353p. Cambridge Studies in Social and Cultural Anthropology Ser., Vol. 7 ISBN:0-521-01720-3, ISBN13: 978-0-521-01720-6. Dewey:301.42/1. LCCN:2006-272607.
Audience: **u,f.**

Goody, Jack **HQ611.G665 2000**
The European Family. Trade Cloth. Blackwell Publishing, Inc. Malden, MA. 1999. 224p. The Making of Europe Ser. ISBN:0-631-20156-4, ISBN13: 978-0-631-20156-4. Dewey:306.85/094. LCCN:99-034410.
Audience: **g,l,u,f.** *Choice, 2000.*

Goody, Jack (Author, Contribution by) **GN484.4**
Production and Reproduction: A Comparative Study of the Domestic Domain. Meyer Fortes, Edmund Leach & Stanley Tambiah (Contribution by). Trade Paper. Cambridge University Press. New York, NY. 1977. 170p. Cambridge Studies in Social and Cultural Anthropology, No.17 ISBN:0-521-29088-0, ISBN13: 978-0-521-29088-3. Dewey:301.42. LCCN:76-004238.
Audience: **u,f.**

Gray, Robert F. & Gulliver, P. **GN480**
The Family Estate in Africa: Studies in the Role of Property in Family Structure and Lineage Continuity. Library Binding. Routledge. New York, NY. 2004. 280p. Routledge Library Editions Ser., :Anthropology and Ethnography, US/Can. Edition Ser. ISBN:0-415-32985-X, ISBN13: 978-0-415-32985-9. Dewey:392.3/096.
Audience: **u,f.**

Griffiths, Anne M. **DT2458.K84G75 1997**
In the Shadow of Marriage: Gender and Justice in an African Community. Trade Cloth. University of Chicago Press. Chicago, IL. 1998. 320p. ISBN:0-226-30873-1, ISBN13: 978-0-226-30873-9. Dewey:305.3096883. LCCN:97-019579.
Audience: **u,f.** *Choice, 1998.*

Hua, Cai & Hustvedt, Asti **DS731.N39H8313 2001**
A Society Without Fathers or Husbands: The Na of China. Trade Cloth. Zone Books. Brooklyn, NY. 2001. 512p. ISBN:1-890951-12-9, ISBN13: 978-1-890951-12-2. Dewey:306.8/089/951. LCCN:99-010528.
Audience: **u,f.** *Choice, 2002.*

Kahn, Susan Martha **KMK1527.K34 2000**
Reproducing Jews: A Cultural Account of Assisted Conception in Israel. Library Binding. Duke University Press. Durham, NC. 2000. viii, 227p. Body, Commodity, Text Ser. ISBN:0-8223-2601-9, ISBN13: 978-0-8223-2601-4. Dewey:306.83. LCCN:00-030856.
Audience: **u,f.** *Choice, 2001.*

Modell, Judith **HV875.55.M643 2001**
A Sealed and Secret Kinship: The Culture of Policies and Practices in American Adoption. Trade Cloth. Berghahn Books, Inc. New York, NY. 2002. 224p. Public Issues in Anthropological Perspectives Ser. ISBN:1-57181-077-3, ISBN13: 978-1-57181-077-9. Dewey:362.73/4/0973. LCCN:2001-049957.
Audience: **u,f.** *Choice, 2003.*

Parkin, R. J. & Stone, Linda (Editors) **GN487.K53 2004**
Kinship and Family: An Anthropological Reader. Trade Paper. Blackwell Publishing, Inc. Malden, MA. 2003. 496p. Blackwell Anthologies in Social and Cultural Anthropology Ser., Vol. 4 ISBN:0-631-22999-X, ISBN13: 978-0-631-22999-5. Dewey:306.85. LCCN:2003-056028.
Audience: **l,u,f.**

Radcliffe-Brown, A. R. & Forde, Daryll (Editors) **GN645.A375 1987**
African Systems of Kinship and Marriage. Paper Text. Routledge. New York, NY. 1994. 400p. ISBN:0-7103-0234-7, ISBN13: 978-0-7103-0234-2. Dewey:306.8/3/096. LCCN:87-146735.
Audience: **l,u,f.**

Schneider, David M. **GN560.U6**
American Kinship: A Cultural Account. Ed. 2. Trade Paper. University of Chicago Press. Chicago, IL. 1980. 148p. ISBN:0-226-73930-9, ISBN13: 978-0-226-73930-4. Dewey:301.42/1/0973. LCCN:79-018185.
Audience: **l,u,f.**

Schneider, David M. **GN487.S36 1984**
A Critique of the Study of Kinship. Trade Paper. University of Michigan Press. Chicago, IL. 1984. 224p. ISBN:0-472-08051-2, ISBN13: 978-0-472-08051-9. Dewey:306.8/3. LCCN:84-005246.
Audience: **u,f.**

Schneider, David Murray **GN480.4 .S37**
Matrilineal Kinship. Paper Text. Textbook Publishers. Temecula, CA. 2003. xx, 761p. ISBN:0-7581-2756-1, ISBN13: 978-0-7581-2756-3. Dewey:392.3.
Audience: **l,u,f.**

Smith, Raymond T. **GN564.C37S65 1995**
The Matrifocal Family: Power, Pluralism and Politics. UK-B Format Paperback. Routledge. New York, NY. 1995. 250p. ISBN:0-415-91215-6, ISBN13: 978-0-415-91215-0. Dewey:306.8/5. LCCN:95-013171.
Audience: **u,f.**

Smith, Raymond T. **HQ602.B7 S6**
Negro Family in British Guiana: Family Structure and Social Status in the Villages. Paper over Boards. Routledge. New York, NY. 2003. 308p. International Library of Sociology Ser., Vol. 66 ISBN:0-415-17576-3, ISBN13: 978-0-415-17576-0. Dewey:301.
Audience: **u,f.**

Stone, Linda (Editor) **GN480.S83 2001**
New Directions in Anthropological Kinship. Book, Other. Rowman & Littlefield Publishers, Inc. Lanham, MD. 2000. 368p. ISBN:0-7425-0107-8, ISBN13: 978-0-7425-0107-2. Dewey:306.83. LCCN:00-040303.
Audience: **l,u,f.**

Strathern, Marilyn **GN487.S767 2005**
Kinship, Law and the Unexpected: Relatives Are Always a Surprise. Trade Cloth. Cambridge University Press. New York, NY. 2005. 240p. ISBN:0-521-84992-6, ISBN13: 978-0-521-84992-0. Dewey:306.83. LCCN:2005-000153.
Audience: **l,u,f.**

Weston, Kath **HQ76.3.U5W48**
Families We Choose: Lesbians, Gays, Kinship. Ed. 2. Trade Paper. Columbia University Press. New York, NY. 1997. 288p. Between Men, Between Women Ser. ISBN:0-231-11093-6, ISBN13: 978-0-231-11093-8. Dewey:306.87. LCCN:90-049349.
Audience: **g,l,u,f.** *Choice, 1991.*

Social and Cultural Anthropology > Legal Anthropology

An-Na'im, Abdullahi A. (Editor) **JC599.A35C85 2002**
Cultural Transformation and Human Rights in Africa. Cloth over Boards. Zed Books, Ltd. London, 2002. 288p. ISBN:1-84277-090-X, ISBN13: 978-1-84277-090-0. Dewey:323.096. LCCN:2002-726605.
Audience: **l,u,f.**

Biolsi, Thomas **KFS3505.5.R67 B56**
Deadliest Enemies: Law and Making the Race Relations on and off Rosebud Reservation. Trade Cloth. University of California Press. Berkeley, CA. 2001. 256p. ISBN:0-520-22078-1, ISBN13: 978-0-520-22078-2. Dewey:342.783/0872. LCCN:00-067498.
Audience: **g,l,u,f.** *Choice, 2002.*

Brown, Michael F. **K1401.B79 2003**
Who Owns Native Culture? Trade Cloth. Harvard University Press. Cambridge, MA. 2003. 336p. ISBN:0-674-01171-6, ISBN13: 978-0-674-01171-7. Dewey:346.04/8. LCCN:2003-044978.
Audience: **g,l,u,f.** *Choice, 2004.*

Greenhouse, Carol J., et al. **KF371.G74 1994**
Law and Community in Three American Towns. Barbara Yngvesson & David M. Engel (Authors). Trade Paper. Cornell University Press. Ithaca, NY. 1994. 240p. ISBN:0-8014-8169-4, ISBN13: 978-0-8014-8169-7. Dewey:340/.115. LCCN:93-044353.
Audience: **l,u,f.** *Choice, 1995.*

Koff, Clea **DT450.435**
The Bone Woman: A Forensic Anthropologist's Search for Truth in Rwanda, Bosnia, and Kosovo. Trade Paper. Random House of Canada, Ltd. Mississauga, ON. 2005. 304p. ISBN:0-676-97607-7, ISBN13: 978-0-676-97607-6. Dewey:364.15/1/0967571.
Audience: **g,l,u,f.**

Lâm, Maivân Clech **K3247.L36 2000**
At the Edge of the State: Indigenous Peoples and Self-Determination. Richard A. Falk (Contribution by). Trade Cloth. Transnational Publishers, Inc. Ardsley, NY. 2000. 300p. Innovation in International Law Ser. ISBN:1-57105-076-0, ISBN13: 978-1-57105-076-2. Dewey:341.26. LCCN:00-027349.
Audience: **g,l,u,f.** *Choice, 2001.*

Maine, Sir, Henry Sumner **D85.L3**
Ancient Law: Its Connection with the Early History of Society, and Its Relation to Modern Ideas. Trade Cloth. Scholarly Publishing Office, University of Michigan Library. Ann Arbor, MI. 2004. ISBN:1-4181-2886-4, ISBN13: 978-1-4181-2886-9. Dewey:340.09.
Audience: **u,f.**

Merry, Sally E. **KF379.M47 1990**
Getting Justice and Getting Even: Legal Consciousness among Working-Class Americans. Trade Cloth. University of Chicago Press. Chicago, IL. 1997. 238p. Language and Legal Discourse Ser. ISBN:0-226-52068-4, ISBN13: 978-0-226-52068-1. Dewey:349.73. LCCN:89-029627.
Audience: **l,u,f.** *Choice, 1991.*

Merry, Sally Engle **HQ1237.M47 2006**
Human Rights and Gender Violence: Translating International Law into Local Justice. Trade Cloth. University of Chicago Press. Chicago, IL. 2005. 264p. Chicago Series in Law and Society Ser. ISBN:0-226-52073-0, ISBN13: 978-0-226-52073-5. Dewey:362.88/082. LCCN:2005-011951.
Audience: **g,l,u,f.**

Nader, Laura **K487.A57L385 1997**
Law in Culture and Society. Trade Paper. University of California Press. Berkeley, CA. 1997. 464p. ISBN:0-520-20833-1, ISBN13: 978-0-520-20833-9. Dewey:340/.115. LCCN:96-034175.
Audience: **u,f.**

Nader, Laura **K487.A57N33 2002**
The Life of the Law: Anthropological Projects. Trade Cloth. University of California Press. Berkeley, CA. 2002. 278p. ISBN:0-520-22988-6, ISBN13: 978-0-520-22988-4. Dewey:340/.115. LCCN:2001-027675.
Audience: **u,f.**

Newman, Katherine S. **K583**
Law and Economic Organization: A Comparative Study of Preindustrial Studies. Trade Cloth. Cambridge University Press. New York, NY. 1983. 276p. ISBN:0-521-24791-8, ISBN13: 978-0-521-24791-7. Dewey:342. LCCN:83-007169.
Audience: **u,f.** B

Pospísil, Leopold **K**
Anthropology of Law: A Comparative Theory. Trade Cloth. Harper & Row Ltd. London, 1971. xiii, 385p. ISBN:0-06-045247-1, ISBN13: 978-0-06-045247-6. Dewey:340.1/15. LCCN:70-154880.
Audience: **l,u,f.**

Price-Cohen, Cynthia (Editor) **K3240.6.H879 1998**
Human Rights of Indigenous Peoples. Trade Paper. Transnational Publishers, Inc. Ardsley, NY. 1998. 462p. ISBN:0-941320-93-6, ISBN13: 978-0-941320-93-1. Dewey:341.4/81. LCCN:98-025991.
Audience: **g,l,u,f.**

Starr, June & Collier, Jane F. (Editors) **K146.H57 1989**
History and Power in the Study of Law: New Directions in Legal Anthropology. Book, Other. Cornell University Press. Ithaca, NY. 1989. 352p. The Anthropology of Contemporary Issues Ser. ISBN:0-8014-2113-6, ISBN13: 978-0-8014-2113-6. Dewey:340/.115. LCCN:88-030258.
Audience: **u,f.**

Wilson, Richard (Editor) **JC571.H769523 2003**
Human Rights in Global Perspective: Anthropological Studies of Rights, Claims and Entitlements. Jon P. Mitchell (Editor, Foreword by). Paper over Boards. Routledge. New York, NY. 2003. 272p. ASA Monographs ISBN:0-415-30409-1, ISBN13: 978-0-415-30409-2. Dewey:323. LCCN:2002-036976.
Audience: **u,f.**

Social and Cultural Anthropology > Political Anthropology

Barth, Fredrik **DS485.S8 B3**
Political Leadership among Swat Pathans. Cloth over Boards. Berg Publishers. Oxford, 1965. 220p. London School of Economics Monographs on Social Anthropology Ser., Vol. 19 ISBN:1-84520-007-1, ISBN13: 978-1-84520-007-7. Dewey:954.9/12.
Audience: **u,f.**

Das, Veena & Poole, Deborah **GN492.A5923 2004**
Anthropology in the Margins of the State. Trade Cloth. School of American Research Press. Santa Fe, NM. 2004. 354p. School of American Research Advanced Seminar Ser. ISBN:1-930618-40-9, ISBN13: 978-1-930618-40-4. Dewey:306.2. LCCN:2003-026005.
Audience: **u,f.**

Di Leonardo, Micaela **GN33.D5 1998**
Exotics at Home: Anthropologies, Others, and American Modernity. Trade Cloth. University of Chicago Press. Chicago, IL. 1998. 464p. Women in Culture and Society Ser. ISBN:0-226-47263-9, ISBN13: 978-0-226-47263-8. Dewey:305.8001. LCCN:97-048475.
Audience: **l,u,f.** *Choice, 1999.*

Engels, Friedrich **HQ518**
Origin of the Family, Private Property, and the State. Ed. 2. Eleanor Burke Leacock (Editor). Trade Paper. International Publishers Company, Inc. New York, NY. 1972. 274p. ISBN:0-7178-0359-7, ISBN13: 978-0-7178-0359-0. Dewey:306.8/5. LCCN:79-184309.
Audience: **l,u,f.** B

Eriksen, Thomas Hylland **GN495.6.E75 2002**
Ethnicity and Nationalism: Anthropological Perspectives. Ed. 2. Trade Cloth. Pluto Press. London, 2002. 224p. Anthropology, Culture, and Society Ser. ISBN:0-7453-1888-6, ISBN13: 978-0-7453-1888-2. Dewey:305.8. LCCN:2002-002245.
Audience: **l,u,f.**

Gledhill, John **GN492.G55**
Power and Its Disguises: Anthropological Perspectives on Politics. Ed. 2. Trade Paper. Pluto Press. London, 2000. 288p. Anthropology, Culture and Society Ser. ISBN:0-7453-1685-9, ISBN13: 978-0-7453-1685-7. Dewey:306.2. LCCN:00-026069.
Audience: **u,f.** *Choice, 1994.*

Gluckman, Max **GN645.G56 2004**
Order and Rebellion in Tribal Africa. Library Binding. Routledge. New York, NY. 2004. 288p. Routledge Library Editions Ser., :Anthropology and Ethnography, US/Can. Edition Ser. ISBN:0-415-32983-3, ISBN13: 978-0-415-32983-5. Dewey:306.2/0967.
Audience: **u,f.**

Gupta, Akhil **GN492.A54 2006**
The Anthropology of the State: A Reader. Aradhana Sharma (Editor). Trade Cloth. Blackwell Publishing, Inc. Malden, MA. 2006. 424p. Blackwell Readers in Anthropology Ser., Vol. 9 ISBN:1-4051-1467-3, ISBN13: 978-1-4051-1467-7. Dewey:306.2. LCCN:2005-013799.
Audience: **g,l,u,f.**

Hansen, Thomas Blom & Stepputat, Finn (Editors) **GN492.S68 2005**
Sovereign Bodies: Citizens, Migrants, and States in the Postcolonial World. Trade Cloth. Princeton University Press. Princeton, NJ. 2005. 360p. ISBN:0-691-12118-4, ISBN13: 978-0-691-12118-5. Dewey:305.5/122. LCCN:2004-054933.
Audience: **u,f.**

Kurtz, Donald V. **GN492.K87 2001**
Political Anthropology: Power and Paradigms. Trade Paper. Westview Press. Boulder, CO. 2001. 272p. ISBN:0-8133-3804-2, ISBN13: 978-0-8133-3804-0. Dewey:306.2. LCCN:00-053179.
Audience: **u,f.** *Choice, 2002.*

Leach, E. R. **DS485.B85L4**
Political Systems of Highland Burma: A Study of Kachin Social Structure. Cloth over Boards. Berg Publishers. Oxford, 1973. 352p. London School of Economics Monographs on Social Anthropology Ser. ISBN:1-84520-055-1, ISBN13: 978-1-84520-055-8. Dewey:320.9/591.
Audience: **u,f.**

Nash, June **HD8039.M72**
We Eat the Mines and the Mines Eat Us: Dependency and Exploitation in Bolivian Tin Mines. Cloth Text. Columbia University Press. New York, NY. 1993. 384p. ISBN:0-231-08050-6, ISBN13: 978-0-231-08050-7. Dewey:331.7/6223453/0984.
Audience: **g,l,u,f.** B

Richards, Paul **GN497.N6 2004**
No Peace, No War: An Anthropology of Contemporary Armed Conflicts. Trade Cloth. Ohio University Press. Athens, OH. 2004. 288p. ISBN:0-8214-1575-1, ISBN13: 978-0-8214-1575-7. Dewey:303.6/6. LCCN:2004-063555.
Audience: **g,l,u,f.**

Sluka, Jeffrey A. (Editor) **HV6431.D433 2000**
Death Squad: The Anthropology of State Terror. Trade Cloth. University of Pennsylvania Press. Philadelphia, PA. 1999. x, 260p. The Ethnography of Political Violence Ser. ISBN:0-8122-3523-1, ISBN13: 978-0-8122-3523-4. Dewey:303.6/25. LCCN:99-034602.
Audience: **g,l,u,f.**

Sponsel, Leslie E. & Gregor, Thomas (Editors) **GN396.A57 1994**
The Anthropology of Peace and Nonviolence. Library Binding. Lynne Rienner Publishers, Inc. Boulder, CO. 1994. 300p. ISBN:1-55587-424-X, ISBN13: 978-1-55587-424-7. Dewey:303.6/1. LCCN:93-040822.
Audience: **l,u,f.**

Vincent, Joan (Editor) **GN492.A593 2002**
The Anthropology of Politics: A Reader in Ethnography, Theory, and Critique. Trade Cloth. Blackwell Publishing, Inc. Malden, MA. 2002. 488p. Anthologies in Social and Cultural Anthropology Ser., Vol. 3 ISBN:0-631-22439-4, ISBN13: 978-0-631-22439-6. Dewey:306.2. LCCN:2001-043232.
Audience: **g,l,u,f.**

Wolf, Eric R. **D208.W64 1982**
Europe and the People Without History. Trade Paper. University of California Press. Berkeley, CA. 1997. 534p. ISBN:0-520-04898-9, ISBN13: 978-0-520-04898-0. Dewey:940.2. LCCN:81-024031.
Audience: **g,l,u,f.** B

Wolf, Eric R. **D445.W8 1999**
Peasant Wars of the Twentieth Century. Trade Paper. University of Oklahoma Press. Norman, OK. 1999. 352p. ISBN:0-8061-3196-9, ISBN13: 978-0-8061-3196-2. Dewey:909.82. LCCN:99-026445.
Audience: **g,l,u,f.**

Wolf, Eric R. **GN345.W643 2001**
Pathways of Power: Building an Anthropology of the Modern World. Sydel Silverman (Editor), Aram A. Yengoyan (Foreword by). Trade Cloth. University of California Press. Berkeley, CA. 2001. 488p. ISBN:0-520-22333-0, ISBN13: 978-0-520-22333-2. Dewey:306. LCCN:00-055969.
Audience: **l,u,f.** *Choice, 2001.*

Social and Cultural Anthropology > Psychological Anthropology

Bock, Philip K. (Editor) **GN502**
Handbook of Psychological Anthropology. Cloth Text. Greenwood Publishing Group, Inc. Portsmouth, NH. 1994. 432p. ISBN:0-313-28433-4, ISBN13: 978-0-313-28433-5. Dewey:155.8. LCCN:93-043434.
Audience: **l,u,f.**

Bock, Philip K. (Editor) **GN502**
Psychological Anthropology. Paper Text. Greenwood Publishing Group, Inc. Portsmouth, NH. 1994. 432p. ISBN:0-275-94956-7, ISBN13: 978-0-275-94956-3. Dewey:155.8. LCCN:93-043434.
Audience: **l,u,f.**

Bock, Philip K. **GN502.B63 1999**
Rethinking Psychological Anthropology: Continuity and Change in the Study of Human Action. Ed. 2. Paper Text. Waveland Press, Inc. Prospect Heights, IL. 1999. 309p. ISBN:1-57766-055-2, ISBN13: 978-1-57766-055-2. Dewey:155.8/2. LCCN:99-234450.
Audience: **l,u,f.**

Devereux, George (Author, Translator) **RC455.4.E8**
Basic Problems of Ethnopsychiatry. Basia M. Gulati (Translator). Trade Cloth. University of Chicago Press. Chicago, IL. 1980. 380p. ISBN:0-226-14355-4, ISBN13: 978-0-226-14355-2. Dewey:616.89. LCCN:79-011104.
Audience: **u,f.**

Hallowell, A. Irving **GN671.C3M37**
Culture and Experience. Paper Text. Waveland Press, Inc. Prospect Heights, IL. 1988. 434p. ISBN:0-88133-368-9, ISBN13: 978-0-88133-368-8. Dewey:306.089973.
Audience: **l,u,f.** B

Ingham, John M. **GN502.I55 1996**
Psychological Anthropology Reconsidered. Trade Cloth. Cambridge University Press. New York, NY. 1996. 320p. Publications of the Society for Psychological Anthropology, No. 8 ISBN:0-521-55107-2, ISBN13: 978-0-521-55107-6. Dewey:155.8. LCCN:95-039730.
Audience: **l,u,f.**

Jahoda, Gustav **GN502.J325 1993**
Crossroads Between Culture and Mind: Continuities and Change in Theories of Human Nature. Trade Cloth. Harvard University Press. Cambridge, MA. 1993. 232p. ISBN:0-674-17775-4, ISBN13: 978-0-674-17775-8. Dewey:302.09. LCCN:92-019501.
Audience: **u,f.** *Choice, 1993.*

Kaplan, Bert **BF698.K33**
Studying Personality Cross: Culturally. Paper Text. Textbook Publishers. Temecula, CA. 2003. 687p. ISBN:0-7581-4511-X, ISBN13: 978-0-7581-4511-6. Dewey:137.082.
Audience: **g,l,u,f.**

Levine, Robert A. (Editor) **BF698.9.C8 L48**
Culture, Behavior, and Personality. Ed. 2. Trade Cloth. Aldine Transaction. Somerset, NJ. 1982. 335p. ISBN:0-202-01167-4, ISBN13: 978-0-202-01167-7. Dewey:155.9/2. LCCN:80-071038.
Audience: **l,u,f.**

Manson, William C. **GN504**
The Psychodynamics of Culture: Abram Kardiner and Neo-Freudian Anthropology. Trade Cloth. Greenwood Publishing Group, Inc. Portsmouth, NH. 1988. 162p. Contributions to the Study of Anthropology Ser., No. 3 ISBN:0-313-26267-5, ISBN13: 978-0-313-26267-8. Dewey:306/.01/9. LCCN:88-017778.
Audience: **l,u,f.**

Nuckolls, Charles W. **GN357.N83 1998**
Culture: A Problem That Cannot Be Solved. Trade Cloth. University of Wisconsin Press. Chicago, IL. 1998. 336p. ISBN:0-299-15890-X, ISBN13: 978-0-299-15890-3. Dewey:306. LCCN:98-006856.
Audience: **l,u,f.**

Rosaldo, Michelle Zimbalist **DS666.I4R67**
Knowledge and Passion. Trade Paper. Cambridge University Press. New York, NY. 1980. 272p. Cambridge Studies in Cultural Systems ISBN:0-521-29562-9, ISBN13: 978-0-521-29562-8. Dewey:305.8/9921. LCCN:79-012632.
Audience: **l,u,f.**

Spindler, George D. (Editor) **GN502**
The Making of Psychological Anthropology. Trade Cloth. University of California Press. Berkeley, CA. 1978. xiv, 665p. ISBN:0-520-03320-5, ISBN13: 978-0-520-03320-7. Dewey:155.8. LCCN:76-024597.
Audience: **l,u,f.**

Spiro, Melford E. **GN635.B8S63 1997**
Gender Ideology and Psychological Reality: An Essay on Cultural Reproduction. Cloth over Boards. Yale University Press. Cumberland, RI. 1997. 240p. ISBN:0-300-07007-1, ISBN13: 978-0-300-07007-1. Dewey:305.3/09591. LCCN:97-003919.
Audience: **u,f.** *Choice, 1998.*

Stigler, James W. (Editor) **GN502.C85 1990**
Cultural Psychology: Essays on Comparative Human Development. Richard A. Schweder & Gilbert S. Herdt (Editors). Trade Paper. Cambridge University Press. New York, NY. 1990. 637p. ISBN:0-521-37804-4, ISBN13: 978-0-521-37804-8. Dewey:155.8. LCCN:88-037008.
Audience: **u,f.** *Choice, 1991.*

Social and Cultural Anthropology > Religion

Allen, Catherine J. **F2230.2.K4A45 2002**
The Hold Life Has: Coca and Cultural Identity in an Andean Community. Ed. 2. Trade Paper. Smithsonian Institution Press. Washington, DC. 2002. 304p. ISBN:1-58834-032-5, ISBN13: 978-1-58834-032-0. Dewey:305.898/323. LCCN:2002-021013.
Audience: **l,u,f.** *Choice, 1989.*

Atran, Scott **BL53.A88 2002**
In Gods We Trust: The Evolutionary Landscape of Religion. Trade Cloth. Oxford University Press, Inc. New York, NY. 2002. 400p. Evolution and Cognition Ser. ISBN:0-19-514930-0, ISBN13: 978-0-19-514930-2. Dewey:200/.1/9. LCCN:2002-074884.
Audience: **l,u,f.**

Boyer, Pascal **BL48.B6438 2001**
Religion Explained. Trade Cloth. Basic Books. New York, NY. 2001. 384p. ISBN:0-465-00695-7, ISBN13: 978-0-465-00695-3. Dewey:200.1. LCCN:00-054661.
Audience: **g,l,u,f.** *Choice, 2002.*

Buckser, Andrew & Glazier, Stephen D. (Editors) **BL639.A58 2003**
The Anthropology of Religious Conversion. Book, Other. Rowman & Littlefield Publishers, Inc. Lanham, MD. 2003. 256p. ISBN:0-7425-1777-2, ISBN13: 978-0-7425-1777-6. Dewey:306.6/91. LCCN:2003-007435.
Audience: **l,u,f.**

Douglas, Mary Tew **GN494**
Purity and Danger: An Analysis of Concepts of Pollution and Taboo. Trade Cloth. Routledge. New York, NY. 1978. viii, 186p. ISBN:0-7100-1299-3, ISBN13: 978-0-7100-1299-9. Dewey:390.
Audience: **u,f.**

Elkin, A. P. **GN666.E43 1994**
Aboriginal Men of High Degree: Initiation and Sorcery in the World's Oldest Tradition. Trade Cloth. Inner Traditions International, Ltd. Rochester, VT. 1993. 224p. ISBN:0-89281-421-7, ISBN13: 978-0-89281-421-3. Dewey:299/.92. LCCN:93-030461.
Audience: **l,u,f.**

Evans-Pritchard, Edward E. **DT155.2.A93E92 1976**
Witchcraft, Oracles and Magic among the Azande. Paper Text. Oxford University Press, Inc. New York, NY. 1976. 260p. ISBN:0-19-874029-8, ISBN13: 978-0-19-874029-2. Dewey:133.4/0967. LCCN:76-375196.
Audience: **u,f.** B

Firth, Raymond **GN470.H35 1996**
Religion: A Humanist Interpretation. Paper over Boards. Routledge. New York, NY. 1995. 256p. ISBN:0-415-12896-X, ISBN13: 978-0-415-12896-4. Dewey:211.6. LCCN:95-009180.
Audience: **l,u,f.** *Choice, 1996.*

Hoehler-Fatton, Cynthia **BR1443.K4H64 1996**
Women of Fire and Spirit: History, Faith, and Gender in Roho Religion in Western Kenya. Cloth Text. Oxford University Press, Inc. New York, NY. 1996. 304p. ISBN:0-19-509790-4, ISBN13: 978-0-19-509790-0. Dewey:289.9. LCCN:95-011563.
Audience: **l,u,f.** *Choice, 1996.*

Holy, Ladislav **DT155.2.B47H65 1991**
Religion and Custom in a Muslim Society: The Berti of Sudan. Meyer Fortes, Jack Goody, Edmund Leach & Stanley Tambiah (Contribution by). Trade Cloth. Cambridge University Press. New York, NY. 1991. 255p. Cambridge Studies in Social and Cultural Anthropology, No. 78 ISBN:0-521-39485-6, ISBN13: 978-0-521-39485-7. Dewey:305.896/50624. LCCN:90-020417.
Audience: **l,u,f.** *Choice, 1992.*

Kehoe, Alice Beck **BL2370.S5K43 2000**
Shamans and Religion: An Anthropological Exploration in Critical Thinking. Paper Text. Waveland Press, Inc. Prospect Heights, IL. 2000. 125p. ISBN:1-57766-162-1, ISBN13: 978-1-57766-162-7. Dewey:291.1/44. LCCN:2001-268737.
Audience: **g,l,u,f.** *Choice, 2001.*

LaBarre, Weston **BL48**
The Ghost Dance: The Origins of Religion. Paper Text. Waveland Press, Inc. Prospect Heights, IL. 1990. 677p. ISBN:0-88133-561-4, ISBN13: 978-0-88133-561-3. Dewey:200.
Audience: **g,l,u,f.**

Lambek, Michael **BL256.R43 2001**
A Reader in the Anthropology of Religion. Trade Paper. Blackwell Publishing, Inc. Malden, MA. 2001. 632p. Anthologies in Social and Cultural Anthropology Ser., Vol. 2 ISBN:0-631-22113-1, ISBN13: 978-0-631-22113-5. Dewey:306.6. LCCN:2001-035008.
Audience: **g,l,u,f.**

Lewis, I. M. **BL626.L48 1989**
Ecstatic Religion: An Anthropological Study of Spirit Possession and Shamanism. Ed. 2. Trade Paper. Routledge. New York, NY. 1988. 208p. ISBN:0-415-00799-2, ISBN13: 978-0-415-00799-3. Dewey:306/.6. LCCN:88-023977.
Audience: **g,l,u,f.** B

Luhrmann, Tanya M. **BF1581.L84 1989**
Persuasions of the Witch's Craft: Ritual Magic in Contemporary England. Trade Cloth. Harvard University Press. Cambridge, MA. 1989. 396p. ISBN:0-674-66323-3, ISBN13: 978-0-674-66323-7. Dewey:133.4/3/0942. LCCN:88-033382.
Audience: **g,l,u,f.** *Choice, 1990.*

Middleton, John & Beidelman, Thomas O. **BL2480.L76**
Lugbara Religion. Trade Cloth. Lit Verlag. Munster, 1999. 344p. ISBN:3-8258-4034-4, ISBN13: 978-3-8258-4034-1. Dewey:306.6.
Audience: **g,l,u,f.**

Miller, Elmer S. **GN21.M52A3 1995**
Nurturing Doubt: From Mennonite Missionary to Anthropologist in the Argentine Chaco. Trade Cloth. University of Illinois Press. Champaign, IL. 1995. 248p. ISBN:0-252-02155-X, ISBN13: 978-0-252-02155-8. LCCN:94-030791.
Audience: **u,f.** *Choice, 1995.*

Mooney, James **E98.R3M6 1991**
The Ghost-Dance Religion and the Sioux Outbreak of 1890. Raymond J. DeMallie (Introduction by). Trade Cloth. University of Nebraska Press. Lincoln, NE. 1991. 531p. ISBN:0-8032-8177-3, ISBN13: 978-0-8032-8177-6. Dewey:299/.77. LCCN:91-024546.
Audience: **u,f.**

Rappaport, Roy A. **BL600.R37 1999**
Ritual and Religion in the Making of Humanity. Keith Hart (Foreword by), Meyer Fortes, Jack Goody, Edmund Leach & Stanley Tambiah (Contribution by). Cloth Text. Cambridge University Press. New York, NY. 1999. 562p. Studies in Social and Cultural Anthropology, No. 110 ISBN:0-521-22873-5, ISBN13: 978-0-521-22873-2. Dewey:291.38. LCCN:98-024494.
Audience: **l,u,f.** *Choice, 1999.*

Simpson, George E. **BL2520**
Black Religions in the New World. Trade Cloth. Columbia University Press. New York, NY. 1978. 415p. ISBN:0-231-04540-9, ISBN13: 978-0-231-04540-7. Dewey:291/.0899607. LCCN:78-016892.
Audience: **g,l,u,f.**

Stoller, Paul & Olkes, Cheryl **DT547.45.S65S76 1987**
In Sorcery's Shadow: A Memoir of Apprenticeship among the Songhay of Niger. Trade Paper. University of Chicago Press. Chicago, IL. 1989. 252p. ISBN:0-226-77543-7, ISBN13: 978-0-226-77543-2. Dewey:306/.08996. LCCN:87-010746.
Audience: **g,l,u,f.** *Choice, 1988.*

Turner, Victor W. **DT963.42**
The Forest of Symbols: Aspects of Ndembu Ritual. Trade Paper. Cornell University Press. Ithaca, NY. 1970. 417p. ISBN:0-8014-9101-0, ISBN13: 978-0-8014-9101-6. Dewey:392/.09689/4. LCCN:67-012308.
Audience: **u,f.**

Van Gennep, Arnold **GN473**
The Rites of Passage. Monika B. Vizedom & Gabrielle L. Caffee (Translators). Trade Paper. University of Chicago Press. Chicago, IL. 1961. 224p. ISBN:0-226-84849-3, ISBN13: 978-0-226-84849-5. Dewey:392. LCCN:59-014321.
Audience: **l,u,f.**

Varisco, Daniel Martin **BP161.3.V37 2005**
Islam Obscured: The Rhetoric of Anthropological Representation. Cloth over Boards. Palgrave Macmillan. New York, NY. 2005. 240p. Contemporary Anthropology of Religion Ser. ISBN:1-4039-6772-5, ISBN13: 978-1-4039-6772-5. Dewey:306.6/97. LCCN:2004-050514.
Audience: **l,u,f.** *Choice, 2006.*

Wallace, Anthony F. **E99.S3**
The Death and Rebirth of the Seneca. Trade Paper. Knopf Publishing Group. New York, NY. 1972. 416p. ISBN:0-394-71699-X, ISBN13: 978-0-394-71699-2. Dewey:970.3.
Audience: **g,l,u,f.**

Walter, Mariko Namba **BL2370.S5**
Shamanism: An Encyclopedia of World Beliefs, Practices, and Culture. Eva Jane Neumann Fridman (Editor). Library Binding. ABC-CLIO, Inc. Santa Barbara, CA. 2004. 800p. ISBN:1-57607-645-8, ISBN13: 978-1-57607-645-3. Dewey:201/.44/03. LCCN:2004-020416.
Audience: **g,l,u,f.** *Choice, 2005.*

Worsley, Peter **BL2620.M4**
The Trumpet Shall Sound: A Study of Cargo Cults in Melanesia. Ed. 2. Trade Paper. Knopf Publishing Group. New York, NY. 1987. 300p. ISBN:0-8052-0156-4, ISBN13: 978-0-8052-0156-7. Dewey:299/.9. LCCN:67-026995.
Audience: **l,u,f.**

Social and Cultural Anthropology > Urban Anthropology

Braidwood, Robert John & Willey, Gordon R. **GN0738.B67**
Courses Toward Urban Life: Archeological Considerations of Some Cultural Alternates. Subscribers Ed. Trade Paper. Books on Demand. Ann Arbor, MI. 386p. Viking Fund Publications in Anthropology, No. 32 ISBN:0-598-22801-2, ISBN13: 978-0-598-22801-7. Dewey:572.082. LCCN:62-006062.
Audience: **u,f.**

Gmelch, George & Zenner, Walter P. (Editors) **GN395.U725 2002**
Urban Life: Readings in the Anthropology of the City. Ed. 4. Paper Text. Waveland Press, Inc. Prospect Heights, IL. 2001. 394p. ISBN:1-57766-194-X, ISBN13: 978-1-57766-194-8. Dewey:307.76. LCCN:2002-277258.
Audience: **l,u,f.**

Hansen, Karen T. **GN657.R4H36 1996**
Keeping House in Lusaka. Trade Cloth. Columbia University Press. New York, NY. 1996. 256p. ISBN:0-231-08142-1, ISBN13: 978-0-231-08142-9. Dewey:307.76/096894. LCCN:96-021351.
Audience: **u.** *Choice, 1997.*

Leeds, Anthony **GN395.L44 1994**
Cities, Classes, and the Social Order. Roger Sanjek (Editor). Book, Other. Cornell University Press. Ithaca, NY. 1994. 272p. The Anthropology of Contemporary Issues Ser. ISBN:0-8014-2957-9, ISBN13: 978-0-8014-2957-6. Dewey:307.76. LCCN:93-038934.
Audience: **l,u,f.**

Sheriff, Robin E. **F2646.9.N4S44 2001**
Dreaming Equality: Color, Race and Racism in Urban Brazil. Trade Cloth. Rutgers University Press. Piscataway, NJ. 2004. 288p. ISBN:0-8135-2999-9, ISBN13: 978-0-8135-2999-8. Dewey:305.896/08153. LCCN:2001-019294.
Audience: **u,f.** *Choice, 2002.*

Stack, Carol B. **E185.86.S697**
All Our Kin: Strategies for Survival in a Black Community. Trade Cloth. HarperCollins Publishers. New York, NY. 1974. xxi, 175p. ISBN:0-06-013974-9, ISBN13: 978-0-06-013974-2. Dewey:301.45/19/6073. LCCN:73-004126.
Audience: **g,l,u,f.**

Young, Michael & Willmott, Peter **HQ616**
Family and Kinship in East London. Trade Paper. University of

California Press. Berkeley, CA. 1992. ISBN:0-520-07897-7, ISBN13: 978-0-520-07897-0. Dewey:306.8/5/094215. LCCN:91-035769.

Audience: **u,f.**

Social and Cultural Anthropology > World Ethnography by Continent > Africa

Barnard, Alan **DT1058.S36B37 1992**
Hunters and Herders of Southern Africa: A Comparative Ethnography of the Khoisan Peoples. Meyer Fortes, Jack Goody, Edmund Leach & Stanley Tambiah (Contribution by). Trade Cloth. Cambridge University Press. New York, NY. 1992. 379p. Cambridge Studies in Social and Cultural Anthropology, No. 85 ISBN:0-521-41188-2, ISBN13: 978-0-521-41188-2. Dewey:305.896/1068. LCCN:91-017705.

Audience: **u,f.**

Caplan, Pat & Topan, Farouk (Editors) **DT423**
Swahili Modernities: Culture, Politics, and Identity on the East Coast of Africa. Cloth Text. Africa World Press. Trenton, NJ. 2003. 270p. ISBN:1-59221-045-7, ISBN13: 978-1-59221-045-9. Dewey:967.604.

Audience: **u,f.**

Eber, Paula Holmes & Holmes-Eber, Paula **HQ1792.Z9**
Daughters of Tunis: Women, Family, and Networks in a Muslim City. Trade Paper. Westview Press. Boulder, CO. 2002. 192p. ISBN:0-8133-3944-8, ISBN13: 978-0-8133-3944-3. Dewey:306/.099611.

Audience: **u,f.**

Evans-Pritchard, Edward E. **DT132**
The Nuer: A Description of the Modes of Livelihood and Political Institutions of a Nilotic People. Cloth Text. Oxford University Press, Inc. New York, NY. 1969. 284p. ISBN:0-19-500322-5, ISBN13: 978-0-19-500322-2. Dewey:306/.09629/3.

Audience: **u,f.**

Gluckman, Max **GN645.G56 2004**
Order and Rebellion in Tribal Africa. Library Binding. Routledge. New York, NY. 2004. 288p. Routledge Library Editions Ser., :Anthropology and Ethnography, US/Can. Edition Ser. ISBN:0-415-32983-3, ISBN13: 978-0-415-32983-5. Dewey:306.2/0967.

Audience: **u,f.**

Grinker, Roy R. & Steiner, Christopher B. **GN645.P47 1996**
Perspectives on Africa: A Reader in Culture, History and Representation. Trade Paper. Blackwell Publishing, Inc. Malden, MA. 1996. 772p. ISBN:1-55786-686-4, ISBN13: 978-1-55786-686-8. Dewey:306/.096. LCCN:96-021537.

Audience: **u,f.**

Gulliver, P. H. **DT433.545.M33**
The Family Herds: A Study of Two Pastoral Tribes in East Africa: The Jie and Turkana. Paper over Boards. Routledge. New York, NY. 2003. 296p. International Library of Sociology Ser., Vol. 126 ISBN:0-415-17646-8, ISBN13: 978-0-415-17646-0. Dewey:305.8/965.

Audience: **u,f.**

Lee, Richard B. & DeVore, Irven **DT797**
Kalahari Hunter-Gatherers: Studies of the !Kung San and Their Neighbors. Trade Paper. iUniverse, Inc. Lincoln, NE. 1999. 432p. ISBN:1-58348-125-7, ISBN13: 978-1-58348-125-7. Dewey:968.711. LCCN:75-028320.

Audience: **l,u,f.**

Ottenberg, Simon **GN645.O75**
Cultures and Societies of Africa. Paper Text. Textbook Publishers. Temecula, CA. 2003. 614p. ISBN:0-7581-5098-9, ISBN13: 978-0-7581-5098-1. Dewey:572.96.

Audience: **g,l,u,f.** B

Ottenberg, Simon & Falola, Toyin **DT515.45.I33O885**
Igbo Art and Culture, and Other Essays. Trade Cloth. Africa World Press. Trenton, NJ. 2006. Classic Authors and Texts on Africa Ser. ISBN:1-59221-441-X, ISBN13: 978-1-59221-441-9. Dewey:306.4/708996332. LCCN:2005-029623.

Audience: **u,f.**

Parkin, David **BL2480.G57P37 1991**
The Sacred Void: Spatial Images of Work and Ritual among the Giriama of Kenya. Meyer Fortes, Edmund Leach, Jack Goody & Stanley Tambiah (Contribution by). Trade Paper. Cambridge University Press. New York, NY. 2006. 282p. Cambridge Studies in Social and Cultural Anthropology Ser. ISBN:0-521-02498-6, ISBN13: 978-0-521-02498-3. Dewey:299/.68395.

Audience: **u,f.** *Choice, 1992.*

Pritchett, James A. **DT3058.N44P75 2001**
The Lunda-Ndembu: Style, Change and Social Transformation in South Central Africa. Trade Paper. University of Wisconsin Press. Chicago, IL. 2001. 424p. ISBN:0-299-17154-X, ISBN13: 978-0-299-17154-4. Dewey:305.896/3977. LCCN:00-012230.

Audience: **u,f.** *Choice, 2002.*

Riesman, Paul **DT555.45.F85R5513**
Freedom in Fulani Social Life: An Introspective Ethnography. Martha Fuller (Translator), Paul Stoller (Foreword by). Trade Paper. University of Chicago Press. Chicago, IL. 1998. 320p. ISBN:0-226-71743-7, ISBN13: 978-0-226-71743-2. Dewey:305.89632206625. LCCN:98-011166.

Audience: **u,f.** B

Schumaker, Lyn **GN657.R4S38 2001**
Africanizing Anthropology: Fieldwork, Networks and the Making of Cultural Knowledge in Central Africa. Trade Cloth. Duke University Press. Durham, NC. 2001. 376p. ISBN:0-8223-2678-7, ISBN13: 978-0-8223-2678-6. Dewey:305.8/0096894. LCCN:2001-028054.

Audience: **l,u,f.** *Choice, 2002.*

Shostak, Marjorie **DT797**
Nisa: The Life and Words of a Kung Woman. Trade Paper. Harvard University Press. Cambridge, MA. 2000. 382p. ISBN:0-674-00432-9, ISBN13: 978-0-674-00432-0. Dewey:306/.08996106811. LCCN:81-004210.

Audience: **g,l,u,f.** B

Stone, Glenn D. **DT515.45.K64S76 1996**
Settlement Ecology: The Social and Spatial Organization of Kofyar Agriculture. Trade Cloth. University of Arizona Press. Tucson, AZ. 1996. 310p. Studies in Human Ecology

ISBN:0-8165-1567-0, ISBN13: 978-0-8165-1567-7.
Dewey:338.1/09669/5. LCCN:96-009997.
Audience: **u,f.** *Choice, 1997.*

Sudarkasa, Niara **DT513**
Where Women Work: A Study of Yoruba Women in the Market Place and in the Home. Trade Paper. University of Michigan, Museum of Anthropology, Publications Department. Ann Arbor, MI. 1973. Anthropological Papers Ser., No. 53 ISBN:0-932206-51-4, ISBN13: 978-0-932206-51-0. Dewey:301.2/08 s 331.4/096.
Audience: **u,f.**

Turnbull, Colin M. **DT650.B36**
The Forest People. Trade Cloth. Peter Smith Publisher, Inc. Magnolia, MA. 1988. ISBN:0-8446-6333-6, ISBN13: 978-0-8446-6333-3. Dewey:305.8/967515.
Audience: **g,l,u,f.**

Turnbull, Colin M. **DT650.B36**
The Mbuti Pygmies: Adaptation and Change in Ituri Forest. Paper Text. Harcourt College Publishers. Fort Worth, TX. 1983. 161p. Case Studies in Cultural Anthropology ISBN:0-03-061537-2, ISBN13: 978-0-03-061537-5. Dewey:305.8/963. LCCN:82-021332.
Audience: **g,l,u,f.**

Wikan, Unni **HN786.C3W55 1996**
Tomorrow, God Willing: Self-Made Destinies in Cairo. Trade Cloth. University of Chicago Press. Chicago, IL. 1996. 352p. ISBN:0-226-89834-2, ISBN13: 978-0-226-89834-6. Dewey:306/.096216. LCCN:95-026658.
Audience: **l,u,f.** *Choice, 1997.*

Wilson, Peter J. **DT469.M277T788 1992**
Freedom by a Hair's Breadth: Tsimihety in Madagascar. Trade Cloth. University of Michigan Press. Chicago, IL. 1993. 208p. ISBN:0-472-10389-X, ISBN13: 978-0-472-10389-8. Dewey:305.89/93. LCCN:92-028344.
Audience: **u,f.** *Choice, 1993.*

Social and Cultural Anthropology > World Ethnography by Continent > Asia

Bosco, Joseph (Editor), et al. **GN17.3.E18**
The Making of Anthropology in East and Southeast Asia. J. S. Eades & Shinji Yamashita (Editors). Trade Cloth. Berghahn Books, Inc. New York, NY. 2004. 384p. Asian Anthropologies Ser. ISBN:1-57181-259-8, ISBN13: 978-1-57181-259-9. Dewey:306/.0959. LCCN:2004-050332.
Audience: **l,u,f.** *Choice, 2005.*

Critchfield, Richard **HD1542.C75 1988**
The Golden Bowl Be Broken: Peasant Life in Four Cultures. Cloth Text. Indiana University Press. Bloomington, IN. 1974. 338p. ISBN:0-253-32554-4, ISBN13: 978-0-253-32554-9. Dewey:305.5/63. LCCN:87-003690.
Audience: **l,u,f.**

Darrah, Charles N. **HD5715.D37 1996**
Learning and Work: An Exploration in Industrial Ethnography. Cloth Text. Garland Publishing, Inc. New York, NY. 1996. 200p. Studies in Education and Culture, No. 8 ISBN:0-8153-1455-8, ISBN13: 978-0-8153-1455-4. Dewey:658.3/124. LCCN:95-042416.
Audience: **l,u,f.**

Early, John D. & Headland, Thomas N. **DS666.A3E37 1998**
Population Dynamics of a Philippine Rain Forest People: The San Ildefonso Agta. Trade Cloth. University Press of Florida. Gainesville, FL. 1998. 224p. ISBN:0-8130-1555-3, ISBN13: 978-0-8130-1555-2. Dewey:304.6/2/089991105991. LCCN:97-041150.
Audience: **u,f.** *Choice, 1998.*

Ekvall, Robert B. **DS786 .E4**
Fields on the Hoof: Nexus of Tibetan Nomadic Pastoralism. Paper Text. Waveland Press, Inc. Prospect Heights, IL. 1983. 100p. ISBN:0-88133-052-3, ISBN13: 978-0-88133-052-6. Dewey:915.15/03.
Audience: **u,f.**

Firth, Raymond **HD9466**
Malay Fishermen. Paper over Boards. Routledge. New York, NY. 2003. 388p. International Library of Sociology E, Vol. 64:The Sociology of Development ISBN:0-415-17574-7, ISBN13: 978-0-415-17574-6. Dewey:338.37.
Audience: **u,f.**

Freedman, Maurice **HQ667**
Chinese Lineage and Society: Fukien and Kwantung. Cloth over Boards. Berg Publishers. Oxford, 1971. 216p. London School of Economics Monographs on Social Anthropology Ser., Vol. 33 ISBN:1-85973-869-9, ISBN13: 978-1-85973-869-6. Dewey:301.44/2/0951245.
Audience: **u,f.**

Howe, Leo **DS647.B2H68 2005**
The Changing World of Bali: Religion, Society and Tourism. Paper over Boards. Routledge. New York, NY. 2005. X, 166p. The Modern Anthropology of South-East Asia Ser. ISBN:0-415-36497-3, ISBN13: 978-0-415-36497-3. Dewey:959.8/604. LCCN:2005-002518.
Audience: **l,u,f.**

King, Victor T. & Wilder, William D. **GN635.S58K55 2003**
The Modern Anthropology of South-East Asia: An Introduction. Paper over Boards. Routledge. New York, NY. 2003. 448p. Modern Anthropology of South-East Asia Ser. ISBN:0-415-29751-6, ISBN13: 978-0-415-29751-6. Dewey:306/.0959. LCCN:2002-068244.
Audience: **g,l,u,f.**

Kondo, Dorinne K. **HD6197.K658 1990**
Crafting Selves: Power, Gender, and Discourses of Identity in a Japanese Workplace. Trade Paper. University of Chicago Press. Chicago, IL. 1990. 354p. ISBN:0-226-45044-9, ISBN13: 978-0-226-45044-5. Dewey:305.420952. LCCN:89-038547.
Audience: **g,u,f.**

Linger, Daniel Touro **DS832.7.B73L56 2001**
No One Home: Brazilian Selves Remade in Japan. Trade Cloth. Stanford University Press. Palo Alto, CA. 2001. xix, 342p. ISBN:0-8047-3910-2, ISBN13: 978-0-8047-3910-8. Dewey:952/.004698. LCCN:2001-020026.
Audience: **l,u,f.**

Moeran, Brian **GN21.M58**
Far Valley: Four Years in Japanese Village. Paper Text. Kodansha International. Tokyo, 1998. 264p. ISBN:4-7700-2301-4, ISBN13: 978-4-7700-2301-8. Dewey:306.092.
Audience: **u,f.**

Nieuwenhuys, Olga **HD6250.5.N52 1994**
Children's Lifeworlds: Gender, Welfare and Labour in the Developing World. Paper over Boards. Routledge. New York, NY. 1994. 256p. ISBN:0-415-09750-9, ISBN13: 978-0-415-09750-5. Dewey:331.310954. LCCN:93-017607.
Audience: **u,f.**

Peters, Emrys L. **DT238.C8P47 1990**
The Bedouin of Cyrenaica: Studies in Personal and Corporate Power. Jack Goody (Editor, Contribution by), Emanuel Marx (Editor), Meyer Fortes, Edmund Leach & Stanley Tambiah (Contribution by). Trade Cloth. Cambridge University Press. New York, NY. 1991. 322p. Cambridge Studies in Social and Cultural Anthropology, No. 72 ISBN:0-521-38561-X, ISBN13: 978-0-521-38561-9. Dewey:306.09612. LCCN:89-048036.
Audience: **l,u,f.** *Choice, 1992.*

Potter, Sulamith Heins **GN635.T4P68**
[e] Family Life in a Northern Thai Village: A Study in the Structural Significance of Women. E-Book. NetLibrary, Inc. Boulder, CO. 1977. ISBN:0-585-34359-4, ISBN13: 978-0-585-34359-4. Dewey:301.42/1/09593.
Audience: **u,f.**

Potter, Sulamith Heins & Potter, Jack M. **HN733.5.P68 1990**
China's Peasants: The Anthropology of a Revolution. Cloth Text. Cambridge University Press. New York, NY. 1990. 358p. ISBN:0-521-35521-4, ISBN13: 978-0-521-35521-6. Dewey:305.5/633/0951. LCCN:89-031420.
Audience: **l,u,f.** *Choice, 1991.*

Racine, Jean-Luc & Viramma, Josiane Racine **DS422.C3V49613 1997**
Viramma: Life of an Untouchable. Will Hobson (Translator). Trade Paper. Analytical Psychology Club of San Francisco, Inc. San Francisco, CA. 1998. 320p. ISBN:1-85984-148-1, ISBN13: 978-1-85984-148-8. Dewey:305.5/68. LCCN:97-039447.
Audience: **g,l,u,f.** *Choice, 1998.*

Stafford, Charles **GN635.C5 S73 1995**
The Roads of Chinese Childhood: Learning and Identification in Angang. Meyer Fortes, Edmund Leach, Jack Goody & Stanley Tambiah (Contribution by). Trade Paper. Cambridge University Press. New York, NY. 2006. 233p. Cambridge Studies in Social and Cultural Anthropology Ser. ISBN:0-521-02656-3, ISBN13: 978-0-521-02656-7. Dewey:305.23/051.
Audience: **u,f.**

Wikan, Unni **HQ1731.Z8S838 1991**
Behind the Veil in Arabia: Women in Oman. Trade Paper. University of Chicago Press. Chicago, IL. 1991. 328p. ISBN:0-226-89683-8, ISBN13: 978-0-226-89683-0. Dewey:305.42/0953. LCCN:81-018622.
Audience: **g,l,u,f.** [B]

Wiser, William & Wiser, Charlotte V. **DS421**
Behind Mud Walls: Seventy-Five Years in a North Indian Village. Susan S. Wadley (Revised by). Trade Paper. University of California Press. Berkeley, CA. 2001. 408p. ISBN:0-520-22710-7, ISBN13: 978-0-520-22710-1. Dewey:954.1/009734. LCCN:63-019178.
Audience: **l,u,f.**

Social and Cultural Anthropology > World Ethnography by Continent > Caribbean Region

Beckwith, Martha W. **F1896.N4B4 1969**
Black Roadways: A Study of Jamaican Folk Life. Trade Cloth. Greenwood Publishing Group, Inc. Portsmouth, NH. 1971. 243p. ISBN:0-8371-1144-7, ISBN13: 978-0-8371-1144-5. Dewey:917.292/03/5. LCCN:69-016597.
Audience: **l,u,f.**

Beriss, David **DC34.5.A46**
Black Skins, French Voices: Caribbean Ethnicity and Activism in Urban France. Trade Paper. Westview Press. Boulder, CO. 2004. 176p. ISBN:0-8133-4254-6, ISBN13: 978-0-8133-4254-2. Dewey:305.8/96044.
Audience: **g,l,u,f.**

Besson, Jean-Louis **F1895.M37B48 2002**
Martha Brae's Two Histories: European Expansion and Caribbean Culture-Building in Jamaica. Trade Cloth. University of North Carolina Press. Chapel Hill, NC. 2002. 424p. ISBN:0-8078-2734-7, ISBN13: 978-0-8078-2734-5. Dewey:972.92. LCCN:2002-006111.
Audience: **l,u,f.** *Choice, 2003.*

Bolles, A. Lynn **HD6113.Z6K553 1996**
Sister Jamaica: A Study of Women, Work and Households in Kingston. Trade Cloth. University Press of America, Inc. Lanham, MD. 1996. 150p. ISBN:0-7618-0211-8, ISBN13: 978-0-7618-0211-2. Dewey:331.4/097292. LCCN:95-046006.
Audience: **l,u,f.** *Choice, 1996.*

Bueno, Maria de Los Reyes Castillo **F1789.N3C37 2000**
Reyita: The Life of a Black Cuban Woman in the Twentieth Century. Daisy Rubiera Castillo (As told to). Library Binding. Duke University Press. Durham, NC. 2000. 168p. ISBN:0-8223-2579-9, ISBN13: 978-0-8223-2579-6. Dewey:972.9106/092 B. LCCN:99-087007.
Audience: **g,l,u,f.**

Clarke, Edith **HQ584**
My Mother Who Fathered Me: A Study of the Families in Three Selected Communities of Jamaica. Trade Paper. University of the West Indies Press. Kingston, 1999. 266p. ISBN:976-640-040-7, ISBN13: 978-976-640-040-8. Dewey:392.3.
Audience: **u,f.**

Fog-Olwig, Karen (Editor) **HN244.A8S6 1995**
Small Islands, Large Questions: Society, Culture and Resistance in the Post-Emancipation Caribbean. Paper over Boards. Taylor & Francis Group. Abingdon, 1995. 200p. Studies in Slave and Post-Slave Societies and Cultures ISBN:0-7146-4576-1, ISBN13: 978-0-7146-4576-6. Dewey:306/.09729. LCCN:95-014437.
Audience: **l,u,f.**

Knight, Franklin W. & Martínez Vergne, Teresita **F1741.C66 2005**
Contemporary Caribbean Cultures and Societies in a Global Context. Trade Cloth. University of North Carolina Press. Chapel Hill, NC. 2005. 304p. ISBN:0-8078-2972-2, ISBN13: 978-0-8078-2972-1. Dewey:972.905/3. LCCN:2005-010529.
Audience: **u,f.** *Choice, 2006.*

Martinez, Samuel **HD5856.H2M37 1995**
Peripheral Migrants: Haitians and Dominican Republic Sugar Plantations. Cloth Text. University of Tennessee Press. Knoxville, TN. 1995. 256p. ISBN:0-87049-901-7, ISBN13: 978-0-87049-901-2. Dewey:331.6/2729407293. LCCN:95-004359.
Audience: **u,f.** *Choice, 1996.*

Martinez-Vergne, Teresita & Knight, Franklin W. (Editors) **F1741.C66 2005**
Contemporary Caribbean Cultures and Societies in a Global Context. Trade Paper, Perfect. University of North Carolina Press. Chapel Hill, NC. 2005. 304p. ISBN:0-8078-5634-7, ISBN13: 978-0-8078-5634-5. Dewey:972.905/3. LCCN:2005-010529.
Audience: **u,f.** *Choice, 2006.*

Maurer, Bill **F2129**
Recharting the Caribbean: Land, Law, and Citizenship in the British Virgin Islands. Trade Paper. University of Michigan Press. Chicago, IL. 2000. 320p. ISBN:0-472-08693-6, ISBN13: 978-0-472-08693-1. Dewey:972.97/25. LCCN:96-051247.
Audience: **u,f.** *Choice, 1998.*

Mintz, Sidney W. **HT1071.M56**
Caribbean Transformations. Cloth Text. Columbia University Press. New York, NY. 1989. 384p. ISBN:0-231-07114-0, ISBN13: 978-0-231-07114-7. Dewey:972.9. LCCN:89-017446.
Audience: **l,u,f.**

Mintz, Sidney W. **HD8039.S86**
Worker in the Cane: A Puerto Rican Life History. Trade Paper. W. W. Norton & Company, Inc. New York, NY. 1974. 320p. ISBN:0-393-00731-6, ISBN13: 978-0-393-00731-2. Dewey:331.763.
Audience: **g,l,u,f.**

Mintz, Sidney W. & Price, Richard **F2191.B55M56 1992**
The Birth of African-American Culture: An Anthropological Perspective. Trade Paper. Beacon Press. Boston, MA. 1992. 144p. ISBN:0-8070-0917-2, ISBN13: 978-0-8070-0917-8. Dewey:305.8960729. LCCN:91-041020.
Audience: **g,l,u,f.**

Olwig, Karen F. **F2084**
Global Culture, Island Identity: Continuity and Change in the Afro-Caribbean Community of Nevis. Trade Paper. Gordon & Breach Publishing Group. New York, NY. 1996. 256p. Studies in Anthropology and History ISBN:3-7186-0624-0, ISBN13: 978-3-7186-0624-5. Dewey:972.973.
Audience: **u,f.**

Price, Richard **F2431.S27A457 1990**
Alabi's World. Trade Paper. Johns Hopkins University Press. Baltimore, MD. 1990. 472p. Johns Hopkins Studies in Atlantic History and Culture Ser. ISBN:0-8018-3956-4, ISBN13: 978-0-8018-3956-6. Dewey:988.3/3. LCCN:89-015488.
Audience: **g,l,u,f.** *Choice, 1991.*

Price, Richard (Editor) **HT1048.P74 1996**
Maroon Societies: Rebel Slave Communities in the Americas. Ed. 3. Trade Paper. Johns Hopkins University Press. Baltimore, MD. 1996. 480p. ISBN:0-8018-5496-2, ISBN13: 978-0-8018-5496-5. Dewey:305.5/67/097. LCCN:96-026927.
Audience: **g,l,u,f.** B

Price, Sally **F2431.S27P74 1993**
Co-wives and Calabashes. Ed. 2. Trade Paper. University of Michigan Press. Chicago, IL. 1993. 264p. Women and Culture Ser. ISBN:0-472-08218-3, ISBN13: 978-0-472-08218-6. Dewey:306/.09883/3. LCCN:92-043700.
Audience: **g,l,u,f.**

Richman, Karen E. **E184.H27R53 2005**
Migration and Vodou. Trade Cloth, Compact Disc. University Press of Florida. Gainesville, FL. 2005. 360p. ISBN:0-8130-2835-3, ISBN13: 978-0-8130-2835-4. Dewey:305.896/97294073. LCCN:2005-041359.
Audience: **g,l,u,f.** *Choice, 2006.*

Rosendahl, Mona **HX160.P35R67 1997**
Inside the Revolution: Everyday Life in Socialist Cuba. Trade Paper. Cornell University Press. Ithaca, NY. 1997. 208p. Anthropology of Contemporary Issues Ser. ISBN:0-8014-8412-X, ISBN13: 978-0-8014-8412-4. Dewey:335.43/47. LCCN:97-016517.
Audience: **g,l,u,f.** *Choice, 1998.*

Wilson, Samuel M. **F1619**
Indigenous People of the Caribbean. Paper Text. University Press of Florida. Gainesville, FL. 1999. 304p. Florida Museum of Natural History Ser., :Ripley P. Bullen ISBN:0-8130-1692-4, ISBN13: 978-0-8130-1692-4. Dewey:972.9/01.
Audience: **g,l,u,f.**

Yelvington, Kevin A. **HN246.Z9P69 1995**
Producing Power: Ethnicity, Gender, and Class in a Caribbean Workplace. Library Binding. Temple University Press. Philadelphia, PA. 1995. 320p. ISBN:1-56639-285-3, ISBN13: 978-1-56639-285-3. Dewey:305.8/00972983. LCCN:94-034679.
Audience: **l,u,f.**

Social and Cultural Anthropology > World Ethnography by Continent > Europe

Arensberg, Conrad Maynadier **GN585.I7 A7**
The Irish Countryman: An Anthropological Study. Trade Cloth. Peter Smith Publisher, Inc. Magnolia, MA. 1990. ISBN:0-8446-1031-3, ISBN13: 978-0-8446-1031-3. Dewey:914.15.
Audience: **l,u,f.** B

Delamont, Sara **D1056.D45 1995**
Appetites and Identities: An Introduction to Social Anthropology of Western Europe. Trade Cloth. Routledge. New York, NY. 1994. 240p. ISBN:0-415-06253-5, ISBN13: 978-0-415-06253-4. Dewey:306.4/094. LCCN:94-009581.
Audience: **g,l,u,f.**

Goddard, Victoria A. (Editor), et al. **GN575.A58 1995**
The Anthropology of Europe: Identities and Boundaries in Conflict. Josep R. Llobera, Cris Shore, John Gledhill, Bruce Kapferer & Barbara Bender (Editors). Cloth over Boards. Berg Publishers. Oxford, 1994. 310p. Explorations in Anthropology Ser. ISBN:0-85496-901-2, ISBN13: 978-0-85496-901-2. Dewey:305.8/0094. LCCN:95-005083.
Audience: **l,u,f.**

Green, Sarah F. **HN650.5.Z9M264 2005**
Notes from the Balkans: Locating Marginality and Ambiguity on the Greek-Albanian Border. Trade Cloth. Princeton University Press. Princeton, NJ. 2005. 320p. Princeton Modern Greek Studies ISBN:0-691-12198-2, ISBN13: 978-0-691-12198-7. Dewey:305.5/6/094953. LCCN:2004-058686.
Audience: **u,f.**

Gulliver, Philip H. & Silverman, Marilyn **DA995.T46G85 1995**
Merchants and Shopkeepers: An Historical Anthropology of an Irish Market Town, 1200-1986. Cloth Text. University of Toronto Press. Toronto, ON. 1995. 464p. Anthropological Horizons Ser. ISBN:0-8020-0644-2, ISBN13: 978-0-8020-0644-8. Dewey:941.8/9. LCCN:95-211277.
Audience: **l,u,f.** *Choice, 1995.*

Hastrup, Kirsten **DL375.H37 1998**
A Place Apart: An Anthropological Study of the Icelandic World. Trade Cloth. Oxford University Press, Inc. New York, NY. 1998. 240p. Oxford Studies in Social and Cultural Anthropology - Cultural Forms ISBN:0-19-823380-9, ISBN13: 978-0-19-823380-0. Dewey:949.12. LCCN:97-039269.
Audience: **l,u,f.**

Just, Roger **GN585.G85J87 2000**
A Greek Island Cosmos: Kinship and Community on Meganisi. Trade Cloth. School of American Research Press. Santa Fe, NM. 2000. 288p. World Anthropology Ser. ISBN:0-933452-72-1, ISBN13: 978-0-933452-72-5. Dewey:301/.09495. LCCN:00-059644.
Audience: **u,f.**

Mendras, Henri & Cole, Alistair **GN585.F8M46 1991**
Social Change in Modern France: Towards a Cultural Anthropology of the Fifth Republic. Cloth Text. Cambridge University Press. New York, NY. 1991. 262p. ISBN:0-521-39108-3, ISBN13: 978-0-521-39108-5. Dewey:306/.0944. LCCN:90-001493.
Audience: **u,f.** *Choice, 1991.*

Mintz, Jerome R. **HX928.C34**
The Anarchists of Casas Viejas. James W. Fernandez (Foreword by). Trade Cloth. Indiana University Press. Bloomington, IN. 2004. 368p. ISBN:0-253-21658-3, ISBN13: 978-0-253-21658-8. Dewey:335/.83/094688. LCCN:2004-266509.
Audience: **u,f.**

Peristiany, J. G. & Pitt-Rivers, Julian (Editors) **HN380.M4 H66 1992**
Honor and Grace in Anthropology. Meyer Fortes, Edmund Leach, Jack Goody & Stanley Tambiah (Contribution by). Trade Paper. Cambridge University Press. New York, NY. 2005. 274p. Cambridge Studies in Social and Cultural Anthropology Ser., Vol. 76 ISBN:0-521-61932-7, ISBN13: 978-0-521-61932-5. Dewey:303.3/72091822. LCCN:2005-279887.
Audience: **u,f.**

Pitt-Rivers, Julian A. **HN590.G73**
The People of the Sierra. Ed. 2. Trade Paper. University of Chicago Press. Chicago, IL. 1972. 260p. ISBN:0-226-67010-4, ISBN13: 978-0-226-67010-2. Dewey:309.1/46/88. LCCN:70-153710.
Audience: **g,l,u,f.**

Silverman, Sydel **DG975.M6736**
The Three Bells of Civilization. Trade Cloth. Columbia University Press. New York, NY. 1975. 304p. ISBN:0-231-03804-6, ISBN13: 978-0-231-03804-1. Dewey:301.29/45/651. LCCN:75-015916.
Audience: **g,l,u,f.**

Stewart, Michael **DX223.S75 1997**
The Time of the Gypsies. Trade Cloth. Westview Press. Boulder, CO. 1997. 320p. Studies in Ethnographic Imagination ISBN:0-8133-3198-6, ISBN13: 978-0-8133-3198-0. Dewey:305.891/4970439. LCCN:97-009001.
Audience: **g,l,u,f.** *Choice, 1998.*

Verdery, Katherine **HD839.T7V47 2003**
The Vanishing Hectare: Property and Value in Postsocialist Transylvania. Trade Paper. Cornell University Press. Ithaca, NY. 2005. 432p. Culture and Society after Socialism Ser. ISBN:0-8014-8869-9, ISBN13: 978-0-8014-8869-6. Dewey:333.3/14984. LCCN:2003-012516.
Audience: **u,f.**

Willis **HD6276.G7W54 2000**
Learning to Labour. Trade Cloth. Ashgate Publishing, Ltd. Aldershot, 1977. 224p. ISBN:1-85742-170-1, ISBN13: 978-1-85742-170-5. Dewey:305.56208351.
Audience: **u,f.**

Social and Cultural Anthropology > World Ethnography by Continent > Australia and the Pacific

Bateson, Gregory **DU740.B3**
Naven: A Survey of the Problems Suggested by a Composite Picture of the Culture of a New Guinea Tribe Drawn from Three Points of View. Ed. 2. Trade Cloth. Stanford University Press. Palo Alto, CA. 1958. xix, 312p. ISBN:0-8047-0519-4, ISBN13: 978-0-8047-0519-6. Dewey:572.995.
Audience: **u,f.**

Brison, Karen J. **DU740.42.B75 1992**
Just Talk: Gossip, Meetings, and Power in a Papua New Guinea Village. Trade Cloth. University of California Press. Berkeley, CA. 1992. 306p. Studies in Melanesian Anthropology, No. 11 ISBN:0-520-07700-8, ISBN13: 978-0-520-07700-3. Dewey:302.30953. LCCN:91-034511.
Audience: **u,f.** *Choice, 1993.*

Broome, Richard **GN666.B77 2002**
Aboriginal Australians. Ed. 3. Trade Paper. Allen & Unwin Pty., Ltd. Crows Nest, NSW. 2002. 336p. ISBN:1-86508-755-6, ISBN13: 978-1-86508-755-9. Dewey:994/.0049915. LCCN:2003-428438.
Audience: **g,l,u,f.**

Denoon, Donald & Meleisea, Malama **DU28.3.C33 1997**
The Cambridge History of the Pacific Islanders. Stewart Firth, Jocelyn Linnekin & Karen Nero (As told tos). Trade Paper. Cambridge University Press. New York, NY. 2004. 539p. ISBN:0-521-00354-7, ISBN13: 978-0-521-00354-4. Dewey:990.
Audience: **g,l,u,f.** *Choice, 1998.*

Firth, Raymond William **GN480**
We, the Tikopia: A Sociological Study of Kinship in Primitive Polynesia. Library Binding. Routledge. New York, NY. 2004.

656p. Routledge Library Editions Ser., :Anthropology and Ethnography, US/Can. Edition Ser. ISBN:0-415-33020-3, ISBN13: 978-0-415-33020-6. Dewey:306/.089994.
Audience: **l,u,f.** *B*

Goodale, Jane C. **GN481**
Tiwi Wives: A Study of the Women of Melville Island, North Australia. Paper Text. Waveland Press, Inc. Prospect Heights, IL. 1994. 368p. ISBN:0-88133-784-6, ISBN13: 978-0-88133-784-6. Dewey:301.41/2/099429.
Audience: **l,u,f.** *B*

Herdt, Gilbert H. & Leavitt, Stephen C. (Editors) **GN663.A53 1998**
Adolescence in Pacific Island Communities. Cloth Text. University of Pittsburgh Press. Pittsburgh, PA. 1998. 344p. ASAO Monograph Ser. ISBN:0-8229-4068-X, ISBN13: 978-0-8229-4068-5. Dewey:305.235/0995. LCCN:98-009053.
Audience: **l,u,f.**

Knauft, Bruce M. **GN668.K53 1999**
From Primitive to Postcolonial in Melanesia and Anthropology. Trade Cloth. University of Michigan Press. Chicago, IL. 1999. 352p. ISBN:0-472-09687-7, ISBN13: 978-0-472-09687-9. Dewey:305.8/00995. LCCN:98-040153.
Audience: **l,u,f.** *Choice, 2000.*

Levy, Robert I. **DU870**
Tahitians: Mind and Experience in the Society Islands. Pierre Heyman (Illustrator). Library Binding. University of Chicago Press. Chicago, IL. 1973. xxviii, 547p. ISBN:0-226-47605-7, ISBN13: 978-0-226-47605-6. Dewey:301.29/96/21. LCCN:73-077136.
Audience: **l,u,f.**

Marshall, Mac **GN671.C3M36 2004**
Namoluk Beyond the Reef: The Transformation of a Micronesian Community. Trade Paper. Westview Press. Boulder, CO. 2004. 192p. Westview Case Studies in Anthropology ISBN:0-8133-4162-0, ISBN13: 978-0-8133-4162-0. Dewey:996.6. LCCN:2005-298361.
Audience: **u,f.**

Mead, Margaret **GN671.S2**
Coming of Age in Samoa. Cloth Text. Amereon, Ltd. Mattituck, NY. 2004. ISBN:0-8488-2716-3, ISBN13: 978-0-8488-2716-8. Dewey:306/.09961/3.
Audience: **g,l,u,f.**

Meggitt, Mervyn J. **DU122.W3 M4**
Desert People: A Study of the Walbiri Aborigines of Central Australia. Paper Text. Textbook Publishers. Temecula, CA. 2003. 348p. ISBN:0-7581-2434-1, ISBN13: 978-0-7581-2434-0. Dewey:301.4420994.
Audience: **l,u,f.**

Merry, Sally Engle & Brenneis, Donald Lawrence **GN673.H3L39 2003**
Law and Empire in the Pacific: Fiji and Hawaii. Trade Cloth. School of American Research Press. Santa Fe, NM. 2004. 314p. ISBN:1-930618-24-7, ISBN13: 978-1-930618-24-4. Dewey:306/.09969. LCCN:2003-021458.
Audience: **u,f.** *Choice, 2004.*

Obeyesekere, Gananath **DU626.O28 1997**
The Apotheosis of Captain Cook: European Mythmaking in the Pacific. Ed. 2. Trade Paper. Princeton University Press. Princeton, NJ. 1997. 336p. ISBN:0-691-05752-4, ISBN13: 978-0-691-05752-1. Dewey:996.902. LCCN:98-149683.
Audience: **g,l,u,f.**

Oliver, Douglas **DU510.O45 2002**
Polynesia in Early Historic Times. Trade Cloth. Bess Press, Inc. Honolulu, HI. 2002. 320p. ISBN:1-57306-149-2, ISBN13: 978-1-57306-149-0. Dewey:919.6.
Audience: **g,l,u,f.** *Choice, 2003.*

Oliver, Douglas L. **GN662.O46 1989**
Oceania: The Native Cultures of Australia and the Pacific Islands. Lois Johnson (Illustrator). Trade Cloth. University of Hawaii Press. Honolulu, HI. 1988. 1264p. ISBN:0-8248-1019-8, ISBN13: 978-0-8248-1019-1. Dewey:306/.099. LCCN:88-029551.
Audience: **g,l,u,f.** *Choice, 1989.*

Powdermaker, Hortense **GN671.B5P68 1979**
Life in Lesu: The Study of a Melanesian Society in New Ireland. Trade Cloth. A M S Press, Inc. New York, NY. ISBN:0-404-15877-3, ISBN13: 978-0-404-15877-4. Dewey:301.29/936. LCCN:76-044778.
Audience: **u,f.**

Schieffelin, Edward L. & Crittenden, Robert **DU740.S34 1991**
Like People You See in a Dream: First Contact in Six Papuan Societies. Trade Paper. Stanford University Press. Palo Alto, CA. 1991. 344p. ISBN:0-8047-1899-7, ISBN13: 978-0-8047-1899-8. Dewey:995.3. LCCN:90-041760.
Audience: **l,u,f.** *Choice, 1991.*

Sillitoe, Paul **GN668.S55 1998**
An Introduction to the Anthropology of Melanesia: Culture and Tradition. Cloth Text. Cambridge University Press. New York, NY. 1998. 280p. ISBN:0-521-58186-9, ISBN13: 978-0-521-58186-8. Dewey:306/.0995. LCCN:97-035251.
Audience: **l,u,f.** *Choice, 1999.*

Swain, Tony **GN666.S93 1993**
A Place for Strangers: Towards a History of Australian Aboriginal Being. Cloth Text. Cambridge University Press. New York, NY. 1993. 315p. ISBN:0-521-43005-4, ISBN13: 978-0-521-43005-0. Dewey:305.8/991. LCCN:92-030379.
Audience: **g,l,u,f.** *Choice, 1994.*

Ward, R. Gerard & Kingdon, Elizabeth (Editors) **HD1120.7.L34 1995**
Land, Custom and Practice in the South Pacific. John Ravenhill (Contribution by). Trade Cloth. Cambridge University Press. New York, NY. 1995. 304p. Asia-Pacific Studies, No. 1 ISBN:0-521-47289-X, ISBN13: 978-0-521-47289-0. Dewey:333.3/24/099. LCCN:95-034425.
Audience: **u,f.**

Watson, Virginia D. **DU740.42.W38 1997**
Anyan's Story: A New Guinea Woman in Two Worlds. Trade Cloth. University of Washington Press. Seattle, WA. 1997. 192p. McLellan Bks. ISBN:0-295-97589-X, ISBN13: 978-0-295-97589-4. Dewey:995.3. LCCN:96-042573.
Audience: **l,u,f.**

Weiner, Annette B. **GN671.N5W43 1988**
The Trobrianders of Papua New Guinea: Case Studies in Cultural Anthropology. George D. Spindler & Louise S. Spindler (Foreword by). Cloth Text. Thomson Wadsworth. Belmont, CA. 1988. 208p. Case Studies in Cultural Anthropology

ISBN:0-03-011919-7, ISBN13: 978-0-03-011919-4. Dewey:306/.0995/3. LCCN:87-018614.
Audience: **g,l,u,f.**

Social and Cultural Anthropology > World Ethnography by Continent > Transnational Phenomena and Complex Societies

Bruner, Edward M. **G156.5.H47B78 2004**
Culture on Tour: Ethnographies of Travel. Trade Cloth. University of Chicago Press. Chicago, IL. 2004. 312p. ISBN:0-226-07762-4, ISBN13: 978-0-226-07762-8. Dewey:306.4/819. LCCN:2004-007653.
Audience: **g,l,u,f.**

Clarke, Kamari Maxine **E194.Y66C53 2004**
Mapping Yorùbá Networks: Power and Agency in the Making of Transnational Communities. Trade Cloth. Duke University Press. Durham, NC. 2004. 384p. ISBN:0-8223-3330-9, ISBN13: 978-0-8223-3330-2. Dewey:305.896/333. LCCN:2004-001301.
Audience: **u,f.** *Choice, 2005.*

Darrah, Charles N. **HD5715.D37 1996**
Learning and Work: An Exploration in Industrial Ethnography. Cloth Text. Garland Publishing, Inc. New York, NY. 1996. 200p. Studies in Education and Culture, No. 8 ISBN:0-8153-1455-8, ISBN13: 978-0-8153-1455-4. Dewey:658.3/124. LCCN:95-042416.
Audience: **l,u,f.**

Forsythe, Diana **GN34.3.I53F67 2001**
Studying Those Who Study Us: An Anthropologist in the World of Artificial Intelligence. David J. Hess (Editor). Trade Cloth. Stanford University Press. Palo Alto, CA. 2001. 271p. Writing Science Ser. ISBN:0-8047-4141-7, ISBN13: 978-0-8047-4141-5. Dewey:306/.01. LCCN:2001-020018.
Audience: **u,f.** *Choice, 2002.*

George, Sheba Mariam **E184.E2G46 2005**
When Women Come First: Gender and Class in Transnational Migration. Trade Cloth. University of California Press. Berkeley, CA. 2005. 276p. ISBN:0-520-24318-8, ISBN13: 978-0-520-24318-7. Dewey:305.48/891411073. LCCN:2004-020977.
Audience: **l,u,f.** *Choice, 2006.*

Levitt, Peggy **JV7395.L48 2001**
The Transnational Villagers. Trade Cloth. University of California Press. Berkeley, CA. 2001. 294p. ISBN:0-520-22811-1, ISBN13: 978-0-520-22811-5. Dewey:304.8/744610729373. LCCN:00-055172.
Audience: **g,l,u,f.**

MacGaffey, Janet & Bazenguissa-Ganga, Remy **HF3911.Z5M33 2000**
Congo-Paris: Transnational Traders on the Margins of the Law. International African Institute Staff (Contribution by). Trade Cloth. Indiana University Press. Bloomington, IN. 2000. xii, 190p. African Issues Ser. ISBN:0-253-33770-4, ISBN13: 978-0-253-33770-2. Dewey:382/.096724/044. LCCN:00-027282.
Audience: **u,f.**

Miles, Ann **F128.9.E28M55 2004**
From Cuenca to Queens: An Anthropological Story of Transnational Migration. Trade Cloth. University of Texas Press. Austin, TX. 2004. 247p. ISBN:0-292-70205-1, ISBN13: 978-0-292-70205-9. Dewey:974.7/230046886. LCCN:2003-007700.
Audience: **u,f.**

Parrenas, Rhacel Salazar **HQ792.P5P37 2005**
Children of Global Migration: Transnational Families and Gendered Woes. Trade Cloth. Stanford University Press. Palo Alto, CA. 2005. 232p. ISBN:0-8047-4944-2, ISBN13: 978-0-8047-4944-2. Dewey:306.85/09599. LCCN:2004-016220.
Audience: **l,u.** *Choice, 2006.*

Rattansi, Ali & Westwood, Sallie (Editors) **D1056.R335 1994**
Racism, Modernity, and Identity on the Western Front. Trade Paper. Blackwell Publishing, Inc. Malden, MA. 1994. 312p. ISBN:0-7456-0942-2, ISBN13: 978-0-7456-0942-3. Dewey:305.8/0094. LCCN:94-034776.
Audience: **u,f.**

Scher, Philip W. **GT4229.T7.S24 2003**
Carnival and the Formation of a Caribbean Transnation. Trade Cloth. University Press of Florida. Gainesville, FL. 2003. xv, 214p. New World Diasporas Ser. ISBN:0-8130-2612-1, ISBN13: 978-0-8130-2612-1. Dewey:394.25/0972983. LCCN:2002-075081.
Audience: **g,l,u,f.** *Choice, 2003.*

Spellman, Kathryn **DA125.I68**
Religion and Nation: Iranian Local and Transnational Networks in Britain. Trade Cloth. Berghahn Books, Inc. New York, NY. 2004. 240p. Studies in Forced Migration, Vol. 11 ISBN:1-57181-576-7, ISBN13: 978-1-57181-576-7. Dewey:305.891/55041. LCCN:2003-063912.
Audience: **l,u,f.** *Choice, 2005.*

Applied Anthropology

Grimes, Kimberly M. & Milgram, B. Lynne (Editors) **HD9999.H362A78 2000**
Artisans and Cooperatives: Developing Alternative Trade for the Global Economy. Trade Cloth. University of Arizona Press. Tucson, AZ. 2000. 208p. ISBN:0-8165-2051-8, ISBN13: 978-0-8165-2051-0. Dewey:306.3/68. LCCN:00-008226.
Audience: **u,f.**

Gwynne, Margaret Anderson **GN397.5.G99 2003**
Applied Anthropology: A Career-Oriented Approach. Trade Paper. Allyn & Bacon, Inc. Boston, MA. 2002. 416p. ISBN:0-205-35866-7, ISBN13: 978-0-205-35866-3. Dewey:301. LCCN:2002-027754.
Audience: **l,u,f.**

Hahn, Robert A. (Editor) **RA427.A58 1999**
Anthropology in Public Health: Bridging Differences in Culture and Society. Trade Paper. Oxford University Press, Inc. New York, NY. 1999. 408p. ISBN:0-19-511955-X, ISBN13: 978-0-19-511955-8. Dewey:306.461. LCCN:98-034571.
Audience: **g,l,u,f.**

Higgins, Patricia J. & Paredes, J. Anthony (Editors) **GN397.5**
Classics of Practicing Anthropology, 1978-1998. Trade Paper. Society for Applied Anthropology. Oklahoma City, OK. 2000.

300p. ISBN:0-9642023-1-X, ISBN13: 978-0-9642023-1-3. Dewey:301/.05.
Audience: **l,u,f.**

McDonald, James H. **GN397.5.A66 2002**
The Applied Anthropology Reader. Trade Paper. Allyn & Bacon, Inc. Boston, MA. 2001. 432p. ISBN:0-205-32491-6, ISBN13: 978-0-205-32491-0. Dewey:301. LCCN:2001-046174.
Audience: **g,l,u,f.**

Nagengast, Carole & Velez-Ibanez, Carlos G. (Editors) **JC423.N344 2004**
Human Rights: The Scholar as Activist. William Schulz (Foreword by). Trade Paper. Society for Applied Anthropology. Oklahoma City, OK. 2004. 237p. ISBN:0-9642023-2-8, ISBN13: 978-0-9642023-2-0. Dewey:321.8.
Audience: **g,l,u,f.**

Nolan, Riall **GN397.5.N63 2003**
Anthropology in Practice. Trade Cloth. Lynne Rienner Publishers, Inc. Boulder, CO. 2003. 200p. Directions in Applied Anthropology Ser., :Adaptations and Innovations ISBN:1-55587-957-8, ISBN13: 978-1-55587-957-0. Dewey:301. LCCN:2002-073968.
Audience: **l,u,f.** *Choice, 2003.*

Sillitoe, Paul (Editor), et al. **GN476.P37 2002**
Participating in Development: Approaches to Indigenous Knowledge. Alan Bicker & Johan Pottier (Editors). Paper over Boards. Routledge. New York, NY. 2002. 288p. ASA Monographs, Vol. 34 ISBN:0-415-25868-5, ISBN13: 978-0-415-25868-5. Dewey:307.1/4. LCCN:2002-021956.
Audience: **u,f.**

Electronic Resources

GN36.U6
The American Folklife Center - Ethnographic Resources related to Folklore, Anthropology, Ethnomusicology, and the Humanities.
http://www.loc.gov/folklife/other.html
Audience: **g,l,u,f.**

GN1
AnthroSource.
http://www.anthrosource.net
Audience: **g,l,u,f.**

CC97.E
Archaeological Resource Guide for Europe.
http://www.let.rug.nl/arge/
Audience: **g,l,u,f.**

GN60
Internet Resources for Physical Anthropology.
http://www2.lib.udel.edu/subj/anth/phys/internet.htm
Audience: **g,l,u,f.**

GN316
Internet Resources for Social and Cultural Anthropology.
http://www2.lib.udel.edu/subj/anth/soccult/internet.htm
Audience: **g,l,u,f.**

Athropology of Food Habits, Cuisine, Drink, and Nutrition

Counihan, Carole (Editor) **GT2853.U5F663 2002**
Food in the USA: Reader. Paper over Boards. Routledge. New York, NY. 2002. 448p. ISBN:0-415-93231-9, ISBN13: 978-0-415-93231-8. Dewey:394.1/2/0973. LCCN:2002-017785.
Audience: **g,l,u,f.**

Counihan, Carole M. & Kaplan, Steven L. **GT2850.F774 1998**
Food and Gender: Identity and Power. Paper over Boards. Gordon & Breach Publishing Group. New York, NY. 1998. 157p. Food in History and Culture Ser., Vol. 1 ISBN:90-5702-573-6, ISBN13: 978-90-5702-573-0. Dewey:363.8.
Audience: **g,l,u,f.**

Counihan, Carole & Van Esterik, Penny **GT2850.F64 1997**
Food and Culture: A Reader. Paper over Boards. Routledge. New York, NY. 1997. 432p. ISBN:0-415-91709-3, ISBN13: 978-0-415-91709-4. Dewey:394.1. LCCN:96-046430.
Audience: **g,l,u,f.**

de Garine, I. & de Garine, Valerie **GT2880.G34 2001**
Drinking: Anthropological Approaches. Trade Cloth. Berghahn Books, Inc. New York, NY. 2001. 272p. The Anthropology of Food and Nutrition Ser., Vol. 4 ISBN:1-57181-315-2, ISBN13: 978-1-57181-315-2. Dewey:394.1/3. LCCN:2001-035608.
Audience: **l,u,f.**

Dettwyler, Katherine **GN655.M22.D48 1994**
Dancing Skeletons: Life and Death in West Africa. Paper Text. Waveland Press, Inc. Prospect Heights, IL. 1994. 172p. ISBN:0-88133-748-X, ISBN13: 978-0-88133-748-8. Dewey:306.4/61. LCCN:94-175193.
Audience: **l,u,f.**

Goodman, Alan H., et al. **GN407.N878 1999**
Nutritional Anthropology: Biocultural Perspectives on Food and Nutrition. Darna L. Dufour & Gretel H. Pelto (Authors). Paper Text. Mayfield Publishing Company. San Francisco, CA. 1999. viii, 392p. ISBN:1-55934-074-6, ISBN13: 978-1-55934-074-8. Dewey:306.4. LCCN:99-016016.
Audience: **u,f.**

Huss-Ashmore, Rebecca (Editor) **HD9017.A2A39 1989**
Contending with Change: African Food Systems in Crisis. Ed. 2. Cloth Text. Gordon & Breach Publishing Group. New York, NY. 1991. 292p. Food and Nutrition in History and Anthropology Ser., Vol. 2 ISBN:2-88124-307-X, ISBN13: 978-2-88124-307-3. Dewey:363.8/096. LCCN:88-025949.
Audience: **u,f.**

Marshall, Mac **GN671.C3 M37**
Weekend Warriors: Alcohol in a Micronesian Culture. Robert B. Edgerton & L. L. Langness (Editors). Paper Text. McGraw-Hill Higher Education. Burr Ridge, IL. 1978. 170p. ISBN:0-87484-455-X, ISBN13: 978-0-87484-455-9. Dewey:362.2/92/09966. LCCN:78-064597.
Audience: **l,u,f.**

Mintz, Sidney W. **GT2869.M56 1986**
Sweetness and Power: The Place of Sugar in Modern History. Trade Paper. Penguin Group (USA) Inc. New York, NY. 1986. 320p. ISBN:0-14-009233-1, ISBN13: 978-0-14-009233-2. Dewey:394.1/2. LCCN:86-000781.
Audience: **g,l,u,f.** *Choice, 1985.*

Mintz, Sidney W. **GT2850.M58 1996**
Tasting Food, Tasting Freedom: Excursions into Eating, Power, and the Past. Trade Paper. Beacon Press. Boston, MA. 1997. 176p. ISBN:0-8070-4629-9, ISBN13: 978-0-8070-4629-6. Dewey:394.1. LCCN:95-047569.
Audience: **g,l,u,f.**

Richards, Audrey I. **DT764.N34R53 2004**
Hunger and Work in a Savage Tribe: A Functional Study of Nutrition among the Southern Bantu. Library Binding. Routledge. New York, NY. 2005. 264p. Routledge Library Editions Ser., :Anthropology and Ethnography, US/Can. Edition Ser. ISBN:0-415-33001-7, ISBN13: 978-0-415-33001-5. Dewey:394.1/08996398.
Audience: **u,f.**

Saggers, Sherry & Gray, Dennis **HV5198.S34 1998**
Dealing with Alcohol: Indigenous Usage in Australia, New Zealand and Canada. Cloth Text. Cambridge University Press. New York, NY. 1998. 248p. ISBN:0-521-62032-5, ISBN13: 978-0-521-62032-1. Dewey:362.292/089. LCCN:98-007278.
Audience: **u.** *Choice, 1999.*

Scheper-Hughes, Nancy **HV1448.B72**
Death Without Weeping: The Violence of Everyday Life in Brazil. Trade Paper. University of California Press. Berkeley, CA. 1993. 628p. ISBN:0-520-07537-4, ISBN13: 978-0-520-07537-5. Dewey:303.60981.
Audience: **u,f.** *Choice, 1993.*

Sutton, David E. **GT2850**
Remembrance of Repasts: An Anthropology of Food and Memory. Cloth over Boards. Berg Publishers. Oxford, 2001. 224p. Materializing Culture Ser. ISBN:1-85973-469-3, ISBN13: 978-1-85973-469-8. Dewey:394.1/2.
Audience: **l,u,f.**

Watson, James L. & Caldwell, Melissa (Editors) **GT2850.C853 2005**
Cultural Politics of Food and Eating. Trade Paper. Blackwell Publishing, Inc. Malden, MA. 2004. 336p. Blackwell Readers in Anthropology Ser., Vol. 8 ISBN:0-631-23093-9, ISBN13: 978-0-631-23093-9. Dewey:394.1/2. LCCN:2004-013999.
Audience: **g,l,u,f.**

Medical Anthropology

Adams, Vincanne **RA413.5.N35A3 1998**
Medical Science and Democratic Truth: Doctors and Revolution in Nepal. Cloth Text. Cambridge University Press. New York, NY. 1998. 263p. Cambridge Studies in Medical Anthropology, No. 6 ISBN:0-521-58486-8, ISBN13: 978-0-521-58486-9. Dewey:306.4/61/095496. LCCN:97-018016.
Audience: **u,f.**

Bailey, Eric J. **RA448**
Medical Anthropology and African American Health. Trade Cloth. Greenwood Publishing Group, Inc. Portsmouth, NH. 2000. 270p. ISBN:0-89789-592-4, ISBN13: 978-0-89789-592-7. Dewey:306.4/61/089/96073. LCCN:99-021244.
Audience: **g,l,u,f.**

Ember, Carol R. & Ember, Melvin (Editors) **RA418.E354 2004**
Encyclopedia of Medical Anthropology: Health and Illness in the World's Cultures. Trade Cloth. Springer. New York, NY. 2003. 2944p. ISBN:0-306-47754-8, ISBN13: 978-0-306-47754-6. Dewey:362.1/03. LCCN:2003-050644.
Audience: **g,l,u,f.**

Farmer, Paul **RA644.A25F37 2006**
AIDS and Accusation: Haiti and Geography of Blame. Ed. 2. Trade Paper. University of California Press. Berkeley, CA. 2006. 338p. Comparative Studies of Health Systems and Medical Care ISBN:0-520-24839-2, ISBN13: 978-0-520-24839-7. Dewey:306.4/61. LCCN:2005-046650.
Audience: **u,f.**

Farmer, Paul **HM821.F37 2003**
Pathologies of Power: Health, Human Rights, and the New War on the Poor. Amartya Sen (Foreword by). Trade Cloth. University of California Press. Berkeley, CA. 2003. 419p. California Series in Public Anthropology, Vol. 4 ISBN:0-520-23550-9, ISBN13: 978-0-520-23550-2. Dewey:305.5/69. LCCN:2002-013311.
Audience: **u,f.** *Choice, 2004.*

Harper, Janice **GN661.M2H37 2002**
Endangered Species: Health, Illness, and Death among Madagascar's People of the Forest. Trade Paper. Carolina Academic Press. Durham, NC. 2002. 296p. Carolina Academic Press Ethnographic Studies in Medical Anthropology ISBN:0-89089-238-5, ISBN13: 978-0-89089-238-1. Dewey:306.4610969. LCCN:2002-107086.
Audience: **u,f.** *Choice, 2003.*

Hsu, Elisabeth **R601.H697 1999**
The Transmission of Chinese Medicine. Cloth Text. Cambridge University Press. New York, NY. 1999. 306p. Cambridge Studies in Medical Anthropology, No. 7 ISBN:0-521-64236-1, ISBN13: 978-0-521-64236-1. Dewey:610.951. LCCN:98-050700.
Audience: **g,l,u,f.**

Laderman, Carol **DS666.I15**
Wives and Midwives: Childbirth and Nutrition in Rural Malaysia. Trade Paper. University of California Press. Berkeley, CA. 1987. 267p. Comparative Studies of Health Systems and Medical Care, Vol. 7 ISBN:0-520-06036-9, ISBN13: 978-0-520-06036-4. Dewey:306.4/61/095951. LCCN:83-047664.
Audience: **u,f.**

Laderman, Carol & Roseman, Marina (Editors) **GR880.P38 1995**
The Performance of Healing. Paper over Boards. Routledge. New York, NY. 1996. 330p. ISBN:0-415-91199-0, ISBN13: 978-0-415-91199-3. Dewey:615.5. LCCN:95-024568.
Audience: **u,f.**

Lindenbaum, Shirley **DU740.42.L56**
Kuru Sorcery: Disease and Danger in the New Guinea Highlands. Robert B. Edgerton & L. L. Langness (Editors). Paper Text. McGraw-Hill Higher Education. Burr Ridge, IL. 1978. xii, 174p. ISBN:0-87484-362-6, ISBN13: 978-0-87484-362-0. Dewey:301.5. LCCN:78-064596.
Audience: **u,f.**

Lock, Margaret (Editor, Contribution by) **RA564.85.P73 1998**
Pragmatic Women and Body Politics. Patricia Alice Kaufert (Editor), Janice Boddy, Ellen Gruenbaum, Soheir A. Morsy, Brooke G. Schoepf, Karina Kielmann & Alan Harwood (Contribution by). Trade Cloth. Cambridge University Press. New York, NY. 1998. 376p. Cambridge Studies in Medical Anthropology, No. 5 ISBN:0-521-62099-6, ISBN13: 978-0-521-62099-4. Dewey:362.1/082. LCCN:97-010263.
Audience: **u,f.**

Martin, Emily **RG103.5.M37 2001**
The Woman in the Body: A Cultural Analysis of Reproduction. Trade Paper. Beacon Press. Boston, MA. 2001. 320p. ISBN:0-8070-4645-0, ISBN13: 978-0-8070-4645-6. Dewey:155.3/33. LCCN:2001-029523.
Audience: **l,u,f.**

McClain, Carol S. (Editor) **GN296.W65 1989**
Women As Healers: Cross-Cultural Perspectives. Paper Text. Rutgers University Press. Piscataway, NJ. 1989. 272p. ISBN:0-8135-1370-7, ISBN13: 978-0-8135-1370-6. Dewey:610/.88042. LCCN:88-016896.
Audience: **g,l,u,f.** *Choice, 1990.*

Moerman, Daniel E. **R726.5.M645 2002**
Meaning, Medicine and the 'Placebo Effect'. Cloth Text. Cambridge University Press. New York, NY. 2002. 186p. Cambridge Studies in Medical Anthropology, Vol. 9 ISBN:0-521-80630-5, ISBN13: 978-0-521-80630-5. Dewey:615.5. LCCN:2002-020167.
Audience: **u,f.** *Choice, 2003.*

Rapp, Rayna **RG628.3.A48R37 1999**
Testing Women, Testing the Fetus: The Social Impact of Amniocentesis in America. UK-B Format Paperback. Routledge. New York, NY. 2000. 376p. Anthropology of Everyday Life Ser. ISBN:0-415-91645-3, ISBN13: 978-0-415-91645-5. Dewey:618.3/204275. LCCN:98-045968.
Audience: **u,f.**

Romanucci-Ross, Lola E. & Moerman, Daniel R. (Editors) **GN296.A63 1997**
The Anthropology of Medicine: From Culture to Method. Ed. 3. Trade Cloth. Greenwood Publishing Group, Inc. Portsmouth, NH. 1997. 416p. ISBN:0-89789-490-1, ISBN13: 978-0-89789-490-6. Dewey:306.4/6. LCCN:96-053993.
Audience: **u,f.**

Sargent, Carolyn F. & Brettell, Caroline B. **RA564.85.G46 1996**
Gender and Health: An International Perspective. Trade Paper. Prentice Hall PTR. Upper Saddle River, NJ. 1995. 370p. ISBN:0-13-079427-9, ISBN13: 978-0-13-079427-7. Dewey:362.1/082. LCCN:95-037457.
Audience: **u,f.**

Sargent, Carolyn F. & Johnson, Thomas M. (Editors) **GN296**
Handbook of Medical Anthropology: Contemporary Theory and Method. Ed. 2. Cloth Text. Greenwood Publishing Group, Inc. Portsmouth, NH. 1996. 584p. ISBN:0-313-29658-8, ISBN13: 978-0-313-29658-1. Dewey:306.4/61. LCCN:95-040052.
Audience: **l,u,f.**

Singer, Merrill & Baer, Hans **GN296.S56 1995**
Critical Medical Anthropology. Trade Cloth. Baywood Publishing Company, Inc. Amityville, NY. 1995. 416p. Critical Approaches in the Health Social Sciences Ser. ISBN:0-89503-124-8, ISBN13: 978-0-89503-124-2. Dewey:306.4/61. LCCN:94-039810.
Audience: **u,f.**

Museum Anthropology

Ames, Michael M. **GN35.A52 1992**
Cannibal Tours and Glass Boxes: The Anthropology of Museums. Ed. 2. Trade Paper. University of British Columbia Press. Vancouver, BC. 1992. "xvi, 212"p. ISBN:0-7748-0391-6, ISBN13: 978-0-7748-0391-5. Dewey:306/.074. LCCN:92-224765.
Audience: **g,l,u,f.**

Bouquet, Mary (Editor) **GN35.A33 2001**
Academic Anthropology and the Museum: Back to the Future. Trade Cloth. Berghahn Books, Inc. New York, NY. 2001. 256p. New Directions in Anthropology Ser. ISBN:1-57181-825-1, ISBN13: 978-1-57181-825-6. Dewey:069/.5. LCCN:00-051932.
Audience: **u,f.**

Bouquet, Mary & Porto, Nuno **AM151.S39 2004**
Science, Magic, and Religion: The Ritual Process of Museum Magic. Trade Cloth. Berghahn Books, Inc. New York, NY. 2004. 288p. New Directions in Anthropology Ser. ISBN:1-57181-520-1, ISBN13: 978-1-57181-520-0. Dewey:069/.5. LCCN:2004-046271.
Audience: **l,u,f.**

Fforde, Cressida (Editor), et al. **CC79.5.H85D43 2002**
The Dead and Their Possessions: Repatriation in Principle, Policy, and Practice. Jane Hubert & Paul Turnbull (Editors). Paper over Boards. Routledge. New York, NY. 2002. 360p. One World Archaeology Ser., Vol. 43 ISBN:0-415-23385-2, ISBN13: 978-0-415-23385-9. Dewey:930.1. LCCN:2001-048189.
Audience: **u,f.**

Gosden, Chris & Knowles, Chantal
Possessing Culture: Museums, Anthropology and German New Guinea. Berg. 2006. ISBN:1-85973-655-6, ISBN13: 978-1-85973-655-5.
Audience: **u,f.**

Hinsley, Curtis M. **GN17.3.U6H56 1994**
The Smithsonian and the American Indian: Making a Moral Anthropology in Victorian America. Trade Paper. Smithsonian Institution Press. Washington, DC. 1994. 320p. ISBN:1-56098-409-0, ISBN13: 978-1-56098-409-2. Dewey:301/.0973. LCCN:80-020193.
Audience: **g,l,u,f.**

Kirshenblatt-Gimblett, Barbara **GN36.U62.B478 1998**
[e] Destination Culture: Tourism, Museums, and Heritage. E-Book. NetLibrary, Inc. Boulder, CO. 1998. ISBN:0-585-29277-9, ISBN13: 978-0-585-29277-9. Dewey:306/.074.
Audience: **g,l,u,f.**

Kreps, Christina F. **AM7.K74 2003**
Liberating Culture: Cross-Cultural Perspectives on Museums, Curation, and Heritage Preservation. Paper over Boards. Routledge. New York, NY. 2003. 176p. Museum Meanings Ser.

ISBN:0-415-25025-0, ISBN13: 978-0-415-25025-2. Dewey:069/.01. LCCN:2002-031776.

Audience: **g,l,u,f.**

Peers, Laura L. & Brown, Alison K. (Editors) **GN35.M88 2003**
Museums and Source Communities: A Routledge Reader. Paper over Boards. Routledge. New York, NY. 2003. 304p. ISBN:0-415-28051-6, ISBN13: 978-0-415-28051-8. Dewey:305.8/0074. LCCN:2002-037123.

Audience: **l,u,f.**

Price, Sally **N5311.P75 2001**
Primitive Art in Civilized Places. Ed. 2. Trade Paper. University of Chicago Press. Chicago, IL. 2002. 176p. ISBN:0-226-68067-3, ISBN13: 978-0-226-68067-5. Dewey:709/.01/1. LCCN:2001-042815.

Audience: **g,l,u,f.**

Stocking, George W. Jr. (Editor) **GN35.O25**
Objects and Others: Essays on Museums and Material Culture. Trade Paper. University of Wisconsin Press. Chicago, IL. 1988. 240p. History of Anthropology Ser., No. 3 ISBN:0-299-10324-2, ISBN13: 978-0-299-10324-8. Dewey:306. LCCN:85-040379.

Audience: **u,f.** *Choice, 1986.*

BUSINESS ADMINISTRATION

In selecting the resources, an attempt is made to focus on the great and essential works in the various disciplines within business. The selection process aims to include works that show the historical development of various fields, the influences that shaped the dominant paradigm, and important alternative views. The items included here will inform the introductory reader or the advanced undergraduate of the comprehensive breadth of all of the major disciplines within business. This collection includes core reference books, monographic works, and electronic resources.

The approach to classification here allows for the inclusion of both practical and scholarly works. Inspired by the ABI Inform index subject classification, the taxonomy reflects the broad range of topics that could be researched in an academic library by undergraduate business students. The subjects are divided into five areas: business environment, management, companies/industries, career/vocational guidance, and business information sources. The business environment section includes such current and important topics as business ethics, globalization, and cross-cultural business. The majority of items selected however are indexed in the broad "management function" subject area. This area includes the disciplines that may often be found in degree concentrations within undergraduate business programs: general management, finance, accounting, operations, human resource management, and marketing. The additional subject areas of companies/industries, career/vocational guidance, and business information sources round out the classification system and results in a pertinent and timely collection that is not dominated only by scholarly and theoretical works.

— Glenn McGuigan

Business Environment

Bagley, Constance E. & Savage, Diane **KF889.B255 2006**
Managers and the Legal Environment: Strategies for the 21st Century. Ed. 5. Cloth Text. Thomson South-Western. Mason, OH. 2005. 1128p. ISBN:0-324-26951-X, ISBN13: 978-0-324-26951-2. Dewey:346.7307. LCCN:2005-925692.
Audience: **u,f.**

Baron, David P. **HD60.B37 2005**
Business and Its Environment. Ed. 5. Trade Paper, Perfect. Prentice Hall PTR. Upper Saddle River, NJ. 2005. 877p. ISBN:0-13-187355-5, ISBN13: 978-0-13-187355-1. Dewey:658.4/08. LCCN:2005-014666.
Audience: **u,f.**

Christensen, Clayton M. **HD53.C49 1997**
The Innovator's Dilemma: When New Technologies Cause Great Firms to Fail. Trade Cloth. Harvard Business School Press. Boston, MA. 1997. 256p. The Management of Innovation and Change Ser. ISBN:0-87584-585-1, ISBN13: 978-0-87584-585-2. Dewey:658. LCCN:96-010894.
Audience: **g,l,u,f.**

Downes, Larry & Mui, Chunka **HD30.2.D68 2000**
Unleashing the Killer App.: Digital Strategies for Market Dominance. Trade Paper. Harvard Business School Press. Boston, MA. 2000. 272p. ISBN:1-57851-261-1, ISBN13: 978-1-57851-261-4. Dewey:658.4/038. LCCN:99-088674.
Audience: **g,l,u,f.** *Choice, 1999.*

Gladwell, Malcolm **HM1033.G53 2000**
The Tipping Point: How Little Things Can Make a Big Difference. Trade Paper. Little Brown & Company. New York, NY. 2002. 304p. ISBN:0-316-34662-4, ISBN13: 978-0-316-34662-7. Dewey:302. LCCN:99-047576.
Audience: **g,l,u,f.**

Government Printing Office Staff **HC101**
Survey of Current Business.
http://www.bea.gov/bea/pubs.htm
Bureau of Economic Analysis.
Audience: **g,l,u,f.**

Grant, R. M. **HD30.28**
Contemporary Strategy Analysis: Concepts, Techniques, Applications. Ed. 5. Trade Cloth. Blackwell Publishing, Inc. Malden, MA. 2005. 560p. ISBN:1-4051-1998-5, ISBN13: 978-1-4051-1998-6. Dewey:658.4/012. LCCN:2004-007696.
Audience: **u,f.**

Kubasek, Nancy K., et al. **KF1600.K83 2005**
Legal Environment of Business: A Critical Thinking Approach. Ed. 4. Bartley A. Brennan & Neil Browne (Authors). Cloth Text. Prentice Hall PTR. Upper Saddle River, NJ. 2005. 888p. ISBN:0-13-149856-8, ISBN13: 978-0-13-149856-3. Dewey:346.7307. LCCN:2004-061122.
Audience: **u,f.**

Porter, Michael E. **HD3611.P654 1998**
The Competitive Advantage of Nations. Trade Cloth. Simon & Schuster. New York, NY. 1998. 896p. ISBN:0-684-84147-9, ISBN13: 978-0-684-84147-2. Dewey:338.6/048. LCCN:98-009584.
Audience: **g,u,f.**

Prestowitz, Clyde & Prestowitz, Clyde V. **HB3730**
Three Billion New Capitalists: The Great Shift of Wealth and Power to the East. Perfect, Paper over Boards, Dust Jacket. Basic Books. New York, NY. 2005. 321p. ISBN:0-465-06281-4, ISBN13: 978-0-465-06281-2. Dewey:330.0112.
Audience: **g,l,u,f.** *Choice, 2005.*

Shapiro, Carol & Varian, Hal R. **HC79.I55S53 1998**
Information Rules: A Strategic Guide to the Network Economy. Trade Cloth. Harvard Business School Press. Boston, MA. 1998. 368p. ISBN:0-87584-863-X, ISBN13: 978-0-87584-863-1. Dewey:658.4/038. LCCN:98-024923.
Audience: **g,l,u,f.**

Surowiecki, James **JC328.2.S87 2003**
The Wisdom of Crowds: Why the Many Are Smarter Than the Few and How Collective Wisdom Shapes Business, Economies, Societies and Nations. Trade Cloth. Doubleday Canada, Ltd. Toronto, ON. 2004. 320p. ISBN:0-385-50386-5, ISBN13: 978-0-385-50386-0. Dewey:303.3/8. LCCN:2003-070095.
Audience: **g,l,u,f.** *Choice, 2004.*

Business Environment > Social Policy

Andreasen, Alan R. **HF5414.A527 2006**
Social Marketing in the 21st Century. Cloth Text. SAGE Publications, Inc. Thousand Oaks, CA. 2005. 280p. ISBN:1-4129-1633-X, ISBN13: 978-1-4129-1633-2. Dewey:361/.0068/8. LCCN:2005-022466.
Audience: **g,l,u,f.**

Kotler, Philip, et al. **HF5414.K67 2002**
Social Marketing: Improving the Quality of Life. Ed. 2. Ned L. Roberto & Nancy R. Lee (Authors). Paper Text. SAGE Publications, Inc. Thousand Oaks, CA. 2002. 456p. ISBN:0-7619-2434-5, ISBN13: 978-0-7619-2434-0. Dewey:658.8. LCCN:2001-007178.
Audience: **g,l,u,f.**

Porter, Michael E. **HD41.P668 1985**
The Competitive Advantage: Creating and Sustaining Superior Performance. Trade Cloth. Simon & Schuster. New York, NY. 1985. 484p. ISBN:0-02-925090-0, ISBN13: 978-0-02-925090-7. Dewey:658. LCCN:83-049518.
Audience: **u,f.**

Porter, Michael E. **HD3611.P654 1990**
The Competitive Advantage of Nations and Their Firms. Trade Cloth. Simon & Schuster. New York, NY. 1990. 896p. ISBN:0-02-925361-6, ISBN13: 978-0-02-925361-8. Dewey:382/.1042. LCCN:89-025632.
Audience: **u,f.** *Choice, 1990.*

Porter, Michael E. **HF1414.P67 1998**
On Competition. Trade Cloth. Harvard Business School Press. Boston, MA. 1998. 496p. Review Book Ser. ISBN:0-87584-795-1, ISBN13: 978-0-87584-795-5. Dewey:382/.1042. LCCN:98-007643.
Audience: **u,f.** *Choice, 1999.*

Schaper, Michael **HB615**
Making Ecopreneurs: Developing Sustainable Entrepreneurship. Trade Cloth. Ashgate Publishing, Ltd. Aldershot, 2005. 276p.

Corporate Social Responsibility Ser. ISBN:0-7546-4491-X, ISBN13: 978-0-7546-4491-0. Dewey:658.4/083. LCCN:2005-015273.

Audience: **l,u.**

Business Environment > Social Policy > Social Trends and Culture

Castro, Barry **HD60.B878 1996**
Business and Society: A Reader in the History, Sociology, and Ethics of Business. Paper Text. Oxford University Press, Inc. New York, NY. 1996. 288p. ISBN:0-19-509566-9, ISBN13: 978-0-19-509566-1. Dewey:658.4/08. LCCN:95-006663.
Audience: **g,u,f.**

Hollender, Jeffrey **HD60**
What Matters Most: How a Small Group of Pioneers Is Teaching Social Responsibility to Big Business, and Why Big Business Is Listening. Trade Paper. Basic Books. New York, NY. 2005. 384p. ISBN:0-465-03086-6, ISBN13: 978-0-465-03086-6. Dewey:658.4/08.
Audience: **g,u,f.** *Choice, 2004.*

Lager, Fred C. **E187.O7K4**
Ben and Jerry's: How Two Real Guys Built a Business with a Social Conscience and a Sense of Humor. Trade Paper. Random House, Inc. New York, NY. 1995. 276p. ISBN:0-517-88370-8, ISBN13: 978-0-517-88370-9. Dewey:973.18.
Audience: **g,u,f.**

Manheim, Jarol B. **HD59.M257 2001**
The Death of a Thousand Cuts: Corporate Campaigns and the Attack on the Corporation. Cloth over Boards. Lawrence Erlbaum Associates, Inc. Mahwah, NJ. 2000. 376p. ISBN:0-8058-3831-7, ISBN13: 978-0-8058-3831-2. Dewey:659.2. LCCN:00-034780.
Audience: **g,l,u,f.** *Choice, 2001.*

Mitroff, Ian I. & Denton, Elizabeth A. **HD4905.M53 1999**
A Spiritual Audit of Corporate America: A Hard Look at Spirituality, Religion, and Values in the Workplace. Trade Cloth. John Wiley & Sons, Inc. Hoboken, NJ. 1999. 288p. ISBN:0-7879-4666-4, ISBN13: 978-0-7879-4666-1. Dewey:261.8/5. LCCN:99-006693.
Audience: **l,u,f.**

Prahalad, C. K., et al. **HD60.H389 2003**
Harvard Business Review on Corporate Responsibility. Michael E. Porter & Charles Handy (Authors). Trade Paper. Harvard Business School Press. Boston, MA. 2003. 208p. The Harvard Business Review Paperback Ser. ISBN:1-59139-274-8, ISBN13: 978-1-59139-274-3. Dewey:658.4/08. LCCN:2003-008219.
Audience: **g,l,u,f.**

Business Environment > Social Policy > Social Trends and Culture > Buiness and Government

Adams, Walter & Brock, James W. **HD2785.A68 2004**
The Bigness Complex: Industry, Labor, and Government in the American Economy. Ed. 2. Trade Paper. Stanford University Press. Palo Alto, CA. 2004. 400p. ISBN:0-8047-4969-8, ISBN13: 978-0-8047-4969-5. Dewey:338.6/44/0973. LCCN:2004-001030.
Audience: **g,l,u,f.**

MacAvoy, Paul W. & Millstein, Ira M. **HD2741.M196 2003**
The Recurrent Crisis in Corporate Governance. Cloth over Boards. Palgrave Macmillan. New York, NY. 2004. 160p. ISBN:1-4039-1666-7, ISBN13: 978-1-4039-1666-2. Dewey:658.4. LCCN:2003-048290.
Audience: **g,l,u,f.** *Choice, 2004.*

Nuechterlein, Jonathan E. & Weiser, Philip J. **HE7781.N84 2005**
Digital Crossroads: American Telecommunications Policy in the Internet Age. Trade Cloth. MIT Press. Cambridge, MA. 2005. 672p. ISBN:0-262-14091-8, ISBN13: 978-0-262-14091-1. Dewey:384/.0973. LCCN:2004-061063.
Audience: **g,l,u,f.** *Choice, 2005.*

Post, James, et al. **HD60 .F72**
Business and Society: Corporate Strategy, Public Policy, and Ethics with PowerWeb and Enron Case. Ed. 10. Anne T. Lawrence & James Weber (Authors). Cloth Text. McGraw-Hill Higher Education. Burr Ridge, IL. 2003. ISBN:0-07-287227-6, ISBN13: 978-0-07-287227-9. Dewey:658.4/08 21.
Audience: **u,f.**

Steiner, John F. & Steiner, George A. **HD60.5.U5 S8 1980B**
Business, Government and Society. Ed. 10. Cloth Text. McGraw-Hill Higher Education. Burr Ridge, IL. 2003. 768p. ISBN:0-07-293943-5, ISBN13: 978-0-07-293943-9. Dewey:658.4/08.
Audience: **u,f.**

Vogel, David **JK467.V643 1996**
Kindred Strangers: The Uneasy Relationship Between Politics and Business in America. Trade Cloth. Princeton University Press. Princeton, NJ. 1996. 426p. Princeton Studies in American Politics ISBN:0-691-02746-3, ISBN13: 978-0-691-02746-3. Dewey:324/.4/0973. LCCN:95-042251.
Audience: **g,l,u,f.**

Business Environment > Social Policy > Social Trends and Culture > Consumer Movement

Ewen, Stuart **HF5813.U6**
Captains of Consciousness: Advertising and the Social Roots of the Consumer Culture. Ed. 25. Trade Paper. Basic Books. New York, NY. 2001. 272p. ISBN:0-465-02155-7, ISBN13: 978-0-465-02155-0. Dewey:306.3/0973/09045.
Audience: **g,u,f.**

Pertschuk, Michael **HC110.C63**
Revolt Against Regulation: The Rise and Pause of the Consumer Movement. Trade Paper. University of California Press. Berkeley, CA. 1983. 192p. ISBN:0-520-05074-6, ISBN13: 978-0-520-05074-7. Dewey:381/.34/0973. LCCN:82-040108.
Audience: **g,u,f.**

Business Environment > Social Policy > Social Trends and Culture > Economic Justice

Laird, Pamela Walker **HD69.S8L35 2005**
Pull: Networking and Success since Benjamin Franklin. Trade Cloth. Harvard University Press. Cambridge, MA. 2006. 464p. Harvard Studies in Business History Ser., Vol. 48 ISBN:0-674-01907-5, ISBN13: 978-0-674-01907-2. Dewey:650.1/3. LCCN:2005-050247.
Audience: **g,l,u,f.** *Choice, 2006.*

Stiglitz, Joseph E. & Charlton, Andrew **HF1413.S85 2005**
Fair Trade for All: How Trade Can Promote Development. Trade Cloth. Oxford University Press, Inc. New York, NY. 2006. 352p. The Initiative for Policy Dialogue Ser. ISBN:0-19-929090-3, ISBN13: 978-0-19-929090-1. Dewey:382/.3. LCCN:2005-027734.
Audience: **l,u.**

Business Environment > Social Policy > Business Ethics

Badaracco, Joseph L. **HF5387.H3748 2003**
Harvard Business Review on Corporate Ethics. Trade Paper. Harvard Business School Press. Boston, MA. 2003. 208p. The Harvard Business Review Paperback Ser. ISBN:1-59139-273-X, ISBN13: 978-1-59139-273-6. Dewey:174/.4. LCCN:2003-008216.
Audience: **g,l,u,f.**

Enderle, Georges **HF5387**
Bibliography of Business Ethics Articles, 1992 - present. http://www.isbee.org/biblio/EthicsArticles.php
Xiaoqing Feng, Donna Kamm and Allie Wilkie. International Society of Business, Economics, and Ethics.
Audience: **l,u,f.**

Frank, Robert H. **HF5387.F737 2004**
What Price the Moral High Ground?: Ethical Dilemmas in Competitive Environments. Trade Cloth. Princeton University Press. Princeton, NJ. 2003. 256p. ISBN:0-691-00672-5, ISBN13: 978-0-691-00672-7. Dewey:174/.4. LCCN:2003-050429.
Audience: **g,l,u,f.** *Choice, 2004.*

Frederick, William C. **HD58.7.F735 1995**
Values, Nature, and Culture in the American Corporation. Trade Paper. Oxford University Press, Inc. New York, NY. 1995. 332p. The Ruffin Series in Business Ethics ISBN:0-19-509674-6, ISBN13: 978-0-19-509674-3. Dewey:302.3/5. LCCN:94-038396.
Audience: **l,u,f.** *Choice, 1996.*

May, Steve (Editor) **HD30.3.C37155 2006**
Case Studies in Organizational Communication: Ethical Perspectives and Practices. Paper Text. SAGE Publications, Inc. Thousand Oaks, CA. 2006. 424p. ISBN:0-7619-2983-5, ISBN13: 978-0-7619-2983-3. Dewey:302.3/5. LCCN:2005-026094.
Audience: **l,u.**

Piper, Thomas R., et al. **HF5387.P56 1993**
Can Ethics Be Taught?: Perspectives, Challenges, and Approaches at the Harvard Business School. Mary C. Gentile & Sharon D. Parks (Authors). Trade Cloth. Harvard Business School Press. Boston, MA. 1993. 208p. ISBN:0-87584-400-6, ISBN13: 978-0-87584-400-8. Dewey:174/.4/071173. LCCN:92-027077.
Audience: **g,u,f.** *Choice, 1993.*

Richardson, John E. **HF5387**
Annual Editions: Business Ethics 06/07. Ed. 18. Paper Text. McGraw-Hill Higher Education. Burr Ridge, IL. 2006. 224p. ISBN:0-07-352837-4, ISBN13: 978-0-07-352837-3. Dewey:174.4 T.
Audience: **g,l,u,f.**

William M. White Business Library, Leeds School of Business, University of Colorado at Boulder **HF5387.5.U5**
BELL: the Business Ethics Links Library - Resources for Research in Business Ethics and Social Responsibility. http://libnet.colorado.edu/Bell/
Gene Hayworth.
Audience: **g,l,u,f.**

Business Environment > Social Policy > Business Ethics > Corporate Social Responsibility

Adams, Walter & Brock, James W. **HD2785.A68 2004**
The Bigness Complex: Industry, Labor, and Government in the American Economy. Ed. 2. Trade Paper. Stanford University Press. Palo Alto, CA. 2004. 400p. ISBN:0-8047-4969-8, ISBN13: 978-0-8047-4969-5. Dewey:338.6/44/0973. LCCN:2004-001030.
Audience: **g,l,u,f.**

Berenson, Alex **HV6768**
The Number: How the Drive for Quarterly Earnings Corrupted Wall Street and Corporate America. E-Book. Random House Adult Trade Publishing Group. New York, NY. 2003. ISBN:1-58836-288-4, ISBN13: 978-1-58836-288-9. Dewey:364.16/8.
Audience: **g,l,u,f.** *Choice, 2004.*

Dienhart, John W. & Curnutt, Jordan **HF5387.D54 1998**
Business Ethics: A Reference Handbook. Library Binding. ABC-CLIO, Inc. Santa Barbara, CA. 1998. 464p. Contemporary Ethical Issues Ser. ISBN:0-87436-863-4, ISBN13: 978-0-87436-863-5. Dewey:174/.4/03. LCCN:98-042277.
Audience: **g,l,u,f.** *Choice, 1999.*

Frederick, William C. **HD60**
Corporation Be Good!: The Story of Corporate Social Responsibility. Dog Ear Publishing. 2006. ISBN:1-59858-103-1, ISBN13: 978-1-59858-103-4.
Audience: **l,u,f.**

Gardner, Howard, et al. **HF5549.5.J63G355**
Good Work: When Excellence and Ethics Meet. Mihaly Csikszentmihalyi & William Damon (Authors). Trade Cloth. Basic Books. New York, NY. 2001. 304p. ISBN:0-465-02607-9, ISBN13: 978-0-465-02607-4. Dewey:174/.4. LCCN:2001-025950.
Audience: **g,l,u,f.** *Choice, 2002.*

Garten, Jeffrey E. **HD57.7.G377 2002**
The Politics of Fortune: A New Agenda for Business Leaders. Trade Cloth. Harvard Business School Press. Boston, MA. 2002. 224p. ISBN:1-57851-878-4, ISBN13: 978-1-57851-878-4. Dewey:658.4/08. LCCN:2002-008472.
Audience: **g,l,u,f.**

Gillan, Stuart L. & Chew, Donald H. **HD2741.C77497 2005**
Corporate Governance at the Crossroads: A Book of Readings. Ed. 6. Paper Text. McGraw-Hill Higher Education. Burr Ridge, IL. 2004. 528p. The McGraw-Hill/Irwin Series in Finance, Insurance, and Real Estate ISBN:0-07-295708-5, ISBN13: 978-0-07-295708-2. Dewey:658.4. LCCN:2003-066489.
Audience: **g,l,u,f.**

Hollender, Jeffrey & Fenichell, Stephen **HD60.H65 2003**
What Matters Most: How a Small Group of Pioneers Is Teaching Social Responsibility to Big Business, and Why Big Business Is Listening. Trade Cloth. Basic Books. New York, NY. 2003. 336p. ISBN:0-7382-0902-3, ISBN13: 978-0-7382-0902-9. Dewey:658.4/08. LCCN:2003-020345.
Audience: **u,f.** *Choice, 2004.*

Kotler, Philip & Lee, Nancy **HD60.K67 2005**
Corporate Social Responsibility: Doing the Most Good for Your Company and Your Cause. Trade Cloth. John Wiley & Sons, Inc. Hoboken, NJ. 2004. 320p. ISBN:0-471-47611-0, ISBN13: 978-0-471-47611-5. Dewey:658.4/08. LCCN:2004-020375.
Audience: **l,u,f.**

Lorsch, Jay W. (Editor), et al. **HD2741**
Restoring Trust in American Business. Leslie Berlowitz & Andy Zelleke (Editors). Trade Paper. MIT Press. Cambridge, MA. 2005. 192p. ISBN:0-262-74027-3, ISBN13: 978-0-262-74027-2. Dewey:658.4/08.
Audience: **g,l,u,f.** *Choice, 2005.*

MacAvoy, Paul W. & Millstein, Ira M. **HD2741.M196 2003**
The Recurrent Crisis in Corporate Governance. Cloth over Boards. Palgrave Macmillan. New York, NY. 2004. 160p. ISBN:1-4039-1666-7, ISBN13: 978-1-4039-1666-2. Dewey:658.4. LCCN:2003-048290.
Audience: **g,l,u,f.** *Choice, 2004.*

Manheim, Jarol B. **HD59.M257 2001**
The Death of a Thousand Cuts: Corporate Campaigns and the Attack on the Corporation. Cloth over Boards. Lawrence Erlbaum Associates, Inc. Mahwah, NJ. 2000. 376p. ISBN:0-8058-3831-7, ISBN13: 978-0-8058-3831-2. Dewey:659.2. LCCN:00-034780.
Audience: **g,l,u,f.** *Choice, 2001.*

Mitroff, Ian I. & Denton, Elizabeth A. **HD4905.M53 1999**
A Spiritual Audit of Corporate America: A Hard Look at Spirituality, Religion, and Values in the Workplace. Trade Cloth. John Wiley & Sons, Inc. Hoboken, NJ. 1999. 288p. ISBN:0-7879-4666-4, ISBN13: 978-0-7879-4666-1. Dewey:261.8/5. LCCN:99-006693.
Audience: **l,u,f.**

Paine, Lynn Sharp **HF5387**
Value Shift: Why Companies Must Merge Social and Financial Imperatives to Achieve Superior Performance. Trade Cloth. McGraw-Hill Companies, The. New York, NY. 2002. 288p. ISBN:0-07-138239-9, ISBN13: 978-0-07-138239-7. Dewey:174/.4.
Audience: **l,u,f.** *Choice, 2003.*

Prahalad, C. K., et al. **HD60.H389 2003**
Harvard Business Review on Corporate Responsibility. Michael E. Porter & Charles Handy (Authors). Trade Paper. Harvard Business School Press. Boston, MA. 2003. 208p. The Harvard Business Review Paperback Ser. ISBN:1-59139-274-8, ISBN13: 978-1-59139-274-3. Dewey:658.4/08. LCCN:2003-008219.
Audience: **g,l,u,f.**

Sayles, Leonard R. & Smith, Cynthia J. **HV6768**
The Rise of the Rogue Executive: How Good Companies Go Bad and How to Stop the Destruction. Trade Cloth. Prentice Hall PTR. Upper Saddle River, NJ. 2005. 288p. ISBN:0-13-147772-2, ISBN13: 978-0-13-147772-8. Dewey:174/.4. LCCN:2005-924352.
Audience: **g,l,u,f.** *Choice, 2006.*

Schaper, Michael **HB615**
Making Ecopreneurs: Developing Sustainable Entrepreneurship. Trade Cloth. Ashgate Publishing, Ltd. Aldershot, 2005. 276p. Corporate Social Responsibility Ser. ISBN:0-7546-4491-X, ISBN13: 978-0-7546-4491-0. Dewey:658.4/083. LCCN:2005-015273.
Audience: **l,u.**

Shaw, William H. (Editor) **HF5387.E836 2002**
Ethics at Work: Basic Readings in Business Ethics. Paper Text. Oxford University Press, Inc. New York, NY. 2002. 190p. ISBN:0-19-513942-9, ISBN13: 978-0-19-513942-6. Dewey:174/.4. LCCN:2002-074883.
Audience: **g,l,u,f.**

Transparency International **JF1081**
☐ Global Corruption Report.
http://www.transparency.org/publications/gcr;
http://bibpurl.oclc.org/web/5476
Ed. 5. Neuman, Georg. Transparency International.
Audience: **g,l,u,f.**

Vogel, David **HD60**
The Market for Virtue: The Potential and Limits of Corporate Social Responsibility. Book, Other. Brookings Institution Press. Washington, DC. 2005. 222p. ISBN:0-8157-9076-7, ISBN13: 978-0-8157-9076-1. Dewey:658.4/08. LCCN:2005-015005.
Audience: **g,l,u,f.** *Choice, 2006.*

Waddock, Sandra; Graves, Samuel **HF5387**
☐ 100 Best Corporate Citizens.
http://www.business-ethics.com/whats_new/100best.html#Article
Ed. 6. KLD Research & Analytics, Inc.. Business Ethics Magazine.
Audience: **g,l,u,f.**

Werhane, P. H. & Freeman, R. Edward **HD30.15.B455**
Business Ethics. Ed. 2. Trade Cloth. Blackwell Publishing, Inc. Malden, MA. 2006. 600p. The Blackwell Encyclopedia of Management Ser., Vol. 2 ISBN:1-4051-0013-3, ISBN13: 978-1-4051-0013-7. Dewey:658/.003 174/.4/03. LCCN:2004-007693.
Audience: **g,l,u,f.**

Business Environment > Social Policy > Business Ethics > Individual Decision Making

Dienhart, John W. & Curnutt, Jordan **HF5387.D54 1998**
Business Ethics: A Reference Handbook. Library Binding. ABC-CLIO, Inc. Santa Barbara, CA. 1998. 464p. Contemporary Ethical Issues Ser. ISBN:0-87436-863-4, ISBN13: 978-0-87436-863-5. Dewey:174/.4/03. LCCN:98-042277.
Audience: **g,l,u,f.** *Choice, 1999.*

Fischman, Wendy, et al. **HD4905.M344 2004**
Making Good: How Young People Cope with Moral Dilemmas at Work. Becca Solomon, Deborah Greenspan & Howard Gardner (Authors). Trade Cloth. Harvard University Press. Cambridge, MA. 2004. 224p. ISBN:0-674-01194-5, ISBN13: 978-0-674-01194-6. Dewey:174. LCCN:2003-058738.
Audience: **g,l,u,f.** *Choice, 2004.*

Gardner, Howard, et al. **HF5549.5.J63G355**
Good Work: When Excellence and Ethics Meet. Mihaly Csikszentmihalyi & William Damon (Authors). Trade Cloth. Basic Books. New York, NY. 2001. 304p. ISBN:0-465-02607-9, ISBN13: 978-0-465-02607-4. Dewey:174/.4. LCCN:2001-025950.
Audience: **g,l,u,f.** *Choice, 2002.*

Novak, Michael **HD4905.N65 1996**
Business as a Calling: Work and the Examined Life. Trade Cloth. Simon & Schuster. New York, NY. 1996. 256p. ISBN:0-684-82748-4, ISBN13: 978-0-684-82748-3. Dewey:306.36. LCCN:96-000482.
Audience: **g,l,u,f.**

Shaw, William H. (Editor) **HF5387.E836 2002**
Ethics at Work: Basic Readings in Business Ethics. Paper Text. Oxford University Press, Inc. New York, NY. 2002. 190p. ISBN:0-19-513942-9, ISBN13: 978-0-19-513942-6. Dewey:174/.4. LCCN:2002-074883.
Audience: **g,l,u,f.**

Werhane, P. H. & Freeman, R. Edward **HD30.15.B455**
Business Ethics. Ed. 2. Trade Cloth. Blackwell Publishing, Inc. Malden, MA. 2006. 600p. The Blackwell Encyclopedia of Management Ser., Vol. 2 ISBN:1-4051-0013-3, ISBN13: 978-1-4051-0013-7. Dewey:658/.003 174/.4/03. LCCN:2004-007693.
Audience: **g,l,u,f.**

Business Environment > Social Policy > Globalization and Social Impact of business

JZ1318
☐ Yale Global Online.
http://yaleglobal.yale.edu/
Audience: **g,l,u,f.**

Bhagwati, Jagdish N. **HF1359.B499 2004**
In Defense of Globalization. Trade Cloth. Oxford University Press, Inc. New York, NY. 2004. 320p. ISBN:0-19-517025-3, ISBN13: 978-0-19-517025-2. Dewey:337. LCCN:2003-023641.
Audience: **g,l,u,f.** *Choice, 2004.*

Friedman, Thomas L. **HF1359.F74 2000**
The Lexus and the Olive Tree: Understanding Globalization. Cloth over Boards. Farrar, Straus & Giroux. New York, NY. 2000. 469p. ISBN:0-374-18552-2, ISBN13: 978-0-374-18552-7. Dewey:337. LCCN:00-029411.
Audience: **l,u.**

Gilpin, Robert **HF1359**
The Challenge of Global Capitalism: The World Economy in the 21st Century. Trade Paper. Princeton University Press. Princeton, NJ. 2002. 408p. ISBN:0-691-09279-6, ISBN13: 978-0-691-09279-9. Dewey:337.
Audience: **u,f.** *Choice, 2000.*

Internet Center for Corruption Research **JF1081**
☐ Corruption Perceptions Index.
http://www.icgg.org/
University of Passau. Internet Center for Corruption Research.
Audience: **l,u,f.**

Irwin, Douglas A. **HF1756.I68 2002**
Free Trade under Fire. Cloth Text. Princeton University Press. Princeton, NJ. 2002. 288p. ISBN:0-691-08843-8, ISBN13: 978-0-691-08843-3. Dewey:382/.71. LCCN:2001-043159.
Audience: **g,l,u,f.** *Choice, 2003.*

Jones, Kent Albert & Jones, Kent **HF1385.J67 2003**
Who's Afraid of the WTO? Trade Cloth. Oxford University Press, Inc. New York, NY. 2004. 248p. ISBN:0-19-516616-7, ISBN13: 978-0-19-516616-3. Dewey:382/.92. LCCN:2003-048292.
Audience: **g,l,u,f.** *Choice, 2004.*

Laurel, Brenda **HC252.5.B73**
Utopian Entrepreneur. Trade Cloth. MIT Press. Cambridge, MA. 2001. 112p. Mediaworks Pamphlets Ser. ISBN:0-262-12244-8, ISBN13: 978-0-262-12244-3. Dewey:338/.04/092 B. LCCN:2001-092089.
Audience: **g,l,u,f.**

Lechner, Frank & Boli, John (Editors) **HF1359**
The Globalization Reader. Ed. 2. Trade Cloth. Blackwell Publishing, Inc. Malden, MA. 2003. 472p. ISBN:1-4051-0279-9, ISBN13: 978-1-4051-0279-7. Dewey:337. LCCN:2003-056025.
Audience: **g,l,u,f.** *Choice, 2000.*

Rivoli, Pietra **HD9969.S6R58 2005**
The Travels of a T-Shirt in the Global Economy: An Economist Examines the Markets, Power and Politics of World Trade. Trade Cloth. John Wiley & Sons, Inc. Hoboken, NJ. 2005. 272p. ISBN:0-471-64849-3, ISBN13: 978-0-471-64849-9. Dewey:382/.45687115. LCCN:2004-025910.
Audience: **g,l,u,f.** *Choice, 2006.*

Steger, Manfred B. **JZ1318**
Globalization: A Very Short Introduction. Ed. 1. Trade Paper. Oxford University Press, Inc. New York, NY. 2003. 168p. Very

Short Introductions Ser., Vol. 86 ISBN:0-19-280359-X, ISBN13: 978-0-19-280359-7. Dewey:303.48/2. LCCN:2003-273144.
Audience: **g,l,u,f.**

Stiglitz, Joseph E. **HF1418.5.S75 2002**
Globalization and Its Discontents. Trade Cloth. W. W. Norton & Company, Inc. New York, NY. 2003. 192p.
ISBN:0-393-05124-2, ISBN13: 978-0-393-05124-7. Dewey:337. LCCN:2002-023148.
Audience: **g,l,u,f.** *Choice, 2002.*

Stiglitz, Joseph E. & Charlton, Andrew **HF1413.S85 2005**
Fair Trade for All: How Trade Can Promote Development. Trade Cloth. Oxford University Press, Inc. New York, NY. 2006. 352p. The Initiative for Policy Dialogue Ser.
ISBN:0-19-929090-3, ISBN13: 978-0-19-929090-1. Dewey:382/.3. LCCN:2005-027734.
Audience: **l,u.**

Vaidya, Ashish K. **HF1359.G5854 2006**
Globalization: Encyclopedia of Trade, Labor, and Politics. Library Binding. ABC-CLIO, Inc. Santa Barbara, CA. 2005. 800p. ISBN:1-57607-826-4, ISBN13: 978-1-57607-826-6. Dewey:337.03. LCCN:2006-012274.
Audience: **g,l,u,f.**

Wolf, Martin **HF1359.W6534 2004**
Why Globalization Works. Cloth over Boards. Yale University Press. Cumberland, RI. 2004. 416p. ISBN:0-300-10252-6, ISBN13: 978-0-300-10252-9. Dewey:337. LCCN:2004-000475.
Audience: **g,l,u,f.** *Choice, 2004.*

World Bank Group **HC59.72.P6**
☐ Globalization.
http://www1.worldbank.org/economicpolicy/globalization/
Audience: **g,l,u,f.**

Yergin, Daniel & Stanislaw, Joseph **HD87.Y47 2002**
The Commanding Heights: The Battle for the World Economy. Trade Paper. Simon & Schuster. New York, NY. 2002. 496p.
ISBN:0-684-83569-X, ISBN13: 978-0-684-83569-3. Dewey:338.9. LCCN:2002-019992.
Audience: **g,l,u,f.**

Business Environment > Social Policy > Globalization and Social Impact of business > Business Etiquette

Axtell, Roger E. **HF5387 .D66**
Do's and Taboos around the World. Trade Paper. John Wiley & Sons, Inc. Hoboken, NJ. 2000. ISBN:0-471-34427-3, ISBN13: 978-0-471-34427-8. Dewey:395/.52.
Audience: **l,u.**

Earley, P. Christopher & Erez, Miriam **HD62.4.E24 1997**
The Transplanted Executive: Why You Need to Understand How Workers in Other Countries See the World Differently. Trade Cloth. Oxford University Press, Inc. New York, NY. 1997. 208p. ISBN:0-19-508795-X, ISBN13: 978-0-19-508795-6. Dewey:658/.049. LCCN:96-009286.
Audience: **u.** *Choice, 1997.*

Gesteland, Richard R. **HF5389**
Cross-Cultural Business-Behaviour: Negotiating, Selling, Sourcing and Managing Across Cultures. Ed. 4. Trade Cloth. Copenhagen Business School Press. Copenhagen, 2005. 351p. ISBN:87-630-0149-7, ISBN13: 978-87-630-0149-6. Dewey:395.52.
Audience: **u.**

Hodge, Sheida **HF5389.H63 2000**
Global Smarts: The Art of Communicating and Deal Making Anywhere in the World. Trade Cloth. John Wiley & Sons, Inc. Hoboken, NJ. 2000. 256p. ISBN:0-471-38246-9, ISBN13: 978-0-471-38246-1. Dewey:395.5/2. LCCN:99-059990.
Audience: **u.**

Leaptrott and Company Staff & Leaptrott, Nan **HF5389.L43 1996**
Rules of the Game: Global Business Protocol. Mass Market. Thomson South-Western. Mason, OH. 1995. 280p. Organizational Behavior Ser. ISBN:0-538-85455-3, ISBN13: 978-0-538-85455-9. Dewey:395/.52. LCCN:95-038856.
Audience: **u.**

Lewis, Richard D. **HF5549.5.M5**
When Cultures Collide: Leading Across Cultures. Ed. 3. Trade Paper. Nicholas Brealey Publishing Ltd. Yarmouth, ME. 2005. 628p. ISBN:1-904838-02-2, ISBN13: 978-1-904838-02-9. Dewey:658/.049. LCCN:2005-022299.
Audience: **u.**

Martin, Jeanette S. & Chaney, Lillian H. **HF5389.M375 2006**
Global Business Etiquette: A Guide to International Communication and Customs. Trade Cloth. Greenwood Publishing Group, Inc. Portsmouth, NH. 2006. 188p. ISBN:0-275-98815-5, ISBN13: 978-0-275-98815-9. Dewey:395.5/2. LCCN:2005-037086.
Audience: **l,u,f.** *Choice, 2006.*

Marx, Elisabeth **HD58.7.M3747**
Breaking Through Culture Shock: What You Need to Succeed in International Business. Trade Paper. Nicholas Brealey Publishing Ltd. Yarmouth, ME. 2001. 252p. ISBN:1-85788-221-0, ISBN13: 978-1-85788-221-6. Dewey:658. LCCN:98-046502.
Audience: **u.** *Choice, 1999.*

Morrison, Terri & Conaway, Wayne A. **HF1416.M78 2001**
Dun and Bradstreet's Guide to Doing Business Around the World. Ed. 2. Trade Paper. Prentice Hall Press. Paramus, NJ. 2000. 512p. ISBN:0-7352-0108-0, ISBN13: 978-0-7352-0108-8. Dewey:658.8/48. LCCN:00-059846.
Audience: **u.** *Choice, 1997.*

Morrison, Terri, et al. **HF5389 .M67**
Kiss, Bow or Shake Hands: How to Do Business in Sixty Countries. Wayne A. Conaway & George Borden (Authors), Hans Koehler (Foreword by). Paper Text. DIANE Publishing Company. Collingdale, PA. 2000. 438p. ISBN:0-7881-9227-2, ISBN13: 978-0-7881-9227-2. Dewey:395/.52.
Audience: **u.**

Nelson, Carl A. **HF5389.N45 1998**
Protocol for Profit: A Manager's Guide to Competing Worldwide. Trade Paper. Thomson Learning. Independence, KY. 1998. 256p. Global Manager Ser. ISBN:1-86152-314-9, ISBN13: 978-1-86152-314-3. Dewey:395.5/2. LCCN:98-218553.
Audience: **u.**

Post, Peggy & Post, Peter **HF5382.7.P68 2005**
Emily Post's the Etiquette Advantage in Business: Personal Skills for Professional Success. Ed. 2. Trade Cloth. HarperCollins Publishers. New York, NY. 2005. 384p. ISBN:0-06-076002-8, ISBN13: 978-0-06-076002-1. Dewey:395.52. LCCN:2005-283037.
Audience: **g,l,u.**

Training Management Corporation Staff **HF5389**
Doing Business Internationally: The Resource for Business and Social Etiquette. Ed. 5. Trade Paper. Princeton Training Press. Princeton, NJ. 1999. 600p. ISBN:1-882390-16-4, ISBN13: 978-1-882390-16-8. Dewey:395.52.
Audience: **g,u,f.**

Business Environment > Social Policy > Women and Minorities in Business

Anderson, Terry H. **HF5549.5.A34A53 2004**
The Pursuit of Fairness: A History of Affirmative Action. Trade Cloth. Oxford University Press, Inc. New York, NY. 2004. 336p. ISBN:0-19-515764-8, ISBN13: 978-0-19-515764-2. Dewey:331.13/3/0973. LCCN:2003-024637.
Audience: **l,u,f.** *Choice, 2005.*

Axtell, Roger E., et al. **G156.5.B86D67 1997**
Do's and Taboos Around the World for Women in Business. Tami Briggs, Margaret Corcoran & Mary Beth Lamb (Authors). Trade Paper. John Wiley & Sons, Inc. Hoboken, NJ. 1997. 272p. ISBN:0-471-14364-2, ISBN13: 978-0-471-14364-2. Dewey:910/.2/02. LCCN:96-035911.
Audience: **g,l,u,f.**

Catalyst Staff **HD6053.A38 1998**
Advancing Women in Business—The Catalyst Guide: Best Practices from the Corporate Leaders. Sheila Wellington (Foreword by). Trade Cloth. John Wiley & Sons, Inc. Hoboken, NJ. 1998. 244p. Jossey Bass Business and Management Ser. ISBN:0-7879-3966-8, ISBN13: 978-0-7879-3966-3. Dewey:650.1. LCCN:97-045394.
Audience: **g,u,f.**

Catalyst **HD69.S8C74 1999**
Creating Women's Networks: A How-to-Guide for Women and Companies. Sheila Wellington (Foreword by). Trade Cloth. John Wiley & Sons, Inc. Hoboken, NJ. 1998. 208p. Business and Management Ser. ISBN:0-7879-4014-3, ISBN13: 978-0-7879-4014-0. Dewey:658.4/9/082. LCCN:98-040255.
Audience: **g,l,u.**

Krismann, Carol H. **HD6054**
Encyclopedia of American Women in Business: From Colonial Times to the Present [Two Volumes], Vol. 2. Cloth Text. Greenwood Publishing Group, Inc. Portsmouth, NH. 2004. 744p. ISBN:0-313-32757-2, ISBN13: 978-0-313-32757-5. Dewey:338.092/2. LCCN:2004-056065.
Audience: **l,u.** *Choice, 2005.*

Kwolek-Folland, Angel **HD6095**
Incorporating Women: A History of Women and Business in the United States. Kenneth Lipartito (Introduction by). Trade Paper. DIANE Publishing Company. Collingdale, PA. 2005. 278p. ISBN:0-7567-8591-X, ISBN13: 978-0-7567-8591-8. Dewey:331.4/0973.
Audience: **g,u,f.**

Laurel, Brenda **HC252.5.B73**
Utopian Entrepreneur. Trade Cloth. MIT Press. Cambridge, MA. 2001. 112p. Mediaworks Pamphlets Ser. ISBN:0-262-12244-8, ISBN13: 978-0-262-12244-3. Dewey:338/.04/092 B. LCCN:2001-092089.
Audience: **g,l,u,f.**

Business Environment > International Trade and Foreign Investment

Aliber, Robert Z. **HG3881.A44 2000**
The New International Money Game. Ed. 6. Trade Cloth. University of Chicago Press. Chicago, IL. 2000. 304p. ISBN:0-226-01396-0, ISBN13: 978-0-226-01396-1. Dewey:332. LCCN:99-055593.
Audience: **g,l,u,f.**

Destler, I. M. **HF1455.D48 2005**
American Trade Politics. Ed. 4. Trade Paper, Perfect. Institute for International Economics. Washington, DC. 2005. 373p. ISBN:0-88132-382-9, ISBN13: 978-0-88132-382-5. Dewey:382/.3/0973. LCCN:2005-043367.
Audience: **g,l,u,f.** *Choice, 2005.*

McCusker, John J. **HF1379.H574 2005**
Economic History of World Trade. Trade Cloth. Thomson Gale. Farmington Hills, MI. 2005. 900p. ISBN:0-02-865840-X, ISBN13: 978-0-02-865840-7. Dewey:382/.09. LCCN:2005-018624.
Audience: **g,l,u,f.**

McNett, Jeanne **HD30.15.B455**
International Management. Ed. 2. Trade Cloth. Blackwell Publishing, Inc. Malden, MA. 2006. 376p. The Blackwell Encyclopedia of Management Ser., Vol. 6 ISBN:0-631-23493-4, ISBN13: 978-0-631-23493-7. Dewey:658/.003 s 658/.049. LCCN:2004-018073.
Audience: **g,l,u,f.**

Neipert, David **K1005.N45 2002**
Law for Global Commerce: A Tour. Trade Paper. Prentice Hall PTR. Upper Saddle River, NJ. 2001. 159p. ISBN:0-13-040873-5, ISBN13: 978-0-13-040873-0. Dewey:346.07. LCCN:2001-036178.
Audience: **g,l,u,f.**

Pomeranz, Kenneth & Topik, Steven **HF352.P58W67 2006**
The World That Trade Created: Society, Culture, and the World Economy 1400 to the Present. Ed. 2. Saddle Stitched, Cloth over Boards. M. E. Sharpe Inc. Armonk, NY. 2005. 287p. Sources and Studies in World History Ser. ISBN:0-7656-1708-0, ISBN13: 978-0-7656-1708-8. Dewey:382/.09. LCCN:2005-018044.
Audience: **l,u,f.**

Porter, Michael E. **HD3611.P654 1990**
The Competitive Advantage of Nations and Their Firms. Trade Cloth. Simon & Schuster. New York, NY. 1990. 896p. ISBN:0-02-925361-6, ISBN13: 978-0-02-925361-8. Dewey:382/.1042. LCCN:89-025632.
Audience: **u,f.** *Choice, 1990.*

Porter, Michael E. **HF1414.P67 1998**
On Competition. Trade Cloth. Harvard Business School Press. Boston, MA. 1998. 496p. Review Book Ser.

ISBN:0-87584-795-1, ISBN13: 978-0-87584-795-5.
Dewey:382/.1042. LCCN:98-007643.
Audience: **u,f.** *Choice, 1999.*

Rivoli, Pietra **HD9969.S6R58 2005**
The Travels of a T-Shirt in the Global Economy: An Economist Examines the Markets, Power and Politics of World Trade. Trade Cloth. John Wiley & Sons, Inc. Hoboken, NJ. 2005. 272p. ISBN:0-471-64849-3, ISBN13: 978-0-471-64849-9. Dewey:382/.45687115. LCCN:2004-025910.
Audience: **g,l,u,f.** *Choice, 2006.*

Shippey, Karla C. **K1401.S528 2001**
A Short Course in International Intellectual Property Rights: Protecting Your Brands, Marks, Copyrights, Patents, Designs, and Related Rights Worldwide. Trade Cloth. World Trade Press. Petaluma, CA. 2001. The Short Course in International Trade Ser. ISBN:1-885073-56-9, ISBN13: 978-1-885073-56-3. Dewey:341.7/58. LCCN:2001-026778.
Audience: **g,l,u,f.**

Stiglitz, Joseph E. **HF1418.5.S75 2002**
Globalization and Its Discontents. Trade Cloth. W. W. Norton & Company, Inc. New York, NY. 2003. 192p. ISBN:0-393-05124-2, ISBN13: 978-0-393-05124-7. Dewey:337. LCCN:2002-023148.
Audience: **g,l,u,f.** *Choice, 2002.*

The World Bank (Created by) **HC79.C7**
Doing Business In 2006: Creating Jobs. Ed. 2006. Trade Paper, Perfect. World Bank Publications. Washington, DC. 2005. 228p. Doing Business Ser. ISBN:0-8213-5749-2, ISBN13: 978-0-8213-5749-1. Dewey:341.754.
Audience: **g,l,u,f.**

Vaidya, Ashish K. **HF1359.G5854 2006**
Globalization: Encyclopedia of Trade, Labor, and Politics. Library Binding. ABC-CLIO, Inc. Santa Barbara, CA. 2005. 800p. ISBN:1-57607-826-4, ISBN13: 978-1-57607-826-6. Dewey:337.03. LCCN:2006-012274.
Audience: **g,l,u,f.**

Valdez, Stephen & Wood, Julian **HG173.V184 2003**
An Introduction to Global Financial Markets. Ed. 4. Trade Cloth. Palgrave Macmillan. New York, NY. 2003. xviii, 403p. ISBN:1-4039-0011-6, ISBN13: 978-1-4039-0011-1. Dewey:332. LCCN:2003-049803.
Audience: **g,l,u,f.**

Wolf, Martin **HF1359.W6534 2004**
Why Globalization Works. Cloth over Boards. Yale University Press. Cumberland, RI. 2004. 416p. ISBN:0-300-10252-6, ISBN13: 978-0-300-10252-9. Dewey:337. LCCN:2004-000475.
Audience: **g,l,u,f.** *Choice, 2004.*

Yergin, Daniel & Stanislaw, Joseph **HD87.Y47 2002**
The Commanding Heights: The Battle for the World Economy. Trade Paper. Simon & Schuster. New York, NY. 2002. 496p. ISBN:0-684-83569-X, ISBN13: 978-0-684-83569-3. Dewey:338.9. LCCN:2002-019992.
Audience: **g,l,u,f.**

Business Environment > International Trade and Foreign Investment > Cross-cultural Business

Adler, Nancy J. **HD58.7.A33 2002**
International Dimensions of Organizational Behavior. Ed. 4. Paper Text. Thomson South-Western. Mason, OH. 2001. 408p. SWC-Management Ser. ISBN:0-324-05786-5, ISBN13: 978-0-324-05786-7. Dewey:658. LCCN:00-046396.
Audience: **g,l,u,f.**

Adler, Nancy J., et al. **HD58.7**
From Boston to Beijing: Managing with a World View. John Szilagyi & Robert Bloom (Authors). Digital, Other. Thomson South-Western. Mason, OH. 2001. 408p. ISBN:0-324-07475-1, ISBN13: 978-0-324-07475-8. Dewey:658.049. LCCN:00-046396.
Audience: **l,u,f.** *Choice, 2002.*

Axtell, Roger E. **HF5387 .D66**
Do's and Taboos around the World. Trade Paper. John Wiley & Sons, Inc. Hoboken, NJ. 2000. ISBN:0-471-34427-3, ISBN13: 978-0-471-34427-8. Dewey:395/.52.
Audience: **l,u.**

Bartlett, Christopher A. & Ghoshal, Sumantra **HD62.4.B36 1998**
Managing Across Borders: The Transnational Solution. Ed. 2. Trade Cloth. Harvard Business School Press. Boston, MA. 1998. 416p. ISBN:0-87584-849-4, ISBN13: 978-0-87584-849-5. Dewey:658.049. LCCN:98-026004.
Audience: **g,l,u,f.** *Choice, 1990.*

DeVries, Mary A. **HF5383**
Internationally Yours: Writing and Communicating Successfully in Today's Global Marketplace. Paper Text. DIANE Publishing Company. Collingdale, PA. 1999. 352p. ISBN:0-7881-6172-5, ISBN13: 978-0-7881-6172-8. Dewey:808/.06665.
Audience: **l,u.**

Earley, P. Christopher **HF5549.5.M5E17 2006**
CQ: Developing Cultural Intelligence at Work. Trade Cloth. Stanford University Press. Palo Alto, CA. 2006. 283p. ISBN:0-8047-4313-4, ISBN13: 978-0-8047-4313-6. Dewey:658.3/008. LCCN:2005-023670.
Audience: **l,u.** *Choice, 2006.*

Geffner, Andrea B. **PE1115.G38 1998**
Barron's ESL Guide to American Business English. Trade Paper. Barron's Educational Series, Inc. Hauppauge, NY. 1998. 320p. ISBN:0-7641-0594-9, ISBN13: 978-0-7641-0594-4. Dewey:428.2/4/02465. LCCN:98-021252.
Audience: **l,u.**

Hofstede, Geert & Hofstede, Gert Jan **HM711**
Cultures and Organizations: Software for the Mind. Ed. 2. Trade Paper. McGraw-Hill Companies, The. New York, NY. 2004. 300p. ISBN:0-07-143959-5, ISBN13: 978-0-07-143959-6. Dewey:306. LCCN:2004-063164.
Audience: **g,l,u,f.** *Choice, 2005.*

Mattock, John **HD62.4**
Cross-Cultural Communication: The Essential Guide to International Business. Ed. 3. Trade Paper, Perfect. Kogan Page, Ltd. London, 2003. 176p. ISBN:0-7494-3922-X, ISBN13: 978-0-7494-3922-4. Dewey:658.1/8. LCCN:2003-000965.
Audience: **l,u.**

McCall, Morgan W. & Hollenbeck, George P. **HD30.4.M42 2002**
Frequent Flyers: Developing Global Executives. Trade Cloth. Harvard Business School Press. Boston, MA. 2002. 288p. ISBN:1-57851-336-7, ISBN13: 978-1-57851-336-9. Dewey:658.4/07124. LCCN:2001-039434.
Audience: **g,l,u,f.**

Peterson, Brooks **HM1211.P47 2004**
Cultural Intelligence: A Guide to Working with People from Other Cultures. Trade Paper. Intercultural Press, Inc. Yarmouth, ME. 2004. 200p. ISBN:1-931930-00-7, ISBN13: 978-1-931930-00-0. Dewey:303.48/2. LCCN:2004-040720.
Audience: **g,l,u,f.**

Porter, Michael E. **HD3611.P654 1990**
The Competitive Advantage of Nations and Their Firms. Trade Cloth. Simon & Schuster. New York, NY. 1990. 896p. ISBN:0-02-925361-6, ISBN13: 978-0-02-925361-8. Dewey:382/.1042. LCCN:89-025632.
Audience: **u,f.** *Choice, 1990.*

Salacuse, Jeswald W. **HD58.6.S246 2003**
The Global Negotiator: Making, Managing and Mending Deals Around the World in the Twenty-First Century. Cloth over Boards. Palgrave Macmillan. New York, NY. 2003. 320p. ISBN:0-312-29339-9, ISBN13: 978-0-312-29339-0. Dewey:658.4/052. LCCN:2002-193099.
Audience: **g,l,u,f.**

Sull, Donald N. & Wang, Yong **HB615.S94 2005**
Made in China: What Western Managers Can Learn from Trailblazing Chinese Entrepreneurs. Book, Other. Harvard Business School Press. Boston, MA. 2005. 256p. ISBN:1-59139-715-4, ISBN13: 978-1-59139-715-1. Dewey:658.4/21. LCCN:2005-000321.
Audience: **g,l,u,f.** *Choice, 2006.*

Thomas, David C. & Inkson, Kerr **GN450.8.T47 2004**
Cultural Intelligence: People Skills for Global Business. Trade Paper. Berrett-Koehler Publishers, Inc. San Francisco, CA. 2004. 225p. ISBN:1-57675-256-9, ISBN13: 978-1-57675-256-2. Dewey:302.3/5. LCCN:2003-063867.
Audience: **l,u.**

Trompenaars, Fons **HD30.55.T76 1998**
Riding the Waves of Culture: Understanding Diversity in Global Business. Ed. 2. Trade Cloth. McGraw-Hill Companies, The. New York, NY. 1997. 416p. ISBN:0-7863-1125-8, ISBN13: 978-0-7863-1125-5. Dewey:658.3/0089. LCCN:97-039551.
Audience: **g,l,u,f.**

Trompenaars, Fons & Woolliams, Peter **HD30.55**
Business Across Cultures. Trade Paper. John Wiley & Sons, Inc. Hoboken, NJ. 2004. 368p. Culture for Business Ser. ISBN:1-84112-474-5, ISBN13: 978-1-84112-474-2. Dewey:650.089. LCCN:2004-298808.
Audience: **g,l,u,f.**

Walker, Danielle Medina & Walker, Thomas **HD31.B7235 2001**
Doing Business Internationally: The Guide to Cross-Cultural Success. Ed. 2. Trade Cloth. McGraw-Hill Companies, The. New York, NY. 2002. 288p. ISBN:0-07-137832-4, ISBN13: 978-0-07-137832-1. Dewey:658/.049. LCCN:2001-054412.
Audience: **g,l,u,f.**

Business Environment > International Trade and Foreign Investment > Foreign investment in the U.S.

Bureau of Economic Analysis, U.S. Department of Commerce **HG4061**
International Economic Accounts.
http://www.bea.gov/bea/di1.htm
Audience: **u,f.**

Center for International Business Education and Research at Michigan State University **HF1379**
Global Edge.
http://globaledge.msu.edu/about_globaledge.asp
Audience: **l,u,f.**

Jensen, N. M. **HG4538.J46 2006**
Institutions, Information and International Capital: A Political Economy of Foreign Direct Investment. Trade Cloth. Princeton University Press. Princeton, NJ. 2006. 224p. ISBN:0-691-12222-9, ISBN13: 978-0-691-12222-9. Dewey:338.8/8. LCCN:2005-014030.
Audience: **g,l,u,f.**

The World Bank **HD82**
World Development Report 2005: Investment Climate, Growth and Poverty. Ed. 2005. Paper Text. World Bank Publications. Washington, DC. 2004. 288p. A World Bank Publication ISBN:0-8213-5682-8, ISBN13: 978-0-8213-5682-1. Dewey:338.9/109051. LCCN:2004-304824.
Audience: **g,l,u,f.**

Business Environment > International Trade and Foreign Investment > U.S Foreign Investment Abroad

Center for International Business Education and Research at Michigan State University **HF1379**
Global Edge.
http://globaledge.msu.edu/about_globaledge.asp
Audience: **l,u,f.**

Jensen, N. M. **HG4538.J46 2006**
Institutions, Information and International Capital: A Political Economy of Foreign Direct Investment. Trade Cloth. Princeton University Press. Princeton, NJ. 2006. 224p. ISBN:0-691-12222-9, ISBN13: 978-0-691-12222-9. Dewey:338.8/8. LCCN:2005-014030.
Audience: **g,l,u,f.**

Moran, Theodore **HD5710.75.D44M67**
Beyond Sweatshops: Foreign Direct Investment and Globalization in Developing Nations. Trade Cloth. Brookings Institution Press. Washington, DC. 2002. 224p. ISBN:0-8157-0616-2, ISBN13: 978-0-8157-0616-8. Dewey:331.1/09172/4. LCCN:2002-003528.
Audience: **g,l,u,f.**

Moran, Theodore, et al. **HG4538.I4654 2005**
Does Foreign Direct Investment Promote Development. Edward Graham & Magnus Blomstrom (Authors). Trade Paper. Institute for International Economics. Washington, DC. 2005. 440p. ISBN:0-88132-381-0, ISBN13: 978-0-88132-381-8. Dewey:338.9. LCCN:2005-043298.
Audience: **g,l,u,f.** *Choice, 2005.*

The World Bank **HD82**
World Development Report 2005: Investment Climate, Growth and Poverty. Ed. 2005. Paper Text. World Bank Publications. Washington, DC. 2004. 288p. A World Bank Publication ISBN:0-8213-5682-8, ISBN13: 978-0-8213-5682-1. Dewey:338.9/109051. LCCN:2004-304824.
Audience: **g,l,u,f.**

United States Department of Commerce **HF1379**
Export.gov.
http://www.export.gov
Audience: **u,f.**

Business Environment > International Trade and Foreign Investment > Treatment of Regions and Individual Countries

HD2756.5
Practical Guide to Foreign Direct Investment in the European Union. Ed. 3. Trade Cloth. Routledge. New York, NY. 2005. 400p. ISBN:1-85743-338-6, ISBN13: 978-1-85743-338-8. Dewey:338.8884.
Audience: **g,u,f.**

Chase, Kerry A. **HF1418.7.C53 2006**
Trading Blocs: States, Firms, and Regions in the World Economy. Trade Cloth. University of Michigan Press. Chicago, IL. 2005. 328p. Michigan Studies in International Political Economy Ser. ISBN:0-472-09906-X, ISBN13: 978-0-472-09906-1. Dewey:382/.9/0904. LCCN:2005-016620.
Audience: **u,f.**

Drabek, Zdenek (Editor) **HF2036.C36 2005**
Can Regional Integration Arrangements Enforce Trade Discipline?: The Story of EU Enlargement. Cloth over Boards. Palgrave Macmillan. New York, NY. 2005. 288p. ISBN:1-4039-4160-2, ISBN13: 978-1-4039-4160-2. Dewey:382/.9142. LCCN:2004-054252.
Audience: **g,u,f.**

Freeman, Nick & Bartels, Frank (Editors) **HG5740.8.A3F87 2004**
The Future of Foreign Investment in Southeast Asia. Paper over Boards. Taylor & Francis Group. Philadelphia, PA. 2004. 304p. RoutledgeCurzon International Business in Asia Ser., Vol. 1 ISBN:0-415-30841-0, ISBN13: 978-0-415-30841-0. Dewey:332.67/3/0959. LCCN:2003-010576.
Audience: **g,u,f.**

Hamilton, Daniel & Quinlan, Joseph **HF1456.5.E8H357 2004**
Partners in Prosperity: The Changing Geography of the Transatlantic Economy. Trade Paper. Center for Transatlantic Relations. Washington, DC. 2004. 220p. ISBN:0-9753325-5-4, ISBN13: 978-0-9753325-5-9. Dewey:337.7304. LCCN:2005-351027.
Audience: **g,f.**

Ito, Takatoshi & Krueger, Anne O. (Editors) **HG5770.5.A3R65 2000**
The Role of Foreign Direct Investment in East Asian Economic Development. Trade Cloth. University of Chicago Press. Chicago, IL. 2000. 389p. Nber-East Asia Seminar on Economics Ser., Vol. 9 ISBN:0-226-38675-9, ISBN13: 978-0-226-38675-1. Dewey:332.67/3/095. LCCN:99-086531.
Audience: **g,u,f.**

Morrison, Andrea M. & Mann, Barbara J. **ZA5050**
International Government Information and Country Information: A Subject Guide. Cloth Text. Greenwood Publishing Group, Inc. Portsmouth, NH. 2004. 312p. How to Find It, How to Use It Ser. ISBN:1-57356-479-6, ISBN13: 978-1-57356-479-3. Dewey:025.04. LCCN:2004-000441.
Audience: **l,u.**

Rae, Ian & Witzel, Morgen (Editors) **HF3836.5.R34 2004**
Singular and Different: Business in China Past, Present and Future. Cloth over Boards. Palgrave Macmillan. New York, NY. 2004. 184p. ISBN:1-4039-1722-1, ISBN13: 978-1-4039-1722-5. Dewey:330.951. LCCN:2003-065675.
Audience: **g,u,f.** *Choice, 2004.*

Ray, Pradeep **HG5732.R32 2005**
FDI and Industrial Organization in Developing Countries: The Challenge of Globalization in India. Trade Cloth. Ashgate Publishing, Ltd. Aldershot, 2005. 292p. ISBN:0-7546-4322-0, ISBN13: 978-0-7546-4322-7. Dewey:338.6/0954. LCCN:2005-013251.
Audience: **g,u,f.**

Shafaeddin, Mehdi **HF2580.9.S53 2005**
Trade Policy at the Crossroads: The Recent Experience of Developing Countries. Paul Streeten (Foreword by). Cloth over Boards. Palgrave Macmillan. New York, NY. 2005. 288p. ISBN:0-333-59559-9, ISBN13: 978-0-333-59559-6. Dewey:382/.3/091724. LCCN:2004-051238.
Audience: **g,u,f.**

The World Bank **HD82**
World Development Report 2005: Investment Climate, Growth and Poverty. Ed. 2005. Paper Text. World Bank Publications. Washington, DC. 2004. 288p. A World Bank Publication ISBN:0-8213-5682-8, ISBN13: 978-0-8213-5682-1. Dewey:338.9/109051. LCCN:2004-304824.
Audience: **g,l,u,f.**

United States Central Intelligence Agency
CIA World Fact Book.
http://www.cia.gov/cia/publications/factbook/index.html
Audience: **l,u.**

Business Environment > International Trade and Foreign Investment > Trade Organizations and Treaties

Barton, John H., et al. **HF1713.E96 2006**
The Evolution of the Trade Regime: Politics, Law and Economics of the Gatt and the Wto. Judith L. Goldstein, Timothy E. Josling & Richard H. Steinberg (Authors). Trade Cloth. Princeton University Press. Princeton, NJ. 2006. 256p. ISBN:0-691-12450-7, ISBN13: 978-0-691-12450-6. Dewey:382/.92. LCCN:2005-045400.
Audience: **g,l,u,f.** *Choice, 2006.*

Hafez, Mohammed Zakirul **HF1717.A785H34 2004**
The Dimensions of Regional Trade Integration in Southeast Asia. Trade Cloth. Transnational Publishers, Inc. Ardsley, NY. 2005. 486p. ISBN:1-57105-184-8, ISBN13: 978-1-57105-184-4. Dewey:382/.9159. LCCN:2004-053682.
Audience: **g,u,f.**

Jones, Kent Albert & Jones, Kent **HF1385.J67 2003**
Who's Afraid of the WTO? Trade Cloth. Oxford University Press, Inc. New York, NY. 2004. 248p. ISBN:0-19-516616-7, ISBN13: 978-0-19-516616-3. Dewey:382/.92. LCCN:2003-048292.
Audience: **g,l,u,f.** *Choice, 2004.*

Moran, Robert T. & Abbott, Jeffrey D. **HF1746**
Uniting North American Business: NAFTA Best Practices. Ed. 2. Trade Paper. Elsevier Science & Technology Books. Saint Louis, MO. 2002. 288p. Managing Cultural Differences Ser. ISBN:0-87719-384-3, ISBN13: 978-0-87719-384-5. Dewey:382/.917. LCCN:2002-020052.
Audience: **g,u,f.**

Narlikar, Amrita **HF1385**
The World Trade Organization: A Very Short Introduction. Trade Paper. Oxford University Press, Inc. New York, NY. 2005. 168p. Very Short Introductions Ser. ISBN:0-19-280608-4, ISBN13: 978-0-19-280608-6. Dewey:382/.92. LCCN:2005-019519.
Audience: **g,l,u,f.**

Porrata-Doria, Rafael **KH736.M47P67 2005**
Mercosur: The Common Market of the Southern Cone. Cloth Text. Carolina Academic Press. Durham, NC. 2005. 240p. Carolina Academic Press Studies on Globalization and Society ISBN:1-59460-010-4, ISBN13: 978-1-59460-010-4. Dewey:337.1/8. LCCN:2005-001655.
Audience: **g,u,f.** *Choice, 2006.*

Vizentini, Paulo Gilberto Fagundes & Wiesebron, Marianne (Editors) **HF1745.F73 2003**
Free Trade for the Americas?: The United States' Push for the FTAA Agreement. Cloth over Boards. Zed Books, Ltd. London, 2004. 256p. ISBN:1-84277-312-7, ISBN13: 978-1-84277-312-3. Dewey:382/.97. LCCN:2003-047926.
Audience: **g,u,f.**

Weintraub, Sidney (Editor) **HF1746.N34 2004**
NAFTA's Impact on North America: The First Decade. Carla A. Hills (Foreword by). Paper Text. Center for Strategic & International Studies. Washington, DC. 2004. 464p. Significant Issues Ser., 26 ISBN:0-89206-451-X, ISBN13: 978-0-89206-451-9. Dewey:382/.917. LCCN:2004-016450.
Audience: **g,u,f.**

Business Environment > Energy / Environment

Freeman, A. Myrick III **HC79.E5F713 2003**
The Measurements of Environmental and Resource Values: Theory and Methods. Ed. 2. Trade Cloth. Resources for the Future. Washington, DC. 2003. 496p. ISBN:1-891853-63-5, ISBN13: 978-1-891853-63-0. Dewey:333.7. LCCN:2002-155435.
Audience: **u,f.** *Choice, 2003.*

Freeman, R. Edward, et al. **HD30.255.F74 2000**
Environmentalism and the New Logic of Business: How Firms Can Be Profitable and Leave Our Children a Living Planet. Jessica Pierce & Richard Dodd (Authors). Trade Cloth. Oxford University Press, Inc. New York, NY. 2000. 160p. ISBN:0-19-508093-9, ISBN13: 978-0-19-508093-3. Dewey:658.4/08. LCCN:99-051545.
Audience: **u,f.**

Hoffman, Andrew J. **HD30.255.H64 2001**
From Heresy to Dogma: An Institutional History of Corporate Environmentalism. Trade Paper. Stanford University Press. Palo Alto, CA. 2001. 320p. Stanford Business Books ISBN:0-8047-4503-X, ISBN13: 978-0-8047-4503-1. Dewey:658.4/08. LCCN:2001-049129.
Audience: **u,f.** *Choice, 2002.*

Lyon, Thomas P. & Maxwell, John W. **HD30.255.L96 2004**
Corporate Environmentalism and Public Policy. Trade Paper. Cambridge University Press. New York, NY. 2004. 308p. ISBN:0-521-60376-5, ISBN13: 978-0-521-60376-8. Dewey:363.7.
Audience: **u,f.**

Newton, Lisa H. **HD30.255.N49 2005**
Business Ethics and the Natural Environment. Trade Paper. Blackwell Publishing, Inc. Malden, MA. 2005. 280p. Foundations of Business Ethics Ser., Vol. 6 ISBN:1-4051-1663-3, ISBN13: 978-1-4051-1663-3. Dewey:174/.4. LCCN:2004-024668.
Audience: **u,f.** *Choice, 2006.*

Porter, Michael E. **HF1414.P67 1998**
On Competition. Trade Cloth. Harvard Business School Press. Boston, MA. 1998. 496p. Review Book Ser. ISBN:0-87584-795-1, ISBN13: 978-0-87584-795-5. Dewey:382/.1042. LCCN:98-007643.
Audience: **u,f.** *Choice, 1999.*

Savitz, Andrew, et al. **HF5386.S346 2006**
Triple Bottom Line: Why the Smartest Companies Are Adopting Sustainability As the New Business Model and What You Need to Know about It. Morgan McVicar & Karl Weber (Authors). Trade Cloth. John Wiley & Sons, Inc. Hoboken, NJ. 2006. 320p. ISBN:0-7879-7907-4, ISBN13: 978-0-7879-7907-2. Dewey:658.4/08. LCCN:2006-012329.
Audience: **u,f.**

Staib, Richard **HD30.255**
Environmental Management and Decision Making for Business. Cloth over Boards. Palgrave Macmillan. New York, NY. 2005. 320p. ISBN:1-4039-4133-5, ISBN13: 978-1-4039-4133-6. Dewey:658.4/03. LCCN:2005-043187.
Audience: **u,f.**

Business Environment > Energy / Environment > Natural Resources

Folmer, Henk (Editor), et al. **HC79.E5P6944 1995**
Principles of Environmental and Resource Economics: A Guide for Students and Decision-Makers. H. Landis Gabel & Hans Opschoor (Editors). Trade Cloth. Edward Elgar Publishing, Inc. Northampton, MA. 1995. 512p. ISBN:1-85898-224-3, ISBN13: 978-1-85898-224-3. Dewey:333.7. LCCN:95-004051.
Audience: **g,u,f.** *Choice, 1996.*

Henning, Daniel H. & Mangun, William R. **HC79.E5H46 1989**
Managing the Environmental Crisis: Incorporating Competing Values in Natural Resource Administration. Lynton K. Caldwell (Foreword by). Paper Text. Duke University Press. Durham, NC. 1989. 378p. ISBN:0-8223-0967-X, ISBN13: 978-0-8223-0967-3. Dewey:363.7. LCCN:89-011886.
Audience: **g,u,f.** *Choice, 1990.*

Krutilla, John V. & Fisher, Anthony C. **HC103.7.K78**
The Economics of Natural Environments: Studies in the Valuation of Commodity and Amenity Resources. Ed. 2. Trade Cloth. Resources for the Future. Washington, DC. 1975. 314p. ISBN:0-8018-1699-8, ISBN13: 978-0-8018-1699-4. Dewey:333.7/0973. LCCN:74-024400.
Audience: **g,u,f.** B

Mangun, William R. & Henning, Daniel H. **HC79.E5H46 1999**
Managing the Environmental Crisis: Incorporating Competing Values in Natural Resource Administration. Ed. 2. Lynton K. Caldwell (Foreword by). Trade Cloth. Duke University Press. Durham, NC. 1999. 416p. ISBN:0-8223-2379-6, ISBN13: 978-0-8223-2379-2. Dewey:363.7. LCCN:99-026267.
Audience: **g,u,f.** *Choice, 2000.*

Mercuro, Nicholas, et al. **GE170.M46 1994**
Ecology, Law and Economics: The Simple Analytics of Natural Resource and Environment Economics. Franklin A. Lopez & Kristian P. Preston (Authors). Trade Paper. University Press of America, Inc. Lanham, MD. 1994. 212p. ISBN:0-8191-9594-4, ISBN13: 978-0-8191-9594-4. Dewey:363.7. LCCN:94-017739.
Audience: **g,u,f.** *Choice, 1995.*

Pennell, Allison A. (Editor), et al. **HD69.P6.P46 1992**
Business and the Environment: A Resource Guide. Lawrence Molinaro Jr. & Patricia E. Choi (Editors). Trade Cloth. Island Press. Washington, DC. 1992. 382p. ISBN:1-55963-159-7, ISBN13: 978-1-55963-159-4. Dewey:016.6584/08. LCCN:91-038369.
Audience: **g,u,f.** *Choice, 1992.*

Portney, Paul & Haas, Ruth B. (Editors) **HC103.7**
Current Issues in Natural Resource Policy. Trade Cloth. Resources for the Future. Washington, DC. 1982. 318p. ISBN:0-8018-2916-X, ISBN13: 978-0-8018-2916-1. Dewey:333.7/0973. LCCN:87-047982.
Audience: **g,u,f.** B

Rothman, Hal K. **GE197.R69 2000**
Saving the Planet: The American Response to the Environment in the Twentieth Century. Book, Other. Ivan R. Dee Publisher. Blue Ridge Summit, PA. 2000. 224p. American Ways Ser. ISBN:1-56663-288-9, ISBN13: 978-1-56663-288-1. Dewey:333.7/2/09730904. LCCN:99-049372.
Audience: **g,u,f.** *Choice, 2000.*

Tisdell, Clement A. **HD75.6**
Natural Resources, Growth and Development: Economics, Ecology and Resource-Scarcity. Trade Cloth. Greenwood Publishing Group, Inc. Portsmouth, NH. 1990. 200p. ISBN:0-275-93479-9, ISBN13: 978-0-275-93479-8. Dewey:333.7/09172/4. LCCN:90-042118.
Audience: **g,u,f.** *Choice, 1991.*

Van den Bergh, Jeroen C. (Editor) **HC79.E5H3284 1999**
Handbook of Environmental and Resource Economics. Trade Cloth. Edward Elgar Publishing, Inc. Northampton, MA. 1999. 1328p. ISBN:1-85898-375-4, ISBN13: 978-1-85898-375-2. Dewey:333.7. LCCN:98-042887.
Audience: **g,u,f.** *Choice, 2000.*

Business Environment > Energy / Environment > Energy Policy

Heinberg, Richar **TJ163.2**
Powerdown: Options and Actions for a Post-Carbon World. Trade Paper. New Society Publishers, Ltd. Gabriola Island, BC. 2004. 288p. ISBN:0-86571-510-6, ISBN13: 978-0-86571-510-3. Dewey:333.7.
Audience: **g,u,f.** *Choice, 2005.*

Kalicki, Jan H. & Goldwyn, David L. **HD9502.U52E4543 2005**
Energy and Security: Toward a New Foreign Policy Strategy. Trade Cloth. Johns Hopkins University Press. Baltimore, MD. 2005. 640p. ISBN:0-8018-8278-8, ISBN13: 978-0-8018-8278-4. Dewey:333.79/0973. LCCN:2005-006082.
Audience: **g,u,f.** *Choice, 2005.*

Morgenstern, Richard D. **HD9502.U52N45 2004**
New Approaches on Energy and the Environment: Policy Advice for the President. Paul R. Portney (Editor). Trade Cloth. Resources for the Future. Washington, DC. 2005. 180p. ISBN:1-933115-00-9, ISBN13: 978-1-933115-00-9. Dewey:333.79/0973/09051. LCCN:2004-018822.
Audience: **g,u,f.** *Choice, 2005.*

Stagliano, Vito A. **HD9502.U52S72 2001**
A Policy of Discontent: The Making of a National Energy Strategy. Trade Cloth. PennWell Corporation. Tulsa, OK. 2001. 446p. ISBN:0-87814-817-5, ISBN13: 978-0-87814-817-2. Dewey:333.79/0973. LCCN:2001-033939.
Audience: **g,u,f.** *Choice, 2002.*

Business Environment > Energy / Environment > Pollution Control

Davies, J. Clarence III & Mazurek, Jan **TD180.D39 1998**
Pollution Control in the United States: Evaluating the System. Trade Paper. Resources for the Future. Washington, DC. 1998. 319p. ISBN:0-915707-88-8, ISBN13: 978-0-915707-88-1. Dewey:363.73. LCCN:97-049246.
Audience: **g,u,f.** *Choice, 1998.*

Leonard, H. Jeffrey **HD75.6 .L46 1988**
Pollution and the Struggle for the World Product: Multinational Corporations, Environment, and International Comparative Advantage. Cloth Text. Cambridge University Press. New York, NY. 1988. 272p. ISBN:0-521-34042-X, ISBN13: 978-0-521-34042-7. Dewey:338.6/042. LCCN:87-017766.
Audience: **g,u,f.** *Choice, 1989.*

Rahm, Dianne **TD1040.T687 2002**
Toxic Waste and Environmental Policy in the 21st Century United States. Paper Text. McFarland & Company, Incorporated Publishers. Jefferson, NC. 2002. 190p. ISBN:0-7864-1202-X, ISBN13: 978-0-7864-1202-0. Dewey:363.72/87. LCCN:86-43090.
Audience: **g,l,u,f.** *Choice, 2002.*

Scruggs, Lyle **HC79.E5S29245 2002**
Sustaining Abundance: Environmental Performance in Industrial Democracies. Trade Cloth. Cambridge University Press. New York, NY. 2003. 268p. Cambridge Studies in Comparative Politics ISBN:0-521-81672-6, ISBN13: 978-0-521-81672-4. Dewey:363.73/5. LCCN:2002-067712.
Audience: **g,u,f.** *Choice, 2003.*

Tietenberg, T. H. **HC110.A4T54 2006**
Emissions Trading: Principles and Practice. Ed. 2. Trade Cloth. Resources for the Future. Washington, DC. 2006. 230p. ISBN:1-933115-30-0, ISBN13: 978-1-933115-30-6. Dewey:363.739/260973. LCCN:2005-033482.
Audience: **g,u,f.** *Choice, 2006.*

Business Environment > Energy / Environment > Green Businesses and Marketing

Coddington, Walter & Florian, Peter **HF5413.C63 1993**
Environmental Marketing: Positive Strategies for Reaching the Green Consumer. Cloth Text. McGraw-Hill Companies, The. New York, NY. 1993. xi, 252p. ISBN:0-07-011599-0, ISBN13: 978-0-07-011599-6. Dewey:658.8/02. LCCN:92-035217.
Audience: **g,u,f.** *Choice, 1993.*

Keenan, Andrea & Georges, Danielle **TH880.G74 2002**
Green Building: Project Planning and Cost Estimating. Trade Cloth. R. S. Means Company, Inc. Kingston, MA. 2002. 350p. Reference Book Publications ISBN:0-87629-659-2, ISBN13: 978-0-87629-659-2. Dewey:690.837. LCCN:2003-266423.
Audience: **l,u,f.**

Laurel, Brenda **HC252.5.B73**
Utopian Entrepreneur. Trade Cloth. MIT Press. Cambridge, MA. 2001. 112p. Mediaworks Pamphlets Ser. ISBN:0-262-12244-8, ISBN13: 978-0-262-12244-3. Dewey:338/.04/092 B. LCCN:2001-092089.
Audience: **g,l,u,f.**

Makower, Joel **HD60.M344 1993**
The E-Factor: Turning Environmental Responsibility into Good, Green Profits. Trade Cloth. Crown Publishing Group. New York, NY. 1993. 291p. ISBN:0-8129-2057-0, ISBN13: 978-0-8129-2057-4. Dewey:658.4/08. LCCN:92-050504.
Audience: **g,u,f.**

Neumayer, Eric **HF1713.N42 2001**
Greening Trade and Investment: Environmental Protection Without Protectionism. Trade Cloth. Earthscan/James & James. London, 2001. 240p. ISBN:1-85383-787-3, ISBN13: 978-1-85383-787-6. Dewey:333.7. LCCN:2001-001379.
Audience: **g,u,f.** *Choice, 2002.*

Prakash, Aseem **GE170 .P69 2000**
Greening the Firm: The Politics of Corporate Environmentalism. Trade Cloth. Cambridge University Press. New York, NY. 2000. 196p. ISBN:0-521-66249-4, ISBN13: 978-0-521-66249-9. Dewey:658.408. LCCN:99-033723.
Audience: **g,u,f.**

Robbins, Peter T. **HD62.4.R58 2001**
Greening the Corporation: Management Strategy and the Environmental Challenge. Trade Cloth. Earthscan/James & James. London, 2001. 240p. ISBN:1-85383-771-7, ISBN13: 978-1-85383-771-5. Dewey:658.4/08. LCCN:2001-002890.
Audience: **g,u,f.** *Choice, 2002.*

Smith, Toby **HF5413.S64 1998**
The Myth of Green Marketing: Tending Our Goats at the Edge of Apocalypse. Trade Paper. University of Toronto Press. Toronto, ON. 1998. 306p. ISBN:0-8020-8035-9, ISBN13: 978-0-8020-8035-6. Dewey:658.8.
Audience: **g,u,f.** *Choice, 1999.*

Business Environment > Energy / Environment > Ethics and Environment

Freeman, R. Edward, et al. **HD30.255.F74 2000**
Environmentalism and the New Logic of Business: How Firms Can Be Profitable and Leave Our Children a Living Planet. Jessica Pierce & Richard Dodd (Authors). Trade Cloth. Oxford University Press, Inc. New York, NY. 2000. 160p. ISBN:0-19-508093-9, ISBN13: 978-0-19-508093-3. Dewey:658.4/08. LCCN:99-051545.
Audience: **u,f.**

Hoffman, Andrew J. **HD30.255.H64 2001**
From Heresy to Dogma: An Institutional History of Corporate Environmentalism. Trade Paper. Stanford University Press. Palo Alto, CA. 2001. 320p. Stanford Business Books ISBN:0-8047-4503-X, ISBN13: 978-0-8047-4503-1. Dewey:658.4/08. LCCN:2001-049129.
Audience: **u,f.** *Choice, 2002.*

Lyon, Thomas P. & Maxwell, John W. **HD30.255.L96 2004**
Corporate Environmentalism and Public Policy. Trade Paper. Cambridge University Press. New York, NY. 2004. 308p. ISBN:0-521-60376-5, ISBN13: 978-0-521-60376-8. Dewey:363.7.
Audience: **u,f.**

Newton, Lisa H. **HD30.255.N49 2005**
Business Ethics and the Natural Environment. Trade Paper. Blackwell Publishing, Inc. Malden, MA. 2005. 280p. Foundations of Business Ethics Ser., Vol. 6 ISBN:1-4051-1663-3, ISBN13: 978-1-4051-1663-3. Dewey:174/.4. LCCN:2004-024668.
Audience: **u,f.** *Choice, 2006.*

Savitz, Andrew, et al. **HF5386.S346 2006**
Triple Bottom Line: Why the Smartest Companies Are Adopting Sustainability As the New Business Model and What You Need to Know about It. Morgan McVicar & Karl Weber (Authors). Trade Cloth. John Wiley & Sons, Inc. Hoboken, NJ. 2006. 320p. ISBN:0-7879-7907-4, ISBN13: 978-0-7879-7907-2. Dewey:658.4/08. LCCN:2006-012329.
Audience: **u,f.**

Staib, Richard **HD30.255**
Environmental Management and Decision Making for Business. Cloth over Boards. Palgrave Macmillan. New York, NY. 2005. 320p. ISBN:1-4039-4133-5, ISBN13: 978-1-4039-4133-6. Dewey:658.4/03. LCCN:2005-043187.
Audience: **u,f.**

Management Function > General Management

Barnard, Chester I. **HD31**
The Functions of the Executive. Ed. 30. K. R. Andrews (Introduction by). Trade Paper. Harvard University Press. Cambridge, MA. 1971. 376p. ISBN:0-674-32803-5, ISBN13: 978-0-674-32803-7. Dewey:658.42. LCCN:68-028690.
Audience: **g,l,u,f.**

Drucker, Peter F. **HD70.U5D7**
The Practice of Management. Trade Paper. HarperCollins Publishers. New York, NY. 1999. ISBN:0-06-662026-0, ISBN13: 978-0-06-662026-8. Dewey:658.
Audience: **g,l,u,f.**

Martin, John D. (Author, Editor) **HD47.3.M37 2000**
Value Based Management: The Corporate Response to the Shareholder Revolution. J. William Petty (Editor). Trade Cloth. Oxford University Press, Inc. New York, NY. 2000. 268p. Financial Management Association Survey and Synthesis Ser. ISBN:0-87584-800-1, ISBN13: 978-0-87584-800-6. Dewey:658. LCCN:00-031910.
Audience: **g,l,u,f.** *Choice, 2001.*

McNett, Jeanne **HD30.15.B455**
International Management. Ed. 2. Trade Cloth. Blackwell Publishing, Inc. Malden, MA. 2006. 376p. The Blackwell Encyclopedia of Management Ser., Vol. 6 ISBN:0-631-23493-4, ISBN13: 978-0-631-23493-7. Dewey:658/.003 s 658/.049. LCCN:2004-018073.
Audience: **g,l,u,f.**

Mintzberg, Henry **HD31**
The Nature of Managerial Work. Trade Paper. Addison-Wesley Educational Publishers, Inc. Boston, MA. 1997. 298p. ISBN:0-06-044556-4, ISBN13: 978-0-06-044556-0. Dewey:658.4. LCCN:72-009400.
Audience: **g,l,f.**

Porter, Michael E. **HD41.P668 1985**
The Competitive Advantage: Creating and Sustaining Superior Performance. Trade Cloth. Simon & Schuster. New York, NY. 1985. 484p. ISBN:0-02-925090-0, ISBN13: 978-0-02-925090-7. Dewey:658. LCCN:83-049518.
Audience: **u,f.** B

Taylor, Frederick Winslow **T58.T38 A3**
The Principles of Scientific Management. Trade Paper. 1st World Publishing, Inc. Fairfield, IA. 2005. 132p. ISBN:1-4218-0440-9, ISBN13: 978-1-4218-0440-8. Dewey:658.5. LCCN:2004195619.
Audience: **g,l,u,f.** B

Management Function > General Management > Managerial Skills

Bartlett, Christopher A. & Ghoshal, Sumantra **HD62.4.B36 1998**
Managing Across Borders: The Transnational Solution. Ed. 2. Trade Cloth. Harvard Business School Press. Boston, MA. 1998. 416p. ISBN:0-87584-849-4, ISBN13: 978-0-87584-849-5. Dewey:658.049. LCCN:98-026004.
Audience: **g,l,u,f.** *Choice, 1990.*

Management Function > General Management > Managerial Skills > Consulting

Buono, Anthony F. **HD69.C6C74 2004**
Creative Consulting: Innovative Perspectives on Management Consulting. Trade Paper. Information Age Publishing, Inc. Greenwich, CT. 2004. xix, 377p. Research in Management Consulting Ser. ISBN:1-59311-240-8, ISBN13: 978-1-59311-240-0. Dewey:001. LCCN:2004-015800.
Audience: **l,u,f.**

Edersheim, Elizabeth Haas **HD69.C6E34 2004**
McKinsey's Marvin Bower: Vision, Leadership, and the Creation of Management Consulting. Trade Cloth. John Wiley & Sons, Inc. Hoboken, NJ. 2004. 305p. ISBN:0-471-65285-7, ISBN13: 978-0-471-65285-4. Dewey:658.46092. LCCN:2004-299600.
Audience: **g,l,u,f.**

Grodzki, Lynn & Allen, Wendy **HD69.C6G74 2005**
The Business and Practice of Coaching: Finding Your Niche, Making Money and Attracting Ideal Clients. Perfect, Paper over Boards, Dust Jacket. W. W. Norton & Company, Inc. New York, NY. 2005. 599p. ISBN:0-393-70462-9, ISBN13: 978-0-393-70462-4. Dewey:001/.68/8. LCCN:2005-047294.
Audience: **g,l,u,f.**

Kipping, Matthias & Engwall, Lars (Editors) **HD69.C6M3655 2002**
Management Consulting: Emergence and Dynamics of a Knowledge Industry. Trade Paper. Oxford University Press, Inc. New York, NY. 2003. 282p. ISBN:0-19-926711-1, ISBN13: 978-0-19-926711-8. Dewey:001.
Audience: **u,f.**

Morgan, Howard, et al. **HD57.7.A77 2004**
The Art and Practice of Leadership Coaching: 50 Top Executive Coaches Reveal Their Secrets. Phil Harkins & Marshall Goldsmith (Authors). Trade Cloth. John Wiley & Sons, Inc. Hoboken, NJ. 2004. 304p. ISBN:0-471-70546-2, ISBN13: 978-0-471-70546-8. Dewey:658.4/092. LCCN:2004-016225.
Audience: **g,l,u,f.**

O'Shea, James & Madigan, Charles **HD69.C6**
Dangerous Company: The Consulting Powerhouses and the Businesses They Save and Ruin. Trade Cloth. DIANE Publishing Company. Collingdale, PA. 2002. 355p. ISBN:0-7567-5600-6, ISBN13: 978-0-7567-5600-0. Dewey:658.4/6.
Audience: **g,l,u,f.**

Phillips, Jack **HD69.C6**
How to Build a Successful Consulting Practice. Trade Paper. McGraw-Hill Companies, The. New York, NY. 2006. 256p. ISBN:0-07-146229-5, ISBN13: 978-0-07-146229-7. Dewey:001/.068.
Audience: **u,f.**

Reeves, Douglas B. **HD69.C6R425 2005**
It's All about the Client: Consulting for Results. Trade Paper. Advanced Learning Press. Denver, CO. 2005. 128p. ISBN:0-9644955-6-2, ISBN13: 978-0-9644955-6-2. Dewey:650.1. LCCN:2005-045371.
Audience: **g,l,u,f.**

Rubin, Frances & Rowley, John **HD69.C6**
Effective Consultancies in Development and Humanitarian Programmes: A Practical Guide. Oxfam GB Staff (Contribution by). Trade Paper. Oxfam Publishing. Oxford, 2005. 112p. Oxfam Skills and Practice Ser. ISBN:0-85598-500-3, ISBN13: 978-0-85598-500-4. Dewey:658.4/6.
Audience: **g,l,u,f.**

Stroh, Linda K. & Johnson, Homer H. **HD69.C6S77 2006**
The Basic Principles of Effective Consulting. Trade Paper. Lawrence Erlbaum Associates, Inc. Mahwah, NJ. 2005. 192p. ISBN:0-8058-5420-7, ISBN13: 978-0-8058-5420-6. Dewey:658.4/6. LCCN:2005-050733.
Audience: **g,l,u,f.**

Thommen, Jean-Paul & Richter, Ansgar **HD69.C6**
Management Consulting Today. Trade Cloth. Betriebswirtschaftlicher Verlag Dr. Th. Gabler GmbH. Wiesbaden, 2005. 200p. ISBN:3-409-12584-1, ISBN13: 978-3-409-12584-0. Dewey:1.068.
Audience: **u,f.**

Toppin, Gilbert & Czerniawska, Fiona **HD69.C6**
Business Consulting: A Guide to How It Works and How to Make It Work. Trade Cloth. Bloomberg Press. New York, NY. 2005. 264p. ISBN:1-86197-702-6, ISBN13: 978-1-86197-702-1. Dewey:658.46.
Audience: **g,l,u,f.**

Walsh, George, et al. **HD9999.I492E58 2004**
Start Your Own Information Consultant Business: Your Step by Step Guide to Success. Ed. 5. Rachel Adelson & Alan Breznick (Authors), Entrepreneur Press Staff (Editor). Trade Paper. Entrepreneur Press. Irvine, CA. 2004. 117p. ISBN:1-932156-73-9, ISBN13: 978-1-932156-73-7. Dewey:001/.068/1. LCCN:2004-046940.
Audience: **g,l,u,f.**

Weiss, Alan **HD69.C6W4613 2005**
Million Dollar Consulting Toolkit: Step-by-Step Guidance, Checklists, Templates, and Samples from the Million Dollar Consultant. Trade Paper, Perfect. John Wiley & Sons, Inc. Hoboken, NJ. 2005. 238p. ISBN:0-471-74027-6, ISBN13: 978-0-471-74027-8. Dewey:658.4/6. LCCN:2005-048974.
Audience: **g,l,u,f.**

WetFeet **HD69.C6**
25 Top Consulting Firms: Wetfeet Insider Guide. Trade Paper, Perfect. WetFeet, Inc. San Francisco, CA. 2006. 130p. ISBN:1-58207-528-X, ISBN13: 978-1-58207-528-0. Dewey:001/.023/73.
Audience: **g,l,u,f.**

Management Function > General Management > Managerial Skills > Creativity in Business

Bennis, Warren & Biederman, Patricia W. **HD58.9**
Organizing Genius. Trade Paper. Perseus Books Group. New York, NY. 1998. 256p. ISBN:0-201-33989-7, ISBN13: 978-0-201-33989-5. Dewey:158.7.
Audience: **u,f.**

Bills, Tim & Genasi, Chris **HD53.B55 2003**
Creative Business: Achieving Your Goals Through Creative Thinking and Action. Trade Paper. Palgrave Macmillan. New York, NY. 2004. 200p. ISBN:0-333-99735-2, ISBN13: 978-0-333-99735-2. Dewey:658.4/063. LCCN:2003-056340.
Audience: **g,l,u,f.**

Cartwright, Roger **HD62.5**
Creating the Entrepreneurial Organization. Trade Paper. John Wiley & Sons, Inc. Hoboken, NJ. 2002. 124p. Express Exec Ser. ISBN:1-84112-247-5, ISBN13: 978-1-84112-247-2. Dewey:658.11.
Audience: **u,f.**

Christensen, Clayton M., et al. **HD30.28.C54 2004**
Seeing What's Next: Using the Theories of Innovation to Predict Industry Change. Scott D. Anthony & Eric A. Roth (Authors). Trade Cloth. Harvard Business School Press. Boston, MA. 2004. 336p. ISBN:1-59139-185-7, ISBN13: 978-1-59139-185-2. Dewey:658.4/0355. LCCN:2004-004399.
Audience: **u,f.** *Choice, 2005.*

Christensen, Clayton M. & Raynor, Michael E. **HD53.C495 2003**
The Innovator's Solution: Creating and Sustaining Successful Growth. Trade Cloth. Harvard Business School Press. Boston, MA. 2003. 288p. ISBN:1-57851-852-0, ISBN13: 978-1-57851-852-4. Dewey:658.4/063. LCCN:2003-014328.
Audience: **u,f.**

Cirque Du Soleil, et al. **PS3604.O5654S76 2006**
The Spark: Igniting the Creative Fire That Lives Within Us All. Lyn Heward & John U. Bacon (Authors), Guy Laliberte (Foreword by). Trade Cloth. Doubleday Publishing. New York,

NY. 2006. 144p. ISBN:0-385-51651-7, ISBN13: 978-0-385-51651-8. Dewey:813/.6. LCCN:2005-053828.
Audience: **g,l,u,f.**

Dangelo, Mark **HD53**
Innovative Relevance: Realigning the Organization for Profit. Trade Paper. iUniverse, Inc. Lincoln, NE. 2005. 258p. ISBN:0-595-34246-9, ISBN13: 978-0-595-34246-4. Dewey:658.16.
Audience: **l,u,f.**

Davenport, Thomas H. & Prusak, Laurence **HD53.D38 2003**
What's the Big Idea?: Creating and Capitalizing on the Best Management Thinking. Trade Cloth. Harvard Business School Press. Boston, MA. 2003. 256p. ISBN:1-57851-931-4, ISBN13: 978-1-57851-931-6. Dewey:658. LCCN:2002-155934.
Audience: **u,f.** *Choice, 2003.*

DeGraff, Jeff & Lawrence, Katherine A. **HD58.8.D438 2002**
[e] Creativity at Work: Developing the Right Practices to Make Innovation Happen. E-Book. John Wiley & Sons, Inc. Hoboken, NJ. 2002. J-B-UMBS Ser. ISBN:0-7879-6653-3, ISBN13: 978-0-7879-6653-9. Dewey:658.4/063.
Audience: **g,l,u,f.**

Drucker Foundation Staff, et al. **HD53.O526 2002**
On Creativity, Innovation, and Renewal: A Leader to Leader Guide. Frances Hesselbein & Rob Johnston (Authors). Trade Cloth. John Wiley & Sons, Inc. Hoboken, NJ. 2002. 176p. J-B Drucker Foundation Ser., Vol. 71 ISBN:0-7879-6067-5, ISBN13: 978-0-7879-6067-4. Dewey:658.4. LCCN:2001-007586.
Audience: **u,f.**

Dudik, Evan Matthew **HD53.D83 2000**
Strategic Renaissance: New Thinking and Innovative Tools to Create Great Corporate Strategies. . . Using Insights from History and Science. Trade Cloth. Amacom. New York, NY. 2000. 259p. ISBN:0-8144-0551-7, ISBN13: 978-0-8144-0551-2. Dewey:658.4/012. LCCN:99-057944.
Audience: **l,u,f.**

Fagerberg, Jan (Editor), et al. **HC79.T4**
The Oxford Handbook of Innovation. David C. Mowery & Richard R. Nelson (Editors). Trade Paper. Oxford University Press, Inc. New York, NY. 2006. 680p. Oxford Handbooks Ser. ISBN:0-19-928680-9, ISBN13: 978-0-19-928680-5. Dewey:658.4063. LCCN:2004-276168.
Audience: **l,u,f.**

Gogatz, Arthur & Mondejar, Reuben **HD53.G64 2004**
Business Creativity: Breaking the Invisible Barriers. Cloth over Boards. Palgrave Macmillan. New York, NY. 2005. 256p. ISBN:1-4039-4509-8, ISBN13: 978-1-4039-4509-9. Dewey:658.4/094. LCCN:2004-056538.
Audience: **u,f.**

Gryskiewicz, Stan & Taylor, Sylvester **BS192.2.A1**
Making Creativity Practical: Innovation That Gets Results. Trade Paper. Center for Creative Leadership. Greensboro, NC. 2003. 31p. ISBN:1-882197-78-X, ISBN13: 978-1-882197-78-1. Dewey:224.1077.
Audience: **g,l,u,f.**

Hamel, Gary **HD538.H353 2002**
Leading the Revolution. Ed. 2. Trade Cloth. Harvard Business School Press. Boston, MA. 2004. 333p. ISBN:1-59139-146-6, ISBN13: 978-1-59139-146-3. Dewey:658.4/012.
Audience: **g,l,u,f.**

Honig, Bruce & Rostain, Alain **HD53.H66 2003**
Creative Collaboration: Simple Tools for Inspired Teamwork. Debbie Woodbury, Ann Gosch & Genevieve Del Rosario (Editors), Ralph Mapson (Illustrator), Nicole Phillips & Rich Lehl (Designed by). Trade Paper. Crisp Publications, Inc. Menlo Park, CA. 2003. 120p. A Fifty-Minute Series Book ISBN:1-56052-687-4, ISBN13: 978-1-56052-687-2. Dewey:658.4/022. LCCN:2003-105054.
Audience: **g,l,u,f.**

Howard, Christopher **HF5386.H845 2005**
Turning Passions into Profits: Three Steps to Wealth and Power. Trade Cloth. John Wiley & Sons, Inc. Hoboken, NJ. 2005. 272p. ISBN:0-471-71856-4, ISBN13: 978-0-471-71856-7. Dewey:650.1/2. LCCN:2004-024102.
Audience: **g,l,u,f.**

Klein, Maury **HB615.K6137 2003**
The Change Makers: From Carnegie to Gates, How the Great Entrepreneurs Transformed Ideas into Industries. Cloth over Boards. Henry Holt & Company. New York, NY. 2003. 336p. ISBN:0-8050-6914-3, ISBN13: 978-0-8050-6914-3. Dewey:338/.04/0973. LCCN:2002-032439.
Audience: **g,l,u,f.**

Kunstler, Barton Lee **HD53.K86 2004**
The Hothouse Effect: Intensify Creativity in Your Organization Using Secrets from History's Most Innovative Communities. Trade Cloth. Amacom. New York, NY. 2003. 256p. ISBN:0-8144-0769-2, ISBN13: 978-0-8144-0769-1. Dewey:658.3/14. LCCN:2003-012012.
Audience: **g,l,u,f.** *Choice, 2004.*

Leonard, Dorothy & Swap, Walter **HD53.L46 2005**
When Sparks Fly: Igniting Creativity in Groups. Trade Paper. Harvard Business School Press. Boston, MA. 2005. 256p. ISBN:1-59139-793-6, ISBN13: 978-1-59139-793-9. Dewey:658.4/036.
Audience: **l,u,f.** *Choice, 2000.*

Martin, Joyce **HD53**
Profiting from Multiple Intelligences in the Workplace. Trade Paper. Crown House Publishing. Carmarthen, 2005. 256p. ISBN:1-904424-65-1, ISBN13: 978-1-904424-65-9. Dewey:658.4/03. LCCN:2004-111449.
Audience: **l,u,f.**

Mattimore, Bryan W. **HD53 .M374 1994**
99 Percent Inspiration: Tips, Tales and Techniques for Liberating Your Business Creativity. Trade Paper. Amacom. New York, NY. 1993. 176p. ISBN:0-8144-7788-7, ISBN13: 978-0-8144-7788-5. Dewey:650.1. LCCN:93-028469.
Audience: **g,l,u,f.**

Morgan, Gareth **HD38.M612 1997**
Imaginization: New Mindsets for Seeing, Organizing and Managing. Book, Other. Berrett-Koehler Publishers, Inc. San Francisco, CA. 1997. 345p. ISBN:1-57675-026-4, ISBN13: 978-1-57675-026-1. Dewey:658.4. LCCN:97-021081.
Audience: **g,l,u,f.**

Nemiro, Jill **HD66.N45 2004**
Creativity in Virtual Teams: Key Components for Success. Trade Paper. John Wiley & Sons, Inc. Hoboken, NJ. 2004. 364p. Collaborative Work Systems Ser. ISBN:0-7879-7114-6, ISBN13: 978-0-7879-7114-4. Dewey:658.4/07124. LCCN:2004-030444.
Audience: **u,f.**

Perelman, Michael **KF2980**
Steal This Idea: Intellectual Property Rights and the Corporate Confiscation of Creativity. Trade Paper. Palgrave Macmillan. New York, NY. 2004. 272p. ISBN:1-4039-6713-X, ISBN13: 978-1-4039-6713-8. Dewey:346.7304/8.
Audience: **g,l,u,f.** *Choice, 2002.*

Peters, Tom **HD53.P48 1999**
The Circle of Innovation: You Can't Shrink Your Way to Greatness. Trade Paper. Knopf Publishing Group. New York, NY. 1999. 544p. ISBN:0-679-75765-1, ISBN13: 978-0-679-75765-8. Dewey:658.406. LCCN:97-074755.
Audience: **g,l,u,f.**

Rich, Jason R. **HD53.R529 2003**
Brain Storm: Tap into Your Creativity to Generate Awesome Ideas and Remarkable Results. Trade Paper. Career Press, Inc. Franklin Lks, NJ. 2003. 192p. ISBN:1-56414-668-5, ISBN13: 978-1-56414-668-7. Dewey:650.1. LCCN:2002-191191.
Audience: **g,l,u,f.**

Schrage, Michael **HD45.S368 2000**
Serious Play: How the World's Best Companies Simulate to Innovate. Trade Cloth. Harvard Business School Press. Boston, MA. 1999. 272p. ISBN:0-87584-814-1, ISBN13: 978-0-87584-814-3. Dewey:658.4/0352. LCCN:99-023757.
Audience: **g,l,u,f.** *Choice, 2000.*

Schwartz, Evan I. **HD53.S39 2004**
Juice: The Creative Fuel That Drives World-Class Inventors. Trade Cloth. Harvard Business School Press. Boston, MA. 2004. 224p. ISBN:1-59139-288-8, ISBN13: 978-1-59139-288-0. Dewey:658.5/75. LCCN:2004-005827.
Audience: **l,u,f.**

Storey, John & Salaman, Graeme **HD45.S845 2004**
Managers of Innovation: Insights into Making Innovation Happen. Trade Paper. Blackwell Publishing, Inc. Malden, MA. 2004. 208p. Management, Organizations, and Business Ser. ISBN:1-4051-2461-X, ISBN13: 978-1-4051-2461-4. Dewey:658.4/063. LCCN:2004-007685.
Audience: **u,f.**

Sutton, Robert I. **HD53 .S883**
Weird Ideas That Work. Trade Paper. Simon & Schuster. New York, NY. 2002. 256p. ISBN:0-7432-2788-3, ISBN13: 978-0-7432-2788-9. Dewey:658.
Audience: **g,l,u,f.**

Syrett, Michel & Lammiman, Jean **HD53.S974 2002**
The Innovative Individual. Trade Paper. John Wiley & Sons, Inc. Hoboken, NJ. 2002. 110p. Express Exec Ser. ISBN:1-84112-317-X, ISBN13: 978-1-84112-317-2. Dewey:658.421.
Audience: **g,l,u,f.**

Management Function > General Management > Managerial Skills > Entrepreneurship

Bagley, Constance E. & Dauchy, Craig E. **KF390.B84B34 2003**
The Entrepreneur's Guide to Business Law. Ed. 2. Paper Text. Thomson South-Western. Mason, OH. 2002. 752p. Business Law Ser. ISBN:0-324-04291-4, ISBN13: 978-0-324-04291-7. Dewey:346.7307. LCCN:2002-067215.
Audience: **u,f.**

Bhide, Amar V. **HD62.5.B49 2003**
The Origin and Evolution of New Businesses. Trade Paper. Oxford University Press, Inc. New York, NY. 2003. 432p. ISBN:0-19-517031-8, ISBN13: 978-0-19-517031-3. Dewey:658.11.
Audience: **l,u,f.**

Boulton, Chris & Turner, Patrick **HB615.B668 2005**
Entrepreneurship. Trade Paper. John Wiley & Sons, Inc. Hoboken, NJ. 2005. 250p. Wiley Executive MBA Ser. ISBN:0-470-82138-8, ISBN13: 978-0-470-82138-1. Dewey:338.04095. LCCN:2005-275559.
Audience: **u,f.**

Collins, Jim & Porras, Jerry I. **HF5386**
Built to Last: Successful Habits of Visionary Companies. Trade Cloth. HarperCollins Publishers. New York, NY. 2004. 368p. ISBN:0-06-056610-8, ISBN13: 978-0-06-056610-4. Dewey:338.7/09.
Audience: **g,l,u,f.**

Crouch, Colin **HB501**
Capitalist Diversity and Change: Recombinant Governance and Institutional Entrepreneurs. Trade Paper. Oxford University Press, Inc. New York, NY. 2005. 192p. ISBN:0-19-928665-5, ISBN13: 978-0-19-928665-2. Dewey:330.12/2. LCCN:2005-020675.
Audience: **u,f.**

Drucker, Peter F. **HB615**
Innovation and Entrepreneurship: Practice and Principles. Ed. 2. Paper Text. Elsevier Science & Technology Books. Saint Louis, MO. 2004. 272p. ISBN:0-7506-4388-9, ISBN13: 978-0-7506-4388-7. Dewey:658.4/21.
Audience: **l,u,f.** B *Choice, 1985.*

Foster, Richard & Kaplan, Sarah **HD58.8 .F687**
Creative Destruction: Why Companies That Are Built to Last Underperform the Market - And How to Successfully Transform Them. Trade Paper. Doubleday Publishing. New York, NY. 2003. 384p. ISBN:0-385-50134-X, ISBN13: 978-0-385-50134-7. Dewey:658.4/06.
Audience: **g,l,u,f.**

Gerber, Michael E. **HD62.7**
The E-Myth Revisited. Trade Paper. HarperCollins Publishers. New York, NY. 2005. 288p. ISBN:0-06-076661-1, ISBN13: 978-0-06-076661-0. Dewey:658.022.
Audience: **g,l,u,f.**

Govindarajan, Vijay & Trimble, Chris **HD62.5.G68 2005**
Ten Rules for Strategic Innovators: From Idea to Execution. Trade Cloth. Harvard Business School Press. Boston, MA. 2005. 288p. ISBN:1-59139-758-8, ISBN13: 978-1-59139-758-8. Dewey:658.4/06. LCCN:2005-014230.
Audience: **l,u,f.**

Harris, Wendy Beech & Beech, Wendy **HC29.H37 2001**
Against All Odds: Ten Entrepreneurs Who Followed Their Hearts and Found Success. Trade Cloth. John Wiley & Sons, Inc. Hoboken, NJ. 2001. 256p. Black Enterprise Ser. ISBN:0-471-37472-5, ISBN13: 978-0-471-37472-5. Dewey:338.04092396073. LCCN:00-043584.
Audience: **g,l,u,f.**

Kaplan, Jack M. **HD62.5.K35 2001**
Getting Started in Entrepreneurship. Trade Paper. John Wiley & Sons, Inc. Hoboken, NJ. 2001. 304p. Getting Started in Ser., Vol. 21 ISBN:0-471-29456-X, ISBN13: 978-0-471-29456-6. Dewey:658.4/21. LCCN:00-047988.
Audience: **g,l,u,f.**

Matthews, Jana B., et al. **HD62.5.M366 2003**
Lessons from the Edge: Survival Skills for Starting and Growing a Company. Jeff Dennis & Peter Economy (Authors). Trade Cloth. Oxford University Press, Inc. New York, NY. 2003. 288p. ISBN:0-19-516825-9, ISBN13: 978-0-19-516825-9. Dewey:658.1/142. LCCN:2003-007970.
Audience: **u,f.**

McGrath, Rita Gunther & MacMillan, Ian C. **HB615.M3735 2000**
Entrepreneurial Mindset: Strategies for Continuously Creating Opportunity in an Age of Uncertainty. Trade Cloth. Harvard Business School Press. Boston, MA. 2000. 368p. ISBN:0-87584-834-6, ISBN13: 978-0-87584-834-1. Dewey:658.4/21. LCCN:00-033514.
Audience: **l,u,f.**

McKnight, Thomas K. **HD62.5.M395 2004**
Will It Fly? How to Know If Your New Business Idea Has Wings... Before You Take the Leap. Trade Paper. Financial Times/Prentice Hall. Paramus, NJ. 2003. 368p. Financial Times Prentice Hall Books ISBN:0-13-046221-7, ISBN13: 978-0-13-046221-3. Dewey:658.11. LCCN:2004-299983.
Audience: **g,l,u,f.**

Meier, David **HD2346.U5M45 2006**
Make Your Life Tax Deductible: Easy Techniques to Reduce Your Taxes and Start Building Wealth Immediately. Trade Paper. McGraw-Hill Companies, The. New York, NY. 2005. 256p. ISBN:0-07-146762-9, ISBN13: 978-0-07-146762-9. Dewey:658.15/92. LCCN:2005-025265.
Audience: **g,l,u,f.**

Miles, Raymond E., et al. **HD69.S8M55 2005**
Collaborative Entrepreneurship: How Communities of Networked Firms Use Continuous Innovation to Create Economic Wealth. Grant Miles & Charles C. Snow (Authors). Saddle Stitched, Cloth over Boards. Stanford University Press. Palo Alto, CA. 2005. 144p. ISBN:0-8047-4801-2, ISBN13: 978-0-8047-4801-8. Dewey:658.4063. LCCN:2005-002979.
Audience: **u,f.**

Moltz, Barry **HD62.5.M64 2003**
You Need to Be a Little Crazy: The Truth about Starting and Growing Your Business. Trade Paper. Kaplan Publishing. Chicago, IL. 2003. 208p. ISBN:0-7931-8018-X, ISBN13: 978-0-7931-8018-9. Dewey:658.1/1. LCCN:2003-014116.
Audience: **g,l,u,f.**

Moore, Dorothy Perrin **HD6072.6.U5M66 2000**
CareerPreneurs: Lessons from Leading Women Entrepreneurs on Building a Career Without Boundaries. Trade Cloth. Consulting Psychologists Press, Inc. Mountain View, CA. 2000. 198p. ISBN:0-89106-144-4, ISBN13: 978-0-89106-144-1. Dewey:658.4/21/0820973. LCCN:00-022628.
Audience: **g,l,u,f.** *Choice, 2001.*

Moss, Wes **HC102.5.A2M67 2005**
Starting from Scratch: Secrets from 21 Ordinary People Who Made the Entrepreneurial Leap. Cloth Text. Kaplan Publishing. Chicago, IL. 2005. 224p. ISBN:1-4195-2106-3, ISBN13: 978-1-4195-2106-5. Dewey:338/.04/092273 B. LCCN:2005-019395.
Audience: **g,l,u,f.**

Sloan, Jeffrey & Sloan, Richard **HD62.5.S576 2005**
StartupNation: America's Leading Entrepreneurial Experts Reveal the Secrets to Building a Blockbuster Business. Trade Paper. Doubleday Publishing. New York, NY. 2005. 304p. ISBN:0-385-51248-1, ISBN13: 978-0-385-51248-0. Dewey:658.1/1. LCCN:2004-065547.
Audience: **l,u,f.**

Sull, Donald N. & Wang, Yong **HB615.S94 2005**
Made in China: What Western Managers Can Learn from Trailblazing Chinese Entrepreneurs. Book, Other. Harvard Business School Press. Boston, MA. 2005. 256p. ISBN:1-59139-715-4, ISBN13: 978-1-59139-715-1. Dewey:658.4/21. LCCN:2005-000321.
Audience: **g,l,u,f.** *Choice, 2006.*

Tracy, Brian S. **HF5386.T8139 2000**
The 100 Absolutely Unbreakable Laws of Business Success. Trade Cloth. Berrett-Koehler Publishers, Inc. San Francisco, CA. 2000. 319p. ISBN:1-57675-107-4, ISBN13: 978-1-57675-107-7. Dewey:650.1. LCCN:00-026693.
Audience: **l,u,f.**

Tracy, Brian S. **HF5386.T8139 2000**
The 100 Absolutely Unbreakable Laws of Business Success. Book, Other. Berrett-Koehler Publishers, Inc. San Francisco, CA. 2001. 336p. ISBN:1-57675-126-0, ISBN13: 978-1-57675-126-8. Dewey:650.1. LCCN:00-026693.
Audience: **l,u,f.**

Vise, David A. & Malseed, Mark **TK5105.885.G66**
The Google Story: Inside the Hottest Business, Media, and Technology Success of Our Time. Trade Paper. Random House Adult Trade Publishing Group. New York, NY. 2006. 336p. ISBN:0-553-38366-3, ISBN13: 978-0-553-38366-9. Dewey:338.7/6102504/0973.
Audience: **g,l,u,f.**

Wallace, Robert **HD62.47.W338 2004**
Strategic Partnerships: An Entrepreneur's Guide to Joint Ventures and Alliances. Cloth Text. Kaplan Publishing. Chicago, IL. 2004. 210p. ISBN:0-7931-8828-8, ISBN13: 978-0-7931-8828-4. Dewey:658/.044. LCCN:2004-012321.
Audience: **u,f.**

Management Function > General Management > Managerial Skills > International Perspectives

Adler, Nancy J., et al. **HD58.7**
From Boston to Beijing: Managing with a World View. John Szilagyi & Robert Bloom (Authors). Digital, Other. Thomson South-Western. Mason, OH. 2001. 408p. ISBN:0-324-07475-1, ISBN13: 978-0-324-07475-8. Dewey:658.049. LCCN:00-046396.
Audience: **l,u,f.** *Choice, 2002.*

Ball **HD62.4 .B34**
International Business: the Challenge of Global Competition. Ed. 9. Video, VHS Format. Glencoe/McGraw-Hill. Columbus, OH. 2004. ISBN:0-07-253801-5, ISBN13: 978-0-07-253801-4. Dewey:658/.049.
Audience: **l,u,f.**

Blenkhorn, David L. & Fleisher, Craig S. (Editors) **HD38**
Competitive Intelligence and Global Business. Trade Cloth. Greenwood Publishing Group, Inc. Portsmouth, NH. 2005. 312p. ISBN:0-275-98140-1, ISBN13: 978-0-275-98140-2. Dewey:658.4/72. LCCN:2004-018110.
Audience: **l,u,f.**

Conklin, David W. (Editor) **HD62.4.C3685 2006**
Cases in the Environment of Business: International Perspectives. Paper Text. SAGE Publications, Inc. Thousand Oaks, CA. 2005. 624p. The Ivey Casebook Ser. ISBN:1-4129-1436-1, ISBN13: 978-1-4129-1436-9. Dewey:658/.049. LCCN:2005-003579.
Audience: **u,f.** *Choice, 2006.*

Doz, Yves L., et al. **HD62.4.D688 2001**
From Global to Metanational: How Companies Win in the Knowledge Economy. Jose Santos & Peter Williamson (Authors). Trade Cloth. Harvard Business School Press. Boston, MA. 2001. 272p. ISBN:0-87584-870-2, ISBN13: 978-0-87584-870-9. Dewey:658.4/038. LCCN:2001-024748.
Audience: **g,l,u,f.**

Govindarajan, Vijay & Gupta, Anil K. **HD62.4.G68 2001**
The Quest for Global Dominance: Transforming Global Presence into Global Competitive Advantage. Trade Cloth. John Wiley & Sons, Inc. Hoboken, NJ. 2001. 320p. ISBN:0-7879-5721-6, ISBN13: 978-0-7879-5721-6. Dewey:658/.049. LCCN:2001-002207.
Audience: **l,u,f.** *Choice, 2002.*

Hartman, Laura P. (Editor), et al. **HF5549**
Rising above Sweatshops: Innovative Approaches to Global Labor Challenges. Denis G. Arnold & Richard E. Wokutch (Editors). Trade Cloth. Greenwood Publishing Group, Inc. Portsmouth, NH. 2003. 440p. ISBN:1-56720-618-2, ISBN13: 978-1-56720-618-0. Dewey:658.3/009172/4. LCCN:2003-052901.
Audience: **l,u,f.** *Choice, 2004.*

Head, Simon **HC106.83**
The New Ruthless Economy: Work and Power in the Digital Age. Trade Paper. Oxford University Press, Inc. New York, NY. 2005. 240p. ISBN:0-19-517983-8, ISBN13: 978-0-19-517983-5. Dewey:330.973.
Audience: **l,u,f.**

Hinds, Pamela & Kiesler, Sara (Editors) **HD51.D57 2002**
Distributed Work. Trade Cloth. MIT Press. Cambridge, MA. 2002. 495p. ISBN:0-262-08305-1, ISBN13: 978-0-262-08305-8. Dewey:658.4/036. LCCN:2001-056237.
Audience: **l,u,f.** *Choice, 2002.*

Hodgetts, Richard M., et al. **HD62.4.H63 2006**
International Management: Culture, Strategy, and Behavior. Ed. 6. Fred Luthans & Jonathan P. Doh (Authors). Trade Cloth. McGraw-Hill Higher Education. Burr Ridge, IL. 2005. 672p. ISBN:0-07-296108-2, ISBN13: 978-0-07-296108-9. Dewey:658.049. LCCN:2004-057945.
Audience: **l,u,f.**

House, Robert J. (Editor), et al. **HD57.7.L4323 2004**
Culture, Leadership, and Organizations: The GLOBE Study of 62 Societies. Paul J. Hanges, Mansour Javidan, Peter W. Dorfman & Vipin Gupta (Editors). Trade Cloth. SAGE Publications, Inc. Thousand Oaks, CA. 2004. 848p. ISBN:0-7619-2401-9, ISBN13: 978-0-7619-2401-2. Dewey:302.3/5. LCCN:2003-024360.
Audience: **u,f.** *Choice, 2005.*

Lan, Yi-Chen & Unhelkar, Bhuvan **HD38.5.G575 2006**
Global Integrated Supply Chain Systems. Trade Paper, Perfect. Idea Group Publishing. Hershey, PA. 2005. 349p. ISBN:1-59140-612-9, ISBN13: 978-1-59140-612-9. Dewey:658.7/2. LCCN:2005-013551.
Audience: **l,u,f.**

Laudicina, Paul A. **HF5351**
World Out of Balance: Navigating Global Risks to Seize Competitive Advantage. Trade Cloth. McGraw-Hill Companies, The. New York, NY. 2004. 256p. ISBN:0-07-143918-8, ISBN13: 978-0-07-143918-3. Dewey:338.5. LCCN:2005-298076.
Audience: **l,u,f.**

Magee, David **HD9710.U54N555 2003**
Turnaround: How Carlos Ghosn Rescued Nissan. Trade Cloth. HarperCollins Publishers. New York, NY. 2003. 256p. ISBN:0-06-051485-X, ISBN13: 978-0-06-051485-3. Dewey:338.7/62922/092. LCCN:2002-035745.
Audience: **g,l,u,f.**

Murtha, Thomas P., et al. **HF5415.153.M87 2001**
Managing New Industry Creation: Global Knowledge Formation and Entrepreneurship in High Technology. Stefanie Ann Lenway & Jeffrey A. Hart (Authors). Trade Cloth. Stanford University Press. Palo Alto, CA. 2001. 280p. Stanford Business Books ISBN:0-8047-4228-6, ISBN13: 978-0-8047-4228-3. Dewey:658.5/75. LCCN:2001-049225.
Audience: **l,u,f.**

Ohmae, Kenichi **HF1418.5.O46 2001**
The Borderless World: Power and Strategy in the Interlinked Economy. Trade Paper. HarperCollins Publishers. New York, NY. 1999. 276p. ISBN:0-88730-967-4, ISBN13: 978-0-88730-967-0. Dewey:339. LCCN:99-012126.
Audience: **g,l,u,f.** *Choice, 1991.*

Ohmae, Kenichi **HD30.28**
The Invisible Continent: Four Strategic Imperatives of the New Economy. Trade Paper. HarperCollins Publishers. New York, NY. 2001. 272p. ISBN:0-06-095742-5, ISBN13: 978-0-06-095742-1. Dewey:658.4/012.
Audience: **g,l,u,f.** *Choice, 2001.*

Ricks, David & Bertola, Giuseppe **HD62.4**
Blunders in International Business. Ed. 4. Trade Paper. Blackwell Publishing, Inc. Malden, MA. 2006. 192p. ISBN:1-4051-3492-5, ISBN13: 978-1-4051-3492-7. Dewey:658/.049. LCCN:2005-057059.
Audience: **u,f.**

Steers, Richard M. & Nardon, Luciara **HD62.4.S736 2006**
Managing in the Global Economy. Trade Paper. M. E. Sharpe Inc. Armonk, NY. 2005. 352p. ISBN:0-7656-1551-7, ISBN13: 978-0-7656-1551-0. Dewey:658/.049. LCCN:2005-007422.
Audience: **l,u,f.**

Stroh, Linda K., et al. **HD30.4.I574 2004**
International Assignments: An Integration of Strategy, Research, and Practice. J. Sewart Black, Mark E. Mendenhall & Hal B. Gregersen (Authors). Trade Paper. Lawrence Erlbaum Associates, Inc. Mahwah, NJ. 2004. 304p. ISBN:0-8058-5050-3, ISBN13: 978-0-8058-5050-5. Dewey:658.4/07. LCCN:2004-050610.
Audience: **l,u,f.**

Thomas, David C. **HD62.4.T488 2002**
Essentials of International Management: A Cross-Cultural Perspective. Paper Text. SAGE Publications, Inc. Thousand Oaks, CA. 2001. 344p. ISBN:0-7619-2181-8, ISBN13: 978-0-7619-2181-3. Dewey:658/.049. LCCN:2001-001626.
Audience: **l,u,f.** *Choice, 2002.*

Yourdon, Edward **HD2365.Y68 2005**
Outsource: Competing in the Global Productivity Race. Trade Cloth. Prentice Hall PTR. Upper Saddle River, NJ. 2004. 304p. ISBN:0-13-147571-1, ISBN13: 978-0-13-147571-7. Dewey:658.4/058. LCCN:2004-108578.
Audience: **g,l,u,f.**

Management Function > General Management > Managerial Skills > Leadership

Allard, Kenneth **HD57.7.A619 2004**
Business As War: Battling for Competitive Advantage. Trade Cloth. John Wiley & Sons, Inc. Hoboken, NJ. 2004. 240p. ISBN:0-471-46854-1, ISBN13: 978-0-471-46854-7. Dewey:658.4. LCCN:2003-020607.
Audience: **l,u,f.**

Bennis, Warren **HD38.2**
On Becoming a Leader: The Leadership Classic. Ed. 2. Trade Paper. Basic Books. New York, NY. 2003. 256p. Art of Mentoring Ser. ISBN:0-7382-0817-5, ISBN13: 978-0-7382-0817-6. Dewey:158/.4. LCCN:2003-100205.
Audience: **g,l,u,f.**

Bennis, Warren (Editor), et al. **HD57.7.F87 2001**
The Future of Leadership: Today's Top Leadership Thinkers Speak to Tomorrow's Leaders. Gretchen M. Spreitzer & Thomas Cummings (Editors). Trade Cloth. John Wiley & Sons, Inc. Hoboken, NJ. 2001. 336p. Jossey Bass Business and Management Ser. ISBN:0-7879-5567-1, ISBN13: 978-0-7879-5567-0. Dewey:658.4/092. LCCN:2001-000575.
Audience: **l,u,f.** *Choice, 2001.*

Buckingham, Marcus & Coffman, Curt **HD38.2.B83 1999**
First, Break All the Rules: What the World's Greatest Managers Do Differently. Trade Cloth. Simon & Schuster. New York, NY. 1999. 272p. ISBN:0-684-85286-1, ISBN13: 978-0-684-85286-7. Dewey:658.4. LCCN:99-019452.
Audience: **l,u,f.**

Charan, Ram, et al. **HD57.7.C474 2001**
The Leadership Pipeline: How to Build the Leadership-Powered Company. Stephen Drotter & James L. Noel (Authors). Trade Cloth. John Wiley & Sons, Inc. Hoboken, NJ. 2000. 272p. ISBN:0-7879-5172-2, ISBN13: 978-0-7879-5172-6. Dewey:658.4/092. LCCN:00-011188.
Audience: **l,u,f.**

Cohen, Allan R. & Bradford, David L. **HD58.9.C64 2005**
Influence Without Authority. Ed. 2. Trade Cloth. John Wiley & Sons, Inc. Hoboken, NJ. 2005. 320p. ISBN:0-471-46330-2, ISBN13: 978-0-471-46330-6. Dewey:658.4/09. LCCN:2004-027078.
Audience: **g,l,u.**

Cohen, William A. **HD57.7.C643 2005**
Secrets of Special Ops Leadership: Dare the Impossible—Achieve the Extraordinary. Trade Cloth. Amacom. New York, NY. 2005. 256p. ISBN:0-8144-0840-0, ISBN13: 978-0-8144-0840-7. Dewey:658.4/092. LCCN:2005-010447.
Audience: **g,l,u.**

Collins, Jim **HD57.7.C645 2001**
Good to Great: Why Some Companies Make the Leap... and Others Don't. Trade Cloth. HarperCollins Publishers. New York, NY. 2001. 320p. ISBN:0-06-662099-6, ISBN13: 978-0-06-662099-2. Dewey:658. LCCN:2001-024818.
Audience: **g,l,u,f.** *Choice, 2002.*

Coughlin, Lin (Editor), et al. **HD57.7.E55 2005**
Enlightened Power: How Women Are Transforming the Practice of Leadership. Ellen Wingard & Keith Hollihan (Editors). Trade Cloth. John Wiley & Sons, Inc. Hoboken, NJ. 2005. 576p. ISBN:0-7879-7787-X, ISBN13: 978-0-7879-7787-0. Dewey:658.4/092/082. LCCN:2005-002449.
Audience: **g,l,u.**

Dalla Costa, John **HF5387.D25 1998**
The Ethical Imperative: Why Moral Leadership Is Good Business. Cloth Text. Addison-Wesley Longman, Inc. Boston, MA. 1998. 368p. ISBN:0-201-33983-8, ISBN13: 978-0-201-33983-3. Dewey:174/.4. LCCN:98-014109.
Audience: **g,l,u,f.** *Choice, 1998.*

Gandossy, Robert P. & Sonnenfeld, Jeffrey A. (Editors) **HD57.7.L4314 2004**
Leadership and Governance from the Inside Out. Trade Cloth. John Wiley & Sons, Inc. Hoboken, NJ. 2004. 320p. ISBN:0-471-67185-1, ISBN13: 978-0-471-67185-5. Dewey:658.4. LCCN:2004-007663.
Audience: **l,u,f.**

Hamel, Gary **HD538.H353 2002**
Leading the Revolution. Ed. 2. Trade Cloth. Harvard Business School Press. Boston, MA. 2004. 333p. ISBN:1-59139-146-6, ISBN13: 978-1-59139-146-3. Dewey:658.4/012.
Audience: **g,l,u,f.**

Harvard Business School Staff (Editor) **HD57.7.R468 2005**
Becoming an Effective Leader. Trade Paper. Harvard Business School Press. Boston, MA. 2005. 192p. The Results Driven Manager Ser. ISBN:1-59139-780-4, ISBN13: 978-1-59139-780-9. Dewey:658.4/092. LCCN:2004-022261.
Audience: **l,u,f.**

Hesselbein, Frances **HD57.7**
The Leader of the Future. Trade Cloth. John Wiley & Sons, Inc. Hoboken, NJ. 2000. 319p. ISBN:0-7879-5320-2, ISBN13: 978-0-7879-5320-1. Dewey:658.4/092.
Audience: **l,u.**

Hesselbein, Frances (Editor), et al. **HD57.7.L4375 2002**
Leading for Innovation: And Organizing for Results. Marshall Goldsmith & Iain Somerville (Editors). Trade Cloth. John Wiley & Sons, Inc. Hoboken, NJ. 2001. 336p. J-B Drucker Foundation Ser., Vol. 10 ISBN:0-7879-5359-8, ISBN13: 978-0-7879-5359-1. Dewey:658.4/092. LCCN:2001-005165.
Audience: **l,u,f.**

Higgins, Monica C. **HD57.7.H528 2005**
Career Imprints: Creating Leaders Across an Industry. Edgar H. Schein (Foreword by). Trade Cloth. John Wiley & Sons, Inc. Hoboken, NJ. 2005. 416p. J-B Warren Bennis Ser. ISBN:0-7879-7751-9, ISBN13: 978-0-7879-7751-1. Dewey:658.4/092. LCCN:2004-030568.
Audience: **l,u.**

House, Robert J. (Editor), et al. **HD57.7.L4323 2004**
Culture, Leadership, and Organizations: The GLOBE Study of 62 Societies. Paul J. Hanges, Mansour Javidan, Peter W. Dorfman & Vipin Gupta (Editors). Trade Cloth. SAGE Publications, Inc. Thousand Oaks, CA. 2004. 848p. ISBN:0-7619-2401-9, ISBN13: 978-0-7619-2401-2. Dewey:302.3/5. LCCN:2003-024360.
Audience: **u,f.** *Choice, 2005.*

Hughes, Richard L. & Beatty, Katherine M. **HD57.7.H84 2005**
Becoming a Strategic Leader: Your Role in Your Organization's Enduring Success. Trade Cloth. John Wiley & Sons, Inc. Hoboken, NJ. 2005. 288p. J-B CCL (Center for Creative Leadership) Ser. ISBN:0-7879-6867-6, ISBN13: 978-0-7879-6867-0. Dewey:658.4/092. LCCN:2004-025830.
Audience: **l,u.**

Kotter, John P. **HD57.7.K66 1990**
A Force for Change: How Leadership Differs from Management. Trade Cloth. Simon & Schuster. New York, NY. 1990. 192p. ISBN:0-02-918465-7, ISBN13: 978-0-02-918465-3. Dewey:658.4/092. LCCN:89-077323.
Audience: **l,u.**

Kotter, John P. **HD58.8.K65 1996**
Leading Change. Trade Cloth. Harvard Business School Press. Boston, MA. 1996. 208p. ISBN:0-87584-747-1, ISBN13: 978-0-87584-747-4. Dewey:658.4/06. LCCN:96-020263.
Audience: **l,u.**

Kouzes, James M. & Posner, Barry Z. **HD57.7.K678 2003**
Credibility: How Leaders Gain and Lose It, Why People Demand It. Ed. 2. Trade Paper. John Wiley & Sons, Inc. Hoboken, NJ. 2003. 384p. J-B Leadership Challenge Ser., :Kouzes/Posner Ser. ISBN:0-7879-6464-6, ISBN13: 978-0-7879-6464-1. Dewey:658.4/092. LCCN:2002-043855.
Audience: **g,l,u.**

Krames, Jeffrey A. **HD58.8**
What the Best CEOs Know: 7 Exceptional Leaders and Their Lessons for Transforming Any Business. Trade Paper, Perfect. McGraw-Hill Companies, The. New York, NY. 2005. 250p. ISBN:0-07-146252-X, ISBN13: 978-0-07-146252-5. Dewey:658.4/06.
Audience: **g,l.**

Maxwell, John C. **HD57.7**
Developing the Leaders Around You: How to Help Others Reach Their Full Potential. Trade Paper, Perfect. Nelson Business. Nashville, TN. 2005. 224p. ISBN:0-7852-8111-8, ISBN13: 978-0-7852-8111-5. Dewey:658.4/092.
Audience: **l,u.**

Menkes, Justin **HD38.2.M4623 2005**
Executive Intelligence: What All Great Leaders Have. Trade Cloth. HarperCollins Publishers. New York, NY. 2005. 336p. ISBN:0-06-078187-4, ISBN13: 978-0-06-078187-3. Dewey:658.4/094. LCCN:2005-049635.
Audience: **l,u,f.**

Pandya, Mukul, et al. **HD57.7**
Nightly Business Report Presents Lasting Leadership: What You Can Learn from the Top 25 Business People of our Times. Knowledge@Wharton Staff, Jeffrey Brown, Sandeep Junnarkar, Robbie Shell & Susan Warner (Authors). Trade Cloth. Wharton School Publishing. Upper Saddle River, NJ. 2004. 256p. ISBN:0-13-153118-2, ISBN13: 978-0-13-153118-5. Dewey:658.4/092. LCCN:2004-109360.
Audience: **l,u.** *Choice, 2005.*

Perseus Publishing Staff **HD31 .B426**
Best Practice: Ideas and Insights from the World's Foremost Business Thinkers. Library Binding. Sagebrush Education Resources. Caledonia, MN. 2003. ISBN:0-613-91251-9, ISBN13: 978-0-613-91251-8. Dewey:658.
Audience: **l,u.**

Sayles, Leonard R. & Smith, Cynthia J. **HV6768**
The Rise of the Rogue Executive: How Good Companies Go Bad and How to Stop the Destruction. Trade Cloth. Prentice Hall PTR. Upper Saddle River, NJ. 2005. 288p. ISBN:0-13-147772-2, ISBN13: 978-0-13-147772-8. Dewey:174/.4. LCCN:2005-924352.
Audience: **g,l,u,f.** *Choice, 2006.*

Segil, Larraine (Editor), et al. **HD69.S8P37 2002**
Partnering: The New Face of Leadership. James Belasco & Marshall Goldsmith (Editors). Trade Cloth. Amacom. New York, NY. 2002. 288p. ISBN:0-8144-0757-9, ISBN13: 978-0-8144-0757-8. Dewey:658. LCCN:2002-011116.
Audience: **l,u.** *Choice, 2003.*

Welch, Jack & Byrne, John A. **HD9697.A3**
Jack: Straight from the Gut. Trade Paper. Warner Books, Inc. New York, NY. 2003. 496p. ISBN:0-446-69068-6, ISBN13: 978-0-446-69068-3. Dewey:338.7/62138/092.
Audience: **g,l,u,f.**

Wheatley, Margaret J. **HD57.7**
Leadership and the New Science: Discovering Order in a Chaotic World. Ed. 2. Trade Paper. Berrett-Koehler Publishers, Inc. San Francisco, CA. 2000. 215p. ISBN:1-57675-119-8, ISBN13: 978-1-57675-119-0. Dewey:500. LCCN:99-016514.
Audience: **l,u.** *Choice, 2000.*

Wills, Garry **HM141**
Certain Trumpets: The Nature of Leadership. Trade Paper. Simon & Schuster. New York, NY. 1995. 336p. ISBN:0-684-80138-8, ISBN13: 978-0-684-80138-4. Dewey:303.3/4. LCCN:94-006526.
Audience: **g,l,u.**

Wren, J. Thomas **HM141.L375 1995**
The Leader's Companion: Insights on Leadership Through the Ages. Trade Paper. Simon & Schuster. New York, NY. 1995. 376p. ISBN:0-02-874091-2, ISBN13: 978-0-02-874091-1. Dewey:303.3/4/09. LCCN:95-002850.
Audience: **g,l,u.**

Management Function > General Management > Managerial Skills > Management Theory

Andriessen, Daniel **HD53.A49 2004**
Making Sense of Intellectual Capital: Designing a Method for the Valuation of Intangibles. Trade Paper. Elsevier Science & Technology Books. Saint Louis, MO. 2003. 456p. ISBN:0-7506-7774-0, ISBN13: 978-0-7506-7774-5. Dewey:658.4/038. LCCN:2003-060685.
Audience: **u,f.**

Berry, Anthony J., et al. **HD31.M29196 2005**
Management Control: Theories, Issues and Performance. Ed. 2. Jane Broadbent & David Otley (Authors). Trade Paper, Saddle Stitched. Palgrave Macmillan. New York, NY. 2005. 350p. ISBN:1-4039-3535-1, ISBN13: 978-1-4039-3535-9. Dewey:658.4/013. LCCN:2004-063622.
Audience: **u,f.**

Buckingham, Marcus & Coffman, Curt **HD38.2.B83 1999**
First, Break All the Rules: What the World's Greatest Managers Do Differently. Trade Cloth. Simon & Schuster. New York, NY. 1999. 272p. ISBN:0-684-85286-1, ISBN13: 978-0-684-85286-7. Dewey:658.4. LCCN:99-019452.
Audience: **l,u,f.**

Chester, Eric **HF5549.2.U5C44 2005**
Getting Them to Give a Damn: How to Get Your Front Line to Care about Your Bottom Line. Trade Paper. Kaplan Publishing. Chicago, IL. 2005. 205p. ISBN:1-4195-0458-4, ISBN13: 978-1-4195-0458-7. Dewey:658.3/14. LCCN:2004-029168.
Audience: **g,l,u.**

Conner, Daryl R. **HD58.8.C6518 1998**
Leading at the Edge of Chaos: How to Create the Nimble Organization. Trade Cloth. John Wiley & Sons, Inc. Hoboken, NJ. 1998. 368p. ISBN:0-471-29557-4, ISBN13: 978-0-471-29557-0. Dewey:658.4/06. LCCN:98-024357.
Audience: **u,f.** *Choice, 1999.*

Cyert, Richard M. & March, James G. **HD30.23.C9 1992**
Behavioral Theory of the Firm. Ed. 2. Trade Paper. Blackwell Publishing, Inc. Malden, MA. 1992. 264p. ISBN:0-631-17451-6, ISBN13: 978-0-631-17451-6. Dewey:658.403. LCCN:91-038300.
Audience: **u,f.**

Davenport, Thomas H. & Prusak, Laurence **HD53.D38 2003**
What's the Big Idea?: Creating and Capitalizing on the Best Management Thinking. Trade Cloth. Harvard Business School Press. Boston, MA. 2003. 256p. ISBN:1-57851-931-4, ISBN13: 978-1-57851-931-6. Dewey:658. LCCN:2002-155934.
Audience: **u,f.** *Choice, 2003.*

Dess, Gregory G. & Picken, Joseph C. **HD58.9.D47 1999**
Beyond Productivity: How Leading Companies Achieve Superior Performance by Leveraging Their Human Capital. Trade Cloth. Amacom. New York, NY. 1999. 244p. ISBN:0-8144-0435-9, ISBN13: 978-0-8144-0435-5. Dewey:658.3. LCCN:98-049319.
Audience: **u,f.** *Choice, 1999.*

Drucker, Peter F. **HD38.25.U6**
The Effective Executive: The Definitive Guide to Getting the Right Things Done. Trade Paper. HarperCollins Publishers. New York, NY. 2006. 208p. HarperBusiness Essentials Ser. ISBN:0-06-083345-9, ISBN13: 978-0-06-083345-9. Dewey:658.4.
Audience: **u,f.**

Drucker, Peter F. **HD58.8**
Managing in a Time of Great Change. Paper Text. Elsevier Science & Technology Books. Saint Louis, MO. 1997. 336p. ISBN:0-7506-3714-5, ISBN13: 978-0-7506-3714-5. Dewey:658.4/06.
Audience: **l,u,f.** *Choice, 1996.*

Drucker, Peter F. **HD62.6**
Managing the Nonprofit Organization. Trade Paper. HarperCollins Publishers. New York, NY. 2006. 256p. ISBN:0-06-085114-7, ISBN13: 978-0-06-085114-9. Dewey:658.0480973.
Audience: **u,f.**

Hagel, John & Brown, John Seely **HD30.28.H323 2005**
Your Next Business Strategy: The Case for Dynamic Friction and Loose Specialization. Trade Cloth. Harvard Business School Press. Boston, MA. 2005. 192p. ISBN:1-59139-720-0, ISBN13: 978-1-59139-720-5. Dewey:658.4/012. LCCN:2005-003559.
Audience: **u,f.**

Hamel, Gary **HD538.H353 2002**
Leading the Revolution. Ed. 2. Trade Cloth. Harvard Business School Press. Boston, MA. 2004. 333p. ISBN:1-59139-146-6, ISBN13: 978-1-59139-146-3. Dewey:658.4/012.
Audience: **g,l,u,f.**

Harvard Business School Staff (Editor) **HF5549.5.E42D428**
Dealing with Difficult People. Trade Paper. Harvard Business School Press. Boston, MA. 2004. 192p. The Results Driven Manger Ser. ISBN:1-59139-634-4, ISBN13: 978-1-59139-634-5. Dewey:658.3/045. LCCN:2004-010149.
Audience: **l,u,f.**

Hesselbein, Frances (Editor), et al. **HD58.8**
The Organization of the Future. Marshall Goldsmith & Richard Beckhard (Editors). Trade Paper. John Wiley & Sons, Inc. Hoboken, NJ. 2000. 400p. J-B Drucker Foundation Ser., Vol. 50 ISBN:0-7879-5203-6, ISBN13: 978-0-7879-5203-7. Dewey:658.4/06. LCCN:96-045826.
Audience: **u,f.**

Kaplan, Robert S. & Norton, David P. **HD56.K35 1996**
The Balanced Scorecard: Translating Strategy into Action. Trade Cloth. Harvard Business School Press. Boston, MA. 1996. 336p. ISBN:0-87584-651-3, ISBN13: 978-0-87584-651-4. Dewey:658.401. LCCN:96-010216.
Audience: **g,l,u,f.** *Choice, 1997.*

Kaplan, Robert S. & Norton, David P. **HD30.28.K3544 2001**
The Strategy-Focused Organization: How Balanced Scorecard Companies Thrive in the New Business Environment. Trade Cloth. Harvard Business School Press. Boston, MA. 2004. 416p. ISBN:1-57851-250-6, ISBN13: 978-1-57851-250-8. Dewey:658.4/012. LCCN:00-033515.
Audience: **g,l,u,f.**

Kemp, Sid **TS156.K4187 2005**
Quality Management Demystified. Trade Paper. McGraw-Hill Professional Publishing. New York, NY. 2005. 320p. ISBN:0-07-144908-6, ISBN13: 978-0-07-144908-3. Dewey:658.4/013. LCCN:2005-054522.
Audience: **l,u.**

Kotter, John P. & Cohen, Dan S. **HD58.8.K645 2002**
The Heart of Change: Real Life Stories of How People Change Their Organizations. Trade Cloth. Harvard Business School Press. Boston, MA. 2002. 208p. ISBN:1-57851-254-9, ISBN13: 978-1-57851-254-6. Dewey:658.4/06. LCCN:2002-001475.
Audience: **g,l.** *Choice, 2003, 2002.*

Latzko, William J. & Saunders, David M. **HD62.15.L38 1995**
Four Days with Dr. Deming: A Strategy for Modern Methods of Management. Trade Paper. Pearson Education. Boston, MA. 1995. 256p. Engineering Process Improvement Ser. ISBN:0-201-63366-3, ISBN13: 978-0-201-63366-5. Dewey:658.5/62. LCCN:94-029252.
Audience: **l,u,f.**

Mosby, David & Weissman, Michael **HF5386.M79 2005**
The Paradox of Excellence: How Great Performance Can Kill Your Business. Trade Cloth. John Wiley & Sons, Inc. Hoboken, NJ. 2005. 224p. ISBN:0-7879-8139-7, ISBN13: 978-0-7879-8139-6. Dewey:658.8/12. LCCN:2005-013190.
Audience: **u,f.**

Niven, Paul R. **HD58.9.N58 2006**
Balanced Scorecard Step-by-Step: Maximizing Performance and Maintaining Results. Ed. 2. Trade Cloth. John Wiley & Sons, Inc. Hoboken, NJ. 2006. 336p. ISBN:0-471-78049-9, ISBN13: 978-0-471-78049-6. Dewey:658.4/013. LCCN:2006-008526.
Audience: **g,l,u,f.**

Peters, Tom **HD58.8**
Liberation Management: Necessary Disorganization for the Nanosecond Nineties. Paper Text. Ballantine Books. New York, NY. 1994. ISBN:0-449-90910-7, ISBN13: 978-0-449-90910-2. Dewey:658.4/063.
Audience: **g,l,u,f.**

Pfeffer, Jeffrey **HF5386.5**
Managing with Power: Politics and Influence in Organizations. Trade Paper. Harvard Business School Press. Boston, MA. 1993. 400p. ISBN:0-87584-440-5, ISBN13: 978-0-87584-440-4. Dewey:658.4/095. LCCN:91-026237.
Audience: **u,f.** *Choice, 1992.*

Porter, Michael, et al. **HD30.28.H3786 2002**
Harvard Business Review on Advances in Strategy. Robert Kaplan, David Norton, Kathy Eisenhardt, Don Sull, Peter Tufano, Orit Gadiesh, James Gilbert & Mohanbir Sawhney (Authors). Trade Paper. Harvard Business School Press. Boston, MA. 2002. 256p. The Harvard Business Review Book Ser. ISBN:1-57851-803-2, ISBN13: 978-1-57851-803-6. Dewey:658.4/012. LCCN:2002-100252.
Audience: **l,u,f.**

Porter, Micheal E. **HD41.P668 1998**
Competitive Advantage: Creating and Sustaining Superior Performance. Trade Cloth. Simon & Schuster. New York, NY. 1998. 592p. ISBN:0-684-84146-0, ISBN13: 978-0-684-84146-5. Dewey:658. LCCN:98-009581.
Audience: **g,l,u,f.**

Quelch, John A. & Deshpande, Rohit (Editors) **HF1416.G554 2004**
The Global Market: Developing a Strategy to Manage Across Borders. Trade Cloth. John Wiley & Sons, Inc. Hoboken, NJ. 2004. 432p. The Jossey-Bass Business & Management Ser. ISBN:0-7879-6857-9, ISBN13: 978-0-7879-6857-1. Dewey:658.8/4. LCCN:2004-003711.
Audience: **u,f.** *Choice, 2005.*

Schermerhorn, John R. **HD31.S33247 2003**
Core Concepts of Management. Ed. 2. Trade Paper. John Wiley & Sons, Inc. Hoboken, NJ. 2003. 304p. ISBN:0-471-23055-3, ISBN13: 978-0-471-23055-7. Dewey:658. LCCN:2003-057658.
Audience: **l.**

Silva, Ajit **HD62.15**
The Ten Commandments of Quality Management: Best Practices to Develop New Leaders and Create a Quality Environment.

Trade Paper. iUniverse, Inc. Lincoln, NE. 2005. 120p. ISBN:0-595-35756-3, ISBN13: 978-0-595-35756-7. Dewey:658.4013.
Audience: **u,f.**

Simmons, Annette **HF5549.S5898 1998**
Territorial Games: Understanding and Ending Turf Wars at Work. Trade Cloth. Amacom. New York, NY. 1997. 208p. ISBN:0-8144-0383-2, ISBN13: 978-0-8144-0383-9. Dewey:658.3. LCCN:97-025819.
Audience: **g,l,f.**

Simon, Herbert A. **HD31.S55 1997**
Administrative Behavior: A Study of Decision-Making Processes in Administrative Organizations. Ed. 4. Trade Paper. Simon & Schuster. New York, NY. 1997. 384p. ISBN:0-684-83582-7, ISBN13: 978-0-684-83582-2. Dewey:658.4. LCCN:96-034148.
Audience: **u,f.**

Sutton, Robert I. **HD53.S883 2002**
Weird Ideas That Work: 11 1/2 Practices for Promoting, Managing and Sustaining Innovation. Trade Cloth. Simon & Schuster. New York, NY. 2001. 240p. ISBN:0-7432-1212-6, ISBN13: 978-0-7432-1212-0. Dewey:658. LCCN:2001-033657.
Audience: **g,l.**

Management Function > General Management > Managerial Skills > Negotiation

Adler, Bill Jr. & Adler, Bill **HD58.6.A35 2005**
How to Negotiate Like a Child: Unlease the Little Monster Within to Get Everything You Want. Trade Cloth. Amacom. New York, NY. 2005. 161p. ISBN:0-8144-7294-X, ISBN13: 978-0-8144-7294-1. Dewey:658.4/052. LCCN:2005-018460.
Audience: **g,l.**

Bazerman, Max H. & Neale, Margaret A. **HD58.6.B39 1993**
Negotiating Rationally. Trade Paper. Simon & Schuster. New York, NY. 1994. 196p. ISBN:0-02-901986-9, ISBN13: 978-0-02-901986-3. Dewey:658.4052. LCCN:91-034205.
Audience: **l,f.**

Brett, Jeanne M. **HD58.6.B74 2001**
Negotiating Globally: How to Negotiate Deals, Resolve Disputes and Make Decisions Across Cultural Boundaries. Trade Cloth. John Wiley & Sons, Inc. Hoboken, NJ. 2001. 288p. Business and Management Ser. ISBN:0-7879-5586-8, ISBN13: 978-0-7879-5586-1. Dewey:658.4/052. LCCN:00-011770.
Audience: **u,f.**

Cohen, Herb **BF637.N4**
Negotiate This!: By Caring, but Not T-H-A-T Much. Trade Paper. Warner Books, Inc. New York, NY. 2006. 400p. ISBN:0-446-69644-7, ISBN13: 978-0-446-69644-9. Dewey:302.3. LCCN:2003-043281.
Audience: **g,l,u,f.**

Felder, Raoul **KF373.F38A33 2004**
Bare-Knuckle Negotiation: Savvy Tips and True Stories from the Master of Give-and-Take. Trade Cloth. John Wiley & Sons, Inc. Hoboken, NJ. 2004. 256p. ISBN:0-471-46333-7, ISBN13: 978-0-471-46333-7. Dewey:347.73/9/092. LCCN:2003-018879.
Audience: **g,l.**

Fisher, Roger & Ury, William L. **BF637.N4F57**
Getting to Yes: Negotiating Agreement Without Giving In. Ed. 2. Bruce Patton (Editor). Trade Paper. Penguin Group (USA) Inc. New York, NY. 1991. 224p. ISBN:0-14-015735-2, ISBN13: 978-0-14-015735-2. Dewey:158.5. LCCN:91-032444.
Audience: **g,l,u,f.** B

Gelfand, Michele J. & Brett, Jeanne M. **BF637.N4H365 2004**
The Handbook of Negotiation: Theoretical Advances and Cross-Cultural Perspectives. Trade Cloth. Stanford University Press. Palo Alto, CA. 2004. 480p. ISBN:0-8047-4586-2, ISBN13: 978-0-8047-4586-4. Dewey:302.3. LCCN:2003-025169.
Audience: **g,l,u,f.** *Choice, 2005.*

Lum, Grande **HD58.6**
The Negotiation Fieldbook. Trade Paper. McGraw-Hill Companies, The. New York, NY. 2004. 204p. ISBN:0-07-144114-X, ISBN13: 978-0-07-144114-8. Dewey:658.4/052. LCCN:2005-281453.
Audience: **g,l,u,f.**

Mayer, Bernard S. **BF637.I48M39 2000**
The Dynamics of Conflict Resolution: A Practitioner's Guide. Trade Cloth. John Wiley & Sons, Inc. Hoboken, NJ. 2000. 288p. ISBN:0-7879-5019-X, ISBN13: 978-0-7879-5019-4. Dewey:303.6/9. LCCN:99-050576.
Audience: **g,l,u,f.**

Morrison, William F. **HD58**
The Savvy Negotiator: Building Win/Win Relationships. Trade Cloth. Greenwood Publishing Group, Inc. Portsmouth, NH. 2005. 220p. ISBN:0-275-98800-7, ISBN13: 978-0-275-98800-5. Dewey:650.1/3. LCCN:2005-020943.
Audience: **u,f.**

Raiffa, Howard, et al. **HD58.6.R342 2003**
Negotiation Analysis: The Science and Art of Collaborative Decision Making. John Richardson & David Metcalfe (Authors). Trade Cloth. Harvard University Press. Cambridge, MA. 2003. 576p. ISBN:0-674-00890-1, ISBN13: 978-0-674-00890-8. Dewey:658.4/052. LCCN:2002-074688.
Audience: **u,f.**

Rousseau, Denise M. **HD6971.R69 2005**
I-Deals: Idiosyncratic Deals Employees Bargain for Themselves. Trade Paper, Perfect. M. E. Sharpe Inc. Armonk, NY. 2005. 261p. ISBN:0-7656-1043-4, ISBN13: 978-0-7656-1043-0. Dewey:650.1. LCCN:2004-026588.
Audience: **g,l,u,f.**

Rusk, Tom & Miller, D. Patrick **BF637.N4 R87**
The Power of Ethical Persuasion: Winning Through Understanding at Work and at Home. Trade Paper. DIANE Publishing Company. Collingdale, PA. 2001. 221p. ISBN:0-7881-9810-6, ISBN13: 978-0-7881-9810-6. Dewey:158/.5.
Audience: **g,l.**

Salacuse, Jeswald W. **HD58.6.S246 2003**
The Global Negotiator: Making, Managing and Mending Deals Around the World in the Twenty-First Century. Cloth over Boards. Palgrave Macmillan. New York, NY. 2003. 320p.

ISBN:0-312-29339-9, ISBN13: 978-0-312-29339-0. Dewey:658.4/052. LCCN:2002-193099.
Audience: **g,l,u,f.**

Shell, G. Richard **BF637.N4S44 2006**
Bargaining for Advantage: Negotiation Strategies for Reasonable People. Ed. 2. Trade Paper. Penguin Group (USA) Inc. New York, NY. 2006. 320p. ISBN:0-14-303697-1, ISBN13: 978-0-14-303697-5. Dewey:302.3. LCCN:2005-056636.
Audience: **u,f.** *Choice, 1999.*

Thomas, Jim **BF637.N4T45 2005**
Negotiate to Win: The 21 Rules for Successful Negotiating. Trade Cloth. HarperCollins Publishers. New York, NY. 2005. 320p. ISBN:0-06-078106-8, ISBN13: 978-0-06-078106-4. Dewey:302.3. LCCN:2005-045711.
Audience: **g,l.**

Volkema, Roger **HD58.6.V648 2006**
Leverage: How to Get It and How to Keep It in Any Negotiation. Trade Paper. Amacom. New York, NY. 2006. 224p. ISBN:0-8144-7326-1, ISBN13: 978-0-8144-7326-9. Dewey:658.4/052. LCCN:2005-023210.
Audience: **u,f.**

Management Function > General Management > Organizational Behavior

Adler, Nancy J. **HD58.7.A33 2002**
International Dimensions of Organizational Behavior. Ed. 4. Paper Text. Thomson South-Western. Mason, OH. 2001. 408p. SWC-Management Ser. ISBN:0-324-05786-5, ISBN13: 978-0-324-05786-7. Dewey:658. LCCN:00-046396.
Audience: **g,l,u,f.**

Hofstede, Geert & Hofstede, Gert Jan **HM711**
Cultures and Organizations: Software for the Mind. Ed. 2. Trade Paper. McGraw-Hill Companies, The. New York, NY. 2004. 300p. ISBN:0-07-143959-5, ISBN13: 978-0-07-143959-6. Dewey:306. LCCN:2004-063164.
Audience: **g,l,u,f.** *Choice, 2005.*

Schein, Edgar H. **HD58.7.S33 2004**
Organizational Culture and Leadership. Ed. 3. Trade Cloth. John Wiley & Sons, Inc. Hoboken, NJ. 2004. 464p. The Jossey-Bass Business & Management Ser. ISBN:0-7879-6845-5, ISBN13: 978-0-7879-6845-8. Dewey:302.3/5. LCCN:2004-002764.
Audience: **g,l,u,f.**

Simon, Herbert A. **HD31.S55 1997**
Administrative Behavior: A Study of Decision-Making Processes in Administrative Organizations. Ed. 4. Trade Paper. Simon & Schuster. New York, NY. 1997. 384p. ISBN:0-684-83582-7, ISBN13: 978-0-684-83582-2. Dewey:658.4. LCCN:96-034148.
Audience: **u,f.**

Management Function > General Management > Organizational Behavior > Agency Theory

Gregory, William A. **KF1345.R48 2001**
The Law of Agency and Partnership. Ed. 3. Trade Cloth. West Publishing Company, College & School Division. Eagan, MN. 2001. 690p. Hornbook Ser. ISBN:0-314-23858-1, ISBN13: 978-0-314-23858-0. Dewey:346.7302/9. LCCN:2001-276602.
Audience: **u,f.**

Hynes, J. Dennis, and Loewenstein, Mark J. **KF1375.Z9 H95 2003**
Agency, Partnership, and the LLC in a Nutshell. Ed. 3. Thomson/West. 2005. West Nutshell Series ISBN:0-314-15894-4, ISBN13: 978-0-314-15894-9.
Audience: **u,f.**

Lane, Jan-Erik **JF1351.L366 2005**
Public Administration and Public Management: The Principal-Agent Perspective. Trade Paper. Routledge. New York, NY. 2005. 304p. ISBN:0-415-37016-7, ISBN13: 978-0-415-37016-5. Dewey:351. LCCN:2005-001274.
Audience: **u,f.**

Rosin, Gary S. & Closen, Michael L. **KF1372**
Agency, Partnerships, and Limited Liability Companies: Cases and Materials. Trade Cloth. Carolina Academic Press. Durham, NC. 2004. ISBN:0-89089-397-7, ISBN13: 978-0-89089-397-5. Dewey:016.34973.
Audience: **u,f.**

Management Function > General Management > Organizational Behavior > Human Resources Management

Analoui **HD58.9 .M45**
Strategic Human Resource Management. Trade Paper. Thomson Learning EMEA, Ltd. London, 2006. 352p. ISBN:1-84480-159-4, ISBN13: 978-1-84480-159-6. Dewey:658.3.
Audience: **u,f.**

Arthur, Diane **HF5549.5.R44A748**
The Employee Recruitment and Retention Handbook. Trade Cloth. Amacom. New York, NY. 2001. xii, 402p. ISBN:0-8144-0552-5, ISBN13: 978-0-8144-0552-9. Dewey:658.3111. LCCN:00-049581.
Audience: **u,f.** *Choice, 2001.*

Aspatore Books Staff **HF5549**
HR Best Practices: Top Human Resources Executives from Prudential Financial, Northrop Grumman, and More on Hiring the Right People and Enhancing Corporate Culture. Trade Paper.

Aspatore Books, Inc. Boston, MA. 2005. Inside the Minds Ser. ISBN:1-59622-153-4, ISBN13: 978-1-59622-153-6. Dewey:658.3.
Audience: **u,f.**

Berman, Evan M., et al. JF1601.H86 2006
Human Resource Management in Public Service: Paradoxes, Processes, and Problems. Ed. 2. James S. Bowman, Jonathan P. West & Montgomery Van Wart (Authors). Cloth Text. SAGE Publications, Inc. Thousand Oaks, CA. 2005. 392p. ISBN:1-4129-0421-8, ISBN13: 978-1-4129-0421-6. Dewey:352.6. LCCN:2004-029458.
Audience: **u,f.**

Blair, Margaret M. (Editor) HF5549.N376 2000
New Relationship: Human Capital in the American Corporation. Trade Paper. Brookings Institution Press. Washington, DC. 2000. 350p. ISBN:0-8157-0901-3, ISBN13: 978-0-8157-0901-5. Dewey:658.3/00973. LCCN:99-050476.
Audience: **u,f.** *Choice, 2000.*

Coffman, Curt & Gonzalez-Molina, Gabriel HD56
Follow This Path: How the World's Greatest Organizations Drive Growth by Unleashing Human Potential. Trade Paper. Warner Books, Inc. New York, NY. 2002. 304p. ISBN:0-446-69035-X, ISBN13: 978-0-446-69035-5. Dewey:658.3/14.
Audience: **l,u,f.**

Dubois, David D. HF5549.C7115 2004
Competency-Based Human Resource Management. Trade Cloth. Consulting Psychologists Press, Inc. Mountain View, CA. 2004. 376p. ISBN:0-89106-174-6, ISBN13: 978-0-89106-174-8. Dewey:658.3. LCCN:2003-023886.
Audience: **u,f.** *Choice, 2004.*

Gilley, Jerry W. & Maycunich, Ann HD58.82.G53 2000
Organizational Learning, Performance and Change: An Introduction to Strategic Human Resource Development. Trade Cloth. Basic Books. New York, NY. 2000. 512p. ISBN:0-7382-0248-7, ISBN13: 978-0-7382-0248-8. Dewey:658.3/124. LCCN:00-102435.
Audience: **g,l.**

Gilson, Stuart C. HD58.8.G555 2001
Creating Value through Corporate Restructuring: Case Studies in Bankruptcies, Buyouts, and Breakups. Trade Cloth. John Wiley & Sons, Inc. Hoboken, NJ. 2001. 528p. Wiley Finance Ser., Vol. 95 ISBN:0-471-40559-0, ISBN13: 978-0-471-40559-7. Dewey:658.1/6. LCCN:2001-023753.
Audience: **u,f.**

Huselid, Mark, et al. HD58.9.B43 2001
The HR Scorecard: Linking People, Strategy, and Performance. Brian Becker & Dave Ulrich (Authors). Trade Cloth. Harvard Business School Press. Boston, MA. 2001. 304p. ISBN:1-57851-136-4, ISBN13: 978-1-57851-136-5. Dewey:658.3. LCCN:00-053945.
Audience: **u,f.**

Jackson, Susan E. (Editor), et al. HD30.2.M3646 2003
Managing Knowledge for Sustained Competitive Advantage: Designing Strategies for Effective Human Resource Management. Michael A. Hitt & Angelo S. DeNisi (Editors). Trade Cloth. John Wiley & Sons, Inc. Hoboken, NJ. 2003. 480p. J-B SIOP Frontiers Ser. ISBN:0-7879-5717-8, ISBN13: 978-0-7879-5717-9. Dewey:658.4/038. LCCN:2002-154863.
Audience: **u,f.**

Kahnweiler, William & Kahnweiler, Jennifer HF5549.K233 2005
Shaping Your HR Role: Succeeding in Today's Organizations. Trade Paper, Perfect. Elsevier Science & Technology Books. Saint Louis, MO. 2005. 264p. ISBN:0-7506-7823-2, ISBN13: 978-0-7506-7823-0. Dewey:658.3. LCCN:2005-040076.
Audience: **u,f.**

Kanter, Rosabeth Moss HD45
Change Masters. Trade Paper. Simon & Schuster. New York, NY. 1985. 432p. ISBN:0-671-52800-9, ISBN13: 978-0-671-52800-3. Dewey:658.314.
Audience: **g,l,u,f.**

Lengnick-Hall, Mark L. & Lengnick-Hall, Cynthia A. HF5549.L46143 2002
Human Resource Management in the Knowledge Economy: New Challenges, New Roles, New Capabilities. Trade Paper. Berrett-Koehler Publishers, Inc. San Francisco, CA. 2002. 210p. ISBN:1-57675-159-7, ISBN13: 978-1-57675-159-6. Dewey:658.3. LCCN:2002-074530.
Audience: **u,f.**

Losey, Mike (Editor), et al. HF5549
The Future of Human Resource Management: 64 Thought Leaders Explore the Critical HR Issues of Today and Tomorrow. Sue Meisinger & Dave Ulrich (Editors). Trade Cloth. John Wiley & Sons, Inc. Hoboken, NJ. 2005. 448p. ISBN:0-471-67791-4, ISBN13: 978-0-471-67791-8. Dewey:658.3. LCCN:2005-278358.
Audience: **l,u,f.**

Mathis, Robert L. & Jackson, John H. HF5549.H7854
Human Resource Management: Essential Perspectives. Ed. 4. Paper Text. Thomson South-Western. Mason, OH. 2006. 220p. ISBN:0-324-36178-5, ISBN13: 978-0-324-36178-0. Dewey:658.3. LCCN:2005-937605.
Audience: **g,l,u,f.**

Reddington, Martin, et al. HF5549
Transforming HR: Creating Value Through People. Mark Williamson & Mark Withers (Authors). Paper Text. Elsevier Science & Technology Books. Saint Louis, MO. 2005. 304p. The HR Series, Ser. ISBN:0-7506-6447-9, ISBN13: 978-0-7506-6447-9. Dewey:658.3. LCCN:2005-296031.
Audience: **l,u,f.**

Rosse, Joseph G. & Levin, Robert A. HF5549.L46278 2001
Talent Flow: A Strategic Approach to Keeping Good Employees, Helping Them Grow, and Letting Them Go. Trade Cloth. John Wiley & Sons, Inc. Hoboken, NJ. 2001. 272p. ISBN:0-7879-4830-6, ISBN13: 978-0-7879-4830-6. Dewey:658.3. LCCN:2001-001764.
Audience: **l,u.**

Salaman, Graeme (Editor), et al. HF5549.S7 2005
Strategic Human Resource Management: Theory and Practice. Ed. 2. John Storey & Jon Billsberry (Editors). Paper Text.

SAGE Publications, Ltd. London, 2005. 360p. ISBN:1-4129-1901-0, ISBN13: 978-1-4129-1901-2. Dewey:658.3. LCCN:2005-926178.

Audience: **u,f.**

Scullion, Hugh & Linehan, Margaret **HF5549.5.E45I5773**
International Human Resource Management: A Critical Text. Trade Paper. Palgrave Macmillan. New York, NY. 2005. 400p. Management, Work and Organisations Ser. ISBN:0-333-74139-0, ISBN13: 978-0-333-74139-9. Dewey:658.3. LCCN:2004-054823.

Audience: **u,f.**

Swart, Juani, et al. **HF5549.5.T7**
Human Resource Development: Strategy and Tactics. Clare Mann, Steve Brown & Alan Price (Authors). Paper Text. Elsevier Science & Technology Books. Saint Louis, MO. 2005. 256p. ISBN:0-7506-6250-6, ISBN13: 978-0-7506-6250-5. Dewey:658.3/124.

Audience: **u,f.**

Tayeb, Monir **HD62.4.T388 2005**
International Human Resource Management. Trade Paper. Oxford University Press, Inc. New York, NY. 2005. 258p. ISBN:0-19-925809-0, ISBN13: 978-0-19-925809-3. Dewey:658.3. LCCN:2004-276465.

Audience: **u,f.**

Ulrich, Dave & Brockbank, Wayne **HF5549.U38 2005**
The HR Value Proposition. Trade Cloth. Harvard Business School Press. Boston, MA. 2005. 304p. ISBN:1-59139-707-3, ISBN13: 978-1-59139-707-6. Dewey:658.3. LCCN:2005-002389.

Audience: **u,f.**

Management Function > General Management > Organizational Behavior > Knowledge Management

Botkin, Jim **HD30.2.B676 1999**
Smart Business: How Knowledge Communities Can Revolutionize Your Company. Trade Cloth. Simon & Schuster. New York, NY. 1999. 304p. ISBN:0-684-85024-9, ISBN13: 978-0-684-85024-5. Dewey:658.4/038. LCCN:99-017727.

Audience: **u,f.**

Buckman, Robert H. **HD30.2**
Building a Knowledge-Driven Organization. Trade Cloth. McGraw-Hill Companies, The. New York, NY. 2004. 300p. ISBN:0-07-138471-5, ISBN13: 978-0-07-138471-1. Dewey:658.4/038.

Audience: **u,f.**

Chatzkel, Jay L. **HD30.2.C743 2003**
Knowledge Capital: How Knowledge-Based Enterprises Really Get Built. Cloth Text. Oxford University Press, Inc. New York, NY. 2003. 432p. ISBN:0-19-516114-9, ISBN13: 978-0-19-516114-4. Dewey:658.4/038. LCCN:2003-001213.

Audience: **u,f.**

Collins, Heidi **HD30.37.C657 2002**
Enterprise Knowledge Portals: Next Generation Portal Solutions for Dynamic Information Access, Better Decision Making and Maximum Results. Trade Cloth. Amacom. New York, NY. 2002. 400p. ISBN:0-8144-0708-0, ISBN13: 978-0-8144-0708-0. Dewey:658.4/038/011. LCCN:2002-009989.

Audience: **u,f.**

Courtney, James F., et al. **HD58.82.I534 2005**
Inquiring Organizations: Moving from Knowledge Management to Wisdom. John D. Haynes & David B. Paradice (Authors). Trade Paper. Idea Group Publishing. Hershey, PA. 2005. 398p. ISBN:1-59140-310-3, ISBN13: 978-1-59140-310-4. Dewey:658.4/038/01. LCCN:2004-023591.

Audience: **u,f.**

Dalkir, Kimiz **HD30.2.D354 2005**
Knowledge Management in Theory and Practice. Cloth Text. Elsevier Science & Technology Books. Saint Louis, MO. 2005. 368p. ISBN:0-7506-7864-X, ISBN13: 978-0-7506-7864-3. Dewey:658.4/038. LCCN:2005-045074.

Audience: **l,u,f.**

Evans, Philip & Wurster, Thomas S. **HC79.I55E93 2000**
Blown to Bits: How the New Economics of Information Transforms Strategy. Trade Cloth. Harvard Business School Press. Boston, MA. 1999. 288p. ISBN:0-87584-877-X, ISBN13: 978-0-87584-877-8. Dewey:658.4/012. LCCN:99-031132.

Audience: **g,l,u,f.**

Lehaney, Brian (Editor) **HD30.2.B477 2003**
Beyond Knowledge Management. Trade Cloth. Idea Group Publishing. Hershey, PA. 2003. 275p. ISBN:1-59140-223-9, ISBN13: 978-1-59140-223-7. Dewey:658.4/038. LCCN:2003-021678.

Audience: **l,u,f.**

Malone, Thomas W. (Editor), et al. **HD30.2.T67 2003**
Organizing Business Knowledge: The MIT Process Handbook. Kevin Crowston & George A. Herman (Editors). Trade Cloth. MIT Press. Cambridge, MA. 2003. 570p. ISBN:0-262-13429-2, ISBN13: 978-0-262-13429-3. Dewey:658.4/038. LCCN:2002-045174.

Audience: **l,u,f.**

Rothberg, Helen & Erickson, G. Scott **HD30.2.R6648 2004**
From Knowledge to Intelligence: Creating Competitive Advantage in the Next Economy. Audio, Other. Elsevier Science & Technology Books. Saint Louis, MO. 2004. 400p. ISBN:0-7506-7762-7, ISBN13: 978-0-7506-7762-2. Dewey:658.4/038. LCCN:2004-050665.

Audience: **u,f.**

Seivert, Sharon & Cavaleri, Steven A. **HD30.2.C43 2005**
Knowledge Leadership: The Art and Science of the Knowledge-Based Organization. Trade Paper. Elsevier Science & Technology Books. Saint Louis, MO. 2005. 376p. KMCI Press Ser. ISBN:0-7506-7840-2, ISBN13: 978-0-7506-7840-7. Dewey:658.4/038. LCCN:2004-028098.

Audience: **u,f.**

Takeuchi, Hirotaka & Nonaka, Ikujiro **HD30.2**
Hitotsubashi on Knowledge Management. Trade Cloth. John

Wiley & Sons, Inc. Hoboken, NJ. 2004. 250p. ISBN:0-470-82074-8, ISBN13: 978-0-470-82074-2. Dewey:658.4/038. LCCN:2004-299100.
Audience: **u,f.**

Thurow, Lester C. **HC110.S3T47**
Building Wealth: The New Rules for Individuals, Companies, and Nations in a Knowledge-Based Economy. Trade Paper. HarperCollins Publishers. New York, NY. 2000. 336p. ISBN:0-88730-952-6, ISBN13: 978-0-88730-952-6. Dewey:332.
Audience: **g,l,u,f.** *Choice, 2000.*

Management Function > General Management > Organizational Behavior > Organizational Learning

Albrecht, Karl **HD30.2.A385 2002**
The Power of Minds at Work: Leveraging the Power of Organizational Intelligence. Trade Cloth. Amacom. New York, NY. 2002. 240p. ISBN:0-8144-0737-4, ISBN13: 978-0-8144-0737-0. Dewey:658.4/038. LCCN:2002-005079.
Audience: **l,u,f.**

Argyris, Chris **HD58.82.A734 1999**
On Organizational Learning. Ed. 2. Trade Paper. Blackwell Publishing, Inc. Malden, MA. 1999. 480p. ISBN:0-631-21309-0, ISBN13: 978-0-631-21309-3. Dewey:658.3/124. LCCN:98-054396.
Audience: **g,l,u,f.**

Bennet, Alex & Bennet, David **HD58.8.B459 2003**
Organizational Survival in the New World: The Intelligent Complex Adaptive System. Trade Cloth. Elsevier Science & Technology Books. Saint Louis, MO. 2003. 391p. KMCI Press Ser. ISBN:0-7506-7712-0, ISBN13: 978-0-7506-7712-7. Dewey:302.3/5. LCCN:2003-057749.
Audience: **u,f.**

Cutcher-Gershenfeld, Joel & Ford, Kevin **HD58.82.C88 2005**
Valuable Disconnects in Organizational Learning Systems: Integrating Bold Visions and Harsh Realities. Trade Cloth. Oxford University Press, Inc. New York, NY. 2005. xiii, 202p. ISBN:7-80195-089-5, ISBN13: 978-7-80195-089-5. Dewey:658.4/038. LCCN:2004-057635.
Audience: **u,f.**

Davenport, Thomas H. & Prusak, Laurence **HD30.23**
Working Knowledge: How Organizations Manage What They Know. Ed. 2. Trade Paper. Harvard Business School Press. Boston, MA. 2000. 224p. ISBN:1-57851-301-4, ISBN13: 978-1-57851-301-7. Dewey:658.4/03. LCCN:97-010781.
Audience: **g,l,u,f.** *Choice, 1998.*

De Geus, Arie **HD31.G438 1997**
The Living Company. Peter M. Senge (Foreword by). Cloth Text. Harvard Business School Press. Boston, MA. 1997. 240p. ISBN:0-87584-782-X, ISBN13: 978-0-87584-782-5. Dewey:658. LCCN:96-048384.
Audience: **g,l,u,f.**

DeLong, David W. **HD58.82.D4 2004**
Lost Knowledge: Confronting the Threat of an Aging Workforce. Trade Cloth. Oxford University Press, Inc. New York, NY. 2004. 268p. ISBN:0-19-517097-0, ISBN13: 978-0-19-517097-9. Dewey:658.3/01. LCCN:2004-041577.
Audience: **g,l,u,f.** *Choice, 2005.*

Dess, Gregory G. & Picken, Joseph C. **HD58.9.D47 1999**
Beyond Productivity: How Leading Companies Achieve Superior Performance by Leveraging Their Human Capital. Trade Cloth. Amacom. New York, NY. 1999. 244p. ISBN:0-8144-0435-9, ISBN13: 978-0-8144-0435-5. Dewey:658.3. LCCN:98-049319.
Audience: **u,f.** *Choice, 1999.*

Dierkes, Meinolf (Editor), et al. **HD58.82**
Handbook of Organizational Learning and Knowledge. Ariane Berthoin Antal, John Child & Ikujiro Nonaka (Editors). Trade Paper. Oxford University Press, Inc. New York, NY. 2003. 1,008p. ISBN:0-19-829582-0, ISBN13: 978-0-19-829582-2. Dewey:658.4.
Audience: **g,l,u,f.**

Dixon, Nancy M. **HD58.82.D585 2000**
Common Knowledge: How Companies Thrive by Sharing What They Know. Trade Cloth. Harvard Business School Press. Boston, MA. 2000. 208p. ISBN:0-87584-904-0, ISBN13: 978-0-87584-904-1. Dewey:658.4/5. LCCN:99-048879.
Audience: **u,f.** *Choice, 2001.*

Fulmer, William E. **HD58.8.F85 2000**
Shaping the Adaptive Organization: Landscapes, Learning and Leadership in Volatile Times. Trade Cloth. Amacom. New York, NY. 2000. 294p. ISBN:0-8144-0546-0, ISBN13: 978-0-8144-0546-8. Dewey:658.4/063. LCCN:99-047659.
Audience: **g,l.**

Gargiulo, Terrence L. **HD30.3.G365 2005**
The Strategic Use of Stories in Organizational Communication and Learning. Trade Paper. M. E. Sharpe Inc. Armonk, NY. 2005. 272p. ISBN:0-7656-1413-8, ISBN13: 978-0-7656-1413-1. Dewey:658.3. LCCN:2004-019153.
Audience: **g,l.**

Garvin, David A. **HD58.8**
Learning in Action: A Guide to Putting the Learning Organization to Work. Trade Paper. Harvard Business School Press. Boston, MA. 2003. 256p. ISBN:1-59139-190-3, ISBN13: 978-1-59139-190-6. Dewey:658.4/06.
Audience: **u,f.**

Gill, Stephen J. **HD58.82**
Organizational Learning. Trade Paper. Human Resource Development Press. Amherst, MA. 2000. 143p. ISBN:0-87425-588-0, ISBN13: 978-0-87425-588-1. Dewey:658.406.
Audience: **g,l.**

Gilley, Jerry W., et al. **HD58.82.G532 2001**
Philosophy and Practice of Organizational Learning, Performance and Change. Peter Dean & Laura L. Bierema (Authors). Trade Paper. Perseus Books Group. New York, NY. 2001. 256p. New Perspectives in Organizational Learning, Performance, and Change Ser. ISBN:0-7382-0461-7, ISBN13: 978-0-7382-0461-1. Dewey:658.4/06. LCCN:2001-094855.
Audience: **g,l.**

Greve, Henrich R. **HD30.23**
Organizational Learning from Performance Feedback: A Behavioral Perspective on Innovation and Change. Trade Paper.

Cambridge University Press. New York, NY. 2003. 226p. ISBN:0-521-53491-7, ISBN13: 978-0-521-53491-8. Dewey:658.403. LCCN:2003-284150.
Audience: **l,u,f.**

Johnson, Spencer **BF637.C4J64 1998**
Who Moved My Cheese?: An Amazing Way to Deal with Change in Your Work and in Your Life. Trade Cloth. Penguin Group (USA) Inc. New York, NY. 1998. 96p. ISBN:0-399-14446-3, ISBN13: 978-0-399-14446-2. Dewey:155.2/4. LCCN:98-015502.
Audience: **g,l,u,f.**

Kikoski, Catherine Kano & Kikoski, John F. **HD30**
The Inquiring Organization: Tacit Knowledge, Conversation, and Knowledge Creation Skills for 21st-Century Organizations. Trade Cloth. Greenwood Publishing Group, Inc. Portsmouth, NH. 2004. 208p. ISBN:1-56720-490-2, ISBN13: 978-1-56720-490-2. Dewey:658.4/038. LCCN:2003-058157.
Audience: **u,f.**

Kirkpatrick, Donald L. & Kirkpatrick, James D. **HF5549.5.T7**
Transferring Learning to Behavior: Using the Four Levels to Improve Performance. Trade Paper. Berrett-Koehler Publishers, Inc. San Francisco, CA. 2005. 182p. ISBN:1-57675-325-5, ISBN13: 978-1-57675-325-5. Dewey:658.3/124. LCCN:2004-062370.
Audience: **l,u,f.**

Klein, David A. **HD53.S77 1998**
The Strategic Management of Intellectual Capital. Audio, Other. Elsevier Science & Technology Books. Saint Louis, MO. 1997. 256p. Knowledge Reader Ser. ISBN:0-7506-9850-0, ISBN13: 978-0-7506-9850-4. Dewey:658.4. LCCN:97-040130.
Audience: **u,f.**

Langer, Arthur M. **HD58.82.L33 2004**
IT and Organizational Learning: Managing Change through Technology and Education. Trade Paper. Routledge. New York, NY. 2004. 304p. ISBN:0-415-94837-1, ISBN13: 978-0-415-94837-1. Dewey:658.4/038. LCCN:2004-011011.
Audience: **u,f.**

Lyles, Marjorie A. & Crossan, Mary **HD58.82.B56 2005**
The Blackwell Handbook of Organizational Learning and Knowledge Management. Mark Easterby-Smith & Amy C. Edmondson (Editors). Trade Paper, Perfect. Blackwell Publishing, Inc. Malden, MA. 2005. 696p. ISBN:1-4051-3304-X, ISBN13: 978-1-4051-3304-3. Dewey:658.3/124.
Audience: **g,l,u,f.**

Marquardt, Michael, et al. **HF5549.M3195 2004**
HRD in the Age of Globalization: A Practical Guide to Workplace Learning in the Third Millennium. Nancy Berger & Peter Loan (Authors). Trade Paper. Basic Books. New York, NY. 2004. 400p. New Perspectives in Organizational Learning, Performance, and Change Ser. ISBN:0-465-04383-6, ISBN13: 978-0-465-04383-5. Dewey:658.3. LCCN:2004-006148.
Audience: **g,l,u,f.** *Choice, 2005.*

Pietersen, Jacques & Pietersen, Willie **HD58.82.P53 2002**
Reinventing Strategy: Using Strategic Learning to Create and Sustain Breakthrough Performance. Trade Cloth. John Wiley & Sons, Inc. Hoboken, NJ. 2002. 288p. ISBN:0-471-06190-5, ISBN13: 978-0-471-06190-8. Dewey:658.4/012. LCCN:2001-006725.
Audience: **u,f.**

Rothwell, William J., et al. **HD58.82.R673 2003**
What CEOs Expect from Corporate Training: Building Workplace Learning and Performance Initiatives That Advance Organizational Goals. John Lindholm & William G. Wallick (Authors). Trade Cloth. Amacom. New York, NY. 2003. 272p. ISBN:0-8144-0679-3, ISBN13: 978-0-8144-0679-3. Dewey:658.3/124. LCCN:2002-011719.
Audience: **u,f.**

Senge, Peter M. **HD 58.9 S46**
The Fifth Discipline: The Art and Practice of the Learning Organization. Trade Paper. Doubleday Publishing. New York, NY. 2006. 464p. ISBN:0-385-51725-4, ISBN13: 978-0-385-51725-6. Dewey:658.4.
Audience: **g,l,u,f.**

Szulanski, Gabriel **HD30.2.S98 2003**
Sticky Knowledge: Barriers to Knowing in the Firm. Paper Text. SAGE Publications, Ltd. London, 2003. 140p. The Strategy Ser. ISBN:0-7619-6143-7, ISBN13: 978-0-7619-6143-7. Dewey:658.4/038. LCCN:2002-109393.
Audience: **u,f.**

Underwood, Jim **HD30.28.U53 2004**
What's Your Corporate IQ?: How the Smartest Companies Learn, Transform, Lead. Cloth Text. Kaplan Publishing. Chicago, IL. 2004. 240p. ISBN:0-7931-8573-4, ISBN13: 978-0-7931-8573-3. Dewey:658. LCCN:2004-009569.
Audience: **g,l,u,f.**

von Krogh, Georg, et al. **HD53.V63 2000**
Enabling Knowledge Creation: How to Unlock the Mystery of Tacit Knowledge and Release the Power of Innovation. Kazuo Ichijo & Ikujiro Nonaka (Authors). Trade Cloth. Oxford University Press, Inc. New York, NY. 2000. 302p. ISBN:0-19-512616-5, ISBN13: 978-0-19-512616-7. Dewey:658.4/038. LCCN:00-020291.
Audience: **u,f.**

Management Function > General Management > Organizational Behavior > Teams in the Workplace

Annunzio, Susan & McGowan, Sharon **HD58.9.A545 2004**
Contagious Success. Trade Cloth. Penguin Group (USA) Inc. New York, NY. 2004. 272p. ISBN:1-59184-060-0, ISBN13: 978-1-59184-060-2. Dewey:658.4. LCCN:2004-053389.
Audience: **g,l,u,f.**

Barner, Robert W. **HD66.B366 2000**
Team Troubleshooter: How to Find and Fix Team Problems. Trade Paper. Consulting Psychologists Press, Inc. Mountain View, CA. 2001. 320p. ISBN:0-89106-151-7, ISBN13: 978-0-89106-151-9. Dewey:658.4/02. LCCN:00-064534.
Audience: **u,f.**

Beatty, Carol A. & Barker Scott, Brenda A. **HD66.B43 2004**
Building Smart Teams: A Roadmap to High Performance. Paper

Text. SAGE Publications, Inc. Thousand Oaks, CA. 2004. 208p. ISBN:0-7619-2956-8, ISBN13: 978-0-7619-2956-7. Dewey:658.4/022. LCCN:2004-003258.
Audience: **u,f.**

Beyerlein, Michael M., et al. **HD69.S8B49 2002**
Beyond Teams: Building the Collaborative Organization. Susan Freedman, Craig McGee & Linda Moran (Authors). Trade Paper. John Wiley & Sons, Inc. Hoboken, NJ. 2002. 272p. Collaborative Work Systems Ser. ISBN:0-7879-6373-9, ISBN13: 978-0-7879-6373-6. Dewey:658.4/02. LCCN:2002-007171.
Audience: **u.**

Collier Cochran, Alice **HF5734.5.C63 2004**
Roberta's Rules of Order: Sail Through Meetings for Stellar Results Without the Gavel. Trade Paper. John Wiley & Sons, Inc. Hoboken, NJ. 2004. 336p. ISBN:0-7879-6423-9, ISBN13: 978-0-7879-6423-8. Dewey:658.4/56. LCCN:2003-026847.
Audience: **u.**

Harvard Business School Press Staff **HD66.L436 2006**
Leading Teams. Anne Donnellon (Contribution by). Trade Paper. Harvard Business School Press. Boston, MA. 2006. 112p. Pocket Mentor Ser. ISBN:1-4221-0184-3, ISBN13: 978-1-4221-0184-1. Dewey:658.4/022. LCCN:2006-001213.
Audience: **g,l,u,f.**

Jones, Robert; Oyung, Robert; Pace, Lise **HD66.J6565 2005**
Working Virtually: Challenges of Virtual Teams. Idea Group Publishing. 2005. ISBN:1-59140-551-3, ISBN13: 978-1-59140-551-1.
Audience: **g,l,u,f.**

Katzenbach, Jon R. & Smith, Douglas K. **HD66.K384 2003**
The Wisdom of Teams: Creating the High-Performance Organization. Trade Paper. HarperCollins Publishers. New York, NY. 2003. 352p. HarperBusiness Essentials Ser. ISBN:0-06-052200-3, ISBN13: 978-0-06-052200-1. Dewey:658.3/128. LCCN:2002-032805.
Audience: **u,f.** *Choice, 1993.*

Lencioni, Patrick M. & Lencioni, Patrick **HD66.L457 2005**
Overcoming the Five Dysfunctions of a Team: A Field Guide for Leaders, Managers, and Facilitators. Trade Paper. John Wiley & Sons, Inc. Hoboken, NJ. 2005. 192p. ISBN:0-7879-7637-7, ISBN13: 978-0-7879-7637-8. Dewey:658.4/022. LCCN:2004-025529.
Audience: **g,l,u,f.**

Leonard, Dorothy & Swap, Walter **HD53.L46 2005**
When Sparks Fly: Igniting Creativity in Groups. Trade Paper. Harvard Business School Press. Boston, MA. 2005. 256p. ISBN:1-59139-793-6, ISBN13: 978-1-59139-793-9. Dewey:658.4/036.
Audience: **l,u,f.** *Choice, 2000.*

Miller, Brian Cole **HD66.M544 2004**
Quick Teambuilding Activities for Busy Managers: 50 Exercises That Get Results in Just 15 Minutes. Trade Paper. Amacom. New York, NY. 2003. 176p. ISBN:0-8144-7201-X, ISBN13: 978-0-8144-7201-9. Dewey:658.4/02. LCCN:2003-011316.
Audience: **g,l,u,f.**

Ostroff, Frank **HD66.O68 1999**
The Horizontal Organization: What the Organization of the Future Actually Looks Like and How It Delivers Value to Customers. Trade Cloth. Oxford University Press, Inc. New York, NY. 1999. 272p. ISBN:0-19-512138-4, ISBN13: 978-0-19-512138-4. Dewey:658.4/02. LCCN:98-009781.
Audience: **u,f.** *Choice, 1999.*

Parker, Glenn M. **HD66 .P346 1996**
Team Players and Teamwork. Trade Paper. John Wiley & Sons, Inc. Hoboken, NJ. 1996. 208p. Management Ser. ISBN:0-7879-0185-7, ISBN13: 978-0-7879-0185-1. Dewey:658.4/036. LCCN:96-160490.
Audience: **g,l,u,f.**

Pearce, Craig L. **HM1261.S53 2003**
Shared Leadership: Reframing the How's and Why's of Leadership. Jay Alden Conger (Editor). Paper Text. SAGE Publications, Inc. Thousand Oaks, CA. 2002. 344p. ISBN:0-7619-2624-0, ISBN13: 978-0-7619-2624-5. Dewey:303.3/4. LCCN:2002-010085.
Audience: **u,f.**

Salas, Eduardo & Fiore, Stephen M. **HD66.T422 2004**
Team Cognition: Understanding the Factors That Drive Process and Performance. Trade Cloth. American Psychological Association. Washington, DC. 2004. 264p. ISBN:1-59147-103-6, ISBN13: 978-1-59147-103-5. Dewey:302.3/5. LCCN:2003-026064.
Audience: **u,f.**

Senge, Peter M. **HD 58.9 S46**
The Fifth Discipline: The Art and Practice of the Learning Organization. Trade Paper. Doubleday Publishing. New York, NY. 2006. 464p. ISBN:0-385-51725-4, ISBN13: 978-0-385-51725-6. Dewey:658.4.
Audience: **g,l,u,f.**

Thomas, Alan G. & LoVuolo, Ralph L.
Innovative Management: Best Practice Guidelines and Templates for Team Planning and Learning in Action. Jeanne C. Hillson (Editor, Contribution by). Paper Text. Learning House Publishing, Inc. Charlestown, MA. 2006. 208p. ISBN:0-9746358-2-0, ISBN13: 978-0-9746358-2-8.
Audience: **g,l,u,f.**

Wellins, Richard S., et al. **HD66**
Inside Teams: How 20 World-Class Organizations Are Winning Through Teamwork. William C. Byham & George R. Dixon (Authors). Trade Paper. John Wiley & Sons, Inc. Hoboken, NJ. 1996. 378p. Business and Management Ser. ISBN:0-7879-0245-4, ISBN13: 978-0-7879-0245-2. Dewey:658.4/02.
Audience: **g,l,u,f.**

West, Michael **HD66.M473 2004**
Motivate Teams, Maximize Success: Effective Strategies for Realizing Your Goals. Trade Paper. Chronicle Books LLC. San Francisco, CA. 2004. 160p. Positive Business Ser. ISBN:0-8118-3695-9, ISBN13: 978-0-8118-3695-1. Dewey:658.4/022. LCCN:2003-055440.
Audience: **g,l,u,f.**

Management Function > General Management > Planning and Strategy

Ansoff, H. Igor **HD30.28.A535 1988**
The New Corporate Strategy. Trade Cloth. John Wiley & Sons, Inc. Hoboken, NJ. 1988. 288p. ISBN:0-471-62950-2, ISBN13: 978-0-471-62950-4. Dewey:658.4/012. LCCN:87-023266.
Audience: **g,l,u,f.** *Choice, 1988.*

Ellis, Joseph H. **HB3730.E55 2005**
Ahead of the Curve: A Commonsense Guide to Forecasting Business and Market Cycles. Trade Cloth. Harvard Business School Press. Boston, MA. 2005. 276p. ISBN:1-59139-691-3, ISBN13: 978-1-59139-691-8. Dewey:330/.01/12. LCCN:2005-012862.
Audience: **g,l,u,f.**

McGahan, Anita M. **HD58.8.M3445 2004**
How Industries Evolve: Understanding the Critical Link Between Strategy and Innovation. Trade Cloth. Harvard Business School Press. Boston, MA. 2004. 256p. ISBN:1-57851-840-7, ISBN13: 978-1-57851-840-1. Dewey:658.4/012. LCCN:2004-011378.
Audience: **g,l,u,f.** *Choice, 2005.*

Peters, Thomas J. & Waterman, Robert H. Jr. **HD70.U5P424 2004**
In Search of Excellence: Lessons from America's Best-Run Companies. Tan (Editor). Trade Paper. HarperCollins Publishers. New York, NY. 2004. 400p. ISBN:0-06-054878-9, ISBN13: 978-0-06-054878-0. Dewey:658/.00973. LCCN:2003-067759.
Audience: **g,l,u,f.**

Porter, Michael E. **HD41.P67 1980**
Competitive Strategy: Techniques for Analyzing Industries and Competitors. Trade Cloth. Simon & Schuster. New York, NY. 1980. 400p. ISBN:0-02-925360-8, ISBN13: 978-0-02-925360-1. Dewey:658. LCCN:80-065200.
Audience: **u,f.** B

Management Function > General Management > Planning and Strategy > Business Planning

Altschuld, James W. & Witkin, Belle Ruth **HD30.28.A388 2000**
From Needs Assessment to Action: Transforming Needs into Solution Strategies. Trade Paper. SAGE Publications, Inc. Thousand Oaks, CA. 1999. 304p. Needs Assessment Ser. ISBN:0-7619-0932-X, ISBN13: 978-0-7619-0932-3. Dewey:658.4/012. LCCN:99-006773.
Audience: **l,u,f.**

Axson, David A. J. & Hackett Group **HD62.15.A96 2003**
Best Practices in Planning and Management Reporting: From Data to Decisions. Trade Cloth. John Wiley & Sons, Inc. Hoboken, NJ. 2003. 304p. ISBN:0-471-22408-1, ISBN13: 978-0-471-22408-2. Dewey:658.4/012. LCCN:2002-153113.
Audience: **u,f.**

Brown, Shona L. & Eisenhardt, Kathleen M. **HD30.28.B7822 1998**
Competing on the Edge: Strategy As Structured Chaos. Trade Cloth. Harvard Business School Press. Boston, MA. 1998. 320p. ISBN:0-87584-754-4, ISBN13: 978-0-87584-754-2. Dewey:658.4/012. LCCN:97-041459.
Audience: **u,f.** *Choice, 1998.*

Chapman, Chris S. **HD30.28**
Controlling Strategy: Management, Accounting, and Performance Measurement. Trade Cloth. Oxford University Press, Inc. New York, NY. 2005. 204p. ISBN:0-19-928323-0, ISBN13: 978-0-19-928323-1. Dewey:658.4012. LCCN:2005-280913.
Audience: **u,f.**

Christensen, Clayton M., et al. **HD30.28.C54 2004**
Seeing What's Next: Using the Theories of Innovation to Predict Industry Change. Scott D. Anthony & Eric A. Roth (Authors). Trade Cloth. Harvard Business School Press. Boston, MA. 2004. 336p. ISBN:1-59139-185-7, ISBN13: 978-1-59139-185-2. Dewey:658.4/0355. LCCN:2004-004399.
Audience: **u,f.** *Choice, 2005.*

Collis, David J., et al. **HD30.28.H3788 1999**
Harvard Business Review on Corporate Strategy. Cynthia A. Montgomery, Michael Goold, Andrew Campbell, C. K. Prahalad, Kenneth Lieberthal & Stuart L. Hart (Authors). Trade Paper. Harvard Business School Press. Boston, MA. 1999. 272p. The Harvard Business Review Paperback Ser. ISBN:1-57851-142-9, ISBN13: 978-1-57851-142-6. Dewey:658.4/012. LCCN:99-018898.
Audience: **l,u,f.**

Formisano, Roger **HD30.28.F67 2003**
The Manager's Guide to Strategy. Trade Paper. McGraw-Hill Companies, The. New York, NY. 2003. 224p. A Briefcase Book Ser. ISBN:0-07-142172-6, ISBN13: 978-0-07-142172-0. Dewey:658.4/012. LCCN:2003-017209.
Audience: **l,u,f.**

Grove, Andrew S. **HD58.8.G765 1999**
Only the Paranoid Survive: How to Exploit the Crisis Points that Challenge Every Company. Trade Paper. Doubleday Publishing. New York, NY. 1999. 240p. ISBN:0-385-48382-1, ISBN13: 978-0-385-48382-7. Dewey:658.406. LCCN:96-013509.
Audience: **u,f.**

Hamel, Gary & Prahalad, C. **HD30.28**
Competing for the Future. Trade Paper. Harvard Business School Press. Boston, MA. 1996. 384p. ISBN:0-87584-716-1, ISBN13: 978-0-87584-716-0. Dewey:658.4/012. LCCN:94-018035.
Audience: **g,l,u,f.** *Choice, 1995.*

Hill, Charles & Jones, Gareth **HD70.U5**
Strategic Management Theory: An Integrated Approach. Ed. 7. Paper Text. Houghton Mifflin College Division. Boston, MA. 2006. 511p. ISBN:0-618-64164-5, ISBN13: 978-0-618-64164-2. Dewey:658.4.
Audience: **u,f.**

Kaplan, Robert S. & Norton, David P. **HD56.K35 1996**
The Balanced Scorecard: Translating Strategy into Action. Trade Cloth. Harvard Business School Press. Boston, MA. 1996. 336p. ISBN:0-87584-651-3, ISBN13: 978-0-87584-651-4. Dewey:658.401. LCCN:96-010216.
Audience: **g,l,u,f.** *Choice, 1997.*

Kaplan, Robert S. & Norton, David P. **HD30.28.K37 2003**
Strategy Maps: Converting Intangible Assets into Tangible Outcomes. Trade Cloth. Harvard Business School Press. Boston, MA. 2004. 324p. ISBN:1-59139-134-2, ISBN13: 978-1-59139-134-0. Dewey:658.4/012. LCCN:2003-024059.
Audience: **u,f.**

Kaplan, Robert S. & Norton, David P. **HD30.28.K3544 2001**
The Strategy-Focused Organization: How Balanced Scorecard Companies Thrive in the New Business Environment. Trade Cloth. Harvard Business School Press. Boston, MA. 2004. 416p. ISBN:1-57851-250-6, ISBN13: 978-1-57851-250-8. Dewey:658.4/012. LCCN:00-033515.
Audience: **g,l,u,f.**

Katsaros, John & Christy, Peter **HB3730**
Getting It Right the First Time: How Innovative Companies Anticipate Demand. Trade Cloth. Greenwood Publishing Group, Inc. Portsmouth, NH. 2005. 176p. ISBN:0-275-98479-6, ISBN13: 978-0-275-98479-3. Dewey:658.4/0355. LCCN:2004-022505.
Audience: **g,l,u,f.** *Choice, 2005.*

Lele, Milind **HF5415.153.L43 2005**
Monopoly Rules: How to Find, Capture, and Control the Most Lucrative Markets in Any Business. Trade Cloth. Alfred A. Knopf Inc. New York, NY. 2005. 224p. ISBN:1-4000-4972-5, ISBN13: 978-1-4000-4972-1. Dewey:658.5/75. LCCN:2005-006404.
Audience: **u,f.**

Lindgren, Mats & Bandhold, Hans **HD30.28.L543 2002**
Scenario Planning: The Link Between Future and Strategy. Cloth over Boards. Palgrave Macmillan. New York, NY. 2003. 240p. ISBN:0-333-99317-9, ISBN13: 978-0-333-99317-0. Dewey:658.4/012. LCCN:2002-193098.
Audience: **u,f.** *Choice, 2003.*

McKenzie, Richard B. **HC79**
Digital Economics: How Information Technology Has Transformed Business Thinking. Trade Cloth. Greenwood Publishing Group, Inc. Portsmouth, NH. 2003. 336p. ISBN:1-56720-644-1, ISBN13: 978-1-56720-644-9. Dewey:338.5. LCCN:2002-028308.
Audience: **u,f.** *Choice, 2004.*

Meyer, Marshall W. **HD58.9.M487 2002**
Rethinking Performance Measurement: Beyond the Balanced Scorecard. Trade Cloth. Cambridge University Press. New York, NY. 2003. 216p. ISBN:0-521-81243-7, ISBN13: 978-0-521-81243-6. Dewey:658.4/01. LCCN:2002-031068.
Audience: **l,u,f.** *Choice, 2003.*

Nair, Mohan **HD56.25.N35 2004**
Essentials of Balanced Scorecard. Trade Paper. John Wiley & Sons, Inc. Hoboken, NJ. 2004. 244p. Essentials Ser. ISBN:0-471-56973-9, ISBN13: 978-0-471-56973-2. Dewey:658.4/012. LCCN:2003-027402.
Audience: **g,l,u,f.**

Niven, Paul R. **HD58.9.N578 2005**
Balanced Scorecard Diagnostics: Maintaining Maximum Performance. Trade Cloth. John Wiley & Sons, Inc. Hoboken, NJ. 2005. 224p. ISBN:0-471-68123-7, ISBN13: 978-0-471-68123-6. Dewey:658.4/01. LCCN:2004-025807.
Audience: **u,f.**

Rogoff, Edward G. **HD30.28.R65 2003**
Bankable Business Plans. Jeff Bezos (Introduction by). Trade Cloth. Thomson South-Western. Mason, OH. 2003. 272p. ISBN:1-58799-163-2, ISBN13: 978-1-58799-163-9. Dewey:658.4/012. LCCN:2002-042982.
Audience: **g,l,u,f.** *Choice, 2004.*

Siedel, George J. **KF390.B84S56 2002**
Using the Law for Competitive Advantage. Trade Cloth. John Wiley & Sons, Inc. Hoboken, NJ. 2002. 224p. J-B-UMBS Ser., Vol. 6 ISBN:0-7879-5623-6, ISBN13: 978-0-7879-5623-3. Dewey:346.7307. LCCN:2001-008352.
Audience: **g,l,u,f.**

Welch, Jack **HD38.2**
Winning. Magdalena Palmer (Translator). Trade Paper. Ediciones B. Barcelona, 2006. 400p. ISBN:84-666-2109-1, ISBN13: 978-84-666-2109-0. Dewey:658.4/09.
Audience: **g,l,u,f.**

Witkin, Belle Ruth & Altschuld, James W. **HD30.28.W595 1995**
Planning and Conducting Needs Assessments: A Practical Guide. Trade Paper. SAGE Publications, Inc. Thousand Oaks, CA. 1995. 328p. ISBN:0-8039-5810-2, ISBN13: 978-0-8039-5810-4. Dewey:658.4012. LCCN:95-016786.
Audience: **g,l,u,f.**

Management Function > General Management > Planning and Strategy > Decision Analysis

Baron, Jonathan **BF441 .B29 2000**
Thinking and Deciding. Ed. 3. Trade Paper. Cambridge University Press. New York, NY. 2000. 576p. ISBN:0-521-65972-8, ISBN13: 978-0-521-65972-7. Dewey:153.4/2. LCCN:00-033670.
Audience: **g,l,u,f.** *Choice, 1989.*

Blenkhorn, David L. & Fleisher, Craig S. (Editors) **HD38**
Competitive Intelligence and Global Business. Trade Cloth. Greenwood Publishing Group, Inc. Portsmouth, NH. 2005. 312p. ISBN:0-275-98140-1, ISBN13: 978-0-275-98140-2. Dewey:658.4/72. LCCN:2004-018110.
Audience: **l,u,f.**

Boardman, Anthony, et al. **HD47.4.C669 2006**
Cost Benefit Analysis: Concepts and Practice. Ed. 3. David Greenberg, Aidan Vining & David Weimer (Authors). Trade Cloth. Prentice Hall PTR. Upper Saddle River, NJ. 2005. 576p. ISBN:0-13-143583-3, ISBN13: 978-0-13-143583-4. Dewey:658.15/54. LCCN:2005-023256.
Audience: **u,f.**

Brown, Rex V. **BF448**
Rational Choice and Judgment: Decision Analysis for the Decider. Trade Cloth. John Wiley & Sons, Inc. Hoboken, NJ. 2005. 245p. Wiley Series in Systems Engineering and Management Ser. ISBN:0-471-20237-1, ISBN13: 978-0-471-20237-0. Dewey:153.8/3. LCCN:2004-059802.
Audience: **u,f.**

Cyert, Richard M. & March, James G. **HD30.23.C9 1992**
Behavioral Theory of the Firm. Ed. 2. Trade Paper. Blackwell Publishing, Inc. Malden, MA. 1992. 264p. ISBN:0-631-17451-6, ISBN13: 978-0-631-17451-6. Dewey:658.403. LCCN:91-038300.
Audience: **u,f.**

Gladwell, Malcolm **BF448.G53 2005**
Blink: The Power of Thinking Without Thinking. Trade Cloth. Little Brown & Company. New York, NY. 2005. 288p. ISBN:0-316-17232-4, ISBN13: 978-0-316-17232-5. Dewey:153.4/4. LCCN:2004-013916.
Audience: **g,l,u,f.** *Choice, 2005.*

Golub, Andrew Lang **HD30.23.G64 1997**
Decision Analysis: An Integrated Approach. Trade Paper. John Wiley & Sons, Inc. Hoboken, NJ. 1997. 256p. ISBN:0-471-15511-X, ISBN13: 978-0-471-15511-9. Dewey:658.4/03. LCCN:96-035433.
Audience: **l,u,f.**

McAfee, R. Preston **HD30.28.M3815 2005**
Competitive Solutions: The Strategist's Toolkit. Trade Paper. Princeton University Press. Princeton, NJ. 2005. 424p. ISBN:0-691-12403-5, ISBN13: 978-0-691-12403-2. Dewey:658.4/012.
Audience: **l,u,f.**

Nutt, Paul C. **HD30.23.N88 1989**
Making Tough Decisions: Tactics for Improving Managerial Decision Making. Trade Cloth. John Wiley & Sons, Inc. Hoboken, NJ. 1989. 612p. Management Series - Public Administration ISBN:1-55542-138-5, ISBN13: 978-1-55542-138-0. Dewey:658.4/03. LCCN:88-046079.
Audience: **g,l,u,f.** *Choice, 1990.*

Puttaswamaiah, K. **HD75.6.C693 2002**
Cost-Benefit Analysis: With Reference to Environment and Ecology. Trade Paper. Transaction Publishers. Somerset, NJ. 2001. 430p. ISBN:0-7658-0706-8, ISBN13: 978-0-7658-0706-9. Dewey:333.7. LCCN:00-062882.
Audience: **u,f.**

Rath, Tom & Clifton, Donald O. **BF204.6**
How Full Is Your Bucket?: Positive Strategies for Work and Life. Trade Cloth. Gallup Press. New York, NY. 2004. 120p. ISBN:1-59562-003-6, ISBN13: 978-1-59562-003-3. Dewey:158.1. LCCN:2004-106559.
Audience: **g,l,u,f.**

Rothberg, Helen & Erickson, G. Scott **HD30.2.R6648 2004**
From Knowledge to Intelligence: Creating Competitive Advantage in the Next Economy. Audio, Other. Elsevier Science & Technology Books. Saint Louis, MO. 2004. 400p. ISBN:0-7506-7762-7, ISBN13: 978-0-7506-7762-2. Dewey:658.4/038. LCCN:2004-050665.
Audience: **u,f.**

Simon, Herbert A. **HD31.S55 1997**
Administrative Behavior: A Study of Decision-Making Processes in Administrative Organizations. Ed. 4. Trade Paper. Simon & Schuster. New York, NY. 1997. 384p. ISBN:0-684-83582-7, ISBN13: 978-0-684-83582-2. Dewey:658.4. LCCN:96-034148.
Audience: **u,f.**

Vibert, Conor **HD30.37**
Competitive Intelligence: A Framework for Web-based Analysis and Decision Making. Trade Cloth. Thomson South-Western. Mason, OH. 2003. 264p. ISBN:0-324-20325-X, ISBN13: 978-0-324-20325-7. Dewey:658.4/72. LCCN:2004-298942.
Audience: **u,f.**

Management Function > General Management > Planning and Strategy > Game Theory

Bacharach, Michael **HB144.B328 2006**
Beyond Individual Choice: Teams and Frames in Game Theory. Natalie Gold & Robert Sugden (Editors). Trade Cloth. Princeton University Press. Princeton, NJ. 2006. 272p. ISBN:0-691-12005-6, ISBN13: 978-0-691-12005-8. Dewey:330/.01/5193. LCCN:2005-049608.
Audience: **u,f.**

Barash, David P. **HM1111**
The Survival Game: How Game Theory Explains the Biology of Cooperation and Competition. Trade Paper. Henry Holt & Company. New York, NY. 2004. 320p. ISBN:0-8050-7699-9, ISBN13: 978-0-8050-7699-8. Dewey:302.
Audience: **l,u,f.**

Binmore, Ken **QA269.B475 2005**
Playing for Real: Game Theory. Trade Cloth. Oxford University Press, Inc. New York, NY. 2007. 764p. ISBN:0-19-530057-2, ISBN13: 978-0-19-530057-4. Dewey:519.3. LCCN:2005-053938.
Audience: **u,f.**

Brams, Steven J. **JA72.5.B73 2004**
Game Theory and Politics. Trade Paper. Dover Publications, Inc. Mineola, NY. 2004. 336p. ISBN:0-486-43497-4, ISBN13: 978-0-486-43497-1. Dewey:320/.01/5193. LCCN:2004-049420.
Audience: **g,l,u,f.**

Kaplow, Louis & Shavell, Steven **K212**
Decision Analysis, Game Theory, and Information. Trade Cloth. Foundation Press. New York, NY. 2004. 488p. ISBN:1-58778-807-1, ISBN13: 978-1-58778-807-9. Dewey:340.1.
Audience: **u,f.**

Kelly, Anthony **HB144.K45 2002**
Decision Making Using Game Theory: An Introduction for Managers. Cloth Text. Cambridge University Press. New York, NY. 2003. 214p. ISBN:0-521-81462-6, ISBN13: 978-0-521-81462-1. Dewey:658.4/0353. LCCN:2002-019217.
Audience: **g,l.**

Miller, James D. **HD30.26.M54 2003**
Game Theory at Work: How to Use Game Theory to Outthink and Outmaneuver Your Competition. Trade Cloth. McGraw-Hill

Companies, The. New York, NY. 2003. 288p. ISBN:0-07-140020-6, ISBN13: 978-0-07-140020-6. Dewey:658.4/0353. LCCN:2002-013681.
Audience: **g,l.**

Montet, Christian & Serra, Daniel **HB144.M66 2003**
Game Theory and Economics. Trade Paper. Palgrave Macmillan. New York, NY. 2003. 520p. ISBN:0-333-61847-5, ISBN13: 978-0-333-61847-9. Dewey:330/.01/5193. LCCN:2002-030258.
Audience: **u,f.**

Sugar, Steve **HD30.26.S84 1998**
Games That Teach: Experiential Activities for Reinforcing Training. Trade Paper. John Wiley & Sons, Inc. Hoboken, NJ. 1998. 192p. ISBN:0-7879-4018-6, ISBN13: 978-0-7879-4018-8. Dewey:652.3/124. LCCN:97-076317.
Audience: **l,u,f.**

Management Function > General Management > Planning and Strategy > Mergers and Acquisitions

Anandalingam, G. & Lucas, Henry C. **HD2746.5.A53 2004**
Beware the Winner's Curse: Victories That Can Sink You and Your Company. Trade Cloth. Oxford University Press, Inc. New York, NY. 2004. 256p. ISBN:0-19-517740-1, ISBN13: 978-0-19-517740-4. Dewey:658.1/62. LCCN:2004-002987.
Audience: **l,u,f.**

Blair, Margaret M. (Editor) **HD2746.5**
The Deal Decade: What Takeovers and Leveraged Buyouts Mean for Corporate Governance. Trade Paper. Brookings Institution Press. Washington, DC. 1993. 390p. ISBN:0-8157-0945-5, ISBN13: 978-0-8157-0945-9. Dewey:338.8/3. LCCN:92-039450.
Audience: **u,f.** *Choice, 1993.*

Burrough, Bryan & Helyar, John **HD2796.R57**
Barbarians at the Gate: The Fall of R. J. R. Nabisco. Trade Paper. HarperCollins Publishers. New York, NY. 2004. 576p. ISBN:0-06-092038-6, ISBN13: 978-0-06-092038-8. Dewey:338.8/3664/00973. LCCN:89-045635.
Audience: **g,l,u,f.**

Burrows, Peter **HD9696.2**
Backfire: Carly Fiorina's High-Stakes Battle for the Soul of Hewlett-Packard. Trade Cloth. John Wiley & Sons, Inc. Hoboken, NJ. 2003. 304p. ISBN:0-471-26765-1, ISBN13: 978-0-471-26765-2. Dewey:338.7/61004165. LCCN:2002-156443.
Audience: **g,l.**

Frankel, Michael E. S. **HD2746.5**
Mergers and Acquisitions Basics: The Key Steps of Acquisitions, Divestitures, and Investments. Trade Cloth. John Wiley & Sons, Inc. Hoboken, NJ. 2005. 320p. ISBN:0-471-67518-0, ISBN13: 978-0-471-67518-1. Dewey:658.1/6. LCCN:2005-002062.
Audience: **u,f.**

Geisst, Charles R. **HG4028.M4G45 2005**
Deals of the Century: Wall Street, Mergers, and the Making of Modern America. Trade Paper. John Wiley & Sons, Inc. Hoboken, NJ. 2005. 330p. ISBN:0-471-73603-1, ISBN13: 978-0-471-73603-5. Dewey:338.8/3/0973.
Audience: **g,l,u,f.**

Gilson, Stuart C. **HD58.8.G555 2001**
Creating Value through Corporate Restructuring: Case Studies in Bankruptcies, Buyouts, and Breakups. Trade Cloth. John Wiley & Sons, Inc. Hoboken, NJ. 2001. 528p. Wiley Finance Ser., Vol. 95 ISBN:0-471-40559-0, ISBN13: 978-0-471-40559-7. Dewey:658.1/6. LCCN:2001-023753.
Audience: **u,f.**

Hindery, Leo & Cauley, Leslie **HD58.6.H56 2003**
The Biggest Game of All: The Inside Strategies, Tactics, and Temperaments That Make Great Dealmakers Great. Trade Cloth. Simon & Schuster. New York, NY. 2003. 272p. ISBN:0-7432-2900-2, ISBN13: 978-0-7432-2900-5. Dewey:658.4/052. LCCN:2002-034670.
Audience: **u,f.**

Kwoka, John E. & White, Lawrence J. (Editors) **HD2795.A64 2003**
The Antitrust Revolution: Economics, Competition, and Policy. Ed. 4. Cloth Text. Oxford University Press, Inc. New York, NY. 2003. 544p. ISBN:0-19-516117-3, ISBN13: 978-0-19-516117-5. Dewey:338.8/5. LCCN:2002-042551.
Audience: **g,l,u,f.**

Lajoux, Alexandra Reed & Nesvold, H. Peter **HD2746.5.L353 2004**
The Art of M&A Structuring. Trade Cloth. McGraw-Hill Companies, The. New York, NY. 2004. 350p. ISBN:0-07-141064-3, ISBN13: 978-0-07-141064-9. Dewey:658.1/62. LCCN:2003-016497.
Audience: **u,f.**

Lees, Stan **HD58.8.L424 2002**
Global Acquisitions: Strategic Integration and the Human Factor. Cloth over Boards. Palgrave Macmillan. New York, NY. 2003. 272p. ISBN:0-333-77629-1, ISBN13: 978-0-333-77629-2. Dewey:658.1/6. LCCN:2002-042496.
Audience: **u,f.**

Mirvis, Philip H., et al. **HD58.8**
To the Desert and Back: The Story of One of the Most Dramatic Business Transformations on Record. Karen Ayas & George Roth (Authors). Trade Cloth. John Wiley & Sons, Inc. Hoboken, NJ. 2003. 272p. ISBN:0-7879-6677-0, ISBN13: 978-0-7879-6677-5. Dewey:338.7/61664/009492. LCCN:2003-002023.
Audience: **g,l.**

Morris, Joseph M. & Gole, William J. **HG4028.M4**
Mergers and Acquisitions: Business Strategies for Accountants. Ed. 2. Trade Paper. John Wiley & Sons, Inc. Hoboken, NJ. 2006. 144p. ISBN:0-471-46471-6, ISBN13: 978-0-471-46471-6. Dewey:657/.96.
Audience: **u,f.**

Munk, Nina **K526**
Fools Rush In: Steve Case, Jerry Levin, and the Unmaking of AOL Time Warner. Trade Paper. HarperCollins Publishers. New York, NY. 2005. 368p. ISBN:0-06-054035-4, ISBN13: 978-0-06-054035-7. Dewey:338.7/61004678.
Audience: **g,l,u,f.**

Oesterle, Dale A. **KF1477.A7O33 2005**
The Law of Mergers and Acquisitions. Ed. 3. Trade Cloth. West Publishing Company, College & School Division. Eagan, MN. 2005. 810p. American Casebook Ser. ISBN:0-314-15391-8, ISBN13: 978-0-314-15391-3. Dewey:346.73/06626. LCCN:2005-278948.
Audience: **u,f.**

Paulson, Ed **HD9696.2.U64.C5 2001**
Inside Cisco: The Real Story of Sustained M&A Growth. Trade Cloth. John Wiley & Sons, Inc. Hoboken, NJ. 2001. 320p. ISBN:0-471-41425-5, ISBN13: 978-0-471-41425-4. Dewey:338.8/36213981/0973. LCCN:2002-265506.
Audience: **g,l,u,f.**

Romanek, Broc & Krus, Cynthia M. **HD2746.5**
Mergers and Acquisitions. Trade Paper. John Wiley & Sons, Inc. Hoboken, NJ. 2002. 116p. Express Exec Ser. ISBN:1-84112-339-0, ISBN13: 978-1-84112-339-4. Dewey:658.1/6.
Audience: **u,f.**

Shenefield, John H. & Stelzer, Irwin M. **KF1650.S53 2001**
The Antitrust Laws: A Primer. Ed. 4. Trade Cloth. National Book Network. Lanham, MD. 2001. 202p. ISBN:0-8447-4154-X, ISBN13: 978-0-8447-4154-3. Dewey:343.73/0721. LCCN:2001-045088.
Audience: **g,l,u,f.** *Choice, 1994.*

Sherman, Andrew J. & Hart, Milledge A. **HD58.8.S484 2006**
Mergers and Acquisitions from A to Z. Ed. 2. Trade Cloth. Amacom. New York, NY. 2006. 288p. ISBN:0-8144-0880-X, ISBN13: 978-0-8144-0880-3. Dewey:658.1/62. LCCN:2005-016449.
Audience: **g,l,u,f.**

Wasserstein, Bruce **HD2746.55.U5W37 2000**
Big Deal: 2000 and Beyond. Ed. 2. Trade Cloth. Warner Books, Inc. New York, NY. 2000. 944p. ISBN:0-446-52642-8, ISBN13: 978-0-446-52642-5. Dewey:338.8/3/0973. LCCN:99-044624.
Audience: **g,u,f.**

Management Function > General Management > Planning and Strategy > Organizational Structure

ABA Coordinating Committee on Nonprofit Governance Staff (Contribution by) **KF1388.5.G85 2005**
Guide to Nonprofit Corporate Governance in the Wake of Sarbanes-Oxley. Trade Paper. American Bar Association. Chicago, IL. 2006. 80p. ISBN:1-59031-567-7, ISBN13: 978-1-59031-567-5. Dewey:346.73/064. LCCN:2005-011947.
Audience: **u,f.**

Ali, Paul & Gregoriou, Greg N. **HD2741.I589 2006**
International Corporate Governance after Sarbanes-Oxley. Trade Cloth. John Wiley & Sons, Inc. Hoboken, NJ. 2006. 608p. Wiley Finance Ser. ISBN:0-471-77592-4, ISBN13: 978-0-471-77592-8. Dewey:658.4. LCCN:2005-026054.
Audience: **u,f.**

Anheier, Helmut K. (Editor) **HG3761.W46 1998**
When Things Go Wrong: Organizational Failures and Breakdowns. Trade Paper. SAGE Publications, Inc. Thousand Oaks, CA. 1999. 328p. ISBN:0-7619-1048-4, ISBN13: 978-0-7619-1048-0. Dewey:658.4. LCCN:98-025537.
Audience: **g,l.**

Ashkenas, Ronald N., et al. **HD58.8.B675 2002**
The Boundaryless Organization: Breaking the Chains of Organizational Structure. Ed. 2. Todd Jick, Steve Kerr & Dave Ulrich (Authors). Trade Cloth. John Wiley & Sons, Inc. Hoboken, NJ. 2002. 384p. Jossey Bass Business and Management Ser. ISBN:0-7879-5943-X, ISBN13: 978-0-7879-5943-2. Dewey:658.4/063. LCCN:2001-006128.
Audience: **l,u,f.**

Berle, Adolf A. Jr. & Means, Gardiner C. **HD2795.B53 1991**
The Modern Corporation and Private Property. Ed. 2. Trade Paper. Transaction Publishers. Somerset, NJ. 1997. 426p. ISBN:0-88738-887-6, ISBN13: 978-0-88738-887-3. Dewey:338.5/024658. LCCN:90-048752.
Audience: **g,l,u,f.**

Cappelli, Peter **HD58.8.C452 1997**
Change at Work. Trade Cloth. Oxford University Press, Inc. New York, NY. 1997. 287p. ISBN:0-19-510327-0, ISBN13: 978-0-19-510327-4. Dewey:658.4/06. LCCN:96-023911.
Audience: **g,l,u,f.** *Choice, 1997.*

Cappelli, Peter **HD31.C3433 1999**
The New Deal at Work: Managing the Market-Driven Workforce. Trade Cloth. Harvard Business School Press. Boston, MA. 1999. 320p. ISBN:0-87584-668-8, ISBN13: 978-0-87584-668-2. Dewey:658.3. LCCN:98-042221.
Audience: **l,u,f.** *Choice, 1999.*

Carey, Dennis & von Weichs, Marie-Caroline **HD38.2.C374 2003**
How to Run a Company: Lessons from Top Leaders of the CEO Academy. Trade Cloth. Crown Publishing Group. New York, NY. 2003. 304p. ISBN:1-4000-4927-X, ISBN13: 978-1-4000-4927-1. Dewey:658.4/2. LCCN:2003-010402.
Audience: **u,f.**

Colley, John L., et al. **HD2741.C77462**
Corporate Governance. Jacqueline L. Doyle, Wallace Stettinius & George Logan (Authors). Trade Paper, Perfect. McGraw-Hill Companies, The. New York, NY. 2005. 256p. ISBN:0-07-146400-X, ISBN13: 978-0-07-146400-0. Dewey:658.4.
Audience: **g,l,u,f.**

Epstein, Marc J. & Birchard, Bill **HD2741.E67 2000**
Counting What Counts: Turning Corporate Accountability to Competitive Advantage. Trade Paper. Basic Books. New York, NY. 2000. 320p. ISBN:0-7382-0313-0, ISBN13: 978-0-7382-0313-3. Dewey:658.4.
Audience: **g,l,u,f.** *Choice, 1999.*

Ernst & Young LLP Staff, et al. **HD2741**
Corporate Governance. Peter Wallace & John Zinkin (Authors). Trade Paper. John Wiley & Sons, Inc. Hoboken, NJ. 2005. 220p. ISBN:0-470-82112-4, ISBN13: 978-0-470-82112-1. Dewey:658.4/0095. LCCN:2005-273779.
Audience: **u,f.**

Fritz, Robert **HD38.F726 1996**
Corporate Tides: The Inescapable Laws of Organizational Structure. Trade Cloth. Berrett-Koehler Publishers, Inc. San Francisco, CA. 1996. 200p. ISBN:1-881052-88-5, ISBN13: 978-1-881052-88-3. Dewey:658.4/063. LCCN:96-015508.
Audience: **u,f.**

Gandossy, Robert P. & Sonnenfeld, Jeffrey A. (Editors) **HD57.7.L4314 2004**
Leadership and Governance from the Inside Out. Trade Cloth. John Wiley & Sons, Inc. Hoboken, NJ. 2004. 320p. ISBN:0-471-67185-1, ISBN13: 978-0-471-67185-5. Dewey:658.4. LCCN:2004-007663.
Audience: **l,u,f.**

Garnaut, Ross, et al. **HC427.92.C42874 2005**
China's Ownership Transformation: Process, Outcomes, Prospects. Ligang Song, Stoyan Tenev & Yang Yao (Authors). Trade Paper, Perfect. World Bank Publications. Washington, DC. 2005. 256p. ISBN:0-8213-6237-2, ISBN13: 978-0-8213-6237-2. Dewey:330.951. LCCN:2005-047501.
Audience: **u,f.** *Choice, 2006.*

Gourevitch, Peter Alexis & Shinn, James **HD2741.G677 2005**
Political Power and Corporate Control: The New Global Politics of Corporate Governance. Trade Cloth. Princeton University Press. Princeton, NJ. 2005. 384p. ISBN:0-691-12291-1, ISBN13: 978-0-691-12291-5. Dewey:338.6+. LCCN:2004-065435.
Audience: **u,f.** *Choice, 2006.*

Green, Scott **HD2745.G74 2005**
Sarbanes-Oxley and the Board of Directors: Techniques and Best Practices for Corporate Governance. Trade Cloth. John Wiley & Sons, Inc. Hoboken, NJ. 2005. 313p. Wiley CIA Exam Review Ser. ISBN:0-471-73608-2, ISBN13: 978-0-471-73608-0. Dewey:658.4/22. LCCN:2005-010214.
Audience: **u,f.**

Hammer, Michael & Champy, James **HD58.8.H356 2003**
Reengineering the Corporation: A Manifesto for Business Revolution. Trade Paper. HarperCollins Publishers. New York, NY. 2004. 272p. HarperBusiness Essentials Ser. ISBN:0-06-055953-5, ISBN13: 978-0-06-055953-3. Dewey:658.4063. LCCN:2004-295374.
Audience: **g,l,u,f.** *Choice, 2002.*

Jacoby, Sanford M. **HD5660.J3J33 2005**
The Embedded Corporation: Corporate Governance and Employment Relations in Japan and the United States. Trade Cloth. Princeton University Press. Princeton, NJ. 2004. 248p. ISBN:0-691-11999-6, ISBN13: 978-0-691-11999-1. Dewey:338.6/0952. LCCN:2004-044328.
Audience: **u,f.** *Choice, 2005.*

Kaen, Fred R. **HD2741.K327 2003**
A Blueprint for Corporate Governance: Strategy, Accountability, and the Preservation of Shareholder Value. Trade Cloth. Amacom. New York, NY. 2002. 256p. ISBN:0-8144-0586-X, ISBN13: 978-0-8144-0586-4. Dewey:658.4. LCCN:2002-014162.
Audience: **g,l,u,f.** *Choice, 2003.*

Karger, Gunther (Author, Editor)
Wall Street and Government Fraud: How They Deceive Us. Trade Paper. Discovery Group. Miami, FL. 2005. 222p. ISBN:0-9645979-3-4, ISBN13: 978-0-9645979-3-8.
Audience: **g,l.**

Keasey, Kevin (Editor), et al. **HD2741.C775 2005**
Corporate Governance: Accountability, Enterprise and International Comparisons. Steve R. Thompson & Michael Wright (Editors). Trade Cloth. John Wiley & Sons, Inc. Hoboken, NJ. 2005. 482p. ISBN:0-470-87030-3, ISBN13: 978-0-470-87030-3. Dewey:338.6. LCCN:2004-023807.
Audience: **u,f.**

Kennedy-Glans, Donna & Schulz, Robert **HF5387.K464 2005**
Corporate Integrity: A Toolkit for Managing Beyond Compliance. Trade Cloth. John Wiley & Sons, Inc. Hoboken, NJ. 2005. 288p. ISBN:0-470-83569-9, ISBN13: 978-0-470-83569-2. Dewey:658.4. LCCN:2005-415648.
Audience: **u,f.**

Krier, Dan **HD2741.K75 2005**
Speculative Management: Stock Market Power and Corporate Change. Paper Text. State University of New York Press. Albany, NY. 2005. 320p. SUNY Series in the Sociology of Work and Organizations ISBN:0-7914-6350-8, ISBN13: 978-0-7914-6350-5. Dewey:338.7. LCCN:2004-045337.
Audience: **u,f.** *Choice, 2006.*

Lorsch, Jay W. (Editor), et al. **HD2741**
Restoring Trust in American Business. Leslie Berlowitz & Andy Zelleke (Editors). Trade Paper. MIT Press. Cambridge, MA. 2005. 192p. ISBN:0-262-74027-3, ISBN13: 978-0-262-74027-2. Dewey:658.4/08.
Audience: **g,l,u,f.** *Choice, 2005.*

MacAvoy, Paul & Millstein, Ira M. **HD2741.M196 2004**
The Recurrent Crisis in Corporate Governance. Trade Paper. Stanford University Press. Palo Alto, CA. 2004. 300p. ISBN:0-8047-5086-6, ISBN13: 978-0-8047-5086-8. Dewey:658.4. LCCN:2004-011644.
Audience: **u,f.**

Nadler, David, et al. **HD58.9.N33 1997**
Competing by Design: The Power of Organizational Architecture. Ed. 2. Michael Tushman & Mark B. Nadler (Authors). Trade Cloth. Oxford University Press, Inc. New York, NY. 1997. 252p. ISBN:0-19-509917-6, ISBN13: 978-0-19-509917-1. Dewey:658.4/02. LCCN:96-041167.
Audience: **l,u,f.**

Niskanen, William A. **HF5658.A24 2005**
After Enron: Lessons for Public Policy. Book, Other. Rowman & Littlefield Publishers, Inc. Lanham, MD. 2005. 384p. ISBN:0-7425-4433-8, ISBN13: 978-0-7425-4433-8. Dewey:338.6/0973. LCCN:2004-024939.
Audience: **u,f.** *Choice, 2006.*

Nofsinger, John R. & Kim, Kenneth **HD2741.K4713 2007**
Corporate Governance. Ed. 2. Trade Paper. Pearson Education.

Boston, MA. 2006. 192p. ISBN:0-13-173534-9, ISBN13: 978-0-13-173534-7. Dewey:338.7/4. LCCN:2006-003612.
Audience: **g,l,u,f.**

Nofsinger, John & Kim, Kenneth **HD2741 .N84**
Infectious Greed: Restoring Confidence in America's Companies. Trade Cloth. DIANE Publishing Company. Collingdale, PA. 2005. 277p. ISBN:0-7567-9535-4, ISBN13: 978-0-7567-9535-1. Dewey:332.63/2042.
Audience: **g,l,u,f.**

Oliver, R. E. **HF5351**
What Is Transparency? Trade Paper. McGraw-Hill Companies, The. New York, NY. 2004. 96p. ISBN:0-07-143548-4, ISBN13: 978-0-07-143548-2. Dewey:174/.4. LCCN:2003-025365.
Audience: **g,l.**

Phillips, Robert **HD2741.P48 2003**
Stakeholder Theory and Organizational Ethics. Trade Cloth. Berrett-Koehler Publishers, Inc. San Francisco, CA. 2003. 200p. ISBN:1-57675-268-2, ISBN13: 978-1-57675-268-5. Dewey:174/.4. LCCN:2003-048112.
Audience: **u,f.** *Choice, 2004.*

Management Function > General Management > Planning and Strategy > Small Business Start-Up

American Bar Association Staff **KF1659.Z9A43 2000**
The American Bar Association Legal Guide for Small Business: Everything a Small-Business Person Must Know, from Start-Up to Employment Laws to Financing and Selling a Business. Trade Paper. Crown Publishing Group. New York, NY. 2000. 544p. ISBN:0-8129-3015-0, ISBN13: 978-0-8129-3015-3. Dewey:343.7307. LCCN:99-086498.
Audience: **g,u,f.**

Ballew, Vincent **HD2346.U5**
Make it Happen: Small business Start-up. Trade Paper. Detroit International Press. Troy, MI. 2005. 142p. ISBN:0-9766622-2-1, ISBN13: 978-0-9766622-2-8. Dewey:338.6420973.
Audience: **g,l.**

Barrow, Colin **HD62.7**
The Complete Small Business Guide: A Sourcebook for New and Small Businesses. Ed. 8. Trade Paper. John Wiley & Sons, Inc. Hoboken, NJ. 2006. 472p. Capstone Reference Ser. ISBN:1-84112-686-1, ISBN13: 978-1-84112-686-9. Dewey:658/.022.
Audience: **g,l,u,f.**

Blackford, Mansel G. **HD2346.U5B56 2003**
A History of Small Business in America. Ed. 2. Trade Cloth. University of North Carolina Press. Chapel Hill, NC. 2003. 272p. The Luther Hartwell Hodges Series on Business, Society, and the State ISBN:0-8078-2780-0, ISBN13: 978-0-8078-2780-2. Dewey:338.6/42/0973. LCCN:2002-151277.
Audience: **g,l,u,f.** *Choice, 2003, 1992.*

Burns, Paul **HD2341.B873 2001**
Entrepreneurship and Small Business. Cloth over Boards. Palgrave Macmillan. New York, NY. 2001. 444p. ISBN:0-333-91473-2, ISBN13: 978-0-333-91473-1. Dewey:658.02/2. LCCN:2001-040653.
Audience: **u,f.**

Gottry, Steve **HD62.7**
Common Sense Business: Starting, Operating, and Growing Your Small Business—in Any Economy!. Trade Paper. HarperCollins Publishers. New York, NY. 2006. 368p. ISBN:0-06-077839-3, ISBN13: 978-0-06-077839-2. Dewey:658.02/2.
Audience: **g,l.**

Holihan, Mary **HF5549.H5237 2006**
365 Answers about Human Resources for the Small Business Owner: What Every Manager Needs to Know about Work Place Law. Paper Text. Atlantic Publishing Company. Ocala, FL. 2006. 288p. ISBN:0-910627-78-9, ISBN13: 978-0-910627-78-8. Dewey:658.3. LCCN:2006-012536.
Audience: **g,l.**

Kirk, Randy W. **HD62.7.K57 2006**
Running a 21st-Century Small Business: The Owner's Guide to Starting and Growing Your Company. Trade Paper. Warner Books, Inc. New York, NY. 2006. 416p. ISBN:0-446-69618-8, ISBN13: 978-0-446-69618-0. Dewey:658.02/2. LCCN:2005-052118.
Audience: **g,l,u,f.**

Lawson, Russell **HD59.L42 2006**
How Using Pr Can Boost Your Business Public Relations for the Small Business. Trade Paper, Perfect. Kogan Page, Ltd. London, 2006. 192p. ISBN:0-7494-4468-1, ISBN13: 978-0-7494-4468-6. Dewey:659.2. LCCN:2005-035382.
Audience: **u,f.**

Little, Kenneth E. **HG4026**
The Complete Idiot's Guide to Finance for Small Business. Trade Paper. Penguin Group (USA) Inc. New York, NY. 2006. 352p. ISBN:1-59257-479-3, ISBN13: 978-1-59257-479-7. Dewey:658.15. LCCN:2005-937200.
Audience: **g,l.**

Marinel, Alan Le **HD62.7**
Start and Run Your Own Business: The Complete Guide to Setting up and Managing a Small Business. Ed. 2. Trade Paper. How To Books. Oxford, 2005. 278p. ISBN:1-85703-988-2, ISBN13: 978-1-85703-988-7. Dewey:658.022.
Audience: **g,l,f.**

Pakroo, Peri **KF1659.Z9**
The Small Business Start-up Kit. Ed. 4. Trade Paper. NOLO. Berkeley, CA. 2006. 384p. ISBN:1-4133-0412-5, ISBN13: 978-1-4133-0412-1. Dewey:346.73/0652. LCCN:2005-055490.
Audience: **g,l,u,f.**

Pinson, Linda & Jinnett, Jerry **HD62.5.P565 2006**
Steps to Small Business Start-Up. Ed. 6. Paper Text. Kaplan Publishing. Chicago, IL. 2006. 272p. ISBN:1-4195-3727-X, ISBN13: 978-1-4195-3727-1. Dewey:658.1/11. LCCN:2006-005651.
Audience: **g,l,u,f.**

Rickman, Cheryl D. **HD62.5**
Small Business Start-Up Workbook: A Step-by-Step Guide to Starting the Business You've Dreamed Of. Trade Paper. How To Books. Oxford, 2006. 270p. ISBN:1-84528-038-5, ISBN13: 978-1-84528-038-3. Dewey:658.11.
Audience: **g,l,u,f.**

Rogak, Lisa **HD62.7**
The Complete Small Business Start-up Guide. Trade Paper. John Wiley & Sons, Inc. Hoboken, NJ. 2004. 256p. ISBN:0-471-67957-7, ISBN13: 978-0-471-67957-8. Dewey:658/.022.
Audience: **g,l,u,f.**

Steingold, Fred **KF1659.A65**
Legal Forms for Starting and Running a Small Business. Ed. 4. Trade Paper. NOLO. Berkeley, CA. 2006. 448p. ISBN:1-4133-0411-7, ISBN13: 978-1-4133-0411-4. Dewey:346.73/06520269. LCCN:2005-055493.
Audience: **g,l,u,f.**

Thomson Gale Staff **HD62.7**
Encyclopedia of Small Business. Ed. 3. Trade Cloth. Thomson Gale. Farmington Hills, MI. 2006. 1,100p. ISBN:0-7876-9112-7, ISBN13: 978-0-7876-9112-7. Dewey:658.02/2. LCCN:2006-022623.
Audience: **g,l,u,f.**

Management Function > Finance

HG1
Finance Site List.
http://fisher.osu.edu/fin/journal/jofsites.htm
Audience: **g,l,u,f.**

HG151
Finance, Wikipedia, the free encyclopedia.
http://en.wikipedia.org/wiki/Finance
Audience: **g,l,u,f.**

HG173
studyfinance.com.
http://www.studyfinance.com/
Audience: **l,u.**

HG151.8
Wachowicz's Web World: Web Sites for Discerning Finance Students.
http://web.utk.edu/~jwachowi/wacho_world.html#Part%20I
Audience: **g,l,u,f.**

Allen, Franklin & Gale, Douglas **HG173.A433 2000**
Comparing Financial Systems. Trade Cloth. MIT Press. Cambridge, MA. 2000. 521p. ISBN:0-262-01177-8, ISBN13: 978-0-262-01177-8. Dewey:332. LCCN:99-030173.
Audience: **u,f.**

Balachandran, M. **Z7164.F5B23 1988**
A Guide to Statistical Sources in Money, Banking, and Finance. Trade Cloth. Greenwood Publishing Group, Inc. Portsmouth, NH. 1987. 128p. ISBN:0-89774-265-6, ISBN13: 978-0-89774-265-8. Dewey:016.332/021. LCCN:87-021941.
Audience: **g,l,u,f.** *Choice, 1988.*

Battilossi, Stefano & Cassis, Youssef (Editors) **HG2974.E9 2002**
European Banks and the American Challenge: Competition and Cooperation in International Banking Under Bretton Woods. Trade Cloth. Oxford University Press, Inc. New York, NY. 2002. 238p. ISBN:0-19-925027-8, ISBN13: 978-0-19-925027-1. Dewey:332.1/5/094. LCCN:2001-055719.
Audience: **u,f.**

Becker, William H. & McClenahan, William M. **HG3754.U5B43 2002**
The Market, the State, and the Export-Import Bank of the United States, 1934-2000. Cloth Text. Cambridge University Press. New York, NY. 2003. 352p. ISBN:0-521-81143-0, ISBN13: 978-0-521-81143-9. Dewey:332.1/54/0973. LCCN:2002-066521.
Audience: **u,f.** *Choice, 2003.*

Benston, George J., et al. **HG2481.P47 1986**
Perspectives on Safe and Sound Banking: Past, Present, and Future. Robert A. Eisenbeis, Paul M. Horvitz, Edward J. Kane & George G. Kaufman (Authors). Trade Cloth. MIT Press. Cambridge, MA. 1986. 352p. Regulation of Economic Activity Ser. ISBN:0-262-02246-X, ISBN13: 978-0-262-02246-0. Dewey:332.1/0973. LCCN:85-023882.
Audience: **u,f.** *Choice, 1986.*

Blinder, Alan S. **HG1811.B554 2004**
The Quiet Revolution: Central Banking Goes Modern. Cloth over Boards. Yale University Press. Cumberland, RI. 2004. 144p. Arthur Okun Memorial Lectures Ser. ISBN:0-300-10087-6, ISBN13: 978-0-300-10087-7. Dewey:332.1/1. LCCN:2003-061371.
Audience: **g,l,u,f.**

Bogle, John C. **HB501.B655 2005**
The Battle for the Soul of Capitalism. Cloth over Boards. Yale University Press. Cumberland, RI. 2005. 288p. ISBN:0-300-10990-3, ISBN13: 978-0-300-10990-0. Dewey:330.12/2/0973. LCCN:2005-013193.
Audience: **g,l,u,f.** *Choice, 2006.*

Chancellor, Edward **HG6005**
Devil Take the Hindmost: A History of Financial Speculation. Trade Paper. Penguin Group (USA) Inc. New York, NY. 2000. 400p. ISBN:0-452-28180-6, ISBN13: 978-0-452-28180-6. Dewey:332.6/3228/09.
Audience: **g,l,u,f.** *Choice, 1999.*

Chew, Donald H. Jr. **HG4011.N44 2001**
The New Corporate Finance. Ed. 3. Paper Text. McGraw-Hill Higher Education. Burr Ridge, IL. 2000. 672p. Series in Finance, Insurance, and Real Estate ISBN:0-07-233973-X, ISBN13: 978-0-07-233973-4. Dewey:658.15. LCCN:00-106022.
Audience: **u,f.**

Choi, Frederick D. S. (Editor) **HF5686.I56H36 2003**
International Finance and Accounting Handbook. Ed. 3. Trade Cloth. John Wiley & Sons, Inc. Hoboken, NJ. 2003. 888p. ISBN:0-471-22921-0, ISBN13: 978-0-471-22921-6. Dewey:657/.96. LCCN:2002-192266.
Audience: **u,f.**

Ellis, Charles D. & Vertin, James R. **HG4928.5.E42 2001**
Wall Street People: True Stories of Today's Masters and Moguls. Trade Cloth. John Wiley & Sons, Inc. Hoboken, NJ.

2001. 360p. ISBN:0-471-23809-0, ISBN13: 978-0-471-23809-6. Dewey:332.6/0973. LCCN:2001-026114.
Audience: **g,l,u,f.**

Ellis, Charles D. & Vertin, James R. **HG4928.5 .E42 2001**
Wall Street People: True Stories of the Great Barons of Finance. Trade Cloth. John Wiley & Sons, Inc. Hoboken, NJ. 2003. 288p. ISBN:0-471-27428-3, ISBN13: 978-0-471-27428-5. Dewey:332.60973.
Audience: **g,l,u,f.**

Friedman, Thomas L. **HM846.F74 2005**
The World Is Flat: A Brief History of the Twenty-First Century. Oliver Wyman (Read by). Cloth over Boards. Farrar, Straus & Giroux. New York, NY. 2005. 496p. ISBN:0-374-29288-4, ISBN13: 978-0-374-29288-1. Dewey:303.48/33. LCCN:2004-028685.
Audience: **g,u,f.** *Choice, 2006.*

Fuerst, Oren & Geiger, Uri **HG4751.F84 2003**
From Concept to Wall Street: A Complete Guide to Entrepreneurship and Venture Capital. Trade Cloth. Financial Times/Prentice Hall. Paramus, NJ. 2002. 352p. ISBN:0-13-034803-1, ISBN13: 978-0-13-034803-6. Dewey:658.15224. LCCN:2003-268062.
Audience: **g,l,u,f.**

Geisst, Charles **HG5129.N5G44 2001**
The Last Partnerships: Inside the Great Wall Street Dynasties. Trade Cloth. McGraw-Hill Companies, The. New York, NY. 2001. 338p. ISBN:0-07-136999-6, ISBN13: 978-0-07-136999-2. Dewey:332.6/0973. LCCN:2001-030374.
Audience: **g,l,u,f.** *Choice, 2001.*

Geisst, Charles R. **HG4028.M4G45 2004**
Deals of the Century: Wall Street, Mergers, and the Making of Modern America. Trade Cloth. John Wiley & Sons, Inc. Hoboken, NJ. 2003. 352p. ISBN:0-471-26397-4, ISBN13: 978-0-471-26397-5. Dewey:338.8/3/0973. LCCN:2003-008868.
Audience: **g,l,u,f.**

Goedhart, Marc, et al. **HG4028.V3**
Valuation: Measuring and Managing the Value of Companies. Ed. 4. Tim Koller, David Wessels & Jeffrey P. Lessard (Authors), McKinsey and Company Staff (Editor). Trade Paper. John Wiley & Sons, Inc. Hoboken, NJ. 2005. 742p. Wiley Finance Ser. ISBN:0-471-70221-8, ISBN13: 978-0-471-70221-4. Dewey:658.15. LCCN:2005-003087.
Audience: **g,u,f.**

Goetzmann, William N. & Rouwenhorst, K. Geert **HG171**
Origins of Value: A Document History of Finance. Trade Cloth. Oxford University Press, Inc. New York, NY. 2005. 416p. ISBN:0-19-517571-9, ISBN13: 978-0-19-517571-4. Dewey:332/.041. LCCN:2005-002394.
Audience: **g,l,u,f.**

Graham, Benjamin **HG4521.G665 2003**
The Intelligent Investor: The Definitive Book on Value Investing. Ed. 4. Jason Zweig (Commentaries by), Warren E. Buffett (Preface by). Trade Paper. HarperCollins Publishers. New York, NY. 2003. 640p. ISBN:0-06-055566-1, ISBN13: 978-0-06-055566-5. LCCN:2003-047894.
Audience: **g,l,u,f.**

Grant, James L. **HG4028.V3**
Foundations of Economic Value Added. Ed. 2. Trade Cloth. John Wiley & Sons, Inc. Hoboken, NJ. 2003. 324p. Frank J. Fabozzi Ser. ISBN:0-471-23483-4, ISBN13: 978-0-471-23483-8. Dewey:332.63/2042. LCCN:2003-269697.
Audience: **u,f.**

Kolb, Robert W. & Overdahl, James A. **HG6024.A3K648 2003**
Financial Derivatives. Ed. 3. Trade Cloth. John Wiley & Sons, Inc. Hoboken, NJ. 2002. 336p. Wiley Finance Ser. ISBN:0-471-23232-7, ISBN13: 978-0-471-23232-2. Dewey:332.64/5. LCCN:2002-014027.
Audience: **g,l,u,f.**

Lewis, Michael M. **HG4928.5.L48 1989**
Liar's Poker: Rising Through the Wreckage on Wall Street. Trade Cloth. W. W. Norton & Company, Inc. New York, NY. 1989. 256p. ISBN:0-393-02750-3, ISBN13: 978-0-393-02750-1. Dewey:332.6/2/0973. LCCN:89-030819.
Audience: **g,l,u,f.**

Markham, Jerry W. **HV6769.M37 2005**
A Financial History of Modern U S Corporate Scandals. Cloth Text. M. E. Sharpe Inc. Armonk, NY. 2005. 768p. ISBN:0-7656-1583-5, ISBN13: 978-0-7656-1583-1. Dewey:364.16/8/0973. LCCN:2005-005562.
Audience: **g,l,u,f.** *Choice, 2006.*

Markham, Jerry W. **HG181.M297 2001**
A Financial History of the United States. Trade Cloth. M. E. Sharpe Inc. Armonk, NY. 2002. 1364p. ISBN:0-7656-0730-1, ISBN13: 978-0-7656-0730-0. Dewey:332/.0973. LCCN:00-054917.
Audience: **g,l,u,f.** *Choice, 2002.*

Melamed, Leo & Tamarkin, Bob **HG6024.A3M437 1996**
Leo Melamed: Escape to the Futures. Trade Cloth. John Wiley & Sons, Inc. Hoboken, NJ. 1996. 480p. ISBN:0-471-11215-1, ISBN13: 978-0-471-11215-0. Dewey:332.6/2/092 B. LCCN:96-015316.
Audience: **g,l,u,f.**

Rosenstreich, Peter **HG3851.R67 2005**
Forex Revolution: An Insider's Guide to the Real World of Foreign Exchange Trading. Trade Cloth. Financial Times/Prentice Hall. Paramus, NJ. 2005. 360p. ISBN:0-13-148690-X, ISBN13: 978-0-13-148690-4. Dewey:332.4/5. LCCN:2005-921697.
Audience: **g,l,u,f.**

Ross, Stephen A. **HG173.R675 2004**
Neoclassical Finance. Trade Cloth. Princeton University Press. Princeton, NJ. 2004. 144p. Princeton Lectures in Finance Ser. ISBN:0-691-12138-9, ISBN13: 978-0-691-12138-3. Dewey:332/.01. LCCN:2004-048901.
Audience: **u,f.**

Shamah, Shani Beverly **HG3853.S53 2003**
A Foreign Exchange Primer. Trade Cloth. John Wiley & Sons, Inc. Hoboken, NJ. 2003. 196p. Wiley Finance Ser. ISBN:0-470-85162-7, ISBN13: 978-0-470-85162-3. Dewey:332.4/5. LCCN:2002-191093.
Audience: **g,l,u,f.**

Shiller, Robert J. **HD61.S55 2003**
The New Financial Order: Risk in the 21st Century. Trade Cloth. Princeton University Press. Princeton, NJ. 2003. 400p. ISBN:0-691-09172-2, ISBN13: 978-0-691-09172-3. Dewey:368. LCCN:2002-042563.
Audience: **g,l,u,f.** *Choice, 2003.*

Shirreff, David **HD61.S47 2004**
Dealing with Financial Risk. Perfect, Paper over Boards, Dust Jacket. Bloomberg Press. New York, NY. 2004. 214p. The Economist Ser. ISBN:1-57660-162-5, ISBN13: 978-1-57660-162-4. Dewey:658.15/5. LCCN:2004-011211.
Audience: **g,l,u,f.**

Useem, Michael **HG4028.C4**
Investor Capitalism: How Money Managers Are Changing the Face of Corporate America. Trade Paper. Basic Books. New York, NY. 1999. 342p. ISBN:0-465-05032-8, ISBN13: 978-0-465-05032-1. Dewey:658.1/52. LCCN:96-007847.
Audience: **g,l,u,f.** *Choice, 1996.*

Wells, Donald R. **HG2563**
The Federal Reserve System: A History. Paper Text. McFarland & Company, Incorporated Publishers. Jefferson, NC. 2004. 224p. ISBN:0-7864-1880-X, ISBN13: 978-0-7864-1880-0. Dewey:332.1/1/0973. LCCN:2004-014714.
Audience: **g,l,u,f.** *Choice, 2005.*

Woodward, Bob **HG2565.W654 2000**
Maestro: Greenspan's Fed and the American Boom. Trade Cloth. Simon & Schuster. New York, NY. 2000. 272p. ISBN:0-7432-0412-3, ISBN13: 978-0-7432-0412-5. Dewey:330.9/73/0928. LCCN:00-052627.
Audience: **g,l,u,f.** *Choice, 2001.*

Wright, Robert E. & Cowen, David J. **HG172.A2W75 2006**
Financial Founding Fathers: The Men Who Made America Rich. Trade Cloth. University of Chicago Press. Chicago, IL. 2006. 216p. ISBN:0-226-91068-7, ISBN13: 978-0-226-91068-0. Dewey:330.973/05/0922. LCCN:2005-026938.
Audience: **g,l,u,f.**

Management Function > Finance > Capital and Debt Management. Corporate Finance

HF5035
EDGAR: SEC Filings & Forms.
http://www.sec.gov/edgar.shtml
Audience: **g,l,u,f.**

HG4574.2
The NASDAQ Stock Market.
http://www.nasdaq.com/
Audience: **g,l,u,f.**

HG4572
NYSE, New York Stock Exchange.
http://www.nyse.com/
Audience: **g,l,u.**

HG173
OSU Virtual Finance Library.
http://fisher.osu.edu/fin/overview.htm
Audience: **g,l,u,f.**

Abramson, Daniel **NA6245.G72L633 2005**
Building the Bank of England: Money, Architecture and Society, 1694-1942. Cloth over Boards. Yale University Press. Cumberland, RI. 2005. 320p. Paul Mellon Centre for Studies in British Art ISBN:0-300-10924-5, ISBN13: 978-0-300-10924-5. Dewey:940.5488. LCCN:2006-278815.
Audience: **g,l,u,f.**

Ackrill, Margaret & Hannah, Leslie **HG2998.B34 A37 2001**
Barclays: The Business of Banking, 1690-1996. Trade Cloth. Cambridge University Press. New York, NY. 2001. 504p. ISBN:0-521-79035-2, ISBN13: 978-0-521-79035-2. Dewey:332.1/5/0941. LCCN:00-025417.
Audience: **g,l,u,f.** *Choice, 2003.*

Adams, James R. **HG2151.A35 1990**
The Big Fix: Inside the S&L Scandal: How an Unholy Alliance of Politics and Money Destroyed America's Banking System. Trade Cloth. John Wiley & Sons, Inc. Hoboken, NJ. 1990. 308p. ISBN:0-471-51535-3, ISBN13: 978-0-471-51535-7. Dewey:364.1/68/0973. LCCN:89-027378.
Audience: **g,l,u,f.**

Alexander, Kern, et al. **K1066.A9154 2004**
Global Governance of Financial Systems: The Legal and Economic Regulation of Systemic Risk. Rahul Dhumale & John Eatwell (Authors). Trade Cloth. Oxford University Press, Inc. New York, NY. 2005. 327p. The CERF Monographs on Finance and the Economy Ser. ISBN:0-19-516698-1, ISBN13: 978-0-19-516698-9. Dewey:346/.082. LCCN:2003-064714.
Audience: **u,f.** *Choice, 2006.*

Amram, Martha (Author, Editor) **HG6024.A3A47 1999**
Real Options: Managing Strategic Investment in an Uncertain World. Nalin Kulatilaka (Editor). Trade Cloth. Oxford University Press, Inc. New York, NY. 1998. 246p. Financial Management Association Survey and Synthesis Ser. ISBN:0-87584-845-1, ISBN13: 978-0-87584-845-7. Dewey:332.64/5. LCCN:98-022392.
Audience: **u,f.** *Choice, 1999.*

Baker, George P. & Smith, George D. **HG4028.M4 B335 1998**
The New Financial Capitalists: Kohlberg Kravis Roberts and the Creation of Corporate Value. Trade Cloth. Cambridge University Press. New York, NY. 1998. 272p. ISBN:0-521-64260-4, ISBN13: 978-0-521-64260-6. Dewey:338.830973. LCCN:98-028007.
Audience: **g,l,u,f.** *Choice, 1999.*

Barth, James R., et al. **K1066.B37 2006**
Rethinking Bank Regulation: Till Angels Govern. Gerard Caprio Jr. & Ross Levine (Authors). Trade Cloth. Cambridge University Press. New York, NY. 2005. 444p. ISBN:0-521-85576-4, ISBN13: 978-0-521-85576-1. Dewey:346/.082. LCCN:2005-028138.
Audience: **u,f.**

Benston, George J. **HG2461.B46 1990**
The Separation of Commercial and Investment Banking: The Glass-Steagall Act Revisited and Reconsidered. Cloth Text. Oxford University Press, Inc. New York, NY. 1990. 276p. ISBN:0-19-520830-7, ISBN13: 978-0-19-520830-6. Dewey:332.1/0973. LCCN:90-006946.
Audience: **u,f.** *Choice, 1991.*

Berman, Karen, et al. **HG4028.B2B42 2005**
The Art of the Financial Statements: A Practical Handbook for Managers. Joe Knight & John Case (Authors). Trade Cloth. Harvard Business School Press. Boston, MA. 2005. 272p. ISBN:1-59139-764-2, ISBN13: 978-1-59139-764-9. Dewey:658.15/11. LCCN:2005-025556.
Audience: **g,l,u,f.** *Choice, 2006.*

Bernstein, Peter L. **HG173**
Capital Ideas: The Improbable Origins of Modern Wall Street. Trade Paper, Perfect. John Wiley & Sons, Inc. Hoboken, NJ. 2005. 360p. ISBN:0-471-73174-9, ISBN13: 978-0-471-73174-0. Dewey:332.632. LCCN:2005-276389.
Audience: **g,l,u,f.**

Billingsley, Randall **HG6024.A3B55 2006**
Understanding Arbitrage: An Intuitive Approach to Financial Analysis. Trade Cloth. Financial Times/Prentice Hall. Paramus, NJ. 2005. 224p. ISBN:0-13-147020-5, ISBN13: 978-0-13-147020-0. Dewey:332.64/5. LCCN:2005-020842.
Audience: **g,l,u,f.**

Brennan, Niamh **HD30.15.B455**
Accounting. Ed. 2. Colin Clubb (Editor). Trade Cloth. Blackwell Publishing, Inc. Malden, MA. 2006. 456p. The Blackwell Encyclopedia of Management Ser., Vol. 1 ISBN:1-4051-1827-X, ISBN13: 978-1-4051-1827-9. Dewey:658/.003 s 657/.03. LCCN:2004-024923.
Audience: **g,l,u,f.**

Cassis, Yves & Cassis, Youssef (Editors) **HG2974 .F56 1992**
Finance and Financiers in European History, 1880-1960. Trade Cloth. Cambridge University Press. New York, NY. 1991. 461p. ISBN:0-521-40024-4, ISBN13: 978-0-521-40024-4. Dewey:332/.094. LCCN:90-019525.
Audience: **g,l,u,f.** *Choice, 1992.*

Chernow, Ron **HG2613.N54**
The House of Morgan: An American Banking Dynasty and the Rise of Modern Finance. Trade Paper. Grove/Atlantic, Inc. New York, NY. 2001. 832p. ISBN:0-8021-3829-2, ISBN13: 978-0-8021-3829-3. Dewey:332.1/2/097471.
Audience: **g,l,u,f.**

Chew, Donald H. **HG4026.5.R48 2003**
The Revolution in Corporate Finance. Ed. 4. Joel M. Stern (Editor). Trade Paper. Blackwell Publishing, Inc. Malden, MA. 2003. 648p. ISBN:1-4051-0781-2, ISBN13: 978-1-4051-0781-5. Dewey:658.15. LCCN:2002-038488.
Audience: **g,l,u,f.** *Choice, 2003.*

Finnerty, John D. & Emery, Douglas R. (Author, Editors) **HG4028.D3F53 2001**
Debt Management: A Practitioner's Guide. Cloth Text. Oxford University Press, Inc. New York, NY. 2001. 430p. Financial Management Association Survey and Synthesis Ser. ISBN:0-87584-617-3, ISBN13: 978-0-87584-617-0. Dewey:658.15/26. LCCN:2001-016792.
Audience: **u,f.**

Fraser, Lyn M. & Ormiston, Aileen **HG4028.B2F73 2003**
Understanding the Corporate Annual Report: Nuts, Bolts and a Few Loose Screws. Trade Paper. Prentice Hall PTR. Upper Saddle River, NJ. 2002. 133p. ISBN:0-13-100431-X, ISBN13: 978-0-13-100431-3. Dewey:332.63/2042. LCCN:2002-073952.
Audience: **g,l,u,f.**

Fridson, Martin S. & Alvarez, Fernando **HF5681**
Financial Statement Analysis: A Practitioner's Guide. Ed. 3. Trade Cloth. John Wiley & Sons, Inc. Hoboken, NJ. 2002. 416p. Wiley Finance Ser., Vol. 76 ISBN:0-471-40915-4, ISBN13: 978-0-471-40915-1. Dewey:657/.3. LCCN:2002-284068.
Audience: **g,l,u,f.**

Fuerst, Oren & Geiger, Uri **HG4751.F84 2003**
From Concept to Wall Street: A Complete Guide to Entrepreneurship and Venture Capital. Trade Cloth. Financial Times/Prentice Hall. Paramus, NJ. 2002. 352p. ISBN:0-13-034803-1, ISBN13: 978-0-13-034803-6. Dewey:658.15224. LCCN:2003-268062.
Audience: **g,l,u,f.**

Goedhart, Marc, et al. **HG4028.V3**
Valuation: Measuring and Managing the Value of Companies. Ed. 4. Tim Koller, David Wessels & Jeffrey P. Lessard (Authors), McKinsey and Company Staff (Editor). Trade Paper. John Wiley & Sons, Inc. Hoboken, NJ. 2005. 742p. Wiley Finance Ser. ISBN:0-471-70221-8, ISBN13: 978-0-471-70221-4. Dewey:658.15. LCCN:2005-003087.
Audience: **g,u,f.**

Hussey, Roger, et al. **HF5681.B2**
International Financial Reporting Standards Desk Reference: Overview, Guide and Dictionary. Wei-Ming Ong & Audra Ong (Authors). Trade Cloth. John Wiley & Sons, Inc. Hoboken, NJ. 2005. 382p. ISBN:0-471-71450-X, ISBN13: 978-0-471-71450-7. Dewey:657.30218. LCCN:2005-275535.
Audience: **u,f.**

Isaacs, Alan (Author, Editor) **HG151**
A Dictionary of Finance and Banking. Ed. 3. John Smullen & Nicholas Hand (Editors). Trade Paper. Oxford University Press, Inc. New York, NY. 2005. 448p. Oxford Paperback Reference Ser. ISBN:0-19-860749-0, ISBN13: 978-0-19-860749-6. Dewey:332/.03. LCCN:2005-274362.
Audience: **g,l,u,f.**

Lease, Ronald C., et al. **HG4028.D5D579 2000**
Dividend Policy: Its Impact on Firm Value. Kose John, Avner Kalay, Uri Loewenstein & Oded H. Sarig (Authors). Cloth Text. Oxford University Press, Inc. New York, NY. 1999. 219p. Financial Management Association Survey and Synthesis Ser. ISBN:0-87584-497-9, ISBN13: 978-0-87584-497-8. Dewey:658.15/5. LCCN:99-028695.
Audience: **u,f.**

Martin, John D. (Author, Editor) **HD47.3.M37 2000**
Value Based Management: The Corporate Response to the Shareholder Revolution. J. William Petty (Editor). Trade Cloth. Oxford University Press, Inc. New York, NY. 2000. 268p. Financial Management Association Survey and Synthesis Ser. ISBN:0-87584-800-1, ISBN13: 978-0-87584-800-6. Dewey:658. LCCN:00-031910.
Audience: **g,l,u,f.** *Choice, 2001.*

McLean, Bethany & Elkind, Peter **HD9502.U54E5763 2003**
Smartest Guys in the Room: The Amazing Rise and Scandalous Fall of Enron. Trade Cloth. Penguin Group (USA) Inc. New York, NY. 2003. 464p. ISBN:1-59184-008-2, ISBN13: 978-1-59184-008-4. Dewey:333.79/0973. LCCN:2003-054944.
Audience: **g,l,u,f.** *Choice, 2004.*

Moore, Michael L. & Outslay, Edmund **KF6445.M66 2000**
U. S. Tax Aspects of Doing Business Abroad. Ed. 5. Paper Text. American Institute of Certified Public Accountants. Jersey City, NJ. 2000. xii, 849p. ISBN:0-87051-291-9, ISBN13: 978-0-87051-291-9. Dewey:343.7305/248. LCCN:99-089702.
Audience: **u,f.**

PricewaterhouseCoopers LLP Staff **HJ2240**
Corporate Taxes 2005—2006: Worldwide Summaries. Trade Paper. John Wiley & Sons, Inc. Hoboken, NJ. 2006. 1000p. ISBN:0-471-74069-1, ISBN13: 978-0-471-74069-8. Dewey:336.2.
Audience: **g,u,f.**

PricewaterhouseCoopers Staff, et al. **HG4028.B2D547 2002**
Building Public Trust: The Future of Corporate Reporting. Samuel A. DiPiazza & Robert G. Eccles (Authors). Trade Cloth. John Wiley & Sons, Inc. Hoboken, NJ. 2002. 208p. ISBN:0-471-26151-3, ISBN13: 978-0-471-26151-3. Dewey:658.1/512. LCCN:2002-510544.
Audience: **g,l,u,f.**

Schilit, Howard M. **HF5681.B2S3243 2002**
Financial Shenanigans: How to Detect Accounting Gimmicks and Fraud in Financial Reports. Ed. 2. Trade Cloth. McGraw-Hill Companies, The. New York, NY. 2002. 240p. ISBN:0-07-138626-2, ISBN13: 978-0-07-138626-5. Dewey:657/.3. LCCN:2002-002879.
Audience: **g,l,u,f.**

Seligman, Joel **HG4910.S4 1995**
The Transformation of Wall Street: A History of the Securities and Exchange Commission and Modern Corporate Finance. Trade Cloth. Northeastern University Press. Boston, MA. 1995. 772p. ISBN:1-55553-231-4, ISBN13: 978-1-55553-231-4. Dewey:354.8/8/0973. LCCN:95-013762.
Audience: **g,l,u,f.** *Choice, 1996.*

Smith, Roy C. & Walter, Ingo **HG3881.S5434 2002**
Global Banking. Ed. 2. Trade Cloth. Oxford University Press, Inc. New York, NY. 2003. 448p. ISBN:0-19-513436-2, ISBN13: 978-0-19-513436-0. Dewey:332.1/5. LCCN:2002-003692.
Audience: **u,f.** *Choice, 2003, 1997.*

Stern, Joel M., et al. **HG4028.V3S83 2001**
The EVA Challenge: Implementing Value-Added Change in an Organization. John S. Shiely & Irwin Ross (Authors). Trade Cloth. John Wiley & Sons, Inc. Hoboken, NJ. 2001. 256p. Finance Ser. ISBN:0-471-40555-8, ISBN13: 978-0-471-40555-9. Dewey:658.15. LCCN:00-047993.
Audience: **g,u,f.**

Tracy, John A. **HF5681.B2**
How to Read a Financial Report: Wringing Vital Signs Out of the Numbers. Ed. 6. Trade Paper. John Wiley & Sons, Inc. Hoboken, NJ. 2004. 216p. ISBN:0-471-47867-9, ISBN13: 978-0-471-47867-6. Dewey:657/.3. LCCN:2004-274182.
Audience: **g,l,u,f.**

Wasserstein, Bruce **HD2746.55.U5W37 2000**
Big Deal: 2000 and Beyond. Ed. 2. Trade Cloth. Warner Books, Inc. New York, NY. 2000. 944p. ISBN:0-446-52642-8, ISBN13: 978-0-446-52642-5. Dewey:338.8/3/0973. LCCN:99-044624.
Audience: **g,u,f.**

Management Function > Finance > Risk Management

HD61
Risk Management - Wikipedia, the free encyclopedia. http://en.wikipedia.org/wiki/Risk_management
Audience: **g,l,u,f.**

Arditti, Fred D. **HG6024.U6A73 1996**
Derivatives: A Comprehensive Resource for Options, Futures, Interest Rate Swaps and Mortgage Securities. Trade Cloth. Harvard Business School Press. Boston, MA. 1996. 416p. Financial Management Association Survey and Synthesis Ser. ISBN:0-87584-560-6, ISBN13: 978-0-87584-560-9. Dewey:332.64/5. LCCN:95-031894.
Audience: **g,l,u,f.** *Choice, 1996.*

Bernstein, Peter L. **HD61.B466 1996**
Against the Gods: The Remarkable Story of Risk. Trade Cloth. John Wiley & Sons, Inc. Hoboken, NJ. 1996. 400p. ISBN:0-471-12104-5, ISBN13: 978-0-471-12104-6. Dewey:368. LCCN:96-033861.
Audience: **g,l,u,f.**

Billingsley, Randall **HG6024.A3B55 2006**
Understanding Arbitrage: An Intuitive Approach to Financial Analysis. Trade Cloth. Financial Times/Prentice Hall. Paramus, NJ. 2005. 224p. ISBN:0-13-147020-5, ISBN13: 978-0-13-147020-0. Dewey:332.64/5. LCCN:2005-020842.
Audience: **g,l,u,f.**

Borge, Dan **HD61.B647 2001**
The Book of Risk. Trade Cloth. John Wiley & Sons, Inc. Hoboken, NJ. 2001. 256p. Investment Ser., Vol. 67 ISBN:0-471-32378-0, ISBN13: 978-0-471-32378-5. Dewey:658.15/5. LCCN:2001-017503.
Audience: **g,l,u,f.**

Lewis, Michael M. **HG4928.5.L48 1989**
Liar's Poker: Rising Through the Wreckage on Wall Street. Trade Cloth. W. W. Norton & Company, Inc. New York, NY. 1989. 256p. ISBN:0-393-02750-3, ISBN13: 978-0-393-02750-1. Dewey:332.6/2/0973. LCCN:89-030819.
Audience: **g,l,u,f.**

Moss, David A. **HD61.M63 2002**
When All Else Fails: Government as the Ultimate Risk Manager. Trade Cloth. Harvard University Press. Cambridge, MA. 2002. 464p. ISBN:0-674-00757-3, ISBN13: 978-0-674-00757-4. Dewey:338.5/0973. LCCN:2002-017111.
Audience: **g,l,u,f.** *Choice, 2003, 2002.*

Shapiro, Sidney A. & Glicksman, Robert L. **KF3775.S53 2003**
Risk Regulation at Risk: Restoring a Pragmatic Approach. Trade Cloth. Stanford University Press. Palo Alto, CA. 2002. 288p. ISBN:0-8047-4593-5, ISBN13: 978-0-8047-4593-2. Dewey:344.73/046. LCCN:2002-009778.
Audience: **g,l,u,f.**

Shiller, Robert J. **HD61.S55 2003**
The New Financial Order: Risk in the 21st Century. Trade Cloth. Princeton University Press. Princeton, NJ. 2003. 400p. ISBN:0-691-09172-2, ISBN13: 978-0-691-09172-3. Dewey:368. LCCN:2002-042563.
Audience: **g,l,u,f.** *Choice, 2003.*

Shirreff, David **HD61.S47 2004**
Dealing with Financial Risk. Perfect, Paper over Boards, Dust Jacket. Bloomberg Press. New York, NY. 2004. 214p. The Economist Ser. ISBN:1-57660-162-5, ISBN13: 978-1-57660-162-4. Dewey:658.15/5. LCCN:2004-011211.
Audience: **g,l,u,f.**

Management Function > Finance > Investment Analysis and Personal Finance

HG5131.C43
CBOE, Chicago Board Options Exhange.
http://www.cboe.com/
Audience: **g,l,u,f.**

HF295
Chicago Board of Trade.
http://www.cbot.com/
Audience: **g,l,u,f.**

HF5035
EDGAR: SEC Filings & Forms.
http://www.sec.gov/edgar.shtml
Audience: **g,l,u,f.**

HG4501
Fool.com: To Educate, Amuse and Enrich.
http://www.fool.com/
Audience: **g,l,u,f.**

HG4009
Hoover's Online.
http://www.hoovers.com
Audience: **g,l,u,f.**

HG4529
Investopedia - Your Source for Investment Education.
http://www.investopedia.com/
Audience: **g,l,u,f.**

HG4501
The Investor's Clearinghouse.
http://www.investoreducation.org/
Audience: **g,l,u,f.**

HG4529
InvestorWords.com.
http://www.investorwords.com/
Audience: **g,l,u,f.**

HG4501
MarketWatch.
http://www.marketwatch.com/
Audience: **g,l,u,f.**

HG4530
Morningstar.
http://www.morningstar.com
Audience: **g,l,u,f.**

HG4574.2
The NASDAQ Stock Market.
http://www.nasdaq.com/
Audience: **g,l,u,f.**

HG4572
NYSE, New York Stock Exchange.
http://www.nyse.com/
Audience: **g,l,u.**

HG173
OSU Virtual Finance Library.
http://fisher.osu.edu/fin/overview.htm
Audience: **g,l,u,f.**

HG4501
Path to Investing.
http://www.pathtoinvesting.org/
Audience: **g,l,f.**

HG173
studyfinance.com.
http://www.studyfinance.com/
Audience: **l,u.**

KF1444
U.S. Securities and Exchange Commission.
http://www.sec.gov/
Audience: **g,l,u,f.**

HG151.8
Yahoo! Finance.
http://finance.yahoo.com/
Audience: **g,l,u,f.**

Aliber, Robert Z. **HG3881.A44 2000**
The New International Money Game. Ed. 6. Trade Cloth. University of Chicago Press. Chicago, IL. 2000. 304p. ISBN:0-226-01396-0, ISBN13: 978-0-226-01396-1. Dewey:332. LCCN:99-055593.
Audience: **g,l,u,f.**

Arditti, Fred D. **HG6024.U6A73 1996**
Derivatives: A Comprehensive Resource for Options, Futures, Interest Rate Swaps and Mortgage Securities. Trade Cloth. Harvard Business School Press. Boston, MA. 1996. 416p. Financial Management Association Survey and Synthesis Ser. ISBN:0-87584-560-6, ISBN13: 978-0-87584-560-9. Dewey:332.64/5. LCCN:95-031894.
Audience: **g,l,u,f.** *Choice, 1996.*

Benz, Christine **HG4530.B45 2005**
Morningstar Guide to Mutual Funds: Five-Star Strategies for Success. Ed. 2. Trade Cloth. John Wiley & Sons, Inc. Hoboken, NJ. 2005. 288p. ISBN:0-471-71832-7, ISBN13: 978-0-471-71832-1. Dewey:332.63/27. LCCN:2005-012595.
Audience: **g,l,u,f.**

Berenson, Alex **HV6768**
The Number: How the Drive for Quarterly Earnings Corrupted Wall Street and Corporate America. E-Book. Random House Adult Trade Publishing Group. New York, NY. 2003. ISBN:1-58836-288-4, ISBN13: 978-1-58836-288-9. Dewey:364.16/8.
Audience: **g,l,u,f.** *Choice, 2004.*

Bernstein, Peter L. **HG173**
Capital Ideas: The Improbable Origins of Modern Wall Street. Trade Paper, Perfect. John Wiley & Sons, Inc. Hoboken, NJ. 2005. 360p. ISBN:0-471-73174-9, ISBN13: 978-0-471-73174-0. Dewey:332.632. LCCN:2005-276389.
Audience: **g,l,u,f.**

Bernstein, Peter L. **GR810.B47 2000**
The Power of Gold: The History of an Obsession. Trade Cloth. John Wiley & Sons, Inc. Hoboken, NJ. 2000. 448p. ISBN:0-471-25210-7, ISBN13: 978-0-471-25210-8. Dewey:398/.365. LCCN:00-036647.
Audience: **g,l,u,f.**

Bernstein, Peter L. & Damodaran, Aswath (Editors) **HG4529.5.I58 1998**
Investment Management. Trade Cloth. John Wiley & Sons, Inc. Hoboken, NJ. 1998. 480p. Frontiers in Finance Ser. ISBN:0-471-19716-5, ISBN13: 978-0-471-19716-4. Dewey:332.6. LCCN:97-043844.
Audience: **u,f.** *Choice, 1998.*

Biggs, Barton **HG4530.B516 2006**
Hedgehogging. Trade Cloth. John Wiley & Sons, Inc. Hoboken, NJ. 2006. 320p. ISBN:0-471-77191-0, ISBN13: 978-0-471-77191-3. Dewey:332.64/5. LCCN:2005-026139.
Audience: **g,l,u,f.**

Billingsley, Randall **HG6024.A3B55 2006**
Understanding Arbitrage: An Intuitive Approach to Financial Analysis. Trade Cloth. Financial Times/Prentice Hall. Paramus, NJ. 2005. 224p. ISBN:0-13-147020-5, ISBN13: 978-0-13-147020-0. Dewey:332.64/5. LCCN:2005-020842.
Audience: **g,l,u,f.**

Blustein, Paul **HC175.B665 2005**
And the Money Kept Rolling In (and Out): Wall Street, the IMF, and the Bankrupting of Argentina. Trade Cloth. PublicAffairs. New York, NY. 2005. 336p. ISBN:1-58648-245-9, ISBN13: 978-1-58648-245-9. Dewey:330.982/07. LCCN:2004-058743.
Audience: **g,l,u,f.** *Choice, 2005.*

Bogle, John C. **HG4530.B633 1999**
Common Sense on Mutual Funds: New Imperatives for the Intelligent Investor. Trade Cloth. John Wiley & Sons, Inc. Hoboken, NJ. 1999. 496p. ISBN:0-471-29543-4, ISBN13: 978-0-471-29543-3. Dewey:332.63/27. LCCN:98-055377.
Audience: **g,l,u,f.**

Brennan, Niamh **HD30.15.B455**
Accounting. Ed. 2. Colin Clubb (Editor). Trade Cloth. Blackwell Publishing, Inc. Malden, MA. 2006. 456p. The Blackwell Encyclopedia of Management Ser., Vol. 1 ISBN:1-4051-1827-X, ISBN13: 978-1-4051-1827-9. Dewey:658/.003 s 657/.03. LCCN:2004-024923.
Audience: **g,l,u,f.**

Buffett, Warren **HG4061.B8372 2001**
The Essays of Warren Buffett: Lessons for Corporate America. Ed. 2. Lawrence Cunningham (Arranged by, Introduction by, Selected by). Trade Paper. Cunningham Group, The. Newton, MA. 2001. 246p. ISBN:0-9664461-1-9, ISBN13: 978-0-9664461-1-1. Dewey:338.6041. LCCN:2001-336907.
Audience: **g,l,u,f.**

Chicago Board of Trade Staff **HG6024.U6C45 2006**
The CBOT Handbook of Futures and Options. Trade Cloth. McGraw-Hill Companies, The. New York, NY. 2006. 480p. ISBN:0-07-145751-8, ISBN13: 978-0-07-145751-4. Dewey:332.64/52. LCCN:2005-027316.
Audience: **g,l,u,f.**

Cottle, S., et al. **HG4529.G7 1988**
Security Analysis. Ed. 5. R. F. Murray & F. E. Block (Authors). Trade Cloth. McGraw-Hill Companies, The. New York, NY. 1988. 658p. ISBN:0-07-013235-6, ISBN13: 978-0-07-013235-1. Dewey:332.63/2. LCCN:87-019990.
Audience: **u,f.**

Downes, John & Goodman, Jordan Elliot **HG173.D66 2003**
Finance and Investment Handbook. Ed. 6. Trade Cloth. Barron's Educational Series, Inc. Hauppauge, NY. 2003. 1400p. ISBN:0-7641-5554-7, ISBN13: 978-0-7641-5554-3. Dewey:332.67/8. LCCN:2002-038595.
Audience: **g,l,u,f.**

Downey, Tom **HG179.D697 2005**
The Standard and Poor's Guide to Personal Finance. Trade Paper. McGraw-Hill Companies, The. New York, NY. 2005. 204p. ISBN:0-07-144741-5, ISBN13: 978-0-07-144741-6. Dewey:332.024. LCCN:2004-028201.
Audience: **g,l,u,f.**

Dreman, David N. **HG6041.D658 1998**
Contrarian Investment Strategies, the Next Generation: Beat the Market Going Against the Crowd. Trade Cloth. Simon & Schuster. New York, NY. 1998. 464p. ISBN:0-684-81350-5, ISBN13: 978-0-684-81350-9. Dewey:332.63/228. LCCN:98-014660.
Audience: **g,l,u,f.**

Ellis, Charles D. (Editor) **HG4522.C57 1989**
Classics: A Treasury of Investment Literature. Cloth Text. McGraw-Hill School Education Group. Columbus, OH. 1988. 250p. ISBN:1-55623-098-2, ISBN13: 978-1-55623-098-1. Dewey:332.6/78. LCCN:88-017609.
Audience: **g,l,u,f.**

Ellis, Charles D. **HG4521.E484 2002**
Winning the Loser's Game: Timeless Strategies for Successful Investing. Ed. 4. Trade Cloth. McGraw-Hill Companies, The. New York, NY. 2002. 144p. ISBN:0-07-138767-6, ISBN13: 978-0-07-138767-5. Dewey:332.6. LCCN:2002-021872.
Audience: **g,l,u,f.**

Ellis, Charles D. & Vertin, James R. (Editors) **HG4522.C57 1991**
Classics: The Most Interesting Ideas and Concepts from the Literature of Investing. Cloth Text. McGraw-Hill School Education Group. Columbus, OH. 1991. 480p. ISBN:1-55623-358-2, ISBN13: 978-1-55623-358-6. Dewey:332.6/78. LCCN:91-002939.
Audience: **g,l,u,f.**

Ellis, Charles D. & Vertin, James R. **HG4910.E463**
The Investor's Anthology: Original Ideas from the Industry's Greatest Minds. Trade Paper. John Wiley & Sons, Inc. Hoboken, NJ. 2001. 320p. ISBN:0-471-41616-9, ISBN13: 978-0-471-41616-6. Dewey:332.6.
Audience: **g,l,u,f.**

Ernst & Young LLP, et al. **HG179.E73 2004**
Ernst and Young's Personal Financial Planning Guide. Ed. 5. Martin Nissenbaum, Barbara J. Raasch & Charles L. Ratner (Authors). Trade Paper. John Wiley & Sons, Inc. Hoboken, NJ. 2004. 540p. ISBN:0-471-68724-3, ISBN13: 978-0-471-68724-5. Dewey:332.024. LCCN:2004-559194.
Audience: **g,l,u,f.**

Evans, David S. & Schmalensee, Richard **HG3755.8.U6E94 2005**
Paying with Plastic: The Digital Revolution in Buying and Borrowing. Ed. 2. Trade Cloth. MIT Press. Cambridge, MA. 2005. 360p. ISBN:0-262-05077-3, ISBN13: 978-0-262-05077-7. Dewey:332.7/65/0973. LCCN:2004-055249.
Audience: **g,l,u,f.** *Choice, 2005.*

Fisher, Philip A. **HG4661.F5 1996**
Common Stocks and Uncommon Profits and Other Writings. Trade Paper. John Wiley & Sons, Inc. Hoboken, NJ. 1996. 288p. Wiley Investment Classic Ser., Vol. 5 ISBN:0-471-11927-X, ISBN13: 978-0-471-11927-2. Dewey:332.6/322. LCCN:95-051449.
Audience: **g,l,u,f.**

Fraser, Lyn M. & Ormiston, Aileen **HG4028.B2F73 2003**
Understanding the Corporate Annual Report: Nuts, Bolts and a Few Loose Screws. Trade Paper. Prentice Hall PTR. Upper Saddle River, NJ. 2002. 133p. ISBN:0-13-100431-X, ISBN13: 978-0-13-100431-3. Dewey:332.63/2042. LCCN:2002-073952.
Audience: **g,l,u,f.**

Fridson, Martin S. & Alvarez, Fernando **HF5681**
Financial Statement Analysis: A Practitioner's Guide. Ed. 3. Trade Cloth. John Wiley & Sons, Inc. Hoboken, NJ. 2002. 416p. Wiley Finance Ser., Vol. 76 ISBN:0-471-40915-4, ISBN13: 978-0-471-40915-1. Dewey:657/.3. LCCN:2002-284068.
Audience: **g,l,u,f.**

Friedman, Jack P., et al. **HD1375.H349 2005**
Real Estate Handbook. Ed. 6. Jack C. Harris & Barry A. Diskin (Authors). Trade Cloth. Barron's Educational Series, Inc. Hauppauge, NY. 2005. 768p. Barron's Educational Ser. ISBN:0-7641-5777-9, ISBN13: 978-0-7641-5777-6. Dewey:333.33. LCCN:2004-062680.
Audience: **g,l,u,f.**

Fuerst, Oren & Geiger, Uri **HG4751.F84 2003**
From Concept to Wall Street: A Complete Guide to Entrepreneurship and Venture Capital. Trade Cloth. Financial Times/Prentice Hall. Paramus, NJ. 2002. 352p. ISBN:0-13-034803-1, ISBN13: 978-0-13-034803-6. Dewey:658.15224. LCCN:2003-268062.
Audience: **g,l,u,f.**

Galbraith, John Kenneth **HB3717 1929.G32 1997**
The Great Crash 1929. Trade Paper. Houghton Mifflin Company Trade & Reference Division. Boston, MA. 1997. 224p. ISBN:0-395-85999-9, ISBN13: 978-0-395-85999-5. Dewey:338.5/4/0973. LCCN:97-022051.
Audience: **g,l,u,f.**

Goedhart, Marc, et al. **HG4028.V3**
Valuation: Measuring and Managing the Value of Companies. Ed. 4. Tim Koller, David Wessels & Jeffrey P. Lessard (Authors), McKinsey and Company Staff (Editor). Trade Paper. John Wiley & Sons, Inc. Hoboken, NJ. 2005. 742p. Wiley Finance Ser. ISBN:0-471-70221-8, ISBN13: 978-0-471-70221-4. Dewey:658.15. LCCN:2005-003087.
Audience: **g,u,f.**

Graham, Benjamin **HG4521.G665 2003**
The Intelligent Investor: The Definitive Book on Value Investing. Ed. 4. Jason Zweig (Commentaries by), Warren E. Buffett (Preface by). Trade Paper. HarperCollins Publishers. New York, NY. 2003. 640p. ISBN:0-06-055566-1, ISBN13: 978-0-06-055566-5. LCCN:2003-047894.
Audience: **g,l,u,f.**

Haight, G. Timothy & Singer, Daniel D. **HD1382.5.H33 2005**
The Real Estate Investment Handbook. Trade Cloth. John Wiley & Sons, Inc. Hoboken, NJ. 2005. 544p. Frank J. Fabozzi Ser. ISBN:0-471-64922-8, ISBN13: 978-0-471-64922-9. Dewey:332.6324. LCCN:2005-275406.
Audience: **g,l,u,f.**

Isaacs, Alan (Author, Editor) **HG151**
A Dictionary of Finance and Banking. Ed. 3. John Smullen & Nicholas Hand (Editors). Trade Paper. Oxford University Press, Inc. New York, NY. 2005. 448p. Oxford Paperback Reference Ser. ISBN:0-19-860749-0, ISBN13: 978-0-19-860749-6. Dewey:332/.03. LCCN:2005-274362.
Audience: **g,l,u,f.**

Kindleberger, Charles P. & Aliber, Robert **HB3722.K56 2005**
Manias, Panics, and Crashes: A History of Financial Crises. Ed. 5. Robert Solow (Foreword by). Trade Paper. John Wiley & Sons, Inc. Hoboken, NJ. 2005. 304p. Wiley Investment Classics Ser. ISBN:0-471-46714-6, ISBN13: 978-0-471-46714-4. Dewey:338.5/42. LCCN:2005-001066.
Audience: **g,l,u,f.**

Kolb, Robert W. & Overdahl, James A. **HG6024.A3K648 2003**
Financial Derivatives. Ed. 3. Trade Cloth. John Wiley & Sons, Inc. Hoboken, NJ. 2002. 336p. Wiley Finance Ser. ISBN:0-471-23232-7, ISBN13: 978-0-471-23232-2. Dewey:332.64/5. LCCN:2002-014027.
Audience: **g,l,u,f.**

Kravetz, Stacy **HF5382.7.K734 2004**
Welcome to the Real World: You've Got an Education, Now Get a Life!. Ed. 2. Trade Paper. W. W. Norton & Company, Inc. New York, NY. 2004. 320p. ISBN:0-393-32480-X, ISBN13: 978-0-393-32480-8. Dewey:650.14. LCCN:2004-557651.
Audience: **l,u.**

Lease, Ronald C., et al. **HG4028.D5D579 2000**
Dividend Policy: Its Impact on Firm Value. Kose John, Avner Kalay, Uri Loewenstein & Oded H. Sarig (Authors). Cloth Text. Oxford University Press, Inc. New York, NY. 1999. 219p. Financial Management Association Survey and Synthesis Ser. ISBN:0-87584-497-9, ISBN13: 978-0-87584-497-8. Dewey:658.15/5. LCCN:99-028695.
Audience: **u,f.**

LeBaron, Dean & Vaitilingam, Romesh **HG4521.L332 2002**
Dean LeBaron's Treasury of Investment Wisdom: 30 Great Investing Minds. Trade Cloth. John Wiley & Sons, Inc. Hoboken, NJ. 2001. 320p. ISBN:0-471-15294-3, ISBN13: 978-0-471-15294-1. Dewey:332.6. LCCN:2001-045556.
Audience: **g,l,u,f.**

Lefèvre, Edwin & Marketplace Books **HG4572**
Reminiscences of a Stock Operator: The Wall Street Classic about the Life and Times of Jesse Livermore. William J. O'Neil (Foreword by). Trade Cloth. John Wiley & Sons, Inc. Hoboken,

NJ. 2004. 253p. ISBN:0-471-67876-7, ISBN13: 978-0-471-67876-2. Dewey:332.6/42/73. LCCN:2004-275015.
Audience: **g,l,u,f.**

Lehmann, Michael B. **HB3743.L44 2005**
The Irwin Guide to Using the Wall Street Journal. Ed. 7. Trade Cloth. McGraw-Hill Companies, The. New York, NY. 2005. 368p. ISBN:0-07-141664-1, ISBN13: 978-0-07-141664-1. Dewey:332.6. LCCN:2004-023293.
Audience: **g,l,u,f.**

Levinson, Marc **HG173.L485 2003**
Guide to Financial Markets. Ed. 3. Perfect, Paper over Boards. Bloomberg Press. New York, NY. 2003. 250p. The Economist Ser. ISBN:1-57660-142-0, ISBN13: 978-1-57660-142-6. Dewey:332.64. LCCN:03-000655.
Audience: **g,l,u,f.**

Levitt, Arthur & Dwyer, Paula **HG4521.L339 2002**
Take on the Street: What Wall Street and Corporate America Don't Want You to Know: What You Can Do to Fight Back. Trade Cloth. Knopf Publishing Group. New York, NY. 2002. 352p. ISBN:0-375-42178-5, ISBN13: 978-0-375-42178-5. Dewey:332.6. LCCN:2002-070422.
Audience: **g,l,u,f.**

Levy, Leon & Linden, Eugene **HG4910.L463 2002**
The Mind of Wall Street: A Legendary Financier on the Perils of Greed and the Mysteries of the Market. Trade Cloth. PublicAffairs. New York, NY. 2002. 240p. ISBN:1-58648-103-7, ISBN13: 978-1-58648-103-2. Dewey:332.6/0973. LCCN:2002-031856.
Audience: **g,l,u,f.**

Lewis, Michael M. **HG4928.5.L48 1989**
Liar's Poker: Rising Through the Wreckage on Wall Street. Trade Cloth. W. W. Norton & Company, Inc. New York, NY. 1989. 256p. ISBN:0-393-02750-3, ISBN13: 978-0-393-02750-1. Dewey:332.6/2/0973. LCCN:89-030819.
Audience: **g,l,u,f.**

Little, Jeffrey B. **HG4910.L54 2004**
Understanding Wall Street. Ed. 4. Trade Paper. McGraw-Hill Companies, The. New York, NY. 2004. 304p. ISBN:0-07-143373-2, ISBN13: 978-0-07-143373-0. Dewey:332.678. LCCN:2004-301326.
Audience: **g,l,u,f.** *Choice, 2004.*

Lowenstein, Roger **HG172.B84L69 1995**
Buffett: The Making of an American Capitalist. Trade Cloth. Random House, Inc. New York, NY. 1995. 512p. ISBN:0-679-41584-X, ISBN13: 978-0-679-41584-8. Dewey:332.6/092 B. LCCN:95-008494.
Audience: **g,l,u,f.** *Choice, 1996.*

Lowenstein, Roger **HG4930.L69 2000**
When Genius Failed: The Rise and Fall of Long-Term Capital Management. Trade Cloth. Random House, Inc. New York, NY. 2000. 288p. ISBN:0-375-50317-X, ISBN13: 978-0-375-50317-7. Dewey:332.6. LCCN:00-028091.
Audience: **g,l,u,f.** *Choice, 2001.*

Malaspina, Margaret A. **HD7105.45.U6M32 2003**
Cracking Your Retirement Nest Egg (Without Scrambling Your Finances): 25 Things You Must Know Before You Tap Your 401(K), IRA, or Other Retirement Savings Plan. Saddle Stitched, Cloth over Boards. Bloomberg Press. New York, NY. 2003. 256p. Bloomberg Personal Bookshelf ISBN:1-57660-126-9, ISBN13: 978-1-57660-126-6. Dewey:332.024/01. LCCN:2002-013470.
Audience: **g,l,u,f.**

Malkiel, Burton Gordon **HG4521.M284 2003**
A Random Walk down Wall Street: The Time Tested Strategy for Successful Investing Completely. Ed. 8. Trade Cloth. W. W. Norton & Company, Inc. New York, NY. 2003. 352p. ISBN:0-393-05782-8, ISBN13: 978-0-393-05782-9. Dewey:332.6. LCCN:2002-153052.
Audience: **g,l,u,f.** *Choice, 2003.*

Matthews, Joseph L. & Matthews Berman, Dorothy **KF3650.M37 2005**
Social Security, Medicare and Government Pensions: Get the Most Out of Your Retirement and Medical Benefits. Ed. 10. Trade Paper. NOLO. Berkeley, CA. 2005. 320p. ISBN:1-4133-0154-1, ISBN13: 978-1-4133-0154-0. Dewey:344.7302/26. LCCN:2004-065446.
Audience: **g,l,u,f.**

McLeavey, Dennis W. & Solnik, Bruno **HG4538.S52 2003**
International Investments. Ed. 5. Trade Cloth. Benjamin-Cummings Publishing Company. San Francisco, CA. 2003. 748p. Addison-Wesley Series in Finance ISBN:0-201-78568-4, ISBN13: 978-0-201-78568-5. Dewey:332.67/3. LCCN:2003-045954.
Audience: **u,f.**

Morris, Kenneth M. & Morris, Virginia B. **HG179**
The Wall Street Journal Guide to Understanding Personal Finance: Mortgages, Banking, Taxes, Investing, Financial Planning, Credit, Paying for Tuition. Ed. 4. Trade Paper. Simon & Schuster, Inc. New York, NY. 2004. 176p. ISBN:0-7432-6632-3, ISBN13: 978-0-7432-6632-1. Dewey:332.024.
Audience: **g,l,u,f.**

Morris, Kenneth M. & Morris, Virginia B. **HG4910.M67 2005**
The Wall Street Journal Guide to Understanding Money and Investing: An Easy-to-Understand, Easy-to-Use Primer That Helps Take the Mystery Out of Money, Indexes, Treasury Bills, Stocks, Commodities, Options, Bonds, Tracking Performance, Risk/Return, Mutual Funds, Futures, and Inflation. Ed. 3. Cherise Davis (Editor). Trade Paper. Simon & Schuster, Inc. New York, NY. 2004. 160p. ISBN:0-7432-6633-1, ISBN13: 978-0-7432-6633-8. Dewey:332.6/0973. LCCN:2004-558017.
Audience: **g,l,u,f.**

Moss, Rita W. **Z7164.C81S7796 2003**
Strauss's Handbook of Business Information: A Guide for Librarians, Students, and Researchers. Ed. 2. Trade Cloth. Libraries Unlimited, Inc. Westport, CT. 2003. 480p. ISBN:1-56308-520-8, ISBN13: 978-1-56308-520-8. Dewey:016.33. LCCN:2003-054569.
Audience: **g,u.** *Choice, 2004.*

Mulford, Charles W. & Comiskey, Eugene E. **HF5681.B2.M75 2002**
The Financial Numbers Game: Detecting Creative Accounting Practices. Trade Cloth. John Wiley & Sons, Inc. Hoboken, NJ. 2002. 408p. ISBN:0-471-37008-8, ISBN13: 978-0-471-37008-6. Dewey:657.3. LCCN:2001-045648.
Audience: **g,l,u,f.** *Choice, 2002.*

Munnell, Alicia H. & Sunden, Annika **HD7105.45.U6M86 2004**
Coming up Short: The Challenge of 401(K) Plans. Trade Cloth. Brookings Institution Press. Washington, DC. 2003. 272p. ISBN:0-8157-5888-X, ISBN13: 978-0-8157-5888-4. Dewey:331.25/2. LCCN:2003-026256.
Audience: **g,l,u,f.**

Nofsinger, John R. **HG4515.15.N643 2005**
The Psychology of Investing. Ed. 2. Trade Paper. Prentice Hall PTR. Upper Saddle River, NJ. 2004. 128p. ISBN:0-13-143270-2, ISBN13: 978-0-13-143270-3. Dewey:332.6/01/9. LCCN:2004-044409.
Audience: **g,l,u,f.**

Poorvu, William J. & Cruikshank, Jeffrey L. **HD1375.P6643 1999**
The Real Estate Game: The Intelligent Guide to Successful Investing and Decision-Making. Trade Cloth. Simon & Schuster. New York, NY. 1999. 336p. ISBN:0-684-85550-X, ISBN13: 978-0-684-85550-9. Dewey:333.33. LCCN:99-032272.
Audience: **g,l,u,f.**

Quinn, Jane Bryant **HG179.Q565 2006**
Smart and Simple Financial Strategies for Busy People. Trade Cloth. Simon & Schuster, Inc. New York, NY. 2006. 256p. ISBN:0-7432-6994-2, ISBN13: 978-0-7432-6994-0. Dewey:332.024. LCCN:2005-057475.
Audience: **g,l,u,f.**

Rosenstreich, Peter **HG3851.R67 2005**
Forex Revolution: An Insider's Guide to the Real World of Foreign Exchange Trading. Trade Cloth. Financial Times/Prentice Hall. Paramus, NJ. 2005. 360p. ISBN:0-13-148690-X, ISBN13: 978-0-13-148690-4. Dewey:332.4/5. LCCN:2005-921697.
Audience: **g,l,u,f.**

Schilit, Howard M. **HF5681.B2S3243 2002**
Financial Shenanigans: How to Detect Accounting Gimmicks and Fraud in Financial Reports. Ed. 2. Trade Cloth. McGraw-Hill Companies, The. New York, NY. 2002. 240p. ISBN:0-07-138626-2, ISBN13: 978-0-07-138626-5. Dewey:657/.3. LCCN:2002-002879.
Audience: **g,l,u,f.**

Scott, David L. **HG4513.S37 2003**
Wall Street Words: An A to Z Guide to Investment Terms for Today's Investor. Ed. 3. Trade Paper. Houghton Mifflin Company Trade & Reference Division. Boston, MA. 2003. 432p. ISBN:0-618-17651-9, ISBN13: 978-0-618-17651-9. Dewey:332.6/03. LCCN:2003-049928.
Audience: **g,l,u,f.**

Shamah, Shani Beverly **HG3853.S53 2003**
A Foreign Exchange Primer. Trade Cloth. John Wiley & Sons, Inc. Hoboken, NJ. 2003. 196p. Wiley Finance Ser. ISBN:0-470-85162-7, ISBN13: 978-0-470-85162-3. Dewey:332.4/5. LCCN:2002-191093.
Audience: **g,l,u,f.**

Shefrin, Hersh **HG4515.15.S53 2002**
Beyond Greed and Fear: Understanding Behavioral Finance and the Psychology of Investing. Ed. 2. Trade Cloth. Oxford University Press, Inc. New York, NY. 1999. 408p. Financial Management Association Survey and Synthesis Ser. ISBN:0-19-516121-1, ISBN13: 978-0-19-516121-2. Dewey:332.6/01/9. LCCN:2002-010047.
Audience: **g,l,u,f.** *Choice, 2003, 2000.*

Shiller, Robert J. **HG4910.S457 2005**
Irrational Exuberance. Ed. 2. Trade Cloth. Princeton University Press. Princeton, NJ. 2005. 344p. ISBN:0-691-12335-7, ISBN13: 978-0-691-12335-6. Dewey:332.63/222/0973. LCCN:2004-024789.
Audience: **g,l,u,f.** *Choice, 2000.*

Shirreff, David **HD61.S47 2004**
Dealing with Financial Risk. Perfect, Paper over Boards, Dust Jacket. Bloomberg Press. New York, NY. 2004. 214p. The Economist Ser. ISBN:1-57660-162-5, ISBN13: 978-1-57660-162-4. Dewey:658.15/5. LCCN:2004-011211.
Audience: **g,l,u,f.**

Shleifer, Andrei **HG4515**
Inefficient Markets: An Introduction to Behavioral Finance. Trade Paper. Oxford University Press, Inc. New York, NY. 2000. 224p. Clarendon Lectures in Economics ISBN:0-19-829227-9, ISBN13: 978-0-19-829227-2. Dewey:332.6.
Audience: **g,l,u,f.**

Siegel, Jeremy J. **HG4661.S52 2005**
The Future for Investors: Why the Tried and the True Triumph over the Bold and the New. Trade Cloth. Crown Publishing Group. New York, NY. 2005. 336p. ISBN:1-4000-8198-X, ISBN13: 978-1-4000-8198-1. Dewey:332.63/22. LCCN:2004-022938.
Audience: **g,l,u,f.**

Siegel, Jeremy J. **HG4661.S53 2002**
Stocks for the Long Run: The Definitive Guide to Financial Market Returns and Long-Term Investment Strategies. Ed. 3. Trade Paper. McGraw-Hill Companies, The. New York, NY. 2002. 388p. ISBN:0-07-137048-X, ISBN13: 978-0-07-137048-6. Dewey:332.63/22. LCCN:2002-002669.
Audience: **g,l,u,f.** *Choice, 2003, 1998, 1995.*

Sindell, Kathleen **HG4501**
Investing Online for Dummies®. Ed. 5. Trade Paper. John Wiley & Sons, Inc. Hoboken, NJ. 2005. 408p. ISBN:0-7645-8456-1, ISBN13: 978-0-7645-8456-5. Dewey:332.6/02854678. LCCN:2005-923224.
Audience: **g,u,f.**

Skeel, David A. **KF1526.S59 2001**
Debt's Dominion: A History of Bankruptcy Law in America. Trade Cloth. Princeton University Press. Princeton, NJ. 2001. 296p. ISBN:0-691-08810-1, ISBN13: 978-0-691-08810-5. Dewey:346.7307/8/09. LCCN:2001-021464.
Audience: **g,l,u,f.**

Smith, B. Mark **HG4551.S568 2003**
The Equity Culture: The Story of the Global Stock Market. Cloth over Boards. Farrar, Straus & Giroux. New York, NY. 2003. 352p. ISBN:0-374-28175-0, ISBN13: 978-0-374-28175-5. Dewey:332.63/2. LCCN:2003-040851.
Audience: **g,l,u,f.** *Choice, 2003.*

Teweles, Richard J. & Bradley, Edward S. **HG4551.T48 1998**
The Stock Market. Ed. 7. Trade Cloth. John Wiley & Sons, Inc. Hoboken, NJ. 1998. 576p. Wiley Investment Ser., Vol. 64

ISBN:0-471-19134-5, ISBN13: 978-0-471-19134-6. Dewey:332.63/2. LCCN:98-015213.
Audience: **g,l,u,f.**

Teweles, Richard J., et al. **HG6046.T45 1999**
The Futures Game: Who Wins, Who Loses, and Why. Ed. 3. Frank J. Jones & Ben Warwick (Authors). Cloth Text. McGraw-Hill Companies, The. New York, NY. 1998. 676p. ISBN:0-07-064757-7, ISBN13: 978-0-07-064757-2. Dewey:332.64/4. LCCN:98-022659.
Audience: **g,l,u,f.**

Thaler, Richard **HG4515.15**
Advances in Behavioral Finance, Vol. 2. Trade Paper. Princeton University Press. Princeton, NJ. 2005. 728p. The Roundtable Series in Behavioral Economics Ser. ISBN:0-691-12175-3, ISBN13: 978-0-691-12175-8. Dewey:332.6019.
Audience: **u,f.**

Thaler, Richard H. (Editor) **HG4515.15.A38 1993**
Advances in Behavioral Finance. Trade Cloth. Russell Sage Foundation. New York, NY. 1993. 544p. ISBN:0-87154-845-3, ISBN13: 978-0-87154-845-0. Dewey:332.6/01/9. LCCN:93-012149.
Audience: **u,f.**

Tobias, Andrew **HG4521.T6 2005**
The Only Investment Guide You'll Ever Need. Ed. 4. Trade Paper. Harcourt Trade Publishers. New York, NY. 2005. 312p. ISBN:0-15-602963-4, ISBN13: 978-0-15-602963-6. Dewey:332.024. LCCN:2004-015705.
Audience: **g,l,u,f.**

Tracy, John A. **HF5681.B2**
How to Read a Financial Report: Wringing Vital Signs Out of the Numbers. Ed. 6. Trade Paper. John Wiley & Sons, Inc. Hoboken, NJ. 2004. 216p. ISBN:0-471-47867-9, ISBN13: 978-0-471-47867-6. Dewey:657/.3. LCCN:2004-274182.
Audience: **g,l,u,f.**

Valdez, Stephen & Wood, Julian **HG173.V184 2003**
An Introduction to Global Financial Markets. Ed. 4. Trade Cloth. Palgrave Macmillan. New York, NY. 2003. xviii, 403p. ISBN:1-4039-0011-6, ISBN13: 978-1-4039-0011-1. Dewey:332. LCCN:2003-049803.
Audience: **g,l,u,f.**

Warren, Elizabeth & Tyagi, Amelia Warren **HG179.W3183 2005**
All Your Worth: The Ultimate Lifetime Money Plan. Trade Cloth. Simon & Schuster. New York, NY. 2005. 304p. ISBN:0-7432-6987-X, ISBN13: 978-0-7432-6987-2. Dewey:332.024. LCCN:2005-042483.
Audience: **g,l,u,f.**

Management Function > Finance > Foreign Exchange Administration

Aliber, Robert Z. **HG3881.A44 2000**
The New International Money Game. Ed. 6. Trade Cloth. University of Chicago Press. Chicago, IL. 2000. 304p. ISBN:0-226-01396-0, ISBN13: 978-0-226-01396-1. Dewey:332. LCCN:99-055593.
Audience: **g,l,u,f.**

Billingsley, Randall **HG6024.A3B55 2006**
Understanding Arbitrage: An Intuitive Approach to Financial Analysis. Trade Cloth. Financial Times/Prentice Hall. Paramus, NJ. 2005. 224p. ISBN:0-13-147020-5, ISBN13: 978-0-13-147020-0. Dewey:332.64/5. LCCN:2005-020842.
Audience: **g,l,u,f.**

Blustein, Paul **HC175.B665 2005**
And the Money Kept Rolling In (and Out): Wall Street, the IMF, and the Bankrupting of Argentina. Trade Cloth. PublicAffairs. New York, NY. 2005. 336p. ISBN:1-58648-245-9, ISBN13: 978-1-58648-245-9. Dewey:330.982/07. LCCN:2004-058743.
Audience: **g,l,u,f.** *Choice, 2005.*

Lowenstein, Roger **HG4930.L69 2000**
When Genius Failed: The Rise and Fall of Long-Term Capital Management. Trade Cloth. Random House, Inc. New York, NY. 2000. 288p. ISBN:0-375-50317-X, ISBN13: 978-0-375-50317-7. Dewey:332.6. LCCN:00-028091.
Audience: **g,l,u,f.** *Choice, 2001.*

Rosenstreich, Peter **HG3851.R67 2005**
Forex Revolution: An Insider's Guide to the Real World of Foreign Exchange Trading. Trade Cloth. Financial Times/Prentice Hall. Paramus, NJ. 2005. 360p. ISBN:0-13-148690-X, ISBN13: 978-0-13-148690-4. Dewey:332.4/5. LCCN:2005-921697.
Audience: **g,l,u,f.**

Shamah, Shani Beverly **HG3853.S53 2003**
A Foreign Exchange Primer. Trade Cloth. John Wiley & Sons, Inc. Hoboken, NJ. 2003. 196p. Wiley Finance Ser. ISBN:0-470-85162-7, ISBN13: 978-0-470-85162-3. Dewey:332.4/5. LCCN:2002-191093.
Audience: **g,l,u,f.**

Smith, Roy C. & Walter, Ingo **HG3881.S5434 2002**
Global Banking. Ed. 2. Trade Cloth. Oxford University Press, Inc. New York, NY. 2003. 448p. ISBN:0-19-513436-2, ISBN13: 978-0-19-513436-0. Dewey:332.1/5. LCCN:2002-003692.
Audience: **u,f.** *Choice, 2003, 1997.*

Management Function > Finance > Pension Fund Management

Matthews, Joseph L. & Matthews Berman, Dorothy **KF3650.M37 2005**
Social Security, Medicare and Government Pensions: Get the Most Out of Your Retirement and Medical Benefits. Ed. 10. Trade Paper. NOLO. Berkeley, CA. 2005. 320p. ISBN:1-4133-0154-1, ISBN13: 978-1-4133-0154-0. Dewey:344.7302/26. LCCN:2004-065446.
Audience: **g,l,u,f.**

McGill, Dan, et al. **HD7105.35.U6**
Fundamentals of Private Pensions. Ed. 8. Kyle N. Brown, John J. Haley & Sylvester Schieber (Authors). Trade Cloth. Oxford University Press, Inc. New York, NY. 2005. 902p. ISBN:0-19-926950-5, ISBN13: 978-0-19-926950-1. Dewey:658.3/253/0973. LCCN:2005-270572.
Audience: **u,f.**

Mitchell, Olivia S. (Editor) **HD4928.N62U62325**
Benefits for the Workplace of the Future. Wharton School, Pension Research Council Staff (Contribution by). Book, Other.

University of Pennsylvania Press. Philadelphia, PA. 2003. 312p. ISBN:0-8122-3708-0, ISBN13: 978-0-8122-3708-5. Dewey:331.2/0973. LCCN:2002-041258.
Audience: **u,f.** *Choice, 2003.*

Munnell, Alicia H. & Sunden, Annika **HD7105.45.U6M86 2004**
Coming up Short: The Challenge of 401(K) Plans. Trade Cloth. Brookings Institution Press. Washington, DC. 2003. 272p. ISBN:0-8157-5888-X, ISBN13: 978-0-8157-5888-4. Dewey:331.25/2. LCCN:2003-026256.
Audience: **g,l,u,f.**

Management Function > Finance > Financial Markets

HG4501
☐ Path to Investing.
http://www.pathtoinvesting.org/
Audience: **g,l,f.**

KF1444
☐ U.S. Securities and Exchange Commission.
http://www.sec.gov/
Audience: **g,l,u,f.**

Aliber, Robert Z. **HG3881.A44 2000**
The New International Money Game. Ed. 6. Trade Cloth. University of Chicago Press. Chicago, IL. 2000. 304p. ISBN:0-226-01396-0, ISBN13: 978-0-226-01396-1. Dewey:332. LCCN:99-055593.
Audience: **g,l,u,f.**

Bagehot, Walter **HG3000.L82B3 1999**
Lombard Street: A Description of the Money Market. Trade Cloth. John Wiley & Sons, Inc. Hoboken, NJ. 1999. 359p. Wiley Investment Classic Ser., Vol. 23 ISBN:0-471-34499-0, ISBN13: 978-0-471-34499-5. Dewey:332/.09421. LCCN:98-051463.
Audience: **u,f.**

Bagehot, Walter **HG3000.L82B3 1999**
Lombard Street: A Description of the Money Market. Trade Paper. John Wiley & Sons, Inc. Hoboken, NJ. 1999. 359p. Wiley Investment Classic Ser., Vol. 22 ISBN:0-471-34536-9, ISBN13: 978-0-471-34536-7. Dewey:332/.09421. LCCN:98-051463.
Audience: **g,l,u,f.**

Baker, George P. & Smith, George D. **HG4028.M4 B335 1998**
The New Financial Capitalists: Kohlberg Kravis Roberts and the Creation of Corporate Value. Trade Cloth. Cambridge University Press. New York, NY. 1998. 272p. ISBN:0-521-64260-4, ISBN13: 978-0-521-64260-6. Dewey:338.830973. LCCN:98-028007.
Audience: **g,l,u,f.** *Choice, 1999.*

Bernstein, Peter L. **HD61.B466 1996**
Against the Gods: The Remarkable Story of Risk. Trade Cloth. John Wiley & Sons, Inc. Hoboken, NJ. 1996. 400p. ISBN:0-471-12104-5, ISBN13: 978-0-471-12104-6. Dewey:368. LCCN:96-033861.
Audience: **g,l,u,f.**

Bernstein, Peter L. **HG173**
Capital Ideas: The Improbable Origins of Modern Wall Street. Trade Paper, Perfect. John Wiley & Sons, Inc. Hoboken, NJ. 2005. 360p. ISBN:0-471-73174-9, ISBN13: 978-0-471-73174-0. Dewey:332.632. LCCN:2005-276389.
Audience: **g,l,u,f.**

Bernstein, Peter L. **GR810.B47 2000**
The Power of Gold: The History of an Obsession. Trade Cloth. John Wiley & Sons, Inc. Hoboken, NJ. 2000. 448p. ISBN:0-471-25210-7, ISBN13: 978-0-471-25210-8. Dewey:398/.365. LCCN:00-036647.
Audience: **g,l,u,f.**

Biggs, Barton **HG4530.B516 2006**
Hedgehogging. Trade Cloth. John Wiley & Sons, Inc. Hoboken, NJ. 2006. 320p. ISBN:0-471-77191-0, ISBN13: 978-0-471-77191-3. Dewey:332.64/5. LCCN:2005-026139.
Audience: **g,l,u,f.**

Blustein, Paul **HC175.B665 2005**
And the Money Kept Rolling In (and Out): Wall Street, the IMF, and the Bankrupting of Argentina. Trade Cloth. PublicAffairs. New York, NY. 2005. 336p. ISBN:1-58648-245-9, ISBN13: 978-1-58648-245-9. Dewey:330.982/07. LCCN:2004-058743.
Audience: **g,l,u,f.** *Choice, 2005.*

Blustein, Paul **HB3808.B58 2001**
The Chastening: Inside the Crisis That Rocked the Global Financial System and Humbled the IMF. Trade Cloth. PublicAffairs. New York, NY. 2001. 448p. ISBN:1-891620-81-9, ISBN13: 978-1-891620-81-2. Dewey:332/.042/095. LCCN:2001-041678.
Audience: **g,l,u,f.** *Choice, 2002.*

Brennan, Niamh **HD30.15.B455**
Accounting. Ed. 2. Colin Clubb (Editor). Trade Cloth. Blackwell Publishing, Inc. Malden, MA. 2006. 456p. The Blackwell Encyclopedia of Management Ser., Vol. 1 ISBN:1-4051-1827-X, ISBN13: 978-1-4051-1827-9. Dewey:658/.003 s 657/.03. LCCN:2004-024923.
Audience: **g,l,u,f.**

Bruck, Connie **HD2746.5.B78 1988**
The Predator's Ball: How the Junk Bond Machine Staked the Corporate Raiders. Children's Board Books. Simon & Schuster. New York, NY. 1988. 448p. ISBN:0-671-61780-X, ISBN13: 978-0-671-61780-6. Dewey:332.63/2/0973. LCCN:88-011572.
Audience: **g,l,u,f.**

Chancellor, Edward **HG6005**
Devil Take the Hindmost: A History of Financial Speculation. Trade Paper. Penguin Group (USA) Inc. New York, NY. 2000. 400p. ISBN:0-452-28180-6, ISBN13: 978-0-452-28180-6. Dewey:332.6/3228/09.
Audience: **g,l,u,f.** *Choice, 1999.*

Davis, E. Philip & Steil, Benn **HG4521.D14 2001**
Institutional Investors. Trade Cloth. MIT Press. Cambridge, MA. 2001. 560p. ISBN:0-262-04192-8, ISBN13: 978-0-262-04192-8. Dewey:332.67/154. LCCN:2001-030280.
Audience: **g,l,u,f.**

Galbraith, John Kenneth **HB3717 1929.G32 1997**
The Great Crash 1929. Trade Paper. Houghton Mifflin Company Trade & Reference Division. Boston, MA. 1997. 224p.

ISBN:0-395-85999-9, ISBN13: 978-0-395-85999-5. Dewey:338.5/4/0973. LCCN:97-022051.
Audience: **g,l,u,f.** B

Geisst, Charles **HG5129.N5G44 2001**
The Last Partnerships: Inside the Great Wall Street Dynasties. Trade Cloth. McGraw-Hill Companies, The. New York, NY. 2001. 338p. ISBN:0-07-136999-6, ISBN13: 978-0-07-136999-2. Dewey:332.6/0973. LCCN:2001-030374.
Audience: **g,l,u,f.** *Choice, 2001.*

Geisst, Charles **HG4572**
Wall Street: From Its Beginnings to the Fall of Enron. Trade Cloth. Oxford University Press, Inc. New York, NY. 2004. 449p. ISBN:0-19-517061-X, ISBN13: 978-0-19-517061-0. Dewey:332.64/273. LCCN:2004-555123.
Audience: **g,l,u,f.**

Gordon, John S. **HG4910.G667 1999**
The Great Game: The Emergence of Wall Street as a World Power, 1653-2000. Trade Cloth. Simon & Schuster. New York, NY. 1999. 320p. ISBN:0-684-83287-9, ISBN13: 978-0-684-83287-6. Dewey:332.64/273. LCCN:00-265068.
Audience: **g,l,u,f.**

Kindleberger, Charles P. & Aliber, Robert **HB3722.K56 2005**
Manias, Panics, and Crashes: A History of Financial Crises. Ed. 5. Robert Solow (Foreword by). Trade Paper. John Wiley & Sons, Inc. Hoboken, NJ. 2005. 304p. Wiley Investment Classics Ser. ISBN:0-471-46714-6, ISBN13: 978-0-471-46714-4. Dewey:338.5/42. LCCN:2005-001066.
Audience: **g,l,u,f.** B

Kolb, Robert W. & Overdahl, James A. **HG6024.A3K648 2003**
Financial Derivatives. Ed. 3. Trade Cloth. John Wiley & Sons, Inc. Hoboken, NJ. 2002. 336p. Wiley Finance Ser. ISBN:0-471-23232-7, ISBN13: 978-0-471-23232-2. Dewey:332.64/5. LCCN:2002-014027.
Audience: **g,l,u,f.**

Levy, Leon & Linden, Eugene **HG4910.L463 2002**
The Mind of Wall Street: A Legendary Financier on the Perils of Greed and the Mysteries of the Market. Trade Cloth. PublicAffairs. New York, NY. 2002. 240p. ISBN:1-58648-103-7, ISBN13: 978-1-58648-103-2. Dewey:332.6/0973. LCCN:2002-031856.
Audience: **g,l,u,f.**

Lewis, Michael M. **HG4928.5.L48 1989**
Liar's Poker: Rising Through the Wreckage on Wall Street. Trade Cloth. W. W. Norton & Company, Inc. New York, NY. 1989. 256p. ISBN:0-393-02750-3, ISBN13: 978-0-393-02750-1. Dewey:332.6/2/0973. LCCN:89-030819.
Audience: **g,l,u,f.**

Little, Jeffrey B. **HG4910.L54 2004**
Understanding Wall Street. Ed. 4. Trade Paper. McGraw-Hill Companies, The. New York, NY. 2004. 304p. ISBN:0-07-143373-2, ISBN13: 978-0-07-143373-0. Dewey:332.678. LCCN:2004-301326.
Audience: **g,l,u,f.** *Choice, 2004.*

Lowenstein, Roger **HG4930.L69 2000**
When Genius Failed: The Rise and Fall of Long-Term Capital Management. Trade Cloth. Random House, Inc. New York, NY. 2000. 288p. ISBN:0-375-50317-X, ISBN13: 978-0-375-50317-7. Dewey:332.6. LCCN:00-028091.
Audience: **g,l,u,f.** *Choice, 2001.*

Rosenstreich, Peter **HG3851.R67 2005**
Forex Revolution: An Insider's Guide to the Real World of Foreign Exchange Trading. Trade Cloth. Financial Times/Prentice Hall. Paramus, NJ. 2005. 360p. ISBN:0-13-148690-X, ISBN13: 978-0-13-148690-4. Dewey:332.4/5. LCCN:2005-921697.
Audience: **g,l,u,f.**

Seligman, Joel **HG4910.S4 1995**
The Transformation of Wall Street: A History of the Securities and Exchange Commission and Modern Corporate Finance. Trade Cloth. Northeastern University Press. Boston, MA. 1995. 772p. ISBN:1-55553-231-4, ISBN13: 978-1-55553-231-4. Dewey:354.8/8/0973. LCCN:95-013762.
Audience: **g,l,u,f.** *Choice, 1996.*

Shamah, Shani Beverly **HG3853.S53 2003**
A Foreign Exchange Primer. Trade Cloth. John Wiley & Sons, Inc. Hoboken, NJ. 2003. 196p. Wiley Finance Ser. ISBN:0-470-85162-7, ISBN13: 978-0-470-85162-3. Dewey:332.4/5. LCCN:2002-191093.
Audience: **g,l,u,f.**

Shiller, Robert J. **HG4910.S457 2005**
Irrational Exuberance. Ed. 2. Trade Cloth. Princeton University Press. Princeton, NJ. 2005. 344p. ISBN:0-691-12335-7, ISBN13: 978-0-691-12335-6. Dewey:332.63/222/0973. LCCN:2004-024789.
Audience: **g,l,u,f.** *Choice, 2000.*

Shiller, Robert J. **HD61.S55 2003**
The New Financial Order: Risk in the 21st Century. Trade Cloth. Princeton University Press. Princeton, NJ. 2003. 400p. ISBN:0-691-09172-2, ISBN13: 978-0-691-09172-3. Dewey:368. LCCN:2002-042563.
Audience: **g,l,u,f.** *Choice, 2003.*

Shirreff, David **HD61.S47 2004**
Dealing with Financial Risk. Perfect, Paper over Boards, Dust Jacket. Bloomberg Press. New York, NY. 2004. 214p. The Economist Ser. ISBN:1-57660-162-5, ISBN13: 978-1-57660-162-4. Dewey:658.15/5. LCCN:2004-011211.
Audience: **g,l,u,f.**

Shleifer, Andrei **HG4515**
Inefficient Markets: An Introduction to Behavioral Finance. Trade Paper. Oxford University Press, Inc. New York, NY. 2000. 224p. Clarendon Lectures in Economics ISBN:0-19-829227-9, ISBN13: 978-0-19-829227-2. Dewey:332.6.
Audience: **g,l,u,f.**

Siegel, Jeremy J. **HG4661.S52 2005**
The Future for Investors: Why the Tried and the True Triumph over the Bold and the New. Trade Cloth. Crown Publishing Group. New York, NY. 2005. 336p. ISBN:1-4000-8198-X, ISBN13: 978-1-4000-8198-1. Dewey:332.63/22. LCCN:2004-022938.
Audience: **g,l,u,f.**

Stewart, James B. **HG4910.S683 1991**
Den of Thieves: The Untold Story of the Men Who Plundered Wall Street and the Chase That Brought Them Down. Trade Cloth. Simon & Schuster. New York, NY. 1991. 496p.

ISBN:0-671-63802-5, ISBN13: 978-0-671-63802-3. Dewey:364.1/68. LCCN:91-028819.
Audience: **g,l,u,f.**

Thaler, Richard H. (Editor) **HG4515.15.A38 1993**
Advances in Behavioral Finance. Trade Cloth. Russell Sage Foundation. New York, NY. 1993. 544p. ISBN:0-87154-845-3, ISBN13: 978-0-87154-845-0. Dewey:332.6/01/9. LCCN:93-012149.
Audience: **u,f.**

Management Function > Finance > Financial Markets > Securities and Derivatives

HG5131.C43
CBOE, Chicago Board Options Exhange.
http://www.cboe.com/
Audience: **g,l,u,f.**

HF295
Chicago Board of Trade.
http://www.cbot.com/
Audience: **g,l,u,f.**

HG4501
Fool.com: To Educate, Amuse and Enrich.
http://www.fool.com/
Audience: **g,l,u,f.**

HG4009
Hoover's Online.
http://www.hoovers.com
Audience: **g,l,u,f.**

HG4529
Investopedia - Your Source for Investment Education.
http://www.investopedia.com/
Audience: **g,l,u,f.**

HG4529
InvestorWords.com.
http://www.investorwords.com/
Audience: **g,l,u,f.**

HG4501
MarketWatch.
http://www.marketwatch.com/
Audience: **g,l,u,f.**

HG4530
Morningstar.
http://www.morningstar.com
Audience: **g,l,u,f.**

HG4574.2
The NASDAQ Stock Market.
http://www.nasdaq.com/
Audience: **g,l,u,f.**

HG4572
NYSE, New York Stock Exchange.
http://www.nyse.com/
Audience: **g,l,u.**

HG173
OSU Virtual Finance Library.
http://fisher.osu.edu/fin/overview.htm
Audience: **g,l,u,f.**

HG151.8
Yahoo! Finance.
http://finance.yahoo.com/
Audience: **g,l,u,f.**

Amram, Martha (Author, Editor) **HG6024.A3A47 1999**
Real Options: Managing Strategic Investment in an Uncertain World. Nalin Kulatilaka (Editor). Trade Cloth. Oxford University Press, Inc. New York, NY. 1998. 246p. Financial Management Association Survey and Synthesis Ser. ISBN:0-87584-845-1, ISBN13: 978-0-87584-845-7. Dewey:332.64/5. LCCN:98-022392.
Audience: **u,f.** *Choice, 1999.*

Arditti, Fred D. **HG6024.U6A73 1996**
Derivatives: A Comprehensive Resource for Options, Futures, Interest Rate Swaps and Mortgage Securities. Trade Cloth. Harvard Business School Press. Boston, MA. 1996. 416p. Financial Management Association Survey and Synthesis Ser. ISBN:0-87584-560-6, ISBN13: 978-0-87584-560-9. Dewey:332.64/5. LCCN:95-031894.
Audience: **g,l,u,f.** *Choice, 1996.*

Berenson, Alex **HV6768**
e The Number: How the Drive for Quarterly Earnings Corrupted Wall Street and Corporate America. E-Book. Random House Adult Trade Publishing Group. New York, NY. 2003. ISBN:1-58836-288-4, ISBN13: 978-1-58836-288-9. Dewey:364.16/8.
Audience: **g,l,u,f.** *Choice, 2004.*

Billingsley, Randall **HG6024.A3B55 2006**
Understanding Arbitrage: An Intuitive Approach to Financial Analysis. Trade Cloth. Financial Times/Prentice Hall. Paramus, NJ. 2005. 224p. ISBN:0-13-147020-5, ISBN13: 978-0-13-147020-0. Dewey:332.64/5. LCCN:2005-020842.
Audience: **g,l,u,f.**

Chancellor, Edward **HG6005**
Devil Take the Hindmost: A History of Financial Speculation. Trade Paper. Penguin Group (USA) Inc. New York, NY. 2000. 400p. ISBN:0-452-28180-6, ISBN13: 978-0-452-28180-6. Dewey:332.6/3228/09.
Audience: **g,l,u,f.** *Choice, 1999.*

Chicago Board of Trade Staff **HG6024.U6C45 2006**
The CBOT Handbook of Futures and Options. Trade Cloth. McGraw-Hill Companies, The. New York, NY. 2006. 480p. ISBN:0-07-145751-8, ISBN13: 978-0-07-145751-4. Dewey:332.64/52. LCCN:2005-027316.
Audience: **g,l,u,f.**

Downes, John & Goodman, Jordan Elliot **HG173.D66 2003**
Finance and Investment Handbook. Ed. 6. Trade Cloth. Barron's Educational Series, Inc. Hauppauge, NY. 2003. 1400p. ISBN:0-7641-5554-7, ISBN13: 978-0-7641-5554-3. Dewey:332.67/8. LCCN:2002-038595.
Audience: **g,l,u,f.**

Isaacs, Alan (Author, Editor) **HG151**
A Dictionary of Finance and Banking. Ed. 3. John Smullen & Nicholas Hand (Editors). Trade Paper. Oxford University Press, Inc. New York, NY. 2005. 448p. Oxford Paperback Reference Ser. ISBN:0-19-860749-0, ISBN13: 978-0-19-860749-6. Dewey:332/.03. LCCN:2005-274362.
Audience: **g,l,u,f.**

Kolb, Robert W. & Overdahl, James A. **HG6024.A3K648 2003**
Financial Derivatives. Ed. 3. Trade Cloth. John Wiley & Sons, Inc. Hoboken, NJ. 2002. 336p. Wiley Finance Ser. ISBN:0-471-23232-7, ISBN13: 978-0-471-23232-2. Dewey:332.64/5. LCCN:2002-014027.
Audience: **g,l,u,f.**

Lefèvre, Edwin & Marketplace Books **HG4572**
Reminiscences of a Stock Operator: The Wall Street Classic about the Life and Times of Jesse Livermore. William J. O'Neil (Foreword by). Trade Cloth. John Wiley & Sons, Inc. Hoboken, NJ. 2004. 253p. ISBN:0-471-67876-7, ISBN13: 978-0-471-67876-2. Dewey:332.6/42/73. LCCN:2004-275015.
Audience: **g,l,u,f.**

Levinson, Marc **HG173.L485 2003**
Guide to Financial Markets. Ed. 3. Perfect, Paper over Boards. Bloomberg Press. New York, NY. 2003. 250p. The Economist Ser. ISBN:1-57660-142-0, ISBN13: 978-1-57660-142-6. Dewey:332.64. LCCN:03-000655.
Audience: **g,l,u,f.**

Mulford, Charles W. & Comiskey, Eugene E. **HF5681.B2.M75 2002**
The Financial Numbers Game: Detecting Creative Accounting Practices. Trade Cloth. John Wiley & Sons, Inc. Hoboken, NJ. 2002. 408p. ISBN:0-471-37008-8, ISBN13: 978-0-471-37008-6. Dewey:657.3. LCCN:2001-045648.
Audience: **g,l,u,f.** *Choice, 2002.*

Shefrin, Hersh **HG4515.15.S53 2002**
Beyond Greed and Fear: Understanding Behavioral Finance and the Psychology of Investing. Ed. 2. Trade Cloth. Oxford University Press, Inc. New York, NY. 1999. 408p. Financial Management Association Survey and Synthesis Ser. ISBN:0-19-516121-1, ISBN13: 978-0-19-516121-2. Dewey:332.6/01/9. LCCN:2002-010047.
Audience: **g,l,u,f.** *Choice, 2003, 2000.*

Shirreff, David **HD61.S47 2004**
Dealing with Financial Risk. Perfect, Paper over Boards, Dust Jacket. Bloomberg Press. New York, NY. 2004. 214p. The Economist Ser. ISBN:1-57660-162-5, ISBN13: 978-1-57660-162-4. Dewey:658.15/5. LCCN:2004-011211.
Audience: **g,l,u,f.**

Siegel, Jeremy J. **HG4661.S53 2002**
Stocks for the Long Run: The Definitive Guide to Financial Market Returns and Long-Term Investment Strategies. Ed. 3. Trade Paper. McGraw-Hill Companies, The. New York, NY. 2002. 388p. ISBN:0-07-137048-X, ISBN13: 978-0-07-137048-6. Dewey:332.63/22. LCCN:2002-002669.
Audience: **g,l,u,f.** *Choice, 2003, 1998, 1995.*

Smith, B. Mark **HG4551.S568 2003**
The Equity Culture: The Story of the Global Stock Market. Cloth over Boards. Farrar, Straus & Giroux. New York, NY. 2003. 352p. ISBN:0-374-28175-0, ISBN13: 978-0-374-28175-5. Dewey:332.63/2. LCCN:2003-040851.
Audience: **g,l,u,f.** *Choice, 2003.*

Smith, Roy C. & Walter, Ingo **HG3881.S5434 2002**
Global Banking. Ed. 2. Trade Cloth. Oxford University Press, Inc. New York, NY. 2003. 448p. ISBN:0-19-513436-2, ISBN13: 978-0-19-513436-0. Dewey:332.1/5. LCCN:2002-003692.
Audience: **u,f.** *Choice, 2003, 1997.*

Tamarkin, Robert A. **HG6049.T35 1993**
Merc: The Emergence of a Global Financial Powerhouse. Trade Cloth. HarperCollins Publishers. New York, NY. 1993. 304p. ISBN:0-88730-516-4, ISBN13: 978-0-88730-516-0. Dewey:332.64/4/0977311. LCCN:92-053335.
Audience: **g,l,u,f.**

Teweles, Richard J. & Bradley, Edward S. **HG4551.T48 1998**
The Stock Market. Ed. 7. Trade Cloth. John Wiley & Sons, Inc. Hoboken, NJ. 1998. 576p. Wiley Investment Ser., Vol. 64 ISBN:0-471-19134-5, ISBN13: 978-0-471-19134-6. Dewey:332.63/2. LCCN:98-015213.
Audience: **g,l,u,f.**

Teweles, Richard J., et al. **HG6046.T45 1999**
The Futures Game: Who Wins, Who Loses, and Why. Ed. 3. Frank J. Jones & Ben Warwick (Authors). Cloth Text. McGraw-Hill Companies, The. New York, NY. 1998. 676p. ISBN:0-07-064757-7, ISBN13: 978-0-07-064757-2. Dewey:332.64/4. LCCN:98-022659.
Audience: **g,l,u,f.**

Valdez, Stephen & Wood, Julian **HG173.V184 2003**
An Introduction to Global Financial Markets. Ed. 4. Trade Cloth. Palgrave Macmillan. New York, NY. 2003. xviii, 403p. ISBN:1-4039-0011-6, ISBN13: 978-1-4039-0011-1. Dewey:332. LCCN:2003-049803.
Audience: **g,l,u,f.**

Management Function > Finance > Financial Markets > Bonds

HF295
☐ Chicago Board of Trade.
http://www.cbot.com/
Audience: **g,l,u,f.**

HG4529
☐ Investopedia - Your Source for Investment Education.
http://www.investopedia.com/
Audience: **g,l,u,f.**

HG4529
☐ InvestorWords.com.
http://www.investorwords.com/
Audience: **g,l,u,f.**

HG4501
☐ MarketWatch.
http://www.marketwatch.com/
Audience: **g,l,u,f.**

HG4530

☐ Morningstar.
http://www.morningstar.com
Audience: **g,l,u,f.**

HG173

☐ OSU Virtual Finance Library.
http://fisher.osu.edu/fin/overview.htm
Audience: **g,l,u,f.**

HG151.8

☐ Yahoo! Finance.
http://finance.yahoo.com/
Audience: **g,l,u,f.**

Arditti, Fred D. **HG6024.U6A73 1996**
Derivatives: A Comprehensive Resource for Options, Futures, Interest Rate Swaps and Mortgage Securities. Trade Cloth. Harvard Business School Press. Boston, MA. 1996. 416p. Financial Management Association Survey and Synthesis Ser. ISBN:0-87584-560-6, ISBN13: 978-0-87584-560-9. Dewey:332.64/5. LCCN:95-031894.
Audience: **g,l,u,f.** *Choice, 1996.*

Billingsley, Randall **HG6024.A3B55 2006**
Understanding Arbitrage: An Intuitive Approach to Financial Analysis. Trade Cloth. Financial Times/Prentice Hall. Paramus, NJ. 2005. 224p. ISBN:0-13-147020-5, ISBN13: 978-0-13-147020-0. Dewey:332.64/5. LCCN:2005-020842.
Audience: **g,l,u,f.**

Downes, John & Goodman, Jordan Elliot **HG173.D66 2003**
Finance and Investment Handbook. Ed. 6. Trade Cloth. Barron's Educational Series, Inc. Hauppauge, NY. 2003. 1400p. ISBN:0-7641-5554-7, ISBN13: 978-0-7641-5554-3. Dewey:332.67/8. LCCN:2002-038595.
Audience: **g,l,u,f.**

Fabozzi, Frank J. **HG4651.H265 2005**
The Handbook of Fixed Income Securities. Ed. 7. Trade Cloth. McGraw-Hill Companies, The. New York, NY. 2005. 1500p. ISBN:0-07-144099-2, ISBN13: 978-0-07-144099-8. Dewey:332.63/2044. LCCN:2004-019507.
Audience: **u,f.**

Homer, Sidney & Leibowitz, Martin L. **HG4936.H65 2004**
Inside the Yield Book: The Classic That Created the Science of Bond Analysis. Saddle Stitched, Cloth over Boards. Bloomberg Press. New York, NY. 2004. 240p. ISBN:1-57660-159-5, ISBN13: 978-1-57660-159-4. Dewey:332.63/23. LCCN:2004-006036.
Audience: **u,f.**

Isaacs, Alan (Author, Editor) **HG151**
A Dictionary of Finance and Banking. Ed. 3. John Smullen & Nicholas Hand (Editors). Trade Paper. Oxford University Press, Inc. New York, NY. 2005. 448p. Oxford Paperback Reference Ser. ISBN:0-19-860749-0, ISBN13: 978-0-19-860749-6. Dewey:332/.03. LCCN:2005-274362.
Audience: **g,l,u,f.**

Levinson, Marc **HG173.L485 2003**
Guide to Financial Markets. Ed. 3. Perfect, Paper over Boards. Bloomberg Press. New York, NY. 2003. 250p. The Economist Ser. ISBN:1-57660-142-0, ISBN13: 978-1-57660-142-6. Dewey:332.64. LCCN:03-000655.
Audience: **g,l,u,f.**

Lewis, Michael M. **HG4928.5.L48 1989**
Liar's Poker: Rising Through the Wreckage on Wall Street. Trade Cloth. W. W. Norton & Company, Inc. New York, NY. 1989. 256p. ISBN:0-393-02750-3, ISBN13: 978-0-393-02750-1. Dewey:332.6/2/0973. LCCN:89-030819.
Audience: **g,l,u,f.**

Shefrin, Hersh **HG4515.15.S53 2002**
Beyond Greed and Fear: Understanding Behavioral Finance and the Psychology of Investing. Ed. 2. Trade Cloth. Oxford University Press, Inc. New York, NY. 1999. 408p. Financial Management Association Survey and Synthesis Ser. ISBN:0-19-516121-1, ISBN13: 978-0-19-516121-2. Dewey:332.6/01/9. LCCN:2002-010047.
Audience: **g,l,u,f.** *Choice, 2003, 2000.*

Shirreff, David **HD61.S47 2004**
Dealing with Financial Risk. Perfect, Paper over Boards, Dust Jacket. Bloomberg Press. New York, NY. 2004. 214p. The Economist Ser. ISBN:1-57660-162-5, ISBN13: 978-1-57660-162-4. Dewey:658.15/5. LCCN:2004-011211.
Audience: **g,l,u,f.**

Smith, Roy C. & Walter, Ingo **HG3881.S5434 2002**
Global Banking. Ed. 2. Trade Cloth. Oxford University Press, Inc. New York, NY. 2003. 448p. ISBN:0-19-513436-2, ISBN13: 978-0-19-513436-0. Dewey:332.1/5. LCCN:2002-003692.
Audience: **u,f.** *Choice, 2003, 1997.*

Valdez, Stephen & Wood, Julian **HG173.V184 2003**
An Introduction to Global Financial Markets. Ed. 4. Trade Cloth. Palgrave Macmillan. New York, NY. 2003. xviii, 403p. ISBN:1-4039-0011-6, ISBN13: 978-1-4039-0011-1. Dewey:332. LCCN:2003-049803.
Audience: **g,l,u,f.**

Management Function > Accounting, Taxation, and Law

HF5667

☐ PCAOB: The Public Company Accounting Oversight Board.
http://www.pcaobus.org/
Audience: **g,l,u,f.**

Eichenwald, Kurt **HD9502.U54E5736 2005**
Conspiracy of Fools: A True Story. Trade Cloth. Broadway Books. New York, NY. 2005. 768p. ISBN:0-7679-1178-4, ISBN13: 978-0-7679-1178-8. Dewey:364.1. LCCN:2004-058216.
Audience: **g,l,u,f.** *Choice, 2005.*

Management Function > Accounting, Taxation, and Law > Accounting

HF5627

☐ AICPA: American Institute of Certified Public Accountants.
http://www.aicpa.org/
Audience: **g,l,u,f.**

HF5626

□ FASB: Financial Accounting Standards Board.
http://www.fasb.org/

Audience: **g,l,u,f.**

HF5667

□ PCAOB: The Public Company Accounting Oversight Board.
http://www.pcaobus.org/

Audience: **g,l,u,f.**

HF5681.T3

□ Tax and Accounting Sites Directory.
http://www.taxsites.com/

Audience: **g,l,u,f.**

Chatfield, Michael & Vangermeersch, Richard (Editors) **HF5605.H573 1996**
The History of Accounting: An Encyclopedia. Paper over Boards. Garland Publishing, Inc. New York, NY. 1996. 680p. Reference Library of the Humanities Ser., Vol. 1573:1826, 1878 ISBN:0-8153-0809-4, ISBN13: 978-0-8153-0809-6. Dewey:657/.09. LCCN:95-020710.
Audience: **g,l,u,f.** *Choice, 1996.*

Chenok, P. B. (Editor) **HF5616.U5C483 2000**
Foundations for the Future: The AICPA from 1980-1995. Trade Cloth. Elsevier Science & Technology Books. Saint Louis, MO. 2000. 224p. Studies in the Development of Accounting Thought Ser., Vol. 2 ISBN:0-7623-0672-6, ISBN13: 978-0-7623-0672-5. Dewey:657/.06/073. LCCN:2001-269656.
Audience: **g,l,u,f.**

Choi, Frederick D. S. (Editor) **HF5686.I56H36 2003**
International Finance and Accounting Handbook. Ed. 3. Trade Cloth. John Wiley & Sons, Inc. Hoboken, NJ. 2003. 888p. ISBN:0-471-22921-0, ISBN13: 978-0-471-22921-6. Dewey:657/.96. LCCN:2002-192266.
Audience: **u,f.**

Garrett, Ian (Editor) **HD30.15.B455**
Finance. Ed. 2. Trade Cloth. Blackwell Publishing, Inc. Malden, MA. 2006. 248p. The Blackwell Encyclopedia of Management Ser., Vol. 4 ISBN:1-4051-1826-1, ISBN13: 978-1-4051-1826-2. Dewey:658/.003 s 658.15/03. LCCN:2004-024922.
Audience: **g,l,u,f.**

Markham, Jerry W. **HV6769.M37 2005**
A Financial History of Modern U S Corporate Scandals. Cloth Text. M. E. Sharpe Inc. Armonk, NY. 2005. 768p. ISBN:0-7656-1583-5, ISBN13: 978-0-7656-1583-1. Dewey:364.16/8/0973. LCCN:2005-005562.
Audience: **g,l,u,f.** *Choice, 2006.*

Oxford University Press (Created by) **HF5621**
Oxford Dictionary of Accounting. Ed. 3. Trade Paper, Perfect. Oxford University Press, Inc. New York, NY. 2005. 416p. Oxford Paperback Reference Ser. ISBN:0-19-280627-0, ISBN13: 978-0-19-280627-7. Dewey:657.003. LCCN:2006-272990.
Audience: **g,l,u,f.**

Previts, Gary J. & Merino, Barbara Dubis **HF5616.U5P724 1998**
History of Accountancy in the United States: The Cultural Significance of Accounting. Paper Text. Ohio State University Press. Columbus, OH. 1997. 577p. Historical Perspectives on Business Enterprise Ser. ISBN:0-8142-0728-6, ISBN13: 978-0-8142-0728-4. Dewey:657/.0973. LCCN:97-024109.
Audience: **g,l,u,f.** *Choice, 1998.*

Management Function > Accounting, Taxation, and Law > Accounting > Accounting Policies and Procedures

HF5626

□ FASB: Financial Accounting Standards Board.
http://www.fasb.org/

Audience: **g,l,u,f.**

HF5667

□ PCAOB: The Public Company Accounting Oversight Board.
http://www.pcaobus.org/

Audience: **g,l,u,f.**

KF1444

□ U.S. Securities and Exchange Commission.
http://www.sec.gov/

Audience: **g,l,u,f.**

Berenson, Alex **HV6768**
[e] The Number: How the Drive for Quarterly Earnings Corrupted Wall Street and Corporate America. E-Book. Random House Adult Trade Publishing Group. New York, NY. 2003. ISBN:1-58836-288-4, ISBN13: 978-1-58836-288-9. Dewey:364.16/8.
Audience: **g,l,u,f.** *Choice, 2004.*

Bragg, Steven M. **HF5635.B818 2005**
Accounting Best Practices. Ed. 4. Trade Cloth. John Wiley & Sons, Inc. Hoboken, NJ. 2005. 464p. ISBN:0-471-72794-6, ISBN13: 978-0-471-72794-1. Dewey:657. LCCN:2005-003022.
Audience: **g,l,u,f.** *Choice, 2001, 2000.*

Bragg, Steven M. **HF5616.U5B713 2005**
[e] The Ultimate Accountants' Reference Including GAAP, IRS and SEC Regulations, Leases, and More. Ed. 2. E-Book. John Wiley & Sons, Inc. Hoboken, NJ. 2005. 680p. ISBN:0-471-69497-5, ISBN13: 978-0-471-69497-7. Dewey:657.0973.
Audience: **g,l,u,f.**

Carmichael, Douglas R. & Rosenfield, Paul H. **HF5621.A22 2003**
Accountants' Handbook, Set. Ed. 10. Trade Paper. John Wiley & Sons, Inc. Hoboken, NJ. 2003. 1808p. ISBN:0-471-26993-X, ISBN13: 978-0-471-26993-9. Dewey:657. LCCN:2002-153108.
Audience: **u,f.**

Financial Accounting Standards Board Staff **HF5616.U5**
2005 Current Text, Vol. 12. Trade Paper. John Wiley & Sons, Inc. Hoboken, NJ. 2005. 0p. ISBN:0-471-73789-5, ISBN13: 978-0-471-73789-6. Dewey:657.021873.
Audience: **u,f.**

Financial Accounting Standards Board Staff **HF5618**
2005 Original Pronouncements, Vol. 13. Trade Paper. John Wiley & Sons, Inc. Hoboken, NJ. 2005. 0p. ISBN:0-471-73791-7, ISBN13: 978-0-471-73791-9. Dewey:657.
Audience: **u,f.**

Fraser, Lyn M. & Ormiston, Aileen **HG4028.B2F73 2003**
Understanding the Corporate Annual Report: Nuts, Bolts and a Few Loose Screws. Trade Paper. Prentice Hall PTR. Upper Saddle River, NJ. 2002. 133p. ISBN:0-13-100431-X, ISBN13: 978-0-13-100431-3. Dewey:332.63/2042. LCCN:2002-073952.
Audience: **g,l,u,f.**

Fridson, Martin S. & Alvarez, Fernando **HF5681**
Financial Statement Analysis: A Practitioner's Guide. Ed. 3. Trade Cloth. John Wiley & Sons, Inc. Hoboken, NJ. 2002. 416p. Wiley Finance Ser., Vol. 76 ISBN:0-471-40915-4, ISBN13: 978-0-471-40915-1. Dewey:657/.3. LCCN:2002-284068.
Audience: **g,l,u,f.**

Haber, Jeffry R. **HF5635.H112 2004**
Accounting Demystified. Trade Paper. Amacom. New York, NY. 2003. 192p. ISBN:0-8144-0790-0, ISBN13: 978-0-8144-0790-5. Dewey:657. LCCN:2003-017265.
Audience: **l,u,f.**

Lexis Nexis Staff, et al. **HF5630.W39 2004**
Auditing and Tax Research. Ed. 6. ACL Staff, Thomas C. Pearson, Alan Reinstein & Thomas Weirich (Authors). Paper Text. Thomson South-Western. Mason, OH. 2004. 256p. ISBN:0-324-30228-2, ISBN13: 978-0-324-30228-8. Dewey:657/.072. LCCN:2004-111826.
Audience: **l,u,f.**

McLean, Bethany & Elkind, Peter **HD9502.U54E5763 2003**
Smartest Guys in the Room: The Amazing Rise and Scandalous Fall of Enron. Trade Cloth. Penguin Group (USA) Inc. New York, NY. 2003. 464p. ISBN:1-59184-008-2, ISBN13: 978-1-59184-008-4. Dewey:333.79/0973. LCCN:2003-054944.
Audience: **g,l,u,f.** *Choice, 2004.*

Mulford, Charles W. & Comiskey, Eugene E. **HF5681.B2.M75 2002**
The Financial Numbers Game: Detecting Creative Accounting Practices. Trade Cloth. John Wiley & Sons, Inc. Hoboken, NJ. 2002. 408p. ISBN:0-471-37008-8, ISBN13: 978-0-471-37008-6. Dewey:657.3. LCCN:2001-045648.
Audience: **g,l,u,f.** *Choice, 2002.*

PricewaterhouseCoopers Staff, et al. **HG4028.B2D547 2002**
Building Public Trust: The Future of Corporate Reporting. Samuel A. DiPiazza & Robert G. Eccles (Authors). Trade Cloth. John Wiley & Sons, Inc. Hoboken, NJ. 2002. 208p. ISBN:0-471-26151-3, ISBN13: 978-0-471-26151-3. Dewey:658.1/512. LCCN:2002-510544.
Audience: **g,l,u,f.**

Schilit, Howard M. **HF5681.B2S3243 2002**
Financial Shenanigans: How to Detect Accounting Gimmicks and Fraud in Financial Reports. Ed. 2. Trade Cloth. McGraw-Hill Companies, The. New York, NY. 2002. 240p. ISBN:0-07-138626-2, ISBN13: 978-0-07-138626-5. Dewey:657/.3. LCCN:2002-002879.
Audience: **g,l,u,f.**

Tracy, John A. **HF5681.B2**
How to Read a Financial Report: Wringing Vital Signs Out of the Numbers. Ed. 6. Trade Paper. John Wiley & Sons, Inc. Hoboken, NJ. 2004. 216p. ISBN:0-471-47867-9, ISBN13: 978-0-471-47867-6. Dewey:657/.3. LCCN:2004-274182.
Audience: **g,l,u,f.**

Williams, Jen R. & Carcillo, Joseph V. **HF5616.U5 M5**
Miller Complete GAAP Library 2006, Vol. 2. Judith Weiss (Contribution by). Trade Paper. C C H, Inc. Riverwoods, IL. 2005. 3200p. ISBN:0-8080-9010-0, ISBN13: 978-0-8080-9010-6. Dewey:657.021873.
Audience: **u,f.**

Management Function > Accounting, Taxation, and Law > Accounting > Auditing

HF5626
FASB: Financial Accounting Standards Board.
http://www.fasb.org/
Audience: **g,l,u,f.**

HF5667
PCAOB: The Public Company Accounting Oversight Board.
http://www.pcaobus.org/
Audience: **g,l,u,f.**

KF1444
U.S. Securities and Exchange Commission.
http://www.sec.gov/
Audience: **g,l,u,f.**

Berenson, Alex **HV6768**
The Number: How the Drive for Quarterly Earnings Corrupted Wall Street and Corporate America. E-Book. Random House Adult Trade Publishing Group. New York, NY. 2003. ISBN:1-58836-288-4, ISBN13: 978-1-58836-288-9. Dewey:364.16/8.
Audience: **g,l,u,f.** *Choice, 2004.*

Carmichael, Douglas R. & Rosenfield, Paul H. **HF5621.A22 2003**
Accountants' Handbook, Set. Ed. 10. Trade Paper. John Wiley & Sons, Inc. Hoboken, NJ. 2003. 1808p. ISBN:0-471-26993-X, ISBN13: 978-0-471-26993-9. Dewey:657. LCCN:2002-153108.
Audience: **u,f.**

Financial Accounting Standards Board Staff **HF5616.U5**
2005 Current Text, Vol. 12. Trade Paper. John Wiley & Sons, Inc. Hoboken, NJ. 2005. 0p. ISBN:0-471-73789-5, ISBN13: 978-0-471-73789-6. Dewey:657.021873.
Audience: **u,f.**

Financial Accounting Standards Board Staff **HF5618**
2005 Original Pronouncements, Vol. 13. Trade Paper. John Wiley & Sons, Inc. Hoboken, NJ. 2005. 0p. ISBN:0-471-73791-7, ISBN13: 978-0-471-73791-9. Dewey:657.
Audience: **u,f.**

Fraser, Lyn M. & Ormiston, Aileen **HG4028.B2F73 2003**
Understanding the Corporate Annual Report: Nuts, Bolts and a Few Loose Screws. Trade Paper. Prentice Hall PTR. Upper

Saddle River, NJ. 2002. 133p. ISBN:0-13-100431-X, ISBN13: 978-0-13-100431-3. Dewey:332.63/2042. LCCN:2002-073952.
Audience: **g,l,u,f.**

Fridson, Martin S. & Alvarez, Fernando **HF5681**
Financial Statement Analysis: A Practitioner's Guide. Ed. 3. Trade Cloth. John Wiley & Sons, Inc. Hoboken, NJ. 2002. 416p. Wiley Finance Ser., Vol. 76 ISBN:0-471-40915-4, ISBN13: 978-0-471-40915-1. Dewey:657/.3. LCCN:2002-284068.
Audience: **g,l,u,f.**

Lexis Nexis Staff, et al. **HF5630.W39 2004**
Auditing and Tax Research. Ed. 6. ACL Staff, Thomas C. Pearson, Alan Reinstein & Thomas Weirich (Authors). Paper Text. Thomson South-Western. Mason, OH. 2004. 256p. ISBN:0-324-30228-2, ISBN13: 978-0-324-30228-8. Dewey:657/.072. LCCN:2004-111826.
Audience: **l,u,f.**

McLean, Bethany & Elkind, Peter **HD9502.U54E5763 2003**
Smartest Guys in the Room: The Amazing Rise and Scandalous Fall of Enron. Trade Cloth. Penguin Group (USA) Inc. New York, NY. 2003. 464p. ISBN:1-59184-008-2, ISBN13: 978-1-59184-008-4. Dewey:333.79/0973. LCCN:2003-054944.
Audience: **g,l,u,f.** *Choice, 2004.*

Mulford, Charles W. & Comiskey, Eugene E. **HF5681.B2.M75 2002**
The Financial Numbers Game: Detecting Creative Accounting Practices. Trade Cloth. John Wiley & Sons, Inc. Hoboken, NJ. 2002. 408p. ISBN:0-471-37008-8, ISBN13: 978-0-471-37008-6. Dewey:657.3. LCCN:2001-045648.
Audience: **g,l,u,f.** *Choice, 2002.*

PricewaterhouseCoopers Staff, et al. **HG4028.B2D547 2002**
Building Public Trust: The Future of Corporate Reporting. Samuel A. DiPiazza & Robert G. Eccles (Authors). Trade Cloth. John Wiley & Sons, Inc. Hoboken, NJ. 2002. 208p. ISBN:0-471-26151-3, ISBN13: 978-0-471-26151-3. Dewey:658.1/512. LCCN:2002-510544.
Audience: **g,l,u,f.**

Schilit, Howard M. **HF5681.B2S3243 2002**
Financial Shenanigans: How to Detect Accounting Gimmicks and Fraud in Financial Reports. Ed. 2. Trade Cloth. McGraw-Hill Companies, The. New York, NY. 2002. 240p. ISBN:0-07-138626-2, ISBN13: 978-0-07-138626-5. Dewey:657/.3. LCCN:2002-002879.
Audience: **g,l,u,f.**

Management Function > Accounting, Taxation, and Law > Accounting > International and Comparative Accounting

HF5626
□ IASB: International Accounting Standards Board.
http://www.iasb.org/
Audience: **g,l,u,f.**

Hussey, Roger, et al. **HF5681.B2**
International Financial Reporting Standards Desk Reference: Overview, Guide and Dictionary. Wei-Ming Ong & Audra Ong (Authors). Trade Cloth. John Wiley & Sons, Inc. Hoboken, NJ. 2005. 382p. ISBN:0-471-71450-X, ISBN13: 978-0-471-71450-7. Dewey:657.30218. LCCN:2005-275535.
Audience: **u,f.**

Management Function > Accounting, Taxation, and Law > Accounting > Managerial (Cost) Accounting

Bragg, Steven M. & Roehl-Anderson, Janice M. **HF5657.4.R63 2004**
The Controller's Function: The Work of the Managerial Accountant. Ed. 3. Trade Paper. John Wiley & Sons, Inc. Hoboken, NJ. 2004. 460p. ISBN:0-471-68330-2, ISBN13: 978-0-471-68330-8. Dewey:658.1511. LCCN:2004-304972.
Audience: **u,f.**

Johnson, H. Thomas & Kaplan, Robert S. **HF5605.J64 1991**
Relevance Lost: The Rise and Fall of Management Accounting. Trade Paper. Harvard Business School Press. Boston, MA. 1990. 272p. ISBN:0-87584-254-2, ISBN13: 978-0-87584-254-7. Dewey:658.1/511/09. LCCN:90-025035.
Audience: **u,f.** *Choice, 1987.*

McKinnon, Sharon M. & Bruns, William J. Jr. **HF5657.4.M38 1992**
The Information Mosaic. Trade Cloth. Harvard Business School Press. Boston, MA. 1992. 300p. Harvard Business School Series in Accounting ISBN:0-87584-317-4, ISBN13: 978-0-87584-317-9. Dewey:658.4/038. LCCN:91-046758.
Audience: **g,l,u,f.** *Choice, 1992.*

Management Function > Accounting, Taxation, and Law > Taxation

HJ2361
□ IRS: Internal Revenue Service.
http://www.irs.gov/
Audience: **g,l,u,f.**

HJ2305
□ Tax - Wikipedia, the free encyclopedia.
http://en.wikipedia.org/wiki/Tax
Audience: **g,l,u,f.**

HF5681.T3
□ Tax and Accounting Sites Directory.
http://www.taxsites.com/
Audience: **g,l,u,f.**

HJ4629
□ The Tax Foundation.
http://www.taxfoundation.org/
Audience: **g,l,u,f.**

Bank, Stephen A. **KF6368**
Business Tax Stories 2005. Trade Paper. Foundation Press. New York, NY. 2005. 321p. ISBN:1-58778-729-6, ISBN13: 978-1-58778-729-4. Dewey:343.73052. LCCN:2005-620503.
Audience: **g,l,u,f.**

Brownlee, W. Elliot **HJ2362.B76 2004**
Federal Taxation in America: A Short History. Ed. 2. Lee H. Hamilton (Contribution by). Cloth Text. Cambridge University Press. New York, NY. 2004. 304p. Woodrow Wilson Center Press Ser. ISBN:0-521-83665-4, ISBN13: 978-0-521-83665-4. Dewey:336.2/00973. LCCN:2003-063904.
Audience: **g,l,u,f.** *Choice, 2004, 1996.*

Ebel, Robert D. (Editor), et al. **HJ2305.E53 2005**
The Encyclopedia of Taxation and Tax Policy. Ed. 2. Joseph J. Cordes & Jane G. Gravelle (Editors). Trade Paper. Urban Institute Press. Washington, DC. 2005. xvii, 499p. ISBN:0-87766-752-7, ISBN13: 978-0-87766-752-0. Dewey:336.2/003. LCCN:2005-020901.
Audience: **g,l,u,f.**

Gale, William G. & Orszag, Peter R. **HJ141**
Taxing the Future: Fiscal Policy in the Bush Administration. Book, Other. Brookings Institution Press. Washington, DC. 2005. 135p. ISBN:0-8157-3119-1, ISBN13: 978-0-8157-3119-1. Dewey:336.
Audience: **l,u,f.**

Gardner, Robert L., et al. **KF241.T38G35 2003**
Tax Research Techniques. Ed. 6. Dave N. Stewart & Ronald G. Worsham (Authors), American Institute of Certified Public Accountants Staff (Contribution by). Trade Cloth. American Institute of Certified Public Accountants. Jersey City, NJ. 2003. x, 273p. ISBN:0-87051-471-7, ISBN13: 978-0-87051-471-5. Dewey:343.7304072. LCCN:2004-268990.
Audience: **g,l,u,f.**

Graetz, Michael J. **HJ4652.G697 1997**
The Decline and Fall of the Income Tax: How to Make Sense of the American Tax Mess and the Flat-Tax Cures That Are Supposed to Fix It. Trade Cloth. W. W. Norton & Company, Inc. New York, NY. 1997. 352p. ISBN:0-393-04061-5, ISBN13: 978-0-393-04061-6. Dewey:336.24/0973. LCCN:96-036159.
Audience: **g,l,u,f.**

Graetz, Michael J. & Shapiro, Ian **HJ5805.G73 2005**
Death by a Thousand Cuts: The Fight over Taxing Inherited Wealth. Trade Cloth. Princeton University Press. Princeton, NJ. 2005. 392p. ISBN:0-691-12293-8, ISBN13: 978-0-691-12293-9. Dewey:336.2/76/0973. LCCN:2004-024431.
Audience: **g,l,u,f.**

Hufbauer, Gary Clyde & Grieco, Paul L. E. **HJ4653.C7H837 2005**
Reforming the US Corporate Tax. Trade Paper. Institute for International Economics. Washington, DC. 2005. 144p. Policy Analyses in International Economics Ser., Vol. 76 ISBN:0-88132-384-5, ISBN13: 978-0-88132-384-9. Dewey:382/.9730494. LCCN:2005-027712.
Audience: **g,l,u,f.**

Johnston, David Cay **HJ2362.J64 2003**
Perfectly Legal: The Secret Campaign to Rig Our Tax System to Benefit the Super Rich—and Cheat Everybody Else. Trade Cloth. Penguin Group (USA) Inc. New York, NY. 2003. 352p. ISBN:1-59184-019-8, ISBN13: 978-1-59184-019-0. Dewey:336.2/00973. LCCN:2003-061660.
Audience: **g,l,u,f.**

Lamb, Margaret (Editor), et al. **HJ2305.T187 2005**
Taxation: An Interdisciplinary Approach to Research. Andrew Lymer, Judith Freedman & Simon James (Editors). Trade Cloth. Oxford University Press, Inc. New York, NY. 2004. 328p. ISBN:0-19-924293-3, ISBN13: 978-0-19-924293-1. Dewey:336.2. LCCN:2005-271081.
Audience: **u,f.**

Lexis Nexis Staff, et al. **HF5630.W39 2004**
Auditing and Tax Research. Ed. 6. ACL Staff, Thomas C. Pearson, Alan Reinstein & Thomas Weirich (Authors). Paper Text. Thomson South-Western. Mason, OH. 2004. 256p. ISBN:0-324-30228-2, ISBN13: 978-0-324-30228-8. Dewey:657/.072. LCCN:2004-111826.
Audience: **l,u,f.**

Murray, Alan S. **KF6289.B57 1988**
Showdown at Gucci Gulch: Lawmakers, Lobbyists, and the Unlikely Triumph of Tax Reform. Peter Osnos (Editor), Jeffrey H. Birnbaum (Introduction by). Trade Paper. Alfred A. Knopf Inc. New York, NY. 1988. 336p. ISBN:0-394-75811-0, ISBN13: 978-0-394-75811-4. Dewey:343.7304. LCCN:87-045971.
Audience: **g,l,u,f.**

PricewaterhouseCoopers LLP Staff **HJ2240**
Corporate Taxes 2005—2006: Worldwide Summaries. Trade Paper. John Wiley & Sons, Inc. Hoboken, NJ. 2006. 1000p. ISBN:0-471-74069-1, ISBN13: 978-0-471-74069-8. Dewey:336.2.
Audience: **g,u,f.**

PricewaterhouseCoopers LLP Staff **HJ2240**
Individual Taxes 2005—2006: Worldwide Summaries. Trade Paper. John Wiley & Sons, Inc. Hoboken, NJ. 2006. 1000p. ISBN:0-471-74070-5, ISBN13: 978-0-471-74070-4. Dewey:336.2.
Audience: **g,u,f.**

Raabe, William A., et al. **KF241.T38W47**
Federal Tax Research. Ed. 7. Gerald E. Whittenburg & Debra L. Sanders (Authors). Cloth Text. Thomson South-Western. Mason, OH. 2005. 572p. ISBN:0-324-30613-X, ISBN13: 978-0-324-30613-2. Dewey:343.7304/072.
Audience: **u,f.**

Rossotti, Charles O. **HJ2361.R667 2005**
Many Unhappy Returns: One Man's Quest to Turn Around the Most Unpopular Organization in America. Trade Cloth. Harvard Business School Press. Boston, MA. 2005. 352p. Leadership for the Common Good Ser. ISBN:1-59139-441-4, ISBN13: 978-1-59139-441-9. Dewey:352.4/4. LCCN:2004-023103.
Audience: **g,l,u,f.** *Choice, 2005.*

Salanié, Bernard **HJ2307.S26 2002**
The Economics of Taxation. Trade Cloth. MIT Press. Cambridge, MA. 2003. 236p. ISBN:0-262-19486-4, ISBN13: 978-0-262-19486-0. Dewey:336.2. LCCN:2002-035596.
Audience: **u,f.**

Slemrod, Joel **HJ2322.A3D64 2000**
Does Atlas Shrug?: The Economic Consequences of Taxing the Rich. Trade Cloth. Harvard University Press. Cambridge, MA. 2000. 532p. ISBN:0-674-00154-0, ISBN13: 978-0-674-00154-1. Dewey:336.24. LCCN:99-057238.
Audience: **u,f.**

Slemrod, Joel (Editor) **HJ2305 .T179 1998**
Tax Policy in the Real World. Trade Paper. Cambridge University Press. New York, NY. 1999. 526p. ISBN:0-521-64644-8, ISBN13: 978-0-521-64644-4. Dewey:336.2. LCCN:98-031981.
Audience: **u,f.** *Choice, 1999.*

Slemrod, Joel & Bakija, Jon **HJ4652.S528 2004**
Taxing Ourselves: A Citizen's Guide to the Debate over Taxes. Ed. 3. Trade Cloth. MIT Press. Cambridge, MA. 2004. 360p. ISBN:0-262-19505-4, ISBN13: 978-0-262-19505-8. Dewey:336.2/05. LCCN:2003-070625.
Audience: **g,l,u,f.**

Steuerle, C. Eugene **HJ2381.S737 2004**
Contemporary U. S. Tax Policy. Trade Paper. Urban Institute Press. Washington, DC. 2004. xiii, 322p. ISBN:0-87766-720-9, ISBN13: 978-0-87766-720-9. Dewey:336/.00973. LCCN:2004-006717.
Audience: **g,l,u,f.** *Choice, 2004.*

Steuerle, Eugene C. **HJ2381 .S74 1991**
The Tax Decade, 1981-1990. Trade Paper. Urban Institute Press. Washington, DC. 1992. 266p. ISBN:0-87766-523-0, ISBN13: 978-0-87766-523-6. Dewey:336.2/00973. LCCN:91-031917.
Audience: **g,l,u,f.** *Choice, 1992.*

The Urban Institute and The Brookings Institution **HJ4629**
Tax Policy Center.
http://www.taxpolicycenter.org/
Audience: **g,l,u,f.**

Thorndike, Joseph & Ventry, Dennis (Editors) **HJ2322.A3T313 2002**
Tax Justice: The Ongoing Debate. Trade Paper. Urban Institute Press. Washington, DC. 2002. ix, 296p. ISBN:0-87766-707-1, ISBN13: 978-0-87766-707-0. Dewey:336.2/9/0973. LCCN:2002-009712.
Audience: **g,l,u,f.** *Choice, 2003.*

Weisman, Steven R. **HJ4652.W556 2002**
The Great Tax Wars: Lincoln to Wilson - The Fierce Battles over Money and Power That Transformed the Nation. Trade Cloth. Simon & Schuster. New York, NY. 2002. 432p. ISBN:0-684-85068-0, ISBN13: 978-0-684-85068-9. Dewey:336.24/2/097309034. LCCN:2002-070486.
Audience: **g,l,u,f.** *Choice, 2003.*

Management Function > Accounting, Taxation, and Law > Taxation > Estate Planning

HJ2250
Tax History Project.
http://www.taxhistory.org/
Audience: **g,l,u,f.**

Management Function > Accounting, Taxation, and Law > Taxation > Institutional Taxation

HJ2250
Tax History Project.
http://www.taxhistory.org/
Audience: **g,l,u,f.**

Moore, Michael L. & Outslay, Edmund **KF6445.M66 2000**
U. S. Tax Aspects of Doing Business Abroad. Ed. 5. Paper Text. American Institute of Certified Public Accountants. Jersey City, NJ. 2000. xii, 849p. ISBN:0-87051-291-9, ISBN13: 978-0-87051-291-9. Dewey:343.7305/248. LCCN:99-089702.
Audience: **u,f.**

Management Function > Accounting, Taxation, and Law > Taxation > Personal Taxation

HJ2250
Tax History Project.
http://www.taxhistory.org/
Audience: **g,l,u,f.**

Management Function > Accounting, Taxation, and Law > Taxation > Public Finance

HJ2250
Tax History Project.
http://www.taxhistory.org/
Audience: **g,l,u,f.**

Management Function > Accounting, Taxation, and Law > Law

KF242.A1
FindLaw.
http://www.findlaw.com/
Audience: **g,l,u,f.**

Anderson, Terry H. **HF5549.5.A34A53 2004**
The Pursuit of Fairness: A History of Affirmative Action. Trade Cloth. Oxford University Press, Inc. New York, NY. 2004. 336p. ISBN:0-19-515764-8, ISBN13: 978-0-19-515764-2. Dewey:331.13/3/0973. LCCN:2003-024637.
Audience: **l,u,f.** *Choice, 2005.*

Bagley, Constance E. & Dauchy, Craig E. **KF390.B84B34 2003**
The Entrepreneur's Guide to Business Law. Ed. 2. Paper Text. Thomson South-Western. Mason, OH. 2002. 752p. Business Law Ser. ISBN:0-324-04291-4, ISBN13: 978-0-324-04291-7. Dewey:346.7307. LCCN:2002-067215.
Audience: **u,f.**

Bank, Stephen A. **KF6368**
Business Tax Stories 2005. Trade Paper. Foundation Press. New York, NY. 2005. 321p. ISBN:1-58778-729-6, ISBN13: 978-1-58778-729-4. Dewey:343.73052. LCCN:2005-620503.
Audience: **g,l,u,f.**

Block, Richard N., et al. **HD8072.5.B57 2002**
Labor Standards in the United States and Canada. Karen Roberts & Ronald O. Clarke (Authors). Trade Paper. W. E. Upjohn Institute for Employment Research. Kalamazoo, MI. 2003. 185p. ISBN:0-88099-235-2, ISBN13: 978-0-88099-235-0. Dewey:331.12/042/0973. LCCN:2002-013604.
Audience: **g,l,u,f.** *Choice, 2003.*

Elias, Stephen & Levinkind, Susan **KF240.E35**
Legal Research: How to Find and Understand the Law. Ed. 13. Richard Stim (Editor). Trade Paper, Perfect. NOLO. Berkeley, CA. 2005. 368p. ISBN:1-4133-0395-1, ISBN13: 978-1-4133-0395-7. Dewey:340.072073.
Audience: **g,l,u,f.**

Elias, Stephen & Stim, Richard **KF2980.E44 2004**
Patent, Copyright and Trademark: An Intellectual Property Desk Reference. Ed. 7. Trade Paper. NOLO. Berkeley, CA. 2004. 570p. ISBN:1-4133-0055-3, ISBN13: 978-1-4133-0055-0. Dewey:346.7304/8. LCCN:2003-070158.
Audience: **g,l,u,f.**

Emerson, Robert W. **KF889.6.H37 2004**
Business Law. Ed. 4. Trade Paper. Barron's Educational Series, Inc. Hauppauge, NY. 2003. 680p. Barron's Business Review Ser. ISBN:0-7641-1984-2, ISBN13: 978-0-7641-1984-2. Dewey:346.7307. LCCN:2003-052487.
Audience: **g,l,u,f.**

Friedman, Lawrence Meir **KF385.A4F7 2002**
American Law in the 20th Century. Cloth over Boards. Yale University Press. Cumberland, RI. 2002. 736p. ISBN:0-300-09137-0, ISBN13: 978-0-300-09137-3. Dewey:349.73. LCCN:2001-003332.
Audience: **g,l,u,f.** *Choice, 2002.*

Goldstein, Paul **KF2994.G654 2003**
Copyright's Highway: From Gutenberg to the Celestial Jukebox. Trade Paper. Stanford University Press. Palo Alto, CA. 2003. x, 238p. ISBN:0-8047-4748-2, ISBN13: 978-0-8047-4748-6. Dewey:346.7304/82. LCCN:2003-007385.
Audience: **g,l,u,f.** *Choice, 2004.*

Gould, William B. IV **KF3369.G68 2004**
A Primer on American Labor Law. Ed. 4. Cloth Text. MIT Press. Cambridge, MA. 2004. 432p. ISBN:0-262-07250-5, ISBN13: 978-0-262-07250-2. Dewey:347.3041. LCCN:2003-070610.
Audience: **g,l,u,f.**

Hans, Valerie P. **KF8972.H267 2000**
Business on Trial: The Civil Jury and Corporate Responsibility. Cloth over Boards. Yale University Press. Cumberland, RI. 2000. 288p. ISBN:0-300-08206-1, ISBN13: 978-0-300-08206-7. Dewey:347.73/752. LCCN:99-087513.
Audience: **g,l,u,f.**

Hogler, Raymond L. **KF3369.H643 2004**
Employment Relations in the United States: Law, Policy, and Practice. Cloth Text. SAGE Publications, Inc. Thousand Oaks, CA. 2003. 312p. ISBN:1-4129-0414-5, ISBN13: 978-1-4129-0414-8. Dewey:344.7301. LCCN:2003-021149.
Audience: **g,l,u,f.** *Choice, 2004.*

Kohn, Stephen M., et al. **KF3471**
Whistleblower Law: A Guide to Legal Protections for Corporate Employees. Michael D. Kohn & David K. Colapinto (Authors). Trade Cloth. Greenwood Publishing Group, Inc. Portsmouth, NH. 2004. 304p. ISBN:0-275-98127-4, ISBN13: 978-0-275-98127-3. Dewey:344.7301/2596. LCCN:2004-052154.
Audience: **g,l,u,f.**

Kwoka, John E. & White, Lawrence J. (Editors) **HD2795.A64 2003**
The Antitrust Revolution: Economics, Competition, and Policy. Ed. 4. Cloth Text. Oxford University Press, Inc. New York, NY. 2003. 544p. ISBN:0-19-516117-3, ISBN13: 978-0-19-516117-5. Dewey:338.8/5. LCCN:2002-042551.
Audience: **g,l,u,f.**

Lander, Guy **KF1446.L36 2004**
What Is Sarbanes-Oxley? Trade Paper. McGraw-Hill Trade. New York, NY. 2003. 114p. ISBN:0-07-143796-7, ISBN13: 978-0-07-143796-7. Dewey:346.73/0666. LCCN:2004-558553.
Audience: **g,l,u,f.**

Lorsch, Jay W. (Editor), et al. **HD2741**
Restoring Trust in American Business. Leslie Berlowitz & Andy Zelleke (Editors). Trade Paper. MIT Press. Cambridge, MA. 2005. 192p. ISBN:0-262-74027-3, ISBN13: 978-0-262-74027-2. Dewey:658.4/08.
Audience: **g,l,u,f.** *Choice, 2005.*

Malaspina, Margaret A. **HD7105.45.U6M32 2003**
Cracking Your Retirement Nest Egg (Without Scrambling Your Finances): 25 Things You Must Know Before You Tap Your 401(K), IRA, or Other Retirement Savings Plan. Saddle Stitched, Cloth over Boards. Bloomberg Press. New York, NY. 2003. 256p. Bloomberg Personal Bookshelf ISBN:1-57660-126-9, ISBN13: 978-1-57660-126-6. Dewey:332.024/01. LCCN:2002-013470.
Audience: **g,l,u,f.**

Markham, Jerry W. **HV6769.M37 2005**
A Financial History of Modern U S Corporate Scandals. Cloth Text. M. E. Sharpe Inc. Armonk, NY. 2005. 768p. ISBN:0-7656-1583-5, ISBN13: 978-0-7656-1583-1. Dewey:364.16/8/0973. LCCN:2005-005562.
Audience: **g,l,u,f.** *Choice, 2006.*

McLean, Bethany & Elkind, Peter **HD9502.U54E5763 2003**
Smartest Guys in the Room: The Amazing Rise and Scandalous Fall of Enron. Trade Cloth. Penguin Group (USA) Inc. New York, NY. 2003. 464p. ISBN:1-59184-008-2, ISBN13: 978-1-59184-008-4. Dewey:333.79/0973. LCCN:2003-054944.
Audience: **g,l,u,f.** *Choice, 2004.*

Nakamura, Robert T. & Church, Thomas W. **HD3616.U46N27 2003**
Taming Regulation: Superfund and the Challenge of Regulatory Reform. Trade Cloth. Brookings Institution Press. Washington, DC. 2003. 192p. ISBN:0-8157-5942-8, ISBN13: 978-0-8157-5942-3. Dewey:363.738/4. LCCN:2003-018458.
Audience: **g,l,u,f.**

National Research Council Staff **KF2979.D54 2000**
The Digital Dilemma: The Future of Intellectual Property in the Information Infrastructure. Trade Paper. National Academies Press. Washington, DC. 2000. xxi, 340p. ISBN:0-309-06499-6, ISBN13: 978-0-309-06499-6. Dewey:346.7304/8. LCCN:99-069855.
Audience: **g,l,u,f.** *Choice, 2000.*

Neipert, David **K1005.N45 2002**
Law for Global Commerce: A Tour. Trade Paper. Prentice Hall PTR. Upper Saddle River, NJ. 2001. 159p. ISBN:0-13-040873-5, ISBN13: 978-0-13-040873-0. Dewey:346.07. LCCN:2001-036178.
Audience: **g,l,u,f.**

Sayles, Leonard R. & Smith, Cynthia J. **HV6768**
The Rise of the Rogue Executive: How Good Companies Go Bad and How to Stop the Destruction. Trade Cloth. Prentice Hall PTR. Upper Saddle River, NJ. 2005. 288p. ISBN:0-13-147772-2, ISBN13: 978-0-13-147772-8. Dewey:174/.4. LCCN:2005-924352.
Audience: **g,l,u,f.** *Choice, 2006.*

Shace, Joseph & Epstein, David G. **KF1355.S52 2002**
Shace and Epstein's Business Structures in a Nutshell. Trade Paper. West Publishing Company, College & School Division. Eagan, MN. 2003. xxvi, 392p. Nutshell Ser. ISBN:0-314-14356-4, ISBN13: 978-0-314-14356-3. Dewey:346.73/065. LCCN:2003-283150.
Audience: **g,l,u,f.**

Shapiro, Sidney A. & Glicksman, Robert L. **KF3775.S53 2003**
Risk Regulation at Risk: Restoring a Pragmatic Approach. Trade Cloth. Stanford University Press. Palo Alto, CA. 2002. 288p. ISBN:0-8047-4593-5, ISBN13: 978-0-8047-4593-2. Dewey:344.73/046. LCCN:2002-009778.
Audience: **g,l,u,f.**

Shenefield, John H. & Stelzer, Irwin M. **KF1650.S53 2001**
The Antitrust Laws: A Primer. Ed. 4. Trade Cloth. National Book Network. Lanham, MD. 2001. 202p. ISBN:0-8447-4154-X, ISBN13: 978-0-8447-4154-3. Dewey:343.73/0721. LCCN:2001-045088.
Audience: **g,l,u,f.** *Choice, 1994.*

Shippey, Karla C. **K1401.S528 2001**
A Short Course in International Intellectual Property Rights: Protecting Your Brands, Marks, Copyrights, Patents, Designs, and Related Rights Worldwide. Trade Cloth. World Trade Press. Petaluma, CA. 2001. The Short Course in International Trade Ser. ISBN:1-885073-56-9, ISBN13: 978-1-885073-56-3. Dewey:341.7/58. LCCN:2001-026778.
Audience: **g,l,u,f.**

Siedel, George J. **KF390.B84S56 2002**
Using the Law for Competitive Advantage. Trade Cloth. John Wiley & Sons, Inc. Hoboken, NJ. 2002. 224p. J-B-UMBS Ser., Vol. 6 ISBN:0-7879-5623-6, ISBN13: 978-0-7879-5623-3. Dewey:346.7307. LCCN:2001-008352.
Audience: **g,l,u,f.**

Skeel, David A. **KF1526.S59 2001**
Debt's Dominion: A History of Bankruptcy Law in America. Trade Cloth. Princeton University Press. Princeton, NJ. 2001. 296p. ISBN:0-691-08810-1, ISBN13: 978-0-691-08810-5. Dewey:346.7307/8/09. LCCN:2001-021464.
Audience: **g,l,u,f.**

Stewart, James B. **HG4910.S683 1991**
Den of Thieves: The Untold Story of the Men Who Plundered Wall Street and the Chase That Brought Them Down. Trade Cloth. Simon & Schuster. New York, NY. 1991. 496p. ISBN:0-671-63802-5, ISBN13: 978-0-671-63802-3. Dewey:364.1/68. LCCN:91-028819.
Audience: **g,l,u,f.**

Sunstein, Cass R. **HD61.S86 2002**
Risk and Reason: Safety, Law, and the Environment. Cloth Text. Cambridge University Press. New York, NY. 2002. 352p. ISBN:0-521-79199-5, ISBN13: 978-0-521-79199-1. Dewey:368. LCCN:2002-020166.
Audience: **g,l,u,f.** *Choice, 2003.*

The World Bank (Created by) **HC79.C7**
Doing Business In 2006: Creating Jobs. Ed. 2006. Trade Paper, Perfect. World Bank Publications. Washington, DC. 2005. 228p. Doing Business Ser. ISBN:0-8213-5749-2, ISBN13: 978-0-8213-5749-1. Dewey:341.754.
Audience: **g,l,u,f.**

Viscusi, W. Kip (Editor) **KF8896.5.R44 2002**
Regulation Through Litigation. Trade Cloth. Brookings Institution Press. Washington, DC. 2002. 352p. ISBN:0-8157-0610-3, ISBN13: 978-0-8157-0610-6. Dewey:347.73/53. LCCN:2002-005335.
Audience: **g,l,u,f.** *Choice, 2003.*

Management Function > Accounting, Taxation, and Law > Law > Intellectual Property

Elias, Stephen & Stim, Richard **KF2980.E44 2004**
Patent, Copyright and Trademark: An Intellectual Property Desk Reference. Ed. 7. Trade Paper. NOLO. Berkeley, CA. 2004. 570p. ISBN:1-4133-0055-3, ISBN13: 978-1-4133-0055-0. Dewey:346.7304/8. LCCN:2003-070158.
Audience: **g,l,u,f.**

Goldstein, Paul **KF2994.G654 2003**
Copyright's Highway: From Gutenberg to the Celestial Jukebox. Trade Paper. Stanford University Press. Palo Alto, CA. 2003. x, 238p. ISBN:0-8047-4748-2, ISBN13: 978-0-8047-4748-6. Dewey:346.7304/82. LCCN:2003-007385.
Audience: **g,l,u,f.** *Choice, 2004.*

National Research Council Staff **KF2979.D54 2000**
The Digital Dilemma: The Future of Intellectual Property in the Information Infrastructure. Trade Paper. National Academies Press. Washington, DC. 2000. xxi, 340p. ISBN:0-309-06499-6, ISBN13: 978-0-309-06499-6. Dewey:346.7304/8. LCCN:99-069855.
Audience: **g,l,u,f.** *Choice, 2000.*

Management Function > Accounting, Taxation, and Law > Law > Regulation

HF5035
☐ EDGAR: SEC Filings & Forms.
http://www.sec.gov/edgar.shtml
Audience: **g,l,u,f.**

HF5626
☐ IASB: International Accounting Standards Board.
http://www.iasb.org/
Audience: **g,l,u,f.**

KF1444
☐ U.S. Securities and Exchange Commission.
http://www.sec.gov/
Audience: **g,l,u,f.**

Berenson, Alex **HV6768**
e The Number: How the Drive for Quarterly Earnings Corrupted Wall Street and Corporate America. E-Book. Random House Adult Trade Publishing Group. New York, NY. 2003. ISBN:1-58836-288-4, ISBN13: 978-1-58836-288-9. Dewey:364.16/8.
Audience: **g,l,u,f.** *Choice, 2004.*

Block, Richard N., et al. **HD8072.5.B57 2002**
Labor Standards in the United States and Canada. Karen Roberts & Ronald O. Clarke (Authors). Trade Paper. W. E. Upjohn Institute for Employment Research. Kalamazoo, MI. 2003. 185p. ISBN:0-88099-235-2, ISBN13: 978-0-88099-235-0. Dewey:331.12/042/0973. LCCN:2002-013604.
Audience: **g,l,u,f.** *Choice, 2003.*

Calomiris, Charles W. **HG2491 .C348 2000**
U. S. Bank Deregulation in Historical Perspective. Trade Cloth. Cambridge University Press. New York, NY. 2000. 392p. ISBN:0-521-58362-4, ISBN13: 978-0-521-58362-6. Dewey:332.1/0973. LCCN:99-040041.
Audience: **g,l,u,f.** *Choice, 2000.*

Goldstein, Fred **HE7631**
The Great Telecom Meltdown. Trade Cloth. Artech House, Inc. Norwood, MA. 2005. 209p. Artech House Telecommunications Library ISBN:1-58053-939-4, ISBN13: 978-1-58053-939-5. Dewey:384.3. LCCN:2005-041036.
Audience: **g,l,u,f.**

Gould, William B. IV **KF3369.G68 2004**
A Primer on American Labor Law. Ed. 4. Cloth Text. MIT Press. Cambridge, MA. 2004. 432p. ISBN:0-262-07250-5, ISBN13: 978-0-262-07250-2. Dewey:347.3041. LCCN:2003-070610.
Audience: **g,l,u,f.**

Handley, John **HE7775.H33 2005**
Telebomb: The Truth Behind the $500-Billion Telecom Bust and What the Industry Must Do to Recover. Trade Cloth. Amacom. New York, NY. 2005. 256p. ISBN:0-8144-0833-8, ISBN13: 978-0-8144-0833-9. Dewey:384/.0973. LCCN:2005-005682.
Audience: **g,l,u,f.**

Lander, Guy **KF1446.L36 2004**
What Is Sarbanes-Oxley? Trade Paper. McGraw-Hill Trade. New York, NY. 2003. 114p. ISBN:0-07-143796-7, ISBN13: 978-0-07-143796-7. Dewey:346.73/0666. LCCN:2004-558553.
Audience: **g,l,u,f.**

MacAvoy, Paul W. & Millstein, Ira M. **HD2741.M196 2003**
The Recurrent Crisis in Corporate Governance. Cloth over Boards. Palgrave Macmillan. New York, NY. 2004. 160p. ISBN:1-4039-1666-7, ISBN13: 978-1-4039-1666-2. Dewey:658.4. LCCN:2003-048290.
Audience: **g,l,u,f.** *Choice, 2004.*

Mulford, Charles W. & Comiskey, Eugene E. **HF5681.B2.M75 2002**
The Financial Numbers Game: Detecting Creative Accounting Practices. Trade Cloth. John Wiley & Sons, Inc. Hoboken, NJ. 2002. 408p. ISBN:0-471-37008-8, ISBN13: 978-0-471-37008-6. Dewey:657.3. LCCN:2001-045648.
Audience: **g,l,u,f.** *Choice, 2002.*

Nakamura, Robert T. & Church, Thomas W. **HD3616.U46N27 2003**
Taming Regulation: Superfund and the Challenge of Regulatory Reform. Trade Cloth. Brookings Institution Press. Washington, DC. 2003. 192p. ISBN:0-8157-5942-8, ISBN13: 978-0-8157-5942-3. Dewey:363.738/4. LCCN:2003-018458.
Audience: **g,l,u,f.**

Nuechterlein, Jonathan E. & Weiser, Philip J. **HE7781.N84 2005**
Digital Crossroads: American Telecommunications Policy in the Internet Age. Trade Cloth. MIT Press. Cambridge, MA. 2005. 672p. ISBN:0-262-14091-8, ISBN13: 978-0-262-14091-1. Dewey:384/.0973. LCCN:2004-061063.
Audience: **g,l,u,f.** *Choice, 2005.*

PricewaterhouseCoopers Staff, et al. **HG4028.B2D547 2002**
Building Public Trust: The Future of Corporate Reporting. Samuel A. DiPiazza & Robert G. Eccles (Authors). Trade Cloth. John Wiley & Sons, Inc. Hoboken, NJ. 2002. 208p. ISBN:0-471-26151-3, ISBN13: 978-0-471-26151-3. Dewey:658.1/512. LCCN:2002-510544.
Audience: **g,l,u,f.**

Schilit, Howard M. **HF5681.B2S3243 2002**
Financial Shenanigans: How to Detect Accounting Gimmicks and Fraud in Financial Reports. Ed. 2. Trade Cloth. McGraw-Hill Companies, The. New York, NY. 2002. 240p. ISBN:0-07-138626-2, ISBN13: 978-0-07-138626-5. Dewey:657/.3. LCCN:2002-002879.
Audience: **g,l,u,f.**

Shapiro, Sidney A. & Glicksman, Robert L. **KF3775.S53 2003**
Risk Regulation at Risk: Restoring a Pragmatic Approach. Trade Cloth. Stanford University Press. Palo Alto, CA. 2002. 288p. ISBN:0-8047-4593-5, ISBN13: 978-0-8047-4593-2. Dewey:344.73/046. LCCN:2002-009778.
Audience: **g,l,u,f.**

Shenefield, John H. & Stelzer, Irwin M. **KF1650.S53 2001**
The Antitrust Laws: A Primer. Ed. 4. Trade Cloth. National Book Network. Lanham, MD. 2001. 202p. ISBN:0-8447-4154-X, ISBN13: 978-0-8447-4154-3. Dewey:343.73/0721. LCCN:2001-045088.
Audience: **g,l,u,f.** *Choice, 1994.*

Sunstein, Cass R. **HD61.S86 2002**
Risk and Reason: Safety, Law, and the Environment. Cloth Text. Cambridge University Press. New York, NY. 2002. 352p.

ISBN:0-521-79199-5, ISBN13: 978-0-521-79199-1. Dewey:368. LCCN:2002-020166.
Audience: **g,l,u,f.** *Choice, 2003.*

The World Bank (Created by) **HC79.C7**
Doing Business In 2006: Creating Jobs. Ed. 2006. Trade Paper, Perfect. World Bank Publications. Washington, DC. 2005. 228p. Doing Business Ser. ISBN:0-8213-5749-2, ISBN13: 978-0-8213-5749-1. Dewey:341.754.
Audience: **g,l,u,f.**

Viscusi, W. Kip (Editor) **KF8896.5.R44 2002**
Regulation Through Litigation. Trade Cloth. Brookings Institution Press. Washington, DC. 2002. 352p. ISBN:0-8157-0610-3, ISBN13: 978-0-8157-0610-6. Dewey:347.73/53. LCCN:2002-005335.
Audience: **g,l,u,f.** *Choice, 2003.*

Vogel, David **JK467.V643 1996**
Kindred Strangers: The Uneasy Relationship Between Politics and Business in America. Trade Cloth. Princeton University Press. Princeton, NJ. 1996. 426p. Princeton Studies in American Politics ISBN:0-691-02746-3, ISBN13: 978-0-691-02746-3. Dewey:324/.4/0973. LCCN:95-042251.
Audience: **g,l,u,f.**

Management Function > Accounting, Taxation, and Law > Law > Legislation

Block, Richard N., et al. **HD8072.5.B57 2002**
Labor Standards in the United States and Canada. Karen Roberts & Ronald O. Clarke (Authors). Trade Paper. W. E. Upjohn Institute for Employment Research. Kalamazoo, MI. 2003. 185p. ISBN:0-88099-235-2, ISBN13: 978-0-88099-235-0. Dewey:331.12/042/0973. LCCN:2002-013604.
Audience: **g,l,u,f.** *Choice, 2003.*

Gould, William B. IV **KF3369.G68 2004**
A Primer on American Labor Law. Ed. 4. Cloth Text. MIT Press. Cambridge, MA. 2004. 432p. ISBN:0-262-07250-5, ISBN13: 978-0-262-07250-2. Dewey:347.3041. LCCN:2003-070610.
Audience: **g,l,u,f.**

Lander, Guy **KF1446.L36 2004**
What Is Sarbanes-Oxley? Trade Paper. McGraw-Hill Trade. New York, NY. 2003. 114p. ISBN:0-07-143796-7, ISBN13: 978-0-07-143796-7. Dewey:346.73/0666. LCCN:2004-558553.
Audience: **g,l,u,f.**

Shenefield, John H. & Stelzer, Irwin M. **KF1650.S53 2001**
The Antitrust Laws: A Primer. Ed. 4. Trade Cloth. National Book Network. Lanham, MD. 2001. 202p. ISBN:0-8447-4154-X, ISBN13: 978-0-8447-4154-3. Dewey:343.73/0721. LCCN:2001-045088.
Audience: **g,l,u,f.** *Choice, 1994.*

Management Function > Accounting, Taxation, and Law > Law > Litigation

Bank, Stephen A. **KF6368**
Business Tax Stories 2005. Trade Paper. Foundation Press. New York, NY. 2005. 321p. ISBN:1-58778-729-6, ISBN13: 978-1-58778-729-4. Dewey:343.73052. LCCN:2005-620503.
Audience: **g,l,u,f.**

Gould, William B. IV **KF3369.G68 2004**
A Primer on American Labor Law. Ed. 4. Cloth Text. MIT Press. Cambridge, MA. 2004. 432p. ISBN:0-262-07250-5, ISBN13: 978-0-262-07250-2. Dewey:347.3041. LCCN:2003-070610.
Audience: **g,l,u,f.**

Hans, Valerie P. **KF8972.H267 2000**
Business on Trial: The Civil Jury and Corporate Responsibility. Cloth over Boards. Yale University Press. Cumberland, RI. 2000. 288p. ISBN:0-300-08206-1, ISBN13: 978-0-300-08206-7. Dewey:347.73/752. LCCN:99-087513.
Audience: **g,l,u,f.**

Viscusi, W. Kip (Editor) **KF8896.5.R44 2002**
Regulation Through Litigation. Trade Cloth. Brookings Institution Press. Washington, DC. 2002. 352p. ISBN:0-8157-0610-3, ISBN13: 978-0-8157-0610-6. Dewey:347.73/53. LCCN:2002-005335.
Audience: **g,l,u,f.** *Choice, 2003.*

Management Function > Operations

Drucker, Peter F. **HD2328.D78 1992**
The New Society: The Anatomy of Industrial Order. Ed. 2. Trade Paper. Transaction Publishers. Somerset, NJ. 1993. 362p. ISBN:1-56000-624-2, ISBN13: 978-1-56000-624-4. Dewey:306.3/6. LCCN:92-005075.
Audience: **u,f.**

Management Function > Operations > Facilities Management

Alexander, Keith (Editor) **TS155.F197 2003**
Facilities Management. UK-B Format Paperback. Routledge. New York, NY. 2004. 184p. ISBN:0-415-32146-8, ISBN13: 978-0-415-32146-4. Dewey:658.2. LCCN:2004-007290.
Audience: **g,u.**

Atkin, Brian & Brooks, Adrian **HD1394.A86 2005**
Total Facilities Management. Ed. 2. Trade Paper, Perfect. Blackwell Publishing, Inc. Malden, MA. 2005. 256p. ISBN:1-4051-2790-2, ISBN13: 978-1-4051-2790-5. Dewey:658.2. LCCN:2004-026966.
Audience: **g,u,f.**

Barrett, P. S. & Baldry, David **HD1394.B37 2003**
Facilities Management. Ed. 2. Trade Paper. Blackwell Publishing, Inc. Malden, MA. 2003. 288p. ISBN:0-632-06445-5,

ISBN13: 978-0-632-06445-8. Dewey:658.2. LCCN:2002-028192.
Audience: **g,l,u.**

Best, Rick (Editor), et al. **TS184**
Workplace Strategies and Facilities Management: Building in Value. Gerard de Valence & Craig Langston (Editors). Paper Text. Elsevier Science & Technology Books. Saint Louis, MO. 2003. 410p. ISBN:0-7506-5150-4, ISBN13: 978-0-7506-5150-9. Dewey:658.2.
Audience: **g,f.**

Booty, Frank (Editor) **TS177**
Facilities Management Handbook. Ed. 2. Trade Paper. Elsevier Science & Technology Books. Saint Louis, MO. 2003. 416p. ISBN:0-7545-2374-8, ISBN13: 978-0-7545-2374-1. Dewey:658.2/00941.
Audience: **g,u,f.**

Langston, Craig & Lauge-Kristensen, Rima **TS177.L36 2002**
Strategic Management of Built Facilities. Paper Text. Elsevier Science & Technology Books. Saint Louis, MO. 2002. 256p. ISBN:0-7506-5440-6, ISBN13: 978-0-7506-5440-1. Dewey:658.2.
Audience: **g,f.**

Reuvid, Jonathan & Hinks, John **HD2365.M36 2002**
[e] Managing Business Support Services: Strategies for Outsourcing and Facilities Management. Ed. 2. E-Book. NetLibrary, Inc. Boulder, CO. 2002. ISBN:0-585-45648-8, ISBN13: 978-0-585-45648-5. Dewey:658.
Audience: **g,f.**

Then, Danny & McGregor, Wes **HF5547.2 .M38**
Facilities Management and the Business of Space. Cloth Text. Elsevier Science & Technology Books. Saint Louis, MO. 1999. 272p. ISBN:0-340-71964-8, ISBN13: 978-0-340-71964-0. Dewey:658.2. LCCN:99-051848.
Audience: **g,u.**

Management Function > Operations > Communications and Information Management > Electronic Commerce (b to b and b to c)

Bussler, Christoph **HF5548.32**
B2B-Integration: Concepts and Architecture. Trade Cloth. Springer. New York, NY. 2003. XXII, 418p. ISBN:3-540-43487-9, ISBN13: 978-3-540-43487-0. Dewey:004.6/2. LCCN:2003-050556.
Audience: **l,u,f.**

Chen, Stephen **HF5548.32**
Strategic Management of E-Business. Ed. 2. Trade Paper. John Wiley & Sons, Inc. Hoboken, NJ. 2004. 384p. ISBN:0-470-87073-7, ISBN13: 978-0-470-87073-0. Dewey:658.8/4. LCCN:2004-007924.
Audience: **l,u,f.**

Epstein, Marc J. **HF5548**
Implementing E-Commerce Strategies: A Guide to Corporate Success after the Dot. Com Bust. Trade Cloth. Greenwood Publishing Group, Inc. Portsmouth, NH. 2004. 224p. ISBN:0-275-98463-X, ISBN13: 978-0-275-98463-2. Dewey:658.8/72. LCCN:2004-049568.
Audience: **l,u,f.** *Choice, 2005.*

Malonis, Jane A. (Editor) **HF5548.32.G35 2002**
Gale Encyclopedia of E-Commerce. Trade Cloth. Thomson Gale. Farmington Hills, MI. 2002. 863p. ISBN:0-7876-5660-7, ISBN13: 978-0-7876-5660-7. Dewey:381/.1. LCCN:2001-055543.
Audience: **g,l,u,f.**

Plunkett, Jack W. **HF5548.32**
Plunkett's E-Commerce and Internet Industry Almanac 2005: Your Reference Source to All Facets of the Internet Business. Trade Paper, CD-ROM. Plunkett Research, Ltd. Houston, TX. 2005. 574p. ISBN:1-59392-022-9, ISBN13: 978-1-59392-022-7. Dewey:658.84.
Audience: **g,l,u,f.**

Shaw, Michael J. (Editor) **HF5548.32**
E-Commerce and the Digital Economy. Trade Cloth. M. E. Sharpe Inc. Armonk, NY. 2005. 304p. Advances in Management Information Systems Ser. ISBN:0-7656-1150-3, ISBN13: 978-0-7656-1150-5. Dewey:658.84.
Audience: **l,u,f.**

Watt, Dougal **HF5548.32**
E-Business Implementation: A Guide to Web Services, EAI, BPI, E-Commerce, Content Management, Portals, and Supporting Technologies. Trade Cloth. Elsevier Science & Technology Books. Saint Louis, MO. 2003. 352p. COMPUTER WEEKLY PROFESSIONAL ISBN:0-7506-5751-0, ISBN13: 978-0-7506-5751-8. Dewey:608/.054678.
Audience: **g,u,f.**

Management Function > Operations > Communications and Information Management > Electronic Security

Conklin, Wm. Arthur, et al. **QA76.9.A25**
Principles of Computer Security: Security and Beyond. Gregory White, Chuck Cothren, Dwayne Williams & Roger L. Davis (Authors). Mixed Media, Trade Paper, CD-ROM. McGraw-Hill Professional Publishing. New York, NY. 2004. 800p. ISBN:0-07-225509-9, ISBN13: 978-0-07-225509-6. Dewey:5.8.
Audience: **l,u,f.**

Easttom II, William & Easttom, Chuck **QA76.9.A25E325 2006**
Computer Security Fundamentals. Trade Paper. Prentice Hall PTR. Upper Saddle River, NJ. 2005. 368p. ISBN:0-13-171129-6, ISBN13: 978-0-13-171129-7. Dewey:5.8. LCCN:2005-299884.
Audience: **l,u,f.**

Kovacich, Gerald **TK5105.59**
The Information Systems Security Officer's Guide: Establishing and Managing an Information Protection Program. Ed. 2. Paper Text. Elsevier Science & Technology Books. Saint Louis, MO. 2003. 361p. ISBN:0-7506-7656-6, ISBN13: 978-0-7506-7656-4. Dewey:005.8. LCCN:2003-276409.
Audience: **g,u,f.**

Krause, Micki **QA76.9.A25**
Information Security Management Handbook, Vol. 3. Ed. 5. Saddle Stitched. Taylor & Francis Group. Abingdon, 2006. 712p. ISBN:0-8493-9561-5, ISBN13: 978-0-8493-9561-1. Dewey:658/.0558.
Audience: **l,u,f.**

Maiwald, Eric **TK5105.59.M362 2004**
Fundamentals of Network Security. Paper Text. McGraw-Hill Osborne. Emeryville, CA. 2003. 672p. Networking Ser. ISBN:0-07-223093-2, ISBN13: 978-0-07-223093-2. Dewey:005.8. LCCN:2004-272654.
Audience: **u,f.**

Tipton, Harold F. & Krause, Micki (Editors) **QA76.9.A25I54165**
Information Security Management Handbook. Ed. 5. Paper over Boards. Taylor & Francis Group. Abingdon, 2003. 2088p. ISBN:0-8493-1997-8, ISBN13: 978-0-8493-1997-6. Dewey:658/.0558. LCCN:2003-061151.
Audience: **l,u,f.**

Tipton, Harold F. & Krause, Micki **QA76.9.A25H36 2004**
Information Security Management Handbook, Vol. 2. Ed. 5. Paper over Boards. Taylor & Francis Group. Abingdon, 2004. 680p. ISBN:0-8493-3210-9, ISBN13: 978-0-8493-3210-4. Dewey:658/.0558. LCCN:2003-061151.
Audience: **l,u,f.**

Management Function > Operations > Communications and Information Management > Hardware

Berger, Arnold S. **QA76.9.C643B47 2005**
Hardware and Computer Organization. Cloth Text. Elsevier Science & Technology Books. Saint Louis, MO. 2005. 512p. Embedded Technology Ser. ISBN:0-7506-7886-0, ISBN13: 978-0-7506-7886-5. Dewey:004.2/2. LCCN:2005-040553.
Audience: **g,u,f.**

Campbell-Kelly, Martin & Aspray, William **QA76.17.C36 2004**
Computer: A History of the Information Machine. Ed. 2. Trade Paper. Westview Press. Boulder, CO. 2004. 360p. The Sloan Technology Ser. ISBN:0-8133-4264-3, ISBN13: 978-0-8133-4264-1. Dewey:004/.09. LCCN:2004-006325.
Audience: **g,l,u,f.** *Choice, 2005.*

Richard III, Golden, et al. **QA76.59**
Fundamentals of Mobile and Pervasive Computing. Frank Adelstein, Sandeep K. S. Gupta & Loren Schwiebert (Authors). Trade Cloth. McGraw-Hill Professional Publishing. New York, NY. 2004. 404p. McGraw-Hill Professional Engineering Ser. ISBN:0-07-141237-9, ISBN13: 978-0-07-141237-7. Dewey:621.3845/6. LCCN:2004-062407.
Audience: **u,f.**

Thompson, Robert Bruce & Thompson, Barbara Fritchman **QA76.5**
PC Hardware in a Nutshell. Ed. 3. Paper Text. O'Reilly Media, Inc. Sebastopol, CA. 2003. 850p. ISBN:0-596-00513-X, ISBN13: 978-0-596-00513-9. Dewey:621.39/16. LCCN:2004-268182.
Audience: **g,l,u,f.**

Management Function > Operations > Communications and Information Management > Management Information Systems

Bernus, P. (Editor), et al. **QA76.9.A73H36 1998**
Handbook on Architectures of Information Systems. K. Mertins, G. Schmidt, M. Shaw & J. Blazewicz (Editors). Trade Cloth. Springer. New York, NY. 1998. IX, 834p. International Handbooks on Information Systems ISBN:3-540-64453-9, ISBN13: 978-3-540-64453-8. Dewey:004.2/2. LCCN:98-026194.
Audience: **u,f.**

Blazewicz, Jacek (Editor), et al. **Z699**
Handbook on Data Management in Information Systems. Wieslaw Kubiak, Tadeusz Morzy & Marek Rusinkiewicz (Editors). Trade Cloth. Springer. New York, NY. 2003. X, 578p. International Handbooks on Information Systems ISBN:3-540-43893-9, ISBN13: 978-3-540-43893-9. Dewey:005.74. LCCN:2003-054771.
Audience: **l,u,f.**

Cadle, James & Yeates, Donald **HD69.P75P72865 2004**
Project Management for Information Systems. Ed. 4. Trade Paper. Financial Times/Prentice Hall. Paramus, NJ. 2004. 448p. ISBN:0-273-68580-5, ISBN13: 978-0-273-68580-7. Dewey:658.4/038/011. LCCN:2004-043345.
Audience: **l,u,f.**

Plunkett, Jack W. **HC79.I55**
Plunkett's Infotech Industry Almanac 2005: The Only Complete Guide to the Technologies and Companies Changing the Way the World Thinks, Works and Shares Information. Trade Paper, CD-ROM. Plunkett Research, Ltd. Houston, TX. 2005. 686p. ISBN:1-59392-024-5, ISBN13: 978-1-59392-024-1. Dewey:338.761.
Audience: **g,l,u,f.**

Ross, Ronald G. **HD30.2.R673 2003**
Principles of the Business Rule Approach. Trade Paper. Addison Wesley Professional. Boston, MA. 2003. 400p. Addison-Wesley Information Technology Ser. ISBN:0-201-78893-4, ISBN13: 978-0-201-78893-8. Dewey:658.4/013. LCCN:2002-151451.
Audience: **u,f.**

Strauss, Steven **T58.64.I5338 2003**
IS Management Handbook. Ed. 8. Carol V. Brown & Heikki Topi (Editors). Paper over Boards. Taylor & Francis Group. Abingdon, 2003. 944p. ISBN:0-8493-1595-6, ISBN13: 978-0-8493-1595-4. Dewey:658.4/038. LCCN:2003-041798.
Audience: **g,l,u,f.**

Ward, John & Peppard, Joe **HF5548.2.W319 2002**
Strategic Planning for Information Systems. Ed. 3. Trade Cloth. John Wiley & Sons, Inc. Hoboken, NJ. 2002. 640p. Series in Information Systems ISBN:0-470-84147-8, ISBN13: 978-0-470-84147-1. Dewey:658.4/038/011. LCCN:2002-284128.
Audience: **u,f.**

Management Function > Operations > Communications and Information Management > Networks and Telecommunications and Internet

Anttalainen, Tarmo **TK5101**
[e] Introduction to Telecommunications Network Engineering. Ed. 2. Trade Cloth, E-Book. Artech House, Inc. Norwood, MA. 2003. 402p. Telecommunications Library ISBN:1-58053-500-3, ISBN13: 978-1-58053-500-7. Dewey:004.6. LCCN:2002-044067.
Audience: **u,f.**

Bates, Regis Bud J. **TK5103.4.B38 2002**
Broadband Telecommunications Handbook. Ed. 2. Trade Paper. McGraw-Hill Professional Publishing. New York, NY. 2002. 805p. Professional Telecom Ser. ISBN:0-07-139851-1, ISBN13: 978-0-07-139851-0. Dewey:384. LCCN:2002-021281.
Audience: **u,f.**

Buchanan, William J. **TK5105.875.I57**
The Complete Handbook of the Internet. Trade Cloth. Springer. New York, NY. 2002. 1645p. ISBN:1-4020-7290-2, ISBN13: 978-1-4020-7290-1. Dewey:004.67/8. LCCN:2002-038937.
Audience: **g,l,u,f.**

Edwards, John **TK5101.E33 2005**
Telecosmos: The Next Great Telecom Revolution. Trade Paper. John Wiley & Sons, Inc. Hoboken, NJ. 2004. 256p. ISBN:0-471-65533-3, ISBN13: 978-0-471-65533-6. Dewey:621.382. LCCN:2004-048081.
Audience: **g,l,u,f.** *Choice, 2005.*

Goldsmith, Jack L. & Wu, Tim **HM851.G65 2006**
Who Controls the Internet?: Illusions of a Borderless World. Trade Cloth. Oxford University Press, Inc. New York, NY. 2006. 272p. ISBN:0-19-515266-2, ISBN13: 978-0-19-515266-1. Dewey:303.48/33. LCCN:2005-027404.
Audience: **l,u.**

Green, James H., et al. **TK5102.5.G73 2001**
The Irwin Handbook of Telecommunications Management. Ed. 3. Joseph T. DiPiro, Terry Schwinghammer, Gary R. Matzke, Michael Posey, Robert L. Talbert, Barbara G. Wells & Gary C. Yee (Authors). Trade Cloth. McGraw-Hill Companies, The. New York, NY. 2001. 875p. ISBN:0-07-137058-7, ISBN13: 978-0-07-137058-5. Dewey:621.382. LCCN:00-050094.
Audience: **u,f.**

Horak, Ray **TK5101**
Communications Systems and Networks. Ed. 3. Trade Paper. John Wiley & Sons, Inc. Hoboken, NJ. 2002. 720p. M&T Bks. ISBN:0-7645-4899-9, ISBN13: 978-0-7645-4899-4. Dewey:621.382. LCCN:2002-108108.
Audience: **l,u,f.**

Kularatna, Nihal & Dias, Dileeka **TK5101.K838 2004**
Essentials of Modern Telecommunications Systems. Trade Cloth. Artech House, Inc. Norwood, MA. 2004. 396p. Artech House Telecommunications Library ISBN:1-58053-491-0, ISBN13: 978-1-58053-491-8. Dewey:621.382. LCCN:2004-047640.
Audience: **g,u,f.** *Choice, 2004.*

Plunkett, Jack W. (Editor) **HD7621**
Plunkett's Telecommunications Industry Almanac 2006: Your Reference Source to the Telecom Business. Trade Paper, CD-ROM. Plunkett Research, Ltd. Houston, TX. 2005. 646p. ISBN:1-59392-032-6, ISBN13: 978-1-59392-032-6. Dewey:384.06.
Audience: **g,l,u,f.**

Wetteroth, Debbra **TK5105.58.W48 2002**
OSI Reference Model for Telecommunications. Paper Text. McGraw-Hill Professional Publishing. New York, NY. 2001. 320p. McGraw-Hill Telecom Professional Ser. ISBN:0-07-138041-8, ISBN13: 978-0-07-138041-6. Dewey:621.38/12. LCCN:2002-265967.
Audience: **u,f.**

Management Function > Operations > Communications and Information Management > Records Management

CCH Editorial Staff **JK468.P76**
Guide to Record Retention Requirements as of August 2005. Paper Text. C C H, Inc. Riverwoods, IL. 2006. 456p. ISBN:0-8080-1385-8, ISBN13: 978-0-8080-1385-3. Dewey:353.00714.
Audience: **g,l,u,f.**

Cox, Richard J. **CD3021**
Closing an Era: Historical Perspectives on Modern Archives and Records Management. Trade Cloth. Greenwood Publishing Group, Inc. Portsmouth, NH. 2000. 272p. New Directions in Information Management Ser., Vol. 35 ISBN:0-313-31331-8, ISBN13: 978-0-313-31331-8. Dewey:025/.0068. LCCN:99-089071.
Audience: **g,l,u,f.**

Montana, John C., et al. **KF1357.5**
The Sarbanes-Oxley Act: Implications for Records Management. J. Edwin Dietel & Cristine S. Martins (Authors). Spiral. A R M A International. Lenexa, KS. 2003. 112p. ISBN:1-931786-16-X, ISBN13: 978-1-931786-16-4. Dewey:651.53.
Audience: **g,l,u,f.**

Penn, Ira A., et al. **JK468.P76R44 1994**
Records Management Handbook. Ed. 2. Gail Pennix & Jim Coulson (Authors). Trade Cloth. Ashgate Publishing, Ltd. Aldershot, 1994. 320p. ISBN:0-566-07510-5, ISBN13: 978-0-566-07510-0. Dewey:354.410071/4. LCCN:93-048279.
Audience: **g,l,u,f.** *Choice, 1989.*

Sampson, Karen L. **HF5736**
Value-Added Records Management: Protecting Corporate Assets, Reducing Business Risks. Ed. 2. Trade Cloth. Greenwood Publishing Group, Inc. Portsmouth, NH. 2002. 304p. ISBN:1-56720-547-X, ISBN13: 978-1-56720-547-3. Dewey:651.5. LCCN:2002-023045.
Audience: **g,l,u,f.**

Management Function > Operations > Production Management

Duncan, Acheson J. **TS156**
Quality Control and Industrial Statistics. Paper Text. Textbook Publishers. Temecula, CA. 2003. 946p. ISBN:0-7581-5186-1, ISBN13: 978-0-7581-5186-5. Dewey:658.5/62/015195.
Audience: **u,f.** B

Greene, James H. **TS155.P74 1997**
Production and Inventory Control Handbook. Ed. 3. Trade Cloth. McGraw-Hill Companies, The. New York, NY. 1997. 1200p. ISBN:0-07-024428-6, ISBN13: 978-0-07-024428-3. Dewey:658.5. LCCN:96-039980.
Audience: **g,u.**

Groover, Mikell P. **TS183.G78**
Fundamentals of Modern Manufacturing: Materials, Processes and Systems. Ed. 3. Trade Cloth. John Wiley & Sons, Inc. Hoboken, NJ. 2006. 1040p. ISBN:0-471-74485-9, ISBN13: 978-0-471-74485-6. Dewey:670.42.
Audience: **l,u.**

Groover, Mikell P. Jr. **TS183.G76 2001**
Automation, Production Systems, and Computer-Integrated Manufacturing. Ed. 2. Cloth Text. Prentice Hall PTR. Upper Saddle River, NJ. 2000. 856p. ISBN:0-13-088978-4, ISBN13: 978-0-13-088978-2. Dewey:670.42/7. LCCN:00-029821.
Audience: **u,f.**

Hanlon, Joseph F., et al. **TS195.H35 1998**
e Handbook of Package Engineering. Ed. 3. Robert J. Kelsey & Hallie E. Forcinio (Authors). E-Book. NetLibrary, Inc. Boulder, CO. 1998. ISBN:0-585-24020-5, ISBN13: 978-0-585-24020-6. Dewey:688.8.
Audience: **g.** B

Mabert, Vincent A. & Jacobs, F. Robert (Editors) **TS176.I5518 1991**
Integrated Production Systems: Design, Planning, Control, and Scheduling. Ed. 4. Paper Text. Engineering & Management Press. Norcross, GA. 1991. 277p. ISBN:0-89806-119-9, ISBN13: 978-0-89806-119-2. Dewey:658.5/03. LCCN:91-031574.
Audience: **u,f.**

Machover, Carl **TS155.6.M316 1996**
CAD-CAM Handbook. Ed. 3. Trade Cloth. McGraw-Hill Companies, The. New York, NY. 1995. 704p. ISBN:0-07-039375-3, ISBN13: 978-0-07-039375-2. Dewey:670.2/85. LCCN:95-025668.
Audience: **u,f.** *Choice, 1996.*

McMillan, Gregory K. & Considine, Douglas M. **TS156.8.P764 1999**
Process/Industrial Instruments and Controls Handbook. Ed. 5. Cloth Text. McGraw-Hill Professional Publishing. New York, NY. 1999. 1200p. ISBN:0-07-012582-1, ISBN13: 978-0-07-012582-7. Dewey:629.8. LCCN:99-029591.
Audience: **g,u.**

Merrill, Harwood F. **HD30.M45 1970**
Classics in Management. Trade Cloth. American Management Association. New York, NY. 1970. xiv, 495p. ISBN:0-8144-5231-0, ISBN13: 978-0-8144-5231-8. Dewey:658/.008. LCCN:74-111466.
Audience: **l,f.** B

Meyers, Fred E. & Stephens, Matthew P. **TS184.M49 2005**
Manufacturing Facilities Design and Material Handling. Ed. 3. Cloth Text. Prentice Hall PTR. Upper Saddle River, NJ. 2004. 528p. ISBN:0-13-112535-4, ISBN13: 978-0-13-112535-3. Dewey:658.2/3. LCCN:2003-069029.
Audience: **g,u.**

Nof, Shimon Y. (Editor) **TS191.8.H36 1999**
Handbook of Industrial Robotics. Ed. 2. Trade Cloth. John Wiley & Sons, Inc. Hoboken, NJ. 1999. 1378p. ISBN:0-471-17783-0, ISBN13: 978-0-471-17783-8. Dewey:670.42/72. LCCN:98-008017.
Audience: **g,u.** B *Choice, 2000, 1985.*

Patrick, Dale R. & Fardo, Stephen **TS156.8.P25 1997**
Industrial Process Control Systems. Ed. 1. Cloth Text. Thomson Delmar Learning. Albany, NY. 1997. 464p. Mechanical Technology Ser. ISBN:0-8273-6386-9, ISBN13: 978-0-8273-6386-1. Dewey:670.42/7. LCCN:96-022104.
Audience: **u.** B

Sawik, Tadeusz **TS155.65.S29 1998**
Production Planning and Scheduling in Flexible Assembly Systems. Trade Cloth. Springer. New York, NY. 1998. XIII, 207p. ISBN:3-540-64998-0, ISBN13: 978-3-540-64998-4. Dewey:658.5. LCCN:98-049870.
Audience: **g,u.**

Tersine, Richard J. **TS160.T4 1994**
Principles of Inventory and Materials Management. Ed. 4. Trade Paper. Prentice Hall PTR. Upper Saddle River, NJ. 1993. 608p. ISBN:0-13-457888-0, ISBN13: 978-0-13-457888-0. Dewey:658.7/87. LCCN:93-001583.
Audience: **l.**

Thornley, Gail (Editor) **T57.85 .T46**
Critical Path Analysis in Practice: Collected Papers on Project Control. Library Binding. Routledge. New York, NY. 2003. 168p. International Behavioural and Social Sciences Ser., Vol. 80:Classics from the Tavistock Press ISBN:0-415-26472-3, ISBN13: 978-0-415-26472-3. Dewey:658.4032.
Audience: **f.**

Management Function > Operations > Production Management > Inventory Management

Apple, James M. **TS178.A63 1991**
Plant Layout and Materials Handling. Library Binding. Krieger Publishing Company. Melbourne, FL. 1991. 496p. ISBN:0-89464-545-5, ISBN13: 978-0-89464-545-7. Dewey:658.7. LCCN:90-048718.
Audience: **u.** B

Broeckelmann, Russ **TS160 .B755 1999**
Inventory Classification Innovation: Paving the Way for Electronic Commerce and Vendor Managed Inventory. Paper over Boards. Saint Lucie Press. Boca Raton, FL. 1998. 256p. APICS Series on Resource Management ISBN:1-57444-237-6, ISBN13: 978-1-57444-237-3. Dewey:658.7/87. LCCN:98-042135.
Audience: **g,u.**

Lewis, Colin D. **TS160.L46 1997**
Demand Forcasting and Inventory Control: A Computer Aided Learning Approach. Trade Cloth. Elsevier Science & Technology Books. Saint Louis, MO. 2000. 176p. ISBN:1-85573-241-6, ISBN13: 978-1-85573-241-4. Dewey:658.7. LCCN:98-227907.
Audience: **u,f.**

Wild, Tony **TS160**
Best Practice in Inventory Management. Trade Cloth. Elsevier Science & Technology Books. Saint Louis, MO. 2000. 204p. ISBN:1-85573-310-2, ISBN13: 978-1-85573-310-7. Dewey:658.7/87.
Audience: **g,u.**

Wild, Tony **HD40**
Improving Inventory Record Accuracy: Getting Your Stock Information Right. Paper Text. Elsevier Science & Technology Books. Saint Louis, MO. 2004. 144p. ISBN:0-7506-5900-9, ISBN13: 978-0-7506-5900-0. Dewey:658.7/87. LCCN:2004-052948.
Audience: **g.**

Management Function > Operations > Production Management > Production Planning and Control

TS192 .T68
Total Productive Maintenance: A Collection of Applications and Thoughts. Trade Paper. American Production & Inventory Control Society, Inc. Alexandria, VA. 1994. 216p. ISBN:0-614-24986-4, ISBN13: 978-0-614-24986-6. Dewey:658.2/7.
Audience: **u,f.**

Bedworth, David D. & Bailey, James E. **TS157.B43 1987**
Integrated Production, Control Systems: Management, Analysis and Design. Ed. 2. Trade Cloth. John Wiley & Sons, Inc. Hoboken, NJ. 1987. 496p. ISBN:0-471-82179-9, ISBN13: 978-0-471-82179-3. Dewey:658.5/0028/5. LCCN:86-023379.
Audience: **g,u.** B

Blecker, Thorsten **TS155.65.I54 2005**
Information and Management Systems for Product Customization. Trade Cloth. Springer. New York, NY. 2004. XXII, 269p. Integrated Series in Information Systems, Vol. 7 ISBN:0-387-23347-4, ISBN13: 978-0-387-23347-5. Dewey:658.5/01/1. LCCN:2004-058922.
Audience: **u.**

Martin, Peter **TS183.M366 2005**
Bottom-Line Automation. Ed. 2. Trade Cloth. ISA. Research Triangle Park, NC. 2005. 211p. ISBN:1-55617-962-6, ISBN13: 978-1-55617-962-4. Dewey:670.42/7. LCCN:2005-023370.
Audience: **g.**

Swift, K. G. & Booker, J. D. **TS183**
Process Selection: From Design to Manufacture. Ed. 2. Paper Text. Elsevier Science & Technology Books. Saint Louis, MO. 2003. 336p. ISBN:0-7506-5437-6, ISBN13: 978-0-7506-5437-1. Dewey:670.42. LCCN:2003-045197.
Audience: **u.**

Management Function > Operations > Production Management > Quality Control

Bell, Steve **TS183.B444 2006**
Lean Enterprise Systems: Using IT for Continuous Improvement. Trade Cloth. John Wiley & Sons, Inc. Hoboken, NJ. 2005. 456p. Wiley Series in Systems Engineering and Management Ser. ISBN:0-471-67784-1, ISBN13: 978-0-471-67784-0. Dewey:658.5. LCCN:2005-048987.
Audience: **u.** *Choice, 2006.*

Goldsby, Thomas J. & Martichenko, Robert **HD38.5.G63 2005**
Lean Six SIGMA Logistics: Strategic Development to Operational Success. Cloth Text. J. Ross Publishing, Inc. Ft. Lauderdale, FL. 2005. 248p. ISBN:1-932159-36-3, ISBN13: 978-1-932159-36-3. Dewey:658.4/013. LCCN:2005-011208.
Audience: **g.**

Hoyle, David **TS156.6**
ISO 9000 Quality Systems Handbook. Ed. 5. Paper Text. Elsevier Science & Technology Books. Saint Louis, MO. 2005. 704p. ISBN:0-7506-6785-0, ISBN13: 978-0-7506-6785-2. Dewey:658.5/62. LCCN:2006-277895.
Audience: **g.**

Hoyle, David (Editor) **TS156.6 .H686 2003**
ISO 9000:2000: An A-Z Guide. Trade Paper. Elsevier Science & Technology Books. Saint Louis, MO. 2002. 155p. ISBN:0-7506-5844-4, ISBN13: 978-0-7506-5844-7. Dewey:658.5/62. LCCN:2002-038518.
Audience: **g.**

Taghizadegan, Salman **HD62.15**
Essentials of Lean Six Sigma. Book, Other. Elsevier Science & Technology Books. Saint Louis, MO. 2006. 304p. ISBN:0-12-370502-9, ISBN13: 978-0-12-370502-0. Dewey:658.562.
Audience: **g,l.**

Zipkin, Paul Herbert **HD40.Z56 2000**
Foundations of Inventory Management. Cloth Text. McGraw-Hill Higher Education. Burr Ridge, IL. 2000. 524p. ISBN:0-256-11379-3, ISBN13: 978-0-256-11379-2. Dewey:658.7/87. LCCN:99-040847.
Audience: **l.**

Management Function > Operations > Supply Chain Management

Boyer, Kenneth K., et al. **HD38.5.B698 2004**
Extending the Supply Chain: How Cutting-Edge Companies Bridge the Critical Last Mile into Customers Homes. Markham T. Frohlich & G. Tomas M. Hult (Authors). Trade Cloth. Amacom. New York, NY. 2004. 288p. ISBN:0-8144-0836-2, ISBN13: 978-0-8144-0836-0. Dewey:658.7/88. LCCN:2004-000846.
Audience: **l,u,f.** *Choice, 2005.*

Gattorna, John (Editor) **HF5415.7.H33 2003**
Gower Handbook of Supply Chain Management. Ed. 5. Trade Cloth. Ashgate Publishing, Ltd. Aldershot, 2003. 720p.

ISBN:0-566-08511-9, ISBN13: 978-0-566-08511-6. Dewey:658.788. LCCN:2002-029488.
Audience: **g,l,u,f.**

IOMA Staff **HD38.5.I59 2002**
The IOMA Handbook of Logistics and Inventory Management. Trade Cloth. John Wiley & Sons, Inc. Hoboken, NJ. 2002. 1056p. ISBN:0-471-44293-3, ISBN13: 978-0-471-44293-6. Dewey:658.5. LCCN:2001-045363.
Audience: **g,l,u,f.**

Kotabe, Masaaki & Mol, Michael J. (Editors) **HD38.5 .G585 2006**
Global Supply Chain Management. P. Buckley, J. Dunning, J. Dyer, R. Feenstra, G. Grossman, R. Handfield & C. Markides (Contribution by). Trade Cloth. Edward Elgar Publishing, Inc. Northampton, MA. 2006. 1040p. The Globalization of the World Economy Ser., Vol. 18 ISBN:1-84542-131-0, ISBN13: 978-1-84542-131-1. Dewey:658.5. LCCN:2006-296691.
Audience: **u,f.**

Long, Douglas **HD38.5.L683 2003**
International Logistics: Global Supply Chain Management -. Trade Cloth. Springer. New York, NY. 2003. 460p. ISBN:1-4020-7453-0, ISBN13: 978-1-4020-7453-0. Dewey:658.7. LCCN:2003-058808.
Audience: **u,f.**

McClellan, Michael **TS155.M3455 2002**
Collaborative Manufacturing: Using Real-Time Information to Support the Supply Chain. Paper over Boards. Saint Lucie Press. Boca Raton, FL. 2002. 264p. APICS Series on Resource Management ISBN:1-57444-341-0, ISBN13: 978-1-57444-341-7. Dewey:658.7/2. LCCN:2002-068208.
Audience: **g,u.**

Mentzer, John T. **HD38.5.M463 2004**
Fundamentals of Supply Chain Management: Twelve Drivers of Competitive Advantage. Paper Text. SAGE Publications, Inc. Thousand Oaks, CA. 2004. 304p. ISBN:0-7619-2908-8, ISBN13: 978-0-7619-2908-6. Dewey:658.7. LCCN:2003-027866.
Audience: **g,l,u,f.**

Plunkett, Jack W. **HE9.U5 P58**
Plunkett's Transportation, Supply Chain and Logistics Industry Almanac: Your Complete Guide to All Facets of the Business of Transportation, Logistics and Supply Chains. Trade Paper, CD-ROM. Plunkett Research, Ltd. Houston, TX. 2004. 617p. ISBN:1-59392-007-5, ISBN13: 978-1-59392-007-4. Dewey:380.5240257.
Audience: **g,l,u.**

Ross, David Frederick **HF5415.13.R649 2004**
Distribution: Planning and Control—Managing in the Era of Supply Chain Management. Ed. 2. Trade Cloth. Springer. New York, NY. 2003. 840p. ISBN:1-4020-7686-X, ISBN13: 978-1-4020-7686-2. Dewey:658.7. LCCN:2003-062058.
Audience: **l,u,f.**

Ross, David F. (Editor) **HD38.5.R6753 2002**
E-Supply Chain Management: Foundations for Maximizing Technology and Achieving Breakthrough Performance. American Production and Inventory Control Society Staff (Contribution by). Saddle Stitched. Saint Lucie Press. Boca Raton, FL. 2002. 384p. St. Lucie Press Series on Resource Management Ser. ISBN:1-57444-324-0, ISBN13: 978-1-57444-324-0. Dewey:658.7/0285. LCCN:2002-031711.
Audience: **l.**

Sethi, Suresh P., et al. **HD38.5.S48 2005**
Inventory and Supply Chain Management with Forecast Updates. Houmin Yan & Hanqin Zhang (Authors). Trade Cloth. Springer. New York, NY. 2005. XVIII, 292p. International Series in Operations Research and Management Science, Vol. 81 ISBN:1-4020-8123-5, ISBN13: 978-1-4020-8123-1. Dewey:658.7/87. LCCN:2005-046552.
Audience: **u,f.**

Waller, Derek **TS155**
Operations Management: A Supply Chain Approach. Ed. 2. Trade Paper. International Thomson Business Press. Boston, MA. 2003. 1088p. ISBN:1-86152-803-5, ISBN13: 978-1-86152-803-2. Dewey:658.5.
Audience: **l,u,f.**

Management Function > Operations > Research and Development

Brethauer, Dale M. **HF5415.153.B74 2002**
New Product Development and Delivery: Ensuring Successful Products Through Integrated Process Management. Trade Cloth. Amacom. New York, NY. 2002. 224p. ISBN:0-8144-0713-7, ISBN13: 978-0-8144-0713-4. Dewey:658.8. LCCN:2001-045907.
Audience: **g,u.**

Ellis, Lynn W. **HF5415.15.E44 1997**
Evaluation of R&D Processes: Effectiveness Through Measurements. Trade Cloth. Artech House, Inc. Norwood, MA. 1997. 257p. ISBN:0-89006-791-0, ISBN13: 978-0-89006-791-8. Dewey:658.5/7. LCCN:96-037126.
Audience: **g,u.**

Nishiguchi, Toshihiro (Editor) **HF5415.153.M334 1996**
Managing Product Development. Trade Cloth. Oxford University Press, Inc. New York, NY. 1996. 318p. ISBN:0-19-507438-6, ISBN13: 978-0-19-507438-3. Dewey:658.5/75. LCCN:96-026530.
Audience: **u,f.**

Management Function > Operations > Management Science. Operations Research

Armstrong, J. Scott (Editor) **H61.4.P75 2001**
Principles of Forecasting: A Handbook for Researchers and Practitioners. Trade Cloth. Springer. New York, NY. 2001. 864p. International Operations Research and Management Science Ser. ISBN:0-7923-7930-6, ISBN13: 978-0-7923-7930-0. Dewey:003/.2. LCCN:00-058719.
Audience: **u,f.**

Armstrong, Stephen **TS155 .A683 2001**
Engineering and Product Development Management: The Holistic Approach. Trade Paper. Cambridge University Press. New York, NY. 2005. 357p. ISBN:0-521-01774-2, ISBN13: 978-0-521-01774-9. Dewey:658.5.
Audience: **l,u,f.**

Blackburn, Joseph **HD9725.T57 1991**
Time-Based Competition: The Next Battle Ground in American Manufacturing. Trade Cloth. McGraw-Hill School Education Group. Columbus, OH. 1990. 240p. APICS Ser. ISBN:1-55623-321-3, ISBN13: 978-1-55623-321-0. Dewey:658.5. LCCN:90-003471.
Audience: **u,f.** *Choice, 1991.*

Brown, Steve **TS155**
Strategic Operations Management. Trade Cloth. Pearson Education, Ltd. Harlow, 2000. ISBN:0-273-63921-8, ISBN13: 978-0-273-63921-3. Dewey:658.5.
Audience: **u,f.**

Easterby-Smith, Mark, et al. **HD30.4**
Management Research: An Introduction. Ed. 2. Richard Thorpe & Andy Lowe (Authors). Cloth Text. SAGE Publications, Ltd. London, 2002. 208p. Series in Management Research, : ISBN:0-7619-7284-6, ISBN13: 978-0-7619-7284-6. Dewey:650/.072.
Audience: **l,u,f.**

Flaherty, M. Therese **HD62.4.F595 1996**
Global Operations Management. Paper Text. McGraw-Hill Higher Education. Burr Ridge, IL. 1996. 608p. Series in Management ISBN:0-07-023716-6, ISBN13: 978-0-07-023716-2. Dewey:658/.049. LCCN:95-046943.
Audience: **l,u,f.**

Flood, Robert L. & Daellenbach, Hans **T56.24 .D34 2002**
The Informed Student Guide to Management Science. Trade Paper. International Thomson Business Press. Boston, MA. 2002. 320p. ISBN:1-86152-542-7, ISBN13: 978-1-86152-542-0. Dewey:658.4/03. LCCN:76-047074.
Audience: **g,l,u.** *Choice, 2002.*

Forrester, Jay W. **HD31 .F573**
Industrial Dynamics. Cloth Text. Productivity Press. University Park, IL. 1991. 284p. ISBN:0-915299-88-7, ISBN13: 978-0-915299-88-1. Dewey:658.403. LCCN:73-089547.
Audience: **u,f.**

Gass, Saul I. & Harris, Carl M. (Editors) **T57.6.E53 2000**
Encyclopedia of Operations Research and Management Science: Centennial Edition. Ed. 2. Trade Cloth. Springer. New York, NY. 2001. 960p. ISBN:0-7923-7827-X, ISBN13: 978-0-7923-7827-3. Dewey:658.4/034/03. LCCN:00-025363.
Audience: **g,l,u,f.**

Hopp, Wallace & Spearman, Mark **TS155.H679 2001**
Factory Physics. Ed. 2. Cloth Text. McGraw-Hill Higher Education. Burr Ridge, IL. 2000. 720p. ISBN:0-256-24795-1, ISBN13: 978-0-256-24795-4. Dewey:658.5. LCCN:99-086385.
Audience: **u,f.**

Lawler, E. L., et al. **QA164.T73 1985**
The Traveling Salesman Problem: A Guided Tour of Combinatorial Optimization. Jan Karel Lenstra, A. H. G. Rinnooy-Kan & D. B. Shmoys (Authors). Trade Cloth. John Wiley & Sons, Inc. Hoboken, NJ. 1985. 476p. Wiley Series in Discrete Mathematics and Optimization, Vol. 12 ISBN:0-471-90413-9, ISBN13: 978-0-471-90413-7. Dewey:511/.6. LCCN:85-003158.
Audience: **g,l,u,f.** B *Choice, 1986.*

Melnyk, Steven A. & Christensen, R. T. (Contribution by) **TS155.M438 2000**
Back to Basics: Your Guide to Manufacturing Excellence. Paper over Boards. Saint Lucie Press. Boca Raton, FL. 2000. 224p. APICS Series on Resource Management ISBN:1-57444-279-1, ISBN13: 978-1-57444-279-3. Dewey:658.5/62. LCCN:99-059099.
Audience: **l,u,f.**

Render, Barry, et al. **HD30.25.R466 2006**
Quantitative Analysis for Management. Ed. 9. Ralph M. Stair & Michael Hanna (Authors). Mixed Media. Pearson Education. Boston, MA. 2005. 752p. ISBN:0-13-185702-9, ISBN13: 978-0-13-185702-5. Dewey:658.4/03.
Audience: **l,u.**

Salvendy, Gavriel (Editor) **T56.23.H36 2001**
Handbook of Industrial Engineering: Technology and Operations Management. Ed. 3. Trade Cloth. John Wiley & Sons, Inc. Hoboken, NJ. 2001. 2832p. ISBN:0-471-33057-4, ISBN13: 978-0-471-33057-8. Dewey:658.5. LCCN:2001-022320.
Audience: **u,f.**

Schonberger, Richard J. **HD31.S3384 2001**
Let's Fix It!: Overcoming the Crisis in Manufacturing. Trade Cloth. Simon & Schuster. New York, NY. 2001. 304p. ISBN:0-7432-1551-6, ISBN13: 978-0-7432-1551-0. Dewey:670/.68. LCCN:2001-050117.
Audience: **l,u.**

Stalk, George **TS157**
Competing Against Time: How Time-Based Competition Is Reshaping Global Markets. Trade Paper. Simon & Schuster. New York, NY. 2003. 304p. ISBN:0-7432-5341-8, ISBN13: 978-0-7432-5341-3. Dewey:658.5/6.
Audience: **u,f.**

Strauss, Steven **HD45.M3295 2001**
Manufacturing Handbook of Best Practices: An Innovation, Productivity, and Quality Focus. Jack B. ReVelle (Editor). Paper over Boards. Saint Lucie Press. Boca Raton, FL. 2001. 472p. St. Lucie Press/APICS Series on Resource Management ISBN:1-57444-300-3, ISBN13: 978-1-57444-300-4. Dewey:658.5. LCCN:2001-048504.
Audience: **u,f.**

Wild, Ray **TS155**
Essentials of Production and Operations Management. Ed. 4. Trade Paper. Continuum International Publishing Group, Ltd. London, 1995. 480p. ISBN:0-304-33130-9, ISBN13: 978-0-304-33130-7. Dewey:658.5.
Audience: **l,u,f.**

Management Function > Human Resource Management

Albrecht, Karl **HM1106.A53 2006**
Social Intelligence: The New Science of Success. Trade Cloth. John Wiley & Sons, Inc. Hoboken, NJ. 2005. 304p. ISBN:0-7879-7938-4, ISBN13: 978-0-7879-7938-6. Dewey:302.1/2. LCCN:2005-025923.
Audience: **g,l,u,f.**

Cartwright, Susan (Editor) **HD30.15.B455**
Human Resource Management. Ed. 2. Trade Cloth. Blackwell Publishing, Inc. Malden, MA. 2006. 488p. The Blackwell

Encyclopedia of Management Ser., Vol. 5 ISBN:1-4051-1697-8, ISBN13: 978-1-4051-1697-8. Dewey:658/.003 s 658.3/003. LCCN:2004-004338.

Audience: **g,l,u,f.**

Cross, Rob & Parker, Andrew **HD69.S8C76 2004**
The Hidden Power of Social Networks: Understanding How Work Really Gets Done in Organizations. Trade Paper. Harvard Business School Press. Boston, MA. 2004. 304p. ISBN:1-59139-270-5, ISBN13: 978-1-59139-270-5. Dewey:658. LCCN:2003-021436.

Audience: **g,l,u,f.** *Choice, 2004.*

Huselid, Mark & Becker, Brian **HF5549.5.P35H87 2005**
Workforce Scorecard. Trade Paper. Harvard Business School Press. Boston, MA. 2005. 288p. ISBN:1-59139-245-4, ISBN13: 978-1-59139-245-3. Dewey:658.3/01. LCCN:2004-023599.

Audience: **g,l,u,f.**

McGregor, Douglas **HF5549.M33956 2006**
The Human Side of Enterprise. Trade Cloth. McGraw-Hill Companies, The. New York, NY. 2005. 256p. ISBN:0-07-146222-8, ISBN13: 978-0-07-146222-8. Dewey:658.3. LCCN:2005-023046.

Audience: **g,l,u,f.**

Management Function > Human Resource Management > Training and Development

McCall, Morgan W. & Hollenbeck, George P. **HD30.4.M42 2002**
Frequent Flyers: Developing Global Executives. Trade Cloth. Harvard Business School Press. Boston, MA. 2002. 288p. ISBN:1-57851-336-7, ISBN13: 978-1-57851-336-9. Dewey:658.4/07124. LCCN:2001-039434.

Audience: **g,l,u,f.**

Management Function > Human Resource Management > Labor Relations

HD8106.5 .U55
Union Management Relations in Canada. Ed. 4. Trade Cloth. Simon & Schuster. New York, NY. 2000. 160p. ISBN:0-201-61408-1, ISBN13: 978-0-201-61408-4. Dewey:331/.0971.

Audience: **u,f.**

Adams, Walter & Brock, James W. **HD2785.A68 2004**
The Bigness Complex: Industry, Labor, and Government in the American Economy. Ed. 2. Trade Paper. Stanford University Press. Palo Alto, CA. 2004. 400p. ISBN:0-8047-4969-8, ISBN13: 978-0-8047-4969-5. Dewey:338.6/44/0973. LCCN:2004-001030.

Audience: **g,l,u,f.**

Amjad, Ali **HD6812.A45 2001**
Labour Legislation and Trade Unions in India and Pakistan. Trade Cloth. Oxford University Press, Inc. New York, NY. 2001. 210p. ISBN:0-19-579572-5, ISBN13: 978-0-19-579572-1. Dewey:344.5401. LCCN:2001-287122.

Audience: **u,f.**

Atleson, James B. **HD8072.A82 1998**
Labor and the Wartime State: Labor Relations and Law During World War II. Trade Paper. University of Illinois Press. Champaign, IL. 1998. 312p. ISBN:0-252-06674-X, ISBN13: 978-0-252-06674-0. Dewey:331/.0973/09044. LCCN:97-021069.

Audience: **g,l,u,f.** *Choice, 1998.*

Ballot, Michael **HD8072.5.B35 1996**
Labor-Management Relations in a Changing Environment. Ed. 2. Trade Cloth. John Wiley & Sons, Inc. Hoboken, NJ. 1995. 656p. Management Ser. ISBN:0-471-11185-6, ISBN13: 978-0-471-11185-6. Dewey:331. LCCN:95-035394.

Audience: **u,f.**

Bamber, Greg (Editor) **HD8720.5.E468 2000**
Employment Relations in the Asia Pacific: Changing Approaches. Trade Paper. Allen & Unwin Pty., Ltd. Crows Nest, NSW. 2000. 288p. ISBN:1-86508-189-2, ISBN13: 978-1-86508-189-2. Dewey:331/.095. LCCN:00-455335.

Audience: **u,f.**

Bean, Ron **HD6971.B368 1994**
Comparative Industrial Relations: An Introduction to Cross-National Perspectives. Ed. 2. Trade Paper. Thomson Learning. Independence, KY. 1994. 256p. ISBN:0-415-07087-2, ISBN13: 978-0-415-07087-4. Dewey:331. LCCN:93-029290.

Audience: **u,f.** B *Choice, 1985.*

Block, Richard N. & Beck, John P. **KF3369.B49 1996**
Labor Law, Industrial Relations and Employee Choice: The State of the Workplace in the 1990's. Daniel H. Kruger (Editor). Paper Text. W. E. Upjohn Institute for Employment Research. Kalamazoo, MI. 1996. 116p. ISBN:0-88099-163-1, ISBN13: 978-0-88099-163-6. Dewey:344.73/01. LCCN:96-026103.

Audience: **u,f.**

Block, Richard N., et al. **HD8072.5.B57 2002**
Labor Standards in the United States and Canada. Karen Roberts & Ronald O. Clarke (Authors). Trade Paper. W. E. Upjohn Institute for Employment Research. Kalamazoo, MI. 2003. 185p. ISBN:0-88099-235-2, ISBN13: 978-0-88099-235-0. Dewey:331.12/042/0973. LCCN:2002-013604.

Audience: **g,l,u,f.** *Choice, 2003.*

Bognanno, Mario F. & Coleman, Charles J. (Editors) **HD5504**
Labor Arbitration in America: The Profession and Practice. Trade Cloth. Greenwood Publishing Group, Inc. Portsmouth, NH. 1992. 200p. ISBN:0-275-94375-5, ISBN13: 978-0-275-94375-2. Dewey:331.891430973. LCCN:92-000399.

Audience: **g,l,u,f.**

Budd, John W. **HD8066.B83 2005**
Labor Relations: Striking a Balance. Cloth Text. McGraw-Hill Higher Education. Burr Ridge, IL. 2004. 568p. ISBN:0-07-284221-0, ISBN13: 978-0-07-284221-0. Dewey:331.88/0973. LCCN:2003-069082.

Audience: **u,f.**

Cherny, Robert W., et al. **HD6510.A45 2004**
American Labor and the Cold War: Grassroots Politics and Postwar Political Culture. William Issel & Kieran Walsh Taylor (Authors). Trade Paper. Rutgers University Press. Piscataway, NJ. 2004. 320p. ISBN:0-8135-3403-8, ISBN13: 978-0-8135-3403-9. Dewey:331.88/0973/09045. LCCN:2003-020095.

Audience: **u,f.**

Clark **HD6508.C6564 2002**
Collective Barganing in the Private Sector. Trade Paper. Cornell University Press. Ithaca, NY. 2002. iv, 380p. Industrial Relations Research Association Ser. ISBN:0-913447-84-6, ISBN13: 978-0-913447-84-0. Dewey:331.89/04/0973. LCCN:2003-271103.
Audience: **u,f.**

Cooper, Bruce S. (Editor) **LB2844**
Labor Relations in Education: An International Perspective. Trade Cloth. Greenwood Publishing Group, Inc. Portsmouth, NH. 1992. 384p. Contributions to the Study of Education Ser., No. 54 ISBN:0-313-26707-3, ISBN13: 978-0-313-26707-9. Dewey:331.88113711. LCCN:91-037121.
Audience: **u,f.**

Crouch, Colin **HD8376.5**
Industrial Relations and European State Traditions. Paper Text. Oxford University Press, Inc. New York, NY. 1994. 428p. ISBN:0-19-827974-4, ISBN13: 978-0-19-827974-7. Dewey:331/.094. LCCN:92-014645.
Audience: **u,f.** *Choice, 1993.*

Deslippe, Dennis A. **HD6079.2.U5D47 2000**
Rights, Not Roses: Unions and the Rise of Working-Class Feminism, 1945 80. Trade Paper. University of Illinois Press. Champaign, IL. 1999. 280p. The Working Class in American History Ser. ISBN:0-252-06834-3, ISBN13: 978-0-252-06834-8. Dewey:331.4/78/0973. LCCN:99-006426.
Audience: **l,u,f.** *Choice, 2000.*

Dundon, Tony & Rollinson, Derek **HD6971**
Employment Relations in Non-Union Firms. Paper over Boards. Routledge. New York, NY. 2004. 200p. Routledge Research in Employment Relations Ser., Vol. 12 ISBN:0-415-31246-9, ISBN13: 978-0-415-31246-2. Dewey:331. LCCN:2003-066691.
Audience: **u,f.**

Eaton, Adrienne E. & Keefe, Jeffrey H. (Editors) **KF3425.E485 1999**
Employment Dispute Resolution and Worker Rights in the Changing Workplace. Book, Other. Industrial Relations Research Association. Champaign, IL. 2000. 305p. Industrial Relations Research Association Ser. ISBN:0-913447-77-3, ISBN13: 978-0-913447-77-2. Dewey:344.7301/89143. LCCN:00-712985.
Audience: **u,f.**

Eberwein, Wilhelm, et al. **HD8376.5.E24 2002**
The Europeanisation of Industrial Relations: National and European Processes in Germany, UK, Italy and France. Jochen Tholen & Joachim Schuster (Authors). Trade Cloth. Ashgate Publishing, Ltd. Aldershot, 2002. 182p. ISBN:0-7546-1892-7, ISBN13: 978-0-7546-1892-8. Dewey:331/.094/09049. LCCN:2001-098450.
Audience: **u,f.**

Epstein, Edward C. **HD6530.5.L33 1989**
Labor, Autonomy and the State in Latin America. Cloth Text. Routledge. New York, NY. 1989. 272p. Thematic Studies in Latin America ISBN:0-04-445331-0, ISBN13: 978-0-04-445331-4. Dewey:322/.2/098. LCCN:88-030377.
Audience: **u,f.** *Choice, 1990.*

Fairris, David **HD8072.5.F34 1997**
Shopfloor Matters: Labor-Management Relations in 20th Century American Manufacturing. Paper over Boards. Routledge. New York, NY. 1997. 256p. Routledge Studies in Business Organization and Networks ISBN:0-415-12123-X, ISBN13: 978-0-415-12123-1. Dewey:331/.047/09730904. LCCN:97-004318.
Audience: **u,f.**

Flood, Lawrence G. (Editor) **HD6508**
Unions and Public Policy: The New Economy, Law, and Democratic Politics, 364. Trade Cloth. Greenwood Publishing Group, Inc. Portsmouth, NH. 1995. 220p. Contributions in Political Science Ser., Vol. 364 ISBN:0-313-29800-9, ISBN13: 978-0-313-29800-4. Dewey:331.88/0973. LCCN:95-022976.
Audience: **u,f.** *Choice, 1996.*

Fossum, John A. **HD8072.5.F67 2006**
Labor Relations. Ed. 9. Cloth Text. McGraw-Hill Companies, The. New York, NY. 2005. 576p. ISBN:0-07-298713-8, ISBN13: 978-0-07-298713-3. Dewey:331/.0973. LCCN:2004-065637.
Audience: **l,u,f.**

Friedman, Clara H. **HD5504.A3F75 1995**
Between Labor and Management. Trade Cloth. Thomson Gale. Farmington Hills, MI. 1995. 200p. Twayne's Oral History Ser. ISBN:0-8057-9101-9, ISBN13: 978-0-8057-9101-3. Dewey:331.89/143/0973. LCCN:94-044559.
Audience: **l,u,f.**

Friedman, Raymond A. **HD6971.5.F75 1994**
Front Stage, Backstage: The Dramatic Structure of Labor Negotions. Trade Cloth. MIT Press. Cambridge, MA. 1994. 271p. Organization Studies, Vol. 10 ISBN:0-262-06167-8, ISBN13: 978-0-262-06167-4. Dewey:331.89. LCCN:93-044591.
Audience: **g,l,u,f.** *Choice, 1994.*

Gavroglou, Stavros P. **HD6515.A8G38 1998**
Labor's Power and Industrial Performance: Automobile Production Regimes in the U. S., Germany, and Japan. Cloth Text. Garland Publishing, Inc. New York, NY. 1998. 352p. Garland Studies in Industrial Productivity ISBN:0-8153-3244-0, ISBN13: 978-0-8153-3244-2. Dewey:331.88/1292. LCCN:98-037453.
Audience: **u,f.**

Gleason, Sandra E. **KF3425.W67 1997**
Workplace Dispute Resolution: Directions for the Twenty-First Century. Trade Paper. Michigan State University Press. East Lansing, MI. 1998. 283p. ISBN:0-87013-436-1, ISBN13: 978-0-87013-436-4. Dewey:344.7301/89. LCCN:97-025092.
Audience: **l,u,f.** *Choice, 1998.*

Golden, Miriam A. **HD5708.5 .G65 1997**
Heroic Defeats: The Politics of Job Loss. Robert H. Bates, Ellen Comisso, Peter Hall, Peter Lange, Joel Samuel Migdal & Helen V. Milner (Contribution by). Trade Paper. Cambridge University Press. New York, NY. 1996. 213p. Studies in Comparative Politics ISBN:0-521-48432-4, ISBN13: 978-0-521-48432-9. Dewey:331.25. LCCN:96-012296.
Audience: **u,f.** *Choice, 1997.*

Gould, William B. IV **KF3369.G68 2004**
A Primer on American Labor Law. Ed. 4. Cloth Text. MIT Press. Cambridge, MA. 2004. 432p. ISBN:0-262-07250-5, ISBN13: 978-0-262-07250-2. Dewey:347.3041. LCCN:2003-070610.
Audience: **g,l,u,f.**

Gross, James A. **HD8072.5.G76 1995**
Broken Promise: The Subversion of U. S. Labor Relations, 1947-1994. Cloth Text. Temple University Press. Philadelphia,

PA. 1995. 416p. Labor and Social Change Ser. ISBN:1-56639-325-6, ISBN13: 978-1-56639-325-6. Dewey:331/.0973. LCCN:94-042510.
Audience: **g,l,u,f.**

Halpern, Martin **HD6508**
Unions, Radicals, and Democratic Presidents: Seeking Social Change in the Twentieth Century. Trade Cloth. Greenwood Publishing Group, Inc. Portsmouth, NH. 2003. 304p. Contributions in American History Ser., Vol. 201 ISBN:0-313-32471-9, ISBN13: 978-0-313-32471-0. Dewey:331.88/0973/0904. LCCN:2003-046967.
Audience: **u,f.** *Choice, 2004.*

Heckscher, Charles C. **HD6508**
The New Unionism: Employee Involvement in the Changing Corporation. Trade Paper. Basic Books. New York, NY. 1989. 320p. ISBN:0-465-05099-9, ISBN13: 978-0-465-05099-4. Dewey:331.88/0973. LCCN:87-047769.
Audience: **u,f.** *Choice, 1988.*

Hirsch, Susan Eleanor **HD8072.5.H57 2003**
After the Strike: A Century of Labor Struggle at Pullman. Trade Cloth. University of Illinois Press. Champaign, IL. 2003. 320p. The Working Class in American Hsitory Ser. ISBN:0-252-02791-4, ISBN13: 978-0-252-02791-8. Dewey:331.7/62523. LCCN:2002-007705.
Audience: **g,l,u,f.** *Choice, 2004.*

Hogler, Raymond L. **KF3369.H643 2004**
Employment Relations in the United States: Law, Policy, and Practice. Cloth Text. SAGE Publications, Inc. Thousand Oaks, CA. 2003. 312p. ISBN:1-4129-0414-5, ISBN13: 978-1-4129-0414-8. Dewey:344.7301. LCCN:2003-021149.
Audience: **g,l,u,f.** *Choice, 2004.*

Jefferys, Steve **HD8430.J44 2003**
Liberté, Égalité and Fraternité at Work: Changing French Employment Relations and Management. Cloth over Boards. Palgrave Macmillan. New York, NY. 2003. 320p. ISBN:0-333-74137-4, ISBN13: 978-0-333-74137-5. Dewey:331/.0944. LCCN:2002-035833.
Audience: **u,f.**

Jenkins, Alan **HD8431.J46 2000**
Employment Relations in France: Evolution and Innovation. Trade Cloth. Springer. New York, NY. 2000. 268p. Studies in Work and Industry ISBN:0-306-46333-4, ISBN13: 978-0-306-46333-4. Dewey:331/.0944. LCCN:00-022118.
Audience: **u,f.**

Jennings, Kenneth M. **GV880**
Swings and Misses: Moribund Labor Relations in Professional Baseball. Trade Cloth. Greenwood Publishing Group, Inc. Portsmouth, NH. 1997. 272p. ISBN:0-275-95797-7, ISBN13: 978-0-275-95797-1. Dewey:331.89/041796357/097. LCCN:97-011085.
Audience: **g,l,u,f.**

Jenson, Jane & Mahon, Rianne (Editors) **HD6508.C39 1993**
The Challenge of Restructuring: North American Labor Movements Respond. Trade Cloth. Temple University Press. Philadelphia, PA. 1993. 488p. Labor and Social Change Ser. ISBN:0-87722-981-3, ISBN13: 978-0-87722-981-0. Dewey:331.88/0973. LCCN:92-020464.
Audience: **u,f.**

Kaufman, Bruce E. & Taras, Daphne Gottlieb (Editors) **HD6971.8.N66 2000**
Nonunion Employee Representation: History, Contemporary Practice and Policy. Cloth Text. M. E. Sharpe Inc. Armonk, NY. 2000. 592p. Issues in Work and Human Resources Ser. ISBN:0-7656-0494-9, ISBN13: 978-0-7656-0494-1. Dewey:331/.01/10973. LCCN:99-032610.
Audience: **u,f.**

Kester, Gerard & Sidibe, Ousmane O. **HD6858.5 .S9513 1997**
Trade Unions and Sustainable Democracy in Africa. Michael Cunningham (Translator). Trade Cloth. Ashgate Publishing, Ltd. Aldershot, 1997. 388p. ISBN:1-84014-323-1, ISBN13: 978-1-84014-323-2. Dewey:322.2/096/09049. LCCN:97-074263.
Audience: **u,f.**

LaCugna, Charles S. **KF3424**
An Introduction to Labor Arbitration. Trade Cloth. Greenwood Publishing Group, Inc. Portsmouth, NH. 1988. 292p. ISBN:0-275-93047-5, ISBN13: 978-0-275-93047-9. Dewey:344.73/0189143. LCCN:88-005810.
Audience: **l,u,f.**

Lipset, Seymour Martin & Meltz, Noah M. **HD6508.L53 2004**
The Paradox of American Unionism: Why Americans Like Unions More Than Canadians Do, but Join Much Less. Thomas A. Kochan (Foreword by). Trade Cloth. Cornell University Press. Ithaca, NY. 2004. 208p. ISBN:0-8014-4200-1, ISBN13: 978-0-8014-4200-1. Dewey:331.88/0973. LCCN:2003-024992.
Audience: **u,f.** *Choice, 2005.*

Lo, Vai Io (Contribution by) **KNC409.L6 1999**
Law and Industrial Relations: China and Japan after World War II. Trade Cloth. Kluwer Law International. Alphen a/d Rijn, 1997. 224p. Studies in Employment and Social Policy ISBN:90-411-1075-5, ISBN13: 978-90-411-1075-6. Dewey:344.5101/88. LCCN:98-036799.
Audience: **u,f.**

Makoto, Kumazawa, et al. **HD8726.5.K772 1996**
Portraits of the Japanese Workplace: Labor Movements, Workers, and Managers. Mark Selden, Andrew Gordon & Mikiso Hane (Authors). Trade Paper. Westview Press. Boulder, CO. 1996. 288p. Social Change in Global Perspective Ser. ISBN:0-8133-1708-8, ISBN13: 978-0-8133-1708-3. Dewey:306.3/6/0952. LCCN:96-015010.
Audience: **u,f.**

Milkman, Ruth & Voss, Kim **HD5708.R43 2004**
Rebuilding Labor: Organizing and Organizers in the New Union Movement. Book, Other. Cornell University Press. Ithaca, NY. 2004. 312p. An ILR Press Book Ser. ISBN:0-8014-4265-6, ISBN13: 978-0-8014-4265-0. Dewey:331.88/0973. LCCN:2004-006703.
Audience: **u,f.**

Murray, R. Emmett **HD8066.M87 1998**
The Lexicon of Labor: More Than 500 Key Terms, Biographical Sketches, and Historical Insights Concerning Labor in America. Thomas Geoghegan (Foreword by). Trade Paper. New Press, The. New York, NY. 1998. 208p. ISBN:1-56584-456-4, ISBN13: 978-1-56584-456-8. Dewey:331/.0973/03. LCCN:98-012783.
Audience: **g,l,u,f.**

Najita, Joyce M. & Stern, James L. (Editors) **HD8005.6.U5C643 2001**
Collective Bargaining in the Public Sector: The Experience of Eight States. Cloth Text. M. E. Sharpe Inc. Armonk, NY. 2001. xiii, 270p. Issues in Work and Human Resources Ser. ISBN:0-7656-0754-9, ISBN13: 978-0-7656-0754-6. Dewey:331.89/04135173. LCCN:2001-018406.
Audience: **u,f.** *Choice, 2002.*

Nolan, Dennis R. **KF3425.N638 1998**
Labor and Employment Arbitration in a Nutshell. Trade Paper. West Publishing Company, College & School Division. Eagan, MN. 1998. 496p. Nutshell Ser. ISBN:0-314-21160-8, ISBN13: 978-0-314-21160-6. Dewey:344.7301/89143. LCCN:98-010054.
Audience: **g,l,u,f.**

Robertson, David Brian **HD6508.R616 2000**
Capital, Labor, and State: The Battle for American Labor Markets from the Civil War to the New Deal. Book, Other. Rowman & Littlefield Publishers, Inc. Lanham, MD. 2000. 320p. ISBN:0-8476-9728-2, ISBN13: 978-0-8476-9728-1. Dewey:331.8/0973/09034. LCCN:99-087953.
Audience: **u,f.** *Choice, 2001.*

Royle, Tony & Towers, Brian **HD6976.H8R69 2002**
Labour Relations in the Global Fast-Food Industry. Trade Paper. Routledge. New York, NY. 2002. 240p. ISBN:0-415-22167-6, ISBN13: 978-0-415-22167-2. Dewey:331/.04164795. LCCN:2001-058181.
Audience: **g,l,u,f.**

Sexton, Patricia Cayo **HD8066.S44 1991**
War on Labor and the Left: Understanding America's Unique Conservatism. Trade Paper. Westview Press. Boulder, CO. 1992. 336p. ISBN:0-8133-1063-6, ISBN13: 978-0-8133-1063-3. Dewey:322/.2/0973. LCCN:91-022028.
Audience: **u,f.**

Slomp, Hans **HD6658**
Between Bargaining and Politics: An Introduction to European Labor Relations. Paper Text. Greenwood Publishing Group, Inc. Portsmouth, NH. 1998. 184p. ISBN:0-275-96466-3, ISBN13: 978-0-275-96466-5. Dewey:322/.2/094. LCCN:96-002205.
Audience: **u,f.** *Choice, 1997.*

Slomp, Hans **HD8374**
Labor Relations in Europe: A History of Issues and Developments, 29. Trade Cloth. Greenwood Publishing Group, Inc. Portsmouth, NH. 1990. 241p. Contributions in Labor Studies Ser., No. 29 ISBN:0-313-26756-1, ISBN13: 978-0-313-26756-7. Dewey:331/.094. LCCN:89-023262.
Audience: **u,f.** *Choice, 1990.*

Stepan-Norris, Judith & Zeitlin, Maurice **HX544.S76 2002**
Left Out: Reds and America's Industrial Unions. Trade Cloth. Cambridge University Press. New York, NY. 2002. 392p. ISBN:0-521-79212-6, ISBN13: 978-0-521-79212-7. Dewey:331.88/33/097309041. LCCN:2001-037655.
Audience: **u,f.** *Choice, 2003.*

Szell, Gyorgy (Editor) **HD8380.7.L33 1991**
Labour Relations in Transition in Eastern Europe. Library Binding. Walter De Gruyter Inc. Ossining, NY. 1991. x, 369p. Studies in Organization, No. 33 ISBN:3-11-012648-6, ISBN13: 978-3-11-012648-8. Dewey:331/.0947. LCCN:91-031137.
Audience: **u,f.**

Troy, Leo **HD6971.5.T76 1999**
Beyond Unions and Collective Bargaining. Cloth Text. M. E. Sharpe Inc. Armonk, NY. 1999. 240p. Issues in Work and Human Resources Ser. ISBN:0-7656-0469-8, ISBN13: 978-0-7656-0469-9. Dewey:331.88. LCCN:99-027840.
Audience: **u,f.** *Choice, 2000.*

University of Hawaii at Manoa, Industrial Relation Staff **HD4839.R612 1994**
Robert's Dictionary of Industrial Relations. Ed. 4. Trade Cloth. B N A Books. Edison, NJ. 1994. 894p. ISBN:0-87179-777-1, ISBN13: 978-0-87179-777-3. Dewey:331/.03. LCCN:93-023280.
Audience: **g,l,u,f.** *Choice, 1994.*

Van Horn, Carl E. & Schaffner, Herbert A. (Author, Editors) **HD8072**
Work in America: An Encyclopedia of History, Policy, and Society. Library Binding. ABC-CLIO, Inc. Santa Barbara, CA. 2003. 750p. ISBN:1-57607-676-8, ISBN13: 978-1-57607-676-7. Dewey:331/.0973/03. LCCN:2003-018708.
Audience: **g,l,u,f.** *Choice, 2004.*

Walton, Richard E., et al. **HD8072.5.W35 1994**
Strategic Negotiations: A Theory of Change in Labor-Management Relations. Joel E. Cutcher-Gershenfeld & Robert B. McKersie (Authors). Trade Cloth. Harvard Business School Press. Boston, MA. 1994. 400p. ISBN:0-87584-551-7, ISBN13: 978-0-87584-551-7. Dewey:331/.0973. LCCN:93-050838.
Audience: **u,f.**

Weir, Robert E. & Hanlan, James P. (Editors) **HD8066**
Historical Encyclopedia of American Labor. Cloth Text. Greenwood Publishing Group, Inc. Portsmouth, NH. 2004. 733p. ISBN:0-313-31840-9, ISBN13: 978-0-313-31840-5. Dewey:331.88/0973/03. LCCN:2003-052847.
Audience: **g,l,u,f.** *Choice, 2004.*

Wever, Kirsten S. **HD8451.W45 1995**
Negotiating Competitiveness: Employment Relations and Organizational Innovation in Germany and the United States. Trade Cloth. Harvard Business School Press. Boston, MA. 1995. 256p. ISBN:0-87584-554-1, ISBN13: 978-0-87584-554-8. Dewey:331/.0943. LCCN:94-039672.
Audience: **u,f.**

Management Function > Human Resource Management > Labor Relations > Unions

Addison, John T. & Schnabel, Claus **HD6350**
International Handbook of Trade Unions. Trade Paper. Edward Elgar Publishing, Inc. Northampton, MA. 2005. 576p. ISBN:1-84542-625-8, ISBN13: 978-1-84542-625-5. Dewey:331.8. LCCN:2003049040.
Audience: **u,f.** *Choice, 2004.*

Anderson, Jervis **E185.97.K5**
A. Philip Randolph: A Biographical Portrait. Trade Paper. University of California Press. Berkeley, CA. 1986. 398p. ISBN:0-520-05505-5, ISBN13: 978-0-520-05505-6. Dewey:323.4/092/4. LCCN:73-012847.
Audience: **g,l,u,f.** ☛

Babson, Steve **HD6515.A82I573 1991**
Building the Union: Skilled Workers and Anglo-Gaelic Immigrants in the Rise of the UAW. Cloth Text. Rutgers University Press. Piscataway, NJ. 1991. 250p. Class and Culture Ser. ISBN:0-8135-1657-9, ISBN13: 978-0-8135-1657-8. Dewey:331.88/1292/097734. LCCN:90-045947.
Audience: **u,f.** *Choice, 1992.*

Barnard, John **HD6515.A82I584 2003**
American Vanguard: The United Auto Workers During the Reuther Years, 1935-1970. Trade Cloth. Wayne State University Press. Detroit, MI. 2003. 480p. ISBN:0-8143-2947-0, ISBN13: 978-0-8143-2947-4. Dewey:331.88/1292/0973. LCCN:2003-017663.
Audience: **u,f.** *Choice, 2005.*

Black, Errol & Silver, Jim **HD6524.B58 2001**
Building a Better World: An Introduction to Trade Unionism in Canada. Trade Cloth. Fernwood Publishing Company, Ltd. Peterborough, ON. 2001. 224p. ISBN:1-55266-051-6, ISBN13: 978-1-55266-051-5. Dewey:331.88/0971. LCCN:2001-409897.
Audience: **g,l,u,f.**

Blatz, Perry K. **HD8039.M62U6148 1994**
Democratic Miners: Work and Labor Relations in the Anthracite Coal Industry, 1875-1925. Cloth Text. State University of New York Press. Albany, NY. 1994. 368p. SUNY Series in American Labor History ISBN:0-7914-1819-7, ISBN13: 978-0-7914-1819-2. Dewey:331.88/122335/0973. LCCN:93-000843.
Audience: **u,f.** *Choice, 1994.*

Booth, Alison L. **HD6664 .B598 1995**
The Economics of the Trade Union. Trade Paper. Cambridge University Press. New York, NY. 1994. 311p. ISBN:0-521-46839-6, ISBN13: 978-0-521-46839-8. Dewey:331.88/0941. LCCN:93-050224.
Audience: **u,f.** *Choice, 1995.*

Boyle, Kevin **HD6515.A82**
The UAW and the Heyday of American Liberalism, 1945-1968. Book, Other. Cornell University Press. Ithaca, NY. 1998. 360p. ISBN:0-8014-8538-X, ISBN13: 978-0-8014-8538-1. Dewey:331.88/1292/0973.
Audience: **u,f.** *Choice, 1996.*

Brexel, Bernadette **HD8055.K7B67 2004**
The Knights of Labor and the Haymarket Riot: The Fight for an Eight-Hour Workday. Library Binding. Rosen Publishing Group, Incorporated, The. New York, NY. 2004. 32p. America's Industrial Society in the Nineteenth Century Ser. ISBN:0-8239-4028-4, ISBN13: 978-0-8239-4028-8. Dewey:977.3/11041. LCCN:2003-001255.
Audience: **u,f.**

Brody, David **HD6508**
In Labor's Cause: Main Themes on the History of the American Worker. Paper Text. Oxford University Press, Inc. New York, NY. 1993. 272p. ISBN:0-19-506791-6, ISBN13: 978-0-19-506791-0. Dewey:331.88/0973. LCCN:92-042134.
Audience: **l,u,f.** *Choice, 1994.*

Bronfenbrenner, Kate (Editor), et al. **HD6490.O72U66 1998**
Organizing to Win: New Research on Union Strategies. Sheldon Friedman, Richard W. Hurd, Rudolph A. Oswald & Ronald L. Seeber (Editors). Trade Paper. Cornell University Press. Ithaca, NY. 1998. 368p. ISBN:0-8014-8446-4, ISBN13: 978-0-8014-8446-9. Dewey:331.89/12. LCCN:97-028827.
Audience: **u,f.** *Choice, 1998.*

Brown, Jonathan C. (Editor) **HD8110.5.W67 1997**
Workers' Control in Latin America. Trade Paper. University of North Carolina Press. Chapel Hill, NC. 1997. 344p. ISBN:0-8078-4666-X, ISBN13: 978-0-8078-4666-7. Dewey:322/.2/098. LCCN:97-001880.
Audience: **u,f.** *Choice, 1998.*

Bruns, Roger **HD6509.C48B78 2005**
Cesar Chavez: A Biography. Trade Cloth. Greenwood Publishing Group, Inc. Portsmouth, NH. 2005. 168p. Greenwood Biographies Ser. ISBN:0-313-33452-8, ISBN13: 978-0-313-33452-8. Dewey:331.88/13/092 B. LCCN:2005-016819.
Audience: **g,l,u,f.**

Cameron, Don **LB2844.53**
The Inside Story of the Teacher Revolution in America. Trade Paper. Scarecrow Press, Inc. Lanham, MD. 2005. 216p. ISBN:1-57886-196-9, ISBN13: 978-1-57886-196-5. Dewey:371.1/00973. LCCN:2004-019439.
Audience: **u,f.**

Chaison, Gary N. **HD6508.C384 2006**
Unions in America. Cloth Text. SAGE Publications, Inc. Thousand Oaks, CA. 2005. 208p. ISBN:1-4129-2671-8, ISBN13: 978-1-4129-2671-3. Dewey:331.88/0973. LCCN:2005-019005.
Audience: **g,l,u,f.**

Chamberlain, Neil W. & Schilling, Jane M. **HD5324 .C42 1973**
Impact of Strikes: Their Social and Economic Costs. Trade Cloth. Greenwood Publishing Group, Inc. Portsmouth, NH. 1973. 257p. Yale Labor and Management Center Ser. ISBN:0-8371-7066-4, ISBN13: 978-0-8371-7066-4. Dewey:331.89/2973. LCCN:73-011841.
Audience: **u,f.**

Chavez, Cesar, et al. **HD6509.C48A25 2002**
The Words of Cesar Chávez. Richard J. Jensen & John C. Hammerback (Authors). Trade Paper. Texas A&M University Press. College Station, TX. 2004. 256p. ISBN:1-58544-170-8, ISBN13: 978-1-58544-170-9. Dewey:331.88/13/092 B. LCCN:2001-006994.
Audience: **g,l,u,f.**

Clarke, Simon & Ashwin, Sarah **HD6735.15.R88 2003**
Russian Trade Unions and Industrial Relations in Transition. Cloth over Boards. Palgrave Macmillan. New York, NY. 2003. 304p. ISBN:0-333-73518-8, ISBN13: 978-0-333-73518-3. Dewey:331.88/0947. LCCN:2002-068332.
Audience: **u,f.**

Coleman, Walter **HV6452.P4 M6**
The Molly Maguire Riots: Industrial Conflict in the Pennsylvania Coal Region. Leon Stein & Philip Taft (Editors). Trade Paper. Ayer Company Publishers, Inc. Manchester, NH. 1997. 189p. American Labor, from Conspiracy to Collective Bargaining Ser., No. 1 ISBN:0-405-02112-7, ISBN13: 978-0-405-02112-1. Dewey:364.14/06. LCCN:78-089726.
Audience: **u,f.**

Craft, Donna & Peck, Terrance W. (Contribution by) **HD6504**
Profiles of American Labor Unions. Ed. 2. Stephen P. Yokich (Foreword by). Trade Cloth. Thomson Gale. Farmington Hills, MI. 1998. 1,650p. ISBN:0-8103-9059-0, ISBN13: 978-0-8103-9059-1. Dewey:331.88/025/73. LCCN:99-161894.
Audience: **g,l,u,f.** *Choice, 1999.*

Daniel, Clete **HD6515.T4D36 2001**
Culture of Misfortune: An Interpretive History of Textile Unionism in the United States. Book, Other. Cornell University Press. Ithaca, NY. 2001. 352p. Cornell Studies in Industrial and Labor Relations, Vol. 34 ISBN:0-8014-3853-5, ISBN13: 978-0-8014-3853-0. Dewey:331.88/177/00973. LCCN:00-011634.
Audience: **u,f.** *Choice, 2002.*

Devault, Ileen A. **HD6079.2.U5D48 2004**
United Apart: Gender and the Rise of Craft Unionism. Book, Other. Cornell University Press. Ithaca, NY. 2004. 240p. ISBN:0-8014-2768-1, ISBN13: 978-0-8014-2768-8. Dewey:331.4/7/0973. LCCN:2004-001134.
Audience: **u,f.** *Choice, 2005.*

Docherty, J. C. **HD4839.D58 2004**
Historical Dictionary of Organized Labor. Ed. 2. Trade Cloth. Scarecrow Press, Inc. Lanham, MD. 2004. 496p. Historical Dictionaries of Religions, Philosophies, and Movements Ser., No. 50 ISBN:0-8108-4911-9, ISBN13: 978-0-8108-4911-2. Dewey:331.88/03. LCCN:2003-021283.
Audience: **g,l,u,f.** *Choice, 2004.*

Dubofsky, Melvyn **HD8072.D848 1994**
The State and Labor in Modern America. Trade Paper. University of North Carolina Press. Chapel Hill, NC. 1994. 342p. ISBN:0-8078-4436-5, ISBN13: 978-0-8078-4436-6. Dewey:331/.0973. LCCN:93-021404.
Audience: **u,f.**

Fine, Sidney **HD5325.A82**
Sit-Down: The General Motors Strike of 1936-1937. Trade Cloth. University of Michigan Press. Chicago, IL. 1969. 472p. ISBN:0-472-32948-0, ISBN13: 978-0-472-32948-9. Dewey:331.881292. LCCN:73-083455.
Audience: **u,f.**

Foner, Philip S. **HD6508 .F57**
History of the Labor Movement: The TUEL, 1925-1929, Vol. 10. Trade Cloth. International Publishers Company, Inc. New York, NY. 1994. ISBN:0-7178-0690-1, ISBN13: 978-0-7178-0690-4. Dewey:331.88/0973.
Audience: **u,f.**

Foner, Philip S. **HD6508.F57 1975**
History of the Labor Movement in the United States: From the Founding of the American Federation of Labor to the Emergence of American Imperialism, Vol. 2. Trade Cloth. International Publishers Company, Inc. New York, NY. 1955. 480p. ISBN:0-7178-0092-X, ISBN13: 978-0-7178-0092-6. Dewey:331.88/0973. LCCN:47-019381.
Audience: **u,f.**

Foner, Philip S. **HD6508 .F57**
History of the Labor Movement in the United States: The AFL in the Progressive Era, 1910-1913. Trade Cloth. International Publishers Company, Inc. New York, NY. 1979. 300p. ISBN:0-7178-0570-0, ISBN13: 978-0-7178-0570-9. Dewey:331.88/0973. LCCN:47-019381.
Audience: **u,f.**

Foner, Philip S. **HD6508 .F57**
History of the Labor Movement in the United States: Postwar Struggles, 1918-1920, Vol. 8. Trade Cloth. International Publishers Company, Inc. New York, NY. 1988. ISBN:0-7178-0653-7, ISBN13: 978-0-7178-0653-9. Dewey:331.88/0973. LCCN:75-315606.
Audience: **u,f.**

Foner, Philip S. **HD6508 .F57**
History of the Labor Movement in the United States: From Colonial Times to the Founding of the American Federation of Labor, Vol. 1. Trade Cloth. International Publishers Company, Inc. New York, NY. 1947. 576p. ISBN:0-7178-0091-1, ISBN13: 978-0-7178-0091-9. Dewey:331.88/0973. LCCN:47-019381.
Audience: **u,f.**

Foner, Philip S. **HD6508 .F57**
A History of the Labor Movement in the United States: 1915-1916, on the Eve of America's Entrance into World War I, Vol. 6. Trade Cloth. International Publishers Company, Inc. New York, NY. 1982. 254p. ISBN:0-7178-0602-2, ISBN13: 978-0-7178-0602-7. Dewey:331.88/0973. LCCN:47-019381.
Audience: **u,f.**

Foner, Philip S. **HD6508 .F57**
History of the Labor Movement in the United States: The Policies and Practices of the AFL, 1900-1909, Vol. 3. Trade Cloth. International Publishers Company, Inc. New York, NY. 1964. 480p. ISBN:0-7178-0093-8, ISBN13: 978-0-7178-0093-3. Dewey:331.88/0973. LCCN:47-019381.
Audience: **u,f.**

Foner, Philip S. **HD6508 .F57**
History of the Labor Movement in the United States: 1914-1918, Vol. 7. Trade Cloth. International Publishers Company, Inc. New York, NY. 1987. 420p. ISBN:0-7178-0638-3, ISBN13: 978-0-7178-0638-6. Dewey:331.88/0973. LCCN:47-019381.
Audience: **u,f.**

Foner, Philip S. **HD6508 .F57**
History of the Labor Movement in the United States: The Industrial Workers of the World. Trade Paper. International Publishers Company, Inc. New York, NY. 1992. 608p. ISBN:0-7178-0396-1, ISBN13: 978-0-7178-0396-5. LCCN:47-019381.
Audience: **u,f.**

Foner, Philip S. **HD6508 .F57**
History of the Labor Movement in the United States: The TUEL to the End of the Gompers Era, Vol. 9. Trade Cloth. International Publishers Company, Inc. New York, NY. 1991. ISBN:0-7178-0673-1, ISBN13: 978-0-7178-0673-7. Dewey:331.88/0973. LCCN:47-019381.
Audience: **u,f.**

Forbath, William **HD6510.F67 1991**
Law and the Shaping of the American Labor Movement. Trade Paper. Harvard University Press. Cambridge, MA. 1991. 230p. ISBN:0-674-51782-2, ISBN13: 978-0-674-51782-0. Dewey:322/.2/0973. LCCN:90-049662.
Audience: **u,f.** *Choice, 1992.*

Fraser, Steven **HD8073.H5F73 1991**
Labor Will Rule: Sidney Hillman and the Rise of American Labor. Trade Cloth. Simon & Schuster. New York, NY. 1991. 600p. ISBN:0-02-910630-3, ISBN13: 978-0-02-910630-3. Dewey:331.88/187/092 B. LCCN:91-006528.
Audience: **u,f.**

Fraser, W. Hamish **HD6664.F757 1999**
A History of British Trade Unionism, 1700-1998. Cloth over Boards. Palgrave Macmillan. New York, NY. 1999. 301p. British Studies ISBN:0-312-21857-5, ISBN13: 978-0-312-21857-7. Dewey:331.8/8/0941. LCCN:98-029187.
Audience: **u,f.** *Choice, 1999.*

Freeman, Joshua Benjamin **HD6515.T7F74 2001**
In Transit: The Transport Workers Union in New York City, 1933-1966: With a New Epilogue. Paper Text. Temple University Press. Philadelphia, PA. 2001. 456p. Labor in Crisis Ser. ISBN:1-56639-922-X, ISBN13: 978-1-56639-922-7. Dewey:331.89/041388/097471. LCCN:2001-034718.
Audience: **u,f.**

Galenson, Walter **PR4650.F70**
The CIO Challenge to the AFL: A History of the American Labor Movement. Trade Cloth. Harvard University Press. Cambridge, MA. 1992. Wertheim Publications in Industrial Relations Ser. ISBN:0-674-13150-9, ISBN13: 978-0-674-13150-7. Dewey:823/.8.
Audience: **u,f.** B

Galenson, Walter **HD6515.C2U5**
The United Brotherhood of Carpenters: The First Hundred Years. Trade Cloth. Harvard University Press. Cambridge, MA. 1983. 454p. Wertheim Publications in Industrial Relations ISBN:0-674-92196-8, ISBN13: 978-0-674-92196-2. Dewey:331.88/19/0973. LCCN:82-023402.
Audience: **g,l,u,f.** B

Gorn, Elliott J. **HD8073.J6G67 2001**
Mother Jones: An American Life. Trade Paper. Farrar, Straus & Giroux. New York, NY. 2001. xiii, 408p. ISBN:0-8090-7093-6, ISBN13: 978-0-8090-7093-0. Dewey:331.88/092 B. LCCN:00-044997.
Audience: **g,l,u,f.** *Choice, 2001.*

Gould, William B. IV **KF3369.G68 2004**
A Primer on American Labor Law. Ed. 4. Cloth Text. MIT Press. Cambridge, MA. 2004. 432p. ISBN:0-262-07250-5, ISBN13: 978-0-262-07250-2. Dewey:347.3041. LCCN:2003-070610.
Audience: **g,l,u,f.**

Green, Harvey **HD5325.P152**
On Strike at Hormel: The Struggle for a Democratic Labor Movement. Trade Cloth. Temple University Press. Philadelphia, PA. 1990. 336p. Labor and Social Change Ser. ISBN:0-87722-635-0, ISBN13: 978-0-87722-635-2. Dewey:331.89/28649/0097761. LCCN:89-004991.
Audience: **u,f.**

Greene, Julie **HD8055.A5 G784 1998**
Pure and Simple Politics: The American Federation of Labor and Political Activism, 1881-1917. Cloth Text. Cambridge University Press. New York, NY. 1998. 306p. ISBN:0-521-43398-3, ISBN13: 978-0-521-43398-3. Dewey:331.88320973. LCCN:97-025547.
Audience: **u,f.**

Griswold del Castillo, Richard & Garcia, Richard A. **HD6509.C48G75 1995**
Cesar Chávez: A Triumph of Spirit. Trade Cloth. University of Oklahoma Press. Norman, OK. 1995. 224p. Oklahoma Western Biographies Ser., Vol. 11 ISBN:0-8061-2758-9, ISBN13: 978-0-8061-2758-3. Dewey:331.88. LCCN:95-015230.
Audience: **g,l,u.** *Choice, 1996.*

Halpern, Martin **HD6515.A82I574 1988**
UAW Politics in the Cold War Era. Cloth Text. State University of New York Press. Albany, NY. 1988. 361p. SUNY Series in American Labor History ISBN:0-88706-671-2, ISBN13: 978-0-88706-671-9. Dewey:322/.2/0973. LCCN:87-013890.
Audience: **u,f.** *Choice, 1989.*

Hinshaw, John **HD8039.I52U545 2002**
Steel and Steelworkers: Race and Class Struggle in Twentieth-Century Pittsburgh. Cloth Text. State University of New York Press. Albany, NY. 2002. 320p. SUNY Series in American Labor History ISBN:0-7914-5225-5, ISBN13: 978-0-7914-5225-7. Dewey:305.9/672/0974886. LCCN:2001-034868.
Audience: **u,f.** *Choice, 2002.*

Hogler, Raymond L. **KF3369.H643 2004**
Employment Relations in the United States: Law, Policy, and Practice. Cloth Text. SAGE Publications, Inc. Thousand Oaks, CA. 2003. 312p. ISBN:1-4129-0414-5, ISBN13: 978-1-4129-0414-8. Dewey:344.7301. LCCN:2003-021149.
Audience: **g,l,u,f.** *Choice, 2004.*

Hyman, Richard **HD6657.H95 2001**
Understanding European Trade Unionism: Between Market, Class and Society. Paper Text. SAGE Publications, Ltd. London, 2001. 208p. Economics Ser. ISBN:0-7619-5221-7, ISBN13: 978-0-7619-5221-3. Dewey:331.88/094. LCCN:2001-269919.
Audience: **u,f.**

Jones, Mary **HD8073.J6A3**
Autobiography of Mother Jones. Perfect. Great Falls Publishing Company. Sykesville, MD. 2003. 140p. ISBN:0-9725431-1-2, ISBN13: 978-0-9725431-1-8. Dewey:331.88/092 B.
Audience: **u,f.**

Juravich, Tom & Bronfenbrenner, Kate **HD5325.A492**
Ravenswood: The Steelworkers' Victory and the Revival of American Labor. Book, Other. Cornell University Press. Ithaca, NY. 1999. 296p. ISBN:0-8014-3633-8, ISBN13: 978-0-8014-3633-8. Dewey:331.892/869142. LCCN:99-017965.
Audience: **u,f.** *Choice, 2000.*

Kawanishi, Hirosuke **HD6490.C612J35 1991**
Enterprise Unionism in Japan. Ross E. Mouer (Translator). Trade Cloth. Kegan Paul International, Ltd. London, 1992. 300p. ISBN:0-7103-0341-6, ISBN13: 978-0-7103-0341-7. Dewey:331.88/34/0952. LCCN:90-005050.
Audience: **u,f.** *Choice, 1993.*

Kenny, Kevin **HV6452.P4M64 1998**
Making Sense of the Molly Maguires. Cloth Text. Oxford University Press, Inc. New York, NY. 1998. 336p. ISBN:0-19-510664-4, ISBN13: 978-0-19-510664-0. Dewey:305.8/9162/073. LCCN:96-053599.
Audience: **u,f.** *Choice, 1998.*

Kimeldorf, Howard **HD6508 .K485 1999**
Battling for American Labor: Wobblies, Craft Workers, and the Making of the Union Movement. Trade Paper. University of California Press. Berkeley, CA. 1999. 256p. ISBN:0-520-21833-7, ISBN13: 978-0-520-21833-8. Dewey:331.88/0973. LCCN:99-018366.
Audience: **u,f.** *Choice, 2000.*

Kubicek, Paul J. **HD6660.7.K8 2004**
Organized Labor in Postcommunist States: From Solidarity to Infirmity. Trade Paper. University of Pittsburgh Press. Pittsburgh, PA. 2004. 288p. Pitt Series in Russian and East European Studies ISBN:0-8229-5856-2, ISBN13: 978-0-8229-5856-7. Dewey:331.88/0947. LCCN:2004-013596.
Audience: **u,f.**

Lambert, Josiah Bartlett **HD8072.5.L357 2005**
If the Workers Took a Notion: The Right to Strike and American Political Development. Trade Paper, Perfect. Cornell University Press. Ithaca, NY. 2005. 259p. ISBN:0-8014-8945-8, ISBN13: 978-0-8014-8945-7. Dewey:331.8/0973. LCCN:2005-008839.
Audience: **u,f.** *Choice, 2006.*

Laslett, John M. (Editor) **HD6515.M616U5584**
The United Mine Workers of America: A Model of Industrial Solidarity? Trade Cloth. Pennsylvania State University Press. University Park, PA. 1996. 1016p. ISBN:0-271-01537-3, ISBN13: 978-0-271-01537-8. Dewey:331.88/122334/0973. LCCN:95-039732.
Audience: **u,f.** *Choice, 1997.*

Laybourn, Keith **HD5365.A6 L39 1993**
The General Strike of 1926. Cloth Text. Manchester University Press. Manchester, 1993. x, 161p. New Frontiers in History Ser. ISBN:0-7190-3865-0, ISBN13: 978-0-7190-3865-5. Dewey:331.89250941. LCCN:93-028180.
Audience: **u,f.**

Levenstein, Harvey A. **HX544 .L45**
Communism, Anticommunism, and the CIO, 91. Trade Cloth. Greenwood Publishing Group, Inc. Portsmouth, NH. 1981. 364p. Contributions in American History Ser., No. 91 ISBN:0-313-22072-7, ISBN13: 978-0-313-22072-2. Dewey:335.43/0973. LCCN:80-000787.
Audience: **u,f.**

Lichtenstein, Nelson **HD8055.C75L5 2003**
Labor's War at Home: The CIO in World War II. Library Binding. Temple University Press. Philadelphia, PA. 2003. 344p. Labor in Crisis Ser. ISBN:1-59213-196-4, ISBN13: 978-1-59213-196-9. Dewey:331.88/33/097309044. LCCN:2002-041625.
Audience: **u,f.** B

Lichtenstein, Nelson **HD8066.L53 2003**
State of the Union: A Century of American Labor. Trade Paper. Princeton University Press. Princeton, NJ. 2003. 352p. Politics and Society in Twentieth Century America Ser. ISBN:0-691-11654-7, ISBN13: 978-0-691-11654-9. Dewey:331/.0973/0904.
Audience: **g,l,u,f.** *Choice, 2002.*

Lichtenstein, Nelson **HD6509.R4L53 1997**
Walter Reuther: The Most Dangerous Man in Detroit. Trade Paper. University of Illinois Press. Champaign, IL. 1997. 608p. ISBN:0-252-06626-X, ISBN13: 978-0-252-06626-9. Dewey:[B]. LCCN:96-033058.
Audience: **u,f.**

Lindsey, Almont **HD5325 .R12**
The Pullman Strike: The Story of a Unique Experiment and of a Great Labor Upheaval. Trade Paper. University of Chicago Press. Chicago, IL. 1994. 393p. ISBN:0-226-48383-5, ISBN13: 978-0-226-48383-2. Dewey:331.892/8523/0977311. LCCN:64-032413.
Audience: **l,u,f.** B

Livesay, Harold C. **HD6509.G6**
Samuel Gompers and Organized Labor in America. Paper Text. Waveland Press, Inc. Prospect Heights, IL. 1993. 195p. ISBN:0-88133-751-X, ISBN13: 978-0-88133-751-8. Dewey:331.88.
Audience: **l,u,f.**

Lynd, Staughton & Lynd, Alice (Editors) **HD6490.O72U654 2000**
The New Rank and File. Book, Other. Cornell University Press. Ithaca, NY. 2000. 288p. ILR Press Bk, ISBN:0-8014-3806-3, ISBN13: 978-0-8014-3806-6. Dewey:331.88/0973. LCCN:00-009146.
Audience: **g,l,u,f.**

MacShane, Denis **HD6735.7**
Solidarity: Poland's Independent Trade Union. Trade Cloth. Spokesman Books. Nottingham, 1982. 172p. ISBN:0-85124-319-3, ISBN13: 978-0-85124-319-1. Dewey:331.88/09438. LCCN:81-016515.
Audience: **u,f.**

Markowitz, Linda **HD6490.O72U6495 2000**
Worker Activism after Successful Union Organizing. Trade Cloth. M. E. Sharpe Inc. Armonk, NY. 1999. 204p. ISBN:0-7656-0492-2, ISBN13: 978-0-7656-0492-7. Dewey:331.87/0973. LCCN:99-023904.
Audience: **u,f.**

Martin, Christopher **P96.T72U66 2004**
Framed! Labor and the Corporate Media. Book, Other. Cornell University Press. Ithaca, NY. 2004. 272p. ISBN:0-8014-4198-6, ISBN13: 978-0-8014-4198-1. Dewey:331.88/0973. LCCN:2003-012870.
Audience: **u,f.** *Choice, 2004.*

Minchin, Timothy J. **HD8083.S9M56 2004**
Fighting Against the Odds: A History of Southern Labor since World War II. Trade Cloth. University Press of Florida. Gainesville, FL. 2005. 240p. New Perspectives on the History of the South Ser. ISBN:0-8130-2790-X, ISBN13: 978-0-8130-2790-6. Dewey:331.88/0975/09045. LCCN:2004-054194.
Audience: **l,u,f.** *Choice, 2005.*

Mort, Jo-Ann (Editor) **HD8055.A5N67 1999**
Not Your Father's Union Movement: Inside the AFL-CIO. Trade Paper. Analytical Psychology Club of San Francisco, Inc. San

Francisco, CA. 1998. xii, 237p. ISBN:1-85984-286-0, ISBN13: 978-1-85984-286-7. Dewey:331.88/0973. LCCN:00-267160.
Audience: **g,l,u,f.**

Murillo, Maria Victoria **HD6653.5 .M87 2001**
Labor Unions, Partisan Coalitions, and Market Reforms in Latin America. Robert H. Bates, Ellen Comisso, Peter Hall, Peter Lange, Joel Samuel Migdal & Helen V. Milner (Contribution by). Trade Paper. Cambridge University Press. New York, NY. 2001. 270p. Studies in Comparative Politics ISBN:0-521-78555-3, ISBN13: 978-0-521-78555-6. Dewey:322.2098. LCCN:00-048631.
Audience: **u,f.** *Choice, 2002.*

Nelson, Bruce **HD6515.S4**
Workers on the Waterfront: Seamen, Longshoremen, and Unionism in the 1930s. Trade Paper. University of Illinois Press. Champaign, IL. 1990. 384p. The Working Class in American History Ser. ISBN:0-252-06144-6, ISBN13: 978-0-252-06144-8. Dewey:331.88/113875/0973. LCCN:87-028749.
Audience: **u,f.** *Choice, 1989.*

Nelson, Daniel **HD8066.N37 1997**
Shifting Fortunes: The Rise and Decline of American Labor, from the 1820s to the Present. Trade Paper. Ivan R. Dee Publisher. Blue Ridge Summit, PA. 1998. 192p. American Ways Ser. ISBN:1-56663-180-7, ISBN13: 978-1-56663-180-8. Dewey:331/.0973. LCCN:97-022108.
Audience: **l,u,f.** *Choice, 1998.*

Ness, Immanuel **HD8085.N53N47 2005**
Immigrants, Unions, and the New U. S. Labor Market. Trade Paper, Perfect. Temple University Press. Philadelphia, PA. 2005. 240p. ISBN:1-59213-041-0, ISBN13: 978-1-59213-041-2. Dewey:331.6/2/097471. LCCN:2004-062559.
Audience: **u,f.** *Choice, 2006.*

Ng, Sek H. & Warner, Malcolm **HD6837.N4 1998**
China's Trade Unions and Management. Cloth over Boards. Palgrave Macmillan. New York, NY. 1998. 219p. Studies on the Chinese Economy ISBN:0-312-21029-9, ISBN13: 978-0-312-21029-8. Dewey:331.88/0951. LCCN:97-027116.
Audience: **u,f.**

Nicholson, Philip Yale **HD8066.N53 2004**
Labor's Story in the United States. Trade Cloth. Temple University Press. Philadelphia, PA. 2004. 376p. Labor in Crisis Ser. ISBN:1-59213-020-8, ISBN13: 978-1-59213-020-7. Dewey:331/.0973/0904. LCCN:2003-066317.
Audience: **g,l,u,f.** *Choice, 2004.*

Nissen, Bruce (Editor) **HD6508**
Unions and Workplace Reorganization. Trade Paper. Wayne State University Press. Detroit, MI. 1999. 224p. ISBN:0-8143-2885-7, ISBN13: 978-0-8143-2885-9. Dewey:331.88/0973. LCCN:97-015001.
Audience: **u,f.** *Choice, 1998.*

Nordlund, Willis J. **HD5325**
Silent Skies: The Air Traffic Controllers' Strike. Trade Cloth. Greenwood Publishing Group, Inc. Portsmouth, NH. 1998. 224p. ISBN:0-275-96188-5, ISBN13: 978-0-275-96188-6. Dewey:331.892/81387740426/. LCCN:97-038545.
Audience: **g,l,u,f.**

Parmet, Robert D. **HD6509.D8P37 2005**
The Master of Seventh Avenue: David Dubinsky and American Labor Movement. Trade Cloth. New York University Press. New York, NY. 2005. 456p. ISBN:0-8147-6711-7, ISBN13: 978-0-8147-6711-5. Dewey:331.88/187/092 B. LCCN:2004-029212.
Audience: **u,f.** *Choice, 2005.*

Peterson, Florence **HD8051.A5 NO.651**
Strikes in the United States, 1880-1936. Trade Cloth. Scholarly Press, Inc. Saint Clair Shores, MI. 1972. 190p. ISBN:0-403-01148-5, ISBN13: 978-0-403-01148-3. Dewey:331.89/29/73. LCCN:70-145232.
Audience: **u,f.**

Phelan, Craig **HD8055**
Grand Master Workman: Terence Powderly and the Knights of Labor. Trade Cloth. Greenwood Publishing Group, Inc. Portsmouth, NH. 2000. 304p. Contributions in Labor Studies ISBN:0-313-30948-5, ISBN13: 978-0-313-30948-9. Dewey:331.88/092 B. LCCN:99-016145.
Audience: **u,f.**

Puddington, Arch **HD6509.K57K57 2005**
Lane Kirkland: Champion of American Labor. Trade Cloth. John Wiley & Sons, Inc. Hoboken, NJ. 2005. 352p. ISBN:0-471-41694-0, ISBN13: 978-0-471-41694-4. Dewey:331.88/092 B. LCCN:2004-008489.
Audience: **l,u,f.**

Reid, Alastair J. **HD6664**
United We Stand: A History of Britain's Trade Unions. Trade Cloth. Penguin Books, Ltd. London, 2004. 496p. ISBN:0-7139-9758-3, ISBN13: 978-0-7139-9758-3. Dewey:331.88/0941. LCCN:2005-360940.
Audience: **g,l,u,f.**

Richards, Andrew J. **HD6668.M6152N357**
Miners on Strike: Class Solidarity and Division in Britain. Cloth over Boards. Berg Publishers. Oxford, 1997. 256p. ISBN:1-85973-172-4, ISBN13: 978-1-85973-172-7. Dewey:331.8/928/22/334. LCCN:96-034875.
Audience: **u,f.**

Robinson, Archie **HD6509.M4 R6 1981**
George Meany and His Times. Trade Cloth. Simon & Schuster. New York, NY. 1982. ISBN:0-671-42163-8, ISBN13: 978-0-671-42163-2. Dewey:331.88/33/0924. LCCN:81-013616.
Audience: **u,f.**

Rosen, Ellen Doree **HD6509.D67R67 2004**
A Wobbly Life: IWW Organizer E. F. Doree. Trade Cloth. Wayne State University Press. Detroit, MI. 2004. 256p. ISBN:0-8143-3202-1, ISBN13: 978-0-8143-3202-3. Dewey:331.88/6/092 B. LCCN:2004-000533.
Audience: **u,f.**

Rosenblum, Jonathan D. **HD5325.M73 1983**
Copper Crucible: How the Arizona Miners' Strike of 1983 Recast Labor-Management Relations. Ed. 2. Trade Paper. Cornell University Press. Ithaca, NY. 1998. 280p. ISBN:0-8014-8554-1, ISBN13: 978-0-8014-8554-1. Dewey:331.89/28223431/0979. LCCN:98-011699.
Audience: **u,f.**

Ross, Fred **HD6509.C48**
Conquering Goliath: Cesar Chávez at the Beginning. Trade Paper. Wayne State University Press. Detroit, MI. 1992.

ISBN:0-8143-2418-5, ISBN13: 978-0-8143-2418-9. Dewey:331.88/13/092 B.
Audience: **g,l,u,f.**

Russell, Thaddeus **HD6509.H6R87 2003**
Out of the Jungle: Jimmy Hoffa and the Remaking of the American Working Class. Trade Paper. Temple University Press. Philadelphia, PA. 2003. 296p. Labor in Crisis Ser. ISBN:1-59213-027-5, ISBN13: 978-1-59213-027-6. Dewey:331.88/11388324/092. LCCN:2002-043556.
Audience: **g,l,u,f.** *Choice, 2002.*

Schain, Martin A. (Editor), et al. **HD6684.C45 1998**
A Century of Organized Labor in France: A Union Movement for the Twenty-First Century? Mark Kesselman & Herrich Chapman (Editors). Cloth over Boards. Palgrave Macmillan. New York, NY. 1998. 274p. Century of Organized Labor in France Ser., Vol. 1 ISBN:0-312-16497-1, ISBN13: 978-0-312-16497-3. Dewey:331.88/0944. LCCN:97-050524.
Audience: **u,f.** *Choice, 1999.*

Schlager, Neil (Editor) **HD4839.S74 2003**
St. James Encyclopedia of Labor History Worldwide: Major Events in Labor History and Their Impact, Set. Trade Cloth. Thomson Gale. Farmington Hills, MI. 2003. 1200p. ISBN:0-7876-5730-1, ISBN13: 978-0-7876-5730-7. Dewey:331.8/03. LCCN:2003-000294.
Audience: **g,l,u,f.**

Shogan, Robert **HD5325.M615S49 2004**
The Battle of Blair Mountain: The Story of America's Largest Labor Uprising. Trade Cloth. Westview Press. Boulder, CO. 2004. 288p. ISBN:0-8133-4096-9, ISBN13: 978-0-8133-4096-8. Dewey:331.892/822334. LCCN:2004-001648.
Audience: **l,u,f.**

Silver, Beverly J. **HD4851.S55 2003**
Forces of Labor: Workers' Movements and Globalization Since 1870. Robert H. Bates, Ellen Comisso, Peter Hall, Peter Lange, Joel Migdal & Helen Milner (Contribution by). Trade Cloth. Cambridge University Press. New York, NY. 2003. 256p. Cambridge Studies in Comparative Politics Ser. ISBN:0-521-81751-X, ISBN13: 978-0-521-81751-6. Dewey:331.1/1/0904. LCCN:2002-031361.
Audience: **u,f.** *Choice, 2003.*

Sloane, Arthur A. **HD6509.H6S56 1991**
Hoffa. Trade Cloth. MIT Press. Cambridge, MA. 1991. 430p. ISBN:0-262-19309-4, ISBN13: 978-0-262-19309-2. Dewey:331.88/11388324/092. LCCN:90-026137.
Audience: **u,f.** *Choice, 1992.*

Smith, Robert Michael **HD5324.S64 2003**
From Blackjacks to Briefcases: A History of Commercialized Strikebreaking and Unionbusting in the United States. Scott Molloy (Contribution by). Trade Cloth. Ohio University Press. Athens, OH. 2003. 192p. ISBN:0-8214-1465-8, ISBN13: 978-0-8214-1465-1. Dewey:331.89/4. LCCN:2002-030809.
Audience: **u,f.** *Choice, 2003.*

Stefancic, David R. **HD8537.N783 S73 1992**
Robotnik: A Short History of the Struggle for Worker Self Management and Free Trade Unions in Poland, 1944-1981. Trade Cloth. Eastern European Monographs. Bradenton, FL. 1992. 109p. ISBN:0-88033-235-2, ISBN13: 978-0-88033-235-4. Dewey:331.809438. LCCN:91-078353.
Audience: **u,f.**

Stolberg, Benjamin **HD8055.C75 S7 1971**
Story of the CIO. Trade Cloth. Ayer Company Publishers, Inc. Manchester, NH. 1974. American Labor Ser., No. 2 ISBN:0-405-02944-6, ISBN13: 978-0-405-02944-8. Dewey:331.88/33/0973. LCCN:77-156426.
Audience: **u,f.**

Taylor, Andrew **HD6668.M6152N3578**
The NUM and British Politics. Trade Cloth. Ashgate Publishing, Ltd. Aldershot, 2003. 282p. ISBN:0-7546-0690-2, ISBN13: 978-0-7546-0690-1. Dewey:331.88/122334. LCCN:2003-045236.
Audience: **u,f.**

Taylor, Andrew **HD8039.M62.G7**
The NUM and British Politics, Vol. 2. Trade Cloth. Ashgate Publishing, Ltd. Aldershot, 2005. 372p. Studies in Labour History Ser. ISBN:0-7546-5333-1, ISBN13: 978-0-7546-5333-2. Dewey:331.88/122334. LCCN:2003-045236.
Audience: **u,f.**

Thorne, Florence C. **HD8073.G6 T5 1969**
Samuel Gompers, American Statesman. Library Binding. Greenwood Publishing Group, Inc. Portsmouth, NH. 1969. 175p. ISBN:0-8371-2293-7, ISBN13: 978-0-8371-2293-9. Dewey:57-2741. LCCN:70-090710.
Audience: **u,f.**

Tillman, Ray M. & Cummings, Michael S. (Editors) **HD6508.T72 1999**
The Transformation of U. S. Unions: Voices, Visions, and Strategies from the Grassroots. Library Binding. Lynne Rienner Publishers, Inc. Boulder, CO. 1999. 250p. ISBN:1-55587-812-1, ISBN13: 978-1-55587-812-2. Dewey:331.88/0973. LCCN:98-045923.
Audience: **u,f.** *Choice, 2000.*

Turner, Lowell (Editor), et al. **HD6508.T87 2001**
Rekindling the Movement: Labor's Quest for Relevance in the 21st Century. Harry C. Katz, Richard W. Hurd & New York State School of Industrial and Labor Relations Staff (Editors). Trade Paper. Cornell University Press. Ithaca, NY. 2001. 416p. Frank W. Pierce Memorial Lectureship and Conference Ser., Vol. 11 ISBN:0-8014-8712-9, ISBN13: 978-0-8014-8712-5. Dewey:331.88/0973. LCCN:00-011823.
Audience: **l,u,f.** *Choice, 2002.*

Von Drehle, David **F128.5.V688 2003**
Triangle: The Fire That Changed America. Trade Paper. Grove/Atlantic, Inc. New York, NY. 2004. 352p. ISBN:0-8021-4151-X, ISBN13: 978-0-8021-4151-4. Dewey:974.7/1041. LCCN:2003-041835.
Audience: **g,l,u,f.**

Walesa, Lech **DK4452.W34A3 1987**
A Way of Hope: An Autobiography. Trade Cloth. Henry Holt & Company. New York, NY. 1987. ISBN:0-8050-0668-0, ISBN13: 978-0-8050-0668-1. Dewey:322/.2/0924 B. LCCN:87-021194.
Audience: **u,f.**

Walesa, Lech **DK4452.W34A3 1992**
The Struggle and the Triumph: An Autobiography. Franklin Philip (Translator), Helen Mahut (Contribution by). Trade Cloth. Arcade Publishing, Inc. New York, NY. 1992. 330p. ISBN:1-55970-149-8, ISBN13: 978-1-55970-149-5. Dewey:943.805/6/092. LCCN:91-035875.
Audience: **u,f.**

Weir, Robert E. **HD8055.K7W45 1996**
Beyond Labor's Veil: The Culture of the Knights of Labor. Cloth Text. Pennsylvania State University Press. University Park, PA. 1996. 770p. ISBN:0-271-01498-9, ISBN13: 978-0-271-01498-2. Dewey:331.88/33/097. LCCN:95-013166.
Audience: **u,f.** *Choice, 1996.*

Weir, Robert E. **HD8055.K7W46 2000**
Knights Unhorsed: Internal Conflict in a Gilded Age Social Movement. Trade Cloth. Wayne State University Press. Detroit, MI. 2001. 288p. ISBN:0-8143-2873-3, ISBN13: 978-0-8143-2873-6. Dewey:331.88/33/0973. LCCN:00-009733.
Audience: **u,f.**

Wheeler, Hoyt N. **HD8072.5.W485 2002**
The Future of the American Labor Movement. Trade Paper. Cambridge University Press. New York, NY. 2002. 278p. ISBN:0-521-89354-2, ISBN13: 978-0-521-89354-1. Dewey:331.88/0973. LCCN:2002-073770.
Audience: **u,f.** *Choice, 2003.*

Winslow, Calvin **HD8039.L82U733 1998**
Waterfront Workers: New Perspectives on Race and Class. Trade Paper. University of Illinois Press. Champaign, IL. 1998. 216p. The Working Class in American History Ser. ISBN:0-252-06691-X, ISBN13: 978-0-252-06691-7. Dewey:331.88/11387544/0973. LCCN:97-033754.
Audience: **u,f.** *Choice, 1999.*

Witwer, David **HD6515.T22I589 2003**
Corruption and Reform in the Teamsters Union. Trade Cloth. University of Illinois Press. Champaign, IL. 2003. 312p. Working Class in American History Ser. ISBN:0-252-02825-2, ISBN13: 978-0-252-02825-0. Dewey:331.88/11388324/0973. LCCN:2002-013118.
Audience: **u,f.** *Choice, 2003.*

Zieger, Robert H. **HD8055.C75Z54 1995**
The CIO, 1935-1955. Trade Cloth. University of North Carolina Press. Chapel Hill, NC. 1995. 520p. ISBN:0-8078-2182-9, ISBN13: 978-0-8078-2182-4. Dewey:331.88/33/09730904. LCCN:94-017949.
Audience: **u,f.** *Choice, 1995.*

Management Function > Human Resource Management > Employee Problems

Bingham, Clara & Gansler, Laura Leedy **KF228.J464**
Class Action: The Landmark Case That Changed Sexual Harassment Law. UK-Trade Paper. Knopf Publishing Group. New York, NY. 2003. 400p. ISBN:0-385-49613-3, ISBN13: 978-0-385-49613-1.
Audience: **g,l,u,f.**

Boland, Mary L. **KF3467.B65 2005**
Sexual Harassment in Workplace. Trade Paper. Sourcebooks, Inc. Naperville, IL. 2005. 304p. ISBN:1-57248-527-2, ISBN13: 978-1-57248-527-3. Dewey:344.7301/133. LCCN:2005-027970.
Audience: **g,l,u,f.**

Cava, Roberta **BF637.C45C38 2004**
Dealing with Difficult People: How to Deal with Nasty Customers, Demanding Bosses and Annoying Co-Workers. Trade Paper. Firefly Books, Ltd. Tonawanda, NY. 2006. 224p. ISBN:1-55297-927-X, ISBN13: 978-1-55297-927-3. Dewey:158.2/6. LCCN:2004-300649.
Audience: **g,l,u.**

Dilts, David A., et al. **HD5115**
Getting Absent Workers Back on the Job: An Analytical Approach. Clarence R. Deitsch & Robert J. Paul (Authors). Trade Cloth. Greenwood Publishing Group, Inc. Portsmouth, NH. 1985. 164p. ISBN:0-89930-025-1, ISBN13: 978-0-89930-025-2. Dewey:658.3/14. LCCN:85-003540.
Audience: **u,f.** *Choice, 1986.*

Fearing, James **HF5549.5.D7F43 2000**
Workplace Intervention: The Bottom Line on Helping Addicted Employees Become Productive Again. Trade Paper. Hazelden Publishing & Educational Services. Center City, MN. 2000. 232p. ISBN:1-56838-520-X, ISBN13: 978-1-56838-520-4. Dewey:658.3/822. LCCN:00-044999.
Audience: **u,f.**

Furnham, Adrian & Taylor, John **HF5549.5.E42F87 2004**
The Dark Side of Behaviour at Work: Understanding and Avoiding Employees Leaving, Thieving and Deceiving. Cloth over Boards. Palgrave Macmillan. New York, NY. 2004. 300p. ISBN:1-4039-3577-7, ISBN13: 978-1-4039-3577-9. Dewey:658.3/045. LCCN:2004-041584.
Audience: **u,f.** *Choice, 2005.*

Geffner, Robert (Editor), et al. **HF5549.5.E43A33 2004**
Aggression in Organizations: Violence, Abuse, and Harassment at Work and in Schools. Mark Braverman, Joseph Galasso & Janessa Marsh (Editors). Trade Cloth. Haworth Press, Incorporated, The. Binghamton, NY. 2005. xxii, 246p. ISBN:0-7890-2841-7, ISBN13: 978-0-7890-2841-9. Dewey:658.4/73. LCCN:2004-027873.
Audience: **u,f.**

Ghodse, Hamid **HF5549.5.D7A33 2004**
Addiction at Work: Tackling Drug Use and Misuse in the Workplace. Trade Cloth. Ashgate Publishing, Ltd. Aldershot, 2005. 278p. Personnel Today/Management Resources Ser. ISBN:0-566-08619-0, ISBN13: 978-0-566-08619-9. Dewey:658.3/822. LCCN:2004-023996.
Audience: **u,f.**

Giacalone, Robert A. & Greenberg, Jerald (Editors) **HF5549.5.E43A58 1996**
Antisocial Behavior in Organizations. Trade Paper. SAGE Publications, Inc. Thousand Oaks, CA. 1996. 213p. ISBN:0-8039-7236-9, ISBN13: 978-0-8039-7236-0. Dewey:158.7. LCCN:96-025241.
Audience: **u,f.**

Harvard Business School Staff (Contribution by) **HF5549.5.E42M35 2004**
When Good People Behave Badly. Trade Paper. Harvard Business School Press. Boston, MA. 2004. 208p. Harvard Business Review Management Dilemas Ser. ISBN:1-59139-504-6, ISBN13: 978-1-59139-504-1. Dewey:658.3/045. LCCN:2004-000445.
Audience: **g,l,u.**

Kelloway, E. Kevin (Editor), et al. **HF5549.5.E43H36 2006**
Handbook of Workplace Violence. Julian Barling & Joseph J. Hurrell Jr. (Editors). Trade Cloth. SAGE Publications, Inc.

Thousand Oaks, CA. 2006. 704p. ISBN:0-7619-3062-0, ISBN13: 978-0-7619-3062-4. Dewey:363.32. LCCN:2005-023062.
Audience: **u,f.**

Kidwell, Roland E. Jr. & Martin, Christopher L (Editors) **HD58.7.M363 2005**
Managing Organizational Deviance. Paper Text. SAGE Publications, Inc. Thousand Oaks, CA. 2004. 376p. ISBN:0-7619-3014-0, ISBN13: 978-0-7619-3014-3. Dewey:658.3/14. LCCN:2004-018460.
Audience: **l,u,f.**

Manzoni, Jean-Francois & Barsoux, Jean-Louis **HF5549.12.M364 2002**
The Set-up-to-Fail Syndrome: How Good Managers Cause Great People to Fail. Trade Cloth. Harvard Business School Press. Boston, MA. 2002. 304p. ISBN:0-87584-949-0, ISBN13: 978-0-87584-949-2. Dewey:658.3/15. LCCN:2002-002904.
Audience: **g,l,u,f.**

Segrave, Kerry **HD6060.3.S43 1994**
The Sexual Harassment of Women in the Workplace, 1600-1993. Library Binding. McFarland & Company, Incorporated Publishers. Jefferson, NC. 1994. 279p. ISBN:0-7864-0007-2, ISBN13: 978-0-7864-0007-2. Dewey:331.4/133/09. LCCN:94-002803.
Audience: **u,f.**

Tunnell, Kenneth D. **HF5549.5.D7T86 2004**
Pissing on Demand: Workplace Drug Testing and the Rise of the Detox Industry. Trade Paper. New York University Press. New York, NY. 2004. 186p. Alternative Criminology Ser. ISBN:0-8147-8281-7, ISBN13: 978-0-8147-8281-1. Dewey:331.25/98. LCCN:2003-020502.
Audience: **g,l,u,f.** *Choice, 2004.*

Management Function > Human Resource Management > Employee Rights

Fersh, Don & Thomas, Peter **KF3469**
Complying with the Americans with Disabilities Act: A Guidebook for Management and People with Disabilities. Robert Kerrey (Foreword by). Trade Cloth. Greenwood Publishing Group, Inc. Portsmouth, NH. 1993. 280p. ISBN:0-89930-714-0, ISBN13: 978-0-89930-714-5. Dewey:344.73/01133. LCCN:92-028478.
Audience: **g,l,u,f.**

Greenspan, Amy L. **KF3455.Z9**
Employer's Guide to Workplace Privacy. Ed. 5. Ringbound. Aspen Publishers, Inc. New York, NY. 2005. 478p. ISBN:0-7355-5409-9, ISBN13: 978-0-7355-5409-2. Dewey:344.7301/2596.
Audience: **g,l,u,f.**

Gross, James A. (Editor) **HD6490.O72U69 2003**
Workers' Rights As Human Rights. Trade Cloth. Cornell University Press. Ithaca, NY. 2003. 272p. ISBN:0-8014-4082-3, ISBN13: 978-0-8014-4082-3. Dewey:331/.01/1. LCCN:2002-156374.
Audience: **u,f.** *Choice, 2004.*

Gutman, Arthur **KF3464**
EEO Law and Personnel Practices. Trade Cloth. SAGE Publications, Inc. Thousand Oaks, CA. 1993. 403p. ISBN:0-8039-5221-X, ISBN13: 978-0-8039-5221-8. Dewey:344.7301/133. LCCN:93-021828.
Audience: **u,f.**

Hunt, James W. & Strongin, Patricia K. **KF3319.H83 1994**
The Law of the Workplace: Rights of Employers and Employees. Ed. 3. Trade Cloth. B N A Books. Edison, NJ. 1994. 318p. Employers' Guides ISBN:0-87179-841-7, ISBN13: 978-0-87179-841-1. Dewey:344.73/01. LCCN:93-038145.
Audience: **g,u,f.**

Jenkins, Rhys Owen (Editor), et al. **HD60.C639 2002**
Corporate Responsibility and Labour Rights: Codes of Conduct in the Global Economy. Ruth Pearson & Gill Seyfang (Editors). Trade Cloth. Earthscan/James & James. London, 2002. 256p. ISBN:1-85383-930-2, ISBN13: 978-1-85383-930-6. Dewey:331.25/98. LCCN:2002-011681.
Audience: **u,f.** *Choice, 2003.*

Kohn, Stephen M., et al. **KF3471.K644 2004**
ⓔ Whistleblower Law: A Guide to Legal Protections for Corporate Employees. Michael D. Kohn & David K. Colapinto (Authors). E-Book. Greenwood Publishing Group, Inc. Portsmouth, NH. 2004. ISBN:0-313-05207-7, ISBN13: 978-0-313-05207-1. Dewey:344.7301/2596.
Audience: **u,f.**

Macdonald, Lynda A. C. **KD667.C65**
Managing E-Mail and Internet Use: A Practical Guide to Employer's Obligations and Employee's Rights. Ed. 2. Trade Paper. Elsevier Science & Technology Books. Saint Louis, MO. 2004. xiii, 380p. ISBN:0-7545-2443-4, ISBN13: 978-0-7545-2443-4. Dewey:343.4109/944. LCCN:2004-444179.
Audience: **u,f.**

Repa, Barbara Kate **KF3455.Z9R47 2005**
Your Rights in the Workplace. Ed. 7. Trade Paper. NOLO. Berkeley, CA. 2005. 560p. ISBN:1-4133-0188-6, ISBN13: 978-1-4133-0188-5. Dewey:344.7301. LCCN:2005-043098.
Audience: **g,l,u,f.**

Wheeler, Hoyt N., et al. **HD6971.8.W5 2004**
Workplace Justice Without Unions. Brian S. Klaas & Douglas M. Mahony (Authors). Trade Paper. W. E. Upjohn Institute for Employment Research. Kalamazoo, MI. 2004. xii, 231p. ISBN:0-88099-312-X, ISBN13: 978-0-88099-312-8. Dewey:331/.01/10973. LCCN:2004-009579.
Audience: **u,f.** *Choice, 2005.*

Management Function > Human Resource Management > Diversity

Carnevale, Anthony P. & Stone, Susan C. **HF5549.5.M5C383 1995**
The American Mosaic: An In-Depth Report on the Future of Diversity at Work. Cloth Text. McGraw-Hill Trade. New York, NY. 1995. 524p. ISBN:0-07-011377-7, ISBN13: 978-0-07-011377-0. Dewey:331.1/1/0973. LCCN:95-012618.
Audience: **u,f.** *Choice, 1996.*

Cheney, George & Barnett, George A. **HD30.3**
International and Multicultural Organizational Communication. Trade Cloth. Hampton Press, Inc. Cresskill, NJ. 2004. 320p. ISBN:1-57273-549-X, ISBN13: 978-1-57273-549-1. Dewey:658.4/5. LCCN:2004-060642.
Audience: **u,f.**

Davila, Arlene M. **HF5415.33.U6 D38**
Latinos, Inc.: The Marketing and Making of a People. Trade Paper. University of California Press. Berkeley, CA. 2001. 304p. ISBN:0-520-22724-7, ISBN13: 978-0-520-22724-8. Dewey:658.8/34/08968073. LCCN:2001-016206.
Audience: **g,l,u,f.** *Choice, 2002.*

DiTomaso, Nancy & Post, Corinne (Editors) **HF5549.5.M5**
Diversity in the Work Force. Trade Cloth. Elsevier Science & Technology Books. Saint Louis, MO. 2004. 318p. ISBN:0-7623-0788-9, ISBN13: 978-0-7623-0788-3. Dewey:306.3/6.
Audience: **u,f.**

Guirdham, Maureen **HF5549.5.C6G84 2005**
Communicating Across Cultures at Work. Ed. 2. Trade Paper. Purdue University Press. West Lafayette, IN. 2005. 360p. ISBN:1-55753-410-1, ISBN13: 978-1-55753-410-1. Dewey:658.4/5. LCCN:2005-017207.
Audience: **g,l,u.**

Hemphill, Hellen & Haines, Ray **HF5549**
Discrimination, Harassment and the Failure of Diversity Training: What to Do Now. Trade Cloth. Greenwood Publishing Group, Inc. Portsmouth, NH. 1997. 152p. ISBN:1-56720-109-1, ISBN13: 978-1-56720-109-3. Dewey:658.3/145. LCCN:97-001702.
Audience: **u,f.**

Henderson, George **HF5549**
Cultural Diversity in the Workplace: Issues and Strategies. Paper Text. Greenwood Publishing Group, Inc. Portsmouth, NH. 1994. 288p. ISBN:0-275-95095-6, ISBN13: 978-0-275-95095-8. Dewey:658.3/041. LCCN:94-002991.
Audience: **u,f.** *Choice, 1995.*

Hopkins, Willie E. **HF5549.5.M5H67 1997**
Ethical Dimensions of Diversity, Vol. 5. Trade Paper. SAGE Publications, Inc. Thousand Oaks, CA. 1997. 200p. Business Ethics Ser. ISBN:0-8039-7289-X, ISBN13: 978-0-8039-7289-6. Dewey:658.3/008. LCCN:96-045797.
Audience: **u,f.** *Choice, 1997.*

Laird, Pamela Walker **HD69.S8L35 2005**
Pull: Networking and Success since Benjamin Franklin. Trade Cloth. Harvard University Press. Cambridge, MA. 2006. 464p. Harvard Studies in Business History Ser., Vol. 48 ISBN:0-674-01907-5, ISBN13: 978-0-674-01907-2. Dewey:650.1/3. LCCN:2005-050247.
Audience: **g,l,u,f.** *Choice, 2006.*

Lancaster, Lynne C. & Stillman, David **HF5549.5.M5L36 2003**
When Generations Collide: Who They Are. Why They Clash. How to Solve the Generational Puzzle at Work. Trade Paper. HarperCollins Publishers. New York, NY. 2003. 384p. ISBN:0-06-662107-0, ISBN13: 978-0-06-662107-4. Dewey:658.3/0084. LCCN:2002-032890.
Audience: **g,l,u,f.** *Choice, 2003.*

Miller, Frederick A. & Katz, Judith H. **HF5549.5.M5M55 2002**
The Inclusion Breakthrough: Unleashing the Real Power of Diversity. Trade Paper. Berrett-Koehler Publishers, Inc. San Francisco, CA. 2002. 220p. ISBN:1-57675-139-2, ISBN13: 978-1-57675-139-8. Dewey:658.3/008. LCCN:2002-021458.
Audience: **g,l,u.** *Choice, 2002.*

Mor Barak, Michàlle **HF5549.5.M5M662 2005**
Managing Diversity: Toward a Globally Inclusive Workplace. Paper Text. SAGE Publications, Inc. Thousand Oaks, CA. 2005. 360p. ISBN:0-7619-2773-5, ISBN13: 978-0-7619-2773-0. Dewey:658.3/008. LCCN:2004-023045.
Audience: **g,l,u,f.** *Choice, 2005.*

Prasad, Pushkala, et al. **HF5549.5.M5M365 1997**
Managing the Organizational Melting Pot: Dilemmas of Workplace Diversity. Albert J. Mills, Michael Elmes & Anshuman Prasad (Authors). Trade Paper. SAGE Publications, Inc. Thousand Oaks, CA. 1997. 403p. ISBN:0-8039-7411-6, ISBN13: 978-0-8039-7411-1. Dewey:658.3/041. LCCN:96-035610.
Audience: **u,f.** *Choice, 1997.*

Prasad, Pushkala (Editor), et al. **HF5549.5.M5**
Handbook of Workplace Diversity. Judith Pringle & Alison M. Konrad (Editors). Trade Cloth. SAGE Publications, Inc. Thousand Oaks, CA. 2006. 568p. ISBN:0-7619-4422-2, ISBN13: 978-0-7619-4422-5. Dewey:658.3008. LCCN:2005-925395.
Audience: **u,f.**

Stockdale, Margaret S. & Crosby, Faye J. (Editors) **HF5549.5.M5P79 2003**
The Psychology and Management of Workplace Diversity. Trade Paper. Blackwell Publishing, Inc. Malden, MA. 2003. 400p. ISBN:1-4051-0096-6, ISBN13: 978-1-4051-0096-0. Dewey:658.3/008. LCCN:2002-156372.
Audience: **u,f.** *Choice, 2004.*

Trompenaars, Fons **HD30.55.T76 1998**
Riding the Waves of Culture: Understanding Diversity in Global Business. Ed. 2. Trade Cloth. McGraw-Hill Companies, The. New York, NY. 1997. 416p. ISBN:0-7863-1125-8, ISBN13: 978-0-7863-1125-5. Dewey:658.3/0089. LCCN:97-039551.
Audience: **g,l,u,f.**

Winfeld, Liz & Spielman, Susan **HD6285.W56 2001**
Straight Talk about Gays in the Workplace. Ed. 2. Trade Cloth. Haworth Press, Incorporated, The. Binghamton, NY. 2005. 185p. Gay and Lesbian Studies ISBN:1-56023-171-8, ISBN13: 978-1-56023-171-4. Dewey:658.3/0086/64. LCCN:00-039712.
Audience: **g,l,u,f.** *Choice, 2001.*

Zemke, Ron, et al. **HF5549.5.M5**
[e] Generations at Work: Managing the Clash of Veterans, Boomers, Xers, Nexters in Your Workplace. Claire Raines & Bob Filipczak (Authors). E-Book. Amacom. New York, NY. 1999. ISBN:0-8144-2474-0, ISBN13: 978-0-8144-2474-2. Dewey:658.3/0084.
Audience: **g,l,u,f.** *Choice, 2000.*

Zweigenhaft, Richard L. & Domhoff, G. William **HN90.E4**
Diversity in the Power Elite: Have Women and Minorities Reached the Top? Trade Paper. Yale University Press. Cumberland, RI. 1999. 224p. ISBN:0-300-08089-1, ISBN13: 978-0-300-08089-6. Dewey:305.5/2/0973. LCCN:97-017541.
Audience: **u,f.** *Choice, 1998.*

Management Function > Human Resource Management > Discrimination

Anderson, Terry H. **HF5549.5.A34A53 2004**
The Pursuit of Fairness: A History of Affirmative Action. Trade Paper. Oxford University Press, Inc. New York, NY. 2005. 344p. ISBN:0-19-518245-6, ISBN13: 978-0-19-518245-3. Dewey:331.13/3/0973. LCCN:2003-024637.
Audience: **g,l,u,f.** *Choice, 2005.*

Becker, Gary Stanley **HD4903.5.U58**
The Economics of Discrimination. Ed. 2. Trade Paper. University of Chicago Press. Chicago, IL. 1971. 178p. Economic Research Studies ISBN:0-226-04116-6, ISBN13: 978-0-226-04116-2. Dewey:331.1/33/0973. LCCN:73-157422.
Audience: **u,f.**

Browne, Irene (Editor) **HD6057.5.U5L37 1999**
African American and Latina Women at Work: Race, Gender and Economic Inequality. Book, Other. Russell Sage Foundation. New York, NY. 1998. 356p. ISBN:0-87154-147-5, ISBN13: 978-0-87154-147-5. Dewey:331.4/089/96073. LCCN:98-019536.
Audience: **u,f.** *Choice, 1999.*

Cherry, Robert D. **HD4903.5.U58C46 2001**
Who Gets the Good Jobs?: Combatting Race and Gender Disparities. Cloth Text. Rutgers University Press. Piscataway, NJ. 2001. xv, 288p. ISBN:0-8135-2920-4, ISBN13: 978-0-8135-2920-2. Dewey:331.13/3. LCCN:00-045684.
Audience: **g,l,u,f.** *Choice, 2001.*

Cotter, Anne-Marie Mooney **K1770.C68 2004**
Gender Injustice: An International Comparative Analysis of Equality in Employment. Trade Cloth. Ashgate Publishing, Ltd. Aldershot, 2004. 306p. ISBN:0-7546-2377-7, ISBN13: 978-0-7546-2377-9. Dewey:344.01/4133. LCCN:2004-000032.
Audience: **u,f.**

Crosby, Faye J. **HF5549.5.A34C76 2004**
Affirmative Action Is Dead: Long Live Affirmative Action. Cloth over Boards. Yale University Press. Cumberland, RI. 2004. 352p. Current Perspectives in Psychology Ser. ISBN:0-300-10129-5, ISBN13: 978-0-300-10129-4. Dewey:331.13/3/0973. LCCN:2003-019187.
Audience: **g,l,u,f.** *Choice, 2004.*

Diamant, Louis & Lee, Jo Ann (Editors) **HQ1075**
The Psychology of Sex, Gender and Jobs: Issues and Solutions. Trade Cloth. Greenwood Publishing Group, Inc. Portsmouth, NH. 2001. 336p. ISBN:0-275-96507-4, ISBN13: 978-0-275-96507-5. Dewey:305.3/0973. LCCN:2001-021164.
Audience: **u,f.** *Choice, 2002.*

Dipboye, Robert & Colella, Adrienne (Editors) **HD4903.D573 2005**
Discrimination at Work: The Psychological and Organizational Bases. Janet L. Barnes-Farrell, Arthur P. Brief & Rebecca M. Butz (Contribution by). Cloth over Boards. Lawrence Erlbaum Associates, Inc. Mahwah, NJ. 2004. 536p. The Organizational Frontiers Ser. ISBN:0-8058-5207-7, ISBN13: 978-0-8058-5207-3. Dewey:331.13/3. LCCN:2004-016293.
Audience: **u,f.** *Choice, 2005.*

Ellis, Alan L. & Riggle, Ellen D. (Editors) **HD6285.5.U6S48 1996**
Sexual Identity on the Job: Issues and Services. Trade Paper. Haworth Press, Incorporated, The. Binghamton, NY. 1996. 108p. Journal of Gay and Lesbian Social Services Ser., Vol. 4, No. 4 ISBN:1-56023-076-2, ISBN13: 978-1-56023-076-2. Dewey:331.5. LCCN:96-020265.
Audience: **g,l,u,f.**

England, Paula **HD6061.2.U6E54 1992**
Comparable Worth: Theories and Evidence. Trade Cloth. Aldine Transaction. Somerset, NJ. 1992. 346p. Social Institutions and Social Change Ser. ISBN:0-202-30348-9, ISBN13: 978-0-202-30348-2. Dewey:331.2/153. LCCN:92-000900.
Audience: **u,f.** *Choice, 1993.*

Epstein, Richard A. **KF3464.E64 1992**
Forbidden Grounds: The Case Against Employment Discrimination Laws. Trade Cloth. Harvard University Press. Cambridge, MA. 1992. 544p. ISBN:0-674-30808-5, ISBN13: 978-0-674-30808-4. Dewey:344.73/01133. LCCN:91-025250.
Audience: **u,f.** *Choice, 1992.*

Fernandez, John **HF5549.5.M5**
Race, Gender and Rhetoric: The True State of Race and Gender Relations in Corporate America. Cloth Text. McGraw-Hill Trade. New York, NY. 1998. 259p. ISBN:0-07-022008-5, ISBN13: 978-0-07-022008-9. Dewey:658.3/0089. LCCN:98-028280.
Audience: **g,l,u,f.**

Goldin, Claudia D. **HD6095.G65 1990**
Understanding the Gender Gap: An Economic History of American Women. Trade Cloth. Oxford University Press, Inc. New York, NY. 1990. 316p. NBER Series on Long-term Factors in Economic Development Ser. ISBN:0-19-505077-0, ISBN13: 978-0-19-505077-6. Dewey:331.4/0973. LCCN:89-033502.
Audience: **u,f.** *Choice, 1990.*

Moreno, Paul D. **KF3464.M665 1997**
From Direct Action to Affirmative Action: Fair Employment Law and Policy in America, 1933-1972. Trade Cloth. Louisiana State University Press. Baton Rouge, LA. 1997. xii, 312p. ISBN:0-8071-2138-X, ISBN13: 978-0-8071-2138-2. Dewey:344.7301/133. LCCN:96-050168.
Audience: **u,f.** *Choice, 1997.*

Moss, Philip & Tilly, Chris **HF5549.5.A34**
Stories Employers Tell: Race, Skill and Hiring in America. Trade Paper. Russell Sage Foundation. New York, NY. 2003. 336p. ISBN:0-87154-632-9, ISBN13: 978-0-87154-632-6. Dewey:331.13/3/0973.
Audience: **u,f.** *Choice, 2001.*

Ryscavage, Paul **HC110.I5R95 1998**
Income Inequality in America: An Analysis of Trends. Daniel J. Mitchell (Foreword by). Cloth Text. M. E. Sharpe Inc. Armonk, NY. 1998. 244p. Issues in Work and Human Resources Ser. ISBN:0-7656-0233-4, ISBN13: 978-0-7656-0233-6. Dewey:339.220973. LCCN:98-023186.
Audience: **u,f.** *Choice, 1999.*

Segrave, Kerry **HD6280.S44 2001**
Age Discrimination by Employers. Paper Text. McFarland & Company, Incorporated Publishers. Jefferson, NC. 2001. 220p. ISBN:0-7864-1010-8, ISBN13: 978-0-7864-1010-1. Dewey:331.3/98. LCCN:2001-030770.
Audience: **g,l,u,f.** *Choice, 2001.*

Shulman, Steven & Darity, William Jr. (Editors) **HD4903.5.U58Q47 1989**
The Question of Discrimination: Racial Inequality in the U. S. Labor Market. Library Binding. Wesleyan University Press. Middletown, CT. 1989. 410p. ISBN:0-8195-5214-3, ISBN13: 978-0-8195-5214-3. Dewey:331.13/3/0973. LCCN:89-005481.
Audience: **u,f.** *Choice, 1990.*

Stith, Anthony **HD4903.5.U58**
Breaking the Glass Ceiling: Sexism and Racism in Corporate America: the Myths, the Realities and the Solutions. Paper Text. Warwick Publishing. Toronto, ON. 1998. 208p. ISBN:1-894020-20-0, ISBN13: 978-1-894020-20-6. Dewey:331.133. LCCN:98-090410.
Audience: **g,l,u,f.**

Stockford, Marjorie A. **KF2849.A4S76 2004**
The Bellwomen: The Story of the Landmark AT&T Sex Discrimination Case. Trade Cloth. Rutgers University Press. Piscataway, NJ. 2004. 256p. ISBN:0-8135-3428-3, ISBN13: 978-0-8135-3428-2. Dewey:344.7301/4133. LCCN:2003-019800.
Audience: **g,l,u,f.** *Choice, 2005.*

Twomey, David P. **KF3464**
Employment Discrimination Law. Ed. 6. Paper Text. Thomson South-Western. Mason, OH. 2004. 384p. ISBN:0-324-27130-1, ISBN13: 978-0-324-27130-0. Dewey:344.7301/133. LCCN:2004-107526.
Audience: **u,f.**

Woo, Deborah **HD8081.A8W66 2000**
Glass Ceilings and Asian Americans: The New Face of Workplace Barriers. Trade Paper. AltaMira Press. Walnut Creek, CA. 2000. 256p. ISBN:0-7425-0335-6, ISBN13: 978-0-7425-0335-9. Dewey:331.6/395/073.
Audience: **u,f.** *Choice, 2001.*

Management Function > Marketing

Andreasen, Alan R. **HF5414.A527 2006**
Social Marketing in the 21st Century. Cloth Text. SAGE Publications, Inc. Thousand Oaks, CA. 2005. 280p. ISBN:1-4129-1633-X, ISBN13: 978-1-4129-1633-2. Dewey:361/.0068/8. LCCN:2005-022466.
Audience: **g,l,u,f.**

Bartels, Robert **HF5415.B36 1976**
The History of Marketing Thought. Trade Cloth. Bow Historical Books. New Providence, NJ. 1976. 327p. ISBN:0-88244-085-3, ISBN13: 978-0-88244-085-9. Dewey:658.8/009. LCCN:75-006015.
Audience: **u,f.** B

Bennett, Peter **HF5415.D4874 1995**
AMA Dictionary of Marketing Terms. Ed. 2. Trade Cloth. McGraw-Hill Companies, The. New York, NY. 1995. 336p. ISBN:0-8442-3598-9, ISBN13: 978-0-8442-3598-1. Dewey:658.8/003. LCCN:94-039784.
Audience: **u,f.** *Choice, 1995.*

Bennett, Roger **HF1416**
International Marketing: Strategy, Planning, Market Entry and Implementation. Ed. 2. Trade Paper. Kogan Page, Ltd. London, 1998. 400p. ISBN:0-7494-2272-6, ISBN13: 978-0-7494-2272-1. Dewey:658.8/48.
Audience: **u,f.** *Choice, 1999.*

Clancy, Kevin J. & Krieg, Peter C. **HF5415.C5277 2000**
Counterintuitive Marketing: Achieve Great Results Using Uncommom Sense. Trade Cloth. Simon & Schuster. New York, NY. 2000. 368p. ISBN:0-684-85555-0, ISBN13: 978-0-684-85555-4. Dewey:658.8. LCCN:00-055109.
Audience: **u.**

Douglas, Edna **HF5415.D73**
Economics of Marketing. Trade Cloth. Harper & Row Ltd. London, 1975. viii, 728p. ISBN:0-06-041695-5, ISBN13: 978-0-06-041695-9. Dewey:380.1. LCCN:75-003527.
Audience: **u,f.** B

Engel, James F. **HF5415.E65 1983**
Promotional Strategy. Ed. 5. Trade Cloth. McGraw-Hill Higher Education. Burr Ridge, IL. 1983. xv, 655p. ISBN:0-256-02846-X, ISBN13: 978-0-256-02846-1. Dewey:658.8/2. LCCN:82-084060.
Audience: **u,f.** B

Govoni, Norman **HF5412.G68 2004**
The Dictionary of Marketing Communications. Cloth Text. SAGE Publications, Inc. Thousand Oaks, CA. 2003. 256p. ISBN:0-7619-2770-0, ISBN13: 978-0-7619-2770-9. Dewey:380.1/03. LCCN:2003-007359.
Audience: **u,f.** *Choice, 2004.*

Heilbrunn, Jeffrey **HF5415.M2982 1995**
AMA Marketing Encyclopedia: Issues and Trends Shaping the Future. Anne Knudsen (Editor). Trade Cloth. McGraw-Hill Trade. New York, NY. 1995. 360p. ISBN:0-8442-3593-8, ISBN13: 978-0-8442-3593-6. Dewey:658/.003. LCCN:94-017747.
Audience: **u,f.** *Choice, 1996.*

Johnson, Winslow **HF5415.13.J5878 2004**
Powerhouse Marketing Plans: 14 Outstanding Real-Life Plans and What You Can Learn from Them to Supercharge Your Own Campaigns. Trade Cloth. Amacom. New York, NY. 2004. 384p. ISBN:0-8144-7219-2, ISBN13: 978-0-8144-7219-4. Dewey:658.8/101. LCCN:2004-006898.
Audience: **u.** *Choice, 2005.*

Kotler, Philip **HF5415.K624 2005**
According to Kotler. Trade Paper. Amacom. New York, NY. 2005. 192p. ISBN:0-8144-7295-8, ISBN13: 978-0-8144-7295-8. Dewey:658.8. LCCN:2005-001422.
Audience: **g,l,u,f.**

Kotler, Philip, et al. **HF5414.K67 2002**
Social Marketing: Improving the Quality of Life. Ed. 2. Ned L. Roberto & Nancy R. Lee (Authors). Paper Text. SAGE Publications, Inc. Thousand Oaks, CA. 2002. 456p. ISBN:0-7619-2434-5, ISBN13: 978-0-7619-2434-0. Dewey:658.8. LCCN:2001-007178.
Audience: **g,l,u,f.**

Levitt, I. M. **HF5415.L482 1986**
Marketing Imagination. Trade Paper. Simon & Schuster. New York, NY. 1986. 238p. ISBN:0-02-919090-8, ISBN13: 978-0-02-919090-6. Dewey:658.8. LCCN:86-000576.
Audience: **g,l,u,f.**

Levy, Sidney J. & Rook, Dennis W. (Editors) **HF5415.1.L48 1999**
Brands, Consumers, Symbols and Research: Sidney J Levy on Marketing. Trade Cloth. SAGE Publications, Inc. Thousand Oaks, CA. 1999. 608p. ISBN:0-7619-1696-2, ISBN13: 978-0-7619-1696-3. Dewey:658.8/243. LCCN:99-006225.
Audience: **u,f.** *Choice, 2000.*

McDonald, Malcolm & Morris, Peter **HF5415.13**
Marketing: A Complete Guide in Pictures. Ed. 2. Paper Text. Elsevier Science & Technology Books. Saint Louis, MO. 2004. 168p. ISBN:0-7506-6198-4, ISBN13: 978-0-7506-6198-0. Dewey:658.8/02.
Audience: **g,l,u.**

Rados, David L. **HF5415**
Marketing for Non-Profit Organizations. Ed. 2. Cloth Text. Greenwood Publishing Group, Inc. Portsmouth, NH. 1996. 480p. ISBN:0-86569-254-8, ISBN13: 978-0-86569-254-1. Dewey:658.8. LCCN:95-013609.
Audience: **u,f.** *Choice, 1996.*

Schmitt, Bernd H. **HF5415.13.S343 1999**
Experiential Marketing: How to Get Customers to Sense, Feel, Think, Act and Relate to Your Company and Brand. Trade Cloth. Simon & Schuster. New York, NY. 1999. 304p. ISBN:0-684-85423-6, ISBN13: 978-0-684-85423-6. Dewey:658.8/27. LCCN:99-018003.
Audience: **g,l,u,f.**

Surowiecki, James **JC328.2.S87 2003**
The Wisdom of Crowds: Why the Many Are Smarter Than the Few and How Collective Wisdom Shapes Business, Economies, Societies and Nations. Trade Cloth. Doubleday Canada, Ltd. Toronto, ON. 2004. 320p. ISBN:0-385-50386-5, ISBN13: 978-0-385-50386-0. Dewey:303.3/8. LCCN:2003-070095.
Audience: **g,l,u,f.** *Choice, 2004.*

Tellis, Gerard J. & Golder, Peter N. **HF5415.1.T45 2002**
Will and Vision: How Latecomers Grow to Dominate Markets. Clayton Christensen (Foreword by). Trade Cloth. McGraw-Hill Companies, The. New York, NY. 2001. 256p. ISBN:0-07-137549-X, ISBN13: 978-0-07-137549-8. Dewey:658.8/00973. LCCN:2001-044001.
Audience: **u,f.** *Choice, 2002.*

Treacy, Michael & Wiersema, Fred **HF5415**
The Discipline of Market Leaders: Choose Your Customers, Narrow Your Focus, Dominate Your Market. Trade Cloth. DIANE Publishing Company. Collingdale, PA. 2001. 208p. ISBN:0-7567-5055-5, ISBN13: 978-0-7567-5055-8. Dewey:658.8.
Audience: **g,u,f.**

Wind, Jerry, et al. **HF5415.1265.W558**
Convergence Marketing: Strategies for Reaching the New Hybrid Consumer. Vijay Mahajan, Robert Gunther & Yoram Wind (Authors). Trade Cloth. Financial Times/Prentice Hall. Paramus, NJ. 2001. 368p. ISBN:0-13-065075-7, ISBN13: 978-0-13-065075-7. Dewey:658.8. LCCN:2002-282225.
Audience: **u,f.**

Management Function > Marketing > Market Research

HF5415
☐ MarketResearch.com.
http://www.marketresearch.com/
Audience: **g,u,f.**

Birn, Robin **HF5415.2**
The International Handbook of Market Research Techniques. Ed. 2. Trade Cloth. Kogan Page, Ltd. London, 2000. 594p. ISBN:0-7494-2616-0, ISBN13: 978-0-7494-2616-3. Dewey:658.8/3.
Audience: **l,u,f.**

Cox, William Edwin **HF5415.2.C68 1979**
Industrial Marketing Research. Trade Cloth. John Wiley & Sons, Inc. Hoboken, NJ. 1979. 468p. ISBN:0-471-03467-3, ISBN13: 978-0-471-03467-4. Dewey:658.8/3/0973. LCCN:78-011480.
Audience: **u,f.**

Crawford, Fred & Mathews, Ryan **HF5415.3**
The Myth of Excellence: Why Great Companies Never Try to Be the Best at Everything. UK-Trade Paper. Crown Publishing Group. New York, NY. 2003. 272p. ISBN:0-609-81001-4, ISBN13: 978-0-609-81001-9. Dewey:658.8/34.
Audience: **u,f.** *Choice, 2002.*

Duboff, Robert S. & Spaeth, Jim **HF5415.2.D83 2000**
Market Research Matters: Tools and Techniques for Aligning Your Business. Trade Cloth. John Wiley & Sons, Inc. Hoboken, NJ. 2000. 312p. ISBN:0-471-36005-8, ISBN13: 978-0-471-36005-6. Dewey:658.8/3. LCCN:00-025183.
Audience: **u,f.** *Choice, 2000.*

Ereaut, Gill (Editor), et al. **HF5415.2.Q25 2002**
Qualitative Market Research: Principle and Practice. Mike Imms & Martin Callingham (Editors). Trade Cloth. SAGE Publications, Inc. Thousand Oaks, CA. 2002. 1112p. ISBN:0-7619-7272-2, ISBN13: 978-0-7619-7272-3. Dewey:658.8/3. LCCN:2002-101993.
Audience: **u,f.** *Choice, 2003.*

Frigstad, David B. **HF5415.2.F73 1995**
Know Your Market: How to Do Low-Cost Market Research. Trade Cloth. PSI Research. Central Point, OR. 1994. 187p. Successful Business Library Ser. ISBN:1-55571-333-5, ISBN13: 978-1-55571-333-1. Dewey:658.8/3. LCCN:94-021353.
Audience: **u,f.** *Choice, 1995.*

Hague, Paul N. & Hague, Nick **HF5415.2**
Market Research in Practice: A Guide to the Basics. Trade Paper, Perfect. Kogan Page, Ltd. London, 2004. 272p. Market Research in Practice Ser. ISBN:0-7494-4180-1, ISBN13: 978-0-7494-4180-7. Dewey:658.8/3. LCCN:2004-002449.
Audience: **g,l.**

McQuarrie, Edward F. **HF5415.2.M383 2006**
The Market Research Toolbox: A Concise Guide for Beginners. Ed. 2. Cloth Text. SAGE Publications, Inc. Thousand Oaks, CA. 2005. 224p. ISBN:1-4129-1318-7, ISBN13: 978-1-4129-1318-8. Dewey:658.8/3. LCCN:2005-006695.
Audience: **u,f.** *Choice, 2005, 1996.*

Myers, John G. **HF5415.2.M945**
Marketing Research and Knowledge Development: An Assessment for Marketing Management. Trade Cloth. Prentice-Hall. Upper Saddle, NJ. 1980. xiv, 306p. ISBN:0-13-557686-5, ISBN13: 978-0-13-557686-1. Dewey:658.8/3973. LCCN:80-013929.
Audience: **u,f.** B

Reid, David A. & Plank, Richard E. (Editors) **HF5415.1263.F86 2003**
Fundamentals of Business Marketing Research: A Guide for University-Level Faculty and Policymakers. Box or Slipcased. Haworth Press, Incorporated, The. Binghamton, NY. 2003. 278p. The Foundation Series in Business Marketing ISBN:0-7890-2311-3, ISBN13: 978-0-7890-2311-7. Dewey:658.8/3. LCCN:2003-016234.
Audience: **u,f.** *Choice, 2004.*

Ritchie, Jane & Lewis, Jane (Editors) **H62**
Qualitative Research Practice: A Guide for Social Science Students and Researchers. Paper Text. SAGE Publications, Ltd. London, 2003. 336p. ISBN:0-7619-7110-6, ISBN13: 978-0-7619-7110-8. Dewey:001.4/2.
Audience: **u,f.** *Choice, 2003.*

Sayre, Shay **HF5415.2.S29 2001**
Qualitative Methods for Marketplace Research. Trade Cloth. SAGE Publications, Inc. Thousand Oaks, CA. 2001. 272p. ISBN:0-7619-2269-5, ISBN13: 978-0-7619-2269-8. Dewey:658.8/3. LCCN:00-012352.
Audience: **u,f.** *Choice, 2001.*

Soares, Eric J. **HF5415**
Cost-Effective Marketing Research: A Guide for Marketing Managers. Trade Cloth. Greenwood Publishing Group, Inc. Portsmouth, NH. 1988. 177p. ISBN:0-89930-278-5, ISBN13: 978-0-89930-278-2. Dewey:658.8/3. LCCN:88-018526.
Audience: **u,f.** *Choice, 1989.*

Stevens, Robert E., et al. **HF5415.2.M35585 1996**
The Marketing Research Guide. Bruce Wrenn, Morris E. Ruddick & Philip K. Sherwood (Authors). Trade Cloth. Haworth Press, Incorporated, The. Binghamton, NY. 1997. 488p. Haworth Marketing Resources Ser. ISBN:1-56024-339-2, ISBN13: 978-1-56024-339-7. Dewey:658.8/3. LCCN:96-019070.
Audience: **g,u,f.** *Choice, 1997.*

Stevens, Robert E., et al. **HF5415.2.M35585 2005**
The Marketing Research Guide. Ed. 2. Bruce Wrenn, Philip K. Sherwood & Morris E. Ruddick (Authors). Trade Cloth. Haworth Press, Incorporated, The. Binghamton, NY. 2005. 489p. ISBN:0-7890-2416-0, ISBN13: 978-0-7890-2416-9. Dewey:658.8/3. LCCN:2005-003578.
Audience: **g,l,u,f.** *Choice, 1997.*

Valdes, Isabel & Seoane, Marta **HC110.C6V347 1995**
The Hispanic Market Handbook. Trade Cloth. Thomson Gale. Farmington Hills, MI. 1995. 488p. Professional Library ISBN:0-8103-8500-7, ISBN13: 978-0-8103-8500-9. Dewey:658.8/348. LCCN:95-003268.
Audience: **u,f.** *Choice, 1995.*

Management Function > Marketing > Market Research > Focus Groups

Bader, Gloria E. & Rossi, Catherine A **H61.28**
Focus Groups: A Step-by-Step Guide. Ed. 3. Trade Paper. Bader Group, The. San Diego, CA. 2002. 6p. ISBN:0-9664708-7-7, ISBN13: 978-0-9664708-7-1. Dewey:300.723.
Audience: **u.**

Dutka, Alan F. **HF5415.3.D88 1994**
AMA Handbook for Customer Satisfaction: A Complete Guide to Research, Planning, and Implementation. Trade Cloth. McGraw-Hill Trade. New York, NY. 1995. 240p. ISBN:0-8442-3454-0, ISBN13: 978-0-8442-3454-0. Dewey:658.8/12. LCCN:92-034249.
Audience: **u.** *Choice, 1994.*

Fern, Edward F. **H61.28.F47 2001**
Advanced Focus Group Research. Trade Cloth. SAGE Publications, Inc. Thousand Oaks, CA. 2001. 264p. ISBN:0-7619-1248-7, ISBN13: 978-0-7619-1248-4. Dewey:001.4/33. LCCN:00-012632.
Audience: **l,u,f.**

Krueger, Richard A. **H61.28.F63 1998**
Analyzing and Reporting Focus Group Results. Trade Paper. SAGE Publications, Inc. Thousand Oaks, CA. 1997. 160p. Focus Group Kit Ser., Vol. 6 ISBN:0-7619-0816-1, ISBN13: 978-0-7619-0816-6. Dewey:001.4/33. LCCN:97-021135.
Audience: **u,f.**

Krueger, Richard A. **HA31.2**
Developing Questions for Focus Groups. Trade Paper. SAGE Publications, Inc. Thousand Oaks, CA. 1997. 128p. Focus Group Kit Ser., Vol. 3 ISBN:0-7619-0819-6, ISBN13: 978-0-7619-0819-7. Dewey:001.4/33.
Audience: **u,f.**

Krueger, Richard A. **HA31.2**
Moderating Focus Groups. Trade Paper. SAGE Publications, Inc. Thousand Oaks, CA. 1997. 136p. Focus Group Kit Ser., Vol. 4 ISBN:0-7619-0821-8, ISBN13: 978-0-7619-0821-0. Dewey:001.4/33.
Audience: **g,u,f.**

Krueger, Richard A. & King, Jean A. **HA31.2**
Involving Community Members in Focus Groups. Trade Paper. SAGE Publications, Inc. Thousand Oaks, CA. 1997. 120p. Focus Group Kit Ser., Vol. 5 ISBN:0-7619-0820-X, ISBN13: 978-0-7619-0820-3. Dewey:001.4/33. LCCN:97-021135.
Audience: **g,u,f.**

Langer, Judith **H61.28.L36 2001**
The Mirrored Window: Focus Groups from a Moderator's Point of View. Trade Cloth. Paramount Market Publishing, Inc. Ithaca, NY. 2001. 272p. ISBN:0-9671439-4-2, ISBN13: 978-0-9671439-4-1. Dewey:658.4036. LCCN:2001-275361.
Audience: **u,f.**

Morgan, David L. **HN29**
The Focus Group Guidebook. Trade Paper. SAGE Publications, Inc. Thousand Oaks, CA. 1997. 120p. Focus Group Kit Ser., Vol. 1 ISBN:0-7619-0818-8, ISBN13: 978-0-7619-0818-0. Dewey:300.7/23. LCCN:97-021135.
Audience: **g,u,f.**

Morgan, David L. **HN29**
Planning Focus Groups. Trade Paper. SAGE Publications, Inc. Thousand Oaks, CA. 1997. 160p. Focus Group Kit Ser., Vol. 2 ISBN:0-7619-0817-X, ISBN13: 978-0-7619-0817-3. Dewey:300.7/23. LCCN:97-021135.
Audience: **u,f.**

Ritchie, Jane & Lewis, Jane (Editors) **H62**
Qualitative Research Practice: A Guide for Social Science Students and Researchers. Cloth Text. SAGE Publications, Inc. Thousand Oaks, CA. 2003. 336p. ISBN:0-7619-7109-2, ISBN13: 978-0-7619-7109-2. Dewey:001.4/2. LCCN:2002-109391.
Audience: **u,f.** *Choice, 2003.*

Management Function > Marketing > Market Research > Forecasting

Crosby, John V. **HF5415.2.C77 2000**
Cycles, Trends, and Turning Points: Practical Marketing and Sales Forecasting Techniques. Trade Cloth. McGraw-Hill Companies, The. New York, NY. 2000. xii, 321p. ISBN:0-8442-3244-0, ISBN13: 978-0-8442-3244-7. Dewey:658.8/02. LCCN:98-034338.
Audience: **u,f.**

Kitchen, Philip J. (Editor) **HF5415.F945 2003**
The Future of Marketing: Critical 21st Century Perspectives. Cloth over Boards. Palgrave Macmillan. New York, NY. 2003. 224p. ISBN:0-333-99286-5, ISBN13: 978-0-333-99286-9. Dewey:658.8/001/12. LCCN:2002-029402.
Audience: **u,f.**

Kress, George J. & Snyder, John **HF5415**
Forecasting and Market Analysis Techniques: A Practical Approach. Trade Cloth. Greenwood Publishing Group, Inc. Portsmouth, NH. 1994. 304p. ISBN:0-89930-835-X, ISBN13: 978-0-89930-835-7. Dewey:658.835. LCCN:93-011890.
Audience: **u,f.** *Choice, 1994.*

Mentzer, John T. & Moon, Mark A. **HF5415.2.M393 2005**
Sales Forecasting Management: A Demand Management Approach. Ed. 2. Paper Text. SAGE Publications, Inc. Thousand Oaks, CA. 2004. 368p. ISBN:1-4129-0571-0, ISBN13: 978-1-4129-0571-8. Dewey:658.8/18. LCCN:2004-016438.
Audience: **u,f.**

Roney, C. W. **HD30**
Assessing the Business Environment: Guidelines for Strategists. Trade Cloth. Greenwood Publishing Group, Inc. Portsmouth, NH. 1999. 288p. ISBN:1-56720-235-7, ISBN13: 978-1-56720-235-9. Dewey:658.4/012. LCCN:99-013716.
Audience: **u,f.** *Choice, 2000.*

Shim, Jae K. **HD30.27.S48 2000**
Strategic Business Forecasting: The Complete Guide to Forecasting Real World Company Performance. Ed. 2. Paper over Boards. Saint Lucie Press. Boca Raton, FL. 2000. 312p. ISBN:1-57444-251-1, ISBN13: 978-1-57444-251-9. Dewey:658.4/0355. LCCN:99-056213.
Audience: **u,f.** *Choice, 2000.*

Management Function > Marketing > Market Research > Surveys

Alreck, Pamela L. & Settle, Robert B. **HN29.A46 2004**
Survey Research Handbook. Ed. 3. Paper Text. McGraw-Hill Higher Education. Burr Ridge, IL. 2003. 496p. McGraw-Hill/Irwin Series in Marketing ISBN:0-07-294548-6, ISBN13: 978-0-07-294548-5. Dewey:300/.72/3. LCCN:2003-066453.
Audience: **u,f.**

Brace, Ian **HF5415.2**
Questionnaire Design: How to Plan, Structure and Write Survey Material for Effective Market Research. Trade Paper, CD-ROM, Mixed Media. Kogan Page, Ltd. London, 2004. 288p. Market Research in Practice Ser. ISBN:0-7494-4181-X, ISBN13: 978-0-7494-4181-4. Dewey:658.8/3. LCCN:2004-010045.
Audience: **g,l,u,f.** *Choice, 2005.*

Bradburn, Norman M., et al. **H62.B63 2004**
Asking Questions: The Definitive Guide to Questionnaire Design — for Market Research, Political Polls, and Social and Health Questionnaires. Brian Wansink & Seymour Sudman (Authors). Trade Paper. John Wiley & Sons, Inc. Hoboken, NJ. 2004. 448p. ISBN:0-7879-7088-3, ISBN13: 978-0-7879-7088-8. Dewey:300/.72/3. LCCN:2004-001683.
Audience: **g,u,f.**

Czaja, Ronald & Blair, Johnny **HA31.2**
Designing Surveys: A Guide to Decisions and Procedures. Ed. 2. Cloth Text. Pine Forge Press. Newbury Park, CA. 2004. 320p. Undergraduate Research Methods and Statistics in the Social Sciences Ser. ISBN:0-7619-2745-X, ISBN13: 978-0-7619-2745-7. Dewey:001.4/33. LCCN:2004-014521.
Audience: **g,u,f.** *Choice, 2005.*

Mediamark Research Inc. **HF5415.2**
Mediamark Reporter. Ed. 2005. Mediamark Research Inc. Mediamark Reporter
Audience: **u,f.**

Management Function > Marketing > Demographics

HF5415.33.U6
Baby Boom: Americans Born 1946 To 1964. Ed. 4. Trade Cloth. New Strategist Publications, Inc. Ithaca, NY. 2004. 400p. American Generations Ser. ISBN:1-885070-51-9, ISBN13: 978-1-885070-51-7. Dewey:305.2.
Audience: **g,l,u,f.** *Choice, 2005.*

HF5415.33.U6
Generation X: Americans Born 1965 to 1976. Ed. 4. Trade Cloth. New Strategist Publications, Inc. Ithaca, NY. 2004. 384p.

American Generations Ser. ISBN:1-885070-52-7, ISBN13: 978-1-885070-52-4.
Audience: **g,l,u,f.** *Choice, 2005.*

HF5415.33.U6
Lifestyle Market Analyst. Standard Rate & Data Service. 2006. Lifestyle Market Analyst
Audience: **g,u,f.**

HQ796
The Millennials: Americans Born 1977 To 1994. Ed. 2. Trade Cloth. New Strategist Publications, Inc. Ithaca, NY. 2004. 402p. American Generations Ser. ISBN:1-885070-53-5, ISBN13: 978-1-885070-53-1. Dewey:305.235.
Audience: **g,l,u,f.** *Choice, 2005.*

HF5438.A34
Sales and Marketing Management: Survey of Buying Power. Ed. 2005. Bill Communications.
Audience: **u,f.**

HA203
Sourcebook of County Demographics. Ed. 15. CACI, Inc. 2003.
Audience: **g,l,u,f.**

Asacker, Tom **HD69.B7A83 2005**
A Clear Eye for Branding: Straight Talk on Today's Most Powerful Business Concept. Trade Paper. Paramount Market Publishing, Inc. Ithaca, NY. 2005. 144p. ISBN:0-9725290-8-X, ISBN13: 978-0-9725290-8-2. Dewey:658.827. LCCN:2005-284483.
Audience: **g,u,f.**

Danziger, Pamela N. **HF5415.32.D36 2004**
Why People Buy Things They Don't Need. Ed. 2. Cloth Text. Paramount Market Publishing, Inc. Ithaca, NY. 2004. 290p. ISBN:0-9725290-4-7, ISBN13: 978-0-9725290-4-4. Dewey:658.8/342. LCCN:2004-302355.
Audience: **g,l,u,f.** *Choice, 2002.*

Davila, Arlene M. **HF5415.33.U6 D38**
Latinos, Inc.: The Marketing and Making of a People. Trade Paper. University of California Press. Berkeley, CA. 2001. 304p. ISBN:0-520-22724-7, ISBN13: 978-0-520-22724-8. Dewey:658.8/34/08968073. LCCN:2001-016206.
Audience: **g,l,u,f.** *Choice, 2002.*

Farley, Reynolds & Haaga, John (Editors) **HA201.122.A45 2005**
The American People: Census 2000. Perfect. Russell Sage Foundation. New York, NY. 2005. 456p. ISBN:0-87154-273-0, ISBN13: 978-0-87154-273-1. Dewey:304.6/0973/021. LCCN:2005-050433.
Audience: **g,l,u,f.**

Faura, Juan **HF5415.32.F38 2004**
The Whole Enchilada: Hispanic Marketing 101. Cloth Text. Paramount Market Publishing, Inc. Ithaca, NY. 2004. 140p. ISBN:0-9725290-5-5, ISBN13: 978-0-9725290-5-1. Dewey:658.8/3468/073. LCCN:2005-278873.
Audience: **u,f.** *Choice, 2005.*

Green, Brent **HF5415.127**
Marketing to Leading-Edge Baby Boomers: Perceptions, Principles, Practices, Predictions. Ed. 2. Kivar (or like). Paramount Market Publishing, Inc. Ithaca, NY. 2005. 350p. ISBN:0-9725290-7-1, ISBN13: 978-0-9725290-7-5. Dewey:658.8.
Audience: **u,f.** *Choice, 2005.*

Harris, Leslie M. (Editor) **HF5415.13**
After Fifty: How the Baby Boom Will Redefine the Mature Market. Cloth Text. Paramount Market Publishing, Inc. Ithaca, NY. 2003. 192p. ISBN:0-9725290-2-0, ISBN13: 978-0-9725290-2-0. Dewey:658.834.
Audience: **g,u,f.** *Choice, 2004.*

Miller, Pepper & Kemp, Herb **HC110.C6.M53 2005**
What's Black about It?: Insights to Increase Your Share of A Changing African-American Market. Kivar (or like). Paramount Market Publishing, Inc. Ithaca, NY. 2005. 144p. ISBN:0-9725290-9-8, ISBN13: 978-0-9725290-9-9. Dewey:658.834.
Audience: **u,f.** *Choice, 2006.*

Mitchell, Susan **HC110.C6M545 2005**
American Generations: Who They Are, How They Live, What They Think. Ed. 5. New Strategist Publications, Inc. Staff (Author, Contribution by). Trade Cloth. New Strategist Publications, Inc. Ithaca, NY. 2005. 500p. ISBN:1-885070-69-1, ISBN13: 978-1-885070-69-2. Dewey:330.973/0931021. LCCN:2005-284140.
Audience: **u,f.** *Choice, 2003, 1998.*

New Strategist Publications, Inc. Staff (Editor) **HN90.P8**
American Attitutdes: What Americans Think about the Issues That Shape Their Lives. Ed. 4. Trade Cloth. New Strategist Publications, Inc. Ithaca, NY. 2005. 346p. ISBN:1-885070-43-8, ISBN13: 978-1-885070-43-2. Dewey:303.38.
Audience: **g,l,u,f.** *Choice, 2005.*

New Strategist Publications, Inc. Staff **HF5415.33.U6**
The American Marketplace: Demographics and Spending Patterns. Ed. 7. Perfect, Paper over Boards. New Strategist Publications, Inc. Ithaca, NY. 2005. 524p. ISBN:1-885070-60-8, ISBN13: 978-1-885070-60-9. Dewey:658.83.
Audience: **l,u,f.**

New Strategist Publications, Inc. Staff **HC110.C6**
Household Spending: Who Spends How Much on What. Ed. 9. Trade Cloth. New Strategist Publications, Inc. Ithaca, NY. 2004. 800p. ISBN:1-885070-67-5, ISBN13: 978-1-885070-67-8. Dewey:339.470973.
Audience: **u,f.**

Nyren, Chuck **HF5823.N85 2005**
Advertising to Baby Boomers. Kivar (or like). Paramount Market Publishing, Inc. Ithaca, NY. 2005. 135p. ISBN:0-9766973-1-9, ISBN13: 978-0-9766973-1-2. Dewey:659.1. LCCN:2005-284327.
Audience: **u,f.**

Siegel, David, et al. **HF5415.32**
Marketing to the New Super Consumer Mom and Kid. Timothy Coffey & Gregory Livingston (Authors). Cloth Text. Paramount Market Publishing, Inc. Ithaca, NY. 2005. 220p. ISBN:0-9766973-2-7, ISBN13: 978-0-9766973-2-9. Dewey:658.8343.
Audience: **g,l,u,f.** *Choice, 2006.*

Valdes, M. Isabel **HC110.C6 V348 2000**
Marketing to American Latinos: A Guide to the In-Culture Approach. Trade Cloth. Paramount Market Publishing, Inc. Ithaca, NY. 2002. 250p. ISBN:0-9671439-2-6, ISBN13: 978-0-9671439-2-7. Dewey:658.8.
Audience: **u,f.** *Choice, 2003.*

Management Function > Marketing > Demographics > Market Segmentation

HF5415.33.U6
Lifestyle Market Analyst. Standard Rate & Data Service. 2006. Lifestyle Market Analyst
Audience: **g,u,f.**

HF5415.3.W67
World Consumer Lifestyles Databook: Key Trends. Ed. 2. Euromonitor International Plc. 2003.
Audience: **u,f.**

Kanner, Bernice **HF5415.32.K36 2004**
Pocketbook Power. Ed. 1. McGraw-Hill. 2004. ISBN:0-07-141860-1, ISBN13: 978-0-07-141860-7.
Audience: **l,u,f.**

Simmons Market Research Bureau **HC110.C6**
Choices III.
http://www.smrb.com/
Ed. 2006. Simmons Market Research Bureau.
Audience: **u,f.**

Zollo, Peter **HF5415.32**
Getting Wiser to Teens. Ed. 2. New Strategist Publications. 2004. ISBN:1-885070-54-3, ISBN13: 978-1-885070-54-8.
Audience: **g,l,u,f.**

Management Function > Marketing > Consumer Behavior

HF5415.3.W67
World Consumer Lifestyles Databook: Key Trends. Ed. 2. Euromonitor International Plc. 2003.
Audience: **u,f.**

Cialdini, Robert B. **BF774.C53 2001**
Influence: Science and Practice. Ed. 4. Trade Paper. Allyn & Bacon, Inc. Boston, MA. 2000. 262p. ISBN:0-321-01147-3, ISBN13: 978-0-321-01147-3. Dewey:153.8/52. LCCN:00-026647.
Audience: **g,l,u,f.**

Curtis P. Haugtvedt, Karen A. Machleit & Richard Yalch **HF5415.32**
Online Consumer Psychology. Lawrence Erlbaum Associates. 2005. Advertising and consumer psychology ISBN:0-8058-5154-2, ISBN13: 978-0-8058-5154-0.
Audience: **u,f.**

Foxall, Gordon R. **HF5415.32.F688 2005**
Understanding Consumer Choice. Palgrave Macmillan. 2005. ISBN:1-4039-1492-3, ISBN13: 978-1-4039-1492-7.
Audience: **u,f.**

Gladwell, Malcolm **HM1033.G53 2000**
The Tipping Point: How Little Things Can Make a Big Difference. Trade Paper. Little Brown & Company. New York, NY. 2002. 304p. ISBN:0-316-34662-4, ISBN13: 978-0-316-34662-7. Dewey:302. LCCN:99-047576.
Audience: **g,l,u,f.**

Johnson, Michael D. & Gustaffson, Anders **HF5415.335.J64 2006**
Improving Customer Satisfaction, Loyalty, and Profit: An Integrated Measurement and Management System. Trade Paper. John Wiley & Sons, Inc. Hoboken, NJ. 2006. 240p. ISBN:0-7879-6469-7, ISBN13: 978-0-7879-6469-6. Dewey:658.8/12.
Audience: **u,f.** *Choice, 2001.*

Kanner, Bernice **HF5415.32.K36 2004**
Pocketbook Power. Ed. 1. McGraw-Hill. 2004. ISBN:0-07-141860-1, ISBN13: 978-0-07-141860-7.
Audience: **l,u,f.**

Mariampolski, Hy **HF5415.2.M3164 2006**
Ethnography for Marketers : A Guide to Consumer Immersion. SAGE Publications. 2006. ISBN:0-7619-6946-2, ISBN13: 978-0-7619-6946-4.
Audience: **u,f.**

Mediamark Research Inc. **HF5415.2**
Mediamark Reporter. Ed. 2005. Mediamark Research Inc. Mediamark Reporter
Audience: **u,f.**

O'Shaughnessy, John **HF5415.3.O84 1987**
Why People Buy. Trade Paper. Oxford University Press, Inc. New York, NY. 1989. 202p. ISBN:0-19-504087-2, ISBN13: 978-0-19-504087-6. Dewey:658.8/342. LCCN:86-012511.
Audience: **g,l,u,f.** *Choice, 1987.*

Peter, J. Paul & Jerry C. Olson **HF5415.3.P468 2005**
Consumer Behavior and Marketing Strategy. Ed. 7. McGraw-Hill. 2005. McGraw-Hill/Irwin Series in Marketing ISBN:0-07-286487-7, ISBN13: 978-0-07-286487-8.
Audience: **l,u.**

Simmons Market Research Bureau **HC110.C6**
Choices III.
http://www.smrb.com/
Ed. 2006. Simmons Market Research Bureau.
Audience: **u,f.**

Zollo, Peter **HF5415.32**
Getting Wiser to Teens. Ed. 2. New Strategist Publications. 2004. ISBN:1-885070-54-3, ISBN13: 978-1-885070-54-8.
Audience: **g,l,u,f.**

Management Function > Marketing > Advertising

HF5801
Advertising Age. Crain Communications, Inc.
Audience: **g,l,u,f.**

HF5801
Adweek. V N U Business Publications.
Audience: **g,l,u,f.**

HF5801
Brandweek: The Newsweekly of Marketing Communications. V N U Business Publications.
Audience: **g,l,u,f.**

HF5826.5
Marketer's Guide to Media. V N U Business Publications. 2005.
Audience: **g,u,f.**

Altman, Dennis, et al. **HF5813.U6**
Advertising and the Business of Brands. Ed. 2. Jim Avery, Beth Barnes, Dennis Ganahl, Robert Gustafson, Joe Bob Hester, Tom Jordan, Alice Kendrick, Carla Lloyd, James Marra, Ann Maxwell, Anthony McGann, Elizabeth Tucker & Jon Wardrip (Authors), Bruce Bendinger (Editor). Perfect. Copy Workshop, The. Chicago, IL. 2004. ISBN:1-887229-18-3, ISBN13: 978-1-887229-18-0. Dewey:659.10973.
Audience: **l,u,f.**

Cappo, Joe **HG4521.R538**
The Future of Advertising: New Media, New Clients, New Consumers in the Post-Television Age. Trade Paper. McGraw-Hill Companies, The. New York, NY. 2005. 256p. ISBN:0-07-146215-5, ISBN13: 978-0-07-146215-0. Dewey:659.1.
Audience: **l,u,f.** *Choice, 2004.*

Curtis P. Haugtvedt, Karen A. Machleit & Richard Yalch **HF5415.32**
Online Consumer Psychology. Lawrence Erlbaum Associates. 2005. Advertising and consumer psychology ISBN:0-8058-5154-2, ISBN13: 978-0-8058-5154-0.
Audience: **u,f.**

Gunter, Barrie, et al. **HQ784.T4G858 2004**
Advertising to Children on TV: Content, Impact, and Regulation. Caroline Oates & Mark Blades (Authors). Cloth over Boards. Lawrence Erlbaum Associates, Inc. Mahwah, NJ. 2004. 224p. ISBN:0-8058-4488-0, ISBN13: 978-0-8058-4488-7. Dewey:302.23/45/083. LCCN:2004-043266.
Audience: **u,f.** *Choice, 2005.*

Hackley, Chris **HF5823**
Advertising and Promotion: Communicating Brands. Paper Text. SAGE Publications, Inc. Thousand Oaks, CA. 2005. 280p. ISBN:0-7619-4154-1, ISBN13: 978-0-7619-4154-5. Dewey:659.1. LCCN:2004-114267.
Audience: **u,f.**

Leiss, William, et al. **HF5827.S63 2005**
Social Communication in Advertising: Persons, Products and Images of Well-being. Ed. 3. Stephen Kline, Sut Jhally & Jackie Botterill (Authors). UK-B Format Paperback. Routledge. New York, NY. 2005. 696p. ISBN:0-415-96676-0, ISBN13: 978-0-415-96676-4. Dewey:659.1/042. LCCN:2005-001364.
Audience: **g,u,f.**

Lewis, Herschell Gordon & Nelson, Carol **HF5823.N36**
Advertising Age: Handbook of Advertising. Rance Crain (Foreword by). Trade Paper. McGraw-Hill Companies, The. New York, NY. 1999. 240p. ISBN:0-8442-2448-0, ISBN13: 978-0-8442-2448-0. Dewey:659.1. LCCN:98-008362.
Audience: **g,l,u,f.**

LexisNexis **HF5805.St7**
The Advertising Red Books. Agencies. LexisNexis. 2005. Red Book
Audience: **g,l,u,f.**

McDonough, John (Editor) **HF5801**
The Advertising Age Encyclopedia of Advertising, Set. Trade Cloth. Fitzroy Dearborn Publishers, Inc. Chicago, IL. 2002. 1958p. ISBN:1-57958-172-2, ISBN13: 978-1-57958-172-5. Dewey:659.1/03. LCCN:2003-270744.
Audience: **g,l,u,f.** *Choice, 2003.*

Segrave, Kerry **HF5831.S44 2005**
Endorsements in Advertising: A Social History. Paper Text. McFarland & Company, Incorporated Publishers. Jefferson, NC. 2005. 239p. ISBN:0-7864-2043-X, ISBN13: 978-0-7864-2043-8. Dewey:659.1/042. LCCN:2005-001968.
Audience: **u,f.**

Strasser, Susan **HF5813.U6S79 2004**
Satisfaction Guaranteed: The Making of the American Mass Market. Trade Paper. Smithsonian Institution Press. Washington, DC. 2004. 348p. ISBN:1-58834-146-1, ISBN13: 978-1-58834-146-4. Dewey:659.1/042/0973.
Audience: **g,u,f.**

Management Function > Marketing > Advertising > Graphic Design

Z119
American Printer: The Graphic Arts Managers Magazine. Primedia Business Magazines & Media, Inc.
Audience: **g,u,f.**

Z119
Graphic Arts Monthly: Applied Technology for the Printing Industry. Reed Business Information.
Audience: **u,f.**

Hoffman, Barry **NC998.5.A1H64 2003**
The Fine Art of Advertising : Irreverent, Irrepressible, Irresistibly Ironic. Stewart, Tabori & Chang. 2002.
Audience: **g,l,u,f.**

Holland, D. K. (Editor) **NC997.D448 2001**
Design Issues: How Graphic Design Informs Society. Trade Paper. Allworth Press. New York, NY. 2001. 272p. ISBN:1-58115-202-7, ISBN13: 978-1-58115-202-9. Dewey:741.6. LCCN:2001-005297.
Audience: **g,l,u,f.** *Choice, 2002.*

O'Neil, Dennis **PN1998.2.O54 2001**
The DC Guide to Writing Comics. Trade Cloth. Watson-Guptill Publications, Inc. New York, NY. 2001. 128p. ISBN:0-8230-1027-9, ISBN13: 978-0-8230-1027-1. Dewey:808/.066741. LCCN:2001-026101.
Audience: **g,l,u,f.**

Management Function > Marketing > Advertising > History

HF5415.153
☐ Productscan.
http://www.productscan.com

Marketing Intelligence Service via Datamonitor, Inc.
Audience: **g,u,f.**

Bader, Sara **HF6125.B33 2005**
Strange Red Cow: And Other Curious Classified Ads from the Past. Trade Cloth. Crown Publishing Group. New York, NY. 2005. 224p. ISBN:1-4000-5120-7, ISBN13: 978-1-4000-5120-5. Dewey:659.13/2. LCCN:2004-030466.
Audience: **g,l,u.**

Brown, Elspeth (Editor), et al. **HM791.C844 2006**
Cultures of Commerce: Representation and American Business Culture, 1877-1960. Catherine Gudis & Marina Moskowitz (Editors). Cloth over Boards. Palgrave Macmillan. New York, NY. 2006. 384p. ISBN:1-4039-7050-5, ISBN13: 978-1-4039-7050-3. Dewey:302.3/50973. LCCN:2005-056289.
Audience: **g,u,f.** *Choice, 2006.*

Heimann, Jim (Editor) **NC998.5.A1**
1900-1919: All-American Ads. Steven Heller (Introduction by). Trade Cloth. Taschen America, LLC. Los Angeles, CA. 2005. 638p. ISBN:3-8228-2512-3, ISBN13: 978-3-8228-2512-9. Dewey:741.67097309041.
Audience: **g,l,u,f.**

Hoffman, Barry **NC998.5.A1H64 2003**
The Fine Art of Advertising : Irreverent, Irrepressible, Irresistibly Ironic. Stewart, Tabori & Chang. 2002.
Audience: **g,l,u,f.**

John W. Hartman Center for Sales, Advertising & Marketing History **HF5813.U6**
☐ Ad* Access.
http://scriptorium.lib.duke.edu/adaccess/
Digital Scriptorium, Rare Book, Manuscript, and Special Collections Library, Duke University.
Audience: **g,l,u,f.**

Kitch, Carolyn **P94.5.W652U655 2001**
Girl on the Magazine Cover: The Origins of Visual Stereotypes in American Mass Media. University of North Carolina Press. 2001.
Audience: **g,l,u,f.**

Lorin, Philippe & Alonso, Cristina **HF5810.A2**
5 Giants of Advertising. Trade Paper. DIANE Publishing Company. Collingdale, PA. 2005. 143p. ISBN:0-7567-8976-1, ISBN13: 978-0-7567-8976-3. Dewey:659.109.
Audience: **g,l,u.**

McFall, Liz **HF5827**
Advertising: A Cultural Economy. Cloth Text. SAGE Publications, Inc. Thousand Oaks, CA. 2004. 224p. Culture, Representation and Identity Ser. ISBN:0-7619-4254-8, ISBN13: 978-0-7619-4254-2. Dewey:659.1/042. LCCN:2003-110017.
Audience: **u,f.**

Penny, Laura **303.3/75/0973**
Your Call Is Important to Us: The Truth about Bullshit. Trade Cloth. Crown Publishing Group. New York, NY. 2005. 256p. ISBN:1-4000-8103-3, ISBN13: 978-1-4000-8103-5. Dewey:HM1231.P46 2005.
Audience: **g,l,u,f.**

Segrave, Kerry **HF5831.S44 2005**
Endorsements in Advertising: A Social History. Paper Text. McFarland & Company, Incorporated Publishers. Jefferson, NC. 2005. 239p. ISBN:0-7864-2043-X, ISBN13: 978-0-7864-2043-8. Dewey:659.1/042. LCCN:2005-001968.
Audience: **u,f.**

University of Illinois Communications Library **HF5813.U6**
☐ University of Illinois Ad Collections Index.
http://www.library.uiuc.edu/cmx/collections/adcollections.htm
Romero, Lisa. University of Illinois at Urbana-Champaign.
Audience: **l,u,f.**

Warlaumont, Hazel G. **ML156**
Advertising in the 60s: Turncoats, Traditionalists, and Waste Makers in America's Turbulent Decade. Praeger. 2001. ISBN:0-275-96932-0, ISBN13: 978-0-275-96932-5.
Audience: **u,f.**

Management Function > Marketing > Brands and Brand Management

T223.V4
Brands and Their Companies. Gale Group. 2004.
Audience: **l,u,f.**

HF5801
Brandweek: The Newsweekly of Marketing Communications. V N U Business Publications.
Audience: **g,l,u,f.**

HF5801
Brandweek: The Newsweekly of Marketing Communications. V N U Business Publications.
Audience: **g,u,f.**

HF5415.153
☐ Productscan.
http://www.productscan.com
Marketing Intelligence Service via Datamonitor, Inc.
Audience: **g,u,f.**

Aaker, David A. **HD69.B7A216 1996**
Building Strong Brands. Trade Cloth. Simon & Schuster. New York, NY. 1995. 400p. ISBN:0-02-900151-X, ISBN13: 978-0-02-900151-6. Dewey:658.8/27. LCCN:95-009238.
Audience: **g,u.**

Advertising Red Books.com
☐ Brand Name Lookup.
http://www.redbooks.com/Nonsub/brand.asp
Lexis-Nexis.
Audience: **g,l,u,f.**

Danesi, Marcel **HD69.B7**
Brands. Trade Paper. Routledge. New York, NY. 2006. 176p. Introductions to Media and Communications Ser. ISBN:0-415-27998-4, ISBN13: 978-0-415-27998-7. Dewey:658.8/27.
Audience: **g,u,f.**

Duffy, Neill & Hooper, Jo **HD69.B7D92 2003**
ⓔ Passion Branding: Harnessing the Power of Emotion to Build Strong Brands. E-Book. John Wiley & Sons, Inc. Hoboken, NJ.

2004. 264p. ISBN:0-470-86940-2, ISBN13: 978-0-470-86940-6. Dewey:658.8/27.

Audience: **l,u,f.**

Gobe, Marc **HD69.B7.G62 2001**
Emotional Branding: The New Paradigm for Connecting Brands to People. Trade Cloth. Allworth Press. New York, NY. 2001. 256p. ISBN:1-58115-078-4, ISBN13: 978-1-58115-078-0. Dewey:658.8/343. LCCN:00-053428.

Audience: **g,u,f.** *Choice, 2002.*

Haig, Matt **HD69.B7H345 2005**
Brand Failures: The Truth about the 100 Biggest Branding Mistakes of All Time. Trade Paper, Perfect. Kogan Page, Ltd. London, 2005. 272p. ISBN:0-7494-4433-9, ISBN13: 978-0-7494-4433-4. Dewey:658.8/27.

Audience: **g,l,u,f.** *Choice, 2003.*

Haig, Matt **HD69.B7H346 2004**
Brand Royalty: How the World's Top 100 Brands Thrive and Survive. Trade Cloth. Kogan Page, Ltd. London, 2004. 320p. ISBN:0-7494-4257-3, ISBN13: 978-0-7494-4257-6. Dewey:658.8/27. LCCN:2004-015322.

Audience: **u,f.** *Choice, 2005.*

McEwen, William J. **HF5415.3**
Married to the Brand: Why Consumers Bond with Some Brands for Life. Trade Cloth. Gallup Press. New York, NY. 2005. 210p. ISBN:1-59562-005-2, ISBN13: 978-1-59562-005-7. Dewey:658.8343.

Audience: **g,u,f.**

Morris, Evan **HD69.B7M667 2004**
From Altoids to Zima: The Surprising Stories Behind 125 Famous Brand Names. Trade Paper. Simon & Schuster, Inc. New York, NY. 2004. 208p. ISBN:0-7432-5797-9, ISBN13: 978-0-7432-5797-8. Dewey:658.8/27. LCCN:2004-052597.

Audience: **g,l,u,f.**

Payne, Michael **GV721**
Olympic Turnaround: How the Olympic Games Stepped Back from the Brink of Extinction to Become the World's Best Known Brand. Trade Cloth. Greenwood Publishing Group, Inc. Portsmouth, NH. 2006. 368p. ISBN:0-275-99030-3, ISBN13: 978-0-275-99030-5. Dewey:796.48. LCCN:2005-032679.

Audience: **l,u.**

Post, Karen **HD69.B7P64 2005**
Brain Tattoos: Creating Unique Brands That Stick in Your Customers' Minds. Trade Paper. Amacom. New York, NY. 2004. 208p. ISBN:0-8144-7234-6, ISBN13: 978-0-8144-7234-7. Dewey:658.8/27. LCCN:2004-014340.

Audience: **g,l,u,f.**

Ries, Al & Ries, Laura **HD69.B7R538 2005**
Origin of Brands: How Product Evolution Creates Endless Possibilities for New Brands. Trade Paper. HarperCollins Publishers. New York, NY. 2005. 320p. ISBN:0-06-057015-6, ISBN13: 978-0-06-057015-6. Dewey:658.827.

Audience: **g,u,f.**

Rivkin, Steve & Sutherland, Fraser **HD69.B7**
The Making of a Name: The Inside Story of the Brands We Buy. Trade Cloth. Oxford University Press, Inc. New York, NY. 2005. 286p. ISBN:0-19-516872-0, ISBN13: 978-0-19-516872-3. Dewey:658.8/27. LCCN:2004-012206.

Audience: **g,u,f.**

Simmons Market Research Bureau **HC110.C6**
Choices III.
http://www.smrb.com/
Ed. 2006. Simmons Market Research Bureau.

Audience: **u,f.**

Swystun, Jeff (Editor) **HD69.B7**
Interbrand's Brand Glossary: The Resource for Branding and Brand Management. Cloth over Boards. Palgrave Macmillan. New York, NY. 2006. 144p. ISBN:1-4039-9809-4, ISBN13: 978-1-4039-9809-5. Dewey:658.827.

Audience: **l,u,f.**

Thomson Gale Staff (Editor) **HF5415.3 .E527**
Encyclopedia of Consumer Brands. Ed. 2. Trade Cloth. Thomson Gale. Farmington Hills, MI. 2006. ISBN:1-55862-227-6, ISBN13: 978-1-55862-227-2. Dewey:658.8/343.

Audience: **g,l,u,f.**

Wheeler, Alina **HD69.B7W44 2006**
Designing Brand Identity: A Complete Guide to Creating, Building, and Maintaining Strong Brands. Ed. 2. Trade Cloth. John Wiley & Sons, Inc. Hoboken, NJ. 2006. 288p. ISBN:0-471-74684-3, ISBN13: 978-0-471-74684-3. Dewey:658.8/27. LCCN:2005-056961.

Audience: **g,u,f.**

Wipperfurth, Alex **HD69.B7W553 2005**
Brand Hijack: Marketing Without Marketing. Trade Cloth. Penguin Group (USA) Inc. New York, NY. 2005. 288p. ISBN:1-59184-078-3, ISBN13: 978-1-59184-078-7. Dewey:658.8/27. LCCN:2004-057391.

Audience: **g,l,u,f.**

Management Function > Marketing > Sales and Selling

HF5438.A34
Sales and Marketing Management: Survey of Buying Power. Ed. 2005. Bill Communications.

Audience: **u,f.**

Cherry, Paul **HF5438.25.C485 2006**
Questions That Sell: The Powerful Process for Discovering What Your Customer Really Wants. Trade Paper. Amacom. New York, NY. 2006. 192p. ISBN:0-8144-7339-3, ISBN13: 978-0-8144-7339-9. Dewey:658.85. LCCN:2005-033216.

Audience: **g,u,f.**

Green, Charles **HF5438.25.G732 2006**
Trust-Based Selling. Trade Cloth. McGraw-Hill Companies, The. New York, NY. 2005. 288p. ISBN:0-07-146194-9, ISBN13: 978-0-07-146194-8. Dewey:658.85. LCCN:2005-031036.

Audience: **g,u,f.**

Hanan, Mack **HF5438.25.H345 2003**
Consultative Selling: The Hanan Formula for High-Margin Sales at High Levels. Ed. 7. Trade Cloth. Amacom. New York, NY. 2003. 256p. ISBN:0-8144-7215-X, ISBN13: 978-0-8144-7215-6. Dewey:658.85. LCCN:2003-019604.

Audience: **g,u,f.**

Miller, William & Zemke, Ron **HF5438.3.M55 2005**
Knock Your Socks Off Prospecting: How to Cold Call, Get Qualified Leads, and Make More Money. Trade Paper, Perfect. Amacom. New York, NY. 2005. 162p. ISBN:0-8144-7285-0, ISBN13: 978-0-8144-7285-9. Dewey:658.8/72. LCCN:2005-000981.
Audience: **g,u,f.**

Sales and marketing management
Survey of Buying Power and Media Markets. Ed. 2005. Bill Communications, Inc.
Audience: **u,f.**

Schwartz, Matthew **HF5438.4.S362 2006**
Fundamentals of Sales Management for the Newly Appointed Sales Manager. Trade Paper. Amacom. New York, NY. 2006. 224p. ISBN:0-8144-0873-7, ISBN13: 978-0-8144-0873-5. Dewey:658.8/1. LCCN:2005-022936.
Audience: **g,u,f.**

Simpkins, Robert A. **HF5438.4.S52 2004**
The Secrets of Great Sales Management: Advanced Strategies for Maximizing Performance. Trade Cloth. Amacom. New York, NY. 2004. 24p. ISBN:0-8144-7238-9, ISBN13: 978-0-8144-7238-5. Dewey:658.8/1. LCCN:2004-004340.
Audience: **g,u,f.**

Super, Carol & Gold, Ronald **HF5438.25.S865 2003**
Selling Without Selling: 4 1/2 Steps to Success. Trade Paper. Amacom. New York, NY. 2003. 208p. ISBN:0-8144-7186-2, ISBN13: 978-0-8144-7186-9. Dewey:658.85. LCCN:2003-011347.
Audience: **g,u,f.**

Management Function > Marketing > Sales and Selling > Customer Relations

Abram, John & Hawkes, Paul **HF5415.5.A26 2003**
[e] The Seven Myths of Customer Management: How to be Customer-Driven Without Being Customer-Led. E-Book. John Wiley & Sons, Inc. Hoboken, NJ. 2005. 236p. ISBN:0-470-85881-8, ISBN13: 978-0-470-85881-3. Dewey:658.8/12.
Audience: **g,l,u,f.**

Barnes, James G. **HF5415.5.B3683 2001**
Secrets of Customer Relationship Management: It's All about How You Make Them Feel. McGraw-Hill. 2000. ISBN:0-07-136253-3, ISBN13: 978-0-07-136253-5.
Audience: **g,u,f.**

Blanchard, Ken, et al. **HF5415.5.B526 2004**
Customer Mania!: It's Never Too Late to Build a Customer-Focused Company. Fred Finch & Jim Ballard (Authors), Fred Hills (Editor). Trade Cloth. Simon & Schuster. New York, NY. 2004. 208p. ISBN:0-7432-7028-2, ISBN13: 978-0-7432-7028-1. Dewey:658.8/12. LCCN:2004-056398.
Audience: **g,l,u,f.**

Blomstermo, Anders (Editor), et al. **HF5415.55**
Managing Customer Relationships on the Internet. Jan Johanson, Angelika Lindstrand & Dharma Deo Sharma (Editors). Trade Cloth. Elsevier Science & Technology Books. Saint Louis, MO. 2005. 318p. International Business and Management Ser. ISBN:0-08-044124-6, ISBN13: 978-0-08-044124-5. Dewey:658.81202854678.
Audience: **g,u,f.**

Gupta, Sunil & Lehmann, Donald **HC79.C6G86 2005**
Managing Customers as Investments: The Strategic Value of Customers in the Long Run. Trade Cloth. Wharton School Publishing. Upper Saddle River, NJ. 2005. 224p. ISBN:0-13-142895-0, ISBN13: 978-0-13-142895-9. Dewey:658.8/12. LCCN:2004-116044.
Audience: **g,u,f.**

Peck, Helen **HF5415.55.R448 1999**
Relationship Marketing: Strategy and Implementation. Butterworth-Heinemann. 1999. ISBN:0-585-22931-7, ISBN13: 978-0-585-22931-7.
Audience: **u,f.**

Pelletier, Ray **HF5415.5.P45 2005**
It's All about Service: How to Lead Your People to Care for Your Customers. Trade Cloth. John Wiley & Sons, Inc. Hoboken, NJ. 2005. 232p. ISBN:0-471-71675-8, ISBN13: 978-0-471-71675-4. Dewey:658.8/12. LCCN:2004-027960.
Audience: **g,u,f.**

Peppers, Don & Rogers, Martha **HF5415.5**
[e] The One to One Manager: Real-World Lessons in Customer Relationship Management. E-Book. John Wiley & Sons, Inc. Hoboken, NJ. 2004. 180p. ISBN:1-84112-651-9, ISBN13: 978-1-84112-651-7. Dewey:658.8/12.
Audience: **g,u,f.**

Reichheld, Frederick F. **HF5415.5.R439 2006**
The Ultimate Question: Driving Good Profits and True Growth. Trade Cloth. Harvard Business School Press. Boston, MA. 2006. 224p. ISBN:1-59139-783-9, ISBN13: 978-1-59139-783-0. Dewey:658.15/54. LCCN:2005-025733.
Audience: **g,u,f.**

Shaw, Colin & Ivens, John **HF5415.5**
Building Great Customer Experiences. Ed. 2. Trade Paper. Palgrave Macmillan. New York, NY. 2004. 288p. ISBN:1-4039-3949-7, ISBN13: 978-1-4039-3949-4. Dewey:658.8/12.
Audience: **g,u,f.**

Management Function > Marketing > Distribution

Bowersox, Donald J. **HF5415.7.B66 1978**
Logistical Management: A Systems Integration of Physical Distribution Management and Materials Management. Trade Cloth. Macmillan Publishing Company, Inc. Old Tappan, NJ. 1978. xii, 528p. ISBN:0-02-313110-1, ISBN13: 978-0-02-313110-3. Dewey:658.7. LCCN:77-004670.
Audience: **u,f.** B

Vega, Gina **HD30.28.V43 2000**
A Passion for Planning: Financials, Operations, Marketing, Management and Ethics. Trade Cloth. University Press of America, Inc. Lanham, MD. 2001. 248p. ISBN:0-7618-1853-7,

ISBN13: 978-0-7618-1853-3. Dewey:658.4/012. LCCN:00-048854.
Audience: **u,f.** *Choice, 2001.*

Management Function > Marketing > Product Planning and Development

Brooke, Michael Z. & Mills, William R. **HF5415.153.B76 2002**
New Product Development: Successful Innovation in the Marketplace. Trade Cloth. Haworth Press, Incorporated, The. Binghamton, NY. 2002. 244p. ISBN:0-7890-1566-8, ISBN13: 978-0-7890-1566-2. Dewey:658.5/75. LCCN:2002-068763.
Audience: **u,f.** *Choice, 2003.*

Clark, Kim B. & Fujimoto, Takahiro **HD9710.A2C57 1991**
Product Development Performance: Strategy, Organization, and Management in the World Auto Industry. Trade Cloth. Harvard Business School Press. Boston, MA. 1991. 350p. ISBN:0-87584-245-3, ISBN13: 978-0-87584-245-5. Dewey:629.2/068/5. LCCN:90-047967.
Audience: **u,f.** *Choice, 1991.*

Dine, B. Joseph II & Gilmore, James H. **HF5415.15.P56 1999**
The Experience Economy: Work Is Theatre and Every Business a Stage. Trade Cloth. Harvard Business School Press. Boston, MA. 1999. 272p. ISBN:0-87584-819-2, ISBN13: 978-0-87584-819-8. Dewey:658.5/6. LCCN:98-033202.
Audience: **u,f.** *Choice, 1999.*

Fisher, Lawrence **HF5415**
Industrial Marketing: An Analytical Approach to Planning and Execution. Ed. 2. Trade Cloth. Random House. London, 1976. xiv, 270p. ISBN:0-220-66292-4, ISBN13: 978-0-220-66292-9. Dewey:658.8. LCCN:77-365309.
Audience: **u,f.** B

Kahn, Kenneth B. **TS170.K34 2001**
Product Planning Essentials. Cloth Text. SAGE Publications, Inc. Thousand Oaks, CA. 2000. 264p. ISBN:0-7619-1998-8, ISBN13: 978-0-7619-1998-8. Dewey:658.5/75. LCCN:00-009514.
Audience: **u,f.** *Choice, 2001.*

Kahn, Kenneth B. (Editor) **HF5415.153.P35 2005**
The PDMA Handbook of New Product Development. Ed. 2. Product Development & Management Association Staff (Contribution by). Trade Cloth. John Wiley & Sons, Inc. Hoboken, NJ. 2004. 640p. ISBN:0-471-48524-1, ISBN13: 978-0-471-48524-7. Dewey:658.5/75. LCCN:2004-002261.
Audience: **u,f.**

Mark, Margaret & Pearson, Carol S. **HF5415.15.M334 2001**
The Hero and the Outlaw: Building Extraordinary Brands Through the Power of Archetypes. Trade Cloth. McGraw-Hill Companies, The. New York, NY. 2001. 384p. ISBN:0-07-136415-3, ISBN13: 978-0-07-136415-7. Dewey:658.827. LCCN:2001-274378.
Audience: **u,f.** *Choice, 2001.*

McDonald, Malcolm & Keegan, Warren J. **HF5415.13.M3154 2002**
Marketing Plans That Work. Ed. 2. Paper Text. Elsevier Science & Technology Books. Saint Louis, MO. 2001. 264p. ISBN:0-7506-7307-9, ISBN13: 978-0-7506-7307-5. Dewey:658.8/02. LCCN:2001-043345.
Audience: **u,f.** *Choice, 2002.*

Onkvisit, Sak & Shaw, John J. **HF5415**
Product Life Cycles and Product Management. Trade Cloth. Greenwood Publishing Group, Inc. Portsmouth, NH. 1989. 172p. ISBN:0-89930-319-6, ISBN13: 978-0-89930-319-2. Dewey:658.5/038. LCCN:88-026509.
Audience: **u,f.** *Choice, 1989.*

Palda, Kristian S. **HF5415**
Pricing Decisions and Marketing Policy. Trade Paper. Prentice-Hall. Upper Saddle, NJ. 1971. x, 116p. ISBN:0-13-699660-4, ISBN13: 978-0-13-699660-6. Dewey:658.8/16/0184. LCCN:78-139413.
Audience: **u,f.** B

Management Function > Marketing > Packaging

Meyers, Herbert M. & Gerstman, Richard **HF5770**
The Visionary Package. Cloth over Boards. Palgrave Macmillan. New York, NY. 2005. 200p. ISBN:1-4039-0677-7, ISBN13: 978-1-4039-0677-9. Dewey:658.8/23. LCCN:2004-057787.
Audience: **u,f.** *Choice, 2005.*

Ware, Leslie **HF5827.8.S45 2001**
Selling It!: The Incredible Shrinking Package and Other Marvels of Modern Marketing. Consumer Reports Books Editors (Editor). Trade Paper. W. W. Norton & Company, Inc. New York, NY. 2002. 196p. ISBN:0-393-32172-X, ISBN13: 978-0-393-32172-2. Dewey:658.8. LCCN:2001-041004.
Audience: **u,f.** *Choice, 2003, 2002.*

Management Function > Marketing > Public Relations

Harris, Thomas L. **HF5415.123.H37 1998**
Value-Added Public Relations: The Secret Weapon of Integrated Marketing. Philip Hotler (Foreword by). Trade Cloth. McGraw-Hill Companies, The. New York, NY. 1998. 336p. ISBN:0-8442-3411-7, ISBN13: 978-0-8442-3411-3. Dewey:659.2. LCCN:97-037323.
Audience: **u,f.** *Choice, 1999.*

Holtz, Shel **HD59.H596 1999**
Public Relations on the Net: Winning Strategies to Inform and Influence the Media, the Investment Community, the Government, the Public, and More!. Trade Paper. Amacom. New York, NY. 1998. xx, 332p. ISBN:0-8144-7987-1, ISBN13: 978-0-8144-7987-2. Dewey:659.2/0285/4678. LCCN:98-008580.
Audience: **u,f.** *Choice, 1999.*

Marchand, Roland **HD59.2 .M368 1998**
Creating the Corporate Soul: The Rise of Public Relations and Corporate Imagery in American Big Business. Trade Cloth. University of California Press. Berkeley, CA. 1998. 470p. Director's Circle Book Ser. ISBN:0-520-08719-4, ISBN13: 978-0-520-08719-4. Dewey:659.2/85. LCCN:97-050098.
Audience: **u,f.** *Choice, 1999.*

Management Function > Marketing > Public Relations > Business-Government Relations

Kennedy, Scott **HD3616.C63K46 2005**
The Business of Lobbying in China. Trade Cloth. Harvard University Press. Cambridge, MA. 2005. 278p. ISBN:0-674-01547-9, ISBN13: 978-0-674-01547-0. Dewey:322/.3/0951. LCCN:2004-054314.
Audience: **u.** *Choice, 2005.*

Wartick, Steven L. & Wood, Donna J. **HD62.4**
International Business and Society. Trade Paper. Blackwell Publishing, Inc. Malden, MA. 2000. 264p. Business Ser. ISBN:1-55786-944-8, ISBN13: 978-1-55786-944-9. Dewey:658/.049. LCCN:97-011926.
Audience: **u.** *Choice, 1998.*

Management Function > Marketing > Public Relations > Image

Manheim, Jarol B. **HD59.M257 2001**
The Death of a Thousand Cuts: Corporate Campaigns and the Attack on the Corporation. Cloth over Boards. Lawrence Erlbaum Associates, Inc. Mahwah, NJ. 2000. 376p. ISBN:0-8058-3831-7, ISBN13: 978-0-8058-3831-2. Dewey:659.2. LCCN:00-034780.
Audience: **g,l,u,f.** *Choice, 2001.*

Marconi, Joe **HF5414.M37 2002**
Cause Marketing. Cloth Text. Kaplan Publishing. Chicago, IL. 2002. 225p. ISBN:0-7931-5258-5, ISBN13: 978-0-7931-5258-2. Dewey:658.8. LCCN:2002-004699.
Audience: **u.** *Choice, 2003.*

Marconi, Joe **HD59.2.M37 1996**
Image Marketing: Using Public Perceptions to Create Awareness and Build Market Share. Trade Cloth. McGraw-Hill Companies, The. New York, NY. 1996. 256p. ISBN:0-8442-3504-0, ISBN13: 978-0-8442-3504-2. Dewey:658.8/001. LCCN:95-046960.
Audience: **u.** *Choice, 1997.*

Management Function > Marketing > Public Relations > Social Responsibility

Bloom, Paul N. & Gundlach, Gregory T. **HF5414.H36 2001**
Handbook of Marketing and Society. Trade Cloth. SAGE Publications, Inc. Thousand Oaks, CA. 2000. 570p. ISBN:0-7619-1626-1, ISBN13: 978-0-7619-1626-0. Dewey:658.8/02. LCCN:00-009055.
Audience: **u,f.** *Choice, 2001.*

Keller, Edward B. & Berry, Jonathan L. **HN65.K43 2003**
The Influentials: One American in Ten Tells the Other Nine How to Vote, Where to Eat, and What to Buy. Trade Cloth. Simon & Schuster. New York, NY. 2003. 368p. ISBN:0-7432-2729-8, ISBN13: 978-0-7432-2729-2. Dewey:303.3/4. LCCN:2002-034671.
Audience: **g,u,f.**

Manheim, Jarol B. **HD59.M257 2001**
The Death of a Thousand Cuts: Corporate Campaigns and the Attack on the Corporation. Cloth over Boards. Lawrence Erlbaum Associates, Inc. Mahwah, NJ. 2000. 376p. ISBN:0-8058-3831-7, ISBN13: 978-0-8058-3831-2. Dewey:659.2. LCCN:00-034780.
Audience: **g,l,u,f.** *Choice, 2001.*

Reeves-Ellington, Richard H. & Anderson, Adele **HF5387.R44 1997**
Business, Commerce, and Social Responsibility: Beyond Agenda. Ed. 4. Trade Cloth. Edwin Mellen Press, The. Lewiston, NY. 1997. 288p. ISBN:0-7734-8442-6, ISBN13: 978-0-7734-8442-9. Dewey:174.4. LCCN:97-037725.
Audience: **u,f.** *Choice, 1998.*

Richter, Judith **HD60.R525 2001**
Holding Corporations Accountable: Corporate Conduct, International Codes and Citizen Action. Cloth over Boards. Zed Books, Ltd. London, 2002. 256p. ISBN:1-85649-983-9, ISBN13: 978-1-85649-983-5. Dewey:658.4/08. LCCN:2001-026998.
Audience: **u,f.** *Choice, 2002.*

Samli, A. Coskun **HF5415**
Social Responsibility in Marketing: A Proactive and Profitable Marketing Management Strategy. Trade Cloth. Greenwood Publishing Group, Inc. Portsmouth, NH. 1992. 224p. ISBN:0-89930-628-4, ISBN13: 978-0-89930-628-5. Dewey:658.8/02. LCCN:92-009810.
Audience: **u,f.** *Choice, 1993.*

Schwartz, Peter & Gibb, Blair **HD60.S39 1999**
When Good Companies Do Bad Things: Responsibility and Risk in an Age of Globalization. Trade Cloth. John Wiley & Sons, Inc. Hoboken, NJ. 1999. 194p. ISBN:0-471-32332-2, ISBN13: 978-0-471-32332-7. Dewey:658.4/08. LCCN:98-031700.
Audience: **l,u,f.** *Choice, 1999.*

Wartick, Steven L. & Wood, Donna J. **HD62.4**
International Business and Society. Trade Paper. Blackwell Publishing, Inc. Malden, MA. 2000. 264p. Business Ser. ISBN:1-55786-944-8, ISBN13: 978-1-55786-944-9. Dewey:658/.049. LCCN:97-011926.
Audience: **u.** *Choice, 1998.*

Management Function > Marketing > Ethics and Marketing

Badaracco, Joseph L. Jr. **HF5387.B32 1997**
Defining Moments: When Managers Must Choose Between Right and Right. Trade Cloth. Harvard Business School Press. Boston, MA. 1997. 160p. ISBN:0-87584-803-6, ISBN13: 978-0-87584-803-7. Dewey:174/.4. LCCN:97-017613.
Audience: **u.** *Choice, 1998.*

Bird, Frederick Bruce **HF5387**
The Muted Conscience: Moral Silence and the Practice of Ethics in Business. Trade Cloth. Greenwood Publishing Group, Inc. Portsmouth, NH. 1996. 280p. ISBN:0-89930-652-7, ISBN13: 978-0-89930-652-0. Dewey:174.4. LCCN:96-000591.
Audience: **u.** *Choice, 1997.*

Davidson, D. Kirk **HF5414.D38 2002**
The Moral Dimension of Marketing: Essays on Business Ethics. Trade Paper. Thomson South-Western. Mason, OH. 2002. 212p. ISBN:0-87757-300-X, ISBN13: 978-0-87757-300-5. Dewey:174/.4. LCCN:2002-074358.
Audience: **u.**

Hayworth, Gene **HF5387**
☐ BELL: the business ethics links library.
http://libnet.colorado.edu/Bell/
Audience: **g,l,u,f.**

Smith, N. Craig & Quelch, John **HD37.C47**
Ethics in Marketing. Paper Text. McGraw-Hill Higher Education. Burr Ridge, IL. 1996. 864p. ISBN:0-256-25903-8, ISBN13: 978-0-256-25903-2. Dewey:174.9/658.
Audience: **u,f.**

Company and Industry Information

Freese, Barbara **TN801**
Coal: A Human History. Trade Cloth. DIANE Publishing Company. Collingdale, PA. 2005. 308p. ISBN:0-7567-9769-1, ISBN13: 978-0-7567-9769-0. Dewey:553.2/4.
Audience: **g,l,u,f.** *Choice, 2003.*

Company and Industry Information > Business History

HC21
☐ EH.Net Encyclopedia of Economic and Business History.
http://www.eh.net/encyclopedia/
Audience: **g,l,u,f.**

HJ2250
☐ Tax History Project.
http://www.taxhistory.org/
Audience: **g,l,u,f.**

Bagehot, Walter **HG3000.L82B3 1999**
Lombard Street: A Description of the Money Market. Trade Paper. John Wiley & Sons, Inc. Hoboken, NJ. 1999. 359p. Wiley Investment Classic Ser., Vol. 22 ISBN:0-471-34536-9, ISBN13: 978-0-471-34536-7. Dewey:332/.09421. LCCN:98-051463.
Audience: **g,l,u,f.**

Berle, Adolf A. Jr. & Means, Gardiner C. **HD2795.B53 1991**
The Modern Corporation and Private Property. Ed. 2. Trade Paper. Transaction Publishers. Somerset, NJ. 1997. 426p. ISBN:0-88738-887-6, ISBN13: 978-0-88738-887-3. Dewey:338.5/024658. LCCN:90-048752.
Audience: **g,l,u,f.**

Blackford, Mansel G. **HD2346.U5B56 2003**
A History of Small Business in America. Ed. 2. Trade Cloth. University of North Carolina Press. Chapel Hill, NC. 2003. 272p. The Luther Hartwell Hodges Series on Business, Society, and the State ISBN:0-8078-2780-0, ISBN13: 978-0-8078-2780-2. Dewey:338.6/42/0973. LCCN:2002-151277.
Audience: **g,l,u,f.** *Choice, 2003, 1992.*

Chandler, Alfred D. Jr. **HD9651.5.C457 2005**
Shaping the Industrial Century: The Remarkable Story of the Evolution of the Modern Chemical and Pharmaceutical Industries. Trade Cloth. Harvard University Press. Cambridge, MA. 2005. 384p. Harvard Studies in Business History Ser., Vol. 46 ISBN:0-674-01720-X, ISBN13: 978-0-674-01720-7. Dewey:338.4/766/00973. LCCN:2004-054320.
Audience: **g,l,u,f.** *Choice, 2005.*

Chernow, Ron **HG2613.N54M6613 1990**
The House of Morgan: An American Banking Family and the Rise of Modern Finance. Trade Cloth. Grove/Atlantic, Inc. New York, NY. 1990. ISBN:0-87113-338-5, ISBN13: 978-0-87113-338-0. Dewey:332.1/2/097471. LCCN:89-017542.
Audience: **g,l,u,f.**

Cortada, James W. **HC110.A9C655 2003**
The Digital Hand: How Computers Changed the Work of American Manufacturing, Transportation, and Retail Industries. Trade Cloth. Oxford University Press, Inc. New York, NY. 2003. 522p. ISBN:0-19-516588-8, ISBN13: 978-0-19-516588-3. Dewey:338.0973. LCCN:2003-012107.
Audience: **g,l,u,f.** *Choice, 2004.*

Cortada, James W. **HC110.I55C67 2005**
The Digital Hand, Volume 2: How Computers Changed the Work of American Financial, Telecommunications, Media, and Entertainment Industries. Trade Cloth. Oxford University Press, Inc. New York, NY. 2005. 672p. ISBN:0-19-516587-X, ISBN13: 978-0-19-516587-6. Dewey:338/.064/0973. LCCN:2004-030363.
Audience: **g,l,u,f.**

Ellis, Charles D. & Vertin, James R. **HG4928.5 .E42 2001**
Wall Street People: True Stories of the Great Barons of Finance. Trade Cloth. John Wiley & Sons, Inc. Hoboken, NJ. 2003. 288p. ISBN:0-471-27428-3, ISBN13: 978-0-471-27428-5. Dewey:332.60973.
Audience: **g,l,u,f.**

Ferguson, Niall **HG1552.A1F46 1998**
The House of Rothschild: Money's Prophets, 1798-1848. Trade Cloth. Penguin Group (USA) Inc. New York, NY. 1998. 688p. ISBN:0-670-85768-8, ISBN13: 978-0-670-85768-5. Dewey:332.1/092/24 B. LCCN:98-044706.
Audience: **g,l,u,f.** *Choice, 1999.*

Friedman, Walter A. **HF5438.4.F75 2004**
Birth of a Salesman: The Transformation of Selling in America. Trade Cloth. Harvard University Press. Cambridge, MA. 2004. 368p. ISBN:0-674-01298-4, ISBN13: 978-0-674-01298-1. Dewey:381/.1/0973. LCCN:2003-065235.
Audience: **g,l,u,f.**

Geisst, Charles **HG4572**
Wall Street: From Its Beginnings to the Fall of Enron. Trade Cloth. Oxford University Press, Inc. New York, NY. 2004. 449p. ISBN:0-19-517061-X, ISBN13: 978-0-19-517061-0. Dewey:332.64/273. LCCN:2004-555123.
Audience: **g,l,u,f.**

Goetzmann, William N. & Rouwenhorst, K. Geert **HG171**
Origins of Value: A Document History of Finance. Trade Cloth. Oxford University Press, Inc. New York, NY. 2005. 416p. ISBN:0-19-517571-9, ISBN13: 978-0-19-517571-4. Dewey:332/.041. LCCN:2005-002394.
Audience: **g,l,u,f.**

Gordon, John S. **HG4910.G667 1999**
The Great Game: The Emergence of Wall Street as a World Power, 1653-2000. Trade Cloth. Simon & Schuster. New York, NY. 1999. 320p. ISBN:0-684-83287-9, ISBN13: 978-0-684-83287-6. Dewey:332.64/273. LCCN:00-265068.
Audience: **g,l,u,f.**

Kindleberger, Charles P. & Aliber, Robert **HB3722.K56 2005**
Manias, Panics, and Crashes: A History of Financial Crises. Ed. 5. Robert Solow (Foreword by). Trade Paper. John Wiley & Sons, Inc. Hoboken, NJ. 2005. 304p. Wiley Investment Classics Ser. ISBN:0-471-46714-6, ISBN13: 978-0-471-46714-4. Dewey:338.5/42. LCCN:2005-001066.
Audience: **g,l,u,f.**

Laird, Pamela Walker **HD69.S8L35 2005**
Pull: Networking and Success since Benjamin Franklin. Trade Cloth. Harvard University Press. Cambridge, MA. 2006. 464p. Harvard Studies in Business History Ser., Vol. 48 ISBN:0-674-01907-5, ISBN13: 978-0-674-01907-2. Dewey:650.1/3. LCCN:2005-050247.
Audience: **g,l,u,f.** *Choice, 2006.*

Markham, Jerry W. **HV6769.M37 2005**
A Financial History of Modern U S Corporate Scandals. Cloth Text. M. E. Sharpe Inc. Armonk, NY. 2005. 768p. ISBN:0-7656-1583-5, ISBN13: 978-0-7656-1583-1. Dewey:364.16/8/0973. LCCN:2005-005562.
Audience: **g,l,u,f.** *Choice, 2006.*

Mason, David **HG2151.M37 2004**
From Building and Loans to Bail Outs: A History of the American Savings and Loan Industry, 1831-1995. Cloth Text. Cambridge University Press. New York, NY. 2004. 362p. ISBN:0-521-82754-X, ISBN13: 978-0-521-82754-6. Dewey:332.3/2/0973. LCCN:2003-069691.
Audience: **g,l,u,f.** *Choice, 2005.*

McCraw, Thomas K. (Introduction by) **HD2785.C4732 1988**
The Essential Alfred Chandler: Essays Toward a Historical Theory of Big Business. Cloth Text. Harvard Business School Press. Boston, MA. 1988. 544p. ISBN:0-87584-176-7, ISBN13: 978-0-87584-176-2. Dewey:338.6/44/0973. LCCN:87-029754.
Audience: **g,l,u,f.** *Choice, 1988.*

McCusker, John J. **HF1379.H574 2005**
Economic History of World Trade. Trade Cloth. Thomson Gale. Farmington Hills, MI. 2005. 900p. ISBN:0-02-865840-X, ISBN13: 978-0-02-865840-7. Dewey:382/.09. LCCN:2005-018624.
Audience: **g,l,u,f.**

Pomeranz, Kenneth & Topik, Steven **HF352.P58W67 2006**
The World That Trade Created: Society, Culture, and the World Economy 1400 to the Present. Ed. 2. Saddle Stitched, Cloth over Boards. M. E. Sharpe Inc. Armonk, NY. 2005. 287p. Sources and Studies in World History Ser. ISBN:0-7656-1708-0, ISBN13: 978-0-7656-1708-8. Dewey:382/.09. LCCN:2005-018044.
Audience: **l,u,f.**

Seligman, Joel **HG4910.S4 1995**
The Transformation of Wall Street: A History of the Securities and Exchange Commission and Modern Corporate Finance. Trade Cloth. Northeastern University Press. Boston, MA. 1995. 772p. ISBN:1-55553-231-4, ISBN13: 978-1-55553-231-4. Dewey:354.8/8/0973. LCCN:95-013762.
Audience: **g,l,u,f.** *Choice, 1996.*

Stewart, James B. **HG4910.S683 1991**
Den of Thieves: The Untold Story of the Men Who Plundered Wall Street and the Chase That Brought Them Down. Trade Cloth. Simon & Schuster. New York, NY. 1991. 496p. ISBN:0-671-63802-5, ISBN13: 978-0-671-63802-3. Dewey:364.1/68. LCCN:91-028819.
Audience: **g,l,u,f.**

Tarbell, Ida **HD9569.S8 T37**
History of the Standard Oil Company. Paper Text. Classic Textbooks. Murrieta, CA. 1904. 368p. ISBN:1-4047-5406-7, ISBN13: 978-1-4047-5406-5. Dewey:338.7/622382/0973.
Audience: **g,l,u,f.**

Weisman, Steven R. **HJ4652.W556 2002**
The Great Tax Wars: Lincoln to Wilson - The Fierce Battles over Money and Power That Transformed the Nation. Trade Cloth. Simon & Schuster. New York, NY. 2002. 432p. ISBN:0-684-85068-0, ISBN13: 978-0-684-85068-9. Dewey:336.24/2/097309034. LCCN:2002-070486.
Audience: **g,l,u,f.** *Choice, 2003.*

Company and Industry Information > Business History > Business and Executive Biographies

Edersheim, Elizabeth Haas **HD69.C6E34 2004**
McKinsey's Marvin Bower: Vision, Leadership, and the Creation of Management Consulting. Trade Cloth. John Wiley & Sons, Inc. Hoboken, NJ. 2004. 305p. ISBN:0-471-65285-7, ISBN13: 978-0-471-65285-4. Dewey:658.46092. LCCN:2004-299600.
Audience: **g,l,u,f.**

Ellis, Charles D. & Vertin, James R. **HG4928.5.E42 2001**
Wall Street People: True Stories of Today's Masters and Moguls. Trade Cloth. John Wiley & Sons, Inc. Hoboken, NJ. 2001. 360p. ISBN:0-471-23809-0, ISBN13: 978-0-471-23809-6. Dewey:332.6/0973. LCCN:2001-026114.
Audience: **g,l,u,f.**

Ellis, Charles D. & Vertin, James R. **HG4928.5 .E42 2001**
Wall Street People: True Stories of the Great Barons of Finance. Trade Cloth. John Wiley & Sons, Inc. Hoboken, NJ. 2003. 288p. ISBN:0-471-27428-3, ISBN13: 978-0-471-27428-5. Dewey:332.60973.
Audience: **g,l,u,f.**

Ferguson, Niall **HG1552.R8F47 1999**
The House of Rothschild: The World's Banker, 1849-1999. Trade Cloth. Penguin Group (USA) Inc. New York, NY. 1999. 608p. ISBN:0-670-88794-3, ISBN13: 978-0-670-88794-1. Dewey:332.1/092/2. LCCN:99-041868.
Audience: **g,l,u,f.**

Lowenstein, Roger **HG172.B84L69 1995**
Buffett: The Making of an American Capitalist. Trade Cloth. Random House, Inc. New York, NY. 1995. 512p.

ISBN:0-679-41584-X, ISBN13: 978-0-679-41584-8.
Dewey:332.6/092 B. LCCN:95-008494.
Audience: **g,l,u,f.** *Choice, 1996.*

Melamed, Leo & Tamarkin, Bob **HG6024.A3M437 1996**
Leo Melamed: Escape to the Futures. Trade Cloth. John Wiley & Sons, Inc. Hoboken, NJ. 1996. 480p. ISBN:0-471-11215-1, ISBN13: 978-0-471-11215-0. Dewey:332.6/2/092 B. LCCN:96-015316.
Audience: **g,l,u,f.**

Wright, Robert E. & Cowen, David J. **HG172.A2W75 2006**
Financial Founding Fathers: The Men Who Made America Rich. Trade Cloth. University of Chicago Press. Chicago, IL. 2006. 216p. ISBN:0-226-91068-7, ISBN13: 978-0-226-91068-0. Dewey:330.973/05/0922. LCCN:2005-026938.
Audience: **g,l,u,f.**

Company and Industry Information > Company Information

HG4009
Hoover's Online.
http://www.hoovers.com
Audience: **g,l,u,f.**

Chernow, Ron **HG2613.N54M6613 1990**
The House of Morgan: An American Banking Family and the Rise of Modern Finance. Trade Cloth. Grove/Atlantic, Inc. New York, NY. 1990. ISBN:0-87113-338-5, ISBN13: 978-0-87113-338-0. Dewey:332.1/2/097471. LCCN:89-017542.
Audience: **g,l,u,f.**

Ewald, William Bragg Jr. **HC102.5.C79**
Trammell Crow: A Legacy of Real Estate Business Innovation. Cloth over Boards. Urban Land Institute. Washington, DC. 2005. 300p. ISBN:0-87420-935-8, ISBN13: 978-0-87420-935-8. Dewey:333.33/092 B. LCCN:2005-922783.
Audience: **g,l,u,f.**

McCraw, Thomas K. (Introduction by) **HD2785.C4732 1988**
The Essential Alfred Chandler: Essays Toward a Historical Theory of Big Business. Cloth Text. Harvard Business School Press. Boston, MA. 1988. 544p. ISBN:0-87584-176-7, ISBN13: 978-0-87584-176-2. Dewey:338.6/44/0973. LCCN:87-029754.
Audience: **g,l,u,f.** *Choice, 1988.*

McLean, Bethany & Elkind, Peter **HD9502.U54E5763 2003**
Smartest Guys in the Room: The Amazing Rise and Scandalous Fall of Enron. Trade Cloth. Penguin Group (USA) Inc. New York, NY. 2003. 464p. ISBN:1-59184-008-2, ISBN13: 978-1-59184-008-4. Dewey:333.79/0973. LCCN:2003-054944.
Audience: **g,l,u,f.** *Choice, 2004.*

Peters, Thomas J. & Waterman, Robert H. Jr. **HD70.U5P424 2004**
In Search of Excellence: Lessons from America's Best-Run Companies. Tan (Editor). Trade Paper. HarperCollins Publishers. New York, NY. 2004. 400p. ISBN:0-06-054878-9, ISBN13: 978-0-06-054878-0. Dewey:658/.00973. LCCN:2003-067759.
Audience: **g,l,u,f.**

Tarbell, Ida **HD9569.S8 T37**
History of the Standard Oil Company. Paper Text. Classic Textbooks. Murrieta, CA. 1904. 368p. ISBN:1-4047-5406-7, ISBN13: 978-1-4047-5406-5. Dewey:338.7/622382/0973.
Audience: **g,l,u,f.**

Company and Industry Information > Industries and Markets (Selected)

Z731
The Bowker Annual Library and Book Trade Almanac 2005-2006. Ed. 50. Trade Cloth. Information Today, Inc. Medford, NJ. 2005. 800p. ISBN:1-57387-216-4, ISBN13: 978-1-57387-216-4. Dewey:20.58.
Audience: **u,f.**

HC102.E53
Encyclopedia of American Industries. Ed. 4. Trade Cloth. Thomson Gale. Farmington Hills, MI. 2004. 3500p. ISBN:0-7876-9061-9, ISBN13: 978-0-7876-9061-8. Dewey:338.0973.
Audience: **g,l,u,f.**

Adams, Walter & Brock, James W. **HD2785.A68 2004**
The Bigness Complex: Industry, Labor, and Government in the American Economy. Ed. 2. Trade Paper. Stanford University Press. Palo Alto, CA. 2004. 400p. ISBN:0-8047-4969-8, ISBN13: 978-0-8047-4969-5. Dewey:338.6/44/0973. LCCN:2004-001030.
Audience: **g,l,u,f.**

Baldasty, Gerald J. **PN4874.S37B35 1999**
E. W. Scripps and the Business of Newspapers. Trade Paper. University of Illinois Press. Champaign, IL. 1999. 232p. History of Communication Ser. ISBN:0-252-06750-9, ISBN13: 978-0-252-06750-1. Dewey:070.5/092 B. LCCN:98-025357.
Audience: **g,l,u,f.** *Choice, 1999.*

Boettcher, Jennifer C. & Gaines, Leonard M. **HC101**
Industry Research Using the Economic Census: How to Find It, How to Use It. Cloth Text. Greenwood Publishing Group, Inc. Portsmouth, NH. 2004. 328p. How to Find It, How to Use It Ser. ISBN:1-57356-351-X, ISBN13: 978-1-57356-351-2. Dewey:338.0973/0072/7. LCCN:2004-008607.
Audience: **l,u,f.** *Choice, 2005.*

Brock, James & Adams, Walter **HC106.S85 2004**
The Structure of American Industry. Ed. 11. Trade Paper. Prentice Hall PTR. Upper Saddle River, NJ. 2004. 336p. ISBN:0-13-143273-7, ISBN13: 978-0-13-143273-4. Dewey:338.6/0973. LCCN:2004-050278.
Audience: **g,l,u,f.** B

Cabell, David W. E. & English, Deborah L. (Editors) **HF5635.C33 2004; H91**
Cabell's Directory of Publishing Opportunities in Accounting. Ed. 9. Perfect. Cabell Publishing Company. Beaumont, TX. 2004. 548p. ISBN:0-911753-22-2, ISBN13: 978-0-911753-22-6. Dewey:330.
Audience: **u,f.**

Cabell, David W. E. & English, Deborah L. (Editors) **Z286.B88; H91**
Cabell's Directory of Publishing Opportunities in Economics and Finance. Ed. 9. Perfect. Cabell Publishing Company. Beaumont, TX. 2004. 1411p. ISBN:0-911753-23-0, ISBN13: 978-0-911753-23-3. Dewey:330.
Audience: **u,f.**

Cabell, David W. E. & English, Deborah L. (Editors) **HD28.C23 2004**
Cabell's Directory of Publishing Opportunities in Management. Ed. 9. Perfect. Cabell Publishing Company. Beaumont, TX. 2004. 2470p. ISBN:0-911753-24-9, ISBN13: 978-0-911753-24-0. Dewey:658.025.
Audience: **u,f.**

Cortada, James W. **HC110.A9C655 2003**
The Digital Hand: How Computers Changed the Work of American Manufacturing, Transportation, and Retail Industries. Trade Cloth. Oxford University Press, Inc. New York, NY. 2003. 522p. ISBN:0-19-516588-8, ISBN13: 978-0-19-516588-3. Dewey:338.0973. LCCN:2003-012107.
Audience: **g,l,u,f.** *Choice, 2004.*

Drucker, Peter F. **HD2328.D78 1992**
The New Society: The Anatomy of Industrial Order. Ed. 2. Trade Paper. Transaction Publishers. Somerset, NJ. 1993. 362p. ISBN:1-56000-624-2, ISBN13: 978-1-56000-624-4. Dewey:306.3/6. LCCN:92-005075.
Audience: **u,f.**

Duetsch, Larry L. (Editor) **HC106.8.I53 2002**
Industry Studies. Ed. 3. Trade Cloth. M. E. Sharpe Inc. Armonk, NY. 2003. 416p. ISBN:0-7656-0963-0, ISBN13: 978-0-7656-0963-2. Dewey:338.0973. LCCN:2002-023102.
Audience: **g,l,u,f.** *Choice, 1999.*

Einsohn, Amy **PN4784.C75 E37 2006**
The Copyeditor's Handbook: A Guide for Book Publishing and Corporate Communications. Ed. 2. Trade Paper. University of California Press. Berkeley, CA. 2005. 573p. ISBN:0-520-24688-8, ISBN13: 978-0-520-24688-1. Dewey:808/.027. LCCN:2005-048579.
Audience: **u,f.**

Epstein, Jason **Z280.E67 2001**
Book Business: Publishing: Past, Present and Future. Trade Cloth. W. W. Norton & Company, Inc. New York, NY. 2001. 128p. ISBN:0-393-04984-1, ISBN13: 978-0-393-04984-8. Dewey:070.5/09. LCCN:00-060079.
Audience: **g,u,f.**

Greco, Albert N. **Z471.G74 2004**
The Book Publishing Industry. Ed. 2. Trade Paper. Lawrence Erlbaum Associates, Inc. Mahwah, NJ. 2004. 400p. ISBN:0-8058-4853-3, ISBN13: 978-0-8058-4853-3. Dewey:070.5/0973. LCCN:2003-069607.
Audience: **g,u,f.**

Information Today, Inc. Staff (Editor) **PN161**
Literary Market Place 2004: The Directory of the American Book Publishing Industry. Trade Paper. Information Today, Inc. Medford, NJ. 2003. "2,200"p. ISBN:1-57387-178-8, ISBN13: 978-1-57387-178-5. Dewey:70.5025.
Audience: **g,l,u,f.**

Manning, Matt **Z471.M36 2004**
Vault Career Guide to Book Publishing. Trade Paper. Vault.com. New York, NY. 2004. 128p. ISBN:1-58131-269-5, ISBN13: 978-1-58131-269-0. Dewey:070.5/02373. LCCN:2004-009490.
Audience: **g,l,u.**

McGahan, Anita M. **HD58.8.M3445 2004**
How Industries Evolve: Understanding the Critical Link Between Strategy and Innovation. Trade Cloth. Harvard Business School Press. Boston, MA. 2004. 256p. ISBN:1-57851-840-7, ISBN13: 978-1-57851-840-1. Dewey:658.4/012. LCCN:2004-011378.
Audience: **g,l,u,f.** *Choice, 2005.*

Meyer, Philip **PN4867.2.M48 2004**
The Vanishing Newspaper: Saving Journalism in the Information Age. Trade Cloth. University of Missouri Press. Columbia, MO. 2004. 272p. ISBN:0-8262-1561-0, ISBN13: 978-0-8262-1561-1. Dewey:071/.3. LCCN:2004-016121.
Audience: **g,u,f.** *Choice, 2005.*

Nasaw, David **Z473.H4N37 2000**
The Chief: The Life of William Randolph Hearst. Trade Cloth. Houghton Mifflin Company Trade & Reference Division. Boston, MA. 2000. 752p. ISBN:0-395-82759-0, ISBN13: 978-0-395-82759-8. Dewey:070.5/092 B. LCCN:99-462122.
Audience: **g,l,u,f.**

Nord, David Paul **PN4855.N67 2001**
Communities of Journalism: A History of American Newspapers and Their Readers. Trade Cloth. University of Illinois Press. Champaign, IL. 2001. 312p. History of Communication Ser. ISBN:0-252-02671-3, ISBN13: 978-0-252-02671-3. Dewey:071/.3/09. LCCN:2001-000370.
Audience: **g,l,u,f.** *Choice, 2002.*

Robinson, Judith **Z473**
The Hearsts: An American Dynasty. Ed. 2. Perfect. Telegraph Hill Press. San Francisco, CA. 2002. 431p. ISBN:0-9643382-1-1, ISBN13: 978-0-9643382-1-0. Dewey:070.5/092 B. LCCN:89-040768.
Audience: **g,l,u,f.** *Choice, 1991.*

Schiffrin, Andre **Z278**
The Business of Books: How the International Conglomerates Took over Publishing and Changed the Way We Read. Trade Cloth. Verso Books. London, 2001. 240p. ISBN:1-85984-763-3, ISBN13: 978-1-85984-763-3. Dewey:070.5/0973/09045.
Audience: **g,u,f.**

Sylvie, George & Witherspoon, Patricia D. **PN4784.M34S98 2002**
Time, Change and the American Newspaper. Trade Paper. Lawrence Erlbaum Associates, Inc. Mahwah, NJ. 2001. 224p. LEA's Communication Ser. ISBN:0-8058-3588-1, ISBN13: 978-0-8058-3588-5. Dewey:070.4/068. LCCN:2001-023583.
Audience: **g,l,u,f.** *Choice, 2002.*

Tifft, Susan E. & Jones, Alex S. **PN4899.N42**
The Trust: The Private and Powerful Family Behind the New York Times. Trade Paper. Little Brown & Company. New York, NY. 2000. 928p. ISBN:0-316-83631-1, ISBN13: 978-0-316-83631-9. Dewey:071/.471.
Audience: **g,l,u,f.** *Choice, 2000.*

Whitelaw, Nancy **Z473.H4W48 2004**
William Randolph Hearst and the American Century. Trade Cloth. Morgan Reynolds Inc. Greensboro, NC. 2004. 128p. Makers of the Media Ser. ISBN:1-931798-35-4, ISBN13: 978-1-931798-35-8. Dewey:070.5/092 B. LCCN:2003-024612.
Audience: **g,l,u.**

Yager, Fred & Yager, Jan **Z471.Y34 2004**
Career Opportunities in the Publishing Industry: A Guide to Careers in Newspapers, Magazines, and Books. Trade Cloth. Facts On File, Inc. New York, NY. 2004. 304p. Career Opportunities Ser. ISBN:0-8160-5140-2, ISBN13: 978-0-8160-5140-3. Dewey:070.5/023/73. LCCN:2003-025279.
Audience: **g,l,u.** *Choice, 2005.*

Company and Industry Information > Industries and Markets (Selected) > General Industry Statistics

HF1016
☐ Current Industrial Reports.
http://www.census.gov/cir/www/
U.S. Census Bureau.
Audience: **l,u,f.**

HC102.E53
Encyclopedia of American Industries. Ed. 2005. Gale Group. 2005. ISBN:0-7876-9061-9, ISBN13: 978-0-7876-9061-8.
Audience: **g,l,u,f.**

HF1016
☐ Industries Statistics.
http://www.census.gov/main/www/industries.html
U.S. Census Bureau.
Audience: **l,u,f.**

HD30.35
☐ Mergent Online Industry Reports.
http://www.mergentonline.com/
Audience: **u,f.**

HD30.35
☐ Plunkett Research Online.
http://www.plunkettresearch.com/
Plunkett Research, Ltd.
Audience: **u,f.**

HD30.35
☐ Plunkett's Research Online.
http://www.plunkettresearchonline.com/Default.aspx
Audience: **u,f.**

HC106.6
☐ Standard & Poor's Industry Surveys Online.
http://www.netadvantage.standardandpoors.com/
Standard & Poor's.
Audience: **l,u,f.**

Amanda Quick **HD2324**
Encyclopedia of Global Industries. Ed. 2003. Gale Group. 2003. ISBN:0-7876-4905-8, ISBN13: 978-0-7876-4905-0.
Audience: **g,l,u,f.**

Robert C. Byrd **HC106.82**
United States Industry and Trade Outlook 1998: Business Forecasts for 350 Industries. United States Government Printing Office. 1998. ISBN:0-16-063703-1, ISBN13: 978-0-16-063703-2.
Audience: **u,f.**

Company and Industry Information > Industries and Markets (Selected) > Advertising and Public Relations

HF5801
Advertising Age. Crain Communications, Inc.
Audience: **g,l,u,f.**

HF5801
Adweek. V N U Business Publications.
Audience: **g,l,u,f.**

HF5801
Brandweek: The Newsweekly of Marketing Communications. V N U Business Publications.
Audience: **g,u,f.**

HF5826.5
Marketer's Guide to Media. V N U Business Publications. 2005.
Audience: **g,u,f.**

HF5415.153
☐ Productscan.
http://www.productscan.com
Marketing Intelligence Service via Datamonitor, Inc.
Audience: **g,u,f.**

LexisNexis **HF5805.St7**
The Advertising Red Books. Agencies. LexisNexis. 2005. Red Book
Audience: **g,l,u,f.**

Plunkett, Jack W. (Editor) **HF5805**
Plunkett's Advertising and Branding Industry Almanac 2006. Trade Paper, CD-ROM. Plunkett Research, Ltd. Houston, TX. 2006. 451p. ISBN:1-59392-042-3, ISBN13: 978-1-59392-042-5. Dewey:659.1.
Audience: **l,u,f.**

Company and Industry Information > Industries and Markets (Selected) > Aerospace and Defense

AY67.5
ⓔ The 2003 World Almanac - US Government and Defense. E-Book. Town Compass, LLC. Seattle, WA. 2003. ISBN:1-930988-84-2, ISBN13: 978-1-930988-84-2. Dewey:317.
Audience: **g,l,u,f.**

Ball, Howard **UA927**
U. S. Homeland Security: A Reference Handbook. Mildred Vasan (Editor). Library Binding. ABC-CLIO, Inc. Santa Barbara, CA. 2005. 288p. Contemporary World Issues Ser.

ISBN:1-85109-803-8, ISBN13: 978-1-85109-803-3. Dewey:353.3/0973. LCCN:2005-021789.
Audience: **g,l,u.**

Ben-Yosef, Eldad **HE9803.A4**
The Evolution of the US Airline Industry: Theory, Strategy and Policy. Trade Cloth. Springer. New York, NY. 2005. X, 298p. Studies in Industrial Organization Ser., Vol. 25 ISBN:0-387-24213-9, ISBN13: 978-0-387-24213-2. Dewey:387.70973. LCCN:2006-274991.
Audience: **u,f.**

Echaore-McDavid, Susan **HD8039.A23E285 2004**
Career Opportunities in Aviation and the Aerospace Industry. Trade Cloth. Facts On File, Inc. New York, NY. 2005. 320p. Career Opportunities Ser. ISBN:0-8160-4649-2, ISBN13: 978-0-8160-4649-2. Dewey:387.7/023. LCCN:2004-004863.
Audience: **g,l,u.**

Global Investment Center Staff **UA23.U478**
U. S. Defense Policy Handbook. Trade Paper. International Business Publications, USA. Washington, DC. 2003. World Investment and Business Library ISBN:0-7397-5952-3, ISBN13: 978-0-7397-5952-3. Dewey:355.033573.
Audience: **u,f.**

Global Investment Center Staff **UC263**
U. S. Department of Defense Handbook. Trade Paper. International Business Publications, USA. Washington, DC. 2003. ISBN:0-7397-6208-7, ISBN13: 978-0-7397-6208-0. Dewey:355.6.
Audience: **g,l,u,f.**

Gunston, Bill **HD 9711 .G86 1993**
World Encyclopedia of Aircraft Manufacturers: From the Wright Brothers to the Present. Trade Cloth. Haynes Publishing PLC. Yeovil, 1993. 240p. ISBN:1-85260-205-8, ISBN13: 978-1-85260-205-5. Dewey:338.4762913303. LCCN:93-078378.
Audience: **g,l,u,f.**

Plunkett, Jack W. (Editor) **HE9803.A2 P58**
Plunkett's Airline, Hotel and Travel Industry Almanac 2006 (E-Book). E-Book, CD-ROM. Plunkett Research, Ltd. Houston, TX. 2005. 463p. ISBN:1-59392-376-7, ISBN13: 978-1-59392-376-1. Dewey:387.7.
Audience: **l,u,f.**

Sacknoff, Scott **HD9711.75.A1 S73**
State of the Space Industry — 2005. Perfect. SpaceBusiness.com. Bethesda, MD. 2005. 56p. ISBN:1-887022-16-3, ISBN13: 978-1-887022-16-3. Dewey:338.4/76294/05.
Audience: **u,f.**

Surgenor, Christopher **HD9711.U6**
Aircraft Maintenance & Engineering Directory 2005. Trade Paper. Air Transport Publications. London, 2005. 364p. ISBN:0-9549179-2-8, ISBN13: 978-0-9549179-2-0. Dewey:338.4762913334025.
Audience: **u,f.**

Taylor, Michael John Haddrick **HD9711.A1**
Flight International World Aircraft and Systems Directory. Ed. 3. Flight International Staff (Contribution by). Trade Cloth. Flight International. Sutton, 2005. iv, 967p. ISBN:0-617-01289-X, ISBN13: 978-0-617-01289-4. Dewey:629.133340294.
Audience: **u,f.**

Company and Industry Information > Industries and Markets (Selected) > Agriculture

HD1769.C468
2002 Census of Agriculture.
http://www.nass.usda.gov/Census_of_Agriculture/index.asp
United States National Agricultural Statistics Service.
Audience: **g,l,u,f.**

Albert R. Mann Library, Cornell University Library **S441**
The Core Historical Literature of Agriculture.
http://chla.mannlib.cornell.edu/
Cornell University Library.
Audience: **g,l,u,f.**

Beierlein, James G., et al. **HD9000.5**
Principles of Agribusiness Management. Ed. 3. Kenneth C. Schneeberger & Donald D. Osburn (Authors). Cloth Text. Waveland Press, Inc. Prospect Heights, IL. 2003. 326p. ISBN:1-57766-267-9, ISBN13: 978-1-57766-267-9. Dewey:630/.68. LCCN:2004-274093.
Audience: **l,u,f.**

Bonanno, Alessandro (Editor), et al. **HD9000.5.F76 1994**
From Columbus to ConAgra: The Globalization of Agriculture and Food. Lawrence Busch, William Friedland, Lourdes Gouveia & Enzo Mingione (Editors). Trade Cloth. University Press of Kansas. Lawrence, KS. 1994. 336p. Rural America Ser. ISBN:0-7006-0660-2, ISBN13: 978-0-7006-0660-3. Dewey:338.1. LCCN:93-046569.
Audience: **g,l,u,f.**

Chapman, Forestine **HD1751**
Agricultural Statistics.
http://purl.access.gpo.gov/GPO/LPS1063
United States Agriculture Department.
Audience: **g,l,u,f.**

Curtis, Patricia A. **KF3875**
A Guide to Food Laws and Regulations. Trade Paper. Blackwell Publishing Professional. Ames, IA. 2005. 248p. ISBN:0-8138-1946-6, ISBN13: 978-0-8138-1946-4. Dewey:344.7304232.
Audience: **g,l,u,f.**

Food and Agriculture Organization (FAO) Staff **HD1421**
FAO Statistical Yearbook, Vol. 1. Trade Paper. Food and Agriculture Organization of the United Nations. Rome, 2005. 360p. ISBN:92-5-005151-4, ISBN13: 978-92-5-005151-2. Dewey:338.1.
Audience: **l,u,f.**

Food and Agriculture Organization of the United Nations Staff (Contribution by) **SB123.57**
The State of Food and Agriculture, 2003-04. CD-ROM, Trade Paper. Food and Agriculture Organization of the United Nations.

Rome, 2004. 224p. ISBN:92-5-105079-1, ISBN13: 978-92-5-105079-8. Dewey:631.5/233/091724.
Audience: **l,u,f.**

Millstone, Eric **HD9000.5.M52 2003**
Penguin Atlas of Food: Who Eats What Where and Why. Trade Paper. Penguin Group (USA) Inc. New York, NY. 2003. 128p. ISBN:0-14-200224-0, ISBN13: 978-0-14-200224-7. Dewey:664. LCCN:2003-266836.
Audience: **g,l,u.**

National Agricultural Library **S494.5.I47**
National Agricultural Library Portal.
http://www.nal.usda.gov/
United States Department of Agriculture.
Audience: **g,l,u,f.**

Seitz, Wesley D., et al. **HD1415.S395 2002**
Economics of Resources, Agriculture and Food. Ed. 2. Gerald C. Nelson & Harold G. Halcrow (Authors). Cloth Text. McGraw-Hill Higher Education. Burr Ridge, IL. 2001. 544p. Agricultural Economics Ser. ISBN:0-07-025958-5, ISBN13: 978-0-07-025958-4. Dewey:338.1. LCCN:2001-031266.
Audience: **l,u.**

Steen, Harold K. **DS822.3.G88 2004**
The U. S. Forest Service: A History. Ed. 2. Trade Cloth. University of Washington Press. Seattle, WA. 2004. 432p. ISBN:0-295-98402-3, ISBN13: 978-0-295-98402-5. Dewey:915.204/31/0092. LCCN:2003-066592.
Audience: **l,u,f.**

Tansey, Geoff & Worsley, Tony **HD9000.5 .T36 1995**
The Food System: A Guide. Trade Paper. Earthscan/James & James. London, 1995. 272p. ISBN:1-85383-277-4, ISBN13: 978-1-85383-277-2. Dewey:363.8.
Audience: **l,u.**

United Nations Timber Committee **HD9765.A2**
Timber Committee Forest Products Statistics.
http://www.unece.org/trade/timber/mis/fp-stats.htm
UNECE Trade and Timber Division.
Audience: **g,l,u,f.**

United States Department of Agriculture **S441**
Agriculture Fact Book.
http://purl.access.gpo.gov/GPO/LPS2942
United States Department of Agriculture.
Audience: **g,l,u,f.**

United States Department of Agriculture Foreign Agricultural Service **HD1769**
Market and Trade Data: Statistical Market Information.
http://www.fas.usda.gov/data.asp
United States Department of Agriculture Foreign Agricultural Service.
Audience: **g,l,u,f.**

United States Department of Agriculture, Agricultural Marketing Service **HD1751.A9184**
Agricultural Marketing Service @ USDA Portal.
http://www.ams.usda.gov/
United States Department of Agriculture, Agricultural Marketing Service.
Audience: **g,l,u,f.**

United States Department of Agriculture, Economic Research Service **S21.A99**
Key Topics Portal.
http://www.ers.usda.gov/Topics/
United States Department of Agriculture, Economic Research Service.
Audience: **g,l,u,f.**

Company and Industry Information > Industries and Markets (Selected) > Airlines

Ben-Yosef, Eldad **HE9803.A4**
The Evolution of the US Airline Industry: Theory, Strategy and Policy. Trade Cloth. Springer. New York, NY. 2005. X, 298p. Studies in Industrial Organization Ser., Vol. 25 ISBN:0-387-24213-9, ISBN13: 978-0-387-24213-2. Dewey:387.70973. LCCN:2006-274991.
Audience: **u,f.**

OptimumFinance.net **TL509**
Airline Industry - Global Best Practices: 2005 Edition. Ed. 2005. E-Book. OptimumFinance.net. Randolph, NJ. 2005. ISBN:1-933414-00-6, ISBN13: 978-1-933414-00-3. Dewey:387.
Audience: **u,f.**

Oum, Tae Hoon, et al. **HE9780.O96 2000**
Globalization and Strategic Alliances: The Case of the Airline Industry. Jong Hun Park & Anming Zhang (Authors). E-Book. NetLibrary, Inc. Boulder, CO. 2000. ISBN:0-585-47403-6, ISBN13: 978-0-585-47403-8. Dewey:658/.044.
Audience: **u,f.**

Pitt, Ivan L. & Norsworthy, J. R. **HE9803.A4P58 1999**
Economics of the U. S. Commercial Airline Industry: Productivity, Technology and Deregulation. Trade Cloth. Springer. New York, NY. 1999. 204p. Transportation Research, Economics and Policy Ser. ISBN:0-7923-8505-5, ISBN13: 978-0-7923-8505-9. Dewey:387.7/1/0973. LCCN:99-020658.
Audience: **u,f.**

Plunkett, Jack W. (Editor) **HE9803.A2 P58**
Plunkett's Airline, Hotel and Travel Industry Almanac 2006. Trade Paper, CD-ROM. Plunkett Research, Ltd. Houston, TX. 2005. 463p. ISBN:1-59392-034-2, ISBN13: 978-1-59392-034-0. Dewey:387.7.
Audience: **l,u,f.**

Plunkett, Jack W. (Editor) **G155.U6**
Plunkett's Airline, Hotel and Travel Industry Trends and Statistics 2006 (Summary). E-Book. Plunkett Research, Ltd. Houston, TX. 2005. 56p. ISBN:1-59392-712-6, ISBN13: 978-1-59392-712-7. Dewey:387.7.
Audience: **l,u,f.**

Van der Linden, R. Robert **HE9763.V36 2002**
Airlines and Air Mail: The Post Office and the Birth of the Commercial Aviation Industry. Trade Cloth. University Press of Kentucky. Lexington, KY. 2002. 400p. ISBN:0-8131-2219-8, ISBN13: 978-0-8131-2219-9. Dewey:383/.144. LCCN:2001-007229.
Audience: **g,l,u,f.** *Choice, 2003, 2002.*

Company and Industry Information > Industries and Markets (Selected) > Alcoholic Beverages and Tabacco

Business Information Agency Staff
Exporters - Alcoholic Beverages Worldwide. Ed. 3. Perfect. Business Information Agency. Arlington, VA. 2004. 350p. ISBN:1-4187-0893-3, ISBN13: 978-1-4187-0893-1.
Audience: **u,f.**

Evans, Janet M. **HF6161.L46**
Alcohol Marketing and Advertising: A Report to Congress by the U. S. Federal Trade Commission. Paper Text. DIANE Publishing Company. Collingdale, PA. 2004. 68p. ISBN:0-7567-4260-9, ISBN13: 978-0-7567-4260-7. Dewey:659.1966310973.
Audience: **u,f.**

Moyer, David B. **HV5735.M68 2004**
The Tobacco Book: A Reference Guide of Facts, Figures, and Quotations about Tobacco. Trade Paper. Sunstone Press. Santa Fe, NM. 2005. 494p. ISBN:0-86534-382-9, ISBN13: 978-0-86534-382-5. Dewey:362.29/6. LCCN:2004-003575.
Audience: **g,l,u,f.**

Pampel, Fred C. **HV5760.P36 2004**
Tobacco Industry and Smoking. Trade Cloth. Facts On File, Inc. New York, NY. 2004. 320p. Library in a Book ISBN:0-8160-5450-9, ISBN13: 978-0-8160-5450-3. Dewey:338.4/767973/0973. LCCN:2003-013236.
Audience: **g,l,u.** *Choice, 2004.*

Plunkett, Jack W. **HD9003 .P57**
Plunkett's Food Industry Almanac 2005: The Only Complete Reference to the Business of Creating and Selling Food, Beverages and Tobacco. Trade Paper, CD-ROM. Plunkett Research, Ltd. Houston, TX. 2005. 544p. ISBN:1-59392-021-0, ISBN13: 978-1-59392-021-0. Dewey:338.1.
Audience: **l,u,f.**

Trolldal, Bjorn **HD9364.C3**
Availability and Sale of Alcohol: Experiences from Canada and the U. S. Trade Paper. Almqvist & Wiksell International. Stockholm, 2005. 112p. Centre for Social Research on Alcohol and Drugs Ser., Vol. 2 ISBN:91-22-02122-1, ISBN13: 978-91-22-02122-3. Dewey:338.47663520971.
Audience: **u,f.**

Company and Industry Information > Industries and Markets (Selected) > Apparel and Footwear

Business Information Agency, Inc. Staff **HD9940.A1**
Industry and Trade, Textile, Apparel, Footwear, U. S. A. Trade Paper. Business Information Agency. Arlington, VA. 2001. 200p. ISBN:1-59064-899-4, ISBN13: 978-1-59064-899-5. Dewey:338.4768708.
Audience: **l,u,f.**

Icon Group International, Inc. Staff (Compiled by) **KJE6762**
The 2006 Report on Footwear. Ringbound, CD-ROM. Icon Group International, Inc. San Diego, CA. 2005. 330p. World Statistical Outlook Cities Ser. ISBN:0-497-24742-9, ISBN13: 978-0-497-24742-3.
Audience: **l,u,f.**

Icon Group International, Inc. Staff (Compiled by) **HD9787.A2**
The 2006-2011 World Outlook for Footwear. Ringbound, CD-ROM. Icon Group International, Inc. San Diego, CA. 2005. 235p. World Statistical Outlook Ser. ISBN:0-497-24422-5, ISBN13: 978-0-497-24422-4. Dewey:338.4768530971.
Audience: **l,u,f.**

Plunkett, Jack W. (Editor) **HD9940.U3**
Plunkett's Apparel and Textiles Industry Almanac 2006. Trade Paper, CD-ROM. Plunkett Research, Ltd. Houston, TX. 2006. ISBN:1-59392-043-1, ISBN13: 978-1-59392-043-2. Dewey:338.
Audience: **l,u,f.**

Company and Industry Information > Industries and Markets (Selected) > Automobile Industry

HD9710.U5 W3
Ward's Automotive Yearbook. Ward's Communications. 2005. ISBN:0-910589-22-4, ISBN13: 978-0-910589-22-2.
Audience: **g,l,u,f.**

HD9710.A1 W373
Ward's world motor vehicle data. Ward's Communications. 2005. ISBN:0-910589-87-9, ISBN13: 978-0-910589-87-1.
Audience: **g,l,u,f.**

Bradsher, Keith **TL230.5.S66**
High and Mighty: The Dangerous Rise of the SUV. Trade Paper. DIANE Publishing Company. Collingdale, PA. 2005. 488p. ISBN:0-7567-8969-9, ISBN13: 978-0-7567-8969-5. Dewey:363.125.
Audience: **g,l,u.**

Brinkley, Douglas G. **HD9710.U52**
Wheels for the World: Henry Ford, His Company, and a Century of Progress. Trade Paper. Penguin Group (USA) Inc. New York, NY. 2004. 880p. ISBN:0-14-200439-1, ISBN13: 978-0-14-200439-5. Dewey:338.7/6292/092 B.
Audience: **g,l,u.**

Conybeare, John A. C. **HD9710.A2C65 2003**
Merging Traffic: The Consolidation of the International Automobile Industry. Book, Other. Rowman & Littlefield Publishers, Inc. Lanham, MD. 2003. 192p. ISBN:0-7425-2828-6, ISBN13: 978-0-7425-2828-4. Dewey:338.8/3629222. LCCN:2003-007758.
Audience: **u,f.** *Choice, 2004.*

Curcio, Vincent **HD9710.U52**
Chrysler: The Life and Times of an Automotive Genius. Trade Paper. DIANE Publishing Company. Collingdale, PA. 2004. 699p. ISBN:0-7567-7165-X, ISBN13: 978-0-7567-7165-2. Dewey:338.7/6292/092 B.
Audience: **l,u,f.**

Farber, David **HD9710.U52S494 2002**
Sloan Rules: Alfred P. Sloan and the Triumph of General Motors. Trade Cloth. University of Chicago Press. Chicago, IL.

2002. 312p. ISBN:0-226-23804-0, ISBN13: 978-0-226-23804-3. Dewey:338.7/62922/092 B. LCCN:2002-004967.
Audience: **g,l,u,f.** *Choice, 2003.*

Flink, James J. **HE5623**
The Automobile Age. Trade Paper. MIT Press. Cambridge, MA. 1990. 472p. ISBN:0-262-56055-0, ISBN13: 978-0-262-56055-9. Dewey:303.4/832.
Audience: **g,l,u,f.**

Hyde, Charles K. **HD9710.U54C467 2003**
Riding the Roller Coaster: A History of the Chrysler Corporation. Trade Cloth. Wayne State University Press. Detroit, MI. 2003. 480p. Great Lakes Books ISBN:0-8143-3091-6, ISBN13: 978-0-8143-3091-3. Dewey:338.7/6292/0973. LCCN:2002-008512.
Audience: **g,l,u,f.** *Choice, 2003.*

Ingrassia, Paul J. **HD9710.U52**
Comeback: The Fall and Rise of the American Automobile Industry. Trade Paper. Simon & Schuster. New York, NY. 1995. 512p. ISBN:0-684-80437-9, ISBN13: 978-0-684-80437-8. Dewey:338.4/7/6292/0973.
Audience: **g,l,u.**

Laux, James M. **HD9710.E82L38 1992**
The European Automobile Industry. Cloth Text. Macmillan Publishing Company, Inc. Old Tappan, NJ. 1992. 250p. ISBN:0-8057-3800-2, ISBN13: 978-0-8057-3800-1. Dewey:338.4/76292/094. LCCN:91-043223.
Audience: **u,f.** *Choice, 1992.*

Luger, Stan **HD9710.U52 L84 2000**
Corporate Power, American Democracy, and the Automobile Industry. Trade Paper. Cambridge University Press. New York, NY. 2005. 216p. ISBN:0-521-02361-0, ISBN13: 978-0-521-02361-0. Dewey:338.4/76292/0973.
Audience: **u,f.**

Maxton, Graeme P. & Wormald, John **HD9710.A2M3863 2004**
Time for a Model Change: Re-Engineering the Global Automotive Industry. Trade Cloth. Cambridge University Press. New York, NY. 2004. 294p. ISBN:0-521-83715-4, ISBN13: 978-0-521-83715-6. Dewey:338.4/7629222. LCCN:2004-045634.
Audience: **u,f.** *Choice, 2006.*

Plunkett, Jack W. **HD9710.U5 P58**
Plunkett's Automobile Industry Almanac 2005: The Only Complete Guide to the Automobile, Truck and Specialty Vehicle Industry. Trade Paper, CD-ROM. Plunkett Research, Ltd. Houston, TX. 2004. 506p. ISBN:1-59392-001-6, ISBN13: 978-1-59392-001-2. Dewey:381.
Audience: **g,l,u,f.**

Riley, Robert Q. **HD9710.A2R55 1994**
Alternative Cars in the 21st Century: A New Personal Transportation Paradigm. Trade Cloth. Society of Automotive Engineers, Inc. Warrendale, PA. 1994. 400p. ISBN:1-56091-519-6, ISBN13: 978-1-56091-519-5. Dewey:338.4/7629222. LCCN:94-019325.
Audience: **g,l,u,f.** *Choice, 1995.*

Sherman, Joe **HD9710.U54.G47557**
In the Rings of Saturn. Trade Cloth. Oxford University Press, Inc. New York, NY. 1993. 346p. ISBN:0-19-507244-8, ISBN13: 978-0-19-507244-0. Dewey:338.762922220973. LCCN:93-012858.
Audience: **g,l,u,f.**

Shimokawa, Koichi S. **HD9710.J32S514 1994**
The Japanese Automobile Industry: A Business History. Trade Cloth. Continuum International Publishing Group, Ltd. London, 1994. 240p. ISBN:0-485-11270-1, ISBN13: 978-0-485-11270-2. Dewey:338.4/7004/0952. LCCN:94-018947.
Audience: **u,f.**

Sloan, Alfred P. Jr. **HD9710.U54**
My Years with General Motors. Peter F. Drucker (Introduction by). Trade Paper. DIANE Publishing Company. Collingdale, PA. 2004. 472p. ISBN:0-7567-8366-6, ISBN13: 978-0-7567-8366-2. Dewey:338.7/6292/0973.
Audience: **u,f.**

Volti, Rudi **TL15**
Cars and Culture: The Life Story of a Technology. Cloth Text. Greenwood Publishing Group, Inc. Portsmouth, NH. 2004. 192p. Greenwood Technographies Ser. ISBN:0-313-32831-5, ISBN13: 978-0-313-32831-2. Dewey:629.222/09. LCCN:2004-053044.
Audience: **g,l,u,f.**

Watts, Steven **HD9710.U52F6684 2005**
The People's Tycoon: Henry Ford and the American Century. Trade Cloth. Knopf Publishing Group. New York, NY. 2005. 640p. ISBN:0-375-40735-9, ISBN13: 978-0-375-40735-2. Dewey:338.7/6292/092. LCCN:2004-048594.
Audience: **g,u,f.** *Choice, 2006.*

Company and Industry Information > Industries and Markets (Selected) > Banking and Financial Services

Bagehot, Walter **HG3000.L82B3 1999**
Lombard Street: A Description of the Money Market. Trade Paper. John Wiley & Sons, Inc. Hoboken, NJ. 1999. 359p. Wiley Investment Classic Ser., Vol. 22 ISBN:0-471-34536-9, ISBN13: 978-0-471-34536-7. Dewey:332/.09421. LCCN:98-051463.
Audience: **g,l,u,f.**

Blinder, Alan S. **HG1811.B554 2004**
The Quiet Revolution: Central Banking Goes Modern. Cloth over Boards. Yale University Press. Cumberland, RI. 2004. 144p. Arthur Okun Memorial Lectures Ser. ISBN:0-300-10087-6, ISBN13: 978-0-300-10087-7. Dewey:332.1/1. LCCN:2003-061371.
Audience: **g,l,u,f.**

Calomiris, Charles W. **HG2491 .C348 2000**
U. S. Bank Deregulation in Historical Perspective. Trade Cloth. Cambridge University Press. New York, NY. 2000. 392p. ISBN:0-521-58362-4, ISBN13: 978-0-521-58362-6. Dewey:332.1/0973. LCCN:99-040041.
Audience: **g,l,u,f.** *Choice, 2000.*

Chernow, Ron **HG2613.N54M6613 1990**
The House of Morgan: An American Banking Family and the Rise of Modern Finance. Trade Cloth. Grove/Atlantic, Inc. New York, NY. 1990. ISBN:0-87113-338-5, ISBN13: 978-0-87113-338-0. Dewey:332.1/2/097471. LCCN:89-017542.
Audience: **g,l,u,f.**

Choi, Frederick D. S. (Editor) **HF5686.I56H36 2003**
International Finance and Accounting Handbook. Ed. 3. Trade Cloth. John Wiley & Sons, Inc. Hoboken, NJ. 2003. 888p. ISBN:0-471-22921-0, ISBN13: 978-0-471-22921-6. Dewey:657/.96. LCCN:2002-192266.
Audience: **u,f.**

Cortada, James W. **HC110.I55C67 2005**
The Digital Hand, Volume 2: How Computers Changed the Work of American Financial, Telecommunications, Media, and Entertainment Industries. Trade Cloth. Oxford University Press, Inc. New York, NY. 2005. 672p. ISBN:0-19-516587-X, ISBN13: 978-0-19-516587-6. Dewey:338/.064/0973. LCCN:2004-030363.
Audience: **g,l,u,f.**

Davis, E. Philip & Steil, Benn **HG4521.D14 2001**
Institutional Investors. Trade Cloth. MIT Press. Cambridge, MA. 2001. 560p. ISBN:0-262-04192-8, ISBN13: 978-0-262-04192-8. Dewey:332.67/154. LCCN:2001-030280.
Audience: **g,l,u,f.**

Ellis, Charles D. & Vertin, James R. **HG4928.5.E42 2001**
Wall Street People: True Stories of Today's Masters and Moguls. Trade Cloth. John Wiley & Sons, Inc. Hoboken, NJ. 2001. 360p. ISBN:0-471-23809-0, ISBN13: 978-0-471-23809-6. Dewey:332.6/0973. LCCN:2001-026114.
Audience: **g,l,u,f.**

Ellis, Charles D. & Vertin, James R. **HG4928.5 .E42 2001**
Wall Street People: True Stories of the Great Barons of Finance. Trade Cloth. John Wiley & Sons, Inc. Hoboken, NJ. 2003. 288p. ISBN:0-471-27428-3, ISBN13: 978-0-471-27428-5. Dewey:332.60973.
Audience: **g,l,u,f.**

Evans, David S. & Schmalensee, Richard **HG3755.8.U6E94 2005**
Paying with Plastic: The Digital Revolution in Buying and Borrowing. Ed. 2. Trade Cloth. MIT Press. Cambridge, MA. 2005. 360p. ISBN:0-262-05077-3, ISBN13: 978-0-262-05077-7. Dewey:332.7/65/0973. LCCN:2004-055249.
Audience: **g,l,u,f.** *Choice, 2005.*

Ferguson, Niall **HG1552.A1F46 1998**
The House of Rothschild: Money's Prophets, 1798-1848. Trade Cloth. Penguin Group (USA) Inc. New York, NY. 1998. 688p. ISBN:0-670-85768-8, ISBN13: 978-0-670-85768-5. Dewey:332.1/092/24 B. LCCN:98-044706.
Audience: **g,l,u,f.** *Choice, 1999.*

Ferguson, Niall **HG1552.R8F47 1999**
The House of Rothschild: The World's Banker, 1849-1999. Trade Cloth. Penguin Group (USA) Inc. New York, NY. 1999. 608p. ISBN:0-670-88794-3, ISBN13: 978-0-670-88794-1. Dewey:332.1/092/2. LCCN:99-041868.
Audience: **g,l,u,f.**

Geisst, Charles **HG5129.N5G44 2001**
The Last Partnerships: Inside the Great Wall Street Dynasties. Trade Cloth. McGraw-Hill Companies, The. New York, NY. 2001. 338p. ISBN:0-07-136999-6, ISBN13: 978-0-07-136999-2. Dewey:332.6/0973. LCCN:2001-030374.
Audience: **g,l,u,f.** *Choice, 2001.*

Geisst, Charles **HG4572**
Wall Street: From Its Beginnings to the Fall of Enron. Trade Cloth. Oxford University Press, Inc. New York, NY. 2004. 449p. ISBN:0-19-517061-X, ISBN13: 978-0-19-517061-0. Dewey:332.64/273. LCCN:2004-555123.
Audience: **g,l,u,f.**

Geisst, Charles R. **HG4028.M4G45 2004**
Deals of the Century: Wall Street, Mergers, and the Making of Modern America. Trade Cloth. John Wiley & Sons, Inc. Hoboken, NJ. 2003. 352p. ISBN:0-471-26397-4, ISBN13: 978-0-471-26397-5. Dewey:338.8/3/0973. LCCN:2003-008868.
Audience: **g,l,u,f.**

Gordon, John S. **HG4910.G667 1999**
The Great Game: The Emergence of Wall Street as a World Power, 1653-2000. Trade Cloth. Simon & Schuster. New York, NY. 1999. 320p. ISBN:0-684-83287-9, ISBN13: 978-0-684-83287-6. Dewey:332.64/273. LCCN:00-265068.
Audience: **g,l,u,f.**

Hafer, R. W. **HG2563**
The Federal Reserve System: An Encyclopedia. Trade Cloth. Greenwood Publishing Group, Inc. Portsmouth, NH. 2005. 488p. ISBN:0-313-32839-0, ISBN13: 978-0-313-32839-8. Dewey:332.1/1/097303. LCCN:2005-006189.
Audience: **g,l,u,f.** *Choice, 2006.*

Homer, Sidney & Sylla, Richard **HG1621**
History of Interest Rates. Ed. 4. Trade Cloth. John Wiley & Sons, Inc. Hoboken, NJ. 2005. 710p. Wiley Finance Ser. ISBN:0-471-73283-4, ISBN13: 978-0-471-73283-9. Dewey:332.809. LCCN:2005-281578.
Audience: **g,l,u,f.** B

Isaacs, Alan (Author, Editor) **HG151**
A Dictionary of Finance and Banking. Ed. 3. John Smullen & Nicholas Hand (Editors). Trade Paper. Oxford University Press, Inc. New York, NY. 2005. 448p. Oxford Paperback Reference Ser. ISBN:0-19-860749-0, ISBN13: 978-0-19-860749-6. Dewey:332/.03. LCCN:2005-274362.
Audience: **g,l,u,f.**

Laurentis, Giacomo De (Editor) **HG1601**
Strategy and Organization of Corporate Banking. Trade Cloth. Springer. New York, NY. 2004. ix, 191p. ISBN:3-540-22797-0, ISBN13: 978-3-540-22797-7. Dewey:332.1/2/068. LCCN:2004-112290.
Audience: **u,f.**

Mason, David **HG2151.M37 2004**
From Building and Loans to Bail Outs: A History of the American Savings and Loan Industry, 1831-1995. Cloth Text. Cambridge University Press. New York, NY. 2004. 362p. ISBN:0-521-82754-X, ISBN13: 978-0-521-82754-6. Dewey:332.3/2/0973. LCCN:2003-069691.
Audience: **g,l,u,f.** *Choice, 2005.*

Seligman, Joel **HG4910.S4 1995**
The Transformation of Wall Street: A History of the Securities and Exchange Commission and Modern Corporate Finance. Trade Cloth. Northeastern University Press. Boston, MA. 1995. 772p. ISBN:1-55553-231-4, ISBN13: 978-1-55553-231-4. Dewey:354.8/8/0973. LCCN:95-013762.
Audience: **g,l,u,f.** *Choice, 1996.*

Smith, Roy C. & Walter, Ingo **HG3881.S5434 2002**
Global Banking. Ed. 2. Trade Cloth. Oxford University Press, Inc. New York, NY. 2003. 448p. ISBN:0-19-513436-2, ISBN13: 978-0-19-513436-0. Dewey:332.1/5. LCCN:2002-003692.
Audience: **u,f.** *Choice, 2003, 1997.*

Wood, John H. **HG2994.W66 2005**
A History of Central Banking in Great Britain and the United States. Michael D. Bordo, Forrest Capie & Angela Redish (Contribution by). Trade Cloth. Cambridge University Press. New York, NY. 2005. 424p. Studies in Macroeconomic History Ser. ISBN:0-521-85013-4, ISBN13: 978-0-521-85013-1. Dewey:332.1/1/0941. LCCN:2004-024984.
Audience: **g,l,u,f.** *Choice, 2005.*

Woodward, Bob **HG2565.W654 2000**
Maestro: Greenspan's Fed and the American Boom. Trade Cloth. Simon & Schuster. New York, NY. 2000. 272p. ISBN:0-7432-0412-3, ISBN13: 978-0-7432-0412-5. Dewey:330.9/73/0928. LCCN:00-052627.
Audience: **g,l,u,f.** *Choice, 2001.*

Company and Industry Information > Industries and Markets (Selected) > Biotechnology and Pharmaceuticals

Barnum, Susan R. **TP248.2.B363**
Biotechnology: An Introduction. Ed. 2. Paper Text. Brooks/Cole. Pacific Grove, CA. 2006. 440p. ISBN:0-495-11205-4, ISBN13: 978-0-495-11205-1. Dewey:660.6.
Audience: **g,l,u.**

Dosi, Giovanni & Mazzucato, Mariana (Editors) **T175**
Knowledge Accumulation and Industry Evolution: The Case of Pharma-Biotech. Trade Cloth. Cambridge University Press. New York, NY. 2006. 464p. ISBN:0-521-85822-4, ISBN13: 978-0-521-85822-9. Dewey:615.19. LCCN:2006-280325.
Audience: **u,f.**

Figeys, Daniel (Editor) **TP248.65.P76**
Industrial Proteomics: Applications for Biotechnology and Pharmaceuticals. Digital, Other. John Wiley & Sons, Inc. Hoboken, NJ. 2005. 320p. Methods of Biochemical Analysis Ser. ISBN:0-471-70375-3, ISBN13: 978-0-471-70375-4. Dewey:660.6/3.
Audience: **u,f.**

Gibson, Mark **HF5549.5**
Technology Transfer: An International Good Practice Guide for Pharmaceuticals and Allied Industries. Trade Cloth. Davis Horwood International Publishers, Limited (DHI). Raleigh, NC. 2005. ISBN:1-930114-78-8, ISBN13: 978-1-930114-78-4. Dewey:658.
Audience: **u,f.**

Grace, Eric S. **TP248.15.G73**
Biotechnology Unzipped: Promises and Realities. Ed. 2. Trade Paper. National Academies Press. Washington, DC. 2005. 256p. ISBN:0-309-09621-9, ISBN13: 978-0-309-09621-8. Dewey:660.6.
Audience: **g,u,f.**

Interdata Staff (Compiled by) **HF1419.I70**
International Directory of Importers - Drugs and Pharmaceuticals. Ringbound. Interdata. Poulsbo, WA. 2002. 269p. ISBN:1-58239-009-6, ISBN13: 978-1-58239-009-3. Dewey:382.5.
Audience: **u,f.**

Knäblein, Jörg & Muller, Rainer H. (Editors) **RM301.M63 2005**
Modern Biopharmaceuticals: Design, Development and Optimization. Trade Cloth. John Wiley & Sons, Inc. Hoboken, NJ. 2005. 2022p. ISBN:3-527-31184-X, ISBN13: 978-3-527-31184-2. Dewey:615.19.
Audience: **u,f.**

McKelvey, Maureen & Orsenigo, Luigi **HD9999.B442**
The Economics of Biotechnology. Trade Cloth. Edward Elgar Publishing, Inc. Northampton, MA. 2006. 968p. ISBN:1-84376-776-7, ISBN13: 978-1-84376-776-3. Dewey:338.476606.
Audience: **u,f.**

Nill KimballR. **TP248.16.F54 2005**
Glossary of Biotechnology and Nanobiotechnology Terms. Ed. 4. Saddle Stitched. C R C Press LLC. Boca Raton, FL. 2005. 416p. No Ser. ISBN:0-8493-6609-7, ISBN13: 978-0-8493-6609-3. Dewey:660.6/03. LCCN:2005-051082.
Audience: **l,u,f.** *Choice, 2006.*

Plunkett, Jack W. **HD9999.B44**
Plunkett's Biotech and Genetics Industry Almanac 2006: The Only Complete Reference to the Business of Biotechnology and Genetic Engineering. Trade Paper, CD-ROM. Plunkett Research, Ltd. Houston, TX. 2005. 560p. ISBN:1-59392-033-4, ISBN13: 978-1-59392-033-3. Dewey:338.4/76606.
Audience: **l,u,f.**

Ratledge, Colin & Kristiansen, Bjorn (Editors) **TP248.2**
Basic Biotechnology. Ed. 3. Cloth Text. Cambridge University Press. New York, NY. 2006. 682p. ISBN:0-521-84031-7, ISBN13: 978-0-521-84031-6. Dewey:660.6.
Audience: **g,l,u.**

Smith, Mickey C., et al. **HD9665.5.P525 2002**
Pharmaceutical Marketing: Principles, Environment, and Practice. E. M. Kolassa, Greg Perkins & Bruce R. Siecker (Authors). Trade Paper. Haworth Press, Incorporated, The. Binghamton, NY. 2002. 372p. ISBN:0-7890-1583-8, ISBN13: 978-0-7890-1583-9. Dewey:615/.19/0688. LCCN:2002-022045.
Audience: **u,f.**

Turner, Tyya N. **HD9999.B44**
Vault Guide to the Top Pharmaceuticals and Biotech Employers. Trade Paper. Vault.com. New York, NY. 2005. 176p. ISBN:1-58131-319-5, ISBN13: 978-1-58131-319-2. Dewey:338.4/76153/025.
Audience: **g,l,u.**

Wing, Bret & Walker, Sharon **TP248.2**
Biotechnology Demystified. Trade Paper. McGraw-Hill Professional Publishing. New York, NY. 2006. 276p. ISBN:0-07-144812-8, ISBN13: 978-0-07-144812-3. Dewey:660.6.
Audience: **g,l,u.**

Wink, Michael (Editor) **TP248.2**
An Introduction to Molecular Biotechnolo: From Molecular Biological Fundmentals to Methoda and Applications in Modern Biotechnology. Trade Paper. John Wiley & Sons, Inc. Hoboken, NJ. 2006. 828p. ISBN:3-527-31412-1, ISBN13: 978-3-527-31412-6. Dewey:660.6.
Audience: **l,u.**

Company and Industry Information > Industries and Markets (Selected) > Broadcasting, Cable, and Film

TK6540.B77
Broadcasting and Cable Yearbook. Ed. 14. RR Bowker. 2006.
Audience: **g,l,u,f.**

HF5826.5
Marketer's Guide to Media. V N U Business Publications. 2005.
Audience: **g,u,f.**

PN1990
Television Week. Crain Communications, Inc.
Audience: **l,u,f.**

TK6540.W67
World Radio Television Handbook. Ed. 15. O. Lund Johansen. 2006.
Audience: **g,l,u,f.**

Cortada, James W. **HC110.I55C67 2005**
The Digital Hand, Volume 2: How Computers Changed the Work of American Financial, Telecommunications, Media, and Entertainment Industries. Trade Cloth. Oxford University Press, Inc. New York, NY. 2005. 672p. ISBN:0-19-516587-X, ISBN13: 978-0-19-516587-6. Dewey:338/.064/0973. LCCN:2004-030363.
Audience: **g,l,u,f.**

Plunkett Research, Ltd **TK6630.P58**
Plunkett's Entertainment and Media Industry Almanac. Ed. 7. Plunkett Research, Ltd. 2005. Plunkett Research, Ltd
Audience: **l,u,f.**

Company and Industry Information > Industries and Markets (Selected) > Chemicals

Chandler, Alfred D. Jr. **HD9651.5.C457 2005**
Shaping the Industrial Century: The Remarkable Story of the Evolution of the Modern Chemical and Pharmaceutical Industries. Trade Cloth. Harvard University Press. Cambridge, MA. 2005. 384p. Harvard Studies in Business History Ser., Vol. 46 ISBN:0-674-01720-X, ISBN13: 978-0-674-01720-7. Dewey:338.4/766/00973. LCCN:2004-054320.
Audience: **g,l,u,f.** *Choice, 2005.*

Spitz, Peter H. **HD9650.5.S69 2003**
The Chemical Industry at the Millenium: Maturity, Restructuring and Globalization. Trade Cloth. AtlasBooks. Ashland, OH. 2005. 400p. ISBN:0-941901-34-3, ISBN13: 978-0-941901-34-5. Dewey:338.4/766. LCCN:2003-010798.
Audience: **g,u,f.**

Company and Industry Information > Industries and Markets (Selected) > Computers: Commercial Services and Internet

Battelle, John **HD9696.8.U64G663**
The Search: How Google and Its Rivals Rewrote the Rules of Business and Transformed Our Culture. Perfect, Paper over Boards, Dust Jacket. Penguin Group (USA) Inc. New York, NY. 2005. 311p. ISBN:1-59184-088-0, ISBN13: 978-1-59184-088-6. Dewey:338.7/6102504/0973. LCCN:2005-047538.
Audience: **g,l,u.** *Choice, 2006.*

Buderi, Robert & Huang, Gregory T. **HD9696.63.A4-U(U.S.)**
Guanxi (the Art of Relationships): Microsoft, China, and Bill Gates's Plan to Win the Road Ahead. Trade Cloth. Simon & Schuster. New York, NY. 2006. 320p. ISBN:0-7432-7322-2, ISBN13: 978-0-7432-7322-0. Dewey:338.8/8710040951. LCCN:2006-042253.
Audience: **g,l,u,f.**

Clark, Jim **HD9696.65.U64**
Netscape Time: The Making of the Billion-Dollar Start-Up That Took on Microsoft. Owen Edwards (As told to). Trade Paper. St. Martin's Press. Gordonville, VA. 2000. 288p. ISBN:0-312-26361-9, ISBN13: 978-0-312-26361-4. Dewey:338.4/7004678/0973.
Audience: **g,l,u,f.**

Klein, Alec **HE7583.U6**
Stealing Time: Steve Case, Jerry Levin, and the Collapse of AOL Time Warner. Trade Paper. Simon & Schuster, Inc. New York, NY. 2004. 352p. ISBN:0-7432-5984-X, ISBN13: 978-0-7432-5984-2. Dewey:338.7/61004678/0973.
Audience: **g,l,u.**

Slater, Robert **HD9696.8.U64C577**
The Eye of the Storm: How John Chambers Steered Cisco Through the Technology Collapse. Trade Cloth. HarperCollins Publishers. New York, NY. 2003. 304p. ISBN:0-06-018887-1, ISBN13: 978-0-06-018887-0. Dewey:338.7/6213981/092. LCCN:2002-027565.
Audience: **g,l,u,f.**

Company and Industry Information > Industries and Markets (Selected) > Computers: Hardware

Dell, Michael & Fredman, Catherine **HD57.7**
Direct from Dell: Strategies That Revolutionized an Industry. Trade Paper. HarperCollins Publishers. New York, NY. 2006. 272p. ISBN:0-06-084572-4, ISBN13: 978-0-06-084572-8. Dewey:658.4/092.
Audience: **l,u,f.**

Company and Industry Information > Industries and Markets (Selected) > Computers: Software

Cortada, James W. **HC110.I55C67 2005**
The Digital Hand, Volume 2: How Computers Changed the Work of American Financial, Telecommunications, Media, and Entertainment Industries. Trade Cloth. Oxford University Press, Inc. New York, NY. 2005. 672p. ISBN:0-19-516587-X, ISBN13: 978-0-19-516587-6. Dewey:338/.064/0973. LCCN:2004-030363.
Audience: **g,l,u,f.**

Heilemann, John **KF228.U5H45**
Pride Before the Fall: The Trials of Bill Gates and the End of the Microsoft Era. Trade Cloth. DIANE Publishing Company. Collingdale, PA. 2001. 246p. ISBN:0-7567-6052-6, ISBN13: 978-0-7567-6052-6. Dewey:338.826100530973.
Audience: **g,l,u,f.**

Manes, Stephen & Andrews, Paul **HD9696.C62G336 1993**
Gates: How Microsoft's Mogul Reinvented an Industry - and Made Himself the Richest Man in America. Trade Cloth. Doubleday Canada, Ltd. Toronto, ON. 1992. 544p. ISBN:0-385-42075-7, ISBN13: 978-0-385-42075-4. Dewey:338.7/610053/092 B. LCCN:92-015994.
Audience: **g,l,u.**

Yost, Jeffrey R. **HD9696**
The Computer Industry. Trade Cloth. Greenwood Publishing Group, Inc. Portsmouth, NH. 2005. 288p. Emerging Industries in the United States Ser. ISBN:0-313-32844-7, ISBN13: 978-0-313-32844-2. Dewey:338.4/7004/0973. LCCN:2005-004196.
Audience: **g,l,u,f.** *Choice, 2005.*

Company and Industry Information > Industries and Markets (Selected) > Construction

Alexander, Barbara T. **HD7293**
☐ The U.S. Homebuilding Industry: A Half Century of Building the American Dream.
http://www.jchs.harvard.edu/publications/markets/balexander_M00-1.pdf
Joint Center for Housing Studies, Harvard University. Joint Center for Housing Studies, Harvard University.
Audience: **l,u,f.**

Burden, Ernest E. **TH9**
Illustrated Dictionary of Building Design and Construction. Trade Paper. McGraw-Hill Companies, The. New York, NY. 2004. 296p. ISBN:0-07-144506-4, ISBN13: 978-0-07-144506-1. Dewey:690.03. LCCN:2004-275924.
Audience: **g,l,u,f.** *Choice, 2005.*

Collier, Nathan S., et al. **HD9715.A2C59 2002**
Construction Funding: The Process of Real Estate Development, Appraisal, and Finance. Ed. 3. Courtland A. Collier & Don A. Halperin (Authors). Trade Cloth. John Wiley & Sons, Inc. Hoboken, NJ. 2001. 384p. ISBN:0-471-39466-1, ISBN13: 978-0-471-39466-2. Dewey:690/.068/1. LCCN:2001-026949.
Audience: **l,u,f.**

Colton, Kent W. **HD7287.3**
Housing in the Twenty-First Century: Achieving Common Ground. Trade Cloth. Harvard University Press. Cambridge, MA. 2003. 528p. Wertheim Publications in Industrial Relations Ser. ISBN:0-674-01093-0, ISBN13: 978-0-674-01093-2. Dewey:363.5/0973.
Audience: **l,u.**

Dewberry, Sidney O., et al. **TA549**
Land Development Handbook. Ed. 2. Davis, Philip C. Champagne & The Dewberry Companies (Authors), Curtis M. Sumner (Editor). Trade Cloth, CD-ROM, Mixed Media. McGraw-Hill Professional Publishing. New York, NY. 2002. 1124p. Handbook Ser. ISBN:0-07-137525-2, ISBN13: 978-0-07-137525-2. Dewey:690. LCCN:2002-279933.
Audience: **l,u,f.**

Federal Deposit Insurance Corporation **HD1361**
☐ Survey of Real Estate Trends.
http://purl.access.gpo.gov/GPO/LPS937
Federal Deposit Insurance Corporation.
Audience: **l,u,f.**

Gould, Frederick E. **TH438.G625 2005**
Managing the Construction Process: Estimating, Scheduling, and Project Control. Ed. 3. Cloth Text. Prentice Hall PTR. Upper Saddle River, NJ. 2004. 400p. ISBN:0-13-113406-X, ISBN13: 978-0-13-113406-5. Dewey:690. LCCN:2003-070721.
Audience: **l,u.**

Grubb & Ellis **HD1361**
☐ Grubb & Ellis Real Estate Forecast.
http://www.grubb-ellis.com/research/
Grubb & Ellis.
Audience: **g,l,u,f.**

Hecht, Bennett L. **HD259**
Developing Affordable Housing: A Practical Guide for Nonprofit Organizations. Ed. 3. Trade Cloth. John Wiley & Sons, Inc. Hoboken, NJ. 2006. 840p. Wiley Nonprofit Law, Finance and Management Ser. ISBN:0-471-74346-1, ISBN13: 978-0-471-74346-0. Dewey:333.73/150973. LCCN:2005-058121.
Audience: **l,u,f.**

Joint Center for Housing Studies, Harvard University **HD7285**
☐ State of the Nation's Housing 2005.
http://www.jchs.harvard.edu/publications/markets/son2005/index.html
Joint Center for Housing Studies, Harvard University.
Audience: **l,u,f.**

Keenan, Andrea & Georges, Danielle **TH880.G74 2002**
Green Building: Project Planning and Cost Estimating. Trade Cloth. R. S. Means Company, Inc. Kingston, MA. 2002. 350p. Reference Book Publications ISBN:0-87629-659-2, ISBN13: 978-0-87629-659-2. Dewey:690.837. LCCN:2003-266423.
Audience: **l,u,f.**

Kibert, Charles **TH880.K53 2005**
Sustainable Construction: Green Building Design and Delivery. Trade Cloth. John Wiley & Sons, Inc. Hoboken, NJ. 2005. 448p. ISBN:0-471-66113-9, ISBN13: 978-0-471-66113-9. Dewey:720/.47. LCCN:2004-014938.
Audience: **g,l,u,f.**

National Association of Home Builders **HA175**
Economic and Housing Data.
http://www.nahb.org/page.aspx/category/sectionID=113
National Association of Home Builders.
Audience: **g,l,u,f.**

National Center for Manufacturing Sciences **HD9715.8**
Construction Industry Compliance Assistance Portal.
http://www.cicacenter.org/
National Center for Manufacturing Sciences.
Audience: **g,l,u,f.**

Ogershok, David & Pray, Richard (Editors) **TH435**
National Construction Estimator. Ed. 54. Trade Paper, CD-ROM. Craftsman Book Company. Carlsbad, CA. 2005. 661p. ISBN:1-57218-159-1, ISBN13: 978-1-57218-159-5. Dewey:692/.5/0973.
Audience: **g,l,u,f.**

Preece, Christopher N. (Editor), et al. **HD9715**
Construction Business Development: Meeting New Challenges, Seeking Opportunities. Krisen Moodley & Paul Smith (Editors). Paper Text. Elsevier Science & Technology Books. Saint Louis, MO. 2003. 216p. ISBN:0-7506-5109-1, ISBN13: 978-0-7506-5109-7. Dewey:624/.068/8. LCCN:2003-052365.
Audience: **l,u,f.**

Thelen Reid and Priest LLP **HD9715**
Construction WebLinks Portal.
http://www.constructionweblinks.com/
Thelen Reid and Priest LLP.
Audience: **g,l,u,f.**

United States Census Bureau **HD9715**
Construction and Housing Publications.
http://www.census.gov/prod/www/abs/cons-hou.html
United States Census Bureau.
Audience: **g,l,u,f.**

United States Census Bureau **HD9715**
Construction Statistics.
http://www.census.gov/const/www/
United States Census Bureau.
Audience: **g,l,u,f.**

United States Green Building Council **NA2542.35**
Industry Research Portal.
http://www.usgbc.org/DisplayPage.aspx?CMSPageID=78&
United States Green Building Council.
Audience: **g,l,u,f.**

Urban Land Institute Staff **HC103.7**
America's Real Estate: Natural Resource, National Legacy. Trade Paper. Urban Land Institute. Washington, DC. 1997. 120p. ISBN:0-87420-796-7, ISBN13: 978-0-87420-796-5. Dewey:333.7/0973. LCCN:97-061514.
Audience: **g,l,u,f.**

Company and Industry Information > Industries and Markets (Selected) > Electric Utilities

HD9685.U4 E33
Statistical Yearbook of the Electric Power Industry. Edison Electric Institute.. 2005.
Audience: **g,l,u,f.**

Hughes, Thomas P. **TK1005.H83**
Networks of Power: Electrification in Western Society, 1880-1930. Trade Paper. Johns Hopkins University Press. Baltimore, MD. 1975. 488p. ISBN:0-8018-4614-5, ISBN13: 978-0-8018-4614-4. Dewey:333.7932. LCCN:82-014858.
Audience: **g,u,f.** B

Company and Industry Information > Industries and Markets (Selected) > Environmental and Waste Management

Berg, David R. & Ferrier, Grant **HD9718.U62 B47**
The U. S. Environmental Industry: Meeting the Challenge: U. S. Industry Faces the 21st Century. Jon Paugh (Editor). Paper Text. DIANE Publishing Company. Collingdale, PA. 2000. 190p. ISBN:0-7881-8401-6, ISBN13: 978-0-7881-8401-7. Dewey:354.73.
Audience: **l,u,f.**

Guttentag, Roger M. **TD794.5.G88 1997**
Recycling and Waste Management Guide to the Internet. Trade Paper. Government Institutes. Blue Ridge Summit, PA. 1997. 267p. ISBN:0-86587-582-0, ISBN13: 978-0-86587-582-1. Dewey:025.06/3637282. LCCN:97-034588.
Audience: **l,u,f.** *Choice, 1998.*

Mason, Robert J. & Mattson, Mark T. **G1201.G3**
Atlas of United States Environmental Issues. Trade Cloth. Macmillan Publishing Company, Inc. Old Tappan, NJ. 1990. 192p. ISBN:0-685-38861-1, ISBN13: 978-0-685-38861-7. Dewey:333.7/0973/022.
Audience: **l,u,f.** *Choice, 1991.*

Middleton, Nick **GF41.M525 2003**
The Global Casino: An Introduction to Environmental Issues. Ed. 3. Trade Cloth. Oxford University Press, Inc. New York, NY. 2003. 448p. An Arnold Publication ISBN:0-340-80949-3, ISBN13: 978-0-340-80949-5. Dewey:304.2/8. LCCN:2004-271618.
Audience: **g,l,u,f.** *Choice, 1996.*

Moseley, Charles J. (Editor) **GE115.B43 1993**
Beacham's Guide to Environmental Issues and Sources, Set. Trade Cloth. Beacham Publishing Corporation. Osprey, FL. 1993. ISBN:0-933833-31-8, ISBN13: 978-0-933833-31-9. Dewey:363.7. LCCN:92-042027.
Audience: **l,u,f.** *Choice, 1993.*

Company and Industry Information > Industries and Markets (Selected) > Extractive Industries (e.g., Petroleum)

Freese, Barbara **TN801**
Coal: A Human History. Trade Cloth. DIANE Publishing Company. Collingdale, PA. 2005. 308p. ISBN:0-7567-9769-1, ISBN13: 978-0-7567-9769-0. Dewey:553.2/4.
Audience: **g,l,u,f.** *Choice, 2003.*

Goodstein, David **TN870.G645 2004**
Out of Gas: The End of the Age of Oil. Trade Cloth. W. W. Norton & Company, Inc. New York, NY. 2004. 128p. ISBN:0-393-05857-3, ISBN13: 978-0-393-05857-4. Dewey:622/.1828. LCCN:2003-010376.
Audience: **g,l,u,f.** *Choice, 2004.*

Yergin, Daniel **HD9560.5**
The Prize: The Epic Quest for Oil, Money and Power. Library Binding. Buccaneer Books, Inc. Cutchogue, NY. 1994. ISBN:1-56849-572-2, ISBN13: 978-1-56849-572-9. Dewey:338.2/7/282/0904.
Audience: **g,l,u,f.**

Company and Industry Information > Industries and Markets (Selected) > Extractive Industries (e.g., Petroleum) > Oil and Gas

TN860
Oil & Gas Journal. PennWell Publisher. 1902.
Audience: **g,u,f.**

Deffeyes, Kenneth S. **TN870.D369 2005**
Beyond Oil: The View from Hubbert's Peak. Cloth over Boards. Farrar, Straus & Giroux. New York, NY. 2005. 224p. ISBN:0-8090-2956-1, ISBN13: 978-0-8090-2956-3. Dewey:333.8/23211. LCCN:2004-116475.
Audience: **g,u,f.** *Choice, 2005.*

PennWell Books **TN865**
2004 International Petroleum Encyclopedia. Trade Cloth. PennWell Corporation. Tulsa, OK. 2004. ISBN:1-59370-028-8, ISBN13: 978-1-59370-028-7. Dewey:665.503.
Audience: **g,l,u,f.**

Company and Industry Information > Industries and Markets (Selected) > Foods and Non-Alcoholic Beverages

HD9003.F578
Thomas Food and Beverage Market Place 2006. Trade Paper. Grey House Publishing. Millerton, NY. 2005. ISBN:1-59237-096-9, ISBN13: 978-1-59237-096-2. Dewey:338.
Audience: **l,u,f.**

Doeg, Colin **HD9000.5.D597 2005**
Crisis Management in the Food and Drinks Industry: A Practical Approach. Ed. 2. Trade Cloth. Springer. New York, NY. 2005. XX, 263p. Practical Approaches to Food Control and Food Quality Ser. ISBN:0-387-23382-2, ISBN13: 978-0-387-23382-6. Dewey:664/.0068/4. LCCN:2004-065092.
Audience: **l,u,f.**

Gottlieb, Richard (Editor) **HD9003**
Food and Beverage Market Place: Suppliers Guide, 2000-01. Ed. 2. Trade Paper. Grey House Publishing. Millerton, NY. 2000. 973p. ISBN:1-891482-34-3, ISBN13: 978-1-891482-34-2. Dewey:338.
Audience: **l,u,f.**

Gottlieb, Richard (Editor) **HD9003**
Thomas Food and Beverage Market Place, 2002/2003. Ed. 2. Trade Paper. Grey House Publishing. Millerton, NY. 2002. 7000p. ISBN:1-930956-95-9, ISBN13: 978-1-930956-95-7. Dewey:338.47664.
Audience: **l,u,f.** *Choice, 2003.*

Michman, Ronald D. & Mazze, Edward M. **HD9005**
The Food Industry Wars: Marketing Triumphs and Blunders. Trade Cloth. Greenwood Publishing Group, Inc. Portsmouth, NH. 1998. 280p. ISBN:1-56720-111-3, ISBN13: 978-1-56720-111-6. Dewey:664/.0068/8. LCCN:97-032992.
Audience: **l,u,f.** *Choice, 1998.*

Schröder, Monika J. A. **TX531**
Food Quality and Consumer Value: Delivering Food That Satisfies. Trade Cloth. Springer. New York, NY. 2003. XVI, 330p. ISBN:3-540-43914-5, ISBN13: 978-3-540-43914-1. Dewey:641.3. LCCN:2003-041538.
Audience: **l,u.** *Choice, 2003.*

Seitz, Wesley D., et al. **HD1415.S395 2002**
Economics of Resources, Agriculture and Food. Ed. 2. Gerald C. Nelson & Harold G. Halcrow (Authors). Cloth Text. McGraw-Hill Higher Education. Burr Ridge, IL. 2001. 544p. Agricultural Economics Ser. ISBN:0-07-025958-5, ISBN13: 978-0-07-025958-4. Dewey:338.1. LCCN:2001-031266.
Audience: **l,u.**

Company and Industry Information > Industries and Markets (Selected) > Healthcare

RA395.A3 H432
Healthcare Trends and Forecasts in 2006: Performance Expectations for the Healthcare Industry. Comb Bound. Healthcare Intelligence Network. Wall, NJ. 2005. 45p. ISBN:1-933402-34-2, ISBN13: 978-1-933402-34-5. Dewey:362.1.
Audience: **l,u,f.**

HD9994.U5 M42
Medical and Healthcare Marketplace Guide. Ed. 18. Paper Text. Dorland Healthcare Information. Philadelphia, PA. 2002. ISBN:1-880874-80-6, ISBN13: 978-1-880874-80-6. Dewey:338.7/61/68176102573.
Audience: **l,u,f.**

Kronenfeld, Jennie J. **RA395.A3K7593 2004**
Healthcare Reform in America: A Reference Handbook. Library Binding. ABC-CLIO, Inc. Santa Barbara, CA. 2004. 300p. Contemporary World Issues Ser. ISBN:1-57607-977-5, ISBN13: 978-1-57607-977-5. Dewey:362.1/0973. LCCN:2004-005417.
Audience: **l,u,f.** *Choice, 2005.*

Company and Industry Information > Industries and Markets (Selected) > Hospitality and Tourism

Allen, Judy **GT3405.A55 2000**
Event Planning: The Ultimate Guide to Successful Meetings, Corporate Events, Fundraising Galas, Conferences, Conventions, Incentives, and Other Special Events. Trade Cloth. John Wiley & Sons, Inc. Hoboken, NJ. 2000. 320p. ISBN:0-471-64412-9, ISBN13: 978-0-471-64412-5. Dewey:394.2/068. LCCN:00-363937.
Audience: **g,u,f.**

Dickinson, Bob & Vladimir, Andy **G550.D53 1996**
Selling the Sea: An Inside Look at the Cruise Industry. Trade Cloth. John Wiley & Sons, Inc. Hoboken, NJ. 1996. 384p. ISBN:0-471-12001-4, ISBN13: 978-0-471-12001-8. Dewey:387.2/430688. LCCN:96-020420.
Audience: **g,l,u.**

Fenich, George G. **TX911.2.M44 2005**
Meetings, Expositions, Events and Conventions: An Introduction to the Industry. Cloth Text. Prentice Hall PTR. Upper Saddle River, NJ. 2004. 544p. ISBN:0-13-112587-7, ISBN13: 978-0-13-112587-2. Dewey:647.94. LCCN:2004-013995.
Audience: **g,l,u.**

Jafari, Jafar (Editor) **G155**
Encyclopedia of Tourism. Trade Paper. Routledge. New York, NY. 2003. 720p. Routledge World Reference Ser. ISBN:0-415-30890-9, ISBN13: 978-0-415-30890-8. Dewey:338.4/791/03.
Audience: **g,l,u.**

Kotler, Phillip R., et al. **TX911.3.M3K68 2005**
Marketing for Hospitality and Tourism. Ed. 4. John T. Bowen & James C. Makens (Authors). Cloth Text. Prentice Hall PTR. Upper Saddle River, NJ. 2005. 960p. ISBN:0-13-119378-3, ISBN13: 978-0-13-119378-9. Dewey:647.94/098/8. LCCN:2005-015341.
Audience: **g,l,u,f.**

Lane, Harold E. & Dupré, Denise **TX911.3.M27**
Hospitality World!: An Introduction. Trade Cloth. John Wiley & Sons, Inc. Hoboken, NJ. 1996. 560p. Hospitality, Travel, and Tourism Ser. ISBN:0-471-28989-2, ISBN13: 978-0-471-28989-0. Dewey:647.9/4/068.
Audience: **l,u.**

Mancini, Marc **G155.A1M263 2003**
Selling Destinations: Geography for the Travel Professional. Ed. 4. Paper Text. Thomson Delmar Learning. Albany, NY. 2003. 560p. ISBN:1-4018-1982-6, ISBN13: 978-1-4018-1982-8. Dewey:338.4/791. LCCN:2003-008416.
Audience: **g,l,u.**

Medlik, S. **G155.A1M397 2003**
Dictionary of Travel, Tourism and Hospitality. Ed. 3. Cloth Text. Elsevier Science & Technology Books. Saint Louis, MO. 2003. 288p. ISBN:0-7506-5650-6, ISBN13: 978-0-7506-5650-4. Dewey:338.4/791/03.
Audience: **g,l,u.** *Choice, 1994.*

Nixon, Judith M. **Z6250 .N59 1993TX911**
Hotel and Restaurant Industries: A Bibliography and Sourcebook. Ed. 2. Trade Cloth. Purdue University, Office of Publications. West Lafayette, IN. 1993. ISBN:0-931682-35-5, ISBN13: 978-0-931682-35-3. Dewey:016.3384/764794. LCCN:93-010578.
Audience: **g,l,u,f.**

Pizam, Abraham (Editor-In-Chief) **TX911.3.M27**
International Encyclopedia of Hospitality Management. Cloth Text. Elsevier Science & Technology Books. Saint Louis, MO. 2005. 736p. ISBN:0-7506-5996-3, ISBN13: 978-0-7506-5996-3. Dewey:647.94.
Audience: **g,l,u,f.** *Choice, 2006.*

Sawin, Philip (Compiled by), et al. **Z6250**
A Literature Guide to the Hospitality Industry. Denise Madland, Mary K. Richards & Jana Reeg Steidenger (Compiled by). Cloth Text. Greenwood Publishing Group, Inc. Portsmouth, NH. 1990. 112p. Bibliographies and Indexes in Economics and Economic History Ser., No. 10 ISBN:0-313-26721-9, ISBN13: 978-0-313-26721-5. Dewey:016.64794. LCCN:90-031740.
Audience: **g,l,u,f.** *Choice, 1990.*

Scarrott, Martin **GV188.S66 1999**
Sport, Leisure and Tourism Information Sources: A Guide for Researchers. Cloth Text. Elsevier Science & Technology Books. Saint Louis, MO. 1999. 256p. ISBN:0-7506-3864-8, ISBN13: 978-0-7506-3864-7. Dewey:026.79. LCCN:99-218933.
Audience: **l,u,f.**

Scott, Joseph **G155.A1**
□ Travel Industry World Yearbook: The Big Picture. http://www.travelbigpicture.com/storyboard1.htm Travel Industry Publishing Company, Inc.
Audience: **g,l,u,f.**

Stipanuk, David M. & Roffman, Harold **TX928.S75 1996**
Hospitality Facilities Management and Design. Trade Paper. Educational Institute of the American Hotel & Motel Association. Lansing, MI. 1996. 509p. ISBN:0-86612-109-9, ISBN13: 978-0-86612-109-5. Dewey:647.94/068/2. LCCN:92-018623.
Audience: **l,u,f.**

Stutts, Alan T. & Wortman, James **TX911.3.M27S78 2006**
Hotel and Lodging Management: An Introduction. Ed. 2. Trade Cloth. John Wiley & Sons, Inc. Hoboken, NJ. 2005. 368p. ISBN:0-471-47447-9, ISBN13: 978-0-471-47447-0. Dewey:647.94/068. LCCN:2004-027109.
Audience: **l,u.**

United States Department of Commerce, International Trade Administration **G155.U6**
□ Office of Travel and Tourism Industries Portal. http://www.tinet.ita.doc.gov/ United States Department of Commerce, International Trade Administration.
Audience: **g,l,u,f.**

Weaver, David B. (Editor) **G156.5.E26E53 2003**
The Encyclopedia of Ecotourism. Trade Paper. Oxford University Press, Inc. New York, NY. 2003. 688p. CABI

Publishing Ser. ISBN:0-85199-682-5, ISBN13: 978-0-85199-682-0. Dewey:338.4/791.
Audience: **g,l,u.**

World Tourism Organization (WTO) Staff **G155.A1**
Compendium of Tourism Statistics. Ed. 25. Trade Paper. World Tourism Organization. 28020 Madrid 16, 2005. 329p. ISBN:92-844-0780-X, ISBN13: 978-92-844-0780-4. Dewey:338.4791021.
Audience: **g,l,u,f.**

Company and Industry Information > Industries and Markets (Selected) > Invesment Services

Aliber, Robert Z. **HG3881.A44 2000**
The New International Money Game. Ed. 6. Trade Cloth. University of Chicago Press. Chicago, IL. 2000. 304p. ISBN:0-226-01396-0, ISBN13: 978-0-226-01396-1. Dewey:332. LCCN:99-055593.
Audience: **g,l,u,f.**

Bernstein, Peter L. **HD61.B466 1996**
Against the Gods: The Remarkable Story of Risk. Trade Cloth. John Wiley & Sons, Inc. Hoboken, NJ. 1996. 400p. ISBN:0-471-12104-5, ISBN13: 978-0-471-12104-6. Dewey:368. LCCN:96-033861.
Audience: **g,l,u,f.**

Bernstein, Peter L. & Damodaran, Aswath (Editors) **HG4529.5.I58 1998**
Investment Management. Trade Cloth. John Wiley & Sons, Inc. Hoboken, NJ. 1998. 480p. Frontiers in Finance Ser. ISBN:0-471-19716-5, ISBN13: 978-0-471-19716-4. Dewey:332.6. LCCN:97-043844.
Audience: **u,f.** *Choice, 1998.*

Biggs, Barton **HG4530.B516 2006**
Hedgehogging. Trade Cloth. John Wiley & Sons, Inc. Hoboken, NJ. 2006. 320p. ISBN:0-471-77191-0, ISBN13: 978-0-471-77191-3. Dewey:332.64/5. LCCN:2005-026139.
Audience: **g,l,u,f.**

Chicago Board of Trade Staff **HG6024.U6C45 2006**
The CBOT Handbook of Futures and Options. Trade Cloth. McGraw-Hill Companies, The. New York, NY. 2006. 480p. ISBN:0-07-145751-8, ISBN13: 978-0-07-145751-4. Dewey:332.64/52. LCCN:2005-027316.
Audience: **g,l,u,f.**

Choi, Frederick D. S. (Editor) **HF5686.I56H36 2003**
International Finance and Accounting Handbook. Ed. 3. Trade Cloth. John Wiley & Sons, Inc. Hoboken, NJ. 2003. 888p. ISBN:0-471-22921-0, ISBN13: 978-0-471-22921-6. Dewey:657/.96. LCCN:2002-192266.
Audience: **u,f.**

Davis, E. Philip & Steil, Benn **HG4521.D14 2001**
Institutional Investors. Trade Cloth. MIT Press. Cambridge, MA. 2001. 560p. ISBN:0-262-04192-8, ISBN13: 978-0-262-04192-8. Dewey:332.67/154. LCCN:2001-030280.
Audience: **g,l,u,f.**

Downes, John & Goodman, Jordan Elliot **HG173.D66 2003**
Finance and Investment Handbook. Ed. 6. Trade Cloth. Barron's Educational Series, Inc. Hauppauge, NY. 2003. 1400p. ISBN:0-7641-5554-7, ISBN13: 978-0-7641-5554-3. Dewey:332.67/8. LCCN:2002-038595.
Audience: **g,l,u,f.**

Ellis, Charles D. & Vertin, James R. **HG4928.5.E42 2001**
Wall Street People: True Stories of Today's Masters and Moguls. Trade Cloth. John Wiley & Sons, Inc. Hoboken, NJ. 2001. 360p. ISBN:0-471-23809-0, ISBN13: 978-0-471-23809-6. Dewey:332.6/0973. LCCN:2001-026114.
Audience: **g,l,u,f.**

Ellis, Charles D. & Vertin, James R. **HG4928.5 .E42 2001**
Wall Street People: True Stories of the Great Barons of Finance. Trade Cloth. John Wiley & Sons, Inc. Hoboken, NJ. 2003. 288p. ISBN:0-471-27428-3, ISBN13: 978-0-471-27428-5. Dewey:332.60973.
Audience: **g,l,u,f.**

Geisst, Charles **HG5129.N5G44 2001**
The Last Partnerships: Inside the Great Wall Street Dynasties. Trade Cloth. McGraw-Hill Companies, The. New York, NY. 2001. 338p. ISBN:0-07-136999-6, ISBN13: 978-0-07-136999-2. Dewey:332.6/0973. LCCN:2001-030374.
Audience: **g,l,u,f.** *Choice, 2001.*

Geisst, Charles **HG4572**
Wall Street: From Its Beginnings to the Fall of Enron. Trade Cloth. Oxford University Press, Inc. New York, NY. 2004. 449p. ISBN:0-19-517061-X, ISBN13: 978-0-19-517061-0. Dewey:332.64/273. LCCN:2004-555123.
Audience: **g,l,u,f.**

Gordon, John S. **HG4910.G667 1999**
The Great Game: The Emergence of Wall Street as a World Power, 1653-2000. Trade Cloth. Simon & Schuster. New York, NY. 1999. 320p. ISBN:0-684-83287-9, ISBN13: 978-0-684-83287-6. Dewey:332.64/273. LCCN:00-265068.
Audience: **g,l,u,f.**

Isaacs, Alan (Author, Editor) **HG151**
A Dictionary of Finance and Banking. Ed. 3. John Smullen & Nicholas Hand (Editors). Trade Paper. Oxford University Press, Inc. New York, NY. 2005. 448p. Oxford Paperback Reference Ser. ISBN:0-19-860749-0, ISBN13: 978-0-19-860749-6. Dewey:332/.03. LCCN:2005-274362.
Audience: **g,l,u,f.**

Seligman, Joel **HG4910.S4 1995**
The Transformation of Wall Street: A History of the Securities and Exchange Commission and Modern Corporate Finance. Trade Cloth. Northeastern University Press. Boston, MA. 1995. 772p. ISBN:1-55553-231-4, ISBN13: 978-1-55553-231-4. Dewey:354.8/8/0973. LCCN:95-013762.
Audience: **g,l,u,f.** *Choice, 1996.*

Smith, B. Mark **HG4551.S568 2003**
The Equity Culture: The Story of the Global Stock Market. Cloth over Boards. Farrar, Straus & Giroux. New York, NY. 2003. 352p. ISBN:0-374-28175-0, ISBN13: 978-0-374-28175-5. Dewey:332.63/2. LCCN:2003-040851.
Audience: **g,l,u,f.** *Choice, 2003.*

Smith, Roy C. & Walter, Ingo **HG3881.S5434 2002**
Global Banking. Ed. 2. Trade Cloth. Oxford University Press, Inc. New York, NY. 2003. 448p. ISBN:0-19-513436-2, ISBN13: 978-0-19-513436-0. Dewey:332.1/5. LCCN:2002-003692.
Audience: **u,f.** *Choice, 2003, 1997.*

Tamarkin, Robert A. **HG6049.T35 1993**
Merc: The Emergence of a Global Financial Powerhouse. Trade Cloth. HarperCollins Publishers. New York, NY. 1993. 304p. ISBN:0-88730-516-4, ISBN13: 978-0-88730-516-0. Dewey:332.64/4/0977311. LCCN:92-053335.
Audience: **g,l,u,f.**

Teweles, Richard J. & Bradley, Edward S. **HG4551.T48 1998**
The Stock Market. Ed. 7. Trade Cloth. John Wiley & Sons, Inc. Hoboken, NJ. 1998. 576p. Wiley Investment Ser., Vol. 64 ISBN:0-471-19134-5, ISBN13: 978-0-471-19134-6. Dewey:332.63/2. LCCN:98-015213.
Audience: **g,l,u,f.**

Company and Industry Information > Industries and Markets (Selected) > Insurance

HG8501
Best's Review. Perfect. A.M. Best Company, Inc. Oldwick, NJ. 2005. ISBN:1-933062-45-2, ISBN13: 978-1-933062-45-7. Dewey:368.
Audience: **g,l,u,f.**

Athearn, James L. **HG8051.A82 1989**
Risk and Insurance. Ed. 6. Trade Cloth. West Publishing Company, College & School Division. Eagan, MN. ISBN:0-314-64063-0, ISBN13: 978-0-314-64063-5. Dewey:368/.01. LCCN:87-033128.
Audience: **u.**

Black, Kenneth Jr. & Skipper, Harold D. Jr. **HG8771.B55 2000**
Life and Health Insurance. Ed. 13. Trade Cloth. Prentice Hall PTR. Upper Saddle River, NJ. 1999. 1072p. Prentice Hall Series in Security and Insurance Ser. ISBN:0-13-891250-5, ISBN13: 978-0-13-891250-5. Dewey:368.300973. LCCN:99-022004.
Audience: **u,f.**

Briys, Eric C. & de Varenne, François **HG8844.B855 2001**
Insurance: From Underwriting to Derivatives. Trade Cloth. John Wiley & Sons, Inc. Hoboken, NJ. 2001. 176p. Wiley Finance Ser. ISBN:0-471-49227-2, ISBN13: 978-0-471-49227-6. Dewey:368/.01. LCCN:2001-033417.
Audience: **u,f.**

Clark, John (Editor) **HG8025.C58 1999**
International Dictionary of Insurance and Finance. Trade Cloth. Fitzroy Dearborn Publishers, Inc. Chicago, IL. 1999. 360p. ISBN:1-57958-161-7, ISBN13: 978-1-57958-161-9. Dewey:368.003. LCCN:99-482831.
Audience: **g,l,u,f.** *Choice, 2000.*

Coombs, Jan **RA413.5.U5C677 2004**
The Rise and Fall of HMOs: An American Health Care Revolution. Trade Cloth. University of Wisconsin Press. Chicago, IL. 2005. 430p. ISBN:0-299-20240-2, ISBN13: 978-0-299-20240-8. Dewey:362.1/042584. LCCN:2004-012819.
Audience: **g,l,u,f.** *Choice, 2006.*

Dorfman, Mark S. **HG8051.D65 2004**
Introduction to Risk Management and Insurance. Ed. 8. Cloth Text. Prentice Hall PTR. Upper Saddle River, NJ. 2004. 608p. ISBN:0-13-144958-3, ISBN13: 978-0-13-144958-9. Dewey:368. LCCN:2003-064699.
Audience: **g,l,u,f.**

Estes, Jack C. **HG1626 .E82 1993**
McGraw-Hill's Compound Interest and Annuity Tables. Ed. 2. Trade Paper. McGraw-Hill Companies, The. New York, NY. 1992. 256p. ISBN:0-07-019686-9, ISBN13: 978-0-07-019686-5. Dewey:332.8/2/0212. LCCN:92-025142.
Audience: **g,l,u,f.**

Folland, Sherman, et al. **RA410.F65 2003**
The Economics of Health and Health Care. Ed. 4. Allen C. Goodman & Miron Stano (Authors). Trade Cloth. Pearson Education. Boston, MA. 2003. 648p. Prentice-Hall Series in Economics ISBN:0-13-100067-5, ISBN13: 978-0-13-100067-4. Dewey:338.4/33621. LCCN:2003-045980.
Audience: **u.**

Rejda, George E. **HG8051.R44 2004**
Principles of Risk Management and Insurance. Ed. 9. Cloth Text. Addison Wesley. Boston, MA. 2004. 784p. Addison-Wesley Series in Finance ISBN:0-321-23687-4, ISBN13: 978-0-321-23687-6. Dewey:368. LCCN:2004-047606.
Audience: **g,l,u,f.**

Rubin, Harvey W. **HG8025.R83 2000**
Dictionary of Insurance Terms. Ed. 4. Trade Paper. Barron's Educational Series, Inc. Hauppauge, NY. 2000. 573p. Business Dictionaries Ser. ISBN:0-7641-1262-7, ISBN13: 978-0-7641-1262-1. Dewey:368/.003. LCCN:99-046788.
Audience: **g,l,u,f.**

Stevens, William S. **RA395.A3H4243 2003**
Health Insurance: Current Issues and Background. Trade Cloth. Nova Science Publishers, Inc. Hauppauge, NY. 2003. 212p. ISBN:1-59033-687-9, ISBN13: 978-1-59033-687-8. Dewey:368.38/2/00973. LCCN:2003-013771.
Audience: **u.**

Thomsett, Michael C. (Compiled by) **HG151.T48 1989**
Insurance Dictionary Illustrated. Library Binding. McFarland & Company, Incorporated Publishers. Jefferson, NC. 1989. 255p. ISBN:0-89950-391-8, ISBN13: 978-0-89950-391-2. Dewey:368/.003/21. LCCN:88-007947.
Audience: **l,u,f.** *Choice, 1989.*

Company and Industry Information > Industries and Markets (Selected) > Paper and Forest Products

Albert R. Mann Library, Cornell University Library **S441**
☐ The Core Historical Literature of Agriculture.
http://chla.mannlib.cornell.edu/
Cornell University Library.
Audience: **g,l,u,f.**

Chapman, Forestine **HD1751**
☐ Agricultural Statistics.
http://purl.access.gpo.gov/GPO/LPS1063
United States Agriculture Department.
Audience: **g,l,u,f.**

Fahl, Ronald J. **Z5991.F33**
North American Forest and Conservation History: A Bibliography. Trade Cloth. Forest History Society, Inc. Durham, NC. 1977. 408p. ISBN:0-87436-235-0, ISBN13: 978-0-87436-235-0. Dewey:016.3337/5/0973. LCCN:76-027306.
Audience: **g,l,u,f.** B

Food and Agriculture Organization (FAO) Staff **HD1421**
FAO Statistical Yearbook, Vol. 1. Trade Paper. Food and Agriculture Organization of the United Nations. Rome, 2005. 360p. ISBN:92-5-005151-4, ISBN13: 978-92-5-005151-2. Dewey:338.1.
Audience: **l,u,f.**

Marchak, M. Patricia **HD9750.5 .M293 1995**
Logging the Globe. Trade Cloth. McGill-Queen's University Press. Montreal, PQ. 1995. 440p. ISBN:0-7735-1345-0, ISBN13: 978-0-7735-1345-7. Dewey:333.7511. LCCN:96-154371.
Audience: **l,u.** *Choice, 1996.*

McDonald, Peter & Lassoie, James P. (Editors) **SD387.D6L58 1996**
The Literature of Forestry and Agroforestry. Book, Other. Cornell University Press. Ithaca, NY. 1996. 456p. The Literature of the Agricultural Sciences Ser. ISBN:0-8014-3181-6, ISBN13: 978-0-8014-3181-4. Dewey:634.9. LCCN:95-039328.
Audience: **l,u.** *Choice, 1996.*

National Agricultural Library **S494.5.I47**
☐ National Agricultural Library Portal.
http://www.nal.usda.gov/
United States Department of Agriculture.
Audience: **g,l,u,f.**

Pierce Colfer, Carol J. & Byron, Yvonne (Editors) **SD247.P46 2001**
People Managing Forests: The Links between Human Well-Being and Sustainability. Trade Cloth. Resources for the Future. Washington, DC. 2001. 464p. ISBN:1-891853-05-8, ISBN13: 978-1-891853-05-0. Dewey:333.75/16/0913. LCCN:2001-019059.
Audience: **l,u.** *Choice, 2002.*

Seitz, Wesley D., et al. **HD1415.S395 2002**
Economics of Resources, Agriculture and Food. Ed. 2. Gerald C. Nelson & Harold G. Halcrow (Authors). Cloth Text. McGraw-Hill Higher Education. Burr Ridge, IL. 2001. 544p. Agricultural Economics Ser. ISBN:0-07-025958-5, ISBN13: 978-0-07-025958-4. Dewey:338.1. LCCN:2001-031266.
Audience: **l,u.**

Sharpe, Grant William, et al. **SD373.I585 2002**
Introduction to Forest and Renewable Resources. Ed. 7. John C. Hendee, Wenonah Sharpe & Clare W. Handee (Authors). Paper Text. McGraw-Hill Higher Education. Burr Ridge, IL. 2002. 560p. McGraw-Hill Series in Forest Resources ISBN:0-07-366172-4, ISBN13: 978-0-07-366172-8. Dewey:634.9. LCCN:2002-067098.
Audience: **l,u.**

Steen, Harold K. **DS822.3.G88 2004**
The U. S. Forest Service: A History. Ed. 2. Trade Cloth. University of Washington Press. Seattle, WA. 2004. 432p. ISBN:0-295-98402-3, ISBN13: 978-0-295-98402-5. Dewey:915.204/31/0092. LCCN:2003-066592.
Audience: **l,u,f.**

United Nations Timber Committee **HD9765.A2**
☐ Timber Committee Forest Products Statistics.
http://www.unece.org/trade/timber/mis/fp-stats.htm
UNECE Trade and Timber Division.
Audience: **g,l,u,f.**

United States Department of Agriculture Foreign Agricultural Service **HD1769**
☐ Market and Trade Data: Statistical Market Information.
http://www.fas.usda.gov/data.asp
United States Department of Agriculture Foreign Agricultural Service.
Audience: **g,l,u,f.**

United States Department of Agriculture, Agricultural Marketing Service **HD1751.A9184**
☐ Agricultural Marketing Service @ USDA Portal.
http://www.ams.usda.gov/
United States Department of Agriculture, Agricultural Marketing Service.
Audience: **g,l,u,f.**

Company and Industry Information > Industries and Markets (Selected) > Retailing: General

Krafft, Manfred & Mantrala, Murali K. (Editors) **HF5429**
Retailing in the 21st Century: Current and Future Trends. Trade Cloth. Springer. New York, NY. 2005. XI, 413p. ISBN:3-540-28399-4, ISBN13: 978-3-540-28399-7. Dewey:658.8/7. LCCN:2005-932316.
Audience: **g,l,u,f.**

Company and Industry Information > Industries and Markets (Selected) > Retailing: Specialty

Birkeland, Peter M. **HF5429.235.U5B57**
Franchising Dreams: The Lure of Entrepreneurship in America. Trade Cloth. University of Chicago Press. Chicago, IL. 2002. 196p. ISBN:0-226-05190-0, ISBN13: 978-0-226-05190-1. Dewey:658.8/708. LCCN:2001-007061.
Audience: **g,l,u,f.**

Krafft, Manfred & Mantrala, Murali K. (Editors) **HF5429**
Retailing in the 21st Century: Current and Future Trends. Trade Cloth. Springer. New York, NY. 2005. XI, 413p. ISBN:3-540-28399-4, ISBN13: 978-3-540-28399-7. Dewey:658.8/7. LCCN:2005-932316.
Audience: **g,l,u,f.**

Spector, Robert **HF5430.S67 2005**
Category Killers: The Retail Revolution and Its Impact on Consumer Culture. Trade Cloth. Harvard Business School Press. Boston, MA. 2005. 256p. ISBN:1-57851-960-8, ISBN13: 978-1-57851-960-6. Dewey:658.8/7. LCCN:2004-012224.
Audience: **g,l,u,f.**

Company and Industry Information > Industries and Markets (Selected) > Restaurants

Cichy, Ronald F. & Hickey, Philip J. **TX911.3.M27R48 2005**
Managing Service in Food and Beverage Operations. Ed. 3. Trade Cloth. Educational Institute of the American Hotel & Motel Association. Lansing, MI. 2005. xvii, 621p. ISBN:0-86612-267-2, ISBN13: 978-0-86612-267-2. Dewey:647.95/068. LCCN:2005-049458.
Audience: **l,u.**

Curtis, Patricia A. **KF3875**
A Guide to Food Laws and Regulations. Trade Paper. Blackwell Publishing Professional. Ames, IA. 2005. 248p. ISBN:0-8138-1946-6, ISBN13: 978-0-8138-1946-4. Dewey:344.7304232.
Audience: **g,l,u,f.**

Hayes, David K. & Ninemeier, Jack D. **TX911.3.M27N566 2005**
Restaurant Operations Management: Principles and Practices. Cloth Text. Prentice Hall PTR. Upper Saddle River, NJ. 2005. 736p. ISBN:0-13-110090-4, ISBN13: 978-0-13-110090-9. Dewey:647.95/068. LCCN:2005-002365.
Audience: **l,u.**

Knight, John R. **TX905.K65 1987**
Knight's Foodservice Dictionary. Charles A. Salter (Editor). Cloth Text. John Wiley & Sons, Inc. Hoboken, NJ. 1987. 384p. Professional Bks. ISBN:0-442-24666-8, ISBN13: 978-0-442-24666-2. Dewey:642/.03/21. LCCN:84-027140.
Audience: **g,l,u,f.**

Millstone, Eric **HD9000.5.M52 2003**
Penguin Atlas of Food: Who Eats What Where and Why. Trade Paper. Penguin Group (USA) Inc. New York, NY. 2003. 128p. ISBN:0-14-200224-0, ISBN13: 978-0-14-200224-7. Dewey:664. LCCN:2003-266836.
Audience: **g,l,u.**

National Restaurant Association **TX943.N38**
Restaurant Industry Forecast. Ed. 2006. National Restaurant Association. 2005. ISBN:1-931400-59-8, ISBN13: 978-1-931400-59-6.
Audience: **g,l,u,f.**

Payne-Palacio, June & Theis, Monica **TX911.3.M27P39 2005**
Introduction to Foodservice. Ed. 10. Cloth Text. Prentice Hall PTR. Upper Saddle River, NJ. 2004. 720p. ISBN:0-13-048903-4, ISBN13: 978-0-13-048903-6. Dewey:647.95/068. LCCN:2004-013327.
Audience: **l,u.**

Rainsford, Peter & Bangs, David H. Jr. **TX911.3.M27R36 2001**
Restaurant Start-up Guide. Ed. 2. Trade Paper. Kaplan Publishing. Chicago, IL. 2000. 224p. ISBN:1-57410-137-4, ISBN13: 978-1-57410-137-9. Dewey:647.95068. LCCN:00-060232.
Audience: **g,l,u.**

Sweeney, Kep **TX911.3.M27S93 2004**
The New Restaurant Entrepreneur: An Inside Look at Restaurant Deal-Making and Other Tales from the Culinary Trenches. Trade Paper. Kaplan Publishing. Chicago, IL. 2004. 224p. ISBN:0-7931-8567-X, ISBN13: 978-0-7931-8567-2. Dewey:647.95/068. LCCN:2004-004599.
Audience: **l,u.**

Walker, John R. & Lundberg, Donald E. **TX911.3.M27W352 2005**
The Restaurant: From Concept to Operation. Ed. 4. Trade Cloth. John Wiley & Sons, Inc. Hoboken, NJ. 2004. 432p. ISBN:0-471-45028-6, ISBN13: 978-0-471-45028-3. Dewey:647.95/068. LCCN:2004-041193.
Audience: **l,u.**

Company and Industry Information > Industries and Markets (Selected) > Miscellaneous Service Industries

Birla, Madan **HE5903.F435B56 2005**
FedEx Delivers: How the World's Leading Shipping Company Keeps Innovating and Outperforming the Competition. Trade Cloth. John Wiley & Sons, Inc. Hoboken, NJ. 2005. 240p. ISBN:0-471-71579-4, ISBN13: 978-0-471-71579-5. Dewey:388/.044. LCCN:2004-028835.
Audience: **g,l,u,f.**

Friedman, Walter A. **HF5438.4.F75 2004**
Birth of a Salesman: The Transformation of Selling in America. Trade Cloth. Harvard University Press. Cambridge, MA. 2004. 368p. ISBN:0-674-01298-4, ISBN13: 978-0-674-01298-1. Dewey:381/.1/0973. LCCN:2003-065235.
Audience: **g,l,u,f.**

Company and Industry Information > Industries and Markets (Selected) > Telecommunications

Cortada, James W. **HC110.I55C67 2005**
The Digital Hand, Volume 2: How Computers Changed the Work of American Financial, Telecommunications, Media, and Entertainment Industries. Trade Cloth. Oxford University Press, Inc. New York, NY. 2005. 672p. ISBN:0-19-516587-X, ISBN13: 978-0-19-516587-6. Dewey:338/.064/0973. LCCN:2004-030363.
Audience: **g,l,u,f.**

Goldstein, Fred **HE7631**
The Great Telecom Meltdown. Trade Cloth. Artech House, Inc. Norwood, MA. 2005. 209p. Artech House Telecommunications Library ISBN:1-58053-939-4, ISBN13: 978-1-58053-939-5. Dewey:384.3. LCCN:2005-041036.
Audience: **g,l,u,f.**

Handley, John **HE7775.H33 2005**
Telebomb: The Truth Behind the $500-Billion Telecom Bust and What the Industry Must Do to Recover. Trade Cloth. Amacom. New York, NY. 2005. 256p. ISBN:0-8144-0833-8, ISBN13: 978-0-8144-0833-9. Dewey:384/.0973. LCCN:2005-005682.
Audience: **g,l,u,f.**

McMaster, Susan E. **HE8815**
The Telecommunications Industry. Cloth Text. Greenwood Publishing Group, Inc. Portsmouth, NH. 2002. 208p. Emerging Industries in the United States Ser. ISBN:0-313-31601-5, ISBN13: 978-0-313-31601-2. Dewey:384.6/0973. LCCN:2002-021628.
Audience: **g,l,u,f.** *Choice, 2003.*

Nuechterlein, Jonathan E. & Weiser, Philip J. **HE7781.N84 2005**
Digital Crossroads: American Telecommunications Policy in the Internet Age. Trade Cloth. MIT Press. Cambridge, MA. 2005. 672p. ISBN:0-262-14091-8, ISBN13: 978-0-262-14091-1. Dewey:384/.0973. LCCN:2004-061063.
Audience: **g,l,u,f.** *Choice, 2005.*

Sterling, Christopher H., et al. **HE7775.S76 2006**
Shaping American Telecommunications: A History of Technology, Policy, and Economics. Phyllis W. Bernt & Martin B. H. Weiss (Authors). Trade Paper. Lawrence Erlbaum Associates, Inc. Mahwah, NJ. 2005. 432p. LEA Telecommunications Ser. ISBN:0-8058-2237-2, ISBN13: 978-0-8058-2237-3. Dewey:384.0973. LCCN:2005-045616.
Audience: **g,l,u,f.** *Choice, 2006.*

Company and Industry Information > Industries and Markets (Selected) > Transportation, Commercial

Z7164
☐ Sources of Information in Transportation.
http://199.79.179.78/ref/biblio/
National Transportation Library.
Audience: **g,l,u,f.**

Darnay, Arsen J. (Editor) **HE203**
Transportation and Public Utilities USA. Trade Cloth. Thomson Gale. Farmington Hills, MI. 1997. 1000p. ISBN:0-7876-1665-6, ISBN13: 978-0-7876-1665-6. Dewey:388.097. LCCN:98-641092.
Audience: **l,u,f.** *Choice, 1998.*

Weiner, Edward **HE308**
Urban Transportation Planning in the United States: An Historical Overview. Trade Cloth. Greenwood Publishing Group, Inc. Portsmouth, NH. 1999. 272p. ISBN:0-275-96329-2, ISBN13: 978-0-275-96329-3. Dewey:388.4/0973. LCCN:98-038286.
Audience: **l,u,f.** *Choice, 1999, 1987.*

Company and Industry Information > Industries and Markets (Selected) > Real Estate

Ewald, William Bragg Jr. **HC102.5.C79**
Trammell Crow: A Legacy of Real Estate Business Innovation. Cloth over Boards. Urban Land Institute. Washington, DC. 2005. 300p. ISBN:0-87420-935-8, ISBN13: 978-0-87420-935-8. Dewey:333.33/092 B. LCCN:2005-922783.
Audience: **g,l,u,f.**

Friedman, Jack P., et al. **HD1375.H349 2005**
Real Estate Handbook. Ed. 6. Jack C. Harris & Barry A. Diskin (Authors). Trade Cloth. Barron's Educational Series, Inc. Hauppauge, NY. 2005. 768p. Barron's Educational Ser. ISBN:0-7641-5777-9, ISBN13: 978-0-7641-5777-6. Dewey:333.33. LCCN:2004-062680.
Audience: **g,l,u,f.**

Haight, G. Timothy & Singer, Daniel D. **HD1382.5.H33 2005**
The Real Estate Investment Handbook. Trade Cloth. John Wiley & Sons, Inc. Hoboken, NJ. 2005. 544p. Frank J. Fabozzi Ser. ISBN:0-471-64922-8, ISBN13: 978-0-471-64922-9. Dewey:332.6324. LCCN:2005-275406.
Audience: **g,l,u,f.**

Malpezzi, Stephen & Green, Richard (Editors) **HD7293.G687 2003**
A Primer on U. S. Housing Markets and Housing Policy. Trade Paper. Urban Institute Press. Washington, DC. 2002. ix, 226p. AREUEA Monograph Ser. ISBN:0-87766-702-0, ISBN13: 978-0-87766-702-5. Dewey:363.5/8/0973. LCCN:2003-017863.
Audience: **g,l,u,f.** *Choice, 2004.*

Poorvu, William J. & Cruikshank, Jeffrey L. **HD1375.P6643 1999**
The Real Estate Game: The Intelligent Guide to Successful Investing and Decision-Making. Trade Cloth. Simon & Schuster. New York, NY. 1999. 336p. ISBN:0-684-85550-X, ISBN13: 978-0-684-85550-9. Dewey:333.33. LCCN:99-032272.
Audience: **g,l,u,f.**

Urban Land Institute Staff **HC103.7**
America's Real Estate: Natural Resource, National Legacy. Trade Paper. Urban Land Institute. Washington, DC. 1997. 120p. ISBN:0-87420-796-7, ISBN13: 978-0-87420-796-5. Dewey:333.7/0973. LCCN:97-061514.
Audience: **g,l,u,f.**

Careers, Personal Skills Development, and Vocational Guidance

Albrecht, Karl **HM1106.A53 2006**
Social Intelligence: The New Science of Success. Trade Cloth. John Wiley & Sons, Inc. Hoboken, NJ. 2005. 304p. ISBN:0-7879-7938-4, ISBN13: 978-0-7879-7938-6. Dewey:302.1/2. LCCN:2005-025923.
Audience: **g,l,u,f.**

Bolles, Richard Nelson **HF382.7**
What Color Is Your Parachute? 2006. Trade Cloth. Ten Speed Press. Berkeley, CA. 2005. 424p. ISBN:1-58008-728-0, ISBN13: 978-1-58008-728-5. Dewey:650.140.
Audience: **g,l,u.**

Brinkerhoff, Derick W. & Brinkerhoff, Jennifer M. **HF5381.B6528 2005**
Working for Change: Making a Career in International Public Service. Trade Paper. Kumarian Press, Inc. Bloomfield, CT. 2005. 240p. ISBN:1-56549-203-X, ISBN13: 978-1-56549-203-5. Dewey:361.2/6/0231724. LCCN:2005-001044.
Audience: **l,u.**

Burnett, Rebecca **QA10.5.B87 2002**
Careers for Number Crunchers and Other Quantitative Types. Ed. 2. Trade Cloth. McGraw-Hill Companies, The. New York, NY. 2002. 192p. Careers for You Ser. ISBN:0-07-138725-0, ISBN13: 978-0-07-138725-5. Dewey:510/.23. LCCN:2002-019975.
Audience: **l,u.**

Decker, Diane C., et al. **HD6273.D43 2006**
First-Job Survival Guide: How to Thrive and Advance in Your New Career. Victoria A. Hoevemeyer & Marianne Rowe-Dimas (Authors). Trade Paper, Perfect. JIST Publishing. Indianapolis, IN. 2005. 214p. ISBN:1-59357-253-0, ISBN13: 978-1-59357-253-2. Dewey:650.1. LCCN:2005-024684.
Audience: **l,u.**

Evans, Gail **HD6053**
Play Like a Man, Win Like a Woman: What Men Know about Success That Women Need to Learn. Trade Paper. Broadway Books. New York, NY. 2001. 208p. ISBN:0-7679-0463-X, ISBN13: 978-0-7679-0463-6. Dewey:650.1/082.
Audience: **g,l,u.**

Farr, Michael **HF5381.F4563 2006**
200 Best Jobs for College Graduates. Ed. 3. Laurence Shatkin (Contribution by). Trade Cloth. JIST Publishing. Indianapolis, IN. 2005. 464p. JIST'S Best Jobs Ser. ISBN:1-59357-241-7, ISBN13: 978-1-59357-241-9. Dewey:331.7/0235. LCCN:2005-012155.
Audience: **l,u.**

Fogg, Neeta P., et al. **HF5382.5.U5F644 2004**
College Majors Handbook with Real Career Paths and Payoffs: The Actual Jobs, Earnings, and Trends for Graduates of 60 College Majors. Ed. 2. Paul E. Harrington & Thomas F. Harrington (Authors). Trade Cloth. JIST Publishing. Indianapolis, IN. 2004. 656p. ISBN:1-59357-074-0, ISBN13: 978-1-59357-074-3. Dewey:331.702/0973. LCCN:2004-007907.
Audience: **l,u.** *Choice, 2005.*

Frankel, Lois P. **HQ1206.F68 2004**
Nice Girls Don't Get the Corner Office: 101 Unconscious Mistakes Women Make That Sabotage Their Careers. Trade Cloth. Warner Books, Inc. New York, NY. 2004. 288p. ISBN:0-446-53132-4, ISBN13: 978-0-446-53132-0. Dewey:158.1/082. LCCN:2003-045084.
Audience: **g,l,u.**

Ghilani, Mary E. **HF5382.7.G49 2005**
Web-Based Career Counseling: A Guide to Internet Resources for Researching a Career and Choosing A Major. Trade Paper, Perfect. University of Scranton Press. Scranton, PA. 2005. 194p. ISBN:1-58966-110-9, ISBN13: 978-1-58966-110-3. Dewey:025.06/331705. LCCN:2005-042229.
Audience: **g,l,u,f.**

Hansen, Randall et al. **HF338.5**
Quintessential Careers: a Career and Job-Hunting Resources Guide.
http://www.quintcareers.com/
Quintessential Careers.
Audience: **g,l,u.**

Harvard Business School Staff (Contribution by) **HD69.C6**
The Harvard Business School Guide to Careers in Management Consulting. Trade Paper. Harvard Business School Press. Boston, MA. 2001. 240p. ISBN:1-57851-581-5, ISBN13: 978-1-57851-581-3. Dewey:658.4/6/023. LCCN:2004-014894.
Audience: **l,u.**

Hayes, Cassandra **HD62.5.H384 2002**
Black Enterprise Guide to Building Your Career. Trade Paper. John Wiley & Sons, Inc. Hoboken, NJ. 2002. 272p. Black Enterprise Books ISBN:0-471-41710-6, ISBN13: 978-0-471-41710-1. Dewey:650.14/089/96073. LCCN:2001-045646.
Audience: **l,u.**

Kao, Patricia & Tien, Susan **HF5382.6.K36 2003**
Vault Guide to Corporate America for Women and Minorities. Trade Paper. Vault.com. New York, NY. 2003. 176p. Vault Career Library ISBN:1-58131-178-8, ISBN13: 978-1-58131-178-5. Dewey:650.1/082. LCCN:2003-007449.
Audience: **g,l,u.**

Kushell, Jennifer **HD62.5.K875 1999**
The Young Entrepreneur's Edge: Using Your Ambition, Independence, and Youth to Launch a Successful Business. Steve Mariotti (Foreword by). Trade Paper. Random House Information Group. New York, NY. 1999. 272p. ISBN:0-375-75349-4, ISBN13: 978-0-375-75349-7. Dewey:658.1/141. LCCN:99-011523.
Audience: **l,u.**

Levit, Alexandra **HF5381.L48 2004**
They Don't Teach Corporate in College: A Twenty-Something's Guide to the Business World. Trade Paper. Career Press, Inc. Franklin Lks, NJ. 2004. 256p. ISBN:1-56414-765-7, ISBN13: 978-1-56414-765-3. Dewey:650.1/084/2. LCCN:2004-051967.
Audience: **l,u.**

Liu, Ying (Editor) **HG173.8**
The Harvard Business School Guide to Careers in Finance. Harvard Business School Staff (Contribution by). Trade Paper. Harvard Business School Press. Boston, MA. 2001. 144p. ISBN:1-57851-580-7, ISBN13: 978-1-57851-580-6. Dewey:332/.023.
Audience: **l,u.**

Novak, Michael **HD4905.N65 1996**
Business as a Calling: Work and the Examined Life. Trade Cloth. Simon & Schuster. New York, NY. 1996. 256p. ISBN:0-684-82748-4, ISBN13: 978-0-684-82748-3. Dewey:306.36. LCCN:96-000482.
Audience: **g,l,u,f.**

Phifer, Paul **HF5382.5.U5P445 2002**
College Majors and Careers: A Resource Guide for Effective Life Planning. Ed. 5. Paper Text. Facts On File, Inc. New York, NY. 2003. 288p. ISBN:0-89434-378-5, ISBN13: 978-0-89434-378-0. Dewey:331.7/02/0973. LCCN:2002-152068.
Audience: **l,u.**

Rabe, Monica **HF5382.55.R33 1997**
Culture Shock! Living and Working Abroad: A Practical Guide. Trade Paper. Graphic Arts Center Publishing Company. Portland, OR. 1997. 250p. Culture Shock! Practical Guides ISBN:1-55868-304-6, ISBN13: 978-1-55868-304-4. Dewey:303.48/2. LCCN:96-077214.
Audience: **l,u.**

Snyder, Kirk **HD6285.S693 2003**
Lavender Road to Success: The Career Guide for the Gay Community. Trade Paper. Ten Speed Press. Berkeley, CA. 2004. 208p. ISBN:1-58008-496-6, ISBN13: 978-1-58008-496-3. Dewey:650.1/086/6. LCCN:2003-011973.
Audience: **g,l,u,f.**

Stevenson, Ollie & Huebler, Dana **HF5381.S775 1997**
The Colorblind Career: What Every African-American, Hispanic-American and Asian-American Needs to Succeed in Today's Tough Job Market. Karen Hansen (Editor). Trade Paper. Peterson's. Lawrenceville, NJ. 1997. 320p. ISBN:1-56079-700-2, ISBN13: 978-1-56079-700-5. Dewey:650.14/089. LCCN:97-010992.
Audience: **g,l,u,f.**

U.S. Department of Labor Staff **HF538.5**
Occupational Outlook Handbook.
http://www.bls.gov/oco/
Bureau of Labor Statistics, U.S. Department of Labor.
Audience: **g,l,u.**

Watkins, Marie & Braun, Linda **LC220.5**
Service-Learning: From Classroom to Community to Career. Trade Paper. JIST Publishing. Indianapolis, IN. 2005. 192p. ISBN:1-55864-150-5, ISBN13: 978-1-55864-150-1. Dewey:361.3. LCCN:2006-277446.
Audience: **l,u.**

Welsh, Kate Shoup **HF5381**
What Can You Do with a Major in Business?: Real People. Real Jobs. Real Rewards. Jennifer A. Horowitz (Contribution by). Trade Paper. John Wiley & Sons, Inc. Hoboken, NJ. 2005. 144p. What Can You Do with a Major In... Ser. ISBN:0-7645-7608-9, ISBN13: 978-0-7645-7608-9. Dewey:331.70235. LCCN:2005-276360.
Audience: **l,u.**

Wertsman, Vladimir F. **HF5382.5.U5**
Career Opportunities for Bilinguals and Multilinguals: A Directory of Resources in Education, Employment, and Business. Ed. 2. Trade Paper. Scarecrow Press, Inc. Lanham, MD. 2002. 353p. ISBN:0-8108-4460-5, ISBN13: 978-0-8108-4460-5. Dewey:410. LCCN:93-034130.
Audience: **l,u.**

Winfeld, Liz & Spielman, Susan **HD6285.W56 2001**
Straight Talk about Gays in the Workplace. Ed. 2. Trade Cloth. Haworth Press, Incorporated, The. Binghamton, NY. 2005. 185p. Gay and Lesbian Studies ISBN:1-56023-171-8, ISBN13: 978-1-56023-171-4. Dewey:658.3/0086/64. LCCN:00-039712.
Audience: **g,l,u,f.** *Choice, 2001.*

Yena, Donna J. **HF5381.Y46 2007**
Career Directions. Ed. 4. Paper Text. McGraw-Hill Companies, The. New York, NY. 2005. 432p. ISBN:0-07-312314-5, ISBN13: 978-0-07-312314-1. Dewey:650.1. LCCN:2005-044387.
Audience: **g,l,u,f.**

Careers, Personal Skills Development, and Vocational Guidance > Job-seeking

HF5382.5.U5 D86
The Career Guide: The Employment Opportunities Directory. Dun & Bradstreet Information Services. 2006. ISBN:1-59274-215-7, ISBN13: 978-1-59274-215-8.
Audience: **g,l,u.**

Adams **HF5382.5.U5**
The National Job Bank 2005. Trade Paper. Adams Media Corporation. Avon, MA. 2004. 1152p. ISBN:1-59337-104-7, ISBN13: 978-1-59337-104-3. Dewey:331.7020973.
Audience: **g,l,u.**

Adams, Bob & Morin, Laura **HF5382.7.A33 1999**
The Complete Resume and Job Search Book for College Students: The A-Z Career Guide for College Students. Ed. 2. Trade Paper. Adams Media Corporation. Avon, MA. 2000. 240p. ISBN:1-58062-136-8, ISBN13: 978-1-58062-136-6. Dewey:650.14. LCCN:98-033179.
Audience: **l,u.**

Anthony, Rebecca J. & Roe, Gerald **LB2331.72 .A58 1998**
The Curriculum Vitae Handbook: How to Present and Promote Your Academic Career. Ed. 2. Trade Paper. Rudi Publishing. San Francisco, CA. 1998. 176p. ISBN:0-945213-26-3, ISBN13: 978-0-945213-26-0. Dewey:378.1/2/02373. LCCN:98-007277.
Audience: **f.**

Block, Jay A. **HF5383.B5342 2003**
101 Best Resumes for Grads. Trade Paper. McGraw-Hill Companies, The. New York, NY. 2002. 233p. ISBN:0-07-139506-7, ISBN13: 978-0-07-139506-9. Dewey:650.14/2. LCCN:2003-268330.
Audience: **l,u.**

Bolles, Mark Emery & Bolles, Richard Nelson **HF5382.7**
Job Hunting on the Internet. Ed. 4. Trade Paper. Ten Speed Press. Berkeley, CA. 2005. 224p. ISBN:1-58008-652-7, ISBN13: 978-1-58008-652-3. Dewey:025.06/65014. LCCN:2005-003418.
Audience: **l,u.**

Bolles, Richard Nelson & Brown, Dale S. **HV1568.5.B65 2001**
Job-Hunting for the So-Called Handicapped: Or People Who Have Disabilities. Ed. 2. Trade Paper. Ten Speed Press. Berkeley, CA. 2004. 160p. ISBN:1-58008-195-9, ISBN13: 978-1-58008-195-5. Dewey:650.14087. LCCN:2001-002799.
Audience: **g,l,u,f.**

Camenson, Blythe **HF5382.5.U5C25196**
Great Jobs for Economics Majors. Trade Paper. McGraw-Hill Companies, The. New York, NY. 2000. 192p. Great Jobs for ... Majors Ser. ISBN:0-658-00222-8, ISBN13: 978-0-658-00222-9. Dewey:330.023/73. LCCN:99-044167.
Audience: **l,u.**

Catto, Susan & Penrith, Deborah **E41**
Live and Work in the U. S. A. and Canada. Ed. 4. Trade Paper. Vacation Work Publications. Oxford, 2005. 436p. Live and Work - Vacation Work Publications ISBN:1-85458-336-0, ISBN13: 978-1-85458-336-9. Dewey:917.0454.
Audience: **g,l,u,f.**

Cosentino, Marc **HD69.C6**
Case in Point: Complete Case Interview Preparation. Burgee Press. 2005. ISBN:0-9710158-2-1, ISBN13: 978-0-9710158-2-1.
Audience: **g,u.**

Crack, Timothy Falcon **HF5549.5.I6**
Heard on the Street: Quantitative Questions from Wall Street Job Interviews. Ed. 9. Perfect. Timothy Crack. Bloomington, IN. 2004. 284p. ISBN:0-9700552-3-4, ISBN13: 978-0-9700552-3-1. Dewey:650.14.
Audience: **g,l,u.**

Cunningham, John R. **HF5382.7.C86 2005**
Get A Job! Interview Survival Skills for College Students. Ed. 3. Paper Text. McGraw-Hill Primis Custom Publishing. Hightstown, NJ. 2005. 212p. ISBN:0-07-353631-8, ISBN13: 978-0-07-353631-6. Dewey:650.14.
Audience: **l,u.**

Darga, Amy (Editor)
Professional Careers Sourcebook. Ed. 7. Trade Cloth. Thomson Gale. Farmington Hills, MI. 2002. 1,000p. ISBN:0-7876-5460-4, ISBN13: 978-0-7876-5460-3. Dewey:331.7102573.
Audience: **g,l,u,f.**

Dikel, Margaret Riley & Roehm, Frances E. **HF5382.7.D54 2006**
Guide to Internet Job Searching 2006-2007. Trade Paper. McGraw-Hill Companies, The. New York, NY. 2006. 288p. ISBN:0-07-147216-9, ISBN13: 978-0-07-147216-6. Dewey:025.06/65014. LCCN:2006-041973.
Audience: **g,l,u,f.**

Dorsey, Jason **HF5382.75.U6D67 1997**
Graduate to Your Perfect Job in 6 Easy Steps. Dee A. Campbell (Editor), Mike Crixell (Contribution by), Brad Armstrong (Introduction by). Trade Paper. Golden Ladder Productions. Austin, TX. 1997. 140p. Golden Ladder Ser., Vol. 1 ISBN:0-9657725-1-9, ISBN13: 978-0-9657725-1-8. Dewey:650.14. LCCN:97-093471.
Audience: **l,u.**

Eggert, Max **HF5549.5.I6**
Perfect Answers to Interview Questions: The Must-Have Guide to Getting That Job!. UK-B Format Paperback. Random House Business Books. London, 2005. 96p. ISBN:1-84413-460-1, ISBN13: 978-1-84413-460-1. Dewey:650.1/4.
Audience: **l,u.**

Farr, Michael **HF5549.5.I6F368 2005**
Next-Day Job Interview: Prepare Tonight and Get the Job Tomorrow. Trade Cloth. JIST Publishing. Indianapolis, IN. 2005. 192p. JIST's Help in a Hurry Ser. ISBN:1-59357-131-3, ISBN13: 978-1-59357-131-3. Dewey:650.14/4. LCCN:2004-030334.
Audience: **g,l,u.**

Farr, Michael J. (Based on a book by) **HF5382.75.U6F37 2004**
The Very Quick Job Search. Ed. 3. Trade Paper. JIST Publishing. Indianapolis, IN. 2003. 544p. ISBN:1-59357-007-4, ISBN13: 978-1-59357-007-1. Dewey:650.14. LCCN:2003-021423.
Audience: **g,l,u.**

Farr, Michael & Kursmark, Louise **HF5383.F315 2005**
15-Minute Cover Letter: Write an Effective Cover Letter Right Now. Trade Cloth. JIST Publishing. Indianapolis, IN. 2005. 192p. ISBN:1-59357-175-5, ISBN13: 978-1-59357-175-7. Dewey:650.14/2. LCCN:2005-005196.
Audience: **g,l,u.**

Finnigan, Dan, et al. **HD6277.F56 2006**
From Learning to Earning: Yahoo! HotJobs Success Strategies for New Grads. Christopher Jones & Marc Karasu (Authors). Trade Paper. Sterling Publishing Co., Inc. New York, NY. 2005. 192p. HotJobs Career Advisors Ser. ISBN:1-4027-2825-5, ISBN13: 978-1-4027-2825-9. Dewey:650.14. LCCN:2005-027115.
Audience: **l,u.**

Fitzwater, Terry **HF5549.5.I6F58 2001**
Preparing for the Behavior-Based Interview: Getting the Job You Want. Brenda Pittsley, Charlotte Bosarge & Debbie Woodbury (Editors), Ralph Mapson (Illustrator), Zach Hooker (Designed by). Trade Paper. Crisp Publications, Inc. Menlo Park, CA. 2001. 96p. Crisp Fifty-Minute Book Ser. ISBN:1-56052-643-2, ISBN13: 978-1-56052-643-8. Dewey:650.14. LCCN:2001-090684.
Audience: **g,l,u.**

Fry, Ron **HF5383.F89 2001**
Your First Resume: For Students and Anyone Preparing to Enter Today's Tough Job Market. Ed. 5. Trade Paper. Thomson Delmar Learning. Albany, NY. 2001. 188p. ISBN:1-56414-583-2, ISBN13: 978-1-56414-583-3. Dewey:650.14. LCCN:2001-035875.
Audience: **l,u.**

Goldberg, Jan **HF5616.U5G643 2005**
Great Jobs for Accounting Majors. Ed. 2. Trade Paper. McGraw-Hill Companies, The. New York, NY. 2005. 192p. ISBN:0-07-143854-8, ISBN13: 978-0-07-143854-4. Dewey:657/.023/73. LCCN:2004-059737.
Audience: **l,u.**

Green, Marianne E. **LC1072.I58**
Internship Success: Real-World, Step-by-Step Advice on Getting the Most Out of Internships. Trade Paper. McGraw-Hill Companies, The. New York, NY. 1998. 192p. ISBN:0-8442-4496-1, ISBN13: 978-0-8442-4496-9. Dewey:331.25/922. LCCN:97-022902.
Audience: **l,u.**

Griffith, Susan **HD6271**
Work Your Way Around the World. Ed. 12. Trade Paper. Vacation Work Publications. Oxford, 2005. 576p. ISBN:1-85458-329-8, ISBN13: 978-1-85458-329-1. Dewey:331.125. LCCN:2005-440594.
Audience: **l,u.**

Hansen, Katharine **HF5383.H278 1998**
Dynamic Cover Letters for New Graduates. Trade Cloth. Ten Speed Press. Berkeley, CA. 2004. 192p. ISBN:0-89815-984-9, ISBN13: 978-0-89815-984-4. Dewey:808/.06665. LCCN:97-051729.
Audience: **l,u.**

Hansen, Katherine **HF5382.7.H354 2000**
A Foot in the Door: Networking Your Way into the Hidden Job Market. Trade Paper. Ten Speed Press. Berkeley, CA. 2004. 192p. ISBN:1-58008-140-1, ISBN13: 978-1-58008-140-5. Dewey:650.14. LCCN:00-710221.
Audience: **g,l,u.**

Hansen, Randall et al. **HF338.5**
☐ Quintessential Careers: a Career and Job-Hunting Resources Guide.
http://www.quintcareers.com/
Quintessential Careers.
Audience: **g,l,u.**

Heiberger, Mary Morris & Vick, Julia Miller **LB2331.72.H45 2001**
The Academic Job Search Handbook. Ed. 3. Book, Other. University of Pennsylvania Press. Philadelphia, PA. 2001. 240p. ISBN:0-8122-1778-0, ISBN13: 978-0-8122-1778-0. Dewey:650.14/088/372. LCCN:2001-027489.
Audience: **u,f.**

Johnson, Jeffrey S. & VGM Career Books Staff **HF5383.V46 2000**
Resumes for Business Management Careers. Ed. 2. Trade Paper. McGraw-Hill Companies, The. New York, NY. 2000. 160p. VGM Professional Resumes Ser. ISBN:0-658-00455-7, ISBN13: 978-0-658-00455-1. Dewey:808/.06665. LCCN:00-038188.
Audience: **g,l,u.**

Kronenfeld, Jennie J. & Whicker, Marcia L. **LB2332.72.K76 1997**
Getting an Academic Job: Strategies for Success, Vol. 17. Trade Paper. SAGE Publications, Inc. Thousand Oaks, CA. 1996. 119p. Survival Skills for Scholars Ser., Vol. 17 ISBN:0-8039-7015-3, ISBN13: 978-0-8039-7015-1. Dewey:378/.0023. LCCN:96-035683.
Audience: **u,f.**

Krueger, Brian D. **HF5382.7.K78 2003**
College Grad Job Hunter. Ed. 5. Trade Paper. Adams Media Corporation. Avon, MA. 2003. 352p. ISBN:1-58062-907-5, ISBN13: 978-1-58062-907-2. Dewey:650.14. LCCN:2004-556469.
Audience: **l,u.**

Kursmark, Louise M. **HF5383.K867 2005**
Best Resumes for College Students and New Grads. Ed. 2. Trade Paper, Perfect. JIST Publishing. Indianapolis, IN. 2005. 234p. ISBN:1-59357-238-7, ISBN13: 978-1-59357-238-9. Dewey:650.142. LCCN:2005-021335.
Audience: **l,u.**

Lambert, Stephen E. **HF5382.7.L347 2003**
Great Jobs for Business Majors. Ed. 2. Trade Paper. McGraw-Hill Companies, The. New York, NY. 2003. 240p. Great Jobs for Ser. ISBN:0-07-140581-X, ISBN13: 978-0-07-140581-2. Dewey:650.14. LCCN:2002-033300.
Audience: **l,u.**

Lauber, Daniel **JK692.L39 1997**
Government Job Finder. Ed. 3. Trade Paper. Planning/Communications. River Forest, IL. 1997. 336p. ISBN:1-884587-05-4, ISBN13: 978-1-884587-05-4. Dewey:353.001/03. LCCN:96-092662.
Audience: **g,l,u.**

Lauber, Daniel & Atkin, Jennifer **HF5382.75.U6 L328**
Nonprofits Job Finder: Where the Jobs Are in Charities and Nonprofits. Ed. 5. Trade Cloth. Planning/Communications. River Forest, IL. 2004. 240p. ISBN:1-884587-26-7, ISBN13: 978-1-884587-26-9. Dewey:331.12/8/0973.
Audience: **g,l,u.**

Lauber, Daniel & Rice, Kraig **HF5549.5.E45**
International Job Finder: Where the Jobs Are Worldwide. Trade Cloth. Planning/Communications. River Forest, IL. 2002. 320p. ISBN:1-884587-10-0, ISBN13: 978-1-884587-10-8. Dewey:650.14. LCCN:98-065911.
Audience: **g,l,u.**

Lurie, Rosanne **HF5383.K4812 2003**
Killer Cover Letters and Resumes! The WetFeet Insider Guide 2004. WetFeet.com (Firm) Staff (Contribution by). Trade Paper. WetFeet, Inc. San Francisco, CA. 2005. 106p. WetFeet Insider Guide Ser. ISBN:1-58207-371-6, ISBN13: 978-1-58207-371-2. Dewey:650.14/2. LCCN:2004-298623.
Audience: **g,l,u.**

Medley, H. Anthony **HF5549.5.I6M35 2005**
Sweaty Palms: The Neglected Art of Being Interviewed. Trade Paper, Perfect. Warner Books, Inc. New York, NY. 2005. 464p. ISBN:0-446-69383-9, ISBN13: 978-0-446-69383-7. Dewey:650.14/4. LCCN:2004-027774.
Audience: **g,l,u.**

Noble, David F. **HF5383.N62 2004**
Gallery of Best Resumes. Ed. 3. Trade Cloth. JIST Publishing. Indianapolis, IN. 2004. 432p. ISBN:1-56370-985-6, ISBN13: 978-1-56370-985-2. Dewey:650.14/2. LCCN:2003-026436.
Audience: **g,l,u.**

Penrith, Deborah (Editor) **HF5382.55**
The Directory of Jobs and Careers Abroad. Ed. 12. Paper Text. Vacation Work Publications. Oxford, 2005. 446p. ISBN:1-85458-317-4, ISBN13: 978-1-85458-317-8. Dewey:331.702.
Audience: **l,u.**

Peterson's **HD6271.2.U5**
Peterson's Internships. Ed. 25. Trade Paper, Perfect. Peterson's. Lawrenceville, NJ. 2004. 764p. ISBN:0-7689-1498-1, ISBN13: 978-0-7689-1498-6. Dewey:331.25922. LCCN:2002-258003.
Audience: **l,u.**

Pigford, Lois **HF5381.P534 2001**
The Successful Interview and Beyond. Paper Text. Thomson Delmar Learning. Albany, NY. 2000. 256p. ISBN:0-7668-2235-4, ISBN13: 978-0-7668-2235-1. Dewey:650.14. LCCN:00-060279.
Audience: **g,l,u.**

Plunkett, Jack W. **HC4057**
The Almanac of American Employers 2006: The Only Complete Guide to America's Hottest, Fastest-Growing Corporate Employers. Trade Paper, CD-ROM. Plunkett Research, Ltd. Houston, TX. 2005. 748p. ISBN:1-59392-045-8, ISBN13: 978-1-59392-045-6. Dewey:331.702.
Audience: **g,l,u.**

Princeton Review Publishing Staff **LC1072.I58I46**
The Internship Bible. Ed. 10. Trade Paper. Random House

Information Group. New York, NY. 2005. 656p. ISBN:0-375-76468-2, ISBN13: 978-0-375-76468-4. Dewey:378 12. LCCN:93-013818.
Audience: **l,u.**

Princeton Review Publishing Staff **HF5382.7.O463 2002**
Job Surfing: Working Abroad. Trade Paper. Random House Information Group. New York, NY. 2002. 352p. Job Surfing Ser. ISBN:0-375-76238-8, ISBN13: 978-0-375-76238-3. Dewey:650.140285. LCCN:2002-510584.
Audience: **l,u.**

Princeton Review Staff **DT20.P76**
Best Entry-Level Jobs, 2005-2006. Trade Paper. Random House Information Group. New York, NY. 2005. 320p. ISBN:0-375-76472-0, ISBN13: 978-0-375-76472-1. Dewey:960.
Audience: **l,u.**

Reuvid, Jonathan **HF5382.55**
Working Abroad: The Complete Guide to Overseas Employment. Ed. 26. Trade Paper. Kogan Page, Ltd. London, 2005. 496p. ISBN:0-7494-4427-4, ISBN13: 978-0-7494-4427-3. Dewey:331.702.
Audience: **l,u.**

Templeton, Mary E. **HF5381 .T26 1997**
Help! My Job Interview Is Tomorrow!: How to Use the Library to Research an Employer. Ed. 2. Trade Cloth. Neal-Schuman Publishers, Inc. New York, NY. 1997. 125p. ISBN:1-55570-271-6, ISBN13: 978-1-55570-271-7. Dewey:650.14. LCCN:96-053655.
Audience: **g,l,u.**

VGM Career Books Staff (Editor) **HF5383.R434 2004**
Resumes for College Students and Recent Graduates. Ed. 3. Trade Paper. McGraw-Hill Companies, The. New York, NY. 2004. 153p. VGM Professional Resumes Ser. ISBN:0-07-143737-1, ISBN13: 978-0-07-143737-0. Dewey:650.14/2. LCCN:2004-040263.
Audience: **l,u.**

Wallace, Richard (Editor) **HF5383.A26 2006**
Adams Cover Letter Almanac. Ed. 2. Trade Paper. Adams Media Corporation. Avon, MA. 2006. 736p. ISBN:1-59337-600-6, ISBN13: 978-1-59337-600-0. Dewey:650.14/2. LCCN:2005-034593.
Audience: **l,u.**

WetFeet.com (Firm) Staff **HF5382.75**
Ace Your Case!: The WetFeet Insider Guide to Consulting Interviews. Ed. 2. Trade Paper. WetFeet, Inc. San Francisco, CA. 2005. 118p. ISBN:1-58207-247-7, ISBN13: 978-1-58207-247-0. Dewey:658.4/6/023.
Audience: **u.**

Woodworth, David **HD6271**
Summer Jobs Abroad 2006. Cloth Text. Vacation Work Publications. Oxford, 2006. 320p. ISBN:1-85458-343-3, ISBN13: 978-1-85458-343-7. Dewey:331.124025.
Audience: **l,u.**

Woodworth, David & Hobbs, Guy (Editors) **HD6271.2.G7J36 2004**
Summer Jobs in Britain 2005. Trade Paper. Vacation Work Publications. Oxford, 2005. 320p. ISBN:1-85458-326-3, ISBN13: 978-1-85458-326-0. Dewey:331.1/24/02541.
Audience: **l,u.**

Yate, Martin **HF5549.5.I6.Y37 2005**
Knock 'Em Dead: The Ultimate Job Seeker's Guide. Ed. 20. Trade Paper, Perfect. Adams Media Corporation. Avon, MA. 2005. 352p. ISBN:1-59337-452-6, ISBN13: 978-1-59337-452-5. Dewey:650.14.
Audience: **g,l,u.**

Careers, Personal Skills Development, and Vocational Guidance > Business Writing and Communications

Alred, Gerald J., et al. **HF5726**
The Business Writer's Handbook. Ed. 8. Walter E. Oliu & Charles T. Brusaw (Authors). Trade Cloth. St. Martin's Press. Gordonville, VA. 2006. 688p. ISBN:0-312-35268-9, ISBN13: 978-0-312-35268-4. Dewey:651.7/03.
Audience: **g,l,u.**

Andrews, Deborah C. & Andrews, William D. **HD30.3.A4593 2004**
Management Communication. Paper Text. Houghton Mifflin College Division. Boston, MA. 2003. 224p. ISBN:0-618-21415-1, ISBN13: 978-0-618-21415-0. Dewey:658.4/5. LCCN:2002-109349.
Audience: **l,u.**

Atkinson, Cliff **HF5718.22.A87 2005**
Beyond Bullet Points: Using Microsoft PowerPoint to Create Presentations That Inform, Motivate, and Inspire. Trade Paper. Microsoft Press. Redmond, WA. 2005. 240p. ISBN:0-7356-2052-0, ISBN13: 978-0-7356-2052-0. Dewey:658.45202856686.
Audience: **g,l,u.**

Bailey, Edward P. Jr. **HF5718.3.B35 1997**
The Plain English Approach to Business Writing. Trade Paper. Oxford University Press, Inc. New York, NY. 1997. 142p. ISBN:0-19-511565-1, ISBN13: 978-0-19-511565-9. Dewey:808/.06665. LCCN:96-045541.
Audience: **g,l,u.**

Basye, Anne **HF5726.B29 1998**
Business Letters Ready to Go!. Diskette, Trade Paper. McGraw-Hill Companies, The. New York, NY. 1998. 192p. Ready to Go! Ser. ISBN:0-8442-3571-7, ISBN13: 978-0-8442-3571-4. Dewey:651.7/5. LCCN:98-009247.
Audience: **g,l,u.**

Bates, Suzanne **HD50.3.B38 2005**
Speak Like a CEO: Secrets for Commanding Attention and Getting Results. Trade Cloth. McGraw-Hill Companies, The. New York, NY. 2005. 240p. ISBN:0-07-145151-X, ISBN13: 978-0-07-145151-2. Dewey:658.4/52. LCCN:2004-026461.
Audience: **l,u.**

Blicq, Ron S. & Moretto, Lisa A. **HF5719.B55 2001**
Writing Reports to Get Results: Quick, Effective, Results Using the Pyramid Method. Ed. 3. Trade Cloth. John Wiley & Sons, Inc. Hoboken, NJ. 2001. 248p. ISBN:0-471-14342-1, ISBN13: 978-0-471-14342-0. Dewey:808/.066651. LCCN:2001-277146.
Audience: **l,u.**

Bly, Robert W. **HF5721.B59 1999**
The Encyclopedia of Business Letters, Fax Memos, and E-Mail. Trade Paper. Career Press, Inc. Franklin Lks, NJ. 1999. 288p. ISBN:1-56414-375-9, ISBN13: 978-1-56414-375-4. Dewey:651.75. LCCN:98-045170.
Audience: **g,l,u.**

Boone, Mary E. **HD30.3.B667 2001**
Managing Interactively: Executing Business Strategy, Improving Communication, and Creating a Knowledge-Sharing Culture. Cloth Text. McGraw-Hill Companies, The. New York, NY. 2000. 322p. ISBN:0-07-135866-8, ISBN13: 978-0-07-135866-8. Dewey:658.4/5. LCCN:2001-274222.
Audience: **l,u.**

Business Department, Carnegie Library of Pittsburgh Staff **HD62.7**
□ Business Plans and Profiles Index: A Subject Guide to Sample Business Plans and Profiles for Specific Business Types. http://www.carnegielibrary.org/subject/business/bplansindex.html
Audience: **g,l,u.**

Carlson, Tony **PN4193.B8C37 2005**
The How of WOW: A Guide to Giving a Speech That Will Positively Blow 'Em Away. Trade Paper. Amacom. New York, NY. 2005. 288p. ISBN:0-8144-7251-6, ISBN13: 978-0-8144-7251-4. Dewey:808.5/1. LCCN:2004-022112.
Audience: **l,u.**

Cleland, Jane K. **HF5726.C56 2003**
Business Writing for Results: How to Create a Sense of Urgency and Increase Response to Your E-Mails, Letters, Proposals, Reports, Newsletters and Websites. Trade Paper. McGraw-Hill Companies, The. New York, NY. 2003. 240p. ISBN:0-07-140570-4, ISBN13: 978-0-07-140570-6. Dewey:651.7/4. LCCN:2002-026329.
Audience: **l,u.**

Cohen, Allan R. & Bradford, David L. **HD58.9.C64 2005**
Influence Without Authority. Ed. 2. Trade Cloth. John Wiley & Sons, Inc. Hoboken, NJ. 2005. 320p. ISBN:0-471-46330-2, ISBN13: 978-0-471-46330-6. Dewey:658.4/09. LCCN:2004-027078.
Audience: **g,l,u.**

Cross, Wilbur L. **HF1001.C68 1999**
Dictionary of Business Terms. Trade Paper. Prentice Hall Press. Paramus, NJ. 1999. 480p. ISBN:0-7352-0099-8, ISBN13: 978-0-7352-0099-9. Dewey:650/.03. LCCN:99-218719.
Audience: **g,l,u.**

Cross, Wilbur L. & Richey, Alice M. **HD30.28.C76 1998**
The Prentice Hall Encyclopedia of Model Business Plans. Trade Cloth. Prentice Hall Press. Paramus, NJ. 1998. 448p. ISBN:0-7352-0024-6, ISBN13: 978-0-7352-0024-1. Dewey:658.4/012. LCCN:98-015279.
Audience: **g,l,u.**

Cunningham, Helen & Greene, Brenda **HF5718.3.C86 2002**
The Business Style Handbook: An A-to-Z Guide for Writing on the Job with Tips from Communications Experts at the Fortune 500. Trade Paper. McGraw-Hill Companies, The. New York, NY. 2002. 240p. ISBN:0-07-138230-5, ISBN13: 978-0-07-138230-4. Dewey:808/.06665. LCCN:2001-044553.
Audience: **g,l,u.**

Cutlip, Scott M., et al. **HM1221.C88 2006**
Effective Public Relations. Ed. 9. Allen H. Center & Glen M. Broom (Authors). Trade Paper, Perfect. Prentice Hall PTR. Upper Saddle River, NJ. 2005. 486p. ISBN:0-13-008200-7, ISBN13: 978-0-13-008200-8. Dewey:659.2. LCCN:2005-016701.
Audience: **l,u.**

DeVries, Mary A. **HF5383**
Internationally Yours: Writing and Communicating Successfully in Today's Global Marketplace. Paper Text. DIANE Publishing Company. Collingdale, PA. 1999. 352p. ISBN:0-7881-6172-5, ISBN13: 978-0-7881-6172-8. Dewey:808/.06665.
Audience: **l,u.**

Earley, P. Christopher **HF5549.5.M5E17 2006**
CQ: Developing Cultural Intelligence at Work. Trade Cloth. Stanford University Press. Palo Alto, CA. 2006. 283p. ISBN:0-8047-4313-4, ISBN13: 978-0-8047-4313-6. Dewey:658.3/008. LCCN:2005-023670.
Audience: **l,u.** *Choice, 2006.*

Economist Books Staff **PN147**
Style Guide. Ed. 9. Trade Cloth. Profile Books Ltd. London, 2005. 160p. ISBN:1-86197-916-9, ISBN13: 978-1-86197-916-2. Dewey:808.042.
Audience: **g,l,u.**

Few, Stephen **HF5718.22**
Show Me the Numbers: Designing Tables and Graphs to Enlighten. Nan Wishner (Editor), Keith Stevenson (Illustrator). Cloth over Boards. Analytics Press. Oakland, CA. 2004. 280p. ISBN:0-9706019-9-9, ISBN13: 978-0-9706019-9-5. Dewey:658.45.
Audience: **l,u.**

Flynn, Nancy **HE7551.F59 2004**
Instant Messaging Rules: A Business Guide to Managing Policies, Security, and Legal Issues for Safe IM Communication. Trade Paper. Amacom. New York, NY. 2004. 224p. ISBN:0-8144-7253-2, ISBN13: 978-0-8144-7253-8. Dewey:651.8/469. LCCN:2004-003413.
Audience: **l,u.**

Geffner, Andrea B. **PE1115.G38 1998**
Barron's ESL Guide to American Business English. Trade Paper. Barron's Educational Series, Inc. Hauppauge, NY. 1998. 320p. ISBN:0-7641-0594-9, ISBN13: 978-0-7641-0594-4. Dewey:428.2/4/02465. LCCN:98-021252.
Audience: **l,u.**

Graham, John W. & Havlick, Wendy **HD30.28.G697 1994**
Mission Statements: A Guide to the Corporate and Nonprofit Sectors. Cloth Text. Garland Publishing, Inc. New York, NY. 1994. 576p. Reference Library of Social Science, Vol. 900 ISBN:0-8153-1297-0, ISBN13: 978-0-8153-1297-0. Dewey:658.4/012. LCCN:94-000540.
Audience: **l,u.** *Choice, 1995.*

Griffin, Jack **HF5718.G748 1998**
How to Say It at Work: Putting Yourself Across with Power Words, Phrases, Body Language and Communication Secrets. Ed. 1. Trade Cloth. Prentice Hall PTR. Upper Saddle River, NJ. 1998. 394p. How to Say It Ser. ISBN:0-13-242546-7, ISBN13: 978-0-13-242546-9. Dewey:658.4/52. LCCN:98-009748.
Audience: **g,l,u.**

Haschak, Paul G. **HD30.285.H37 1998**
Corporate Statements: The Official Missions, Goals, Principles and Philosophies of over 900 Countries. Cloth Text. McFarland & Company, Incorporated Publishers. Jefferson, NC. 1998. 336p. ISBN:0-7864-0342-X, ISBN13: 978-0-7864-0342-4. Dewey:338.7. LCCN:97-40509.
Audience: **l,u.**

Herrmann, Keith R. **HF5718.22.H47 2001**
[e] Visualizing Your Business: Let Graphics Tell the Story. E-Book. John Wiley & Sons, Inc. Hoboken, NJ. 2001. ISBN:0-471-15102-5, ISBN13: 978-0-471-15102-9. Dewey:658.4/5.
Audience: **l,u.**

Kroeger, Otto, et al. **BF698.9.O3K68 2002**
Type Talk at Work: How the 16 Personality Types Determine Your Success on the Job. Janet M. Thuesen & Hile Rutledge (Authors). UK-Trade Paper. Dell Publishing. New York, NY. 2002. 416p. ISBN:0-440-50928-9, ISBN13: 978-0-440-50928-8. Dewey:155.2/64. LCCN:2001-058421.
Audience: **l,u.**

Langford-Wood, Naomi & Salter, Brian **HF5718.L368 2003**
Critical Corporate Communications: A Best Practice Blueprint. Trade Paper. John Wiley & Sons, Inc. Hoboken, NJ. 2003. 192p. Fast-Track Ser. ISBN:0-470-84763-8, ISBN13: 978-0-470-84763-3. Dewey:658.45. LCCN:2003-283026.
Audience: **l,u.**

Lanham, Richard A. **PE1479.B87L36 1999**
Revising Business Prose. Ed. 4. Trade Paper. Longman Publishing. Boston, MA. 1999. 117p. ISBN:0-205-30944-5, ISBN13: 978-0-205-30944-3. Dewey:808/.066651. LCCN:99-027672.
Audience: **l,u.**

Lewis, Herschell Gordon **HF5825.L44 1999**
On the Art of Writing Copy: The Best of Print, Broadcast, Internet, Direct Mail. Ed. 2. Trade Paper. Amacom. New York, NY. 1999. 424p. ISBN:0-8144-7031-9, ISBN13: 978-0-8144-7031-2. Dewey:659.1/32. LCCN:99-043415.
Audience: **l,u.**

Marsh, Charles, et al. **PE1479.B87M35 2005**
Strategic Writing: Multimedia Writing for Public Relations, Advertising, Sales and Marketing, and Business Communication. David Guth & Bonnie Poovey Short (Authors). Trade Paper. Allyn & Bacon, Inc. Boston, MA. 2004. 272p. ISBN:0-205-40573-8, ISBN13: 978-0-205-40573-2. Dewey:808/.06665. LCCN:2004-044491.
Audience: **l,u.**

May, Steve (Editor) **HD30.3.C37155 2006**
Case Studies in Organizational Communication: Ethical Perspectives and Practices. Paper Text. SAGE Publications, Inc. Thousand Oaks, CA. 2006. 424p. ISBN:0-7619-2983-5, ISBN13: 978-0-7619-2983-3. Dewey:302.3/5. LCCN:2005-026094.
Audience: **l,u.**

McLeary, Joseph Webb, et al. **HF5718.22.B9 2000**
By the Numbers: Using Facts and Figures to Get Your Projects, Plans and Ideas Approved. Richard Haasnoot, Joyce McLeary & Susan Drake (Authors). Trade Cloth. Amacom. New York, NY. 2000. xvii, 286p. ISBN:0-8144-0499-5, ISBN13: 978-0-8144-0499-7. Dewey:658.4/5. LCCN:99-059434.
Audience: **l,u.**

Millar, Dan Pyle & Heath, Robert L. (Editors) **HD49.R47 2003**
Responding to Crisis: A Rehetorical Approach to Crisis Communication. Cloth over Boards. Lawrence Erlbaum Associates, Inc. Mahwah, NJ. 2003. 392p. Lea's Communication Ser. ISBN:0-8058-4059-1, ISBN13: 978-0-8058-4059-9. Dewey:658.4/056. LCCN:2003-052859.
Audience: **l,u.**

Miller, Jane E. **T11.M485 2004**
The Chicago Guide to Writing about Numbers. Trade Cloth. University of Chicago Press. Chicago, IL. 2004. 312p. Chicago Guides to Writing, Editing, and Publishing Ser. ISBN:0-226-52630-5, ISBN13: 978-0-226-52630-0. Dewey:808/.0665. LCCN:2004-000204.
Audience: **g,l,u,f.** *Choice, 2005.*

Mindell, Phyllis **HF5718.M553 2001**
A Woman's Guide to the Language of Success. Trade Cloth. Prentice Hall PTR. Upper Saddle River, NJ. 2001. 256p. ISBN:0-13-028672-9, ISBN13: 978-0-13-028672-7. Dewey:650.1. LCCN:00-048328.
Audience: **g,l,u.**

Morrison, Terri **HF5389 .M67 2006**
Kiss, Bow, or Shake Hands: The Bestselling Guide to Doing Business in More Than 60 Countries. Ed. 2. Wayne A. Conaway (Editor). Trade Paper. Adams Media Corporation. Avon, MA. 2006. 592p. ISBN:1-59337-368-6, ISBN13: 978-1-59337-368-9. Dewey:395.5/2. LCCN:2006-013587.
Audience: **l,u.**

Munter, Mary & Haley, Thea **HF5718.M86 2005**
Guide to Managerial Communication. Ed. 7. Trade Paper. Prentice Hall PTR. Upper Saddle River, NJ. 2005. 208p. ISBN:0-13-146704-2, ISBN13: 978-0-13-146704-0. Dewey:658.4/5. LCCN:2005-042190.
Audience: **l,u.**

Murphy, Patrick E. **HF5387.E37 1998**
Eighty Exemplary Ethics Statements. Trade Paper. University of Notre Dame Press. Notre Dame, IN. 1998. xv, 243p. ISBN:0-268-00939-2, ISBN13: 978-0-268-00939-7. Dewey:174/.4. LCCN:97-028411.
Audience: **l,u.**

Pallister, John, et al. **HF1001 .C63 2006**
A Dictionary of Business and Management. Ed. 4. John Daintith & Jonathan Law (Authors). Trade Paper. Oxford University Press, Inc. New York, NY. 2006. 576p. Oxford Paperback Reference Ser. ISBN:0-19-280648-3, ISBN13: 978-0-19-280648-2. Dewey:650.03. LCCN:2006-040130.
Audience: **g,l,u.**

Pearce, Lynne (Editor) **HD62.7.B865**
Business Plans Handbook, Vol. 11. Ed. 11. Gale Group (Created by). Saddle Stitched, Cloth over Boards. Thomson Gale. Farmington Hills, MI. 2005. 459p. ISBN:0-7876-6681-5, ISBN13: 978-0-7876-6681-1. Dewey:658.4012.
Audience: **l,u.**

Perseus Publishing Staff **HF1001.U45 2003**
The Ultimate Business Dictionary: Defining the World of Work. Trade Paper. Basic Books. New York, NY. 2003. 672p. ISBN:0-7382-0821-3, ISBN13: 978-0-7382-0821-3. Dewey:330./03. LCCN:2003-282078.
Audience: **g,l,u.**

Pindsdorf, Marion K. **HD59.2.P55 1998**
Communicating When Your Company Is under Siege. Ed. 2. Trade Cloth. Fordham University Press. Bronx, NY. 1999. 171p. ISBN:0-8232-1783-3, ISBN13: 978-0-8232-1783-0. Dewey:380.1/456753/09797. LCCN:98-038612.
Audience: **l,u.** *Choice, 1999.*

Pinson, Linda **HD30.28.P5 2005**
Anatomy of a Business Plan: A Step-by-Step Guide to Building a Business and Securing Your Company's Future. Ed. 6. Trade Paper. Kaplan Publishing. Chicago, IL. 2004. 304p. ISBN:0-7931-9192-0, ISBN13: 978-0-7931-9192-5. Dewey:658.4/012. LCCN:2004-014728.
Audience: **l,u.**

Post, Peggy & Post, Peter **HF5382.7.P68 2005**
Emily Post's the Etiquette Advantage in Business: Personal Skills for Professional Success. Ed. 2. Trade Cloth. HarperCollins Publishers. New York, NY. 2005. 384p. ISBN:0-06-076002-8, ISBN13: 978-0-06-076002-1. Dewey:395.52. LCCN:2005-283037.
Audience: **g,l,u.**

Pugh, David G. & Bacon, Terry R. **HF5718.5.P84 2005**
Powerful Proposals: How to Give Your Business the Winning Edge. Trade Cloth. Amacom. New York, NY. 2004. 256p. ISBN:0-8144-7232-X, ISBN13: 978-0-8144-7232-3. Dewey:658.4/53. LCCN:2004-018327.
Audience: **l,u.**

Putnam, Linda L. & Jablin, Fredric M. **HD30.3.H3575**
The New Handbook of Organizational Communication: Advances in Theory, Research, and Methods. Paper Text. SAGE Publications, Inc. Thousand Oaks, CA. 2004. 944p. ISBN:1-4129-1525-2, ISBN13: 978-1-4129-1525-0. Dewey:658.45. LCCN:00-010051.
Audience: **l,u.**

Sabin, William A. **PE1479.B87S23 2005**
The Gregg Reference Manual: A Manual of Style, Grammar, Usage, and Formatting. Ed. 10. Cloth Text. McGraw-Hill Higher Education. Burr Ridge, IL. 2004. 704p. ISBN:0-07-293653-3, ISBN13: 978-0-07-293653-7. Dewey:808/.042. LCCN:2004-040335.
Audience: **g,l,u.**

Schwarz, Roger **HD30.3.S373 2002**
The Skilled Facilitator: A Comprehensive Resource for Consultants, Facilitators, Managers, Trainers, and Coaches. Ed. 2. Trade Cloth. John Wiley & Sons, Inc. Hoboken, NJ. 2002. 432p. Jossey Bass Business and Management Ser. ISBN:0-7879-4723-7, ISBN13: 978-0-7879-4723-1. Dewey:658.3124. LCCN:2002-007934.
Audience: **l,u,f.**

Tufte, Edward R. **QA276.3.T83 2001**
The Visual Display of Quantitative Information. Ed. 2. Cloth Text. Graphics Press. Cheshire, CT. 2001. 197p. ISBN:0-9613921-4-2, ISBN13: 978-0-9613921-4-7. Dewey:001.4/226. LCCN:2001-271866.
Audience: **g,l,u,f.**

Weick, Karl E. **HD57.7.W447 2001**
Making Sense of the Organization. Trade Paper. Blackwell Publishing, Inc. Malden, MA. 2000. 496p. ISBN:0-631-22319-3, ISBN13: 978-0-631-22319-1. Dewey:158.7. LCCN:00-034327.
Audience: **l,u.**

Weissman, Jerry **HF5718.22.W45 2006**
Presenting to Win: The Art of Telling Your Story. Trade Paper. Prentice Hall PTR. Upper Saddle River, NJ. 2006. 336p. ISBN:0-13-187510-8, ISBN13: 978-0-13-187510-4. Dewey:651.7/3.
Audience: **l,u.**

Wempen, Faithe **QA76.76.A65**
PowerPoint Advanced Presentation Techniques. Trade Paper. John Wiley & Sons, Inc. Hoboken, NJ. 2004. 600p. ISBN:0-7645-6881-7, ISBN13: 978-0-7645-6881-7. Dewey:006.6. LCCN:2004-301777.
Audience: **l,u.**

Wilder, Claudyne & Rotondo, Jennifer **HF5718.22.W55 2002**
Point, Click and Wow!: A Quick Guide to Brilliant Laptop Presentations. Ed. 2. Trade Paper. John Wiley & Sons, Inc. Hoboken, NJ. 2002. 256p. ISBN:0-7879-5669-4, ISBN13: 978-0-7879-5669-1. Dewey:658.4/5. LCCN:2001-005073.
Audience: **l,u.**

Zelazny, Gene **HF5718.22.Z45 2001**
Say It with Charts: The Executive's Guide to Visual Communication. Ed. 4. Trade Cloth. McGraw-Hill Companies, The. New York, NY. 2001. 225p. ISBN:0-07-136997-X, ISBN13: 978-0-07-136997-8. Dewey:658.4/5. LCCN:00-046464.
Audience: **l,u.**

Careers, Personal Skills Development, and Vocational Guidance > Business Mathematics

Bluman, Allan G. **HF5691.B666 2006**
Business Math Demystified. Trade Paper. McGraw-Hill Professional Publishing. New York, NY. 2006. 390p. ISBN:0-07-146470-0, ISBN13: 978-0-07-146470-3. Dewey:650.01/513. LCCN:2006-042034.
Audience: **g,l,u.**

Bragg, Steven M. **HF5691.B73 2002**
[e] Business Ratios and Formulas: A Comprehensive Guide. E-Book. John Wiley & Sons, Inc. Hoboken, NJ. 2003. 352p. ISBN:0-471-46348-5, ISBN13: 978-0-471-46348-1. Dewey:650.01/513.
Audience: **g,l,u,f.** *Choice, 2003.*

Cleaves, Cheryl S. & Hobbs, Margie J. **HF5691.C53 2004**
Business Math. Ed. 7. Trade Cloth. Prentice Hall PTR. Upper Saddle River, NJ. 2004. xxi, 858p. ISBN:0-13-114283-6, ISBN13: 978-0-13-114283-1. Dewey:650/.01/513. LCCN:2004-040139.
Audience: **g,l,u.**

Dowling, Edward T. **HF5691.L64 1993**
Schaum's Outline of Mathematical Methods for Business and Economics. Paper Text. McGraw-Hill Companies, The. New York, NY. 1992. 384p. Schaum's ISBN:0-07-017697-3, ISBN13: 978-0-07-017697-3. Dewey:650.01513. LCCN:92-011962.
Audience: **g,l,u.**

Few, Stephen **HF5718.22**
Show Me the Numbers: Designing Tables and Graphs to Enlighten. Nan Wishner (Editor), Keith Stevenson (Illustrator). Cloth over Boards. Analytics Press. Oakland, CA. 2004. 280p. ISBN:0-9706019-9-9, ISBN13: 978-0-9706019-9-5. Dewey:658.45.
Audience: **l,u.**

Fridson, Martin S. & Alvarez, Fernando **HF5681.B2F772 2002**
Financial Statement Analysis: A Practitioner's Guide. Ed. 3. Trade Paper. John Wiley & Sons, Inc. Hoboken, NJ. 2002. 432p. Wiley Finance Ser., Vol. 78 ISBN:0-471-40917-0, ISBN13: 978-0-471-40917-5. Dewey:657/.3. LCCN:2002-279146.
Audience: **l,u.**

Friedlob, G. Thomas & Welton, Ralph E. **HF5681.B2F773 2001**
Keys to Reading an Annual Report. Ed. 3. Trade Paper. Barron's Educational Series, Inc. Hauppauge, NY. 2001. 192p. Barron's Business Keys Ser. ISBN:0-7641-1306-2, ISBN13: 978-0-7641-1306-2. Dewey:657/.3. LCCN:00-056451.
Audience: **l,u.**

Garrity, Peter **HF5691.G317 2000**
The Fast Forward MBA in Business Math. Trade Paper. John Wiley & Sons, Inc. Hoboken, NJ. 1999. 342p. Fast Forward MBA Ser. ISBN:0-471-31503-6, ISBN13: 978-0-471-31503-2. Dewey:650/.01/513. LCCN:00-269077.
Audience: **g,l,u.**

Haeussler, Ernest F., et al. **QA300.H328 2005**
Introductory Mathematical Analysis for Business, Economics and the Life and Social Sciences. Ed. 11. Richard S. Paul & R. J. Wood (Authors). Cloth Text. Prentice Hall PTR. Upper Saddle River, NJ. 2004. 1056p. ISBN:0-13-113948-7, ISBN13: 978-0-13-113948-0. Dewey:515/.1. LCCN:2004-044607.
Audience: **g,l,u.**

Huettenmueller, Rhonda **QA303.2.H838 2006**
Business Calculus Demystified. Trade Paper. McGraw-Hill Professional Publishing. New York, NY. 2005. 384p. ISBN:0-07-145157-9, ISBN13: 978-0-07-145157-4. Dewey:515. LCCN:2005-058377.
Audience: **g,l,u.**

Intriligator, Michael D. **HB74.M3I57 2002**
Mathematical Optimization and Economic Theory. Ed. 2. Trade Paper. Society for Industrial & Applied Mathematics. Philadelphia, PA. 2002. xix, 508p. Classics in Applied Mathematics Ser., Vol. 39 ISBN:0-89871-511-3, ISBN13: 978-0-89871-511-8. Dewey:330/.01/5193. LCCN:2002-017640.
Audience: **u.**

Lipsman, Ron **HG179 .L525**
[e] You Can Do the Math: Overcome Your Math Phobia and Make Better Financial Decisions. E-Book. Greenwood Publishing Group, Inc. Portsmouth, NH. 2004. 216p. ISBN:0-313-01757-3, ISBN13: 978-0-313-01757-5. Dewey:332.024/001/51.
Audience: **g,l.**

Luderer, Bernd, et al. **HB135.L83 2005**
Mathematical Formulas for Economists. Ed. 2. Volker Nollau & Klaus Vetters (Authors). Trade Paper. Springer. New York, NY. 2005. x, 188p. ISBN:3-540-27916-4, ISBN13: 978-3-540-27916-7. Dewey:330.01/5195. LCCN:2005-928964.
Audience: **l,u.** *Choice, 2006.*

McCusker, John J. **HB235.U6M39 2001**
How Much Is That in Real Money?: A Historical Commodity Price Index for Use As a Deflator of Money Values in the Economy of the United States. Ed. 2. Trade Paper. American Antiquarian Society. Worcester, MA. 2001. 142p. ISBN:1-929545-01-0, ISBN13: 978-1-929545-01-8. Dewey:332.4/973. LCCN:2001-022075.
Audience: **g,l,u,f.**

McLeary, Joseph Webb, et al. **HF5718.22.B9 2000**
By the Numbers: Using Facts and Figures to Get Your Projects, Plans and Ideas Approved. Richard Haasnoot, Joyce McLeary & Susan Drake (Authors). Trade Cloth. Amacom. New York, NY. 2000. xvii, 286p. ISBN:0-8144-0499-5, ISBN13: 978-0-8144-0499-7. Dewey:658.4/5. LCCN:99-059434.
Audience: **l,u.**

Muksian, Robert **HG1621.M857 2003**
Mathematics of Interest Rates, Insurance, Social Security, and Pensions. Cloth Text. Prentice Hall PTR. Upper Saddle River, NJ. 2002. 351p. ISBN:0-13-009425-0, ISBN13: 978-0-13-009425-4. Dewey:332.8/2/0151. LCCN:2002-034632.
Audience: **g,l,u,f.**

Rosser, M. J. **HB135.R665 2003**
Basic Mathematics for Economists. Ed. 2. Trade Paper. Routledge. New York, NY. 2003. 528p. ISBN:0-415-26784-6, ISBN13: 978-0-415-26784-7. Dewey:510.2/4339. LCCN:2002-031813.
Audience: **l,u.**

Searle, Shayle R. & Willett, Lois Schertz **HB135.S38 2001**
Matrix Algebra for Applied Economics. Trade Cloth. John Wiley & Sons, Inc. Hoboken, NJ. 2001. 432p. Wiley Series in Probability and Statistics, Vol. 349 ISBN:0-471-32207-5, ISBN13: 978-0-471-32207-8. Dewey:330/.01/5129434. LCCN:2001-026759.
Audience: **l,u.**

Stutely, Richard **HF5691.S694 2003**
Numbers Guide: The Essentials of Business Numeracy. Ed. 5. Saddle Stitched, Cloth over Boards. Bloomberg Press. New York, NY. 2003. 256p. The Economist Ser. ISBN:1-57660-144-7, ISBN13: 978-1-57660-144-0. Dewey:650/.01/513. LCCN:03-005901.
Audience: **g,l,u.**

Thorndike, David **HG1626**
Thorndike Encyclopedia of Banking and Financial Tables. Trade Cloth. Warren, Gorham & Lamont, Inc. New York, NY. 1991.

1792p. ISBN:0-7913-0801-4, ISBN13: 978-0-7913-0801-1. Dewey:332.8/0212. LCCN:87-050721.
Audience: **g,l,u,f.**

Tracy, John A. **HF5681.B2**
How to Read a Financial Report: Wringing Vital Signs Out of the Numbers. Ed. 6. Trade Paper. John Wiley & Sons, Inc. Hoboken, NJ. 2004. 216p. ISBN:0-471-47867-9, ISBN13: 978-0-471-47867-6. Dewey:657/.3. LCCN:2004-274182.
Audience: **g,l,u,f.**

Weiglin, Peter C. **HF5415.W364 2002**
Survival Math for Marketers. Paper Text. SAGE Publications, Inc. Thousand Oaks, CA. 2002. 144p. ISBN:0-7619-1632-6, ISBN13: 978-0-7619-1632-1. Dewey:658/.001/51. LCCN:2002-005204.
Audience: **l,u.** *Choice, 2003.*

Weintraub, E. Roy **HB135.W437 2002**
How Economics Became a Mathematical Science. Trade Paper. Duke University Press. Durham, NC. 2002. 312p. Science and Cultural Theory Ser. ISBN:0-8223-2871-2, ISBN13: 978-0-8223-2871-1. Dewey:330/.01/51. LCCN:2001-007280.
Audience: **l,u.**

Careers, Personal Skills Development, and Vocational Guidance > Management Education

Alsop, Ronald & Wall Street Journal Staff (Editors) **HF1106**
The Wall Street Journal Guide to the Top Business Schools 2006. Trade Paper. Bantam Books. New York, NY. 2005. 496p. ISBN:0-375-72098-7, ISBN13: 978-0-375-72098-7. Dewey:650.0711.
Audience: **g,l,u,f.**

Argyris, Chris (Contribution by), et al. **HD38.2.H3744 2004**
Harvard Business Review on Developing Leaders: Ideas with Impact. Warren G. Bennis & Robert J. Thomas (Contribution by). Trade Paper. Harvard Business School Press. Boston, MA. 2004. 208p. Harvard Business Review Paperback Ser. ISBN:1-59139-500-3, ISBN13: 978-1-59139-500-3. Dewey:658.4/07124. LCCN:2003-023489.
Audience: **g,u,f.**

Bickerstaffe, George **HF1111.B53 2004**
Which MBA?: A Critical Guide to the World's Best MBAs. Ed. 16. Trade Paper. Financial Times/Prentice Hall. Paramus, NJ. 2005. 568p. ISBN:0-273-69536-3, ISBN13: 978-0-273-69536-3. Dewey:658/.00711.
Audience: **g,l,u.**

Cameron, Sheila **HF1111.C27 2004**
The MBA Handbook: Skills for Mastering Management. Ed. 5. Trade Paper. Pearson Education, Ltd. Harlow, 2005. 432p. ISBN:0-273-68467-1, ISBN13: 978-0-273-68467-1. Dewey:658. LCCN:2004-053232.
Audience: **g,l,u,f.**

Crainer, Stuart & Dearlove, Des **HF1131**
Gravy Training: Inside the Shadowy World of Business Schools. Trade Paper. John Wiley & Sons, Inc. Hoboken, NJ. 1998. 288p. ISBN:1-900961-68-7, ISBN13: 978-1-900961-68-4. Dewey:650/.071173.
Audience: **g,l,u,f.**

Daniel, Carter A. **HF1111.D36 1998**
MBA: The First Century. Trade Cloth. Bucknell University Press. Cranbury, NJ. 1998. 336p. ISBN:0-8387-5362-0, ISBN13: 978-0-8387-5362-0. Dewey:650/.071/173. LCCN:97-025110.
Audience: **l,u,f.**

Educational Testing Service **HF1118**
Official Guide for GMAT Review. Ed. 11. Educational Testing Service. 2005. ISBN:0-9765709-0-4, ISBN13: 978-0-9765709-0-5.
Audience: **g,u.**

Erck, Dan, et al. **HF1131.A135 2004**
65 Successful Harvard Business School Application Essays: With Analysis by the Staff of the Harbus, the Harvard Business School Newspaper. Pavel Swiatek & The Harbus (Authors). Trade Paper. St. Martin's Press. Gordonville, VA. 2004. 240p. ISBN:0-312-33448-6, ISBN13: 978-0-312-33448-2. Dewey:808/.06665. LCCN:2004-049743.
Audience: **g,u,f.**

Lichtenthal, J. David (Editor) **HF5415.1263.F857**
Fundamentals of Business Marketing Education: A Guide for University-Level Faculty and Policy Makers. Box or Slipcased. Haworth Press, Incorporated, The. Binghamton, NY. 2004. xviii, 298p. ISBN:0-7890-0121-7, ISBN13: 978-0-7890-0121-4. Dewey:658.8/0071/1. LCCN:2003-016230.
Audience: **g,f.**

Locke, Robert & Schöne, Katja **HF1140**
The Entrepreneurial Shift: Americanization in European High-Technology Management Education. Trade Cloth. Cambridge University Press. New York, NY. 2004. 264p. ISBN:0-521-84010-4, ISBN13: 978-0-521-84010-1. Dewey:658.007114. LCCN:2005-299162.
Audience: **g,u,f.**

Lorange, Peter (Editor) **HF1111.L67 2002**
New Vision for Management Education: Leadership Challenges. Ed. 2. Cloth Text. Elsevier Science & Technology Books. Saint Louis, MO. 2002. 400p. ISBN:0-08-044034-7, ISBN13: 978-0-08-044034-7. Dewey:650/.071/1. LCCN:2002-070424.
Audience: **g,u,f.**

Merritt, Jennifer **HF1111**
BusinessWeek Guide to the Best Business Schools. Ed. 8. Trade Paper. McGraw-Hill Companies, The. New York, NY. 2003. 432p. ISBN:0-07-141521-1, ISBN13: 978-0-07-141521-7. Dewey:650/.071/173. LCCN:2003-007869.
Audience: **g,l,u,f.**

Miller, Eugene & Pollack, Neuman F. **HF1131**
Guide to Graduate Business Schools. Ed. 14. Trade Paper, Perfect. Barron's Educational Series, Inc. Hauppauge, NY. 2005. 832p. ISBN:0-7641-3198-2, ISBN13: 978-0-7641-3198-1. Dewey:650.071173.
Audience: **g,l,u,f.**

Mintzberg, Henry **HD30.4**
Managers Not MBAs: A Hard Look at the Soft Practice of Managing and Management Development. Trade Cloth. Financial Times/Prentice Hall. Paramus, NJ. 2004. 480p.

ISBN:0-273-66324-0, ISBN13: 978-0-273-66324-9. Dewey:658/.0071/1. LCCN:2004-047203.
Audience: **g,u,f.** *Choice, 2004.*

Montauk, Richard **HF1111.M66 2005**
How to Get into the Top MBA Programs. Ed. 3. Trade Paper, Perfect. Prentice Hall Press. Paramus, NJ. 2005. 672p. ISBN:0-7352-0390-3, ISBN13: 978-0-7352-0390-7. Dewey:658/.0071/1. LCCN:2005-279291.
Audience: **g,l,u.**

Navarro, Peter **HF1106.W55 2005**
What the Best MBAs Know: How to Apply the Greatest Ideas Taught in the Best Business Schools. Trade Cloth. McGraw-Hill Companies, The. New York, NY. 2005. 304p. ISBN:0-07-142275-7, ISBN13: 978-0-07-142275-8. Dewey:658. LCCN:2004-018239.
Audience: **g,l,u,f.**

Piper, Thomas R., et al. **HF5387.P56 1993**
Can Ethics Be Taught?: Perspectives, Challenges, and Approaches at the Harvard Business School. Mary C. Gentile & Sharon D. Parks (Authors). Trade Cloth. Harvard Business School Press. Boston, MA. 1993. 208p. ISBN:0-87584-400-6, ISBN13: 978-0-87584-400-8. Dewey:174/.4/071173. LCCN:92-027077.
Audience: **g,u,f.** *Choice, 1993.*

Rugman, Alan M. (Editor) **HF1131**
Leadership in International Business Education and Research. Trade Cloth. Elsevier Science & Technology Books. Saint Louis, MO. 2003. 356p. Research in Global Strategic Management Ser., Vol. 8 ISBN:0-7623-1038-3, ISBN13: 978-0-7623-1038-8. Dewey:658.0071173. LCCN:2004-271193.
Audience: **g,f.**

Witzel, Morgen **HF1111.W58 2001**
How to Get an MBA. Trade Paper. Routledge. New York, NY. 2001. 208p. Routledge Study Guides Ser. ISBN:0-415-22817-4, ISBN13: 978-0-415-22817-6. Dewey:650/.071/173. LCCN:00-056024.
Audience: **g,l,u.**

Wolfe, Joseph & Keys, J. Bernard (Editors) **HF1106.B945 1997**
Business Simulations, Games and Experiential Learning in International Business Education. Trade Cloth. Haworth Press, Incorporated, The. Binghamton, NY. 1997. 122p. Journal of Teachings in International Business Monograph Ser., Vol. 8, No. 4 ISBN:0-7890-0041-5, ISBN13: 978-0-7890-0041-5. Dewey:650/.071/5. LCCN:97-000758.
Audience: **g,u,f.**

Wolverton, Mimi & Penley, Larry Edward (Editors) **HF1131**
Elite MBA Programs at Public Universities: How a Dozen Innovative Schools Are Redefining Business Education. Trade Cloth. Greenwood Publishing Group, Inc. Portsmouth, NH. 2004. 264p. ISBN:0-275-97811-7, ISBN13: 978-0-275-97811-2. LCCN:2004-017679.
Audience: **g,u,f.**

World Resources Institute Staff **HD30.255**
Beyond Grey Pinstripes 2001: Preparing MBAs for Social and Environmental Stewardship. Trade Cloth. World Resources Institute. Washington, DC. 2001. 28p. ISBN:1-56973-488-7, ISBN13: 978-1-56973-488-9. Dewey:330.
Audience: **g,u,f.**

Careers, Personal Skills Development, and Vocational Guidance > Management Education > Case Method

Barbazette, Jean **LB1029.C37B37 2004**
Instant Case Studies: How to Design, Adapt, and Use Case Studies in Training. Trade Cloth. John Wiley & Sons, Inc. Hoboken, NJ. 2003. 336p. ISBN:0-7879-6885-4, ISBN13: 978-0-7879-6885-4. Dewey:658.3/124. LCCN:2003-016270.
Audience: **g,u,f.**

Bruner, Robert F. **LB1029.C37**
Socrates' Muse: Reflections on Effective Case Discussion Leadership. Ed. 4. Trade Paper. McGraw-Hill Higher Education. Burr Ridge, IL. 2002. 236p. ISBN:0-07-248566-3, ISBN13: 978-0-07-248566-0. Dewey:370.711.
Audience: **f.**

Christensen, C. Roland **LB2331**
Education for Judgment: The Artistry of Discussion Leadership. Trade Paper. Harvard Business School Press. Boston, MA. 1992. 320p. ISBN:0-87584-365-4, ISBN13: 978-0-87584-365-0. Dewey:378.1/77.
Audience: **f.**

Erskine, James A., et al. **HF1118**
Teaching with Cases. Ed. 2. Michiel R. Leenders & L. A. Mauffette-Leenders (Authors). Trade Paper. University of Western Ontario. London, ON. 1998. ISBN:0-7714-2087-0, ISBN13: 978-0-7714-2087-0. Dewey:658/.0071/1.
Audience: **f.**

Ghemawat, Pankaj **HD30.26.G47 1997**
Games Businesses Play: Cases and Models. Trade Cloth. MIT Press. Cambridge, MA. 1997. 255p. ISBN:0-262-07182-7, ISBN13: 978-0-262-07182-6. Dewey:658.4/0353. LCCN:97-007564.
Audience: **l,u,f.**

Harvard Business Review Staff **HF1131 .C48**
Teaching and the Case Method. Ed. 3. Trade Paper. McGraw-Hill Companies, The. New York, NY. 1994. 416p. ISBN:0-07-103602-4, ISBN13: 978-0-07-103602-3. Dewey:650/.071/2.
Audience: **f.**

Heath John Staff **HF1118**
Teaching and Writing Case Studies. Trade Paper. Unknown UK Publisher. New Providence, NJ. ISBN:0-907815-02-2, ISBN13: 978-0-907815-02-0. Dewey:658.00722.
Audience: **f.**

Leenders, Michiel R., James A. Erskine and Louise A. Mauffette-Leenders **HD30.4**
Writing Cases. Ed. 4. Richard Ivey School of Business, University of Western Ontario. 2001. ISBN:0-7714-2270-9, ISBN13: 978-0-7714-2270-6.
Audience: **g,u,f**

Lynn, Laurence E. Jr. **LB1029.C37L96 1998**
Teaching and Learning with Cases: A Guidebook. Paper Text. CQ Press. Washington, DC. 1998. 192p. Public Administration and Public Policy Ser. ISBN:1-56643-066-6, ISBN13: 978-1-56643-066-1. Dewey:371.39. LCCN:98-025376.
Audience: **l,u,f.** *Choice, 1999.*

Naumes, William & Naumes, Margaret J. **LB1029.C37N38 2006**
The Art and Craft of Case Writing. Ed. 2. Cloth Text. M. E. Sharpe Inc. Armonk, NY. 2006. 296p. ISBN:0-7656-1681-5, ISBN13: 978-0-7656-1681-4. Dewey:371.39. LCCN:2005-025021.
Audience: **l,u,f.**

Ronstadt, Robert C. **HF1118**
Art of Case Analysis: How to Improve Performance by Developing Better Case Analysis Skills. Ed. 3. Trade Paper. Lord Publishing, Inc. Austin, TX. 1994. ISBN:0-685-69348-1, ISBN13: 978-0-685-69348-3. Dewey:658.0072.
Audience: **l,u,f.**

WetFeet.com (Firm) Staff **HF5382.75**
Ace Your Case!: The WetFeet Insider Guide to Consulting Interviews. Ed. 2. Trade Paper. WetFeet, Inc. San Francisco, CA. 2005. 118p. ISBN:1-58207-247-7, ISBN13: 978-1-58207-247-0. Dewey:658.4/6/023.
Audience: **u.**

Careers, Personal Skills Development, and Vocational Guidance > Management Education > Research and Statistical Methods

Barbuto, Domenica M. **HG151.7.B37 1995**
The International Financial Statistics Locator: A Research and Information Guide. Cloth Text. Garland Publishing, Inc. New York, NY. 1994. 352p. Research and Information Guides in Business, Industry, and Economic Institutions Ser., Vol. 11:Garland Reference Library of Social Science Ser. ISBN:0-8153-1483-3, ISBN13: 978-0-8153-1483-7. Dewey:016.332. LCCN:94-019999.
Audience: **g,u,f.** *Choice, 1995.*

Boettcher, Jennifer C. & Gaines, Leonard M. **HC101**
Industry Research Using the Economic Census: How to Find It, How to Use It. Cloth Text. Greenwood Publishing Group, Inc. Portsmouth, NH. 2004. 328p. How to Find It, How to Use It Ser. ISBN:1-57356-351-X, ISBN13: 978-1-57356-351-2. Dewey:338.0973/0072/7. LCCN:2004-008607.
Audience: **l,u,f.** *Choice, 2005.*

Buglear, John **HD30.25**
Quantitative Methods for Business: The A to Z of QM. Paper Text. Elsevier Science & Technology Books. Saint Louis, MO. 2004. 704p. ISBN:0-7506-5898-3, ISBN13: 978-0-7506-5898-0. Dewey:658/.00151. LCCN:2005-275777.
Audience: **u,f.**

Chapman, Karen J. **Z7164.C83C46 1989**
The Commodities Price Locator. Trade Cloth. Greenwood Publishing Group, Inc. Portsmouth, NH. 1989. 168p. ISBN:0-89774-366-0, ISBN13: 978-0-89774-366-2. Dewey:016.33264/4. LCCN:88-029371.
Audience: **g,u,f.** *Choice, 1989.*

Chapman, Karen J. **Z7164.C18C47 1988**
Investment Statistics Locator. Trade Cloth. Greenwood Publishing Group, Inc. Portsmouth, NH. 1988. 192p. ISBN:0-89774-367-9, ISBN13: 978-0-89774-367-9. Dewey:332.6/0973. LCCN:87-024746.
Audience: **g,u,f.** *Choice, 1988.*

Cohen, Steve (Editor), et al. **LB1029.S53V57 2005**
Virtual Decisions: Digital Simulations for Teaching Reasoning in the Social Sciences and Humanities. Kent E. Portney, Dean Rehberger & Carolyn Thorsen (Editors), Victor Asal, Jeremy Bailenson & James Blascovich (Contribution by). Cloth over Boards. Lawrence Erlbaum Associates, Inc. Mahwah, NJ. 2005. 304p. ISBN:0-8058-4994-7, ISBN13: 978-0-8058-4994-3. Dewey:300/.71. LCCN:2004-060682.
Audience: **u,f.**

Frumkin, Norman **HC103.F9 2006**
Guide to Economic Indicators. Ed. 4. Cloth Text. M. E. Sharpe Inc. Armonk, NY. 2005. 304p. ISBN:0-7656-1646-7, ISBN13: 978-0-7656-1646-3. Dewey:330.973/0021. LCCN:2005-013951.
Audience: **g,l,u,f.** *Choice, 2000, 1995, 1990.*

Gildersleeve, Rich **HF5681.R25G55 1999**
Winning Business: How to Use Financial Analysis and Benchmarks to Outscore Your Competition. Trade Paper. Elsevier Science & Technology Books. Saint Louis, MO. 1999. 330p. ISBN:0-88415-898-5, ISBN13: 978-0-88415-898-1. Dewey:658.15/5. LCCN:99-013911.
Audience: **g,u,f.**

Hardy, Melissa A. & Bryman, Alan E. (Editors) **H62**
Handbook of Data Analysis. Trade Cloth. SAGE Publications, Inc. Thousand Oaks, CA. 2004. 728p. ISBN:0-7619-6652-8, ISBN13: 978-0-7619-6652-4. Dewey:300.7/2. LCCN:2003-101541.
Audience: **g,u,f.**

Holland, Bart K. **QA273.15.H65 2002**
What Are the Chances?: Voodoo Deaths, Office Gossip and Other Adventures in Probability. Trade Cloth. Johns Hopkins University Press. Baltimore, MD. 2002. 160p. ISBN:0-8018-6941-2, ISBN13: 978-0-8018-6941-9. Dewey:519.2. LCCN:2001-005687.
Audience: **g,l,u,f.** *Choice, 2002.*

Jaffe, Abram J., et al. **HA29.S65574 1998**
Misused Statistics. Ed. 2. Herbert F. Spirer & Louise Spirer (Authors). Paper over Boards. Marcel Dekker Inc. New York, NY. 1998. 280p. Popular Statistics Ser., Vol. 7 ISBN:0-8247-0211-5, ISBN13: 978-0-8247-0211-3. Dewey:300/.1/5195. LCCN:98-025625.
Audience: **g,l,u,f.**

Keller, Gerald **HD30.215K45 2005**
Statistics for Management and Economics (Ise). Ed. 7. Trade Cloth. Brooks/Cole. Pacific Grove, CA. 2005. 1054p. ISBN:0-495-01339-0, ISBN13: 978-0-495-01339-6. Dewey:519.5. LCCN:2004-115362.
Audience: **g,l,u.**

Kemp, Steven M. & Kemp, Sid **HF1017**
Business Statistics Demystified. Trade Paper. McGraw-Hill Professional Publishing. New York, NY. 2004. 380p. ISBN:0-07-144024-0, ISBN13: 978-0-07-144024-0. Dewey:519.5. LCCN:2004-301317.
Audience: **g,l,u.**

Mendenhall, William, et al. **HF1017.M45 2001**
A Brief Course in Business Statistics. Ed. 2. Robert J. Beaver & Barbara M. Beaver (Authors). Cloth Text. Brooks/Cole. Pacific Grove, CA. 2000. 720p. ISBN:0-534-38130-8, ISBN13: 978-0-534-38130-1. Dewey:519.5. LCCN:00-030850.
Audience: **g,l,u.**

Miller, Jane E. **T11.M485 2004**
The Chicago Guide to Writing about Numbers. Trade Cloth. University of Chicago Press. Chicago, IL. 2004. 312p. Chicago Guides to Writing, Editing, and Publishing Ser. ISBN:0-226-52630-5, ISBN13: 978-0-226-52630-0. Dewey:808/.0665. LCCN:2004-000204.
Audience: **g,l,u,f.** *Choice, 2005.*

Oakshott, Les **HD30.215**
Essential Quantitative Methods for Business, Management and Finance. Ed. 3. Trade Paper. Palgrave Macmillan. New York, NY. 2006. 512p. ISBN:1-4039-4991-3, ISBN13: 978-1-4039-4991-2. Dewey:650.01/513. LCCN:2006-040724.
Audience: **g,l,u.**

Ragsdale, Cliff T. **T57.62**
Spreadsheet Modeling and Decision Analysis. Ed. 4. Cloth Text. Thomson South-Western. Mason, OH. 2004. ISBN:0-324-32177-5, ISBN13: 978-0-324-32177-7. Dewey:658.4/03/0285554.
Audience: **g,l,u,f.**

Riche, Martha Farnsworth (Editor) **HA201.122.W48 2003**
Who What and Where of America: Understanding the Census Results. Trade Cloth. Bernan Associates. Lanham, MD. 2003. 1296p. County and City Extra Ser. ISBN:0-89059-763-4, ISBN13: 978-0-89059-763-7. Dewey:317.3. LCCN:2004-272494.
Audience: **g,l,u,f.** *Choice, 2004.*

Schwab, Donald P. **HD30.4.S38 2004**
Research Methods for Organizational Studies. Ed. 2. Cloth over Boards. Lawrence Erlbaum Associates, Inc. Mahwah, NJ. 2004. 352p. ISBN:0-8058-4727-8, ISBN13: 978-0-8058-4727-7. Dewey:302.3/5/072. LCCN:2004-013167.
Audience: **l,u,f.**

Tennent, John & Friend, Graham **HG4026**
Guide to Business Modelling. Ed. 2. Trade Cloth. Bloomberg Press. New York, NY. 2005. 281p. ISBN:1-86197-915-0, ISBN13: 978-1-86197-915-5. Dewey:650.
Audience: **g,l,u.**

Travers, Max **H62.T635 2001**
Qualitative Research Through Case Studies. Paper Text. SAGE Publications, Ltd. London, 2001. 208p. Introducing Qualitative Methods Ser. ISBN:0-7619-6806-7, ISBN13: 978-0-7619-6806-1. Dewey:001.4/32. LCCN:2001-131812.
Audience: **u,f.**

United States Census Bureau, Systems Support Division **HA37**
□ Statistical Agencies (International). http://www.census.gov/main/www/stat_int.html
Audience: **g,l,u,f.**

University of Auckland Library **HA155**
□ OFFSTATS: Official Statistics on the Web. http://www.library.auckland.ac.nz/subjects/stats/offstats/ University of Auckland Library.
Audience: **g,l,u,f.**

Weiers, Ronald M. **HF1017.W45 2005**
Introduction to Business Statistics. Ed. 5. Cloth Text. Thomson South-Western. Mason, OH. 2004. 1008p. ISBN:0-534-46521-8, ISBN13: 978-0-534-46521-6. Dewey:519.5. LCCN:2004-100655.
Audience: **g,l,u.**

Williams, David **QA273 .W626 2001**
Weighing the Odds: A Course in Probability and Statistics. Trade Paper. Cambridge University Press. New York, NY. 2001. 566p. ISBN:0-521-00618-X, ISBN13: 978-0-521-00618-7. Dewey:519.2. LCCN:2001-025435.
Audience: **l,u.** *Choice, 2002.*

Zeisel, Hans & Kaye, D. H. **KF320.S73Z45 1997**
Prove It with Figures: Empirical Methods in Law and Litigation. J. B. Weinstein (Foreword by). Trade Cloth. Springer. New York, NY. 1997. xxiii, 353p. Statistics for Social Science and Public Policy Ser. ISBN:0-387-94892-9, ISBN13: 978-0-387-94892-8. Dewey:349.73/07/27. LCCN:97-009827.
Audience: **g,l,u,f.**

Business Information Sources

HC21
□ EH.Net Encyclopedia of Economic and Business History. http://www.eh.net/encyclopedia/
Audience: **g,l,u,f.**

HC102.E53
Encyclopedia of American Industries. Ed. 4. Trade Cloth. Thomson Gale. Farmington Hills, MI. 2004. 3500p. ISBN:0-7876-9061-9, ISBN13: 978-0-7876-9061-8. Dewey:338.0973.
Audience: **g,l,u,f.**

Alfoldi, Jeanette **HG2563 .K449 1999**
Global Directory of Private Banking. Trade Cloth. Richmond Law & Tax Ltd. Richmond, 2005. 497p. ISBN:1-904501-12-5, ISBN13: 978-1-904501-12-1. Dewey:332.123025.
Audience: **u,f.**

Barbuto, Domenica M. **HG151.7.B37 1995**
The International Financial Statistics Locator: A Research and Information Guide. Cloth Text. Garland Publishing, Inc. New York, NY. 1994. 352p. Research and Information Guides in Business, Industry, and Economic Institutions Ser., Vol. 11:Garland Reference Library of Social Science Ser. ISBN:0-8153-1483-3, ISBN13: 978-0-8153-1483-7. Dewey:016.332. LCCN:94-019999.
Audience: **g,u,f.** *Choice, 1995.*

Berkman, Robert I. **HF54.56.B4685 2004**
The Skeptical Business Searcher: The Information Advisor's Guide to Evaluating Web Data, Sites, and Sources. Reva Basch (Foreword by). Trade Paper. Information Today, Inc. Medford, NJ. 2005. 288p. ISBN:0-910965-66-8, ISBN13: 978-0-910965-66-8. Dewey:025.06/338. LCCN:2003-020692.
Audience: **g,l,u,f.** *Choice, 2005.*

Boettcher, Jennifer C. & Gaines, Leonard M. **HC101**
Industry Research Using the Economic Census: How to Find It, How to Use It. Cloth Text. Greenwood Publishing Group, Inc. Portsmouth, NH. 2004. 328p. How to Find It, How to Use It Ser. ISBN:1-57356-351-X, ISBN13: 978-1-57356-351-2. Dewey:338.0973/0072/7. LCCN:2004-008607.
Audience: **l,u,f.** *Choice, 2005.*

Cartwright, Susan (Editor) **HD30.15.B455**
Human Resource Management. Ed. 2. Trade Cloth. Blackwell Publishing, Inc. Malden, MA. 2006. 488p. The Blackwell Encyclopedia of Management Ser., Vol. 5 ISBN:1-4051-1697-8, ISBN13: 978-1-4051-1697-8. Dewey:658/.003 s 658.3/003. LCCN:2004-004338.
Audience: **g,l,u,f.**

Daniells, Lorna M. **Z7164.C81.D16 1993**
Business Information Sources. Ed. 3. Trade Cloth. University of California Press. Berkeley, CA. 1993. 725p. ISBN:0-520-08180-3, ISBN13: 978-0-520-08180-2. Dewey:016.33. LCCN:92-041827.
Audience: **g,f.** B *Choice, 1994.*

Dienhart, John W. & Curnutt, Jordan **HF5387.D54 1998**
Business Ethics: A Reference Handbook. Library Binding. ABC-CLIO, Inc. Santa Barbara, CA. 1998. 464p. Contemporary Ethical Issues Ser. ISBN:0-87436-863-4, ISBN13: 978-0-87436-863-5. Dewey:174/.4/03. LCCN:98-042277.
Audience: **g,l,u,f.** *Choice, 1999.*

Elias, Stephen & Levinkind, Susan **KF240.E35**
Legal Research: How to Find and Understand the Law. Ed. 13. Richard Stim (Editor). Trade Paper, Perfect. NOLO. Berkeley, CA. 2005. 368p. ISBN:1-4133-0395-1, ISBN13: 978-1-4133-0395-7. Dewey:340.072073.
Audience: **g,l,u,f.**

Elias, Stephen & Stim, Richard **KF2980.E44 2004**
Patent, Copyright and Trademark: An Intellectual Property Desk Reference. Ed. 7. Trade Paper. NOLO. Berkeley, CA. 2004. 570p. ISBN:1-4133-0055-3, ISBN13: 978-1-4133-0055-0. Dewey:346.7304/8. LCCN:2003-070158.
Audience: **g,l,u,f.**

Harvard Business Reference Staff **Z7164.C81H37 1999**
1999 Harvard Business School Core Collection: An Author, Title and Subject Guide. Paper Text. Harvard Business School Press. Boston, MA. 1999. 464p. ISBN:0-87584-888-5, ISBN13: 978-0-87584-888-4. Dewey:16.658. LCCN:97-027683.
Audience: **g,f.**

Karp, Rashelle S. (Editor) **Z675**
The Basic Business Library: Core Resources. Ed. 4. Bernard S. Schlessinger (Editor-In-Chief). Cloth Text. Greenwood Publishing Group, Inc. Portsmouth, NH. 2002. 304p. ISBN:1-57356-512-1, ISBN13: 978-1-57356-512-7. Dewey:016.0276/9. LCCN:2002-025349.
Audience: **g,f.** *Choice, 2003.*

Lavin, Michael **HF5356 .L36**
Business Information: How to Find It, How to Use It. Ed. 3. Cloth Text. Greenwood Publishing Group, Inc. Portsmouth, NH. 2001. 560p. ISBN:1-57356-212-2, ISBN13: 978-1-57356-212-6. Dewey:650/.072.
Audience: **g,u,f.**

Lavin, Michael R. **HA2011990AR**
Understanding the Census: A Guide for Marketers, Planners, Grant-Writers and Other Data Users. Trade Cloth. Greenwood Publishing Group, Inc. Portsmouth, NH. 1996. 560p. ISBN:0-89774-995-2, ISBN13: 978-0-89774-995-4. Dewey:304.6/0723. LCCN:96-146991.
Audience: **g,u,f.** *Choice, 1996.*

Maier, Ernest (Editor), et al. **Z675.B8B87 1996**
Business Library and How to Use It: A Guide to Sources and Research Strategies for Information on Business and Management. Anthony Faria, Peter Kaatrude & Elizabeth Wood (Editors). Library Binding. Omnigraphics, Inc. Detroit, MI. 1996. 330p. ISBN:0-7808-0026-5, ISBN13: 978-0-7808-0026-7. Dewey:027.6/9. LCCN:94-012700.
Audience: **l,u.** *Choice, 1996.*

McCusker, John J. **HF1379.H574 2005**
Economic History of World Trade. Trade Cloth. Thomson Gale. Farmington Hills, MI. 2005. 900p. ISBN:0-02-865840-X, ISBN13: 978-0-02-865840-7. Dewey:382/.09. LCCN:2005-018624.
Audience: **g,l,u,f.**

McNett, Jeanne **HD30.15.B455**
International Management. Ed. 2. Trade Cloth. Blackwell Publishing, Inc. Malden, MA. 2006. 376p. The Blackwell Encyclopedia of Management Ser., Vol. 6 ISBN:0-631-23493-4, ISBN13: 978-0-631-23493-7. Dewey:658/.003 s 658/.049. LCCN:2004-018073.
Audience: **g,l,u,f.**

Moss, Rita W. **Z7164.C81S7796 2003**
Strauss's Handbook of Business Information: A Guide for Librarians, Students, and Researchers. Ed. 2. Trade Cloth. Libraries Unlimited, Inc. Westport, CT. 2003. 480p. ISBN:1-56308-520-8, ISBN13: 978-1-56308-520-8. Dewey:016.33. LCCN:2003-054569.
Audience: **g,u.** *Choice, 2004.*

Pagell, Ruth A. & Halperin, Michael **HF54.5**
International Business Information: How to Find It, How to Use It. Paper Text. Glenlake Publishing Company, Limited, The. Chicago, IL. 2001. 450p. ISBN:1-888998-83-0, ISBN13: 978-1-888998-83-2. Dewey:016.33.
Audience: **g,u,f.** *Choice, 1994.*

Perseus Publishing Staff (Editor) **HD38.15.B878 2002**
Business: The Ultimate Resource. Daniel Goleman (Introduction by). Trade Cloth. Basic Books. New York, NY. 2002. 2208p. ISBN:0-7382-0242-8, ISBN13: 978-0-7382-0242-6. Dewey:650. LCCN:2003-001075.
Audience: **g,u,f.** *Choice, 2003.*

Thorndike, David **HG1626**
Thorndike Encyclopedia of Banking and Financial Tables. Trade Cloth. Warren, Gorham & Lamont, Inc. New York, NY. 1991. 1792p. ISBN:0-7913-0801-4, ISBN13: 978-0-7913-0801-1. Dewey:332.8/0212. LCCN:87-050721.
Audience: **g,l,u,f.**

Vaidya, Ashish K. **HF1359.G5854 2006**
Globalization: Encyclopedia of Trade, Labor, and Politics. Library Binding. ABC-CLIO, Inc. Santa Barbara, CA. 2005. 800p. ISBN:1-57607-826-4, ISBN13: 978-1-57607-826-6. Dewey:337.03. LCCN:2006-012274.
Audience: **g,l,u,f.**

Werhane, P. H. & Freeman, R. Edward **HD30.15.B455**
Business Ethics. Ed. 2. Trade Cloth. Blackwell Publishing, Inc. Malden, MA. 2006. 600p. The Blackwell Encyclopedia of Management Ser., Vol. 2 ISBN:1-4051-0013-3, ISBN13: 978-1-4051-0013-7. Dewey:658/.003 174/.4/03. LCCN:2004-007693.
Audience: **g,l,u,f.**

White, Gary W. (Editor) **HD30.37.C67 2003**
The Core Business Web: A Guide to Key Information Resources. Trade Cloth. Haworth Press, Incorporated, The. Binghamton, NY. 2003. 325p. Journal of Business and Finance Librarianship Ser., Vol. 8 ISBN:0-7890-2094-7, ISBN13: 978-0-7890-2094-9. Dewey:025.06/65. LCCN:2003-005541.
Audience: **g,u,f.**

Woy, James (Editor) **HF5353**
Encyclopedia of Business Information Sources. Ed. 19. Trade Cloth. Thomson Gale. Farmington Hills, MI. 2004. 1200p. ISBN:0-7876-6891-5, ISBN13: 978-0-7876-6891-4. Dewey:016.33.
Audience: **g,u,f.**

Zagorsky, Jay L. **HD30.2.Z337 2003**
Business Information: Finding and Using Data in the Digital Age. Paper Text. McGraw-Hill Higher Education. Burr Ridge, IL. 2002. 288p. The McGraw-Hill/Irwin Series Operations and Decision Sciences ISBN:0-07-250770-5, ISBN13: 978-0-07-250770-6. Dewey:658/.05. LCCN:2002-025453.
Audience: **l,u.** *Choice, 2003.*

ECONOMICS

This section included materials related to the study of economics per se, and is classified in a system loosely based on the Journal of Economic Literature (JEL) classification system. Materials and classification take into account the growth of interdisciplinary inquiry in economics since the publication of BCL3 in 1988, e.g., socio-economics and the psychology of economics. The works of major theorists and practitioners are present in representative rather than comprehensive titles. This section represents a collection sufficient for basic study of the discipline of economics at the undergraduate level, as well as providing support for other allied disciplines, e.g. business administration. Excluded from this section are the sorts of comparative and industry studies which predominated in BCL3.

— Gwyneth Crowley

General Economics

Becker, William E. & Watts, Michael (Editors) **HB74.8.T4 1998**
Teaching Economics to Undergraduates: Alternatives to Chalk and Talk. R. Bartlett, W. Baumol, W. L. Hansen, P. Kennedy, M. Lage, C. Noussair, A. R. Sanderson, J. Siegfried, K. Sosin & M. Treglia (Contribution by). Trade Cloth. Edward Elgar Publishing, Inc. Northampton, MA. 1999. 296p. ISBN:1-85898-972-8, ISBN13: 978-1-85898-972-3. Dewey:330/.071/173. LCCN:98-048149.
Audience: **f.** *Choice, 1999.*

Bowmaker, Simon W. (Editor) **HB171.5**
Economics Uncut: A Complete Guide to Life, Death and Misadventure. S. W. Bowmaker, S. Cameron, L. Friedberg, D. D. Friedman, J. A. Goddard, R.D. Johnson, L. Kahane & S. A. Kossoudji (Contribution by). Trade Cloth. Edward Elgar Publishing, Inc. Northampton, MA. 2006. 488p. ISBN:1-84376-362-1, ISBN13: 978-1-84376-362-8. Dewey:306.3.
Audience: **g,l,u,f.**

Canterbery, E. Ray **HB75.C25 2003**
The Making of Economics: The Foundation. Ed. 4. Trade Cloth. World Scientific Publishing Company, Inc. Hackensack, NJ. 2003. 250p. ISBN:981-238-324-7, ISBN13: 978-981-238-324-2. Dewey:330/.09. LCCN:2003-045072.
Audience: **l,u,f.**

Cleaver, Tony **HB171.C655 2004**
Economics: The Basics. Paper over Boards. Routledge. New York, NY. 2004. 240p. The Basics Ser. ISBN:0-415-31411-9, ISBN13: 978-0-415-31411-4. Dewey:330. LCCN:2004-002732.
Audience: **g,l,u,f.**

Colander, David C. & Holt, Richard P. F. **HB76.C65 2004**
The Changing Face of Economics: Conversations with Cutting Edge Economists. John Barkley Rosser (Editor). Trade Cloth. University of Michigan Press. Chicago, IL. 2004. 368p. ISBN:0-472-09877-2, ISBN13: 978-0-472-09877-4. Dewey:330/.092/2. LCCN:2004-007728.
Audience: **g,l,u,f.** *Choice, 2005.*

Etzioni, Amitai **JC330.15.E866 2004**
The Common Good. Trade Cloth. Polity Press. Cambridge, 2004. 256p. ISBN:0-7456-3266-1, ISBN13: 978-0-7456-3266-7. Dewey:320/.01/1. LCCN:2003-019620.
Audience: **l,u,f.**

Etzioni, Amitai **HB99.3**
The Moral Dimension: Toward a New Economics. Trade Paper. Simon & Schuster. New York, NY. 1990. 314p. ISBN:0-02-909901-3, ISBN13: 978-0-02-909901-8. Dewey:330.1/55.
Audience: **g,l,u,f.** *Choice, 1989.*

Granovetter, Mark S. & Swedberg, Richard **HM548.S64 2001**
The Sociology of Economic Life. Ed. 2. Trade Paper. Westview Press. Boulder, CO. 2001. 544p. ISBN:0-8133-9764-2, ISBN13: 978-0-8133-9764-1. Dewey:306.3. LCCN:2001-026823.
Audience: **g,u,f.**

Levitt, Steven D. & Dubner, Stephen J. **HB74.P8**
Freakonomics: A Rogue Economist Explores the Hidden Side of Everything. Trade Paper. Penguin Books Canada, Ltd. Toronto, ON. 2006. 256p. ISBN:0-14-101901-8, ISBN13: 978-0-14-101901-7. Dewey:330.
Audience: **g,l,u,f.** *Choice, 2005.*

McCloskey, Deirdre N. **HQ77.8.M39A3 2000**
Crossing: A Memoir. Trade Paper. University of Chicago Press. Chicago, IL. 2000. 282p. ISBN:0-226-55669-7, ISBN13: 978-0-226-55669-7. Dewey:305.9/066.
Audience: **g,l,u,f.** *Choice, 2000.*

McCloskey, Deirdre N. **HB71.M38 1998**
The Rhetoric of Economics. Ed. 2. Trade Paper. University of Wisconsin Press. Chicago, IL. 1998. 248p. Rhetoric of the Human Sciences Ser. ISBN:0-299-15814-4, ISBN13: 978-0-299-15814-9. Dewey:330. LCCN:97-037740.
Audience: **l,u,f.** *Choice, 1998.*

McCloskey, Deirdre N. **HB87.M34 1996**
The Vices of Economists: The Virtues of the Bourgeoisie. Trade Cloth. Amsterdam University Press. Amsterdam, 1997. 135p. ISBN:90-5356-244-3, ISBN13: 978-90-5356-244-4. Dewey:330. LCCN:97-143404.
Audience: **l,u,f.**

Olson, Paulette I. & Emami, Zohren **HB74.8.O45 2002**
Engendering Economics: Conversations with Women Economists in the United States. Paper over Boards. Routledge. New York, NY. 2002. 288p. ISBN:0-415-20555-7, ISBN13: 978-0-415-20555-9. Dewey:330/.082/0973. LCCN:2001-048405.
Audience: **l,u,f.**

O'Rourke, P. J. **PN6231.E295O76 1998**
Eat the Rich: A Treatise on Economics. Trade Cloth. Grove/Atlantic, Inc. New York, NY. 1998. 272p. ISBN:0-87113-719-4, ISBN13: 978-0-87113-719-7. Dewey:330/.02/07. LCCN:98-027100.
Audience: **g,l,u,f.**

Pressman, Steven **HB76.P74 2006**
Fifty Major Economists. Ed. 2. Paper over Boards. Routledge. New York, NY. 2006. XXIII, 329p. ISBN:0-415-36648-8, ISBN13: 978-0-415-36648-9. LCCN:2005-025713.
Audience: **g,l,u,f.**

Pressman, Steven **HB76.P74 1999**
Fifty Major Economists: A Reference Guide. Paper over Boards. Routledge. New York, NY. 1999. 208p. Key Concepts Ser. ISBN:0-415-13480-3, ISBN13: 978-0-415-13480-4. Dewey:330/.092/2 B. LCCN:98-033133.
Audience: **g,l,u,f.**

Roberts, Russell **PS3618.O3159I58 2002**
The Invisible Heart: An Economic Romance. Trade Paper. MIT Press. Cambridge, MA. 2002. 282p. ISBN:0-262-68135-8, ISBN13: 978-0-262-68135-3. Dewey:813/.6. LCCN:00-055402.
Audience: **g,l,u,f.** *Choice, 2001.*

Robinson, Joan **HB171**
Economic Heresies: Some Old-Fashioned Questions in Economic Theory. Paper Text. Basic Books. New York, NY. 1973. 528p. ISBN:0-465-09515-1, ISBN13: 978-0-465-09515-5. Dewey:330. LCCN:71-147012.
Audience: **l,u,f.**

Samuels, Warren J. (Editor) **HB87.N49 1992**
New Horizons in Economic Thought: Appraisals of Leading Economists. Trade Cloth. Edward Elgar Publishing, Inc. Northampton, MA. 1992. 320p. ISBN:1-85278-379-6, ISBN13: 978-1-85278-379-2. Dewey:330.1. LCCN:91-040184.
Audience: **l,u,f.** *Choice, 1993.*

Skousen, Mark & Taylor, Kenna C. **HB171.5**
Puzzles and Paradoxes in Economics. Trade Paper. Edward Elgar Publishing, Inc. Northampton, MA. 1998. 232p. ISBN:1-84064-049-9, ISBN13: 978-1-84064-049-6. Dewey:330. LCCN:96-042202.
Audience: **u,f.**

Sowell, Thomas **HB171.S713 2003**
Basic Economics: A Citizen's Guide to the Economy. Cloth Text. Basic Books. New York, NY. 2003. 448p. ISBN:0-465-08145-2, ISBN13: 978-0-465-08145-5. Dewey:330. LCCN:2003-013778.
Audience: **g,l,u,f.** *Choice, 2004, 2001.*

Stiglitz, Joseph E. & Walsh, Carl E. **HB171.5.S884 2005**
Economics. Ed. 4. Trade Cloth. W. W. Norton & Company, Inc. New York, NY. 2005. 830p. ISBN:0-393-92622-2, ISBN13: 978-0-393-92622-4. Dewey:330. LCCN:2005-055518.
Audience: **g,l,u,f.**

Szenberg, Michael, et al. **HB119.S25**
Paul Samuelson: On Being an Economist. Aron Gottesman & Lall Ramrattan (Authors), Joseph Stiglitz (Foreword by). Book, Other. Jorge Pinto Books. New York, NY. 2005. ISBN:0-9742615-3-X, ISBN13: 978-0-9742615-3-9. Dewey:330.092.
Audience: **g,l,u,f.**

Szenberg, Michael (Editor) **HB76.P37 1998**
Passion and Craft: Economists at Work. Paul Anthony Samuelson (Foreword by). Trade Cloth. University of Michigan Press. Chicago, IL. 1999. 336p. ISBN:0-472-09685-0, ISBN13: 978-0-472-09685-5. Dewey:330/.092/2. LCCN:98-027739.
Audience: **l,u,f.** *Choice, 1999.*

Watts, Michael (Editor, Commentaries by) **PN51**
The Literary Book of Economics. Trade Cloth. ISI Books. Wilmington, DE. 2003. 450p. ISBN:1-932236-02-3, ISBN13: 978-1-932236-02-6. Dewey:808.8/0353. LCCN:2003-102918.
Audience: **g,l,u,f.** *Choice, 2004.*

General Economics > Dictionaries. Handbooks

Aghion, Philippe & Durlauf, Steven N. (Editors) **338.9**
Handbook of Economic Growth. Trade Cloth. Elsevier Science & Technology Books. Saint Louis, MO. 2005. 1138p. Handbooks in Economics Ser., Vol. 1A ISBN:0-444-52041-4, ISBN13: 978-0-444-52041-8. Dewey:338.9.
Audience: **l,u,f.**

Amman, Hans M. (Editor), et al. **HB135.H356 1996**
Handbook of Computational Economics. David A. Kendrick & John Rust (Editors). Trade Cloth. Elsevier Science & Technology Books. Saint Louis, MO. 1996. 832p. Handbooks in Economics Ser., Vol. 1 ISBN:0-444-89857-3, ISBN13: 978-0-444-89857-9. Dewey:330/.01/5195. LCCN:96-012806.
Audience: **u,f.**

Amstrong, M. & Porter, R. H. (Editors) **HD2326**
Handbook of Industrial Organization. Trade Cloth. Elsevier Science & Technology Books. Saint Louis, MO. 2002. Handbooks in Economics Ser., Vol. 3 ISBN:0-444-82435-9, ISBN13: 978-0-444-82435-6. Dewey:338.6.
Audience: **u,f.**

Andreff, Wladimir **GV716.H37 2005**
Handbook on Economics of Sport. Trade Cloth. Edward Elgar Publishing, Inc. Northampton, MA. 2006. 832p. Elgar Original Reference Ser. ISBN:1-84376-608-6, ISBN13: 978-1-84376-608-7. Dewey:338.4/7796. LCCN:2005-050622.
Audience: **l,u,f.**

Annesley, Claire (Editor) **D9**
A Political and Economic Dictionary of Western Europe. Paper over Boards. Routledge. New York, NY. 2005. 344p. Political and Economic Dictionaries Ser. ISBN:1-85743-214-2, ISBN13: 978-1-85743-214-5. Dewey:940.03. LCCN:2005-282392.
Audience: **g,l,u,f.**

Arrow, Kenneth Joseph **HB135**
Handbook of Mathematical Economics, Vol. 1. Ed. 6. Michael D. Intriligator (Editor). Trade Cloth. Elsevier Science & Technology Books. Saint Louis, MO. 1987. 398p. Handbooks in Economics Ser., No. 1 ISBN:0-444-86126-2, ISBN13: 978-0-444-86126-9. Dewey:330/.01/51. LCCN:81-002820.
Audience: **u,f.**

Arrow, Kenneth Joseph **HB135**
Handbook of Mathematical Economics, Set. Michael D. Intriligator (Editor). Trade Cloth. Elsevier. New York, NY. 1986. xvii, 378p. Handbooks in Economics Ser., No. 1 ISBN:0-444-86054-1, ISBN13: 978-0-444-86054-5. Dewey:330/.01/51. LCCN:81-002820.
Audience: **u,f.**

Arrow, Kenneth Joseph & Intriligator, Michael D. (Volume Editors) **HB135**
Handbook of Mathematical Economics, Vol. 3. Ed. 3. Trade Cloth. Elsevier Science & Technology Books. Saint Louis, MO. 1986. 486p. Handbooks in Economics Ser. ISBN:0-444-86128-9, ISBN13: 978-0-444-86128-3. Dewey:330/.01/51.
Audience: **u,f.**

Arrow, Kenneth J. (Editor), et al. **HB846.8.H36 2002**
Handbook of Social Choice and Welfare, Vol. 1. Amartya Sen & K. Suzumura (Editors). Trade Cloth. Elsevier Science & Technology Books. Saint Louis, MO. 2002. 680p. Handbooks in Economics Ser., Bk. 19 ISBN:0-444-82914-8, ISBN13: 978-0-444-82914-6. Dewey:330.12/6. LCCN:2002-072211.
Audience: **u,f.**

Ashenfelter, Orley C. & Card, David (Editors) **HD5706**
Handbook of Labor Economics. Book, Other. Elsevier Science & Technology Books. Saint Louis, MO. 1999. 2674p. Handbooks in Economics Ser. ISBN:0-444-82289-5, ISBN13: 978-0-444-82289-5. Dewey:331.12.
Audience: **u,f.**

Ashenfelter, Orley C. & Card, David (Editors) **HD5706**
Handbook of Labor Economics, Vol. 3. Ed. 2. Trade Cloth. Elsevier Science & Technology Books. Saint Louis, MO. 1999. 956p. Handbooks in Economics Ser. ISBN:0-444-50188-6, ISBN13: 978-0-444-50188-2. Dewey:331.12.
Audience: **u,f.**

Ashenfelter, Orley C. & Card, David (Editors) **HD5706**
Handbook of Labor Economics, Vol. 3A. Ed. 2. Trade Cloth. Elsevier Science & Technology Books. Saint Louis, MO. 1999. 930p. Handbooks in Economics Ser. ISBN:0-444-50187-8, ISBN13: 978-0-444-50187-5. Dewey:331.12.
Audience: **u,f.**

Ashenfelter, Orley C. & Card, David (Editors) **HD5706**
Handbook of Labor Economics, Vol. 3C. Ed. 2. Trade Cloth. Elsevier Science & Technology Books. Saint Louis, MO. 1999. 800p. Handbooks in Economics Ser. ISBN:0-444-50189-4, ISBN13: 978-0-444-50189-9. Dewey:331.12.
Audience: **u,f.**

Atkinson, A. B. & Bourguignon, F. (Editors) **HB523.H358 2000**
Handbook of Income Distribution, Vol. 1. Ed. 2. Trade Cloth. Elsevier Science & Technology Books. Saint Louis, MO. 2000. 938p. Handbooks in Economics Ser. ISBN:0-444-81631-3, ISBN13: 978-0-444-81631-3. Dewey:339.2. LCCN:00-709379.
Audience: **l,u,f.**

Auerbach, Alan J. **HJ141**
Handbook of Public Economics, Vol. 4. M. Feldstein (Editor). Trade Cloth. Elsevier Science & Technology Books. Saint Louis, MO. 2002. 702p. Handbooks in Economics Ser. ISBN:0-444-82315-8, ISBN13: 978-0-444-82315-1. Dewey:336.
Audience: **u,f.**

Auerbach, Alan J. & Feldstein, Martin (Editors) **HC256.6**
Handbook of Public Economics, Vol. 2. Ed. 4. Trade Cloth. Elsevier Science & Technology Books. Saint Louis, MO. 1987. 644p. Handbooks in Economics Ser., II ISBN:0-444-87908-0, ISBN13: 978-0-444-87908-0. Dewey:336. LCCN:85-199148.
Audience: **u,f.**

Auerbach, Alan J. & Feldstein, Martin (Editors) **HJ141.H36 1999**
Handbook of Public Economics, Vol. I. Ed. 4. Trade Cloth. Elsevier Science & Technology Books. Saint Louis, MO. 1985. 502p. Handbooks in Economics Ser. ISBN:0-444-87612-X, ISBN13: 978-0-444-87612-6. Dewey:336. LCCN:99-028028.
Audience: **u,f.**

Auerbach, Alan J. & Feldstein, Martin (Editors) **HJ141.H36 2002**
Handbook of Public Economics. Trade Cloth. Elsevier Science & Technology Books. Saint Louis, MO. 2002. 674p. Handbooks in Economics Ser., Vol. 3 ISBN:0-444-82314-X, ISBN13: 978-0-444-82314-4. Dewey:336. LCCN:99-028028.
Audience: **u,f.**

Auerbach, Alan J. & Feldstein, Martin **HJ141.H36 1985**
Handbook of Public Economics, Vol. 1, June 1985. Trade Cloth. Elsevier. New York, NY. 1988. xvii, 484p. ISBN:0-444-87667-7, ISBN13: 978-0-444-87667-6. Dewey:336. LCCN:85-199148.
Audience: **u,f.**

Aumann, R. J. & Hart, S. R. (Editors) **HB144.H36 1992**
Handbook of Game Theory with Economic Applications, Vol. 1. Ed. 3. Trade Cloth. Elsevier Science & Technology Books. Saint Louis, MO. 1992. 760p. Handbooks in Economics Ser., Vol. 11 ISBN:0-444-88098-4, ISBN13: 978-0-444-88098-7. Dewey:519.3. LCCN:91-038429.
Audience: **u,f.**

Aumann, R. J. & Hart, S. R. (Editors) **HB144 .H36 1992**
Handbook of Game Theory with Economic Applications. Ed. 2. Trade Cloth. Elsevier Science & Technology Books. Saint Louis, MO. 1994. 818p. Handbooks in Economics Ser., Vol. 11 ISBN:0-444-89427-6, ISBN13: 978-0-444-89427-4. Dewey:519.3. LCCN:91-038429.
Audience: **u,f.**

Aumann, Robert J. & Hart, Sergiu (Editors) **QA269**
Handbook of Game Theory with Economic Applications, Vol. 3. Trade Cloth. Elsevier Science & Technology Books. Saint Louis, MO. 2002. 890p. Handbooks in Economics Ser. ISBN:0-444-89428-4, ISBN13: 978-0-444-89428-1. Dewey:519.3.
Audience: **u,f.**

Backhaus, Jurgen G. **K487.E3Z945 2005**
The Elgar Companion to Law and Economics. Ed. 2. Trade Cloth. Edward Elgar Publishing, Inc. Northampton, MA. 2005. 800p. Elgar original Reference Ser. ISBN:1-84542-032-2, ISBN13: 978-1-84542-032-1. Dewey:340/.11. LCCN:2004-048850.
Audience: **g,l,u,f.**

Bastiat, Frederic **HF1713.B3313 1996**
Economic Sophisms. Henry Hazlitt (Introduction by). Trade Paper. Foundation for Economic Education, Inc. Irvington-on-Hudson, NY. 1996. 291p. ISBN:0-910614-14-8, ISBN13: 978-0-910614-14-6. Dewey:343.705/6. LCCN:95-083126.
Audience: **l,u,f.**

Baumol, William J. & Blinder, Alan S. **HB171.5**
Economics: Principles and Policy, 2004 Update. Ed. 9. Cloth Text. Thomson South-Western. Mason, OH. 2004. 816p. ISBN:0-324-20163-X, ISBN13: 978-0-324-20163-5. Dewey:330. LCCN:2004-103711.
Audience: **l,u,f.**

Beaud, Michel & Dostaler, Gilles **HB87.B4313 1997**
Economic Thought since Keynes: A History and Dictionary of Major Economists. Trade Paper. Routledge. New York, NY.

1997. 512p. ISBN:0-415-16454-0, ISBN13: 978-0-415-16454-2. Dewey:330/.0922. LCCN:97-012823.
Audience: **l,u,f.**

Beaud, Michel & Dostaler, Gilles **HB87.B4313 1995**
Economic Thought since Keynes: A History and Dictionary of Major Economists. Trade Cloth. Edward Elgar Publishing, Inc. Northampton, MA. 1995. 512p. ISBN:1-85278-667-1, ISBN13: 978-1-85278-667-0. Dewey:330/.0922. LCCN:93-050629.
Audience: **g,l,u,f.**

Berlin, Howard M. **HG216.B465 2005**
World Monetary Units: An Historical Dictionary, Country by Country. Cloth Text. McFarland & Company, Incorporated Publishers. Jefferson, NC. 2005. 237p. ISBN:0-7864-2080-4, ISBN13: 978-0-7864-2080-3. Dewey:332.4/03. LCCN:2005-025416.
Audience: **g,l,u,f.**

Blaug, Mark **HB76.B55 1998**
Great Economists since Keynes: An Introduction to the Lives and Works of One Hundred Modern Economists. Ed. 2. Trade Cloth. Edward Elgar Publishing, Inc. Northampton, MA. 1998. 328p. ISBN:1-85898-692-3, ISBN13: 978-1-85898-692-0. Dewey:[B]. LCCN:97-037217.
Audience: **l,u,f.**

Chenery, Hollis B. (Editor), et al. **HD82**
Handbook of Development Economics, Vol. 3A. Ed. 2. T. N. Srinivasan & J. R. Behrman (Editors). Trade Cloth. Elsevier Science & Technology Books. Saint Louis, MO. 1995. 766p. Handbooks in Economics Ser. ISBN:0-444-82301-8, ISBN13: 978-0-444-82301-4. Dewey:338.9. LCCN:87-034960.
Audience: **u,f.**

Chenery, Hollis B. (Editor), et al. **HD82**
Handbook of Development Economics, Vol. 3B. Ed. 2. T. N. Srinivasan & J. R. Behrman (Editors). Trade Cloth. Elsevier Science & Technology Books. Saint Louis, MO. 1995. 618p. Handbooks in Economics Ser. ISBN:0-444-82302-6, ISBN13: 978-0-444-82302-1. Dewey:338.9. LCCN:87-034960.
Audience: **u,f.**

Cheshire, P. C. & Mills, E. S. (Editors) **HB171.5**
Handbook of Regional and Urban Economics: Applied Urban Economics. Trade Cloth. Elsevier Science & Technology Books. Saint Louis, MO. 1999. 800p. Handbooks in Economics Ser., III ISBN:0-444-82138-4, ISBN13: 978-0-444-82138-6. Dewey:330.
Audience: **u,f.**

Circa Reference Staff **DJK51**
A Political and Economic Dictionary of Eastern Europe. Ed. 2. Paper over Boards. Routledge. New York, NY. 2005. 500p. ISBN:1-85743-334-3, ISBN13: 978-1-85743-334-0.
Audience: **g,l,u,f.**

Constantinides, G. M. (Editor), et al. **HG173.H345 2003**
Handbook of the Economics of Finance: Corporate Finance. M. Harris & R. M. Stulz (Editors). Trade Cloth. Elsevier Science & Technology Books. Saint Louis, MO. 2003. 654p. Handbooks in Economics Ser., 21 ISBN:0-444-51362-0, ISBN13: 978-0-444-51362-5. Dewey:332. LCCN:2003-063077.
Audience: **u,f.**

Constantinides, G. M. (Editor), et al. **HG173.H345 2003**
Handbook of the Economics of Finance: Financial Markets and Asset Pricing. M. Harris & R. M. Stulz (Editors). Trade Cloth. Elsevier Science & Technology Books. Saint Louis, MO. 2003. 694p. Handbooks in Economics Ser., 21 ISBN:0-444-51363-9, ISBN13: 978-0-444-51363-2. Dewey:332. LCCN:2003-063077.
Audience: **u,f.**

Constantinides, G. M. (Editor), et al. **HG173.H345 2003**
Handbook of the Economics of Finance. M. Harris & Rene M. Stulz (Editors). Trade Cloth. Elsevier Science & Technology Books. Saint Louis, MO. 2003. 1685p. Handbooks in Economics Ser., Bk. 21 ISBN:0-444-50298-X, ISBN13: 978-0-444-50298-8. Dewey:332. LCCN:2003-063077.
Audience: **u,f.**

Culyer, A. J. & Newhouse, J. P. (Editors) **RA410.H255 2000**
Handbook of Health Economics. Trade Cloth. Elsevier Science & Technology Books. Saint Louis, MO. 2000. 1996p. Handbooks in Economics Ser. ISBN:0-444-82290-9, ISBN13: 978-0-444-82290-1. Dewey:338.4/33621. LCCN:2001-275530.
Audience: **u,f.**

Culyer, A. J. & Newhouse, J. P. (Editors) **RA410.H255 2000**
Handbook of Health Economics, Vol. 1A. Ed. 3. Trade Cloth. Elsevier Science & Technology Books. Saint Louis, MO. 2000. 1000p. Handbooks in Economics Ser. ISBN:0-444-50470-2, ISBN13: 978-0-444-50470-8. Dewey:338.4/33621. LCCN:2001-275530.
Audience: **l,u,f.**

Culyer, A. J. & Newhouse, J. P. (Editors) **RA410.H255 2000**
Handbook of Health Economics, Vol. 1B. Ed. 3. Trade Cloth. Elsevier Science & Technology Books. Saint Louis, MO. 2000. 1132p. Handbooks in Economics Ser. ISBN:0-444-50471-0, ISBN13: 978-0-444-50471-5. Dewey:338.4/33621. LCCN:2001-275530.
Audience: **l,u,f.**

Darnell, Adrian C. **HB139**
A Dictionary of Econometrics. Trade Paper. Edward Elgar Publishing, Inc. Northampton, MA. 1996. 480p. ISBN:1-85898-328-2, ISBN13: 978-1-85898-328-8. Dewey:330/.015195/03. LCCN:93-039138.
Audience: **g,l,u,f.** *Choice, 1994.*

Derks, Scott **HB235.U6V35 2004**
The Value of a Dollar: 1860-2004. Ed. 3. Trade Cloth. Grey House Publishing. Millerton, NY. 2004. 600p. ISBN:1-59237-074-8, ISBN13: 978-1-59237-074-0. Dewey:338.5/2/0973. LCCN:2005-270058.
Audience: **g,l,u,f.** *Choice, 2005.*

Derks, Scott & Smith, Tony **HB235.U6**
The Value of a Dollar: 1600-1865. Trade Cloth. Grey House Publishing. Millerton, NY. 2005. 436p. ISBN:1-59237-094-2, ISBN13: 978-1-59237-094-8. Dewey:338.5/2/0973. LCCN:2006-275331.
Audience: **g,l,u,f.** *Choice, 2006.*

Friedman, Benjamin M. & Hahn, F. H. (Editors) **HG221.H24 1990**
Handbook of Monetary Economics, Vol. 1. Ed. 4. Trade Cloth.

Elsevier Science & Technology Books. Saint Louis, MO. 1990. 766p. Handbooks in Economics Ser., No. 8 ISBN:0-444-88025-9, ISBN13: 978-0-444-88025-3. Dewey:332.4. LCCN:90-006983.
Audience: **u,f.**

Friedman, Benjamin M. & Hahn, F. H. (Editors) **HG221.H24 1990**
Handbook of Monetary Economics, Vol. 2. Ed. 4. Trade Cloth. Elsevier Science & Technology Books. Saint Louis, MO. 1999. 620p. Handbooks in Economics Ser., No. 8 ISBN:0-444-88026-7, ISBN13: 978-0-444-88026-0. Dewey:332.4. LCCN:90-006983.
Audience: **u,f.**

Gardner, B. L. & Rausser, G. C. **HD1415.H313**
Handbook of Agricultural Economics, Vol. 1. Trade Cloth. Elsevier Science & Technology Books. Saint Louis, MO. 2001. 1400p. Handbooks in Economics Ser. ISBN:0-444-82588-6, ISBN13: 978-0-444-82588-9. Dewey:338.1. LCCN:2001-032603.
Audience: **u,f.**

Gardner, Bruce L. & Rausser, Gordon C. (Editors) **HD1415.H313**
Handbook of Agricultural Economics, Vol. 2. Trade Cloth. Elsevier Science & Technology Books. Saint Louis, MO. 2002. 1124p. ISBN:0-444-51081-8, ISBN13: 978-0-444-51081-5. Dewey:338.1. LCCN:2001-032603.
Audience: **u,f.**

Gerard-Varet, L.A. (Editor), et al. **HM548**
Handbook of the Economics of Giving, Altruism and Reciprocity: Foundations. Serge-Christophe Kolm & Jean Mercier Ythier (Editors). Trade Cloth. Elsevier Science & Technology Books. Saint Louis, MO. 2006. 948p. Handbooks in Economics Ser. ISBN:0-444-50697-7, ISBN13: 978-0-444-50697-9. Dewey:330.1.
Audience: **u,f.**

Gertler, Mark **HB172.5.N39 2005**
NBER Macroeconomics Annual 2004. Kenneth Rogoff (Editor). Trade Paper. MIT Press. Cambridge, MA. 2005. 432p. NBER Macroeconomics Annual Ser. ISBN:0-262-57229-X, ISBN13: 978-0-262-57229-3. Dewey:339.05.
Audience: **l,u,f.**

Greenwald, Douglas (Editor) **HB61.E55 1994**
The McGraw-Hill Encyclopedia of Economics. Ed. 2. Trade Cloth. McGraw-Hill Companies, The. New York, NY. 1993. 1120p. ISBN:0-07-024410-3, ISBN13: 978-0-07-024410-8. Dewey:330/.03. LCCN:93-009805.
Audience: **g,l,u,f.** *Choice, 1994.*

Griliches, Zvi & Intriligator, Michael D. (Editors) **HB139**
Handbook of Econometrics, Vol. 2. Ed. 6. Trade Cloth. Elsevier Science & Technology Books. Saint Louis, MO. 1987. 716p. Handbooks in Economics Ser. ISBN:0-444-86186-6, ISBN13: 978-0-444-86186-3. Dewey:330.015195. LCCN:83-002396.
Audience: **g,l,u,f.**

Grossman, G. M. & Rogoff, K. (Editors) **HF1359**
Handbook of International Economics, Vol. 3. Ed. 2. Trade Cloth. Elsevier Science & Technology Books. Saint Louis, MO. 1995. 898p. Handbooks in Economics Ser., Vol. 3 ISBN:0-444-81547-3, ISBN13: 978-0-444-81547-7. Dewey:337.
Audience: **u,f.**

Grossman, Gene M. & Rogoff, Kenneth S. (Editors) **HF1411.H257 1997**
Handbook of International Economics, Vol. 3. Ed. 3. Trade Cloth. Elsevier Science & Technology Books. Saint Louis, MO. 1997. 900p. Handbooks in Economics Ser. ISBN:0-444-82864-8, ISBN13: 978-0-444-82864-4. Dewey:337. LCCN:97-038457.
Audience: **u,f.**

Gwartney, James D. **HB95 .G89**
Economic Freedom of the World, 2005. Trade Paper. Cato Institute. Washington, DC. 2005. 220p. ISBN:1-930865-77-5, ISBN13: 978-1-930865-77-8. Dewey:330.122.
Audience: **g,l,u,f.**

Hartley, Keith & Sandler, Todd (Editors) **HB195.H26 1995**
Handbook of Defense Economics, Vol. 1. Trade Cloth. Elsevier Science & Technology Books. Saint Louis, MO. 1995. 626p. Handbooks in Economics Ser., Vol. 12 ISBN:0-444-81887-1, ISBN13: 978-0-444-81887-4. Dewey:338.4/7355. LCCN:95-040584.
Audience: **u,f.**

Heckman, J. J. & Leamer, E. E. (Editors) **HB139**
Handbook of Econometrics, Vol. 6. Trade Cloth. Elsevier. New York, NY. 2001. Handbooks in Economics Ser. ISBN:0-444-50631-4, ISBN13: 978-0-444-50631-3. Dewey:330/.015195.
Audience: **u,f.**

Heckman, J. J. & Leamer, E. E. (Editors) **HB139**
Handbook of Econometrics, Vol. 5. Trade Cloth. Elsevier Science & Technology Books. Saint Louis, MO. 2001. 740p. Handbooks in Economics Ser., Vol. V ISBN:0-444-82340-9, ISBN13: 978-0-444-82340-3. Dewey:330/.015195.
Audience: **l,u,f.**

Henderson, V. & Thisse, J. F. (Editors) **HB171.5**
Handbook of Regional and Urban Economics: Cities and Geography, Vol. 4. Trade Cloth. Elsevier Science & Technology Books. Saint Louis, MO. 2004. 1082p. Handbooks in Economics Ser. ISBN:0-444-50967-4, ISBN13: 978-0-444-50967-3. Dewey:330.
Audience: **u,f.**

Hildenbrand, W. & Sonnenschein, H. (Editors) **HB135**
Handbook of Mathematical Economics, Vol. 4. Trade Cloth. Elsevier Science & Technology Books. Saint Louis, MO. 1991. 754p. Handbooks in Economics Ser. ISBN:0-444-87461-5, ISBN13: 978-0-444-87461-0. Dewey:330.1543.
Audience: **u,f.**

Hoare, Jim & Pares, Susan (Editors) **D518.1**
A Political and Economic Dictionary of East Asia. Paper over Boards. Routledge. New York, NY. 2005. 336p. The Europa Political and Economic Dictionaries Ser. ISBN:1-85743-258-4,

ISBN13: 978-1-85743-258-9. Dewey:950.03. LCCN:2005-281339.

Audience: **g,l,u,f.**

Jones, Derek C. (Editor) **HC79.T4**
New Economy Handbook. Trade Cloth. Elsevier Science & Technology Books. Saint Louis, MO. 2003. 1118p. ISBN:0-12-389172-8, ISBN13: 978-0-12-389172-3. Dewey:330.9/049. LCCN:2003-107468.

Audience: **l,u,f.**

Jones, Ronald W. & Kenen, Peter B. (Editors) **HF1411**
Handbook of International Economics: International Trade. Ed. 5. Trade Cloth. Elsevier Science & Technology Books. Saint Louis, MO. 1988. 646p. Sub-Series of Handbooks in Economics ISBN:0-444-86792-9, ISBN13: 978-0-444-86792-6. Dewey:337.

Audience: **u,f.**

Jones, Ronald W. & Kenen, Peter B. (Editors) **HF1411 .H257**
Handbook of International Economics: International Monetary Economics and Finance. Ed. 3. Trade Paper. Elsevier Science & Technology Books. Saint Louis, MO. 1988. 636p. Handbooks in Economics Ser., No. 3 ISBN:0-444-70421-3, ISBN13: 978-0-444-70421-4. Dewey:337.

Audience: **u,f.**

Jones, Ronald W. & Kenen, Peter B. (Editors) **HF1359**
Handbook of International Economics: International Trade. Ed. 3. Trade Paper. Elsevier Science & Technology Books. Saint Louis, MO. 1988. 646p. Handbooks in Economics Ser., No. 3 ISBN:0-444-70422-1, ISBN13: 978-0-444-70422-1. Dewey:337.

Audience: **u,f.**

Jones, Ronald W. & Kenen, Peter B. (Editors) **HF1411**
Handbook of International Economics: International Monetary Economics and Finance. Ed. 5. Trade Cloth. Elsevier Science & Technology Books. Saint Louis, MO. 1988. 635p. Sub-Series of Handbooks in Economics ISBN:0-444-86793-7, ISBN13: 978-0-444-86793-3. Dewey:337.

Audience: **u,f.**

Judd, Kenneth L. & Tesfatsion, Leigh (Editors) **HB135**
Handbook of Computational Economics: Agent-Based Computational Economics. Trade Cloth. Elsevier Science & Technology Books. Saint Louis, MO. 2006. 904p. ISBN:0-444-51253-5, ISBN13: 978-0-444-51253-6. Dewey:330.015195.

Audience: **u,f.**

Kaish, Stanley (Editor), et al. **HB74.P8H36 1986**
Handbook of Behavioral Economics: Behavioral Decision Making, Vol. 1, Pt. A: Behavioral Microeconomics. Benjamin Gilad, Roger Frantz, Harinder Singh & James A. Gerber (Editors). Trade Cloth. Elsevier Science & Technology Books. Saint Louis, MO. 1999. 376p. ISBN:0-89232-700-6, ISBN13: 978-0-89232-700-3. Dewey:330/01/9. LCCN:86-010315.

Audience: **u,f.**

Khan, Muhammad Akram **HB61.K46 2003**
Islamic Economics and Finance: A Glossary. Ed. 2. Paper over Boards. Routledge. New York, NY. 2003. 208p. Routledge International Studies in Money and Banking, Vol. 23 ISBN:0-415-31888-2, ISBN13: 978-0-415-31888-4. Dewey:330/.03. LCCN:2002-037125.

Audience: **g,l,u,f.**

Kneese, Allen V. & Sweeney, J. L. (Editors) **HD9502.A2 H257**
Handbook of Natural Resource and Energy, Vol. 3. Trade Cloth. Elsevier Science & Technology Books. Saint Louis, MO. 1993. 630p. Handbooks in Economics Ser., Vol. 6 ISBN:0-444-87800-9, ISBN13: 978-0-444-87800-7. Dewey:333.7. LCCN:85-010322.

Audience: **u,f.**

Kneese, Allen V. & Sweeney, J. L. (Editors) **HC59**
Handbook of Natural Resource and Energy Economics, Vol. 1. Ed. 3. Trade Cloth. Elsevier Science & Technology Books. Saint Louis, MO. 1985. 486p. Handbooks in Economics Ser. ISBN:0-444-87644-8, ISBN13: 978-0-444-87644-7. Dewey:333.7. LCCN:85-019322.

Audience: **u,f.**

Kneese, Allen V. & Sweeney, J. L. (Editors) **HC79.E5**
Handbook of Natural Resource and Energy Economics: Handbooks in Economics, Six, 2. Trade Cloth. Elsevier Science & Technology Books. Saint Louis, MO. 1985. ISBN:0-685-09922-9, ISBN13: 978-0-685-09922-3. Dewey:333.7.

Audience: **u,f.**

Kneese, Allen V. & Sweeney, J. L. (Editors) **HD9502.A2H257 1985**
Handbook of Natural Resource and Energy Economics: Handbooks in Economics, Six, Set. Trade Cloth. Elsevier Science & Technology Books. Saint Louis, MO. 1985. xxiii, 462p. ISBN:0-444-87646-4, ISBN13: 978-0-444-87646-1. Dewey:333.7. LCCN:85-010322.

Audience: **u,f.**

Kneese, Allen V. & Sweeney, J. L. (Editors) **HC59**
Handbook of Natural Resource and Energy Economics, Vol. 2. Ed. 2. Trade Cloth. Elsevier Science & Technology Books. Saint Louis, MO. 1985. 308p. Handbooks in Economics Ser., Vol. 6 ISBN:0-444-87645-6, ISBN13: 978-0-444-87645-4. Dewey:333.7. LCCN:85-010322.

Audience: **u,f.**

Kolm, Serge-Christophe & Mercier Ythier, Jean (Editors) **HB171**
Handbook of the Economics of Giving, Altruism and Reciprocity: Applications. Trade Cloth. Elsevier Science & Technology Books. Saint Louis, MO. 2006. 752p. ISBN:0-444-52145-3, ISBN13: 978-0-444-52145-3. Dewey:330.1.

Audience: **u,f.**

Majumdar, Sumit (Editor), et al. **HE7631**
Handbook of Telecommunications Economics: Technology Evolution and the Internet. Ingo Vogelsang & Martin Cave (Editors). Trade Cloth. Elsevier Science & Technology Books. Saint Louis, MO. 2006. 684p. Handbook of Telecommunications Economics Ser. ISBN:0-444-51423-6, ISBN13: 978-0-444-51423-3. Dewey:384.

Audience: **u,f.**

McCann, Charles R. (Editor) **HB71**
The Elgar Dictionary of Economic Quotations. Trade Cloth. Edward Elgar Publishing, Inc. Northampton, MA. 2004. 328p. ISBN:1-84064-820-1, ISBN13: 978-1-84064-820-1. Dewey:330. LCCN:2003-049103.
Audience: **g,l,u,f.** *Choice, 2004.*

Mills, E. S. (Editor) **HT391**
Handbook of Regional and Urban Economics: Urban Economics. Ed. 3. Trade Cloth. Elsevier Science & Technology Books. Saint Louis, MO. 1987. 638p. Handbooks in Economics Ser. ISBN:0-444-87970-6, ISBN13: 978-0-444-87970-7. Dewey:330.9173/2.
Audience: **u,f.**

Mitra, Subrata (Editor) **DS341**
A Political and Economic Dictionary of South Asia. Paper over Boards. Routledge. New York, NY. 2005. 464p. ISBN:1-85743-210-X, ISBN13: 978-1-85743-210-7. Dewey:954.003.
Audience: **g,l,u,f.**

Mäler, Karl-Göran & Vincent, Jeffrey R. (Editors) **HC79.E5**
Handbook of Environmental Economics: Economywide and International Environmental Issues. Trade Cloth. Elsevier Science & Technology Books. Saint Louis, MO. 2005. 556p. ISBN:0-444-51146-6, ISBN13: 978-0-444-51146-1. Dewey:333.7.
Audience: **u,f.**

Mäler, Karl-Göran & Vincent, Jeffrey R. (Editors) **HC79.E5**
Handbook of Environmental Economics: Valuing Environmental Changes. Audio, Other. Elsevier Science & Technology Books. Saint Louis, MO. 2005. 642p. ISBN:0-444-51145-8, ISBN13: 978-0-444-51145-4. Dewey:333.7.
Audience: **u,f.**

Newman, Peter (Editor) **HB61**
The New Palgrave Dictionary of Economics and the Law. Cloth over Boards. Palgrave Macmillan. New York, NY. 1998. 2210p. ISBN:1-56159-215-3, ISBN13: 978-1-56159-215-9. Dewey:330/.03.
Audience: **g,l,u,f.** *Choice, 1999.*

Nijkamp, Peter (Editor) **HT321**
Handbook of Urban and Regional Economics. Ed. 3. Trade Cloth. Elsevier Science & Technology Books. Saint Louis, MO. 1987. 728p. Handbooks in Economics Ser., No. 7 ISBN:0-444-87969-2, ISBN13: 978-0-444-87969-1. Dewey:330.9173/2. LCCN:86-016538.
Audience: **u,f.**

Nijkamp, Peter & Mills, E. S. **HT321**
Handbook of Regional and Urban Economics: Volumes One and Two. Trade Cloth. Elsevier. New York, NY. 1987. xxiii, 1323p. ISBN:0-444-87971-4, ISBN13: 978-0-444-87971-4. Dewey:330. LCCN:86-016538.
Audience: **u,f.**

Pesaran, M. Hashem & Schmidt, Peter (Editors) **HB172**
Handbook of Applied Econometrics: Microeconomics. Trade Paper. Blackwell Publishing, Inc. Malden, MA. 1999. 464p. Handbooks in Economics Ser. ISBN:0-631-21633-2, ISBN13: 978-0-631-21633-9. Dewey:338.5/015195.
Audience: **l,u,f.**

Rosenzweig, M. R. & Stark, O. (Editors) **HB849.41.H36 1997**
Handbook of Population and Family Economics, Vol. IB. Ed. 2. Trade Cloth. Elsevier Science & Technology Books. Saint Louis, MO. 1997. 707p. Handbooks in Economics Ser., Vol. 14 ISBN:0-444-82646-7, ISBN13: 978-0-444-82646-6. Dewey:304.6. LCCN:98-201816.
Audience: **u,f.**

Rosenzweig, M. R. & Stark, O. (Editors) **HB849.41.H36 1997**
Handbook of Population and Family Economics, Vols. 1A & 1B. Book, Other. Elsevier Science & Technology Books. Saint Louis, MO. 1997. 1422p. Handbooks in Economics Ser., Vol. 14 ISBN:0-444-89647-3, ISBN13: 978-0-444-89647-6. Dewey:304.6. LCCN:98-201816.
Audience: **u,f.**

Rosenzweig, M. R. & Stark, O. (Editors) **HB849.41.H36 1997**
Handbook of Population and Family Economics, Vol. IA. Ed. 2. Trade Cloth. Elsevier Science & Technology Books. Saint Louis, MO. 1997. 708p. Handbooks in Economics Ser., Vol. 14 ISBN:0-444-82645-9, ISBN13: 978-0-444-82645-9. Dewey:304.6. LCCN:98-201816.
Audience: **u,f.**

Rutherford, Donald **HB61.R92 2002**
Dictionary of Economics. Ed. 2. Paper over Boards. Routledge. New York, NY. 2002. 704p. ISBN:0-415-25090-0, ISBN13: 978-0-415-25090-0. Dewey:330/.03. LCCN:2002-069946.
Audience: **g,l,u,f.**

Schmalensee, Richard & Willig, Robert D. (Editors) **HD2326.H28 1989**
Handbook of Industrial Organization, Vol. 1. Trade Cloth. Elsevier Science & Technology Books. Saint Louis, MO. 1989. 986p. Handbooks in Economics Ser., No. 10 ISBN:0-444-70434-5, ISBN13: 978-0-444-70434-4. Dewey:338.6. LCCN:88-025138.
Audience: **u,f.** *Choice, 1990.*

Schmalensee, Richard & Willig, Robert D. (Editors) **HD2326.H28 1989**
Handbook of Industrial Organization, Vol. 2. Ed. 6. Trade Cloth. Elsevier Science & Technology Books. Saint Louis, MO. 1989. 632p. Handbooks in Economics Ser., No. 10 ISBN:0-444-70435-3, ISBN13: 978-0-444-70435-1. Dewey:338.6. LCCN:88-025138.
Audience: **u,f.** *Choice, 1990.*

Schmalensee, Richard & Willig, Robert D. (Editors) **HD2326.H28 1989**
Handbook of Industrial Organization, Set, Vols. 1 & 2. Trade Cloth. Elsevier. New York, NY. 1989. Handbooks in Economics Ser., No. 10 ISBN:0-444-70436-1, ISBN13: 978-0-444-70436-8. Dewey:338.6. LCCN:88-025138.
Audience: **u,f.** *Choice, 1990.*

Seddon, David & Zeilig, Leo (Editors) **DT31**
A Political and Economic Dictionary of Africa. Paper over Boards. Routledge. New York, NY. 2005. 536p. Political and Economic Dictionaries Ser. ISBN:1-85743-213-4, ISBN13: 978-1-85743-213-8. Dewey:960.03. LCCN:2006-365944.
Audience: **g,l,u,f.**

Segura, Julio **HB61.E66 2004**
Ebook: An Eponymous Dictionary of Economics: A Guide to Laws and Theorems Named after Economists. Carlos Rodriguez Braun (Editor). E-Book. Edward Elgar Publishing, Inc. Northampton, MA. 2005. 384p. ISBN:1-84542-360-7, ISBN13: 978-1-84542-360-5. Dewey:330/.03.
Audience: **g,l,u,f.**

Srinivasan, T. N. (Editor), et al. **HF1025**
Handbook of Development Economics, Vols. 3A & 3B. J. R. Behrman & Hollis B. Chenery (Editors). Trade Cloth. Elsevier Science & Technology Books. Saint Louis, MO. 1995. 1376p. Handbooks in Economics Ser. ISBN:0-444-88481-5, ISBN13: 978-0-444-88481-7. Dewey:330.9. LCCN:87-034960.
Audience: **u,f.**

Taylor, J. B. & Woodford, Michael (Editors) **HB172.5.H356 1999**
Handbook of Macroeconomics, Vol. 15. Ed. 2. Trade Cloth. Elsevier Science & Technology Books. Saint Louis, MO. 1999. 810p. Handbooks in Economics Ser. ISBN:0-444-50156-8, ISBN13: 978-0-444-50156-1. Dewey:339. LCCN:00-701196.
Audience: **u,f.**

Taylor, J. B. & Woodford, Michael (Editors) **HB172.5.H356 1999**
Handbook of Macroeconomics, Vol. 1B. Ed. 2. Trade Cloth. Elsevier Science & Technology Books. Saint Louis, MO. 1999. 562p. Handbooks in Economics Ser. ISBN:0-444-50157-6, ISBN13: 978-0-444-50157-8. Dewey:339. LCCN:00-701196.
Audience: **u,f.**

Taylor, J. B. & Woodford, Michael (Editors) **HB172.5.H356 1999**
Handbook of Macroeconomics. Trade Cloth. Elsevier Science & Technology Books. Saint Louis, MO. 1999. 1960p. Handbooks in Economics Ser. ISBN:0-444-82528-2, ISBN13: 978-0-444-82528-5. Dewey:339. LCCN:00-701196.
Audience: **u,f.**

Taylor, J. B. & Woodford, Michael (Editors) **HB172.5.H356 1999**
Handbook of Macroeconomics, Vol. 15. Trade Cloth. Elsevier Science & Technology Books. Saint Louis, MO. 1999. 588p. Handbooks in Economics Ser. ISBN:0-444-50158-4, ISBN13: 978-0-444-50158-5. Dewey:339. LCCN:00-701196.
Audience: **u,f.**

Vincent, Jeffrey R. & Mäler, Karl-Göran (Editors) **HC79.E5**
Handbook of Environmental Economics: Environmental Degradation and Institutional Responses. Trade Cloth. Elsevier Science & Technology Books. Saint Louis, MO. 2003. 572p. Handbooks in Economics Ser. ISBN:0-444-50063-4, ISBN13: 978-0-444-50063-2. Dewey:333.7. LCCN:2003-043913.
Audience: **u,f.**

Zenios, S. A. & Ziemba, W. T. (Editors) **HG1615.25**
Handbook of Asset and Liability Management: Theory and Methodology. Trade Cloth. Elsevier Science & Technology Books. Saint Louis, MO. 2006. 508p. ISBN:0-444-50875-9, ISBN13: 978-0-444-50875-1. Dewey:332.10681.
Audience: **u,f.**

General Economics > Encyclopedias

Cate, Thomas (Editor), et al. **HB99.7.E528 1997**
An Encyclopedia of Keynesian Economics. Geoff Harcourt & David C. Colander (Editors). Trade Cloth. Edward Elgar Publishing, Inc. Northampton, MA. 1997. 672p. ISBN:1-85898-145-X, ISBN13: 978-1-85898-145-1. Dewey:330.15/6/03. LCCN:96-023171.
Audience: **g,l,u,f.** *Choice, 1998.*

Eatwell, John (Editor), et al. **HB61**
The New Palgrave: A Dictionary of Economics. Murray Milgate & Peter Newman (Editors). Trade Cloth. Pan Macmillan. London, 1987. 3200p. ISBN:0-333-37235-2, ISBN13: 978-0-333-37235-7. Dewey:330.0321. LCCN:87-001946.
Audience: **g,l,u,f.**

Forsyth, Tim (Editor) **HD82.E547 2005**
Encyclopedia of International Development. Paper over Boards. Routledge. New York, NY. 2004. 856p. ISBN:0-415-25342-X, ISBN13: 978-0-415-25342-0. Dewey:338.9/003. LCCN:2004-050985.
Audience: **g,l,u,f.** *Choice, 2005.*

Johansen, Bruce E. (Editor) **E98**
The Encyclopedia of Native American Economic History. Cloth Text. Greenwood Publishing Group, Inc. Portsmouth, NH. 1999. 320p. ISBN:0-313-30623-0, ISBN13: 978-0-313-30623-5. Dewey:330.973/008997. LCCN:98-025733.
Audience: **g,l,u,f.** *Choice, 1999.*

Jones, R. J. Barry **HF1359.R68 2001**
Ebook: Routledge Encyclopedia of International Political Economy. E-Book. Routledge. New York, NY. 2001. ISBN:0-203-44016-1, ISBN13: 978-0-203-44016-2. Dewey:337/.03.
Audience: **g,l,u,f.** *Choice, 2001.*

Mokyr, Joel (Editor) **HC15**
The Oxford Encyclopedia of Economic History, Set. Trade Cloth. Oxford University Press, Inc. New York, NY. 2003. 2806p. ISBN:0-19-510507-9, ISBN13: 978-0-19-510507-0. Dewey:330/.03. LCCN:2003-008992.
Audience: **g,l,u,f.** *Choice, 2004.*

O'Connor, David E. **HF1359O28 2006**
Encyclopedia of the Global Economy: A Guide for Students and Researchers. Trade Cloth. Greenwood Publishing Group, Inc. Portsmouth, NH. 2005. ISBN:0-313-33585-0, ISBN13: 978-0-313-33585-3. Dewey:330.03. LCCN:2005-025481.
Audience: **g,l,u,f.**

O'Hara, Phillip Anthony **HB61.E554 2001**
Encyclopedia of Political Economy. Trade Paper. Routledge. New York, NY. 2001. ISBN:0-415-24187-1, ISBN13: 978-0-415-24187-8. Dewey:330/.03. LCCN:00-042491.
Audience: **g,l,u,f.**

Rowley, Charles Kershaw & Schneider, Friedrich (Editors) **H41.E57 2003**
Encyclopedia of Public Choice. Trade Cloth. Springer. New York, NY. 2004. 1000p. ISBN:0-7923-8607-8, ISBN13: 978-0-7923-8607-0. Dewey:320/.6/03. LCCN:2003-046109.
Audience: **l,u,f.** *Choice, 2004.*

Snowdon, Brian & Vane, Howard R. **HB1725**
An Encyclopedia of Macroeconomics. Trade Paper. Edward Elgar Publishing, Inc. Northampton, MA. 2005. 752p. Elgar

Original Reference Ser. ISBN:1-84542-180-9, ISBN13: 978-1-84542-180-9. Dewey:339.
Audience: **g,l,u,f.** *Choice, 2003.*

Snowdon, Brian & Vane, Howard R. (Editors) **HB172.5.E55 2003**
An Encyclopedia of Macroeconomics. Trade Cloth. Edward Elgar Publishing, Inc. Northampton, MA. 2003. 752p. ISBN:1-84064-387-0, ISBN13: 978-1-84064-387-9. Dewey:339. LCCN:2002-026392.
Audience: **g,l,u,f.** *Choice, 2003.*

Zafirovski, Milan **HM548**
International Encyclopedia of Economic Sociology. Jens Beckert (Editor). Paper over Boards. Routledge. New York, NY. 2005. XXII, 778p. ISBN:0-415-28673-5, ISBN13: 978-0-415-28673-2. Dewey:306.3.
Audience: **g,l,u,f.**

General Economics > Biographical

Arestis, Philip & Sawyer, Malcolm C. (Editors) **HB76.B5 2000**
A Biographical Dictionary of Dissenting Economists. Ed. 2. Trade Cloth. Edward Elgar Publishing, Inc. Northampton, MA. 2001. 736p. ISBN:1-85898-560-9, ISBN13: 978-1-85898-560-2. Dewey:330/.092/2 B. LCCN:00-034824.
Audience: **g,l,u,f.** *Choice, 2001, 1993.*

Blaug, Mark & Vane, Howard R. (Editors) **HB75**
Who's Who in Economics. Ed. 4. Trade Cloth. Edward Elgar Publishing, Inc. Northampton, MA. 2003. 1,000p. ISBN:1-84064-992-5, ISBN13: 978-1-84064-992-5. Dewey:330/.092/2 B. LCCN:2003-276034.
Audience: **g,l,u,f.** *Choice, 2000.*

Cicarelli, James & Cicarelli, Julianne **HB76**
Distinguished Women Economists. Cloth Text. Greenwood Publishing Group, Inc. Portsmouth, NH. 2003. 272p. ISBN:0-313-30331-2, ISBN13: 978-0-313-30331-9. Dewey:330/.092/2. LCCN:2003-049136.
Audience: **g,l,u,f.** *Choice, 2004.*

Dimand, Robert W. (Editor), et al. **HB76.B535 2000**
A Biographical Dictionary of Women Economists. Mary Ann Dimand & Evelyn L. Forget (Editors). Trade Cloth. Edward Elgar Publishing, Inc. Northampton, MA. 2000. 520p. ISBN:1-85278-964-6, ISBN13: 978-1-85278-964-0. Dewey:330/.0922. LCCN:00-028842.
Audience: **l,u,f.** *Choice, 2001.*

Dimand, Robert W., et al. **HB76**
A Biographical Dictionary of Women Economists. Mary Ann Dimand & Evelyn L. Forget (Authors). Trade Paper. Edward Elgar Publishing, Inc. Northampton, MA. 2004. 520p. Elgar Original Reference Ser. ISBN:1-84376-902-6, ISBN13: 978-1-84376-902-6. Dewey:330/.0922.
Audience: **g,l,u,f.** *Choice, 2001.*

Fawcett, Millicent **JN979 .F26**
What I Remember. Trade Paper. University Press of the Pacific. Miami, FL. 2004. 284p. ISBN:1-4102-1170-3, ISBN13: 978-1-4102-1170-5. Dewey:324/.3/0924.
Audience: **l,u,f.**

Froelich, Paul **HX0276.L86F7**
Rosa Luxemburg: Her Life and Work. Johanna Hoornweg (Translator). Trade Paper. Books on Demand. Ann Arbor, MI. 352p. ISBN:0-8357-3521-4, ISBN13: 978-0-8357-3521-6. Dewey:335.430924. LCCN:72-081776.
Audience: **u,f.**

Galbraith, John Kenneth **HB119.G33A3 2004**
Interviews with John Kenneth Galbraith. J. Ron Stanfield & Jacqueline Bloom Stanfield (Editors). Trade Cloth. University Press of Mississippi. Jackson, MS. 2004. xxi, 247p. Conversations with Public Intellectuals Ser. ISBN:1-57806-610-7, ISBN13: 978-1-57806-610-0. Dewey:330/.092. LCCN:2003-060093.
Audience: **g,l,u,f.**

Heertje, Arnold (Editor) **HB72**
The Makers of Modern Economics, Vol. 4. Trade Cloth. Edward Elgar Publishing, Inc. Northampton, MA. 1999. 192p. ISBN:1-85898-787-3, ISBN13: 978-1-85898-787-3. Dewey:330/.01. LCCN:92-029859.
Audience: **g,l,u,f.**

Heertje, Arnold **HB72**
The Makers of Modern Economics. Paper Text. Prentice Hall PTR. Upper Saddle River, NJ. 1994. 208p. ISBN:0-13-302233-1, ISBN13: 978-0-13-302233-9. Dewey:330/.01.
Audience: **g,l,u,f.**

Heertje, Arnold (Editor) **HB72**
The Makers of Modern Economics, Vol. 3. F. M. Fisher, C. Freeman, P. Groenewegen, K. Lancaster, M. Shubik & G. Tullock (Contribution by). Trade Cloth. Edward Elgar Publishing, Inc. Northampton, MA. 1997. 160p. ISBN:1-85898-546-3, ISBN13: 978-1-85898-546-6. Dewey:330/.01.
Audience: **g,l,u,f.**

Keynes, John Maynard **DA574.A1**
Essays in Biography, Vol. 10. Donald E. Moggridge (Editor). Cloth Text. Cambridge University Press. New York, NY. 1978. 472p. The Collected Writings of John Maynard Keynes Ser. ISBN:0-521-22102-1, ISBN13: 978-0-521-22102-3. Dewey:920.042.
Audience: **l,u,f.**

Martineau, Harriet **PR4984.M5Z5**
Harriet Martineau's Autobiography, Vol. 2. Ed. 3. Trade Paper. Books on Demand. Ann Arbor, MI. 518p. ISBN:0-598-01207-9, ISBN13: 978-0-598-01207-4. Dewey:823/.8.
Audience: **u,f.**

McKenzie, Norman & McKenzie, Jeanne (Editors) **HX244.7.W42A33 2000**
The Diaries of Beatrice Webb. Lynn Knight (Abridged by), Hermoine Lee (Preface by). Cloth Text. Northeastern University Press. Boston, MA. 2001. xxv, 630p. ISBN:1-55553-483-X, ISBN13: 978-1-55553-483-7. Dewey:335/.14/092 B. LCCN:2001-022252.
Audience: **u,f.**

Nettl, J. P. **HX273.L83.N4 1969**
Rosa Luxemburg. Trade Cloth. Oxford University Press, Inc. New York, NY. 1969. xvii, 557p. ISBN:0-19-281040-5, ISBN13: 978-0-19-281040-3. Dewey:335.43/092/4 B. LCCN:76-463973.
Audience: **u,f.**

Polkinghorn, Bette & Thomson, Dorothy L. **HB76.P65 1999**
Adam Smith's Daughters: Eight Prominent Women Economists from the Eighteenth Century to the Present. Trade Cloth. Edward Elgar Publishing, Inc. Northampton, MA. 1999. 144p. ISBN:1-85898-084-4, ISBN13: 978-1-85898-084-3. Dewey:330/.092/2 B. LCCN:98-022239.
Audience: **l,u,f.**

General Methodology

Abell, Peter (Editor) **HM24.R34 1991**
Rational Choice Theory. Cloth Text. Edward Elgar Publishing, Inc. Northampton, MA. 1991. 432p. Schools of Thought in Sociology Ser., No. 8 ISBN:1-85278-321-4, ISBN13: 978-1-85278-321-1. Dewey:301/.01. LCCN:91-009912.
Audience: **u,f.**

Aghion, Philippe & Durlauf, Steven N. (Editors) **338.9**
Handbook of Economic Growth. Trade Cloth. Elsevier Science & Technology Books. Saint Louis, MO. 2005. 1138p. Handbooks in Economics Ser., Vol. 1A ISBN:0-444-52041-4, ISBN13: 978-0-444-52041-8. Dewey:338.9.
Audience: **l,u,f.**

Akerlof, George A. **HB71 .A34 1984**
An Economic Theorist's Book of Tales: Essays That Entertain the Consequences of New Assumptions in Economic Theory. Trade Cloth. Cambridge University Press. New York, NY. 1984. 206p. ISBN:0-521-26323-9, ISBN13: 978-0-521-26323-8. Dewey:330.1. LCCN:84-003225.
Audience: **g,l,u,f.**

Backhouse, Roger **HB87 .B23**
A History of Modern Economic Analysis. Trade Paper. Blackwell Publishing, Inc. Malden, MA. 1997. 536p. ISBN:0-631-18745-6, ISBN13: 978-0-631-18745-5. Dewey:330/.09.
Audience: **l,u,f.**

Bentham, Jeremy **HB539 .B5**
Defence of Usury. Trade Paper. Kessinger Publishing, LLC. Whitefish, MT. 2004. ISBN:1-4192-1550-7, ISBN13: 978-1-4192-1550-6. Dewey:332.8/3.
Audience: **u,f.**

Biddle, J. E. (Editor), et al. **HB75**
Research in the History of Economic Thought and Methodology, Vol. 23, Set. R. B. Emmett & W. J. Samuels (Editors). Trade Cloth. Elsevier Science & Technology Books. Saint Louis, MO. 2005. 350p. ISBN:0-7623-1171-1, ISBN13: 978-0-7623-1171-2. Dewey:330/.09.
Audience: **l,u,f.**

Blaug, Mark **HB75 .B664 1997**
Economic Theory in Retrospect. Ed. 5. Cloth Text. Cambridge University Press. New York, NY. 1997. 751p. ISBN:0-521-57153-7, ISBN13: 978-0-521-57153-1. Dewey:330/.01/09. LCCN:95-026743.
Audience: **g,l,u,f.**

Blaug, Mark **HB76.B55 1998**
Great Economists since Keynes: An Introduction to the Lives and Works of One Hundred Modern Economists. Ed. 2. Trade Cloth. Edward Elgar Publishing, Inc. Northampton, MA. 1998. 328p. ISBN:1-85898-692-3, ISBN13: 978-1-85898-692-0. Dewey:[B]. LCCN:97-037217.
Audience: **l,u,f.**

Blaug, Mark (Editor) **HB119.V4**
Irving Fisher (1867-1947), Arthur Hadley (1856-1930), Ragnar Frisch (1895-1973), Friedrich von Hayek (1899-1992), Allyn Young (1876-1929), Ugo Mazzola (1863-1899). Trade Cloth. Edward Elgar Publishing, Inc. Northampton, MA. 1992. 242p. Pioneers in Economics Ser., Vol. 41 ISBN:1-85278-505-5, ISBN13: 978-1-85278-505-5. Dewey:330.092.
Audience: **u,f.**

Blaug, Mark **HB131 .B56 1992**
The Methodology of Economics: Or, How Economists Explain. Ed. 2. John Pencavel (Contribution by). Trade Paper. Cambridge University Press. New York, NY. 1992. 314p. Surveys of Economic Literature Ser. ISBN:0-521-43678-8, ISBN13: 978-0-521-43678-6. Dewey:330.01. LCCN:92-004375.
Audience: **l,u,f.**

Boland, Lawrence A. **HB131.B65 1989**
The Methodology of Economic Model Building: Methodology after Samuelson. Cloth Text. Routledge. New York, NY. 1989. 224p. ISBN:0-415-00014-9, ISBN13: 978-0-415-00014-7. Dewey:330/.01/8. LCCN:88-023919.
Audience: **u,f.** *Choice, 1989.*

Brue, Stanley L. & McConnell, Campbell R. **HB171.B778 2007**
Essentials of Economics. Cloth Text. McGraw-Hill Companies, The. New York, NY. 2005. 496p. ISBN:0-07-301967-4, ISBN13: 978-0-07-301967-3. Dewey:330. LCCN:2005-049644.
Audience: **g,l,u,f.**

Buchanan, James M. **HB199.B82 1999**
Cost and Choice: An Inquiry in Economic Theory. Geoffrey Brennan, Hartmut Kleimt & Robert D. Tollison (Foreword by). Trade Cloth. Liberty Fund, Inc. Indianapolis, IN. 1999. 96p. The Collected Works of James M. Buchanan, Vol. 6 ISBN:0-86597-223-0, ISBN13: 978-0-86597-223-0. Dewey:338.5/1. LCCN:98-032143.
Audience: **u,f.**

Caldwell, Bruce **HB131.C37 1994**
Beyond Positivism: Economic Methodology in the Twentieth Century. Ed. 2. Trade Paper. Routledge. New York, NY. 1994. 304p. ISBN:0-415-10911-6, ISBN13: 978-0-415-10911-6. Dewey:330.1. LCCN:93-048811.
Audience: **u,f.**

Caldwell, Bruce J. (Editor) **HB107.M54**
Carl Menger and His Legacy in Economics. Cloth Text. Duke University Press. Durham, NC. 1990. 407p. ISBN:0-8223-1087-2, ISBN13: 978-0-8223-1087-7. Dewey:330.1.
Audience: **l,u,f.**

Cirillo, R. **DS126.5.P44**
Economics of Vilfredo Pareto. Trade Cloth. Taylor & Francis Group. Abingdon, 1979. 148p. ISBN:0-7146-3100-0, ISBN13: 978-0-7146-3100-4. Dewey:320.9/5694.
Audience: **u,f.**

Colander, David C. **HB171.5.C788 2006**
Economics. Ed. 6. Cloth Text. McGraw-Hill Higher Education. Burr Ridge, IL. 2005. 936p. ISBN:0-07-297883-X, ISBN13: 978-0-07-297883-4. Dewey:330. LCCN:2005-043868.
Audience: **g,l,u,f.**

Creedy, John **HB75.C836 1999**
The History of Economic Analysis: Selected Essays by John Creedy. Trade Cloth. Edward Elgar Publishing, Inc. Northampton, MA. 1999. 360p. ISBN:1-85898-908-6, ISBN13: 978-1-85898-908-2. Dewey:330/.09. LCCN:98-029698.
Audience: **u,f.**

Dobbin, Frank (Editor) **HM548.N49 2004**
The New Economic Sociology: A Reader. Trade Cloth. Princeton University Press. Princeton, NJ. 2004. 520p. ISBN:0-691-04905-X, ISBN13: 978-0-691-04905-2. Dewey:306.3. LCCN:2003-060037.
Audience: **l,u,f.**

Dooley, Peter **HB206.D66 2005**
Labour Theory of Value. Paper over Boards. Routledge. New York, NY. 2005. 272p. Routledge Frontiers of Political Economy Ser. ISBN:0-415-32821-7, ISBN13: 978-0-415-32821-0. Dewey:338.5/21. LCCN:2004-025763.
Audience: **l,u,f.**

Ekelund, Robert B. Jr. & Hebert, Robert F. **HB75**
A History of Economic Theory and Method. Ed. 4. Cloth Text. Waveland Press, Inc. Prospect Heights, IL. 2004. 602p. ISBN:1-57766-381-0, ISBN13: 978-1-57766-381-2. Dewey:330.09.
Audience: **l,u,f.**

Fisher, Irving **HB0171**
Elementary Principles of Economics. Trade Paper. Books on Demand. Ann Arbor, MI. 579p. ISBN:0-598-44439-4, ISBN13: 978-0-598-44439-4. Dewey:330. LCCN:15-019767.
Audience: **u,f.**

Frisch, Ragnar **HB201**
New Methods of Measuring Marginal Utility. Library Binding. Porcupine Press, Inc. Philadelphia, PA. 1978. 142p. ISBN:0-87991-863-2, ISBN13: 978-0-87991-863-7. Dewey:330.15/7. LCCN:78-015136.
Audience: **u,f.**

Griffin, Dale (Editor), et al. **BF447.H48 2002**
Heuristics and Biases: The Psychology of Intuitive Judgment. Daniel Kahneman & Thomas Gilovich (Editors). Trade Paper. Cambridge University Press. New York, NY. 2002. 874p. ISBN:0-521-79679-2, ISBN13: 978-0-521-79679-8. Dewey:153.4. LCCN:2001-037860.
Audience: **u,f.**

Heilbroner, Robert L. **HB75.H375 1996**
Teachings from the Worldly Philosophy. Trade Cloth. W. W. Norton & Company, Inc. New York, NY. 1996. 352p. ISBN:0-393-03919-6, ISBN13: 978-0-393-03919-1. Dewey:330. LCCN:95-037470.
Audience: **g,l,u,f.** *Choice, 1996.*

Hoover, Kevin D. **HB172.5 .H659 2001**
The Methodology of Empirical Macroeconomics. Trade Cloth. Cambridge University Press. New York, NY. 2001. 198p. ISBN:0-521-80272-5, ISBN13: 978-0-521-80272-7. Dewey:339. LCCN:2001-018480.
Audience: **l,u,f.**

Kahneman, Daniel (Editor), et al. **BF441 .J8 1982**
Judgment under Uncertainty: Heuristics and Biases. Paul Slovic & Amos Tversky (Editors). Trade Paper. Cambridge University Press. New York, NY. 1982. 544p. ISBN:0-521-28414-7, ISBN13: 978-0-521-28414-1. Dewey:153.4/6. LCCN:81-010042.
Audience: **u,f.**

Khalil, Elias L. (Editor) **HB131.I577 2001**
Dewey, Pragmatism and Economic Methodology. Paper over Boards. Routledge. New York, NY. 2004. 400p. Routledge INEM Advances in Economic Methodology Ser., Vol. 3 ISBN:0-415-70014-0, ISBN13: 978-0-415-70014-6. Dewey:330/.092. LCCN:2003-058654.
Audience: **u,f.**

Loasby, Brian J. **HB87.L58 1989**
The Mind and Method of the Economist: A Critical Appraisal of Major Economists in the 20th Century. Cloth Text. Edward Elgar Publishing, Inc. Northampton, MA. 1989. 248p. ISBN:1-85278-124-6, ISBN13: 978-1-85278-124-8. Dewey:330/.0922. LCCN:89-001492.
Audience: **l,u,f.**

Locke, John & Fraser, Alexander Campbell **B12902004**
An Essay Concerning Human Understanding. Trade Paper. Barnes & Noble, Inc. New York, NY. 2004. xxxvii, 642p. ISBN:0-7607-6049-7, ISBN13: 978-0-7607-6049-9. Dewey:121. LCCN:2006-271042.
Audience: **l,u,f.**

Logan, Deborah Anna & Sanders, Valerie (Editors) **DA535 .M377**
Collected Letters of Harriet Martineau. Trade Cloth. Pickering & Chatto Publishers, Ltd. London, 2006. 2000p. ISBN:1-85196-804-0, ISBN13: 978-1-85196-804-6. Dewey:942.081.
Audience: **l,u,f.**

Mair, Douglas & Miller, Anne **HB90.M63 1991**
A Modern Guide to Economic Thought: An Introduction to Comparative Schools of Thought in Economics. Cloth Text. Edward Elgar Publishing, Inc. Northampton, MA. 1991. 304p. ISBN:1-85278-323-0, ISBN13: 978-1-85278-323-5. Dewey:330.1. LCCN:91-018139.
Audience: **g,l,u,f.** *Choice, 1992.*

Marcet, Jane H. **HB161 .M335**
John Hopkins's Notions on Political Economy. Ed. 3. Trade Cloth. Scholar's Bookshelf. Cranbury, NJ. 1981. ISBN:0-678-01192-3, ISBN13: 978-0-678-01192-8. Dewey:330. LCCN:68-056251.
Audience: **u,f.**

Mayer, Thomas **HB131.M39 1993**
Truth Versus Precision in Economics. Trade Cloth. Edward Elgar Publishing, Inc. Northampton, MA. 1992. 208p. Advances in Economic Methodology Ser. ISBN:1-85278-546-2, ISBN13: 978-1-85278-546-8. Dewey:330. LCCN:92-025821.
Audience: **u,f.** *Choice, 1993.*

Nelson, Julie A. **HB72.N445 2006**
Economics for Humans. Trade Cloth. University of Chicago Press. Chicago, IL. 2006. 164p. ISBN:0-226-57202-1, ISBN13: 978-0-226-57202-4. Dewey:174. LCCN:2005-034406.
Audience: **l,u,f.**

Newman, Lex (Editor) **B1294.C36 2006**
The Cambridge Companion to Locke's Essay Concerning Human Understanding. Cloth Text. Cambridge University Press. New York, NY. 2007. 480p. ISBN:0-521-83433-3, ISBN13: 978-0-521-83433-9. Dewey:121. LCCN:2006-011712.
Audience: **l,u,f.**

North, Douglass Cecil **HB97.3.N67 2005**
Understanding the Process of Economic Change. Trade Cloth. Princeton University Press. Princeton, NJ. 2005. 208p. Princeton Economic History of the Western World Ser. ISBN:0-691-11805-1, ISBN13: 978-0-691-11805-5. Dewey:330.1. LCCN:2004-049131.
Audience: **g,l,u,f.** *Choice, 2005.*

O'Rourke, P. J. **PN6231.E295O76 1998**
Eat the Rich: A Treatise on Economics. Trade Cloth. Grove/Atlantic, Inc. New York, NY. 1998. 272p. ISBN:0-87113-719-4, ISBN13: 978-0-87113-719-7. Dewey:330/.02/07. LCCN:98-027100.
Audience: **g,l,u,f.**

Parente, Stephen L. & Prescott, Edward C. **HD75.P375 2000**
Barriers to Riches. Trade Cloth. MIT Press. Cambridge, MA. 2000. 184p. Walras-Pareto Lectures ISBN:0-262-16193-1, ISBN13: 978-0-262-16193-0. Dewey:338.9. LCCN:00-025414.
Audience: **u,f.** *Choice, 2001.*

Payson, Steven **HF5415.157.P39 1994**
Quality Measurement in Economics: New Perspectives on the Evolution of Goods and Services. Trade Cloth. Edward Elgar Publishing, Inc. Northampton, MA. 1994. 256p. ISBN:1-85278-926-3, ISBN13: 978-1-85278-926-8. Dewey:658.562. LCCN:93-028612.
Audience: **u,f.** *Choice, 1994.*

Polanyi, Karl **HC53.P6 2001**
The Great Transformation: The Political and Economic Origins of Our Time. Ed. 2. Trade Paper. Beacon Press. Boston, MA. 2001. 328p. ISBN:0-8070-5643-X, ISBN13: 978-0-8070-5643-1. Dewey:330.9. LCCN:00-064156.
Audience: **l,u.**

Ray, Larry (Editor) **HM22.G3S53 1991**
Formal Sociology: The Work of Georg Simmel. Cloth Text. Edward Elgar Publishing, Inc. Northampton, MA. 1991. 358p. Schools of Thought in Sociology Ser. ISBN:1-85278-298-6, ISBN13: 978-1-85278-298-6. Dewey:301/.0943. LCCN:90-020465.
Audience: **l,u,f.**

Reinert, Kenneth A. **HF1411.R4198 2005**
Windows on the World Economy with Economic Applications. Cloth Text. Thomson South-Western. Mason, OH. 2004. 456p. ISBN:0-03-031399-6, ISBN13: 978-0-03-031399-8. Dewey:337. LCCN:2003-114662.
Audience: **l,u,f.**

Rima, Ingrid H. **HB75.R46 2000**
Development of Economic Analysis. Ed. 6. Paper over Boards. Routledge. New York, NY. 2000. 608p. ISBN:0-415-23296-1, ISBN13: 978-0-415-23296-8. Dewey:330/.09. LCCN:00-038255.
Audience: **u,f.**

Robinson, Joan **HB33.R6**
Collected Economic Papers. Cambridge, Ma.: MIT Press. 1980. ISBN:0-262-18099-5, ISBN13: 978-0-262-18099-3.
Audience: **u,f.**

Robinson, Joan **HB71**
Economic Philosophy. Trade Paper. Aldine Transaction. Somerset, NJ. 2006. 150p. ISBN:0-202-30908-8, ISBN13: 978-0-202-30908-8. Dewey:330.1. LCCN:2006-048146.
Audience: **l,u,f.**

Robinson, Joan **HB171**
Further Contributions to Modern Economics. Trade Paper. Blackwell Publishing, Inc. Malden, MA. xiv, 202p. ISBN:0-631-12634-1, ISBN13: 978-0-631-12634-8. Dewey:330.
Audience: **u,f.**

Ruccio, David F. & Amariglio, Jack **HB87.R83 2003**
Postmodern Moments in Modern Economics. Trade Cloth. Princeton University Press. Princeton, NJ. 2003. 376p. ISBN:0-691-05870-9, ISBN13: 978-0-691-05870-2. Dewey:330.1. LCCN:2002-193066.
Audience: **u,f.** *Choice, 2004.*

Samuelson, Paul Anthony **HB33.S2**
The Collected Scientific Papers of Paul A. Samuelson. Cambridge, Mass., M.I.T. Press. 1966. ISBN:0-262-19022-2, ISBN13: 978-0-262-19022-0.
Audience: **u,f.**

Samuelson, Paul Anthony **HB171.5**
The Collected Scientific Papers of Paul Samuelson, Vol. 1. Trade Cloth. MIT Press. Cambridge, MA. 1966. 781p. ISBN:0-262-19021-4, ISBN13: 978-0-262-19021-3. Dewey:330.
Audience: **u,f.**

Samuelson, Paul Anthony **HB171.5**
The Collected Scientific Papers of Paul Samuelson, Vol. 2. Trade Cloth. MIT Press. Cambridge, MA. 1966. 1050p. Collected Scientific Papers of Paul Samuelson, Vol. 2 ISBN:0-262-19022-2, ISBN13: 978-0-262-19022-0. Dewey:330.
Audience: **u,f.**

Samuelson, Paul Anthony **HB171**
The Collected Scientific Papers of Paul Samuelson, Vol. 4. Trade Cloth. MIT Press. Cambridge, MA. 1978. 991p. ISBN:0-262-19167-9, ISBN13: 978-0-262-19167-8. Dewey:330. LCCN:65-028408.
Audience: **u,f.**

Samuelson, Paul Anthony **HB171**
The Collected Scientific Papers of Paul Samuelson, Vol. 3. Trade Cloth. MIT Press. Cambridge, MA. 1972. 942p. Collected Scientific Papers of Paul Samuelson, Vol. 3 ISBN:0-262-19080-X, ISBN13: 978-0-262-19080-0. Dewey:330. LCCN:65-028408.
Audience: **u,f.**

Samuelson, Paul Anthony **HB171**
Economics from the Heart: A Samuelson Sampler. Trade Paper. Thomas Horton & Daughters. Glen Ridge, NJ. 1983.

ISBN:0-913878-30-8, ISBN13: 978-0-913878-30-9. Dewey:330. LCCN:82-023318.

Audience: **g,l,u,f.**

Samuelson, Paul Anthony **HB135**
Foundations of Economic Analysis. Trade Paper. Harvard University Press. Cambridge, MA. 1983. 632p. Economic Studies, No. 80 ISBN:0-674-31303-8, ISBN13: 978-0-674-31303-3. Dewey:330/.01/51. LCCN:82-021304.

Audience: **g,l,u,f.**

Samuelson, Paul Anthony **HB171**
The Collected Scientific Papers of Paul Samuelson, Vol. 5. Kate Crowley (Editor). Trade Cloth. MIT Press. Cambridge, MA. 1986. 1064p. ISBN:0-262-19251-9, ISBN13: 978-0-262-19251-4. Dewey:330. LCCN:65-028408.

Audience: **u,f.**

Samuelson, Paul Anthony **HB119.P38 2001**
Paul Samuelson and the Foundations of Modern Economics. K. Puttaswamaiah (Editor). Trade Cloth. Transaction Publishers. Somerset, NJ. 2002. 265p. ISBN:0-7658-0114-0, ISBN13: 978-0-7658-0114-2. Dewey:330.1. LCCN:2001-041598.

Audience: **l,u,f.**

Shackleton, J. R. (Editor) **HB171.N497 1990**
New Thinking in Economics. Cloth Text. Edward Elgar Publishing, Inc. Northampton, MA. 1990. 256p. ISBN:1-85278-341-9, ISBN13: 978-1-85278-341-9. Dewey:330. LCCN:90-041645.

Audience: **u,f.**

Szenberg, Michael & Ramrattan, Lall (Editors) **HB87.N487 2004**
New Frontiers in Economics. Paul A. Samuelson (Foreword by). Cloth Text. Cambridge University Press. New York, NY. 2004. 336p. ISBN:0-521-83686-7, ISBN13: 978-0-521-83686-9. Dewey:330/.09/04. LCCN:2003-065442.

Audience: **u,f.**

Tinbergen, Jan **HB199**
Economic Policy: Principles and Design. Trade Cloth. Elsevier Science & Technology Books. Saint Louis, MO. 1956. 276p. Contributions to Economic Analysis Ser., Vol. 10 ISBN:0-7204-3129-8, ISBN13: 978-0-7204-3129-2. Dewey:338.9.

Audience: **u,f.**

Tinbergen, Jan **HB0179**
Selected Papers. L. H. Klaassen (Editor). Trade Paper. Books on Demand. Ann Arbor, MI. 134p. ISBN:0-598-50751-5, ISBN13: 978-0-598-50751-8. Dewey:330.08. LCCN:59-007582.

Audience: **u,f.**

Veblen, Thorstein B. & Ardzrooni, Leon **HB34.V38 1998**
Essays in Our Changing Order. Trade Paper. Transaction Publishers. Somerset, NJ. 1997. 470p. ISBN:1-56000-964-0, ISBN13: 978-1-56000-964-1. Dewey:330. LCCN:97-024839.

Audience: **u,f.**

von Mises, Ludwig **HB71.V65 2006**
Ultimate Foundation of Economic Science: An Essay on Method. Ed. 2. Trade Cloth. Liberty Fund, Inc. Indianapolis, IN. 2006. 124p. ISBN:0-86597-638-4, ISBN13: 978-0-86597-638-2. Dewey:330.01. LCCN:2005-033274.

Audience: **u,f.**

Walras, Leon **HB173.W2313 2004**
Studies in Applied Economics: Theory of the Production of Social Wealth. Trade Cloth. Routledge. New York, NY. 2004. lxvii, 417p. ISBN:0-415-34617-7, ISBN13: 978-0-415-34617-7. Dewey:330.1. LCCN:2004-050934.

Audience: **u,f.**

Wong, Stanley **HB801**
The Foundations of Paul Samuelson's Revealed Preference Theory: A Study by the Method of Rational Reconstruction. Trade Cloth. Routledge. New York, NY. 1978. x, 148p. ISBN:0-7100-8643-1, ISBN13: 978-0-7100-8643-3. Dewey:339.4/7. LCCN:78-040600.

Audience: **u,f.**

Wood, John Cunningham & McLure, Michael **HB119.S25P378 2005**
Paul A. Samuelson. Paper over Boards. Routledge. New York, NY. 2005. 408p. Critical Assessments of Contemporary Economists Ser. ISBN:0-415-31061-X, ISBN13: 978-0-415-31061-1. Dewey:330/.092. LCCN:2004-046791.

Audience: **l,u,f.**

Wood, John C. & Woods, Ronald N. (Editors) **HB119.S25P378 1989**
Paul A. Samuelson: Critical Assessments, Set. Paper over Boards. Routledge. New York, NY. 1989. 1360p. ISBN:0-415-02002-6, ISBN13: 978-0-415-02002-2. Dewey:330.15/5. LCCN:88-037899.

Audience: **u,f.**

Zeitz, Paul **QA63**
The Art and Craft of Problem Solving. Ed. 2. Trade Paper. John Wiley & Sons, Inc. Hoboken, NJ. 2006. 384p. ISBN:0-471-78901-1, ISBN13: 978-0-471-78901-7. Dewey:153.4/3. LCCN:2006-049698.

Audience: **l,u,f.**

Econometrics. Mathematical Economics

Adda, Jerome & Cooper, Russell W. **HB135.D935 2003**
Dynamic Economics: Quantitative Methods and Applications. Trade Cloth. MIT Press. Cambridge, MA. 2003. 296p. ISBN:0-262-01201-4, ISBN13: 978-0-262-01201-0. Dewey:330/.01/5195. LCCN:2003-042126.

Audience: **u,f.**

Amman, Hans M. (Editor), et al. **HB135.H356 1996**
Handbook of Computational Economics. David A. Kendrick & John Rust (Editors). Trade Cloth. Elsevier Science & Technology Books. Saint Louis, MO. 1996. 832p. Handbooks in Economics Ser., Vol. 1 ISBN:0-444-89857-3, ISBN13: 978-0-444-89857-9. Dewey:330/.01/5195. LCCN:96-012806.

Audience: **u,f.**

Antelman, Gordon **QA279.5.A58 1997**
Elementary Bayesian Statistics. Albert Madansky & Robert McCulloch (Editors). Trade Cloth. Edward Elgar Publishing, Inc. Northampton, MA. 1997. 480p. ISBN:1-85898-504-8, ISBN13: 978-1-85898-504-6. Dewey:519.5/42. LCCN:97-014359.

Audience: **l,u,f.** *Choice, 1998.*

Arellano, Manuel **HB139**
Panel Data Econometrics. Trade Paper. Oxford University Press, Inc. New York, NY. 2003. 244p. Advanced Texts in Econometrics ISBN:0-19-924529-0, ISBN13: 978-0-19-924529-1. Dewey:330.015195. LCCN:2004-270169.
Audience: **u,f.**

Arrow, Kenneth Joseph & Hahn, F. H. **HB74.M3 A75**
General Competitive Analysis. Ed. 3. Trade Cloth. Elsevier Science & Technology Books. Saint Louis, MO. 1977. 452p. Advanced Textbooks in Economics, Vol. 12 ISBN:0-7204-0750-8, ISBN13: 978-0-7204-0750-1. Dewey:330/.01/82.
Audience: **u,f.**

Arrow, Kenneth Joseph **HB135**
Handbook of Mathematical Economics, Vol. 1. Ed. 6. Michael D. Intriligator (Editor). Trade Cloth. Elsevier Science & Technology Books. Saint Louis, MO. 1987. 398p. Handbooks in Economics Ser., No. 1 ISBN:0-444-86126-2, ISBN13: 978-0-444-86126-9. Dewey:330/.01/51. LCCN:81-002820.
Audience: **u,f.**

Arrow, Kenneth Joseph & Intriligator, Michael D. (Volume Editors) **HB135**
Handbook of Mathematical Economics, Vol. 3. Ed. 3. Trade Cloth. Elsevier Science & Technology Books. Saint Louis, MO. 1986. 486p. Handbooks in Economics Ser. ISBN:0-444-86128-9, ISBN13: 978-0-444-86128-3. Dewey:330/.01/51.
Audience: **u,f.**

Backhouse, Roger E. & Salanti, Andrea (Editors) **HB172.5**
Macroeconomics and the Real World: Econometric Techniques and Macroeconomic, Vol. 1. Trade Cloth. Oxford University Press, Inc. New York, NY. 2001. 310p. ISBN:0-19-829795-5, ISBN13: 978-0-19-829795-6. Dewey:339/.015195.
Audience: **l,u,f.**

Backhouse, Roger E. & Salanti, Andrea (Editors) **HB172.5**
Macroeconomics and the Real World: Keynesian Economics, Unemployment, and Policy, Vol. 2. Trade Cloth. Oxford University Press, Inc. New York, NY. 2001. 312p. ISBN:0-19-829796-3, ISBN13: 978-0-19-829796-3. Dewey:339. LCCN:00-057111.
Audience: **u,f.**

Baltagi, Badi H. (Editor) **HB139**
A Companion to Theoretical Econometrics. Trade Paper. Blackwell Publishing, Inc. Malden, MA. 2003. 736p. ISBN:1-4051-0676-X, ISBN13: 978-1-4051-0676-4. Dewey:330/.015195.
Audience: **u,f.**

Baltagi, Badi H. **HB139**
Econometric Analysis of Panel Data. Ed. 3. Trade Cloth. John Wiley & Sons, Inc. Hoboken, NJ. 2002. 1728p. ISBN:0-471-26730-9, ISBN13: 978-0-471-26730-0. Dewey:330/.01/5195. LCCN:00-043811.
Audience: **u,f.**

Barnett, William A. (Editor), et al. **HB139 .I566 1995**
Nonlinear Econometric Modeling in Time Series: Proceedings of the Eleventh International Symposium in Economic Theory. David F. Hendry, Svend Hylleberg, Timo Terasvirta, Dag Tjostheim & Allan Wurtz (Editors). Trade Cloth. Cambridge University Press. New York, NY. 2000. 240p. International Symposia in Economic Theory and Econometrics Ser., No. 11 ISBN:0-521-59424-3, ISBN13: 978-0-521-59424-0. Dewey:330/.01/5195. LCCN:99-034095.
Audience: **u,f.**

Bhagat, Sanjai & Jefferis, Richard H. Jr. **HD2741.B48 2002**
The Econometrics of Corporate Governance Studies. Trade Cloth. MIT Press. Cambridge, MA. 2002. 128p. ISBN:0-262-02517-5, ISBN13: 978-0-262-02517-1. Dewey:658.4. LCCN:2001-056203.
Audience: **u,f.**

Bjerkholt, Olav (Editor) **HB139.F677 1995**
Foundations of Modern Econometrics: The Selected Essays of Ragnar Frisch. Trade Cloth. Edward Elgar Publishing, Inc. Northampton, MA. 1995. 1,072p. Economists of the Twentieth Century Ser. ISBN:1-85278-840-2, ISBN13: 978-1-85278-840-7. Dewey:330/.01/5195. LCCN:95-016389.
Audience: **u,f.**

Boumans, Marcel **HB135.B68 2005**
How Economists Model the World into Numbers. Paper over Boards. Routledge. New York, NY. 2005. 224p. Routledge INEM Advances in Economic Methodology Ser. ISBN:0-415-34621-5, ISBN13: 978-0-415-34621-4. Dewey:330/.01/5195. LCCN:2004-012725.
Audience: **g,l,u,f.**

Brooks, Chris **HG173 .B76 2002**
Introductory Econometrics for Finance. Cloth Text. Cambridge University Press. New York, NY. 2002. 728p. ISBN:0-521-79018-2, ISBN13: 978-0-521-79018-5. Dewey:332/.01/5195. LCCN:2001-037930.
Audience: **g,u,f.**

Caldwell, Bruce **HB131.C37 1994**
Beyond Positivism: Economic Methodology in the Twentieth Century. Ed. 2. Trade Paper. Routledge. New York, NY. 1994. 304p. ISBN:0-415-10911-6, ISBN13: 978-0-415-10911-6. Dewey:330.1. LCCN:93-048811.
Audience: **u,f.**

Campbell, John Y., et al. **HG4523.C27 1997**
The Econometrics of Financial Markets. Andrew W. Lo, Archie C. Mackinlay & A. Craig MacKinlay (Authors). Trade Cloth. Princeton University Press. Princeton, NJ. 1996. 630p. ISBN:0-691-04301-9, ISBN13: 978-0-691-04301-2. Dewey:332/.09414. LCCN:96-027868.
Audience: **u,f.**

Caputo, Michael R. **HB135.C27 2005**
Foundations of Dynamic Economic Analysis: Optimal Control Theory and Applications. Trade Cloth. Cambridge University Press. New York, NY. 2005. 592p. ISBN:0-521-84272-7, ISBN13: 978-0-521-84272-3. Dewey:330/.01/515642. LCCN:2004-046568.
Audience: **u,f.**

Cournot, Augustin **HB74.M3**
Researches into the Mathematical Principles of the Theory of Wealth. Trade Cloth. Scholar's Bookshelf. Cranbury, NJ. 1971. xxv, 213p. Reprints of Economic Classics Ser. ISBN:0-678-00066-2, ISBN13: 978-0-678-00066-3. Dewey:330.1/6. LCCN:73-028986.
Audience: **u,f.**

Cramer, Jan Salomon **HB141.C722 2003**
Logit Models from Economics and Other Fields. Ed. 2. Trade Cloth. Cambridge University Press. New York, NY. 2003. 184p. ISBN:0-521-81588-6, ISBN13: 978-0-521-81588-8. Dewey:330/.01/5195. LCCN:2002-041450.
Audience: **l,u,f.**

Culyer, A. J. & Newhouse, J. P. (Editors) **RA410.H255 2000**
Handbook of Health Economics, Vol. 1A. Ed. 3. Trade Cloth. Elsevier Science & Technology Books. Saint Louis, MO. 2000. 1000p. Handbooks in Economics Ser. ISBN:0-444-50470-2, ISBN13: 978-0-444-50470-8. Dewey:338.4/33621. LCCN:2001-275530.
Audience: **l,u,f.**

Culyer, A. J. & Newhouse, J. P. (Editors) **RA410.H255 2000**
Handbook of Health Economics, Vol. 1B. Ed. 3. Trade Cloth. Elsevier Science & Technology Books. Saint Louis, MO. 2000. 1132p. Handbooks in Economics Ser. ISBN:0-444-50471-0, ISBN13: 978-0-444-50471-5. Dewey:338.4/33621. LCCN:2001-275530.
Audience: **l,u,f.**

Darnell, Adrian C. **HB139**
A Dictionary of Econometrics. Trade Paper. Edward Elgar Publishing, Inc. Northampton, MA. 1996. 480p. ISBN:1-85898-328-2, ISBN13: 978-1-85898-328-8. Dewey:330/.015195/03. LCCN:93-039138.
Audience: **g,l,u,f.** *Choice, 1994.*

Davidson, Russell & MacKinnon, James G. **HB139**
Estimation and Inference in Econometrics. Cloth Text. Oxford University Press, Inc. New York, NY. 1993. 894p. ISBN:0-19-506011-3, ISBN13: 978-0-19-506011-9. Dewey:330.015195. LCCN:92-012048.
Audience: **u,f.**

Diebolt, Claude, et al. **HB172.5.N497 2005**
New Trends in Macroeconomics. Catherine Kyrtsou & Olivier Darné (Authors). Trade Cloth. Springer. New York, NY. 2005. xiv, 238p. ISBN:7-83540-214-9, ISBN13: 978-7-83540-214-8. Dewey:339. LCCN:2005-929196.
Audience: **l,u,f.**

Dorfman, Robert, et al. **HB135.D67 1987**
Linear Programming and Economic Analysis. Paul Anthony Samuelson & Robert M. Solow (Authors). Trade Paper. Dover Publications, Inc. Mineola, NY. 1987. 525p. ISBN:0-486-65491-5, ISBN13: 978-0-486-65491-1. Dewey:330/.0724. LCCN:87-024382.
Audience: **u,f.**

Dow, Sheila C. & Hillard, John (Editors) **HB139.P675 2002**
Post Keynesian Econometrics, Microeconomics and the Theory of the Firm: Beyond Keynes, Vol. 1. Trade Cloth. Edward Elgar Publishing, Inc. Northampton, MA. 2002. 288p. ISBN:1-85898-584-6, ISBN13: 978-1-85898-584-8. Dewey:338.5. LCCN:2001-054781.
Audience: **u,f.**

Engle, R. F. (Editor) **HB141.A69 1995**
Arch: Selected Readings. Trade Cloth. Oxford University Press, Inc. New York, NY. 1995. 424p. Advanced Texts in Econometrics ISBN:0-19-877431-1, ISBN13: 978-0-19-877431-0. Dewey:330/.01/5195. LCCN:95-012837.
Audience: **u,f.**

Engle, R. F. **HB139.L66 1991**
Long-Run Economic Relationships: Readings in Cointegration. Paper Text. Oxford University Press, Inc. New York, NY. 1992. 308p. Advanced Texts in Econometrics ISBN:0-19-828339-3, ISBN13: 978-0-19-828339-3. Dewey:330/.01/5195. LCCN:91-010092.
Audience: **u,f.**

Engle, R. F. & McFadden, D. L. (Editors) **HB139**
Handbook of Econometrics, Vol. 4. Ed. 4. Trade Cloth. Elsevier Science & Technology Books. Saint Louis, MO. 1994. 1078p. Handbooks in Economics Ser., Vol. 2 ISBN:0-444-88766-0, ISBN13: 978-0-444-88766-5. Dewey:330.015195.
Audience: **u,f.**

Fisher, Irving **HB119.F5.A25 1996**
100% Money. Trade Cloth. Pickering & Chatto Publishers, Ltd. London, 1996. vi, 312p. The Works of Irving Fisher ISBN:1-85196-236-0, ISBN13: 978-1-85196-236-5. Dewey:330 S. LCCN:96-012211.
Audience: **u,f.**

Fisher, Irving **HB119.F5.A25 1996**
Booms and Depressions. Trade Cloth. Pickering & Chatto Publishers, Ltd. London, 1996. vi, 351p. The Works of Irving Fisher ISBN:1-85196-235-2, ISBN13: 978-1-85196-235-8. Dewey:330 S. LCCN:96-012210.
Audience: **u,f.**

Fisher, Irving **HB119.F5.A25 1996**
Contributions to the Theory and Practice of Public Finance. Trade Cloth. Pickering & Chatto Publishers, Ltd. London, 1996. vi, 537p. The Works of Irving Fisher ISBN:1-85196-237-9, ISBN13: 978-1-85196-237-2. Dewey:330 S. LCCN:96-012212.
Audience: **u,f.**

Fisher, Irving **HB0171**
Elementary Principles of Economics. Trade Paper. Books on Demand. Ann Arbor, MI. 579p. ISBN:0-598-44439-4, ISBN13: 978-0-598-44439-4. Dewey:330. LCCN:15-019767.
Audience: **u,f.**

Fisher, Irving **HB135.F57 1991**
Mathematical Investigations in the Theory of Value and Prices: Appreciation and Interest. Library Binding. Scholar's Bookshelf. Cranbury, NJ. 1991. 226p. Reprints of Economic Classics Ser. ISBN:0-678-01456-6, ISBN13: 978-0-678-01456-1. Dewey:330/.01/51. LCCN:90-004603.
Audience: **u,f.**

Fisher, Irving **HB501**
The Nature of Capital and Income. Trade Cloth. Simon Publications, Inc. 2003. 427p. ISBN:1-932512-05-5, ISBN13: 978-1-932512-05-2. Dewey:332/.041. LCCN:28-019914.
Audience: **u,f.**

Fisher, Irving **HB0539.F54**
The Rate of Interest: Its Nature, Determination and Relation to Economic Phenomena. Trade Paper. Books on Demand. Ann Arbor, MI. 465p. ISBN:0-598-98884-X, ISBN13: 978-0-598-98884-3. Dewey:332.82. LCCN:73-006195.
Audience: **u,f.**

Fisher, Irving **HD0539**
The Theory of Interest: As Determined by Impatience to Spend and Opportunity to Invest It. Trade Paper. Books on Demand. Ann Arbor, MI. 626p. ISBN:0-598-54237-X, ISBN13: 978-0-598-54237-3. Dewey:330 S. LCCN:30-008152.
Audience: **u,f.**

Fisher, Irving **HB119.F5A25 1996**
The Works of Irving Fisher, Set. William J. Barber & James Tobin (Editors). Trade Cloth. Pickering & Chatto Publishers, Ltd. London, 1997. 6240p. Masters Ser. ISBN:1-85196-225-5, ISBN13: 978-1-85196-225-9. Dewey:330. LCCN:96-021156.
Audience: **u,f.**

Fisher, Irving **HB119.F5E27 1999**
The Economics of Irving Fisher: Reviewing the Scientific Work of a Great Economist. Hans-Edi Loef & Hans G. Monissen (Editors). Trade Cloth. Edward Elgar Publishing, Inc. Northampton, MA. 1999. 368p. ISBN:1-84064-037-5, ISBN13: 978-1-84064-037-3. Dewey:330.1. LCCN:98-050845.
Audience: **u,f.**

Fomby, Thomas & Terrell, Dek **HB141**
Econometric Analysis of Financial and Economic Time Series Part A. R. Carter Hill (Contribution by). Trade Cloth. Elsevier Science & Technology Books. Saint Louis, MO. 2006. 406p. ISBN:0-7623-1274-2, ISBN13: 978-0-7623-1274-0. Dewey:330.015195.
Audience: **u,f.**

Franses, Philip Hans **HB139**
[e] A Concise Introduction to Econometrics: An Intuitive Guide. E-Book. Cambridge University Press. New York, NY. 2005. ISBN:0-511-03062-2, ISBN13: 978-0-511-03062-8. Dewey:330/.01/5195.
Audience: **l,u,f.** *Choice, 2003.*

Franses, Philip Hans **HB139.F722 2002**
A Concise Introduction to Econometrics: An Intuitive Guide. Cloth Text. Cambridge University Press. New York, NY. 2002. 130p. ISBN:0-521-81769-2, ISBN13: 978-0-521-81769-1. Dewey:330/.01/5195. LCCN:2002-067380.
Audience: **l,u,f.** *Choice, 2003.*

Geanakoplos, John **HB171**
Celebrating Irving Fisher: The Legacy of a Great Economist. Robert W. Dimand (Editor). Trade Paper. Blackwell Publishing, Inc. Malden, MA. 2005. 320p. ISBN:1-4051-3307-4, ISBN13: 978-1-4051-3307-4. Dewey:330.1.
Audience: **l,u,f.**

Gertler, Mark **HB172.5.N39 2005**
NBER Macroeconomics Annual 2004. Kenneth Rogoff (Editor). Trade Paper. MIT Press. Cambridge, MA. 2005. 432p. NBER Macroeconomics Annual Ser. ISBN:0-262-57229-X, ISBN13: 978-0-262-57229-3. Dewey:339.05.
Audience: **l,u,f.**

Ghysels, Eric & Osborn, Denise R. **HB139 .G49 2001**
The Econometric Analysis of Seasonal Time Series. Thomas J. Sargent (Foreword by), Christian Gourieroux, Peter C. B. Phillips & Michael Wickens (Contribution by). Trade Cloth. Cambridge University Press. New York, NY. 2001. 250p. Themes in Modern Econometrics Ser. ISBN:0-521-56260-0, ISBN13: 978-0-521-56260-7. Dewey:330/.01/5195. LCCN:00-063070.
Audience: **u,f.**

Goldberger, Arthur S. **HB139.G634 1991**
A Course in Econometrics. Trade Cloth. Harvard University Press. Cambridge, MA. 1991. 437p. ISBN:0-674-17544-1, ISBN13: 978-0-674-17544-0. Dewey:330/.01/5195. LCCN:90-042284.
Audience: **l,u,f.**

Gong, Gang & Semmler, Willi **HB172.5.G66 2005**
Stochastic Dynamic Macroeconomics: Theory, Numerics, and Empirical Evidence. Trade Cloth. Oxford University Press, Inc. New York, NY. 2006. 212p. ISBN:0-19-530162-5, ISBN13: 978-0-19-530162-5. Dewey:339/.01/51922. LCCN:2005-049870.
Audience: **u,f.**

Gourieroux, Christian & Jasiak, Joann **HB139.G685 2001**
Financial Econometrics: Problems, Models, and Methods. Trade Cloth. Princeton University Press. Princeton, NJ. 2001. 528p. Princeton Series in Finance ISBN:0-691-08872-1, ISBN13: 978-0-691-08872-3. Dewey:330/.01/5195. LCCN:2001-036264.
Audience: **u,f.**

Gourieroux, Christian **HB139 .G6813 2000**
Econometrics of Qualitative Dependent Variables. Paul B. Klassen (Translator), Peter C. B. Phillips, Michael Wickens, Eric Ghysels & Richard J. Smith (Contribution by). Trade Cloth. Cambridge University Press. New York, NY. 2000. 384p. Themes in Modern Econometrics Ser. ISBN:0-521-33149-8, ISBN13: 978-0-521-33149-4. Dewey:330/.01/5195. LCCN:00-029263.
Audience: **u,f.**

Granger, Clive **HB141 .G728 1999**
Empirical Modeling in Economics: Specification and Evaluation. Trade Paper. Cambridge University Press. New York, NY. 1999. 112p. ISBN:0-521-77825-5, ISBN13: 978-0-521-77825-1. Dewey:330.015118. LCCN:00-700407.
Audience: **u,f.**

Granger, Clive W. J. **HB139 .G69 2001**
Essays in Econometrics: Collected Papers of Clive W. J. Granger. Eric Ghysels, Norman R. Swanson & Mark W. Watson (Editors), Andrew Chesher & Matthew Jackson (Contribution by). Quantity Pack, Trade Cloth. Cambridge University Press. New York, NY. 2001. 944p. Econometric Society Monographs, Vols. 32 & 33 ISBN:0-521-80407-8, ISBN13: 978-0-521-80407-3. Dewey:330/.01/5195. LCCN:00-034306.
Audience: **u,f.**

Granger, Clive **HB141 .G728 1999**
Empirical Modeling in Economics: Specification and Evaluation. Geoff Harcourt (Foreword by). Cloth Text. Cambridge University Press. New York, NY. 1999. 108p. ISBN:0-521-66208-7, ISBN13: 978-0-521-66208-6. Dewey:330.015118. LCCN:00-700407.
Audience: **u,f.**

Granger, Clive **HB141**
[e] Empirical Modeling in Economics: Specification and Evaluation. Geoff Harcourt (Foreword by). E-Book. Cambridge University Press. New York, NY. 2005. ISBN:0-511-03367-2, ISBN13: 978-0-511-03367-4. Dewey:330.015118.
Audience: **u,f.**

Greene, William H. **HB139.G74 2002**
Econometric Analysis. Ed. 5. Cloth Text. Prentice Hall PTR. Upper Saddle River, NJ. 2002. 1026p. ISBN:0-13-066189-9, ISBN13: 978-0-13-066189-0. Dewey:330/.01/5195. LCCN:2002-029308.
Audience: **l,u,f.**

Griliches, Zvi & Intriligator, Michael D. (Editors) **HB139**
Handbook of Econometrics, Vol. 2. Ed. 6. Trade Cloth. Elsevier Science & Technology Books. Saint Louis, MO. 1987. 716p. Handbooks in Economics Ser. ISBN:0-444-86186-6, ISBN13: 978-0-444-86186-3. Dewey:330.015195. LCCN:83-002396.
Audience: **g,l,u,f.**

Guesnerie, Roger **HB3732.G84 2005**
Assessing Rational Expectations: Eductive Stability in Economics. Trade Cloth. MIT Press. Cambridge, MA. 2005. 416p. ISBN:0-262-07258-0, ISBN13: 978-0-262-07258-8. Dewey:339.5/01/51. LCCN:2004-057855.
Audience: **l,u,f.**

Gujarati **HB139.G85 2006**
Essentials of Econometrics. Ed. 3. Trade Cloth. McGraw-Hill School Education Group. Columbus, OH. 2005. 544p. ISBN:0-07-297092-8, ISBN13: 978-0-07-297092-0. Dewey:330/.01/5195. LCCN:2004-058825.
Audience: **g,l,u,f.**

Gujarati, Damodar N. **HB139.G84 2003**
Basic Econometrics. Ed. 4. Trade Cloth. McGraw-Hill Companies, The. New York, NY. 2003. xxix, 1002p. ISBN:0-07-112342-3, ISBN13: 978-0-07-112342-6. Dewey:330/.01/5195. LCCN:2001-099577.
Audience: **g,l,u,f.**

Hamouda, Omar F. & Rowley, J. C. (Editors) **HB139**
Econometric Exploration and Diagnosis. Trade Cloth. Edward Elgar Publishing, Inc. Northampton, MA. 1997. 512p. Foundations of Probability, Econometrics and Economic Games Ser., Vol. 6 ISBN:1-85898-438-6, ISBN13: 978-1-85898-438-4. Dewey:330.015195. LCCN:96-054038.
Audience: **u,f.**

Hamouda, Omar F. & Rowley, J. C. (Editors) **HB139.F678 1997**
Expected Utility, Fair Gambles and Rational Choice. Trade Cloth. Edward Elgar Publishing, Inc. Northampton, MA. 1997. 528p. Foundations of Probability, Econometrics and Economic Games Ser., Vol. 1 ISBN:1-85898-433-5, ISBN13: 978-1-85898-433-9. Dewey:330/.01/5195. LCCN:96-054038.
Audience: **u,f.**

Hamouda, Omar F. & Rowley, J. C. (Editors) **HB139.F678 1997**
Foundations of Probability, Econometrics and Economic Games, Vols. 1-10. D. Ellsberg, R. M. Hogarth, J. B. Kadane, B. O. Koopmans, E. L. Lehmann, D. F. Nicholls, H. Rubin, T. J. Sargent, L. H. Summers & C. R. Wymer (Contribution by). Trade Cloth. Edward Elgar Publishing, Inc. Northampton, MA. 1997. 5024p. ISBN:1-85898-370-3, ISBN13: 978-1-85898-370-7. Dewey:330/.01/5195. LCCN:96-054038.
Audience: **l,u,f.**

Hayashi, Fumio **HB139.H39 2000**
Econometrics. Trade Cloth. Princeton University Press. Princeton, NJ. 2000. 704p. ISBN:0-691-01018-8, ISBN13: 978-0-691-01018-2. Dewey:330/.01/5195. LCCN:00-034665.
Audience: **l,u,f.**

Heckman, J. J. & Leamer, E. E. (Editors) **HB139**
Handbook of Econometrics, Vol. 5. Trade Cloth. Elsevier Science & Technology Books. Saint Louis, MO. 2001. 740p. Handbooks in Economics Ser., Vol. V ISBN:0-444-82340-9, ISBN13: 978-0-444-82340-3. Dewey:330/.015195.
Audience: **l,u,f.**

Heij, Christiaan, et al. **HB139**
Econometric Methods with Applications in Business and Economics. Paul de Boer, Philip Hans Franses, Teun Kloek & Herman K. van Dijk (Authors). Trade Cloth. Oxford University Press, Inc. New York, NY. 2004. 814p. ISBN:0-19-926801-0, ISBN13: 978-0-19-926801-6. Dewey:330.015195. LCCN:2004-301166.
Audience: **l,f.**

Hendry, David F. **HB141.H46 2000**
Econometrics: Alchemy or Science? Ed. 2. Trade Paper. Oxford University Press, Inc. New York, NY. 2001. 560p. ISBN:0-19-829354-2, ISBN13: 978-0-19-829354-5. Dewey:333/.01/5195. LCCN:2001-265783.
Audience: **u,f.**

Hendry, David F. & Morgan, Mary S. (Editors) **HB139 .F676 1995**
The Foundations of Econometric Analysis. Trade Cloth. Cambridge University Press. New York, NY. 1995. 574p. ISBN:0-521-38043-X, ISBN13: 978-0-521-38043-0. Dewey:330/.015195. LCCN:93-050840.
Audience: **l,u,f.** *Choice, 1996.*

Hendry, David F. & Morgan, Mary S. **HB139 .F676 1995**
The Foundations of Econometric Analysis. Trade Paper. Cambridge University Press. New York, NY. 1997. 574p. ISBN:0-521-58870-7, ISBN13: 978-0-521-58870-6. Dewey:330/.015195.
Audience: **u,f.** *Choice, 1996.*

Hess, Peter N. **HB135.H48 2002**
Using Mathematics in Economic Analysis. Trade Cloth. Prentice Hall PTR. Upper Saddle River, NJ. 2001. 604p. Prentice-Hall Series in Economics ISBN:0-13-020026-3, ISBN13: 978-0-13-020026-6. Dewey:330/.01/51. LCCN:2001-034018.
Audience: **g,l,u,f.**

Hildenbrand, Werner **HB87.E24 2001**
Economics Essays: A Festschrift for Werner Heldenbrand. Gerard Debreu, Wilhelm Neuefeind & Walter Trockel (Editors). Cloth Text. Springer. New York, NY. 2001. 371p. ISBN:3-540-41882-2, ISBN13: 978-3-540-41882-5. Dewey:330. LCCN:2001-020859.
Audience: **u,f.**

Hill, R. Carter, et al. **HB139.H548 2001**
Undergraduate Econometrics. Ed. 2. William E. Griffiths & George G. Judge (Authors). Trade Cloth. John Wiley & Sons,

Inc. Hoboken, NJ. 2000. 424p. ISBN:0-471-33184-8, ISBN13: 978-0-471-33184-1. Dewey:330.015195. LCCN:00-042295.
Audience: **g,l,u,f.**

Hoover, Kevin D. (Editor) **HB172.5.M325 1995**
Macroeconometrics: Developments, Tensions and Prospects. Trade Cloth. Springer. New York, NY. 1995. 596p. Recent Economic Thought Ser. ISBN:0-7923-9589-1, ISBN13: 978-0-7923-9589-8. Dewey:339. LCCN:95-016697.
Audience: **u,f.**

Hsiao, Cheng **HB139.H75 2002**
Analysis of Panel Data. Ed. 2. Peter Hammond, Alberto Holly, Andrew Chesher & Matthew Jackson (Contribution by). Trade Cloth. Cambridge University Press. New York, NY. 2003. 382p. Econometric Society Monographs, No. 34 ISBN:0-521-81855-9, ISBN13: 978-0-521-81855-1. Dewey:330/.01/5195. LCCN:2002-023348.
Audience: **u,f.**

Jansen, Eilev S., et al. **HB172.5.E27 2005**
The Econometrics of Macroeconomic Modelling. Gunnar Bardsen, Oyvind Eitrheim & Ragnar Nymoen (Authors). Trade Cloth. Oxford University Press, Inc. New York, NY. 2005. 360p. Advanced Texts in Econometrics Ser. ISBN:0-19-924649-1, ISBN13: 978-0-19-924649-6. Dewey:339.01/5195. LCCN:2005-299990.
Audience: **l,u,f.**

Jorgenson, Dale W. **HB241**
Econometrics: Economic Growth in the Information Age. Trade Cloth. MIT Press. Cambridge, MA. 2002. 492p. ISBN:0-262-10094-0, ISBN13: 978-0-262-10094-6. Dewey:330/.01/5195. LCCN:99-046138.
Audience: **u,f.**

Jorgenson, Dale W. **HB241.J67 2000**
Econometrics and the Cost of Capital, Vol. 2. Lawrence J. Lau (Editor). Trade Cloth. MIT Press. Cambridge, MA. 2000. 450p. ISBN:0-262-10083-5, ISBN13: 978-0-262-10083-0. Dewey:330/.01/5195. LCCN:99-046138.
Audience: **u,f.**

Judd, Kenneth L. **HB137.J83 1998**
Numerical Methods in Economics. Trade Cloth. MIT Press. Cambridge, MA. 1998. 633p. ISBN:0-262-10071-1, ISBN13: 978-0-262-10071-7. Dewey:330/.01/5195. LCCN:98-013591.
Audience: **l,u,f.**

Kalecki, Michal **HB74.M3.K32**
Theory of Economic Dynamics. London : Routledge. 2003. Routledge Library Editions.; The Economics Series ISBN:0-415-31373-2, ISBN13: 978-0-415-31373-5.
Audience: **u,f.**

Karlqvist, Anders, et al. **HT391**
Spatial Interaction Theory and Planning Models. L. Lundqvist, J. Weibull & Folke Snickars (Authors). Trade Cloth. Elsevier Science & Technology Books. Saint Louis, MO. 1978. 388p. Studies in Regional Science and Urban Economics, Vol. 3 ISBN:0-444-85182-8, ISBN13: 978-0-444-85182-6. Dewey:330.9/172/4.
Audience: **u,f.**

Kendrick, David, et al. **HB135 .K465**
Computational Economics. Ruben P. Mercado & Hans M. Amman (Authors). Trade Cloth. Princeton University Press. Princeton, NJ. 2005. 456p. ISBN:0-691-12549-X, ISBN13: 978-0-691-12549-7. Dewey:330.0151.
Audience: **l,u,f.**

Kennedy, Peter **HB139.K45 2003**
A Guide to Econometrics. Ed. 5. Trade Paper. MIT Press. Cambridge, MA. 2003. 500p. ISBN:0-262-61183-X, ISBN13: 978-0-262-61183-1. Dewey:330/.028. LCCN:2002-045179.
Audience: **g,l,u,f.**

Kennedy, Peter **HB139.K45 1998**
[e] A Guide to Econometrics. Ed. 4. E-Book. NetLibrary, Inc. Boulder, CO. 1998. ISBN:0-585-20203-6, ISBN13: 978-0-585-20203-7. Dewey:330/.028.
Audience: **g,l,u,f.**

Kennedy, Peter **HB139.K45 2003**
A Guide to Econometrics. Ed. 5. Trade Cloth. MIT Press. Cambridge, MA. 2003. 500p. ISBN:0-262-11280-9, ISBN13: 978-0-262-11280-2. Dewey:330/.028. LCCN:2002-045179.
Audience: **g,l,u,f.**

Keuzenkamp, Hugo A. **HB139 .K48 2000**
Probability, Econometrics and Truth: The Methodology of Econometrics. Trade Cloth. Cambridge University Press. New York, NY. 2000. 322p. ISBN:0-521-55359-8, ISBN13: 978-0-521-55359-9. Dewey:330.015195. LCCN:99-058732.
Audience: **u,f.**

Klein, Ingo & Mittnik, Stefan (Editors) **HB141.C6596 2003**
Contributions to Modern Econometrics: From Data Analysis to Economic Policy. Trade Cloth. Springer. New York, NY. 2002. 296p. Dynamic Modeling in Econometrics in Economics and Finance Ser., Vol. 4 ISBN:1-4020-7334-8, ISBN13: 978-1-4020-7334-2. Dewey:330/.01/5195. LCCN:2002-040746.
Audience: **u,f.**

Kmenta, Jan **HB139.K56 1997**
Elements of Econometrics. Ed. 2. Trade Cloth. University of Michigan Press. Chicago, IL. 1997. 800p. ISBN:0-472-10886-7, ISBN13: 978-0-472-10886-2. Dewey:330/.01/82. LCCN:97-021688.
Audience: **g,l,u,f.**

Kreps, David M. (Editor), et al. **HB139.A35 2003**
Advances in Economics and Econometrics: Theory and Applications, Eighth World Congress. Kenneth Frank Wallis, Mathias Dewatripont, Lars Peter Hansen & Stephen J. Turnovsky (Editors), Econometric Society, World Congress Staff, Andrew Chesher & Matthew Jackson (Contribution by). Trade Cloth. Cambridge University Press. New York, NY. 2003. 392p. Econometric Society Monographs, Vol. 1 ISBN:0-521-81872-9, ISBN13: 978-0-521-81872-8. Dewey:330. LCCN:2002-071258.
Audience: **u,f.**

Leamer, Edward E. **HB139.L42 1994**
Sturdy Econometrics. Trade Cloth. Edward Elgar Publishing, Inc. Northampton, MA. 1994. 392p. Economists of the Twentieth Century Ser. ISBN:1-85278-802-X, ISBN13: 978-1-85278-802-5. Dewey:330/.01/5195. LCCN:94-004208.
Audience: **u,f.**

Long, Frank (Editor) **HD82**
Ragnar Frisch: Economic Planning Studies. Jan Tinbergen (Introduction by). Library Binding. Springer. New York, NY.

1975. 213p. International Studies in Economics and Econometrics Ser., No. 8 ISBN:90-277-0245-4, ISBN13: 978-90-277-0245-6. Dewey:338.9. LCCN:75-044219.
Audience: **u,f.**

Lucas, Robert E. Jr. & Sargent, Thomas J. (Editors) **HB139**
Rational Expectations and Econometric Practice, 2. Trade Paper. University of Minnesota Press. Minneapolis, MN. 1981. 776p. ISBN:0-8166-1071-1, ISBN13: 978-0-8166-1071-6. Dewey:330/.028. LCCN:80-024602.
Audience: **u,f.**

Luce, Mary Frances, et al. **HF5415.32**
Emotional Decisions: Trade off Difficulty and Coping in Consumer Choice. James R. Bettman & John W. Payne (Authors). Trade Paper. University of Chicago Press. Chicago, IL. 2001. 209p. Monographs of the Journal of Consumer Research ISBN:0-226-53433-2, ISBN13: 978-0-226-53433-6. Dewey:658.8342.
Audience: **u,f.**

Maddala, G. S. **HB139.M348 1994**
Econometric Methods and Applications. Trade Cloth. Edward Elgar Publishing, Inc. Northampton, MA. 1994. 1,168p. Economists of the Twentieth Century Ser. ISBN:1-85278-804-6, ISBN13: 978-1-85278-804-9. Dewey:330/.01/5195. LCCN:93-042454.
Audience: **u,f.**

Mallios, William S. **HG4515.2.M35 2000**
The Anatomy of Sports Forecasting: Modeling Parallels Between Sports Gambling and Financial Markets. Trade Cloth. Springer. New York, NY. 1999. 312p. ISBN:0-7923-7713-3, ISBN13: 978-0-7923-7713-9. Dewey:332.6. LCCN:99-049247.
Audience: **u,f.**

McCann, Charles R. Jr. (Editor) **QA273.18.E34 1996**
F. Y. Edgeworth: Writings in Probability, Statistics and Economics, Set. Trade Cloth. Edward Elgar Publishing, Inc. Northampton, MA. 1996. 1,664p. Elgar Mini Ser. ISBN:1-85898-238-3, ISBN13: 978-1-85898-238-0. Dewey:330/.01. LCCN:95-044045.
Audience: **u,f.**

Mittelhammer, Ron C., et al. **HB139 .M575 2000**
Econometric Foundations. George G. Judge & Douglas J. Miller (Authors). Mixed Media, Cloth Text, CD-ROM. Cambridge University Press. New York, NY. 2000. 784p. ISBN:0-521-62394-4, ISBN13: 978-0-521-62394-0. Dewey:330/.01/5195. LCCN:99-040040.
Audience: **u,f.**

Morgan, Mary S. **HB139.M66 1990**
The History of Econometric Ideas. Craufurd D. Goodwin (Contribution by). Trade Paper. Cambridge University Press. New York, NY. 1991. 312p. Historical Perspectives on Modern Economics Ser. ISBN:0-521-42465-8, ISBN13: 978-0-521-42465-3. Dewey:330.015195.
Audience: **l,u,f.**

Mortensen, Dale T. **HD6061**
Wage Dispersion: Why Are Similar Workers Paid Differently? Trade Paper. MIT Press. Cambridge, MA. 2005. 160p. Zeuthen Lectures ISBN:0-262-63319-1, ISBN13: 978-0-262-63319-2. Dewey:331.2101.
Audience: **g,l,u,f.**

Murray, Michael P. **HB139.M877 2006**
Econometrics: A Modern Introduction. Saddle Stitched, Cloth over Boards. Addison Wesley. Boston, MA. 2005. 929p. ISBN:0-321-11361-6, ISBN13: 978-0-321-11361-0. Dewey:330/.01/5195. LCCN:2005-018586.
Audience: **l,u,f.**

Nerlove, Marc **H61.26.N47 2002**
Essays in Panel Data Econometrics. Cloth Text. Cambridge University Press. New York, NY. 2002. 382p. ISBN:0-521-81534-7, ISBN13: 978-0-521-81534-5. Dewey:330/.01/5195. LCCN:2002-073479.
Audience: **u,f.**

Novshek, William **HB135**
Mathematics for Economists. Ed. 2. Trade Cloth. Elsevier Science & Technology Books. Saint Louis, MO. 2005. 350p. Economic Theory, Econometrics, and Mathematical Economics Ser. ISBN:0-12-522568-7, ISBN13: 978-0-12-522568-7. Dewey:330.0151.
Audience: **g,l,u,f.**

Patterson, Kerry & Mills, Terence C. (Editors) **HB139**
Palgrave Handbook of Econometrics: Econometric Theory. Cloth over Boards. Palgrave Macmillan. New York, NY. 2006. 800p. ISBN:1-4039-4155-6, ISBN13: 978-1-4039-4155-8. Dewey:330/.01/5195. LCCN:2005-050049.
Audience: **l,u,f.**

Pesaran, M. Hashem & Schmidt, Peter (Editors) **HB172**
Handbook of Applied Econometrics: Microeconomics. Trade Paper. Blackwell Publishing, Inc. Malden, MA. 1999. 464p. Handbooks in Economics Ser. ISBN:0-631-21633-2, ISBN13: 978-0-631-21633-9. Dewey:338.5/015195.
Audience: **l,u,f.**

Pindyck, Robert S. & Rubinfeld, Daniel L. **HB3730.P54 1998**
Econometric Models and Economic Forecasts. Ed. 4. Cloth Text. McGraw-Hill Companies, The. New York, NY. 1997. 700p. ISBN:0-07-050208-0, ISBN13: 978-0-07-050208-6. Dewey:330/.015195. LCCN:97-010357.
Audience: **l,u,f.**

Plasmans, Joseph **HB139**
Modern Linear and Nonlinear Econometrics. Trade Cloth. Springer. New York, NY. 2006. XXII, 382p. Dynamic Modeling and Econometrics in Economics and Finance Ser. ISBN:0-387-25760-8, ISBN13: 978-0-387-25760-0. Dewey:330.015195.
Audience: **u,f.**

Plasmans, Joseph, et al. **HJ275**
Dynamic Modeling of Monetary and Fiscal Cooperation among Nations. Jacob Engwerda, Bas van Aarle, Giovanni di Bartolomeo & Tomasz Michalak (Authors). Trade Cloth. Springer. New York, NY. 2006. XVI, 324p. Dynamic Modeling and Econometrics in Economics and Finance Ser. ISBN:0-387-27884-2, ISBN13: 978-0-387-27884-1. Dewey:336.185.
Audience: **u,f.**

Poirier, Dale J. **HB137.P645 1995**
Intermediate Statistics and Econometrics: A Comparative Approach. Trade Cloth. MIT Press. Cambridge, MA. 1995.

731p. ISBN:0-262-16149-4, ISBN13: 978-0-262-16149-7. Dewey:330/.01/5195. LCCN:94-028184.
Audience: **l,u,f.**

Poitras, Geoffrey **HG173.P54 2006**
Pioneers of Financial Economics: Contributions Prior to Irving Fisher. Trade Cloth. Edward Elgar Publishing, Inc. Northampton, MA. 2006. 288p. ISBN:1-84542-381-X, ISBN13: 978-1-84542-381-0. Dewey:332. LCCN:2005-049498.
Audience: **l,u,f.**

Pudney, Stephen **HB801.P78 1989**
Modelling Individual Choice: The Econometrics of Corners, Kinks and Holes. Cloth Text. Blackwell Publishing, Inc. Malden, MA. 1989. 352p. ISBN:0-631-14589-3, ISBN13: 978-0-631-14589-9. Dewey:338.5/212/0724. LCCN:88-023356.
Audience: **l,u,f.**

Qin, Duo **HB139.Q3 1993**
The Formation of Econometrics: A Historical Perspective. Trade Cloth. Oxford University Press, Inc. New York, NY. 1993. 234p. ISBN:0-19-828388-1, ISBN13: 978-0-19-828388-1. Dewey:330/.015195/09. LCCN:93-018799.
Audience: **l,u,f.** *Choice, 1994.*

Ramanathan, Ramu **HB139.R337 2002**
Introductory Econometrics with Applications. Ed. 5. Trade Cloth. Harcourt College Publishers. Fort Worth, TX. 2002. xvi, 688p. Harcourt Series in Economics ISBN:0-03-034186-8, ISBN13: 978-0-03-034186-1. Dewey:330/.015195. LCCN:2001-092277.
Audience: **l,u,f.**

Renshaw, Geoff & Ireland, Norman J. **HB135.R46 2005**
Maths for Economics. Paper Text. Oxford University Press, Inc. New York, NY. 2005. 908p. ISBN:0-19-926746-4, ISBN13: 978-0-19-926746-0. Dewey:510.2433. LCCN:2005-280909.
Audience: **g,l,u,f.**

Rima, Ingrid H. (Editor) **HB135.M423 1995**
Measurement, Quantification and Economic Analysis: Numeracy in Economics. Paper over Boards. Routledge. New York, NY. 1995. 480p. ISBN:0-415-08915-8, ISBN13: 978-0-415-08915-9. Dewey:330/.01/51. LCCN:94-014956.
Audience: **u,f.**

Robinson, Peter M. **HB141.R62 2003**
Time Series with Long Memory. Trade Paper. Oxford University Press, Inc. New York, NY. 2003. 392p. Advanced Texts in Econometrics ISBN:0-19-925730-2, ISBN13: 978-0-19-925730-0. Dewey:330/.01/51932. LCCN:2002-035565.
Audience: **u,f.**

Romer, David **HB172.5.R66 2006**
Advanced Macroeconomics. Ed. 3. Cloth Text. McGraw-Hill Higher Education. Burr Ridge, IL. 2005. 696p. ISBN:0-07-287730-8, ISBN13: 978-0-07-287730-4. Dewey:339. LCCN:2005-041697.
Audience: **u,f.**

Rothman, Philip (Editor) **HB141.N658 1999**
Nonlinear Time Series Analysis of Economic and Financial Data. Trade Cloth. Springer. New York, NY. 1999. 396p. ISBN:0-7923-8379-6, ISBN13: 978-0-7923-8379-6. Dewey:330/.01/5195. LCCN:98-045191.
Audience: **u,f.**

Ruud, Paul A. **HB139.R88 2000**
An Introduction to Classical Econometric Theory. Cloth Text. Oxford University Press, Inc. New York, NY. 2000. 976p. ISBN:0-19-511164-8, ISBN13: 978-0-19-511164-4. Dewey:330/.01/5195. LCCN:99-089456.
Audience: **l,u,f.**

Samuelson, Paul Anthony **HB135**
Foundations of Economic Analysis. Trade Cloth. Harvard University Press. Cambridge, MA. 1983. 632p. Economic Studies, No. 80 ISBN:0-674-31301-1, ISBN13: 978-0-674-31301-9. Dewey:330/.01/51. LCCN:82-021304.
Audience: **u,f.**

Searle, Shayle R. & Willett, Lois Schertz **HB135.S38 2001**
Matrix Algebra for Applied Economics. Trade Cloth. John Wiley & Sons, Inc. Hoboken, NJ. 2001. 432p. Wiley Series in Probability and Statistics, Vol. 349 ISBN:0-471-32207-5, ISBN13: 978-0-471-32207-8. Dewey:330/.01/5129434. LCCN:2001-026759.
Audience: **l,u.**

Sellekaerts, Willy (Editor) **HB139**
Econometrics and Economic Theory: Essays in Honour of Jan Tinbergen. Trade Cloth. M. E. Sharpe Inc. Armonk, NY. 1974. 300p. ISBN:0-87332-056-5, ISBN13: 978-0-87332-056-6. Dewey:330/.028. LCCN:73-092709.
Audience: **u,f.**

Simon, Carl P. & Blume, Lawrence E. **HB135**
Mathematics for Economists. Trade Cloth. W. W. Norton & Company, Inc. New York, NY. 1994. 954p. ISBN:0-393-95733-0, ISBN13: 978-0-393-95733-4. Dewey:510.2/4339. LCCN:93-024962.
Audience: **l,u,f.**

Simon, Carl P. & Blume, Lawrence E. **HB135**
Mathematics for Economists: Answers Pamphlet. Paper Text. W. W. Norton & Company, Inc. New York, NY. 1994. ISBN:0-393-96083-8, ISBN13: 978-0-393-96083-9. Dewey:510/.24339. LCCN:93-024962.
Audience: **l,u,f.**

Stigum, Bernt P. **HB139**
Econometrics and the Philosophy of Economics: Theory-Data Confrontations in Economics. Trade Paper. Princeton University Press. Princeton, NJ. 2003. 856p. ISBN:0-691-11300-9, ISBN13: 978-0-691-11300-5. Dewey:330/.01/5195. LCCN:2003-106662.
Audience: **u,f.**

Stock, James H. & Watson, Mark W. **HB139.S765 2003**
Introduction to Econometrics. Mixed Media. Addison-Wesley Longman, Inc. Boston, MA. 2002. 696p. ISBN:0-201-71595-3, ISBN13: 978-0-201-71595-8. Dewey:330.01/5195. LCCN:2002-071217.
Audience: **u,f.**

Stock, James H. & Watson, Mark W. **HB139.S765 2006**
Introduction to Econometrics. Ed. 2. Cloth Text. Addison-Wesley Longman, Inc. Boston, MA. 2006. 840p. ISBN:0-321-27887-9, ISBN13: 978-0-321-27887-6. Dewey:330.01/5195. LCCN:2006-018388.
Audience: **u,f.**

Stokey, Nancy L. & Lucas, Robert E. Jr. **HB135.S7455 1989**
Recursive Methods in Economic Dynamics. Trade Cloth. Harvard University Press. Cambridge, MA. 1989. 616p. ISBN:0-674-75096-9, ISBN13: 978-0-674-75096-8. Dewey:330/.01/51. LCCN:88-037681.
Audience: **u,f.**

Studenmund, A. H. **HB139.S795 2005**
Using Econometrics: A Practical Guide. Ed. 5. Cloth Text. Addison-Wesley Longman, Inc. Boston, MA. 2005. 656p. The Addison-Wesley Series in Economics ISBN:0-321-31649-5, ISBN13: 978-0-321-31649-3. Dewey:330/.01/5195. LCCN:2005-013040.
Audience: **g,l,u,f.**

Tinbergen, Jan **HB139**
Econometrics. Paper over Boards. Routledge. New York, NY. 2004. 272p. ISBN:0-415-32138-7, ISBN13: 978-0-415-32138-9. Dewey:330/.015195.
Audience: **u,f.**

Tinbergen, Jan; Bos, Hendricus Cornelis **HB71.T5**
Mathematical models of economic growth. New York, McGraw-Hill. 1962. Economics handbook series
Audience: **u,f.**

Tobin, J. **HB801**
Essays in Economics: Consumption and Econometrics. Trade Cloth. Elsevier Science & Technology Books. Saint Louis, MO. 1975. 492p. ISBN:0-444-10684-7, ISBN13: 978-0-444-10684-1. Dewey:330/.028. LCCN:70-183276.
Audience: **u,f.**

Tsay, Ruey S. **HA30.3 T76**
Analysis of Financial Time Series. Trade Cloth. John Wiley & Sons, Inc. Hoboken, NJ. 2003. ISBN:0-471-26410-5, ISBN13: 978-0-471-26410-1. Dewey:332/.01/51955.
Audience: **u,f.**

van Den Berg, Richard **HB135**
At the Origins of Mathematical Economics: The Contribution of A. N. Isnard. Paper over Boards. Routledge. New York, NY. 2005. 480p. Routledge Studies in the History of Economics Ser. ISBN:0-415-30649-3, ISBN13: 978-0-415-30649-2. Dewey:330.15/43/092 B. LCCN:2005-003569.
Audience: **u,f.**

Verbeek, Marno **HB139**
A Guide to Modern Econometrics. Ed. 2. Trade Paper. John Wiley & Sons, Inc. Hoboken, NJ. 2004. 446p. ISBN:0-470-85773-0, ISBN13: 978-0-470-85773-1. Dewey:330/.01/5195. LCCN:2004-004222.
Audience: **l,u,f.**

Verbeek, Marno **HB139.V465 2004**
[e] A Guide to Modern Econometrics. Ed. 2. E-Book. John Wiley & Sons, Inc. Hoboken, NJ. 2005. 446p. ISBN:0-470-85774-9, ISBN13: 978-0-470-85774-8. Dewey:330/.01/5195.
Audience: **l,u,f.**

Vohra, Rakesh **HB135.V636 2004**
Advanced Mathematical Economics. Paper over Boards. Routledge. New York, NY. 2005. 208p. Routledge Advanced Texts in Economics and Finance Ser. ISBN:0-415-70007-8, ISBN13: 978-0-415-70007-8. Dewey:330/.01/513. LCCN:2004-050813.
Audience: **u,f.**

Wansbeek, Tom J. & Meijer, Erik **HB139.W36 2000**
[e] Measurement Error and Latent Variables in Econometrics. E-Book. NetLibrary, Inc. Boulder, CO. 2000. ISBN:0-585-48959-9, ISBN13: 978-0-585-48959-9. Dewey:330.015195.
Audience: **u,f.**

White, Halbert **HB139.W5 2001**
Asymptotic Theory for Econometricians. Ed. 2. Cloth Text. Elsevier Science & Technology Books. Saint Louis, MO. 2000. 264p. Economic Theory, Econometrics and Mathematical Economics Ser. ISBN:0-12-746652-5, ISBN13: 978-0-12-746652-1. Dewey:330/.01/5195. LCCN:00-107735.
Audience: **u,f.**

Wilcox, Jarrod W. **HG4515.3**
Investing by the Numbers. John Y. Campbell (Foreword by). Trade Cloth. John Wiley & Sons, Inc. Hoboken, NJ. 1999. 358p. Frank J. Fabozzi Ser., Vol. 49 ISBN:1-883249-54-6, ISBN13: 978-1-883249-54-0. Dewey:332.60151.
Audience: **g,l,u,f.**

Wooldridge, Jeffrey M. **HB171.5**
Basic Econometrics. Trade Cloth. Thomson South-Western. Mason, OH. 2005. Econometrics Ser. ISBN:0-538-85009-4, ISBN13: 978-0-538-85009-4. Dewey:330.
Audience: **l,u,f.**

Wooldridge, Jeffrey M. **HB139.W663 2001**
Econometric Analysis of Cross Section and Panel Data. Trade Cloth. MIT Press. Cambridge, MA. 2001. 740p. ISBN:0-262-23219-7, ISBN13: 978-0-262-23219-7. Dewey:330.015195. LCCN:2001-044263.
Audience: **u,f.**

Wooldridge, Jeffrey M. **HB139.W665 2002**
Introductory Econometrics: A Modern Approach. Ed. 2. Cloth Text. Thomson South-Western. Mason, OH. 2002. 896p. ISBN:0-324-11364-1, ISBN13: 978-0-324-11364-8. Dewey:330/.01/5195. LCCN:2002-070585.
Audience: **l,u,f.**

Yatchew, Adonis **HB139.Y38 2003**
Semiparametric Regression for the Applied Econometrician. Trade Cloth. Cambridge University Press. New York, NY. 2003. 234p. Themes in Modern Econometrics Ser. ISBN:0-521-81283-6, ISBN13: 978-0-521-81283-2. Dewey:330/.01/519536. LCCN:2002-041002.
Audience: **u,f.**

Econometrics. Mathematical Economics > General Equilibrium

Ackerman, Frank & Nadal, Alejandro **HB145**
The Perfect Impossibility of General Equilibrium Theory. Paper over Boards. Routledge. New York, NY. 2004. 240p. Routledge Frontiers of Political Economy Ser., Vol. 62 ISBN:0-415-70001-9, ISBN13: 978-0-415-70001-6. Dewey:339.5. LCCN:2004-040955.
Audience: **l,u,f.**

Arrow, Kenneth Joseph **HM251**
Social Choice and Individual Values. Ed. 2. Trade Paper. Yale University Press. Cumberland, RI. 1970. 138p. Cowles Foundation Monograph Ser., No. 12 ISBN:0-300-01364-7, ISBN13: 978-0-300-01364-1. Dewey:301.1.
Audience: **l,u,f.**

Borglin, Anders & Tvede, M. V. **QA297**
Economic Dynamics and General Equilibrium: Time and Uncertainty. Trade Cloth. Springer. New York, NY. 2004. XII, 396p. ISBN:3-540-00265-0, ISBN13: 978-3-540-00265-9. Dewey:330/.01/5195. LCCN:2003-069143.
Audience: **l,u,f.**

Dimand, Robert (Editor, Introduction by) **HF1379.O75 2004**
General Equilibrium in International Trade: The Origins of International Economics. Paper over Boards. Routledge. New York, NY. 2004. 440p. Origins of International Economics Ser., Vol. 7 ISBN:0-415-31562-X, ISBN13: 978-0-415-31562-3. Dewey:382. LCCN:2003-060550.
Audience: **l,u,f.**

Walsh, Vivian & Gram, Harvey N. **HB145**
Classical and Neoclassical Theories of General Equilibrium. Joan Robinson (Introduction by). Cloth Text. Oxford University Press, Inc. New York, NY. 1979. 442p. ISBN:0-19-502674-8, ISBN13: 978-0-19-502674-0. Dewey:330.15/43. LCCN:78-031129.
Audience: **u,f.**

Econometrics. Mathematical Economics > Simultaneous Equation Models. Multiple Variables

Boyce, William E. & DiPrima, Richard C. **QA371**
WIE Elementary Differential Equations and Boundary Value Problems, Textbook and Student Solutions Manual. Ed. 8. Trade Cloth. John Wiley & Sons, Inc. Hoboken, NJ. 2004. 1078p. ISBN:0-471-69767-2, ISBN13: 978-0-471-69767-1.
Audience: **u,f.**

Stewart, James **QA303.2.S737 2005**
Multivariable Calculus: Concepts and Contexts. Ed. 3. Cloth Text. Brooks/Cole. Pacific Grove, CA. 2004. ISBN:0-534-41002-2, ISBN13: 978-0-534-41002-5. Dewey:515. LCCN:2004-113997.
Audience: **u,f.**

Econometrics. Mathematical Economics > Panel Data

Baltagi, Badi H. **HB139**
Econometric Analysis of Panel Data. Ed. 3. Trade Cloth. John Wiley & Sons, Inc. Hoboken, NJ. 2002. 1728p. ISBN:0-471-26730-9, ISBN13: 978-0-471-26730-0. Dewey:330/.01/5195. LCCN:00-043811.
Audience: **u,f.**

Hsiao, Cheng **HB139.H75 2002**
Analysis of Panel Data. Ed. 2. Peter Hammond, Alberto Holly, Andrew Chesher & Matthew Jackson (Contribution by). Trade Cloth. Cambridge University Press. New York, NY. 2003. 382p. Econometric Society Monographs, No. 34 ISBN:0-521-81855-9, ISBN13: 978-0-521-81855-1. Dewey:330/.01/5195. LCCN:2002-023348.
Audience: **u,f.**

Wooldridge, Jeffrey M. **HB139.W663 2001**
Econometric Analysis of Cross Section and Panel Data. Trade Cloth. MIT Press. Cambridge, MA. 2001. 740p. ISBN:0-262-23219-7, ISBN13: 978-0-262-23219-7. Dewey:330.015195. LCCN:2001-044263.
Audience: **u,f.**

Econometrics. Mathematical Economics > Time-Series

Enders, Walter **HB139.E55 2003**
Applied Econometric Time Series. Ed. 2. Trade Cloth. John Wiley & Sons, Inc. Hoboken, NJ. 2003. 480p. Wiley Series in Probability and Statistics ISBN:0-471-23065-0, ISBN13: 978-0-471-23065-6. Dewey:330/.01/519232. LCCN:2003-053787.
Audience: **l,u,f.**

Granger, C. W. (Editor) **HB3730**
Forecasting Economic Time Series. Trade Cloth. Elsevier Science & Technology Books. Saint Louis, MO. 1977. xii, 333p. Economic Theory and Mathematical Economics Ser. ISBN:0-12-295150-6, ISBN13: 978-0-12-295150-3. Dewey:338.5/442. LCCN:76-009156.
Audience: **u,f.**

Granger, C. W. & Hatanaka, Michio **HB199**
Spectral Analysis of Economic Time Series. Trade Cloth. Princeton University Press. Princeton, NJ. 1964. 320p. Mathematical Economics Studies, Vol. 1 ISBN:0-691-04177-6, ISBN13: 978-0-691-04177-3. Dewey:330.182.
Audience: **u,f.**

Karlin, Samuel (Editor), et al. **HB139**
Studies in Econometrics, Time Series and Multivariate Statistics: Monograph. Takeshi Amemiya & Leo Goodman (Editors). Trade Cloth. Elsevier Science & Technology Books. Saint Louis, MO. 1983. ISBN:0-12-398750-4, ISBN13: 978-0-12-398750-1. Dewey:330/.028.
Audience: **u,f.**

Tsay, Ruey S. **HA30.3 T76**
Analysis of Financial Time Series. Trade Cloth. John Wiley & Sons, Inc. Hoboken, NJ. 2003. ISBN:0-471-26410-5, ISBN13: 978-0-471-26410-1. Dewey:332/.01/51955.
Audience: **u,f.**

Econometrics. Mathematical Economics > Modeling/Forecasting

Barnett, William A. (Editor), et al. **HB139 .I566 1995**
Nonlinear Econometric Modeling in Time Series: Proceedings of the Eleventh International Symposium in Economic Theory. David F. Hendry, Svend Hylleberg, Timo Terasvirta, Dag Tjostheim & Allan Wurtz (Editors). Trade Cloth. Cambridge

University Press. New York, NY. 2000. 240p. International Symposia in Economic Theory and Econometrics Ser., No. 11 ISBN:0-521-59424-3, ISBN13: 978-0-521-59424-0. Dewey:330/.01/5195. LCCN:99-034095.
Audience: **u,f.**

Duraiappah, Anantha Kumar **HD75.6.D865 2003**
Computational Models in the Economics of Environment and Development. Trade Cloth. Kluwer Law International. Alphen a/d Rijn, 2003. 248p. Economy and Environment Ser., Vol. 27 ISBN:1-4020-1773-1, ISBN13: 978-1-4020-1773-5. Dewey:333.7/01/519. LCCN:2003-064067.
Audience: **l,u,f.**

Eeckhoudt, Louis, et al. **HB615.E44 2005**
Economic and Financial Decisions under Risk. Christian Gollier & Harris Schlesinger (Authors). Trade Cloth. Princeton University Press. Princeton, NJ. 2005. 244p. ISBN:0-691-09655-4, ISBN13: 978-0-691-09655-1. Dewey:338.5. LCCN:2004-058689.
Audience: **l,u,f.**

Granger, Clive **HB141 .G728 1999**
Empirical Modeling in Economics: Specification and Evaluation. Geoff Harcourt (Foreword by). Cloth Text. Cambridge University Press. New York, NY. 1999. 108p. ISBN:0-521-66208-7, ISBN13: 978-0-521-66208-6. Dewey:330.015118. LCCN:00-700407.
Audience: **u,f.**

Granger, Clive **HB141**
[e] Empirical Modeling in Economics: Specification and Evaluation. Geoff Harcourt (Foreword by). E-Book. Cambridge University Press. New York, NY. 2005. ISBN:0-511-03367-2, ISBN13: 978-0-511-03367-4. Dewey:330.015118.
Audience: **u,f.**

Granger, Clive & Terasvirta, Timo **HB139**
Modelling Nonlinear Economic Relationships. Trade Paper. Oxford University Press, Inc. New York, NY. 1993. 198p. Advanced Texts in Econometrics ISBN:0-19-877320-X, ISBN13: 978-0-19-877320-7. Dewey:330.015195.
Audience: **u,f.**

Jorgenson, Dale W. **HB241.J67 2000**
Econometrics: Econometric Modeling of Producer Behavior. Trade Cloth. MIT Press. Cambridge, MA. 2000. 460p. ISBN:0-262-10082-7, ISBN13: 978-0-262-10082-3. Dewey:330/.01/5195. LCCN:99-046138.
Audience: **u,f.**

Mallios, William S. **HG4515.2.M35 2000**
The Anatomy of Sports Forecasting: Modeling Parallels Between Sports Gambling and Financial Markets. Trade Cloth. Springer. New York, NY. 1999. 312p. ISBN:0-7923-7713-3, ISBN13: 978-0-7923-7713-9. Dewey:332.6. LCCN:99-049247.
Audience: **u,f.**

Pindyck, Robert S. & Rubinfeld, Daniel L. **HB3730.P54 1998**
Econometric Models and Economic Forecasts. Ed. 4. Cloth Text. McGraw-Hill Companies, The. New York, NY. 1997. 700p. ISBN:0-07-050208-0, ISBN13: 978-0-07-050208-6. Dewey:330/.015195. LCCN:97-010357.
Audience: **l,u,f.**

Econometrics. Mathematical Economics > Game Theory

Norman, George & LaManna, Manfred (Editors) **HD2326.N42 1992**
The New Industrial Economics: Recent Developments in Industrial Organization, Oligopoly and Game Theory. Cloth Text. Edward Elgar Publishing, Inc. Northampton, MA. 1992. 272p. ISBN:1-85278-139-4, ISBN13: 978-1-85278-139-2. Dewey:338.8. LCCN:91-028153.
Audience: **u,f.** *Choice, 1993.*

Osborne, Martin J. & Rubinstein, Ariel **HB144.O733 1994**
A Course in Game Theory. Trade Paper. MIT Press. Cambridge, MA. 1994. 368p. ISBN:0-262-65040-1, ISBN13: 978-0-262-65040-3. Dewey:658.4/0353. LCCN:94-008308.
Audience: **u,f.**

Princeton University Conference Staff **QA0269.P75**
Recent Advances in Game Theory. Trade Paper. Books on Demand. Ann Arbor, MI. 290p. ISBN:0-598-77661-3, ISBN13: 978-0-598-77661-7. Dewey:519.3. LCCN:62-005290.
Audience: **u,f.**

Rubinstein, Ariel **HB144.G375 1990**
Game Theory in Economics. Trade Cloth. Edward Elgar Publishing, Inc. Northampton, MA. 1990. 680p. The International Library of Critical Writings in Economics, Vol. 5 ISBN:1-85278-169-6, ISBN13: 978-1-85278-169-9. Dewey:330/.01/5193. LCCN:90-037730.
Audience: **u,f.**

Sundaram, Rangarajan K. **QA402.5 .S837 1996**
A First Course in Optimization Theory. Trade Cloth. Cambridge University Press. New York, NY. 1996. 357p. ISBN:0-521-49719-1, ISBN13: 978-0-521-49719-0. Dewey:330/.0151. LCCN:95-022878.
Audience: **u,f.**

Systems

Engels, Friedrich **HB501.M5E48**
Engels on Capital: Synopsis, Reviews, and Supplementary Material. Leonard Emil Mins (Editor and Translator). New York, International Publishers. 1974.
Audience: **l,u,f.**

Kuran, Timur **HB126.4.K87 2004**
Islam and Mammon: The Economic Predicaments of Islamism. Trade Cloth. Princeton University Press. Princeton, NJ. 2004. 232p. ISBN:0-691-11510-9, ISBN13: 978-0-691-11510-8. Dewey:330.917/67. LCCN:2003-060094.
Audience: **l,u,f.** *Choice, 2005.*

Lutz, Mark A. **HB72.L874 1999**
Economics for the Common Good: Two Centuries of Social Economic Thought in the Humanistic Tradition. Paper over Boards. Routledge. New York, NY. 1999. 320p. Advances in Social Economics Ser. ISBN:0-415-14312-8, ISBN13: 978-0-415-14312-7. Dewey:330/.01. LCCN:99-222946.
Audience: **l,u,f.**

Pressman, Steven **HB76.P74 2006**
Fifty Major Economists. Ed. 2. Paper over Boards. Routledge. New York, NY. 2006. XXIII, 329p. ISBN:0-415-36648-8, ISBN13: 978-0-415-36648-9. LCCN:2005-025713.
Audience: **g,l,u,f.**

Systems > History

Bastiat, Frederic **HB163 .B32**
Essays on Political Economy. Trade Paper. University Press of the Pacific. Miami, FL. 2004. 420p. ISBN:1-4102-1307-2, ISBN13: 978-1-4102-1307-5. Dewey:330.
Audience: **u,f.**

Beaud, Michel & Dostaler, Gilles **HB87.B4313 1997**
Economic Thought since Keynes: A History and Dictionary of Major Economists. Trade Paper. Routledge. New York, NY. 1997. 512p. ISBN:0-415-16454-0, ISBN13: 978-0-415-16454-2. Dewey:330/.0922. LCCN:97-012823.
Audience: **l,u,f.**

Biddle, J. E. (Editor), et al. **HB75**
Research in the History of Economic Thought and Methodology, Vol. 23, Set. R. B. Emmett & W. J. Samuels (Editors). Trade Cloth. Elsevier Science & Technology Books. Saint Louis, MO. 2005. 350p. ISBN:0-7623-1171-1, ISBN13: 978-0-7623-1171-2. Dewey:330/.09.
Audience: **l,u,f.**

Blackwell, Ron (Editor), et al. **HB72**
Economics as Worldly Philosophy: Essays in Political and Historical Economics in Honour of Robert Heilbroner. Jaspal Chatha & Edward J. Nell (Editors). Trade Cloth. Palgrave Macmillan Ltd. Basingstoke, 1993. 370p. ISBN:0-333-49477-6, ISBN13: 978-0-333-49477-6. Dewey:330.01. LCCN:92-002547.
Audience: **l,u,f.**

Blaug, Mark **HB75 .B664 1997**
Economic Theory in Retrospect. Ed. 5. Cloth Text. Cambridge University Press. New York, NY. 1997. 751p. ISBN:0-521-57153-7, ISBN13: 978-0-521-57153-1. Dewey:330/.01/09. LCCN:95-026743.
Audience: **g,l,u,f.**

Blaug, Mark **HB76 .B54**
Great Economists Before Keynes: An Introduction to the Lives and Works of One Hundred Great Economists of the Past. Trade Cloth. Edward Elgar Publishing, Inc. Northampton, MA. 1997. 304p. ISBN:1-85898-571-4, ISBN13: 978-1-85898-571-8. Dewey:330/.092/2.
Audience: **g,l,u,f.**

Blaug, Mark **HB76.B55 1998**
Great Economists since Keynes: An Introduction to the Lives and Works of One Hundred Modern Economists. Ed. 2. Trade Cloth. Edward Elgar Publishing, Inc. Northampton, MA. 1998. 328p. ISBN:1-85898-692-3, ISBN13: 978-1-85898-692-0. Dewey:[B]. LCCN:97-037217.
Audience: **l,u,f.**

Boulding, Kenneth E. & Mukerjee, Tapan (Editors) **HC51.B65 1972**
Economic Imperialism: A Book of Readings. Trade Cloth. University of Michigan Press. Chicago, IL. 1972. xviii, 338p. ISBN:0-472-16830-4, ISBN13: 978-0-472-16830-9. Dewey:330.9. LCCN:74-146490.
Audience: **l,u,f.**

Bourdieu, Pierre **HM548**
The Social Structures of the Economy. Trade Cloth. Polity Press. Cambridge, 2005. 180p. ISBN:0-7456-2539-8, ISBN13: 978-0-7456-2539-3. Dewey:306.3. LCCN:2005-620708.
Audience: **l,u,f.**

Buchanan, James M. **HB0171.B86**
Fiscal Theory and Political Economy: Selected Essays. Trade Paper. Books on Demand. Ann Arbor, MI. 207p. ISBN:0-598-16843-5, ISBN13: 978-0-598-16843-6. Dewey:330. LCCN:60-050887.
Audience: **u,f.**

Clark, John **HB171 .C59**
The Philosophy of Wealth: Economic Principles Newly Formulated. Trade Paper. University Press of the Pacific. Miami, FL. 2004. 252p. ISBN:1-4102-1322-6, ISBN13: 978-1-4102-1322-8. Dewey:330.15/5.
Audience: **u,f.**

Clark, John Bates **HB171**
Essentials of Economic Theory as Applied to Modern Problems of Industry and Public Policy. Trade Cloth. Library Reprints, Inc. Temecula, CA. 1907. 566p. ISBN:0-7222-2665-9, ISBN13: 978-0-7222-2665-0. Dewey:330.1.
Audience: **u,f.**

Commons, John Rogers **HB171.C77 1970**
The Economics of Collective Action. Trade Cloth. University of Wisconsin Press. Chicago, IL. 1970. xxi, 382p. ISBN:0-299-05360-1, ISBN13: 978-0-299-05360-4. Dewey:330.1. LCCN:69-017328.
Audience: **u,f.**

Conrad, Alfred H.; Meyer, John Robert **HC53.C57**
The Economics of Slavery, and Other Studies in Econometric History. Chicago, Aldine Pub. Co.. 1964.
Audience: **u,f.**

Creedy, John **HB75.C836 1999**
The History of Economic Analysis: Selected Essays by John Creedy. Trade Cloth. Edward Elgar Publishing, Inc. Northampton, MA. 1999. 360p. ISBN:1-85898-908-6, ISBN13: 978-1-85898-908-2. Dewey:330/.09. LCCN:98-029698.
Audience: **u,f.**

Dobb, Maurice **HC51**
Studies in the Development of Capitalism. Trade Paper. International Publishers Company, Inc. New York, NY. 1964. 415p. ISBN:0-7178-0197-7, ISBN13: 978-0-7178-0197-8. Dewey:330.9. LCCN:74-013744.
Audience: **l,u,f.**

Dobb, Maurice Herbert **HB0171**
On Economic Theory and Socialism: Collected Papers. Trade Paper. Books on Demand. Ann Arbor, MI. 301p. ISBN:0-598-39938-0, ISBN13: 978-0-598-39938-0. Dewey:330.81. LCCN:55-013844.
Audience: **u,f.**

Eucken, W. **HB171 .E7913 1992**
The Foundations of Economics: History and Theory in the Analysis of Economic Reality. Cloth Text. Springer. New York, NY. 1992. 342p. ISBN:0-387-55189-1, ISBN13: 978-0-387-55189-0. Dewey:330.
Audience: **u,f.**

Fawcett, Millicent Garrett **HB171.5 .F27**
Political Economy for Beginners. Trade Paper. University Press of the Pacific. Miami, FL. 2004. 264p. ISBN:1-4102-1318-8, ISBN13: 978-1-4102-1318-1. Dewey:330.
Audience: **l,u,f.**

Fawcett, Millicent Garrett **HB171.5 .F28**
Tales in Political Economy. Trade Paper. University Press of the Pacific. Miami, FL. 2004. 116p. ISBN:1-4102-1303-X, ISBN13: 978-1-4102-1303-7. Dewey:330.
Audience: **l,u,f.**

Fawcett, Millicent Garrett & Fawcett, Henry **AC8 .F3**
Essays and Lectures on Social and Political Subjects. Trade Paper. University Press of the Pacific. Miami, FL. 2004. 380p. ISBN:1-4102-1292-0, ISBN13: 978-1-4102-1292-4. Dewey:081.
Audience: **u,f.**

Galbraith, John Kenneth **HB75.G27**
The Age of Uncertainty. Trade Cloth. Houghton Mifflin Company. New York, NY. 1977. 365p. ISBN:0-395-24900-7, ISBN13: 978-0-395-24900-0. Dewey:330/.09. LCCN:76-026965.
Audience: **g,l,u,f.**

Galbraith, John Kenneth **HB119.G33**
A Life in Our Times: Memoirs. Trade Paper. Ballantine Books. New York, NY. 1982. ISBN:0-345-30323-7, ISBN13: 978-0-345-30323-3. Dewey:330/.092/4.
Audience: **g,l,u,f.**

George, Henry **HB171**
The Science of Political Economy. Trade Cloth. Robert Schalkenbach Foundation. New York, NY. 1992. 545p. ISBN:0-911312-51-X, ISBN13: 978-0-911312-51-5. Dewey:330.1. LCCN:81-005939.
Audience: **u,f.**

George, Henry **HB171**
Social Problems. Trade Paper. Adamant Media. Chestnut Hill, MA. 2000. 252p. ISBN:1-4021-9814-0, ISBN13: 978-1-4021-9814-4. Dewey:304.
Audience: **l,u,f.**

Heilbroner, Robert L. **HB76.H4 1999**
The Worldly Philosophers: The Lives, Times and Ideas of the Great Economic Thinkers. Ed. 7. Trade Paper. Simon & Schuster. New York, NY. 1999. 368p. ISBN:0-684-86214-X, ISBN13: 978-0-684-86214-9. Dewey:330.1/092/2. LCCN:99-014050.
Audience: **g,l,u,f.**

Heilbroner, Robert L. & Milberg, William **HC51.H44 2001**
The Making of Economic Society. Ed. 11. Trade Paper. Prentice Hall PTR. Upper Saddle River, NJ. 2001. 224p. ISBN:0-13-091050-3, ISBN13: 978-0-13-091050-9. Dewey:330. LCCN:2001-021124.
Audience: **l,u.**

Hicks, John Richard **HB171**
Capital and Growth. Trade Cloth. Oxford University Press, Inc. New York, NY. 1972. ISBN:0-19-828150-1, ISBN13: 978-0-19-828150-4. Dewey:330.1.
Audience: **u,f.**

Hicks, John Richard **HB171.H6343**
Economic Perspectives: Further Essays on Money and Growth. Trade Cloth. Oxford University Press, Inc. New York, NY. 1977. 220p. ISBN:0-19-828407-1, ISBN13: 978-0-19-828407-9. Dewey:330. LCCN:77-005770.
Audience: **u,f.**

Hicks, John Richard **HC26.H5**
A Theory of Economic History. Trade Cloth. Oxford University Press, Inc. New York, NY. 1969. ix, 181p. ISBN:0-19-828247-8, ISBN13: 978-0-19-828247-1. Dewey:330/.09. LCCN:70-437823.
Audience: **u,f.**

Hicks, John Richard **HB171**
Value and Capital: An Inquiry into Some Fundamental Principles of Economic Theory. Ed. 2. Paper Text. Oxford University Press, Inc. New York, NY. 1975. 352p. ISBN:0-19-828269-9, ISBN13: 978-0-19-828269-3. Dewey:330.
Audience: **u,f.**

Jones, Eric L. **HD79.J65 2000**
Growth Recurring: Economic Change in World History. Ed. 2. Trade Cloth. University of Michigan Press. Chicago, IL. 2000. 296p. Economics, Cognition, and Society Ser. ISBN:0-472-09728-8, ISBN13: 978-0-472-09728-9. Dewey:338.9. LCCN:00-037740.
Audience: **l,u,f.** *Choice, 1988.*

Kaldor, Nicholas **HB171.K28 1980**
Collected Economic Essays: Essays on Economic Stability and Growth. Trade Cloth. Holmes & Meier Publishers, Inc. Teaneck, NJ. 1980. 312p. ISBN:0-8419-0452-9, ISBN13: 978-0-8419-0452-1. Dewey:332.4/6. LCCN:80-018145.
Audience: **u,f.**

Kaldor, Nicholas **HB171.K2852 1981**
Collected Economic Essays: Essays on Value and Distribution. Trade Cloth. Holmes & Meier Publishers, Inc. Teaneck, NJ. 1980. 238p. ISBN:0-8419-0451-0, ISBN13: 978-0-8419-0451-4. Dewey:332.4/6. LCCN:81-006523.
Audience: **u,f.**

Lutz, Mark A. **HB72.L874 1999**
Economics for the Common Good: Two Centuries of Social Economic Thought in the Humanistic Tradition. Paper over Boards. Routledge. New York, NY. 1999. 320p. Advances in Social Economics Ser. ISBN:0-415-14312-8, ISBN13: 978-0-415-14312-7. Dewey:330/.01. LCCN:99-222946.
Audience: **l,u,f.**

Martineau, Harriet **PR4984.M5 Z463**
Harriet Martineaus's Autobiography, Vol. 1. Trade Paper. Kessinger Publishing, LLC. Whitefish, MT. 2005. ISBN:1-4179-7016-2, ISBN13: 978-1-4179-7016-2. Dewey:823/.8.
Audience: **g,l,u,f.**

Medema, Steven G. & Samuels, Warren J. **HB87.M35 2001**
Historians of Economics and Economic Thought: The Construction of Disciplinary Memory. Paper over Boards. Routledge. New York, NY. 2001. 384p. Routledge Studies in the

History of Economics Ser. ISBN:0-415-18581-5, ISBN13: 978-0-415-18581-3. Dewey:330/.09. LCCN:2001-019459.
Audience: **l,u,f.**

Modigliani, Franco **HB171**
Collected Papers of Franco Modigliani: Essays in Macroeconomics. Andrew B. Abel & Simon Johnson (Editors). Trade Cloth. MIT Press. Cambridge, MA. 1980. 480p. Collected Papers of Franco Modigliani, Vol. 1 ISBN:0-262-13150-1, ISBN13: 978-0-262-13150-6. Dewey:330. LCCN:78-021041.
Audience: **u,f.**

Myrdal, Gunnar **HB171**
The Political Element in the Development of Economic Theory. Paper Text. Textbook Publishers. Temecula, CA. 2003. xvii, 248p. ISBN:0-7581-4602-7, ISBN13: 978-0-7581-4602-1. Dewey:330.1.
Audience: **u,f.**

Myrdal, Gunnar **HB171**
The Political Element in the Development of Economic Theory, Vol. 29. Paper over Boards. Routledge. New York, NY. 2003. 268p. International Library of Sociology Ser. ISBN:0-415-17530-5, ISBN13: 978-0-415-17530-2. Dewey:330.1.
Audience: **u,f.**

North, Douglass Cecil **HB97.3.N67 2005**
Understanding the Process of Economic Change. Trade Cloth. Princeton University Press. Princeton, NJ. 2005. 208p. Princeton Economic History of the Western World Ser. ISBN:0-691-11805-1, ISBN13: 978-0-691-11805-5. Dewey:330.1. LCCN:2004-049131.
Audience: **g,l,u,f.** *Choice, 2005.*

Pigou, Arthur C. **HC57 .P48 1979B**
Economics in Practice: Six Lectures on Current Issues. Trade Cloth. Hyperion Press, Inc. Westport, CT. 1991. ISBN:0-88355-707-X, ISBN13: 978-0-88355-707-5. Dewey:330. LCCN:78-059035.
Audience: **l,u,f.**

Pigou, Arthur C. **HB171 .P58 1978**
Employment and Equilibrium: A Theoretical Discussion. Ed. 2. Library Binding. Scholar's Bookshelf. Cranbury, NJ. 1978. ix, 283p. ISBN:0-678-01224-5, ISBN13: 978-0-678-01224-6. Dewey:330.1. LCCN:76-052397.
Audience: **u,f.**

Polanyi, Karl **HC53.P6 2001**
The Great Transformation: The Political and Economic Origins of Our Time. Ed. 2. Trade Paper. Beacon Press. Boston, MA. 2001. 328p. ISBN:0-8070-5643-X, ISBN13: 978-0-8070-5643-1. Dewey:330.9. LCCN:00-064156.
Audience: **l,u.**

Polanyi, Karl **HC31.P6**
Trade and Market in the Early Empires: Economies in History and Theory. Arensberg, Conrad Maynadier (Editor); Pearson, Harry W. (Editor). Glencoe, Ill. : Free Press ; [s.l.] : Falcon's Wing Press. 1986.
Audience: **l,u,f.**

Polanyi, Karl **HB75**
Primitive, Archaic and Modern Economies: Essays of Karl Polanyi. George Dalton (Editor). Trade Paper. Beacon Press. Boston, MA. 1971. ISBN:0-8070-4793-7, ISBN13: 978-0-8070-4793-4. Dewey:330.1.
Audience: **u,f.**

Robbins, Lionel C. **HC57.R57 1971**
Great Depression. Trade Cloth. Ayer Company Publishers, Inc. Manchester, NH. 1977. xiv, 238p. Select Bibliographies Reprint Ser. ISBN:0-8369-5711-3, ISBN13: 978-0-8369-5711-2. Dewey:330.9/04. LCCN:75-150198.
Audience: **u,f.**

Robbins, Lionel **HB71.R58 1984**
The Nature and Significance of Economic Science. William Baumol (Introduction by). Trade Cloth. New York University Press. New York, NY. 1984. 200p. ISBN:0-8147-7389-3, ISBN13: 978-0-8147-7389-5. Dewey:330. LCCN:84-003416.
Audience: **l,u,f.**

Samuels, Warren J. (Editor), et al. **HB75.E774 2004**
Essays in the History of Economics. Willie Henderson, Kirk D. Johnson & Marianne Johnson (Editors). Paper over Boards. Routledge. New York, NY. 2004. 368p. Routledge Studies in the History of Economics Ser., Vol. 67 ISBN:0-415-70006-X, ISBN13: 978-0-415-70006-1. Dewey:330/.09. LCCN:2003-069534.
Audience: **u,f.**

Samuelson, Paul Anthony **HB171.5**
Study Guide to Accompany Economics. Ed. 17. Paper Text. McGraw-Hill Higher Education. Burr Ridge, IL. 2000. 448p. ISBN:0-07-237225-7, ISBN13: 978-0-07-237225-0.
Audience: **l,u.**

Schumpeter, Joseph Alois **HB76**
Ten Great Economists: From Marx to Keynes. Trade Paper. Simon Publications, Inc. 2003. 301p. ISBN:1-932512-09-8, ISBN13: 978-1-932512-09-0. Dewey:330.0922. LCCN:52-040824.
Audience: **g,l,u,f.**

Schumpeter, Joseph Alois **HB75.S456 1994**
History of Economic Analysis: With a New Introduction. Mark Perlman (Introduction by). Paper Text. Oxford University Press, Inc. New York, NY. 1996. 1320p. ISBN:0-19-510559-1, ISBN13: 978-0-19-510559-9. Dewey:330/.09. LCCN:95-044189.
Audience: **l,u,f.**

Stigler, George J. **HB85.S668 1994**
Production and Distribution Theories. Douglas Irwin (Introduction by). Trade Paper. Transaction Publishers. Somerset, NJ. 1994. 392p. ISBN:1-56000-710-9, ISBN13: 978-1-56000-710-4. Dewey:330.1. LCCN:93-036977.
Audience: **u,f.**

Veblen, Thorstein **H61**
Portable Veblen. Max Lerner (Editor). Trade Paper. Penguin Group (USA) Inc. New York, NY. 1976. vii, 632p. Portable

Library, No. 36 ISBN:0-14-015036-6, ISBN13: 978-0-14-015036-0. Dewey:300/.1.
Audience: **l,u,f.**

Weber, Max **HC31.W42213 1976**
The Agrarian Sociology of Ancient Civilizations. Trade Cloth. Bow Historical Books. New Providence, NJ. 1976. 421p. ISBN:0-902308-08-4, ISBN13: 978-0-902308-08-4. Dewey:330.9/01. LCCN:76-370998.
Audience: **l,u,f.**

Zein-Elabdin, Eiman O. & Charusheela, S. (Editors) **HB72.P637 2004**
Postcolonialism Meets Economics. Paper over Boards. Routledge. New York, NY. 2003. 304p. Economics As Social Theory Ser. ISBN:0-415-28725-1, ISBN13: 978-0-415-28725-8. Dewey:330/.01. LCCN:2003-046991.
Audience: **u,f.**

Systems > History > European

Barnett, Vincent **HB113.A2**
A History of Russian Economic Thought. Paper over Boards. Routledge. New York, NY. 2005. 176p. ISBN:0-415-35264-9, ISBN13: 978-0-415-35264-2. Dewey:330/.0947. LCCN:2005-004840.
Audience: **l,u,f.**

Blaug, Mark **HB103**
Ricardian Economics: A Historical Study, 8—8. Trade Cloth. Greenwood Publishing Group, Inc. Portsmouth, NH. 1973. 269p. Yale Studies in Economics Ser. ISBN:0-8371-6982-8, ISBN13: 978-0-8371-6982-8. Dewey:330.094209. LCCN:73-009208.
Audience: **u,f.**

Campbell, R. H. & Skinner, Andrew S. **HB103.S6.C35 1982**
Adam Smith. Trade Cloth. St. Martin's Press. Gordonville, VA. 1982. 231p. ISBN:0-312-00423-0, ISBN13: 978-0-312-00423-1. Dewey:330.15/3. LCCN:82-003308.
Audience: **l,u,f.**

Cannan, Edwin **HB103.A2 C2**
A History of the Theories of Production and Distribution in English Political Economy from 1776 To 1848. Trade Cloth. Continuum International Publishing Group, Ltd. London, 1999. 438p. ISBN:1-85506-789-7, ISBN13: 978-1-85506-789-9. Dewey:330.
Audience: **u,f.**

Coats, A. W. **HB75**
On the History of Economic Thought: British and American Economic Essays, Vol. 1. Paper over Boards. Routledge. New York, NY. 1992. 512p. British and American Economic Essays Ser. ISBN:0-415-06715-4, ISBN13: 978-0-415-06715-7. Dewey:330.09. LCCN:91-047898.
Audience: **l,u,f.**

Feiwel, George R. **HB113.K28.F43**
The Intellectual Capital of Michal Kalecki: A Study in Economic Theory and Policy. Trade Cloth. University of Tennessee Press. Knoxville, TN. 1975. xxii, 583p. ISBN:0-87049-161-X, ISBN13: 978-0-87049-161-0. Dewey:330.15/6. LCCN:74-022487.
Audience: **u,f.**

Galbraith, John Kenneth **HB119.G33.A34**
A Life in Our Times: Memoirs. Trade Cloth. Houghton Mifflin Company. New York, NY. 1981. 576p. ISBN:0-395-30509-8, ISBN13: 978-0-395-30509-6. Dewey:330/.092/4. LCCN:80-027373.
Audience: **g,l,u,f.**

Gray, John **HB101.H39 G73**
Hayek on Liberty. Trade Cloth. Blackwell Publishing, Inc. Malden, MA. ISBN:0-85520-710-8, ISBN13: 978-0-85520-710-6.
Audience: **l,u,f.**

Hansen, Ejvind Damsgaard **HC240.H3195 2001**
European Economic History: From Mercantilism to Maastricht and Beyond. Trade Cloth. Copenhagen Business School Press. Copenhagen, 2001. 529p. European Studies ISBN:87-630-0017-2, ISBN13: 978-87-630-0017-8. Dewey:330.94. LCCN:2001-542958.
Audience: **l,u,f.**

Harris, Seymour E. (Editor) **HB119.S35**
Schumpeter, Social Scientist. Trade Cloth. Ayer Company Publishers, Inc. Manchester, NH. 1977. Essay Index Reprint Ser. ISBN:0-8369-1138-5, ISBN13: 978-0-8369-1138-1. Dewey:923.373. LCCN:71-080387.
Audience: **g,l,u,f.**

Harrod, Roy F. **HB99.7**
The Life of John Maynard Keynes. Ed. 2. Trade Cloth. Scholar's Bookshelf. Cranbury, NJ. 1969. xvi, 674p. ISBN:0-678-00459-5, ISBN13: 978-0-678-00459-3. Dewey:330.15/6. LCCN:68-030524.
Audience: **l,u,f.**

Harrop, Jeffrey **HC241.2.H3935 1992**
The Political Economy of Integration in the European Community. Ed. 2. Cloth Text. Edward Elgar Publishing, Inc. Northampton, MA. 1992. 304p. ISBN:1-85278-590-X, ISBN13: 978-1-85278-590-1. Dewey:337.1/42. LCCN:91-028216.
Audience: **l,u,f.** *Choice, 1990.*

Harrop, Jeffrey **HC241.2.H3935 1989**
The Political Economy of Integration in the European Community. Cloth Text. Edward Elgar Publishing, Inc. Northampton, MA. 1989. 224p. ISBN:1-85278-008-8, ISBN13: 978-1-85278-008-1. Dewey:337.1/42. LCCN:88-016590.
Audience: **l,u,f.** *Choice, 1990.*

Hayek, Friedrich A. **B1606**
John Stuart Mill and Harriet Taylor: Their Correspondence and Subsequent Marriage. Library Binding. Richard West. Philadelphia, PA. 1979. ISBN:0-8492-5349-7, ISBN13: 978-0-8492-5349-2. Dewey:921.2.
Audience: **u,f.**

Hollander, Samuel **HB103.S6 H65**
The Economics of Adam Smith. Trade Cloth. University of Toronto Press. Toronto, ON. 1973. 320p. Studies in Classical

Political Economy Ser. ISBN:0-8020-1811-4, ISBN13: 978-0-8020-1811-3. Dewey:330.15/3. LCCN:72-185717.
Audience: **l,u,f.**

Hollander, Samuel **HB103.R5.H72**
The Economics of David Ricardo. Cloth Text. University of Toronto Press. Toronto, ON. 1979. xiv, 759p. Studies in Classical Political Economy Ser. ISBN:0-8020-5438-2, ISBN13: 978-0-8020-5438-8. Dewey:330.15/3. LCCN:79-004392.
Audience: **u,f.**

Jevons, W. Stanley (William Stanley) **HB103.J5 A4 1972**
Papers and Correspondence of William Stanley Jevons: Vol.1, Biography and Personal Journal. Black, Robert Denis Collison (Editor); Könekamp, Rosamond (Editor). London : Macmillan [for] the Royal Economic Society. 1972.
Audience: **u,f.**

Johnson, Edgar A. **HB103.A3 J6**
Predecessors of Adam Smith: The Growth of British Economic Thought. Trade Cloth. Scholar's Bookshelf. Cranbury, NJ. 1965. xiii, 423p. ISBN:0-678-00115-4, ISBN13: 978-0-678-00115-8. Dewey:330.1. LCCN:65-025860.
Audience: **u,f.**

Koot, Gerard M. **HB103.A2K65 1987**
English Historical Economics, 1870-1926: The Rise of Economic History and Neo-Mercantilism. Trade Cloth. Cambridge University Press. New York, NY. 1988. 288p. Historical Perspectives on Modern Economics Ser. ISBN:0-521-32854-3, ISBN13: 978-0-521-32854-8. Dewey:330/.0941. LCCN:87-011592.
Audience: **u,f.** *Choice, 1988.*

Martin, Andrew & Ross, George (Editors) **HG925.E974 2004**
Euros and Europeans: Monetary Integration and the European Model of Society. Cloth Text. Cambridge University Press. New York, NY. 2004. 398p. ISBN:0-521-83570-4, ISBN13: 978-0-521-83570-1. Dewey:332.4/94. LCCN:2003-069666.
Audience: **g,l,u,f.**

Moggridge, Donald E. **HB99.7**
John Maynard Keynes. Trade Cloth. Peter Smith Publisher, Inc. Magnolia, MA. 1983. ISBN:0-8446-5975-4, ISBN13: 978-0-8446-5975-6. Dewey:330.15/6.
Audience: **g,l,u,f.**

Mokyr, Joel (Editor) **HC254.5.B88 1999**
British Industrial Revolution: An Economic Perspective. Ed. 2. Trade Paper. Westview Press. Boulder, CO. 1998. 366p. ISBN:0-8133-3389-X, ISBN13: 978-0-8133-3389-2. Dewey:338/.0941. LCCN:98-045108.
Audience: **l,f.**

Ormrod, David **HF3505.O76 2002**
The Rise of Commercial Empires: England and the Netherlands in the Age of Mercantilism, 1650-1770. Charles Feinstein, Patrick O'Brien, Barry Supple, Peter Temin & Gianni Toniolo (Contribution by). Trade Cloth. Cambridge University Press. New York, NY. 2003. 420p. Cambridge Studies in Modern Economic History ISBN:0-521-81926-1, ISBN13: 978-0-521-81926-8. Dewey:382/.09410492. LCCN:2002-074191.
Audience: **u,f.** *Choice, 2003.*

Pappe, H. O. **B1607**
John Stuart Mill and the Harriet Taylor Myth. Paper Text. Textbook Publishers. Temecula, CA. 2003. 51p. ISBN:0-7581-8360-7, ISBN13: 978-0-7581-8360-6. Dewey:192.
Audience: **l,u.**

Pareto, Vilfredo **HB177.P2913**
Manual of political economy. New York, A.M. Kelley. 1971. ISBN:0-678-00881-7, ISBN13: 978-0-678-00881-2.
Audience: **l,u,f.**

Passfield, et al. **HD6664**
The History of Trade Unionism. Sidney James Webb & Beatrice Webb (Authors). Trade Cloth. Library Reprints, Inc. Temecula, CA. 1902. 784p. ISBN:0-7222-2723-X, ISBN13: 978-0-7222-2723-7. Dewey:331.880941.
Audience: **u,f.**

Raphael, D. D. **HB103.S6R27 1985**
Adam Smith. Trade Cloth. Oxford University Press, Inc. New York, NY. 1985. viii, 120p. Past Masters Ser. ISBN:0-19-287559-0, ISBN13: 978-0-19-287559-4. Dewey:330.15/3/0924. LCCN:84-020629.
Audience: **l,u,f.** *Choice, 1985.*

Riesman, David **HB119.V4R5 1995**
Thorstein Veblen. Stjepan G. Mestrovic (Introduction by). Trade Paper. Transaction Publishers. Somerset, NJ. 1995. 287p. ISBN:1-56000-776-1, ISBN13: 978-1-56000-776-0. Dewey:330/.092. LCCN:94-031537.
Audience: **u,f.**

Schumpeter, Joseph Alois **HD75**
The Theory of Economic Development: An Inquiry into Profits, Capital, Credit, Interest and the Business Cycle. Redvers Opies (Translator), John E. Elliott (Introduction by). Trade Paper. Transaction Publishers. Somerset, NJ. 1982. 244p. Social Science Classics Ser. ISBN:0-87855-698-2, ISBN13: 978-0-87855-698-4. Dewey:330.1. LCCN:79-067059.
Audience: **u,f.**

Skinner, Andrew S. **HB103.S6S56 1996**
A System of Social Science: Papers Relating to Adam Smith. Ed. 2. Trade Cloth. Oxford University Press, Inc. New York, NY. 1996. 304p. ISBN:0-19-823334-5, ISBN13: 978-0-19-823334-3. Dewey:300/.92. LCCN:95-040597.
Audience: **u,f.**

Veblen, Thorstein **HB119.A2 V42 1973**
Essays, reviews, and reports; previously uncollected writings. Dorfman, Joseph (Editor). Clifton [N.J.] A.M. Kelley. 1973. ISBN:0-678-00960-0, ISBN13: 978-0-678-00960-4.
Audience: **u,f.**

von Mises, Ludwig **HB171.V63 2006**
Human Action: A Treatise on Economics. Bettina B. Greaves (Editor). Trade Paper. Liberty Fund, Inc. Indianapolis, IN. 2006. 1050p. ISBN:0-86597-631-7, ISBN13: 978-0-86597-631-3. Dewey:330. LCCN:2005-025025.
Audience: **u,f.**

von Mises, Ludwig **HB71**
Epistemological Problems of Economics. Ed. 3. Jorg Guido Hulsmann (Introduction by). Laminated. Ludwig von Mises Institute. Auburn, AL. 2003. 341p. ISBN:0-945466-36-6, ISBN13: 978-0-945466-36-9. Dewey:330/.01/8.
Audience: **u,f.**

Walker, Donald A. (Editor) **HB118.W34 J33 1983**
William Jaffe's Essays on Walras. Trade Cloth. Cambridge University Press. New York, NY. 1983. 391p. ISBN:0-521-25142-7, ISBN13: 978-0-521-25142-6. Dewey:330.15/7. LCCN:82-022001.
Audience: **u,f.**

Walras, Leon **HB173.W2213 2003**
Elements of Pure Economics, or the Theory of Social Wealth. Paper over Boards. Routledge. New York, NY. 2003. 624p. Routledge Library Editions Ser., Vol. 40:Economics, US/Can. Edition Ser. ISBN:0-415-31340-6, ISBN13: 978-0-415-31340-7. Dewey:330.
Audience: **u,f.**

Weber, Max **HB175**
The Theory of Social and Economic Organization. Trade Paper. Simon & Schuster. New York, NY. 1997. 448p. ISBN:0-684-83640-8, ISBN13: 978-0-684-83640-9. Dewey:330.1.
Audience: **g,l,u,f.**

Wrigley, Chris (Editor) **HD8391.H57 1996**
A History of British Industrial Relations, 1939-1979: Industrial Relations in a Declining Economy. Trade Cloth. Edward Elgar Publishing, Inc. Northampton, MA. 1996. 256p. ISBN:1-85278-892-5, ISBN13: 978-1-85278-892-6. Dewey:331/.0941. LCCN:95-032813.
Audience: **u,f.** *Choice, 1996.*

Systems > History > American

Bernanke, Ben S. **HB3717**
Essays on the Great Depression. Trade Cloth. Princeton University Press. Princeton, NJ. 2000. 320p. ISBN:0-691-01698-4, ISBN13: 978-0-691-01698-6. Dewey:338.5/42. LCCN:99-041738.
Audience: **g,l,u,f.**

Bordo, Michael D. (Editor), et al. **HB3717 1929**
The Defining Moment: The Great Depression and the American Economy in the Twentieth Century. Claudia Goldin & Eugene N. White (Editors). Trade Cloth. University of Chicago Press. Chicago, IL. 1997. 492p. National Bureau of Economic Research Project Report ISBN:0-226-06589-8, ISBN13: 978-0-226-06589-2. Dewey:338.5/42. LCCN:97-029751.
Audience: **l,u,f.**

Brown, E. Carey & Solow, Robert (Editors) **HB119.S25.P38 1983**
Paul Samuelson and Modern Economic Theory. Cloth Text. McGraw-Hill Companies, The. New York, NY. 1983. 350p. ISBN:0-07-059667-0, ISBN13: 978-0-07-059667-2. Dewey:330. LCCN:82-020343.
Audience: **l,u,f.**

Eichengreen, Barry J. **HG3881.J33 1996**
Golden Fetters: The Gold Standard and the Great Depression, 1919-1939. Trade Paper. Oxford University Press, Inc. New York, NY. 1996. 480p. NBER Series on Long-Term Factors in Economic Development ISBN:0-19-510113-8, ISBN13: 978-0-19-510113-3. Dewey:332.4/222. LCCN:95-032227.
Audience: **u,f.** *Choice, 1992.*

Etzioni, Amitai **HC106.8.E89 1983**
An Immodest Agenda: Rebuilding America Before the 21st Century. Cloth Text. McGraw-Hill Companies, The. New York, NY. 1982. 464p. New Press Ser. ISBN:0-07-019723-7, ISBN13: 978-0-07-019723-7. Dewey:306/.0973. LCCN:82-007136.
Audience: **g,l,u,f.**

Feiwel, George R. (Editor) **HB119.S25**
Samuelson and Neo-Classical Economics. Trade Cloth. Springer. New York, NY. 1982. 372p. Recent Economic Thought Ser. ISBN:0-89838-069-3, ISBN13: 978-0-89838-069-9. Dewey:330.15/5. LCCN:81-001211.
Audience: **u,f.**

Galbraith, John Kenneth **HC106.5.G32 1998**
The Affluent Society. Ed. 40. Trade Paper. Houghton Mifflin Company Trade & Reference Division. Boston, MA. 1998. 288p. ISBN:0-395-92500-2, ISBN13: 978-0-395-92500-3. Dewey:330.1. LCCN:98-046513.
Audience: **g,l,u,f.**

Galbraith, John Kenneth **HC106**
Economics and the Art of Controversy. Library Binding. Hippocrene Books, Inc. New York, NY. 1980. 111p. ISBN:0-374-92972-6, ISBN13: 978-0-374-92972-5. Dewey:338.973.
Audience: **l,u,f.**

Galbraith, John Kenneth **HC106.6.G35 1978**
The New Industrial State. Ed. 3. Trade Cloth. Houghton Mifflin Company. New York, NY. 1978. xxiv, 438p. ISBN:0-395-25712-3, ISBN13: 978-0-395-25712-8. Dewey:338.0973. LCCN:78-006310.
Audience: **g,l,u,f.**

Hall, Thomas E. & Ferguson, J. David **HB3717 1929**
The Great Depression: An International Disaster of Perverse Economic Policies. Trade Cloth. University of Michigan Press. Chicago, IL. 1998. 216p. ISBN:0-472-09667-2, ISBN13: 978-0-472-09667-1. Dewey:338.5/42. LCCN:97-021196.
Audience: **l,u,f.** *Choice, 1998.*

Hamilton, Alexander **HC105.H35**
Papers on Public Credit, Commerce and Finance. New York, Liberal Arts Press. 1957. The American heritage series,; no. 18
Audience: **l,u,f.**

Hoover, Herbert **HC106.3**
American Ideals vs. the New Deal. Library Binding. Reprint Services Company. Temecula, CA. 1993. 96p. History of the United States Ser. ISBN:0-7812-4918-X, ISBN13: 978-0-7812-4918-8. Dewey:330.9/73/0917.
Audience: **g,l,u,f.**

Leontief, Wassily **HB142**
Input-Output Economics. Ed. 2. Cloth Text. Oxford University Press, Inc. New York, NY. 1986. 436p. ISBN:0-19-503525-9, ISBN13: 978-0-19-503525-4. Dewey:339.2/3. LCCN:84-029449.
Audience: **u,f.**

Leontief, Wassily **HC106.3**
The Structure of the American Economy 1919-1939: An Empirical Application of Equilibrium Analysis. Ed. 2. Cloth Text. M. E. Sharpe Inc. Armonk, NY. 1977. 264p. ISBN:0-87332-087-5, ISBN13: 978-0-87332-087-0. Dewey:330.9/73/091. LCCN:76-017415.
Audience: **l,u,f.**

Madden, Kirsten & Seitz, Janet **Z7164.E2**
A Bibliography of Female Economic Thought to 1940. Paper over Boards. Routledge. New York, NY. 2004. 560p. Routledge Studies in the History of Economics Ser., Vol. 64 ISBN:0-415-23817-X, ISBN13: 978-0-415-23817-5. Dewey:016.33/009/034. LCCN:2003-058782.
Audience: **g,l,u,f.**

Myrdal, Gunnar **HC106.5.M9**
Challenge to Affluence. New York: Pantheon. 1963.
Audience: **l,u,f.**

Temin, Peter **HB3717 1929**
Lessons from the Great Depression. Trade Paper. MIT Press. Cambridge, MA. 1991. 210p. Lionel Robbins Lectures ISBN:0-262-70044-1, ISBN13: 978-0-262-70044-3. Dewey:330.9/0437. LCCN:89-034040.
Audience: **g,l,u,f.** *Choice, 1990.*

Veblen, Thorstein **HC106.3 .V4**
The Engineers and the Price System. Trade Paper. Kessinger Publishing, LLC. Whitefish, MT. 2004. ISBN:1-4191-6096-6, ISBN13: 978-1-4191-6096-7. Dewey:338.
Audience: **u,f.**

Veblen, Thorstein B. **HC106**
Absentee Ownership and Business Enterprise in Recent Times: The Case of America. Trade Cloth. Scholar's Bookshelf. Cranbury, NJ. 1964. v, 445p. Reprints of Economic Classics Ser. ISBN:0-678-00048-4, ISBN13: 978-0-678-00048-9. Dewey:330.973. LCCN:63-023516.
Audience: **u,f.**

Systems > Capitalist

Bowles, Samuel, et al. **HB171.5.B6937 2005**
Understanding Capitalism: Competition, Command, and Change. Ed. 3. Richard Edwards & Frank Roosevelt (Authors). Cloth Text. Oxford University Press, Inc. New York, NY. 2005. 608p. ISBN:0-19-513864-3, ISBN13: 978-0-19-513864-1. Dewey:330.12/2. LCCN:2004-024955.
Audience: **u,f.**

Cornwall, John & Cornwall, Wendy A. **HC54 .C73 2001**
Capitalist Development in the Twentieth Century: An Evolutionary-Keynesian Analysis. Phyllis Deane, Gautam Mathur & Joan Robinson (Contribution by). Trade Cloth. Cambridge University Press. New York, NY. 2001. 302p. Modern Cambridge Economics Ser. ISBN:0-521-34149-3, ISBN13: 978-0-521-34149-3. Dewey:330.122. LCCN:00-069752.
Audience: **l,u,f.**

De Vroey, Michel **HB145**
Equilibrium and Disequilibrium: From Adam Smith to Robert Lucas. Trade Cloth. Routledge. New York, NY. 2005. 256p. Studies in the History of Economics ISBN:0-415-20311-2, ISBN13: 978-0-415-20311-1. Dewey:330.1/57.
Audience: **u,f.**

Diamond, Larry & Plattner, Marc F. (Editors) **JF51**
Capitalism, Socialism, and Democracy Revisited. Trade Cloth. Johns Hopkins University Press. Baltimore, MD. 1993. 152p. A Journal of Democracy Bks. ISBN:0-8018-4746-X, ISBN13: 978-0-8018-4746-2. Dewey:320.3. LCCN:93-004362.
Audience: **u,f.**

Friedman, Milton **HB501.F7 2002**
Capitalism and Freedom. Ed. 40. Trade Cloth. University of Chicago Press. Chicago, IL. 2002. 230p. ISBN:0-226-26420-3, ISBN13: 978-0-226-26420-2. Dewey:330.12/2. LCCN:2002-067530.
Audience: **l,u,f.**

Galbraith, John Kenneth **HB501**
American Capitalism: The Concept of Countervailing Power. Trade Paper. Transaction Publishers. Somerset, NJ. 1993. 208p. ISBN:1-56000-674-9, ISBN13: 978-1-56000-674-9. Dewey:330.1/22/0973.
Audience: **u,f.**

Hamilton, Gary **HC427**
Commerce and Capitalism in Chinese Societies: Organisation of Chinese Economics. Paper over Boards. Routledge. New York, NY. 2006. XIV, 322p. ISBN:0-415-15704-8, ISBN13: 978-0-415-15704-9. Dewey:330.951. LCCN:2005-028808.
Audience: **l,u,f.**

Heilbroner, Robert L. **HB501.H397 1976**
Business Civilization in Decline. Trade Cloth. W. W. Norton & Company, Inc. New York, NY. 1976. 128p. ISBN:0-393-05571-X, ISBN13: 978-0-393-05571-9. Dewey:330.12/2. LCCN:75-033367.
Audience: **l,u,f.**

Heilbroner, Robert L. **HB501**
The Nature and Logic of Capitalism. Trade Paper. W. W. Norton & Company, Inc. New York, NY. 1986. 225p. ISBN:0-393-95529-X, ISBN13: 978-0-393-95529-3. Dewey:330.12/2.
Audience: **l,u,f.** *Choice, 1986.*

Hicks, John Richard **HB501**
Capital and Time: A Neo-Austrian Theory. Trade Paper. Oxford University Press, Inc. New York, NY. 1987. 228p. ISBN:0-19-877286-6, ISBN13: 978-0-19-877286-6. Dewey:339.
Audience: **u,f.**

Kautsky, Karl **HB97.5 .M333313 1979**
The Economic Doctrines of Karl Marx. H. J. Stenning (Translator). Trade Cloth. Hyperion Press, Inc. Westport, CT. 1991. 252p. ISBN:0-88355-888-2, ISBN13: 978-0-88355-888-1. Dewey:335.4/12. LCCN:79-001583.
Audience: **l,u,f.**

Keech, William R. **JK271 .K318 1995**
Economic Politics: The Costs of Democracy. Trade Cloth. Cambridge University Press. New York, NY. 1995. 255p. ISBN:0-521-46206-1, ISBN13: 978-0-521-46206-8. Dewey:338.9. LCCN:94-011813.
Audience: **l,u,f.**

Lippit, Victor **HB501.L525 2005**
Capitalism. Paper over Boards. Routledge. New York, NY. 2005. 224p. Routledge Frontiers of Political Economy Ser. ISBN:0-415-27394-3, ISBN13: 978-0-415-27394-7. Dewey:330.12/2. LCCN:2004-026545.
Audience: **l,u,f.**

Loasby, Brian J. **HB87.L58 1989**
The Mind and Method of the Economist: A Critical Appraisal of Major Economists in the 20th Century. Cloth Text. Edward Elgar Publishing, Inc. Northampton, MA. 1989. 248p. ISBN:1-85278-124-6, ISBN13: 978-1-85278-124-8. Dewey:330/.0922. LCCN:89-001492.
Audience: **l,u,f.**

Marx, Karl **HX39.5**
Capital: A Critique of Political Economy. David Fernbach (Translator), Ernest Mandel (Introduction by). Trade Paper. Penguin Group (USA) Inc. New York, NY. 1993. 1088p. Capital Ser., Vol. 3 ISBN:0-14-044570-6, ISBN13: 978-0-14-044570-1. Dewey:335.4. LCCN:92-023876.
Audience: **l,u,f.**

Nee, Victor & Swedberg, Richard (Editors) **HB501.E2565 2005**
Economic Sociology of Capitalism. Trade Cloth. Princeton University Press. Princeton, NJ. 2005. 496p. ISBN:0-691-11957-0, ISBN13: 978-0-691-11957-1. Dewey:306.3/42. LCCN:2004-043151.
Audience: **g,l,u,f.**

Systems > Capitalist > Preclassical/Pre-1798/Phisiocrats/Mercantilists

Blaug, Mark (Editor) **HB105.Q5F73 1991**
Francois Quesnay, (1694-1774), Vols. 1 & 2. Trade Cloth. Edward Elgar Publishing, Inc. Northampton, MA. 1991. 656p. Pioneers in Economics Ser., Vol. 10 ISBN:1-85278-472-5, ISBN13: 978-1-85278-472-0. Dewey:330.15/2. LCCN:90-026870.
Audience: **u,f.**

Bury, R. G. (Editor) **B395**
Symposium of Plato. Ed. 2. Trade Cloth. Aris & Phillips. Oxford, 1991. lxxviii, 179p. Classical Texts Ser. ISBN:0-85270-039-3, ISBN13: 978-0-85270-039-6. Dewey:184.
Audience: **u,f.**

Cantillon, Richard **HB153.C313 2001**
Essays on the Nature of Commerce in General. Anthony Brewer (Introduction by). Trade Paper. Transaction Publishers. Somerset, NJ. 2001. 188p. ISBN:0-7658-0499-9, ISBN13: 978-0-7658-0499-0. Dewey:330. LCCN:99-021222.
Audience: **u,f.**

Ekelund, Robert B. Jr. & Tollison, Robert D. **HB91.E42 1997**
Politicized Economies: Monarchy, Monopoly, and Mercantilism. Cloth Text. Texas A&M University Press. College Station, TX. 1997. 320p. Texas A&M University Economics Ser., Vol. 14 ISBN:0-89096-745-8, ISBN13: 978-0-89096-745-4. Dewey:382/.3/0940903. LCCN:96-038971.
Audience: **u,f.** *Choice, 1997.*

Groenewegen, P. D. **HB83.G76 2002**
Eighteenth Century Economics. Paper over Boards. Routledge. New York, NY. 2002. 448p. Routledge Studies in the History of Economics, Vol. 55 ISBN:0-415-27940-2, ISBN13: 978-0-415-27940-6. Dewey:330/.09/033. LCCN:2002-068314.
Audience: **u,f.**

Guillet de Monthoux, Pierre **HD30.5.G85 1993**
The Moral Philosophy of Management: From Quesnay to Keynes. Cloth Text. M. E. Sharpe Inc. Armonk, NY. 1993. 328p. Studies in Socio-Economics ISBN:1-56324-081-5, ISBN13: 978-1-56324-081-2. Dewey:658.001. LCCN:93-016576.
Audience: **u,f.** *Choice, 1994.*

Hansen, Ejvind Damsgaard **HC240.H3195 2001**
European Economic History: From Mercantilism to Maastricht and Beyond. Trade Cloth. Copenhagen Business School Press. Copenhagen, 2001. 529p. European Studies ISBN:87-630-0017-2, ISBN13: 978-87-630-0017-8. Dewey:330.94. LCCN:2001-542958.
Audience: **l,u,f.**

Heckscher, Eli F. **HF1025**
Mercantilism. Mendel Shapiro (Translator). Paper over Boards. Routledge. New York, NY. 1997. 944p. Critical Concepts Ser. ISBN:0-415-11357-1, ISBN13: 978-0-415-11357-1. Dewey:330.9.
Audience: **u,f.**

Heertje, Arnold **HB76**
The Makers of Modern Economics, Vol. 2. Trade Paper. Edward Elgar Publishing Ltd. Cheltenham, ISBN:1-85898-293-6, ISBN13: 978-1-85898-293-9. Dewey:330/.01.
Audience: **l,u,f.**

Heertje, Arnold (Editor) **HB72**
The Makers of Modern Economics, Vol. 2. Trade Cloth. Edward Elgar Publishing, Inc. Northampton, MA. 1995. 192p. ISBN:1-85898-237-5, ISBN13: 978-1-85898-237-3. Dewey:330/.01. LCCN:92-029859.
Audience: **l,u,f.**

Hutchison, Terence Wilmot **HB83.H8**
Before Adam Smith: The Emergence of Political Economy 1662-1776. Trade Cloth. Ashgate Publishing, Ltd. Aldershot, 1993. 480p. Modern Revivals in Economics Ser. ISBN:0-7512-0237-1, ISBN13: 978-0-7512-0237-3. Dewey:330/.09/032.
Audience: **u,f.** *Choice, 1989.*

Jaffe, W. **HB105.W3 A4**
Correspondence of Leon Walras. Trade Cloth. Elsevier. New York, NY. 1965. 2100p. ISBN:0-7204-8376-X, ISBN13: 978-0-7204-8376-5. Dewey:330.157.
Audience: **u,f.**

Koot, Gerard M. **HB103.A2K65 1987**
English Historical Economics, 1870-1926: The Rise of Economic History and Neo-Mercantilism. Trade Cloth. Cambridge University Press. New York, NY. 1988. 288p. Historical Perspectives on Modern Economics Ser. ISBN:0-521-32854-3, ISBN13: 978-0-521-32854-8. Dewey:330/.0941. LCCN:87-011592.
Audience: **u,f.** *Choice, 1988.*

Locke, John **HG661.L62**
Further Considerations Concerning Raising the Value of Money. Trade Paper. Kessinger Publishing, LLC. Whitefish, MT. 2004. ISBN:1-4191-2133-2, ISBN13: 978-1-4191-2133-3.
Audience: **u,f.**

Locke, John **JC153.L85**
Natural Liberty and Civil Government: The Two Treatises on the Art of Ruling Humanity. Trade Cloth. Institute for Economic

& Political World Strategic Studies. Albuquerque, NM. 1991. 257p. ISBN:0-86722-246-8, ISBN13: 978-0-86722-246-3. Dewey:354.42.
Audience: **u,f.**

Locke, John **BR120**
The Reasonableness of Christianity, with A Discourse of Miracles, and Part of a Third Letter Concerning Toleration. Paper Text. Textbook Publishers. Temecula, CA. 2003. 102p. ISBN:0-7581-3514-9, ISBN13: 978-0-7581-3514-8. Dewey:230.
Audience: **g,l,u,f.** B

Locke, John **HG937.L74 1989**
Several Papers Relating to Money, Interest and Trade, Etc. Trade Cloth. Scholar's Bookshelf. Cranbury, NJ. 1989. 328p. Reprints of Economic Classics Ser. ISBN:0-678-00334-3, ISBN13: 978-0-678-00334-3. Dewey:332.4/941. LCCN:87-017243.
Audience: **u,f.**

Locke, John **JC153.L63 2005**
Two Treatises of Government: In the Former, the False Principles and Foundation of Sir Robert Filmer, and His Followers Are Detected and Overthrown: The Latter Is an Essay Concerning the True Original, Extent, and End of Civil-Government. Trade Cloth. Lawbook Exchange, Limited, The. Clark, NJ. 2005. 358p. ISBN:1-58477-602-1, ISBN13: 978-1-58477-602-4. Dewey:320/.01. LCCN:2004-030387.
Audience: **u,f.**

Locke, John **BD161**
An Essay Concerning Human Understanding, Set. Alexander C. Fraser (Editor). Trade Cloth. Peter Smith Publisher, Inc. Magnolia, MA. 1959. ISBN:0-8446-2478-0, ISBN13: 978-0-8446-2478-5. Dewey:121.
Audience: **u,f.**

Locke, John **B1270**
Of the Conduct of the Understanding. Francis W. Garforth (Editor). Trade Paper. Books on Demand. Ann Arbor, MI. 1966. 144p. Classics in Education Ser., Vol. 31 ISBN:0-7837-8878-9, ISBN13: 978-0-7837-8878-4. Dewey:001.2. LCCN:66-020498.
Audience: **u,f.**

Locke, John **HG937.L735 1990**
Locke on Money, Vol. 1. Patrick H. Kelly (Editor). Trade Cloth. Oxford University Press, Inc. New York, NY. 1991. 358p. Clarendon Edition of the Works of John Locke Ser. ISBN:0-19-824546-7, ISBN13: 978-0-19-824546-9. Dewey:332.4/942. LCCN:90-007880.
Audience: **u,f.**

Locke, John **HG937.L735 1990**
Locke on Money, Vol. 2. Patrick H. Kelly (Editor). Trade Cloth. Oxford University Press, Inc. New York, NY. 1991. 330p. Clarendon Edition of the Works of John Locke Ser. ISBN:0-19-824837-7, ISBN13: 978-0-19-824837-8. Dewey:332.4/942. LCCN:90-007880.
Audience: **u,f.**

Locke, John **JC0153.L79**
Locke's Second Treatise of Civil Government: An Essay Concerning the True Original, Extent, and End of Civil Government. Lester De Koster (Editor). Trade Paper. Books on Demand. Ann Arbor, MI. 83p. ISBN:0-598-19474-6, ISBN13: 978-0-598-19474-9. Dewey:320/.01. LCCN:78-001657.
Audience: **u,f.**

Locke, John **BR1610**
Two Treatises of Government and a Letter Concerning Toleration. Ian Shapiro (Editor). Cloth over Boards. Yale University Press. Cumberland, RI. 2003. 384p. Rethinking the Western Tradition Ser. ISBN:0-300-10017-5, ISBN13: 978-0-300-10017-4. Dewey:261.72. LCCN:2004-271163.
Audience: **u,f.**

Locke, John **JC153**
Treatise of Civil Government and a Letter Concerning Toleration. Ed. 3. Charles L. Sherman (Editor). Trade Paper. Irvington Publishers. New York, NY. 1965. 224p. ISBN:0-89197-519-5, ISBN13: 978-0-89197-519-9. Dewey:320/.01.
Audience: **u,f.**

Locke, John **LB475.L6S65**
Some Thoughts Concerning Education. John W. Yolton & Jean S. Yolton (Editors). Trade Paper. Oxford University Press, Inc. New York, NY. 2000. 346p. Clarendon Edition of the Works of John Locke Ser. ISBN:0-19-825016-9, ISBN13: 978-0-19-825016-6. Dewey:370.1.
Audience: **u,f.** *Choice, 1990.*

Magnusson, Lars (Editor) **HB91.M4 1994**
Mercantilism, Set. Paper over Boards. Routledge. New York, NY. 1996. 1384p. Critical Concepts in the History of Economics Ser. ISBN:0-415-11600-7, ISBN13: 978-0-415-11600-8. Dewey:330.1513. LCCN:94-033823.
Audience: **u,f.**

McCulloch, John R. **HB161**
Treatises and Essays on Subjects Connected with Economical Policy: With Biographical Sketches of Quesnay, Adam Smith and Ricardo. Trade Cloth. Scholar's Bookshelf. Cranbury, NJ. 1967. vii, 487p. Reprints of Economic Classics Ser. ISBN:0-678-00255-X, ISBN13: 978-0-678-00255-1. Dewey:330/.08. LCCN:67-020088.
Audience: **u,f.**

Mun, Thomas **HF3505.4 .M9 1986**
England's Treasure by Forraign Trade. Trade Cloth. Scholar's Bookshelf. Cranbury, NJ. 1986. vii, 88p. Reprints of Economic Classics Ser. ISBN:0-678-06274-9, ISBN13: 978-0-678-06274-6. Dewey:382/.0941. LCCN:86-007467.
Audience: **u,f.**

Petty, William **HB151**
The Economic Writings of Sir William Petty. Charles H. Hull (Editor). Trade Cloth. Scholar's Bookshelf. Cranbury, NJ. 1986. xci, 700p. Reprints of Economic Classics Ser. ISBN:0-678-00029-8, ISBN13: 978-0-678-00029-8. Dewey:330. LCCN:63-023521.
Audience: **u,f.**

Plato **PA4279**
The Philebus of Plato. Robert G. Bury (Editor). Trade Cloth. Ayer Company Publishers, Inc. Manchester, NH. 1977. The Philosophy of Plato and Aristotle Ser. ISBN:0-405-04834-3, ISBN13: 978-0-405-04834-0. Dewey:171/.4. LCCN:72-009284.
Audience: **u,f.**

Pressman, Steven **HB153.Q582P74 1994**
Quesnay's "Tableau Economique": A Critique and Reassessment. Library Binding. Scholar's Bookshelf. Cranbury, NJ. 1994. x, 198p. ISBN:0-678-01471-X, ISBN13: 978-0-678-01471-4. Dewey:330.15/2. LCCN:94-021389.
Audience: **u,f.**

Quesnay, Francois **HB153 .M6813**
The Economical Table: An Attempt Toward Ascertaining and Exhibiting the Source, Progress and Employment of Riches. Trade Cloth. Institute for Economic & Financial Research. Albuquerque, NM. 1988. 257p. ISBN:0-86654-274-4, ISBN13: 978-0-86654-274-6. Dewey:330.15/2.
Audience: **u,f.**

Quesnay, Francois **QB173**
The Economical Table. Trade Paper. University Press of the Pacific. Miami, FL. 2004. 256p. ISBN:1-4102-1554-7, ISBN13: 978-1-4102-1554-3.
Audience: **u,f.**

Quesnay, Francois **HB153.Q55713**
Quesnay's Tableau Economique. Trade Cloth. Macmillan Publishing Company, Inc. Old Tappan, NJ. 1972. ISBN:0-333-11173-7, ISBN13: 978-0-333-11173-4. Dewey:330.15/2. LCCN:78-157694.
Audience: **u,f.**

Steuart-Denham, James **HB0151.S7**
An Inquiry into the Principles of Political Economy, Vol. 1. Trade Paper. Books on Demand. Ann Arbor, MI. 668p. ISBN:0-598-73878-9, ISBN13: 978-0-598-73878-3. Dewey:330.1. LCCN:51-009456.
Audience: **u,f.**

Vaggi, Gianni **HB105.Q5V34 1987**
The Economics of Francois Quesnay. Cloth Text. Duke University Press. Durham, NC. 1987. xiii, 247p. ISBN:0-8223-0757-X, ISBN13: 978-0-8223-0757-0. Dewey:330.15/2. LCCN:87-003549.
Audience: **u,f.**

Walker, Donald A. (Editor) **HB118.W34 J33 1983**
William Jaffe's Essays on Walras. Trade Cloth. Cambridge University Press. New York, NY. 1983. 391p. ISBN:0-521-25142-7, ISBN13: 978-0-521-25142-6. Dewey:330.15/7. LCCN:82-022001.
Audience: **u,f.**

Walras, Leon **HB173.W2213 2003**
Elements of Pure Economics, or the Theory of Social Wealth. Paper over Boards. Routledge. New York, NY. 2003. 624p. Routledge Library Editions Ser., Vol. 40:Economics, US/Can. Edition Ser. ISBN:0-415-31340-6, ISBN13: 978-0-415-31340-7. Dewey:330.
Audience: **u,f.**

Systems > Capitalist > Classical

Bentham, Jeremy **HB161**
Jeremy Bentham's Economic Writings. Werner Stark (Editor). Paper over Boards. Routledge. New York, NY. 2003. 1440p. ISBN:0-415-31866-1, ISBN13: 978-0-415-31866-2. Dewey:330/.01.
Audience: **u,f.**

Bowley, Marian **HB103.S4B6 2003**
Nassau Senior and Classical Economics. Paper over Boards. Routledge. New York, NY. 2003. 360p. Routledge Library Editions Ser., Vol. 24:Economics, US/Can. Edition Ser. ISBN:0-415-31323-6, ISBN13: 978-0-415-31323-0. Dewey:330.1/53.
Audience: **u,f.**

Brauer, Jurgen & Dunne, Paul J. **HD9743.A2A76 2004**
Arms Trade and Economic Development: Theory and Policy in Offsets. Paper over Boards. Routledge. New York, NY. 2004. 352p. Routledge Studies in Defence and Peace Economics, Vol. 8 ISBN:0-415-33106-4, ISBN13: 978-0-415-33106-7. Dewey:382/.456234. LCCN:2004-048122.
Audience: **l,u,f.**

Cairnes, John Elliott **HB161.C123 2003**
John Elliot Cairnes: Collected Works. Thomas A. Boylan & Tadhg Foley (Editors). Paper over Boards. Routledge. New York, NY. 2003. 2368p. ISBN:0-415-31219-1, ISBN13: 978-0-415-31219-6. Dewey:330. LCCN:2003-047219.
Audience: **l,u,f.**

Dobb, Maurice H. **HB171**
Theories of Value and Distribution since Adam Smith: Ideology and Economic Theory. Trade Paper. Cambridge University Press. New York, NY. 1975. 295p. ISBN:0-521-09936-6, ISBN13: 978-0-521-09936-3. Dewey:330.1. LCCN:72-088619.
Audience: **u,f.**

Forget, Evelyn & Peart, Sandra (Editors) **HB94.R44 2000**
Reflections on the Classical Canon in Economics: Essays in Honor of Samuel Hollander. Paper over Boards. Routledge. New York, NY. 2000. 544p. Studies in the History of Economics, Vol. 41 ISBN:0-415-20801-7, ISBN13: 978-0-415-20801-7. Dewey:330.15/3. LCCN:00-036595.
Audience: **l,u,f.**

Heertje, Arnold **HB76**
The Makers of Modern Economics, Vol. 2. Trade Paper. Edward Elgar Publishing Ltd. Cheltenham, ISBN:1-85898-293-6, ISBN13: 978-1-85898-293-9. Dewey:330/.01.
Audience: **l,u,f.**

Hollander, Samuel **HB103.S6**
Classical Economics. Trade Paper. University of Toronto Press. Toronto, ON. 1993. 740p. ISBN:0-8020-7764-1, ISBN13: 978-0-8020-7764-6. Dewey:330.15/3. LCCN:92-095047.
Audience: **u,f.**

Hollander, Samuel **HB103.S6**
The Economics of John Stuart Mill, Set. Trade Cloth. University of Toronto Press. Toronto, ON. 1985. 1843p. ISBN:0-8020-5671-7, ISBN13: 978-0-8020-5671-9. Dewey:330.15/3.
Audience: **u,f.** *Choice, 1986.*

Hollander, Samuel **HB71.H69 1998**
The Literature of the Political Economy. Ed. 2. Paper over Boards. Routledge. New York, NY. 1997. 432p. ISBN:0-415-11429-2, ISBN13: 978-0-415-11429-5. Dewey:016.33. LCCN:97-011430.
Audience: **u,f.**

Hoover, Kevin D. (Editor) **HB172.5**
The New Classical Macroeconomics, Set. Trade Cloth. Edward Elgar Publishing, Inc. Northampton, MA. 1992. 1,856p. The International Library of Critical Writings in Economics, Vol. 19 ISBN:1-85278-572-1, ISBN13: 978-1-85278-572-7. Dewey:339.
Audience: **l,u,f.**

Hume, David **HB161 .H84 1972**
Writings on Economics. Eugene Rotwein (Editor, Introduction by). Trade Cloth. Ayer Company Publishers, Inc. Manchester,

NH. 1977. Essay Index Reprint Ser. ISBN:0-8369-2907-1, ISBN13: 978-0-8369-2907-2. Dewey:330/.08. LCCN:72-003303.
Audience: **l,u,f.**

Kurz, Heinz D. & Salvadori, Neri (Editors) **HB94.E42 1998**
The Elgar Companion to Classical Economics, Set. R. Arena, P. Groenewegen, G. Harcourt, S. Metcalfe, D. O'Brien, Paul Anthony Samuelson, B. Schefold, A. Skimmer, I. Steedman & P. Sylos Labini (Contribution by). Trade Cloth. Edward Elgar Publishing, Inc. Northampton, MA. 1998. 1,056p. ISBN:1-85898-282-0, ISBN13: 978-1-85898-282-3. Dewey:330.15/3. LCCN:97-035419.
Audience: **l,u,f.**

Kurz, Heinz-Dieter & Salvadori, Neri **HB98.2.K87 2003**
Classical Economics and Modern Theory: Studies in Long-Period Analysis. Paper over Boards. Routledge. New York, NY. 2003. 352p. Studies in the History of Economics, Vol. 63 ISBN:0-415-36952-5, ISBN13: 978-0-415-36952-7. Dewey:330.15/3. LCCN:2002-037167.
Audience: **l,u,f.**

Malthus, Thomas Robert **HB161 .M22 1986**
Definitions in Political Economy: Preceded by an Inquiry into the Rules Which Ought to Guide Political Economists in the Definition and Use of Their Terms. Morton Paglin (Introduction by). Trade Cloth. Scholar's Bookshelf. Cranbury, NJ. 1986. xvi, 261p. Reprints of Economic Classics Ser. ISBN:0-678-00018-2, ISBN13: 978-0-678-00018-2. Dewey:330.15/3. LCCN:86-007468.
Audience: **l,u,f.**

Marcet, Jane **QC23**
Conversations in Natural Philosophy, 1826. Trade Paper. Albert Saifer Publisher. Watchung, NJ. 1998. 220p. ISBN:0-87556-862-9, ISBN13: 978-0-87556-862-1. Dewey:530.
Audience: **l,u,f.**

Martineau, Harriet **PR4984.M5I44 2004**
Illustrations of Political Economy: Selected Tales. Deborah Anna Logan (Editor). Trade Paper. Broadview Press. Peterborough, ON. 2004. 350p. Broadview Editions Ser. ISBN:1-55111-441-0, ISBN13: 978-1-55111-441-5. Dewey:823/.8. LCCN:2005-544534.
Audience: **g,l,u,f.**

Marx, Karl **HB97.5.M33313 1995**
The Poverty of Philosophy. H. Quelch (Translator), Friedrich Engels (Produced by). Trade Cloth. Prometheus Books, Publishers. Amherst, NY. 1995. 227p. Great Books in Philosophy ISBN:0-87975-977-1, ISBN13: 978-0-87975-977-3. Dewey:335.4/12. LCCN:95-011391.
Audience: **l,u,f.**

O'Brien, D. P. **HB85.O27 2004**
The Classical Economists Revisited. Ed. 2. Trade Cloth. Princeton University Press. Princeton, NJ. 2004. 432p. ISBN:0-691-11939-2, ISBN13: 978-0-691-11939-7. Dewey:330.15/3. LCCN:2003-064106.
Audience: **l,u,f.** *Choice, 2005.*

Smith, Adam **AC7; HB103.S6**
The Glasgow Edition of the Works and Correpondence of Adam Smith, Set. Trade Paper. Liberty Fund, Inc. Indianapolis, IN. 1982. 3311p. ISBN:0-86597-369-5, ISBN13: 978-0-86597-369-5. Dewey:330.15/3/0924.
Audience: **u,f.**

Sowell, Thomas **HB94.S69 2006**
On Classical Economics. Cloth over Boards. Yale University Press. Cumberland, RI. 2006. 320p. ISBN:0-300-11316-1, ISBN13: 978-0-300-11316-7. Dewey:330.15/3. LCCN:2005-026877.
Audience: **l,u,f.**

Walsh, Vivian & Gram, Harvey N. **HB145**
Classical and Neoclassical Theories of General Equilibrium. Joan Robinson (Introduction by). Cloth Text. Oxford University Press, Inc. New York, NY. 1979. 442p. ISBN:0-19-502674-8, ISBN13: 978-0-19-502674-0. Dewey:330.15/43. LCCN:78-031129.
Audience: **u,f.**

Systems > Capitalist > Classical > Adam Smith

Aspromourgos, Tony **HB94.A85 1996**
On the Origins of Classical Economics: Distribution and Value from William Petty to Adam Smith. Paper over Boards. Routledge. New York, NY. 1995. 240p. Studies in the History of Economics ISBN:0-415-12878-1, ISBN13: 978-0-415-12878-0. Dewey:330.1/53. LCCN:95-021628.
Audience: **u,f.**

Brown, Maurice **HB103.S6B76 1988**
Adam Smith's Economics: Its Place in the Development of Economic Thought. Library Binding. Routledge. New York, NY. 1988. 208p. ISBN:0-7099-5079-9, ISBN13: 978-0-7099-5079-0. Dewey:330.15/3. LCCN:88-000425.
Audience: **u,f.**

Campbell, R. H. & Skinner, Andrew S. **HB103.S6.C35 1982**
Adam Smith. Trade Cloth. St. Martin's Press. Gordonville, VA. 1982. 231p. ISBN:0-312-00423-0, ISBN13: 978-0-312-00423-1. Dewey:330.15/3. LCCN:82-003308.
Audience: **l,u,f.**

Copley, Stephen & Sutherland, Kathryn (Editors) **HB161.S66914 1995**
Adam Smith's Wealth of Nations: New Interdisciplinary Essays. Cloth Text. Manchester University Press. Manchester, 1995. xiii, 205p. Texts in Culture Ser. ISBN:0-7190-3942-8, ISBN13: 978-0-7190-3942-3. Dewey:330.1/53. LCCN:94-016671.
Audience: **u,f.**

Fitzgibbons, Athol **HB103.S6F58 1995**
Adam Smith's System of Liberty, Wealth, and Virtue: The Moral and Political Foundations of the Wealth of Nations. Trade Cloth. Oxford University Press, Inc. New York, NY. 1995. 222p.

ISBN:0-19-828923-5, ISBN13: 978-0-19-828923-4. Dewey:330.15/3. LCCN:94-042603.
Audience: **u,f.** *Choice, 1996.*

Fleischacker, Samuel **HB103.S6F59 2004**
On Adam Smith's Wealth of Nations: A Philosophical Companion. Trade Cloth. Princeton University Press. Princeton, NJ. 2004. 352p. ISBN:0-691-11502-8, ISBN13: 978-0-691-11502-3. Dewey:330.15/3. LCCN:2003-042889.
Audience: **l,u,f.** *Choice, 2004.*

Fleischacker, Samuel **HB103.S6F59 2005**
On Adam Smith's Wealth of Nations: A Philosophical Companion. Trade Paper. Princeton University Press. Princeton, NJ. 2005. 352p. ISBN:0-691-12390-X, ISBN13: 978-0-691-12390-5. Dewey:330.15/3.
Audience: **l,u,f.** *Choice, 2004.*

Fry, Michael (Editor) **HB103.S6A6275 1992**
Adam Smith's Legacy: His Place in the Development of Modern Economics. Paper over Boards. Routledge. New York, NY. 1992. 224p. ISBN:0-415-06164-4, ISBN13: 978-0-415-06164-3. Dewey:330.15/3. LCCN:91-025698.
Audience: **u,f.**

Ginzberg, Eli **HB103.S6G56 2002**
Adam Smith and the Founding of Market Economics. Trade Paper. Transaction Publishers. Somerset, NJ. 2002. 265p. ISBN:0-7658-0949-4, ISBN13: 978-0-7658-0949-0. Dewey:330.15/3. LCCN:2002-072673.
Audience: **l,u,f.**

Happle, Stephen K. **HB171.5**
Economics, an Examination of Scarcity: Adam Smith's Micro to Current U. S. Macro. Paper Text. Thomas Horton & Daughters. Glen Ridge, NJ. 2000. 210p. ISBN:0-913878-62-6, ISBN13: 978-0-913878-62-0. Dewey:330.
Audience: **u,f.**

Hollander, Samuel **HB103.S6 H65**
The Economics of Adam Smith. Trade Cloth. University of Toronto Press. Toronto, ON. 1973. 320p. Studies in Classical Political Economy Ser. ISBN:0-8020-1811-4, ISBN13: 978-0-8020-1811-3. Dewey:330.15/3. LCCN:72-185717.
Audience: **l,u,f.**

Malloy, Robin P. & Evensky, Jerry (Editors) **K235**
Adam Smith and the Philosophy of Law and Economics. Paper Text. Springer. New York, NY. 1995. 235p. Law and Philosophy Library, No. 20 ISBN:0-7923-3425-6, ISBN13: 978-0-7923-3425-5. Dewey:340/.1.
Audience: **u,f.**

Malloy, Robin P. & Evensky, Jerry (Editors) **K487.E3Z93 1994**
Adam Smith and the Philosophy of Law and Economics. Trade Cloth. Springer Dordrecht. Dordrecht, 1994. 240p. Law and Philosophy Library, Vol. 20 ISBN:0-7923-2796-9, ISBN13: 978-0-7923-2796-7. Dewey:340/.1. LCCN:94-009710.
Audience: **u,f.**

Minowitz, Peter **HB72.M53 1993**
Profits, Priests, and Princes: Adam Smith's Emancipation of Economics from Politics and Religion. Trade Cloth. Stanford University Press. Palo Alto, CA. 1993. 364p. ISBN:0-8047-2166-1, ISBN13: 978-0-8047-2166-0. Dewey:330.15/3. LCCN:93-018798.
Audience: **u,f.** *Choice, 1994.*

O'Driscoll, Gerald P. Jr. (Editor) **HB103.S6**
Adam Smith and Modern Political Economy: Bicentennial Essays on The Wealth of Nations. Cloth Text. Blackwell Publishing Professional. Ames, IA. 1979. 182p. ISBN:0-8138-1900-8, ISBN13: 978-0-8138-1900-6. Dewey:330.15/3.
Audience: **u,f.**

O'Driscoll, Gerald P. Jr. (Editor) **HB0103.S6A62**
Adam Smith and Modern Political Economy: Bicentennial Essays on the Wealth of Nations. Trade Paper. Books on Demand. Ann Arbor, MI. 197p. ISBN:0-8357-6757-4, ISBN13: 978-0-8357-6757-6. Dewey:330.15/3. LCCN:78-010181.
Audience: **u,f.**

Otteson, James R. **HB501.O824 2002**
Adam Smith's Marketplace of Life. Trade Cloth. Cambridge University Press. New York, NY. 2002. 352p. ISBN:0-521-81625-4, ISBN13: 978-0-521-81625-0. Dewey:174. LCCN:2002-023867.
Audience: **u,f.** *Choice, 2003.*

Pack, Spencer J. **HB501.P125 1991**
Capitalism As a Moral System: Adam Smith's Critique of the Free Market Economy. Cloth Text. Edward Elgar Publishing, Inc. Northampton, MA. 1991. 208p. ISBN:1-85278-442-3, ISBN13: 978-1-85278-442-3. Dewey:330.12/2. LCCN:90-028093.
Audience: **u,f.** *Choice, 1992.*

Rae, John **B3376.W564**
Life of Adam Smith. Jacob Viner (Introduction by). Trade Cloth. Scholar's Bookshelf. Cranbury, NJ. 1965. xv, 449p. Reprints of Economic Classics Ser. ISBN:0-678-00101-4, ISBN13: 978-0-678-00101-1. Dewey:192. LCCN:63-023522.
Audience: **u,f.**

Raphael, D. D. **HB103.S6R27 1985**
Adam Smith. Paper Text. Oxford University Press, Inc. New York, NY. 1985. 128p. Past Masters Ser. ISBN:0-19-287558-2, ISBN13: 978-0-19-287558-7. Dewey:330.15/3/0924. LCCN:84-020629.
Audience: **g,l,u,f.** *Choice, 1985.*

Ross, Ian S. **HB103.S6R67 1995**
The Life of Adam Smith. Trade Cloth. Oxford University Press, Inc. New York, NY. 1995. 524p. ISBN:0-19-828821-2, ISBN13: 978-0-19-828821-3. Dewey:330.1/53/092. LCCN:95-012836.
Audience: **u,f.** *Choice, 1996.*

Skinner, Andrew S. & Wilson, Thomas **HB103.S6**
Essays on Adam Smith. Trade Cloth. Oxford University Press, Inc. New York, NY. 1976. xvi, 647p. ISBN:0-19-828191-9, ISBN13: 978-0-19-828191-7. Dewey:330.15/3.
Audience: **u,f.**

Smith, Adam **BJ1005.S6 2000**
The Theory of Moral Sentiments. Trade Cloth. Prometheus Books, Publishers. Amherst, NY. 2004. 546p. Great Books in

Philosophy ISBN:1-57392-800-3, ISBN13: 978-1-57392-800-7. Dewey:170. LCCN:99-087819.
Audience: **g,l,u,f.**

Smith, Adam **HB103.S6**
Wealth of Nations. Trade Cloth. Amereon, Ltd. Mattituck, NY. ISBN:0-8488-1170-4, ISBN13: 978-0-8488-1170-9. Dewey:330.15/3.
Audience: **g,l,u,f.**

Smith, Adam **B3376.W564**
Essays on Philosophical Subjects, with Dugald Stewart's Account of Adam Smith. W. P. Wightman, J. C. Bryce & Ian S. Ross (Editors). Trade Cloth. Oxford University Press, Inc. New York, NY. 1980. 368p. The Glasgow Edition of the Works and Correspondence of Adam Smith Ser. ISBN:0-19-828187-0, ISBN13: 978-0-19-828187-0. Dewey:192. LCCN:79-040614.
Audience: **u,f.**

Smith, Craig **JC574.S53 2005**
Adam Smiths Political Philosophy: The Invisible Hand and Spontaneous Order. Paper over Boards. Routledge. New York, NY. 2005. 208p. Routledge Studies in Social and Political Thought Ser. ISBN:0-415-36094-3, ISBN13: 978-0-415-36094-4. Dewey:320.51/2/092. LCCN:2005-003077.
Audience: **l,u,f.**

Stirati, Antonella **HD4909.S7513 1994**
The Theory of Wages in Classical Economics: A Study of Adam Smith, David Ricardo and Their Contemporaries. Trade Cloth. Edward Elgar Publishing, Inc. Northampton, MA. 1994. 240p. ISBN:1-85278-710-4, ISBN13: 978-1-85278-710-3. Dewey:331.2/101. LCCN:93-042452.
Audience: **u,f.** *Choice, 1994.*

Winch, D. **JC176.S63**
Adam Smith's Politics. Trade Cloth. Cambridge University Press. New York, NY. 1978. 216p. Cambridge Studies in the History and Theory of Politics ISBN:0-521-21827-6, ISBN13: 978-0-521-21827-6. Dewey:320.5/092/4. LCCN:77-082525.
Audience: **u,f.**

Young, Jeffrey T. **HB103.S6Y677 1997**
Economics as a Moral Science: The Political Economy of Adam Smith. Trade Cloth. Edward Elgar Publishing, Inc. Northampton, MA. 1997. 240p. ISBN:1-85898-267-7, ISBN13: 978-1-85898-267-0. Dewey:330.15/3. LCCN:97-023203.
Audience: **u,f.** *Choice, 1998.*

Systems > Capitalist > Classical > David Ricardo

Hollander, Samuel **HB103.R5.H72**
The Economics of David Ricardo. Cloth Text. University of Toronto Press. Toronto, ON. 1979. xiv, 759p. Studies in Classical Political Economy Ser. ISBN:0-8020-5438-2, ISBN13: 978-0-8020-5438-8. Dewey:330.15/3. LCCN:79-004392.
Audience: **u,f.**

Hollander, Samuel **HB103.R5H723 1995**
Ricardo, the New View. Paper over Boards. Routledge. New York, NY. 1995. 384p. Collected Essays Ser., Vol. 1 ISBN:0-415-11582-5, ISBN13: 978-0-415-11582-7. Dewey:330.1/53. LCCN:96-007939.
Audience: **u,f.**

Ricardo, David **HB161**
Economic Essays. Trade Paper. University Press of the Pacific. Miami, FL. 2002. 148p. ISBN:1-4102-0186-4, ISBN13: 978-1-4102-0186-7. Dewey:330.
Audience: **u,f.**

Ricardo, David **HB161**
The Economic Philosophy of David Ricardo As a Textbook Which Far Surpasses Anything Employed in Our Schools Today. Trade Cloth. Institute for Economic & Financial Research. Albuquerque, NM. 1991. 426p. ISBN:0-86654-319-8, ISBN13: 978-0-86654-319-4. Dewey:330.153.
Audience: **u,f.**

Ricardo, David **HG0944.R5**
The High Price of Bullion: A Proof of Depreciation of Bank Notes. Trade Paper. Books on Demand. Ann Arbor, MI. 462p. ISBN:0-598-73942-4, ISBN13: 978-0-598-73942-1. Dewey:330. LCCN:64-003195.
Audience: **u,f.**

Ricardo, David **HG938**
Minor Papers on the Currency Question, 1809-1823. Trade Cloth. Ayer Company Publishers, Inc. Manchester, NH. 1979. ISBN:0-405-10624-6, ISBN13: 978-0-405-10624-8. Dewey:332.4/941.
Audience: **u,f.**

Ricardo, David
The Principles of Economic Analysis, Set. Trade Cloth. Institute for Economic & Financial Research. Albuquerque, NM. 1987. 267p. ISBN:0-86654-236-1, ISBN13: 978-0-86654-236-4.
Audience: **l,u,f.**

Ricardo, David **HB103.S6**
The Principles of Political Economy and Taxation. Ed. 3. Trade Paper. Janus Publishing Company. Colchester, 2002. 314p. ISBN:1-902835-15-8, ISBN13: 978-1-902835-15-0. Dewey:330.15/3.
Audience: **u,f.**

Ricardo, David
The Theory of Precious Metals and of Money. Trade Cloth. Foundation for Classical Reprints, The. Albuquerque, NM. 1989. 120p. ISBN:0-89901-383-X, ISBN13: 978-0-89901-383-1.
Audience: **u,f.**

Ricardo, David **HB161**
The Works and Correspondence of David Ricardo, Vol. 1-11. Trade Paper. Liberty Fund, Inc. Indianapolis, IN. 2004. 4624p. ISBN:0-86597-976-6, ISBN13: 978-0-86597-976-5. Dewey:330.15/13/092.
Audience: **u,f.**

Ricardo, David **HB161.R4812**
The Works and Correspondence of David Ricardo: Notes on Malthus. Trade Paper. Liberty Fund, Inc. Indianapolis, IN. 2004. 463p. ISBN:0-86597-966-9, ISBN13: 978-0-86597-966-6. Dewey:330.81.
Audience: **u,f.**

Ricardo, David **HB161 .R4812**
The Works and Correspondence of David Ricardo: Letters, 1810-1815. Trade Paper. Liberty Fund, Inc. Indianapolis, IN. 2004. 353p. ISBN:0-86597-970-7, ISBN13: 978-0-86597-970-3. Dewey:330.15/13/092.
Audience: **u,f.**

Ricardo, David **HB161 .R4812**
The Works and Correspondence of David Ricardo: Letters, 1816-1818. Trade Paper. Liberty Fund, Inc. Indianapolis, IN. 2004. 394p. ISBN:0-86597-971-5, ISBN13: 978-0-86597-971-0. Dewey:330.15/13/092.
Audience: **u,f.**

Ricardo, David **HB161.R4812**
The Works and Correspondence of David Ricardo: Speeches and Evidence. Trade Paper. Liberty Fund, Inc. Indianapolis, IN. 2004. 534p. ISBN:0-86597-969-3, ISBN13: 978-0-86597-969-7. Dewey:330.81.
Audience: **u,f.**

Ricardo, David **HB161.R4812**
The Works and Correspondence of David Ricardo: Pamphlets and Papers, 1815-1823. Trade Paper. Liberty Fund, Inc. Indianapolis, IN. 2004. 422p. ISBN:0-86597-968-5, ISBN13: 978-0-86597-968-0. Dewey:330.81.
Audience: **u,f.**

Ricardo, David **HB161 .R4812**
The Works and Correspondence of David Ricardo: Letters, 1819-June 1821. Trade Paper. Liberty Fund, Inc. Indianapolis, IN. 2004. 403p. ISBN:0-86597-972-3, ISBN13: 978-0-86597-972-7. Dewey:330.15/13/092.
Audience: **u,f.**

Ricardo, David **HB161 .R4812**
The Works and Correspondence of David Ricardo: Biographical Miscellany. Trade Paper. Liberty Fund, Inc. Indianapolis, IN. 2004. 424p. ISBN:0-86597-974-X, ISBN13: 978-0-86597-974-1. Dewey:330.15/13/092.
Audience: **u,f.**

Ricardo, David **HB103.S6**
The Works and Correspondence of David Ricardo: General Index. Trade Paper. Liberty Fund, Inc. Indianapolis, IN. 2004. 114p. ISBN:0-86597-975-8, ISBN13: 978-0-86597-975-8. Dewey:330.15/3.
Audience: **u,f.**

Ricardo, David **HB161 .R4812**
The Works and Correspondence of David Ricardo: Letters, July 1821-1823. Trade Paper. Liberty Fund, Inc. Indianapolis, IN. 2004. 408p. ISBN:0-86597-973-1, ISBN13: 978-0-86597-973-4. Dewey:330.15/13/092.
Audience: **u,f.**

Ricardo, David **HB161.R4812**
The Works and Correspondence of David Ricardo: Pamphlets and Papers, 1809-1811. Trade Paper. Liberty Fund, Inc. Indianapolis, IN. 2004. 437p. ISBN:0-86597-967-7, ISBN13: 978-0-86597-967-3. Dewey:330.81.
Audience: **u,f.**

Ricardo, David & Dobb, M. H. **HB161.R4812 2004**
The Works and Correspondence of David Ricardo: Principles of Political Economy and Taxation. Piero Sraffa (Editor). Trade Paper. Liberty Fund, Inc. Indianapolis, IN. 2004. 447p. ISBN:0-86597-965-0, ISBN13: 978-0-86597-965-9. Dewey:330.15/13/092. LCCN:2002-016222.
Audience: **u,f.**

Ricardo, David, et al. **HB103.R5R53 2004**
Letters of David Ricardo to Thomas Robert Malthus, 1810-1823. T. R. Malthus & James Bonar (Authors). Trade Cloth. Martino Publishing. Mansfield Centre, CT. 2004. ISBN:1-57898-485-8, ISBN13: 978-1-57898-485-5. Dewey:330.15/3. LCCN:2003-064874.
Audience: **u,f.**

Ricardo, David & McCulloch, J. R. **HB161.R48 1999**
The Works of David Ricardo, Esq., M. P.: With a Notice of the Life and Writings of the Author [1846]. Trade Cloth. Lawbook Exchange, Limited, The. Clark, NJ. 2000. 617p. ISBN:1-58477-028-7, ISBN13: 978-1-58477-028-2. Dewey:330.15/3. LCCN:99-039612.
Audience: **u,f.**

Ricardo, David **HB161.R4812**
The Works and Correspondence of David Ricardo: Principles of Political Economy, Vol. 1. P. Sraffa (Editor). Trade Paper. Cambridge University Press. New York, NY. 1981. 447p. ISBN:0-521-28505-4, ISBN13: 978-0-521-28505-6. Dewey:330.81.
Audience: **u,f.**

Systems > Capitalist > Classical > Thomas Malthus

Elwell, Frank W. **HB863.E49 2001**
A Commentary on Malthus' 1798 Essay on Population As Social Theory. Trade Cloth. Edwin Mellen Press, The. Lewiston, NY. 2001. 324p. Mellen Studies in Sociology, Vol. 26 ISBN:0-7734-7669-5, ISBN13: 978-0-7734-7669-1. Dewey:304.6. LCCN:00-058724.
Audience: **u,f.**

Hollander, Samuel (Editor) **HB871**
Malthus' Essay on Population. Ed. 6. Library Binding. Routledge. New York, NY. 1996. 5970p. History of British Economic Thought Ser. ISBN:0-415-14304-7, ISBN13: 978-0-415-14304-2. Dewey:304.6.
Audience: **u,f.**

James, Patricia **HB863**
Population Malthus: His Life and Times. Trade Cloth. Routledge. New York, NY. 1979. xv, 524p. ISBN:0-7100-0266-1, ISBN13: 978-0-7100-0266-2. Dewey:330.15/3. LCCN:79-040584.
Audience: **u,f.**

Malthus, Thomas Robert **HB871**
An Essay on the Principle of Population. Trade Cloth. Prometheus Books, Publishers. Amherst, NY. 1998. 410p. Great Minds Ser. ISBN:1-57392-255-2, ISBN13: 978-1-57392-255-5. Dewey:304.6. LCCN:98-031693.
Audience: **l,u,f.**

Malthus, Thomas Robert **HB401**
An Inquiry into the Nature and Progress of Rent and the Principles by Which It Is Regulated. Trade Cloth. Library Reprints, Inc. Temecula, CA. 1815. 61p. ISBN:0-7222-2673-X, ISBN13: 978-0-7222-2673-5. Dewey:333.5.
Audience: **u,f.**

Malthus, Thomas Robert **HB401.M19 1969**
Inquiry into the Nature and Progress of Rent and the Principles by Which It Is Regulated: A Greenwood Archival Edition.

Library Binding. Greenwood Publishing Group, Inc. Portsmouth, NH. 1970. 61p. ISBN:0-8371-2362-3, ISBN13: 978-0-8371-2362-2. Dewey:333.5. LCCN:69-013984.
Audience: **u,f.**

Malthus, Thomas Robert **HB201.M297 1989**
The Measure of Value Stated and Illuminated. Trade Cloth. Scholar's Bookshelf. Cranbury, NJ. 1989. v, 81p. Reprints of Economic Classics Ser. ISBN:0-678-00603-2, ISBN13: 978-0-678-00603-0. Dewey:332.4/1. LCCN:87-017246.
Audience: **u,f.**

Malthus, Thomas Robert **HC255**
The Pamphlets of Thomas Robert Malthus, 1800-1817. Library Binding. Scholar's Bookshelf. Cranbury, NJ. 1970. v, 320p. Reprints of Economic Classics Ser. ISBN:0-678-00646-6, ISBN13: 978-0-678-00646-7. Dewey:330.942. LCCN:77-117389.
Audience: **u,f.**

Malthus, Thomas Robert **HB861 .E7**
Population: The First Essay. Trade Paper. University of Michigan Press. Chicago, IL. 1959. 160p. Ann Arbor Paperbacks Ser. ISBN:0-472-06031-7, ISBN13: 978-0-472-06031-3. Dewey:301.32.
Audience: **l,u,f.**

Malthus, Thomas Robert **HB871**
An Essay on the Principle of Population. Philip Appleman (Editor). Paper Text. W. W. Norton & Company, Inc. New York, NY. 1976. 256p. Critical Editions Ser. ISBN:0-393-09202-X, ISBN13: 978-0-393-09202-8. Dewey:304.6.
Audience: **g,l,u,f.**

Malthus, Thomas Robert **HB161.M25 1987**
Principles of Political Economy, Set. John Pullen (Editor). Quantity Pack, Trade Cloth. Cambridge University Press. New York, NY. 1990. 1147p. ISBN:0-521-24775-6, ISBN13: 978-0-521-24775-7. Dewey:304.6. LCCN:87-009372.
Audience: **u,f.**

Malthus, Thomas Robert **HB161**
The Occasional Papers on Population and Political Economy from Contemporary Journals. Bernard Semmel (Editor). Trade Cloth. Burt Franklin Publisher. New York, NY. 1963. ISBN:0-8337-2197-6, ISBN13: 978-0-8337-2197-6. Dewey:308.1.
Audience: **u,f.**

Malthus, Thomas Robert **HB861 .E7 1992**
An Essay on the Principle of Population, or a View of Its Past and Present Effects on Human Happiness: With an Inquiry into Our Prospects Respecting the Future Removal or Mitigation of the Evils Which it Occasions. Donald Winch (Editor). Cloth Text. Cambridge University Press. New York, NY. 1992. 426p. Texts in the History of Political Thought ISBN:0-521-41954-9, ISBN13: 978-0-521-41954-3. Dewey:304.6. LCCN:91-038432.
Audience: **u,f.**

Marx, Karl & Engels, Friedrich **HB863.M253 1971**
Marx and Engels on the Population Bomb. Ronald L. Meek (Editor), S. Weissman (Introduction by). Trade Paper. Ramparts Press. Forestville, CA. 1971. 215p. ISBN:0-87867-002-5, ISBN13: 978-0-87867-002-4. Dewey:301.3/1. LCCN:71-132220.
Audience: **l,u,f.**

Mill, John Stuart **HB161 .M645**
Essays on Some Unsettled Questions of Political Economy. Trade Paper. Kessinger Publishing, LLC. Whitefish, MT. 2004. ISBN:1-4191-1840-4, ISBN13: 978-1-4191-1840-1. Dewey:330.15/3.
Audience: **u,f.**

Petersen, William **HB863.P47**
Malthus. Trade Cloth. Harvard University Press. Cambridge, MA. 1979. vi, 302p. ISBN:0-674-54425-0, ISBN13: 978-0-674-54425-3. Dewey:301.32/092/4. LCCN:78-031479.
Audience: **l,u,f.**

Systems > Capitalist > Classical > John Stuart Mill

Hollander, Samuel **HB103.S6**
The Economics of John Stuart Mill, Set. Trade Cloth. University of Toronto Press. Toronto, ON. 1985. 1843p. ISBN:0-8020-5671-7, ISBN13: 978-0-8020-5671-9. Dewey:330.15/3.
Audience: **u,f.** *Choice, 1986.*

Mill, John Stuart **B1606**
Autobiography of John Stuart Mill. Trade Paper. Columbia University Press. New York, NY. 1960. 240p. ISBN:0-231-08506-0, ISBN13: 978-0-231-08506-9. Dewey:190. LCCN:24-027691.
Audience: **g,l,u,f.**

Mill, John Stuart **HB161 .M645**
Essays on Some Unsettled Questions of Political Economy. Trade Paper. Kessinger Publishing, LLC. Whitefish, MT. 2004. ISBN:1-4191-1840-4, ISBN13: 978-1-4191-1840-1. Dewey:330.15/3.
Audience: **u,f.**

Mill, John Stuart **HQ1154.M476 2001**
The Subjection of Women. Edward Alexander (Editor). Trade Paper. Transaction Publishers. Somerset, NJ. 2001. 216p. ISBN:0-7658-0766-1, ISBN13: 978-0-7658-0766-3. Dewey:305.4/09. LCCN:00-054386.
Audience: **g,u,f.**

Mill, John Stuart **B1603.U873M54 1998**
Utilitarianism. Roger Crisp (Editor). Paper Text. Oxford University Press, Inc. New York, NY. 1998. 164p. Oxford Philosophical Texts ISBN:0-19-875163-X, ISBN13: 978-0-19-875163-2. Dewey:171/.5. LCCN:97-031037.
Audience: **u,f.**

Mill, John Stuart (Editor) **HB161.J75 2004**
Principles of Political Economy with Some of Their Applications to Social Philosophy. Stephen Nathanson (Abridged by, Introduction by). Trade Cloth. Hackett Publishing Company, Inc. Indianapolis, IN. 2004. 309p. Hackett Classics Ser. ISBN:0-87220-714-5, ISBN13: 978-0-87220-714-1. Dewey:330.15/3. LCCN:2003-056869.
Audience: **l,u,f.**

Mill, John Stuart **HB72**
Principles of Political Economy: And Chapters on Socialism. Jonathan Riley (Editor, Introduction by). Trade Paper. Oxford University Press, Inc. New York, NY. 1999. 512p. Oxford World's Classics Ser. ISBN:0-19-283672-2, ISBN13: 978-0-19-283672-4. Dewey:330/.01.
Audience: **u,f.**

Mill, John Stuart **JC585.M6 2004**
On Liberty. C. L. Ten (Introduction by). Book, Other. Rowman & Littlefield Publishers, Inc. Lanham, MD. 2005. 180p. ISBN:0-7425-4247-5, ISBN13: 978-0-7425-4247-1. Dewey:323.44. LCCN:2004-015989.
Audience: **u,f.** *Choice, 2003.*

Morales, Maria H. **HQ1596.J64 2004**
Mill's the Subjection of Women: Critical Essays. Book, Other. Rowman & Littlefield Publishers, Inc. Lanham, MD. 2004. 232p. Critical Essays on the Classics Ser. ISBN:0-7425-3517-7, ISBN13: 978-0-7425-3517-6. Dewey:305.42/0941. LCCN:2004-013907.
Audience: **l,u,f.**

Robson, John M. **JC223.M66**
Improvement of Mankind: The Social and Political Thought of John Stuart Mill. Trade Cloth. University of Toronto Press. Toronto, ON. 1968. ISBN:0-8020-1529-8, ISBN13: 978-0-8020-1529-7. Dewey:300/.924. LCCN:68-140051.
Audience: **u,f.**

Schwartz, Pedro **KF8745.S8**
The New Political Economy of J. S. Mill. Trade Cloth. Duke University Press. Durham, NC. 1973. 331p. ISBN:0-8223-0277-2, ISBN13: 978-0-8223-0277-3. Dewey:923.473. LCCN:72-088518.
Audience: **u,f.**

Stigler, George J. **HB171**
Essays in the History of Economics. Library Binding. University of Chicago Press. Chicago, IL. 1965. viii, 392p. Phoenix Ser. ISBN:0-226-77426-0, ISBN13: 978-0-226-77426-8. Dewey:330.109. LCCN:65-014426.
Audience: **u,f.**

Systems > Capitalist > Classical > Says

Hollander, S **HB105.S25H65 2005**
Jean-Baptiste Say and the Classical Canon in Economics: The British Connection in French Classicism. Paper over Boards. Routledge. New York, NY. 2005. XIV, 322p. Routledge Studies in the History of Economics Ser. ISBN:0-415-32338-X, ISBN13: 978-0-415-32338-3. Dewey:330.15/3. LCCN:2004-016597.
Audience: **l,u,f.**

Systems > Capitalist > Neoclassical

Clark, John Bates **HB501**
Capital and Its Earnings. Trade Paper. University Press of the Pacific. Miami, FL. 2003. 72p. ISBN:1-4102-0578-9, ISBN13: 978-1-4102-0578-0. Dewey:332/.041.
Audience: **u,f.**

Clark, John Bates **HB771**
The Distribution of Wealth: A Theory of Wages, Interest and Profits. Trade Paper. University Press of the Pacific. Miami, FL. 2002. 476p. ISBN:1-4102-0155-4, ISBN13: 978-1-4102-0155-3. Dewey:339.2.
Audience: **u,f.**

Clark, John Bates **HB771**
The Distribution of Wealth and Universal Economic Laws. Trade Cloth. Institute for Economic & Political World Strategic Studies. Albuquerque, NM. 1988. 455p. ISBN:0-86654-243-4, ISBN13: 978-0-86654-243-2. Dewey:339.2.
Audience: **u,f.**

Clark, John Bates **HB171**
Essentials of Economic Theory as Applied to Modern Problems of Industry and Public Policy. Trade Cloth. Library Reprints, Inc. Temecula, CA. 1907. 566p. ISBN:0-7222-2665-9, ISBN13: 978-0-7222-2665-0. Dewey:330.1.
Audience: **u,f.**

Clark, John Bates **HB171**
The Philosophy of Wealth: Economic Principles Newly Formulated. Trade Cloth. Library Reprints, Inc. Temecula, CA. 1894. 236p. ISBN:0-7222-2666-7, ISBN13: 978-0-7222-2666-7. Dewey:330.15/5.
Audience: **u,f.**

Edgeworth, Francis Y. **HB74.M3 E3**
Mathematical Psychics: An Essay on the Application of Mathematics to the Moral Sciences. Trade Cloth. Scholar's Bookshelf. Cranbury, NJ. 1967. viii, 150p. Reprints of Economic Classics Ser. ISBN:0-678-00308-4, ISBN13: 978-0-678-00308-4. Dewey:330.0182. LCCN:67-028410.
Audience: **u,f.**

Edgeworth, Francis Y. **HB135.E3 1995**
Mathematical Psychics and Other Essays: Commentaries by Marshall, Jevons and Keynes. Paper Text. James & Gordon. Mountain Center, CA. 1995. 192p. Foundations of Mathematical Economics Ser., :Commentaries by Cairnes, Marshall, Newcomb, Leslie and Wicksteed ISBN:1-887585-03-6, ISBN13: 978-1-887585-03-3. Dewey:330/.01/51. LCCN:95-078026.
Audience: **u,f.**

Edgeworth, Francis Y. **HB33 .E32**
Papers Relating to Political Economy. Library Binding. Burt Franklin Publisher. New York, NY. 1970. Research and Source Works, No. 493 ISBN:0-8337-1000-1, ISBN13: 978-0-8337-1000-0. Dewey:330/.08. LCCN:71-122226.
Audience: **u,f.**

Ferguson, Charles E. **HB103.S6**
The Neoclassical Theory of Production and Distribution. Trade Cloth. Cambridge University Press. New York, NY. 1969. 402p. ISBN:0-521-07453-3, ISBN13: 978-0-521-07453-7. Dewey:330.153. LCCN:75-092248.
Audience: **u,f.**

Heertje, Arnold **HB76**
The Makers of Modern Economics, Vol. 2. Trade Paper. Edward Elgar Publishing Ltd. Cheltenham, ISBN:1-85898-293-6, ISBN13: 978-1-85898-293-9. Dewey:330/.01.
Audience: **l,u,f.**

Heertje, Arnold (Editor) **HB72**
The Makers of Modern Economics, Vol. 2. Trade Cloth. Edward Elgar Publishing, Inc. Northampton, MA. 1995. 192p. ISBN:1-85898-237-5, ISBN13: 978-1-85898-237-3. Dewey:330/.01. LCCN:92-029859.
Audience: **l,u,f.**

Patinkin, Don & Leith, J. Clark **HB99.7.K3817 1978**
Keynes, Cambridge and the General Theory. Trade Cloth.

University of Toronto Press. Toronto, ON. 1978. xii, 182p. ISBN:0-8020-2296-0, ISBN13: 978-0-8020-2296-7. Dewey:330.15/6. LCCN:78-320853.
Audience: **u,f.**

Ricketts, Martin **HB98.2.N44 1988**
Neoclassical Microeconomics, Vol. I. Cloth Text. Edward Elgar Publishing, Inc. Northampton, MA. 1988. 384p. ISBN:1-85278-112-2, ISBN13: 978-1-85278-112-5. Dewey:338.5. LCCN:88-016345.
Audience: **l,u,f.**

Walsh, Vivian & Gram, Harvey N. **HB145**
Classical and Neoclassical Theories of General Equilibrium. Joan Robinson (Introduction by). Cloth Text. Oxford University Press, Inc. New York, NY. 1979. 442p. ISBN:0-19-502674-8, ISBN13: 978-0-19-502674-0. Dewey:330.15/43. LCCN:78-031129.
Audience: **u,f.**

Systems > Capitalist > Neoclassical > Marshall

Groenewegen, Peter & Marshall, Alfred **HC255 .M387 SUPPL.**
Official Papers of Alfred Marshall: A Supplement. Trade Cloth. Cambridge University Press. New York, NY. 1996. 372p. ISBN:0-521-55185-4, ISBN13: 978-0-521-55185-4. Dewey:330.9/41/081. LCCN:95-030972.
Audience: **u,f.**

Marshall, Alfred **HB171**
Elements of Economics of Industry. Trade Paper. Simon Publications, Inc. 2003. 416p. ISBN:1-932512-13-6, ISBN13: 978-1-932512-13-7. Dewey:330. LCCN:02-019708.
Audience: **u,f.**

Marshall, Alfred **HD2326 .M3**
Industry and Trade: A Study of Industrial Technique and Business Organization; and of Their Influences on the Conditions of Various Classes and Nations. Trade Paper. University Press of the Pacific. Miami, FL. 2003. 488p. ISBN:1-4102-0469-3, ISBN13: 978-1-4102-0469-1. Dewey:338.6.
Audience: **u,f.**

Marshall, Alfred **HD2326**
Industry and Trade: A Study of Industrial Technique and Business Organization; and of Their Influences on the Conditions of Various Classes and Nations - Volume I, Vol. 1. Trade Paper. University Press of the Pacific. Miami, FL. 2003. 420p. ISBN:1-4102-0468-5, ISBN13: 978-1-4102-0468-4. Dewey:338/.09.
Audience: **u,f.**

Marshall, Alfred **HG230.3.M357 2003**
Money, Credit, and Commerce. Trade Paper. Prometheus Books, Publishers. Amherst, NY. 2004. 475p. Great Minds Ser. ISBN:1-59102-036-0, ISBN13: 978-1-59102-036-3. Dewey:332.4. LCCN:2002-037037.
Audience: **u,f.**

Marshall, Alfred **HC255**
Official Papers. Trade Cloth. Greenwood Publishing Group, Inc. Portsmouth, NH. 1979. 428p. ISBN:0-313-21110-8, ISBN13: 978-0-313-21110-2. Dewey:330.9/41/081. LCCN:78-010179.
Audience: **u,f.**

Marshall, Alfred **HB171.5.M289 1997**
Principles of Economics. Trade Cloth. Prometheus Books, Publishers. Amherst, NY. 1997. 342p. Great Minds Ser. ISBN:1-57392-140-8, ISBN13: 978-1-57392-140-4. Dewey:330. LCCN:97-003368.
Audience: **u,f.**

Marshall, Alfred **HF1007**
The Pure Theory of Foreign Trade and the Pure Theory of Domestic Values. Library Binding. Scholar's Bookshelf. Cranbury, NJ. 1975. 65p. Reprints of Economic Classics Ser. ISBN:0-678-01194-X, ISBN13: 978-0-678-01194-2. Dewey:382. LCCN:73-022013.
Audience: **u,f.**

Marshall, Alfred **HB171**
The Early Economic Writings of Alfred Marshall, 1867-1890. Whitaker, John K. (John King) (Editor). New York : Free Press. 1975.
Audience: **u,f.**

Marshall, Alfred & Marshall, Mary P. **HB171 .M342**
Economics of Industry: 1879 Edition. Ed. 18. D. P. O'Brien (Introduction by). Trade Paper. Continuum International Publishing Group, Ltd. London, 1996. 248p. Key Texts Ser., :Classic Studies in the History of Ideas ISBN:1-85506-320-4, ISBN13: 978-1-85506-320-4. Dewey:330.
Audience: **l,u,f.**

Marshall, Alfred **HB98 .M3**
Memorials of Alfred Marshall. A. C. Pigou (Editor). Trade Cloth. Scholar's Bookshelf. Cranbury, NJ. 1966. ix, 518p. Reprints of Economic Classics Ser. ISBN:0-678-00197-9, ISBN13: 978-0-678-00197-4. Dewey:330.08. LCCN:66-024415.
Audience: **u,f.**

Marshall, Alfred **HB119.V4**
The Correspondence of Alfred Marshall, Economist, Set. John K. Whitaker (Editor). Quantity Pack, Trade Cloth. Cambridge University Press. New York, NY. 1996. 416p. ISBN:0-521-55889-1, ISBN13: 978-0-521-55889-1. Dewey:330/.092.
Audience: **u,f.**

Systems > Capitalist > Neoclassical > Fisher

Fisher, Irving **HB119.F5.A25 1996**
100% Money. Trade Cloth. Pickering & Chatto Publishers, Ltd. London, 1996. vi, 312p. The Works of Irving Fisher ISBN:1-85196-236-0, ISBN13: 978-1-85196-236-5. Dewey:330 S. LCCN:96-012211.
Audience: **u,f.**

Fisher, Irving **HB501**
The Nature of Capital and Income. Trade Cloth. Simon Publications, Inc. 2003. 427p. ISBN:1-932512-05-5, ISBN13: 978-1-932512-05-2. Dewey:332/.041. LCCN:28-019914.
Audience: **u,f.**

Fisher, Irving **HB119.F5.A25 1996**
The Theory of Interest. Trade Cloth. Pickering & Chatto Publishers, Ltd. London, 1996. v, 612p. The Works of Irving Fisher ISBN:1-85196-234-4, ISBN13: 978-1-85196-234-1. Dewey:330 S. LCCN:96-012209.
Audience: **u,f.**

Fisher, Irving **HB119.F5A25 1996**
The Works of Irving Fisher, Set. William J. Barber & James Tobin (Editors). Trade Cloth. Pickering & Chatto Publishers, Ltd. London, 1997. 6240p. Masters Ser. ISBN:1-85196-225-5, ISBN13: 978-1-85196-225-9. Dewey:330. LCCN:96-021156.
Audience: **u,f.**

Fisher, Irving **HB119.F5E27 1999**
The Economics of Irving Fisher: Reviewing the Scientific Work of a Great Economist. Hans-Edi Loef & Hans G. Monissen (Editors). Trade Cloth. Edward Elgar Publishing, Inc. Northampton, MA. 1999. 368p. ISBN:1-84064-037-5, ISBN13: 978-1-84064-037-3. Dewey:330.1. LCCN:98-050845.
Audience: **u,f.**

Geanakoplos, John **HB171**
Celebrating Irving Fisher: The Legacy of a Great Economist. Robert W. Dimand (Editor). Trade Paper. Blackwell Publishing, Inc. Malden, MA. 2005. 320p. ISBN:1-4051-3307-4, ISBN13: 978-1-4051-3307-4. Dewey:330.1.
Audience: **l,u,f.**

Systems > Capitalist > Keynesian

Backhouse, Roger E. & Salanti, Andrea (Editors) **HB172.5**
Macroeconomics and the Real World: Keynesian Economics, Unemployment, and Policy, Vol. 2. Trade Cloth. Oxford University Press, Inc. New York, NY. 2001. 312p. ISBN:0-19-829796-3, ISBN13: 978-0-19-829796-3. Dewey:339. LCCN:00-057111.
Audience: **u,f.**

Ferguson, Charles E. **HB103.S6**
The Neoclassical Theory of Production and Distribution. Trade Cloth. Cambridge University Press. New York, NY. 1969. 402p. ISBN:0-521-07453-3, ISBN13: 978-0-521-07453-7. Dewey:330.153. LCCN:75-092248.
Audience: **u,f.**

Harcourt, G. C. **HB99.7**
50 Years a Keynesian and Other Essays. Trade Paper. Palgrave Macmillan. New York, NY. 2006. 364p. ISBN:1-4039-8760-2, ISBN13: 978-1-4039-8760-0. Dewey:330.156. LCCN:00-040462.
Audience: **l,u,f.**

Laidler, David **HB99.7 .L28 1999**
Fabricating the Keynesian Revolution: Studies of the Inter-War Literature on Money, the Cycle and Unemployment. Craufurd D. Goodwin (Contribution by). Trade Cloth. Cambridge University Press. New York, NY. 1999. 396p. Historical Perspectives on Modern Economics Ser. ISBN:0-521-64173-X, ISBN13: 978-0-521-64173-9. Dewey:330.156. LCCN:98-038614.
Audience: **l,u,f.**

Leeson, Robert (Editor) **HB119.F84K49 2003**
Keynes, Chicago and Friedman. Milton Friedman (Preface by). Trade Cloth. Pickering & Chatto Publishers, Ltd. London, 2003. 944p. ISBN:1-85196-767-2, ISBN13: 978-1-85196-767-4. Dewey:330.15. LCCN:2002-030351.
Audience: **u,f.**

Leijonhufvud, Axel **HB99.7**
On Keynesian Economics and the Economics of Keynes: A Study in Monetary Theory. Cloth Text. Oxford University Press, Inc. New York, NY. 1968. 466p. ISBN:0-19-500948-7, ISBN13: 978-0-19-500948-4. Dewey:330.156.
Audience: **l,u,f.**

Mankiw, N. Gregory & Romer, David (Editors) **HB99.7.N88 1991**
New Keynesian Economics: Coordination Failures and Real Rigidities. Trade Paper. MIT Press. Cambridge, MA. 1991. 462p. Readings in Economics Ser. ISBN:0-262-63134-2, ISBN13: 978-0-262-63134-1. Dewey:330.15/6. LCCN:90-006358.
Audience: **u,f.**

Mankiw, N. Gregory & Romer, David (Editors) **HB99.7.N88 1991**
New Keynesian Economics: Imperfect Competition and Sticky Prices. Trade Paper. MIT Press. Cambridge, MA. 1991. 444p. Readings in Economics Ser. ISBN:0-262-63133-4, ISBN13: 978-0-262-63133-4. Dewey:330.15/6. LCCN:90-006358.
Audience: **u,f.**

Patinkin, Don **HB99.7.P26 1982**
Anticipations of the General Theory and Other Essays on Keynes. Trade Cloth. University of Chicago Press. Chicago, IL. 1997. 304p. ISBN:0-226-64873-7, ISBN13: 978-0-226-64873-6. Dewey:330.15/6. LCCN:81-021929.
Audience: **u,f.**

Patinkin, Don **HB99.7.P27**
Keynes' Monetary Thought: A Study of Its Development. Trade Cloth. Duke University Press. Durham, NC. 1976. viii, 160p. ISBN:0-8223-0360-4, ISBN13: 978-0-8223-0360-2. Dewey:332.4/01. LCCN:75-040630.
Audience: **u,f.**

Patinkin, Don & Leith, J. Clark **HB99.7.K3817 1978**
Keynes, Cambridge and the General Theory. Trade Cloth. University of Toronto Press. Toronto, ON. 1978. xii, 182p. ISBN:0-8020-2296-0, ISBN13: 978-0-8020-2296-7. Dewey:330.15/6. LCCN:78-320853.
Audience: **u,f.**

Shaw, G. K. **HB99.7.S46 1988**
Keynesian Economics: The Permanent Revolution. Cloth Text. Edward Elgar Publishing, Inc. Northampton, MA. 1988. 168p. ISBN:1-85278-098-3, ISBN13: 978-1-85278-098-2. Dewey:330.15/6. LCCN:88-004017.
Audience: **u,f.**

Systems > Capitalist > Keynesian > J. M. Keynes

Allan, Walter (Editor) **HB99.7**
A Critique of Keynesian Economics. Cloth Text. Palgrave Macmillan. New York, NY. 1993. xvii, 247p. ISBN:0-312-08554-0, ISBN13: 978-0-312-08554-4. Dewey:330.156. LCCN:92-018932.
Audience: **u,f.**

Ambrosi, Gerhard Michael **HB99.7.A39 2003**
Keynes, Pigou and Cambridge Keynesians: Authenticity and Analytical Perpective in the Keynes-Classics Debate. Cloth over Boards. Palgrave Macmillan. New York, NY. 2004. 464p. ISBN:0-333-63390-3, ISBN13: 978-0-333-63390-8. Dewey:330.15/3. LCCN:2003-050455.
Audience: **u,f.**

Asimakopulos, Athanasios **HB99.7.K38 A85 1991**
Keynes's General Theory and Accumulation. Phyllis Deane, Gautam Mathur & Joan Robinson (Contribution by). Trade Paper. Cambridge University Press. New York, NY. 1991. 225p. Modern Cambridge Economics Ser. ISBN:0-521-36815-4, ISBN13: 978-0-521-36815-5. Dewey:330.15/6. LCCN:90-041557.
Audience: **l,u,f.** *Choice, 1992.*

Backhouse, Roger **HB99.7.K364**
Keynes: Contemporary Responses to the General Theory. Ed. 2. Paper Text. Saint Augustine's Press, Inc. South Bend, IN. 2000. 267p. Key Issues Ser., Vol. 21 ISBN:1-890318-28-0, ISBN13: 978-1-890318-28-4. Dewey:330.1/56. LCCN:99-039475.
Audience: **u,f.**

Backhouse, Roger & Bateman, Bradley (Editors) **HB103.K47**
The Cambridge Companion to Keynes. Cloth Text. Cambridge University Press. New York, NY. 2006. 342p. Cambridge Companions to Philosophy Ser. ISBN:0-521-84090-2, ISBN13: 978-0-521-84090-3. Dewey:330.156092.
Audience: **g,l,u,f.**

Bateman, Bradley W. & Davis, John B. (Editors) **HB103.K47K385 1991**
Keynes and Philosophy: Essays on the Origins of Keyne's Thought. Trade Cloth. Edward Elgar Publishing, Inc. Northampton, MA. 1991. 176p. ISBN:1-85278-306-0, ISBN13: 978-1-85278-306-8. Dewey:330.15/6. LCCN:90-046812.
Audience: **u,f.** *Choice, 1991.*

Blaug, Mark **HB103.A3K473 1990**
John Maynard Keynes: Life, Ideas, Legacy. Trade Cloth. Palgrave Macmillan. New York, NY. 1990. 104p. ISBN:0-312-04890-4, ISBN13: 978-0-312-04890-7. Dewey:330.15/6 B. LCCN:90-008446.
Audience: **g,l,u,f.** *Choice, 1991.*

Blaug, Mark (Editor) **HB103.K47J64 1991**
John Maynard Keynes, 1883-1946, Set. Trade Cloth. Edward Elgar Publishing, Inc. Northampton, MA. 1991. 1,104p. Pioneers in Economics Ser., Vol. 46 ISBN:1-85278-510-1, ISBN13: 978-1-85278-510-9. Dewey:330.15/6 B. LCCN:91-015828.
Audience: **l,u,f.**

Buchanan, J. M., et al. **HC256.5**
The Consequences of Mr. Keynes: An Analysis of the Misuse of Economic Theory for Political Profiteering, with Proposals for Constitutional Disciplines. John Burton & R. Wagner (Authors). Trade Paper. Transatlantic Arts, Inc. Albuquerque, NM. 1978. 88p. Hobart Paperback Ser., No. 78 ISBN:0-255-36110-6, ISBN13: 978-0-255-36110-1. Dewey:330.9/41/085.
Audience: **u,f.**

Cammarosano, Joseph R. **HF1411.C323 1987**
The Contributions of John Maynard Keynes to Foreign Trade Theory and Policy, 1909-1946. Stuart Bruchey (Editor). Library Binding. Garland Publishing, Inc. New York, NY. 1987. 437p. Foreign Economic Policy of the United States Ser. ISBN:0-8240-8076-9, ISBN13: 978-0-8240-8076-1. Dewey:382.1/04. LCCN:87-023775.
Audience: **u,f.**

Carabelli, Anna M. **HB99.7.C37 1988**
On Keynes's Method. Donald E. Moggridge (Foreword by). Cloth Text. Palgrave Macmillan. New York, NY. 1988. 400p. ISBN:0-312-01913-0, ISBN13: 978-0-312-01913-6. Dewey:330.15/6. LCCN:87-035617.
Audience: **u,f.**

Chick, Victoria **HB103.K47C46 1992**
On Money, Method and Keynes: Selected Essays by Victoria Chick. Philip Arestis & Sheila C. Dow (Editors). Cloth Text. Palgrave Macmillan. New York, NY. 1992. 240p. ISBN:0-312-06815-8, ISBN13: 978-0-312-06815-8. Dewey:330.15/6. LCCN:91-025838.
Audience: **u,f.**

Clarke, Peter **HB103.K47C528 1998**
The Keynesian Revolution and Its Economic Consequences: Selected Essays by Peter Clarke. Trade Cloth. Edward Elgar Publishing, Inc. Northampton, MA. 1998. 240p. ISBN:1-85898-590-0, ISBN13: 978-1-85898-590-9. Dewey:330.15/6. LCCN:97-029957.
Audience: **u,f.**

Coddington, Alan **HB99.7.C6 2003**
Keynesian Economics: The Search for First Principles. Paper over Boards. Routledge. New York, NY. 2003. 152p. Routledge Library Editions Ser., Vol. 65:Economics, US/Can. Edition Ser. ISBN:0-415-31368-6, ISBN13: 978-0-415-31368-1. Dewey:330.1/56.
Audience: **l,u,f.**

Davis, John B. **HB103.K47 D38 1994**
Keynes's Philosophical Development. Trade Cloth. Cambridge University Press. New York, NY. 1994. 210p. ISBN:0-521-41902-6, ISBN13: 978-0-521-41902-4. Dewey:330.15/6. LCCN:93-050564.
Audience: **u,f.**

De Carvalho, Fernando J. **HB99.7.C38 1992**
Mr. Keynes and the Post Keynesians: Principles of Macroeconomics for a Monetary Production Economy. Trade Cloth. Edward Elgar Publishing, Inc. Northampton, MA. 1992. 256p. New Directions in Modern Economics Ser.

ISBN:1-85278-653-1, ISBN13: 978-1-85278-653-3. Dewey:330.15/6. LCCN:92-001108.
Audience: **l,u,f.** *Choice, 1993.*

Dimand, Robert **HB87**
The Origins of the Keynesian Revolution. Trade Cloth. Edward Elgar Publishing, Inc. Northampton, MA. 1992. 224p. ISBN:1-85278-645-0, ISBN13: 978-1-85278-645-8. Dewey:330.15.
Audience: **u,f.**

Dow, Sheila C. & Earl, Peter E. **HG221**
Money Matters: A Keynesian Approach to Monetary Economics. Trade Paper. Blackwell Publishing, Inc. Malden, MA. viii, 270p. ISBN:0-85520-485-0, ISBN13: 978-0-85520-485-3. Dewey:332.4/01.
Audience: **u,f.**

Dow, Sheila C. & Hillard, John (Editors) **HB99.7.K38K485 2002**
Keynes, Uncertainty and the Global Economy: Beyond Keynes, Vol. 2. Trade Cloth. Edward Elgar Publishing, Inc. Northampton, MA. 2002. 336p. In Association with the Post Keynesian Economics Study Group ISBN:1-85898-797-0, ISBN13: 978-1-85898-797-2. Dewey:330.1. LCCN:2001-057495.
Audience: **f.**

Dow, Sheila & Hillard, John (Editors) **HB99.7.K38K476 1995**
Keynes, Knowledge and Uncertainty. Trade Cloth. Edward Elgar Publishing, Inc. Northampton, MA. 1995. 448p. ISBN:1-85278-873-9, ISBN13: 978-1-85278-873-5. Dewey:330.15/6. LCCN:94-037307.
Audience: **f.**

European Society for the History of Economic Thoug **HB99.7.I567 1999**
The Impact of Keynes on Economics in the 20th Century. Luigi L. Pasinetti & Bertram Schefold (Editors). Trade Cloth. Edward Elgar Publishing, Inc. Northampton, MA. 1999. 272p. ISBN:1-85898-861-6, ISBN13: 978-1-85898-861-0. Dewey:330.15/6. LCCN:98-034329.
Audience: **u,f.**

Fender, John **HB99.7**
Understanding Keynes: An Analysis of the General Theory. Trade Cloth. John Wiley & Sons, Inc. Hoboken, NJ. 1981. 160p. ISBN:0-470-27197-3, ISBN13: 978-0-470-27197-1. Dewey:330.15/6. LCCN:81-003385.
Audience: **u,f.**

Frazer, William **HB119**
The Legacy of Keynes and Friedman: Economic Analysis, Money, and Ideology. Trade Cloth. Greenwood Publishing Group, Inc. Portsmouth, NH. 1994. 304p. ISBN:0-275-94731-9, ISBN13: 978-0-275-94731-6. Dewey:330.1. LCCN:93-023490.
Audience: **u,f.**

Garretsen, Harry **HB99.7.G377 1992**
Keynes, Coordination and Beyond: The Development of Macroeconomic and Monetary Theory since 1945. Trade Cloth. Edward Elgar Publishing, Inc. Northampton, MA. 1992. 240p. ISBN:1-85278-620-5, ISBN13: 978-1-85278-620-5. Dewey:339. LCCN:92-007337.
Audience: **u,f.** *Choice, 1993.*

Gerrard, Bill & Hillard, John (Editors) **HB103.K47P46 1992**
The Philosophy and Economics of J. M. Keynes. Trade Cloth. Edward Elgar Publishing, Inc. Northampton, MA. 1992. 272p. ISBN:1-85278-400-8, ISBN13: 978-1-85278-400-3. Dewey:330.156. LCCN:91-037688.
Audience: **u,f.**

Hamouda, O. G. & Smithin, J. (Editors) **HB99.7**
Keynes and Public Policy after Fifty Years: Theories and Method, Vol. 2. Trade Cloth. Edward Elgar Publishing, Inc. Northampton, MA. 1988. 432p. ISBN:1-85278-004-5, ISBN13: 978-1-85278-004-3. Dewey:330.15/6.
Audience: **u,f.**

Hamouda, Omar F. & Smithin, John N. (Editors) **HB99.7**
Keynes and Public Policy after Fifty Years: Economics and Policy, Vol. 1. Trade Cloth. Edward Elgar Publishing, Inc. Northampton, MA. 1988. 432p. ISBN:1-85278-003-7, ISBN13: 978-1-85278-003-6. Dewey:330.15/6.
Audience: **u,f.**

Harcourt, G. C. & Riach, P. A. (Editors) **HB99.7.S43 1997**
A Second Edition of the General Theory, Vol. 1. Ed. 2. Paper over Boards. Routledge. New York, NY. 1997. 560p. ISBN:0-415-14942-8, ISBN13: 978-0-415-14942-6. Dewey:330.1/56. LCCN:96-003293.
Audience: **u,f.**

Harcourt, Geoffrey C. (Editor) **HB99.7.K38**
Keynes and His Contemporaries. Cloth Text. Palgrave Macmillan. New York, NY. 1985. 172p. ISBN:0-312-45184-9, ISBN13: 978-0-312-45184-4. Dewey:330.15/6. LCCN:85-008269.
Audience: **l,u,f.**

Harrod, Roy F. **HB103.K47**
The Life of John Maynard Keynes. Trade Paper. W. W. Norton & Company, Inc. New York, NY. 1983. 696p. ISBN:0-393-30024-2, ISBN13: 978-0-393-30024-6. Dewey:330.15/6. LCCN:82-014378.
Audience: **g,l,u,f.**

Hayek, Friedrich A. **HB99.7**
A Tiger by the Tail: The Keynesian Legacy of Inflation. Trade Paper. Cato Institute. Washington, DC. 1979. 157p. Cato Papers, No. 6 ISBN:0-932790-06-2, ISBN13: 978-0-932790-06-4. Dewey:330.15/6.
Audience: **l,u,f.**

Helm, Dieter R. (Editor) **HC256.6**
The Economic Borders of the State. Paper Text. Oxford University Press, Inc. New York, NY. 1992. 332p. ISBN:0-19-828606-6, ISBN13: 978-0-19-828606-6. Dewey:338.9.
Audience: **u,f.**

Hillard, John (Editor) **HB99.7.J15 1988**
J. M. Keynes in Retrospect: The Legacy of the Keynesian Revolution. Trade Cloth. Edward Elgar Publishing, Inc. Northampton, MA. 1988. 240p. ISBN:1-85278-012-6, ISBN13: 978-1-85278-012-8. Dewey:330.15/6. LCCN:87-032976.
Audience: **l,u,f.**

Johnson, Elizabeth S. & Johnson, Harry G. **HB99.7**
The Shadow of Keynes: Understanding Keynes, Cambridge, and Keynesian Economics. Paper Text. University of Chicago Press. Chicago, IL. 1982. ISBN:0-226-40149-9, ISBN13: 978-0-226-40149-2. Dewey:330.15/6. LCCN:78-056338.
Audience: **u,f.**

Keynes, John Maynard **HB171.K44**
The Collected Writings of John Maynard Keynes. [London] Macmillan; [New York] St. Martin's Press, for the Royal Economic Society. 1971. ISBN:0-333-10738-1, ISBN13: 978-0-333-10738-6.
Audience: **u,f.**

Keynes, John Maynard **HC57.K45 1963**
Essays in Persuasion. New York, Norton. 1963.
Audience: **l,u,f.**

Leeson, Robert (Editor) **HB119.F84K49 2003**
Keynes, Chicago and Friedman. Milton Friedman (Preface by). Trade Cloth. Pickering & Chatto Publishers, Ltd. London, 2003. 944p. ISBN:1-85196-767-2, ISBN13: 978-1-85196-767-4. Dewey:330.15. LCCN:2002-030351.
Audience: **u,f.**

Littleboy, Bruce **HB99.7.L58 1990**
On Interpreting Keynes: A Study in Reconciliation. Paper over Boards. Routledge. New York, NY. 1991. 352p. ISBN:0-415-04475-8, ISBN13: 978-0-415-04475-2. Dewey:330.15/6. LCCN:90-008400.
Audience: **u,f.** *Choice, 1991.*

Marzola, Alessandra & Silva, Francesco (Editors) **HB103.K47J6313 1994**
John Maynard Keynes: Language and Method. Trade Cloth. Edward Elgar Publishing, Inc. Northampton, MA. 1994. 256p. Advances in Economic Methodology Ser. ISBN:1-85278-923-9, ISBN13: 978-1-85278-923-7. Dewey:330.15/6. LCCN:93-033302.
Audience: **u,f.**

McCann, Charles R. **HB99.7.M4 1998**
John Maynard Keynes: Critical Responses. Paper over Boards. Routledge. New York, NY. 1998. 1720p. ISBN:0-415-15193-7, ISBN13: 978-0-415-15193-1. Dewey:330.156. LCCN:97-012924.
Audience: **u,f.**

Meltzer, Allan H. **HB99.7.K38 M45 1988**
Keynes's Monetary Theory: A Different Interpretation. Trade Paper. Cambridge University Press. New York, NY. 2005. 352p. ISBN:0-521-02275-4, ISBN13: 978-0-521-02275-0. Dewey:332.4/01.
Audience: **u,f.** *Choice, 1989.*

Mini, Piero V. **HB103.K47M53 1994**
John Maynard Keynes: A Study in the Psychology of Original Work. Trade Cloth. Palgrave Macmillan. New York, NY. 1994. viii, 254p. ISBN:0-312-12137-7, ISBN13: 978-0-312-12137-2. Dewey:330.15/6. LCCN:93-048289.
Audience: **u,f.**

Moggridge, Donald E. (Editor) **HB103.K47 K4**
Keynes: Aspects of the Man and His Work. Cloth Text. Palgrave Macmillan. New York, NY. 1974. 112p. ISBN:0-312-45185-7, ISBN13: 978-0-312-45185-1. Dewey:330.15/6.
Audience: **u,f.**

Moggridge, Donald E. **HB103.K47**
Maynard Keynes: An Economists' Biography. Trade Paper. Routledge. New York, NY. 1995. 992p. ISBN:0-415-12711-4, ISBN13: 978-0-415-12711-0. Dewey:330.1/56/092.
Audience: **l,u,f.**

Nell, Edward J. **HB99.7 .N457 1998**
The General Theory of Transformational Growth: Keynes after Sraffa. Trade Paper. Cambridge University Press. New York, NY. 2005. 814p. ISBN:0-521-02359-9, ISBN13: 978-0-521-02359-7. Dewey:330.15/6.
Audience: **u,f.**

O'Donnell, R. M. **HB103.K47O36 1989**
Keynes: Philosophy, Economics and Politics: The Philosophical Foundations of Keynes's Thought and Their Influence on His Economics. Cloth Text. Palgrave Macmillan. New York, NY. 1989. 256p. ISBN:0-312-03578-0, ISBN13: 978-0-312-03578-5. Dewey:330.15/6. LCCN:89-032732.
Audience: **l,u,f.** *Choice, 1990.*

Peden, G. C. **HB103.K47P39 1988**
Keynes, the Treasury and British Economic Policy. Trade Paper. Macmillan Publishers Ltd. London, 1988. 96p. Studies in Economic and Social History ISBN:0-333-36272-1, ISBN13: 978-0-333-36272-3. Dewey:338.941. LCCN:88-183412.
Audience: **u,f.**

Peden, George **HC256.3**
Keynes and His Critics: Treasury Responses to the Keynesian Revolution, 1925-1946. Trade Cloth. Oxford University Press, Inc. New York, NY. 2005. 388p. Records of Social and Economic History, New Ser. ISBN:0-19-726322-4, ISBN13: 978-0-19-726322-8. Dewey:338.941009043. LCCN:2005-295408.
Audience: **u,f.**

Pigou, Arthur C. **HB99.7.K38**
Keynes's General Theory: A Retrospective View. Library Binding. Scholar's Bookshelf. Cranbury, NJ. 1978. 68p. Reprints of Economic Classics Ser. ISBN:0-678-01225-3, ISBN13: 978-0-678-01225-3. Dewey:330.15/6. LCCN:76-057702.
Audience: **u,f.**

Raffaelli, Tiziano **HB103.M3R33 2003**
Marshall's Evolutionary Economics. Paper over Boards. Routledge. New York, NY. 2002. 192p. Routledge Studies in the History of Economics, Vol. 59 ISBN:0-415-25989-4, ISBN13: 978-0-415-25989-7. Dewey:330.15/7/092. LCCN:2002-028472.
Audience: **u,f.**

Raphael, D. D., et al. **HB103.A2T48 1997**
Three Great Economists: Smith, Malthus, Keynes. Donald Winch & Robert Skidelsky (Authors). Paper Text. Oxford University Press, Inc. New York, NY. 1997. 392p. Past Masters

Ser. ISBN:0-19-287694-5, ISBN13: 978-0-19-287694-2. Dewey:330.092. LCCN:96-036196.
Audience: **l,u,f.**

Schumpeter, Joseph Alois **HB76**
Ten Great Economists: From Marx to Keynes. Trade Paper. Simon Publications, Inc. 2003. 301p. ISBN:1-932512-09-8, ISBN13: 978-1-932512-09-0. Dewey:330.0922. LCCN:52-040824.
Audience: **g,l,u,f.**

Sharma, Soumitra (Editor) **HB99.7.J638 1998**
John Maynard Keyness: Keynesianism into the Twenty-First Century. P. Arestis, Z. Baletic, I. Ban, D. Benic, J. Chen, V. Chick, E. V. Fitzgerald & J. K. Gailbraith (Contribution by). Trade Cloth. Edward Elgar Publishing, Inc. Northampton, MA. 1998. 288p. ISBN:1-85898-653-2, ISBN13: 978-1-85898-653-1. Dewey:330.15/6. LCCN:97-029928.
Audience: **u,f.**

Shaw, G. K. **HB99.7.S46 1988**
Keynesian Economics: The Permanent Revolution. Cloth Text. Edward Elgar Publishing, Inc. Northampton, MA. 1988. 168p. ISBN:1-85278-098-3, ISBN13: 978-1-85278-098-2. Dewey:330.15/6. LCCN:88-004017.
Audience: **u,f.**

Skidelsky, Robert (Editor) **HB99.7**
The End of the Keynesian Era. Cloth Text. Holmes & Meier Publishers, Inc. Teaneck, NJ. 1977. ISBN:0-8419-0329-8, ISBN13: 978-0-8419-0329-6. Dewey:330.15/6. LCCN:77-008878.
Audience: **u,f.**

Skidelsky, Robert **HB99.7**
John Maynard Keynes: The Economist As Savior, 1920-1937. Trade Cloth. Penguin Group (USA) Inc. New York, NY. 1994. 768p. ISBN:0-7139-9110-0, ISBN13: 978-0-7139-9110-9. Dewey:330.156.
Audience: **l,u,f.** *Choice, 1994.*

Skidelsky, Robert **PL788.4.G4E3 2001**
John Maynard Keynes: Fighting for Freedom 1937-1946. Trade Cloth. Penguin Group (USA) Inc. New York, NY. 2001. 576p. ISBN:0-670-03022-8, ISBN13: 978-0-670-03022-4. Dewey:895.6/314. LCCN:2001-017748.
Audience: **l,u,f.** *Choice, 2002.*

Skidelsky, Robert **HB103.K47S57 1986**
John Maynard Keynes: Hopes Betrayed, 1883-1920. Trade Cloth. Penguin Group (USA) Inc. New York, NY. 1986. 480p. ISBN:0-670-40810-7, ISBN13: 978-0-670-40810-8. Dewey:330.15/6 B. LCCN:86-001514.
Audience: **l,u,f.** *Choice, 1986.*

Steele, Gerry **HG221.S749 2001**
Keynes and Hayek: Money Economy. Paper over Boards. Routledge. New York, NY. 2001. 240p. Foundations of the Market Economy Ser. ISBN:0-415-25138-9, ISBN13: 978-0-415-25138-9. Dewey:332.4. LCCN:2001-019570.
Audience: **u,f.**

Stewart, Michael **HB99.7**
Keynes and After. Ed. 3. Trade Paper. Penguin Group (USA) Inc. New York, NY. 1986. 240p. ISBN:0-14-022646-X, ISBN13: 978-0-14-022646-1. Dewey:330.1/56.
Audience: **l,u,f.**

Thirlwall, A. P. (Editor) **HG3881 .K46**
Keynes and International Monetary Relations: The Second Keynes Seminar Held at University of Kent at Canterbury, 1974. Cloth Text. Palgrave Macmillan. New York, NY. 1976. 115p. ISBN:0-312-45255-1, ISBN13: 978-0-312-45255-1. Dewey:332.4/5. LCCN:75-044515.
Audience: **u,f.**

Toye, John **HB103.K47T69 2000**
Keynes on Population. Trade Cloth. Oxford University Press, Inc. New York, NY. 2000. 272p. ISBN:0-19-829362-3, ISBN13: 978-0-19-829362-0. Dewey:304.6. LCCN:00-022358.
Audience: **u,f.**

Ventelou, Bruno **HB99.7**
Millennial Keynes: An Introduction to the Origin, Development, and Later Currents of Keynesian Thought. Gregory P. Nowell (Editor, Translator). Trade Cloth. M. E. Sharpe Inc. Armonk, NY. 2004. 224p. ISBN:0-7656-1516-9, ISBN13: 978-0-7656-1516-9. Dewey:330.15/6. LCCN:2003-070437.
Audience: **u,f.** *Choice, 2005.*

Ventelou, Bruno **HB99.7.V42613 2004**
Millennial Keynes: An Introduction to the Origin, Development, and Later Currents of Keynesian Thought. Gregory P. Nowell (Editor, Translator). Trade Cloth. M. E. Sharpe Inc. Armonk, NY. 2004. 224p. ISBN:0-7656-0670-4, ISBN13: 978-0-7656-0670-9. Dewey:330.15/6. LCCN:2003-070437.
Audience: **u,f.** *Choice, 2005.*

Vicarelli, Fausto **HC240**
Keynes: The Instability of Capitalism. Trade Cloth. University of Pennsylvania Press. Philadelphia, PA. 1984. 208p. ISBN:0-8122-7914-X, ISBN13: 978-0-8122-7914-6. Dewey:330.12/2/0924. LCCN:83-014801.
Audience: **u,f.**

Victor, R. F. **HB103.K47 V5**
John Maynard Keynes: Father of Modern Economics. D. Steve Rahmas (Editor). Library Binding. SamHar Press. Charlotteville, NY. 1972. 32p. Outstanding Personalities Ser., No. 17 ISBN:0-87157-517-5, ISBN13: 978-0-87157-517-3. Dewey:330.15/6.
Audience: **l,u,f.**

Wood, John C. (Editor) **HB99.7.J636**
John Maynard Keynes: Critical Assessments, Vol. 38115. Paper over Boards. Routledge. New York, NY. 1994. 2344p. Critical Assessments Ser. ISBN:0-415-11413-6, ISBN13: 978-0-415-11413-4. Dewey:330.15/6. LCCN:93-047996.
Audience: **u,f.**

Yamaguchi, Kaoru **HB135.Y335 1988**
Beyond Walras, Keynes and Marx. Cloth Text. Peter Lang Publishing, Inc. New York, NY. 1988. 360p. Synthesis in

Economic Theory Toward a New Social Design Ser. ISBN:0-8204-0762-3, ISBN13: 978-0-8204-0762-3. Dewey:330.1. LCCN:88-002919.
Audience: **u,f.**

Systems > Capitalist > Keynesian > Schumpeter

HX72.S383.S38X 1981
Schumpeter's Vision: Capitalism, Socialism, and Democracy after 40 Years. Trade Cloth. Greenwood Publishing Group, Inc. Portsmouth, NH. 1981. xvi, 208p. ISBN:0-03-060276-9, ISBN13: 978-0-03-060276-4. Dewey:335. LCCN:86-673514.
Audience: **u,f.**

Brouwer, Maria **HB119.S35B76 1991**
Schumpeterian Puzzles: Technological Competition and Economic Evolution. Trade Cloth. University of Michigan Press. Chicago, IL. 1991. 272p. ISBN:0-472-10254-0, ISBN13: 978-0-472-10254-9. Dewey:330.1. LCCN:91-002822.
Audience: **u,f.**

Cantner, Uwe (Editor), et al. **HC79.T4**
Entrepreneurship, the New Economy and Public Policy: Schumpeterian Perspectives. Elias Dinopoulos & Robert F. Lanzilloti (Editors). Trade Cloth. Springer. New York, NY. 2004. vi, 345p. ISBN:3-540-22613-3, ISBN13: 978-3-540-22613-0. Dewey:338/.064. LCCN:2004-113933.
Audience: **u,f.**

Clemence, Richard Vernon & Doody, Francis S. **HB0119.S35C5**
The Schumpeterian System. Trade Paper. Books on Demand. Ann Arbor, MI. 127p. ISBN:0-598-99124-7, ISBN13: 978-0-598-99124-9. Dewey:330.092. LCCN:50-004879.
Audience: **u,f.**

Eliasson, Gunnar K. (Editor), et al. **HC79.T4M52 1998**
Microfoundations of Economic Growth: A Schumpeterian Perspective. Christopher Green & Charles R. McCann (Editors). Cloth over Boards. University of Michigan Press. Chicago, IL. 1998. 456p. International Schumpeter Society Ser. ISBN:0-472-10904-9, ISBN13: 978-0-472-10904-3. Dewey:338.064. LCCN:98-005012.
Audience: **u,f.**

Frisch, Helmut **HB119.S35**
Schumpeterian Economics. Trade Cloth. Greenwood Publishing Group, Inc. Portsmouth, NH. 1983. 208p. ISBN:0-275-90982-4, ISBN13: 978-0-275-90982-6. Dewey:330/.092/4.
Audience: **u,f.**

Harris, Seymour E. (Editor) **HB119.S35**
Schumpeter, Social Scientist. Trade Cloth. Ayer Company Publishers, Inc. Manchester, NH. 1977. Essay Index Reprint Ser. ISBN:0-8369-1138-5, ISBN13: 978-0-8369-1138-1. Dewey:923.373. LCCN:71-080387.
Audience: **g,l,u,f.**

Heertje, Arnold & Perlman, Mark (Editors) **HB119.S35E96 1990**
Evolving Technology and Market Structure: Studies in Schumpeterian Economics. Trade Cloth. University of Michigan Press. Chicago, IL. 1991. 360p. The International Schumpeter Society Ser. ISBN:0-472-10192-7, ISBN13: 978-0-472-10192-4. Dewey:330/.092. LCCN:90-044520.
Audience: **u,f.**

Lee, Yeonwoo **HC110.I52L44 2002**
Schumpeterian Dynamics and Metropolitan-Scale Productivity. Trade Cloth. Ashgate Publishing, Ltd. Aldershot, 2003. 152p. Bruton Center for Development Studies Ser. ISBN:0-7546-3426-4, ISBN13: 978-0-7546-3426-3. Dewey:338/.06/0973. LCCN:2002-028133.
Audience: **u,f.**

Oakley, Allen **HB119.S35O25 1990**
Schumpeter's Theory of Capitalist Motion: A Critical Exposition and Reassessment. Cloth Text. Edward Elgar Publishing, Inc. Northampton, MA. 1990. 272p. ISBN:1-85278-055-X, ISBN13: 978-1-85278-055-5. Dewey:338.9. LCCN:90-038634.
Audience: **l,u,f.** *Choice, 1991.*

Scherer, F. M. **HC79.T4S33 1984**
Innovation and Growth: Schumpeterian Perspectives. Trade Paper. MIT Press. Cambridge, MA. 1986. 310p. ISBN:0-262-69102-7, ISBN13: 978-0-262-69102-4. Dewey:338/.06.
Audience: **u,f.**

Schumpeter, Joseph Alois **HB3711.S39 2006**
Business Cycles: A Theoretical, Historical, and Statistical Analysis of the Capitalist Process. Trade Cloth. Martino Publishing. Mansfield Centre, CT. 2005. 1122p. ISBN:1-57898-556-0, ISBN13: 978-1-57898-556-2. Dewey:338.5/42. LCCN:2005-047854.
Audience: **l,u,f.**

Schumpeter, Joseph Alois **HX86.S38 1994**
[e] Capitalism, Socialism and Democracy. E-Book. NetLibrary, Inc. Boulder, CO. 1994. ISBN:0-585-46039-6, ISBN13: 978-0-585-46039-0. Dewey:330.12/2/0904.
Audience: **u,f.**

Schumpeter, Joseph Alois **HD75**
The Theory of Economic Development: An Inquiry into Profits, Capital, Credit, Interest and the Business Cycle. Redvers Opies (Translator), John E. Elliott (Introduction by). Trade Paper. Transaction Publishers. Somerset, NJ. 1982. 244p. Social Science Classics Ser. ISBN:0-87855-698-2, ISBN13: 978-0-87855-698-4. Dewey:330.1. LCCN:79-067059.
Audience: **u,f.**

Schumpeter, Joseph Alois **HB75.S456 1994**
History of Economic Analysis: With a New Introduction. Mark Perlman (Introduction by). Paper Text. Oxford University Press, Inc. New York, NY. 1996. 1320p. ISBN:0-19-510559-1, ISBN13: 978-0-19-510559-9. Dewey:330/.09. LCCN:95-044189.
Audience: **l,u,f.**

Systems > Capitalist > Keynesian > Jeremy Bentham

Bentham, Jeremy **HB161**
Jeremy Bentham's Economic Writings. Werner Stark (Editor). Paper over Boards. Routledge. New York, NY. 2003. 1440p. ISBN:0-415-31866-1, ISBN13: 978-0-415-31866-2. Dewey:330/.01.
Audience: **u,f.**

Systems > Capitalist > Keynesian > Jevons

Jevons, W. Stanley **HG221**
Money and the Mechanism of Exchange. Trade Paper. University Press of the Pacific. Miami, FL. 2002. 364p. ISBN:1-4102-0119-8, ISBN13: 978-1-4102-0119-5. Dewey:332.4.
Audience: **u,f.**

Jevons, W. Stanley **HB98**
The Theory of Political Economy. Trade Cloth. Palgrave Macmillan. New York, NY. 2001. liv, 267p. ISBN:0-333-80417-1, ISBN13: 978-0-333-80417-9. Dewey:330.157.
Audience: **u,f.**

Jevons, William Stanley **BC108**
Elementary Lessons in Logic: Deductive and Inductive. Trade Cloth. Library Reprints, Inc. Temecula, CA. 1965. ISBN:0-7222-2055-3, ISBN13: 978-0-7222-2055-9. Dewey:160.
Audience: **l,u.**

Jevons, William Stanley **HG221**
Investigations in Currency and Finance. Trade Cloth. Library Reprints, Inc. Temecula, CA. 1884. 428p. ISBN:0-7222-2753-1, ISBN13: 978-0-7222-2753-4. Dewey:332.41.
Audience: **u,f.**

Jevons, William Stanley **Q175**
Principles Science, Set. Trade Cloth. Continuum International Publishing Group, Ltd. London, 1999. 976p. ISBN:1-85506-757-9, ISBN13: 978-1-85506-757-8. Dewey:160.
Audience: **u,f.**

Jevons, William Stanley **KD3009.J48 2001**
The State in Relation to Labour. Trade Paper. Transaction Publishers. Somerset, NJ. 2002. 190p. ISBN:0-7658-0867-6, ISBN13: 978-0-7658-0867-7. Dewey:344.4101. LCCN:2001-027311.
Audience: **u,f.**

Jevons, Willian Stanley **HB98**
Writings on Economics. Bert Mosselmans & Michael V. White (Introduction by). Trade Paper. Palgrave Macmillan. New York, NY. 2002. 3344p. ISBN:0-333-80416-3, ISBN13: 978-0-333-80416-2. Dewey:330.1/57.
Audience: **u,f.**

Systems > Capitalist > Monetarist

Brunner, Karl & Meltzer, Allan H. **HG230.3.B78 1997**
Money and the Economy: Issues in Monetary Analysis. Trade Cloth. Cambridge University Press. New York, NY. 1993. 411p. Raffaele Mattiloi Lectures on the History of Economic Thought ISBN:0-521-44542-6, ISBN13: 978-0-521-44542-9. Dewey:332.4/01. LCCN:93-017996.
Audience: **u,f.**

Systems > Capitalist > Monetarist > Friedman

HB119.F84
Milton Friedman. Trade Paper. Liberty Fund, Inc. Indianapolis, IN. 2005. 73p. The Intellectual Portrait Ser. ISBN:0-86597-596-5, ISBN13: 978-0-86597-596-5. Dewey:330/.092/4.
Audience: **u,f.**

Friedman, Milton **HB501.F7 2002**
Capitalism and Freedom. Ed. 40. Trade Cloth. University of Chicago Press. Chicago, IL. 2002. 230p. ISBN:0-226-26420-3, ISBN13: 978-0-226-26420-2. Dewey:330.12/2. LCCN:2002-067530.
Audience: **l,u,f.**

Friedman, Milton **HB33**
Essays in Positive Economics. Trade Paper. University of Chicago Press. Chicago, IL. 1966. 334p. ISBN:0-226-26403-3, ISBN13: 978-0-226-26403-5. Dewey:330.1. LCCN:53-003533.
Audience: **l,u,f.**

Friedman, Milton **HB98.3.F74 1990**
Monetarist Economics. Cloth Text. Blackwell Publishing, Inc. Malden, MA. 1990. 256p. IEA Masters of Modern Economics Ser. ISBN:0-631-17111-8, ISBN13: 978-0-631-17111-9. Dewey:330.1. LCCN:89-078251.
Audience: **l,u,f.**

Friedman, Milton **HG230.3.F75 1994**
Money Mischief: Episodes in Monetary History. Trade Paper. Harcourt Trade Publishers. New York, NY. 1994. 304p. Harvest Book Ser. ISBN:0-15-661930-X, ISBN13: 978-0-15-661930-1. Dewey:332.4/6. LCCN:94-158555.
Audience: **u,f.**

Friedman, Milton (Editor) **HG0221.F87**
Studies in the Quantity Theory of Money. Trade Paper. Books on Demand. Ann Arbor, MI. 271p. A Phoenix Book Ser., Vol. 561 ISBN:0-608-09303-3, ISBN13: 978-0-608-09303-1. Dewey:332.4. LCCN:56-010999.
Audience: **u,f.**

Friedman, Milton (Editor) **HG221**
Studies in the Quantity Theory of Money. Paper Text. University of Chicago Press. Chicago, IL. 1992. ISBN:0-226-26406-8, ISBN13: 978-0-226-26406-6. Dewey:332.4. LCCN:56-010999.
Audience: **u,f.**

Friedman, Milton **HB801 .F7**
Theory of the Consumption Function. Cloth Text. Princeton University Press. Princeton, NJ. 1957. 260p. General Ser., No. 63 ISBN:0-691-04182-2, ISBN13: 978-0-691-04182-7. Dewey:339.4.
Audience: **u,f.**

Friedman, Milton **HB171.5**
Bright Promises, Dismal Performance: An Economist's Protest. William R. Allen (Introduction by). Trade Paper. Harcourt Trade Publishers. New York, NY. 1983. 404p. Harvest Book Ser. ISBN:0-15-614161-2, ISBN13: 978-0-15-614161-1. Dewey:330. LCCN:82-021390.
Audience: **u,f.**

Friedman, Milton & Friedman, Rose D. **HB501.F72 1990**
Free to Choose: A Personal Statement. Trade Paper. Harcourt Trade Publishers. New York, NY. 1990. 360p.
ISBN:0-15-633460-7, ISBN13: 978-0-15-633460-0.
Dewey:330.12/2. LCCN:90-036179.
Audience: **g,l,u,f.**

Friedman, Milton & Friedman, Rose D. **HB119.A3F75 1998**
Two Lucky People: Memoirs. Trade Cloth. University of Chicago Press. Chicago, IL. 1998. 667p. ISBN:0-226-26414-9, ISBN13: 978-0-226-26414-1. Dewey:330/.092/273 B. LCCN:97-048951.
Audience: **g,l,u,f.** *Choice, 1998.*

Gordon, Robert J. & Friedman, Milton **HG221**
Milton Friedman's Monetary Framework: A Debate with His Critics. Trade Cloth. University of Chicago Press. Chicago, IL. 1974. xii, 192p. ISBN:0-226-26407-6, ISBN13: 978-0-226-26407-3. Dewey:332.4/01. LCCN:73-092599.
Audience: **u,f.**

Hadjimatheou, George **HB801.H245 1987**
Consumer Economics after Keynes: Theory and Evidence of the Consumption Function. Cloth Text. Palgrave Macmillan. New York, NY. 1987. 224p. ISBN:0-312-00478-8, ISBN13: 978-0-312-00478-1. Dewey:339.4/7. LCCN:87-009427.
Audience: **u,f.** *Choice, 1987.*

Hammond, J. Daniel (Editor) **HB119.F84L44 1999**
The Intellectual Legacy of Milton Friedman, Set. Trade Cloth. Edward Elgar Publishing, Inc. Northampton, MA. 1999. 1,192p. Intellectual Legacies in Modern Economics Ser., Vol. 2
ISBN:1-85898-423-8, ISBN13: 978-1-85898-423-0.
Dewey:330/.092 B. LCCN:99-014858.
Audience: **l,u,f.**

Hammond, J. Daniel **HB119.F84 H36 1996**
Theory and Measurement: Causality Issues in Milton Friedman's Monetary Economics. Trade Cloth. Cambridge University Press. New York, NY. 1996. 256p. Historical Perspectives on Modern Economics Ser. ISBN:0-521-55205-2, ISBN13: 978-0-521-55205-9. Dewey:332. LCCN:95-019324.
Audience: **u,f.**

Hammond, J. Daniel **HB119.F84 H36 1996**
Theory and Measurement: Causality Issues in Milton Friedman's Monetary Economics. Craufurd D. Goodwin (Contribution by). Trade Paper. Cambridge University Press. New York, NY. 2005. 248p. Historical Perspectives on Modern Economics Ser.
ISBN:0-521-02264-9, ISBN13: 978-0-521-02264-4. Dewey:332.
Audience: **u,f.**

Hirsch, Abraham & De Marchi, Neil **HB119.F84H57 1990**
Milton Friedman: Economics in Theory and Practice. Trade Cloth. University of Michigan Press. Chicago, IL. 1990. 336p.
ISBN:0-472-10175-7, ISBN13: 978-0-472-10175-7.
Dewey:330.1. LCCN:89-020266.
Audience: **l,u,f.** *Choice, 1990.*

Hirsch, Abraham & De Marchi, Neil **HB171**
Milton Friedman: Economics in Theory and Practice. Trade Paper. University of Michigan Press. Chicago, IL. 1992. 336p.
ISBN:0-472-08167-5, ISBN13: 978-0-472-08167-7.
Dewey:330.1. LCCN:89-020266.
Audience: **u,f.** *Choice, 1990.*

Leeson, Robert (Editor) **HB119.F84K49 2003**
Keynes, Chicago and Friedman. Milton Friedman (Preface by). Trade Cloth. Pickering & Chatto Publishers, Ltd. London, 2003. 944p. ISBN:1-85196-767-2, ISBN13: 978-1-85196-767-4.
Dewey:330.15. LCCN:2002-030351.
Audience: **u,f.**

Modigliani, Franco & Friedman, Milton **HG540**
The Monetarist Controversy: A Seminar Discussion. Trade Paper. University Press of the Pacific. Miami, FL. 2005. 52p.
ISBN:1-4102-2098-2, ISBN13: 978-1-4102-2098-1.
Dewey:332.4973.
Audience: **u,f.**

Systems > Capitalist > Post-Keynesian

Dow, Sheila C. & Hillard, John (Editors) **HB139.P675 2002**
Post Keynesian Econometrics, Microeconomics and the Theory of the Firm: Beyond Keynes, Vol. 1. Trade Cloth. Edward Elgar Publishing, Inc. Northampton, MA. 2002. 288p.
ISBN:1-85898-584-6, ISBN13: 978-1-85898-584-8.
Dewey:338.5. LCCN:2001-054781.
Audience: **u,f.**

Downward, Paul **HB221.D64 1999**
Pricing Theory in Post-Keynesian Economics: A Realist Approach. Trade Cloth. Edward Elgar Publishing, Inc. Northampton, MA. 1999. 240p. New Directions in Modern Economics Ser. ISBN:1-85898-791-1, ISBN13: 978-1-85898-791-0. Dewey:338.5/2. LCCN:98-006257.
Audience: **l,u,f.**

Eichner, Alfred S. (Editor) **HB171**
A Guide to Post-Keynesian Economics. Joan Robinson (Introduction by). Cloth Text. M. E. Sharpe Inc. Armonk, NY. 1979. 216p. ISBN:0-87332-142-1, ISBN13: 978-0-87332-142-6. Dewey:330.1. LCCN:79-001971.
Audience: **l,u,f.**

King, J. E. (Editor) **HB99.7**
The Elgar Companion to Post Keynesian Economics. Trade Cloth. Edward Elgar Publishing, Inc. Northampton, MA. 2003. 424p. ISBN:1-84064-630-6, ISBN13: 978-1-84064-630-6.
Dewey:330.15. LCCN:2003-044802.
Audience: **l,u,f.** *Choice, 2004.*

Kurihara, Kenneth K. (Editor) **HB87**
Post-Keynesian Economics. Paper over Boards. Routledge. New York, NY. 2003. 464p. Routledge Library Editions Ser., Vol. 71:Economics, US/Can. Edition Ser. ISBN:0-415-31376-7, ISBN13: 978-0-415-31376-6. Dewey:330.1.
Audience: **l,u,f.**

Lavoie, Marc (Editor) **HB99.7.L35 1992**
Foundations of Post-Keynesian Economic Analysis. Trade Cloth. Edward Elgar Publishing, Inc. Northampton, MA. 1992. 480p. New Directions in Modern Economics Ser.
ISBN:1-85278-322-2, ISBN13: 978-1-85278-322-8.
Dewey:330.15/6. LCCN:93-191429.
Audience: **l,u,f.**

Lee, Frederic S. **HB221.L45 1998**
Post Keynesian Price Theory. Phyllis Deane, Gautam Mathur & Joan Robinson (Contribution by). Trade Cloth. Cambridge University Press. New York, NY. 1999. 288p. Modern Cambridge Economics Ser. ISBN:0-521-32870-5, ISBN13: 978-0-521-32870-8. Dewey:338.521. LCCN:97-049242.
Audience: **l,u,f.**

Wray, L. Randall **HG226.3.W73 1990**
Money and Credit in Capitalist Economies: The Endogenous Money Approach. Cloth Text. Edward Elgar Publishing, Inc. Northampton, MA. 1990. 352p. ISBN:1-85278-356-7, ISBN13: 978-1-85278-356-3. Dewey:332.4/14. LCCN:90-013856.
Audience: **u,f.** *Choice, 1991.*

Systems > Capitalist > New Classical

Hoover, Kevin D. (Editor) **HB119.L83L44 1999**
The Economic Legacy of Robert Lucas, Jr. Trade Cloth. Edward Elgar Publishing, Inc. Northampton, MA. 1999. 1,648p. Intellectual Legacies in Modern Economics Ser., Vol. 3 ISBN:1-85898-387-8, ISBN13: 978-1-85898-387-5. Dewey:330.1. LCCN:99-030946.
Audience: **u,f.**

Klamer, Arjo **HB172.5**
Conversations with Economists: New Classical Economists and Opponents Speak Out on the Current Controversy in Macroeconomics. Book, Other. Rowman & Littlefield Publishers, Inc. Lanham, MD. 1984. 278p. ISBN:0-86598-155-8, ISBN13: 978-0-86598-155-3. Dewey:339.
Audience: **l,u,f.**

Klamer, Arjo **HB172.5.C66 1984**
Conversations with Economists: New Classical Economists and Opponents Speak Out on the Current Controversy in Macroeconomics. Trade Cloth. Rowman & Littlefield Publishers, Inc. Lanham, MD. 1984. 278p. ISBN:0-86598-146-9, ISBN13: 978-0-86598-146-1. Dewey:339. LCCN:83-017765.
Audience: **l,u,f.**

Lucas, Robert E. Jr. **HD75.L824 2004**
Lectures on Economic Growth. Trade Paper. Harvard University Press. Cambridge, MA. 2004. 224p. ISBN:0-674-01601-7, ISBN13: 978-0-674-01601-9. Dewey:338.9.
Audience: **u,f.**

Lucas, Robert E. Jr. **HB172.5**
Models of Business Cycles. Trade Paper. Blackwell Publishing, Inc. Malden, MA. 1989. 128p. ISBN:0-631-14791-8, ISBN13: 978-0-631-14791-6. Dewey:338.5/42/0724. LCCN:86-017622.
Audience: **u,f.**

Lucas, Robert E. Jr. & Sargent, Thomas J. (Editors) **HB139**
Rational Expectations and Econometric Practice. Trade Cloth. University of Minnesota Press. Minneapolis, MN. 1981. 776p. ISBN:0-8166-0916-0, ISBN13: 978-0-8166-0916-1. Dewey:330/.028. LCCN:80-024602.
Audience: **u,f.**

Van Zijp, Rudy **HC79.I5**
Austrian and New Classical Business Cycle Theories: A Comparative Study Through the Method of Rational Reconstruction. Trade Cloth. Edward Elgar Publishing, Inc. Northampton, MA. 1993. 272p. ISBN:1-85278-674-4, ISBN13: 978-1-85278-674-8. Dewey:339.3.
Audience: **l,u,f.**

Systems > Capitalist > Evolutionary

Andersen, Esben S. **HB97.3.A53 1996**
Evolutionary Economics: Post-Schumpeterian Contributions. Ed. 2. Trade Paper. Routledge. New York, NY. 1996. 238p. ISBN:1-85567-383-5, ISBN13: 978-1-85567-383-0. Dewey:330.1/5. LCCN:96-012690.
Audience: **u,f.**

Magnusson, Lars (Editor) **HB171**
Evolutionary and Neo-Schumpeterian Approaches to Economics. Trade Cloth. Springer. New York, NY. 1994. 340p. Recent Economic Thought Ser. ISBN:0-7923-9385-6, ISBN13: 978-0-7923-9385-6. Dewey:330.1. LCCN:93-005059.
Audience: **l,u,f.**

Myrdal, Gunnar **HB171**
The Political Element in the Development of Economic Theory. Paper Text. Textbook Publishers. Temecula, CA. 2003. xvii, 248p. ISBN:0-7581-4602-7, ISBN13: 978-0-7581-4602-1. Dewey:330.1.
Audience: **u,f.**

Nelson, Richard R. & Winter, Sidney G. **HB71**
An Evolutionary Theory of Economic Change. Trade Cloth. Harvard University Press. Cambridge, MA. 1982. 400p. ISBN:0-674-27227-7, ISBN13: 978-0-674-27227-9. Dewey:338.9/001. LCCN:81-013455.
Audience: **u,f.**

Systems > Capitalist > Evolutionary > Austrian Tradition

Alter, Max **HB107.M54A78 1990**
Carl Menger and the Origins of Austrian Economics. Trade Paper. Westview Press. Boulder, CO. 1990. 256p. ISBN:0-8133-0945-X, ISBN13: 978-0-8133-0945-3. Dewey:330.15/7/092. LCCN:89-037661.
Audience: **l,u,f.** *Choice, 1991.*

Bellet, Michel, et al. **HB501**
Evolution of the Market Process. Sandye Gloria-Palermo & Abdallah Zouzche (Authors). Paper over Boards. Routledge. New York, NY. 2004. 344p. Foundations of the Market Economy Ser., Vol. 70 ISBN:0-415-31683-9, ISBN13: 978-0-415-31683-5. Dewey:330.15/7. LCCN:2004-046729.
Audience: **f.**

Bohm-Bawerk, Eugen von **HB501**
Capital and Interest. Trade Cloth. Libertarian Press, Inc. Grove City, PA. 1959. ISBN:0-910884-08-0, ISBN13: 978-0-910884-08-2. Dewey:330.15.
Audience: **u,f.**

Bohm-Bawerk, Eugen von **HB501**
Further Essays on Capital and Interest, Vol. 3. Trade Cloth. Libertarian Press, Inc. Grove City, PA. 1959. 246p. ISBN:0-910884-11-0, ISBN13: 978-0-910884-11-2. Dewey:330.122. LCCN:58-005555.
Audience: **u,f.**

Bohm-Bawerk, Eugen von **HB501**
History and Critique of Interest Theories, Vol. 1. Trade Cloth. Libertarian Press, Inc. Grove City, PA. 1959. 490p. ISBN:0-910884-09-9, ISBN13: 978-0-910884-09-9. Dewey:332.809. LCCN:58-005555.
Audience: **u,f.**

Bohm-Bawerk, Eugen von **HB175 .B647**
Shorter Classics. Trade Paper. Libertarian Press, Inc. Grove City, PA. 1962. 370p. ISBN:0-910884-12-9, ISBN13: 978-0-910884-12-9. Dewey:330.
Audience: **u,f.**

Bohm-Bawerk, Eugen von & Hilferding, Rudolph **HB501.M37**
Karl Marx and the Close of His System: Bohm-Bawerk's Criticism of Marx. Paul M. Sweezy (Editor). Trade Paper. Porcupine Press, Inc. Philadelphia, PA. 1984. xxx, 224p. ISBN:0-87991-250-2, ISBN13: 978-0-87991-250-5. Dewey:335.4.
Audience: **u,f.**

Bohm-Bawerk, Eugen von **HB501**
The Positive Theory of Capital. William Smart (Translator). Trade Cloth. Ayer Company Publishers, Inc. Manchester, NH. 1977. Select Bibliographies Reprint Ser. ISBN:0-8369-6604-X, ISBN13: 978-0-8369-6604-6. Dewey:332/.041. LCCN:70-175689.
Audience: **u,f.**

Colonna, M. & Hagemann, Harald (Editors) **HG221.E254 1994**
The Economics of F. A. Hayek. Trade Cloth. Edward Elgar Publishing, Inc. Northampton, MA. 1994. 512p. ISBN:1-85278-545-4, ISBN13: 978-1-85278-545-1. Dewey:330.1. LCCN:93-042575.
Audience: **l,u,f.**

Hayek, Friedrich A. **HG229 .H3**
Prices and Production. Ed. 2. Trade Cloth. Scholar's Bookshelf. Cranbury, NJ. 1967. xiv, 162p. ISBN:0-678-06515-2, ISBN13: 978-0-678-06515-0. Dewey:338.52/2. LCCN:67-019586.
Audience: **u,f.**

Hayek, Friedrich A. **HG221.H346 1984**
Money, Capital and Fluctuations: Early Essays. R. K. McCloughry (Editor). Library Binding. University of Chicago Press. Chicago, IL. 1993. 196p. ISBN:0-226-32092-8, ISBN13: 978-0-226-32092-2. Dewey:332.4. LCCN:84-000227.
Audience: **u,f.**

Horowitz, Steven **HB98.H67 2000**
Microfoundations and Macroeconomics: An Austrian Perspective. Paper over Boards. Routledge. New York, NY. 2000. 288p. Foundations of the Market Economy Ser., Vol. 2 ISBN:0-415-19762-7, ISBN13: 978-0-415-19762-5. Dewey:330.15/7. LCCN:00-036890.
Audience: **l,u,f.**

Menger, Carl **HB175**
Investigations into the Method of the Social Sciences. Trade Paper. Libertarian Press, Inc. Grove City, PA. 1996. 234p. ISBN:0-910884-30-7, ISBN13: 978-0-910884-30-3. Dewey:330.072.
Audience: **u,f.**

Menger, Carl **HB171**
Principles of Economics. Trade Paper. Libertarian Press, Inc. Grove City, PA. 1994. 328p. ISBN:0-910884-27-7, ISBN13: 978-0-910884-27-3. Dewey:330.1.
Audience: **u,f.**

Menger, Carl
The Theory of Money, Price and Exchange. Trade Cloth. American Institute for Psychological Research, The. Albuquerque, NM. 1990. 127p. ISBN:0-89266-687-0, ISBN13: 978-0-89266-687-4.
Audience: **u,f.**

Menger, Carl **HB203**
The Theory of Value. Trade Cloth. Foundation for Classical Reprints, The. Albuquerque, NM. 1984. 131p. ISBN:0-89901-133-0, ISBN13: 978-0-89901-133-2. Dewey:335.412.
Audience: **u,f.**

Van Zijp, Rudy **HC79.I5**
Austrian and New Classical Business Cycle Theories: A Comparative Study Through the Method of Rational Reconstruction. Trade Cloth. Edward Elgar Publishing, Inc. Northampton, MA. 1993. 272p. ISBN:1-85278-674-4, ISBN13: 978-1-85278-674-8. Dewey:339.3.
Audience: **l,u,f.**

Vaughn, Karen I. **HB98 .V38 1994**
Austrian Economics in America: The Migration of a Tradition. Craufurd D. Goodwin (Contribution by). Trade Paper. Cambridge University Press. New York, NY. 1998. 214p. Historical Perspectives on Modern Economics Ser. ISBN:0-521-63765-1, ISBN13: 978-0-521-63765-7. Dewey:330.1/57/0973.
Audience: **u,f.**

Systems > Capitalist > Evolutionary > Schumpeter

HX72.S383.S38X 1981
Schumpeter's Vision: Capitalism, Socialism, and Democracy after 40 Years. Trade Cloth. Greenwood Publishing Group, Inc. Portsmouth, NH. 1981. xvi, 208p. ISBN:0-03-060276-9, ISBN13: 978-0-03-060276-4. Dewey:335. LCCN:86-673514.
Audience: **u,f.**

Brouwer, Maria **HB119.S35B76 1991**
Schumpeterian Puzzles: Technological Competition and Economic Evolution. Trade Cloth. University of Michigan Press. Chicago, IL. 1991. 272p. ISBN:0-472-10254-0, ISBN13: 978-0-472-10254-9. Dewey:330.1. LCCN:91-002822.
Audience: **u,f.**

Cantner, Uwe (Editor), et al. **HC79.T4**
Entrepreneurship, the New Economy and Public Policy: Schumpeterian Perspectives. Elias Dinopoulos & Robert F. Lanzilloti (Editors). Trade Cloth. Springer. New York, NY. 2004. vi, 345p. ISBN:3-540-22613-3, ISBN13: 978-3-540-22613-0. Dewey:338/.064. LCCN:2004-113933.
Audience: **u,f.**

Clemence, Richard Vernon & Doody, Francis S. **HB0119.S35C5**
The Schumpeterian System. Trade Paper. Books on Demand. Ann Arbor, MI. 127p. ISBN:0-598-99124-7, ISBN13: 978-0-598-99124-9. Dewey:330.092. LCCN:50-004879.
Audience: **u,f.**

Eliasson, Gunnar K. (Editor), et al. **HC79.T4M52 1998**
Microfoundations of Economic Growth: A Schumpeterian Perspective. Christopher Green & Charles R. McCann (Editors). Cloth over Boards. University of Michigan Press. Chicago, IL. 1998. 456p. International Schumpeter Society Ser. ISBN:0-472-10904-9, ISBN13: 978-0-472-10904-3. Dewey:338.064. LCCN:98-005012.
Audience: **u,f.**

Frisch, Helmut **HB119.S35**
Schumpeterian Economics. Trade Cloth. Greenwood Publishing Group, Inc. Portsmouth, NH. 1983. 208p. ISBN:0-275-90982-4, ISBN13: 978-0-275-90982-6. Dewey:330/.092/4.
Audience: **u,f.**

Harris, Seymour E. (Editor) **HB119.S35**
Schumpeter, Social Scientist. Trade Cloth. Ayer Company Publishers, Inc. Manchester, NH. 1977. Essay Index Reprint Ser. ISBN:0 8369-1138-5, ISBN13: 978-0-8369-1138-1. Dewey:923.373. LCCN:71-080387.
Audience: **g,l,u,f.**

Heertje, Arnold & Perlman, Mark (Editors) **HB119.S35E96 1990**
Evolving Technology and Market Structure: Studies in Schumpeterian Economics. Trade Cloth. University of Michigan Press. Chicago, IL. 1991. 360p. The International Schumpeter Society Ser. ISBN:0-472-10192-7, ISBN13: 978-0-472-10192-4. Dewey:330/.092. LCCN:90-044520.
Audience: **u,f.**

Kleinknecht, Alfred **HB3729.K58 1986**
Innovation Patterns in Crisis and Prosperity: Schumpeter's Long Cycle Reconsidered. Jan Tinbergen (Foreword by). Cloth Text. Palgrave Macmillan. New York, NY. 1987. 256p. ISBN:0-312-41816-7, ISBN13: 978-0-312-41816-8. Dewey:338.001. LCCN:86-006466.
Audience: **u,f.**

Lee, Yeonwoo **HC110.I52L44 2002**
Schumpeterian Dynamics and Metropolitan-Scale Productivity. Trade Cloth. Ashgate Publishing, Ltd. Aldershot, 2003. 152p. Bruton Center for Development Studies Ser. ISBN:0-7546-3426-4, ISBN13: 978-0-7546-3426-3. Dewey:338/.06/0973. LCCN:2002-028133.
Audience: **u,f.**

Scherer, F. M. **HC79.T4S33 1984**
Innovation and Growth: Schumpeterian Perspectives. Trade Paper. MIT Press. Cambridge, MA. 1986. 310p. ISBN:0-262-69102-7, ISBN13: 978-0-262-69102-4. Dewey:338/.06.
Audience: **u,f.**

Schumpeter, Joseph Alois **HX86.S38 1994**
[e] Capitalism, Socialism and Democracy. E-Book. NetLibrary, Inc. Boulder, CO. 1994. ISBN:0-585-46039-6, ISBN13: 978-0-585-46039-0. Dewey:330.12/2/0904.
Audience: **u,f.**

Schumpeter, Joseph Alois **HD75**
The Theory of Economic Development: An Inquiry into Profits, Capital, Credit, Interest and the Business Cycle. Redvers Opies (Translator), John E. Elliott (Introduction by). Trade Paper. Transaction Publishers. Somerset, NJ. 1982. 244p. Social Science Classics Ser. ISBN:0-87855-698-2, ISBN13: 978-0-87855-698-4. Dewey:330.1. LCCN:79-067059.
Audience: **u,f.**

Schumpeter, Joseph Alois **HB75.S456 1994**
History of Economic Analysis: With a New Introduction. Mark Perlman (Introduction by). Paper Text. Oxford University Press, Inc. New York, NY. 1996. 1320p. ISBN:0-19-510559-1, ISBN13: 978-0-19-510559-9. Dewey:330/.09. LCCN:95-044189.
Audience: **l,u,f.**

Systems > Socialist

Barnett, Vincent **HB113.A2**
A History of Russian Economic Thought. Paper over Boards. Routledge. New York, NY. 2005. 176p. ISBN:0-415-35264-9, ISBN13: 978-0-415-35264-2. Dewey:330/.0947. LCCN:2005-004840.
Audience: **l,u,f.**

Diamond, Larry & Plattner, Marc F. (Editors) **JF51**
Capitalism, Socialism, and Democracy Revisited. Trade Cloth. Johns Hopkins University Press. Baltimore, MD. 1993. 152p. A Journal of Democracy Bks. ISBN:0-8018-4746-X, ISBN13: 978-0-8018-4746-2. Dewey:320.3. LCCN:93-004362.
Audience: **u,f.**

Tinbergen, Jan **HD82**
Central Planning. Trade Cloth. Elliot's Books. Northford, CT. 1964. ISBN:0-685-30608-9, ISBN13: 978-0-685-30608-6. Dewey:338.9.
Audience: **u,f.**

Systems > Socialist > Marx

Arthur, C. J. **HB501.M37A75 2003**
The New Dialectic and Marx's Capital. Trade Paper. Brill Academic Publishers. Leiden, 2003. vii, 264p. Historical Materialism Book Ser., Vol. 1 ISBN:90-04-13643-6, ISBN13: 978-90-04-13643-4. Dewey:335.4/112. LCCN:2003-065432.
Audience: **u,f.**

Fine, Ben & Saad-Filho, Alfredo **HB97.5.F55 2003**
Marx's Capital. Ed. 4. Trade Cloth. Pluto Press. London, 2003. 216p. ISBN:0-7453-2050-3, ISBN13: 978-0-7453-2050-2. Dewey:335.41. LCCN:2003-017296.
Audience: **u,f.**

Fromm, Erich **HX39.5.F7 2004**
Marx's Concept of Man. Trade Paper. Continuum International Publishing Group, Ltd. London, 2005. 224p. ISBN:0-8264-7791-7, ISBN13: 978-0-8264-7791-0. Dewey:128. LCCN:2005-295475.
Audience: **l,u,f.**

Heilbroner, Robert L. **HX73**
Marxism: For and Against. Trade Cloth. W. W. Norton & Company, Inc. New York, NY. 1980. 186p.

ISBN:0-393-01307-3, ISBN13: 978-0-393-01307-8.
Dewey:335.4. LCCN:79-020385.
Audience: **l,u,f.**

Luxemburg, Rosa **HB501**
The Accumulation of Capital. Ed. 2. Trade Paper. Routledge. New York, NY. 2003. 496p. Classics Ser. ISBN:0-415-30445-8, ISBN13: 978-0-415-30445-0. Dewey:332/.041. LCCN:2003-001500.
Audience: **u,f.**

Luxemburg, Rosa & Bukharin, Nikolai I. **HB0501.L9813**
The Accumulation of Capital: An Anti-Critique Imperialism and the Accumulation of Capital. Rudolf Wichmann (Translator), Kenneth J. Tarbuck (Introduction by). Trade Paper. Books on Demand. Ann Arbor, MI. 299p. ISBN:0-8357-6001-4, ISBN13: 978-0-8357-6001-0. Dewey:330.122. LCCN:72-081768.
Audience: **u,f.**

Luxemburg, Rosa & Graf, William David **HX273**
Selected Political Writings [of] Rosa Luxemburg. Robert Looker (Introduction by). Trade Cloth. Random House. London, 1972. 309p. ISBN:0-224-00619-3, ISBN13: 978-0-224-00619-4. Dewey:335.4/08.
Audience: **u,f.**

Luxemburg, Rosa, et al. **B809.8**
The Rosa Luxemburg Reader. Peter Hudis & Kevin Anderson (Authors). Trade Cloth. Monthly Review Press. New York, NY. 2004. 447p. ISBN:1-58367-104-8, ISBN13: 978-1-58367-104-7. Dewey:335.4/092. LCCN:2004-001533.
Audience: **u,f.** *Choice, 2005.*

Luxemburg, Rosa **HB501 .L942**
Accumulation of Capital. Joan Robinson (Introduction by). Trade Paper. Monthly Review Press. New York, NY. 1964. ISBN:0-85345-059-5, ISBN13: 978-0-85345-059-7. Dewey:330.15. LCCN:64-016176.
Audience: **l,u,f.**

Marx, Karl **HB203.M31313 1999**
Capital: Theories of Surplus Value, Vol. 4. Trade Cloth. Prometheus Books, Publishers. Amherst, NY. 2004. 1,605p. Great Minds Ser. ISBN:1-57392-777-5, ISBN13: 978-1-57392-777-2. Dewey:335.4/12. LCCN:99-042497.
Audience: **u,f.**

Marx, Karl **HB301 .M3813**
Wage Labour and Capital. Trade Paper. Kessinger Publishing, LLC. Whitefish, MT. 2004. ISBN:1-4191-9297-3, ISBN13: 978-1-4191-9297-5. Dewey:331.
Audience: **u,f.**

Marx, Karl **HB501.M3393**
Pre-capitalist economic formations. Hobsbawm, E. J. (Editor). New York, International Publishers. 1965.
Audience: **u,f.**

Marx, Karl **HB203.M315**
A history of economic theories. Kautsky, Karl (Editor); McCarthy, Terence (Translator). New York, Langland Press. 1952.
Audience: **l,u,f.**

Marx, Karl & Engels, Friedrich **HX276**
The Communist Manifesto. Gareth Stedman Jones (Notes by). Trade Paper. Penguin Group (USA) Inc. New York, NY. 2002. 304p. Classics Ser. ISBN:0-14-044757-1, ISBN13: 978-0-14-044757-6. Dewey:335.4/22. LCCN:2003-265747.
Audience: **g,l,u,f.**

McLellan, David **HX39.5**
Karl Marx: A Biography. Ed. 4. Cloth over Boards. Palgrave Macmillan. New York, NY. 2006. 512p. ISBN:1-4039-9729-2, ISBN13: 978-1-4039-9729-6. Dewey:335.4092 B. LCCN:2006-043372.
Audience: **g,l,u,f.**

Moseley, Fred (Editor) **HG220.A2M347 2004**
Marx's Theory of Money: Modern Appraisals. Cloth over Boards. Palgrave Macmillan. New York, NY. 2005. 288p. ISBN:1-4039-3641-2, ISBN13: 978-1-4039-3641-7. Dewey:332.4/01. LCCN:2004-056078.
Audience: **u,f.**

Munck, Ronaldo **HX44.5.M86 2001**
Marx@2000: Late Marxist Perspectives. Ed. 2. Trade Paper. Zed Books, Ltd. London, 2002. 176p. ISBN:1-84277-083-7, ISBN13: 978-1-84277-083-2. Dewey:335.4. LCCN:2001-026992.
Audience: **u,f.**

Oakley, Allen **HB97.5**
Marx's Critique of Political Economy: Intellectual Sources and Evolution, Vol. 1. Paper over Boards. Routledge. New York, NY. 2003. 288p. Routledge Library Editions Ser., Vol. 34:Economics, US/Can. Edition Ser. ISBN:0-415-31334-1, ISBN13: 978-0-415-31334-6. Dewey:335.4/12.
Audience: **u,f.**

Robinson, Joan **HB97.5.R6 1990**
An Essay on Marxian Economics. Ed. 2. Trade Paper. Porcupine Press, Inc. Philadelphia, PA. 1991. xxiv, 104p. ISBN:0-87991-270-7, ISBN13: 978-0-87991-270-3. Dewey:335.41. LCCN:90-007216.
Audience: **u,f.**

Rockmore, Tom **B3305.M74R57 2002**
Marx after Marxism: The Philosophy of Karl Marx. Trade Paper. Blackwell Publishing, Inc. Malden, MA. 2003. 248p. ISBN:0-631-23190-0, ISBN13: 978-0-631-23190-5. Dewey:193. LCCN:2001-052685.
Audience: **g,u,f.** *Choice, 2003, 2002.*

Rosdolsky, Roman **HB97.5.R6613**
The Making of Marx's Capital. Pete Burgess (Translator). Trade Paper. Pluto Press. London, 2005. 488p. ISBN:0-7453-2321-9, ISBN13: 978-0-7453-2321-3. Dewey:335.4/1.
Audience: **u,f.**

Spargo, John **HB501.M5**
Karl Marx: His Life and Work. Trade Paper. University Press of the Pacific. Miami, FL. 2003. 428p. ISBN:1-4102-0760-9, ISBN13: 978-1-4102-0760-9. Dewey:335.41.
Audience: **g,u,f.**

Sweezy, Paul M. **HB501.M5**
Theory of Capitalist Development. Trade Paper. Monthly Review Press. New York, NY. 1968. 400p. ISBN:0-85345-079-X, ISBN13: 978-0-85345-079-5. Dewey:335.41. LCCN:64-021234.
Audience: **u,f.**

Uchida, Hiroshi (Editor) **HB97.5**
Marx for the 21st Century. Paper over Boards. Routledge. New York, NY. 2005. 208p. Routledge Frontiers of Political Economy Ser. ISBN:0-415-30530-6, ISBN13: 978-0-415-30530-3. Dewey:335.4. LCCN:2005-000891.
Audience: **g,l,u,f.**

Wheen, Francis **B3305.M74**
Karl Marx: A Life. Trade Paper. W. W. Norton & Company, Inc. New York, NY. 2001. 448p. ISBN:0-393-32157-6, ISBN13: 978-0-393-32157-9. Dewey:335.4/092 B.
Audience: **g,l,u,f.** *Choice, 2000.*

Wolff, Robert P. **HB501.M37W65 1984**
Understanding Marx: A Reconstructive and Critique of Capital. Marshall Cohen (Editor). Trade Cloth. Princeton University Press. Princeton, NJ. 1985. 245p. Studies in Moral, Political, and Legal Philosophy ISBN:0-691-07678-2, ISBN13: 978-0-691-07678-2. Dewey:335.4/1. LCCN:84-042908.
Audience: **u,f.**

Systems > Socialist > Lenin

Lenin, V. I. **HX418.5**
The State and Revolution. Trade Paper. Kessinger Publishing, LLC. Whitefish, MT. 2004. ISBN:1-4192-8347-2, ISBN13: 978-1-4192-8347-5. Dewey:320.5323.
Audience: **u,f.**

Systems > Comparative

Kuran, Timur **HB126.4.K87 2006**
Islam and Mammon: The Economic Predicaments of Islamism. Trade Paper. Princeton University Press. Princeton, NJ. 2005. 232p. ISBN:0-691-12629-1, ISBN13: 978-0-691-12629-6. Dewey:330.917/67.
Audience: **u,f.** *Choice, 2005.*

Landes, David S. **HC240.Z9W45 1999**
The Wealth and Poverty of Nations: Why Some Are So Rich and Some So Poor. Trade Paper. W. W. Norton & Company, Inc. New York, NY. 1999. 672p. ISBN:0-393-31888-5, ISBN13: 978-0-393-31888-3. Dewey:330.1/6. LCCN:97-027508.
Audience: **l,u,f.** *Choice, 1998.*

Morris, Cynthia T. & Adelman, Irma **HC0051.M645**
Comparative Patterns of Economic Development, 1850-1914. Trade Paper. Books on Demand. Ann Arbor, MI. 592p. Johns Hopkins Studies in Development ISBN:0-608-07406-3, ISBN13: 978-0-608-07406-1. Dewey:338.9/009. LCCN:87-045480.
Audience: **l,u,f.** *Choice, 1988.*

Rosser, John Barkley & Rosser, Marina V. **HB90.R67 2004**
Comparative Economics in a Transforming World Economy. Ed. 2. Trade Cloth. MIT Press. Cambridge, MA. 2004. 672p. ISBN:0-262-18234-3, ISBN13: 978-0-262-18234-8. Dewey:337. LCCN:2003-059363.
Audience: **l,u,f.**

Tinbergen, Jan **HD82**
Centralization and Decentralization in Economic Policy. Trade Cloth. Greenwood Publishing Group, Inc. Portsmouth, NH. 1981. 80p. Contributions to Economic Analysis Ser., No. 6 ISBN:0-313-23077-3, ISBN13: 978-0-313-23077-6. Dewey:338.9. LCCN:81-002723.
Audience: **u,f.**

Macroeconomics and Monetary Economics

Balderston, Theo (Editor) **HB3717 1929.W67 2002**
The World Economy and National Economies in the Interwar Slump. Cloth over Boards. Palgrave Macmillan. New York, NY. 2003. 272p. ISBN:0-333-73864-0, ISBN13: 978-0-333-73864-1. Dewey:330.9/043. LCCN:2002-026949.
Audience: **l,u,f.**

Begg, David K. **HB0172.5.B43**
The Rational Expectations Revolution in Macroeconomics: Theories and Evidence. Trade Paper. Books on Demand. Ann Arbor, MI. 303p. ISBN:0-608-06039-9, ISBN13: 978-0-608-06039-2. Dewey:339/.0724. LCCN:82-047785.
Audience: **u,f.**

Blaug, Mark, et al. **HG226.6.Q36 1995**
The Quantity Theory of Money: From Locke to Keynes and Friedman. Walter A. Eltis, Denis O'Brien, Don Patinkin, Robert Skidelpsky & Geoffrey Wood (Authors). Trade Cloth. Edward Elgar Publishing, Inc. Northampton, MA. 1995. 152p. ISBN:1-85898-177-8, ISBN13: 978-1-85898-177-2. Dewey:332.4/01. LCCN:94-040621.
Audience: **u,f.**

Bordo, Michael D. & Schwartz, Anna J. (Editors) **HG297.R44 1984**
A Retrospective on the Classical Gold Standard, 1821-1931. Trade Cloth. University of Chicago Press. Chicago, IL. 1984. 689p. Conference Report / National Bureau of Economic Research Ser. ISBN:0-226-06590-1, ISBN13: 978-0-226-06590-8. Dewey:332.4/222. LCCN:84-002440.
Audience: **u,f.**

Bresciani-Turroni, Constantino **HG220.A2**
Monetary Economics. Ed. 2. Paper over Boards. Routledge. New York, NY. 2003. 472p. Routledge Library Editions Ser., Vol. 84:Economics, US/Can. Edition Ser. ISBN:0-415-31392-9, ISBN13: 978-0-415-31392-6. Dewey:332.4/1/0943/09041.
Audience: **l,u,f.**

Dow, Sheila C. & Earl, Peter E. **HG221**
Money Matters: A Keynesian Approach to Monetary Economics. Trade Paper. Blackwell Publishing, Inc. Malden, MA. viii, 270p. ISBN:0-85520-485-0, ISBN13: 978-0-85520-485-3. Dewey:332.4/01.
Audience: **u,f.**

Friedman, Milton **HB171.5.F75**
Price Theory: A Provisional Text. Chicago, Ill.: Aldine. 1975.
Audience: **l,u.**

Friedman, Milton (Editor) **HG221**
Studies in the Quantity Theory of Money. Paper Text. University of Chicago Press. Chicago, IL. 1992. ISBN:0-226-26406-8, ISBN13: 978-0-226-26406-6. Dewey:332.4. LCCN:56-010999.
Audience: **u,f.**

Friedman, Milton & Schwartz, A. J. **HG538**
Monetary History of the United States, 1867-1960. Trade Paper. Princeton University Press. Princeton, NJ. 1971. 888p. National Bureau of Economic Research Ser., No. B.12 ISBN:0-691-00354-8, ISBN13: 978-0-691-00354-2. Dewey:332.4/973/09034.
Audience: **g,l,u,f.**

Friedman, Milton & Schwartz, Anna J. **HG501**
Monetary Statistics of the United States: Estimates, Sources, Methods. Trade Cloth. National Bureau of Economic Research, Inc. Cambridge, MA. 1970. 654p. Business Cycles Ser., No. 20 ISBN:0-87014-210-0, ISBN13: 978-0-87014-210-9. Dewey:332.4/973. LCCN:78-085410.
Audience: **l,u,f.**

Friedman, Milton & Schwartz, Anna J. **HG939**
Monetary Trends in the United States and the United Kingdom: Their Relation to Income, Prices, and Interest Rates, 1867-1975. Library Binding. University of Chicago Press. Chicago, IL. 1994. xxxii, 664p. National Bureau of Economic Research Monographs ISBN:0-226-26409-2, ISBN13: 978-0-226-26409-7. Dewey:332.4/941. LCCN:81-016273.
Audience: **u,f.**

Gordon, Robert J. & Friedman, Milton **HG221**
Milton Friedman's Monetary Framework: A Debate with His Critics. Trade Cloth. University of Chicago Press. Chicago, IL. 1974. xii, 192p. ISBN:0-226-26407-6, ISBN13: 978-0-226-26407-3. Dewey:332.4/01. LCCN:73-092599.
Audience: **u,f.**

Hayek, Friedrich A. **HG229 .H3**
Prices and Production. Ed. 2. Trade Cloth. Scholar's Bookshelf. Cranbury, NJ. 1967. xiv, 162p. ISBN:0-678-06515-2, ISBN13: 978-0-678-06515-0. Dewey:338.52/2. LCCN:67-019586.
Audience: **u,f.**

Hayek, Friedrich A. **HG221.H346 1984**
Money, Capital and Fluctuations: Early Essays. R. K. McCloughry (Editor). Library Binding. University of Chicago Press. Chicago, IL. 1993. 196p. ISBN:0-226-32092-8, ISBN13: 978-0-226-32092-2. Dewey:332.4. LCCN:84-000227.
Audience: **u,f.**

Hicks, J. R. **HB801.H48 1986**
A Revision of Demand Theory. Paper Text. Oxford University Press, Inc. New York, NY. 1986. 206p. ISBN:0-19-828550-7, ISBN13: 978-0-19-828550-2. Dewey:338.5/212. LCCN:86-154241.
Audience: **u,f.**

Johnson, Harry G. & Swoboda, Alexander K. **HG205 1970.A15 1973A**
The Economics of Common Currencies. Trade Cloth. Harvard University Press. Cambridge, MA. 1973. 302p. ISBN:0-674-23226-7, ISBN13: 978-0-674-23226-6. Dewey:332.4/5. LCCN:73-076382.
Audience: **u,f.**

Laidler, David **HB99.7 .L28 1999**
Fabricating the Keynesian Revolution: Studies of the Inter-War Literature on Money, the Cycle and Unemployment. Craufurd D. Goodwin (Contribution by). Trade Cloth. Cambridge University Press. New York, NY. 1999. 396p. Historical Perspectives on Modern Economics Ser. ISBN:0-521-64173-X, ISBN13: 978-0-521-64173-9. Dewey:330.156. LCCN:98-038614.
Audience: **l,u,f.**

Lucas, Robert E. Jr. **HD75.L824 2004**
Lectures on Economic Growth. Trade Paper. Harvard University Press. Cambridge, MA. 2004. 224p. ISBN:0-674-01601-7, ISBN13: 978-0-674-01601-9. Dewey:338.9.
Audience: **u,f.**

Lucas, Robert E. Jr. & Sargent, Thomas J. (Editors) **HB139**
Rational Expectations and Econometric Practice. Trade Cloth. University of Minnesota Press. Minneapolis, MN. 1981. 776p. ISBN:0-8166-0916-0, ISBN13: 978-0-8166-0916-1. Dewey:330/.028. LCCN:80-024602.
Audience: **u,f.**

Marshall, Alfred **HG230.3.M357 2003**
Money, Credit, and Commerce. Trade Paper. Prometheus Books, Publishers. Amherst, NY. 2004. 475p. Great Minds Ser. ISBN:1-59102-036-0, ISBN13: 978-1-59102-036-3. Dewey:332.4. LCCN:2002-037037.
Audience: **u,f.**

Marx, Karl **HB203**
Theories of Surplus Value. Trade Paper. Beekman Books, Inc. Wappingers Falls, NY. 1970. 508p. ISBN:0-8464-0920-8, ISBN13: 978-0-8464-0920-5. Dewey:330.1.
Audience: **u,f.**

Marx, Karl **HB301 .M3813**
Wage Labour and Capital. Trade Paper. Kessinger Publishing, LLC. Whitefish, MT. 2004. ISBN:1-4191-9297-3, ISBN13: 978-1-4191-9297-5. Dewey:331.
Audience: **u,f.**

Mayer, Thomas **HG501.M39 1990**
Monetarism and Macroeconomic Policy. Cloth Text. Edward Elgar Publishing, Inc. Northampton, MA. 1990. 208p. ISBN:1-85278-088-6, ISBN13: 978-1-85278-088-3. Dewey:339.5/3/0973. LCCN:90-041728.
Audience: **u,f.** *Choice, 1991.*

Merton, Robert C. **HB172**
Continuous -Time Finance. Paul Anthony Samuelson (Foreword by). Trade Paper. Blackwell Publishing, Inc. Malden, MA. 1992. 752p. Macroeconomics and Finance Ser. ISBN:0-631-18508-9, ISBN13: 978-0-631-18508-6. Dewey:338.5.
Audience: **u,f.**

Morley, Richard **HB172.5.M66 1988**
The Macroeconomics of Open Economies: An Introduction to Aggregate Behavior and Policy. Cloth Text. Edward Elgar Publishing, Inc. Northampton, MA. 1988. 224p. ISBN:1-85278-070-3, ISBN13: 978-1-85278-070-8. Dewey:339. LCCN:88-001197.
Audience: **l,u,f.**

Mundell, Robert **HG221**
Monetary Theory: Inflation, Interest and Growth in the World Economy. Cloth Text. Scott, Foresman & Company. Glenview, IL. 1971. ISBN:0-87620-586-4, ISBN13: 978-0-87620-586-0. Dewey:332.4/01. LCCN:74-123615.
Audience: **u,f.**

Myrdal, Gunnar **HG221**
Monetary Equilibrium. Trade Cloth. Scholar's Bookshelf. Cranbury, NJ. 1965. xi, 214p. Reprints of Economic Classics Ser. ISBN:0-678-00092-1, ISBN13: 978-0-678-00092-2. Dewey:332.401. LCCN:65-023216.
Audience: **u,f.**

Okun, Arthur M. **HB172.5**
Prices and Quantities: A Macroeconomic Analysis. Trade Paper. Brookings Institution Press. Washington, DC. 1981. 367p. ISBN:0-8157-6479-0, ISBN13: 978-0-8157-6479-3. Dewey:339. LCCN:80-070076.
Audience: **u,f.**

Robinson, Joan **HB201.R6 1969**
The Economics of Imperfect Competition. Ed. 2. Trade Cloth. Macmillan Publishing Company, Inc. Old Tappan, NJ. 1969. xx, 352p. ISBN:0-333-08362-8, ISBN13: 978-0-333-08362-8. Dewey:338.6048. LCCN:77-415316.
Audience: **u,f.**

Solomon, Robert **HG3881**
The International Monetary System. Trade Cloth. HarperCollins Publishers. New York, NY. 1982. 452p. ISBN:0-06-015004-1, ISBN13: 978-0-06-015004-4. Dewey:332.4/5. LCCN:81-048156.
Audience: **g,l,u.**

Stigler, George J. & Kindahl, James K. **HB235.U6**
Behavior of Industrial Prices. Cloth Text. National Bureau of Economic Research, Inc. Cambridge, MA. 1970. 220p. General Ser., No. 90 ISBN:0-87014-216-X, ISBN13: 978-0-87014-216-1. Dewey:338.52/0973. LCCN:79-121003.
Audience: **u,f.**

Stokey, Nancy L. & Lucas, Robert E. Jr. **HB135.S7455 1989**
Recursive Methods in Economic Dynamics. Trade Cloth. Harvard University Press. Cambridge, MA. 1989. 616p. ISBN:0-674-75096-9, ISBN13: 978-0-674-75096-8. Dewey:330/.01/51. LCCN:88-037681.
Audience: **u,f.**

Tobin, James **HB171**
Asset Accumulation and Economic Activity: Reflections on Contemporary Macroeconomic Theory. Trade Paper. University of Chicago Press. Chicago, IL. 1982. 116p. ISBN:0-226-80502-6, ISBN13: 978-0-226-80502-3. Dewey:339. LCCN:80-012844.
Audience: **u,f.**

Tobin, James **HB171**
Essays in Economics: Theory and Policy. Trade Cloth. MIT Press. Cambridge, MA. 1982. 736p. ISBN:0-262-20042-2, ISBN13: 978-0-262-20042-4. Dewey:330. LCCN:81-020784.
Audience: **u,f.**

Tobin, James **HB171.T629 1996**
Essays in Economics: National and International. Trade Cloth. MIT Press. Cambridge, MA. 1996. 760p. ISBN:0-262-20101-1, ISBN13: 978-0-262-20101-8. Dewey:330. LCCN:95-023522.
Audience: **u,f.**

Tobin, James **HB34.T622 1987**
Essays in Economics: Macroeconomics. Trade Cloth. MIT Press. Cambridge, MA. 1987. 526p. ISBN:0-262-20062-7, ISBN13: 978-0-262-20062-2. Dewey:339. LCCN:86-021157.
Audience: **u,f.**

Tobin, James **HD5724**
Full Employment and Growth: Further Keynesian Essays on Policy. Trade Paper. Edward Elgar Publishing, Inc. Northampton, MA. 1998. 328p. ISBN:1-85898-774-1, ISBN13: 978-1-85898-774-3. Dewey:339.5/0973. LCCN:95-031937.
Audience: **u,f.**

Tobin, James **HC106.5 .T57**
National Economic Policy. Trade Paper. Yale University Press. Cumberland, RI. 1966. ISBN:0-300-00243-2, ISBN13: 978-0-300-00243-0. Dewey:338.973.
Audience: **u,f.**

Tobin, James **HC106.6**
The New Economics One Decade Older. Trade Cloth. Princeton University Press. Princeton, NJ. 1974. 100p. Eliot Janeway Lectures in Historical Economics ISBN:0-691-04205-5, ISBN13: 978-0-691-04205-3. Dewey:330.9/73/092. LCCN:73-016763.
Audience: **u,f.**

Tobin, James **HB99.7**
Policies for Prosperity: Essays in a Keynesian Mode. Peter M. Jackson (Editor). Trade Paper. MIT Press. Cambridge, MA. 1989. 528p. ISBN:0-262-70036-0, ISBN13: 978-0-262-70036-8. Dewey:330.15/6.
Audience: **u,f.** *Choice, 1988.*

Ugur, Mehmet **HB172.5.U35 2001**
An Open Economy Macroeconomics Reader. Paper over Boards. Routledge. New York, NY. 2002. 568p. ISBN:0-415-25331-4, ISBN13: 978-0-415-25331-4. Dewey:339. LCCN:2001-048168.
Audience: **l,u.**

Wicksell, Knut **HG229 .W52**
Interest and Prices: A Study of the Causes Regulating the Value of Money. B. F. Kahn (Translator). Trade Cloth. Scholar's Bookshelf. Cranbury, NJ. 1965. xxi, 219p. Reprints of Economic Classics Ser. ISBN:0-678-00086-7, ISBN13: 978-0-678-00086-1. Dewey:332.4. LCCN:65-016993.
Audience: **l,u,f.**

Zarembka, Paul & Soederberg, Susanne (Editors) **HB501**
Neoliberalism in Crisis, Accumulation, and Rosa Luxemburg's Legacy. Trade Cloth. Elsevier Science & Technology Books. Saint Louis, MO. 2004. 306p. Research in Political Economy Ser. ISBN:0-7623-1098-7, ISBN13: 978-0-7623-1098-2. Dewey:332/.041.
Audience: **u,f.**

Macroeconomics and Monetary Economics > Models

Backhouse, Roger **HB172.5**
Interpreting Macroeconomics: Explorations in the History of Economic Thought. Trade Paper. Routledge. New York, NY. 1996. 256p. ISBN:0-415-15360-3, ISBN13: 978-0-415-15360-7. Dewey:339.
Audience: **l,u,f.**

Bergstrom, Abram R. (Editor) **HG0229.S73**
Stability and Inflation: A Volume of Essays to Honour the Memory of A. W. H. Phillips. Trade Paper. Books on Demand. Ann Arbor, MI. 341p. ISBN:0-8357-4318-7, ISBN13: 978-0-8357-4318-1. Dewey:332.41. LCCN:77-004420.
Audience: **l,u,f.**

Blackwell, Ron (Editor), et al. **HB72**
Economics as Worldly Philosophy: Essays in Political and Historical Economics in Honour of Robert Heilbroner. Jaspal Chatha & Edward J. Nell (Editors). Trade Cloth. Palgrave Macmillan Ltd. Basingstoke, 1993. 370p. ISBN:0-333-49477-6, ISBN13: 978-0-333-49477-6. Dewey:330.01. LCCN:92-002547.
Audience: **l,u,f.**

Boumans, Marcel **HB135.B68 2005**
How Economists Model the World into Numbers. Paper over Boards. Routledge. New York, NY. 2005. 224p. Routledge INEM Advances in Economic Methodology Ser. ISBN:0-415-34621-5, ISBN13: 978-0-415-34621-4. Dewey:330/.01/5195. LCCN:2004-012725.
Audience: **g,l,u,f.**

Brunner, K. & Meltzer, A. H. (Editors) **HB3730**
Stabilization of the Domestic and International Economy. Trade Cloth. Elsevier. New York, NY. 1977. Carnegie-Rochester Conference Ser., Vol. 5 ISBN:0-7204-0709-5, ISBN13: 978-0-7204-0709-9. Dewey:339.5.
Audience: **l,u,f.**

Bugge, Anna, et al. **HD6052.A76 1995**
Women's Work and Wages: A Selection of Papers from the 15th Arne Ryde Symposium on Economics of Gender and Family in Honor of Anna Bugge and Knut Wicksell. Knut Wicksell, Christina Jonung & Inga Persson (Authors). Paper over Boards. Routledge. New York, NY. 1998. 272p. Routledge Research in Gender and Society Ser. ISBN:0-415-14903-7, ISBN13: 978-0-415-14903-7. Dewey:331.4. LCCN:97-020424.
Audience: **u,f.**

Diebolt, Claude, et al. **HB172.5.N497 2005**
New Trends in Macroeconomics. Catherine Kyrtsou & Olivier Darné (Authors). Trade Cloth. Springer. New York, NY. 2005. xiv, 238p. ISBN:7-83540-214-9, ISBN13: 978-7-83540-214-8. Dewey:339. LCCN:2005-929196.
Audience: **l,u,f.**

Harrop, Jeffrey **HC241.2.H3935 1992**
The Political Economy of Integration in the European Community. Ed. 2. Cloth Text. Edward Elgar Publishing, Inc. Northampton, MA. 1992. 304p. ISBN:1-85278-590-X, ISBN13: 978-1-85278-590-1. Dewey:337.1/42. LCCN:91-028216.
Audience: **l,u,f.** *Choice, 1990.*

Hoover, Kevin D. **HB172.5 .H658 2001**
Causality in Macroeconomics. Trade Cloth. Cambridge University Press. New York, NY. 2001. 326p. ISBN:0-521-45217-1, ISBN13: 978-0-521-45217-5. Dewey:339. LCCN:00-049351.
Audience: **l,u,f.**

Jansen, Eilev S., et al. **HB172.5.E27 2005**
The Econometrics of Macroeconomic Modelling. Gunnar Bardsen, Oyvind Eitrheim & Ragnar Nymoen (Authors). Trade Cloth. Oxford University Press, Inc. New York, NY. 2005. 360p. Advanced Texts in Econometrics Ser. ISBN:0-19-924649-1, ISBN13: 978-0-19-924649-6. Dewey:339.01/5195. LCCN:2005-299990.
Audience: **l,u,f.**

Kasper, Sherryl **HB95.K27 2002**
The Revival of Laissez-Faire in American Macroeconomic Theory: A Case Study of Its Pioneers. Trade Cloth. Edward Elgar Publishing, Inc. Northampton, MA. 2003. 192p. ISBN:1-84064-606-3, ISBN13: 978-1-84064-606-1. Dewey:339/.01. LCCN:2002-024583.
Audience: **l,u,f.**

Leijonhufvud, Axel **HB172.5**
Information and Coordination: Essays in Macroeconomic Theory. Trade Cloth. Oxford University Press, Inc. New York, NY. 1981. x, 388p. ISBN:0-19-502814-7, ISBN13: 978-0-19-502814-0. Dewey:339.3/01. LCCN:80-015166.
Audience: **l,u,f.**

Leijonhufvud, Axel **HB172.5.L45 2000**
Macroeconomic Instability and Coordination: Selected Essays of Axel Leijonhufvud. Trade Cloth. Edward Elgar Publishing, Inc. Northampton, MA. 2001. 392p. Economists of the Twentieth Century Ser. ISBN:1-85278-967-0, ISBN13: 978-1-85278-967-1. Dewey:339. LCCN:00-034121.
Audience: **l,u,f.**

McCulloch, John R. **HB161**
Treatises and Essays on Subjects Connected with Economical Policy: With Biographical Sketches of Quesnay, Adam Smith and Ricardo. Trade Cloth. Scholar's Bookshelf. Cranbury, NJ. 1967. vii, 487p. Reprints of Economic Classics Ser. ISBN:0-678-00255-X, ISBN13: 978-0-678-00255-1. Dewey:330/.08. LCCN:67-020088.
Audience: **u,f.**

Mody, Ashoka & Pattilo, Catherine (Editors) **HC79.P6**
Macroeconomics Policies and Poverty. Paper over Boards. Routledge. New York, NY. 2005. 400p. Routledge Studies in the Modern World Economy Ser. ISBN:0-415-70071-X, ISBN13: 978-0-415-70071-9. Dewey:339.4/6. LCCN:2005-002522.
Audience: **l,u,f.**

Phelps, Edmund S. **HB172.5.P458 1990**
Seven Schools of Macroeconomic Thought: The Arne Ryde Memorial Lectures. Trade Cloth. Oxford University Press, Inc. New York, NY. 1990. 124p. ISBN:0-19-828333-4, ISBN13: 978-0-19-828333-1. Dewey:339. LCCN:89-049214.
Audience: **l,u,f.**

Plasmans, Joseph, et al. **HJ275**
Dynamic Modeling of Monetary and Fiscal Cooperation among Nations. Jacob Engwerda, Bas van Aarle, Giovanni di Bartolomeo & Tomasz Michalak (Authors). Trade Cloth. Springer. New York, NY. 2006. XVI, 324p. Dynamic Modeling and Econometrics in Economics and Finance Ser. ISBN:0-387-27884-2, ISBN13: 978-0-387-27884-1. Dewey:336.185.
Audience: **u,f.**

Rodrik, Dani (Editor, Introduction by) **HD73.I52 2003**
In Search of Prosperity: Analytic Narratives on Economic Growth. Trade Cloth. Princeton University Press. Princeton, NJ. 2003. 520p. ISBN:0-691-09268-0, ISBN13: 978-0-691-09268-3. Dewey:338.9. LCCN:2002-072854.
Audience: **l,u,f.**

Snowdon, Brian & Vane, Howard R. **HB172.5.S648 1999**
Conversations with Leading Economists: Interpreting Modern Macroeconomics. Trade Cloth. Edward Elgar Publishing, Inc. Northampton, MA. 1999. 384p. ISBN:1-85898-942-6, ISBN13: 978-1-85898-942-6. Dewey:339. LCCN:99-012890.
Audience: **g,l,u,f.** *Choice, 2000.*

Snowdon, Brian & Vane, Howard R. (Editors) **HB172.5.R44 1997**
Reflections on the Development of Modern Macroeconomics. Roger Backhouse, Keith Shaw, Thomas Mayer, Patrick Minford, Cillian Ryan, Andrew Mullineux & Huw Dixon (Contribution by). Trade Cloth. Edward Elgar Publishing, Inc. Northampton, MA. 1998. 256p. ISBN:1-85898-342-8, ISBN13: 978-1-85898-342-4. Dewey:339. LCCN:97-023219.
Audience: **u,f.**

Taylor, J. Edward & Adelman, Irma **HT431 .T39 1996**
Village Economies: The Design, Estimation, and Use of Villagewide Economic Models. Elise H. Golan, Blane D. Lewis, Katherine Ralston, Shankar Subramanian & Erik Thorbecke (Contribution by). Trade Cloth. Cambridge University Press. New York, NY. 1996. 276p. ISBN:0-521-55012-2, ISBN13: 978-0-521-55012-3. Dewey:338/.091734. LCCN:95-043030.
Audience: **u,f.**

Wicksell, Knut **HB201.W6313 1970**
Value, Capital and Rent. S. H. Frowein (Translator). Trade Cloth. Scholar's Bookshelf. Cranbury, NJ. 1970. 180p. Reprints of Economic Classics Ser. ISBN:0-678-00652-0, ISBN13: 978-0-678-00652-8. Dewey:330.1. LCCN:68-058668.
Audience: **l,u.**

Wicksell, Knut **HG229 .W52**
Interest and Prices: A Study of the Causes Regulating the Value of Money. B. F. Kahn (Translator). Trade Cloth. Scholar's Bookshelf. Cranbury, NJ. 1965. xxi, 219p. Reprints of Economic Classics Ser. ISBN:0-678-00086-7, ISBN13: 978-0-678-00086-1. Dewey:332.4. LCCN:65-016993.
Audience: **l,u,f.**

Wicksell, Knut **HB34**
Selected Papers on Economic Theory. Erik Lindhal (Editor). Trade Cloth. Scholar's Bookshelf. Cranbury, NJ. 1969. 292p. Reprints of Economic Classics Ser. ISBN:0-678-00493-5, ISBN13: 978-0-678-00493-7. Dewey:330.1. LCCN:68-058667.
Audience: **u,f.**

Wicksell, Knut **HB179**
Lectures on Political Economy: Money. Lionel Robbins (Editor, Introduction by), E. Classen (Translator). Trade Cloth. Scholar's Bookshelf. Cranbury, NJ. 1967. 246p. Reprints of Economic Classics Ser. ISBN:0-678-06533-0, ISBN13: 978-0-678-06533-4. Dewey:330.1. LCCN:67-028341.
Audience: **u,f.**

Wicksell, Knut & Sandelin, Bo **HB34.W48213 1999**
Knut Wicksell: Essays in Economics. Paper over Boards. Routledge. New York, NY. 1997. 288p. ISBN:0-415-15512-6, ISBN13: 978-0-415-15512-0. Dewey:330. LCCN:96-009038.
Audience: **u,f.**

Wilson, J. S. G. **HG220.A2**
Monetary Economics. Paper over Boards. Routledge. New York, NY. 2003. 360p. Routledge Library Editions Ser., Vol. 87:Economics, US/Can. Edition Ser. ISBN:0-415-31395-3, ISBN13: 978-0-415-31395-7. Dewey:332.4.
Audience: **l,u,f.**

Macroeconomics and Monetary Economics > Models > General

Snowdon, Brian & Vane, Howard R. **HB172.5.S653 2005**
Modern Macroeconomics. Trade Cloth. Edward Elgar Publishing, Inc. Northampton, MA. 2005. 832p. ISBN:1-84376-394-X, ISBN13: 978-1-84376-394-9. Dewey:339. LCCN:2004-054072.
Audience: **g,l,u,f.** *Choice, 2005.*

Snowdon, Brian, et al. **HB172.5.S65 1994**
A Modern Guide to Macroeconomics: An Introduction to Competing Schools of Thought. Howard Vane & Peter Wynarczyk (Authors). Trade Paper. Edward Elgar Publishing, Inc. Northampton, MA. 1995. 480p. ISBN:1-85278-882-8, ISBN13: 978-1-85278-882-7. Dewey:339. LCCN:94-006255.
Audience: **l,u,f.** *Choice, 1995.*

Macroeconomics and Monetary Economics > Marxian/Sraffian/Institutional/ Evolutionary

Grupp, Hariolf **HD45.G78 1998**
Foundations of the Economics of Innovation: Theory, Measurement and Practice. Christopher Freeman (Preface by). Trade Cloth. Edward Elgar Publishing, Inc. Northampton, MA. 1998. 544p. ISBN:1-85898-716-4, ISBN13: 978-1-85898-716-3. Dewey:338/.064. LCCN:98-005817.
Audience: **u,f.**

Robinson, Joan **HB97.5.R6 1990**
An Essay on Marxian Economics. Ed. 2. Trade Paper. Porcupine Press, Inc. Philadelphia, PA. 1991. xxiv, 104p. ISBN:0-87991-270-7, ISBN13: 978-0-87991-270-3. Dewey:335.41. LCCN:90-007216.
Audience: **u,f.**

Macroeconomics and Monetary Economics > Marxian/Sraffian/Institutional/ Evolutionary > Keynes/Post-Keynesian

Arestis, Philip & Chick, Victoria (Editors) **HB171**
Recent Developments in Post Keynesian Economics. Trade Cloth. Edward Elgar Publishing, Inc. Northampton, MA. 1992. 224p. Post Keynesian Economics Study Group Ser. ISBN:1-85278-412-1, ISBN13: 978-1-85278-412-6. Dewey:330.1. LCCN:91-041165.
Audience: **l,u,f.**

Cornwall, John & Cornwall, Wendy **HB501**
ⓔ Capitalist Development in the Twentieth Century: An Evolutionary-Keynesian Analysis. Phyllis Deane, Gautam Mathur & Joan Robinson (Contribution by). E-Book. Cambridge

University Press. New York, NY. Modern Cambridge Economics Ser. ISBN:0-511-15310-4, ISBN13: 978-0-511-15310-5. Dewey:330.122.
Audience: **u,f.**

De Carvalho, Fernando J. **HB99.7.C38 1992**
Mr. Keynes and the Post Keynesians: Principles of Macroeconomics for a Monetary Production Economy. Trade Cloth. Edward Elgar Publishing, Inc. Northampton, MA. 1992. 256p. New Directions in Modern Economics Ser. ISBN:1-85278-653-1, ISBN13: 978-1-85278-653-3. Dewey:330.15/6. LCCN:92-001108.
Audience: **l,u,f.** *Choice, 1993.*

Lee, Frederic S. **HB201**
Post Keynesian Price Theory. Phyllis Deane, Gautam Mathur & Joan Robinson (Contribution by). E-Book. Cambridge University Press. New York, NY. Modern Cambridge Economics Ser. ISBN:0-511-15214-0, ISBN13: 978-0-511-15214-6. Dewey:338.521.
Audience: **u,f.**

Macroeconomics and Monetary Economics > Business Cycles/Economic Growth/Prices

Abramovitz, Moses **HC106 .A33 1989**
Thinking about Growth: And Other Essays on Economic Growth and Welfare. Louis Galambos & Robert Gallmam (Contribution by). Cloth Text. Cambridge University Press. New York, NY. 1989. 400p. Studies in Economic History and Policy: The United States in the Twentieth Century ISBN:0-521-33396-2, ISBN13: 978-0-521-33396-2. Dewey:338.973. LCCN:88-018902.
Audience: **u,f.** *Choice, 1990.*

Acemoglu, Daron (Editor) **HD72**
Recent Developments in Growth Theory. P. Aghion, E. Helpman, P. Howitt, C. I. Jones, S. Johnson, P. J. Krussel, J. Robinson & J. Ventura (Contribution by). Trade Cloth. Edward Elgar Publishing, Inc. Northampton, MA. 2004. 1,368p. The International Library of Critical Writings in Economics Ser., Vol. 179 ISBN:1-84376-259-5, ISBN13: 978-1-84376-259-1. Dewey:338.9/001. LCCN:2004-042272.
Audience: **l,u,f.**

Adelman, Irma **HB171**
Theories of Economic Growth and Development. Trade Paper. Stanford University Press. Palo Alto, CA. 1961. viii, 164p. ISBN:0-8047-0084-2, ISBN13: 978-0-8047-0084-9. Dewey:3301.
Audience: **l,u,f.**

Alesina, Alberto, et al. **HB3711**
Political Cycles and the Macroeconomy. Nouriel Roubini & Gerald D. Cohen (Authors). Trade Paper. MIT Press. Cambridge, MA. 1997. 302p. ISBN:0-262-51094-4, ISBN13: 978-0-262-51094-3. Dewey:338.5/4.
Audience: **u,f.**

Allen, Roy E. **HB3722.A36 1994**
Financial Crises and Recession in the Global Economy. Trade Cloth. Edward Elgar Publishing, Inc. Northampton, MA. 1994. 200p. Studies in International Political Economy ISBN:1-85278-997-2, ISBN13: 978-1-85278-997-8. Dewey:338.5/42. LCCN:93-050632.
Audience: **l,u,f.** *Choice, 2000, 1995.*

Allen, Roy E. **HB3722**
The Political Economy of Financial Crises. Trade Cloth. Edward Elgar Publishing, Inc. Northampton, MA. 2004. 1,120p. The International Library of Writings on the New Global Economy Ser., Vol. 5 ISBN:1-84376-106-8, ISBN13: 978-1-84376-106-8. Dewey:338.5/42. LCCN:2004-053039.
Audience: **l,u,f.**

Barro, Robert J. **HD75.B365 1997**
Determinants of Economic Growth: A Cross-Country Empirical Study. Trade Cloth. MIT Press. Cambridge, MA. 1997. 160p. Lionel Robbins Lectures ISBN:0-262-02421-7, ISBN13: 978-0-262-02421-1. Dewey:338.9. LCCN:96-050235.
Audience: **u,f.** *Choice, 1997.*

Barro, Robert J. **HB172.5**
Money, Expectations, and Business Cycles: Essays in Macroeconomics. Trade Cloth. Elsevier Science & Technology Books. Saint Louis, MO. 1981. 371p. Economic Theory, Econometrics and Mathematical Economics Ser. ISBN:0-12-079550-7, ISBN13: 978-0-12-079550-5. Dewey:339. LCCN:80-001770.
Audience: **u,f.**

Bauer, P. T. **HD82 .B328 1972**
Dissent on Development: Studies and Debates in Development Economics. Trade Cloth. Harvard University Press. Cambridge, MA. 1972. 550p. ISBN:0-674-21281-9, ISBN13: 978-0-674-21281-7. Dewey:330.9/172/4. LCCN:70-189158.
Audience: **u,f.**

Bauer, Peter T. **HD82.B333 1984**
Reality and Rhetoric: Studies in the Economics of Development. Cambridge, Mass.: Harvard University Press. 1984. ISBN:0-674-74946-4, ISBN13: 978-0-674-74946-7.
Audience: **u,f.**

Bauer, Peter T. **HD82.B332**
The Economics of Under-Developed Countries. Yamey, Basil S.. [Chicago] University of Chicago Press. 1957. The Cambridge economic handbooks
Audience: **u,f.**

Bauer, Peter T. **HC59**
Economic Analysis and Policy in Underdeveloped Countries, 4. Joseph J. Spengler (Foreword by). Trade Cloth. Greenwood Publishing Group, Inc. Portsmouth, NH. 1981. 145p. Duke University Commonwealth-Studies Center Publications, No. 4 ISBN:0-313-23272-5, ISBN13: 978-0-313-23272-5. Dewey:330.904. LCCN:81-013361.
Audience: **u,f.**

Belongia, Michael T. & Garfinkel, Michelle R. (Editors) **HB3743**
The Business Cycle: Theories and Evidence, Proceedings of the Sixteenth Annual Economic Policy Conference of the Federal Reserve Bank of St. Louis. Trade Cloth. Springer. New York, NY. 1992. 240p. ISBN:0-7923-9239-6, ISBN13: 978-0-7923-9239-2. Dewey:338.5420973. LCCN:92-011616.
Audience: **l,u,f.**

Bhagwati, Jagdish N. & Grossman, Gene M. (Editors) **HD82.B468 1985**
Essays in Development Economic: Dependence and Interdependence. Trade Cloth. MIT Press. Cambridge, MA. 1985. 416p. ISBN:0-262-02230-3, ISBN13: 978-0-262-02230-9. Dewey:338.9. LCCN:85-011343.
Audience: **u,f.**

Bhagwati, Jagdish N. **HD82.B468 1985**
Essays in Developmental Economics: Wealth and Poverty. Gene M. Grossman (Editor). Trade Cloth. MIT Press. Cambridge, MA. 1985. 400p. ISBN:0-262-02229-X, ISBN13: 978-0-262-02229-3. Dewey:338.9. LCCN:85-011343.
Audience: **u,f.**

Birner, Jack (Editor), et al. **HB101.H39F16 2001**
F. A. Hayek As a Political Economist: Economic Analysis and Values. Pierre Garrouste & Thierry Aimar (Editors). Paper over Boards. Routledge. New York, NY. 2001. 256p. Routledge Studies in the History of Economics Ser. ISBN:0-415-22622-8, ISBN13: 978-0-415-22622-6. Dewey:330/.092. LCCN:2001-019941.
Audience: **u,f.**

Dixit, Avinash **HD75**
The Theory of Equilibrium Growth. Cloth Text. Oxford University Press, Inc. New York, NY. 1976. 214p. ISBN:0-19-877080-4, ISBN13: 978-0-19-877080-0. Dewey:339.5.
Audience: **u,f.**

Dobb, Maurice Herbert **HD82.D54 1969**
An Essay on Economic Growth and Planning. Trade Cloth. Monthly Review Press. New York, NY. 1969. vii, 119p. ISBN:0-85345-110-9, ISBN13: 978-0-85345-110-5. Dewey:338.9. LCCN:78-087281.
Audience: **u,f.**

Dorfman, Robert, et al. **HB135.D67 1987**
Linear Programming and Economic Analysis. Paul Anthony Samuelson & Robert M. Solow (Authors). Trade Paper. Dover Publications, Inc. Mineola, NY. 1987. 525p. ISBN:0-486-65491-5, ISBN13: 978-0-486-65491-1. Dewey:330/.0724. LCCN:87-024382.
Audience: **u,f.**

Easterlin, Richard A. **HD82**
Growth Triumphant: The Twenty-First Century in Historical Perspective. Trade Paper. University of Michigan Press. Chicago, IL. 1998. 216p. Economics, Cognition, and Society Ser. ISBN:0-472-08553-0, ISBN13: 978-0-472-08553-8. Dewey:338.9.
Audience: **u,f.** *Choice, 1997.*

Easterly, William **HC59.7**
The Elusive Quest for Growth: Economists' Adventures and Misadventures in the Tropics. Trade Paper. MIT Press. Cambridge, MA. 2002. 356p. ISBN:0-262-55042-3, ISBN13: 978-0-262-55042-0. Dewey:338.9/009172/4. LCCN:00-068382.
Audience: **u,f.** *Choice, 2001.*

Eden, Lorraine & Dobson, Wendy **HD2741.G6893 2005**
Governance, Multinationals, and Growth. Trade Cloth. Edward Elgar Publishing, Inc. Northampton, MA. 2005. 400p. New Horizons in International Business Ser. ISBN:1-84376-909-3, ISBN13: 978-1-84376-909-5. Dewey:658/.049. LCCN:2005-043238.
Audience: **l,u,f.**

Eliasson, Gunnar K. (Editor), et al. **HC79.T4M52 1998**
Microfoundations of Economic Growth: A Schumpeterian Perspective. Christopher Green & Charles R. McCann (Editors). Cloth over Boards. University of Michigan Press. Chicago, IL. 1998. 456p. International Schumpeter Society Ser. ISBN:0-472-10904-9, ISBN13: 978-0-472-10904-3. Dewey:338.064. LCCN:98-005012.
Audience: **u,f.**

Fisher, Irving **HB119.F5.A25 1996**
Booms and Depressions. Trade Cloth. Pickering & Chatto Publishers, Ltd. London, 1996. vi, 351p. The Works of Irving Fisher ISBN:1-85196-235-2, ISBN13: 978-1-85196-235-8. Dewey:330 S. LCCN:96-012210.
Audience: **u,f.**

Galbraith, John Kenneth **HB3717 1929.G32 1997**
The Great Crash 1929. Trade Paper. Houghton Mifflin Company Trade & Reference Division. Boston, MA. 1997. 224p. ISBN:0-395-85999-9, ISBN13: 978-0-395-85999-5. Dewey:338.5/4/0973. LCCN:97-022051.
Audience: **g,l,u,f.** B

Greiner, Alfred, et al. **HD75.5.G752 2005**
The Forces of Economic Growth: A Time Series Perspective. Willi Semmler & Gang Gong (Authors). Trade Cloth. Princeton University Press. Princeton, NJ. 2004. 208p. ISBN:0-691-11918-X, ISBN13: 978-0-691-11918-2. Dewey:330/.01/51955. LCCN:2004-044534.
Audience: **l,u,f.**

Hansen, Alvin H. **HB3711.H315 2003**
Fiscal Policy and Business Cycles. Paper over Boards. Routledge. New York, NY. 2003. 464p. Routledge Library Editions Ser., Vol. 16:Economics, US/Can. Edition Ser. ISBN:0-415-31314-7, ISBN13: 978-0-415-31314-8. Dewey:330.1.
Audience: **l,u,f.**

Harvie, Charles & Lee, Boon-Chye (Editors) **HD2346.E18S87 2004**
Sustainable Growth and Performance in East Asia, Bk.. III. Trade Cloth. Edward Elgar Publishing, Inc. Northampton, MA. 2005. 392p. Studies of Small and Medium Size Enterprises in East Asia, Vol. 3 ISBN:1-84064-808-2, ISBN13: 978-1-84064-808-9. Dewey:338.6/42/095. LCCN:2004-058626.
Audience: **l,u,f.**

Hayek, Friedrich A. **HD82.H38 1994**
The Road to Serfdom. Ed. 50. Milton Friedman (Introduction by). Trade Cloth. University of Chicago Press. Chicago, IL. 1994. 320p. ISBN:0-226-32059-6, ISBN13: 978-0-226-32059-5. Dewey:338.9. LCCN:94-027675.
Audience: **l,u,f.**

Heilbroner, Robert L. **HD82.H388**
Between Capitalism and Socialism: Essays in Political Economics. Trade Cloth. Random House, Inc. New York, NY. 1970. xviii, 294p. ISBN:0-394-41665-1, ISBN13: 978-0-394-41665-6. Dewey:330.1. LCCN:79-117700.
Audience: **l,u,f.**

Heilbroner, Robert L. **HD82 .H39**
Great Ascent: The Struggle for Economic Development in Our Time. Mass Market. HarperCollins Publishers. New York, NY. 1985. ISBN:0-06-133030-2, ISBN13: 978-0-06-133030-8. Dewey:338.9.
Audience: **g,l,u,f.**

Kaldor, Nicholas **HD82.K3 1980**
Essays on Economic Policy. New York: Holmes & Meier. 1980. ISBN:0-8419-0453-7, ISBN13: 978-0-8419-0453-8.
Audience: **u,f.**

Kalecki, Michal **HB3711.K27 2003**
Essays in the Theory of Economic Fluctuations. Paper over Boards. Routledge. New York, NY. 2003. 160p. Routledge Library Editions Ser., Vol. 69:Economics, US/Can. Edition Ser. ISBN:0-415-31372-4, ISBN13: 978-0-415-31372-8. Dewey:330.1.
Audience: **l,u,f.**

Kalecki, Michal **HG3711**
Studies in the Theory of Business Cycles, 1933-39. Ada Kaleca (Translator), Joan Robinson (Introduction by). Trade Cloth. Scholar's Bookshelf. Cranbury, NJ. 1969. xii, 71p. ISBN:0-678-06269-2, ISBN13: 978-0-678-06269-2. Dewey:338.54. LCCN:66-031550.
Audience: **l,u,f.**

Kindleberger, Charles P. **HB3711**
The World in Depression, 1929-1939. Trade Paper. University of California Press. Berkeley, CA. 1986. 355p. History of the World Economy in the Twentieth Century Ser., Vol. 4 ISBN:0-520-05592-6, ISBN13: 978-0-520-05592-6. Dewey:338.5/4.
Audience: **g,l,u,f.** *Choice, 1986.*

Kindleberger, Charles P. & Aliber, Robert **HB3722.K56 2005**
Manias, Panics, and Crashes: A History of Financial Crises. Ed. 5. Robert Solow (Foreword by). Trade Paper. John Wiley & Sons, Inc. Hoboken, NJ. 2005. 304p. Wiley Investment Classics Ser. ISBN:0-471-46714-6, ISBN13: 978-0-471-46714-4. Dewey:338.5/42. LCCN:2005-001066.
Audience: **g,l,u,f.** B

Krugman, Paul **HB3716.K76 1999**
The Return of Depression Economics. Trade Cloth. W. W. Norton & Company, Inc. New York, NY. 1999. 192p. ISBN:0-393-04839-X, ISBN13: 978-0-393-04839-1. Dewey:338.5/42. LCCN:99-012965.
Audience: **l,u,f.** *Choice, 1999.*

Kydland, Finn E. (Editor) **HB3711.B934 1995**
Business Cycle Theory. Trade Cloth. Edward Elgar Publishing, Inc. Northampton, MA. 1995. 548p. The International Library of Critical Writings in Economics, Vol. 58 ISBN:1-85278-751-1, ISBN13: 978-1-85278-751-6. Dewey:338.5/42. LCCN:95-030411.
Audience: **u,f.**

Landau, Ralph (Editor), et al. **HD75.M674 1996**
The Mosaic of Economic Growth. Timothy Taylor & Gavin Wright (Editors). Trade Cloth. Stanford University Press. Palo Alto, CA. 1996. 512p. ISBN:0-8047-2599-3, ISBN13: 978-0-8047-2599-6. Dewey:338.9. LCCN:95-022572.
Audience: **l,u,f.**

Levy, Frank **HC110.I5L47 1998**
The New Dollars and Dreams: American Incomes and Economic Change. Trade Cloth. Russell Sage Foundation. New York, NY. 1998. 256p. ISBN:0-87154-514-4, ISBN13: 978-0-87154-514-5. Dewey:339.2/0973. LCCN:98-020635.
Audience: **g,l,u,f.** *Choice, 1999.*

Lucas, Robert E. Jr. **HB172.5**
Models of Business Cycles. Trade Paper. Blackwell Publishing, Inc. Malden, MA. 1989. 128p. ISBN:0-631-14791-8, ISBN13: 978-0-631-14791-6. Dewey:338.5/42/0724. LCCN:86-017622.
Audience: **u,f.**

Lucas, Robert E. Jr. **HB3711**
Studies in Business-Cycle Theory. Trade Paper. MIT Press. Cambridge, MA. 1983. 300p. ISBN:0-262-62044-8, ISBN13: 978-0-262-62044-4. Dewey:338.542.
Audience: **u,f.**

Lucas, Robert E. Jr. **HB3711.L83**
Studies in Business-Cycle Theory. Cloth Text. MIT Press. Cambridge, MA. 1981. 256p. ISBN:0-262-12089-5, ISBN13: 978-0-262-12089-0. Dewey:338.542. LCCN:81-000692.
Audience: **u,f.**

MacKay, Charles **AZ999**
Memoirs of Extraordinary Popular Delusions and the Madness of Crowds: The Essential Library Edition. Trade Paper. Xlibris Corporation. Philadelphia, PA. 2001. 370p. ISBN:0-7388-4309-1, ISBN13: 978-0-7388-4309-4. Dewey:1.96.
Audience: **l,u,f.**

Mallaby, Sebastian **HG3881.5.W57**
The World's Banker: A Story of Failed States, Financial Crises, and the Wealth and Poverty of Nations. Trade Paper. Penguin Group (USA) Inc. New York, NY. 2006. 496p. ISBN:0-14-303679-3, ISBN13: 978-0-14-303679-1. Dewey:332.1532.
Audience: **g,l,u,f.** *Choice, 2005.*

Mirrlees, J. **HD82**
Models of Economic Growth: Proceedings of a Conference Held by the International Economic Association at Jerusalem. N. H. Stern (Editor). Trade Cloth. John Wiley & Sons, Inc. Hoboken, NJ. 1973. 372p. ISBN:0-470-60918-4, ISBN13: 978-0-470-60918-7. Dewey:330.9/172/4. LCCN:73-000531.
Audience: **u,f.**

Mortensen, Dale T. **HD6061**
Wage Dispersion: Why Are Similar Workers Paid Differently? Trade Paper. MIT Press. Cambridge, MA. 2005. 160p. Zeuthen Lectures ISBN:0-262-63319-1, ISBN13: 978-0-262-63319-2. Dewey:331.2101.
Audience: **g,l,u,f.**

Myrdal, Gunnar **HD82.M9 1958**
[Development and Underdevelopment] Rich Lands and Poor: The Road to World Prosperity. New York: Harper. 1958.
Audience: **l,u,f.**

Robinson, Joan **HG4521.R66 1985**
The Accumulation of Capital. Ed. 3. Trade Paper. Porcupine Press, Inc. Philadelphia, PA. 1986. xvi, 440p. ISBN:0-87991-260-X, ISBN13: 978-0-87991-260-4. Dewey:330.1. LCCN:85-012465.
Audience: **u,f.**

Schumpeter, Joseph Alois **HB3711.S39 2006**
Business Cycles: A Theoretical, Historical, and Statistical Analysis of the Capitalist Process. Trade Cloth. Martino Publishing. Mansfield Centre, CT. 2005. 1122p. ISBN:1-57898-556-0, ISBN13: 978-1-57898-556-2. Dewey:338.5/42. LCCN:2005-047854.
Audience: **l,u,f.**

Schumpeter, Joseph Alois **HD75**
The Theory of Economic Development: An Inquiry into Profits, Capital, Credit, Interest and the Business Cycle. Redvers Opies (Translator), John E. Elliott (Introduction by). Trade Paper. Transaction Publishers. Somerset, NJ. 1982. 244p. Social Science Classics Ser. ISBN:0-87855-698-2, ISBN13: 978-0-87855-698-4. Dewey:330.1. LCCN:79-067059.
Audience: **u,f.**

Shiller, Robert J. **HG4910.S457 2000**
[e] Irrational Exuberance. E-Book. Princeton University Press. Princeton, NJ. ISBN:1-4008-1339-5, ISBN13: 978-1-4008-1339-1. Dewey:332.63/222/0973.
Audience: **g,l,u,f.** *Choice, 2000.*

Snowdon, Brian **HB172.5.S647 2003**
Conversations on Growth, Stability and Trade: An Historical Perspective. Trade Cloth. Edward Elgar Publishing, Inc. Northampton, MA. 2003. 512p. ISBN:1-84064-995-X, ISBN13: 978-1-84064-995-6. Dewey:339. LCCN:2002-075239.
Audience: **l,u,f.**

Solow, R. **HB501**
Capital Theory and the Rate of Return. Trade Cloth. Elsevier. New York, NY. 1971. ISBN:0-7204-3404-1, ISBN13: 978-0-7204-3404-0. Dewey:332.
Audience: **u,f.**

Solow, Robert **HD82.S593 2000**
Growth Theory: An Exposition. Ed. 2. Paper Text. Oxford University Press, Inc. New York, NY. 2000. 218p. ISBN:0-19-510903-1, ISBN13: 978-0-19-510903-0. Dewey:338.9. LCCN:99-048779.
Audience: **u,f.** *Choice, 2000.*

Solow, Robert M. & Taylor, John B. **HG540.A37 1995**
Inflation, Unemployment and Monetary Policy. Trade Cloth. MIT Press. Cambridge, MA. 1997. 136p. ISBN:0-262-19397-3, ISBN13: 978-0-262-19397-9. Dewey:332.4/973. LCCN:97-014979.
Audience: **u,f.**

Tinbergen, Jan **HD82 .T519**
The Design of Development. Trade Paper. Johns Hopkins University Press. Baltimore, MD. 1974. 128p. World Bank Research Publications ISBN:0-8018-0633-X, ISBN13: 978-0-8018-0633-9. Dewey:338.91.
Audience: **u,f.**

Tinbergen, Jan **HB3711.T483**
The Dynamics of Business Cycles: A Study in Economic Fluctuations. Trade Paper. Books on Demand. Ann Arbor, MI. 376p. ISBN:0-598-16824-9, ISBN13: 978-0-598-16824-5. Dewey:330.1. LCCN:50-006578.
Audience: **u,f.**

Tinbergen, Jan (Editor) **HD82 .T53**
On the Theory of Economic Policy. Trade Cloth. Elsevier Science & Technology Books. Saint Louis, MO. 1952. 78p. Contributions to Economic Analysis Ser., Vol. 1 ISBN:0-7204-3130-1, ISBN13: 978-0-7204-3130-8. Dewey:338.01.
Audience: **u,f.**

Tinbergen, Jan **JX1975**
Statistical Testing of Business-Cycle Theories. Trade Cloth. Agathon Press. Bronx, NY. 1968. 254p. ISBN:0-87586-009-5, ISBN13: 978-0-87586-009-1. Dewey:338.54/01/82. LCCN:68-016357.
Audience: **u,f.**

Willett, Thomas D. (Editor) **HB3743.P67 1988**
Political Business Cycles: The Political Economy of Money, Inflation, and Unemployment. Axel Leijonhufvud (Foreword by). Cloth Text. Duke University Press. Durham, NC. 1988. xxii, 521p. Duke Press Policy Studies ISBN:0-8223-0824-X, ISBN13: 978-0-8223-0824-9. Dewey:338.5/42/0973. LCCN:88-007148.
Audience: **l,u,f.** *Choice, 1989.*

Macroeconomics and Monetary Economics > Consumption/Investment/Savings

Evans, David S. & Schmalensee, Richard **HG3755.8.U6E94 2005**
Paying with Plastic: The Digital Revolution in Buying and Borrowing. Ed. 2. Trade Cloth. MIT Press. Cambridge, MA. 2005. 360p. ISBN:0-262-05077-3, ISBN13: 978-0-262-05077-7. Dewey:332.7/65/0973. LCCN:2004-055249.
Audience: **g,l,u,f.** *Choice, 2005.*

Garrison, Roger W. **HG220.A2G37 2001**
[e] Time and Money: The Macroeconomics of Capital Structure. E-Book. Routledge. New York, NY. 2000. ISBN:0-203-32038-7, ISBN13: 978-0-203-32038-9. Dewey:339.5/3.
Audience: **u,f.**

Hadjimatheou, George **HB801.H245 1987**
Consumer Economics after Keynes: Theory and Evidence of the Consumption Function. Cloth Text. Palgrave Macmillan. New York, NY. 1987. 224p. ISBN:0-312-00478-8, ISBN13: 978-0-312-00478-1. Dewey:339.4/7. LCCN:87-009427.
Audience: **u,f.** *Choice, 1987.*

Keister, Lisa A. **HC110.W4K44 2005**
Getting Rich: America's New Rich and How They Got That Way. Cloth Text. Cambridge University Press. New York, NY. 2005. 320p. ISBN:0-521-82970-4, ISBN13: 978-0-521-82970-0. Dewey:339.2/2/0973. LCCN:2005-000241.
Audience: **l,u,f.** *Choice, 2005.*

Levy, Frank **HC110.I5L47 1998**
The New Dollars and Dreams: American Incomes and Economic Change. Trade Cloth. Russell Sage Foundation. New York, NY. 1998. 256p. ISBN:0-87154-514-4, ISBN13: 978-0-87154-514-5. Dewey:339.2/0973. LCCN:98-020635.
Audience: **g,l,u,f.** *Choice, 1999.*

Luxemburg, Rosa **HB501.L94213 2003**
[e] The Accumulation of Capital. E-Book. Taylor & Francis Group. Philadelphia, PA. ISBN:0-203-36186-5, ISBN13: 978-0-203-36186-3. Dewey:332/.041.
Audience: **l,u,f.**

Perrotta, Cosimo **HB801**
Consumption As an Investment. Paper over Boards. Routledge. New York, NY. 2004. 400p. Routledge Studies in the History of Economics Ser., Vol. 71 ISBN:0-415-30619-1, ISBN13: 978-0-415-30619-5. Dewey:339.4/7. LCCN:2004-048162.
Audience: **l,u,f.**

Steedman, Ian **HB801.S775 2001**
Consumption Takes Time: Implications for Economic Theory. Paper over Boards. Routledge. New York, NY. 2004. 176p. The Graz Schumpeter Lectures, Vol. 4 ISBN:0-415-25099-4, ISBN13: 978-0-415-25099-3. Dewey:339.4/7. LCCN:00-062812.
Audience: **u,f.**

Warneryd, Karl Erik **HB822.W37 1999**
The Psychology of Saving: A Study on Economic Psychology. Trade Cloth. Edward Elgar Publishing, Inc. Northampton, MA. 1999. 400p. ISBN:1-84064-016-2, ISBN13: 978-1-84064-016-8. Dewey:332/.0415/019. LCCN:98-031080.
Audience: **u,f.** *Choice, 1999.*

Wiggin, Addison & Bonner, William **HB3722**
Empire of Debt: The Rise of an Epic Financial Crisis. Trade Cloth. John Wiley & Sons, Inc. Hoboken, NJ. 2005. 384p. ISBN:0-471-73902-2, ISBN13: 978-0-471-73902-9. Dewey:336.3/4/0973. LCCN:2005-023682.
Audience: **g,l,u,f.**

Macroeconomics and Monetary Economics > Central Banking and Monetary Policy/Interest Rates

Allen, Roy E. **HB3722**
The Political Economy of Financial Crises. Trade Cloth. Edward Elgar Publishing, Inc. Northampton, MA. 2004. 1,120p. The International Library of Writings on the New Global Economy Ser., Vol. 5 ISBN:1-84376-106-8, ISBN13: 978-1-84376-106-8. Dewey:338.5/42. LCCN:2004-053039.
Audience: **l,u,f.**

Bellet, Michel, et al. **HB501**
Evolution of the Market Process. Sandye Gloria-Palermo & Abdallah Zouzche (Authors). Paper over Boards. Routledge. New York, NY. 2004. 344p. Foundations of the Market Economy Ser., Vol. 70 ISBN:0-415-31683-9, ISBN13: 978-0-415-31683-5. Dewey:330.15/7. LCCN:2004-046729.
Audience: **f.**

Bernanke, Ben S., et al. **HG229.I457 1999**
Inflation Targeting: Lessons from the International Experience. Thomas Laubach, Frederic S. Mishkin & Adam S. Posen (Authors). Cloth Text. Princeton University Press. Princeton, NJ. 1998. 392p. ISBN:0-691-05955-1, ISBN13: 978-0-691-05955-6. Dewey:332.4/1. LCCN:98-039632.
Audience: **l,u,f.** *Choice, 1999.*

Bernanke, Ben S. & Woodford, Michael (Editors) **HG229.I45636 2004**
The Inflation -Targeting Debate. Trade Cloth. University of Chicago Press. Chicago, IL. 2005. 468p. National Bureau of Economic Research Conference Reports ISBN:0-226-04471-8, ISBN13: 978-0-226-04471-2. Dewey:332.4/1. LCCN:2004-055352.
Audience: **l,u,f.**

Cohen, Benjamin J. **HG3881.C5854 2004**
The Future of Money. Trade Cloth. Princeton University Press. Princeton, NJ. 2003. 312p. ISBN:0-691-11665-2, ISBN13: 978-0-691-11665-5. Dewey:332/.042. LCCN:2003-045983.
Audience: **g,l,u,f.**

Fisher, Irving **HB501**
The Nature of Capital and Income. Trade Cloth. Simon Publications, Inc. 2003. 427p. ISBN:1-932512-05-5, ISBN13: 978-1-932512-05-2. Dewey:332/.041. LCCN:28-019914.
Audience: **u,f.**

Fisher, Irving **HB119.F5.A25 1996**
The Theory of Interest. Trade Cloth. Pickering & Chatto Publishers, Ltd. London, 1996. v, 612p. The Works of Irving Fisher ISBN:1-85196-234-4, ISBN13: 978-1-85196-234-1. Dewey:330 S. LCCN:96-012209.
Audience: **u,f.**

Greider, William **HG2563.G72 1989**
Secrets of the Temple: How the Federal Reserve Runs the Country. Trade Paper. Simon & Schuster. New York, NY. 1989. 800p. ISBN:0-671-67556-7, ISBN13: 978-0-671-67556-1. Dewey:332.1/1/0973. LCCN:88-026696.
Audience: **g,l,u,f.** *Choice, 1988.*

Hansen, Alvin H. **HB3711.H315 2003**
Fiscal Policy and Business Cycles. Paper over Boards. Routledge. New York, NY. 2003. 464p. Routledge Library Editions Ser., Vol. 16:Economics, US/Can. Edition Ser. ISBN:0-415-31314-7, ISBN13: 978-0-415-31314-8. Dewey:330.1.
Audience: **l,u,f.**

Krooss, Herman E. (Editor) **HG2461 .K76**
A Documentary History of Banking and Currency in the United States. Paul Anthony Samuelson (Introduction by). Trade Paper. Chelsea House Publishers. Langhorne, PA. 1971. 1592p. ISBN:0-87754-460-3, ISBN13: 978-0-87754-460-9. Dewey:332/.0973.
Audience: **g,l,u,f.**

Mahadeva, Lavan & Sinclair, Peter **HG230.3.H69 2004**
How Monetary Policy Works. Paper over Boards. Routledge. New York, NY. 2004. 464p. Central Bank Governors' Symposium Ser. ISBN:0-415-34351-8, ISBN13: 978-0-415-34351-0. Dewey:339.5/3. LCCN:2004-046763.
Audience: **g,l,u,f.**

Mankiw, N. Gregory (Editor) **HG540.M653 1994**
Monetary Policy. Trade Cloth. University of Chicago Press. Chicago, IL. 1994. 356p. National Bureau of Economic Research Studies in Income and Wealth Ser. ISBN:0-226-50308-9, ISBN13: 978-0-226-50308-0. Dewey:332.4/973. LCCN:94-016029.
Audience: **u,f.**

Mayer, Thomas **HG501.M39 1990**
Monetarism and Macroeconomic Policy. Cloth Text. Edward Elgar Publishing, Inc. Northampton, MA. 1990. 208p. ISBN:1-85278-088-6, ISBN13: 978-1-85278-088-3. Dewey:339.5/3/0973. LCCN:90-041728.
Audience: **u,f.** *Choice, 1991.*

Mundell, Robert A. **HG0588.M7**
The Dollar and the Policy Mix: 1971. Trade Paper. Books on Demand. Ann Arbor, MI. 34p. Essays in International Ffnance Ser., No. 85 ISBN:0-598-38661-0, ISBN13: 978-0-598-38661-8. Dewey:332. LCCN:70-165467.
Audience: **u,f.**

Rogers, Colin D. **HG221 .R683 1989**
Money, Interest and Capital: A Study in the Foundations of Monetary Theory. Phyllis Deane, Gautam Mathur & Joan Robinson (Contribution by). Trade Paper. Cambridge University Press. New York, NY. 1989. 336p. Modern Cambridge Economics Ser. ISBN:0-521-35956-2, ISBN13: 978-0-521-35956-6. Dewey:332.4. LCCN:88-020364.
Audience: **l,u,f.** *Choice, 1990.*

Public

Alesina, Alberto & Rosenthal, Howard **HB3743 .A45 1995**
Partisan Politics, Divided Government, and the Economy. Trade Cloth. Cambridge University Press. New York, NY. 1995. 298p. Political Economy of Institutions and Decisions Ser. ISBN:0-521-43029-1, ISBN13: 978-0-521-43029-6. Dewey:338.5/42. LCCN:93-048512.
Audience: **u,f.** *Choice, 1995.*

Alesina, Alberto & Spolaore, Enrico **JC364.A39 2003**
The Size of Nations. Trade Cloth. MIT Press. Cambridge, MA. 2003. 272p. ISBN:0-262-01204-9, ISBN13: 978-0-262-01204-1. Dewey:320.1. LCCN:2003-051201.
Audience: **u.** *Choice, 2004.*

Buchanan, James M. **HJ193.B83 1999**
Demand and Supply of Public Goods, Vol. 5. Geoffrey Brennan, Hartmut Kleimt & Robert D. Tollison (Foreword by). Trade Cloth. Liberty Fund, Inc. Indianapolis, IN. 1999. 202p. The Collected Works of James M. Buchanan, Vol. 5 ISBN:0-86597-221-4, ISBN13: 978-0-86597-221-6. Dewey:336. LCCN:98-043536.
Audience: **u,f.**

Feldstein, Martin **RA981.A3**
Hospital Costs and Health Insurance. Trade Cloth. Harvard University Press. Cambridge, MA. 1981. 336p. ISBN:0-674-40675-3, ISBN13: 978-0-674-40675-9. Dewey:338.4/336211/0973. LCCN:80-018226.
Audience: **u,f.**

Fisher, Irving **HB119.F5.A25 1996**
Contributions to the Theory and Practice of Public Finance. Trade Cloth. Pickering & Chatto Publishers, Ltd. London, 1996. vi, 537p. The Works of Irving Fisher ISBN:1-85196-237-9, ISBN13: 978-1-85196-237-2. Dewey:330 S. LCCN:96-012212.
Audience: **u,f.**

Gruchy, Allan G. **HD99**
The Reconstruction of Economics: An Analysis of the Fundamentals of Institutional Economics. Donald R. Stabile & Norton T. Dodge (Preface by). Trade Cloth. Greenwood Publishing Group, Inc. Portsmouth, NH. 1987. 193p. Contributions in Economics and Economic History Ser., No. 71 ISBN:0-313-25679-9, ISBN13: 978-0-313-25679-0. Dewey:330. LCCN:86-025721.
Audience: **u,f.**

Hamermesh, Daniel S. **HD7096.U5**
Jobless Pay and the Economy. Trade Cloth. Johns Hopkins University Press. Baltimore, MD. 1977. 126p. Policy Studies in Employment and Welfare, No. 29 ISBN:0-8018-1927-X, ISBN13: 978-0-8018-1927-8. Dewey:368.4/4/00973. LCCN:76-047369.
Audience: **u,f.**

Hubbard, R. Glenn **HG173**
Money, the Financial System, and the Economy Plus Myeconlab Student Access Kit. Ed. 5. Book, Other. Addison-Wesley Longman, Inc. Boston, MA. 2004. 0p. ISBN:0-321-24639-X, ISBN13: 978-0-321-24639-4. Dewey:332.1.
Audience: **l,u,f.**

Kohler, Peter A. & Zacher, Hans F. **HD7091.E86 1982**
The Evolution of Social Insurance, Eighteen Eighty-One to Nineteen Eighty-One: Studies of Great Britain, France, Switzerland, Austria, and Germany. Cloth Text. Palgrave Macmillan. New York, NY. 1982. 500p. ISBN:0-312-27285-5, ISBN13: 978-0-312-27285-2. Dewey:368.4. LCCN:81-023258.
Audience: **g,u,f.**

Leach, John **HB171.5.L372 2004**
A Course in Public Economics. Cloth Text. Cambridge University Press. New York, NY. 2003. 434p. ISBN:0-521-82877-5, ISBN13: 978-0-521-82877-2. Dewey:330. LCCN:2003-046123.
Audience: **g,l,u,f.**

McGovern, George **HD7125.M255 2005**
Social Security and the Golden Age: An Essay on the New American Demographic. Trade Paper, Perfect. Fulcrum Publishing. Golden, CO. 2005. 76p. ISBN:1-55591-589-2, ISBN13: 978-1-55591-589-6. Dewey:368.4/300973. LCCN:2005-027907.
Audience: **l,u,f.**

Musgrave, Richard Abel **HJ141.M796 1986**
Public Finance in a Democratic Society: Collected Papers of Richard A. Musgrave, Vol. 1. New York : New York University Press. 1986. ISBN:0-8147-5428-7, ISBN13: 978-0-8147-5428-3.
Audience: **u,f.**

Musgrave, Richard Abel **HJ141.M8**
The Theory of Public Finance: A Study in Public Economy. New York, McGraw-Hill. 1959.
Audience: **u,f.**

Myers, Margaret G. **HJ9145**
A Financial History of the United States. Trade Cloth. Columbia University Press. New York, NY. 1970. xi, 451p. ISBN:0-231-02442-8, ISBN13: 978-0-231-02442-6. Dewey:332/.0973. LCCN:70-104900.
Audience: **g,l,u,f.**

Vickrey, William **HJ141**
Public Economics: Selected Papers by William Vickrey. Richard Arnott, Kenneth Arrow, Anthony B. Atkinson & Jacques H. Drèze (Editors). Trade Paper. Cambridge University Press. New York, NY. 1997. 569p. ISBN:0-521-59763-3, ISBN13: 978-0-521-59763-0. Dewey:336.
Audience: **u,f.**

Public > Government Taxation and Expenditure

HJ2051 .A59
The Budget of the United States Government Fiscal Year 2006. Ed. 2006. Perfect. Claitor's Publishing Division. Baton Rouge, LA. 2005. ISBN:1-59804-000-6, ISBN13: 978-1-59804-000-5. Dewey:353.007/22.
Audience: **g,l,u,f.**

Dixit, Avinash K. **HD87.D588 2004**
Lawlessness and Economics: Alternative Modes of Governance. Trade Cloth. Princeton University Press. Princeton, NJ. 2004. 176p. The Gorman Lectures in Economics ISBN:0-691-11486-2, ISBN13: 978-0-691-11486-6. Dewey:330.1. LCCN:2003-068992.
Audience: **l,u,f.**

Kaldor, Nicholas **HD9579.G5**
An Expenditure Tax. Cloth Text. Ashgate Publishing, Ltd. Aldershot, 1993. 256p. Modern Revivals in Economics Ser. ISBN:0-7512-0249-5, ISBN13: 978-0-7512-0249-6. Dewey:336.2713.
Audience: **u,f.**

Scholes, Myron S., et al. **KF6450.S33 2004**
Taxes and Business Strategy: A Planning Approach. Ed. 3. Merle M. Erickson, Edward L. Maydew, Terrence J. Shevlin & Mark A. Wolfson (Authors). Cloth Text. Prentice Hall PTR. Upper Saddle River, NJ. 2004. 576p. ISBN:0-13-146553-8, ISBN13: 978-0-13-146553-4. Dewey:343.7305/268. LCCN:2003-069004.
Audience: **l,u.**

Thurow, Lester C. **HJ2381.T53**
The Impact of Taxes on the American Economy. New York: Praeger. 1971.
Audience: **g,u,f.**

United States.; Bureau of the Budget **HJ2051.A5974**
The Federal Budget in Brief, July 1950/June 1951. [Washington : U.S. G.P.O.]. 1950.
Audience: **u,f.**

Vickrey, William S. **HJ2326**
Agenda for Progressive Taxation. Trade Cloth. Scholar's Bookshelf. Cranbury, NJ. 1972. ISBN:0-678-00617-2, ISBN13: 978-0-678-00617-7. Dewey:336.2/93. LCCN:73-107919.
Audience: **l,u,f.**

Microeconomics

Coman, Katharine **HC103**
The Industrial History of the United States. Trade Cloth. Ayer Company Publishers, Inc. Manchester, NH. 1973. Big Business, :Economic Power in a Free Society Ser. ISBN:0-405-05080-1, ISBN13: 978-0-405-05080-0. Dewey:330.9/73. LCCN:73-001999.
Audience: **g,l,u,f.**

McFadden, D. & Fuss, M. **HB241**
Production Economics: A Dual Approach to Theory and Applications. Trade Cloth. Elsevier. New York, NY. 1978. xx, 482p. Contributions to Economic Analysis Ser., Vols. 110 & 111 ISBN:0-444-85014-7, ISBN13: 978-0-444-85014-0. Dewey:338/.001. LCCN:78-019128.
Audience: **u,f.**

North, Douglass Cecil **HB99.5 .N67 1990**
Institutions, Institutional Change and Economic Performance. Randall Calvert & Thrainn Eggertsson (Contribution by). Trade Cloth. Cambridge University Press. New York, NY. 1990. 159p. Political Economy of Institutions and Decisions Ser. ISBN:0-521-39416-3, ISBN13: 978-0-521-39416-1. Dewey:302.3/5. LCCN:90-001673.
Audience: **l,u,f.** *Choice, 1991.*

Ricketts, Martin **HB98.2.N44 1988**
Neoclassical Microeconomics, Vol. I. Cloth Text. Edward Elgar Publishing, Inc. Northampton, MA. 1988. 384p. ISBN:1-85278-112-2, ISBN13: 978-1-85278-112-5. Dewey:338.5. LCCN:88-016345.
Audience: **l,u,f.**

Simon, Herbert A. (Author, Preface by) **HB172 .S5648 1997**
An Empirically-Based Microeconomics. Trade Cloth. Cambridge University Press. New York, NY. 1998. 235p. Raffaele Mattioli Lectures Ser., No. 10 ISBN:0-521-62412-6, ISBN13: 978-0-521-62412-1. Dewey:338.5. LCCN:98-232318.
Audience: **u,f.**

Smith, Vernon L. **HD52 .S6**
Investment and Production: A Study in the Theory of the Capital-Using Enterprise. Trade Cloth. Harvard University Press. Cambridge, MA. 1961. 352p. Harvard Economic Studies, No. 117 ISBN:0-674-46500-8, ISBN13: 978-0-674-46500-8. Dewey:338.01. LCCN:61-007395.
Audience: **u,f.**

Microeconomics > Concepts

Hayek, Friedrich A. **HB72**
Individualism and Economic Order. Trade Paper. University of Chicago Press. Chicago, IL. 1996. 280p. ISBN:0-226-32093-6, ISBN13: 978-0-226-32093-9. Dewey:330/.01. LCCN:48-004149.
Audience: **u,f.**

Pareto, Vilfredo **HB30.F59**
The Foundations of Contemporary and Historical Sociology. Trade Cloth. Institute for Economic & Financial Research. Albuquerque, NM. 1985. 156p. ISBN:0-86654-147-0, ISBN13: 978-0-86654-147-3. Dewey:330.947103.
Audience: **l,u,f.**

Pareto, Vilfredo **DG417**
The Historical Theory of the Ruling Class. Trade Cloth. American Classical College Press. Albuquerque, NM. 1979. The Most Meaningful Classics in World Culture Ser. ISBN:0-89266-193-3, ISBN13: 978-0-89266-193-0. Dewey:945.
Audience: **l,u,f.**

Pareto, Vilfredo **HM59**
Irrational Forces Contributing to the Ondulatory and Neurotic Course of History: The Theory of the Residues and of the Derivations. Trade Cloth. Institute for Economic & Political World Strategic Studies. Albuquerque, NM. 1990. 486p. ISBN:0-86722-233-6, ISBN13: 978-0-86722-233-3. Dewey:301.
Audience: **u,f.**

Pareto, Vilfredo **H1.A123**
The Organization of the Social System and the Compositon of the Social Forces, Set. Trade Cloth. American Classical College Press. Albuquerque, NM. 1984. 226p. ISBN:0-89266-474-6, ISBN13: 978-0-89266-474-0. Dewey:300.5.
Audience: **l,u,f.**

Pareto, Vilfredo **HB109.P3; HC302**
Pareto's Italian Letters. Trade Cloth. Foundation for Classical Reprints, The. Albuquerque, NM. 1981. 97p. ISBN:0-89901-371-6, ISBN13: 978-0-89901-371-8. Dewey:301.
Audience: **u,f.**

Pareto, Vilfredo
The Plutocratic Cycle in the Economic and Historical Growth of Mankind. Trade Cloth. Institute for Economic & Political World Strategic Studies. Albuquerque, NM. 1984. 147p. ISBN:0-86722-092-9, ISBN13: 978-0-86722-092-6.
Audience: **u,f.**

Pareto, Vilfredo
The Political and Historical Theory of the Elites. Trade Cloth. Foundation for Classical Reprints, The. Albuquerque, NM. 1987. 127p. ISBN:0-89901-296-5, ISBN13: 978-0 89901-296-4.
Audience: **l,u,f.**

Pareto, Vilfredo
Political Non-Logical Conduct and Theories Transcending Experience. Cloth Text. Institute for Economic & Political World Strategic Studies. Albuquerque, NM. 1990. 550p. ISBN:0-86722-231-X, ISBN13: 978-0-86722-231-9.
Audience: **u,f.**

Pareto, Vilfredo
The Problem of Leadership and the Conflict Between the Rational and the Irrational Forces in the Stream of History, Set. Trade Cloth. Institute for Economic & Political World Strategic Studies. Albuquerque, NM. 1990. 497p. ISBN:0-86722-229-8, ISBN13: 978-0-86722-229-6.
Audience: **u,f.**

Pareto, Vilfredo **HM141**
The Rise and Fall of the Elites: An Application of Theoretical Sociology. Lewis A. Coser & Walter W. Powell (Editors), Hans L. Zetterberg (Introduction by). Library Binding. Ayer Company Publishers, Inc. Manchester, NH. 1980. Perennial Works in Sociology ISBN:0-405-12110-5, ISBN13: 978-0-405-12110-4. Dewey:301.44/92. LCCN:79-007011.
Audience: **l,u,f.**

Pareto, Vilfredo **HM59**
The Mind and Society, Set. Arthur Livingston (Editor), Andrew Bongiorno (Translator). Trade Cloth. A M S Press, Inc. New York, NY. Studies in Fascism, :Ideology and Practice ISBN:0-404-16990-2, ISBN13: 978-0-404-16990-9. Dewey:301. LCCN:78-063704.
Audience: **u,f.**

Pareto, Vilfredo **HM101**
The Transformation of Democracy. Charles Powers (Editor), Renata Girola (Translator). Trade Paper. Transaction Publishers. Somerset, NJ. 1984. 93p. ISBN:0-87855-949-3, ISBN13: 978-0-87855-949-7. Dewey:303.4. LCCN:83-018089.
Audience: **u,f.**

Stigler, George J. **HB85.S668 1994**
Production and Distribution Theories. Douglas Irwin (Introduction by). Trade Paper. Transaction Publishers. Somerset, NJ. 1994. 392p. ISBN:1-56000-710-9, ISBN13: 978-1-56000-710-4. Dewey:330.1. LCCN:93-036977.
Audience: **u,f.**

Tinbergen, Jan **HB601 .T56**
Income Differences. Trade Paper. Elsevier Science & Technology Books. Saint Louis, MO. 1976. Professor Dr. F. De Vries Lectures, Vol. 10 ISBN:0-444-11054-2, ISBN13: 978-0-444-11054-1. Dewey:339.2.
Audience: **u,f.**

Tinbergen, Jan **HC79.I5 T39**
Income Distribution. Trade Cloth. Elsevier Science & Technology Books. Saint Louis, MO. 1975. 170p. ISBN:0-444-10832-7, ISBN13: 978-0-444-10832-6. Dewey:339.2. LCCN:74-030921.
Audience: **u,f.**

Varian, H. R. **HB172.V34 2005**
Intermediate Microeconomics: A Modern Approach. Ed. 7. Trade Cloth. W. W. Norton & Company, Inc. New York, NY. 2005. 778p. ISBN:0-393-92702-4, ISBN13: 978-0-393-92702-3. Dewey:338.5. LCCN:2005-055483.
Audience: **u,f.**

Microeconomics > Consumption/Consumer Behavior

Blackwell, Roger **HF5415.32 .E53**
Consumer Behavior. Ed. 10. Cloth Text. Thomson Delmar Learning. Albany, NY. 2005. 832p. ISBN:0-324-27197-2, ISBN13: 978-0-324-27197-3. Dewey:658.8/342.
Audience: **l,u,f.**

Bowles, Samuel **HB172.B67 2003**
Microeconomics: Behavior, Institutions, and Evolution. Trade Cloth. Princeton University Press. Princeton, NJ. 2003. 560p. The Roundtable Series in Behavioral Economics ISBN:0-691-09163-3, ISBN13: 978-0-691-09163-1. Dewey:338.5. LCCN:2003-049841.
Audience: **u,f.**

Camerer, Colin (Editor), et al. **HB74.P8A375 2003**
Advances in Behavioral Economics. George Loewenstein & Matthew Rabin (Editors). Trade Cloth. Princeton University Press. Princeton, NJ. 2003. 776p. The Roundtable Series in Behavioral Economics ISBN:0-691-11681-4, ISBN13: 978-0-691-11681-5. Dewey:330/.01/9. LCCN:2003-044481.
Audience: **l,u,f.**

Commons, John R. **JC327**
A Sociological View of Sovereignty: A Series of Articles in the American Journal of Sociology, 1899-1900. Trade Cloth. Scholar's Bookshelf. Cranbury, NJ. 1967. xiv, 107p. Reprints of Economic Classics Ser. ISBN:0-678-00090-5, ISBN13: 978-0-678-00090-8. Dewey:320.11. LCCN:64-017405.
Audience: **u,f.**

Dimitri, Nicola (Editor, Translator), et al. **HB74.P8C64 2003**
Cognitive Processes and Economic Behaviour. Marcello Basili

& Itzhak Gilboa (Editor, Translators). Paper over Boards. Routledge. New York, NY. 2003. 264p. Routledge Siena Studies in Political Economy ISBN:0-415-32005-4, ISBN13: 978-0-415-32005-4. Dewey:330/.01/9. LCCN:2003-046535.
Audience: **l,u,f.**

Figart, Deborah M. **HD4917.F54 2004**
Living Wage Movements: Global Perspectives. Paper over Boards. Routledge. New York, NY. 2004. 256p. Routledge Frontiers of Political Economy Ser., Vol. 58 ISBN:0-415-32002-X, ISBN13: 978-0-415-32002-3. Dewey:331.2/3. LCCN:2003-066692.
Audience: **l,u,f.**

Friedman, Milton **HB801 .F7**
Theory of the Consumption Function. Cloth Text. Princeton University Press. Princeton, NJ. 1957. 260p. General Ser., No. 63 ISBN:0-691-04182-2, ISBN13: 978-0-691-04182-7. Dewey:339.4.
Audience: **u,f.**

Garman, E. Thomas **HC110.C6G37 2006**
Consumer Economics Issues in America. Ed. 9. Cloth Text. Thomson Learning. Independence, KY. 2005. 576p. ISBN:0-7593-5262-3, ISBN13: 978-0-7593-5262-9. Dewey:381.30973. LCCN:2005-930774.
Audience: **g,l,u,f.**

Guesnerie, Roger **HB3732.G84 2005**
Assessing Rational Expectations: Eductive Stability in Economics. Trade Cloth. MIT Press. Cambridge, MA. 2005. 416p. ISBN:0-262-07258-0, ISBN13: 978-0-262-07258-8. Dewey:339.5/01/51. LCCN:2004-057855.
Audience: **l,u,f.**

Hadjimatheou, George **HB801.H245 1987**
Consumer Economics after Keynes: Theory and Evidence of the Consumption Function. Cloth Text. Palgrave Macmillan. New York, NY. 1987. 224p. ISBN:0-312-00478-8, ISBN13: 978-0-312-00478-1. Dewey:339.4/7. LCCN:87-009427.
Audience: **u,f.** *Choice, 1987.*

Haworth, J. T. & Veal, Anthony James (Editors) **HD6951**
Work and Leisure. Paper over Boards. Routledge. New York, NY. 2005. 256p. ISBN:0-415-25057-9, ISBN13: 978-0-415-25057-3. Dewey:306.3/6. LCCN:2004-009692.
Audience: **l,u,f.**

Perrotta, Cosimo **HB801**
Consumption As an Investment. Paper over Boards. Routledge. New York, NY. 2004. 400p. Routledge Studies in the History of Economics Ser., Vol. 71 ISBN:0-415-30619-1, ISBN13: 978-0-415-30619-5. Dewey:339.4/7. LCCN:2004-048162.
Audience: **l,u,f.**

Pixley, Jocelyn **HG101.P59 2004**
Emotions in Finance: Distrust and Uncertainty in Global Markets. Cloth Text. Cambridge University Press. New York, NY. 2004. 228p. ISBN:0-521-82785-X, ISBN13: 978-0-521-82785-0. Dewey:332/.042/019. LCCN:2004-020922.
Audience: **l,u,f.**

Shiller, Robert J. **HG4910.S457 2000**
[e] Irrational Exuberance. E-Book. Princeton University Press. Princeton, NJ. ISBN:1-4008-1339-5, ISBN13: 978-1-4008-1339-1. Dewey:332.63/222/0973.
Audience: **g,l,u,f.** *Choice, 2000.*

Simon, Herbert, et al. **HD30.23**
Economics, Bounded Rationality and the Cognitive Revolution. Massimo Edigi, Robin Marris & Ricardon Viale (Authors). Trade Cloth. Edward Elgar Publishing, Inc. Northampton, MA. 1992. 240p. ISBN:1-85278-425-3, ISBN13: 978-1-85278-425-6. Dewey:658.403. LCCN:91-042473.
Audience: **u,f.**

Sullivan, Teresa A., et al. **HG3766.S79 1999**
As We Forgive Our Debtors: Bankruptcy and Consumer Credit in America. Elizabeth Warren & Jay L. Westbrook (Authors). Trade Cloth. Beard Books, Inc. Chevy Chase, MD. 1999. 370p. ISBN:1-893122-15-8, ISBN13: 978-1-893122-15-4. Dewey:332.7/5/0973. LCCN:99-016954.
Audience: **g,l,u,f.** *Choice, 1990.*

Veblen, Thorstein **HG173**
Fisher's Capital and Income. Trade Paper. Kessinger Publishing, LLC. Whitefish, MT. 2004. ISBN:1-4191-1984-2, ISBN13: 978-1-4191-1984-2. Dewey:332.
Audience: **l,u,f.**

Veblen, Thorstein **D16.9**
The Later Marxism. Trade Paper. Kessinger Publishing, LLC. Whitefish, MT. 2004. ISBN:1-4191-6885-1, ISBN13: 978-1-4191-6885-7. Dewey:335.4119.
Audience: **u,f.**

Veblen, Thorstein **HB103.S6**
The Preconceptions of Economic Science. Trade Paper. Kessinger Publishing, LLC. Whitefish, MT. 2004. ISBN:1-4191-7851-2, ISBN13: 978-1-4191-7851-1. Dewey:330.153.
Audience: **l,u,f.**

Veblen, Thorstein **HD2326 .V4**
The Vested Interests and the Common Man. Trade Paper. Kessinger Publishing, LLC. Whitefish, MT. 2004. ISBN:1-4191-8668-X, ISBN13: 978-1-4191-8668-4. Dewey:330.1.
Audience: **l,u,f.**

Veblen, Thorstein B. **HC106**
Absentee Ownership and Business Enterprise in Recent Times: The Case of America. Trade Cloth. Scholar's Bookshelf. Cranbury, NJ. 1964. v, 445p. Reprints of Economic Classics Ser. ISBN:0-678-00048-4, ISBN13: 978-0-678-00048-9. Dewey:330.973. LCCN:63-023516.
Audience: **u,f.**

Veblen, Thorstein B. **HC106.3**
The Engineers and the Price System. Trade Cloth. Library Reprints, Inc. Temecula, CA. 1921. 169p. ISBN:0-7222-2685-3, ISBN13: 978-0-7222-2685-8. Dewey:338.
Audience: **l,u,f.**

Veblen, Thorstein B. **LA226**
The Higher Learning in America: A Memorandum on the Conduct of Universities by Business Men. Trade Cloth. Scholar's Bookshelf. Cranbury, NJ. 1965. viii, 286p. Reprints of Economic Classics Ser. ISBN:0-678-00055-7, ISBN13: 978-0-678-00055-7. Dewey:378.73. LCCN:65-015956.
Audience: **u,f.**

Veblen, Thorstein B. **JX1952**
An Inquiry into the Nature of Peace: And the Terms of Its Perpetuation. Trade Cloth. Scholar's Bookshelf. Cranbury, NJ.

1964. xiii, 367p. Reprints of Economic Classics Ser. ISBN:0-678-00052-2, ISBN13: 978-0-678-00052-6. Dewey:177. LCCN:63-023512.

Audience: **u,f.**

Veblen, Thorstein B. **HB831.V4 1998**
The Theory of the Leisure Class. Trade Cloth. Prometheus Books, Publishers. Amherst, NY. 1998. 411p. Great Minds Ser. ISBN:1-57392-219-6, ISBN13: 978-1-57392-219-7. Dewey:305.5. LCCN:98-016549.

Audience: **u,f.**

Veblen, Thorstein B. **HB34 .V38**
Essays in Our Changing Order: A Posthumous Collection of Papers from Periodicals. Leon Ardzrooni (Editor). Trade Cloth. Scholar's Bookshelf. Cranbury, NJ. 1964. 476p. Reprints of Economic Classics Ser. ISBN:0-678-00049-2, ISBN13: 978-0-678-00049-6. Dewey:330.81. LCCN:63-023514.

Audience: **u,f.**

Veblen, Thorstein B. **DD220**
Imperial Germany and the Industrial Revolution. Joseph Dorfman (Introduction by). Trade Cloth. Scholar's Bookshelf. Cranbury, NJ. 1964. xxi, 343p. Reprints of Economic Classics Ser. ISBN:0-678-00050-6, ISBN13: 978-0-678-00050-2. Dewey:943.08. LCCN:63-023510.

Audience: **u,f.**

Veblen, Thorstein B. **TS171**
The Instinct of Workmanship and the State of the Industrial Arts. Joseph Dorfman (Introduction by). Trade Cloth. Scholar's Bookshelf. Cranbury, NJ. 1964. xiii, 355p. Reprints of Economic Classics Ser. ISBN:0-678-00051-4, ISBN13: 978-0-678-00051-9. Dewey:745.2. LCCN:63-023515.

Audience: **u,f.**

Veblen, Thorstein B. **HF5351**
The Theory of Business Enterprise. Joseph Dorfman (Preface by), James H. Tufts (Contribution by). Trade Cloth. Scholar's Bookshelf. Cranbury, NJ. 1965. xx, 400p. Reprints of Economic Classics Ser. ISBN:0-678-00056-5, ISBN13: 978-0-678-00056-4. Dewey:330. LCCN:65-015957.

Audience: **u,f.**

Veblen, Thorstein B. **JZ5560.V43 1998**
The Nature of Peace. Warren J. Samuels (Introduction by). Trade Paper. Transaction Publishers. Somerset, NJ. 1997. 367p. ISBN:1-56000-973-X, ISBN13: 978-1-56000-973-3. Dewey:327.1/72. LCCN:97-049871.

Audience: **u,f.**

Veblen, Thorstein B. **HB34.V4 1990**
The Place of Science in Modern Civilization. Warren J. Samuels (Introduction by). Trade Paper. Transaction Publishers. Somerset, NJ. 1990. 539p. ISBN:0-88738-808-6, ISBN13: 978-0-88738-808-8. Dewey:330. LCCN:89-030458.

Audience: **g,l,u,f.**

Warneryd, Karl Erik **HB822.W37 1999**
The Psychology of Saving: A Study on Economic Psychology. Trade Cloth. Edward Elgar Publishing, Inc. Northampton, MA. 1999. 400p. ISBN:1-84064-016-2, ISBN13: 978-1-84064-016-8. Dewey:332/.0415/019. LCCN:98-031080.

Audience: **u,f.** *Choice, 1999.*

Wong, Stanley **HB801**
Foundations of Paul Samuelson's Revealed Preference Theory. Ed. 2. Paper over Boards. Routledge. New York, NY. 2005. 176p. Routledge INEM Advances in Economic Methodology Ser. ISBN:0-415-31157-8, ISBN13: 978-0-415-31157-1. Dewey:339.4/7. LCCN:2005-049787.

Audience: **u,f.**

Microeconomics > Market Structure and Pricing

Amihud, Yakov (Editor) **HD52.5**
Bidding and Auctioning for Procurement and Allocation: Proceedings of a Conference at the Center for Applied Economics, New York University. Trade Cloth. New York University Press. New York, NY. 1975. 220p. ISBN:0-8147-0558-8, ISBN13: 978-0-8147-0558-2. Dewey:658.7/2/0184. LCCN:75-027104.

Audience: **u,f.**

Bowles, Samuel **HB172.B67 2003**
Microeconomics: Behavior, Institutions, and Evolution. Trade Cloth. Princeton University Press. Princeton, NJ. 2003. 560p. The Roundtable Series in Behavioral Economics ISBN:0-691-09163-3, ISBN13: 978-0-691-09163-1. Dewey:338.5. LCCN:2003-049841.

Audience: **u,f.**

Fisher, Irving **HB135.F57 1991**
Mathematical Investigations in the Theory of Value and Prices: Appreciation and Interest. Library Binding. Scholar's Bookshelf. Cranbury, NJ. 1991. 226p. Reprints of Economic Classics Ser. ISBN:0-678-01456-6, ISBN13: 978-0-678-01456-1. Dewey:330/.01/51. LCCN:90-004603.

Audience: **u,f.**

O'Rourke, P. J. **PN6231.E295O76 1998**
Eat the Rich: A Treatise on Economics. Trade Cloth. Grove/Atlantic, Inc. New York, NY. 1998. 272p. ISBN:0-87113-719-4, ISBN13: 978-0-87113-719-7. Dewey:330/.02/07. LCCN:98-027100.

Audience: **g,l,u,f.**

Robinson, Joan **HB33**
Collected Economic Papers of Joan Robinson - Index. Cloth Text. MIT Press. Cambridge, MA. 1980. ISBN:0-262-18099-5, ISBN13: 978-0-262-18099-3. Dewey:330.

Audience: **l,u,f.**

Wu, Chi-Yuen **HG3821.W85 2003**
An Outline of International Price Theories. Paper over Boards. Routledge. New York, NY. 2003. 392p. Routledge Library Editions Ser., Vol. 64:Economics, US/Can. Edition Ser. ISBN:0-415-31366-X, ISBN13: 978-0-415-31366-7. Dewey:338.5/2.

Audience: **u,f.**

Microeconomics > Competition

Bowles, Samuel, et al. **HB171.5.B6937 2005**
Understanding Capitalism: Competition, Command, and Change. Ed. 3. Richard Edwards & Frank Roosevelt (Authors). Cloth Text. Oxford University Press, Inc. New York, NY. 2005. 608p. ISBN:0-19-513864-3, ISBN13: 978-0-19-513864-1. Dewey:330.12/2. LCCN:2004-024955.

Audience: **u,f.**

Clark, John Bates **HB771**
The Distribution of Wealth: A Theory of Wages, Interest and Profits. Trade Paper. University Press of the Pacific. Miami, FL. 2002. 476p. ISBN:1-4102-0155-4, ISBN13: 978-1-4102-0155-3. Dewey:339.2.
Audience: **u,f.**

Dixit, Avinash K. **HD87.D588 2004**
Lawlessness and Economics: Alternative Modes of Governance. Trade Cloth. Princeton University Press. Princeton, NJ. 2004. 176p. The Gorman Lectures in Economics ISBN:0-691-11486-2, ISBN13: 978-0-691-11486-6. Dewey:330.1. LCCN:2003-068992.
Audience: **l,u,f.**

Dobbs, Lou **HF5549.5.M3**
Exporting America: Why Corporate Greed Is Shipping American Jobs Overseas. Trade Paper. Warner Books, Inc. New York, NY. 2006. 208p. ISBN:0-446-69509-2, ISBN13: 978-0-446-69509-1. Dewey:331.13/72.
Audience: **l,u,f.**

Kleit, Andrew N. (Editor) **HD3611**
Antitrust and Competition Policy. Trade Cloth. Edward Elgar Publishing, Inc. Northampton, MA. 2005. 672p. Business Economics Ser., Vol. 2 ISBN:1-84376-319-2, ISBN13: 978-1-84376-319-2. Dewey:338.8/5. LCCN:2005-043329.
Audience: **l,u,f.**

Lambsdorff, Johann Graf, et al. **HB99.5.L36 2004**
The New Institutional Economics of Corruption. Markus Taube & Matthias Schramm (Authors). Paper over Boards. Routledge. New York, NY. 2004. 272p. Routledge Frontiers of Political Economy Ser., Vol. 64 ISBN:0-415-33368-7, ISBN13: 978-0-415-33368-9. Dewey:330. LCCN:2004-046797.
Audience: **u,f.**

Pigou, Arthur C. **HB99.3 .P58 1978**
The Economics of Welfare. Ed. 4. Trade Cloth. A M S Press, Inc. New York, NY. ISBN:0-404-14583-3, ISBN13: 978-0-404-14583-5. Dewey:330.15/5. LCCN:75-041213.
Audience: **l,u,f.**

Robinson, Joan **HB33**
Collected Economic Papers of Joan Robinson - Index. Cloth Text. MIT Press. Cambridge, MA. 1980. ISBN:0-262-18099-5, ISBN13: 978-0-262-18099-3. Dewey:330.
Audience: **l,u,f.**

Robinson, Joan **HB201 .R6**
Economics of Imperfect Competition. Cloth Text. Palgrave Macmillan. New York, NY. 1969. ISBN:0-312-23380-9, ISBN13: 978-0-312-23380-8. Dewey:330.1/62.
Audience: **l,u,f.**

Shubik, Martin **HB0771**
Strategy and Market Structure: Competition, Oligopoly and the Theory of Games. Trade Paper. Books on Demand. Ann Arbor, MI. 406p. ISBN:0-598-67945-6, ISBN13: 978-0-598-67945-1. Dewey:338.522. LCCN:58-014221.
Audience: **u,f.**

Microeconomics > Monopoly/Oligopoly

Kleit, Andrew N. (Editor) **HD3611**
Antitrust and Competition Policy. Trade Cloth. Edward Elgar Publishing, Inc. Northampton, MA. 2005. 672p. Business Economics Ser., Vol. 2 ISBN:1-84376-319-2, ISBN13: 978-1-84376-319-2. Dewey:338.8/5. LCCN:2005-043329.
Audience: **l,u,f.**

Norman, George & LaManna, Manfred (Editors) **HD2326.N42 1992**
The New Industrial Economics: Recent Developments in Industrial Organization, Oligopoly and Game Theory. Cloth Text. Edward Elgar Publishing, Inc. Northampton, MA. 1992. 272p. ISBN:1-85278-139-4, ISBN13: 978-1-85278-139-2. Dewey:338.8. LCCN:91-028153.
Audience: **u,f.** *Choice, 1993.*

Microeconomics > Employment/Unemployment

Adelman, Irma **HB523**
Dynamics and Income Distribution: Selected Essays of Irma Adelman, Vol. 2. Trade Cloth. Edward Elgar Publishing, Inc. Northampton, MA. 1995. 432p. Economists of the Twentieth Century Ser. ISBN:1-85898-052-6, ISBN13: 978-1-85898-052-2. Dewey:339.2. LCCN:94-048924.
Audience: **l,u,f.**

Bertola, Giuseppe, et al. **HB523.B47 2006**
Income Distribution in Macroeconomic Models. Reto Foellmi & Josef Zweimuller (Authors). Trade Cloth. Princeton University Press. Princeton, NJ. 2005. 416p. ISBN:0-691-12171-0, ISBN13: 978-0-691-12171-0. Dewey:339.2/01/51. LCCN:2005-048825.
Audience: **l,u,f.**

Cross, Rod (Editor) **HD5707.5 .N383 1995**
The Natural Rate of Unemployment: Reflections on 25 Years of the Hypothesis. Olivier J. Blanchard (Preface by). Trade Paper. Cambridge University Press. New York, NY. 1995. 398p. ISBN:0-521-48330-1, ISBN13: 978-0-521-48330-8. Dewey:331.13/72. LCCN:94-020097.
Audience: **u,f.**

Dobbs, Lou **HF5549.5.M3**
Exporting America: Why Corporate Greed Is Shipping American Jobs Overseas. Trade Paper. Warner Books, Inc. New York, NY. 2006. 208p. ISBN:0-446-69509-2, ISBN13: 978-0-446-69509-1. Dewey:331.13/72.
Audience: **l,u,f.**

Figart, Deborah M. **HD4917.F54 2004**
Living Wage Movements: Global Perspectives. Paper over Boards. Routledge. New York, NY. 2004. 256p. Routledge Frontiers of Political Economy Ser., Vol. 58 ISBN:0-415-32002-X, ISBN13: 978-0-415-32002-3. Dewey:331.2/3. LCCN:2003-066692.
Audience: **l,u,f.**

Hellinger, Stephen H. & Hellinger, Douglas A. **HD5730.5.A6**
Unemployment and the Multinationals: A Strategy for Technological Change in Latin America. Barbara Ward (Foreword by). Trade Cloth. Associated Faculty Press, Inc. New York, NY. 1976. viii, 158p. ISBN:0-8046-9126-6, ISBN13: 978-0-8046-9126-0. Dewey:331.1/098. LCCN:76-008484.
Audience: **l,u,f.**

Killingsworth, Mark R. **HD6061.2.U6K56 1990**
The Economics of Comparable Worth. Paper Text. W. E. Upjohn Institute for Employment Research. Kalamazoo, MI. 1990. 306p. ISBN:0-88099-085-6, ISBN13: 978-0-88099-085-1. Dewey:331.2/153. LCCN:89-025044.
Audience: **l,u,f.** *Choice, 1990.*

Levitan, Sar A., et al. **HC110.I5 L468 1993**
Working but Poor: America's Contradiction. Ed. 2. Frank Gallo & Issac Shapiro (Authors). Trade Cloth. Johns Hopkins University Press. Baltimore, MD. 1993. 168p. ISBN:0-8018-4574-2, ISBN13: 978-0-8018-4574-1. Dewey:362.5/0973. LCCN:92-034719.
Audience: **g,l,u,f.** *Choice, 1988.*

Levy, Frank & Murnane, Richard J. **HD6331.L48 2004**
The New Division of Labor: How Computers Are Creating the Next Job Market. Trade Cloth. Princeton University Press. Princeton, NJ. 2004. 200p. ISBN:0-691-11972-4, ISBN13: 978-0-691-11972-4. Dewey:331.1. LCCN:2003-065497.
Audience: **l,u,f.** *Choice, 2004.*

Robinson, Joan **HB171 .R63 1980**
Essays in the Theory of Employment. Trade Cloth. Hyperion Press, Inc. Westport, CT. 1985. ISBN:0-88355-812-2, ISBN13: 978-0-88355-812-6. Dewey:331/.01. LCCN:78-014138.
Audience: **u,f.**

Robinson, Joan **HB99.7 .R6**
Introduction to the Theory of Employment. Ed. 2. Cloth Text. Palgrave Macmillan. New York, NY. 1969. ISBN:0-312-43435-9, ISBN13: 978-0-312-43435-9. Dewey:330.15/6.
Audience: **u,f.**

Labor and Demographic

Abbott, Edith **HD6095 .A6**
Women in Industry. Library Binding. Reprint Services Company. Temecula, CA. 1993. 408p. ISBN:0-7812-5241-5, ISBN13: 978-0-7812-5241-6. Dewey:331.4/0973.
Audience: **u,f.**

Adelman, Irma & Morris, Cynthia T. **HC59.7**
Economic Growth and Social Equity in Developing Countries. Trade Paper. Stanford University Press. Palo Alto, CA. 1973. xiv, 260p. ISBN:0-8047-0888-6, ISBN13: 978-0-8047-0888-3. Dewey:338.91/172/4. LCCN:73-080616.
Audience: **l,u,f.**

Becker, Gary S. **HD4903.5.U58**
The Economics of Discrimination. Ed. 2. Trade Cloth. University of Chicago Press. Chicago, IL. 1971. x, 167p. ISBN:0-226-04115-8, ISBN13: 978-0-226-04115-5. Dewey:331.1/33/0973. LCCN:57-008578.
Audience: **l,u,f.**

Bertola, Giuseppe, et al. **HB523.B47 2006**
Income Distribution in Macroeconomic Models. Reto Foellmi & Josef Zweimuller (Authors). Trade Cloth. Princeton University Press. Princeton, NJ. 2005. 416p. ISBN:0-691-12171-0, ISBN13: 978-0-691-12171-0. Dewey:339.2/01/51. LCCN:2005-048825.
Audience: **l,u,f.**

Blau, Francine D. **HD6061**
Equal Pay in the Office. Trade Cloth. Lexington Books. Lanham, MD. 1977. ISBN:0-669-01003-0, ISBN13: 978-0-669-01003-9. Dewey:331.4/2/0973. LCCN:76-055077.
Audience: **u,f.**

Brue, Stanley L., et al. **HD4901.M15 2006**
Contemporary Labor Economics. Ed. 7. Campbell R. McConnell & David Macpherson (Authors). Cloth Text. McGraw-Hill Companies, The. New York, NY. 2005. 640p. ISBN:0-07-297860-0, ISBN13: 978-0-07-297860-5. Dewey:331. LCCN:2004-058186.
Audience: **g,l,u,f.**

Brunner, K. F. & Meltzer, A. (Editors) **HD5701.6**
Phillips Curve and Labor Markets. Trade Cloth. Elsevier. New York, NY. 1976. 164p. ISBN:0-444-11007-0, ISBN13: 978-0-444-11007-7. Dewey:331.12/0724.
Audience: **u,f.**

Cahuc, Pierre & Zylberberg, André **HD4901.C24 2004**
Labor Economics. Trade Cloth. MIT Press. Cambridge, MA. 2004. 872p. ISBN:0-262-03316-X, ISBN13: 978-0-262-03316-9. Dewey:331. LCCN:2003-067181.
Audience: **l,u,f.**

Danziger, Sheldon H. & Weinberg, Daniel H. (Editors) **HC110.P63F54 1986**
Fighting Poverty: What Works and What Doesn't. Trade Cloth. Harvard University Press. Cambridge, MA. 1986. 448p. ISBN:0-674-30085-8, ISBN13: 978-0-674-30085-9. Dewey:362.5/8/0973. LCCN:85-024848.
Audience: **g,l,u,f.** *Choice, 1986.*

DeLaat, Jacqueline **HD6060.5.U5D45 1999**
Gender in the Workplace: A Case Study Approach. Cloth Text. SAGE Publications, Inc. Thousand Oaks, CA. 1999. 112p. ISBN:0-7619-1478-1, ISBN13: 978-0-7619-1478-5. Dewey:306.3/6150973. LCCN:98-058080.
Audience: **l,u,f.**

Dooley, Peter **HB206.D66 2005**
Labour Theory of Value. Paper over Boards. Routledge. New York, NY. 2005. 272p. Routledge Frontiers of Political Economy Ser. ISBN:0-415-32821-7, ISBN13: 978-0-415-32821-0. Dewey:338.5/21. LCCN:2004-025763.
Audience: **l,u,f.**

Fernie, Sue & Metcalf, David (Editors) **HD6664.T72335 2005**
Trade Unions: Resurgence or Decline? Paper over Boards. Routledge. New York, NY. 2005. XVIII, 270p. Future of Trade Unions in Modern Britain Ser. ISBN:0-415-28411-2, ISBN13: 978-0-415-28411-0. Dewey:331.88/0941. LCCN:2004-029209.
Audience: **l,u,f.**

Gutek, Barbara A. **HD6060.3.G88**
Sex and the Workplace: The Impact of Sexual Behavior and Harassment on Women, Men, and Organizations. Trade Paper.

Books on Demand. Ann Arbor, MI. 238p. A Joint Publication in the Jossey-Bass Social and Behavioral Science Series and the Jossey-Bass Management Ser. ISBN:0-608-21673-9, ISBN13: 978-0-608-21673-7. Dewey:305.4/3. LCCN:85-045054.
Audience: **l,u,f.** *Choice, 1986.*

Hartmann, Heidi I. **HD6061.2.U6C653 1985**
Comparable Worth: New Directions for Research. E-Book. NetLibrary, Inc. Boulder, CO. 1985. ISBN:0-585-14284-X, ISBN13: 978-0-585-14284-5. Dewey:331.2/1.
Audience: **u,f.**

Heckman, James J. & Singer, Burton S. (Editors) **HD5706.L66 1985**
Longitudinal Analysis of Labor Market Data. Cloth Text. Cambridge University Press. New York, NY. 1985. 432p. Econometric Society Monographs, No. 10 ISBN:0-521-30453-9, ISBN13: 978-0-521-30453-5. Dewey:331.12/01/5195. LCCN:84-023253.
Audience: **u,f.**

Herman, Bohuslav & Tinbergen, Jan **HF499 .H45**
The Optimal International Division of Labour: A WEP Study. Trade Cloth. International Labour Office. Washington, DC. 1975. ISBN:92-2-101286-7, ISBN13: 978-92-2-101286-3. Dewey:331.1/18.
Audience: **u,f.**

Hicks, John Richard, Sir **HD4909.H5 1964**
The Theory of Wages. Ed. 2. New York: St Martin's Press. 1964.
Audience: **u,f.**

International Labour Office **HD5706**
World Labour Report 2000: Income Security and Social Protection in a Changing World. Geneva: ILO. 2000. ISBN:92-2-110831-7, ISBN13: 978-92-2-110831-3.
Audience: **l,u,f.**

Kreps, Juanita & Clark, Robert **HD8072.K777**
Sex, Age, and Work: The Changing Composition of the Labor Force. Trade Paper. Books on Demand. Ann Arbor, MI. 110p. Policy Studies in Employment and Welfare, Vol. 23 ISBN:0-608-06052-6, ISBN13: 978-0-608-06052-1. Dewey:331.0973. LCCN:75-034452.
Audience: **l,u,f.**

Levitan, Sar A., et al. **HC110.I5 L468 1993**
Working but Poor: America's Contradiction. Ed. 2. Frank Gallo & Issac Shapiro (Authors). Trade Cloth. Johns Hopkins University Press. Baltimore, MD. 1993. 168p. ISBN:0-8018-4574-2, ISBN13: 978-0-8018-4574-1. Dewey:362.5/0973. LCCN:92-034719.
Audience: **g,l,u,f.** *Choice, 1988.*

Levy, Frank **HC110.I5L47 1998**
The New Dollars and Dreams: American Incomes and Economic Change. Trade Cloth. Russell Sage Foundation. New York, NY. 1998. 256p. ISBN:0-87154-514-4, ISBN13: 978-0-87154-514-5. Dewey:339.2/0973. LCCN:98-020635.
Audience: **g,l,u,f.** *Choice, 1999.*

Levy, Frank & Murnane, Richard J. **HD6331.L48 2004**
The New Division of Labor: How Computers Are Creating the Next Job Market. Trade Cloth. Princeton University Press. Princeton, NJ. 2004. 200p. ISBN:0-691-11972-4, ISBN13: 978-0-691-11972-4. Dewey:331.1. LCCN:2003-065497.
Audience: **l,u,f.** *Choice, 2004.*

Mortensen, Dale T. **HD6061**
Wage Dispersion: Why Are Similar Workers Paid Differently? Trade Paper. MIT Press. Cambridge, MA. 2005. 160p. Zeuthen Lectures ISBN:0-262-63319-1, ISBN13: 978-0-262-63319-2. Dewey:331.2101.
Audience: **g,l,u,f.**

Nahuis, Richard **HC79.I5N34 2003**
Knowledge, Inequality and Growth in the New Economy. Trade Cloth. Edward Elgar Publishing, Inc. Northampton, MA. 2004. 400p. ISBN:1-84376-323-0, ISBN13: 978-1-84376-323-9. Dewey:331.2/2. LCCN:2003-048537.
Audience: **u,f.**

National Research Council Staff **HD6061.2.U6.W65**
Women, Work, and Wages: Equal Pay for Jobs of Equal Value. Trade Paper. National Academies Press. Washington, DC. 1981. 148p. ISBN:0-309-03177-X, ISBN13: 978-0-309-03177-6. Dewey:331.2/1. LCCN:81-082863.
Audience: **l,u,f.**

Passfield, et al. **HD6664**
The History of Trade Unionism. Sidney James Webb & Beatrice Webb (Authors). Trade Cloth. Library Reprints, Inc. Temecula, CA. 1902. 784p. ISBN:0-7222-2723-X, ISBN13: 978-0-7222-2723-7. Dewey:331.880941.
Audience: **u,f.**

Petty, William **HB3584.L6 P4**
Essays on Mankind and Political Arithmetic. Trade Paper. Kessinger Publishing, LLC. Whitefish, MT. 2004. ISBN:1-4191-1837-4, ISBN13: 978-1-4191-1837-1. Dewey:301.32942.
Audience: **u,f.**

Pigou, Arthur C. **HD5706 .P47**
Theory of Unemployment. Trade Cloth. Scholar's Bookshelf. Cranbury, NJ. 1981. ISBN:0-678-05079-1, ISBN13: 978-0-678-05079-8. Dewey:331.1/37/01. LCCN:67-024752.
Audience: **u,f.**

Reskin, Barbara F. & Hartmann, Heidi I. **HD6060.5.U5W66 1986**
Women's Work, Men's Work: Sex Segregation on the Job. E-Book. NetLibrary, Inc. Boulder, CO. 1986. ISBN:0-585-24096-5, ISBN13: 978-0-585-24096-1. Dewey:331.4133097.
Audience: **l,u,f.**

Ross, Andrew **HD4909.R66 2004**
Low Pay High Profile: The Global Push for Fair Labor. Trade Cloth. New Press, The. New York, NY. 2004. 256p. ISBN:1-56584-919-1, ISBN13: 978-1-56584-919-8. Dewey:331.2/15. LCCN:2003-061554.
Audience: **u,f.**

Spence, A. Michael **HD5707**
Market Signaling: Informational Transfer in Hiring and Related Screening Processes. Trade Cloth. Harvard University Press. Cambridge, MA. 1974. 224p. Harvard Economic Studies, No. 143 ISBN:0-674-54990-2, ISBN13: 978-0-674-54990-6. Dewey:331.1/1. LCCN:73-083419.
Audience: **u,f.**

Treiman, Donald J. & Hartmann, Heidi I. **HD6061.2.U6W65**
[e] Women, Work, and Wages: Equal Pay for Jobs of Equal Value. E-Book. NetLibrary, Inc. Boulder, CO. 1981. ISBN:0-585-14470-2, ISBN13: 978-0-585-14470-2. Dewey:331.2/1.
Audience: **l,u,f.**

Vargas, Zaragosa **HD8081.M6V36 2004**
Labor Rights Are Civil Rights: Mexican American Workers in Twentieth-Century America. Trade Cloth. Princeton University Press. Princeton, NJ. 2004. 368p. Politics and Society in Twentieth-Century America Ser. ISBN:0-691-11546-X, ISBN13: 978-0-691-11546-7. Dewey:331.6/272073/0904. LCCN:2004-042852.
Audience: **l,u,f.**

Zalk, Sue R. & Gordon-Kelter, Janice (Editors) **HQ1190.R49 1991**
Revolutions in Knowledge: Feminism in the Social Sciences. Trade Paper. Westview Press. Boulder, CO. 1992. 170p. ISBN:0-8133-0584-5, ISBN13: 978-0-8133-0584-4. Dewey:305.42. LCCN:91-027461.
Audience: **l,u,f.**

International

Balasubramanyam, V. N. **HC435.B294 2001**
Conversations with Indian Economists. Cloth over Boards. Palgrave Macmillan. New York, NY. 2001. 213p. ISBN:0-333-77774-3, ISBN13: 978-0-333-77774-9. Dewey:338.954. LCCN:00-044629.
Audience: **l,u,f.**

Barnett, Vincent **HB113.A2**
A History of Russian Economic Thought. Paper over Boards. Routledge. New York, NY. 2005. 176p. ISBN:0-415-35264-9, ISBN13: 978-0-415-35264-2. Dewey:330/.0947. LCCN:2005-004840.
Audience: **l,u,f.**

Bhagwati, Jagdish N. (Editor) **HF1411**
The New International Economic Order: The North-South Debate. Cloth Text. MIT Press. Cambridge, MA. 1977. xiv, 390p. ISBN:0-262-02126-9, ISBN13: 978-0-262-02126-5. Dewey:337/.09172/2. LCCN:77-007062.
Audience: **l,u,f.**

Bhagwati, Jagdish N. **HB171.5**
A Stream of Windows: Unsettling Reflections on Trade, Immigration and Democracy. Trade Paper. MIT Press. Cambridge, MA. 1999. 531p. ISBN:0-262-52265-9, ISBN13: 978-0-262-52265-6. Dewey:330.
Audience: **l,u,f.**

Bhagwati, Jagdish N. **HF1359**
Writings on International Economics. V. N. Balasubramanyam (Editor). Paper Text. Oxford University Press, Inc. New York, NY. 1999. 628p. Oxford India Paperbacks Ser. ISBN:0-19-564755-6, ISBN13: 978-0-19-564755-6. Dewey:337.
Audience: **u,f.**

Bhagwati, Jagdish N. **HF1411**
Essays in International Economic Theory: The International Factor Mobility. Robert Feenstra (Editor). Trade Paper. MIT Press. Cambridge, MA. 1986. 576p. ISBN:0-262-52121-0, ISBN13: 978-0-262-52121-5. Dewey:337.
Audience: **u,f.**

Bhagwati, Jagdish N. **HF1411**
Essays in International Economic Theory: The Theory of Commercial Policy. Robert Feenstra (Editor). Trade Paper. MIT Press. Cambridge, MA. 1986. 644p. ISBN:0-262-52120-2, ISBN13: 978-0-262-52120-8. Dewey:337.
Audience: **u,f.**

Bordo, Michael D. (Editor) **HG203.M69 1989**
Money, History, and International Finance: Essays in Honor of Anna J. Schwartz. Trade Cloth. University of Chicago Press. Chicago, IL. 1989. 279p. National Bureau of Economic Research Conference Report Ser. ISBN:0-226-06593-6, ISBN13: 978-0-226-06593-9. Dewey:332.4. LCCN:88-039779.
Audience: **u,f.**

Brunner, K. & Meltzer, A. H. (Editors) **HB3730**
Stabilization of the Domestic and International Economy. Trade Cloth. Elsevier. New York, NY. 1977. Carnegie-Rochester Conference Ser., Vol. 5 ISBN:0-7204-0709-5, ISBN13: 978-0-7204-0709-9. Dewey:339.5.
Audience: **l,u,f.**

Buck, Philip W. **HB91**
Politics of Mercantilism. Library Binding. Hippocrene Books, Inc. New York, NY. 1964. ISBN:0-374-91083-9, ISBN13: 978-0-374-91083-9. Dewey:330.151.
Audience: **u,f.**

Dimand, Robert W. **HF1379.O75 2004**
The Origins of International Economics, Vol. 1. Paper over Boards. Routledge. New York, NY. 2004. 400p. Origins of International Economics Ser. ISBN:0-415-31556-5, ISBN13: 978-0-415-31556-2. Dewey:382. LCCN:2003-060550.
Audience: **l,u,f.**

Dimand, Robert (Editor, Introduction by) **HF1379.O75 2004**
International Exchange Rates: The Origins of International Economics, Vol. 8. Paper over Boards. Routledge. New York, NY. 2004. 448p. Origins of International Economics Ser., Vol. 8 ISBN:0-415-31563-8, ISBN13: 978-0-415-31563-0. Dewey:382. LCCN:2003-060550.
Audience: **l,u,f.**

Eichengreen, Barry J. **HG3881 .E346 1990**
Elusive Stability: Essays in the History of International Finance, 1919-1939. Michael D. Bordo, Forrest Capie & Angela Redish (Contribution by). Trade Cloth. Cambridge University Press. New York, NY. 1990. 347p. Studies in Monetary and Financial History ISBN:0-521-36538-4, ISBN13: 978-0-521-36538-3. Dewey:332/.042/0904. LCCN:89-007189.
Audience: **u,f.** *Choice, 1990.*

Harrop, Jeffrey **HC241.2.H3935 1989**
The Political Economy of Integration in the European Community. Cloth Text. Edward Elgar Publishing, Inc. Northampton, MA. 1989. 224p. ISBN:1-85278-008-8, ISBN13: 978-1-85278-008-1. Dewey:337.1/42. LCCN:88-016590.
Audience: **l,u,f.** *Choice, 1990.*

Malinvaud, Edmond **HD82.I45 1979**
Economic Growth and Resources: Proceedings of the Fifth World Congress of the International Economic Association held in Tokyo, Japan, 1977. St. Martin's Press. 1979. ISBN:0-312-23314-0, ISBN13: 978-0-312-23314-3.
Audience: **l,u,f.**

Myrdal, Gunnar **HF1411**
Beyond the Welfare State: Economic Planning and Its International Implications. Trade Cloth. Greenwood Publishing Group, Inc. Portsmouth, NH. 1982. 287p. ISBN:0-313-23697-6, ISBN13: 978-0-313-23697-6. Dewey:338.91. LCCN:82-015819.
Audience: **l,u,f.**

O'Brien, Thomas J. **HG3881.O263 2005**
International Financial Economics: Corporate Decisions in Global Markets. Ed. 2. Trade Cloth. Oxford University Press, Inc. New York, NY. 2005. 316p. ISBN:0-19-517504-2, ISBN13: 978-0-19-517504-2. Dewey:658.15/99. LCCN:2004-025888.
Audience: **l,u,f.**

Stiglitz, Joseph E. **HC59.I5**
The Roaring 90s: A New History of the World's Most Prosperous Decade. Trade Cloth. Penguin Books, Ltd. London, 2003. 352p. ISBN:0-7139-9722-2, ISBN13: 978-0-7139-9722-4. Dewey:330.973/0929.
Audience: **g,l,u,f.** *Choice, 2004.*

Tinbergen, Jan **HF1411**
International Economic Integration. Ed. 2. Trade Cloth. Elsevier. New York, NY. 1965. ISBN:0-444-40573-9, ISBN13: 978-0-444-40573-9. Dewey:338.91.
Audience: **u,f.**

Tinbergen, Jan **JX1395**
The Rio Report: Reshaping the International Order: a Report to the Club of Rome Coordinator. Mass Market. Penguin Group (USA) Inc. New York, NY. 1977. ISBN:0-451-07708-3, ISBN13: 978-0-451-07708-0. Dewey:341.2.
Audience: **l,u,f.**

Tinbergen, Jan **HD82.T54**
Shaping the World Economy: Suggestions for an International Economicy Policy. New York : The Twentieth Century Fund. 1964.
Audience: **l,u,f.**

International > Trade

Aggarwal, Vinod K., et al. **HF1480.5.S77 2004**
The Strategic Dynamics of Latin American Trade. Ralph H. Espach & Joseph S. Tulchin (Authors). Trade Cloth. Stanford University Press. Palo Alto, CA. 2004. 368p. ISBN:0-8047-4899-3, ISBN13: 978-0-8047-4899-5. Dewey:382/.3/098. LCCN:2003-024441.
Audience: **l,u,f.**

Andersson, Ake E. & Andersson, David E. **HT388.G38 2000**
Gateways to the Global Economy. Trade Cloth. Edward Elgar Publishing, Inc. Northampton, MA. 2000. 416p. ISBN:1-84064-389-7, ISBN13: 978-1-84064-389-3. Dewey:382/.63. LCCN:00-037619.
Audience: **l,u,f.** *Choice, 2001.*

Batra, Ravi **HF1455**
The Myth of Free Trade: The Pooring of America. Trade Paper. Simon & Schuster. New York, NY. 1996. 288p. ISBN:0-684-83355-7, ISBN13: 978-0-684-83355-2. Dewey:382./710. LCCN:93-035764.
Audience: **l,u,f.**

Bhagwati, Jagdish N. **HF1713**
Free Trade Today. Trade Paper. Princeton University Press. Princeton, NJ. 2003. 144p. ISBN:0-691-11730-6, ISBN13: 978-0-691-11730-0. Dewey:382.7/1.
Audience: **g,u,f.**

Bhagwati, Jagdish N. (Editor) **HF1411.O497 2002**
Going Alone: The Case for Relaxed Reciprocity in Freeing Trade. Trade Cloth. MIT Press. Cambridge, MA. 2002. 592p. ISBN:0-262-02521-3, ISBN13: 978-0-262-02521-8. Dewey:337. LCCN:2002-016513.
Audience: **u,f.**

Bhagwati, Jagdish N. (Editor), et al. **HF1418.7.T73 1999**
Trading Blocs: Alternative Approaches to Analyzing Preferential Trade Agreements. Pravin Krishna & Arvind Panagariya (Editors), Paul Krugman & Lawrence H. Summers (Contribution by). Trade Cloth. MIT Press. Cambridge, MA. 1999. 606p. ISBN:0-262-02450-0, ISBN13: 978-0-262-02450-1. Dewey:382/.91. LCCN:98-030485.
Audience: **u,f.**

Bhagwati, Jagdish N., et al. **HF1379.B5 1998**
Lectures on International Trade. Ed. 2. Arvind Panagariya & T. N. Srinivasan (Authors). Trade Cloth. MIT Press. Cambridge, MA. 1998. 628p. ISBN:0-262-02443-8, ISBN13: 978-0-262-02443-3. Dewey:382. LCCN:98-010303.
Audience: **l,u,f.**

Brauer, Jurgen & Dunne, Paul J. **HD9743.A2A76 2004**
Arms Trade and Economic Development: Theory and Policy in Offsets. Paper over Boards. Routledge. New York, NY. 2004. 352p. Routledge Studies in Defence and Peace Economics, Vol. 8 ISBN:0-415-33106-4, ISBN13: 978-0-415-33106-7. Dewey:382/.456234. LCCN:2004-048122.
Audience: **l,u,f.**

Cardwell, Michael (Editor), et al. **K3870.A944 2003**
Agriculture and International Trade: Law, Policy, and the WTO. Margaret R. Grossman, C. P. Rodgers, M. N. Cardwell, C. Rogers & M. R. Grossman (Editors). Cloth Text. Oxford University Press, Inc. New York, NY. 2004. 352p. CABI Publishing Ser. ISBN:0-85199-663-9, ISBN13: 978-0-85199-663-9. Dewey:341.7/5471. LCCN:2003-004769.
Audience: **l,u,f.**

Chua, Amy **HF1359.C524 2003**
World on Fire: How Exporting Free Market Democracy Breeds Ethnic Hatred and Global Instability. Trade Cloth. Doubleday Publishing. New York, NY. 2002. 352p. ISBN:0-385-50302-4, ISBN13: 978-0-385-50302-0. Dewey:303.6. LCCN:2002-067676.
Audience: **g,l,u,f.** *Choice, 2003.*

Dimand, Robert (Editor, Introduction by) **HF1379.O75 2004**
Classical Theory of the Gains from Trade: The Origins of International Economics. Paper over Boards. Routledge. New

York, NY. 2004. 536p. Origins of International Economics Ser., Vol. 2 ISBN:0-415-31557-3, ISBN13: 978-0-415-31557-9. Dewey:382. LCCN:2003-060550.
Audience: **l,u,f.**

Dimand, Robert (Editor, Introduction by) **HF1379.O75 2004**
Developments in International Trade Theory: The Origins of International Economics. Paper over Boards. Routledge. New York, NY. 2004. 400p. Origins of International Economics Ser., Vol. 10 ISBN:0-415-31565-4, ISBN13: 978-0-415-31565-4. Dewey:382. LCCN:2003-060550.
Audience: **l,u,f.**

Dimand, Robert (Editor, Introduction by) **HF1379.O75 2004**
General Equilibrium in International Trade: The Origins of International Economics. Paper over Boards. Routledge. New York, NY. 2004. 440p. Origins of International Economics Ser., Vol. 7 ISBN:0-415-31562-X, ISBN13: 978-0-415-31562-3. Dewey:382. LCCN:2003-060550.
Audience: **l,u,f.**

Dimand, Robert (Editor, Introduction by) **HF1379.O75 2004**
Neoclassical Theory of International Trade: The Origins of International Economics. Paper over Boards. Routledge. New York, NY. 2004. 392p. Origins of International Economics Ser., Vol. 3 ISBN:0-415-31558-1, ISBN13: 978-0-415-31558-6. Dewey:382. LCCN:2003-060550.
Audience: **l,u,f.**

Driver, Rebecca & Thoenissen, C. **HG3821.E93 2004**
Exchange Rates, Capital Flows and Policy. Peter Sinclair (Editor). Paper over Boards. Routledge. New York, NY. 2004. 432p. Routledge International Studies in Money and Banking, Vol. 30 ISBN:0-415-35263-0, ISBN13: 978-0-415-35263-5. Dewey:332.4/56. LCCN:2004-053186.
Audience: **l,u,f.**

Feenstra, Robert C. **HF1379.F44 2003**
Advanced International Trade: Theory and Evidence. Trade Cloth. Princeton University Press. Princeton, NJ. 2003. 496p. ISBN:0-691-11410-2, ISBN13: 978-0-691-11410-1. Dewey:382/.01. LCCN:2003-048604.
Audience: **l,u,f.**

Feenstra, Robert C. (Editor), et al. **HF1411.P59116 1996**
The Political Economy of Trade Policy: Papers in Honor of Jagdish Bhagwati. Gene M. Grossman & Douglas A. Irwin (Editors), Paul Krugman, T. N. Srinivasan & Paul Anthony Samuelson (Contribution by). Trade Cloth. MIT Press. Cambridge, MA. 1996. 314p. ISBN:0-262-06186-4, ISBN13: 978-0-262-06186-5. Dewey:382/.3. LCCN:96-002479.
Audience: **u,f.**

Hamilton, Gary **HC427**
Commerce and Capitalism in Chinese Societies: Organisation of Chinese Economics. Paper over Boards. Routledge. New York, NY. 2006. XIV, 322p. ISBN:0-415-15704-8, ISBN13: 978-0-415-15704-9. Dewey:330.951. LCCN:2005-028808.
Audience: **l,u,f.**

Hessler, Julie **HF5429.6.S63H47 2004**
A Social History of Soviet Trade: Trade Policy, Retail Practices, and Consumption, 1917-1953. Trade Cloth. Princeton University Press. Princeton, NJ. 2004. 384p. ISBN:0-691-11492-7, ISBN13: 978-0-691-11492-7. Dewey:381/.1/094709041. LCCN:2003-048612.
Audience: **l,u,f.** *Choice, 2004.*

Horwich, George & Samuelson, Paul Anthony (Editors) **HB171**
Trade, Stability, and Macroeconomics: Essays in Honor of Lloyd A. Metzler. Trade Cloth. Elsevier Science & Technology Books. Saint Louis, MO. 1974. Economic Theory and Mathematical Economics Ser. ISBN:0-12-356750-5, ISBN13: 978-0-12-356750-5. Dewey:339.
Audience: **u,f.**

Irwin, Douglas A. **HF1756.I68 2002**
Free Trade under Fire. Cloth Text. Princeton University Press. Princeton, NJ. 2002. 288p. ISBN:0-691-08843-8, ISBN13: 978-0-691-08843-3. Dewey:382/.71. LCCN:2001-043159.
Audience: **g,l,u,f.** *Choice, 2003.*

Martijn, Jan K. **HG3823.M38 1993**
Exchange-Rate Veriability and Trade: Essays on the Impact of Exchange-Rate Variability on Trade Policy and Trade Flows. Trade Paper. Purdue University Press. West Lafayette, IN. 1993. 275p. Tinbergen Institute Research Ser. ISBN:90-5170-089-X, ISBN13: 978-90-5170-089-3. Dewey:332.45. LCCN:93-165196.
Audience: **u,f.**

Mun, Thomas **HF3508.E2 M9 1971**
A Discourse of Trade, from England unto the East-Indies. Trade Cloth. Scholar's Bookshelf. Cranbury, NJ. 1971. 58p. Reprints of Economic Classics Ser. ISBN:0-678-00873-6, ISBN13: 978-0-678-00873-7. Dewey:382/.0942/0598. LCCN:68-030534.
Audience: **u,f.**

Navaretti, Giorgio Barba & Venables, Anthony J. **HD2755.5.B368 2005**
Multinational Firms in the World Economy. Trade Cloth. Princeton University Press. Princeton, NJ. 2004. 336p. ISBN:0-691-11920-1, ISBN13: 978-0-691-11920-5. Dewey:338.8/8. LCCN:2004-050592.
Audience: **l,u,f.**

Nelson, Douglas R. & Vandenbussche, Hylke (Editors) **HF1425**
The WTO and Anti-Dumping. J. Anderson, B. Blonigen, R. Feinberg, J. M. Finger, B. Hoekman, C. Krupp, M. Leidy, T. Prusa, R. Staiger & R. Willig (Contribution by). Trade Cloth. Edward Elgar Publishing, Inc. Northampton, MA. 2005. 1,248p. Critical Perspectives on the Global Trading System and the Wto Ser., Vol. 7 ISBN:1-84376-602-7, ISBN13: 978-1-84376-602-5. Dewey:382/.63. LCCN:2005-049499.
Audience: **l,u,f.**

Rima, Ingrid H. (Editor) **HF1359**
The Political Economy of Global Restructuring: Economic Organization and Production, Vol. 1. Trade Cloth. Edward Elgar Publishing, Inc. Northampton, MA. 1993. 256p. ISBN:1-85278-638-8, ISBN13: 978-1-85278-638-0. Dewey:337. LCCN:93-012027.
Audience: **u,f.** *Choice, 1994.*

Sampson, Gary & Whalley, John (Editors) **HF1385**
The WTO, Trade and the Environment. W. Antweiler, J. Bhagwati, B. Copeland, G. Grossman, A. Krueger, R. E. B. Lucas & T. N. Srinivasan (Contribution by). Trade Cloth. Edward Elgar Publishing, Inc. Northampton, MA. 2005. 736p.

Critical Perspectives on the Global Trading System and the Wto Ser., Vol. 5 ISBN:1-84376-839-9, ISBN13: 978-1-84376-839-5. Dewey:382/.92. LCCN:2005-043326.

Audience: **u,f.**

Sellekaerts, Willy (Editor) **HF1359**
International Trade and Finance: Essays in Honour of Jan Tinbergen. Trade Cloth. M. E. Sharpe Inc. Armonk, NY. 1974. ISBN:0-87332-054-9, ISBN13: 978-0-87332-054-2. Dewey:337. LCCN:73-092710.

Audience: **u,f.**

Snowdon, Brian **HB172.5.S647 2003**
Conversations on Growth, Stability and Trade: An Historical Perspective. Trade Cloth. Edward Elgar Publishing, Inc. Northampton, MA. 2003. 512p. ISBN:1-84064-995-X, ISBN13: 978-1-84064-995-6. Dewey:339. LCCN:2002-075239.

Audience: **l,u,f.**

Streissler, Erich W. **HG3821.S77 2002**
Exchange Rates and International Finance Markets: An Asset-Theoretic Perspective with Schumpeterian Innovation. Paper over Boards. Routledge. New York, NY. 2002. 160p. The Graz Schumpeter Lectures, Vol. 5 ISBN:0-415-27746-9, ISBN13: 978-0-415-27746-4. Dewey:332.4/56. LCCN:2001-051063.

Audience: **u,f.**

Taussig, Frank W. **HF1756.T34 1971**
Some Aspects of the Tariff Question: An Examination of the Development of American Industries Under Protection. Trade Cloth. A M S Press, Inc. New York, NY. 1971. xiii, 499p. ISBN:0-404-06348-9, ISBN13: 978-0-404-06348-1. Dewey:382/.7. LCCN:72-137297.

Audience: **u,f.**

United Nations Development Programme Staff **HD72**
Human Development Report 2005: International Cooperation at a Crossroads: Aid, Trade and Security in an Unequal World. Trade Paper. Oxford University Press, Inc. New York, NY. 2005. 388p. ISBN:0-19-530511-6, ISBN13: 978-0-19-530511-1. Dewey:338.9.

Audience: **g,l,u,f.** *Choice, 2006.*

Wonnacott, Ronald J. & Wonnacott, Gordon P. **HF1766 .W6**
Free Trade Between the United States and Canada: The Potential Economic Effects. Trade Cloth. Harvard University Press. Cambridge, MA. 1967. 450p. Harvard Economic Studies, No. 129 ISBN:0-674-31900-1, ISBN13: 978-0-674-31900-4. Dewey:382/.09/71073. LCCN:67-017323.

Audience: **l,u,f.**

International > Economic Development

Adelman, Irma & Morris, Cynthia T. **HC59.7**
Economic Growth and Social Equity in Developing Countries. Trade Paper. Stanford University Press. Palo Alto, CA. 1973. xiv, 260p. ISBN:0-8047-0888-6, ISBN13: 978-0-8047-0888-3. Dewey:338.91/172/4. LCCN:73-080616.

Audience: **l,u,f.**

Adelman, Irma & Morris, Cynthia T. **HC0059.7.A73**
Society, Politics, and Economic Development: A Quantitative Approach. Trade Paper. Books on Demand. Ann Arbor, MI. 317p. ISBN:0-608-06037-2, ISBN13: 978-0-608-06037-8. Dewey:338.9009172. LCCN:67-021582.

Audience: **l,u,f.**

Adelman, Irma & Thorbecke, Erik (Editors) **HD0082**
The Theory and Design of Economic Development. Trade Paper. Books on Demand. Ann Arbor, MI. 438p. ISBN:0-598-25705-5, ISBN13: 978-0-598-25705-5. Dewey:338.9. LCCN:66-023004.

Audience: **l,u,f.**

Allen, G. C. & Donnithorne, Audrey G. **HD82**
Development Economics. Paper over Boards. Routledge. New York, NY. 2003. 328p. Routledge Library Editions Ser., Vol. 2:Economics, US/Can. Edition Ser. ISBN:0-415-31296-5, ISBN13: 978-0-415-31296-7. Dewey:338.9.

Audience: **l,u,f.**

Bird, Graham (Editor) **HJ8899.T48 1989**
Third World Debt: The Search for a Solution. Trade Cloth. Edward Elgar Publishing, Inc. Northampton, MA. 1989. 256p. ISBN:1-85278-162-9, ISBN13: 978-1-85278-162-0. Dewey:336.3/435/091724. LCCN:89-017072.

Audience: **l,u,f.**

Black, Richard & White, Howard (Editors) **HD82.T327 2003**
Targeting Development. Paper over Boards. Routledge. New York, NY. 2003. 384p. Studies in Development Economics, Vol. 36 ISBN:0-415-30376-1, ISBN13: 978-0-415-30376-7. Dewey:362.5/56/091724. LCCN:2003-047096.

Audience: **l,u,f.**

Brauer, Jurgen & Dunne, Paul J. **HD9743.A2A76 2004**
Arms Trade and Economic Development: Theory and Policy in Offsets. Paper over Boards. Routledge. New York, NY. 2004. 352p. Routledge Studies in Defence and Peace Economics, Vol. 8 ISBN:0-415-33106-4, ISBN13: 978-0-415-33106-7. Dewey:382/.456234. LCCN:2004-048122.

Audience: **l,u,f.**

Cypher, James M. & Dietz, James L. **HD75**
The Process of Economic Development. Ed. 2. Paper over Boards. Routledge. New York, NY. 2004. 568p. ISBN:0-415-25415-9, ISBN13: 978-0-415-25415-1. Dewey:338.9. LCCN:2003-058553.

Audience: **l,u,f.**

De Kadt, Emanuel & Williams, Gavin (Editors) **HM548**
Sociology and Development. Library Binding. Routledge. New York, NY. 2003. 392p. International Behavioural and Social Sciences Ser., Vol. 106:Classics from the Tavistock Press ISBN:0-415-26498-7, ISBN13: 978-0-415-26498-3. Dewey:306.3.

Audience: **l,u,f.**

Ghatak, Subrata **HD72**
Introduction to Development Economics. Ed. 4. Paper over Boards. Routledge. New York, NY. 2003. 480p.

ISBN:0-415-28075-3, ISBN13: 978-0-415-28075-4. Dewey:338.9. LCCN:2004-351624.
Audience: **l,u,f.**

Hall, Derek R. **G155.A1T589525 2003**
Tourism and Transition: Governance, Transformation and Development. Cloth Text. CAB International. Wallingford, 2004. 252p. CABI Publishing Ser. ISBN:0-85199-748-1, ISBN13: 978-0-85199-748-3. Dewey:338.4/791. LCCN:2003-020954.
Audience: **l,u,f.**

Hamilton, Gary **HC427**
Commerce and Capitalism in Chinese Societies: Organisation of Chinese Economics. Paper over Boards. Routledge. New York, NY. 2006. XIV, 322p. ISBN:0-415-15704-8, ISBN13: 978-0-415-15704-9. Dewey:330.951. LCCN:2005-028808.
Audience: **l,u,f.**

Harvie, Charles & Lee, Boon-Chye (Editors) **HD2346.E18S87 2004**
Sustainable Growth and Performance in East Asia, Bk.. III. Trade Cloth. Edward Elgar Publishing, Inc. Northampton, MA. 2005. 392p. Studies of Small and Medium Size Enterprises in East Asia, Vol. 3 ISBN:1-84064-808-2, ISBN13: 978-1-84064-808-9. Dewey:338.6/42/095. LCCN:2004-058626.
Audience: **l,u,f.**

Henshall Momsen, Janet **HQ1240.5.D44M657**
Gender and Development. Ed. 2. Paper over Boards. Routledge. New York, NY. 2003. 288p. Routledge Perspectives on Development Ser. ISBN:0-415-26689-0, ISBN13: 978-0-415-26689-5. Dewey:305.3/09172/4. LCCN:2003-008539.
Audience: **l,u,f.**

Kalecki, Michal **HC59.7**
Essays on Developing Economies. Joan Robinson (Introduction by). Cloth Text. Brill Academic Publishers, Inc. Boston, MA. 1976. 208p. ISBN:0-391-00524-3, ISBN13: 978-0-391-00524-2. Dewey:330.9172/4. LCCN:75-040308.
Audience: **l,u,f.**

Kambhampati, Uma S. **HC59.7.K255 2004**
Development and the Developing World. Trade Cloth. Polity Press. Cambridge, 2004. 312p. ISBN:0-7456-1550-3, ISBN13: 978-0-7456-1550-9. Dewey:338.9/009172/4. LCCN:2003-017316.
Audience: **l,u,f.**

Leontief, Wassily **HC60.L443**
The Future of the World Economy: A United Nations Study. Trade Cloth. Oxford University Press, Inc. New York, NY. 1977. 118p. ISBN:0-19-502232-7, ISBN13: 978-0-19-502232-2. Dewey:338/.09. LCCN:77-072024.
Audience: **l,u,f.**

Lewis, Paul (Editor) **HB131.L48 2004**
Transforming Economics: Perspectives on the Critical Realist Project. Paper over Boards. Routledge. New York, NY. 2004. 336p. Economics As Social Theory Ser. ISBN:0-415-36966-5, ISBN13: 978-0-415-36966-4. Dewey:330/.01. LCCN:2004-046854.
Audience: **l,u,f.**

Lewis, W. Arthur **HD82**
Development Economics. Paper over Boards. Routledge. New York, NY. 2003. 208p. Routledge Library Editions Ser., Vol. 6:Economics, US/Can. Edition Ser. ISBN:0-415-31300-7, ISBN13: 978-0-415-31300-1. Dewey:338.9.
Audience: **l,u,f.**

Lewis, W. Arthur **HD82**
Development Economics. Paper over Boards. Routledge. New York, NY. 2003. 456p. Routledge Library Editions Ser., Vol. 7:Economics, US/Can. Edition Ser. ISBN:0-415-31301-5, ISBN13: 978-0-415-31301-8. Dewey:338.9.
Audience: **l,u.**

Little & Mirlees **HD47.L49**
Project Appraisal and Planning for Developing Countries. Cloth Text. Basic Books. New York, NY. 1974. xii, 388p. ISBN:0-465-06412-4, ISBN13: 978-0-465-06412-0. Dewey:309.2/12/091724. LCCN:73-091075.
Audience: **u,f.**

Lucas, Robert E. B. **JV6118.L83 2005**
International Migration and Economic Development: Lessons from Low-Income Countries. Trade Cloth. Edward Elgar Publishing, Inc. Northampton, MA. 2005. 384p. ISBN:1-84542-383-6, ISBN13: 978-1-84542-383-4. Dewey:337. LCCN:2005-046188.
Audience: **l,u,f.**

Maxwell, Daniel G. & Barrett, Christopher B. **HV696.F6B375 2005**
Food Aid after Fifty Years: Recasting its Role. Paper over Boards. Routledge. New York, NY. 2005. 336p. Priorities for Development Economics Ser. ISBN:0-415-70124-4, ISBN13: 978-0-415-70124-2. Dewey:363.8/56/0973. LCCN:2004-023634.
Audience: **g,l,u,f.** *Choice, 2006.*

Morris, Cynthia T. & Adelman, Irma **HC0051.M645**
Comparative Patterns of Economic Development, 1850-1914. Trade Paper. Books on Demand. Ann Arbor, MI. 592p. Johns Hopkins Studies in Development ISBN:0-608-07406-3, ISBN13: 978-0-608-07406-1. Dewey:338.9/009. LCCN:87-045480.
Audience: **l,u,f.** *Choice, 1988.*

Myrdal, Gunnar **HC59.7**
Challenge of World Poverty: A World Poverty Program in Outline. Trade Cloth. Knopf Publishing Group. New York, NY. 1970. ISBN:0-394-41895-6, ISBN13: 978-0-394-41895-7. Dewey:338.91/172/4. LCCN:78-079797.
Audience: **l,u,f.**

Nahuis, Richard **HC79.I5N34 2003**
Knowledge, Inequality and Growth in the New Economy. Trade Cloth. Edward Elgar Publishing, Inc. Northampton, MA. 2004. 400p. ISBN:1-84376-323-0, ISBN13: 978-1-84376-323-9. Dewey:331.2/2. LCCN:2003-048537.
Audience: **u,f.**

Parente, Stephen L. & Prescott, Edward C. **HD82**
Barriers to Riches. Trade Paper. MIT Press. Cambridge, MA.

2002. 184p. Walras-Pareto Lectures ISBN:0-262-66130-6, ISBN13: 978-0-262-66130-0. Dewey:338.9.
Audience: **u,f.** *Choice, 2001.*

Power, Marcus **HF1021**
Rethinking Development Geographies. Paper over Boards. Routledge. New York, NY. 2003. 288p. ISBN:0-415-25078-1, ISBN13: 978-0-415-25078-8. Dewey:338.9. LCCN:2002-155680.
Audience: **u,f.**

Ramsamy, Edward **HC60**
World Bank and Urban Development: From Projects to Policy. Paper over Boards. Routledge. New York, NY. 2006. XVIII, 229p. Routledge Studies in Development and Society Ser. ISBN:0-415-34439-5, ISBN13: 978-0-415-34439-5. Dewey:338.9009173/2. LCCN:2005-033644.
Audience: **l,u,f.**

Robinson, Joan **HC59.7**
Aspects of Development and Underdevelopment. Trade Cloth. Cambridge University Press. New York, NY. 1979. 170p. Modern Cambridge Economics Ser. ISBN:0-521-22637-6, ISBN13: 978-0-521-22637-0. Dewey:330.9/172/4. LCCN:78-025610.
Audience: **u,f.**

Robinson, Joan **HB171 .R628**
Essays in the Theory of Economic Growth. Cloth Text. Palgrave Macmillan. New York, NY. 1969. ISBN:0-312-26390-2, ISBN13: 978-0-312-26390-4. Dewey:330.1.
Audience: **u,f.**

Roitman, Janet L. **HJ3069.R64 2005**
Fiscal Disobedience: An Anthropology of Economic Regulation in Central Africa. Trade Cloth. Princeton University Press. Princeton, NJ. 2004. 216p. In-Formation Ser. ISBN:0-691-11869-8, ISBN13: 978-0-691-11869-7. Dewey:330.96711. LCCN:2003-069017.
Audience: **u,f.**

Root, Hilton L. **HD87.R66 2006**
Capital and Collusion: The Political Logic of Global Economic Development. Trade Cloth. Princeton University Press. Princeton, NJ. 2005. 280p. ISBN:0-691-12407-8, ISBN13: 978-0-691-12407-0. Dewey:338.9/009172/4. LCCN:2005-045830.
Audience: **u,f.** *Choice, 2006.*

Sellekaerts, Willy (Editor) **HF1025**
Economic Development and Planning: Essays in Honour of Jan Tinbergen. Trade Cloth. M. E. Sharpe Inc. Armonk, NY. 1974. 288p. ISBN:0-87332-055-7, ISBN13: 978-0-87332-055-9. Dewey:330.9. LCCN:73-092712.
Audience: **u,f.**

Tinbergen, Jan **HD7533.A3**
Some Principles of Regional Planning. Trade Paper. Books on Demand. Ann Arbor, MI. 23p. Nederlandsch Economisch Institute, Rotterdam Publication Ser., No. 21 ISBN:0-598-56338-5, ISBN13: 978-0-598-56338-5. Dewey:338.9.
Audience: **u,f.**

Ward, Barbara (Editor), et al. **HC59.7**
Widening Gap: Development in the 1970's. J. D. Runnalls & Lenore D'Anjou (Editors). Trade Cloth. Columbia University Press. New York, NY. 1971. xii, 372p. ISBN:0-231-03538-1, ISBN13: 978-0-231-03538-5. Dewey:330.9/1724. LCCN:75-151617.
Audience: **u,f.**

Wolfe, J. N. (Editor) **HB201 .V349**
Value, Capital and Growth. Trade Paper. Transaction Publishers. Somerset, NJ. 2006. 563p. ISBN:0-202-30846-4, ISBN13: 978-0-202-30846-3. Dewey:330. LCCN:2005-046696.
Audience: **u,f.**

World Bank Staff **HD82**
World Development Report 2004: Making Services Work for Poor People. Ed. 2004. Trade Cloth. World Bank Publications. Washington, DC. 2003. 288p. A World Bank Publication ISBN:0-8213-5537-6, ISBN13: 978-0-8213-5537-4. Dewey:338.9/109051.
Audience: **g,l,u,f.** *Choice, 2004.*

World Bank Staff **HD82**
World Development Report 2006: Equity and Development. Ed. 2006. Trade Paper. World Bank Publications. Washington, DC. 2005. 24p. World Development Report ISBN:0-8213-6251-8, ISBN13: 978-0-8213-6251-8. Dewey:338.9109051.
Audience: **g,l,u,f.** *Choice, 2006.*

International > Globalization

Allen, Roy E. **HB3722.A36 1994**
Financial Crises and Recession in the Global Economy. Trade Cloth. Edward Elgar Publishing, Inc. Northampton, MA. 1994. 200p. Studies in International Political Economy ISBN:1-85278-997-2, ISBN13: 978-1-85278-997-8. Dewey:338.5/42. LCCN:93-050632.
Audience: **l,u,f.** *Choice, 2000, 1995.*

Allen, Roy E. **HB3722**
The Political Economy of Financial Crises. Trade Cloth. Edward Elgar Publishing, Inc. Northampton, MA. 2004. 1,120p. The International Library of Writings on the New Global Economy Ser., Vol. 5 ISBN:1-84376-106-8, ISBN13: 978-1-84376-106-8. Dewey:338.5/42. LCCN:2004-053039.
Audience: **l,u,f.**

Andersson, Ake E. & Andersson, David E. **HT388.G38 2000**
Gateways to the Global Economy. Trade Cloth. Edward Elgar Publishing, Inc. Northampton, MA. 2000. 416p. ISBN:1-84064-389-7, ISBN13: 978-1-84064-389-3. Dewey:382/.63. LCCN:00-037619.
Audience: **l,u,f.** *Choice, 2001.*

Barry Jones, R. **HB91.J66 1986**
Conflict and Control in the World Economy: Contemporary Economic Realism and Neo-Mercantilism. Cloth Text. Brill Academic Publishers, Inc. Boston, MA. 1986. 288p. ISBN:0-391-03413-8, ISBN13: 978-0-391-03413-6. Dewey:338.9. LCCN:86-000219.
Audience: **l,u,f.** *Choice, 1986.*

Batra, Ravi **HF1455**
The Myth of Free Trade: The Pooring of America. Trade Paper. Simon & Schuster. New York, NY. 1996. 288p. ISBN:0-684-83355-7, ISBN13: 978-0-684-83355-2. Dewey:382./710. LCCN:93-035764.
Audience: **l,u,f.**

Beck, Ulrich & Willms, Johannes **HM1266.B42513 2004**
Conversations with Ulrich Beck. Trade Cloth. Polity Press. Cambridge, 2003. 240p. ISBN:0-7456-2823-0, ISBN13: 978-0-7456-2823-3. Dewey:301. LCCN:2003-008590.
Audience: **g,l,u,f.**

Bellofiore, Riccardo (Editor) **HD5701.3.G575 1999**
Global Money, Capital Restructuring and the Changing Patterns of Labour. Trade Cloth. Edward Elgar Publishing, Inc. Northampton, MA. 1999. 224p. ISBN:1-85898-848-9, ISBN13: 978-1-85898-848-1. Dewey:331.12. LCCN:99-014861.
Audience: **l,u,f.**

Campbell, John L. **HM826.C36 2004**
Institutional Change and Globalization. Trade Cloth. Princeton University Press. Princeton, NJ. 2004. 264p. ISBN:0-691-08920-5, ISBN13: 978-0-691-08920-1. Dewey:302.3/5. LCCN:2004-042851.
Audience: **l,u,f.**

Chua, Amy **HF1359.C524 2003**
World on Fire: How Exporting Free Market Democracy Breeds Ethnic Hatred and Global Instability. Trade Cloth. Doubleday Publishing. New York, NY. 2002. 352p. ISBN:0-385-50302-4, ISBN13: 978-0-385-50302-0. Dewey:303.6. LCCN:2002-067676.
Audience: **g,l,u,f.** *Choice, 2003.*

Cohen, Benjamin J. **HG3881.C5854 2004**
The Future of Money. Trade Cloth. Princeton University Press. Princeton, NJ. 2003. 312p. ISBN:0-691-11665-2, ISBN13: 978-0-691-11665-5. Dewey:332/.042. LCCN:2003-045983.
Audience: **g,l,u,f.**

Dimand, Robert (Editor, Introduction by) **HF1379.O75 2004**
The German Transfer Problem and International Capital Movements: The Origins of International Economics. Paper over Boards. Routledge. New York, NY. 2004. 520p. Origins of International Economics Ser., Vol. 5 ISBN:0-415-31560-3, ISBN13: 978-0-415-31560-9. Dewey:382. LCCN:2003-060550.
Audience: **l,u,f.**

Dobbs, Lou **HF5549.5.M3**
Exporting America: Why Corporate Greed Is Shipping American Jobs Overseas. Trade Paper. Warner Books, Inc. New York, NY. 2006. 208p. ISBN:0-446-69509-2, ISBN13: 978-0-446-69509-1. Dewey:331.13/72.
Audience: **l,u,f.**

Eden, Lorraine & Dobson, Wendy **HD2741.G6893 2005**
Governance, Multinationals, and Growth. Trade Cloth. Edward Elgar Publishing, Inc. Northampton, MA. 2005. 400p. New Horizons in International Business Ser. ISBN:1-84376-909-3, ISBN13: 978-1-84376-909-5. Dewey:658/.049. LCCN:2005-043238.
Audience: **l,u,f.**

Irwin, Douglas A. **HF1756.I68 2002**
Free Trade under Fire. Cloth Text. Princeton University Press. Princeton, NJ. 2002. 288p. ISBN:0-691-08843-8, ISBN13: 978-0-691-08843-3. Dewey:382/.71. LCCN:2001-043159.
Audience: **g,l,u,f.** *Choice, 2003.*

Isard, Peter **HB3722.I83 2004**
Globalization and the International Financial System: What's Wrong and What Can Be Done. Cloth Text. Cambridge University Press. New York, NY. 2004. 384p. ISBN:0-521-84389-8, ISBN13: 978-0-521-84389-8. Dewey:332/.042. LCCN:2004-049269.
Audience: **l,u,f.**

Levy-Livermore, Amnon (Editor) **HF1359.H353 1998**
Handbook on the Globalization of the World Economy. Trade Cloth. Edward Elgar Publishing, Inc. Northampton, MA. 1998. 776p. ISBN:1-85898-467-X, ISBN13: 978-1-85898-467-4. Dewey:337. LCCN:97-044513.
Audience: **l,u,f.** *Choice, 1998.*

Lury, Celia **HD69.B7L87 2004**
Brands: The Logos of the Global Economy. Paper over Boards. Routledge. New York, NY. 2004. 208p. International Library of Sociology Ser. ISBN:0-415-25182-6, ISBN13: 978-0-415-25182-2. Dewey:658.8/27. LCCN:2004-002706.
Audience: **g,l,u,f.**

Milanovic, Branko **HC79.I5M55 2005**
Worlds Apart: Measuring International and Global Inequality. Trade Cloth. Princeton University Press. Princeton, NJ. 2005. 240p. ISBN:0-691-12110-9, ISBN13: 978-0-691-12110-9. Dewey:330.9. LCCN:2004-058312.
Audience: **l,u,f.** *Choice, 2005.*

Navaretti, Giorgio Barba & Venables, Anthony J. **HD2755.5.B368 2005**
Multinational Firms in the World Economy. Trade Cloth. Princeton University Press. Princeton, NJ. 2004. 336p. ISBN:0-691-11920-1, ISBN13: 978-0-691-11920-5. Dewey:338.8/8. LCCN:2004-050592.
Audience: **l,u,f.**

Pixley, Jocelyn **HG101.P59 2004**
Emotions in Finance: Distrust and Uncertainty in Global Markets. Cloth Text. Cambridge University Press. New York, NY. 2004. 228p. ISBN:0-521-82785-X, ISBN13: 978-0-521-82785-0. Dewey:332/.042/019. LCCN:2004-020922.
Audience: **l,u,f.**

Root, Hilton L. **HD87.R66 2006**
Capital and Collusion: The Political Logic of Global Economic Development. Trade Cloth. Princeton University Press. Princeton, NJ. 2005. 280p. ISBN:0-691-12407-8, ISBN13: 978-0-691-12407-0. Dewey:338.9/009172/4. LCCN:2005-045830.
Audience: **u,f.** *Choice, 2006.*

Ross, Andrew **HD4909.R66 2004**
Low Pay High Profile: The Global Push for Fair Labor. Trade Cloth. New Press, The. New York, NY. 2004. 256p. ISBN:1-56584-919-1, ISBN13: 978-1-56584-919-8. Dewey:331.2/15. LCCN:2003-061554.
Audience: **u,f.**

Rowe, James K. & Lipschutz, Ronnie D. **JZ1318.L57 2005**
Globalization, Governmentiality and Global Politics: Regulation for the Rest of Us? Paper over Boards. Routledge. New York, NY. 2005. XVIII, 254p. Routledge/RIPE Studies in Global Political Economy ISBN:0-415-70159-7, ISBN13: 978-0-415-70159-4. Dewey:303.48/2. LCCN:2005-000632.
Audience: **u,f.**

Sandoval, Armbruster **HD6539.O33A76 2004**
Globalization and Cross-Border Labor Solidarity in the Americas: The Anti-Sweatshop Movement and the Struggle for Social Justice. Paper over Boards. Routledge. New York, NY. 2004. 240p. ISBN:0-415-94956-4, ISBN13: 978-0-415-94956-9. Dewey:331.25. LCCN:2004-009989.
Audience: **u,f.**

Stiglitz, Joseph E. **HF1359**
Globalization and Its Discontents. Trade Paper. Penguin Books Canada, Ltd. Toronto, ON. 2003. 320p. ISBN:0-14-101038-X, ISBN13: 978-0-14-101038-0. Dewey:337.
Audience: **g,l,u,f.** *Choice, 2002.*

Stilgitz, Joseph E. (Author, Afterword by) **HF1418.5.S75 2002**
Globalization and Its Discontents. Trade Paper. W. W. Norton & Company, Inc. New York, NY. 2003. 304p. ISBN:0-393-32439-7, ISBN13: 978-0-393-32439-6. Dewey:337. LCCN:2002-023148.
Audience: **g,l,u,f.**

Suter, Keith **JZ1318**
In Defence of Globalisation. Trade Paper. University of New South Wales Press. Sydney, NSW. 2000. 64p. ISBN:0-86840-475-6, ISBN13: 978-0-86840-475-2. Dewey:330.9.
Audience: **l,u,f.**

Vreeland, James (Editor), et al. **HG3881.G5768 2005**
Globalization and the Nation State: The Impact of the IMF and the World Bank. Stephen Kosack & Gustav Ranis (Editors). Paper over Boards. Routledge. New York, NY. 2005. 464p. Routledge Studies in the Modern World Economy Ser., Vol. 52 ISBN:0-415-70086-8, ISBN13: 978-0-415-70086-3. Dewey:332.1/52. LCCN:2004-017568.
Audience: **l,u,f.**

International > Relations

Chatterji, Manas (Editor), et al. **HC79.D4E267 1994**
The Economics of International Security: Essays in Honour of Jan Tinbergen. Henk Jager & Annemarie Rima (Editors). Trade Cloth. Palgrave Macmillan. New York, NY. 1994. 304p. ISBN:0-312-12018-4, ISBN13: 978-0-312-12018-4. Dewey:338.4/76233. LCCN:93-034313.
Audience: **u,f.** *Choice, 1995.*

Chua, Amy **HF1359.C524 2003**
World on Fire: How Exporting Free Market Democracy Breeds Ethnic Hatred and Global Instability. Trade Cloth. Doubleday Publishing. New York, NY. 2002. 352p. ISBN:0-385-50302-4, ISBN13: 978-0-385-50302-0. Dewey:303.6. LCCN:2002-067676.
Audience: **g,l,u,f.** *Choice, 2003.*

Etzioni, Amitai **JZ1480.E89 2004**
From Empire to Community: A New Approach to International Relations. Cloth over Boards. Palgrave Macmillan. New York, NY. 2004. 272p. ISBN:1-4039-6535-8, ISBN13: 978-1-4039-6535-6. Dewey:327.73. LCCN:2003-064013.
Audience: **g,l,u.** *Choice, 2005.*

Nelson, Douglas R. & Vandenbussche, Hylke (Editors) **HF1425**
The WTO and Anti-Dumping. J. Anderson, B. Blonigen, R. Feinberg, J. M. Finger, B. Hoekman, C. Krupp, M. Leidy, T. Prusa, R. Staiger & R. Willig (Contribution by). Trade Cloth. Edward Elgar Publishing, Inc. Northampton, MA. 2005. 1,248p. Critical Perspectives on the Global Trading System and the Wto Ser., Vol. 7 ISBN:1-84376-602-7, ISBN13: 978-1-84376-602-5. Dewey:382/.63. LCCN:2005-049499.
Audience: **l,u,f.**

Rowe, James K. & Lipschutz, Ronnie D. **JZ1318.L57 2005**
Globalization, Governmentiality and Global Politics: Regulation for the Rest of Us? Paper over Boards. Routledge. New York, NY. 2005. XVIII, 254p. Routledge/RIPE Studies in Global Political Economy ISBN:0-415-70159-7, ISBN13: 978-0-415-70159-4. Dewey:303.48/2. LCCN:2005-000632.
Audience: **u,f.**

Tinbergen, Jan **HB846.T56 1990**
World Security and Equity. Trade Cloth. Edward Elgar Publishing, Inc. Northampton, MA. 1990. 144p. ISBN:1-85278-187-4, ISBN13: 978-1-85278-187-3. Dewey:361.6/1. LCCN:89-023686.
Audience: **u,f.**

Tinbergen, Jan, et al. **JX1395.R42 1977**
Reshaping the International Order: A Report to the Club of Rome. Antony J. Dolman & Jan Van Ettinger (Authors), Reshaping the International Order (Project) Staff (Contribution by). Trade Cloth. Random House. London, 1977. 325p. ISBN:0-09-129051-1, ISBN13: 978-0-09-129051-1. Dewey:327/.17. LCCN:78-315934.
Audience: **g,l,u,f.**

Tinbergen, Jan & Fischer, Dietrich **HB846.T55 1987**
Warfare and Welfare: Integrating Security Policy into Socio-Economic Policy. Cloth Text. Palgrave Macmillan. New York, NY. 1987. 203p. ISBN:0-312-00957-7, ISBN13: 978-0-312-00957-1. Dewey:303.4/82. LCCN:87-009625.
Audience: **l,u,f.**

United Nations Development Programme Staff **HD72**
Human Development Report 2005: International Cooperation at a Crossroads: Aid, Trade and Security in an Unequal World. Trade Paper. Oxford University Press, Inc. New York, NY. 2005. 388p. ISBN:0-19-530511-6, ISBN13: 978-0-19-530511-1. Dewey:338.9.
Audience: **g,l,u,f.** *Choice, 2006.*

Financial Economics

Bellofiore, Riccardo (Editor) **HD5701.3.G575 1999**
Global Money, Capital Restructuring and the Changing Patterns of Labour. Trade Cloth. Edward Elgar Publishing, Inc. Northampton, MA. 1999. 224p. ISBN:1-85898-848-9, ISBN13: 978-1-85898-848-1. Dewey:331.12. LCCN:99-014861.
Audience: **l,u,f.**

Bennis, Warren G. & Thomas, Robert J. **HM141**
Geeks and Geezers: How Era, Values, and Defining Moments Shape Leaders. Trade Paper. Harvard Business School Press.

Boston, MA. 2007. 256p. ISBN:1-4221-0281-5, ISBN13: 978-1-4221-0281-7. Dewey:303.3/4.
Audience: **l,u,f.** *Choice, 2003.*

Budd, Leslie & Harris, Lisa **HF5548.32.E1866 2004**
E-Economy: Rhetoric or Business Reality? Paper over Boards. Routledge. New York, NY. 2004. 248p. Routledge E-Business Ser., Vol. 4 ISBN:0-415-33954-5, ISBN13: 978-0-415-33954-4. Dewey:381/.142. LCCN:2004-003417.
Audience: **g,l,u,f.**

Dimand, Robert (Editor, Introduction by) **HF1379.O75 2004**
The German Transfer Problem and International Capital Movements: The Origins of International Economics. Paper over Boards. Routledge. New York, NY. 2004. 520p. Origins of International Economics Ser., Vol. 5 ISBN:0-415-31560-3, ISBN13: 978-0-415-31560-9. Dewey:382. LCCN:2003-060550.
Audience: **l,u,f.**

Driver, Rebecca & Thoenissen, C. **HG3821.E93 2004**
Exchange Rates, Capital Flows and Policy. Peter Sinclair (Editor). Paper over Boards. Routledge. New York, NY. 2004. 432p. Routledge International Studies in Money and Banking, Vol. 30 ISBN:0-415-35263-0, ISBN13: 978-0-415-35263-5. Dewey:332.4/56. LCCN:2004-053186.
Audience: **l,u,f.**

Eden, Lorraine & Dobson, Wendy **HD2741.G6893 2005**
Governance, Multinationals, and Growth. Trade Cloth. Edward Elgar Publishing, Inc. Northampton, MA. 2005. 400p. New Horizons in International Business Ser. ISBN:1-84376-909-3, ISBN13: 978-1-84376-909-5. Dewey:658/.049. LCCN:2005-043238.
Audience: **l,u,f.**

Eeckhoudt, Louis, et al. **HB615.E44 2005**
Economic and Financial Decisions under Risk. Christian Gollier & Harris Schlesinger (Authors). Trade Cloth. Princeton University Press. Princeton, NJ. 2005. 244p. ISBN:0-691-09655-4, ISBN13: 978-0-691-09655-1. Dewey:338.5. LCCN:2004-058689.
Audience: **l,u,f.**

Evans, David S. & Schmalensee, Richard **HG3755.8.U6E94 2005**
Paying with Plastic: The Digital Revolution in Buying and Borrowing. Ed. 2. Trade Cloth. MIT Press. Cambridge, MA. 2005. 360p. ISBN:0-262-05077-3, ISBN13: 978-0-262-05077-7. Dewey:332.7/65/0973. LCCN:2004-055249.
Audience: **g,l,u,f.** *Choice, 2005.*

Hellinger, Stephen H. & Hellinger, Douglas A. **HD5730.5.A6**
Unemployment and the Multinationals: A Strategy for Technological Change in Latin America. Barbara Ward (Foreword by). Trade Cloth. Associated Faculty Press, Inc. New York, NY. 1976. viii, 158p. ISBN:0-8046-9126-6, ISBN13: 978-0-8046-9126-0. Dewey:331.1/098. LCCN:76-008484.
Audience: **l,u,f.**

Hubbard, R. Glenn **HG173**
Money, the Financial System, and the Economy Plus Myeconlab Student Access Kit. Ed. 5. Book, Other. Addison-Wesley Longman, Inc. Boston, MA. 2004. 0p. ISBN:0-321-24639-X, ISBN13: 978-0-321-24639-4. Dewey:332.1.
Audience: **l,u,f.**

Isard, Peter **HB3722.I83 2004**
Globalization and the International Financial System: What's Wrong and What Can Be Done. Cloth Text. Cambridge University Press. New York, NY. 2004. 384p. ISBN:0-521-84389-8, ISBN13: 978-0-521-84389-8. Dewey:332/.042. LCCN:2004-049269.
Audience: **l,u,f.**

Kindleberger, Charles P. & Aliber, Robert **HB3722.K56 2005**
Manias, Panics, and Crashes: A History of Financial Crises. Ed. 5. Robert Solow (Foreword by). Trade Paper. John Wiley & Sons, Inc. Hoboken, NJ. 2005. 304p. Wiley Investment Classics Ser. ISBN:0-471-46714-6, ISBN13: 978-0-471-46714-4. Dewey:338.5/42. LCCN:2005-001066.
Audience: **g,l,u,f.** B

Lambsdorff, Johann Graf, et al. **HB99.5.L36 2004**
The New Institutional Economics of Corruption. Markus Taube & Matthias Schramm (Authors). Paper over Boards. Routledge. New York, NY. 2004. 272p. Routledge Frontiers of Political Economy Ser., Vol. 64 ISBN:0-415-33368-7, ISBN13: 978-0-415-33368-9. Dewey:330. LCCN:2004-046797.
Audience: **u,f.**

Lengwiler, Yvan **HG173.L46 2004**
Microfoundations of Financial Economics: An Introduction to General Equilibrium Asset Pricing. Trade Cloth. Princeton University Press. Princeton, NJ. 2004. 272p. Princeton Series in Finance ISBN:0-691-11315-7, ISBN13: 978-0-691-11315-9. Dewey:332/.01/5195. LCCN:2003-066415.
Audience: **g,l,u,f.**

Lo, Andrew W. (Editor) **HG4636.M367 1997**
Market Efficiency: Stock Market Behavior in Theory and Practice. F. Black, A. Cowles, F. Fama, S. Grossman, R. Roll & Paul Anthony Samuelson (Contribution by). Trade Cloth. Edward Elgar Publishing, Inc. Northampton, MA. 1997. 1,224p. The International Library of Critical Writings in Economics, No. 3 ISBN:1-85898-161-1, ISBN13: 978-1-85898-161-1. Dewey:332.63/222. LCCN:97-003805.
Audience: **u,f.**

O'Brien, Thomas J. **HG3881.O263 2005**
International Financial Economics: Corporate Decisions in Global Markets. Ed. 2. Trade Cloth. Oxford University Press, Inc. New York, NY. 2005. 316p. ISBN:0-19-517504-2, ISBN13: 978-0-19-517504-2. Dewey:658.15/99. LCCN:2004-025888.
Audience: **l,u,f.**

Payson, Steven **HF5415.157.P39 1994**
Quality Measurement in Economics: New Perspectives on the Evolution of Goods and Services. Trade Cloth. Edward Elgar Publishing, Inc. Northampton, MA. 1994. 256p. ISBN:1-85278-926-3, ISBN13: 978-1-85278-926-8. Dewey:658.562. LCCN:93-028612.
Audience: **u,f.** *Choice, 1994.*

Pelzmann, Linda **HB74.P8 P36**
Wirtschaftspsychologie: Behavioral Economics. Behavioral Finance. Arbeitswelt. Ed. 4. Jan Tinbergen (Introduction by).

Trade Paper. Springer. New York, NY. 2006. XLII, 342p. ISBN:3-211-30846-6, ISBN13: 978-3-211-30846-2. Dewey:330.019.

Audience: **u,f.**

Poitras, Geoffrey **HG173.P54 2006**
Pioneers of Financial Economics: Contributions Prior to Irving Fisher. Trade Cloth. Edward Elgar Publishing, Inc. Northampton, MA. 2006. 288p. ISBN:1-84542-381-X, ISBN13: 978-1-84542-381-0. Dewey:332. LCCN:2005-049498.

Audience: **l,u,f.**

Rima, Ingrid H. (Editor) **HF1359**
The Political Economy of Global Restructuring: Economic Organization and Production, Vol. 1. Trade Cloth. Edward Elgar Publishing, Inc. Northampton, MA. 1993. 256p. ISBN:1-85278-638-8, ISBN13: 978-1-85278-638-0. Dewey:337. LCCN:93-012027.

Audience: **u,f.** *Choice, 1994.*

Ross, Stephen A. **HG173.R675 2004**
Neoclassical Finance. Trade Cloth. Princeton University Press. Princeton, NJ. 2004. 144p. Princeton Lectures in Finance Ser. ISBN:0-691-12138-9, ISBN13: 978-0-691-12138-3. Dewey:332/.01. LCCN:2004-048901.

Audience: **u,f.**

Shiller, Robert J. **HG4915**
Irrational Exuberance. Ed. 2. Trade Paper. Doubleday Publishing. New York, NY. 2006. 336p. ISBN:0-7679-2363-4, ISBN13: 978-0-7679-2363-7. Dewey:332.63/222/0973.

Audience: **g,l,u,f.** *Choice, 2000.*

Smith, Vernon L. **HG4551.M54 2002B**
Experimental Economics: How We Can Build Better Financial Markets. Ross M. Miller (Foreword by). Trade Paper. John Wiley & Sons, Inc. Hoboken, NJ. 2005. 314p. ISBN:0-471-70625-6, ISBN13: 978-0-471-70625-0. Dewey:332.642. LCCN:2005-297240.

Audience: **u,f.**

Streissler, Erich W. **HG3821.S77 2002**
Exchange Rates and International Finance Markets: An Asset-Theoretic Perspective with Schumpeterian Innovation. Paper over Boards. Routledge. New York, NY. 2002. 160p. The Graz Schumpeter Lectures, Vol. 5 ISBN:0-415-27746-9, ISBN13: 978-0-415-27746-4. Dewey:332.4/56. LCCN:2001-051063.

Audience: **u,f.**

Tsay, Ruey S. **HA30.3 T76**
Analysis of Financial Time Series. Trade Cloth. John Wiley & Sons, Inc. Hoboken, NJ. 2003. ISBN:0-471-26410-5, ISBN13: 978-0-471-26410-1. Dewey:332/.01/51955.

Audience: **u,f.**

Whitman, Marina von Neumann **HG3881.W47**
International and Interregional Payments Adjustment: A Synthetic View. Trade Paper. Books on Demand. Ann Arbor, MI. 42p. Princeton Studies in International Finance, No. 19 ISBN:0-598-35725-4, ISBN13: 978-0-598-35725-0. Dewey:332.1/52. LCCN:67-016270.

Audience: **u,f.**

Health/Education/Welfare/Poverty

Adelman, Irma **HB523**
Dynamics and Income Distribution: Selected Essays of Irma Adelman, Vol. 2. Trade Cloth. Edward Elgar Publishing, Inc. Northampton, MA. 1995. 432p. Economists of the Twentieth Century Ser. ISBN:1-85898-052-6, ISBN13: 978-1-85898-052-2. Dewey:339.2. LCCN:94-048924.

Audience: **l,u,f.**

Allen, Vernon L. **HC79.P6.A56**
Psychological Factors in Poverty. Trade Cloth. Markham Publishing Company. Chicago, IL. 1970. viii, 392p. ISBN:0-8410-5003-1, ISBN13: 978-0-8410-5003-7. Dewey:155.9/2. LCCN:70-111978.

Audience: **l,u,f.**

Batra, Ravi **HF1455**
The Myth of Free Trade: The Pooring of America. Trade Paper. Simon & Schuster. New York, NY. 1996. 288p. ISBN:0-684-83355-7, ISBN13: 978-0-684-83355-2. Dewey:382./710. LCCN:93-035764.

Audience: **l,u,f.**

Blank, Rebecca M. **HV95.B59 1996**
It Takes a Nation: A New Agenda for Fighting Poverty. Cloth Text. Princeton University Press. Princeton, NJ. 1996. 372p. ISBN:0-691-02675-0, ISBN13: 978-0-691-02675-6. Dewey:362.5/8/0973. LCCN:96-008671.

Audience: **l,u,f.** *Choice, 1998.*

Bowles, Samuel (Editor), et al. **HC79.I5.U515 2005**
Unequal Chances: Family Background and Economic Success. Herbert Gintis & Melissa Osborne Groves (Editors). Trade Cloth. Princeton University Press. Princeton, NJ. 2005. 304p. ISBN:0-691-11930-9, ISBN13: 978-0-691-11930-4. Dewey:339.2/2. LCCN:2004-050521.

Audience: **l,u,f.** *Choice, 2005.*

Culyer, A. J. & Newhouse, J. P. (Editors) **RA410.H255 2000**
Handbook of Health Economics, Vol. 1A. Ed. 3. Trade Cloth. Elsevier Science & Technology Books. Saint Louis, MO. 2000. 1000p. Handbooks in Economics Ser. ISBN:0-444-50470-2, ISBN13: 978-0-444-50470-8. Dewey:338.4/33621. LCCN:2001-275530.

Audience: **l,u,f.**

Culyer, A. J. & Newhouse, J. P. (Editors) **RA410.H255 2000**
Handbook of Health Economics, Vol. 1B. Ed. 3. Trade Cloth. Elsevier Science & Technology Books. Saint Louis, MO. 2000. 1132p. Handbooks in Economics Ser. ISBN:0-444-50471-0, ISBN13: 978-0-444-50471-5. Dewey:338.4/33621. LCCN:2001-275530.

Audience: **l,u,f.**

Danziger, Sheldon H. & Weinberg, Daniel H. (Editors) **HC110.P63F54 1986**
Fighting Poverty: What Works and What Doesn't. Trade Cloth. Harvard University Press. Cambridge, MA. 1986. 448p. ISBN:0-674-30085-8, ISBN13: 978-0-674-30085-9. Dewey:362.5/8/0973. LCCN:85-024848.

Audience: **g,l,u,f.** *Choice, 1986.*

Darity, William A. Jr. & Myers, Samuel L. Jr. **HD4903.5.U58D37 1998**
Persistent Disparity: Race and Economic Inequality in the U. S. since 1945. Trade Cloth. Edward Elgar Publishing, Inc. Northampton, MA. 1998. 208p. ISBN:1-85898-658-3, ISBN13: 978-1-85898-658-6. Dewey:331.13/3/097309045. LCCN:97-030626.
Audience: **g,l,u,f.** *Choice, 1999.*

Drewnowski, Jan **HN25**
On Measuring and Planning the Quality of Life. J. Tinbergen (Introduction by). Paper Text. Walter de Gruyter GmbH & Co. KG. Berlin, 1974. xiii, 148p. Publications of the Institute of Social Studies Ser., No. 11 ISBN:90-279-2701-4, ISBN13: 978-90-279-2701-9. Dewey:301/.0723.
Audience: **u,f.**

Dreze, Jean & Sen, Amartya **HD9018.D44 D74**
Hunger and Public Action. Paper Text. Oxford University Press, Inc. New York, NY. 1991. 392p. WIDER Studies in Development Economics ISBN:0-19-828365-2, ISBN13: 978-0-19-828365-2. Dewey:363.8/52/091724.
Audience: **u,f.** *Choice, 1991.*

Ehrenreich, Barbara **HD5708.55.U6E47 2005**
Bait and Switch: The (Futile) Pursuit of the American Dream. Cloth over Boards. Henry Holt & Company. New York, NY. 2005. 256p. ISBN:0-8050-7606-9, ISBN13: 978-0-8050-7606-6. Dewey:650.14/086/22. LCCN:2005-047916.
Audience: **g,l,u,f.** *Choice, 2006.*

Figart, Deborah M. **HD4917.F54 2004**
Living Wage Movements: Global Perspectives. Paper over Boards. Routledge. New York, NY. 2004. 256p. Routledge Frontiers of Political Economy Ser., Vol. 58 ISBN:0-415-32002-X, ISBN13: 978-0-415-32002-3. Dewey:331.2/3. LCCN:2003-066692.
Audience: **l,u,f.**

Galbraith, John Kenneth **HC79.P6**
The Nature of Mass Poverty. Trade Paper. iUniverse, Inc. Lincoln, NE. 2001. 164p. ISBN:1-58348-419-1, ISBN13: 978-1-58348-419-7. Dewey:339.46.
Audience: **l,u,f.**

Keister, Lisa A. **HC110.W4K44 2005**
Getting Rich: America's New Rich and How They Got That Way. Cloth Text. Cambridge University Press. New York, NY. 2005. 320p. ISBN:0-521-82970-4, ISBN13: 978-0-521-82970-0. Dewey:339.2/2/0973. LCCN:2005-000241.
Audience: **l,u,f.** *Choice, 2005.*

Kreps, Juanita M. **HD6279.K74**
Lifetime Allocation of Work and Income: Essays in the Economics of Aging. Trade Cloth. Duke University Press. Durham, NC. 1971. 170p. ISBN:0-8223-0249-7, ISBN13: 978-0-8223-0249-0. Dewey:331.3. LCCN:74-161355.
Audience: **u,f.**

Kyrk, Hazel **HQ535**
The Family in the American Economy. Paper Text. University of Chicago Press. Chicago, IL. 1976. Midway Reprint Ser. ISBN:0-226-46621-3, ISBN13: 978-0-226-46621-7. Dewey:306.850973. LCCN:53-012266.
Audience: **l,u,f.**

Landes, David S. **HC240.Z9W45 1999**
The Wealth and Poverty of Nations: Why Some Are So Rich and Some So Poor. Trade Paper. W. W. Norton & Company, Inc. New York, NY. 1999. 672p. ISBN:0-393-31888-5, ISBN13: 978-0-393-31888-3. Dewey:330.1/6. LCCN:97-027508.
Audience: **l,u,f.** *Choice, 1998.*

Landes, David S. **HC240.Z9W45 1998**
The Wealth and Poverty of Nations: Why Some Are So Rich and Some So Poor. Trade Cloth. W. W. Norton & Company, Inc. New York, NY. 1998. 544p. ISBN:0-393-04017-8, ISBN13: 978-0-393-04017-3. Dewey:330.1/6. LCCN:97-027508.
Audience: **u,f.** *Choice, 1998.*

Levitan, Sar A., et al. **HC110.I5 L468 1993**
Working but Poor: America's Contradiction. Ed. 2. Frank Gallo & Issac Shapiro (Authors). Trade Cloth. Johns Hopkins University Press. Baltimore, MD. 1993. 168p. ISBN:0-8018-4574-2, ISBN13: 978-0-8018-4574-1. Dewey:362.5/0973. LCCN:92-034719.
Audience: **g,l,u,f.** *Choice, 1988.*

Levy, Frank **HC110.I5L47 1998**
The New Dollars and Dreams: American Incomes and Economic Change. Trade Cloth. Russell Sage Foundation. New York, NY. 1998. 256p. ISBN:0-87154-514-4, ISBN13: 978-0-87154-514-5. Dewey:339.2/0973. LCCN:98-020635.
Audience: **g,l,u,f.** *Choice, 1999.*

Lipton, Michael **HC79.P6.L56 1977**
Why Poor People Stay Poor: Urban Bias in World Development. Trade Cloth. Harvard University Press. Cambridge, MA. 1977. 467p. ISBN:0-674-95238-3, ISBN13: 978-0-674-95238-6. Dewey:301.44/1. LCCN:76-023584.
Audience: **l,u,f.**

Lucas, Robert E. B. **JV6118.L83 2005**
International Migration and Economic Development: Lessons from Low-Income Countries. Trade Cloth. Edward Elgar Publishing, Inc. Northampton, MA. 2005. 384p. ISBN:1-84542-383-6, ISBN13: 978-1-84542-383-4. Dewey:337. LCCN:2005-046188.
Audience: **l,u,f.**

Mallaby, Sebastian **HG3881.5.W57**
The World's Banker: A Story of Failed States, Financial Crises, and the Wealth and Poverty of Nations. Trade Paper. Penguin Group (USA) Inc. New York, NY. 2006. 496p. ISBN:0-14-303679-3, ISBN13: 978-0-14-303679-1. Dewey:332.1532.
Audience: **g,l,u,f.** *Choice, 2005.*

Maxwell, Daniel G. & Barrett, Christopher B. **HV696.F6B375 2005**
Food Aid after Fifty Years: Recasting its Role. Paper over Boards. Routledge. New York, NY. 2005. 336p. Priorities for Development Economics Ser. ISBN:0-415-70124-4, ISBN13: 978-0-415-70124-2. Dewey:363.8/56/0973. LCCN:2004-023634.
Audience: **g,l,u,f.** *Choice, 2006.*

Mayer, Susan & Peterson, Paul E. (Editors) **LC66.E23 1999**
Earning and Learning: How Schools Matter. Trade Paper. Brookings Institution Press. Washington, DC. 1999. 365p. ISBN:0-8157-5529-5, ISBN13: 978-0-8157-5529-6. Dewey:306.43/2. LCCN:99-006383.
Audience: **g,l,u,f.** *Choice, 2000.*

McMurrer, Daniel P. & Sawhill, Isabel V. **HN90.S65M34 1998**
Getting Ahead: Economic and Social Mobility in America. Library Binding. Urban Institute Press. Washington, DC. 1998. 130p. ISBN:0-87766-673-3, ISBN13: 978-0-87766-673-8. Dewey:350.5/13/0973. LCCN:97-049260.
Audience: **l,u,f.**

Milanovic, Branko **HC79.I5M55 2005**
Worlds Apart: Measuring International and Global Inequality. Trade Cloth. Princeton University Press. Princeton, NJ. 2005. 240p. ISBN:0-691-12110-9, ISBN13: 978-0-691-12110-9. Dewey:330.9. LCCN:2004-058312.
Audience: **l,u,f.** *Choice, 2005.*

Mody, Ashoka & Pattilo, Catherine (Editors) **HC79.P6**
Macroeconomics Policies and Poverty. Paper over Boards. Routledge. New York, NY. 2005. 400p. Routledge Studies in the Modern World Economy Ser. ISBN:0-415-70071-X, ISBN13: 978-0-415-70071-9. Dewey:339.4/6. LCCN:2005-002522.
Audience: **l,u,f.**

Mortensen, Dale T. **HD6061**
Wage Dispersion: Why Are Similar Workers Paid Differently? Trade Paper. MIT Press. Cambridge, MA. 2005. 160p. Zeuthen Lectures ISBN:0-262-63319-1, ISBN13: 978-0-262-63319-2. Dewey:331.2101.
Audience: **g,l,u,f.**

Moynihan, Daniel P. **HC110.P63**
Maximum Feasible Misunderstanding. Trade Cloth. Simon & Schuster. New York, NY. 1970. xxi, 218p. ISBN:0-02-922000-9, ISBN13: 978-0-02-922000-9. Dewey:362.5/0973. LCCN:69-018005.
Audience: **g,l,u,f.**

Nussbaum, Martha C. & Sen, Amartya (Editors) **HN25.Q33 1993**
The Quality of Life. Trade Paper. Oxford University Press, Inc. New York, NY. 1993. 480p. WIDER Studies in Development Economics ISBN:0-19-828797-6, ISBN13: 978-0-19-828797-1. Dewey:306. LCCN:91-042030.
Audience: **u,f.** *Choice, 1994.*

Rivlin, Alice M. **HJ3258.A2.R57 1992**
Reviving the American Dream: The Economy, the States, and the Federal Government. Trade Cloth. Brookings Institution Press. Washington, DC. 1992. 196p. ISBN:0-8157-7476-1, ISBN13: 978-0-8157-7476-1. Dewey:336.73. LCCN:92-016631.
Audience: **g,u,f.** *Choice, 1992.*

Ross, Heather L. & Sawhill, Isabel V. **HQ536**
Time of Transition: The Growth of Families Headed by Women. Trade Paper. University Press of America, Inc. Lanham, MD. 1975. 233p. ISBN:0-87766-148-0, ISBN13: 978-0-87766-148-1. Dewey:306.8.
Audience: **l,u,f.** B

Sachs, Jeffrey D. **HC59.72.P6**
The End of Poverty: Economic Possibilities for Our Time. Bono (Foreword by). Trade Paper. Penguin Group (USA) Inc. New York, NY. 2006. 416p. ISBN:0-14-303658-0, ISBN13: 978-0-14-303658-6. Dewey:339.4/6/091724.
Audience: **g,l,u,f.** *Choice, 2005.*

Schneider, Michael **HB251**
The Distribution of Wealth. Trade Cloth. Edward Elgar Publishing, Inc. Northampton, MA. 2004. 168p. ISBN:1-84064-814-7, ISBN13: 978-1-84064-814-0. Dewey:339.2/2. LCCN:2004-042270.
Audience: **u,f.** *Choice, 2005.*

Schultz, Theodore W. (Editor) **HQ728.E3**
The Economics of the Family: Marriage, Children, and Human Capital. Library Binding. University of Chicago Press. Chicago, IL. 1992. x, 584p. ISBN:0-226-74085-4, ISBN13: 978-0-226-74085-0. Dewey:301.42. LCCN:73-081484.
Audience: **l,u,f.**

Sen, Amartya **HB846.S46 1997**
Choice, Welfare, and Measurement. Trade Paper. Harvard University Press. Cambridge, MA. 1997. 480p. ISBN:0-674-12778-1, ISBN13: 978-0-674-12778-4. Dewey:330.15/56. LCCN:97-014986.
Audience: **u,f.**

Sen, Amartya **HM251**
Collective Choice and Social Welfare. Ed. 4. Trade Cloth. Elsevier Science & Technology Books. Saint Louis, MO. 1984. 226p. Advanced Textbooks in Economics, Vol. 11 ISBN:0-444-85127-5, ISBN13: 978-0-444-85127-7. Dewey:301.1.
Audience: **u,f.**

Sen, Amartya **HB99.3**
Commodities and Capabilities. Trade Paper. Oxford University Press, Inc. New York, NY. 1999. 102p. ISBN:0-19-565038-7, ISBN13: 978-0-19-565038-9. Dewey:330.15/5.
Audience: **u,f.**

Sen, Amartya **HC79.F3**
Poverty and Famines: An Essay on Entitlement and Deprivation. Paper Text. Oxford University Press, Inc. New York, NY. 1983. 270p. ISBN:0-19-828463-2, ISBN13: 978-0-19-828463-5. Dewey:363.8. LCCN:80-042191.
Audience: **u,f.**

Sen, Amartya **HD6978.S73 1987**
The Standard of Living. Geoffrey Hawthorn (Editor). Trade Paper. Cambridge University Press. New York, NY. 1988. 139p. Tanner Lectures in Human Values Ser. ISBN:0-521-36840-5, ISBN13: 978-0-521-36840-7. Dewey:339.47. LCCN:86-018832.
Audience: **u,f.**

Thurow, Lester C. **HC0110.P6T5**
Poverty and Discrimination. Trade Paper. Books on Demand. Ann Arbor, MI. 228p. Studies in Social Economics ISBN:0-608-13531-3, ISBN13: 978-0-608-13531-1. Dewey:362.50973. LCCN:69-018825.
Audience: **l,u,f.**

Tinbergen, Jan **HB171.5**
Production, Income and Welfare: The Search for an Optimal Social Order. Trade Cloth. University of Nebraska Press. Lincoln, NE. 1985. xiv, 210p. ISBN:0-8032-4412-6, ISBN13: 978-0-8032-4412-2. Dewey:330. LCCN:84-028042.
Audience: **u,f.** *Choice, 1985.*

Tinbergen, Jan, et al. **HB99.3**
Optimum Social Welfare and Productivity: A Comparative View. Abram Bergson, Fritz Machlup & Oskar Morgenstern (Authors).

Trade Cloth. New York University Press. New York, NY. 1972. 208p. Moskowitz Lectures ISBN:0-8147-8155-1, ISBN13: 978-0-8147-8155-5. Dewey:330.15/5. LCCN:72-094083.
Audience: **u,f.**

Tinbergen, Jan & Fischer, Dietrich **HB846.T55 1987**
Warfare and Welfare: Integrating Security Policy into Socio-Economic Policy. Cloth Text. Palgrave Macmillan. New York, NY. 1987. 203p. ISBN:0-312-00957-7, ISBN13: 978-0-312-00957-1. Dewey:303.4/82. LCCN:87-009625.
Audience: **l,u,f.**

Ward, Barbara **HD0082.W3**
Towards a World of Plenty? Trade Paper. Books on Demand. Ann Arbor, MI. 79p. The Sir Robert Falconer Lectures / University of Toronto, Vol. 1963 ISBN:0-598-18323-X, ISBN13: 978-0-598-18323-1. Dewey:338.9. LCCN:64-003047.
Audience: **l,u,f.**

Wiggin, Addison & Bonner, William **HB3722**
Empire of Debt: The Rise of an Epic Financial Crisis. Trade Cloth. John Wiley & Sons, Inc. Hoboken, NJ. 2005. 384p. ISBN:0-471-73902-2, ISBN13: 978-0-471-73902-9. Dewey:336.3/4/0973. LCCN:2005-023682.
Audience: **g,l,u,f.**

Wise, David A. (Editor) **HQ1064.U5I89 1990**
Issues in the Economics of Aging. Trade Cloth. University of Chicago Press. Chicago, IL. 1990. 403p. National Bureau of Economic Research Project Report ISBN:0-226-90297-8, ISBN13: 978-0-226-90297-5. Dewey:305.26. LCCN:90-011035.
Audience: **u,f.**

Zalk, Sue R. & Gordon-Kelter, Janice (Editors) **HQ1190.R49 1991**
Revolutions in Knowledge: Feminism in the Social Sciences. Trade Paper. Westview Press. Boulder, CO. 1992. 170p. ISBN:0-8133-0584-5, ISBN13: 978-0-8133-0584-4. Dewey:305.42. LCCN:91-027461.
Audience: **l,u,f.**

Zamagni, Stefano (Editor) **HB201.E26 1995**
The Economics of Altruism. Trade Cloth. Edward Elgar Publishing, Inc. Northampton, MA. 1995. 484p. The International Library of Critical Writings in Economics, Vol. 48 ISBN:1-85278-953-0, ISBN13: 978-1-85278-953-4. Dewey:330. LCCN:94-044344.
Audience: **l,u,f.**

Agricultural/Land/Environmental/Energy Economics

Allen, Robert C. **HC335.A655 2003**
Farm to Factory: A Reinterpretation of the Soviet Industrial Revolution. Trade Cloth. Princeton University Press. Princeton, NJ. 2003. 264p. The Princeton Economic History of the Western World Ser. ISBN:0-691-00696-2, ISBN13: 978-0-691-00696-3. Dewey:330.947/0842. LCCN:2002-042718.
Audience: **l,u,f.** *Choice, 2004.*

Andersen, Lykke E., et al. **SD418.3.B6**
[e] The Dynamics of Deforestation and Economic Growth in the Brazilian Amazon. Clive W. J. Granger, Eustaquio J. Reis, Diana Weinhold & Sven Wunder (Authors). E-Book. Cambridge University Press. New York, NY. 2004. ISBN:0-511-05821-7, ISBN13: 978-0-511-05821-9. Dewey:333.75/137/0981.
Audience: **u,f.**

Atkinson, Giles, et al. **HC79.E5M4 1997**
Measuring Sustainable Development: Macroeconomics and the Environment. Richard Dubourg, Kirk Hamilton, Mohan Munasinghe, David Pearce & Carlos Young (Authors). Trade Cloth. Edward Elgar Publishing, Inc. Northampton, MA. 1997. 272p. ISBN:1-85898-572-2, ISBN13: 978-1-85898-572-5. Dewey:338.9. LCCN:96-039592.
Audience: **l,u,f.** *Choice, 1998.*

Barton, Jonathan **HC79.E5**
Environmental Regulation in the New Global Economy: The Impact on Industry and Competitiveness. Trade Paper. Edward Elgar Publishing, Inc. Northampton, MA. 2004. 368p. ISBN:1-84376-845-3, ISBN13: 978-1-84376-845-6. Dewey:333.7.
Audience: **l,u,f.**

Beck, Ulrich & Willms, Johannes **HM1266.B42513 2004**
Conversations with Ulrich Beck. Trade Cloth. Polity Press. Cambridge, 2003. 240p. ISBN:0-7456-2823-0, ISBN13: 978-0-7456-2823-3. Dewey:301. LCCN:2003-008590.
Audience: **g,l,u,f.**

Bergstrom, John C., et al. **HD111**
Land Use Problems and Conflicts: Causes, Consequences and Solutions. Stephan J. Goetz & James S. Shortle (Authors). Paper over Boards. Routledge. New York, NY. 2004. 384p. Routledge Explorations in Environmental Economics Ser., Vol. 2 ISBN:0-415-70028-0, ISBN13: 978-0-415-70028-3. Dewey:333.73/13/0973. LCCN:2004-050983.
Audience: **l,u,f.**

Brown, Lester Russell **HD75.6.S734 2001**
State of the World 2001: A Worldwatch Institute Report on Progress Toward a Sustainable Society. Ed. 18. The Worldwatch Institute Staff (Contribution by). Trade Paper. Earthscan Canada. Toronto, ON. 2001. xx, 275p. ISBN:1-85383-769-5, ISBN13: 978-1-85383-769-2. Dewey:333.7/2. LCCN:2001-369493.
Audience: **g,l,u,f.**

Cardwell, Michael (Editor), et al. **K3870.A944 2003**
Agriculture and International Trade: Law, Policy, and the WTO. Margaret R. Grossman, C. P. Rodgers, M. N. Cardwell, C. Rogers & M. R. Grossman (Editors). Cloth Text. Oxford University Press, Inc. New York, NY. 2004. 352p. CABI Publishing Ser. ISBN:0-85199-663-9, ISBN13: 978-0-85199-663-9. Dewey:341.7/5471. LCCN:2003-004769.
Audience: **l,u,f.**

Duraiappah, Anantha Kumar **HD75.6.D865 2003**
Computational Models in the Economics of Environment and Development. Trade Cloth. Kluwer Law International. Alphen a/d Rijn, 2003. 248p. Economy and Environment Ser., Vol. 27 ISBN:1-4020-1773-1, ISBN13: 978-1-4020-1773-5. Dewey:333.7/01/519. LCCN:2003-064067.
Audience: **l,u,f.**

Geist, Helmut (Editor) **GF90**
Our Earth's Changing Land: An Encyclopedia of Land-Use and Land-Cover Change. Cloth Text. Greenwood Publishing Group, Inc. Portsmouth, NH. 2005. 792p. ISBN:0-313-32704-1,

ISBN13: 978-0-313-32704-9. Dewey:333.7. LCCN:2005-019212.
Audience: **g,l,u,f.** *Choice, 2006.*

Jones, Samantha & Carswell, Grace (Editors) **HC59.72.E5E24 2004**
The Earthscan Reader in Environment, Development and Rural Livelihoods. Trade Cloth. Earthscan/James & James. London, 2004. 368p. ISBN:1-84407-052-2, ISBN13: 978-1-84407-052-7. Dewey:333.7. LCCN:2004-011585.
Audience: **l,u,f.**

Lewis, W. Arthur **HD82**
Development Economics. Paper over Boards. Routledge. New York, NY. 2003. 456p. Routledge Library Editions Ser., Vol. 7:Economics, US/Can. Edition Ser. ISBN:0-415-31301-5, ISBN13: 978-0-415-31301-8. Dewey:338.9.
Audience: **l,u.**

Marchant, Mary A. & Williamson, Handy Jr. (Editors) **HD9005.A63 1994**
Achieving Diversity: The Status and Progress of Women and African Americans in the Agricultural Economics Profession. Paper over Boards. Garland Publishing, Inc. New York, NY. 1994. 248p. Studies on Industrial Productivity ISBN:0-8153-1537-6, ISBN13: 978-0-8153-1537-7. Dewey:331.4/813381/0973. LCCN:93-039458.
Audience: **u,f.**

Moore, Keith M. **HC1000.Z65C66 2004**
Conflict, Social Capital, and Managing Natural Resources: A West African Case Study. SANREM Staff (Contribution by). Cloth Text. CAB International. Wallingford, 2005. 278p. CABI Publishing Ser. ISBN:0-85199-948-4, ISBN13: 978-0-85199-948-7. Dewey:333.7/0966. LCCN:2004-012409.
Audience: **u,f.**

Power, Marcus **HF1021**
Rethinking Development Geographies. Paper over Boards. Routledge. New York, NY. 2003. 288p. ISBN:0-415-25078-1, ISBN13: 978-0-415-25078-8. Dewey:338.9. LCCN:2002-155680.
Audience: **u,f.**

Sampson, Gary & Whalley, John (Editors) **HF1385**
The WTO, Trade and the Environment. W. Antweiler, J. Bhagwati, B. Copeland, G. Grossman, A. Krueger, R. E. B. Lucas & T. N. Srinivasan (Contribution by). Trade Cloth. Edward Elgar Publishing, Inc. Northampton, MA. 2005. 736p. Critical Perspectives on the Global Trading System and the Wto Ser., Vol. 5 ISBN:1-84376-839-9, ISBN13: 978-1-84376-839-5. Dewey:382/.92. LCCN:2005-043326.
Audience: **u,f.**

Simmons, Matthew R. **HD9576.S33**
Twilight in the Desert: The Coming Saudi Oil Shock and the World Economy. Trade Paper. John Wiley & Sons, Inc. Hoboken, NJ. 2006. 464p. ISBN:0-471-79018-4, ISBN13: 978-0-471-79018-1. Dewey:338.2/728/09538.
Audience: **g,l,u,f.**

Smith, V. L. (Editor) **HC55**
The Economics of Natural and Environmental Resources. Cloth Text. Gordon & Breach Publishing Group. New York, NY. 1977. 506p. ISBN:0-677-15040-7, ISBN13: 978-0-677-15040-6. Dewey:333.7/0724. LCCN:73-093135.
Audience: **l,u,f.**

Urban and Rural Economics

Domencich, T. **HE336.C5**
Urban Travel Demand. Trade Cloth. Elsevier. New York, NY. 1975. 215p. Contributions to Economic Analysis Ser., Vol. 93 ISBN:0-444-10830-0, ISBN13: 978-0-444-10830-2. Dewey:388.4/131/4. LCCN:74-030936.
Audience: **u,f.**

Ramsamy, Edward **HC60**
World Bank and Urban Development: From Projects to Policy. Paper over Boards. Routledge. New York, NY. 2006. XVIII, 229p. Routledge Studies in Development and Society Ser. ISBN:0-415-34439-5, ISBN13: 978-0-415-34439-5. Dewey:338.9009173/2. LCCN:2005-033644.
Audience: **l,u,f.**

Wheeler, Stephen & Beatley, Timothy (Editors) **HT166.S9135 2004**
The Sustainable Urban Development Reader. Paper over Boards. Routledge. New York, NY. 2004. 392p. The Routledge Urban Reader Ser. ISBN:0-415-31186-1, ISBN13: 978-0-415-31186-1. Dewey:307.1/216. LCCN:2003-015200.
Audience: **l,u,f.**

Cultural Economics. Social Economics

Balak, Benjamin **HB171**
McCloskey's Economic Thought: The Rhetoric of an Economist. Paper over Boards. Routledge. New York, NY. 2005. X, 142p. Routledge INEM Advances in Economic Methodology Ser. ISBN:0-415-31682-0, ISBN13: 978-0-415-31682-8. Dewey:174. LCCN:2005-004314.
Audience: **l,u,f.**

Barley, Stephen R. & Kunda, Gideon **HD8039.I372U63 2004**
Gurus, Hired Guns, and Warm Bodies: Itinerant Experts in a Knowledge Economy. Trade Cloth. Princeton University Press. Princeton, NJ. 2004. 352p. ISBN:0-691-11943-0, ISBN13: 978-0-691-11943-4. Dewey:331.2. LCCN:2003-068993.
Audience: **l,u,f.**

Coats, A. W. **HB75**
The Sociology and Professionalization of Economics: British and American Economic Essays. Paper over Boards. Routledge. New York, NY. 1993. 656p. ISBN:0-415-06716-2, ISBN13: 978-0-415-06716-4. Dewey:330.09. LCCN:93-016563.
Audience: **l,u,f.**

Coulomb, Fanny **HB195**
Economic Theories of Peace and War. Paper over Boards. Routledge. New York, NY. 2004. 320p. Routledge Studies in Defense Economics Ser. ISBN:0-415-28408-2, ISBN13: 978-0-415-28408-0. Dewey:330/.01. LCCN:2003-063848.
Audience: **l,u,f.**

Dobbin, Frank (Editor) **HM548.N49 2004**
The New Economic Sociology: A Reader. Trade Cloth. Princeton University Press. Princeton, NJ. 2004. 520p. ISBN:0-691-04905-X, ISBN13: 978-0-691-04905-2. Dewey:306.3. LCCN:2003-060037.
Audience: **l,u,f.**

Etzioni, Amitai **HM35.E888 1999**
Essays in Socio-Economics. Cloth Text. Springer. New York, NY. 1999. 193p. Studies in Economic Ethics and Philosophy ISBN:3-540-64466-0, ISBN13: 978-3-540-64466-8. Dewey:306.3. LCCN:98-032344.
Audience: **u,f.**

Etzioni, Amitai & Lawrence, Paul R. (Editors) **HM548**
Socio-Economics: Toward a New Synthesis. Paper Text. M. E. Sharpe Inc. Armonk, NY. 1993. 288p. Studies in Socio-Economics ISBN:0-87332-686-5, ISBN13: 978-0-87332-686-5. Dewey:306.3. LCCN:90-040462.
Audience: **u,f.** *Choice, 1992.*

Fawcett, Millicent Garrett **HB171.5 .F27**
Political Economy for Beginners. Trade Paper. University Press of the Pacific. Miami, FL. 2004. 264p. ISBN:1-4102-1318-8, ISBN13: 978-1-4102-1318-1. Dewey:330.
Audience: **l,u,f.**

Fawcett, Millicent Garrett **HB171.5 .F28**
Tales in Political Economy. Trade Paper. University Press of the Pacific. Miami, FL. 2004. 116p. ISBN:1-4102-1303-X, ISBN13: 978-1-4102-1303-7. Dewey:330.
Audience: **l,u,f.**

Fawcett, Millicent Garrett & Fawcett, Henry **AC8 .F3**
Essays and Lectures on Social and Political Subjects. Trade Paper. University Press of the Pacific. Miami, FL. 2004. 380p. ISBN:1-4102-1292-0, ISBN13: 978-1-4102-1292-4. Dewey:081.
Audience: **u,f.**

Friedman, Milton **HG0501.F74**
Monetary Trends in the United States and the United Kingdom, Their Relation to Income, Prices, and Interest Rates, 1867-1975. Trade Paper. Books on Demand. Ann Arbor, MI. 696p. National Bureau of Economic Research Monographs ISBN:0-608-09302-5, ISBN13: 978-0-608-09302-4. Dewey:332.4973. LCCN:81-016273.
Audience: **l,u,f.**

Heintz, James, et al. **HC103.F59 2000**
The Ultimate Field Guide to the U. S. Economy: A Compact and Irreverent Guide to Economic Life in America. Nancy Folbre & Center for Popular Economics Staff (Authors). Trade Paper. New Press, The. New York, NY. 2000. 224p. ISBN:1-56584-578-1, ISBN13: 978-1-56584-578-7. Dewey:330.973. LCCN:99-048804.
Audience: **g,l,u.**

Huntington, Samuel P. & Harrison, Lawrence E. (Editors) **HM681.C85 2000**
Culture Matters: How Values Shape Human Progress. Paper Text. Basic Books. New York, NY. 2001. 384p. ISBN:0-465-03176-5, ISBN13: 978-0-465-03176-4. Dewey:306. LCCN:00-022951.
Audience: **l,u,f.**

Kalecki, Michal **HC59.7**
Essays on Developing Economies. Joan Robinson (Introduction by). Cloth Text. Brill Academic Publishers, Inc. Boston, MA. 1976. 208p. ISBN:0-391-00524-3, ISBN13: 978-0-391-00524-2. Dewey:330.9172/4. LCCN:75-040308.
Audience: **l,u,f.**

Kamien, Morton I. & Schwartz, Nancy Lou **HC79.T4 K3**
Market Structure and Innovation. John Pencavel (Contribution by). Trade Paper. Cambridge University Press. New York, NY. 1982. 256p. Cambridge Surveys of Economic Literature Ser. ISBN:0-521-29385-5, ISBN13: 978-0-521-29385-3. Dewey:338/.06. LCCN:81-012254.
Audience: **u,f.**

King, J. E. **HB99.7**
A History of Post Keynesian Economics since 1936. Trade Paper. Edward Elgar Publishing, Inc. Northampton, MA. 2004. 328p. Awarded Choice Outstanding Academic Title for 2002 Ser. ISBN:1-84376-650-7, ISBN13: 978-1-84376-650-6. Dewey:330.1/56.
Audience: **g,l,u,f.** *Choice, 2003, 2002.*

Kreps, Juanita & Clark, Robert **HD8072.K777**
Sex, Age, and Work: The Changing Composition of the Labor Force. Trade Paper. Books on Demand. Ann Arbor, MI. 110p. Policy Studies in Employment and Welfare, Vol. 23 ISBN:0-608-06052-6, ISBN13: 978-0-608-06052-1. Dewey:331.0973. LCCN:75-034452.
Audience: **l,u,f.**

Latsis, Spiro J. (Editor) **HB131**
Method and Appraisal in Economics. Cloth Text. Cambridge University Press. New York, NY. 1976. 238p. ISBN:0-521-21076-3, ISBN13: 978-0-521-21076-8. Dewey:330/.01/8. LCCN:75-044581.
Audience: **u,f.**

Lin, Nan **HM741.L56 2001**
Social Capital: A Theory of Social Structure and Action. Mark Granovetter (Contribution by). Cloth Text. Cambridge University Press. New York, NY. 2001. 292p. Structural Analysis in the Social Sciences Ser., No. 19 ISBN:0-521-47431-0, ISBN13: 978-0-521-47431-3. Dewey:302.4. LCCN:00-036289.
Audience: **u,f.**

Martineau, Harriet **PR4984.M5I44 2004**
Illustrations of Political Economy: Selected Tales. Deborah Anna Logan (Editor). Trade Paper. Broadview Press. Peterborough, ON. 2004. 350p. Broadview Editions Ser. ISBN:1-55111-441-0, ISBN13: 978-1-55111-441-5. Dewey:823/.8. LCCN:2005-544534.
Audience: **g,l,u,f.**

McGuire, C. B. & Radner, Roy (Editors) **HD30.23.D378 1986**
Decision and Organization. Ed. 2. Trade Paper. University of Minnesota Press. Minneapolis, MN. 1987. 400p. ISBN:0-8166-1365-6, ISBN13: 978-0-8166-1365-6. Dewey:658.4/033. LCCN:86-011407.
Audience: **u,f.**

Myrdal, Gunnar **HB179.S8M9713 2005**
The Essential Gunnar Myrdal. Orjan Appelqvist & Stellan Andersson (Editors). Trade Cloth. New Press, The. New York, NY. 2005. 416p. The New Press Essential Ser. ISBN:1-56584-601-X, ISBN13: 978-1-56584-601-2. Dewey:330.1. LCCN:2004-052116.
Audience: **l,u,f.**

Nelson, Julie A. **HB72.N445 2006**
Economics for Humans. Trade Cloth. University of Chicago Press. Chicago, IL. 2006. 164p. ISBN:0-226-57202-1, ISBN13: 978-0-226-57202-4. Dewey:174. LCCN:2005-034406.
Audience: **l,u,f.**

O'Driscoll, Gerald P., et al. **HB98.O372 1996**
[e] The Economics of Time and Ignorance. Mario J. Rizzo & Roger W. Garrison (Authors). E-Book. Routledge. New York, NY. 1996. ISBN:0-203-00674-7, ISBN13: 978-0-203-00674-0. Dewey:330.15/7.
Audience: **u,f.**

Parsons, Talcott & Smelser, Neil J. **HM548**
Economy and Society: A Study in the Integration of Economic and Social Theory, Vol. 26. Paper over Boards. Routledge. New York, NY. 2003. 344p. International Library of Sociology Ser. ISBN:0-415-17527-5, ISBN13: 978-0-415-17527-2. Dewey:306.3.
Audience: **l,u,f.**

Polanyi, Karl **HB75**
Primitive, Archaic and Modern Economies: Essays of Karl Polanyi. George Dalton (Editor). Trade Paper. Beacon Press. Boston, MA. 1971. ISBN:0-8070-4793-7, ISBN13: 978-0-8070-4793-4. Dewey:330.1.
Audience: **u,f.**

Rima, Ingrid H. (Editor) **HB103.R63J65 1991**
The Joan Robinson Legacy. Cloth Text. M. E. Sharpe Inc. Armonk, NY. 1991. 296p. ISBN:0-87332-611-3, ISBN13: 978-0-87332-611-7. Dewey:330.1/092. LCCN:90-028932.
Audience: **l,u,f.**

Robinson, Joan **HB171**
The Accumulation of Capital. Ed. 3. Library Binding. Porcupine Press, Inc. Philadelphia, PA. 1986. xvi, 440p. ISBN:0-87991-266-9, ISBN13: 978-0-87991-266-6. Dewey:330.1. LCCN:85-012465.
Audience: **l,u,f.**

Robinson, Joan **HB171**
Contributions to Modern Economics. Trade Cloth. Blackwell Publishing, Inc. Malden, MA. xxii, 274p. ISBN:0-631-19220-4, ISBN13: 978-0-631-19220-6. Dewey:330.
Audience: **l,u,f.**

Robinson, Joan **HC256.5 .R644**
Economics: An Awkward Corner. Paper Text. Routledge. New York, NY. 1965. ISBN:0-04-330080-4, ISBN13: 978-0-04-330080-0. Dewey:330.
Audience: **l,u,f.**

Robinson, Joan **HB201 .R6**
Economics of Imperfect Competition. Cloth Text. Palgrave Macmillan. New York, NY. 1969. ISBN:0-312-23380-9, ISBN13: 978-0-312-23380-8. Dewey:330.1/62.
Audience: **l,u,f.**

Robinson, Joan **HB97.5.R6 1990**
An Essay on Marxian Economics. Ed. 2. Trade Paper. Porcupine Press, Inc. Philadelphia, PA. 1991. xxiv, 104p. ISBN:0-87991-270-7, ISBN13: 978-0-87991-270-3. Dewey:335.41. LCCN:90-007216.
Audience: **u,f.**

Robinson, Joan **HB171 .R63 1980**
Essays in the Theory of Employment. Trade Cloth. Hyperion Press, Inc. Westport, CT. 1985. ISBN:0-88355-812-2, ISBN13: 978-0-88355-812-6. Dewey:331/.01. LCCN:78-014138.
Audience: **u,f.**

Robinson, Joan **HB171**
Further Contributions to Modern Economics. Trade Paper. Blackwell Publishing, Inc. Malden, MA. xiv, 202p. ISBN:0-631-12634-1, ISBN13: 978-0-631-12634-8. Dewey:330.
Audience: **u,f.**

Robinson, Joan **HB171 .R644 1979B**
The Generalization of the General Theory and Other Essays. Cloth Text. Palgrave Macmillan. New York, NY. 1980. ISBN:0-312-31963-0, ISBN13: 978-0-312-31963-2. Dewey:330.1. LCCN:79-015275.
Audience: **u,f.**

Robinson, Joan **HB99.7 .R6**
Introduction to the Theory of Employment. Ed. 2. Cloth Text. Palgrave Macmillan. New York, NY. 1969. ISBN:0-312-43435-9, ISBN13: 978-0-312-43435-9. Dewey:330.15/6.
Audience: **u,f.**

Robinson, Joan **HB171**
The Rate of Interest and Other Essays. Trade Cloth. Hyperion Press, Inc. Westport, CT. 1986. ISBN:0-88355-959-5, ISBN13: 978-0-88355-959-8. Dewey:330. LCCN:79-051867.
Audience: **u,f.**

Robinson, Joan **HB171 .R6443 1981**
What Are the Questions?: Other Essays. Trade Cloth. M. E. Sharpe Inc. Armonk, NY. 1981. 244p. ISBN:0-87332-199-5, ISBN13: 978-0-87332-199-0. Dewey:330. LCCN:80-028062.
Audience: **u,f.**

Robinson, Joan **HB171**
Joan Robinson: Economic Writings. Ed. 2. G. C. Harcourt & Prue Kerr (Introduction by). Trade Paper. Palgrave Macmillan. New York, NY. 2004. 2363p. ISBN:0-333-97707-6, ISBN13: 978-0-333-97707-1. Dewey:330.1.
Audience: **u,f.**

Rogers, Colin D. **HG221 .R683 1989**
Money, Interest and Capital: A Study in the Foundations of Monetary Theory. Phyllis Deane, Gautam Mathur & Joan Robinson (Contribution by). Trade Paper. Cambridge University Press. New York, NY. 1989. 336p. Modern Cambridge Economics Ser. ISBN:0-521-35956-2, ISBN13: 978-0-521-35956-6. Dewey:332.4. LCCN:88-020364.
Audience: **l,u,f.** *Choice, 1990.*

Romano, Mary A. **HM22.G8W3927 1998**
Beatrice Webb (1858-1943) - The Socialist with a Sociological Imagination. Trade Cloth. Edwin Mellen Press, The. Lewiston, NY. 1998. 152p. Studies in Sociology, Vol. 17 ISBN:0-7734-8312-8, ISBN13: 978-0-7734-8312-5. Dewey:335/.14/092 B. LCCN:98-027079.
Audience: **u,f.**

Simon, Carl P. & Witte, Ann D. **HJ2348**
Beating the System: The Underground Economy. Trade Cloth. Greenwood Publishing Group, Inc. Portsmouth, NH. 1982. 320p. ISBN:0-86569-105-3, ISBN13: 978-0-86569-105-6. Dewey:364.1/33. LCCN:81-012846.
Audience: **g,l,u,f.**

Sullivan, Teresa A., et al. **HG3766.S794 2000**
The Fragile Middle Class: Americans in Debt. Elizabeth Warren & Jay Lawrence Westbrook (Authors). Cloth over Boards. Yale University Press. Cumberland, RI. 2000. 400p. ISBN:0-300-07960-5, ISBN13: 978-0-300-07960-9. Dewey:332.7/5/0673. LCCN:99-041894.
Audience: **g,l,u,f.** *Choice, 2000.*

Swedberg, Richard **HM35.S93 1990**
Economics and Sociology: Conversations with Economists and Sociologists. Trade Cloth. Princeton University Press. Princeton, NJ. 1990. 376p. ISBN:0-691-04248-9, ISBN13: 978-0-691-04248-0. Dewey:300. LCCN:89-010964.
Audience: **l,u,f.**

Swonk, Diane **HC103.S94 2003**
The Passionate Economist: Finding the Power and Humanity Behind the Numbers. Trade Cloth. John Wiley & Sons, Inc. Hoboken, NJ. 2003. 288p. ISBN:0-471-26996-4, ISBN13: 978-0-471-26996-0. Dewey:330.973. LCCN:2002-153259.
Audience: **l,u,f.**

Taylor, J. Edward & Adelman, Irma **HT431 .T39 1996**
Village Economies: The Design, Estimation, and Use of Villagewide Economic Models. Elise H. Golan, Blane D. Lewis, Katherine Ralston, Shankar Subramanian & Erik Thorbecke (Contribution by). Trade Cloth. Cambridge University Press. New York, NY. 1996. 276p. ISBN:0-521-55012-2, ISBN13: 978-0-521-55012-3. Dewey:338/.091734. LCCN:95-043030.
Audience: **u,f.**

Turner, Marjorie S. **HB103.R63T87 1989**
Joan Robinson and the Americans. Cloth Text. M. E. Sharpe Inc. Armonk, NY. 1989. 336p. ISBN:0-87332-533-8, ISBN13: 978-0-87332-533-2. Dewey:330.1/092/4. LCCN:88-030858.
Audience: **l,u,f.** *Choice, 1989.*

Turner, Marjorie S. **HB103.K47T87 1993**
Nicholas Kaldor and the Real World. Cloth Text. M. E. Sharpe Inc. Armonk, NY. 1993. 254p. ISBN:1-56324-147-1, ISBN13: 978-1-56324-147-5. Dewey:330/.092. LCCN:93-021759.
Audience: **l,u,f.** *Choice, 1994.*

Wallace, Phyllis A., et al. **HD6053**
Black Women in the Labor Force. Linda Datcher & Julianne Malveaux (Authors). Trade Paper. MIT Press. Cambridge, MA. 1982. 182p. ISBN:0-262-73063-4, ISBN13: 978-0-262-73063-1. Dewey:331.4.
Audience: **l,u,f.**

Walsh, Vivian & Gram, Harvey N. **HB145**
Classical and Neoclassical Theories of General Equilibrium. Joan Robinson (Introduction by). Cloth Text. Oxford University Press, Inc. New York, NY. 1979. 442p. ISBN:0-19-502674-8, ISBN13: 978-0-19-502674-0. Dewey:330.15/43. LCCN:78-031129.
Audience: **u,f.**

Ward, Barbara **HD0082.W3**
Towards a World of Plenty? Trade Paper. Books on Demand. Ann Arbor, MI. 79p. The Sir Robert Falconer Lectures / University of Toronto, Vol. 1963 ISBN:0-598-18323-X, ISBN13: 978-0-598-18323-1. Dewey:338.9. LCCN:64-003047.
Audience: **l,u,f.**

Ward, Barbara (Editor), et al. **HC59.7**
Widening Gap: Development in the 1970's. J. D. Runnalls & Lenore D'Anjou (Editors). Trade Cloth. Columbia University Press. New York, NY. 1971. xii, 372p. ISBN:0-231-03538-1, ISBN13: 978-0-231-03538-5. Dewey:330.9/1724. LCCN:75-151617.
Audience: **u,f.**

Webb, Beatrice **HX246**
My Apprenticeship. Trade Paper. Penguin Books, Ltd. London, 1971. 432p. ISBN:0-14-003220-7, ISBN13: 978-0-14-003220-8. Dewey:335/.00924.
Audience: **l,u,f.**

Whitman, Marina V. **HD2785.W46 1999**
New World, New Rules: The Changing Role of the American Corporation. Trade Cloth. Harvard Business School Press. Boston, MA. 1999. 272p. ISBN:0-87584-858-3, ISBN13: 978-0-87584-858-7. Dewey:338.7/0973. LCCN:98-045835.
Audience: **u,f.** *Choice, 1999.*

Zein-Elabdin, Eiman O. & Charusheela, S. (Editors) **HB72.P637 2004**
Postcolonialism Meets Economics. Paper over Boards. Routledge. New York, NY. 2003. 304p. Economics As Social Theory Ser. ISBN:0-415-28725-1, ISBN13: 978-0-415-28725-8. Dewey:330/.01. LCCN:2003-046991.
Audience: **u,f.**

Experimental Economics

Isaac, R. Mark & Smith, Vernon L. (Editors) **HB1**
Research in Experimental Economics, Vol. 3. Trade Cloth. Elsevier Science & Technology Books. Saint Louis, MO. 1986. 248p. ISBN:0-89232-337-X, ISBN13: 978-0-89232-337-1. Dewey:330/.05.
Audience: **u,f.**

Isaac, R. Mark & Smith, Vernon L. (Editors) **HB1**
Research in Experimental Economics, Vol. 1. Trade Cloth. Elsevier Science & Technology Books. Saint Louis, MO. 1979. 374p. ISBN:0-89232-030-3, ISBN13: 978-0-89232-030-1. Dewey:330/.05.
Audience: **u,f.**

Isaac, R. Mark & Smith, Vernon L. (Editors) **HB1**
Research in Experimental Economics, Vol. 2. Trade Cloth. Elsevier Science & Technology Books. Saint Louis, MO. 1983. 250p. ISBN:0-89232-263-2, ISBN13: 978-0-89232-263-3. Dewey:330/.05.
Audience: **u,f.**

Levitt, Steven D. & Dubner, Stephen J. **HB74.P8**
Freakonomics: A Rogue Economist Explores the Hidden Side of Everything. Trade Paper. Penguin Books Canada, Ltd. Toronto, ON. 2006. 256p. ISBN:0-14-101901-8, ISBN13: 978-0-14-101901-7. Dewey:330.
Audience: **g,l,u,f.** *Choice, 2005.*

Nee, Victor & Swedberg, Richard (Editors) **HB501.E2565 2005**
Economic Sociology of Capitalism. Trade Cloth. Princeton University Press. Princeton, NJ. 2005. 496p.

ISBN:0-691-11957-0, ISBN13: 978-0-691-11957-1. Dewey:306.3/42. LCCN:2004-043151.
Audience: **g,l,u,f.**

Smith, Vernon L. **HB131 .S6 1991**
Papers in Experimental Economics. Trade Paper. Cambridge University Press. New York, NY. 2006. 827p. ISBN:0-521-02465-X, ISBN13: 978-0-521-02465-5. Dewey:330.
Audience: **u,f.**

Smith, Vernon L. **HG4551.M54 2002B**
Experimental Economics: How We Can Build Better Financial Markets. Ross M. Miller (Foreword by). Trade Paper. John Wiley & Sons, Inc. Hoboken, NJ. 2005. 314p. ISBN:0-471-70625-6, ISBN13: 978-0-471-70625-0. Dewey:332.642. LCCN:2005-297240.
Audience: **u,f.**

Cognitive Economics

Arrow, Kenneth Joseph **HM251**
Social Choice and Individual Values. Ed. 2. Trade Paper. Yale University Press. Cumberland, RI. 1970. 138p. Cowles Foundation Monograph Ser., No. 12 ISBN:0-300-01364-7, ISBN13: 978-0-300-01364-1. Dewey:301.1.
Audience: **l,u,f.**

Bourgine, Paul & Nadal, Jean-Pierre (Editors) **HB74.P8**
[e] Cognitive Economics: An Interdisciplinary Approach. E-Book. Springer. New York, NY. 2005. ISBN:3-540-24708-4, ISBN13: 978-3-540-24708-1. Dewey:330/.019.
Audience: **l,u,f.**

Dimitri, Nicola (Editor, Translator), et al. **HB74.P8C64 2003**
Cognitive Processes and Economic Behaviour. Marcello Basili & Itzhak Gilboa (Editor, Translators). Paper over Boards. Routledge. New York, NY. 2003. 264p. Routledge Siena Studies in Political Economy ISBN:0-415-32005-4, ISBN13: 978-0-415-32005-4. Dewey:330/.01/9. LCCN:2003-046535.
Audience: **l,u,f.**

Egidi, Massimo & Rizzello, Salvatore (Editors) **HB74.P8**
Cognitive Economics. Trade Cloth. Edward Elgar Publishing, Inc. Northampton, MA. 2004. 1,296p. The International Library of Critical Writings in Economics, Vol. 169 ISBN:1-84064-780-9, ISBN13: 978-1-84064-780-8. Dewey:330/.01/9. LCCN:2003-061592.
Audience: **l,u,f.**

Glimcher, Paul W. **QP360.5.G565 2003**
[e] Decisions, Uncertainty, and the Brain: The Science of Neuroeconomics. E-Book. NetLibrary, Inc. Boulder, CO. 2003. ISBN:0-585-44496-X, ISBN13: 978-0-585-44496-3. Dewey:153.
Audience: **u,f.**

Kahneman, Daniel & Tversky, Amos (Editors) **HD30.23 .C469 2000**
Choices, Values, and Frames. Trade Paper. Cambridge University Press. New York, NY. 2000. 860p. ISBN:0-521-62749-4, ISBN13: 978-0-521-62749-8. Dewey:658.4/03. LCCN:99-059883.
Audience: **l,u,f.**

Leahy, Robert L. **RC480.5.L369 2003**
Psychology and the Economic Mind: Cognitive Processes Conceptualization. Trade Cloth. Springer Publishing Company, Inc. New York, NY. 2003. 232p. ISBN:0-8261-5042-X, ISBN13: 978-0-8261-5042-4. Dewey:658.4/03/019. LCCN:2002-075751.
Audience: **u,f.**

Nadal, Jean-Pierre **HB171**
Cognitive Economics: An Interdisciplinary Approach. Paul Bourgine (Editor). Trade Cloth. Springer. New York, NY. 2004. XIV, 479p. ISBN:3-540-40468-6, ISBN13: 978-3-540-40468-2. Dewey:330/.019.
Audience: **l,u,f.**

Rizzello, Salvatore (Editor) **HB131.C64 2003**
Cognitive Developments in Economics. Paper over Boards. Routledge. New York, NY. 2003. 416p. Routledge Frontiers of Political Economy Ser., Vol. 48 ISBN:0-415-30620-5, ISBN13: 978-0-415-30620-1. Dewey:330/.01. LCCN:2003-043149.
Audience: **u,f.**

Ross, Don **HB71.R67 2005**
Economic Theory and Cognitive Science: Microexplanation. Trade Cloth. MIT Press. Cambridge, MA. 2005. 384p. Bradford Bks. ISBN:0-262-18246-7, ISBN13: 978-0-262-18246-1. Dewey:330.1. LCCN:2004-059216.
Audience: **u,f.**

Simon, Herbert, et al. **HD30.23**
Economics, Bounded Rationality and the Cognitive Revolution. Massimo Edigi, Robin Marris & Ricardon Viale (Authors). Trade Cloth. Edward Elgar Publishing, Inc. Northampton, MA. 1992. 240p. ISBN:1-85278-425-3, ISBN13: 978-1-85278-425-6. Dewey:658.403. LCCN:91-042473.
Audience: **u,f.**

Turner, Mark **H61**
Cognitive Dimensions of Social Science: The Way We Think about Politics, Economics, Law, and Society. Trade Paper. Oxford University Press, Inc. New York, NY. 2003. 192p. ISBN:0-19-516539-X, ISBN13: 978-0-19-516539-5. Dewey:300.
Audience: **g,l,u,f.**

Feminist Economics

Agarwal, Bina, et al. **HQ1381.A33 2005**
Amartya Sen's Work and Ideas: A Gender Perspective. Jane Humphries & Ingrid Robeyns (Authors). Trade Paper. Routledge. New York, NY. 2005. ISBN:0-415-37320-4, ISBN13: 978-0-415-37320-3. Dewey:330/.082. LCCN:2005-050608.
Audience: **l,u,f.**

Albelda, Randy P. & Tilly, Chris **HV95.A5988 1997**
Glass Ceilings and Bottomless Pits: Women's Work, Women's Poverty. Trade Cloth. South End Press. Cambridge, MA. 1997. 221p. Women's Studies ISBN:0-89608-566-X, ISBN13: 978-0-89608-566-4. Dewey:362.83/086/942. LCCN:97-017419.
Audience: **l,u,f.** *Choice, 1998.*

American Assembly Staff **HQ1381.W64**
Women and the American Economy: A Look to the 1980s. Juanita M. Kreps (Editor). Trade Paper. Books on Demand. Ann Arbor, MI. 187p. A Spectrum Book Ser. ISBN:0-598-15591-0, ISBN13: 978-0-598-15591-7. Dewey:331.4/0973. LCCN:76-004105.
Audience: **l,u,f.**

Barker, Drucilla K. & Feiner, Susan F. **HQ1381.B365 2004**
Liberating Economics: Feminist Perspectives on Families, Work, and Globalization. Trade Cloth. University of Michigan Press. Chicago, IL. 2004. 208p. ISBN:0-472-09843-8, ISBN13: 978-0-472-09843-9. Dewey:330/.082. LCCN:2004-015058.
Audience: **l,u,f.** *Choice, 2005.*

Bergmann, Barbara R. **HQ1426.B429 2005**
The Economic Emergence of Women. Ed. 2. Cloth over Boards. Palgrave Macmillan. New York, NY. 2005. 272p. ISBN:0-312-21941-5, ISBN13: 978-0-312-21941-3. Dewey:305.43/0973. LCCN:2005-040556.
Audience: **l,u,f.** *Choice, 1987.*

Blau, Francine D., et al. **HQ1421.B56 2006**
The Economics of Women, Men, and Work. Ed. 5. Marianne A. Ferber & Anne E. Winkler (Authors). Trade Paper. Prentice Hall PTR. Upper Saddle River, NJ. 2005. 464p. ISBN:0-13-185154-3, ISBN13: 978-0-13-185154-2. Dewey:305.42/0973. LCCN:2005-005877.
Audience: **l,u,f.**

Cole, Margaret Isabel Postgate **HX0246.W37C6**
Beatrice Webb. Trade Paper. Books on Demand. Ann Arbor, MI. 246p. ISBN:0-598-59296-2, ISBN13: 978-0-598-59296-5. Dewey:923.342. LCCN:46-003961.
Audience: **u,f.**

Costin, Lela B. **HV28.A2C67 2003**
Two Sisters for Social Justice: A Biography of Grace and Edith Abbott. Trade Paper. University of Illinois Press. Champaign, IL. 2003. 344p. ISBN:0-252-07155-7, ISBN13: 978-0-252-07155-3. Dewey:361/.922 B. LCCN:2003-276359.
Audience: **u,f.**

DeLaat, Jacqueline **HD6060.5.U5D45 1999**
Gender in the Workplace: A Case Study Approach. Cloth Text. SAGE Publications, Inc. Thousand Oaks, CA. 1999. 112p. ISBN:0-7619-1478-1, ISBN13: 978-0-7619-1478-5. Dewey:306.3/6150973. LCCN:98-058080.
Audience: **l,u,f.**

Dimand, Mary Ann (Editor), et al. **HB74.8.W66 1995**
Women of Value: Feminist Essays on the History of Women in Economics. Robert W. Dimand & Evelyn L. Forget (Editors). Trade Cloth. Edward Elgar Publishing, Inc. Northampton, MA. 1995. 240p. ISBN:1-85278-959-X, ISBN13: 978-1-85278-959-6. Dewey:330/.082. LCCN:95-007191.
Audience: **u,f.** *Choice, 1996.*

Fawcett, Millicent **JN979 .F26**
What I Remember. Trade Paper. University Press of the Pacific. Miami, FL. 2004. 284p. ISBN:1-4102-1170-3, ISBN13: 978-1-4102-1170-5. Dewey:324/.3/0924.
Audience: **l,u,f.**

Fawcett, Millicent Garrett **JN0979.F3**
The Women's Victory- and after: Personal Reminiscences, 1911-1918. Trade Paper. Books on Demand. Ann Arbor, MI. 196p. ISBN:0-598-81472-8, ISBN13: 978-0-598-81472-2. Dewey:324.6230941. LCCN:22-008628.
Audience: **l,u,f.**

Ferber, Marianne A. & Nelson, Julie A. (Editors) **HQ1190.F447 2003**
Feminist Economics Today: Beyond Economic Man. Trade Cloth. University of Chicago Press. Chicago, IL. 2003. 218p. ISBN:0-226-24206-4, ISBN13: 978-0-226-24206-4. Dewey:330/.082. LCCN:2003-006766.
Audience: **u,f.** *Choice, 2004.*

Figart, Deborah M., et al. **HD4975**
Living Wages, Equal Wages: Gender and Labour Market Policies in the United States. Ellen Mutari & Marilyn Power (Authors). Paper over Boards. Routledge. New York, NY. 2002. 272p. Routledge Advances in Feminist Economics Ser. ISBN:0-415-27390-0, ISBN13: 978-0-415-27390-9. Dewey:331.2/1/0973.
Audience: **l,u,f.** *Choice, 2003.*

Folbre, Nancy **HC110.C6**
The Invisible Heart: Economics and Family Values. Trade Paper. New Press, The. New York, NY. 2002. 288p. ISBN:1-56584-747-4, ISBN13: 978-1-56584-747-7. Dewey:306.3/0973.
Audience: **g,l,u,f.** *Choice, 2001.*

Folbre, Nancy (Editor), et al. **HB171.5**
Women's Work in the World Economy. Barbara Bergmann & Bina Agarwal (Editors). Trade Cloth. Palgrave Macmillan Ltd. Basingstoke, 1992. 304p. ISBN:0-333-53725-4, ISBN13: 978-0-333-53725-1. Dewey:330.
Audience: **g,l,u,f.**

Gibson-Graham, J. K. **HB501.G447 2006**
The End of Capitalism (As We Knew It): A Feminist Critique of Political Economy. Trade Paper. University of Minnesota Press. Minneapolis, MN. 2006. 348p. ISBN:0-8166-4805-0, ISBN13: 978-0-8166-4805-4. Dewey:330.12/2. LCCN:2005-023230.
Audience: **l,u,f.**

Hartsock, Nancy C. **HM131.H32 1983**
Money, Sex and Power: Toward a Feminist Historical Materialism. Trade Cloth. University Press of New England. Lebanon, NH. 1983. 320p. Series in Feminist Theory ISBN:0-582-28279-9, ISBN13: 978-0-582-28279-7. Dewey:303.3/3. LCCN:82-017157.
Audience: **l,u,f.**

Henshall Momsen, Janet **HQ1240.5.D44M657**
Gender and Development. Ed. 2. Paper over Boards. Routledge. New York, NY. 2003. 288p. Routledge Perspectives on Development Ser. ISBN:0-415-26689-0, ISBN13: 978-0-415-26689-5. Dewey:305.3/09172/4. LCCN:2003-008539.
Audience: **l,u,f.**

Hewitson, Gillian J. **HQ1381.H48 1999**
Feminist Economics: Interrogating the Masculinity of Rational Economic Man. Trade Cloth. Edward Elgar Publishing, Inc. Northampton, MA. 1999. 288p. ISBN:1-85898-946-9, ISBN13: 978-1-85898-946-4. Dewey:330/.082. LCCN:98-038336.
Audience: **u,f.** *Choice, 2000.*

Kreps, Juanita **HD6095**
Sex in the Marketplace. Trade Cloth. Johns Hopkins University Press. Baltimore, MD. 1971. 108p. Policy Studies in Employment and Welfare Ser. ISBN:0-8018-1278-X, ISBN13: 978-0-8018-1278-1. Dewey:331.4/0973. LCCN:75-155165.
Audience: **l,u,f.**

Kuiper, Edith & Barker, Drucilla K. **HQ1381.F462 2005**
Feminist Economics and the World Bank: History, Theory, and Policy. Ed. 2. Trade Paper. Routledge. New York, NY. 2005. 256p. ISBN:0-415-76381-9, ISBN13: 978-0-415-76381-3. Dewey:330/.082. LCCN:2005-007856.
Audience: **l,u,f.**

Kuiper, Edith & Sap, Jolande **HQ1190.O94 1995**
[e] Out of the Margin: Feminist Perspectives on Economics. E-Book. Taylor & Francis Group. Philadelphia, PA. ISBN:0-203-98374-2, ISBN13: 978-0-203-98374-4. Dewey:305.42/01.
Audience: **l,u,f.**

Madden, Kirsten & Seitz, Janet **Z7164.E2**
A Bibliography of Female Economic Thought to 1940. Paper over Boards. Routledge. New York, NY. 2004. 560p. Routledge Studies in the History of Economics Ser., Vol. 64 ISBN:0-415-23817-X, ISBN13: 978-0-415-23817-5. Dewey:016.33/009/034. LCCN:2003-058782.
Audience: **g,l,u,f.**

McKay, Ailsa **HD7165**
Future of Social Security: A Feminist Economics Perspective. Paper over Boards. Routledge. New York, NY. 2005. 272p. Routledge Frontiers of Political Economy Ser. ISBN:0-415-34436-0, ISBN13: 978-0-415-34436-4. Dewey:362.5/82. LCCN:2004-029294.
Audience: **g,l,u,f.**

Olson, Paulette I. & Emami, Zohren **HB74.8.O45 2002**
Engendering Economics: Conversations with Women Economists in the United States. Paper over Boards. Routledge. New York, NY. 2002. 288p. ISBN:0-415-20555-7, ISBN13: 978-0-415-20555-9. Dewey:330/.082/0973. LCCN:2001-048405.
Audience: **l,u,f.**

Zalk, Sue R. & Gordon-Kelter, Janice (Editors) **HQ1190.R49 1991**
Revolutions in Knowledge: Feminism in the Social Sciences. Trade Paper. Westview Press. Boulder, CO. 1992. 170p. ISBN:0-8133-0584-5, ISBN13: 978-0-8133-0584-4. Dewey:305.42. LCCN:91-027461.
Audience: **l,u,f.**

EDUCATION

The field of education is more comprehensively represented in RCL than in BCL3. Using the Library of Congress subject classification scheme as a general base, and modifying it to reflect more current trends, a taxonomy of education was created. Excluded from consideration within the education category are topics such as medical education and children's literature, which we believe are covered elsewhere (medicine and literature, respectively). The education taxonomy developed for this project reflects the impact of technology on education, the political aspects of high-stakes testing, initiatives such as No Child Left Behind, and recognition of changes in family and social structures since the 1988.

The education section also recognizes that university extension has merged into distance education and learning in much of the literature. Therefore the area of university extension is no longer included as a separate category. Traditional areas such as history and philosophy of education reflect more of an American focus than in previous editions where Plato's theories or European development of universities were emphasized. New philosophers such as Paulo Freire are incorporated into the content of the database. With an increase in attention to different needs of various populations, and of special services, areas such as multicultural education have been expanded as has special education.

While Web sites were incorporated where relevant, a conscious decision was made to exclude videos and other multi-media material in general. Because education incorporates training in some areas, the huge quantity of videos would be overwhelming. Excellent directories already exist to provide access to these types of materials and should be consulted.

Selection of materials for inclusion were made by subject selectors practicing in the field of education and/or librarianship. Selectors assumed that most colleges will have programs in elementary and secondary education. These selections reflect the needs of a college audience in seeking information about a diversity of educational subjects related to learning, teaching, and intellectual growth.

— Nancy O'Brien and Kate Corby

Education and Training of Teachers and Administrators

Boreen, Jean, et al. **LB1731.4.B67 2003**
Mentoring Across Boundaries: Helping Beginning Teachers Succeed in Challenging Situations. Donna Niday & Mary K. Johnson (Authors). Trade Paper. Stenhouse Publishers. Portland, ME. 2003. 224p. ISBN:1-57110-377-5, ISBN13: 978-1-57110-377-2. Dewey:370/.71/5. LCCN:2003-050692.
Audience: **u,f.** *Choice, 2004.*

Boreen, Jean, et al. **LB1731.4.M4655 2000**
Mentoring Beginning Teachers: Guiding, Reflecting, Coaching. Donna Niday, Mary Johnson & Joseph Potts (Authors), Philippa Stratton (Editor). Trade Paper. Stenhouse Publishers. Portland, ME. 2000. 144p. ISBN:1-57110-309-0, ISBN13: 978-1-57110-309-3. Dewey:370/.71/5. LCCN:99-051645.
Audience: **u,f.** *Choice, 2000.*

Borrowman, Merle L. **LB1715 .B66**
The Liberal and Technical in Teacher Education: A Historical Survey of American Thought. Paper Text. Textbook Publishers. Temecula, CA. 2003. xiii, 247p. ISBN:0-7581-3229-8, ISBN13: 978-0-7581-3229-1. Dewey:370/.73/0973.
Audience: **g.** B

Costigan, Arthur T., et al. **LB2806.22.C67 2004**
Learning to Teach in an Age of Accountability. Margaret Crocco & Karen Kepler Zumwalt (Authors), David Milton Gerwin (Editor). Cloth over Boards. Lawrence Erlbaum Associates, Inc. Mahwah, NJ. 2004. 288p. The Studies in Curriculum Theory Ser. ISBN:0-8058-4707-3, ISBN13: 978-0-8058-4707-9. Dewey:371.1. LCCN:2004-043633.
Audience: **l,u.** *Choice, 2005.*

Dangel, Julie Rainer **LC46.3**
Research on Alternative and Non-Traditional Education: Teacher Education Yearbook XIII. Trade Paper. Scarecrow Press, Inc. Lanham, MD. 2005. 256p. ISBN:1-57886-237-X, ISBN13: 978-1-57886-237-5. Dewey:371.04.
Audience: **u,f.** *Choice, 2005.*

Duffy, Mary Lou & Forgan, James W. **LC3969.45.D84 2005**
Mentoring New Special Education Teachers: A Guide for Mentors and Program Developers. Trade Cloth. SAGE Publications, Inc. Thousand Oaks, CA. 2004. 184p. 1-off Ser. ISBN:0-7619-3133-3, ISBN13: 978-0-7619-3133-1. Dewey:371.9. LCCN:2004-018165.
Audience: **f.** *Choice, 2005.*

Goldblatt, Patricia F. & Smith, Deirdre (Editors) **LB1025.3.C39 2005**
Cases for Teacher Development: Preparing for the Classroom. Cloth Text. SAGE Publications, Inc. Thousand Oaks, CA. 2005. 280p. ISBN:1-4129-1366-7, ISBN13: 978-1-4129-1366-9. Dewey:371.102. LCCN:2004-025365.
Audience: **l,u,f.** *Choice, 2005.*

Leavitt, Howard B. (Editor) **LB1707**
Issues and Problems in Teacher Education: An International Handbook. Cloth Text. Greenwood Publishing Group, Inc. Portsmouth, NH. 1992. 312p. ISBN:0-313-25991-7, ISBN13: 978-0-313-25991-3. Dewey:370.71. LCCN:91-033503.
Audience: **g,l,u,f.** *Choice, 1993.*

Levin, Barbara B. **LB1731.L474 2003**
Case Studies of Teacher Development: An In-Depth Look at How Thinking about Pedagogy Develops over Time. Cloth over Boards. Lawrence Erlbaum Associates, Inc. Mahwah, NJ. 2002. 320p. The Studies in Curriculum Theory Ser. ISBN:0-8058-4197-0, ISBN13: 978-0-8058-4197-8. Dewey:370/.71/173. LCCN:2002-019618.
Audience: **u,f.** *Choice, 2003.*

Novak, John (Editor) **LB1715.D45 1994**
Democratic Teacher Education: Programs, Processes, Problems, and Prospects. Cloth Text. State University of New York Press. Albany, NY. 1994. 262p. SUNY Series in Democracy and Education ISBN:0-7914-1927-4, ISBN13: 978-0-7914-1927-4. Dewey:370.71/0973. LCCN:93-026763.
Audience: **l,f.** *Choice, 1994.*

Parsad, Basmat & Lewis, Laurie **LB1731**
Teacher Preparation and Professional Development: 2000. http://nces.ed.gov/pubs2001/2001088.pdf
Westat, Elizabeth Farris and Bernard Greene (Authors). National Center for Education Statistics.
Audience: **g.**

Portner, Hal **LB1731.4.P67 2002**
Mentoring New Teachers. Ed. 2. Trade Cloth. Corwin Press. Thousand Oaks, CA. 2002. 120p. ISBN:0-7619-4631-4, ISBN13: 978-0-7619-4631-1. Dewey:371.102. LCCN:2002-007684.
Audience: **f.** *Choice, 1999.*

Roth, Wolff-Michael & Tobin, Kenneth George **LB1731.R65 2002**
At the Elbow of Another: Learning to Teach by Coteaching. Trade Paper. Peter Lang Publishing, Inc. New York, NY. 2001. xxv, 340p. ISBN:0-8204-5567-9, ISBN13: 978-0-8204-5567-9. Dewey:371.14/8. LCCN:2001-029274.
Audience: **u,f.** *Choice, 2003, 2002.*

Sarason, Seymour B. **LB1715.S24 1993**
The Case for Change: Rethinking the Preparation of Educators. Trade Cloth. John Wiley & Sons, Inc. Hoboken, NJ. 1993. 317p. Education-Higher Education Ser. ISBN:1-55542-504-6, ISBN13: 978-1-55542-504-3. Dewey:370.71/0973. LCCN:92-029937.
Audience: **g,f.**

Schoonmaker, Frances **LB1715.S33 2002**
Growing up Teaching: Kay's Journey. Cloth Text. Teachers College Press, Teachers College, Columbia University. New York, NY. 2002. 276p. ISBN:0-8077-4271-6, ISBN13: 978-0-8077-4271-6. Dewey:370/.71/1. LCCN:2002-020296.
Audience: **g,l,u,f.** *Choice, 2003.*

Schwebel, Sara L., et al. **LB2157.A3S9 2002**
The Student Teacher's Handbook. Ed. 4. David C. Schwebel, Bernice L. Schwebel & Carol R. Schwebel (Authors). Cloth over Boards. Lawrence Erlbaum Associates, Inc. Mahwah, NJ. 2001. 304p. The Studies in Curriculum Theory Ser. ISBN:0-8058-3928-3, ISBN13: 978-0-8058-3928-9. Dewey:370/.71. LCCN:2001-033001.
Audience: **u.**

Teachers College Press **LB2154.A3P75 2005**
Professional Development Schools: Schools for Developing a Profession. Trade Paper, Perfect. Teachers College Press, Teachers College, Columbia University. New York, NY. 2005.

228p. ISBN:0-8077-4592-8, ISBN13: 978-0-8077-4592-2. Dewey:370/.71/1. LCCN:2005-043068.
Audience: **f.** *Choice, 2005.*

Trubowitz, Sidney & Robins, Maureen Picard **LB1731.4.T78 2003**
The Good Teacher Mentor: Setting the Standard for Support and Success. Trade Cloth. Teachers College Press, Teachers College, Columbia University. New York, NY. 2003. x, 133p. ISBN:0-8077-4388-7, ISBN13: 978-0-8077-4388-1. Dewey:370/.71/55. LCCN:2003-054022.
Audience: **f.** *Choice, 2004.*

Wong, Rosemary T. **LB1775.2**
The First Days of School: How to Be an Effective Teacher. Ed. 3. Harry K. Wong (Based on a movie by). Cloth Text. Harry K. Wong Publications. Mountain View, CA. 2004. xiv, 338p. ISBN:0-9629360-6-5, ISBN13: 978-0-9629360-6-7. Dewey:371.102. LCCN:2003-109628.
Audience: **l,u.**

Education and Training of Teachers and Administrators > Certification of Teachers

LB1771
☐ Certification Requirements for 50 States.
http://www.uky.edu/Education/TEP/usacert.html
University of Kentucky. College of Education.
Audience: **g,l,u,f.**

LB1771
☐ Standards and National Board Certification.
http://www.nbpts.org/standards/nbcert.cfm
National Board for Professional Teaching Standards.
Audience: **g,l,u,f.**

LB1771
☐ State Contacts for Alternative Teacher Education.
http://www.ncei.com/State-alt-contact.htm
National Center for Education Information.
Audience: **g,l,u,f.**

Council for Exceptional Children Staff (Contribution by) **LC3969.45.C69 2003**
What Every Special Educator Must Know: The Ethics, Standards, and Guidelines for Special Educators. Ed. 5. Trade Cloth. Council for Exceptional Children. Arlington, VA. 2003. ISBN:0-86586-993-6, ISBN13: 978-0-86586-993-6. Dewey:379.1/57. LCCN:2003-070002.
Audience: **u,f.**

Feistritzer, C. Emily & Chester, David T. **LB1771 .A45**
Alternative Teacher Certification, A State-by-State Analysis: 1998-1999 Edition. Ed. 9. Trade Paper. National Center for Education Information. Washington, DC. 1998. 426p. ISBN:1-928665-00-4, ISBN13: 978-1-928665-00-7. Dewey:379.
Audience: **g,l,u,f.**

Mack-Kirschner, Adrienne **LB1771.M27 2003**
The Teacher's Guide to National Board Certification: Unpacking the Standards. Trade Paper. Heinemann. Portsmouth, NH. 2003. 128p. ISBN:0-325-00549-4, ISBN13: 978-0-325-00549-2. Dewey:379.1/57. LCCN:2002-014464.
Audience: **l,u.**

Smylie, Mark A. & Miretzky, Debra (Editors) **LB5**
Developing the Teacher Workforce. Trade Cloth. University of Chicago Press. Chicago, IL. 2004. 320p. National Society for the Study of Education Yearbooks Ser. ISBN:0-226-76718-3, ISBN13: 978-0-226-76718-5. Dewey:371.14.
Audience: **u,f.**

U. S. News and World Report Staff **LB2165.W47 2004**
U. S. News Ultimate Guide to Becoming a Teacher. Trade Paper. Sourcebooks, Inc. Naperville, IL. 2004. 528p. ISBN:1-4022-0291-1, ISBN13: 978-1-4022-0291-9. Dewey:371.1/0023/73. LCCN:2004-012729.
Audience: **g,l,u.** *Choice, 2005.*

Education and Training of Teachers and Administrators > Professional Aspects of Teaching and School Administration

LB1707
☐ Characteristics of Public School Teachers' Professional Development Activities: 1999-2000.
http://nces.ed.gov/pubs2005/2005030.pdf
National Center for Education Statistics.
Audience: **l,u,f.**

Carnegie Forum on Education and the Economy Staff **LB1775.C34 1986**
A Nation Prepared: Teachers for the 21st Century: the Report of the Task Force on Teaching As a Profession, Carnegie Forum on Education and the Economy, May 1986. Trade Cloth. Forum, The. Santa Fe, NM. 1986. ix, 135p. ISBN:0-9616685-0-4, ISBN13: 978-0-9616685-0-1. Dewey:371.1/00973. LCCN:86-011743.
Audience: **g,l,u.** BCL3

Heck, Shirley F. & Williams, C. Ray **LB1775.H42 1984**
ⓔ The Complex Roles of the Teacher: An Ecological Perspective. E-Book. NetLibrary, Inc. Boulder, CO. 1984. ISBN:0-585-35539-8, ISBN13: 978-0-585-35539-9. Dewey:371.1/02.
Audience: **l,u,f.**

Jimerson, Lorna **LC5146**
☐ The Competitive Disadvantage: Teacher Compensation in Rural America.
http://www.ruraledu.org/docs/teacher_pay.pdf
Rural School and Community Trust.
Audience: **l,u.**

Johnson, Susan Moore **LB1775 .J546**
Teachers at Work: Achieving Success in Our Schools. Paper Text. DIANE Publishing Company. Collingdale, PA. 2000. 395p. ISBN:0-7881-6860-6, ISBN13: 978-0-7881-6860-4. Dewey:371.11/02.
Audience: **l,u,f.**

King, James R. **LB1775.8.K56 1998**
Uncommon Caring: Learning from Men Who Teach in the Primary Grades. Trade Cloth. Teachers College Press, Teachers College, Columbia University. New York, NY. 1998. 168p. Early Childhood Education Ser. ISBN:0-8077-3740-2, ISBN13: 978-0-8077-3740-8. Dewey:372.11. LCCN:98-003464.
Audience: **u,f.**

Lipka, Richard P. & Brinthaupt, Thomas M. (Editors) **LB1775.2.R65 1999**
The Role of Self in Teacher Development. Cloth Text. State University of New York Press. Albany, NY. 1998. 256p. SUNY Series, Studying the Self ISBN:0-7914-4015-X, ISBN13: 978-0-7914-4015-5. Dewey:371.1/0023. LCCN:98-008361.
Audience: **u,f.** *Choice, 1999.*

Miller, Janet L. **LB1775.M615 1990**
Creating Spaces and Finding Voices: Teachers Collaborating for Empowerment. Paper Text. State University of New York Press. Albany, NY. 1990. 204p. SUNY Series in Teacher Preparation and Development ISBN:0-7914-0282-7, ISBN13: 978-0-7914-0282-5. Dewey:371.1/02/0973. LCCN:89-036216.
Audience: **u,f.** *Choice, 1991.*

Roehrig, Alysia D., et al. **LB2844.1.N4R62 2002**
Stories of Beginning Teachers: First Year Challenges and Beyond. Michael Pressley & Denise A. Talotta (Authors). Trade Cloth. University of Notre Dame Press. Notre Dame, IN. 2002. 256p. The Notre Dame Alliance for Catholic Education Ser. ISBN:0-268-01777-8, ISBN13: 978-0-268-01777-4. Dewey:371.1. LCCN:2001-005495.
Audience: **l,u.** *Choice, 2003.*

Rogers, Dwight L. & Babinski, Leslie M. **LB2844.1.N4R63 2002**
From Isolation to Conversation: Supporting New Teachers' Development. Cloth Text. State University of New York Press. Albany, NY. 2002. 160p. Teacher Preparation and Development Ser. ISBN:0-7914-5335-9, ISBN13: 978-0-7914-5335-3. Dewey:371.102. LCCN:2001-049460.
Audience: **l,u,f.** *Choice, 2002.*

Sargent, Paul **LB1776.2.S27 2001**
Real Men or Real Teachers?: Contradictions in the Lives of Men Elementary School Teachers. Trade Paper. Men's Studies Press. Oakdale, TN. 2001. 248p. ISBN:0-9671794-3-2, ISBN13: 978-0-9671794-3-8. Dewey:372.11/0081/0973. LCCN:00-049552.
Audience: **g,l,u,f.** *Choice, 2002.*

Singer, Harvey **LB2844.1.N4S56 2003**
A New Teacher's Guide: Surviving Your First Year. Book, Other. Scarecrow Press, Inc. Lanham, MD. 2003. 192p. ISBN:0-8108-4573-3, ISBN13: 978-0-8108-4573-2. Dewey:371.1. LCCN:2002-011766.
Audience: **g,l,u,f.** *Choice, 2003.*

Wilke, Rebecca Lynn **LB2844.1.N4W54 2003**
The First Days of Class: A Practical Guide for the Beginning Teacher. Trade Cloth. Corwin Press. Thousand Oaks, CA. 2002. 152p. ISBN:0-7619-3812-5, ISBN13: 978-0-7619-3812-5. Dewey:371.1. LCCN:2002-010062.
Audience: **u,f.** *Choice, 2003.*

Education and Training of Teachers and Administrators > Teacher Training in Universities and Colleges

LB1715
☐ American Association of Colleges for Teacher Education.
http://www.aacte.org/
American Association of Colleges for Teacher Education.
Audience: **g,l,u,f.**

LB1715
☐ National Council for Accreditation of Teacher Education.
http://www.ncate.org/
National Council for Accreditation of Teacher Education..
Audience: **f.**

Bondy, Elizabeth & Ross, Dorene D. (Editors) **LB1716.F6P74 2005**
Preparing for Inclusive Teaching: Meeting the Challenges of Teacher Education Reform. Cloth Text. State University of New York Press. Albany, NY. 2005. 288p. ISBN:0-7914-6357-5, ISBN13: 978-0-7914-6357-4. Dewey:370/.71/1. LCCN:2004-048186.
Audience: **u,f.** *Choice, 2005.*

Cochran-Smith, Marilyn & Zeichner, Ken (Editors) **LB1715.A47 2006**
Studying Teacher Education: The Report of the AERA Panel on Research and Teacher Education. Patricia Brady, Renee T. Clift & Hillary Conklin (Contribution by). Cloth over Boards. Lawrence Erlbaum Associates, Inc. Mahwah, NJ. 2005. 816p. ISBN:0-8058-5592-0, ISBN13: 978-0-8058-5592-0. Dewey:370/.71/1. LCCN:2005-011015.
Audience: **u,f.** *Choice, 2005.*

Goodlad, John I. **LB1715**
Educational Renewal: Better Teachers, Better Schools. Trade Paper. John Wiley & Sons, Inc. Hoboken, NJ. 1998. 336p. Education Ser. ISBN:0-7879-4422-X, ISBN13: 978-0-7879-4422-3. Dewey:370.71/0973.
Audience: **g,u,f.** *Choice, 1994.*

Graham, Peg & Hudson-Ross, Sally (Editors) **LB1731.4.T45 1999**
Teacher - Mentor: A Dialogue for Collaborative Learning. Trade Cloth. Teachers College Press, Teachers College, Columbia University. New York, NY. 1999. 208p. Practitioner Inquiry Ser. ISBN:0-8077-3794-1, ISBN13: 978-0-8077-3794-1. Dewey:373.1102/0973. LCCN:98-039674.
Audience: **u,f.** *Choice, 1999.*

Griffin, Gary A. (Editor) **LB1715.G75 2002**
Rethinking Standards Through Teacher Preparation Partnerships. Paper Text. State University of New York Press. Albany, NY. 2002. ix, 221p. ISBN:0-7914-5440-1, ISBN13: 978-0-7914-5440-4. Dewey:370/.71/1. LCCN:2002-019098.
Audience: **g,l,u,f.** *Choice, 2003.*

Grossman, Pamela **PE68.U5G76 1990**
The Making of a Teacher: Teacher Knowledge and Teacher Education. Cloth Text. Teachers College Press, Teachers College, Columbia University. New York, NY. 1990. 200p. The Series on School Reform ISBN:0-8077-3048-3, ISBN13: 978-0-8077-3048-5. Dewey:420/.71/273. LCCN:90-038509.
Audience: **l,u,f.** *Choice, 1991.*

Modoc Press Staff & American Association of Colleges for Teacher Education Staff (Contribution by) **LB1715.T424 2004**
Teacher Education Programs in the United States: A Guide. Book, Other. Greenwood Publishing Group, Inc. Portsmouth, NH. 2004. 488p. Ace/Praeger Series on Higher Education Ser. ISBN:0-275-98156-8, ISBN13: 978-0-275-98156-3. Dewey:370/.71/1. LCCN:2004-014776.
Audience: **l,u.** *Choice, 2005.*

Vavrus, Michael J. **LB1731.V38 2002**
Transforming the Multicultural Education of Teachers: Theory, Research, and Practice. Cloth Text. Teachers College Press, Teachers College, Columbia University. New York, NY. 2002. 256p. ISBN:0-8077-4261-9, ISBN13: 978-0-8077-4261-7. Dewey:370/.71/5. LCCN:2002-067316.
Audience: **u,f.** *Choice, 2003.*

School Administration and Organization

LB2817.3
The Comparative Guide to American Elementary and Secondary Schools 2004. Trade Cloth. Grey House Publishing. Millerton, NY. 2004. 2,300p. ISBN:1-59237-047-0, ISBN13: 978-1-59237-047-4. Dewey:371.01/0973.
Audience: **g.**

LB2831
☐ The Key Work of School Boards.
http://www.nsba.org/keywork2/
National School Boards Association.
Audience: **g,l,u,f.**

Berends, Mark, et al. **LB2822.82.I44 2001**
Implementation and Performance in New American Schools: Three Years into Scale Up. Sheila Nataraj Kirby, Scott Naftel & Christopher McKelvey (Authors). Trade Paper. RAND Corporation, The. Santa Monica, CA. 2000. 260p. ISBN:0-8330-2902-9, ISBN13: 978-0-8330-2902-7. Dewey:371.2/00973. LCCN:00-062770.
Audience: **u,f.** *Choice, 2001.*

Burrup, Percy E., et al. **LB2825.B86 2001**
Financing Education in a Climate of Change. Ed. 8. Vern Brimley & Rulon R. Garfield (Authors). Cloth Text. Allyn & Bacon, Inc. Boston, MA. 2001. 432p. ISBN:0-205-33235-8, ISBN13: 978-0-205-33235-9. Dewey:371.2/06/0973. LCCN:2001-022229.
Audience: **u,f.** B

Center on Reinventing Public Education. Daniel J. Evans School of Public Affairs. University of Washington **LB2806.36**
☐ A Study of Charter School Accountability.
http://www.ed.gov/pubs/chartacct/index.html
Melissa Cast. United States. Department of Education.
Audience: **g,l,u,f.**

Clinchy, Evans (Editor) **LB2822.82.C76 2000**
Creating New Schools: How Small Schools Are Changing American Education. Trade Cloth. Teachers College Press, Teachers College, Columbia University. New York, NY. 2000. 240p. ISBN:0-8077-3877-8, ISBN13: 978-0-8077-3877-1. Dewey:371.01. LCCN:99-048170.
Audience: **g,l,u,f.** *Choice, 2000.*

Comer, James P., et al. **LB2805**
Child by Child: The Comer Process for Change in Education. Maurice Falk, Michael Ben-Avie, Norris M. Haynes & Edward T. Joyner (Authors), Lois Jean White (Foreword by). Cloth Text. Teachers College Press, Teachers College, Columbia University. New York, NY. 1999. 336p. ISBN:0-8077-3869-7, ISBN13: 978-0-8077-3869-6. Dewey:371.2/00973.
Audience: **g,l,u,f.** *Choice, 2000.*

Coons, John E. & Sugarman, Stephen D. **LB1027.9.C68 1999**
Education by Choice: The Case for Family Control. Trade Paper. Educator's International Press, Inc. Troy, NY. 1999. 290p. ISBN:1-891928-02-3, ISBN13: 978-1-891928-02-4. Dewey:379.1/11/0973. LCCN:99-010059.
Audience: **g.** B

Earle, Jason & Kruse, Sharon D. **LB2806.E27 1999**
Organizational Literacy for Educators. Trade Paper. Lawrence Erlbaum Associates, Inc. Mahwah, NJ. 1999. 272p. Topics in Educational Leadership Ser. ISBN:0-8058-2639-4, ISBN13: 978-0-8058-2639-5. Dewey:371.2/00973. LCCN:98-029684.
Audience: **l,u,f.** *Choice, 1999.*

Hassel, Bryan C. **LB2806.36.H37 1999**
The Charter School Challenge: Avoiding the Pitfalls, Fulfilling the Promise. Book, Other. Brookings Institution Press. Washington, DC. 1999. 193p. ISBN:0-8157-3512-X, ISBN13: 978-0-8157-3512-0. Dewey:371.01. LCCN:98-058132.
Audience: **g,l,u.** *Choice, 1999.*

Hess, Frederick M. **LB2822.82.H49 2004**
Common Sense School Reform. Cloth over Boards. Palgrave Macmillan. New York, NY. 2004. 272p. ISBN:1-4039-6353-3, ISBN13: 978-1-4039-6353-6. Dewey:371.2. LCCN:2003-190057.
Audience: **g,u,f.** *Choice, 2004.*

March, James G; Olsen, Johan P
Ambiguity and Choice in Organizations. Ed. 2. Oxford University Press, Inc. 1985. ISBN:82-00-01960-8, ISBN13: 978-82-00-01960-2.
Audience: **u,f.** B

McMeekin, Robert **LB2822.8**
Incentives to Improve Education: A New Perspective. Trade Cloth. Edward Elgar Publishing, Inc. Northampton, MA. 2003. 224p. ISBN:1-84376-068-1, ISBN13: 978-1-84376-068-9. Dewey:371.2. LCCN:2002-034710.
Audience: **g,u,f.** *Choice, 2003.*

Melissa Cast **LB2801.A1**
☐ Clearinghouse on Educational Policy and Management.
http://cepm.uoregon.edu/
Clearinghouse on Educational Policy and Management.
Audience: **l,u,f.**

Melissa Cast **LB2825**
☐ School Spending: The Business of Education.
http://www.asbj.com/schoolspending/
American School Board Journal.
Audience: **g,u,f.**

Quade, Quentin **LB2825.Q24 1996**
Financing Education: The Struggle Between Governmental Monopoly and Parental Control. Trade Cloth. Transaction Publishers. Somerset, NJ. 1996. 166p. ISBN:1-56000-255-7, ISBN13: 978-1-56000-255-0. Dewey:379.1/222/0973. LCCN:96-017333.
Audience: **g,l,u,f.** *Choice, 1997.*

Richardson, Michael D., et al. **LB2831.92.R53 1993**
School Principals and Change. Paula M. Short & Robert L. Prickett (Authors). Paper over Boards. Garland Publishing, Inc. New York, NY. 1993. 288p. Source Books on Education, Vol.

33 ISBN:0-8153-0383-1, ISBN13: 978-0-8153-0383-1. Dewey:371.20120973. LCCN:92-028436.
Audience: **l,u,f.** *Choice, 1993.*

Rofes, Eric E. & Stulberg, Lisa M. (Editors) **LB2806.36.E42 2004**
The Emancipatory Promise of Charter Schools: Toward a Progressive Politics of School Choice. Herbert Gintis (Foreword by). Cloth Text. State University of New York Press. Albany, NY. 2004. 304p. ISBN:0-7914-6235-8, ISBN13: 978-0-7914-6235-5. Dewey:371.01. LCCN:2003-068663.
Audience: **u,f.** *Choice, 2005.*

Sarason, Seymour B. **LB2806.36.S27 1998**
Charter Schools: Another Flawed Educational Reform? Trade Cloth. Teachers College Press, Teachers College, Columbia University. New York, NY. 1998. 128p. The Series on School Reform ISBN:0-8077-3785-2, ISBN13: 978-0-8077-3785-9. Dewey:371.01. LCCN:98-011732.
Audience: **g,l,u,f.** *Choice, 1999.*

Sergiovanni, Thomas **LB2805.S518 1994**
Building Community in Schools. Trade Cloth. John Wiley & Sons, Inc. Hoboken, NJ. 1993. 222p. The Jossey-Bass Education Ser. ISBN:1-55542-571-2, ISBN13: 978-1-55542-571-5. Dewey:371.2/00973. LCCN:93-019582.
Audience: **u,f.** *Choice, 1994.*

Sirotnik, Kenneth A. **LB2806.22.H65 2004**
Holding Accountability Accountable: What Ought to Matter in Public Education. Trade Cloth. Teachers College Press, Teachers College, Columbia University. New York, NY. 2004. 216p. Series on School Reform ISBN:0-8077-4465-4, ISBN13: 978-0-8077-4465-9. Dewey:379.1/58. LCCN:2003-066895.
Audience: **u,f.** *Choice, 2004.*

Slavin, Robert E. & Madden, Nancy A. (Editors) **LB2822.8.S88 2001**
Success for All: Research and Reform in Elementary Education. Cloth over Boards. Lawrence Erlbaum Associates, Inc. Mahwah, NJ. 2001. 248p. ISBN:0-8058-3810-4, ISBN13: 978-0-8058-3810-7. Dewey:372. LCCN:00-044248.
Audience: **l,u,f.** *Choice, 2001.*

Stecher, Brian & Kirby, Sheila Nataraj (Editors) **LB28.06.22**
Organizational Improvement and Accountability.
http://www.rand.org/pubs/monographs/2004/RAND_MG136.pdf
Rand Corporation.
Audience: **u,f.**

Trump, Kenneth S. **LB2866.5.T78 2000**
Classroom Killers? Hallway Hostages?: How Schools Can Prevent and Manage School Crises. Trade Paper. Corwin Press. Thousand Oaks, CA. 2000. 184p. ISBN:0-7619-7511-X, ISBN13: 978-0-7619-7511-3. Dewey:371.7/82/0973. LCCN:00-008379.
Audience: **g,l,u,f.** *Choice, 2001.*

Ward, James G. & Anthony, Patricia (Editors) **LB2825.W43 1992**
Who Pays for Student Diversity?: Population Changes and Educational Policy. Trade Cloth. Corwin Press. Thousand Oaks, CA. 1992. 280p. School Finance Ser. ISBN:0-8039-4019-X, ISBN13: 978-0-8039-4019-2. Dewey:379.20973. LCCN:91-035594.
Audience: **l,u,f.** *Choice, 1992.*

Warren, Donald R. **LB2807**
To Enforce Education: A History of the Founding Years of the United States Office of Education. Trade Cloth. Greenwood Publishing Group, Inc. Portsmouth, NH. 1985. 239p. ISBN:0-313-25213-0, ISBN13: 978-0-313-25213-6. Dewey:379.73. LCCN:73-008209.
Audience: **l,u,f.** B

School Administration and Organization > Administrative Personnel

Beck, Lynn G. & Murphy, Joseph **LB2831.93.B43 1993**
Understanding the Principalship: Metaphorical Themes, 1920s-1990s. Cloth Text. Teachers College Press, Teachers College, Columbia University. New York, NY. 1992. 272p. ISBN:0-8077-3208-7, ISBN13: 978-0-8077-3208-3. Dewey:371.2012. LCCN:92-028071.
Audience: **l,u,f.** *Choice, 1993.*

Brunner, C. Cryss (Editor) **LB2831.72.S23 1999**
Sacred Dreams: Women and the Superintendency. Cloth Text. State University of New York Press. Albany, NY. 1999. 288p. SUNY Series in Women in Education ISBN:0-7914-4159-8, ISBN13: 978-0-7914-4159-6. Dewey:371.2/011. LCCN:98-036545.
Audience: **u,f.** *Choice, 1999.*

Carlton, Patrick W. **LB2831.92**
Oral History of the Principalship.
http://scholar.lib.vt.edu/faculty_archives/principalship/
Virginia Tech New Media Center.
Audience: **g.**

Edson, Sakre K. **LB2831.62.E33 1988**
Pushing the Limits: The Female Administrative Aspirant. Cloth Text. State University of New York Press. Albany, NY. 1988. 299p. SUNY Series in Educational Leadership ISBN:0-88706-556-2, ISBN13: 978-0-88706-556-9. Dewey:371.2/0088042. LCCN:87-001893.
Audience: **u,f.** *Choice, 1988.*

Gates, Susan M., & Ringel, Jeanne S. **LB2831.82**
Who is Leading Our Schools? An Overview of School Administrators and Their Careers.
http://www.rand.org/publications/MR/MR1679/
Santibanez, Chung Catherine H., and Ross, Karen (Authors). Rand.
Audience: **u,f.**

Johnson, Susan Moore **LB2831.72**
Leading to Change: The Challenge of the New Superintendency. Trade Cloth. John Wiley & Sons, Inc. Hoboken, NJ. 1996. 352p. ISBN:0-7879-0214-4, ISBN13: 978-0-7879-0214-8. Dewey:371.2/011. LCCN:96-004460.
Audience: **u,f.** *Choice, 1996.*

Jones, Bruce Anthony (Editor) **LB2805.E3475 2000**
Educational Leadership: Policy Dimensions in the 21st Century, 1. Trade Cloth. Greenwood Publishing Group, Inc. Portsmouth, NH. 2000. x, 176p. Educational Policy in the 21st Century Ser. ISBN:1-56750-488-4, ISBN13: 978-1-56750-488-0. Dewey:379.73. LCCN:99-046145.
Audience: **g,l,u,f.** *Choice, 2000.*

Lipham, James M., et al. **LB2831.92.L57 1985**
The Principalship. Robb E. Rankin & James A. Hoeh Jr. (Authors). Cloth Text. Longman Publishing Group. White Plains, NY. 1985. 335p. ISBN:0-582-28581-X, ISBN13: 978-0-582-28581-1. Dewey:371.2/012/0973. LCCN:84-021858.
Audience: **u,f.** BCL3

National Association of Elementary School Principals **LB2831.92**
[Web] National Association of Elementary School Principals.
http://www.naesp.org/
Audience: **g,l,u,f.**

Richardson, Michael D., et al. **LB2831.92.R53 1993**
School Principals and Change. Paula M. Short & Robert L. Prickett (Authors). Paper over Boards. Garland Publishing, Inc. New York, NY. 1993. 288p. Source Books on Education, Vol. 33 ISBN:0-8153-0383-1, ISBN13: 978-0-8153-0383-1. Dewey:371.20120973. LCCN:92-028436.
Audience: **l,u,f.** *Choice, 1993.*

Rothstein, Stanley W. & Garubo, Raymond C. **LB2806**
Supportive Supervision in Schools: A Guide for Teachers and Administrators. Cloth Text. Greenwood Publishing Group, Inc. Portsmouth, NH. 1998. 176p. The Greenwood Educator's Reference Collection ISBN:0-313-29652-9, ISBN13: 978-0-313-29652-9. Dewey:371.2/03. LCCN:97-021993.
Audience: **g,l,u,f.** *Choice, 1998.*

Roza, Marguerite & Celio, Mary Beth **LB2831.92**
[Web] A Matter of Definition: Is there truly a shortage of school principals?
http://www.crpe.org/pubs/pdf/mroza_princshortagewb.pdf
Harvey, James and Wishon, Susan (Authors). Center on Reinventing Public Education.
Audience: **u,f.**

Sergiovanni, Thomas **LB2831.72**
Leadership for the Schoolhouse: How Is It Different? Why Is It Important? Trade Paper. John Wiley & Sons, Inc. Hoboken, NJ. 2000. 232p. ISBN:0-7879-5542-6, ISBN13: 978-0-7879-5542-7. Dewey:371.2/011. LCCN:95-009405.
Audience: **g,l,u,f.** *Choice, 1996.*

Tyack, David B. & Hansot, Elisabeth **LB2805**
Managers of Virtue: Public School Leadership in America, 1820-1980. Trade Paper. Basic Books. New York, NY. 1986. 320p. ISBN:0-465-04374-7, ISBN13: 978-0-465-04374-3. Dewey:371.2/00973. LCCN:81-022923.
Audience: **g,l,u.**

Wolcott, Harry F. **LB2831.92.W64 2003**
The Man in the Principal's Office. Trade Paper. AltaMira Press. Walnut Creek, CA. 2003. 356p. ISBN:0-7591-0529-4, ISBN13: 978-0-7591-0529-4. Dewey:372.12/012. LCCN:2003-050278.
Audience: **g,l,u.**

School Administration and Organization > Teaching Personnel, Work Conditions

American Federation of Teachers **HD6483**
[Web] AFT: A Union of Professionals.
http://www.aft.org/
American Federation of Teachers, AFL-CIO.
Audience: **g.**

Brandt, Richard M. **LB2842.2.B7 1990**
Incentive Pay and Career Ladders for Today's Teachers: A Study of Current Programs and Practices. Cloth Text. State University of New York Press. Albany, NY. 1990. 286p. SUNY Series in Educational Leadership ISBN:0-7914-0399-8, ISBN13: 978-0-7914-0399-0. Dewey:331.2/813711/00973. LCCN:89-048220.
Audience: **u,f.** *Choice, 1991.*

Brimelow, Peter **LB2844.53.U6**
The Worm in the Apple: How the Teacher Unions Are Destroying American Education. Trade Paper. HarperCollins Publishers. New York, NY. 2004. 320p. ISBN:0-06-009662-4, ISBN13: 978-0-06-009662-5. Dewey:331.88/113711/00973.
Audience: **g.** *Choice, 2003.*

Golin, Steve **LB2844.47.U62N494**
The Newark Teacher Strikes: Hopes on the Line. Trade Cloth. Rutgers University Press. Piscataway, NJ. 2002. 336p. ISBN:0-8135-3057-1, ISBN13: 978-0-8135-3057-4. Dewey:331.892/813711. LCCN:2001-048608.
Audience: **g,l,u,f.** *Choice, 2003.*

Goodlad, John I. (Editor), et al. **LB1779**
The Moral Dimensions of Teaching. Roger Soder & Kenneth A. Sirotnik (Editors). Trade Paper. John Wiley & Sons, Inc. Hoboken, NJ. 1993. 368p. Education-Higher Education Ser. ISBN:1-55542-637-9, ISBN13: 978-1-55542-637-8. Dewey:174/.9372. LCCN:89-028755.
Audience: **f.** *Choice, 1990.*

Grumet, Madeleine R. **LB2837.G78 1988**
Bitter Milk: Women and Teaching. Trade Paper. University of Massachusetts Press. Amherst, MA. 1988. 248p. ISBN:0-87023-613-X, ISBN13: 978-0-87023-613-6. Dewey:371.1/0088041/0973. LCCN:87-022679.
Audience: **g,l,u,f.** *Choice, 1989.*

Hoffman, Nancy (Editor) **LB2837.W65 1981**
Woman's "True" Profession: Voices from the History of Teaching. Trade Cloth. Feminist Press at The City University of New York. New York, NY. 1981. 352p. Women's Lives-Women's Work Ser. ISBN:0-912670-93-2, ISBN13: 978-0-912670-93-5. Dewey:371.1/00973. LCCN:80-023329.
Audience: **g,l.** BCL3

Ingersoll, Richard M. **LB1775.2.I555 2003**
Who Controls Teacher's Work?: Power and Accountability in America's Schools. Trade Cloth. Harvard University Press. Cambridge, MA. 2003. 366p. ISBN:0-674-00922-3, ISBN13: 978-0-674-00922-6. Dewey:371.1. LCCN:2002-027274.
Audience: **l,u,f.** *Choice, 2003.*

Irwin, Judith W. **LB2805.I7 1996**
Empowering Ourselves and Transforming Schools: Educators Making a Difference. Cloth Text. State University of New York Press. Albany, NY. 1996. 352p. SUNY Series in Teacher Preparation and Development ISBN:0-7914-3103-7, ISBN13: 978-0-7914-3103-0. Dewey:371.2/00973. LCCN:95-051392.
Audience: **g,u,f.** *Choice, 1997.*

Kissen, Rita M. **LB2844.1.G39K57 1996**
The Last Closet: The Real Lives of Lesbian and Gay Teachers. Trade Cloth. Heinemann. Portsmouth, NH. 1996. 198p. ISBN:0-435-07005-3, ISBN13: 978-0-435-07005-2. Dewey:371.1/008/664. LCCN:96-4128.
Audience: **g,l,u.** *Choice, 1997.*

National Education Association **LB2832.2**
Status of the American Public School Teacher 2000-2002.
http://www.nea.org/edstats/images/status.pdf
National Education Association.
Audience: **g,l,u.**

National Staff Development Council **LB1775.2**
National Staff Development Council.
http://www.nsdc.org/
Melissa Cast. National Staff Development Council.
Audience: **l,u,f.**

Nolan, James L. Jr. & Meister, Denise G. **LB1777.2.N64 2000**
Teachers and Educational Change: The Lived Experience of Secondary School Restructuring. Cloth Text. State University of New York Press. Albany, NY. 2000. xi, 237p. Series in Restructuring and School Change ISBN:0-7914-4699-9, ISBN13: 978-0-7914-4699-7. Dewey:373.11/06. LCCN:00-026563.
Audience: **u,f.** *Choice, 2001.*

Podair, Jerald E. **LB2844.47.U62N4867**
The Strike That Changed New York: Blacks, Whites, and the Ocean Hill-Brownsville Crisis. Cloth over Boards. Yale University Press. Cumberland, RI. 2002. 288p. ISBN:0-300-08122-7, ISBN13: 978-0-300-08122-0. Dewey:331.892/813711. LCCN:2002-004315.
Audience: **u,f.** *Choice, 2003.*

Prentice, Alison & Theobald, Marjorie R. (Editors) **LB2837.W68 1991**
Women Who Taught: Perspectives on the History of Women and Teaching. Trade Cloth. University of Toronto Press. Toronto, ON. 1991. 304p. ISBN:0-8020-2745-8, ISBN13: 978-0-8020-2745-0. Dewey:371.1/0082. LCCN:92-226267.
Audience: **g,l,u,f.** *Choice, 1991.*

Selden, David **LB2844.53.U6**
The Teacher Rebellion. Trade Paper. Howard University Press. Washington, DC. 2003. 272p. ISBN:0-88258-235-6, ISBN13: 978-0-88258-235-1. Dewey:331.88/113711/00973.
Audience: **g,l,u.** B

Shedd, Joseph B. & Bacharach, Samuel B. **LB2805.S579 1991**
Tangled Hierarchies: Teachers As Professionals and the Management of Schools. Trade Cloth. John Wiley & Sons, Inc. Hoboken, NJ. 1991. 240p. Education-Higher Education Ser. ISBN:1-55542-342-6, ISBN13: 978-1-55542-342-1. Dewey:371.2/00973. LCCN:90-026937.
Audience: **g,l,u,f.** *Choice, 1991.*

Urban, Wayne J. **LB2844.53.U6U69 2000**
Gender, Race, and the National Education Association: Professionalism and Its Limitations. Cloth Text. Routledge. New York, NY. 2000. 304p. Studies in the History of Education Ser. ISBN:0-8153-3816-3, ISBN13: 978-0-8153-3816-1. Dewey:370. LCCN:00-711333.
Audience: **g,f.**

School Administration and Organization > Classroom Management and Discipline

KF4159.S364 2004
School Violence: From Discipline to Due Process. Trade Paper, Perfect. American Bar Association. Chicago, IL. 2005. 239p. ISBN:1-59031-465-4, ISBN13: 978-1-59031-465-4. Dewey:344.730793. LCCN:2004-023759.
Audience: **u,f.**

Alexandrowicz, Harry J. **LB1775.A414 2001**
Testing Your Mettle: Tough Problems and Real-World Solutions for Middle and High School Teachers. Trade Cloth. Corwin Press. Thousand Oaks, CA. 2001. 152p. One-Off Ser. ISBN:0-7619-7752-X, ISBN13: 978-0-7619-7752-0. Dewey:371.1/02/4. LCCN:00-011238.
Audience: **u.**

Bender, William N. **LB301.46**
Relational Discipline: Strategies for in-Your-Face Kids. Allyn & Bacon, Inc. 2002. ISBN:0-205-30633-0, ISBN13: 978-0-205-30633-6.
Audience: **g,l,u.**

Burden, Paul R. **LB3013.B876 2000**
Powerful Classroom Management Strategies: Motivating Students to Learn. Trade Cloth. Corwin Press. Thousand Oaks, CA. 2000. 176p. One-Off Ser. ISBN:0-7619-7562-4, ISBN13: 978-0-7619-7562-5. Dewey:371.102/4. LCCN:99-050711.
Audience: **u.**

Evertson, Carolyn & Weinstein, Carol S. (Editors) **LB3013.H336 2006**
Handbook of Classroom Management: Research, Practice, and Contemporary Issues. Miriam Ben-Peretz, Hank Bohanon-Edmonson, Victor Battistich & Cheryl Mason Bolick (Contribution by). Cloth over Boards. Lawrence Erlbaum Associates, Inc. Mahwah, NJ. 2006. 1352p. ISBN:0-8058-4753-7, ISBN13: 978-0-8058-4753-6. Dewey:371.102/4. LCCN:2005-030877.
Audience: **u,f.**

Greene, Ross W. **HQ773.G73 2005**
The Explosive Child: A New Approach for Understanding and Parenting Easily Frustrated, Chronically Inflexible Children. Trade Paper. HarperCollins Publishers. New York, NY. 2005. 320p. ISBN:0-06-077939-X, ISBN13: 978-0-06-077939-9. Dewey:649/.153.
Audience: **g,l,u,f.**

Hyman, Irwin A. **Z5055.B88B873A**
School Discipline and School Violence: The Teacher Variance Approach. Trade Paper. Allyn & Bacon, Inc. Boston, MA. 1997. ISBN:0-205-27023-9, ISBN13: 978-0-205-27023-1. Dewey:371.5.
Audience: **u.**

Hyman, Irwin A. & Snook, Pamela A. **LB3013.H897 1999**
Dangerous Schools: What We Can Do about the Physical and Emotional Abuse to Our Children. Trade Cloth. John Wiley & Sons, Inc. Hoboken, NJ. 1999. 288p. ISBN:0-7879-4363-0, ISBN13: 978-0-7879-4363-9. Dewey:371.7/8. LCCN:98-058074.
Audience: **g,l,u,f.**

Hymes, James L. **LB3011.H95**
Behavior and Misbehavior: A Teacher's Guide to Action. Paper Text. Textbook Publishers. Temecula, CA. 2003. 140p. ISBN:0-7581-5919-6, ISBN13: 978-0-7581-5919-9. Dewey:371.5.
Audience: **u.**

Kerr, Mary Margaret & Nelson, C. Michael **LB3013.K47 2005**
Strategies for Addressing Behavior Problems in the Classrooms. Ed. 5. Trade Paper. Prentice Hall PTR. Upper Saddle River, NJ. 2005. 416p. ISBN:0-13-117986-1, ISBN13: 978-0-13-117986-8. Dewey:371.5/3. LCCN:2005-000192.
Audience: **u.**

Kohn, Alfie **LB3011.K64 2001**
Beyond Discipline: From Compliance to Community. Trade Paper. Prentice Hall PTR. Upper Saddle River, NJ. 2000. 166p. Merrill Education/ASCD College Textbook Ser. ISBN:0-13-093050-4, ISBN13: 978-0-13-093050-7. Dewey:371.5. LCCN:00-068108.
Audience: **u,f.** *Choice, 1997.*

Kohn, Alfie **BF505.R48**
Punished by Rewards: The Trouble with Gold Stars, Incentive Plans. Library Binding. Replica Books. Bridgewater, NJ. 1999. 412p. ISBN:0-7351-0138-8, ISBN13: 978-0-7351-0138-8. Dewey:153.8/5.
Audience: **g,l,u,f.**

Levin, James & Nolan, James F. **LB3013.L48 2003**
What Every Teacher Should Know about Classroom Management. Trade Paper. Allyn & Bacon, Inc. Boston, MA. 2002. ISBN:0-205-38064-6, ISBN13: 978-0-205-38064-0. Dewey:371.
Audience: **u.**

Lindberg, Jill A., et al. **LB3013.L54 2005**
Common-Sense Classroom Management for Middle and High School Teachers: Surviving September and Beyond in the Secondary Classroom. April M. Swick & Dianne Evans Kelley (Authors). Trade Cloth. SAGE Publications, Inc. Thousand Oaks, CA. 2004. 128p. 1-off Ser. ISBN:0-7619-3159-7, ISBN13: 978-0-7619-3159-1. Dewey:373.1102/4. LCCN:2004-015953.
Audience: **u.**

Marzano, Robert J., et al. **LB3013.H36 2005**
A Handbook for Classroom Management That Works. Barbara B. Gaddy, Maria C. Foseid, Mark P. Foseid & Jana S. Marzano (Authors). Trade Paper. Association for Supervision & Curriculum Development. Alexandria, VA. 2005. 181p. ISBN:1-4166-0236-4, ISBN13: 978-1-4166-0236-1. Dewey:371.102/4. LCCN:2005-024849.
Audience: **l,u.**

Partin, Ronald L. **LB3013**
Classroom Teacher's Survival Guide: Practical Strategies, Management Techniques, and Reproducibles for New and Experienced Teachers. Ed. 2. Trade Paper. John Wiley & Sons, Inc. Hoboken, NJ. 2004. 400p. J-B Ed Ser., :Survival Guides ISBN:0-7879-7253-3, ISBN13: 978-0-7879-7253-0. Dewey:371.1/024. LCCN:2005-270574.
Audience: **u.**

Rozalski, Michael E. **LB3013.3.S379 2004**
School Violence Intervention: A Practical Handbook. Ed. 2. Arnold P. Goldstein & Jane Close Conoley (Editors). Cloth over Boards. Guilford Publications, Inc. New York, NY. 2004. 544p. ISBN:1-57230-671-8, ISBN13: 978-1-57230-671-4. Dewey:371.7/82. LCCN:2004-010564.
Audience: **g,l,u.**

Shore, Kenneth **LB3012.S533 2003**
Elementary Teacher's Discipline Problem Solver: A Practical A-Z Guide for Managing Classroom Behavior Problems. Trade Paper. John Wiley & Sons, Inc. Hoboken, NJ. 2003. 320p. ISBN:0-7879-6599-5, ISBN13: 978-0-7879-6599-0. Dewey:372.15. LCCN:2003-015227.
Audience: **u.**

Stewart, John **RJ506.B44**
Beyond Time Out: A Practical Guide to Understanding and Serving Students with Behavioral Impairments in the Public Schools. Ed. 2. Cloth Text. Hastings Clinical Associates. Gorham, ME. 2002. 192p. ISBN:0-9702657-2-7, ISBN13: 978-0-9702657-2-2. Dewey:371.1024.
Audience: **u.**

Wolfgang, Charles H. **LB3012.W65 2005**
Solving Discipline and Classroom Management Problems: Methods and Models for Today's Teachers. Ed. 6. Trade Paper. John Wiley & Sons, Inc. Hoboken, NJ. 2004. 352p. ISBN:0-471-65387-X, ISBN13: 978-0-471-65387-5. Dewey:371.5. LCCN:2004-042233.
Audience: **u.**

School Administration and Organization > Classroom Management and Discipline > Textbooks

American Association for the Advancement of Science **Q183.3A1**
☐ Project 2061 Textbook Evaluations. http://www.project2061.org/publications/textbook/default.htm American Association for the Advancement of Science.
Audience: **u.**

Daniels, Harvey & Zemelman, Steven **LB1050.455.D36 2004**
Subjects Matter: Every Teacher's Guide to Content-Area Reading. Trade Paper. Heinemann. Portsmouth, NH. 2004. 288p. ISBN:0-325-00595-8, ISBN13: 978-0-325-00595-9. Dewey:428.4/071/2. LCCN:2003-024143.
Audience: **l,u.**

Giordano, Gerard **LB3047.G56 2001**
Twentieth-Century Textbook Wars: A History of Advocacy and Opposition. Trade Paper. Peter Lang Publishing, Inc. New York, NY. 2001. 216p. History of Schools and Schooling Ser. ISBN:0-8204-5228-9, ISBN13: 978-0-8204-5228-9. Dewey:379.1/56/09730904. LCCN:00-062952.
Audience: **g,l,u,f.**

Moreau, Joseph **E175.85.M67 2004**
Schoolbook Nation: Conflicts over American History Textbooks from the Civil War to the Present. Trade Paper. University of Michigan Press. Chicago, IL. 2004. 404p. ISBN:0-472-03053-1, ISBN13: 978-0-472-03053-8. Dewey:973/.071/273. LCCN:2003-007212.
Audience: **g,l,u,f.** *Choice, 2004.*

Nietz, John Alfred **PJ5054.G728**
Old Textbooks: Spelling, Grammar, Reading, Arithmetic, Geography, American History, Civil Government, Physiology, Penmanship, Art, Music, As Taught in the Common Schools from Colonial Days To 1900. I. Paper Text. Textbook Publishers. Temecula, CA. 2003. vii, 364p. ISBN:0-7581-1606-3, ISBN13: 978-0-7581-1606-2. Dewey:892.4/36.
Audience: **u,f.**

School Administration and Organization > Classroom Management and Discipline > Tests, Measurements, Evaluation, and Examinations

American Educational Research Association, et al. **LB3051.A693 1999**
Standards for Educational and Psychological Testing. American Psychological Association; National Council on Measurement in Education; Joint Committee on Standards for Educational and Psychological Testing (U.S.) (Authors). American Educational Research Association. 1999. ISBN:0-935302-25-5, ISBN13: 978-0-935302-25-7.
Audience: **l,u,f.**

Andrews, Jac J. W. (Volume Editor), et al. **LB3051.H31985 2001**
Handbook of Psychoeducational Assessment: A Practical Handbook. Henry L. Janzen & Donald H. Saklofske (Volume Editors), Gary D. Phye (Contribution by). Trade Cloth. Elsevier Science & Technology Books. Saint Louis, MO. 2002. 512p. Educational Psychology Ser. ISBN:0-12-058570-7, ISBN13: 978-0-12-058570-0. Dewey:370.15. LCCN:2001-086089.
Audience: **u,f.** *Choice, 2002.*

Angelo, Thomas A. & Cross, K. Patricia **LB2822.75 .A54**
Classroom Assessment Techniques: A Handbook for College Teachers. Trade Paper. John Wiley & Sons, Inc. Hoboken, NJ. 2005. ISBN:0-7879-8236-9, ISBN13: 978-0-7879-8236-2. Dewey:378.1/25 20.
Audience: **u,f.**

Arter, Judith, et al. **LC1034.A78 2001**
Scoring Rubrics in the Classroom: Using Performance Criteria for Assessing and Improving Student Performance. Northwest Regional Educational Laboratory Staff & Jay McTighe (Authors). Trade Cloth. Corwin Press. Thousand Oaks, CA. 2000. 208p. Experts in Assessment Kit Ser. ISBN:0-7619-7574-8, ISBN13: 978-0-7619-7574-8. Dewey:371.27/0973. LCCN:00-009504.
Audience: **u.**

Banta, Trudy W. (Editor) **LB2822.75**
Hallmarks of Effective Outcomes Assessment: Assessment Update Collections. Trade Paper. John Wiley & Sons, Inc. Hoboken, NJ. 2004. 72p. Assessment Update Special Collections ISBN:0-7879-7288-6, ISBN13: 978-0-7879-7288-2. Dewey:379.15.
Audience: **u,f.**

Bracey, Gerald W. **LA212 .B66 1995**
Final Exam: A Study of the Perpetual Scrutiny of American Education: Historical Perspectives on Assessment, Standards, Outcomes, and Criticism of U. S. Schools. Cloth Text. Agency for Instructional Technology. Bloomington, IN. 1995. 256p. ISBN:0-7842-0807-7, ISBN13: 978-0-7842-0807-6. Dewey:370.973. LCCN:95-061639.
Audience: **g,l,u,f.** *Choice, 1996.*

Bracey, Gerald W. **Z232.E5**
Put to the Test: An Educator's and Consumer's Guide to Standardized Testing. Trade Paper. Phi Delta Kappa Educational Foundation. Bloomington, IN. 1998. 80p. ISBN:0-87367-528-2, ISBN13: 978-0-87367-528-4. Dewey:686.20922.
Audience: **g,l,u.**

Brookhart, Susan M. & AEHE Staff **LB2822.75.B76 1999**
The Art and Science of Classroom Assessment: The Missing Part of Pedagogy, 27. Trade Paper. John Wiley & Sons, Inc. Hoboken, NJ. 1999. 132p. ASHE-ERIC Higher Education Reports, Vol. 27 ISBN:1-878380-89-3, ISBN13: 978-1-878380-89-0. Dewey:378.16. LCCN:99-063955.
Audience: **u,f.** *Choice, 2000.*

Center for Education Staff & National Research Council Staff **LB3051.K59 2001**
Knowing What Students Know: The Science and Design of Educational Assessment. James W. Pellegrino, Naomi Chudowsky & Robert Glaser (Editors). Trade Cloth. National Academies Press. Washington, DC. 2001. 382p. ISBN:0-309-07272-7, ISBN13: 978-0-309-07272-4. Dewey:371.26/1. LCCN:2001-003876.
Audience: **u,f.**

Chapman, Carolyn & King, Rita S. **LB3051.C4483 2005**
Differentiated Assessment Strategies: One Tool Doesn't Fit All. Trade Cloth. SAGE Publications, Inc. Thousand Oaks, CA. 2004. 248p. 1-off Ser. ISBN:0-7619-8890-4, ISBN13: 978-0-7619-8890-8. Dewey:371.26. LCCN:2004-018751.
Audience: **u,f.**

Chicago Board of Education **LB2831**
Instructional Intranet—Chicago Public Schools—Assessments. http://intranet.cps.k12.il.us/Assessments/ Chicago Board of Education.
Audience: **u.**

Dunn, Dana, et al. **BF77.M385 2004**
Measuring Up: Educational Assessment Challenges and Practices for Psychology. Chandra Mehrotra & Jane S. Halonen (Authors). Trade Cloth. American Psychological Association.

Washington, DC. 2004. 312p. ISBN:1-59147-108-7, ISBN13: 978-1-59147-108-0. Dewey:150/.71. LCCN:2004-004235.
Audience: **l,u,f.** *Choice, 2005.*

Educational Testing Service **LB3051**
☐ ETS.
http://www.ets.org/
Audience: **u,f.**

Elford, George W. **LB3051.E456 2002**
Beyond Standardized Testing: Better Information for School Accountability and Management. Trade Cloth. Scarecrow Press, Inc. Lanham, MD. 2002. 128p. ISBN:0-8108-4386-2, ISBN13: 978-0-8108-4386-8. Dewey:371.26/2. LCCN:2002-005356.
Audience: **g,l,u,f.** *Choice, 2003.*

Firestone, William A. (Editor), et al. **LB3051.A592 2004**
The Ambiguity of Teaching to the Test: Standards, Assessment, and Educational Reform. Lora Frances Monfils & Roberta Y. Schorr (Editors), Sylvia Bulgar, Katrina E. Bulkley & Gregory A. Camilli (Contribution by). Trade Paper. Lawrence Erlbaum Associates, Inc. Mahwah, NJ. 2004. 264p. ISBN:0-8058-4569-0, ISBN13: 978-0-8058-4569-3. Dewey:371.26/4. LCCN:2003-054587.
Audience: **u,f.** *Choice, 2004.*

Glasgow, Jackie (Editor) **LB1631.5.S78 2002**
Standards-Based Activities with Scoring Rubrics: Middle and High School English Performance-Based Portfolios. Trade Cloth. Eye On Education, Inc. Larchmont, NY. 2002. ISBN:1-930556-28-4, ISBN13: 978-1-930556-28-7. Dewey:428/.0076. LCCN:2001-051221.
Audience: **u.**

Glasgow, Jackie (Editor) **LB1631.5.S78 2002**
Standards-Based Activities with Scoring Rubrics: Middle and High School English Performance-Based Projects. Trade Cloth. Eye On Education, Inc. Larchmont, NY. 2002. ISBN:1-930556-29-2, ISBN13: 978-1-930556-29-4. Dewey:428/.0076. LCCN:2001-051221.
Audience: **u.**

Hebert, Elizabeth A. **LB1029.P67H43 2001**
The Power of Portfolios: What Children Can Teach Us about Learning and Assessment. Trade Paper. John Wiley & Sons, Inc. Hoboken, NJ. 2001. 176p. The Jossey-Bass Education Ser. ISBN:0-7879-5871-9, ISBN13: 978-0-7879-5871-8. Dewey:372.127. LCCN:2001-003792.
Audience: **g,l,u,f.** *Choice, 2002.*

Johnson, David W. & Johnson, Roger T. **LB1032.J592 2004**
Assessing Students in Groups: Promoting Group Responsibility and Individual Accountability. Trade Cloth. Corwin Press. Thousand Oaks, CA. 2004. 224p. Experts in Assessment Ser. ISBN:0-7619-3946-6, ISBN13: 978-0-7619-3946-7. Dewey:371.39/5. LCCN:2003-017595.
Audience: **u,f.**

Jones, M. Gail, et al. **LB3051.J584 2003**
The Unintended Consequences of High-Stakes Testing. Brett D. Jones & Tracy Hargroves (Authors). Book, Other. Rowman & Littlefield Publishers, Inc. Lanham, MD. 2003. 192p. ISBN:0-7425-2627-5, ISBN13: 978-0-7425-2627-3. Dewey:371.26/4. LCCN:2002-153819.
Audience: **g,l,u,f.** *Choice, 2004.*

Keeves, John P. (Editor) **LB1028.E3184 1997**
Educational Research, Methodology and Measurement: An International Handbook. Ed. 2. Trade Cloth. Elsevier Science & Technology Books. Saint Louis, MO. 1997. 964p. Resources in Education Ser. ISBN:0-08-042710-3, ISBN13: 978-0-08-042710-2. Dewey:370/.7. LCCN:96-052173.
Audience: **u,f.** *Choice, 1998.*

Kohn, Alfie **LB3060.3.K64 2000**
The Case Against Standardized Testing: Raising the Scores, Ruining the Schools. Trade Paper. Heinemann. Portsmouth, NH. 2000. 104p. ISBN:0-325-00325-4, ISBN13: 978-0-325-00325-2. Dewey:371.26/2/0973. LCCN:00-57245.
Audience: **g.**

Langer, Georgea M., et al. **LB3051.L34 2003**
Collaborative Analysis of Student Work: Improving Teaching and Learning. Amy B. Colton & Loretta S. Goff (Authors). Trade Paper. Association for Supervision & Curriculum Development. Alexandria, VA. 2003. 215p. ISBN:0-87120-784-2, ISBN13: 978-0-87120-784-5. Dewey:371.26/4. LCCN:2003-011032.
Audience: **u,f.**

Lemann, Nicholas **LB3051.L44 2000**
The Big Test: The Secret History of the American Meritocracy. Trade Paper. Farrar, Straus & Giroux. New York, NY. 2000. 406p. ISBN:0-374-52751-2, ISBN13: 978-0-374-52751-8. Dewey:371.26/0973. LCCN:2001-268120.
Audience: **g,l,u,f.** *Choice, 2000.*

Marzano, Robert J. & Kendall, John S. **LB3060.83.M378 1998**
Implementing Standards-Based Education. Trade Cloth. National Education Association. Annapolis Junction, MD. 1998. 90p. Student Assessment Ser. ISBN:0-8106-2072-3, ISBN13: 978-0-8106-2072-8. Dewey:379.1/58/0973. LCCN:98-043678.
Audience: **u,f.**

National Center for Fair and Open Testing **LB3051**
☐ FairTest.
http://www.fairtest.org/index.htm
Assessment Reform Network.
Audience: **g,u.**

Popham, James W. **LB3051.P61433 2003**
Test Better, Teach Better: The Instructional Role of Assessment. Trade Paper. Association for Supervision & Curriculum Development. Alexandria, VA. 2003. 144p. ISBN:0-87120-667-6, ISBN13: 978-0-87120-667-1. Dewey:371.26/2. LCCN:2003-011511.
Audience: **u,f.** *Choice, 2004.*

Sandoval, Jonathan H. (Editor), et al. **LB3060.8.T47 1998**
Test Interpretation and Diversity: Achieving Equity in Assessment. Craig L. Frisby, Kurt F. Geisinger, Julia Ramos-Grenier & Janice Dowd Scheuneman (Editors). Trade Cloth. American Psychological Association. Washington, DC. 1998. 436p. ISBN:1-55798-509-X, ISBN13: 978-1-55798-509-5. Dewey:371.26/01/3. LCCN:98-026487.
Audience: **g,u,f.** *Choice, 1999.*

Scott, David (Editor) **LB3051.C865 2001**
Curriculum and Assessment. Paper Text. Greenwood Publishing Group, Inc. Portsmouth, NH. 2000. 200p. International Perspectives on Curriculum Studies, Vol. 1

ISBN:1-56750-521-X, ISBN13: 978-1-56750-521-4.
Dewey:375/.001. LCCN:00-026073.
Audience: **u,f.** *Choice, 2001.*

Sever, Dave **LB3051.S395 2004**
Dancing with Data to Improve Learning. Trade Paper. Scarecrow Press, Inc. Lanham, MD. 2004. 88p.
ISBN:1-57886-171-3, ISBN13: 978-1-57886-171-2.
Dewey:379.1/58. LCCN:2004-011639.
Audience: **u,f.**

Shapiro, Edward S. **LB1029.R4S5 2004**
Academic Skills Problems: Direct Assessment and Intervention. Ed. 3. Trade Cloth. Guilford Publications, Inc. New York, NY. 2004. 370p. Guilford School Practitioner Ser.
ISBN:1-57230-977-6, ISBN13: 978-1-57230-977-7.
Dewey:372.4/3. LCCN:2004-010860.
Audience: **u,f.**

Smith, Jeffrey K., et al. **LB3051.S586 2001**
Natural Classroom Assessment: Designing Seamless Instruction and Assessment. Lisa F. Smith & Richard De Lisi (Authors). Trade Cloth. Corwin Press. Thousand Oaks, CA. 2000. 144p. Experts in Assessment Kits Ser. ISBN:0-7619-7586-1, ISBN13: 978-0-7619-7586-1. Dewey:371.27. LCCN:00-008997.
Audience: **u,f.**

Sternberg, Robert J. & Grigorenko, Elena **LB1134 .S74 2002**
Dynamic Testing: The Nature and Measurement of Learning Potential. Trade Cloth. Cambridge University Press. New York, NY. 2001. 230p. ISBN:0-521-77128-5, ISBN13: 978-0-521-77128-3. Dewey:153.9/4. LCCN:2001-025402.
Audience: **u,f.** *Choice, 2003.*

Thomas B. Fordham Foundation **LB3051**
☐ Testing and Accountability.
http://www.edexcellence.net/foundation/topic/topic.cfm?topic=Testing%20%26%20Accountability
Thomas B. Fordham Foundation.
Audience: **u,f.**

Tileston, Donna E. Walker **LB3051.T564 2004**
What Every Teacher Should Know about Student Assessment. Trade Paper. Corwin Press. Thousand Oaks, CA. 2003. 136p.
ISBN:0-7619-3123-6, ISBN13: 978-0-7619-3123-2.
Dewey:371.26. LCCN:2003-010240.
Audience: **u.**

Wappingers Central School District **LC1035**
☐ Developing Educational Standards.
http://edstandards.org/Standards.html
Audience: **u,f.**

Wiggins, Grant P. **LB3051**
Assessing Student Performance: Exploring the Purpose and Limits of Testing. Trade Paper. John Wiley & Sons, Inc. Hoboken, NJ. 1999. 336p. ISBN:0-7879-5047-5, ISBN13: 978-0-7879-5047-7. Dewey:371.2/64.
Audience: **u,f.** *Choice, 1994.*

Wiggins, Grant P. **LB3051.W495 1998**
Educative Assessment: Designing Assessments to Inform and Improve Student Performance. Trade Paper. John Wiley & Sons, Inc. Hoboken, NJ. 1998. 384p. Education Ser.
ISBN:0-7879-0848-7, ISBN13: 978-0-7879-0848-5.
Dewey:371.26. LCCN:97-049935.
Audience: **u,f.** *Choice, 1999.*

Wilde, Sandra **LB3051.W4966 2002**
Testing and Standards: A Brief Encyclopedia. Trade Paper. Heinemann. Portsmouth, NH. 2002. 120p. ISBN:0-325-00360-2, ISBN13: 978-0-325-00360-3. Dewey:371.26/4.
LCCN:2002-004352.
Audience: **g,l.**

Willingham, Warren W. & Cole, Nancy S. (Editors) **LB3051.W4996 1997**
Gender and Fair Assessment. Cloth over Boards. Lawrence Erlbaum Associates, Inc. Mahwah, NJ. 1997. 424p.
ISBN:0-8058-2331-X, ISBN13: 978-0-8058-2331-8.
Dewey:371.26/01/3. LCCN:96-039932.
Audience: **u,f.** *Choice, 1997.*

Zenderland, Leila **BF431 .Z46 1998**
Measuring Minds: Henry Herbert Goddard and the Origins of American Intelligence Testing. Mitchell G. Ash & William R. Woodward (Contribution by). Trade Cloth. Cambridge University Press. New York, NY. 1998. 478p. Cambridge Studies in the History of Psychology ISBN:0-521-44373-3, ISBN13: 978-0-521-44373-9. Dewey:153.9/3/097309041.
LCCN:97-006101.
Audience: **u,f.** *Choice, 1998.*

School Administration and Organization > Classroom Management and Discipline > Schedules

Gainey, Donald D. & Brucato, John M. **LB3032.2.G35 1999**
Questions and Answers about Block Scheduling: An Implementation Guide. Trade Cloth. Eye On Education, Inc. Larchmont, NY. 1999. 250p. ISBN:1-883001-68-4, ISBN13: 978-1-883001-68-1. Dewey:371.2/42. LCCN:98-054128.
Audience: **u,f.**

Hottenstein, David S. **LB3032.H68 1998**
Intensive Scheduling: Restructuring America's Secondary Schools Through Time Management. Trade Cloth. Corwin Press. Thousand Oaks, CA. 1998. 120p. One-Off Ser.
ISBN:0-8039-6653-9, ISBN13: 978-0-8039-6653-6.
Dewey:373.12/42/0973. LCCN:97-045259.
Audience: **u,f.**

Lybbert, Blair **LB3032.2.L93 1998**
Transforming Learning with Block Scheduling: A Guide for Principals. Trade Cloth. Corwin Press. Thousand Oaks, CA. 1998. 104p. Educational Innovation Ser. ISBN:0-8039-6657-1, ISBN13: 978-0-8039-6657-4. Dewey:371.2/42.
LCCN:98-009075.
Audience: **u.**

Marshak, David **LB3032.2.M38 2001**
Improving Teaching in the High School Block Period. Trade Paper. Scarecrow Press, Inc. Lanham, MD. 2001. 192p.
ISBN:0-8108-3923-7, ISBN13: 978-0-8108-3923-6.
Dewey:373.12/42/0973. LCCN:00-064090.
Audience: **u,f.**

McCullough, Laura L. & Tanner, Brenda M. **LB3051.M46246 2001**
Assessment in the Block: The Link to Instruction. Trade Paper. Eye On Education, Inc. Larchmont, NY. 2001. xii, 135p. Teaching in the Block Ser. ISBN:1-930556-07-1, ISBN13: 978-1-930556-07-2. Dewey:371.26. LCCN:00-063603.
Audience: **u,f.**

Porter, Carol **LB1631.P63 2002**
What Do I Teach for 90 Minutes?: Creating a Successful Block-Scheduled English Classroom. Trade Paper. National Council of Teachers of English. Urbana, IL. 2002. xii, 187p. ISBN:0-8141-5653-3, ISBN13: 978-0-8141-5653-7. Dewey:428/.0071/2. LCCN:2002-001435.
Audience: **u.**

Queen, J. Allen **LB3032.2.Q85 2002**
The Block Scheduling Handbook. Trade Cloth. Corwin Press. Thousand Oaks, CA. 2002. 272p. One-Off Ser. ISBN:0-7619-4525-3, ISBN13: 978-0-7619-4525-3. Dewey:371.2/42. LCCN:2002-005184.
Audience: **u,f.**

Rettig, Michael D. & Canady, Robert Lynn **LB3032.2.R48 2000**
Scheduling Strategies for Middle Schools. Trade Cloth. Eye On Education, Inc. Larchmont, NY. 2000. xviii, 262p. ISBN:1-883001-67-6, ISBN13: 978-1-883001-67-4. Dewey:373.12/42. LCCN:99-059277.
Audience: **u,f.**

Robbins, Pam, et al. **LB3032.2.R63 2000**
Thinking Inside the Block Schedule: Strategies for Teaching in Extended Periods of Time. Lynne E. Herndon & Gayle Gregory (Authors). Trade Cloth. Corwin Press. Thousand Oaks, CA. 2000. 224p. One-Off Ser. ISBN:0-8039-6782-9, ISBN13: 978-0-8039-6782-3. Dewey:371.2/42. LCCN:99-006885.
Audience: **u,f.**

School Facilities

LB3221
Creating Connections: The CEFPI Guide for Educational Facility Planning. Ringbound, CD-ROM. CEFPI. Scottsdale, AZ. 2004. ISBN:0-9753483-0-2, ISBN13: 978-0-9753483-0-7. Dewey:371.6.
Audience: **u,f.**

NA6600
Educational Facilities. Trade Cloth. Links Internacional. Barcelona, 2002. 180p. ISBN:84-89861-69-2, ISBN13: 978-84-89861-69-5. Dewey:727.3.
Audience: **g,u,f.**

LB3218.A1
The Language of School Design: Design Patterns for 21st Century Schools. Trade Paper. Designshare, Inc. Minneapolis, MN. 2005. 136p. ISBN:0-9762670-0-4, ISBN13: 978-0-9762670-0-3. Dewey:371.620973.
Audience: **g,l,u.**

Biehle, James T., et al. **Q183.U6B54 1999**
NSTA Guide to School Science Facilities. LaMoine L. Motz & Sandra S. West (Authors), National Science Teachers Association Staff (Contribution by). Trade Cloth. National Science Teachers Association. Arlington, VA. 1999. vi, 100p. ISBN:0-87355-174-5, ISBN13: 978-0-87355-174-8. Dewey:371.6/23. LCCN:00-687935.
Audience: **u,f.**

Kowalski, Theodore J. **LB3218.A1K638 2002**
Planning and Managing School Facilities. Ed. 2. Trade Cloth. Greenwood Publishing Group, Inc. Portsmouth, NH. 2001. 296p. ISBN:0-89789-770-6, ISBN13: 978-0-89789-770-9. Dewey:371.6/8/0973. LCCN:2001-037652.
Audience: **g,u,f.**

Student Life (Including Organizations and Activities)

CBS News Staff **HQ796.C65 2000**
[Ebook] The Class of 2000: The Definitive Survey of the New Generation. Dan Rather (Preface by). E-Book. Simon & Schuster. New York, NY. 2000. ISBN:0-7432-1209-6, ISBN13: 978-0-7432-1209-0. Dewey:305.235.
Audience: **g.**

Fashola, Olatokunbo S. **LB3605.F37 2002**
Building Effective Afterschool Programs. Trade Paper. Corwin Press. Thousand Oaks, CA. 2001. 136p. One-Off Ser. ISBN:0-7619-7878-X, ISBN13: 978-0-7619-7878-7. Dewey:371.8/9/0973. LCCN:2001-001654.
Audience: **l,u,f.**

Gregory, Dennis E. **LJ34.G74 2003**
The Administration of Fraternal Organizations on North American Campuses: A Pattern for the New Millennium. Trade Paper. College Administration Publications, Inc. Asheville, NC. 2003. xxviii, 425p. The Higher Education Administration Ser. ISBN:0-912557-27-3, ISBN13: 978-0-912557-27-4. Dewey:378.1/985/097. LCCN:2003-063330.
Audience: **u,f.**

Klesse, Edward J. **LB3605.K54 2004**
Student Activities in Today's Schools: Essential Learning for All Youth. Trade Paper. Scarecrow Press, Inc. Lanham, MD. 2004. 264p. ISBN:1-57886-087-3, ISBN13: 978-1-57886-087-6. Dewey:371.8/9. LCCN:2003-023553.
Audience: **g,l,u,f.**

Larson, Reed & Eccles, Jacquelynne S. (Editors) **LB3605.O74 2004**
Organized Activities As Contexts of Development: Extracurricular Activities, After-School and Community Programs. Amy L. Anderson, Megan L. Babkes & Dale A. Blyth (Contribution by). Trade Paper. Lawrence Erlbaum Associates, Inc. Mahwah, NJ. 2005. 568p. ISBN:0-8058-4431-7, ISBN13: 978-0-8058-4431-3. Dewey:371.8/9. LCCN:2003-062650.
Audience: **u,f.**

Nuwer, Hank **LJ51**
Wrongs of Passage: Fraternities, Sororities, Hazing, and Binge Drinking. Trade Paper. Indiana University Press. Bloomington, IN. 2001. 352p. ISBN:0-253-21498-X, ISBN13: 978-0-253-21498-0. Dewey:378.1/98/55.
Audience: **g.**

Ross, Lawrence C. Jr. & Kensington Publishing Corporation Staff **LC2781.7.R68 2000**
The Divine Nine: The History of African-American Fraternities and Sororities in America. Trade Cloth. Kensington Publishing Corporation. New York, NY. 2000. xiii, 465p. ISBN:1-57566-491-7, ISBN13: 978-1-57566-491-0. Dewey:378.1/9855/08996073. LCCN:99-063482.
Audience: **u,f.**

Sheldon, Henry D. **LA229 .S5**
Student Life and Customs. Trade Cloth. Ayer Company Publishers, Inc. Manchester, NH. 1975. American Education, :Its Men, Institutions, and Ideas, Series 1 ISBN:0-405-01470-8, ISBN13: 978-0-405-01470-3. Dewey:378.1/98/0973. LCCN:70-089233.
Audience: **g,l,u,f.**

Higher Education > Institutions of Higher Education

LB2331.6
☐ CHEA web site.
http://www.chea.org/
Audience: **f.**

L901
☐ College and University Rankings.
http://www.library.uiuc.edu/edx/rankings.htm
Audience: **g,u.**

LB1044.87
☐ Copyright and Fair Use in the Classroom, on the Internet, and the World Wide Web.
http://www.umuc.edu/library/copy.html
Audience: **f.**

LB2331.62
☐ Measuring Up.
http://measuringup.highereducation.org/default.cfm
Audience: **f.**

L901
☐ Peterson's Education Portal.
http://www.petersons.com/
Peterson's.
Audience: **l.**

L901
☐ The Top American Research Universities.
http://thecenter.ufl.edu/research2004.html
Audience: **f.**

Astin, Alexander W. **LA229**
What Matters in College: Four Critical Years Revisited. Trade Paper. John Wiley & Sons, Inc. Hoboken, NJ. 1997. 512p. ISBN:0-7879-0838-X, ISBN13: 978-0-7879-0838-6. Dewey:378.198.
Audience: **f.**

Barzun, Jacques **LA226.B27 1993**
The American University: How It Runs, Where It Is Going. Ed. 2. Herbert I. London (Introduction by). Trade Paper. University of Chicago Press. Chicago, IL. 1993. 356p. ISBN:0-226-03845-9, ISBN13: 978-0-226-03845-2. Dewey:378.1550973. LCCN:92-028479.
Audience: **f.** B

Birnbaum, Robert **LA227.3**
Maintaining Diversity in Higher Education. Trade Cloth. John Wiley & Sons, Inc. Hoboken, NJ. 1983. 227p. Higher Education Ser. ISBN:0-87589-574-3, ISBN13: 978-0-87589-574-1. Dewey:378.73. LCCN:83-048156.
Audience: **g,l,u,f.**

Bloom, Allan **LA227.3.B584 1988**
Closing of the American Mind. Trade Paper. Simon & Schuster. New York, NY. 1988. 400p. ISBN:0-671-65715-1, ISBN13: 978-0-671-65715-4. Dewey:378.73.
Audience: **g.**

Bogue, E. Grady **LB2806.22.B64**
The Evidence for Quality: Strengthening the Tests of Academic and Administrative Effectiveness. Trade Paper. Books on Demand. Ann Arbor, MI. 355p. The Jossey-Bass Higher and Adult Education Ser. ISBN:0-608-21520-1, ISBN13: 978-0-608-21520-4. Dewey:379.1/54. LCCN:91-032020.
Audience: **u,f.**

Bok, Derek C. **LB2331.53**
Beyond the Ivory Tower: Social Responsibilities of the Modern University. Trade Paper. Harvard University Press. Cambridge, MA. 1984. 328p. ISBN:0-674-06898-X, ISBN13: 978-0-674-06898-8. Dewey:378/.103. LCCN:81-020278.
Audience: **u,f.** B

Bowen, Howard R. **LA227.4.B68 1997**
Investment in Learning: The Individual and Social Value of American Higher Education. Ed. 2. Trade Paper. Johns Hopkins University Press. Baltimore, MD. 1997. 536p. ISBN:0-8018-5530-6, ISBN13: 978-0-8018-5530-6. Dewey:378.73. LCCN:96-045438.
Audience: **f.** B

Boyer, Ernest L. & Carnegie Foundation for the Advancement of Teaching Staff **LA227.3 .B678 1988**
College: The Undergraduate Experience in America. Trade Paper. John Wiley & Sons, Inc. Hoboken, NJ. 1997. 328p. ISBN:0-06-091458-0, ISBN13: 978-0-06-091458-5. Dewey:378.73. LCCN:97-033424.
Audience: **g,f.**

Brubacher, John S. **LB2324**
On the Philosophy of Higher Education. Trade Cloth. John Wiley & Sons, Inc. Hoboken, NJ. 1990. 186p. Higher Education Ser. ISBN:0-87589-536-0, ISBN13: 978-0-87589-536-9. Dewey:378/.001. LCCN:82-048076.
Audience: **u,f.** B

Chamberlain, Mariam K. **LC1752**
Women in Academe: Progress and Prospects. Trade Paper. Russell Sage Foundation. New York, NY. 1991. 448p. ISBN:0-87154-218-8, ISBN13: 978-0-87154-218-2. Dewey:376/.973.
Audience: **l,u,f.** *Choice, 1989.*

Chu, Donald A. **GV351.C484 1989**
The Character of American Higher Education and Intercollegiate Sport. Trade Paper. State University of New York Press. Albany, NY. 1989. 252p. SUNY Series in Frontiers of Education ISBN:0-88706-793-X, ISBN13: 978-0-88706-793-8. Dewey:796/.07/1173. LCCN:87-034015.
Audience: **l,u,f.**

Conant, James Bryant **F855.2.M5C45**
The Citadel of Learning. Paper Text. Textbook Publishers. Temecula, CA. 2003. 79p. ISBN:0-7581-0082-5, ISBN13: 978-0-7581-0082-5. Dewey:979.5/0046872073.
Audience: **u,f.**

Harvard University. **LA210**
Committee on the Objectives of General Education in a Free Society.
General Education in a Free Society. Harvard University Press. 1945.
Audience: **f.**

Horowitz, Helen L. **LA229.H569 1988**
Campus Life: Undergraduate Cultures from the End of the Eighteenth Century to the Present. Trade Paper. University of Chicago Press. Chicago, IL. 1988. 348p. ISBN:0-226-35373-7, ISBN13: 978-0-226-35373-9. Dewey:378/.198/0973. LCCN:87-030226.
Audience: **f.** *Choice, 1987.*

Hutchins, Robert M. **LA226 .H85 1995**
The Higher Learning in America. Ed. 2. Harry S. Ashmore (Introduction by). Trade Paper. Transaction Publishers. Somerset, NJ. 1995. 141p. ISBN:1-56000-808-3, ISBN13: 978-1-56000-808-8. Dewey:378.73. LCCN:94-041613.
Audience: **l,u,f.**

Jencks, Christopher & **LA226 .J4 1977**
Riesman, David
The Academic Revolution. Martin A. Trow (Foreword by). Paper Text. University of Chicago Press. Chicago, IL. 1996. 606p. ISBN:0-226-39628-2, ISBN13: 978-0-226-39628-6. Dewey:378.73. LCCN:76-151838.
Audience: **u,f.** B

Jenkins, Hugh M. **LB2376**
Educating Students from Other Nations: American Colleges and Universities in International Educational Interchange. Trade Cloth. John Wiley & Sons, Inc. Hoboken, NJ. 1983. 387p. Higher Education Ser. ISBN:0-87589-559-X, ISBN13: 978-0-87589-559-8. Dewey:370.19/621. LCCN:82-049043.
Audience: **l,u,f.**

Kerr, Clark **LB2325.K43 2001**
The Uses of the University. Ed. 5. Trade Paper. Harvard University Press. Cambridge, MA. 2001. 286p. The Godkin Lectures on the Essentials of Free Government and the Duties of the Citizen Ser. ISBN:0-674-00532-5, ISBN13: 978-0-674-00532-7. Dewey:378. LCCN:00-053942.
Audience: **u,f.** B

Long, Edward L. Jr. **LB2324 .L66 1992**
Higher Education As a Moral Enterprise. Trade Paper. Georgetown University Press. Washington, DC. 1992. 224p. ISBN:0-87840-531-3, ISBN13: 978-0-87840-531-2. Dewey:378/.014. LCCN:92-013886.
Audience: **u,f.**

Meiklejohn, Alexander **LD6096**
The Experimental College. Trade Cloth. Ayer Company Publishers, Inc. Manchester, NH. 1977. American Education Ser., :No. 2 ISBN:0-405-03712-0, ISBN13: 978-0-405-03712-2. Dewey:378.775/84. LCCN:75-165724.
Audience: **l,u,f.**

Newman, John Henry **LB2321.N54 1996**
The Idea of a University. Frank M. Turner (Editor), Martha M. Garland (Contribution by). Trade Paper. Yale University Press. Cumberland, RI. 1996. 400p. Rethinking the Western Tradition Ser. ISBN:0-300-06405-5, ISBN13: 978-0-300-06405-6. Dewey:378/.01. LCCN:95-038832.
Audience: **l,u,f.** B

Nisbet, Robert A. & **LA226.N56 1996**
Himmelfard, Gertrude
The Degradation of the Academic Dogma. Trade Paper. Transaction Publishers. Somerset, NJ. 1996. 252p. ISBN:1-56000-915-2, ISBN13: 978-1-56000-915-3. Dewey:378.73. LCCN:96-020341.
Audience: **u.**

O'Brien, George Dennis **LA228.O37 1998**
All the Essential Half-Truths about Higher Education. Trade Cloth. University of Chicago Press. Chicago, IL. 1998. 266p. ISBN:0-226-61654-1, ISBN13: 978-0-226-61654-4. Dewey:378.7/3. LCCN:97-014479.
Audience: **l,u,f.** *Choice, 1998.*

Olevnik, Peter P., et al. **LA226**
American Higher Education: A Guide to Reference Sources, 12. Sarah Hammond, Gregory M. Toth & Chang W. Chan (Authors), Betty W. Chan (Contribution by), Philip G. Altbach (Foreword by). Cloth Text. Greenwood Publishing Group, Inc. Portsmouth, NH. 1993. 232p. Bibliographies and Indexes in Education Ser., No. 12 ISBN:0-313-27749-4, ISBN13: 978-0-313-27749-8. Dewey:016.37873. LCCN:93-025015.
Audience: **l,u,f.** *Choice, 1994.*

Pascarella, Ernest T. & **LA229.P34 1991**
Terenzini, Patrick T.
How College Affects Students: Findings and Insights from Twenty Years of Research. Kenneth A. Feldman (Foreword by). Trade Paper. John Wiley & Sons, Inc. Hoboken, NJ. 1991. 920p. Higher and Adult Education Ser. ISBN:1-55542-338-8, ISBN13: 978-1-55542-338-4. Dewey:378.1/98/0973. LCCN:90-046068.
Audience: **g,l,u.** *Choice, 1991.*

Rosovsky, Henry **L901**
University: An Owner's Manual. Trade Paper. W. W. Norton & Company, Inc. New York, NY. 1991. 309p. ISBN:0-393-30783-2, ISBN13: 978-0-393-30783-2. Dewey:378.7/3. LCCN:89-009466.
Audience: **u,f.**

Sanford, Nevitt **GV351**
The American College: A Psychological and Social Interpretation of the Higher Learning. Paper Text. Textbook Publishers. Temecula, CA. 2003. xvi, 1084p. ISBN:0-7581-0495-2, ISBN13: 978-0-7581-0495-3. Dewey:796.071173.
Audience: **f.** B

Slaughter, Sheila A. & **LC67.62.S62 2004**
Rhoades, Gary
Academic Capitalism and the New Economy: Markets, State, and Higher Education. Trade Cloth. Johns Hopkins University Press. Baltimore, MD. 2004. 384p. ISBN:0-8018-7949-3, ISBN13: 978-0-8018-7949-4. Dewey:338.4/337873. LCCN:2003-024783.
Audience: **u,f.** *Choice, 2005.*

Smith, Huston **LB2321.S57 1971**
The Purposes of Higher Education. Arthur H. Compton (Foreword by). Library Binding. Greenwood Publishing Group, Inc. Portsmouth, NH. 1971. 218p. ISBN:0-8371-4698-4, ISBN13: 978-0-8371-4698-0. Dewey:378/.01. LCCN:76-138130.
Audience: **l,u,f.**

Snow, C. P. **AZ361 .S56 1969B**
The Two Cultures. Stefan Collini (Introduction by). Trade Paper. Cambridge University Press. New York, NY. 1993. 181p. A Canto Book Ser. ISBN:0-521-45730-0, ISBN13: 978-0-521-45730-9. Dewey:001. LCCN:93-243498.
Audience: **u,f.**

Thelin, John R. **GV351.T43**
Games Colleges Play: Scandal and Reform in Intercollegiate Athletics. Trade Paper. Johns Hopkins University Press. Baltimore, MD. 1996. 272p. ISBN:0-8018-5504-7, ISBN13: 978-0-8018-5504-7. Dewey:796.071173.
Audience: **g,l,u,f.** *Choice, 1995.*

Whitehead, Alfred North **LB875**
The Aims of Education. Trade Paper. Simon & Schuster. New York, NY. 1967. 165p. ISBN:0-02-935180-4, ISBN13: 978-0-02-935180-2. Dewey:370.4. LCCN:29-010164.
Audience: **g,l,u,f.**

Young, Richard B. **LA227.4.Y68 1997**
No Neutral Ground: Standing by the Values We Prize in Higher Education. Trade Cloth. John Wiley & Sons, Inc. Hoboken, NJ. 1997. 231p. ISBN:0-7879-0800-2, ISBN13: 978-0-7879-0800-3. Dewey:378.73. LCCN:96-035693.
Audience: **l,u,f.**

Higher Education > Institutions of Higher Education > Private

Breneman, David W. **LB2342.B74 1994**
Liberal Arts Colleges: Thriving, Surviving, or Endangered? Trade Paper. Brookings Institution Press. Washington, DC. 1994. 184p. ISBN:0-8157-1061-5, ISBN13: 978-0-8157-1061-5. Dewey:378/.04/0973. LCCN:93-046086.
Audience: **g,f.** *Choice, 1994.*

Drewry, Henry N. & Doermann, Humphrey **LC2781**
Stand and Prosper: Private Black Colleges and Their Students. Trade Paper. Princeton University Press. Princeton, NJ. 2003. 368p. ISBN:0-691-11632-6, ISBN13: 978-0-691-11632-7. Dewey:378.7/3/08996073.
Audience: **l,u,f.**

Gleason, Philip **LC501.G56 1995**
Contending with Modernity: Catholic Higher Education in the Twentieth Century. Trade Cloth. Oxford University Press, Inc. New York, NY. 1995. 448p. ISBN:0-19-509828-5, ISBN13: 978-0-19-509828-0. Dewey:377/.82. LCCN:95-010330.
Audience: **l,u,f.** *Choice, 1996.*

Ingram, Richard T. **LB2341.I532 1993**
Governing Independent Colleges and Universities: A Handbook for Trustees, Chief Executives and Other Campus Leaders. Trade Cloth. John Wiley & Sons, Inc. Hoboken, NJ. 1993. 528p. ISBN:1-55542-567-4, ISBN13: 978-1-55542-567-8. Dewey:378.1/00973. LCCN:93-019511.
Audience: **f.**

Sanford, Nevitt **GV351**
The American College: A Psychological and Social Interpretation of the Higher Learning. Paper Text. Textbook Publishers. Temecula, CA. 2003. xvi, 1084p. ISBN:0-7581-0495-2, ISBN13: 978-0-7581-0495-3. Dewey:796.071173.
Audience: **f.** ℬ

Simpson, Ronald D. & Frost, Susan H. **LA227.4.S56 1993**
Inside College: Undergraduate Education for the Future. Cloth Text. Perseus Books Group. New York, NY. 1993. 302p. ISBN:0-306-44504-2, ISBN13: 978-0-306-44504-0. Dewey:378.73. LCCN:93-027880.
Audience: **l,u,f.** *Choice, 1994.*

Higher Education > Institutions of Higher Education > Public

LB2328.2
☐ American Association of State Colleges and Universities. http://www.aascu.org/
Audience: **f.**

Ingram, Richard T. **LB2341.I5325 1993**
Governing Public Colleges and Universities: A Handbook for Trustees, Chief Executives and Other Campus Leaders. Trade Cloth. John Wiley & Sons, Inc. Hoboken, NJ. 1993. 512p. ISBN:1-55542-566-6, ISBN13: 978-1-55542-566-1. Dewey:378.1/00973. LCCN:93-019512.
Audience: **f.** *Choice, 1994.*

Higher Education > Institutions of Higher Education > Community colleges

LB2328
☐ American Association of Community Colleges. http://www.aacc.nche.edu/
Audience: **f.**

Brint, Steven & Karabel, Jerome **LA226.B74 1989**
The Diverted Dream: Community Colleges and the Promise of Educational Opportunity in America, 1900-1985. Trade Paper. Oxford University Press, Inc. New York, NY. 1991. 336p. ISBN:0-19-504816-4, ISBN13: 978-0-19-504816-2. Dewey:378.73. LCCN:89-002891.
Audience: **f.** *Choice, 1990.*

Cohen, Arthur M. & Brawer, Florence B. **LB2328.C55 2002**
The American Community College. Ed. 4. Trade Cloth. John Wiley & Sons, Inc. Hoboken, NJ. 2002. 536p. Jossey-Bass Higher and Adult Education Ser. ISBN:0-7879-6011-X, ISBN13: 978-0-7879-6011-7. Dewey:378/.052. LCCN:2002-004710.
Audience: **l,u,f.** ℬ

Dougherty, Kevin James **LB2328.15.U6D68 1994**
ⓔ The Contradictory College: The Conflicting Origins, Impacts, and Futures of the Community College. E-Book. NetLibrary, Inc. Boulder, CO. 1994. ISBN:0-585-06261-7, ISBN13: 978-0-585-06261-7. Dewey:378/.052/0973.
Audience: **l,u,f.**

Gaither, Gerald H. **LB2341.M77 1998**
The Multicampus System: Perspectives on Practice and Prospects. Paper over Boards. Stylus Publishing, LLC. Sterling, VA. 1999. 208p. ISBN:1-57922-016-9, ISBN13: 978-1-57922-016-7. Dewey:378.73. LCCN:98-040753.
Audience: **u,f.**

Higher Education > Teaching Personnel, Academic Freedom, Work Conditions

LC72
□ AAUP web site.
http://www.aaup.org/
Audience: **f.**

LB1778
□ Chronicle Careers.
http://chronicle.com/jobs/
Audience: **f.**

Axelrod, Joseph **LB2331**
The University Teacher As Artist. Trade Cloth. John Wiley & Sons, Inc. Hoboken, NJ. 1973. 256p. Higher Education Ser. ISBN:0-87589-183-7, ISBN13: 978-0-87589-183-5. Dewey:001.3/07/1173. LCCN:73-003773.
Audience: **u,f.**

Barzun, Jacques **LB2331.B374 1986**
Teacher in America. Trade Paper. University Press of America, Inc. Lanham, MD. 1986. 328p. ISBN:0-8191-5447-4, ISBN13: 978-0-8191-5447-7. Dewey:378/.12/0973. LCCN:86-015853.
Audience: **g,l,u,f.** B

Blau, Peter **LB2341.B54 1994**
The Organization of Academic Work. Ed. 2. Trade Paper. Transaction Publishers. Somerset, NJ. 1994. 324p. ISBN:1-56000-756-7, ISBN13: 978-1-56000-756-2. Dewey:378.73. LCCN:94-007215.
Audience: **u,f.**

Bowen, Howard R; Schuster, Jack H **LB2331.72.B67 1986**
American Professors: A National Resource Imperiled. Oxford University Press, Inc. 1986. ISBN:0-19-503693-X, ISBN13: 978-0-19-503693-0.
Audience: **u,f.**

Boyer, Ernest L. & Glassick, Charles E. **LA227.3 .B694**
Scholarship Assessed and Reconsidered Set. Trade Paper. John Wiley & Sons, Inc. Hoboken, NJ. 2003. 304p. ISBN:0-7879-7476-5, ISBN13: 978-0-7879-7476-3. Dewey:378.73.
Audience: **f.**

Brookfield, Stephen D. & Preskill, Stephen **LB2331.B679 2005**
Discussion as a Way of Teaching: Tools and Techniques for Democratic Classrooms. Ed. 2. Trade Cloth. John Wiley & Sons, Inc. Hoboken, NJ. 2005. 336p. ISBN:0-7879-7808-6, ISBN13: 978-0-7879-7808-2. Dewey:378.1/2. LCCN:2005-008307.
Audience: **u,f.**

Buckley, William F. Jr. **LD6309 .B8 1977**
God and Man at Yale: The Superstitions of "Academic Freedom". Ed. 50. John Chamberlain (Introduction by). Trade Paper. Regnery Publishing, Incorporated, An Eagle Publishing Company. Washington, DC. 2005. 240p. ISBN:0-89526-692-X, ISBN13: 978-0-89526-692-7. Dewey:378.746/8. LCCN:79-108308.
Audience: **u,f.**

Caplan, Paula **LB2332.3.C37 1993**
Lifting a Ton of Feathers: A Woman's Guide to Surviving in the Academic World. Trade Paper. University of Toronto Press. Toronto, ON. 1993. 271p. ISBN:0-8020-7411-1, ISBN13: 978-0-8020-7411-9. Dewey:378.1/2/082. LCCN:93-093082.
Audience: **l,u,f.** *Choice, 1994.*

Carnegie Commission on Higher Education, et al. **LA227.3.L33**
The Divided Academy. Everett C. Ladd & Seymour Martin Lipset (Authors). Trade Cloth. McGraw-Hill Companies, The. New York, NY. 1975. 407p. ISBN:0-07-010112-4, ISBN13: 978-0-07-010112-8. Dewey:378.1/2. LCCN:74-017247.
Audience: **u,f.** B

Eble, Kenneth E. & McKeachie, Wilbert J. **LB2331.73.M6E24 1985**
Improving Undergraduate Education Through Faculty Development: An Analysis of Effective Programs and Practices. Trade Cloth. John Wiley & Sons, Inc. Hoboken, NJ. 1985. 266p. Higher Education Ser. ISBN:0-87589-643-X, ISBN13: 978-0-87589-643-4. Dewey:370/.7/124. LCCN:84-043027.
Audience: **f.**

Finkelstein, Martin J. **LB2331.72.F5**
The American Academic Profession: A Synthesis of Social Scientific Inquiry since World War II. Trade Paper. Books on Demand. Ann Arbor, MI. 301p. ISBN:0-608-09672-5, ISBN13: 978-0-608-09672-8. Dewey:378/.12/0973. LCCN:84-003613.
Audience: **f.**

Fortunato, Ray T. & Waddell, D. Geneva **LB2342.7**
Personnel Administration in Higher Education: Handbook of Faculty and Staff Personnel Practices. Trade Cloth. John Wiley & Sons, Inc. Hoboken, NJ. 1981. 408p. Higher Education Ser. ISBN:0-87589-506-9, ISBN13: 978-0-87589-506-2. Dewey:378/.11/0973. LCCN:81-047769.
Audience: **f.**

Furniss, W. Todd & Graham, Patricia A. (Editors) **LC1756 .W66**
Women in Higher Education. Trade Cloth. American Council on Education. Washington, DC. 1974. 325p. ISBN:0-8268-1421-2, ISBN13: 978-0-8268-1421-0. Dewey:376/.65. LCCN:73-022230.
Audience: **u,f.**

Glazer-Raymo, Judith **LB2332.3**
Shattering the Myths: Women in Academe. Trade Paper. Johns Hopkins University Press. Baltimore, MD. 2001. 256p. ISBN:0-8018-6641-3, ISBN13: 978-0-8018-6641-8. Dewey:378.12082.
Audience: **u,f.**

Higher Education > Scholarships, Grants, Student Financial Aid

LB2337.2
Federal School Code List.
http://www.fafsa.ed.gov/fotw0506/fslookup.htm
Audience: **l.**

LB2337.2
SRA International Grants Web.
http://www.srainternational.org/newweb/grantsweb/index.cfm
Audience: **f.**

College Entrance Examination Board **LB2342**
College Costs and Financial Aid Handbook. College Entrance Examination Board. 2005.
Audience: **l.**

Ehrenberg, Ronald G. **LB2342**
Tuition Rising: Why College Costs So Much. Trade Paper. Harvard University Press. Cambridge, MA. 2002. 336p. ISBN:0-674-00988-6, ISBN13: 978-0-674-00988-2. Dewey:378.3/8/0973.
Audience: **u,f.**

Grants Program Staff **LB2338**
Directory of Research Grants 2005. Cloth Text. Greenwood Publishing Group, Inc. Portsmouth, NH. 2004. 912p. Directory of Research Grants Ser. ISBN:1-57356-598-9, ISBN13: 978-1-57356-598-1. Dewey:139.95.
Audience: **f.**

McPherson, Michael S. & Schapiro, Morton Owen **LB2337.4**
The Student Aid Game: Meeting Need and Rewarding Talent in American Higher Education. Trade Paper. Princeton University Press. Princeton, NJ. 1998. 176p. ISBN:0-691-00536-2, ISBN13: 978-0-691-00536-2. Dewey:378.3/0973.
Audience: **u,f.** *Choice, 1998.*

Palgrave Macmillan Staff (Editor) **LB2338.G7 2004**
The Grants Register 2005: The Complete Guide to Postgraduate Funding Worldwide, Twenty-Third Edition. Trade Cloth. Palgrave Macmillan. New York, NY. 2004. 1120p. ISBN:1-4039-2116-4, ISBN13: 978-1-4039-2116-1. Dewey:378.3/3. LCCN:2004-003978.
Audience: **u,f.** *Choice, 2004.*

Higher Education > Administration and Finance

Chait, Richard P., et al. **LB2342.5 .C43 1993**
The Effective Board of Trustees. Thomas P. Holland & Barbara E. Taylor (Authors). Trade Cloth. Greenwood Publishing Group, Inc. Portsmouth, NH. 1991. 144p. American Council on Education Series on Higher Education ISBN:0-89774-806-9, ISBN13: 978-0-89774-806-3. Dewey:378.1/011. LCCN:92-043362.
Audience: **u,f.**

Delworth, Ursula & Hanson, Gary R. **LB2343.S795 1989**
Student Services: A Handbook for the Profession. Ed. 2. Trade Cloth. John Wiley & Sons, Inc. Hoboken, NJ. 1989. 680p. Higher Education Ser. ISBN:1-55542-148-2, ISBN13: 978-1-55542-148-9. Dewey:378/.194. LCCN:88-046086.
Audience: **u,f.**

Ehrle, Elwood B. & Bennett, John B. **LB2341.E49 1987**
Managing the Academic Enterprise: Case Studies for Deans and Provosts. Trade Cloth. Simon & Schuster. New York, NY. 1987. 224p. ACE-Oryx Series on Higher Education ISBN:0-02-902640-7, ISBN13: 978-0-02-902640-3. Dewey:378/.1/00973. LCCN:87-007877.
Audience: **f.**

Hopkins, David S. P. & Massy, William F. **LB2341 .H59**
Planning Models for Colleges and Universities. Trade Cloth. Stanford University Press. Palo Alto, CA. 1981. 572p. ISBN:0-8047-1023-6, ISBN13: 978-0-8047-1023-7. Dewey:378/.107. LCCN:78-066176.
Audience: **f.**

Keller, George **LB2341**
Academic Strategy: The Management Revolution in American Higher Education. Richard M. Cyert (Foreword by). Trade Paper. Johns Hopkins University Press. Baltimore, MD. 1991. 224p. ISBN:0-8018-3030-3, ISBN13: 978-0-8018-3030-3. Dewey:378.73. LCCN:82-049256.
Audience: **u,f.**

Kennedy, Donald **LA227.4.K465 1997**
Academic Duty. Trade Cloth. Harvard University Press. Cambridge, MA. 1997. 320p. ISBN:0-674-00222-9, ISBN13: 978-0-674-00222-7. Dewey:378.73. LCCN:97-013210.
Audience: **f.** *Choice, 1998.*

Kerr, Clark & Gade, Marian L. **LB2341 .K44**
The Many Lives of Academic Presidents: Association of Governing Boards and Universities and Colleges. Trade Cloth. Association of Governing Boards of Universities & Colleges. Washington, DC. 1986. 260p. ISBN:0-318-21457-1, ISBN13: 978-0-318-21457-3. Dewey:378/.111.
Audience: **f.**

Rowland, A. Westley **LB2342.8.H36 1986**
Handbook of Institutional Advancement: A Modern Guide to Executive Management, Institutional Relations, Fund Raising, Alumni Administration, Government Relations, Publications, Periodicals, and Enrollment Management. Ed. 2. Trade Cloth. John Wiley & Sons, Inc. Hoboken, NJ. 1986. 832p. Higher and Adult Education Ser. ISBN:0-87589-689-8, ISBN13: 978-0-87589-689-2. Dewey:659.2/937873. LCCN:85-045912.
Audience: **f.**

Shulman, James Lawrence & Bowen, William G. **GV351**
The Game of Life: College Sports and Educational Values. Trade Paper. Princeton University Press. Princeton, NJ. 2002.

494p. ISBN:0-691-09619-8, ISBN13: 978-0-691-09619-3. Dewey:796.04/3/0973.
Audience: **g,l,u,f.** *Choice, 2001.*

Tucker, Allan (Editor) **LB2341.T78 1992**
Chairing the Academic Department: Leadership among Peers. Library Binding. Macmillan Publishing Company, Inc. Old Tappan, NJ. 1992. ISBN:0-02-897425-5, ISBN13: 978-0-02-897425-5. Dewey:378.1/11. LCCN:91-031292.
Audience: **f.**

Wilson, Logan **LB1778.2.W55 1995**
The Academic Man: A Study in the Sociology of a Profession. Philip G. Altbach (Introduction by). Trade Paper. Transaction Publishers. Somerset, NJ. 1995. 248p. ISBN:1-56000-810-5, ISBN13: 978-1-56000-810-1. Dewey:378.1/2. LCCN:94-041612.
Audience: **u,f.** BCL3

Higher Education > Entrance Requirements. College Choice

Bowen, William G. & Bok, Derek **LB2351.2**
The Shape of the River: Long-Term Consequences of Considering Race in College and University Admissions. Glenn C. Loury (Foreword by). Trade Paper. Princeton University Press. Princeton, NJ. 2000. 538p. ISBN:0-691-05019-8, ISBN13: 978-0-691-05019-5. Dewey:378.1/61/0973.
Audience: **g,u,f.** *Choice, 1999.*

College Entrance Examination Board **LB2351.A1**
The College Handbook. College Entrance Examination Board. 2005.
Audience: **u.**

Hossler, Don, et al. **LB2350.5.H634 1999**
[Ebook] Going to College: How Social, Economic, and Educational Factors Influence the Decisions Students Make. Jack L. Schmit & Nick Vesper (Authors). E-Book. Johns Hopkins University Press. Baltimore, MD. 192p. ISBN:0-8018-7034-8, ISBN13: 978-0-8018-7034-7. Dewey:378.1/61.
Audience: **l,u,f.**

Jacobs, Bonita C. **LB2360.3.C65 2004**
The College Transfer Student in America: The Forgotten Student. American Association of Collegiate Registrars and Admissions Officers Staff (Contribution by). Trade Cloth. American Association of Collegiate Registrars & Admissions Officers. Washington, DC. 2004. v, 230p. ISBN:1-57858-058-7, ISBN13: 978-1-57858-058-3. Dewey:378.1/69. LCCN:2003-025981.
Audience: **l,u,f.**

Kahlenberg, Richard D. (Editor) **LC4823.A54 2004**
America's Untapped Resource: Low-Income Students in Higher Education. Trade Paper. Century Foundation, The. New York, NY. 2003. 188p. ISBN:0-87078-485-4, ISBN13: 978-0-87078-485-9. Dewey:378.1/9826942. LCCN:2003-023798.
Audience: **u,f.**

Lavin, David E. & Hyllegard, David **LD3835.L375 1996**
Changing the Odds: Open Admissions and the Life Chances of the Disadvantaged. Cloth over Boards. Yale University Press. Cumberland, RI. 1996. 304p. ISBN:0-300-06328-8, ISBN13: 978-0-300-06328-8. Dewey:370.1/934/09747. LCCN:95-031948.
Audience: **l,u,f.** *Choice, 1996.*

Higher Education > Curriculum

LB2361
[Web] World Lecture Hall. http://web.austin.utexas.edu/wlh/
Audience: **u.**

Applebee, Arthur N. **LB1570.A67 1996**
Curriculum as Conversation: Transforming Traditions of Teaching and Learning. Trade Paper. University of Chicago Press. Chicago, IL. 1996. 158p. ISBN:0-226-02123-8, ISBN13: 978-0-226-02123-2. Dewey:375/.00973. LCCN:95-042694.
Audience: **u,f.** *Choice, 1996.*

Carnegie Foundation for the Advancement of Teaching Staff **LB2361.5.C37 1977**
Missions of the College Curriculum: A Contemporary Review with Suggestions: a Commentary of the Carnegie Foundation for the Advancement of Teaching. Trade Cloth. John Wiley & Sons, Inc. Hoboken, NJ. 1977. xvii, 322p. ISBN:0-87589-360-0, ISBN13: 978-0-87589-360-0. Dewey:378.1/99/0973. LCCN:77-084320.
Audience: **u,f.** BCL3

Carnochan, W. B. **LB2361.5**
The Battleground of the Curriculum: Liberal Education and American Experience. Trade Paper. Stanford University Press. Palo Alto, CA. 1994. 188p. ISBN:0-8047-2364-8, ISBN13: 978-0-8047-2364-0. Dewey:378.1/99/0973.
Audience: **u,f.** *Choice, 1994.*

Gaff, Jerry G. **LC985.G34 1991**
New Life for the College Curriculum: Assessing Achievements and Furthering Progress in the Reform of General Education. Ed. 2. Trade Cloth. John Wiley & Sons, Inc. Hoboken, NJ. 1991. 272p. Higher and Adult Education Ser. ISBN:1-55542-392-2, ISBN13: 978-1-55542-392-6. Dewey:378.1/99. LCCN:91-019068.
Audience: **u,f.** *Choice, 1992.*

Harvard University. Committee on the Objectives of General Education in a Free Society. **LA210**
General Education in a Free Society. Harvard University Press. 1945.
Audience: **f.**

Levine, Arthur **LB2361.5**
Handbook on Undergraduate Curriculum: Prepared for the Carnegie Council on Policy Studies in Higher Education. Trade Cloth. John Wiley & Sons, Inc. Hoboken, NJ. 1978. 697p. Higher Education Ser. ISBN:0-87589-376-7, ISBN13: 978-0-87589-376-1. Dewey:378/.199/0973. LCCN:78-050893.
Audience: **u,f.** BCL3

Levine, Arthur & Weingart, John R. **LA0227.L4**
Reform of Undergraduate Education. Trade Cloth. Books on Demand. Ann Arbor, MI. 176p. Jossey-Bass Higher Education Ser. ISBN:0-8357-9343-5, ISBN13: 978-0-8357-9343-8. Dewey:378.73. LCCN:73-007154.
Audience: **u,f.**

Stark, Joan S. & Lattuca, Lisa R. **LB2361.5.S73 1996**
Shaping the College Curriculum: Academic Plans in Action. Cloth Text. Allyn & Bacon, Inc. Boston, MA. 1996. 462p. ISBN:0-205-16706-3, ISBN13: 978-0-205-16706-7. Dewey:378.1/99/0973. LCCN:95-044529.
Audience: **u,f.**

Higher Education > Graduate and Professional Education

L901
☐ America's Best Graduate Schools. http://www.usnews.com/usnews/edu/beyond/bchome.htm
Audience: **u.**

Bok, Derek C. **LA227.3**
Higher Learning. Trade Cloth. Harvard University Press. Cambridge, MA. 1986. 208p. ISBN:0-674-39175-6, ISBN13: 978-0-674-39175-8. Dewey:378.73. LCCN:86-009876.
Audience: **g,f.**

Curry, Lynn & Wergin, Jon F. **LC1059.C87 1993**
Educating Professionals: Responding to New Expectations for Competence and Accountability. Trade Cloth. John Wiley & Sons, Inc. Hoboken, NJ. 1993. 379p. Higher and Adult Education Ser. ISBN:1-55542-523-2, ISBN13: 978-1-55542-523-4. Dewey:378/.013. LCCN:92-041686.
Audience: **f.**

Marsh, Peter (Editor) **LD5231.C66 1988**
Contesting the Boundaries of Liberal and Professional Education: The Syracuse Experiment. Cloth Text. Syracuse University Press. Syracuse, NY. 1988. 280p. ISBN:0-8156-2428-X, ISBN13: 978-0-8156-2428-8. Dewey:378/.199/0974766. LCCN:87-033635.
Audience: **u,f.**

National Research Council Staff **Q180.U5R387 1995**
Research-Doctorate Programs in the United States: Continuity and Change. Marvin Goldberger, Brendan A. Maher & Pamela E. Flatteau (Editors). Cloth Text. National Academies Press. Washington, DC. 1995. 768p. ISBN:0-309-05094-4, ISBN13: 978-0-309-05094-4. Dewey:378.1/553/0973. LCCN:95-035154.
Audience: **u,f.** *Choice, 1996.*

Higher Education > Academic Degrees

Brown, David **LB2390.B76 1995**
Degrees of Control: A Sociology of Educational Expansion and Occupational Credentialism. Trade Cloth. Teachers College Press, Teachers College, Columbia University. New York, NY. 1995. 492p. ISBN:0-8077-3452-7, ISBN13: 978-0-8077-3452-0. Dewey:378.2/4/0973. LCCN:95-013196.
Audience: **u,f.** *Choice, 1996.*

College Entrance Examination Board **L901**
Index of Majors and Graduate Degrees. College Entrance Examination Board. 2005.
Audience: **u.**

Higher Education > State and Federal policy

LB2331.62
☐ State Policy Inventory Database Online. http://www.wiche.edu/policy/SPIDO/
Audience: **f.**

Callan, Patrick M. & Finney, Joni E. (Editors) **LB2342.P785 1997**
Public and Private Financing of Higher Education: Shaping Public Policy for the Future. Trade Cloth. Greenwood Publishing Group, Inc. Portsmouth, NH. 1997. 264p. American Council on Education Series on Higher Education ISBN:1-57356-116-9, ISBN13: 978-1-57356-116-7. Dewey:379.1/214/0973. LCCN:97-029457.
Audience: **u,f.**

Chang, Mitchell (Editor), et al. **LC212.42.C66 2003**
A Compelling Interest: Examining the Evidence on Racial Dynamics in Colleges and Universities. Daria Witt, James Jones & Kenji Hakuta (Editors). Cloth Text. Stanford University Press. Palo Alto, CA. 2003. xv, 246p. ISBN:0-8047-4034-8, ISBN13: 978-0-8047-4034-0. Dewey:378.1/9829. LCCN:2002-151608.
Audience: **l,u,f.**

Cook, Constance E. **LC173.C66 1998**
Lobbying for Higher Education: How Colleges and Universities Influence Federal Policy. Trade Paper. Vanderbilt University Press. Nashville, TN. 1998. 272p. ISBN:0-8265-1317-4, ISBN13: 978-0-8265-1317-5. Dewey:379.1/18/0973. LCCN:98-008885.
Audience: **u,f.** *Choice, 1999.*

Finney, Joni E., et al. **LC173.D47 1999**
Designing State Higher Education Systems for a New Century. Richard C. Richardson, Kathy R. Bracco & Patrick M. Callan (Authors). Trade Cloth. Greenwood Publishing Group, Inc. Portsmouth, NH. 1998. 232p. American Council on Education Series on Higher Education ISBN:1-57356-174-6, ISBN13: 978-1-57356-174-7. Dewey:378.73. LCCN:98-042300.
Audience: **u,f.**

Johnstone, D. Bruce **LB2341.98.F85 1993**
The Funding of Higher Education: International Perspectives. Philip G. Altbach (Editor). Cloth Text. Garland Publishing, Inc. New York, NY. 1993. 336p. Studies in Higher Education Library of Sociology, Vol. 1 ISBN:0-8153-1335-7, ISBN13: 978-0-8153-1335-9. Dewey:378.02. LCCN:93-007388.
Audience: **u,f.** *Choice, 1994.*

Rosenzweig, Robert M. **L901**
The Political University: Policy, Politics, and Presidential Leadership in the American Research University. Trade Paper. Johns Hopkins University Press. Baltimore, MD. 2001. 240p. ISBN:0-8018-6819-X, ISBN13: 978-0-8018-6819-1. Dewey:378.7/3. LCCN:97-025109.
Audience: **u,f.** *Choice, 1998.*

Van De Graaff, John H., et al. **LA132**
Academic Power: Patterns of Authority in Seven National Systems of Higher Education. Burton R. Clark, Dorotea Furth, Dietrich Goldschmidt & Donald F. Wheeler (Authors). Trade Cloth. Greenwood Publishing Group, Inc. Portsmouth, NH.

1978. 217p. Praeger Special Studies ISBN:0-275-90318-4, ISBN13: 978-0-275-90318-3. Dewey:370.19/5. LCCN:78-017172.

Audience: **u,f.**

Special Forms of Education > Home Schooling

Cooper, Bruce S. **LC40.H669 2005**
Homeschooling in Full View: A Reader. Trade Cloth. Information Age Publishing, Inc. Greenwich, CT. 2005. xix, 253p. ISBN:1-59311-339-0, ISBN13: 978-1-59311-339-1. Dewey:371.04/2. LCCN:2005-009103.
Audience: **g,l.**

Farenga, Patrick & Holt, John **LC37.H66 2003**
Teach Your Own: The John Holt Book of Home Schooling. Trade Paper. Basic Books. New York, NY. 2003. 368p. ISBN:0-7382-0694-6, ISBN13: 978-0-7382-0694-3. Dewey:649.6/8. LCCN:2003-101364.
Audience: **g,l,u,f.**

Home School Legal Defense Association **LC40**
☐ HSLDA: Home School Legal Defense Association. http://www.hslda.org
HSLDA.
Audience: **g,l,u,f.**

Klicka, Christopher J. **KF4221.K56 2002**
The Right to Home School: A Guide to the Law on Parents' Rights in Education. Carolina Academic Press. 2002. ISBN:0-89089-623-2, ISBN13: 978-0-89089-623-5.
Audience: **g,l,u,f.**

National Home Education Research Institute **LC40**
☐ NHERI: National Home Education Resource Institute. http://www.nheri.org
NHERI.
Audience: **g,l,u,f.**

Penn-Nabrit, Paula **LC40.P45 2003**
Morning by Morning: How We Home-Schooled Our African-American Sons to the Ivy League. Trade Cloth. Random House Adult Trade Publishing Group. New York, NY. 2003. 304p. ISBN:0-375-50774-4, ISBN13: 978-0-375-50774-8. Dewey:371.04/2. LCCN:2002-033051.
Audience: **g,l,f.**

Ray, Brian D. **LC40.R39 1997**
Strengths of Their Own - Home Schoolers Across America: Academic Achievement, Family Characteristics, and Longitudinal Traits. Trade Paper. National Home Education Research Institute. Salem, OR. 1997. 160p. ISBN:0-9657554-0-1, ISBN13: 978-0-9657554-0-5. Dewey:371.04/2/0973. LCCN:97-091643.
Audience: **g,l,u,f.**

Stevens, Mitchell L. **LC40**
Kingdom of Children: Culture and Controversy in the Homeschooling Movement. Trade Paper. Princeton University Press. Princeton, NJ. 2003. 248p. Princeton Studies in Cultural Sociology Ser. ISBN:0-691-11468-4, ISBN13: 978-0-691-11468-2. Dewey:371/.042/0973.
Audience: **g,l,u,f.** *Choice, 2002.*

Van Galen, Jane (Editor), et al. **LC40.H66 1991**
Home Schooling: Political, Historical, and Pedagogical Perspectives. Mary A. Pitman & Kathryn M. Borman (Editors). Book, Other. Greenwood Publishing Group, Inc. Portsmouth, NH. 1991. 224p. Social and Policy Issues in Education Ser., Vol. 2 ISBN:0-89391-706-0, ISBN13: 978-0-89391-706-7. Dewey:649/.68. LCCN:90-025723.
Audience: **l,u,f.** *Choice, 1991.*

Special Forms of Education > Private schools. Boarding Schools

Bassett, Patrick F. & Thorn, Craig (Illustrators) **LC49**
Looking Ahead: Independent School Issues and Answers. Ed. 2. Trade Paper. Avocus Publishing, Inc. Gilsum, NH. 2003. 272p. ISBN:1-890765-10-4, ISBN13: 978-1-890765-10-1. Dewey:371/.02/0973.
Audience: **g,l,u,f.**

Beadie, Nancy & Tolley, Kimberly (Editors) **LC49.C47 2002**
Chartered Schools: Two Hundred Years of Independent Academies in United States, 1727-1925. Trade Cloth. Routledge. New York, NY. 2002. 384p. Studies in the History of Education ISBN:0-415-93118-5, ISBN13: 978-0-415-93118-2. Dewey:371.02/0973. LCCN:2001-051102.
Audience: **g,l,u,f.**

Benveniste, Luis, et al. **LB2806.36.R68 2002**
All Else Equal: Are Public and Private Schools Different? Martin Carnoy & Richard Rothstein (Authors). Trade Cloth. Routledge. New York, NY. 2002. 224p. ISBN:0-415-93196-7, ISBN13: 978-0-415-93196-0. Dewey:371.01/0973. LCCN:2002-026714.
Audience: **g,l,u,f.**

Crosier, Louis M. (Editor) **LC58.4.C37 1991**
Casualties of Privilege: Essays on Prep Schools' Hidden Culture. Trade Paper. Avocus Publishing, Inc. Gilsum, NH. 1991. 153p. ISBN:0-9627671-0-7, ISBN13: 978-0-9627671-0-4. Dewey:373.2/22. LCCN:90-084618.
Audience: **g,l,u,f.**

Hillman, Tim & Thorn, Craig IV (Editors) **LC58.7**
Far and Wide: Cultural Diversity in American Boarding Schools. Trade Paper. Avocus Publishing, Inc. Gilsum, NH. 1997. 182p. ISBN:0-9627671-8-2, ISBN13: 978-0-9627671-8-0. Dewey:373.
Audience: **g,l,u,f.**

Kane, Pearl R. **LC49.I53 1991**
Independent Schools, Independent Thinkers. Trade Cloth. John Wiley & Sons, Inc. Hoboken, NJ. 1992. 446p. Education-Higher Education Ser. ISBN:1-55542-398-1, ISBN13: 978-1-55542-398-8. Dewey:371/.02/0973. LCCN:91-027073.
Audience: **l,u,f.** *Choice, 1992.*

Kingston, Paul W. & Lewis, Lionel S. (Editors) **LC4941.H54 1990**
The High Status Track: Studies of Elite Schools and Stratification. Paper Text. State University of New York Press. Albany, NY. 1990. 261p. SUNY Series in Frontiers of Education

ISBN:0-7914-0011-5, ISBN13: 978-0-7914-0011-1. Dewey:371.96/2/0973. LCCN:89-031600.
Audience: **l,u,f.** *Choice, 1990.*

McKeever, Daniel (Editor) **L901.H3**
The Handbook of Private Schools: An Annual Descriptive Survey of Independent Education. Ed. 86. Porter Sargent Staff (Compiled by). Trade Cloth. Porter Sargent Publishers, Inc. Boston, MA. 2005. 1472p. Handbook Ser. ISBN:0-87558-154-4, ISBN13: 978-0-87558-154-5. Dewey:373. LCCN:15-012869.
Audience: **g,l,u,f.**

Peshkin, Alan **LC58.4.P58 2000**
Permissible Advantage?: The Moral Consequences of Elite Schooling. E-Book. NetLibrary, Inc. Boulder, CO. 2001. ISBN:0-585-36548-2, ISBN13: 978-0-585-36548-0. Dewey:373.2/22.
Audience: **g,l,u,f.**

Thorn, Craig (Editor) **LC58.4**
Second Home: Life in a Boarding School. Ed. 2. Trade Paper. Avocus Publishing, Inc. Gilsum, NH. 2002. 224p. ISBN:1-890765-09-0, ISBN13: 978-1-890765-09-5. Dewey:373.222.
Audience: **g,l,u,f.**

Social Aspects of Education

LB5.N25
National Society for the Study of Education (NSSE). http://www.nsse-chicago.org/
Audience: **u,f.**

McLaren, Peter **LC196.5.U6M345 2007**
Life in Schools: An Introduction to Critical Pedagogy in the Foundations of Education. Ed. 5. Trade Paper. Allyn & Bacon, Inc. Boston, MA. 2006. 352p. ISBN:0-205-50181-8, ISBN13: 978-0-205-50181-6. Dewey:370.11/5. LCCN:2006-041623.
Audience: **l,u,f.**

Rury, John L. **LA205.R67 2005**
Education and Social Change: Themes in the History of American Schooling. Ed. 2. Other. Lawrence Erlbaum Associates, Inc. Mahwah, NJ. 2004. ISBN:1-4106-1180-9, ISBN13: 978-1-4106-1180-2. Dewey:370/.973.
Audience: **l,u,f.** *Choice, 2002.*

Social Aspects of Education > Economic Aspects of Education

Belfield, Clive R. **LC65**
Economic Principles for Education: Theory and Evidence. Trade Paper. Edward Elgar Publishing, Inc. Northampton, MA. 2003. 272p. ISBN:1-84376-273-0, ISBN13: 978-1-84376-273-7. Dewey:338.4/737.
Audience: **u,f.** *Choice, 2001.*

Berg, Ivar **LC66.B47 2003**
Education and Jobs: The Great Training Robbery. Paper Text. Eliot Werner Publications, Inc. Clinton Corners, NY. 2003. 266p. Foundations of Sociology Ser. ISBN:0-9712427-5-5, ISBN13: 978-0-9712427-5-3. Dewey:331.1/142. LCCN:2001-099685.
Audience: **u,f.**

Checchi, Daniele **LC65**
The Economics of Education: Human Capital, Family Background and Inequality. Trade Cloth. Cambridge University Press. New York, NY. 2006. 290p. ISBN:0-521-79310-6, ISBN13: 978-0-521-79310-0. Dewey:379.2.
Audience: **u,f.**

Gould, Eric **LC67.62.G68 2003**
The University in a Corporate Culture. Cloth over Boards. Yale University Press. Cumberland, RI. 2003. 272p. ISBN:0-300-08706-3, ISBN13: 978-0-300-08706-2. Dewey:338.4/3378. LCCN:2002-014242.
Audience: **u,f.**

Gradstein, Mark, et al. **LC65.G73 2004**
The Political Economy of Education: Implications for Growth and Inequality. Moshe Justman & Volker Meier (Authors). Trade Cloth. MIT Press. Cambridge, MA. 2004. 176p. CESifo Book Ser. ISBN:0-262-07256-4, ISBN13: 978-0-262-07256-4. Dewey:338.4/337. LCCN:2004-040293.
Audience: **u,f.**

Heijke, Hans & Muysken, Joan (Editors) **LC67.E9E38 2000**
Education and Training in a Knowledge Based Economy. Trade Cloth. Palgrave Macmillan. New York, NY. 2000. 331p. Applied Econometrics Association Ser. ISBN:0-312-23569-0, ISBN13: 978-0-312-23569-7. Dewey:331.25/92/094. LCCN:00-031117.
Audience: **g,l,u,f.**

Machin, Stephen & Vignoles, Anna **LC67.G7W43 2005**
What's the Good of Education?: The Economics of Education in the UK. Trade Paper. Princeton University Press. Princeton, NJ. 2005. 272p. ISBN:0-691-11734-9, ISBN13: 978-0-691-11734-8. Dewey:370/.941. LCCN:2004-062442.
Audience: **l,u,f.**

Social Aspects of Education > Education and the State

Arons, Stephen **LC72.2.A76 1986**
Compelling Belief: The Culture of American Schooling. Trade Paper. University of Massachusetts Press. Amherst, MA. 1986. 240p. ISBN:0-87023-524-9, ISBN13: 978-0-87023-524-5. Dewey:370/.973. LCCN:85-028818.
Audience: **g,l,u,f.**

Bascia, Nina (Editor), et al. **LC71 .I489 2005**
International Handbook of Educational Policy. Alister Cumming, Amanda Datnow, Kenneth Leithwood & David Livingstone (Editors). Trade Cloth. Springer. New York, NY. 2005. xlv,1114p. Springer International Handbooks of Education Ser., Vol. 13 ISBN:1-4020-3189-0, ISBN13: 978-1-4020-3189-2. Dewey:379. LCCN:2005-296775.
Audience: **u,f.**

Cuban, Larry & Tyack, David B. **LA216.T92 1995**
Tinkering Toward Utopia: A Century of Public School Reform. Trade Cloth. Harvard University Press. Cambridge, MA. 1995. 192p. ISBN:0-674-89282-8, ISBN13: 978-0-674-89282-8. Dewey:371/.01/097309. LCCN:94-047545.
Audience: **g,l,u,f.** *Choice, 1996.*

Demetrion, George **LC149.7.D416 2004**
Conflicting Paradigms in Adult Literacy Education: In Quest of a U.S. Democratic Politics of Literacy. Trade Cloth. Lawrence Erlbaum Associates, Inc. Mahwah, NJ. 2004. 336p. ISBN:0-8058-4623-9, ISBN13: 978-0-8058-4623-2. Dewey:374/.012/0973. LCCN:2004-050677.
Audience: **u,f.** *Choice, 2005.*

Greenawalt, Kent **LC111.G68 2004**
Does God Belong in Public Schools? Trade Cloth. Princeton University Press. Princeton, NJ. 2004. 296p. ISBN:0-691-12111-7, ISBN13: 978-0-691-12111-6. Dewey:379.28/0973. LCCN:2004-045779.
Audience: **g,l,u,f.** *Choice, 2005.*

Henderson, John Cleaves **LC89**
Thomas Jefferson's Views on Public Education. Trade Cloth. Library Reprints, Inc. Temecula, CA. 1890. 387p. ISBN:0-7222-2934-8, ISBN13: 978-0-7222-2934-7. Dewey:370/.924.
Audience: **g,l,u,f.** B

Tyack, David **LC191.4.T93 2003**
Seeking Common Ground: Public Schools in a Diverse Society. Trade Cloth. Harvard University Press. Cambridge, MA. 2004. 256p. ISBN:0-674-01198-8, ISBN13: 978-0-674-01198-4. Dewey:379.73. LCCN:2003-049921.
Audience: **g,l,u,f.** *Choice, 2004.*

Wiggin, Gladys Anna **PN2035.B6**
Education and Nationalism: An Historical Interpretation of American Education. Paper Text. Textbook Publishers. Temecula, CA. 2003. 518p. ISBN:0-7581-8558-8, ISBN13: 978-0-7581-8558-7. Dewey:792.03.
Audience: **g,l,u,f.** B

Wirt, Frederick M. & Kirst, Michael W. **LC89.W56 1997**
The Political Dynamics of American Education. Trade Cloth. McCutchan Publishing Corporation. Richmond, CA. 1997. 356p. ISBN:0-8211-2273-8, ISBN13: 978-0-8211-2273-0. Dewey:379.73. LCCN:97-070792.
Audience: **g,l,u,f.**

Social Aspects of Education > Education and the State > Academic Freedom

Aby, Stephen H. & Kuhn, James C. (Compiled by) **LC72**
Academic Freedom: A Guide to the Literature. Cloth Text. Greenwood Publishing Group, Inc. Portsmouth, NH. 2000. 240p. Bibliographies and Indexes in Education Ser., Vol. 20 ISBN:0-313-30386-X, ISBN13: 978-0-313-30386-9. Dewey:378.1/21. LCCN:99-059136.
Audience: **l,u,f.** *Choice, 2000.*

Brown, Jean E. (Editor, Introduction by) **LC72.2.P74 1994**
Preserving Intellectual Freedom: Fighting Censorship in Our Schools. Trade Cloth. National Council of Teachers of English. Urbana, IL. 1994. xv, 252p. ISBN:0-8141-3671-0, ISBN13: 978-0-8141-3671-3. Dewey:379.1/55. LCCN:94-019860.
Audience: **g,l,u.**

DeGeorge, Richard **LB2335.7.D4 1997**
Academic Freedom and Tenure: Ethical Issues. Book, Other. Rowman & Littlefield Publishers, Inc. Lanham, MD. 1997. 300p. Issues in Academic Ethics Ser., No. 41 ISBN:0-8476-8331-1, ISBN13: 978-0-8476-8331-4. Dewey:378.1/21. LCCN:96-039513.
Audience: **g,l,u,f.** *Choice, 1998.*

Hofstadter, Richard **LC72.2.H64 1996**
Academic Freedom in the Age of the College. Roger L. Geiger (Introduction by). Trade Paper. Transaction Publishers. Somerset, NJ. 1995. 284p. ISBN:1-56000-860-1, ISBN13: 978-1-56000-860-6. Dewey:378.1/21. LCCN:95-021463.
Audience: **l,u,f.**

Kahn, Sharon E. & Pavlich, Dennis J. (Editors) **LC72.A417 2000**
Academic Freedom and the Inclusive University. Cloth Text. University of British Columbia Press. Vancouver, BC. 2000. 192p. ISBN:0-7748-0807-1, ISBN13: 978-0-7748-0807-1. Dewey:378.1/21. LCCN:2001-430725.
Audience: **g,l,u,f.**

McGuinness, Kevin **LC72.5.G7M35 2002**
Approaches to Academic Freedom and Related Issues. Trade Cloth. Edwin Mellen Press, The. Lewiston, NY. 2002. 316p. Studies in Education, Vol. 72 ISBN:0-7734-7061-1, ISBN13: 978-0-7734-7061-3. Dewey:371.1/04. LCCN:2002-025053.
Audience: **u,f.**

Menand, Louis **LC72.2**
The Future of Academic Freedom. Trade Paper. University of Chicago Press. Chicago, IL. 1998. 250p. ISBN:0-226-52005-6, ISBN13: 978-0-226-52005-6. Dewey:378.1/21.
Audience: **g,l,u,f.**

Poch, Robert K. & AEHE Staff **LC72.2**
Academic Freedom in American Higher Education: Rights, Responsibilities, and Limitations, Vol. 22. Jonathan D. Fife (Editor, Foreword by). Trade Paper. John Wiley & Sons, Inc. Hoboken, NJ. 2000. 110p. ASHE-ERIC Higher Education Reports, No. 94-4 ISBN:1-878380-25-7, ISBN13: 978-1-878380-25-8. Dewey:378.1/21.
Audience: **g,l,u,f.**

Social Aspects of Education > Education and the State > School Choice. Vouchers

Fuller, Bruce **LB2806.36.I57 2000**
Inside Charter Schools: The Paradox of Radical Decentralization. Trade Cloth. Harvard University Press. Cambridge, MA. 2001. 304p. ISBN:0-674-00325-X, ISBN13: 978-0-674-00325-5. Dewey:371.01. LCCN:00-056713.
Audience: **g,l,u,f.** *Choice, 2001.*

Godwin, R. Kenneth & Kemerer, Frank R. **LB1027.9.G63 2002**
School Choice Tradeoffs: Liberty, Equity, and Diversity. Trade Cloth. University of Texas Press. Austin, TX. 2002. 335p. ISBN:0-292-72842-5, ISBN13: 978-0-292-72842-4. Dewey:379.1/11/0973. LCCN:2001-005081.
Audience: **u,f.** *Choice, 2002.*

Howell, William G. & Peterson, Paul E. **LC89**
The Education Gap: Vouchers and Urban Schools. Trade Paper.

Brookings Institution Press. Washington, DC. 2005. 310p. ISBN:0-8157-3685-1, ISBN13: 978-0-8157-3685-1. Dewey:379.1110973091732. LCCN:2006-277846.
Audience: **g,l,u,f.**

Levin, Henry M. **LB2806.36.P49 2001**
Privatizing Education: Can the School Marketplace Deliver Freedom of Choice, Efficiency, Equity, and Social Cohesion? Trade Paper. Westview Press. Boulder, CO. 2001. 384p. ISBN:0-8133-6640-2, ISBN13: 978-0-8133-6640-1. Dewey:379. LCCN:00-054656.
Audience: **g,l,u,f.** *Choice, 2002.*

Petrovich, Janice & Wells, Amy Stuart (Editors) **LC213.2.B75 2005**
Bringing Equity Back: Research for a New Era in American Educational Policy. Alison R. Bernstein (Foreword by), Wendy Puriefoy (Afterword by). Trade Cloth. Teachers College Press, Teachers College, Columbia University. New York, NY. 2005. 350p. ISBN:0-8077-4576-6, ISBN13: 978-0-8077-4576-2. Dewey:379.260973. LCCN:2004-063670.
Audience: **g,l,u,f.** *Choice, 2006.*

Weil, Danny **LB2828.8.W45 2002**
School Vouchers and Privatization: A Reference Handbook. Library Binding. ABC-CLIO, Inc. Santa Barbara, CA. 2003. 320p. Contemporary Education Issues Ser. ISBN:1-57607-346-7, ISBN13: 978-1-57607-346-9. Dewey:379.1/11. LCCN:2002-153378.
Audience: **g,l,u,f.** *Choice, 2003.*

Wells, Amy Stuart **LB1027.9 .W45 1993**
Time to Choose: America at the Crossroads of School Choice Policy. Trade Cloth. Farrar, Straus & Giroux. New York, NY. 1993. ISBN:0-8090-3439-5, ISBN13: 978-0-8090-3439-0. Dewey:371/.01. LCCN:93-015080.
Audience: **g,l,u,f.**

Wolfe, Alan **LB1027.9**
Issues: School Choice.
http://www.bc.edu/bc_org/research/rapl/issues/schoolchoice/index.html
The Boisi Center for Religion & American Public Life at Boston College.
Audience: **g,l,u,f.**

Social Aspects of Education > Education and the State > Public School Issues (Including Religious Instruction)

LC111
Religion & Public Schools.
http://pewforum.org/religion-schools/
The Pew Forum on Religion & Public Life.
Audience: **g,l,u,f.**

LC401
Religion in the Public Schools: A Joint Statement of Current Law.
http://www.ed.gov/Speeches/04-1995/prayer.html
U. S. Department of Education.
Audience: **g,l,u,f.**

LC401
Religious Liberty: Religious Liberty in Public Schools.
http://www.firstamendmentcenter.org/rel_liberty/publicschools/Index.aspx
First Admendment Center.
Audience: **g,l,u,f.**

OABITAR, (Objectivity, Accuracy, and Balance In Teaching About Religion) **BL42.5.U5**
Teaching About Religion: Worldview Education.
http://www.teachingaboutreligion.org
OABITAR.
Audience: **g,l,u,f.**

Social Aspects of Education > Compulsory Education. Attendance. Dropouts

Farrell, Edwin **LA229.F36 1990**
Hanging in and Dropping Out: Voices of At-Risk High School Students. Trade Paper. Teachers College Press, Teachers College, Columbia University. New York, NY. 1990. 280p. ISBN:0-8077-3003-3, ISBN13: 978-0-8077-3003-4. Dewey:373.18/1. LCCN:89-028620.
Audience: **g,u,f.** *Choice, 1991.*

Kelly, Deirdre **LC5551.K44 1993**
Last Chance High: How Girls and Boys Drop in and Out of Alternative Schools. Trade Cloth. Yale University Press. Cumberland, RI. 1993. 296p. ISBN:0-300-05272-3, ISBN13: 978-0-300-05272-5. Dewey:373.129130973. LCCN:92-041978.
Audience: **g,u,f.** *Choice, 1994.*

Natriello, Gary **LC4091.N39 1990**
Schooling Disadvantaged Children: Racing Against Catastrophe. Cloth Text. Teachers College Press, Teachers College, Columbia University. New York, NY. 1990. 272p. ISBN:0-8077-3015-7, ISBN13: 978-0-8077-3015-7. Dewey:371.96/7/0973. LCCN:89-077441.
Audience: **g,l,u,f.** *Choice, 1990.*

Orfield, Gary (Editor) **LC146.6.D763 2004**
Dropouts in America: Confronting the Graduation Rate Crisis. Trade Paper. Harvard Education Publishing Group (H E P G). Cambridge, MA. 2004. 306p. ISBN:1-891792-53-9, ISBN13: 978-1-891792-53-3. Dewey:373.12/913. LCCN:2004-108772.
Audience: **g,l,u,f.** *Choice, 2005.*

Roderick, Melissa **LC144**
The Path to Dropping Out: Evidence for Intervention. Trade Cloth. Greenwood Publishing Group, Inc. Portsmouth, NH. 1993. 240p. ISBN:0-86569-206-8, ISBN13: 978-0-86569-206-0. Dewey:373.29130974485. LCCN:92-042905.
Audience: **g,u,f.** *Choice, 1994.*

Social Aspects of Education > Literacy

LC149
Literacy Web.
http://www.literacy.uconn.edu
Audience: **g,l,u,f.**

Brisk, Maria E. & Harrington, Margaret M. **LC3731.B684 2000**
Literacy and Bilingualism: A Handbook for All Teachers. Trade Paper. Lawrence Erlbaum Associates, Inc. Mahwah, NJ. 1999.

184p. ISBN:0-8058-3165-7, ISBN13: 978-0-8058-3165-8. Dewey:370.117/5/0973. LCCN:99-031664.
Audience: **u.** *Choice, 2000.*

Dickinson, David K. & Neuman, Susan B. (Editors) **LB1139.5.L35H37 2005**
Handbook of Early Literacy Research, Vol. 2. Ed. 2. Trade Cloth. Guilford Publications, Inc. New York, NY. 2005. 468p. ISBN:1-59385-184-7, ISBN13: 978-1-59385-184-2. Dewey:372.6.
Audience: **u,f.**

Flood, James (Editor), et al. **P91.3.H36**
Handbook of Research on Teaching Literacy Through the Communicative and Visual Arts: Sponsored by the International Reading Association. Shirley Brice Heath & Diane Lapp (Editors). Trade Paper. Lawrence Erlbaum Associates, Inc. Mahwah, NJ. 2004. 936p. ISBN:0-8058-5379-0, ISBN13: 978-0-8058-5379-7. Dewey:302.207.
Audience: **g,l,u,f.**

Hladczuk, Sharon (Compiled by), et al. **Z5814**
General Issues in Literacy - Illiteracy in the World: A Bibliography. John Hladczuk, Allan Hladczuk & William Eller (Compiled by). Cloth Text. Greenwood Publishing Group, Inc. Portsmouth, NH. 1990. 435p. Bibliographies and Indexes in Education Ser., Vol. 8 ISBN:0-313-27327-8, ISBN13: 978-0-313-27327-8. Dewey:016.374/012. LCCN:89-028646.
Audience: **g,l,u,f.** *Choice, 1990.*

Social Aspects of Education > Educational Sociology

Apple, Michael W. **LC89.A814 1996**
Cultural Politics and Education. Cloth Text. Teachers College Press, Teachers College, Columbia University. New York, NY. 1996. 176p. John Dewey Lectures, Vol. 5 ISBN:0-8077-3504-3, ISBN13: 978-0-8077-3504-6. Dewey:370.1/9/0941. LCCN:95-036212.
Audience: **l,u,f.** *Choice, 1996.*

Apple, Michael W. **LC191.4.A65 1995**
Education and Power. Ed. 2. Trade Cloth. Routledge. New York, NY. 1995. 248p. ISBN:0-415-91309-8, ISBN13: 978-0-415-91309-6. Dewey:370.1/934. LCCN:95-000541.
Audience: **l,u,f.**

Apple, Michael W. **LC191.4.A66 2004**
Ideology and Curriculum. Ed. 3. Trade Cloth. Routledge. New York, NY. 2004. 264p. ISBN:0-415-94911-4, ISBN13: 978-0-415-94911-8. Dewey:306.47. LCCN:2003-027158.
Audience: **l,u,f.** B

Callejo-Perez, David M. **LC189.P39 2004**
Pedagogy of Place: Seeing Space As Cultural Education. Judith J. Slater & Stephen M. Fain (Editors). Trade Cloth. Peter Lang Publishing, Inc. New York, NY. 2003. xxvii, 231p. ISBN:0-8204-6910-6, ISBN13: 978-0-8204-6910-2. Dewey:370.11/5. LCCN:2003-011173.
Audience: **u,f.**

Dreeben, Robert **LC191.D7 2002**
On What Is Learned in School. Paper Text. Eliot Werner Publications, Inc. Clinton Corners, NY. 2002. 194p. Foundations of Sociology Ser. ISBN:0-9719587-0-X, ISBN13: 978-0-9719587-0-8. Dewey:306.43/0973. LCCN:2002-104250.
Audience: **u,f.** B

Freire, Paolo **LC191.8.L29F74 2005**
Education for Critical Consciousness. Trade Paper. Continuum International Publishing Group, Ltd. London, 2005. 160p. Continuum Impacts Ser. ISBN:0-8264-7795-X, ISBN13: 978-0-8264-7795-8. Dewey:306.43. LCCN:2005-273061.
Audience: **g,l,u,f.**

Shor, Ira **LC191.4.S54 1986**
Culture Wars: School and Society in the Conservative Restoration 1969-1984. Trade Cloth. Routledge. New York, NY. 1986. xvii, 238p. ISBN:0-7102-0637-2, ISBN13: 978-0-7102-0637-4. Dewey:370.19. LCCN:85-002305.
Audience: **u,f.** B *Choice, 1986.*

Social Aspects of Education > Educational Sociology > Discrimination in Education

Armor, David J. **KF4155.A87 1995**
Forced Justice: School Desegregation and the Law. Trade Cloth. Oxford University Press, Inc. New York, NY. 1995. 284p. ISBN:0-19-509012-8, ISBN13: 978-0-19-509012-3. Dewey:344.73/0798. LCCN:94-013497.
Audience: **l,u,f.**

Banks, James A. & Banks, Cherry A. McGee **LC1099.3.H35 2002**
Handbook of Research on Multicultural Education. Ed. 2. Trade Cloth. John Wiley & Sons, Inc. Hoboken, NJ. 2003. 1120p. ISBN:0-7879-5915-4, ISBN13: 978-0-7879-5915-9. Dewey:370.117. LCCN:2002-156022.
Audience: **g,l,u,f.** *Choice, 2004, 1995.*

Brown, Les **LC213.2.B76 1985**
Justice, Morality, and Education: A New Focus in Ethics in Education. Trade Cloth. Bow Historical Books. New Providence, NJ. 1985. xiv, 366p. ISBN:0-312-44948-8, ISBN13: 978-0-312-44948-3. Dewey:370.19/0973. LCCN:85-002457.
Audience: **g,l,u,f.** B

Fife, Brian L. **LC214.2.F57 1997**
School Desegregation in the Twenty-First Century: The Focus Must Change. Trade Cloth. Edwin Mellen Press, The. Lewiston, NY. 1997. 146p. Symposium Ser., Vol. 41 ISBN:0-7734-8725-5, ISBN13: 978-0-7734-8725-3. Dewey:379.2/63/0973. LCCN:96-051742.
Audience: **u,f.**

Grant, Carl A. & Sleeter, Christine E. **LC213.22.M53G73 1996**
After the School Bell Rings. Ed. 2. Trade Cloth. Taylor & Francis Group. Philadelphia, PA. 1996. 280p. ISBN:0-7507-0558-2, ISBN13: 978-0-7507-0558-5. Dewey:370.19/0977. LCCN:96-012657.
Audience: **l,u,f.** B *Choice, 1986.*

Hochschild, Jennifer & Scovronick, Nathan **LC89.H63 2003**
The American Dream and the Public Schools. Trade Cloth. Oxford University Press, Inc. New York, NY. 2003. 320p.

ISBN:0-19-515278-6, ISBN13: 978-0-19-515278-4. Dewey:371.01/0973. LCCN:2002-027848.
Audience: **g,l,u,f.** *Choice, 2003.*

King, Joyce E. (Editor) **LC2699.B53 2005**
Black Education: A Transformative Research and Action Agenda for the New Century. Gloria Ladson Billings, Grace Lee Boggs & A. Wade Boykin (Contribution by). Perfect, Paper over Boards. Lawrence Erlbaum Associates, Inc. Mahwah, NJ. 2005. 443p. ISBN:0-8058-5457-6, ISBN13: 978-0-8058-5457-2. Dewey:370/.8996. LCCN:2004-060676.
Audience: **l,u,f.** *Choice, 2006.*

Knaus, Christopher **LC212.2.K57 2006**
Race, Racism, and Multiraciality in American Education. Trade Cloth. Academica Press, LLC. Bethesda, MD. 2005. 264p. ISBN:1-930901-96-8, ISBN13: 978-1-930901-96-4. Dewey:371.82900973. LCCN:2005-021781.
Audience: **u,f.**

Orfield, Gary, et al. **LC212.62.O72 1996**
Dismantling Desegregation: The Quiet Reversal of Brown vs. Board of Education. Susan E. Eaton & Harvard Project on School Desegregation (Authors). Trade Cloth. New Press, The. New York, NY. 1996. 448p. ISBN:1-56584-305-3, ISBN13: 978-1-56584-305-9. Dewey:370.19/342/0973. LCCN:95-025315.
Audience: **g,l,u,f.** *Choice, 1997.*

Pizarro, Marcos **LC2688.L7P59 2005**
Chicanas and Chicanos in School: Racial Profiling, Identity Battles, and Empowerment. Trade Cloth. University of Texas Press. Austin, TX. 2005. 320p. The Louann Atkins Temple Women & Culture Ser., Bk. 11 ISBN:0-292-70636-7, ISBN13: 978-0-292-70636-1. Dewey:373.1829/6872/073. LCCN:2004-020252.
Audience: **g,l,u,f.**

Pottker, Janice & Fishel, Andrew (Editors) **LC212.2.S48 1977**
Sex Bias in the Schools: The Research Evidence. Trade Cloth. Fairleigh Dickinson University Press. Cranbury, NJ. 1976. 571p. ISBN:0-8386-1464-7, ISBN13: 978-0-8386-1464-8. Dewey:376. LCCN:74-000200.
Audience: **u,f.** B

Rist, Ray C. (Author, Introduction by) **LC2771.R57 2002**
The Urban School: A Factory for Failure. Ed. 2. Trade Paper. Transaction Publishers. Somerset, NJ. 2002. 261p. ISBN:0-7658-0938-9, ISBN13: 978-0-7658-0938-4. Dewey:306.43. LCCN:2002-022502.
Audience: **u,f.**

U. S. Office of Education Staff & Coleman, James S. **LC213.2 .C64 1979**
Equality of Educational Opportunity. Lewis A. Coser & Walter W. Powell (Editors). Library Binding. Ayer Company Publishers, Inc. Manchester, NH. 1980. Perennial Works in Sociology ISBN:0-405-12088-5, ISBN13: 978-0-405-12088-6. Dewey:370.19/342. LCCN:79-006990.
Audience: **g,l,u,f.**

Wells, Amy Stuart & Crain, Robert L. **LC214.23.S22W45 1997**
Stepping over the Color Line: African-American Students in White Suburban Schools. Cloth over Boards. Yale University Press. Cumberland, RI. 1997. 392p. ISBN:0-300-06760-7, ISBN13: 978-0-300-06760-6. Dewey:379.2/63/0977865. LCCN:96-043906.
Audience: **l,u,f.** *Choice, 1997.*

Yarmolinsky, Adam, et al. **LC214.2**
Race and Schooling in the City. Lance M. Liebman & Corinne S. Schelling (Authors). Trade Cloth. Harvard University Press. Cambridge, MA. 1981. 291p. ISBN:0-674-74577-9, ISBN13: 978-0-674-74577-3. Dewey:370.19/342. LCCN:80-020424.
Audience: **g,l,u,f.** B

Ybarra, Raul E. & López, Nancy **LC2669.C74 2004**
Creating Alternative Discourses in the Education of Latinos and Latinas: A Reader. Trade Cloth. Peter Lang Publishing, Inc. New York, NY. 2004. 254p. ISBN:0-8204-6801-0, ISBN13: 978-0-8204-6801-3. Dewey:371.829/68073. LCCN:2003-019415.
Audience: **g,l,u,f.**

Social Aspects of Education > Educational Sociology > Gender Differences in Education

Datnow, Amanda & Hubbard, Lea (Editors) **LB3067.3.G46 2002**
Gender in Policy and Practice: Perspectives on Single-Sex and Coeducational Schooling. Trade Cloth. Routledge. New York, NY. 2002. 344p. Sociology in Education Ser. ISBN:0-415-93270-X, ISBN13: 978-0-415-93270-7. Dewey:371.822. LCCN:2002-069886.
Audience: **l,u,f.**

Dziech, Billie W. & Hawkins, Michael W. **LC212.862.D957 1998**
Sexual Harassment in Higher Education: Reflections and New Perspectives. Philip Altbach (Editor). Cloth Text. Garland Publishing, Inc. New York, NY. 1998. 224p. Garland Studies in Higher Education, Vol. 12 ISBN:0-8153-2036-1, ISBN13: 978-0-8153-2036-4. Dewey:306.43. LCCN:98-014229.
Audience: **l,u,f.**

Francis, Becky & Skelton, Christine **LC212.9.I59 2001**
Investigating Gender: Contemporary Perspectives in Education. Trade Cloth. McGraw-Hill Education. Maidenhead, 2002. 240p. ISBN:0-335-20788-X, ISBN13: 978-0-335-20788-6. Dewey:305.3. LCCN:2001-036255.
Audience: **u,f.**

Kelly, Gail P. (Editor) **LC1411**
International Handbook of Women's Education. Cloth Text. Greenwood Publishing Group, Inc. Portsmouth, NH. 1989. 672p. ISBN:0-313-25638-1, ISBN13: 978-0-313-25638-7. Dewey:376. LCCN:88-034730.
Audience: **g,l,u,f.** *Choice, 1990.*

Riordan, Cornelius H. **LB3066.R56 1990**
Girls and Boys in School: Together or Separate? Cloth Text. Teachers College Press, Teachers College, Columbia University. New York, NY. 1989. 200p. ISBN:0-8077-2993-0, ISBN13: 978-0-8077-2993-9. Dewey:372. LCCN:89-038053.
Audience: **l,u,f.** *Choice, 1991.*

Sadker, David M. & Sadker, Myra P. **LC197**
Failing at Fairness: How America's Schools Cheat Girls. Trade Paper. Simon & Schuster. New York, NY. 1995. 368p. ISBN:0-684-80073-X, ISBN13: 978-0-684-80073-8. Dewey:370.19/345. LCCN:93-011586.
Audience: **g,l,u,f.** *Choice, 1994.*

Solomon, Barbara M. **LC1752**
In the Company of Educated Women: A History of Women and Higher Education in America. Trade Paper. Yale University Press. Cumberland, RI. 1986. 298p. ISBN:0-300-03639-6, ISBN13: 978-0-300-03639-8. Dewey:376/.973. LCCN:84-019681.
Audience: **u,f.** BCL3 *Choice, 1985.*

Weis, Lois & Fine, Michelle (Editors) **LC212.2.B49 2005**
Beyond Silenced Voices: Class, Race, and Gender in United States Schools. Ed. 2. Cloth Text. State University of New York Press. Albany, NY. 2005. 336p. ISBN:0-7914-6461-X, ISBN13: 978-0-7914-6461-8. Dewey:371.82. LCCN:2004-062592.
Audience: **l,u,f.** *Choice, 1993.*

Social Aspects of Education > Educational Sociology > Educational Equity

Web: Center for Research on Education, Diversity & Excellence (CREDE).
http://crede.org
Audience: **u,f.**

Betts, Julian & Loveless, Tom (Editors) **LB1027.9.G475 2005**
Getting Choice Right: Ensuring Equity and Efficiency in Education Policy. Trade Cloth. Brookings Institution Press. Washington, DC. 2005. 240p. ISBN:0-8157-5332-2, ISBN13: 978-0-8157-5332-2. Dewey:379.1/11. LCCN:2005-027078.
Audience: **g,l,u,f.**

England, Crystal **LC213.2.E54 2005**
Divided We Fail: Issues of Equity in American Schools. Trade Paper. Heinemann. Portsmouth, NH. 2005. 160p. ISBN:0-325-00723-3, ISBN13: 978-0-325-00723-6. Dewey:379.2/6. LCCN:2004-020393.
Audience: **g,l,u,f.**

Finn, Patrick J. **LC5051**
Literacy with an Attitude: Educating Working-Class Children in Their Own Self-Interest. Paper Text. State University of New York Press. Albany, NY. 1999. 243p. ISBN:0-7914-4286-1, ISBN13: 978-0-7914-4286-9. Dewey:370.8/623/0973. LCCN:99-026086.
Audience: **l,u,f.** *Choice, 2000.*

Jacob, E. & Cathie Jordan (Editors) **LC3731**
Minority Education: Anthropological Perspectives. Greenwood Publishing Group, Inc. 1993. Social and Policy Issues in Education Ser. ISBN:0-89391-868-7, ISBN13: 978-0-89391-868-2.
Audience: **l,u,f.**

Kozol, Jonathan **LC4091**
Savage Inequalities: Children in America's Schools. Trade Paper. HarperCollins Publishers. New York, NY. 1992. 272p. ISBN:0-06-097499-0, ISBN13: 978-0-06-097499-2. Dewey:371.96/7. LCCN:92-052636.
Audience: **g,l,u,f.**

Linkon, Sherry L. (Editor) **LC5051.L494 1999**
Teaching Working Class. Trade Paper. University of Massachusetts Press. Amherst, MA. 1999. 336p. ISBN:1-55849-188-0, ISBN13: 978-1-55849-188-5. Dewey:378.1/9826/23. LCCN:98-032258.
Audience: **u,f.** *Choice, 2000.*

Petrovich, Janice & Wells, Amy Stuart (Editors) **LC213.2.B75 2005**
Bringing Equity Back: Research for a New Era in American Educational Policy. Alison R. Bernstein (Foreword by), Wendy Puriefoy (Afterword by). Trade Cloth. Teachers College Press, Teachers College, Columbia University. New York, NY. 2005. 350p. ISBN:0-8077-4576-6, ISBN13: 978-0-8077-4576-2. Dewey:379.260973. LCCN:2004-063670.
Audience: **g,l,u,f.** *Choice, 2006.*

Samarco, C. Vincent **LC5051**
Reflections from the Wrong Side of the Tracks: Class, Identity, and the Working Class Experience in Academe. Trade Cloth. Rowman & Littlefield Publishers, Inc. Lanham, MD. 2005. 256p. ISBN:0-7425-3511-8, ISBN13: 978-0-7425-3511-4. Dewey:378.1/98623.
Audience: **g,l,u,f.**

Yinger, John (Editor) **LB2825.H38 2004**
Helping Children Left Behind: State Aid and the Pursuit of Educational Equity. Trade Cloth. MIT Press. Cambridge, MA. 2004. 392p. ISBN:0-262-24046-7, ISBN13: 978-0-262-24046-8. Dewey:379.2/6. LCCN:2003-066825.
Audience: **g,l,u,f.** *Choice, 2005.*

Social Aspects of Education > Educational Sociology > Anthropology of Education

Greene, Maxine **LB45.G68**
Landscapes of Learning. Trade Paper. Teachers College Press, Teachers College, Columbia University. New York, NY. 1978. 362p. ISBN:0-8077-2534-X, ISBN13: 978-0-8077-2534-4. Dewey:370.19/3. LCCN:78-006571.
Audience: **g,l,u,f.** BCL3

Jacob, E. & Cathie Jordan (Editors) **LC3731**
Minority Education: Anthropological Perspectives. Greenwood Publishing Group, Inc. 1993. Social and Policy Issues in Education Ser. ISBN:0-89391-868-7, ISBN13: 978-0-89391-868-2.
Audience: **l,u,f.**

Levinson, Bradley A. U. (Editor), et al. **LC191.S267 2000**
Schooling the Symbolic Animal: Social and Cultural Dimensions of Education. Kathryn M. Borman & Margaret Eisenhart (Editors). Book, Other. Rowman & Littlefield Publishers, Inc.

Lanham, MD. 2000. 408p. ISBN:0-7425-0119-1, ISBN13: 978-0-7425-0119-5. Dewey:306.43. LCCN:00-040286.
Audience: **l,u,f.** *Choice, 2001.*

Peshkin, Alan **LB1567**
Growing up American: Schooling and the Survival of Community. University of Chicago Press: Chicago. 1978. ISBN:0-226-66196-2, ISBN13: 978-0-226-66196-4.
Audience: **g,l,u,f.**

Spindler, George D. (Editor) **LB45.E237 1997**
Education and Cultural Process: Anthropological Approaches. Ed. 3. Paper Text. Waveland Press, Inc. Prospect Heights, IL. 1997. 561p. ISBN:0-88133-958-X, ISBN13: 978-0-88133-958-1. Dewey:306.43. LCCN:98-115988.
Audience: **l,u,f.**

Social Aspects of Education > Community and the School

Constantino, Steven M. **LC225.3.C65 2003**
Engaging All Families: Creating a Positive School Culture by Putting Research into Practice. Book, Other. Scarecrow Press, Inc. Lanham, MD. 2003. 160p. ISBN:1-57886-062-8, ISBN13: 978-1-57886-062-3. Dewey:371.19/2. LCCN:2003-009342.
Audience: **g,l,u.** *Choice, 2004.*

Crowson, Robert L. & Driscoll, Mary Erina **LC221.C78 2003**
School Community Relations,Under Reform. Ed. 3. Finch Andrew J., Berk, Robert J. (Authors). Mccutchan Pub Corp. 2003. ISBN:0-8211-0234-6, ISBN13: 978-0-8211-0234-3.
Audience: **l,u,f.**

Konzal, Jean L. & Dodd, Anne Wescott **LC221.D62 2002**
How Communities Build Stonger Schools: Stories, Strategies, and Promising Practices for Educating Every Child. Trade Cloth. Palgrave Macmillan. New York, NY. 2002. 368p. ISBN:0-312-23891-6, ISBN13: 978-0-312-23891-9. Dewey:371.19. LCCN:2002-022040.
Audience: **g,l,u,f.** *Choice, 2003.*

Lightfoot, Sara Lawrence **LC225**
Worlds Apart: Relationships between Families and Schools. New York: Basic Books. 1978. ISBN:0-465-09244-6, ISBN13: 978-0-465-09244-4.
Audience: **g,l,u.**

Salowe, Allen E. **LC221.S25 2003**
Schools for Our Time: The Local Classroom in an Uncertain World. Trade Paper. Scarecrow Press, Inc. Lanham, MD. 2003. 224p. ISBN:0-8108-4709-4, ISBN13: 978-0-8108-4709-5. Dewey:371.19/0973. LCCN:2002-154846.
Audience: **g,l,u.** *Choice, 2004.*

Types of Education

Cohen, Jonathan (Editor) **LB1072.E38 1999**
Educating Minds and Hearts: Social Emotional Learning and the Passage into Adolescence: A Guide for Educators. Trade Cloth. Teachers College Press, Teachers College, Columbia University. New York, NY. 1999. 462p. ISBN:0-8077-3839-5, ISBN13: 978-0-8077-3839-9. Dewey:370.15/3. LCCN:98-050479.
Audience: **u,f.** *Choice, 1999.*

Types of Education > Humanistic and Liberal Education

☐ Lifetime of Color.
http://www.sanford-artedventures.com/
Audience: **g,l,u,f.**

Gardner, Howard **BF432.3**
Intelligence Reframed: Multiple Intelligences for the 21st Century. Trade Paper. Basic Books. New York, NY. 2000. 304p. ISBN:0-465-02611-7, ISBN13: 978-0-465-02611-1. Dewey:153.9. LCCN:99-042468.
Audience: **g,l,u,f.** *Choice, 2000.*

Johnson, Michael L. **LA209.2.J64 1993**
Education on the Wild Side: Learning for the Twenty-First Century. Trade Cloth. University of Oklahoma Press. Norman, OK. 1993. 338p. Oklahoma Project for Discourse and Theory Ser., Vol. 12 ISBN:0-8061-2546-2, ISBN13: 978-0-8061-2546-6. Dewey:370.120973. LCCN:93-012365.
Audience: **g,u,f.** *Choice, 1994.*

Moulakis, Athanasios **LC1011.M76 1993**
Beyond Utility: Liberal Education for a Technological Age. Cloth Text. University of Missouri Press. Columbia, MO. 1993. 184p. ISBN:0-8262-0929-7, ISBN13: 978-0-8262-0929-0. Dewey:370.1120973. LCCN:93-027212.
Audience: **g,u,f.** *Choice, 1994.*

National Endowment for the Humanities **TK5105.875.I57**
☐ EDSITEment.
http://edsitement.neh.gov
Audience: **g,l,u,f.**

Pelikan, Jaroslav J. **LB2321.P383 1992**
The Idea of the University: A Reexamination. Cloth over Boards. Yale University Press. Cumberland, RI. 1992. 288p. ISBN:0-300-05725-3, ISBN13: 978-0-300-05725-6. Dewey:378. LCCN:92-002928.
Audience: **g,u,f.** *Choice, 1992.*

Simmons, Tracy Lee **LC1011**
Climbing Parnassus: A New Apologia for Greek and Latin. William F. Buckley Jr. (Foreword by). Trade Cloth. ISI Books. Wilmington, DE. 2002. 286p. ISBN:1-882926-73-0, ISBN13: 978-1-882926-73-2. Dewey:373.24/2. LCCN:2001-097019.
Audience: **g,l,u,f.** *Choice, 2002.*

Types of Education > Competency Based Education

Evers, Frederick & Rush, James **LC1032.E84 1998**
The Bases of Competence: Skills for Lifefong Learning and Employability. Berdrow, Iris (Authors). Jossey-Bass. 1998. ISBN:0-7879-0921-1, ISBN13: 978-0-7879-0921-5.
Audience: **g,l,u,f.**

Zmuda, Allison & Tomaino, Mary **LB1607.5.Z68 2001**
The Competent Classroom: Aligning High School Curriculum, Standards and Assessment - A Creative Teaching Guide. Trade Paper. Teachers College Press, Teachers College, Columbia University. New York, NY. 2001. xx, 119p. School Reform Ser., Vol. 31 ISBN:0-8077-4022-5, ISBN13: 978-0-8077-4022-4. Dewey:373.1102/0973. LCCN:00-050314.
Audience: **g,u,f.** *Choice, 2001.*

Zigler, Edward F. (Editor), et al. **LB1139.35.P55C48**
Children's Play: The Roots of Reading. Dorothy G. Singer & Sandra J. Bishop-Josef (Editors). Trade Paper, Perfect. Zero To Three Press. Washington, DC. 2004. 200p. ISBN:0-943657-75-X, ISBN13: 978-0-943657-75-2. Dewey:155. LCCN:2003-027631.
Audience: **u,f.** *Choice, 2004.*

Types of Education > Basic Education (Including Basic Skills Education)

LC151
☐ National Institute for Literacy (NIFL).
http://www.nifl.gov
Audience: **g,l,u,f.**

Cheryl Grossman **LC5215**
☐ National Center for the Study of Adult Learning and Literacy (NCSALL).
http://www.ncsall.net
National Center for the Study of Adult Learning and Literacy.
Audience: **g,l,u,f.**

Demetrion, George **LC149.7.D416 2004**
Conflicting Paradigms in Adult Literacy Education: In Quest of a U.S. Democratic Politics of Literacy. Trade Cloth. Lawrence Erlbaum Associates, Inc. Mahwah, NJ. 2004. 336p. ISBN:0-8058-4623-9, ISBN13: 978-0-8058-4623-2. Dewey:374/.012/0973. LCCN:2004-050677.
Audience: **u,f.** *Choice, 2005.*

Huerta-Macias, Ana **LC149**
Workforce Education for Latinos: Politics, Programs, and Practices. Trade Cloth. Greenwood Publishing Group, Inc. Portsmouth, NH. 2002. 160p. ISBN:0-89789-808-7, ISBN13: 978-0-89789-808-9. Dewey:374.1829/68073. LCCN:2001-037912.
Audience: **u,f.** *Choice, 2002.*

Morris, G.S. Don & Stiehl, Jim (Authors) **GV443.M66 1998**
Changing Kids' Games. Human Kinetics. 1999. ISBN:0-88011-691-9, ISBN13: 978-0-88011-691-6.
Audience: **g,l,u,f.**

Purcell-Gates, Victoria, et al. **LC151.P86 2004**
Print Literacy Development: Uniting Cognitive and Social Practice Theories. Erik Jacobson & Sophie Degener (Authors). Trade Cloth. Harvard University Press. Cambridge, MA. 2004. 218p. ISBN:0-674-01518-5, ISBN13: 978-0-674-01518-0. Dewey:302.2/244. LCCN:2004-052606.
Audience: **u,f.** *Choice, 2005.*

Stevenson, Howard Jr. (Editor) **E185**
Playing with Anger: Teaching Coping Skills to African American Boys through Athletics and Culture. Trade Cloth. Greenwood Publishing Group, Inc. Portsmouth, NH. 2003. 224p. Race and Ethnicity in Psychology Ser. ISBN:0-275-97517-7, ISBN13: 978-0-275-97517-3. Dewey:305.235. LCCN:2002-044996.
Audience: **g,u,f.** *Choice, 2004.*

Types of Education > Career and Vocational Education

HF5382.5.U5
☐ America's Career InfoNet.
http://www.acinet.org
U.S. Department of Labor.
Audience: **g.**

HF5382.5.U5
☐ Occupational Outlook Handbook.
http://www.bls.gov/oco/
U.S. Department of Labor. Bureau of Labor Statistics.
Audience: **g.**

American Society for Training and Development Staff (Contribution by) **HD58.82.A88 2004**
ASTD 2004 Competency Study: Mapping the Future: New Workplace Learning and Performance Competencies. Trade Cloth. American Society for Training & Development. Alexandria, VA. 2004. xxvi, 142p. ISBN:1-56286-368-1, ISBN13: 978-1-56286-368-5. Dewey:658.3124. LCCN:2004-092794.
Audience: **u,f.**

Bills, David B. **LC191.4.B53 2004**
Sociology of Education and Work. Trade Paper. Blackwell Publishing, Inc. Malden, MA. 2004. 264p. ISBN:0-631-22363-0, ISBN13: 978-0-631-22363-4. Dewey:306.43. LCCN:2003-024828.
Audience: **l,u.** *Choice, 2005.*

Cheryl Grossman **LC1041**
☐ ACTE online (Association for Career and Technical Education).
http://www.acteonline.org
Association for Career and Technical Education.
Audience: **u,f.**

Craig, Robert L. **HF5549.5.T7T6648**
The ASTD Training and Development Handbook: A Guide to Human Resource Development. Ed. 4. Trade Cloth, CD-ROM. McGraw-Hill Companies, The. New York, NY. 1996. 1088p. McGraw-Hill Training Ser. ISBN:0-07-013359-X, ISBN13: 978-0-07-013359-4. Dewey:658.3/124. LCCN:96-004177.
Audience: **g.** *Choice, 1997.*

Evans, Karen (Editor), et al. **HD58.82.W675 2002**
Working to Learn: Transforming Learning in the Workplace. Phil Hodkinson & Lorna Unwin (Editors). Cloth Text. Kogan Page, Ltd. London, 2002. 256p. ISBN:0-7494-3685-9, ISBN13: 978-0-7494-3685-8. Dewey:658.3/124. LCCN:2002-511392.
Audience: **u,f.**

Gonon, Philipp (Editor) **LC1506.E85G45 2001**
Gender Perspectives on Vocational Education: Historical, Cultural, and Policy Aspects. Trade Cloth. Peter Lang Publishing, Inc. New York, NY. 2001. 332p. ISBN:3-906763-87-0, ISBN13: 978-3-906763-87-3. Dewey:370.11/3/094. LCCN:2001-038012.
Audience: **u,f.**

Gordon, Howard R. D. **LC1045 .G67 2003**
The History and Growth of Vocational Education in America. Ed. 2. Paper Text. Waveland Press, Inc. Prospect Heights, IL. 2002. 302p. ISBN:1-57766-260-1, ISBN13: 978-1-57766-260-0. Dewey:370.11/3/0973. LCCN:2003-267435.
Audience: **l,u.**

Grubb, W. Norton & Lazerson, Marvin **LC66.G78 2004**
The Education Gospel: The Economic Power of Schooling. Trade Cloth. Harvard University Press. Cambridge, MA. 2004. 334p. ISBN:0-674-01537-1, ISBN13: 978-0-674-01537-1. Dewey:338.4/737. LCCN:2004-052298.
Audience: **g,l.** *Choice, 2005.*

Grubb, W. Norton & Ryan, Paul **LC1044.G78 1999**
The Roles of Evaluation for Vocational Education and Training: Plain Talk in the Field of Dreams. Trade Cloth. Kogan Page, Ltd. London, 2000. 208p. ISBN:0-7494-3070-2, ISBN13: 978-0-7494-3070-2. Dewey:370.1/13. LCCN:99-495025.
Audience: **u,f.**

Hake, Kathryn **HF5382.5.U5**
Vocational Information Center.
http://www.khake.com
Cheryl Grossman.
Audience: **g.**

Huerta-Macias, Ana **LC149**
Workforce Education for Latinos: Politics, Programs, and Practices. Trade Cloth. Greenwood Publishing Group, Inc. Portsmouth, NH. 2002. 160p. ISBN:0-89789-808-7, ISBN13: 978-0-89789-808-9. Dewey:374.1829/68073. LCCN:2001-037912.
Audience: **u,f.** *Choice, 2002.*

Kantor, Harvey & Tyack, David B. (Editors) **LC1045.W6 1982**
Work, Youth, and Schooling: Historical Perspectives on Vocationalism in American Education. Trade Cloth. Stanford University Press. Palo Alto, CA. 1982. 367p. ISBN:0-8047-1121-6, ISBN13: 978-0-8047-1121-0. Dewey:370.11/3/0973. LCCN:81-050788.
Audience: **u,f.** B

Kliebard, Herbert M. **LB1570.K587 1999**
Schooled to Work: Vocationalism and the American Curriculum, 1876-1946. Trade Cloth. Teachers College Press, Teachers College, Columbia University. New York, NY. 1999. 312p. ISBN:0-8077-3867-0, ISBN13: 978-0-8077-3867-2. Dewey:370.11/3/0973. LCCN:99-021307.
Audience: **u,f.** *Choice, 2000.*

Lauglo, Jon & Maclean, Rupert (Contribution by) **LC1043.V626 2005**
Vocationalisation of Secondary Education Revisited. Trade Cloth. Springer. New York, NY. 2005. xxii,376p. Technical and Vocational Education and Training Ser., Vol. 1 ISBN:1-4020-3031-2, ISBN13: 978-1-4020-3031-4. Dewey:373. LCCN:2005-283573.
Audience: **u,f.**

Miller, Melvin D. **LC1045 .M64**
Principles and a Philosophy for Vocational Education. Trade Cloth. Center on Education & Training for Employment. Columbus, OH. 1985. 250p. ISBN:0-318-17790-0, ISBN13: 978-0-318-17790-8. Dewey:370.11/3/0973.
Audience: **l,u,f.**

Power, Paul W. **HD7255.P68 2006**
A Guide to Vocational Assessment. Ed. 4. Trade Cloth. PRO-ED, Inc. Austin, TX. 2005. xxv, 375p. ISBN:1-4164-0138-5, ISBN13: 978-1-4164-0138-4. Dewey:362.4/0484. LCCN:2005-015072.
Audience: **l,u,f.**

Pryor, Frederic L. & Schaffer, David L. **HD5724 .P78 1999**
Who's Not Working and Why: Employment, Cognitive Skills, Wages, and the Changing U. S. Labor Market. Trade Paper. Cambridge University Press. New York, NY. 2000. 320p. ISBN:0-521-79439-0, ISBN13: 978-0-521-79439-8. Dewey:331.12/0973. LCCN:98-039048.
Audience: **u,f.** *Choice, 1999.*

Pucel, David J. **LC1045.P77 2001**
Beyond Vocational Education: Career Majors, Tech Prep, Schools Within Schools, Magnet Schools and Academies. Trade Paper. Eye On Education, Inc. Larchmont, NY. 2001. xi, 161p. ISBN:1-930556-04-7, ISBN13: 978-1-930556-04-1. Dewey:373.01/13. LCCN:00-055154.
Audience: **g,l,u,f.**

Rosenbaum, James E. **LC1045.R77 2001**
Beyond College for All: Career Paths for the Forgotten Half. Trade Cloth. Russell Sage Foundation. New York, NY. 2001. 300p. American Sociological Association Rose Series in Sociology ISBN:0-87154-727-9, ISBN13: 978-0-87154-727-9. Dewey:331.11/423. LCCN:2001-041783.
Audience: **g,l,u,f.** *Choice, 2002.*

Rossett, Allison **HF5549.5.T7R643 2002**
The ASTD e-Learning Handbook: Best Practices, Strategies and Case Studies for an Emerging Field. Trade Cloth. McGraw-Hill Companies, The. New York, NY. 2001. 500p. ISBN:0-07-138796-X, ISBN13: 978-0-07-138796-5. Dewey:658.3/124/02854678. LCCN:2002-265903.
Audience: **g,l,u.**

Stasz, Cathleen, et al. **LC1045.S67 2003**
Efforts to Improve the Quality of Vocational Education in Secondary Schools: Impact of Federal and State Policies. Susan J. Bodilly & Sarah Remes (Authors). Trade Paper. RAND Corporation, The. Santa Monica, CA. 2003. 222p. ISBN:0-8330-3357-3, ISBN13: 978-0-8330-3357-4. Dewey:373.246. LCCN:2003-004697.
Audience: **u,f.**

Strathdee, Robert **HV1421.S77 2004**
Remaking Social Networks: the Emergence of Embeddedness in Vocational Training. Trade Cloth. Ashgate Publishing, Ltd. Aldershot, 2005. 220p. Voices in Development Management Ser. ISBN:0-7546-3815-4, ISBN13: 978-0-7546-3815-5. Dewey:362.7/083. LCCN:2004-062397.
Audience: **u,f.**

Wakefield, Suzy Mygatt (Editor) **LB1620.5**
Unfocused Kids: Helping Students to Focus on Their Education and Career Plans: A Resource for Educators. Trade Paper. Counseling & Psychological Services, Inc. Tucson, AZ. 2004. 526p. ISBN:1-56109-105-7, ISBN13: 978-1-56109-105-8. Dewey:373.14/2. LCCN:2004-043169.
Audience: **l,u.**

Walsh, W. Bruce & Heppner, Mary J. (Editors) **HF5382.6.H36 2005**
Handbook of Career Counseling for Women. Ed. 2. Nancy E. Betz, Kathleen J. Bieschke & Rosie P. Bingham (Contribution by). Cloth over Boards. Lawrence Erlbaum Associates, Inc. Mahwah, NJ. 2005. 560p. Contemporary Topics in Vocational Psychology Ser. ISBN:0-8058-4888-6, ISBN13: 978-0-8058-4888-5. Dewey:331.702/082. LCCN:2005-040062.
Audience: **u,f.** *Choice, 2006.*

Walsh, W. Bruce & Savickas, Mark (Editors) **HF5381.H1335 2005**
Handbook of Vocational Psychology: Theory, Research, and Practice. Ed. 3. Steven D. Brown, Timothy R. Elliott & Gary D. Gottfredson (Contribution by). Cloth over Boards. Lawrence Erlbaum Associates, Inc. Mahwah, NJ. 2005. 480p. Contemporary Topics in Vocational Psychology Ser. ISBN:0-8058-4517-8, ISBN13: 978-0-8058-4517-4. Dewey:158.6. LCCN:2004-030573.
Audience: **u,f.**

Winch, Christopher **LC1042.5.W56 2000**
Education, Work and Social Capital: Towards a New Conception of Vocational Training. Paper over Boards. Routledge. New York, NY. 2000. 240p. International Studies in the Philosophy of Education, Vol. 11 ISBN:0-415-20434-8, ISBN13: 978-0-415-20434-7. Dewey:370.11/3/01. LCCN:00-035311.
Audience: **u,f.** *Choice, 2001.*

Types of Education > Moral, Religious, and Character Education

Howe, Leland W. **LC268.H67**
Personalizing Education: Values Clarification and Beyond. Trade Cloth. Hart Publishing Company. Great Falls, VA. 1975. 574p. ISBN:0-8055-1138-5, ISBN13: 978-0-8055-1138-3. Dewey:370.11/4. LCCN:74-027697.
Audience: **g,l,u,f.** B

Nash, Robert J. **LC311.N27 1997**
Answering the "Virtuecrats": A Moral Conversation on Character Education. Trade Cloth. Teachers College Press, Teachers College, Columbia University. New York, NY. 1997. 224p. Advances in Contemporary Educational Thought Ser. ISBN:0-8077-3670-8, ISBN13: 978-0-8077-3670-8. Dewey:370.11/4. LCCN:97-023123.
Audience: **g,l,u,f.** *Choice, 1998.*

Simon, Katherine G. **LC311.S49 2003**
Moral Questions in the Classroom: How to Get Kids to Think Deeply about Real Life and Their School Work. Trade Paper. Yale University Press. Cumberland, RI. 2003. 304p. ISBN:0-300-10168-6, ISBN13: 978-0-300-10168-3. Dewey:373/.0114/0973.
Audience: **g,l,u,f.** *Choice, 2002.*

Smagorinsky, Peter & Taxel, Joel (Editors) **LC311.S549 2005**
The Discourse of Character Education: Culture Wars in the Classroom. Saddle Stitched, Cloth over Boards. Lawrence Erlbaum Associates, Inc. Mahwah, NJ. 2005. 395p. ISBN:0-8058-5126-7, ISBN13: 978-0-8058-5126-7. Dewey:370.114. LCCN:2004-056420.
Audience: **l,u,f.** *Choice, 2005.*

Types of Education > Moral, Religious, and Character Education > Moral, Character Education

LC291
☐ Studies in Moral Development and Education: Developing Fairness and Concern for Others.
http://tigger.uic.edu/~lnucci/MoralEd/
University of Illinois at Chicago, College of Education.
Audience: **l,u,f.**

Durkheim, Emile **LC262.D813 2002**
Moral Education: A Study in the Theory and Application of the Sociology of Education. Trade Paper. Dover Publications, Inc. Mineola, NY. 2002. 304p. ISBN:0-486-42498-7, ISBN13: 978-0-486-42498-9. Dewey:370.11/4. LCCN:2002-073827.
Audience: **l,u,f.** B

Huitt, W. **LC291**
☐ Moral and Character Development.
http://chiron.valdosta.edu/whuitt/col/morchr/morchr.html
Valdosta State University, Valdosta, GA.
Audience: **l,u,f.**

Hunter, James Davison **LC311.H86 2000**
The Death of Character: Moral Education in an Age Without Good or Evil. Trade Cloth. Basic Books. New York, NY. 2000. 336p. ISBN:0-465-04730-0, ISBN13: 978-0-465-04730-7. Dewey:370.11/4. LCCN:00-027937.
Audience: **l,u,f.**

McClellan, B. Edward **LC311.M38 1999**
Moral Education in America: Schools and the Shaping of Character from Colonial Times to the Present. Trade Cloth. Teachers College Press, Teachers College, Columbia University. New York, NY. 1999. 370p. ISBN:0-8077-3821-2, ISBN13: 978-0-8077-3821-4. Dewey:370.11/4. LCCN:99-013652.
Audience: **g,l,u,f.** *Choice, 1999.*

Noddings, Nel **LC268.N56 2002**
Educating Moral People: A Caring Alternative to Character Education. Trade Cloth. Teachers College Press, Teachers College, Columbia University. New York, NY. 2001. xiv, 170p. ISBN:0-8077-4169-8, ISBN13: 978-0-8077-4169-6. Dewey:370.11/4. LCCN:2001-053438.
Audience: **g,l,u,f.** *Choice, 2002.*

Purpel, David E. & McLaurin, William M. **LA217.P874 2004**
Reflections on the Moral and Spiritual Crisis in Education. Trade Paper. Peter Lang Publishing, Inc. New York, NY. 2004. xii, 298p. Counterpoints Ser., :Studies in the Postmodern Theory of Education ISBN:0-8204-6846-0, ISBN13: 978-0-8204-6846-4. Dewey:370.11/4/0973. LCCN:2004-002450.
Audience: **g,l,u,f.**

Types of Education > Moral, Religious, and Character Education > Religious Education

Benne, Robert **LC427.B45 2001**
Quality with Soul: How Six Premier Colleges and Universities Keep Faith with Their Religious Traditions. Trade Paper. William B. Eerdmans Publishing Company. Grand Rapids, MI. 2001. 232p. ISBN:0-8028-4704-8, ISBN13: 978-0-8028-4704-1. Dewey:378/.071. LCCN:00-065423.
Audience: **g,l,u,f.**

Blumhofer, Edith Waldvogel (Editor) **LC111.R46 2002**
Religion, Education and the American Experience: Reflections on Religion and American Public Life. Trade Cloth. University of Alabama Press. Tuscaloosa, AL. 2002. 256p. Religion and American Culture Ser. ISBN:0-8173-1146-7, ISBN13: 978-0-8173-1146-9. Dewey:379.2/8/0973. LCCN:2002-002309.
Audience: **l,u,f.** *Choice, 2003.*

Dovre, Paul J. (Editor) **LC428.H37 2002**
The Future of Religious Colleges. Trade Paper. William B. Eerdmans Publishing Company. Grand Rapids, MI. 2002. 379p. ISBN:0-8028-4955-5, ISBN13: 978-0-8028-4955-7. Dewey:378/.071/0973. LCCN:2002-023817.
Audience: **g,l,u,f.**

Erricker, Clive & Erricker, Jane **BL42.E75 2000**
Reconstructing Religious, Spiritual and Moral Education. Paper over Boards. Routledge. New York, NY. 2000. 224p. ISBN:0-415-18946-2, ISBN13: 978-0-415-18946-0. Dewey:291.7/5. LCCN:00-022587.
Audience: **l,u,f.** *Choice, 2001.*

Fraser, James W. **LC111.F68 1999**
Between Church and State: Religion and Public Education in a Multicultural America, 1600-2000. Cloth over Boards. Palgrave Macmillan. New York, NY. 1999. 252p. ISBN:0-312-21636-X, ISBN13: 978-0-312-21636-8. Dewey:379.2/8/0973. LCCN:98-055303.
Audience: **g,l,u,f.** *Choice, 2000.*

Greenawalt, Kent **LC111.G68 2004**
Does God Belong in Public Schools? Trade Cloth. Princeton University Press. Princeton, NJ. 2004. 296p. ISBN:0-691-12111-7, ISBN13: 978-0-691-12111-6. Dewey:379.28/0973. LCCN:2004-045779.
Audience: **g,l,u,f.** *Choice, 2005.*

Jacobsen, Douglas G. & Jacobsen, Rhonda Hustedt **LC383.J33 2004**
Scholarship and Christian Faith: Enlarging the Conversation. Martin E. Marty (Foreword by). Trade Cloth. Oxford University Press, Inc. New York, NY. 2004. 208p. ISBN:0-19-517038-5, ISBN13: 978-0-19-517038-2. Dewey:378/.071. LCCN:2003-008369.
Audience: **g,l,u,f.**

Jeynes, William **LC428.J49 2003**
Religion, Education, and Academic Success. Trade Cloth. Information Age Publishing, Inc. Greenwich, CT. 2003. xii, 266p. Research on Religion and Education Ser. ISBN:1-931576-53-X, ISBN13: 978-1-931576-53-6. Dewey:371.07. LCCN:2003-013825.
Audience: **l,u,f.**

Marty, Martin E. & Moore, Jonathan **LC111.M32 2000**
Education, Religion, and the Common Good: Advancing a Distinctly American Conversation about Religion's Role in Our Shared Life. Trade Cloth. John Wiley & Sons, Inc. Hoboken, NJ. 2000. 176p. ISBN:0-7879-5033-5, ISBN13: 978-0-7879-5033-0. Dewey:379.2/8/0973. LCCN:00-009152.
Audience: **g,l,u,f.**

Nash, Robert J. **BL85.N27 2001**
Religious Pluralism In The Academy: Opening The Dialogue. Trade Paper. Peter Lang Publishing, Inc. New York, NY. 2001. 232p. Studies in Education and Spirituality, Vol. 2 ISBN:0-8204-5592-X, ISBN13: 978-0-8204-5592-1. Dewey:291.1/72/071173. LCCN:2001-022294.
Audience: **g,l,u,f.**

Noddings, Nel **LC405.N63 1993**
Educating for Intelligent Belief or Unbelief. Cloth Text. Teachers College Press, Teachers College, Columbia University. New York, NY. 1993. 176p. John Dewey Lectures ISBN:0-8077-3272-9, ISBN13: 978-0-8077-3272-4. Dewey:377.10973. LCCN:93-019098.
Audience: **l,u,f.**

Nord, Warren A. **LC111.N67 1995**
Religion and American Education: Rethinking a National Dilemma. Trade Paper. University of North Carolina Press. Chapel Hill, NC. 1995. 502p. H. Eugene and Lillian Youngs Lehman Ser. ISBN:0-8078-4478-0, ISBN13: 978-0-8078-4478-6. Dewey:377/.1/0973. LCCN:94-004589.
Audience: **g,l,u,f.** *Choice, 1995.*

Provenzo, Eugene F. Jr. **LC111.P83 1990**
Religious Fundamentalism and American Education: The Battle for the Public Schools. Cloth Text. State University of New York Press. Albany, NY. 1990. 134p. SUNY Series in Frontiers of Education ISBN:0-7914-0217-7, ISBN13: 978-0-7914-0217-7. Dewey:371/.01/0973. LCCN:89-004456.
Audience: **g,l,u,f.** *Choice, 1990.*

Types of Education > Moral, Religious, and Character Education > Religious Education > Christian Schooling

Bryk, Anthony S., et al. **LC501.B624 1993**
Catholic Schools and the Common Good. Valerie E. Lee & Peter B. Holland (Authors). Trade Cloth. Harvard University Press. Cambridge, MA. 1993. 416p. ISBN:0-674-10310-6, ISBN13: 978-0-674-10310-8. Dewey:377.8273. LCCN:92-032312.
Audience: **g,l,u,f.** *Choice, 1994.*

Gallin, Alice **LC501**
Negotiating Identity: Catholic Higher Education since 1960. Trade Cloth. University of Notre Dame Press. Notre Dame, IN. 2001. 288p. ISBN:0-268-01491-4, ISBN13: 978-0-268-01491-9. Dewey:378/.071/273. LCCN:99-088281.
Audience: **g,l,u,f.**

Hughes, Richard T. & Adrian, William B. (Editors) **LC427.M63 1996**
Models for Christian Higher Education: Strategies for Success in the Twenty-First Century. Trade Paper. William B. Eerdmans Publishing Company. Grand Rapids, MI. 1997. 470p. ISBN:0-8028-4121-X, ISBN13: 978-0-8028-4121-6. Dewey:371.071. LCCN:96-037653.
Audience: **l,u,f.**

Peshkin, Alan **LC621**
God's Choice: The Total World of a Fundamentalist Christian School. Trade Paper. University of Chicago Press. Chicago, IL. 1988. 360p. ISBN:0-226-66199-7, ISBN13: 978-0-226-66199-5. Dewey:377/.0973. LCCN:85-024524.
Audience: **l,u,f.** B

Rose, Susan D. **LC586.F85R67 1988**
Keeping Them Out of the Hands of Satan: Evangelical Schooling in America. Routledge. 1990. ISBN:0-415-90004-2, ISBN13: 978-0-415-90004-1.
Audience: **g,l,u,f.**

Vryhof, Steven C. **LC531**
Between Memory and Vision: The Case for Faith-Based Schooling. Trade Paper. William B. Eerdmans Publishing Company. Grand Rapids, MI. 2003. 208p. ISBN:0-8028-4932-6, ISBN13: 978-0-8028-4932-8. Dewey:371.071. LCCN:2003-061113.
Audience: **g,l,u,f.**

Wilson, Douglas **LC1023.W55 2002**
The Case for Classical Christian Education. Trade Paper. Crossway Books. Wheaton, IL. 2005. 224p. ISBN:1-58134-384-1, ISBN13: 978-1-58134-384-7. Dewey:370.11/2. LCCN:2002-002732.
Audience: **g,l,u,f.**

Types of Education > Moral, Religious, and Character Education > Religious Education > Other Religious Education

LC903
☐ Muslim Schools, Education, Children and Family Life. http://www.islamfortoday.com/schools.htm
Islam for Today.
Audience: **g,l.**

Daun, Holger **LC904.E39 2004**
Educational Strategies among Muslims in the Context of Globalization: Some National Case Studies. Trade Cloth. Brill Academic Publishers. Leiden, 2004. viii, 288p. Muslim Minorities Ser., Vol. 3 ISBN:90-04-13675-4, ISBN13: 978-90-04-13675-5. Dewey:371.077. LCCN:2004-040770.
Audience: **l,u,f.**

Gartner, Lloyd P. (Editor) **LC0741.G35**
Jewish Education in the United States: A Documentary History. Trade Paper. Books on Demand. Ann Arbor, MI. 243p. Classics in Education Ser., No. 41 ISBN:0-608-15645-0, ISBN13: 978-0-608-15645-3. Dewey:371.98. LCCN:73-112708.
Audience: **g,l,u,f.** B

Hartung, Jan-Peter & Reifeld, Helmut (Editors) **BP43.I48I75 2006**
Islamic Education, Diversity and National Identity: Dini Madaris in India Post 9/11. Cloth Text. SAGE Publications India Pvt, Ltd. New Delhi, 2006. 320p. ISBN:0-7619-3432-4, ISBN13: 978-0-7619-3432-5. Dewey:297.7/7/0954. LCCN:2005-019718.
Audience: **g,l,u,f.**

Parker-Jenkins, Marie, et al. **LC431**
In Good Faith: Schools, Religion and Public Funding. Dimitra Hartas & Barrie A. Irving (Authors). Trade Paper. Ashgate Publishing, Ltd. Aldershot, 2004. 254p. ISBN:0-7546-3351-9, ISBN13: 978-0-7546-3351-8. Dewey:379.2/8/0941. LCCN:2004-006138.
Audience: **l,u,f.**

Peters, Shawn Francis **KF228.Y63P48 2003**
The Yoder Case: Religious Freedom, Education, and Parental Rights. Trade Cloth. University Press of Kansas. Lawrence, KS. 2003. viii, 200p. Landmark Law Cases and American Society Ser. ISBN:0-7006-1272-6, ISBN13: 978-0-7006-1272-7. Dewey:342.73/0852. LCCN:2003-007159.
Audience: **g,l,u,f.** *Choice, 2004.*

Scheffler, Israel (Editor), et al. **LC719.V57 2003**
Visions of Jewish Education. Seymour Fox & Daniel Marom (Editors). Cloth Text. Cambridge University Press. New York, NY. 2003. 366p. ISBN:0-521-82147-9, ISBN13: 978-0-521-82147-6. Dewey:371.82992/4. LCCN:2002-041244.
Audience: **g,l,u,f.** *Choice, 2004.*

Types of Education > Multicultural Education (General)

LC219
☐ Institute for Urban and Minority Education. http://iume.tc.columbia.edu/default.asp
Audience: **g,l,f.**

Appelbaum, Peter **LC1099.3.A66 2002**
Multicultural and Diversity Education: A Reference Handbook. Danny Weil (Editor). Library Binding. ABC-CLIO, Inc. Santa Barbara, CA. 2002. 191p. Contemporary Education Issues Ser. ISBN:1-57607-264-9, ISBN13: 978-1-57607-264-6. Dewey:370.117. LCCN:2002-011678.
Audience: **g.** *Choice, 2003.*

Banks, James A. & Banks, Cherry A. McGee **LC1099.3.H35 2002**
Handbook of Research on Multicultural Education. Ed. 2. Trade Cloth. John Wiley & Sons, Inc. Hoboken, NJ. 2003. 1120p. ISBN:0-7879-5915-4, ISBN13: 978-0-7879-5915-9. Dewey:370.117. LCCN:2002-156022.
Audience: **g,l,u,f.** *Choice, 2004, 1995.*

Chang, Mitchell (Editor), et al. **LC212.42.C66 2003**
A Compelling Interest: Examining the Evidence on Racial Dynamics in Colleges and Universities. Daria Witt, James Jones & Kenji Hakuta (Editors). Cloth Text. Stanford University Press. Palo Alto, CA. 2003. xv, 246p. ISBN:0-8047-4034-8, ISBN13: 978-0-8047-4034-0. Dewey:378.1/9829. LCCN:2002-151608.
Audience: **l,u,f.**

Delpit, Lisa **LC1099.3.D45 1995**
Other People's Children: Cultural Conflict in the Classroom. Trade Cloth. New Press, The. New York, NY. 1995. 224p. ISBN:1-56584-179-4, ISBN13: 978-1-56584-179-6. Dewey:370.19/6. LCCN:94-069571.
Audience: **g.** *Choice, 1995.*

Dilg, Mary **LC1099.3.D55 1999**
Race and Culture in the Classroom: Teaching and Learning Through Multicultural Education. Trade Cloth. Teachers College Press, Teachers College, Columbia University. New York, NY. 1999. 144p. ISBN:0-8077-3823-9, ISBN13: 978-0-8077-3823-8. Dewey:370.117/0973. LCCN:98-055473.
Audience: **u.** *Choice, 2000.*

Kugler, Eileen Gale **LC1099.3.K84 2002**
Debunking the Middle-Class Myth: Why Diverse Schools Are Good for All Kids. Trade Cloth. Scarecrow Press, Inc. Lanham, MD. 2002. 192p. ISBN:0-8108-4511-3, ISBN13: 978-0-8108-4511-4. Dewey:370.117/0973. LCCN:2002-008700.
Audience: **g,l,u,f.** *Choice, 2003.*

Lynch, James (Editor), et al. **LC1099.C815 1992**
Education for Cultural Diversity: Convergence and Divergence. Celia Modgil & Sohan Modgil (Editors). Paper over Boards. Taylor & Francis Group. Philadelphia, PA. 1992. 488p. Cultural Diversity and the Schools Ser., Vol. 1 ISBN:1-85000-989-9, ISBN13: 978-1-85000-989-4. Dewey:370.1934. LCCN:91-038686.
Audience: **u,f.** *Choice, 1993.*

Ramsey, Patricia G., et al. **LC1099.3.R35 2002**
Multicultural Education: A Source Book. Ed. 2. Edwina B. Vold & Leslie Williams (Authors). Cloth Text. Garland Publishing, Inc. New York, NY. 2002. 312p. Source Books on Education ISBN:0-8153-1744-1, ISBN13: 978-0-8153-1744-9. Dewey:370.117. LCCN:2002-068312.
Audience: **u.** *Choice, 1989.*

Tiedt, Pamela L. & Tiedt, Iris M. **LC1099.3.T54 2005**
Multicultural Teaching: A Handbook of Activities, Information, and Resources. Ed. 7. Trade Paper, Perfect. Allyn & Bacon, Inc. Boston, MA. 2005. 406p. ISBN:0-205-45117-9, ISBN13: 978-0-205-45117-3. Dewey:370.117/0973. LCCN:2005-045800.
Audience: **g,l,u,f.**

Types of Education > Multicultural Education (General) > Gay, Lesbian, Bisexual, Transgendered

LC192.6
Gay Lesbian Straight Education Network. http://www.glsen.org/
Audience: **g,l,u,f.**

Besner, Hilda F. & Spungin, Charlotte I. **LC192.6.B47 1995**
Gay and Lesbian Students: Understanding Their Needs. UK-B Format Paperback. Taylor & Francis Group. Philadelphia, PA. 1995. 174p. ISBN:1-56032-338-8, ISBN13: 978-1-56032-338-9. Dewey:370.19/345. LCCN:95-012727.
Audience: **g,l.** *Choice, 1996.*

Blount, Jackie M. **LC192.6.B56 2004**
Fit to Teach: Same-Sex Desire, Gender, and School Work in the Twentieth Century. Cloth Text. State University of New York Press. Albany, NY. 2004. 272p. ISBN:0-7914-6267-6, ISBN13: 978-0-7914-6267-6. Dewey:371.1/0086/64. LCCN:2004-041624.
Audience: **u.** *Choice, 2005.*

Harbeck, Karen M. **LC192.6.H37 1997**
Gay and Lesbian Educators: Personal Freedoms - Public Constraints. Trade Cloth. Amethyst Press & Productions. Malden, MA. 1997. 500p. ISBN:1-889393-48-7, ISBN13: 978-1-889393-48-3. Dewey:371.1/0086/64. LCCN:96-085545.
Audience: **g,l.** *Choice, 1997.*

Harris, Mary B. (Editor) **LC2575.S36 1997**
School Experiences of Gay and Lesbian Youth: The Invisible Minority. Trade Paper. Haworth Press, Incorporated, The. Binghamton, NY. 1998. 115p. Journal of Gay and Lesbian Social Services Ser., Vol. 7, No. 4 ISBN:1-56023-109-2, ISBN13: 978-1-56023-109-7. Dewey:371.826/64. LCCN:97-041783.
Audience: **u,f.** *Choice, 1998.*

Kissen, Rita M. **LB2844.1.G39K57 1996**
The Last Closet: The Real Lives of Lesbian and Gay Teachers. Trade Cloth. Heinemann. Portsmouth, NH. 1996. 198p. ISBN:0-435-07005-3, ISBN13: 978-0-435-07005-2. Dewey:371.1/008/664. LCCN:96-4128.
Audience: **g,l,u.** *Choice, 1997.*

Letts, William J. IV & Sears, James T. (Editors) **LC192.6.Q85 1999**
Queering Elementary Education: Advancing the Dialogue about Sexualities and Schooling. Book, Other. Rowman & Littlefield Publishers, Inc. Lanham, MD. 1999. 320p. Curriculum, Cultures, and (Homo)sexualities Ser. ISBN:0-8476-9368-6, ISBN13: 978-0-8476-9368-9. Dewey:371/.01/1. LCCN:99-023762.
Audience: **g,l,u,f.** *Choice, 2000.*

Types of Education > Multicultural Education (General) > African Americans

Ballard, Allen **LC2741**
The Education of Black Folk: The Afro-American Struggle for Knowledge in White America. Trade Paper. iUniverse, Inc. Lincoln, NE. 2004. 188p. ISBN:0-595-31766-9, ISBN13: 978-0-595-31766-0. Dewey:378.73.
Audience: **g,l,u,f.**

Bullock, Henry A. **LC2801.B9**
A History of Negro Education in the South: From 1619 to the Present. Trade Paper. Books on Demand. Ann Arbor, MI. 355p. ISBN:0-7837-2057-2, ISBN13: 978-0-7837-2057-9. Dewey:370/.975. LCCN:67-020873.
Audience: **g,l,u,f.**

Clark, Reginald M. **LC3731**
Family Life and School Achievement: Why Poor Black Children Succeed or Fail. Trade Paper. University of Chicago Press. Chicago, IL. 1984. 264p. ISBN:0-226-10770-1, ISBN13: 978-0-226-10770-7. Dewey:371.97/00973. LCCN:83-003481.
Audience: **u,f.** B

Florence, Namulundah **LB885.H626F56 1998**
A Critical Analysis of Bell Hooks' Engaged Pedagogy: A Transgressive Education for the Development of Critical Consciousness. Trade Cloth. Greenwood Publishing Group, Inc. Portsmouth, NH. 1998. 280p. Critical Studies in Education and Culture ISBN:0-89789-564-9, ISBN13: 978-0-89789-564-4. Dewey:370.115. LCCN:98-011065.
Audience: **u.** *Choice, 1999.*

Hale, Janice E. **E185.86.H23 1994**
Unbank the Fire: Visions for the Education of African American Children. Trade Paper. Johns Hopkins University Press. Baltimore, MD. 1968. 264p. ISBN:0-8018-4822-9, ISBN13: 978-0-8018-4822-3. Dewey:370/.089/96073. LCCN:94-002864.
Audience: **l,u,f.** *Choice, 1995.*

Hale, Janice E. **LC277.H34 1986**
Black Children: Their Roots, Culture, and Learning Styles. Ed. 2. Asa G. Hilliard (Foreword by). Trade Paper. Johns Hopkins University Press. Baltimore, MD. 1992. 240p. ISBN:0-8018-3383-3, ISBN13: 978-0-8018-3383-0. Dewey:371.8/2. LCCN:86-045459.
Audience: **u,f.** B

Institute for the Study of Educational Policy Staf **LC2781.H68 1976**
Equal Educational Opportunity for Blacks in U. S. Higher Education: An Assessment. Trade Paper. Howard University Press. Washington, DC. 2003. xxxiii, 330p. ISBN:0-88258-072-8, ISBN13: 978-0-88258-072-2. Dewey:378. LCCN:75-043488.
Audience: **u,f.** B

Jackson, Cynthia L. **LC2741.J33 2001**
e African American Education: A Reference Handbook. E-Book. ABC-CLIO, Inc. Santa Barbara, CA. 2002. xv, 294p. Contemporary Education Issues Ser. ISBN:1-57607-566-4, ISBN13: 978-1-57607-566-1. Dewey:370/.89/96073. LCCN:2001-000347.
Audience: **g.** *Choice, 2001.*

King, Joyce E. (Editor) **LC2699.B53 2005**
Black Education: A Transformative Research and Action Agenda for the New Century. Gloria Ladson Billings, Grace Lee Boggs & A. Wade Boykin (Contribution by). Perfect, Paper over Boards. Lawrence Erlbaum Associates, Inc. Mahwah, NJ. 2005. 443p. ISBN:0-8058-5457-6, ISBN13: 978-0-8058-5457-2. Dewey:370/.8996. LCCN:2004-060676.
Audience: **l,u,f.** *Choice, 2006.*

Kohl, Herbert R. **LC2803.N5 K6 1988**
36 Children. Trade Paper. Penguin Group (USA) Inc. New York, NY. 1988. 224p. ISBN:0-452-26463-4, ISBN13: 978-0-452-26463-2. Dewey:370.19344097471.
Audience: **g,l,u,f.** B

Ladson-Billings, Gloria **LC2717.L33 1994**
The Dreamkeepers: Successful Teachers of African-American Children. Trade Paper. John Wiley & Sons, Inc. Hoboken, NJ. 1997. 208p. ISBN:0-7879-0338-8, ISBN13: 978-0-7879-0338-1. Dewey:370/.8996073. LCCN:94-010316.
Audience: **l,u.**

Morgan, Harry **LC2741**
Historical Perspectives on the Education of Black Children. Trade Cloth. Greenwood Publishing Group, Inc. Portsmouth, NH. 1995. 256p. ISBN:0-275-95071-9, ISBN13: 978-0-275-95071-2. Dewey:371.97/96/073. LCCN:94-042843.
Audience: **u,f.** *Choice, 1996.*

Murrell, Peter C. Jr. **LC2731.M87 2002**
African-Centered Pedagogy: Developing Schools of Achievement for African American Children. Trade Paper. State University of New York Press. Albany, NY. 2002. 256p. The Social Context of Education Ser. ISBN:0-7914-5292-1, ISBN13: 978-0-7914-5292-9. Dewey:371.829/96073. LCCN:2001-049178.
Audience: **u.** *Choice, 2002.*

Paley, Vivian G. **LB1140.3.P356 1995**
Kwanzaa and Me: A Teacher's Story. Trade Cloth. Harvard University Press. Cambridge, MA. 1995. 152p. ISBN:0-674-50585-9, ISBN13: 978-0-674-50585-8. Dewey:372.21. LCCN:94-025002.
Audience: **u.** *Choice, 1995.*

Paley, Vivian Gussin **LC2771.P34 2000**
White Teacher. Trade Paper. Harvard University Press. Cambridge, MA. 2000. 160p. ISBN:0-674-00273-3, ISBN13: 978-0-674-00273-9. Dewey:371.8299/073. LCCN:99-058993.
Audience: **g,l,u,f.** B

Rist, Ray C. (Author, Introduction by) **LC2771.R57 2002**
The Urban School: A Factory for Failure. Ed. 2. Trade Paper. Transaction Publishers. Somerset, NJ. 2002. 261p. ISBN:0-7658-0938-9, ISBN13: 978-0-7658-0938-4. Dewey:306.43. LCCN:2002-022502.
Audience: **u,f.**

Sowell, Thomas **LC2801.S64 1986**
Education, Assumptions vs. History: Collected Papers. Trade Paper. Hoover Institution Press. Stanford, CA. 1985. 203p. Publication Ser., No. 311 ISBN:0-8179-8112-8, ISBN13: 978-0-8179-8112-9. Dewey:370.19/34/0973. LCCN:85-018131.
Audience: **g,l,u,f.** B

Tatum, Beverly Daniel **E185.625**
Why Are All the Black Kids Sitting Together in the Cafeteria?: And Other Conversations about Race. Trade Paper. Basic Books. New York, NY. 2002. 320p. Art of Mentoring Ser. ISBN:0-465-08361-7, ISBN13: 978-0-465-08361-9. Dewey:305.8/00973. LCCN:2003-270044.
Audience: **g.**

Thompson, Gail L. **LC2771.T56 2004**
Through Ebony Eyes: What Teachers Need to Know but Are Afraid to Ask about African American Students. Trade Cloth. John Wiley & Sons, Inc. Hoboken, NJ. 2004. 352p. ISBN:0-7879-7061-1, ISBN13: 978-0-7879-7061-1. LCCN:2003-027616.
Audience: **u.** *Choice, 2005.*

Thompson, Gail L. **LC2731**
What African American Parents Want Educators to Know. Trade Cloth. Greenwood Publishing Group, Inc. Portsmouth, NH. 2003. 232p. ISBN:0-89789-893-1, ISBN13: 978-0-89789-893-5. Dewey:371.829/96073. LCCN:2002-029888.
Audience: **u.** *Choice, 2004.*

Woodson, Carter Godwin **HS310.Z6**
The Mis-education of the Negro. Daryl Michael Scott (Editor);

V. P. Franklin (Foreword by). ASALH Press. 2005. ISBN:0-9768111-0-3, ISBN13: 978-0-9768111-0-7.
Audience: **g,l,u,f.**

Types of Education > Multicultural Education (General) > Asian Americans

LC903

☐ Arab World and Islamic Resources. http://www.awaironline.org
Audience: **g.**

Nakanishi, Donald T. & Nishida, Tina Y. (Editors) **LC2632.A85 1995**
The Asian American Educational Experience: A Sourcebook for Teachers and Students. Trade Paper. Routledge. New York, NY. 1994. 424p. ISBN:0-415-90872-8, ISBN13: 978-0-415-90872-6. Dewey:371.97/073. LCCN:94-016361.
Audience: **g.**

Walker-Moffat, Wendy **LC3501.H56W35 1995**
The Other Side of the Asian American Success Story. Trade Cloth. John Wiley & Sons, Inc. Hoboken, NJ. 1995. 240p. Education Ser. ISBN:0-7879-0122-9, ISBN13: 978-0-7879-0122-6. Dewey:371.9795. LCCN:95-021568.
Audience: **u.** *Choice, 1996.*

Weinberg, Meyer **LC2632.W45 1997**
Asian-American Education: Historical Background and Current Realities. Cloth over Boards. Lawrence Erlbaum Associates, Inc. Mahwah, NJ. 1997. 352p. ISBN:0-8058-2775-7, ISBN13: 978-0-8058-2775-0. Dewey:371.82995/073. LCCN:97-008974.
Audience: **l,u.**

Types of Education > Multicultural Education (General) > Hispanic Americans

Cordasco, Francesco & Bucchioni, Eugene **E184.P85**
The Puerto Rican Community and Its Children on the Mainland: A Source Book for Teachers, Social Workers and Other Professionals. Ed. 3. Trade Cloth. Scarecrow Press, Inc. Lanham, MD. 1982. 469p. ISBN:0-8108-1506-0, ISBN13: 978-0-8108-1506-3. Dewey:305.8/687295/073. LCCN:81-021250.
Audience: **g,l,u,f.** B

Garcia, Eugene E. **LC2669.G37 2001**
Hispanic Education in the United States: Raices y Alas. Trade Cloth. Rowman & Littlefield Publishers, Inc. Lanham, MD. 2001. 320p. Critical Issues in Contemporary American Education Ser. ISBN:0-7425-1076-X, ISBN13: 978-0-7425-1076-0. Dewey:371.829/68073. LCCN:00-054434.
Audience: **l,u.** *Choice, 2002.*

Gonzalez, Maria Luisa (Editor), et al. **LC2669**
Educating Latino Students: A Guide to Successful Practice. Ana Huerta-Macias & Josefina Villamil Tinajero (Editors). Trade Paper. Scarecrow Press, Inc. Lanham, MD. 2002. 385p. ISBN:0-8108-4377-3, ISBN13: 978-0-8108-4377-6. Dewey:371.82968.
Audience: **g.** *Choice, 1998.*

Nieto, Sonia (Editor) **LC2692.P82 2000**
Puerto Rican Students in U. S. Schools. Alicia Nieto, Hipolito Baez & Diana Caballero (Contribution by). Trade Paper. Lawrence Erlbaum Associates, Inc. Mahwah, NJ. 2000. 368p. Sociocultural, Political, and Historical Studies in Education ISBN:0-8058-2765-X, ISBN13: 978-0-8058-2765-1. Dewey:371.82968/7295. LCCN:99-047154.
Audience: **u,f.** *Choice, 2000.*

Trueba, Enrique T. **E184.S75T78 1998**
Latinos Unidos: From Cultural Diversity to the Politics of Solidarity. George Spindler (Foreword by). Trade Cloth. Rowman & Littlefield Publishers, Inc. Lanham, MD. 1999. 216p. Critical Perspectives Ser., Vol. 110 ISBN:0-8476-8596-9, ISBN13: 978-0-8476-8596-7. Dewey:305.868. LCCN:98-008617.
Audience: **l,u.** *Choice, 1999.*

Trumbull, Elise **LC1099.3.B74 2001**
Bridging Cultures Between Home and School: A Guide for Teachers with Special Focus on Immigrant Latino Families. Trade Paper. Lawrence Erlbaum Associates, Inc. Mahwah, NJ. 2001. 184p. ISBN:0-8058-3519-9, ISBN13: 978-0-8058-3519-9. Dewey:370.117/0973. LCCN:00-051404.
Audience: **u,f.** *Choice, 2002.*

Valdés, Guadalupe **PE1129.S8V26 2001**
Learning and Not Learning English: Latino Students in American Schools. Trade Cloth. Teachers College Press, Teachers College, Columbia University. New York, NY. 2001. xiv, 177p. ISBN:0-8077-4106-X, ISBN13: 978-0-8077-4106-1. Dewey:428/.0071/073. LCCN:00-054495.
Audience: **u,f.** *Choice, 2001.*

Valencia, Richard R. (Editor) **LC2683.C47 2002**
Chicano School Failure and Success: Past, Present, and Future. Ed. 2. Paper over Boards. Routledge. New York, NY. 2002. 416p. ISBN:0-415-25773-5, ISBN13: 978-0-415-25773-2. Dewey:373.1/2913089/68. LCCN:2002-021959.
Audience: **l,u.** *Choice, 2003.*

Types of Education > Multicultural Education (General) > Native Americans

Adams, David W. **E97.5.A35 1995**
Education for Extinction: American Indians and the Boarding School Experience, 1875-1928. Trade Cloth. University Press of Kansas. Lawrence, KS. 1997. 408p. ISBN:0-7006-0735-8, ISBN13: 978-0-7006-0735-8. Dewey:371.97/97. LCCN:95-007638.
Audience: **l,u.** *Choice, 1996.*

Cajete, Gregory **E96.C35 1994**
Look to the Mountain: An Ecology of Indigenous Education. Trade Paper. Kivaki Press, Inc. Skyland, NC. 1993. 248p. ISBN:1-882308-65-4, ISBN13: 978-1-882308-65-1. Dewey:370.897073. LCCN:94-175203.
Audience: **l,u,f.**

Child, Brenda J., et al. **E97.5.R46 2000**
Away from Home: American Indian Boarding School Experience, 1879-2000. Ed. 2. K. Tsianina Lomawaima & Heard Museum Staff (Authors). Trade Paper. Heard Museum, The. Phoenix, AZ. 2000. 144p. ISBN:0-934351-62-7, ISBN13: 978-0-934351-62-1. Dewey:371.829/97. LCCN:2004-047416.
Audience: **g.** *Choice, 2001.*

Mihesuah, Devon A. & Wilson, Angela Cavender **E97.I464 2004**
Indigenizing the Academy: Native Scholars and Scholarship on Natives. Trade Paper. University of Nebraska Press. Lincoln, NE. 2005. 240p. Contemporary Indigenous Issues Ser. ISBN:0-8032-8292-3, ISBN13: 978-0-8032-8292-6. Dewey:378.1/982997. LCCN:2003-020064.
Audience: **u,f.** *Choice, 2005.*

Reyhner, Jon Allan & Eder, Jeanne Oyawin **E97.R49 2004**
American Indian Education: A History. Trade Cloth. University of Oklahoma Press. Norman, OK. 2004. 368p. ISBN:0-8061-3593-X, ISBN13: 978-0-8061-3593-9. Dewey:371.829/97. LCCN:2003-063420.
Audience: **g,l,u,f.** *Choice, 2005.*

Senese, Guy B. **E97**
Self-Determination and the Social Education of Native Americans. Trade Cloth. Greenwood Publishing Group, Inc. Portsmouth, NH. 1991. 248p. ISBN:0-275-93776-3, ISBN13: 978-0-275-93776-8. Dewey:370/.8997. LCCN:90-020011.
Audience: **u,f.** *Choice, 1992.*

Types of Education > Multicultural Education (General) > Immigrants or Ethnic and Linguistic Minorities

Brisk, Maria E. & Harrington, Margaret M. **LC3731.B684 2000**
Literacy and Bilingualism: A Handbook for All Teachers. Trade Paper. Lawrence Erlbaum Associates, Inc. Mahwah, NJ. 1999. 184p. ISBN:0-8058-3165-7, ISBN13: 978-0-8058-3165-8. Dewey:370.117/5/0973. LCCN:99-031664.
Audience: **u.** *Choice, 2000.*

Garcia, Eugene E. **LC3731.G35 2004**
Teaching and Learning in Two Languages: Bilingualism and Schooling in the United States. Perfect, Paper over Boards. Teachers College Press, Teachers College, Columbia University. New York, NY. 2005. 199p. Multicultural Education Ser. ISBN:0-8077-4537-5, ISBN13: 978-0-8077-4537-3. Dewey:370.117. LCCN:2004-062042.
Audience: **u.** *Choice, 2005.*

Jacob, E. & Cathie Jordan (Editors) **LC3731**
Minority Education: Anthropological Perspectives. Greenwood Publishing Group, Inc. 1993. Social and Policy Issues in Education Ser. ISBN:0-89391-868-7, ISBN13: 978-0-89391-868-2.
Audience: **l,u,f.**

Kluwin, Thomas N. (Editor), et al. **HV2551 .T68 1992**
Toward Effective Public School Programs for Deaf Students: Context, Process and Outcomes. Donald F. Moores & Martha G. Gaustad (Editors). Trade Paper. Teachers College Press, Teachers College, Columbia University. New York, NY. 1992. 272p. Special Education Ser. ISBN:0-8077-3159-5, ISBN13: 978-0-8077-3159-8. Dewey:371.91/2/0973. LCCN:92-002932.
Audience: **g.** *Choice, 1993.*

Olivas, Michael A. **LC3727.O43**
The Dilemma of Access: Minorities in Two Year Colleges. Trade Paper. Howard University Press. Washington, DC. 2003. xv, 259p. ISBN:0-88258-079-5, ISBN13: 978-0-88258-079-1. Dewey:378.1/543/0973. LCCN:79-002575.
Audience: **u,f.** B

Rader, Debra & Sittig, Linda Harris **LB1575.R33 2003**
New Kid in School: Using Literature to Help Children in Transition. Trade Cloth. Teachers College Press, Teachers College, Columbia University. New York, NY. 2003. xi, 185p. ISBN:0-8077-4315-1, ISBN13: 978-0-8077-4315-7. Dewey:372.64/044. LCCN:2002-038432.
Audience: **u.** *Choice, 2004.*

Sadowski, Michael (Editor) **LC3731.T387 2004**
Teaching Immigrant and Second-Language Students: Strategies for Success. Trade Paper. Harvard Education Publishing Group (H E P G). Cambridge, MA. 2004. 132p. ISBN:1-891792-51-2, ISBN13: 978-1-891792-51-9. Dewey:428.0071. LCCN:2004-108774.
Audience: **l,u.** *Choice, 2005.*

Santa Ana, Otto **LC3731.T65 2003**
Tongue Tied: The Lives of Multilingual Children in Public Education. Book, Other. Rowman & Littlefield Publishers, Inc. Lanham, MD. 2004. 336p. ISBN:0-7425-2383-7, ISBN13: 978-0-7425-2383-8. Dewey:370.117. LCCN:2003-022739.
Audience: **u.** *Choice, 2004.*

Trumbull, Elise **LC1099.3.B74 2001**
Bridging Cultures Between Home and School: A Guide for Teachers with Special Focus on Immigrant Latino Families. Trade Paper. Lawrence Erlbaum Associates, Inc. Mahwah, NJ. 2001. 184p. ISBN:0-8058-3519-9, ISBN13: 978-0-8058-3519-9. Dewey:370.117/0973. LCCN:00-051404.
Audience: **u,f.** *Choice, 2002.*

Valdés, Guadalupe **PE1129.S8V26 2001**
Learning and Not Learning English: Latino Students in American Schools. Trade Cloth. Teachers College Press, Teachers College, Columbia University. New York, NY. 2001. xiv, 177p. ISBN:0-8077-4106-X, ISBN13: 978-0-8077-4106-1. Dewey:428/.0071/073. LCCN:00-054495.
Audience: **u,f.** *Choice, 2001.*

Types of Education > Comparative and International Education

Alexander, Robin J. **LB43.A44 2001**
Culture and Pedagogy: International Comparisons in Primary Education. Trade Paper. Blackwell Publishing, Inc. Malden, MA. 2001. 668p. ISBN:0-631-22051-8, ISBN13: 978-0-631-22051-0. Dewey:372. LCCN:00-057908.
Audience: **u,f.** *Choice, 2001.*

Altbach, Phillip G. **LB2322.2.A48 1998**
Comparative Higher Education: Knowledge, the University, and Development. Trade Cloth. Greenwood Publishing Group, Inc. Portsmouth, NH. 1998. 248p. Contemporary Studies in Social and Policy Issues in Education ISBN:1-56750-380-2, ISBN13: 978-1-56750-380-7. Dewey:378. LCCN:97-049237.
Audience: **g,l,u,f.** *Choice, 1999.*

Anderson-Levitt, Kathryn M. (Editor) **LB45.L56 2003**
Local Meanings, Global Schooling: Anthropology and World Culture Theory. Cloth over Boards. Palgrave Macmillan. New York, NY. 2003. 272p. ISBN:1-4039-6162-X, ISBN13: 978-1-4039-6162-4. Dewey:306.43. LCCN:2002-033307.
Audience: **u,f.** *Choice, 2004.*

Arnove, Robert F. (Editor), et al. **LB43.E46 1992**
Emergent Issues in Education: Comparative Perspectives. Philip G. Altbach & Gail P. Kelly (Editors). Cloth Text. State University of New York Press. Albany, NY. 1992. 363p. SUNY Series in Frontiers of Education ISBN:0-7914-1031-5, ISBN13: 978-0-7914-1031-8. Dewey:370.19/5. LCCN:91-004328.
Audience: **u,f.** *Choice, 1992.*

Arnove, Robert F. & Torres, Carlos Alberto (Editors) **LB43.C68 2003**
Comparative Education: The Dialectic of the Global and the Local. Ed. 2. Book, Other. Rowman & Littlefield Publishers, Inc. Lanham, MD. 2003. 504p. ISBN:0-7425-2380-2, ISBN13: 978-0-7425-2380-7. Dewey:370/.9. LCCN:2003-007673.
Audience: **g,l,u,f.** *Choice, 2000.*

Baker, David & LeTendre, Gerald K. **LB43.B25 2005**
National Differences, Global Similarities: World Culture and the Future of Schooling. Trade Cloth. Stanford University Press. Palo Alto, CA. 2005. 248p. ISBN:0-8047-5020-3, ISBN13: 978-0-8047-5020-2. Dewey:370/.9. LCCN:2004-027281.
Audience: **u,f.** *Choice, 2005.*

Banks, James A. (Editor) **LC1099.B45 2003**
Diversity and Citizenship Education: Global Perspectives. Trade Cloth. John Wiley & Sons, Inc. Hoboken, NJ. 2003. 528p. The Jossey-Bass Education Ser. ISBN:0-7879-6651-7, ISBN13: 978-0-7879-6651-5. Dewey:372.83/2. LCCN:2003-007302.
Audience: **g,l,u,f.** *Choice, 2004.*

Cushner, Kenneth H. (Editor) **LC1099.I5958 1998**
International Perspectives on Intercultural Education. Cloth over Boards. Lawrence Erlbaum Associates, Inc. Mahwah, NJ. 1998. 400p. ISBN:0-8058-2745-5, ISBN13: 978-0-8058-2745-3. Dewey:370.117. LCCN:98-017268.
Audience: **u,f.** *Choice, 1999.*

Ginsburg, Mark **LA217.2.U53 1991**
Understanding Educational Reform in Global Context: Economy, Ideology and the State. Cloth Text. Garland Publishing, Inc. New York, NY. 1991. 424p. Reference Books in International Education, Vol. 22 ISBN:0-8240-6896-3, ISBN13: 978-0-8240-6896-7. Dewey:370. LCCN:91-003812.
Audience: **g,l,u,f.** *Choice, 1992.*

Hayden, Mary & Thompson, Jeff (Editors) **LB1090.I58 1998**
International Education: Principles and Practice. Ed. 2. Trade Paper. Kogan Page, Ltd. London, 2001. 240p. ISBN:0-7494-3616-6, ISBN13: 978-0-7494-3616-2. Dewey:370.116. LCCN:2001-275940.
Audience: **u,f.**

Hayden, Mary (Editor), et al. **LC1090.I5553 2002**
International Education in Practice: Dimensions for Schools and International Schools. Jeff Thompson & George Walker (Editors). Trade Paper. Kogan Page, Ltd. London, 2002. 240p. ISBN:0-7494-3835-5, ISBN13: 978-0-7494-3835-7. Dewey:370.116. LCCN:2002-512631.
Audience: **u,f.** *Choice, 2003.*

Husén, Torsten & Postlethwaite, T. Neville (Editors) **LB15.I569 1994**
The International Encyclopedia of Education, Set. Ed. 2. Trade Cloth. Elsevier Science & Technology Books. Saint Louis, MO. 1994. 7740p. ISBN:0-08-041046-4, ISBN13: 978-0-08-041046-3. Dewey:370/.3/21. LCCN:94-003059.
Audience: **g,l,u,f.** B *Choice, 1994, 1986.*

Kauffmann, Norman L., et al. **LB2376.K38 1992**
Students Abroad: Strangers at Home: Education for a Global Society. Judith N. Martin, Henry D. Weaver & Judy Weaver (Authors). Trade Paper. Intercultural Press, Inc. Yarmouth, ME. 1992. 208p. ISBN:0-933662-94-7, ISBN13: 978-0-933662-94-0. Dewey:370.19/6. LCCN:91-038527.
Audience: **g,l,u,f.** *Choice, 1992.*

Kelly, Gail P. (Editor) **LC1411**
International Handbook of Women's Education. Cloth Text. Greenwood Publishing Group, Inc. Portsmouth, NH. 1989. 672p. ISBN:0-313-25638-1, ISBN13: 978-0-313-25638-7. Dewey:376. LCCN:88-034730.
Audience: **g,l,u,f.** *Choice, 1990.*

Leavitt, Howard B. (Editor) **LB1707**
Issues and Problems in Teacher Education: An International Handbook. Cloth Text. Greenwood Publishing Group, Inc. Portsmouth, NH. 1992. 312p. ISBN:0-313-25991-7, ISBN13: 978-0-313-25991-3. Dewey:370.71. LCCN:91-033503.
Audience: **g,l,u,f.** *Choice, 1993.*

Postlethwaite, T. Neville (Editor) **LB43.I584 1995**
International Encyclopedia of National Systems of Education. Ed. 2. Trade Cloth. Elsevier Science & Technology Books. Saint Louis, MO. 1995. 1050p. Resources in Education Ser. ISBN:0-08-042302-7, ISBN13: 978-0-08-042302-9. Dewey:370.19/5. LCCN:95-034436.
Audience: **g,l,u,f.** *Choice, 1997.*

Reagan, Timothy G. **LB43.R43 2004**
Non-Western Educational Traditions: Indigenous Approaches to Educational Thought and Practice. Ed. 3. Trade Paper. Lawrence Erlbaum Associates, Inc. Mahwah, NJ. 2004. 320p. The Sociocultural, Political, and Historical Studies in Education Ser. ISBN:0-8058-4857-6, ISBN13: 978-0-8058-4857-1. Dewey:370.9. LCCN:2004-559149.
Audience: **g,l,u,f.**

Spring, Joel H. **LC191.S686 1998**
e Education and the Rise of the Global Economy. E-Book.

NetLibrary, Inc. Boulder, CO. 1998. ISBN:0-585-11896-5, ISBN13: 978-0-585-11896-3. Dewey:379.
Audience: **g,l,u,f.** *Choice, 1999.*

Spring, Joel H. **LC1090.S67 2004**
How Educational Ideologies Are Shaping Global Society: Intergovernmental Organizations, NGO's, and the Decline of the Nation-State. Cloth over Boards. Lawrence Erlbaum Associates, Inc. Mahwah, NJ. 2004. 232p. Sociocultural, Political, and Historical Studies in Education ISBN:0-8058-4915-7, ISBN13: 978-0-8058-4915-8. Dewey:370.116. LCCN:2004-041155.
Audience: **g,l,u,f.** *Choice, 2004.*

Tye, Barbara Benham & Tye, Kenneth A. **LC1090.T97 1992**
Global Education: A Study of School Change. Cloth Text. State University of New York Press. Albany, NY. 1992. 273p. SUNY Series in Theory, Research, and Practice ISBN:0-7914-1041-2, ISBN13: 978-0-7914-1041-7. Dewey:375/.0082/0979496. LCCN:91-019045.
Audience: **g,l,u,f.** *Choice, 1992.*

Vestal, Theodore M. **LC1099**
International Education: Its History and Promise for Today. Robert Leestma (Foreword by). Trade Cloth. Greenwood Publishing Group, Inc. Portsmouth, NH. 1994. 224p. ISBN:0-275-94759-9, ISBN13: 978-0-275-94759-0. Dewey:370.196. LCCN:93-023478.
Audience: **g,l,u,f.** *Choice, 1995.*

Woodill, Gary (Editor), et al. **LB1139.23.I68 1992**
International Handbook of Early Childhood Education. Judith Bernhard & Lawrence Prochner (Editors). Paper over Boards. Garland Publishing, Inc. New York, NY. 1992. 576p. ISBN:0-8240-4939-X, ISBN13: 978-0-8240-4939-3. Dewey:372.21. LCCN:92-023846.
Audience: **l,u,f.** *Choice, 1993.*

Types of Education > Education in Developing Countries

Daniel, John (Editor), et al. **ND623.M67**
Academic Freedom: Education and Human Rights, Vol. 3. Ed. 3. Frederick De Vlaming, Nigel Hartley & Manfred Nowak (Editors). Trade Cloth. Zed Books, Ltd. London, 1995. 256p. World University Service Series on Academic Freedom ISBN:1-85649-301-6, ISBN13: 978-1-85649-301-7. Dewey:759.5.
Audience: **g,l,u,f.** *Choice, 1995.*

Kelly, David H. & Kelly, Gail P. **Z5815.D44K44 1989**
Women's Education in the Third World: An Annotated Bibliography. Trade Cloth. Garland Publishing, Inc. New York, NY. 1989. 482p. ISBN:0-8240-8634-1, ISBN13: 978-0-8240-8634-3. Dewey:016.375. LCCN:89-032058.
Audience: **g,l,u,f.** *Choice, 1989.*

Kelly, Gail P. (Editor) **LC1411**
International Handbook of Women's Education. Cloth Text. Greenwood Publishing Group, Inc. Portsmouth, NH. 1989. 672p. ISBN:0-313-25638-1, ISBN13: 978-0-313-25638-7. Dewey:376. LCCN:88-034730.
Audience: **g,l,u,f.** *Choice, 1990.*

Lockheed, Marlaine E. & Verspoor, Adriaan M. **LC2608.L63 1991**
Improving Primary Education in Developing Countries. Cloth Text. Oxford University Press, Inc. New York, NY. 1992. 452p. ISBN:0-19-520872-2, ISBN13: 978-0-19-520872-6. Dewey:372.9172/4. LCCN:91-030421.
Audience: **g,l,u,f.** *Choice, 1992.*

Perraton, H. D. **LC5808.D48P47 2000**
Open and Distance Learning in Developing World. Paper over Boards. Routledge. New York, NY. 2000. 240p. Routledge Studies in Distance Education Ser. ISBN:0-415-19418-0, ISBN13: 978-0-415-19418-1. Dewey:371.3/5/091724. LCCN:99-016902.
Audience: **g,l,u,f.** *Choice, 2000.*

Rondinelli, Dennis A., et al. **LC2605.R66 1990**
Planning Education Reforms in Developing Countries: The Contingency Approach. John Middleton & Adriaan M. Verspoor (Authors). Cloth Text. Duke University Press. Durham, NC. 1990. 225p. ISBN:0-8223-0966-1, ISBN13: 978-0-8223-0966-6. Dewey:379.1/54/091724. LCCN:89-036234.
Audience: **u,f.** *Choice, 1990.*

Scrase, Timothy **LC191.8.D44S63 1996**
Social Justice and Third World Education, Vol. 37. Edward R. Beauchamp (Editor). Cloth Text. Garland Publishing, Inc. New York, NY. 1996. 245p. Reference Books in International Education ISBN:0-8153-1168-0, ISBN13: 978-0-8153-1168-3. Dewey:370.11/5/091724. LCCN:96-020094.
Audience: **g,l,u,f.** *Choice, 1997.*

Types of Education > Rural Education. Urban Education

Anyon, Jean **LC5133.N39A59 1997**
Ghetto Schooling: A Political Economy of Urban Educational Reform. Trade Cloth. Teachers College Press, Teachers College, Columbia University. New York, NY. 1997. 240p. ISBN:0-8077-3663-5, ISBN13: 978-0-8077-3663-0. Dewey:370/.9173/2. LCCN:97-026507.
Audience: **g,l,u.**

Check, Joseph W. **LC5131**
Politics, Language, and Culture: A Critical Look at Urban School Reform. Trade Cloth. Greenwood Publishing Group, Inc. Portsmouth, NH. 2002. 240p. Series in Language and Ideology ISBN:0-89789-647-5, ISBN13: 978-0-89789-647-4. Dewey:370/.9173/2. LCCN:2002-021576.
Audience: **u,f.**

Corbett, H. Dickson, et al. **LC5131.C62 2002**
Effort and Excellence in Urban Classrooms: Expecting, and Getting, Success with All Students. Bruce L. Wilson & Belinda Williams (Authors). Cloth Text. Teachers College Press, Teachers College, Columbia University. New York, NY. 2002. 192p. ISBN:0-8077-4217-1, ISBN13: 978-0-8077-4217-4. Dewey:370/.9173/2. LCCN:2001-060366.
Audience: **u,f.** *Choice, 2003, 2002.*

Cuban, Larry & Usdan, Michael D. (Editors) **LC5131.P69 2002**
Powerful Reforms with Shallow Roots: Improving America's Urban Schools. Cloth Text. Teachers College Press, Teachers

College, Columbia University. New York, NY. 2002. 192p. ISBN:0-8077-4293-7, ISBN13: 978-0-8077-4293-8. Dewey:370/.9173/2. LCCN:2002-027128.
Audience: **g,l,u,f.** *Choice, 2003.*

Galbraith, Michael W. (Editor) **LC5146**
Education in the Rural American Community: A Lifelong Process. Trade Paper. Krieger Publishing Company. Melbourne, FL. 1996. 398p. ISBN:1-57524-029-7, ISBN13: 978-1-57524-029-9. Dewey:370.19/346/0973.
Audience: **l,u.**

Henig, Jeffrey R. **LC5131.C586 1999**
The Color of School Reform: Race, Politics and the Challenge of Urban Education. Cloth Text. Princeton University Press. Princeton, NJ. 1999. 320p. ISBN:0-691-01634-8, ISBN13: 978-0-691-01634-4. Dewey:370/.9173/2. LCCN:99-011258.
Audience: **u,f.**

Hess, Frederick M. **LC5131.H44 1998**
Spinning Wheels: The Politics of Urban School Reform. Trade Cloth. Brookings Institution Press. Washington, DC. 1998. 210p. ISBN:0-8157-3636-3, ISBN13: 978-0-8157-3636-3. Dewey:370/.9173/2. LCCN:98-025373.
Audience: **u,f.** *Choice, 1999.*

Kozol, Jonathan **LC4091**
Savage Inequalities: Children in America's Schools. Trade Paper. HarperCollins Publishers. New York, NY. 1992. 272p. ISBN:0-06-097499-0, ISBN13: 978-0-06-097499-2. Dewey:371.96/7. LCCN:92-052636.
Audience: **g,l,u,f.**

Kozol, Jonathan **LC212.62K69 2005**
The Shame of the Nation: The Restoration of Apartheid Schooling in America. Trade Cloth. Crown Publishing Group. New York, NY. 2005. 416p. ISBN:1-4000-5244-0, ISBN13: 978-1-4000-5244-8. Dewey:379.2/63/0973. LCCN:2005-008626.
Audience: **g,l,u,f.** *Choice, 2006.*

Lopez, Nancy **LC5101.L66 2002**
Hopeful Girls Troubled Boys: Race and Gender Disparity in Urban Education. Paper over Boards. Routledge. New York, NY. 2002. 224p. ISBN:0-415-93074-X, ISBN13: 978-0-415-93074-1. Dewey:370/.9173/2. LCCN:2002-011253.
Audience: **g,u.** *Choice, 2004.*

Meier, Daniel **LB1025.3.M45 1997**
Learning in Small Moments: Life in an Urban Classroom. Cloth Text. Teachers College Press, Teachers College, Columbia University. New York, NY. 1997. 176p. Practitioners Inquiry Ser., Vol. 3 ISBN:0-8077-3627-9, ISBN13: 978-0-8077-3627-2. Dewey:371.1/02. LCCN:96-040291.
Audience: **l,u.**

Noguera, Pedro **LC5131.N64 2003**
City Schools and the American Dream: Reclaiming the Promise of Public Education. Trade Cloth. Teachers College Press, Teachers College, Columbia University. New York, NY. 2003. xvi, 189p. ISBN:0-8077-4382-8, ISBN13: 978-0-8077-4382-9. Dewey:371/.009173/2. LCCN:2003-053342.
Audience: **g.**

Peshkin, Alan **LB1567**
Growing up American: Schooling and the Survival of Community. University of Chicago Press: Chicago. 1978. ISBN:0-226-66196-2, ISBN13: 978-0-226-66196-4.
Audience: **g,l,u,f.**

Popkewitz, Thomas S. **LB1715.P58 1998**
Struggling for the Soul: The Politics of Schooling and the Construction of the Teacher. Trade Cloth. Teachers College Press, Teachers College, Columbia University. New York, NY. 1998. 176p. ISBN:0-8077-3729-1, ISBN13: 978-0-8077-3729-3. Dewey:371.1/00973. LCCN:97-052181.
Audience: **u.**

Ravitch, Diane & Viteritti, Joseph P. (Editors) **LC5131.N29 1997**
New Schools for a New Century: The Redesign of Urban Education. Cloth over Boards. Yale University Press. Cumberland, RI. 1997. 336p. ISBN:0-300-07046-2, ISBN13: 978-0-300-07046-0. Dewey:370/.973/091732. LCCN:96-039929.
Audience: **u,f.** *Choice, 1998.*

Rothstein, Stanley W. (Editor) **LC5131**
Handbook of Schooling in Urban America. Cloth Text. Greenwood Publishing Group, Inc. Portsmouth, NH. 1993. 440p. ISBN:0-313-28412-1, ISBN13: 978-0-313-28412-0. Dewey:370.193480973. LCCN:93-009323.
Audience: **g,u,f.** *Choice, 1994.*

Rymes, Betsy **LC5131.R96 2001**
Conversational Borderlands: Talk with Troubled Teens in an Urban School. Trade Cloth. Teachers College Press, Teachers College, Columbia University. New York, NY. 2001. x, 193p. Language and Literacy Ser. ISBN:0-8077-4130-2, ISBN13: 978-0-8077-4130-6. Dewey:373.12/913. LCCN:2001-027751.
Audience: **u.** *Choice, 2002.*

Types of Education > Special Education. Exceptional Children and Youth

Alexander, Kern & Hunter, Richard C. (Editors) **LC3965 .A36 2004**
Administering Special Education: In Pursuit of Dignity and Autonomy. Trade Cloth. Elsevier Science & Technology Books. Saint Louis, MO. 2004. 264p. Advances in Educational Administration Ser. ISBN:0-7623-1145-2, ISBN13: 978-0-7623-1145-3. Dewey:371.9068.
Audience: **u,f.**

Cavallaro, Claire C. & Haney, Michele **LC1201.C38 1999**
Preschool Inclusion. Trade Cloth. Paul H. Brookes Publishing Company. Baltimore, MD. 1999. 320p. ISBN:1-55766-419-6, ISBN13: 978-1-55766-419-8. Dewey:371.9/0472. LCCN:99-011264.
Audience: **g,l,u.**

Council for Exceptional Children Staff (Contribution by) **LC3969.45.C69 2003**
What Every Special Educator Must Know: The Ethics, Standards, and Guidelines for Special Educators. Ed. 5. Trade

Cloth. Council for Exceptional Children. Arlington, VA. 2003. ISBN:0-86586-993-6, ISBN13: 978-0-86586-993-6. Dewey:379.1/57. LCCN:2003-070002.
Audience: **u,f.**

Feldman, Maurice (Editor) **BF713**
Early Intervention: The Essential Readings. Trade Paper. Blackwell Publishing, Inc. Malden, MA. 2003. 368p. Essential Readings in Developmental Psychology Ser. ISBN:1-4051-1168-2, ISBN13: 978-1-4051-1168-3. Dewey:618.92/8905. LCCN:2003-004193.
Audience: **u,f.** *Choice, 2004.*

Gallagher, James J., et al. **LC4015**
Educating Exceptional Children. Ed. 11. Nicholas J. Anastasiow, Mary Ruth Coleman & Samuel Kirk (Authors). Paper Text. Houghton Mifflin College Division. Boston, MA. 2005. 557p. ISBN:0-618-47389-0, ISBN13: 978-0-618-47389-2. Dewey:371.9.
Audience: **l,u,f.**

Hunt, Nancy & Marshall, Kathleen **LC3965.H86 2002**
Exceptional Children and Youth: An Introduction to Special Education. Ed. 3. Cloth Text. Houghton Mifflin College Division. Boston, MA. 2001. 521p. ISBN:0-618-11650-8, ISBN13: 978-0-618-11650-8. Dewey:371.9. LCCN:2001-131509.
Audience: **l.**

Kalyanpur, Maya & Harry, Beth **LC3969.K35 1999**
Culture in Special Education: Building Reciprocal Family-Professional Relationships. Paper Text. Paul H. Brookes Publishing Company. Baltimore, MD. 1999. 192p. ISBN:1-55766-376-9, ISBN13: 978-1-55766-376-4. Dewey:371.9/04. LCCN:99-026339.
Audience: **u,f.**

Kostelnick, Marjorie, et al. **LC4019.3.C45 2002**
Children with Special Needs: Lessons for Early Childhood Professionals. Esther Onaga, Barbara Rohde & Alice Whiren (Authors). Trade Cloth. Teachers College Press, Teachers College, Columbia University. New York, NY. 2001. 208p. ISBN:0-8077-4160-4, ISBN13: 978-0-8077-4160-3. Dewey:371.9/0472. LCCN:2001-041574.
Audience: **g,l.** *Choice, 2002.*

Lynch, Eleanor W. & Hanson, Marci J. (Editors) **HV888.5.D48 2004**
Developing Cross-Cultural Competence: A Guide for Working with Children and Their Families. Ed. 3. Trade Paper. Paul H. Brookes Publishing Company. Baltimore, MD. 2004. 608p. ISBN:1-55766-744-6, ISBN13: 978-1-55766-744-1. Dewey:362.7/086/930973. LCCN:2004-009543.
Audience: **u,f.**

Mazurek, Kas & Winzer, M. A. **LC3981.S594 2000**
Special Education in the 21st Century: Issues of Inclusion and Reform. Trade Cloth. Gallaudet University Press. Washington, DC. 2000. 272p. ISBN:1-56368-100-5, ISBN13: 978-1-56368-100-4. Dewey:371.9/0973. LCCN:00-061705.
Audience: **u,f.** *Choice, 2001.*

Nordlund, Marcie **LB1031.N64 2003**
Differentiated Instruction: Meeting the Educational Needs of All Students in Your Classroom. Trade Paper. Scarecrow Press, Inc. Lanham, MD. 2003. 112p. ISBN:0-8108-4702-7, ISBN13: 978-0-8108-4702-6. Dewey:371.39/4. LCCN:2002-044667.
Audience: **u,f.** *Choice, 2004.*

Pierangelo, Roger **LC3965.P54 2003**
The Special Educator's Book of Lists. Ed. 2. Trade Paper. John Wiley & Sons, Inc. Hoboken, NJ. 2003. 640p. J-B Ed Ser., :Book of Lists ISBN:0-7879-6593-6, ISBN13: 978-0-7879-6593-8. Dewey:371.9. LCCN:2002-155181.
Audience: **g,l,u.**

Pierangelo, Roger & Giuliani, George A. **LC4019.P53 1998**
Special Educator's Complete Guide to 109 Diagnostic Tests: How to Select and Interpret Tests, Use Results in IEPs and Remediate Specific Difficulties. Trade Paper. John Wiley & Sons, Inc. Hoboken, NJ. 1998. 352p. ISBN:0-87628-893-X, ISBN13: 978-0-87628-893-1. Dewey:371.9/04. LCCN:97-046821.
Audience: **g,u,f.**

Porter Sargent Staff (Editor) **LC4007.D5**
The Directory for Exceptional Children: A Listing of Educational and Training Facilities. Ed. 15. Trade Cloth. Porter Sargent Publishers, Inc. Boston, MA. 2004. 1104p. Handbook Ser. ISBN:0-87558-150-1, ISBN13: 978-0-87558-150-7. Dewey:371.92. LCCN:54-004975.
Audience: **g,l,u,f.**

Reynolds, Arthur J. **HV743.C5R48 2000**
Success in Early Intervention: The Chicago Child-Parent Centers. Cloth Text. University of Nebraska Press. Lincoln, NE. 2000. 266p. Child, Youth, and Family Services Ser. ISBN:0-8032-3936-X, ISBN13: 978-0-8032-3936-4. Dewey:362.7/086/940977311. LCCN:99-045985.
Audience: **u,f.** *Choice, 2001.*

Reynolds, Cecil R. & Fletcher-Janzen, Elaine (Editors) **LC3957**
Concise Encyclopedia of Special Education: A Reference for the Education of the Handicapped and Other Exceptional Children and Adults. Ed. 2. Trade Paper. John Wiley & Sons, Inc. Hoboken, NJ. 2004. 1062p. ISBN:0-471-65251-2, ISBN13: 978-0-471-65251-9. Dewey:371.9/03. LCCN:2004-014539.
Audience: **g,l,u,f.** *Choice, 2002.*

Reynolds, Cecil R. & Fletcher-Janzen, Elaine **LC4007.E53 2000**
Encyclopedia of Special Education: A Reference for the Education of the Handicapped and Other Exceptional Children and Adults. Ed. 2. Trade Cloth. John Wiley & Sons, Inc. Hoboken, NJ. 1999. 670p. ISBN:0-471-25324-3, ISBN13: 978-0-471-25324-2. Dewey:371.9/03. LCCN:99-015333.
Audience: **g,l,u,f.**

Sandall, Susan, et al. **LC4019.2**
DEC Recommended Practices: A Comprehensive Guide for Practical Application. Mary Louise Hemmeter, Barbara J. Smith & Mary E. McLean (Authors). Perfect. Sopris West Educational Services. Longmont, CO. 2004. 318p. ISBN:1-59318-423-9, ISBN13: 978-1-59318-423-0. Dewey:371.90472. LCCN:2006-271526.
Audience: **g,u,f.**

Shapiro, Arthur **LC1201**
Everybody Belongs: Changing Negative Attitudes Towards Classmates with Disabilities. Trade Paper. Garland Publishing, Inc. New York, NY. 2000. 360p. Critical Education Practice Ser. ISBN:0-8153-3960-7, ISBN13: 978-0-8153-3960-1. Dewey:306.432.
Audience: **g,u,f.**

The Alliance for Technology Access Staff **HV1569.5.A45 2004**
Computer Resources for People with Disabilities: A Guide to Assistive Technologies, Tools, and Resources for People of All Ages. Ed. 4. Stephen W. Hawking (Foreword by). Trade Cloth. Hunter House, Inc. Alameda, CA. 2004. 384p. ISBN:0-89793-433-4, ISBN13: 978-0-89793-433-6. Dewey:004/.087. LCCN:2004-002782.
Audience: **g,u.** *Choice, 2005.*

Vergason, Glenn A. & Anderegg, M. L. **LC3957.D53 1997**
Dictionary of Special Education and Rehabilitation. Ed. 4. Paper Text. Love Publishing Company. Denver, CO. 1997. 244p. ISBN:0-89108-243-3, ISBN13: 978-0-89108-243-9. Dewey:371.9/03. LCCN:95-082151.
Audience: **g,l,u,f.** *Choice, 1997.*

Types of Education > Special Education. Exceptional Children and Youth > Gifted Children and Youth

Borland, James H. (Editor) **LC3993.R48 2003**
Rethinking Gifted Education. Trade Cloth. Teachers College Press, Teachers College, Columbia University. New York, NY. 2003. 304p. Education and Psychology of the Gifted Ser. ISBN:0-8077-4304-6, ISBN13: 978-0-8077-4304-1. Dewey:371.95. LCCN:2002-042987.
Audience: **g,u.** *Choice, 2004.*

Ford, Donna Y. **LC3993.9.F66 1996**
Reversing Underachievement among Gifted Black Students: Promising Practices and Programs. Cloth Text. Teachers College Press, Teachers College, Columbia University. New York, NY. 1996. 256p. Education and Psychology of the Gifted Ser., Vol. 11 ISBN:0-8077-3536-1, ISBN13: 978-0-8077-3536-7. Dewey:371.95/6. LCCN:95-052527.
Audience: **u,f.** *Choice, 1997.*

Ford, Donna Y. & Harris, J. John **LC3993.9.F658 1999**
Multicultural Gifted Education. Paper Text. Council for Exceptional Children. Arlington, VA. 1999. 250p. Education and Psychology of the Gifted Ser. ISBN:0-8077-3850-6, ISBN13: 978-0-8077-3850-4. Dewey:371.95/0973. LCCN:98-056046.
Audience: **u,f.** *Choice, 1999.*

Gallagher, James J. & Gallagher, Shelagh A. **LC3993.9.G35 1994**
Teaching the Gifted Child. Ed. 4. Cloth Text. Allyn & Bacon, Inc. Boston, MA. 1994. 480p. ISBN:0-205-14828-X, ISBN13: 978-0-205-14828-8. Dewey:371.95. LCCN:93-036642.
Audience: **u,f.**

Heller, K. A. (Editor), et al. **LC3993.I596 2000**
International Handbook of Giftedness and Talent. Ed. 2. F. J. Mönks, R. Subotnik & R. J. Sternberg (Editors). Trade Cloth. Elsevier Science & Technology Books. Saint Louis, MO. 2000. 950p. ISBN:0-08-043796-6, ISBN13: 978-0-08-043796-5. Dewey:371.9/5. LCCN:00-035438.
Audience: **u,f.** *Choice, 2001.*

Karnes, Frances A. & Bean, Suzanne M. (Editors) **LC3993.M48 2005**
Methods and Materials for Teaching the Gifted. Ed. 2. Trade Cloth. Prufrock Press. Waco, TX. 2005. 734p. ISBN:1-59363-022-0, ISBN13: 978-1-59363-022-5. Dewey:371.95. LCCN:2004-018969.
Audience: **u,f.**

Maker, C. June & Nielson, Aleene B. **LC3993.M29 1996**
Curriculum Development and Teaching Strategies for Gifted Learners. Ed. 2. Cloth Text. PRO-ED, Inc. Austin, TX. 1996. 345p. ISBN:0-89079-631-9, ISBN13: 978-0-89079-631-3. Dewey:371.95/3. LCCN:95-009020.
Audience: **g,u.** *Choice, 1997.*

Neihart, Maureen **HQ773.5**
The Social and Emotional Development of Gifted Children: What Do We Know? Sally M. Reis, Nancy M. Robinson & Sidney M. Moon (Editors). Trade Cloth. Prufrock Press. Waco, TX. 2002. 322p. ISBN:1-882664-77-9, ISBN13: 978-1-882664-77-1. Dewey:155.455.
Audience: **u,f.**

Pendarvis, Edwina D., et al. **LC3993.9.H69 1995**
Out of Our Minds: Anti-Intellectualism and Talent Development in American Schooling. Aimee Howley & Craig B. Howley (Authors). Cloth Text. Teachers College Press, Teachers College, Columbia University. New York, NY. 1995. 288p. Education and Psychology of the Gifted Ser., Vol. 9 ISBN:0-8077-3417-9, ISBN13: 978-0-8077-3417-9. Dewey:371.95/0973. LCCN:94-044979.
Audience: **u,f.** *Choice, 1996.*

Smutny, Joan F. (Editor) **LC3993.22.D47 2003**
Designing and Developing Programs for Gifted Students. Trade Cloth. Corwin Press. Thousand Oaks, CA. 2002. 200p. ISBN:0-7619-3852-4, ISBN13: 978-0-7619-3852-1. Dewey:371.95/0973. LCCN:2002-013045.
Audience: **g,u,f.** *Choice, 2003.*

Smutny, Joan Franklin **LC3993.22.S475 2003**
Gifted Education: Promising Practices. Perfect. Phi Delta Kappa Educational Foundation. Bloomington, IN. 2003. 200p. ISBN:0-87367-845-1, ISBN13: 978-0-87367-845-2. Dewey:371.95. LCCN:2003-100181.
Audience: **u.** *Choice, 2003.*

VanTassel-Baska, Joyce & Reis, Sally M. (Editors) **LC3993.9.C89 2004**
Curriculum for Gifted and Talented Students. Trade Paper. Corwin Press. Thousand Oaks, CA. 2003. 208p. Essential Readings in Gifted Education Ser., Vol. 4 ISBN:0-7619-8874-2, ISBN13: 978-0-7619-8874-8. Dewey:371.95/3. LCCN:2003-020158.
Audience: **g,u,f.** *Choice, 2004.*

Types of Education > Special Education. Exceptional Children and Youth > Children and Youth with Disabilities (Including Learning Disabilities)

LC4704.6
The Complete Learning Disabilities Directory 2005. Trade Paper, CD-ROM. Grey House Publishing. Millerton, NY. 2005. 900p. ISBN:1-59237-092-6, ISBN13: 978-1-59237-092-4. Dewey:371.9.
Audience: **g,l,u,f.**

Accardo, Pasquale J. (Editor), et al. **RJ135.A26 2002**
Dictionary of Developmental Disabilities Terminology. Ed. 2. Barbara Y. Whitman & Shirley K. Behr (Editors). Trade Cloth, CD-ROM. Paul H. Brookes Publishing Company. Baltimore, MD. 2002. 472p. ISBN:1-55766-593-1, ISBN13: 978-1-55766-593-5. Dewey:618.92/85889/003. LCCN:2002-016091.
Audience: **g,l,u,f.** *Choice, 2003.*

Anastopoulos, Arthur D. & Shelton, Terri L. **RJ506.H9A593 2001**
Assessing Attention-Deficit/Hyperactivity Disorder. Trade Cloth. Springer. New York, NY. 2001. 348p. Topics in Social Psychiatry Ser. ISBN:0-306-46388-1, ISBN13: 978-0-306-46388-4. Dewey:618.92/8589. LCCN:00-049780.
Audience: **g,u,f.** *Choice, 2001.*

Beukelman, David R. & Mirenda, Pat **RC423.B477 2005**
Augmentative and Alternative Communication: Supporting Children and Adults with Complex Communication Needs. Ed. 3. Trade Cloth. Paul H. Brookes Publishing Company. Baltimore, MD. 2005. 672p. ISBN:1-55766-684-9, ISBN13: 978-1-55766-684-0. Dewey:616.85/503. LCCN:2005-011941.
Audience: **u,f.**

Bradley, Renee (Editor), et al. **LC4704.I34 2002**
Identification of Learning Disabilities: Research to Practice. Louis C. Danielson & Daniel P. Hallahan (Editors), Alfredo J. Artiles, Barbara D. Bateman & Virginia W. Berninger (Contribution by). Cloth over Boards. Lawrence Erlbaum Associates, Inc. Mahwah, NJ. 2002. 888p. LEA Series on Special Education and Disability ISBN:0-8058-4447-3, ISBN13: 978-0-8058-4447-4. Dewey:371.92/6. LCCN:2002-066822.
Audience: **u,f.** *Choice, 2003.*

Brown, Fredda & Snell, Martha **LC4031.I572 2006**
Instruction of Students with Severe Disabilities. Ed. 6. Cloth Text. Prentice Hall PTR. Upper Saddle River, NJ. 2005. 672p. ISBN:0-13-114335-2, ISBN13: 978-0-13-114335-7. Dewey:371.91/0973. LCCN:2005-005089.
Audience: **u,f.**

Downing, June E. **LC4028.D694 2005**
Teaching Literacy to Students with Significant Disabilities: Strategies for the K-12 Inclusive Classroom. Trade Cloth. Corwin Press. Thousand Oaks, CA. 2005. 192p. ISBN:0-7619-8878-5, ISBN13: 978-0-7619-8878-6. Dewey:371.9/0446. LCCN:2004-022984.
Audience: **u,f.** *Choice, 2005.*

Downing, June E., et al. **LC4031.D69 2002**
Including Students with Severe and Multiple Disabilities in Typical Classrooms: Practical Strategies for Teachers. Ed. 2. Joanne Eichinger & MaryAnn Demchak (Authors). Trade Cloth. Paul H. Brookes Publishing Company. Baltimore, MD. 2002. xvii, 267p. ISBN:1-55766-519-2, ISBN13: 978-1-55766-519-5. Dewey:371.9/043. LCCN:2001-035260.
Audience: **u,f.**

Hammill, Donald D. & Bartel, Nettie R. **LC4704.H35 2004**
Teaching Students with Learning and Behavior Problems: Managing Mild-To-Moderate Difficulties in Resource and Inclusive Settings. Ed. 7. Trade Cloth. PRO-ED, Inc. Austin, TX. 2004. viii, 444p. ISBN:0-89079-928-8, ISBN13: 978-0-89079-928-4. Dewey:371.9. LCCN:2003-060298.
Audience: **l,u.**

Harwell, Joan M. **LC4704.H378 2001**
Complete Learning Disabilities Handbook: Ready-to-Use Strategies and Activities for Teaching Students with Learning Disabilities. Ed. 2. Trade Paper. John Wiley & Sons, Inc. Hoboken, NJ. 2001. 400p. ISBN:0-13-032562-7, ISBN13: 978-0-13-032562-4. Dewey:371.9. LCCN:2001-028152.
Audience: **g,l,u,f.**

Koegel, Robert L. **LC4717.5.T42 1995**
Teaching Children with Autism: Strategies for Initiating Positive Interactions and Improving Learning Opportunities. Lynn K. Koegel (Editor). Trade Paper. Paul H. Brookes Publishing Company. Baltimore, MD. 1995. 272p. ISBN:1-55766-180-4, ISBN13: 978-1-55766-180-7. Dewey:371.94. LCCN:94-045943.
Audience: **u,f.**

Lerner, Janet W. **LC4704.L48 2003**
Learning Disabilities: Theories, Diagnosis, and Teaching Strategies. Ed. 9. Cloth Text. Houghton Mifflin College Division. Boston, MA. 2002. 575p. ISBN:0-618-22405-X, ISBN13: 978-0-618-22405-0. Dewey:371.92/6. LCCN:2001-133299.
Audience: **u,f.** B

Marschark, Marc, et al. **HV2437.M27 2002**
Educating Deaf Students: From Research to Practice. Harry G. Lang & John A. Albertini (Authors). Trade Cloth. Oxford University Press, Inc. New York, NY. 2001. 304p. ISBN:0-19-512139-2, ISBN13: 978-0-19-512139-1. Dewey:371.91/2. LCCN:00-140070.
Audience: **u,f.** *Choice, 2003.*

Marschark, Marc & Spencer, Patricia Elizabeth (Editors) **HV2380.O88 2003**
Oxford Handbook of Deaf Studies, Language, and Education. Cloth Text. Oxford University Press, Inc. New York, NY. 2003. 528p. ISBN:0-19-514997-1, ISBN13: 978-0-19-514997-5. Dewey:362.4/2. LCCN:2002-010496.
Audience: **u,f.** *Choice, 2003.*

Orelove, Fred P. (Editor), et al. **LC4015**
Educating Children with Multiple Disabilities: A Collaborative Approach. Ed. 4. Dick Sobsey & Roesanne K. Silberman (Editors). Paper Text. Paul H. Brookes Publishing Company. Baltimore, MD. 2004. 544p. ISBN:1-55766-710-1, ISBN13: 978-1-55766-710-6. Dewey:371.9. LCCN:2004-005333.
Audience: **u,f.**

Rafalovich, Adam **RJ506.H9R34 2004**
Framing ADHD Children: A Critical Examination of the History, Discourse, and Everyday Experience of Attention Deficit/Hyperactivity Disorder. Book, Other. Lexington Books. Lanham, MD. 2004. 208p. ISBN:0-7391-0747-X, ISBN13: 978-0-7391-0747-8. Dewey:616.85/89. LCCN:2004-003005.
Audience: **u,f.** *Choice, 2005.*

Sternberg, Robert J. & Grigorenko, Elena **LC 4704 S79 1999**
Our Labeled Children: What Every Parent and Teacher Needs to Know about Learning Disabilities. Trade Paper. Basic Books. New York, NY. 2000. 304p. ISBN:0-7382-0365-3, ISBN13: 978-0-7382-0365-2. Dewey:371.9. LCCN:99-064772.
Audience: **g,l,u.** *Choice, 2000.*

Thacker, John **LC4803.G7T43 2001**
Educating Children with Emotional and Behavioural Difficulties: Inclusive Practice in Mainstream Schools. Paper over Boards. Routledge. New York, NY. 2001. 168p. School Concerns Ser. ISBN:0-415-23050-0, ISBN13: 978-0-415-23050-6. Dewey:371.93. LCCN:2001-049063.
Audience: **u,f.** *Choice, 2003.*

Turkington, Carol & Harris, Joseph **LC4704.5.T86 2006**
The Encyclopedia of Learning Disabilities. Ed. 2. Trade Cloth. Facts On File, Inc. New York, NY. 2006. 320p. Library of Health and Living Ser. ISBN:0-8160-6399-0, ISBN13: 978-0-8160-6399-4. Dewey:371.9/03. LCCN:2005-053045.
Audience: **g,l,u,f.** *Choice, 2003.*

Wehmeyer, Michael L., et al. **LC4631.T43 2002**
Teaching Students with Mental Retardation: Providing Access to the General Curriculum. Deanna J. Sands, Earle Knowlton & Elizabeth B. Kozleski (Authors). Trade Cloth. Paul H. Brookes Publishing Company. Baltimore, MD. 2001. 352p. ISBN:1-55766-528-1, ISBN13: 978-1-55766-528-7. Dewey:371.92/8. LCCN:2001-037585.
Audience: **u,f.**

Wong, Bernice Y. L. (Editor) **LC4704.L376 2004**
Learning about Learning Disabilities. Ed. 3. Cloth Text. Elsevier Science & Technology Books. Saint Louis, MO. 2004. 656p. ISBN:0-12-762533-X, ISBN13: 978-0-12-762533-1. Dewey:371.9. LCCN:2004-008886.
Audience: **g,l,u.**

Types of Education > Adult and Continuing Education

Apps, Jerold W. **LC5225.A34A67 1994**
Leadership for the Emerging Age: Transforming Practice in Adult and Continuing Education. Trade Cloth. John Wiley & Sons, Inc. Hoboken, NJ. 1994. 254p. Jossey-Bass Higher and Adult Education Ser. ISBN:0-7879-0036-2, ISBN13: 978-0-7879-0036-6. Dewey:374/.12. LCCN:94-027619.
Audience: **u,f.** *Choice, 1995.*

Brookfield, Stephen D. **BF441 .B79 1987B**
Developing Critical Thinkers: Challenging Adults to Explore Alternative Ways of Thinking and Acting. Trade Paper. McGraw-Hill Education. Maidenhead, 1987. 312p. ISBN:0-335-15551-0, ISBN13: 978-0-335-15551-4. Dewey:153.4/2/071. LCCN:90-138171.
Audience: **u,f.**

Cervero, Ron M. & Wilson, Arthur L. **LC5225.S64P69 2001**
Power in Practice: Adult Education and the Struggle for Knowledge and Power in Society. E-Book. John Wiley & Sons, Inc. Hoboken, NJ. 2001. ISBN:0-7879-5860-3, ISBN13: 978-0-7879-5860-2. Dewey:374.
Audience: **u,f.**

Cheryl Grossman **LC5215**
ALADIN: Adult Learning Documentation and Information Network.
http://www.unesco.org/education/aladin/
United Nations Educational, Cultural and Scientific Organization (UNESCO) Institute for Education.
Audience: **g,u,f.**

Cheryl Grossman **LB1027.23**
infed.
http://www.infed.org
infed.org.
Audience: **g,u,f.**

Cheryl Grossman **LC151**
National Adult Literacy Database.
http://www.nald.ca
National Adult Literacy Database, Inc.
Audience: **g,l,u,f.**

Cheryl Grossman **LC5215**
National Center for the Study of Adult Learning and Literacy (NCSALL).
http://www.ncsall.net
National Center for the Study of Adult Learning and Literacy.
Audience: **g,l,u,f.**

Coben, Diana (Editor), et al. **QA11.P535 2000**
Perspectives on Adults Learning Mathematics: Research and Practice. John L. O'Donoghue & Gail E. FitzSimons (Editors). Trade Cloth. Springer. New York, NY. 2000. 376p. Mathematics Education Library, Vol. 21 ISBN:0-7923-6415-5, ISBN13: 978-0-7923-6415-3. Dewey:510/.71/5. LCCN:00-033084.
Audience: **u,f.**

Cross, K. Patricia **LC5219**
Adults as Learners: Increasing Participation and Facilitating Learning. Trade Paper. John Wiley & Sons, Inc. Hoboken, NJ. 1992. 336p. Classics Ser. ISBN:1-55542-445-7, ISBN13: 978-1-55542-445-9. Dewey:374. LCCN:80-026985.
Audience: **g,l.**

Crowther, Jim & Sutherland, Peter (Editors) **LC5215.L496 2006**
Lifelong Learning: Concepts and Contexts. Paper over Boards. Routledge. New York, NY. 2005. 272p. ISBN:0-415-35372-6, ISBN13: 978-0-415-35372-4. Dewey:374. LCCN:2005-011157.
Audience: **g,l,u.**

Drago-Severson, Eleanor **LC5251.D72 2004**
Becoming Adult Learners: Principles and Practices for Effective Development. Trade Cloth. Teachers College Press, Teachers College, Columbia University. New York, NY. 2004. xv, 223p.

ISBN:0-8077-4485-9, ISBN13: 978-0-8077-4485-7. Dewey:374/.012/0973. LCCN:2004-046096.
Audience: **u,f.** *Choice, 2005.*

Edwards, Richard (Editor), et al. **LC5225.A36**
Supporting Lifelong Learning: Making Policy Work. Nod Miller, Nick Small & Alan Tait (Editors). Paper over Boards. Routledge. New York, NY. 2001. 232p. ISBN:0-415-25930-4, ISBN13: 978-0-415-25930-9. Dewey:374.
Audience: **g,l,u,f.** *Choice, 2003, 2002.*

Elias, John L. & Merriam, Sharan B. **LC5219.E46 2005**
Philosophical Foundations of Adult Education. Ed. 3. Trade Cloth. Krieger Publishing Company. Melbourne, FL. 2005. 298p. ISBN:1-57524-254-0, ISBN13: 978-1-57524-254-5. Dewey:374/.001. LCCN:2004-048721.
Audience: **g,l.**

English, Leona M. (Editor) **LC5211.I56 2005**
International Encyclopedia of Adult Education. Cloth over Boards. Palgrave Macmillan. New York, NY. 2005. 384p. ISBN:1-4039-1735-3, ISBN13: 978-1-4039-1735-5. Dewey:374/.003. LCCN:2004-059171.
Audience: **g.** *Choice, 2005.*

Findsen, Brian **LC5225.L42F56 2004**
Learning Later. Trade Cloth. Krieger Publishing Company. Melbourne, FL. 2004. 184p. ISBN:1-57524-218-4, ISBN13: 978-1-57524-218-7. Dewey:374. LCCN:2004-043846.
Audience: **l,u.** *Choice, 2005.*

Galbraith, Michael W. (Editor) **LC5225.L42A35 2004**
Adult Learning Methods: A Guide for Effective Instruction. Ed. 3. Cloth Text. Krieger Publishing Company. Melbourne, FL. 2004. 498p. ISBN:1-57524-232-X, ISBN13: 978-1-57524-232-3. Dewey:374/.1102. LCCN:2003-054669.
Audience: **g,l,f.**

Harrison, Roger (Editor) **LC5225.L42S86 2002**
Supporting Lifelong Learning: Perspective on Learning, Vol. 1. Paper over Boards. Routledge. New York, NY. 2001. 232p. ISBN:0-415-25926-6, ISBN13: 978-0-415-25926-2. Dewey:374. LCCN:2001-041848.
Audience: **g,l,u,f.** *Choice, 2002.*

Herman, Lee & Mandell, Alan **LC5225.M45H47 2004**
From Teaching to Mentoring in Adult Education: The Integration of Principle and Practice. Paper over Boards. Taylor & Francis Group. Philadelphia, PA. 2003. 240p. ISBN:0-415-26617-3, ISBN13: 978-0-415-26617-8. Dewey:374. LCCN:2003-013095.
Audience: **l,u,f.**

Holton, Elwood F. III, et al. **LC5225.L42K56 2005**
Adult Learner: The Definitive Classic in Adult Education and Human Resource Development. Ed. 6. Malcolm S. Knowles & Richard A. Swanson (Authors). Paper Text. Elsevier Science & Technology Books. Saint Louis, MO. 2005. 390p. ISBN:0-7506-7837-2, ISBN13: 978-0-7506-7837-7. Dewey:374. LCCN:2004-024356.
Audience: **g,l.**

Houle, Cyril O. **LC5251.H69 1992**
The Literature of Adult Education: A Bibliographic Essay. Trade Cloth. John Wiley & Sons, Inc. Hoboken, NJ. 1992. 441p. Higher and Adult Education Ser. ISBN:1-55542-470-8, ISBN13: 978-1-55542-470-1. Dewey:016.374/973. LCCN:92-012659.
Audience: **u,f.** *Choice, 1993.*

Jarvis, Peter **LC5215.J37 2004**
Adult Education and Lifelong Learning: Theory and Practice. Ed. 3. Paper over Boards. Taylor & Francis Group. Philadelphia, PA. 2004. 392p. ISBN:0-415-31492-5, ISBN13: 978-0-415-31492-3. Dewey:374. LCCN:2003-027165.
Audience: **u,f.**

Jarvis, Peter **LC5211**
International Dictionary of Adult and Continuing Education. Ed. 2. Trade Paper. Kogan Page, Ltd. London, 2002. 208p. ISBN:0-7494-3736-7, ISBN13: 978-0-7494-3736-7. Dewey:374/.003. LCCN:2003-265740.
Audience: **g,l,u,f.**

King, Kathleen P. **LC5225.L42K54 2005**
Bringing Transformative Learning to Life. Cloth Text. Krieger Publishing Company. Melbourne, FL. 2005. 224p. ISBN:1-57524-253-2, ISBN13: 978-1-57524-253-8. Dewey:374. LCCN:2004-042326.
Audience: **u,f.** *Choice, 2005.*

Knowles, Malcolm S. **LC5251**
A History of the Adult Education Movement in the United States. Trade Cloth. Krieger Publishing Company. Melbourne, FL. 1994. 442p. ISBN:0-89464-872-1, ISBN13: 978-0-89464-872-4. Dewey:374.973.
Audience: **g,l.**

Knox, Alan B. **LC5225.A75K66 2002**
Evaluation for Continuing Education: A Comprehensive Guide to Success. Trade Cloth. John Wiley & Sons, Inc. Hoboken, NJ. 2002. 352p. Jossey-Bass Higher and Adult Education Ser. ISBN:0-7879-6143-4, ISBN13: 978-0-7879-6143-5. Dewey:374/.12. LCCN:2002-001867.
Audience: **u,f.**

Merriam, Sharan B. & Caffarella, Rosemary S. **LC5225.L42M47 1999**
Learning in Adulthood: A Comprehensive Guide. Ed. 2. Trade Cloth. John Wiley & Sons, Inc. Hoboken, NJ. 1998. 528p. Education Ser. ISBN:0-7879-1043-0, ISBN13: 978-0-7879-1043-3. Dewey:374. LCCN:98-025498.
Audience: **g,l.** *Choice, 1991.*

Mezirow, Jack & Jack Meizirow and Associates Staff **LB1059.M49 2000**
Learning as Transformation: Critical Perspectives on a Theory in Progress. Trade Cloth. John Wiley & Sons, Inc. Hoboken, NJ. 2000. 416p. Higher and Adult Education Ser. ISBN:0-7879-4845-4, ISBN13: 978-0-7879-4845-0. Dewey:370.15/23. LCCN:00-009158.
Audience: **u,f.** *Choice, 2001.*

Reeve, Fiona (Editor), et al. **LC5225.L42S86 2002**
Supporting Lifelong Learning: Organising Learning. Marion Cartwright & Richard Edwards (Editors). Paper over Boards. Routledge. New York, NY. 2001. 232p. ISBN:0-415-25928-2, ISBN13: 978-0-415-25928-6. Dewey:374. LCCN:2001-041848.
Audience: **g,l,u,f.** *Choice, 2003, 2002.*

Smith, M. Cecil & Pourchot, Thomas (Editors) **LC5225.P78A48 1998**
Adult Learning and Development: Perspectives from Educational Psychology. Trade Paper. Lawrence Erlbaum Associates, Inc. Mahwah, NJ. 1998. 288p. The Educational Psychology Ser. ISBN:0-8058-2524-X, ISBN13: 978-0-8058-2524-4. Dewey:374/.001/9. LCCN:97-030926.
Audience: **l,u,f.** *Choice, 1998.*

Stein, David, et al. **LC5225.L42**
The New Update on Adult Learning Theory: New Directions for Adult and Continuing Education. Susan Imel & Phillip Owenby (Authors), Sharan B. Merriam (Editor). Trade Paper. John Wiley & Sons, Inc. Hoboken, NJ. 2001. 112p. J-B ACE Single Issue Adult and Continuing Education Ser. ISBN:0-7879-5773-9, ISBN13: 978-0-7879-5773-5. Dewey:374.
Audience: **g,l.**

Tapia, John E. **LC6551.T27 1997**
Circuit Chautauqua: From Rural Education to Popular Entertainment in Early Twentieth Century America. Robert A. McCown (Foreword by). Cloth Text. McFarland & Company, Incorporated Publishers. Jefferson, NC. 1997. 240p. ISBN:0-7864-0213-X, ISBN13: 978-0-7864-0213-7. Dewey:791.1/0973. LCCN:96-41623.
Audience: **u,f.**

Taylor, Kathleen, et al. **LC5225.L42T39 2000**
Developing Adult Learners: Strategies for Teachers and Trainers. Catherine Marienau & Morris Fiddler (Authors). Trade Cloth. John Wiley & Sons, Inc. Hoboken, NJ. 2000. 416p. Higher and Adult Education Ser. ISBN:0-7879-4573-0, ISBN13: 978-0-7879-4573-2. Dewey:374/.13. LCCN:00-008478.
Audience: **l,u.** *Choice, 2001.*

Tight, Malcolm **LC5215.T57 2003**
Key Concepts in Adult Education and Training. Ed. 2. Trade Paper. Routledge. New York, NY. 2003. 208p. ISBN:0-415-27579-2, ISBN13: 978-0-415-27579-8. Dewey:374/.1. LCCN:2002-031664.
Audience: **g,l.** *Choice, 1997.*

Vella, Jane **LB1025.3**
Dialogue Education at Work: A Case Book. Trade Cloth. John Wiley & Sons, Inc. Hoboken, NJ. 2003. 368p. Jossey-Bass Higher and Adult Education Ser. ISBN:0-7879-6473-5, ISBN13: 978-0-7879-6473-3. Dewey:370.11/5. LCCN:2003-012215.
Audience: **l,u,f.** *Choice, 2004.*

Vella, Jane Kathryn **LC5225.L42V45 2002**
Learning to Listen, Learning to Teach: The Power of Dialogue in Educating Adults. Ed. 2. Trade Paper. John Wiley & Sons, Inc. Hoboken, NJ. 2002. 288p. Jossey-Bass Higher and Adult Education Ser. ISBN:0-7879-5967-7, ISBN13: 978-0-7879-5967-8. Dewey:374. LCCN:2002-003807.
Audience: **u,f.**

Types of Education > Distance Education

Berge, Zane L. & Clark, Thomas A. **LC5803.C65V58 2005**
Virtual Schools: Planning for Success. Trade Cloth. Teachers College Press, Teachers College, Columbia University. New York, NY. 2005. 256p. ISBN:0-8077-4572-3, ISBN13: 978-0-8077-4572-4. Dewey:371.358. LCCN:2004-059826.
Audience: **g,f.** *Choice, 2005.*

Birnbaum, Barry W. **LC5800.B57 2001**
Foundations and Practices in the Use of Distance Education. Trade Cloth. Edwin Mellen Press, The. Lewiston, NY. 2002. 168p. Studies in Education, Vol. 66 ISBN:0-7734-7196-0, ISBN13: 978-0-7734-7196-2. Dewey:378.1/75. LCCN:2001-051188.
Audience: **u,f.**

Clarke, Steve & Coakes, Elayne **HD58.82.E53 2006**
ⓔ Encyclopedia of Support Services and Distance Education. Mary Hricko (Editor). E-Book. Idea Group Publishing. Hershey, PA. 2005. 600p. ISBN:1-59140-558-0, ISBN13: 978-1-59140-558-0. Dewey:658.4/038. LCCN:2005-013816.
Audience: **g,l,u,f.**

Discenza, Richard (Editor), et al. **LC5800.D47 2001**
The Design and Management of Effective Distance Learning Programs. Caroline Howard & Karen Schenk (Editors). Trade Cloth. Idea Group Publishing. Hershey, PA. 2002. 312p. ISBN:1-930708-20-3, ISBN13: 978-1-930708-20-4. Dewey:371.3/5. LCCN:2001-039269.
Audience: **g,f.**

DiStefano, Anna (Editor), et al. **LC5211.E52 2004**
Encyclopedia of Distributed Learning. Kjell Erik Rudestam & Robert J. Silverman (Editors). Trade Cloth. SAGE Publications, Inc. Thousand Oaks, CA. 2003. 576p. ISBN:0-7619-2451-5, ISBN13: 978-0-7619-2451-7. Dewey:374/.003. LCCN:2003-015573.
Audience: **g.** *Choice, 2004.*

Driscoll, Margaret & Carliner, Saul **HF5549.5.T7D73 2005**
Advanced Web-Based Training Strategies: Unlocking Instructionally Sound Online Learning. Trade Cloth. John Wiley & Sons, Inc. Hoboken, NJ. 2005. 500p. ISBN:0-7879-6979-6, ISBN13: 978-0-7879-6979-0. Dewey:658.3/124/02854678. LCCN:2004-025825.
Audience: **u,f.**

Horton, William K. **LB1044.87.H69 2001**
Evaluating E-Learning. Trade Paper. American Society for Training & Development. Alexandria, VA. 2001. 136p. ISBN:1-56286-300-2, ISBN13: 978-1-56286-300-5. Dewey:371.3344678. LCCN:2001-117681.
Audience: **u,f.**

Howard, Caroline (Editor) **LC5800**
Encyclopedia of Distance Learning, Vol. 1. Trade Cloth. Idea Group Publishing. Hershey, PA. 2005. 2,500p. ISBN:1-59140-555-6, ISBN13: 978-1-59140-555-9. Dewey:371.35/03. LCCN:2005-004507.
Audience: **g,l,u,f.** *Choice, 2005.*

Johnson, Judith L. **LC5805.J64 2003**
Distance Education: The Complete Guide to Design, Delivery, and Improvement. Trade Cloth. Teachers College Press, Teachers College, Columbia University. New York, NY. 2003. x, 230p. ISBN:0-8077-4374-7, ISBN13: 978-0-8077-4374-4. Dewey:371.3/5/0973. LCCN:2003-044045.
Audience: **g,u,f.**

Khan, Badrul Huda **LC5803.C65K53 2005**
Managing E-Learning: Design, Delivery, Implementation, and Evaluation. Trade Cloth. Idea Group Publishing. Hershey, PA. 2005. 250p. ISBN:1-59140-634-X, ISBN13: 978-1-59140-634-1. Dewey:371.3/58. LCCN:2005-004526.
Audience: **u,f.**

Maeroff, Gene I. **LC5803.C65M34 2003**
A Classroom of One: How Online Learning Is Changing Our Schools and Colleges. Cloth over Boards. Palgrave Macmillan. New York, NY. 2003. 320p. ISBN:1-4039-6085-2, ISBN13: 978-1-4039-6085-6. Dewey:371.3/5. LCCN:2002-041042.
Audience: **g,l,u,f.** *Choice, 2004.*

McPherson, Maggie & Nunes, Miguel Baptista **LC5800**
Developing Innovation in Online Learning: An Action Research Framework. Trade Cloth. Kogan Page, Ltd. London, 2003. 224p. Open and Flexible Learning Ser. ISBN:0-7494-4035-X, ISBN13: 978-0-7494-4035-0. Dewey:371.33/4.
Audience: **g,l,u,f.**

Melton, Reginald F. **LC5800 .M458 2002**
Planning and Developing Open and Distance Learning: A Framework for Quality. Paper over Boards. Routledge. New York, NY. 2002. 240p. Studies in Distance Education ISBN:0-415-25480-9, ISBN13: 978-0-415-25480-9. Dewey:371.35.
Audience: **u,f.**

Moore, Michael G. & Anderson, William (Editors) **LC5800.H36 2003**
Handbook of Distance Education. Cloth over Boards. Lawrence Erlbaum Associates, Inc. Mahwah, NJ. 2003. 896p. ISBN:0-8058-3924-0, ISBN13: 978-0-8058-3924-1. Dewey:371.3/58. LCCN:2002-152189.
Audience: **g,l,u,f.** *Choice, 2003.*

O'Neil, Harold F. **LC5800.W54 2005**
What Works in Distance Learning: Guidelines. Trade Cloth. Information Age Publishing, Inc. Greenwich, CT. 2005. v, 144p. ISBN:1-59311-261-0, ISBN13: 978-1-59311-261-5. Dewey:371.35. LCCN:2004-025837.
Audience: **u,f.**

Palloff, Rena M. **LC5803.C65 P35**
Virtual Student: A Profile and Guide to Working with Online Learners. Library Binding. Sagebrush Education Resources. Caledonia, MN. 2003. ISBN:0-613-91247-0, ISBN13: 978-0-613-91247-1. Dewey:371.3/5.
Audience: **f.**

Reisman, Sorel (Editor), et al. **LC5803.C65E54 2003**
Electronic Learning Communities: Issues and Practices. John G. Flores & Denzil Edge (Editors). Trade Cloth. Information Age Publishing, Inc. Greenwich, CT. 2003. xix, 565p. ISBN:1-931576-97-1, ISBN13: 978-1-931576-97-0. Dewey:371.3/58. LCCN:2003-000183.
Audience: **u,f.**

Zucker, Andrew A. & Kozma, Robert **LC5803.C65.Z83 2003**
The Virtual High School: Teaching Generation V. Cloth Text. Teachers College Press, Teachers College, Columbia University. New York, NY. 2003. 176p. ISBN:0-8077-4287-2, ISBN13: 978-0-8077-4287-7. Dewey:373.133/4. LCCN:2002-028978.
Audience: **g,l,u,f.**

Education (General)

L11
▭ ERIC (Education Resources Information Center). http://eric.ed.gov
Audience: **g,l,u,f.**

L11
▭ U.S. Department of Education. http://www.ed.gov
Audience: **g,l,u,f.**

Collins, John W. & O'Brien, Nancy Patricia (Editors) **LB15**
The Greenwood Dictionary of Education. Greenwood. 2003. ISBN:0-89774-860-3, ISBN13: 978-0-89774-860-5.
Audience: **g.**

Guthrie, James W. (Editor) **LB15.E47 2003**
The Encyclopedia of Education. Ed. 2. Gale. 2003. ISBN:0-02-865596-6, ISBN13: 978-0-02-865596-3.
Audience: **l,u,f.**

Hayes, William **LC89**
Are We Still a Nation at Risk Two Decades Later? Scarecrow. 2005. ISBN:1-57886-179-9, ISBN13: 978-1-57886-179-8.
Audience: **g,l,u,f.**

Husén, Torsten & Postlethwaite, T. Neville (Editors) **LB15.I569 1994**
The International Encyclopedia of Education, Set. Ed. 2. Trade Cloth. Elsevier Science & Technology Books. Saint Louis, MO. 1994. 7740p. ISBN:0-08-041046-4, ISBN13: 978-0-08-041046-3. Dewey:370/.3/21. LCCN:94-003059.
Audience: **g,l,u,f.** B *Choice, 1994, 1986.*

National Center for Education Statistics **L112**
▭ Condition of Education.
http://nces.ed.gov/pubsearch/pubsinfo.asp?pubid=2005094
U.S. Dept. of Education. Institute for Education Sciences.
Audience: **g,l,u,f.**

National Center for Education Statistics **L11**
▭ Digest of Education Statistics.
http://purl.access.gpo.gov/GPO/LPS6878
Washington, D.C.: U.S. Dept. of Education. Institute of Education Sciences.
Audience: **g.**

National Center for Education Statistics **LA209.2**
▭ National Center for Education Statistics.
http://nces.ed.gov/
Washington, D.C.: U.S. Dept. of Education. Institute of Education Sciences.
Audience: **g.**

National Commission on Excellence in Education **LA217.U49 1984**
A Nation at Risk: The Full Account. U.S.A. Research, Inc. 1994. ISBN:0-917191-02-1, ISBN13: 978-0-917191-02-2.
Audience: **g,l,u,f.**

U.S. Department of Education **L901**
Education Resource Organizations Directory (EROD). http://bcol02.ed.gov/Programs/EROD/
Audience: **g.**

Ulich, Robert (Editor) **LB41**
Three Thousand Years of Educational Wisdom: Selections from Great Documents. iUniverse, Inc. 1999. ISBN:1-58348-537-6, ISBN13: 978-1-58348-537-8.
Audience: **l.**

United States. National Commission on Excellence in Education **LA217**
A Nation at Risk: the Imperative for Educational Reform: a Report to the Nation and the Secretary of Education, United States Department of Education.
http://www.ed.gov/pubs/NatAtRisk/title.html
Audience: **g.**

Philosophy of Education

LB5.N25
National Society for the Study of Education (NSSE). http://www.nsse-chicago.org/
Audience: **u,f.**

Blake, Nigel (Editor) **LB14.7.B57 2002**
The Blackwell Guide to the Philosophy of Education. Trade Paper. Blackwell Publishing, Inc. Malden, MA. 2002. 432p. Blackwell Philosophy Guides Ser., Vol. 9 ISBN:0-631-22119-0, ISBN13: 978-0-631-22119-7. Dewey:370/.1. LCCN:2002-066430.
Audience: **u,f.** *Choice, 2003.*

Blake, Nigel (Editor) **LB1.7**
The Blackwell Guide to the Philosophy of Education. Blackwell. 2003. Blackwell Philosophy Guides ISBN:0-631-22119-0, ISBN13: 978-0-631-22119-7.
Audience: **g,l,u,f.**

Burns, Hobert Warren **LB675.N45C8**
Philosophy of Education: Essays and Commentaries. Paper Text. Textbook Publishers. Temecula, CA. 2003. 442p. ISBN:0-7581-4700-7, ISBN13: 978-0-7581-4700-4. Dewey:282/.092.
Audience: **u,f.**

Carr, Wilfred (editor) **LB1.7**
Routledgefalmer Reader in the Philosophy of Education. Ed. 3. Taylor and Francis. 2005. Readers in Education ISBN:0-415-34571-5, ISBN13: 978-0-415-34571-2.
Audience: **g,l.**

Chambliss, J. J. (Editor) **LB17.P485 1996**
Philosophy of Education: An Encyclopedia. Cloth Text. Garland Publishing, Inc. New York, NY. 1996. 736p. ISBN:0-8153-1177-X, ISBN13: 978-0-8153-1177-5. Dewey:370/.1. LCCN:96-018393.
Audience: **l,u,f.** *Choice, 1997.*

Gallagher, Shaun **LB14.7**
Hermeneutics and Education. Paper Text. State University of New York Press. Albany, NY. 1992. 402p. SUNY Series in Contemporary Continental Philosophy ISBN:0-7914-1176-1, ISBN13: 978-0-7914-1176-6. Dewey:370/.1. LCCN:91-037120.
Audience: **u,f.** *Choice, 1993.*

Hirst, Paul H. & White, Patricia **LB7.P5432 1998**
The Philosophy of Education: Major Themes in the Analytic Tradition. Paper over Boards. Routledge. New York, NY. 1998. 1712p. Major Writings in Education Ser. ISBN:0-415-12944-3, ISBN13: 978-0-415-12944-2. Dewey:370/.1. LCCN:97-030748.
Audience: **u,f.**

McDonough, Kevin & Feinberg, Walter (Editors) **LC1091.E3843 2003**
Education and Citizenship in Liberal-Democratic Societies: Teaching for Cosmopolitan Values and Collective Identities. Oxford University Press. 2003. ISBN:0-19-925366-8, ISBN13: 978-0-19-925366-1.
Audience: **u,f.**

Perkinson, Henry J. **LA205.P45 1987**
Two Hundred Years of American Educational Thought. Trade Paper. University Press of America, Inc. Lanham, MD. 1987. 342p. ISBN:0-8191-6124-1, ISBN13: 978-0-8191-6124-6. Dewey:370/.973. LCCN:86-033960.
Audience: **u,f.** E

Postman, Neil **CB430**
Building a Bridge to 18th Century. Trade Paper. Knopf Publishing Group. New York, NY. 2000. 224p. ISBN:0-375-70127-3, ISBN13: 978-0-375-70127-6. Dewey:909.825.
Audience: **u,f.**

Postman, Neil **LA217.2**
The End of Education: Redefining the Value of Schools. Trade Paper. Alfred A. Knopf Inc. New York, NY. 1996. 224p. Vintage Ser. ISBN:0-679-75031-2, ISBN13: 978-0-679-75031-4. Dewey:370/.973.
Audience: **u,f.** *Choice, 1996.*

Postman, Neil **LA217.2**
Teaching As a Subversive Activity. Trade Paper. Dell Publishing. New York, NY. 1971. ISBN:0-385-29009-8, ISBN13: 978-0-385-29009-8. Dewey:370/.973.
Audience: **g,l,u,f.**

Power, Edward J. **LB14.7.P68 1995**
Educational Philosophy: A History from the Ancient World to Modern America. Cloth Text. Garland Publishing, Inc. New York, NY. 1995. 256p. Garland Reference Library of Social Science, Vol. 3 ISBN:0-8153-1971-1, ISBN13: 978-0-8153-1971-9. Dewey:370/.1/09. LCCN:95-024265.
Audience: **u,f.** *Choice, 1996.*

Reed, Ronald F. **LB14.7**
Philosophical Documents in Education. Paper Text. Addison-Wesley Longman, Inc. Boston, MA. 1995. ISBN:0-8013-1725-8, ISBN13: 978-0-8013-1725-5. Dewey:370/.1.
Audience: **u,f.**

Rorty, Amelie **LB41.P572 1998**
Philosophers on Education. Paper over Boards. Routledge. New York, NY. 1998. 496p. ISBN:0-415-19130-0, ISBN13: 978-0-415-19130-2. Dewey:370/.1. LCCN:98-004865.
Audience: **u.**

Winch, Christopher & Gingell, John **LB15.W54 1999**
Key Concepts in the Philosophy of Education. Paper over Boards. Routledge. New York, NY. 1999. 296p. Key Guides ISBN:0-415-17303-5, ISBN13: 978-0-415-17303-2. Dewey:370.1. LCCN:00-267717.
Audience: **l.** *Choice, 2000.*

History of Education

Warren, Donald R. **LB2807**
To Enforce Education: A History of the Founding Years of the United States Office of Education. Trade Cloth. Greenwood Publishing Group, Inc. Portsmouth, NH. 1985. 239p. ISBN:0-313-25213-0, ISBN13: 978-0-313-25213-6. Dewey:379.73. LCCN:73-008209.
Audience: **l,u,f.** BCL3

History of Education > General Education by Period, Level, and Type (Public or private)

LT6
[Web] 19th Century Schoolbooks. http://digital.library.pitt.edu/nietz/
Audience: **l,u,f.**

LA212.S353
[CD/DVD-ROM] School: The Story of American Public Education Series. Video, VHS Format. Films Media Group. Princeton, NJ. 2001. Dewey:370/.973.
Audience: **g,l,u,f.**

Adler, Mortimer J. **LA210**
Paideia Proposal. Reinforced. Simon & Schuster. New York, NY. 1998. 96p. ISBN:0-684-84188-6, ISBN13: 978-0-684-84188-5. Dewey:370.973.
Audience: **g.**

Angus, David & Mirel, Jeffery **LA222.A543 1999**
The Failed Promise of the American High School, 1890-1995. Cloth Text. Teachers College Press, Teachers College, Columbia University. New York, NY. 1999. 272p. ISBN:0-8077-3843-3, ISBN13: 978-0-8077-3843-6. Dewey:373.73. LCCN:99-017345.
Audience: **u,f.** *Choice, 1999.*

Astuto, Terry A., et al. **LA217.2.R68 1994**
Roots of Reform: Challenging the Assumptions That Control Change in Education. David L. Clark, Anne-Marie Read & Kathleen McGree (Authors). Trade Cloth. Phi Delta Kappa Educational Foundation. Bloomington, IN. 1994. 108p. ISBN:0-87367-464-2, ISBN13: 978-0-87367-464-5. Dewey:370/.973. LCCN:94-065000.
Audience: **u,f.**

Avrich, Paul **LB1029.F7**
The Modern School Movement: Anarchism and Education in the United States. Trade Paper. AK Press. Edinburgh, 2005. 400p. ISBN:1-904859-09-7, ISBN13: 978-1-904859-09-3. Dewey:371.040973. LCCN:2004-110808.
Audience: **u,f.** BCL3

Bailyn, Bernard **LA0206.B3**
Education in the Forming of American Society: Needs and Opportunities for Study. Trade Paper. Books on Demand. Ann Arbor, MI. 159p. Needs and Opportunities for Study Ser. ISBN:0-7837-0280-9, ISBN13: 978-0-7837-0280-3. Dewey:370.973. LCCN:60-051488.
Audience: **u,f.** BCL3

Barth, Roland S. **LB1060**
Learning by Heart. Trade Paper. John Wiley & Sons, Inc. Hoboken, NJ. 2004. 272p. ISBN:0-7879-7223-1, ISBN13: 978-0-7879-7223-3. Dewey:371.102.
Audience: **g.** *Choice, 2001.*

Barth, Roland S. **LA217.2**
Improving Schools from Within: Teachers, Parents, and Principals Can Make the Difference. Theodore R. Sizer (Foreword by). Trade Paper. John Wiley & Sons, Inc. Hoboken, NJ. 1991. 224p. Education-Higher Education Ser. ISBN:1-55542-368-X, ISBN13: 978-1-55542-368-1. Dewey:371/.01/0973. LCCN:89-043460.
Audience: **g.** *Choice, 1990.*

Bereday, George Z. & Volpicelli, Luigi (Editors) **LA209.2 .B45 1977**
Public Education in America: A New Interpretation of Purpose and Practice. Trade Cloth. Greenwood Publishing Group, Inc. Portsmouth, NH. 1977. 212p. ISBN:0-8371-9702-3, ISBN13: 978-0-8371-9702-9. Dewey:370/.973. LCCN:77-023510.
Audience: **u,f.**

Berliner, David C. & Biddle, Bruce J. **LA217.2.B46 1995**
The Manufactured Crisis: Myths, Fraud and the Attack on America's Public Schools. Trade Cloth. Addison-Wesley Longman, Inc. Boston, MA. 1995. 432p. ISBN:0-201-40957-7, ISBN13: 978-0-201-40957-4. Dewey:371/.01/0973. LCCN:95-003271.
Audience: **g.**

Bowen, James **LA11**
History of Western Education—Civilization of Europe: 6th to 16th Century, Vol. 2. Paper over Boards. Routledge. New York, NY. 2003. 528p. ISBN:0-415-30293-5, ISBN13: 978-0-415-30293-7. Dewey:370.9/1821.
Audience: **u,f.**

Bowen, James **LA11**
History of Western Education—The Ancient World: Orient and Mediterranean 2000 B. C.-A. D. 1054, Vol. 1. Paper over Boards. Routledge. New York, NY. 2003. 424p. ISBN:0-415-30292-7, ISBN13: 978-0-415-30292-0. Dewey:370.9/1821.
Audience: **u,f.**

Bowen, James **LA11**
History of Western Education—The Modern West: Europe and the New World, Vol. 3. Paper over Boards. Routledge. New York, NY. 2003. 664p. ISBN:0-415-30294-3, ISBN13: 978-0-415-30294-4. Dewey:370.9/1821.
Audience: **u,f.**

Boyd, William **LA13.B48 1975**
The History of Western Education. Ed. 11. Trade Cloth. A & C Black. London, 1975. xii, 517p. ISBN:0-7136-1600-8, ISBN13: 978-0-7136-1600-2. Dewey:370.94. LCCN:76-357730.
Audience: **u,f.**

Bracey, Gerald W. **LA217.2.B73 2004**
Setting the Record Straight: Responses to Misconceptions about Public Education in the United States. Ed. 2. Trade Paper. Heinemann. Portsmouth, NH. 2004. 232p. ISBN:0-325-00594-X, ISBN13: 978-0-325-00594-2. Dewey:371.01/0973. LCCN:2004-010979.
Audience: **u,f.** *Choice, 1997.*

Burg, David F. **LA186.B87 1998**
Encyclopedia of Student and Youth Movements. Trade Cloth. Facts On File, Inc. New York, NY. 1998. 304p. ISBN:0-8160-3375-7, ISBN13: 978-0-8160-3375-1. Dewey:371.8/1. LCCN:97-032408.
Audience: **g.** *Choice, 1999.*

Callahan, Raymond E. **PR6011.O58Z65**
Education and the Cult of Efficiency: A Study of the Social Forces That Have Shaped the Administration of the Public Schools. Paper Text. Textbook Publishers. Temecula, CA. 2003. 273p. ISBN:0-7581-2426-0, ISBN13: 978-0-7581-2426-5. Dewey:823.912.
Audience: **u,f.**

Carnoy, Martin **LA212.C34**
Education As Cultural Imperialism. Trade Cloth. David McKay Company, Inc. New York, NY. 1974. 378p. ISBN:0-679-30246-8, ISBN13: 978-0-679-30246-9. Dewey:370.19/3/0903. LCCN:73-093964.
Audience: **u.** B

Clinchy, Evans **LA217.2.T73 1997**
Transforming Public Education: A New Course for America's Future. Cloth Text. Teachers College Press, Teachers College, Columbia University. New York, NY. 1996. 224p. ISBN:0-8077-3569-8, ISBN13: 978-0-8077-3569-5. Dewey:371/.01/0973. LCCN:96-003467.
Audience: **u,f.**

Compayre, Gabriel **LA177.C7**
Abelard and the Origin and Early History of the Universities. Trade Cloth. A M S Press, Inc. New York, NY. 1969. BCL Ser., II ISBN:0-404-01639-1, ISBN13: 978-0-404-01639-5. Dewey:189. LCCN:75-090094.
Audience: **u,f.**

Conant, James B. **LA209**
Education in a Divided World: The Function of the Public Schools in Our Unique Society. Trade Cloth. Greenwood Publishing Group, Inc. Portsmouth, NH. 1970. 249p. ISBN:0-8371-2548-0, ISBN13: 978-0-8371-2548-0. Dewey:370/.973. LCCN:78-094580.
Audience: **u,f.** B

Cookson, Peter W. Jr. (Editor), et al. **LA135**
International Handbook of Educational Reform. Alan R. Sadovnik & Susan F. Semel (Editors). Cloth Text. Greenwood Publishing Group, Inc. Portsmouth, NH. 1992. 640p. ISBN:0-313-27277-8, ISBN13: 978-0-313-27277-6. Dewey:370. LCCN:91-030586.
Audience: **u.** *Choice, 1993.*

Coombs, Philip H. **LA132.C64 1985**
The World Crisis in Education: A View from the Eighties. Cloth Text. Oxford University Press, Inc. New York, NY. 1985. 368p. ISBN:0-19-503502-X, ISBN13: 978-0-19-503502-5. Dewey:370. LCCN:84-005713.
Audience: **u,f.** B

Cremin, Lawrence **LA0210.C67**
The Genius of American Education. Trade Paper. Books on Demand. Ann Arbor, MI. 132p. Horace Mann Lectures, 1965 ISBN:0-608-12760-4, ISBN13: 978-0-608-12760-6. Dewey:370.110973. LCCN:65-028146.
Audience: **u,f.**

Cuban, Larry **LA217.2**
How Teachers Taught: Constancy and Change in American Classrooms, 1890-1990. Ed. 2. Trade Cloth. Teachers College Press, Teachers College, Columbia University. New York, NY. 1993. 700p. Research on Teaching Ser. ISBN:0-8077-3227-3, ISBN13: 978-0-8077-3227-4. Dewey:370/.973. LCCN:92-031867.
Audience: **u,f.** B

Cuban, Larry **LA217.2.C83 2003**
Why Is It So Hard to Get Good Schools? Cloth Text. Teachers College Press, Teachers College, Columbia University. New York, NY. 2002. 112p. ISBN:0-8077-4295-3, ISBN13: 978-0-8077-4295-2. Dewey:371.01/0973. LCCN:2002-027126.
Audience: **g,l,u,f.**

Cuban, Larry & Shipps, Dorothy (Editors) **LA212.R42 2000**
Reconstructing the Common Good in Education: Coping with Intractable American Dilemmas. Cloth Text. Stanford University Press. Palo Alto, CA. 2000. xvi, 283p. ISBN:0-8047-3862-9, ISBN13: 978-0-8047-3862-0. Dewey:370/.973. LCCN:00-027258.
Audience: **g.** *Choice, 2001.*

Cuban, Larry & Tyack, David B. **LA216.T92 1995**
Tinkering Toward Utopia: A Century of Public School Reform. Trade Cloth. Harvard University Press. Cambridge, MA. 1995. 192p. ISBN:0-674-89282-8, ISBN13: 978-0-674-89282-8. Dewey:371/.01/097309. LCCN:94-047545.
Audience: **g,l,u,f.** *Choice, 1996.*

Cubberley, Ellwood P. (Editor) **LA205.C82 1970**
Readings in Public Education in the United States: A Collection of Sources and Readings to Illustrate the History of Educational Practice and Progress in the United States. Library Binding. Greenwood Publishing Group, Inc. Portsmouth, NH. 1986. xviii, 534p. ISBN:0-8371-3912-0, ISBN13: 978-0-8371-3912-8. Dewey:370/.973. LCCN:79-104258.
Audience: **u,f.**

Cubberley, Ellwood Patterson **LA0205.C8**
Public Education in the United States. Trade Paper. Books on Demand. Ann Arbor, MI. 554p. ISBN:0-598-82327-1, ISBN13: 978-0-598-82327-4. Dewey:370.973. LCCN:34-002426.
Audience: **u,f.**

De Ridder-Symoens, Hilde (Editor) **LA177 .U53 1991**
A History of the University in Europe: Universities in the Middle Ages. Trade Cloth. Cambridge University Press. New York, NY. 1991. 534p. A History of the University in Europe Ser. ISBN:0-521-36105-2, ISBN13: 978-0-521-36105-7. Dewey:378.4/09/02. LCCN:90-033558.
Audience: **u,f.**

De Ridder-Symoens, Hilde (Editor) **LA179 .U55 1995**
A History of the University in Europe: Universities in Early Modern Europe (1500-1800). Walter Rüegg (Contribution by). Trade Paper. Cambridge University Press. New York, NY. 2003. 719p. A History of the University in Europe Ser., Vol. 2 ISBN:0-521-54114-X, ISBN13: 978-0-521-54114-5. Dewey:378.4.
Audience: **u,f.**

Dobson, John F. **LA71**
Ancient Education and Its Meaning for Us. Trade Cloth. Rowman & Littlefield Publishers, Inc. Lanham, MD. 1930. 0p. Our Debt to Greece and Rome Ser. ISBN:0-8154-0060-8, ISBN13: 978-0-8154-0060-8. Dewey:370.93. LCCN:63-010297.
Audience: **l,u.**

Education Atlas **LA9**
Education Atlas: History of Education. http://www.educationatlas.com/history-of-education.html
Audience: **f.**

Engel, Michael **LA217.2.E533 2000**
The Struggle for Control of Public Education: Market Ideology vs. Democratic Values. Trade Cloth. Temple University Press. Philadelphia, PA. 2000. xi, 223p. ISBN:1-56639-740-5, ISBN13: 978-1-56639-740-7. Dewey:371.01/0973. LCCN:99-034615.
Audience: **u,f.** *Choice, 2000.*

Fass, Paula S. **LA217.2**
Outside In: Minorities and the Transformation of American Education. Trade Paper. Oxford University Press, Inc. New York, NY. 1991. 336p. ISBN:0-19-507135-2, ISBN13: 978-0-19-507135-1. Dewey:370/.973.
Audience: **u,f.** *Choice, 1990.*

Flexner, Abraham **LA184.F54 1994**
Universities: American, English, German. Clark Kerr (Introduction by). Trade Paper. Transaction Publishers. Somerset, NJ. 1994. 381p. ISBN:1-56000-737-0, ISBN13: 978-1-56000-737-1. Dewey:378. LCCN:94-002280.
Audience: **u,f.**

Franciosi, Robert J. **LA212**
The Rise and Fall of American Public Schools: The Political Economy of Public Education in the 20th Century. Trade Cloth. Greenwood Publishing Group, Inc. Portsmouth, NH. 2004. 264p. ISBN:0-275-97687-4, ISBN13: 978-0-275-97687-3. Dewey:371.01/0973. LCCN:2004-003012.
Audience: **u.** *Choice, 2005.*

Fraser, Ronald, et al. **LA186.A16 1988**
1968: A Student Generation in Revolt. Daniel Bertaux, Bret Eynon, Ron Grele, Beatrix LeWita, Daniele Linhart, Luisa Passerini, Jochen Staadt & Annemarie Troger (Authors). Trade Paper. Knopf Publishing Group. New York, NY. 1988. 368p. ISBN:0-679-73953-X, ISBN13: 978-0-679-73953-1. Dewey:378/.1981. LCCN:87-046058.
Audience: **g.**

Gaither, Milton **LA205.G35 2003**
American Educational History Revisited: A Critique of Progress. Cloth Text. Teachers College Press, Teachers College, Columbia University. New York, NY. 2002. 216p. Reflective History Ser. ISBN:0-8077-4290-2, ISBN13: 978-0-8077-4290-7. Dewey:370/.973. LCCN:2002-074033.
Audience: **f.** *Choice, 2003.*

Gibboney, Richard A. **LA210.G49 1994**
The Stone Trumpet: A Story of Practical School Reform, 1960-1990. Paper Text. State University of New York Press. Albany, NY. 1994. 306p. SUNY Series in Democracy and Education ISBN:0-7914-2010-8, ISBN13: 978-0-7914-2010-2. Dewey:370/.973/09045. LCCN:93-042681.
Audience: **u.** *Choice, 1995.*

Gold, Alice Ross **LA186.G59**
Fists and Flowers: A Social Psychological Interpretation of Student Dissent. Trade Cloth. Elsevier Science & Technology Books. Saint Louis, MO. 1976. 204p. ISBN:0-12-287650-4, ISBN13: 978-0-12-287650-9. Dewey:378.1/98/1. LCCN:75-019640.
Audience: **u,f.**

Goodlad, John I. **LA210.G626 1997**
In Praise of Education. Cloth Text. Teachers College Press, Teachers College, Columbia University. New York, NY. 1997. 192p. John Dewey Lectures ISBN:0-8077-3621-X, ISBN13: 978-0-8077-3621-0. Dewey:370/.973. LCCN:97-002885.
Audience: **u,f.** *Choice, 1997.*

Goodlad, John I., et al. **LC213.2**
Education for Everyone: Agenda for Education in a Democracy. Corinne Mantle-Bromley & Stephen John Goodlad (Authors). Trade Cloth. John Wiley & Sons, Inc. Hoboken, NJ. 2004. 208p. ISBN:0-7879-7224-X, ISBN13: 978-0-7879-7224-0. Dewey:370.9/73. LCCN:2003-026852.
Audience: **u,f.** *Choice, 2004.*

Gordon, David T. (Editor) **LC89.N2 2003**
A Nation Reformed?: American Education Twenty Years after a Nation at Risk. Patricia Albjerg Graham (Foreword by). Cloth Text. Harvard Education Publishing Group (H E P G). Cambridge, MA. 2003. 227p. ISBN:1-891792-09-1, ISBN13: 978-1-891792-09-0. Dewey:379.73. LCCN:2002-114347.
Audience: **u,f.**

Graham, Patricia Albjerg **LA209.G65 2005**
Schooling America: How the Public Schools Meet the Nation's Changing Needs. Trade Cloth. Oxford University Press, Inc. New York, NY. 2005. 287p. ISBN:0-19-517222-1, ISBN13: 978-0-19-517222-5. Dewey:370/.973/094. LCCN:2005-008495.
Audience: **g,l,u.**

Graves, Frank P. **LA31 .G7**
A History of Education Before the Middle Ages. Trade Cloth. Library Reprints, Inc. Temecula, CA. 1909. 304p. ISBN:0-7222-2893-7, ISBN13: 978-0-7222-2893-7. Dewey:370.9.
Audience: **u,f.**

Graves, Frank P. **LA96**
A History of Education During the Middle Ages and the Transition of Modern Times. Trade Cloth. Library Reprints, Inc. Temecula, CA. 1910. 328p. ISBN:0-7222-2895-3, ISBN13: 978-0-7222-2895-1. Dewey:370.94.
Audience: **u,f.**

Gutek, Gerald L. **LA11.G8 1995**
A History of the Western Educational Experience. Ed. 2. Paper Text. Waveland Press, Inc. Prospect Heights, IL. 1995. 558p. ISBN:0-88133-818-4, ISBN13: 978-0-88133-818-8. Dewey:370/.9. LCCN:95-154245.
Audience: **u,f.**

Hammack, Floyd M. **LA222.C555 2004**
The Comprehensive High School Today. Trade Cloth. Teachers College Press, Teachers College, Columbia University. New York, NY. 2004. viii, 157p. The Series on School Reform ISBN:0-8077-4456-5, ISBN13: 978-0-8077-4456-7. Dewey:373.73. LCCN:2003-070258.
Audience: **f.** *Choice, 2005.*

Herbst, Jurgen **LA5**
Bibliography of the History of American Education. http://www.zzbw.uni-hannover.de/HerbstStart.htm
Audience: **u,f.**

Herbst, Jurgen **LA222.H386 1996**
The Once and Future School: Three Hundred and Fifty Years of American Secondary Education. Trade Paper. Routledge. New York, NY. 1996. 280p. ISBN:0-415-91194-X, ISBN13: 978-0-415-91194-8. Dewey:373.73. LCCN:96-024908.
Audience: **g,l,u,f.** *Choice, 1997.*

Hirsch, E. D. Jr. **LA210.H57 1999**
The Schools We Need: And Why We Don't Have Them. Trade Paper. Doubleday Publishing. New York, NY. 1999. 336p. ISBN:0-385-49524-2, ISBN13: 978-0-385-49524-0. Dewey:370/.973. LCCN:99-028096.
Audience: **g,l,u,f.**

History of Education Society **LA11**
H-Education. http://www.h-net.org/%7Eeduc/
Audience: **f.**

Holt, John **LA217.H6 2005**
The Underachieving School. Patrick Farenga (Foreword by). Trade Paper, Perfect. Sentient Publications. Boulder, CO. 2005. 147p. ISBN:1-59181-038-8, ISBN13: 978-1-59181-038-4. Dewey:370/.973. LCCN:2005-019421.
Audience: **g,l,u,f.**

Husen, Torsten **LC75.H87 1986**
The Learning Society Revisited. Trade Cloth. Pergamon Press. Kidlington, 1986. 296p. ISBN:0-08-032660-9, ISBN13: 978-0-08-032660-3. Dewey:370.19. LCCN:85-029683.
Audience: **u,f.**

Hutchins, Robert Maynard **LA216.C28**
The University of Utopia. Paper Text. Textbook Publishers. Temecula, CA. 2003. 103p. ISBN:0-7581-2429-5, ISBN13: 978-0-7581-2429-6. Dewey:371.2.
Audience: **u,f.** *B*

Illich, Ivan **LA 210 I4 1996**
Deschooling Society: Social Questions. Trade Paper. Marion Boyars Publishers, Inc. New York, NY. 1999. 150p. ISBN:0-7145-0879-9, ISBN13: 978-0-7145-0879-5. Dewey:370.1.
Audience: **g,l,u,f.**

Jossey-Bass Inc. Staff **LA216.J67 2001**
The Jossey-Bass Reader on School Reform. Trade Paper. John Wiley & Sons, Inc. Hoboken, NJ. 2001. 552p. The Jossey-Bass Education Ser. ISBN:0-7879-5524-8, ISBN13: 978-0-7879-5524-3. Dewey:370/.973. LCCN:00-011528.
Audience: **u.**

Kaestle, Carl **LA215.K33 1983**
Pillars of the Republic: Common Schools and American Society, 1780-1860. Eric Foner (Editor). Trade Paper. Farrar, Straus & Giroux. New York, NY. 1983. 282p. American Century Ser. ISBN:0-8090-0154-3, ISBN13: 978-0-8090-0154-5. Dewey:371/.01/0973. LCCN:82-021163.
Audience: **u,f.** *B*

Karier, Clarence J. **LA205.K3 1986**
The Individual, Society, and Education: A History of American Educational Ideas. Ed. 2. Trade Cloth. University of Illinois Press. Champaign, IL. 1986. 472p. ISBN:0-252-01290-9, ISBN13: 978-0-252-01290-7. Dewey:370/.973. LCCN:85-024547.
Audience: **u,f.** *B*

Kohn, Alfie **LA217.2.K65 2004**
What Does It Mean to Be Well-Educated?: And More Essays on Standards, Grading, and Other Follies. Trade Paper. Beacon Press. Boston, MA. 2004. 208p. ISBN:0-8070-3267-0, ISBN13: 978-0-8070-3267-1. Dewey:370/.973. LCCN:2003-020744.
Audience: **g,l,u,f.**

Kozol, Jonathan **LA217.2**
On Being a Teacher. Trade Paper. Oneworld Publications. Oxford, 1994. 192p. ISBN:1-85168-065-9, ISBN13: 978-1-85168-065-8. Dewey:371.102.
Audience: **g,l,u,f.** *B*

Krug, Edward A. **LA0222.K7**
The Shaping of the American High School, 1880-1920, Vol. 1. Trade Paper. Books on Demand. Ann Arbor, MI. 504p. Exploration Series in Education Ser. ISBN:0-608-07007-6, ISBN13: 978-0-608-07007-0. Dewey:373.73. LCCN:64-012801.
Audience: **u,f.**

Krug, Edward A. **LA0222.K7**
The Shaping of the American High School, 1920-1941, Vol. 2. Trade Paper. Books on Demand. Ann Arbor, MI. 391p. Exploration Series in Education Ser. ISBN:0-608-07008-4, ISBN13: 978-0-608-07008-7. Dewey:373.73. LCCN:64-012801.
Audience: **u,f.**

Laurie, Simon S. **LA31**
Historical Survey of Pre-Christian Education. Ed. 2. Trade Cloth. A M S Press, Inc. New York, NY. ISBN:0-404-03889-1, ISBN13: 978-0-404-03889-2. Dewey:370/.93. LCCN:79-124596.
Audience: **u,f.** *B*

Leonard, George **LA210**
Education and Ecstasy: With the Great School Reform Hoax. Cloth Text. North Atlantic Books. Berkeley, CA. 1987. 288p. ISBN:1-55643-007-8, ISBN13: 978-1-55643-007-7. Dewey:379.73.
Audience: **u,f.**

Macedo, Stephen **LA217.2.M33 2000**
Diversity and Distrust: Civic Education in a Multicultural Democracy. Trade Cloth. Harvard University Press. Cambridge, MA. 2000. 368p. ISBN:0-674-21311-4, ISBN13: 978-0-674-21311-1. Dewey:320.4. LCCN:99-041461.
Audience: **u,f.**

Meier, Deborah **LA217.2**
The Power of Their Ideas: Lessons from America from a Small School in Harlem. Trade Paper. Beacon Press. Boston, MA. 2002. 208p. ISBN:0-8070-3113-5, ISBN13: 978-0-8070-3113-1. Dewey:372.1/0421/0973.
Audience: **f.**

Meyer, Adolph E. **LA126**
Development of Education in the Twentieth Century. Ed. 2. Trade Cloth. Greenwood Publishing Group, Inc. Portsmouth, NH. 1969. 609p. ISBN:0-8371-2838-2, ISBN13: 978-0-8371-2838-2. Dewey:370/.9/04. LCCN:75-097332.
Audience: **u,f.**

Mondale, Sarah & Patton, Sarah B. (Editors) **LA212 .S353**
School: The Story of American Public Education. Meryl Streep (Foreword by). Trade Paper. Beacon Press. Boston, MA. 2002. 256p. ISBN:0-8070-4221-8, ISBN13: 978-0-8070-4221-2. Dewey:370/.973.
Audience: **g,l,u,f.**

Nasaw, David **LA217.2**
Schooled to Order: A Social History of Public Schooling in the United States. Trade Paper. Oxford University Press, Inc. New York, NY. 1981. 302p. ISBN:0-19-502892-9, ISBN13: 978-0-19-502892-8. Dewey:371/.01/0973.
Audience: **u,f.** B

Pangle, Lorraine S. & Pangle, Thomas L. **LA206 .P36**
The Learning of Liberty: The Educational Ideas of the American Founders. Trade Cloth. University Press of Kansas. Lawrence, KS. 2004. 370p. American Political Thought Ser. ISBN:0-7006-0746-3, ISBN13: 978-0-7006-0746-4. Dewey:370/.1. LCCN:92-029956.
Audience: **u,f.**

Perkinson, Henry J. **LA209.2.P422 1995**
The Imperfect Panacea: American Faith in Education. Ed. 4. Paper Text. McGraw-Hill Higher Education. Burr Ridge, IL. 1995. 256p. ISBN:0-07-049371-5, ISBN13: 978-0-07-049371-1. Dewey:370/.973. LCCN:94-040277.
Audience: **u,f.**

Perkinson, Henry J. **LA132**
Learning from Our Mistakes: A Reinterpretation of Twentieth-Century Educational Theory. Trade Cloth. Greenwood Publishing Group, Inc. Portsmouth, NH. 1984. 224p. Contributions to the Study of Education Ser., No. 14 ISBN:0-313-24239-9, ISBN13: 978-0-313-24239-7. Dewey:370.1. LCCN:83-026670.
Audience: **u,f.** B

Perkinson, Henry J. **LA205.P45 1987**
Two Hundred Years of American Educational Thought. Trade Paper. University Press of America, Inc. Lanham, MD. 1987. 342p. ISBN:0-8191-6124-1, ISBN13: 978-0-8191-6124-6. Dewey:370/.973. LCCN:86-033960.
Audience: **u,f.** B

Peterson, Paul E. **LA216**
The Politics of School Reform, 1870-1940. Trade Paper. University of Chicago Press. Chicago, IL. 1985. 252p. ISBN:0-226-66295-0, ISBN13: 978-0-226-66295-4. Dewey:370/.973. LCCN:85-001042.
Audience: **u,f.**

Peterson, Paul E. (Editor) **LA217.2.O87 2003**
Our Schools and Our Future: Are We Still at Risk? John E. Chubb (Contribution by). Trade Cloth. Hoover Institution Press. Stanford, CA. 2003. 338p. Publication Ser., No. 516:Studies of Nationalities ISBN:0-8179-3921-0, ISBN13: 978-0-8179-3921-2. Dewey:370/.973. LCCN:2002-191907.
Audience: **g,u,f.** *Choice, 2003.*

Popham, W. James **LA217.2.P65 2004**
America's Failing Schools: How Parents and Teachers Can Cope with No Child Left Behind. Paper over Boards. Taylor & Francis Group. Philadelphia, PA. 2004. 168p. ISBN:0-415-94947-5, ISBN13: 978-0-415-94947-7. Dewey:379.73. LCCN:2005-008214.
Audience: **g,l,u,f.**

Ravitch, Diane **LA216**
Left Back: A Century of Battles over School Reform. Trade Paper. Simon & Schuster. New York, NY. 2001. 560p. ISBN:0-7432-0326-7, ISBN13: 978-0-7432-0326-5. Dewey:370.973.
Audience: **g,u,f.**

Ravitch, Diane **LA217.2**
The Schools We Deserve: Reflections on the Educational Crisis of Our Time. Trade Paper. Basic Books. New York, NY. 1987. 352p. ISBN:0-465-07234-8, ISBN13: 978-0-465-07234-7. Dewey:370/.973. LCCN:84-045303.
Audience: **g,u,f.** B

Ravitch, Diane **LA209.2**
Troubled Crusade: American Education, 1945-1980. Trade Paper. Basic Books. New York, NY. 1985. 400p. ISBN:0-465-08757-4, ISBN13: 978-0-465-08757-0. Dewey:370/.973.
Audience: **g,u,f.**

Reese, William J. **LA212.R423 2005**
America's Public Schools: From the Common School to "No Child Left Behind". Trade Cloth. Johns Hopkins University Press. Baltimore, MD. 2005. 376p. The American Moment Ser. ISBN:0-8018-8195-1, ISBN13: 978-0-8018-8195-4. Dewey:371.01/0973/09. LCCN:2004-029625.
Audience: **u,f.** *Choice, 2006.*

Reese, William J. **LA222.R39 1995**
The Origins of the American High School. Cloth over Boards. Yale University Press. Cumberland, RI. 1995. 352p. ISBN:0-300-06384-9, ISBN13: 978-0-300-06384-4. Dewey:373.7/3. LCCN:94-024975.
Audience: **u,f.** *Choice, 1996.*

Rury, John L. **LA205.R67 2005**
Education and Social Change: Themes in the History of American Schooling. Ed. 2. Other. Lawrence Erlbaum Associates, Inc. Mahwah, NJ. 2004. ISBN:1-4106-1180-9, ISBN13: 978-1-4106-1180-2. Dewey:370/.973.
Audience: **l,u,f.** *Choice, 2002.*

Rüegg, Walter (Editor) **LA627.U55 2004**
A History of the University in Europe: Universities in the Nineteenth and Early Twentieth Centuries (1800-1945). Trade Cloth. Cambridge University Press. New York, NY. 2004. 772p. A History of the University in Europe Ser., Vol. 3 ISBN:0-521-36107-9, ISBN13: 978-0-521-36107-1. Dewey:378.4/09/034. LCCN:2003-065688.
Audience: **u,f.**

Sarason, Seymour B. **LA210.S34 1996**
Revisiting "The Culture of the School and the Problem of Change". Cloth Text. Teachers College Press, Teachers College, Columbia University. New York, NY. 1996. 416p. School Reform Ser., Vol. 12 ISBN:0-8077-3544-2, ISBN13: 978-0-8077-3544-2. Dewey:370.19/3/0973. LCCN:96-002143.
Audience: **u,f.**

Sarason, Seymour Bernard **LA217.2.S26 2002**
Educational Reform: A Self Scrutinizing Memoir. Cloth Text. Teachers College Press, Teachers College, Columbia University. New York, NY. 2002. 304p. ISBN:0-8077-4244-9, ISBN13: 978-0-8077-4244-0. Dewey:370/.973. LCCN:2001-060376.
Audience: **u,f.**

Scheffler, Israel **LA132.S328 1985**
Of Human Potential. Trade Cloth. Routledge. New York, NY. 1985. 141p. ISBN:0-7102-0571-6, ISBN13: 978-0-7102-0571-1. Dewey:370/.1. LCCN:85-002140.
Audience: **u,f.** B

Scheffler, Israel **LB885.S34R43 1989**
Reason and Teaching. Trade Cloth. Hackett Publishing Company, Inc. Indianapolis, IN. 1981. 214p. ISBN:0-87220-085-X, ISBN13: 978-0-87220-085-2. Dewey:370.1. LCCN:72-086641.
Audience: **u,f.** B

Schugurensky, Daniel **LA91**
History of Education: Selected Moments of the 20th Century. http://fcis.oise.utoronto.ca/~daniel_schugurensky/assignment1/
Audience: **g,l,u,f.**

Sexton, Patricia Cayo **PR6007.U76Z75**
Education and Income: Inequalities of Opportunity in Our Public Schools. Paper Text. Textbook Publishers. Temecula, CA. 2003. xxi, 298p. ISBN:0-7581-0852-4, ISBN13: 978-0-7581-0852-4. Dewey:823.912.
Audience: **u,f.** B

Sharpes, Donald K. **LA11.S44 2002**
Advanced Educational Foundations for Teachers: The History, Philosophy and Culture of Schooling. Cloth Text. Garland Publishing, Inc. New York, NY. 2001. 544p. ISBN:0-8153-3860-0, ISBN13: 978-0-8153-3860-4. Dewey:370/.9. LCCN:2001-019471.
Audience: **u,f.**

Sizer, Theodore R. **LA222**
Horace's Compromise: The Dilemma of the American High School. Trade Paper. Houghton Mifflin Company Trade & Reference Division. Boston, MA. 2004. 272p. ISBN:0-618-51606-9, ISBN13: 978-0-618-51606-3. Dewey:373.73. LCCN:2004-559154.
Audience: **u,f.**

Sizer, Theodore R. **LA222.S544**
Horace's School: Redesigning the American High School. Trade Paper. Houghton Mifflin Company Trade & Reference Division. Boston, MA. 1997. 256p. ISBN:0-395-75534-4, ISBN13: 978-0-395-75534-1. Dewey:373.73.
Audience: **u,f.** *Choice, 1992.*

Sizer, Theodore R. **LB1607 .S54 1976**
Secondary Schools at the Turn of the Century. Trade Cloth. Greenwood Publishing Group, Inc. Portsmouth, NH. 1976. 304p. ISBN:0-8371-8972-1, ISBN13: 978-0-8371-8972-7. Dewey:373.73. LCCN:76-043028.
Audience: **u,f.** B

Sloan, Douglas (Author, Editor) **LA0205.S57**
The Great Awakening and American Education: A Documentary History. Trade Paper. Books on Demand. Ann Arbor, MI. 283p. Classics in Education Ser., No. 46 ISBN:0-598-16827-3, ISBN13: 978-0-598-16827-6. Dewey:370/.973. LCCN:72-091270.
Audience: **u,f.** B

Smith, William Jr. **LA31.S63**
Ancient Education. Trade Cloth. Philosophical Library, Inc. New York, NY. 1955. ISBN:0-8022-1602-1, ISBN13: 978-0-8022-1602-1. Dewey:370/.93.
Audience: **u,f.**

Spring, Joel H. **LA205.S64 2005**
The American School, 1642-2004. Ed. 6. Paper Text. McGraw-Hill Higher Education. Burr Ridge, IL. 2004. 512p. ISBN:0-07-287566-6, ISBN13: 978-0-07-287566-9. Dewey:370/.973. LCCN:2003-068649.
Audience: **u,f.**

Spring, Joel H. **LC89.S664 1976**
The Sorting Machine: National Educational Policy since 1945. Trade Cloth. David McKay Company, Inc. New York, NY. 1976. vi, 309p. ISBN:0-679-30304-9, ISBN13: 978-0-679-30304-6. Dewey:379.73. LCCN:75-043801.
Audience: **u,f.** B

Ulich, Robert (Editor) **LB41**
Three Thousand Years of Educational Wisdom: Selections from Great Documents. iUniverse, Inc. 1999. ISBN:1-58348-537-6, ISBN13: 978-1-58348-537-8.
Audience: **l.**

Urban, Wayne J. & Wagoner, Jennings L. **LA205**
American Education: A History with the McGraw-Hill Foundations of Education Timeline. Ed. 3. Trade Paper. McGraw-Hill Higher Education. Burr Ridge, IL. 2003. 400p. ISBN:0-07-287835-5, ISBN13: 978-0-07-287835-6. Dewey:370/.973.
Audience: **l,u.**

Vinovskis, Maris A. **LA212.V56 1995**
Education, Society, and Economic Opportunity: A Historical Perspective on Persistent Issues. Cloth over Boards. Yale University Press. Cumberland, RI. 1995. 256p. ISBN:0-300-06269-9, ISBN13: 978-0-300-06269-4. Dewey:370/.973/09. LCCN:95-005892.
Audience: **u,f.** *Choice, 1996.*

Vinovskis, Maris A. **LA217.2.L43 1995**
Learning from the Past: What History Teaches Us about School Reform. Diane Ravitch (Editor). Trade Paper. Johns Hopkins University Press. Baltimore, MD. 1989. 400p. ISBN:0-8018-4921-7, ISBN13: 978-0-8018-4921-3. Dewey:370/.973. LCCN:94-027015.
Audience: **g,u,f.** *Choice, 1995.*

Wagner, Tony **LA222.W25 2000**
How Schools Change: Lessons from Three Communities. Ed. 2. Trade Paper. Routledge. New York, NY. 2000. 320p. ISBN:0-415-92763-3, ISBN13: 978-0-415-92763-5. Dewey:373.73. LCCN:00-047021.
Audience: **u,f.** *Choice, 2001.*

Wagner, Tony **LA217.2**
Making the Grade: Reinventing America's Schools. Trade Paper. Routledge. New York, NY. 2003. 176p. ISBN:0-415-92762-5, ISBN13: 978-0-415-92762-8. Dewey:370.9/73.
Audience: **u,f.** *Choice, 2002.*

History of Education > History of Higher Education

Altbach, Philip G. **LA229.A69 1997**
Student Politics in America: A Historical Analysis. Trade Paper. Transaction Publishers. Somerset, NJ. 1997. 292p. Foundations of Higher Education Ser. ISBN:1-56000-944-6, ISBN13: 978-1-56000-944-3. Dewey:378.1/98/10973. LCCN:97-000597.
Audience: **f.**

Altbach, Philip G., et al. **LA227.4.A45 2005**
American Higher Education in the Twenty-First Century: Social, Political, and Economic Challenges. Ed. 2. Robert Oliver Berdahl & Patricia J. Gumport (Authors). Trade Cloth. Johns Hopkins University Press. Baltimore, MD. 2005. 568p. ISBN:0-8018-8034-3, ISBN13: 978-0-8018-8034-6. Dewey:378.73. LCCN:2004-013766.
Audience: **g,f.** *Choice, 1999.*

Altbach, Philip G. (Author, Editor), et al. **LA227.4.I5 2001**
In Defense of American Higher Education. Patricia J. Gumport & D. Bruce Johnstone (Author, Editors). Trade Cloth. Johns Hopkins University Press. Baltimore, MD. 2001. 376p. ISBN:0-8018-6654-5, ISBN13: 978-0-8018-6654-8. Dewey:378.73. LCCN:00-011291.
Audience: **f.**

American Council on Education Staff **LA226 A65 2006**
American Universities and Colleges. Ed. 17. Cloth Text. Greenwood Publishing Group, Inc. Portsmouth, NH. 2006. 1744p. ACE/Praeger Series on Higher Education Ser. ISBN:0-275-98745-0, ISBN13: 978-0-275-98745-9. Dewey:378.73/05.
Audience: **g,l,u,f.**

Astin, Alexander W. **LA229**
What Matters in College: Four Critical Years Revisited. Trade Paper. John Wiley & Sons, Inc. Hoboken, NJ. 1997. 512p. ISBN:0-7879-0838-X, ISBN13: 978-0-7879-0838-6. Dewey:378.198.
Audience: **f.**

Barzun, Jacques **LA226.B27 1993**
The American University: How It Runs, Where It Is Going. Ed. 2. Herbert I. London (Introduction by). Trade Paper. University of Chicago Press. Chicago, IL. 1993. 356p. ISBN:0-226-03845-9, ISBN13: 978-0-226-03845-2. Dewey:378.1550973. LCCN:92-028479.
Audience: **f.** B

Berube, Michael & Nelson, Cary (Editors) **LA227.4.H544 1994**
Higher Education under Fire: Politics, Economics and the Crisis of the Humanities. Paper over Boards. Routledge. New York, NY. 1994. 400p. ISBN:0-415-90805-1, ISBN13: 978-0-415-90805-4. Dewey:378.73. LCCN:94-017598.
Audience: **f.**

Bogue, E. Grady & Aper, Jeffery **LA227.4.B66 2000**
Exploring the Heritage of American Higher Education: The Evolution of Philosophiy and Policy. Trade Cloth. Greenwood Publishing Group, Inc. Portsmouth, NH. 1999. 272p. American Council on Education Series on Higher Education ISBN:1-57356-310-2, ISBN13: 978-1-57356-310-9. Dewey:378.73. LCCN:99-049294.
Audience: **f.**

Bok, Derek C. **LA227.3**
Higher Learning. Trade Cloth. Harvard University Press. Cambridge, MA. 1986. 208p. ISBN:0-674-39175-6, ISBN13: 978-0-674-39175-8. Dewey:378.73. LCCN:86-009876.
Audience: **g,f.**

Bowen, Howard R. **LA227.4.B68 1997**
Investment in Learning: The Individual and Social Value of American Higher Education. Ed. 2. Trade Paper. Johns Hopkins University Press. Baltimore, MD. 1997. 536p. ISBN:0-8018-5530-6, ISBN13: 978-0-8018-5530-6. Dewey:378.73. LCCN:96-045438.
Audience: **f.** B

Boyer, Ernest L. & Carnegie Foundation for the Advancement of Teaching Staff **LA227.3 .B678 1988**
College: The Undergraduate Experience in America. Trade Paper. John Wiley & Sons, Inc. Hoboken, NJ. 1997. 328p. ISBN:0-06-091458-0, ISBN13: 978-0-06-091458-5. Dewey:378.73. LCCN:97-033424.
Audience: **g,f.**

Boyer, Ernest L. & Glassick, Charles E. **LA227.3 .B694**
Scholarship Assessed and Reconsidered Set. Trade Paper. John Wiley & Sons, Inc. Hoboken, NJ. 2003. 304p. ISBN:0-7879-7476-5, ISBN13: 978-0-7879-7476-3. Dewey:378.73.
Audience: **f.**

Brint, Steven & Karabel, Jerome **LA226.B74 1989**
The Diverted Dream: Community Colleges and the Promise of Educational Opportunity in America, 1900-1985. Trade Paper. Oxford University Press, Inc. New York, NY. 1991. 336p. ISBN:0-19-504816-4, ISBN13: 978-0-19-504816-2. Dewey:378.73. LCCN:89-002891.
Audience: **f.** *Choice, 1990.*

Brubacher, John S. & Rudy, Willis **LA226.B75 1997**
Higher Education in Transition: A History of American Colleges and Universities. Ed. 4. Trade Paper. Transaction Publishers. Somerset, NJ. 1997. 564p. Foundations of Higher Education Ser. ISBN:1-56000-917-9, ISBN13: 978-1-56000-917-7. Dewey:378.73. LCCN:96-053075.
Audience: **f.**

Cohen, Arthur M. **LA226.C66 1998**
The Shaping of American Higher Education: Emergence and Growth of the Contemporary System. Trade Cloth. John Wiley & Sons, Inc. Hoboken, NJ. 1998. 512p. Health and Psychology Ser. ISBN:0-7879-1029-5, ISBN13: 978-0-7879-1029-7. Dewey:378.73. LCCN:98-011854.
Audience: **f.**

Cohen, Robert **LA229**
When the Old Left Was Young: Student Radicals and America's First Mass Student Movement, 1929-1941. Trade Paper. Oxford University Press, Inc. New York, NY. 1997. 454p. ISBN:0-19-511136-2, ISBN13: 978-0-19-511136-1. Dewey:378.1/9/81/0973.
Audience: **u,f.**

Conant, James Bryant **F855.2.M5C45**
The Citadel of Learning. Paper Text. Textbook Publishers. Temecula, CA. 2003. 79p. ISBN:0-7581-0082-5, ISBN13: 978-0-7581-0082-5. Dewey:979.5/0046872073.
Audience: **u,f.**

Cross, K. Patricia **LA227.3.C76**
Beyond the Open Door. Trade Cloth. John Wiley & Sons, Inc. Hoboken, NJ. 1971. xviii, 200p. ISBN:0-87589-111-X, ISBN13: 978-0-87589-111-8. Dewey:378.1/05/60973. LCCN:77-170212.
Audience: **f.** B

D'Souza, Dinesh **LA227.4.D77 1991**
Illiberal Education: The Politics of Race and Sex on Campus. Trade Cloth. Simon & Schuster. New York, NY. 1991. 336p. ISBN:0-02-908100-9, ISBN13: 978-0-02-908100-6. Dewey:370.19/342. LCCN:90-047055.
Audience: **l,u,f.** *Choice, 1991.*

Geiger, Louis G. **LA228**
Higher Education in a Maturing Democracy. Trade Cloth. Greenwood Publishing Group, Inc. Portsmouth, NH. 1977. 92p. ISBN:0-8371-9550-0, ISBN13: 978-0-8371-9550-6. Dewey:378.73. LCCN:77-002203.
Audience: **f.**

Geiger, Roger L. (Editor) **LA227.1.A64 2000**
American College in the Nineteenth Century. Cloth Text. Vanderbilt University Press. Nashville, TN. 2000. ix, 363p. Vanderbilt Issues in Higher Education ISBN:0-8265-1336-0, ISBN13: 978-0-8265-1336-6. Dewey:378.73. LCCN:00-008025.
Audience: **u,f.**

Gilbert, Marc Jason (Editor) **LA229**
The Vietnam War on Campus: Other Voices, More Distant Drums. Trade Cloth. Greenwood Publishing Group, Inc. Portsmouth, NH. 2000. 280p. ISBN:0-275-96909-6, ISBN13: 978-0-275-96909-7. Dewey:378.1/981. LCCN:99-086097.
Audience: **f.** *Choice, 2001.*

Graham, Hugh Davis & Diamond, Nancy **LA227.4.G73 1997**
The Rise of American Research Universities: Elites and Challengers in the Postwar Era. Trade Cloth. Johns Hopkins University Press. Baltimore, MD. 1997. 328p. ISBN:0-8018-5425-3, ISBN13: 978-0-8018-5425-5. Dewey:378.73/09/045. LCCN:96-030432.
Audience: **f.** *Choice, 1997.*

Heineman, Kenneth J. **LA229.H39 2001**
Put Your Bodies upon the Wheels: Student Revolt in the 1960s. Book, Other. Ivan R. Dee Publisher. Blue Ridge Summit, PA. 2001. 256p. American Ways Ser. ISBN:1-56663-351-6, ISBN13: 978-1-56663-351-2. Dewey:378.1/981/0973. LCCN:00-049371.
Audience: **g,l.** *Choice, 2001.*

Hersh, Richard H. & Merrow, John (Editors) **LA227.4.D45 2005**
Declining by Degrees: Higher Education at Risk. Tom Wolfe (Foreword by). Cloth over Boards. Palgrave Macmillan. New York, NY. 2005. 256p. ISBN:1-4039-6921-3, ISBN13: 978-1-4039-6921-7. Dewey:378.73. LCCN:2005-043024.
Audience: **g,u,f.** *Choice, 2006.*

Hofstadter, Richard **QC176.O38**
American Higher Education, a Documentary History. Paper Text. Textbook Publishers. Temecula, CA. 2003. ISBN:0-7581-2423-6, ISBN13: 978-0-7581-2423-4. Dewey:530.4/1.
Audience: **l,u.**

Horowitz, Helen L. **LA229.H569 1988**
Campus Life: Undergraduate Cultures from the End of the Eighteenth Century to the Present. Trade Paper. University of Chicago Press. Chicago, IL. 1988. 348p. ISBN:0-226-35373-7, ISBN13: 978-0-226-35373-9. Dewey:378/.198/0973. LCCN:87-030226.
Audience: **f.** *Choice, 1987.*

Kolodny, Annette **LA227.4.K65 1998**
Failing the Future: A Dean Looks at Higher Education in the 21st Century. Trade Cloth. Duke University Press. Durham, NC. 1998. 312p. ISBN:0-8223-2186-6, ISBN13: 978-0-8223-2186-6. Dewey:378.7/3. LCCN:97-037781.
Audience: **g,l,u,f.** *Choice, 1998.*

Levine, Arthur (Editor) **LA227.4**
Higher Learning in America, 1980-2000. Trade Paper. Johns Hopkins University Press. Baltimore, MD. 1975. 408p. ISBN:0-8018-4861-X, ISBN13: 978-0-8018-4861-2. Dewey:378.73. LCCN:93-019746.
Audience: **f.**

Lucas, Christopher J. **LA226.L83 2006**
American Higher Education: A History. Ed. 2. Trade Paper. Palgrave Macmillan. New York, NY. 2006. 416p. ISBN:1-4039-7289-3, ISBN13: 978-1-4039-7289-7. Dewey:378.73/09. LCCN:2005-056468.
Audience: **u,f.**

Marsden, George M **LA226.M34 1994**
The Soul of the American University: From Protestant Establishment to Established Non-Belief. Oxford University Press, Inc. 1994. ISBN:0-19-507046-1, ISBN13: 978-0-19-507046-0.
Audience: **g,l,u,f.**

Miller, Richard E. **LA227.4.M555 1998**
As If Learning Mattered: Reforming Higher Education. Book, Other. Cornell University Press. Ithaca, NY. 1998. 264p. ISBN:0-8014-3483-1, ISBN13: 978-0-8014-3483-9. Dewey:378.73. LCCN:97-039221.
Audience: **f.** *Choice, 1999.*

Newman, Frank, et al. **LA227.4.N494 2004**
The Future of Higher Education: Rhetoric, Reality, and the Risks of the Market. Lara Couturier & Jamie Scurry (Authors). Trade Cloth. John Wiley & Sons, Inc. Hoboken, NJ. 2004. 304p. ISBN:0-7879-6972-9, ISBN13: 978-0-7879-6972-1. Dewey:378.73. LCCN:2004-006400.
Audience: **f.**

Nisbet, Robert A. & Himmelfard, Gertrude **LA226.N56 1996**
The Degradation of the Academic Dogma. Trade Paper. Transaction Publishers. Somerset, NJ. 1996. 252p. ISBN:1-56000-915-2, ISBN13: 978-1-56000-915-3. Dewey:378.73. LCCN:96-020341.
Audience: **u.**

Novak, Steven J. **LA0229.N68**
The Rights of Youth: American Colleges and Student Revolt, 1798-1815. Trade Paper. Books on Demand. Ann Arbor, MI. 230p. ISBN:0-7837-5939-8, ISBN13: 978-0-7837-5939-5. Dewey:378.1/98/1. LCCN:76-043109.
Audience: **f.** B

Pascarella, Ernest T. & Terenzini, Patrick T. **LA229.P34 2005**
How College Affects Students: A Third Decade of Research. Ed. 2. Trade Cloth. John Wiley & Sons, Inc. Hoboken, NJ. 2005. 848p. ISBN:0-7879-1044-9, ISBN13: 978-0-7879-1044-0. Dewey:378.1/98/0973. LCCN:2004-021981.
Audience: **f.**

Reuben, Julie A. **LA227.1.R48 1996**
The Making of the Modern University: Intellectual Transformation and the Marginalization of Morality. Trade Paper. University of Chicago Press. Chicago, IL. 1996. 374p. ISBN:0-226-71020-3, ISBN13: 978-0-226-71020-4. Dewey:378.73. LCCN:96-012267.
Audience: **u,f.** *Choice, 1997.*

Rhodes, Frank Harold Trevor **LA227.4.R49 2001**
The Creation of the Future: The Role of the American University. Trade Cloth. Cornell University Press. Ithaca, NY. 2001. 288p. ISBN:0-8014-3937-X, ISBN13: 978-0-8014-3937-7. Dewey:378.73. LCCN:2001-002214.
Audience: **f.**

Riesman, David **LA226.J4 2002**
The Academic Revolution. Christopher Jencks (Introduction by). Trade Paper. Transaction Publishers. Somerset, NJ. 2001. 580p. ISBN:0-7658-0115-9, ISBN13: 978-0-7658-0115-9. Dewey:378.73. LCCN:2001-041588.
Audience: **u,f.** B

Robson, David W. **LA227**
Educating Republicans: The College in the Era of the American Revolution, 1750-1800. Trade Cloth. Greenwood Publishing Group, Inc. Portsmouth, NH. 1985. 272p. Contributions to the Study of Education Ser., No. 15 ISBN:0-313-24606-8, ISBN13: 978-0-313-24606-7. Dewey:378.73. LCCN:84-022436.
Audience: **u,f.** *Choice, 1986.*

Ross, Earle D. **LA226.R65**
Democracy's College: The Land-Grant Movement in the Formative Stage. Trade Cloth. Ayer Company Publishers, Inc. Manchester, NH. 1973. American Education, :Its Men, Institutions, and Ideas, Series 1 ISBN:0-405-01463-5, ISBN13: 978-0-405-01463-5. Dewey:379/.123. LCCN:74-089226.
Audience: **f.**

Ruben, Brent D. **LA227.4.R83 2004**
Pursuing Excellence in Higher Education: Eight Fundamental Challenges. Trade Cloth. John Wiley & Sons, Inc. Hoboken, NJ. 2003. 464p. Jossey-Bass Higher and Adult Education Ser. ISBN:0-7879-6204-X, ISBN13: 978-0-7879-6204-3. Dewey:378.73. LCCN:2003-011190.
Audience: **f.**

Rudolph, Frederick **LA226.R72 1990**
The American College and University: A History. John R. Thelin (Introduction by). Trade Paper. University of Georgia Press. Athens, GA. 1991. 616p. ISBN:0-8203-1284-3, ISBN13: 978-0-8203-1284-2. Dewey:378.73. LCCN:90-040967.
Audience: **u,f.** B

Sanford, Nevitt **GV351**
The American College: A Psychological and Social Interpretation of the Higher Learning. Paper Text. Textbook Publishers. Temecula, CA. 2003. xvi, 1084p. ISBN:0-7581-0495-2, ISBN13: 978-0-7581-0495-3. Dewey:796.071173.
Audience: **f.** B

Schwartz, John A. **LA11**
☐ History and Archival Resources in Higher Education. http://www.higher-ed.org/history.htm
Audience: **f.**

Thelin, John R. **LA226.T45 2004**
A History of American Higher Education. Trade Cloth. Johns Hopkins University Press. Baltimore, MD. 2004. 448p. ISBN:0-8018-7855-1, ISBN13: 978-0-8018-7855-8. Dewey:378.73. LCCN:2003-012878.
Audience: **g,l,u,f.** *Choice, 2005.*

Tierney, William G. **LA227.4 .R45 1999**
The Responsive University: Restructuring for High Performance. Trade Paper. Johns Hopkins University Press. Baltimore, MD. 1999. 192p. ISBN:0-8018-6260-4, ISBN13: 978-0-8018-6260-1. Dewey:378.73.
Audience: **f.** *Choice, 1998.*

Unger, Irwin **LA229.U47**
The Movement: A History of the American New Left, 1959-1972. Trade Cloth. Dodd, Mead & Company, U. S.. London, 1974. viii, 217p. ISBN:0-396-06940-1, ISBN13: 978-0-396-06940-9. Dewey:322.4/4/0973. LCCN:73-021168.
Audience: **g,l,u,f.** B

United States. President's Commission on Campus Unrest **LA229.A54 1970**
Report of the President's Commission on Campus Unrest: Including the Killings at Jackson State and Kent State Tragedy. Trade Cloth. Ayer Company Publishers, Inc. Manchester, NH. 1970. 537p. ISBN:0-405-01712-X, ISBN13: 978-0-405-01712-4. Dewey:378.1/98/1. LCCN:71-139710.
Audience: **g,l,u,f.** B

Veysey, Laurence R. **LA226.V47**
The Emergence of the American University. Trade Paper. University of Chicago Press. Chicago, IL. 1970. 520p. ISBN:0-226-85456-6, ISBN13: 978-0-226-85456-4. Dewey:378.73. LCCN:65-024427.
Audience: **u,f.**

William M. McDonald and Associates Staff & McDonald, William M. (Editors) **LA229**
Creating Campus Community: In Search of Ernest Boyer's Legacy. Parker J. Palmer (Afterword by, Foreword by). Trade Paper. John Wiley & Sons, Inc. Hoboken, NJ. 2002. 240p. ISBN:0-7879-5700-3, ISBN13: 978-0-7879-5700-1. Dewey:378.1/98. LCCN:2002-000938.
Audience: **f.**

History of Education > By Place (Non-U.S. Regions or Countries)

Akenson, Donald Harman **LA643**
A Mirror to Kathleen's Face: Education in Independent Ireland, 1922-1960. Trade Cloth. McGill-Queen's University Press. Montreal, PQ. 1975. 240p. ISBN:0-7735-0203-3, ISBN13: 978-0-7735-0203-1. Dewey:372.9/417. LCCN:76-356281.
Audience: **u,f.**

Anderson, R. D. Jr. **LA627**
European Universities from the Enlightenment to 1914. Trade Cloth. Oxford University Press, Inc. New York, NY. 2004. 346p. ISBN:0-19-820660-7, ISBN13: 978-0-19-820660-6. Dewey:378.409033. LCCN:2005-295584.
Audience: **u,f.**

Anderson, Robert D. **LA651.A53 1995**
Education and the Scottish People, 1750-1918. Trade Cloth. Oxford University Press, Inc. New York, NY. 1995. 348p. ISBN:0-19-820515-5, ISBN13: 978-0-19-820515-9. Dewey:370/.9411/0903. LCCN:94-049084.
Audience: **u,f.**

Axelrod, Paul **LA411.7.A94 1994**
The Promise of Schooling: Education in Canada, 1800-1914. Cloth over Boards. University of Toronto Press. Toronto, ON. 1997. 160p. Themes in Canadian Social History Ser. ISBN:0-8020-0825-9, ISBN13: 978-0-8020-0825-1. Dewey:370/.971/09034. LCCN:97-159155.
Audience: **u,f.**

Axelrod, Paul & Reid, John G. (Editors) **LA417.Y68 1989**
Youth, University, and Canadian Society: Essays in the Social History of Higher Education. Trade Cloth. McGill-Queen's University Press. Montreal, PQ. 1989. 416p. ISBN:0-7735-0685-3, ISBN13: 978-0-7735-0685-5. Dewey:378.71. LCCN:90-114792.
Audience: **u,f.**

Baker, David & LeTendre, Gerald K. **LB43.B25 2005**
National Differences, Global Similarities: World Culture and the Future of Schooling. Trade Cloth. Stanford University Press. Palo Alto, CA. 2005. 248p. ISBN:0-8047-5020-3, ISBN13: 978-0-8047-5020-2. Dewey:370/.9. LCCN:2004-027281.
Audience: **u,f.** *Choice, 2005.*

Benner, Dietrich & Lenzen, Dieter (Editors) **LA622.E3812 1996**
Education for the New Europe. Trade Cloth. Berghahn Books, Inc. New York, NY. 1996. 192p. ISBN:1-57181-074-9, ISBN13: 978-1-57181-074-8. Dewey:370/.94. LCCN:95-031517.
Audience: **u,f.**

Björk, Christopher **LA1271.B56 2005**
Indonesian Education: Teachers, Schools, and Central Bureaucracy. Paper over Boards. Routledge. New York, NY. 2005. 206p. East Asia History, Politics, Sociology and Culture Ser. ISBN:0-415-97444-5, ISBN13: 978-0-415-97444-8. Dewey:370/.9598. LCCN:2005-005708.
Audience: **u,f.**

Brickman, William W. **LA621.B74 1985**
Educational Roots and Routes in Western Europe. Trade Paper. Emeritus Incorporated, Publisher. Cherry Hill, NJ. 1986. viii, 404p. ISBN:0-943694-01-9, ISBN13: 978-0-943694-01-6. Dewey:370/.94. LCCN:85-070176.
Audience: **u,f.**

Britton, John A. (Editor) **LA541.M577 1994**
Molding Their Hearts and Minds: Education, Communications and Social Change in Latin America. Book, Other. Rowman & Littlefield Publishers, Inc. Lanham, MD. 1997. 248p. Jaguar Books on Latin America, No. 4 ISBN:0-8420-2489-1, ISBN13: 978-0-8420-2489-1. Dewey:370/.98. LCCN:93-041937.
Audience: **u,f.**

Brock, Colin & Clarkson, Donald (Editors) **LA436**
Education in Central America and the Caribbean. Library Binding. Routledge. New York, NY. 1988. 256p. ISBN:0-415-00569-8, ISBN13: 978-0-415-00569-2. Dewey:370/.9728.
Audience: **f.** *Choice, 1990.*

Brockliss, Laurence **LB2362.F8B76 1987**
French Higher Education in the Seventeenth and Eighteenth Centuries: A Cultural History. Cloth Text. Oxford University Press, Inc. New York, NY. 1987. 440p. ISBN:0-19-821988-1, ISBN13: 978-0-19-821988-0. Dewey:378/.199/0944. LCCN:86-012686.
Audience: **u,f.** *Choice, 1988.*

Copley, Terence **LC410.G7**
Spiritual Development in the State School: A Perspective on Worship and Spirituality in the Education System of England and Wales. Trade Cloth. University of Exeter Press. Exeter, 2000. 176p. ISBN:0-85989-600-5, ISBN13: 978-0-85989-600-9. Dewey:291.7/5/0942.
Audience: **u,f.**

Coulby, David & Jones, Crispin **LC93.A2C68 2001**
Education and Warfare in Europe. Trade Cloth. Ashgate Publishing, Ltd. Aldershot, 2001. 166p. ISBN:0-7546-1204-X, ISBN13: 978-0-7546-1204-9. Dewey:379.4. LCCN:2001-088801.
Audience: **g,l,u,f.**

Daglish, Neil D. **LC93.G7D34 1996**
Education Policy-Making in England and Wales: The Crucible Years, 1895-1911. Paper over Boards. Woburn Press. Andover,

1996. 496p. The Woburn Education Ser. ISBN:0-7130-0200-X, ISBN13: 978-0-7130-0200-3. Dewey:379.42/09/041. LCCN:95-044531.

Audience: **u,f.**

Dent, H. C. **LA631.D385 1977**
Education in England and Wales. Trade Cloth. Hodder General Publishing Division. London, 1977. iv, 171p. ISBN:0-340-21489-9, ISBN13: 978-0-340-21489-3. Dewey:370/.942. LCCN:78-318147.

Audience: **u,f.** B

Digby, Anne **LA631.7.D53 1981**
Children, School, and Society in Nineteenth-Century England. Trade Cloth. Macmillan Publishing Company, Inc. Old Tappan, NJ. 1981. 258p. ISBN:0-333-24678-0, ISBN13: 978-0-333-24678-8. Dewey:370.19/3/0942. LCCN:82-100863.

Audience: **u,f.** B

Drijvers, Jan Willem & MacDonald, A. A. (Editors) **LA31.C46 1995**
Centres of Learning: Learning and Location in Pre-Modern Europe and the Near East. Trade Cloth. Brill Academic Publishers, Inc. Boston, MA. 1995. xiv, 340p. Studies in Intellectual History, Vol. 61 ISBN:90-04-10193-4, ISBN13: 978-90-04-10193-7. Dewey:370/.93. LCCN:94-046806.

Audience: **u,f.**

Duke, Benjamin C. O. **LA1312**
The Japanese School: Lessons for Industrial America. Clark Kerr & James M. Hestor (Foreword by), Edwin O. Reischauer (Introduction by). Trade Cloth. Greenwood Publishing Group, Inc. Portsmouth, NH. 1986. 265p. ISBN:0-275-92053-4, ISBN13: 978-0-275-92053-1. Dewey:370/.952. LCCN:86-005002.

Audience: **g,l,u,f.** B

Epstein, Irving (Editor) **LA1131.82.C544 1991**
Chinese Education: Problems, Policies, and Prospects. Paper over Boards. Garland Publishing, Inc. New York, NY. 1991. 536p. Books in International Education, Vol. 20 ISBN:0-8240-4382-0, ISBN13: 978-0-8240-4382-7. Dewey:370/.951. LCCN:90-021938.

Audience: **u,f.** *Choice, 1991.*

Feingold, Mordechai **LA173**
History of Universities. Trade Cloth. Oxford University Press, Inc. New York, NY. 2005. 244p. ISBN:0-19-928928-X, ISBN13: 978-0-19-928928-8. Dewey:378.009.

Audience: **u,f.**

Feingold, Mordechai & Navarro-Brotons, Victor (Editors) **Q125.2.U55 2006**
Universities and Science in the Early Modern Period. Trade Cloth. Springer. New York, NY. 2006. viii, 309p. ISBN:1-4020-3974-3, ISBN13: 978-1-4020-3974-4. Dewey:509.024.

Audience: **u,f.**

Feldman, Jonathan **F1436.8.U6F45 1989**
Universities in the Business of Repression: The Academic-Military-Industrial Complex in Central America. Trade Cloth. South End Press. Cambridge, MA. 1989. 382p. Latina/O and Latin American Studies ISBN:0-89608-355-1, ISBN13: 978-0-89608-355-4. Dewey:303.4/8273/0728. LCCN:89-004156.

Audience: **l,u,f.**

Field, John **LA622.F54 1998**
European Dimensions: Education, Training and the European Union. Trade Paper. Jessica Kingsley Ltd. London, 1997. 224p. Higher Education Policy Ser. ISBN:1-85302-432-5, ISBN13: 978-1-85302-432-0. Dewey:370/.94. LCCN:96-036550.

Audience: **u,f.**

Fitzpatrick, Sheila **LA831.8 .F56**
The Commissariat of Enlightenment: Soviet Organization of Education and the Arts under Lunacharsky, October 1917-1921. Trade Paper. Cambridge University Press. New York, NY. 2002. 406p. Cambridge Russian, Soviet and Post-Soviet Studies ISBN:0-521-52438-5, ISBN13: 978-0-521-52438-4. Dewey:370.94709041.

Audience: **u,f.**

Fitzpatrick, Sheila **LA831.8**
Education and Social Mobility in the Soviet Union 1921-1934. Trade Paper. Cambridge University Press. New York, NY. 2002. 365p. Cambridge Russian, Soviet and Post-Soviet Studies ISBN:0-521-89423-9, ISBN13: 978-0-521-89423-4. Dewey:379.4/7/09042.

Audience: **u,f.**

Grendler, Paul F. **LA797.G74 2001**
The Universities of the Italian Renaissance. Trade Cloth. Johns Hopkins University Press. Baltimore, MD. 2002. 616p. ISBN:0-8018-6631-6, ISBN13: 978-0-8018-6631-9. Dewey:378.45. LCCN:00-011287.

Audience: **u,f.** *Choice, 2002.*

Guo, Yugui **LB2822.75.G86 2005**
Asia's Educational Edge: Current Achievements in Japan, Korea, Taiwan, China, and India. Book, Other. Lexington Books. Lanham, MD. 2005. 290p. ISBN:0-7391-0737-2, ISBN13: 978-0-7391-0737-9. Dewey:370/.95. LCCN:2004-016985.

Audience: **l,u,f.**

Hans, Nicholas **LA831 .H353**
The Russian Tradition in Education. Trade Cloth. Greenwood Publishing Group, Inc. Portsmouth, NH. 1973. 196p. ISBN:0-8371-6914-3, ISBN13: 978-0-8371-6914-9. Dewey:370/.947. LCCN:73-007104.

Audience: **u,f.**

Hartung, Jan-Peter & Reifeld, Helmut (Editors) **BP43.I48I75 2006**
Islamic Education, Diversity and National Identity: Dini Madaris in India Post 9/11. Cloth Text. SAGE Publications India Pvt, Ltd. New Delhi, 2006. 320p. ISBN:0-7619-3432-4, ISBN13: 978-0-7619-3432-5. Dewey:297.7/7/0954. LCCN:2005-019718.

Audience: **g,l,u,f.**

Hayhoe, Ruth **LA1133.H39 1989**
China's Universities and the Open Door. Cloth Text. M. E. Sharpe Inc. Armonk, NY. 1989. 264p. ISBN:0-87332-501-X, ISBN13: 978-0-87332-501-1. Dewey:378.51. LCCN:88-018347.

Audience: **u,f.** *Choice, 1989.*

Hayhoe, Ruth **LA1133.H388 1996**
China's Universities, 1895-1995: A Century of Cultural Conflict. Cloth Text. Garland Publishing, Inc. New York, NY. 1996. 328p. Studies in Higher Education, No. 4 ISBN:0-8153-1859-6, ISBN13: 978-0-8153-1859-0. Dewey:378.51/09/04. LCCN:95-044021.

Audience: **u,f.** *Choice, 1996.*

Holmes, Brian, et al. **LC116.S68H65 1995**
Russian Education: Tradition and Transition. Gerald H. Read & Natalya Voskresenskaya (Authors). Cloth Text. Garland Publishing, Inc. New York, NY. 1995. 400p. Reference Books in International Education, Vol. 27, Reference Library of Social Science, Vol. 26 ISBN:0-8153-1169-9, ISBN13: 978-0-8153-1169-0. Dewey:370/.947. LCCN:94-008442.
Audience: **u,f.**

Houston, R. A. **LA621.4**
Literacy in Early Modern Europe: Its Growth, Uses and Impact, 1500-1800. Ed. 2. Trade Paper. Longman Publishing Group. White Plains, NY. 2002. 312p. ISBN:0-582-36810-3, ISBN13: 978-0-582-36810-1. Dewey:370.9/4/0903.
Audience: **u,f.**

Hu, Shi Ming & Seifman, Eli (Editors) **LA1131.T64**
Toward a New World Outlook: A Documentary History of Education in the People's Republic of China, 1949-1976. Trade Cloth. A M S Press, Inc. New York, NY. 1976. xx, 335p. Asian Studies, No. 2 ISBN:0-404-15401-8, ISBN13: 978-0-404-15401-1. Dewey:370'.951. LCCN:76-023977.
Audience: **u,f.**

Kozol, Jonathan **LA486.K69**
Children of the Revolution: A Yankee Teacher in the Cuban Schools. Trade Cloth. Dell Publishing. New York, NY. 1978. xxi, 245p. ISBN:0-440-00982-0, ISBN13: 978-0-440-00982-5. Dewey:370/.97291. LCCN:78-018522.
Audience: **g,l,u,f.**

LeTendre, Gerald K. (Editor) **LA1312.C64 1999**
Competitor or Ally?: Japan's Role in American Educational Debates. Merry White, Ineko Tsuchida, Catherine C. Lewis, David McConnell, Hidetada Shimizu, Hua Yang, Kangmin Zeng & David Baker (Contribution by). Cloth Text. Garland Publishing, Inc. New York, NY. 1999. 200p. Reference Books in International Education, No. 45 ISBN:0-8153-3273-4, ISBN13: 978-0-8153-3273-2. Dewey:370/.952. LCCN:00-552170.
Audience: **l,u,f.**

Lorey, David E. **LA427.L67**
The University System and Economic Development in Mexico since 1929. Trade Cloth. Stanford University Press. Palo Alto, CA. 1993. 288p. ISBN:0-8047-2124-6, ISBN13: 978-0-8047-2124-0. Dewey:378.72/09/043. LCCN:93-020289.
Audience: **u,f.**

Lulat, Y. G-M. **LA1503**
A History of African Higher Education from Antiquity to the Present: A Critical Synthesis. Trade Cloth. Greenwood Publishing Group, Inc. Portsmouth, NH. 2005. 640p. Studies in Higher Education Ser. ISBN:0-313-32061-6, ISBN13: 978-0-313-32061-3. Dewey:378.6/09. LCCN:2004-028717.
Audience: **u,f.** *Choice, 2006.*

Maaba, Brown, et al. **LG468.5**
Education in Exile: SOMAFCO, the African National Congress School in Tanzania, 1978-1992. Loyiso Pulumani & Sean Morrow (Authors). Trade Paper. Human Sciences Research Council. Pretoria, 2005. 94p. ISBN:0-7969-2051-6, ISBN13: 978-0-7969-2051-5. Dewey:371/.009678. LCCN:2004-448312.
Audience: **u,f.**

Mays, Annabelle **LA849.57.P43 2000**
Challenge and Change in Education: The Experience of the Baltic States in the 1990's. Bryan T. Peck (Editor). Trade Cloth. Nova Science Publishers, Inc. Hauppauge, NY. 2000. 246p. ISBN:1-56072-852-3, ISBN13: 978-1-56072-852-8. Dewey:370/.9479. LCCN:2001-267529.
Audience: **u,f.**

Mickelson, Roslyn Arlin **HV887.B8C475 2000**
Children on the Streets of the Americas: Globalization, Homelessness Education in Brazil, Cuba and the United States. Trade Paper. Routledge. New York, NY. 2000. 304p. ISBN:0-415-92322-0, ISBN13: 978-0-415-92322-4. Dewey:362.74. LCCN:99-022989.
Audience: **u,f.**

Miller, Errol **LA476.E376 1998**
Educational Reform in the Commonwealth Caribbean. Trade Cloth. Organization of American States. Washington, DC. 1998. Educational Ser. ISBN:0-8270-3640-X, ISBN13: 978-0-8270-3640-6. Dewey:370/.9729. LCCN:98-035796.
Audience: **u,f.**

Milligan, Jeffrey Ayala **LC94**
Islamic Identity, Postcoloniality, and Educational Policy: Schooling and Ethno-Religious Conflict in the Southern Philippines. Cloth over Boards. Palgrave Macmillan. New York, NY. 2005. 240p. ISBN:1-4039-6351-7, ISBN13: 978-1-4039-6351-2. Dewey:371.82829709599. LCCN:2005-296447.
Audience: **u,f.**

Milloy, John **E96.5**
A National Crime: The Canadian Government and the Residential School System, 1879-1986. Trade Paper. University of Manitoba Press. Winnipeg, MB. 1999. 424p. Manitoba Studies in Native History Ser. ISBN:0-88755-646-9, ISBN13: 978-0-88755-646-3. Dewey:371.829/97071.
Audience: **u,f.**

Misnad, Sheikha **LA1101.M57**
Development of Modern Education in the Gulf. Trade Cloth. Evergreen Book Distributors. Los Angeles, CA. 1985. 386p. ISBN:0-685-14920-X, ISBN13: 978-0-685-14920-1. Dewey:370/.953/6.
Audience: **u,f.**

Nsamenang, A. Bame **HQ792.A35N73 2004**
Cultures of Human Development and Education: Challenge to Growing up African. Trade Cloth. Nova Science Publishers, Inc. Hauppauge, NY. 2005. 192p. ISBN:1-59454-187-6, ISBN13: 978-1-59454-187-2. Dewey:305.231/096. LCCN:2004-021765.
Audience: **u,f.**

Okano, Kaori & Tsuchiya, Motonori **LA1312 .O426 1999**
Education in Contemporary Japan: Inequality and Diversity. Harumi Befu, Roger Goodman, Michio Muramatsu, Wolfgang Seifert, Yoshio Sugimoto & Chizuko Ueno (Contribution by). Cloth Text. Cambridge University Press. New York, NY. 1999. 286p. Contemporary Japanese Society Ser. ISBN:0-521-62252-2, ISBN13: 978-0-521-62252-3. Dewey:370/.952. LCCN:98-043666.
Audience: **u,f.** *Choice, 1999.*

Orme, Nicholas **LA2141**
Education in the West of England, 1066-1548. Trade Paper. University of Exeter Press. Exeter, 2003. 254p. South-West Studies ISBN:0-85989-707-9, ISBN13: 978-0-85989-707-5. Dewey:370/.9423.
Audience: **u,f.**

Orme, Nicholas **LA631.3**
Medieval Schools: Roman Britain to Renaissance England. Cloth over Boards. Yale University Press. Cumberland, RI. 2006. 432p. ISBN:0-300-11102-9, ISBN13: 978-0-300-11102-6. Dewey:370.942/09031. LCCN:2006-004516.
Audience: **u,f.**

Osborn, Marilyn, et al. **LB3602**
A World of Difference? Elizabeth McNess, Patricia Broadfoot, Claire Planel, Birte Ravn & Pat Triggs (Authors). Cloth Text. McGraw-Hill Education. Maidenhead, 2003. 224p. ISBN:0-335-21102-X, ISBN13: 978-0-335-21102-9. Dewey:306.4/3.
Audience: **l,u,f.**

Osborne, Robert D. **LA669.63.O73 1995**
Higher Education in Ireland: North and South. Trade Paper. Jessica Kingsley Ltd. London, 1996. 182p. Higher Education Policy Ser., No. 33 ISBN:1-85302-379-5, ISBN13: 978-1-85302-379-8. Dewey:378.4/15. LCCN:96-157046.
Audience: **u,f.**

Paterson, Lindsay **LA651.82**
Scottish Education in the Twentieth Century. Trade Paper. Edinburgh University Press. Edinburgh, 2003. 256p. ISBN:0-7486-1590-3, ISBN13: 978-0-7486-1590-2. Dewey:370.94110904. LCCN:2003-501535.
Audience: **u,f.**

Pedersen, Olaf **LA627 .P4313 1997**
The First Universities: Studium Generale and the Origins of University Education in Europe. Richard North (Translator). Trade Cloth. Cambridge University Press. New York, NY. 1998. 326p. ISBN:0-521-59431-6, ISBN13: 978-0-521-59431-8. Dewey:378.4/09/02. LCCN:97-007037.
Audience: **u,f.**

Pepper, Suzanne **LA1131.82.P47 1996**
Radicalism and Education Reform in 20th-Century China: The Search for an Ideal Development Model. Trade Paper. Cambridge University Press. New York, NY. 2000. 622p. ISBN:0-521-77860-3, ISBN13: 978-0-521-77860-2. Dewey:370/.951/09047.
Audience: **u,f.** *Choice, 1997.*

Platt, Brian **LC94.J3P53 2004**
Burning and Building: Schooling and State Formation in Japan, 1750-1890. Trade Cloth. Harvard University Press. Cambridge, MA. 2004. 352p. Harvard East Asian Monographs, Vol. 237 ISBN:0-674-01396-4, ISBN13: 978-0-674-01396-4. Dewey:379.52/09/034. LCCN:2004-003854.
Audience: **u,f.** *Choice, 2005.*

Prentice, Alison **MLCM 2006/10092**
The School Promoters: Education and Social Class in Mid-Nineteenth Century Upper Canada. Trade Paper. University of Toronto Press. Toronto, ON. 2004. 192p. Canadian Social History Ser. ISBN:0-8020-8692-6, ISBN13: 978-0-8020-8692-1. Dewey:370/.9713/09034. LCCN:2004-299371.
Audience: **u,f.**

Prescott, Laurence E. **PQ8180.1.R77Z85 2000**
Without Hatreds or Fears: Jorge Artel and the Struggle for Black Literacy Expression in Colombia. Trade Cloth. Wayne State University Press. Detroit, MI. 2000. 298p. African American Life Ser. ISBN:0-8143-2751-6, ISBN13: 978-0-8143-2751-7. Dewey:868. LCCN:99-039371.
Audience: **u,f.** *Choice, 2001.*

Ringer, Fritz K. **LA727.R47 1990**
The Decline of the German Mandarins: The German Academic Community, 1890-1933. Trade Paper. Wesleyan University Press. Middletown, CT. 1990. 548p. ISBN:0-8195-6235-1, ISBN13: 978-0-8195-6235-7. Dewey:301.445. LCCN:90-050315.
Audience: **u,f.** B

Roesgaard, Marie H. **LA1312 .R62 1998**
Moving Mountains: Japanese Education Reform. Trade Paper. Aarhus Universitetsforlag. DK-8200 Aarhus N, 1998. 264p. Acta Jutlandica 73:1 Ser., Vol. 71:Humanities Ser. ISBN:87-7288-477-0, ISBN13: 978-87-7288-477-6. Dewey:370. LCCN:98-189528.
Audience: **u,f.**

Rohlen, Thomas P. & LeTendre, Gerald K. (Editors) **LB1025.3.R64 1996**
Teaching and Learning in Japan. Trade Cloth. Cambridge University Press. New York, NY. 1996. 405p. ISBN:0-521-49587-3, ISBN13: 978-0-521-49587-5. Dewey:371.3/0952. LCCN:95-013941.
Audience: **u,f.**

Schell, Patience A. **LC505**
Church and State Education in Revolutionary Mexico City. Trade Cloth. University of Arizona Press. Tucson, AZ. 2003. 290p. ISBN:0-8165-2198-0, ISBN13: 978-0-8165-2198-2. Dewey:371.071/27253. LCCN:2003-005509.
Audience: **u,f.**

Seddon, Terri **LA2101.S43 1994**
Context and Beyond: Reframing the Theory and Practice of Education. Library Binding. Taylor & Francis Group. Philadelphia, PA. 1994. 230p. ISBN:0-7507-0181-1, ISBN13: 978-0-7507-0181-5. Dewey:370/.994. LCCN:93-045397.
Audience: **u,f.**

Seeberg, Vilma **LA1131.82.S44 2000**
The Rhetoric and Reality of Mass Education in Mao's China. Trade Cloth. Edwin Mellen Press, The. Lewiston, NY. 2000. 592p. Chinese Studies, Vol. 14 ISBN:0-7734-7638-5, ISBN13: 978-0-7734-7638-7. Dewey:370/.951. LCCN:00-041833.
Audience: **u,f.**

Sehoole, M.T. **LC180.S6S45 2005**
Democratizing Higher Education Policy: Constraints of Reform in Post-Apartheid South Africa. Paper over Boards. Routledge. New York, NY. 2005. 250p. RoutledgeFalmer Studies in Higher Education Ser. ISBN:0-415-97445-3, ISBN13: 978-0-415-97445-5. Dewey:378.68. LCCN:2005-005709.
Audience: **u,f.**

Silver, Harold **LC178**
Higher Education and Opinion Making in Twentieth-Century England. Paper over Boards. Woburn Press. Andover, 2003. 276p. The Woburn Education Ser. ISBN:0-7130-0231-X, ISBN13: 978-0-7130-0231-7. Dewey:378.42/09/04. LCCN:2003-047938.
Audience: **u,f.**

Silver, Harold & Silver, Pamela **LC4091 .S48 1991**
An Educational War on Poverty: American and British Policy-Making 1960-1980. Trade Cloth. Cambridge University Press. New York, NY. 1991. 459p. ISBN:0-521-38149-5, ISBN13: 978-0-521-38149-9. Dewey:379.41/0973. LCCN:90-020583.
Audience: **u,f.**

Solis, Jose **LA501**
Public School Reform in Puerto Rico: Sustaining Colonial Models of Development, 60. Greenwood Press. 1994. ISBN:0-313-28978-6, ISBN13: 978-0-313-28978-1.
Audience: **u,f.**

Tibawi, Abdul Latif **LA1491.T5**
Islamic Education: Its Traditions and Modernization into the Arab National Systems. Trade Cloth. Luzac Oriental Ltd. Corsham, 1972. 256p. ISBN:0-7189-0161-4, ISBN13: 978-0-7189-0161-5. Dewey:370/.917/671. LCCN:73-159526.
Audience: **u,f.**

Toth, Istvan Gyorgy **LC156.H9T6813 2000**
Literacy and Written Culture in Early Modern Central Europe. Trade Cloth. Central European University Press. Herndon, VA. 2000. 266p. ISBN:963-9116-85-8, ISBN13: 978-963-9116-85-6. Dewey:302.2/244. LCCN:2001-017221.
Audience: **u,f.** *Choice, 2001.*

Unger, Jonathan **LA1134.C35**
Education under Mao: Class and Competition in Canton Schools, 1960-1980. Trade Paper. Kegan Paul International, Ltd. London, 1982. 308p. ISBN:0-231-05299-5, ISBN13: 978-0-231-05299-3. Dewey:370/.951/27. LCCN:81-015470.
Audience: **u,f.**

United States.Congress. Senate. Committee on Appropriations. Subcommittee on Departments of Labor, Health and Human Services, Education, and Related Agencies **HV6431**
Palestinian Education: Teaching for Peace or War?: Hearing Before a Subcommittee of the Committee Appropriations, United States Senate, One Hundred Eighth Congress, First Session, Special Hearing, October 30, 2003, Washington, DC. http://frwebgate.access.gpo.gov/cgi-bin/getdoc.cgi?dbname=108_senate_hearings&docid=f:90712.pdf
U.S. G.P.O.. ISBN:0-16-071246-7, ISBN13: 978-0-16-071246-3.
Audience: **u,f.**

World Bank Staff (Contribution by) **LA568.T47 2003**
Tertiary Education in Colombia: Paving the Way for Reform. Trade Paper. World Bank Publications. Washington, DC. 2003. 228p. A World Bank Country Study Ser. ISBN:0-8213-5466-3, ISBN13: 978-0-8213-5466-7. Dewey:378.861. LCCN:2003-045008.
Audience: **u,f.**

Zameret, Zvi **LC3747.I75T7313 2002**
The Melting Pot in Israel: The Commission of Inquiry Concerning the Education of Immigrant Children During the Early Years of the State. Paper Text. State University of New York Press. Albany, NY. 2002. 320p. SUNY Series in Israeli Studies ISBN:0-7914-5256-5, ISBN13: 978-0-7914-5256-1. Dewey:303.48/2/095694. LCCN:2001-049303.
Audience: **u,f.**

History of Education > Biography

Allitt, Patrick **E175.8.A505 2004**
I'm the Teacher, You're the Student: A Semester in the University Classroom. Trade Cloth. University of Pennsylvania Press. Philadelphia, PA. 2004. 256p. ISBN:0-8122-3821-4, ISBN13: 978-0-8122-3821-1. Dewey:378.1/2/092. LCCN:2004-042047.
Audience: **g,l,u,f.**

Ashton-Warner, Sylvia (Author, Author) **LC3501.M3A8 1986**
Teacher. Trade Paper. Simon & Schuster. New York, NY. 1986. 224p. A Touchstone Book Ser. ISBN:0-671-61768-0, ISBN13: 978-0-671-61768-4. Dewey:371.97/9916. LCCN:85-027962.
Audience: **g,l,u,f.**

Collins, Marva & Tamarkin, Civia **LA2317.C62A3 1990**
Marva Collins' Way: Returning to Excellence in Education. Ed. 2. Alex Haley (Foreword by). Trade Paper. Penguin Group (USA) Inc. New York, NY. 1990. 256p. ISBN:0-87477-572-8, ISBN13: 978-0-87477-572-3. Dewey:372.11/092 B. LCCN:82-010516.
Audience: **g,l,u,f.**

Goodlad, John I. **LB885.G66 2004**
Romances with Schools: A Life of Education. Trade Cloth. McGraw-Hill Companies, The. New York, NY. 2004. 256p. ISBN:0-07-143212-4, ISBN13: 978-0-07-143212-2. Dewey:370/.92 B. LCCN:2003-024623.
Audience: **g.**

Johnston, James Scott **LB875.D5J65 2006**
Inquiry and Education: John Dewey and the Quest for Democracy. Cloth Text. State University of New York Press. Albany, NY. 2006. 288p. SUNY Series in Philosophy of Education ISBN:0-7914-6723-6, ISBN13: 978-0-7914-6723-7. Dewey:370/.1. LCCN:2005-020657.
Audience: **l,f.**

Keller, Helen **HV1624**
Teacher: Anne Sullivan Macy. Trade Cloth. Greenwood Publishing Group, Inc. Portsmouth, NH. 1985. 256p. ISBN:0-313-24738-2, ISBN13: 978-0-313-24738-5. Dewey:371.91/1/0924 B. LCCN:84-025274.
Audience: **g,l,u,f.**

Klein, Ann G. **BF109.H6K57 2002**
A Forgotten Voice: A Biography of Leta Stetter Hollingworth. Trade Paper. Great Potential Press, Inc. Scottsdale, AZ. 2002. 264p. ISBN:0-910707-53-7, ISBN13: 978-0-910707-53-4. Dewey:150/.92 B. LCCN:2002-012772.
Audience: **u,f.** *Choice, 2003.*

Kohl, Herbert R. **LA2317.K64**
Growing Minds. Trade Paper. HarperCollins Publishers. New York, NY. 1989. 192p. ISBN:0-06-132089-7, ISBN13: 978-0-06-132089-7. Dewey:371.102.
Audience: **l,u,f.**

Lillard, Angeline Stoll **LB1029.M75L53 2005**
Montessori: The Science Behind the Genius. Trade Cloth. Oxford University Press, Inc. New York, NY. 2005. 419p. ISBN:0-19-516868-2, ISBN13: 978-0-19-516868-6. Dewey:371.39/2. LCCN:2004-057580.
Audience: **u,f.** *Choice, 2006.*

Lord, John **LA2317.W5 L6**
The Life of Emma Willard. Trade Cloth. New Library Press.Net. Murrieta, CA. 2003. 351p. ISBN:0-7950-4500-X, ISBN13: 978-0-7950-4500-4. Dewey:370.92.
Audience: **u,f.**

Mack-Kirschner, Adrienne **LB1025.3.M334 2004**
Powerful Classroom Stories from Accomplished Teachers: Stories from the Classrooms of Accomplished Teachers. Trade Cloth. Corwin Press. Thousand Oaks, CA. 2003. 216p. 1-Off Ser. ISBN:0-7619-3911-3, ISBN13: 978-0-7619-3911-5. Dewey:371.102. LCCN:2003-012432.
Audience: **l,u,f.** *Choice, 2004.*

McCourt, Frank **LA2383.C52**
Teacher Man: A Memoir. Saddle Stitched, Cloth over Boards, Dust Jacket. Simon & Schuster. New York, NY. 2005. 389p. ISBN:0-7432-8966-8, ISBN13: 978-0-7432-8966-5. Dewey:371.10092 B.
Audience: **g,l,u,f.**

Ohles, Frederik M., et al. **LA2311**
Biographical Dictionary of Modern American Educators. Shirley G. Ohles & John Ramsay (Authors). Cloth Text. Greenwood Publishing Group, Inc. Portsmouth, NH. 1997. 448p. ISBN:0-313-29133-0, ISBN13: 978-0-313-29133-3. Dewey:370/.92/2 B. LCCN:97-006413.
Audience: **l,u,f.** *Choice, 1998.*

Ohles, John F. (Editor) **LA2311**
Biographical Dictionary of American Educators, Vol. 2. Cloth Text. Greenwood Publishing Group, Inc. Portsmouth, NH. 1978. li, 1666p. ISBN:0-8371-9895-X, ISBN13: 978-0-8371-9895-8. Dewey:370/.92/2. LCCN:77-084750.
Audience: **l,u,f.**

Ohles, John F. (Editor) **LA2311**
Biographical Dictionary of American Educators. Cloth Text. Greenwood Publishing Group, Inc. Portsmouth, NH. 1978. 1666p. ISBN:0-8371-9893-3, ISBN13: 978-0-8371-9893-4. Dewey:370/.92/2. LCCN:77-084750.
Audience: **l,u,f.**

Ohles, John F. (Editor) **LA2311**
Biographical Dictionary of American Educators, Vol. 3. Cloth Text. Greenwood Publishing Group, Inc. Portsmouth, NH. 1978. li, 1666p. ISBN:0-8371-9896-8, ISBN13: 978-0-8371-9896-5. Dewey:370/.92/2. LCCN:77-084750.
Audience: **l,u,f.**

Paul, James L. & Smith, Terry Jo (Editors) **LC196.S6994 2000**
Stories Out of School: Memories and Reflections on Care and Cruelty in the Classroom. Trade Cloth. Greenwood Publishing Group, Inc. Portsmouth, NH. 2000. xii, 162p. Contemporary Studies in Social and Policy Issues in Education ISBN:1-56750-476-0, ISBN13: 978-1-56750-476-7. Dewey:370.11/5. LCCN:99-036571.
Audience: **g,l,u,f.** *Choice, 2001.*

Peltzman, Barbara R. **LB1139**
Pioneers of Early Childhood Education: A Bio-Bibliographical Guide. Cloth Text. Greenwood Publishing Group, Inc. Portsmouth, NH. 1998. 160p. ISBN:0-313-30404-1, ISBN13: 978-0-313-30404-0. Dewey:372.21/092/2. LCCN:97-026907.
Audience: **l,u,f.** *Choice, 1998.*

Smith, L. Glenn & Smith, Joan K. **LB17**
Lives in Education: A Narrative of People and Ideas. Ed. 2. Trade Paper. Lawrence Erlbaum Associates, Inc. Mahwah, NJ. 1995. 472p. ISBN:0-8058-8008-9, ISBN13: 978-0-8058-8008-3. Dewey:370.922. LCCN:92-050028.
Audience: **g,l,u,f.**

Theory and Practice of Education

LB1028.27.U6
□ Educator's Reference Desk.
http://www.eduref.org
Audience: **g,l,u,f.**

LC149
□ Literacy Web.
http://www.literacy.uconn.edu
Audience: **g,l,u,f.**

Alexander, Robin J. **LB43.A44 2001**
Culture and Pedagogy: International Comparisons in Primary Education. Trade Paper. Blackwell Publishing, Inc. Malden, MA. 2001. 668p. ISBN:0-631-22051-8, ISBN13: 978-0-631-22051-0. Dewey:372. LCCN:00-057908.
Audience: **u,f.** *Choice, 2001.*

American Education Research Association **LB15 .E48**
Encyclopedia of Educational Research. Ed. 7. Trade Cloth. Thomson Gale. Farmington Hills, MI. 2001. ISBN:0-02-864945-1, ISBN13: 978-0-02-864945-0. Dewey:370/.3.
Audience: **g,l,u,f.**

Anderson, Lorin W., et al. **LB17.T29 2001**
A Taxonomy for Learning, Teaching and Assessing: A Revision of Bloom's Taxonomy of Educational Objectives. David R. Krathwohl & Peter W. Airasian (Authors), Benjamin Samuel Bloom (Contribution by). Trade Cloth. Allyn & Bacon, Inc. Boston, MA. 2000. 384p. ISBN:0-321-08405-5, ISBN13: 978-0-321-08405-7. Dewey:370/.1. LCCN:00-063423.
Audience: **u,f.**

Arnove, Robert F. & Torres, Carlos Alberto (Editors) **LB43.C68 2003**
Comparative Education: The Dialectic of the Global and the Local. Ed. 2. Book, Other. Rowman & Littlefield Publishers, Inc. Lanham, MD. 2003. 504p. ISBN:0-7425-2380-2, ISBN13: 978-0-7425-2380-7. Dewey:370/.9. LCCN:2003-007673.
Audience: **g,l,u,f.** *Choice, 2000.*

Blake, Nigel (Editor) **LB14.7.B57 2002**
The Blackwell Guide to the Philosophy of Education. Trade Paper. Blackwell Publishing, Inc. Malden, MA. 2002. 432p. Blackwell Philosophy Guides Ser., Vol. 9 ISBN:0-631-22119-0, ISBN13: 978-0-631-22119-7. Dewey:370/.1. LCCN:2002-066430.
Audience: **u,f.** *Choice, 2003.*

Blake, Nigel, et al. **LB14**
Thinking Again: Education after Postmodernism. Paul Smeyers, Paul Standish & Richard Smith (Authors). Trade Cloth. Greenwood Publishing Group, Inc. Portsmouth, NH. 1998. 224p.

Critical Studies in Education and Culture ISBN:0-89789-511-8, ISBN13: 978-0-89789-511-8. Dewey:370.1. LCCN:97-027886.
Audience: **u,f.** *Choice, 1998.*

Burns, Hobert Warren **LB675.N45C8**
Philosophy of Education: Essays and Commentaries. Paper Text. Textbook Publishers. Temecula, CA. 2003. 442p. ISBN:0-7581-4700-7, ISBN13: 978-0-7581-4700-4. Dewey:282/.092.
Audience: **u,f.**

Chambliss, J. J. (Editor) **LB17.P485 1996**
Philosophy of Education: An Encyclopedia. Cloth Text. Garland Publishing, Inc. New York, NY. 1996. 736p. ISBN:0-8153-1177-X, ISBN13: 978-0-8153-1177-5. Dewey:370/.1. LCCN:96-018393.
Audience: **l,u,f.** *Choice, 1997.*

Davis, Brent **LB14.7.D38 2004**
Inventions of Teaching: A Genealogy. Cloth over Boards. Lawrence Erlbaum Associates, Inc. Mahwah, NJ. 2004. 256p. The Studies in Curriculum Theory Ser. ISBN:0-8058-5038-4, ISBN13: 978-0-8058-5038-3. Dewey:371.102/01. LCCN:2003-061552.
Audience: **u,f.** *Choice, 2004.*

Dejnozka, Edward L., et al. **LB15**
American Educators' Encyclopedia. Ed. 2. David E. Kapel, Charles S. Gifford & Marilyn B. Kapel (Authors). Cloth Text. Greenwood Publishing Group, Inc. Portsmouth, NH. 1991. 752p. ISBN:0-313-25269-6, ISBN13: 978-0-313-25269-3. Dewey:370/.3. LCCN:90-041510.
Audience: **g,l,u,f.**

Eby, Frederick (Editor) **LB7.E3**
Early Protestant Educators. Trade Cloth. A M S Press, Inc. New York, NY. BCL Ser. I ISBN:0-404-02238-3, ISBN13: 978-0-404-02238-9. Dewey:370.1/08. LCCN:76-149656.
Audience: **u,f.**

Egan, Kieran **LB41.E382 1999**
Children's Minds, Talking Rabbits and Clockwork: Changes - Essays on Education. Cloth Text. Teachers College Press, Teachers College, Columbia University. New York, NY. 1999. 216p. Critical Issues in Curriculum Ser. ISBN:0-8077-3808-5, ISBN13: 978-0-8077-3808-5. Dewey:370.11. LCCN:98-037458.
Audience: **l,u,f.** *Choice, 1999.*

Egan, Kieran **LB14.7**
The Educated Mind: How Cognitive Tools Shape Our Understanding. Trade Paper. University of Chicago Press. Chicago, IL. 1998. 310p. ISBN:0-226-19039-0, ISBN13: 978-0-226-19039-6. Dewey:370/.1.
Audience: **u,f.**

Finkel, Donald L. & Arney, William Ray **LB14.7.F56 1995**
Educating for Freedom: The Paradox of Pedagogy. Cloth Text. Rutgers University Press. Piscataway, NJ. 1995. 260p. Rose Series of the American Sociological Association ISBN:0-8135-2201-3, ISBN13: 978-0-8135-2201-2. Dewey:370/.1. LCCN:94-025231.
Audience: **u,f.** *Choice, 1996.*

Gallagher, Shaun **LB14.7**
Hermeneutics and Education. Paper Text. State University of New York Press. Albany, NY. 1992. 402p. SUNY Series in Contemporary Continental Philosophy ISBN:0-7914-1176-1, ISBN13: 978-0-7914-1176-6. Dewey:370/.1. LCCN:91-037120.
Audience: **u,f.** *Choice, 1993.*

Goodlad, John I. **LB41.G65 1994**
What Schools Are For. Ed. 2. Trade Paper. Phi Delta Kappa Educational Foundation. Bloomington, IN. 1994. 144p. ISBN:0-87367-467-7, ISBN13: 978-0-87367-467-6. Dewey:370/.11. LCCN:94-066515.
Audience: **g,l,u,f.**

Hare, William **LB41.H285**
Open-Mindedness and Education. Trade Paper. McGill-Queen's University Press. Montreal, PQ. 1993. 178p. ISBN:0-7735-0411-7, ISBN13: 978-0-7735-0411-0. Dewey:370.1.
Audience: **u,f.**

Hawkins, David B. **LB41.H34**
The Informed Vision: Essays on Learning and Human Nature. Perfect. Agathon Press. Bronx, NY. 2002. 248p. ISBN:0-87586-177-6, ISBN13: 978-0-87586-177-7. Dewey:370.
Audience: **u,f.**

Hirst, Paul H. & White, Patricia **LB7.P5432 1998**
The Philosophy of Education: Major Themes in the Analytic Tradition. Paper over Boards. Routledge. New York, NY. 1998. 1712p. Major Writings in Education Ser. ISBN:0-415-12944-3, ISBN13: 978-0-415-12944-2. Dewey:370/.1. LCCN:97-030748.
Audience: **u,f.**

Lawton, Denis & Gordon, Peter **LB14.7.L39 2002**
A History of Western Educational Ideas. Paper over Boards. Woburn Press. Andover, 2002. 256p. The Woburn Education Ser. ISBN:0-7130-0219-0, ISBN13: 978-0-7130-0219-5. Dewey:370/.1. LCCN:2001-057514.
Audience: **u,f.** *Choice, 2003.*

Noble, Keith A. (Editor, Compiled by) **LB7.I65 1995**
The International Education Quotations Encyclopedia. Paper Text. McGraw-Hill Education. Maidenhead, 1995. 400p. ISBN:0-335-19394-3, ISBN13: 978-0-335-19394-3. Dewey:370. LCCN:94-036312.
Audience: **g,l,u,f.** *Choice, 1996.*

Noddings, Nel **LB41.N55 2003**
Happiness and Education. Cloth Text. Cambridge University Press. New York, NY. 2003. 316p. ISBN:0-521-80763-8, ISBN13: 978-0-521-80763-0. Dewey:370/.1. LCCN:2002-041547.
Audience: **u,f.** *Choice, 2004.*

O'Brien, Nancy P. & Fabiano, Emily S. **Z5811.C798 1991**
Core List of Books and Journals in Education. Trade Cloth. Greenwood Publishing Group, Inc. Portsmouth, NH. 1991. 136p. ISBN:0-89774-559-0, ISBN13: 978-0-89774-559-8. Dewey:016.37. LCCN:90-042404.
Audience: **u,f.** *Choice, 1991.*

Palmer, Joy A. (Editor) **LB17.F56 2001**
Fifty Major Thinkers on Education: From Confucious to Dewey. Paper over Boards. Routledge. New York, NY. 2001. 272p. Key Guides ISBN:0-415-23125-6, ISBN13: 978-0-415-23125-1. Dewey:370/.92/2 B. LCCN:2001-019309.
Audience: **u,f.** *Choice, 2002.*

Palmer, Joy A. (Editor) **LB17.F57 2001**
Fifty Modern Thinkers on Education: From Piaget to the Present Day. Trade Paper. Routledge. New York, NY. 2001. 320p. Key Guides ISBN:0-415-22409-8, ISBN13: 978-0-415-22409-3. Dewey:370/.92/2 B. LCCN:2001-019308.
Audience: **u,f.** *Choice, 2002.*

Power, Edward J. **LB14.7.P68 1995**
Educational Philosophy: A History from the Ancient World to Modern America. Cloth Text. Garland Publishing, Inc. New York, NY. 1995. 256p. Garland Reference Library of Social Science, Vol. 3 ISBN:0-8153-1971-1, ISBN13: 978-0-8153-1971-9. Dewey:370/.1/09. LCCN:95-024265.
Audience: **u,f.** *Choice, 1996.*

Reed, Ronald F. **LB14.7**
Philosophical Documents in Education. Paper Text. Addison-Wesley Longman, Inc. Boston, MA. 1995. ISBN:0-8013-1725-8, ISBN13: 978-0-8013-1725-5. Dewey:370/.1.
Audience: **u,f.**

Rorty, Amelie **LB41.P572 1998**
Philosophers on Education. Paper over Boards. Routledge. New York, NY. 1998. 496p. ISBN:0-415-19130-0, ISBN13: 978-0-415-19130-2. Dewey:370/.1. LCCN:98-004865.
Audience: **u.**

Sirotnik, Kenneth A. & Soder, Roger (Editors) **LB7.B396 1999**
The Beat of a Different Drummer: Essays on Educational Renewal in Honor of John I. Goodlad. Cloth Text. Peter Lang Publishing, Inc. New York, NY. 1999. XVI, 318p. ISBN:0-8204-3797-2, ISBN13: 978-0-8204-3797-2. Dewey:370/.973. LCCN:98-044638.
Audience: **u,f.**

Taylor, James S. **LB14.7.T39 1998**
[Ebook] Poetic Knowledge: The Recovery of Education. E-Book. NetLibrary, Inc. Boulder, CO. 1998. ISBN:0-585-05600-5, ISBN13: 978-0-585-05600-5. Dewey:370/.1.
Audience: **u,f.** *Choice, 1998.*

Unger, Harlow G. **LB17.U54 2001**
Encyclopedia of American Education, Set. Ed. 2. Trade Cloth. Facts On File, Inc. New York, NY. 2001. 1392p. Facts on File Library of American History ISBN:0-8160-4344-2, ISBN13: 978-0-8160-4344-6. Dewey:370.97303. LCCN:2001-017475.
Audience: **g,l,u,f.** *Choice, 2002.*

Whitehead, Alfred North **LB41**
The Organisation of Thought, Educational and Scientific. Trade Cloth. Greenwood Publishing Group, Inc. Portsmouth, NH. 1974. 228p. ISBN:0-8371-3448-X, ISBN13: 978-0-8371-3448-2. Dewey:370/.8. LCCN:76-106727.
Audience: **u,f.** [BCL3]

Winch, Christopher & Gingell, John **LB15.W54 1999**
Key Concepts in the Philosophy of Education. Paper over Boards. Routledge. New York, NY. 1999. 296p. Key Guides ISBN:0-415-17303-5, ISBN13: 978-0-415-17303-2. Dewey:370.1. LCCN:00-267717.
Audience: **l.** *Choice, 2000.*

Zoch, Paul A. **LB14.7.I63 2004**
Doomed to Fail: The Built-in Defects of American Education. Book, Other. Ivan R. Dee Publisher. Blue Ridge Summit, PA. 2004. 272p. ISBN:1-56663-567-5, ISBN13: 978-1-56663-567-7. Dewey:370/.1/0973. LCCN:2003-066529.
Audience: **g,l,u,f.** *Choice, 2005.*

Theory and Practice of Education > Systems of Individual Educators

Addis, Cameron **LB695.J42A33 2002**
Jefferson's Vision for Education, 1760-1845. Trade Paper. Peter Lang Publishing, Inc. New York, NY. 2002. 254p. History of Schools and Schooling Ser., Vol. 29 ISBN:0-8204-5755-8, ISBN13: 978-0-8204-5755-0. Dewey:370/.1. LCCN:2001-038904.
Audience: **u,f.** *Choice, 2004.*

Ball, Stephen J. (Editor) **LB880.F682F68 1990**
Foucault and Education: Disciplines and Knowledge. Cloth Text. Routledge. New York, NY. 1990. 224p. ISBN:0-415-04710-2, ISBN13: 978-0-415-04710-4. Dewey:370.1. LCCN:89-049384.
Audience: **u,f.** *Choice, 1991.*

Barrow, Robin **LB85.P7**
Plato and Education. Trade Cloth. Routledge. New York, NY. 1976. xi, 83p. Students Library of Education ISBN:0-7100-8343-2, ISBN13: 978-0-7100-8343-2. Dewey:370/.1. LCCN:76-367059.
Audience: **l,u,f.** [BCL3]

Bauman, Richard W. **LB85.A72B38 1998**
Aristotle's Logic of Education. Trade Cloth. Peter Lang Publishing, Inc. New York, NY. 1998. 240p. New Perspectives in Philosophical Scholarship Ser. ISBN:0-8204-4007-8, ISBN13: 978-0-8204-4007-1. Dewey:370/.1. LCCN:97-048799.
Audience: **u,f.** *Choice, 1999.*

Beineke, John A. **LB875.K54B44 1997**
And There Were Giants in the Land: The Life of William Heard Kilpatrick. Trade Paper. Peter Lang Publishing, Inc. New York, NY. 1998. xx,500p. History of Schools and Schooling Ser., Vol. 5 ISBN:0-8204-3773-5, ISBN13: 978-0-8204-3773-6. Dewey:370/.92 B. LCCN:97-008539.
Audience: **u,f.** *Choice, 1999.*

Bestor, Arthur E. **LB875.B345 1985**
Educational Wastelands: The Retreat from Learning in Our Public Schools. Ed. 2. Clarence J. Karier & Foster McMurray (Contribution by). Trade Cloth. University of Illinois Press. Champaign, IL. 1985. 304p. ISBN:0-252-01226-7, ISBN13: 978-0-252-01226-6. Dewey:370/.973. LCCN:85-001014.
Audience: **l,u,f.** [BCL3] *Choice, 1986.*

Bode, Boyd H. **LB875.B518**
Progressive Education at the Crossroads. Trade Cloth. Ayer Company Publishers, Inc. Manchester, NH. 1972. 128p. American Education Ser., :No. 2 ISBN:0-405-03696-5, ISBN13: 978-0-405-03696-5. Dewey:370.1. LCCN:71-165707.
Audience: **u,f.**

Boyd, William **LB518 .B66**
Educational Theory of Jean Jacques Rousseau. Trade Cloth. Russell & Russell Publishers. New York, NY. 1963. ISBN:0-8462-0359-6, ISBN13: 978-0-8462-0359-9. Dewey:370.1. LCCN:63-015150.
Audience: **u,f.** *B*

Boydston, Jo Ann (Editor) **LB875.D5.G83**
Guide to the Works of John Dewey. Trade Paper. Southern Illinois University Press. Carbondale, IL. 1972. 413p. Arcturus Books Paperbacks ISBN:0-8093-0561-5, ISBN13: 978-0-8093-0561-2. Dewey:191. LCCN:70-112383.
Audience: **g,u,f.** *B*

Brameld, Theodore Burghard Hurt **LB0875.B715**
Education for the Emerging Age. Trade Paper. Books on Demand. Ann Arbor, MI. 284p. ISBN:0-598-72096-0, ISBN13: 978-0-598-72096-2. Dewey:370.1. LCCN:60-015207.
Audience: **u,f.**

Breault, Donna Adair & Breault, Rick (Editors) **LB875.D5E96 2005**
Experiencing Dewey: Insights for Today's Classroom. David T. Hansen (Foreword by). Trade Cloth. Kappa Delta Pi, International Honor Society in Education. Indianapolis, IN. 2005. 176p. ISBN:0-912099-42-9, ISBN13: 978-0-912099-42-2. Dewey:370/.1. LCCN:2005-007771.
Audience: **l,u,f.**

Broudy, Harry S. **LB1025.2**
The Uses of Schooling. Cloth Text. Routledge. New York, NY. 1988. 160p. ISBN:0-415-00176-5, ISBN13: 978-0-415-00176-2. Dewey:370/.1. LCCN:87-015753.
Audience: **u,f.** *Choice, 1988.*

Bruner, Jerome S. **LB17**
Process of Education. Trade Paper. Harvard University Press. Cambridge, MA. 1976. 127p. ISBN:0-674-71001-0, ISBN13: 978-0-674-71001-6. Dewey:370. LCCN:60-015235.
Audience: **u,f.** *B*

Bruner, Jerome S. **LB1025.3**
Toward a Theory of Instruction. Trade Paper. Harvard University Press. Cambridge, MA. 1966. 192p. Belknap Press Ser. ISBN:0-674-89701-3, ISBN13: 978-0-674-89701-4. Dewey:371.1/02. LCCN:66-013179.
Audience: **l,u,f.** *B*

Carbone, Peter F. **LB885.R73.C37 1977**
The Social and Educational Thought of Harold Rugg. Trade Cloth. Duke University Press. Durham, NC. 1977. xiii, 217p. ISBN:0-8223-0355-8, ISBN13: 978-0-8223-0355-8. Dewey:370/.92/4. LCCN:75-036176.
Audience: **u,f.** *B*

Childs, John Lawrence **LB0875**
American Pragmatism and Education, an Interpretation and Criticism. Trade Paper. Books on Demand. Ann Arbor, MI. 384p. ISBN:0-598-57849-8, ISBN13: 978-0-598-57849-5. Dewey:370.1. LCCN:56-006061.
Audience: **u,f.** *B*

Clarke, Mark A. **LB885.C5235P53 2003**
A Place to Stand: Essays for Educators in Troubled Times. Trade Paper. University of Michigan Press. Chicago, IL. 2003. 264p. Surviving Innovation Ser., Vol. 1 ISBN:0-472-08879-3, ISBN13: 978-0-472-08879-9. Dewey:370/.1. LCCN:2002-015816.
Audience: **l,u,f.**

Combs, Arthur W. **LB1025.2**
Myths in Education: Beliefs That Hinder Progress and Their Alternatives. Trade Cloth. Allyn & Bacon, Inc. Boston, MA. 1979. xii, 240p. ISBN:0-205-06021-8, ISBN13: 978-0-205-06021-4. Dewey:370/.1. LCCN:78-017338.
Audience: **l,u,f.** *B*

Comenius, Johann Amos **LB695.J4C6**
Analytical Didactic: Translated from the Latin with Introd. and Notes. Paper Text. Textbook Publishers. Temecula, CA. 2003. xvii, 239p. ISBN:0-7581-2480-5, ISBN13: 978-0-7581-2480-7. Dewey:379.73.
Audience: **u,f.**

Conant, James Bryant **N85.R42**
Thomas Jefferson and the Development of American Public Education. Paper Text. Textbook Publishers. Temecula, CA. 2003. x, 164p. ISBN:0-7581-2643-3, ISBN13: 978-0-7581-2643-6. Dewey:707.
Audience: **u,f.** *B*

Connell, W. F. **E185.97.W4**
The Educational Thought and Influence of Matthew Arnold, Vol. 223. Paper over Boards. Routledge. New York, NY. 2003. 320p. International Library of Sociology Ser. ISBN:0-415-17761-8, ISBN13: 978-0-415-17761-0. Dewey:370.9/2.
Audience: **u,f.** *B*

Conrad, David R. **LB885.M722.C66**
Education for Transformation: Implications in Lewis Mumford's Ecohumanism. Trade Cloth. E T C Publications. Palm Springs, CA. 1976. 230p. ISBN:0-88280-030-2, ISBN13: 978-0-88280-030-1. Dewey:370.1. LCCN:75-025867.
Audience: **u,f.** *B*

Culler, A. Dwight **LB695**
The Imperial Intellect: A Study of Newman's Educational Ideal. Paper Text. Textbook Publishers. Temecula, CA. 2003. xiii, 327p. ISBN:0-7581-0067-1, ISBN13: 978-0-7581-0067-2. Dewey:370.4.
Audience: **u,f.**

Curren, Randall R. **LB85.A7C87 2000**
Aristotle on the Necessity of Public Education. Book, Other. Rowman & Littlefield Publishers, Inc. Lanham, MD. 2000. 296p. ISBN:0-8476-9672-3, ISBN13: 978-0-8476-9672-7. Dewey:370/.1. LCCN:00-036922.
Audience: **l,u,f.** *Choice, 2001.*

Dennis, Lawrence J. (Editor) **LB885.C662D45 1989**
George S. Counts and Charles A. Beard: Collaborators for Change. Cloth Text. State University of New York Press. Albany, NY. 1989. 192p. SUNY Series, the Philosophy of Education ISBN:0-88706-992-4, ISBN13: 978-0-88706-992-5. Dewey:370/.92/2. LCCN:88-020153.
Audience: **u,f.** *Choice, 1990.*

Dennis, Lawrence J. & Eaton, William E. (Editors) **LB885.C66 1980**
George S. Counts: Educator for a New Age. Trade Cloth. Southern Illinois University Press. Carbondale, IL. 1980. 167p.

ISBN:0-8093-0954-8, ISBN13: 978-0-8093-0954-2. Dewey:370/.092/4. LCCN:79-028182.
Audience: **u,f.** BCL3

Dewey, John **LB875**
Democracy and Education. Perfect, Trade Paper. Digireads.com. Stilwell, KS. 2005. 209p. ISBN:1-4209-2504-0, ISBN13: 978-1-4209-2504-3. Dewey:370.1.
Audience: **g,u,f.**

Dewey, John **LB875**
Experience and Education. Ed. 60. Trade Cloth. Kappa Delta Pi, International Honor Society in Education. Indianapolis, IN. 1998. 194p. ISBN:0-912099-34-8, ISBN13: 978-0-912099-34-7. Dewey:370/.1.
Audience: **g,u,f.**

Dewey, John **LB875**
Ebook The School and Society. E-Book. Digireads.com. Stilwell, KS. 2004. ISBN:1-4209-0332-2, ISBN13: 978-1-4209-0332-4. Dewey:370.4.
Audience: **g,u,f.**

Dewey, John **LB875; B945.D43**
The Collected Works of John Dewey, 1882-1953: (Windows). Jo Ann Boydston & Larry Hickman (Editors). Trade Cloth. Intelex Corporation. Charlottesville, VA. Past Masters Ser. ISBN:1-57085-118-2, ISBN13: 978-1-57085-118-6. Dewey:16.191.
Audience: **u,f.**

Dewey, John **LB41**
Education Today. Joseph Rather (Editor). Library Binding. Century Bookbindery. Philadelphia, PA. 1986. 373p. ISBN:0-89984-560-6, ISBN13: 978-0-89984-560-9. Dewey:370/.8.
Audience: **g,u,f.** BCL3

Downs, Robert B. **LB638.D68**
Friedrich Froebel. Library Binding. Thomson Gale. Farmington Hills, MI. 1978. 126p. World Leaders Ser. ISBN:0-8057-7668-0, ISBN13: 978-0-8057-7668-3. Dewey:370/.92/4. LCCN:77-013512.
Audience: **u,f.** BCL3

Downs, Robert B. **LB627.D68**
Heinrich Pestalozzi. Library Binding. Thomson Gale. Farmington Hills, MI. 1975. 147p. World Leaders Ser. ISBN:0-8057-3560-7, ISBN13: 978-0-8057-3560-4. Dewey:370/.92/4. LCCN:74-014554.
Audience: **u,f.** BCL3

Eisner, Elliot W. **LB885.E37A3 1998**
The Kind of Schools We Need: Personal Essays. Trade Paper. Heinemann. Portsmouth, NH. 1998. 240p. ISBN:0-325-00029-8, ISBN13: 978-0-325-00029-9. Dewey:370/.973. LCCN:98-24114.
Audience: **g,u,f.**

Elkind, David **LB1590.3**
Child Development and Education: A Piagetian Perspective. Paper Text. Oxford University Press, Inc. New York, NY. 1976. 304p. ISBN:0-19-502069-3, ISBN13: 978-0-19-502069-4. Dewey:370.15/2.
Audience: **u,f.** BCL3

Fishman, Stephen M. & McCarthy, Lucille P. **LB875.D5F57 1998**
John Dewey and the Challenge of Classroom Practice. Trade Paper. Teachers College Press, Teachers College, Columbia University. New York, NY. 1998. 382p. Practitioner Inquiry Ser. ISBN:0-8077-3726-7, ISBN13: 978-0-8077-3726-2. Dewey:370/.1. LCCN:98-005308.
Audience: **g,u,f.** *Choice, 1998.*

Florence, Namulundah **LB885.H662F56 1998**
Ebook Bell Hooks' Engaged Pedagogy: A Transgressive Education for Critical Consciousness. E-Book. NetLibrary, Inc. Boulder, CO. 1998. ISBN:0-585-38950-0, ISBN13: 978-0-585-38950-9. Dewey:370/.11/5.
Audience: **u,f.**

Franklin, Benjamin **LB0575**
Educational Views of Benjamin Franklin. Thomas Woody (Editor). Trade Paper. Books on Demand. Ann Arbor, MI. 290p. ISBN:0-598-53426-1, ISBN13: 978-0-598-53426-2. Dewey:370.81. LCCN:31-012966.
Audience: **u,f.** BCL3

Fraser, Stewart **LB0675.J79F8**
Jullien's Plan for Comparative Education 1816-1817. Trade Paper. Books on Demand. Ann Arbor, MI. 170p. ISBN:0-598-35538-3, ISBN13: 978-0-598-35538-6. Dewey:370.81. LCCN:64-012484.
Audience: **u,f.** BCL3

Freire, Paulo **LB880.F732P432 1994**
Pedagogy of Hope: Reliving Pedagogy of the Oppressed. Trade Cloth. Continuum International Publishing Group, Ltd. London, 1994. 192p. ISBN:0-8264-0590-8, ISBN13: 978-0-8264-0590-6. Dewey:370.1. LCCN:76-015651.
Audience: **u,f.** *Choice, 1995.*

Freire, Paulo **LB880.F73P4313 2000**
Pedagogy of the Oppressed. Ed. 30. Trade Paper. Continuum International Publishing Group, Ltd. London, 2000. 192p. ISBN:0-8264-1276-9, ISBN13: 978-0-8264-1276-8. Dewey:379. LCCN:00-030304.
Audience: **u,f.** BCL3

Freire, Paulo **LB880.F73P76413 2006**
Teachers As Cultural Workers: Letters to Those Who Dare Teach with New Essays by Shirley Steinberg, Joe Kincheloe, and Peter McClaren. Trade Paper. Westview Press. Boulder, CO. 2005. 240p. ISBN:0-8133-4329-1, ISBN13: 978-0-8133-4329-7. Dewey:306.43.
Audience: **u,f.**

Gadotti, Moacir **LB880.G24 1996**
Pedagogy of Praxis: A Dialectical Philosophy of Education. John Milton (Translator), Paulo Freire (Preface by). Cloth Text. State University of New York Press. Albany, NY. 1996. 216p. SUNY Series in Teacher Empowerment and School Reform ISBN:0-7914-2935-0, ISBN13: 978-0-7914-2935-8. Dewey:370.1. LCCN:95-032347.
Audience: **u,f.** *Choice, 1997.*

Gagne, Robert M., et al. **LB1028.38.G34 2005**
Principles of Instructional Design. Ed. 5. Walter W. Wager, Katharine Golas & John M. Keller (Authors). Cloth Text. Thomson Wadsworth. Belmont, CA. 2004. 408p. ISBN:0-534-58284-2, ISBN13: 978-0-534-58284-5. Dewey:371.3. LCCN:2004-104325.
Audience: **u,f.**

Gardner, Howard **LB885.G37D48 2005**
Development and Education of Mind. Trade Paper. Routledge. New York, NY. 2005. x, 270p. ISBN:0-415-36728-X, ISBN13: 978-0-415-36728-8. Dewey:370.1.
Audience: **u,f.**

Gardner, Howard **LB885.G37**
The Disciplined Mind: Beyond Facts and Standardized Tests, the K-12 Education That Every Child Deserves. Trade Paper. Penguin Group (USA) Inc. New York, NY. 2000. 304p. ISBN:0-14-029624-7, ISBN13: 978-0-14-029624-2. Dewey:370/.1.
Audience: **g,u,f.**

Giroux, Henry A. & Epstein, Seymour **LB885**
Theory and Resistance in Education: Towards a Pedagogy for the Opposition. Ed. 2. Paolo Freire (Foreword by), Stanley Aronowitz (Preface by). Paper Text. Greenwood Publishing Group, Inc. Portsmouth, NH. 2001. 320p. Critical Studies in Education and Culture ISBN:0-89789-796-X, ISBN13: 978-0-89789-796-9. Dewey:370.115. LCCN:2001-025177.
Audience: **u,f.**

Greene, Maxine **LB885 .G68**
Teacher As Stranger: Educational Psychology for the Modern Age. Trade Cloth. Thomson Wadsworth. Belmont, CA. 1973. 256p. ISBN:0-534-00205-6, ISBN13: 978-0-534-00205-3. Dewey:370.1. LCCN:72-087809.
Audience: **l,u,f.** *B*

Gutek, Gerald L. **LB628**
Pestalozzi and Education. Trade Paper. Waveland Press, Inc. Prospect Heights, IL. 1999. 178p. ISBN:1-57766-091-9, ISBN13: 978-1-57766-091-0. Dewey:370.1.
Audience: **u,f.**

Hainstock, Elizabeth G. **LB1029.M75H35 1997**
The Essential Montessori: An Introduction to the Woman, the Writings, the Method and the Movement. Ed. 2. Trade Paper. Penguin Group (USA) Inc. New York, NY. 1997. 144p. ISBN:0-452-27796-5, ISBN13: 978-0-452-27796-0. Dewey:371.3/92. LCCN:96-049711.
Audience: **g,l,u,f.**

Henry, Jules **LB885.H43 1972**
Jules Henry on Education. Trade Cloth. Random House, Inc. New York, NY. 1972. 183p. ISBN:0-394-48030-9, ISBN13: 978-0-394-48030-5. Dewey:370.19/3. LCCN:75-037047.
Audience: **u,f.** *B*

Heslep, Robert D. **LB885**
Philosophical Thinking in Educational Practice. Trade Cloth. Greenwood Publishing Group, Inc. Portsmouth, NH. 1997. 200p. ISBN:0-275-95495-1, ISBN13: 978-0-275-95495-6. Dewey:370/.1. LCCN:96-053935.
Audience: **u,f.** *Choice, 1998.*

Holt, John **LB885.H64F74 1995**
Freedom and Beyond. Trade Paper. Heinemann. Portsmouth, NH. 1995. 272p. Innovators in Education Ser. ISBN:0-86709-367-6, ISBN13: 978-0-86709-367-4. Dewey:370/.1. LCCN:95-31345.
Audience: **u,f.**

Hunter, Robin **LB1051**
Madeline Hunter's Mastery Teaching: Increasing Instructional Effectiveness in Elementary and Secondary Schools. Trade Cloth. Corwin Press. Thousand Oaks, CA. 2004. 176p. 1-Off Ser. ISBN:0-7619-3929-6, ISBN13: 978-0-7619-3929-0. Dewey:371.102. LCCN:2004-004625.
Audience: **u,f.**

Hutchins, Robert M. **LB875.H96 1972**
The Conflict in Education in a Democratic Society. Cloth Text. Greenwood Publishing Group, Inc. Portsmouth, NH. 1972. 112p. ISBN:0-8371-5693-9, ISBN13: 978-0-8371-5693-4. Dewey:370.1. LCCN:77-138117.
Audience: **u,f.** *B*

Jones, Howard M. **LB885.J6 1969**
Reflections on Learning. Trade Cloth. Ayer Company Publishers, Inc. Manchester, NH. 1977. 97p. Essay Index Reprint Ser. ISBN:0-8369-0022-7, ISBN13: 978-0-8369-0022-4. Dewey:370.1. LCCN:69-017580.
Audience: **u,f.** *B*

Kant, Immanuel **LB675.K18513 1971**
Educational Theory of Immanuel Kant. Edward F. Buchner (Editor). Trade Cloth. A M S Press, Inc. New York, NY. 1971. 309p. ISBN:0-404-03628-7, ISBN13: 978-0-404-03628-7. Dewey:370.1. LCCN:71-137251.
Audience: **u,f.**

Kramer, Rita **LB775.M8K7 1988**
Maria Montessori: A Biography. Anna Freud (Foreword by). Trade Paper. Da Capo Press, Inc. Cambridge, MA. 2000. 418p. Radcliffe Biography Ser. ISBN:0-201-09227-1, ISBN13: 978-0-201-09227-1. Dewey:372.13/0924. LCCN:88-022287.
Audience: **g,l,u,f.** *B*

Lerner, Max **QC702 .G37**
Education and a Radical Humanism: Notes Toward a Theory of the Educational Crisis. Paper Text. Textbook Publishers. Temecula, CA. 2003. 63p. ISBN:0-7581-7364-4, ISBN13: 978-0-7581-7364-5. Dewey:370.10973.
Audience: **u,f.** *B*

Lifton, Betty J. **LB775.K6272L53 1988**
The King of Children: A Portrait of Janusz Korczak. Trade Cloth. Farrar, Straus & Giroux. New York, NY. 1988. 448p. ISBN:0-374-18124-1, ISBN13: 978-0-374-18124-6. Dewey:370/.92/4 B. LCCN:87-009288.
Audience: **u,f.** *Choice, 1988.*

Lillard, Paula P. **LB775.M8**
Montessori: A Modern Approach. Trade Paper. Knopf Publishing Group. New York, NY. 1988. 192p. ISBN:0-8052-0920-4, ISBN13: 978-0-8052-0920-4. Dewey:371.3. LCCN:78-163334.
Audience: **l,u,f.**

Locke, John **LB475.L6S65**
Some Thoughts Concerning Education. John W. Yolton & Jean S. Yolton (Editors). Trade Paper. Oxford University Press, Inc. New York, NY. 2000. 346p. Clarendon Edition of the Works of John Locke Ser. ISBN:0-19-825016-9, ISBN13: 978-0-19-825016-6. Dewey:370.1.
Audience: **u,f.** *Choice, 1990.*

Mackenzie, Hettie Millicent Hughes **LB675.H4.M3 1971**
Hegel's Educational Theory and Practice. Library Binding. M. S. G. Haskell House. Brooklyn, NY. 1971. xxi, 192p. Studies in Philosophy, No. 40 ISBN:0-8383-1118-0, ISBN13: 978-0-8383-1118-9. Dewey:370.1/0924. LCCN:79-122985.
Audience: **u,f.** *B*

Mann, Horace **LB885.L422**
The Republic and the School: Horace Mann on the Education of Free Men. Paper Text. Textbook Publishers. Temecula, CA. 2003. 112p. ISBN:0-7581-3236-0, ISBN13: 978-0-7581-3236-9. Dewey:370.10973.
Audience: **u,f.**

Maritain, Jacques **LB775**
Education at the Crossroads. Trade Paper. Yale University Press. Cumberland, RI. 1960. 132p. Terry Lectures ISBN:0-300-00163-0, ISBN13: 978-0-300-00163-1. Dewey:370.1.
Audience: **u,f.** B

McPeck, John E., et al. **LB885.M35T43 1990**
Teaching Critical Thinking. Richard P. Paul, Harvey Siegel & Stephen P. Norris (Authors), Michael Scriven (Foreword by). Paper over Boards. Routledge. New York, NY. 1990. 176p. Philosophy of Education Research Library ISBN:0-415-90225-8, ISBN13: 978-0-415-90225-0. Dewey:370.15/2. LCCN:89-029791.
Audience: **u,f.** *Choice, 1991.*

Meiklejohn, Alexander **LB41.M485 2005**
Education Between Two Worlds. Reginald D. Archambault (Foreword by). Trade Paper, Perfect. Aldine Transaction. Somerset, NJ. 2005. 337p. ISBN:0-202-30813-8, ISBN13: 978-0-202-30813-5. Dewey:370/.1. LCCN:2005-052023.
Audience: **u,f.** B

Messerli, Jonathan **LB695.M35.M4**
Horace Mann, a Biography. Trade Cloth. Random House Children's Books. New York, NY. 1972. xviii, 604p. ISBN:0-394-42920-6, ISBN13: 978-0-394-42920-5. Dewey:370/.92/4. LCCN:78-154905.
Audience: **u,f.** B

Mill, John Stuart **LB0675.M517**
John Stuart Mill on Education. Francis W. Garforth (Editor). Trade Paper. Books on Demand. Ann Arbor, MI. 247p. Classics in Education Ser., Vol. 43 ISBN:0-598-09839-9, ISBN13: 978-0-598-09839-9. Dewey:370.19. LCCN:75-155230.
Audience: **u,f.** B

Montagu, Ashley **LB885 .M6 1973**
Education and Human Relations. Trade Cloth. Greenwood Publishing Group, Inc. Portsmouth, NH. 1973. 191p. ISBN:0-8371-6659-4, ISBN13: 978-0-8371-6659-9. Dewey:370.19/3. LCCN:72-011333.
Audience: **u,f.** B

Montessori, Maria **LB775.M8**
Discovery of the Child. Paper Text. ABC-CLIO, Inc. Santa Barbara, CA. 1990. 349p. The Clio Montessori Ser. ISBN:1-85109-086-X, ISBN13: 978-1-85109-086-0. Dewey:371.392.
Audience: **g,u,f.**

Montessori, Maria **LB775**
The Secret of Childhood. Trade Paper. Ballantine Books. New York, NY. 1982. 240p. ISBN:0-345-30583-3, ISBN13: 978-0-345-30583-1. Dewey:66-20175.
Audience: **g,u,f.**

Montessori, Maria **LB775 .M7863**
Spontaneous Activity in Education. Trade Paper. Education System Publisher. Hemet, CA. 1984. 384p. A Basic Montessori Library ISBN:0-916011-02-X, ISBN13: 978-0-916011-02-4. Dewey:372.
Audience: **l,u,f.** B

Montessori, Maria & Hunt, J. **LB775**
The Montessori Method. Trade Paper. Kessinger Publishing, LLC. Whitefish, MT. 2005. ISBN:1-4179-2468-3, ISBN13: 978-1-4179-2468-4. Dewey:372.
Audience: **g,l,u,f.**

Mulcahy, D. G. **LB885**
Knowledge, Gender, and Schooling: The Feminist Educational Thought of Jane Roland Martin. Trade Cloth. Greenwood Publishing Group, Inc. Portsmouth, NH. 2002. 232p. Critical Studies in Education and Culture ISBN:0-89789-875-3, ISBN13: 978-0-89789-875-1. Dewey:370/.1. LCCN:2001-058322.
Audience: **u,f.**

Nash, Paul **LB0880.N29**
Authority and Freedom in Education: An Introduction to the Philosophy of Education. Trade Paper. Books on Demand. Ann Arbor, MI. 352p. ISBN:0-8357-5900-8, ISBN13: 978-0-8357-5900-7. Dewey:370.1. LCCN:66-017624.
Audience: **u,f.** B

Nelson, Adam R. **LB875.M332N45 2001**
Education and Democracy: The Meaning of Alexander Meiklejohn, 1872-1964. Trade Cloth. University of Wisconsin Press. Chicago, IL. 2001. xix, 416p. ISBN:0-299-17140-X, ISBN13: 978-0-299-17140-7. Dewey:370/.92 B. LCCN:00-011979.
Audience: **u,f.** *Choice, 2002.*

Nietzsche, Friedrich **LB775.N547N53 2004**
On the Future of Our Educational Institutions. Michael W. Grenke (Editor, Translator). Trade Cloth. Saint Augustine's Press, Inc. South Bend, IN. 2004. 200p. William of Moerbeke Translation Ser. ISBN:1-58731-601-3, ISBN13: 978-1-58731-601-2. Dewey:370/.1. LCCN:2004-000797.
Audience: **u,f.**

Niu, Xiaodong **LB875.D5N58 1994**
Education East and West: The Influence of Mao Zedong and John Dewey. Trade Cloth. International Scholars Publications. Lanham, MD. 1994. 195p. ISBN:1-883255-57-0, ISBN13: 978-1-883255-57-2. Dewey:370/.1. LCCN:94-007854.
Audience: **u,f.**

Olssen, Mark **LB880**
Michel Foucault: Materialism and Education. Trade Cloth. Greenwood Publishing Group, Inc. Portsmouth, NH. 1999. 216p. Critical Studies in Education and Culture ISBN:0-89789-587-8, ISBN13: 978-0-89789-587-3. Dewey:370/.1. LCCN:98-049933.
Audience: **u,f.** *Choice, 2000.*

Paringer, William Andrew **LB875.D5P37 1990**
John Dewey and the Paradox of Liberal Reform. Cloth Text. State University of New York Press. Albany, NY. 1990. 215p. SUNY Series in Global Conflict and Peace Education ISBN:0-7914-0253-3, ISBN13: 978-0-7914-0253-5. Dewey:370/.1/092 B. LCCN:89-077669.
Audience: **u,f.** *Choice, 1991.*

Pass, Susan **LB775.P49P37 2004**
Parallel Paths to Constructivism: Jean Piaget and Lev Vygotsky. Trade Cloth. Information Age Publishing, Inc. Greenwich, CT. 2004. xviii, 143p. ISBN:1-59311-146-0, ISBN13: 978-1-59311-146-5. Dewey:370.15/23. LCCN:2004-009776.
Audience: **u,f.**

Peters, Michael A. **LB775.H44122H45 2002**
Heidegger, Education and Modernity. Book, Other. Rowman & Littlefield Publishers, Inc. Lanham, MD. 2002. 288p. ISBN:0-7425-0886-2, ISBN13: 978-0-7425-0886-6. Dewey:370/.1. LCCN:2002-024820.
Audience: **u,f.**

Phillips, Norman R. **LB885.P53.Q44 1978**
The Quest for Excellence. Trade Cloth. Philosophical Library, Inc. New York, NY. 1978. viii, 179p. ISBN:0-8022-2220-X, ISBN13: 978-0-8022-2220-6. Dewey:370.1. LCCN:77-087940.
Audience: **u,f.**

Piaget, Jean **LB1051**
Science of Education and the Psychology of the Child. Trade Paper. Penguin Group (USA) Inc. New York, NY. 1976. 186p. ISBN:0-14-004377-2, ISBN13: 978-0-14-004377-8. Dewey:370.15. LCCN:76-026177.
Audience: **u,f.**

Popkewitz, Thomas S. & Brennan, Marie **LB880.F682F685 1998**
Foucault's Challenge: Discourse, Knowledge, and Power in Education. Trade Cloth. Teachers College Press, Teachers College, Columbia University. New York, NY. 1997. 408p. ISBN:0-8077-3677-5, ISBN13: 978-0-8077-3677-7. Dewey:370/.1. LCCN:97-034270.
Audience: **u,f.**

Provenzo, Eugene F. Jr. **LB875.D83D833 2002**
Du Bois on Education. Trade Paper. AltaMira Press. Walnut Creek, CA. 2002. 344p. ISBN:0-7591-0200-7, ISBN13: 978-0-7591-0200-2. Dewey:370/.8996/073. LCCN:2002-003241.
Audience: **g,u,f.** *Choice, 2003.*

Read, Herbert Edward **QD502**
Education Through Art. Paper Text. Textbook Publishers. Temecula, CA. 2003. xxiv, 328p. ISBN:0-7581-6664-8, ISBN13: 978-0-7581-6664-7. Dewey:541.36.
Audience: **l,u,f.**

Redden, John D. **LB875 .R43**
Catholic Philosophy of Education. Trade Cloth. Glencoe/McGraw-Hill. Columbus, OH. 1956. ISBN:0-02-826320-0, ISBN13: 978-0-02-826320-5. Dewey:370.1.
Audience: **g,u,f.**

Roberts, Peter **LB880.F732R62 2000**
Education, Literacy, and Humanization: Exploring the Work of Paulo Freire. E-Book. NetLibrary, Inc. Boulder, CO. 2000. ISBN:0-585-39423-7, ISBN13: 978-0-585-39423-7. Dewey:370/.1.
Audience: **u,f.**

Ross, Ralph (Introduction by) **LB875**
Middle Works of John Dewey, 1899-1924: 1920. Trade Cloth. Southern Illinois University Press. Carbondale, IL. 1988. 346p. ISBN:0-8093-1435-5, ISBN13: 978-0-8093-1435-5. Dewey:370.1. LCCN:76-007231.
Audience: **u,f.**

Russell, Bertrand **LB775.R8**
Education and the Good Life. Trade Paper. Kessinger Publishing, LLC. Whitefish, MT. 2004. ISBN:0-7661-8161-8, ISBN13: 978-0-7661-8161-8. Dewey:370.1.
Audience: **l,u,f.**

Russell, Bertrand **LC191**
Education and the Social Order. Trade Paper. Routledge. New York, NY. 1988. 160p. ISBN:0-415-07916-0, ISBN13: 978-0-415-07916-7. Dewey:370.19/3.
Audience: **l,u,f.**

Scheffler, Israel **LB0885.S34**
Conditions of Knowledge: An Introduction to Epistemology and Education. Trade Paper. Books on Demand. Ann Arbor, MI. 127p. Midway Reprints Ser. ISBN:0-608-09038-7, ISBN13: 978-0-608-09038-2. Dewey:121. LCCN:78-054987.
Audience: **u,f.**

Sidorkin, Alexander M. **LB885.S53B497 1999**
Beyond Discourse: Education, the Self, and Dialogue. Cloth Text. State University of New York Press. Albany, NY. 1999. 160p. ISBN:0-7914-4247-0, ISBN13: 978-0-7914-4247-0. Dewey:370/.1. LCCN:98-042634.
Audience: **u,f.**

Simon, Louis **LB775.S6665 S5 1974**
Shaw on Education. Library Binding. Greenwood Publishing Group, Inc. Portsmouth, NH. 1974. 290p. ISBN:0-8371-7245-4, ISBN13: 978-0-8371-7245-3. Dewey:370.1/092/4. LCCN:73-016953.
Audience: **u,f.**

Simpson, Douglas J., et al. **LB875.D5J64 2005**
John Dewey and the Art of Teaching: Toward Reflective and Imaginative Practice. Michael J. B. Jackson & Judy C. Aycock (Authors). Cloth Text. SAGE Publications, Inc. Thousand Oaks, CA. 2004. 232p. ISBN:1-4129-0902-3, ISBN13: 978-1-4129-0902-0. Dewey:370/.1. LCCN:2004-016440.
Audience: **g,u,f.** *Choice, 2005.*

Smith, Philip L. **LB0885.S5717**
The Problem of Values in Educational Thought. Trade Paper. Books on Demand. Ann Arbor, MI. 1982. 102p. ISBN:0-608-00025-6, ISBN13: 978-0-608-00025-1. Dewey:370/.1. LCCN:81-023650.
Audience: **u,f.**

Spangler, Mary M. **LB85.A7S73 1998**
Aristotle on Teaching. Trade Paper. University Press of America, Inc. Lanham, MD. 1998. 244p. ISBN:0-7618-1211-3, ISBN13: 978-0-7618-1211-1. Dewey:371.102. LCCN:98-026328.
Audience: **l,u,f.** *Choice, 1999.*

Spencer, Herbert **LB14.7**
Education: Intellectual, Moral, and Physical. Trade Paper. University Press of the Pacific. Miami, FL. 2002. 248p. ISBN:0-89875-783-5, ISBN13: 978-0-89875-783-5. Dewey:370.1.
Audience: **u,f.**

Spencer, Herbert **LB0675.S79K3**
Herbert Spencer on Education. Andreas M. Kazamias (Editor). Trade Paper. Books on Demand. Ann Arbor, MI. 239p. Classics in Education Ser., Vol. 30 ISBN:0-598-12077-7, ISBN13: 978-0-598-12077-9. Dewey:370.12. LCCN:66-017068.
Audience: **u,f.** BCL3

Steedman, Carolyn **LB775.M3172S74 1990**
Childhood, Culture, and Class in Britain: Margaret McMillan, 1860-1931. Paper Text. Rutgers University Press. Piscataway, NJ. 1990. 335p. ISBN:0-8135-1540-8, ISBN13: 978-0-8135-1540-3. Dewey:372.41. LCCN:89-029176.
Audience: **u,f.** *Choice, 1991.*

Titone, Connie **LB575.M1162T575 2004**
Gender Equality in the Philosophy of Education: Catharine Macaulay's Forgotten Contribution. Trade Paper. Peter Lang Publishing, Inc. New York, NY. 2004. 192p. Counterpoints Ser., :Studies in the Postmodern Theory of Education ISBN:0-8204-5174-6, ISBN13: 978-0-8204-5174-9. Dewey:370/.1. LCCN:2003-027814.
Audience: **u,f.**

Tolstoy, Leo **LB675.T62T65 2000**
Tolstoy As Teacher: Leo Tolstoy's Writings on Education. Bob Blaisdell (Editor), Christopher Edgar (Translator). Trade Paper. Teachers & Writers Collaborative. New York, NY. 2000. 246p. ISBN:0-915924-96-X, ISBN13: 978-0-915924-96-7. Dewey:370/.1. LCCN:99-033215.
Audience: **u,f.** *Choice, 2000.*

Turnbull, George (Editor) **LB575.T87T86 2003**
Observations upon Liberal Education. Terrence O. Moore (Editor, Introduction by). Trade Cloth. Liberty Fund, Inc. Indianapolis, IN. 2003. 442p. Natural Law and Enlightenment Classics Ser. ISBN:0-86597-411-X, ISBN13: 978-0-86597-411-1. Dewey:370.11/2. LCCN:2002-034059.
Audience: **u,f.**

Weber, Lillian & Alberty, Beth **LB885.W33W33 1997**
Looking Back and Thinking Forward: Reexaminations of Teaching and Schooling. Trade Cloth. Teachers College Press, Teachers College, Columbia University. New York, NY. 1997. 216p. ISBN:0-8077-3674-0, ISBN13: 978-0-8077-3674-6. Dewey:370/.1. LCCN:97-020829.
Audience: **l,u,f.** *Choice, 1998.*

Whitehead, Alfred North **LB875**
The Aims of Education. Trade Paper. Simon & Schuster. New York, NY. 1967. 165p. ISBN:0-02-935180-4, ISBN13: 978-0-02-935180-2. Dewey:370.4. LCCN:29-010164.
Audience: **g,l,u,f.**

Theory and Practice of Education > Teaching (Principles and Practice)

☐ Center for Research on Education, Diversity & Excellence (CREDE).
http://crede.org
Audience: **u,f.**

LB1555
☐ edHelper.com.
http://edhelper.com
Audience: **g,l,u,f.**

LC149
☐ Literacy Web.
http://www.literacy.uconn.edu
Audience: **g,l,u,f.**

Banner, James M. Jr. & Cannon, Harold C. **LB1025.3**
The Elements of Teaching. Trade Paper. Yale University Press. Cumberland, RI. 1999. 160p. ISBN:0-300-07855-2, ISBN13: 978-0-300-07855-8. Dewey:371.1/02. LCCN:96-034227.
Audience: **u,f.** *Choice, 1997.*

Barell, John **LB1027.44.B37 2003**
Developing More Curious Minds. Trade Cloth. Association for Supervision & Curriculum Development. Alexandria, VA. 2003. 244p. ISBN:0-87120-719-2, ISBN13: 978-0-87120-719-7. Dewey:371.39. LCCN:2002-151117.
Audience: **u,f.** *Choice, 2004.*

Belmonte, Dominic **LB1025.3.B455 2003**
Teaching from the Deep End: Succeeding with Today's Classroom Challenges. Trade Cloth. Corwin Press. Thousand Oaks, CA. 2003. 136p. ISBN:0-7619-3848-6, ISBN13: 978-0-7619-3848-4. Dewey:371.102. LCCN:2002-154677.
Audience: **u,f.** *Choice, 2004.*

Berk, Ronald A. **LB1027.B472 2002**
Humor as an Instructional Defibrillator: Evidence-Based Techniques in Teaching and Assessment. Trade Paper. Stylus Publishing. Ridley Park, PA. 2002. 320p. ISBN:1-57922-063-0, ISBN13: 978-1-57922-063-1. Dewey:371.3/02/07. LCCN:2002-006866.
Audience: **u,f.** *Choice, 2003.*

Bickman, Martin **LB1027.23.B53 2003**
Minding American Education: Reclaiming the Tradition of Active Learning. Trade Cloth. Teachers College Press, Teachers College, Columbia University. New York, NY. 2003. ix, 182p. ISBN:0-8077-4353-4, ISBN13: 978-0-8077-4353-9. Dewey:370/.973. LCCN:2002-041615.
Audience: **l,u,f.** *Choice, 2004.*

Blacker, David J. **LB1025.3.B58 1997**
Dying to Teach: The Educator's Search for Immortality. Trade Cloth. Teachers College Press, Teachers College, Columbia University. New York, NY. 1997. 388p. Advances in Contemporary Educational Thought Ser. ISBN:0-8077-3592-2, ISBN13: 978-0-8077-3592-3. Dewey:371.102/01. LCCN:96-040843.
Audience: **u,f.**

Briggs, Leslie J. (Editor), et al. **LB1028.38.I57 1991**
Instructional Design: Principles and Applications. Ed. 2. Kent L. Gustafson & Murray H. Tillman (Editors). Trade Cloth. Educational Technology Publications, Inc. Englewood Cliffs, NJ. 1991. 512p. ISBN:0-87778-230-X, ISBN13: 978-0-87778-230-8. Dewey:371.3. LCCN:90-023255.
Audience: **u,f.** BCL3

Brighouse, Harry **LB1027.9**
School Choice and Social Justice. Trade Paper. Oxford University Press, Inc. New York, NY. 2003. 232p.

ISBN:0-19-925787-6, ISBN13: 978-0-19-925787-4. Dewey:379.2/6.
Audience: **l,u,f.** *Choice, 2001.*

Brookfield, Stephen D. & Preskill, Stephen **LB2331.B679 2005**
Discussion as a Way of Teaching: Tools and Techniques for Democratic Classrooms. Ed. 2. Trade Cloth. John Wiley & Sons, Inc. Hoboken, NJ. 2005. 336p. ISBN:0-7879-7808-6, ISBN13: 978-0-7879-7808-2. Dewey:378.1/2. LCCN:2005-008307.
Audience: **u,f.**

Bruner, Jerome S. **LB1051.B736 1996**
Culture of Education. Trade Cloth. Harvard University Press. Cambridge, MA. 1996. 240p. ISBN:0-674-17952-8, ISBN13: 978-0-674-17952-3. Dewey:370.1/5. LCCN:95-046844.
Audience: **l,u.**

Combs, Arthur W. **LB1025.3**
A Personal Approach to Teaching: Beliefs That Make a Difference. Cloth Text. Allyn & Bacon, Inc. Boston, MA. 1981. 200p. ISBN:0-205-07604-1, ISBN13: 978-0-205-07604-8. Dewey:371.1/02.
Audience: **l,u,f.**

Coppola, Eileen M. **LB1028.5.C628 2004**
Powering Up: Learning to Teach Well with Technology. Richard F. Elmore (Foreword by). Perfect, Paper over Boards. Teachers College Press, Teachers College, Columbia University. New York, NY. 2004. 189p. ISBN:0-8077-4499-9, ISBN13: 978-0-8077-4499-4. Dewey:371.33/4. LCCN:2004-051650.
Audience: **u,f.** *Choice, 2005.*

Dill, David D. **LB1025.2.W46 1990**
What Teachers Need to Know: The Knowledge, Skills and Values Essential to Good Teaching. Trade Cloth. John Wiley & Sons, Inc. Hoboken, NJ. 1990. 280p. Education-Higher Education Ser. ISBN:1-55542-226-8, ISBN13: 978-1-55542-226-4. Dewey:371.1/02. LCCN:89-048337.
Audience: **l,u,f.** *Choice, 1990.*

Egan, Kieran **LB1025.3.E37 2005**
An Imaginative Approach to Teaching. Trade Cloth. John Wiley & Sons, Inc. Hoboken, NJ. 2005. 272p. ISBN:0-7879-7157-X, ISBN13: 978-0-7879-7157-1. Dewey:371.102. LCCN:2004-020703.
Audience: **l,u,f.** *Choice, 2005.*

Flanders, Ned A. **LB1027.F555**
Analyzing Teaching Behavior. Trade Cloth. Addison-Wesley Longman, Inc. Boston, MA. 1970. xvi, 448p. Education Ser. ISBN:0-201-02052-1, ISBN13: 978-0-201-02052-6. Dewey:371.1. LCCN:70-104967.
Audience: **u,f.**

Gage, Nathaniel L. **LB1025.2.G29**
The Scientific Basis of the Art of Teaching. Trade Paper. Teachers College Press, Teachers College, Columbia University. New York, NY. 1978. 215p. ISBN:0-8077-2537-4, ISBN13: 978-0-8077-2537-5. Dewey:371.1/02. LCCN:78-006250.
Audience: **u,f.**

Gardner, Robert **LB1025.3**
On Trying to Teach: The Mind in Correspondence. Trade Paper. Analytic Press. Hillsdale, NJ. 1997. 174p. ISBN:0-88163-281-3, ISBN13: 978-0-88163-281-1. Dewey:217.012. LCCN:94-028731.
Audience: **u,f.**

Glasgow, Neal A. & Hicks, Cathy **LB1025.3.G516 2003**
What Successful Teachers Do: 91 Research-Based Classroom Strategies for New and Veteran Teachers. Trade Cloth. Corwin Press. Thousand Oaks, CA. 2002. 232p. 1-Off Ser. ISBN:0-7619-4573-3, ISBN13: 978-0-7619-4573-4. Dewey:371.102. LCCN:2002-011244.
Audience: **l,u,f.** *Choice, 2003.*

Goldfarb, Brian **LB1043.G57 2002**
Visual Pedagogy: Media Cultures in and Beyond the Classroom. Trade Cloth. Duke University Press. Durham, NC. 2002. 264p. ISBN:0-8223-2936-0, ISBN13: 978-0-8223-2936-7. Dewey:371.335. LCCN:2002-001692.
Audience: **u,f.** *Choice, 2003.*

Goodman, Paul **LB1025**
Compulsory Mis-Education. Trade Paper. Books on Demand. Ann Arbor, MI. 191p. ISBN:0-598-55285-5, ISBN13: 978-0-598-55285-3. Dewey:370.1. LCCN:64-024538.
Audience: **g,u,f.**

Hargreaves, Andy **LB1025.3.H366 2003**
Teaching in the Knowledge Society: Education in the Age of Insecurity. Trade Cloth. Teachers College Press, Teachers College, Columbia University. New York, NY. 2003. x, 230p. Professional Learning Ser. ISBN:0-8077-4360-7, ISBN13: 978-0-8077-4360-7. Dewey:371.102. LCCN:2002-035459.
Audience: **u,f.** *Choice, 2003.*

Hebert, Elizabeth A. **LB1029.P67H43 2001**
The Power of Portfolios: What Children Can Teach Us about Learning and Assessment. Trade Paper. John Wiley & Sons, Inc. Hoboken, NJ. 2001. 176p. The Jossey-Bass Education Ser. ISBN:0-7879-5871-9, ISBN13: 978-0-7879-5871-8. Dewey:372.127. LCCN:2001-003792.
Audience: **g,l,u,f.** *Choice, 2002.*

Henig, Jeffrey **LB1027.9.H46 1994**
Rethinking School Choice: Limits of the Market Metaphor. Cloth Text. Princeton University Press. Princeton, NJ. 1994. 287p. ISBN:0-691-03347-1, ISBN13: 978-0-691-03347-1. Dewey:371.01. LCCN:93-005411.
Audience: **g,u,f.** *Choice, 1994.*

Hess, Frederick M. & Finn, Chester E. Jr. (Editors) **LB1027.9.L43 2004**
Leaving No Child Behind?: Options for Kids in Failing Schools. Cloth over Boards. Palgrave Macmillan. New York, NY. 2004. 320p. ISBN:1-4039-6588-9, ISBN13: 978-1-4039-6588-2. Dewey:379.1/11. LCCN:2004-046722.
Audience: **g.** *Choice, 2005.*

Highet, Gilbert **LB1025.H63 1989**
The Art of Teaching. Trade Paper. Knopf Publishing Group. New York, NY. 1989. 288p. ISBN:0-679-72314-5, ISBN13: 978-0-679-72314-1. Dewey:371.1/02. LCCN:88-040505.
Audience: **l,u,f.**

Hill, Anne **LB1775.H46 2005**
Making Sense of Methods in the Classroom: A Pedagogical Presence. Book, Other. Rowman & Littlefield Education. Lanham, MD. 2005. 164p. ISBN:1-57886-315-5, ISBN13: 978-1-57886-315-0. Dewey:371.102. LCCN:2005-016825.
Audience: **l,u,f.**

Jay, Joelle Kristin **LB1025.3.J39 2003**
Quality Teaching: Reflection as the Heart of Practice. Trade Paper. Scarecrow Press, Inc. Lanham, MD. 2003. 224p. ISBN:0-8108-4715-9, ISBN13: 978-0-8108-4715-6. Dewey:371.102. LCCN:2002-154949.
Audience: **u,f.** *Choice, 2004.*

Johnson, Elaine B. **LB1027.J545 2002**
Contextual Teaching and Learning: What It Is and Why It's Here to Stay. Trade Cloth. Corwin Press. Thousand Oaks, CA. 2001. 208p. ISBN:0-7619-7864-X, ISBN13: 978-0-7619-7864-0. Dewey:371.102. LCCN:2001-002907.
Audience: **l,u,f.** *Choice, 2002.*

Kennedy, Mary M. (Editor) **LB1025.3.T43 1991**
Teaching Academic Subjects to Diverse Learners: What Teachers Need to Know. Trade Paper. Teachers College Press, Teachers College, Columbia University. New York, NY. 1991. 312p. ISBN:0-8077-3089-0, ISBN13: 978-0-8077-3089-8. Dewey:371.1/02. LCCN:91-003814.
Audience: **u,f.** *Choice, 1992.*

Kohl, Herbert R. **LB1025.2.K62 1986**
On Teaching. Trade Paper. Knopf Publishing Group. New York, NY. 1986. 192p. ISBN:0-8052-0801-1, ISBN13: 978-0-8052-0801-6. Dewey:371.1/02. LCCN:71-009131.
Audience: **g,u,f.**

Mack-Kirschner, Adrienne **LB1025.3.M334 2004**
Powerful Classroom Stories from Accomplished Teachers: Stories from the Classrooms of Accomplished Teachers. Trade Cloth. Corwin Press. Thousand Oaks, CA. 2003. 216p. 1-Off Ser. ISBN:0-7619-3911-3, ISBN13: 978-0-7619-3911-5. Dewey:371.102. LCCN:2003-012432.
Audience: **l,u,f.** *Choice, 2004.*

Meyers, Chet & Jones, Thomas B. **LB1027.23.M49 1993**
Promoting Active Learning: Strategies for the College Classroom. Trade Cloth. John Wiley & Sons, Inc. Hoboken, NJ. 1993. 224p. Higher and Adult Education Ser. ISBN:1-55542-524-0, ISBN13: 978-1-55542-524-1. Dewey:378.1/25. LCCN:92-041685.
Audience: **f.**

National Endowment for the Humanities **TK5105.875.I57**
☐ EDSITEment. http://edsitement.neh.gov
Audience: **g,l,u,f.**

Newton, Douglas P. **LB1025.3.N495 2000**
Teaching for Understanding: What It Is and How to Do It. Paper over Boards. Routledge. New York, NY. 2000. 208p. ISBN:0-415-22790-9, ISBN13: 978-0-415-22790-2. Dewey:371.102. LCCN:99-055457.
Audience: **l,u,f.** *Choice, 2001.*

O'Reilley, Mary Rose **LB1025.3.O74 1998**
Radical Presence: Teaching as Contemplative Practice. Parker J. Palmer (Foreword by). Trade Paper. Heinemann. Portsmouth, NH. 1998. 64p. ISBN:0-86709-427-3, ISBN13: 978-0-86709-427-5. Dewey:808/.042/0715. LCCN:97-044855.
Audience: **f.**

Oser, Fritz K. **LB1025.3.E35 1992**
Effective and Responsible Teaching: The New Synthesis. Andreas Dick & Jean-Luc Patry (Editors). Trade Cloth. John Wiley & Sons, Inc. Hoboken, NJ. 1992. 488p. Education-Higher Education Ser. ISBN:1-55542-449-X, ISBN13: 978-1-55542-449-7. Dewey:371.1/02. LCCN:92-011511.
Audience: **u,f.** *Choice, 1993.*

Preskill, Stephen L. & Jacobvitz, Robin S. **LB1775**
Stories of Teaching: A Foundation for Educational Renewal. Trade Paper. Prentice Hall PTR. Upper Saddle River, NJ. 2000. 213p. ISBN:0-13-921248-5, ISBN13: 978-0-13-921248-2. Dewey:371.102.
Audience: **l,u,f.**

Rogoff, Barbara, et al. **LB1027.23.C63 2001**
Learning Together: Children and Adults in a School Community. Carolyn Goodman-Turkanis & Leslee Bartlett (Authors). Trade Cloth. Oxford University Press, Inc. New York, NY. 2001. 260p. ISBN:0-19-509753-X, ISBN13: 978-0-19-509753-5. Dewey:370.15/23. LCCN:00-064971.
Audience: **u,f.** *Choice, 2001.*

Sarason, Seymour B. **LB1025.3.S273 1999**
Teaching as a Performing Art. Maxine Greene (Foreword by). Trade Cloth. Teachers College Press, Teachers College, Columbia University. New York, NY. 1999. 192p. ISBN:0-8077-3891-3, ISBN13: 978-0-8077-3891-7. Dewey:371.102. LCCN:99-034549.
Audience: **l,u,f.** *Choice, 2000.*

Semel, Susan F. & Sadovnik, Alan R. **LB1027.3.S33 1999**
"Schools of Tomorrow," Schools of Today: What Happened to Progressive Education. Trade Paper. Peter Lang Publishing, Inc. New York, NY. 1999. xxviii, 448p. History of Schools and Schooling Ser., Vol. 8 ISBN:0-8204-2666-0, ISBN13: 978-0-8204-2666-2. Dewey:371.04/0973. LCCN:98-030470.
Audience: **g,u,f.** *Choice, 1999.*

Shulman, Lee S. **LB1027.S475 2004**
The Wisdom of Practice: Essays on Teaching, Learning, and Learning to Teach. Trade Cloth. John Wiley & Sons, Inc. Hoboken, NJ. 2004. 608p. Jossey-Bass Higher and Adult Education Ser. ISBN:0-7879-7200-2, ISBN13: 978-0-7879-7200-4. Dewey:371.102. LCCN:2003-025429.
Audience: **u,f.** *Choice, 2004.*

Spreyer, Leon **LB1025.3.S69 2002**
Teaching Is an Art: An A-Z Handbook for Successful Teaching in Middle Schools and High Schools. Trade Cloth. Corwin Press. Thousand Oaks, CA. 2002. 200p. ISBN:0-7619-4518-0,

ISBN13: 978-0-7619-4518-5. Dewey:371.102.
LCCN:2002-005183.
Audience: **l,u,f.** *Choice, 2003.*

Stronge, James **LB1025.3.S789 2002**
Qualities of Effective Teachers. Trade Paper. Association for Supervision & Curriculum Development. Alexandria, VA. 2002. 130p. ISBN:0-87120-663-3, ISBN13: 978-0-87120-663-3. Dewey:371.102. LCCN:2002-004844.
Audience: **u,f.** *Choice, 2003.*

Tharp, Roland G. & Gallimore, Ronald G. **LB1025.2 .T446 1988**
Rousing Minds to Life: Teaching, Learning, and Schooling in Social Context. Trade Cloth. Cambridge University Press. New York, NY. 1989. 336p. ISBN:0-521-36234-2, ISBN13: 978-0-521-36234-4. Dewey:371.1/02. LCCN:88-020224.
Audience: **u,f.** *Choice, 1989.*

Torp, Linda & Sage, Sara **LB1027.42.T67 2002**
Problems As Possibilities: Problem-Based Learning for K-16 Education. Ed. 2. Trade Paper. Association for Supervision & Curriculum Development. Alexandria, VA. 2002. 129p. ISBN:0-87120-574-2, ISBN13: 978-0-87120-574-2. Dewey:375/.001. LCCN:2001-006219.
Audience: **l,u,f.**

Yelon, Stephen L. **LB1025.3.Y45 1996**
Powerful Principles of Instruction. Paper Text. Allyn & Bacon, Inc. Boston, MA. 1995. 299p. ISBN:0-8013-1643-X, ISBN13: 978-0-8013-1643-2. Dewey:371.1/02. LCCN:95-010866.
Audience: **l,u,f.** *Choice, 1996.*

Theory and Practice of Education > Teaching (Principles and Practice) > Individual and Group Instruction

LB1555

edHelper.com.
http://edhelper.com
Audience: **g,l,u,f.**

Lifetime of Color.
http://www.sanford-artedventures.com/
Audience: **g,l,u,f.**

Bartolome, Lilia I. **LB1033.5.B37 1998**
Misteaching of Academic Discourses: The Politics of Language in the Classroom. Trade Paper. Westview Press. Boulder, CO. 1998. 160p. The Edge Ser., :Critical Studies in Education Theory ISBN:0-8133-3144-7, ISBN13: 978-0-8133-3144-7. Dewey:370.1/4/0973. LCCN:98-009693.
Audience: **u,f.** *Choice, 1998.*

Briggs, Dennie **LB1031**
A Class of Their Own: When Children Teach Children. Trade Cloth. Greenwood Publishing Group, Inc. Portsmouth, NH. 1998. 144p. ISBN:0-89789-550-9, ISBN13: 978-0-89789-550-7. Dewey:371.394. LCCN:97-041000.
Audience: **l,u,f.** *Choice, 1999.*

Brophy, Jere E. & Good, Thomas L. **LB1033**
Teacher-Student Relationships: Causes and Consequences. Trade Paper. Holt, Rinehart & Winston. Austin, TX. 1974. xvi, 400p. ISBN:0-03-085749-X, ISBN13: 978-0-03-085749-2. Dewey:371.1/02. LCCN:73-014740.
Audience: **l,u,f.** B

Brown, Nina W. **LB1032.B74 2000**
Creating High Performance Classroom Groups. Cloth Text. Taylor & Francis Group. Philadelphia, PA. 2000. 256p. Source Bks on Education Ser. ISBN:0-8153-3689-6, ISBN13: 978-0-8153-3689-1. Dewey:378.1/795. LCCN:00-028336.
Audience: **l,u,f.** *Choice, 2001.*

Bruffee, Kenneth A. **LB1032.B76 1999**
Collaborative Learning: Higher Education, Interdependence, and the Authority of Knowledge. Ed. 2. Trade Cloth. Johns Hopkins University Press. Baltimore, MD. 1999. 344p. ISBN:0-8018-5973-5, ISBN13: 978-0-8018-5973-1. Dewey:371.39/5. LCCN:98-075126.
Audience: **l,u,f.** *Choice, 1994.*

Cohen, Elizabeth G. (Editor), et al. **LB1032.T42 2004**
Teaching Cooperative Learning: The Challenge for Teacher Education. Celeste M. Brody & Mara Sapon-Shevin (Editors). Cloth Text. State University of New York Press. Albany, NY. 2004. xiii, 234p. ISBN:0-7914-5969-1, ISBN13: 978-0-7914-5969-0. Dewey:371.39/5. LCCN:2003-045654.
Audience: **l,u,f.** *Choice, 2005.*

Gregory, Gayle H. & Chapman, Carolyn **LB1031.G74 2002**
Differentiated Instructional Strategies: One Size Doesn't Fit All. Trade Cloth. Corwin Press. Thousand Oaks, CA. 2001. 160p. ISBN:0-7619-4550-4, ISBN13: 978-0-7619-4550-5. Dewey:371.39/4. LCCN:2001-005120.
Audience: **l,u,f.**

Gregory, Gayle H. & Kuzmich, Lin **LB1031.G733 2004**
Data Driven Differentiation in the Standards-Based Classroom. Trade Cloth. Corwin Press. Thousand Oaks, CA. 2004. 224p. 1-Off Ser. ISBN:0-7619-3157-0, ISBN13: 978-0-7619-3157-7. Dewey:371.39/4. LCCN:2003-024016.
Audience: **l,u,f.**

Jacobs, George M., et al. **LB1032.J34 2002**
The Teacher's Sourcebook for Cooperative Learning: Practical Techniques, Basic Principles, and Frequently Asked Questions. Michael A. Power & Wan Inn Loh (Authors). Trade Cloth. Corwin Press. Thousand Oaks, CA. 2002. 184p. ISBN:0-7619-4608-X, ISBN13: 978-0-7619-4608-3. Dewey:371.3. LCCN:2002-000152.
Audience: **l,u,f.**

Keefe, James W. & Jenkins, John M. **LB1031**
Personalized Instruction: Changing Classroom Practice. Trade Paper. Eye On Education, Inc. Larchmont, NY. 2000. 225p. ISBN:1-883001-86-2, ISBN13: 978-1-883001-86-5. Dewey:371.34/9.
Audience: **l,u,f.** *Choice, 2000.*

Manke, Mary Phillips **LB1033 .M2123 1997**
Classroom Power Relations: Understanding Student-Teacher Interaction. Trade Paper. Lawrence Erlbaum Associates, Inc.

Mahwah, NJ. 1997. 176p. ISBN:0-8058-2496-0, ISBN13: 978-0-8058-2496-4. Dewey:371.102/3. LCCN:97-012619.
Audience: **l,u,f.** *Choice, 1998.*

Michaelsen, Larry K. (Editor), et al. **LB1032**
Team-Based Learning: A Transformative Use of Small Groups. Arletta B. Knight & L. Dee Fink (Editors). Trade Cloth. Greenwood Publishing Group, Inc. Portsmouth, NH. 2002. 304p. ISBN:0-89789-863-X, ISBN13: 978-0-89789-863-8. Dewey:371.39/5. LCCN:2002-038103.
Audience: **u,f.**

National Endowment for the Humanities **TK5105.875.I57**
EDSITEment.
http://edsitement.neh.gov
Audience: **g,l,u,f.**

Nordlund, Marcie **LB1031.N64 2003**
Differentiated Instruction: Meeting the Educational Needs of All Students in Your Classroom. Trade Paper. Scarecrow Press, Inc. Lanham, MD. 2003. 112p. ISBN:0-8108-4702-7, ISBN13: 978-0-8108-4702-6. Dewey:371.39/4. LCCN:2002-044667.
Audience: **u,f.** *Choice, 2004.*

Rios, Francisco A. (Editor) **LB1033.T26 1996**
Teacher Thinking in Cultural Contexts. Cloth Text. State University of New York Press. Albany, NY. 1996. 400p. SUNY Series in the Social Context of Education ISBN:0-7914-2881-8, ISBN13: 978-0-7914-2881-8. Dewey:371.1/023. LCCN:95-051310.
Audience: **u,f.** *Choice, 1996.*

Roberts, Tim S. **LB1032.C575 2005**
Computer-Supported Collaborative Learning in Higher Education. Trade Cloth. Idea Group Publishing. Hershey, PA. 2004. 300p. ISBN:1-59140-408-8, ISBN13: 978-1-59140-408-8. Dewey:378.1/758. LCCN:2004-003755.
Audience: **u,f.**

Schmuck, Richard A. & Schmuck, Patricia A. **LB1032.S35 2000**
Group Processes in the Classroom. Ed. 8. Paper Text. McGraw-Hill Higher Education. Burr Ridge, IL. 2000. 352p. ISBN:0-07-232287-X, ISBN13: 978-0-07-232287-3. Dewey:371.39/5. LCCN:00-032897.
Audience: **u,f.** B

Sharan, Shlomo (Editor) **LB1032**
Cooperative Learning: Research and Theory. Book, Other. Greenwood Publishing Group, Inc. Portsmouth, NH. 1990. 328p. ISBN:0-275-92887-X, ISBN13: 978-0-275-92887-2. Dewey:371.1/48. LCCN:89-036649.
Audience: **l,u,f.** *Choice, 1990.*

Shulman, Judith, et al. **LB1032.G769 1998**
Groupwork in Diverse Classrooms: A Casebook for Educators. Rachel A. Lotan & Jennifer A. Whitcomb (Authors). Trade Paper. Teachers College Press, Teachers College, Columbia University. New York, NY. 1998. 120p. ISBN:0-8077-3701-1, ISBN13: 978-0-8077-3701-9. Dewey:371.39/5. LCCN:97-033507.
Audience: **l,u,f.** *Choice, 1998.*

Simon, Sidney B., et al. **LB1033.R37**
Values and Teaching: Working with Values in the Classroom. Merrill Harmin & Louis E. Raths (Authors). Paper Text. Values Press. Hadley, MA. 1991. ISBN:1-880424-01-0, ISBN13: 978-1-880424-01-8. Dewey:370.19334.
Audience: **u,f.**

Tomlinson, Carol Ann **LB1031**
The Differentiated Classroom: Responding to the Needs of All Learners. Trade Paper. Prentice Hall PTR. Upper Saddle River, NJ. 2004. 144p. ISBN:0-13-119502-6, ISBN13: 978-0-13-119502-8. Dewey:371.39/4.
Audience: **u,f.**

Tomlinson, Carol A. & Allan, Susan D. **LB1031.T66 2000**
Leadership for Differentiating Schools and Classrooms. Trade Paper. Association for Supervision & Curriculum Development. Alexandria, VA. 2000. viii, 168p. ISBN:0-87120-502-5, ISBN13: 978-0-87120-502-5. Dewey:371.39/4. LCCN:00-011252.
Audience: **u,f.** *Choice, 2001.*

Topping, Keith J. **LB1031.5.T66 2000**
Peer Assisted Learning: A Practical Guide for Teachers. Trade Cloth. Brookline Books, Inc. Newton Upper Falls, MA. 2001. 168p. ISBN:1-57129-085-0, ISBN13: 978-1-57129-085-4. Dewey:371.39/4. LCCN:00-012343.
Audience: **u,f.**

Topping, Keith & Ehly, Stewart (Editors) **LB1031.5.P44 1998**
Peer-Assisted Learning. Cloth over Boards. Lawrence Erlbaum Associates, Inc. Mahwah, NJ. 1998. 392p. ISBN:0-8058-2501-0, ISBN13: 978-0-8058-2501-5. Dewey:371.39/4. LCCN:98-020777.
Audience: **u,f.**

Theory and Practice of Education > Teaching (Principles and Practice) > Educational Technology

Abbott, Chris **LB1028.5.A215 2000**
Information Communication Technology: Changing Education. Paper over Boards. Routledge. New York, NY. 2001. 144p. Master Classes in Education Ser. ISBN:0-7507-0951-0, ISBN13: 978-0-7507-0951-4. Dewey:371.33/09. LCCN:00-042486.
Audience: **u,f.**

Baule, Steven **LB1028.3.B39 2001**
Technology Planning for Effective Teaching and Learning. Ed. 2. Trade Cloth. Linworth Publishing, Inc. Worthington, OH. 2001. 160p. Professional Growth Ser. ISBN:1-58683-032-5, ISBN13: 978-1-58683-032-8. Dewey:371.33. LCCN:00-066399.
Audience: **u,f.**

Birnbaum, Barry W. **LC3969.5.B57 1999**
Connecting Special Education and Technology for the 21st Century. Trade Cloth. Edwin Mellen Press, The. Lewiston, NY. 1999. 132p. Studies in Education, Vol. 45 ISBN:0-7734-7991-0, ISBN13: 978-0-7734-7991-3. Dewey:371.9/0285. LCCN:99-033111.
Audience: **g,l,u,f.**

Coppola, Eileen M. **LB1028.5.C628 2004**
Powering Up: Learning to Teach Well with Technology. Richard F. Elmore (Foreword by). Perfect, Paper over Boards. Teachers College Press, Teachers College, Columbia University. New York, NY. 2004. 189p. ISBN:0-8077-4499-9, ISBN13: 978-0-8077-4499-4. Dewey:371.33/4. LCCN:2004-051650.
Audience: **u,f.** *Choice, 2005.*

Cuban, Larry **LB1028.5.C77 2001**
Oversold and Underused: Computers in Classrooms, 1980-2000. Trade Cloth. Harvard University Press. Cambridge, MA. 2001. 256p. ISBN:0-674-00602-X, ISBN13: 978-0-674-00602-7. Dewey:371.33/4. LCCN:2001-020420.
Audience: **g,l,u,f.** *Choice, 2002.*

Cuban, Larry **LB1028.3.C8 1985**
Teachers and Machines: The Classroom Use of Technology since 1920. Trade Paper. Teachers College Press, Teachers College, Columbia University. New York, NY. 1985. 205p. ISBN:0-8077-2792-X, ISBN13: 978-0-8077-2792-8. Dewey:371.3/07/8. LCCN:85-014789.
Audience: **g,l,u,f.** B

Darbyshire, Paul **LB1028.3.I563 2004**
Instructional Technologies: Cognitive Aspects of Online Programs. Trade Cloth. Idea Group Publishing. Hershey, PA. 2004. 274p. ISBN:1-59140-565-3, ISBN13: 978-1-59140-565-8. Dewey:371.33/4. LCCN:2004-003769.
Audience: **u,f.**

Dowling, Carolyn & Kwok-Wing Lai (Editors) **LB1028.3.I334 2003**
Information and Communication Technology and the Teacher of the Future. Trade Cloth. Springer. New York, NY. 2003. 322p. IFIP International Federation for Information Processing Ser., Vol. 260 ISBN:1-4020-7604-5, ISBN13: 978-1-4020-7604-6. Dewey:371.33. LCCN:2003-058874.
Audience: **f.**

Eastmond, Nick
A Global View of Instructional Technology for the 21st Century. Trade Cloth. Libraries Unlimited, Inc. Westport, CT. 2003. 220p. Instructional Technology Ser. ISBN:1-56308-941-6, ISBN13: 978-1-56308-941-1.
Audience: **g,u,f.**

George Lucas Educational Foundation Staff **LB2822.82.E393 2002**
Edutopia: Success Stories for Learning in the Digital Age. Sara Armstrong & Milton Chen (Editors), George Lucas (Introduction by). Trade Paper. John Wiley & Sons, Inc. Hoboken, NJ. 2002. 320p. ISBN:0-7879-6082-9, ISBN13: 978-0-7879-6082-7. Dewey:371.33/4. LCCN:2001-007993.
Audience: **g,l,u,f.** *Choice, 2002.*

Glandon, Shan **LB1028.4**
Integrating Technology: Effective Tools for Collaboration. Trade Cloth. Linworth Publishing, Inc. Worthington, OH. 2002. 160p. Professional Growth Ser. ISBN:1-58683-055-4, ISBN13: 978-1-58683-055-7. Dewey:27.8.
Audience: **u,f.**

Green, Timothy D. & Brown, Abbie **LB1028.4.G76 2002**
Multimedia Projects in the Classroom: A Guide to Development and Evaluation. Trade Cloth. Corwin Press. Thousand Oaks, CA. 2002. 72p. ISBN:0-7619-7852-6, ISBN13: 978-0-7619-7852-7. Dewey:371.33/467. LCCN:2001-005328.
Audience: **l,u,f.**

Heineke, Walt & Willis, Jerry (Editors) **LB1028.3 .M484 2001**
Methods of Evaluating Educational Technology. Cloth Text. Information Age Publishing, Inc. Greenwich, CT. 2001. 323p. Research Methods for Educational Technology ISBN:1-930608-57-8, ISBN13: 978-1-930608-57-3. Dewey:371.33.
Audience: **f.**

Howell, Joseph H. & Dunnivant, Stephen W. **LB1028.3.H673 2000**
Technology for Teachers: Mastering New Media and Portfolio Development. Trade Cloth. McGraw-Hill Companies, The. New York, NY. 2000. xx, 133p. ISBN:0-07-235547-6, ISBN13: 978-0-07-235547-5. Dewey:005.369. LCCN:2001-280085.
Audience: **u,f.**

International Society for Technology in Education Staff **LB3060.83**
National Educational Technology Standards for Teachers: Preparing Teachers to Use Technology. Trade Cloth. International Society for Technology in Education. Eugene, OR. 2002. 371p. ISBN:1-56484-173-1, ISBN13: 978-1-56484-173-5. Dewey:371.334. LCCN:2001-097951.
Audience: **u,f.**

Ivers, Karen S. **LB1028.5.I87 2003**
A Teacher's Guide to Using Technology in the Classroom. Trade Cloth. Libraries Unlimited, Inc. Westport, CT. 2003. 168p. ISBN:1-59158-074-9, ISBN13: 978-1-59158-074-4. Dewey:371.33. LCCN:2003-273307.
Audience: **l,u.**

Januszewski, Alan **LB1028.3**
Educational Technology: The Development of a Concept. Library Binding. Sagebrush Education Resources. Caledonia, MN. 2001. ISBN:0-613-91268-3, ISBN13: 978-0-613-91268-6. Dewey:371.33.
Audience: **g.**

Jonassen, David H. (Editor) **LB1028.3.H355 2001**
Handbook of Research for Educational Communications and Technology: A Project of the Association for Educational Communications and Technology. Ed. 2. Association for Educational Communications and Technology Staff, Brock S. Allen, Gary J. Anglin & Eun-Ok Baek (Contribution by). Cloth over Boards. Lawrence Erlbaum Associates, Inc. Mahwah, NJ. 2003. 1224p. ISBN:0-8058-4145-8, ISBN13: 978-0-8058-4145-9. Dewey:371.33/072. LCCN:2003-015730.
Audience: **g,l,u,f.** *Choice, 2004.*

McKenzie, Walter **LB1028.3.M397 2004**
Standards-Based Lessons for Tech-Savvy Students: A Multiple Intelligences Approach. Trade Cloth. Linworth Publishing, Inc. Worthington, OH. 2004. 136p. ISBN:1-58683-125-9, ISBN13: 978-1-58683-125-7. Dewey:371.33. LCCN:2003-026304.
Audience: **g,l,u,f.**

Means, Barbara, et al. **LB1028.3.M413 2001**
The Connected School: Technology and Learning in High School. William R. Penuel & Christine Padilla (Authors). Trade

Cloth. John Wiley & Sons, Inc. Hoboken, NJ. 2001. 272p. The Jossey-Bass Education Ser. ISBN:0-7879-5953-7, ISBN13: 978-0-7879-5953-1. Dewey:373.1/334. LCCN:2001-004678.
Audience: **u.**

Mehlinger, Howard D. & Powers, Susan M. **LB1707.M43 2002**
Technology and Teacher Education: A Guide for Educators and Policy Makers. Paper Text. Houghton Mifflin College Division. Boston, MA. 2001. 340p. College Teaching Ser. ISBN:0-618-07199-7, ISBN13: 978-0-618-07199-9. Dewey:370/.71/14. LCCN:2001-131528.
Audience: **u,f.**

Naidu, Som **LC5800**
E-Learning: Technology and the Development of Learning and Teaching. Cloth Text. Kogan Page, Ltd. London, 2003. 352p. Open and Distance Learning Ser. ISBN:0-7494-3776-6, ISBN13: 978-0-7494-3776-3. Dewey:378.173. LCCN:2002-152260.
Audience: **u,f.**

Orey, Michael, et al. **LB1028.3**
Educational Media and Technology Yearbook: 2006. V. J. McClendon & Robert Maribe Branch (Authors). Trade Cloth. Libraries Unlimited, Inc. Westport, CT. 2006. 440p. Education Media Yearbook Ser. ISBN:1-59158-362-4, ISBN13: 978-1-59158-362-2. Dewey:371.3/07/8.
Audience: **u,f.**

Reksten, Linda E. **LB1028.3.R44 2000**
Using Technology to Increase Student Learning. Trade Cloth. Corwin Press. Thousand Oaks, CA. 2000. 176p. Technology Ser. ISBN:0-8039-6813-2, ISBN13: 978-0-8039-6813-4. Dewey:371.33. LCCN:99-050607.
Audience: **u,f.**

Roblyer, Margaret D. **LB1028.3.R595 2006**
Integrating Educational Technology into Teaching. Ed. 4. Trade Paper. Prentice Hall PTR. Upper Saddle River, NJ. 2005. 480p. ISBN:0-13-119572-7, ISBN13: 978-0-13-119572-1. Dewey:371.33. LCCN:2005-001244.
Audience: **l,u,f.**

Rogers, Patricia L. (Editor) **LB1028.38.D49 2001**
Designing Instruction for Technology-Enhanced Learning. Trade Cloth. Idea Group Publishing. Hershey, PA. 2001. 286p. ISBN:1-930708-28-9, ISBN13: 978-1-930708-28-0. Dewey:371.33. LCCN:2001-039615.
Audience: **u,f.** *Choice, 2003, 2002.*

Rothwell, William J., et al. **HD5715.2**
Handbook of Training Technologies: An Introductory Guide to Facilitating Learning with Technology — From Planning to Evaluation. Jessica Li, Marilynn Butler, Daryl Hunt, Cecilia Maldonado & Karen Peters (Authors), D. J. King Stern (As told to). Trade Cloth. John Wiley & Sons, Inc. Hoboken, NJ. 2006. 592p. Tech Training Ser. ISBN:0-7879-7159-6, ISBN13: 978-0-7879-7159-5. Dewey:658.3/124. LCCN:2006-011520.
Audience: **g,l,u,f.**

Saettler, L. Paul **LB1028.3.S22 2005**
The Evolution of American Educational Technology. Ed. 3. Trade Cloth. Lawrence Erlbaum Associates, Inc. Mahwah, NJ. 2005. 448p. ISBN:0-8058-4057-5, ISBN13: 978-0-8058-4057-5. Dewey:371.33. LCCN:2004-058342.
Audience: **g,l,u,f.**

Tomei, Lawrence A. (Editor) **LB1028.5.C478 2003**
Challenges of Teaching with Technology Across the Curriculum: Issues and Solutions. Trade Cloth. Idea Group Publishing. Hershey, PA. 2002. 340p. ISBN:1-59140-109-7, ISBN13: 978-1-59140-109-4. Dewey:371.33/4. LCCN:2002-014192.
Audience: **g,l,u,f.**

Tomei, Lawrence A. **LB1028.3.T36 2005**
Taxonomy for the Technology Domain. Trade Cloth. Idea Group Publishing. Hershey, PA. 2005. 296p. ISBN:1-59140-524-6, ISBN13: 978-1-59140-524-5. Dewey:371.33. LCCN:2004-023607.
Audience: **u,f.**

Vrasidas, Charalambos & Glass, Gene V. (Editors) **LB1028.3.P74 2005**
Preparing Teachers to Teach with Technology. Trade Cloth. Information Age Publishing, Inc. Greenwich, CT. 2005. xviii, 397p. Current Perspectives on Applied Information Technologies Ser. ISBN:1-59311-161-4, ISBN13: 978-1-59311-161-8. Dewey:371.33. LCCN:2005-013170.
Audience: **u,f.**

Wenglinsky, Harold **LB1028.3.W42 2005**
Using Technology Wisely: The Keys to Success in Schools. Trade Cloth. Teachers College Press, Teachers College, Columbia University. New York, NY. 2005. 112p. The TEC Ser. ISBN:0-8077-4584-7, ISBN13: 978-0-8077-4584-7. Dewey:371.33. LCCN:2005-041704.
Audience: **g,u,f.**

Whitehead, Bruce M., et al. **LB1028.3.W48 2003**
Planning for Technology: A Guide for Administrtors, Technology Coordinators and Curriculum Leaders. Devon F. N. Jensen & Floyd Boschee (Authors). Trade Cloth. Corwin Press. Thousand Oaks, CA. 2002. 256p. ISBN:0-7619-4595-4, ISBN13: 978-0-7619-4595-6. Dewey:371.33. LCCN:2002-007155.
Audience: **u,f.**

Zhao, Yong (Editor) **LB1028.3.W44 2003**
What Should Teachers Know about Technology: Perspectives and Practices. Trade Cloth. Information Age Publishing, Inc. Greenwich, CT. 2003. xviii, 164p. ISBN:1-59311-037-5, ISBN13: 978-1-59311-037-6. Dewey:371.33. LCCN:2003-005926.
Audience: **g,u,f.**

Theory and Practice of Education > Teaching (Principles and Practice) > Student Guidance and Counseling

Cohen, Jeffrey J. & Fish, Marian C. **LB1027.55.C64 1993**
Handbook of School-Based Interventions: Resolving Student Problems and Promoting Healthy Educational Environments. Trade Cloth. John Wiley & Sons, Inc. Hoboken, NJ. 1993. 544p. Social and Behavioral Science Ser. ISBN:1-55542-549-6, ISBN13: 978-1-55542-549-4. Dewey:371.4/6. LCCN:93-003619.
Audience: **g,l.**

Kantor, Harvey & Tyack, David B. (Editors) **LC1045.W6 1982**
Work, Youth, and Schooling: Historical Perspectives on Vocationalism in American Education. Trade Cloth. Stanford University Press. Palo Alto, CA. 1982. 367p. ISBN:0-8047-1121-6, ISBN13: 978-0-8047-1121-0. Dewey:370.11/3/0973. LCCN:81-050788.
Audience: **u,f.**

Lawrence-Lightfoot, Sara **LB1048.5**
The Essential Conversation: What Parents and Teachers Can Learn from Each Other. Trade Paper. Ballantine Books. New York, NY. 2004. 288p. ISBN:0-345-47580-1, ISBN13: 978-0-345-47580-0. Dewey:371.19/2.
Audience: **g.**

Lazerson, Marvin & Grubb, W. Norton (Editors) **LC1045.L36**
American Education and Vocationalism: A Documentary History, 1870-1970. Trade Paper. Books on Demand. Ann Arbor, MI. 1974. 189p. Classics in Education Ser., Vol. 48 ISBN:0-7837-8951-3, ISBN13: 978-0-7837-8951-4. Dewey:370.11/3/0973. LCCN:73-087511.
Audience: **l,u,f.**

Lee, Courtland C. (Editor) **LB1027.5.C653 1995**
Counseling for Diversity: A Guide for School Counselors and Related Professionals. Ed. 1. Trade Paper. Allyn & Bacon, Inc. Boston, MA. 1994. 208p. ISBN:0-205-15321-6, ISBN13: 978-0-205-15321-3. Dewey:371.4/0973. LCCN:94-002860.
Audience: **u,f.** *Choice, 1994.*

Mierzwik, Diane **LB1048.5.M54 2004**
Quick and Easy Ways to Connect with Students and Their Parents, Grades K-8: Improving Student Achievement Through Parent Involvement. Trade Cloth. Corwin Press. Thousand Oaks, CA. 2004. 152p. ISBN:0-7619-3179-1, ISBN13: 978-0-7619-3179-9. Dewey:372.13. LCCN:2004-000415.
Audience: **u,f.**

Miller, Melvin D. **LC1045 .M64**
Principles and a Philosophy for Vocational Education. Trade Cloth. Center on Education & Training for Employment. Columbus, OH. 1985. 250p. ISBN:0-318-17790-0, ISBN13: 978-0-318-17790-8. Dewey:370.11/3/0973.
Audience: **l,u,f.**

Philips, Beeman N. **LB1027.55.P48 1990**
School Psychology at a Turning Point: Ensuring a Bright Future for the Profession. Trade Cloth. John Wiley & Sons, Inc. Hoboken, NJ. 1990. 328p. Social and Behavioral Science Ser. ISBN:1-55542-195-4, ISBN13: 978-1-55542-195-3. Dewey:370.15. LCCN:89-027510.
Audience: **g,l.** *Choice, 1990.*

Pitcher, Gayle D. & Poland, Scott **LB1027.55 P53**
Crisis Intervention in the Schools. Cloth over Boards. Guilford Publications, Inc. New York, NY. 1992. 246p. School Practitioner Ser. ISBN:0-89862-364-2, ISBN13: 978-0-89862-364-2. Dewey:371.7. LCCN:92-001417.
Audience: **f.**

Pollard, Andrew (Editor), et al. **LC1047.G7E37 1988**
Education, Training and the New Vocationalism: Experience and Policy. June Purvis & Geoffrey Walford (Editors). Library Binding. McGraw-Hill Education. Maidenhead, 1988. 192p. ISBN:0-335-15845-5, ISBN13: 978-0-335-15845-4. Dewey:370.11/3/0941. LCCN:88-001687.
Audience: **l,u.**

Power, Paul W. **HD7255.P68 2006**
A Guide to Vocational Assessment. Ed. 4. Trade Cloth. PRO-ED, Inc. Austin, TX. 2005. xxv, 375p. ISBN:1-4164-0138-5, ISBN13: 978-1-4164-0138-4. Dewey:362.4/0484. LCCN:2005-015072.
Audience: **l,u,f.**

Rosenbaum, James E. **LC1045.R77 2001**
Beyond College for All: Career Paths for the Forgotten Half. Trade Cloth. Russell Sage Foundation. New York, NY. 2001. 300p. American Sociological Association Rose Series in Sociology ISBN:0-87154-727-9, ISBN13: 978-0-87154-727-9. Dewey:331.11/423. LCCN:2001-041783.
Audience: **g,l,u,f.** *Choice, 2002.*

Rudney, Gwen L. **LC226.R83 2006**
Every Teacher's Guide to Working with Parents. Trade Cloth. Corwin Press. Thousand Oaks, CA. 2005. 128p. ISBN:1-4129-1774-3, ISBN13: 978-1-4129-1774-2. Dewey:371.103. LCCN:2005-008040.
Audience: **g,l,u,f.**

Sandoval, Jonathan (Editor) **LB1027.55.C74 2001**
Handbook of Crisis Counseling, Intervention, and Prevention in the Schools. Ed. 2. Cloth over Boards. Lawrence Erlbaum Associates, Inc. Mahwah, NJ. 2001. 448p. ISBN:0-8058-3615-2, ISBN13: 978-0-8058-3615-8. Dewey:371.7/13. LCCN:2001-031552.
Audience: **f.**

Stevenson, Robert G. (Editor) **LB1027.55.W42 1994**
What Will We Do?: Preparing a School Community to Cope with Crises. Cloth Text. Baywood Publishing Company, Inc. Amityville, NY. 1994. 224p. Death, Value and Meaning Ser. ISBN:0-89503-151-5, ISBN13: 978-0-89503-151-8. Dewey:371.4/6/0973. LCCN:94-005217.
Audience: **g,l.** *Choice, 1994.*

Strain, Phillip S. (Editor) **LB3013**
The Utilization of Classroom Peers As Behavior Change Agents. Trade Cloth. Springer. New York, NY. 1981. 378p. Applied Clinical Psychology Ser. ISBN:0-306-40618-7, ISBN13: 978-0-306-40618-8. Dewey:371.1/02. LCCN:81-001733.
Audience: **l,u.**

Wakefield, Suzy Mygatt (Editor) **LB1620.5**
Unfocused Kids: Helping Students to Focus on Their Education and Career Plans: A Resource for Educators. Trade Paper. Counseling & Psychological Services, Inc. Tucson, AZ. 2004. 526p. ISBN:1-56109-105-7, ISBN13: 978-1-56109-105-8. Dewey:373.14/2. LCCN:2004-043169.
Audience: **l,u.**

Walsh, W. Bruce & Heppner, Mary J. (Editors) **HF5382.6.H36 2005**
Handbook of Career Counseling for Women. Ed. 2. Nancy E. Betz, Kathleen J. Bieschke & Rosie P. Bingham (Contribution by). Cloth over Boards. Lawrence Erlbaum Associates, Inc. Mahwah, NJ. 2005. 560p. Contemporary Topics in Vocational Psychology Ser. ISBN:0-8058-4888-6, ISBN13: 978-0-8058-4888-5. Dewey:331.702/082. LCCN:2005-040062.
Audience: **u,f.** *Choice, 2006.*

Webster-Stratton, Carolyn **BF721.W347 1999**
How to Promote Children's Social and Emotional Competence. Cloth Text. Paul Chapman Publishing. London, 2000. 336p. ISBN:0-7619-6500-9, ISBN13: 978-0-7619-6500-8. Dewey:372.1102/4. LCCN:2001-268847.
Audience: **u,f.**

Theory and Practice of Education > Teaching (Principles and Practice) > Reading (General)

LC149
☐ Literacy Web.
http://www.literacy.uconn.edu
Audience: **g,l,u,f.**

LC151
☐ National Institute for Literacy (NIFL).
http://www.nifl.gov
Audience: **g,l,u,f.**

Beard, Roger **LB1050.2.R424 1999**
Reading Development and the Teaching of Reading: A Psychological Perspective. Jane Oakhill (Editor). Trade Paper. Blackwell Publishing, Inc. Malden, MA. 1999. 264p. ISBN:0-631-20682-5, ISBN13: 978-0-631-20682-8. Dewey:428/.4. LCCN:99-010517.
Audience: **u,f.** *Choice, 2000.*

Guthrie, John T. & Givermann, Donna E. (Editors) **LB1573.E654 1999**
Engaged in Reading: Processes, Practices and Policy Implications. Trade Paper. Teachers College Press, Teachers College, Columbia University. New York, NY. 1999. 272p. Language and Literacy Ser. ISBN:0-8077-3816-6, ISBN13: 978-0-8077-3816-0. Dewey:428.4/071/073. LCCN:98-040022.
Audience: **g,l,u,f.** *Choice, 1999.*

Kamil, Michael L. (Editor), et al. **LB1050.H278 1996**
Handbook of Reading Research. Peter B. Mosenthal, P. David Pearson & Rebecca Barr (Editors), Peter Afflerbach, Patricia A. Alexander & Donna E. Alvermann (Contribution by). Cloth over Boards. Lawrence Erlbaum Associates, Inc. Mahwah, NJ. 2000. 1024p. Handbook of Reading Research Ser., Vol. III ISBN:0-8058-2398-0, ISBN13: 978-0-8058-2398-1. Dewey:428.4072. LCCN:83-026838.
Audience: **g,l,u,f.** *Choice, 2000.*

Kucer, Stephen B. **LB1576.K83 2005**
Dimensions of Literacy: A Conceptual Base for Teaching Reading and Writing in School Settings. Ed. 2. Cloth over Boards. Lawrence Erlbaum Associates, Inc. Mahwah, NJ. 2004. 368p. ISBN:0-8058-4940-8, ISBN13: 978-0-8058-4940-0. Dewey:428.6. LCCN:2004-016811.
Audience: **u,f.**

Murphy, Sharon, et al. **LB1050.46.F72 1998**
Fragile Evidence: A Critique of Reading Assessment. Patrick Shannon, Peter Johnston & Jane Hansen (Authors). Trade Cloth. Lawrence Erlbaum Associates, Inc. Mahwah, NJ. 1998. 224p. ISBN:0-8058-2529-0, ISBN13: 978-0-8058-2529-9. Dewey:428.4/076. LCCN:97-042352.
Audience: **u,f.** *Choice, 1999.*

Purcell-Gates, Victoria, et al. **LC151.P86 2004**
Print Literacy Development: Uniting Cognitive and Social Practice Theories. Erik Jacobson & Sophie Degener (Authors). Trade Cloth. Harvard University Press. Cambridge, MA. 2004. 218p. ISBN:0-674-01518-5, ISBN13: 978-0-674-01518-0. Dewey:302.2/244. LCCN:2004-052606.
Audience: **u,f.** *Choice, 2005.*

Verhoeven, Ludo T. & Snow, Catherine E. (Editors) **LB1050.2.V47 2001**
Literacy and Motivation: Reading Engagement in Individuals and Groups. Cloth over Boards. Lawrence Erlbaum Associates, Inc. Mahwah, NJ. 2001. 336p. ISBN:0-8058-3193-2, ISBN13: 978-0-8058-3193-1. Dewey:302.2/244. LCCN:00-051393.
Audience: **g,u,f.** *Choice, 2001.*

Zigler, Edward F. (Editor), et al. **LB1139.35.P55C48**
Children's Play: The Roots of Reading. Dorothy G. Singer & Sandra J. Bishop-Josef (Editors). Trade Paper, Perfect. Zero To Three Press. Washington, DC. 2004. 200p. ISBN:0-943657-75-X, ISBN13: 978-0-943657-75-2. Dewey:155. LCCN:2003-027631.
Audience: **u,f.** *Choice, 2004.*

Educational Research

LB1028.25.U6
Ethical Standards of the American Educational Research Association: Cases and Commentary. American Educational Research Association. 2002. ISBN:0-935302-28-X, ISBN13: 978-0-935302-28-8.
Audience: **u,f.**

LB5.N25
☐ National Society for the Study of Education (NSSE).
http://www.nsse-chicago.org/
Audience: **u,f.**

PR2848.K6
Review of Research in Education. Trade Cloth. American Educational Research Association. Washington, DC. ISBN:0-317-31936-1, ISBN13: 978-0-317-31936-1. Dewey:821.3.
Audience: **u,f.**

American Education Research Association **LB15 .E48**
Encyclopedia of Educational Research. Ed. 7. Trade Cloth. Thomson Gale. Farmington Hills, MI. 2001. ISBN:0-02-864945-1, ISBN13: 978-0-02-864945-0. Dewey:370/.3.
Audience: **g,l,u,f.**

American Education Research Association **LB1570.H264 1992**
Handbook of Research on Curriculum. Trade Cloth. Simon & Schuster. New York, NY. 1992. 1088p. ISBN:0-02-900385-7, ISBN13: 978-0-02-900385-5. Dewey:375/.00973. LCCN:91-012373.
Audience: **g,u,f.** *Choice, 1992.*

Chang, Mitchell (Editor), et al. **LC212.42.C66 2003**
A Compelling Interest: Examining the Evidence on Racial Dynamics in Colleges and Universities. Daria Witt, James Jones & Kenji Hakuta (Editors). Cloth Text. Stanford University Press. Palo Alto, CA. 2003. xv, 246p. ISBN:0-8047-4034-8, ISBN13: 978-0-8047-4034-0. Dewey:378.1/9829. LCCN:2002-151608.
Audience: **l,u,f.**

Cochran-Smith, Marilyn & Zeichner, Ken (Editors) **LB1715.A47 2006**
Studying Teacher Education: The Report of the AERA Panel on Research and Teacher Education. Patricia Brady, Renee T. Clift & Hillary Conklin (Contribution by). Cloth over Boards. Lawrence Erlbaum Associates, Inc. Mahwah, NJ. 2005. 816p. ISBN:0-8058-5592-0, ISBN13: 978-0-8058-5592-0. Dewey:370/.71/1. LCCN:2005-011015.
Audience: **u,f.** *Choice, 2005.*

Freed, Melvyn N., et al. **LB1028**
The Educator's Desk Reference: (EDR) A Sourcebook of Educational Information and Research. Ed. 2. Robert K. Hess & Joseph M. Ryan (Authors). Trade Cloth. Greenwood Publishing Group, Inc. Portsmouth, NH. 2002. 584p. American Council on Education/Praeger Series on Higher Education ISBN:1-57356-359-5, ISBN13: 978-1-57356-359-8. Dewey:370/.7/2. LCCN:2002-025344.
Audience: **g,l,u,f.** *Choice, 2003.*

Jaeger, Richard M. (Editor) **LB1028.C577 1997**
Complementary Methods for Research in Education. Ed. 2. Tom Barone (Contribution by). Trade Cloth. American Educational Research Association. Washington, DC. 1997. ISBN:0-935302-19-0, ISBN13: 978-0-935302-19-6. Dewey:370/.7/8. LCCN:97-070925.
Audience: **u,f.**

Jones, Lyle V. & Olkin, Ingram **LB2822.75**
The Nation's Report Card: Evolution and Perspectives. Bloomington, IN: Phi Delta Kappa Educational Foundation in cooperation with the American Educational Research Association 2004. ISBN:0-87367-848-6, ISBN13: 978-0-87367-848-3.
Audience: **u,f.**

Keeves, John P. (Editor) **LB1028.E3184 1997**
Educational Research, Methodology and Measurement: An International Handbook. Ed. 2. Trade Cloth. Elsevier Science & Technology Books. Saint Louis, MO. 1997. 964p. Resources in Education Ser. ISBN:0-08-042710-3, ISBN13: 978-0-08-042710-2. Dewey:370/.7. LCCN:96-052173.
Audience: **u,f.** *Choice, 1998.*

Kincheloe, Joe L. **LB1028.25.U6K56 2002**
Teachers As Researchers: Qualitative Inquiry As a Path to Empowerment. Ed. 2. Paper over Boards. Routledge. New York, NY. 2002. 304p. Teacher's Library ISBN:0-415-27645-4, ISBN13: 978-0-415-27645-0. Dewey:370/.78073. LCCN:2002-026985.
Audience: **u.**

King, Joyce E. (Editor) **LC2699.B53 2005**
Black Education: A Transformative Research and Action Agenda for the New Century. Gloria Ladson Billings, Grace Lee Boggs & A. Wade Boykin (Contribution by). Perfect, Paper over Boards. Lawrence Erlbaum Associates, Inc. Mahwah, NJ. 2005. 443p. ISBN:0-8058-5457-6, ISBN13: 978-0-8058-5457-2. Dewey:370/.8996. LCCN:2004-060676.
Audience: **l,u,f.** *Choice, 2006.*

Lagemann, Ellen Condliffe **LB1028.25.U6L33 2002**
An Elusive Science: The Troubling History of Education Research. Trade Paper. University of Chicago Press. Chicago, IL. 2002. 320p. ISBN:0-226-46773-2, ISBN13: 978-0-226-46773-3. Dewey:370.7/2/073. LCCN:99-086832.
Audience: **u,f.** *Choice, 2000.*

Lomax, Richard G. **QA276.12.L67 2001**
Statistical Concepts for Education and the Behavioral Sciences. Cloth over Boards. Lawrence Erlbaum Associates, Inc. Mahwah, NJ. 2000. 528p. ISBN:0-8058-2749-8, ISBN13: 978-0-8058-2749-1. Dewey:519.5. LCCN:99-055432.
Audience: **u,f.** *Choice, 2001.*

Richardson, Virginia (Editor) **LB1028.H315 2001**
Handbook of Research on Teaching. Ed. 4. American Educational Research Association Staff (Contribution by). Trade Cloth. American Educational Research Association. Washington, DC. 2001. xiii, 1278p. ISBN:0-935302-26-3, ISBN13: 978-0-935302-26-4. Dewey:370/.7/2. LCCN:2001-045075.
Audience: **g,l,u,f.**

Smith, John K. **H61.S5885 1989**
The Nature of Social and Educational Inquiry: Empiricism vs. Interpretation. Trade Cloth. Greenwood Publishing Group, Inc. Portsmouth, NH. 1989. 200p. ISBN:0-89391-514-9, ISBN13: 978-0-89391-514-8. Dewey:300/.1. LCCN:89-006613.
Audience: **u,f.** *Choice, 1990.*

Tomal, Daniel R. **LB1028.24.T66 2003**
Action Research for Educators. Trade Paper. Scarecrow Press, Inc. Lanham, MD. 2003. 160p. ISBN:0-8108-4613-6, ISBN13: 978-0-8108-4613-5. Dewey:370/.7/2. LCCN:2002-012991.
Audience: **l,u,f.** *Choice, 2004.*

Educational Psychology. Child Study

Axline, Virginia M. **RJ505.P6A94 1989**
Play Therapy. Trade Paper. Elsevier - Health Sciences Division. Philadelphia, PA. 1989. 360p. ISBN:0-443-04061-3, ISBN13: 978-0-443-04061-0. Dewey:618.92/89/1653. LCCN:88-028552.
Audience: **f.**

Bandura, Albert **LB1051**
Social Learning Theory. Ed. 1. Trade Paper. Pearson Education. Boston, MA. 1976. 247p. ISBN:0-13-816744-3, ISBN13: 978-0-13-816744-8. Dewey:153.1/5. LCCN:76-043024.
Audience: **l,u.** B

Banner, James M. Jr. & Cannon, Harold C. **LB1060.B36 1999**
The Elements of Learning. Cloth over Boards. Yale University Press. Cumberland, RI. 1999. 200p. ISBN:0-300-07836-6, ISBN13: 978-0-300-07836-7. Dewey:378.1/70281. LCCN:98-050161.
Audience: **u,f.** *Choice, 2000.*

Bereiter, Carl **LB1057.B47 2002**
Education and Mind in the Knowledge Age. Cloth over Boards. Lawrence Erlbaum Associates, Inc. Mahwah, NJ. 2002. 536p. ISBN:0-8058-3942-9, ISBN13: 978-0-8058-3942-5. Dewey:370.15/23. LCCN:2001-033887.
Audience: **u,f.** *Choice, 2002.*

Berliner, David C. & Calfee, Robert C. (Editors) **LB1051.H2354 1996**
Handbook of Research on Educational Psychology. Trade Cloth. Thomson Gale. Farmington Hills, MI. 1996. 1200p. ISBN:0-02-897089-6, ISBN13: 978-0-02-897089-9. Dewey:370.15. LCCN:95-043348.
Audience: **f.** *Choice, 1997.*

Bower, Gordon H. & Hilgard, Ernest J. **BF318.H55 1981**
Theories of Learning. Ed. 5. Cloth Text. Prentice Hall PTR. Upper Saddle River, NJ. 1997. 647p. Century Psychology Ser. ISBN:0-13-914432-3, ISBN13: 978-0-13-914432-5. Dewey:153.1/5. LCCN:80-019396.
Audience: **l,u.** B

Bracken, Bruce A. (Editor) **LB3051**
The Psychoeducational Assessment of Preschool Children. Ed. 3. Cloth over Boards. Lawrence Erlbaum Associates, Inc. Mahwah, NJ. 2004. 496p. ISBN:0-8058-5327-8, ISBN13: 978-0-8058-5327-8. Dewey:372.12/6.
Audience: **u,f.**

Brown, Cheryl Render & Cookson, Catherine (Editors) **LB1137.P5547 2002**
Play in Practice: Case Studies in Young Children's Play. Trade Paper. Redleaf Press. Saint Paul, MN. 2004. 176p. Topics in Early Childhood Education Ser. ISBN:1-929610-09-2, ISBN13: 978-1-929610-09-9. Dewey:155.4/18. LCCN:2002-017820.
Audience: **f.** *Choice, 2002.*

Bruner, Jerome S. **LB1051.B736 1996**
Culture of Education. Trade Cloth. Harvard University Press. Cambridge, MA. 1996. 240p. ISBN:0-674-17952-8, ISBN13: 978-0-674-17952-3. Dewey:370.1/5. LCCN:95-046844.
Audience: **l,u.**

Cohen, Jonathan (Editor) **LB1072.E38 1999**
Educating Minds and Hearts: Social Emotional Learning and the Passage into Adolescence: A Guide for Educators. Trade Cloth. Teachers College Press, Teachers College, Columbia University. New York, NY. 1999. 462p. ISBN:0-8077-3839-5, ISBN13: 978-0-8077-3839-9. Dewey:370.15/3. LCCN:98-050479.
Audience: **u,f.** *Choice, 1999.*

Cropley, Arthur **LB1060**
Creativity in Education and Learning: A Guide for Teachers and Educators. Trade Paper. Kogan Page, Ltd. London, 2001. 192p. ISBN:0-7494-3447-3, ISBN13: 978-0-7494-3447-2. Dewey:370.1/523.
Audience: **l,u,f.** *Choice, 2002.*

Davis, Meredith, et al. **LB1062.D475 1997**
Design As a Catalyst for Learning. Peter Hawley, Bernard McMullan & Gertrude Spilka (Authors). Trade Paper. Association for Supervision & Curriculum Development. Alexandria, VA. 1998. 147p. ISBN:0-87120-284-0, ISBN13: 978-0-87120-284-0. Dewey:370.15/2. LCCN:97-043361.
Audience: **u,f.** *Choice, 1999.*

Dewey, John **GB451.J6**
The Child and the Curriculum and the School and Society. Trade Cloth. Library Reprints, Inc. Temecula, CA. 1902. 31p. ISBN:0-7222-2930-5, ISBN13: 978-0-7222-2930-9. Dewey:551.46.
Audience: **u,f.**

Donaldson, Margaret **BF723.C5**
Children's Minds. Trade Paper. W. W. Norton & Company, Inc. New York, NY. 1979. ISBN:0-393-95101-4, ISBN13: 978-0-393-95101-1. Dewey:155.4/13.
Audience: **l,u.** B

Elliot, Alison J. **LB1139.L3 E44 1981**
Child Language. S. R. Anderson, J. Bresnan, B. Comrie, W. Dressler & C. J. Ewen (Contribution by). Trade Paper. Cambridge University Press. New York, NY. 1981. 200p. Textbooks in Linguistics ISBN:0-521-29556-4, ISBN13: 978-0-521-29556-7. Dewey:401/.9. LCCN:80-041240.
Audience: **u,f.** B

Elliott, Stephen, et al. **LB1055**
School Psychology: Essentials of Theory and Practice. Ed. 2. Cecil Reynolds & Thomas Kratochwill (Authors). Trade Cloth. John Wiley & Sons Canada, Ltd. Mississauga, ON. 2005. 450p. ISBN:0-471-42614-8, ISBN13: 978-0-471-42614-1. Dewey:370.15.
Audience: **g,l,u.**

Gardner, Howard **LB885.G37D48 2005**
Development and Education of Mind. Trade Paper. Routledge. New York, NY. 2005. x, 270p. ISBN:0-415-36728-X, ISBN13: 978-0-415-36728-8. Dewey:370.1.
Audience: **u,f.**

Goodwin, William Lawrence **LB1115.G635**
Handbook for Measurement and Evaluation in Early Childhood Education. Trade Cloth. John Wiley & Sons, Inc. Hoboken, NJ. 1980. xviii, 632p. ISBN:0-87589-440-2, ISBN13: 978-0-87589-440-9. Dewey:372.1/2/6. LCCN:79-088768.
Audience: **u.** B

Hart, Betty & Risley, Todd R. **LB1139.L3H279 1995**
Meaningful Differences in the Everyday Experience of Young American Children. Trade Cloth, Box or Slipcased. Paul H. Brookes Publishing Company. Baltimore, MD. 1995. 304p. ISBN:1-55766-197-9, ISBN13: 978-1-55766-197-5. Dewey:401/.93. LCCN:95-003939.
Audience: **g,u.** *Choice, 1996.*

Hatch, J. Amos (Editor) **LB1119**
Qualitative Research in Early Childhood Settings. Trade Cloth. Greenwood Publishing Group, Inc. Portsmouth, NH. 1995. 272p. ISBN:0-275-94921-4, ISBN13: 978-0-275-94921-1. Dewey:372.21/072. LCCN:94-032916.
Audience: **u,f.** *Choice, 1995.*

Heath, Shirley Brice **LB1139.L3 H37 1983**
Ways with Words: Language, Life and Work in Communities and Classrooms. Trade Paper. Cambridge University Press. New York, NY. 1983. 448p. ISBN:0-521-27319-6, ISBN13: 978-0-521-27319-0. Dewey:372.6. LCCN:82-022062.
Audience: **u,f.**

Hill, Winfred F. **BF318.H553 2001**
Learning: A Survey of Psychological Interpretations. Ed. 7. Trade Paper. Allyn & Bacon, Inc. Boston, MA. 2001. 224p. ISBN:0-321-05676-0, ISBN13: 978-0-321-05676-4. Dewey:153.1/5. LCCN:2001-033386.
Audience: **l,u.**

Holt, John **LB1060.H64 1995**
How Children Learn. Trade Paper. Da Capo Press, Inc. Cambridge, MA. 1995. 320p. Classics in Child Development Ser. ISBN:0-201-48404-8, ISBN13: 978-0-201-48404-5. Dewey:371.102. LCCN:95-000402.
Audience: **l,u.**

Hull, Clark L. **LB1063.M3 1970**
Mathematico-Deductive Theory of Rote Learning: A Study in Scientific Methodology. Library Binding. Greenwood Publishing Group, Inc. Portsmouth, NH. 1970. xii, 329p. ISBN:0-8371-3126-X, ISBN13: 978-0-8371-3126-9. Dewey:153.1/522. LCCN:74-095126.
Audience: **u,f.**

Hullfish, Henry G. & Smith, Phillip G. **LB1062 .H8 1978**
Reflective Thinking: The Method of Education. Trade Cloth. Greenwood Publishing Group, Inc. Portsmouth, NH. 1978. 273p. ISBN:0-313-20005-X, ISBN13: 978-0-313-20005-2. Dewey:370.1. LCCN:77-016064.
Audience: **f.**

Isaacs, Nathan & Isaacs, Susan S. **BF723.C5**
Intellectual Growth in Young Children. Library Binding. Routledge. New York, NY. 1999. 384p. International Library of Psychology ISBN:0-415-20991-9, ISBN13: 978-0-415-20991-5. Dewey:155.4/13/4.
Audience: **l,u.**

James, William **LB 1051 .J341 1907**
Talks to Teachers on Psychology and to Students on Some of Life's Ideals. Library Binding. Reprint Services Company. Temecula, CA. 1992. Notable American Authors Ser. ISBN:0-7812-3475-1, ISBN13: 978-0-7812-3475-7. Dewey:370.15.
Audience: **u,f.**

Jersild, Arthur Thomas **LB1117.J43**
In Search of Self: An Exploration of the Role of the School in Promoting Self-Understanding. Trade Paper. Books on Demand. Ann Arbor, MI. 159p. A Publication of the Horace Mann-Lincoln Institute of School Experimentation, Teachers College, Columbia University Ser. ISBN:0-598-11514-5, ISBN13: 978-0-598-11514-0. Dewey:370.15. LCCN:52-012030.
Audience: **u,f.**

Jones, Richard M. **LB14.7**
Fantasy and Feeling in Education. Trade Cloth. New York University Press. New York, NY. 1968. ISBN:0-8147-0220-1, ISBN13: 978-0-8147-0220-8. Dewey:370.1. LCCN:68-029430.
Audience: **u,f.**

Kearsley,Greg **LB17**
Explorations in Learning & Instruction: The Theory Into Practice Database.
http://tip.psychology.org/
Audience: **u,f.**

Kessler, Rachael **LB1072.K48 2000**
The Soul of Education: Helping Students Find Connection, Compassion and Character at School. Trade Paper. Association for Supervision & Curriculum Development. Alexandria, VA. 2000. xiii, 181p. ISBN:0-87120-373-1, ISBN13: 978-0-87120-373-1. Dewey:373.17/82. LCCN:99-050911.
Audience: **u.** *Choice, 2001.*

Kozulin, Alex (Editor), et al. **LB1051.V943 2003**
Vygotsky's Educational Theory in Cultural Context. Vladimir Ageyev, Suzanne Miller & Boris Gindis (Editors), John Seely Brown, Christian Heath & Roy Pea (Contribution by). Trade Cloth. Cambridge University Press. New York, NY. 2003. 492p. Learning in Doing Ser. ISBN:0-521-82131-2, ISBN13: 978-0-521-82131-5. Dewey:370.15/23. LCCN:2002-042902.
Audience: **f.** *Choice, 2004.*

Lapan, Maureen & Houghton, Raymond **LB1060 .L36 1995**
Learning and Intelligence: Conversations with Skinner and Wheeler. Trade Cloth. Irish Academic Press. Dublin, 1995. 142p. ISBN:0-7165-2584-4, ISBN13: 978-0-7165-2584-4. Dewey:370.1523. LCCN:96-136450.
Audience: **u,f.** *Choice, 1996.*

Lenneberg, Eric H. (Editor) **LB1139.L3**
New Directions in the Study of Language. Trade Paper. MIT Press. Cambridge, MA. 1966. ISBN:0-262-62005-7, ISBN13: 978-0-262-62005-5. Dewey:158.8.
Audience: **u,f.**

Lytle, Donald E. (Editor) **LB1137**
Play and Educational Theory and Practice. Trade Cloth. Greenwood Publishing Group, Inc. Portsmouth, NH. 2003. 352p. Play and Culture Studies, Vol. 5 ISBN:1-56750-684-4, ISBN13: 978-1-56750-684-6. Dewey:155.4/18. LCCN:2002-028309.
Audience: **u,f.** *Choice, 2004.*

Miller, George A. **LB1139.L3.M56**
Spontaneous Apprentices: Children and Language. Trade Cloth. The Seabury Press, Inc. New York, NY. 1977. xxvii, 188p. ISBN:0-8164-9330-8, ISBN13: 978-0-8164-9330-2. Dewey:372.6. LCCN:77-008677.
Audience: **u,f.**

Miller, Gloria E. **LB1051**
Handbook of Psychology, Educational Psychology, Vol. 7. William M. Reynolds (Editor), Irving B. Weiner (Editor-In-Chief). Trade Cloth. John Wiley & Sons, Inc. Hoboken, NJ. 2003. 688p. ISBN:0-471-38406-2, ISBN13: 978-0-471-38406-9. Dewey:150. LCCN:2002-066380.
Audience: **g,l,u.**

Miller, Neal E. & Dollard, John **LB1069 .M5 1979**
Social Learning and Imitation. Trade Cloth. Greenwood Publishing Group, Inc. Portsmouth, NH. 1979. 341p.

ISBN:0-313-20714-3, ISBN13: 978-0-313-20714-3. Dewey:153.1/5. LCCN:78-023728.
Audience: **u,f.** BCL3

Moerk, Ernst L. **LB1139.L3.M655 1983**
The Mother of Eve: As a First Language Teacher. Lewis P. Lipsitt (Editor). Trade Cloth. Greenwood Publishing Group, Inc. Portsmouth, NH. 1984. 160p. Monographs on Infancy Ser., Vol. 3 ISBN:0-89391-162-3, ISBN13: 978-0-89391-162-1. Dewey:372.6. LCCN:82-016358.
Audience: **u,f.** BCL3

Mowrer, Orval Hobart **LB1051 .M737**
Learning Theory and Behavior. Paper Text. Textbook Publishers. Temecula, CA. 2003. 555p. ISBN:0-7581-0484-7, ISBN13: 978-0-7581-0484-7. Dewey:153.1/5.
Audience: **g,l.** BCL3

Mowrer, Orval Hobart **LB1051 .M75**
Learning Theory and the Symbolic Processes. Paper Text. Textbook Publishers. Temecula, CA. 2003. 473p. ISBN:0-7581-0346-8, ISBN13: 978-0-7581-0346-8. Dewey:154.4.
Audience: **g,l.** BCL3

Murphy, Gardner **LB1055**
Freeing Intelligence Through Teaching: A Dialectic of the Rational and the Personal. Library Binding. Greenwood Publishing Group, Inc. Portsmouth, NH. 1977. ISBN:0-8371-9593-4, ISBN13: 978-0-8371-9593-3. Dewey:370.15/2. LCCN:77-004217.
Audience: **l,u.** BCL3

Neuman, Susan B. & Dickinson, David K. (Editors) **LB1139.5.L35H37 2001**
Handbook of Early Literacy Research, Vol. 1. Cloth over Boards. Guilford Publications, Inc. New York, NY. 2001. 494p. ISBN:1-57230-653-X, ISBN13: 978-1-57230-653-0. Dewey:372.6. LCCN:2001-033004.
Audience: **u,f.** *Choice, 2002.*

Novak, Joseph D. **LB1060.N677 1998**
Learning, Creating, and Using Knowledge: Concept Maps As Facilitative Tools in Schools and Corporations. Cloth over Boards. Lawrence Erlbaum Associates, Inc. Mahwah, NJ. 1998. 264p. ISBN:0-8058-2625-4, ISBN13: 978-0-8058-2625-8. Dewey:370.1523. LCCN:97-033965.
Audience: **l,u,f.** *Choice, 1998.*

Petraglia, Joseph **LB1062.P42 1998**
Reality by Design: The Rhetoric and Technology of Authenticity in Education. Cloth over Boards. Lawrence Erlbaum Associates, Inc. Mahwah, NJ. 1998. 208p. Rhetoric, Knowledge and Society Ser. ISBN:0-8058-2041-8, ISBN13: 978-0-8058-2041-6. Dewey:370/.1. LCCN:97-028104.
Audience: **u,f.** *Choice, 1998.*

Piaget, Jean **LB1117 .P5**
The Moral Judgment of the Child. Marjorie Gabain (Translator). Trade Paper. Simon & Schuster. New York, NY. 1965. 416p. ISBN:0-02-925240-7, ISBN13: 978-0-02-925240-6. Dewey:155.41825.
Audience: **u,f.**

Piaget, Jean, et al. **LB1139.G4 P53 1981**
The Child's Conception of Geometry. Barbel Inhelder & Alina Szeminska (Authors). Trade Paper. W. W. Norton & Company, Inc. New York, NY. 1981. 432p. ISBN:0-393-00057-5, ISBN13: 978-0-393-00057-3. Dewey:155.4/13. LCCN:81-004752.
Audience: **u,f.**

Reilly, Mary (Editor) **LB1137.R44**
Play as Exploratory Learning: Studies of Curiosity Behavior. Trade Paper. Books on Demand. Ann Arbor, MI. 1974. 317p. ISBN:0-608-01448-6, ISBN13: 978-0-608-01448-7. Dewey:155.4/18. LCCN:72-098044.
Audience: **u,f.**

Reynolds, Cecil R. & Gutkin, Terry B. (Editors) **LB1051.H2356 1999**
The Handbook of School Psychology. Ed. 3. Trade Cloth. John Wiley & Sons, Inc. Hoboken, NJ. 1998. 1216p. ISBN:0-471-12205-X, ISBN13: 978-0-471-12205-0. Dewey:370.15. LCCN:98-017618.
Audience: **g,l,u.**

Rogers, Carl Ransom & Freiberg, H. Jerome **LB1051 .R636 1994**
Freedom to Learn. Ed. 3. Trade Paper. Prentice Hall PTR. Upper Saddle River, NJ. 1994. 352p. ISBN:0-02-403121-6, ISBN13: 978-0-02-403121-1. Dewey:370.15. LCCN:93-034791.
Audience: **l,u.**

Rosenthal, Robert & Jacobson, Lenore **LB1131 .R585 1992**
Pygmalion in the Classroom: Teacher Expectation and Pupils' Intellectual Development. Trade Paper. Irvington Publishers. New York, NY. 1989. 265p. ISBN:0-8290-1768-2, ISBN13: 978-0-8290-1768-7. Dewey:372.12/64. LCCN:82-023289.
Audience: **l,u.**

Sapora, Allen Victor Heimback **LB1137 .S24**
The Theory of Play and Recreation. Paper Text. Textbook Publishers. Temecula, CA. 2003. 558p. ISBN:0-7581-4693-0, ISBN13: 978-0-7581-4693-9. Dewey:790.
Audience: **g,l,u.** BCL3

Singley, Mark K. & Anderson, John R. **LB1059.S523 1989**
The Transfer of Cognitive Skill. Trade Cloth. Harvard University Press. Cambridge, MA. 1989. 320p. Cognitive Science Ser., No. 9 ISBN:0-674-90340-4, ISBN13: 978-0-674-90340-1. Dewey:370.15. LCCN:88-028404.
Audience: **g,l,u.** *Choice, 1990.*

Strahan, David B. **LB1072.S87 1997**
Mindful Learning: Teaching Self-Discipline and Academic Accomplishment. Trade Paper. Carolina Academic Press. Durham, NC. 1997. 224p. ISBN:0-89089-932-0, ISBN13: 978-0-89089-932-8. Dewey:370.15/23. LCCN:97-037448.
Audience: **g,l,u.** *Choice, 1998.*

Thorndike, Edward L. **LB1051**
The Principles of Teaching Based on Psychology. Library Binding. Routledge. New York, NY. 1999. 308p. International Library of Psychology ISBN:0-415-21012-7, ISBN13: 978-0-415-21012-6. Dewey:370.15.
Audience: **u,f.**

Thorndike, Edward Lee **LB1051**
Educational Psychology. Trade Cloth. Ayer Company Publishers, Inc. Manchester, NH. 1978. American Education, :Its Men, Institutions, and Ideas, Series 1 ISBN:0-405-01484-8, ISBN13: 978-0-405-01484-0. Dewey:370.15. LCCN:72-089247.
Audience: **u,f.** B

Thorndike, Edward Lee **LB1051 .T53 1971**
Fundamentals of Learning. Trade Cloth. A M S Press, Inc. New York, NY. ISBN:0-404-06429-9, ISBN13: 978-0-404-06429-7. Dewey:153.1/5. LCCN:72-137270.
Audience: **u,f.** B

Thorndike, Edward Lee, et al. **BF431 .T45 1973**
The Measurement of Intelligence. E. O. Bregman & M. V. Cobb (Authors). Trade Cloth. Ayer Company Publishers, Inc. Manchester, NH. 1976. Classics in Psychology Ser. ISBN:0-405-05165-4, ISBN13: 978-0-405-05165-4. Dewey:153.9/3. LCCN:73-002993.
Audience: **u,f.**

Wall, William Douglas **LB1115.W217**
Constructive Education for Children. Trade Cloth. Larousse Harrap Publishers. London, 1975. xv, 349p. ISBN:92-3-101195-2, ISBN13: 978-92-3-101195-5. Dewey:372. LCCN:76-356490.
Audience: **l,u.** B

Woodill, Gary (Editor), et al. **LB1139.23.I68 1992**
International Handbook of Early Childhood Education. Judith Bernhard & Lawrence Prochner (Editors). Paper over Boards. Garland Publishing, Inc. New York, NY. 1992. 576p. ISBN:0-8240-4939-X, ISBN13: 978-0-8240-4939-3. Dewey:372.21. LCCN:92-023846.
Audience: **l,u,f.** *Choice, 1993.*

Zigler, Edward F. (Editor), et al. **LB1139.35.P55C48**
Children's Play: The Roots of Reading. Dorothy G. Singer & Sandra J. Bishop-Josef (Editors). Trade Paper, Perfect. Zero To Three Press. Washington, DC. 2004. 200p. ISBN:0-943657-75-X, ISBN13: 978-0-943657-75-2. Dewey:155. LCCN:2003-027631.
Audience: **u,f.** *Choice, 2004.*

Zimmerman, Barry J. & Schunk, Dale H. (Editors) **LB1051.E36214 2003**
Educational Psychology: A Century of Contributions: A Project of Division 15 (educational Psychology) of the American Psychological Society. Lorin W. Anderson, J. William Asher & David C. Berliner (Contribution by). Cloth over Boards. Lawrence Erlbaum Associates, Inc. Mahwah, NJ. 2002. 504p. ISBN:0-8058-3681-0, ISBN13: 978-0-8058-3681-3. Dewey:370.15. LCCN:2002-010674.
Audience: **u,f.** *Choice, 2004.*

Education by Level (Includes Teaching of Individual Subjects)

LB1555
edHelper.com.
http://edhelper.com
Audience: **g,l,u,f.**

LB1715
National Educational Technology Standards.
http://cnets.iste.org/
International Society for Technology in Education.
Audience: **l,u,f.**

American Council on the Teaching of Foreign Languages **LB1578**
National Standards for Foreign Language Education.
http://www.actfl.org/i4a/pages/index.cfm?pageid=3392
Audience: **u,f.**

ArtsEdge—The National Arts and Education Network **NX280**
Standards (Art Education).
http://artsedge.kennedy-center.org/teach/standards.cfm
ArtsEdge; Marcopolo; MCI Foundation.
Audience: **u,f.**

Kendall, John S. and Marzano, Robert J. **LB3060.83**
Content Knowledge: A Compendium of Standards and Benchmarks for K-12 Education.
http://www.mcrel.org/standards-benchmarks/
Mid-Continent Research for Education and Learning (McREL).
Audience: **g.**

National Academy of Sciences **Q183.3A1**
National Science Education Standards.
http://www.nap.edu/readingroom/books/nses/html/
National Academy of Sciences.
Audience: **u,f.**

National Center for History **D16.3**
National Standards for History Basic Edition.
http://nchs.ucla.edu/standards/
National Center for History.
Audience: **u,f.**

National Council for Accreditation of Teacher Education (NCATE)
Program Standards and Report Forms.
http://www.ncate.org/public/programStandards.asp?ch=4
Audience: **g.**

National Council for the Social Studies **LB1584**
Expectations of Excellence: Curriculum Standards for Social Studies.
http://www.socialstudies.org/standards/
National Council for the Social Studies.
Audience: **u,f.**

National Council of Teachers of Mathematics **QA11.5**
Principles & Standards for School Mathematics. http://standards.nctm.org/
National Council of Teachers of Mathematics.
Audience: **u,f.**

National Geographic Society **G74**
National Geography Standards. http://www.nationalgeographic.com/resources/ngo/education/standardslist.html
National Geographic Society.
Audience: **u,f.**

Education by Level (Includes Teaching of Individual Subjects) > Primary Education

Barone, Diane M., et al. **LB1139.5.R43B36 2004**
Teaching Early Literacy: Development, Assessment, and Instruction. Shelley Hong Xu & Marla H. Mallette (Authors). Cloth over Boards. Guilford Publications, Inc. New York, NY. 2004. 246p. ISBN:1-59385-107-3, ISBN13: 978-1-59385-107-1. Dewey:372.4. LCCN:2004-017181.
Audience: **l,u.** *Choice, 2005.*

Block, Cathy Collins, et al. **LB1525.L36 2001**
Learning to Read: Lessons from Exemplary First-Grade Classrooms. Richard L. Allington, Lesley Mandel Morrow, Michael Pressley & Ruth Wharton-McDonald (Authors). Cloth over Boards. Guilford Publications, Inc. New York, NY. 2001. 242p. Solving Problems in the Teaching of Literacy Ser. ISBN:1-57230-648-3, ISBN13: 978-1-57230-648-6. Dewey:372.4. LCCN:2001-018802.
Audience: **g,l.** *Choice, 2002.*

Carr, Janine C. **LB1576.C31714 1999**
A Child Went Forth: Reflective Teaching with Young Readers and Writers. Trade Paper. Heinemann. Portsmouth, NH. 1999. 390p. ISBN:0-325-00171-5, ISBN13: 978-0-325-00171-5. Dewey:372.6/044. LCCN:99-29498.
Audience: **g,l,u,f.** *Choice, 2000.*

Clements, Douglas H. (Editor), et al. **QA135.6.E57 2003**
Engaging Young Children in Mathematics: Standards for Pre-School and Kindergarten Mathematics Education. Julie Sarama & Ann-Marie DiBiase (Editors). Cloth over Boards. Lawrence Erlbaum Associates, Inc. Mahwah, NJ. 2003. 488p. The Studies in Mathematical Thinking and Learning Ser. ISBN:0-8058-4210-1, ISBN13: 978-0-8058-4210-4. Dewey:372.7. LCCN:2002-192834.
Audience: **u,f.** *Choice, 2004.*

Craft, Anna **LB1062.C73 2000**
Creativity Across the Primary Curriculum: Framing and Developing Practice. E-Book. NetLibrary, Inc. Boulder, CO. 2000. ISBN:0-585-45730-1, ISBN13: 978-0-585-45730-7. Dewey:370.15/7.
Audience: **g,l,u,f.**

Dyson, Anne Haas **LB1139.L3D97 2003**
The Brothers and Sisters Learn to Write: Popular Literacies in Childhood and School Cultures. Cloth Text. Teachers College Press, Teachers College, Columbia University. New York, NY. 2002. 264p. ISBN:0-8077-4281-3, ISBN13: 978-0-8077-4281-5. Dewey:302.2/244. LCCN:2002-073565.
Audience: **l,u,f.** *Choice, 2003.*

Dyson, Anne Haas **LB1529.U5.D97 1993**
Social Worlds of Children Learning to Write in an Urban Primary School. Cloth Text. Teachers College Press, Teachers College, Columbia University. New York, NY. 1993. 288p. Language and Literacy Ser. ISBN:0-8077-3296-6, ISBN13: 978-0-8077-3296-0. Dewey:372.6. LCCN:93-025086.
Audience: **l,u,f.** *Choice, 1994.*

Flood, James & Anders, Patricia (Editors) **LC151.L48214 2005**
Literacy Development of Students in Urban Schools: Research and Policy. Trade Cloth. International Reading Association. Newark, DE. 2005. ISBN:0-87207-543-5, ISBN13: 978-0-87207-543-6. Dewey:302.2/244. LCCN:2004-024968.
Audience: **g,l,u,f.** *Choice, 2005.*

Gallas, Karen **LB1139.L3.G34 1994**
The Languages of Learning: How Children Talk, Write, Dance, Draw and Sing Their Understanding of the World. Cloth Text. Teachers College Press, Teachers College, Columbia University. New York, NY. 1994. 192p. Language and Literacy Ser. ISBN:0-8077-3306-7, ISBN13: 978-0-8077-3306-6. Dewey:372.6. LCCN:93-036505.
Audience: **u,f.** *Choice, 1994.*

Gangi, Jane M. **PS490.G36 2004**
Encountering Children's Literature: An Arts Approach. Trade Paper. Allyn & Bacon, Inc. Boston, MA. 2003. 360p. ISBN:0-205-39240-7, ISBN13: 978-0-205-39240-7. Dewey:809/.89282. LCCN:2003-046387.
Audience: **g,u.** *Choice, 2004.*

Hall, Susan T. **LC311.H33 2000**
Using Picture Storybooks to Teach Character Education. Paper Text. Greenwood Publishing Group, Inc. Portsmouth, NH. 2000. 232p. Using Picture Books to Teach Ser. ISBN:1-57356-349-8, ISBN13: 978-1-57356-349-9. Dewey:370.11/4. LCCN:00-009664.
Audience: **g,u.** *Choice, 2001.*

Hart-Hewins, Linda & Wells, Jan **LB1525.H26 1999**
Better Books! Better Readers!: How to Choose, Use and Level Books for Children in the Primary Grades. Trade Paper. Harbour Publishing Company, Ltd. Madeira Park, BC. 1999. 152p. ISBN:1-55138-105-2, ISBN13: 978-1-55138-105-3. Dewey:372.4. LCCN:99-010632.
Audience: **g,l,u.**

McEwan, Elaine K. **LB1573.M1667 2002**
Teach Them ALL to Read: Catching the Kids Who Fall Through the Cracks. Trade Cloth. Corwin Press. Thousand Oaks, CA. 2002. 225p. ISBN:0-7619-4502-4, ISBN13: 978-0-7619-4502-4. Dewey:372.4. LCCN:2001-008016.
Audience: **g,u.** *Choice, 2003.*

McLane, Joan B. & McNamee, Gillian D. **LB1139.L3M3348 1990**
Early Literacy. Trade Cloth. Harvard University Press. Cambridge, MA. 1990. 160p. The Developing Child Ser. ISBN:0-674-22164-8, ISBN13: 978-0-674-22164-2. Dewey:372.6. LCCN:89-027082.
Audience: **g,u.** *Choice, 1990.*

Meek, Margaret **LB1050.M42 1982**
Learning to Read. Trade Cloth. Random House. London, 1982. 192p. ISBN:0-370-30154-4, ISBN13: 978-0-370-30154-9. Dewey:428.4. LCCN:83-670127.
Audience: **g,u,f.** B

Meier, Daniel **LB1140.5.L3M45 2000**
Scribble Scrabble, Learning to Read and Write: Success with Diverse Teachers, Children and Families. Trade Paper. Teachers College Press, Teachers College, Columbia University. New York, NY. 2000. 248p. ISBN:0-8077-3882-4, ISBN13: 978-0-8077-3882-5. Dewey:372.6. LCCN:99-048786.
Audience: **g,u.** *Choice, 2000.*

National Research Council Staff & Alberts, Betty **LB1139.5.R43S83 1999**
Starting Out Right: A Guide to Promoting Children's Reading Success. M. Susan Burns (Editor), Bruce Alberts (Foreword by). Trade Paper. National Academies Press. Washington, DC. 1999. 192p. ISBN:0-309-06410-4, ISBN13: 978-0-309-06410-1. Dewey:372.1. LCCN:98-025492.
Audience: **u,f.** *Choice, 1999.*

Rathvon, Natalie **LB1525.75.R38 2004**
Early Reading Assessment: A Practitioner's Handbook. Cloth over Boards. Guilford Publications, Inc. New York, NY. 2004. 612p. ISBN:1-57230-984-9, ISBN13: 978-1-57230-984-5. Dewey:372.48. LCCN:2003-017065.
Audience: **u,f.** *Choice, 2005.*

Slavin, Robert E. (Editor), et al. **LB1139.25.P76 1994**
Preventing Early School Failure: Research, Policy, and Practice. Ed. 1. Nancy L. Karweit & Barbara A. Wasik (Editors). Paper Text. Allyn & Bacon, Inc. Boston, MA. 1993. 256p. ISBN:0-205-13991-4, ISBN13: 978-0-205-13991-0. Dewey:372.21/0973. LCCN:93-016546.
Audience: **u,f.** *Choice, 1994.*

Sornson, Robert (Editor) **LB1139.23.P74 2001**
Preventing Early Learning Failure. Association for Supervision and Curriculum Development Staff (Contribution by). Trade Paper. Association for Supervision & Curriculum Development. Alexandria, VA. 2001. vi, 193p. ISBN:0-87120-510-6, ISBN13: 978-0-87120-510-0. Dewey:372.21. LCCN:2001-001200.
Audience: **g,u.** *Choice, 2002.*

Vacca, Richard T., et al. **LB1573.V32 2006**
Reading and Learning to Read. Ed. 6. Linda C. Burkey, Mary K. Gove, Lisa A. Lenhart, Christine A. McKeon & Jo Anne L. Vacca (Authors). Cloth Text. Allyn & Bacon, Inc. Boston, MA. 2005. 656p. ISBN:0-205-43154-2, ISBN13: 978-0-205-43154-0. Dewey:372.4. LCCN:2004-065071.
Audience: **l,u.**

Education by Level (Includes Teaching of Individual Subjects) > Elementary

Adams, Marilyn J. **LB1050.A258 1990**
Beginning to Read: Thinking and Learning about Print. Trade Cloth. MIT Press. Cambridge, MA. 1990. 480p. ISBN:0-262-01112-3, ISBN13: 978-0-262-01112-9. Dewey:372.4. LCCN:89-013716.
Audience: **f.** *Choice, 1990.*

Allen, Jo Beth (Editor) **LC196.5.U6C53 1999**
Class Actions: Teaching for Social Justice in Elementary and Middle School. Cloth Text. Teachers College Press, Teachers College, Columbia University. New York, NY. 1999. 192p. ISBN:0-8077-3857-3, ISBN13: 978-0-8077-3857-3. Dewey:370.11/5/0973. LCCN:98-055471.
Audience: **u,f.**

Allington, Richard L. & Johnston, Peter H. **LB1573.A47 2002**
Reading to Learn: Lessons from Exemplary Fourth-Grade Classrooms. Cloth over Boards. Guilford Publications, Inc. New York, NY. 2002. 254p. Solving Problems in the Teaching of Literacy Ser. ISBN:1-57230-763-3, ISBN13: 978-1-57230-763-6. Dewey:372.4. LCCN:2002-024461.
Audience: **g,l,u,f.** *Choice, 2002.*

American Education Research Association **LB1570.H264 1992**
Handbook of Research on Curriculum. Trade Cloth. Simon & Schuster. New York, NY. 1992. 1088p. ISBN:0-02-900385-7, ISBN13: 978-0-02-900385-5. Dewey:375/.00973. LCCN:91-012373.
Audience: **g,u,f.** *Choice, 1992.*

Anderson, Paul S. & Lapp, Diane K. **LB1576**
Language Skills in Elementary Education. Ed. 4. Trade Paper. Prentice Hall PTR. Upper Saddle River, NJ. 1996. 496p. ISBN:0-02-303170-0, ISBN13: 978-0-02-303170-0. Dewey:372.6/044. LCCN:86-016363.
Audience: **u.** B

Apple, Michael, et al. **LB2806.15**
Curriculum Studies: The Reconceptionalization (Curriculum Theorizing:The Reconceptualists). Maxine Greene & Herb Kliebard (Authors), William Pinar (Editor). Trade Paper. Educator's International Press, Inc. Troy, NY. 2000. 470p. ISBN:1-891928-08-2, ISBN13: 978-1-891928-08-6. Dewey:375/.001. LCCN:00-027803.
Audience: **u,f.**

Applebee, Arthur N. **LB1570.A67 1996**
Curriculum as Conversation: Transforming Traditions of Teaching and Learning. Trade Paper. University of Chicago Press. Chicago, IL. 1996. 158p. ISBN:0-226-02123-8, ISBN13: 978-0-226-02123-2. Dewey:375/.00973. LCCN:95-042694.
Audience: **u,f.** *Choice, 1996.*

Arnold, Roslyn **LB1139.W7A74 1991**
Writing Development: Magic in the Brain. Trade Paper. McGraw-Hill Education. Maidenhead, 1991. 160p. English, Language and Education Ser. ISBN:0-335-15195-7, ISBN13: 978-0-335-15195-0. Dewey:372.6/23. LCCN:90-027371.
Audience: **g,u.** *Choice, 1992.*

Ballenger, Cynthia (Editor) **LB1576.R44 2004**
Regarding Children's Words: Teacher Research on Language and Literacy. Brookline Teacher Researcher Seminar Staff (Contribution by). Trade Cloth. Teachers College Press, Teachers College, Columbia University. New York, NY. 2003. 192p. The Practitioner Inquiry Ser. ISBN:0-8077-4402-6, ISBN13: 978-0-8077-4402-4. Dewey:372.6. LCCN:2003-061152.
Audience: **l,u,f.** *Choice, 2005.*

Bauer, Caroline Feller **LB1042**
Caroline Feller Bauer's New Handbook for Storytellers. Lynn Bredeson (Illustrator). Trade Cloth. American Library Association. Chicago, IL. 1995. 550p. ISBN:0-8389-0664-8, ISBN13: 978-0-8389-0664-4. Dewey:372.64/2. LCCN:93-014959.
Audience: **g,u.**

Bettelheim, Bruno & Zelan, Karen **LB1050.B47 1982**
On Learning to Read: The Child's Fascination with Meaning. Trade Cloth. Alfred A. Knopf Inc. New York, NY. 1981. x, 306p. ISBN:0-394-51592-7, ISBN13: 978-0-394-51592-2. Dewey:428.407. LCCN:81-047492.
Audience: **u.** B

Blough, Glenn O. & Schwartz, Julius **LB1585.3.B55 1990**
Elementary School Science and How to Teach It. Ed. 8. Cloth Text. Thomson Wadsworth. Belmont, CA. 1990. 688p. ISBN:0-03-031312-0, ISBN13: 978-0-03-031312-7. Dewey:372.3/5044. LCCN:89-015288.
Audience: **u.** B

Bricker, David C. **LB1584.B67 1989**
Classroom Life as Civic Education: Individual Achievement and Student Cooperation in Schools. Trade Paper. Teachers College Press, Teachers College, Columbia University. New York, NY. 1989. 152p. Professional Ethics in Education Ser., No. 2 ISBN:0-8077-2959-0, ISBN13: 978-0-8077-2959-5. Dewey:372.83/2044. LCCN:89-031615.
Audience: **g,u.** *Choice, 1990.*

Burns, Marilyn **QA135.5.B83963 2000**
About Teaching Mathematics: A K-8 Resource. Ed. 2. Trade Paper. Math Solutions Publications. Sausalito, CA. 2000. 348p. ISBN:0-941355-25-X, ISBN13: 978-0-941355-25-4. Dewey:372.7. LCCN:00-036177.
Audience: **g,u.**

Campbell, Patricia S. & Scott-Kassner, Carol **MT1.C226 2002**
Music in Childhood: From Preschool Through the Elementary Grades. Ed. 2. Spiral. Thomson Wadsworth. Belmont, CA. 2001. 448p. ISBN:0-534-58554-X, ISBN13: 978-0-534-58554-9. Dewey:372.87044. LCCN:2001-048347.
Audience: **u,f.**

Carin, Arthur A. **LB1585.C28 1997**
Teaching Science Through Discovery. Ed. 8. Trade Cloth. Prentice Hall PTR. Upper Saddle River, NJ. 1996. 272p. ISBN:0-13-234089-5, ISBN13: 978-0-13-234089-2. Dewey:372.3/5044. LCCN:96-027830.
Audience: **g,u.** B

Carlson, Maura O'Brien, et al. **LB1585.C29 2003**
Weaving Science Inquiry and Continuous Assessment: Using Formative Assessment to Improve Learning. Gregg E. Humphrey & Karen S. Reinhardt (Authors). Trade Cloth. Corwin Press. Thousand Oaks, CA. 2003. 152p. One-Off Ser. ISBN:0-7619-4589-X, ISBN13: 978-0-7619-4589-5. Dewey:372.3/5044. LCCN:2003-004594.
Audience: **u.** *Choice, 2004.*

Chall, Jeanne S. **LB1573.C438 1996**
Learning to Read: The Great Debate. Ed. 2. Cloth Text. Harcourt College Publishers. Fort Worth, TX. 1995. 512p. ISBN:0-15-503080-9, ISBN13: 978-0-15-503080-0. Dewey:372.4/1. LCCN:95-079648.
Audience: **u,f.**

Cohen, Jonathan (Editor) **LB1072.C35 2001**
Caring Classrooms/Intelligent Schools: The Social Emotional Education of Young Children. Trade Cloth. Teachers College Press, Teachers College, Columbia University. New York, NY. 2001. xvi, 219p. Social Emotional Learning Ser. ISBN:0-8077-4058-6, ISBN13: 978-0-8077-4058-3. Dewey:372.01/9. LCCN:00-066989.
Audience: **u,f.** *Choice, 2002.*

Cohen, Jonathan (Editor) **LB1072.E38 1999**
Educating Minds and Hearts: Social Emotional Learning and the Passage into Adolescence: A Guide for Educators. Trade Cloth. Teachers College Press, Teachers College, Columbia University. New York, NY. 1999. 462p. ISBN:0-8077-3839-5, ISBN13: 978-0-8077-3839-9. Dewey:370.15/3. LCCN:98-050479.
Audience: **u,f.** *Choice, 1999.*

Cunningham, Patricia M. & Allington, Richard L. **LB1576.C855 2006**
Classrooms That Work: They Can All Read and Write. Ed. 4. Trade Paper. Allyn & Bacon, Inc. Boston, MA. 2006. 320p. ISBN:0-205-49394-7, ISBN13: 978-0-205-49394-4. Dewey:372.6/044. LCCN:2005-058601.
Audience: **g,u.**

Doll, Ronald C. **LB2806.15.D65 1996**
Curriculum Improvement: Decision Making and Process. Ed. 9. Cloth Text. Allyn & Bacon, Inc. Boston, MA. 1995. 544p. ISBN:0-205-16457-9, ISBN13: 978-0-205-16457-8. Dewey:375/.001/0973. LCCN:94-048644.
Audience: **u,f.** B

Eisner, Elliot W. **LB1590.3.E37 1994**
Cognition and Curriculum Reconsidered. Ed. 2. Cloth Text. Teachers College Press, Teachers College, Columbia University. New York, NY. 1994. 120p. ISBN:0-8077-3311-3, ISBN13: 978-0-8077-3311-0. Dewey:375/.006. LCCN:94-000320.
Audience: **u,f.**

Eisner, Elliot W. **LB1570**
The Educational Imagination: On the Design and Education of School Programs. Ed. 2. Cloth Text. Prentice Hall PTR. Upper Saddle River, NJ. 1985. 352p. ISBN:0-02-332110-5, ISBN13: 978-0-02-332110-8. Dewey:375/.001/0973. LCCN:83-026754.
Audience: **u,f.** B

Erickson, H. Lynn **LB1570.E74 2001**
Stirring the Head, Heart, and Soul: Redefining Curriculum and Instruction, Vol. 6. Ed. 2. Trade Cloth. Corwin Press. Thousand Oaks, CA. 2000. 256p. ISBN:0-8039-6884-1, ISBN13: 978-0-8039-6884-4. Dewey:375.00973. LCCN:00-009940.
Audience: **u,f.** *Choice, 1995.*

Evans, Ronald W. **LB1584.E95 2004**
The Social Studies Wars: What Should We Teach the Children? Trade Cloth. Teachers College Press, Teachers College, Columbia University. New York, NY. 2004. 224p.

ISBN:0-8077-4420-4, ISBN13: 978-0-8077-4420-8. Dewey:300/.71. LCCN:2003-060188.
Audience: **u,f.** *Choice, 2004.*

Farstrup, Alan E. & Samuels, S. Jay (Editors) **LB1050.W435 2002**
What Research Has to Say about Reading Instruction. Ed. 3. Trade Cloth. International Reading Association. Newark, DE. 2002. viii, 440p. ISBN:0-87207-177-4, ISBN13: 978-0-87207-177-3. Dewey:428.4. LCCN:2002-001759.
Audience: **u,f.**

Faunce, Roland Cleo **LB1555 .F3**
Developing the Core Curriculum. Paper Text. Textbook Publishers. Temecula, CA. 2003. 386p. ISBN:0-7581-5908-0, ISBN13: 978-0-7581-5908-3. Dewey:375.
Audience: **u,f.**

Flood, James (Editor), et al. **LB1576.H234 2003**
Handbook of Research on Teaching the English Language Arts: Sponsored by the International Reading Association and the National Council of Teachers of English. Ed. 2. Diane Lapp, James R. Squire & Julie M. Jensen (Editors), JoBeth Allen, Donna E. Alvermann & Arthur Applebee (Contribution by). Cloth over Boards. Lawrence Erlbaum Associates, Inc. Mahwah, NJ. 2002. 1120p. ISBN:0-8058-3786-8, ISBN13: 978-0-8058-3786-5. Dewey:428/.007073. LCCN:2002-011444.
Audience: **u,f.** *Choice, 2003.*

Foshay, Arthur W. **LB2806.15.F66 2000**
The Curriculum: Purpose, Substance, Practice. Trade Cloth. Teachers College Press, Teachers College, Columbia University. New York, NY. 2000. 112p. ISBN:0-8077-3936-7, ISBN13: 978-0-8077-3936-5. Dewey:375/.001/0973. LCCN:99-053667.
Audience: **u,f.** *Choice, 2001.*

Friedl, Alfred E. & Koontz, Trish Yourst **LB1585**
Teaching Science to Children: An Inquiry Approach. Ed. 6. Paper Text. McGraw-Hill Higher Education. Burr Ridge, IL. 2004. 480p. ISBN:0-07-256395-8, ISBN13: 978-0-07-256395-5. Dewey:372.3/5044. LCCN:2004-108551.
Audience: **g,u.**

Gallagher, Kelly **LB1050.45.G34 2004**
Deeper Reading: Comprehending Challenging Texts, 4-12. Trade Paper. Stenhouse Publishers. Portland, ME. 2004. 224p. ISBN:1-57110-384-8, ISBN13: 978-1-57110-384-0. Dewey:372.47. LCCN:2004-052469.
Audience: **u,f.** *Choice, 2005.*

Garcia, Jesus & Michaelis, John U. **LB1584.G33 2000**
Social Studies for Children: A Guide to Basic Instruction. Ed. 12. Cloth Text. Allyn & Bacon, Inc. Boston, MA. 2000. 480p. ISBN:0-205-28316-0, ISBN13: 978-0-205-28316-3. Dewey:372.83/044. LCCN:00-060901.
Audience: **g,u.**

Gollnick, Donna M. & Chinn, Philip C. **LC1099.3.G65 2006**
Multicultural Education in a Pluralistic Society. Ed. 7. Trade Paper. Prentice Hall PTR. Upper Saddle River, NJ. 2005. 432p. ISBN:0-13-119719-3, ISBN13: 978-0-13-119719-0. Dewey:370.117. LCCN:2005-041552.
Audience: **g,u.**

Gunning, Thomas G. **LB1573 .G93 2004**
Creating Literacy Instruction for All Students. Ed. 5. Cloth Text. Allyn & Bacon, Inc. Boston, MA. 2004. 672p. ISBN:0-205-41036-7, ISBN13: 978-0-205-41036-1. Dewey:372.6. LCCN:2004-040982.
Audience: **g,u.**

Guthrie, John T. (Editor), et al. **LB1573.E655 2000**
Engaging Young Readers: Promoting Achievement and Motivation. Mariam Jean Dreher & Linda Baker (Editors). Cloth over Boards. Guilford Publications, Inc. New York, NY. 2000. 328p. Solving Problems in the Teaching of Literacy Ser. ISBN:1-57230-554-1, ISBN13: 978-1-57230-554-0. Dewey:428.4. LCCN:99-056748.
Audience: **u.** *Choice, 2000.*

Harmon, Deborah A. & Jones, Toni Stokes **LA219**
Elementary Education: A Reference Handbook. Danny Weil (Editor). Saddle Stitched, Cloth over Boards. ABC-CLIO, Inc. Santa Barbara, CA. 2005. 261p. Contemporary Education Issues Ser. ISBN:1-57607-942-2, ISBN13: 978-1-57607-942-3. Dewey:372. LCCN:2005-004578.
Audience: **g,l.** *Choice, 2005.*

Harris, Albert J. & Sipay, Edward R. **LB1050.53.H37 1990**
How to Increase Reading Ability: A Guide to Developmental and Remedial Methods. Ed. 9. Trade Cloth. Allyn & Bacon, Inc. Boston, MA. 1990. 926p. ISBN:0-8013-0246-3, ISBN13: 978-0-8013-0246-6. Dewey:371.91/4. LCCN:89-038901.
Audience: **g,u.**

Hebert, Elizabeth A. **LB1029.P67H43 2001**
The Power of Portfolios: What Children Can Teach Us about Learning and Assessment. Trade Paper. John Wiley & Sons, Inc. Hoboken, NJ. 2001. 176p. The Jossey-Bass Education Ser. ISBN:0-7879-5871-9, ISBN13: 978-0-7879-5871-8. Dewey:372.127. LCCN:2001-003792.
Audience: **g,l,u,f.** *Choice, 2002.*

Heilman, Arthur W. **LB1573.3.H44 2006**
Phonics in Proper Perspective. Ed. 10. Trade Paper, Perfect. Prentice Hall PTR. Upper Saddle River, NJ. 2005. 152p. ISBN:0-13-117798-2, ISBN13: 978-0-13-117798-7. Dewey:372.46/5. LCCN:2004-061069.
Audience: **g,u.**

Heilman, Arthur W., et al. **LB1573.H325 2002**
Principles and Practices of Teaching Reading. Ed. 10. Timothy R. Blair & William H. Rupley (Authors). Trade Paper. Prentice Hall PTR. Upper Saddle River, NJ. 2001. 608p. ISBN:0-13-042083-2, ISBN13: 978-0-13-042083-1. Dewey:372.4. LCCN:2001-030323.
Audience: **g,u.**

Holland, Kathleen E., et al. **LB1575.5.U5.J68 1993**
Journeying: Children Responding to Literature. Rachael A. Hungerford & Shirley B. Ernst (Authors). Trade Paper. Heinemann. Portsmouth, NH. 1993. 326p. ISBN:0-435-08758-4, ISBN13: 978-0-435-08758-6. Dewey:372.64/0973. LCCN:93-12655.
Audience: **u,f.** *Choice, 1994.*

Holt, John **LB3063.H627 1995**
How Children Fail. Trade Paper. Da Capo Press, Inc. Cambridge, MA. 1995. 320p. Classics in Child Development Ser. ISBN:0-201-48402-1, ISBN13: 978-0-201-48402-1. Dewey:371.2/8. LCCN:95-000404.
Audience: **g,u.**

Huck, Charlotte S., et al. **LB1575.5.U5 H79**
Children's Literature in the Elementary School with Litlinks. Ed. 8. Barbara Kiefer, Susan Hepler & Janet Hickman (Authors). CD-ROM, Cloth Text, Mixed Media. McGraw-Hill Higher Education. Burr Ridge, IL. 2003. ISBN:0-07-287841-X, ISBN13: 978-0-07-287841-7. Dewey:372.64.
Audience: **g,u.**

Hurst, Beth **LB1050.44.C74 2002**
Creating Independent Readers: Developing Word Recognition Skills in K-12 Classrooms. Perfect. Holcomb Hathaway, Inc. Scottsdale, AZ. 2001. 150p. ISBN:1-890871-36-2, ISBN13: 978-1-890871-36-9. Dewey:428.4. LCCN:2001-039110.
Audience: **l,u.** *Choice, 2002.*

Jacobs, Heidi Hayes (Editor) **LB2806.15.G48 2004**
Getting Results with Curriculum Mapping. Trade Paper. Association for Supervision & Curriculum Development. Alexandria, VA. 2004. 182p. ISBN:0-87120-999-3, ISBN13: 978-0-87120-999-3. Dewey:375/.001. LCCN:2004-016184.
Audience: **l,u.** *Choice, 2005.*

Kearney, Nolan Charles **PN1998.A3D37**
Elementary School Objectives: A Report Prepared for the Mid. Paper Text. Textbook Publishers. Temecula, CA. 2003. 189p. ISBN:0-7581-4321-4, ISBN13: 978-0-7581-4321-1. Dewey:791.43/0232/0924.
Audience: **u,f.** B

Kessler, Rachael **LB1072.K48 2000**
The Soul of Education: Helping Students Find Connection, Compassion and Character at School. Trade Paper. Association for Supervision & Curriculum Development. Alexandria, VA. 2000. xiii, 181p. ISBN:0-87120-373-1, ISBN13: 978-0-87120-373-1. Dewey:373.17/82. LCCN:99-050911.
Audience: **u.** *Choice, 2001.*

Kucer, Stephen B. **LB1576.K83 2005**
Dimensions of Literacy: A Conceptual Base for Teaching Reading and Writing in School Settings. Ed. 2. Cloth over Boards. Lawrence Erlbaum Associates, Inc. Mahwah, NJ. 2004. 368p. ISBN:0-8058-4940-8, ISBN13: 978-0-8058-4940-0. Dewey:428.6. LCCN:2004-016811.
Audience: **u,f.**

Lewis, Catherine C. **LB1140.25.J3 L48**
Educating Hearts and Minds: Reflections on Japanese Preschool and Elementary Education. Trade Paper. Cambridge University Press. New York, NY. 1995. 261p. ISBN:0-521-45832-3, ISBN13: 978-0-521-45832-0. Dewey:372.952. LCCN:94-007524.
Audience: **g,l,u,f.** *Choice, 1995.*

Ma, Liping **QA135.5.M22 1999**
Knowing and Teaching Elementary Mathematics: Teachers' Understanding of Fundamental Mathematics in China and the United States. Cloth over Boards. Lawrence Erlbaum Associates, Inc. Mahwah, NJ. 1999. 192p. The Studies in Mathematical Thinking and Learning ISBN:0-8058-2908-3, ISBN13: 978-0-8058-2908-2. Dewey:372.7/0973. LCCN:99-017342.
Audience: **u,f.** *Choice, 1999.*

Mallett, Margaret **LB1576.M3627 1999**
Young Researchers: Informational Reading and Writing in the Early and Primary Years. Paper over Boards. Routledge. New York, NY. 1999. 224p. ISBN:0-415-21657-5, ISBN13: 978-0-415-21657-9. Dewey:372.6. LCCN:99-013532.
Audience: **g,f.** *Choice, 2000.*

Marzano, Robert J. **LB1025.3.H364 2001**
A Handbook for Classroom Instruction That Works. Trade Cloth. Association for Supervision & Curriculum Development. Alexandria, VA. 2001. 378p. ISBN:0-87120-522-X, ISBN13: 978-0-87120-522-3. Dewey:371.3. LCCN:2001-004896.
Audience: **g,u.**

McCardle, Peggy & Chhabra, Vinita (Editors) **LB1050.6.V65 2004**
The Voice of Evidence in Reading Research. Trade Cloth. Paul H. Brookes Publishing Company. Baltimore, MD. 2004. 384p. ISBN:1-55766-672-5, ISBN13: 978-1-55766-672-7. Dewey:428/.4/072. LCCN:2003-068583.
Audience: **g,u,f.**

McDonald, Nan & Fisher, Douglas **LB1537**
Developing Arts Loving Readers: Top 10 Questions Teachers Are Asking about Integrated Arts Education. Trade Cloth. Scarecrow Press, Inc. Lanham, MD. 2002. 208p. ISBN:0-8108-4453-2, ISBN13: 978-0-8108-4453-7. Dewey:372.5.
Audience: **u,f.** *Choice, 2003.*

McNeil, John D. **LB2806.15**
Curriculum: A Comprehensive Introduction. Ed. 5. Trade Cloth. John Wiley & Sons, Inc. Hoboken, NJ. 1996. 480p. ISBN:0-471-36470-3, ISBN13: 978-0-471-36470-2. Dewey:375/.001.
Audience: **u,f.**

Morris, G. S. Don & Stiehl, Jim **GV443.M66 1998**
Changing Kids' Games. Ed. 2. Trade Paper. Human Kinetics Publishers. Champaign, IL. 1998. 16p. ISBN:0-88011-691-9, ISBN13: 978-0-88011-691-6. Dewey:372.1/337. LCCN:98-027142.
Audience: **g,l,u.** *Choice, 1999.*

National Writing Project Staff & Nagin, Carl **PE1405.U6 N38 2003**
Because Writing Matters: Improving Student Writing in Our Schools. Trade Cloth. John Wiley & Sons, Inc. Hoboken, NJ. 2003. 160p. The Jossey-Bass Education Ser. ISBN:0-7879-6562-6, ISBN13: 978-0-7879-6562-4. Dewey:372.623. LCCN:2002-155027.
Audience: **g,l,u.** *Choice, 2003.*

Newton, Douglas P. **LB1585.N44 2002**
Talking Sense in Science: Helping Children Understand Through Talk. Trade Paper. Routledge. New York, NY. 2001. 192p. ISBN:0-415-25351-9, ISBN13: 978-0-415-25351-2. Dewey:372.3/5044. LCCN:2001-031913.
Audience: **l,u.** *Choice, 2002.*

Paley, Vivian G. **LB1140.3.P356 1995**
Kwanzaa and Me: A Teacher's Story. Trade Cloth. Harvard University Press. Cambridge, MA. 1995. 152p. ISBN:0-674-50585-9, ISBN13: 978-0-674-50585-8. Dewey:372.21. LCCN:94-025002.
Audience: **u.** *Choice, 1995.*

Paris, Scott G. & Stahl, Steven A. (Editors) **LB1050.45.C87 2004**
Children's Reading Comprehension and Assessment. Alison H. Paris, Allan & Richard C. Anderson (Contribution by). Cloth over Boards. Lawrence Erlbaum Associates, Inc. Mahwah, NJ. 2005. 440p. Center for Improvement of Early Reading Ser. ISBN:0-8058-4655-7, ISBN13: 978-0-8058-4655-3. Dewey:372.47. LCCN:2004-052067.
Audience: **u,f.**

Parker, Walter **LB1584.J3 2005**
Social Studies in Elementary Education. Ed. 12. Cloth Text. Prentice Hall PTR. Upper Saddle River, NJ. 2004. 528p. ISBN:0-13-113936-3, ISBN13: 978-0-13-113936-7. Dewey:372.83/044/0973. LCCN:2003-063260.
Audience: **g,u.**

Pinar, William F. **LB1570.U434 1995**
Understanding Curriculum: An Introduction to the Study of Historical and Contemporary Curriculum Discourses. Trade Paper. Peter Lang Publishing, Inc. New York, NY. 1995. xviii;1143p. Counterpoints of Education Ser., Vol. 17:Studies in the Postmodern Theory of Education ISBN:0-8204-2601-6, ISBN13: 978-0-8204-2601-3. Dewey:375/.00973. LCCN:94-044009.
Audience: **u,f.**

Pinar, William F. (Editor) **LB2806.15.I595 2003**
International Handbook of Curriculum Research. Tadahiko Abiko, Frida Diaz Barriga Arceo & Shigeru Asanuma (Contribution by). Cloth over Boards. Lawrence Erlbaum Associates, Inc. Mahwah, NJ. 2003. 712p. Studies in Curriculum Theory ISBN:0-8058-3222-X, ISBN13: 978-0-8058-3222-8. Dewey:375/.0007/2. LCCN:2002-026368.
Audience: **g,u,f.** *Choice, 2004.*

Pressley, Michael **LB1573.P72 2006**
Reading Instruction That Works, Third Edition: The Case for Balanced Teaching. Ed. 3. Cloth over Boards. Guilford Publications, Inc. New York, NY. 2005. 469p. Solving Problems in Teaching of Literacy Ser. ISBN:1-59385-229-0, ISBN13: 978-1-59385-229-0. Dewey:372.41. LCCN:2005-022680.
Audience: **g,u,f.**

Rader, Debra & Sittig, Linda Harris **LB1575.R33 2003**
New Kid in School: Using Literature to Help Children in Transition. Trade Cloth. Teachers College Press, Teachers College, Columbia University. New York, NY. 2003. xi, 185p. ISBN:0-8077-4315-1, ISBN13: 978-0-8077-4315-7. Dewey:372.64/044. LCCN:2002-038432.
Audience: **u.** *Choice, 2004.*

Roney, R. Craig **LB1042.R64 2001**
The Story Performance Handbook. Trade Paper. Lawrence Erlbaum Associates, Inc. Mahwah, NJ. 2000. 208p. ISBN:0-8058-3628-4, ISBN13: 978-0-8058-3628-8. Dewey:808.5/43. LCCN:00-034759.
Audience: **u.** *Choice, 2001.*

Ross, Raymon R. **LB1042.R67 1996**
Storyteller. Ed. 3. Trade Paper. August House Publishers, Inc. Atlanta, GA. 1997. 224p. ISBN:0-87483-451-1, ISBN13: 978-0-87483-451-2. Dewey:808.543. LCCN:96-017345.
Audience: **g,u.**

Schiro, Michael Stephen **QA135.6.S42 2004**
Oral Storytelling and Teaching Mathematics: Pedagogical and Multicultural Perspectives. Cloth Text. SAGE Publications, Inc. Thousand Oaks, CA. 2004. 280p. ISBN:0-7619-3009-4, ISBN13: 978-0-7619-3009-9. Dewey:372.7/044. LCCN:2003-026081.
Audience: **u.** *Choice, 2005.*

Schubert, William H. **NX303.R44 2000**
Reflections from the Heart of Educational Inquiry: Understanding Curriculum and Teaching through the Arts. George Willis, Elliot W. Eisner & Max Van Manen (Editors). Trade Paper. Educator's International Press, Inc. Troy, NY. 2000. 388p. ISBN:1-891928-09-0, ISBN13: 978-1-891928-09-3. Dewey:707/.1/273. LCCN:00-062285.
Audience: **u,f.**

Sedgwick, Fred **PR2987.S39 1999**
Shakespeare and Young Learner. Paper over Boards. Routledge. New York, NY. 1999. 176p. ISBN:0-415-17468-6, ISBN13: 978-0-415-17468-8. Dewey:822.3/3. LCCN:98-050231.
Audience: **u,f.** *Choice, 2000.*

Silliman, Elaine R. & Wilkinson, Louise Cherry (Editors) **LB1576.L2932 2004**
Language and Literacy Learning in Schools. Cloth over Boards. Guilford Publications, Inc. New York, NY. 2004. 366p. Challenges in Language and Literacy Ser. ISBN:1-59385-065-4, ISBN13: 978-1-59385-065-4. Dewey:372.6. LCCN:2004-014031.
Audience: **u,f.** *Choice, 2005.*

Slavin, Robert E. & Madden, Nancy A. (Editors) **LB2822.8.S88 2001**
Success for All: Research and Reform in Elementary Education. Cloth over Boards. Lawrence Erlbaum Associates, Inc. Mahwah, NJ. 2001. 248p. ISBN:0-8058-3810-4, ISBN13: 978-0-8058-3810-7. Dewey:372. LCCN:00-044248.
Audience: **l,u,f.** *Choice, 2001.*

Strickland, Dorothy S. & Alvermann, Donna E. **LB1631.B7644 2004**
Bridging the Literacy Achievement Gap, Grades 4-12. Trade Cloth. Teachers College Press, Teachers College, Columbia University. New York, NY. 2004. ix, 294p. ISBN:0-8077-4487-5, ISBN13: 978-0-8077-4487-1. Dewey:428.4/071. LCCN:2004-043965.
Audience: **g,l,u,f.** *Choice, 2004.*

Szymusiak, Karen & Sibberson, Franki **LB1573.45.S99 2001**
Beyond Leveled Books: Supporting Transitional Readers in Grades 2-5. Trade Paper. Stenhouse Publishers. Portland, ME. 2001. 144p. ISBN:1-57110-330-9, ISBN13: 978-1-57110-330-7. Dewey:372.4. LCCN:00-066136.
Audience: **g,u.** *Choice, 2002.*

Tanner, Daniel & Tanner, Laurel N. **LB1570.T23 2006**
Curriculum Development: Theory into Practice. Ed. 4. Cloth Text. Prentice Hall PTR. Upper Saddle River, NJ. 2006. 576p.

ISBN:0-13-086473-0, ISBN13: 978-0-13-086473-4. Dewey:375/.001. LCCN:2005-026920.
Audience: **u,f.** *B*

Taylor, Barbara (Editor), et al. **LB1050.45.R443 2000**
Reading for Meaning: Fostering Comprehension in the Middle Grades. Michael F. Graves & Paul van den Broek (Editors). Trade Cloth. Teachers College Press, Teachers College, Columbia University. New York, NY. 1999. 216p. Language and Literacy Ser. ISBN:0-8077-3897-2, ISBN13: 978-0-8077-3897-9. Dewey:428.4/3/0712. LCCN:99-045904.
Audience: **u,f.** *Choice, 2000.*

Thier, Marlene & Daviss, Bennett **LB1585.3.T487 2002**
The New Science Literacy: Using Language Skills to Help Students Learn Science. Trade Paper. Heinemann. Portsmouth, NH. 2002. 216p. ISBN:0-325-00459-5, ISBN13: 978-0-325-00459-4. Dewey:507.1. LCCN:2001-007441.
Audience: **u,f.** *Choice, 2003.*

Thornton, Stephen J. **LB1584.T47 2004**
Teaching Social Studies That Matters: Curriculum for Active Learning. Nel Noddings (Foreword by). Perfect, Paper over Boards. Teachers College Press, Teachers College, Columbia University. New York, NY. 2004. 127p. ISBN:0-8077-4523-5, ISBN13: 978-0-8077-4523-6. Dewey:300/.71. LCCN:2004-053730.
Audience: **g,l,u,f.**

Thorton, Stephen J. & Flinders, David J. (Editors) **LB1570.C957 2004**
The Curriculum Studies Reader. Ed. 2. Paper over Boards. Taylor & Francis Group. Philadelphia, PA. 2004. 376p. ISBN:0-415-94522-4, ISBN13: 978-0-415-94522-6. Dewey:375/.000973. LCCN:2004-004905.
Audience: **u,f.**

Topping, Donna Hooker & McManus, Roberta Ann **LB1050.455.T68 2002**
Real Reading, Real Writing: Content-Area Strategies. Trade Paper. Heinemann. Portsmouth, NH. 2002. 208p. ISBN:0-325-00428-5, ISBN13: 978-0-325-00428-0. Dewey:428.4/07/1. LCCN:2001-059365.
Audience: **g,u,f.** *Choice, 2003.*

Trelease, Jim **LB1573.5**
Read Aloud Handbook. Ed. 5. Trade Cloth. Peter Smith Publisher, Inc. Magnolia, MA. 2004. ISBN:0-8446-7234-3, ISBN13: 978-0-8446-7234-2. Dewey:372.6.
Audience: **g,u.**

Tyler, Ralph W. **LB1570**
Basic Principles of Curriculum and Instruction. Trade Paper. University of Chicago Press. Chicago, IL. 2003. 134p. ISBN:0-226-82031-9, ISBN13: 978-0-226-82031-6. Dewey:375.
Audience: **u,f.** *B*

Vacca, Richard T. & Vacca, Jo Anne L. **LB1050.455**
Content Area Reading: Literacy and Learning Across the Curriculum, MyLabSchool Edition. Ed. 8. Mixed Media. Allyn & Bacon, Inc. Boston, MA. 2004. 496p. ISBN:0-205-46029-1, ISBN13: 978-0-205-46029-8. Dewey:428.4/3.
Audience: **u,f.**

Victor, Edward & Kellough, Richard D. **LB1585.V46 2004**
Science K-8: An Integrated Approach. Ed. 10. Cloth Text. Prentice Hall PTR. Upper Saddle River, NJ. 2003. 576p. ISBN:0-13-098881-2, ISBN13: 978-0-13-098881-2. Dewey:372.3/5. LCCN:2002-038050.
Audience: **u.**

Weil, Danny & Kincheloe, Joe L. (Editors) **LB1590**
Critical Thinking and Learning: An Encyclopedia for Parents and Teachers. Cloth Text. Greenwood Publishing Group, Inc. Portsmouth, NH. 2004. 544p. ISBN:0-313-32389-5, ISBN13: 978-0-313-32389-8. Dewey:370.15/2. LCCN:2003-052848.
Audience: **u,f.** *Choice, 2004.*

Williams, Nancy S. **LB1050.5.W48945 2004**
Using Literature to Support Skills and Critical Discussion for Struggling Readers: Grades 3-9. Trade Paper. Scarecrow Press, Inc. Lanham, MD. 2004. 200p. ISBN:1-57886-096-2, ISBN13: 978-1-57886-096-8. Dewey:372.43. LCCN:2003-023552.
Audience: **u.** *Choice, 2004.*

Wood, Terry Lee (Editor), et al. **QA135.6.B49 2001**
Beyond Classical Pedagogy: Teaching Elementary School Mathematic. Barbara Scott Nelson & Janet Warfield (Editors). Cloth over Boards. Lawrence Erlbaum Associates, Inc. Mahwah, NJ. 2001. 320p. The Studies in Mathematical Thinking and Learning ISBN:0-8058-3570-9, ISBN13: 978-0-8058-3570-0. Dewey:372.7. LCCN:2001-016100.
Audience: **u,f.** *Choice, 2002.*

Wormeli, Rick **LB1623.W67 2001**
Meet Me in the Middle: Becoming an Accomplished Middle-Level Teacher. Trade Paper. Stenhouse Publishers. Portland, ME. 2001. 264p. ISBN:1-57110-328-7, ISBN13: 978-1-57110-328-4. Dewey:373.1102. LCCN:2001-031173.
Audience: **g,l,u.** *Choice, 2002.*

Zemelman, Steven **CS49**
History Comes Home: Family Stories Across the Curriculum. Library Binding. Sagebrush Education Resources. Caledonia, MN. 1999. ISBN:0-613-70596-3, ISBN13: 978-0-613-70596-7. Dewey:929/.1/071273.
Audience: **u,f.** *Choice, 2000.*

Education by Level (Includes Teaching of Individual Subjects) > Secondary Education

American Social History Project **E175.8**
☐ History Matters.
http://historymatters.gmu.edu/
Center for Media and Learning (Graduate Center, CUNY).
Audience: **g,l,u,f.**

Barrell, Barrie R. C. **LB1631.T283 2004**
Teaching English Today: Advocating Change in the Secondary Curriculum. Trade Cloth. Teachers College Press, Teachers College, Columbia University. New York, NY. 2004. 168p. ISBN:0-8077-4478-6, ISBN13: 978-0-8077-4478-9. Dewey:428/.0071/273. LCCN:2004-043966.
Audience: **u,f.** *Choice, 2004.*

Barton, Roy **Q181**
Teaching Secondary Science with ICT. Cloth Text. McGraw-Hill Education. Maidenhead, 2004. 176p. ISBN:0-335-20863-0, ISBN13: 978-0-335-20863-0.
Audience: **u,f.**

Conant, James Bryant **JQ1508.H78**
The American High School Today: A First Report to Interested Citizens. Paper Text. Textbook Publishers. Temecula, CA. 2003. xiii, 140p. ISBN:0-7581-8684-3, ISBN13: 978-0-7581-8684-3. Dewey:320.951.
Audience: **u,f.**

Cornell University **Q183.3A1**
Math and Science Gateway.
http://www.tc.cornell.edu/CTC-Main/Services/Education/Gateways/Math_and_Science/
Cornell University.
Audience: **g,u,f.**

George, Paul S. & Alexander, William M. **LB1623.G38 2003**
The Exemplary Middle School. Ed. 3. Cloth Text. Thomson Wadsworth. Belmont, CA. 2002. 648p. ISBN:0-534-53948-3, ISBN13: 978-0-534-53948-1. Dewey:373.236. LCCN:2002-112466.
Audience: **u,f.**

Grant, S. G. **D16.3.G73 2003**
History Lessons: Teaching, Learning, and Testing in U. S. High School Classrooms. Cloth over Boards. Lawrence Erlbaum Associates, Inc. Mahwah, NJ. 2003. 248p. ISBN:0-8058-4502-X, ISBN13: 978-0-8058-4502-0. Dewey:907/.1/273. LCCN:2002-192833.
Audience: **u,f.** *Choice, 2004.*

Hines, Maxwell S. (Contribution by) **Q183.3.A1.M85 2000**
Multicultural Science Education: Theory, Practice, and Promise. Trade Paper. Peter Lang Publishing, Inc. New York, NY. 2003. "xiv, 217"p. Counterpoints Ser. ISBN:0-8204-4540-1, ISBN13: 978-0-8204-4540-3. Dewey:507/.1073. LCCN:99-043781.
Audience: **u,f.** *Choice, 2004.*

Howes, Elaine V. **Q130.H69 2002**
Connecting Girls and Science: Constructivism, Feminism, and Science Education Reform. Trade Cloth. Teachers College Press, Teachers College, Columbia University. New York, NY. 2002. 176p. Ways of Knowing in Science and Mathematics Ser. ISBN:0-8077-4211-2, ISBN13: 978-0-8077-4211-2. Dewey:500/.82. LCCN:2001-060390.
Audience: **u,f.** *Choice, 2002.*

Library of Congress **F175.8**
The Learning Page—American Memory Collection.
http://lcweb2.loc.gov/ammem/ndlpedu/lessons/index.html
Audience: **l,u,f.**

Lipsitz, Joan **LB1623**
Successful Schools for Young Adolescents. Trade Paper. Transaction Publishers. Somerset, NJ. 2002. 230p. ISBN:0-87855-947-7, ISBN13: 978-0-87855-947-3. Dewey:373.2/36. LCCN:83-009139.
Audience: **u,f.**

Lynch, Sharon J. **LB1585.3.L96 2000**
Equity and Science Education Reform. Cloth over Boards. Lawrence Erlbaum Associates, Inc. Mahwah, NJ. 2000. 312p. ISBN:0-8058-3248-3, ISBN13: 978-0-8058-3248-8. Dewey:507.1. LCCN:99-038080.
Audience: **u,f.** *Choice, 2000.*

National Middle School Association Staff (Contribution by) **LB1623.5.T55 2003**
This We Believe: Successful Schools for Young Adolescents: A Position Paper of the National Middle School Association. Trade Paper. National Middle School Association. Westerville, OH. 2003. xi, 51p. ISBN:1-56090-142-X, ISBN13: 978-1-56090-142-6. Dewey:373.2/36. LCCN:2003-044251.
Audience: **u.**

Peshkin, Alan **LB1567**
Growing up American: Schooling and the Survival of Community. University of Chicago Press: Chicago. 1978. ISBN:0-226-66196-2, ISBN13: 978-0-226-66196-4.
Audience: **g,l,u,f.**

Scott, Janelle T. **LB1027.9.S28 2005**
School Choice and Diversity: What the Evidence Says. Trade Cloth. Teachers College Press, Teachers College, Columbia University. New York, NY. 2005. 192p. ISBN:0-8077-4599-5, ISBN13: 978-0-8077-4599-1. Dewey:379.1/11/0973. LCCN:2005-043958.
Audience: **g,l,u.**

Sizer, Theodore R. **LB1607 .S54 1976**
Secondary Schools at the Turn of the Century. Trade Cloth. Greenwood Publishing Group, Inc. Portsmouth, NH. 1976. 304p. ISBN:0-8371-8972-1, ISBN13: 978-0-8371-8972-7. Dewey:373.73. LCCN:76-043028.
Audience: **u,f.**

Smrekar, Claire & Goldring, Ellen **LB2818.S57 1999**
School Choice in Urban America: Magnet Schools and the Pursuit of Equity. Trade Cloth. Teachers College Press, Teachers College, Columbia University. New York, NY. 1999. 390p. ISBN:0-8077-3829-8, ISBN13: 978-0-8077-3829-0. Dewey:373.24/1/0973. LCCN:98-052041.
Audience: **u,f.**

Tolley, Kimberly **Q183.3.A1 T66**
Science Education of American Girls: A Historical Perspective. Library Binding. Sagebrush Education Resources. Caledonia, MN. 2002. ISBN:0-613-91163-6, ISBN13: 978-0-613-91163-4. Dewey:507.1/073.
Audience: **u,f.**

Trowbridge, Leslie W., et al. **Q183.3.A1T76 2004**
Teaching Secondary School Science: Strategies for Developing Scientific Literacy. Ed. 8. Rodger W. Bybee & Janet Carlson-Powell (Authors). Trade Paper. Prentice Hall PTR. Upper Saddle River, NJ. 2003. 464p. ISBN:0-13-099234-8, ISBN13: 978-0-13-099234-5. Dewey:507/.1/2. LCCN:2003-054128.
Audience: **u.**

Wellington, Jerry **Q181.W4416 2000**
Teaching and Learning Secondary Science: Contemporary Issues and Practical Approaches. Trade Paper. Routledge. New York, NY. 2000. 296p. ISBN:0-415-21403-3, ISBN13: 978-0-415-21403-2. Dewey:507/.1/2. LCCN:99-016842.
Audience: **u,f.** *Choice, 2000.*

Education by Level (Includes Teaching of Individual Subjects) > Kindergarten

McGee, Lea M. & Richgels, Donald J. **LB1140.5.L3M36 2003**
Designing Early Literacy Programs: Strategies for at-Risk Preschool and Kindergarten Children. Trade Paper. Guilford Publications, Inc. New York, NY. 2003. 214p. ISBN:1-57230-890-7, ISBN13: 978-1-57230-890-9. Dewey:372.6. LCCN:2003-004009.
Audience: **l,u,f.** *Choice, 2004.*

Wollons, Roberta Lyn (Editor) **LB1199.K58 2000**
Kindergartens and Cultures: The Global Diffusion of an Idea. Cloth over Boards. Yale University Press. Cumberland, RI. 2000. 312p. ISBN:0-300-07788-2, ISBN13: 978-0-300-07788-9. Dewey:372.21/8/09. LCCN:99-059627.
Audience: **l,u,f.** *Choice, 2000.*

Education by Level (Includes Teaching of Individual Subjects) > Early Childhood Education

Barone, Diane M. & Morrow, Lesley Mandel (Editors) **LB1139.5.R43L58 2002**
Literacy and Young Children: Research-Based Practices. Cloth over Boards. Guilford Publications, Inc. New York, NY. 2002. 318p. Solving Problems in the Teaching of Literacy Ser. ISBN:1-57230-820-6, ISBN13: 978-1-57230-820-6. Dewey:372.4. LCCN:2002-010221.
Audience: **f.** *Choice, 2003.*

Bloom, Lois **LB1139.L3.B596 1993**
The Transition from Infancy to Language: Acquiring the Power of Expression. Trade Cloth. Cambridge University Press. New York, NY. 1993. 364p. ISBN:0-521-44031-9, ISBN13: 978-0-521-44031-8. Dewey:401.9/3. LCCN:92-047407.
Audience: **f.** *Choice, 1994.*

Bruce, Tina **LB1139.2**
Developing Learning in Early Childhood. Cloth Text. Paul Chapman Publishing. London, 2004. 248p. Zero to Eight Ser. ISBN:0-7619-4175-4, ISBN13: 978-0-7619-4175-0. Dewey:372.21. LCCN:2003-106582.
Audience: **l,u,f.** *Choice, 2004.*

Chen, Jie-Qi & Horsch, Patricia (Translators) **LB1139.27.I3C44 2003**
Effective Partnering for School Change: Improving Early Childhood Education in Urban Classrooms. Trade Cloth. Teachers College Press, Teachers College, Columbia University. New York, NY. 2003. 176p. ISBN:0-8077-4414-X, ISBN13: 978-0-8077-4414-7. Dewey:372.21/09773/11. LCCN:2003-060098.
Audience: **g,u.** *Choice, 2004.*

Clay, Marie M. **LB1139.5.L35**
By Different Paths to Common Outcomes. Trade Cloth. Teaching Resource Center. San Diego, CA. 2000. 278p. Dewey:302.2/244.
Audience: **u.** *Choice, 1999.*

DeVries, Rheta **LB1139.4.D49 2002**
Developing Constructivist Early Childhood Curriculum: Practical Principles and Activities. Trade Cloth. Teachers College Press, Teachers College, Columbia University. New York, NY. 2001. 256p. ISBN:0-8077-4121-3, ISBN13: 978-0-8077-4121-4. Dewey:372.19. LCCN:2001-026689.
Audience: **u,f.** *Choice, 2002.*

Dickinson, David K. & Neuman, Susan B. (Editors) **LB1139.5.L35H37 2005**
Handbook of Early Literacy Research, Vol. 2. Ed. 2. Trade Cloth. Guilford Publications, Inc. New York, NY. 2005. 468p. ISBN:1-59385-184-7, ISBN13: 978-1-59385-184-2. Dewey:372.6.
Audience: **u,f.**

Ferreiro, Emilia **P118**
Literacy Before Schooling. Cloth Text. Heinemann. Portsmouth, NH. 1982. xii, 289p. ISBN:0-435-08202-7, ISBN13: 978-0-435-08202-4. Dewey:401/.9. LCCN:82-015839.
Audience: **g,u.** B

Gandini, Lella & Edwards, Carolyn Pope (Editors) **LB1139.3.I8B26 2001**
Bambini: The Italian Approach to Infant/Toddler Care. Trade Cloth. Teachers College Press, Teachers College, Columbia University. New York, NY. 2000. xv, 237p. Early Childhood Education Ser., Vol. 77 ISBN:0-8077-4009-8, ISBN13: 978-0-8077-4009-5. Dewey:649/.1/0945. LCCN:00-044117.
Audience: **u,f.** *Choice, 2001.*

Goldstein, Lisa **LB1139.25.G65 1997**
Teaching with Love: A Feminist Approach to Early Childhood Education. Trade Paper. Peter Lang Publishing, Inc. New York, NY. 1997. 200p. Rethinking Childhood Ser., No. 1 ISBN:0-8204-3481-7, ISBN13: 978-0-8204-3481-0. Dewey:372.21. LCCN:96-036581.
Audience: **g,u.** *Choice, 1998.*

Hall, Nigel (Editor), et al. **LC149**
Handbook of Early Childhood Literacy. Joanne Larson & Jackie Marsh (Editors). Trade Cloth. SAGE Publications, Inc. Thousand Oaks, CA. 2003. 464p. ISBN:0-7619-7437-7, ISBN13: 978-0-7619-7437-6. Dewey:372.6. LCCN:2002-108284.
Audience: **u,f.**

Hart, Betty & Risley, Todd R. **LB1139.L3H279 1995**
Meaningful Differences in the Everyday Experience of Young American Children. Trade Cloth, Box or Slipcased. Paul H. Brookes Publishing Company. Baltimore, MD. 1995. 304p. ISBN:1-55766-197-9, ISBN13: 978-1-55766-197-5. Dewey:401/.93. LCCN:95-003939.
Audience: **g,u.** *Choice, 1996.*

Hauser-Cram, Penny, et al. **LB1139.25.E27 1991**
Early Education in the Public Schools: Lessons from a Comprehensive Birth-to-Kindergarten Program. Donald E. Pierson, Deborah K. Walker & Terrance Tivnan (Authors). Trade Cloth. John Wiley & Sons, Inc. Hoboken, NJ. 1991. 288p. Education and Social and Behavioral Science Ser. ISBN:1-55542-328-0, ISBN13: 978-1-55542-328-5. Dewey:372.21/09744/7. LCCN:90-022972.
Audience: **g,u.** *Choice, 1991.*

Howes, Carollee & Ritchie, Sharon **LB1139.23.H69 2002**
A Matter of Trust: Connecting Teachers and Learners in the Early Childhood Classroom. Cloth Text. Teachers College Press, Teachers College, Columbia University. New York, NY. 2002. 192p. ISBN:0-8077-4265-1, ISBN13: 978-0-8077-4265-5. Dewey:372.21. LCCN:2002-021759.
Audience: **l,u,f.** *Choice, 2003.*

Hyson, Marilou **LB1139.4.H97 2003**
The Emotional Development of Young Children: Building an Emotion-Centered Curriculum. Ed. 2. Trade Paper. Teachers College Press, Teachers College, Columbia University. New York, NY. 2003. 308p. ISBN:0-8077-4342-9, ISBN13: 978-0-8077-4342-3. Dewey:372.19. LCCN:2003-054001.
Audience: **u,f.**

Isenberg, Joan P. & Jalongo, Mary Renck (Editors) **LB1139.25.M353 2003**
Major Trends and Issues in Early Childhood Education: Challenges, Controversies, and Insights. Ed. 2. Trade Cloth. Teachers College Press, Teachers College, Columbia University. New York, NY. 2003. xiii, 208p. ISBN:0-8077-4351-8, ISBN13: 978-0-8077-4351-5. Dewey:372.21. LCCN:2002-040927.
Audience: **l,u.**

Kagan, Sharon Lynn **LB5.N25 90th, pt. 1 LB1139.25**
The Care and Education of America's Young Children: Obstacles and Opportunities. National Society for the Study of Education. 1991. Yearbook of the National Society for the Study of Education
Audience: **l,u,f.**

Kraus International Publications Staff, ; Freidus, Helen **LB1139.4.E175 1993**
Early Childhood Curriculum Resource Handbook. Kraus International Publications Staff (Editor) ; Helen Freidus (Introduction by). Kraus International Publications. 1993. ISBN:0-527-20809-4, ISBN13: 978-0-527-20809-7.
Audience: **g.**

Landsmann, Liliana Tolchinsky **LB1139.W7T65 2003**
The Cradle of Culture and What Children Know about Writing and Numbers Before Being Taught. Cloth over Boards. Lawrence Erlbaum Associates, Inc. Mahwah, NJ. 2003. 288p. The Developing Mind Ser. ISBN:0-8058-3843-0, ISBN13: 978-0-8058-3843-5. Dewey:302.2/244. LCCN:2002-073214.
Audience: **u,f.** *Choice, 2003.*

Mallory, Bruce & New, Rebecca **LB1139.25.D58 1994**
Diversity and Developmentally Appropriate Practice in Early Childhood Education: Challenges for Early Childhood Education. Cloth Text. Teachers College Press, Teachers College, Columbia University. New York, NY. 1993. 304p. Early Childhood Education Ser. ISBN:0-8077-3300-8, ISBN13: 978-0-8077-3300-4. Dewey:372.21. LCCN:93-011912.
Audience: **u,f.** *Choice, 1994.*

Neuman, Susan B. & Dickinson, David K. (Editors) **LB1139.5.L35H37 2001**
Handbook of Early Literacy Research, Vol. 1. Cloth over Boards. Guilford Publications, Inc. New York, NY. 2001. 494p. ISBN:1-57230-653-X, ISBN13: 978-1-57230-653-0. Dewey:372.6. LCCN:2001-033004.
Audience: **u,f.** *Choice, 2002.*

Roskos, Kathleen & Christie, James F. (Editors) **LB1140.35.P55P557**
Play and Literacy in Early Childhood: Research from Multiple Perspectives. Cloth over Boards. Lawrence Erlbaum Associates, Inc. Mahwah, NJ. 1999. 304p. ISBN:0-8058-2964-4, ISBN13: 978-0-8058-2964-8. Dewey:372.21. LCCN:99-047474.
Audience: **l,u,f.** *Choice, 2000.*

Saracho, Olivia N. & Spodek, Bernard (Editors) **LB1139.4.C66 2002**
Contemporary Influences in Early Childhood Curriculum. Trade Cloth. Information Age Publishing, Inc. Greenwich, CT. 2002. xii, 277p. Contemporary Perspectives in Early Childhood Education Ser. ISBN:1-930608-27-6, ISBN13: 978-1-930608-27-6. Dewey:372.19. LCCN:2001-007270.
Audience: **u,f.**

Saracho, Olivia N. & Spodek, Bernard (Editors) **LB1139.35.P55.M85**
Multiple Perspectives on Play in Early Childhood Education. Cloth Text. State University of New York Press. Albany, NY. 1998. 323p. SUNY Series, Early Childhood Education, :Inquiries and Insights ISBN:0-7914-3615-2, ISBN13: 978-0-7914-3615-8. Dewey:155.4/18. LCCN:97-012087.
Audience: **f.** *Choice, 1998.*

Seefeldt, Carol (Editor) **LB1139.4.E17 1992**
Early Childhood Curriculum: A Review of Current Research. Ed. 2. Cloth Text. Teachers College Press, Teachers College, Columbia University. New York, NY. 1992. 640p. Early Childhood Education Ser. ISBN:0-8077-3196-X, ISBN13: 978-0-8077-3196-3. Dewey:372.19. LCCN:92-018816.
Audience: **u,f.** *Choice, 1993.*

Stegelin, Dolores A. & Borman, Kathyrn M. (Editors) **LB1139.25.E265 1992**
Early Childhood Education: Policy Issues for the 1990s. Trade Cloth. Greenwood Publishing Group, Inc. Portsmouth, NH. 1992. 240p. Social and Policy Issues in Education Ser. ISBN:0-89391-797-4, ISBN13: 978-0-89391-797-5. Dewey:372.21/0973. LCCN:92-003171.
Audience: **g,l,u.** *Choice, 1992.*

Tobin, Joseph J. (Editor) **LB1139.25.M36 1997**
Making a Place for Pleasure in Early Childhood Education. Cloth over Boards. Yale University Press. Cumberland, RI. 1997. 264p. ISBN:0-300-06968-5, ISBN13: 978-0-300-06968-6. Dewey:372.2/1. LCCN:96-041890.
Audience: **f.** *Choice, 1997.*

Williams, Leslie R. & Fromberg, Doris P. (Editors) **LB1139.25.E53 1992**
Encyclopedia of Early Childhood Education, Set. Cloth Text. Garland Publishing, Inc. New York, NY. 1992. 536p. ISBN:0-8240-4626-9, ISBN13: 978-0-8240-4626-2. Dewey:372.2103. LCCN:92-004579.
Audience: **g,l,u,f.** *Choice, 1992.*

Woodill, Gary (Editor), et al. **LB1139.23.I68 1992**
International Handbook of Early Childhood Education. Judith Bernhard & Lawrence Prochner (Editors). Paper over Boards. Garland Publishing, Inc. New York, NY. 1992. 576p. ISBN:0-8240-4939-X, ISBN13: 978-0-8240-4939-3. Dewey:372.21. LCCN:92-023846.
Audience: **l,u,f.** *Choice, 1993.*

Education by Level (Includes Teaching of Individual Subjects) > Preschool Education. Nursery Schools

Anbar, Ada **LB1140**
The Secret of Natural Readers: How Preschool Children Learn to Read. Trade Cloth. Greenwood Publishing Group, Inc. Portsmouth, NH. 2004. 232p. ISBN:0-275-98424-9, ISBN13: 978-0-275-98424-3. Dewey:372.4. LCCN:2004-050586.
Audience: **g,l.** *Choice, 2005.*

Beatty, Barbara **LB1140.23.B43 1995**
Preschool Education in America: The Culture of Young Children from the Colonial Era to the Present. Cloth over Boards. Yale University Press. Cumberland, RI. 1995. 272p. ISBN:0-300-06027-0, ISBN13: 978-0-300-06027-0. Dewey:372.2/1/0973. LCCN:94-041347.
Audience: **g,l,u,f.** *Choice, 1996.*

DeRoche, Edward F. & Williams, Mary M. **LC311.D47 2001**
Educating Hearts and Minds: A Comprehensive Character Education Framework. Ed. 2. Trade Cloth. Corwin Press. Thousand Oaks, CA. 2000. 232p. ISBN:0-7619-7689-2, ISBN13: 978-0-7619-7689-9. Dewey:370.11/4/0973. LCCN:00-009508.
Audience: **u,f.**

Lewis, Catherine C. **LB1140.25.J3 L48**
Educating Hearts and Minds: Reflections on Japanese Preschool and Elementary Education. Trade Paper. Cambridge University Press. New York, NY. 1995. 261p. ISBN:0-521-45832-3, ISBN13: 978-0-521-45832-0. Dewey:372.952. LCCN:94-007524.
Audience: **g,l,u,f.** *Choice, 1995.*

National Research Council Staff & Committee on Early Childhood Pedagogy Staff **LB1140.23.N38 2001**
Eager to Learn: Educating Our Preschoolers. Barbara T. Bowman, M. Suzanne Donovan & M. Susan Burns (Editors). Trade Cloth. National Academies Press. Washington, DC. 2000. 464p. ISBN:0-309-06836-3, ISBN13: 978-0-309-06836-9. Dewey:372.21/0973. LCCN:00-011192.
Audience: **g,l,u,f.** *Choice, 2001.*

Olfman, Sharna (Editor) **LB1139**
All Work and No Play....: How Educational Reforms Are Harming Our Preschoolers. Trade Cloth. Greenwood Publishing Group, Inc. Portsmouth, NH. 2003. 224p. Childhood in America Ser. ISBN:0-275-97768-4, ISBN13: 978-0-275-97768-9. Dewey:372.21. LCCN:2003-053621.
Audience: **g,l,u,f.** *Choice, 2004.*

Paley, Vivian G. **LB1140.3.P35 1990**
The Boy Who Would Be a Helicopter. Robert Coles (Foreword by). Trade Cloth. Harvard University Press. Cambridge, MA. 1990. 176p. ISBN:0-674-08030-0, ISBN13: 978-0-674-08030-0. Dewey:372.11/02. LCCN:87-023091.
Audience: **g,u.** *Choice, 1990.*

Tobin, Joseph J., et al. **LB1140.25.J3T63 1989**
Preschool in Three Cultures: Japan, China and the United States. David Y. Wu & Dana H. Davidson (Authors). Trade Cloth. Yale University Press. Cumberland, RI. 1989. 240p. ISBN:0-300-04235-3, ISBN13: 978-0-300-04235-1. Dewey:372/.21/0951. LCCN:88-020904.
Audience: **g,l,u,f.** *Choice, 1989.*

GEOGRAPHY

Geography required a focus on GIS-related technologies and spatial analysis more than before. However, works that follow along the lines of the history and general subject areas of geography, as well as specific works that cover a range of sub-discipline areas such a political geography and physical geography, were emphasized. Every attempt was made to include the best works in fields such as geomorphology or human geography and cultural studies. Moreover, reference works that are essential for undergraduate work, such as atlases, have been given a great deal of coverage.

Problematic areas are in geographies of ancient and medieval times, as well as texts on exploration. More materials were available in physical, human, and technological areas of geography. In addition to this, many texts (especially in GIS and associated fields) were at a more advanced level. Too many works at the undergraduate levels provide for a minimal coverage of these areas, so the decision was made to include more advanced texts.

Almost all items chosen were found in print and every effort was made to find the most recent texts in the field, expect were texts were considered to be essential no matter how old.

— James Boxall

General

G3700

☐ Geodata.Gov U.S. maps and Data. http://purl.access.gpo.gov/GPO/LPS36094 Office of Management and Budget.
Audience: **g,l,u,f.**

Abler, Ronald (Introduction by) **JC263.A69A3**
Guide to Programs in Geography in the United States and Canada 2001-2002. Trade Paper. Association of American Geographers. Washington, DC. 2001. ISBN:0-89291-259-6, ISBN13: 978-0-89291-259-9. Dewey:320.5/092.
Audience: **g.**

Cresswell, Tim **GF21**
Place: A Short Introduction. Trade Cloth. Blackwell Publishing, Inc. Malden, MA. 2004. 168p. Short Introductions to Geography Ser. ISBN:1-4051-0671-9, ISBN13: 978-1-4051-0671-9. Dewey:304.2/3. LCCN:2003-021515.
Audience: **g,l,u.**

De Blij, Harm J. **GF503.D4 2005**
Why Geography Matters: Three Challenges Facing America: Climate Change, the Rise of China, and Global Terrorism. Trade Cloth. Oxford University Press, Inc. New York, NY. 2005. 320p. ISBN:0-19-518301-0, ISBN13: 978-0-19-518301-6. Dewey:909.83. LCCN:2004-030369.
Audience: **g,l,u,f.** *Choice, 2006.*

Dorling, Danny **GF551**
Human Geography of the UK. Cloth Text. SAGE Publications, Inc. Thousand Oaks, CA. 2005. 216p. ISBN:0-7619-4135-5, ISBN13: 978-0-7619-4135-4. Dewey:304.2/0941. LCCN:2004-094667.
Audience: **l,u,f.**

Hoare, Anthony **G62.D53 1995**
Diffusing Geography: Essays for Peter Haggett. Andrew Cliff, Peter Gould & Nigel Thrift (Editors). Trade Cloth. Blackwell Publishing, Inc. Malden, MA. 1995. 448p. IBG Special Publications ISBN:0-631-19534-3, ISBN13: 978-0-631-19534-4. Dewey:910. LCCN:94-031610.
Audience: **u,f.**

Johnston, R. J. (Editor), et al. **G128.G474 2002**
Geographies of Global Change: Remapping the World. Ed. 2. Peter J. Taylor & Michael Watts (Editors). Trade Paper. Blackwell Publishing, Inc. Malden, MA. 2002. 544p. ISBN:0-631-22286-3, ISBN13: 978-0-631-22286-6. Dewey:910. LCCN:2002-022136.
Audience: **l,u,f.**

Unwin, Tim **G80 .U58 1992**
The Place of Geography. Ed. 1. Trade Paper. Prentice Hall PTR. Upper Saddle River, NJ. 1996. 288p. ISBN:0-582-05107-X, ISBN13: 978-0-582-05107-2. Dewey:910. LCCN:92-023369.
Audience: **l,u,f.**

World Bank Staff **HC59.7.W6593**
World Development Report 1978-2006 with Selected World Development Indicators 2005: Indexed Omnibus. Ed. 2005. CD-ROM. World Bank Publications. Washington, DC. 2005. World Development Report ISBN:0-8213-6252-6, ISBN13: 978-0-8213-6252-5. Dewey:31.
Audience: **g,l,u,f.**

Reference > Dictionaries

G63.H68 1997

ⓔ The Houghton Mifflin Dictionary of Geography: Places and Peoples of the World. E-Book. NetLibrary, Inc. Boulder, CO. 1997. ISBN:0-585-10946-X, ISBN13: 978-0-585-10946-6. Dewey:910/.3.
Audience: **g,l,u,f.**

Calhoun, Craig (Editor) **H41.D53 2001**
Dictionary of the Social Sciences. Trade Cloth. Oxford University Press, Inc. New York, NY. 2002. 582p. ISBN:0-19-512371-9, ISBN13: 978-0-19-512371-5. Dewey:300/.3. LCCN:00-068151.
Audience: **g,l,u.** *Choice, 2002.*

Clark, Audrey N. **G63 .C562 2003**
The Penguin Dictionary of Geography. Ed. 3. Trade Paper. Penguin Group (USA) Inc. New York, NY. 2003. 480p. Penguin Reference Bks. ISBN:0-14-051505-4, ISBN13: 978-0-14-051505-3. Dewey:910/.3. LCCN:2003-276042.
Audience: **g.** *Choice, 2004, 1999.*

Douglas, Ian (Editor), et al. **G116.C645**
Companion Encyclopedia of Geography: The Environment and Humankind. Richard Huggett & Mike Robinson (Editors). Trade Paper. Routledge. New York, NY. 2002. 1056p. Routledge World Reference Ser. ISBN:0-415-27750-7, ISBN13: 978-0-415-27750-1. Dewey:910.3.
Audience: **g,l,u,f.** *Choice, 1997.*

Forsyth, Tim (Editor) **HD82.E547 2005**
Encyclopedia of International Development. Paper over Boards. Routledge. New York, NY. 2004. 856p. ISBN:0-415-25342-X, ISBN13: 978-0-415-25342-0. Dewey:338.9/003. LCCN:2004-050985.
Audience: **g,l,u,f.** *Choice, 2005.*

Goudie, Andrew S. **GB10.D53 2000**
The Dictionary of Physical Geography. Ed. 3. David S. Thomas (Editor). Trade Paper. Blackwell Publishing, Inc. Malden, MA. 2000. 624p. ISBN:0-631-20473-3, ISBN13: 978-0-631-20473-2. Dewey:910/.02/03. LCCN:99-049818.
Audience: **g,l,u,f.** *Choice, 2001.*

Gregory, Derek & Pratt, Geraldine **GF4.D52 2000**
The Dictionary of Human Geography. Ed. 4. R. J. Johnston, David Smith & Michael Watts (Editors). Trade Paper. Blackwell Publishing, Inc. Malden, MA. 2000. 976p. ISBN:0-631-20561-6, ISBN13: 978-0-631-20561-6. Dewey:304.2/03/21. LCCN:00-022964.
Audience: **g,l,u,f.** B *Choice, 1994.*

Mayhew, Susan **G63**
A Dictionary of Geography. Ed. 3. Trade Paper. Oxford University Press, Inc. New York, NY. 2004. 560p. Oxford Paperback Reference Ser. ISBN:0-19-860673-7, ISBN13: 978-0-19-860673-4. Dewey:910/.3. LCCN:2004-058035.
Audience: **g,l,u,f.** *Choice, 1997.*

Merriam-Webster, Inc. Staff **G103.5.W42 1997**
Merriam-Webster's Geographical Dictionary. Ed. 3. Trade Cloth. Merriam-Webster, Inc. Springfield, MA. 2001. 1392p.

ISBN:0-87779-546-0, ISBN13: 978-0-87779-546-9. Dewey:910/.3. LCCN:96-052365.
Audience: **g,l,u,f.**

Park, Ken **AY67.N5**
The World Almanac and Book of Facts 2005. Trade Cloth. World Almanac Books. New York, NY. 2004. 1008p. ISBN:0-88687-939-6, ISBN13: 978-0-88687-939-6. Dewey:31.02.
Audience: **g,l,u,f.**

Small, John, et al. **G116**
A Modern Dictionary of Geography. Ed. 4. Michael Witherick & Simon Ross (Authors). Paper Text. Oxford University Press, Inc. New York, NY. 2001. 304p. An Arnold Publication Ser. ISBN:0-340-76210-1, ISBN13: 978-0-340-76210-3. Dewey:910.3.
Audience: **g,l,u,f.**

Thomson Gale Staff (Contribution by) **G103.5**
Worldmark Encyclopedia of the Nations. Ed. 11. Trade Cloth. Thomson Gale. Farmington Hills, MI. 2003. 3460p. ISBN:0-7876-7330-7, ISBN13: 978-0-7876-7330-7. Dewey:910/.3. LCCN:2004-266420.
Audience: **g,l,u,f.** *Choice, 2001.*

Turner, Barry (Editor) **JA51.S7 2005**
The Statesman's Yearbook: The Politics, Cultures and Economies of the World. Ed. 142. Saddle Stitched, Cloth over Boards, Dust Jacket. Palgrave Macmillan. New York, NY. 2005. 2112p. ISBN:1-4039-1482-6, ISBN13: 978-1-4039-1482-8. Dewey:909.8305.
Audience: **g,l,u,f.**

Reference > Gazetteers

E155
☐ GNIS Geographic Names Information System: Digital Gazetteer.
http://purl.access.gpo.gov/GPO/LPS1507
U.S. Geological Survey, Nation Mapping Division.
Audience: **g,l,u,f.**

Brabner, J. H. F. (Editor) **DA640**
The Comprehensive Gazetteer of England and Wales, Set. Library Binding. Routledge. New York, NY. 1997. 2218p. Early Sources in Reference Ser. ISBN:0-415-16095-2, ISBN13: 978-0-415-16095-7. Dewey:914.2/003.
Audience: **g,l,u,f.**

Cohen, Saul B. **E35.C65 2000**
The Columbia Gazetteer of North America. Trade Cloth. Columbia University Press. New York, NY. 2000. 1250p. ISBN:0-231-11990-9, ISBN13: 978-0-231-11990-0. Dewey:917/.003. LCCN:00-027512.
Audience: **g,l,u,f.** *Choice, 2001.*

Cohen, Saul B. **G103.5.C645 1998**
The Columbia Gazetteer of the World. Ed. 2. Trade Cloth. Columbia University Press. New York, NY. 1998. 3578p. ISBN:0-231-11040-5, ISBN13: 978-0-231-11040-2. Dewey:910/.3. LCCN:98-071262.
Audience: **g,l,u,f.** *Choice, 1998.*

Hellmann, Paul T. **E154.H45 2005**
Historical Gazetteer of the United States. Paper over Boards. Routledge. New York, NY. 2004. 888p. ISBN:0-415-93948-8, ISBN13: 978-0-415-93948-5. Dewey:911/.73. LCCN:2004-011421.
Audience: **g,l,u,f.** *Choice, 2005.*

Hobson, Archie **E154 .C36 1995**
The Cambridge Gazetteer of the USA and Canada: A Dictionary of Places. Trade Cloth. Cambridge University Press. New York, NY. 1995. 783p. ISBN:0-521-41579-9, ISBN13: 978-0-521-41579-8. Dewey:970. LCCN:96-025630.
Audience: **g.** *Choice, 1996.*

General Works

Cutter, Susan (Editor), et al. **G70.P74 2004**
Presidential Musings from the Meridian: Reflections on the Nature of Geography. Janice Monk & M. Duane Nellis (Editors), Douglas Richardson (Preface by). Trade Cloth. West Virginia University Press. Morgantown, WV. 2004. 276p. ISBN:0-937058-89-0, ISBN13: 978-0-937058-89-3. Dewey:910. LCCN:2004-114161.
Audience: **u,f.**

de Blij, H. J. **G116.D42 1995 SUPPL.**
The Earth, Student's Companion: An Introduction to its Physical and Human Geography. Ed. 4. Trade Paper. John Wiley & Sons, Inc. Hoboken, NJ. 1995. 167p. ISBN:0-471-14219-0, ISBN13: 978-0-471-14219-5. Dewey:910. LCCN:96-132868.
Audience: **l,u,f.**

Janelle, Donald G. **G128**
WorldMinds: Geographical Perspectives on 100 Problems. Barney Warf & Kathy Hansen (Editors). Trade Cloth. Springer. New York, NY. 2004. 660p. ISBN:1-4020-1612-3, ISBN13: 978-1-4020-1612-7. Dewey:910. LCCN:2004-274988.
Audience: **g,l,u,f.**

Johnston, R. J. (Editor), et al. **G99**
A Century of British Geography. Michael Williams & Ron Johnston (Editors), British Academy Staff (Contribution by). Trade Cloth. Oxford University Press, Inc. New York, NY. 2003. 692p. British Academy Centenary Monographs ISBN:0-19-726286-4, ISBN13: 978-0-19-726286-3. Dewey:910.71041. LCCN:2003-278562.
Audience: **u,f.** *Choice, 2004.*

Johnston, Ron **GF41**
Geography and Geographers: Anglo-American Human Geography since 1945. Ed. 6. Trade Paper. Oxford University Press, Inc. New York, NY. 2004. 542p. A Hodder Arnold Publication ISBN:0-340-80860-8, ISBN13: 978-0-340-80860-3. Dewey:304.2. LCCN:2004-303953.
Audience: **u,f.** *Choice, 2005.*

Livingstone, David N. **G80 .L54 1993**
The Geographical Tradition: Episodes in the History of a Contested Enterprise. Trade Paper. Blackwell Publishing, Inc. Malden, MA. 1992. 448p. ISBN:0-631-18586-0, ISBN13: 978-0-631-18586-4. Dewey:910.9. LCCN:92-015681.
Audience: **u,f.** *Choice, 1993.*

Mayhew, Robert J. **DA600.M295 2000**
Enlightenment Geography: The Political Languages of British Geography, 1650-1850. Cloth over Boards. Palgrave Macmillan. New York, NY. 2000. 334p. Studies in Modern History Ser. ISBN:0-312-23475-9, ISBN13: 978-0-312-23475-1. Dewey:910.9/41. LCCN:00-027247.
Audience: **u,f.** *Choice, 2001.*

Monmonier, Mark **G108.7.M66 1996**
How to Lie with Maps. Ed. 2. Trade Paper. University of Chicago Press. Chicago, IL. 1996. 222p. ISBN:0-226-53421-9, ISBN13: 978-0-226-53421-3. Dewey:910/.0148. LCCN:95-032199.
Audience: **g,l,u,f.**

Pickles, John **GA105.3.P52 2004**
A History of Spaces: Cartographic Reason, Mapping, and the Geo-Coded World. Paper over Boards. Routledge. New York, NY. 2003. 256p. ISBN:0-415-14497-3, ISBN13: 978-0-415-14497-1. Dewey:526. LCCN:2003-008283.
Audience: **l,u,f.**

Rischar Davis, Pat **G1021**
Geographic Literacy: Maps for Memorization. Ed. 3. Trade Cloth. Walch Publishing. Portland, ME. 2001. 214p. ISBN:0-8251-4272-5, ISBN13: 978-0-8251-4272-7. Dewey:912.
Audience: **g,l,u,f.**

Timmerman, Peter (Editor) **GE10**
Encyclopedia of Global Environmental Change, Social and Economic Dimensions of Global Environmental Change, Vol. 5. Trade Cloth. John Wiley & Sons, Inc. Hoboken, NJ. 2003. 688p. ISBN:0-470-85364-6, ISBN13: 978-0-470-85364-1. Dewey:363.7003.
Audience: **g,l,u,f.**

Tuan, Yi-Fu **BF299.S5**
Space and Place: The Perspective of Experience. Book, Other. University of Minnesota Press. Minneapolis, MN. 1979. 248p. ISBN:0-8166-0884-9, ISBN13: 978-0-8166-0884-3. Dewey:153.7/52. LCCN:77-072910.
Audience: **g,l,u,f.**

Philosophy

Baker, Alan R. H. (Author, Contribution by) **G141**
Geography and History: Bridging the Divide. Richard Dennis & Deryck Holdworth (Contribution by). Cloth Text. Cambridge University Press. New York, NY. 2003. 296p. Cambridge Studies in Historical Geography, Vol. 36 ISBN:0-521-24683-0, ISBN13: 978-0-521-24683-5. Dewey:911. LCCN:2003-046037.
Audience: **g,l,u,f.** *Choice, 2004.*

Buttel, Frederick H. & McMichael, Philip David (Editors) **N75**
New Directions in the Sociology of Global Development. Trade Cloth. Elsevier Science & Technology Books. Saint Louis, MO. 2005. 346p. ISBN:0-7623-1250-5, ISBN13: 978-0-7623-1250-4. Dewey:306.3.
Audience: **u,f.**

Castree, Noel, et al. **G128**
Questioning Geography: Fundamental Debates. Douglas Sherman, Alisdair Rogers & Gareth Schott (Authors). Trade Paper. Blackwell Publishing, Inc. Malden, MA. 2005. 328p. ISBN:1-4051-0192-X, ISBN13: 978-1-4051-0192-9. Dewey:910. LCCN:2005-008544.
Audience: **u,f.**

Febvre, Lucien & Bataillon, Lionel **GF13**
A Geographical Introduction to History: An Introduction to Human Geography. Trade Cloth. Kegan Paul International, Ltd. London, 2003. 256p. ISBN:0-7103-0844-2, ISBN13: 978-0-7103-0844-3. Dewey:304.2/09.
Audience: **u,f.**

Goodchild, Michael F. & Janelle, Donald G. (Editors) **HA30.6.S665 2003**
Spatially Integrated Social Science. Trade Cloth. Oxford University Press, Inc. New York, NY. 2004. 480p. Spatial Information Systems Ser. ISBN:0-19-515270-0, ISBN13: 978-0-19-515270-8. Dewey:300/.1/5195. LCCN:2002-156669.
Audience: **l,u,f.**

Hartshorne, Richard **G70.H32**
Perspective on the Nature of Geography. Paper Text. Textbook Publishers. Temecula, CA. 2003. 201p. ISBN:0-7581-5500-X, ISBN13: 978-0-7581-5500-9. Dewey:910.
Audience: **l,u,f.**

Inkpen, Robert (Editor) **GB21.I55 2005**
Science, Philosophy and Physical Geography. Paper over Boards. Routledge. New York, NY. 2004. 176p. ISBN:0-415-27953-4, ISBN13: 978-0-415-27953-6. Dewey:910/.02. LCCN:2004-012957.
Audience: **u,f.**

Livingstone, David N. & Withers, Charles W. J. (Editors) **G70.G4419 2005**
Geography and Revolution. Trade Cloth. University of Chicago Press. Chicago, IL. 2005. 440p. ISBN:0-226-48733-4, ISBN13: 978-0-226-48733-5. Dewey:910/.01. LCCN:2005-003443.
Audience: **u,f.**

Peet, Richard **G70.P375 1998**
Modern Geographic Thought: Richard Peet. Trade Paper. Blackwell Publishing, Inc. Malden, MA. 1998. 352p. ISBN:1-55786-378-4, ISBN13: 978-1-55786-378-2. Dewey:910/.01. LCCN:97-027639.
Audience: **u,f.**

Proctor, James D. **G70.G4433 1999**
Geography and Ethics: Journeys in a Moral Terrain. David M. Smith (Editor). Paper over Boards. Routledge. New York, NY. 1999. 320p. ISBN:0-415-18968-3, ISBN13: 978-0-415-18968-2. Dewey:910/.01. LCCN:98-047914.
Audience: **f.**

Taylor, D. R. **GA108.7.P65 1998**
Policy Issues in Modern Cartography. Trade Cloth. Elsevier Science & Technology Books. Saint Louis, MO. 1998. 286p. Modern Cartography Ser. ISBN:0-08-043111-9, ISBN13: 978-0-08-043111-6. Dewey:526. LCCN:98-025805.
Audience: **u,f.**

Methodology

Bennison, George M. & Moseley, Keith **QE601**
An Introduction to Geological Structures and Maps. Ed. 7.

Trade Paper. Oxford University Press, Inc. New York, NY. 2003. 176p. An Arnold Publication ISBN:0-340-80956-6, ISBN13: 978-0-340-80956-3. Dewey:551.8/022/3.
Audience: **l,u,f.**

Bobrowsky, P. T. **QE36**
Geoenvironmental Mapping: Method, Theory and Practice. Paper over Boards. Taylor & Francis Group. Abingdon, 2001. 750p. ISBN:90-5410-487-2, ISBN13: 978-90-5410-487-2. Dewey:550.0223. LCCN:2001-052525.
Audience: **g,l,u,f.**

Fotheringham, A. Stewart, et al. **G70.3.F68 2000**
Quantitative Geography: Perspectives on Spatial Data Analysis. Chris Brunsdon & Martin Charlton (Authors). Paper Text. SAGE Publications, Ltd. London, 2000. 288p. ISBN:0-7619-5948-3, ISBN13: 978-0-7619-5948-9. Dewey:910.2/85. LCCN:00-698468.
Audience: **u,f.**

Hay, Iain **G70.H35 2002**
Communicating in Geography and the Environmental Sciences. Ed. 2. Trade Paper. Oxford University Press, Inc. New York, NY. 2003. 256p. ISBN:0-19-551557-9, ISBN13: 978-0-19-551557-2. Dewey:333.7/068. LCCN:2003-267417.
Audience: **g,l,u,f.**

Hay, Iain (Editor) **GF26**
Qualitative Research Methods in Human Geography. Ed. 2. Trade Paper. Oxford University Press, Inc. New York, NY. 2005. 468p. ISBN:0-19-555079-X, ISBN13: 978-0-19-555079-5. Dewey:304.2042. LCCN:2005-281863.
Audience: **u,f.**

Holloway, Sarah (Editor), et al. **G105**
Key Concepts in Geography. Stephen Rice & Gill Valentine (Editors). Cloth Text. SAGE Publications, Ltd. London, 2003. 360p. ISBN:0-7619-7388-5, ISBN13: 978-0-7619-7388-1. Dewey:910/.014. LCCN:2002-112358.
Audience: **l,u,f.**

Northey, Margot & Knight, David B. **Q223**
Making Sense: A Student's Guide to Research and Writing: Geography and Environmental Sciences. Ed. 2. Trade Paper. Oxford University Press, Inc. New York, NY. 2004. 264p. ISBN:0-19-542099-3, ISBN13: 978-0-19-542099-9. Dewey:808/.06691.
Audience: **l,u,f.**

Rogerson, Peter **G70.3**
Statistical Methods for Geography. Cloth Text. SAGE Publications, Inc. Thousand Oaks, CA. 2001. 248p. Geography/Quantitative Methods Ser. ISBN:0-7619-6287-5, ISBN13: 978-0-7619-6287-8. Dewey:910/.21.
Audience: **l,u,f.**

Rogerson, Peter A. **G70.3**
Statistical Methods for Geography: A Student's Guide. Ed. 2. Cloth Text. SAGE Publications, Ltd. London, 2006. 320p. ISBN:1-4129-0795-0, ISBN13: 978-1-4129-0795-8. Dewey:910.015195. LCCN:2005-930121.
Audience: **l,u.**

Rowland, Don **HB871**
Demographic Methods and Concepts. Paper Text. Oxford University Press, Inc. New York, NY. 2003. 546p. ISBN:0-19-875263-6, ISBN13: 978-0-19-875263-9. Dewey:304.6072. LCCN:2003-542918.
Audience: **l,u,f.**

Siegel, Jacob S. & Swanson, David A. (Editors) **HB848**
The Methods and Materials of Demography: Condensed Edition. Ed. 2. Cloth Text. Elsevier Science & Technology Books. Saint Louis, MO. 2004. 819p. ISBN:0-12-641955-8, ISBN13: 978-0-12-641955-9. Dewey:304.6. LCCN:2003-103000.
Audience: **u,f.**

Slocum, Terry A., et al. **GA105.3**
Thematic Cartography and Geographic Visualization. Ed. 2. Robert B. McMaster, Fritz C. Kessler & Hugh H. Howard (Authors). Cloth Text. Prentice Hall PTR. Upper Saddle River, NJ. 2004. 528p. Prentice Hall Series in Geographic Information Science ISBN:0-13-035123-7, ISBN13: 978-0-13-035123-4. Dewey:526. LCCN:2004-002166.
Audience: **l,u,f.**

Wolfer, Loreen
Real Research: Conducting and Evaluating Research in the Social Sciences. Trade Paper. Allyn & Bacon, Inc. Boston, MA. 2006. 576p. ISBN:0-205-41662-4, ISBN13: 978-0-205-41662-2.
Audience: **g,l,u,f.**

Geographical Education

Butt, Graham **G72**
Continuum Studies in Geography Education: Continuum Guide to Geography Education. Trade Paper. Continuum International Publishing Group, Ltd. London, 2005. 232p. ISBN:0-8264-7746-1, ISBN13: 978-0-8264-7746-0. Dewey:910.7/1.
Audience: **u,f.**

de Blij, H. J. **G116.D42 1995 SUPPL.**
The Earth, Student's Companion: An Introduction to its Physical and Human Geography. Ed. 4. Trade Paper. John Wiley & Sons, Inc. Hoboken, NJ. 1995. 167p. ISBN:0-471-14219-0, ISBN13: 978-0-471-14219-5. Dewey:910. LCCN:96-132868.
Audience: **l,u,f.**

Fisher, Chris & Binns, Tony (Editors) **G73.I87 2000**
Issues in Geography Teaching. Trade Paper. Routledge. New York, NY. 2000. 336p. Issues in Subject Teaching Ser. ISBN:0-415-23077-2, ISBN13: 978-0-415-23077-3. Dewey:910/.71. LCCN:00-020762.
Audience: **u,f.**

Gabler, Robert E. (Author, Editor) **G0073.H3**
A Handbook for Geography Teachers. Trade Paper. Books on Demand. Ann Arbor, MI. 281p. Geographic Education Ser., No. 6 ISBN:0-598-19581-5, ISBN13: 978-0-598-19581-4. Dewey:910.
Audience: **u,f.**

Gerber, Rodney (Editor) **G73.I663 2002**
International Handbook on Geographical Education. Trade Cloth. Springer. New York, NY. 2002. 368p. Geojournal Library, Vol. 73 ISBN:1-4020-1019-2, ISBN13: 978-1-4020-1019-4. Dewey:910/.71. LCCN:2002-040555.
Audience: **u,f.**

Gerber, Rodney & Williams, Michael (Editors) **GF26.G47 2002**
Geography, Culture and Education. Trade Cloth. Springer. New York, NY. 2002. 260p. Geojournal Library, Vol. 71 ISBN:1-4020-0878-3, ISBN13: 978-1-4020-0878-8. Dewey:910/.71. LCCN:2002-032155.
Audience: **u,f.**

Kneale, Pauline E. **G116**
Study Skills for Geography Students: A Practical Guide. Ed. 2. Trade Paper. Oxford University Press, Inc. New York, NY. 2003. 304p. An Arnold Publication ISBN:0-340-81031-9, ISBN13: 978-0-340-81031-6. Dewey:910.7/11. LCCN:2004-353868.
Audience: **g,l,u,f.**

Geography History > Ancient

G128
Geographie Generale. Leather. French & European Publications, Inc. New York, NY. 1966. ISBN:0-320-05918-9, ISBN13: 978-0-320-05918-6. Dewey:910.
Audience: **l,u,f.**

Clarke, Katherine A. **DG77.C577 1999**
Between Geography and History: Hellenistic Constructions of the Roman World. Trade Cloth. Oxford University Press, Inc. New York, NY. 2000. 420p. Oxford Classical Monographs ISBN:0-19-924003-5, ISBN13: 978-0-19-924003-6. Dewey:937. LCCN:99-023235.
Audience: **u,f.** *Choice, 2000.*

Nicolet, Claude **G86.N5313 1990**
Space, Geography, and Politics in the Early Roman Empire. Trade Cloth. University of Michigan Press. Chicago, IL. 1991. 276p. Thomas Spencer Jerome Lectures ISBN:0-472-10096-3, ISBN13: 978-0-472-10096-5. Dewey:913.7. LCCN:90-048168.
Audience: **u,f.** *Choice, 1992.*

Ptolemy, Claudius **GA105.3**
Ptolemy's Geography: An Annotated Translation of the Theoretical Chapters. J. L. Berggren & Alexander Jones (Translators). Trade Paper. Princeton University Press. Princeton, NJ. 2001. 216p. ISBN:0-691-09259-1, ISBN13: 978-0-691-09259-1. Dewey:912.3.
Audience: **u,f.**

Scott, James M. **BS1830.J8 S45 2001**
Geography in Early Judaism and Christianity: The Book of Jubilees. John Court (Contribution by). Trade Cloth. Cambridge University Press. New York, NY. 2002. 346p. Society for New Testament Studies Monograph Ser. ISBN:0-521-80812-X, ISBN13: 978-0-521-80812-5. Dewey:229/.911. LCCN:2001-035282.
Audience: **u,f.**

Geography History > Modern

Abler, Ronald F. (Editor), et al. **G70.G446 1992**
Geography's Inner Worlds: Pervasive Themes in Contemporary American Geography. Melvin G. Marcus & Judy M. Olson (Editors). Cloth Text. Rutgers University Press. Piscataway, NJ. 1992. 440p. ISBN:0-8135-1829-6, ISBN13: 978-0-8135-1829-9. Dewey:910/.01. LCCN:91-043478.
Audience: **l,u,f.** *Choice, 1993.*

Baker, Alan R. H. (Author, Contribution by) **G141**
Geography and History: Bridging the Divide. Deryck Holdworth & Richard Dennis (Contribution by). Trade Paper. Cambridge University Press. New York, NY. 2003. 296p. Cambridge Studies in Historical Geography, Vol. 36 ISBN:0-521-28885-1, ISBN13: 978-0-521-28885-9. Dewey:911. LCCN:2003-046037.
Audience: **g,l,u,f.** *Choice, 2004.*

Beazley, Charles Raymond **G89 .B38**
The Dawn of Modern Geography: A History of Exploration and Geographical Science. Trade Cloth. Library Reprints, Inc. Temecula, CA. ISBN:0-7222-6411-9, ISBN13: 978-0-7222-6411-9. Dewey:910.9.
Audience: **l,u,f.** B

Benko, Georges & Strohmayer, Ulf **GF21.S69 1997**
Space and Social Theory: Interpreting Modernity and Postmodernity. Trade Cloth. Blackwell Publishing, Inc. Malden, MA. 1997. 416p. Institute of British Geographers Special Publications ISBN:0-631-19466-5, ISBN13: 978-0-631-19466-8. Dewey:304.2/01. LCCN:96-025628.
Audience: **u,f.**

Bennett, Robert & Estall, Robert (Editors) **G128.G57 1991**
Global Change and Challenge: Geography for the 1990s. Trade Paper. Routledge. New York, NY. 1991. 280p. ISBN:0-415-00143-9, ISBN13: 978-0-415-00143-4. Dewey:910. LCCN:90-027303.
Audience: **l,u,f.** *Choice, 1992.*

Crone, G. R. **G98 .C7**
Modern Geographers: An Outline of Progress in Geography since 1800 A. D. Paper Text. Textbook Publishers. Temecula, CA. 2003. 55p. ISBN:0-7581-4498-9, ISBN13: 978-0-7581-4498-0. Dewey:910.9.
Audience: **u,f.**

Dikshit, R. D. **G80**
Geographical Thought: A Contextual History of Ideas. Trade Cloth. Prentice Hall India Pvt., Ltd. New Delhi, 2003. 312p. ISBN:81-203-1182-5, ISBN13: 978-81-203-1182-4. Dewey:910.9.
Audience: **l,u,f.**

Fritze, Ronald H. **G400**
New Worlds: The Great Voyages of Discovery, 1400-1600. Trade Cloth. Sutton Publishing, Ltd. Stroud, 2003. 256p. ISBN:0-7509-2346-6, ISBN13: 978-0-7509-2346-0. Dewey:910/.9024.
Audience: **g,l,u,f.** *Choice, 2003.*

Johnston, R. J. **G116 .C43 1993**
The Challenge for Geography: A Changing World, a Changing Discipline. Trade Paper. Blackwell Publishing, Inc. Malden, MA. 1993. 264p. ISBN:0-631-18714-6, ISBN13: 978-0-631-18714-1. Dewey:910. LCCN:92-025239.
Audience: **l,u,f.**

Johnston, R. J. (Editor), et al. **G99**
A Century of British Geography. Michael Williams & Ron Johnston (Editors), British Academy Staff (Contribution by). Trade Cloth. Oxford University Press, Inc. New York, NY. 2003. 692p. British Academy Centenary Monographs ISBN:0-19-726286-4, ISBN13: 978-0-19-726286-3. Dewey:910.71041. LCCN:2003-278562.
Audience: **u,f.** *Choice, 2004.*

Johnston, Ron **GF41**
Geography and Geographers: Anglo-American Human Geography since 1945. Ed. 6. Trade Paper. Oxford University Press, Inc. New York, NY. 2004. 542p. A Hodder Arnold Publication ISBN:0-340-80860-8, ISBN13: 978-0-340-80860-3. Dewey:304.2. LCCN:2004-303953.
Audience: **u,f.** *Choice, 2005.*

Martin, Geoffrey J. **G80.M38 2004**
All Possible Worlds: A History of Geographical Ideas. Ed. 4. Trade Cloth. Oxford University Press, Inc. New York, NY. 2005. 605p. ISBN:0-19-516870-4, ISBN13: 978-0-19-516870-9. Dewey:910/.9. LCCN:2004-057559.
Audience: **u,f.** *Choice, 2005.*

Rawling, Eleanor M., et al. **G76.5.I8**
Geography into the Twenty-First Century. Ed. 1. Richard A. Daugherty & Adrianna J. Kezar (Authors). Trade Paper. John Wiley & Sons, Inc. Hoboken, NJ. 1999. 422p. ISBN:0-471-96236-8, ISBN13: 978-0-471-96236-6. Dewey:910.7/041. LCCN:95-052309.
Audience: **g,l,u,f.**

Schulten, Susan **G96.S36 2001**
The Geographical Imagination in America, 1880-1950. Trade Cloth. University of Chicago Press. Chicago, IL. 2001. 330p. ISBN:0-226-74055-2, ISBN13: 978-0-226-74055-3. Dewey:917. LCCN:00-010159.
Audience: **l,u,f.** *Choice, 2001.*

Smith, Neil **G69.B75 S65 2003**
American Empire: Roosevelt's Geographer and the Prelude to Globalization. Trade Cloth. University of California Press. Berkeley, CA. 2003. 570p. California Studies in Critical Human Geography, Vol. 9 ISBN:0-520-23027-2, ISBN13: 978-0-520-23027-9. Dewey:910/.92 B. LCCN:2002-011192.
Audience: **u,f.** *Choice, 2003.*

West, Robert C. (Author, Translator) **G62 .P52 1990**
Pioneers of Modern Geography: Translations Pertaining to German Geographers of the Late Nineteenth and Early Twentieth Centuries, 28. Paper Text. Geoscience Publications, Department of Geography & Anthropology. Baton Rouge, LA. 1990. 200p. Geoscience and Man Ser., Vol. 28 ISBN:0-938909-52-5, ISBN13: 978-0-938909-52-1. Dewey:910/.92/243 B. LCCN:90-081472.
Audience: **u,f.**

Exploration

Albanese, Denise **PR438.S35A43 1996**
New Science, New World. Library Binding. Duke University Press. Durham, NC. 1996. 264p. ISBN:0-8223-1759-1, ISBN13: 978-0-8223-1759-3. Dewey:820.9/356. LCCN:95-047757.
Audience: **g,l,u,f.** *Choice, 1997.*

Bridges, Roy; Hair, P E **G161.H2 2nd ser.,**
Compassing the Vast Glove of the Earth. Roy Bridges (Editor) ; P. E. Hair (Editor). Hakluyt Society. 1998. Hakluyt Society Second Ser. ISBN:0-904180-44-1, ISBN13: 978-0-904180-44-2.
Audience: **g,l,u,f.**

Davies, Wayne K. **G640.D295 2003**
Writing Geographical Exploration: Thomas James and the Northwest Passage 1631-33. Trade Cloth. University of Alberta Press. Georgetown, ON. 2004. 316p. ISBN:1-55238-062-9, ISBN13: 978-1-55238-062-8. Dewey:910/.9163/27. LCCN:2004-401078.
Audience: **g,l,u,f.** *Choice, 2005.*

Fiennes, Ranulph **G875.S35 F54**
Race to the Pole: Tragedy, Heroism, and Scott's Antarctic Quest. Trade Paper, Perfect. Hyperion Press. New York, NY. 2005. 484p. ISBN:0-7868-8858-X, ISBN13: 978-0-7868-8858-0. Dewey:919.8/904/092 B.
Audience: **g,l,u,f.** *Choice, 2005.*

Fleming, Fergus (As told by) **G80**
Off the Map: Tales of Endurance and Exploration. Trade Paper. Grove/Atlantic, Inc. New York, NY. 2006. 528p. ISBN:0-8021-4272-9, ISBN13: 978-0-8021-4272-6. Dewey:910/.9.
Audience: **g,l,u,f.**

Fleming, Fergus & Merullo, Annabel (Editors) **G80**
The Explorer's Eye: First-Hand Accounts of Adventure and Exploration. Michael Palin (Introduction by). Trade Cloth. Overlook Press, The. New York, NY. 2005. 264p. ISBN:1-58567-766-3, ISBN13: 978-1-58567-766-5. Dewey:910.409.
Audience: **g,l,u,f.**

Fogg, G. E. **G860 .F64 1992**
A History of Antarctic Science. Margaret Thatcher (Foreword by), L. C. Bliss, A. C. Clarke, D. J. Drewry, M. A. P. Renouf, D. W. H. Walton & P. J. Williams (Contribution by). Trade Paper. Cambridge University Press. New York, NY. 2005. 505p. Studies in Polar Research Ser. ISBN:0-521-67337-2, ISBN13: 978-0-521-67337-2. Dewey:507.20989.
Audience: **l,u,f.** *Choice, 1993.*

Hall, Richard **DS340.H35 1998**
Empires of the Monsoon. Trade Paper. HarperCollins World. New York, NY. 1998. xxiii, 575p. ISBN:0-00-638083-2, ISBN13: 978-0-00-638083-2. Dewey:909/.09824. LCCN:97-174392.
Audience: **g,l,u,f.**

Harmon, Daniel E. **E131.H37 2003**
The Early French Explorers of North America. Library Binding. Mason Crest Publishers. Broomall, PA. 2002. 64p. Exploration and Discovery Ser. ISBN:1-59084-044-5, ISBN13: 978-1-59084-044-3. Dewey:970.01/8. LCCN:2002-008527.
Audience: **g,l,u,f.**

Hayes, Derek **G1201.S1**
America Discovered: A Historical Atlas of North American Exploration. Trade Paper. Douglas & McIntyre, Ltd. Vancouver, BC. 2004. 224p. ISBN:1-55365-049-2, ISBN13: 978-1-55365-049-2. Dewey:911/.73.
Audience: **g,l,u,f.** *Choice, 2006.*

Hayes, Derek **F1060.7.M1783H39**
First Crossing: Alexander Mackenzie, His Expedition Across North America and the Opening of the Continent. Trade Cloth. Douglas & McIntyre, Ltd. Vancouver, BC. 2001. 320p. ISBN:1-55054-866-2, ISBN13: 978-1-55054-866-2. Dewey:917.1204/1. LCCN:2001-431098.
Audience: **g,l,u,f.**

Hayes, Derek **G2862.N6S12 H3 2001**
Historical Atlas of the North Pacific Ocean: Maps of Discovery and Scientific Exploration, 1500-2000. Trade Cloth. Sasquatch Books. Seattle, WA. 2002. 224p. ISBN:1-57061-311-7, ISBN13: 978-1-57061-311-1. Dewey:911/.164/4. LCCN:2001-031368.
Audience: **g,l,u,f.**

Irwin, Geoffrey **GN871.178 1994**
The Prehistoric Exploration and Colonisation of the Pacific. Trade Paper. Cambridge University Press. New York, NY. 1994. 248p. ISBN:0-521-47651-8, ISBN13: 978-0-521-47651-5. Dewey:990.
Audience: **u,f.** *Choice, 1993.*

Leacock, Stephen **N5345.L55**
The Dawn of Canadian History: A Chronicle of Aboriginal Canada and the Coming of the White Man. Trade Cloth. IndyPublish.com. Cambridge, MA. 2002. 120p. ISBN:1-58827-291-5, ISBN13: 978-1-58827-291-1. Dewey:709.56.
Audience: **g,l,u,f.**

McGhee, Robert **G606.M39 2004**
The Last Imaginary Place: A Human History of the Arctic World. Saddle Stitched, Cloth over Boards, Dust Jacket. Oxford University Press, Inc. New York, NY. 2005. 296p. ISBN:0-19-518368-1, ISBN13: 978-0-19-518368-9. Dewey:909/.0913. LCCN:2004-066296.
Audience: **g,l,u,f.** *Choice, 2006.*

Phillips, J. R. **G89.P48 1998**
The Medieval Expansion of Europe. Ed. 2. Trade Paper. Oxford University Press, Inc. New York, NY. 1998. 342p. ISBN:0-19-820740-9, ISBN13: 978-0-19-820740-5. Dewey:910/.9. LCCN:99-179710.
Audience: **l,u.** *Choice, 1989.*

Pope, Peter E. **E129.C1 P67 1997**
The Many Landfalls of John Cabot. Trade Paper. University of Toronto Press. Toronto, ON. 1997. 400p. ISBN:0-8020-7150-3, ISBN13: 978-0-8020-7150-7. Dewey:970.01/7/092. LCCN:98-112689.
Audience: **g,l,u,f.** *Choice, 1998.*

Redwood, David **G1036.S12 A8 2001**
Atlas of Exploration. Trade Cloth. Fitzroy Dearborn Publishers, Inc. Chicago, IL. 2001. 256p. ISBN:1-57958-311-3, ISBN13: 978-1-57958-311-8. Dewey:910.9.
Audience: **g,l,u,f.**

Richardson, Brian W. **G246.C7R45 2005**
Longitude and Empire: How Captain Cook's Voyages Changed the World. Trade Cloth. University of British Columbia Press. Vancouver, BC. 2005. 256p. ISBN:0-7748-1189-7, ISBN13: 978-0-7748-1189-7. Dewey:910/.92. LCCN:2005-472150.
Audience: **g,l,u,f.** *Choice, 2006.*

Ross, M. J. **G635.R6R67 1994**
Polar Pioneers: John Ross and James Clark Ross. Clive Holland (Foreword by). Trade Cloth. McGill-Queen's University Press. Montreal, PQ. 1994. 464p. ISBN:0-7735-1234-9, ISBN13: 978-0-7735-1234-4. Dewey:919.8/04. LCCN:95-170373.
Audience: **g,l,u,f.** *Choice, 1995.*

Seymour, M. J. **D210**
The Transformation of the North Atlantic World, 1492-1763: An Introduction. Trade Cloth. Greenwood Publishing Group, Inc. Portsmouth, NH. 2004. 272p. Studies in Military History and International Affairs Ser. ISBN:0-275-97380-8, ISBN13: 978-0-275-97380-3. Dewey:909.08. LCCN:2004-014020.
Audience: **g,l,u,f.** *Choice, 2005.*

Waldman, Carl & Wexler, Alan **G63**
Encyclopedia of Exploration: The Explorers. Trade Cloth. Facts On File, Inc. New York, NY. 2004. 1424p. ISBN:0-8160-4678-6, ISBN13: 978-0-8160-4678-2. Dewey:910/.3.
Audience: **g,l,u,f.**

Whitfield, Peter **G81.W47 1998**
New Found Lands: Maps in the History of Exploration. Paper over Boards. Routledge. New York, NY. 1998. 208p. ISBN:0-415-92026-4, ISBN13: 978-0-415-92026-1. Dewey:912/.09. LCCN:97-047767.
Audience: **g,l,u,f.** *Choice, 1998.*

Atlases > General

National Atals of the United States of America.
http://purl.access.gpo.gov/GPO/LPS13575
U.S. Geological Survey, Nation Mapping Division.
Audience: **g,l,u,f.**

Aharoni, Yohanan, et al. **G2230.A2 1993**
Bible Atlas. Ed. 3. Michael Avi-Yonah, Anson F. Rainey & Ze'ev Safrai (Authors). Trade Cloth. John Wiley & Sons, Inc. Hoboken, NJ. 1993. 224p. ISBN:0-02-500605-3, ISBN13: 978-0-02-500605-8. Dewey:912'.56. LCCN:77-004313.
Audience: **g,l,u,f.** *Choice, 1993.*

de Blij, H. J. **G1105**
Atlas of North America. Trade Cloth. Oxford University Press, Inc. New York, NY. 2005. 320p. ISBN:0-19-516993-X, ISBN13: 978-0-19-516993-5. Dewey:912.7.
Audience: **g,l,u,f.** *Choice, 2005.*

HarperCollins UK Staff **G1021**
The Times Comprehensive Atlas of the World. Ed. 11. Trade Cloth. HarperCollins Publishers. New York, NY. 2005. 544p. ISBN:0-00-715720-7, ISBN13: 978-0-00-715720-4. Dewey:912.19.
Audience: **g.**

London Times Staff, London Times **G1021.T5**
The Times Atlas of the World: Comprehensive Edition. Ed. 10. Trade Cloth. Crown Publishing Group. New York, NY. 1999.

544p. ISBN:0-8129-3265-X, ISBN13: 978-0-8129-3265-2. Dewey:912. LCCN:99-027273.
Audience: **g,l,u,f.**

National Geographic Society Staff **G1021**
Atlas of the World. Ed. 8. Trade Cloth. National Geographic Society. Washington, DC. 2004. 416p. ISBN:0-7922-7543-8, ISBN13: 978-0-7922-7543-5. LCCN:89-162237.
Audience: **g,l,u,f.**

Oxford University Press (Created by) **G1021**
Oxford World Atlas. Saddle Stitched, Cloth over Boards. Oxford University Press, Inc. New York, NY. 2005. 561p. ISBN:0-19-522045-5, ISBN13: 978-0-19-522045-2. Dewey:912.
Audience: **g,l,u,f.**

Oxford University Press Staff **G1021**
Atlas of the World. Ed. 12. Trade Cloth. Oxford University Press, Inc. New York, NY. 2004. 448p. ISBN:0-19-522147-8, ISBN13: 978-0-19-522147-3. Dewey:912.
Audience: **g,l,u,f.** *Choice, 2004, 2002, 1993.*

Oxford University Press Staff (Editor) **G1021.G4337 2003**
New Concise World Atlas. Trade Cloth. Oxford University Press, Inc. New York, NY. 2003. 288p. ISBN:0-19-521983-X, ISBN13: 978-0-19-521983-8. Dewey:912. LCCN:2003-057201.
Audience: **g,l,u,f.** *Choice, 2004.*

Rand McNally Inc. Staff, et al. **G1021 .P22**
World Atlas: Featuring Maps from the Rand McNally Goode's World Atlas. Ed. 2. Jon Malinowski & Eugene Palka (Authors). Trade Paper. John Wiley & Sons, Inc. Hoboken, NJ. 2005. 201p. ISBN:0-471-70691-4, ISBN13: 978-0-471-70691-5. Dewey:912.
Audience: **g,l,u,f.**

Atlases > Historic

Collins UK Staff **G1030**
Collins Atlas of Military History. Trade Paper. HarperCollins Publishers. New York, NY. 2006. 192p. ISBN:0-06-084997-5, ISBN13: 978-0-06-084997-9. Dewey:911.
Audience: **g.**

Dorling Kindersley Publishing Staff **G1030 .D6 2005**
World History Atlas. Jeremy Black (Editor). Trade Cloth. Dorling Kindersley Publishing, Inc. New York, NY. 2005. 320p. ISBN:0-7566-0967-4, ISBN13: 978-0-7566-0967-2. Dewey:911.
Audience: **g,l,u,f.**

Farrington, Karen **G1030**
Historical Atlas of Empires: From 4000 BC to the 21st Century. Trade Cloth. Mercury Books Limited.. London, 2004. 192p. ISBN:1-904668-02-X, ISBN13: 978-1-904668-02-2. Dewey:909.0712.
Audience: **g,l,u,f.**

Gilbert, Martin **E179.5**
The Routledge Atlas of American History. Ed. 5. Trade Paper. Routledge. New York, NY. 2005. 184p. Routledge Historical Atlases Ser. ISBN:0-415-35903-1, ISBN13: 978-0-415-35903-0. Dewey:911.73.
Audience: **g,l,u,f.**

Gilbert, Martin (Author, Author) **G2236**
The Routledge Atlas of the Arab-Israeli Conflict. Ed. 8. Trade Paper, Perfect. Routledge. New York, NY. 2005. 187p. Routledge Historical Atlases Ser. ISBN:0-415-35900-7, ISBN13: 978-0-415-35900-9. Dewey:911.56.
Audience: **g,l,u,f.**

Haywood, John **G141**
The Penguin Historical Atlas of Ancient Civilizations. Simon Hall (Editor). Trade Paper. Penguin Group (USA) Inc. New York, NY. 2005. 144p. ISBN:0-14-101448-2, ISBN13: 978-0-14-101448-7. Dewey:911.0901.
Audience: **g,l,u.**

Hull, Caroline & Jotischky, Andrew **G141**
The Penguin Historical Atlas of the Medieval World. Simon Hall & John Haywood (Editors). Trade Paper. Penguin Group (USA) Inc. New York, NY. 2005. 144p. ISBN:0-14-101449-0, ISBN13: 978-0-14-101449-4. Dewey:911.0902.
Audience: **g,l,u,f.**

Konstam, Angus **D151**
Historical Atlas of the Crusades. Warren Lapworth & Neil Williams (Editors). Trade Cloth. Mercury Books Limited.. London, 2004. 192p. ISBN:1-904668-00-3, ISBN13: 978-1-904668-00-8. Dewey:911/.4.
Audience: **g,l,u,f.**

Nash, Gary B. **E179.5**
Atlas of American History. Ed. 4. Trade Cloth. Facts On File, Inc. New York, NY. 2006. 336p. ISBN:0-8160-5952-7, ISBN13: 978-0-8160-5952-2. Dewey:911/.73. LCCN:2006-015915.
Audience: **g,l,u,f.**

Nicolle, David **DS36.57**
Historical Atlas of the Rise of Islam. Trade Cloth. Mercury Books Limited.. London, 2004. 192p. ISBN:1-904668-17-8, ISBN13: 978-1-904668-17-6. Dewey:911.1/767.
Audience: **g,l,u,f.**

Overy, Richard **G1035**
Collins Atlas of 20th Century History. Trade Paper. HarperCollins Publishers. New York, NY. 2006. 192p. ISBN:0-06-089072-X, ISBN13: 978-0-06-089072-8. Dewey:911.0904.
Audience: **g,l,u,f.**

Ramen, Fred **E35.R36 2005**
A Historical Atlas of North America Before Columbus. Library Binding. Rosen Publishing Group, Incorporated, The. New York, NY. 2005. 64p. The United States, Historical Atlases of the Growth of a New Nation Ser. ISBN:1-4042-0203-X, ISBN13: 978-1-4042-0203-0. Dewey:911/.7. LCCN:2004-041877.
Audience: **g,l,u,f.**

Story, Ronald **G1038.H52 2005**
Historical Atlas of World War Two. Trade Cloth. Oxford University Press, Inc. New York, NY. 2005. 128p. ISBN:0-19-518219-7, ISBN13: 978-0-19-518219-4. Dewey:940.540223.
Audience: **g,l,u,f.**

Wexler, Alan **G1201.S1**
Atlas of Westward Expansion. Molly Braun (Illustrator). Trade Paper. DIANE Publishing Company. Collingdale, PA. 2006. 240p. ISBN:0-7567-9968-6, ISBN13: 978-0-7567-9968-7. Dewey:911/.73.
Audience: **g,l,u,f.**

Woodworth, Steven E. & Winkle, Kenneth J. **E468.W754 2004**
Atlas of the Civil War. James M. McPherson (Foreword by). Trade Cloth. Oxford University Press, Inc. New York, NY. 2004. 400p. ISBN:0-19-522131-1, ISBN13: 978-0-19-522131-2. Dewey:973.7. LCCN:2004-053112.
Audience: **g,l,u,f.** *Choice, 2005.*

Atlases > Subject

Boyd, Andrew **G1035 .B6 1998**
An Atlas of World Affairs. Ed. 10. Paper over Boards. Routledge. New York, NY. 1998. 256p. ISBN:0-415-10670-2, ISBN13: 978-0-415-10670-2. Dewey:911. LCCN:97-022867.
Audience: **g,l,u,f.**

Christopher, A. J. **G1046**
The Atlas of States: Global Change, 1900-2000. Trade Cloth. John Wiley & Sons, Inc. Hoboken, NJ. 1999. 286p. ISBN:0-471-98613-5, ISBN13: 978-0-471-98613-3. Dewey:909. LCCN:99-019391.
Audience: **g.**

Cohn-Sherbok, Daniel **G1030.C559 1994**
Atlas of Jewish History. Paper over Boards. Routledge. New York, NY. 1994. 232p. ISBN:0-415-08684-1, ISBN13: 978-0-415-08684-4. Dewey:909.04924. LCCN:93-015018.
Audience: **g,l,u,f.** *Choice, 1994.*

Goetzmann, William H. & Williams, Glyndwr **G1106.S12 G6 1992**
The Atlas of North American Exploration: From the Norse Voyages to the Race to the Pole. Trade Paper. University of Oklahoma Press. Norman, OK. 1998. 224p. ISBN:0-8061-3058-X, ISBN13: 978-0-8061-3058-3. Dewey:911.7.
Audience: **g,l,u,f.**

McKitterick, Rosamond (Editor) **D117.M35 2004**
Atlas of the Medieval World. Trade Cloth. Oxford University Press, Inc. New York, NY. 2004. 304p. ISBN:0-19-522158-3, ISBN13: 978-0-19-522158-9. Dewey:909.07/022/3. LCCN:2004-056816.
Audience: **g,l,u,f.**

O'Brien, Patrick K. (Editor) **D21.5.A89 2002**
Concise Atlas of World History. Trade Cloth. Oxford University Press, Inc. New York, NY. 2002. 312p. ISBN:0-19-521921-X, ISBN13: 978-0-19-521921-0. Dewey:911. LCCN:2002-728410.
Audience: **g,l,u,f.** *Choice, 2003.*

Parker, Steve **GB611**
Atlas of the World's Deserts. Trade Cloth. Fitzroy Dearborn Publishers, Inc. Chicago, IL. 2003. 192p. ISBN:1-57958-310-5, ISBN13: 978-1-57958-310-1. Dewey:551.4/15. LCCN:2003-054706.
Audience: **g,l,u,f.**

Redwood, David **G1036.S12 A8 2001**
Atlas of Exploration. Trade Cloth. Fitzroy Dearborn Publishers, Inc. Chicago, IL. 2001. 256p. ISBN:1-57958-311-3, ISBN13: 978-1-57958-311-8. Dewey:910.9.
Audience: **g,l,u,f.**

Smallman-Raynor, Matthew **G1046**
World Atlas of Epidemic Diseases. Trade Cloth. Oxford University Press, Inc. New York, NY. 2004. 224p. An Arnold Publication ISBN:0-340-76171-7, ISBN13: 978-0-340-76171-7. Dewey:614.4/2/0223.
Audience: **g,l,u,f.**

Smith, Dan **G1021**
The Penguin State of the World Atlas. Ed. 7. Trade Paper. Penguin Group (USA) Inc. New York, NY. 2003. 144p. ISBN:0-14-200318-2, ISBN13: 978-0-14-200318-3. Dewey:912.
Audience: **g,l,u,f.**

Regions > United States

Acs, Zoltan & Armington, Catherine **HB615.A32 2006**
Entrepreneurship, Geography, and American Economic Growth. Trade Cloth. Cambridge University Press. New York, NY. 2006. 262p. ISBN:0-521-84322-7, ISBN13: 978-0-521-84322-5. Dewey:338/.040973. LCCN:2005-025468.
Audience: **u,f.**

Arreola, Daniel D. (Editor) **E184.S75H5843 2004**
Hispanic Spaces, Latino Places: Community and Cultural Diversity in Contemporary America. Trade Cloth. University of Texas Press. Austin, TX. 2004. 344p. ISBN:0-292-70267-1, ISBN13: 978-0-292-70267-7. Dewey:304.2/089/68073. LCCN:2004-007746.
Audience: **u,f.**

Berry, Brian J.L. & Wheeler, James (Editors) **GF503.U73 2005**
Urban Geography in America, 1950-2000: Paradigms and Personalities. Paper over Boards. Routledge. New York, NY. 2005. 408p. ISBN:0-415-95190-9, ISBN13: 978-0-415-95190-6. Dewey:307.76/0973. LCCN:2004-029780.
Audience: **l,u,f.**

Davis, Donald Edward **F217.A65D38 2006**
Homeplace Geography: Essays for Appalachia. Trade Paper. Mercer University Press. Macon, GA. 2006. 224p. ISBN:0-88146-014-1, ISBN13: 978-0-88146-014-8. Dewey:974. LCCN:2006-001478.
Audience: **u,f.**

de Souza Briggs, Xavier (Editor) **HD7288.76.U5G46 2005**
The Geography of Opportunity: Race and Housing Choice in Metropolitan America. William Julius Wilson (Foreword by). Trade Paper, Perfect. Brookings Institution Press. Washington, DC. 2005. 353p. ISBN:0-8157-0873-4, ISBN13: 978-0-8157-0873-5. Dewey:363.59900973. LCCN:2005-009628.
Audience: **u,f.** *Choice, 2006.*

Earle, Carville **G1201.S1**
The American Way: A Geographical History of Crisis and Recovery. Trade Paper. Rowman & Littlefield Publishers, Inc.

Lanham, MD. 2005. 472p. ISBN:0-8476-8713-9, ISBN13: 978-0-8476-8713-8. Dewey:911/.73.
Audience: **u,f.** *Choice, 2004.*

Frazier, John W. & Margai, Florence M. **E184.A1M8165 2003**
Multicultural Geographies: The Changing Racial/Ethnic Patterns of the United States. Perfect. Global Academic Publishing. Binghamton, NY. 2003. 310p. ISBN:1-58684-045-2, ISBN13: 978-1-58684-045-7. Dewey:305.8/00973. LCCN:2003-018494.
Audience: **u,f.**

Gaile, Gary L. & Willmott, Cort J. **G99.2**
Geography in America at the Dawn of the 21st Century. Trade Paper. Oxford University Press, Inc. New York, NY. 2006. 848p. ISBN:0-19-929586-7, ISBN13: 978-0-19-929586-9. Dewey:910.7073.
Audience: **g,l,u,f.** *Choice, 2004.*

Gallagher, Michael **DS247.A13G345 2005**
Gulf States. Library Binding, Paper over Boards. Smart Apple Media. North Mankato, MN. 2005. 44p. ISBN:1-58340-608-5, ISBN13: 978-1-58340-608-3. Dewey:953.6. LCCN:2005-043054.
Audience: **u,f.**

Golden, Nancy **E161.3.G65 2004**
Exploring the United States with the Five Themes of Geography. Trade Cloth. Rosen Publishing Group, Incorporated, The. New York, NY. 2005. 24p. Library of the Western Hemisphere ISBN:1-4042-2670-2, ISBN13: 978-1-4042-2670-8. Dewey:917.3. LCCN:2003-021591.
Audience: **g,l,u,f.**

Hartman, Monte **F595.3.H37 2005**
America's 100th Meridian: A Plains Journey. William Kittredge (Contribution by). Trade Cloth. Texas Tech University Press. Lubbock, TX. 2006. 176p. Plains Histories Ser. ISBN:0-89672-561-8, ISBN13: 978-0-89672-561-4. Dewey:917.804. LCCN:2005-018092.
Audience: **g,l,u,f.**

Hayes, Derek **G1201.S1**
America Discovered: A Historical Atlas of North American Exploration. Trade Paper. Douglas & McIntyre, Ltd. Vancouver, BC. 2004. 224p. ISBN:1-55365-049-2, ISBN13: 978-1-55365-049-2. Dewey:911/.73.
Audience: **g,l,u,f.** *Choice, 2006.*

Henry, Mark & Armstrong, Leslie (Editors) **SB486.M35M36 2004**
Mapping the Future of America's National Parks: Stewardship Through Geographic Information Systems. Trade Paper. ESRI, Inc. Redlands, CA. 2004. 175p. ISBN:1-58948-080-5, ISBN13: 978-1-58948-080-3. Dewey:917.3. LCCN:2004-008093.
Audience: **g,l,u,f.**

Jordan-Bychkov, Terry **GF41**
My Kind of Geography. Trade Cloth. Center for American Places, Inc. Staunton, VA. 2007. 96p. Center for American Places - My Kind of ... Ser. ISBN:1-930066-47-3, ISBN13: 978-1-930066-47-2. Dewey:301.34.
Audience: **l,u,f.**

McKnight, Tom L. **E161.3.M35 2003**
Regional Geography of the United States and Canada. Ed. 4. Trade Paper. Prentice Hall PTR. Upper Saddle River, NJ. 2003. 528p. ISBN:0-13-101473-0, ISBN13: 978-0-13-101473-2. Dewey:917.3. LCCN:2003-023174.
Audience: **g,l,u,f.**

Menendez, Albert J. **JK524.M48 2005**
The Geography of Presidential Elections in the United States, 1868-2004. Cloth Text. McFarland & Company, Incorporated Publishers. Jefferson, NC. 2005. 358p. ISBN:0-7864-2217-3, ISBN13: 978-0-7864-2217-3. Dewey:324.973/09. LCCN:2005-004744.
Audience: **g,l,u,f.**

National Geographic Society Staff **G1201.S1F5 2004**
National Geographic Historical Atlas of the United States. Ron Fisher (Text by). Trade Cloth. National Geographic Society. Washington, DC. 2004. 224p. ISBN:0-7922-6131-3, ISBN13: 978-0-7922-6131-5. Dewey:911/.73. LCCN:2004-050421.
Audience: **g,l,u,f.** *Choice, 2005.*

Nolt, John **GE155.A58N65 2005**
/A Land Imperiled: The Declining Health of the Southern Appalachian Bioregion. Trade Paper, Perfect. University of Tennessee Press. Knoxville, TN. 2005. 375p. Outdoor Tennessee Ser. ISBN:1-57233-326-X, ISBN13: 978-1-57233-326-0. Dewey:333.95/137/0975. LCCN:2004-028991.
Audience: **u,f.** *Choice, 2005.*

Otterstrom, Samuel **HT123.G43 2004**
A Geographical History of United States City-Systems: From Frontier to the Urban Transformation. Trade Cloth. Edwin Mellen Press, The. Lewiston, NY. 2004. 265p. Mellen Studies in Geography Ser., Vol. 10 ISBN:0-7734-6521-9, ISBN13: 978-0-7734-6521-3. Dewey:307.76. LCCN:2004-040188.
Audience: **u,f.**

Platt, Rutherford H. **KF5698.P588 2004**
Land Use and Society: Geography, Law, and Public Policy. Ed. 2. Paper Text. Island Press. Washington, DC. 2004. 488p. ISBN:1-55963-685-8, ISBN13: 978-1-55963-685-8. Dewey:346.7304/5. LCCN:2003-024791.
Audience: **u,f.**

Schein, Richard H. **E184.A1L256 2006**
Landscapes of Race in United States. Paper over Boards. Routledge. New York, NY. 2006. 272p. ISBN:0-415-94994-7, ISBN13: 978-0-415-94994-1. Dewey:305.800973. LCCN:2005-033020.
Audience: **g,l,u,f.**

Stanley, George Edward **E49.2.E95S73 2005**
The European Settlement of North America (1492-1754). Library Binding. Gareth Stevens Inc. Milwaukee, WI. 2005. 48p. ISBN:0-8368-5824-7, ISBN13: 978-0-8368-5824-2. Dewey:970.02. LCCN:2004-061597.
Audience: **g,l,u,f.**

Regions > Mexico and Latin America

Adams, John A. **HF1456**
Bordering the Future: The Impact of Mexico on the United States. Trade Cloth. Greenwood Publishing Group, Inc. Portsmouth, NH. 2006. 184p. ISBN:1-56720-637-9, ISBN13: 978-1-56720-637-1. Dewey:337.72073. LCCN:2005-032301.
Audience: **g,l,u,f.**

Cimoli, Mario (Editor) **HC140.T4D48 2000**
Developing Innovation Systems: Mexico in a Global Context. Cloth Text. Routledge. New York, NY. 2005. 336p. Science, Technology and the International Political Economy Ser. ISBN:0-8264-4768-6, ISBN13: 978-0-8264-4768-5. Dewey:338.972. LCCN:00-035835.
Audience: **u,f.**

Coerver, Don, et al. **F1234.C67 2004**
Mexico: An Encyclopedia of Contemporary Culture and History. Suzanne B. Pasztor & Robert Buffington (Authors). E-Book. ABC-CLIO, Inc. Santa Barbara, CA. 2004. xxiv, 621p. ISBN:1-85109-517-9, ISBN13: 978-1-85109-517-9. Dewey:972.08203. LCCN:2004-014738.
Audience: **g,l,u,f.** *Choice, 2005.*

Craib, Raymond B. **F1228.9.C73 2004**
Cartographic Mexico: A History of State Fixations and Fugitive Landscapes. Trade Cloth. Duke University Press. Durham, NC. 2004. 288p. Latin America Otherwise Ser. ISBN:0-8223-3405-4, ISBN13: 978-0-8223-3405-7. Dewey:911/.72. LCCN:2004-009140.
Audience: **g,l,u,f.** *Choice, 2005.*

Otero, Gerardo (Editor) **HC135**
Mexico in Transition: Neoliberal Globalism, the State and Civil Society. Cloth over Boards. Zed Books, Ltd. London, 2004. 288p. Globalization and the Semi-Periphery Ser., :Impacts, Opposition, Alternatives Ser. ISBN:1-84277-358-5, ISBN13: 978-1-84277-358-1. Dewey:338.9'72. LCCN:2005-295293.
Audience: **u,f.**

Randall, Laura (Editor) **HC135.C44 2005**
Changing Structure of Mexico: Political, Social, and Economic Prospects. Ed. 2. Cloth Text. M. E. Sharpe Inc. Armonk, NY. 2006. 512p. Columbia University Seminar Ser. ISBN:0-7656-1404-9, ISBN13: 978-0-7656-1404-9. Dewey:972.08/4. LCCN:2004-029098.
Audience: **u,f.**

Ross, John **F1208.R828 2002**
Mexico in Focus: A Guide to the People, Politics, and Culture. Trade Cloth. Interlink Publishing Group, Inc. Northampton, MA. 2004. 100p. In Focus Guides ISBN:1-56656-421-2, ISBN13: 978-1-56656-421-2. Dewey:972. LCCN:2001-008044.
Audience: **l,u,f.**

Trigg, Heather B. **F799.T75 2005**
From Household to Empire: Society and Economy in Early Colonial New Mexico. Trade Cloth. University of Arizona Press. Tucson, AZ. 2005. 264p. ISBN:0-8165-2444-0, ISBN13: 978-0-8165-2444-0. Dewey:978.9/02. LCCN:2004-023680.
Audience: **u,f.**

Regions > Europe

Adams, Simon **DR36.A3 2005**
The Balkans. Library Binding, Paper over Boards. Smart Apple Media. North Mankato, MN. 2005. 44p. ISBN:1-58340-603-4, ISBN13: 978-1-58340-603-8. Dewey:949.6. LCCN:2004-056456.
Audience: **g,l,u,f.**

Berentsen, William H. (Editor) **D900.E97 1997**
Contemporary Europe: A Geographic Analysis. Ed. 7. Trade Cloth. John Wiley & Sons, Inc. Hoboken, NJ. 1997. 688p. ISBN:0-471-58336-7, ISBN13: 978-0-471-58336-3. Dewey:914. LCCN:96-037342.
Audience: **g,l,u,f.**

Berezin, Mabel & Schain, Martin (Editors) **JN12.R458 2004**
Europe Without Borders: Remapping Territory, Citizenship, and Identity in a Transnational Age. Trade Paper. Johns Hopkins University Press. Baltimore, MD. 2004. 336p. ISBN:0-8018-7437-8, ISBN13: 978-0-8018-7437-6. Dewey:306.2/094. LCCN:2003-006212.
Audience: **g,l,u,f.** *Choice, 2004.*

Frankland, E. Gene **D424**
Global Studies: Europe. Ed. 9. Paper Text. McGraw-Hill Higher Education. Burr Ridge, IL. 2005. 320p. ISBN:0-07-319874-9, ISBN13: 978-0-07-319874-3. Dewey:940.
Audience: **g,l,u,f.**

Gowland, D. A., et al. **D1055.E84 2006**
The European Mosaic: Contemporary Politics, Economics, and Culture. Ed. 3. Richard Dunphy & Charlotte Lythe (Authors). Trade Paper. Longman Publishing. Boston, MA. 2006. 624p. ISBN:0-582-47370-5, ISBN13: 978-0-582-47370-6. Dewey:940.55. LCCN:2005-053916.
Audience: **u,f.**

Konstam, Angus **DC235**
Historical Atlas of the Napoleonic Era. Trade Cloth. Mercury Books Limited.. London, 2004. 192p. ISBN:1-904668-04-6, ISBN13: 978-1-904668-04-6. Dewey:940.27.
Audience: **g,l,u,f.**

Koster, Eduard A. (Editor) **GB171**
Physical Geography of Western Europe. Trade Cloth. Oxford University Press, Inc. New York, NY. 2005. 472p. Oxford Regional Environments Ser. ISBN:0-19-927775-3, ISBN13: 978-0-19-927775-9. Dewey:914.02. LCCN:2005-299486.
Audience: **l,u,f.**

Miyares, Ines M., et al. **G128**
World Cultures and Geography: Western Hemisphere and Europe. Mark C. Schug & Charles S. White (Authors). Trade Cloth. McDougal Littell Inc. Evanston, IL. 2005. ISBN:0-618-37759-X, ISBN13: 978-0-618-37759-6. Dewey:910.
Audience: **g,l,u,f.**

Mouritzen, Hans & Wivel, Anders **HC241.2**
The Geopolitics of Euro-Atlantic Intergration. Paper over Boards. Routledge. New York, NY. 2005. 272p. Europe and the Nation State Ser., Vol. 9 ISBN:0-415-28280-2, ISBN13: 978-0-415-28280-2. Dewey:341.242/2. LCCN:2005-042840.
Audience: **u,f.**

Tsoukalis, Loukas **JN30**
What Kind of Europe? Trade Paper. Oxford University Press, Inc. New York, NY. 2005. 260p. ISBN:0-19-927948-9, ISBN13: 978-0-19-927948-7. Dewey:341.242/2. LCCN:2005-278203.
Audience: **l,u,f.** *Choice, 2004.*

White, George W. **JC311.W463 2004**
Nation, State, and Territory: Origins, Evolutions, and Relationships. Ed. 2. Book, Other. Rowman & Littlefield Publishers, Inc. Lanham, MD. 2004. 304p. ISBN:0-7425-3025-6,

ISBN13: 978-0-7425-3025-6. Dewey:320.1. LCCN:2004-014114.
Audience: **l,u,f.**

Regions > Africa

African Development Bank Staff (Contribution by) **HC800.A1A354 2005**
African Development Report 2005. Trade Paper. Oxford University Press, Inc. New York, NY. 2006. 336p. ISBN:0-19-928084-3, ISBN13: 978-0-19-928084-1. Dewey:338.96005.
Audience: **l,u,f.**

Binns, Tony (Author, Editor) **GF0701.P46S**
People and Environment in Africa. Trade Paper. Books on Demand. Ann Arbor, MI. 286p. ISBN:0-598-02815-3, ISBN13: 978-0-598-02815-0. Dewey:304.2/096. LCCN:94-038627.
Audience: **l,u,f.**

Cline-Cole, Reginald & Robson, Elsbeth **HC1000.W476 2005**
West African Worlds, Paths Through Socio-Economic Change, Livelihoods and Development. Trade Paper. Prentice Hall PTR. Upper Saddle River, NJ. 2005. 296p. DARG Regional Development Ser., No. 6 ISBN:0-13-025949-7, ISBN13: 978-0-13-025949-3. Dewey:338.966. LCCN:2004-043193.
Audience: **u,f.**

Fox, Roddy & Rowntree, Kate (Editors) **DT1728.G46 2000**
The Geography of South Africa in a Changing World. Paper Text. Oxford University Press, Inc. New York, NY. 2000. 544p. ISBN:0-19-571682-5, ISBN13: 978-0-19-571682-5. Dewey:916.8. LCCN:00-291591.
Audience: **g,l,u,f.** *Choice, 2001.*

Howard, Allen M. & Shain, Richard M. **GF701.S65 2005**
The Spatial Factor in African History: The Relationship of the Social, Material, and Perceptual. Trade Paper. Brill Academic Publishers. Leiden, 2004. 300p. African Social Studies Ser., Vol. 8 ISBN:90-04-13913-3, ISBN13: 978-90-04-13913-8. Dewey:304.2/3/096. LCCN:2004-058586.
Audience: **u,f.**

Kyambalesa, Henry & Houngnikpo, Mathurin C. **HC800**
Economic Integration and Development in Africa. Trade Cloth. Ashgate Publishing Company. Williston, VT. 2006. 222p. ISBN:0-7546-4603-3, ISBN13: 978-0-7546-4603-7. Dewey:337.167. LCCN:2005-935868.
Audience: **u,f.**

Lyons, Tanya & Pye, Geralyn **HC800.A558 2005**
Africa on a Global Stage. Trade Cloth. Africa World Press. Trenton, NJ. 2005. ISBN:1-59221-387-1, ISBN13: 978-1-59221-387-0. Dewey:960.3/3. LCCN:2005-024846.
Audience: **g,l,u,f.**

Mitchell, Peter (Editor) **DT14.P46 2006**
Peoples and Cultures of Africa. Trade Cloth. Facts On File, Inc. New York, NY. 2006. 672p. ISBN:0-8160-6260-9, ISBN13: 978-0-8160-6260-7. Dewey:960. LCCN:2006-040011.
Audience: **g,l,u,f.**

Warburton, Christopher **HC800.W368 2005**
The Evolution of Crises and Underdevelopment in Africa. Trade Paper. University Press of America, Inc. Lanham, MD. 2005. 158p. ISBN:0-7618-3208-4, ISBN13: 978-0-7618-3208-9. Dewey:330.96. LCCN:2005-924859.
Audience: **u,f.**

Regions > Asia

Bregel, Yuri **G2202.21.S1 B7 2003**
An Historical Atlas of Central Asia. Trade Cloth. Brill Academic Publishers. Leiden, 2003. xii, 110p. Asian Studies ISBN:90-04-12321-0, ISBN13: 978-90-04-12321-2. Dewey:911/.58. LCCN:2003-055011.
Audience: **g,l,u,f.** *Choice, 2004.*

Chapman, Graham P. & Baker, Kathleen M. (Editors) **DS5.92 .C45 1992**
The Changing Geography of Asia. Trade Paper. Routledge. New York, NY. 1992. 288p. ISBN:0-415-05708-6, ISBN13: 978-0-415-05708-0. Dewey:915. LCCN:91-044801.
Audience: **l,u.**

Gupta, Avijit (Editor) **DS521.62**
The Physical Geography of Southeast Asia. Trade Cloth. Oxford University Press, Inc. New York, NY. 2005. 464p. Oxford Regional Environments Ser. ISBN:0-19-924802-8, ISBN13: 978-0-19-924802-5. Dewey:915.9'02. LCCN:2005-298036.
Audience: **l,u,f.** *Choice, 2005.*

Hill, Ronald **GF668.H55 2004**
Southeast Asia: People, Land and Economy. Trade Paper. Allen & Unwin Pty., Ltd. Crows Nest, NSW. 2002. 328p. ISBN:1-86508-517-0, ISBN13: 978-1-86508-517-3. Dewey:915.9.
Audience: **g,l,u,f.**

Rigg, Jonathan **DS521.62.R542 2002**
Southeast Asia: The Human Landscape of Modernization and Development. Ed. 2. Paper over Boards. Routledge. New York, NY. 2002. 408p. ISBN:0-415-25639-9, ISBN13: 978-0-415-25639-1. Dewey:959. LCCN:2002-031816.
Audience: **u,f.**

Weightman, Barbara A. **DS335.W37 2005**
Dragons and Tigers: A Geography of South, East, and Southeast Asia. Ed. 2. Trade Cloth. John Wiley & Sons, Inc. Hoboken, NJ. 2005. 464p. ISBN:0-471-63084-5, ISBN13: 978-0-471-63084-5. Dewey:915. LCCN:2005-027689.
Audience: **g,l,u,f.**

Regions > Oceania and Antarctica

D'Arcy, Paul **DU28.D37 2006**
The People of the Sea: Environment, Identity, and History in Oceania. Trade Cloth. University of Hawaii Press. Honolulu, HI. 2005. 304p. ISBN:0-8248-2959-X, ISBN13: 978-0-8248-2959-9. Dewey:995. LCCN:2005-029353.
Audience: **g,l,u,f.**

Darian-Smith, Kate **DU96.D355 2005**
Australia, Antarctica, and the Pacific. Library Binding, Paper over Boards. Gareth Stevens Inc. Milwaukee, WI. 2006. 64p. Continents of the World Ser. ISBN:0-8368-5912-X, ISBN13: 978-0-8368-5912-6. Dewey:994. LCCN:2005-042110.
Audience: **g,l,u,f.**

Frost, Alan **DA16.F76 2003**
The Global Reach of Empire: Britain's Maritime Expansion in the Indian and Pacific Oceans, 1764-1814. Cloth over Boards. Melbourne University Publishing. Carlton, VIC. 2003. 96p. ISBN:0-522-85050-2, ISBN13: 978-0-522-85050-5. Dewey:909/.0964. LCCN:2003-374221.
Audience: **u,f.**

Goodwin, Bill **DU23.5**
South Pacific. Ed. 10. Trade Paper. John Wiley & Sons, Inc. Hoboken, NJ. 2006. 480p. ISBN:0-471-76980-0, ISBN13: 978-0-471-76980-4. Dewey:919.5/04.
Audience: **g.**

Hampton, David **DU96.H36 2006**
Australia. Trade Cloth. Sea-To-Sea Publications. North Mankato, MN. 2006. Living In- Ser. ISBN:1-59771-041-5, ISBN13: 978-1-59771-041-1. Dewey:994. LCCN:2005-057547.
Audience: **g.**

Hema Maps Staff (Author, Illustrator) **DU405**
New Zealand: Aotearoa — Land of the Long White Cloud. Trade Cloth. New Zealand Visitor Publications, Ltd. Nelson, 2006. 492p. ISBN:1-877339-21-0, ISBN13: 978-1-877339-21-9. Dewey:919.30014.
Audience: **g.**

Hillstrom, Kevin & Hillstrom, Laurie Collier **GE160.S645H55 2003**
[e] Australia, Oceania, and Antarctica: A Continental Overview of Environmental Issues. E-Book. ABC-CLIO, Inc. Santa Barbara, CA. 2003. xxvi, 269p. The World's Environments Ser. ISBN:1-57607-695-4, ISBN13: 978-1-57607-695-8. Dewey:363.7/0099. LCCN:2003-020748.
Audience: **g,l,u,f.**

Lansdown, Richard (Editor) **DU28.S83 2006**
Strangers in the South Seas: The Idea of the Pacific in Western Thought. Trade Cloth. University of Hawaii Press. Honolulu, HI. 2006. 496p. ISBN:0-8248-3042-3, ISBN13: 978-0-8248-3042-7. Dewey:995. LCCN:2005-034632.
Audience: **g,l,u,f.**

Lockwood, Victoria S. **GN663.G56 2004**
Globalization and Culture Change in the Pacific Islands. Trade Paper. Prentice Hall PTR. Upper Saddle River, NJ. 2003. 493p. Exploring Cultures Ser. ISBN:0-13-042173-1, ISBN13: 978-0-13-042173-9. Dewey:306/.0995. LCCN:2003-049816.
Audience: **l,u,f.**

Mitchell, B. R. **HA4675.M552 2003**
International Historical Statistics: Africa, Asia and Oceania, 1750-2002. Ed. 4. Cloth over Boards. Palgrave Macmillan. New York, NY. 2003. 1144p. ISBN:0-333-99412-4, ISBN13: 978-0-333-99412-2. Dewey:310. LCCN:2002-035523.
Audience: **g,l,u,f.** *Choice, 2004.*

Moran, Michael **DU744**
Beyond the Coral Sea: Travels in the Old Empires of the South-West Pacific. Trade Paper. HarperCollins Publishers Ltd. London, 2004. 432p. ISBN:0-00-655235-8, ISBN13: 978-0-00-655235-2. Dewey:919.504.
Audience: **u,f.**

Rodgers, Hilary, et al. **DU870**
Tahiti and French Polynesia. Ed. 6. Jean-Bernard Carillet & Tony Wheeler (Authors). Trade Paper. Lonely Planet Publications. Oakland, CA. 2003. 288p. ISBN:1-74059-229-8, ISBN13: 978-1-74059-229-1. Dewey:919.6/2/04.
Audience: **g,l,u,f.**

Sturman, Andrew & Tapper, Nigel **QC992.A1**
The Weather and Climate of Australia and New Zealand. Ed. 2. Trade Paper. Oxford University Press, Inc. New York, NY. 2006. 520p. ISBN:0-19-558466-X, ISBN13: 978-0-19-558466-0. Dewey:551.6994. LCCN:2006-279364.
Audience: **l,u,f.** *Choice, 1997.*

Thomas, Nicholas **G420.C65T56 2003**
Cook: The Extraordinary Sea Voyages of Captain James Cook. Cloth over Boards. Walker & Company. New York, NY. 2004. 468p. ISBN:0-8027-1412-9, ISBN13: 978-0-8027-1412-1. Dewey:910/.92 B. LCCN:2003-057648.
Audience: **g,l,u,f.** *Choice, 2004.*

Cartography

Dent, Borden D. **GA105.3.D45 1999**
Cartography: Thematic Map Design with Arcview GIS Software. Ed. 5. Mixed Media, Trade Cloth, CD-ROM. McGraw-Hill Higher Education. Burr Ridge, IL. 2002. 448p. ISBN:0-07-282202-3, ISBN13: 978-0-07-282202-1. Dewey:526.
Audience: **l,u.**

Jacob, Christian **GA201.J3313 2006**
The Sovereign Map: Theoretical Approaches in Cartography throughout History. Edward H. Dahl (Editor), Tom Conley (Translator). Trade Cloth. University of Chicago Press. Chicago, IL. 2006. 464p. ISBN:0-226-38953-7, ISBN13: 978-0-226-38953-0. Dewey:526. LCCN:2005-014228.
Audience: **u,f.**

Klinghoffer, Arthur J. **GA201.K54 2006**
The Power of Projections: How Maps Reflect Global Politics and History. Trade Cloth. Greenwood Publishing Group, Inc. Portsmouth, NH. 2006. 208p. ISBN:0-275-99135-0, ISBN13: 978-0-275-99135-7. Dewey:912. LCCN:2006-001247.
Audience: **l,u,f.**

Liu, Lin & Madej **GA102.4.E4M32 2001**
Cartographic Design Using Arcview GIS. Trade Paper. Thomson Delmar Learning. Albany, NY. 2000. 384p. ISBN:1-56690-187-1, ISBN13: 978-1-56690-187-1. Dewey:526/.0285. LCCN:99-058421.
Audience: **l,u.**

Monmonier, Mark **JK1341.M66 2001**
Bushmanders and Bullwinkles: How Politicians Manipulate Electronic Maps and Census Data to Win Elections. Trade Cloth. University of Chicago Press. Chicago, IL. 2001. 216p. ISBN:0-226-53424-3, ISBN13: 978-0-226-53424-4. Dewey:328.73/073455. LCCN:00-060727.
Audience: **g,l,u,f.** *Choice, 2002.*

Monmonier, Mark **G108.7.M66 1996**
How to Lie with Maps. Ed. 2. Trade Paper. University of Chicago Press. Chicago, IL. 1996. 222p. ISBN:0-226-53421-9, ISBN13: 978-0-226-53421-3. Dewey:910/.0148. LCCN:95-032199.
Audience: **g,l,u,f.**

Monmonier, Mark **PN4888.M37M66 1989**
Maps with the News: The Development of American Journalistic Cartography. Trade Cloth. University of Chicago Press. Chicago, IL. 1989. 348p. ISBN:0-226-53411-1, ISBN13: 978-0-226-53411-4. Dewey:070.4/449912. LCCN:88-023829.
Audience: **g,l,u,f.** *Choice, 1990.*

Monmonier, Mark **GA115.M66 2004**
Rhumb Lines and Map Wars: A Social History of the Mercator Projection. Trade Cloth. University of Chicago Press. Chicago, IL. 2004. 256p. ISBN:0-226-53431-6, ISBN13: 978-0-226-53431-2. Dewey:526/.82. LCCN:2003-027614.
Audience: **g,l,u,f.**

Monmonier, Mark **TK7882.E2**
Spying with Maps: Surveillance Technologies and the Future of Privacy. Trade Paper. University of Chicago Press. Chicago, IL. 2004. 250p. ISBN:0-226-53428-6, ISBN13: 978-0-226-53428-2. Dewey:621.389/28.
Audience: **g,l,u,f.**

Monmonier, Mark S. **G105.M66 2006**
From Squaw Tit to Whorehouse Meadow: How Maps Name, Claim, and Inflame. Trade Cloth. University of Chicago Press. Chicago, IL. 2006. 230p. ISBN:0-226-53465-0, ISBN13: 978-0-226-53465-7. Dewey:910/.01/4. LCCN:2005-014683.
Audience: **g,l,u,f.**

Peterson, M. P. (Editor) **GA102.4.E4 M365**
Maps and the Internet. Trade Paper. Elsevier Science & Technology Books. Saint Louis, MO. 2005. 470p. ISBN:0-08-044944-1, ISBN13: 978-0-08-044944-9. Dewey:526/.0285/4678.
Audience: **g,l,u,f.**

Taylor, D. R. F. (Editor) **GA139.5**
Cybercartography: Theory and Practice. Trade Cloth. Elsevier Science & Technology Books. Saint Louis, MO. 2006. 594p. Modern Cartography Ser. ISBN:0-444-51629-8, ISBN13: 978-0-444-51629-9. Dewey:526/.0285/67.
Audience: **u,f.**

Geographic Information Systems

Bernhardsen, Tor **G70.212.B473 2001**
Geographic Information Systems: An Introduction. Ed. 3. Trade Cloth. John Wiley & Sons, Inc. Hoboken, NJ. 2002. 448p. ISBN:0-471-41968-0, ISBN13: 978-0-471-41968-6. Dewey:910/.285. LCCN:2001-046661.
Audience: **l,u,f.**

Bettinger, Pete & Wing, Michael G. **SD387.R4B48 2004**
Geographic Information Systems: Applications in Forestry and Natural Resources Management. Paper Text. McGraw-Hill Higher Education. Burr Ridge, IL. 2003. 240p. ISBN:0-07-256242-0, ISBN13: 978-0-07-256242-2. Dewey:634.9/028. LCCN:2003-056175.
Audience: **u,f.**

Boots, B. N. (Editor), et al. **G70.212.M59 2002**
Modelling Geographical Systems: Statistical and Computational Applications. Atsuyuki Okabe & Richard Thomas (Editors). Trade Cloth. Springer. New York, NY. 2003. 376p. Geojournal Library, Vol. 70 ISBN:1-4020-0821-X, ISBN13: 978-1-4020-0821-4. Dewey:910/.285. LCCN:2002-031643.
Audience: **u,f.**

Brewer, Cynthia A. **GA105.3B74 2005**
Designing Better Maps: A Guide for GIS Users. Trade Paper. ESRI, Inc. Redlands, CA. 2005. 220p. ISBN:1-58948-089-9, ISBN13: 978-1-58948-089-6. Dewey:526. LCCN:2005-007987.
Audience: **l,u,f.**

Chainey, Spencer & Ratcliffe, Jerry **HV7936.C88C48 2005**
GIS and Crime Mapping. Trade Paper. John Wiley & Sons, Inc. Hoboken, NJ. 2005. 442p. Mastering GIS Ser., :Technol, Applications and Mgmnt Ser. ISBN:0-470-86099-5, ISBN13: 978-0-470-86099-1. Dewey:363.25. LCCN:2004-028500.
Audience: **l,u.**

Chandra, A. M. **G70.4 .C53 2006**
Remote Sensing and Geographic Information System. Trade Cloth. Alpha Science International, Ltd. Oxford, 2005. 250p. ISBN:1-84265-278-8, ISBN13: 978-1-84265-278-7. Dewey:621.3678.
Audience: **l,u.**

Chrisman, Nicholas **TJ163.12**
GIS Technology, Maps, Society. Paper over Boards. Routledge. New York, NY. 2007. 240p. ISBN:0-415-94427-9, ISBN13: 978-0-415-94427-4. Dewey:621.
Audience: **l.**

Clarke, Graham & Stillwell, John (Editors) **G70.212**
Applied GIS and Spatial Analysis. Trade Cloth. John Wiley & Sons, Inc. Hoboken, NJ. 2003. 420p. ISBN:0-470-84409-4, ISBN13: 978-0-470-84409-0. Dewey:910/.285. LCCN:2003-049478.
Audience: **u,f.**

Conolly, James & Lake, Mark **CC79.G46**
Geographical Information Systems in Archaeology. Graeme Barker, Peter Bogucki & Elizabeth Slater (Contribution by). Cloth Text. Cambridge University Press. New York, NY. 2006. 358p. Cambridge Manuals in Archaeology Ser. ISBN:0-521-79330-0, ISBN13: 978-0-521-79330-8. Dewey:930.10285.
Audience: **u,f.**

Davis, David E. **G70.212 .D383**
GIS for Everyone: Exploring Your Neighborhood and Your World with a Geographic I. Library Binding. Sagebrush Education Resources. Caledonia, MN. 2003. ISBN:0-613-91415-5, ISBN13: 978-0-613-91415-4. Dewey:910/.285.
Audience: **g,l,u,f.**

DeMers, Michael N. **G70.212 .D383**
Basics of Geographical Information Systems. Trade Cloth. John Wiley & Sons, Inc. Hoboken, NJ. 2004. 375p. ISBN:0-471-15215-3, ISBN13: 978-0-471-15215-6. Dewey:910.
Audience: **l.**

DeMers, Michael N. **G70.212.D46 2005**
Fundamentals of Geographic Information Systems. Ed. 3. Trade Cloth. John Wiley & Sons, Inc. Hoboken, NJ. 2004. 480p.

ISBN:0-471-20491-9, ISBN13: 978-0-471-20491-6. Dewey:910/.285. LCCN:2004-042236.
Audience: **l.** *Choice, 1997.*

Forer, Pip (Editor), et al. **G70.2**
Advances in GIS Research. Anthony Yeh & Jiangbang He (Editors). Trade Cloth. Springer. New York, NY. 2005. 800p. ISBN:3-540-43456-9, ISBN13: 978-3-540-43456-6. Dewey:025.06/91.
Audience: **u,f.**

Gorr, Wilpen & Kurland, Kristen S. **G70.212G74 2005**
Gis Tutorial: A Workbook for Arcview 9. 0. Spiral. ESRI, Inc. Redlands, CA. 2005. 368p. ISBN:1-58948-127-5, ISBN13: 978-1-58948-127-5. Dewey:910/.285. LCCN:2005-014578.
Audience: **l,u.**

Gregory, Ian N. **D16.117**
A Place in History: A Guide to Using GIS in Historical Research. Trade Paper. Oxbow Books, Ltd. Oxford, 2003. 88p. The Arts and Humanities Data Service Guides to Good Practice Ser. ISBN:1-84217-036-8, ISBN13: 978-1-84217-036-6. Dewey:907.2/3.
Audience: **l,u,f.**

Hall-Wallace, Michelle K., et al. **GB656.2.R34**
Exploring Water Resources: GIS Investigations for the Earth Sciences. Ed. 2. C. Scott Walker, Larry P. Kendall, Anne Huth & Jennifer A. Weeks (Authors). Paper Text. Brooks/Cole. Pacific Grove, CA. 2006. 176p. ISBN:0-495-11512-6, ISBN13: 978-0-495-11512-0. Dewey:551.48/028.
Audience: **u,f.**

Halls, Peter, et al. **GE45**
GIS for Ecologists and Environmental Scientists. Colin McClean & Geraldine Newton-Cross (Authors). Trade Paper. John Wiley & Sons, Inc. Hoboken, NJ. 2006. 320p. ISBN:0-470-84797-2, ISBN13: 978-0-470-84797-8. Dewey:333.70285.
Audience: **u,f.**

Harmon, John E. & Anderson, Steven J. **G70.212.H36 2003**
The Design and Implementation of Geographic Information Systems. Trade Cloth. John Wiley & Sons, Inc. Hoboken, NJ. 2003. 272p. ISBN:0-471-20488-9, ISBN13: 978-0-471-20488-6. Dewey:910/.285. LCCN:2002-032425.
Audience: **l,u,f.**

Harrington, J. W. **G128**
Geography and Technology. Stanley D. Brunn & Susan L. Cutter (Editors). Trade Cloth. Springer. New York, NY. 2004. 649p. ISBN:1-4020-1857-6, ISBN13: 978-1-4020-1857-2. Dewey:910/.0285. LCCN:2003-070348.
Audience: **g,l,u,f.**

Kennedy, Michael **G70.212.K47 2006**
Introducing Geographic Information Systems with ArcGIS. Trade Paper. John Wiley & Sons, Inc. Hoboken, NJ. 2006. 624p. ISBN:0-471-79229-2, ISBN13: 978-0-471-79229-1. Dewey:910.285. LCCN:2006-000886.
Audience: **g,l,u.**

Knowles, Anne Kelly (Editor) **G70.212.P38 2002**
Past Time, Past Place: GIS for History. Trade Paper. ESRI, Inc. Redlands, CA. 2002. 250p. ISBN:1-58948-032-5, ISBN13: 978-1-58948-032-2. Dewey:910/.285. LCCN:2002-002688.
Audience: **l,u,f.** *Choice, 2003.*

Lee, Jay & Wong, David W. S. **G70.212L43 2005**
Statistical Analysis of Geographic Information with ArcView GIS and ArcGIS. Trade Cloth. John Wiley & Sons, Inc. Hoboken, NJ. 2005. 464p. ISBN:0-471-46899-1, ISBN13: 978-0-471-46899-8. Dewey:910/.285. LCCN:2005-005178.
Audience: **u,f.**

LeGates, Richard **HT391.L45 2005**
Thinking Globally, Acting Regionally: GIS and Data Visualization for Social Science and Public Policy Research. Trade Paper. ESRI, Inc. Redlands, CA. 2005. 538p. ISBN:1-58948-124-0, ISBN13: 978-1-58948-124-4. Dewey:307.1/2/0285. LCCN:2005-010160.
Audience: **l,u,f.**

Liu, Lin & Madej **GA102.4.E4M32 2001**
Cartographic Design Using Arcview GIS. Trade Paper. Thomson Delmar Learning. Albany, NY. 2000. 384p. ISBN:1-56690-187-1, ISBN13: 978-1-56690-187-1. Dewey:526/.0285. LCCN:99-058421.
Audience: **l,u.**

Longley, Paul A., et al. **G70.212.G44553 2005**
[e] Geographic Information Systems and Science. Ed. 2. Michael F. Goodchild, David J. Maguire & David W. Rhind (Authors). E-Book. John Wiley & Sons, Inc. Hoboken, NJ. 2006. 536p. ISBN:0-470-87002-8, ISBN13: 978-0-470-87002-0. Dewey:910/.285.
Audience: **l,u,f.**

Longley, Paul A. (Editor), et al. **G70212**
Geographical Information Systems: Principles, Techniques, Management and Applications. Ed. 2. Michael F. Goodchild, David J. Maguire & David W. Rhind (Editors). Trade Paper. John Wiley & Sons, Inc. Hoboken, NJ. 2005. 404p. ISBN:0-471-73545-0, ISBN13: 978-0-471-73545-8. Dewey:910.285. LCCN:2006-295632.
Audience: **l,u,f.**

Maantay, Juliana & Ziegler, John **HT153.M314 2006**
GIS for the Urban Environment. John Pickles (Foreword by). Trade Paper. ESRI, Inc. Redlands, CA. 2006. 600p. ISBN:1-58948-082-1, ISBN13: 978-1-58948-082-7. Dewey:307.760285. LCCN:2006-013778.
Audience: **u,f.**

Malone, Lyn, et al. **G70.212.M2833 2003**
Community Geography: GIS in Action. Anita M. Palmer & Christine Voigt (Authors). Trade Paper. ESRI, Inc. Redlands, CA. 2003. 200p. ISBN:1-58948-051-1, ISBN13: 978-1-58948-051-3. Dewey:910/.285. LCCN:2003-009537.
Audience: **l,u,f.**

Mitchell, Andy **G70.212 .M58 1999**
The ESRI Guide to GIS Analysis: Geographic Patterns and Relationships. Trade Paper. ESRI, Inc. Redlands, CA. 1999. 250p. ISBN:1-879102-06-4, ISBN13: 978-1-879102-06-4. Dewey:910/.285. LCCN:2004-400242.
Audience: **l,u,f.**

Mitchell, Andy **G70.212**
The ESRI Guide to GIS Analysis: Spatial Measurements and Statistics. Trade Paper. ESRI, Inc. Redlands, CA. 2005. 252p. ISBN:1-58948-116-X, ISBN13: 978-1-58948-116-9. Dewey:910.285.
Audience: **l,u,f.**

Ormsby, Tim, et al. **G70.212.G489 2004**
Getting to Know ArcGIS Desktop: The Basics of ArcView, ArcEditor, and ArcInfo Updated for ArcGIS 9. Ed. 2. Eileen Napoleon & Robert Burke (Authors). Trade Paper. ESRI, Inc. Redlands, CA. 2004. 588p. Getting to Know Series Ser. ISBN:1-58948-083-X, ISBN13: 978-1-58948-083-4. Dewey:910/.285/53. LCCN:2004-015629.
Audience: **l,u,f.**

Pamuk, Ayse **HT166.P333 2006**
Mapping Global Cities: GIS Methods in Urban Analysis. Trade Paper. ESRI, Inc. Redlands, CA. 2006. 350p. ISBN:1-58948-143-7, ISBN13: 978-1-58948-143-5. Dewey:307.1/2160285. LCCN:2006-010177.
Audience: **u,f.**

Pick, James B. **HD30.213.G46 2005**
Geographic Information Systems in Business. Trade Paper. Idea Group Publishing. Hershey, PA. 2004. 300p. ISBN:1-59140-400-2, ISBN13: 978-1-59140-400-2. Dewey:910/.285. LCCN:2004-003754.
Audience: **u,f.**

Schuurman, Nadine **G70.212.S38 2003**
Gis: A Short Introduction. Trade Cloth. Blackwell Publishing, Inc. Malden, MA. 2004. 184p. Short Introductions to Geography Ser. ISBN:0-631-23532-9, ISBN13: 978-0-631-23532-3. Dewey:910/.285. LCCN:2003-005917.
Audience: **g,l,u,f.** *Choice, 2005.*

Stefanakis, Emmanuel
Geographic Databases and GIS. Trade Cloth. Springer. New York, NY. 2006. 400p. ISBN:3-540-22491-2, ISBN13: 978-3-540-22491-4.
Audience: **l,u,f.**

Steinberg, Steven J. & Steinberg, Sheila L. **H62.S7542 2006**
Geographic Information Systems for the Social Sciences: Investigating Space and Place. Cloth Text. SAGE Publications, Inc. Thousand Oaks, CA. 2005. 272p. ISBN:0-7619-2872-3, ISBN13: 978-0-7619-2872-0. Dewey:300/.285. LCCN:2005-007114.
Audience: **l,u,f.**

United Nations, Statistical Division Staff (Contribution by) **HA31.25 .H36 2000**
Handbook on Geographic Information Systems and Digital Mapping. Trade Paper. United Nations Publications. New York, NY. 2005. 208p. Studies in Methods, No. 79 ISBN:92-1-161426-0, ISBN13: 978-92-1-161426-8. Dewey:1.433. LCCN:2001-335487.
Audience: **l,u,f.**

Wilson, John & Fotheringham, Stewart (Editors) **G70.2**
Handbook of Geographic Information Science. Trade Paper. Blackwell Publishing, Inc. Malden, MA. 2007. 496p. ISBN:1-4051-0796-0, ISBN13: 978-1-4051-0796-9. Dewey:910.285.
Audience: **l,u,f.**

Wilson, John & Fotheringham, Stewart (Editors) **G70.2**
The Handbook of Geographical Information Science. Trade Cloth. Blackwell Publishing, Inc. Malden, MA. 2007. 496p. ISBN:1-4051-0795-2, ISBN13: 978-1-4051-0795-2. Dewey:910.285.
Audience: **l,u,f.**

Remote Sensing

Arnold, Robert H. **TR810**
Interpretation of Airphotos and Remotely Sensed Imagery. Spiral. Waveland Press, Inc. Prospect Heights, IL. 2004. 250p. ISBN:1-57766-353-5, ISBN13: 978-1-57766-353-9. Dewey:778.3/5/078.
Audience: **l,u,f.**

Campbell, James B. **G70.4.C23 2002**
Introduction to Remote Sensing. Ed. 3. Cloth over Boards. Guilford Publications, Inc. New York, NY. 2002. 621p. ISBN:1-57230-640-8, ISBN13: 978-1-57230-640-0. Dewey:621.36/78. LCCN:2001-058581.
Audience: **l,u,f.** *Choice, 1997.*

Chandra, A. M. **G70.4 .C53 2006**
Remote Sensing and Geographic Information System. Trade Cloth. Alpha Science International, Ltd. Oxford, 2005. 250p. ISBN:1-84265-278-8, ISBN13: 978-1-84265-278-7. Dewey:621.3678.
Audience: **l,u.**

Ehlers, Manfred & Michel, Ulrich **GE45.R44S65 2003**
Remote Sensing for Environmental Monitoring, GIS Applications, and Geology III. Trade Paper. S P I E-International Society for Optical Engineering. Bellingham, WA. 2004. 562p. Proceedings of SPIE Ser. ISBN:0-8194-5122-3, ISBN13: 978-0-8194-5122-4. Dewey:621.36/78. LCCN:2004-302624.
Audience: **u,f.**

Frouin, Robert J., et al. **GC10.4.R4O265 2003**
Ocean Remote Sensing and Imaging, II. Gary D. Gilbert & Delu Pan (Authors). Trade Paper. S P I E-International Society for Optical Engineering. Bellingham, WA. 2003. viii, 260p. ISBN:0-8194-5028-6, ISBN13: 978-0-8194-5028-9. Dewey:551.46. LCCN:2004-270694.
Audience: **u,f.**

Gupta, R. P. **QE33.2.R4G86 1990**
Remote Sensing Geology. Ed. 2. Cloth Text. Springer. New York, NY. 2002. 655p. ISBN:0-387-52805-9, ISBN13: 978-0-387-52805-2. Dewey:550/.28. LCCN:90-010309.
Audience: **u,f.**

Jong, Steven M. de & Meer, Freek D. van der (Editors) **G70.4 .J66 2004**
Remote Sensing Image Analysis: Including the Spatial Domain. Mixed Media. Springer. New York, NY. 2006. XV, 359p. ISBN:1-4020-2559-9, ISBN13: 978-1-4020-2559-4. Dewey:621.3678.
Audience: **u,f.**

Lillesand, Thomas M., et al. **G70.4.L54 2003**
Remote Sensing and Image Interpretation. Ed. 5. Jonathan W. Chipman & Ralph W. Kiefer (Authors). Trade Cloth. John Wiley

& Sons, Inc. Hoboken, NJ. 2003. 784p. ISBN:0-471-15227-7, ISBN13: 978-0-471-15227-9. Dewey:621.36/78. LCCN:2004-270046.
Audience: **u,f.**

Malthus, T. J. **QE33.2**
Environmental Remote Sensing. Trade Paper. John Wiley & Sons, Inc. Hoboken, NJ. 2004. 224p. Modules in Environmental Science Ser. ISBN:0-471-98566-X, ISBN13: 978-0-471-98566-2. Dewey:550/.28.
Audience: **u,f.**

Martin, Seelye **GC10.4.R4M375 2004**
An Introduction to Ocean Remote Sensing. Cloth Text. Cambridge University Press. New York, NY. 2004. 454p. ISBN:0-521-80280-6, ISBN13: 978-0-521-80280-2. Dewey:551.46/028. LCCN:2003-061380.
Audience: **u,f.** *Choice, 2005.*

Mather, Paul M. **G70.4.M38 2004**
Computer Processing of Remotely-Sensed Images: An Introduction. Ed. 3. Trade Cloth. John Wiley & Sons, Inc. Hoboken, NJ. 2004. 442p. ISBN:0-470-84918-5, ISBN13: 978-0-470-84918-7. Dewey:621.36/78. LCCN:2004-005079.
Audience: **u,f.**

McCoy, Roger M. **G70.4.M39 2005**
Field Methods in Remote Sensing. Cloth over Boards. Guilford Publications, Inc. New York, NY. 2004. 159p. ISBN:1-59385-080-8, ISBN13: 978-1-59385-080-7. Dewey:526. LCCN:2004-019785.
Audience: **u,f.**

Richards, John A. & Jia, Xiuping **G70.4**
Remote Sensing Digital Image Analysis: An Introduction. Ed. 4. Trade Cloth. Springer. New York, NY. 2005. XXV, 439p. ISBN:3-540-25128-6, ISBN13: 978-3-540-25128-6. Dewey:621.3678. LCCN:2005-926341.
Audience: **u,f.**

Stein, Alfred (Editor), et al. **G70.4**
Spatial Statistics for Remote Sensing. Freek D. Van der Meer & Ben Gorte (Editors). Trade Paper. Springer. New York, NY. 2002. 300p. Remote Sensing and Digital Image Processing Ser. ISBN:1-4020-0551-2, ISBN13: 978-1-4020-0551-0. Dewey:621.36/78.
Audience: **u,f.**

Ustin, Susan L. **TK8315**
Remote Sensing for Natural Resource Management and Environmental Monitoring, Vol. 4. Ed. 3. Trade Cloth. John Wiley & Sons, Inc. Hoboken, NJ. 2004. 768p. Manual of Remote Sensing - Third Edition Ser., Vol. 4 ISBN:0-471-31793-4, ISBN13: 978-0-471-31793-7. Dewey:621.3/678. LCCN:2004-295308.
Audience: **u,f.**

Surveying

Ariel, Avraham & Berger, Nora Ariel **QB207**
Plotting the Globe: Stories of Meridians, Parallels, and the International Date Line. Trade Cloth. Greenwood Publishing Group, Inc. Portsmouth, NH. 2005. 248p. Explorations in World Maritime History Ser. ISBN:0-275-98895-3, ISBN13: 978-0-275-98895-1. Dewey:526/.6. LCCN:2005-019178.
Audience: **g,l,u,f.** *Choice, 2006.*

Fischer, Irene **QB280.5**
Geodesy? What's That?: My Personal Involvement in the Age-Old Quest for the Size and Shape of the Earth. Trade Paper. iUniverse, Inc. Lincoln, NE. 2005. 397p. ISBN:0-595-36399-7, ISBN13: 978-0-595-36399-5. Dewey:526.30944.
Audience: **u,f.**

Ghilani, Chuck, et al. **TA545**
Elementary Surveying: An Introduction to Geomatics. Ed. 11. Paul Wolf, Dave Taylor & Virgina Rometty (Authors). Trade Cloth. Prentice Hall PTR. Upper Saddle River, NJ. 2005. 944p. ISBN:0-13-148189-4, ISBN13: 978-0-13-148189-3. Dewey:526.9.
Audience: **u,f.**

Hoare, Michael Rand **QB281.H53 2004**
The Quest for the True Figure of the Earth: Ideas and Expeditions in Four Centuries of Geodesy. Trade Cloth. Ashgate Publishing Company. Williston, VT. 2005. 288p. Science, Technology, and Culture, 1700-1945 Ser. ISBN:0-7546-5020-0, ISBN13: 978-0-7546-5020-1. Dewey:526/.1/09. LCCN:2004-026903.
Audience: **l,u,f.**

Hofmann-Wellenhof, Bernhard, et al. **QB281.H545 2005**
Physical Geodesy. Ed. 2. Norbert Kuhtreiber & Helmut Moritz (Authors). Trade Paper. Springer. New York, NY. 2005. XVII, 403p. ISBN:3-211-23584-1, ISBN13: 978-3-211-23584-3. Dewey:526/.1. LCCN:2005-925135.
Audience: **u,f.**

Kavanagh, Barry F. **TA545.K368 2003**
Geomatics. Trade Cloth. Prentice Hall PTR. Upper Saddle River, NJ. 2002. 589p. ISBN:0-13-032289-X, ISBN13: 978-0-13-032289-0. Dewey:526.9. LCCN:2002-019752.
Audience: **l,u,f.**

Kavanagh, Barry F. **TA545.K37 2006**
Surveying: Principles and Applications. Ed. 7. Trade Cloth. Prentice Hall PTR. Upper Saddle River, NJ. 2005. 816p. ISBN:0-13-118862-3, ISBN13: 978-0-13-118862-4. Dewey:526.9. LCCN:2004-062470.
Audience: **u,f.**

McCormac, Jack C. **TA545.M17 2004**
Surveying. Ed. 5. Trade Cloth. John Wiley & Sons, Inc. Hoboken, NJ. 2003. 480p. ISBN:0-471-23758-2, ISBN13: 978-0-471-23758-7. Dewey:526.9. LCCN:2004-268944.
Audience: **u,f.**

Global Positioning Systems

Cooke, Donald **G109.5.C645 2005**
Fun with GPS. Trade Paper, Perfect. ESRI, Inc. Redlands, CA. 2005. 160p. ISBN:1-58948-087-2, ISBN13: 978-1-58948-087-2. Dewey:910/.285. LCCN:2004-029575.
Audience: **g,l.**

El-Rabbany, Ahmed **G109.5.E6 2002**
Introduction to GPS: The Global Positioning System.

E-Book. Artech House, Inc. Norwood, MA. 2002. 196p. ISBN:1-58053-547-X, ISBN13: 978-1-58053-547-2. Dewey:910/.285.
Audience: **l,u.**

Featherstone, Steve **GV191.623.F43 2004**
Outdoor Guide to Using Your GPS. Trade Paper. Quayside. Chanhassen, MN. 2004. 192p. ISBN:1-58923-145-7, ISBN13: 978-1-58923-145-0. Dewey:910/.285. LCCN:2004-004623.
Audience: **l,u,f.**

Grubbs, Bruce **G109.5.G78 2005**
Basic Essentials Using GPS. Ed. 2. Trade Paper, Perfect. Globe Pequot Press, The. Guilford, CT. 2005. 80p. Basic Essentials Ser. ISBN:0-7627-3421-3, ISBN13: 978-0-7627-3421-4. Dewey:910/.285. LCCN:2005-040339.
Audience: **l,u.**

Kaplan, Elliott D. (Author, Editor) **G109.5.K36 2006**
Understanding GPS: Principles and Applications. Ed. 2. Christopher Hegarty (Editor). Trade Cloth. Artech House, Inc. Norwood, MA. 2005. 726p. Artech House Mobile Communications Ser. ISBN:1-58053-894-0, ISBN13: 978-1-58053-894-7. Dewey:623.89/3. LCCN:2005-056270.
Audience: **l,u,f.**

Leick, Alfred **TA595.5**
GPS Satellite Surveying. Ed. 3. Trade Cloth. John Wiley & Sons, Inc. Hoboken, NJ. 2003. 464p. ISBN:0-471-05930-7, ISBN13: 978-0-471-05930-1. Dewey:526.9/82. LCCN:2003-049651.
Audience: **l,u,f.**

Spencer, John, et al. **G109.5.G56 2003**
Global Positioning System: A Field Guide for the Social Sciences. Brian Frizzelle, Philip Page & John Vogler (Authors). Trade Paper. Blackwell Publishing, Inc. Malden, MA. 2003. 232p. ISBN:1-4051-0185-7, ISBN13: 978-1-4051-0185-1. Dewey:910/.285. LCCN:2002-152561.
Audience: **l,u,f.** *Choice, 2004.*

Physical Geography > Geology

Chernicoff, Stanley & Whitney, Donna **QE28.2.C48 2002**
Geology: An Introduction to Physical Geology. Ed. 3. Paper Text. Houghton Mifflin College Division. Boston, MA. 2001. xxiv, 648p. ISBN:0-618-11815-2, ISBN13: 978-0-618-11815-1. Dewey:551. LCCN:2001-131484.
Audience: **l.**

Hamblin, W. Kenneth & Christiansen, Eric H. **QE28.2**
Earth's Dynamic Systems. Ed. 10. Trade Paper. Prentice Hall PTR. Upper Saddle River, NJ. 2003. 816p. ISBN:0-13-142066-6, ISBN13: 978-0-13-142066-3. Dewey:550. LCCN:2003-054839.
Audience: **l,u.**

Plummer, Charles C., et al. **QE28.2.P58 2007**
Physical Geology. Ed. 11. Diane H. Carlson & David McGeary (Authors). Trade Cloth. McGraw-Hill Companies, The. New York, NY. 2005. xxi, 617p. ISBN:0-07-282692-4, ISBN13: 978-0-07-282692-0. Dewey:550. LCCN:2005-024100.
Audience: **l.**

Physical Geography > Topography

TA545
Geodetic and Topographic Surveying. Library Binding. Gordon Press Publishers. New York, NY. 1991. ISBN:0-8490-4122-8, ISBN13: 978-0-8490-4122-8. Dewey:526.9.
Audience: **u,f.**

American Society of Civil Engineers Staff **TA590.T699 2000**
Topographic Surveying. Trade Cloth. American Society of Civil Engineers. Reston, VA. 1999. 104p. Technical Engineering and Design Guides as Adapted from the U. S. Army Corps of Engineers Ser., No. 29 ISBN:0-7844-0374-0, ISBN13: 978-0-7844-0374-7. Dewey:526.9/8. LCCN:99-049722.
Audience: **l,u,f.**

Bohme, R. (Compiled by) **Z6028; GA300**
Inventory of World Topographic Mapping: The International Cartographic Association. Trade Cloth. Elsevier Science & Technology Books. Saint Louis, MO. 1993. 1186p. ISBN:0-08-042414-7, ISBN13: 978-0-08-042414-9. Dewey:16.912.
Audience: **g,l,u,f.**

Hranicky, W. Jack **GA105.3**
Using USGS Topographic Maps, Vol. 20. Trade Paper. Archeological Society of Virginia Press of The Archeological Society of Virginia. Richmond, VA. 1990. 80p. ISBN:1-884626-18-1, ISBN13: 978-1-884626-18-0. Dewey:912.014.
Audience: **l,u.**

Mahaney, Ian F. **GA130.M365 2007**
Reading Topographic Maps. Library Binding. Rosen Publishing Group, Incorporated, The. New York, NY. 2007. ISBN:1-4042-3454-3, ISBN13: 978-1-4042-3454-3. Dewey:912/.014. LCCN:2005-026344.
Audience: **g,l,u,f.**

Salisbury, Rollin D. **GA0151**
The Interpretation of Topographic Maps: A Laboratory Manual for Use in Connection with the Topographic Maps of the United States Geological Survey. to Accompany Courses in Physiography. Trade Paper. Books on Demand. Ann Arbor, MI. 72p. ISBN:0-598-63131-3, ISBN13: 978-0-598-63131-2. Dewey:912. LCCN:22-011683.
Audience: **g,l,u,f.**

Physical Geography > Geomorphology

Burt, T. **GB400.4**
Geomorphological Techniques. Ed. 3. Trade Cloth. Routledge. New York, NY. 2006. 576p. ISBN:0-415-34187-6, ISBN13: 978-0-415-34187-5. Dewey:551.4/072.
Audience: **u,f.**

Evans, David J. A. (Editor) **GB401.5**
Geomorphology: Critical Concepts in Geography. Paper over Boards. Routledge. New York, NY. 2004. 2800p. Critical Concepts Ser. ISBN:0-415-27608-X, ISBN13: 978-0-415-27608-5. Dewey:551.41. LCCN:2003-069539.
Audience: **l,u,f.**

Evans, David J. A. **GB401.5**
Geomorphology, Vol. 3. Paper over Boards. Routledge. New York, NY. 2004. 584p. Critical Concepts in Geography Ser. ISBN:0-415-27611-X, ISBN13: 978-0-415-27611-5. Dewey:551.41. LCCN:2003-069539.
Audience: **u,f.**

Ford, Derek C. & Williams, Paul **GB600 .F66**
Karst Hydrogeology and Geomorphology. Trade Cloth. John Wiley & Sons, Inc. Hoboken, NJ. 2007. 568p. ISBN:0-470-84996-7, ISBN13: 978-0-470-84996-5. Dewey:551.44/7. LCCN:2006-029323.
Audience: **g,l,u,f.**

Goudie, Andrew (Editor) **GB400.3.E53 2003**
Encyclopedia of Geomorphology. Mario Panizza (Foreword by). Paper over Boards. Routledge. New York, NY. 2003. 1200p. ISBN:0-415-27298-X, ISBN13: 978-0-415-27298-8. Dewey:551.41/03. LCCN:2005-440494.
Audience: **l,u,f.** *Choice, 2004.*

Gutierrez Elorza, M. **GB447.G88 2005**
Climatic Geomorphology. Trade Paper. Elsevier Science & Technology Books. Saint Louis, MO. 2005. 774p. Developments in Earth Surface Processes Ser. ISBN:0-444-52128-3, ISBN13: 978-0-444-52128-6. Dewey:551.41.
Audience: **u,f.**

Hubbard, Bryn & Glasser, Neil F. **GB2402.3.H64 2005**
Field Techniques in Glaciology and Glacial Geomorphology. Trade Paper, Perfect. John Wiley & Sons, Inc. Hoboken, NJ. 2005. 412p. ISBN:0-470-84427-2, ISBN13: 978-0-470-84427-4. Dewey:551.31/072/3. LCCN:2004-028501.
Audience: **u,f.**

Kondolf, G. Mathias & Piégay, Hervé (Editors) **GB562.T66 2003**
[e] Tools in Fluvial Geomorphology. E-Book. John Wiley & Sons, Inc. Hoboken, NJ. 2005. 696p. ISBN:0-470-86832-5, ISBN13: 978-0-470-86832-4. Dewey:551.3/5.
Audience: **u,f.**

Owens, Philip N. & Slaymaker, Olav **GB501.2**
Mountain Geomorphology. Trade Paper, Perfect. Oxford University Press, Inc. New York, NY. 2004. 313p. A Hodder Arnold Publication ISBN:0-340-76417-1, ISBN13: 978-0-340-76417-6. Dewey:551.43/2. LCCN:2004-463410.
Audience: **u,f.** *Choice, 2005.*

Thornbury, William D. **QE601**
Principles of Geomorphology. Paper Text. Textbook Publishers. Temecula, CA. 2003. 618p. ISBN:0-7581-0453-7, ISBN13: 978-0-7581-0453-3. Dewey:551.4.
Audience: **g,l,u,f.** B

Physical Geography > Hydrology

Bennett, Sean J. & Simon, Andrew **GB562.R56 2004**
Riparian Vegetation and Fluvial Geomorphology. Trade Cloth. American Geophysical Union. Washington, DC. 2004. viii, 282p. Water Science and Application Ser., Vol. 8 ISBN:0-87590-357-6, ISBN13: 978-0-87590-357-6. Dewey:551.44/2. LCCN:2004-043683.
Audience: **u,f.**

Brinkworth, Brian **QH541.5.C7B75 2006**
Life in a Coral Reef. Library Binding. Rosen Publishing Group, Incorporated, The. New York, NY. 2006. 16p. ISBN:1-4042-3342-3, ISBN13: 978-1-4042-3342-3. Dewey:578.77/89. LCCN:2005-011882.
Audience: **u,f.**

Bronmark, Christer & Hansson, Lars-Anders **QH96.B724 2005**
Biology of Lakes and Ponds. Ed. 2. Trade Cloth. Oxford University Press, Inc. New York, NY. 2005. 300p. Biology of Habitats Ser. ISBN:0-19-851612-6, ISBN13: 978-0-19-851612-5. Dewey:577.63. LCCN:2004-025884.
Audience: **u,f.**

Brown, Antony & Quine, Timothy **GB1201.2.F59 1999**
Fluvial Processes and Environmental Change. Trade Cloth. John Wiley & Sons, Inc. Hoboken, NJ. 1999. 426p. British Geomorphological Research Group Symposia Ser. ISBN:0-471-98548-1, ISBN13: 978-0-471-98548-8. Dewey:551.48/3. LCCN:98-037167.
Audience: **u,f.**

Cote, Isabelle & Reynolds, John (Editors) **QH75**
Coral Reef Conservation. Guy Cowlishaw, Rosie Woodroffe, John Gittleman & Michael Samways (Contribution by). Cloth Text. Cambridge University Press. New York, NY. 2006. 588p. Conservation Biology Ser. ISBN:0-521-85536-5, ISBN13: 978-0-521-85536-5. Dewey:578.7789.
Audience: **u,f.**

Davis, Richard A. & FitzGerald, Duncan **GB451.2.D385 2003**
Beaches and Coasts. Trade Cloth. Blackwell Publishing, Inc. Malden, MA. 2003. 448p. ISBN:0-632-04308-3, ISBN13: 978-0-632-04308-8. Dewey:551.45/7. LCCN:2002-151119.
Audience: **l,u,f.** *Choice, 2004.*

Day, Trevor **GC21.5.D385 2003**
Exploring the Ocean: The Physical Ocean; Life in the Ocean; Uses of the Ocean; Index. Trade Cloth. Oxford University Press, Inc. New York, NY. 2003. 256p. ISBN:0-19-515738-9, ISBN13: 978-0-19-515738-3. Dewey:551.46. LCCN:2002-042583.
Audience: **l,u,f.**

Dodson, Stanley I. **GB1603.2.D63 2005**
Introduction to Limnology. Cloth Text. McGraw-Hill Higher Education. Burr Ridge, IL. 2004. 416p. ISBN:0-07-287935-1, ISBN13: 978-0-07-287935-3. Dewey:551.48. LCCN:2003-060397.
Audience: **u,f.**

Dyer, Keith R. **GC97.D93 1997**
Estuaries: A Physical Introduction. Ed. 2. Trade Cloth. John Wiley & Sons, Inc. Hoboken, NJ. 2002. 210p. ISBN:0-471-97470-6, ISBN13: 978-0-471-97470-3. Dewey:551.4/609. LCCN:97-014903.
Audience: **u,f.** B

Ferguson, Charlene **QH541.5.C7A74 2005**
Are the World's Coral Reefs Threatened? Trade Paper. Thomson Gale. Farmington Hills, MI. 2005. 110p. ISBN:0-7377-2698-9, ISBN13: 978-0-7377-2698-5. Dewey:333.95/22. LCCN:2004-053918.
Audience: **l,u,f.**

Follows, Mick & Oguz, Temel (Editors) **GC117.C37**
The Ocean Carbon Cycle and Climate: Proceedings of the NATO Asi on Ocean Carbon Cycle and Climate, Ankara, Turkey, from 5 to 16 August 2002. Trade Paper. Springer. New York, NY. 2004. XII, 395p. NATO Science Ser., Vol. 40:Earth and Environmental Sciences 29 ISBN:1-4020-2086-4, ISBN13: 978-1-4020-2086-5. Dewey:551.46/6.
Audience: **u,f.**

Fraser, Lauchlan H. & Keddy, Paul A. (Editors) **QH541.5.M3W67 2005**
The World's Largest Wetlands: Ecology and Conservation. Trade Cloth. Cambridge University Press. New York, NY. 2005. 498p. ISBN:0-521-83404-X, ISBN13: 978-0-521-83404-9. Dewey:577.68. LCCN:2005-296813.
Audience: **u,f.** *Choice, 2006.*

Haslam, S. M. **QH87.3.H38 2003**
[e] Understanding Wetlands: Fen, Bog, and Marsh. E-Book. Taylor & Francis Group. Philadelphia, PA. ISBN:0-203-63418-7, ISBN13: 978-0-203-63418-9. Dewey:577.68.
Audience: **u,f.**

Imberger, Jorg (Editor) **GB1603.2 .P48 1998**
Physical Processes in Lakes and Oceans. Trade Cloth. American Geophysical Union. Washington, DC. 1998. 662p. Coastal and Estuarine Studies, Vol. 54 ISBN:0-87590-268-5, ISBN13: 978-0-87590-268-5. Dewey:551.48/2. LCCN:98-041142.
Audience: **u,f.**

Jochum, Markus & Murtugudde, Raghu (Editors) **GC11.2**
Physical Oceanography: Developments Since 1950. Trade Cloth. Springer. New York, NY. 2006. xii, 250p. ISBN:0-387-30261-1, ISBN13: 978-0-387-30261-4. Dewey:551.46. LCCN:2005-935458.
Audience: **u,f.**

Jumars, Peter A. **QH541.5.S3.J85 1993**
Concepts in Biological Oceanography: An Interdisciplinary Primer. Trade Cloth. Oxford University Press, Inc. New York, NY. 1993. 360p. ISBN:0-19-506732-0, ISBN13: 978-0-19-506732-3. Dewey:574.5/2636. LCCN:92-039069.
Audience: **u,f.** *Choice, 1993.*

Knauss, John A. **GC150.5.K6**
Introduction to Physical Oceanography. Ed. 2. Paper Text. Waveland Press, Inc. Prospect Heights, IL. 2005. 309p. ISBN:1-57766-429-9, ISBN13: 978-1-57766-429-1. Dewey:551.46.
Audience: **l,u.** [BCL3]

Lalli, Carol M. & Parsons, Timothy **QH91.16**
Biological Oceanography: An Introduction. Ed. 2. Paper Text. Elsevier Science & Technology Books. Saint Louis, MO. 1997. 320p. ISBN:0-7506-3384-0, ISBN13: 978-0-7506-3384-0. Dewey:574.92. LCCN:96-042139.
Audience: **u,f.** *Choice, 1994.*

Majumdar, Shyamal K. (Editor), et al. **GC150.5.O24 1994**
The Oceans: Physical-Chemical Dynamics and Human Impact. G. S. Miller, E. W. Miller, Robert F. Schmalz, G. S. Forbes & A. A. Panah (Editors). Trade Cloth. Pennsylvania Academy of Science. Easton, PA. 1994. x, 498p. ISBN:0-945809-10-7, ISBN13: 978-0-945809-10-4. Dewey:551.46. LCCN:94-067523.
Audience: **u,f.**

Miller, Charles B. **QH541.5.S3M55 2003**
Biological Oceanography. Trade Paper. Blackwell Publishing, Inc. Malden, MA. 2003. 416p. ISBN:0-632-05536-7, ISBN13: 978-0-632-05536-4. Dewey:577.7. LCCN:2003-004622.
Audience: **u,f.** *Choice, 2004.*

Mills, Eric L. **QH91.25.M55 1989**
Biological Oceanography: An Early History, Eighteen Seventy to Nineteen Sixty. Book, Other. Cornell University Press. Ithaca, NY. 1989. 368p. A Comstock Bk. ISBN:0-8014-2340-6, ISBN13: 978-0-8014-2340-6. Dewey:574.92/09. LCCN:89-033048.
Audience: **u,f.** *Choice, 1990.*

National Geographic Society Staff **G9096.C22**
National Geographic World Physical/Ocean Floor. Trade Paper. MapQuest.com, Inc. Mountville, PA. 1998. ISBN:1-57262-332-2, ISBN13: 978-1-57262-332-3. Dewey:551.46084.
Audience: **g,l,u,f.**

Nordstrom, Karl F. (Author, Editor) **GC0097.E79**
Estuarine Shores: Evolution, Environments, and Human Alterations. Charles T. Roman (Editor). Trade Paper. Books on Demand. Ann Arbor, MI. 510p. ISBN:0-598-00289-8, ISBN13: 978-0-598-00289-1. Dewey:574.5/26365. LCCN:96-012984.
Audience: **u,f.** *Choice, 1998.*

Postma, G. & Oti, M. N. **GB591 .G46**
Geology of Deltas. Paper over Boards. Taylor & Francis Group. Abingdon, 1995. 322p. ISBN:90-5410-614-X, ISBN13: 978-90-5410-614-2. Dewey:551.456.
Audience: **u,f.**

Pye, K. & Allen, J. R. L. (Editors) **GB450**
Coastal and Estuarine Environments: Sedimentology, Geomorphology and Geoarchaeology. Trade Cloth. Geological Society Publishing House. Bath, 2000. 470p. Special Publication Ser., No. 175 ISBN:1-86239-070-3, ISBN13: 978-1-86239-070-6. Dewey:551.4/57.
Audience: **u,f.**

Robinson, Allan R. & Brink, Kenneth H. **GC11.S4**
The Global Coastal Ocean: Interdisciplinary Regional Studies and Syntheses. Trade Cloth. Harvard University Press. Cambridge, MA. 2006. 840p. The Sea Ser. ISBN:0-674-01527-4, ISBN13: 978-0-674-01527-2. Dewey:551.46.
Audience: **u,f.**

Rothschild, Bruce J. (Editor) **QH541.5.S3 N375 1987**
Toward a Theory on Biological-Physical Interactions in the World Ocean. Trade Cloth. Springer London, Ltd. Guildford,

1988. 658p. NATO Science Series C ISBN:90-277-2765-1, ISBN13: 978-90-277-2765-7. Dewey:574.5/2636. LCCN:88-008950.

Audience: **u,f.**

Sale, Peter F. (Editor) **QL620.45.C67 2002**
Coral Reef Fishes: Dynamics and Diversity in a Complex Ecosystem. Ed. 2. Cloth Text. Elsevier Science & Technology Books. Saint Louis, MO. 2002. 549p. ISBN:0-12-615185-7, ISBN13: 978-0-12-615185-5. Dewey:597.177/89. LCCN:2001-096577.

Audience: **u,f.**

Sarmiento, Jorge Louis & Gruber, Nicolas **GC116S27 2006**
Ocean Biogeochemical Dynamics. Trade Cloth. Princeton University Press. Princeton, NJ. 2006. 464p. ISBN:0-691-01707-7, ISBN13: 978-0-691-01707-5. Dewey:551.46/6. LCCN:2005-050465.

Audience: **u,f.**

Somervill, Barbara A. **QH96.S66 2004**
Rivers, Streams, Lakes, and Ponds. Trade Cloth. Tradition Publishing Company. Maple Plain, MN. 2004. ISBN:1-59187-047-X, ISBN13: 978-1-59187-047-0. Dewey:577.6. LCCN:2004-009384.

Audience: **l,u,f.**

Spalding, Mark **QH541.5.C7**
Reefs at Risk: A Map-Based Indicator of Threats to the World's Coral Reefs. Library Binding. Sagebrush Education Resources. Caledonia, MN. 2002. ISBN:0-613-92367-7, ISBN13: 978-0-613-92367-5. Dewey:577.789.

Audience: **l,u,f.**

Spalding, Mark D., et al. **GB461 .S72 2001**
World Atlas of Coral Reefs. Edmund P. Green & Corinna Ravilious (Authors). Trade Cloth. University of California Press. Berkeley, CA. 2001. 424p. ISBN:0-520-23255-0, ISBN13: 978-0-520-23255-6. Dewey:577.7/89/0223. LCCN:2001-018243.

Audience: **g,l,u,f.** *Choice, 2002.*

Spray, Sharon L. **QH541.5.M3W4655 2003**
Wetlands. Karen L. McGlothlin (Editor). Book, Other. Rowman & Littlefield Publishers, Inc. Lanham, MD. 2004. 216p. Exploring Environmental Challenges Ser. ISBN:0-7425-2568-6, ISBN13: 978-0-7425-2568-9. Dewey:333.91/816. LCCN:2003-020408.

Audience: **u,f.** *Choice, 2004.*

Tiner, Ralph W. **QH104.5.N58**
In Search of Swampland: A Wetland Sourcebook and Field Guide. Ed. 2. Trade Paper. Rutgers University Press. Piscataway, NJ. 2005. 336p. ISBN:0-8135-3681-2, ISBN13: 978-0-8135-3681-1. Dewey:578.768/0974.

Audience: **u,f.**

Valk, Arnoud van der **QH541.5.M3**
The Biology of Freshwater Wetlands. Trade Cloth. Oxford University Press, Inc. New York, NY. 2006. 192p. Biology of Habitats Ser. ISBN:0-19-852539-7, ISBN13: 978-0-19-852539-4. Dewey:577.68. LCCN:2005-026314.

Audience: **u,f.**

Wangersky, Peter J. (Volume Editor) **QD31.H335**
Estuaries, Vol. 5, Pts. H. Mixed Media. Springer. New York, NY. 2006. XVI, 305p. ISBN:3-540-00270-7, ISBN13: 978-3-540-00270-3. Dewey:628.168. LCCN:90-009690.

Audience: **u,f.**

Wangersky, Peter J. (Editor) **QD31.H335 VOL.5**
Marine Chemistry. Trade Cloth. Springer. New York, NY. 2000. XIV, 230p. The Handbook of Environmental Chemistry Ser., Vol. 5 ISBN:3-540-66020-8, ISBN13: 978-3-540-66020-0. Dewey:628.168. LCCN:90-009690.

Audience: **u,f.**

Woodroffe, Colin D. **GB451.2.W65 2002**
Coasts: Form, Process and Evolution. Cloth Text. Cambridge University Press. New York, NY. 2002. 638p. ISBN:0-521-81254-2, ISBN13: 978-0-521-81254-2. Dewey:551.45/7. LCCN:2002-017418.

Audience: **u,f.**

Wright, Dawn J. & Bartlett, Darius J. **GC10.4.R4M37 2000**
[e] Marine and Coastal Geographical Information Systems. E-Book. NetLibrary, Inc. Boulder, CO. 2000. ISBN:0-585-45559-7, ISBN13: 978-0-585-45559-4. Dewey:551.46/0028.

Audience: **u,f.**

Physical Geography > Climatology

ACIA - Arctic Climate Impact Assessment **QC994.8.A695 2005**
Arctic Climate Impact Assessment - Scientific Report. Trade Cloth. Cambridge University Press. New York, NY. 2005. 1046p. ISBN:0-521-86509-3, ISBN13: 978-0-521-86509-8. Dewey:551.690911/3. LCCN:2006-272652.

Audience: **u,f.**

Ahrens, C. Donald **QC861.2.A3**
Meteorology Today. Ed. 8. Cloth Text. Brooks/Cole. Pacific Grove, CA. 2006. 608p. ISBN:0-495-11005-1, ISBN13: 978-0-495-11005-7. Dewey:551.5.

Audience: **l,u,f.**

Carbone, Greg **N**
Exercises for Weather and Climate. Ed. 6. Trade Paper. Pearson Education. Boston, MA. 2006. 224p. ISBN:0-13-149701-4, ISBN13: 978-0-13-149701-6. Dewey:551.6.

Audience: **l.**

Chambers, Frank & Ogle, Michael (Editors) **QC981.8.C5C5185 2002**
Climate Change: Critical Concepts in the Environment and Physical Geography. Paper over Boards. Routledge. New York, NY. 2002. 1600p. Critical Concepts Ser. ISBN:0-415-27656-X, ISBN13: 978-0-415-27656-6. Dewey:551.6. LCCN:2002-075144.

Audience: **l,u,f.**

Grove, Jean M. **QC981.8.I23G76 2004**
Little Ice Ages: Ancient and Modern. Ed. 2. Paper over Boards. Routledge. New York, NY. 2004. 432p. Routledge Studies in Physical Geography and Environment, Vol. 5

ISBN:0-415-33422-5, ISBN13: 978-0-415-33422-8. Dewey:551.6/09. LCCN:2003-016884.
Audience: **g,l,u,f.**

Intergovernmental Panel on Climate Change (Editor) **QC981.8.C5I57 2005**
Safeguarding the Ozone Layer and the Global Climate System: Special Report of the Intergovernmental Panel on Climate Change. Trade Paper. Cambridge University Press. New York, NY. 2005. 486p. ISBN:0-521-68206-1, ISBN13: 978-0-521-68206-0. Dewey:363.73875. LCCN:2006-295591.
Audience: **l,u,f.**

Linden, Eugene **QC981.8.C5L567 2006**
The Winds of Change: Climate, Weather, and the Destruction of Civilizations. Trade Cloth. Simon & Schuster. New York, NY. 2006. 320p. ISBN:0-684-86352-9, ISBN13: 978-0-684-86352-8. Dewey:551.609/01. LCCN:2005-054434.
Audience: **l,u,f.** *Choice, 2006.*

Lovejoy, Thomas E. & Hannah, Lee (Editors) **QC981.8.C5**
Climate Change and Biodiversity. Trade Paper. Yale University Press. Cumberland, RI. 2006. 440p. ISBN:0-300-11980-1, ISBN13: 978-0-300-11980-0. Dewey:577.2/2. LCCN:2004-043536.
Audience: **u,f.** *Choice, 2005.*

Low, Pak Sum (Editor) **QC991.A1**
Climate Change and Africa. Trade Paper. Cambridge University Press. New York, NY. 2006. 411p. ISBN:0-521-02995-3, ISBN13: 978-0-521-02995-7. Dewey:551.696.
Audience: **l,u,f.**

Maury, Matthew Fontaine **GC11.2.M38 2003**
The Physical Geography of the Sea and Its Meteorology. Trade Paper. Dover Publications, Inc. Mineola, NY. 2003. 480p. ISBN:0-486-43248-3, ISBN13: 978-0-486-43248-9. Dewey:551.46. LCCN:2003-055663.
Audience: **l,u,f.**

Pearce, Fred **QC981.8.C5**
With Speed and Violence: Why Scientists Fear Tipping Points in Climate Change. Trade Cloth. Beacon Press. Boston, MA. 2007. 288p. ISBN:0-8070-8576-6, ISBN13: 978-0-8070-8576-9. Dewey:551.6. LCCN:2006-019901.
Audience: **u,f.**

Sinnott-Armstrong, Walter & Howarth, Richard B. (Editors) **GE149**
Perspectives on Climate Change: Science, Economics, Politics, Ethics. Trade Cloth. Elsevier Science & Technology Books. Saint Louis, MO. 2006. 328p. ISBN:0-7623-1271-8, ISBN13: 978-0-7623-1271-9. Dewey:363.73874.
Audience: **u,f.**

Weisse, Ralf & Storch, Hans v.
Marine Climate Change: Ocean Waves, Storms and Surges in the Perspective of Climate Change. Trade Cloth. Springer. New York, NY. 2005. 200p. Springer Praxis Books / Environmental Sciences Ser. ISBN:3-540-25316-5, ISBN13: 978-3-540-25316-7.
Audience: **l,u,f.**

Physical Geography > Biogeography

Coker, Paddy & Ganderton, Paul **QH84.C614 2005**
Environmental Biogeography. Trade Paper. Pearson Education. Boston, MA. 2005. 308p. ISBN:0-582-31829-7, ISBN13: 978-0-582-31829-8. Dewey:577. LCCN:2005-042998.
Audience: **u,f.**

Cox, C. Barry & Moore, Peter D. **QH84.C65 2005**
Biogeography: An Ecological and Evolutionary Approach. Ed. 7. Trade Paper. Blackwell Publishing, Inc. Malden, MA. 2005. 440p. ISBN:1-4051-1898-9, ISBN13: 978-1-4051-1898-9. Dewey:578/.09. LCCN:2004-009770.
Audience: **u,f.**

Leibold, Mathew A. (Editor), et al. **QH541.15.S62M48 2005**
Metacommunities: Spatial Dynamics and Ecological Communities. Marcel Holyoak & Robert D. Holt (Editors). Trade Cloth. University of Chicago Press. Chicago, IL. 2005. 520p. ISBN:0-226-35063-0, ISBN13: 978-0-226-35063-9. Dewey:577. LCCN:2005-002196.
Audience: **u,f.**

Lomolino, Mark V. & Heaney, Lawrence R. **QH84.F76 2004**
Frontiers of Biogeography: New Directions in the Geography of Nature. Trade Cloth. Sinauer Associates, Inc. Sunderland, MA. 2004. 410p. ISBN:0-87893-479-0, ISBN13: 978-0-87893-479-9. Dewey:578/.09. LCCN:2004-021324.
Audience: **u,f.** *Choice, 2005.*

Lomolino, Mark V. (Editor), et al. **QH84.F68 2004**
Foundations of Biogeography: Classic Papers with Commentaries. Dov F. Sax & James H. Brown (Editors). Trade Cloth. University of Chicago Press. Chicago, IL. 2004. 1328p. ISBN:0-226-49236-2, ISBN13: 978-0-226-49236-0. Dewey:578/.09. LCCN:2003-018272.
Audience: **u,f.**

Riddle, Brett R., et al. **QH84.B76 2005**
Biogeography. Ed. 3. James H. Brown & Mark V. Lomolino (Authors). Trade Cloth. Sinauer Associates, Inc. Sunderland, MA. 2005. 560p. ISBN:0-87893-062-0, ISBN13: 978-0-87893-062-3. Dewey:578/.09. LCCN:2005-014443.
Audience: **l,u,f.**

Sax, Dov F. (Editor), et al. **QH353.S29 2005**
Species Invasions: Insights into Ecology, Evolution, and Biogeography. John J. Stachowicz & Steven D. Gaines (Editors). Trade Paper. Sinauer Associates, Inc. Sunderland, MA. 2005. 380p. ISBN:0-87893-811-7, ISBN13: 978-0-87893-811-7. Dewey:577/.18. LCCN:2005-013019.
Audience: **u,f.**

Hazards and Disasters

Alexander, David **GB5014.A46 2000**
Confronting Catastrophe: New Perspectives on Natural Disasters. Paper Text. Oxford University Press, Inc. New York, NY. 2000. 288p. ISBN:0-19-521696-2, ISBN13: 978-0-19-521696-7. Dewey:363.34. LCCN:00-044076.
Audience: **l,u,f.**

Burton, Ian, et al. **GB5014**
The Environment As Hazard. Ed. 2. Robert W. Kates & Gilbert F. White (Authors). Trade Paper. Guilford Publications, Inc. New York, NY. 1993. 290p. ISBN:0-89862-159-3, ISBN13: 978-0-89862-159-4. Dewey:363.3/4. LCCN:92-033125.
Audience: **l,u,f.** B

Glade, T. **QE599.2**
Landslide Hazard and Risk. Thomas Glade, Malcolm G. Anderson & Michael J. Crozier (Editors). Trade Cloth. John Wiley & Sons, Inc. Hoboken, NJ. 2005. 824p. ISBN:0-471-48663-9, ISBN13: 978-0-471-48663-3. Dewey:551.3/07. LCCN:2004-016991.
Audience: **u,f.**

Kates, Robert William **H0031**
Hazard and Choice Perception in Flood Plain Management. Trade Paper. Books on Demand. Ann Arbor, MI. 175p. Department of Geography Research Paper Ser. ISBN:0-598-51904-1, ISBN13: 978-0-598-51904-7. Dewey:627.4. LCCN:62-021379.
Audience: **u,f.**

Smith, Keith **GB5014.S6 2004**
Environmental Hazards: Assessing Risk and Reducing Disaster. Ed. 4. Paper over Boards. Routledge. New York, NY. 2004. 324p. Physical Environment Ser. ISBN:0-415-31803-3, ISBN13: 978-0-415-31803-7. Dewey:363.34. LCCN:2003-021969.
Audience: **l,u,f.** *Choice, 1992.*

Urban Geography

Badcock, Blair **HT371**
Making Sense of Cities. Trade Paper. Oxford University Press, Inc. New York, NY. 2002. 352p. A Hodder Arnold Publication ISBN:0-340-74224-0, ISBN13: 978-0-340-74224-2. Dewey:307.76. LCCN:2003-268506.
Audience: **u,f.**

Conzen, M. R. G. & Conzen, Michael P. **HT371**
Thinking about Urban Form: Papers on Urban Morphology, 1932-1998. Trade Cloth. Peter Lang Publishing, Inc. New York, NY. 2005. 310p. ISBN:3-03-910276-1, ISBN13: 978-3-03-910276-1. Dewey:307.76. LCCN:2004-061562.
Audience: **u,f.**

Hall, Tim **GF125.H35 2006**
Urban Geography. Ed. 3. Trade Paper. Routledge. New York, NY. 2006. XIV, 202p. Routledge Contemporary Human Geography Ser. ISBN:0-415-34446-8, ISBN13: 978-0-415-34446-3. Dewey:910/.9173/2. LCCN:2005-020301.
Audience: **l,u,f.**

Holloway, Julian (Editor), et al. **HT119.C68 2006**
Cosmopolitan Urbanism. Jon Binnie, Craig Young & Steve Millington (Editors). Paper over Boards. Routledge. New York, NY. 2006. XII, 260p. ISBN:0-415-34491-3, ISBN13: 978-0-415-34491-3. Dewey:307.76. LCCN:2005-013886.
Audience: **u,f.**

Kaplan Staff, et al. **GF125.K37 2004**
Wie Urban Geography International Edition. Steven Holloway, Dave H. Kaplan & James O. Wheeler (Authors). Trade Cloth. John Wiley & Sons, Inc. Hoboken, NJ. 2004. 504p. ISBN:0-471-45158-4, ISBN13: 978-0-471-45158-7. Dewey:307.76 T. LCCN:2004-298933.
Audience: **u,f.**

Kenny, Judith T. & Fyfe, Nicholas (Editors) **GF125**
The Urban Geography Reader. Perfect, Paper over Boards. Routledge. New York, NY. 2005. XIV, 410p. Routledge Urban Readers Ser. ISBN:0-415-30701-5, ISBN13: 978-0-415-30701-7. Dewey:307.76. LCCN:2004-018547.
Audience: **l,u,f.**

Neill, William J. V. **HT166.N4218 2004**
Urban Planning and Cultural Identity. Paper over Boards. Routledge. New York, NY. 2003. 272p. The RTPI Library, Vol. 6 ISBN:0-415-19747-3, ISBN13: 978-0-415-19747-2. Dewey:307.1/216. LCCN:2003-008576.
Audience: **u,f.**

Ravetz, Joe, et al. **HT241**
Environment and the City. Joe Howe, Clive George & Peter Roberts (Authors). Cloth Text. Routledge. New York, NY. 2007. 248p. Routledge Introductions to Environment Ser. ISBN:0-415-30246-3, ISBN13: 978-0-415-30246-3. Dewey:307.1/416.
Audience: **l,u,f.**

Short, John Rennie **HT151.S477 1996**
The Urban Order: An Introduction to Urban Geography. Trade Cloth. Blackwell Publishing, Inc. Malden, MA. 1996. 512p. ISBN:1-55786-360-1, ISBN13: 978-1-55786-360-7. Dewey:307.7/6. LCCN:95-000307.
Audience: **l,u,f.**

Rural Geography

Grigg, David B. **S495.G79 1995**
An Introduction to Agricultural Geography. Ed. 2. Trade Paper. Routledge. New York, NY. 1995. 240p. ISBN:0-415-08443-1, ISBN13: 978-0-415-08443-7. Dewey:338.1/09. LCCN:94-012681.
Audience: **u,f.** B

Hart, John Fraser **GF127.H38 1998**
The Rural Landscape. Trade Cloth. Johns Hopkins University Press. Baltimore, MD. 1998. 416p. ISBN:0-8018-5717-1, ISBN13: 978-0-8018-5717-1. Dewey:333.76. LCCN:97-028553.
Audience: **g,l,u,f.** *Choice, 1998.*

Roberts, Brian K. **GF127.R62 1996**
Landscapes of Settlement: Prehistory to the Present. Paper over Boards. Routledge. New York, NY. 1996. 200p. ISBN:0-415-11967-7, ISBN13: 978-0-415-11967-2. Dewey:307.7/2/09. LCCN:95-022435.
Audience: **l,u,f.**

Robinson, G. M. **S494.5.G46R63 2003**
Geographies of Agriculture: Globalisation, Restructuring, and Sustainability. Trade Paper. Pearson Education. Boston, MA. 2003. 352p. ISBN:0-582-35662-8, ISBN13: 978-0-582-35662-7. Dewey:338.1/09. LCCN:2003-049882.
Audience: **u,f.**

Rumney, Thomas A. **Z5074.G45R86 2005**
The Study of Agricultural Geography: A Scholarly Guide and Bibliography. Trade Cloth. Scarecrow Press, Inc. Lanham, MD. 2005. 816p. ISBN:0-8108-5702-2, ISBN13: 978-0-8108-5702-5. Dewey:016.63/09. LCCN:2005-019598.
Audience: **u,f.**

Woods, Michael **HN49.C6**
Rural Geography: Processes, Responses and Experiences in Rural Restructuring. Paper Text. SAGE Publications, Inc. Thousand Oaks, CA. 2005. 352p. ISBN:0-7619-4761-2, ISBN13: 978-0-7619-4761-5. Dewey:333.7615091722. LCCN:2004-095884.
Audience: **u,f.**

Human Geography > General

Anderson, Timothy **GF41**
Introduction to Human Geography: A World-Systems Approach. Trade Paper. Kendall/Hunt Publishing Company. Dubuque, IA. 2005. 118p. ISBN:0-7575-2076-6, ISBN13: 978-0-7575-2076-1. Dewey:304.2.
Audience: **l,u,f.**

Blij, H. J. de, et al. **GF41.D4 2006**
Human Geography: People, Place, and Culture. Ed. 8. Alexander B. Murphy & Erin Fouberg (Authors). Trade Cloth. John Wiley & Sons, Inc. Hoboken, NJ. 2006. 528p. ISBN:0-471-67951-8, ISBN13: 978-0-471-67951-6. Dewey:304.2.
Audience: **g,l,u,f.**

Cloke, Paul J. (Editor), et al. **GF41**
Envisioning Human Geographies. Mark Goodwin & Philip Crang (Editors). Trade Paper. Oxford University Press, Inc. New York, NY. 2004. 262p. An Arnold Publication ISBN:0-340-72012-3, ISBN13: 978-0-340-72012-7. Dewey:304.2090501. LCCN:2004-401890.
Audience: **u,f.**

Goodall, Brian **GF4.G66 1987**
Facts on File Dictionary of Human Geography. Trade Cloth. Facts On File, Inc. New York, NY. 9999. 528p. ISBN:0-8160-1738-7, ISBN13: 978-0-8160-1738-6. Dewey:910/.03/21. LCCN:86-029232.
Audience: **g,l,u,f.** *Choice, 1987.*

Gregory, Derek (Editor) **GF41**
Human Geography. Trade Cloth. SAGE Publications, Inc. Thousand Oaks, CA. 2007. 1664p. ISBN:1-4129-0369-6, ISBN13: 978-1-4129-0369-1. Dewey:304.2.
Audience: **l,u,f.**

Hay, Iain (Editor) **GF26**
Qualitative Research Methods in Human Geography. Ed. 2. Trade Paper. Oxford University Press, Inc. New York, NY. 2005. 468p. ISBN:0-19-555079-X, ISBN13: 978-0-19-555079-5. Dewey:304.2042. LCCN:2005-281863.
Audience: **u,f.**

Hoggart, Keith, et al. **GF21.H66 2002**
Researching Human Geography. Loretta Lees & Anna Davies (Authors). Cloth Text. Oxford University Press, Inc. New York, NY. 2002. 368p. A Hodder Arnold Publication ISBN:0-340-67674-4, ISBN13: 978-0-340-67674-5. Dewey:304.2. LCCN:2002-277714.
Audience: **l,u,f.**

Knox, Paul L. & Marston, Sallie A. **GF41.K56 2006**
Places and Regions in Global Context: Human Geography. Ed. 4. Cloth Text. Prentice Hall PTR. Upper Saddle River, NJ. 2006. 560p. ISBN:0-13-149705-7, ISBN13: 978-0-13-149705-4. Dewey:304.2. LCCN:2005-036389.
Audience: **g,l,u,f.**

Norton, William **GF41**
Human Geography. Ed. 4. Cloth Text. Oxford University Press, Inc. New York, NY. 2001. 446p. ISBN:0-19-541641-4, ISBN13: 978-0-19-541641-1. Dewey:304.2.
Audience: **l,u,f.**

Paul Cloke, Professor, et al. **GF41**
Introducing Human Geographies. Ed. 2. Dr Philip Crang & Professor Mark Goodwin (Authors). Trade Paper. Hodder Education. London, 2005. 576p. A Hodder Arnold Publication ISBN:0-340-88276-X, ISBN13: 978-0-340-88276-4. Dewey:304.2.
Audience: **u,f.**

Rogerson Staff
Human Geography: An Introduction. Trade Paper. Polity Press. Cambridge, 2006. ISBN:0-7456-2003-5, ISBN13: 978-0-7456-2003-9. Dewey:304.2.
Audience: **g,u,f.**

Warf, Barney (Editor) **GF4**
Encyclopedia of Human Geography. Trade Cloth. SAGE Publications, Inc. Thousand Oaks, CA. 2006. 584p. ISBN:0-7619-8858-0, ISBN13: 978-0-7619-8858-8. Dewey:304.203. LCCN:2005-036239.
Audience: **g,l,u,f.**

Human Geography > Regional

D21
Regional Surveys of the World 2006. Ed. 5. Trade Cloth. Routledge. New York, NY. 2005. 0p. ISBN:1-85743-320-3, ISBN13: 978-1-85743-320-3. Dewey:909.83.
Audience: **g,l,u,f.**

Bradshaw, Michael J. **G116.B72 2007**
Contemporary World Regional Geography: Global Connections, Local Voices. Ed. 2. Trade Cloth. McGraw-Hill Companies, The. New York, NY. 2005. xx, 599p. ISBN:0-07-282683-5, ISBN13: 978-0-07-282683-8. Dewey:910. LCCN:2005-022876.
Audience: **l,u,f.**

Clawson, David L., et al. **G128**
World Regional Geography. Ed. 9. Merrill L. Johnson, Douglas L. Johnson, Viola F. Haarmann, Christopher A. Airriess, Robert L. Argenbright, Samuel A. Aryeetey-Attoh, Bella Bychkova Jordan, William C. Rowe & Jack F. Williams (Authors). Cloth Text. Prentice Hall PTR. Upper Saddle River, NJ. 2006. 736p. ISBN:0-13-149703-0, ISBN13: 978-0-13-149703-0. Dewey:330.9. LCCN:2006-009284.
Audience: **g,l,u.**

Galdman, Imogen **DK288**
Eastern Europe, Russia and Central Asia 2005. Ed. 5. Paper over Boards. Taylor & Francis Group. Abingdon, 2004. 768p. Regional Surveys of the World Ser. ISBN:1-85743-273-8,

ISBN13: 978-1-85743-273-2. Dewey:947/.086. LCCN:2004-016313.
Audience: **l,u,f.**

Hobbs, Joseph J. **G128**
Fundamentals of World Regional Geography. Paper Text. Brooks/Cole. Pacific Grove, CA. 2006. 464p. ISBN:0-495-10999-1, ISBN13: 978-0-495-10999-0. Dewey:910.
Audience: **g,l,u,f.**

Isard, Walter **HT388.I84 2003**
History of Regional Science and the Regional Science Association International: The Beginnings and Early History. Trade Cloth. Springer. New York, NY. 2003. X, 267p. ISBN:3-540-00934-5, ISBN13: 978-3-540-00934-4. Dewey:338.9. LCCN:2003-052912.
Audience: **u,f.**

Kent, Robert B. **F1408.9.K46 2006**
Latin America: Regions and People. Cloth over Boards. Guilford Publications, Inc. New York, NY. 2006. 422p. Texts in Regional Geography Ser. ISBN:1-59385-269-X, ISBN13: 978-1-59385-269-6. Dewey:918. LCCN:2005-027886.
Audience: **g,l,u,f.**

McKnight, Tom L. **E161.3.M35 2003**
Regional Geography of the United States and Canada. Ed. 4. Trade Paper. Prentice Hall PTR. Upper Saddle River, NJ. 2003. 528p. ISBN:0-13-101473-0, ISBN13: 978-0-13-101473-2. Dewey:917.3. LCCN:2003-023174.
Audience: **g,l,u,f.**

Ostergren, Robert Clifford & Rice, John G. **HC240.O35 2004**
The Europeans: A Geography of People, Culture, and Environment. Trade Paper. Guilford Publications, Inc. New York, NY. 2004. 386p. Texts in Regional Geography Ser. ISBN:0-89862-272-7, ISBN13: 978-0-89862-272-0. Dewey:940. LCCN:2003-027822.
Audience: **g,l,u,f.** *Choice, 2005.*

Spero, Joshua B. **DK4450.S68 2004**
Bridging the European Divide: Middle Power Politics and Regional Security Dilemmas. Book, Other. Rowman & Littlefield Publishers, Inc. Lanham, MD. 2004. 360p. ISBN:0-7425-3553-3, ISBN13: 978-0-7425-3553-4. Dewey:327.4/009/049. LCCN:2004-002715.
Audience: **u,f.**

Stock, Robert **DT351.9.S76 2004**
Africa South of the Sahara: A Geographical Interpretation. Ed. 2. Trade Paper. Guilford Publications, Inc. New York, NY. 2004. 479p. Texts in Regional Geography Ser. ISBN:1-57230-868-0, ISBN13: 978-1-57230-868-8. Dewey:916.7. LCCN:2004-002113.
Audience: **l,u,f.**

Yeung, Yue-man & Li, Xiaojian **H62.5.H6**
China's Western Development: The Role of the State in Historical and Regional Perspective. Trade Cloth. Chinese University of Hong Kong - Hong Kong Institute of Asia-Pacific Studies, The. Shatin, N.T., 2004. 36p. Shanghai-Hong Kong Development Institute Ocasional Paper Ser. ISBN:962-441-810-1, ISBN13: 978-962-441-810-1. Dewey:338.951.
Audience: **g,l,u,f.**

Human Geography > Development Studies

African Development Bank Staff (Contribution by) **HC800.A1A354 2005**
African Development Report 2005. Trade Paper. Oxford University Press, Inc. New York, NY. 2006. 336p. ISBN:0-19-928084-3, ISBN13: 978-0-19-928084-1. Dewey:338.96005.
Audience: **l,u,f.**

Akroyd, H. David **HN49.C6**
Agriculture and Rural Development Planning: A Process in Transition. University of London, School of Oriental and African Studies Staff (Contribution by). Trade Cloth. Ashgate Publishing, Ltd. Aldershot, 2003. 238p. King's SOAS Studies in Development Geography ISBN:0-7546-3693-3, ISBN13: 978-0-7546-3693-9. Dewey:307.1/412/091724. LCCN:2003-050265.
Audience: **u,f.**

Gallup, John Luke, et al. **HC125.G255 2003**
Is Geography Destiny?: Lessons from Latin America. Alejandro Gaviria & Eduardo Lora (Authors). Trade Paper. World Bank Publications. Washington, DC. 2003. 188p. Latin American Development Forum Ser. ISBN:0-8213-5451-5, ISBN13: 978-0-8213-5451-3. Dewey:330.98. LCCN:2003-043288.
Audience: **u,f.** *Choice, 2004.*

Hilpert, Ulrich (Editor) **HC79.D5**
The Regionalization of Internationalized Innovation: Locations for Advanced Industrial Development and Disparities in Participation. Paper over Boards. Routledge. New York, NY. 2003. 272p. Studies in the Modern World Economy ISBN:0-415-21730-X, ISBN13: 978-0-415-21730-9. Dewey:338.9. LCCN:2003-046978.
Audience: **u,f.**

Jensen, Ole B. & Richardson, Tim **HD108.6**
Making European Space: Mobility, Power and Territorial Identity. UK-B Format Paperback. Routledge. New York, NY. 2003. 312p. ISBN:0-415-29193-3, ISBN13: 978-0-415-29193-4. Dewey:333.7/313.
Audience: **l,u,f.**

Kanbur, S. M. Ravi, et al. **HC415.P5S62 2005**
Spatial Disparities in Human Development: Perspectives from Asia. Anthony Venables & Guang-Hua Wan (Authors). Trade Paper. United Nations University Press. Tokyo, 2005. 344p. ISBN:92-808-1122-3, ISBN13: 978-92-808-1122-3. Dewey:339.2/2095. LCCN:2005-029098.
Audience: **u,f.**

Lagendijk, Arnoud & Oinas, Päivi **HC79.D5L34 2005**
Proximity, Distance, and Diversity: Issues on Economic Interaction and Local Development. Trade Cloth. Ashgate Publishing, Ltd. Aldershot, 2005. 344p. Ashgate Economic Geography Ser. ISBN:0-7546-4074-4, ISBN13: 978-0-7546-4074-5. Dewey:338.9. LCCN:2004-025182.
Audience: **u,f.**

Low, Linda (Editor) **HC460.5.D482 2004**
Developmental States: Relevancy, Redundancy or Reconfiguration? Trade Cloth. Nova Science Publishers, Inc. Hauppauge, NY. 2005. 239p. ISBN:1-59454-143-4, ISBN13: 978-1-59454-143-8. Dewey:330.95. LCCN:2004-015038.
Audience: **u,f.**

M'Gonigle, Michael & Starke, Justine **PR9199.3.O35**
Planet U: Sustaining the World, Reinventing the University. Trade Paper. Consortium Book Sales & Distribution. Saint Paul, MN. 2006. 288p. ISBN:0-86571-557-2, ISBN13: 978-0-86571-557-8. Dewey:813.54.
Audience: **f.**

Okigbo, Charl **HD76.D475 2003**
Development and Communication in Africa. Book, Other. Rowman & Littlefield Publishers, Inc. Lanham, MD. 2003. 264p. ISBN:0-7425-2745-X, ISBN13: 978-0-7425-2745-4. Dewey:384/.096. LCCN:2003-021595.
Audience: **u,f.**

Potter, Robert B., et al. **HF1021**
Geographies of Development. Ed. 2. Tony Binns, Jennifer A. Elliott & David Smith (Authors). Trade Paper. Prentice Hall PTR. Upper Saddle River, NJ. 2005. 528p. ISBN:0-13-060569-7, ISBN13: 978-0-13-060569-6. Dewey:338.9.
Audience: **u,f.**

Smith, David Marshall **HT388.L44 2004**
Geographies and Moralities: International Perspectives on Justice, Development and Place. Roger Lee (Editor). Trade Cloth. Blackwell Publishing, Inc. Malden, MA. 2004. 336p. RGS-IBG Book Ser. ISBN:1-4051-1636-6, ISBN13: 978-1-4051-1636-7. Dewey:305.5. LCCN:2004-006261.
Audience: **u,f.**

Soesastro, Hadi & Findlay, Christopher C. **HC412**
Reshaping the Asia Pacific Economic Order. Trade Cloth. Routledge. New York, NY. 2005. 288p. Pacific Trade and Development Conference Ser. ISBN:0-415-34985-0, ISBN13: 978-0-415-34985-7. Dewey:337.1/5. LCCN:2005-014082.
Audience: **u,f.**

Thomas Vinod **HC187**
Development in the Land of Contrasts. Trade Paper. World Bank Publications. Washington, DC. 2006. 176p. ISBN:0-8213-6455-3, ISBN13: 978-0-8213-6455-0. Dewey:338.981. LCCN:2006-276454.
Audience: **l,u,f.**

Yu, Eden S H & Kwan, Yum K **HC427.95.C75 2004**
Critical Issues in China's Growth and Development. Trade Cloth. Ashgate Publishing, Ltd. Aldershot, 2005. 320p. The Chinese Economy Ser. ISBN:0-7546-4270-4, ISBN13: 978-0-7546-4270-1. Dewey:330.951. LCCN:2004-018316.
Audience: **l,u,f.**

Human Geography > Economic Geography

El-Khawas, Mohamed A. & Ndumbe, J. Anyu **JQ1875.E5 2005**
Democracy, Diamonds and Oil: Politics in Today's Africa. Trade Cloth. Nova Science Publishers, Inc. Hauppauge, NY. 2006. 119p. ISBN:1-59454-821-8, ISBN13: 978-1-59454-821-5. Dewey:320.96. LCCN:2005-031767.
Audience: **l,u,f.**

Glassmeier Amy **HC110.P6G543 2006**
Atlas of Poverty in America. Trade Paper. Routledge. New York, NY. 2005. 128p. ISBN:0-415-95336-7, ISBN13: 978-0-415-95336-8. Dewey:339.4/6097309045. LCCN:2005-028141.
Audience: **g,l,u,f.**

Karim, Kahn Fazle **HC440.5**
Economic Geography. Trade Paper. Oxford University Press, Inc. New York, NY. 2006. 256p. ISBN:0-19-579957-7, ISBN13: 978-0-19-579957-6. Dewey:338.95491.
Audience: **l,u,f.**

Marcel, Valerie & Mitchell, John V. **HD9578**
Oil Titans: National Oil Companies in the Middle East. Book, Other. Brookings Institution Press. Washington, DC. 2005. 256p. ISBN:0-8157-5474-4, ISBN13: 978-0-8157-5474-9. Dewey:338.7/66550956. LCCN:2006-004279.
Audience: **g,l,u,f.**

Masson, Paul R. & Pattillo, Catherine **HG1325.M377 2004**
The Monetary Geography of Africa. Trade Cloth. Brookings Institution Press. Washington, DC. 2004. 217p. ISBN:0-8157-5500-7, ISBN13: 978-0-8157-5500-5. Dewey:332.4/96. LCCN:2004-020089.
Audience: **u,f.**

Rhoads, Robert A. **LC67.68.N67U55 2006**
The University, the State, and the Market: The Political Economy of Globalization in the Americas. Trade Paper. Stanford University Press. Palo Alto, CA. 2005. 400p. ISBN:0-8047-5169-2, ISBN13: 978-0-8047-5169-8. Dewey:338.4/3378. LCCN:2005-017982.
Audience: **f.**

Scott, Allen J. **HF1025.S362 2006**
Geography and Economy. Trade Cloth. Oxford University Press, Inc. New York, NY. 2006. 192p. Clarendon Lectures in Geography and Environmental Studies ISBN:0-19-928430-X, ISBN13: 978-0-19-928430-6. Dewey:330.9. LCCN:2005-025981.
Audience: **l,u,f.**

Tickell, Adam (Editor), et al. **HF1025**
Politics and Practice in Economic Geography. Eric Sheppard, Jamie Peck & Trevor Barnes (Editors). Cloth Text. SAGE Publications, Ltd. London, 2007. 288p. ISBN:1-4129-0785-3, ISBN13: 978-1-4129-0785-9. Dewey:330.9.
Audience: **u,f.**

Vertova, Giovanna **HF1359**
Changing Economic Geography Of Globalization. Paper over Boards. Routledge. New York, NY. 2005. XVIII, 254p. ISBN:0-415-35398-X, ISBN13: 978-0-415-35398-4. Dewey:330.9/051/1. LCCN:2005-019374.
Audience: **u,f.**

Human Geography > Cultural Geography

Blunt, Alison (Editor) **GF41**
Cultural Geography in Practice. Trade Cloth. Oxford University Press, Inc. New York, NY. 2004. 352p. A Hodder Arnold Publication ISBN:0-340-80769-5, ISBN13: 978-0-340-80769-9. Dewey:910. LCCN:2004-272414.
Audience: **l,u,f.**

Crang, Mike **CF43.C73 2004**
Cultural Geography. Ed. 2. Paper Text. Routledge. New York, NY. 2006. 312p. Routledge Contemporary Human Geography Ser. ISBN:0-415-25212-1, ISBN13: 978-0-415-25212-6. Dewey:304.2.
Audience: **g,l,u,f.**

Doherty, Gillian & Claybourne, Anna **GN333**
Peoples of the World. Library Binding. EDC Publishing. Tulsa, OK. 2004. 96p. Encyclopedias Ser. ISBN:1-58086-345-0, ISBN13: 978-1-58086-345-2. Dewey:305.8.
Audience: **g,l,u,f.**

Pain, Rachel, et al. **GF45.I57 2001**
Introducing Social Geographies. Michael Burke, Duncan Fuller, Jamie Gough, Robert Macfarlane & Graham Mowl (Authors). Cloth Text. Oxford University Press, Inc. New York, NY. 2001. 320p. An Arnold Publication Ser. ISBN:0-340-72005-0, ISBN13: 978-0-340-72005-9. Dewey:304.2.
Audience: **u,f.**

Sperling, Michael B. & Sack, Amy **HQ1170.G44 2005**
Geographies of Muslim Women: Gender, Religion, and Space. Ghazi-Walid Falah & Caroline Nagel (Editors). UK-B Format Paperback. Guilford Publications, Inc. New York, NY. 2005. 337p. ISBN:1-57230-134-1, ISBN13: 978-1-57230-134-4. Dewey:305.48/697. LCCN:2004-028841.
Audience: **u,f.** *Choice, 2006.*

Wallach, Bret **GF41.W354 2005**
Understanding the Cultural Landscape. Cloth over Boards. Guilford Publications, Inc. New York, NY. 2005. 406p. ISBN:1-59385-120-0, ISBN13: 978-1-59385-120-0. Dewey:304.2. LCCN:2004-024793.
Audience: **l,u,f.**

Whatmore, Sarah **GF41**
Cultural Geography: Critical Concepts in the Social Sciences. Nigel Thrift (Editor). Paper over Boards. Routledge. New York, NY. 2005. 1600p. Critical Concepts in the Social Sciences Ser. ISBN:0-415-28502-X, ISBN13: 978-0-415-28502-5. Dewey:304.2. LCCN:2004-050834.
Audience: **l,u,f.**

WYLIE **QH75**
Landscape. Trade Paper. Routledge. New York, NY. 2007. 256p. Key Ideas in Geography Ser. ISBN:0-415-34144-2, ISBN13: 978-0-415-34144-8. Dewey:304.2.
Audience: **g,l,u,f.**

Human Geography > Historical

Edwards, Jess **GA793.6.A1E39 2005**
Making Space in the Early Modern Atlantic World. Paper over Boards. Routledge. New York, NY. 2005. X, 166p. Routledge Studies in Renaissance Literature and Culture Ser. ISBN:0-415-32341-X, ISBN13: 978-0-415-32341-3. Dewey:526/.0942/09032. LCCN:2005-000800.
Audience: **u,f.**

Galloway, J. H. **HD9100.5.G29 2005**
The Sugar Cane Industry: An Historical Geography from its Origins To 1914. Alan R. H. Baker, Richard Dennis & Deryck Holdworth (Contribution by). Trade Paper. Cambridge University Press. New York, NY. 2005. 280p. Cambridge Studies in Historical Geography Ser., Vol. 12 ISBN:0-521-02219-3, ISBN13: 978-0-521-02219-4. Dewey:338.476336109.
Audience: **u,f.**

Hall, Carolyn & Brignoli, Hector Perez **G1551.S1**
Historical Atlas of Central America. Trade Paper. University of Oklahoma Press. Norman, OK. 2005. 336p. ISBN:0-8061-3038-5, ISBN13: 978-0-8061-3038-5. Dewey:911/.728.
Audience: **g,l,u,f.** *Choice, 2004.*

Matless, David **DA566.4**
Landscape and Englishness. Trade Paper. Reaktion Books, Ltd. London, 2005. 368p. Reaktion Books - Picturing History Ser. ISBN:1-86189-097-4, ISBN13: 978-1-86189-097-9. Dewey:942/.082.
Audience: **g.**

Prentice-Hall Staff **G1030.P75 2005**
The Prentice Hall Atlas of Western Civilization. Trade Paper. Prentice Hall PTR. Upper Saddle River, NJ. 2004. 112p. ISBN:0-13-193262-4, ISBN13: 978-0-13-193262-3. Dewey:909.09812.
Audience: **g,l,u,f.**

Seaver, Kirsten A. **GA308.Z6S43 2004**
Maps, Myths, and Men: The Story of the Vinland Map. Trade Cloth. Stanford University Press. Palo Alto, CA. 2004. 504p. ISBN:0-8047-4962-0, ISBN13: 978-0-8047-4962-6. Dewey:912. LCCN:2004-001197.
Audience: **g,l,u,f.** *Choice, 2005.*

Short, Brian **DA570 .S47 1997**
Land and Society in Edwardian Britain. Alan R. H. Baker, Richard Dennis & Deryck Holdworth (Contribution by). Trade Paper. Cambridge University Press. New York, NY. 2005. 398p. Cambridge Studies in Historical Geography Ser., Vol. 25 ISBN:0-521-02177-4, ISBN13: 978-0-521-02177-7. Dewey:333/.00941.
Audience: **u,f.** *Choice, 1998.*

Weightman, Barbara A. **DS335.W37 2005**
Dragons and Tigers: A Geography of South, East, and Southeast Asia. Ed. 2. Trade Cloth. John Wiley & Sons, Inc. Hoboken, NJ. 2005. 464p. ISBN:0-471-63084-5, ISBN13: 978-0-471-63084-5. Dewey:915. LCCN:2005-027689.
Audience: **g,l,u,f.**

White, George W. **JC311.W463 2004**
Nation, State, and Territory: Origins, Evolutions, and Relationships. Ed. 2. Book, Other. Rowman & Littlefield Publishers, Inc. Lanham, MD. 2004. 304p. ISBN:0-7425-3025-6, ISBN13: 978-0-7425-3025-6. Dewey:320.1. LCCN:2004-014114.
Audience: **l,u,f.**

Human Geography > Geopolitics

Brodsgaard, Kjeld Erik & Heurlin, Bertel (Editors) **DS779.27**
China's Place in Global Geopolitics: Domestic, Regional and International Challenges. Paper over Boards. Taylor & Francis Group. Philadelphia, PA. 2004. 216p. ISBN:0-7007-1532-0, ISBN13: 978-0-7007-1532-9. Dewey:327.9/51.
Audience: **g,l,u,f.**

Dodds, Klaus **JC319.D56 2005**
Global Geopolitics: A Critical Introduction. Trade Paper. Prentice Hall PTR. Upper Saddle River, NJ. 2004. 272p. ISBN:0-273-68609-7, ISBN13: 978-0-273-68609-5. Dewey:320.1/2. LCCN:2004-058279.
Audience: **l,u,f.**

Flint, Colin **JC319**
Introduction to Geopolitics. Paper over Boards. Routledge. New York, NY. 2006. XVI, 240p. ISBN:0-415-34494-8, ISBN13: 978-0-415-34494-4. Dewey:320.1/2. LCCN:2005-033530.
Audience: **u,f.**

Greer, Scott L. (Editor) **JC355.T38 2005**
Territory, Democracy, and Justice: Regionalism and Federalism in Western Democracies. Cloth over Boards. Palgrave Macmillan. New York, NY. 2006. 288p. ISBN:1-4039-9501-X, ISBN13: 978-1-4039-9501-8. Dewey:321.02. LCCN:2005-050929.
Audience: **u,f.**

Le Billon, Philippe (Editor) **HD9560.5.G425 2004**
Geopolitics of Resource Wars: Resource Dependence, Governance and Violence. Paper over Boards. Routledge. New York, NY. 2005. 280p. Cass Studies in Geopolitics ISBN:0-7146-5604-6, ISBN13: 978-0-7146-5604-5. Dewey:355/.033. LCCN:2003-026623.
Audience: **u,f.**

LIM **DS518.1.L49 2005**
Geopolitics of East Asia. Trade Paper. Routledge. New York, NY. 2005. 208p. ISBN:0-415-36030-7, ISBN13: 978-0-415-36030-2. Dewey:320.12095.
Audience: **u,f.**

Marfleet, Philip **HV640.M333 2006**
Refugees in a Global Era. Cloth over Boards. Palgrave Macmillan. New York, NY. 2005. 272p. ISBN:0-333-77783-2, ISBN13: 978-0-333-77783-1. Dewey:305.9/06914. LCCN:2005-056102.
Audience: **l,u,f.**

Mouritzen, Hans & Wivel, Anders **HC241.2**
The Geopolitics of Euro-Atlantic Intergration. Paper over Boards. Routledge. New York, NY. 2005. 272p. Europe and the Nation State Ser., Vol. 9 ISBN:0-415-28280-2, ISBN13: 978-0-415-28280-2. Dewey:341.242/2. LCCN:2005-042840.
Audience: **u,f.**

Nayar, Baldev Raj **JZ1318**
Geopolitics of Globalization: The Consequences for Development. Trade Cloth. Oxford University Press, Inc. New York, NY. 2006. 313p. ISBN:0-19-567202-X, ISBN13: 978-0-19-567202-2. Dewey:327. LCCN:2005-386467.
Audience: **u,f.**

Sedelmeier, Ulrich & Schimmelfennig, Frank (Editors) **JN30.P6533 2005**
The Politics of European Union Enlargement: Theoretical Approaches. Paper over Boards. Routledge. New York, NY. 2005. XIV, 306p. Routledge Advances in European Politics Ser., Vol. 30 ISBN:0-415-36129-X, ISBN13: 978-0-415-36129-3. Dewey:341.242/2. LCCN:2004-028648.
Audience: **u,f.**

Slater, David **JZ1251.S58 2004**
Geopolitics and the Post-Colonial: Rethinking North-South Relations. Trade Cloth. Blackwell Publishing, Inc. Malden, MA. 2004. 296p. ISBN:0-631-21452-6, ISBN13: 978-0-631-21452-6. Dewey:327.101. LCCN:2004-008267.
Audience: **u,f.** *Choice, 2005.*

Tuathail, Gearsid S., et al. **JC319.G646 2006**
Geopolitical Reader. Ed. 2. Simon Dalby & Paul Routledge (Authors). Paper over Boards. Routledge. New York, NY. 2005. XIV, 306p. ISBN:0-415-34147-7, ISBN13: 978-0-415-34147-9. Dewey:320.1/2. LCCN:2005-019590.
Audience: **l,u,f.**

JOURNALISM AND COMMUNICATION

This section contains works pertinent to the study of communication and print and broadcast journalism including: advertising, mass media, public opinion, public relations and telecommunication. In addition to works on theory and criticism are works more practical in nature and intended for the professional preparation of future media professionals.

The collection of titles reflects the multi-disciplinary nature of communication and journalism as well as how the field has developed and changed since BCL3 was published. The Journalism section now includes titles on law and ethics, online graphics and design and special topics such as investigative journalism, sports journalism, war reporting, convergent journalism, and the role of the Internet in print and broadcast journalism. The Communication section reflects the importance of the mass media on society and in the undergraduate curriculum; and the significance of new media and technology in areas such as telecommunication, advertising, and mass media.

— Lisa Romero

Journalism > History and Criticism

Brennan, Elizabeth A. & Clarage, Elizabeth C. **AS911.P8.B74 1999**
Who's Who of Pulitzer Prize Winners. Seymour Topping (Foreword by). Cloth Text. Greenwood Publishing Group, Inc. Portsmouth, NH. 1998. 688p. ISBN:1-57356-111-8, ISBN13: 978-1-57356-111-2. Dewey:070.9/22. LCCN:98-044979.
Audience: **g,l,u,f.** *Choice, 1999.*

Hachten, William A. **PN4855**
Troubles of Journalism: A Critical Look at What's Right and Wrong with the Press. Ed. 3. Cloth over Boards. Lawrence Erlbaum Associates, Inc. Mahwah, NJ. 2004. 216p. LEA's Communication Ser. ISBN:0-8058-5166-6, ISBN13: 978-0-8058-5166-3. Dewey:071/.3. LCCN:2004-304970.
Audience: **l,u,f.** *Choice, 2005.*

Inglis, Fred **PN4751.I54 2002**
People's Witness: The Journalist in Modern Politics. Cloth over Boards. Yale University Press. Cumberland, RI. 2002. 432p. ISBN:0-300-09327-6, ISBN13: 978-0-300-09327-8. Dewey:070.4/4932. LCCN:2002-101098.
Audience: **u,f.**

Kerrane, Kevin & Yagoda, Ben (Editors) **PN6014.A76**
The Art of Fact: A Historical Anthology of Literary Journalism. Trade Paper. Simon & Schuster. New York, NY. 1998. 560p. ISBN:0-684-84630-6, ISBN13: 978-0-684-84630-9. Dewey:081.
Audience: **l,u,f.**

Knightley, Phillip **PN4784.W37K58 2004**
The First Casualty: The War Correspondent as Hero and Myth-Maker from the Crimea to Iraq. Ed. 3. Trade Paper. Johns Hopkins University Press. Baltimore, MD. 2004. 608p. ISBN:0-8018-8030-0, ISBN13: 978-0-8018-8030-8. Dewey:070.4/333. LCCN:2004-010945.
Audience: **l,u,f.**

Read, Donald **PN5111.R4R43 1999**
The Power of News: The History of Reuters. Ed. 2. Trade Cloth. Oxford University Press, Inc. New York, NY. 1999. 558p. ISBN:0-19-820768-9, ISBN13: 978-0-19-820768-9. Dewey:070.4/35. LCCN:98-036926.
Audience: **g,l,u,f.** *Choice, 1993.*

Stephens, Mitchell **PN4801**
A History of News: From Oral Culture to the Information Age. Ed. 2. Paper Text. Thomson Wadsworth. Belmont, CA. 1996. 353p. ISBN:0-15-501857-4, ISBN13: 978-0-15-501857-0. Dewey:070/.9.
Audience: **g,l,u,f.**

Treglown, Jeremy & Bennett, Bridget (Editors) **PR63.G78 1998**
Grub Street and the Ivory Tower: Literary Journalism and Literary Scholarship from Fielding to the Internet. Trade Cloth. Oxford University Press, Inc. New York, NY. 1999. 304p. ISBN:0-19-818413-1, ISBN13: 978-0-19-818413-3. Dewey:801/.95/0941. LCCN:98-026114.
Audience: **g,u,f.**

Weingarten, Marc **PS366.R44W45 2005**
The Gang That Wouldn't Write Straight: Wolfe, Thompson, Didion and the New Journalism Revolution. Trade Cloth. Crown Publishing Group. New York, NY. 2005. 336p. ISBN:1-4000-4914-8, ISBN13: 978-1-4000-4914-1. Dewey:818/.540809. LCCN:2005-015378.
Audience: **u,f.**

Zelizer, Barbie **PN4731.Z45 2004**
Taking Journalism Seriously: News and the Academy. Trade Cloth. SAGE Publications, Inc. Thousand Oaks, CA. 2004. 296p. ISBN:0-8039-7313-6, ISBN13: 978-0-8039-7313-8. Dewey:070. LCCN:2003-025694.
Audience: **u,f.**

Journalism > History and Criticism > Specific Countries

Altschull, J. Herbert **PN4731.A389 1990**
From Milton to McLuhan: The Ideas Behind American Journalism. Trade Paper. Allyn & Bacon, Inc. Boston, MA. 1990. 384p. ISBN:0-582-28562-3, ISBN13: 978-0-582-28562-0. Dewey:070.4/01. LCCN:90-030932.
Audience: **u,f.** *Choice, 1990.*

Andrews, Alexander **PN5114.A6**
The History of British Journalism, from the Foundation of the Newspaper Press in England, to the Repeal of the Stamp Act in 1855. Paper Text. Classic Books. Murrieta, CA. 2001. ISBN:0-7426-9271-X, ISBN13: 978-0-7426-9271-8. Dewey:72.
Audience: **u,f.** B

Aumente, Jerome, et al. **PN5355.E852E19 1999**
Eastern European Journalism: Before, During and after Communism. Peter Gross, Ray Hiebert, Owen Johnson & Dean Mills (Authors), David L. Paletz (Editor). Paper Text. Hampton Press, Inc. Cresskill, NJ. 1999. 224p. Communication Ser., :Political Communication ISBN:1-57273-178-8, ISBN13: 978-1-57273-178-3. Dewey:077. LCCN:99-027158.
Audience: **u,f.**

Ayalon, Ami **PN5359.A93 1995**
The Press in the Arab Middle East: A History. Trade Cloth. Oxford University Press, Inc. New York, NY. 1995. 314p. Studies in Middle Eastern History ISBN:0-19-508780-1, ISBN13: 978-0-19-508780-2. Dewey:079/.17/4927. LCCN:94-009482.
Audience: **u,f.** *Choice, 1995.*

Berry, Neil **PN5122.B47 2002**
Articles of Faith: The Story of British Intellectual Journalism. Trade Paper. Waywiser Press, The. London, 2003. 272p. ISBN:1-904130-08-9, ISBN13: 978-1-904130-08-6. Dewey:070.41902241.
Audience: **u,f.**

Burgh, Hugo de **PN5364.D4 2003**
The Chinese Journalist: Mediating Information in the World's Most Populous Country. Paper over Boards. Routledge. New York, NY. 2003. 264p. ISBN:0-415-30573-X, ISBN13: 978-0-415-30573-0. Dewey:079/.51/0904. LCCN:2003-003693.
Audience: **u,f.**

Campbell, W. Joseph **PN4784**
Yellow Journalism: Puncturing the Myths, Defining the Legacies. Book, Other. Greenwood Publishing Group, Inc. Portsmouth, NH. 2001. 248p. ISBN:0-275-96686-0, ISBN13: 978-0-275-96686-7. Dewey:071/.3/0904. LCCN:00-058024.
Audience: **u,f.** *Choice, 2001.*

Cray, Ed (Editor), et al. **PN4726.A48 2003**
American Datelines: Major News Stories from Colonial Times to the Present. Jonathan Kotler & Miles Beller (Editors). Trade Paper. University of Illinois Press. Champaign, IL. 2003. 440p. ISBN:0-252-07116-6, ISBN13: 978-0-252-07116-4. Dewey:071/.3. LCCN:2002-027190.
Audience: **l,u.**

Fedler, Fred **PN4864.F43 2000**
Lessons from the Past. Trade Paper. Waveland Press, Inc. Prospect Heights, IL. 1999. 250p. ISBN:1-57766-067-6, ISBN13: 978-1-57766-067-5. Dewey:071/.3/09034. LCCN:00-699775.
Audience: **l,u.**

Harnett, Richard M. & Ferguson, Billy G. **PN4841.U66H37 2001**
Unipress: United Press International: Covering the 20th Century. Trade Cloth. Fulcrum Publishing. Golden, CO. 2004. 384p. ISBN:1-55591-481-0, ISBN13: 978-1-55591-481-3. Dewey:070.4/35. LCCN:2002-151742.
Audience: **l,u,f.**

Harrison, S L **PN4871.H27 2002**
Cavalcade of Journalists 1900-2000. Wolf Den Books. 2002. ISBN:0-9708035-1-6, ISBN13: 978-0-9708035-1-1.
Audience: **l,u.**

Jamieson, Kathleen Hall & Waldman, Paul **PN4888.O25J36 2003**
The Press Effect: Politicians, Journalists, and the Stories That Shape the Political World. E-Book. Oxford University Press, Inc. New York, NY. ISBN:0-19-518438-6, ISBN13: 978-0-19-518438-9. Dewey:071.3.
Audience: **u,f.**

Leonard, Thomas C. **PN4888.P6L46 1986**
The Power of the Press: The Birth of American Political Reporting. Trade Cloth. Oxford University Press, Inc. New York, NY. 1986. 288p. ISBN:0-19-503719-7, ISBN13: 978-0-19-503719-7. Dewey:071/.3. LCCN:85-021621.
Audience: **u,f.**

Mindich, David T. **PN4888.O25 M56**
Just the Facts. Trade Paper. New York University Press. New York, NY. 2000. 200p. ISBN:0-8147-5614-X, ISBN13: 978-0-8147-5614-0. Dewey:071/.3.
Audience: **l,u.**

Mongerson, Paul **PN4888.P6M68 1997**
The Power Press: Its Impact on America and What You Can Do about It. Trade Paper. Fulcrum Publishing. Golden, CO. 1997. 224p. ISBN:1-55591-347-4, ISBN13: 978-1-55591-347-2. Dewey:071/.3. LCCN:97-026223.
Audience: **l,u.**

Olasky, Marvin N. **PN4801.O4 1991**
Central Ideas in the Development of American Journalism: A Narrative History. Cloth Text. Lawrence Erlbaum Associates, Inc. Mahwah, NJ. 1990. 208p. ISBN:0-8058-0893-0, ISBN13: 978-0-8058-0893-3. Dewey:071/.3. LCCN:90-040153.
Audience: **u,f.** *Choice, 1991.*

Pride, Armistead S. & Wilson, Clint C. II **PN4882.5.P75 1997**
A History of the Black Press. Trade Paper. Howard University Press. Washington, DC. 1997. 344p. ISBN:0-88258-192-9, ISBN13: 978-0-88258-192-7. Dewey:071.308. LCCN:97-002791.
Audience: **l,u,f.**

Salwen, Micheal B. & Garrison, Bruce **PN4930.S24 1991**
Latin American Journalism. Paper Text. Lawrence Erlbaum Associates, Inc. Mahwah, NJ. 1991. 240p. Communication Textbook Ser., :Journalism ISBN:0-8058-0768-3, ISBN13: 978-0-8058-0768-4. Dewey:079/.8. LCCN:91-013964.
Audience: **u,f.** *Choice, 1992.*

Serrin, Judith & Serrin, William (Editors) **HN65.M83 2001**
Muckraking!: The Journalism That Changed America. Trade Paper. New Press, The. New York, NY. 2002. 468p. ISBN:1-56584-681-8, ISBN13: 978-1-56584-681-4. Dewey:306/.0973/0904. LCCN:2001-037061.
Audience: **l,u.**

Sinclair, Upton **PN4867.S5 2003**
The Brass Check: A Study of American Journalism. Trade Cloth. University of Illinois Press. Champaign, IL. 2002. 480p. ISBN:0-252-02805-8, ISBN13: 978-0-252-02805-2. Dewey:071/.3. LCCN:2002-069557.
Audience: **l,u.**

Sloan, W. David (Compiled by) **Z6951**
American Journalism History: An Annotated Bibliography. Cloth Text. Greenwood Publishing Group, Inc. Portsmouth, NH. 1989. 359p. Bibliographies and Indexes in Mass Media and Communications Ser., No. 1 ISBN:0-313-26350-7, ISBN13: 978-0-313-26350-7. Dewey:016.071/3. LCCN:88-035800.
Audience: **l,u.** *Choice, 1989.*

Sloan, W. David & Parcell, Lisa Mullikin (Editors) **PN4853.A48 2002**
American Journalism: History, Principles, Practices. Paper Text. McFarland & Company, Incorporated Publishers. Jefferson, NC. 2002. 384p. ISBN:0-7864-1371-9, ISBN13: 978-0-7864-1371-3. Dewey:071/.3. LCCN:2001-008468.
Audience: **l,u.** *Choice, 2003, 2002.*

Streitmatter, Rodger **PN4888.P6**
Mightier Than the Sword: How the News Media Have Shaped American History. Trade Paper. Westview Press. Boulder, CO. 1998. 304p. ISBN:0-8133-3211-7, ISBN13: 978-0-8133-3211-6. Dewey:070.4/49324/0973.
Audience: **l,u.** *Choice, 1997.*

Streitmatter, Rodger **PN4888.U5S77 2001**
Voices of Revolution: The Dissident Press in America. Trade Cloth. Columbia University Press. New York, NY. 2001. 340p. ISBN:0-231-12248-9, ISBN13: 978-0-231-12248-1. Dewey:071/.3. LCCN:2001-017099.
Audience: **l,u,f.** *Choice, 2002.*

Journalism > History and Criticism > Specific Periods

Bernstein, Carl & Woodward, Bob **E 860 B47**
All the President's Men. Trade Paper. Simon & Schuster. New York, NY. 2005. 352p. ISBN:1-4165-2291-3, ISBN13: 978-1-4165-2291-1. Dewey:320.973.
Audience: **l,u.** B

Hudson, Frederic **PN4855**
Journalism in the United States from 1690 to 1872, Set. Library Binding. Routledge. New York, NY. 2000. 840p. American Journalism 1690-1940 Ser. ISBN:0-415-24142-1, ISBN13: 978-0-415-24142-7. Dewey:071/.09.
Audience: **u,f.**

Hudson, Frederick, et al. **PN4908**
American Journalism 1690-1940, Set. Alfred McClung Lee & Frank Luther Mott (Authors). Library Binding. Routledge. New York, NY. 2000. 2434p. American Journalism 1690-1940 Ser. ISBN:0-415-22888-3, ISBN13: 978-0-415-22888-6. Dewey:071/.09.
Audience: **l,u.**

Italia, Iona **PR769.I83 2005**
Rise of Literary Journalism in the Eighteenth-Century: Anxious Employment. Paper over Boards. Routledge. New York, NY. 2005. 224p. Routledge Studies in Eighteenth-Century Literature, Vol. 3 ISBN:0-415-34392-5, ISBN13: 978-0-415-34392-3. Dewey:828/.50809. LCCN:2004-059850.
Audience: **u,f.**

Journalism > Law and Ethics

Berry, William E. **PN4751.L37 1995**
Last Rights: Revisiting Four Theories of the Press. John C. Nerone & Robert W. McChesney (Editors). Trade Cloth. University of Illinois Press. Champaign, IL. 1995. 224p. History of Communication Ser. ISBN:0-252-02180-0, ISBN13: 978-0-252-02180-0. Dewey:070/.01. LCCN:95-003566.
Audience: **l,u,f.** *Choice, 1996.*

Christians, Clifford G., et al. **P94.M36 2005**
Media Ethics: Cases and Moral Reasoning. Ed. 7. Mark B. Fackler, Kathy Brittain McKee, Kim B. Rotzoll & Robert H. Woods (Authors). Trade Paper. Allyn & Bacon, Inc. Boston, MA. 2004. 336p. ISBN:0-205-41845-7, ISBN13: 978-0-205-41845-9. Dewey:170. LCCN:2004-049783.
Audience: **l,u,f.**

Christians, Clifford G. & Traber, Michael (Editors) **P94.C5716 1997**
Communication Ethics and Universal Values. Trade Cloth. SAGE Publications, Inc. Thousand Oaks, CA. 1997. 400p. ISBN:0-7619-0584-7, ISBN13: 978-0-7619-0584-4. Dewey:174. LCCN:96-051209.
Audience: **l,u,f.**

Dennis, Everette E. (Editor), et al. **HN90**
Media Freedom and Accountability. Donald M. Gillmor & Theodore L. Glasser (Editors). Trade Cloth. Greenwood Publishing Group, Inc. Portsmouth, NH. 1989. 220p. Contributions to the Study of Mass Media and Communications Ser., No. 14 ISBN:0-313-26727-8, ISBN13: 978-0-313-26727-7. Dewey:302.23/0973. LCCN:89-002148.
Audience: **l,u,f.** *Choice, 1990.*

Goldstein, Tom **PN4888.E8 G6 1985**
The News at Any Cost: How Journalists Compromise Their Ethics to Shape the News. Trade Cloth. Simon & Schuster. New York, NY. 1985. 252p. ISBN:0-671-49960-2, ISBN13: 978-0-671-49960-0. Dewey:174/.9097. LCCN:85-008171.
Audience: **l,u,f.** *Choice, 1985.*

Hindman, Elizabeth B. **KF4774**
Rights vs. Responsibilities: The Supreme Court and the Media, 50. Book, Other. Greenwood Publishing Group, Inc. Portsmouth, NH. 1997. 200p. Contributions to the Study of Mass Media and Communications Ser., Vol. 50 ISBN:0-313-29922-6, ISBN13: 978-0-313-29922-3. Dewey:342.73/0853. LCCN:96-038794.
Audience: **l,u,f.** *Choice, 1997.*

Hixson, Richard F. **KF2765**
Mass Media and the Constitution: An Encyclopedia of Supreme Court Decisions. Ed. 2. John W. Johnson (Editor). Cloth Text. Garland Publishing, Inc. New York, NY. 9999. 700p. American Law and Society Ser. ISBN:0-8153-1384-5, ISBN13: 978-0-8153-1384-7. Dewey:343.73/0994.
Audience: **l,u,f.** *Choice, 1989.*

Hohenberg, John **PN4735 .H6**
Free Press - Free People: The Best Cause. Trade Cloth. Columbia University Press. New York, NY. 1971. ISBN:0-231-03315-X, ISBN13: 978-0-231-03315-2. Dewey:323.44/5. LCCN:70-133912.
Audience: **l,u,f.**

Hulteng, John L. **PN4756.H8 1985**
The Messenger's Motivcs: Ethical Problems of the News Media. Ed. 2. Paper Text. Prentice Hall PTR. Upper Saddle River, NJ. 1984. 272p. ISBN:0-13-577487-X, ISBN13: 978-0-13-577487-8. Dewey:174/.9097. LCCN:84-006878.
Audience: **l,u,f.**

Knowlton, Steven R. & Parsons, Patrick R. (Editors) **PN4888**
The Journalist's Moral Compass: Basic Principles. Trade Cloth. Greenwood Publishing Group, Inc. Portsmouth, NH. 1993. 272p. ISBN:0-275-94537-5, ISBN13: 978-0-275-94537-4. Dewey:174.9097. LCCN:93-004256.
Audience: **l,u,f.** *Choice, 1994.*

Lambeth, Edmund B. **PN4756**
Committed Journalism: An Ethic for the Profession. Ed. 2. Cloth Text. Indiana University Press. Bloomington, IN. 1992. 256p. ISBN:0-253-33220-6, ISBN13: 978-0-253-33220-2. Dewey:174/.9097. LCCN:91-032569.
Audience: **l,u,f.** *Choice, 1986.*

Lewis, Anthony **KF228.W42**
Make No Law: The Sullivan Case and the First Amendment. Trade Paper. Knopf Publishing Group. New York, NY. 1992. 368p. ISBN:0-679-73939-4, ISBN13: 978-0-679-73939-5. Dewey:345.73/0256. LCCN:92-050104.
Audience: **l,u,f.** *Choice, 1991.*

Merrill, John C. **PN4731.M44 1990**
The Imperative of Freedom: A Philosophy of Journalistic Autonomy. Ed. 2. Trade Cloth. University Press of America, Inc. Lanham, MD. 1990. 246p. ISBN:0-932088-45-7, ISBN13: 978-0-932088-45-1. Dewey:070/.01. LCCN:90-030407.
Audience: **l,u,f.**

Meyer, Philip **PN4756.M45 1991**
Ethical Journalism: A Guide for Students, Practitioners and Consumers. Trade Paper. University Press of America, Inc. Lanham, MD. 1993. 272p. ISBN:0-8191-8332-6, ISBN13: 978-0-8191-8332-3. Dewey:174/.9097. LCCN:91-024392.
Audience: **l,u.** *Choice, 1987.*

Miraldi, Robert **PN4888**
Muckraking and Objectivity: Journalism's Colliding Traditions, 18. Trade Cloth. Greenwood Publishing Group, Inc. Portsmouth, NH. 1990. 184p. Contributions to the Study of Mass Media and Communications Ser., No. 18 ISBN:0-313-27298-0, ISBN13: 978-0-313-27298-1. Dewey:174/.9097. LCCN:89-026010.
Audience: **l,u,f.** *Choice, 1990.*

Moore, Roy L. **KF2750.M66 1998**
Mass Communication Law and Ethics. Ed. 2. Cloth over Boards. Lawrence Erlbaum Associates, Inc. Mahwah, NJ. 1999. 696p. LEA's Communication Ser. ISBN:0-8058-2599-1, ISBN13: 978-0-8058-2599-2. Dewey:343.73099. LCCN:98-036329.
Audience: **l,u,f.** *Choice, 1994.*

Sableman, Mark **KF2750.S33 1997**
More Speech, Not Less: Communications Law in the Information Age. Paul Simon (Foreword by). Trade Cloth. Southern Illinois University Press. Carbondale, IL. 1997. 272p. ISBN:0-8093-2135-1, ISBN13: 978-0-8093-2135-3. Dewey:343.7309/9. LCCN:96-053449.
Audience: **l,u,f.** *Choice, 1998.*

Seib, Philip **PN4781**
Campaigns and Conscience: The Ethics of Political Journalism. Trade Cloth. Greenwood Publishing Group, Inc. Portsmouth, NH. 1994. 176p. Series in Political Communication ISBN:0-275-94623-1, ISBN13: 978-0-275-94623-4. Dewey:174/.9097. LCCN:93-037023.
Audience: **l,u,f.** *Choice, 1994.*

Siebert, Fredrick S., et al. **PN4731 .S49 1973**
Four Theories of the Press: The Authoritarian, Libertarian, Social Responsibility and Soviet Communist Concepts of What the Press Should Be. Theodore B. Peterson & Wilbur L. Schramm (Authors). Trade Cloth. Ayer Company Publishers, Inc. Manchester, NH. 1977. Essay Index Reprint Ser. ISBN:0-8369-8173-1, ISBN13: 978-0-8369-8173-5. Dewey:070/.01. LCCN:72-013275.
Audience: **l,u,f.** B

Smith, Ron F. **PN4888.E8G66 2003**
Groping for Ethics in Journalism. Ed. 5. Trade Cloth. Blackwell Publishing Professional. Ames, IA. 2003. ix, 422p. ISBN:0-8138-1088-4, ISBN13: 978-0-8138-1088-1. Dewey:174/.9097. LCCN:2003-005402.
Audience: **l,u,f.**

Ward, Stephen J. A. **PN4756**
The Invention of Journalism Ethics: The Path to Objectivity and Beyond. Trade Cloth. McGill-Queen's University Press. Montreal, PQ. 2004. 368p. McGill-Queen's Studies in the History of Ideas, Vol. 38 ISBN:0-7735-2810-5, ISBN13: 978-0-7735-2810-9. Dewey:174/.90704. LCCN:2005-541280.
Audience: **l,u,f.** *Choice, 2006.*

Journalism > Special Topics

Alexander, S. L. **KF9223.5.A915 2003**
Covering the Courts: A Handbook for Journalists. Ed. 2. Book, Other. Rowman & Littlefield Publishers, Inc. Lanham, MD. 2003. 184p. ISBN:0-7425-2021-8, ISBN13: 978-0-7425-2021-9. Dewey:347.73/12. LCCN:2002-014812.
Audience: **l,u.**

Arnold, R. Douglas **PN4888.P6A76 2004**
Congress, the Press, and Political Accountability. Trade Cloth. Princeton University Press. Princeton, NJ. 2004. 304p. ISBN:0-691-11710-1, ISBN13: 978-0-691-11710-2. Dewey:070.4/49320973. LCCN:2003-055535.
Audience: **u,f.** *Choice, 2005.*

Buddenbaum, Judith **PN4888.R44 B83 1998**
Reporting the News about Religion: An Introduction for Journalists. Paper Text. Blackwell Publishing Professional. Ames, IA. 1998. 240p. ISBN:0-8138-2977-1, ISBN13: 978-0-8138-2977-7. Dewey:070.4/492. LCCN:98-003005.
Audience: **l,u,f.**

Carruthers, Susan L. **P96.W35C37 1999**
The Media at War: Communication and Conflict in the Twentieth Century. Trade Paper. Palgrave Macmillan. New York, NY. 2000. 333p. ISBN:0-312-22801-5, ISBN13: 978-0-312-22801-9. Dewey:070.4/4935502. LCCN:99-037492.
Audience: **l,u,f.**

Connelly, Mark & Welch, David (Editors) **UB275**
War and the Media: Reportage and Propaganda, 1900-2003. Cloth over Boards, Trade Cloth. I. B. Tauris & Company, Ltd. London, 2005. 256p. ISBN:1-86064-959-9, ISBN13: 978-1-86064-959-2. Dewey:355.34. LCCN:2005-362122.
Audience: **l,u,f.** *Choice, 2006.*

Copeland, David A. (Editor-In-Chief) **D25.G84 2005**
The Greenwood Library of American War Reporting. Cloth Text. Greenwood Publishing Group, Inc. Portsmouth, NH. 2005. 4504p. ISBN:0-313-33435-8, ISBN13: 978-0-313-33435-1. Dewey:973. LCCN:2005-010122.
Audience: **l,u,f.** *Choice, 2006.*

Dennis, Everette E. & Snyder, Robert W. **PN4738.C68 1998**
Covering Congress. Trade Paper. Transaction Publishers. Somerset, NJ. 1997. 170p. ISBN:1-56000-946-2, ISBN13: 978-1-56000-946-7. Dewey:070.4/49324/0973. LCCN:97-005091.
Audience: **l,u,f.** *Choice, 1998.*

Eisenstock, Alan **GV742.3.E58 2001**
Sports Talk: A Journey Inside the World of Sports Talk Radio. Trade Cloth. Simon & Schuster. New York, NY. 2001. 272p. ISBN:0-7434-0694-X, ISBN13: 978-0-7434-0694-9. Dewey:070.4/49796/092. LCCN:2001-034026.
Audience: **l,u.**

Emery, Michael **PN4874.E7A3 1995**
On the Front Lines: Following America's Foreign Correspondents Across the Twentieth Century. Trade Cloth. American University. Washington, DC. 1995. 448p. ISBN:1-879383-36-5, ISBN13: 978-1-879383-36-4. Dewey:070.4/332.0922. LCCN:95-004254.
Audience: **l,u,f.** *Choice, 1996.*

Fink, Conrad C. **PN4784.C7F49 2000**
Bottom Line Writing: Reporting the Sense of Dollars. Trade Cloth. Blackwell Publishing Professional. Ames, IA. 2000. 247p. ISBN:0-8138-2286-6, ISBN13: 978-0-8138-2286-0. Dewey:070.4/4933. LCCN:99-053360.
Audience: **l,u,f.**

Fink, Conrad C. **PN4784.S6F56 2001**
Sportswriting: The Lively Game. Trade Cloth. Blackwell Publishing Professional. Ames, IA. 2001. xii, 304p. ISBN:0-8138-2246-7, ISBN13: 978-0-8138-2246-4. Dewey:070.4/49796. LCCN:00-063472.
Audience: **l,u.**

Frome, Michael **PN4888.E65F76 1998**
Green Ink: An Introduction to Environmental Journalism. Trade Paper. University of Utah Press. Salt Lake City, UT. 1998. 195p. ISBN:0-87480-582-1, ISBN13: 978-0-87480-582-6. Dewey:070.4/493637. LCCN:98-038062.
Audience: **l,u,f.** *Choice, 1999.*

Hallin, Daniel C. **DS559.46.H35 1986**
The Uncensored War: The Media and Vietnam. Trade Cloth. Oxford University Press, Inc. New York, NY. 1986. 292p. ISBN:0-19-503814-2, ISBN13: 978-0-19-503814-9. Dewey:959.704/38. LCCN:85-021409.
Audience: **u,f.** *Choice, 1986.*

Hennessy, Brendan **PN4784.F37**
Writing Feature Articles. Ed. 4. Paper Text. Elsevier Science & Technology Books. Saint Louis, MO. 2005. 416p. ISBN:0-240-51691-5, ISBN13: 978-0-240-51691-2. Dewey:808.06607.
Audience: **u,f.**

Lipschultz, Jeremy Harris & Hilt, Michael L. **PN4888.C8L57 2002**
Crime and Local Television News: Dramatic, Breaking, and Live from the Scene. Chris W. Allen (Contribution by). Cloth over Boards. Lawrence Erlbaum Associates, Inc. Mahwah, NJ. 2002. 184p. LEA's Communication Ser. ISBN:0-8058-3620-9, ISBN13: 978-0-8058-3620-2. Dewey:070.4/49364. LCCN:2001-057761.
Audience: **u,f.** *Choice, 2002.*

Lowes, Mark D. **PN4914.S65L69 1999**
Inside the Sports Pages: Work Routines, Professional Ideologies, and the Manufacture of Sports News. Robert A. Stebbins (Foreword by). Trade Cloth. University of Toronto Press. Toronto, ON. 1999. 352p. ISBN:0-8020-4359-3, ISBN13: 978-0-8020-4359-7. Dewey:070.4/49796. LCCN:00-703942.
Audience: **u,f.** *Choice, 1999.*

Moeller, Susan D. **PN4888.D57M64 1999**
e Compassion Fatigue: How the Media Sell Disease, Famine, War, and Death. E-Book. Routledge. New York, NY. 1999. ISBN:0-203-90035-9, ISBN13: 978-0-203-90035-2. Dewey:070.4/4936334.
Audience: **u,f.**

Simpson, Roger & Coté, William E. **PN4784.D57C68 2006**
Covering Violence: A Guide to Ethical Reporting about Victims and Trauma. Ed. 2. Trade Cloth. Columbia University Press. New York, NY. 2006. 305p. ISBN:0-231-13392-8, ISBN13: 978-0-231-13392-0. Dewey:070.4/33. LCCN:2005-034515.
Audience: **u,f.**

Smith, Perry M. **PN4888.T4S64 1991**
How CNN Fought the War: A View from the Inside. Trade Cloth. Carol Publishing Group. Secaucus, NJ. 1991. 256p. ISBN:1-55972-083-2, ISBN13: 978-1-55972-083-0. Dewey:070.4/499567043. LCCN:91-025990.
Audience: **l,u,f.**

Sylvester, Judith L. & Huffman, Suzanne **DS79.76.S954 2004**
Reporting from the Front: The Media and the Military. Book, Other. Rowman & Littlefield Publishers, Inc. Lanham, MD. 2004. 280p. ISBN:0-7425-3059-0, ISBN13: 978-0-7425-3059-1. Dewey:070.4/4995670443. LCCN:2004-011766.
Audience: **u,f.** *Choice, 2005.*

West, Bernadette M., et al. **PN4888.E65R46 2003**
The Reporter's Environmental Handbook. Ed. 3. M. Jane Lewis, Michael R. Greenberg, David B. Sachsman & Renee M. Rogers (Authors). Trade Cloth. Rutgers University Press. Piscataway, NJ. 2003. 304p. ISBN:0-8135-3286-8, ISBN13: 978-0-8135-3286-8. Dewey:070 4/493637. LCCN:2002-037014.
Audience: **u,f.** *Choice, 2004.*

Wilstein, Steve **PN4784.S6.W66 2002**
e Sports Writing Handbook. E-Book. McGraw-Hill Companies, The. New York, NY. 2001. ISBN:0-07-138973-3, ISBN13: 978-0-07-138973-0. Dewey:808/.066796.
Audience: **u,f.**

Wykes, Maggie **PN4784.C88W95 2000**
News, Crime and Culture. Trade Cloth. Pluto Press. London, 2001. 248p. ISBN:0-7453-1331-0, ISBN13: 978-0-7453-1331-3. Dewey:070.4/49364. LCCN:99-037924.
Audience: **u,f.**

Journalism > Special Topics > International Reporting

Gilboa, Eytan (Editor) **PN4784.F6M39 2002**
Media and Conflict: Framing Issues, Making Policy, Shaping Opinions. Trade Cloth. Transnational Publishers, Inc. Ardsley, NY. 2002. 362p. ISBN:1-57105-270-4, ISBN13: 978-1-57105-270-4. Dewey:070.4/332. LCCN:2002-020300.
Audience: **u,f.**

Hannerz, Ulf **PN4784.F6H35 2003**
Foreign News: Exploring the World of Foreign Correspondents. Trade Cloth. University of Chicago Press. Chicago, IL. 2004. 296p. The Lewis Henry Morgan Lectures ISBN:0-226-31574-6, ISBN13: 978-0-226-31574-4. Dewey:070.4/332. LCCN:2003-011743.
Audience: **u,f.**

Paterson, Chris & Sreberny, Annabelle (Editors) **PN4784.F6**
International News in the 21st Century. Trade Paper, Saddle Stitched. University of Luton Press. Luton, 2004. 304p. ISBN:1-86020-596-8, ISBN13: 978-1-86020-596-5. Dewey:070.4/332. LCCN:2005-440779.
Audience: **u,f.**

Robinson, Piers **PN4784.T4R63 2002**
CNN Effect: Myth of News Media Foreign Policy and Intervention. Paper over Boards. Routledge. New York, NY. 2002. 192p. ISBN:0-415-25904-5, ISBN13: 978-0-415-25904-0. Dewey:070.1/95. LCCN:2002-069888.
Audience: **u,f.**

van Ginneken, Jaap **PN4784.F6G5513 1998**
Understanding Global News: A Critical Introduction. Cloth Text. SAGE Publications, Ltd. London, 1998. 256p. Mass Ser. ISBN:0-7619-5708-1, ISBN13: 978-0-7619-5708-9. Dewey:070.4/332. LCCN:97-061880.
Audience: **u,f.**

Wasburn, Philo C. **PN4784**
The Social Construction of International News: We're Talking about Them, They're Talking about Us. Trade Cloth. Greenwood Publishing Group, Inc. Portsmouth, NH. 2002. 208p. Praeger Series in Political Communication ISBN:0-275-97810-9, ISBN13: 978-0-275-97810-5. Dewey:070.4/332. LCCN:2002-067934.
Audience: **u,f.** *Choice, 2003.*

Journalism > Special Topics > Investigative Reporting

Aucoin, James L. **PN4888.I56A83 2006**
The Evolution of American Investigative Journalism. Trade Cloth. University of Missouri Press. Columbia, MO. 2005. 256p. ISBN:0-8262-1615-3, ISBN13: 978-0-8262-1615-1. Dewey:070.4/3/0973. LCCN:2005-022114.
Audience: **l,u,f.** *Choice, 2006.*

De Burgh, Hugo (Editor) **PN4781.I57 2000**
Investigative Journalism: Context and Practice. Paper over Boards. Routledge. New York, NY. 2000. 336p. ISBN:0-415-19053-3, ISBN13: 978-0-415-19053-4. Dewey:070.4/3. LCCN:99-043659.
Audience: **l,u,f.**

DeFleur, Margaret H. **PN4781.D39 1997**
Computer-Assisted Investigative Reporting. Cloth Text. Lawrence Erlbaum Associates, Inc. Mahwah, NJ. 1997. 272p. LEA's Communication Ser. ISBN:0-8058-2162-7, ISBN13: 978-0-8058-2162-8. Dewey:070.4/3. LCCN:96-051568.
Audience: **u,f.**

Gaines, William **PN4781.G27 1998**
Investigative Reporting for Print and Broadcast. Ed. 2. Paper Text. Thomson Wadsworth. Belmont, CA. 1998. 320p. Mass Communication Ser. ISBN:0-8304-1469-X, ISBN13: 978-0-8304-1469-7. Dewey:070.4/3. LCCN:97-013079.
Audience: **u,f.**

Greenwald, Marilyn & Bernt, Joseph (Editors) **PN4888.I56B49 2000**
The Big Chill: Investigative Reporting in the Current Media Environment. Trade Cloth. Blackwell Publishing Professional. Ames, IA. 1999. 280p. ISBN:0-8138-2805-8, ISBN13: 978-0-8138-2805-3. Dewey:071/.3. LCCN:99-042993.
Audience: **u,f.**

Raphael, Chad **PN1992.8.D6R36 2005**
Investigated Reporting: Muckrakers, Regulators and the Struggle over Television Documentary. Trade Cloth. University of Illinois Press. Champaign, IL. 2005. 304p. The History of Communication Ser. ISBN:0-252-03010-9, ISBN13: 978-0-252-03010-9. Dewey:070.4/3/0973. LCCN:2005-002625.
Audience: **u,f.**

Weinberg, Steve, et al. **PN4781.R38 2002**
The Investigative Reporter's Handbook: A Guide to Documents, Databases and Techniques. Ed. 4. Len Bruzzese & Brant Houston (Authors). Cloth over Boards. Bedford/Saint Martin's. New York, NY. 2002. 589p. ISBN:0-312-24823-7, ISBN13: 978-0-312-24823-9. Dewey:070.4/3. LCCN:2001-095266.
Audience: **u,f.**

Journalism > Special Topics > Literary Journalism

Harrington, Walt (Editor) **PN4784.F37I58 1997**
Intimate Journalism: The Art and Craft of Reporting Everyday Life. Cloth Text. SAGE Publications, Inc. Thousand Oaks, CA. 1997. 376p. ISBN:0-7619-0586-3, ISBN13: 978-0-7619-0586-8. Dewey:070.4/4. LCCN:96-045840.
Audience: **u,f.**

Journalism > Special Topics > Sports Journalism

Andrews, Phil **PN4784.S6**
Sports Journalism: A Practical Introduction. Cloth Text. SAGE Publications, Inc. Thousand Oaks, CA. 2005. 192p. ISBN:1-4129-0270-3, ISBN13: 978-1-4129-0270-0. Dewey:070.4/49796. LCCN:2005-298394.
Audience: **l,u.**

Bender, Gary & Johnson, Michael L. **GV742.3.B46 1994**
Call of the Game: What Really Goes on in the Broadcast Booth. Trade Cloth. Bonus Books, Inc. Chicago, IL. 1994. 263p. ISBN:1-56625-013-7, ISBN13: 978-1-56625-013-9. Dewey:070.4/49796. LCCN:94-026463.
Audience: **g,l,u.**

Gumpert, Gary & Drucker, Susan J. (Editors) **GV867.64.T35 2001**
Take Me Out to the Ballgame: Communicating Baseball. Cloth Text. Hampton Press, Inc. Cresskill, NJ. 2001. 448p. Communication Ser., :Communication and Public Space ISBN:1-57273-301-2, ISBN13: 978-1-57273-301-5. Dewey:070.4/49796357/0973. LCCN:2001-039879.
Audience: **u,f.**

Halberstam, David **GV742.3 .H35 1999**
Sports on New York Radio: A Play-by-Play History. Trade Cloth. McGraw-Hill Companies, The. New York, NY. 1999. 432p. ISBN:1-57028-197-1, ISBN13: 978-1-57028-197-6. Dewey:070.4/49796/097471. LCCN:98-046621.
Audience: **g,l,u,f.**

Schultz, Bradley **PN4784.S6**
Sports Media: Reporting, Producing, and Planning. Ed. 2. Paper Text. Elsevier Science & Technology Books. Saint Louis, MO. 2005. 296p. ISBN:0-240-80731-6, ISBN13: 978-0-240-80731-7. Dewey:070.449796.
Audience: **u,f.**

Journalism > Print Journalism

Emery, Michael, et al. **PN4855.E6 2000**
The Press and America: An Interpretive History of the Mass Media. Ed. 9. Edwin Emery & Nancy L. Roberts (Authors). Trade Cloth. Allyn & Bacon, Inc. Boston, MA. 1999. 698p. ISBN:0-205-29557-6, ISBN13: 978-0-205-29557-9. Dewey:071/.3. LCCN:99-044295.
Audience: **l,u,f.**

Freedom House Staff **PN4736.F742 2004**
Freedom of the Press 2004: A Global Survey of Media Independence. Book, Other. Rowman & Littlefield Publishers, Inc. Lanham, MD. 2004. 216p. Freedom of the Press Ser. ISBN:0-7425-3648-3, ISBN13: 978-0-7425-3648-7. Dewey:323.44/5. LCCN:2005-295341.
Audience: **g,l,u,f.** *Choice, 2005.*

Lamb, Chris **E183.L36 2004**
Drawn to Extremes: The Use and Abuse of Editorial Cartoons in the United States. Trade Cloth. Kegan Paul International, Ltd. London, 2004. 288p. ISBN:0-231-13066-X, ISBN13: 978-0-231-13066-0. Dewey:070.4/42. LCCN:2004-048220.
Audience: **g,u,f.** *Choice, 2005.*

Lawson, Joseph Chappell H. **PN4748.M4 L39 2002**
Building the Fourth Estate: Democratization and the Rise of a Free Press in Mexico. Trade Cloth. University of California Press. Berkeley, CA. 2002. 336p. ISBN:0-520-23170-8, ISBN13: 978-0-520-23170-2. Dewey:323.44/5/0972. LCCN:2002-000715.
Audience: **u,f.** *Choice, 2003.*

Steel, Ronald **PN4874.L45S8 1998**
Walter Lippmann and the American Century. Trade Paper. Transaction Publishers. Somerset, NJ. 1999. 669p. ISBN:0-7658-0464-6, ISBN13: 978-0-7658-0464-8. Dewey:070.4/092/4. LCCN:98-029026.
Audience: **l,u,f.** B

Journalism > Print Journalism > Graphics and Design

Barnhurst, Kevin G. **Z246**
Seeing the Newspaper. Ed. 1. Trade Cloth. St. Martin's Press. Gordonville, VA. 1994. 240p. ISBN:0-312-11058-8, ISBN13: 978-0-312-11058-1. Dewey:686.2/252.
Audience: **l,u,f.**

Brown, Joshua **PN4834 .B76 2002**
Beyond the Lines: Pictorial Reporting, Everyday Life, and the Crisis of Gilded-Age America. Trade Cloth. University of California Press. Berkeley, CA. 2002. 384p. ISBN:0-520-23103-1, ISBN13: 978-0-520-23103-0. Dewey:071/.3/09034. LCCN:2002-000714.
Audience: **l,u,f.** *Choice, 2003.*

Frost, Chris **Z253.3.F76 2003**
Designing for Newspapers and Magazines. Paper over Boards. Routledge. New York, NY. 2003. 192p. Media Skills Ser. ISBN:0-415-29026-0, ISBN13: 978-0-415-29026-5. Dewey:686.2/252. LCCN:2002-154486.
Audience: **l,u,f.**

The Society of News Design Staff (Editor) **Z253.5**
The Best of Newspaper Design. Ed. 26. Paper over Boards. Quayside. Chanhassen, MN. 2005. 272p. Best of Newspaper Design Ser. ISBN:1-59253-169-5, ISBN13: 978-1-59253-169-1. Dewey:686.2252.
Audience: **g,l,u,f.**

Journalism > Print Journalism > Graphics and Design > Photojournalism

Chapnick, Howard **TR820.C5235 1994**
Truth Needs No Ally: Inside Photojournalism. Trade Cloth. University of Missouri Press. Columbia, MO. 1994. 384p. ISBN:0-8262-0954-8, ISBN13: 978-0-8262-0954-2. Dewey:778.9/907049. LCCN:94-006737.
Audience: **l,u,f.**

Journalism > Print Journalism > Magazines

Magazine Publishers of America.
http://www.magazine.org/
Magazine Publishers of America.
Audience: **g,l,u,f.**

Augspurger, Michael **HF3031.A94 2004**
An Economy of Abundant Beauty: Fortune Magazine and Depression America. Book, Other. Cornell University Press. Ithaca, NY. 2004. 336p. ISBN:0-8014-4204-4, ISBN13: 978-0-8014-4204-9. Dewey:306.3/42/097309044. LCCN:2004-006698.
Audience: **l,u,f.** *Choice, 2005.*

Baughman, James L. **PN4874.L76B38 2001**
Henry R. Luce and the Rise of the American News Media. Trade Paper. Johns Hopkins University Press. Baltimore, MD. 2001. 296p. ISBN:0-8018-6716-9, ISBN13: 978-0-8018-6716-3. Dewey:070.5/092 B. LCCN:00-053469.
Audience: **l,u,f.** *Choice, 1988.*

Doss, Erika Lee (Editor) **PN4900.L55L55 2001**
Looking at Life Magazine. Trade Cloth. Smithsonian Institution Press. Washington, DC. 2001. 272p. ISBN:1-56098-989-0, ISBN13: 978-1-56098-989-9. Dewey:051. LCCN:2001-017006.
Audience: **g,l,u,f.**

Mott, Frank L. **PN4877 .M63**
A History of American Magazines: 1885-1905. Trade Cloth. Harvard University Press. Cambridge, MA. 1957. 914p. ISBN:0-674-39553-0, ISBN13: 978-0-674-39553-4. Dewey:051/.09. LCCN:39-002823.
Audience: **g,l,u,f.**

Okker, Patricia **PS1774.H2Z83 1995**
Our Sister Editors: Sarah J. Hale and the Tradition of Nineteenth-Century American Women Editors. Trade Cloth. University of Georgia Press. Athens, GA. 1995. 280p. ISBN:0-8203-1686-5, ISBN13: 978-0-8203-1686-4. Dewey:070.4/8347/092 B. LCCN:94-015269.
Audience: **l,u,f.** *Choice, 1995.*

Peterson, Theodore B. **PN4877.P4**
Magazines in the Twentieth Century. Ed. 2. Trade Paper. Books on Demand. Ann Arbor, MI. 498p. ISBN:0-8357-6199-1, ISBN13: 978-0-8357-6199-4. Dewey:51.09. LCCN:64-018668.
Audience: **g,l,u,f.**

Riley, Sam G. (Editor) **PN4871.A47 1988**
American Magazine Journalists, 1741-1850. Cloth Text. Thomson Gale. Farmington Hills, MI. 1988. 430p. Dictionary of Literary Biography Ser., Vol. 73 ISBN:0-8103-4551-X, ISBN13: 978-0-8103-4551-5. Dewey:070/.92/2. LCCN:88-017586.
Audience: **g,l,u,f.** *Choice, 1989.*

Riley, Sam G. (Editor) **PN4871.A474 1989**
American Magazine Journalists, 1850-1900. Cloth Text. Thomson Gale. Farmington Hills, MI. 1988. 387p. Dictionary of Literary Biography Ser., Vol. 79 ISBN:0-8103-4557-9, ISBN13: 978-0-8103-4557-7. Dewey:070/.92/2 B. LCCN:88-031930.
Audience: **g,l,u,f.** *Choice, 1989.*

Schneirov, Matthew **PN4877.S36 1994**
The Dream of a New Social Order: Popular Magazines in America, 1893-1914. Trade Cloth. Columbia University Press. New York, NY. 1994. 357p. ISBN:0-231-08290-8, ISBN13: 978-0-231-08290-7. Dewey:051/.09034. LCCN:94-012534.
Audience: **g,l,u,f.** *Choice, 1995.*

Singleton, Marvin K. **PN4900.A55S5**
H. L. Mencken and the American Mercury Adventure. Trade Paper. Books on Demand. Ann Arbor, MI. 284p. ISBN:0-608-12809-0, ISBN13: 978-0-608-12809-2. Dewey:51. LCCN:62-010053.
Audience: **g,l,u,f.**

Tebbel, John W. & Zuckerman, Mary E. **PN4832.T43 1991**
The Magazine in America, 1741-1990. Trade Cloth. Oxford University Press, Inc. New York, NY. 1991. 448p. ISBN:0-19-505127-0, ISBN13: 978-0-19-505127-8. Dewey:051/.09. LCCN:90-007874.
Audience: **g,l,u,f.** *Choice, 1992.*

Yagoda, Ben **PN4899.N42**
About Town: The New Yorker and the World It Made. Trade Cloth. DIANE Publishing Company. Collingdale, PA. 2002. 478p. ISBN:0-7567-5634-0, ISBN13: 978-0-7567-5634-5. Dewey:071.4/71.
Audience: **g,l,u,f.** *Choice, 2001.*

Zuckerman, Mary E. **PN4879**
A History of Popular Women's Magazines in the United States, 1792-1995. Book, Other. Greenwood Publishing Group, Inc. Portsmouth, NH. 1998. 296p. Contributions in Women's Studies, Vol. 165 ISBN:0-313-30675-3, ISBN13: 978-0-313-30675-4. Dewey:051/.082. LCCN:97-045646.
Audience: **g,l,u,f.** *Choice, 1999.*

Journalism > Print Journalism > Newspapers

PN4888.P6

☐ Newspaper Association of America.
http://www.naa.org
Audience: **g,l,u,f.**

Ashley, Perry J. **PN4871.A52 1984**
American Newspaper Journalists, 1926-1950. Cloth Text. Thomson Gale. Farmington Hills, MI. 1984. 424p. Dictionary of Literary Biography Ser., Vol. 29 ISBN:0-8103-1707-9, ISBN13: 978-0-8103-1707-9. Dewey:070/.92/2 B. LCCN:84-008182.
Audience: **g,l,u,f.**

Clark, Roy Peter & Scanlan, Christopher **PN4726.A485 2006**
America's Best Newspaper Writing: A Collection of ASNE Prizewinners. Ed. 2. Trade Paper. Bedford/Saint Martin's. New York, NY. 2005. 368p. ISBN:0-312-44367-6, ISBN13: 978-0-312-44367-2. Dewey:081. LCCN:2005-928578.
Audience: **g,l,u,f.**

Conolly-Smith, Peter **E184.G3C652 2004**
Translating America: An Immigrant Press Visualizes American Popular Culture, 1895-1918. Trade Cloth. Smithsonian Institution Press. Washington, DC. 2004. 272p. ISBN:1-58834-167-4, ISBN13: 978-1-58834-167-9. Dewey:305.83/1073/09041. LCCN:2003-057262.
Audience: **g,l,u,f.** *Choice, 2005.*

Graham, Katharine **Z473.G696 1997**
Personal History. Trade Cloth. Alfred A. Knopf Inc. New York, NY. 1997. 656p. ISBN:0-394-58585-2, ISBN13: 978-0-394-58585-7. Dewey:070.9/2. LCCN:96-049638.
Audience: **g,l,u,f.**

Griffith, Sally Fore **PN4874.W52**
Home Town News: William Allen White and the Emporia Gazette. Trade Cloth. Random House Value Publishing. New York, NY. 1992. ISBN:0-517-08520-8, ISBN13: 978-0-517-08520-2. Dewey:818/.5209.
Audience: **g,l,u,f.**

Halberstam, David **PN4888.P6H3 2000**
The Powers That Be. Trade Paper. University of Illinois Press. Champaign, IL. 2000. 792p. ISBN:0-252-06941-2, ISBN13: 978-0-252-06941-3. Dewey:071/.3. LCCN:00-032592.
Audience: **g,l,u,f.** B

Ireland, Alleyne **PN4874.P8I7**
Adventure with a Genius: Recollections of Joseph Pulitzer. Trade Cloth. Johnson Reprint Corporation. New York, NY. 1969. American Studies ISBN:0-384-25945-6, ISBN13: 978-0-384-25945-4. Dewey:70.92.
Audience: **g,l,u,f.**

Ireland, Alleyne **PN4874.P8 I7**
Joseph Pulitzer. Library Binding. Havertown Books. Havertown, PA. 1977. ISBN:0-686-19812-3, ISBN13: 978-0-686-19812-3. Dewey:70.92.
Audience: **g,l,u,f.**

Jackson, Gordon S. **PN5474.J33 1993**
Breaking Story: South African Press. Trade Paper. Westview Press. Boulder, CO. 1993. 308p. ISBN:0-8133-8453-2, ISBN13: 978-0-8133-8453-5. Dewey:079.68. LCCN:92-038861.
Audience: **u,f.** *Choice, 1994.*

Lee, Alfred McClung **PN4908**
The Daily Newspaper in America: The Evolution of a Social Instrument, Set. Library Binding. Routledge. New York, NY. 2000. 812p. American Journalism 1690-1940 Ser. ISBN:0-415-24143-X, ISBN13: 978-0-415-24143-4. Dewey:071/.09.
Audience: **g,l,u,f.** B

Leff, Laurel **D804.7.P73L44 2005**
Buried by the Times: The Holocaust and America's Most Important Newspaper. Cloth Text. Cambridge University Press. New York, NY. 2005. 442p. ISBN:0-521-81287-9, ISBN13: 978-0-521-81287-0. Dewey:070.4/499405318. LCCN:2004-018271.
Audience: **g,l,u,f.** *Choice, 2005.*

Martin, Shannon E. & Copeland, David A. (Editors) **PN4731**
The Function of Newspapers in Society: A Global Perspective. John C. Merrill (Foreword by). Trade Cloth. Greenwood Publishing Group, Inc. Portsmouth, NH. 2003. 192p. ISBN:0-275-97398-0, ISBN13: 978-0-275-97398-8. Dewey:070.1/72/09. LCCN:2002-029765.
Audience: **u,f.** *Choice, 2004.*

Meyer, Philip **PN4867.2.M48 2004**
The Vanishing Newspaper: Saving Journalism in the Information Age. Trade Paper. University of Missouri Press. Columbia, MO. 2005. 272p. ISBN:0-8262-1568-8, ISBN13: 978-0-8262-1568-0. Dewey:071/.3. LCCN:2004-016121.
Audience: **g,l,u,f.** *Choice, 2005.*

Mott, Frank Luther **PN4908**
A History of Newspapers in the United States Through 250 Years, 1690-1940, Set. Library Binding. Routledge. New York, NY. 2000. 782p. American Journalism 1690-1940 Ser. ISBN:0-415-24144-8, ISBN13: 978-0-415-24144-1. Dewey:071/.09.
Audience: **l,u,f.**

Nasaw, David **Z473.H4N37 2000**
The Chief: The Life of William Randolph Hearst. Trade Cloth. Houghton Mifflin Company Trade & Reference Division. Boston, MA. 2000. 752p. ISBN:0-395-82759-0, ISBN13: 978-0-395-82759-8. Dewey:070.5/092 B. LCCN:99-462122.
Audience: **g,l,u,f.**

Nemeth, Neil **PN4784**
News Ombudsmen in North America: Assessing an Experiment in Social Responsibility. Trade Cloth. Greenwood Publishing Group, Inc. Portsmouth, NH. 2003. 184p. Contributions to the Study of Mass Media and Communications Ser., Vol. 67 ISBN:0-313-32136-1, ISBN13: 978-0-313-32136-8. Dewey:070.92/273. LCCN:2003-053027.
Audience: **g,l,u,f.** *Choice, 2004.*

Robinson, Judith **Z473**
The Hearsts: An American Dynasty. Ed. 2. Perfect. Telegraph Hill Press. San Francisco, CA. 2002. 431p. ISBN:0-9643382-1-1, ISBN13: 978-0-9643382-1-0. Dewey:070.5/092 B. LCCN:89-040768.
Audience: **g,l,u,f.** *Choice, 1991.*

Simmons, Charles A. **PN4882.5.S57 1998**
The African American Press: A History of News Coverage During National Crises, with Special Reference to Four Black Newspapers, 1827-1965. Cloth Text. McFarland & Company, Incorporated Publishers. Jefferson, NC. 1997. 205p. ISBN:0-7864-0387-X, ISBN13: 978-0-7864-0387-5. Dewey:071/.3/08996073. LCCN:97-40233.
Audiencc: **g,l,u,f.** *Choice, 1998.*

Sloan, Bill **PN4888.T3S57 2001**
I Watched a Wild Hog Eat My Baby!: A Colorful History of Tabloids and Their Cultural Impact. Trade Cloth. Prometheus Books, Publishers. Amherst, NY. 2001. 251p. ISBN:1-57392-902-6, ISBN13: 978-1-57392-902-8. Dewey:071/.3. LCCN:00-045878.
Audience: **g,l,u,f.**

Smith, Richard N. **PN4874.M48395 1997**
Colonel: The Life and Legend of Robert R. McCormick, 1880-1955. Trade Cloth. Houghton Mifflin Company. New York, NY. 1997. 480p. ISBN:0-395-53379-1, ISBN13: 978-0-395-53379-6. Dewey:070.5/092 B. LCCN:97-005875.
Audience: **g,l,u,f.** *Choice, 1997.*

Smythe, Ted Curtis **PN4855**
The Gilded Age Press, 1865-1900. Trade Cloth. Greenwood Publishing Group, Inc. Portsmouth, NH. 2003. 256p. The History of American Journalism Ser., Vol. 4 ISBN:0-313-30080-1, ISBN13: 978-0-313-30080-6. Dewey:071/.3/09034. LCCN:2003-042071.
Audience: **g,l,u,f.** *Choice, 2004.*

Squires, James D. **PN4888.P6**
Read All about It!: The Corporate Takeover of America's Newspapers. Trade Cloth. Random House Value Publishing. New York, NY. 1995. ISBN:0-517-15312-2, ISBN13: 978-0-517-15312-3. Dewey:071/.3.
Audience: **l,u,f.** *Choice, 1993.*

Swanberg, W. A. **Z473.H4S83**
Citizen Hearst, a Biography of William Randolph Hearst. Paper Text. Textbook Publishers. Temecula, CA. 2003. 555p. ISBN:0-7581-4073-8, ISBN13: 978-0-7581-4073-9. Dewey:070.5/092.
Audience: **l,u,f.** B

Tifft, Susan E. & Jones, Alex S. **Z473.N44**
The Trust: The Private and Powerful Family behind the New York Times. Trade Cloth. DIANE Publishing Company. Collingdale, PA. 2005. 870p. ISBN:0-7567-8712-2, ISBN13: 978-0-7567-8712-7. Dewey:071/.471.
Audience: **g,l,u,f.**

Vogel, Todd (Editor) **PN4882.5.B59 2001**
The Black Press: New Literary and Historical Essays. Cloth Text. Rutgers University Press. Piscataway, NJ. 2001. 256p. ISBN:0-8135-3004-0, ISBN13: 978-0-8135-3004-8. Dewey:071/.3/08996073. LCCN:2001-019292.
Audience: **g,l,u,f.** *Choice, 2002.*

Wallace, Aurora **2005006712**
Newspapers and the Making of Modern America: A History. Trade Cloth. Greenwood Publishing Group, Inc. Portsmouth, NH. 2005. 224p. ISBN:0-313-32320-8, ISBN13: 978-0-313-32320-1. Dewey:071/.3/0904. LCCN:2005-006712.
Audience: **g,l,u,f.** *Choice, 2006.*

Journalism > Print Journalism > Reporting and Editing

Brooks, Brian S., et al. **PN4778.B3 2004**
The Art of Editing: In the Age of Convergence. Ed. 8. James L. Pinson & Jack Zanville Sissors (Authors). Cloth Text. Allyn & Bacon, Inc. Boston, MA. 2004. 432p. ISBN:0-205-41826-0, ISBN13: 978-0-205-41826-8. Dewey:808/.06607. LCCN:2004-050357.
Audience: **l,u,f.**

Garlock, David (Editor) **PN4726.P815 2003**
Pulitzer Prize Feature Stories: America's Best Writing, 1979-2003. Ed. 2. Trade Cloth. Blackwell Publishing Professional. Ames, IA. 2003. xii, 809p. ISBN:0-8138-2545-8, ISBN13: 978-0-8138-2545-8. Dewey:070.4/4/0973. LCCN:2003-010358.
Audience: **g,l,u,f.**

Gelb, Arthur **PN4874.T444**
City Room. Trade Paper. Penguin Group (USA) Inc. New York, NY. 2004. 672p. ISBN:0-425-19831-6, ISBN13: 978-0-425-19831-5. Dewey:070.92 B.
Audience: **l,u,f.** *Choice, 2004.*

Goldstein, Norm (Editor) **PN4783**
The Associated Press Stylebook: And Briefing on Media Law. Trade Paper. Basic Books. New York, NY. 2007. 400p. ISBN:0-465-00489-X, ISBN13: 978-0-465-00489-8. Dewey:808.06607.
Audience: **g,l,u,f.**

Knudson, Jerry W. **PN4775.K54 2000**
In the News: American Journalists View Their Craft. Book, Other. Rowman & Littlefield Publishers, Inc. Lanham, MD. 2001. 256p. ISBN:0-8420-2760-2, ISBN13: 978-0-8420-2760-1. Dewey:071/.3. LCCN:99-036464.
Audience: **l,u,f.**

Willis, Jim **PN4771.W55 2003**
The Human Journalist: Reporters, Perspectives, and Emotions. Paper Text. Greenwood Publishing Group, Inc. Portsmouth, NH. 2003. 176p. ISBN:0-275-97307-7, ISBN13: 978-0-275-97307-0. Dewey:070.4/01/9. LCCN:2003-053566.
Audience: **l,u,f.** *Choice, 2004.*

Journalism > Broadcast Journalism

Baran, Stanley J. & Wallis, Roger **PN4784.F6W27 1990**
The Known World of Broadcast News: International News and the Electronic Media. Trade Paper. Routledge. New York, NY. 1990. 288p. A Comedia Bk. ISBN:0-415-03604-6, ISBN13: 978-0-415-03604-7. Dewey:070.1/9. LCCN:89-049327.
Audience: **l,u,f.**

Boyd, Douglas R. **PN1990.6.A65B69 1999**
Broadcasting in the Arab World: A Survey of the Electronic Media in the Middle East. Ed. 3. Trade Cloth. Blackwell Publishing Professional. Ames, IA. 1999. 412p. ISBN:0-8138-0467-1, ISBN13: 978-0-8138-0467-5. Dewey:384.54/09174927. LCCN:99-037250.
Audience: **g,l,u,f.**

Gross, Larry (Editor), et al. **PN4756**
Image Ethics: The Moral Rights of Subjects in Photographs, Film, and Television. John Stuart Katz & Jay Ruby (Editors). Paper Text. Oxford University Press, Inc. New York, NY. 1991. 400p. Communication and Society Ser. ISBN:0-19-506780-0, ISBN13: 978-0-19-506780-4. Dewey:174.9/097. LCCN:88-004203.
Audience: **u,f.**

Harrison, Jackie **PN4731**
News. Paper over Boards. Routledge. New York, NY. 2006. 304p. Routledge Introductions to Media and Communications Ser. ISBN:0-415-31949-8, ISBN13: 978-0-415-31949-2. Dewey:070.4. LCCN:2005-020196.
Audience: **g,l,u.**

Hilmes, Michele **HE8689.8**
Only Connect: Cultural Hist of Broadcasting in U. S. W/Infotrac. Ed. 2. Paper Text. Thomson Wadsworth. Belmont, CA. 2006. 440p. ISBN:0-495-05036-9, ISBN13: 978-0-495-05036-0. Dewey:384.54/0973. LCCN:2005-935697.
Audience: **l,u.**

Katz, Elihu & Wedell, George **HE8689.95.K37**
Broadcasting in the Third World: Promise and Performance. Trade Cloth. Harvard University Press. Cambridge, MA. 1978. 320p. ISBN:0-674-08341-5, ISBN13: 978-0-674-08341-7. Dewey:384.54/09172/4. LCCN:77-008282.
Audience: **u,f.** B

Paulu, Burton **HE8689.9.E22.P38**
Radio and Television Broadcasting in Eastern Europe. Trade Cloth. University of Minnesota Press. Minneapolis, MN. 1974. xi, 592p. ISBN:0-8166-0721-4, ISBN13: 978-0-8166-0721-1. Dewey:384.54/0947. LCCN:74-079505.
Audience: **u,f.** B

Scannell, Paddy (Editor) **P96.L34 B76 1991**
Broadcast Talk, Vol. 5. Trade Paper. SAGE Publications, Ltd. London, 1991. 224p. Media, Culture and Society Ser. ISBN:0-8039-8375-1, ISBN13: 978-0-8039-8375-5. Dewey:302.23. LCCN:91-052965.
Audience: **l,u.**

Scannell, Paddy **P91.S297 1996**
Radio, TV and Modern Life: A Phenomenology of Broadcasting. Trade Cloth. Blackwell Publishing, Inc. Malden, MA. 1996. 208p. ISBN:0-631-19874-1, ISBN13: 978-0-631-19874-1. Dewey:302.2/3. LCCN:96-013393.
Audience: **l,u.**

Smith, F. Leslie, et al. **HE8689.8.S63 1998**
Perspectives on Radio and Television: Telecommunication in the United States. Ed. 4. John W. Wright II & David H. Ostroff (Authors). Cloth over Boards. Lawrence Erlbaum Associates, Inc. Mahwah, NJ. 1998. 748p. Communication Ser. ISBN:0-8058-2092-2, ISBN13: 978-0-8058-2092-8. Dewey:384.54/0973. LCCN:99-160204.
Audience: **u,f.**

Sterling, Christopher H. & Kittross, John M. **HE8689.8.S73 2002**
e Stay Tuned: A History of American Broadcasting. Ed. 3. E-Book. NetLibrary, Inc. Boulder, CO. 2002. xxx, 975p. LEA's Communication Ser. ISBN:0-585-39926-3, ISBN13: 978-0-585-39926-3. Dewey:384.54/0973. LCCN:2001-040808.
Audience: **u,f.**

Willis, Jim **PN4797**
The Shadow World: Life Between the News Media and Reality. Trade Cloth. Greenwood Publishing Group, Inc. Portsmouth, NH. 1991. 272p. ISBN:0-275-93424-1, ISBN13: 978-0-275-93424-8. Dewey:070.4/3. LCCN:90-040802.
Audience: **u,f.** *Choice, 1991.*

Journalism > Broadcast Journalism > Documentary

Aitken, Ian (Editor) **PN1995.9.D6E53 2005**
Encyclopedia of the Documentary Film. Paper over Boards. Routledge. New York, NY. 2005. 1968p. ISBN:1-57958-445-4, ISBN13: 978-1-57958-445-0. Dewey:070.1/8. LCCN:2005-046519.
Audience: **l,u.** *Choice, 2006.*

Beattie, Keith **PN1995.9.D6B384 2004**
Documentary Screens: Non-Fiction Film and Television. Cloth over Boards. Palgrave Macmillan. New York, NY. 2004. 224p. ISBN:0-333-74116-1, ISBN13: 978-0-333-74116-0. Dewey:070.1/8. LCCN:2004-042736.
Audience: **l,u,f.**

Boyle, Deirdre **PN1992.945.B68 1997**
Subject to Change: Guerrilla Television Revisited. Trade Cloth. Oxford University Press, Inc. New York, NY. 1997. 304p. ISBN:0-19-504334-0, ISBN13: 978-0-19-504334-1. Dewey:791.45/0973/09046. LCCN:96-033448.
Audience: **l,u,f.** *Choice, 1997.*

Curtin, Michael **PN1992.8.D6C87 1995**
Redeeming the Wasteland: Television Documentary and Cold War Politics. Cloth Text. Rutgers University Press. Piscataway, NJ. 1995. 350p. Communications, Media and Culture Ser. ISBN:0-8135-2221-8, ISBN13: 978-0-8135-2221-0. Dewey:070.1/95. LCCN:95-012436.
Audience: **l,u,f.** *Choice, 1996.*

Gaines, Jane & Renov, Michael (Editors) **PN1995.9.D6C535 1999**
Collecting Visible Evidence. Book, Other. University of Minnesota Press. Minneapolis, MN. 1999. ix, 339p. Visible Evidence Ser., Vol. 6 ISBN:0-8166-3135-2, ISBN13: 978-0-8166-3135-3. Dewey:070.1/8. LCCN:99-014043.
Audience: **l,u,f.**

Rosenthal, Alan **PN1995.9.D6R65 1996**
Writing, Directing, and Producing Documentary Films and Videos. Trade Cloth. Southern Illinois University Press. Carbondale, IL. 1996. 320p. ISBN:0-8093-2014-2, ISBN13: 978-0-8093-2014-1. Dewey:070.1/8. LCCN:95-017159.
Audience: **u,f.**

Journalism > Broadcast Journalism > Radio

Briggs, Asa **PN1990.6.G7 B75**
The History of Broadcasting in the United Kingdom. Trade Cloth. Oxford University Press, Inc. New York, NY. 1995. 3424p. ISBN:0-19-215966-6, ISBN13: 978-0-19-215966-3. Dewey:384.54/0941.
Audience: **l,u,f.**

Browne, Donald R. **HE8697**
International Radio Broadcasting: The Limits of the Limitless Medium. Trade Cloth. Greenwood Publishing Group, Inc. Portsmouth, NH. 1982. 369p. ISBN:0-275-90767-8, ISBN13: 978-0-275-90767-9. Dewey:384.54. LCCN:81-022707.
Audience: **l,u,f.** B

Crook, Tim **PN4784.R2C76 1998**
International Radio Journalism. Paper over Boards. Routledge. New York, NY. 1998. 320p. Communication and Society Ser. ISBN:0-415-09672-3, ISBN13: 978-0-415-09672-0. Dewey:070.1/94. LCCN:97-016886.
Audience: **l,u,f.**

Lewis, Peter & Booth, Jerry (Editors) **HE8675.L49 1990**
The Invisible Medium: Commercial, Public and Community Radio. Trade Cloth. Howard University Press. Washington, DC. 1990. 250p. ISBN:0-88258-032-9, ISBN13: 978-0-88258-032-6. Dewey:384.54. LCCN:90-004357.
Audience: **l,u,f.** *Choice, 1991.*

Nicholas, Sian **D810.P7G765 1996**
The Echo of War: Home Front Propaganda and the Wartime BBC 1939-1945. Cloth Text. Manchester University Press. Manchester, 1997. 240p. ISBN:0-7190-4608-4, ISBN13: 978-0-7190-4608-7. Dewey:940.5/4886/41. LCCN:95-032668.
Audience: **l,u,f.** *Choice, 1996.*

Scannell, Paddy & Cardiff, David **PN1991.3.G7S28 1991**
A Social History of British Broadcasting, 1922-1939: Serving the Nation. Trade Cloth. Blackwell Publishing, Inc. Malden, MA. 1991. 400p. ISBN:0-631-17543-1, ISBN13: 978-0-631-17543-8. Dewey:302.23/44/0941. LCCN:90-035295.
Audience: **l,u,f.** *Choice, 1992.*

Sterling, Christopher H. (Editor) **TK6544.M84 2004**
Encyclopedia of Radio, Set. Cloth Text. Routledge. New York, NY. 2003. 1696p. ISBN:1-57958-249-4, ISBN13: 978-1-57958-249-4. Dewey:384.54/03. LCCN:2003-015683.
Audience: **l,u.** *Choice, 2004.*

Journalism > Broadcast Journalism > Reporting and Editing

Arnold, George T. **PN4783.A76 2002**
Media Writer's Handbook: A Guide to Common Editing and Writing Problems. Ed. 3. Paper Text. McGraw-Hill Higher Education. Burr Ridge, IL. 2002. 312p. ISBN:0-07-248195-1, ISBN13: 978-0-07-248195-2. Dewey:808/.027. LCCN:2002-071787.
Audience: **l,u.**

Boyd, Andrew **PN4784.B75B69 2001**
Broadcast Journalism. Ed. 5. Paper Text. Elsevier Science & Technology Books. Saint Louis, MO. 2000. 448p. ISBN:0-240-51571-4, ISBN13: 978-0-240-51571-7. Dewey:070.1/94. LCCN:00-064672.
Audience: **u,f.**

Callahan, Christopher **PN4729.3.C35 2002**
A Journalist's Guide to the Internet: The Net As a Reporting Tool. Ed. 2. Trade Paper. Allyn & Bacon, Inc. Boston, MA. 2002. 144p. ISBN:0-205-35098-4, ISBN13: 978-0-205-35098-8. Dewey:070.4/0285. LCCN:2002-018411.
Audience: **l,u.**

Houston, Brant **PN4784.E5**
Computer-Assisted Reporting: A Practical Guide. Trade Paper. Bedford/Saint Martin's. New York, NY. 2003. 246p. ISBN:0-312-41149-9, ISBN13: 978-0-312-41149-7. Dewey:070.4/0285.
Audience: **l,u.**

Kalbfeld, Brad **PN4783.K35 2001**
Associated Press Broadcast News Handbook. Paper Text. McGraw-Hill Companies, The. New York, NY. 2000. 480p. Associated Press Ser. ISBN:0-07-136388-2, ISBN13: 978-0-07-136388-4. Dewey:808/.06607. LCCN:00-048698.
Audience: **l,u,f.**

Lanson, Jerry & Fought, Barbara Croll **PN4781.L37 1999**
News in a New Century: Reporting in an Age of Converging Media. Paper Text. Pine Forge Press. Newbury Park, CA. 1999. 360p. ISBN:0-7619-8506-9, ISBN13: 978-0-7619-8506-8. Dewey:070.4/3. LCCN:98-025449.
Audience: **l,u,f.**

MacDonald, Ronald **PN4784.B75M24 1994**
A Broadcast News Manual of Style. Ed. 2. Trade Paper. Allyn & Bacon, Inc. Boston, MA. 2002. 384p. ISBN:0-8013-1110-1, ISBN13: 978-0-8013-1110-9. Dewey:808/.02. LCCN:93-006072.
Audience: **l,u,f.** *Choice, 1994.*

Missouri Group Staff, et al. **PN4781.N4 2005**
News Reporting and Writing. Ed. 8. Brian S. Brooks, George Kennedy, Daryl R. Moen & Don Ranly (Authors). Trade Paper. Bedford/Saint Martin's. New York, NY. 2004. 608p. ISBN:0-312-41646-6, ISBN13: 978-0-312-41646-1. Dewey:070.4/3. LCCN:2004-101847.
Audience: **l,u.**

Schwartz, Jerry R. **PN4781.S395 2002**
Associated Press Reporting Handbook. Trade Paper. McGraw-Hill Companies, The. New York, NY. 2001. 264p. Associated Press Ser. ISBN:0-07-137217-2, ISBN13: 978-0-07-137217-6. Dewey:070.4/3. LCCN:2002-277588.
Audience: **l,u,f.**

Stephens, Mitchell & Olson, Beth **PN4784.B75S7 2005**
Broadcast News. Ed. 4. Paper Text. Thomson Wadsworth. Belmont, CA. 2004. 448p. Wadsworth Series in Broadcast and Production ISBN:0-534-59570-7, ISBN13: 978-0-534-59570-8. Dewey:070.1/9. LCCN:2004-108372.
Audience: **l,u,f.**

Journalism > Broadcast Journalism > Television

Arlen, Michael J. **PN1992.3.U5A9 1997**
Living Room War. Robert J. Thompson (Editor). Trade Paper. Syracuse University Press. Syracuse, NY. 1997. xii, 242p. Television Ser. ISBN:0-8156-0466-1, ISBN13: 978-0-8156-0466-2. Dewey:791.45/0973. LCCN:97-003070.
Audience: **l,u,f.** B

Baum, Matthew A. **PN4888.T4B34 2003**
Soft News Goes to War: Public Opinion and American Foreign Policy in the New Media Age. Trade Cloth. Princeton University Press. Princeton, NJ. 2003. 344p. ISBN:0-691-11586-9, ISBN13: 978-0-691-11586-3. Dewey:070.1950973. LCCN:2002-044718.
Audience: **l,u,f.** *Choice, 2004.*

Carter, Cynthia, et al. **PN4784.W7N48 1998**
News, Gender and Power. Gill Branston & Stuart Allan (Authors). Paper over Boards. Routledge. New York, NY. 1998. 320p. ISBN:0-415-17015-X, ISBN13: 978-0-415-17015-4. Dewey:070.4/082. LCCN:98-012179.
Audience: **l,u,f.**

Collins, Scott **PN4888.T4C65 2004**
Crazy Like a Fox: The Inside Story of How Fox News Beat CNN. Trade Cloth. Penguin Group (USA) Inc. New York, NY. 2004. 288p. ISBN:1-59184-029-5, ISBN13: 978-1-59184-029-9. Dewey:070.4/3/0973. LCCN:2003-068955.
Audience: **g,l,u,f.** *Choice, 2004.*

Donovan, Robert J. & Scherer, Raymond L. **PN4888.T4 D66 1992**
Unsilent Revolution: Television News and American Public Life, 1948-1991. Lee H. Hamilton (Contribution by). Trade Paper. Cambridge University Press. New York, NY. 1992. 369p. Woodrow Wilson Center Ser. ISBN:0-521-42862-9, ISBN13: 978-0-521-42862-0. Dewey:070.195. LCCN:91-041189.
Audience: **l,u,f.** *Choice, 1992.*

Fry, Katherine **PN4888.T4F78 2003**
Constructing the Heartland: Television News and Natural Disaster. Trade Cloth. Hampton Press, Inc. Cresskill, NJ. 2003. xiv, 171p. The Hampton Press Communication Ser. ISBN:1-57273-516-3, ISBN13: 978-1-57273-516-3. Dewey:070.1/95. LCCN:2003-051112.
Audience: **l,u,f.**

Hallin, Daniel C. **PN4888.T4H35 1994**
We Keep America on Top of the World: Television Journalism and the Public Sphere. Trade Paper. Routledge. New York, NY. 1993. 200p. Communication and Society Ser. ISBN:0-415-09143-8, ISBN13: 978-0-415-09143-5. Dewey:070.195. LCCN:93-021867.
Audience: **l,u,f.**

Hamilton, James T. **PN4888.T4H355 2004**
All the News That's Fit to Sell: How the Market Transforms Information into News. Trade Cloth. Princeton University Press. Princeton, NJ. 2003. 344p. ISBN:0-691-11680-6, ISBN13: 978-0-691-11680-8. Dewey:070.1/95. LCCN:2003-042894.
Audience: **l,u,f.**

Hess, Stephen **PN4784.F6H47 1996**
International News and Foreign Correspondents. Trade Cloth. Brookings Institution Press. Washington, DC. 1995. 209p. Newswork Ser., Vol. 5 ISBN:0-8157-3630-4, ISBN13: 978-0-8157-3630-1. Dewey:070.433. LCCN:95-041808.
Audience: **l,u,f.** *Choice, 1996.*

Jensen, Klaus **PN4784.T4N48 1998**
News of the World: World Cultures Look at Television News. Cloth Text. Routledge. New York, NY. 1998. 248p. Research in Cultural and Media Studies ISBN:0-415-16107-X, ISBN13: 978-0-415-16107-7. Dewey:070.1/95. LCCN:97-047559.
Audience: **l,u,f.**

Langer, John **PN4784.T4L29 1998**
Tabloid Television: Popular Journalism and the "Other News". Paper over Boards. Routledge. New York, NY. 1997. 200p.

Communication and Society Ser. ISBN:0-415-06636-0, ISBN13: 978-0-415-06636-5. Dewey:070.1/95. LCCN:97-012734.
Audience: **l,u,f.**

Lynch, Marc **JQ1850.A91L93 2006**
Voices of the New Arab Public: Iraq, Al-Jazeera and Middle East Politics Today. Trade Cloth. Columbia University Press. New York, NY. 2005. 320p. ISBN:0-231-13448-7, ISBN13: 978-0-231-13448-4. Dewey:306.2/0917/492709051. LCCN:2005-049677.
Audience: **l,u,f.** *Choice, 2006.*

MacGregor, Brent **PN4784.T4M23 1997**
Live, Direct and Biased?: Making Television News in the Satellite Age. Paper Text. Oxford University Press, Inc. New York, NY. 1997. 238p. A Hodder Arnold Publication Ser. ISBN:0-340-66225-5, ISBN13: 978-0-340-66225-0. Dewey:070.1/95. LCCN:96-037949.
Audience: **l,u,f.**

Miles, Hugh **HE8700.9.Q22M55 2005**
Al Jazeera: The Inside Story of the Arab News Channel That Is Challenging the West. Trade Cloth. Grove/Atlantic, Inc. New York, NY. 2005. 320p. ISBN:0-8021-1789-9, ISBN13: 978-0-8021-1789-2. Dewey:070.4/3/09174927. LCCN:2004-054064.
Audience: **g,l,u,f.** *Choice, 2005.*

Newcomb, Horace (Editor) **PN1992.18.E53 2005**
Encyclopedia of Television. Ed. 2. Library Binding. Fitzroy Dearborn Publishers, Inc. Chicago, IL. 2004. 2800p. ISBN:1-57958-394-6, ISBN13: 978-1-57958-394-1. Dewey:384.55/03. LCCN:2004-003947.
Audience: **l,u.** *Choice, 2005, 1997.*

Robinson, Piers **PN4784.T4R63 2002**
CNN Effect: Myth of News Media Foreign Policy and Intervention. Trade Paper. Routledge. New York, NY. 2002. 192p. ISBN:0-415-25905-3, ISBN13: 978-0-415-25905-7. Dewey:070.1/95. LCCN:2002-069888.
Audience: **l,u,f.**

Communication > Mass Media

PN1993.4

☐ The Internet Movie Database.
http://www.imdb.com/
Audience: **g.**

P91

☐ Library Resources for Communication Studies.
http://www.lib.washington.edu/subject/communications/lrcs/
Audience: **g,l,u,f.**

Bourgault, Louise M. **P92.A46B68 1995**
Mass Media in Sub-Saharan Africa. Trade Cloth. Indiana University Press. Bloomington, IN. 1995. 320p. ISBN:0-253-31250-7, ISBN13: 978-0-253-31250-1. Dewey:302.23/0967. LCCN:94-027829.
Audience: **u,f.** *Choice, 1996.*

Fox, Elizabeth & Waisbord, Silvio R. (Editors) **P95.82.L29L38 2002**
Latin Politics, Global Media. Trade Cloth. University of Texas Press. Austin, TX. 2002. 227p. ISBN:0-292-72536-1, ISBN13: 978-0-292-72536-2. Dewey:302.23/098. LCCN:2001-048064.
Audience: **u,f.**

Gunaratne, Shelton A. (Editor) **P92.A7H36 2000**
Handbook of the Media in Asia. Trade Cloth. SAGE Publications, Inc. Thousand Oaks, CA. 2000. 732p. ISBN:0-7619-9427-0, ISBN13: 978-0-7619-9427-5. Dewey:302.23095. LCCN:00-021783.
Audience: **u,f.**

Hafez, Kai & Paletz, David L. (Editors) **P92.M5M374 2001**
Mass Media and Society in the Middle East. Cloth Text. Hampton Press, Inc. Cresskill, NJ. 2001. x, 249p. Communication Ser., :Political Communication ISBN:1-57273-303-9, ISBN13: 978-1-57273-303-9. Dewey:302.23/0956. LCCN:00-053557.
Audience: **u,f.** *Choice, 2002.*

Johnston, Donald H. (Editor) **P87.5**
Encyclopedia of International Media and Communications, Set. Trade Cloth. Elsevier Science & Technology Books. Saint Louis, MO. 2003. 2733p. ISBN:0-12-387670-2, ISBN13: 978-0-12-387670-6. Dewey:302.23/03. LCCN:2003-100764.
Audience: **g,l,u,f.** *Choice, 2003.*

Kelly, Mary J. (Editor), et al. **P92.E9**
The Media in Europe: The Euromedia Handbook. Ed. 3. Gianpietro Mazzoleni & Denis McQuail (Editors). Paper Text. SAGE Publications, Inc. Thousand Oaks, CA. 2004. 288p. ISBN:0-7619-4132-0, ISBN13: 978-0-7619-4132-3. Dewey:302.23/094. LCCN:2003-101546.
Audience: **u,f.** *Choice, 2004.*

Communication > Mass Media > History

Blanchard, Margaret A. (Editor) **P92.U5H55 1998**
History of the Mass Media in the United States: An Encyclopedia. Trade Cloth. Fitzroy Dearborn Publishers, Inc. Chicago, IL. 1998. 700p. ISBN:1-57958-012-2, ISBN13: 978-1-57958-012-4. Dewey:302.23/0973/03. LCCN:98-233183.
Audience: **l,u.** *Choice, 1999.*

Briggs, Asa & Burke, Peter **P90.B695 2005**
Social History of the Media: From Gutenburg to the Internet. Ed. 2. Trade Cloth. Polity Press. Cambridge, 2005. 400p. ISBN:0-7456-3511-3, ISBN13: 978-0-7456-3511-8. Dewey:302.2309. LCCN:2006-271137.
Audience: **l,u,f.** *Choice, 2006.*

Crowley, David & Heyer, Paul **P90.C62945 2007**
Communication in History: Technology, Culture, Society. Ed. 5. Trade Paper. Allyn & Bacon, Inc. Boston, MA. 2006. 368p. ISBN:0-205-48388-7, ISBN13: 978-0-205-48388-4. Dewey:302.209. LCCN:2006-043220.
Audience: **g,l,u,f.**

Hartley, John **P96.A83H37 1992**
The Politics of Pictures: The Creation of the Public in the Age of Popular Media. Paper over Boards. Routledge. New York, NY. 1993. 256p. ISBN:0-415-01541-3, ISBN13: 978-0-415-01541-7. Dewey:302.23. LCCN:91-047601.
Audience: **u,f.**

Marvin, Carolyn **HE7775**
When Old Technologies Were New: Thinking about Electric Communication in the Late Nineteenth Century. Paper Text. Oxford University Press, Inc. New York, NY. 1990. 272p. ISBN:0-19-506341-4, ISBN13: 978-0-19-506341-7. Dewey:384.0973. LCCN:86-033339.
Audience: **u,f.**

Peters, John Durham **P90**
Speaking into the Air: A History of the Idea of Communication. Trade Paper. University of Chicago Press. Chicago, IL. 2001. 304p. ISBN:0-226-66277-2, ISBN13: 978-0-226-66277-0. Dewey:302.2/01.
Audience: **u,f.** *Choice, 2000.*

Communication > Mass Media > Criticism

Alterman, Eric **PN4784.O24.A44 2004**
[e] What Liberal Media?: The Truth about Bias and the News. E-Book. Recorded Books, LLC. Prince Frederick, MD. ISBN:1-4175-7426-7, ISBN13: 978-1-4175-7426-1. Dewey:302.23.
Audience: **u,f.**

Berger, Arthur A. **P90.B413 1995**
Essentials of Mass Communication Theory. Trade Paper. SAGE Publications, Inc. Thousand Oaks, CA. 1995. 224p. ISBN:0-8039-7357-8, ISBN13: 978-0-8039-7357-2. Dewey:302.2/3. LCCN:95-011882.
Audience: **u,f.** *Choice, 1995.*

Brooks, Brian S., et al. **P96.A86T45 2004**
Telling the Story: The Convergence of Print, Broadcast, and Online Media. Ed. 2. George Kennedy, Daryl R. Moen & Don Ranly (Authors), Missouri Group Staff (Contribution by). Trade Paper. Bedford/Saint Martin's. New York, NY. 2003. 394p. ISBN:0-312-40906-0, ISBN13: 978-0-312-40906-7. Dewey:808.066302. LCCN:2003-107541.
Audience: **l,u.**

Curran, James & **P94.6**
Gurevitch, Michael (Editors)
Mass Media and Society. Ed. 4. Trade Paper. Hodder Education. London, 2005. 408p. A Hodder Arnold Publication ISBN:0-340-88499-1, ISBN13: 978-0-340-88499-7. Dewey:302.2/3.
Audience: **l,u,f.**

Dates, Jannette L. & **P94.5.A372 U574 1993**
Barlow, William (Editors)
Split Image: African Americans in the Mass Media. Ed. 2. Trade Paper. Howard University Press. Washington, DC. 1993. ISBN:0-88258-179-1, ISBN13: 978-0-88258-179-8. Dewey:302.23/089/96073. LCCN:92-047367.
Audience: **u,f.**

Davis, Jane **PS173**
The White Image in the Black Mind: A Study of African American Literature. Trade Cloth. Greenwood Publishing Group, Inc. Portsmouth, NH. 2000. 184p. Contributions in Afro-American and African Studies Ser., No. 194 ISBN:0-313-30464-5, ISBN13: 978-0-313-30464-4. Dewey:810.9/896073. LCCN:99-036173.
Audience: **u,f.** *Choice, 2000.*

Douglas, Susan J. **P94.5.W65**
Where the Girls Are: Growing up Female with the Mass Media. Trade Paper. Crown Publishing Group. New York, NY. 1995. 368p. ISBN:0-8129-2530-0, ISBN13: 978-0-8129-2530-2. Dewey:302.2/3/082.
Audience: **u,f.** *Choice, 1995.*

Downing, John, et al. **P90**
Questioning the Media: A Critical Introduction. Ed. 2. Ali Mohammadi & Annabelle Sreberny-Mohammadi (Authors). Cloth Text. SAGE Publications, Inc. Thousand Oaks, CA. 1995. 400p. ISBN:0-8039-7199-0, ISBN13: 978-0-8039-7199-8. Dewey:302.2/3.
Audience: **u,f.**

Gross, Larry P. **P94.5.G38G76 2001**
Up from Invisibility: Lesbians, Gay Men, and the Media in America. Trade Cloth. Columbia University Press. New York, NY. 2001. 320p. Between Men, Between Women Ser. ISBN:0-231-11952-6, ISBN13: 978-0-231-11952-8. Dewey:305.9/0664/0973. LCCN:2001-042140.
Audience: **g,u,f.**

Kitch, Carolyn **P94.5.W652U655 2001**
The Girl on the Magazine Cover: The Origins of Visual Stereotypes in American Mass Media. Trade Cloth. University of North Carolina Press. Chapel Hill, NC. 2001. 272p. ISBN:0-8078-2653-7, ISBN13: 978-0-8078-2653-9. Dewey:302.23/082/0973. LCCN:2001-027415.
Audience: **u,f.** *Choice, 2002.*

Lester, Paul Martin & **P96.S74I45 2003**
Ross, Susan Dente (Editors)
Images That Injure: Pictorial Stereotypes in the Media. Ed. 2. Trade Cloth. Greenwood Publishing Group, Inc. Portsmouth, NH. 2003. 336p. ISBN:0-275-97845-1, ISBN13: 978-0-275-97845-7. Dewey:303.3/85. LCCN:2003-042941.
Audience: **u,f.**

MacKinnon, Kenneth **HQ1090**
Representing Men: Maleness and Masculinity in the Media. Trade Paper. Oxford University Press, Inc. New York, NY. 2003. 144p. An Arnold Publication ISBN:0-340-80833-0, ISBN13: 978-0-340-80833-7. Dewey:305.31. LCCN:2004-540747.
Audience: **u,f.**

McChesney, Robert W. **P95.82.U6M38 1999**
Rich Media, Poor Democracy: Communication Politics in Dubious Times. Trade Cloth. University of Illinois Press. Champaign, IL. 1999. 448p. History of Communication Ser. ISBN:0-252-02448-6, ISBN13: 978-0-252-02448-1. Dewey:302.23/0973. LCCN:98-058055.
Audience: **u,f.** *Choice, 2000.*

McLuhan, Marshall **P90.M26 2003**
Understanding Media: The Extensions of Man (Critical Edition). Terrence Gordon (Editor). Trade Cloth. Gingko Press, Inc. Corte

Madera, CA. 2005. 640p. ISBN:1-58423-073-8, ISBN13: 978-1-58423-073-1. Dewey:302.23. LCCN:2003-012174.
Audience: **u,f.**

Postman, Neil **P94.P63 1986**
Amusing Ourselves to Death: Public Discourse in the Age of Show Business. Trade Paper. Penguin Group (USA) Inc. New York, NY. 1986. 192p. ISBN:0-14-009438-5, ISBN13: 978-0-14-009438-1. Dewey:302.234. LCCN:86-009513.
Audience: **u,f.** *Choice, 1986.*

Singer, Dorothy G. & Singer, Jerome L. (Editors) **HQ784**
Handbook of Children and the Media. Trade Paper. SAGE Publications, Inc. Thousand Oaks, CA. 2002. 784p. ISBN:0-7619-1955-4, ISBN13: 978-0-7619-1955-1. Dewey:302.23/45/083.
Audience: **u,f.** *Choice, 2001.*

Communication > Mass Media > Ethics

Day, Louis A. **P94**
Ethics in Media Communications: Cases and Controversies. Ed. 3. Paper Text. Thomson Wadsworth. Belmont, CA. 1999. 448p. Mass Communication ISBN:0-534-56187-X, ISBN13: 978-0-534-56187-1. Dewey:175. LCCN:99-011387.
Audience: **l,u,f.**

Denton, Robert E. Jr. (Editor) **JA85**
Political Communication Ethics: An Oxymoron? Paper Text. Greenwood Publishing Group, Inc. Portsmouth, NH. 2000. 288p. Series in Political Communication ISBN:0-275-96483-3, ISBN13: 978-0-275-96483-2. Dewey:324/.01/4. LCCN:99-055872.
Audience: **l,u,f.**

Japp, Phyllis M., et al. **P94.C5725 2005**
Communication Ethics, Media, and Popular Culture. Mark Meister & Debra K. Japp (Authors). Trade Cloth. Peter Lang Publishing, Inc. New York, NY. 2005. vi, 309p. ISBN:0-8204-7119-4, ISBN13: 978-0-8204-7119-8. Dewey:175. LCCN:2004-027922.
Audience: **l,u.**

Wilkins, Lee & Coleman, Renita **PN4756.W56 2005**
The Moral Media: How Journalists Reason about Ethics. Lee Seow Ting (Contribution by). Trade Paper. Lawrence Erlbaum Associates, Inc. Mahwah, NJ. 2004. 184p. LEA's Communication Ser. ISBN:0-8058-4475-9, ISBN13: 978-0-8058-4475-7. Dewey:174/.90704. LCCN:2004-050053.
Audience: **l,u,f.**

Wulfemeyer, K. Tim & Buckalew, James K. **P90**
Mass Media in the New Millennium: Structures, Functions, Issues and Ethics. Ed. 3. Trade Paper. Kendall/Hunt Publishing Company. Dubuque, IA. 2005. 388p. ISBN:0-7575-1683-1, ISBN13: 978-0-7575-1683-2. Dewey:302.23.
Audience: **u,f.**

Communication > Mass Media > Print Media

Affe, Robert B. **PN4833.I62 2005**
Internet Newspapers: The Making of a Mainstream Medium. Xigen Li (Editor), Erik P. Bucy, Zhanwei Cao & Jinmyung Choi (Contribution by). Cloth over Boards. Lawrence Erlbaum Associates, Inc. Mahwah, NJ. 2006. 328p. LEA's Communication Ser. ISBN:0-8058-5416-9, ISBN13: 978-0-8058-5416-9. Dewey:0701/72. LCCN:2005-040575.
Audience: **u,f.**

Kipphan, Helmut (Editor) **Z244**
Handbook of Print Media: Technologies and Production Methods. Mixed Media. Springer. New York, NY. 2006. XX, 1207p. ISBN:3-540-33570-6, ISBN13: 978-3-540-33570-2. Dewey:686.2.
Audience: **u,f.**

Lamb, Chris **E183.L36 2004**
Drawn to Extremes: The Use and Abuse of Editorial Cartoons in the United States. Trade Paper. Columbia University Press. New York, NY. 2006. 288p. ISBN:0-231-13067-8, ISBN13: 978-0-231-13067-7. Dewey:070.4/42. LCCN:2004-048220.
Audience: **u,f.** *Choice, 2005.*

Martin, Shannon E. & Copeland, David A. (Editors) **PN4731**
The Function of Newspapers in Society: A Global Perspective. John C. Merrill (Foreword by). Trade Cloth. Greenwood Publishing Group, Inc. Portsmouth, NH. 2003. 192p. ISBN:0-275-97398-0, ISBN13: 978-0-275-97398-8. Dewey:070.1/72/09. LCCN:2002-029765.
Audience: **u,f.** *Choice, 2004.*

Communication > Mass Media > Broadcast Media

Baughman, James L. **P92.U5B345 2006**
The Republic of Mass Culture: Journalism, Filmmaking, and Broadcasting in America since 1941. Ed. 3. Trade Cloth. Johns Hopkins University Press. Baltimore, MD. 2006. 320p. The American Moment Ser. ISBN:0-8018-8315-6, ISBN13: 978-0-8018-8315-6. Dewey:302.23/0973/0945. LCCN:2005-018128.
Audience: **u,f.** *Choice, 1992.*

Hilmes, Michele **PN1990.6.U5H497 2003**
Connections: A Broadcast History Reader. Paper Text. Thomson Wadsworth. Belmont, CA. 2002. 392p. Radio/TV/Film Ser. ISBN:0-534-55217-X, ISBN13: 978-0-534-55217-6. Dewey:384.54/0973. LCCN:2002-111516.
Audience: **l,u.**

Mindich, David T. Z. **PN4731.M49 2004**
Tuned Out: Why Americans under 40 Don't Follow the News. Cloth Text. Oxford University Press, Inc. New York, NY. 2004. 192p. ISBN:0-19-516140-8, ISBN13: 978-0-19-516140-3. Dewey:302.23/083. LCCN:2004-046938.
Audience: **l,u,f.** *Choice, 2005.*

Schechter, Danny **P90.S337 1997**
The More You Watch, the Less You Know: News Wars - (Sub)Merged Hopes - Media Adventures. Jackson Brown Jr. &

Robert W. McChesney (Foreword by). Trade Cloth. Seven Stories Press. New York, NY. 2004. 0p. ISBN:1-888363-40-1, ISBN13: 978-1-888363-40-1. Dewey:302.2/3. LCCN:97-000502.
Audience: **u,f.**

Sommerville, C. John **PN4888.O25S66 1999**
How the News Makes Us Dumb: The Death of Wisdom in an Information Society. Trade Paper. InterVarsity Press. Downers Grove, IL. 1999. 155p. ISBN:0-8308-2203-8, ISBN13: 978-0-8308-2203-4. Dewey:302.23/0973. LCCN:99-010870.
Audience: **u,f.**

Sproule, J. Michael **HM263 .S648 1997**
Propaganda and Democracy: The American Experience of Media and Mass Persuasion. Kenneth Short, Garth Jowett & David Culbert (Contribution by). Trade Paper. Cambridge University Press. New York, NY. 2005. 352p. Cambridge Studies in the History of Mass Communication Ser. ISBN:0-521-02200-2, ISBN13: 978-0-521-02200-2. Dewey:303.3/75/0973.
Audience: **u,f.**

Swan, Karen (Editor), et al. **HQ784.T4S63 1998**
Social Learning from Broadcast Television. Carla Meskill, Steven DeMaio & Robert Muffoletto (Editors). Cloth Text. Hampton Press, Inc. Cresskill, NJ. 1998. 160p. Media, Education, Culture, Technology Ser. ISBN:1-57273-096-X, ISBN13: 978-1-57273-096-0. Dewey:302.23/45/083. LCCN:98-005190.
Audience: **u,f.**

Umphlett, Wiley Lee **E169.12.U47 2006**
From Television to the Internet: Postmodern Visions of American Media Culture in the Twentieth Century. Trade Cloth. Fairleigh Dickinson University Press. Cranbury, NJ. 2006. 460p. ISBN:0-8386-4080-X, ISBN13: 978-0-8386-4080-7. Dewey:302.230973/0904. LCCN:2005-023494.
Audience: **u,f.**

Communication > Mass Media > Broadcast Media > Radio

Boddy, William **PN1991.3.U6**
New Media and Public Imagination: Launching Radio, Television, and Digital Media in the United States. Trade Cloth. Oxford University Press, Inc. New York, NY. 2004. 184p. Oxford Television Studies ISBN:0-19-871146-8, ISBN13: 978-0-19-871146-9. Dewey:384.54/0973. LCCN:2004-302992.
Audience: **u,f.** *Choice, 2005.*

Hutchby, Ian **HE8689**
Media Talk: Language and Interaction on Radio and Television. Cloth Text. McGraw-Hill Education. Maidenhead, 2005. 200p. ISBN:0-335-20996-3, ISBN13: 978-0-335-20996-5. Dewey:302.234. LCCN:2006-277430.
Audience: **l,u,f.**

Sterling, Christopher H. (Editor) **TK6544.M84 2004**
The Museum of Broadcast Communications Encyclopedia of Radio. Museum of Broadcast Communications Staff (Contribution by). Trade Cloth. Fitzroy Dearborn Publishers, Inc. Chicago, IL. 2004. xxvi, 1921p. ISBN:1-57958-429-2, ISBN13: 978-1-57958-429-0. Dewey:384.54/03. LCCN:2003-015683.
Audience: **l,u,f.**

Communication > Mass Media > Broadcast Media > Television

Ang, Ien **HE8700.66.U6A54 1990**
Desperately Seeking the Audience. Trade Paper. Routledge. New York, NY. 1991. 216p. ISBN:0-415-05270-X, ISBN13: 978-0-415-05270-2. Dewey:384.55/1. LCCN:90-008312.
Audience: **u,f.** *Choice, 1991.*

Brooks, Tim & Marsh, Earle **PN1992.18.B68 2003**
The Complete Directory to Prime Time Network TV Shows, 1946-Present. Ed. 8. Trade Paper. Ballantine Books. New York, NY. 2003. 1616p. ISBN:0-345-45542-8, ISBN13: 978-0-345-45542-0. Dewey:791.45/75/0973. LCCN:2003-105447.
Audience: **l,u,f.** B

Doherty, Thomas Patrick **PN1992.6.D64 2003**
Cold War, Cool Medium: Television, McCarthyism, and American Culture. Trade Cloth. Chinese University of Hong Kong, The. Hong Kong SAR, 2003. 320p. ISBN:0-231-12952-1, ISBN13: 978-0-231-12952-7. Dewey:791.45/658. LCCN:2003-051501.
Audience: **u,f.** *Choice, 2004.*

Marc, David **PN1992.3.U5M26 1996**
Demographic Vistas: Television in American Culture. Ed. 2. Book, Other. University of Pennsylvania Press. Philadelphia, PA. 1996. 272p. ISBN:0-8122-1560-5, ISBN13: 978-0-8122-1560-1. Dewey:302.2/345/0973. LCCN:95-050889.
Audience: **u,f.** B

Newcomb, Horace **PN1992.3.U5T42 2006**
Television: The Critical View. Ed. 7. Paper Text. Oxford University Press, Inc. New York, NY. 2006. 688p. ISBN:0-19-530116-1, ISBN13: 978-0-19-530116-8. Dewey:791.45/0973. LCCN:2005-050881.
Audience: **l,u,f.**

Newcomb, Horace **PN1992.18.E53 2005**
Encyclopedia of Television. Ed. 2. Museum of Broadcast Communications Staff (Contribution by). Trade Cloth. Fitzroy Dearborn Publishers, Inc. Chicago, IL. 2005. xxxii, 2697p. ISBN:1-57958-456-X, ISBN13: 978-1-57958-456-6. Dewey:384.55/03. LCCN:2004-003947.
Audience: **l,u,f.** *Choice, 2005, 1997.*

Communication > Mass Media > Broadcast Media > Technology

Lawson-Borders, Gracie **P96.T422U6357 2005**
Media Organizations and Convergence: Case Studies of Media Convergence Pioneers. Cloth over Boards. Lawrence Erlbaum Associates, Inc. Mahwah, NJ. 2005. 224p. LEA's Communication Ser. ISBN:0-8058-5197-6, ISBN13: 978-0-8058-5197-7. Dewey:302.23. LCCN:2005-049488.
Audience: **u,f.**

Meadow, Charles T. **P96.T42M4 1998**
Ink into Bits: A Web of Converging Media. Trade Paper. Scarecrow Press, Inc. Lanham, MD. 1998. 304p.

ISBN:0-8108-3507-X, ISBN13: 978-0-8108-3507-8. Dewey:302.23. LCCN:98-016854.
Audience: **l,u.** *Choice, 1999.*

Oren, Tasha G. & Petro, Patrice **P96.T42G58 2004**
Global Currents: Media and Technology Now. Paper Text, Library Binding. Rutgers University Press. Piscataway, NJ. 2004. 256p. New Directions in International Studies ISBN:0-8135-3479-8, ISBN13: 978-0-8135-3479-4. Dewey:302.23. LCCN:2004-000299.
Audience: **l,u,f.**

P., Taylor **P96.T42H369 2005**
Digital Concepts: The Cultural Context Of New Information Technologies. Paper over Boards. Routledge. New York, NY. 2005. 224p. ISBN:0-415-25184-2, ISBN13: 978-0-415-25184-6. Dewey:302.23. LCCN:2005-006357.
Audience: **u,f.**

Pavlik, John V. **P96.T42P38 1998**
New Media Technology: Cultural and Commercial Perspectives. Ed. 2. Trade Paper. Allyn & Bacon, Inc. Boston, MA. 1997. 450p. ISBN:0-205-27093-X, ISBN13: 978-0-205-27093-4. Dewey:302.23. LCCN:97-037599.
Audience: **u,f.**

Sconce, Jeffrey **P96.T42S37 2000**
Haunted Media: Electronic Presence from Telegraphy to Television. Library Binding. Duke University Press. Durham, NC. 2000. x, 257p. Console-Ing Passions Ser. ISBN:0-8223-2553-5, ISBN13: 978-0-8223-2553-6. Dewey:302.23/09. LCCN:00-029387.
Audience: **l,u,f.** *Choice, 2001.*

van Dijk, Jan **HE7631**
The Network Society: Social Aspects of New Media. Ed. 2. Cloth Text. SAGE Publications, Ltd. London, 2005. 304p. ISBN:1-4129-0867-1, ISBN13: 978-1-4129-0867-2. Dewey:302.23. LCCN:2005-930238.
Audience: **l,u,f.**

Winston, Brian **P96.T42W49 1998**
Media Technology and Society: A History from the Telegraph to the Internet. Paper over Boards. Routledge. New York, NY. 1998. 392p. ISBN:0-415-14229-6, ISBN13: 978-0-415-14229-8. Dewey:302.23. LCCN:97-034781.
Audience: **l,u,f.** *Choice, 1999.*

Communication > Mass Media > New Media

D16.117

□ Center for History and New Media. http://chnm.gmu.edu/
Audience: **g,l,u,f.**

Bolter, Jay David & Grusin, Richard **P96.T42B59 1998**
Remediation: Understanding New Media. Trade Paper. MIT Press. Cambridge, MA. 2000. 310p. ISBN:0-262-52279-9, ISBN13: 978-0-262-52279-3. Dewey:302.2223. LCCN:98-025672.
Audience: **u,f.** *Choice, 1999.*

Flew, Terry **P96T42F58 2005**
New Media: An Introduction. Ed. 2. Trade Paper. Oxford University Press, Inc. New York, NY. 2005. 302p. ISBN:0-19-555041-2, ISBN13: 978-0-19-555041-2. Dewey:302.23. LCCN:2005-541184.
Audience: **l,u.**

Jones, Steve (Editor) **QA76.575.E5368 2003**
Encyclopedia of New Media: An Essential Reference Guide to Communication and Technology. Trade Cloth. SAGE Publications, Inc. Thousand Oaks, CA. 2002. 544p. ISBN:0-7619-2382-9, ISBN13: 978-0-7619-2382-4. Dewey:302.23/4/03. LCCN:2002-013229.
Audience: **l,u,f.** *Choice, 2003.*

Manovich, Lev **P90**
The Language of New Media. Trade Paper. MIT Press. Cambridge, MA. 2002. 352p. Leonardo Book Ser. ISBN:0-262-63255-1, ISBN13: 978-0-262-63255-3. Dewey:302.2.
Audience: **l,u,f.**

Tabbi, Joseph & Wutz, Michael (Editors) **PN212**
Reading Matters: Narrative in the New Media Ecology. Book, Other. Cornell University Press. Ithaca, NY. 1997. 328p. ISBN:0-8014-3366-5, ISBN13: 978-0-8014-3366-5. Dewey:809/.923. LCCN:97-016216.
Audience: **u,f.** *Choice, 1998.*

Communication > Telecommunications

Botto, Francis **TK5103.2.B68 2002**
Encyclopedia of Wireless Telecommunications. Trade Paper. McGraw-Hill Professional Publishing. New York, NY. 2002. 512p. McGraw-Hill Telecommunications Ser. ISBN:0-07-139025-1, ISBN13: 978-0-07-139025-5. Dewey:621.382/03. LCCN:2002-021273.
Audience: **l,u,f.** *Choice, 2003.*

Bracken, James K. & Sterling, Christopher H. **TK5102.7.B73**
Telecommunications Research Resources: An Annotated Guide. Trade Cloth. Lawrence Erlbaum Associates, Inc. Mahwah, NJ. 1999. LEA's Communication Ser. ISBN:0-8058-3636-5, ISBN13: 978-0-8058-3636-3. Dewey:384/.072.
Audience: **l,u,f.**

Crandall, Robert W. **HE7781.C667 2005**
Competition and Chaos: U. S. Telecommunications since the 1996 Telecom ACT. Trade Paper, Perfect. Brookings Institution Press. Washington, DC. 2005. 212p. ISBN:0-8157-1617-6, ISBN13: 978-0-8157-1617-4. Dewey:384/.0973. LCCN:2005-001648.
Audience: **u,f.** *Choice, 2006.*

Jones, Steve (Editor) **QA76.575.E5368 2003**
Encyclopedia of New Media: An Essential Reference Guide to Communication and Technology. Trade Cloth. SAGE Publications, Inc. Thousand Oaks, CA. 2002. 544p. ISBN:0-7619-2382-9, ISBN13: 978-0-7619-2382-4. Dewey:302.23/4/03. LCCN:2002-013229.
Audience: **l,u,f.** *Choice, 2003.*

Katz, Harry C. (Editor) **HD6976.T24**
Telecommunications: Restructuring Work and Employment Relations Worldwide. Trade Cloth. Cornell University Press.

Ithaca, NY. 1996. 393p. IRL Press Book, No. 32 ISBN:0-614-16952-6, ISBN13: 978-0-614-16952-2. Dewey:331/.041384.
Audience: **l,f.** *Choice, 1997.*

Mody, Bella (Editor), et al. **HE8635.T44 1995**
Telecommunications Politics: Ownership and Control of the Information Highway in Developing Countries. Johannes M. Bauer & Joseph D. Straubhaar (Editors). Cloth over Boards. Lawrence Erlbaum Associates, Inc. Mahwah, NJ. 1995. 360p. LEA's Telecommunications Ser. ISBN:0-8058-1752-2, ISBN13: 978-0-8058-1752-2. Dewey:384/.09172/4. LCCN:94-047647.
Audience: **u,f.** *Choice, 1996.*

Muller, Nathan J. **TK5102.M85 2002**
Desktop Encyclopedia of Telecommunications. Ed. 3. Trade Paper. McGraw-Hill Professional Publishing. New York, NY. 2002. 1100p. Telecommunications Ser. ISBN:0-07-138148-1, ISBN13: 978-0-07-138148-2. Dewey:384/.03. LCCN:2002-279913.
Audience: **l,u,f.** *Choice, 2000.*

Noam, Eli **HE8084.N63 1992**
Telecommunications in Europe. Cloth Text. Oxford University Press, Inc. New York, NY. 1992. 536p. Communication and Society Ser. ISBN:0-19-507052-6, ISBN13: 978-0-19-507052-1. Dewey:384/.094. LCCN:90-022969.
Audience: **u,f.** *Choice, 1993.*

Nuechterlein, Jonathan E. & Weiser, Philip J. **HE7781.N84 2005**
Digital Crossroads: American Telecommunications Policy in the Internet Age. Trade Cloth. MIT Press. Cambridge, MA. 2005. 672p. ISBN:0-262-14091-8, ISBN13: 978-0-262-14091-1. Dewey:384/.0973. LCCN:2004-061063.
Audience: **g,l,u,f.** *Choice, 2005.*

Olufs, Dick W. 3rd **HE7781.O38 1998**
The Making of Telecommunication Policy. Trade Cloth. Lynne Rienner Publishers, Inc. Boulder, CO. 1998. 214p. Explorations in Public Policy Ser. ISBN:1-55587-707-9, ISBN13: 978-1-55587-707-1. Dewey:302.2. LCCN:98-007499.
Audience: **u,f.** *Choice, 1999.*

Saracco, Roberto, et al. **HE7631.S2713 1999**
The Disappearance of Telecommunications. Jeffrey R. Harrow & Robert Weihmayer (Authors). Trade Paper. John Wiley & Sons, Inc. Hoboken, NJ. 2000. 174p. ISBN:0-7803-5387-0, ISBN13: 978-0-7803-5387-9. Dewey:384. LCCN:99-052048.
Audience: **l,u,f.** *Choice, 2000.*

Schmandt, Jurgen (Editor), et al. **HE7781**
Telecommunications Policy and Economic Development: The New State Role. Frederick Williams & Robert H. Wilson (Editors). Trade Cloth. Greenwood Publishing Group, Inc. Portsmouth, NH. 1989. 317p. ISBN:0-275-93399-7, ISBN13: 978-0-275-93399-9. Dewey:384/.068. LCCN:89-016148.
Audience: **u,f.** *Choice, 1990.*

Schmidt, Susanne K. & Werle, Raymund **TK5101.S244 1998**
Coordinating Technology: Studies in the International Standardization of Telecommunications. Trade Cloth. MIT Press. Cambridge, MA. 1997. 324p. Inside Technology Ser. ISBN:0-262-19393-0, ISBN13: 978-0-262-19393-1. Dewey:389/.6. LCCN:97-026080.
Audience: **u,f.** *Choice, 1998.*

Zajas, Jay J. & Church, Olive D. **HF5541.T4Z35 1997**
Applying Telecommunications and Technology from a Global Business Perspective. Trade Cloth. Haworth Press, Incorporated, The. Binghamton, NY. 1997. 378p. ISBN:0-7890-0115-2, ISBN13: 978-0-7890-0115-3. Dewey:658.8/4. LCCN:96-048936.
Audience: **u,f.** *Choice, 1998.*

Communication > Telecommunications > History

Brock, Gerald W. **TK5101.B6883 2003**
The Second Information Revolution. Trade Cloth. Harvard University Press. Cambridge, MA. 2003. 336p. ISBN:0-674-01178-3, ISBN13: 978-0-674-01178-6. Dewey:384/.0973. LCCN:2003-044973.
Audience: **l,u.** *Choice, 2004.*

Brock, Gerald W. **HE7775**
Telecommunication Policy for the Information Age: From Monopoly to Competition. Trade Paper. Harvard University Press. Cambridge, MA. 1998. 336p. ISBN:0-674-87326-2, ISBN13: 978-0-674-87326-1. Dewey:384/.0973.
Audience: **l,u,f.** *Choice, 1995.*

Hook, Diana H., et al. **Z5640.H66**
Origins of Cyberspace: A Library on the History of Computing and Computer-Related Telecommunications. Jeremy M. Norman & Michael R. Williams (Authors). Trade Cloth. Norman Publishing. Novato, CA. 2001. x, 670p. ISBN:0-930405-85-4, ISBN13: 978-0-930405-85-4. Dewey:004/.09. LCCN:2001-042742.
Audience: **l,u.** *Choice, 2002.*

Huurdeman, Anton A. **TK5102.2.H88 2003**
The Worldwide History of Telecommunications. Trade Cloth. John Wiley & Sons, Inc. Hoboken, NJ. 2003. 652p. ISBN:0-471-20505-2, ISBN13: 978-0-471-20505-0. Dewey:384. LCCN:2002-027240.
Audience: **l,u.** *Choice, 2004.*

Jensen, Peter R. **TK5102.2.J46 2000**
[e] From the Wireless to the Web: The Evolution of Telecommunications, 1901-2001. E-Book. NetLibrary, Inc. Boulder, CO. 2000. ISBN:0-585-35542-8, ISBN13: 978-0-585-35542-9. Dewey:382/09 22.
Audience: **l,u.**

Lebow, Irwin **TK5102.2.L43 1995**
Information Highways and Byways: From the Telegraph to the 21st Century. Trade Paper. IEEE Computer Society Press. Los Alamitos, CA. 1995. 326p. ISBN:0-7803-1073-X, ISBN13: 978-0-7803-1073-5. Dewey:302.2/09034. LCCN:94-045457.
Audience: **l,u.** *Choice, 1996.*

Oslin, George P. **HE7631 .O82**
The Story of Telecommunications: From the Deep South to the Top of the Big Apple. Trade Paper. Mercer University Press. Macon, GA. 1999. ISBN:0-86554-659-2, ISBN13: 978-0-86554-659-2. Dewey:384.
Audience: **l,u.**

Sterling, Christopher H. **Z5834.T4S74 2000**
History of Telecommunications Technology: An Annotated Bibliography. Trade Cloth. Scarecrow Press, Inc. Lanham, MD. 2000. 352p. ISBN:0-8108-3781-1, ISBN13: 978-0-8108-3781-2. Dewey:016.621382. LCCN:00-024823.
Audience: **l,u,f.** *Choice, 2001.*

Sterling, Christopher H., et al. **HE7775.S76 2006**
Shaping American Telecommunications: A History of Technology, Policy, and Economics. Phyllis W. Bernt & Martin B. H. Weiss (Authors). Trade Paper. Lawrence Erlbaum Associates, Inc. Mahwah, NJ. 2005. 432p. LEA Telecommunications Ser. ISBN:0-8058-2237-2, ISBN13: 978-0-8058-2237-3. Dewey:384.0973. LCCN:2005-045616.
Audience: **g,l,u,f.** *Choice, 2006.*

Temin, Peter **HE8846.A55**
The Fall of the Bell System: A Study in Prices and Politics. Louis Galambos (As told to). Trade Paper. Cambridge University Press. New York, NY. 1989. 398p. ISBN:0-521-38929-1, ISBN13: 978-0-521-38929-7. Dewey:384.6/065/73.
Audience: **l,u,f.** *Choice, 1988.*

Communication > Telecommunications > Telegraph and Telephony

Baark, Erik **HE8424**
Lightning Wires: The Telegraph and China's Technological Modernization, 1860-1890, 6. Trade Cloth. Greenwood Publishing Group, Inc. Portsmouth, NH. 1997. 240p. Contributions in Asian Studies, No. 6 ISBN:0-313-30011-9, ISBN13: 978-0-313-30011-0. Dewey:384.1/0951. LCCN:96-024217.
Audience: **u,f.**

Beauchamp, K. G. **TK5115 .B43 2001**
A History of Telegraphy: Its Technology and Application. Trade Cloth. Institution of Engineering and Technology (IET). Edison, NJ. 2001. 408p. History of Technology Ser., No. 26 ISBN:0-85296-792-6, ISBN13: 978-0-85296-792-8. Dewey:621.38309. LCCN:2001-089897.
Audience: **u,f.** *Choice, 2002.*

Coe, Lewis **TK5115 .C54 2003**
The Telegraph: A History of Morse's Invention and Its Predecessors in the United States. Paper Text. McFarland & Company, Incorporated Publishers. Jefferson, NC. 2003. 192p. ISBN:0-7864-1808-7, ISBN13: 978-0-7864-1808-4. Dewey:621.383. LCCN:92-53597.
Audience: **l,u.** *Choice, 1993.*

Downey, Gregory J. **HE9753.D69 2002**
Telegraph Messenger Boys: Labor Communication and Technology, 1850-1950. Paper over Boards. Routledge. New York, NY. 2002. 240p. ISBN:0-415-93108-8, ISBN13: 978-0-415-93108-3. Dewey:384.1/4. LCCN:2002-283357.
Audience: **u,f.**

Lubrano, Annteresa **HE7631.L83 1997**
The Telegraph: How Technology Innovation Caused Social Change. Stuart Bruchey (Editor). Cloth Text. Garland Publishing, Inc. New York, NY. 1997. 205p. Studies on Industrial Productivity ISBN:0-8153-3001-4, ISBN13: 978-0-8153-3001-1. Dewey:384.1/09. LCCN:97-025292.
Audience: **l,u.**

McKnight, Lee W. (Editor), et al. **TK5105.8865.I57 2001**
Internet Telephony. William Lehr & David D. Clark (Editors). Trade Cloth. MIT Press. Cambridge, MA. 2001. 390p. ISBN:0-262-13385-7, ISBN13: 978-0-262-13385-2. Dewey:004.6. LCCN:00-050012.
Audience: **l,u.** *Choice, 2001.*

Standage, Tom **HE7631.S677 1998**
The Victorian Internet: The Remarkable Story of the Telegraph and the Nineteenth Century's On-Line Pioneers. Trade Cloth. Walker & Company. New York, NY. 1998. 224p. ISBN:0-8027-1342-4, ISBN13: 978-0-8027-1342-1. Dewey:384.1/09. LCCN:98-024959.
Audience: **g,l,u,f.**

Communication > Telecommunications > Cable and Satellite

Bartlett, Eugene R. **TK5105.B358 1995**
[e] Cable Communications: Building the Information Infrastructure. E-Book. McGraw-Hill Companies, The. New York, NY. 2001. ISBN:0-07-136966-X, ISBN13: 978-0-07-136966-4. Dewey:621.3/981.
Audience: **u,f.** *Choice, 1996.*

Chartrand, Mark R. **TK5104.C47 2003**
Satellite Communications for the Nonspecialist. Trade Cloth. S P I E-International Society for Optical Engineering. Bellingham, WA. 2003. 450p. SPIE Press Monograph Ser., Vol. 128 ISBN:0-8194-5185-1, ISBN13: 978-0-8194-5185-9. Dewey:621.382/5. LCCN:2003-064648.
Audience: **l,u.** *Choice, 2004.*

Inglis, Andrew F. & Luther, Arch **TK5104.I53 1997**
Satellite Technology: An Introduction. Ed. 2. Paper Text. Elsevier Science & Technology Books. Saint Louis, MO. 1997. 152p. ISBN:0-240-80295-0, ISBN13: 978-0-240-80295-4. Dewey:384.5/1. LCCN:97-014869.
Audience: **l,u.** *Choice, 1991.*

Mullen, Megan Gwynne **HE8700.72.U6M85 2003**
The Rise of Cable Programming in the United States: Revolution or Evolution? Trade Cloth. University of Texas Press. Austin, TX. 2003. 252p. Texas Film and Media Studies ISBN:0-292-75272-5, ISBN13: 978-0-292-75272-6. Dewey:384.55/532/0973. LCCN:2002-011029.
Audience: **u,f.** *Choice, 2003.*

Rees, David W. E. **TK5104.R44 1990**
Satellite Communications: The First Quarter Century of Service. Trade Cloth. John Wiley & Sons, Inc. Hoboken, NJ. 1990. 329p. Wiley Series in Telecommunications and Signal Processing, Vol. 7 ISBN:0-471-62243-5, ISBN13: 978-0-471-62243-7. Dewey:384.5/1. LCCN:88-033948.
Audience: **l,u.** *Choice, 1990.*

Roddy, Dennis **TK5104.R627 2006**
Satellite Communications. Ed. 4. Cloth Text. McGraw-Hill Professional Publishing. New York, NY. 2006. 636p. ISBN:0-07-146298-8, ISBN13: 978-0-07-146298-3. Dewey:621.382/5. LCCN:2005-058387.
Audience: **u,f.**

Communication > Telecommunications > Computer Networks

Clark, Martin P. **TK5102.5.C53 1997**
Networks and Telecommunications: Design and Operation. Ed. 2. Trade Cloth. John Wiley & Sons, Inc. Hoboken, NJ. 1997. 958p. ISBN:0-471-97346-7, ISBN13: 978-0-471-97346-1. Dewey:621.382. LCCN:97-009248.
Audience: **u,f.**

Schwartz, Mischa **TK5103.2.S37 2004**
Mobile Wireless Communications. Trade Cloth. Cambridge University Press. New York, NY. 2004. 470p. ISBN:0-521-84347-2, ISBN13: 978-0-521-84347-8. Dewey:621.3845/6. LCCN:2004-049268.
Audience: **u,f.** *Choice, 2005.*

Stallings, William **TK5105.S73 2003**
Data and Computer Communications. Ed. 7. Cloth Text. Prentice Hall PTR. Upper Saddle River, NJ. 2003. 864p. ISBN:0-13-100681-9, ISBN13: 978-0-13-100681-2. Dewey:004.6. LCCN:2003-051281.
Audience: **u,f.**

Tanenbaum, Andrew **TK5105.5.T36 2002**
Computer Networks. Ed. 4. Trade Cloth. Prentice Hall PTR. Upper Saddle River, NJ. 2002. 912p. ISBN:0-13-066102-3, ISBN13: 978-0-13-066102-9. Dewey:004.6. LCCN:2002-029263.
Audience: **u,f.**

Watts, Duncan J., et al. **QA845**
The Structure and Dynamics of Networks. Mark Newman & Albert-Laszlo Barabási (Authors). Trade Cloth. Princeton University Press. Princeton, NJ. 2006. 624p. Princeton Studies in Complexity Ser. ISBN:0-691-11356-4, ISBN13: 978-0-691-11356-2. Dewey:003.
Audience: **u,f.**

Communication > Telecommunications > Digitization and Convergence

Carlson, A. Bruce, et al. **TK5102.5.C3 2002**
Communication Systems. Ed. 4. P. B. Crilly & Janet Rutledge (Authors). Cloth Text. McGraw-Hill Higher Education. Burr Ridge, IL. 2001. 864p. Electrical Engineering Ser. ISBN:0-07-011127-8, ISBN13: 978-0-07-011127-1. Dewey:621.382/23. LCCN:2001-030273.
Audience: **u,f.**

Greenblatt, David **TK5105.8865**
The Call Heard 'Round the World: VoIP and the Quest for Convergence. Trade Cloth. Amacom. New York, NY. 2002. 256p. ISBN:0-8144-0752-8, ISBN13: 978-0-8144-0752-3. Dewey:004.6. LCCN:2003-001035.
Audience: **u,f.** *Choice, 2004.*

Haykin, Simon **TK5101.H37 2000**
Communication Systems. Ed. 4. Trade Cloth. John Wiley & Sons, Inc. Hoboken, NJ. 2000. 840p. ISBN:0-471-17869-1, ISBN13: 978-0-471-17869-9. Dewey:621.382. LCCN:99-042977.
Audience: **u,f.**

Jenkins, Henry **P94.65.U6J46 2006**
Convergence Culture. Trade Cloth. New York University Press. New York, NY. 2006. 336p. ISBN:0-8147-4281-5, ISBN13: 978-0-8147-4281-5. Dewey:302.230973. LCCN:2006-007358.
Audience: **l,u,f.**

Meadow, Charles T. **P96.T42M4 1998**
Ink into Bits: A Web of Converging Media. Trade Paper. Scarecrow Press, Inc. Lanham, MD. 1998. 304p. ISBN:0-8108-3507-X, ISBN13: 978-0-8108-3507-8. Dewey:302.23. LCCN:98-016854.
Audience: **l,u.** *Choice, 1999.*

Muller, Nathan J. **TK5105.8865.M85 2000**
IP Convergence: The Next Revolution in Telecommunications. Trade Cloth. Artech House, Inc. Norwood, MA. 1999. 502p. Telecommunications Library ISBN:1-58053-012-5, ISBN13: 978-1-58053-012-5. Dewey:621.382/12. LCCN:99-045837.
Audience: **u,f.**

Owen, Bruce M. **HE8700.8.O826 1999**
The Internet Challenge to Television. Trade Cloth. Harvard University Press. Cambridge, MA. 1999. 384p. ISBN:0-674-87299-1, ISBN13: 978-0-674-87299-8. Dewey:384.55/0973. LCCN:98-039236.
Audience: **u,f.** *Choice, 1999.*

Stanley, William D. & Harrington, Richard F. **TK5101.A1**
Electronic Communication Systems. Trade Cloth. Prentice Hall PTR. Upper Saddle River, NJ. 2001. ISBN:0-13-353764-1, ISBN13: 978-0-13-353764-2. Dewey:621.38.
Audience: **u,f.** B

Communication > Theory

PN6121
☐ American Rhetoric.
http://www.americanrhetoric.com/speechbank.htm
Audience: **g,l,u,f.**

☐ Speeches and Speechmakers.
http://www.uiowa.edu/~commstud/resources/speech.html
Audience: **g,l,u,f.**

Anderson, Rob (Editor), et al. **P95.455.D54 2003**
Dialogue: Theorizing Difference in Communication Studies. Leslie A. Baxter & Kenneth N. Cissna (Editors). Paper Text. SAGE Publications, Inc. Thousand Oaks, CA. 2003. 344p. ISBN:0-7619-2671-2, ISBN13: 978-0-7619-2671-9. Dewey:302.3/46. LCCN:2003-011937.
Audience: **u,f.** *Choice, 2004.*

Berger, Arthur Asa **P90.B413 1995**
e Essentials of Mass Communication Theory. E-Book. NetLibrary, Inc. Boulder, CO. 1995. ISBN:0-585-25132-0, ISBN13: 978-0-585-25132-5. Dewey:302.23.
Audience: **l,u,f.**

Cortese, Anthony **P95.54.C67 2006**
Opposing Hate Speech. Richard Delgado (Foreword by). Trade Cloth. Greenwood Publishing Group, Inc. Portsmouth, NH. 2005. 248p. ISBN:0-275-98427-3, ISBN13: 978-0-275-98427-4. Dewey:302.2/242. LCCN:2005-019176.
Audience: **l,u,f.** *Choice, 2006.*

Danesi, Marcel (Editor) **P87.5.D36 2000**
Encyclopedic Dictionary of Semiotics, Media and Communication. Cloth over Boards. University of Toronto Press. Toronto, ON. 2000. 400p. Toronto Studies in Semiotics ISBN:0-8020-4783-1, ISBN13: 978-0-8020-4783-0. Dewey:302.2/03. LCCN:2001-274016.
Audience: **l,u,f.** *Choice, 2001.*

Firth, Alan **P37**
Spoken Discourse and Social Interaction. Trade Paper. Oxford University Press, Inc. New York, NY. 2006. 320p. A Hodder Arnold Publication ISBN:0-340-74184-8, ISBN13: 978-0-340-74184-9. Dewey:401.9.
Audience: **u,f.**

Gelber, Katharine **P95.54.G45 2002**
Speaking Back: The Free Speech Versus Hate Speech Debate. Trade Cloth. John Benjamins Publishing Company. Philadelphia, PA. 2002. xiv, 177p. Discourse Approaches to Politics, Society, and Culture Ser., Vol. 1 ISBN:1-58811-188-1, ISBN13: 978-1-58811-188-3. Dewey:302.2/242. LCCN:2002-016316.
Audience: **l,u,f.** *Choice, 2003.*

Glenn, Phillip J. **P95.45.G57 2003**
Laughter in Interaction. Paul Drew, Marjorie Harness Goodwin, John J. Gumperz & Deborah Schiffrin (Contribution by). Trade Cloth. Cambridge University Press. New York, NY. 2003. 202p. Studies in Interactional Sociolinguistics Ser. ISBN:0-521-77206-0, ISBN13: 978-0-521-77206-8. Dewey:302.3/46. LCCN:2002-041682.
Audience: **l,u.** *Choice, 2004.*

Goffman, Erving **P95.G58 1981**
Forms of Talk. Book, Other. University of Pennsylvania Press. Philadelphia, PA. 1981. 344p. University of Pennsylvania Publications in Conduct and Communication ISBN:0-8122-1112-X, ISBN13: 978-0-8122-1112-2. Dewey:001.54/2. LCCN:80-052806.
Audience: **l,u,f.** B

Hovland, Carl Iver **P90**
Communication and Persuasion: Psychological Studies of Opinion Change,. Paper Text. Textbook Publishers. Temecula, CA. 2003. xii, 315p. ISBN:0-7581-0148-1, ISBN13: 978-0-7581-0148-8. Dewey:808.
Audience: **u,f.**

Hybels, Saundra & Weaver, Richard L. **P95.H9 2006**
Communicating Effectively. Ed. 8. Trade Cloth. McGraw-Hill Companies, The. New York, NY. 2006. ISBN:0-07-319347-X, ISBN13: 978-0-07-319347-2. Dewey:302.2/242. LCCN:2005-054036.
Audience: **l,u,f.**

Jones, Susan, et al. **LB1555**
Talking, Listening and Learning. Debra Myhill & Rosemary Hopper (Authors). Trade Paper. McGraw-Hill Education. Maidenhead, 2005. 160p. ISBN:0-335-21744-3, ISBN13: 978-0-335-21744-1. Dewey:372.137.
Audience: **l,u,f.**

Kaul, Asha **HF5718.22.K38 2005**
The Effective Presentation: Talk Your Way to Success. Paper Text. SAGE Publications India Pvt, Ltd. New Delhi, 2005. 244p. ISBN:0-7619-3413-8, ISBN13: 978-0-7619-3413-4. Dewey:658.4/52. LCCN:2005-019717.
Audience: **g,l,u.**

Kostelnick, Charles & Hassett, Michael **P93.5.K67 2003**
Shaping Information: The Rhetoric of Visual Conventions. Trade Cloth. Southern Illinois University Press. Carbondale, IL. 2003. 288p. ISBN:0-8093-2502-0, ISBN13: 978-0-8093-2502-3. Dewey:302.23. LCCN:2002-151536.
Audience: **l,u,f.** *Choice, 2004.*

Lindfors, Judith Wells **P95.52.L56 1999**
[e] Children's Inquiry: Using Language to Make Sense of the World. E-Book. NetLibrary, Inc. Boulder, CO. 1999. ISBN:0-585-25264-5, ISBN13: 978-0-585-25264-3. Dewey:306.44.
Audience: **u,f.**

McKerrow, Raymie E. & Gronbeck, Bruce **PN4121**
Principles and Types of Public Speaking. Ed. 16. Cloth Text. Allyn & Bacon, Inc. Boston, MA. 2006. 464p. ISBN:0-205-45621-9, ISBN13: 978-0-205-45621-5. Dewey:808.5/1. LCCN:2006-050316.
Audience: **l,u.**

Richards, Jack C., et al. **PE1128.R46 2005**
Person to Person: Communicative Speaking and Listening Skills. Ed. 3. David Bycina & Ingrid Wisniewska (Authors). Trade Paper. Oxford University Press, Inc. New York, NY. 2005. 124p. ISBN:0-19-430215-6, ISBN13: 978-0-19-430215-9. Dewey:428.3/4. LCCN:2004-065481.
Audience: **l,u.**

Sawyer, R. Keith **P95**
Improvised Dialogue: Emergence and Creativity in Conversation. Trade Cloth. Greenwood Publishing Group, Inc. Portsmouth, NH. 2002. 280p. Publications in Creativity Research ISBN:1-56750-677-1, ISBN13: 978-1-56750-677-8. Dewey:302.3/46. LCCN:2002-018672.
Audience: **l,u,f.** *Choice, 2003.*

Schement, Jorge Reina (Editor) **P87.5.E53 2001**
Encyclopedia of Communication and Information. Trade Cloth. Thomson Gale. Farmington Hills, MI. 1905. 1161p. ISBN:0-02-865386-6, ISBN13: 978-0-02-865386-0. Dewey:302.2/03. LCCN:2001-031220.
Audience: **g,l,u,f.** *Choice, 2002.*

Shachtman, Tom **P95.S49 1995**
The Inarticulate Society: Eloquence and Culture in America. Trade Cloth. Simon & Schuster. New York, NY. 1995. 296p. ISBN:0-02-928375-2, ISBN13: 978-0-02-928375-2. Dewey:302.2/242. LCCN:95-013611.
Audience: **u,f.** *Choice, 1995.*

Tracy, Karen **P95.T7 2002**
Everyday Talk: Building and Reflecting Identities. Trade Paper. Guilford Publications, Inc. New York, NY. 2002. 230p. Guilford Communication Ser. ISBN:1-57230-789-7, ISBN13: 978-1-57230-789-6. Dewey:302.2/242. LCCN:2002-005598.
Audience: **l,u.** *Choice, 2003.*

Tsesis, Alexander **P95.54.T778 2002**
Destructive Messages: How Hate Speech Paves the Way for Harmful Social Movements. Trade Cloth. New York University Press. New York, NY. 2002. 256p. Critical America Ser. ISBN:0-8147-8272-8, ISBN13: 978-0-8147-8272-9. Dewey:320.5/6/014. LCCN:2002-004197.
Audience: **l,u,f.** *Choice, 2003.*

Watson, James & Hill, Anne **P87.5.W38 2003**
Dictionary of Media and Communication Studies. Ed. 6. Trade Paper. Oxford University Press, Inc. New York, NY. 2003. 368p. An Arnold Publication ISBN:0-340-80829-2, ISBN13: 978-0-340-80829-0. Dewey:302.2/03. LCCN:2003-283639.
Audience: **l,u,f.** *Choice, 2004.*

Webb, Jennifer & Schirato, Tony **P93.5**
Understanding the Visual. Paper Text. SAGE Publications, Inc. Thousand Oaks, CA. 2004. 240p. ISBN:1-4129-0157-X, ISBN13: 978-1-4129-0157-4. Dewey:302.2. LCCN:2004-102662.
Audience: **l,u,f.** *Choice, 2005.*

Wright, Russell O. **P92.U5W75 2004**
Chronology of Communication in the United States. Paper Text. McFarland & Company, Incorporated Publishers. Jefferson, NC. 2004. 184p. ISBN:0-7864-2019-7, ISBN13: 978-0-7864-2019-3. Dewey:302.2/0973. LCCN:2004-022966.
Audience: **g,l,u,f.** *Choice, 2005.*

Communication > Theory > Nonverbal Communication

Danesi, Marcello **P99.D36 1999**
Of Cigarettes, High Heels and Other Interesting Things: An Introduction to Semiotics. Trade Paper. Palgrave Macmillan. New York, NY. 1999. 192p. Semaphores and Signs Ser. ISBN:0-312-21450-2, ISBN13: 978-0-312-21450-0. Dewey:302.2. LCCN:99-017390.
Audience: **g,l,u.** *Choice, 1999.*

Eco, Umberto **P99 E28**
[e] The Role of the Reader: Explorations in the Semiotics of Texts (Advances in Semiotics Ser.). E-Book. Indiana University Press. Bloomington, IN. 1994. 288p. Advances in Semiotics Ser. ISBN:0-253-20318-X, ISBN13: 978-0-253-20318-2. Dewey:801.9/5. LCCN:78-018299.
Audience: **u,f.** B

Eco, Umberto **P99.E3**
A Theory of Semiotics. Trade Paper. Indiana University Press. Bloomington, IN. 1978. 368p. Advances in Semiotics Ser. ISBN:0-253-20217-5, ISBN13: 978-0-253-20217-8. Dewey:001.51. LCCN:74-022833.
Audience: **u,f.** B

Horn, Laurence R. & Ward, Gregory L. (Editors) **P99.4.P72H35 2004**
The Handbook of Pragmatics. Trade Cloth. Blackwell Publishing, Inc. Malden, MA. 2004. 864p. Blackwell Handbooks in Linguistics, Vol. 16 ISBN:0-631-22547-1, ISBN13: 978-0-631-22547-8. Dewey:306.44. LCCN:2003-016284.
Audience: **g,l,u.** *Choice, 2004.*

Knapp, Mark L. & Hall, Judith A. **BF637.N66K63 2006**
Nonverbal Communication in Human Interaction. Ed. 6. Paper Text. Thomson Wadsworth. Belmont, CA. 2005. 504p. ISBN:0-534-62563-0, ISBN13: 978-0-534-62563-4. Dewey:158/.2. LCCN:2004-116430.
Audience: **u,f.** B

Manusov, Valerie Lynn (Editor) **P99.5.S58 2004**
The Sourcebook of Nonverbal Measures: Going Beyond Words. Walid A. Afifi, Peter A. Andersen & Krystyna S. Aune (Contribution by). Cloth over Boards. Lawrence Erlbaum Associates, Inc. Mahwah, NJ. 2004. 522p. ISBN:0-8058-4746-4, ISBN13: 978-0-8058-4746-8. Dewey:302.2/22. LCCN:2003-049454.
Audience: **u,f.** *Choice, 2005.*

Manusov, Valerie & Patterson, Miles L. (Editors) **BF637.N66S24 2006**
The SAGE Handbook of Nonverbal Communication. Trade Cloth. SAGE Publications, Inc. Thousand Oaks, CA. 2006. 616p. ISBN:1-4129-0404-8, ISBN13: 978-1-4129-0404-9. Dewey:302.2/22. LCCN:2006-004826.
Audience: **g,l,u,f.**

Poyatos, Fernando **P99.5.P694 2001**
Nonverbal Communication Across Disciplines: Culture, Sensory Interaction, Speech, Conversation, Vol. 1. Trade Cloth. John Benjamins Publishing Company. Philadelphia, PA. 2002. xxvi, 371p. ISBN:1-55619-753-5, ISBN13: 978-1-55619-753-6. Dewey:302.2/22. LCCN:2001-052813.
Audience: **u,f.**

Riggio, Ronald E. & Feldman, Robert S. (Editors) **P99.5.C58 2003**
Applications of Nonverbal Communication. Peter Blanck, Andrew Christensen & Celine Douilliez (Contribution by). Cloth over Boards. Lawrence Erlbaum Associates, Inc. Mahwah, NJ. 2005. 328p. The Claremont Symposium on Applied Social Psychology Ser. ISBN:0-8058-4334-5, ISBN13: 978-0-8058-4334-7. Dewey:302.2/22. LCCN:2004-050673.
Audience: **u,f.**

Sebeok, Thomas A. **P99.S323 2001**
Global Semiotics. Trade Cloth. Indiana University Press. Bloomington, IN. 2001. 272p. Advances in Semiotics Ser. ISBN:0-253-33957-X, ISBN13: 978-0-253-33957-7. Dewey:401/.41. LCCN:00-143857.
Audience: **g,u,f.** *Choice, 2002.*

Communication > Theory > Political Communication

Brader, Ted **JA74.5.B69 2006**
Campaigning for Hearts and Minds: How Emotional Appeals in Political Ads Work. Trade Cloth. University of Chicago Press. Chicago, IL. 2005. 280p. Studies in Communication, Media, and Public Opinion Ser. ISBN:0-226-06988-5, ISBN13: 978-0-226-06988-3. Dewey:324.7/3. LCCN:2005-009159.
Audience: **u,f.** *Choice, 2006.*

Brader, Ted **JA74.5.B69 2006**
Campaigning for Hearts and Minds: How Emotional Appeals in Political Ads Work. Trade Paper, Perfect. University of Chicago Press. Chicago, IL. 2006. 280p. Studies in Communication, Media, and Public Opinion Ser. ISBN:0-226-06989-3, ISBN13: 978-0-226-06989-0. Dewey:324.7/3. LCCN:2005-009159.
Audience: **u,f.** *Choice, 2006.*

K., Voltmer **P95.8**
Mass Media and New Democracies. Paper over Boards. Routledge. New York, NY. 2006. 240p. Routledge/ECPR Studies

in European Political Science, Vol. 42 ISBN:0-415-33779-8, ISBN13: 978-0-415-33779-3. Dewey:302.23. LCCN:2005-010413.
Audience: **u,f.**

Lilleker, Darren G. **JA85.L55**
Key Concepts in Political Communication. Cloth Text. SAGE Publications, Ltd. London, 2006. 224p. ISBN:1-4129-1830-8, ISBN13: 978-1-4129-1830-5. Dewey:320.014. LCCN:2005-928592.
Audience: **l,u.**

McChesney, Robert W. **P95.82.U6M378 2004**
The Problem of the Media: U. S. Communication Politics in the Twenty-First Century. Trade Paper. Monthly Review Press. New York, NY. 2004. 367p. ISBN:1-58367-105-6, ISBN13: 978-1-58367-105-4. Dewey:302.23/0973. LCCN:2003-026386.
Audience: **l,u,f.** *Choice, 2004.*

Communication > Theory > Propaganda

Cull, Nicholas J., et al. **HM1231**
Propaganda and Mass Persuasion: A Historical Encyclopedia, 1500 to the Present. David Culbert & David Welch (Authors). Library Binding. ABC-CLIO, Inc. Santa Barbara, CA. 2003. 479p. ISBN:1-57607-820-5, ISBN13: 978-1-57607-820-4. Dewey:303.3/75. LCCN:2003-009513.
Audience: **g,l,u.** *Choice, 2004.*

Cunningham, Stanley B. **HM1231**
The Idea of Propaganda: A Reconstruction. Trade Cloth. Greenwood Publishing Group, Inc. Portsmouth, NH. 2002. 248p. ISBN:0-275-97445-6, ISBN13: 978-0-275-97445-9. Dewey:303.3/75. LCCN:2001-051368.
Audience: **u,f.** *Choice, 2003.*

Ellul, Jacques **HM263 .E413 1973**
Propaganda: The Formation of Men's Attitudes. Trade Cloth. Knopf Publishing Group. New York, NY. 1973. 352p. ISBN:0-394-71874-7, ISBN13: 978-0-394-71874-3. Dewey:301.15/4. LCCN:72-008053.
Audience: **u,f.**

Communication > Theory > Public Opinion

HM261
☐ PollingReport.com.
http://www.pollingreport.com/
Audience: **g,l,u,f.**

Alvarez, R. Michael & Brehm, John **HM1236.A46 2002**
Hard Choices, Easy Answers: Values, Information, and American Public Opinion. Trade Paper. Princeton University Press. Princeton, NJ. 2002. 264p. ISBN:0-691-09635-X, ISBN13: 978-0-691-09635-3. Dewey:303.3/8/0973. LCCN:2001-050023.
Audience: **u,f.** *Choice, 2003.*

Geer, John G. **HM1236.P83 2004**
Public Opinion, Polling, and Democracy Around the World: A Historical Encyclopedia. Library Binding. ABC-CLIO, Inc. Santa Barbara, CA. 2004. 700p. ISBN:1-57607-911-2, ISBN13: 978-1-57607-911-9. Dewey:303.3/8. LCCN:2004-011691.
Audience: **g,l,u,f.** *Choice, 2005.*

Lewis, Justin **HM1236.L48 2001**
Constructing Public Opinion: How Political Elites Do What They Like and Why We Seem to Go along with It. Trade Paper. Columbia University Press. New York, NY. 2001. 240p. ISBN:0-231-11767-1, ISBN13: 978-0-231-11767-8. Dewey:303.3/8. LCCN:00-063924.
Audience: **l,u,f.** *Choice, 2001.*

Lippmann, Walter **HM261.L75 2004**
Public Opinion. Trade Paper. Dover Publications, Inc. Mineola, NY. 2004. 240p. ISBN:0-486-43703-5, ISBN13: 978-0-486-43703-3. Dewey:303.3/8. LCCN:2004-050241.
Audience: **g,l,u,f.**

Stearns, Peter N. **HM1236**
Global Outrage: The Origins and Impact of World Opinion from the 1780s to the 21st Century. Trade Cloth. Oneworld Publications. Oxford, 2005. 256p. ISBN:1-85168-364-X, ISBN13: 978-1-85168-364-2. Dewey:303.38.
Audience: **u,f.** *Choice, 2005.*

Communication > Theory > Technology and Communication

Allison, Juliann Emmons (Editor) **HM851.T45 2002**
Technology, Development, and Democracy: International Conflict and Cooperation in the Information Age. Paper Text. State University of New York Press. Albany, NY. 2002. 320p. SUNY Series in Global Politics ISBN:0-7914-5214-X, ISBN13: 978-0-7914-5214-1. Dewey:303.48/33. LCCN:2001-031123.
Audience: **l,u,f.** *Choice, 2003.*

Crumlish, Christina **HM851**
The Power of Many: How the Living Web Is Transforming Politics, Business and Everyday Life. Trade Cloth. Sybex, Inc. Alameda, CA. 2004. 272p. ISBN:0-7821-4346-6, ISBN13: 978-0-7821-4346-1. Dewey:303.48/33. LCCN:2004-109414.
Audience: **l,u,f.** *Choice, 2005.*

Howard, Philip & Jones, Steve (Editors) **HM851.S655 2004**
Society Online: The Internet in Context. Paper Text. SAGE Publications, Inc. Thousand Oaks, CA. 2003. 384p. ISBN:0-7619-2708-5, ISBN13: 978-0-7619-2708-2. Dewey:303.48/33. LCCN:2003-008611.
Audience: **l,u,f.** *Choice, 2004.*

Mosco, Vincent **HM851.M667 2005**
The Digital Sublime: Myth, Power, and Cyberspace. Trade Paper, Perfect. MIT Press. Cambridge, MA. 2005. 232p. ISBN:0-262-63329-9, ISBN13: 978-0-262-63329-1. Dewey:303.48/33.
Audience: **u,f.** *Choice, 2004.*

Porter, Beth **HM851**
The Net Effect. Trade Paper. Intellect, Ltd. Bristol, 2003. 190p. ISBN:1-84150-849-7, ISBN13: 978-1-84150-849-8. Dewey:303.48/33.
Audience: **l,u,f.** *Choice, 2002.*

Sunstein, Cass **HM851.S87 2001**
Republic.com. Trade Cloth. Princeton University Press. Princeton, NJ. 2001. 232p. ISBN:0-691-07025-3, ISBN13: 978-0-691-07025-4. Dewey:303.48/33. LCCN:00-045331.
Audience: **l,u,f.** *Choice, 2001.*

Communication > Advertising

HF5823

☐ Advertising Principles.
http://fourps.wharton.upenn.edu/advertising/
Audience: **g,l,u,f.**

HF5823

☐ Texas Advertising.
http://advertising.utexas.edu/research/
Audience: **l,u,f.**

Cappo, Joe **HG4521.R538 2003**
The Future of Advertising: New Media, New Clients, New Consumers in the Post-Television Age. Trade Cloth. McGraw-Hill Companies, The. New York, NY. 2003. 260p. ISBN:0-07-140315-9, ISBN13: 978-0-07-140315-3. Dewey:659.1. LCCN:2003-041335.
Audience: **u,f.** *Choice, 2004.*

Jones, John Philip (Editor) **HF5823.I59 2000**
International Advertising: Realities and Myths. Trade Paper. SAGE Publications, Inc. Thousand Oaks, CA. 1999. 424p. ISBN:0-7619-1245-2, ISBN13: 978-0-7619-1245-3. Dewey:659.1. LCCN:99-006528.
Audience: **g,l,u,f.** *Choice, 2000.*

McDonough, John (Editor) **HF5801**
The Advertising Age Encyclopedia of Advertising, Set. Trade Cloth. Fitzroy Dearborn Publishers, Inc. Chicago, IL. 2002. 1958p. ISBN:1-57958-172-2, ISBN13: 978-1-57958-172-5. Dewey:659.1/03. LCCN:2003-270744.
Audience: **g,l,u,f.** *Choice, 2003.*

O'Shaughnessy, John **HF5822.O84 2003**
Persuasion in Advertising. Paper over Boards. Routledge. New York, NY. 2003. 232p. ISBN:0-415-32223-5, ISBN13: 978-0-415-32223-2. Dewey:659.1/01/9. LCCN:2003-011531.
Audience: **u,f.**

Williams, Jerome D. (Editor), et al. **HF5822.W495 2004**
Diversity in Advertising: Broadening the Scope of Research Directions. Wei-Na Lee & Curtis P. Haugtvedt (Editors), Swee Hoon Ang, Osei Appiah & Jaques G. Bloem (Contribution by). Cloth over Boards. Lawrence Erlbaum Associates, Inc. Mahwah, NJ. 2004. 472p. Advertising and Consumer Psychology Ser. ISBN:0-8058-4794-4, ISBN13: 978-0-8058-4794-9. Dewey:659.1/08. LCCN:2003-022327.
Audience: **u,f.**

Communication > Advertising > History

HF5823

☐ Ad* Access.
http://scriptorium.lib.duke.edu/adaccess/
Audience: **l,u,f.**

HF5813.U6

☐ Emergence of Advertising in America: 1850-1920.
http://scriptorium.lib.duke.edu/eaa/
Audience: **l,u,f.**

Fox, Stephen R. **HF5813.U6F66 1997**
The Mirror Makers: A History of American Advertising and Its Creators. Trade Paper. University of Illinois Press. Champaign, IL. 1997. 416p. ISBN:0-252-06659-6, ISBN13: 978-0-252-06659-7. Dewey:659.1/0973. LCCN:97-009235.
Audience: **u,f.**

Hill, Daniel D. **HF5813.U6H55 2002**
Advertising to the American Woman, 1900-1999. Trade Cloth. Ohio State University Press. Columbus, OH. 2002. xi, 329p. ISBN:0-8142-0890-8, ISBN13: 978-0-8142-0890-8. Dewey:659.1/082/0973. LCCN:2001-052085.
Audience: **u,f.** *Choice, 2002.*

Marchand, Roland **HF5813.U6M26 1986**
Advertising the American Dream: Making Way for Modernity, 1920-1940. Trade Paper. University of California Press. Berkeley, CA. 1986. xxii, 448p. ISBN:0-520-05885-2, ISBN13: 978-0-520-05885-9. Dewey:659.1/0973. LCCN:84-028082.
Audience: **u,f.** B *Choice, 1986.*

Norris, James D. **HF5813**
Advertising and the Transformation of American Society, 1865-1920, Vol. 110. Trade Cloth. Greenwood Publishing Group, Inc. Portsmouth, NH. 1990. 224p. Contributions in Economics and Economic History Ser. ISBN:0-313-26801-0, ISBN13: 978-0-313-26801-4. Dewey:659.1/042/097309034. LCCN:90-002760.
Audience: **u,f.** *Choice, 1991.*

Reichert, Tom **HF5827.85.R45 2003**
The Erotic History of Advertising. Trade Paper. Prometheus Books, Publishers. Amherst, NY. 2003. 300p. ISBN:1-59102-085-9, ISBN13: 978-1-59102-085-1. Dewey:659.1/042. LCCN:2003-043207.
Audience: **u,f.** *Choice, 2003.*

Samuel, Lawrence R. **HF6146.T42S25 2001**
Brought to You By: Postwar Television Advertising and the American Dream. Trade Paper. University of Texas Press. Austin, TX. 2002. 288p. ISBN:0-292-77763-9, ISBN13: 978-0-292-77763-7. Dewey:659.14/3/0973. LCCN:2001-018114.
Audience: **u,f.** *Choice, 2002.*

Sivulka, Juliann **HF5813.U6S55 1997**
Soap, Sex, and Cigarettes: A Cultural History of American Advertising. Ed. 1. Paper Text. Thomson Wadsworth. Belmont, CA. 1997. 464p. Mass Communication Ser. ISBN:0-534-51593-2, ISBN13: 978-0-534-51593-5. Dewey:659/.1/0973. LCCN:96-051949.
Audience: **u,f.**

Communication > Advertising > Criticism

Berger, Arthur Asa **HF5823.B438 2003**
Ads, Fads, and Consumer Culture: Advertising's Impact on American Character and Society. Ed. 2. Book, Other. Rowman & Littlefield Publishers, Inc. Lanham, MD. 2003. 216p. ISBN:0-7425-2723-9, ISBN13: 978-0-7425-2723-2. Dewey:659.1/042/0973. LCCN:2003-008536.
Audience: **u,f.** *Choice, 2004.*

Cortese, Anthony J. **HF5823.C5977 1999**
Provocateur: Images of Women and Minorities in Advertising. Book, Other. Rowman & Littlefield Publishers, Inc. Lanham,

MD. 1999. 176p. ISBN:0-8476-9174-8, ISBN13: 978-0-8476-9174-6. Dewey:659.1/042. LCCN:99-014501.
Audience: **u,f.** *Choice, 2000.*

Gunter, Barrie, et al. **HQ784.T4G858 2004**
Advertising to Children on TV: Content, Impact, and Regulation. Caroline Oates & Mark Blades (Authors). Cloth over Boards. Lawrence Erlbaum Associates, Inc. Mahwah, NJ. 2004. 224p. ISBN:0-8058-4488-0, ISBN13: 978-0-8058-4488-7. Dewey:302.23/45/083. LCCN:2004-043266.
Audience: **u,f.** *Choice, 2005.*

Communication > Advertising > Advertising Management and Planning

Cooper, Alan (Editor) **HF5823.H583 1997**
How to Plan Advertising. Ed. 2. Trade Paper. Continuum International Publishing Group, Ltd. London, 1997. 160p. ISBN:0-304-70143-2, ISBN13: 978-0-304-70143-8. Dewey:659.1/11. LCCN:98-118533.
Audience: **u.**

Czerniawski, Richard D. & Maloney, Michael W. **HF6161.B4C94 1999**
Creating Brand Loyalty: The Management of Power Positioning and Really Great Advertising. Trade Paper. Amacom. New York, NY. 1999. 240p. ISBN:0-8144-0501-0, ISBN13: 978-0-8144-0501-7. Dewey:658.8/343. LCCN:99-026211.
Audience: **u,f.** *Choice, 2000.*

Mooij, Marieke K. de **HF5415.127.M66 2005**
Global Marketing and Advertising: Understanding Cultural Paradoxes. Ed. 2. Cloth Text. SAGE Publications, Inc. Thousand Oaks, CA. 2005. 288p. ISBN:1-4129-1475-2, ISBN13: 978-1-4129-1475-8. Dewey:658.8/02. LCCN:2004-026086.
Audience: **u,f.** *Choice, 2005.*

Percy, Larry & Elliott, Richard **HF5438.5**
Strategic Advertising Management. Ed. 2. Paper Text. Oxford University Press, Inc. New York, NY. 2005. 320p. ISBN:0-19-927489-4, ISBN13: 978-0-19-927489-5. Dewey:659.1. LCCN:2005-012353.
Audience: **u.**

Wood, Douglas J. **KF1614**
Please Be Ad-Vised: The Legal Reference Guide for the Advertising Executive. Ed. 4. Perfect. Association of National Advertisers, Inc. New York, NY. 2003. ISBN:1-56318-028-6, ISBN13: 978-1-56318-028-6. Dewey:343.082.
Audience: **u.**

Communication > Advertising > Campaigns

HF5837
☐ Ad Council Campaigns.
http://www.adcouncil.org/default.aspx?id=15
Audience: **l,u,f.**

Designers and Art Directors Association Staff **HF5825**
Copy Writer's Bible. Trade Cloth. RotoVision SA. Hove, 2000. 180p. ISBN:2-88046-593-1, ISBN13: 978-2-88046-593-3. Dewey:659.1/32.
Audience: **l,u.**

Garfield, Bob **HF5823.G27 2004**
And Now a Few Words from Me: Advertising's Leading Critic Lays down the Law, Once and for All. Trade Paper. McGraw-Hill Companies, The. New York, NY. 2004. 204p. ISBN:0-07-144122-0, ISBN13: 978-0-07-144122-3. Dewey:659.1.
Audience: **l,u.**

Pricken, Mario **NC997**
Creative Advertising: Ideas and Techniques from the World's Best Campaigns. Trade Paper. Thames & Hudson. New York, NY. 2004. 264p. ISBN:0-500-28476-8, ISBN13: 978-0-500-28476-6. Dewey:659.1. LCCN:2001-096432.
Audience: **l,u.**

Schultz, Don E. & Barnes, Beth **HF5823.S3636 1995**
Strategic Advertising Campaigns. Ed. 4. Trade Cloth. McGraw-Hill Trade. New York, NY. 1994. 384p. ISBN:0-8442-3015-4, ISBN13: 978-0-8442-3015-3. Dewey:659.1/13. LCCN:93-042796.
Audience: **l,u.**

Twitchell, James B. **HF5811.T9 2002**
Twenty Ads That Shook the World: The Century's Most Groundbreaking Advertising and How It Changed Us All. Trade Paper. Crown Publishing Group. New York, NY. 2001. 240p. ISBN:0-609-80723-4, ISBN13: 978-0-609-80723-1. Dewey:659.1.
Audience: **u,f.**

West, Nancy Martha **HF6161.P36W47 2000**
Kodak and the Lens of Nostalgia. Trade Cloth. University Press of Virginia. Charlottesville, VA. 2000. xviii, 242p. Cultural Frames, Framing Culture Ser. ISBN:0-8139-1958-4, ISBN13: 978-0-8139-1958-4. Dewey:659.1/977131. LCCN:99-055371.
Audience: **u,f.** *Choice, 2001.*

Communication > Advertising > Audience Analysis/Media Planning

Azzaro, Marian, et al. **HF5415 B.A99 2004**
Strategic Media Decisions: Understanding the Business End of the Advertising Business. Dan Binder, Robb Clawson, Carla Lloyd, Mary Alice Shaver & Olaf Werder (Authors), Bruce Bendinger & Aylward Patrick (Editors). Paper Text. Copy Workshop, The. Chicago, IL. 2004. 544p. ISBN:1-887229-17-5, ISBN13: 978-1-887229-17-3. Dewey:658.8. LCCN:2006-278549.
Audience: **l,u.**

Donnelly, William J. **P95.815.D66**
Planning Media. Paper Text. Prentice Hall PTR. Upper Saddle River, NJ. 1996. ISBN:0-13-567876-5, ISBN13: 978-0-13-567876-3. Dewey:659.
Audience: **l,u.**

Katz, Helen E. **HF5826.5.K38 2003**
The Media Handbook. Ed. 2. Cloth over Boards. Lawrence Erlbaum Associates, Inc. Mahwah, NJ. 2003. 200p. LEA's

Communication Ser. ISBN:0-8058-4267-5, ISBN13: 978-0-8058-4267-8. Dewey:659. LCCN:2002-035398.
Audience: **l,u.** *Choice, 2003.*

Kelley, Larry D. & Jugenheimer, Donald W. **HF5826.5.K45 2004**
Advertising Media Planning: A Brand Management Approach. Cloth Text. M. E. Sharpe Inc. Armonk, NY. 2003. 152p. ISBN:0-7656-1309-3, ISBN13: 978-0-7656-1309-7. Dewey:659.1/11. LCCN:2003-050600.
Audience: **l,u.** *Choice, 2004.*

Surmanek, Jim **HF5826.5.S86 1996**
Media Planning: A Practical Guide. Ed. 3. E-Book. NetLibrary, Inc. Boulder, CO. 1996. ISBN:0-585-13998-9, ISBN13: 978-0-585-13998-2. Dewey:659.1/11.
Audience: **l,u.**

Communication > Advertising > Creative Strategy

Backer, Bill **HD38 .B185 1993**
The Care and Feeding of Ideas. Trade Cloth. Crown Publishing Group. New York, NY. 1993. 320p. ISBN:0-8129-1969-6, ISBN13: 978-0-8129-1969-1. Dewey:658.4/063. LCCN:92-038389.
Audience: **l,u.**

Dru, Jean-Marie **HF6178.D78 1996**
Disruption: Overturning Conventions and Shaking up the Marketplace. Trade Cloth. John Wiley & Sons, Inc. Hoboken, NJ. 1996. 256p. Adweek Magazine Ser., Vol. 1 ISBN:0-471-16565-4, ISBN13: 978-0-471-16565-1. Dewey:153.3/5. LCCN:96-021256.
Audience: **l,u.** *Choice, 1997.*

Paetro, Maxine **HF5828.4.P33 2002**
How to Put Your Book Together and Get a Job in Advertising: 21st Century Edition. Ed. 21. Trade Paper. Copy Workshop, The. Chicago, IL. 2002. 257p. ISBN:1-887229-13-2, ISBN13: 978-1-887229-13-5. Dewey:659.1/023. LCCN:2004-274248.
Audience: **u.**

Weir, Walter **HF5825 .W397 1993**
How to Create Interest-Evoking, Sales-Inducing, Non-Irritating Advertising. Gordon E. Miracle (Foreword by). Trade Paper. Haworth Press, Incorporated, The. Binghamton, NY. 2003. 213p. ISBN:1-56024-239-6, ISBN13: 978-1-56024-239-0. Dewey:659.1. LCCN:91-034585.
Audience: **u.**

Williams, Robin & Tollett, John **Z246**
Robin Williams Design Workshop. Ed. 2. Trade Paper. Peachpit Press. Berkeley, CA. 2006. 320p. ISBN:0-321-44176-1, ISBN13: 978-0-321-44176-8. Dewey:686.22544.
Audience: **u.**

Young, James Webb **HF5825**
A Technique for Producing Ideas. Trade Paper. McGraw-Hill Companies, The. New York, NY. 2003. 64p. ISBN:0-07-141094-5, ISBN13: 978-0-07-141094-6. Dewey:153.2. LCCN:2005-297213.
Audience: **u.**

Communication > Advertising > Technologies

Adams, R. **HF6146.I58A33 2003**
WWW.Advertising: Advertising and Marketing on the World Wide Web. Trade Cloth. Watson-Guptill Publications, Inc. New York, NY. 2003. 192p. Design Directories Ser. ISBN:0-8230-5861-1, ISBN13: 978-0-8230-5861-7. Dewey:659.14. LCCN:2002-117050.
Audience: **l,u.** *Choice, 2003.*

Janoschka, Anja **HF6146.I58**
Web Advertising: New Forms of Communication on the Internet. Trade Cloth. John Benjamins Publishing Company. Amsterdam, 2004. 244p. ISBN:90-272-5374-9, ISBN13: 978-90-272-5374-3. Dewey:659.14/4. LCCN:2004-055441.
Audience: **l,u.**

Stafford, Marla R. & Faber, Ronald J. (Editors) **HF6146.I58A39 2004**
Advertising, Promotion, and New Media. Cloth Text. M. E. Sharpe Inc. Armonk, NY. 2004. 392p. ISBN:0-7656-1315-8, ISBN13: 978-0-7656-1315-8. Dewey:659.14/4. LCCN:2004-004069.
Audience: **u.** *Choice, 2005.*

Communication > Public Relations

Heath, Robert L. (Editor) **HD59.E48 2005**
Encyclopedia of Public Relations. Trade Cloth. SAGE Publications, Inc. Thousand Oaks, CA. 2004. 1128p. ISBN:0-7619-2733-6, ISBN13: 978-0-7619-2733-4. Dewey:659.2/03. LCCN:2004-009256.
Audience: **l,u.** *Choice, 2005.*

Sriramesh, Krishnamurthy & Vereciec, Dejan (Editors) **HM1221.G57 2003**
The Global Public Relations Handbook: Theory, Research, and Practice. Cloth over Boards. Lawrence Erlbaum Associates, Inc. Mahwah, NJ. 2003. 600p. LEA's Communication Ser. ISBN:0-8058-3922-4, ISBN13: 978-0-8058-3922-7. Dewey:659.2. LCCN:2003-048349.
Audience: **l,u,f.**

Communication > Public Relations > History

Cutlip, Scott M. **HM263.C784 1995**
Public Relations History: From the 17th to the 20th Century. Cloth Text. Lawrence Erlbaum Associates, Inc. Mahwah, NJ. 1995. 320p. LEA's Communication Ser. ISBN:0-8058-1779-4, ISBN13: 978-0-8058-1779-9. Dewey:659.2. LCCN:95-013889.
Audience: **l,u,f.**

Ewen, Stuart **HM263.E849 1996**
PR!: A Social History of Spin. Trade Paper. Basic Books. New York, NY. 1998. 496p. ISBN:0-465-06179-6, ISBN13: 978-0-465-06179-2. Dewey:659.2/09.
Audience: **l,u,f.** *Choice, 1997.*

Tye, Larry **HD59.6.U6T94**
The Father of Spin: Edward L. Bernays and the Birth of Public Relations. Trade Paper. DIANE Publishing Company. Collingdale, PA. 2005. 290p. ISBN:0-7567-8825-0, ISBN13: 978-0-7567-8825-4. Dewey:659.2.
Audience: **l,u,f.**

Communication > Public Relations > Criticism

Mickey, Thomas J. **HM1221.M52 2003**
Deconstructing Public Relations: Public Relations Criticism. Trade Paper. Lawrence Erlbaum Associates, Inc. Mahwah, NJ. 2002. 176p. LEA's Communication Ser. ISBN:0-8058-3749-3, ISBN13: 978-0-8058-3749-0. Dewey:659.2. LCCN:2001-054848.
Audience: **u,f.**

Communication > Public Relations > Campaigns

Gregory, Anne **HD59**
Planning and Managing a PR Campaign: A Step by Step Guide. Ed. 2. Trade Paper, Perfect. Kogan Page, Ltd. London, 2001. 192p. Public Relations in Practice Ser. ISBN:0-7494-2991-7, ISBN13: 978-0-7494-2991-1. Dewey:659.2.
Audience: **u,f.**

Marchand, Roland **HD59.2.M368 1998**
Creating the Corporate Soul: The Rise of Public Relations and Corporate Imagery in American Big Business. Trade Paper. University of California Press. Berkeley, CA. 2001. 474p. ISBN:0-520-22688-7, ISBN13: 978-0-520-22688-3. Dewey:659.2/85. LCCN:97-050098.
Audience: **u,f.** *Choice, 1999.*

Communication > Public Relations > Practice

Fearn-Banks, Kathleen **HD59.F37**
Crisis Communications: A Casebook Approach. Ed. 2. Trade Cloth. Lawrence Erlbaum Associates, Inc. Mahwah, NJ. 2002. 192p. Lea's Communication Ser. ISBN:0-8058-3920-8, ISBN13: 978-0-8058-3920-3. Dewey:659.2.
Audience: **u,f.** *Choice, 1996.*

LAW

This section recognizes law as a discipline of study at the undergraduate level as well as a reality in students' everyday lives. As such, it includes general interest and scholarly works and selected practical aids designed to help students effectively deal with legal issues they may encounter during their college years.

In his introduction to The Oxford Companion to American Law, Kermit Hall states that "law is best understood as a system of social choice, one in which government provides for the allocation of resources, the legitimate use of violence, and the structuring of social relationships." The aim of this collection is to provide undergraduate students with that type of understanding. The focus is on United States law, recognizing that the United States is the focus of most undergraduate law courses and acknowledging the limits of college library budgets. The collection consists of core reference books and legal websites, general interest and scholarly monographs, and practical guides. It includes classic works cited in BCL3, a few other retrospective titles and a selection of the most important works published since 1988. Titles were chosen primarily for their balanced perspective on the topic; when a single perspective is presented, an effort was made to include a title with an alternative view. Only a few of the most authoritative and appropriate websites were included. The taxonomy reflects the organization of the "K" (law) section of the Library of Congress Classification schedule.

— Mary Gilles

Law (General) > Law in General

Kritzer, Herbert M. (Editor) **K48.L44 2002**
Legal Systems of the World: A Political, Social, and Cultural Encyclopedia, Set. Library Binding. ABC-CLIO, Inc. Santa Barbara, CA. 2002. 1883p. ISBN:1-57607-231-2, ISBN13: 978-1-57607-231-8. Dewey:340.03. LCCN:2002-002659.
Audience: **g,l,u.**

Walker, David M. (Editor) **K48**
Oxford Companion to Law. Trade Cloth. Oxford University Press, Inc. New York, NY. 1980. 1366p. ISBN:0-19-866110-X, ISBN13: 978-0-19-866110-8. Dewey:340/.09181/2. LCCN:79-040846.
Audience: **g.**

Law (General) > History of Law. Biography. Anthropology

Berman, Harold J. **K230**
Law and Revolution: The Formation of the Western Legal Tradition. Trade Cloth. Harvard University Press. Cambridge, MA. 1983. 672p. ISBN:0-674-51774-1, ISBN13: 978-0-674-51774-5. Dewey:340. LCCN:82-015747.
Audience: **g.** ***B***

Berman, Harold J. **K150**
Law and Revolution II: The Impact of the Protestant Reformations on the Western Legal Tradition. Trade Cloth. Harvard University Press. Cambridge, MA. 2004. 544p. ISBN:0-674-01195-3, ISBN13: 978-0-674-01195-3. Dewey:349.4/09. LCCN:2004-301872.
Audience: **g.** *Choice, 2004.*

Bohannan, Paul (Editor) **GN497**
Law and Warfare: Studies in the Anthropology of Conflict. Trade Paper. University of Texas Press. Austin, TX. 1976. 455p. Sourcebooks in Anthropology, No. 1 ISBN:0-292-74617-2, ISBN13: 978-0-292-74617-6. Dewey:301.6/3. LCCN:75-044033.
Audience: **u,f.**

Fuller, Lon L. **KI50**
Anatomy of the Law. Trade Cloth. Greenwood Publishing Group, Inc. Portsmouth, NH. 1977. 122p. ISBN:0-8371-8622-6, ISBN13: 978-0-8371-8622-1. Dewey:340. LCCN:76-036095.
Audience: **u,f.**

Gluckman, Max **K370**
Politics, Law and Ritual in Tribal Society. Trade Paper. Aldine Transaction. Somerset, NJ. 2006. 371p. ISBN:0-202-30860-X, ISBN13: 978-0-202-30860-9. Dewey:306.2. LCCN:2006-042893.
Audience: **u,f.**

Hoebel, E. Adamson **KF8228**
The Law of Primitive Man: A Study in Comparative Legal Dynamics. Trade Paper. Harvard University Press. Cambridge, MA. 2006. 372p. ISBN:0-674-02362-5, ISBN13: 978-0-674-02362-8. Dewey:340.5/2. LCCN:2006-043725.
Audience: **g.**

MacDowell, Douglas M. **KL4115.A75**
The Law in Classical Athens. Trade Paper. Cornell University Press. Ithaca, NY. 1986. 280p. Aspects of Greek and Roman Life Ser. ISBN:0-8014-9365-X, ISBN13: 978-0-8014-9365-2. Dewey:340.5/3/85. LCCN:78-054141.
Audience: **u,f.** ***B***

Maine, Henry Sumner **D85.L3**
Ancient Law: Its Connection with the Early History of Society and Its Relation to Modern Ideas. Ed. 7. Trade Cloth. Gaunt, Inc. Holmes Beach, FL. 1998. ix, 415p. ISBN:1-56169-421-5, ISBN13: 978-1-56169-421-1. Dewey:364.
Audience: **g.**

Nader, Laura **K487.A57L385 1997**
Law in Culture and Society. Trade Paper. University of California Press. Berkeley, CA. 1997. 464p. ISBN:0-520-20833-1, ISBN13: 978-0-520-20833-9. Dewey:340/.115. LCCN:96-034175.
Audience: **u,f.**

Pound, Roscoe **K230.P67 I58 1986**
Interpretations of Legal History. Trade Cloth. Gaunt, Inc. Holmes Beach, FL. 1986. 198p. Cambridge Studies in English Legal History ISBN:0-912004-50-9, ISBN13: 978-0-912004-50-1. Dewey:340/.09. LCCN:85-081797.
Audience: **g.** ***B***

Vinogradoff, Paul **LAW**
Roman Law in Medieval Europe. Trade Cloth. Gaunt, Inc. Holmes Beach, FL. 1994. xvi, 155p. ISBN:1-56169-103-8, ISBN13: 978-1-56169-103-6. Dewey:340/.094.
Audience: **u,f.** ***B***

Watson, Alan **K150.W37 2000**
The Evolution of Western Private Law. Trade Cloth. Johns Hopkins University Press. Baltimore, MD. 2000. 344p. ISBN:0-8018-6484-4, ISBN13: 978-0-8018-6484-1. Dewey:340/.09. LCCN:00-055274.
Audience: **u,f.**

Winfield, Percy H. **KD530**
Chief Sources of English Legal History. Bernard D. Reams (Editor), Roscoe Pond (Introduction by). Trade Cloth. William S. Hein & Company, Inc. Buffalo, NY. 2001. 374p. Historical Reprints in Law and Jurisprudence Ser. ISBN:0-89941-255-6, ISBN13: 978-0-89941-255-9. Dewey:340.0942. LCCN:74-187697.
Audience: **u,f.**

Law (General) > Jurisprudence. Philosophy and Theory

Cardozo, Benjamin N. **K**
The Growth of the Law. Arthur L. Corbin (Foreword by). Trade Cloth. Greenwood Publishing Group, Inc. Portsmouth, NH. 1973. 145p. ISBN:0-8371-6953-4, ISBN13: 978-0-8371-6953-8. Dewey:340.1. LCCN:73-008154.
Audience: **u,f.** ***B***

Cohen, Felix S. **LAW**
Ethical Systems and Legal Ideals: An Essay on the Foundations of Legal Criticism. Trade Cloth. Greenwood Publishing Group, Inc. Portsmouth, NH. 1976. 303p. ISBN:0-8371-8643-9, ISBN13: 978-0-8371-8643-6. Dewey:174/.3. LCCN:75-040440.
Audience: **u,f.** ***B***

Dworkin, Ronald M. **K237.D86 1986**
Law's Empire. Trade Cloth. Harvard University Press. Cambridge, MA. 1986. 488p. ISBN:0-674-51835-7, ISBN13: 978-0-674-51835-3. Dewey:340. LCCN:85-028566.
Audience: **g.** *Choice, 1986.*

Dworkin, Ronald M. (Editor) **K246 .P45**
The Philosophy of Law. Paper Text. Oxford University Press, Inc. New York, NY. 1977. 192p. Oxford Readings in Philosophy Ser. ISBN:0-19-875022-6, ISBN13: 978-0-19-875022-2. Dewey:340.1. LCCN:77-356204.
Audience: **l,u.**

Fuller, Lon L. **K'**
The Morality of Law. Trade Cloth. Yale University Press. Cumberland, RI. 2004. "xi, 262"p. Storrs Lectures on Jurisprudence Ser. ISBN:0-300-00472-9, ISBN13: 978-0-300-00472-4. Dewey:340.112. LCCN:72-093579.
Audience: **u,f.** **B**

Hart, H. L. **K237.H3**
The Concept of Law. Ed. 2. Paper Text. Oxford University Press, Inc. New York, NY. 1997. 328p. Clarendon Law Ser. ISBN:0-19-876123-6, ISBN13: 978-0-19-876123-5. Dewey:340.1.
Audience: **l,u.**

Kelly, John M. **K215.E53K45 1992**
A Short History of Western Legal Theory. Paper Text. Oxford University Press, Inc. New York, NY. 1992. 488p. ISBN:0-19-876243-7, ISBN13: 978-0-19-876243-0. Dewey:340/.1. LCCN:91-036905.
Audience: **l,u.** *Choice, 1993.*

Newman, Peter (Editor) **HB61**
The New Palgrave Dictionary of Economics and the Law. Cloth over Boards. Palgrave Macmillan. New York, NY. 1998. 2210p. ISBN:1-56159-215-3, ISBN13: 978-1-56159-215-9. Dewey:330/.03.
Audience: **g,l,u,f.** *Choice, 1999.*

Pound, Roscoe **K230.P67I58 2003**
An Introduction to the Philosophy of Law [1922]. Trade Cloth. Lawbook Exchange, Limited, The. Clark, NJ. 2003. 307p. ISBN:1-58477-327-8, ISBN13: 978-1-58477-327-6. Dewey:340/.1. LCCN:2002-044351.
Audience: **u,f.**

Pound, Roscoe **KF394.P613 1999**
The Spirit of the Common Law. Neil Hamilton & Mathias A. Jaren (Introduction by). Trade Paper. Transaction Publishers. Somerset, NJ. 1998. 224p. ISBN:1-56000-942-X, ISBN13: 978-1-56000-942-9. Dewey:340.5/7. LCCN:98-024171.
Audience: **u,f.** **B**

Sunstein, Cass R. **K487.E3S86 1997**
Free Markets and Social Justice. Trade Paper. Oxford University Press, Inc. New York, NY. 1999. 416p. ISBN:0-19-510273-8, ISBN13: 978-0-19-510273-4. Dewey:330.12/2. LCCN:96-005503.
Audience: **g.** *Choice, 1997.*

Sunstein, Cass R. **K213.S86 1996**
Legal Reasoning and Political Conflict. Trade Cloth. Oxford University Press, Inc. New York, NY. 1996. 240p. ISBN:0-19-510082-4, ISBN13: 978-0-19-510082-2. Dewey:340.1/1. LCCN:95-025265.
Audience: **g.** *Choice, 1996.*

Law (General) > Comparative Law. International Uniform Law

Abraham, Henry J. **K2100.A725 1998**
The Judicial Process: An Introductory Analysis of the Courts of the United States, England, and France. Ed. 7. Trade Paper. Oxford University Press, Inc. New York, NY. 1998. 474p. ISBN:0-19-509987-7, ISBN13: 978-0-19-509987-4. Dewey:347.01. LCCN:97-027311.
Audience: **l,u.** **B**

Brownlie, Ian & Goodwin-Gill, Guy S. (Editors) **K3238.A1B76 2002**
Basic Documents on Human Rights. Ed. 4. Trade Paper. Oxford University Press, Inc. New York, NY. 2002. 650p. ISBN:0-19-924944-X, ISBN13: 978-0-19-924944-2. Dewey:341.4/8. LCCN:2002-025227.
Audience: **u,f.** **B**

Fox, James R. **KZ1161.F69 2003**
Dictionary of International and Comparative Law. Ed. 3. Trade Cloth. Oceana Publications. Dobbs Ferry, NY. 2003. 369p. ISBN:0-379-21501-2, ISBN13: 978-0-379-21501-4. Dewey:341/.03. LCCN:2003-101369.
Audience: **u,f.** *Choice, 1993.*

Gibson, John S. **K3239.3.G53 1996**
Dictionary of International Human Rights Law. Trade Cloth. Scarecrow Press, Inc. Lanham, MD. 1996. 272p. ISBN:0-8108-3118-X, ISBN13: 978-0-8108-3118-6. Dewey:341.4/81/03. LCCN:95-047066.
Audience: **g.** *Choice, 1997.*

Gillespie, Alexander **K3585.4.G55 1997**
International Environmental Law, Policy and Ethics. Trade Cloth. Oxford University Press, Inc. New York, NY. 1998. 232p. ISBN:0-19-826562-X, ISBN13: 978-0-19-826562-7. Dewey:341.7/62. LCCN:97-019430.
Audience: **u,f.** *Choice, 1998.*

Glenn, H. Patrick **K583**
Legal Traditions of the World: Sustainable Diversity in Law. Ed. 2. Paper Text. Oxford University Press, Inc. New York, NY. 2004. 428p. ISBN:0-19-926088-5, ISBN13: 978-0-19-926088-1. Dewey:340.2. LCCN:2004-558586.
Audience: **u,f.**

Hall, Jerome **K5018.H35 2005**
General Principles of Criminal Law. Ed. 2. Cloth Text. Lawbook Exchange, Limited, The. Clark, NJ. 2005. 654p. ISBN:1-58477-498-3, ISBN13: 978-1-58477-498-3. Dewey:345. LCCN:2004-053810.
Audience: **u,f.** **B**

Holmes, Oliver Wendell **K588.H65 2004**
The Common Law. Cloth Text. Lawbook Exchange, Limited, The. Clark, NJ. 2005. 438p. ISBN:1-58477-499-1, ISBN13: 978-1-58477-499-0. Dewey:340.5/7. LCCN:2004-053807.
Audience: **u,f.**

Jackson, John H. **K4602.2 1997**
The World Trading System: Law and Policy of International Economic Relations. Ed. 2. Trade Cloth. MIT Press. Cambridge, MA. 1997. 504p. ISBN:0-262-10061-4, ISBN13: 978-0-262-10061-8. Dewey:341.7/543. LCCN:97-015310.
Audience: **u,f.**

Kuper, Leo **HV6322.7**
Genocide: Its Political Use in the Twentieth Century. Trade Paper. Yale University Press. Cumberland, RI. 1983. 256p. ISBN:0-300-03120-3, ISBN13: 978-0-300-03120-1. Dewey:364.1/51/0904. LCCN:81-016151.
Audience: **u,f.**

Lessig, Lawrence **K1401.L47 2001**
The Future of Ideas: The Fate of the Commons in a Connected World. Trade Cloth. Random House, Inc. New York, NY. 2001. 368p. ISBN:0-375-50578-4, ISBN13: 978-0-375-50578-2. Dewey:346.04/8/0285. LCCN:2001-031968.
Audience: **g.** *Choice, 2002.*

Maddex, Robert L. **K3165.M33 2001**
Constitutions of the World. Ed. 2. Trade Cloth. CQ Press. Washington, DC. 2001. 440p. ISBN:1-56802-682-X, ISBN13: 978-1-56802-682-4. Dewey:342/.029. LCCN:2001-280083.
Audience: **u,f.**

Morsink, Johannes **K3238.31948.M67 1999**
The Universal Declaration of Human Rights: Origins and Intent. Trade Cloth. University of Pennsylvania Press. Philadelphia, PA. 1999. 392p. Pennsylvania Studies in Human Rights ISBN:0-8122-3474-X, ISBN13: 978-0-8122-3474-9. Dewey:341.4/81/09. LCCN:98-041468.
Audience: **g.** *Choice, 1999.*

Mower, A. Glenn Jr. **K3240**
The United States, the United Nations, and Human Rights: The Eleanor Roosevelt and Jimmy Carter Eras, 4. Trade Cloth. Greenwood Publishing Group, Inc. Portsmouth, NH. 1979. 215p. Studies in Human Rights, No. 4 ISBN:0-313-21090-X, ISBN13: 978-0-313-21090-7. Dewey:341.48/1. LCCN:78-022134.
Audience: **g,u,f.** B

Robertson, A. H. & **HN400.P8**
Moon, Nick
Opinion Polls: History, Theory and Practice. Cloth over Boards. Manchester University Press. Manchester, 1999. 240p. Political Analyses Ser. ISBN:0-7190-4223-2, ISBN13: 978-0-7190-4223-2. Dewey:303.3/8/0941.
Audience: **g.**

Schabas, William A. **K5104**
The Abolition of the Death Penalty in International Law. Ed. 3. Trade Cloth. Cambridge University Press. New York, NY. 2002. 506p. ISBN:0-521-81491-X, ISBN13: 978-0-521-81491-1. Dewey:345/.0773. LCCN:96-029108.
Audience: **u,f.** *Choice, 1998.*

Stone, Christopher D. **K3478.S764 1996**
Should Trees Have Standing?: And Other Essays on Law, Morals and the Environment. Trade Paper. Oceana Publications. Dobbs Ferry, NY. 1996. 181p. ISBN:0-379-21381-8, ISBN13: 978-0-379-21381-2. Dewey:344/.046. LCCN:96-035448.
Audience: **l,u.**

Weber, Max **K559 .W4313**
Max Weber on Law in Economy and Society. Max R. Shils (Editor), B. Y. Edward (Translator). Trade Cloth. Harvard University Press. Cambridge, MA. 1954. 437p. Twentieth Century Legal Philosophy Ser., No. 6 ISBN:0-674-55651-8, ISBN13: 978-0-674-55651-5. Dewey:330.1. LCCN:54-005023.
Audience: **g.**

Wigmore, John H. **K583 .W54**
A Panorama of the World's Legal Systems, Set. Trade Cloth. Gaunt, Inc. Holmes Beach, FL. 1992. 1206p. ISBN:1-56169-003-1, ISBN13: 978-1-56169-003-9. Dewey:340.2.
Audience: **l,u.**

United Kingdom and Ireland

Blackstone, William **KD660.B52 2003**
(Translator)
Commentaries on the Laws of England: In Four Books, 2. Ed. 3. Thomas McIntyre Cooley (Revised by). Trade Cloth. Lawbook Exchange, Limited, The. Clark, NJ. 2003. 1202p. ISBN:1-58477-361-8, ISBN13: 978-1-58477-361-0. Dewey:348.42/02. LCCN:2003-053970.
Audience: **u,f.**

Dawson, John P. **KJC3673.D39 1999**
A History of Lay Judges, 1960. Trade Cloth. Lawbook Exchange, Limited, The. Clark, NJ. 1999. viii, [2], 310p. ISBN:1-886363-69-2, ISBN13: 978-1-886363-69-4. Dewey:347.41/014. LCCN:98-050812.
Audience: **u,f.**

Levy, Leonard W. **KD7505.Z9**
The Palladium of Justice: Origins of Trial by Jury. Trade Cloth. Ivan R. Dee Publisher. Blue Ridge Summit, PA. 1999. 128p. ISBN:1-56663-259-5, ISBN13: 978-1-56663-259-1. Dewey:345.42/075. LCCN:99-012923.
Audience: **l,u.** *Choice, 2000.*

Madden, Frederick **KD5025**
(Editor)
The End of Empire: Dependencies since 1948: The West Indies, British Honduras, Hong Kong, Fiji, Cyprus, Gibraltar and the Falklands Select Documents on the Constitutional History of the British Empire and Commonwealth. Cloth Text. Greenwood Publishing Group, Inc. Portsmouth, NH. 2000. 600p. Documents in Imperial History Ser., No. 8 ISBN:0-313-29072-5, ISBN13: 978-0-313-29072-5. Dewey:342/.11241024. LCCN:00-030882.
Audience: **g.**

Madden, Frederick & **KD5025**
Darwin, John (Editors)
The Dependent Empire, 1900-1948: Colonies, Protectorates and Mandates Select Documents on the Constitutional History of the British Empire and Commonwealth, Vol. 7. Cloth Text. Greenwood Publishing Group, Inc. Portsmouth, NH. 1994. 912p. Documents in Imperial History Ser., Vol. 7 ISBN:0-313-27318-9, ISBN13: 978-0-313-27318-6. Dewey:325.3141. LCCN:84-021213.
Audience: **g.**

Madden, Frederick & **KD5025**
Darwin, John (Editors)
The Dominions and India since 1900: Select Documents on the Constitutional History of the British Empire and Commonwealth. Cloth Text. Greenwood Publishing Group, Inc.

Portsmouth, NH. 1993. 906p. Documents in Imperial History Ser. ISBN:0-313-27317-0, ISBN13: 978-0-313-27317-9. Dewey:325.9141. LCCN:84-021213.

Audience: **g.**

Madden, Frederick & Fieldhouse, David (Editors) **KD5025**
The Dependent Empire and Ireland, 1840-1900: Advance and Retreat in Representative Self-Government - Select Documents on the Constitutional History of the British Empire and Commonwealth, Vol. V. Trade Cloth. Greenwood Publishing Group, Inc. Portsmouth, NH. 1991. 864p. Documents in Imperial History Ser., No. 5 ISBN:0-685-54256-4, ISBN13: 978-0-685-54256-9. Dewey:325.9141.

Audience: **g.**

Plucknett, Theodore F. T. **KD671.P58 2001**
A Concise History of the Common Law [1956]. Ed. 5. Trade Cloth. Lawbook Exchange, Limited, The. Clark, NJ. 2001. 830p. ISBN:1-58477-137-2, ISBN13: 978-1-58477-137-1. Dewey:340.5/7/0942. LCCN:00-067821.

Audience: **u,f.**

Pollock, Frederick & Maitland, Frederic William **KD532.P64 1996**
The History of English Law Before the Time of Edward I 1898, Set. Ed. 2. Trade Cloth. Lawbook Exchange, Limited, The. Clark, NJ. 1996. 706p. ISBN:1-886363-22-6, ISBN13: 978-1-886363-22-9. Dewey:349.42. LCCN:96-016003.

Audience: **u,f.**

Radzinowicz, Leon & Hood, Roger G. **HV9649.E5R34 1990**
A History of English Law and Its Administration from 1750: Victorian and Edwardian England: The Emergence of Penal Policy. Trade Paper. Oxford University Press, Inc. New York, NY. 1991. 856p. ISBN:0-19-825663-9, ISBN13: 978-0-19-825663-2. Dewey:364.6/0942/09034. LCCN:90-047889.

Audience: **u,f.**

Robertson, Agnes J. **KD548 .R63 1986**
Anglo-Saxon Charters. Ed. 2. Trade Cloth. Gaunt, Inc. Holmes Beach, FL. 1986. 580p. Cambridge Studies in English Legal History ISBN:0-912004-51-7, ISBN13: 978-0-912004-51-8. Dewey:942.01. LCCN:85-081803.

Audience: **u,f.**

Street, Harry **KD**
Freedom, the Individual and the Law. Ed. 3. Trade Paper. Penguin Group (USA) Inc. New York, NY. 1977. 328p. ISBN:0-14-020646-9, ISBN13: 978-0-14-020646-3. Dewey:342/.42/085. LCCN:77-379989.

Audience: **l,u.** BCL3

World Legal Information Institute **KF242.A1**
[Web] World LII.
http://www.worldlii.org/

Audience: **u,f.**

Canada

Gall, Gerald L. **KE444.G34 1995**
The Canadian Legal System. Ed. 4. Trade Cloth. Carswell. Toronto, ON. 1995. 480p. ISBN:0-459-55376-3, ISBN13: 978-0-459-55376-0. Dewey:349.71. LCCN:96-108919.

Audience: **g.**

Glick, Leslie Alan **KDZ944.A41992**
Understanding the North American Free Trade Agreement: Legal and Business Consequences of NAFTA. Trade Cloth. Kluwer Law International. Alphen a/d Rijn, 1993. 110p. ISBN:90-6544-689-3, ISBN13: 978-90-6544-689-3. Dewey:343.7/087. LCCN:92-045137.

Audience: **u,f.**

World Legal Information Institute **KF242.A1**
[Web] World LII.
http://www.worldlii.org/

Audience: **u,f.**

United States > Bibliography. Reference Works

Evans, Patricia R. **KF101.6.B57 1983**
Supreme Court of the United States, 1789-1980: An Index to Opinions Arranged by Justice. Linda A. Blandford (Translator). Library Binding. Kraus International Publications. Hackensack, NJ. 1983. xvii, 503p. ISBN:0-527-27952-8, ISBN13: 978-0-527-27952-3. Dewey:347.7301402648. LCCN:82-048981.

Audience: **l,u,f.** BCL3

Garner, Bryan A. **KF156.B53 2004**
Black's Law Dictionary, Deluxe. Ed. 8. Trade Cloth. West Publishing Company, College & School Division. Eagan, MN. 2006. 1738p. ISBN:0-314-15234-2, ISBN13: 978-0-314-15234-3. Dewey:340.03. LCCN:2004-616324.

Audience: **u,f.**

Garner, Bryan A. **KF156.G367 1995**
A Dictionary of Modern Legal Usage. Ed. 2. Cloth Text. Oxford University Press, Inc. New York, NY. 1995. 984p. ISBN:0-19-507769-5, ISBN13: 978-0-19-507769-8. Dewey:340/.03. LCCN:95-003863.

Audience: **g.** *Choice, 1996, 1988.*

Garza, Hedda (Compiled by) **KF27.J8**
The Watergate Investigation Index: House Judiciary Committee Hearings and Report on Impeachment. Fred L. Israel (Introduction by). Book, Other. Rowman & Littlefield Publishers, Inc. Lanham, MD. 1985. 261p. ISBN:0-8420-2186-8, ISBN13: 978-0-8420-2186-9. Dewey:364.1/32/0973. LCCN:85-002040.

Audience: **l,u,f.** *Choice, 1985.*

Hanson, Carol R., et al. **K3240.4.H847 1999**
Human Rights: The Essential Reference. Ralph Wilde & Carol Devine (Authors), Hilary Poole (Editor). Cloth Text. Greenwood

Publishing Group, Inc. Portsmouth, NH. 1999. 304p. ISBN:1-57356-205-X, ISBN13: 978-1-57356-205-8. Dewey:323. LCCN:99-024395.
Audience: **g.** *Choice, 1999.*

Janosik, Robert J. (Editor) **KF154.E53 1987**
Encyclopedia of the American Judicial System: Studies of the Principal Institutions, Set. Trade Cloth. Thomson Gale. Farmington Hills, MI. 1987. 1420p. ISBN:0-684-17807-9, ISBN13: 978-0-684-17807-3. Dewey:349.73/0321. LCCN:87-004742.
Audience: **u,f.** *Choice, 1987.*

Law Library of Congress **KF352**
☐ A Century of Lawmaking.
http://memory.loc.gov/ammem/amlaw/lawhome.html
Law Library of Congress.
Audience: **u.**

Lehman, Jeffrey & Phelps, Shirelle **KF154.W47 2004**
West's Encyclopedia of American Law. Ed. 2. Trade Cloth. Thomson Gale. Farmington Hills, MI. 2004. 7000p. ISBN:0-7876-6367-0, ISBN13: 978-0-7876-6367-4. Dewey:349.73/03. LCCN:2004-004918.
Audience: **g,l,u.** *Choice, 2005.*

Library of Congress **KF51**
☐ Thomas - Treaties.
http://thomas.loc.gov/home/treaties/treaties.html
Audience: **u,f.**

Organization of American States **KDZ10**
☐ Treaties and Agreements OAS.
http://www.oas.org/main/main.asp?sLang=E&sLink=http://www.oas.org/DIL/treaties_and_agreements.htm
Organization of American States.
Audience: **u.**

Renstrom, Peter G. **KF156.R46 1991**
The American Law Dictionary. Library Binding. ABC-CLIO, Inc. Santa Barbara, CA. 1990. 308p. Clio Dictionaries in Political Science Ser. ISBN:0-87436-226-1, ISBN13: 978-0-87436-226-8. Dewey:348.73/03. LCCN:90-024114.
Audience: **u.** *Choice, 1991.*

United States Department of State **J83**
☐ International Agreements.
http://foia.state.gov/SearchColls/CollsSearch.asp
United States Department of State.
Audience: **u.**

United States Department of State **KZ235**
☐ Treaties In Force.
http://www.state.gov/s/l/treaties/
United States Department of State.
Audience: **u.**

United States. Supreme Court.
☐ United States reports. vol. 150- , 1893-.
http://www.findlaw.com/casecode/supreme.html
United States Government Printing Office.
Audience: **l,u,f.**

United States > Collections

Bickel, Alexander M. **LAW**
Unpublished Opinions of Mr. Justice Brandeis: The Supreme Court at Work. P. A. Freund (Introduction by). Trade Paper. University of Chicago Press. Chicago, IL. 1967. Court and the Constitution Ser. ISBN:0-226-04602-8, ISBN13: 978-0-226-04602-0. Dewey:347.99 347.972. LCCN:67-012001.
Audience: **g.**

Countryman, Vern (Editor) **KF213.D6.C63**
The Douglas Opinions. Trade Cloth. Random House, Inc. New York, NY. 1977. xiv, 465p. ISBN:0-394-49795-3, ISBN13: 978-0-394-49795-2. Dewey:342/.73/085. LCCN:76-053485.
Audience: **u,f.** B

Frank, Jerome D. **KF213.F67K7 1977**
A Man's Reach: The Philosophy of Judge Jerome Frank. Barbara F. Kristein (Editor). Trade Cloth. Greenwood Publishing Group, Inc. Portsmouth, NH. 1977. xxvii, 450p. ISBN:0-8371-9669-8, ISBN13: 978-0-8371-9669-5. Dewey:340.1. LCCN:77-007288.
Audience: **g.**

Frankfurter, Felix **KF213.F68 K8**
Of Law and Life and Other Things That Matter: Papers and Addresses of Felix Frankfurter, 1956-1963. Philip B. Kurland (Editor). Trade Cloth. Harvard University Press. Cambridge, MA. 1965. ISBN:0-674-63100-5, ISBN13: 978-0-674-63100-7. Dewey:340.082. LCCN:65-013221.
Audience: **l,u.**

Hand, Learned **H85**
The Spirit of Liberty. Ed. 3. Irving Dilliard (Editor). Paper Text. University of Chicago Press. Chicago, IL. 1977. xxxi, 311p. ISBN:0-226-31544-4, ISBN13: 978-0-226-31544-7. Dewey:301.
Audience: **g.**

Law Library of Congress **KF352**
☐ A Century of Lawmaking.
http://memory.loc.gov/ammem/amlaw/lawhome.html
Law Library of Congress.
Audience: **u.**

United States > Criminal Trials

KF220
☐ Slaves and the courts, 1740-1860.
http://memory.loc.gov/ammem/sthtml/
Library of Congress..
Audience: **l,u,f.**

KF224.R33.U53 1984
The United States of America V. Trade Cloth. University Publications of America. Bethesda, MD. 1984. xxvii, 482p. ISBN:0-89093-590-4, ISBN13: 978-0-89093-590-3. Dewey:345.73/0274. LCCN:83-025929.
Audience: **g.** B

Boyle, Kevin **KF224.S8B69 2004**
Arc of Justice: A Saga of Race, Civil Rights, and Murder in the Jazz Age. Trade Cloth. Henry Holt & Company. New York, NY. 2004. 432p. ISBN:0-8050-7145-8, ISBN13: 978-0-8050-7145-0. Dewey:345.73/02523/0977434. LCCN:2004-047352.
Audience: **g.**

Carter, Dan T. **KF224.S34**
Scottsboro: A Tragedy of the American South. Paper Text. Louisiana State University Press. Baton Rouge, LA. 1979. 512p. ISBN:0-8071-0498-1, ISBN13: 978-0-8071-0498-9. Dewey:345/.761/0253. LCCN:79-001090.
Audience: **g.**

Frank, Jerome & Frank, Barbara **KF220.F7 1971**
Not Guilty. Paper Text. Da Capo Press, Inc. Cambridge, MA. 1971. 261p. Civil Liberties in American History Ser. ISBN:0-306-70072-7, ISBN13: 978-0-306-70072-9. Dewey:345/.73/05. LCCN:72-138495.
Audience: **g.** B

Goldstein, Robert J. **KF224.J64G65 2000**
Flag Burning and Free Speech: The Case of Texas vs. Johnson. Trade Cloth. University Press of Kansas. Lawrence, KS. 2000. xviii, 270p. Landmark Law Cases and American Society Ser. ISBN:0-7006-1053-7, ISBN13: 978-0-7006-1053-2. Dewey:342.73/0853. LCCN:00-041165.
Audience: **g.** *Choice, 2001.*

Jacobs, James B., et al. **KF224.M2J33 1994**
Busting the Mob: The United States vs. Cosa Nostra. Christopher Panarella & Jay Worthington (Authors). Trade Cloth. New York University Press. New York, NY. 1994. 292p. ISBN:0-8147-4195-9, ISBN13: 978-0-8147-4195-5. Dewey:345.73/02. LCCN:94-027470.
Audience: **u,f.** *Choice, 1995.*

Knappman, Edward W. (Editor), et al. **KF220.G74 2002**
Great American Trials. Ed. 2. Stephen G. Christianson & Lisa Olson Paddock (Editors). Trade Cloth. Thomson Gale. Farmington Hills, MI. 2001. 800p. ISBN:0-7876-4901-5, ISBN13: 978-0-7876-4901-2. Dewey:347.73/7 347.3077. LCCN:2003-267032.
Audience: **g,l.**

Larson, Edward J. **KF224.S3L37 1997**
Summer for the Gods: The Scopes Trial and America's Continuing Debate over Science and Religion. Trade Cloth. Basic Books. New York, NY. 1997. 336p. ISBN:0-465-07509-6, ISBN13: 978-0-465-07509-6. Dewey:345.73/0288. LCCN:97-009648.
Audience: **g.** *Choice, 1997.*

Linder, Douglas O. **KF220**
☐ Famous Trials.
http://www.law.umkc.edu/faculty/projects/ftrials/ftrials.htm University of Missouri-Kansas City Law School..
Audience: **l,u.**

Moran, Jeffrey P. **KF224.S3M67 2002**
The Scopes Trial: A Brief History with Documents. Trade Paper. Bedford/Saint Martin's. New York, NY. 2002. 230p. The Bedford Series in History and Culture Ser. ISBN:0-312-24919-5, ISBN13: 978-0-312-24919-9. LCCN:2001-093634.
Audience: **l,u.**

Radosh, Ronald & Milton, Joyce **KF224.R6.R32 1983**
The Rosenberg File: A Search for the Truth. Trade Cloth. Henry Holt & Company. New York, NY. 1983. 703p. ISBN:0-03-049036-7, ISBN13: 978-0-03-049036-1. Dewey:347.305/231. LCCN:82-015569.
Audience: **g.** B

Russell, Francis **KF224.S2.R85**
Tragedy in Dedham; the Story of the Sacco-Vanzetti Case. Trade Cloth. McGraw-Hill Companies, The. New York, NY. 1971. xxiii, 480p. ISBN:0-07-054342-9, ISBN13: 978-0-07-054342-3. Dewey:345/.73/02523. LCCN:76-154839.
Audience: **g.** B

Schuetz, Janice & Snedaker, Kathryn H. **KF220.S38 1988**
Communication and Litigation: Case Studies of Famous Trials. Peter E. Kane (Foreword by). Cloth Text. Southern Illinois University Press. Carbondale, IL. 1988. 304p. ISBN:0-8093-1456-8, ISBN13: 978-0-8093-1456-0. Dewey:347.73/7. LCCN:87-035654.
Audience: **l,u.** *Choice, 1989.*

Sirica, John J. **E860**
To Set the Record Straight: The Break-in, the Tapes, the Conspirators, the Pardon. Trade Cloth. W. W. Norton & Company, Inc. New York, NY. 1979. 394p. ISBN:0-393-01234-4, ISBN13: 978-0-393-01234-7. Dewey:364.1/323/0973. LCCN:79-010039.
Audience: **g.** B

Stern, Kenneth S. **KF224.B36S74 1994**
Loud Hawk: The United States vs. the American Indian Movement. Trade Cloth. University of Oklahoma Press. Norman, OK. 1994. 384p. ISBN:0-8061-2587-X, ISBN13: 978-0-8061-2587-9. Dewey:345.7307. LCCN:93-006175.
Audience: **g,l,u,f.**

Thomas, Brook **KF223.P56P58 1997**
Plessy vs. Ferguson: A Brief History with Documents. Trade Paper. Bedford/Saint Martin's. New York, NY. 1996. 205p. The Bedford Series in History and Culture ISBN:0-312-13743-5, ISBN13: 978-0-312-13743-4. LCCN:96-084942.
Audience: **l,u.**

Ungar, Sanford J. **KF224.N39U54 1989**
The Papers and the Papers: An Account of the Legal and Political Battle Over the Pentagon Papers. Cloth Text. Columbia University Press. New York, NY. 1989. ISBN:0-231-06948-0, ISBN13: 978-0-231-06948-9. Dewey:342.73/0853. LCCN:88-038764.
Audience: **g.**

Zenger, John Peter **KF223**
The Trial of Peter Zenger. Vincent Buranelli (Editor). Trade Cloth. Greenwood Publishing Group, Inc. Portsmouth, NH. 1975. 152p. ISBN:0-8371-8444-4, ISBN13: 978-0-8371-8444-9. Dewey:345.747/0231. LCCN:75-031814.
Audience: **u,f.**

United States > Civil Trials

Fisher, Franklin M., et al. **KF1890.C6**
Folded, Spindled and Mutilated: The Economics of U. S. vs IBM. John McGowan & Joen Greenwood (Authors),

Schmalensee (Editor), Carl Kaysen (Introduction by). Trade Cloth. MIT Press. Cambridge, MA. 1983. 435p. Regulation of Economic Activity Ser., No. 7 ISBN:0-262-06086-8, ISBN13: 978-0-262-06086-8. Dewey:347.303/72. LCCN:83-000935.
Audience: **u,f.** B

Friendly, Fred **KF228.N35.F73**
Minnesota Rag: The Dramatic Story of the Landmark Supreme Court Case That Gave New Meaning to Freedom of the Press. Trade Cloth. Random House, Inc. New York, NY. 1981. 243p. ISBN:0-394-50752-5, ISBN13: 978-0-394-50752-1. Dewey:342.73/0853/0264. LCCN:80-006018.
Audience: **g.** B

Hull, N. E. H. & Hoffer, Peter Charles **KF228**
Roe vs. Wade: The Abortion Rights Controversy in American History. Trade Cloth. University Press of Kansas. Lawrence, KS. 2001. xii, 316p. Landmark Law Cases and American Society Ser. ISBN:0-7006-1142-8, ISBN13: 978-0-7006-1142-3. Dewey:342.73/084. LCCN:2001-001785.
Audience: **g.** *Choice, 2002.*

Jaworski, Leon **KF228.U5.J3**
The Right and the Power. Trade Cloth. Reader's Digest Press. New York, NY. 1976. 305p. ISBN:0-88349-102-8, ISBN13: 978-0-88349-102-7. Dewey:345/.73/0232. LCCN:76-022594.
Audience: **g.** B

Long, Carolyn N. **KF228.O74L66 2000**
Religious Freedom and Indian Rights: The Case of Oregon vs. Smith. Trade Cloth. University Press of Kansas. Lawrence, KS. 2000. xii, 324p. Landmark Law Cases and American Society Ser. ISBN:0-7006-1063-4, ISBN13: 978-0-7006-1063-1. Dewey:342.73/0852. LCCN:00-043652.
Audience: **g,u,f.** *Choice, 2001.*

Martin, Waldo E. **KF228.B76B76 1998**
Brown vs. Board of Education: A Brief History with Documents. Trade Paper. Bedford/Saint Martin's. New York, NY. 1998. 253p. Brown Vs. Board of Education Ser., Vol. 1 ISBN:0-312-11152-5, ISBN13: 978-0-312-11152-6. Dewey:344.73/0798. LCCN:97-074964.
Audience: **l,u.**

Pringle, Peter **KF226.P75 1998**
Cornered: Big Tobacco at the Bar of Justice. Trade Cloth. Henry Holt & Company. New York, NY. 1997. 288p. ISBN:0-8050-4292-X, ISBN13: 978-0-8050-4292-4. Dewey:346.7303/8. LCCN:97-047008.
Audience: **g.**

Rudenstine, David **KF228.N52 R84 1996**
The Day the Presses Stopped: A History of the Pentagon Papers Case. Trade Cloth. University of California Press. Berkeley, CA. 1996. 278p. ISBN:0-520-08672-4, ISBN13: 978-0-520-08672-2. Dewey:345.73/0231. LCCN:95-044464.
Audience: **l,u.** *Choice, 1996.*

Woloch, Nancy **KF228.M85W65 1996**
Muller Vs. Oregon: A Brief History with Documents. Trade Paper. Bedford/Saint Martin's. New York, NY. 1996. 206p. The Bedford Series in History and Culture ISBN:0-312-08586-9, ISBN13: 978-0-312-08586-5. Dewey:344.7301/4. LCCN:95-083525.
Audience: **l,u.**

United States > Legal Research. Legal Composition

KF245 .U54 2005
The Bluebook: A Uniform System of Citation. Ed. 18. Harvard Law Review Association.. 2005.
Audience: **u,f.**

Berring **KF240.B45 2005**
Finding the Law 2005. Ed. 12. Trade Paper. West Publishing Company, College & School Division. Eagan, MN. 2005. xv, 443p. American Casebook Ser. ISBN:0-314-14579-6, ISBN13: 978-0-314-14579-6. Dewey:340.072/073. LCCN:2005-618989.
Audience: **l,u.**

Elias, Stephen & Levinkind, Susan **KF240.E35**
Legal Research: How to Find and Understand the Law. Ed. 12. Trade Paper. NOLO. Berkeley, CA. 2004. 368p. ISBN:1-4133-0058-8, ISBN13: 978-1-4133-0058-1. Dewey:340.072073. LCCN:2003-065177.
Audience: **g.**

Goehlert, Robert U. & Martin, Fenton S. **KF240.G63 1989**
Congress and Law-Making: Researching the Legislative Process. Ed. 2. Library Binding. ABC-CLIO, Inc. Santa Barbara, CA. 1988. 306p. ISBN:0-87436-509-0, ISBN13: 978-0-87436-509-2. Dewey:328.73/077/072. LCCN:88-022355.
Audience: **u,f.**

Olson, Kent **KF240.O365 1999**
Legal Information: How to Find It, How to Use It. Book, Other. Greenwood Publishing Group, Inc. Portsmouth, NH. 1998. 342p. How to Find It, How to Use It Ser. ISBN:0-89774-961-8, ISBN13: 978-0-89774-961-9. Dewey:340/.07/2073. LCCN:98-046517.
Audience: **g.** *Choice, 1999.*

Price, Miles O., et al. **KF240.P7**
Effective Legal Research. Ed. 4. Harry Bitner & Shirley R. Bysiewicz (Authors). Trade Cloth. Aspen Publishers, Inc. New York, NY. 1979. 672p. ISBN:0-316-71832-7, ISBN13: 978-0-316-71832-5. Dewey:340/.07/2073.
Audience: **u,f.**

United States > Legal Education

Llewellyn, Karl N. **KF283**
Bramble Bush: On Our Law and Its Study. Cloth Text. Oceana Publications. Dobbs Ferry, NY. 1981. 192p. ISBN:0-379-20738-9, ISBN13: 978-0-379-20738-5. Dewey:340/.071173. LCCN:51-001727.
Audience: **g,l,u.** B

Margolis, Wendy (Editor), et al. **KF272**
ABA-LSAC Official Guide to ABA-Approved Law Schools 2006. Bonnie Gordon, Joe Puskarz & David Rosenlieb (Editors). Trade Paper, Perfect. Law School Admission Council. Newtown, PA. 2005. 854p. ISBN:0-9760245-1-9, ISBN13: 978-0-9760245-1-4. Dewey:340.0711.
Audience: **l,u.** *Choice, 2005.*

Research and Education Association Staff **KF285.Z9V47 1998**
LSAT: The Best Test Preparation for the Law School Admission Test with Software. Trade Paper. Research & Education Association. Piscataway, NJ. 2003. 656p. Test Prep Ser. ISBN:0-87891-471-4, ISBN13: 978-0-87891-471-5. LCCN:98-067988.
Audience: **g.**

Vanderbilt, Arthur T. **KF352.A2V35**
Studying Law: Selections from the Writings of Albert J. Beveridge, John Maxcy Zane, Munroe Smith and Others . . . Paper Text. Textbook Publishers. Temecula, CA. 2003. viii, 753p. ISBN:0-7581-0656-4, ISBN13: 978-0-7581-0656-8. Dewey:340.82.
Audience: **g.** B

United States > Legal Profession

Abel, Richard L. **KF297.A756 1989**
American Lawyers. Trade Cloth. Oxford University Press, Inc. New York, NY. 1989. 424p. ISBN:0-19-505140-8, ISBN13: 978-0-19-505140-7. Dewey:340/.023/73. LCCN:88-022522.
Audience: **l,u.** *Choice, 1990.*

Arron, Deborah L. **KF297.A875**
What Can You Do with a Law Degree?: A Lawyer's Guide to Career Alternatives. Library Binding. Sagebrush Education Resources. Caledonia, MN. 2003. ISBN:0-613-92393-6, ISBN13: 978-0-613-92393-4. Dewey:340/.023/73.
Audience: **g,l,u.**

Glendon, Mary Ann **KF320.L4**
A Nation under Lawyers: How the Crisis in the Legal System Is Transforming American Society. Trade Paper. Harvard University Press. Cambridge, MA. 1996. 352p. ISBN:0-674-60138-6, ISBN13: 978-0-674-60138-3. Dewey:340.02373.
Audience: **g.**

Warren, Charles **KF352**
A History of the American Bar. Trade Paper. Beard Books, Inc. Chevy Chase, MD. 1999. 602p. Law Classic Ser. ISBN:1-893122-26-3, ISBN13: 978-1-893122-26-0. Dewey:340.
Audience: **u,f.** B

United States > History of United States Law

Bloomfield, Maxwell **KF366**
American Lawyers in a Changing Society, 1776-1876. Trade Cloth. Harvard University Press. Cambridge, MA. 1976. 425p. Studies in Legal History ISBN:0-674-02910-0, ISBN13: 978-0-674-02910-1. Dewey:340.1/15/0973. LCCN:75-014172.
Audience: **g.** B

Friedman, Lawrence M. **KF352.F7 2005**
A History of American Law. Ed. 3. Trade Paper. Simon & Schuster. New York, NY. 2005. 640p. ISBN:0-684-86988-8, ISBN13: 978-0-684-86988-9. Dewey:349.73/09. LCCN:2005-042451.
Audience: **g.** B

Gilmore, Grant **KF352**
Ages of American Law. Trade Paper. Yale University Press. Cumberland, RI. 1979. 154p. The Storrs Lectures Ser. ISBN:0-300-02352-9, ISBN13: 978-0-300-02352-7. Dewey:340/.0973. LCCN:76-049988.
Audience: **u,f.** B

Hall, Kermit L. **KF352.H35 1989**
The Magic Mirror: Law in American History. Trade Cloth. Oxford University Press, Inc. New York, NY. 1989. 416p. ISBN:0-19-504459-2, ISBN13: 978-0-19-504459-1. Dewey:349.73. LCCN:88-015138.
Audience: **u,f.** *Choice, 1989.*

Hoffer, Peter C. **KF361.H63 1998**
Law and People in Colonial America. Ed. 2. Trade Cloth. Johns Hopkins University Press. Baltimore, MD. 1998. 216p. ISBN:0-8018-5822-4, ISBN13: 978-0-8018-5822-2. Dewey:349.73. LCCN:97-030937.
Audience: **u,f.** *Choice, 1992.*

Horwitz, Morton J. **KF366.H6 1992**
The Transformation of American Law, 1780-1860. Trade Cloth. Oxford University Press, Inc. New York, NY. 1992. 384p. ISBN:0-19-507829-2, ISBN13: 978-0-19-507829-9. Dewey:346/.73/009033. LCCN:92-003464.
Audience: **g.**

Law Library of Congress **KF352**
☐ A Century of Lawmaking.
http://memory.loc.gov/ammem/amlaw/lawhome.html
Law Library of Congress.
Audience: **u.**

Novak, William J. **KF366.N68 1996**
The People's Welfare: Law and Regulation in Nineteenth-Century America. Trade Cloth. University of North Carolina Press. Chapel Hill, NC. 1996. 408p. Studies in Legal History ISBN:0-8078-2292-2, ISBN13: 978-0-8078-2292-0. Dewey:349.73/09/034. LCCN:95-051850.
Audience: **g.** *Choice, 1997.*

Pound, Roscoe (Editor) **KF352.A2**
The Formative Era of American Law. Trade Cloth. Gaunt, Inc. Holmes Beach, FL. 2002. 188p. ISBN:1-56169-801-6, ISBN13: 978-1-56169-801-1. Dewey:340.0973.
Audience: **u,f.** B

Schwartz, Bernard **KF352.S35**
The Law in America. Trade Cloth. McGraw-Hill Companies, The. New York, NY. 1974. 396p. ISBN:0-07-055678-4, ISBN13: 978-0-07-055678-2. Dewey:340/.0973. LCCN:74-005287.
Audience: **g.** B

Urofsky, Melvin I. **KF350.D633 2002**
Documents of American Constitutional and Legal History: From the Age of Industrialization to the Present. Ed. 2. Paper Text. Oxford University Press, Inc. New York, NY. 2001. 583p. ISBN:0-19-512872-9, ISBN13: 978-0-19-512872-7. Dewey:342.73/029. LCCN:2001-021142.
Audience: **l,u.**

Urofsky, Melvin I. & Finkelman, Paul (Editors) **KF350.D633 2002**
Documents of American Constitutional and Legal History: From the Founding Through the Age of Industrialization. Ed. 2. Paper

Text. Oxford University Press, Inc. New York, NY. 2001. 560p. ISBN:0-19-512870-2, ISBN13: 978-0-19-512870-3. Dewey:342.73029. LCCN:2001-021142.
Audience: **l,u.**

United States > History of United States Law > 20th Century Legal Biography

Dees, Morris **KF373.D43A3 1991**
A Season for Justice: The Life and Times of Civil Rights Lawyer Morris Dees. Trade Cloth. Simon & Schuster. New York, NY. 1991. 320p. ISBN:0-684-19189-X, ISBN13: 978-0-684-19189-8. Dewey:342.75/085/092. LCCN:90-022600.
Audience: **g.** *Choice, 1991.*

Gunther, Gerald **KF373.H29G76 1994**
Learned Hand: The Man and the Judge. Lewis F. Powell Jr. (Foreword by). Trade Cloth. Alfred A. Knopf Inc. New York, NY. 1994. xxi, 818p. ISBN:0-394-58807-X, ISBN13: 978-0-394-58807-0. Dewey:347.73/22/34 B 347.3. LCCN:93-022868.
Audience: **g.** *Choice, 1994.*

Hill, Anita **KF373.H46A3 1997**
Speaking Truth to Power. Trade Cloth. Doubleday Publishing. New York, NY. 1997. 368p. ISBN:0-385-47625-6, ISBN13: 978-0-385-47625-6. Dewey:[B]. LCCN:97-001316.
Audience: **g.**

Turow, Scott **KF373.T88A33**
One L: The Turbulent True Story of a First Year at Harvard Law School. Trade Paper. Warner Books, Inc. New York, NY. 1997. 288p. ISBN:0-446-67378-1, ISBN13: 978-0-446-67378-5. Dewey:340/.07/117444. LCCN:97-061016.
Audience: **g.** B

United States > Philosophy. General and Comprehensive Works

Dworkin, Ronald M. **KF380.D85 1985**
A Matter of Principle. Trade Cloth. Harvard University Press. Cambridge, MA. 1985. 448p. ISBN:0-674-55460-4, ISBN13: 978-0-674-55460-3. Dewey:340/.1. LCCN:84-025122.
Audience: **g.** B *Choice, 1985.*

Fishman, Stephen **KF390.5.C6F57 2004**
Web and Software Development: A Legal Guide. Ed. 4. Trade Paper, CD-ROM, Book, Other. NOLO. Berkeley, CA. 2004. 568p. ISBN:1-4133-0087-1, ISBN13: 978-1-4133-0087-1. Dewey:346.7304/8. LCCN:2004-049536.
Audience: **g.**

Friedman, Lawrence Meir **KF385.A4F7 2002**
American Law in the 20th Century. Cloth over Boards. Yale University Press. Cumberland, RI. 2002. 736p. ISBN:0-300-09137-0, ISBN13: 978-0-300-09137-3. Dewey:349.73. LCCN:2001-003332.
Audience: **g,l,u,f.** *Choice, 2002.*

Gray, John Chipman **K235**
The Nature and Sources of the Law. Ed. 2. Trade Cloth. Gaunt, Inc. Holmes Beach, FL. 2000. xvii,. 348p. ISBN:1-56169-582-3, ISBN13: 978-1-56169-582-9. Dewey:340/.1.
Audience: **g.** B

Hawke, Constance S. **KF390.5.C6H39 2001**
Computer and Internet Use on Campus: A Legal Guide to Issues of Intellectual Property, Free Speech, and Privacy. Trade Paper. John Wiley & Sons, Inc. Hoboken, NJ. 2000. 192p. Higher and Adult Education Ser. ISBN:0-7879-5516-7, ISBN13: 978-0-7879-5516-8. Dewey:343.7309/944. LCCN:00-009572.
Audience: **g.** *Choice, 2001.*

Horwitz, Morton J. **KF380.H67 1992**
The Transformation of American Law, 1870-1960: The Crisis of Legal Orthodoxy. Trade Cloth. Oxford University Press, Inc. New York, NY. 1992. 384p. ISBN:0-19-507024-0, ISBN13: 978-0-19-507024-8. Dewey:349.73. LCCN:91-030273.
Audience: **g.** *Choice, 1992.*

Howard, Philip K. **KF384.H69**
The Death of Common Sense: How Law Is Suffocating America. Trade Cloth. Random House Value Publishing. New York, NY. 1998. ISBN:0-517-31696-X, ISBN13: 978-0-517-31696-2. Dewey:349.73.
Audience: **g.** *Choice, 1995.*

Irving, J.D., Shae (Editor) **KF387.N65 2005**
Nolo's Encyclopedia of Everyday Law: Answers to Your Most Frequently Asked Legal Questions. Ed. 6. Trade Paper, Perfect. NOLO. Berkeley, CA. 2005. 490p. ISBN:1-4133-0189-4, ISBN13: 978-1-4133-0189-2. Dewey:349.73.
Audience: **g.**

Johnson, John W. (Editor) **KF385.A4J64 2001**
Historic U. S. Court Cases: An Encyclopedia, Set. Ed. 2. Paper over Boards. Routledge. New York, NY. 2001. 1128p. American Law and Society Ser. ISBN:0-415-93019-7, ISBN13: 978-0-415-93019-2. Dewey:349.73/0264. LCCN:2001-031651.
Audience: **l,u.** *Choice, 2002.*

Kent, James **KF385.K433 1989**
Commentaries on American Law. Ed. 12. Oliver W. Holmes Jr. (Editor). Trade Cloth. William S. Hein & Company, Inc. Buffalo, NY. 1989. ISBN:0-8377-2338-8, ISBN13: 978-0-8377-2338-9. Dewey:349.73. LCCN:89-048822.
Audience: **u,f.** B

Leiter, Richard A. **KF386.N38 2005**
National Survey of State Laws. Ed. 5. Trade Cloth. Thomson Gale. Farmington Hills, MI. 2004. 700p. ISBN:0-7876-7361-7, ISBN13: 978-0-7876-7361-1. Dewey:349.73.
Audience: **g,l,u,f.**

Levi, Edward H. **K3171**
An Introduction to Legal Reasoning. Trade Paper. University of Chicago Press. Chicago, IL. 1962. 112p. ISBN:0-226-47408-9, ISBN13: 978-0-226-47408-3. Dewey:340.1/1. LCCN:49-011213.
Audience: **u,f.**

Lieberman, Jethro K. **KF380.L53 1983**
The Litigious Society. Cloth Text. Basic Books. New York, NY. 1981. 212p. ISBN:0-465-04134-5, ISBN13: 978-0-465-04134-3. Dewey:346.7303. LCCN:80-068181.
Audience: **g.** B

Norwick, Kenneth P. & Chasen, Jerry S. **KF390.A96N67 1992**
The Rights of Authors, Artists, and Other Creative People: The Basic ACLU Guide to Author and Artist Rights. Ed. 2. Trade Cloth. Southern Illinois University Press. Carbondale, IL. 1992.

307p. American Civil Liberties Union Handbook Ser. ISBN:0-8093-1773-7, ISBN13: 978-0-8093-1773-8. Dewey:344.73/017617. LCCN:91-023721.
Audience: **g.**

Posner, Richard A. **K487.E3P67 2002**
Economic Analysis of Law. Ed. 6. Cloth Text. Aspen Publishers, Inc. New York, NY. 2002. xx, 747p. ISBN:0-7355-3474-8, ISBN13: 978-0-7355-3474-2. Dewey:349.73. LCCN:2002-028047.
Audience: **l,u.** BCL3

Scheingold, Stuart A. **K370**
The Politics of Rights: Lawyers, Public Policy and Political Change. Trade Paper. Yale University Press. Cumberland, RI. 1975. 224p. ISBN:0-300-01811-8, ISBN13: 978-0-300-01811-0. Dewey:340.1/15. LCCN:74-079972.
Audience: **u,f.** BCL3

United States > Special Branches of United States Civil Law > Law of Persons. Family Law

Friedman, Lawrence M. **KF505.F75 2005**
Private Lives: Families, Individuals, and the Law. Trade Cloth. Harvard University Press. Cambridge, MA. 2005. 240p. ISBN:0-674-01562-2, ISBN13: 978-0-674-01562-3. Dewey:346.7301/5. LCCN:2004-047519.
Audience: **g.** *Choice, 2005.*

Goldstein, Joseph, et al. **KF547.G64**
Before the Best Interests of the Child. Anna Freud & Albert J. Solnit (Authors). Trade Cloth. Simon & Schuster. New York, NY. 1980. xii, 288p. ISBN:0-02-912220-1, ISBN13: 978-0-02-912220-4. Dewey:344.03/27. LCCN:79-064249.
Audience: **g.** BCL3

Gostin, Larry (Editor) **KF540.A75S87 1990**
[Ebook] Surrogate Motherhood: Politics and Privacy. E-Book. Indiana University Press. Bloomington, IN. 1990. 384p. Medical Ethics Ser. ISBN:0-253-32604-4, ISBN13: 978-0-253-32604-1. Dewey:346.7301/7. LCCN:89-045474.
Audience: **g.** *Choice, 1990.*

Hartog, Hendrik **KF510.H37 2000**
Man and Wife in America: A History. Trade Cloth. Harvard University Press. Cambridge, MA. 2000. 416p. ISBN:0-674-00262-8, ISBN13: 978-0-674-00262-3. Dewey:346.7301/63/09. LCCN:99-056466.
Audience: **g.** *Choice, 2000.*

Hauser, Barbara R. (Editor) **KF478.W674 1996**
Women's Legal Guide: A Comprehensive Guide to Legal Issues Affecting Every Woman. Roberta C. Ramo (Foreword by). Trade Paper. Fulcrum Publishing. Golden, CO. 1996. 544p. ISBN:1-55591-303-2, ISBN13: 978-1-55591-303-8. Dewey:346.7301/34. LCCN:95-046893.
Audience: **g.** *Choice, 1996.*

Kennedy, Randall **KF538**
Interracial Intimacies: Sex, Marriage, Identity, and Adoption. Trade Paper. Knopf Publishing Group. New York, NY. 2004. 688p. ISBN:0-375-70264-4, ISBN13: 978-0-375-70264-8. Dewey:346.7301/6.
Audience: **g.** *Choice, 2003.*

Levit, Nancy **KF475.L48 1998**
The Gender Line: Men, Women, and the Law. Trade Cloth. New York University Press. New York, NY. 1998. 320p. Critical America Ser. ISBN:0-8147-5121-0, ISBN13: 978-0-8147-5121-3. Dewey:305.3. LCCN:97-045398.
Audience: **g,l,u,f.** *Choice, 1998.*

Levy, Robert M. & Rubenstein, Leonard S. **KF480.L48 1996**
The Rights of People with Mental Disabilities: The Authoritative ACLU Guide to the Rights of People with Mental Illness and Mental Retardation. Trade Cloth. Southern Illinois University Press. Carbondale, IL. 1996. 424p. American Civil Liberties Union Handbook Ser. ISBN:0-8093-1989-6, ISBN13: 978-0-8093-1989-3. Dewey:346.7301/38. LCCN:95-036408.
Audience: **l,u.**

MacKinnon, Catharine A. **KF478.M26 2004**
Women's Lives, Men's Laws. Trade Cloth. Harvard University Press. Cambridge, MA. 2005. 576p. ISBN:0-674-01540-1, ISBN13: 978-0-674-01540-1. Dewey:342.7308/78. LCCN:2004-052086.
Audience: **g.** *Choice, 2005.*

Mason, Mary A. **KF547.M37 1994**
From Father's Property to Children's Rights: The History of Child Custody in the United States. Trade Cloth. Columbia University Press. New York, NY. 1994. 256p. ISBN:0-231-08046-8, ISBN13: 978-0-231-08046-0. Dewey:346.7301/7. LCCN:93-034524.
Audience: **u,f.** *Choice, 1994.*

Morris, Thomas D. **KF482.M67 1996**
Southern Slavery and the Law, 1619-1860. Trade Cloth. University of North Carolina Press. Chapel Hill, NC. 1996. 592p. Studies in Legal History ISBN:0-8078-2238-8, ISBN13: 978-0-8078-2238-8. Dewey:342.73/087. LCCN:95-006565.
Audience: **g.** *Choice, 1996.*

Roth, Rachel **KF481.R67 2000**
Making Women Pay: The Hidden Costs of Fetal Rights. Book, Other. Cornell University Press. Ithaca, NY. 1999. 264p. ISBN:0-8014-3607-9, ISBN13: 978-0-8014-3607-9. Dewey:342.73/085. LCCN:99-044982.
Audience: **g,l,u,f.** *Choice, 2000.*

Strasser, Mark P. **KF539.S77 1997**
Legally Wed: Same-Sex Marriage and the Constitution. Book, Other. Cornell University Press. Ithaca, NY. 1997. 256p. ISBN:0-8014-3406-8, ISBN13: 978-0-8014-3406-8. Dewey:346.7301/6. LCCN:96-050344.
Audience: **g,l,u,f.** *Choice, 1997.*

United States > Special Branches of United States Civil Law > Real Property. Land Law

Portman, Janet & Stewart, Marcia **KF590.Z9P673 2005**
Renters' Rights: Legal Basics. Ed. 4. Trade Paper. NOLO. Berkeley, CA. 2005. 272p. ISBN:1-4133-0150-9, ISBN13: 978-1-4133-0150-2. Dewey:346.7304/34. LCCN:2004-065444.
Audience: **g.**

Vose, Clement E. **KF662.Z9 V67**
Caucasians Only: The Supreme Court, the NAACP, and the Restrictive Covenant Cases. Paper Text. Textbook Publishers. Temecula, CA. 2003. xi, 296p. ISBN:0-7581-2647-6, ISBN13: 978-0-7581-2647-4.
Audience: **g.** B

United States > Special Branches of United States Civil Law > Trusts. Estates

Clifford, Denis **KF755.Z9C54 2005**
Nolo's Simple Will Book. Ed. 6. Trade Paper, CD-ROM, Book, Other. NOLO. Berkeley, CA. 2005. 288p. ISBN:1-4133-0360-9, ISBN13: 978-1-4133-0360-5. Dewey:346.7305/4. LCCN:2005-047764.
Audience: **g.**

United States > Special Branches of United States Civil Law > Contracts

Rohwer, Claude D. & Skroki, Anthony M. **KF801.Z9R62 2000**
Contracts in a Nutshell. Ed. 5. Trade Paper. West Publishing Company, College & School Division. Eagan, MN. 2000. xxxi, 639p. Nutshell Ser. ISBN:0-314-23814-X, ISBN13: 978-0-314-23814-6. Dewey:346.7302. LCCN:00-269359.
Audience: **l,u.**

United States > Special Branches of United States Civil Law > Torts

Kionka, Edward J. **KF1250.Z9K53 2005**
Torts in a Nutshell. Ed. 4. Trade Paper. West Publishing Company, College & School Division. Eagan, MN. 2005. 515p. ISBN:0-314-15219-9, ISBN13: 978-0-314-15219-0. Dewey:346.7303. LCCN:2005-282462.
Audience: **u,f.**

White, G. Edward **KF1249.W48 2002**
Tort Law in America: An Intellectual History. Ed. 2. Trade Cloth. Oxford University Press, Inc. New York, NY. 2003. 424p. ISBN:0-19-513964-X, ISBN13: 978-0-19-513964-8. Dewey:346.7303/09. LCCN:2002-071544.
Audience: **g.**

United States > Special Branches of United States Civil Law > Torts > Privacy

DeCew, Judith W. **KF1262.D43 1997**
In Pursuit of Privacy: Law, Ethics, and the Rise of Technology. Book, Other. Cornell University Press. Ithaca, NY. 1997. 208p. ISBN:0-8014-3380-0, ISBN13: 978-0-8014-3380-1. Dewey:342.73/0858. LCCN:97-005409.
Audience: **l,u.**

O'Brien, David M. **KF1262.O25**
Privacy, Law, and Public Policy. Trade Cloth. Greenwood Publishing Group, Inc. Portsmouth, NH. 1979. xiv, 262p. ISBN:0-03-050406-6, ISBN13: 978-0-03-050406-8. Dewey:342/.73/085. LCCN:79-014131.
Audience: **u,f.** B

Rosen, Jeffrey **KF1262.R67 2000**
The Unwanted Gaze: The Destruction of Privacy in America. Trade Cloth. Random House, Inc. New York, NY. 2000. 288p. ISBN:0-679-44546-3, ISBN13: 978-0-679-44546-3. Dewey:342.73/0858. LCCN:99-056498.
Audience: **g.** *Choice, 2001.*

United States > Special Branches of United States Civil Law > Torts > Libel. Slander

Jones, William K. **KF1266.J66 2003**
Insult to Injury: Libel, Slander and Invasion of Privacy. Trade Cloth. University Press of Colorado. Boulder, CO. 2003. 388p. ISBN:0-87081-742-6, ISBN13: 978-0-87081-742-7. Dewey:346.7303/4. LCCN:2003-008786.
Audience: **u,f.** *Choice, 2004.*

Lawhorne, Clifton O. & Long, Howard R. **KF1266.A7.L38**
The Supreme Court and Libel. Trade Cloth. Southern Illinois University Press. Carbondale, IL. 1981. 176p. New Horizons in Journalism Ser. ISBN:0-8093-0998-X, ISBN13: 978-0-8093-0998-6. Dewey:346.7303/4. LCCN:80-021161.
Audience: **u,f.** B

Lewis, Anthony **KF1266.L48 1991**
Make No Law: The Sullivan Case and the First Amendment. Trade Cloth. Random House, Inc. New York, NY. 1991. 368p. ISBN:0-394-58774-X, ISBN13: 978-0-394-58774-5. Dewey:345.73/0256. LCCN:91-006618.
Audience: **g.** *Choice, 1991.*

United States > Special Branches of United States Civil Law > Torts > Government Torts

Jacobs, Clyde E. **KF1322 .J3**
The Eleventh Amendment and Sovereign Immunity. Trade Cloth. Greenwood Publishing Group, Inc. Portsmouth, NH. 1972. 216p. Contributions in American History Ser., No. 19 ISBN:0-8371-6058-8, ISBN13: 978-0-8371-6058-0. Dewey:342/.73/088. LCCN:71-149959.
Audience: **u,f.** B

Noonan, John T. Jr. **KF1322**
Narrowing the Nation's Power: The Supreme Court Sides with the States. Trade Paper. University of California Press. Berkeley, CA. 2003. 212p. ISBN:0-520-24068-5, ISBN13: 978-0-520-24068-1. Dewey:342.73/088. LCCN:2002-019473.
Audience: **u,f.**

United States > Special Branches of United States Civil Law > Business Corporations. Securities Law

Hovenkamp, Herbert **KF1414.H68 1991**
Enterprise and American Law, 1836-1937. Trade Cloth. Harvard University Press. Cambridge, MA. 1991. 456p. ISBN:0-674-25748-0, ISBN13: 978-0-674-25748-1. Dewey:343.73/08/09. LCCN:90-048564.
Audience: **g.**

Stone, Christopher D. **KF1416.S7**
Where the Law Ends: The Social Control of Corporate Behavior. Trade Cloth. HarperCollins Publishers. New York, NY. 1975. xiii, 273p. ISBN:0-06-014133-6, ISBN13: 978-0-06-014133-2. Dewey:346/.73/066. LCCN:74-020415.
Audience: **l,u.**

United States > Special Branches of United States Civil Law > Insolvency and Bankruptcy

Skeel, David A. **KF1526.S59 2001**
Debt's Dominion: A History of Bankruptcy Law in America. Trade Cloth. Princeton University Press. Princeton, NJ. 2001. 296p. ISBN:0-691-08810-1, ISBN13: 978-0-691-08810-5. Dewey:346.7307/8/09. LCCN:2001-021464.
Audience: **g,l,u,f.**

United States > Special Branches of United States Civil Law > Regulation of Trade, Commerce, Industry

American Bar Association Staff **KF1659.Z9A43 2000**
The American Bar Association Legal Guide for Small Business: Everything a Small-Business Person Must Know, from Start-Up to Employment Laws to Financing and Selling a Business. Trade Paper. Crown Publishing Group. New York, NY. 2000. 544p. ISBN:0-8129-3015-0, ISBN13: 978-0-8129-3015-3. Dewey:343.7307. LCCN:99-086498.
Audience: **g,u,f.**

Bork, Robert H. **KF1649.B67**
The Antitrust Paradox. Cloth Text. Basic Books. New York, NY. 1978. xi, 462p. ISBN:0-465-00369-9, ISBN13: 978-0-465-00369-3. Dewey:343/.73/072. LCCN:77-074573.
Audience: **g.**

Letwin, William **KF1649 .L4 1980**
Law and Economic Policy in America: The Evolution of the Sherman Antitrust Act. Trade Cloth. Greenwood Publishing Group, Inc. Portsmouth, NH. 1980. 304p. ISBN:0-313-22651-2, ISBN13: 978-0-313-22651-9. Dewey:343.73/072. LCCN:80-021868.
Audience: **u,f.**

Litan, Robert E. & Nordhaus, William D. **KF1600**
Reforming Federal Regulation. Trade Paper. Yale University Press. Cumberland, RI. 1983. 206p. Yale FastBack Ser., No. 27 ISBN:0-300-03107-6, ISBN13: 978-0-300-03107-2. Dewey:347.302/66. LCCN:83-003622.
Audience: **g.**

Shenefield, John H. & Stelzer, Irwin M. **KF1650.S53 2001**
The Antitrust Laws: A Primer. Ed. 4. Trade Cloth. National Book Network. Lanham, MD. 2001. 202p. ISBN:0-8447-4154-X, ISBN13: 978-0-8447-4154-3. Dewey:343.73/0721. LCCN:2001-045088.
Audience: **g,l,u,f.** *Choice, 1994.*

Steingold, Fred S. **KF1659.Z9S76 2006**
Legal Guide for Starting and Running a Small Business. Ed. 9. Trade Paper. NOLO. Berkeley, CA. 2006. 480p. ISBN:1-4133-0513-X, ISBN13: 978-1-4133-0513-5. Dewey:346.73/0652. LCCN:2006-046427.
Audience: **g.**

United States > Special Branches of United States Civil Law > Regulation of Trade, Commerce, Industry > Mining

Tank, Ronald W. **KF1819**
Legal Aspects of Geology. Trade Paper. Basic Books. New York, NY. 1983. 596p. ISBN:0-306-41215-2, ISBN13: 978-0-306-41215-8. Dewey:347.303/77. LCCN:83-002246.
Audience: **l,u.**

United States > Special Branches of United States Civil Law > Regulation of Trade, Commerce, Industry > Transportation and Communication

Brown, David Wayne **KF2231.Z9B76 2003**
Beat Your Ticket: Go to Court and Win!. Ed. 3. Trade Paper. NOLO. Berkeley, CA. 2003. 224p. ISBN:0-87337-950-0, ISBN13: 978-0-87337-950-2. Dewey:345.73/0247. LCCN:2003-059355.
Audience: **g.**

Campbell, Douglas S. **KF2750**
The Supreme Court and the Mass Media: Selected Cases, Summaries, and Analyses. Trade Cloth. Greenwood Publishing Group, Inc. Portsmouth, NH. 1990. 248p. ISBN:0-275-93421-7, ISBN13: 978-0-275-93421-7. Dewey:343.73/099. LCCN:89-026567.
Audience: **u,f.** *Choice, 1991.*

Cavazos, Edward A. & Morin, Gavino **KF2765.C38 1994**
Cyberspace and the Law: Your Rights and Duties in the on-Line World. Trade Paper. MIT Press. Cambridge, MA. 1994. 220p. ISBN:0-262-53123-2, ISBN13: 978-0-262-53123-8. Dewey:343.7309/944. LCCN:94-012356.
Audience: **g,l,u,f.**

Denniston, Lyle W. **KF2750**
The Reporter and the Law: Techniques of Covering the Courts. Trade Cloth. Columbia University Press. New York, NY. 1992.

289p. ISBN:0-231-08030-1, ISBN13: 978-0-231-08030-9. Dewey:070.4/49/34705. LCCN:92-015053.
Audience: **u,f.** *B*

Devol, Kenneth S. **KF2750.A7M37 1990**
Mass Media and the Supreme Court. Ed. 4. Trade Paper. Hastings House Daytrips Publishers. Winter Park, FL. 1990. 450p. ISBN:0-8038-9305-1, ISBN13: 978-0-8038-9305-4. Dewey:343.73/099. LCCN:95-102360.
Audience: **l,u.**

Hixson, Richard F. **KF2750.A59H58 1989**
Mass Media and the Constitution: An Encyclopedia of Supreme Court Decisions. Trade Cloth. Garland Publishing, Inc. New York, NY. 1989. 552p. American Law and Society Ser. ISBN:0-8240-7947-7, ISBN13: 978-0-8240-7947-5. Dewey:343.73/0994. LCCN:88-025069.
Audience: **l,u.** *Choice, 1989.*

Huber, Peter W. **KF2765.H83 1997**
Abolish the FCC: Common Law Telecosm. Trade Cloth. Oxford University Press, Inc. New York, NY. 1997. 288p. ISBN:0-19-511614-3, ISBN13: 978-0-19-511614-4. Dewey:343.7309/94. LCCN:97-003345.
Audience: **g.**

Katsh, M. Ethan **KF2765.K37 1989**
The Electronic Media and the Transformation of Law. Trade Cloth. Oxford University Press, Inc. New York, NY. 1989. 356p. ISBN:0-19-504590-4, ISBN13: 978-0-19-504590-1. Dewey:343.73/0994. LCCN:88-025576.
Audience: **l,u.**

Krasnow, Erwin G., et al. **KF2840.K7 1982**
The Politics of Broadcast Regulation. Ed. 3. Lawrence D. Longley & Herbert A. Terry (Authors). Paper Text. St. Martin's Press. Gordonville, VA. 1982. 304p. ISBN:0-312-62653-3, ISBN13: 978-0-312-62653-2. Dewey:343.73/09945. LCCN:81-051850.
Audience: **l,u.** *B*

Miller, George H. **KF2355.A4**
Railroads and the Granger Laws. Trade Cloth. University of Wisconsin Press. Chicago, IL. 1971. 308p. ISBN:0-299-05870-0, ISBN13: 978-0-299-05870-8. Dewey:385/.0973. LCCN:75-138059.
Audience: **u,f.**

Minow, Newton & Lamay, Craig **KF2840.M56 1995**
Abandoned in the Wasteland: Children, Television, and the First Amendment. Trade Paper. Farrar, Straus & Giroux. New York, NY. 1995. 224p. ISBN:0-8090-2311-3, ISBN13: 978-0-8090-2311-0. Dewey:343.73099/46. LCCN:95-001113.
Audience: **g.**

Paul, James C. & Schwartz, Murray L. **KF2737**
Federal Censorship: Obscenity in the Mail. Trade Cloth. Greenwood Publishing Group, Inc. Portsmouth, NH. 1977. 368p. ISBN:0-8371-9818-6, ISBN13: 978-0-8371-9818-7. Dewey:344/.73/0531. LCCN:77-010978.
Audience: **u,f.** *B*

Pember, Don R. & Calvert, Clay **KF2750**
Mass Media Law, 2007/2008 Edition with PowerWeb. Ed. 15. Mixed Media, Paper Text. McGraw-Hill Higher Education. Burr Ridge, IL. 2006. ISBN:0-07-327898-X, ISBN13: 978-0-07-327898-8. Dewey:343.099.
Audience: **l,u.**

Ray, William B. **KF2765.1.R39 1990**
Federal Communications Commission: The Ups and Downs of Radio-TV Regulation. Trade Cloth. Blackwell Publishing Professional. Ames, IA. 1989. 214p. ISBN:0-8138-0227-X, ISBN13: 978-0-8138-0227-5. Dewey:343.73099/45. LCCN:89-015330.
Audience: **g,l,u.** *Choice, 1990.*

Sableman, Mark **KF2750.S33 1997**
More Speech, Not Less: Communications Law in the Information Age. Paul Simon (Foreword by). Trade Cloth. Southern Illinois University Press. Carbondale, IL. 1997. 272p. ISBN:0-8093-2135-1, ISBN13: 978-0-8093-2135-3. Dewey:343.7309/9. LCCN:96-053449.
Audience: **l,u,f.** *Choice, 1998.*

Stockford, Marjorie A. **KF2849.A4S76 2004**
The Bellwomen: The Story of the Landmark AT&T Sex Discrimination Case. Trade Cloth. Rutgers University Press. Piscataway, NJ. 2004. 256p. ISBN:0-8135-3428-3, ISBN13: 978-0-8135-3428-2. Dewey:344.7301/4133. LCCN:2003-019800.
Audience: **g,l,u,f.** *Choice, 2005.*

United States > Special Branches of United States Civil Law > Regulation of Trade, Commerce, Industry > Professions. Medical Jurisprudence

DeVries, Raymond G. **KF2915.M5D48 1996**
Making Midwives Legal: Childbirth, Medicine, and the Law. Paper Text. Ohio State University Press. Columbus, OH. 1996. 232p. Women and Health Ser. ISBN:0-8142-0703-0, ISBN13: 978-0-8142-0703-1. Dewey:344.73/0415. LCCN:96-006312.
Audience: **l,u.**

Weiler, Paul C. **KF2905.3.W37 1991**
Medical Malpractice on Trial. Trade Cloth. Harvard University Press. Cambridge, MA. 1991. 240p. ISBN:0-674-56120-1, ISBN13: 978-0-674-56120-5. Dewey:346.7303/32. LCCN:90-015600.
Audience: **g.**

United States > Intellectual Property. Copyright. Trademarks

Aoki, Keith, et al. **KF2994**
Bound by Law: Tales from the Public Domain: by Day a Filmmaker, by Night She Fought for Fair Use!. Jamie Boyle & Jennifer Jenkins (Authors). Trade Paper. Soft Skull Press, Inc. Brooklyn, NY. 2006. 96p. ISBN:1-933368-37-3, ISBN13: 978-1-933368-37-5. Dewey:346.730482.
Audience: **g.**

Branscomb, Anne W. **KF4772**
Who Owns Information?: From Privacy to Public Access. Trade Paper. Basic Books. New York, NY. 1995. 256p. ISBN:0-465-09144-X, ISBN13: 978-0-465-09144-7. Dewey:342.73/0853. LCCN:93-044348.
Audience: **g,l,u,f.** *Choice, 1994.*

Elias, Stephen **KF3180.Z9E43 2005**
Trademark: Legal Care for Your Business and Product Name. Ed. 7. Trade Paper, Perfect. NOLO. Berkeley, CA. 2005. 384p. ISBN:1-4133-0358-7, ISBN13: 978-1-4133-0358-2. Dewey:346.7304/88. LCCN:2005-047766.
Audience: **g.**

Fishman, Stephen **KF3024.C6F57 2001**
Copyright Your Software. Ed. 3. Trade Paper, CD-ROM, Book, Other. NOLO. Berkeley, CA. 2001. 288p. ISBN:0-87337-719-2, ISBN13: 978-0-87337-719-5. Dewey:346.7304/82. LCCN:2001-030263.
Audience: **g.**

Goldstein, Paul **KF2994.G654 2003**
Copyright's Highway: From Gutenberg to the Celestial Jukebox. Trade Paper. Stanford University Press. Palo Alto, CA. 2003. x, 238p. ISBN:0-8047-4748-2, ISBN13: 978-0-8047-4748-6. Dewey:346.7304/82. LCCN:2003-007385.
Audience: **g,l,u,f.** *Choice, 2004.*

Hoffmann, Gretchen McCord **KF3030.1.Z9H644 2005**
Copyright in Cyberspace 2: Questions and Answers for Librarians. Trade Cloth. Neal-Schuman Publishers, Inc. New York, NY. 2005. 260p. ISBN:1-55570-517-0, ISBN13: 978-1-55570-517-6. Dewey:346.7304/82. LCCN:2004-018238.
Audience: **g,l,u,f.**

Lessig, Lawrence **KF2979.L47 2004**
Free Culture: How Big Media Uses Technology and the Law to Lock down Culture and Control Creativity. Trade Cloth. Penguin Group (USA) Inc. New York, NY. 2004. 368p. ISBN:1-59420-006-8, ISBN13: 978-1-59420-006-9. Dewey:343.7309/9. LCCN:2003-063276.
Audience: **g.** *Choice, 2004.*

McSherry, Corynne **KF2979.M37 2001**
Who Owns Academic Work?: Battling for Control of Intellectual Property. Trade Cloth. Harvard University Press. Cambridge, MA. 2001. 288p. ISBN:0-674-00629-1, ISBN13: 978-0-674-00629-4. Dewey:346.7304/8. LCCN:2001-024463.
Audience: **g.**

Strong, William S. **KF2994.S75 1999**
The Copyright Book: A Practical Guide. Ed. 5. Trade Cloth. MIT Press. Cambridge, MA. 1999. 386p. ISBN:0-262-19419-8, ISBN13: 978-0-262-19419-8. Dewey:346.7304/82. LCCN:99-022332.
Audience: **g.** B

United States > Labor Law

Bailey, Stephen K. **KF6055**
Congress Makes a Law: The Story Behind the Employment Act of 1946. Trade Cloth. Greenwood Publishing Group, Inc. Portsmouth, NH. 1980. 282p. ISBN:0-313-22407-2, ISBN13: 978-0-313-22407-2. Dewey:344.73/0102632. LCCN:80-012550.
Audience: **u,f.**

Blanck, Peter David (Editor) **KF3469.E48 2000**
Employment, Disability, and the Americans with Disabilities Act: Issues in Law, Public Policy, and Research. Trade Cloth. Northwestern University Press. Evanston, IL. 2000. 488p. Psychosocial Issues Ser. ISBN:0-8101-1688-X, ISBN13: 978-0-8101-1688-7. Dewey:344.7301/59. LCCN:00-008840.
Audience: **u,f.** *Choice, 2001.*

Devaney, Dennis, et al. **KF3431.T46 1999**
Union Violence: The Record and the Response of the Courts, Legislators and NLBR. Armand J. Thieblot Jr., Thomas R. Haggard & Herbert R. Northrup (Authors). Trade Paper. John M. Olin Institute for Employment Practice & Policy. Fairfax, VA. 1999. xv, 506p. Labor Relations and Public Policy Ser., Vol. 25 ISBN:1-891496-10-7, ISBN13: 978-1-891496-10-3. Dewey:344.73018. LCCN:00-713607.
Audience: **u,f.**

Gould, William B. IV **KF3369.G68 2004**
A Primer on American Labor Law. Ed. 4. Cloth Text. MIT Press. Cambridge, MA. 2004. 432p. ISBN:0-262-07250-5, ISBN13: 978-0-262-07250-2. Dewey:347.3041. LCCN:2003-070610.
Audience: **g,l,u,f.**

Greene, Kathanne W. **KF3464**
Affirmative Action and Principles of Justice: Contributions in Legal Studies. Trade Cloth. Greenwood Publishing Group, Inc. Portsmouth, NH. 1989. 195p. Contributions in Legal Studies ISBN:0-313-26678-6, ISBN13: 978-0-313-26678-2. Dewey:344.73/01133. LCCN:89-002121.
Audience: **u,f.** *Choice, 1990.*

Gregory, Raymond F. **KF3467.G74 2004**
Unwelcome and Unlawful: Sexual Harassment in the American Workplace. Trade Cloth. Cornell University Press. Ithaca, NY. 2004. 288p. ISBN:0-8014-4250-8, ISBN13: 978-0-8014-4250-6. Dewey:344.7301/4133. LCCN:2003-023063.
Audience: **g.** *Choice, 2004.*

Gross, James A. **KF3372.G76**
The Making of the National Labor Relations Board: A Study in Economics, Politics, and the Law, 1933-1937. Cloth Text. State University of New York Press. Albany, NY. 1974. 265p. ISBN:0-87395-270-7, ISBN13: 978-0-87395-270-5. Dewey:353.008/3. LCCN:74-005284.
Audience: **l,u.** B

Hubbartt, William S. **KF3455.H83 1998**
The New Battle over Workplace Privacy: Safe Practices to Minimize Conflict, Confusion and Litigation. Trade Cloth. Amacom. New York, NY. 1998. 224p. ISBN:0-8144-0357-3, ISBN13: 978-0-8144-0357-0. Dewey:344.7301. LCCN:97-038669.
Audience: **u,f.** *Choice, 1998.*

Kranz, Rachel **KF3464.K73 2002**
Affirmative Action. Trade Cloth. Facts On File, Inc. New York, NY. 2002. 304p. Library in a Book ISBN:0-8160-4733-2, ISBN13: 978-0-8160-4733-8. Dewey:342.73/087. LCCN:2001-058595.
Audience: **g,l,u.** *Choice, 2003.*

MacKinnon, Catharine A. **HD6095**
Sexual Harassment of Working Women: A Case of Sex Discrimination. Thomas I. Emerson (Foreword by). Trade Paper. Yale University Press. Cumberland, RI. 1979. 326p. Fastback Ser., No. 19 ISBN:0-300-02299-9, ISBN13: 978-0-300-02299-5. Dewey:306.7. LCCN:78-009645.
Audience: **u,f.** B

Moreno, Paul D. **KF3464.M665 1997**
From Direct Action to Affirmative Action: Fair Employment Law and Policy in America, 1933-1972. Trade Cloth. Louisiana State University Press. Baton Rouge, LA. 1997. xii, 312p. ISBN:0-8071-2138-X, ISBN13: 978-0-8071-2138-2. Dewey:344.7301/133. LCCN:96-050168.
Audience: **u,f.** *Choice, 1997.*

Nelson, Robert L. & Bridges, William P. **KF3464 .N45 1999**
Legalizing Gender Inequality: Courts, Markets and Unequal Pay for Women in America. Mark Granovetter (Contribution by). Trade Paper. Cambridge University Press. New York, NY. 1999. 410p. Structural Analysis in the Social Sciences Ser., No. 16 ISBN:0-521-62750-8, ISBN13: 978-0-521-62750-4. Dewey:331.21530973. LCCN:98-038432.
Audience: **l,u.**

Outten, Wayne N., et al. **KF3319.3**
The Rights of Employees and Union Members: The Basic ACLU Guide to the Rights of Employees and Union Members. Ed. 2. Robert J. Rabin & Lisa R. Lipman (Authors). Trade Cloth. Southern Illinois University Press. Carbondale, IL. 1994. 604p. American Civil Liberties Union Handbook Ser. ISBN:0-8093-1913-6, ISBN13: 978-0-8093-1913-8. Dewey:347.304126. LCCN:93-016895.
Audience: **l,u.**

Perritt, Henry H. **KF3469.P47 2003**
Americans with Disabilities Act Handbook. Ed. 4. Trade Cloth. Aspen Publishers, Inc. New York, NY. 2003. ISBN:0-7355-3638-4, ISBN13: 978-0-7355-3638-8. Dewey:344.73/0159. LCCN:2003-265473.
Audience: **u,f.**

Prasow, Paul & Peters, Edward **KF3408 .P7 1983**
Arbitration and Collective Bargaining. Ed. 2. Cloth Text. McGraw-Hill Companies, The. New York, NY. 1983. 480p. ISBN:0-07-050674-4, ISBN13: 978-0-07-050674-9. Dewey:344.73/0189143. LCCN:82-017203.
Audience: **l,u.**

Ruben, Alan Miles (Editor) **KF3424.E53 2003**
Elkouri and Elkouri: How Arbitration Works. Ed. 6. Trade Cloth. B N A Books. Edison, NJ. 2003. 1,828p. ISBN:1-57018-335-X, ISBN13: 978-1-57018-335-5. Dewey:344.7301/81943. LCCN:2003-063598.
Audience: **u,f.**

Sunstein, Cass R. **KF3300.S86 1990**
After the Rights Revolution: Reconceiving the Regulatory State. Trade Cloth. Harvard University Press. Cambridge, MA. 1990. 296p. ISBN:0-674-00908-8, ISBN13: 978-0-674-00908-0. Dewey:344.73. LCCN:89-078254.
Audience: **g.** *Choice, 1991.*

Tomlins, Christopher L. **KF3369 .T65 1993**
Law, Labor, and Ideology in the Early American Republic. Trade Paper. Cambridge University Press. New York, NY. 1993. 426p. ISBN:0-521-43857-8, ISBN13: 978-0-521-43857-5. Dewey:347.3041. LCCN:92-017452.
Audience: **u,f.**

Weiss, Donald H. **KF3457.W45 2004**
Fair, Square and Legal: Safe Hiring, Managing, and Firing Practices to Keep You and Your Company Out of Court. Ed. 4. Trade Cloth. Amacom. New York, NY. 2004. 384p. ISBN:0-8144-0813-3, ISBN13: 978-0-8144-0813-1. Dewey:658.3/11. LCCN:2003-024532.
Audience: **g.**

Wood, Stephen B. **KF3552.W6**
Constitutional Politics in the Progressive Era: Child Labor and the Law. Trade Paper. Books on Demand. Ann Arbor, MI. 336p. ISBN:0-608-13451-1, ISBN13: 978-0-608-13451-2. Dewey:331.3/1/0973. LCCN:67-025525.
Audience: **g.**

United States > Social Insurance

Stevens, Robert Bocking **KF3643.8**
Income Security: Statutory History of the United States. Trade Cloth. McGraw-Hill Companies, The. New York, NY. 1970. ISBN:0-07-055683-0, ISBN13: 978-0-07-055683-6. Dewey:344/.73/02.
Audience: **l,u,f.**

United States > Human Reproduction

Ball, Howard **KF3760.B35 2004**
Supreme Court and the Intimate Lives of Americans: Birth, Sex, Marriage, Childrearing, and Death. Trade Paper. New York University Press. New York, NY. 2004. 278p. ISBN:0-8147-9863-2, ISBN13: 978-0-8147-9863-8. Dewey:344.7/3/0419.
Audience: **u,f.**

Cohen, Sherrill & Taub, Nadine (Editors) **KF3771.R46 1989**
Reproductive Laws for the 1990s. Book, Other. Humana Press. Totowa, NJ. 1988. 482p. Contemporary Issues in Biomedicine, Ethics and Society Ser. ISBN:0-89603-157-8, ISBN13: 978-0-89603-157-9. Dewey:344.73/0419. LCCN:88-025867.
Audience: **u,f.** *Choice, 1989.*

Colker, Ruth **KF3771.C65 1992**
Abortion and Dialogue: Pro-Choice, Pro-Life and American Law. Trade Cloth. Indiana University Press. Bloomington, IN. 1992. 200p. ISBN:0-253-31393-7, ISBN13: 978-0-253-31393-5. Dewey:344.73/0546. LCCN:91-046603.
Audience: **l,u.** *Choice, 1993.*

Devins, Neal **KF3771.D48 1996**
Shaping Constitutional Values: Elected Government, the Supreme Court, and the Abortion Debate. Trade Paper. Johns Hopkins University Press. Baltimore, MD. 1973. 224p. Interpreting American Politics Ser. ISBN:0-8018-5285-4, ISBN13: 978-0-8018-5285-5. Dewey:342.73. LCCN:95-039584.
Audience: **u,f.** *Choice, 1997.*

Garrow, David J. **KF3771.G37 1998**
Liberty and Sexuality: The Right to Privacy and the Making of Roe vs. Wade. Ed. 2. Trade Paper. University of California Press. Berkeley, CA. 1998. 1056p. ISBN:0-520-21302-5, ISBN13: 978-0-520-21302-9. Dewey:342.73/0858. LCCN:97-052173.
Audience: **g,l,u,f.** *Choice, 1994.*

Hull, N. E. H., et al. **KF3771.A937 2004**
The Abortion Rights Controversy in America: A Legal Reader. William James Hoffer & Peter Charles Hoffer (Authors). Trade

Cloth. University of North Carolina Press. Chapel Hill, NC. 2004. 376p. ISBN:0-8078-2873-4, ISBN13: 978-0-8078-2873-1. Dewey:342.7308/4. LCCN:2003-027750.
Audience: **g.** *Choice, 2005.*

Judges, Donald P. **KF3771 .J83 1993**
Hard Choices, Lost Voices: How the Abortion Conflict Has Divided America, Distorted Constitutional Rights, and Damaged the Courts. Trade Cloth. Ivan R. Dee Publisher. Blue Ridge Summit, PA. 1993. 352p. ISBN:1-56663-016-9, ISBN13: 978-1-56663-016-0. Dewey:363.4/6. LCCN:92-044593.
Audience: **g.**

Rubin, Eva R. (Editor) **KF3771**
The Abortion Controversy: A Documentary History. Cloth Text. Greenwood Publishing Group, Inc. Portsmouth, NH. 1994. 336p. Primary Documents in American History and Contemporary Issues Ser., Vol. 1 ISBN:0-313-28476-8, ISBN13: 978-0-313-28476-2. Dewey:363.4/6/0973. LCCN:93-025068.
Audience: **l,u.**

United States > Public Health. Medical Legislation

Annas, George J. **KF3823.A96 2003**
The Rights of Patients: The Authoritative ACLU Guide to the Rights of Patients. Ed. 3. Trade Paper. Southern Illinois University Press. Carbondale, IL. 2004. 432p. An American Civil Liberties Union Handbook Ser. ISBN:0-8093-2515-2, ISBN13: 978-0-8093-2515-3. Dewey:344.73/03211. LCCN:2003-004765.
Audience: **u,f.**

Dolgin, Janet L. **KF3830.D65 1997**
Defining the Family: Law, Technology, and Reproduction in an Uneasy Age. Trade Cloth. New York University Press. New York, NY. 1997. 289p. ISBN:0-8147-1859-0, ISBN13: 978-0-8147-1859-9. Dewey:346.7301/7. LCCN:96-035617.
Audience: **u,f.** *Choice, 1997.*

Dworkin, Roger B. **KF3821.D87 1996**
[e] Limits: The Role of the Law in Bioethical Decision Making. E-Book. Indiana University Press. Bloomington, IN. 1996. 224p. Medical Ethics Ser. ISBN:0-253-33075-0, ISBN13: 978-0-253-33075-8. Dewey:344.73/041. LCCN:95-050697.
Audience: **u,f.** *Choice, 1997.*

Frost, Lynda E. & Bonnie, Richard J. (Editors) **KF3828.E94 2001**
The Evolution of Mental Health Law. Trade Cloth. American Psychological Association. Washington, DC. 2001. xiv, 336p. Law and Public Policy Ser., :Psychology and the Social Sciences ISBN:1-55798-746-7, ISBN13: 978-1-55798-746-4. Dewey:344.73/044. LCCN:2001-018897.
Audience: **u,f.**

Glick, Henry R. **KF3827.E87**
The Right to Die: Policy Innovation and Its Consequences. Trade Paper. Columbia University Press. New York, NY. 1994. 238p. ISBN:0-231-07639-8, ISBN13: 978-0-231-07639-5. Dewey:344.73/04197.
Audience: **g.** *Choice, 1993.*

Lazarus, Richard J. **KF3775.L398 2004**
The Making of Environmental Law. Trade Cloth. University of Chicago Press. Chicago, IL. 2004. 334p. ISBN:0-226-47037-7, ISBN13: 978-0-226-47037-5. Dewey:344.7304/6. LCCN:2004-002971.
Audience: **u,f.**

Rubenstein, William B., et al. **KF3803.A54R83 1996**
The Rights of People Who Are HIV Positive: The Basic ACLU Guide to the Rights of People Living with HIV Disease and AIDS. Ruth Eisenberg & Lawrence O. Gostin (Authors). Trade Cloth. Southern Illinois University Press. Carbondale, IL. 1996. 448p. ISBN:0-8093-1992-6, ISBN13: 978-0-8093-1992-3. Dewey:344.73/04369792. LCCN:95-052122.
Audience: **g.**

Schneider, Carl E. (Editor) **KF3827.E87L39 2000**
Law at the End of Life: The Supreme Court and Assisted Suicide. Trade Cloth. University of Michigan Press. Chicago, IL. 2000. 376p. ISBN:0-472-11157-4, ISBN13: 978-0-472-11157-2. Dewey:344.73/04197. LCCN:00-034388.
Audience: **u,f.** *Choice, 2001.*

Urofsky, Melvin I. **KF3827.E87U755 2000**
Lethal Judgments: Assisted Suicide and American Law. Trade Cloth. University Press of Kansas. Lawrence, KS. 2000. xii, 176p. Landmark Law Cases and American Society Ser. ISBN:0-7006-1010-3, ISBN13: 978-0-7006-1010-5. Dewey:344.73/04197. LCCN:99-053549.
Audience: **g.** *Choice, 2000.*

Webber, David W. **KF3803.A54A94 1997**
AIDS and the Law. Ed. 3. Trade Cloth, Box or Slipcased. John Wiley & Sons, Inc. Hoboken, NJ. 1997. 1394p. Civil Rights Library ISBN:0-471-13542-9, ISBN13: 978-0-471-13542-5. Dewey:344.73/04369792. LCCN:97-011007.
Audience: **u,f.** *Choice, 1998.*

United States > Veterinary Laws. Animals

Francione, Gary L. **KF3841.F73 1995**
Animals, Property, and the Law. William M. Kunstler (Foreword by). Cloth Text. Temple University Press. Philadelphia, PA. 1995. 368p. Ethics and Action Ser. ISBN:1-56639-283-7, ISBN13: 978-1-56639-283-9. Dewey:346.7304/6954. LCCN:94-026263.
Audience: **l,u.**

United States > Food, Drugs, Tobacco, Cosmetics, Alcohol

Erlen, Jonathon & Spillane, Joseph F. **KF3885.E75 2004**
Federal Drug Control: The Evolution of Policy and Practice. Cloth Text. Haworth Press, Incorporated, The. Binghamton, NY. 2004. 228p. ISBN:0-7890-1891-8, ISBN13: 978-0-7890-1891-5. Dewey:344.73/04233. LCCN:2003-016037.
Audience: **u,f.** *Choice, 2005.*

Evans, Rod L. & Berent, Irwin M. (Editors) **KF3890 .D79 1992**
Drug Legalization: For and Against. Linus Pauling (Introduction

by). Trade Paper. Open Court Publishing Company. Chicago, IL. 1992. 355p. For and Against Ser., Vol. 1 ISBN:0-8126-9184-9, ISBN13: 978-0-8126-9184-9. Dewey:364.1/77/0973. LCCN:92-001626.

Audience: **l,u.**

Hamm, Richard F. **KF3919.H35 1995**
Shaping the Eighteenth Amendment: Temperance Reform, Legal Culture, and the Polity, 1880-1920. Trade Cloth. University of North Carolina Press. Chapel Hill, NC. 1995. 352p. Studies in Legal History ISBN:0-8078-4493-4, ISBN13: 978-0-8078-4493-9. Dewey:344.73/0541. LCCN:94-017948.

Audience: **g.** *Choice, 1995.*

Kessler, David **HD9130.5**
Question of Intent: A Great American Battle with a Deadly Industry. Trade Paper. PublicAffairs. New York, NY. 2002. 512p. ISBN:1-58648-121-5, ISBN13: 978-1-58648-121-6. Dewey:338.1/7371. LCCN:00-034152.

Audience: **g.**

Lindesmith, Alfred R. **KF3890 .L5**
The Addict and the Law. Trade Cloth. Indiana University Press. Bloomington, IN. 1965. 352p. ISBN:0-253-10050-X, ISBN13: 978-0-253-10050-4. Dewey:343.57. LCCN:64-018821.

Audience: **u,f.** B

Nolan, James L. **KF3890.N65 2001**
Reinventing Justice: The American Drug Court Movement. Cloth Text. Princeton University Press. Princeton, NJ. 2001. 264p. Studies in Cultural Sociology ISBN:0-691-07452-6, ISBN13: 978-0-691-07452-8. Dewey:364.1/77. LCCN:00-051677.

Audience: **l,u.** *Choice, 2001.*

United States > Public Safety. Firearms, Hazardous Materials, Explosives

Bogus, Carl T. (Editor) **KF3941**
The Second Amendment in Law and History: Historians and Constitutional Scholars on the Right to Bear Arms. Trade Cloth. DIANE Publishing Company. Collingdale, PA. 2005. 358p. ISBN:0-7567-8899-4, ISBN13: 978-0-7567-8899-5. Dewey:344.73/0533.

Audience: **g.** *Choice, 2002.*

Bosso, Christopher J. **KF27**
Pesticides and Politics: The Life Cycle of a Public Issue. Trade Paper. University of Pittsburgh Press. Pittsburgh, PA. 1988. 312p. Series in Policy and Institutional Studies ISBN:0-8229-5418-4, ISBN13: 978-0-8229-5418-7. Dewey:344.73/04633. LCCN:86-019245.

Audience: **l,u,f.** *Choice, 1987.*

Cottrol, Robert J. (Editor) **KF3941.A7G86 1994**
Gun Control and the Constitution: Sources and Explorations on the Second Amendment. Trade Paper. Garland Publishing, Inc. New York, NY. 1994. 480p. ISBN:0-8153-1666-6, ISBN13: 978-0-8153-1666-4. Dewey:344.73/0533. LCCN:94-015079.

Audience: **l,u.**

Utter, Glenn H. **KF3941.A68U88 2000**
Encyclopedia of Gun Control and Gun Rights. Cloth Text. Greenwood Publishing Group, Inc. Portsmouth, NH. 1999. 384p. ISBN:1-57356-172-X, ISBN13: 978-1-57356-172-3. Dewey:363.3/3/097303. LCCN:99-043449.

Audience: **g.** *Choice, 2000.*

United States > Control of Social Activities. Amusements, Sports, Gaming

Wong, Glenn M. **KF3989**
Essentials of Sports Law. Ed. 3. Cloth Text. Greenwood Publishing Group, Inc. Portsmouth, NH. 2002. 832p. ISBN:0-275-97121-X, ISBN13: 978-0-275-97121-2. Dewey:344.73/099. LCCN:2001-058043.

Audience: **l,u.**

United States > Education

Alexander, Kern & Alexander, M. David **KF4118.A39 2005**
American Public School Law. Ed. 6. Cloth Text. Thomson Wadsworth. Belmont, CA. 2004. 1104p. ISBN:0-534-27424-2, ISBN13: 978-0-534-27424-5. Dewey:344.73/071. LCCN:2004-102424.

Audience: **l,u.** B

Armor, David J. **KF4155.A87 1995**
Forced Justice: School Desegregation and the Law. Trade Cloth. Oxford University Press, Inc. New York, NY. 1995. 284p. ISBN:0-19-509012-8, ISBN13: 978-0-19-509012-3. Dewey:344.73/0798. LCCN:94-013497.

Audience: **l,u,f.**

Bell, Derrick **KF4155.B38 2004**
Silent Covenants: Brown v. Board of Education and the Unfulfilled Hopes for Racial Reform. Trade Cloth. Oxford University Press, Inc. New York, NY. 2004. 240p. ISBN:0-19-517272-8, ISBN13: 978-0-19-517272-0. Dewey:344.73/0798. LCCN:2003-027447.

Audience: **g.** *Choice, 2004.*

Carpenter, Linda J. & Acosta, Vivian R. **KF4166.C37 2004**
Title IX. Trade Cloth. Human Kinetics Publishers. Champaign, IL. 2004. 28p. ISBN:0-7360-4239-3, ISBN13: 978-0-7360-4239-0. Dewey:344.73/099. LCCN:2004-009221.

Audience: **g,l,u,f.**

Cate, Fred H. **KF4150.C34 1998**
The Internet and the First Amendment: Schools and Sexually Explicit Expressions. Trade Paper. Phi Delta Kappa Educational Foundation. Bloomington, IN. 1998. 109p. ISBN:0-87367-398-0, ISBN13: 978-0-87367-398-3. Dewey:344.73/0793. LCCN:97-075653.

Audience: **l,u,f.** *Choice, 1998.*

Cottrol, Robert J. (Editor, Translator), et al. **KF4155.B758 2003**
Brown vs. Board of Education: Caste, Culture, and the Constitution. Raymond T. Diamond & Leland Ware (Editor, Translators). Trade Cloth. University Press of Kansas. Lawrence, KS. 2003. xii,292p. Landmark Law Cases and American Society Ser. ISBN:0-7006-1288-2, ISBN13: 978-0-7006-1288-8. Dewey:344.73/0798. LCCN:2003-013217.

Audience: **g.** *Choice, 2004.*

Dwyer, James G. **KF4137.D98 2002**
Vouchers Within Reason: A Child-Centered Approach to Education Reform. Book, Other. Cornell University Press. Ithaca, NY. 2001. 256p. ISBN:0-8014-3948-5, ISBN13: 978-0-8014-3948-3. Dewey:379.1/11/0973. LCCN:2001-002973.
Audience: **u,f.** *Choice, 2002.*

Edwards, Newton **KF4119**
Courts and the Public Schools. Ed. 3. Lee O. Garber (Editor). Library Binding. University of Chicago Press. Chicago, IL. 1971. xviii, 710p. ISBN:0-226-18606-7, ISBN13: 978-0-226-18606-1. Dewey:344/.73/071. LCCN:72-130308.
Audience: **l,u,f.** B

Fellman, David (Editor) **KF4118.F44 1976**
Supreme Court and Education. Ed. 3. Paper Text. Teachers College Press, Teachers College, Columbia University. New York, NY. 1976. xxii, 323p. Classics in Education Ser. ISBN:0-8077-2511-0, ISBN13: 978-0-8077-2511-5. Dewey:344/.73/071. LCCN:76-014495.
Audience: **l,u,f.** B

Fischer, Louis, et al. **KF4175.Z9F55 2003**
Teachers and the Law. Ed. 6. David Schimmel & Leslie Stellman (Authors). Trade Paper. Allyn & Bacon, Inc. Boston, MA. 2002. 461p. ISBN:0-321-08210-9, ISBN13: 978-0-321-08210-7. Dewey:344.73/078. LCCN:2002-074577.
Audience: **l,u.**

Haynes, Charles C., et al. **KF4124.5.F57 2003**
The First Amendment in Schools. Sam Chaltain, John E. Ferguson Jr., David L. Hudson Jr. & Oliver Thomas (Authors). Trade Paper. Association for Supervision & Curriculum Development. Alexandria, VA. 2003. 205p. ISBN:0-87120-777-X, ISBN13: 978-0-87120-777-7. Dewey:342.73/085. LCCN:2003-002637.
Audience: **u,f.**

Hogan, John C. **KF4119**
The Schools, the Courts, and the Public Interest. Ed. 2. Cloth Text. Simon & Schuster. New York, NY. 1985. 224p. ISBN:0-669-07662-7, ISBN13: 978-0-669-07662-2. Dewey:347.304/7. LCCN:83-049011.
Audience: **l,u.**

Irons, Peter H. **KF4155**
Jim Crow's Children: The Broken Promise of the Brown Decision. Trade Paper. Penguin Group (USA) Inc. New York, NY. 2004. 400p. ISBN:0-14-200375-1, ISBN13: 978-0-14-200375-6. Dewey:344.73/0798.
Audience: **g.**

Jaeger, Paul T.; Bowman, Cynthia Ann **KF4210**
Disability Matters: Legal and Pedagogical Issues of Disability in Education. Bergin & Garvey. 2002. ISBN:0-89789-909-1, ISBN13: 978-0-89789-909-3.
Audience: **u,f.**

Kaplin, William A. & Lee, Barbara A. **KF4225**
The Law of Higher Education. Ed. 4. Trade Cloth. John Wiley & Sons, Inc. Hoboken, NJ. 2006. 840p. ISBN:0-7879-8656-9, ISBN13: 978-0-7879-8656-8. Dewey:344.73/074.
Audience: **g.**

Klicka, Christopher J. **KF4221.K56 2002**
The Right to Home School: A Guide to the Law on Parents' Rights in Education. Ed. 3. Trade Paper. Carolina Academic Press. Durham, NC. 2002. 224p. ISBN:0-89089-623-2, ISBN13: 978-0-89089-623-5. Dewey:344.73/07. LCCN:2001-098199.
Audience: **u,f.**

Kluger, Richard **KF4155.K55 2004**
Simple Justice: The History of Brown vs Board of Education and Black America's Struggle For Equality. Trade Cloth. Knopf Publishing Group. New York, NY. 2004. 880p. ISBN:0-375-41477-0, ISBN13: 978-0-375-41477-0. Dewey:344.73/0798. LCCN:2003-026732.
Audience: **g.**

Layman, Nancy S. **KF4155.L39 1994**
Sexual Harassment in American Secondary Schools: A Legal Guide for Administrators, Teachers, and Students. Trade Paper. Contemporary Research Associates. Dallas, TX. 1993. 207p. ISBN:0-935061-52-5, ISBN13: 978-0-935061-52-9. Dewey:344.73/0798. LCCN:93-011323.
Audience: **g,l,u,f.** *Choice, 1995.*

McCarthy, Martha M., et al. **KF4119.M388 2004**
Legal Rights of Teachers and Students. Nelda H. Cambron-McCabe & Stephen B. Thomas (Authors). Trade Paper. Allyn & Bacon, Inc. Boston, MA. 2003. 336p. ISBN:0-205-35449-1, ISBN13: 978-0-205-35449-8. Dewey:344.73/078. LCCN:2003-051824.
Audience: **l,u.**

Patterson, James T. **E468.9**
Brown v. Board of Education: A Civil Rights Milestone and Its Troubled Legacy. Trade Paper. Oxford University Press, Inc. New York, NY. 2002. 318p. Pivotal Moments in American History Ser. ISBN:0-19-515632-3, ISBN13: 978-0-19-515632-4. Dewey:973.7/1.
Audience: **g.** *Choice, 2001.*

Peterson, Paul E. (Editor) **KF4137.F88 2003**
The Future of School Choice. Trade Cloth. Hoover Institution Press. Stanford, CA. 2003. xi, 268p. ISBN:0-8179-3952-0, ISBN13: 978-0-8179-3952-6. Dewey:379.1/11/0973. LCCN:2003-056770.
Audience: **g,l,u,f.** *Choice, 2004.*

Raskin, Jamin B. **KF4150.A7R37 2003**
We the Students: Supreme Court Cases for and about Students. Ed. 2. Trade Cloth. CQ Press. Washington, DC. 2003. 304p. ISBN:1-56802-797-4, ISBN13: 978-1-56802-797-5. Dewey:344.73/079. LCCN:2003-001206.
Audience: **u,f.**

Ravitch, Frank S. **KF4162**
School Prayer and Discrimination: The Civil Rights of Religious Minorities and Dissenters. Paper Text. Northeastern University Press. Boston, MA. 2001. 288p. ISBN:1-55553-477-5, ISBN13: 978-1-55553-477-6. Dewey:344.73/09796.
Audience: **g,l,u.** *Choice, 2000.*

Rothstein **KF4210**
Special Education Law. Ed. 3. Trade Paper. Longman Publishing Group. White Plains, NY. 2001. ISBN:0-8013-1963-3, ISBN13: 978-0-8013-1963-1. Dewey:344.73/0791.
Audience: **u,f.**

Russo, Charles J. (Editor) **KF4102.5**
The Yearbook of Education Law, 2001. Trade Cloth. Education Law Association (ELA). Dayton, OH. 2002. ISBN:1-56534-102-3, ISBN13: 978-1-56534-102-9. Dewey:379.73.
Audience: **u,f.**

Sarat, Austin **KF4155.A2R33 1997**
Race, Law, and Culture: Reflections on Brown vs. Board of Education. Trade Paper. Oxford University Press, Inc. New York, NY. 1997. 256p. ISBN:0-19-510622-9, ISBN13: 978-0-19-510622-0. Dewey:340.1/15/0973. LCCN:96-033875.
Audience: **l,u.** *Choice, 1997.*

Siegel, Lawrence M. **KF4209.3.Z9S57 2005**
The Complete IEP Guide: How to Advocate for Your Special Ed Child. Ed. 4. Trade Paper, Perfect. NOLO. Berkeley, CA. 2005. 300p. ISBN:1-4133-0199-1, ISBN13: 978-1-4133-0199-1. Dewey:371.9/0973. LCCN:2005-051824.
Audience: **g.**

Smith, Michael C. & Fossey, Richard W. **KF9219**
Crime on Campus: Legal Issues and Campus Administration. Ed. 2. Trade Paper. Greenwood Publishing Group, Inc. Portsmouth, NH. 1995. 272p. American Council on Education Series on Higher Education ISBN:1-57356-355-2, ISBN13: 978-1-57356-355-0. Dewey:345.73/02/08837.
Audience: **u,f.**

Taylor, Bonnie B. **KF4117.T39 1996**
Education and the Law: A Dictionary. Library Binding. ABC-CLIO, Inc. Santa Barbara, CA. 1996. 288p. Contemporary Legal Issues Ser. ISBN:0-87436-813-8, ISBN13: 978-0-87436-813-0. Dewey:344.73/07/03. LCCN:96-045171.
Audience: **g,l,u,f.** *Choice, 1997.*

Whitman, Mark **KF4155.B758 2004**
Brown vs. Board of Education: A Documentary History. Ed. 50. Trade Paper. Markus Wiener Publishers, Inc. Princeton, NJ. 2004. 220p. ISBN:1-55876-330-9, ISBN13: 978-1-55876-330-2. Dewey:344.73/0798. LCCN:2003-026120.
Audience: **g.**

United States > Science and the Arts

De Grazia, Edward & Newman, Roger K. **PN1994.A2**
Banned Films: Movies, Censors and the First Amendment. Trade Cloth. R. R. Bowker LLC. New Providence, NJ. 1982. 532p. ISBN:0-8352-1509-1, ISBN13: 978-0-8352-1509-1. Dewey:791.43. LCCN:82-004314.
Audience: **l,u,f.**

Foerstel, Herbert N. **KF4315.F64 2004**
Refuge of a Scoundrel: The Patriot Act in Libraries. Trade Cloth. Libraries Unlimited, Inc. Westport, CT. 2004. 232p. ISBN:1-59158-139-7, ISBN13: 978-1-59158-139-0. Dewey:344.73/092. LCCN:2003-065950.
Audience: **u,f.**

Goldberg, Steven **KF4270.G65 1994**
Culture Clash: Law and Science in America. Trade Cloth. New York University Press. New York, NY. 1994. 255p. ISBN:0-8147-3057-4, ISBN13: 978-0-8147-3057-7. Dewey:344.73/095. LCCN:94-012247.
Audience: **u,f.** *Choice, 1995.*

Minow, Mary & Lipinski, Tomas A. **KF4315.M56 2003**
The Library's Legal Answer Book. Trade Paper. American Library Association. Chicago, IL. 2003. 372p. ISBN:0-8389-0828-4, ISBN13: 978-0-8389-0828-0. Dewey:344.73/092. LCCN:2002-008095.
Audience: **u,f.**

Peck, Robert B. **KF4315.P43 2000**
Libraries, the First Amendment and Cyberspace: What You Need to Know. Trade Paper. American Library Association. Chicago, IL. 2000. 216p. ISBN:0-8389-0773-3, ISBN13: 978-0-8389-0773-3. Dewey:025.04. LCCN:99-039455.
Audience: **u,f.**

Randall, Richard S. **PN1994**
Censorship of the Movies: The Social and Political Control of a Mass Medium. Trade Cloth. University of Wisconsin Press. Chicago, IL. 1968. 296p. ISBN:0-299-04731-8, ISBN13: 978-0-299-04731-3. Dewey:791.43. LCCN:68-014035.
Audience: **l,u,f.**

United States > Constitutional Law > Sources

☐ Constitution of the United States.
http://www.gpoaccess.gov/constitution/index.html
U.S. Govt. Printing Office.
Audience: **g,l,u,f.**

KF4530
☐ U.S. State Constitutions and Web Sites.
http://www.constitution.org/cons/usstcons.htm
Audience: **g,l,u,f.**

Kaminski, John P. (Editor) **KF4502**
☐ The Documentary History of the Ratification of the Constitution.
http://www.wisconsinhistory.org/ratification/
Saladino, Gaspare J. (Editor); Leffler, Richard (Editor); Schoenleber, Charles H. (Editor); Hogan, Margaret A. (Editor). Wisconsin Historical Society.
Audience: **l,u,f.**

Yale Law School **E173**
☐ The Avalon Project at Yale Law School: Documents in Law, History and Diplomacy.
http://www.yale.edu/lawweb/avalon/avalon.htm
The Avalon Project at Yale Law School.
Audience: **l,u,f.**

United States > Constitutional Law > Sources > General Works

Ackerman, Bruce A. **KF4541.A8 1991**
We the People: Foundations, Vol. 1. Cloth Text. Harvard University Press. Cambridge, MA. 1991. 369p.

ISBN:0-674-94840-8, ISBN13: 978-0-674-94840-2. Dewey:342.73/029. LCCN:91-010725.
Audience: **l,u.** *Choice, 1992.*

Ackerman, Bruce A. **KF4541**
We the People: Transformations. Trade Cloth. Harvard University Press. Cambridge, MA. 1998. 538p. We the People Ser. ISBN:0-674-94847-5, ISBN13: 978-0-674-94847-1. Dewey:342.7/3/029. LCCN:91-010725.
Audience: **l,u.** *Choice, 1999.*

Amar, Akhil Reed **KF4541.A87 2005**
America's Constitution: A Biography. Trade Cloth. Random House, Inc. New York, NY. 2005. 672p. ISBN:1-4000-6262-4, ISBN13: 978-1-4000-6262-1. Dewey:342.7302/9. LCCN:2004-061464.
Audience: **g.** *Choice, 2006.*

Corwin, Edward S. **JK 33 C819**
The "Higher Law" Background of American Constitutional Law. C. Rossiter (Preface by). Book, Other. Cornell University Press. Ithaca, NY. 1955. 101p. ISBN:0-8014-9012-X, ISBN13: 978-0-8014-9012-5. Dewey:342.73.
Audience: **u,f.**

Crosskey, William W. & Jeffrey, William Jr. **KF4541**
Politics and the Constitution in the History of the United States. Trade Cloth. University of Chicago Press. Chicago, IL. 1980. 2025p. ISBN:0-226-12134-8, ISBN13: 978-0-226-12134-5. Dewey:342.73/029.
Audience: **u,f.**

Farrand, Max **KF4541.F3**
The Framing of the Constitution of the United States. Trade Paper. Beard Books, Inc. Chevy Chase, MD. 2000. 281p. Law Classic Ser. ISBN:1-58798-054-1, ISBN13: 978-1-58798-054-1. Dewey:320.09.
Audience: **u,f.** B

Gillespie, Michael A. & Lienesch, Michael (Editors) **KF4541.A2R37 1989**
Ratifying the Constitution. Forrest McDonald (Foreword by), W. Carey McWilliams (Afterword by). Trade Cloth. University Press of Kansas. Lawrence, KS. 1989. xiv, 418p. ISBN:0-7006-0402-2, ISBN13: 978-0-7006-0402-9. Dewey:342.73/029. LCCN:89-030118.
Audience: **g,l,u,f.** *Choice, 1990.*

Goldwin, Robert A. **KF4541.G65 1997**
From Parchment to Power: How James Madison Used the Bill of Rights to Save the Constitution. Trade Cloth. American Enterprise Institute for Public Policy Research. Washington, DC. 1998. 225p. ISBN:0-8447-4012-8, ISBN13: 978-0-8447-4012-6. Dewey:342.73/029. LCCN:96-051947.
Audience: **l,u.** *Choice, 1997.*

Levy, Leonard W. **KF4541.A2L3735 1995**
Seasoned Judgments: Constitutional Rights and American History. Trade Cloth. Transaction Publishers. Somerset, NJ. 1996. 444p. ISBN:1-56000-170-4, ISBN13: 978-1-56000-170-6. Dewey:342.73/029. LCCN:94-011046.
Audience: **u,f.** *Choice, 1995.*

Levy, Leonard W. (Author, Editor) **KF4541.E88 1987**
Essays on the Making of the Constitution. Ed. 2. Paper Text. Oxford University Press, Inc. New York, NY. 1987. 350p. ISBN:0-19-504902-0, ISBN13: 978-0-19-504902-2. Dewey:342/.7308. LCCN:86-016255.
Audience: **l,u.**

Lutz, Donald S. **KF4541.L87 1988**
The Origins of American Constitutionalism. Paper Text. Louisiana State University Press. Baton Rouge, LA. 1988. 178p. ISBN:0-8071-1506-1, ISBN13: 978-0-8071-1506-0. Dewey:342.73/029. LCCN:88-006415.
Audience: **g,l,u,f.** *Choice, 1989.*

Murphy, Paul L. **KF4541**
Constitution in Crisis Times, 1918-1969. Cloth Text. HarperCollins Publishers. New York, NY. 1972. xix, 570p. New American Nation Ser. ISBN:0-06-013118-7, ISBN13: 978-0-06-013118-0. Dewey:342/.73/029. LCCN:70-156570.
Audience: **g.** B

Rakove, Jack N. **KF4541.R35 1996**
Original Meanings: Politics and Ideas in the Making of the Constitution. Trade Cloth. Alfred A. Knopf Inc. New York, NY. 1996. 448p. ISBN:0-394-57858-9, ISBN13: 978-0-394-57858-3. Dewey:342.7/3/029. LCCN:95-044550.
Audience: **g,l,u,f.** *Choice, 1996.*

Reid, John P. **KF4541.R45 1988**
The Concept of Liberty in the Age of the American Revolution. Trade Cloth. University of Chicago Press. Chicago, IL. 1987. 232p. ISBN:0-226-70896-9, ISBN13: 978-0-226-70896-6. Dewey:323.44/09. LCCN:87-014971.
Audience: **u,f.** *Choice, 1988.*

Schwartz, Bernard **KF4541 .S35**
From Confederation to Nation: The American Constitution, 1835-1877. Trade Cloth. Johns Hopkins University Press. Baltimore, MD. 1981. 256p. ISBN:0-8018-1464-2, ISBN13: 978-0-8018-1464-8. Dewey:342/.73/029. LCCN:72-012353.
Audience: **u,f.** B

Simon, James F. **KF4541.S53 2002**
What Kind of Nation: Thomas Jefferson, John Marshall, and the Epic Struggle to Create a United States. Trade Cloth. Simon & Schuster. New York, NY. 2002. 352p. ISBN:0-684-84870-8, ISBN13: 978-0-684-84870-9. Dewey:342.73/029. LCCN:2001-055027.
Audience: **g.** *Choice, 2003, 2002.*

Urofsky, Melvin I. & Finkelman, Paul **KF4541.U76 2002**
A March of Liberty: A Constitutional History of the United States: From the Founding to 1890, Vol. I. Ed. 2. Cloth Text. Oxford University Press, Inc. New York, NY. 2001. 576p. ISBN:0-19-512634-3, ISBN13: 978-0-19-512634-1. Dewey:342.73/029. LCCN:2001-037041.
Audience: **l,u.**

Urofsky, Melvin I. & Finkelman, Paul **KF4541.U76 2002**
A March of Liberty: A Constitutional History of the United States: From 1877 to the Present, Vol. II. Ed. 2. Cloth Text. Oxford University Press, Inc. New York, NY. 2001. 624p. ISBN:0-19-512636-X, ISBN13: 978-0-19-512636-5. Dewey:342.73/029. LCCN:2001-037041.
Audience: **l,u.**

VanBurkleo, Sandra F. (Editor), et al. **KF4541.C5895 2002**
Constitutionalism and American Culture: Writing the New Constitutional History. Kermit Hall & Robert J. Kaczorowski (Editors). Trade Cloth. University Press of Kansas. Lawrence, KS. 2004. xxiv, 440p. ISBN:0-7006-1153-3, ISBN13: 978-0-7006-1153-9. Dewey:342.73/029. LCCN:2001-005036.
Audience: **g.** *Choice, 2003, 2002.*

United States > Constitutional Law > Sources > Special Topics

Fehrenbacher, Don E. **KF4545**
The Dred Scott Case: Its Significance in American Law and Politics. Trade Paper. Oxford University Press, Inc. New York, NY. 2001. 756p. ISBN:0-19-514588-7, ISBN13: 978-0-19-514588-5. Dewey:342.7/3087.
Audience: **g.**

Finkelman, Paul **KF4545.S5F558 1997**
Dred Scott V. Sandford: A Brief History with Documents. Trade Paper. Bedford/Saint Martin's. New York, NY. 1997. 240p. The Bedford Series in History and Culture ISBN:0-312-11594-6, ISBN13: 978-0-312-11594-4. Dewey:342.73/087. LCCN:96-086769.
Audience: **l,u.**

Finkelman, Paul **KF390.A4**
An Imperfect Union: Slavery, Federalism, and Comity. Trade Paper. University of North Carolina Press. Chapel Hill, NC. 1981. xii, 378p. Studies in Legal History ISBN:0-8078-4066-1, ISBN13: 978-0-8078-4066-5. Dewey:346/.73/013. LCCN:79-027526.
Audience: **u,f.**

Finkelman, Paul (Editor) **E302 .J442 1994**
Slavery and the Law. Trade Cloth. Rowman & Littlefield Publishers, Inc. Lanham, MD. 1997. 476p. ISBN:0-945612-36-2, ISBN13: 978-0-945612-36-0. Dewey:342.73/087 347.30287. LCCN:93-040661.
Audience: **g.**

Morris, Thomas D. **KF4545.S5**
Free Men All: The Personal Liberty Laws of the North, 1780-1861. Trade Cloth. Johns Hopkins University Press. Baltimore, MD. 1966. 265p. ISBN:0-8018-1505-3, ISBN13: 978-0-8018-1505-8. Dewey:342.73/085. LCCN:73-008126.
Audience: **u,f.**

Vorenberg, Michael **E453 .V67 2001**
Final Freedom: The Civil War, the Abolition of Slavery, and the Thirteenth Amendment. Christopher Tomlins, C. Cullen & Joseph Needham (Contribution by). Trade Cloth. Cambridge University Press. New York, NY. 2001. 324p. Historical Studies in American Law and Society ISBN:0-521-65267-7, ISBN13: 978-0-521-65267-4. Dewey:973.714. LCCN:00-063028.
Audience: **g.** *Choice, 2002.*

United States > Constitutional Law > Constitutional Law. General Works

Arkes, Hadley **KF4541**
Beyond the Constitution. Trade Paper. Princeton University Press. Princeton, NJ. 1992. 288p. ISBN:0-691-02554-1, ISBN13: 978-0-691-02554-4. Dewey:342.73/029. LCCN:90-030788.
Audience: **l,u.** *Choice, 1991.*

Corwin, Edward S. **KF4550**
Edward S. Corwin's, Constitution and What It Means Today. Ed. 14. Harold W. Chase & Craig R. Ducat (Editors). Trade Cloth. Princeton University Press. Princeton, NJ. 1978. 374p. ISBN:0-691-09240-0, ISBN13: 978-0-691-09240-9. Dewey:347.302. LCCN:78-053809.
Audience: **l,u.**

Currie, David P. **KF4541**
The Constitution in the Supreme Court: The Second Century, 1888-1986. Trade Paper. University of Chicago Press. Chicago, IL. 1994. 682p. ISBN:0-226-13112-2, ISBN13: 978-0-226-13112-2. Dewey:342.73/029.
Audience: **u,f.** *Choice, 1991.*

Currie, David P. **KF4550.C87**
The Constitution in the Supreme Court: The First Hundred Years, 1789-1888. Trade Paper. University of Chicago Press. Chicago, IL. 1992. 518p. ISBN:0-226-13109-2, ISBN13: 978-0-226-13109-2. Dewey:342.73.
Audience: **g.** *Choice, 1986.*

Dahl, Robert A. **KF4552**
How Democratic Is the American Constitution? Ed. 2. Trade Paper. Yale University Press. Cumberland, RI. 2003. 240p. Castle Lectures Ser. ISBN:0-300-09524-4, ISBN13: 978-0-300-09524-1. Dewey:342.7/302. LCCN:2003-106483.
Audience: **g.**

Dworkin, Ronald M. **KF4552.D96 1996**
Freedom's Law: The Moral Reading of the American Constitution. Trade Cloth. Harvard University Press. Cambridge, MA. 1996. 416p. ISBN:0-674-31927-3, ISBN13: 978-0-674-31927-1. Dewey:342.73/085. LCCN:95-042193.
Audience: **g.** *Choice, 1996.*

Fallon, Richard H. **KF4550.F35 2004**
The Dynamic Constitution: An Introduction to American Constitutional Law. Trade Cloth. Cambridge University Press. New York, NY. 2004. 358p. ISBN:0-521-84094-5, ISBN13: 978-0-521-84094-1. Dewey:342.73. LCCN:2004-043578.
Audience: **g.** *Choice, 2005.*

Finkelman, Paul & Urofsky, Melvin I. **KF4549.F56 2003**
Landmark Decisions of the United States Supreme Court. Trade Cloth. CQ Press. Washington, DC. 2002. 704p. ISBN:1-56802-720-6, ISBN13: 978-1-56802-720-3. Dewey:347.73/26. LCCN:2002-153035.
Audience: **u,f.**

Fisher, Louis **KF4550.F57 1988**
Constitutional Dialogues: Interpretation As Political Process. Trade Cloth. Princeton University Press. Princeton, NJ. 1988. 272p. ISBN:0-691-07780-0, ISBN13: 978-0-691-07780-2. Dewey:342.73/024. LCCN:88-009629.
Audience: **g.** *Choice, 1989.*

Hall, Kermit L. (Editor) **KF4548.O97 1999**
The Oxford Guide to United States Supreme Court Decisions. Trade Paper. Oxford University Press, Inc. New York, NY. 2001. 448p. ISBN:0-19-513924-0, ISBN13: 978-0-19-513924-2. Dewey:348.73/48. LCCN:98-008747.
Audience: **g.**

Levy, Leonard W. & Karst, Kenneth L. (Editors) **KF4548.E53 2000**
Encyclopedia of the American Constitution, Set. Ed. 2. Trade Cloth. Thomson Gale. Farmington Hills, MI. 1905. xlvi, 3164p. ISBN:0-02-864880-3, ISBN13: 978-0-02-864880-4. Dewey:342.73. LCCN:00-029203.
Audience: **g.** *Choice, 2001, 1987.*

Lieberman, Jethro K. **KF4548 .L54 1999**
A Practical Companion to the Constitution: How the Supreme Court Has Ruled on Issues from Abortion to Zoning. Trade Paper. University of California Press. Berkeley, CA. 1999. 812p. ISBN:0-520-21280-0, ISBN13: 978-0-520-21280-0. Dewey:342.73/02. LCCN:98-018427.
Audience: **g.**

Richards, David **KF4550.R475 1989**
Foundations of American Constitutionalism. Trade Cloth. Oxford University Press, Inc. New York, NY. 1989. 332p. ISBN:0-19-505939-5, ISBN13: 978-0-19-505939-7. Dewey:342.73/02. LCCN:89-003025.
Audience: **l,u.** *Choice, 1990.*

Rubenfeld, Jed **KF4550.R83 2005**
Revolution by Judiciary: The Structure of American Constitutional Law. Trade Cloth. Harvard University Press. Cambridge, MA. 2005. 252p. ISBN:0-674-01715-3, ISBN13: 978-0-674-01715-3. Dewey:342.73. LCCN:2005-040211.
Audience: **g.** *Choice, 2006.*

Tarr, G. Alan **KF4550.Z95T37 1998**
Understanding State Constitutions. Cloth Text. Princeton University Press. Princeton, NJ. 1998. 264p. ISBN:0-691-01112-5, ISBN13: 978-0-691-01112-7. Dewey:342.73/02. LCCN:98-012782.
Audience: **l,u.** *Choice, 1999.*

Tribe, Laurence H. **KF4550.T785 2000**
American Constitutional Law, Vol. I. Ed. 3. Trade Cloth. Foundation Press. New York, NY. 2000. 1470p. University Textbook Ser. ISBN:1-56662-714-1, ISBN13: 978-1-56662-714-6. Dewey:342.73. LCCN:00-265932.
Audience: **g,u.**

United States > Constitutional Law > Constitution Amendment

Caplan, Russell L. **KF4555.C35 1988**
Constitutional Brinksmanship: Amending the Constitution by National Convention. Trade Cloth. Oxford University Press, Inc. New York, NY. 1988. 264p. ISBN:0-19-505573-X, ISBN13: 978-0-19-505573-3. Dewey:342.73/0292. LCCN:88-001529.
Audience: **l,u.** *Choice, 1989.*

Kyvig, David E. **KF4555.K98 1996**
Explicit and Authentic Acts: Amending the U. S. Constitution, 1776-1995. Trade Cloth. University Press of Kansas. Lawrence, KS. 1998. 624p. ISBN:0-7006-0792-7, ISBN13: 978-0-7006-0792-1. Dewey:342.73/029. LCCN:97-027152.
Audience: **l,u.** *Choice, 1997.*

Vile, John R. **KF4557.V555 2003**
Encyclopedia of Constitutional Amendments: Proposed Amendments, and Amending Issues, 1789-2002. Ed. 2. Library Binding. ABC-CLIO, Inc. Santa Barbara, CA. 2003. 635p. ISBN:1-85109-428-8, ISBN13: 978-1-85109-428-8. Dewey:342.73/03. LCCN:2003-001839.
Audience: **g.** *Choice, 2003.*

United States > Constitutional Law > Separation of Powers. Delegation of Powers. Judicial Review

Arthur, John **KF4575.A97 1995**
Words That Bind: Judicial Review and the Grounds of Modern Constitutional Theory. Trade Paper. Westview Press. Boulder, CO. 1994. 236p. ISBN:0-8133-2349-5, ISBN13: 978-0-8133-2349-7. Dewey:347.73/12. LCCN:94-029699.
Audience: **g,l,u.** *Choice, 1995.*

Beard, Charles A. **KF4575.B39 2006**
The Supreme Court and the Constitution. Trade Paper. Dover Publications, Inc. Mineola, NY. 2006. 160p. ISBN:0-486-44779-0, ISBN13: 978-0-486-44779-7. Dewey:347.73/26. LCCN:2005-054771.
Audience: **g.**

Berger, Raoul **KF4570.B47**
Executive Privilege: A Constitutional Myth. Trade Cloth. Harvard University Press. Cambridge, MA. 1974. 384p. Studies in Legal History ISBN:0-674-27425-3, ISBN13: 978-0-674-27425-9. Dewey:353.03/2. LCCN:73-093837.
Audience: **g.** B

Black, Charles Lund **RT84.5**
The People and the Court: Judicial Review in a Democracy. Paper Text. Textbook Publishers. Temecula, CA. 2003. 238p. ISBN:0-7581-9032-8, ISBN13: 978-0-7581-9032-1. Dewey:610.7301.
Audience: **g.** B

Bobbitt, Philip **KF4575**
Constitutional Fate. Trade Cloth. Oxford University Press, Inc. New York, NY. 2006. 304p. ISBN:0-19-518947-7, ISBN13: 978-0-19-518947-6. Dewey:347.73/12.
Audience: **g.**

Fisher, Louis **KF4565.F57 1997**
Constitutional Conflicts Between Congress and the President. Ed. 4. Trade Paper. University Press of Kansas. Lawrence, KS. 1997. 358p. ISBN:0-7006-0816-8, ISBN13: 978-0-7006-0816-4. Dewey:342.73/044. LCCN:96-035569.
Audience: **u.** B *Choice, 1997.*

Friedman, Leon (Editor) **KF4570.A7**
United States vs. Nixon: The President Before the Supreme Court. Alan Weston (Introduction by). Trade Cloth. Chelsea House Publishers. Langhorne, PA. 1974. 644p. ISBN:0-8352-0802-8, ISBN13: 978-0-8352-0802-4. Dewey:342/.73/062. LCCN:74-016403.
Audience: **u,f.** B

Haines, Charles Grove **KF4575.H29**
The American Doctrine of Judicial Supremacy. Paper Text. Textbook Publishers. Temecula, CA. 2003. 705p.

ISBN:0-7581-4356-7, ISBN13: 978-0-7581-4356-3.
Dewey:347/.73.
Audience: **g.** *B*

Nelson, William E. **KF4575.N45 2000**
Marbury vs. Madison: The Origins and Legacy of Judicial Review. Trade Cloth. University Press of Kansas. Lawrence, KS. 2000. xii, 142p. Landmark Law Cases and American Society Ser. ISBN:0-7006-1061-8, ISBN13: 978-0-7006-1061-7. Dewey:347.73/12. LCCN:00-043472.
Audience: **g.** *Choice, 2001.*

Perry, Michael J. **KF4550**
The Constitution in the Courts: Law or Politics? Trade Paper. Oxford University Press, Inc. New York, NY. 1996. 288p. ISBN:0-19-510464-1, ISBN13: 978-0-19-510464-6. Dewey:347.3/02.
Audience: **l,u.** *Choice, 1994.*

United States > Constitutional Law > Federal-State Relations. Contract Clause

Cooley, Thomas M. **KF4600.C6 1999**
A Treatise on the Constitutional Limitations Which Rest upon the Legislative Power of the States of the American Union 1868. Trade Cloth. Lawbook Exchange, Limited, The. Clark, NJ. 1999. 767p. ISBN:1-886363-92-7, ISBN13: 978-1-886363-92-2. Dewey:342.73. LCCN:99-020589.
Audience: **u,f.**

Shapiro, David L. **KF4600.S53 1995**
Federalism: A Dialogue. Trade Cloth. Northwestern University Press. Evanston, IL. 1995. 154p. ISBN:0-8101-1262-0, ISBN13: 978-0-8101-1262-9. Dewey:342.73/042. LCCN:95-008595.
Audience: **u,f.** *Choice, 1996.*

Wiecek, William M. **KF4600.W55**
Guarantee Clause of the U. S. Constitution. Trade Cloth. Cornell University Press. Ithaca, NY. 1972. 335p. Studies in Civil Liberty Ser. ISBN:0-8014-0671-4, ISBN13: 978-0-8014-0671-3. Dewey:342/.73/02. LCCN:73-162542.
Audience: **u,f.** *B*

United States > Constitutional Law > Civil and Political Rights and Liberties > General Works. The Bill of Rights

KF4750

☐ Amendments to the Constitution.
http://lcweb2.loc.gov/const/amend.html
Library of Congress.
Audience: **g,l,u,f.**

Abraham, Henry Julian & Perry, Barbara A. **KF4749.A73 2003**
Freedom and the Court: Civil Rights and Liberties in the United States. Ed. 8. Trade Cloth. University Press of Kansas. Lawrence, KS. 2003. xiv, 554p. ISBN:0-7006-1261-0, ISBN13: 978-0-7006-1261-1. Dewey:342.73/085. LCCN:2003-005819.
Audience: **g.**

Alderman, Ellen & Kennedy, Caroline **KF4749**
In Our Defense: The Bill of Rights in Action. Trade Paper. HarperCollins Publishers. New York, NY. 1992. 432p. ISBN:0-380-71720-4, ISBN13: 978-0-380-71720-0. Dewey:342.73/085. LCCN:90-048844.
Audience: **g.** *Choice, 1991.*

Amar, Akhil R. **KF4750.A436 1998**
The Bill of Rights: Creation and Reconstruction. Cloth over Boards. Yale University Press. Cumberland, RI. 1998. 430p. ISBN:0-300-07379-8, ISBN13: 978-0-300-07379-9. Dewey:342.7/3/085. LCCN:97-038370.
Audience: **g.** *Choice, 1999.*

Douglas, William O. **KF4749**
The Right of the People. Trade Cloth. Greenwood Publishing Group, Inc. Portsmouth, NH. 1980. 238p. ISBN:0-313-22640-7, ISBN13: 978-0-313-22640-3. Dewey:342.73/085. LCCN:80-019135.
Audience: **u,f.** *B*

Glendon, Mary Ann **KF4749.G54 1991**
Rights Talk: The Impoverishment of American Political Discourse. Trade Cloth. Simon & Schuster. New York, NY. 1991. 288p. ISBN:0-02-911825-5, ISBN13: 978-0-02-911825-2. Dewey:342.73/085. LCCN:91-013723.
Audience: **g.**

Hand, Learned **KF4750 .H27**
Bill of Rights. Trade Cloth. Harvard University Press. Cambridge, MA. 1958. 88p. Oliver Wendell Holmes Lectures, 1958 ISBN:0-674-07300-2, ISBN13: 978-0-674-07300-5. Dewey:342.73. LCCN:58-008248.
Audience: **g.** *B*

Henkin, Louis **KF4749**
The Age of Rights. Trade Paper. Columbia University Press. New York, NY. 1996. 224p. ISBN:0-231-06445-4, ISBN13: 978-0-231-06445-3. Dewey:342.73/085. LCCN:89-035555.
Audience: **u,f.** *Choice, 1990.*

Irons, Peter H. **KF4748.I76 1988**
The Courage of Their Convictions: Sixteen Americans Who Fought Their Way to the Supreme Court. Trade Cloth. Simon & Schuster. New York, NY. 1988. 380p. ISBN:0-02-915670-X, ISBN13: 978-0-02-915670-4. Dewey:342.73/085. LCCN:88-021406.
Audience: **g.** *Choice, 1989.*

Karst, Kenneth L. **KF4749**
Law's Promise, Law's Expression: Visions of Power in the Politics of Race, Gender, and Religion. Trade Paper. Yale University Press. Cumberland, RI. 1995. 334p. ISBN:0-300-06507-8, ISBN13: 978-0-300-06507-7. Dewey:342.73/085.
Audience: **u,f.** *Choice, 1994.*

Konvitz, Milton R. (Editor) **KF4748**
Bill of Rights Reader: Leading Constitutional Cases. Ed. 5. Trade Cloth. Cornell University Press. Ithaca, NY. 1973. 747p. ISBN:0-8014-0783-4, ISBN13: 978-0-8014-0783-3. Dewey:342/.73/0850264. LCCN:79-038389.
Audience: **g.** *B*

Levy, Leonard W. **KF4749**
Origins of the Bill of Rights. Trade Paper. Yale University Press. Cumberland, RI. 2001. 320p. Contemporary Law Ser. ISBN:0-300-08901-5, ISBN13: 978-0-300-08901-1. Dewey:342.73/085.
Audience: **g.**

Peck, Robert S. **KF4749.P38 1991**
The Bill of Rights and the Politics of Interpretation. Lippert (Editor). Trade Paper. West Publishing Company, College & School Division. Eagan, MN. 1991. 371p. ISBN:0-314-90881-1, ISBN13: 978-0-314-90881-0. Dewey:342.73/085. LCCN:91-021982.
Audience: **l,u.** *Choice, 1992.*

Perry, Michael J. **KF4749**
The Constitution, the Courts, and Human Rights: An Inquiry into the Legitimacy of Constitutional Policymaking by the Judiciary. Trade Paper. Yale University Press. Cumberland, RI. 1984. 242p. ISBN:0-300-03238-2, ISBN13: 978-0-300-03238-3. Dewey:347.302/85. LCCN:82-040164.
Audience: **u,f.** B

Pritchett, C. Herman **LAW**
Civil Liberties and the Vinson Court. Paper Text. Textbook Publishers. Temecula, CA. 2003. xi, 296p. ISBN:0-7581-2520-8, ISBN13: 978-0-7581-2520-0. Dewey:323.4.
Audience: **g.** B

Rehnquist, William H. **KF4749**
All the Laws but One: Civil Liberties in Wartime. Trade Paper. Alfred A. Knopf Inc. New York, NY. 2000. 288p. ISBN:0-679-76732-0, ISBN13: 978-0-679-76732-9. Dewey:342.73/085.
Audience: **g.** *Choice, 1999.*

Reid, John P. **KF4749.R45 1986**
Constitutional History of the American Revolution: The Authority to Tax. Cloth Text. University of Wisconsin Press. Chicago, IL. 1987. 384p. ISBN:0-299-11290-X, ISBN13: 978-0-299-11290-5. Dewey:342.73/085. LCCN:87-008256.
Audience: **g.** *Choice, 1988.*

Reid, John P. **KF4749**
Constitutional History of the American Revolution: The Authority of Law. Trade Cloth. University of Wisconsin Press. Chicago, IL. 1993. 288p. ISBN:0-299-13980-8, ISBN13: 978-0-299-13980-3. Dewey:342.73/085. LCCN:86-040058.
Audience: **g.** *Choice, 1994.*

Reid, John P. **KF4749.R45 1986**
Constitutional History of the American Revolution: The Authority of Rights. Cloth Text. University of Wisconsin Press. Chicago, IL. 1987. 400p. ISBN:0-299-10870-8, ISBN13: 978-0-299-10870-0. Dewey:342.73/085. LCCN:86-040058.
Audience: **g.** *Choice, 1987.*

Reid, John P. **KF4749.R45 1986**
Constitutional History of the American Revolution: The Authority to Legislate. Trade Cloth. University of Wisconsin Press. Chicago, IL. 1991. 508p. ISBN:0-299-13070-3, ISBN13: 978-0-299-13070-1. Dewey:342.73/085. LCCN:91-050326.
Audience: **g.** *Choice, 1992.*

Savage, David **KF474**
The Supreme Court and Individual Rights. Ed. 4. Trade Cloth. CQ Press. Washington, DC. 2004. 416p. ISBN:1-56802-887-3, ISBN13: 978-1-56802-887-3. Dewey:342.73/085 347.30285. LCCN:2004-273178.
Audience: **u,f.**

Schwartz, Bernard (Editor) **KF4744 1980**
Roots of the Bill of Rights: An Illustrated Source Book of American Freedom. Trade Paper. Chelsea House Publishers. Langhorne, PA. 1981. 1265p. ISBN:0-87754-207-4, ISBN13: 978-0-87754-207-0. Dewey:342.73/029. LCCN:80-022931.
Audience: **l,u.**

United States > Constitutional Law > Civil and Political Rights and Liberties > Civil Rights of Particular Groups

Ancheta, Angelo N. **KF4757.A75A53 1998**
Race, Rights and the Asian American Experience. Trade Cloth. Rutgers University Press. Piscataway, NJ. 1998. xv, 209p. ISBN:0-8135-2463-6, ISBN13: 978-0-8135-2463-4. Dewey:342.73/0873. LCCN:97-024855.
Audience: **l,u,f.** *Choice, 1998.*

Bender, Steven W. **KF4757.5.L38B46 2003**
Greasers and Gringos: Latinos, Law, and the American Imagination. Trade Cloth. New York University Press. New York, NY. 2003. 320p. Critical America Ser. ISBN:0-8147-9887-X, ISBN13: 978-0-8147-9887-4. Dewey:342.73/0873. LCCN:2003-014980.
Audience: **g.**

Berger, Morroe **KF4757 .B4 1978**
Equality by Statute. Library Binding. Hippocrene Books, Inc. New York, NY. 1978. ISBN:0-374-90606-8, ISBN13: 978-0-374-90606-1. Dewey:342/.73/085. LCCN:77-027250.
Audience: **l,u.**

Chang, Robert S. **KF4757.5.A75C48 1999**
Disoriented: Asian Americans, Law and the Nation State. Trade Cloth. New York University Press. New York, NY. 1999. 248p. Critical America Ser. ISBN:0-8147-1521-4, ISBN13: 978-0-8147-1521-5. Dewey:342.73/0873. LCCN:98-058131.
Audience: **l,u,f.** *Choice, 2000.*

Delgado, Richard & Stefancic, Jean (Editors) **KF4755.C75 1999**
Critical Race Theory: The Cutting Edge. Ed. 2. Trade Cloth. Temple University Press. Philadelphia, PA. 2000. 704p. ISBN:1-56639-713-8, ISBN13: 978-1-56639-713-1. Dewey:305.8. LCCN:99-020596.
Audience: **u,f.**

Edley, Christopher Jr. **KF4755.5.E33 1996**
Not All Black and White: Affirmative Action and American Values. Trade Cloth. Farrar, Straus & Giroux. New York, NY. 1996. xix, 294p. ISBN:0-8090-2955-3, ISBN13: 978-0-8090-2955-6. Dewey:342.73/0873. LCCN:96-021397.
Audience: **g.** *Choice, 1997.*

Eskridge, William N. Jr. (Editor) **KF4545.S5**
Gaylaw: Challenging the Apartheid of the Closet. Trade Paper. Harvard University Press. Cambridge, MA. 2002. 480p. ISBN:0-674-00804-9, ISBN13: 978-0-674-00804-5. Dewey:342.73/087.
Audience: **g.** *Choice, 2000.*

Friedman, Leon (Editor) **KF4757.A5**
Southern Justice. Library Binding. Greenwood Publishing Group, Inc. Portsmouth, NH. 1976. 306p. ISBN:0-8371-8489-4, ISBN13: 978-0-8371-8489-0. Dewey:342/.73/085. LCCN:75-033296.
Audience: **g.**

Gerstmann, Evan **KF4754.5.G47 1999**
The Constitutional Underclass: Gays, Lesbians, and the Failure of Class-Based Equal Protection. Trade Cloth. University of Chicago Press. Chicago, IL. 1999. 206p. ISBN:0-226-28859-5, ISBN13: 978-0-226-28859-8. Dewey:342.73/087. LCCN:98-011679.
Audience: **u,f.** *Choice, 1999.*

Higginbotham, A. Leon Jr. **KF4545.S5**
In the Matter of Color: Race and the American Legal Process: The Colonial Period, Vol. 1. Trade Paper. Oxford University Press, Inc. New York, NY. 1980. 544p. ISBN:0-19-502745-0, ISBN13: 978-0-19-502745-7. Dewey:342/.73/087. LCCN:76-051713.
Audience: **g.** B

Higginbotham, A. Leon Jr. **KF4757**
Shades of Freedom: Racial Politics and Presumptions of the American Legal Process Race. Trade Paper. Oxford University Press, Inc. New York, NY. 1998. 336p. ISBN:0-19-512288-7, ISBN13: 978-0-19-512288-6. Dewey:342.7/3/0873.
Audience: **g.**

Hunter, Nan D., et al. **KF4754.5.Z9 H86**
The Rights of Lesbians, Gay Men, Bisexuals, and Transgender People: The Authoritative ACLU Guide to the Rights of Lesbians, Gay Men, Bisexuals, and Transgender People. Ed. 4. Courtney G. Joslin & Sharon M. McGowan (Authors). Trade Paper. New York University Press. New York, NY. 2004. 240p. ISBN:0-8147-3679-3, ISBN13: 978-0-8147-3679-1. Dewey:342.73/087.
Audience: **u,f.**

Klarman, Michael J. **KF4757.K58 2003**
From Jim Crow to Civil Rights: The Supreme Court and the Struggle for Racial Equality. Cloth Text. Oxford University Press, Inc. New York, NY. 2004. 672p. ISBN:0-19-512903-2, ISBN13: 978-0-19-512903-8. Dewey:342.73/0873. LCCN:2003-000515.
Audience: **g.** *Choice, 2004.*

Kull, Andrew **KF4755.5.K85**
The Color-Blind Constitution. Trade Paper. Harvard University Press. Cambridge, MA. 1998. 320p. ISBN:0-674-14293-4, ISBN13: 978-0-674-14293-0. Dewey:347.302873.
Audience: **g.**

Lively, Donald E. **KF4755**
The Constitution and Race. Trade Cloth. Greenwood Publishing Group, Inc. Portsmouth, NH. 1992. 208p. ISBN:0-275-93914-6, ISBN13: 978-0-275-93914-4. Dewey:347.30287. LCCN:91-030280.
Audience: **g.** *Choice, 1992.*

Loevy, Robert D. (Editor) **KF4757.C59 1997**
The Civil Rights Act of 1964: The Passage of the Law That Ended Racial Segregation. Hubert H. Humphrey, Joseph L. Rauh Jr. & John G. Stewart (Contribution by). Paper Text. State University of New York Press. Albany, NY. 1997. 380p. SUNY Series in Afro-American Studies ISBN:0-7914-3362-5, ISBN13: 978-0-7914-3362-1. Dewey:342.73/0873. LCCN:97-000687.
Audience: **l,u.** *Choice, 1998.*

Lopez, Ian F. **KF4755.H36 1996**
White by Law: The Legal Construction of Race. Trade Cloth. New York University Press. New York, NY. 1996. 296p. Critical America Ser. ISBN:0-8147-5099-0, ISBN13: 978-0-8147-5099-5. Dewey:342.73/0873. LCCN:95-032465.
Audience: **u,f.** *Choice, 1996.*

McClain, Charles J. **KF4757.5.C47M37**
In Search of Equality: The Chinese Struggle Against Discrimination in Nineteenth-Century America. Trade Paper. University of California Press. Berkeley, CA. 1996. 396p. ISBN:0-520-20514-6, ISBN13: 978-0-520-20514-7. Dewey:347.30613. LCCN:93-004942.
Audience: **l,u.** *Choice, 1994.*

Moran, Rachel F. **HQ1031**
Interracial Intimacy: The Regulation of Race and Romance. Trade Paper. University of Chicago Press. Chicago, IL. 2003. 232p. ISBN:0-226-53663-7, ISBN13: 978-0-226-53663-7. Dewey:305.8/00973.
Audience: **u,f.** *Choice, 2002.*

Nelson, William E. **KF4757.N45 1988**
The Fourteenth Amendment: From Political Principle to Judicial Doctrine. Trade Cloth. Harvard University Press. Cambridge, MA. 1988. 288p. ISBN:0-674-31625-8, ISBN13: 978-0-674-31625-6. Dewey:342.73/085. LCCN:87-035226.
Audience: **g.** *Choice, 1989.*

Pinello, Daniel R. **KF4754.5.P56 2003**
Gay Rights and American Law. Trade Cloth. Cambridge University Press. New York, NY. 2003. 366p. ISBN:0-521-81274-7, ISBN13: 978-0-521-81274-0. Dewey:342.73/087. LCCN:2002-041555.
Audience: **u,f.** *Choice, 2004.*

Spann, Girardeau A. **KF4757**
Race Against the Court: The Supreme Court and Minorities in Contemporary America. Trade Cloth. New York University Press. New York, NY. 1993. 272p. ISBN:0-8147-7963-8, ISBN13: 978-0-8147-7963-7. Dewey:347.302873. LCCN:92-031343.
Audience: **u,f.** *Choice, 1993.*

Stewart, Chuck **KF4754.5.A68S74 2001**
Homosexuality and the Law: A Dictionary. Library Binding. ABC-CLIO, Inc. Santa Barbara, CA. 2001. 429p. Contemporary Legal Issues Ser. ISBN:1-57607-267-3, ISBN13: 978-1-57607-267-7. Dewey:346.7301/3. LCCN:2001-001344.
Audience: **l,u.** *Choice, 2001.*

Tushnet, Mark V. **KF4749**
Making Civil Rights Law: Thurgood Marshall and the Supreme Court, 1936-1961. Trade Paper. Oxford University Press, Inc.

New York, NY. 1996. 416p. ISBN:0-19-510468-4, ISBN13: 978-0-19-510468-4. Dewey:347.3/0285.
Audience: **l,u.** *Choice, 1994.*

Valencia, Reynaldo Anaya **KF4757.5.M4M49 2004**
Mexican Americans and the Law: El Pueblo Unido Jamás Ser Vencido!. Trade Cloth. University of Arizona Press. Tucson, AZ. 2004. 197p. The Mexican American Experience Ser. ISBN:0-8165-2279-0, ISBN13: 978-0-8165-2279-8. Dewey:342.73/0873. LCCN:2003-015701.
Audience: **u,f.** *Choice, 2005.*

United States > Constitutional Law > Civil and Political Rights and Liberties > Sex Discrimination. Race Discrimination

Cushman, Clare **KF4758.A7S87 2001**
Supreme Court Decisions and Women's Rights: Milestones to Equality. Trade Cloth. CQ Press. Washington, DC. 2000. 320p. ISBN:1-56802-613-7, ISBN13: 978-1-56802-613-8. Dewey:342.73/0878. LCCN:00-064527.
Audience: **u,f.**

Eisaguirre, Lynne **KF4758.E36 1997**
Sexual Harassment. Ed. 2. Mildred Vasan (Editor). Library Binding. ABC-CLIO, Inc. Santa Barbara, CA. 1997. 283p. Contemporary World Issues Ser. ISBN:0-87436-971-1, ISBN13: 978-0-87436-971-7. Dewey:342.73/0878. LCCN:97-035489.
Audience: **l,u.** *Choice, 1994.*

Eisenstein, Zillah R. **KF4758.E38 1988**
The Female Body and the Law. Trade Cloth. University of California Press. Berkeley, CA. 1989. 280p. ISBN:0-520-06309-0, ISBN13: 978-0-520-06309-9. Dewey:346.7301/34. LCCN:88-027890.
Audience: **l,u.** *Choice, 1989.*

Jackson, Donald W. **KF4764.J33 1992**
Even the Children of Strangers: Equality under the U. S. Constitution. Trade Paper. University Press of Kansas. Lawrence, KS. 1992. xii, 284p. ISBN:0-7006-0548-7, ISBN13: 978-0-7006-0548-4. Dewey:342.73/085. LCCN:92-006098.
Audience: **g,l,u.** *Choice, 1993.*

Kaminer, Wendy **KF4758.K35 1990**
A Fearful Freedom: Women's Flight from Equality. Trade Cloth. Addison-Wesley Longman, Inc. Boston, MA. 1990. xvi, 250p. ISBN:0-201-09234-4, ISBN13: 978-0-201-09234-9. Dewey:342.73/0878. LCCN:89-028509.
Audience: **g,l,u,f.** *Choice, 1990.*

Pennock, James Roland & Chapman, John W. (Editors) **KF4765.A75.D8**
Due Process. Trade Cloth. New York University Press. New York, NY. 1977. 362p. Nomos Ser., Vol. 18 ISBN:0-8147-6569-6, ISBN13: 978-0-8147-6569-2. Dewey:347/.73. LCCN:76-040511.
Audience: **u,f.**

Pole, J. R. **KF4764.P64 1993**
The Pursuit of Equality in American History. Ed. 2. Trade Cloth. University of California Press. Berkeley, CA. 1993. 498p. ISBN:0-520-07987-6, ISBN13: 978-0-520-07987-8. Dewey:170.973. LCCN:92-012928.
Audience: **u,f.**

VanBurkleo, Sandra F. **KF4758.V36 2001**
Belonging to the World: Women's Rights and American Constitutional Culture. Trade Paper. Oxford University Press, Inc. New York, NY. 2001. 432p. Bicentennial Essays on the Bill of Rights Ser. ISBN:0-19-506972-2, ISBN13: 978-0-19-506972-3. Dewey:323.3/4/0973. LCCN:00-029349.
Audience: **l,u.** *Choice, 2002.*

United States > Constitutional Law > Civil and Political Rights and Liberties > Freedom of Expression

Anastaplo, George **KF4770**
The Constitutionalist: Notes on the First Amendment. Trade Paper. Lexington Books. Lanham, MD. 2005. 888p. ISBN:0-7391-1099-3, ISBN13: 978-0-7391-1099-7. Dewey:342/.73/085.
Audience: **g.**

Barron, Jerome A. **KF4774.B36**
Freedom of the Press for Whom?: The Right of Access to Mass Media. Trade Paper. Books on Demand. Ann Arbor, MI. 383p. ISBN:0-608-17137-9, ISBN13: 978-0-608-17137-1. Dewey:323.44/3/0973. LCCN:72-075387.
Audience: **u,f.**

Bezanson, Randall P. **KF4770.A7B49 2003**
How Free Can the Press Be? Trade Cloth. University of Illinois Press. Champaign, IL. 2003. 272p. The History of Communication Ser. ISBN:0-252-02866-X, ISBN13: 978-0-252-02866-3. Dewey:342.73/0853. LCCN:2003-002148.
Audience: **g.** *Choice, 2004.*

Boyer, Paul S. **KF4775.B6 2002**
Purity in Print: Book Censorship in America from the Gilded Age to the Computer Age. Ed. 2. Trade Paper. University of Wisconsin Press. Chicago, IL. 2002. 400p. Print Culture History in Modern America Ser. ISBN:0-299-17584-7, ISBN13: 978-0-299-17584-9. Dewey:363.3/1/0973. LCCN:2002-001066.
Audience: **u,f.**

Curry, Richard O. (Editor) **KF4770 .F76**
Freedom at Risk: Secrecy, Censorship, and Repression in the 1980s. Trade Paper. Temple University Press. Philadelphia, PA. 1989. 448p. ISBN:0-87722-660-1, ISBN13: 978-0-87722-660-4. Dewey:342.73/0853.
Audience: **l,u.**

Dickerson, Donna L. **KF4774**
The Course of Tolerance: Freedom of the Press in Nineteenth-Century America. Trade Cloth. Greenwood Publishing Group, Inc. Portsmouth, NH. 1990. 272p. Contributions to the Study of Mass Media and Communications Ser., No. 24 ISBN:0-313-27534-3, ISBN13: 978-0-313-27534-0. Dewey:342.73/0853. LCCN:90-038525.
Audience: **u,f.** *Choice, 1991.*

Downs, Donald A. **KF4772.D69 1985**
Nazis in Skokie: Freedom, Community, and the First Amendment. Paper Text. University of Notre Dame Press. Notre Dame, IN. 1985. 272p. ISBN:0-268-00968-6, ISBN13: 978-0-268-00968-7. Dewey:322.4/4/097731. LCCN:84-040294.
Audience: **g,l,u,f.** *Choice, 1985.*

Eldridge, Larry D. **KF4772.E39**
A Distant Heritage: The Growth of Free Speech in Early America. Trade Paper. New York University Press. New York, NY. 1995. 216p. ISBN:0-8147-2195-8, ISBN13: 978-0-8147-2195-7. Dewey:347.302853.
Audience: **u,f.** *Choice, 1994.*

Finkelman, Paul (Editor) **KF4783.A68R45 2000**
Religion and American Law: An Encyclopedia. Trade Cloth. Garland Publishing, Inc. New York, NY. 1999. 624p. Reference Library of the Humanities, Vol. 1548 ISBN:0-8153-0750-0, ISBN13: 978-0-8153-0750-1. Dewey:342.73/0852. LCCN:99-057222.
Audience: **u,f.** *Choice, 2000.*

Fisher, Louis **KF4783**
Religious Liberty in America: Political Safeguards. Trade Cloth. University Press of Kansas. Lawrence, KS. 2004. xii, 266p. ISBN:0-7006-1201-7, ISBN13: 978-0-7006-1201-7. Dewey:342.73/0852. LCCN:2002-004616.
Audience: **g.** *Choice, 2003.*

Greenawalt, Kent **KF4772**
Fighting Words: Individuals, Communities, and Liberties of Speech. Trade Paper. Princeton University Press. Princeton, NJ. 1996. 202p. ISBN:0-691-02600-9, ISBN13: 978-0-691-02600-8. Dewey:342.73/0853. LCCN:94-042501.
Audience: **l,u.** *Choice, 1995.*

Haiman, Franklyn S. **KF4783.H345 2003**
Religious Expression and the American Constitution. Trade Cloth. Michigan State University Press. East Lansing, MI. 2003. 272p. Rhetoric and Public Affairs Ser. ISBN:0-87013-691-7, ISBN13: 978-0-87013-691-7. Dewey:342.7308/53. LCCN:2003-018527.
Audience: **g.** *Choice, 2004.*

Haiman, Franklyn S. & Haiman, Franklyn Saul **KF4772.H345**
Speech and Law in a Free Society. Trade Paper. Books on Demand. Ann Arbor, MI. 1981. 509p. ISBN:0-608-04452-0, ISBN13: 978-0-608-04452-1. Dewey:347.302/853. LCCN:81-007546.
Audience: **l,u.** *B*

Harer, John B. **KF4770.Z9.H3 1992**
Intellectual Freedom: A Reference Handbook. Library Binding. ABC-CLIO, Inc. Santa Barbara, CA. 1992. 313p. Contemporary World Issues Ser. ISBN:0-87436-669-0, ISBN13: 978-0-87436-669-3. Dewey:342.73/0853. LCCN:92-035565.
Audience: **l,u.** *Choice, 1993.*

Kalven, Harry Jr. **KF4772.K35 1988**
A Worthy Tradition: Freedom of Speech in America. Jamie Kalven (Editor). Trade Cloth. HarperCollins Publishers. New York, NY. 1988. 704p. ISBN:0-06-015810-7, ISBN13: 978-0-06-015810-1. Dewey:342.73/0853. LCCN:87-045059.
Audience: **g,l,u,f.** *Choice, 1988.*

Levy, Leonard W. **Z658.U5**
Emergence of a Free Press. Trade Paper. Oxford University Press, Inc. New York, NY. 1987. 416p. ISBN:0-19-504240-9, ISBN13: 978-0-19-504240-5. Dewey:342.7308/53.
Audience: **g.** *B* *Choice, 1985.*

Levy, Leonard W. **KF4774.F74 1996**
Freedom of the Press from Zenger to Jefferson. Trade Paper. Carolina Academic Press. Durham, NC. 1996. 496p. ISBN:0-89089-837-5, ISBN13: 978-0-89089-837-6. Dewey:342.73/0853. LCCN:95-069528.
Audience: **l,u.**

MacKinnon, Catharine A. **KF4772.M33 1993**
Only Words. Trade Cloth. Harvard University Press. Cambridge, MA. 1993. 160p. ISBN:0-674-63933-2, ISBN13: 978-0-674-63933-1. Dewey:342.7/3/085. LCCN:93-013600.
Audience: **g.** *Choice, 1994.*

Nelson, Harold N. (Editor) **KF4774.A75 F7**
Freedom of the Press from Hamilton to the Warren Court. Trade Cloth. Macmillan Publishing Company, Inc. Old Tappan, NJ. 1967. ISBN:0-672-51005-7, ISBN13: 978-0-672-51005-2. Dewey:323.4450973. LCCN:66-022578.
Audience: **l,u.**

Powe, Lucas A. Jr. **KF4774.P68 1987**
American Broadcasting and the First Amendment. Trade Cloth. University of California Press. Berkeley, CA. 1987. 312p. ISBN:0-520-05918-2, ISBN13: 978-0-520-05918-4. Dewey:343.73/0998. LCCN:86-019254.
Audience: **u,f.** *Choice, 1987.*

Powe, Lucas A. Jr. **KF4774.P69 1991**
The Fourth Estate and the Constitution: Freedom of the Press in America. Trade Cloth. University of California Press. Berkeley, CA. 1991. 350p. ISBN:0-520-07290-1, ISBN13: 978-0-520-07290-9. Dewey:342.73/0853. LCCN:90-045465.
Audience: **l,u.** *Choice, 1991.*

Rabban, David M. **KF4772 .R33 1997**
Free Speech in Its Forgotten Years, 1870-1920. Christopher L. Tomlins (Contribution by). Trade Cloth. Cambridge University Press. New York, NY. 1997. 416p. Historical Studies in American Law and Society ISBN:0-521-62013-9, ISBN13: 978-0-521-62013-0. Dewey:970. LCCN:97-015281.
Audience: **u,f.** *Choice, 1998.*

Shiell, Timothy C. **KF4772.S445 1998**
Campus Hate Speech on Trial. Trade Cloth. University Press of Kansas. Lawrence, KS. 1998. 216p. ISBN:0-7006-0889-3, ISBN13: 978-0-7006-0889-8. Dewey:342.73/0853. LCCN:98-010847.
Audience: **g,l,u,f.** *Choice, 1998.*

Shiffrin, Steven H. **KF4772.S45 1990**
The First Amendment, Democracy, and Romance. Trade Cloth. Harvard University Press. Cambridge, MA. 1990. 296p. ISBN:0-674-30275-3, ISBN13: 978-0-674-30275-4. Dewey:342.73/0853. LCCN:89-028967.
Audience: **l,u.** *Choice, 1991.*

Smith, Jeffery A. **KF4774.S644 1999**
War and Press Freedom: The Problem of Prerogative Power. Trade Paper. Oxford University Press, Inc. New York, NY. 1999. 336p. ISBN:0-19-509946-X, ISBN13: 978-0-19-509946-1. Dewey:342.73/0853. LCCN:97-037755.
Audience: **l,u.** *Choice, 2000.*

Witte, John Jr. **KF4783.Z9W58 2004**
Religion and the American Constitutional Experiment: Essential Rights and Liberties. Ed. 2. Trade Paper. Westview Press.

Boulder, CO. 2004. 352p. ISBN:0-8133-4231-7, ISBN13: 978-0-8133-4231-3. Dewey:342.7308/52. LCCN:2004-012100.
Audience: **g.** *Choice, 2000.*

Wolfson, Nicholas **KF4772**
Hate Speech, Sex Speech, Free Speech. Trade Cloth. Greenwood Publishing Group, Inc. Portsmouth, NH. 1997. 184p. ISBN:0-275-95770-5, ISBN13: 978-0-275-95770-4. Dewey:342.73/0853. LCCN:96-044680.
Audience: **l,u,f.** *Choice, 1997.*

United States > Constitutional Law > Civil and Political Rights and Liberties > Control of Individuals

Ball, Howard **KF4850.B35 2004**
The USA Patriot Act: A Reference Handbook. Mildred Vasan (Editor). Library Binding. ABC-CLIO, Inc. Santa Barbara, CA. 2004. 266p. Contemporary World Issues Ser. ISBN:1-85109-722-8, ISBN13: 978-1-85109-722-7. Dewey:345.73/02. LCCN:2004-005430.
Audience: **g,l,u.** *Choice, 2005.*

Carliner, David, et al. **KF4800.R54 1990**
The Rights of Aliens and Refugees: The Basic ACLU Guide to Alien and Refugee Rights. Ed. 2. Arthur C. Hilton, Lucas Guttentag & Wade J. Henderson (Authors). Trade Paper. Southern Illinois University Press. Carbondale, IL. 1990. 240p. American Civil Liberties Union Handbook Ser. ISBN:0-8093-1598-X, ISBN13: 978-0-8093-1598-7. Dewey:342.73/083. LCCN:89-011570.
Audience: **l,u.**

Cole, David **KF4800.C58 2003**
Enemy Aliens: Double Standards and Constitutional Freedoms in the War on Terrorism. Trade Cloth. New Press, The. New York, NY. 2003. 256p. ISBN:1-56584-800-4, ISBN13: 978-1-56584-800-9. Dewey:323.3/291/0973. LCCN:2003-050966.
Audience: **g.**

Cole, David **KF4850.C65 2006**
Terrorism and the Constitution: Sacrificing Civil Liberties in the Name of National Security. Ed. 3. Trade Paper. New Press, The. New York, NY. 2006. 256p. ISBN:1-56584-939-6, ISBN13: 978-1-56584-939-6. Dewey:343.7301. LCCN:2006-273542.
Audience: **g.** *Choice, 2003.*

Johnson, Kevin R. **KF4819.J64 2004**
The Huddled Masses Myth: Immigration and Civil Rights. Library Binding. Temple University Press. Philadelphia, PA. 2003. 272p. ISBN:1-59213-205-7, ISBN13: 978-1-59213-205-8. Dewey:342.73/082. LCCN:2003-050792.
Audience: **u,f.** *Choice, 2004.*

Ngai, Mae M. **KF4800.N485 2005**
Impossible Subjects: Illegal Aliens and the Making of Modern America. Trade Paper. Princeton University Press. Princeton, NJ. 2005. 400p. Politics and Society in Twentieth Century America Ser. ISBN:0-691-12429-9, ISBN13: 978-0-691-12429-2. Dewey:342.73/083.
Audience: **l,u,f.** *Choice, 2004.*

United States > Constitutional Law > Church and State

Anglim, Christopher Thomas **KF4865.A68A54 1999**
Religion and the Law: A Dictionary. Library Binding. ABC-CLIO, Inc. Santa Barbara, CA. 2000. xv, 451p. Contemporary Legal Issues Ser. ISBN:1-57607-028-X, ISBN13: 978-1-57607-028-4. Dewey:342.73/0852/03. LCCN:99-032889.
Audience: **g,l,u.** *Choice, 2000.*

Gedicks, Frederick M. **KF4865.G43 1995**
The Rhetoric of Church and State: A Critical Analysis of Religion Clause Jurisprudence. Cloth Text. Duke University Press. Durham, NC. 1995. 184p. ISBN:0-8223-1654-4, ISBN13: 978-0-8223-1654-1. Dewey:342.73/0852. LCCN:95-010337.
Audience: **g,l,u,f.** *Choice, 1996.*

Hitchcock, James **KF4865.H58 2004**
The Supreme Court and Religion in American Life: From Higher Law to Sectarian Scruples. Trade Cloth. Princeton University Press. Princeton, NJ. 2004. 272p. New Forum Bks. ISBN:0-691-11923-6, ISBN13: 978-0-691-11923-6. Dewey:342.7308/52. LCCN:2004-040722.
Audience: **l,u.** *Choice, 2005.*

Hitchcock, James **KF4865.H58 2004**
The Supreme Court and Religion in American Life: The Odyssey of the Religion Clauses. Trade Cloth. Princeton University Press. Princeton, NJ. 2004. 232p. New Forum Bks. ISBN:0-691-11696-2, ISBN13: 978-0-691-11696-9. Dewey:342.7308/52. LCCN:2004-040722.
Audience: **l,u.** *Choice, 2005.*

United States > Constitutional Law > Initiative, Referendum, Recall

Magleby, David **KF4881**
Direct Legislation: Voting on Ballot Propositions in the United States. Trade Paper. Johns Hopkins University Press. Baltimore, MD. 2001. 284p. ISBN:0-8018-6980-3, ISBN13: 978-0-8018-6980-8. Dewey:328/.2.
Audience: **u,f.**

Waters, M. Dane **KF4881.A4 2003**
The Initiative and Referendum Almanac: A Comprehensive Reference Guide to the Initiative and Referendum Process. Trade Paper. Carolina Academic Press. Durham, NC. 2003. 654p. ISBN:0-89089-969-X, ISBN13: 978-0-89089-969-4. Dewey:328.273. LCCN:2003-105098.
Audience: **g,l,u,f.** *Choice, 2004.*

United States > Constitutional Law > Election Law

KF4910
☐ Nomination and Election of the President and Vice President of the United States, Including the Manner of Selecting Delegates to National Political Conventions.
http://www.gpoaccess.gov/serialset/cdocuments/index.html
U. S. G. P. O..
Audience: **g,l,u,f.**

Ball, Howard, et al. **KF4893**
Compromised Compliance: Implementation of the 1965 Voting Rights Act, 66. Dale Krane & Thomas P. Lauth (Authors). Trade Cloth. Greenwood Publishing Group, Inc. Portsmouth, NH. 1982. 300p. Contributions in Political Science Ser., No. 66 ISBN:0-313-22037-9, ISBN13: 978-0-313-22037-1. Dewey:342.73/072/0269. LCCN:81-006342.
Audience: **u,f.** *B*

Elliott, Ward E. **KF4891.E43**
The Rise of Guardian Democracy: The Supreme Court's Role in Voting Rights Disputes, 1845-1969. Trade Cloth. Harvard University Press. Cambridge, MA. 1974. 368p. Political Studies ISBN:0-674-77156-7, ISBN13: 978-0-674-77156-7. Dewey:342/.73/07. LCCN:73-090611.
Audience: **u,f.** *B*

Gillette, William **KF4893.Z9G5 1969**
The Right to Vote: Politics and the Passage of the 15th Amendment. Trade Cloth. Johns Hopkins University Press. Baltimore, MD. 1965. 480p. Studies in Historical and Political Science, 83rd Series (1965) ISBN:0-8018-0218-0, ISBN13: 978-0-8018-0218-8. Dewey:324.73. LCCN:74-094492.
Audience: **u,f.** *B*

Grofman, Bernard N. & Davidson, Chandler (Editors) **KF4893.C66 1992**
Controversies in Minority Voting: The Voting Rights Act in Perspective. Trade Cloth. Brookings Institution Press. Washington, DC. 1992. 376p. ISBN:0-8157-1750-4, ISBN13: 978-0-8157-1750-8. Dewey:342.73/072. LCCN:92-007370.
Audience: **u,f.** *Choice, 1992.*

Hamilton, Charles V. **KF4893.H34**
The Bench and the Ballot; Southern Federal Judges and Black Voters. Trade Cloth. Oxford University Press, Inc. New York, NY. 1973. xii, 258p. ISBN:0-19-501718-8, ISBN13: 978-0-19-501718-2. Dewey:342/.75/07. LCCN:73-082668.
Audience: **u,f.** *B*

Ryden, David K. **KF4886.A5U17 2002**
The U. S. Supreme Court and the Electoral Process. Ed. 2. Trade Paper. Georgetown University Press. Washington, DC. 2002. 384p. ISBN:0-87840-886-X, ISBN13: 978-0-87840-886-3. Dewey:342.73/07. LCCN:2002-019496.
Audience: **g.** *Choice, 2001.*

United States > Constitutional Law > The Legislative Branch. Congress. Powers

Johnson Charles W.; Ney, Robert **KF4945.Z9**
🖵 How Our Laws Are Made.
http://thomas.loc.gov/home/lawsmade.toc.html
United States Government Printing Office.
Audience: **g.**

Redman, Eric **KF4980.R4 2001**
The Dance of Legislation. Trade Cloth. University of Washington Press. Seattle, WA. 2003. 317p. ISBN:0-295-98023-0, ISBN13: 978-0-295-98023-2. Dewey:328.73/077. LCCN:00-062896.
Audience: **g.** *B*

Wormuth, Francis D. & Firmage, Edwin B. **KF4941.W67 1989**
To Chain the Dog of War: The War Power of Congress in History and Law. Ed. 2. Trade Paper. University of Illinois Press. Champaign, IL. 1989. 376p. ISBN:0-252-06068-7, ISBN13: 978-0-252-06068-7. Dewey:342.73/062. LCCN:88-020808.
Audience: **u,f.** *Choice, 1986.*

United States > Constitutional Law > The Legislative Branch. Congress. Powers > Impeachment

Berger, Raoul **KF5060**
Impeachment: The Constitutional Problems, Enlarged Edition. Ed. 2. Trade Paper. Harvard University Press. Cambridge, MA. 1999. 359p. ISBN:0-674-44478-7, ISBN13: 978-0-674-44478-2. Dewey:342.73062. LCCN:73-075055.
Audience: **g.**

Gerhardt, Michael J. **KF4958.G47 2000**
The Federal Impeachment Process: A Constitutional and Historical Analysis. Ed. 2. Trade Paper. University of Chicago Press. Chicago, IL. 2000. 271p. ISBN:0-226-28957-5, ISBN13: 978-0-226-28957-1. Dewey:342.73/068. LCCN:99-038736.
Audience: **g.** *Choice, 1996.*

Hoffer, Peter C. & Hull, N. E. **KF4958**
Impeachment in America, 1635-1805. Cloth over Boards. Yale University Press. Cumberland, RI. 1984. 326p. ISBN:0-300-03053-3, ISBN13: 978-0-300-03053-2. Dewey:353.9/3993/09. LCCN:83-019772.
Audience: **g.** *B*

United States > Constitutional Law > The Executive Branch. Presidency

Black, Charles L. Jr. **KF5075.Z9B55 1998**
Impeachment: A Handbook. Cloth over Boards. Yale University Press. Cumberland, RI. 1998. 96p. Yale Fastback Ser. ISBN:0-300-07954-0, ISBN13: 978-0-300-07954-8. Dewey:342.7/3/05. LCCN:98-088356.
Audience: **u,f.**

Cooper, Phillip J. **KF5053.C578 2002**
By Order of the President: The Use and Abuse of Executive Direct Action. Trade Cloth. University Press of Kansas. Lawrence, KS. 2004. 320p. Studies in Government and Public Policy ISBN:0-7006-1179-7, ISBN13: 978-0-7006-1179-9. Dewey:342.73/06. LCCN:2001-008168.
Audience: **g.** *Choice, 2003.*

Corwin, Edward S. **KF5051.C6 1984**
The President: Office and Powers. Ed. 5. Randall W. Bland, Theodore T. Hindson & Jack W. Peltason (Editors). Cloth Text. New York University Press. New York, NY. 1984. 600p. ISBN:0-8147-1390-4, ISBN13: 978-0-8147-1390-7. Dewey:353.031. LCCN:84-000993.
Audience: **l,u.** *B*

Finkelman, Paul & Field van Tassel, Emily **KF5075.V36 1999**
Impeachable Offenses: A Documentary History from 1787 to the Present. Trade Cloth. CQ Press. Washington, DC. 1999. 326p. ISBN:1-56802-479-7, ISBN13: 978-1-56802-479-0. Dewey:342.73/062. LCCN:98-054337.
Audience: **u,f.** *Choice, 1999.*

Fisher, Louis **KF5060.F57 2004**
Presidential War Power. Ed. 2. Trade Cloth. University Press of Kansas. Lawrence, KS. 2004. xvi, 318p. ISBN:0-7006-1332-3, ISBN13: 978-0-7006-1332-8. Dewey:342.73/062. LCCN:2004-001962.
Audience: **g.** *Choice, 1995.*

Gillman, Howard **KF5074.2.G55 2001**
The Votes That Counted: How the Court Decided the 2000 Presidential Election. Trade Cloth. University of Chicago Press. Chicago, IL. 2001. 325p. ISBN:0-226-29407-2, ISBN13: 978-0-226-29407-0. Dewey:324.973/0929. LCCN:2001-003077.
Audience: **g.**

Johnson, Charles A. & Brickman, Danette **KF5107.5.J64 2001**
Independent Counsel: The Law and the Investigations. Trade Cloth. CQ Press. Washington, DC. 2001. 250p. ISBN:1-56802-508-4, ISBN13: 978-1-56802-508-7. Dewey:345.73/01. LCCN:2001-002592.
Audience: **u,f.** *Choice, 2002.*

Labovitz, John R. **KF5075**
Presidential Impeachment. Cloth over Boards. Yale University Press. Cumberland, RI. 1978. 281p. ISBN:0-300-02213-1, ISBN13: 978-0-300-02213-1. Dewey:342/.73/062. LCCN:77-076300.
Audience: **u,f.** B

Mayer, Kenneth R. **KF5053.M39 2001**
With the Stroke of a Pen: Executive Orders and Presidential Power. Cloth Text. Princeton University Press. Princeton, NJ. 2001. 298p. ISBN:0-691-01204-0, ISBN13: 978-0-691-01204-9. Dewey:342.73/062. LCCN:00-064264.
Audience: **l,u.** *Choice, 2001.*

Posner, Richard A. **KF5076.C57P67 1999**
An Affair of State: The Investigation, Impeachment, and Trial of President Clinton. Trade Cloth. Harvard University Press. Cambridge, MA. 1999. 288p. ISBN:0-674-00080-3, ISBN13: 978-0-674-00080-3. Dewey:342.73/062. LCCN:99-024307.
Audience: **g.** *Choice, 2000.*

Stern, Gary M. & Halperin, Morton H. (Editors) **KF5060**
The U. S. Constitution and the Power to Go to War: Historical and Current Perspectives. Trade Cloth. Greenwood Publishing Group, Inc. Portsmouth, NH. 1993. 208p. Contributions in Military Studies, No. 150 ISBN:0-313-28958-1, ISBN13: 978-0-313-28958-3. Dewey:347.30262. LCCN:93-015840.
Audience: **u,f.** *Choice, 1994.*

Sunstein, Cass R. & Epstein, Richard A. (Editors) **KF5074.2.V68 2001**
The Vote: Bush, Gore, and the Supreme Court. Trade Paper. University of Chicago Press. Chicago, IL. 2001. 232p. ISBN:0-226-21307-2, ISBN13: 978-0-226-21307-1. Dewey:324.973/0929. LCCN:2001-037805.
Audience: **u,f.**

Tushnet, Mark (Editor) **KF5060.C58 2005**
The Constitution in Wartime: Beyond Alarmism and Complacency. Trade Cloth. Duke University Press. Durham, NC. 2005. 256p. Constitutional Conflicts Ser. ISBN:0-8223-3456-9, ISBN13: 978-0-8223-3456-9. Dewey:342.730628. LCCN:2004-015809.
Audience: **g.** *Choice, 2005.*

United States > Constitutional Law > The Judiciary. Judicial Power

Agresto, John **KF5130.A93**
The Supreme Court and Constitutional Democracy. Trade Paper. Cornell University Press. Ithaca, NY. 1984. 192p. ISBN:0-8014-9277-7, ISBN13: 978-0-8014-9277-8. Dewey:347.302/52. LCCN:83-045928.
Audience: **u,f.** B

Berger, Raoul **KF4558 14TH.B47 1997**
Government by Judiciary: The Transformation of the Fourteenth Amendment. Ed. 2. Forrest McDonald (Foreword by). Trade Cloth. Liberty Fund, Inc. Indianapolis, IN. 1997. 555p. ISBN:0-86597-143-9, ISBN13: 978-0-86597-143-1. Dewey:342.73/085. LCCN:96-016162.
Audience: **u,f.** B

Bork, Robert H. **KF5130.B59 1991**
The Tempting of America: The Political Seduction of the Law. Trade Paper. Simon & Schuster. New York, NY. 1991. 464p. ISBN:0-671-73014-2, ISBN13: 978-0-671-73014-7. Dewey:347.30712. LCCN:90-019275.
Audience: **g.** *Choice, 1990.*

Burt, Robert A. **KF5130.B87 1992**
The Constitution in Conflict. Trade Cloth. Harvard University Press. Cambridge, MA. 1992. 488p. ISBN:0-674-16536-5, ISBN13: 978-0-674-16536-6. Dewey:347.73/12. LCCN:91-028107.
Audience: **g.** *Choice, 1992.*

Ellis, Richard E. **KF5130 .E44**
The Jeffersonian Crisis: Courts and Politics in the Young Republic. Trade Cloth. Oxford University Press, Inc. New York, NY. 1971. 390p. ISBN:0-19-501390-5, ISBN13: 978-0-19-501390-0. Dewey:320.9/73/046.
Audience: **l,u.** B

Nagal, Robert F. **KF5130.N34 1994**
Judicial Power and American Character: Censoring Ourselves in an Anxious Age. Trade Cloth. Oxford University Press, Inc. New York, NY. 1994. 198p. ISBN:0-19-508901-4, ISBN13: 978-0-19-508901-1. Dewey:347.73/12. LCCN:93-041891.
Audience: **l,u.** *Choice, 1995.*

United States > Local Government

Zimmerman, Joseph F. **KF5300**
State-Local Relations: A Partnership Approach. Ed. 2. Paper Text. Greenwood Publishing Group, Inc. Portsmouth, NH. 1995. 272p. ISBN:0-275-95235-5, ISBN13: 978-0-275-95235-8. Dewey:342.73/042. LCCN:95-002209.
Audience: **u,f.**

United States > Administrative Organization and Procedure

Bryner, Gary C. & Thompson, Dennis L. (Editors) **KF5407.A5C66 1988**
The Constitution and the Regulation of Society. Cloth Text. State University of New York Press. Albany, NY. 1988. 258p. ISBN:0-88706-851-0, ISBN13: 978-0-88706-851-5. Dewey:342.73/02. LCCN:88-000457.
Audience: **l,u.** *Choice, 1989.*

Congressional Quarterly, Inc. **KF5406.A15 F4**
Federal regulatory directory. Ed. 12. Congressional Quarterly, Inc. 2006. ISBN:1-56802-975-6, ISBN13: 978-1-56802-975-7.
Audience: **u,f.**

Harris, Richard A. & Milkis, Sidney M. **KF5407.H37 1996**
The Politics of Regulatory Change: A Tale of Two Agencies. Ed. 2. Paper Text. Oxford University Press, Inc. New York, NY. 1996. 432p. ISBN:0-19-508191-9, ISBN13: 978-0-19-508191-6. Dewey:353/.072/09. LCCN:95-032845.
Audience: **l,u.** *Choice, 1989.*

Kerwin, Cornelius M. **KF5411.K47 2003**
Rulemaking: How Government Agencies Write Law and Make Policy. Ed. 3. Perfect. CQ Press. Washington, DC. 2003. 300p. ISBN:1-56802-780-X, ISBN13: 978-1-56802-780-7. Dewey:342.73066. LCCN:2003-000264.
Audience: **g.**

Robinson, Glen O. **KF5402.R63 1991**
American Bureaucracy: Public Choice and Public Law. Trade Cloth. University of Michigan Press. Chicago, IL. 1991. 256p. ISBN:0-472-10243-5, ISBN13: 978-0-472-10243-3. Dewey:342.73/06. LCCN:91-015395.
Audience: **u,f.** *Choice, 1991.*

United States > Public Property: General Works. Water Resources. Public Land

Archer, Jack H., et al. **KF5627.P83 1994**
The Public Trust Doctrine and the Management of America's Coasts. Donald L. Conners, Kenneth Laurence, Sarah Chapin Columbia & Robert Bowen (Authors), Jan Stevens (Foreword by). Cloth Text. University of Massachusetts Press. Amherst, MA. 1994. 208p. ISBN:0-87023-898-1, ISBN13: 978-0-87023-898-7. Dewey:346.7304/6917. LCCN:93-048759.
Audience: **l,u,f.** *Choice, 1995.*

Bean, Michael J. & Rowland, Melanie J. **KF5640**
The Evolution of National Wildlife Law. Ed. 3. Trade Cloth. Greenwood Publishing Group, Inc. Portsmouth, NH. 1997. 568p. ISBN:0-275-95988-0, ISBN13: 978-0-275-95988-3. Dewey:346.7304/69516. LCCN:97-008860.
Audience: **l,u.**

Czech, Brian, et al. **KF5640.C99 2001**
The Endangered Species Act: History, Conservation Biology and Public Policy. Paul R. Krausman & Center for American Places Staff (Authors). Trade Paper. Johns Hopkins University Press. Baltimore, MD. 2001. 232p. ISBN:0-8018-6504-2, ISBN13: 978-0-8018-6504-6. Dewey:346.7304/69522. LCCN:00-008847.
Audience: **u,f.** *Choice, 2002.*

Donahue, Debra L. **KF5505.A68D66 1998**
Conservation and the Law. Library Binding. ABC-CLIO, Inc. Santa Barbara, CA. 1998. 347p. Contemporary Legal Issues Ser. ISBN:0-87436-771-9, ISBN13: 978-0-87436-771-3. Dewey:346.7304/4/03. LCCN:98-020225.
Audience: **g,l,u.** *Choice, 1999.*

Goldfarb, William **KF5569.G65 1988**
Water Law. Ed. 2. Trade Cloth, Box or Slipcased. Lewis Publishers. Boca Raton, FL. 1988. 304p. ISBN:0-87371-111-4, ISBN13: 978-0-87371-111-1. Dewey:346.7304/691. LCCN:87-035553.
Audience: **l,u.**

MacDonnell, Lawrence J. & Bates, Sarah F. (Editors) **KF5505.N385 1993**
Natural Resources Policy and Law: Trends and Directions. John Firor (Foreword by), Natural Resources Law Center Staff (Other Primary Creator). Trade Cloth. Island Press. Washington, DC. 1993. 255p. ISBN:1-55963-245-3, ISBN13: 978-1-55963-245-4. Dewey:346.73/044. LCCN:93-008388.
Audience: **l,u.**

Petersen, Shannon C. **KF5640.P48 2002**
Acting for Endangered Species: The Statutory Ark. Trade Cloth. University Press of Kansas. Lawrence, KS. 2002. xiv, 168p. Development of Western Resources Ser. ISBN:0-7006-1172-X, ISBN13: 978-0-7006-1172-0. Dewey:346.7304/69522. LCCN:2001-007417.
Audience: **g.** *Choice, 2002.*

Simon, David J. (Editor) **KF5635.O95 1988**
Our Common Lands: Defending the National Parks. Joseph L. Sax (Foreword by). Trade Cloth. Island Press. Washington, DC. 1988. 582p. ISBN:0-933280-58-0, ISBN13: 978-0-933280-58-8. Dewey:346.7304/6783. LCCN:88-016977.
Audience: **l,u.** *Choice, 1989.*

Wilkinson, Charles F. **KF5505.W55 1992**
Crossing the Next Meridian: Land, Water, and the Future of the West. Trade Cloth. Island Press. Washington, DC. 1992. 389p. ISBN:1-55963-150-3, ISBN13: 978-1-55963-150-1. Dewey:346.7804/4. LCCN:92-016869.
Audience: **g.** *Choice, 1993.*

United States > Regional and City Planning. Zoning. Building

Meltz, Robert, et al. **KF5698.M45 1999**
The Takings Issue: Constitutional Limits on Land Use Control and Environmental Regulation. Dwight Merriam & Rick Frank (Authors), Fred Bosselman (Foreword by). Trade Cloth. Island Press. Washington, DC. 1998. 624p. ISBN:1-55963-380-8, ISBN13: 978-1-55963-380-2. Dewey:346.7304/5. LCCN:98-034885.
Audience: **u,f.**

Platt, Rutherford H. **KF5698.P588 2004**
Land Use and Society: Geography, Law, and Public Policy. Ed. 2. Cloth Text. Island Press. Washington, DC. 2004. 488p. ISBN:1-55963-684-X, ISBN13: 978-1-55963-684-1. Dewey:346.7304/5. LCCN:2003-024791.
Audience: **u,f.**

United States > Government Property. Public Records

KF5753.Z9
Your Right to Federal Records: Questions and Answers on the Freedom of Information Act and the Privacy Act. http://www.pueblo.gsa.gov/cic%5Ftext/fed%5Fprog/foia/foia.pdf U.S. Dept. of Justice, GSA Office of Citizen Services and Communications, Federal Citizen Information Center
Audience: **g.**

O'Brien, David M. **KF5753.O24**
The Public's Right to Know: The Supreme Court and the First Amendment. Trade Cloth. Greenwood Publishing Group, Inc. Portsmouth, NH. 1981. x, 205p. ISBN:0-03-058029-3, ISBN13: 978-0-03-058029-1. Dewey:342.73/0853. LCCN:81-000988.
Audience: **g.**

United States > Government Measures in Time of War, National Emergency, or Economic Crisis

Bazyler, Michael J. **KF6075.B39 2003**
Holocaust Justice: The Battle for Restitution in America's Courts. Trade Cloth. New York University Press. New York, NY. 2003. 416p. ISBN:0-8147-9903-5, ISBN13: 978-0-8147-9903-1. Dewey:940.53/18144. LCCN:2002-154298.
Audience: **u,f.** *Choice, 2003.*

United States > Public Finance. Taxation

Conlan, Timothy J., et al. **KF6276.558.A16C66**
Taxing Choices. Margaret T. Wrightson & David R. Beam (Authors). Trade Cloth. Congressional Quarterly, Inc. Washington, DC. 1989. 275p. ISBN:0-87187-480-6, ISBN13: 978-0-87187-480-1. Dewey:343.7304. LCCN:89-017353.
Audience: **g.**

Department of the Treasury Internal Revenue Service **KF6369**
Your Federal Income Tax for Individuals. http://www.irs.gov/pub/irs-pdf/p17.pdf Treasury Dept., Bureau of Internal Revenue.
Audience: **g.**

Jurinski, James John **KF6289.J87 2000**
Tax Reform: A Reference Handbook. Mildred Vasan (Editor). Library Binding. ABC-CLIO, Inc. Santa Barbara, CA. 2000. 0250p. Contemporary World Issues Ser. ISBN:1-57607-157-X, ISBN13: 978-1-57607-157-1. Dewey:343.7304. LCCN:00-010924.
Audience: **g,l.** *Choice, 2001.*

United States > National Defense. Military Law

Fisher, Louis **KF7661.F57 2005**
Military Tribunals and Presidential Power: American Revolution to the War on Terrorism. Trade Paper. University Press of Kansas. Lawrence, KS. 2005. 296p. ISBN:0-7006-1376-5, ISBN13: 978-0-7006-1376-2. Dewey:343.73/0143. LCCN:2004-025521.
Audience: **g.** *Choice, 2005.*

Irons, Peter H. **KF7224.5**
Justice at War: The Story of the Japanese-American Internment Cases. Trade Paper. University of California Press. Berkeley, CA. 1993. 432p. ISBN:0-520-08312-1, ISBN13: 978-0-520-08312-7. LCCN:92-037238.
Audience: **l,u,f.**

Rossiter, Clinton **KF5060**
The Supreme Court and the Commander in Chief. Richard P. Longaker (Editor). Trade Paper. Cornell University Press. Ithaca, NY. 1976. 280p. ISBN:0-8014-9161-4, ISBN13: 978-0-8014-9161-0. Dewey:347.302/62. LCCN:76-012815.
Audience: **l,u.**

United States > Indians

Deloria, Vine Jr. & DeMallie, Raymond J. **KF82021999**
Documents of American Indian Diplomacy: Treaties, Agreements, and Conventions, 1775-1979. Trade Cloth. University of Oklahoma Press. Norman, OK. 1999. 1536p. Legal History of North America Ser., Vol. 4 ISBN:0-8061-3118-7, ISBN13: 978-0-8061-3118-4. Dewey:342.73/0872. LCCN:98-045365.
Audience: **g,u,f.** *Choice, 2000.*

Fine-Dare, Kathleen S. **KF8210.A57F56 2002**
Grave Injustice: The American Indian Repatriation Movement and NAGPRA. Trade Paper. University of Nebraska Press. Lincoln, NE. 2002. 250p. Fourth World Rising Ser. ISBN:0-8032-6908-0, ISBN13: 978-0-8032-6908-8. Dewey:323.1/197073/09. LCCN:2002-020016.
Audience: **g,u,f.** *Choice, 2003.*

Grossman, Mark & ABC-CLIO Inc. Staff, Inc **KF8203.36.G76 1996**
The Native American Rights Movement. Library Binding. ABC-CLIO, Inc. Santa Barbara, CA. 1996. 498p. Clio Companions Ser. ISBN:0-87436-822-7, ISBN13: 978-0-87436-822-2. Dewey:342.73/0872. LCCN:96-036782.
Audience: **g,l,u.** *Choice, 1997.*

Harring, Sidney L. **KF8205 .H37 1994**
Crow Dog's Case: American Indian Sovereignty, Tribal Law, and United States Law in the Nineteenth Century. Frederick Hoxie & Neal Salisbury (Contribution by). Trade Paper. Cambridge University Press. New York, NY. 1994. 317p. Cambridge Studies in North American Indian History ISBN:0-521-46715-2, ISBN13: 978-0-521-46715-5. Dewey:347.30613.
Audience: **u,f.** *Choice, 1994.*

Johansen, Bruce E. (Editor) **KF8204**
The Encyclopedia of Native American Legal Tradition. Charles

R. Cloud (Foreword by). Cloth Text. Greenwood Publishing Group, Inc. Portsmouth, NH. 1998. 424p. ISBN:0-313-30167-0, ISBN13: 978-0-313-30167-4. Dewey:346.7301/3. LCCN:97-021994.
Audience: **g,u,f.** *Choice, 1998.*

Kappler, Charles J. (Editor) **KF8203**
☐ Indian Affairs: Laws and Treaties. http://digital.library.okstate.edu/Kappler/ Oklahoma State University Library.
Audience: **u,f.**

Mason, W. Dale **E78.N65**
Indian Gaming: Tribal Sovereignty and American Politics. Trade Paper. University of Oklahoma Press. Norman, OK. 2000. 320p. ISBN:0-8061-3260-4, ISBN13: 978-0-8061-3260-0. Dewey:795/.089/97.
Audience: **g,u,f.**

Norgren, Jill **KF8208.N67 2004**
The Cherokee Cases: Two Landmark Federal Decisions in the Fight for Sovereignty. Trade Paper. University of Oklahoma Press. Norman, OK. 2004. 224p. ISBN:0-8061-3606-5, ISBN13: 978-0-8061-3606-6. Dewey:346.7304/32/08997557. LCCN:2003-063412.
Audience: **u,f.**

Olson, James S. (Editor) **KF8210**
Encyclopedia of American Indian Civil Rights. Mark M. Baxter, Jason M. Tetzloff & Darren Pierson (Editor-In-Chiefs). Cloth Text. Greenwood Publishing Group, Inc. Portsmouth, NH. 1997. 448p. ISBN:0-313-29338-4, ISBN13: 978-0-313-29338-2. Dewey:323.1/197073/03. LCCN:96-035352.
Audience: **g.** *Choice, 1998.*

Pevar, Stephen L. **KF8210.C5**
The Rights of Indians and Tribes: The Authoritative ACLU Guide to Indian and Tribal Rights, Third Edition. Ed. 3. Trade Paper. New York University Press. New York, NY. 2004. 448p. ISBN:0-8147-6718-4, ISBN13: 978-0-8147-6718-4. Dewey:342.73087.
Audience: **g,l,u,f.**

Prucha, Francis P. **JX235.9**
American Indian Treaties: The History of a Political Anomaly. Trade Paper. University of California Press. Berkeley, CA. 1997. 578p. ISBN:0-520-20895-1, ISBN13: 978-0-520-20895-7. Dewey:341/.026673. LCCN:93-036297.
Audience: **g,l,u,f.** *Choice, 1995.*

Strickland, Rennard F. & Wilkinson, Charles F. (Editors) **KF8205.C6 1982**
Felix S. Cohen's Handbook of Federal Indian Law. Trade Cloth, Mixed Media, Book, Other. LEXIS Publishing. Charlottesville, VA. 1982. 950p. ISBN:0-87215-413-0, ISBN13: 978-0-87215-413-1. Dewey:342.73/0872. LCCN:81-086229.
Audience: **u,f.**

Washburn, Wilcomb E. **KF8205.W38 1995**
Red Man's Land/White Man's Law: The Past and Present Status of the American Indian. Ed. 2. Trade Paper. University of Oklahoma Press. Norman, OK. 1995. 320p. ISBN:0-8061-2740-6, ISBN13: 978-0-8061-2740-8. Dewey:346.7301/3. LCCN:94-038444.
Audience: **g,u,f.**

Wilkins, David E. **KF8205.W527 1997**
American Indian Sovereignty and the U. S. Supreme Court: The Masking of Justice. Trade Paper. University of Texas Press. Austin, TX. 1997. 421p. ISBN:0-292-79109-7, ISBN13: 978-0-292-79109-1. Dewey:342.73/0872. LCCN:97-001988.
Audience: **u,f.** *Choice, 1998.*

Wilkinson, Charles F. **KF8205.W53 1987**
American Indians, Time and the Law: Historical Rights at the Bar of the Supreme Court. Trade Cloth. Yale University Press. Cumberland, RI. 1987. 256p. ISBN:0-300-03589-6, ISBN13: 978-0-300-03589-6. Dewey:342.73/0872. LCCN:86-009164.
Audience: **u,f.** *Choice, 1987.*

Wunder, John R. **KF8205**
Retained by the People: A History of American Indians and the Bill of Rights. New York :; Oxford University Press. 1994. Bicentennial essays on the Bill of Rights ISBN:0-19-505562-4, ISBN13: 978-0-19-505562-7.
Audience: **u,f.**

United States > Courts. Procedure

Canon, Bradley C. & Johnson, Charles A. **KF8700.J63 1999**
Judicial Policies: Implementation and Impact. Ed. 2. Trade Paper. CQ Press. Washington, DC. 1998. 200p. ISBN:1-56802-306-5, ISBN13: 978-1-56802-306-9. Dewey:347.73. LCCN:98-034687.
Audience: **u,f.**

Carp, Robert A. & Stidham, Ronald **KF8719.C33 2001**
The Federal Courts. Ed. 4. Trade Paper. CQ Press. Washington, DC. 2001. xiv, 258p. ISBN:1-56802-591-2, ISBN13: 978-1-56802-591-9. Dewey:347.73/2. LCCN:2001-023139.
Audience: **g,l.** *Choice, 1986.*

Goldfarb, Ronald **KF8725.G65 1998**
TV or Not TV: Television, Justice, and the Courts. Trade Cloth. New York University Press. New York, NY. 1998. 238p. ISBN:0-8147-3112-0, ISBN13: 978-0-8147-3112-3. Dewey:347.7/3/5. LCCN:97-045289.
Audience: **l,u,f.** *Choice, 1998.*

Kairys, David & Cramer, Rene (Editors) **KF8700.P65 1998**
The Politics of Law: A Progressive Critique. Ed. 3. Trade Paper. Basic Books. New York, NY. 1998. 752p. ISBN:0-465-05959-7, ISBN13: 978-0-465-05959-1. Dewey:349.73. LCCN:97-046000.
Audience: **u.**

Karlen, Delmar **KF8720**
Citizen in Court: Litigant, Witness, Juror, Judge. Paper Text. Da Capo Press, Inc. Cambridge, MA. 1974. 211p. American Constitutional and Legal History Ser ISBN:0-306-70614-8, ISBN13: 978-0-306-70614-1. Dewey:347/.73/5. LCCN:73-019739.
Audience: **g.**

Murphy, Walter F., et al. **KF8700.A7C67 2006**
Courts, Judges, and Politics. Ed. 6. C. Herman Pritchett, Lee Epstein & Jack Knight (Authors). Paper Text. McGraw-Hill

Higher Education. Burr Ridge, IL. 2005. 816p. ISBN:0-07-297705-1, ISBN13: 978-0-07-297705-9. Dewey:347.73/1. LCCN:2005-041570.
Audience: **l,u.**

United States > Courts. Procedure > Supreme Court > History

Abraham, Henry J. **KF8742.A72 1999**
Justices, Presidents and Senators: A History of the U. S. Supreme Court Appointments from Washington to Clinton. Ed. 4. Book, Other. Rowman & Littlefield Publishers, Inc. Lanham, MD. 1999. 448p. ISBN:0-8476-9604-9, ISBN13: 978-0-8476-9604-8. Dewey:347.73/2634. LCCN:99-023000.
Audience: **g.** *Choice, 2000.*

Cooper, Phillip J. **KF8742.C66 1995**
Battles on the Bench: Conflict Inside the Supreme Court. Trade Cloth. University Press of Kansas. Lawrence, KS. 1999. xii, 288p. ISBN:0-7006-0737-4, ISBN13: 978-0-7006-0737-2. Dewey:347.73/26. LCCN:95-031618.
Audience: **l,u.** *Choice, 1996.*

Garraty, John A. **KF8742.A5**
Quarrels That Have Shaped the Constitution. Trade Paper. HarperCollins Publishers. New York, NY. 1989. 400p. ISBN:0-06-132084-6, ISBN13: 978-0-06-132084-2. Dewey:342.7302/9.
Audience: **g.**

Hall, Kermit, et al. **KF8742.A35O93 2005**
The Oxford Companion to the Supreme Court of the United States. Ed. 2. James W. Ely & Joel B. Grossman (Authors). Trade Cloth. Oxford University Press, Inc. New York, NY. 2005. 1272p. ISBN:0-19-517661-8, ISBN13: 978-0-19-517661-2. Dewey:347.73/26/03. LCCN:2004-029463.
Audience: **g.** *Choice, 2005.*

Leuchtenburg, William E. **KF8742.L48 1995**
The Supreme Court Reborn: Constitutional Revolution in the Age of Roosevelt. Trade Cloth. Oxford University Press, Inc. New York, NY. 1995. 368p. ISBN:0-19-508613-9, ISBN13: 978-0-19-508613-3. Dewey:347.73/26/09. LCCN:94-011840.
Audience: **g.** *Choice, 1995.*

Martin, Fenton S. & Goehlert, Robert **KF8741.A1.M36 1992**
How to Research the Supreme Court. Cloth Text. Congressional Quarterly, Inc. Washington, DC. 1992. 140p. ISBN:0-87187-697-3, ISBN13: 978-0-87187-697-3. Dewey:016.34773/26. LCCN:91-046903.
Audience: **g,l,u.** *Choice, 1992.*

McCloskey, Robert G. **KF8742.M296 2005**
The American Supreme Court. Ed. 4. Sanford Levinson (Revised by). Trade Cloth. University of Chicago Press. Chicago, IL. 2004. 344p. The Chicago History of American Civilization Ser. ISBN:0-226-55681-6, ISBN13: 978-0-226-55681-9. Dewey:347.73/26. LCCN:2004-009456.
Audience: **u,f.**

O'Brien, David M. **KF8742.O27 2005**
Storm Center: The Supreme Court in American Politics. Ed. 7. Trade Paper. W. W. Norton & Company, Inc. New York, NY. 2005. xxi, 439p. ISBN:0-393-92704-0, ISBN13: 978-0-393-92704-7. Dewey:347.73/26. LCCN:2004-063647.
Audience: **l,u.** *Choice, 1986.*

O'Connor, Sandra Day **KF8742.O274 2003**
The Majesty of the Law: Reflections of a Supreme Court Justice. Trade Cloth. Random House, Inc. New York, NY. 2003. 352p. ISBN:0-375-50925-9, ISBN13: 978-0-375-50925-4. Dewey:347.73/26. LCCN:2002-068210.
Audience: **g.** *Choice, 2003.*

Perry, Barbara A. **KF8742**
The Priestly Tribe: The Supreme Court's Image in the American Mind. Abner J. Mikva (Foreword by). Trade Cloth. Greenwood Publishing Group, Inc. Portsmouth, NH. 1999. 184p. ISBN:0-275-96598-8, ISBN13: 978-0-275-96598-3. Dewey:347.73/26. LCCN:99-013438.
Audience: **u,f.** *Choice, 2000.*

Perry, H. W. **KF8742.P3365 1991**
Deciding to Decide: Agenda Setting in the United States Supreme Court. Trade Cloth. Harvard University Press. Cambridge, MA. 1992. 326p. ISBN:0-674-19442-X, ISBN13: 978-0-674-19442-7. Dewey:347.73/26. LCCN:91-014002.
Audience: **g.** *Choice, 1992.*

Rehnquist, William H. **KF8742.R47 2001**
The Supreme Court: A New Edition of the Chief Justice's Classic History. Trade Cloth. Alfred A. Knopf Inc. New York, NY. 2001. 320p. ISBN:0-375-40943-2, ISBN13: 978-0-375-40943-1. Dewey:347.73/26/09. LCCN:00-044362.
Audience: **g.** *Choice, 2001.*

Savage, David G. & Biskupic, Joan **KF8742.W567 2004**
Guide to the U.S. Supreme Court. Ed. 4. Trade Cloth. CQ Press. Washington, DC. 2004. xii, 1272p. ISBN:1-56802-744-3, ISBN13: 978-1-56802-744-9. Dewey:347.73/26. LCCN:2004-001572.
Audience: **g,l,u,f.** *Choice, 2004.*

Schwartz, Bernard **KF8742**
Decision: How the Supreme Court Decides Cases. Trade Paper. Oxford University Press, Inc. New York, NY. 1997. 288p. ISBN:0-19-511800-6, ISBN13: 978-0-19-511800-1. Dewey:347.3/0735/2. LCCN:98-106278.
Audience: **g.** *Choice, 1996.*

Schwartz, Bernard **KF8742**
A History of the Supreme Court. Trade Paper. Oxford University Press, Inc. New York, NY. 1995. 480p. ISBN:0-19-509387-9, ISBN13: 978-0-19-509387-2. Dewey:347.732609. LCCN:92-044097.
Audience: **g.**

Segal, Jeffrey A. & Spaeth, Harold J. **KF8742.S43 2002**
The Supreme Court and the Attitudinal Model Revisited. Trade Cloth. Cambridge University Press. New York, NY. 2002. 480p. ISBN:0-521-78351-8, ISBN13: 978-0-521-78351-4. Dewey:347.73/26. LCCN:2001-052978.
Audience: **u,f.** *Choice, 2003.*

Semonche, John E. **KF8742.S444 1998**
Keeping the Faith: A Cultural History of the U. S. Supreme Court. Trade Cloth. Rowman & Littlefield Publishers, Inc. Lanham, MD. 1998. 499p. ISBN:0-8476-8985-9, ISBN13: 978-0-8476-8985-9. Dewey:347.73/26. LCCN:97-032481.
Audience: **g.** *Choice, 1998.*

Yarbrough, Tinsley E. **KF8742.Y37 2000**
The Rehnquist Court and the Constitution. Trade Cloth. Oxford University Press, Inc. New York, NY. 2000. 320p. ISBN:0-19-510346-7, ISBN13: 978-0-19-510346-5. Dewey:347.73/26. LCCN:99-018538.
Audience: **g.** *Choice, 2000.*

United States > Courts. Procedure > Supreme Court > Biography

☐ Judges of the United States Courts Biographical Directory of Federal Judges.
http://air.fjc.gov/public/home.nsf/hisj
Federal Judicial Center.
Audience: **l,u,f.**

Baker, Leonard **KF8745.M3.B3**
John Marshall: A Life in Law. Trade Cloth. Macmillan Publishing Company, Inc. Old Tappan, NJ. 1974. x, 845p. ISBN:0-02-506360-X, ISBN13: 978-0-02-506360-0. Dewey:347/.73/2634. LCCN:73-002751.
Audience: **g.**

Ball, Howard **KF8745.B55B298 1996**
Hugo L. Black: Cold Steel Warrior. Trade Cloth. Oxford University Press, Inc. New York, NY. 1996. 328p. ISBN:0-19-507814-4, ISBN13: 978-0-19-507814-5. Dewey:347.73/2634 B. LCCN:95-014107.
Audience: **g.** *Choice, 1997.*

Ball, Howard & Cooper, Phillip J. **KF8744**
Of Power and Right: Hugo Black, William O. Douglas and America's Constitutional Revolution. Trade Cloth. Replica Books. Bridgewater, NJ. 2000. 382p. ISBN:0-7351-0282-1, ISBN13: 978-0-7351-0282-8. Dewey:347.73/2634.
Audience: **u,f.**

Beth, Loren P. **KF8745.H3.B47 1992**
John Marshall Harlan: The Last Whig Justice. Library Binding. University Press of Kentucky. Lexington, KY. 1992. 328p. ISBN:0-8131-1778-X, ISBN13: 978-0-8131-1778-2. Dewey:347.73/2634. LCCN:91-036140.
Audience: **u,f.** *Choice, 1992.*

Bland, Randall W. **KF8745.M34**
Private Pressure on Public Law: The Legal Career of Justice Thurgood Marshall, 1934-1991. Trade Paper. University Press of America, Inc. Lanham, MD. 1993. 250p. ISBN:0-8191-8736-4, ISBN13: 978-0-8191-8736-9. Dewey:347.73/2634. LCCN:92-034835.
Audience: **g.**

Bowen, Catherine D. **KF8745.H6 B65**
Yankee from Olympus: Justice Holmes and His Family. Library Binding. Buccaneer Books, Inc. Cutchogue, NY. 1989. 455p. ISBN:0-89966-636-1, ISBN13: 978-0-89966-636-5. Dewey:923.473.
Audience: **g.**

Bradley, Craig (Editor) **KF8745**
The Rehnquist Legacy. Trade Cloth. Cambridge University Press. New York, NY. 2005. 414p. ISBN:0-521-85919-0, ISBN13: 978-0-521-85919-6. Dewey:347.732634092. LCCN:2006-272892.
Audience: **u,f.** *Choice, 2006.*

Brisbin, Richard A. Jr. **KF8745.S33B75 1997**
Justice Antonin Scalia and the Conservative Revival. Trade Cloth. Johns Hopkins University Press. Baltimore, MD. 1996. 488p. ISBN:0-8018-5432-6, ISBN13: 978-0-8018-5432-3. Dewey:347.30735. LCCN:96-022883.
Audience: **u,f.** *Choice, 1997.*

Cushman, Claire (Editor) **KF8744.S86 1995**
The Supreme Court Justices: Illustrated Biographies, 1789-1995. Ed. 2. Cloth Text. Congressional Quarterly, Inc. Washington, DC. 1996. 588p. ISBN:1-56802-127-5, ISBN13: 978-1-56802-127-0. Dewey:347.73/2634 B. LCCN:93-001446.
Audience: **u,f.**

Douglas, William O. **KF8745.D6A43 2000**
Nature's Justice: Writings of William O. Douglas. James M. O'Fallon (Editor). Trade Cloth. Oregon State University Press. Corvallis, OR. 2000. x, 310p. Northwest Readers Ser. ISBN:0-87071-482-1, ISBN13: 978-0-87071-482-5. Dewey:347.73/2634. LCCN:00-009322.
Audience: **g.** *Choice, 2001.*

Ely, James W. **KF8745.F8E44 1995**
The Chief Justiceship of Melville W. Fuller, 1888-1910. Cloth Text. University of South Carolina Press. Columbia, SC. 1995. 250p. ISBN:1-57003-018-9, ISBN13: 978-1-57003-018-5. Dewey:347.73/2634 B. LCCN:94-018691.
Audience: **u,f.** *Choice, 1995.*

Frankfurter, Felix **KF8745.F7 P45**
Felix Frankfurter Reminisces. Paper Text. Textbook Publishers. Temecula, CA. 2003. 310p. ISBN:0-7581-4883-6, ISBN13: 978-0-7581-4883-4. Dewey:347/.73/2634.
Audience: **u,f.**

Friedman, Leon & Israel, Fred L. (Editors) **KF8744.F75 1995**
The Justices of the United States Supreme Court, 1789-1995: Their Lives and Major Opinions. Benno C. Schmidt (Preface by). Trade Paper. Chelsea House Publishers. Langhorne, PA. 1995. ISBN:0-7910-3225-6, ISBN13: 978-0-7910-3225-1. Dewey:347.73/2634 B. LCCN:94-004171.
Audience: **l,u.**

Gerber, Scott D. **KF8745.T48G47 1998**
First Principles: The Jurisprudence of Clarence Thomas. Trade Cloth. New York University Press. New York, NY. 1998. 281p. ISBN:0-8147-3099-X, ISBN13: 978-0-8147-3099-7. Dewey:347.73/2634. LCCN:98-025524.
Audience: **u,f.** *Choice, 1999.*

Greenhouse, Linda **KF8745.B555G74 2005**
Becoming Justice Blackmun: Harry Blackmun's Supreme Court Journey. Trade Cloth. Henry Holt & Company. New York, NY. 2005. 288p. ISBN:0-8050-7791-X, ISBN13: 978-0-8050-7791-9. Dewey:347.73/2634. LCCN:2004-063772.
Audience: **g.**

Hirsch, H. N. **KF8745.F7.H57**
The Enigma of Felix Frankfurter. Cloth Text. Basic Books. New York, NY. 1981. 320p. ISBN:0-465-01979-X, ISBN13: 978-0-465-01979-3. Dewey:347.73/2634. LCCN:80-068184.
Audience: **g.**

Hobson, Charles F. **KF8745.M3H63 1996**
The Great Chief Justice: John Marshall and the Rule of Law. Paper Text. University Press of Kansas. Lawrence, KS. 1996.

xvi, 256p. American Political Thought Ser.
ISBN:0-7006-0788-9, ISBN13: 978-0-7006-0788-4.
Dewey:347.73/2634 B. LCCN:96-011195.
Audience: **g.** *Choice, 1997.*

Holmes, Justice **KF8745.H6 A434**
Holmes-Pollock Letters: The Correspondence of Mr. Justice Holmes and Sir Frederick Pollock, 1874-1932. Trade Cloth. Harvard University Press. Cambridge, MA. 2002. 686p.
ISBN:0-674-40550-1, ISBN13: 978-0-674-40550-9.
Dewey:347.732634.
Audience: **g.**

Howard, J. Woodford Jr. **KF8745.M8 H6**
Mr. Justice Murphy: A Political Biography. Trade Cloth. Princeton University Press. Princeton, NJ. 1968. 590p.
ISBN:0-691-09213-3, ISBN13: 978-0-691-09213-3.
Dewey:347.99/73. LCCN:68-011444.
Audience: **l,u.**

Howe, Mark D. (Editor) **KF8745.H6 A453**
Holmes-Laski Letters, the Correspondence of Justice Oliver Wendell Holmes and Harold J. Laski, 1916-1935, 2. Trade Cloth. Simon & Schuster. New York, NY. 1963.
ISBN:0-689-70098-9, ISBN13: 978-0-689-70098-9. Dewey:923.
LCCN:63-024385.
Audience: **l,u.**

Howe, Mark D. **KF8745.H6 H65**
Justice Oliver Wendell Holmes: The Shaping Years, 1841-1870. Trade Cloth. Harvard University Press. Cambridge, MA. 1957. 344p. ISBN:0-674-49500-4, ISBN13: 978-0-674-49500-5.
Dewey:923.473.
Audience: **g.**

Howe, Mark D. **KF8745.H6 H65**
Justice Oliver Wendell Holmes: The Proving Years, 1870-1882. Trade Cloth. Harvard University Press. Cambridge, MA. 1963.
ISBN:0-674-49501-2, ISBN13: 978-0-674-49501-2.
Dewey:923.473.
Audience: **g.**

Hutchinson, Dennis J. **KF8745.W48H88 1998**
The Man Who Once Was Whizzer White. Trade Cloth. Simon & Schuster. New York, NY. 1998. 592p. ISBN:0-684-82794-8, ISBN13: 978-0-684-82794-0. Dewey:347.73/2634 B.
LCCN:97-047302.
Audience: **g.**

Jeffries, John C. Jr. **KF8745.P69J44 2001**
Justice Lewis F. Powell, Jr. Trade Cloth. Fordham University Press. Bronx, NY. 2001. 690p. ISBN:0-8232-2109-1, ISBN13: 978-0-8232-2109-7. Dewey:347.73/2634 B. LCCN:00-050383.
Audience: **g.**

Kalman, Laura **KF8745.F65K35 1990**
Abe Fortas: A Biography. Cloth over Boards. Yale University Press. Cumberland, RI. 1990. 544p. ISBN:0-300-04669-3, ISBN13: 978-0-300-04669-4. Dewey:347.73/2634 B.
LCCN:90-031482.
Audience: **u,f.** *Choice, 1991.*

Kaufman, Andrew L. **KF8745.C3K38 1998**
Cardozo. Trade Cloth. Harvard University Press. Cambridge, MA. 1998. 744p. ISBN:0-674-09645-2, ISBN13: 978-0-674-09645-5. Dewey:[B]. LCCN:97-029729.
Audience: **g.** *Choice, 1998.*

Maltz, Earl M. **KF8745.B76M35 2000**
Chief Justiceship of Warren Burger, 1969-1986: A Provocative Interpretation of the Burger Court. Trade Cloth. University of South Carolina Press. Columbia, SC. 2000. xvi, 307p. Chief Justiceships of the United States Supreme Court Ser.
ISBN:1-57003-335-8, ISBN13: 978-1-57003-335-3.
Dewey:347.73/2634. LCCN:00-008049.
Audience: **u,f.** *Choice, 2000.*

Mason, Alpheus T. **E762**
William Howard Taft: Chief Justice. Trade Paper. University Press of America, Inc. Lanham, MD. 1983. 354p.
ISBN:0-8191-3091-5, ISBN13: 978-0-8191-3091-4.
Dewey:973.91/2/0924. LCCN:83-006461.
Audience: **g.**

Maveety, Nancy **KF8745.O25M38 1996**
Justice Sandra Day O'Connor: Strategist on the Supreme Court. Trade Cloth. Rowman & Littlefield Publishers, Inc. Lanham, MD. 2002. 160p. Studies in American Constitutionalism
ISBN:0-8476-8194-7, ISBN13: 978-0-8476-8194-5.
Dewey:347.73/2634. LCCN:95-052533.
Audience: **g.**

McClellan, James **KF8745.S83M34 1990**
Joseph Story and the American Constitution: A Study in Political and Legal Thought. Stephen B. Presser (Foreword by). Trade Cloth. University of Oklahoma Press. Norman, OK. 1990. 448p. ISBN:0-8061-0971-8, ISBN13: 978-0-8061-0971-8.
Dewey:342.73/0092. LCCN:75-160499.
Audience: **u,f.**

Murphy, Bruce A. **KF8744.M87**
The Brandeis-Frankfurter Connection: The Secret Political Activities of Two Supreme Court Justices. Trade Cloth. Oxford University Press, Inc. New York, NY. 1982. 473p.
ISBN:0-19-503122-9, ISBN13: 978-0-19-503122-5.
Dewey:347.73/2634. LCCN:82-002104.
Audience: **g.**

Murphy, Bruce Allen **KF8745.D6M87 2002**
Wild Bill: The Legend and Life of William O. Douglas. Trade Cloth. Random House, Inc. New York, NY. 2003. 736p.
ISBN:0-394-57628-4, ISBN13: 978-0-394-57628-2.
Dewey:347.73/2634 B. LCCN:2002-023114.
Audience: **g.** *Choice, 2003.*

Newman, Roger K. **KF8745.B55N49 1994**
Hugo Black: A Biography. Trade Cloth. Knopf Publishing Group. New York, NY. 1994. 944p. ISBN:0-679-43180-2, ISBN13: 978-0-679-43180-0. Dewey:347.73/2634 B.
LCCN:94-010233.
Audience: **u,f.** *Choice, 1995.*

Newmyer, R. Kent **KF8745.M3N49 2001**
John Marshall and the Heroic Age of the Supreme Court. Trade Cloth. Louisiana State University Press. Baton Rouge, LA. 2001. 568p. Southern Biography Ser. ISBN:0-8071-2701-9, ISBN13: 978-0-8071-2701-8. Dewey:347.73/2634 B.
LCCN:2001-001766.
Audience: **u,f.** *Choice, 2002.*

Newmyer, R. Kent **KF8745.S83N48**
Supreme Court Justice Joseph Story: Statesman of the Old Republic. Trade Paper. University of North Carolina Press.

Chapel Hill, NC. 1986. 512p. Studies in Legal History ISBN:0-8078-4164-1, ISBN13: 978-0-8078-4164-8. Dewey:347.73/2634 B. LCCN:84-011886.
Audience: **g.**

Novick, Sheldon M. **KF8745.H6N69 1989**
Honorable Justice: The Life of Oliver Wendell Holmes. Trade Cloth. Aspen Publishers, Inc. New York, NY. 1989. 512p. ISBN:0-316-61325-8, ISBN13: 978-0-316-61325-5. Dewey:347.73/2634 B. LCCN:89-031651.
Audience: **g.** *Choice, 1990.*

Pollack, Jack **KF8745.W3.P64**
Earl Warren: The Judge Who Changed America. Trade Cloth. Prentice-Hall. Upper Saddle, NJ. 1979. viii, 386p. ISBN:0-13-222315-5, ISBN13: 978-0-13-222315-7. Dewey:347/.73/2634. LCCN:78-024234.
Audience: **l,u.**

Pratt, Walter F. **KF8742.P73 1999**
The Supreme Court under Chief Justice Edward Douglass White, 1910-1921. Trade Cloth. University of South Carolina Press. Columbia, SC. 1999. 352p. Chief Justiceships of the United States Supreme Court Ser. ISBN:1-57003-309-9, ISBN13: 978-1-57003-309-4. Dewey:347.73/26/09. LCCN:99-006156.
Audience: **u,f.** *Choice, 2000.*

Rosenkranz, E. Joshua & Schwartz, Bernard (Editors) **KF8745.B68R43 1997**
Reason and Passion: Justice Brennan's Enduring Influence. Trade Cloth. W. W. Norton & Company, Inc. New York, NY. 1997. 320p. ISBN:0-393-04110-7, ISBN13: 978-0-393-04110-1. Dewey:347.73/2634 B. LCCN:96-043133.
Audience: **g.** *Choice, 1998.*

Ross, Michael A. **KF8745.M5R67 2003**
Justice of Shattered Dreams: Samuel Freeman Miller and the Supreme Court During the Civil War Era. Trade Cloth. Louisiana State University Press. Baton Rouge, LA. 2004. 360p. Conflicting Worlds Ser. ISBN:0-8071-2868-6, ISBN13: 978-0-8071-2868-8. Dewey:347.73/26. LCCN:2003-002069.
Audience: **g.** *Choice, 2004.*

Schwartz, Bernard **KF8745.W3**
Super Chief: Earl Warren and His Supreme Court, A Judicial Biography. Trade Cloth. New York University Press. New York, NY. 1983. 864p. ISBN:0-8147-7825-9, ISBN13: 978-0-8147-7825-8. Dewey:347.307/2634/0924. LCCN:82-018868.
Audience: **g.**

Simon, James F. **KF8744.S563 1989**
The Antagonists: Hugo Black, Felix Frankfurter and Civil Liberties in Modern America. Trade Cloth. Simon & Schuster. New York, NY. 1989. 312p. ISBN:0-671-47797-8, ISBN13: 978-0-671-47797-4. Dewey:347.73/2634 B. LCCN:89-035485.
Audience: **g,l,u,f.**

Smith, Jean E. **KF8745.M3S63 1996**
John Marshall: Definer of a Nation. Cloth over Boards. Henry Holt & Company. New York, NY. 1996. 752p. ISBN:0-8050-1389-X, ISBN13: 978-0-8050-1389-4. Dewey:347.73/2634 B. LCCN:96-015072.
Audience: **g.**

Strum, Philippa **KF8745.B67**
Louis D. Brandeis: Justice for the People. Trade Cloth. Harvard University Press. Cambridge, MA. 1984. 536p. ISBN:0-674-53921-4, ISBN13: 978-0-674-53921-1. Dewey:347.307/2634/0924. LCCN:83-018653.
Audience: **g.**

Swisher, Carl B. **KF8745.F5**
Stephen J. Field: Craftsman of the Law. Robert G. McCloskey (Introduction by). Paper Text. University of Chicago Press. Chicago, IL. 1969. Court and the Constitution Ser. ISBN:0-226-78747-8, ISBN13: 978-0-226-78747-3. Dewey:923.473.
Audience: **g.**

Tushnet, Mark V. **KF8745.M34T87 1997**
Making Constitutional Law: Thurgood Marshall and the Supreme Court, 1961-1991. Trade Cloth. Oxford University Press, Inc. New York, NY. 1997. 256p. ISBN:0-19-509314-3, ISBN13: 978-0-19-509314-8. Dewey:342.7/3/0092. LCCN:96-025548.
Audience: **l,u.** *Choice, 1997.*

Urofsky, Melvin I. **KF8742.U76 1997**
Division and Discord: The Supreme Court under Stone and Vinson, 1941-1953. Cloth Text. University of South Carolina Press. Columbia, SC. 1997. 350p. Chief Justiceships of the United States Supreme Court Ser. ISBN:1-57003-120-7, ISBN13: 978-1-57003-120-5. Dewey:347.30735. LCCN:96-025392.
Audience: **l,u.** *Choice, 1997.*

Urofsky, Melvin I. & Levy, David W. (Editors) **KF8745.B67A44 1991**
Half Brother, Half Son: The Letters of Louis D. Brandeis to Felix Frankfurter. Trade Cloth. University of Oklahoma Press. Norman, OK. 1991. 736p. ISBN:0-8061-2303-6, ISBN13: 978-0-8061-2303-5. Dewey:347.73/14/092. LCCN:90-049279.
Audience: **l,u.** *Choice, 1991.*

Warren, Earl **KF8754**
The Memoirs of Chief Justice Earl Warren. Trade Paper. Madison Books, Inc. New York, NY. 2001. 432p. ISBN:1-56833-234-3, ISBN13: 978-1-56833-234-5. Dewey:347.7322.
Audience: **g.**

White, G. Edward **KF8744.W5 1988**
The American Judicial Tradition: Profiles of Leading American Judges. Trade Paper. Oxford University Press, Inc. New York, NY. 1988. 576p. ISBN:0-19-505685-X, ISBN13: 978-0-19-505685-3. Dewey:347.73/2634. LCCN:88-017914.
Audience: **u,f.**

White, G. Edward **KF8745.M34**
Earl Warren: A Public Life. Trade Paper. Oxford University Press, Inc. New York, NY. 1987. 440p. ISBN:0-19-504936-5, ISBN13: 978-0-19-504936-7. Dewey:347.73/2634.
Audience: **g.**

Williams, Juan **KF8745.M34W55 1998**
Thurgood Marshall: American Revolutionary. Trade Cloth. Crown Publishing Group. New York, NY. 1998. 480p. ISBN:0-8129-2028-7, ISBN13: 978-0-8129-2028-4. Dewey:347.73/2634 B. LCCN:98-009735.
Audience: **g.** *Choice, 1999.*

United States > Courts. Procedure > Supreme Court > Criticism

Blasi, Vincent **KF8742**
The Burger Court: The Counter-Revolution That Wasn't. Anthony Lewis (Foreword by). Trade Cloth. Yale University Press. Cumberland, RI. 1983. 320p. ISBN:0-300-02941-1, ISBN13: 978-0-300-02941-3. Dewey:347.307/26/09. LCCN:83-005828.
Audience: **g.**

Faille, Christopher C. **KF8748**
The Decline and Fall of the Supreme Court: Living Out the Nightmare of the Federalists. William C. Olson (Foreword by). Trade Cloth. Greenwood Publishing Group, Inc. Portsmouth, NH. 1995. 224p. ISBN:0-275-94826-9, ISBN13: 978-0-275-94826-9. Dewey:347.73/2634. LCCN:94-013733.
Audience: **u,f.** *Choice, 1995.*

Frankfurter, Felix & Landis, James M. **KF8742**
The Business of the Supreme Court: A Study in the Federal Judicial System. Trade Cloth. Gaunt, Inc. Holmes Beach, FL. 1993. 362p. ISBN:1-56169-025-2, ISBN13: 978-1-56169-025-1. Dewey:347.73/26. LCCN:92-075951.
Audience: **u,f.**

Irons, Peter **KF8748.I76 1994**
Brennan vs. Rehnquist: The Battle for the Constitution. Trade Cloth. Alfred A. Knopf Inc. New York, NY. 1994. 400p. ISBN:0-679-42436-9, ISBN13: 978-0-679-42436-9. Dewey:342.73. LCCN:94-007708.
Audience: **g.** *Choice, 1995.*

Kahn, Ronald **KF8748.K38 1994**
The Supreme Court and Constitutional Theory, 1953-1993. Trade Cloth. University Press of Kansas. Lawrence, KS. 1995. 326p. ISBN:0-7006-0666-1, ISBN13: 978-0-7006-0666-5. Dewey:347.73/26. LCCN:93-039805.
Audience: **u,f.** *Choice, 1994.*

Keck, Thomas M. **KF8748.K43 2004**
The Most Activist Supreme Court in History: The Road to Modern Judicial Conservatism. Trade Paper. University of Chicago Press. Chicago, IL. 2004. 370p. ISBN:0-226-42885-0, ISBN13: 978-0-226-42885-7. Dewey:347.73/26. LCCN:2004-005108.
Audience: **u,f.** *Choice, 2005.*

Kurland, Philip B. **KF8742**
Politics, the Constitution and the Warren Court. Paper Text. University of Chicago Press. Chicago, IL. 1973. ISBN:0-226-46407-5, ISBN13: 978-0-226-46407-7. Dewey:347/.73/26. LCCN:74-124734.
Audience: **g.**

Mason, Alpheus T. **KF4748**
The Supreme Court from Taft to Burger. Ed. 3. Trade Cloth. Louisiana State University Press. Baton Rouge, LA. 1979. 352p. ISBN:0-8071-0468-X, ISBN13: 978-0-8071-0468-2. Dewey:347/.73/2609. LCCN:78-019084.
Audience: **u,f.**

Mendelson, Wallace **KF8744.M4**
Justices Black and Frankfurter: Conflict in the Court. Ed. 2. Trade Paper. Books on Demand. Ann Arbor, MI. 165p. ISBN:0-608-13409-0, ISBN13: 978-0-608-13409-3. Dewey:347.732634. LCCN:61-005781.
Audience: **g.**

Pacelle, Richard L. Jr. **KF8742**
Role of the Supreme Court in American Politics: The Least Dangerous Branch? Trade Paper. Westview Press. Boulder, CO. 2001. 204p. Dilemmas in American Politics Ser. ISBN:0-8133-6753-0, ISBN13: 978-0-8133-6753-8. Dewey:347.7/326.
Audience: **l,u.** *Choice, 2002.*

Rostow, Eugene V. **KF8748**
The Sovereign Prerogative: The Supreme Court and the Quest for Law. Paper Text. Textbook Publishers. Temecula, CA. 2003. 318p. ISBN:0-7581-0081-7, ISBN13: 978-0-7581-0081-8. Dewey:347.9973.
Audience: **g.**

United States > Courts. Procedure > Courts of Appeal

Bass, Jack **KF8752 5TH.B3 1990**
Unlikely Heroes. Trade Paper. University of Alabama Press. Tuscaloosa, AL. 1990. 362p. ISBN:0-8173-0491-6, ISBN13: 978-0-8173-0491-1. Dewey:342.73/085/0975. LCCN:89-078036.
Audience: **g.**

Scheuerman, William E. **KF8752**
Learned Hand's Court. Trade Cloth. Johns Hopkins University Press. Baltimore, MD. 1987. 128p. ISBN:0-8018-1214-3, ISBN13: 978-0-8018-1214-9. Dewey:347/.73/24. LCCN:73-097491.
Audience: **u,f.**

Songer, Donald R., et al. **KF8750.S66 2000**
Continuity and Change on the United States Courts of Appeals. Reginald S. Sheehan & Susan B. Haire (Authors). Trade Cloth. University of Michigan Press. Chicago, IL. 2000. 200p. ISBN:0-472-11158-2, ISBN13: 978-0-472-11158-9. Dewey:347.73/24. LCCN:00-037735.
Audience: **u,f.** *Choice, 2001.*

United States > Courts. Procedure > Civil Procedure

Abramson, Jeffrey **KF8972.A727 2000**
We, the Jury: The Jury System and the Ideal of Democracy. Trade Paper. Harvard University Press. Cambridge, MA. 2000. 350p. ISBN:0-674-00430-2, ISBN13: 978-0-674-00430-6. Dewey:347.730752. LCCN:00-040771.
Audience: **l,u,f.**

Bergman, Paul **KF8841.B47 2005**
Represent Yourself in Court: How to Prepare and Try a Winning Case. Ed. 5. Trade Paper. NOLO. Berkeley, CA. 2005. 544p. ISBN:1-4133-0369-2, ISBN13: 978-1-4133-0369-8. Dewey:347.73/504. LCCN:2005-054724.
Audience: **g.**

Hastie, Reid, et al. **KF8972.H3 2002**
Inside the Jury (1983). Steven Penrod & Nancy Pennington (Authors). Trade Cloth. Lawbook Exchange, Limited, The. Clark, NJ. 2002. viii, 277p. ISBN:1-58477-269-7, ISBN13: 978-1-58477-269-9. Dewey:347.73/752. LCCN:2002-025963.
Audience: **l,u.**

Litan, Robert E. (Editor) **KF8972**
Verdict: Assessing the Civil Jury System. Trade Paper. Brookings Institution Press. Washington, DC. 1993. 542p. ISBN:0-8157-5281-4, ISBN13: 978-0-8157-5281-3. Dewey:347.73/0752. LCCN:93-009389.
Audience: **l,u.** *Choice, 1994.*

Szasz, Thomas **KF9242.S94 1988**
Psychiatric Justice. Trade Paper. Syracuse University Press. Syracuse, NY. 1988. 304p. ISBN:0-8156-0231-6, ISBN13: 978-0-8156-0231-6. Dewey:345.73/04. LCCN:88-031859.
Audience: **g.**

United States > Criminal Law. Criminal Procedure > Criminal Law. General

Joughin, Louis; Morgan, Edmund Morris **KF9219**
The Legacy of Sacco and Vanzetti. Princeton, N.J.: Princeton University Press. 1978. ISBN:0-691-04656-5, ISBN13: 978-0-691-04656-3.
Audience: **l,u.**

Robinson, Paul H. **KF9218.R634 1999**
Would You Convict?: 17 Cases That Challenged the Law. Trade Paper. New York University Press. New York, NY. 2001. 256p. ISBN:0-8147-7531-4, ISBN13: 978-0-8147-7531-8. Dewey:345.73. LCCN:99-006451.
Audience: **u,f.** *Choice, 2000.*

United States > Criminal Law. Criminal Procedure > Administration of Criminal Justice

Friedman, Lawrence M. **KF9223.F75 1993**
Crime and Punishment in American History. Trade Cloth. Basic Books. New York, NY. 1993. 592p. ISBN:0-465-01461-5, ISBN13: 978-0-465-01461-3. Dewey:345.73/05. LCCN:92-054517.
Audience: **g,l,u.** *Choice, 1994.*

Kennedy, Randall **KF9223.K43 1997**
Race, Crime and the Law. Trade Cloth. Random House, Inc. New York, NY. 1997. 624p. ISBN:0-679-43881-5, ISBN13: 978-0-679-43881-6. Dewey:345.73/05. LCCN:96-046534.
Audience: **g.**

Uviller, H. Richard **KF9223.U88 1996**
Virtual Justice: The Flawed Prosecution of Crime in America. Cloth over Boards. Yale University Press. Cumberland, RI. 1996. 336p. ISBN:0-300-06483-7, ISBN13: 978-0-300-06483-4. Dewey:349.7/3. LCCN:95-038687.
Audience: **u,f.** *Choice, 1996.*

United States > Criminal Law. Criminal Procedure > Punishment. Penalties

Bedau, Hugo Adam **HV8699.U5**
The Death Penalty in America: Current Controversies. Trade Paper. Oxford University Press, Inc. New York, NY. 1998. 544p. ISBN:0-19-512286-0, ISBN13: 978-0-19-512286-2. Dewey:364.6/6/0973. LCCN:96-007028.
Audience: **g.**

Berger, Raoul **KF9227.C2**
Death Penalties: The Supreme Court's Obstacle Course. Trade Cloth. Replica Books. Bridgewater, NJ. 2000. 252p. ISBN:0-7351-0248-1, ISBN13: 978-0-7351-0248-4. Dewey:347.305/773.
Audience: **g.**

Foley, Michael A. **KF9227**
Arbitrary and Capricious: The Supreme Court, the Constitution, and the Death Penalty. Trade Cloth. Greenwood Publishing Group, Inc. Portsmouth, NH. 2003. 264p. ISBN:0-275-97587-8, ISBN13: 978-0-275-97587-6. Dewey:345.73/0773. LCCN:2003-042853.
Audience: **u,f.** *Choice, 2004.*

Henderson, Harry **KF9227.C2F53 2000**
Capital Punishment. Trade Cloth. Facts On File, Inc. New York, NY. 2000. 300p. Library in a Book ISBN:0-8160-4193-8, ISBN13: 978-0-8160-4193-0. Dewey:345.73/0773. LCCN:00-028775.
Audience: **g,l.** *Choice, 2001.*

Meltsner, Michael **KF9227.C2.M4**
Cruel and Unusual: The Supreme Court and Capital Punishment. Trade Cloth. Random House, Inc. New York, NY. 1973. xii, 338p. ISBN:0-394-47231-4, ISBN13: 978-0-394-47231-7. Dewey:345/.73/077. LCCN:73-003990.
Audience: **g.**

Sarat, Austin (Editor) **HV8699.U5**
The Killing State: Capital Punishment in Law, Politics, and Culture. Trade Paper. Oxford University Press, Inc. New York, NY. 2001. 276p. ISBN:0-19-514602-6, ISBN13: 978-0-19-514602-8. Dewey:364.6/6/0973.
Audience: **l,u.** *Choice, 1999.*

United States > Criminal Law. Criminal Procedure > Particular Offenses > Offenses Against the Person. Sexual Offenses

Butler, J. Douglas & Walbert, David F. (Editors) **KF9315.A93 1992**
Abortion, Medicine and the Law. Ed. 4. Library Binding. Facts On File, Inc. New York, NY. 1992. 912p. ISBN:0-8160-2535-5, ISBN13: 978-0-8160-2535-0. Dewey:363.4/6. LCCN:91-043021.
Audience: **g.** *Choice, 1993, 1987.*

Cohen, Jean L. **KF9325.C64 2004**
Regulating Intimacy: A New Legal Paradigm. Trade Paper. Princeton University Press. Princeton, NJ. 2004. 304p. ISBN:0-691-11789-6, ISBN13: 978-0-691-11789-8. Dewey:342.73/0858.
Audience: **l,u.**

Dworkin, Ronald M. **KF9315.D85 1993**
Life's Dominion: An Argument about Abortion, Euthanasia, and Individual Freedom. Trade Cloth. Alfred A. Knopf Inc. New York, NY. 1993. 273p. ISBN:0-394-58941-6, ISBN13: 978-0-394-58941-1. Dewey:344.73/0419. LCCN:92-054800.
Audience: **g.** *Choice, 1993.*

Forell, Caroline **KF9325.F67 2000**
Law of Her Own: The Reasonable Woman as a Measure of Man. Trade Cloth. New York University Press. New York, NY. 2000. 261p. ISBN:0-8147-2676-3, ISBN13: 978-0-8147-2676-1. Dewey:345.73/04. LCCN:99-006811.
Audience: **u,f.** *Choice, 2000.*

Jacobs, James B. & Potter, Kimberly **KF9345**
Hate Crimes: Criminal Law and Identity Politics. Trade Paper. Oxford University Press, Inc. New York, NY. 2000. 222p. Studies in Crime and Public Policy ISBN:0-19-514054-0, ISBN13: 978-0-19-514054-5. Dewey:345.73/025.
Audience: **g.**

McDonagh, Eileen **HQ767.5.U5M373 1996**
Breaking the Abortion Deadlock: From Choice to Consent. Trade Paper. Oxford University Press, Inc. New York, NY. 1996. 294p. ISBN:0-19-509142-6, ISBN13: 978-0-19-509142-7. Dewey:179.7/6. LCCN:95-025899.
Audience: **l,u.** *Choice, 1997.*

Mohr, James C. **KF9315.M6**
Abortion in America: The Origins and Evolution of National Policy, 1800-1900. Trade Cloth. Oxford University Press, Inc. New York, NY. 1978. "xii, 331"p. ISBN:0-19-502249-1, ISBN13: 978-0-19-502249-0. Dewey:344/.73/041. LCCN:77-009430.
Audience: **g.**

Schneider, Elizabeth M. **KF9322.S36 2000**
Battered Women and Feminist Lawmaking and the Struggle for Equality. Cloth over Boards. Yale University Press. Cumberland, RI. 2000. 332p. ISBN:0-300-08343-2, ISBN13: 978-0-300-08343-9. Dewey:362.82/92. LCCN:00-036784.
Audience: **u,f.** *Choice, 2001.*

Schulhofer, Stephen J. **KF9325.S38 1998**
Unwanted Sex: The Culture of Intimidation and the Failure of Law. Trade Cloth. Harvard University Press. Cambridge, MA. 1998. 336p. ISBN:0-674-57648-9, ISBN13: 978-0-674-57648-3. Dewey:345.73/0253. LCCN:98-018020.
Audience: **g.**

Tong, Rosemarie **KF9325**
Women, Sex and the Law. Book, Other. Rowman & Littlefield Publishers, Inc. Lanham, MD. 1989. 216p. New Feminist Perspectives Ser. ISBN:0-8476-7231-X, ISBN13: 978-0-8476-7231-8. Dewey:345.73/0253. LCCN:83-016001.
Audience: **g.**

Tribe, Laurence H. **HQ767.5.U5T73 1992**
Abortion: The Clash of Absolutes. Ed. 2. Trade Paper. W. W. Norton & Company, Inc. New York, NY. 1992. 334p. ISBN:0-393-30956-8, ISBN13: 978-0-393-30956-0. Dewey:363.4/6. LCCN:93-111762.
Audience: **g.**

Walker, Samuel **KF9345**
Hate Speech: The History of an American Controversy. Trade Cloth. University of Nebraska Press. Lincoln, NE. 1994. 217p. ISBN:0-8032-9751-3, ISBN13: 978-0-8032-9751-7. Dewey:347.302853. LCCN:93-005389.
Audience: **g.** *Choice, 1994.*

United States > Criminal Law. Criminal Procedure > Particular Offenses > Offenses Against Property

Benson, Michael L. & Cullen, Francis T. **KF9351.B46 1998**
Combating Corporate Crime: Local Prosecutors at Work. Kip Schlegel & David Weisburd (Contribution by). Cloth Text. Northeastern University Press. Boston, MA. 1998. 312p. Series on White-Collar and Organized Crime ISBN:1-55553-353-1, ISBN13: 978-1-55553-353-3. Dewey:345.73/0268. LCCN:97-045999.
Audience: **u,f.** *Choice, 1998.*

United States > Criminal Law. Criminal Procedure > Particular Offenses > Contempt of Congress. Contempt of Court

Goldfarb, Ronald L. **KF9415**
The Contempt Power. Cloth Text. Columbia University Press. New York, NY. 1963. 366p. ISBN:0-231-02654-4, ISBN13: 978-0-231-02654-3. Dewey:345.730234. LCCN:63-020342.
Audience: **g.**

United States > Criminal Law. Criminal Procedure > Particular Offenses > Obscenity

Clor, Harry M. **KF9444.C53**
Obscenity and Public Morality: Censorship in a Liberal Society. Trade Paper. Books on Demand. Ann Arbor, MI. 326p. Midway Reprint Ser. ISBN:0-598-05676-9, ISBN13: 978-0-598-05676-4. Dewey:098.1.
Audience: **g.**

Haney, Robert W. **KF9444**
Comstockery in America: Patterns of Censorship and Control. Paper Text. Da Capo Press, Inc. Cambridge, MA. 1974. 199p. Civil Liberties in American History Ser. ISBN:0-306-70654-7, ISBN13: 978-0-306-70654-7. Dewey:363.3/1/0973. LCCN:74-001241.
Audience: **l,u.**

Rembar, Charles, et al. **KF9444**
The End of Obscenity: The Trials of Lady Chatterley, Tropic of Cancer and Fanny Hill. D. H. Lawrence & Henry Miller (Authors). Trade Paper. HarperCollins Publishers. New York, NY. 1986. 544p. ISBN:0-06-097061-8, ISBN13: 978-0-06-097061-1. Dewey:347.305/274/0924. LCCN:86-045137.
Audience: **g.**

United States > Criminal Law. Criminal Procedure > Particular Offenses > Trafficking in Persons

Langum, David J. **KF9449.L36 1994**
Crossing over the Line: Legislating Morality and the Mann Act. Trade Cloth. University of Chicago Press. Chicago, IL. 1994. 324p. Chicago Series on Sexuality, History and Society ISBN:0-226-46880-1, ISBN13: 978-0-226-46880-8. Dewey:306.74/2/0973. LCCN:94-013292.
Audience: **g.** *Choice, 1995.*

United States > Criminal Law. Criminal Procedure > Criminal Procedure

Amar, Akhil R. **KF9619.A72196 1997**
Constitution and Criminal Procedure: First Principles. Cloth over Boards. Yale University Press. Cumberland, RI. 1997. 288p. ISBN:0-300-06678-3, ISBN13: 978-0-300-06678-4. Dewey:345.73/05. LCCN:96-021079.
Audience: **u,f.** *Choice, 1997.*

Bergman, Paul & Berman-Barrett, Sara J. **KF9619.6.B47 2005**
The Criminal Law Handbook: Know Your Rights, Survive the System. Ed. 7. Trade Paper. NOLO. Berkeley, CA. 2005. 640p. ISBN:1-4133-0356-0, ISBN13: 978-1-4133-0356-8. Dewey:345.73/05. LCCN:2005-047762.
Audience: **g.**

Cutler, Brian L. & Penrod, Steven D. **KF9672 .C87 1995**
Mistaken Identification: The Eyewitness, Psychology and the Law. Trade Paper. Cambridge University Press. New York, NY. 1995. 300p. ISBN:0-521-44572-8, ISBN13: 978-0-521-44572-6. Dewey:363.2/58. LCCN:94-045187.
Audience: **u,f.** *Choice, 1996.*

Dash, Samuel **KF9630.D37 2004**
The Intruders: Unreasonable Searches and Seizures from King John to John Ashcroft. Trade Cloth. Rutgers University Press. Piscataway, NJ. 2004. 208p. ISBN:0-8135-3409-7, ISBN13: 978-0-8135-3409-1. Dewey:345.73/0522. LCCN:2003-018835.
Audience: **g.** *Choice, 2005.*

Diffie, Whitfield & Landau, Susan **KF9670.D54 1998**
Privacy on the Line: The Politics of Wiretapping and Encryption. Trade Cloth. MIT Press. Cambridge, MA. 1998. 352p. ISBN:0-262-04167-7, ISBN13: 978-0-262-04167-6. Dewey:342.73/0858. LCCN:97-042347.
Audience: **u,f.** *Choice, 1998.*

Fisher, George **KF9654.F57 2003**
Plea Bargaining's Triumph: A History of Plea Bargaining in America. Trade Cloth. Stanford University Press. Palo Alto, CA. 2003. 416p. ISBN:0-8047-4459-9, ISBN13: 978-0-8047-4459-1. Dewey:347.73/72. LCCN:2002-012185.
Audience: **u,f.** *Choice, 2004.*

Kalven, Harry Jr. & Zeisel, Hans **KF9680**
The American Jury. Paper Text. University of Chicago Press. Chicago, IL. 1994. xx, 560p. ISBN:0-226-42318-2, ISBN13: 978-0-226-42318-0. Dewey:347.73752. LCCN:70-149361.
Audience: **g.**

Leo, Richard A. & Thomas, George C. III (Editors) **KF9625.M57 1998**
The Miranda Debate: Law, Justice, and Policing. Cloth Text. Northeastern University Press. Boston, MA. 1998. 352p. Series on White-Collar and Organized Crime ISBN:1-55553-338-8, ISBN13: 978-1-55553-338-0. Dewey:346.73/056. LCCN:98-009496.
Audience: **g,l,u,f.**

Levy, Leonard W. **KF9747.L48 1996**
A License to Steal: The Forfeiture of Property. Trade Cloth. University of North Carolina Press. Chapel Hill, NC. 1995. 700p. ISBN:0-8078-2242-6, ISBN13: 978-0-8078-2242-5. Dewey:345.73/0522. LCCN:95-014497.
Audience: **g.** *Choice, 1996.*

Levy, Leonard W. **KF9668.L48 1999**
Origins of the Fifth Amendment: The Right Against Self-Incrimination. Book, Other. Ivan R. Dee Publisher. Blue Ridge Summit, PA. 1999. 576p. ISBN:1-56663-270-6, ISBN13: 978-1-56663-270-6. Dewey:345.73/056. LCCN:99-034149.
Audience: **g.**

Lewis, Anthony **KF224.M54**
Gideon's Trumpet. Library Binding. Sagebrush Education Resources. Caledonia, MN. 1989. ISBN:0-8085-0206-9, ISBN13: 978-0-8085-0206-7. Dewey:345.73/056.
Audience: **g.**

Loftus, Elizabeth F. **KF9672.L63 1996**
Eyewitness Testimony. Trade Paper. Harvard University Press. Cambridge, MA. 1996. 272p. ISBN:0-674-28777-0, ISBN13: 978-0-674-28777-8. Dewey:345.7/3/066. LCCN:95-051176.
Audience: **g.**

McGough, Lucy S. **KF9672.M37 1994**
Child Witnesses: Fragile Voices in the American Legal System. Cloth over Boards. Yale University Press. Cumberland, RI. 1994. 352p. ISBN:0-300-05748-2, ISBN13: 978-0-300-05748-5. Dewey:347.3/0766/083. LCCN:93-049769.
Audience: **u,f.** *Choice, 1995.*

Pyle, Christopher H. **KF9635.P95 2001**
Extradition, Politics and Human Rights. Trade Cloth. Temple University Press. Philadelphia, PA. 2001. x, 445p. ISBN:1-56639-822-3, ISBN13: 978-1-56639-822-0. Dewey:345.73/052. LCCN:00-039283.
Audience: **u,f.** *Choice, 2002.*

Rosenheim, Margaret K. (Editor) **HV9104**
Pursuing Justice for the Child. Library Binding. University of Chicago Press. Chicago, IL. 1992. xix, 361p. Studies in Crime and Justice ISBN:0-226-72789-0, ISBN13: 978-0-226-72789-9. Dewey:364.6. LCCN:75-043238.
Audience: **g.**

Schlossman, Steven L. **KF9709.S3**
Love and the American Delinquent: The Theory and Practice of "Progressive" Juvenile Justice, 1825-1920. Library Binding.

University of Chicago Press. Chicago, IL. 1994. xii, 303p. ISBN:0-226-73857-4, ISBN13: 978-0-226-73857-4. Dewey:345/.73/08. LCCN:76-017699.
Audience: **g.**

White, Welsh S. **KF9625.W48 2001**
Miranda's Waning Protections: Police Interrogation Practices after Dickerson. Trade Cloth. University of Michigan Press. Chicago, IL. 2001. 240p. ISBN:0-472-11172-8, ISBN13: 978-0-472-11172-5. Dewey:345.73/056. LCCN:2001-002078.
Audience: **l,u,f.** *Choice, 2002.*

United States > States, A-W

Hoffer, Peter C. **KFM2478.8.W5H64 1998**
The Devil's Disciples: The Makers of the Salem Witchcraft Trials. Trade Paper. Johns Hopkins University Press. Baltimore, MD. 1998. 296p. ISBN:0-8018-5201-3, ISBN13: 978-0-8018-5201-5. Dewey:345.744/50288. LCCN:95-031432.
Audience: **u,f.** *Choice, 1996.*

Konig, David T. **KFM2999.E8.K66**
Law and Society in Puritan Massachusetts: Essex County, 1629-1692. Trade Cloth. University of North Carolina Press. Chapel Hill, NC. 1979. xxi, 215p. Studies in Legal History ISBN:0-8078-1336-2, ISBN13: 978-0-8078-1336-2. Dewey:340/.09744. LCCN:78-026685.
Audience: **l,u,f.**

Nelson, William E. **KJV3721**
Americanization of the Common Law: The Impact of Legal Change on Massachusetts Society, 1760-1830. Trade Paper. University of Georgia Press. Athens, GA. 1994. 288p. ISBN:0-8203-1587-7, ISBN13: 978-0-8203-1587-4. Dewey:347.44. LCCN:74-021231.
Audience: **g.**

Schwarz, Philip J. **KFV2801.6.S55S386**
Slave Laws in Virginia. Trade Cloth. University of Georgia Press. Athens, GA. 1996. xvi, 253p. Studies in the Legal History of the South ISBN:0-8203-1831-0, ISBN13: 978-0-8203-1831-8. Dewey:342.755/087. LCCN:96-001010.
Audience: **u,f.** *Choice, 1997.*

United States > Confederate States of America

Lee, Charles R. Jr. **KFZ9000**
The Confederate Constitutions. Trade Cloth. Greenwood Publishing Group, Inc. Portsmouth, NH. 1974. 225p. ISBN:0-8371-7201-2, ISBN13: 978-0-8371-7201-9. Dewey:342.7502. LCCN:73-016628.
Audience: **u,f.**

Latin America

Cornell Legal Information Institute **KF242.A1**
Law by Source: Global.
http://www.law.cornell.edu/world/
Cornell Law School.
Audience: **u.**

Law Library of Congress **KF242.A1**
Global Legal Information Network GLIN.
http://www.glin.gov/
Law Library of Congress.
Audience: **u.**

Organization of American States **KDZ10**
Treaties and Agreements OAS.
http://www.oas.org/main/main.asp?sLang=E&sLink=http://www.oas.org/DIL/treaties_and_agreements.htm
Organization of American States.
Audience: **u.**

South America

Cornell Legal Information Institute **KF242.A1**
Law by Source: Global.
http://www.law.cornell.edu/world/
Cornell Law School.
Audience: **u.**

Law Library of Congress **KF242.A1**
Global Legal Information Network GLIN.
http://www.glin.gov/
Law Library of Congress.
Audience: **u.**

Europe

Cornell Legal Information Institute **KF242.A1**
Law by Source: Global.
http://www.law.cornell.edu/world/
Cornell Law School.
Audience: **u.**

Council of Europe **KZ625.3**
European Treaty Series (ETS).
http://conventions.coe.int/Treaty/EN/v3MenuTraites.asp
Council of Europe.
Audience: **u,f.**

European Commission Delegation to the United States **HC240.E7**
European Union A to Z Index.
http://www.eurunion.org/infores/euindex.htm
European Commission.
Audience: **u.**

European Parliament **KJC383**
Legislative Observatory.
http://www.europarl.eu.int/oeil/
Audience: **u.**

European Union **KJC383**
EurLex.
http://europa.eu.int/eur-lex/lex/en/index.htm
European Union.
Audience: **u.**

Law Library of Congress **KF242.A1**
Global Legal Information Network GLIN.
http://www.glin.gov/
Law Library of Congress.
Audience: **u.**

World Legal Information Institute **KF242.A1**
World LII.
http://www.worldlii.org/
Audience: **u,f.**

Eurasia

Cornell Legal Information Institute **KF242.A1**
Law by Source: Global.
http://www.law.cornell.edu/world/
Cornell Law School.
Audience: **u.**

Law Library of Congress **KF242.A1**
Global Legal Information Network GLIN.
http://www.glin.gov/
Law Library of Congress.
Audience: **u.**

Middle-East. Southwest Asia

Cornell Legal Information Institute **KF242.A1**
Law by Source: Global.
http://www.law.cornell.edu/world/
Cornell Law School.
Audience: **u.**

Law Library of Congress **KF242.A1**
Global Legal Information Network GLIN.
http://www.glin.gov/
Law Library of Congress.
Audience: **u.**

South Asia. Southeast Asia. East Asia

Alford, William P. **KNN1155.A958 1995**
To Steal a Book Is an Elegant Offense: Intellectual Property Law in Chinese Civilization. Trade Cloth. Stanford University Press. Palo Alto, CA. 1995. xiii, 222p. Studies in East Asian Law ISBN:0-8047-2270-6, ISBN13: 978-0-8047-2270-4. Dewey:346.5104/8. LCCN:94-015742.
Audience: **l,u,f.** *Choice, 1995.*

Ch'u Tung-Tsu **KNN122 .Q313 1980**
Law and Society in Traditional China. Trade Cloth. Hyperion Press, Inc. Westport, CT. 1987. ISBN:0-88355-905-6, ISBN13: 978-0-88355-905-5. Dewey:349.51/09. LCCN:79-001602.
Audience: **l,u.**

Cohen, Jerome A. (Editor) **KNQ4610.C64**
The Criminal Process in the People's Republic of China, 1949-1963: An Introduction. Trade Cloth. Harvard University Press. Cambridge, MA. 1968. 722p. Harvard Studies in East Asian Law, No. 2 ISBN:0-674-17650-2, ISBN13: 978-0-674-17650-8. Dewey:345.51. LCCN:68-014252.
Audience: **g.** B

Cornell Legal Information Institute **KF242.A1**
Law by Source: Global.
http://www.law.cornell.edu/world/
Cornell Law School.
Audience: **u.**

Haley, John O. **KNX68**
Authority Without Power: Law and the Japanese Paradox. Trade Paper. Oxford University Press, Inc. New York, NY. 1994. 268p. Studies on Law and Social Control ISBN:0-19-509257-0, ISBN13: 978-0-19-509257-8. Dewey:349.52.
Audience: **l,u.**

Law Library of Congress **KF242.A1**
Global Legal Information Network GLIN.
http://www.glin.gov/
Law Library of Congress.
Audience: **u.**

Lubman, Stanley B. **KNQ470.L83 1999**
Bird in a Cage: Legal Reform in China after Mao. Trade Cloth. Stanford University Press. Palo Alto, CA. 2000. xxii, 447p. ISBN:0-8047-3664-2, ISBN13: 978-0-8047-3664-0. Dewey:340.30951. LCCN:99-027415.
Audience: **u,f.**

Tung, Fei **KNQ42.G36 G74**
A Great Trial in Chinese History: The Trial of the Lin Biao and Jiang Qing Counter-Revolutionary Cliques, Nov. 1980-Jan. 1981. Trade Paper. University Press of the Pacific. Miami, FL. 2003. 256p. ISBN:1-4102-1035-9, ISBN13: 978-1-4102-1035-7. Dewey:345.51/0231 345.1052.
Audience: **g.**

Africa

Cornell Legal Information Institute **KF242.A1**
Law by Source: Global.
http://www.law.cornell.edu/world/
Cornell Law School.
Audience: **u.**

Law Library of Congress **KF242.A1**
Global Legal Information Network GLIN.
http://www.glin.gov/
Law Library of Congress.
Audience: **u.**

World Legal Information Institute **KF242.A1**
World LII.
http://www.worldlii.org/
Audience: **u,f.**

Australia. New Zealand

Cornell Legal Information Institute **KF242.A1**
Law by Source: Global.
http://www.law.cornell.edu/world/
Cornell Law School.
Audience: **u.**

Law Library of Congress **KF242.A1**
Global Legal Information Network GLIN.
http://www.glin.gov/
Law Library of Congress.
Audience: **u.**

World Legal Information Institute **KF242.A1**
World LII.
http://www.worldlii.org/
Audience: **u,f.**

Pacific Island Jurisdictions

Cornell Legal Information Institute **KF242.A1**
Law by Source: Global.
http://www.law.cornell.edu/world/
Cornell Law School.
Audience: **u.**

World Legal Information Institute **KF242.A1**
World LII.
http://www.worldlii.org/
Audience: **u,f.**

Law of Nations

Arthur W. Diamond Law Library, Columia University **JC571**
Human and Constitutional Rights.
http://www.hrcr.org/
Arthur W. Diamond Law Library.
Audience: **u.**

Boczek, Boleslaw Adam **KZ1161.B63 2005**
International Law: A Dictionary. Perfect, Paper over Boards. Scarecrow Press, Inc. Lanham, MD. 2005. 475p. Dictionaries of International Law Ser., No. 2 ISBN:0-8108-5078-8, ISBN13: 978-0-8108-5078-1. Dewey:341.03. LCCN:2004-017288.
Audience: **g.** *Choice, 2005.*

Cornell Legal Information Institute **KF242.A1**
Law by Source: Global.
http://www.law.cornell.edu/world/
Cornell Law School.
Audience: **u.**

Dag Hammarskjold Library, United Nations **JZ5010**
United Nations Documentation: Research Guide.
http://www.un.org/Depts/dhl/resguide/
United Nations.
Audience: **u.**

International Tribunal for the Law of the Sea **KZA5200**
International Tribunal for the Law of the Sea.
http://www.itlos.org/start2_en.html
Audience: **u.**

Law Library of Congress **KF242.A1**
Global Legal Information Network GLIN.
http://www.glin.gov/
Law Library of Congress.
Audience: **u.**

Library of Congress **KF51**
Thomas - Treaties.
http://thomas.loc.gov/home/treaties/treaties.html
Audience: **u,f.**

Organization of American States **KDZ10**
Treaties and Agreements OAS.
http://www.oas.org/main/main.asp?sLang=E&sLink=http://www.oas.org/DIL/treaties_and_agreements.htm
Organization of American States.
Audience: **u.**

Phillips, Charles & Axelrod, Alan **KZ1160.P48 2005**
Encyclopedia of Historical Treaties and Alliances. Ed. 2. Trade Cloth. Facts On File, Inc. New York, NY. 2005. 1136p. ISBN:0-8160-6075-4, ISBN13: 978-0-8160-6075-7. Dewey:341.3/7/09. LCCN:2005-040003.
Audience: **g.**

United Nations **Z6481**
Official Documents of the United Nations. United Nations.
Audience: **u,f.**

United Nations **JZ4935**
United Nations Bibliographic Information System UNBisNet.
http://unbisnet.un.org/
Audience: **u.**

United Nations **KZ172**
United Nations Treaty Collection.
http://untreaty.un.org/English/treaty.asp
United Nations.
Audience: **u.**

United States Department of State **J83**
International Agreements.
http://foia.state.gov/SearchColls/CollsSearch.asp
United States Department of State.
Audience: **u.**

United States Department of State **KZ235**
Treaties In Force.
http://www.state.gov/s/l/treaties/
United States Department of State.
Audience: **u.**

University of Minnesota Law Library **JC571**
University of Minnesota Human Rights Library.
http://www1.umn.edu/humanrts/
University of Minnesota.
Audience: **u.**

World Legal Information Institute **KF242.A1**
World LII.
http://www.worldlii.org/
Audience: **u,f.**

Law of Nations > War Crimes Trials

Conot, Robert E. **K5301**
Justice at Nuremberg. Trade Paper. Avalon Publishing Group. New York, NY. 1984. 594p. ISBN:0-88184-032-7, ISBN13: 978-0-88184-032-2. Dewey:341.6/9.
Audience: **g.**

Falk, Richard A. **JX6731.W3.F3**
Crimes of War; a Legal, Political-Documentary, and Psychological Inquiry into the Responsibility of Leaders, Citizens, and Soldiers for Criminal Acts in Wars. Trade Cloth. Random House, Inc. New York, NY. 1971. 590p. ISBN:0-394-41415-2, ISBN13: 978-0-394-41415-7. Dewey:341/.69. LCCN:73-127540.
Audience: **u,f.**

Minear, Richard H. **KZ1181.M56 2001**
Victors' Justice: The Tokyo War Crimes Trial. Trade Paper. Center for Chinese Studies Publications. Ann Arbor, MI. 2001. xxiii, 229p. Michigan Classics in Japanese Studies, Vol. 22 ISBN:1-929280-06-8, ISBN13: 978-1-929280-06-3. LCCN:2001-028237.
Audience: **u,f.**

Sprecher, Drexel A. **KZ1176.S68 1999**
Inside the Nuremberg Trial: A Prosecutor's Comprehensive Account. Claiborne Pell & William E. Jackson (Preface by). Trade Cloth. University Press of America, Inc. Lanham, MD. 1999. 1626p. ISBN:0-7618-1284-9, ISBN13: 978-0-7618-1284-5. Dewey:341.6/9. LCCN:98-031583.
Audience: **g.** *Choice, 1999.*

Willis, James F. **JX5433.W54 1982**
Prologue to Nuremberg: The Politics and Diplomacy of Punishing War Criminals of the First World War. Trade Cloth. Greenwood Publishing Group, Inc. Portsmouth, NH. 1982. 292p. Contributions in Legal Studies Ser., No. 20 ISBN:0-313-21454-9, ISBN13: 978-0-313-21454-7. Dewey:341.6/9/02684321. LCCN:81-001055.
Audience: **g.**

Law of Nations > 20th Century

Bozeman, Adda B. **JX3110.B6.F85**
Future of Law in a Multicultural World. Trade Cloth. Princeton University Press. Princeton, NJ. 1971. xvii, 229p. ISBN:0-691-05643-9, ISBN13: 978-0-691-05643-2. Dewey:340/.2. LCCN:78-131127.
Audience: **l,u.**

Brierly, James L. **JX1974.7**
The Law of Nations: An Introduction to the International Law of Peace. Ed. 6. Humphrey Waldock (Editor). Cloth Text. Oxford University Press, Inc. New York, NY. 1978. 460p. ISBN:0-19-825105-X, ISBN13: 978-0-19-825105-7. Dewey:341.7/3.
Audience: **l,u.**

Brownlie, Ian **K3150**
Principles of Public International Law. Ed. 6. Paper Text. Oxford University Press, Inc. New York, NY. 2003. 794p. ISBN:0-19-926071-0, ISBN13: 978-0-19-926071-3. Dewey:341. LCCN:2004-269816.
Audience: **g.**

Kelsen, Hans **KZ3375.K45A37 2003**
Principles of International Law [1952]. Trade Cloth. Lawbook Exchange, Limited, The. Clark, NJ. 2003. 480p. ISBN:1-58477-325-1, ISBN13: 978-1-58477-325-2. Dewey:341. LCCN:2003-047462.
Audience: **u,f.**

Tuck, Richard **KZ1242**
The Rights of War and Peace: Political Thought and the International Order from Grotius to Kant. Trade Paper. Oxford University Press, Inc. New York, NY. 2001. 252p. ISBN:0-19-924814-1, ISBN13: 978-0-19-924814-8. Dewey:341/.09.
Audience: **g.** *Choice, 2000.*

Law of Nations > 21st Century

Aust, Anthony **KZ3410.A94 2005**
A Handbook of International Law. Trade Cloth. Cambridge University Press. New York, NY. 2005. 554p. ISBN:0-521-82349-8, ISBN13: 978-0-521-82349-4. Dewey:341. LCCN:2005-012925.
Audience: **u,f.** *Choice, 2006.*

Joyner, Christopher C. **KZ3410.J69 2005**
International Law in the 21st Century: Rules for Global Governance. Book, Other. Rowman & Littlefield Publishers, Inc. Lanham, MD. 2005. 384p. New Millennium Books in International Studies ISBN:0-7425-0008-X, ISBN13: 978-0-7425-0008-2. Dewey:341/.09/05. LCCN:2004-016705.
Audience: **g.** *Choice, 2005.*

Murphy, John F. **KF4581**
The United States and the Rule of Law in International Affairs. Cloth Text. Cambridge University Press. New York, NY. 2004. 378p. ISBN:0-521-82256-4, ISBN13: 978-0-521-82256-5. Dewey:341/.0973. LCCN:2003-069747.
Audience: **l,u.**

Law of Nations > United Nations

Joyner, Christopher C. (Editor) **KZ4993 .U55 1997**
The United Nations and International Law. Ed. 2. Cloth Text. Cambridge University Press. New York, NY. 1997. 500p. ISBN:0-521-58379-9, ISBN13: 978-0-521-58379-4. Dewey:341.2/3. LCCN:96-043488.
Audience: **l,u.** *Choice, 1998.*

Law of Nations > Law of the Sea

The International Tribunal for the Law of the Sea.
http://www.itlos.org/start2_en.html
ITLOS.

Audience: **u,f.**

Borgese, Elisabeth M. (Editor) **JX4408**
Pacem in Maribus. Trade Cloth. W. Clement Stone, P M A Communications, Inc. Northbrook, IL. 1972. ISBN:0-396-06417-5, ISBN13: 978-0-396-06417-6. Dewey:341.44. LCCN:72-003140.

Audience: **u,f.**

Division for Ocean Affairs and the Law of the Sea, United Nations **KZA5200**
Oceans and Law of the Sea.
http://www.un.org/Depts/los/index.htm
United Nations.

Audience: **u,f.**

McDougal, Myres Smith **KZA1145**
The Public Order of the Oceans: A Contemporary International Law of the Sea,. Paper Text. Textbook Publishers. Temecula, CA. 2003. xxv, 1226p. ISBN:0-7581-0094-9, ISBN13: 978-0-7581-0094-8. Dewey:341.4/5.

Audience: **g.**

OceanLaw **KZA5200**
Internet Guide to International Fisheries Law.
http://www.intfish.net/

Audience: **u,f.**

Sohn, Louis B. & Gustafson, Kristen **JX4422.U5S64 1984**
The Law of the Sea in a Nutshell. Trade Paper. West Publishing Company, College & School Division. Eagan, MN. 1984. 264p. Nutshell Ser. ISBN:0-314-82348-4, ISBN13: 978-0-314-82348-9. Dewey:341.4/5. LCCN:84-007469.

Audience: **l,u.**

Law of Nations > Law of War and Neutrality

Best, Geoffrey **JX4508.B47 1994**
War and Law since 1945. Trade Cloth. Oxford University Press, Inc. New York, NY. 1994. 456p. ISBN:0-19-821991-1, ISBN13: 978-0-19-821991-0. Dewey:341.6. LCCN:94-007716.

Audience: **l,u.** *Choice, 1995.*

Howard, Michael C. (Editor) **JX4511.R47**
Restraints on War: Studies in the Limitation of Armed Conflict. Trade Cloth. Oxford University Press, Inc. New York, NY. 1979. 182p. ISBN:0-19-822545-8, ISBN13: 978-0-19-822545-4. Dewey:341.6. LCCN:79-309945.

Audience: **u,f.**

Stone, Julius **JX4511**
Legal Controls of International Conflict: A Treatise on the Dynamics of Disputes. Paper Text. Textbook Publishers. Temecula, CA. 2003. lv, 903p. ISBN:0-7581-4794-5, ISBN13: 978-0-7581-4794-3. Dewey:341.3.

Audience: **g.**

Wilson, Heather A. **JX4511**
International Law and the Use of Force by National Liberation Movements. Trade Paper. Oxford University Press, Inc. New York, NY. 1990. 220p. ISBN:0-19-825662-0, ISBN13: 978-0-19-825662-5. Dewey:341.6.

Audience: **l,u.** *Choice, 1989.*

POLITICAL SCIENCE

Developing the political science section of RCL affords us the luxury of adapting the Library of Congress (LC) taxonomy to a structure that more closely parallels the undergraduate curriculum. Accordingly, entries are arranged under the four main subfields of Political Theory, American Politics, Comparative Government, and International Relations. There is also a heading for General Works on Political Science.

The taxonomy and selections reflect the growing interdisciplinarity of Political Science, including public policy topics such as minorities and politics, sustainable development, and mass media. The International Relations section is new since 1988, and incorporates timely topics such as terrorism, globalization, and global health in addition to relations between countries and international organizations.

The obsolete LC classification JX was divided between Law, and Political Science/International Relations. Non-technical law resources are included in Political Science as they relate to American government, political issues, and international relations. We also selected for LC class HX, Socialism and Communism, as part of Political Theory/Forms of the State.

The Political Science section includes a number of free web sites to enable college libraries to enrich their collections. We selected sites both to provide alternatives to high-cost print publications and to increase ease of access. It is important to note, too, that some government documents are available only online.

The selectors strove to choose scholarly, updated materials on the latest issues while retaining classic works important for a foundation in Political Science.

— Catherine Shreve

Political Science: General

Z7163

PAIS International & PAIS Archive. Cambridge Scientific Abstracts (CSA).

Audience: **l,u,f.**

Z7163

Worldwide Political Science Abstracts. Cambridge Scientific Abstracts (CSA).

Audience: **l,u,f.**

Political Science: General > Government Documents > United States

J951

☐ Congressional Record.
http://www.gpoaccess.gov/crecord/index.html

Audience: **g,l,u,f.**

ZA4755.U6

☐ Core Documents of U.S. Democracy.
http://www.gpoaccess.gov/coredocs.html

Audience: **g,l,u,f.**

U.S. Government Accountability Office (GAO)

☐ GAO Reports.
http://www.gpoaccess.gov/gaoreports/index.html

Audience: **g,u,f.**

Central Intelligence Agency

☐ CIA Declassified Documents.
http://www.foia.cia.gov/search_options.asp

Audience: **g,l,u,f.**

Chairman of the Council of Economic Advisors **HC106.5**

☐ Economic Report of the President.
http://www.gpoaccess.gov/eop/index.html

Audience: **g,l,u,f.**

Federal Register Office

☐ The United States Government Manual.
http://www.gpoaccess.gov/gmanual/index.html

Audience: **g,l,u,f.**

House Committee on Ways and Means

☐ The Green Book: Background Material and Data on Programs Within the Jurisdiction of the House Committee on Ways and Means.
http://www.gpoaccess.gov/wmprints/green/index.html

Audience: **g,u,f.**

Joint Committee on Printing

☐ Congressional Record Index.
http://www.gpoaccess.gov/cri/index.html

Audience: **g,l,u,f.**

Joint Committee on Printing **E185.97.K5**

☐ The Congressional Directory.
http://www.gpoaccess.gov/cdirectory/index.html

Audience: **g,l,u,f.**

Library of Congress **JF511**

☐ American Memory: A Century of Lawmaking for a New Nation.
http://memory.loc.gov/ammem/amlaw/lawhome.html

Audience: **g,l,u,f.**

Library of Congress

☐ THOMAS.
http://thomas.loc.gov/

Audience: **g,l,u,f.**

National Archives and Records Administration (NARA) **J80**

☐ Public Papers of the Presidents of the United States.
http://www.gpoaccess.gov/pubpapers/index.html

Audience: **g,l,u,f.**

National Archives and Records Administration (NARA)

☐ Weekly Compilation of Presidental Statements.
http://www.gpoaccess.gov/wcomp/index.html

Audience: **g,l,u,f.**

National Archives and Records Administration's (NARA) Office of the Federal Register (OFR) **KF70**

☐ Code of Federal Regulations (CFR).
http://www.gpoaccess.gov/cfr/index.html

Audience: **g,u,f.**

National Commission on Terrorist Attacks Against the United States **HV6432**

☐ The 9-11 Commission Report: Final Report of the National Commission on Terrorist Attacks Upon the United States, Official Government Edition.
http://www.gpoaccess.gov/911/index.html

Audience: **g,l,u,f.**

National Security Agency

☐ National Security Agency Declassification Initiatives.
http://www.nsa.gov/public/publi00003.cfm

Audience: **g,l,u,f.**

Office of Management and Budget **HJ2051**

☐ Budget of the United States Government.
http://www.gpoaccess.gov/usbudget/index.html

Audience: **g,l,u,f.**

Office of the Federal Register, National Archives and Records Administration **KF70**

☐ Federal Register.
http://www.gpoaccess.gov/fr/index.html

Audience: **g,l,u,f.**

Office of the Law Revision Counsel of the U.S. House of Representatives **KF61**

☐ United States Code.
http://www.gpoaccess.gov/uscode/index.html

Audience: **g,u,f.**

U.S. Census Bureau **HA202**
☐ Statistical Abstract of the United States.
http://www.census.gov/statab/www/
Audience: **g,l,u,f.**

U.S. Census Bureau **HA201.12**
☐ United States Census 2000.
http://www.census.gov/main/www/cen2000.html
Audience: **g,l,u,f.**

U.S. Department of State **JX1407**
☐ Foreign Relations of the United States.
http://www.state.gov/r/pa/ho/frus/
Audience: **g,l,u,f.**

U.S. Government Printing Office **Z1223.Z7**
☐ Catalog of U.S. Government Publications.
http://catalog.gpo.gov/F
Audience: **g,l,u,f.**

Political Science: General > Government Documents > International

Center for World Indigenous Studies
☐ Fourth World Documentation Project.
http://www.cwis.org/fwdp/
Audience: **g,l,u,f.**

European Union **JN30**
☐ Europa: Gateway to the European Union.
http://europa.eu.int/index_en.htm
Audience: **g,l,u,f.**

United Nations **Z6485**
☐ Offical Documents of the United Nations.
http://documents.un.org/welcome.asp?language=E
Audience: **g,l,u,f.**

University of Michigan Documents Center **ZA5050**
☐ Foreign Government Resources on the Web.
http://www.lib.umich.edu/govdocs/foreign.html
Audience: **g,l,u,f.**

Political Science: General > Reference Works

JA86
Style Manual for Political Science. Trade Paper. American Political Science Association. Washington, DC. 2001. ISBN:1-878147-33-1, ISBN13: 978-1-878147-33-2. Dewey:808.027.
Audience: **l,u,f.**

Bentley, Arthur F. **JA66.B4 1994**
The Process of Government: A Study of Social Pressures. Ed. 3. Thelma Z. Lavine (Introduction by). Trade Paper. Transaction Publishers. Somerset, NJ. 1995. 533p. ISBN:1-56000-778-8, ISBN13: 978-1-56000-778-4. Dewey:320. LCCN:94-021410.
Audience: **g,l,u.**

Clarke, Paul Barry & Foweraker, Joe **JC423.E54 2001**
Encyclopedia of Democratic Thought. Paper over Boards. Routledge. New York, NY. 2001. 768p. ISBN:0-415-19396-6, ISBN13: 978-0-415-19396-2. Dewey:321.8/03. LCCN:00-045740.
Audience: **g,l,u,f.** *Choice, 2002.*

Fagan, Patrick **H61**
☐ Working Paper Sites of Political Science.
http://www.workingpapers.org/
Audience: **u,f.**

Green, Stephen W. & Ernest, Douglas J. (Editors) **Z7161.I543 2005**
Information Sources in Political Science. Ed. 5. Library Binding. ABC-CLIO, Inc. Santa Barbara, CA. 2005. 250p. ISBN:1-57607-104-9, ISBN13: 978-1-57607-104-5. Dewey:016.32. LCCN:2005-014121.
Audience: **l,u,f.** *Choice, 2006.*

Huntington, Samuel P. **JA66**
Political Order in Changing Societies. Trade Paper. Yale University Press. Cumberland, RI. 2006. 512p. The Henry L. Stimson Lectures Ser. ISBN:0-300-11620-9, ISBN13: 978-0-300-11620-5. Dewey:320/.011.
Audience: **l,u,f.** B

Jay, Antony (Editor) **PN6084.P6**
Oxford Dictionary of Political Quotations. Ed. 3. Trade Cloth. Oxford University Press, Inc. New York, NY. 2006. 560p. ISBN:0-19-280616-5, ISBN13: 978-0-19-280616-1. Dewey:320.03. LCCN:2006-298031.
Audience: **g,l,u,f.**

Kogan, Maurice & Hawksworth, Mary (Editors) **JA61.C66 1991**
Encyclopedia of Government and Politics, Set. Paper over Boards. Routledge. New York, NY. 1992. 1312p. Companion Encyclopedias Ser. ISBN:0-415-03092-7, ISBN13: 978-0-415-03092-2. Dewey:320/.03. LCCN:91-030399.
Audience: **g,l,u,f.** *Choice, 1993.*

McLean, Iain & McMillan, Alistair **JA61**
The Concise Oxford Dictionary of Politics. Ed. 2. Trade Paper. Oxford University Press, Inc. New York, NY. 2003. 618p. Oxford Paperback Reference Ser. ISBN:0-19-280276-3, ISBN13: 978-0-19-280276-7. Dewey:320/.03. LCCN:2003-278300.
Audience: **g,l,u,f.**

Robertson, David (Editor) **JA61.R63 2002**
The Dictionary of Modern Politics. Ed. 3. Paper over Boards. Taylor & Francis Group. Philadelphia, PA. 2002. 512p. ISBN:1-85743-093-X, ISBN13: 978-1-85743-093-6. Dewey:320/.03. LCCN:2002-727972.
Audience: **g,l,u,f.** *Choice, 2003.*

Shafritz, Jay M. **H97**
Dictionary of Public Policy and Administration. Trade Cloth. Westview Press. Boulder, CO. 2004. 320p. ISBN:0-8133-4261-9, ISBN13: 978-0-8133-4261-0. Dewey:320.6/03. LCCN:2004-008455.
Audience: **g,l,u,f.** *Choice, 2005.*

Political Science: General > Research Methods

H61.3

☐ Inter-university Consortium for Political and Social Research (ICPSR).
http://www.icpsr.umich.edu/
University of Michigan.
Audience: **u,f.**

Agresti, Alan & Finlay, Barbara **QA276.12.A34 1997**
Statistical Methods for the Social Sciences. Ed. 3. Cloth Text. Prentice Hall PTR. Upper Saddle River, NJ. 1997. 643p. ISBN:0-13-526526-6, ISBN13: 978-0-13-526526-0. Dewey:519.5/024/3. LCCN:96-038408.
Audience: **l,u.**

Johnson, Janet Buttolph & Reynolds, H. T. **JA71.J55 2005**
Political Science Research Methods. Ed. 5. Trade Paper. CQ Press. Washington, DC. 2004. 493p. ISBN:1-56802-874-1, ISBN13: 978-1-56802-874-3. Dewey:320/.072. LCCN:2004-016102.
Audience: **l,u.**

King, Gary, et al. **H61.K5437 1994**
Designing Social Inquiry: Scientific Inference in Qualitative Research. Robert O. Keohane & Sidney Verba (Authors). Trade Paper. Princeton University Press. Princeton, NJ. 1994. 258p. ISBN:0-691-03471-0, ISBN13: 978-0-691-03471-3. Dewey:300/.72. LCCN:93-039283.
Audience: **u,f.** *Choice, 1994.*

Lasswell, Harold Dwight **JA71.L3 2005**
The Future of Political Science. Jay Stanley (Introduction by). Trade Paper, Perfect. Transaction Publishers. Somerset, NJ. 2005. 276p. ISBN:0-202-30829-4, ISBN13: 978-0-202-30829-6. Dewey:320. LCCN:2005-050634.
Audience: **l,u,f.** B

Political Science: General > Relations to Other Subjects > Political Psychology

Alford, C. Fred **HM133.A45 1994**
Group Psychology and Political Theory. Cloth over Boards. Yale University Press. Cumberland, RI. 1994. 240p. ISBN:0-300-05958-2, ISBN13: 978-0-300-05958-8. Dewey:302.3/4. LCCN:94-006774.
Audience: **u,f.** *Choice, 1995.*

√**Amstutz, Mark R.** **JC571.A48 2004**
The Healing of Nations: The Promise and Limits of Political Forgiveness. Book, Other. Rowman & Littlefield Publishers, Inc. Lanham, MD. 2004. 296p. ISBN:0-7425-3581-9, ISBN13: 978-0-7425-3581-7. Dewey:323.4/9. LCCN:2004-001064.
Audience: **l,u,f.** *Choice, 2005.*

Bangura, Abdul Karim, et al. **JA75.7.P646 1996**
Political Behavior. Dawit Isayas, Gerald Smith & Michael O. Thomas (Authors). Trade Cloth. University Press of America, Inc. Lanham, MD. 1996. 176p. ISBN:0-7618-0222-3, ISBN13: 978-0-7618-0222-8. Dewey:306.2. LCCN:95-039480.
Audience: **u.**

Barner-Barry, Carol & Rosenwein, Robert **JA74.5 .B37**
Psychological Perspectives on Politics. Paper Text. Waveland Press, Inc. Prospect Heights, IL. 1991. 342p. ISBN:0-88133-619-X, ISBN13: 978-0-88133-619-1. Dewey:320/.01/9.
Audience: **l,u.**

Cottam, Martha L., et al. **JA74.5.C665 2004**
Introduction to Political Psychology. Beth Dietz-Uhler, Elena M. Mastors & Thomas Preston (Authors). Trade Paper. Lawrence Erlbaum Associates, Inc. Mahwah, NJ. 2004. 360p. ISBN:0-8058-3770-1, ISBN13: 978-0-8058-3770-4. Dewey:320/.01/9. LCCN:2003-025976.
Audience: **l,u,f.**

Davies, James C. **JA74.5 .D38 1978**
Human Nature in Politics: The Dynamics of Political Behavior. Trade Cloth. Greenwood Publishing Group, Inc. Portsmouth, NH. 1978. 403p. ISBN:0-8371-9870-4, ISBN13: 978-0-8371-9870-5. Dewey:320/.01/9. LCCN:77-013870.
Audience: **l,u.**

Feldman, Ofer & Valenty, Linda O. (Editors) **BF698**
Profiling Political Leaders: Cross-Cultural Studies of Personality and Behavior. Trade Cloth. Greenwood Publishing Group, Inc. Portsmouth, NH. 2001. 320p. ISBN:0-275-97036-1, ISBN13: 978-0-275-97036-9. Dewey:303.3/4/019. LCCN:00-052866.
Audience: **u,f.** *Choice, 2002.*

Goff, Patricia M. & Dunn, Kevin C. (Editor, Translators) **JA74.5.I35 2004**
Identity and Global Politics: Theoretical and Empirical Elaborations. Cloth over Boards. Palgrave Macmillan. New York, NY. 2004. 284p. Culture and Religion in International Relations Ser. ISBN:1-4039-6379-7, ISBN13: 978-1-4039-6379-6. Dewey:306.2. LCCN:2003-058036.
Audience: **u,f.** *Choice, 2004.*

Jost, John T. & Sidanius, James (Editors) **JA74.5**
Political Psychology: Essential Readings. Paper over Boards. Routledge. New York, NY. 2004. 512p. Key Readings in Social Psychology Ser. ISBN:1-84169-069-4, ISBN13: 978-1-84169-069-8. Dewey:320/.01/9. LCCN:2003-010695.
Audience: **l,u.**

Kuklinski, Jim (Editor) **JA74.5 .T43 2002**
Thinking about Political Psychology. Cloth Text. Cambridge University Press. New York, NY. 2002. 366p. Studies in Political Psychology and Public Opinion ISBN:0-521-59377-8, ISBN13: 978-0-521-59377-9. Dewey:320/.01/9. LCCN:2001-035589.
Audience: **l,u.** *Choice, 2003.*

√**Ludwig, Arnold M.** **JC330.3.L83 2001**
King of the Mountain: The Nature of Political Leadership. Trade Cloth. University Press of Kentucky. Lexington, KY. 2002. 432p. ISBN:0-8131-2233-3, ISBN13: 978-0-8131-2233-5. Dewey:303.3/4. LCCN:2001-007227.
Audience: **g,l,u.** *Choice, 2003, 2002.*

McDermott, Rose **JA74.5.M4 2004**
Political Psychology in International Relations. Trade Cloth. University of Michigan Press. Chicago, IL. 2004. 320p. Analytical Perspectives on Politics Ser. ISBN:0-472-09701-6, ISBN13: 978-0-472-09701-2. Dewey:327.1/01/9. LCCN:2003-026180.
Audience: **l,u.**

Robin, Corey **JA74.5R48 2004**
Fear: The History of a Political Idea. Trade Cloth. Oxford University Press, Inc. New York, NY. 2004. 326p. ISBN:0-19-515702-8, ISBN13: 978-0-19-515702-4. Dewey:320/.01/9. LCCN:2004-006813.
Audience: **g,l,u.** *Choice, 2005.*

Sears, David O. (Editor), et al. **JA74.5.H355 2003**
Oxford Handbook of Political Psychology. Leonie Huddy & Robert L. Jervis (Editors). Paper Text. Oxford University Press, Inc. New York, NY. 2003. 832p. ISBN:0-19-516220-X, ISBN13: 978-0-19-516220-2. Dewey:320/.01/9. LCCN:2002-012893.
Audience: **g,l,u,f.**

Political Science: General > Relations to Other Subjects > Political Sociology

Habermas, Jürgen **K372.H3313 1996**
Between Facts and Norms: Contributions to a Discourse Theory of Law and Democracy. William Rehg (Translator). Trade Cloth. MIT Press. Cambridge, MA. 1996. 631p. Studies in Contemporary German Social Thought ISBN:0-262-08243-8, ISBN13: 978-0-262-08243-3. Dewey:340.1/15. LCCN:95-040229.
Audience: **u,f.** *Choice, 1997.*

Mappes, Thomas A. & Zembaty, Jane S. **HM216.M27 1997**
Social Ethics: Morality and Social Policy. Ed. 5. Trade Paper. McGraw-Hill Higher Education. Burr Ridge, IL. 1996. 544p. ISBN:0-07-040143-8, ISBN13: 978-0-07-040143-3. Dewey:170. LCCN:96-007924.
Audience: **l,u,f.**

Parekh, Bhikhu C. **HM1271**
Rethinking Multiculturalism: Cultural Diversity and Political Theory. Ed. 2. Cloth over Boards. Palgrave Macmillan. New York, NY. 2006. 432p. ISBN:1-4039-4452-0, ISBN13: 978-1-4039-4452-8. Dewey:305.8/001. LCCN:2005-053018.
Audience: **l,u,f.** *Choice, 2001.*

Reed, Adolph Jr. **E885 .R437 2000**
Class Notes: Posing as Politics and Other Thoughts on the American Scene. Trade Cloth. New Press, The. New York, NY. 2000. 240p. ISBN:1-56584-482-3, ISBN13: 978-1-56584-482-7. Dewey:320.973/09/049. LCCN:2003-389317.
Audience: **g,u,f.**

Schofield, Norman **JA77**
Architects of Political Change: Constitutional Quandaries and Social Choice Theory. Randall Calvert & Thrainn Eggertsson (Contribution by). Trade Cloth. Cambridge University Press. New York, NY. 2006. 336p. Political Economy of Institutions and Decisions Ser. ISBN:0-521-83202-0, ISBN13: 978-0-521-83202-1. Dewey:320.97301. LCCN:2006-004120.
Audience: **u,f.**

Spencer, Herbert **JC571.S75 1969**
The Man Versus the State: With Four Essays on Politics and Society. Trade Cloth. Penguin Group (USA) Inc. New York, NY. 1969. 350p. ISBN:0-14-040010-9, ISBN13: 978-0-14-040010-6. Dewey:320.5/1. LCCN:77-540711.
Audience: **l,u,f.** B

Political Science: General > Relations to Other Subjects > Ethics and Politics

LeBow, Richard Ned **UA10.5.L43 2003**
The Tragic Vision of Politics: Ethics, Interests and Orders. Cloth Text. Cambridge University Press. New York, NY. 2003. 424p. ISBN:0-521-82753-1, ISBN13: 978-0-521-82753-9. Dewey:172/.4. LCCN:2002-041445.
Audience: **u,f.** *Choice, 2004.*

Niebuhr, Reinhold **HM665.N5 2001**
Moral Man and Immoral Society: A Study in Ethics and Politics. Langdon B. Gilkey (Introduction by). Trade Cloth. Westminster John Knox Press. Louisville, KY. 2004. 320p. Library of Theological Ethics ISBN:0-664-22474-1, ISBN13: 978-0-664-22474-5. Dewey:301. LCCN:2003-267709.
Audience: **l,u,f.** B

Sorokin, Pitirim A. & Lunden, Walter A. **HM216 .S59**
Power and Morality. Trade Cloth. Porter Sargent Publishers, Inc. Boston, MA. 1959. Extending Horizons Ser. ISBN:0-87558-032-7, ISBN13: 978-0-87558-032-6. Dewey:301.155.
Audience: **l,u.**

Thomas, Ward **JZ1306.T48 2001**
The Ethics of Destruction: Norms and Force in International Relations. Book, Other. Cornell University Press. Ithaca, NY. 2001. 240p. Cornell Studies in Security Affairs ISBN:0-8014-3819-5, ISBN13: 978-0-8014-3819-6. Dewey:172/.4. LCCN:2001-000054.
Audience: **u,f.** *Choice, 2002.*

Valls, Andrew (Editor) **JZ1306.E88 2000**
Ethics in International Affairs: Theories and Cases. Virginia Held (Foreword by). Book, Other. Rowman & Littlefield Publishers, Inc. Lanham, MD. 2000. 264p. ISBN:0-8476-9156-X, ISBN13: 978-0-8476-9156-2. Dewey:172/.4. LCCN:99-057384.
Audience: **u,f.** *Choice, 2000.*

Valls, Andrew **JZ1306.E88 2000**
Ethics in International Affairs: Theories and Cases. Virginia Held (Foreword by). Trade Paper. Rowman & Littlefield Publishers, Inc. Lanham, MD. 2000. xx, 241p. ISBN:0-8476-9157-8, ISBN13: 978-0-8476-9157-9. Dewey:172/.4. LCCN:99-057384.
Audience: **g,l,u.** *Choice, 2000.*

Wapner, Paul & Falk, Richard A. **JZ1242.P75 2000**
Principled World Politics: The Challenge of Normative International Relations at the Millennium. Lester E. Ruiz (Editor). Book, Other. Rowman & Littlefield Publishers, Inc. Lanham, MD. 2000. 416p. ISBN:0-7425-0065-9, ISBN13: 978-0-7425-0065-5. Dewey:327.1/01. LCCN:99-053985.
Audience: **u,f.** *Choice, 2000.*

Political Science: General > Relations to Other Subjects > Politics and Literature

Lazarus, Neil (Editor) **PN56.C63C36 2004**
The Cambridge Companion to Postcolonial Literary Studies. Cloth Text. Cambridge University Press. New York, NY. 2004. 350p. Cambridge Companions to Literature Ser. ISBN:0-521-82694-2, ISBN13: 978-0-521-82694-5. Dewey:809/.93358. LCCN:2004-040754.
Audience: **u,f.** *Choice, 2005.*

Lye, Colleen **PS159.A85L94 2004**
America's Asia: Racial Form and American Literature, 1893-1945. Trade Cloth. Princeton University Press. Princeton, NJ. 2004. 368p. ISBN:0-691-11418-8, ISBN13: 978-0-691-11418-7. Dewey:810.9/325. LCCN:2004-042066.
Audience: **u,f.** *Choice, 2005.*

Pordzik, Ralph **PR9084.P67 2001**
The Quest for Postcolonial Utopia: A Comparative Introduction to the Utopian Novel in the New English Literatures. Cloth Text. Peter Lang Publishing, Inc. New York, NY. 2001. 199p. Studies of World Literature in English, Vol. 10 ISBN:0-8204-5193-2, ISBN13: 978-0-8204-5193-0. Dewey:823/.91409372. LCCN:00-064766.
Audience: **l,u,f.**

Roberts, Nora Ruth **PS228.R34R63 1996**
Three Radical Women Writers: Class and Gender in Meridel le Sueur, Tillie Olsen, and Josephine Herbst. Cloth Text. Garland Publishing, Inc. New York, NY. 1996. 224p. Gender and Genre in Literature Ser., Vol. 06 ISBN:0-8153-0330-0, ISBN13: 978-0-8153-0330-5. Dewey:810.9/9287/0904. LCCN:95-043538.
Audience: **u,f.**

Political Science: General > Relations to Other Subjects > History

Bruni, Frank **E903 .B78 2002**
Ambling into History: The Unlikely Odyssey of George W. Bush. Trade Cloth. Thorndike Press. Waterville, ME. 2002. 414p. Americana Ser. ISBN:0-7862-4406-2, ISBN13: 978-0-7862-4406-5. Dewey:973.931/092. LCCN:2002-067602.
Audience: **g,l,u,f.**

Carter, Gregg Lee **HV7436.G8783 2002**
Guns in American Society: An Encyclopedia of History, Politics, Culture, and the Law, Set. Library Binding. ABC-CLIO, Inc. Santa Barbara, CA. 2002. 850p. ISBN:1-57607-268-1, ISBN13: 978-1-57607-268-4. Dewey:363.3/3/097303. LCCN:2002-014682.
Audience: **g,l,u,f.** *Choice, 2003.*

Ciment, James (Editor) **D843.E46 1999**
Encyclopedia of Conflicts since World War II. Cloth Text. M. E. Sharpe Inc. Armonk, NY. 1999. 1400p. ISBN:0-7656-8004-1, ISBN13: 978-0-7656-8004-4. Dewey:909.82/5. LCCN:98-028374.
Audience: **g,l,u,f.** *Choice, 1999.*

Connally, Nellie & Herskowitz, Mickey **E842.9.C66 2003**
From Love Field: Our Final Hours with President John F. Kennedy. Trade Cloth. Rugged Land. New York, NY. 2003. 240p. ISBN:1-59071-014-2, ISBN13: 978-1-59071-014-2. Dewey:976.4'063'092. LCCN:2003-108905.
Audience: **g,l,u,f.**

Cyr, Arthur I. **E840.C9 1997**
After the Cold War: American Foreign Policy in Europe and Asia. Trade Cloth. New York University Press. New York, NY. 1997. 208p. ISBN:0-8147-1559-1, ISBN13: 978-0-8147-1559-8. Dewey:327.73. LCCN:96-040848.
Audience: **u,f.** *Choice, 1997.*

Ellis, Joseph J. **E302.5.E45 2000**
Founding Brothers: The Revolutionary Generation. Trade Cloth. Thomson Gale. Farmington Hills, MI. 2001. xii, 457p. ISBN:1-58724-006-8, ISBN13: 978-1-58724-006-5. Dewey:973.4/0922. LCCN:00-069490.
Audience: **g,l,u.** *Choice, 2001.*

Finkelman, Paul & Wallenstein, Peter (Editors) **E183.E48 2001**
The Encyclopedia of American Political History. Trade Cloth. CQ Press. Washington, DC. 2000. 555p. ISBN:1-56802-511-4, ISBN13: 978-1-56802-511-7. Dewey:973/.03. LCCN:00-066812.
Audience: **g,l,u,f.** *Choice, 2001.*

Foner, Eric & Brown, Joshua **E668.F655 2005**
Forever Free: The Story of Emancipation and Reconstruction. Trade Cloth. Alfred A. Knopf Inc. New York, NY. 2005. 304p. ISBN:0-375-40259-4, ISBN13: 978-0-375-40259-3. Dewey:973.8. LCCN:2005-040706.
Audience: **g,l,u,f.**

Freeman, Joanne B. **E310.F85 2001**
Affairs of Honor: National Politics in the New Republic. Cloth over Boards. Yale University Press. Cumberland, RI. 2001. 400p. ISBN:0-300-08877-9, ISBN13: 978-0-300-08877-9. Dewey:306.2/0973/09034. LCCN:2001-000915.
Audience: **u,f.** *Choice, 2002.*

Gellman, Irwin F. **E856**
The Contender: Richard Nixon: The Congress Years, 1946-1952. Trade Cloth. DIANE Publishing Company. Collingdale, PA. 1999. 590p. ISBN:0-7567-6009-7, ISBN13: 978-0-7567-6009-0. Dewey:973.924/092 B.
Audience: **u,f.** *Choice, 2000.*

Gerdes, Louise (Editor) **D843.C57724 2003**
The Cold War. Library Binding. Thomson Gale. Farmington Hills, MI. 2003. 144p. ISBN:0-7377-0869-7, ISBN13: 978-0-7377-0869-1. Dewey:909.82/5. LCCN:2002-034718.
Audience: **g,l,u,f.**

Gilbert, Martin **DA566.9.C5**
Churchill and America. Trade Cloth. McClelland & Stewart. Toronto, ON. 2005. 528p. ISBN:0-7710-3354-0, ISBN13: 978-0-7710-3354-4. Dewey:941.084/092.
Audience: **g,u,f.**

Gill, LaVerne M. **E840.6.G55 1997**
African American Women in Congress. Cloth Text. Rutgers University Press. Piscataway, NJ. 1997. 256p. ISBN:0-8135-2352-4, ISBN13: 978-0-8135-2352-1. Dewey:328.73/092/2 B. LCCN:96-029294.
Audience: **g,l,u.**

Goldberg, Robert A. **E748.G64G65 1995**
Barry Goldwater. Cloth over Boards. Yale University Press. Cumberland, RI. 1995. 478p. ISBN:0-300-06261-3, ISBN13: 978-0-300-06261-8. Dewey:973.9/2/092. LCCN:94-046848.
Audience: **g,u,f.** *Choice, 1996.*

Goldstone, Jack **JC491.E63**
The Encyclopedia of Political Revolutions. Paper over Boards. Fitzroy Dearborn Publishers, Inc. Chicago, IL. 1999. 580p. ISBN:1-57958-122-6, ISBN13: 978-1-57958-122-0. Dewey:903.
Audience: **g,l,u.** *Choice, 1999.*

Graham, Hugh Davis **JC599.U5G685 1990**
The Civil Rights Era: Origins and Development of National Policy, 1960-1972. Oxford University Press, Inc. 1990. ISBN:0-19-504531-9, ISBN13: 978-0-19-504531-4.
Audience: **g,u,f.**

Helms, Jesse **E840.8.H44A3 2005**
Here's Where I Stand: A Memoir. Trade Cloth. Random House Adult Trade Publishing Group. New York, NY. 2005. 336p. ISBN:0-375-50884-8, ISBN13: 978-0-375-50884-4. Dewey:328.73/092 B. LCCN:2005-042795.
Audience: **g,l,u,f.**

Hogan, Michael J. **E813.H58 1998**
A Cross of Iron: Harry S. Truman and the Origins of the National Security State, 1945-1954. Cloth Text. Cambridge University Press. New York, NY. 1998. 554p. ISBN:0-521-64044-X, ISBN13: 978-0-521-64044-2. Dewey:973.9/18. LCCN:98-015865.
Audience: **f.**

Hogan, Michael J. (Editor) **D860 .E56 1992**
The End of the Cold War: Its Meaning and Implications. Cloth Text. Cambridge University Press. New York, NY. 1992. 312p. ISBN:0-521-43128-X, ISBN13: 978-0-521-43128-6. Dewey:327.09045. LCCN:92-004603.
Audience: **u,f.**

Johnson, Haynes **E885.J63**
The Best of Times: America in the Clinton Years. Trade Cloth. DIANE Publishing Company. Collingdale, PA. 2004. 610p. ISBN:0-7567-7912-X, ISBN13: 978-0-7567-7912-2. Dewey:973.929.
Audience: **g,u,f.** *Choice, 2002.*

Kaiser, David E. **DS558.K35 2000**
American Tragedy: Kennedy, Johnson, and the Origins of the Vietnam War. Trade Cloth. Harvard University Press. Cambridge, MA. 2000. 576p. Belknap Press Ser. ISBN:0-674-00225-3, ISBN13: 978-0-674-00225-8. Dewey:959.704/3373. LCCN:99-052925.
Audience: **g,u,f.** *Choice, 2000.*

Kauffman, Bill **E743.K36 1995**
America First!: Its History, Culture and Politics. Gore Vidal (Foreword by). Trade Cloth. Prometheus Books, Publishers. Amherst, NY. 1995. 296p. ISBN:0-87975-956-9, ISBN13: 978-0-87975-956-8. Dewey:320.5/4/0973. LCCN:95-010449.
Audience: **l,u,f.**

Lee, Francis Graham **KF4865**
Church-State Relations. Cloth Text. Greenwood Publishing Group, Inc. Portsmouth, NH. 2002. 456p. Major Issues in American History Ser. ISBN:0-313-31096-3, ISBN13: 978-0-313-31096-6. Dewey:342.73/0852. LCCN:2001-050112.
Audience: **g,l.** *Choice, 2002.*

Major, Patrick & Mitter, Rana (Editor, Translators) **D843.A383 2003**
Across the Blocs: Exploring Comparative Cold War Cultural and Social History. Paper over Boards. Taylor & Francis Group. Abingdon, 2003. 160p. ISBN:0-7146-5581-3, ISBN13: 978-0-7146-5581-9. Dewey:909.82/5. LCCN:2003-013159.
Audience: **u,f.** *Choice, 2004.*

Marty, Martin E. & Moore, Jonathan **LC111.M32 2000**
Education, Religion, and the Common Good: Advancing a Distinctly American Conversation about Religion's Role in Our Shared Life. Trade Cloth. John Wiley & Sons, Inc. Hoboken, NJ. 2000. 176p. ISBN:0-7879-5033-5, ISBN13: 978-0-7879-5033-0. Dewey:379.2/8/0973. LCCN:00-009152.
Audience: **g,l,u,f.**

McGreevy, John T. **BX1406.3.M36 2003**
Catholicism and American Freedom: A History from Slavery to Abortion. Trade Cloth. W. W. Norton & Company, Inc. New York, NY. 2003. 448p. ISBN:0-393-04760-1, ISBN13: 978-0-393-04760-8. Dewey:282/.73. LCCN:2002-154389.
Audience: **g,l,u,f.** *Choice, 2003.*

Miller, Russell **D810.S7.M478 2002**
Behind the Lines: The Oral History of Special Operations in World War II. Cloth over Boards. St. Martin's Press. Gordonville, VA. 2002. 256p. ISBN:0-312-26642-1, ISBN13: 978-0-312-26642-4. Dewey:940.54/8641/092. LCCN:2002-727133.
Audience: **g,u,f.**

O'Neill, William L. **E839.O5 1971**
Coming Apart: An Informal History of America in the 1960's. Trade Cloth. Crown Publishing Group. New York, NY. 1974. 480p. ISBN:0-8129-0190-8, ISBN13: 978-0-8129-0190-0. Dewey:973.923. LCCN:79-152098.
Audience: **g,l,u.** B

Pepper, William F. **HV6278**
An Act of State: The Execution of Martin Luther King Jr. Trade Cloth. Verso Books. London, 2003. 320p. ISBN:1-85984-695-5, ISBN13: 978-1-85984-695-7. Dewey:364.1/524/092. LCCN:2002-025908.
Audience: **g,l,u,f.** *Choice, 2003.*

Phillips, Kevin **JK2249.P48 1994**
The Arrogant Capital: Washington, Wall Street, and the Frustrations of American Politics. Trade Cloth. Little Brown & Company. New York, NY. 1994. xviii, 231p. ISBN:0-316-70618-3, ISBN13: 978-0-316-70618-6. Dewey:320.973. LCCN:94-010035.
Audience: **g,l,u,f.**

Quirk, William J. & Bridwell, R. Randall **HT690.U6Q57 1992**
Abandoned: The Betrayal of the American Middle Class since World War II. Trade Cloth. Madison Books, Inc. New York, NY. 1992. 468p. ISBN:0-8191-8459-4, ISBN13: 978-0-8191-8459-7. Dewey:305.550973. LCCN:92-005166.
Audience: **g,u,f.**

Roberts, Cokie **E176.R63 2004**
Founding Mothers: The Women Who Raised Our Nation. Trade Cloth. HarperCollins Publishers. New York, NY. 2004. 384p. ISBN:0-06-009025-1, ISBN13: 978-0-06-009025-8. Dewey:973.3/092/2 B. LCCN:2004-042873.
Audience: **g,l,u,f.**

Robinson, Jo Ann Ooiman (Editor) **JC599**
Affirmative Action: A Documentary History. Cloth Text. Greenwood Publishing Group, Inc. Portsmouth, NH. 2001. 464p. Primary Documents in American History and Contemporary Issues Ser. ISBN:0-313-30169-7, ISBN13: 978-0-313-30169-8. Dewey:331.13/3/0973. LCCN:00-049508.
Audience: **g,l,u,f.**

Roosevelt, Eleanor & Black, Allida M. **E807.1.R48A3 1999**
Courage in a Dangerous World: The Political Writings of Eleanor Roosevelt. Trade Cloth. Columbia University Press. New York, NY. 1999. 360p. ISBN:0-231-11180-0, ISBN13: 978-0-231-11180-5. Dewey:973.917/092. LCCN:98-033807.
Audience: **g,u,f.** *Choice, 1999.*

Savage, Barbara D. **E185.61.S32 1999**
Broadcasting Freedom: Radio War and the Politics of Race, 1938-1948. Trade Cloth. University of North Carolina Press. Chapel Hill, NC. 1999. 408p. John Hope Franklin Series in African American History and Cult Ser. ISBN:0-8078-2477-1, ISBN13: 978-0-8078-2477-1. Dewey:305.8/00973. LCCN:98-048030.
Audience: **u,f.** *Choice, 1999.*

Schwarzmantel, J. J. **JA83.S367 1998**
The Age of Ideology: Political Ideologies from the American Revolution to Postmodern Times. Trade Cloth. New York University Press. New York, NY. 1998. 304p. ISBN:0-8147-8095-4, ISBN13: 978-0-8147-8095-4. Dewey:320.5. LCCN:97-025893.
Audience: **u,f.** *Choice, 1999.*

Skeen, C. Edward **E341.S57 2003**
1816: America Rising. Trade Cloth. University Press of Kentucky. Lexington, KY. 2003. 320p. ISBN:0-8131-2271-6, ISBN13: 978-0-8131-2271-7. Dewey:973.5/1. LCCN:2003-007863.
Audience: **u,f.** *Choice, 2004.*

Sobel, Robert **E792.S64 1998**
Coolidge: An American Enigma. Trade Cloth. Regnery Publishing, Incorporated, An Eagle Publishing Company. Washington, DC. 1998. 517p. ISBN:0-89526-410-2, ISBN13: 978-0-89526-410-7. Dewey:973.91/5/092. LCCN:98-014826.
Audience: **g,l,u,f.**

Talbott, Strobe & Chanda, Nayan (Editors) **HV6432.A43**
The Age of Terror: America and the World after September 11. Trade Cloth. DIANE Publishing Company. Collingdale, PA. 2003. 232p. ISBN:0-7567-6831-4, ISBN13: 978-0-7567-6831-7. Dewey:973.931.
Audience: **g,l,u,f.** *Choice, 2002.*

Vila, Bryan & Morris, Cynthia (Editors) **HV8699**
Capital Punishment in the United States: A Documentary History. Cloth Text. Greenwood Publishing Group, Inc. Portsmouth, NH. 1997. 384p. Primary Documents in American History and Contemporary Issues Ser. ISBN:0-313-29942-0, ISBN13: 978-0-313-29942-1. Dewey:364.66/0973. LCCN:96-051137.
Audience: **g,l,u,f.**

West, John G. Jr. & Maclean, Iain **BL2525.E52 1999**
Encyclopedia of Religion in American Politics. Jeffrey D. Schultz (Editor), Helen Thomas (Foreword by). Cloth Text. Greenwood Publishing Group, Inc. Portsmouth, NH. 1998. 424p. The American Political Landscape Ser., Vol. 2 ISBN:1-57356-130-4, ISBN13: 978-1-57356-130-3. Dewey:322/.1/097303. LCCN:98-047223.
Audience: **g,l,u,f.** *Choice, 1999.*

Political Science: General > Relations to Other Subjects > Political Economy

Blyth, Mark **JC574.2.U6B59 2002**
Great Transformations: Economic Ideas and Institutional Change in the Twentieth Century. Trade Paper. Cambridge University Press. New York, NY. 2002. 296p. ISBN:0-521-01052-7, ISBN13: 978-0-521-01052-8. Dewey:320.51309485. LCCN:2002-067685.
Audience: **l,u,f.** *Choice, 2003.*

Haggard, Stephan & Kaufman, Robert R. **JC423.H29 1995**
The Political Economy of Democratic Transitions. Trade Paper. Princeton University Press. Princeton, NJ. 1995. 406p. ISBN:0-691-02775-7, ISBN13: 978-0-691-02775-3. Dewey:338.9. LCCN:94-049595.
Audience: **l,u,f.** *Choice, 1996.*

Political Science: General > Relations to Other Subjects > Geopolitics

Agnew, John **JC319.A44 2002**
Making Political Geography. Trade Paper. Oxford University Press, Inc. New York, NY. 2002. 256p. Human Geography in the Making Ser. ISBN:0-340-75955-0, ISBN13: 978-0-340-75955-4. Dewey:320.1/2. LCCN:2003-266522.
Audience: **g,l,u.** *Choice, 2003.*

Anderson, Ewan (Editor) **JC319**
Global Geopolitical Flashpoints: An Atlas of Conflict. Trade Cloth. Fitzroy Dearborn Publishers, Inc. Chicago, IL. 2000. 391p. ISBN:1-57958-137-4, ISBN13: 978-1-57958-137-4. Dewey:320.
Audience: **g,l,u,f.** *Choice, 2001.*

Anderson, Malcolm **JC323.A63 1997**
Frontiers: Territory and State Formation in the Modern World. Trade Paper. Polity Press. Cambridge, 1997. 272p. ISBN:0-7456-2008-6, ISBN13: 978-0-7456-2008-4. Dewey:320.1/2. LCCN:97-029548.
Audience: **l,u.** *Choice, 1996.*

Cohen, Saul Bernard **JC319.C62 2002**
Geopolitics of the World System. Book, Other. Rowman & Littlefield Publishers, Inc. Lanham, MD. 2002. 480p. Regional Geographies for a New Era Ser. ISBN:0-8476-9907-2, ISBN13: 978-0-8476-9907-0. Dewey:320.1/2. LCCN:2002-000615.
Audience: **g,l,u.** *Choice, 2003.*

Dodds, Klaus J. & Atkinson, David **JC319.G483 2000**
Geopolitical Traditions: Critical Histories of Century of Political Thought. Trade Paper. Routledge. New York, NY. 2000. 416p. Critical Geographies Ser., Vol. 7 ISBN:0-415-17249-7, ISBN13: 978-0-415-17249-3. Dewey:327.1/09/04. LCCN:99-044347.
Audience: **l,u,f.** *Choice, 2001.*

Fuller, Graham E. & Lesser, Ian O. **DS35.74.E85F85 1995**
Sense of Siege: The Geopolitics of Islam and the West. Trade Paper. Westview Press. Boulder, CO. 1995. 208p. A RAND Study Ser. ISBN:0-8133-2149-2, ISBN13: 978-0-8133-2149-3. Dewey:297. LCCN:95-131078.
Audience: **g,l,u,f.**

Otuathail, Gearoid, et al. **JC319.G49 1998**
The Geopolitics Reader. Simon Dalby & Paul Routledge (Authors). Trade Paper. Routledge. New York, NY. 1998. 344p. ISBN:0-415-16271-8, ISBN13: 978-0-415-16271-5. Dewey:302.1/2. LCCN:97-013460.
Audience: **l,u.** *Choice, 1999.*

Toft, Monica Duffy **JC328.6.T64 2003**
The Geography of Ethnic Violence: Identity, Interests, and the Indivisibility of Territory. Trade Cloth. Princeton University Press. Princeton, NJ. 2003. 256p. ISBN:0-691-11354-8, ISBN13: 978-0-691-11354-8. Dewey:303.6. LCCN:2002-042463.
Audience: **l,u,f.** *Choice, 2004.*

White, George W. **JC311.W463 2004**
Nation, State, and Territory: Origins, Evolutions, and Relationships. Ed. 2. Book, Other. Rowman & Littlefield Publishers, Inc. Lanham, MD. 2004. 304p. ISBN:0-7425-3025-6, ISBN13: 978-0-7425-3025-6. Dewey:320.1. LCCN:2004-014114.
Audience: **l,u,f.**

Political Theory > History of Political Thought

Okin, Susan Moller **HQ1122**
Women in Western Political Thought. Trade Paper. Princeton University Press. Princeton, NJ. 1979. 384p. ISBN:0-691-02191-0, ISBN13: 978-0-691-02191-1. Dewey:305.4/2/01. LCCN:79-084004.
Audience: **l,u,f.**

Popper, Karl R. **JA71**
The Open Society and Its Enemies. Ed. 5. Other. Princeton University Press. Princeton, NJ. 1966. ISBN:0-318-55362-7, ISBN13: 978-0-318-55362-7. Dewey:320/.01.
Audience: **g,l,u.**

Popper, Karl R. **B63**
The High Tide of Prophecy. Trade Paper. Princeton University Press. Princeton, NJ. 1971. 432p. Open Society and Its Enemies Ser., Vol. II ISBN:0-691-01972-X, ISBN13: 978-0-691-01972-7. Dewey:320.01.
Audience: **l,u,f.**

Strauss, Leo & Cropsey, Joseph (Editors) **JA81.H58 1987**
History of Political Philosophy. Ed. 3. Trade Paper. University of Chicago Press. Chicago, IL. 2003. 980p. ISBN:0-226-77710-3, ISBN13: 978-0-226-77710-8. Dewey:320/.01. LCCN:86-030775.
Audience: **l,u.** BCL3

Political Theory > Ancient

Annas, Julia **JC71.P6 1981**
An Introduction to Plato's Republic. Paper Text. Oxford University Press, Inc. New York, NY. 1981. 384p. ISBN:0-19-827429-7, ISBN13: 978-0-19-827429-2. Dewey:321.07. LCCN:80-041901.
Audience: **g,l,u.** BCL3

Aristotle **JC71.A41K49 1999**
Aristotle: Politics. David Keyt (Translator, Commentaries by). Trade Cloth. Oxford University Press, Inc. New York, NY. 1999. 284p. Clarendon Aristotle Ser. ISBN:0-19-823535-6, ISBN13: 978-0-19-823535-4. Dewey:320/.01/1. LCCN:98-043637.
Audience: **l,u.**

Aristotle **JC71.A41A75513 1997**
Politics, Vol. 5-6, Bks. VII and VIII. Richard Kraut (Translator, Commentaries by). Trade Cloth. Oxford University Press, Inc. New York, NY. 1998. 240p. Clarendon Aristotle Ser. ISBN:0-19-875113-3, ISBN13: 978-0-19-875113-7. Dewey:320.01/1. LCCN:97-011500.
Audience: **l,u.** BCL3 *Choice, 1987.*

Aristotle **JC71.A7A75 1990**
Aristotle's Politics: A Critical Reader. Fred D. Miller Jr. & David Keyt (Editors). Trade Paper. Blackwell Publishing, Inc. Malden, MA. 1991. 380p. ISBN:1-55786-098-X, ISBN13: 978-1-55786-098-9. Dewey:320/.01/1. LCCN:90-035094.
Audience: **l,u.** *Choice, 1992.*

Aristotle **JC71.A41R6 1995**
Politics, Bks. III and IV. Ed. 2. Richard Robinson (Translator, Commentaries by, Introduction by), David Keyt (Supplement by). Trade Cloth. Oxford University Press, Inc. New York, NY. 1996. 186p. Clarendon Aristotle Ser. ISBN:0-19-823591-7, ISBN13: 978-0-19-823591-0. Dewey:320/.01/1. LCCN:97-158552.
Audience: **l,u.**

Aristotle **JC71.A41S3 1995**
Politics, Bks. I & II. Trevor J. Saunders (Translator, Commentaries by). Trade Cloth. Oxford University Press, Inc. New York, NY. 1996. 210p. Clarendon Aristotle Ser. ISBN:0-19-824892-X, ISBN13: 978-0-19-824892-7. Dewey:320/.01/1. LCCN:95-009279.
Audience: **l,u.**

Barker, Ernest **JC73 .B23**
Greek Political Theory, Plato and His Predecessors. Paper Text. Textbook Publishers. Temecula, CA. 2003. 468p. ISBN:0-7581-8199-X, ISBN13: 978-0-7581-8199-2. Dewey:320.938.
Audience: **g,l.** BCL3

Barker, Ernest **JC73.B25 1959**
Political Thought of Plato and Aristotle. Trade Cloth. Russell & Russell Publishers. New York, NY. 1959. 559p. ISBN:0-8462-0772-9, ISBN13: 978-0-8462-0772-6. Dewey:320.938. LCCN:59-007621.
Audience: **g,l.** BCL3

Davis, Michael **JC71.A7D35 1996**
The Politics of Philosophy: A Commentary on Aristotle's Politics. Trade Cloth. Rowman & Littlefield Publishers, Inc. Lanham, MD. 1996. 176p. ISBN:0-8476-8205-6, ISBN13: 978-0-8476-8205-8. Dewey:320/.01/1. LCCN:95-048150.
Audience: **g,l,u.** *Choice, 1996.*

De Coulanges, Numa D. & Fustel de Coulanges, Numa Denis **JC51.F95 1980**
The Ancient City: A Study on the Religion, Laws, and Institutions of Greece and Rome. S. C. Humphreys & Arnaldo D. Momigliano (Foreword by). Trade Paper. Johns Hopkins University Press. Baltimore, MD. 1992. 416p. ISBN:0-8018-2304-8, ISBN13: 978-0-8018-2304-6. Dewey:938. LCCN:79-003703.
Audience: **u,f.** B

Finley, Moses **JC51 .F55 1983**
Politics in the Ancient World. Trade Paper. Cambridge University Press. New York, NY. 1983. 168p. ISBN:0-521-27570-9, ISBN13: 978-0-521-27570-5. Dewey:320.938. LCCN:83-001771.
Audience: **g,l,u,f.** B

Foster, Michael Beresford **JC0071.P6F6**
The Political Philosophies of Plato and Hegel. Trade Paper. Books on Demand. Ann Arbor, MI. 222p. ISBN:0-598-93976-8, ISBN13: 978-0-598-93976-0. Dewey:321.07. LCCN:35-014095.
Audience: **u,f.** B

Greenidge, A. H. J. **KKE2101.G74**
A Handbook of Greek Constitutional History. Trade Paper. Kessinger Publishing, LLC. Whitefish, MT. 2004. ISBN:1-4179-1052-6, ISBN13: 978-1-4179-1052-6. Dewey:949.5.
Audience: **g,l,u,f.** B

Griffin, Miriam D. (Editor) **DS777.A567**
Seneca: A Philosopher in Politics. Paper Text. Oxford University Press, Inc. New York, NY. 1992. 532p. ISBN:0-19-814774-0, ISBN13: 978-0-19-814774-9. Dewey:320.5/092/4.
Audience: **l,u,f.** B

Hall, Robert **JC71.P6**
Plato. Geraint Parry (Editor). Paper over Boards. Routledge. New York, NY. 2004. 180p. Political Thinkers Ser., Vol. 9 ISBN:0-415-32691-5, ISBN13: 978-0-415-32691-9. Dewey:320.01.
Audience: **l,u,f.**

Kochin, Michael S. **JC71.K63 2002**
Gender and Rhetoric in Plato's Political Thought. Trade Cloth. Cambridge University Press. New York, NY. 2002. 174p. ISBN:0-521-80852-9, ISBN13: 978-0-521-80852-1. Dewey:320/.01. LCCN:2001-052480.
Audience: **u,f.** *Choice, 2003.*

Kraut, Richard (Editor) **B395 .C28 1992**
The Cambridge Companion to Plato. Cloth Text. Cambridge University Press. New York, NY. 1992. 576p. Cambridge Companions to Philosophy Ser. ISBN:0-521-43018-6, ISBN13: 978-0-521-43018-0. Dewey:184. LCCN:92-004991.
Audience: **g,u,f.** *Choice, 1993.*

Kraut, Richard **JC11**
Socrates and the State. Trade Paper. Princeton University Press. Princeton, NJ. 1987. 350p. ISBN:0-691-02241-0, ISBN13: 978-0-691-02241-3. Dewey:320.1/01. LCCN:83-017113.
Audience: **l,u,f.** B

Millar, Fergus **JC88.M55 2002**
The Roman Republic in Political Thought. Perfect. University Press of New England. Lebanon, NH. 2002. 240p. Menahem Stern Jerusalem Lectures ISBN:1-58465-199-7, ISBN13: 978-1-58465-199-4. Dewey:320.437/07/204. LCCN:2001-008177.
Audience: **l,u.**

Morrall, John B. **JC71.A7 M67**
Aristotle. Cloth Text. Routledge. New York, NY. 1977. Political Thinkers Ser. ISBN:0-04-320121-0, ISBN13: 978-0-04-320121-3. Dewey:320.01. LCCN:78-303863.
Audience: **l,u.**

Ophir, Adi **JC71.P6O64 1991**
e Plato's Invisible Cities: Discourse and Power in the Republic. E-Book. Routledge. New York, NY. 1991. ISBN:0-203-00734-4, ISBN13: 978-0-203-00734-1. Dewey:321/.07.
Audience: **u,f.** *Choice, 1992.*

Plato & Bloom, Allan **JC71 .P35 1991B**
Republic of Plato. Ed. 2. Trade Paper. Basic Books. New York, NY. 1991. 512p. ISBN:0-465-06934-7, ISBN13: 978-0-465-06934-7. Dewey:321/.07. LCCN:91-189634.
Audience: **l,u,f.**

Plato **JC71.P513 2004**
Republic. Ed. 3. C. D. C. Reeve (Introduction by). Trade Paper. Hackett Publishing Company, Inc. Indianapolis, IN. 2004. 358p. ISBN:0-87220-736-6, ISBN13: 978-0-87220-736-3. Dewey:321/.07. LCCN:2004-013418.
Audience: **g,l,u,f.** B *Choice, 2005.*

Reeve, C. D. **JC71.P6**
Philosopher - Kings: The Argument of Plato's "Republic". Paper Text. Princeton University Press. Princeton, NJ. 1992. 400p. ISBN:0-691-02094-9, ISBN13: 978-0-691-02094-5. Dewey:321/.07.
Audience: **u,f.** *Choice, 1989.*

Rhodes, P. J. **JC71.A41**
A Commentary on the Aristotelian Athenaion Politeia. Ed. 2. Paper Text. Oxford University Press, Inc. New York, NY. 1993. 822p. ISBN:0-19-814942-5, ISBN13: 978-0-19-814942-2. Dewey:320.9385.
Audience: **l,u,f.** B

Salkever, Stephen G. **JC71.A7S25 1990**
Finding the Mean: Theory and Practice in Aristotelian Political Philosophy. Trade Cloth. Princeton University Press. Princeton, NJ. 1990. 328p. ISBN:0-691-07803-3, ISBN13: 978-0-691-07803-8. Dewey:320.1/01. LCCN:89-028742.
Audience: **u,f.** *Choice, 1991.*

Stalley, R. F. **K3169.S725 1983**
An Introduction to Plato's Laws. Trade Cloth. Hackett Publishing Company, Inc. Indianapolis, IN. 1983. 220p. ISBN:0-915145-84-7, ISBN13: 978-0-915145-84-3. Dewey:340/.109. LCCN:83-010850.
Audience: **l,u.** B

Tigerstedt, E. N. **B395 .T53**
Interpreting Plato. Paper Text. Coronet Books. Philadelphia, PA. 1977. 158p. ISBN:91-22-00090-9, ISBN13: 978-91-22-00090-7. Dewey:184. LCCN:77-482110.
Audience: **l,u.**

Von Fritz, Kurt **JC81.P767 F7 1975**
The Theory of the Mixed Constitution in Antiquity: A Critical Analysis of Polybuis Political Ideas. Trade Cloth. Ayer Company Publishers, Inc. Manchester, NH. 1979. Roman History Ser. ISBN:0-405-07082-9, ISBN13: 978-0-405-07082-2. Dewey:320.1/5. LCCN:75-007318.
Audience: **u,f.**

White, Nicholas P. **JC71.P6.W47**
A Companion to Plato's Republic. Trade Cloth. Hackett Publishing Company, Inc. Indianapolis, IN. 1979. 283p. ISBN:0-915144-56-5, ISBN13: 978-0-915144-56-3. Dewey:321/.07. LCCN:78-070043.
Audience: **l,u.** B

Political Theory > Medieval

Aquinas, Thomas **JC121.T42 2002**
Aquinas: Political Writings. R. W. Dyson (Editor, Translator). Cloth Text. Cambridge University Press. New York, NY. 2002. 360p. Cambridge Texts in the History of Political Thought Ser. ISBN:0-521-37569-X, ISBN13: 978-0-521-37569-6. Dewey:320. LCCN:2002-025748.
Audience: **g,u.**

Black, Antony **JA82 .B53 1992**
Political Thought in Europe, 1250-1450. Trade Cloth. Cambridge University Press. New York, NY. 1992. 223p. Cambridge Medieval Textbooks ISBN:0-521-38451-6, ISBN13: 978-0-521-38451-3. Dewey:320/.09. LCCN:91-025110.
Audience: **l,u.**

Blythe, James M. **JA82.B59 1992**
Ideal Government and the Mixed Constitution in the Middle Ages. Trade Cloth. Princeton University Press. Princeton, NJ. 1992. 365p. ISBN:0-691-03167-3, ISBN13: 978-0-691-03167-5. Dewey:320/.09/02. LCCN:91-021104.
Audience: **l,u,f.** *Choice, 1992.*

Burns, J. H. (Editor) **JA82 .C27 1988**
The Cambridge History of Medieval Political Thought C. 350-C. 1450. Trade Cloth. Cambridge University Press. New York, NY. 1988. 816p. The Cambridge History of Political Thought Ser. ISBN:0-521-24324-6, ISBN13: 978-0-521-24324-7. Dewey:320/.01. LCCN:87-006601.
Audience: **l.** *Choice, 1989.*

Coulborn, Rushton (Editor) **JC111 .C6**
Feudalism in History. Trade Cloth. Shoe String Press, Inc. North Haven, CT. 1965. xiv, 438p. ISBN:0-208-00274-X, ISBN13: 978-0-208-00274-7. Dewey:321.3. LCCN:65-024506.
Audience: **l,u,f.** B

Finnis, John (Editor) **JC121.T453F55 1998**
Aquinas: Moral, Political, and Legal Theory. Trade Paper. Oxford University Press, Inc. New York, NY. 1998. 408p. Founders of Modern Political and Social Thought Ser. ISBN:0-19-878085-0, ISBN13: 978-0-19-878085-4. Dewey:320.092. LCCN:97-051411.
Audience: **u,f.**

Gilby, Thomas **JC0121.T5G5**
The Political Thought of Thomas Aquinas. Paper Text. Textbook Publishers. Temecula, CA. 2003. 357p. ISBN:0-7581-2501-1, ISBN13: 978-0-7581-2501-9. Dewey:320.15.
Audience: **u,f.** B

John of Salisbury **JC121 .J6**
The Statesman's Book of John of Salisbury, Being the Fourth, Fifth, and Sixth Books, and Selections from the Seventh and Eighth Books, of the Policraticus. Paper Text. Textbook Publishers. Temecula, CA. 2003. xc, 410p. ISBN:0-7581-4334-6, ISBN13: 978-0-7581-4334-1. Dewey:320.01.
Audience: **u,f.**

Marsilius of Padua **JC121**
Marsilius of Padua: The Defender of the Peace. Annabel S. Brett (Editor), Raymond Guess & Quentin Skinner (Contribution by). Cloth Text. Cambridge University Press. New York, NY. 2005. 640p. Cambridge Texts in the History of Political Thought Ser. ISBN:0-521-78332-1, ISBN13: 978-0-521-78332-3. Dewey:320.1. LCCN:2006-296106.
Audience: **l,u.**

McGrade, Arthur Stephen **JA71**
The Political Thought of William Ockham. Trade Paper. Cambridge University Press. New York, NY. 2002. 283p. Cambridge Studies in Medieval Life and Thought Ser., :Third Ser. ISBN:0-521-52224-2, ISBN13: 978-0-521-52224-3. Dewey:320/.01.
Audience: **u,f.** B

Morrall, John B. **JA82**
Political Thought in Medieval Times. Trade Paper. University of Toronto Press. Toronto, ON. 1980. 152p. Mediaeval Academy Reprints for Teaching Ser., Vol. 7 ISBN:0-8020-6413-2, ISBN13: 978-0-8020-6413-4. Dewey:320/.09/02.
Audience: **l,u.** B

Okin, Susan Moller **HQ1122**
Women in Western Political Thought. Trade Paper. Princeton University Press. Princeton, NJ. 1979. 384p. ISBN:0-691-02191-0, ISBN13: 978-0-691-02191-1. Dewey:305.4/2/01. LCCN:79-084004.
Audience: **l,u,f.**

Popper, Karl R. **B63**
The High Tide of Prophecy. Trade Paper. Princeton University Press. Princeton, NJ. 1971. 432p. Open Society and Its Enemies Ser., Vol. II ISBN:0-691-01972-X, ISBN13: 978-0-691-01972-7. Dewey:320.01.
Audience: **l,u,f.**

von Heyking, John **JC121.A8H48 2001**
Augustine and Politics as Longing in the World. Trade Cloth. University of Missouri Press. Columbia, MO. 2001. xvi, 278p. ISBN:0-8262-1349-9, ISBN13: 978-0-8262-1349-5. Dewey:320/.092. LCCN:2001-027169.
Audience: **u,f.** *Choice, 2002.*

Political Theory > Modern

Ansell-Pearson, Keith **JC233.N52 A56 1994**
An Introduction to Nietzsche as Political Thinker: The Perfect Nihilist. Trade Paper. Cambridge University Press. New York,

NY. 1994. 263p. ISBN:0-521-42721-5, ISBN13: 978-0-521-42721-0. Dewey:320.01. LCCN:93-005504.
Audience: **g,l.** *Choice, 1995.*

Arendt, Hannah **JC251.A74 2005**
The Promise of Politics: From Theory to Practice. Trade Cloth. Knopf Publishing Group. New York, NY. 2005. 256p. ISBN:0-8052-4213-9, ISBN13: 978-0-8052-4213-3. Dewey:320.5. LCCN:2004-061403.
Audience: **u,f.**

Barrow, Clyde W. **JC251.B32 1993**
Critical Theories of the State: Marxist, Neo-Marxist, Post-Marxist. Trade Cloth. University of Wisconsin Press. Chicago, IL. 1993. 256p. ISBN:0-299-13710-4, ISBN13: 978-0-299-13710-6. Dewey:320.1. LCCN:92-034761.
Audience: **l,u.** *Choice, 1994.*

Brod, Harry **JC233.H46B76 1992**
Hegel's Philosophy of Politics: Idealism, Identity, and Modernity. Trade Paper. Westview Press. Boulder, CO. 1992. 216p. ISBN:0-8133-8526-1, ISBN13: 978-0-8133-8526-6. Dewey:320.01. LCCN:91-040678.
Audience: **l,u.** *Choice, 1993.*

Claeys, Gregory **JC178.V2C58 1989**
Thomas Paine: Social and Political Thought. Trade Paper. Routledge. New York, NY. 1989. 256p. ISBN:0-04-445090-7, ISBN13: 978-0-04-445090-0. Dewey:320.5/1/092. LCCN:89-016531.
Audience: **g,l,u.** *Choice, 1990.*

Cook, Ian **JC223.M66C66 1998**
Reading Mill: Studies in Political Theory. Cloth over Boards. Palgrave Macmillan. New York, NY. 1998. 208p. ISBN:0-312-21204-6, ISBN13: 978-0-312-21204-9. Dewey:320/.092. LCCN:97-041421.
Audience: **l,u,f.** *Choice, 1998.*

de Tocqueville, Alexis **JC229.T775 2002**
The Tocqueville Reader: A Life in Letters and Politics. Olivier Zunz & Alan S. Kahan (Editors). Trade Paper. Blackwell Publishing, Inc. Malden, MA. 2002. 384p. ISBN:0-631-21546-8, ISBN13: 978-0-631-21546-2. Dewey:320/.092. LCCN:2002-020851.
Audience: **g,l,u.** *Choice, 2003.*

Detwiler, Bruce **JC233.N52D48 1990**
Nietzsche and the Politics of Aristocratic Radicalism. Trade Cloth. University of Chicago Press. Chicago, IL. 1999. 252p. ISBN:0-226-14354-6, ISBN13: 978-0-226-14354-5. Dewey:305.5/2. LCCN:89-000375.
Audience: **u,f.** *Choice, 1991.*

Dewey, John **JC251.D47 1991**
Public and Its Problems. Trade Paper. Swallow Press. Athens, OH. 1954. 242p. ISBN:0-8040-0254-1, ISBN13: 978-0-8040-0254-7. Dewey:321.8. LCCN:76-178242.
Audience: **g,l,u,f.**

Duchacek, Ivo D. **JC355.D7 1987**
Comparative Federalism: The Territorial Dimension of Politics. Trade Cloth. University Press of America, Inc. Lanham, MD. 1987. 382p. Constitutional Government in Theory and Practice Ser. ISBN:0-8191-5741-4, ISBN13: 978-0-8191-5741-6. Dewey:321/.02. LCCN:86-024697.
Audience: **l,u,f.**

Ellis, Elisabeth **JC181.K4E45 2005**
Kant's Politics: Provisional Theory for an Uncertain World. Cloth over Boards. Yale University Press. Cumberland, RI. 2005. 272p. ISBN:0-300-10120-1, ISBN13: 978-0-300-10120-1. Dewey:320/.092. LCCN:2004-055299.
Audience: **l,u,f.** *Choice, 2005.*

Engster, Daniel **JC139.E54 2001**
Divine Sovereignty: The Origins of Modern State Power. Trade Cloth. Northern Illinois University Press. DeKalb, IL. 2003. 265p. ISBN:0-87580-275-3, ISBN13: 978-0-87580-275-6. Dewey:320.1. LCCN:2001-030463.
Audience: **l,u,f.** *Choice, 2002.*

Finocchiaro, Maurice A. **JC265.M65F56 1999**
Beyond Right and Left: Democratic Elitism in Mosca and Gramsci. Cloth over Boards. Yale University Press. Cumberland, RI. 1999. 314p. Italian Literature and Thought Ser. ISBN:0-300-07535-9, ISBN13: 978-0-300-07535-9. Dewey:320.5/0945. LCCN:98-008642.
Audience: **u,f.** *Choice, 1999.*

Franco, Paul **JC257.O244F72 2004**
Michael Oakeshott: An Introduction. Cloth over Boards. Yale University Press. Cumberland, RI. 2004. 224p. ISBN:0-300-10404-9, ISBN13: 978-0-300-10404-2. Dewey:320/.092. LCCN:2004-009252.
Audience: **l,u.** *Choice, 2005.*

Harris, Ian **JC153.L87 H37 1994**
The Mind of John Locke: A Study of Political Theory in Its Intellectual Setting. Trade Paper. Cambridge University Press. New York, NY. 1998. 449p. ISBN:0-521-63872-0, ISBN13: 978-0-521-63872-2. Dewey:320/.01.
Audience: **l,u,f.** *Choice, 1995.*

Hegel, Georg Wilhelm Fredrich **JC233 .H44613 1999**
Hegel: Political Writings. Lawrence Dickey & H. B. Nisbet (Editors), Raymond Geuss & Quentin Skinner (Contribution by). Trade Paper. Cambridge University Press. New York, NY. 1999. 414p. Texts in the History of Political Thought ISBN:0-521-45975-3, ISBN13: 978-0-521-45975-4. Dewey:320.101. LCCN:98-044357.
Audience: **l,u,f.** *Choice, 2000.*

Hobbes, Thomas **JC153.H65 1998**
The Leviathan. J. C. Gaskin (Editor, Introduction by, Notes by). Trade Paper. Oxford University Press, Inc. New York, NY. 1998. 576p. Oxford World's Classics Ser. ISBN:0-19-283498-3, ISBN13: 978-0-19-283498-0. Dewey:320.1. LCCN:99-178169.
Audience: **g,l,u,f.**

Josephson, Peter **JC153.J67 2002**
The Great Art of Government: Locke's Use of Consent. Trade Cloth. University Press of Kansas. Lawrence, KS. 2002. 378p. ISBN:0-7006-1169-X, ISBN13: 978-0-7006-1169-0. Dewey:320.1/1. LCCN:2001-007731.
Audience: **l,u,f.** *Choice, 2003.*

Jowitt, Kenneth **JC474.J69 1992**
New World Disorder: The Leninist Extinction. Trade Cloth. University of California Press. Berkeley, CA. 1992. 345p. ISBN:0-520-07762-8, ISBN13: 978-0-520-07762-1. Dewey:321.9/2. LCCN:91-028260.
Audience: **l,u,f.** *Choice, 1992.*

Lamberti, Jean-Claude **JC229.T8L35313 1989**
Tocqueville and the Two Democracies. Arthur Goldhammer (Translator). Trade Cloth. Harvard University Press. Cambridge, MA. 1989. 323p. ISBN:0-674-89435-9, ISBN13: 978-0-674-89435-8. Dewey:321.8. LCCN:88-018758.
Audience: **l,u,f.** *Choice, 1989.*

Locke, John **JC153 .L8 1988**
Locke: Two Treatises of Government. Ed. 3. Peter Laslett (Editor), Raymond Geuss & Quentin Skinner (Contribution by). Trade Cloth. Cambridge University Press. New York, NY. 1988. 480p. Texts in the History of Political Thought ISBN:0-521-35448-X, ISBN13: 978-0-521-35448-6. Dewey:320. LCCN:87-033783.
Audience: **g,l,u,f.**

Machiavelli, Niccolo **JC143.M163 2003**
Discourses on Livy. Julia Conaway Bondanella & Peter Bondanella (Translator, Introduction by, Notes by). Trade Paper. Oxford University Press, Inc. New York, NY. 2003. 448p. Oxford World's Classics Ser. ISBN:0-19-280473-1, ISBN13: 978-0-19-280473-0. Dewey:937/.02.
Audience: **u,f.** *Choice, 1996.*

Machiavelli, Niccolo **JC143.M38 2005**
The Prince. George Bull (Translator). Trade Paper. Penguin Group (USA) Inc. New York, NY. 2005. 128p. Great Ideas Ser. ISBN:0-14-303633-5, ISBN13: 978-0-14-303633-3. Dewey:320/.01. LCCN:2005-047730.
Audience: **g,l,u,f.** B

Machiavelli, Niccolo **JC143.M38 1998**
The Prince. Ed. 2. Harvey C. Mansfield Jr. (Translator). Trade Paper. University of Chicago Press. Chicago, IL. 1998. 184p. ISBN:0-226-50044-6, ISBN13: 978-0-226-50044-7. Dewey:320/.01. LCCN:98-005772.
Audience: **g,l.** B

Manent, Pierre **JC229.T8M3213 1996**
Tocqueville and the Nature of Democracy. John Waggoner (Translator), Harvey C. Mansfield Jr. (Introduction by). Book, Other. Rowman & Littlefield Publishers, Inc. Lanham, MD. 1996. 166p. ISBN:0-8476-8116-5, ISBN13: 978-0-8476-8116-7. Dewey:320/.092. LCCN:95-038604.
Audience: **l,u.** *Choice, 1996.*

Mansfield, Harvey C. Jr. **JC143.M4M355 1996**
Machiavelli's Virtue. Trade Cloth. University of Chicago Press. Chicago, IL. 1996. 460p. ISBN:0-226-50368-2, ISBN13: 978-0-226-50368-4. Dewey:320/.092. LCCN:95-024115.
Audience: **g,l,u,f.** *Choice, 1996.*

Marx, Karl **JC233 .M29213 1994**
Marx: Early Political Writings. Joseph J. O'Malley (Editor), Richard A. Davis (Assisted by), Raymond Geuss & Quentin Skinner (Contribution by). Trade Paper. Cambridge University Press. New York, NY. 1994. 230p. Texts in the History of Political Thought ISBN:0-521-34994-X, ISBN13: 978-0-521-34994-9. Dewey:306.2. LCCN:93-031207.
Audience: **g,l,u,f.**

Myers, Peter C. **JC153.L87M94 1998**
Our Only Star and Compass: Locke and the Struggle for Political Rationality. Book, Other. Rowman & Littlefield Publishers, Inc. Lanham, MD. 1999. 288p. ISBN:0-8476-9099-7, ISBN13: 978-0-8476-9099-2. Dewey:320.1/01. LCCN:98-036862.
Audience: **l,u,f.** *Choice, 1999.*

Oakeshott, Michael **JC153.H66 2000**
Hobbes on Civil Association. Paul Franco (Foreword by). Trade Paper. Liberty Fund, Inc. Indianapolis, IN. 2000. 184p. ISBN:0-86597-291-5, ISBN13: 978-0-86597-291-9. Dewey:320/.01. LCCN:00-035410.
Audience: **l,u,f.**

Orwin, Clifford & Tarcov, Nathan (Editors) **JC179.R9L44 1997**
The Legacy of Rousseau. Trade Paper. University of Chicago Press. Chicago, IL. 1997. 345p. ISBN:0-226-63856-1, ISBN13: 978-0-226-63856-0. Dewey:320.1. LCCN:96-008908.
Audience: **g,l,u,f.** *Choice, 1997.*

Pontuso, James F. **JC273.H37P66 2004**
Vaclav Havel: Civic Responsibility in the Postmodern Age. Book, Other. Rowman & Littlefield Publishers, Inc. Lanham, MD. 2004. 192p. Twentieth-Century Political Thinkers Ser. ISBN:0-7425-2256-3, ISBN13: 978-0-7425-2256-5. Dewey:943.7105/092. LCCN:2004-003265.
Audience: **g,l,u,f.**

Rousseau, Jean-Jacques **JC179.R8613 2003**
On the Social Contract. G. D. H. Cole (Translator). Trade Paper. Dover Publications, Inc. Mineola, NY. 2003. 112p. Dover Thrift Editions Ser. ISBN:0-486-42692-0, ISBN13: 978-0-486-42692-1. Dewey:320.1/1. LCCN:2002-034820.
Audience: **g,l,u,f.**

Rousseau, Jean-Jacques **JC336**
The Social Contract and Discourses. G. D. Cole (Translator), J. H. Brumfitt & John C. Hall (Revised by), Alan Ryan (Introduction by). Trade Cloth. Alfred A. Knopf Inc. New York, NY. 1993. 416p. Everyman's Library, Vol. 162 ISBN:0-679-42302-8, ISBN13: 978-0-679-42302-7. Dewey:320.1/1. LCCN:93-022368.
Audience: **g,l,u,f.**

Rousseau, Jean-Jacques **JC179.R7 1987**
Basic Political Writings. Donald A. Cress (Translator), Peter Gay (Introduction by). Trade Paper. Hackett Publishing Company, Inc. Indianapolis, IN. 1987. 249p. HPC Classics Ser. ISBN:0-87220-047-7, ISBN13: 978-0-87220-047-0. Dewey:320/.01. LCCN:87-023610.
Audience: **g,l,u,f.**

Sapiro, Virginia **JC176.W65S27 1992**
A Vindication of Political Virtue: The Political Theory of Mary Wollstonecraft. Trade Paper. University of Chicago Press. Chicago, IL. 1992. 394p. ISBN:0-226-73491-9, ISBN13: 978-0-226-73491-0. Dewey:323.34092. LCCN:91-038426.
Audience: **l,u,f.** *Choice, 1993.*

Sassoon, Anne Showstack **JC265.G68S27 1987**
Gramsci's Politics. Ed. 2. Trade Paper. University of Minnesota Press. Minneapolis, MN. 1988. 318p. ISBN:0-8166-1648-5, ISBN13: 978-0-8166-1648-0. Dewey:320.5/315/0924. LCCN:87-016595.
Audience: **l,u.** B

Sheldon, Garrett Ward **JC211.M35**
The Political Philosophy of James Madison. Trade Paper. Johns Hopkins University Press. Baltimore, MD. 2003. 160p. ISBN:0-8018-7106-9, ISBN13: 978-0-8018-7106-1. Dewey:321.8/092.
Audience: **g,l,u,f.** *Choice, 2001.*

Villa, Dana (Editor) **JC251.A74 C22 2000**
The Cambridge Companion to Hannah Arendt. Trade Paper. Cambridge University Press. New York, NY. 2000. 305p. Companions to Philosophy Ser. ISBN:0-521-64571-9, ISBN13: 978-0-521-64571-3. Dewey:320.5/092. LCCN:00-021835.
Audience: **g,l,u,f.** *Choice, 2001.*

Walling, Karl-Friedrich **JC176.H27W35 1999**
Republican Empire: Alexander Hamilton on War and Free Government. Trade Cloth. University Press of Kansas. Lawrence, KS. 1999. xii, 356p. American Political Thought Ser. ISBN:0-7006-0970-9, ISBN13: 978-0-7006-0970-3. Dewey:321.8/6. LCCN:99-019716.
Audience: **l,u,f.** *Choice, 2000.*

Westbrook, Robert B. **JC251.D48W47 1991**
John Dewey and American Democracy. Book, Other. Cornell University Press. Ithaca, NY. 1991. 608p. ISBN:0-8014-2560-3, ISBN13: 978-0-8014-2560-8. Dewey:320/.01. LCCN:90-055712.
Audience: **g,l,u,f.** *Choice, 1991.*

Wolin, Sheldon S. **DC36.98**
Tocqueville Between Two Worlds: The Making of a Political and Theoretical Life. Trade Paper. Princeton University Press. Princeton, NJ. 2003. 664p. ISBN:0-691-11454-4, ISBN13: 978-0-691-11454-5. Dewey:320/.092.
Audience: **u,f.** *Choice, 2002.*

Political Theory > Modern > By Country, A-Z > United States

Alperovitz, Gar **JK1726.A428 2004**
America Beyond Capitalism: Reclaiming Our Wealth, Our Liberty, and Our Democracy. Trade Cloth. John Wiley & Sons, Inc. Hoboken, NJ. 2004. 336p. ISBN:0-471-66730-7, ISBN13: 978-0-471-66730-8. Dewey:330.973. LCCN:2004-003617.
Audience: **l,u,f.**

Rorty, Richard McKay **HN90.R3R636 1998**
Achieving Our Country: Leftist Thought in Twentieth-Century America. Trade Cloth. Harvard University Press. Cambridge, MA. 1998. 172p. The William E. Massey Sr. Lectures in the History of American Civilization Ser. ISBN:0-674-00311-X, ISBN13: 978-0-674-00311-8. Dewey:303.48/4. LCCN:97-043210.
Audience: **l,u,f.**

Weinstein, James **HX83.W43 2003**
The Long Detour: The History and Future of the American Left. Trade Paper. Westview Press. Boulder, CO. 2004. 304p. ISBN:0-8133-4251-1, ISBN13: 978-0-8133-4251-1. Dewey:335/.00973. LCCN:2003-000941.
Audience: **g,l,u,f.** *Choice, 2004.*

Political Theory > Theories of State

DeLamotte, Eugenia **HX843.7.D43D45 2004**
Gates of Freedom: Voltairine de Cleyre and the Revolution of the Mind. Trade Cloth. University of Michigan Press. Chicago, IL. 2004. 348p. ISBN:0-472-09867-5, ISBN13: 978-0-472-09867-5. Dewey:335/.83/092 B. LCCN:2004-006183.
Audience: **u,f.** *Choice, 2005.*

Giddens, Anthony **HX73.G54 2000**
The Third Way and Its Critics. Trade Paper. Polity Press. Cambridge, 2000. 200p. ISBN:0-7456-2450-2, ISBN13: 978-0-7456-2450-1. Dewey:320.5/31. LCCN:99-086002.
Audience: **g,l,u,f.** *Choice, 2000.*

Johnston, David **JC571.J57 1994**
The Idea of a Liberal Theory. Trade Cloth. Princeton University Press. Princeton, NJ. 1994. 216p. ISBN:0-691-03381-1, ISBN13: 978-0-691-03381-5. Dewey:320.5/1. LCCN:94-004089.
Audience: **l,u,f.** *Choice, 1995.*

Kropotkin, Peter **HX833.K7213 2001**
Anarchism: A Collection of Revolutionary Writings. Trade Paper. Dover Publications, Inc. Mineola, NY. 2002. 320p. ISBN:0-486-41955-X, ISBN13: 978-0-486-41955-8. Dewey:335/.83. LCCN:2001-047465.
Audience: **u,f.**

Kropotkin, Peter **HX833.K744 1995**
Evolution and Environment. Trade Paper. Black Rose Books. Montreal, PQ. 1995. 225p. Collected Works of Peter Kropotkin ISBN:1-895431-44-1, ISBN13: 978-1-895431-44-5. Dewey:116. LCCN:95-076810.
Audience: **u,f.**

Kropotkin, Peter **HX833.K745 1993**
Fugitive Writings. George Woodcock (Introduction by). Trade Cloth. Black Rose Books. Montreal, PQ. 1993. 240p. ISBN:1-895431-43-3, ISBN13: 978-1-895431-43-8. Dewey:320.5/7. LCCN:93-070389.
Audience: **u,f.**

Oakeshott, Michael **JC153.H66 2000**
Hobbes on Civil Association. Paul Franco (Foreword by). Trade Paper. Liberty Fund, Inc. Indianapolis, IN. 2000. 184p. ISBN:0-86597-291-5, ISBN13: 978-0-86597-291-9. Dewey:320/.01. LCCN:00-035410.
Audience: **l,u,f.**

Okin, Susan Moller **HQ1122**
Women in Western Political Thought. Trade Paper. Princeton University Press. Princeton, NJ. 1979. 384p. ISBN:0-691-02191-0, ISBN13: 978-0-691-02191-1. Dewey:305.4/2/01. LCCN:79-084004.
Audience: **l,u,f.**

Popper, Karl R. **B63**
The High Tide of Prophecy. Trade Paper. Princeton University Press. Princeton, NJ. 1971. 432p. Open Society and Its Enemies Ser., Vol. II ISBN:0-691-01972-X, ISBN13: 978-0-691-01972-7. Dewey:320.01.
Audience: **l,u,f.**

Political Theory > Theories of State > Nationalism

Anderson, Benedict R. O'G. **JC311.A656 1991**
Imagined Communities: Reflections on the Origin and Spread of Nationalism. Ed. 2. Trade Cloth. Verso Books. London, 1991. 240p. ISBN:0-86091-546-8, ISBN13: 978-0-86091-546-1. Dewey:320.5/4. LCCN:91-010900.
Audience: **l,u,f.**

Apter, David E. **JQ2951.A99B843 1997**
The Political Kingdom in Uganda: A Study in Bureaucratic Nationalism. Ed. 3. Trade Paper. Irish Academic Press. Dublin, 1997. 592p. ISBN:0-7146-4234-7, ISBN13: 978-0-7146-4234-5. Dewey:306.2/09676. LCCN:97-013495.
Audience: **u,f.** *Choice, 1998.*

Armstrong, John A. **JC0311.A843.**
Nations Before Nationalism. Trade Paper. Books on Demand. Ann Arbor, MI. 447p. ISBN:0-7837-0287-6, ISBN13: 978-0-7837-0287-2. Dewey:320.5/4/09. LCCN:81-012988.
Audience: **l,u,f.**

Canovan, Margaret **JC311.C337 1996**
Nationhood and Political Theory. Trade Cloth. Edward Elgar Publishing, Inc. Northampton, MA. 1996. 168p. ISBN:1-85278-852-6, ISBN13: 978-1-85278-852-0. Dewey:320.5/4. LCCN:95-031939.
Audience: **l,u,f.** *Choice, 1996.*

Cocks, Joan **JC311.C6135 2002**
Passion and Paradox: Intellectuals Confront the National Question. Trade Paper. Princeton University Press. Princeton, NJ. 2002. 234p. ISBN:0-691-07468-2, ISBN13: 978-0-691-07468-9. Dewey:320.54/01. LCCN:2001-038755.
Audience: **u,f.** *Choice, 2003.*

Connor, Walker **GN380**
Ethnonationalism: The Quest for Understanding. Trade Paper. Princeton University Press. Princeton, NJ. 1993. 248p. ISBN:0-691-02563-0, ISBN13: 978-0-691-02563-6. Dewey:323.1/1. LCCN:93-017829.
Audience: **g,l,u,f.** *Choice, 1994.*

Day, Graham & Thompson, Andrew **JC311.D34 2004**
Theorizing Nationalism: Debates and Issues in Social Theory. Trade Paper. Palgrave Macmillan. New York, NY. 2005. 240p. ISBN:0-333-96265-6, ISBN13: 978-0-333-96265-7. Dewey:320.54/01. LCCN:2004-054707.
Audience: **g,l,u,f.** *Choice, 2005.*

Fawn, Rick (Editor) **JC311.I33 2003**
Ideology and National Identity in Post-Communist Foreign Policy. Paper over Boards. Taylor & Francis Group. Abingdon, 2003. 160p. ISBN:0-7146-5517-1, ISBN13: 978-0-7146-5517-8. Dewey:327/.09171/7. LCCN:2003-017673.
Audience: **l,u,f.** *Choice, 2004.*

Forman, Michael H. **JC311.F564 1998**
Nationalism and the International Labor Movement: The Idea of the Nation in Socialist and Anarchist Theory. Trade Paper. Pennsylvania State University Press. University Park, PA. 1998. 374p. ISBN:0-271-01727-9, ISBN13: 978-0-271-01727-3. Dewey:320.53/1. LCCN:97-007117.
Audience: **l,u,f.**

Gellner, Ernest **JC311.G47 1994**
Encounters with Nationalism. Trade Paper. Blackwell Publishing, Inc. Malden, MA. 1995. 224p. ISBN:0-631-19481-9, ISBN13: 978-0-631-19481-1. Dewey:320.5/4. LCCN:94-001737.
Audience: **g,l,u,f.** *Choice, 1995.*

Gellner, Ernest **JC311.G475 1997**
Nationalism. Trade Cloth. New York University Press. New York, NY. 1997. 272p. ISBN:0-8147-3113-9, ISBN13: 978-0-8147-3113-0. Dewey:320.54. LCCN:97-033629.
Audience: **l,u,f.**

Guibernau, Montserrat **JC311.G783 1999**
Nations Without States. Trade Paper. Polity Press. Cambridge, 1999. 224p. ISBN:0-7456-1801-4, ISBN13: 978-0-7456-1801-2. Dewey:320.54/09/049. LCCN:99-022431.
Audience: **u,f.** *Choice, 2000.*

Habermas, Jürgen **JC311.H2213 2001**
The Postnational Constellation: Political Essays. Max Pensky (Editor, Translator, Introduction by). Trade Cloth. MIT Press. Cambridge, MA. 2001. 216p. Studies in Contemporary German Social Thought ISBN:0-262-08297-7, ISBN13: 978-0-262-08297-6. Dewey:320.1/01. LCCN:00-048963.
Audience: **l,u,f.**

Hall, John A. (Editor) **JC311 .S77 1998**
The State of the Nation: Ernest Gellner and the Theory of Nationalism. Trade Paper. Cambridge University Press. New York, NY. 1998. 328p. ISBN:0-521-63366-4, ISBN13: 978-0-521-63366-6. Dewey:320.54/01. LCCN:97-052663.
Audience: **l,u,f.** *Choice, 1999.*

Hobsbawm, E. J. **JC311 .H577 1992**
Nations and Nationalism since 1780: Programme, Myth, Reality. Ed. 2. Trade Paper. Cambridge University Press. New York, NY. 1992. 214p. A Canto Book Ser. ISBN:0-521-43961-2, ISBN13: 978-0-521-43961-9. Dewey:320.5/4. LCCN:92-014949.
Audience: **g,l,u,f.**

Ignatieff, Michael **JC311.I42 1994**
Blood and Belonging: Journeys into the New Nationalism. Trade Cloth. Farrar, Straus & Giroux. New York, NY. 1994. 263p. ISBN:0-374-11440-4, ISBN13: 978-0-374-11440-4. Dewey:320.5/4. LCCN:93-030954.
Audience: **g,l,u,f.**

Karl, Rebecca E. **JC311.K32 2002**
Staging the World: Chinese Nationalism at the Turn of the 20th Century. Trade Paper. Duke University Press. Durham, NC. 2002. 320p. Asia-Pacific Ser. ISBN:0-8223-2867-4, ISBN13: 978-0-8223-2867-4. Dewey:320.54/0951/09034. LCCN:2001-054468.
Audience: **l,u,f.** *Choice, 2002.*

Marx, Anthony W. **JC311**
Faith in Nation: Exclusionary Origins of Nationalism. Trade Paper. Oxford University Press, Inc. New York, NY. 2005. 288p. ISBN:0-19-518259-6, ISBN13: 978-0-19-518259-0. Dewey:320.54/094. LCCN:2002-022449.
Audience: **u,f.**

McKim, Robert & McMahan, Jeff (Editors) **JC311.M588 1997**
The Morality of Nationalism. Paper Text. Oxford University Press, Inc. New York, NY. 1997. 384p. ISBN:0-19-510392-0, ISBN13: 978-0-19-510392-2. Dewey:172. LCCN:96-021168.
Audience: **g,l,u,f.** *Choice, 1998.*

Miller, David **JC311.M475 1995**
On Nationality. Trade Cloth. Oxford University Press, Inc. New York, NY. 1995. 220p. Oxford Political Theory Ser. ISBN:0-19-828047-5, ISBN13: 978-0-19-828047-7. Dewey:320.5/4/01. LCCN:95-017966.
Audience: **l,u,f.** *Choice, 1996.*

Motyl, Alexander J. (Editor-In-Chief) **JC311.E4996 2001**
Encyclopedia of Nationalism, Set. Trade Cloth. Elsevier Science & Technology Books. Saint Louis, MO. 2000. 1529p.

ISBN:0-12-227230-7, ISBN13: 978-0-12-227230-1. Dewey:320.54/03. LCCN:00-102545.
Audience: **g,l,u,f.** *Choice, 2001.*

Ozkirimli, Umut **JC311.O93 2000**
Theories of Nationalism: A Critical Introduction. Fred Halliday (Foreword by). Trade Paper. Palgrave Macmillan. New York, NY. 2000. 266p. ISBN:0-312-22942-9, ISBN13: 978-0-312-22942-9. Dewey:320.5/4. LCCN:99-042150.
Audience: **g,l,u.** *Choice, 2000.*

Poole, Ross **JC311.P662 1999**
Nation and Identity. Paper over Boards. Routledge. New York, NY. 1999. 224p. Ideas Ser. ISBN:0-415-12622-3, ISBN13: 978-0-415-12622-9. Dewey:320.54. LCCN:99-023022.
Audience: **l,u,f.** *Choice, 2000.*

Poole, Ross **JC311.P662 1999**
Nation and Identity. Trade Paper. Routledge. New York, NY. 1999. 224p. Ideas Ser. ISBN:0-415-12623-1, ISBN13: 978-0-415-12623-6. Dewey:320.54. LCCN:99-023022.
Audience: **l,u,f.** *Choice, 2000.*

Skrentny, John D. **JC312**
The Minority Rights Revolution. Trade Paper. Harvard University Press. Cambridge, MA. 2004. 496p. ISBN:0-674-01618-1, ISBN13: 978-0-674-01618-7. Dewey:323.1/73.
Audience: **l,u,f.** *Choice, 2003.*

Smith, Anthony D. **JC311.N5388 1998**
Nationalism and Modernism: A Critical Survey of Recent Theories of Nations and Nationalism. Paper over Boards. Routledge. New York, NY. 1998. 288p. ISBN:0-415-06340-X, ISBN13: 978-0-415-06340-1. Dewey:320.54/01. LCCN:98-018648.
Audience: **l,u.** *Choice, 1999.*

Smith, Anthony & Hutchinson, John (Editors) **JC311.N295 1994**
Nationalism. Paper Text. Oxford University Press, Inc. New York, NY. 1995. 392p. Oxford Readers Ser. ISBN:0-19-289260-6, ISBN13: 978-0-19-289260-7. Dewey:320.5/4. LCCN:94-017708.
Audience: **g,l,u.** *Choice, 1995.*

Suzman, Mark **JC311.S9 1999**
Ethnic Nationalism and State Power: The Rise of Irish Nationalism, Afrikaner Nationalism and Zionism. Cloth over Boards. Palgrave Macmillan. New York, NY. 1999. 244p. ISBN:0-312-22028-6, ISBN13: 978-0-312-22028-0. Dewey:320.5/4. LCCN:98-047533.
Audience: **l,u,f.** *Choice, 2000.*

Political Theory > Theories of State > Political Geography

Agnew, John **JC319.A44 2002**
Making Political Geography. Trade Paper. Oxford University Press, Inc. New York, NY. 2002. 256p. Human Geography in the Making Ser. ISBN:0-340-75955-0, ISBN13: 978-0-340-75955-4. Dewey:320.1/2. LCCN:2003-266522.
Audience: **g,l,u.** *Choice, 2003.*

Anderson, Ewan (Editor) **JC319**
Global Geopolitical Flashpoints: An Atlas of Conflict. Trade Cloth. Fitzroy Dearborn Publishers, Inc. Chicago, IL. 2000. 391p. ISBN:1-57958-137-4, ISBN13: 978-1-57958-137-4. Dewey:320.
Audience: **g,l,u,f.** *Choice, 2001.*

Anderson, Malcolm **JC323.A63 1997**
Frontiers: Territory and State Formation in the Modern World. Trade Paper. Polity Press. Cambridge, 1997. 272p. ISBN:0-7456-2008-6, ISBN13: 978-0-7456-2008-4. Dewey:320.1/2. LCCN:97-029548.
Audience: **l,u.** *Choice, 1996.*

Cohen, Saul Bernard **JC319.C62 2002**
Geopolitics of the World System. Book, Other. Rowman & Littlefield Publishers, Inc. Lanham, MD. 2002. 480p. Regional Geographies for a New Era Ser. ISBN:0-8476-9906-4, ISBN13: 978-0-8476-9906-3. Dewey:320.1/2. LCCN:2002-000615.
Audience: **l,u.** *Choice, 2003.*

Cohen, Saul Bernard **JC319.C62 2002**
Geopolitics of the World System. Book, Other. Rowman & Littlefield Publishers, Inc. Lanham, MD. 2002. 480p. Regional Geographies for a New Era Ser. ISBN:0-8476-9907-2, ISBN13: 978-0-8476-9907-0. Dewey:320.1/2. LCCN:2002-000615.
Audience: **g,l,u.** *Choice, 2003.*

Dodds, Klaus J. & Atkinson, David **JC319.G483 2000**
Geopolitical Traditions: Critical Histories of Century of Political Thought. Trade Paper. Routledge. New York, NY. 2000. 416p. Critical Geographies Ser., Vol. 7 ISBN:0-415-17249-7, ISBN13: 978-0-415-17249-3. Dewey:327.1/09/04. LCCN:99-044347.
Audience: **l,u,f.** *Choice, 2001.*

Flint, Colin (Author, Editor) **JC319.G445 2004**
The Geography of War and Peace: From Death Camps to Diplomats. Trade Paper. Oxford University Press, Inc. New York, NY. 2004. 480p. ISBN:0-19-516209-9, ISBN13: 978-0-19-516209-7. Dewey:303.6/6. LCCN:2003-019427.
Audience: **g,l,u,f.** *Choice, 2005.*

Fuller, Graham E. & Lesser, Ian O. **DS35.74.E85F85 1995**
Sense of Siege: The Geopolitics of Islam and the West. Trade Paper. Westview Press. Boulder, CO. 1995. 208p. A RAND Study Ser. ISBN:0-8133-2149-2, ISBN13: 978-0-8133-2149-3. Dewey:297. LCCN:95-131078.
Audience: **g,l,u,f.**

Gottmann, Jean **JC319.G66**
e The Significance of Territory. E-Book. NetLibrary, Inc. Boulder, CO. 1973. ISBN:0-585-27089-9, ISBN13: 978-0-585-27089-0. Dewey:320.1/2.
Audience: **l,u,f.**

Mellor, Roy **JC319.M56 1989**
Nation, State and Territory: A Political Geography. Trade Cloth. Routledge. New York, NY. 1989. 240p. ISBN:0-415-02287-8, ISBN13: 978-0-415-02287-3. Dewey:320.1/2. LCCN:88-023900.
Audience: **l,u.** *Choice, 1990.*

Migdal, Joel S. (Editor) **JC323.B677 2004**
Boundaries and Belonging: States and Societies in the Struggle to Shape Identities and Local Practices. Trade Cloth. Cambridge University Press. New York, NY. 2004. 374p.

ISBN:0-521-83566-6, ISBN13: 978-0-521-83566-4. Dewey:320.1/2. LCCN:2003-061210.
Audience: **l,u,f.** *Choice, 2005.*

Otuathail, Gearoid, et al. **JC319.G49 1998**
The Geopolitics Reader. Simon Dalby & Paul Routledge (Authors). Trade Paper. Routledge. New York, NY. 1998. 344p. ISBN:0-415-16271-8, ISBN13: 978-0-415-16271-5. Dewey:302.1/2. LCCN:97-013460.
Audience: **l,u.** *Choice, 1999.*

Sukhwal, B. L. & Sukhwal, Lilawati **Z6004.P7.S85 1992**
Political Geography: A Comprehensive Systematic Bibliography. Trade Cloth. A M S Press, Inc. New York, NY. 1992. xx, 715p. International Studies, No. 1 ISBN:0-404-63151-7, ISBN13: 978-0-404-63151-2. Dewey:016.3201/2. LCCN:91-057956.
Audience: **g,l,u,f.** *Choice, 1997.*

Toft, Monica Duffy **JC328.6.T64 2003**
The Geography of Ethnic Violence: Identity, Interests, and the Indivisibility of Territory. Trade Cloth. Princeton University Press. Princeton, NJ. 2003. 256p. ISBN:0-691-11354-8, ISBN13: 978-0-691-11354-8. Dewey:303.6. LCCN:2002-042463.
Audience: **l,u,f.** *Choice, 2004.*

White, George W. **JC311.W463 2004**
Nation, State, and Territory: Origins, Evolutions, and Relationships. Ed. 2. Book, Other. Rowman & Littlefield Publishers, Inc. Lanham, MD. 2004. 304p. ISBN:0-7425-3025-6, ISBN13: 978-0-7425-3025-6. Dewey:320.1. LCCN:2004-014114.
Audience: **l,u,f.**

Political Theory > Theories of State > Sovereignty

Bartelson, Jens **JC327 .B245 1995**
A Genealogy of Sovereignty. Thomas J. Biersteker, Chris Brown, Philip G. Cerny, Joseph Grieco, A. J. R. Groom, Steve Smith, Richard Higgott, G. John Ikenberry, Caroline Kennedy-Pipe & Steve Lamy (Contribution by). Trade Paper. Cambridge University Press. New York, NY. 1995. 329p. Studies in International Relations, 39 ISBN:0-521-47888-X, ISBN13: 978-0-521-47888-5. Dewey:320.1 5. LCCN:94-030053.
Audience: **l,u,f.** *Choice, 1996.*

Bukovansky, Mlada **JC327.B764 2002**
Legitimacy and Power Politics: The American and French Revolutions in International Political Culture. Trade Cloth. Princeton University Press. Princeton, NJ. 2002. 272p. Princeton Studies in International History and Politics ISBN:0-691-07434-8, ISBN13: 978-0-691-07434-4. Dewey:306.2/0944/09033. LCCN:2001-055407.
Audience: **l,u,f.** *Choice, 2003.*

Cusimano-Love, Maryann K. **JX1395**
Beyond Sovereignty: Issues for a Global Agenda. Ed. 3. Paper Text. Thomson Wadsworth. Belmont, CA. 2006. 360p. ISBN:0-495-09026-3, ISBN13: 978-0-495-09026-7. Dewey:327.
Audience: **g,l,u,f.**

Cusimano-Love, Maryann K. **JC362.B4 2002**
Beyond Sovereignty: Issues for a Global Agenda. Ed. 2. Paper Text. Thomson Wadsworth. Belmont, CA. 2002. 384p. ISBN:0-534-60893-0, ISBN13: 978-0-534-60893-4. Dewey:327. LCCN:2002-284136.
Audience: **g,l,u.**

Derrida, Jacques **JC497.D47 2005**
Rogues: Two Essays on Reason. Trade Paper. Stanford University Press. Palo Alto, CA. 2004. 200p. ISBN:0-8047-4951-5, ISBN13: 978-0-8047-4951-0. Dewey:320.1. LCCN:2004-016072.
Audience: **u,f.** *Choice, 2005.*

Duara, Prasenjit **JC311.D83 2003**
Sovereignty and Authenticity: Manchukuo and the East Asian Modern. Book, Other. Rowman & Littlefield Publishers, Inc. Lanham, MD. 2003. 320p. State and Society in East Asia Ser. ISBN:0-7425-2577-5, ISBN13: 978-0-7425-2577-1. Dewey:320.54/095. LCCN:2002-151157.
Audience: **u,f.** *Choice, 2003.*

Engster, Daniel **JC139.E54 2001**
Divine Sovereignty: The Origins of Modern State Power. Trade Cloth. Northern Illinois University Press. DeKalb, IL. 2003. 265p. ISBN:0-87580-275-3, ISBN13: 978-0-87580-275-6. Dewey:320.1. LCCN:2001-030463.
Audience: **l,u,f.** *Choice, 2002.*

Hunter, Ian & Saunders, David (Editors) **JC327.N39 2002**
Natural Law and Civil Sovereignty: Moral Right and State Authority in Early Modern Political Thought. Trade Cloth. Palgrave Macmillan. New York, NY. 2002. 272p. ISBN:0-333-96459-4, ISBN13: 978-0-333-96459-0. Dewey:340/.112. LCCN:2001-058505.
Audience: **u,f.** *Choice, 2003.*

Niebuhr, Reinhold **JC325 .N5**
The Structure of Nations and Empires: A Study of the Recurring Patterns and Problems of the Political Order in Relation to the Unique Problems of the Nuclear Age. Paper Text. Textbook Publishers. Temecula, CA. 2003. xi, 306p. ISBN:0-7581-4059-2, ISBN13: 978-0-7581-4059-3. Dewey:327/.11.
Audience: **u,f.** B

Sassen, Saskia **JC327.S27 1996**
Losing Control?: Sovereignty in the Age of Globalization. Trade Cloth. Columbia University Press. New York, NY. 1996. 128p. University Seminars/Leonard Hastings Schoff Memorial Lecture Ser. ISBN:0-231-10608-4, ISBN13: 978-0-231-10608-5. Dewey:320.1/5. LCCN:96-022691.
Audience: **l,u,f.** *Choice, 1997.*

Spruyt, Hendrik **JC327**
The Sovereign State and Its Competitors: An Analysis of Systems Change. Trade Paper. Princeton University Press. Princeton, NJ. 1996. 300p. Princeton Studies in International History and Politics Ser. ISBN:0-691-02910-5, ISBN13: 978-0-691-02910-8. Dewey:320.1/5/09.
Audience: **l,u,f.**

Political Theory > Theories of State > Consent of the Governed

Bay, Christian & Walker, Charles C. **JC328.3**
Civil Disobedience: Theory and Practice. Trade Paper. Black Rose Books. Montreal, PQ. 1975. 50p. ISBN:0-919618-56-1, ISBN13: 978-0-919618-56-5. Dewey:323.4.
Audience: **l,u.**

Hirst, Paul Q. (Editor) **JC328.2.P58 1989**
The Pluralist Theory of the State: Selected Writings of G. D. H. Cole, J. N. Figgis, and H. J. Laski. Cloth Text. Routledge. New York, NY. 1989. 240p. ISBN:0-415-03370-5, ISBN13: 978-0-415-03370-1. Dewey:320/.01/1. LCCN:89-032066.
Audience: **g,l,u,f.** *Choice, 1991.*

Josephson, Peter **JC153.J67 2002**
The Great Art of Government: Locke's Use of Consent. Trade Cloth. University Press of Kansas. Lawrence, KS. 2002. 378p. ISBN:0-7006-1169-X, ISBN13: 978-0-7006-1169-0. Dewey:320.1/1. LCCN:2001-007731.
Audience: **l,u,f.** *Choice, 2003.*

Sunstein, Cass R. **JC328.3.S93 2005**
Why Societies Need Dissent. Trade Paper. Harvard University Press. Cambridge, MA. 2005. 256p. Oliver Wendell Holmes Lectures ISBN:0-674-01768-4, ISBN13: 978-0-674-01768-9. Dewey:303.48/4.
Audience: **l,u,f.** *Choice, 2004.*

White, James B. **JC328.2.W55 1994**
Acts of Hope: Creating Authority in Literature, Law, and Politics. Trade Cloth. University of Chicago Press. Chicago, IL. 1994. 368p. ISBN:0-226-89510-6, ISBN13: 978-0-226-89510-9. Dewey:303.3/6. LCCN:94-008877.
Audience: **u,f.** *Choice, 1995.*

Political Theory > Theories of State > Revolutions. Political Violence

Arendt, Hannah **JC491**
Crises of the Republic: Lying in Politics, Civil Disobedience, on Violence, Thoughts on Politics and Revolution. Trade Paper. Harcourt Trade Publishers. New York, NY. 1972. 252p. ISBN:0-15-623200-6, ISBN13: 978-0-15-623200-5. Dewey:306. LCCN:72-187703.
Audience: **u,f.**

Arendt, Hannah **JC491**
On Revolution. Trade Cloth. Greenwood Publishing Group, Inc. Portsmouth, NH. 1982. 352p. ISBN:0-313-23493-0, ISBN13: 978-0-313-23493-4. Dewey:301.6/333. LCCN:82-006266.
Audience: **u,f.** B

Arendt, Hannah **HM291**
On Violence. Trade Paper. Harcourt Trade Publishers. New York, NY. 1970. 120p. Harvest Book Ser. ISBN:0-15-669500-6, ISBN13: 978-0-15-669500-8. Dewey:301. LCCN:74-095867.
Audience: **u,f.**

Berghahn, Volker R. **JC328.6.B4713 2002**
Europe in the Era of Two World Wars: From Militarism and Genocide to Civil Society, 1900-1950. Trade Cloth. Princeton University Press. Princeton, NJ. 2005. 176p. ISBN:0-691-12003-X, ISBN13: 978-0-691-12003-4. Dewey:940.5. LCCN:2005-043241.
Audience: **g,l,u,f.**

Bob, Clifford **JC328.5.B63 2005**
The Marketing of Rebellion: Insurgents, Media and International Activism. Douglas McAdam, Sidney Tarrow & Charles Tilly (Contribution by). Cloth Text. Cambridge University Press. New York, NY. 2005. 254p. Cambridge Studies in Contentious Politics ISBN:0-521-84570-X, ISBN13: 978-0-521-84570-0. Dewey:322.4. LCCN:2004-024987.
Audience: **l,u,f.** *Choice, 2005.*

Goodwin, Jeff **JC491 .G64 2001**
No Other Way Out: States and Revolutionary Movements, 1945-1991. Robert H. Bates, Ellen Comisso, Peter Hall, Peter Lange, Joel Samuel Migdal & Helen V. Milner (Contribution by). Cloth Text. Cambridge University Press. New York, NY. 2001. 428p. Studies in Comparative Politics ISBN:0-521-62069-4, ISBN13: 978-0-521-62069-7. Dewey:322.4/2. LCCN:00-058585.
Audience: **l,u,f.** *Choice, 2002.*

Grundy, Kenneth W. & Weinstein, Michael A. **JC328.6.G78**
Ideologies of Violence. Trade Paper. Macmillan Publishing Company, Inc. Old Tappan, NJ. 1974. vii, 117p. ISBN:0-675-08835-6, ISBN13: 978-0-675-08835-0. Dewey:301.6/33. LCCN:73-091055.
Audience: **u,f.** B

Katz, Mark N. **JC491.R48656 2001**
Revolution: The International Dimensions. Paper Text. CQ Press. Washington, DC. 2000. xii, 323p. ISBN:1-56802-553-X, ISBN13: 978-1-56802-553-7. Dewey:303.6/4. LCCN:00-010482.
Audience: **g,l,u,f.** *Choice, 2001.*

Monga, Celestin **JQ1879.A15M6613 1996**
The Anthropology of Anger: Civil Society and Democracy in Africa. Trade Cloth. Lynne Rienner Publishers, Inc. Boulder, CO. 1996. 219p. ISBN:1-55587-644-7, ISBN13: 978-1-55587-644-9. Dewey:347.73/5. LCCN:96-007588.
Audience: **l,u,f.** *Choice, 1997.*

O'Kane, Rosemary H. **JC491.O44 1991**
The Revolutionary Reign of Terror: The Role of Violence in Political Change. Cloth Text. Edward Elgar Publishing, Inc. Northampton, MA. 1991. 320p. ISBN:1-85278-082-7, ISBN13: 978-1-85278-082-1. Dewey:321.09/4. LCCN:91-009171.
Audience: **l,u,f.** *Choice, 1992.*

Rapoport, David C. & Weinberg, Leonard (Author, Editors) **JC328.6.D45 2001**
The Democratic Experience and Political Violence. Paper over Boards. Taylor & Francis Group. Abingdon, 2001. 384p. Political Violence Ser., Vol. 9 ISBN:0-7146-5150-8, ISBN13: 978-0-7146-5150-7. Dewey:303.6/2. LCCN:00-065973.
Audience: **l,u,f.** *Choice, 2002.*

Rupesinghe, Kumar **JQ2951.A2C66 1989**
Conflict Resolution in Uganda. Trade Cloth. Ohio University Press. Athens, OH. 1989. 316p. ISBN:0-8214-0929-8, ISBN13: 978-0-8214-0929-9. Dewey:967.6/104. LCCN:89-030799.
Audience: **l,u,f.** *Choice, 1990.*

Toft, Monica Duffy **JC328.6.T64 2003**
The Geography of Ethnic Violence: Identity, Interests, and the Indivisibility of Territory. Trade Cloth. Princeton University

Press. Princeton, NJ. 2003. 256p. ISBN:0-691-11354-8, ISBN13: 978-0-691-11354-8. Dewey:303.6. LCCN:2002-042463.
Audience: **l,u,f.** *Choice, 2004.*

Wickham-Crowley, Timothy P. **JC491.W53 1992**
Guerrillas and Revolution in Latin America: A Comparative Study of Insurgents and Regimes since 1956. Trade Paper. Princeton University Press. Princeton, NJ. 1993. 444p. ISBN:0-691-02336-0, ISBN13: 978-0-691-02336-6. Dewey:321.09/4/098. LCCN:91-015141.
Audience: **l,u,f.** *Choice, 1992.*

Wilkinson, Paul **JC328.6.W54 1986**
Terrorism and the Liberal State. Ed. 2. Cloth Text. New York University Press. New York, NY. 1986. 336p. ISBN:0-8147-9206-5, ISBN13: 978-0-8147-9206-3. Dewey:322.4/2. LCCN:85-015303.
Audience: **l,u,f.** B

Wilkinson, Paul **HV6431.W564 2001**
Terrorism vs. Democracy: The Liberal State Response. Trade Paper. Routledge. New York, NY. 2000. 272p. Political Violence Ser., Vol. 9 ISBN:0-7146-8165-2, ISBN13: 978-0-7146-8165-8. Dewey:363.3/2. LCCN:00-047530.
Audience: **l,u,f.** *Choice, 2001.*

Political Theory > Theories of State > Patriotism

Klosko, George **JC329.5.K567 2005**
Political Obligations. Trade Cloth. Oxford University Press, Inc. New York, NY. 2005. 276p. ISBN:0-19-925620-9, ISBN13: 978-0-19-925620-4. Dewey:320/.01/1. LCCN:2004-027325.
Audience: **u,f.**

Parenti, Michael **JZ1480.P36 2004**
Superpatriotism. Trade Paper. City Lights Books. San Francisco, CA. 2004. 120p. ISBN:0-87286-433-2, ISBN13: 978-0-87286-433-7. Dewey:323.6/5/0973. LCCN:2004-009556.
Audience: **g,l,u,f.**

Political Theory > Theories of State > Power

Chabal, Patrick **JQ1872.C48 1994**
Power in Africa: An Essay in Political Interpretation. Trade Paper. Palgrave Macmillan. New York, NY. 1993. 321p. ISBN:0-312-09954-1, ISBN13: 978-0-312-09954-1. Dewey:320.96. LCCN:93-032786.
Audience: **u,f.** *Choice, 1992.*

Delmas, Philippe **JC421**
The Rosy Future of War. Trade Paper. Simon & Schuster. New York, NY. 1999. 256p. ISBN:0-684-87042-8, ISBN13: 978-0-684-87042-7. Dewey:320.9/049. LCCN:97-004177.
Audience: **l,u,f.** *Choice, 1997.*

Engster, Daniel **JC139.E54 2001**
Divine Sovereignty: The Origins of Modern State Power. Trade Cloth. Northern Illinois University Press. DeKalb, IL. 2003. 265p. ISBN:0-87580-275-3, ISBN13: 978-0-87580-275-6. Dewey:320.1. LCCN:2001-030463.
Audience: **l,u,f.** *Choice, 2002.*

Florini, Ann **JC337.F56 2003**
The Coming Democracy: New Rules for Running a New World. Trade Cloth. Island Press. Washington, DC. 2003. 272p. ISBN:1-55963-289-5, ISBN13: 978-1-55963-289-8. Dewey:306.2. LCCN:2002-153428.
Audience: **g,l,u,f.** *Choice, 2004.*

Friedberg, Aaron L. **JC330.F74 2000**
In the Shadow of the Garrison State: America's Anti-Statism and Its Cold War Grand Strategy. Cloth Text. Princeton University Press. Princeton, NJ. 2000. 416p. Princeton Studies in International History and Politics ISBN:0-691-07865-3, ISBN13: 978-0-691-07865-6. Dewey:320.1/01. LCCN:99-053043.
Audience: **l,u,f.** *Choice, 2000.*

Hall, John A. & Trentmann, Frank (Editors) **JC337.C549 2004**
Civil Society: A Reader in History, Theory, and Global Politics. Cloth over Boards. Palgrave Macmillan. New York, NY. 2005. 272p. ISBN:1-4039-1542-3, ISBN13: 978-1-4039-1542-9. Dewey:300. LCCN:2004-056071.
Audience: **l,u.** *Choice, 2006.*

Jackman, Robert W. **JC330 .J33 1993**
Power Without Force: The Political Capacity of Nation States. Trade Paper. University of Michigan Press. Chicago, IL. 1993. 208p. Analytical Perspectives on Politics Ser. ISBN:0-472-08236-1, ISBN13: 978-0-472-08236-0. Dewey:303.3/3. LCCN:93-024362.
Audience: **l,u,f.**

Kaldor, Mary **JC337.K35 2003**
Global Civil Society: An Answer to War. Trade Paper. Polity Press. Cambridge, 2003. 200p. ISBN:0-7456-2758-7, ISBN13: 978-0-7456-2758-8. Dewey:300. LCCN:2002-014306.
Audience: **l,u,f.** *Choice, 2004.*

Kandeh, Jimmy D. **JQ2998.A38C584 2004**
Coups from Below: Armed Subalterns and State Power in West Africa. Cloth over Boards. Palgrave Macmillan. New York, NY. 2004. 272p. ISBN:1-4039-6715-6, ISBN13: 978-1-4039-6715-2. Dewey:332/.5/0966. LCCN:2004-049755.
Audience: **u,f.** *Choice, 2006.*

Keane, John **JC337.K433 2003**
Global Civil Society? Ian Shapiro, Russell Hardin, Stephen Holmes & Jeffrey Isaac (Contribution by). Trade Paper. Cambridge University Press. New York, NY. 2003. 234p. Contemporary Political Theory Ser. ISBN:0-521-89462-X, ISBN13: 978-0-521-89462-3. Dewey:320.11. LCCN:2003-277622.
Audience: **l,u,f.** *Choice, 2004.*

Powell, Robert **JZ1242.P68 1999**
In the Shadow of Power: States and Strategies in International Politics. Trade Paper. Princeton University Press. Princeton, NJ. 1999. 318p. ISBN:0-691-00457-9, ISBN13: 978-0-691-00457-0. Dewey:327.1/01. LCCN:99-012207.
Audience: **l,u,f.** *Choice, 2000.*

Rosecrance, Richard **JC330.R66 1999**
The Rise of the Virtual State: Wealth and Power in the Coming Century. Trade Cloth. Basic Books. New York, NY. 1999. 304p. ISBN:0-465-07141-4, ISBN13: 978-0-465-07141-8. Dewey:337. LCCN:99-046146.
Audience: **l,u,f.** *Choice, 2000.*

Rosenblum, Nancy L. & Post, Robert C. (Editors) **JC336.C5645 2002**
Civil Society and Government. Trade Paper. Princeton University Press. Princeton, NJ. 2001. 418p. Ethikon Series in Comparative Ethics ISBN:0-691-08802-0, ISBN13: 978-0-691-08802-0. Dewey:301. LCCN:2001-050010.
Audience: **g,l,u.** *Choice, 2002.*

Rotenstreich, Nathan **JC330.R673 1988**
Order and Might. Paper Text. State University of New York Press. Albany, NY. 1988. 238p. SUNY Series in Philosophy ISBN:0-88706-630-5, ISBN13: 978-0-88706-630-6. Dewey:303.3/3. LCCN:87-009980.
Audience: **l,u,f.** *Choice, 1988.*

Political Theory > Theories of State > Symbolism. National Emblems

Smith, Whitney **JC345.S57**
Flags Through the Ages and Across the World. Trade Cloth. McGraw-Hill Companies, The. New York, NY. 1975. 357p. ISBN:0-07-059093-1, ISBN13: 978-0-07-059093-9. Dewey:929.9. LCCN:75-012602.
Audience: **g,l,u,f.** B

Political Theory > Theories of State > Utopianism. Utopias

Buber, Martin **HX36.B8413 1996**
Paths in Utopia. R. F. C. Hull (Translator). Trade Cloth. Syracuse University Press. Syracuse, NY. 1996. 152p. The Martin Buber Library ISBN:0-8156-0421-1, ISBN13: 978-0-8156-0421-1. Dewey:335/.02. LCCN:96-032897.
Audience: **u,f.** B

Fox, Alistair **HX810.5.Z6F68 1993**
Utopia: An Elusive Vision. Trade Cloth. Macmillan Publishing Company, Inc. Old Tappan, NJ. 1992. 160p. Twayne's Masterworks Studies, Vol. 103 ISBN:0-8057-9419-0, ISBN13: 978-0-8057-9419-9. Dewey:335/.02. LCCN:92-023396.
Audience: **g,l,u,f.** *Choice, 1993.*

Goodwin, Barbara (Editor) **HX806.P47 2001**
The Philosophy of Utopia. Trade Paper. Taylor & Francis Group. Abingdon, 2001. 272p. ISBN:0-7146-8169-5, ISBN13: 978-0-7146-8169-6. Dewey:335/.02. LCCN:00-012153.
Audience: **g,l,u,f.** *Choice, 2001.*

Goodwin, Barbara (Editor) **HX806.P47 2001**
The Philosophy of Utopia. Paper over Boards. Taylor & Francis Group. Abingdon, 2001. 272p. ISBN:0-7146-5153-2, ISBN13: 978-0-7146-5153-8. Dewey:335/.02. LCCN:00-012153.
Audience: **u,f.** *Choice, 2001.*

Goodwin, Barbara & Taylor, Keith W. **JC71.P6**
The Politics of Utopia: A Study in Theory and Practice. Cloth Text. Palgrave Macmillan. New York, NY. 1983. 300p. ISBN:0-312-62933-8, ISBN13: 978-0-312-62933-5. Dewey:321/.07. LCCN:82-021556.
Audience: **l,u,f.**

Grant, H. Roger **HX656.S6G73 1988**
Spirit Fruit: A Gentle Utopia. Trade Cloth. Northern Illinois University Press. DeKalb, IL. 1988. 217p. ISBN:0-87580-137-4, ISBN13: 978-0-87580-137-7. Dewey:335/.973. LCCN:88-005352.
Audience: **g,l,u,f.** *Choice, 1989.*

Kesten, Seymour R. **HX654.K46 1993**
Utopian Episodes: Daily Life in Experimental Colonies Dedicated to Changing the World. Cloth Text. Syracuse University Press. Syracuse, NY. 1993. 296p. Utopianism and Communitarianism Ser. ISBN:0-8156-2593-6, ISBN13: 978-0-8156-2593-3. Dewey:335/.12. LCCN:92-040186.
Audience: **l,u,f.** *Choice, 1994.*

Kolmerten, Carol A. **HX696.O9K65 1998**
Women in Utopia: The Ideology of Gender in the American Owenite Communities. Trade Paper. Syracuse University Press. Syracuse, NY. 1998. 209p. ISBN:0-8156-0555-2, ISBN13: 978-0-8156-0555-3. Dewey:335/.973/09034. LCCN:98-019270.
Audience: **l,u,f.** *Choice, 1990.*

Kuhlmann, Hilke **HX806.K84 2004**
Living Walden Two: B. F. Skinner's Behaviorist Utopia and Experimental Communities. Trade Cloth. University of Illinois Press. Champaign, IL. 2005. 264p. ISBN:0-252-02962-3, ISBN13: 978-0-252-02962-2. Dewey:307.77/0973. LCCN:2004-020463.
Audience: **g,l,u,f.** *Choice, 2006.*

Leslie, Marina **HX806.L47 1998**
Renaissance Utopias and the Problem of History. Book, Other. Cornell University Press. Ithaca, NY. 1998. 208p. ISBN:0-8014-3400-9, ISBN13: 978-0-8014-3400-6. Dewey:321/.07. LCCN:98-017865.
Audience: **u,f.** *Choice, 1999.*

Levitas, Ruth **HX806.L48 1990**
The Concept of Utopia. Cloth Text. Syracuse University Press. Syracuse, NY. 1991. 224p. ISBN:0-8156-2513-8, ISBN13: 978-0-8156-2513-1. Dewey:321.07. LCCN:90-010069.
Audience: **l,u,f.** *Choice, 1991.*

Miller, Timothy **HX653.M55 1998**
The Quest for Utopia in Twentieth Century America. Trade Cloth. Syracuse University Press. Syracuse, NY. 1998. 254p. Peace and Conflict Resolution Studies ISBN:0-8156-2775-0, ISBN13: 978-0-8156-2775-3. Dewey:335/.12/09730904. LCCN:97-048903.
Audience: **g,l,u,f.**

More, Thomas **HX810.5.E54 2001**
Utopia. Clarence H. Miller (Translator, Introduction by). Cloth over Boards. Yale University Press. Cumberland, RI. 2001. 202p. Yale Nota Bene Ser. ISBN:0-300-08428-5, ISBN13: 978-0-300-08428-3. Dewey:321/.07. LCCN:00-044917.
Audience: **g,l,u,f.** *Choice, 2001.*

Morris, William **HX811.M67 2004**
News from Nowhere. Trade Paper. Dover Publications, Inc. Mineola, NY. 2004. 208p. ISBN:0-486-43427-3, ISBN13: 978-0-486-43427-8. Dewey:321/.07. LCCN:2003-068754.
Audience: **g,l,u,f.**

Pitzer, Donald E. (Editor) **HX653.A63 1997**
America's Communal Utopias. Paul S. Boyer (Foreword by). Trade Paper. University of North Carolina Press. Chapel Hill,

NC. 1997. 560p. ISBN:0-8078-4609-0, ISBN13: 978-0-8078-4609-4. Dewey:335/.9/0973. LCCN:96-010889.
Audience: **l,u,f.** *Choice, 1997.*

Shostak, Arthur B. (Editor) **HX806.V49 2003**
Viable Utopian Ideas: Shaping a Better World. Trade Cloth. M. E. Sharpe Inc. Armonk, NY. 2003. 312p. ISBN:0-7656-1104-X, ISBN13: 978-0-7656-1104-8. Dewey:335/.02. LCCN:2002-036588.
Audience: **g,l,u,f.** *Choice, 2003.*

Skinner, Burrhus Frederic **PR6019.O9**
Walden Two. Trade Paper. Hackett Publishing Company, Inc. Indianapolis, IN. 2005. 301p. ISBN:0-87220-778-1, ISBN13: 978-0-87220-778-3. Dewey:823/.9/1.
Audience: **g,l,u,f.**

Sutton, Robert P. **HX632.S87 1994**
Les Icariens: The Utopian Dream in Europe and America. Trade Cloth. University of Illinois Press. Champaign, IL. 1994. 216p. Statue of Liberty-Ellis Island Centennial Ser. ISBN:0-252-02067-7, ISBN13: 978-0-252-02067-4. Dewey:335/.02. LCCN:93-008609.
Audience: **u,f.** *Choice, 1995.*

Political Theory > Forms of the State

Cleyre, Voltairine de **HX843.7**
Exquisite Rebel: The Essays of Voltairine de Cleyre — Anarchist, Feminist, Genius. Sharon Presley & Crispin Sartwell (Editors). Cloth Text. State University of New York Press. Albany, NY. 2005. 224p. ISBN:0-7914-6093-2, ISBN13: 978-0-7914-6093-1. Dewey:335/.83/092. LCCN:2004-059138.
Audience: **u,f.** *Choice, 2005.*

Goodin, Robert E., et al. **JC479 .R4 1999**
The Real Worlds of Welfare Capitalism. Bruce Headey, Ruud Muffels & Henk-Jan Dirven (Authors). Trade Paper. Cambridge University Press. New York, NY. 1999. 368p. ISBN:0-521-59639-4, ISBN13: 978-0-521-59639-8. Dewey:361.65. LCCN:98-049778.
Audience: **l,u,f.** *Choice, 2000.*

Kassem, Maye **JQ3881.K37 2004**
Egyptian Politics: The Dynamics of Authoritarian Rule. Paper Text. Lynne Rienner Publishers, Inc. Boulder, CO. 2004. 230p. ISBN:1-58826-247-2, ISBN13: 978-1-58826-247-9. Dewey:320.962. LCCN:2003-060297.
Audience: **l,u,f.** *Choice, 2005.*

Parsa, Misagh **JC491.P36 2000**
States, Ideologies and Social Revolutions: A Comparative Analysis of Iran, Nicaragua and the Philippines. Cloth Text. Cambridge University Press. New York, NY. 2000. 336p. ISBN:0-521-77337-7, ISBN13: 978-0-521-77337-9. Dewey:303.6/4. LCCN:99-087457.
Audience: **u,f.** *Choice, 2001.*

Schumpeter, Joseph Alois **HX40**
Capitalism, Socialism and Democracy. Ed. 5. Tom Bottomore (Introduction by). Trade Cloth. Allen & Unwin, Ltd. London, 1976. xiv, 437p. ISBN:0-04-335031-3, ISBN13: 978-0-04-335031-7. Dewey:330.12/2/0904. LCCN:77-364732.
Audience: **l,u,f.** B

Political Theory > Forms of the State > Islamic State

Ayubi, Nazih **JC49**
Political Islam: Religion and Politics in the Arab World. Trade Paper. Routledge. New York, NY. 1993. 304p. ISBN:0-415-10385-1, ISBN13: 978-0-415-10385-5. Dewey:297.1977.
Audience: **g,l,u,f.**

Esposito, John L. & Voll, John O. **JC49.E76 1996**
Islam and Democracy. Trade Paper. Oxford University Press, Inc. New York, NY. 1996. 240p. ISBN:0-19-510816-7, ISBN13: 978-0-19-510816-3. Dewey:320.917/671/09045. LCCN:95-042339.
Audience: **l,u,f.** *Choice, 1996.*

Hashmi, Sohail H. (Editor) **JC49.I766 2002**
Islamic Political Ethics: Civil Society, Pluralism, and Conflict. Jack Miles (Foreword by). Trade Cloth. Princeton University Press. Princeton, NJ. 2002. 264p. The Ethikon Series in Comparative Ethics ISBN:0-691-11309-2, ISBN13: 978-0-691-11309-8. Dewey:172. LCCN:2002-025293.
Audience: **l,u,f.** *Choice, 2003.*

Piscatori, James P. **JC49.P57 1986**
Islam in a World of Nation-States. Trade Paper. Cambridge University Press. New York, NY. 1986. 206p. ISBN:0-521-33867-0, ISBN13: 978-0-521-33867-7. Dewey:322/.1/0917671. LCCN:86-008275.
Audience: **g,l,u,f.**

Political Theory > Forms of the State > Ancient > Greece

De Romilly, Jacqueline **JC51.R56**
The Rise and Fall of States According to Greek Authors. Trade Paper. University of Michigan Press. Chicago, IL. 1991. 112p. Thomas Spencer Jerome Lectures ISBN:0-472-08152-7, ISBN13: 978-0-472-08152-3. Dewey:320.1. LCCN:75-031054.
Audience: **u,f.** B

Herman Hansen, Mogens **JC75.D36H3613 1999**
Athenian Democracy in the Age of Demosthenes: Structure, Principles and Ideology. Trade Paper. University of Oklahoma Press. Norman, OK. 1999. 496p. ISBN:0-8061-3143-8, ISBN13: 978-0-8061-3143-6. Dewey:321.8/0938/5. LCCN:98-046468.
Audience: **l,u,f.**

Jones, A. H. M. **JC79.A8J6 1986**
Athenian Democracy. Trade Paper. Johns Hopkins University Press. Baltimore, MD. 1981. 208p. ISBN:0-8018-3380-9, ISBN13: 978-0-8018-3380-9. Dewey:320.938/5. LCCN:86-045460.
Audience: **u,f.** B

McGlew, James F. **JC75.D4M38 1993**
Tyranny and Political Culture in Ancient Greece. Book, Other. Cornell University Press. Ithaca, NY. 1993. 232p. ISBN:0-8014-2787-8, ISBN13: 978-0-8014-2787-9. Dewey:321.60938. LCCN:93-015653.
Audience: **g,l,u,f.** *Choice, 1994.*

Ostwald, Martin **KL4361.5**
From Popular Sovereignty to the Sovereignty of Law: Law, Society, and Politics in Fifth Century Athens. Trade Cloth. University of California Press. Berkeley, CA. 1989. 500p. ISBN:0-520-06798-3, ISBN13: 978-0-520-06798-1. Dewey:342.495/12. LCCN:85-000690.
Audience: **u,f.** *Choice, 1988.*

Sinclair, R. K. **JC79 .A8 S56**
Democracy and Participation in Athens. Trade Paper. Cambridge University Press. New York, NY. 1991. 269p. ISBN:0-521-42389-9, ISBN13: 978-0-521-42389-2. Dewey:320.938. LCCN:87-013174.
Audience: **g,l,u,f.** *Choice, 1988.*

Stockton, David **JC79.A8S74 1990**
The Classical Athenian Democracy. Trade Paper. Oxford University Press, Inc. New York, NY. 1990. 214p. ISBN:0-19-872136-6, ISBN13: 978-0-19-872136-9. Dewey:321.8/0938/5. LCCN:89-023028.
Audience: **u,f.** *Choice, 1991.*

Political Theory > Forms of the State > Ancient > Rome. Byzantine Empire

Hopkins, Keith **HN490.E4**
Death and Renewal: Sociological Studies in Roman History. Trade Paper. Cambridge University Press. New York, NY. 1985. 304p. ISBN:0-521-27117-7, ISBN13: 978-0-521-27117-2. Dewey:305.52.
Audience: **u,f.**

Lintott, Andrew **JC88.L588 1999**
The Constitution of the Roman Republic. Trade Cloth. Oxford University Press, Inc. New York, NY. 1999. 310p. ISBN:0-19-815068-7, ISBN13: 978-0-19-815068-8. Dewey:342.3/7/029. LCCN:98-030456.
Audience: **l,u.** *Choice, 1999.*

Sherwin-White, Adrian Nicholas **JC0085.C5S5**
The Roman Citizenship. Trade Paper. Books on Demand. Ann Arbor, MI. 324p. ISBN:0-598-98362-7, ISBN13: 978-0-598-98362-6. Dewey:323.6/09376. LCCN:40-011806.
Audience: **l,u.**

Talbert, Richard J. **JC85.S4**
The Senate of Imperial Rome. Trade Cloth. Princeton University Press. Princeton, NJ. 1984. 576p. ISBN:0-691-05400-2, ISBN13: 978-0-691-05400-1. Dewey:328/.3/0937. LCCN:83-042580.
Audience: **l,u.** B

Political Theory > Forms of the State > Medieval

Althoff, Gerd **HN445.A67513 2004**
Family, Friends and Followers: Political and Social Bonds in Early Medieval Europe. Christopher Carroll (Translator). Cloth Text. Cambridge University Press. New York, NY. 2004. 206p. ISBN:0-521-77054-8, ISBN13: 978-0-521-77054-5. Dewey:305.5/0943/0902. LCCN:2003-055818.
Audience: **u,f.** *Choice, 2005.*

Blythe, James M. **JA82.B59 1992**
Ideal Government and the Mixed Constitution in the Middle Ages. Trade Cloth. Princeton University Press. Princeton, NJ. 1992. 365p. ISBN:0-691-03167-3, ISBN13: 978-0-691-03167-5. Dewey:320/.09/02. LCCN:91-021104.
Audience: **l,u,f.** *Choice, 1992.*

Burns, J. H. (Editor) **JA82 .C27 1988**
The Cambridge History of Medieval Political Thought C. 350-C. 1450. Trade Cloth. Cambridge University Press. New York, NY. 1988. 816p. The Cambridge History of Political Thought Ser. ISBN:0-521-24324-6, ISBN13: 978-0-521-24324-7. Dewey:320/.01. LCCN:87-006601.
Audience: **l.** *Choice, 1989.*

Coulborn, Rushton (Editor) **JC111 .C6**
Feudalism in History. Trade Cloth. Shoe String Press, Inc. North Haven, CT. 1965. xiv, 438p. ISBN:0-208-00274-X, ISBN13: 978-0-208-00274-7. Dewey:321.3. LCCN:65-024506.
Audience: **l,u,f.** B

Downing, Brian M. **JN7.D69 1991**
The Military Revolution and Political Change: Origins of Democracy and Autocracy in Early Modern Europe. Trade Cloth. Princeton University Press. Princeton, NJ. 1992. 314p. ISBN:0-691-07886-6, ISBN13: 978-0-691-07886-1. Dewey:940.1. LCCN:91-018723.
Audience: **l,u,f.** *Choice, 1992.*

Muldoon, James **JC359.M86 1999**
Empire and Order: The Concept of Empire, 800-1800. Cloth over Boards. Palgrave Macmillan. New York, NY. 1999. 219p. Studies in Modern History Ser. ISBN:0-312-22226-2, ISBN13: 978-0-312-22226-0. Dewey:325.3/2/09. LCCN:99-013305.
Audience: **u,f.** *Choice, 2000.*

Tilly, Charles **JN94.A2T54 1990**
Coercion, Capital, and European States, AD 990-1990. Cloth Text. Blackwell Publishing, Inc. Malden, MA. 1990. 288p. ISBN:1-55786-067-X, ISBN13: 978-1-55786-067-5. Dewey:940. LCCN:89-017730.
Audience: **u,f.** *Choice, 1990.*

Vinogradoff, Paul **LAW**
Roman Law in Medieval Europe. Trade Cloth. Gaunt, Inc. Holmes Beach, FL. 1994. xvi, 155p. ISBN:1-56169-103-8, ISBN13: 978-1-56169-103-6. Dewey:340/.094.
Audience: **u,f.** B

Political Theory > Forms of the State > Modern

Corlett, William **JC325**
Community Without Unity: A Politics of Derridean Extravagance. Paper Text. Duke University Press. Durham, NC. 1993. 280p. Post-Contemporary Interventions Ser. ISBN:0-8223-1335-9, ISBN13: 978-0-8223-1335-9. Dewey:320.5. LCCN:89-001120.
Audience: **u,f.**

Finocchiaro, Maurice A. **JC265.M65F56 1999**
Beyond Right and Left: Democratic Elitism in Mosca and Gramsci. Cloth over Boards. Yale University Press. Cumberland, RI. 1999. 314p. Italian Literature and Thought Ser.

ISBN:0-300-07535-9, ISBN13: 978-0-300-07535-9. Dewey:320.5/0945. LCCN:98-008642.
Audience: **u,f.** *Choice, 1999.*

Goldman, Harvey **JC263.W42.G65 1992**
Politics, Death, and the Devil: Self and Power in Max Weber and Thomas Mann. Trade Cloth. University of California Press. Berkeley, CA. 1992. 400p. ISBN:0 520 07750 4, ISBN13: 978-0-520-07750-8. Dewey:306.2. LCCN:91-036815.
Audience: **u,f.** *Choice, 1993.*

Hegel, Georg Wilhelm Fredrich **JC233 .H44613 1999**
Hegel: Political Writings. Lawrence Dickey & H. B. Nisbet (Editors), Raymond Geuss & Quentin Skinner (Contribution by). Trade Paper. Cambridge University Press. New York, NY. 1999. 414p. Texts in the History of Political Thought ISBN:0-521-45975-3, ISBN13: 978-0-521-45975-4. Dewey:320.101. LCCN:98-044357.
Audience: **l,u,f.** *Choice, 2000.*

Lijphart, Arend **JC330**
Democracy in Plural Societies: A Comparative Exploration. Trade Paper. Yale University Press. Cumberland, RI. 1980. 258p. ISBN:0-300-02494-0, ISBN13: 978-0-300-02494-4. Dewey:321.8. LCCN:77-076311.
Audience: **l,u,f.**

Machiavelli, Niccolo **JC143.M163 2003**
Discourses on Livy. Julia Conaway Bondanella & Peter Bondanella (Translator, Introduction by, Notes by). Trade Paper. Oxford University Press, Inc. New York, NY. 2003. 448p. Oxford World's Classics Ser. ISBN:0-19-280473-1, ISBN13: 978-0-19-280473-0. Dewey:937/.02.
Audience: **u,f.** *Choice, 1996.*

Myers, Peter C. **JC153.L87M94 1998**
Our Only Star and Compass: Locke and the Struggle for Political Rationality. Book, Other. Rowman & Littlefield Publishers, Inc. Lanham, MD. 1999. 288p. ISBN:0-8476-9099-7, ISBN13: 978-0-8476-9099-2. Dewey:320.1/01. LCCN:98-036862.
Audience: **l,u,f.** *Choice, 1999.*

Sapiro, Virginia **JC176.W65S27 1992**
A Vindication of Political Virtue: The Political Theory of Mary Wollstonecraft. Trade Paper. University of Chicago Press. Chicago, IL. 1992. 394p. ISBN:0-226-73491-9, ISBN13: 978-0-226-73491-0. Dewey:323.34092. LCCN:91-038426.
Audience: **l,u,f.** *Choice, 1993.*

Strauss, Leo **JC153.H66 S7**
The Political Philosophy of Hobbes, Its Basis and Its Genesis. Paper Text. Textbook Publishers. Temecula, CA. 2003. xx, 172p. ISBN:0-7581-2487-2, ISBN13: 978-0-7581-2487-6. Dewey:320.1.
Audience: **u,f.**

Political Theory > Forms of the State > Imperialism

Bell, Morag (Editor), et al. **JC359.G46 1995**
Geography and Imperialism, 1820-1940. Robin Butlin & Michael Heffernan (Editors). Cloth Text. Manchester University Press. Manchester, 1995. xiii, 338p. Studies in Imperialism ISBN:0-7190-3934-7, ISBN13: 978-0-7190-3934-8. Dewey:910. LCCN:94-041730.
Audience: **l,u,f.** *Choice, 1996.*

Chilcote, Ronald H. **JC359.P58 2000**
The Political Economy of Imperialism: Critical Appraisals. Book, Other. Rowman & Littlefield Publishers, Inc. Lanham, MD. 2000. 272p. ISBN:0-7425-1010-7, ISBN13: 978-0-7425-1010-4. Dewey:338.9. LCCN:00-059065.
Audience: **l,u,f.** *Choice, 2001.*

Political Theory > Forms of the State > Monarchy

Burns, J. H. **JC375.B87 1992**
Lordship, Kingship, and Empire: The Idea of Monarchy, 1400-1525 (The Carlyle Lectures 1988). Trade Cloth. Oxford University Press, Inc. New York, NY. 1992. 192p. Carlyle Lectures ISBN:0-19-820206-7, ISBN13: 978-0-19-820206-6. Dewey:321.6/094. LCCN:91-042781.
Audience: **u,f.** *Choice, 1993.*

Spellman, W. M. & Spellman, William **JC375 .S64 2001**
Monarchies 1000-2000. Trade Cloth. Reaktion Books, Ltd. London, 2004. 320p. Globalities Ser. ISBN:1-86189-087-7, ISBN13: 978-1-86189-087-0. Dewey:321.6/09. LCCN:00-051329.
Audience: **g,l,u,f.** *Choice, 2002.*

Zmora, Hillay (Contribution by) **JC375.Z58 2000**
Monarchy, Aristocracy, and the State in Europe 1300-1800. Paper over Boards. Routledge. New York, NY. 2000. 176p. Historical Connections Ser. ISBN:0-415-24107-3, ISBN13: 978-0-415-24107-6. Dewey:320.94/09/03. LCCN:00-032311.
Audience: **l,u,f.** *Choice, 2001.*

Political Theory > Forms of the State > Democracy

Alperovitz, Gar **JK1726.A428 2004**
America Beyond Capitalism: Reclaiming Our Wealth, Our Liberty, and Our Democracy. Trade Cloth. John Wiley & Sons, Inc. Hoboken, NJ. 2004. 336p. ISBN:0-471-66730-7, ISBN13: 978-0-471-66730-8. Dewey:330.973. LCCN:2004-003617.
Audience: **l,u,f.**

Barber, Benjamin R. **JK1726 .B27 1998**
A Passion for Democracy: American Essays. Trade Paper. Princeton University Press. Princeton, NJ. 2000. 306p. ISBN:0-691-05024-4, ISBN13: 978-0-691-05024-9. Dewey:320.473.
Audience: **g,l,u,f.** *Choice, 1999.*

Barber, Benjamin R. **JC423.B243 2004**
Strong Democracy: Participatory Politics for a New Age. Ed. 20. Trade Paper. University of California Press. Berkeley, CA. 2004. 325p. ISBN:0-520-24233-5, ISBN13: 978-0-520-24233-3. Dewey:321.8.
Audience: **g,l,u,f.** B

Barney, Darin **JC423.B2613 2000**
Prometheus Wired: The Hope for Democracy in the Age of Network Technology. Trade Paper. University of Chicago Press. Chicago, IL. 2001. 354p. ISBN:0-226-03746-0, ISBN13: 978-0-226-03746-2. Dewey:321.8. LCCN:00-023239.
Audience: **g,l,u,f.** *Choice, 2001.*

Beetham, David **JC423.B324 1999**
Democracy and Human Rights. Trade Paper. Polity Press. Cambridge, 1999. 240p. ISBN:0-7456-2315-8, ISBN13: 978-0-7456-2315-3. Dewey:321.8. LCCN:98-052192.
Audience: **l,u,f.**

Bermeo, Nancy Gina **JC337.B47 2003**
Ordinary People in Extraordinary Times: The Citizenry and the Breakdown of Democracy. Trade Cloth. Princeton University Press. Princeton, NJ. 2003. 272p. ISBN:0-691-08969-8, ISBN13: 978-0-691-08969-0. Dewey:306.2. LCCN:2002-035472.
Audience: **l,u,f.** *Choice, 2005.*

Boix, Carles **JC423.B6255 2003**
Democracy and Redistribution. Robert H. Bates, Ellen Comisso, Joel Migdal, Helen Milner, Martin Klein, Peter Lange & Peter Hall (Contribution by). Trade Paper. Cambridge University Press. New York, NY. 2003. 280p. Cambridge Studies in Comparative Politics ISBN:0-521-53267-1, ISBN13: 978-0-521-53267-9. Dewey:320/.6. LCCN:2002-041689.
Audience: **l,u,f.** *Choice, 2005.*

Bratton, Michael & Walle, Nicholas van de **JQ1879.A15 B73 1997**
Democratic Experiments in Africa: Regime Transitions in Comparative Perspective. Robert H. Bates, Ellen Comisso, Peter Hall, Peter Lange, Joel Migdal & Helen Milner (Contribution by). Trade Paper. Cambridge University Press. New York, NY. 1997. 329p. Studies in Comparative Politics ISBN:0-521-55612-0, ISBN13: 978-0-521-55612-5. Dewey:321.8/0967. LCCN:96-034865.
Audience: **l,u,f.** *Choice, 1998.*

Burns, Nancy, et al. **JK1764.B87 2001**
The Private Roots of Public Action: Gender, Equality, and Political Participation. Kay Lehman Schlozman & Sidney Verba (Authors). Trade Paper. Harvard University Press. Cambridge, MA. 2001. 480p. ISBN:0-674-00660-7, ISBN13: 978-0-674-00660-7. Dewey:323/.042/0973. LCCN:2001-024928.
Audience: **l,u,f.** *Choice, 2002.*

Carothers, Thomas **JC421.C246 1999**
Aiding Democracy Abroad: The Learning Curve. Trade Cloth. Carnegie Endowment for International Peace. Washington, DC. 1999. x, 411p. ISBN:0-87003-168-6, ISBN13: 978-0-87003-168-7. Dewey:321.8/071. LCCN:99-045358.
Audience: **l,u,f.**

Clarke, Paul Barry & Foweraker, Joe **JC423.E54 2001**
Encyclopedia of Democratic Thought. Paper over Boards. Routledge. New York, NY. 2001. 768p. ISBN:0-415-19396-6, ISBN13: 978-0-415-19396-2. Dewey:321.8/03. LCCN:00-045740.
Audience: **g,l,u,f.** *Choice, 2002.*

Conteh-Morgan, Earl **JQ1879**
Democratization in Africa: The Theory and Dynamics of Political Transitions. Trade Cloth. Greenwood Publishing Group, Inc. Portsmouth, NH. 1997. 208p. ISBN:0-275-95780-2, ISBN13: 978-0-275-95780-3. Dewey:320.967/09/045. LCCN:96-033193.
Audience: **l,u.** *Choice, 1997.*

Crotty, William (Editor) **JC423.D46 2005**
Democratic Development and Political Terrorism: The Global Perspective. Trade Cloth. Northeastern University Press. Boston, MA. 2004. 544p. Northeastern Series on Democratization and Political Development ISBN:1-55553-625-5, ISBN13: 978-1-55553-625-1. Dewey:303.6/25. LCCN:2004-009740.
Audience: **l,u,f.** *Choice, 2005.*

Dahl, Robert A. **JC423.D2478**
Democracy and Its Critics. Trade Paper. Yale University Press. Cumberland, RI. 1991. 397p. ISBN:0-300-04938-2, ISBN13: 978-0-300-04938-1. Dewey:321.8.
Audience: **l,u,f.** *Choice, 1990.*

Dahl, Robert A. **JC423 .D249**
Dilemmas of Pluralist Democracy: Autonomy vs. Control. Trade Paper. Yale University Press. Cumberland, RI. 1983. 232p. Studies in Political Science, No. 31 ISBN:0-300-03076-2, ISBN13: 978-0-300-03076-1. Dewey:321.8. LCCN:81-016111.
Audience: **l,u,f.**

Dahl, Robert Alan **JC423.D249 1982**
e Dilemmas of Pluralist Democracy: Autonomy Vs. Control. E-Book. NetLibrary, Inc. Boulder, CO. 1982. ISBN:0-585-34879-0, ISBN13: 978-0-585-34879-7. Dewey:321.8.
Audience: **l,u,f.**

Dewey, John **PQ7087.E5L378**
Freedom and Culture. Trade Cloth. Prometheus Books, Publishers. Amherst, NY. 1989. 134p. Great Books in Philosophy ISBN:0-87975-560-1, ISBN13: 978-0-87975-560-7. Dewey:862/.608098. LCCN:89-062323.
Audience: **g,l,u,f.**

Downs, Anthony **JF1351.D65**
An Economic Theory of Democracy. Trade Paper. Books on Demand. Ann Arbor, MI. 322p. ISBN:0-598-84640-9, ISBN13: 978-0-598-84640-2. Dewey:351. LCCN:57-010571.
Audience: **u,f.** B

Estlund, David M. (Editor) **JC423.D43976 2001**
Democracy. Trade Paper. Blackwell Publishing, Inc. Malden, MA. 2001. 352p. Readings in Philosophy Ser., Vol. 4 ISBN:0-631-22104-2, ISBN13: 978-0-631-22104-3. Dewey:321.8. LCCN:2001-037589.
Audience: **g,l,u,f.**

Fiorina, Morris P., et al. **JK1726.N45 2005**
The New American Democracy. Ed. 4. D. Stephen Voss, Bertram Johnson & Paul E. Peterson (Authors). Trade Paper. Longman Publishing Group. White Plains, NY. 2004. 720p. ISBN:0-321-21000-X, ISBN13: 978-0-321-21000-5. Dewey:320.473. LCCN:2004-022541.
Audience: **l,u,f.**

Fishkin, James S. **JC423.F63 1991**
Democracy and Deliberation: New Directions for Democratic Reform. Cloth over Boards. Yale University Press. Cumberland, RI. 1991. 172p. ISBN:0-300-05161-1, ISBN13: 978-0-300-05161-2. Dewey:321.8. LCCN:91-024929.
Audience: **l,u,f.** *Choice, 1992.*

Fung, Archon **JC423**
Deepening Democracy: Institutional Innovations in Empowered Participatory Governance, Vol. 4. Trade Paper. Analytical Psychology Club of San Francisco, Inc. San Francisco, CA. 2003. 224p. ISBN:1-85984-466-9, ISBN13: 978-1-85984-466-3. Dewey:321.8.
Audience: **g,l,u,f.**

Gaubatz, Kurt Taylor **JC421.G255 1999**
Elections and War: The Electoral Incentive in the Democratic Politics of War and Peace. Trade Cloth. Stanford University Press. Palo Alto, CA. 1999. 224p. ISBN:0-8047-3566-2, ISBN13: 978-0-8047-3566-7. Dewey:324.9. LCCN:99-017333.
Audience: **l,u,f.** *Choice, 2000.*

Gutmann, Amy & Thompson, Dennis **JC423.G925 1996**
Democracy and Disagreement. Trade Cloth. Harvard University Press. Cambridge, MA. 1996. 432p. ISBN:0-674-19765-8, ISBN13: 978-0-674-19765-7. Dewey:321.8/0973. LCCN:96-013732.
Audience: **l,u,f.** *Choice, 1997.*

Gutmann, Amy & Thompson, Dennis **JC423.G9255 2004**
Why Deliberative Democracy? Trade Paper. Princeton University Press. Princeton, NJ. 2004. 256p. ISBN:0-691-12019-6, ISBN13: 978-0-691-12019-5. Dewey:321.8. LCCN:2004-040048.
Audience: **l,u,f.**

Haggard, Stephan & Kaufman, Robert R. **JC423.H29 1995**
The Political Economy of Democratic Transitions. Trade Paper. Princeton University Press. Princeton, NJ. 1995. 406p. ISBN:0-691-02775-7, ISBN13: 978-0-691-02775-3. Dewey:338.9. LCCN:94-049595.
Audience: **l,u,f.** *Choice, 1996.*

Hardt, Michael & Negri, Antonio **JC423.H364 2004**
Multitude: War and Democracy in the Age of Empire. Trade Cloth. Penguin Group (USA) Inc. New York, NY. 2004. 448p. ISBN:1-59420-024-6, ISBN13: 978-1-59420-024-3. Dewey:321.8. LCCN:2004-044463.
Audience: **l,u,f.** *Choice, 2005.*

Held, David **JC423.H466 1995**
Democracy and the Global Order: From the Modern State to Cosmopolitan Governance. Trade Paper. Stanford University Press. Palo Alto, CA. 1996. 336p. ISBN:0-8047-2687-6, ISBN13: 978-0-8047-2687-0. Dewey:321.8. LCCN:95-070941.
Audience: **l,u,f.** *Choice, 1996.*

Hollifield, James F. & Jillson, Calvin C. **JC421.P358 2000**
Pathways to Democracy: The Political Economy of Democratic Transitions. Trade Paper. Routledge. New York, NY. 1999. 344p. ISBN:0-415-92434-0, ISBN13: 978-0-415-92434-4. Dewey:320.9049. LCCN:99-035009.
Audience: **u,f.**

Keenan, Alan **JC423.K363 2002**
The Democratic Question. Paper Text. Stanford University Press. Palo Alto, CA. 2003. 256p. ISBN:0-8047-3865-3, ISBN13: 978-0-8047-3865-1. Dewey:321.8. LCCN:2002-005862.
Audience: **l,u,f.** *Choice, 2003.*

Keenan, Alan **JC423.K363 2002**
The Democratic Question. Cloth Text. Stanford University Press. Palo Alto, CA. 2003. 288p. ISBN:0-8047-3747-9, ISBN13: 978-0-8047-3747-0. Dewey:321.8. LCCN:2002-005862.
Audience: **l,u,f.** *Choice, 2003.*

Ketcham, Ralph Louis **JC423.K4128 2004**
The Idea of Democracy in the Modern ERA. Trade Cloth. University Press of Kansas. Lawrence, KS. 2004. xii, 196p. ISBN:0-7006-1334-X, ISBN13: 978-0-7006-1334-2. Dewey:321.8. LCCN:2004-005383.
Audience: **l,u,f.** *Choice, 2005.*

Kirdar, Uner & Silk, Leonard **JC423.W64 1994**
A World Fit for People: Thinkers from Many Countries Address the Political, Economic, and Social Problems of Our Time. Trade Cloth. New York University Press. New York, NY. 1994. 503p. ISBN:0-8147-4648-9, ISBN13: 978-0-8147-4648-6. Dewey:909.82/9. LCCN:93-008945.
Audience: **g,l,u,f.** *Choice, 1994.*

Kis, Janos **JC423.K53713 2002**
Constitutional Democracy. Trade Cloth. Central European University Press. Herndon, VA. 2003. 340p. ISBN:963-9241-32-6, ISBN13: 978-963-9241-32-9. Dewey:321.8. LCCN:2002-014606.
Audience: **u,f.** *Choice, 2004.*

Lakoff, Sanford **JC423.L295 1996**
Democracy: History, Theory, Practice. Trade Paper. Westview Press. Boulder, CO. 1996. 400p. ISBN:0-8133-3228-1, ISBN13: 978-0-8133-3228-4. Dewey:321.8. LCCN:96-024373.
Audience: **g,l.** *Choice, 1997.*

Levine, Andrew **JC423**
Liberal Democracy: A Critique of Its Theory. Trade Cloth. Columbia University Press. New York, NY. 1981. 272p. ISBN:0-231-05250-2, ISBN13: 978-0-231-05250-4. Dewey:321.8/01. LCCN:81-001204.
Audience: **l,u,f.**

Lijphart, Arend **JC330**
Democracy in Plural Societies: A Comparative Exploration. Trade Paper. Yale University Press. Cumberland, RI. 1980. 258p. ISBN:0-300-02494-0, ISBN13: 978-0-300-02494-4. Dewey:321.8. LCCN:77-076311.
Audience: **l,u,f.**

Lijphart, Arend **JC421.L542 1999**
Patterns of Democracy: Government Forms and Performance in Thirty-Six Countries. Trade Paper. Yale University Press. Cumberland, RI. 1999. 368p. ISBN:0-300-07893-5, ISBN13: 978-0-300-07893-0. Dewey:320.3. LCCN:99-012365.
Audience: **l,u,f.** *Choice, 2000.*

Lijphart, Arend & Waisman, Carlos H. (Editors) **JL966.I57 1996**
Institutional Design in New Democracies: Eastern Europe and Latin America. Trade Paper. Westview Press. Boulder, CO. 1996. 288p. Latin America in Global Perspective Ser. ISBN:0-8133-2109-3, ISBN13: 978-0-8133-2109-7. Dewey:324.6/3/09049. LCCN:96-006133.
Audience: **u,f.**

Linz, Juan J. & Stepan, Alfred **JC421 .L56 1996**
Problems of Democratic Transition and Consolidation: Southern Europe, South America and Post-Communist Europe. Trade Paper. Johns Hopkins University Press. Baltimore, MD. 1981. 504p. ISBN:0-8018-5158-0, ISBN13: 978-0-8018-5158-2. Dewey:321.8/09/045. LCCN:95-043462.
Audience: **u,f.**

Lipset, Seymour Martin & Lakin, Jason M. **JC421.L57 2004**
The Democratic Century. Trade Cloth. University of Oklahoma Press. Norman, OK. 2004. 480p. The Julian J. Rothbaum Distinguished Lecture Ser., Vol. 9 ISBN:0-8061-3618-9, ISBN13: 978-0-8061-3618-9. Dewey:321.8/09/04. LCCN:2004-041231.
Audience: **g,l,u,f.** *Choice, 2005.*

Mackie, Gerry **JC423.M1583 2003**
Democracy Defended. Ian Shapiro, Russell Hardin, Stephen Holmes, Jeffrey Isaac, John Keane, Elizabeth Kiss, Susan Okin, Phillip Pettit & Phillipe Van Parijs (Contribution by). Trade Paper. Cambridge University Press. New York, NY. 2003. 500p. Contemporary Political Theory Ser. ISBN:0-521-53431-3, ISBN13: 978-0-521-53431-4. Dewey:321.8. LCCN:2003-048469.
Audience: **g,l,u,f.** *Choice, 2004.*

Mbaku, John M. & Ihonvbere, Julius O. (Editors) **JQ1875.M83 1995**
Multiparty Democracy and Political Change: Constraints to Democratization in Africa. Trade Cloth. Ashgate Publishing, Ltd. Aldershot, 1998. 354p. ISBN:1-84014-379-7, ISBN13: 978-1-84014-379-9. Dewey:320.96/09/049. LCCN:97-077172.
Audience: **l,u,f.**

Nie, Norman H., et al. **JK1764.N54 1996**
Education and Democratic Citizenship in America. Jane Junn & Kenneth Stehlik-Barry (Authors). Trade Paper. University of Chicago Press. Chicago, IL. 1996. 290p. ISBN:0-226-58389-9, ISBN13: 978-0-226-58389-1. Dewey:306.2. LCCN:95-026657.
Audience: **g,l,u,f.** *Choice, 1997.*

Paehlke, Robert **JC423.P222 2004**
Democracy's Dilemma: Environment, Social Equity, and the Global Economy. Trade Paper. MIT Press. Cambridge, MA. 2004. 316p. ISBN:0-262-66188-8, ISBN13: 978-0-262-66188-1. Dewey:306.2.
Audience: **l,u,f.** *Choice, 2003.*

Przeworski, Adam (Author, Contribution by) **JC423 .D46 2000**
Democracy and Development: Political Institutions and Well-Being in the World, 1950-1990. Michael E. Alvarez, Jose Antonio Cheibub & Fernando Limongi (Authors). Trade Paper. Cambridge University Press. New York, NY. 2000. 336p. Cambridge Studies in the Theory of Democracy ISBN:0-521-79379-3, ISBN13: 978-0-521-79379-7. Dewey:338.9/009/045. LCCN:00-709713.
Audience: **l,u,f.**

Riker, William H. **JC423**
Liberalism Against Populism: A Confrontation Between the Theory of Democracy and the Theory of Social Choice. Paper Text. Waveland Press, Inc. Prospect Heights, IL. 1988. 311p. ISBN:0-88133-367-0, ISBN13: 978-0-88133-367-1. Dewey:320.011.
Audience: **g,l,u,f.**

Salih, Mohamed Abdel Rahim M. **JQ1879.A15.S25 2001**
African Democracies and African Politics. Trade Paper. Pluto Press. London, 2001. 224p. Human Security in the Global Economy Ser. ISBN:0-7453-1724-3, ISBN13: 978-0-7453-1724-3. Dewey:320.96. LCCN:00-012647.
Audience: **g,l,u.** *Choice, 2002.*

Sanford, George **JN6760**
Democratic Government in Poland: Constitutional Politics since 1989. Cloth over Boards. Palgrave Macmillan. New York, NY. 2002. 280p. ISBN:0-333-77475-2, ISBN13: 978-0-333-77475-5. Dewey:320.9438. LCCN:2002-020059.
Audience: **l,u,f.** *Choice, 2003.*

Schaffer, Frederic C. **JQ3396.A91**
Democracy in Translation: Understanding Politics in an Unfamiliar Culture. Trade Paper. Cornell University Press. Ithaca, NY. 2000. 192p. Wilder House Series in Politics, History, and Culture Ser. ISBN:0-8014-8691-2, ISBN13: 978-0-8014-8691-3. Dewey:320.9663.
Audience: **l,u,f.**

Schumpeter, Joseph Alois **HX40**
Capitalism, Socialism and Democracy. Ed. 5. Tom Bottomore (Introduction by). Trade Cloth. Allen & Unwin, Ltd. London, 1976. xiv, 437p. ISBN:0-04-335031-3, ISBN13: 978-0-04-335031-7. Dewey:330.12/2/0904. LCCN:77-364732.
Audience: **l,u,f.** B

Siegle, Joe, et al. **JC423.H3734 2004**
The Democracy Advantage: How Democracies Promote Prosperity and Peace. Michael Weinstein & Morton H. Halperin (Authors), George Soros (Foreword by). Paper over Boards. Routledge. New York, NY. 2004. 312p. ISBN:0-415-95052-X, ISBN13: 978-0-415-95052-7. Dewey:321.8. LCCN:2004-009571.
Audience: **g,l,u,f.**

Snyder, Jack L. **JC421.S557 2000**
From Voting to Violence: Democratization and Nationalist Conflict. Trade Paper. W. W. Norton & Company, Inc. New York, NY. 2000. 384p. ISBN:0-393-97481-2, ISBN13: 978-0-393-97481-2. Dewey:320.54/09/049. LCCN:99-049208.
Audience: **l,u,f.**

Spragens, Thomas A. Jr. **JC423.S75 1990**
Reason and Democracy. Paper Text. Duke University Press. Durham, NC. 1990. 295p. ISBN:0-8223-1068-6, ISBN13: 978-0-8223-1068-6. Dewey:321.8. LCCN:89-071474.
Audience: **u,f.** *Choice, 1991.*

Stone, Geoffrey **JC591.S76 2004**
Perilous Times: Free Speech in Wartime from the Sedition Act of 1798 to the War on Terrorism. Trade Cloth. W. W. Norton & Company, Inc. New York, NY. 2004. 800p. ISBN:0-393-05880-8, ISBN13: 978-0-393-05880-2. Dewey:323.44/3/0973. LCCN:2004-017871.
Audience: **l,u,f.** *Choice, 2005.*

Talisse, Robert B. **JC574.T35 2004**
Democracy after Liberalism: Pragmatism and Deliberative Politics. Trade Paper. Routledge. New York, NY. 2004. 176p. ISBN:0-415-95019-8, ISBN13: 978-0-415-95019-0. Dewey:321.8. LCCN:2004-008431.
Audience: **l,u,f.**

Taras, Ray & Castle, Marjorie **JN6766.C37 2002**
Democracy in Poland. Ed. 2. Trade Paper. Westview Press. Boulder, CO. 2002. 312p. ISBN:0-8133-3935-9, ISBN13: 978-0-8133-3935-1. Dewey:320.9438. LCCN:2002-002968.
Audience: **g,l,u,f.**

Terchek, Ronald & Conte, Thomas C. (Editors) **JC423.T398 2001**
Theories of Democracy: A Reader. Book, Other. Rowman & Littlefield Publishers, Inc. Lanham, MD. 2001. 400p. ISBN:0-8476-9724-X, ISBN13: 978-0-8476-9724-3. Dewey:321.8. LCCN:2001-019692.
Audience: **l.**

Tulchin, Joseph S. & Brown, Amelia (Editors) **JC423.D466 2002**
Democratic Governance and Social Inequality. Trade Paper. Lynne Rienner Publishers, Inc. Boulder, CO. 2002. 200p. ISBN:1-58826-028-3, ISBN13: 978-1-58826-028-4. Dewey:321.8. LCCN:2001-048643.
Audience: **l,u,f.** *Choice, 2003.*

Verba, Sidney & Nie, Norman H. **JK1764.V467 1987**
Participation in America: Political Democracy and Social Equality. Trade Paper. University of Chicago Press. Chicago, IL. 2004. 452p. ISBN:0-226-85296-2, ISBN13: 978-0-226-85296-6. Dewey:323/.042/0973. LCCN:87-010825.
Audience: **g,l,u,f.** B

Weart, Spencer R. **JC421.W43 1998**
Never at War: Why Democracies Will Not Fight One Another. Cloth over Boards. Yale University Press. Cumberland, RI. 1998. 430p. ISBN:0-300-07017-9, ISBN13: 978-0-300-07017-0. Dewey:327.1/7. LCCN:98-002664.
Audience: **g,l,u,f.** *Choice, 1999.*

Wittman, Donald A. **JC423 .W499**
The Myth of Democratic Failure: Why Political Institutions Are Efficient. Trade Paper. University of Chicago Press. Chicago, IL. 1997. 240p. American Politics and Political Economy Ser. ISBN:0-226-90423-7, ISBN13: 978-0-226-90423-8. Dewey:321.8. LCCN:94-046186.
Audience: **l,u,f.** *Choice, 1996.*

Young, Iris Marion **JC578.Y68 1990**
Justice and the Politics of Difference. Trade Paper. Princeton University Press. Princeton, NJ. 1990. 294p. ISBN:0-691-02315-8, ISBN13: 978-0-691-02315-1. Dewey:320/.011. LCCN:90-036988.
Audience: **u,f.**

Political Theory > Forms of the State > Socialism

HX36.A87 1991
Atlas of Communism. Trade Cloth. Macmillan Publishing Company, Inc. Old Tappan, NJ. 1991. 256p. ISBN:0-685-38864-6, ISBN13: 978-0-685-38864-8. Dewey:335.43/09.
Audience: **l,u,f.**

Abrams, Bradley F. **HX528.A25 2004**
The Struggle for the Soul of the Nation: Czech Culture and the Rise of Communism. Book, Other. Rowman & Littlefield Publishers, Inc. Lanham, MD. 2004. 372p. The Harvard Cold War Studies Book ISBN:0-7425-3023-X, ISBN13: 978-0-7425-3023-2. Dewey:943.704. LCCN:2003-026054.
Audience: **l,u,f.** *Choice, 2004.*

Azicri, Max & Deal, Elsie (Editors) **HX158.5.C85 2004**
Cuban Socialism in a New Century. Trade Cloth. University Press of Florida. Gainesville, FL. 2004. 424p. Contemporary Cuba Ser. ISBN:0-8130-2763-2, ISBN13: 978-0-8130-2763-0. Dewey:335.43/47. LCCN:2004-055474.
Audience: **l,u,f.** *Choice, 2005.*

Bronner, Stephen Eric **HX73.B76 2000**
Socialism Unbound. Ed. 2. Trade Paper. Westview Press. Boulder, CO. 2000. 264p. Interventions Ser., :Theory and Contemporary Politics ISBN:0-8133-6776-X, ISBN13: 978-0-8133-6776-7. Dewey:335.4. LCCN:00-048471.
Audience: **g,l,u,f.**

Denitch, Bogdan Denis **HX365.5.A6D46 1990**
Limits and Possibilities: The Crisis of Yugoslav Socialism and State Socialist Systems. Cloth Text. University of Minnesota Press. Minneapolis, MN. 1990. 192p. ISBN:0-8166-1843-7, ISBN13: 978-0-8166-1843-9. Dewey:335/.009497. LCCN:90-033751.
Audience: **l,u,f.** *Choice, 1991.*

Goldman, Emma **HX843.7.G65 E427**
Emma Goldman: A Documentary History of the American Years. Candace Falk, Barry Pateman & Jessica M. Moran (Editors). Trade Cloth. University of California Press. Berkeley, CA. 2003. 696p. Emma Goldman Ser., :A Documentary History of the American Years Ser. ISBN:0-520-08670-8, ISBN13: 978-0-520-08670-8. Dewey:335/.83/092 B. LCCN:2002-028943.
Audience: **g,l,u,f.** *Choice, 2003.*

Harrington, Michael **HX36.H36**
Socialism. Trade Cloth. Saturday Review Press. New York, NY. 1972. 436p. ISBN:0-8415-0141-6, ISBN13: 978-0-8415-0141-6. Dewey:335. LCCN:76-154260.
Audience: **g,l,u,f.** B

Harrington, Michael **HX44.H35 1990**
Socialism: Past and Future. Irving Howe (Introduction by). Trade Paper. Penguin Group (USA) Inc. New York, NY. 1990. 32p. ISBN:0-452-26504-5, ISBN13: 978-0-452-26504-2. Dewey:335/.001/12. LCCN:90-038957.
Audience: **g,l,u,f.** *Choice, 1990.*

Kaminski, Bartlomiej **HX315.7.A6K36 1991**
The Collapse of State Socialism: The Case of Poland. Trade Paper. Princeton University Press. Princeton, NJ. 1991. 252p. ISBN:0-691-02335-2, ISBN13: 978-0-691-02335-9. Dewey:335.43/09438. LCCN:90-021737.
Audience: **l,u,f.** *Choice, 1992.*

Lenin, V. I. **HX314 .L342 1989**
What Is to Be Done? Joe Fineberg & George Hanna (Translators), Robert Service (Introduction by). Trade Paper. Penguin Group (USA) Inc. New York, NY. 1990. 272p. ISBN:0-14-018126-1, ISBN13: 978-0-14-018126-5. Dewey:335.43.
Audience: **g,l,u,f.**

Levine, Andrew **HX73.L46 1988**
Arguing for Socialism. Ed. 2. Paper Text. Analytical Psychology Club of San Francisco, Inc. San Francisco, CA. 1988. 240p.

ISBN:0-86091-918-8, ISBN13: 978-0-86091-918-6. Dewey:335.43. LCCN:88-006080.
Audience: **l,u,f.**

Levine, Andrew **HX73**
A Future for Marxism?: Althusser, the Analytical Turn and the Revival of Socialist Theory. Trade Paper. Pluto Press. London, 2003. 192p. ISBN:0-7453-1987-4, ISBN13: 978-0-7453-1987-2. Dewey:335.4. LCCN:2003-269811.
Audience: **l,u,f.** *Choice, 2003.*

Lipset, Seymour Martin & Marks, Gary **HX83.L55 2000**
It Didn't Happen Here: Why Socialism Failed in the United States. Trade Cloth. W. W. Norton & Company, Inc. New York, NY. 2000. 384p. ISBN:0-393-04098-4, ISBN13: 978-0-393-04098-2. Dewey:335/.00973. LCCN:00-021489.
Audience: **g,l,u,f.** *Choice, 2000.*

Martin, Bill & Avakian, Bob **HX73.A88 2005**
Marxism and the Call of the Future: Conversations on Ethics, History, and Politics. Trade Paper. Open Court Publishing Company. Chicago, IL. 2005. 350p. Creative Marxism Ser., Vol. 2 ISBN:0-8126-9579-8, ISBN13: 978-0-8126-9579-3. Dewey:335.4. LCCN:2004-030777.
Audience: **u,f.** *Choice, 2006.*

Marx, Karl, et al. **HX39.5**
The Communist Manifesto: Karl Marx and Friedrich Engels: Edited and Translated by L.M. Findlay. Friedrich Engels & L. M. Findlay (Authors). Trade Paper. Broadview Press. Peterborough, ON. 2004. 190p. ISBN:1-55111-333-3, ISBN13: 978-1-55111-333-3. Dewey:335.4/22.
Audience: **g,l,u,f.**

Marx, Karl & Engels, Friedrich **HX39.5**
Birth of the Communist Manifesto. Dirk J. Struik (Editor). Trade Paper. International Publishers Company, Inc. New York, NY. 1994. 224p. ISBN:0-7178-0320-1, ISBN13: 978-0-7178-0320-0. Dewey:335.42/2. LCCN:77-148513.
Audience: **g,l,u,f.** *B*

Marx, Karl & Tucker, Robert C. **HX39.5**
The Marx-Engels Reader. Ed. 2. David P. McLellan (Editor). Trade Paper. W. W. Norton & Company, Inc. New York, NY. 1978. 788p. ISBN:0-393-09040-X, ISBN13: 978-0-393-09040-6. Dewey:335.4.
Audience: **g,l,u,f.**

Muravchik, Joshua **HX36.M87 2002**
Heaven on Earth: The Rise and Fall of Socialism. Trade Cloth. Encounter Books. New York, NY. 2003. 418p. ISBN:1-893554-45-7, ISBN13: 978-1-893554-45-0. Dewey:335/.009. LCCN:2001-055681.
Audience: **l,u,f.** *Choice, 2003.*

Ollman, Bertell **HX39.5.O55 2003**
Dance of the Dialectic: Steps in Marx's Method. Trade Cloth. University of Illinois Press. Champaign, IL. 2003. 248p. ISBN:0-252-02832-5, ISBN13: 978-0-252-02832-8. Dewey:335.4/11. LCCN:2002-151570.
Audience: **u,f.** *Choice, 2004.*

Ollman, Bertell **HX39.5.O55 2003**
Dance of the Dialectic: Steps in Marx's Method. Trade Paper. University of Illinois Press. Champaign, IL. 2003. 248p. ISBN:0-252-07118-2, ISBN13: 978-0-252-07118-8. Dewey:335.4/11. LCCN:2002-151570.
Audience: **u,f.** *Choice, 2004.*

Paul, Ellen Frankel (Editor), et al. **HX44.5.A38 2003**
After Socialism, Vol. 20, Pt. 1. Fred Dycus Miller & Jeffrey Paul (Editors). Trade Paper. Cambridge University Press. New York, NY. 2003. 326p. Social Philosophy and Policy Ser. ISBN:0-521-53498-4, ISBN13: 978-0-521-53498-7. Dewey:335.43. LCCN:2002-035151.
Audience: **l,u,f.**

Przeworski, Adam **HX73**
Capitalism and Social Democracy. Trade Cloth. Cambridge University Press. New York, NY. 1985. 277p. Studies in Marxism and Social Theory ISBN:0-521-26742-0, ISBN13: 978-0-521-26742-7. Dewey:320.5/315. LCCN:84-019891.
Audience: **l,u,f.**

Sassoon, Donald **HX238.5**
One Hundred Years of Socialism: The West European Left in the Twentieth Century. Trade Cloth. New Press, The. New York, NY. 1997. 992p. ISBN:1-56584-373-8, ISBN13: 978-1-56584-373-8. Dewey:320.5/31/094.
Audience: **l,u,f.** *Choice, 1997.*

Schumpeter, Joseph Alois **HX40**
Capitalism, Socialism and Democracy. Ed. 5. Tom Bottomore (Introduction by). Trade Cloth. Allen & Unwin, Ltd. London, 1976. xiv, 437p. ISBN:0-04-335031-3, ISBN13: 978-0-04-335031-7. Dewey:330.12/2/0904. LCCN:77-364732.
Audience: **l,u,f.** *B*

Silber, Irwin **HX36.S545 1994**
Socialism: What Went Wrong?: An Inquiry into the Theoretical and Historical Sources of the Socialist Crisis. Pluto Press. 1994. ISBN:0-7453-0715-9, ISBN13: 978-0-7453-0715-2.
Audience: **u,f.**

Skidelsky, Robert J. **HX44.5.S55 1996**
The Road from Serfdom: The Economic and Political Consequences of the End of Communism. Trade Cloth. Penguin Group (USA) Inc. New York, NY. 1996. 224p. ISBN:0-7139-9122-4, ISBN13: 978-0-7139-9122-2. Dewey:338.9. LCCN:95-038459.
Audience: **g,l,u,f.** *Choice, 1996.*

Sorel, Georges **HX72.S674 1987**
From Georges Sorel: Essays in Socialism and Philosophy, Vol. I. John L. Stanley (Editor, Translator). Trade Paper. Transaction Publishers. Somerset, NJ. 1987. 402p. ISBN:0-88738-654-7, ISBN13: 978-0-88738-654-1. Dewey:335. LCCN:86-030758.
Audience: **l,u,f.**

Political Theory > Forms of the State > Communist State

Abrams, Bradley F. **HX528.A25 2004**
The Struggle for the Soul of the Nation: Czech Culture and the Rise of Communism. Book, Other. Rowman & Littlefield Publishers, Inc. Lanham, MD. 2004. 372p. The Harvard Cold

War Studies Book ISBN:0-7425-3023-X, ISBN13: 978-0-7425-3023-2. Dewey:943.704. LCCN:2003-026054.
Audience: **l,u,f.** *Choice, 2004.*

Alexander, Robert J. **HX517**
International Maoism in the Developing World. Trade Cloth. Greenwood Publishing Group, Inc. Portsmouth, NH. 1999. 360p. ISBN:0-275-96149-4, ISBN13: 978-0-275-96149-7. Dewey:335.43/45/091724. LCCN:98-047813.
Audience: **l,u,f.** *Choice, 2000.*

Barany, Zoltan & Volgyes, Ivan (Editors) **HX240.7.A6L44 1995**
The Legacies of Communism in Eastern Europe. Trade Paper. Johns Hopkins University Press. Baltimore, MD. 1995. 352p. ISBN:0-8018-4998-5, ISBN13: 978-0-8018-4998-5. Dewey:335.43. LCCN:94-043245.
Audience: **g,l,u,f.** *Choice, 1996.*

Crossman, Richard (Editor) **HX72.G62 2001**
The God That Failed. David Engerman (Foreword by). Trade Paper. Columbia University Press. New York, NY. 2001. 272p. ISBN:0-231-12395-7, ISBN13: 978-0-231-12395-2. Dewey:320.53/22/0922. LCCN:2001-032546.
Audience: **g,l,u,f.**

Dawisha, Karen & Parrott, Bruce (Editors) **JC359.E53 1997**
The End of Empire?: The Transformation of the U.S.S.R. in Comparative Perspective. Cloth Text. M. E. Sharpe Inc. Armonk, NY. 1996. 390p. International Politics of Eurasia Ser. ISBN:1-56324-368-7, ISBN13: 978-1-56324-368-4. Dewey:321.9/2/0947. LCCN:96-021985.
Audience: **l,u,f.** *Choice, 1997.*

Denitch, Bogdan Denis **HX365.5.A6D46 1990**
Limits and Possibilities: The Crisis of Yugoslav Socialism and State Socialist Systems. Cloth Text. University of Minnesota Press. Minneapolis, MN. 1990. 192p. ISBN:0-8166-1843-7, ISBN13: 978-0-8166-1843-9. Dewey:335/.009497. LCCN:90-033751.
Audience: **l,u,f.** *Choice, 1991.*

Eckstein, Susan Eva **HX158.5.E35 2003**
Back from the Future: Cuba under Castro. Ed. 2. Alejandro Portes (Foreword by). Trade Paper. Routledge. New York, NY. 2003. 352p. ISBN:0-415-94794-4, ISBN13: 978-0-415-94794-7. Dewey:338.97291. LCCN:2003-011941.
Audience: **l,u,f.** *Choice, 1994.*

Gilberg, Trond **HX550.N3G53 1990**
Nationalism and Communism in Romania: The Rise and Fall of Ceausescu's Personal Dictatorship. Cloth Text. Westview Press. Boulder, CO. 1990. 289p. Special Studies on the Soviet Union and Eastern Europe ISBN:0-8133-7497-9, ISBN13: 978-0-8133-7497-0. Dewey:306.2/09498. LCCN:89-025056.
Audience: **u,f.** *Choice, 1991.*

Gill, Graeme J. & Pitty, Roderic **JN6598.K7.G5237 1997**
Power in the Party: The Organization of Power and Central-Republican Relations in the CPSU. Trade Cloth. Bow Historical Books. New Providence, NJ. 1997. 240p. ISBN:0-333-66656-9, ISBN13: 978-0-333-66656-2. Dewey:947/.085. LCCN:96-034345.
Audience: **l,u,f.**

Hoberman, J. **HX40.H5673 1998**
The Red Atlantis: Communist Culture in the Absence of Communism. Trade Cloth. Temple University Press. Philadelphia, PA. 2000. 326p. Culture and the Moving Image Ser. ISBN:1-56639-643-3, ISBN13: 978-1-56639-643-1. Dewey:335.43/097. LCCN:98-016178.
Audience: **l,u,f.** *Choice, 1999.*

Kaminski, Bartlomiej **HX315.7.A6K36 1991**
The Collapse of State Socialism: The Case of Poland. Trade Paper. Princeton University Press. Princeton, NJ. 1991. 252p. ISBN:0-691-02335-2, ISBN13: 978-0-691-02335-9. Dewey:335.43/09438. LCCN:90-021737.
Audience: **l,u,f.** *Choice, 1992.*

Kelley, Robin D. **HX91.A2K45 1990**
Hammer and Hoe: Alabama Communists During the Great Depression. Trade Paper. University of North Carolina Press. Chapel Hill, NC. 1990. 392p. Fred W. Morrison Series in Southern Studies ISBN:0-8078-4288-5, ISBN13: 978-0-8078-4288-1. Dewey:324.2761/075/09042. LCCN:90-050018.
Audience: **g,l,u,f.** *Choice, 1991.*

Lenin, V. I. **HX314**
The State and Revolution: Marxist Teaching about the Theory of the State and the Tasks of the Proletariat in the Revolution. Trade Cloth. Greenwood Publishing Group, Inc. Portsmouth, NH. 1978. 104p. ISBN:0-313-20351-2, ISBN13: 978-0-313-20351-0. LCCN:78-002228.
Audience: **g,l,u,f.**

Lenin, V. I. **HX314 .L342 1989**
What Is to Be Done? Joe Fineberg & George Hanna (Translators), Robert Service (Introduction by). Trade Paper. Penguin Group (USA) Inc. New York, NY. 1990. 272p. ISBN:0-14-018126-1, ISBN13: 978-0-14-018126-5. Dewey:335.43.
Audience: **g,l,u,f.**

Malia, Martin E. **HX311.5**
The Soviet Tragedy: A History of Socialism in Russia 1917-1991. Trade Paper. Simon & Schuster. New York, NY. 1995. 592p. ISBN:0-684-82313-6, ISBN13: 978-0-684-82313-3. Dewey:321.9/2/09470904. LCCN:93-050128.
Audience: **l,u,f.**

Marcuse, Herbert **HX313**
Soviet Marxism: A Critical Analysis. Trade Paper. Columbia University Press. New York, NY. 1985. 271p. ISBN:0-231-08379-3, ISBN13: 978-0-231-08379-9. Dewey:335.43/0947. LCCN:57-010943.
Audience: **l,u,f.** B

Martin, Bill & Avakian, Bob **HX73.A88 2005**
Marxism and the Call of the Future: Conversations on Ethics, History, and Politics. Trade Paper. Open Court Publishing Company. Chicago, IL. 2005. 350p. Creative Marxism Ser., Vol. 2 ISBN:0-8126-9579-8, ISBN13: 978-0-8126-9579-3. Dewey:335.4. LCCN:2004-030777.
Audience: **u,f.** *Choice, 2006.*

Marx, Karl, et al. **HX39.5**
The Communist Manifesto: Karl Marx and Friedrich Engels: Edited and Translated by L.M. Findlay. Friedrich Engels & L. M. Findlay (Authors). Trade Paper. Broadview Press.

Peterborough, ON. 2004. 190p. ISBN:1-55111-333-3, ISBN13: 978-1-55111-333-3. Dewey:335.4/22.
Audience: **g,l,u,f.**

Marx, Karl & Engels, Friedrich **HX39.5**
Birth of the Communist Manifesto. Dirk J. Struik (Editor). Trade Paper. International Publishers Company, Inc. New York, NY. 1994. 224p. ISBN:0-7178-0320-1, ISBN13: 978-0-7178-0320-0. Dewey:335.42/2. LCCN:77-148513.
Audience: **g,l,u,f.** B

McCollum, James K. **HX373.5.M38 1998**
Is Communism Dead Forever? Trade Cloth. University Press of America, Inc. Lanham, MD. 1998. 178p. ISBN:0-7618-1259-8, ISBN13: 978-0-7618-1259-3. Dewey:335.43/09498. LCCN:98-039211.
Audience: **g,l,u,f.**

McDermott, Kevin & Agnew, Jeremy **HX11.I5M38 1997**
The Comintern: A History of International Communism from Lenin to Stalin. Trade Cloth. Palgrave Macmillan. New York, NY. 1996. 304p. ISBN:0-312-16277-4, ISBN13: 978-0-312-16277-1. Dewey:324.1/75. LCCN:96-019746.
Audience: **g,l,u,f.** *Choice, 1997.*

Okey, Robin **DJK50**
The Demise of Communist East Europe: 1989 in Context. Trade Paper. Oxford University Press, Inc. New York, NY. 2004. 240p. A Hodder Arnold Publication ISBN:0-340-74057-4, ISBN13: 978-0-340-74057-6. Dewey:947/.0009045. LCCN:2005-272438.
Audience: **g,l,u,f.** *Choice, 2005.*

O'Neil, Patrick **JN2191.S92O646 1998**
Revolution from Within: The Hungarian Socialist Workers' Party and the Collapse of Communism. Trade Cloth. Edward Elgar Publishing, Inc. Northampton, MA. 1998. 288p. Studies of Communism in Transition ISBN:1-85898-766-0, ISBN13: 978-1-85898-766-8. Dewey:324.2439/074/09048. LCCN:97-035438.
Audience: **l,u,f.** *Choice, 1998.*

Parenti, Michael **HX44.5.P35 1997**
Blackshirts and Reds: Rational Fascism and the Overthrow of Communism. Trade Paper. City Lights Books. San Francisco, CA. 1997. 208p. ISBN:0-87286-329-8, ISBN13: 978-0-87286-329-3. Dewey:335.4/3. LCCN:97-000119.
Audience: **l,u,f.**

Pipes, Richard **HX36.P495 2003**
Communism: A History. Trade Paper. Random House Adult Trade Publishing Group. New York, NY. 2003. 192p. ISBN:0-8129-6864-6, ISBN13: 978-0-8129-6864-4. Dewey:335.43.
Audience: **g,l,u,f.** *Choice, 2002.*

Saxonberg, Steven **HX240.7.A6**
Fall: A Comparative Study of the End of Communism in Czechoslovakia, East Germany, Hungary and Poland. Cloth Text. Gordon & Breach Publishing Group. New York, NY. 2000. 452p. International Studies in Global Change ISBN:90-5823-097-X, ISBN13: 978-90-5823-097-3. Dewey:320.532.
Audience: **g,l,u,f.** *Choice, 2001.*

Solomon, Mark **HX83.S665 1998**
The Cry Was Unity: Communists and African Americans, 1917-1936. Trade Paper. University Press of Mississippi. Jackson, MS. 1998. 400p. ISBN:1-57806-095-8, ISBN13: 978-1-57806-095-5. Dewey:335.43/089/96073. LCCN:98-016013.
Audience: **l,u,f.** *Choice, 1999.*

Steger, Manfred B. & Carver, Terrell **HX274.7.E53E42 1999**
Engels after Marx. Trade Cloth. Pennsylvania State University Press. University Park, PA. 1999. 264p. ISBN:0-271-01891-7, ISBN13: 978-0-271-01891-1. Dewey:335.4/092. LCCN:99-022631.
Audience: **g,l,u,f.** *Choice, 1999.*

Tismaneanu, Vladimir **JN9639.A53 T57 2003**
Stalinism for All Seasons: A Political History of Romanian Communism. Trade Cloth. University of California Press. Berkeley, CA. 2003. 400p. Societies and Culture in East-Central Europe Ser., Vol. 11 ISBN:0-520-23747-1, ISBN13: 978-0-520-23747-6. Dewey:324.2498/075. LCCN:2002-154941.
Audience: **g,l,u,f.** *Choice, 2004.*

Walder, Andrew G. **HX260.5.A6W36 1995**
e The Waning of the Communist State: Economic Origins of Political Decline in China and Hungary. E-Book. NetLibrary, Inc. Boulder, CO. 1995. ISBN:0-585-04386-8, ISBN13: 978-0-585-04386-9. Dewey:335.43/09439.
Audience: **l,u,f.**

Walicki, Andrzej **HX73**
Marxism and the Leap to the Kingdom of Freedom: The Rise and Fall of the Communist Utopia. Trade Paper. Stanford University Press. Palo Alto, CA. 1997. 654p. ISBN:0-8047-3164-0, ISBN13: 978-0-8047-3164-5. Dewey:320.5/315.
Audience: **l,u,f.** *Choice, 1995.*

Political Theory > Forms of the State > Totalitarianism. Fascism

Altemeyer, Bob **JC481.A48 1996**
The Authoritarian Specter. Trade Cloth. Harvard University Press. Cambridge, MA. 1996. 384p. ISBN:0-674-05305-2, ISBN13: 978-0-674-05305-2. Dewey:320.5/3. LCCN:97-015548.
Audience: **l,u,f.** *Choice, 1997.*

Arendt, Hannah **JC480.A74 2004**
The Origins of Totalitarianism. Trade Cloth. Knopf Publishing Group. New York, NY. 2004. 704p. ISBN:0-8052-4225-2, ISBN13: 978-0-8052-4225-6. Dewey:320.53. LCCN:2003-060749.
Audience: **l,u,f.** B

Arendt, Hannah **JC480**
The Origins of Totalitarianism. Trade Paper. Harcourt Trade Publishers. New York, NY. 1973. 576p. Harvest Book Ser., Vol. 244 ISBN:0-15-670153-7, ISBN13: 978-0-15-670153-2. Dewey:320.53. LCCN:68-003757.
Audience: **l,u,f.** B

Derrida, Jacques **JC497.D47 2005**
Rogues: Two Essays on Reason. Trade Paper. Stanford University Press. Palo Alto, CA. 2004. 200p.

ISBN:0-8047-4951-5, ISBN13: 978-0-8047-4951-0. Dewey:320.1. LCCN:2004-016072.
Audience: **u,f.** *Choice, 2005.*

Gregor, A. James **JC491.G674 2000**
The Faces of Janus: Marxism and Fascism in the Twentieth Century. Cloth over Boards. Yale University Press. Cumberland, RI. 2000. 256p. ISBN:0-300-07827-7, ISBN13: 978-0-300-07827-5. Dewey:320.53/09/04. LCCN:99-028711.
Audience: **u,f.** *Choice, 2000.*

Jones, William David **HX273.J66 1999**
Lost Debate: German Socialist Intellectuals and Totalitarianism. Trade Paper. University of Illinois Press. Champaign, IL. 1999. 384p. ISBN:0-252-06796-7, ISBN13: 978-0-252-06796-9. Dewey:335/.00943/0904. LCCN:98-058029.
Audience: **l,u,f.** *Choice, 2000.*

Kasza, Gregory J. **JC481.K34 1995**
The Conscription Society: Administered Mass Organizations. Cloth over Boards. Yale University Press. Cumberland, RI. 1995. 232p. ISBN:0-300-06242-7, ISBN13: 978-0-300-06242-7. Dewey:321.9/09/04. LCCN:94-041148.
Audience: **l,u,f.** *Choice, 1996.*

Laqueur, Walter **JC481.L34 1996**
Fascism: Past, Present, Future. Trade Cloth. Oxford University Press, Inc. New York, NY. 1996. 272p. ISBN:0-19-509245-7, ISBN13: 978-0-19-509245-5. Dewey:320.5/33/09. LCCN:95-017612.
Audience: **g,l,u,f.** *Choice, 1996.*

Mosse, George L. **JC481.M63 1998**
The Fascist Revolution: Toward a General Theory of Fascism. Trade Cloth. Howard Fertig Inc. New York, NY. 1999. 248p. ISBN:0-86527-432-0, ISBN13: 978-0-86527-432-7. Dewey:320.53/3. LCCN:98-016770.
Audience: **l,u,f.** *Choice, 1999.*

Parenti, Michael **HX44.5.P35 1997**
Blackshirts and Reds: Rational Fascism and the Overthrow of Communism. Trade Paper. City Lights Books. San Francisco, CA. 1997. 208p. ISBN:0-87286-329-8, ISBN13: 978-0-87286-329-3. Dewey:335.4/3. LCCN:97-000119.
Audience: **l,u,f.**

Paxton, Robert O. **D424**
The Anatomy of Fascism. Trade Paper. Knopf Publishing Group. New York, NY. 2005. 336p. ISBN:1-4000-3391-8, ISBN13: 978-1-4000-3391-1. Dewey:940.5.
Audience: **l,u,f.** *Choice, 2004.*

Payne, Stanley G. **JC481.P375 1995**
A History of Fascism, 1914-1945. Trade Cloth. University of Wisconsin Press. Chicago, IL. 1996. 632p. ISBN:0-299-14870-X, ISBN13: 978-0-299-14870-6. Dewey:320.5/33/09. LCCN:95-016723.
Audience: **g,l,u.** *Choice, 1996.*

Shenfield, Stephen D. **JC481.S478 2001**
Russian Fascism: Traditions, Tendencies, Movements. Trade Cloth. M. E. Sharpe Inc. Armonk, NY. 2001. 324p. ISBN:0-7656-0634-8, ISBN13: 978-0-7656-0634-1. Dewey:320.53/3/0947. LCCN:00-059536.
Audience: **l,u,f.** *Choice, 2001.*

Strong, George V. **JN2012.3.S85 1998**
Seedtime for Fascism: The Disintegration of Austrian Political Culture, 1867-1918. Cloth Text. M. E. Sharpe Inc. Armonk, NY. 1998. 224p. ISBN:0-7656-0189-3, ISBN13: 978-0-7656-0189-6. Dewey:306.2/09436/09034. LCCN:97-030245.
Audience: **l,u,f.** *Choice, 1998.*

Wolin, Richard **JC481.W65 2004**
The Seduction of Unreason: The Intellectual Romance with Fascism from Nietzsche to Postmodernism. Trade Cloth. Princeton University Press. Princeton, NJ. 2004. 404p. ISBN:0-691-11464-1, ISBN13: 978-0-691-11464-4. Dewey:335.6. LCCN:2003-057955.
Audience: **l,u,f.** *Choice, 2005.*

Political Theory > Forms of the State > Corporate State

Saul, John Ralston **JC478.S38 1997**
The Unconscious Civilization. Trade Cloth. Simon & Schuster. New York, NY. 1997. 208p. ISBN:0-684-83257-7, ISBN13: 978-0-684-83257-9. Dewey:909/.09821. LCCN:96-041910.
Audience: **l,u,f.** *Choice, 1997.*

Wiarda, Howard J. **JC478.W53 1997**
Corporatism and Comparative Politics: The Other Great Ism. Paper Text. M. E. Sharpe Inc. Armonk, NY. 1996. 212p. Comparative Politics Ser. ISBN:1-56324-716-X, ISBN13: 978-1-56324-716-3. Dewey:320.1. LCCN:96-021990.
Audience: **l,u,f.** *Choice, 1997.*

Political Theory > Purpose, Functions and Relations of the State

Bronner, Stephen Eric & Thompson, Michael J. (Editors) **JC574.L65 2005**
The Logos Reader: Rational Radicalism and the Future of Politics. Trade Cloth. University Press of Kentucky. Lexington, KY. 2005. 384p. ISBN:0-8131-2368-2, ISBN13: 978-0-8131-2368-4. Dewey:320.51. LCCN:2005-025882.
Audience: **u,f.**

Dombrowski, Daniel A. **JC574.D63 2001**
Rawls and Religion: The Case for Political Liberalism. Paper Text. State University of New York Press. Albany, NY. 2001. 224p. ISBN:0-7914-5012-0, ISBN13: 978-0-7914-5012-3. Dewey:322/.1/092. LCCN:00-046420.
Audience: **l,u,f.** *Choice, 2001.*

Duncan, Craig & Machan, Tibor R. **JC585.D83 2005**
Libertarianism: For and Against. Martha Nussbaum (Foreword by). Saddle Stitched, Cloth over Boards. Rowman & Littlefield Publishers, Inc. Lanham, MD. 2005. 167p. ISBN:0-7425-4258-0, ISBN13: 978-0-7425-4258-7. Dewey:320.51/2. LCCN:2004-027526.
Audience: **g,l.** *Choice, 2006.*

Galston, William A. **JC574.G372 2005**
The Practice of Liberal Pluralism. Trade Paper. Cambridge University Press. New York, NY. 2004. 216p. ISBN:0-521-54963-9, ISBN13: 978-0-521-54963-9. Dewey:320.51/3. LCCN:2004-046567.
Audience: **l,u,f.** *Choice, 2005.*

Galston, William A. **JC571 .G255 1991**
Liberal Purposes: Goods, Virtues, and Diversity in the Liberal State. Douglas MacLean (Contribution by). Trade Paper. Cambridge University Press. New York, NY. 1991. 348p. Studies in Philosophy and Public Policy ISBN:0-521-42250-7, ISBN13: 978-0-521-42250-5. Dewey:320.5/1. LCCN:90-025355.
Audience: **l,u,f.** *Choice, 1992.*

Gaus, Gerald F. **JC574.G38 1996**
Justificatory Liberalism: An Essay on Epistemology and Political Theory. Trade Paper. Oxford University Press, Inc. New York, NY. 1996. 390p. Oxford Political Theory Ser. ISBN:0-19-509440-9, ISBN13: 978-0-19-509440-4. Dewey:320.5/13. LCCN:94-049138.
Audience: **u,f.**

Green, John C. (Editor), et al. **JC573.2.U6P73 2000**
Prayers in the Precincts: The Christian Right in the 1998 Elections. Mark J. Rozell & Clyde Wilcox (Editors). Trade Cloth. Georgetown University Press. Washington, DC. 2000. 324p. ISBN:0-87840-774-X, ISBN13: 978-0-87840-774-3. Dewey:320.52/0973. LCCN:99-036840.
Audience: **g,l,u,f.** *Choice, 2000.*

Habermas, Jürgen **JA71**
The New Conservatism: Cultural Criticism and the Historians' Debate. ShierryWeber Nicholson (Editor, Translator). Trade Paper. MIT Press. Cambridge, MA. 1991. 306p. Studies in Contemporary German Social Thought ISBN:0-262-58107-8, ISBN13: 978-0-262-58107-3. Dewey:320.5.
Audience: **l,u,f.**

Johnston, David **JC571.J57 1994**
The Idea of a Liberal Theory. Trade Cloth. Princeton University Press. Princeton, NJ. 1994. 216p. ISBN:0-691-03381-1, ISBN13: 978-0-691-03381-5. Dewey:320.5/1. LCCN:94-004089.
Audience: **l,u,f.** *Choice, 1995.*

Katznelson, Ira **JC574.K37 1996**
Liberalism's Crooked Circle: Letters to Adam Michnik. Cloth Text. Princeton University Press. Princeton, NJ. 1996. 232p. ISBN:0-691-03438-9, ISBN13: 978-0-691-03438-6. Dewey:320.5/1. LCCN:95-043184.
Audience: **g,l,u,f.** *Choice, 1996.*

Kekes, John **JC573.K44 1998**
A Case for Conservatism. Book, Other. Cornell University Press. Ithaca, NY. 2001. 256p. ISBN:0-8014-8552-5, ISBN13: 978-0-8014-8552-7. Dewey:32.52. LCCN:98-008358.
Audience: **l,u,f.** *Choice, 1999.*

Kristol, Irving **JC573.2.U6K75 1999**
Neoconservatism: The Autobiography of an Idea. Trade Paper. Ivan R. Dee Publisher. Blue Ridge Summit, PA. 1999. 516p. ISBN:1-56663-228-5, ISBN13: 978-1-56663-228-7. Dewey:973.92. LCCN:98-045126.
Audience: **l,u,f.** *Choice, 1996.*

Mehta, Uday Singh **JC574.2.G7M44 1999**
Liberalism and Empire: A Study in Nineteenth-Century British Liberal Thought. Trade Paper. University of Chicago Press. Chicago, IL. 1999. 245p. ISBN:0-226-51882-5, ISBN13: 978-0-226-51882-4. Dewey:320.5/13/0941. LCCN:98-040812.
Audience: **l,u,f.**

Nozick, Robert **JC571**
Anarchy, State, and Utopia. Trade Paper. Basic Books. New York, NY. 1977. 384p. ISBN:0-465-09720-0, ISBN13: 978-0-465-09720-3. Dewey:320.1/01. LCCN:73-091081.
Audience: **g,l,u,f.**

Rawls, John **JC578.R37 1993**
Political Liberalism. Trade Cloth. Columbia University Press. New York, NY. 1993. 464p. John Dewey Lectures, Vol. 4 ISBN:0-231-05248-0, ISBN13: 978-0-231-05248-1. Dewey:320.51. LCCN:92-043224.
Audience: **u,f.** *Choice, 1993.*

Skrentny, John D. **JC312**
The Minority Rights Revolution. Trade Paper. Harvard University Press. Cambridge, MA. 2004. 496p. ISBN:0-674-01618-1, ISBN13: 978-0-674-01618-7. Dewey:323.1/73.
Audience: **l,u,f.** *Choice, 2003.*

Spencer, Herbert **JC571.S75 1969**
The Man Versus the State: With Four Essays on Politics and Society. Trade Cloth. Penguin Group (USA) Inc. New York, NY. 1969. 350p. ISBN:0-14-040010-9, ISBN13: 978-0-14-040010-6. Dewey:320.5/1. LCCN:77-540711.
Audience: **l,u,f.** B

Strauss, Leo **JC574.S76 1995**
Liberalism Ancient and Modern. Allan Bloom (Foreword by). Trade Paper. University of Chicago Press. Chicago, IL. 1995. 283p. ISBN:0-226-77689-1, ISBN13: 978-0-226-77689-7. Dewey:320.5/1. LCCN:95-021951.
Audience: **g,l,u,f.**

Talisse, Robert B. **JC574.T35 2004**
Democracy after Liberalism: Pragmatism and Deliberative Politics. Trade Paper. Routledge. New York, NY. 2004. 176p. ISBN:0-415-95019-8, ISBN13: 978-0-415-95019-0. Dewey:321.8. LCCN:2004-008431.
Audience: **l,u,f.**

Walzer, Michael **JC574.W393 2005**
Politics and Passion: Toward a More Egalitarian Liberalism. Cloth over Boards. Yale University Press. Cumberland, RI. 2005. 208p. ISBN:0-300-10328-X, ISBN13: 978-0-300-10328-1. Dewey:320.51/3. LCCN:2004-017635.
Audience: **l,u,f.** *Choice, 2005.*

Wolff, Robert P. **JC571 .W86 1998**
In Defense of Anarchism. Trade Paper. University of California Press. Berkeley, CA. 1998. 116p. ISBN:0-520-21573-7, ISBN13: 978-0-520-21573-3. Dewey:335.83. LCCN:98-016131.
Audience: **l,u,f.**

Political Theory > Purpose, Functions and Relations of the State > Political Leadership

Bienen, Henry S. & de Walle, Nicolas van **JC330.3.B54 1991**
Of Time and Power: Leadership Duration in the Modern World. Trade Cloth. Stanford University Press. Palo Alto, CA. 1991. 232p. ISBN:0-8047-1863-6, ISBN13: 978-0-8047-1863-9. Dewey:303.3/4. LCCN:90-042377.
Audience: **l,u,f.** *Choice, 1991.*

Brush, Lisa D. **JC330.B75 2003**
Gender and Governance. Trade Paper. AltaMira Press. Walnut Creek, CA. 2003. 168p. Gender Lens Ser. ISBN:0-7591-0142-6, ISBN13: 978-0-7591-0142-5. Dewey:306.4/842. LCCN:2003-008501.
Audience: **l,u,f.** *Choice, 2004.*

Post, Jerrold M. (Editor) **JC330.3**
The Psychological Assessment of Political Leaders: With Profiles of Saddam Hussein and Bill Clinton. Trade Paper. University of Michigan Press. Chicago, IL. 2005. 480p. ISBN:0-472-06838-5, ISBN13: 978-0-472-06838-8. Dewey:320/.01/9.
Audience: **l,u,f.**

Post, Jerrold M. **JC330.3.P68 2004**
Leaders and Their Followers in a Dangerous World: The Psychology of Political Behavior. Alexander George (Foreword by). Trade Cloth. Cornell University Press. Ithaca, NY. 2004. 320p. Psychoanalysis and Social Theory Ser. ISBN:0-8014-4169-2, ISBN13: 978-0-8014-4169-1. Dewey:320/.01/9. LCCN:2003-021237.
Audience: **l,u,f.** *Choice, 2005.*

Political Theory > Purpose, Functions and Relations of the State > Human Rights

Afshari, Reza **JC599.I65A38 2001**
Human Rights in Iran. Book, Other. University of Pennsylvania Press. Philadelphia, PA. 2001. 384p. Studies in Human Rights ISBN:0-8122-3605-X, ISBN13: 978-0-8122-3605-7. Dewey:323/.0955. LCCN:2001-033037.
Audience: **g,l,u.** *Choice, 2002.*

Edmundson, William A. **JC571.E42 2004**
An Introduction to Rights. Cloth Text. Cambridge University Press. New York, NY. 2004. 240p. Cambridge Introductions to Philosophy and Law Ser. ISBN:0-521-80398-5, ISBN13: 978-0-521-80398-4. Dewey:323. LCCN:2003-059594.
Audience: **g,l,u.** *Choice, 2005.*

Eldridge, Philip J. **JC599.A785E45 2002**
The Politics of Human Rights in Southeast Asia. Paper over Boards. Routledge. New York, NY. 2001. 256p. Politics in Asia Ser. ISBN:0-415-21429-7, ISBN13: 978-0-415-21429-2. Dewey:323/.0959. LCCN:2001-048183.
Audience: **l,u,f.** *Choice, 2003.*

Falk, Richard A. **JC585.F35 2000**
Human Rights Horizons: The Pursuit of Justice in a Globalizing World. Trade Paper. Routledge. New York, NY. 2000. 288p. ISBN:0-415-92513-4, ISBN13: 978-0-415-92513-6. Dewey:323. LCCN:99-088210.
Audience: **g,l,u,f.** *Choice, 2001.*

Gewirth, Alan **JC571.G437 1996**
The Community of Rights. Trade Paper. University of Chicago Press. Chicago, IL. 1998. 396p. ISBN:0-226-28881-1, ISBN13: 978-0-226-28881-9. Dewey:323/01. LCCN:95-033026.
Audience: **l,u,f.** *Choice, 1996.*

Hawkins, Darren G. **JC599.C5H38 2002**
International Human Rights and Authoritarian Rule in Chile. Cloth Text. University of Nebraska Press. Lincoln, NE. 2002. 261p. Human Rights in International Perspective Ser., Vol. 6 ISBN:0-8032-2404-4, ISBN13: 978-0-8032-2404-9. Dewey:323/.0983/09047. LCCN:2001-044597.
Audience: **l,u,f.** *Choice, 2003.*

Hershberg, Eric **JC599.L3C66 1996**
Constructing Democracy: Human Rights, Citizenship and Society in Latin America. Elizabeth Jelin (Editor). Trade Paper. Westview Press. Boulder, CO. 1996. 256p. ISBN:0-8133-2439-4, ISBN13: 978-0-8133-2439-5. Dewey:323/.098. LCCN:95-050932.
Audience: **l,u,f.**

Howard, Rhoda E. **JC599.A36H68 1986**
Human Rights in Commonwealth Africa. Trade Cloth. Rowman & Littlefield Publishers, Inc. Lanham, MD. 1986. 264p. ISBN:0-8476-7433-9, ISBN13: 978-0-8476-7433-6. Dewey:323.4/096. LCCN:86-003860.
Audience: **g,l,u,f.** *Choice, 1987.*

Human Rights Watch Staff **JC571.S63 1995**
Slaughter among Neighbors: Political Origins of Communal Violence. Trade Paper. Yale University Press. Cumberland, RI. 1995. 192p. ISBN:0-300-06544-2, ISBN13: 978-0-300-06544-2. Dewey:323.1/1. LCCN:95-023132.
Audience: **u,f.** *Choice, 1996.*

Human Rights Watch Staff **JC571.S63 1995**
Slaughter among Neighbors: Political Origins of Communal Violence. Trade Cloth. Yale University Press. Cumberland, RI. 1995. 192p. ISBN:0-300-06496-9, ISBN13: 978-0-300-06496-4. Dewey:323.1/1. LCCN:95-023132.
Audience: **l,u,f.** *Choice, 1996.*

Ignatieff, Michael (Editor) **JC599.U5A494 2005**
American Exceptionalism and Human Rights. Trade Paper. Princeton University Press. Princeton, NJ. 2005. 392p. ISBN:0-691-11648-2, ISBN13: 978-0-691-11648-8. Dewey:323/.0973. LCCN:2004-060764.
Audience: **g,l,u,f.** *Choice, 2006.*

Ignatieff, Michael & Appiah, Anthony **JC571.I39 2003**
Human Rights as Politics and Idolatry. Amy Gutmann (Editor, Introduction by). Paper Text. Princeton University Press. Princeton, NJ. 2003. 216p. University Center for Human Values Ser. ISBN:0-691-11474-9, ISBN13: 978-0-691-11474-3. Dewey:323. LCCN:2001-032102.
Audience: **u,f.** *Choice, 2002.*

Ishay, Micheline **JC571 .I73 2004**
The History of Human Rights: From Ancient Times to the Globalization Era. Trade Paper. University of California Press. Berkeley, CA. 2004. 460p. ISBN:0-520-23497-9, ISBN13: 978-0-520-23497-0. Dewey:323/.09. LCCN:2003-012769.
Audience: **g,l,u,f.** *Choice, 2005.*

Juviler, Peter H. **JC599.F6J88 1998**
Freedom's Ordeal: The Struggle for Human Rights and Democracy in Post-Soviet States. Book, Other. University of Pennsylvania Press. Philadelphia, PA. 1997. 312p. Pennsylvania Studies in Human Rights ISBN:0-8122-3418-9, ISBN13: 978-0-8122-3418-3. Dewey:323/.0947/09049. LCCN:97-022400.
Audience: **l,u,f.** *Choice, 1998.*

Kent, Ann **JC599.C6K46 1993**
Between Freedom and Subsistence: China and Human Rights. Paper Text. Oxford University Press, Inc. New York, NY. 1995. 308p. ISBN:0-19-585521-3, ISBN13: 978-0-19-585521-0. Dewey:323.490951. LCCN:92-019756.
Audience: **g,l,u,f.**

Kent, Ann **JC599.C6K48 1999**
China, the United Nations, and Human Rights: The Limits of Compliance. Book, Other. University of Pennsylvania Press. Philadelphia, PA. 1999. 336p. Pennsylvania Studies in Human Rights ISBN:0-8122-1681-4, ISBN13: 978-0-8122-1681-3. Dewey:323/.0951. LCCN:99-012228.
Audience: **l,u,f.** *Choice, 2000.*

Langley, Winston E. **JC571**
Encyclopedia of Human Rights Issues since 1945. Cloth Text. Greenwood Publishing Group, Inc. Portsmouth, NH. 1999. 424p. ISBN:0-313-30163-8, ISBN13: 978-0-313-30163-6. Dewey:323/.03. LCCN:98-030498.
Audience: **g,l,u,f.** *Choice, 2000.*

Lauren, Paul G. **JC571.L285 1998**
Evolution of International Human Rights: Visions Seen. Trade Paper. University of Pennsylvania Press. Philadelphia, PA. 1998. 396p. Pennsylvania Studies in Human Rights ISBN:0-8122-1521-4, ISBN13: 978-0-8122-1521-2. Dewey:341.4/81/09. LCCN:98-015215.
Audience: **g,l,u,f.** *Choice, 1999.*

Maritain, Jacques **JC571.M348 2001**
Natural Law: Reflections on Theory and Practice. William Sweet (Editor). Trade Paper. Saint Augustine's Press, Inc. South Bend, IN. 2001. 106p. ISBN:1-890318-68-X, ISBN13: 978-1-890318-68-0. Dewey:171/.2. LCCN:00-012976.
Audience: **u,f.**

Markell, Patchen **JC575.M37 2003**
Bound by Recognition. Trade Paper. Princeton University Press. Princeton, NJ. 2003. 320p. ISBN:0-691-11382-3, ISBN13: 978-0-691-11382-1. Dewey:320/.01. LCCN:2002-193062.
Audience: **l,u,f.** *Choice, 2004.*

Mertus, Julie **JC571.M444 2004**
Bait and Switch: Human Rights and U. S. Foreign Policy. Paper over Boards. Routledge. New York, NY. 2004. 280p. Global Horizons Ser. ISBN:0-415-94850-9, ISBN13: 978-0-415-94850-0. Dewey:323/.0973. LCCN:2003-022338.
Audience: **g,l,u,f.**

Monshipouri, Mahmood **JC599.M53.M66 1998**
Islamism, Secularism and Human Rights in the Middle East. Library Binding. Lynne Rienner Publishers, Inc. Boulder, CO. 1998. 270p. ISBN:1-55587-782-6, ISBN13: 978-1-55587-782-8. Dewey:323/.0956. LCCN:98-009424.
Audience: **l,u,f.** *Choice, 1998.*

Moseley, Alexander & Norman, Richard (Editors) **JC571.H768834 2002**
Human Rights and Military Intervention. Society for Applied Philosophy Staff (Contribution by). Trade Cloth. Ashgate Publishing, Ltd. Aldershot, 2002. 296p. ISBN:0-7546-0867-0, ISBN13: 978-0-7546-0867-7. Dewey:341.5/84. LCCN:2002-022546.
Audience: **g,l,u,f.** *Choice, 2003.*

O'Flaherty, Michael & Gisvold, Gregory **JC599.B67P67 1998**
Post-War Protection of Human Rights in Bosnia and Herzegovina. Trade Cloth. Kluwer Law International. Alphen a/d Rijn, 1998. 336p. International Studies in Human Rights ISBN:90-411-1020-8, ISBN13: 978-90-411-1020-6. Dewey:341.4/81. LCCN:98-007588.
Audience: **l,u,f.**

Orend, Brian **JC571**
Human Rights: Concept and Context. Trade Paper. Broadview Press. Peterborough, ON. 2002. 272p. ISBN:1-55111-436-4, ISBN13: 978-1-55111-436-1. Dewey:323. LCCN:2002-728227.
Audience: **l,u.** *Choice, 2002.*

Schatzberg, Michael G. **JC599.Z282L577 1988**
The Dialectics of Oppression in Zaire. Trade Cloth. Indiana University Press. Bloomington, IN. 1988. 208p. ISBN:0-253-31703-7, ISBN13: 978-0-253-31703-2. Dewey:323.4/9/0967513. LCCN:87-046093.
Audience: **u,f.** *Choice, 1989.*

Sikkink, Kathryn **JC599.L3S55 2004**
Mixed Messages: U.S. Human Rights Policy and Latin America. Book, Other. Cornell University Press. Ithaca, NY. 2004. 272p. ISBN:0-8014-4270-2, ISBN13: 978-0-8014-4270-4. Dewey:323/.098. LCCN:2004-007159.
Audience: **l,u,f.** *Choice, 2005.*

Singer, Beth J. **JC571 .S628 1993**
Operative Rights. Paper Text. State University of New York Press. Albany, NY. 1993. 218p. ISBN:0-7914-1658-5, ISBN13: 978-0-7914-1658-7. Dewey:323. LCCN:92-039758.
Audience: **u,f.**

Talbott, William **JC571.T1445 2005**
Which Rights Should Be Universal? Trade Cloth. Oxford University Press, Inc. New York, NY. 2005. 232p. ISBN:0-19-517347-3, ISBN13: 978-0-19-517347-5. Dewey:323/.01. LCCN:2004-052064.
Audience: **g,l,u.** *Choice, 2005.*

Tu, Weiming & De Bary, William Theodore (Editors) **JC599.C6C66 1997**
Confucianism and Human Rights. Trade Paper. Columbia University Press. New York, NY. 1999. 408p. ISBN:0-231-10937-7, ISBN13: 978-0-231-10937-6. Dewey:323/.0951. LCCN:97-014687.
Audience: **u,f.**

Walzer, Michael **JC571.W147 1997**
On Toleration. Cloth over Boards. Yale University Press. Cumberland, RI. 1997. 144p. The Castle Lectures in Ethics, Politics, and Economics ISBN:0-300-07019-5, ISBN13: 978-0-300-07019-4. Dewey:305.8. LCCN:96-047779.
Audience: **l,u,f.** *Choice, 1997.*

Zuckert, Michael P. **JC571**
Natural Rights Republic: Studies in the Foundation of the American Political Tradition. Paper Text. University of Notre Dame Press. Notre Dame, IN. 1999. 305p. Frank M. Covey, Jr., Loyola Lectures in Political Analysis ISBN:0-268-01487-6, ISBN13: 978-0-268-01487-2. Dewey:323.01. LCCN:96-009756.
Audience: **g,l,u,f.**

Political Theory > Purpose, Functions and Relations of the State > Equality. Justice

Broadbent, Ed (Editor) **JC575.D45 2001**
Democratic Equality: What Went Wrong? Trade Paper. University of Toronto Press. Toronto, ON. 2001. 442p. ISBN:0-8020-8332-3, ISBN13: 978-0-8020-8332-6. Dewey:323. LCCN:2001-273369.
Audience: **g,l,u,f.** *Choice, 2002.*

Campbell, Tom **JC578.C42 2001**
Justice. Ed. 2. Trade Paper, Perfect. Palgrave Macmillan. New York, NY. 2000. 283p. Issues in Political Theory Ser. ISBN:0-312-23620-4, ISBN13: 978-0-312-23620-5. Dewey:320/.01/1. LCCN:00-062596.
Audience: **g,l,u,f.**

Dworkin, Ronald M. **JC575.D86 2000**
Sovereign Virtue: The Theory and Practice of Equality. Trade Cloth. Harvard University Press. Cambridge, MA. 2000. 528p. ISBN:0-674-00219-9, ISBN13: 978-0-674-00219-7. Dewey:305. LCCN:00-020071.
Audience: **l,u,f.** *Choice, 2000.*

Fogel, Robert William **JC575.F64 2000**
The Fourth Great Awakening and the Future of Egalitarianism: The Political Realignment of the 1990s and the Fate of Egalitarianism. Trade Cloth. University of Chicago Press. Chicago, IL. 2000. 383p. ISBN:0-226-25662-6, ISBN13: 978-0-226-25662-7. Dewey:305/.0973. LCCN:99-089987.
Audience: **l,u,f.** *Choice, 2000.*

Goodwin, Barbara **JC578**
Justice by Lottery. Ed. 2. Trade Paper, Perfect. Imprint Academic. Exeter, 2005. 269p. ISBN:1-84540-025-9, ISBN13: 978-1-84540-025-5. Dewey:323.01.
Audience: **g,l,u,f.**

Markell, Patchen **JC575.M37 2003**
Bound by Recognition. Trade Paper. Princeton University Press. Princeton, NJ. 2003. 320p. ISBN:0-691-11382-3, ISBN13: 978-0-691-11382-1. Dewey:320/.01. LCCN:2002-193062.
Audience: **l,u,f.** *Choice, 2004.*

Nagel, Thomas **JC575.N25 1991**
Equality and Partiality. Cloth Text. Oxford University Press, Inc. New York, NY. 1991. 208p. ISBN:0-19-506967-6, ISBN13: 978-0-19-506967-9. Dewey:320/.01/1. LCCN:90-019428.
Audience: **l,u,f.**

Rawls, John **JC578.R36925 1999**
Collected Papers. Trade Cloth. Harvard University Press. Cambridge, MA. 1999. 672p. ISBN:0-674-13739-6, ISBN13: 978-0-674-13739-4. Dewey:320/.01/1. LCCN:98-055932.
Audience: **l,u,f.** *Choice, 1999.*

Rawls, John **JC578.R37 2005**
Political Liberalism. Ed. 2. Trade Paper. Edinburgh University Press. Edinburgh, 2005. 576p. Columbia Classics in Philosophy Ser. ISBN:0-231-13089-9, ISBN13: 978-0-231-13089-9. Dewey:320.51. LCCN:2004-058205.
Audience: **u,f.** *Choice, 1993.*

Rawls, John **JC578.R38 1999**
A Theory of Justice. Trade Paper. Harvard University Press. Cambridge, MA. 1999. 560p. ISBN:0-674-00078-1, ISBN13: 978-0-674-00078-0. Dewey:320/.01/1. LCCN:99-029110.
Audience: **l,u,f.** B *Choice, 2000.*

Rawls, John **JC578.R38 2005**
A Theory of Justice. Trade Paper. Harvard University Press. Cambridge, MA. 2005. 560p. ISBN:0-674-01772-2, ISBN13: 978-0-674-01772-6. Dewey:320/.01/1. LCCN:2004-060697.
Audience: **g,l,u,f.** B *Choice, 2000.*

Rawls, John **JC578.R3693 2001**
Justice as Fairness: A Restatement. Ed. 2. Erin Kelly (Editor). Trade Paper. Harvard University Press. Cambridge, MA. 2001. 240p. ISBN:0-674-00511-2, ISBN13: 978-0-674-00511-2. Dewey:320/.01/1. LCCN:00-065034.
Audience: **g,l,u,f.** *Choice, 2001.*

Rawls, John **JC578.R3693 2001**
Justice as Fairness: A Restatement. Ed. 2. Erin Kelly (Editor). Trade Cloth. Harvard University Press. Cambridge, MA. 2001. 240p. ISBN:0-674-00510-4, ISBN13: 978-0-674-00510-5. Dewey:320/.01/1. LCCN:00-065034.
Audience: **l,u,f.** *Choice, 2001.*

Rosen, Allen D. **JC181.K4R65 1993**
Kant's Theory of Justice. Book, Other. Cornell University Press. Ithaca, NY. 1993. 240p. ISBN:0-8014-2757-6, ISBN13: 978-0-8014-2757-2. Dewey:320.01. LCCN:93-025807.
Audience: **l,u,f.** *Choice, 1994.*

Sen, Amartya **JC578**
Inequality Reexamined. Trade Paper. Harvard University Press. Cambridge, MA. 1995. 224p. ISBN:0-674-45256-9, ISBN13: 978-0-674-45256-5. Dewey:320/.011.
Audience: **l,u,f.** *Choice, 1993.*

Sterba, James P. **JC578.J87 2003**
Justice: Alternative Political Perspectives. Ed. 4. Paper Text. Thomson Wadsworth. Belmont, CA. 2002. 368p. ISBN:0-534-60219-3, ISBN13: 978-0-534-60219-2. Dewey:320/.01/1. LCCN:2002-066172.
Audience: **l,u,f.**

Walzer, Michael **JC574.W393 2005**
Politics and Passion: Toward a More Egalitarian Liberalism. Cloth over Boards. Yale University Press. Cumberland, RI. 2005. 208p. ISBN:0-300-10328-X, ISBN13: 978-0-300-10328-1. Dewey:320.51/3. LCCN:2004-017635.
Audience: **l,u,f.** *Choice, 2005.*

Walzer, Michael **JC578**
Spheres of Justice: A Defense of Pluralism and Equality. Trade Paper. Basic Books. New York, NY. 1984. 364p. ISBN:0-465-08189-4, ISBN13: 978-0-465-08189-9. Dewey:320/.011. LCCN:82-072409.
Audience: **l,u,f.** B

Young, Iris Marion **JC578.Y68 1990**
Justice and the Politics of Difference. Trade Paper. Princeton University Press. Princeton, NJ. 1990. 294p. ISBN:0-691-02315-8, ISBN13: 978-0-691-02315-1. Dewey:320/.011. LCCN:90-036988.
Audience: **u,f.**

Zucker, Ross **JC423 .Z83 2001**
Democratic Distributive Justice. Trade Cloth. Cambridge University Press. New York, NY. 2000. 336p. ISBN:0-521-79033-6, ISBN13: 978-0-521-79033-8. Dewey:330.1. LCCN:00-023631.
Audience: **l,u,f.** *Choice, 2001.*

Political Theory > Purpose, Functions and Relations of the State > Liberty

Bay, Christian **JC585**
The Structure of Freedom. Trade Paper. Stanford University Press. Palo Alto, CA. 1970. xii, 419p. ISBN:0-8047-0540-2, ISBN13: 978-0-8047-0540-0. Dewey:323.44. LCCN:58-010475.
Audience: **l,u,f.**

Benn, Stanley I. **JC585 .B378 1988**
A Theory of Freedom. Trade Paper. Cambridge University Press. New York, NY. 1988. 352p. ISBN:0-521-34802-1, ISBN13: 978-0-521-34802-7. Dewey:123/.5. LCCN:87-037492.
Audience: **g,l,u,f.** *Choice, 1989.*

Berlin, Isaiah **JC585.B418 2002**
Liberty: Incorporating Four Essays on Liberty. Ed. 2. Henry Hardy (Editor). Paper Text. Oxford University Press, Inc. New York, NY. 2002. 416p. ISBN:0-19-924989-X, ISBN13: 978-0-19-924989-3. Dewey:323.44. LCCN:2002-283107.
Audience: **l,u,f.**

Brown, Cynthia (Editor) **JC599.U5L63 2003**
Lost Liberties: Ashcroft and the Assault on Personal Freedom. Aryeh Neier (Introduction by). Trade Paper. New Press, The. New York, NY. 2003. 320p. ISBN:1-56584-829-2, ISBN13: 978-1-56584-829-0. Dewey:323.4/9/0973. LCCN:2003-052716.
Audience: **g,l,u,f.** *Choice, 2004.*

Corradi, Juan E. (Editor), et al. **JC599.S57F43 1992**
Fear at the Edge: State Terror and Resistance in Latin America. Patricia W. Fagen & Manuel A. Garretón (Editors). Trade Paper. University of California Press. Berkeley, CA. 1992. 308p. ISBN:0-520-07705-9, ISBN13: 978-0-520-07705-8. Dewey:303.6/25. LCCN:91-030628.
Audience: **l,u,f.** *Choice, 1993.*

Etzioni, Amitai **JC596.2.U5**
The Limits of Privacy. Trade Paper. Basic Books. New York, NY. 2000. 288p. ISBN:0-465-04090-X, ISBN13: 978-0-465-04090-2. Dewey:323.4/48/0973. LCCN:98-047082.
Audience: **u,f.** *Choice, 1999.*

Fiss, Owen M. **JC591.F57 1996**
Liberalism Divided: Freedom of Speech and the Many Uses of State Power. Trade Paper. Westview Press. Boulder, CO. 1996. 208p. ISBN:0-8133-2485-8, ISBN13: 978-0-8133-2485-2. Dewey:323.44/3. LCCN:95-046272.
Audience: **l,u,f.** *Choice, 1996.*

Flathman, Richard E. **JC571.F523 1992**
Willful Liberalism: Voluntarism and Individuality in Political Theory and Practice. Book, Other. Cornell University Press. Ithaca, NY. 1992. 256p. ISBN:0-8014-9955-0, ISBN13: 978-0-8014-9955-5. Dewey:320.5/12. LCCN:91-055559.
Audience: **l,u,f.** *Choice, 1992.*

Garfinkel, Simson **JC596.2.U5G37 2001**
Database Nation: The Death of Privacy in the 21st Century. Paper Text. O'Reilly Media, Inc. Sebastopol, CA. 2000. 325p. ISBN:0-596-00105-3, ISBN13: 978-0-596-00105-6. Dewey:323.44/8/0973. LCCN:99-058637.
Audience: **g,l,u,f.** *Choice, 2000.*

Gellner, Ernest **JC336.G45 1994**
Conditions of Liberty: Civil Society and Its Rivals. Trade Cloth. Penguin Group (USA) Inc. New York, NY. 1994. 240p. ISBN:0-7139-9114-3, ISBN13: 978-0-7139-9114-7. Dewey:323.4/4. LCCN:94-239736.
Audience: **l,u,f.** *Choice, 1995.*

Hehir, Bryan, et al. **JZ1480.L53 2004**
Liberty and Power: A Dialogue on Religion and U. S. Foreign Policy in an Unjust World. Michael Walzer, Charles Krauthammer, Louise Richardson & Shibley Telhami (Authors). Trade Paper. Brookings Institution Press. Washington, DC. 2004. 119p. The Pew Forum Dialogues on Religion and Public Life Ser. ISBN:0-8157-3545-6, ISBN13: 978-0-8157-3545-8. Dewey:205/.624. LCCN:2004-019511.
Audience: **l,u,f.**

Kirby, William C. (Editor) **JC599.C6R43 2004**
Realms of Freedom in Modern China. Trade Cloth. Stanford University Press. Palo Alto, CA. 2003. 416p. The Making of Modern Freedom Ser. ISBN:0-8047-4878-0, ISBN13: 978-0-8047-4878-0. Dewey:323/.0951. LCCN:2003-009924.
Audience: **g,l,u,f.** *Choice, 2004.*

Mill, John Stuart **JC585.M76 2003**
On Liberty. David Bromwich & George Kateb (Editors). Cloth over Boards. Yale University Press. Cumberland, RI. 2003. 272p. Rethinking the Western Tradition Ser. ISBN:0-300-09608-9, ISBN13: 978-0-300-09608-8. Dewey:323.44. LCCN:2002-006676.
Audience: **g,l,u,f.** *Choice, 2003.*

Mill, John Stuart **JC585.M74 1998**
On Liberty and Other Essays. John M. Gray (Editor, Introduction by, Notes by). Trade Paper. Oxford University Press, Inc. New York, NY. 1998. 628p. Oxford World's Classics Ser. ISBN:0-19-283384-7, ISBN13: 978-0-19-283384-6. Dewey:323.44. LCCN:98-199211.
Audience: **g,l,u,f.**

Sen, Amartya **JC585.S473 1999**
Development as Freedom. Trade Paper. Oxford University Press, Inc. New York, NY. 2001. 382p. ISBN:0-19-289330-0, ISBN13: 978-0-19-289330-7. Dewey:330/.01. LCCN:2001-274375.
Audience: **l,u,f.**

Soley, Lawrence **JC591.S65 2002**
Censorship, Inc.: The Corporate Threat to Free Speech in the United States. Trade Paper. Monthly Review Press. New York, NY. 2002. 384p. ISBN:1-58367-066-1, ISBN13: 978-1-58367-066-8. Dewey:323.44/3/0973. LCCN:2002-007530.
Audience: **l,u,f.** *Choice, 2003.*

Thompson, C. Bradley **JC585.T49 1998**
John Adams and the Spirit of Liberty. Trade Cloth. University Press of Kansas. Lawrence, KS. 1998. xx, 340p. American Political Thought Ser. ISBN:0-7006-0915-6, ISBN13: 978-0-7006-0915-4. Dewey:323.4/4. LCCN:98-017730.
Audience: **g,l,u.**

Political Theory > Purpose, Functions and Relations of the State > United States

Andrew, John **JC573.2.U6A53 1997**
The Other Side of the '60s: Young Americans for Freedom and the Rise of Conservative Politics. Paper Text. Rutgers University Press. Piscataway, NJ. 1997. 280p. Perspectives on the Sixties Ser. ISBN:0-8135-2401-6, ISBN13: 978-0-8135-2401-6. Dewey:320.52/0973. LCCN:96-048088.
Audience: **g,l,u,f.** *Choice, 1998.*

Bjerre-Poulsen, Niels **JC573.2.U 6B54 2002**
Right Face: Organizing the American Conservative Movement 1945-65. Trade Cloth. Museum Tusculanum Press. Copenhagen S, 2002. 333p. ISBN:87-7289-720-1, ISBN13: 978-87-7289-720-2. Dewey:320.52/0973/09045. LCCN:2003-537807.
Audience: **u,f.** *Choice, 2003.*

Dunn, Charles W. & Woodard, J. David **JC573.2.U6D85 2003**
The Conservative Tradition in America. Ed. 3. Book, Other. Rowman & Littlefield Publishers, Inc. Lanham, MD. 2003. 240p. ISBN:0-7425-2234-2, ISBN13: 978-0-7425-2234-3. Dewey:320.5/2/0973. LCCN:2003-269455.
Audience: **l,u.** *Choice, 1997.*

Halper, Stefan & Clarke, Jonathan **JC573.2.U6H34 2004**
America Alone: The Neo-Conservatives and the Global Order. Trade Cloth. Cambridge University Press. New York, NY. 2004. 382p. ISBN:0-521-83834-7, ISBN13: 978-0-521-83834-4. Dewey:320.520973. LCCN:2004-040795.
Audience: **l,u,f.** *Choice, 2005.*

Kristol, Irving **JC573.2.U6K75 1999**
Neoconservatism: The Autobiography of an Idea. Trade Paper. Ivan R. Dee Publisher. Blue Ridge Summit, PA. 1999. 516p. ISBN:1-56663-228-5, ISBN13: 978-1-56663-228-7. Dewey:973.92. LCCN:98-045126.
Audience: **l,u,f.** *Choice, 1996.*

Murphy, Paul V. **JC573.2.U6M87 2001**
The Rebuke of History: The Southern Agrarians and American Conservative Thought. Trade Cloth. University of North Carolina Press. Chapel Hill, NC. 2001. 368p. ISBN:0-8078-2630-8, ISBN13: 978-0-8078-2630-0. Dewey:320.52/0973/0904. LCCN:2001-027128.
Audience: **l,u,f.** *Choice, 2002.*

Pincus, Fred L. **JC599.U5P478 2003**
Reverse Discrimination: Dismantling a Myth. Library Binding. Lynne Rienner Publishers, Inc. Boulder, CO. 2003. 175p. ISBN:1-58826-101-8, ISBN13: 978-1-58826-101-4. Dewey:305/.0973. LCCN:2003-041425.
Audience: **g,l,u.** *Choice, 2004.*

Skrentny, John D. **JC312**
The Minority Rights Revolution. Trade Paper. Harvard University Press. Cambridge, MA. 2004. 496p. ISBN:0-674-01618-1, ISBN13: 978-0-674-01618-7. Dewey:323.1/73.
Audience: **l,u,f.** *Choice, 2003.*

Thompson, C. Bradley **JC585.T49 1998**
John Adams and the Spirit of Liberty. Trade Cloth. University Press of Kansas. Lawrence, KS. 1998. xx, 340p. American Political Thought Ser. ISBN:0-7006-0915-6, ISBN13: 978-0-7006-0915-4. Dewey:323.4/4. LCCN:98-017730.
Audience: **g,l,u.**

American Government and Politics

JK1021
CQ Electronic Library. Congressional Quarterly Press.
Audience: **l,u,f.**

AP1
LexisNexis Academic. LexisNexis.
Audience: **g,l,u,f.**

Common Cause **JK1118**
☐ Common Cause.
http://www.commoncause.org/site/pp.asp?c=dkLNK1MQIwG&b=186966
Audience: **g,l,u,f.**

Ehrenhalt, Alan **JK1717.E36 1991**
United States of Ambition: Politicians, Power, and the Pursuit of Office. Trade Cloth. Random House, Inc. New York, NY. 1991. vii, 309p. ISBN:0-8129-1894-0, ISBN13: 978-0-8129-1894-6. Dewey:324/.0973. LCCN:90-046243.
Audience: **g,l,u,f.** *Choice, 1991.*

Ginsberg, Benjamin **JK276.G55 2005**
We the People: An Introduction to American Politics. Ed. 5. Cloth Text. W. W. Norton & Company, Inc. New York, NY. 2005. xxviii, 790p. ISBN:0-393-92620-6, ISBN13: 978-0-393-92620-0. Dewey:320.473. LCCN:2004-058309.
Audience: **g,l,u.**

Grossman, Mark (Editor) **JK2249.G767 2003**
Political Corruption in America: An Encyclopedia of Scandals, Power, and Greed. Library Binding. ABC-CLIO, Inc. Santa Barbara, CA. 2003. 400p. ISBN:1-57607-060-3, ISBN13: 978-1-57607-060-4. Dewey:973/.03. LCCN:2003-013127.
Audience: **g,l.** *Choice, 2004.*

Hill, Kathleen Thompson & Hill, Gerald N. **JK9.H54 2001**
The Facts on File Dictionary of American Politics. Trade Cloth. Facts On File, Inc. New York, NY. 2001. 448p. ISBN:0-8160-4519-4, ISBN13: 978-0-8160-4519-8. Dewey:320.973/03. LCCN:2001-018770.
Audience: **g,l,u,f.** *Choice, 2002.*

American Government and Politics > History of American Government

KF35
☐ A Century of Lawmaking for a New Nation: U.S. Congressional Documents and Debates, 1774-1875.
http://memory.loc.gov/ammem/amlaw/lawhome.html
Library of Congress.
Audience: **g,l,u,f.**

Brands, H. W. **E382.B83 2005**
Andrew Jackson: His Life and Times. Trade Cloth. Doubleday Canada, Ltd. Toronto, ON. 2005. 640p. ISBN:0-385-50738-0, ISBN13: 978-0-385-50738-7. Dewey:973.5/6/092. LCCN:2005-042178.
Audience: **g,l,u,f.** *Choice, 2006.*

Chernow, Ron **E302.6.H2C48 2004**
Alexander Hamilton. Trade Cloth. Penguin Group (USA) Inc. New York, NY. 2004. 832p. ISBN:1-59420-009-2, ISBN13: 978-1-59420-009-0. Dewey:973.4/092 B. LCCN:2003-065641.
Audience: **g,l,u,f.** *Choice, 2005.*

de Tocqueville, Alexis **JC85.C7**
Democracy in America. J. P. Mayer (Editor), George Lawrence (Translator). Trade Paper. HarperCollins Publishers. New York, NY. 1988. 800p. ISBN:0-06-091522-6, ISBN13: 978-0-06-091522-3. Dewey:320.9/3 21. LCCN:88-045111.
Audience: **g,l,u,f.** *Choice, 2001.*

Elkins, Stanley M. & McKitrick, Eric L. **E310.E45 1993**
The Age of Federalism. Trade Cloth. Oxford University Press, Inc. New York, NY. 1993. 938p. ISBN:0-19-506890-4, ISBN13: 978-0-19-506890-0. Dewey:973.4. LCCN:92-033660.
Audience: **g,l,u,f.** *Choice, 1994.*

Hyneman, Charles S. & Lutz, Donald S. (Editors) **JK113.A716 1983**
American Political Writing During the Founding Era - 1780-1805, Vol. 1 and 2. Trade Cloth. Liberty Fund, Inc. Indianapolis, IN. 1983. 1447p. ISBN:0-86597-038-6, ISBN13: 978-0-86597-038-0. LCCN:82-024884.
Audience: **l,u,f.**

Jennings, Francis **E210 .J43 2000**
The Creation of America: Through Revolution to Empire. Cloth Text. Cambridge University Press. New York, NY. 2000. 400p. ISBN:0-521-66255-9, ISBN13: 978-0-521-66255-0. Dewey:973.3. LCCN:99-054612.
Audience: **g,l,u,f.** *Choice, 2001.*

Keneally, Thomas **E457.K424 2003**
Lincoln. Trade Cloth. Penguin Group (USA) Inc. New York, NY. 2002. 192p. Penguin Lives Ser. ISBN:0-670-03175-5, ISBN13: 978-0-670-03175-7. Dewey:973.7092. LCCN:2003-268078.
Audience: **g,l,u,f.**

Kurain, George T. (Editor), et al. **JK9.H57 1998**
A Historical Guide to the U. S. Government. Joseph P. Harahan, Morton Keller & Donald F. Kettl (Editors). Trade Cloth. Oxford University Press, Inc. New York, NY. 1998. 760p. ISBN:0-19-510230-4, ISBN13: 978-0-19-510230-7. Dewey:320.9/73. LCCN:97-047442.
Audience: **g,l,u,f.** *Choice, 1998.*

Library of Congress **JF511**
☐ American Memory: A Century of Lawmaking for a New Nation.
http://memory.loc.gov/ammem/amlaw/lawhome.html
Audience: **g,l,u,f.**

McDonald, Forrest **E210**
E Pluribus Unum: The Formation of the American Republic, 1776-1790. Ed. 2. Trade Cloth. Liberty Fund, Inc. Indianapolis, IN. 1979. 386p. ISBN:0-913966-58-4, ISBN13: 978-0-913966-58-7. Dewey:973.3. LCCN:79-004130.
Audience: **g,l,u,f.**

Okin, Susan Moller **HQ1122**
Women in Western Political Thought. Trade Paper. Princeton University Press. Princeton, NJ. 1979. 384p. ISBN:0-691-02191-0, ISBN13: 978-0-691-02191-1. Dewey:305.4/2/01. LCCN:79-084004.
Audience: **l,u,f.**

Popper, Karl R. **B63**
The High Tide of Prophecy. Trade Paper. Princeton University Press. Princeton, NJ. 1971. 432p. Open Society and Its Enemies Ser., Vol. II ISBN:0-691-01972-X, ISBN13: 978-0-691-01972-7. Dewey:320.01.
Audience: **l,u,f.**

Roberts, Cokie **E176.R63 2004**
Founding Mothers: The Women Who Raised Our Nation. Trade Cloth. HarperCollins Publishers. New York, NY. 2004. 384p. ISBN:0-06-009025-1, ISBN13: 978-0-06-009025-8. Dewey:973.3/092/2 B. LCCN:2004-042873.
Audience: **g,l,u,f.**

Wood, Gordon S. **JA84.U5W6 1998**
The Creation of the American Republic, 1776-1787. Trade Cloth. University of North Carolina Press. Chapel Hill, NC. 1998. 675p. Published for the Omohundro Institute of Early American History and Culture Ser. ISBN:0-8078-2422-4, ISBN13: 978-0-8078-2422-1. Dewey:973.3. LCCN:71-078861.
Audience: **g,l,u,f.**

American Government and Politics > History of American Government > Colonial Period

Adams, James T. **F7**
The Founding of New England. Trade Paper. Simon Publications, Inc. 2001. 482p. History of New England Ser., Vol. 1 ISBN:1-931313-50-4, ISBN13: 978-1-931313-50-6. Dewey:974. LCCN:21-009397.
Audience: **f.**

Andrews, Charles McLean **E188**
The Colonial Period of American History. Yale University Press. 1964.
Audience: **l,u,f.**

Eccles, William J. & Cooke, Jacob E. (Editors) **E45.E53 1993**
Encyclopedia of the North American Colonies, Set. Trade Cloth. Thomson Gale. Farmington Hills, MI. 1993. 2397p. ISBN:0-684-19269-1, ISBN13: 978-0-684-19269-7. Dewey:940/.03. LCCN:93-007609.
Audience: **g,l,u.** *Choice, 1994.*

Jensen, Merrill **E195.J4 2004**
The Founding of a Nation: A History of the American Revolution, 1763-1776. Trade Cloth. Hackett Publishing Company, Inc. Indianapolis, IN. 2004. 735p. ISBN:0-87220-706-4, ISBN13: 978-0-87220-706-6. Dewey:973.27. LCCN:2003-056880.
Audience: **l,u,f.** B

Kammen, Michael G. **E195**
A Rope of Sand: The Colonial Agents, British Politics, and the American Revolution. Cornell University Press. 1968.
Audience: **f.**

Osgood, Herbert L. **E191.O83**
American Colonies in the Seventeenth Century, Vol. 2. Trade Cloth. Peter Smith Publisher, Inc. Magnolia, MA. 1981. ISBN:0-8446-1333-9, ISBN13: 978-0-8446-1333-8. Dewey:973.2.
Audience: **u,f.**

Osgood, Herbert Levi **LA228.C66**
The American Colonies in the Eighteenth Century. Paper Text. Textbook Publishers. Temecula, CA. 2003. ISBN:0-7581-6766-0, ISBN13: 978-0-7581-6766-8. Dewey:378.73.
Audience: **u,f.**

Rossiter, Clinton **E188**
The First American Revolution: The American Colonies on the Eve of Independence. Trade Paper. Harcourt Trade Publishers. New York, NY. 1956. 266p. ISBN:0-15-631121-6, ISBN13: 978-0-15-631121-2. Dewey:973.2. LCCN:56-013741.
Audience: **g,l,u.**

American Government and Politics > History of American Government > Declaration of Independence

JK141.D62
☐ Documents from the Continental Congress and the Constitutional Convention, 1774-1789.
http://memory.loc.gov/ammem/collections/continental/
Library of Congress.
Audience: **l,u,f.**

Becker, Carl L. **JK128**
Declaration of Independence: A Study in the History of Political Ideas. Trade Paper. Knopf Publishing Group. New York, NY. 1958. 320p. ISBN:0-394-70060-0, ISBN13: 978-0-394-70060-1. Dewey:342.73 973.313.
Audience: **g,l,u,f.**

Eidelberg, Paul **JK128.E35**
On the Silence of the Declaration of Independence. Cloth Text. University of Massachusetts Press. Amherst, MA. 1976. 148p. ISBN:0-87023-216-9, ISBN13: 978-0-87023-216-9. Dewey:320.5/0973. LCCN:76-008759.
Audience: **g,l,u,f.**

American Government and Politics > History of American Government > Constitution

JK141.D62
☐ Documents from the Continental Congress and the Constitutional Convention, 1774-1789.
http://memory.loc.gov/ammem/collections/continental/
Library of Congress.
Audience: **l,u,f.**

Anastaplo, George **E457.2 .A54 1999**
Abraham Lincoln and His Times: A Constitutional Biography. Trade Cloth. Rowman & Littlefield Publishers, Inc. Lanham, MD. 1999. 400p. ISBN:0-8476-9431-3, ISBN13: 978-0-8476-9431-0. Dewey:973.7/092. LCCN:99-014721.
Audience: **g,l,u,f.** *Choice, 2000.*

Beard, Charles Austin **KF4753.B43 2004**
An Economic Interpretation of the Constitution of the United States. Trade Paper. Dover Publications, Inc. Mineola, NY. 2004. 336p. ISBN:0-486-43365-X, ISBN13: 978-0-486-43365-3. Dewey:330.973/04. LCCN:2004-041429.
Audience: **g,l,u,f.**

Belz, Herman **E457.2.B38 1997**
Abraham Lincoln: Constitutionalism and Equal Rights in the Civil War Era. Trade Cloth. Fordham University Press. Bronx, NY. 1997. 265p. The North's Civil War Ser., No. 2: ISBN:0-8232-1768-X, ISBN13: 978-0-8232-1768-7. Dewey:973.7. LCCN:97-009935.
Audience: **l,u,f.** *Choice, 1998.*

Hamilton, Alexander, James Madison and John Jay **JK155**
☐ The Federalist.
http://www.constitution.org/fed/federa00.htm
Audience: **g,l,u,f.**

Kenyon, Cecelia M. (Editor) **KF4515O**
The Antifederalists. Trade Paper. Macmillan Publishing Company, Inc. Old Tappan, NJ. 1966. ISBN:0-672-60052-8, ISBN13: 978-0-672-60052-4. Dewey:342.73/024. LCCN:65-023008.
Audience: **g,l,u,f.**

Main, Jackson Turner **JK116M2 2004**
The Antifederalists. Ed. 2. Trade Paper. University of North Carolina Press. Chapel Hill, NC. 2004. 336p. Published for the Omohundro Institute of Early American History and Culture, Williamsburg, Virginia Ser. ISBN:0-8078-5544-8, ISBN13: 978-0-8078-5544-7. Dewey:321.020973. LCCN:2004-270380.
Audience: **g,l,u,f.**

McLaughlin, Andrew Cunningham **JK54.M3 2002**
The Foundations of American Constitutionalism [1932]. Trade Cloth. Lawbook Exchange, Limited, The. Clark, NJ. 2002. 183p. ISBN:1-58477-227-1, ISBN13: 978-1-58477-227-9. Dewey:973.4. LCCN:2002-024228.
Audience: **g,l,u,f.**

Rutland, Robert A. **JK168**
The Birth of the Bill of Rights, 1776-1791. Paper Text. Textbook Publishers. Temecula, CA. 2003. vi, 243p. ISBN:0-7581-5401-1, ISBN13: 978-0-7581-5401-9. Dewey:323.4.
Audience: **l,u.**

American Government and Politics > History of American Government > Suffrage

Baker, Jean H. (Editor) **JK1896.V67 2002**
Votes for Women: The Struggle for Suffrage Revisited. Trade Paper. Oxford University Press, Inc. New York, NY. 2002. 214p.

Viewpoints on American Culture Ser. ISBN:0-19-513017-0, ISBN13: 978-0-19-513017-1. Dewey:324.6/23/0973. LCCN:2001-036768.
Audience: **g,l,u,f.** *Choice, 2003, 2002.*

Graham, Sara H. **JK1896.G693 1996**
Women Suffrage and the New Democracy. Cloth over Boards. Yale University Press. Cumberland, RI. 1996. 256p. ISBN:0-300-06346-6, ISBN13: 978-0-300-06346-2. Dewey:324.6/2/082. LCCN:96-018148.
Audience: **l,u,f.** *Choice, 1997.*

Green, Elna C. **JK1896.G695 1997**
Southern Strategies: Southern Women and the Woman Suffrage Question. Trade Paper. University of North Carolina Press. Chapel Hill, NC. 1997. 312p. ISBN:0-8078-4641-4, ISBN13: 978-0-8078-4641-4. Dewey:324.6/23/0975. LCCN:96-036992.
Audience: **l,u,f.** *Choice, 1997.*

Keyssar, Alexander **JK1846 .K48**
Right to Vote: The Contested History of Democracy in the United States. Trade Paper. Basic Books. New York, NY. 2001. 512p. ISBN:0-465-02969-8, ISBN13: 978-0-465-02969-3. Dewey:324.620973.
Audience: **g,l,u,f.** *Choice, 2001.*

Lumsden, Linda J. **JK1896.L86 1997**
Rampant Women: Suffragists and the Right of Assembly. Cloth Text. University of Tennessee Press. Knoxville, TN. 1997. 320p. ISBN:0-87049-986-6, ISBN13: 978-0-87049-986-9. Dewey:324.6/23/0973. LCCN:97-004627.
Audience: **l,u,f.** *Choice, 1998.*

Perman, Michael **JK1929.A2P47 2001**
Struggle for Mastery: Disfranchisement in the South, 1888-1908. Trade Paper. University of North Carolina Press. Chapel Hill, NC. 2001. 416p. Fred W. Morrison Series in Southern Studies ISBN:0-8078-4909-X, ISBN13: 978-0-8078-4909-5. Dewey:324.6/2/097509034. LCCN:00-041773.
Audience: **l,u,f.** *Choice, 2001.*

Stuhler, Barbara **JK1881**
For the Public Record: A Documentary History of the League of Women Voters. Trade Cloth. Greenwood Publishing Group, Inc. Portsmouth, NH. 2000. 360p. Contributions in American Studies, No. 108 ISBN:0-313-25316-1, ISBN13: 978-0-313-25316-4. Dewey:324.6/23/0973. LCCN:99-022094.
Audience: **g,l,u,f.** *Choice, 2000.*

Terborg-Penn, Rosalyn **JK1896.T47 1998**
African American Women in the Struggle for the Vote, 1850-1920. Trade Paper. Indiana University Press. Bloomington, IN. 1998. 224p. Blacks in the Diaspora Ser. ISBN:0-253-21176-X, ISBN13: 978-0-253-21176-7. Dewey:324.6/23/08996073. LCCN:97-041896.
Audience: **g,l,u,f.** *Choice, 1998.*

Walters, Ronald W. **JK1924.W343 2005**
Freedom Is Not Enough: Black Voters, Black Candidates, and American Presidential Politics. Trade Cloth. Rowman & Littlefield Publishers, Inc. Lanham, MD. 2005. 256p. American Political Challenges Ser. ISBN:0-7425-3837-0, ISBN13: 978-0-7425-3837-5. Dewey:324.6/2/08996073. LCCN:2005-008343.
Audience: **g,l,u,f.** *Choice, 2006.*

American Government and Politics > History of American Government > Confederate States of America

Ash, Stephen V. **E487.A83 1995**
When the Yankees Came: Chaos and Conflict in the Occupied South, 1861-1865. Trade Cloth. University of North Carolina Press. Chapel Hill, NC. 1995. 328p. Civil War America Ser., : ISBN:0-8078-2223-X, ISBN13: 978-0-8078-2223-4. Dewey:973.7/13. LCCN:94-049525.
Audience: **g,l,u,f.** *Choice, 1996.*

Baggett, James Alex **E487.B34 2002**
The Scalawags: Southern Dissenters in the Civil War and Reconstruction. Trade Cloth. Louisiana State University Press. Baton Rouge, LA. 2003. xvi, 323p. ISBN:0-8071-2798-1, ISBN13: 978-0-8071-2798-8. Dewey:975/.03. LCCN:2002-001390.
Audience: **g,l,u,f.** *Choice, 2003.*

Ballard, Michael B. **E477.61.B35 1986**
A Long Shadow: Jefferson Davis and the Final Days of the Confederacy. Trade Cloth. University Press of Mississippi. Jackson, MS. 1986. 230p. ISBN:0-87805-295-X, ISBN13: 978-0-87805-295-0. Dewey:973.7/38. LCCN:86-005650.
Audience: **g,l,u,f.** *Choice, 1987.*

Beringer, Richard E., et al. **E487.W48 1986**
Why the South Lost the Civil War. William N. Still Jr., Archer Jones & Herman Hattaway (Authors). Cloth Text. University of Georgia Press. Athens, GA. 1986. 608p. History Book Club Selection ISBN:0-8203-0815-3, ISBN13: 978-0-8203-0815-9. Dewey:973.7/13. LCCN:85-008638.
Audience: **g,l,u,f.** *Choice, 1986.*

Blackett, R. J. M. **E469.8.B66 2001**
Divided Hearts: Britain and the American Civil War. Trade Cloth. Louisiana State University Press. Baton Rouge, LA. 2000. xiii, 273p. ISBN:0-8071-2595-4, ISBN13: 978-0-8071-2595-3. Dewey:973.7. LCCN:00-009794.
Audience: **g,l,u,f.** *Choice, 2001.*

Boritt, Gabor S. **E464 .W48 1992**
Why the Confederacy Lost. James M. McPherson (Contribution by). Cloth Text. Oxford University Press, Inc. New York, NY. 1992. 224p. ISBN:0-19-507405-X, ISBN13: 978-0-19-507405-5. Dewey:973.7. LCCN:91-044291.
Audience: **g,l,u,f.**

Clark, John Elwood Jr. **E491.C58 2001**
Railroads in the Civil War: The Impact of Management on Victory and Defeat. Trade Cloth. Louisiana State University Press. Baton Rouge, LA. 2001. 296p. Conflicting Worlds Ser. ISBN:0-8071-2726-4, ISBN13: 978-0-8071-2726-1. Dewey:973.7/42. LCCN:2001-002452.
Audience: **g,l,u,f.** *Choice, 2002.*

Clinton, Catherine **E628.C58 1995**
Tara Revisited: Women, War, and the Plantation Legend. Henry Louis Gates Jr. (Foreword by). Trade Cloth. Abbeville Press, Inc. New York, NY. 1995. 240p. ISBN:1-55859-491-4, ISBN13: 978-1-55859-491-3. Dewey:973.7/15042. LCCN:94-039218.
Audience: **g,l,u,f.** *Choice, 1995.*

Cooper, William J. Jr. **E467.1.D26C66 2000**
Jefferson Davis, American. Trade Cloth. Alfred A. Knopf Inc. New York, NY. 2000. 784p. ISBN:0-394-56916-4, ISBN13: 978-0-394-56916-1. Dewey:973.7/13/092 B. LCCN:00-062006.
Audience: **g,l,u,f.** *Choice, 2001.*

Current, Richard Nelson & Escott, Paul D. (Editors) **E487.E55 1993**
Encyclopedia of the Confederacy, Set. Trade Cloth. Thomson Gale. Farmington Hills, MI. 1993. 1916p. ISBN:0-13-275991-8, ISBN13: 978-0-13-275991-5. Dewey:973.7/13. LCCN:93-004133.
Audience: **g,l,u.** *Choice, 1994.*

Davis, Burke **E487**
The Long Surrender. Trade Cloth. Random House, Inc. New York, NY. 1985. 316p. ISBN:0-394-52083-1, ISBN13: 978-0-394-52083-4. Dewey:973.7/13. LCCN:83-042767.
Audience: **g,l,u,f.** *Choice, 1985.*

Davis, William C. **E459.D274 1994**
A Government of Our Own: The Making of the Confederacy. Trade Cloth. Simon & Schuster. New York, NY. 1994. 550p. ISBN:0-02-907735-4, ISBN13: 978-0-02-907735-1. Dewey:973.7/13. LCCN:94-015205.
Audience: **g,l,u.**

Davis, William C. **E468.9**
An Honorable Defeat: The Last Days of the Confederate Government. Trade Cloth. Harcourt Trade Publishers. New York, NY. 2001. 512p. ISBN:0-15-100702-0, ISBN13: 978-0-15-100702-8. Dewey:973.7/1.
Audience: **g,l,u,f.** *Choice, 2002.*

Davis, William C. **E487.D278 2002**
Look Away!: A History of the Confederate States of America. Trade Cloth. Simon & Schuster. New York, NY. 2002. 512p. ISBN:0-684-86585-8, ISBN13: 978-0-684-86585-0. Dewey:973.7/13. LCCN:2001-059778.
Audience: **g,l,u,f.** *Choice, 2002.*

Durham, Roger S. (Editor) **HD6515.M62U556 2000**
The Blues in Gray: The Civil War Journal of William Daniel Dixon and the Republican Blues Daybook. Trade Cloth. University of Tennessee Press. Knoxville, TN. 2005. 424p. Voices of the Civil War Ser. ISBN:1-57233-101-1, ISBN13: 978-1-57233-101-3. Dewey:362.1/088/622. LCCN:00-009341.
Audience: **g,l,u,f.** *Choice, 2001.*

Durrill, Wayne K. **E573.9.D87 1990**
War of Another Kind: A Southern Community in the Great Rebellion. Trade Cloth. Oxford University Press, Inc. New York, NY. 1990. 304p. ISBN:0-19-506007-5, ISBN13: 978-0-19-506007-2. Dewey:975.6/03. LCCN:89-036159.
Audience: **g,l,u,f.** *Choice, 1990.*

Faust, Drew G. **E487.F38 1988**
The Creation of Confederate Nationalism: Ideology and Identity in the Civil War South. Cloth Text. Louisiana State University Press. Baton Rouge, LA. 1988. xiii, 110p. Walter Lynwood Fleming Lectures in Southern History ISBN:0-8071-1509-6, ISBN13: 978-0-8071-1509-1. Dewey:973.7/42. LCCN:88-009036.
Audience: **u,f.**

Faust, Drew G. **E628.F35 1996**
Mothers of Invention: Women of the Slaveholding South in the American Civil War. Trade Cloth. University of North Carolina Press. Chapel Hill, NC. 1996. 326p. Fred W. Morrison Series in Southern Studies ISBN:0-8078-2255-8, ISBN13: 978-0-8078-2255-5. Dewey:973.7/15042. LCCN:95-008896.
Audience: **g,l,u,f.** *Choice, 1996.*

Faust, Drew Gilpin **F213.F25 1992**
Southern Stories: Slaveholders in Peace and War. Cloth Text. University of Missouri Press. Columbia, MO. 1992. 264p. ISBN:0-8262-0865-7, ISBN13: 978-0-8262-0865-1. Dewey:306.3620973. LCCN:92-020632.
Audience: **g,l,u,f.** *Choice, 1993.*

Foster, Gaines M. **F215.F694 1987**
Ghosts of the Confederacy: Defeat, the Lost Cause and the Emergence of the New South, 1865 to 1913. Trade Cloth. Oxford University Press, Inc. New York, NY. 1987. 320p. ISBN:0-19-504213-1, ISBN13: 978-0-19-504213-9. Dewey:975/.041. LCCN:86-011420.
Audience: **g,u,f.** *Choice, 1987.*

Fowler, William M. Jr. **E591.F77 1990**
Under Two Flags: The American Navy in the Civil War. Trade Cloth. W. W. Norton & Company, Inc. New York, NY. 1990. 352p. ISBN:0-393-02859-3, ISBN13: 978-0-393-02859-1. Dewey:973.7/5. LCCN:89-029462.
Audience: **g,l,u,f.** *Choice, 1991.*

Freehling, William W. **E487.F83**
The South vs. the South: How Anti-Confederate Southerners Shaped the Course of the Civil War. Trade Cloth. Oxford University Press, Inc. New York, NY. 2001. 256p. ISBN:0-19-513027-8, ISBN13: 978-0-19-513027-0. Dewey:973.7.
Audience: **g,l,u,f.**

Gallagher, Gary W. **E487.G26 1997**
The Confederate War: How Popular Will Nationalism, and Millitary Strategy Could Not Stave off Defeat. Trade Cloth. Harvard University Press. Cambridge, MA. 1997. 232p. ISBN:0-674-16055-X, ISBN13: 978-0-674-16055-2. Dewey:973.7/13. LCCN:97-002495.
Audience: **g,u,f.**

Genovese, Eugene D. **E449.G3724 1998**
A Consuming Fire: The Fall of the Confederacy in the Mind of the White Christian South. Trade Cloth. University of Georgia Press. Athens, GA. 1999. 176p. Mercer University Lamar Memorial Lectures, No. 41 ISBN:0-8203-2046-3, ISBN13: 978-0-8203-2046-5. Dewey:261.8/34567/09750903. LCCN:98-019482.
Audience: **g,u,f.** *Choice, 1999.*

Glaathar, Joseph T. **E470 .G53 1994**
Partners in Command: The Relationships Between Leaders in the Civil War. Trade Cloth. Simon & Schuster. New York, NY. 1993. 304p. ISBN:0-02-911817-4, ISBN13: 978-0-02-911817-7. Dewey:973.73. LCCN:93-025954.
Audience: **g,l,u,f.**

Hattaway, Herman & Beringer, Richard E. **E467.1.D26H38 2002**
Jefferson Davis, Confederate President. Trade Cloth. University Press of Kansas. Lawrence, KS. 2002. xxiv, 542p.

ISBN:0-7006-1170-3, ISBN13: 978-0-7006-1170-6. Dewey:973.7/13/092. LCCN:2001-007131.
Audience: **l,u,f.** *Choice, 2003.*

Horwitz, Tony **E468.9.H78 2000**
Confederates in the Attic: Dispatches from the Unfinished Civil War. Trade Cloth. Thorndike Press. Waterville, ME. 2000. 559p. American History Ser. ISBN:0-7838-9077-X, ISBN13: 978-0-7838-9077-7. Dewey:973.7. LCCN:00-036970.
Audience: **g,u,f.**

Hubbs, G. Ward **F334.G7H83 2003**
Guarding Greensboro: A Confederate Company in the Making of a Southern Community. Trade Cloth. University of Georgia Press. Athens, GA. 2005. 336p. ISBN:0-8203-2505-8, ISBN13: 978-0-8203-2505-7. Dewey:976.1/43. LCCN:2002-154239.
Audience: **g,l,u,f.** *Choice, 2004.*

Inscoe, John C. & McKinney, Gordon B. **E524.I54 2000**
The Heart of Confederate Appalachia: Western North Carolina in the Civil War. Trade Cloth. University of North Carolina Press. Chapel Hill, NC. 2000. 384p. Civil War America Ser., : ISBN:0-8078-2544-1, ISBN13: 978-0-8078-2544-0. Dewey:973.7/456. LCCN:99-056658.
Audience: **f.** *Choice, 2000.*

Jones, Howard **E469.J57 1997**
Union in Peril: The Crisis over British Intervention in the Civil War. Trade Cloth. University of Nebraska Press. Lincoln, NE. 1997. 302p. ISBN:0-8032-7597-8, ISBN13: 978-0-8032-7597-3. Dewey:973.7/21. LCCN:96-049131.
Audience: **g,l,u,f.** *Choice, 1993.*

Jones, Wilmer L. **E467.J79 2000**
After the Thunder: Fourteen Men Who Shaped Post-Civil War America. Trade Cloth. Taylor Trade Publishing. Blue Ridge Summit, PA. 2000. 368p. ISBN:0-87833-176-X, ISBN13: 978-0-87833-176-5. Dewey:973.7/092/2 B. LCCN:99-055775.
Audience: **g,l,u,f.**

Jones, Wilmer L. **E467**
Generals in Blue and Gray. Trade Cloth. Greenwood Publishing Group, Inc. Portsmouth, NH. 2004. 850p. ISBN:0-275-98322-6, ISBN13: 978-0-275-98322-2. Dewey:973.7/3/092 B. LCCN:2004-052153.
Audience: **g,l,u,f.** *Choice, 2005.*

Luraghi, Raimondo **E596.L8713 1996**
A History of the Confederate Navy. Trade Cloth. Naval Institute Press. Annapolis, MD. 1996. 552p. ISBN:1-55750-527-6, ISBN13: 978-1-55750-527-9. Dewey:973.7/57. LCCN:95-049315.
Audience: **g,l,u,f.** *Choice, 1997.*

Mackey, Robert Russell **E470.45.M13 2004**
The Uncivil War: Irregular Warfare in the Upper South, 1861-1865. Trade Cloth. University of Oklahoma Press. Norman, OK. 2004. 304p. Campaigns and Commanders Ser., Vol. 5 ISBN:0-8061-3624-3, ISBN13: 978-0-8061-3624-0. Dewey:973.7/3. LCCN:2004-043541.
Audience: **u,f.** *Choice, 2005.*

McPherson, James M. **E492.3.M38 1997**
For Cause and Comrades: Why Men Fought in the Civil War. Trade Cloth. Oxford University Press, Inc. New York, NY. 1997. 256p. ISBN:0-19-509023-3, ISBN13: 978-0-19-509023-9. Dewey:973.7. LCCN:96-024760.
Audience: **g,l,u,f.** *Choice, 1997.*

Moneyhon, Carl H. **E553.9.M65 1994**
Impact of the Civil War and Reconstruction on Arkansas: Persistence in the Midst of Ruin. Cloth Text. Louisiana State University Press. Baton Rouge, LA. 1993. 336p. ISBN:0-8071-1840-0, ISBN13: 978-0-8071-1840-5. Dewey:976.705. LCCN:93-026080.
Audience: **l,u,f.** *Choice, 1994.*

Neely, Mark E. Jr. **E487.N44 1999**
Southern Rights: Political Prisoners and the Myth of Confederate Constitutionalism. Trade Cloth. University Press of Virginia. Charlottesville, VA. 1999. vii, 212p. Nation Divided Ser. ISBN:0-8139-1894-4, ISBN13: 978-0-8139-1894-5. Dewey:973.7/72. LCCN:99-025230.
Audience: **u,f.** *Choice, 2000.*

Paquette, Robert Louis & Ferieger, Louis A. (Editors) **E441.S646 2000**
Slavery, Secession and Southern History. Trade Cloth. University Press of Virginia. Charlottesville, VA. 2000. xvi, 229p. ISBN:0-8139-1951-7, ISBN13: 978-0-8139-1951-5. Dewey:975/.00496. LCCN:99-045449.
Audience: **g,l,u,f.** *Choice, 2000.*

Pearce, George F. **F319.P4P36 2000**
Pensacola During the Civil War: A Thorn in the Side of the Confederacy. Trade Cloth. University Press of Florida. Gainesville, FL. 2000. 304p. Florida History and Culture Ser. ISBN:0-8130-1770-X, ISBN13: 978-0-8130-1770-9. Dewey:975.9/99. LCCN:99-043001.
Audience: **g,l,u,f.** *Choice, 2000.*

Pfanz, Donald **E467.1.E86P44 1998**
Richard S. Ewell: A Soldier's Life. Trade Cloth. University of North Carolina Press. Chapel Hill, NC. 1998. 680p. Civil War America Ser., : ISBN:0-8078-2389-9, ISBN13: 978-0-8078-2389-7. Dewey:973.7/3. LCCN:97-021473.
Audience: **g,l,u,f.** *Choice, 1998.*

Rable, George C. **E487.R18 1994**
The Confederate Republic: A Revolution Against Politics. Trade Cloth. University of North Carolina Press. Chapel Hill, NC. 1994. 430p. Civil War America Ser. ISBN:0-8078-2144-6, ISBN13: 978-0-8078-2144-2. Dewey:973.7/13. LCCN:93-036491.
Audience: **f.** *Choice, 1994.*

Robinson, Armstead L. **E453.R63 2005**
Bitter Fruits of Bondage: The Demise of Slavery and the Collapse of the Confederacy, 1861-1865. Trade Cloth. University Press of Virginia. Charlottesville, VA. 2004. 352p. Carter G. Woodson Institute Ser. ISBN:0-8139-2309-3, ISBN13: 978-0-8139-2309-3. Dewey:973.7/13. LCCN:2004-010080.
Audience: **g,l,u,f.** *Choice, 2005.*

Rosen, Robert N. **F220.J5R67 2000**
The Jewish Confederates. Trade Cloth. University of South Carolina Press. Columbia, SC. 2000. xxiii, 517p. ISBN:1-57003-363-3, ISBN13: 978-1-57003-363-6. Dewey:975.004/924. LCCN:00-009492.
Audience: **u,f.** *Choice, 2001.*

Rubin, Anne S. **E487.R925 2005**
A Shattered Nation: The Rise and Fall of the Confederacy, 1861-1868. Trade Cloth. University of North Carolina Press. Chapel Hill, NC. 2005. 352p. Civil War America Ser. ISBN:0-8078-2928-5, ISBN13: 978-0-8078-2928-8. Dewey:973.7/13. LCCN:2004-018013.
Audience: **g,l,u,f.** *Choice, 2005.*

Schultz, Jane E. **E621.S35 2004**
Women at the Front: Hospital Workers in Civil War America. Trade Cloth. University of North Carolina Press. Chapel Hill, NC. 2004. 328p. Civil War America Ser. ISBN:0-8078-2867-X, ISBN13: 978-0-8078-2867-0. Dewey:973.7/76/082. LCCN:2003-024944.
Audience: **g,l,u,f.** *Choice, 2005.*

Surdam, David G. **E600.S87 2001**
Northern Naval Superiority and the Economics of the American Civil War. Trade Cloth. University of South Carolina Press. Columbia, SC. 2001. xiv, 286p. Studies in Maritime History ISBN:1-57003-407-9, ISBN13: 978-1-57003-407-7. Dewey:973.7/57. LCCN:2001-000743.
Audience: **g,l,u,f.** *Choice, 2002.*

Thomas, Emory M. **E467.1.L4T48 1995**
Robert E. Lee: A Biography. Trade Cloth. W. W. Norton & Company, Inc. New York, NY. 1995. 576p. ISBN:0-393-03730-4, ISBN13: 978-0-393-03730-2. Dewey:973.7/3/092. LCCN:95-010522.
Audience: **g,l,u,f.** *Choice, 1995.*

Wert, Jeffry D. **E467.1.L55 W46 1993**
General James Longstreet: The Confederacy's Most Controversial Soldier. Trade Cloth. Simon & Schuster. New York, NY. 1993. 384p. ISBN:0-671-70921-6, ISBN13: 978-0-671-70921-1. Dewey:973.7/3/092. LCCN:93-028953.
Audience: **g,l,u,f.**

Wise, Stephen R. **E591**
Lifeline of the Confederacy: Blockade Running During the Civil War. William N. Still Jr. (Editor). Trade Cloth. University of South Carolina Press. Columbia, SC. 1991. 414p. Studies in Maritime History ISBN:0-87249-799-2, ISBN13: 978-0-87249-799-3. Dewey:973.7/5. LCCN:88-020524.
Audience: **g,l,u,f.** *Choice, 1989.*

Woodworth, Steven E. **E467.1.D26W8 1995**
Davis and Lee at War. Trade Cloth. University Press of Kansas. Lawrence, KS. 2004. xiv, 410p. Modern War Studies ISBN:0-7006-0718-8, ISBN13: 978-0-7006-0718-1. Dewey:973.7/3. LCCN:95-022706.
Audience: **g,l,u,f.** *Choice, 1996.*

Woodworth, Steven E. (Editor) **E607.L69 2002**
The Loyal, True and Brave: America's Civil War Soldiers. Book, Other. Rowman & Littlefield Publishers, Inc. Lanham, MD. 2002. 222p. ISBN:0-8420-2930-3, ISBN13: 978-0-8420-2930-8. Dewey:973.7/42. LCCN:2001-054151.
Audience: **g,l,u,f.** *Choice, 2002.*

Woodworth, Steven E. **E487.W8 1999**
No Band of Brothers: Problems of the Rebel High Command. Herman Hattaway & Jon L. Wakelyn (Contribution by). Trade Cloth. University of Missouri Press. Columbia, MO. 1999. 208p. Shades of Blue and Gray Ser. ISBN:0-8262-1255-7, ISBN13: 978-0-8262-1255-9. Dewey:973.7/3. LCCN:99-035480.
Audience: **g,l,u,f.** *Choice, 2000.*

American Government and Politics > History of American Government > New Deal

Barber, William J. **HC106.8**
From New Era to New Deal: Herbert Hoover, the Economists, and American Economic Policy, 1921-1933. Craufurd D. Goodwin (Contribution by). Trade Paper. Cambridge University Press. New York, NY. 1989. 256p. Historical Perspectives on Modern Economics Ser. ISBN:0-521-36737-9, ISBN13: 978-0-521-36737-0. Dewey:330.973/0915.
Audience: **u,f.** *Choice, 1986.*

Chafe, William Henry **E806.M63 2002**
The Achievement of American Liberalism: The New Deal and Its Legacies. Trade Cloth. Columbia University Press. New York, NY. 2002. 350p. ISBN:0-231-11212-2, ISBN13: 978-0-231-11212-3. Dewey:973.917. LCCN:2002-073366.
Audience: **g,u,f.** *Choice, 2003.*

Hamby, Alonzo L. **E806.H293 2004**
For the Survival of Democracy: Franklin Roosevelt and the World Crisis of the 1930's. Trade Cloth. Simon & Schuster. New York, NY. 2003. 512p. ISBN:0-684-84340-4, ISBN13: 978-0-684-84340-7. Dewey:909.82/3. LCCN:2003-061807.
Audience: **f.**

Milkis, Sidney M. & Mileur, Jerome M. (Editors) **JC574.2.U6N48 2002**
The New Deal and the Triumph of Liberalism. Trade Cloth. University of Massachusetts Press. Amherst, MA. 2002. 304p. The Political Development of the American Nation Ser., :Studies in Politics and History ISBN:1-55849-320-4, ISBN13: 978-1-55849-320-9. Dewey:973.917. LCCN:2001-055501.
Audience: **u,f.** *Choice, 2003.*

Patterson, James T. **E806.P365 1981**
Congressional Conservatism and the New Deal: The Growth of the Conservative Coalition in Congress, 1933 to 1939. Trade Cloth. Greenwood Publishing Group, Inc. Portsmouth, NH. 1981. 369p. ISBN:0-313-22676-8, ISBN13: 978-0-313-22676-2. Dewey:353.03/72. LCCN:81-004195.
Audience: **u,f.**

Schlesinger, Arthur M. Jr. **E806.S344 2003**
The Coming of the New Deal: 1933-1935, the Age of Roosevelt. Trade Paper. Houghton Mifflin Company Trade & Reference Division. Boston, MA. 2003. 688p. The Age of Roosevelt Ser., Vol. 2 ISBN:0-618-34086-6, ISBN13: 978-0-618-34086-6. Dewey:973.917/092. LCCN:2003-047859.
Audience: **u,f.**

Zinn, Howard (Editor) **E806.N425 2003**
New Deal Thought. Trade Cloth. Hackett Publishing Company, Inc. Indianapolis, IN. 2003. 431p. ISBN:0-87220-686-6, ISBN13: 978-0-87220-686-1. Dewey:320.973. LCCN:2003-056164.
Audience: **u,f.**

American Government and Politics > Federal Government

Ackerman, Bruce **E331.A15 2005**
The Failure of the Founding Fathers: Jefferson, Marshall, and the Rise of Presidential Democracy. Trade Cloth. Harvard

University Press. Cambridge, MA. 2005. 400p. ISBN:0-674-01866-4, ISBN13: 978-0-674-01866-2. Dewey:320.973/09/034. LCCN:2005-047034.
Audience: **g,u,f.** *Choice, 2006.*

Anton, Thomas J. **JK325**
American Federalism and Public Policy: How the System Works. Trade Cloth. Temple University Press. Philadelphia, PA. 1988. 320p. ISBN:0-87722-577-X, ISBN13: 978-0-87722-577-5. Dewey:321.02097. LCCN:88-017553.
Audience: **g,l,u.** *Choice, 1989.*

Beamer, Glenn **HJ2053.A1B4 1999**
Creative Politics: Taxes and Public Goods in a Federal System. Trade Cloth. University of Michigan Press. Chicago, IL. 1999. 192p. ISBN:0-472-11020-9, ISBN13: 978-0-472-11020-9. Dewey:336.2/00973. LCCN:98-058121.
Audience: **u,f.** *Choice, 2000.*

Beer, Samuel Hutchison **JK325.B38 1993**
To Make a Nation: The Rediscovery of American Federalsim. Trade Cloth. Harvard University Press. Cambridge, MA. 1993. xxi, 474p. ISBN:0-674-60212-9, ISBN13: 978-0-674-60212-0. Dewey:321.02/0973. LCCN:92-012077.
Audience: **g,l,u,f.**

Benedict, Stephen **NX735.P83 1991**
Public Money and the Muse: Essays on Government Funding for the Arts. Trade Cloth. W. W. Norton & Company, Inc. New York, NY. 1991. 288p. ISBN:0-393-03015-6, ISBN13: 978-0-393-03015-0. Dewey:353/.0085/4. LCCN:91-009348.
Audience: **g,u,f.** *Choice, 1991.*

Brown-John, C. Lloyd (Editor) **JF751.C43 1988**
Centralizing and Decentralizing Trends in Federal States. Trade Cloth. University Press of America, Inc. Lanham, MD. 1988. 418p. ISBN:0-8191-6895-5, ISBN13: 978-0-8191-6895-5. Dewey:321.02. LCCN:88-000099.
Audience: **u,f.** *Choice, 1988.*

Calder, James D. **HV9950**
The Origins and Development of Federal Crime Control Policy: Herbert Hoover's Initiatives. Trade Cloth. Greenwood Publishing Group, Inc. Portsmouth, NH. 1993. 328p. ISBN:0-275-94284-8, ISBN13: 978-0-275-94284-7. Dewey:363.20973. LCCN:93-020298.
Audience: **g,l,u,f.** *Choice, 1994.*

Cammisa, Anne M. **JK325**
Governments as Interest Groups: Intergovernmental Lobbying and the Federal System. Trade Cloth. Greenwood Publishing Group, Inc. Portsmouth, NH. 1995. 176p. ISBN:0-275-94962-1, ISBN13: 978-0-275-94962-4. Dewey:320.8/0973. LCCN:95-014428.
Audience: **u,f.** *Choice, 1996.*

Chisman, Forrest & Pifer, Alan **HN59.2.C46 1987**
Government for the People: The Federal Role: What It Is, What It Should Be. Trade Cloth. W. W. Norton & Company, Inc. New York, NY. 1987. 316p. ISBN:0-393-02491-1, ISBN13: 978-0-393-02491-3. Dewey:361.6/1/0973. LCCN:87-018767.
Audience: **g,l,u.** *Choice, 1988.*

Clayton, Cornell W. (Editor) **KF299.G6G68 1995**
Government Lawyers: The Federal Legal Bureaucracy and Presidential Politics. Trade Cloth. University Press of Kansas. Lawrence, KS. 1995. 288p. Studies in Government and Public Policy ISBN:0-7006-0706-4, ISBN13: 978-0-7006-0706-8. Dewey:353.008/8. LCCN:95-006288.
Audience: **u,f.** *Choice, 1995.*

Conlan, Timothy J. **JK325.C617 1988**
New Federalism: Intergovernmental Reform from Nixon to Reagan. Samuel Hutchison Beer (Introduction by). Trade Cloth. Brookings Institution Press. Washington, DC. 1988. 274p. ISBN:0-8157-1540-4, ISBN13: 978-0-8157-1540-5. Dewey:321.02/0973. LCCN:88-027621.
Audience: **u,f.** *Choice, 1989.*

Conley, Patrick T. & Kaminski, John P. (Editors) **KF4541.C585 1988**
The Constitution and the States: The Role of the Original Thirteen in the Framing and Adoption of the Federal Constitution. Warren E. Burger (Foreword by), Paul J. Scudiere (Introduction by). Trade Cloth. Rowman & Littlefield Publishers, Inc. Lanham, MD. 1988. 352p. ISBN:0-945612-02-8, ISBN13: 978-0-945612-02-5. Dewey:342.73/029. LCCN:88-009028.
Audience: **g,l,u,f.** *Choice, 1989.*

Cornell, Saul **E310.C79 1999**
The Other Founders: Anti-Federalism and the Dissenting Tradition in America, 1788-1828. Trade Paper. University of North Carolina Press. Chapel Hill, NC. 1999. 352p. Published for the Omohundro Institute of Early American History and Culture, Williamsburg, Virginia Ser. ISBN:0-8078-4786-0, ISBN13: 978-0-8078-4786-2. Dewey:320.473/049. LCCN:99-013685.
Audience: **u,f.** *Choice, 2000.*

Critchlow, Donald T. **HQ763.6.U5C75 1999**
Intended Consequences: Birth Control, Abortion and the Federal Government in Modern America. Trade Cloth. Oxford University Press, Inc. New York, NY. 1999. 320p. ISBN:0-19-504657-9, ISBN13: 978-0-19-504657-1. Dewey:363.9/6/0973. LCCN:98-013691.
Audience: **g,l,u,f.**

Drake, Frederick D. & Nelson, Lynn R. (Editors) **JK311**
States' Rights and American Federalism: A Documentary History. Cloth Text. Greenwood Publishing Group, Inc. Portsmouth, NH. 1999. 264p. Primary Documents in American History and Contemporary Issues Ser. ISBN:0-313-30573-0, ISBN13: 978-0-313-30573-3. Dewey:320.473. LCCN:99-021705.
Audience: **g,l,u,f.**

Dye, Thomas R. **JK325.D94 1990**
American Federalism: Competition among Governments. Trade Cloth. Simon & Schuster. New York, NY. 1989. 240p. ISBN:0-669-21475-2, ISBN13: 978-0-669-21475-8. Dewey:321.02/0973. LCCN:89-037585.
Audience: **g,l,u,f.** *Choice, 1990.*

Edling, Max M. **KF4541.E28 2003**
A Revolution in Favor of Government: Origins of the U. S. Constitution and the Making of the American State. Trade Cloth. Oxford University Press, Inc. New York, NY. 2003. 347p.

ISBN:0-19-514870-3, ISBN13: 978-0-19-514870-1. Dewey:342.73/029. LCCN:2002-152079.
Audience: **u,f.** *Choice, 2004.*

Freedman, Eric M. **KF9011.F74 2001**
Habeas Corpus: Rethinking the Great Writ of Liberty. Trade Cloth. New York University Press. New York, NY. 2002. 254p. ISBN:0-8147-2717-4, ISBN13: 978-0-8147-2717-1. Dewey:345.7/3/056. LCCN:2001-003912.
Audience: **u,f.** *Choice, 2002.*

Goering, John M. **HD7293.H584 1986**
Housing Desegregation and Federal Policy. Trade Cloth. University of North Carolina Press. Chapel Hill, NC. 1986. xii, 344p. Urban and Regional Policy and Development Studies ISBN:0-8078-1707-4, ISBN13: 978-0-8078-1707-0. Dewey:363.5/1. LCCN:86-001404.
Audience: **u,f.** *Choice, 1987.*

Gutmann, Amy (Editor) **HV91.D462 1988**
Democracy and the Welfare State. Trade Cloth. Princeton University Press. Princeton, NJ. 1988. 352p. Studies from the Project on the Federal Social Role ISBN:0-691-07756-8, ISBN13: 978-0-691-07756-7. Dewey:361.6/5. LCCN:87-036055.
Audience: **u,f.** *Choice, 1988.*

Hamm, Mark S. **HV6432.H365 1997**
Apocalypse in Oklahoma: Waco and Ruby Ridge Revenged. Trade Cloth. Northeastern University Press. Boston, MA. 1997. 352p. ISBN:1-55553-300-0, ISBN13: 978-1-55553-300-7. Dewey:320.55/3. LCCN:96-052897.
Audience: **g,l,u,f.** *Choice, 1997.*

Harriger, Katy J. **KF4568.H37 1992**
Independent Justice: The Federal Special Prosecutor in American Politics. Trade Cloth. University Press of Kansas. Lawrence, KS. 1992. x, 266p. ISBN:0-7006-0535-5, ISBN13: 978-0-7006-0535-4. Dewey:345.73/01. LCCN:91-039258.
Audience: **u,f.** *Choice, 1992.*

Harris, Charles W. **JK2716.H37 1995**
Congress and the Governance of the Nation's Capital: The Conflict of Federal and Local Interests. Trade Cloth. Georgetown University Press. Washington, DC. 1994. 312p. ISBN:0-87840-563-1, ISBN13: 978-0-87840-563-3. Dewey:320.8/09753. LCCN:94-011006.
Audience: **u,f.** *Choice, 1995.*

Hart, John **JK518.H36 1987**
The Presidential Branch. Cloth Text. Elsevier Science & Technology Books. Saint Louis, MO. 1987. 250p. Government and Politics Ser. ISBN:0-08-030939-9, ISBN13: 978-0-08-030939-2. Dewey:353.03/1. LCCN:86-023743.
Audience: **u,f.** *Choice, 1988.*

Hays, R. Allen **HD7293.H394 1995**
The Federal Government and Urban Housing: Ideology and Change in Public Policy. Ed. 2. Cloth Text. State University of New York Press. Albany, NY. 1995. 333p. ISBN:0-7914-2325-5, ISBN13: 978-0-7914-2325-7. Dewey:363.5/8/0973. LCCN:94-028755.
Audience: **u,f.** *Choice, 1986.*

Ippolito, Dennis S. **HJ2051.I66 1990**
Uncertain Legacies: Federal Budget Policy from Roosevelt Through Reagan. Cloth Text. University Press of Virginia. Charlottesville, VA. 1990. 352p. ISBN:0-8139-1287-3, ISBN13: 978-0-8139-1287-5. Dewey:353.0072/2/09043. LCCN:90-036590.
Audience: **g,u,f.** *Choice, 1991.*

Kenyon, Daphne A. & Kincaid, John (Editors) **JK325.C57 1991**
Competition among States and Local Governments: Efficiency and Equity in American Federalism. Library Binding. Urban Institute Press. Washington, DC. 1991. 302p. ISBN:0-87766-516-8, ISBN13: 978-0-87766-516-8. Dewey:321.02/0973. LCCN:91-012344.
Audience: **u,f.** *Choice, 1992.*

Killenbeck, Mark R. **KF4600.T356 2000**
The Tenth Amendment and State Sovereignty: Constitutional History and Contemporary Issues. Book, Other. Rowman & Littlefield Publishers, Inc. Lanham, MD. 2001. 224p. ISBN:0-7425-1879-5, ISBN13: 978-0-7425-1879-7. Dewey:342.73/042. LCCN:2001-048917.
Audience: **u,f.** *Choice, 2002.*

King, David C. **JK1029.K56 1997**
Turf Wars: How Congressional Committees Claim Jurisdiction. Trade Cloth. University of Chicago Press. Chicago, IL. 1997. 222p. American Politics and Political Economy Ser. ISBN:0-226-43623-3, ISBN13: 978-0-226-43623-4. Dewey:328.73/0765. LCCN:96-053058.
Audience: **u,f.** *Choice, 1998.*

King, Desmond **JK723.A34K56 1995**
Separate and Unequal: Black Americans and the U. S. Federal Government. Trade Cloth. Oxford University Press, Inc. New York, NY. 1995. 366p. ISBN:0-19-828016-5, ISBN13: 978-0-19-828016-3. Dewey:331.6/3/96073. LCCN:95-005865.
Audience: **g,l,u,f.** *Choice, 1996.*

Leab, Daniel J. **F159.P653C85 2000**
I Was a Communist for the F. B. I.: The Unhappy Life and Times of Matt Cvetic. Trade Cloth. Pennsylvania State University Press. University Park, PA. 2000. xii, 170p. ISBN:0-271-02053-9, ISBN13: 978-0-271-02053-2. Dewey:974.8/8604/092 B. LCCN:00-035660.
Audience: **g,u,f.** *Choice, 2001.*

Lemco, Jonathan **JC355**
Political Stability in Federal Governments. Trade Cloth. Greenwood Publishing Group, Inc. Portsmouth, NH. 1991. 224p. ISBN:0-275-93854-9, ISBN13: 978-0-275-93854-3. Dewey:321.02. LCCN:91-006777.
Audience: **u,f.** *Choice, 1992.*

Levy, Alan H. **NX735.L48 1997**
Government and the Arts: Debates over Federal Support of the Arts in America from George Washington to Jesse Helms. Trade Cloth. University Press of America, Inc. Lanham, MD. 1997. 160p. ISBN:0-7618-0674-1, ISBN13: 978-0-7618-0674-5. Dewey:700/.973. LCCN:96-052505.
Audience: **g,l,u,f.** *Choice, 1997.*

MacManus, Susan A **JK1673.M33 1992**
Doing Business with the Government: Federal, State, Local and Foreign Purchasing Practices for Every Business and Public Institution. Paragon House Publishers. 1992. ISBN:1-55778-515-5, ISBN13: 978-1-55778-515-2.
Audience: **g,u,f.**

Mann, Alfred K. **Q127.U5M36 2000**
For Better or for Worse: The Marriage of Science and Government in the United States. Trade Cloth. Columbia University Press. New York, NY. 2000. ISBN:0-231-11707-8, ISBN13: 978-0-231-11707-4. Dewey:509.73. LCCN:00-060120.
Audience: **u,f.** *Choice, 2001.*

Muncy, Mitchell S. (Editor) **KF5130.A75E53 1997**
The End of Democracy?: The Judicial Usurpation of Politics. Richard J. Neuhaus, William Bennett & Robert Bork (Contribution by). Trade Cloth. Spence Publishing Company. Dallas, TX. 1997. 303p. ISBN:1-890626-03-1, ISBN13: 978-1-890626-03-7. Dewey:340/.115. LCCN:97-022959.
Audience: **u,f.** *Choice, 1998.*

Mutch, Robert E. **KF4920**
Campaigns, Congress and the Courts: The Making of Federal Campaign Finance Laws. Trade Cloth. Greenwood Publishing Group, Inc. Portsmouth, NH. 1988. 237p. ISBN:0-275-92784-9, ISBN13: 978-0-275-92784-4. Dewey:342.73/078. LCCN:87-030874.
Audience: **u,f.** *Choice, 1988.*

Nagel, Robert F. **KF4600.N34 2001**
The Implosion of American Federalism. Cloth Text. Oxford University Press, Inc. New York, NY. 2001. 224p. ISBN:0-19-514317-5, ISBN13: 978-0-19-514317-1. Dewey:320.473. LCCN:00-053759.
Audience: **u,f.** *Choice, 2002.*

New York University School of Law Staff & Kaczorowski, Robert J. **KF4757.K33 1985**
The Politics of Judicial Interpretation: The Federal Courts, Department of Justice and Civil Rights, 1866-1876. Library Binding. Oceana Publications. Dobbs Ferry, NY. 1985. 241p. New York University School of Law, Linden Studies in Legal History ISBN:0-379-20818-0, ISBN13: 978-0-379-20818-4. Dewey:342.73/0873. LCCN:85-002894.
Audience: **u,f.** *Choice, 1986.*

Nice, David C. **JK325**
Federalism: The Politics of Intergovernmental Relations. Cloth Text. Palgrave Macmillan. New York, NY. 1986. 256p. ISBN:0-312-28550-7, ISBN13: 978-0-312-28550-0. Dewey:321.02/0973. LCCN:86-060643.
Audience: **u,f.** B *Choice, 1987.*

Onuf, Peter S. & Sadosky, Leonard J. **E331.O58 2001**
Jeffersonian America. Trade Cloth. Blackwell Publishing, Inc. Malden, MA. 2001. 280p. Problems in American History Ser., Vol. 5 ISBN:1-55786-922-7, ISBN13: 978-1-55786-922-7. Dewey:320.973/09/034. LCCN:2001-025984.
Audience: **l,u,f.** *Choice, 2002.*

Peterson, Paul E. **JK325.P477 1995**
The Price of Federalism. Trade Cloth. Brookings Institution Press. Washington, DC. 1995. 239p. Twentieth Century Bks. ISBN:0-8157-7024-3, ISBN13: 978-0-8157-7024-4. Dewey:321.02/0973. LCCN:95-013773.
Audience: **u,f.** *Choice, 1995.*

Peterson, Paul E., et al. **JK325**
When Federalism Works. Barry G. Rabe & Kenneth K. Wong (Authors). Trade Cloth. Brookings Institution Press. Washington, DC. 2000. 243p. ISBN:0-8157-7020-0, ISBN13: 978-0-8157-7020-6. Dewey:353.0072/5. LCCN:86-024467.
Audience: **u,f.** *Choice, 1987.*

Redish, Martin H. **KF4600.R43 1995**
The Constitution As Political Structure. Trade Cloth. Oxford University Press, Inc. New York, NY. 1995. 238p. ISBN:0-19-507060-7, ISBN13: 978-0-19-507060-6. Dewey:342.73/02. LCCN:93-042364.
Audience: **u,f.** *Choice, 1995.*

Riccucci, Norma M. **JK723.E9R53 1995**
Unsung Heroes: Federal Execucrats Making a Difference. Trade Cloth. Georgetown University Press. Washington, DC. 1995. 266p. ISBN:0-87840-592-5, ISBN13: 978-0-87840-592-3. Dewey:331.7/95/092273. LCCN:95-007073.
Audience: **g,l,u.** *Choice, 1996.*

Rivlin, Alice M. **HJ3258.A2.R57 1992**
Reviving the American Dream: The Economy, the States, and the Federal Government. Trade Cloth. Brookings Institution Press. Washington, DC. 1992. 196p. ISBN:0-8157-7476-1, ISBN13: 978-0-8157-7476-1. Dewey:336.73. LCCN:92-016631.
Audience: **g,u,f.** *Choice, 1992.*

Roche, George **LB2342.4.U6R63 1994**
The Fall of the Ivory Tower: Government Funding, Corruption and the Bankrupting of Higher Education. Trade Cloth. Regnery Publishing, Incorporated, An Eagle Publishing Company. Washington, DC. 1994. 320p. ISBN:0-89526-487-0, ISBN13: 978-0-89526-487-9. Dewey:379.0973. LCCN:93-047561.
Audience: **g,u,f.** *Choice, 1995.*

Rosentraub, Mark S. (Editor) **HT123**
Urban Policy Problems: Federal Policy and Institutional Change. Trade Cloth. Greenwood Publishing Group, Inc. Portsmouth, NH. 1986. 270p. ISBN:0-275-92120-4, ISBN13: 978-0-275-92120-0. Dewey:307.7/6/0973. LCCN:86-000596.
Audience: **u,f.** *Choice, 1986.*

Rossum, Ralph A. **KF4600.R67 2001**
Federalism, the Supreme Court and the Seventeenth Amendment: The Irony of Constitutional Democracy. Trade Cloth. Lexington Books. Lanham, MD. 2001. 312p. ISBN:0-7391-0285-0, ISBN13: 978-0-7391-0285-5. Dewey:320.473/049. LCCN:2001-038133.
Audience: **g,l,u,f.** *Choice, 2002.*

Scherer, Nancy **KF8776.S34 2005**
Scoring Points: Politicians, Activists, and the Lower Federal Court Appointment Process. Trade Cloth. Stanford University Press. Palo Alto, CA. 2005. x, 272p. ISBN:0-8047-4948-5, ISBN13: 978-0-8047-4948-0. Dewey:347.73/2034. LCCN:2005-004650.
Audience: **u,f.** *Choice, 2006.*

Sky, Theodore **HJ7537.S55 2003**
To Provide for the General Welfare: A History of the Federal Spending Power. Trade Cloth. University of Delaware Press. Newark, DE. 2004. 448p. ISBN:0-87413-793-4, ISBN13: 978-0-87413-793-4. Dewey:343.73/034. LCCN:2003-001364.
Audience: **g,l,u,f.** *Choice, 2004.*

Stoker, Robert P. **JK325.S79 1991**
Reluctant Partners: Implementing Federal Policy. Cloth Text. University of Pittsburgh Press. Pittsburgh, PA. 1992. 232p.

Policy and Institutional Studies ISBN:0-8229-3688-7, ISBN13: 978-0-8229-3688-6. Dewey:321.02/0973. LCCN:91-050112.
Audience: **u,f.** *Choice, 1992.*

Teaford, Jon C. **JK311.T43 2002**
The Rise of the States: Evolution of American State Government. Trade Cloth. Johns Hopkins University Press. Baltimore, MD. 2002. 280p. The Johns Hopkins University Studies in Historical and Political Science, Vol. 120 ISBN:0-8018-6888-2, ISBN13: 978-0-8018-6888-7. Dewey:320.473/049/0904. LCCN:2001-003739.
Audience: **l,u,f.** *Choice, 2003.*

Tully, James **JF1061 .T85 1995**
Strange Multiplicity: Constitutionalism in an Age of Diversity. Cambridge University Press. 1995. The Seeley Lectures ISBN:0-521-47117-6, ISBN13: 978-0-521-47117-6.
Audience: **u,f.**

Wakelyn, Jon L. **E302**
Birth of the Bill of Rights: Encyclopedia of the Antifederalists. Cloth Text. Greenwood Publishing Group, Inc. Portsmouth, NH. 2004. 430p. ISBN:0-313-31739-9, ISBN13: 978-0-313-31739-2. Dewey:973.4/092/2 B. LCCN:2004-047546.
Audience: **g,l,u,f.** *Choice, 2005.*

Weir, Margaret (Editor), et al. **HN65.P635 1988**
The Politics of Social Policy in the United States. Ann S. Orloff & Theda Skocpol (Editors). Trade Cloth. Princeton University Press. Princeton, NJ. 1988. 500p. Studies from the Project on the Federal Social Role ISBN:0-691-09436-5, ISBN13: 978-0-691-09436-6. Dewey:361.6/1/0973. LCCN:87-025702.
Audience: **u,f.** *Choice, 1988.*

Wilkins, David E. & Lomawaima, K. Tsianina **KF8205.W533 2001**
Uneven Grounds: American Indian Sovereignty and Federal Law. Trade Cloth. University of Oklahoma Press. Norman, OK. 2001. vi, 326p. ISBN:0-8061-3351-1, ISBN13: 978-0-8061-3351-5. Dewey:323.1/197073. LCCN:2001-027138.
Audience: **u,f.** *Choice, 2002.*

Williams, Walter **HN60.W55 1998**
Honest Numbers and Democracy: Social Policy Analysis in the White House, Congress and the Federal Agencies. Trade Cloth. Georgetown University Press. Washington, DC. 1998. 292p. ISBN:0-87840-670-0, ISBN13: 978-0-87840-670-8. Dewey:306/.0973. LCCN:97-037972.
Audience: **u,f.** *Choice, 1998.*

Williamson, Richard S. **JK325.W47 1990**
Reagan's Federalism: His Efforts to Decentralize Government. Trade Cloth. University Press of America, Inc. Lanham, MD. 1989. 250p. ISBN:0-8191-7534-X, ISBN13: 978-0-8191-7534-2. Dewey:321.02/0973. LCCN:89-035578.
Audience: **g,l,u,f.** *Choice, 1991.*

American Government and Politics > Federal Government > Executive Branch

Borrelli, Mary Anne (Editor) **JK611.B67 2002**
The President's Cabinet: Gender, Power, and Representation. Library Binding. Lynne Rienner Publishers, Inc. Boulder, CO. 2002. 275p. ISBN:1-58826-094-1, ISBN13: 978-1-58826-094-9. Dewey:352.24/0973. LCCN:2002-023157.
Audience: **u,f.** *Choice, 2003.*

Borrelli, Mary Anne & Martin, Janet M. **JK721.O85 1997**
The Other Elites: Women, Politics, and Power in the Executive Branch. Trade Cloth. Lynne Rienner Publishers, Inc. Boulder, CO. 1997. 280p. ISBN:1-55587-658-7, ISBN13: 978-1-55587-658-6. Dewey:331.4/8135/0000973. LCCN:96-043234.
Audience: **u,f.**

Center for Gifted Education Staff **JK528.R56 2003**
The Road to the White House: Electing the American President. Trade Paper. Kendall/Hunt Publishing Company. Dubuque, IA. 2002. 384p. ISBN:0-7872-9348-2, ISBN13: 978-0-7872-9348-2. Dewey:324.973/0071/2. LCCN:2003-277219.
Audience: **g,l,u,f.**

Clift, Eleanor & Brazaitis, Tom **JK516.C524 2003**
Madam President: Women Blazing the Leadership Trail. Trade Paper. Routledge. New York, NY. 2003. 366p. Women and Politics Ser. ISBN:0-415-93432-X, ISBN13: 978-0-415-93432-9. Dewey:324/.082/0973. LCCN:2002-011136.
Audience: **u,f.**

Congressional Quarterly, Inc. Staff **JK552.C33 1997**
Cabinets and Counselors: The President and the Executive Branch. Ed. 2. Cloth Text. Congressional Quarterly, Inc. Washington, DC. 1997. 205p. ISBN:1-56802-309-X, ISBN13: 978-1-56802-309-0. Dewey:351.73. LCCN:97-001606.
Audience: **g,l,u,f.**

Congressional Quarterly, Inc. Staff **JK524.S45 1997**
Selecting the President: From 1789 to 1996. Cloth Text. Congressional Quarterly, Inc. Washington, DC. 1997. 240p. ISBN:1-56802-312-X, ISBN13: 978-1-56802-312-0. Dewey:324.6/3/0973. LCCN:97-006398.
Audience: **g,l,u,f.**

Eisinger, Robert M. **JK516.E37 2002**
The Evolution of Presidential Polling. Cloth Text. Cambridge University Press. New York, NY. 2003. 228p. ISBN:0-521-81680-7, ISBN13: 978-0-521-81680-9. Dewey:324. LCCN:2002-022283.
Audience: **u,f.** *Choice, 2003.*

Genovese, Michael A. **JK516.G49 2001**
The Power of the American Presidency, 1789-2000. Cloth Text. Oxford University Press, Inc. New York, NY. 2000. 288p. ISBN:0-19-512544-4, ISBN13: 978-0-19-512544-3. Dewey:352.23/0973. LCCN:99-040993.
Audience: **g,l,u,f.**

Gilmour, Robert S. & Halley, Alexis A. **JK585.W48 1994**
Who Makes Public Policy?: The Struggle for Control Between Congress and the Executive. Paper Text. CQ Press. Washington, DC. 1994. 400p. Public Administration and Public Policy Ser. ISBN:1-56643-004-6, ISBN13: 978-1-56643-004-3. Dewey:320.473/04. LCCN:93-034362.
Audience: **l,u,f.** *Choice, 1995.*

Hooton, Cornell G. **JK468.P64H66 1997**
Executive Governance: Presidental Administrations and Policy Change in the Federal Bureaucracy. Cloth Text. M. E. Sharpe Inc. Armonk, NY. 1997. 272p. Bureaucracies, Public Administration, and Public Policy Ser. ISBN:0-7656-0048-X, ISBN13: 978-0-7656-0048-6. Dewey:324.6/3/0973. LCCN:96-047879.
Audience: **u,f.** *Choice, 1998.*

Kellerman, Barbara & Barilleaux, Ryan J. **JK570.K45 1990**
The President As World Leader. Paper Text. St. Martin's Press. Gordonville, VA. 1990. 216p. ISBN:0-312-03603-5, ISBN13: 978-0-312-03603-4. Dewey:327.73/09045. LCCN:89-063906.
Audience: **g,l,u,f.**

Kelley, Christopher S. (Editor) **JK511.E93 2006**
Executing the Constitution: Putting the President Back into the Constitution. Book, Other. State University of New York Press. Albany, NY. 2006. x, 256p. SUNY Series in American Constitutionalism ISBN:0-7914-6727-9, ISBN13: 978-0-7914-6727-5. Dewey:352.23/5/0973. LCCN:2005-021345.
Audience: **u,f.**

Kerbel, Matthew Robert **JK516.K393 1991**
Beyond Persuasion: Organizational Efficiency and Presidential Power. Cloth Text. State University of New York Press. Albany, NY. 1991. 214p. SUNY Series on the Presidency, :Contemporary Issues ISBN:0-7914-0693-8, ISBN13: 978-0-7914-0693-9. Dewey:353.03/23. LCCN:90-042324.
Audience: **u,f.** *Choice, 1992.*

Kessler, Francis P. **JK516**
The Dilemmas of Presidential Leadership: Of Caretakers and Kings. Paper Text. Prentice Hall PTR. Upper Saddle River, NJ. 1982. 404p. ISBN:0-13-214593-6, ISBN13: 978-0-13-214593-0. Dewey:353.03/22. LCCN:81-010731.
Audience: **l,u,f.**

Martin, Janet M. **JK721.M34 2003**
The American Presidency and Women: Promise, Performance, and Illusion. Trade Cloth. Texas A&M University Press. College Station, TX. 2003. 416p. Joseph V. Hughes, Jr., and Holly O. Hughes Series in the Presidency and Leadership Studies, No. 15 ISBN:1-58544-245-3, ISBN13: 978-1-58544-245-4. Dewey:352.3/082/0973. LCCN:2002-014492.
Audience: **u,f.** *Choice, 2004.*

Mezey, Michael L. **JK585.M49 1989**
Congress, the President, and Public Policy. Cloth Text. Westview Press. Boulder, CO. 1989. 255p. ISBN:0-8133-0493-8, ISBN13: 978-0-8133-0493-9. Dewey:353.03/23. LCCN:89-032834.
Audience: **g,l,u,f.** *Choice, 1990.*

Milkis, Sidney M. **JK2261.M55 1993**
The President and the Parties: The Transformation of the American Party System since the New Deal. Cloth Text. Oxford University Press, Inc. New York, NY. 1993. 424p. ISBN:0-19-506620-0, ISBN13: 978-0-19-506620-3. Dewey:324.27300904. LCCN:92-042965.
Audience: **l,u,f.**

Milkis, Sidney M. & Nelson, Michael **JK511.M56 1994**
The American Presidency: Origins and Development, 1776-1993. Ed. 2. Paper Text. Congressional Quarterly, Inc. Washington, DC. 1994. 489p. ISBN:0-87187-766-X, ISBN13: 978-0-87187-766-6. Dewey:353.03/13. LCCN:93-043358.
Audience: **g,l,u,f.**

Peters, Charles & Nelson, Michael **JK421**
The Culture of Bureaucracy. Paper Text. Harcourt College Publishers. Fort Worth, TX. 1979. x, 278p. ISBN:0-03-044216-8, ISBN13: 978-0-03-044216-2. Dewey:353.01/08. LCCN:78-011051.
Audience: **l,u.**

Pfiffner, James P. **JK518.M36 1990**
Managerial Presidency. Paper Text. Harcourt Trade Publishers. New York, NY. 1991. 384p. ISBN:0-534-13194-8, ISBN13: 978-0-534-13194-4. Dewey:352.23/0973. LCCN:89-025183.
Audience: **g,u.**

Pfiffner, James P. **JK511.P47 1998**
The Modern Presidency. Ed. 2. Trade Cloth. Palgrave Macmillan. New York, NY. 1997. 258p. ISBN:0-312-21015-9, ISBN13: 978-0-312-21015-1. Dewey:973.92. LCCN:97-080009.
Audience: **l,u,f.** *Choice, 1994.*

Polsby, Nelson W. **JK1061.P6 1986**
Congress and the Presidency. Ed. 4. Paper Text. Prentice Hall PTR. Upper Saddle River, NJ. 1985. 304p. ISBN:0-13-167719-5, ISBN13: 978-0-13-167719-7. Dewey:320.473. LCCN:85-019326.
Audience: **l,u.**

Rudalevige, Andrew **JK585.R83 2002**
Managing the President's Program: Presidential Leadership and Legislative Policy Formulation. Trade Cloth. Princeton University Press. Princeton, NJ. 2002. 320p. Princeton Studies in American Politics ISBN:0-691-09071-8, ISBN13: 978-0-691-09071-9. Dewey:352.25/6/0973. LCCN:2001-051038.
Audience: **u,f.**

Schroedel, Jean Reith **JK305.S45 1994**
Congress, the President, and Policymaking: A Historical Analysis. Cloth Text. M. E. Sharpe Inc. Armonk, NY. 1994. 224p. American Political Institutions and Public Policy Ser. ISBN:1-56324-176-5, ISBN13: 978-1-56324-176-5. Dewey:320.4/04/0973. LCCN:93-028578.
Audience: **u,f.** *Choice, 1994.*

Schumaker, Paul D. & Loomis, Burdett A. (Editors) **JK528.C44 2002**
Choosing a President: The Electoral College and Beyond. Trade Paper. CQ Press. Washington, DC. 2002. 228p. ISBN:1-889119-53-9, ISBN13: 978-1-889119-53-3. Dewey:324.6/3/0973. LCCN:2001-005749.
Audience: **g,l,u,f.**

Shull, Steven A. & Shaw, Thomas C. **JK585.S44 1999**
Explaining Congressional-Presidential Relations: A Multiple Perspective Approach. Cloth Text. State University of New York Press. Albany, NY. 1999. 224p. SUNY Series on the Presidency, :Contemporary Issues ISBN:0-7914-4273-X, ISBN13: 978-0-7914-4273-9. Dewey:328.73/07456. LCCN:98-045327.
Audience: **u,f.** *Choice, 2000.*

Spitzer, Robert J. **JK586.S67 1988**
The Presidential Veto. Louis Fisher (Foreword by). Cloth Text. State University of New York Press. Albany, NY. 1988. 181p. SUNY Series in Leadership Studies ISBN:0-88706-802-2,

ISBN13: 978-0-88706-802-7. Dewey:353.03/72. LCCN:88-002119.
Audience: **u,f.** *Choice, 1989.*

Thompson, Kenneth W. (Editor) **JK516**
The American Presidency: Principles and Problems. Trade Cloth. University Press of America, Inc. Lanham, MD. 1983. 108p. ISBN:0-8191-3350-7, ISBN13: 978-0-8191-3350-2. Dewey:353.03/1. LCCN:82-045217.
Audience: **l,u,f.**

Warshaw, Shirley Anne **JK611.W37 1996**
Powersharing: White House-Cabinet Relations in the Modern Presidency. Cloth Text. State University of New York Press. Albany, NY. 1996. 380p. SUNY Series on the Presidency, :Contemporary Issues ISBN:0-7914-2869-9, ISBN13: 978-0-7914-2869-6. Dewey:353.04. LCCN:95-016871.
Audience: **u,f.** *Choice, 1996.*

Waterman, Richard W. **JK516.W376 2003**
The Changing American Presidency. Mass Market. Atomic Dog Publishing, Inc. Cincinnati, OH. 2003. 416p. ISBN:1-59260-030-1, ISBN13: 978-1-59260-030-4. Dewey:352.23/0973. LCCN:2002-113374.
Audience: **g,l,u,f.**

Watson, Robert P. & Gordon, Ann (Editors) **JK524.A77 2002**
Anticipating Madam President. Library Binding. Lynne Rienner Publishers, Inc. Boulder, CO. 2002. 260p. ISBN:1-58826-137-9, ISBN13: 978-1-58826-137-3. Dewey:324/.0973. LCCN:2002-073942.
Audience: **u,f.** *Choice, 2004.*

American Government and Politics > Federal Government > Executive Branch > President

Fisher, Louis **KF4565.F57 1991**
Constitutional Conflicts Between Congress and the President. Ed. 3. Trade Cloth. University Press of Kansas. Lawrence, KS. 1991. xvi, 328p. ISBN:0-7006-0490-1, ISBN13: 978-0-7006-0490-6. Dewey:342.73/044. LCCN:91-002240.
Audience: **u,f.** B *Choice, 1997.*

Fisher, Louis **KF4565.F57 1997**
Constitutional Conflicts Between Congress and the President. Ed. 4. Trade Cloth. University Press of Kansas. Lawrence, KS. 1997. 358p. ISBN:0-7006-0815-X, ISBN13: 978-0-7006-0815-7. Dewey:342.73/044. LCCN:96-035569.
Audience: **u,f.** B *Choice, 1997.*

Hersman, Rebecca K. C. **JZ1480.H47 2000**
Friends and Foes: How Congress and the President Really Make Foreign Policy. Trade Cloth. Brookings Institution Press. Washington, DC. 2000. ix, 142p. ISBN:0-8157-3566-9, ISBN13: 978-0-8157-3566-3. Dewey:353.1/3/0973. LCCN:00-008811.
Audience: **g,u,f.** *Choice, 2001.*

Kaplan, Leonard V. & Moran, Beverly I. (Editors) **E886.2.A44 2001**
Aftermath: The Clinton Impeachment and the Presidency in the Age of Political Spectacle. Trade Cloth. New York University Press. New York, NY. 2001. 384p. Critical America Ser. ISBN:0-8147-4742-6, ISBN13: 978-0-8147-4742-1. Dewey:973.929. LCCN:2001-001549.
Audience: **u,f.** *Choice, 2002.*

Nelson, Lyle Emerson **E176.1.N44 2002**
American Presidents: Year by Year. Trade Cloth. M. E. Sharpe Inc. Armonk, NY. 2004. 832p. ISBN:0-7656-8046-7, ISBN13: 978-0-7656-8046-4. Dewey:973/.09/9 B. LCCN:2002-030898.
Audience: **g,l,u,f.** *Choice, 2004.*

Posner, Richard A. **KF5076.C57P67 1999**
An Affair of State: The Investigation, Impeachment, and Trial of President Clinton. Trade Cloth. Harvard University Press. Cambridge, MA. 1999. 288p. ISBN:0-674-00080-3, ISBN13: 978-0-674-00080-3. Dewey:342.73/062. LCCN:99-024307.
Audience: **g.** *Choice, 2000.*

Schroedel, Jean Reith **JK305.S45 1994**
Congress, the President, and Policymaking: A Historical Analysis. Cloth Text. M. E. Sharpe Inc. Armonk, NY. 1994. 224p. American Political Institutions and Public Policy Ser. ISBN:1-56324-176-5, ISBN13: 978-1-56324-176-5. Dewey:320.4/04/0973. LCCN:93-028578.
Audience: **u,f.** *Choice, 1994.*

Smyrl, Marc **KF5060.S57 1988**
Conflict or Codetermination: The Congress, the President, and the Power to Make War. Trade Cloth. HarperCollins Publishers. New York, NY. 1988. 232p. ISBN:0-88730-310-2, ISBN13: 978-0-88730-310-4. Dewey:342.73/052. LCCN:88-019237.
Audience: **u,f.** *Choice, 1989.*

Sobel, Robert **E792.S64 1998**
Coolidge: An American Enigma. Trade Cloth. Regnery Publishing, Incorporated, An Eagle Publishing Company. Washington, DC. 1998. 517p. ISBN:0-89526-410-2, ISBN13: 978-0-89526-410-7. Dewey:973.91/5/092. LCCN:98-014826.
Audience: **g,l,u,f.**

Spitzer, Robert **JK585.S654 1992**
The President and Congress: Executive Hegemony at the Crossroads of American Government. Trade Cloth. Temple University Press. Philadelphia, PA. 1992. 320p. ISBN:1-56639-016-8, ISBN13: 978-1-56639-016-3. Dewey:320.473. LCCN:92-014781.
Audience: **u,f.** *Choice, 1993.*

Stid, Daniel D. **E766.S85 1998**
The President As Statesman: Woodrow Wilson and the Constitution. Trade Cloth. University Press of Kansas. Lawrence, KS. 2004. 244p. American Political Thought Ser. ISBN:0-7006-0884-2, ISBN13: 978-0-7006-0884-3. Dewey:973.91/3/092. LCCN:97-050019.
Audience: **u,f.** *Choice, 1998.*

Watson, W. Martin & Markman, Sherwin **E847.W38 2004**
Chief of Staff: Lyndon Johnson and His Presidency. Cloth over Boards. St. Martin's Press. Gordonville, VA. 2004. 368p. ISBN:0-312-28504-3, ISBN13: 978-0-312-28504-3. Dewey:973.923/092 B. LCCN:2004-046787.
Audience: **g,l,u,f.**

Wicker, Tom & Schlesinger, Arthur M. Jr. **E682.T74 2002**
Dwight D. Eisenhower. Cloth over Boards. Henry Holt & Company. New York, NY. 2002. 176p. The American Presidents

Ser. ISBN:0-8050-6907-0, ISBN13: 978-0-8050-6907-5. Dewey:973.8/3/092 B. LCCN:2002-069577.
Audience: **g,l,u,f.**

American Government and Politics > Federal Government > Executive Branch > Cabinet

Cohen, Jeffrey E. **JK611 .C64 1988**
The Politics of the U. S. Cabinet: Representation in the Executive Branch, 1789-1984. Trade Cloth. University of Pittsburgh Press. Pittsburgh, PA. 1988. 224p. Series in Policy and Institutional Studies ISBN:0-8229-3584-8, ISBN13: 978-0-8229-3584-1. Dewey:353.04. LCCN:89-002008.
Audience: **u,f.** *Choice, 1989.*

Regan, Donald T. **E877**
For the Record: From Wall Street to Washington. Trade Cloth. Random House Value Publishing. New York, NY. 1990. ISBN:0-517-02882-4, ISBN13: 978-0-517-02882-7. Dewey:973.927/092/4.
Audience: **g,u,f.**

Sobel, Robert & Sicilia, David B. (Editors) **E176**
The United States Executive Branch: A Biographical Directory of Heads of State and Cabinet Officials. Cloth Text. Greenwood Publishing Group, Inc. Portsmouth, NH. 2003. 688p. ISBN:0-313-31134-X, ISBN13: 978-0-313-31134-5. Dewey:351.73/092/2 B. LCCN:2002-028434.
Audience: **g,l,u,f.** *Choice, 2004.*

American Government and Politics > Federal Government > Executive Branch > Departments and Agencies

Barzelay, Michael & Amajani, Babak J. **JK6141.B37 1992**
Breaking Through Bureaucracy: A New Vision for Managing in Government. Alan Altshuler (Foreword by). Trade Cloth. University of California Press. Berkeley, CA. 1992. 237p. ISBN:0-520-07800-4, ISBN13: 978-0-520-07800-0. Dewey:353.977601. LCCN:91-039396.
Audience: **u,f.**

Lovinger, King F. (Compiled by) **JK411.L68 1987**
The Federal Government Subject Guide. Library Binding. McFarland & Company, Incorporated Publishers. Jefferson, NC. 1987. 149p. ISBN:0-89950-238-5, ISBN13: 978-0-89950-238-0. Dewey:353/.00025. LCCN:86-043179.
Audience: **g,l,u.**

Steigman, Andrew L. **JX1706.Z5S74 1985**
The Foreign Service of the United States: First Line of Defense. Cloth Text. Westview Press. Boulder, CO. 1985. 263p. Federal Departments, Agencies, and Systems Ser. ISBN:0-8133-0167-X, ISBN13: 978-0-8133-0167-9. Dewey:353.0089/09. LCCN:85-005078.
Audience: **u,f.** *Choice, 1986.*

Walton, Hanes Jr. **E185.615.W325 1988**
When the Marching Stopped: The Politics of Civil Rights Regulatory Agencies. Mary F. Berry (Introduction by). Cloth Text. State University of New York Press. Albany, NY. 1988. 263p. SUNY Series in Afro-American Studies ISBN:0-88706-687-9, ISBN13: 978-0-88706-687-0. Dewey:353.0081/1. LCCN:87-007081.
Audience: **u,f.** *Choice, 1989.*

Zwirn, Jerrold (Compiled by) **Z1223**
Accessing U. S. Government Information: Subject Guide to Jurisdiction of the Executive and Legislative Branches. Ed. 2. Cloth Text. Greenwood Publishing Group, Inc. Portsmouth, NH. 1996. 200p. Bibliographies and Indexes in Law and Political Science Ser., No. 24 ISBN:0-313-29765-7, ISBN13: 978-0-313-29765-6. Dewey:015.73/053. LCCN:95-038638.
Audience: **g,l,u,f.** *Choice, 1996.*

American Government and Politics > Federal Government > Legislative Branch. Congress

JK1108
LexisNexis Congressional. LexisNexis.
Audience: **g,l,u,f.**

Ahuja, Sunil & Dewhirst, Robert E. **JK19682000A**
The Roads to Congress 2000. Ed. 2. Paper Text. Thomson Wadsworth. Belmont, CA. 2001. 240p. ISBN:0-534-52692-6, ISBN13: 978-0-534-52692-4. Dewey:324.9773/0929. LCCN:2001-026225.
Audience: **l,u,f.**

Baker, Ross K. **JK1061.B33 1995**
House and Senate. Ed. 2. Paper Text. W. W. Norton & Company, Inc. New York, NY. 1995. 249p. ISBN:0-393-96318-7, ISBN13: 978-0-393-96318-2. Dewey:328.73. LCCN:95-005367.
Audience: **g,l,u,f.** *Choice, 1990.*

CQ Staff (Editor) **JK9.K73 2001**
American Congressional Dictionary. Ed. 3. Trade Cloth. CQ Press. Washington, DC. 2001. 288p. ISBN:1-56802-611-0, ISBN13: 978-1-56802-611-4. Dewey:328.73/003. LCCN:2001-001840.
Audience: **g,l,u,f.** *Choice, 2001.*

Dodd, Lawrence C. (Editor) **JK1021.C558 2004**
Congress Reconsidered. Ed. 8. Trade Paper. CQ Press. Washington, DC. 2004. 494p. ISBN:1-56802-859-8, ISBN13: 978-1-56802-859-0. Dewey:328.73. LCCN:2004-026308.
Audience: **l,u,f.**

Frantzich, Stephen E. & Schier, Steven E. **JK1041.F68 1995**
Congress: Games and Strategies. Trade Paper. McGraw-Hill Higher Education. Burr Ridge, IL. 1995. 336p. ISBN:0-697-14633-2, ISBN13: 978-0-697-14633-5. Dewey:328.73. LCCN:94-070434.
Audience: **l,u,f.**

Gill, LaVerne M. **E840.6.G55 1997**
African American Women in Congress. Cloth Text. Rutgers University Press. Piscataway, NJ. 1997. 256p. ISBN:0-8135-2352-4, ISBN13: 978-0-8135-2352-1. Dewey:328.73/092/2 B. LCCN:96-029294.
Audience: **g,l,u.**

Gimpel, James G. **JK2356.G55 1996**
Legislating Revolution: The Contract with America in Its First 100 Days. Trade Paper. Longman Publishing. Boston, MA. 1995. 224p. ISBN:0-205-18887-7, ISBN13: 978-0-205-18887-1. Dewey:324.2734/09/049. LCCN:95-038907.
Audience: **g,l,u,f.**

Gordon, Stacy B. **JK1991.5.C2G67 2004**
Campaign Contributions and Legislative Voting: A New Approach. Paper over Boards. Routledge. New York, NY. 2004. 224p. ISBN:0-415-94977-7, ISBN13: 978-0-415-94977-4. Dewey:328.794/0775. LCCN:2004-011917.
Audience: **u,f.**

Grofman, Bernard N. (Editor) **JK1140.L44 1996**
Legislative Term Limits: Public Choice Perspectives. Trade Cloth. Springer. New York, NY. 1996. 416p. Studies in Public Choice Ser., Vol. 10 ISBN:0-7923-9702-9, ISBN13: 978-0-7923-9702-1. Dewey:328.73/073. LCCN:95-052837.
Audience: **u,f.**

Harris, Fred R. **JK1161.H26 1993**
Deadlock or Decision: The U. S. Senate and the Rise of National Politics. Paper Text. Oxford University Press, Inc. New York, NY. 1993. 360p. Twentieth Century Fund Books ISBN:0-19-508026-2, ISBN13: 978-0-19-508026-1. Dewey:328.73/071. LCCN:92-043279.
Audience: **u,f.**

Harris, Fred R. **JK1021.H37 1995**
In Defense of Congress. Paper Text. Thomson Wadsworth. Belmont, CA. 1994. 177p. ISBN:0-312-09456-6, ISBN13: 978-0-312-09456-0. Dewey:328.73/07/0904. LCCN:94-062735.
Audience: **l,u,f.** *Choice, 1995.*

Jacobson, Gary C. **JK1067.J3 1991**
The Politics of Congressional Elections. Ed. 3. Trade Paper. Addison-Wesley Educational Publishers, Inc. Boston, MA. 1997. 280p. ISBN:0-06-500075-7, ISBN13: 978-0-06-500075-7. Dewey:324.973. LCCN:91-015314.
Audience: **l,u,f.**

Kahn, Kim Fridkin & Kenney, Patrick J. **JK2281.K24 1999**
The Spectacle of U. S. Senate Campaigns. Cloth Text. Princeton University Press. Princeton, NJ. 1999. 256p. ISBN:0-691-00504-4, ISBN13: 978-0-691-00504-1. Dewey:324.7/0973. LCCN:98-032011.
Audience: **u,f.** *Choice, 2000.*

Kenney, Patrick J. & Kahn, Kim Fridkin **JK2281.K239 2004**
No Holds Barred: Negativity in United States Senate Campaigns. Trade Paper. Prentice Hall PTR. Upper Saddle River, NJ. 2003. 144p. Real Politics in America Ser. ISBN:0-13-097760-8, ISBN13: 978-0-13-097760-1. Dewey:324.7/0973. LCCN:2003-015025.
Audience: **l,u,f.**

King-Meadows, Tyson & Schaller, Thomas F. **JK2488.K56 2006**
Devolution and Black State Legislators: Challenges and Choices in the 21st Century. Book, Other. State University of New York Press. Albany, NY. 2006. SUNY Series in African American Studies ISBN:0-7914-6729-5, ISBN13: 978-0-7914-6729-9. Dewey:328.73/0089/96073. LCCN:2005-014018.
Audience: **u,f.**

Kousser, Thad **JK2488.K68 2004**
Term Limits and the Dismantling of State Legislative Professionalism. Cloth Text. Cambridge University Press. New York, NY. 2004. 288p. ISBN:0-521-83985-8, ISBN13: 978-0-521-83985-3. Dewey:328.73/073. LCCN:2004-051842.
Audience: **u,f.**

Mann, Thomas E. & Ornstein, Norman J. **JK1140.C62 1994**
Congress, the Press, and the Public. Trade Paper. Brookings Institution Press. Washington, DC. 1994. 212p. ISBN:0-8157-5461-2, ISBN13: 978-0-8157-5461-9. Dewey:070.4/4932873. LCCN:94-026580.
Audience: **g,l,u,f.** *Choice, 1995.*

Mann, Thomas E. & Ornstein, Norman J. **JK1140.C62 1994**
Congress, the Press, and the Public. Trade Cloth. Brookings Institution Press. Washington, DC. 1994. 212p. ISBN:0-8157-5462-0, ISBN13: 978-0-8157-5462-6. Dewey:070.4/4932873. LCCN:94-026580.
Audience: **g,l,u,f.** *Choice, 1995.*

Martin, Fenton S. & Goehlert, Robert **JK1108.M349 1996**
How to Research Congress. Cloth Text. Congressional Quarterly, Inc. Washington, DC. 1996. 107p. ISBN:0-87187-870-4, ISBN13: 978-0-87187-870-0. Dewey:328.73/0072. LCCN:96-003867.
Audience: **g,l,u,f.** *Choice, 1996.*

Menifield, Charles E. & Shaffer, Stephen D. (Editors) **JK2488.P65 2005**
Politics in the New South: Representation of African Americans in Southern State Legislatures. Cloth Text. State University of New York Press. Albany, NY. 2005. 320p. SUNY Series in African American Studies ISBN:0-7914-6531-4, ISBN13: 978-0-7914-6531-8. Dewey:328.75/092/396073. LCCN:2004-062577.
Audience: **l,u,f.** *Choice, 2006.*

Moncrief, Gary F., et al. **JK2488.M664 2001**
Who Runs for the Legislature? Peverill Squire & Malcolm Edwin Jewell (Authors). Trade Paper. Prentice Hall PTR. Upper Saddle River, NJ. 2000. 144p. Real Politics in America Ser. ISBN:0-13-026608-6, ISBN13: 978-0-13-026608-8. Dewey:328.73/073. LCCN:00-058015.
Audience: **g,l,u.**

Patterson, Kelly D. & Shea, Daniel **JK1021.C67 2000**
Contemplating the People's Branch: Legislative Dynamics in the Twenty First Century. Paper Text. Prentice Hall PTR. Upper Saddle River, NJ. 2000. 360p. ISBN:0-13-040160-9, ISBN13: 978-0-13-040160-1. Dewey:328.73. LCCN:99-057666.
Audience: **l,u.**

Pomper, Gerald M. (Editor) **JK5262001**
The Election of 2000: Reports and Interpretations. Trade Paper. CQ Press. Washington, DC. 2001. 232p. ISBN:1-889119-46-6, ISBN13: 978-1-889119-46-5. Dewey:324.973/0929. LCCN:2001-000342.
Audience: **g,l,u,f.** *Choice, 2001.*

Rieselbach, Leroy N. **JK1061.R48 1995**
Congressional Politics: The Evolving Legislative System. Ed. 2. Trade Paper. Westview Press. Boulder, CO. 1995. 500p. Transforming American Politics Ser. ISBN:0-8133-2458-0, ISBN13: 978-0-8133-2458-6. Dewey:328.73. LCCN:94-038589.
Audience: **u,f.**

Ripley, Randall B. & Lindsay, James M. (Editors) **JK1081.C658 1993**
Congress Resurgent: Foreign and Domestic Policy on Capitol Hill. Trade Cloth. University of Michigan Press. Chicago, IL. 1993. 352p. Mershon Center Series on International Security and Foreign Policy ISBN:0-472-09533-1, ISBN13: 978-0-472-09533-9. Dewey:327.73/07658. LCCN:93-016033.
Audience: **u,f.** *Choice, 1994.*

Rosenthal, Alan **JK2495.R66 2004**
Heavy Lifting: The Job of the American Legislature. Trade Paper. CQ Press. Washington, DC. 2004. 262p. ISBN:1-56802-734-6, ISBN13: 978-1-56802-734-0. Dewey:328.73. LCCN:2004-010182.
Audience: **l,u,f.**

Schneier, Edward V. & Gross, Bertram M. **JK1096.S36 1993**
Legislative Strategy: Shaping Public Policy. Paper Text. Thomson Wadsworth. Belmont, CA. 1993. 289p. ISBN:0-312-05192-1, ISBN13: 978-0-312-05192-1. Dewey:328.73. LCCN:92-050020.
Audience: **l,u.** *Choice, 1993.*

Schroedel, Jean Reith **JK305.S45 1994**
Congress, the President, and Policymaking: A Historical Analysis. Cloth Text. M. E. Sharpe Inc. Armonk, NY. 1994. 224p. American Political Institutions and Public Policy Ser. ISBN:1-56324-176-5, ISBN13: 978-1-56324-176-5. Dewey:320.4/04/0973. LCCN:93-028578.
Audience: **u,f.** *Choice, 1994.*

Shea, Daniel M. **JK2276.S47 1995**
Transforming Democracy: Legislative Campaign Committees and Political Parties. Cloth Text. State University of New York Press. Albany, NY. 1995. 238p. ISBN:0-7914-2551-7, ISBN13: 978-0-7914-2551-0. Dewey:324.2747. LCCN:94-032958.
Audience: **u,f.**

Smith, Steven S., et al. **JK1041.S65 2005**
The American Congress. Ed. 4. Jason M. Roberts & Ryan J. Vander Wielen (Authors). Cloth Text. Cambridge University Press. New York, NY. 2005. 458p. ISBN:0-521-85676-0, ISBN13: 978-0-521-85676-8. Dewey:328.73. LCCN:2005-011723.
Audience: **g,l,u.**

Weisberg, Herbert F. **JK5261988M**
Democracy's Feast: Elections in America. Paper Text. Seven Bridges Press, LLC. New York, NY. 1995. 370p. American Politics Ser. ISBN:1-56643-011-9, ISBN13: 978-1-56643-011-1. Dewey:324.973/0928. LCCN:94-046140.
Audience: **l,u,f.** *Choice, 1995.*

American Government and Politics > Federal Government > Legislative Branch. Congress > Powers

Burgess, Susan R. **KF8700.B87 1991**
Contest for Constitutional Authority: The Abortion and War Powers Debates. Trade Cloth. University Press of Kansas. Lawrence, KS. 1992. xiv, 178p. ISBN:0-7006-0522-3, ISBN13: 978-0-7006-0522-4. Dewey:342.73. LCCN:91-034979.
Audience: **u,f.** *Choice, 1992.*

Cox, Andrew & Kirby, Stephen **UA647.C83 1986**
Congress, Parliament and Defence: The Impact of Legislative Reform on Defence Accountability in Britain and America. Cloth Text. Palgrave Macmillan. New York, NY. 1986. 246p. ISBN:0-312-16243-X, ISBN13: 978-0-312-16243-6. Dewey:355/.033/541. LCCN:86-003812.
Audience: **u,f.** *Choice, 1987.*

Devins, Neal & Whittington, Keith E. **KF4550.C568 2005**
Congress and the Constitution. Trade Cloth. Duke University Press. Durham, NC. 2005. 320p. Constitutional Conflicts Ser. ISBN:0-8223-3586-7, ISBN13: 978-0-8223-3586-3. Dewey:342.7302. LCCN:2005-006505.
Audience: **u,f.** *Choice, 2005.*

Farrier, Jasmine **JK1021.F37 2004**
Passing the Buck: Congress, the Budget, and Deficits. Trade Cloth. University Press of Kentucky. Lexington, KY. 2004. 320p. ISBN:0-8131-2335-6, ISBN13: 978-0-8131-2335-6. Dewey:328.73/0778. LCCN:2004-010629.
Audience: **g,u,f.** *Choice, 2005.*

Fisher, Louis **JK305.F53 2000**
Congressional Abdication on War and Spending. Trade Cloth. Texas A&M University Press. College Station, TX. 2000. xv, 220p. Joseph V. Hughes, Jr., and Holly O. Hughes Series in the Presidency and Leadership Studies, Vol. 7 ISBN:0-89096-950-7, ISBN13: 978-0-89096-950-2. Dewey:328.73/074. LCCN:00-027191.
Audience: **u,f.** *Choice, 2001.*

Fisher, Louis **KF4565.F57 1997**
Constitutional Conflicts Between Congress and the President. Ed. 4. Trade Cloth. University Press of Kansas. Lawrence, KS. 1997. 358p. ISBN:0-7006-0815-X, ISBN13: 978-0-7006-0815-7. Dewey:342.73/044. LCCN:96-035569.
Audience: **u,f.** *Choice, 1997.*

Harrison, Robert **JK1041.H37 2004**
Congress, Progressive Reform, and the New American State. Trade Cloth. Cambridge University Press. New York, NY. 2004. 310p. ISBN:0-521-82789-2, ISBN13: 978-0-521-82789-8. Dewey:320/.6/097309041. LCCN:2003-055310.
Audience: **u,f.** *Choice, 2004.*

Hersman, Rebecca K. C. **JZ1480.H47 2000**
Friends and Foes: How Congress and the President Really Make Foreign Policy. Trade Cloth. Brookings Institution Press. Washington, DC. 2000. ix, 142p. ISBN:0-8157-3566-9, ISBN13: 978-0-8157-3566-3. Dewey:353.1/3/0973. LCCN:00-008811.
Audience: **g,u,f.** *Choice, 2001.*

Jones, Charles O. **JK305.J64 1999**
Clinton and Congress, 1993-1996: Risk, Restoration, and Reelection. Trade Cloth. University of Oklahoma Press. Norman, OK. 1999. 240p. Julian J. Rothbaum Distinguished Lecture Ser., Vol. 7 ISBN:0-8061-3164-0, ISBN13: 978-0-8061-3164-1. Dewey:320.973/09/049z. LCCN:99-010985.
Audience: **u,f.** *Choice, 2000.*

Landsberg, Brian K. **KF154.M35 2004**
Major Acts of Congress. Trade Cloth. Thomson Gale. Farmington Hills, MI. 2003. ISBN:0-02-865751-9, ISBN13: 978-0-02-865751-6. Dewey:348.73/22. LCCN:2003-018747.
Audience: **g,l,u,f.** *Choice, 2004.*

Merry, Henry J. **KF4930**
The Constitutional System: The Group Character of the Elected Institutions. Trade Cloth. Greenwood Publishing Group, Inc. Portsmouth, NH. 1986. 225p. ISBN:0-275-92185-9, ISBN13: 978-0-275-92185-9. Dewey:342.73/044. LCCN:86-015162.
Audience: **u,f.** *Choice, 1987.*

Peterson, Mark A. **JK585.P48 1990**
Legislating Together: The White House and Capitol Hill from Eisenhower to Reagan. Trade Cloth. Harvard University Press. Cambridge, MA. 1990. 352p. ISBN:0-674-52415-2, ISBN13: 978-0-674-52415-6. Dewey:320.473. LCCN:89-071618.
Audience: **u,f.** *Choice, 1991.*

Raven-Hansen, Peter (Editor) **KF5060**
First Use of Nuclear Weapons: Under the Constitution, Who Decides? Trade Cloth. Greenwood Publishing Group, Inc. Portsmouth, NH. 1987. 259p. Contributions in Legal Studies Ser., No. 38 ISBN:0-313-25520-2, ISBN13: 978-0-313-25520-5. Dewey:342.73/062. LCCN:86-033655.
Audience: **u,f.** *Choice, 1988.*

Schoenbrod, David **KF5411.S36 1993**
Power Without Responsibility: How Congress Abuses the People Through Delegation. Trade Cloth. Yale University Press. Cumberland, RI. 1993. 264p. ISBN:0-300-05363-0, ISBN13: 978-0-300-05363-0. Dewey:347.30266. LCCN:93-013260.
Audience: **g,l,u,f.** *Choice, 1994.*

Schroedel, Jean Reith **JK305.S45 1994**
Congress, the President, and Policymaking: A Historical Analysis. Cloth Text. M. E. Sharpe Inc. Armonk, NY. 1994. 224p. American Political Institutions and Public Policy Ser. ISBN:1-56324-176-5, ISBN13: 978-1-56324-176-5. Dewey:320.4/04/0973. LCCN:93-028578.
Audience: **u,f.** *Choice, 1994.*

Spitzer, Robert **JK585.S654 1992**
The President and Congress: Executive Hegemony at the Crossroads of American Government. Trade Cloth. Temple University Press. Philadelphia, PA. 1992. 320p. ISBN:1-56639-016-8, ISBN13: 978-1-56639-016-3. Dewey:320.473. LCCN:92-014781.
Audience: **u,f.** *Choice, 1993.*

Stern, Gary M. & Halperin, Morton H. (Editors) **KF5060**
The U. S. Constitution and the Power to Go to War: Historical and Current Perspectives. Trade Cloth. Greenwood Publishing Group, Inc. Portsmouth, NH. 1993. 208p. Contributions in Military Studies, No. 150 ISBN:0-313-28958-1, ISBN13: 978-0-313-28958-3. Dewey:347.30262. LCCN:93-015840.
Audience: **u,f.** *Choice, 1994.*

Wormuth, Francis D., et al. **KF4941.W67 1985**
To Chain the Dog of War: The War Power of Congress in History and Law. Edwin B. Firmage & Francis Butler (Authors). Library Binding. Southern Methodist University Press. Dallas, TX. 1987. 360p. ISBN:0-87074-206-X, ISBN13: 978-0-87074-206-4. Dewey:342.73/062. LCCN:85-014249.
Audience: **u,f.** *Choice, 1986.*

American Government and Politics > Federal Government > Legislative Branch. Congress > Procedures

KF4992
☐ The House Practice: A Guide to the Rules, Precedents and Procedures of the House.
http://www.gpoaccess.gov/hpractice/index.html
U.S. Government Printing Office.
Audience: **g,l,u,f.**

Miller, Ann
☐ Legislation Into Law.
http://docs.lib.duke.edu/federal/guides/LandL1st.html
Duke University.
Audience: **g,l,u.**

Oleszek, Walter J. **JK1096.O43 1996**
Congressional Procedures and the Policy Process. Ed. 4. Cloth Text. Congressional Quarterly, Inc. Washington, DC. 1995. 373p. ISBN:0-87187-704-X, ISBN13: 978-0-87187-704-8. Dewey:328.73. LCCN:95-031596.
Audience: **g,l,u,f.** BCL3 *Choice, 1996.*

United States Senate
☐ Rules and Procedure.
http://www.senate.gov/reference/reference_index_subjects/Rules_and_Procedure_vrd.htm
Audience: **g,l,u,f.**

American Government and Politics > Federal Government > Legislative Branch. Congress > House of Representatives

KF4992
☐ The House Practice: A Guide to the Rules, Precedents and Procedures of the House.
http://www.gpoaccess.gov/hpractice/index.html
U.S. Government Printing Office.
Audience: **g,l,u,f.**

Bach, Stanley J. & Smith, Steven S. **KF4992.B33 1988**
Managing Uncertainty in the House of Representatives: Adaptation and Innovation in Special Rules. Trade Cloth. Brookings Institution Press. Washington, DC. 1988. 154p. ISBN:0-8157-0742-8, ISBN13: 978-0-8157-0742-4. Dewey:328.73/05. LCCN:88-030424.
Audience: **u,f.** *Choice, 1989.*

Cook, Timothy **JK1447.C66 1989**
Making Laws and Making News: Media Strategies in the U. S. House of Representatives. Trade Cloth. Brookings Institution Press. Washington, DC. 1989. 240p. ISBN:0-8157-1558-7, ISBN13: 978-0-8157-1558-0. Dewey:328.73/0731. LCCN:89-022271.
Audience: **u,f.** *Choice, 1990.*

DeGregorio, Christine A. **JK1319.D44 1997**
Networks of Champions: Leadership, Access and Advisory in the U. S. House of Representatives. Trade Cloth. University of Michigan Press. Chicago, IL. 1997. 304p. ISBN:0-472-10762-3, ISBN13: 978-0-472-10762-9. Dewey:324/.4/092273. LCCN:96-039404.
Audience: **u,f.** *Choice, 1997.*

Herrick, Rebekah **JK1379**
Fashioning the More Ethical Representative: The Impact of Ethics Reforms in the U. S. House of Representatives. Trade Cloth. Greenwood Publishing Group, Inc. Portsmouth, NH. 2003. 168p. ISBN:0-275-98018-9, ISBN13: 978-0-275-98018-4. Dewey:328.73/072. LCCN:2003-042096.
Audience: **l,u,f.** *Choice, 2004.*

Hibbing, John R. **JK1319.H53 1991**
Congressional Careers: Contours of Life in the U. S. House of Representatives. Trade Paper. University of North Carolina Press. Chapel Hill, NC. 1991. 230p. ISBN:0-8078-4340-7, ISBN13: 978-0-8078-4340-6. Dewey:328.73/073/0922 B. LCCN:91-000182.
Audience: **l,u,f.** *Choice, 1992.*

Kennon, Donald R. **Z7165.U5K45 1985**
The Speakers of the U. S. House of Representatives: A Bibliography, Seventeen Eighty-Nine to Nineteen Eighty-Four. Trade Cloth. Johns Hopkins University Press. Baltimore, MD. 1986. 360p. Studies in Historical and Political Science, No. 1 ISBN:0-8018-2786-8, ISBN13: 978-0-8018-2786-0. Dewey:016.32873/0762. LCCN:85-045047.
Audience: **l,u,f.** *Choice, 1986.*

Palazzolo, Daniel J. **JK1411.P35 1992**
The Speaker and the Budget: Leadership in the Post-Reform House of Representatives. Cloth Text. University of Pittsburgh Press. Pittsburgh, PA. 1992. 272p. Series in Policy and Institutional Studies ISBN:0-8229-3715-8, ISBN13: 978-0-8229-3715-9. Dewey:353.0072221. LCCN:92-011903.
Audience: **u,f.** *Choice, 1993.*

Peters, Ronald W. Jr. **JK1411.S64 1994**
The Speaker: Leadership in the U. S. House of Representatives. Trade Cloth. Congressional Education Associates. Washington, DC. 1994. 325p. ISBN:0-87187-947-6, ISBN13: 978-0-87187-947-9. Dewey:328.73/0762. LCCN:94-044151.
Audience: **l,u,f.** *Choice, 1995.*

Sinclair, Barbara **JK1411.S55 1995**
Legislators, Leaders, and Lawmaking: The U. S. House of Representatives in the Postreform Era. Trade Cloth. Johns Hopkins University Press. Baltimore, MD. 1981. 352p. ISBN:0-8018-4955-1, ISBN13: 978-0-8018-4955-8. Dewey:328.73/0762. LCCN:94-033953.
Audience: **u,f.** *Choice, 1995.*

Wawro, Gregory **JK1319.W38 2000**
Legislative Entrepreneurship in the U.S. House of Representatives. Cloth over Boards. University of Michigan Press. Chicago, IL. 2000. 208p. Michigan Studies in Political Analysis ISBN:0-472-11153-1, ISBN13: 978-0-472-11153-4. Dewey:328.73/077. LCCN:00-023486.
Audience: **u,f.** *Choice, 2001.*

Zimmerman, Joseph F. & Rule, Wilma (Editors) **JK1319**
The U. S. House of Representatives: Reform or Rebuild? Trade Cloth. Greenwood Publishing Group, Inc. Portsmouth, NH. 2000. 248p. ISBN:0-275-96579-1, ISBN13: 978-0-275-96579-2. Dewey:328.73/0704. LCCN:99-053472.
Audience: **u,f.** *Choice, 2001.*

American Government and Politics > Federal Government > Legislative Branch. Congress > Senate

Baker, Ross K. **JK1061.B33 1989**
House and Senate. Trade Cloth. W. W. Norton & Company, Inc. New York, NY. 1989. 237p. ISBN:0-393-02706-6, ISBN13: 978-0-393-02706-8. Dewey:328.73. LCCN:89-003194.
Audience: **g,l,u,f.** *Choice, 1990.*

Binder, Sarah A. & Smith, Steven S. **JK1161.B56 1997**
Politics or Principle?: Filibustering in the United States Senate. Trade Cloth. Brookings Institution Press. Washington, DC. 1997. 247p. ISBN:0-8157-0952-8, ISBN13: 978-0-8157-0952-7. Dewey:328.73/071. LCCN:96-025372.
Audience: **g,l,u,f.**

Campbell, Colton C. & Rae, Nicol C. (Editors) **JK1161.C66 2001**
The Contentious Senate: Partisanship, Ideology and the Myth of Cool Judgement. Book, Other. Rowman & Littlefield Publishers, Inc. Lanham, MD. 2000. 224p. ISBN:0-7425-0115-9, ISBN13: 978-0-7425-0115-7. Dewey:328.73/01. LCCN:00-059055.
Audience: **u,f.** *Choice, 2001.*

Evans, C. Lawrence **JK1239.E93 1991**
Leadership in Committee: A Comparative Analysis of Leadership Behavior in the U. S. Senate. Trade Cloth. University of Michigan Press. Chicago, IL. 1991. 224p. ISBN:0-472-10237-0, ISBN13: 978-0-472-10237-2. Dewey:328.73/071. LCCN:91-021272.
Audience: **u,f.** *Choice, 1992.*

Fenno, Richard F. Jr. **JK1161.F46 1991**
Learning to Legislate. Trade Cloth. Congressional Quarterly, Inc. Washington, DC. 1991. 300p. ISBN:0-87187-628-0, ISBN13: 978-0-87187-628-7. Dewey:328.73/0731. LCCN:91-004038.
Audience: **g,l,u,f.** *Choice, 1992.*

Greenberg, Ellen **JK1067.G74 1996**
The House and Senate Explained: The People's Guide to Congress. Trade Cloth. W. W. Norton & Company, Inc. New York, NY. 1996. 192p. ISBN:0-393-03984-6, ISBN13: 978-0-393-03984-9. Dewey:328.73/003. LCCN:96-012291.
Audience: **g,l,u.**

Gronke, Paul **JK1967.G76 2000**
The Electorate, the Campaign, and the Office: A Unified Approach to Senate and House Elections. Trade Cloth. University of Michigan Press. Chicago, IL. 2000. 216p. ISBN:0-472-11131-0, ISBN13: 978-0-472-11131-2. Dewey:324.973/092. LCCN:00-031520.
Audience: **u,f.** *Choice, 2001.*

Kubiak, Greg D. **JK1991.K83 1994**
The Gilded Dome: The U. S. Senate and Campaign Finance Reform. Trade Cloth. University of Oklahoma Press. Norman, OK. 1994. 288p. ISBN:0-8061-2621-3, ISBN13: 978-0-8061-2621-0. Dewey:324.7/8/0973. LCCN:93-045027.
Audience: **g,u,f.** *Choice, 1994.*

Loomis, Burdett A. (Editor) **JK1161.E77 2000**
Esteemed Colleagues: Civility and Deliberation in the U. S. Senate. Trade Cloth. Brookings Institution Press. Washington, DC. 2000. 264p. ISBN:0-8157-5294-6, ISBN13: 978-0-8157-5294-3. Dewey:328.73/071. LCCN:00-010381.
Audience: **g,u,f.** *Choice, 2001.*

Malsberger, John W. **JK1161.M34 2000**
From Obstruction to Moderation: The Transformation of Senate Conservatism, 1938-1952. Trade Cloth. Susquehanna University Press. Cranbury, NJ. 2000. 320p. ISBN:1-57591-026-8, ISBN13: 978-1-57591-026-0. Dewey:328.73/0775. LCCN:99-040422.
Audience: **u,f.** *Choice, 2001.*

Rossum, Ralph A. **KF4600.R67 2001**
Federalism, the Supreme Court and the Seventeenth Amendment: The Irony of Constitutional Democracy. Trade Cloth. Lexington Books. Lanham, MD. 2001. 312p. ISBN:0-7391-0285-0, ISBN13: 978-0-7391-0285-5. Dewey:320.473/049. LCCN:2001-038133.
Audience: **g,l,u,f.** *Choice, 2002.*

Schiller, Wendy J. **JK1161.S35 2000**
Partners and Rivals: Representation in U. S. Senate Delegations. Cloth Text. Princeton University Press. Princeton, NJ. 2000. 192p. ISBN:0-691-04886-X, ISBN13: 978-0-691-04886-4. Dewey:328.73/071. LCCN:99-059302.
Audience: **u,f.** *Choice, 2000.*

Smith, Steven S. **JK1096.S58 1989**
Call to Order: Floor Politics in the House and Senate. Trade Cloth. Brookings Institution Press. Washington, DC. 1989. 270p. ISBN:0-8157-8014-1, ISBN13: 978-0-8157-8014-4. Dewey:328.73/077. LCCN:89-009802.
Audience: **g,l,u,f.** *Choice, 1990.*

United States Senate
Rules and Procedure.
http://www.senate.gov/reference/reference_index_subjects/Rules_and_Procedure_vrd.htm
Audience: **g,l,u,f.**

Whalen, Thomas J. **F71.W49 2000**
Kennedy Versus Lodge: The 1952 Massachusetts Senate Race. Robert Dallek (Foreword by). Trade Cloth. Northeastern University Press. Boston, MA. 2000. xii, 216p. ISBN:1-55553-462-7, ISBN13: 978-1-55553-462-2. Dewey:324.9744/043. LCCN:00-033235.
Audience: **g,u,f.** *Choice, 2001.*

Wirls, Daniel & Wirls, Stephen **JK1161.W57 2003**
The Invention of the United States Senate. Trade Cloth. Johns Hopkins University Press. Baltimore, MD. 2004. 288p. Interpreting American Politics Ser. ISBN:0-8018-7438-6, ISBN13: 978-0-8018-7438-3. Dewey:328.73/071. LCCN:2003-006241.
Audience: **u,f.** *Choice, 2004.*

American Government and Politics > Federal Government > Judicial Branch

Judicial Branch. Paper Text. Peoples Publishing Group, Incorporated, The. Saddle Brook, NJ. Dewey:320.4.
Audience: **g,l,u.**

K3367
The Judicial Branch. Video, VHS Format, Trade Paper. Schlessinger Media. Wynnewood, PA. 2002. United States Government Ser. Dewey:347.73.
Audience: **u,f.**

Beier, Anne **KF8742.Z9B45 2004**
The Supreme Court and the Judicial Branch. Library Binding. Rosen Publishing Group, Incorporated, The. New York, NY. 2004. 32p. A Primary Source Library of American Citizenship ISBN:0-8239-4478-6, ISBN13: 978-0-8239-4478-1. Dewey:347.73/26. LCCN:2003-013365.
Audience: **g,l,u.**

Cambridge Educational (Produced by) **KF8700**
The Judicial Branch of Government. DVD. Films Media Group. Princeton, NJ. 1995. ISBN:0-7365-6216-8, ISBN13: 978-0-7365-6216-4. Dewey:347.7306.
Audience: **l,u.**

Carp, Robert A. & Stidham, Ronald **KF8719.C33 2001**
The Federal Courts. Ed. 4. Trade Paper. CQ Press. Washington, DC. 2001. xiv, 258p. ISBN:1-56802-591-2, ISBN13: 978-1-56802-591-9. Dewey:347.73/2. LCCN:2001-023139.
Audience: **g,l.** *Choice, 1986.*

Carp, Robert A., et al. **KF8700.C37 2004**
Judicial Process in America. Ed. 6. Ronald Stidham & Kenneth L. Manning (Authors). Trade Paper. CQ Press. Washington, DC. 2004. 425p. ISBN:1-56802-828-8, ISBN13: 978-1-56802-828-6. Dewey:347.73/1. LCCN:2003-026621.
Audience: **g,l,u,f.** *Choice, 2001.*

Giddens-White, Bryon **KF8742.Z9G53 2006**
Our Government: The Supreme Court and the Judicial Branch. Trade Cloth. Heinemann Library. Chicago, IL. 2005. 32p. ISBN:1-4034-6603-3, ISBN13: 978-1-4034-6603-7. Dewey:347.73/26. LCCN:2005-008666.
Audience: **g,l,u.**

Hall, Kermit L. (Editor) **KF8700.J83 2005**
The Judicial Branch. Saddle Stitched, Cloth over Boards, Dust Jacket. Oxford University Press, Inc. New York, NY. 2005. 579p. Institutions of American Democracy Ser. ISBN:0-19-517172-1, ISBN13: 978-0-19-517172-3. Dewey:347.73. LCCN:2005-017853.
Audience: **g,l,u,f.**

Hall, Kermit L. & McGuire, Kevin T. (Editors) **KF8700 .J83**
Institutions of American Democracy: The Judicial Branch. Trade Paper. Oxford University Press, Inc. New York, NY. 2006. 624p. ISBN:0-19-530917-0, ISBN13: 978-0-19-530917-1. Dewey:347.73.
Audience: **u,f.**

Powers, Stephen & Rothman, Stanley **KF5130.P69 2002**
[e] The Least Dangerous Branch?: Consequences of Judicial Activism. E-Book. Greenwood Publishing Group, Inc. Portsmouth, NH. ISBN:0-313-01226-1, ISBN13: 978-0-313-01226-6. Dewey:347.73/1.
Audience: **u,f.** *Choice, 2003.*

Powers, Stephen & Rothman, Stanley **KF5130**
The Least Dangerous Branch?: Consequences of Judicial Activism. Smith College, Center for the Study of Social and Political Change Staff (Contribution by). Trade Cloth. Greenwood Publishing Group, Inc. Portsmouth, NH. 2002. 232p. ISBN:0-275-97536-3, ISBN13: 978-0-275-97536-4. Dewey:347.73/1. LCCN:2002-025311.
Audience: **u,f.** *Choice, 2003.*

Scholastic, Inc. Staff (Contribution by) **JK40**
Our Nation's Government: Judicial Branch. Trade Cloth. Scholastic, Inc. New York, NY. 1998. ISBN:0-590-26622-5, ISBN13: 978-0-590-26622-2. Dewey:320.473.
Audience: **g,l,u.**

Tobin, Robert **KF8736.T63 2004**
Creating the Judicial Branch: The Unfinished Reform. Trade Paper. iUniverse, Inc. Lincoln, NE. 2004. 314p. ISBN:0-595-32277-8, ISBN13: 978-0-595-32277-0. Dewey:347.731. LCCN:2005-281834.
Audience: **u,f.**

American Government and Politics > Federal Government > Judicial Branch > Supreme Court

Abraham, Henry J. **KF8742.A72 1992**
Justices and Presidents: A Political History of Appointments to the Supreme Court. Ed. 3. Trade Cloth. Oxford University Press, Inc. New York, NY. 1992. 480p. ISBN:0-19-506557-3, ISBN13: 978-0-19-506557-2. Dewey:347.73/2634. LCCN:91-010117.
Audience: **g,l,u,f.** *Choice, 1992.*

Abraham, Henry J. **KF8742.A72 1999**
Justices, Presidents and Senators: A History of the U. S. Supreme Court Appointments from Washington to Clinton. Ed. 4. Book, Other. Rowman & Littlefield Publishers, Inc. Lanham, MD. 1999. 448p. ISBN:0-8476-9604-9, ISBN13: 978-0-8476-9604-8. Dewey:347.73/2634. LCCN:99-023000.
Audience: **g.** *Choice, 2000.*

Ackerman, Bruce **E331.A15 2005**
The Failure of the Founding Fathers: Jefferson, Marshall, and the Rise of Presidential Democracy. Trade Cloth. Harvard University Press. Cambridge, MA. 2005. 400p. ISBN:0-674-01866-4, ISBN13: 978-0-674-01866-2. Dewey:320.973/09/034. LCCN:2005-047034.
Audience: **g,u,f.** *Choice, 2006.*

Atkinson, David N. **KF8744.A98 1999**
Leaving the Bench: Supreme Court Justices at the End. Trade Cloth. University Press of Kansas. Lawrence, KS. 1999. xiv, 248p. ISBN:0-7006-0946-6, ISBN13: 978-0-7006-0946-8. Dewey:347.73/2634. LCCN:98-054752.
Audience: **u,f.** *Choice, 1999.*

Banks, Christopher P. & Green, John C. (Editors) **KF8742.S55 2001**
Superintending Democracy: The Courts and the Political Process. Trade Cloth. University of Akron Press, The. Akron, OH. 2001. 396p. Series on Law, Politics, and Society ISBN:1-884836-72-0, ISBN13: 978-1-884836-72-5. Dewey:342.73/07. LCCN:2001-000480.
Audience: **u,f.** *Choice, 2002.*

Behuniak, Susan M. **KF3823.B44 1999**
Caring Jurisprudence: Listening to Patients at the Supreme Court. Book, Other. Rowman & Littlefield Publishers, Inc. Lanham, MD. 1999. 208p. ISBN:0-8476-9454-2, ISBN13: 978-0-8476-9454-9. Dewey:344.73/041. LCCN:99-016198.
Audience: **u,f.** *Choice, 2000.*

Brenner, Saul & Spaeth, Harold J. **KF8742.S59 1990**
Studies in U. S. Supreme Court Behavior. Trade Cloth. Garland Publishing, Inc. New York, NY. 1990. 352p. ISBN:0-8240-8243-5, ISBN13: 978-0-8240-8243-7. Dewey:347.73/26/09. LCCN:90-002848.
Audience: **u,f.** *Choice, 1991.*

Brigham, John **KF8742.B73 1987**
The Cult of the Court. Trade Cloth. Temple University Press. Philadelphia, PA. 1987. 248p. ISBN:0-87722-486-2, ISBN13: 978-0-87722-486-0. Dewey:347.73/26. LCCN:86-030179.
Audience: **g,u,f.** *Choice, 1988.*

Brisbin, Richard A. Jr. **KF8745.S33B75 1997**
Justice Antonin Scalia and the Conservative Revival. Trade Cloth. Johns Hopkins University Press. Baltimore, MD. 1996. 488p. ISBN:0-8018-5432-6, ISBN13: 978-0-8018-5432-3. Dewey:347.30735. LCCN:96-022883.
Audience: **u,f.** *Choice, 1997.*

Burgess, Susan R. **KF8700.B87 1991**
Contest for Constitutional Authority: The Abortion and War Powers Debates. Trade Cloth. University Press of Kansas. Lawrence, KS. 1992. xiv, 178p. ISBN:0-7006-0522-3, ISBN13: 978-0-7006-0522-4. Dewey:342.73. LCCN:91-034979.
Audience: **u,f.** *Choice, 1992.*

Comiskey, Michael **KF8742.C63 2004**
Seeking Justices: The Judging of Supreme Court Nominees. Trade Cloth. University Press of Kansas. Lawrence, KS. 2004. 256p. ISBN:0-7006-1346-3, ISBN13: 978-0-7006-1346-5. Dewey:347.73/2634. LCCN:2004-013285.
Audience: **u,f.** *Choice, 2005.*

Cooper, Phillip J. **KF8742.C66 1995**
Battles on the Bench: Conflict Inside the Supreme Court. Trade Cloth. University Press of Kansas. Lawrence, KS. 1999. xii, 288p. ISBN:0-7006-0737-4, ISBN13: 978-0-7006-0737-2. Dewey:347.73/26. LCCN:95-031618.
Audience: **l,u.** *Choice, 1996.*

Cortner, Richard C. **KF224.B76C67 1986**
A "Scottsboro" Case in Mississippi: The Supreme Court and Brown vs. Mississippi. Trade Cloth. University Press of Mississippi. Jackson, MS. 1986. 192p. ISBN:0-87805-284-4, ISBN13: 978-0-87805-284-4. Dewey:345.73/02523. LCCN:85-020174.
Audience: **g,l,u,f.** *Choice, 1986.*

Currie, David P. **KF4550.C87 1985**
The Constitution in the Supreme Court: The First Hundred Years, 1789-1888. Trade Cloth. University of Chicago Press. Chicago, IL. 1995. xiv, 506p. ISBN:0-226-13108-4, ISBN13: 978-0-226-13108-5. Dewey:342.73. LCCN:85-001205.
Audience: **u,f.** *Choice, 1986.*

Currie, David P. **KF4550.C873 1990**
The Constitution in the Supreme Court: The Second Century, 1888-1986. Trade Cloth. University of Chicago Press. Chicago, IL. 1990. 682p. ISBN:0-226-13111-4, ISBN13: 978-0-226-13111-5. Dewey:342.73/029. LCCN:90-034143.
Audience: **u,f.** *Choice, 1991.*

Davis, Richard **KF8742.D383 2005**
Electing Justice: Fixing the Supreme Court Nomination Process. Trade Cloth. Oxford University Press, Inc. New York, NY. 2005. 224p. ISBN:0-19-518109-3, ISBN13: 978-0-19-518109-8. Dewey:347.73/2634. LCCN:2004-015898.
Audience: **u,f.** *Choice, 2006.*

Dworkin, Ronald (Editor) **KF5074.2**
A Badly Flawed Election: Debating Bush v. Gore, the Supreme Court and the American Democracy. Trade Cloth. New Press, The. New York, NY. 2002. 352p. ISBN:1-56584-737-7, ISBN13: 978-1-56584-737-8. Dewey:342.73/075. LCCN:2002-019759.
Audience: **g,l,u,f.**

Eastland, Terry **KF4783.A7**
Religious Liberty in the Supreme Court: Cases That Define the Debate over Church and State. Trade Cloth. Ethics & Public Policy Center. Lanham, MD. 1993. 512p. ISBN:0-89633-178-4, ISBN13: 978-0-89633-178-5. Dewey:342.73/0852;.
Audience: **u,f.**

Eastland, Terry (Editor) **KF4550.B375 1995**
Benchmarks: Great Constitutional Controversies in the Supreme Court. Griffin Bell (Introduction by). Trade Cloth. William B. Eerdmans Publishing Company. Grand Rapids, MI. 1994. 152p. ISBN:0-8028-3771-9, ISBN13: 978-0-8028-3771-4. Dewey:342.73/02. LCCN:94-043332.
Audience: **l,u,f.** *Choice, 1996.*

Epstein, Lee **KF8748.E67 1985**
Conservatives in Court. Cloth Text. University of Tennessee Press. Knoxville, TN. 1985. 216p. ISBN:0-87049-449-X, ISBN13: 978-0-87049-449-9. Dewey:347.73/26. LCCN:84-015287.
Audience: **u,f.** *Choice, 1985.*

Faigman, David L. **KF8748.F27 2004**
Laboratory of Justice: The Supreme Court's 200-Year Struggle to Integrate Science and the Law. Cloth over Boards. Henry Holt & Company. New York, NY. 2004. 432p. ISBN:0-8050-7274-8, ISBN13: 978-0-8050-7274-7. Dewey:347.73/26. LCCN:2003-057049.
Audience: **g,l,u,f.**

Fallon, Richard H. Jr. **KF8742.F35 2001**
Implementing the Constitution. Trade Cloth. Harvard University Press. Cambridge, MA. 2001. 208p. ISBN:0-674-00464-7, ISBN13: 978-0-674-00464-1. Dewey:347.73/262. LCCN:00-063477.
Audience: **u,f.** *Choice, 2001.*

Ferren, John M. & Rutledge, Wiley **KF8745.R87F47 2004**
Salt of the Earth, Conscience of the Court: The Story of Justice Wiley Rutledge. Trade Cloth. University of North Carolina Press. Chapel Hill, NC. 2004. 576p. ISBN:0-8078-2866-1, ISBN13: 978-0-8078-2866-3. Dewey:347.73/2634 B. LCCN:2003-027752.
Audience: **g,l,u,f.** *Choice, 2005.*

Fireside, Harvey **KF223.P56**
Separate but Unequal: Homer Plessy and the Supreme Court Decision that Legalized Racism. Trade Cloth. Avalon Publishing Group. New York, NY. 2003. 336p. ISBN:0-7867-1293-7, ISBN13: 978-0-7867-1293-9. Dewey:342.73.
Audience: **g,l,u,f.** *Choice, 2004.*

Foskett, Ken **KF8745.T48J83 2004**
Judging Thomas: The Life and Times of Clarence Thomas. Trade Cloth. HarperCollins Publishers. New York, NY. 2004. 352p. ISBN:0-06-052721-8, ISBN13: 978-0-06-052721-1. Dewey:347.73/2634 B. LCCN:2004-044935.
Audience: **g,l,u,f.**

Friedelbaum, Stanley H. **KF8748**
The Rehnquist Court: In Pursuit of Judicial Conservatism, 76. Trade Cloth. Greenwood Publishing Group, Inc. Portsmouth, NH. 1993. 184p. Contributions in Legal Studies Ser., No. 76 ISBN:0-313-27990-X, ISBN13: 978-0-313-27990-4. Dewey:347.30735. LCCN:93-014122.
Audience: **u,f.** *Choice, 1994.*

Galub, Arthur **KF8742.S9155**
The Burger Court, 1968-1984, Vol. 9. Trade Cloth. Associated Faculty Press, Inc. New York, NY. 1986. Supreme Court in American Life Ser. ISBN:0-86733-064-3, ISBN13: 978-0-86733-064-9. Dewey:347.73/26/09 s. LCCN:85-015735.
Audience: **u,f.** *Choice, 1987.*

Garbus, Martin **KF8742**
Courting Disaster: The Supreme Court and the Unmaking of American Law. Trade Cloth. DIANE Publishing Company. Collingdale, PA. 2005. 322p. ISBN:0-7567-9281-9, ISBN13: 978-0-7567-9281-7. Dewey:347.73/26/09.
Audience: **g,u,f.**

Gitenstein, Mark **KF8742.G57 1992**
Matters of Principle: America's Rejection of the Bork Nomination to the Supreme Court of the United States. Trade Cloth. Simon & Schuster, Inc. New York, NY. 1992. 384p. ISBN:0-671-67424-2, ISBN13: 978-0-671-67424-3. Dewey:347.73/2634. LCCN:92-026149.
Audience: **g,u,f.**

Greenhouse, Linda **KF8745.B555G74 2005**
Becoming Justice Blackmun: Harry Blackmun's Supreme Court Journey. Trade Cloth. Henry Holt & Company. New York, NY. 2005. 288p. ISBN:0-8050-7791-X, ISBN13: 978-0-8050-7791-9. Dewey:347.73/2634. LCCN:2004-063772.
Audience: **g.**

Greenya, John **KF8745.M34**
Silent Justice: The Clarence Thomas Story. Trade Cloth. DIANE Publishing Company. Collingdale, PA. 2005. 313p. ISBN:0-7567-8572-3, ISBN13: 978-0-7567-8572-7. Dewey:347.73/2634 B.
Audience: **g,l,u,f.**

Hall, Kermit, et al. **KF8742.A35O93 2005**
The Oxford Companion to the Supreme Court of the United States. Ed. 2. James W. Ely & Joel B. Grossman (Authors). Trade Cloth. Oxford University Press, Inc. New York, NY. 2005. 1272p. ISBN:0-19-517661-8, ISBN13: 978-0-19-517661-2. Dewey:347.73/26/03. LCCN:2004-029463.
Audience: **g.** *Choice, 2005.*

Hammond, Phillip E., et al. **KF4783.H36 2004**
Religion on Trial: How Supreme Court Trends Threaten Freedom of Conscience in America. David W. Machacek & Eric Michael Mazur (Authors). Trade Cloth. AltaMira Press. Walnut Creek, CA. 2004. 200p. ISBN:0-7591-0600-2, ISBN13: 978-0-7591-0600-0. Dewey:342.7308/52. LCCN:2003-021821.
Audience: **g,l,u,f.** *Choice, 2004.*

Irons, Peter **KF8748.I76 1994**
Brennan vs. Rehnquist: The Battle for the Constitution. Trade Cloth. Alfred A. Knopf Inc. New York, NY. 1994. 400p. ISBN:0-679-42436-9, ISBN13: 978-0-679-42436-9. Dewey:342.73. LCCN:94-007708.
Audience: **g.** *Choice, 1995.*

Irons, Peter H. **KF4748.I76 1988**
The Courage of Their Convictions: Sixteen Americans Who Fought Their Way to the Supreme Court. Trade Cloth. Simon & Schuster. New York, NY. 1988. 380p. ISBN:0-02-915670-X, ISBN13: 978-0-02-915670-4. Dewey:342.73/085. LCCN:88-021406.
Audience: **g.** *Choice, 1989.*

Johnson, Timothy Russell **KF8742.J64 2004**
Oral Arguments and Decision Making on the United States Supreme Court. Cloth Text. State University of New York Press. Albany, NY. 2004. 192p. SUNY Series in American Constitutionalism ISBN:0-7914-6103-3, ISBN13: 978-0-7914-6103-7. Dewey:347.73/2651. LCCN:2003-059535.
Audience: **u,f.** *Choice, 2005.*

Joseph, Joel D. **KF4549.J67 1987**
Black Mondays: Worst Decisions of the U. S. Supreme Court. Trade Cloth. National Press Books. Washington, DC. 1987. 286p. ISBN:0-915765-44-6, ISBN13: 978-0-915765-44-7. Dewey:347.73/26. LCCN:87-014051.
Audience: **l,u,f.**

Jost, Kenneth & CQ Editors **KF8742.A35S8 1998**
The Supreme Court A to Z. Ed. 2. Trade Cloth. CQ Press. Washington, DC. 1998. 584p. American Government A to Z Ser. ISBN:1-56802-357-X, ISBN13: 978-1-56802-357-1. Dewey:347.73/26/03. LCCN:98-038585.
Audience: **g,l,u,f.** *Choice, 1999.*

Katzmann, Robert A. **KF8700.K37 1997**
Courts and Congress. Trade Cloth. Brookings Institution Press. Washington, DC. 1997. 163p. ISBN:0-8157-4866-3, ISBN13: 978-0-8157-4866-3. Dewey:347.73/2. LCCN:96-051298.
Audience: **u,f.** *Choice, 1997.*

Keck, Thomas M. **KF8748.K43 2004**
The Most Activist Supreme Court in History: The Road to Modern Judicial Conservatism. Trade Cloth. University of Chicago Press. Chicago, IL. 2004. 370p. ISBN:0-226-42884-2, ISBN13: 978-0-226-42884-0. Dewey:347.73/26. LCCN:2004-005108.
Audience: **u,f.** *Choice, 2005.*

Klarman, Michael J. **KF4757.K58 2003**
From Jim Crow to Civil Rights: The Supreme Court and the Struggle for Racial Equality. Cloth Text. Oxford University Press, Inc. New York, NY. 2004. 672p. ISBN:0-19-512903-2, ISBN13: 978-0-19-512903-8. Dewey:342.73/0873. LCCN:2003-000515.
Audience: **g.** *Choice, 2004.*

Kloppenberg, Lisa A. **KF8748.K58 2001**
Playing It Safe: How the Supreme Court Sidesteps Hard Cases and Stunts the Development of Law. Trade Cloth. New York University Press. New York, NY. 2001. 320p. Critical America Ser. ISBN:0-8147-4740-X, ISBN13: 978-0-8147-4740-7. Dewey:347.73/26. LCCN:2001-001059.
Audience: **u,f.** *Choice, 2002.*

Lanier, Drew Noble **KF8742.L364 2003**
Of Time and Judicial Behavior: United States Supreme Court Agenda-Setting and Decision-Making, 1888-1997. Trade Cloth. Susquehanna University Press. Cranbury, NJ. 2003. 280p. ISBN:1-57591-067-5, ISBN13: 978-1-57591-067-3. Dewey:347.73/26/09. LCCN:2002-155202.
Audience: **u,f.** *Choice, 2004.*

Lasser, William **KF8742.L38 1988**
The Limits of Judicial Power: The Supreme Court in American Politics. Trade Cloth. University of North Carolina Press. Chapel Hill, NC. 1988. x, 354p. ISBN:0-08-078181-0, ISBN13: 978-0-08-078181-5. Dewey:347.73/26/09. LCCN:88-040141.
Audience: **u,f.** *Choice, 1989.*

Lazarus, Edward **KF8742.L39 1998**
Closed Chambers: The First Eyewitness Account of the Epic Struggles Inside the Supreme Court. Trade Cloth. Crown Publishing Group. New York, NY. 1998. 576p. ISBN:0-8129-2402-9, ISBN13: 978-0-8129-2402-2. Dewey:347.73/16. LCCN:97-035708.
Audience: **g,l,u.** *Choice, 1998.*

Leahy, James E. **KF4749.L4**
Liberty, Justice and Equality: How These Constitutional Guarantees Have Been Shaped by United States Supreme Court Decisions since 1789. Trade Cloth. DIANE Publishing Company. Collingdale, PA. 2003. 205p. ISBN:0-7567-9002-6, ISBN13: 978-0-7567-9002-8. Dewey:347.30285.
Audience: **l,u,f.** *Choice, 1993.*

Lively, Donald E. **KF4549**
Landmark Supreme Court Cases: A Reference Guide. Cloth Text. Greenwood Publishing Group, Inc. Portsmouth, NH. 1999. 384p. ISBN:0-313-30602-8, ISBN13: 978-0-313-30602-0. Dewey:342.73/00264. LCCN:98-044220.
Audience: **g,l,u,f.** *Choice, 2000.*

Maltese, John A. **KF8742.M26 1995**
The Selling of Supreme Court Nominees. Trade Cloth. Johns Hopkins University Press. Baltimore, MD. 1980. 216p. Interpreting American Politics Ser. ISBN:0-8018-5102-5, ISBN13: 978-0-8018-5102-5. Dewey:347.7/3/26/34. LCCN:95-003536.
Audience: **u,f.** *Choice, 1996.*

Maltz, Earl M. **KF8745.B76M35 2000**
Chief Justiceship of Warren Burger, 1969-1986: A Provocative Interpretation of the Burger Court. Trade Cloth. University of South Carolina Press. Columbia, SC. 2000. xvi, 307p. Chief Justiceships of the United States Supreme Court Ser.

ISBN:1-57003-335-8, ISBN13: 978-1-57003-335-3. Dewey:347.73/2634. LCCN:00-008049.
Audience: **u,f.** *Choice, 2000.*

Marcosson, Samuel A. **KF8742.M27 2002**
Original Sin: Clarence Thomas and the Failure of the Constitutional Conservatives. Trade Cloth. New York University Press. New York, NY. 2002. 232p. Critical America Ser. ISBN:0-8147-5640-9, ISBN13: 978-0-8147-5640-9. Dewey:347.73/26. LCCN:2001-008462.
Audience: **u,f.** *Choice, 2002.*

McDowell, Gary L. **KF8700.M37 1988**
Curbing the Courts: The Constitution and the Limits of Judicial Power. Trade Cloth. Louisiana State University Press. Baton Rouge, LA. 1988. xiv, 214p. ISBN:0-8071-1339-5, ISBN13: 978-0-8071-1339-4. Dewey:347.73/1. LCCN:87-024139.
Audience: **u,f.** *Choice, 1988.*

McGuigan, Patrick B. & Weyrich, Dawn M. **KF8742.M33 1990**
Ninth Justice: The Fight for Bork. R. H. Bork Jr. (Contribution by). Trade Cloth. University Press of America, Inc. Lanham, MD. 1993. 348p. ISBN:0-942522-15-X, ISBN13: 978-0-942522-15-0. Dewey:347.73/26/092. LCCN:89-023661.
Audience: **u,f.** *Choice, 1990.*

McKeever, Robert J. **KF8742.M35 1995**
Raw Judicial Power?: The Supreme Court and American Society. Ed. 2. Cloth Text. Manchester University Press. Manchester, 1996. 256p. ISBN:0-7190-4873-7, ISBN13: 978-0-7190-4873-9. Dewey:347.3/0735. LCCN:95-030875.
Audience: **u,f.** *Choice, 1994.*

Miller, Anita (Editor) **KF8745.T48U55 1994**
Complete Transcripts of the Clarence Thomas-Anita Hill Hearings: October 11, 12, 13, 1991. Nina Totenberg (Preface by). Trade Cloth. Academy Chicago Publishers, Ltd. Chicago, IL. 1994. 450p. ISBN:0-89733-408-6, ISBN13: 978-0-89733-408-2. Dewey:347.73/2634. LCCN:94-015891.
Audience: **u,f.**

Nelson, William E. **KF4575.N45 2000**
Marbury vs. Madison: The Origins and Legacy of Judicial Review. Trade Cloth. University Press of Kansas. Lawrence, KS. 2000. xii, 142p. Landmark Law Cases and American Society Ser. ISBN:0-7006-1061-8, ISBN13: 978-0-7006-1061-7. Dewey:347.73/12. LCCN:00-043472.
Audience: **g.** *Choice, 2001.*

Newman, Roger K. **KF8745.B55N49 1994**
Hugo Black: A Biography. Trade Cloth. Knopf Publishing Group. New York, NY. 1994. 944p. ISBN:0-679-43180-2, ISBN13: 978-0-679-43180-0. Dewey:347.73/2634 B. LCCN:94-010233.
Audience: **u,f.** *Choice, 1995.*

Noonan, John Thomas **KF1322 .N66 2002**
Narrowing the Nation's Power: The Supreme Court Sides with the States. Trade Cloth. University of California Press. Berkeley, CA. 2002. 208p. ISBN:0-520-23574-6, ISBN13: 978-0-520-23574-8. Dewey:342.73/088. LCCN:2002-019473.
Audience: **u,f.** *Choice, 2003.*

O'Brien, David M. **KF8742.O27 1993**
Storm Center: The Supreme Court in American Politics. Ed. 3. Trade Cloth. W. W. Norton & Company, Inc. New York, NY. 1993. 404p. ISBN:0-393-03521-2, ISBN13: 978-0-393-03521-6. Dewey:347.73/26. LCCN:92-017079.
Audience: **g,l,u,f.** *Choice, 1986.*

Peretti, Terri J. **KF4575.P466 1999**
In Defense of a Political Court. Cloth Text. Princeton University Press. Princeton, NJ. 1999. 384p. ISBN:0-691-00905-8, ISBN13: 978-0-691-00905-6. Dewey:342.73. LCCN:99-012206.
Audience: **u,f.** *Choice, 2000.*

Perry, Barbara A. **KF8742**
A Representative Supreme Court?: The Impact of Race, Religion, and Gender on Appointments. Trade Cloth. Greenwood Publishing Group, Inc. Portsmouth, NH. 1991. 176p. Contributions in Legal Studies Ser., No. 66 ISBN:0-313-27777-X, ISBN13: 978-0-313-27777-1. Dewey:347.73/2634. LCCN:91-014336.
Audience: **u,f.** *Choice, 1992.*

Perry, H. W. **KF8742.P3365 1991**
Deciding to Decide: Agenda Setting in the United States Supreme Court. Trade Cloth. Harvard University Press. Cambridge, MA. 1992. 326p. ISBN:0-674-19442-X, ISBN13: 978-0-674-19442-7. Dewey:347.73/26. LCCN:91-014002.
Audience: **g.** *Choice, 1992.*

Perry, Michael J. **KF4575.P47 1994**
The Constitution in the Courts: Law or Politics? Cloth Text. Oxford University Press, Inc. New York, NY. 1994. 288p. ISBN:0-19-508347-4, ISBN13: 978-0-19-508347-7. Dewey:347.3/02. LCCN:93-018539.
Audience: **u,f.** *Choice, 1994.*

Pickerill, J. Mitchell **KF4945.P53 2004**
Constitutional Deliberation in Congress: The Impact of Judicial Review in a Separated System. Trade Cloth. Duke University Press. Durham, NC. 2004. 224p. Constitutional Conflicts Ser. ISBN:0-8223-3235-3, ISBN13: 978-0-8223-3235-0. Dewey:347.73/12. LCCN:2003-012570.
Audience: **u,f.** *Choice, 2005.*

Quirk, William J. & Bridwell, R. Randall **KF8748.Q57 1995**
Judicial Dictatorship. Trade Cloth. Transaction Publishers. Somerset, NJ. 1996. 143p. ISBN:1-56000-225-5, ISBN13: 978-1-56000-225-3. Dewey:347.73/12. LCCN:95-000821.
Audience: **u,f.** *Choice, 1995.*

Robarge, David Scott **KF8745**
A Chief Justice's Progress: John Marshall from Revolutionary Virginia to the Supreme Court. Trade Cloth. Greenwood Publishing Group, Inc. Portsmouth, NH. 2000. 400p. Contributions in American History Ser., No. 185 ISBN:0-313-30858-6, ISBN13: 978-0-313-30858-1. Dewey:347.73/2634 B. LCCN:99-033829.
Audience: **g,l,u,f.** *Choice, 2000.*

Ross, Michael A. **KF8745.M5R67 2003**
Justice of Shattered Dreams: Samuel Freeman Miller and the Supreme Court During the Civil War Era. Trade Cloth. Louisiana State University Press. Baton Rouge, LA. 2004. 360p. Conflicting Worlds Ser. ISBN:0-8071-2868-6, ISBN13: 978-0-8071-2868-8. Dewey:347.73/26. LCCN:2003-002069.
Audience: **g.** *Choice, 2004.*

Rowan, Carl Thomas **E185.61**
Dream Makers, Dream Breakers: The World of Justice Thurgood Marshall. Trade Cloth. Welcome Rain Publishers. New York,

NY. 2003. 480p. ISBN:1-56649-235-1, ISBN13: 978-1-56649-235-5. Dewey:323.1/196073/0922.
Audience: **g,l,u,f.** *Choice, 1993.*

Savage, David G. & Biskupic, Joan **KF8742.W567 2004**
Guide to the U.S. Supreme Court. Ed. 4. Trade Cloth. CQ Press. Washington, DC. 2004. 1,440p. ISBN:1-56802-743-5, ISBN13: 978-1-56802-743-2. Dewey:347.73/26. LCCN:2004-001572.
Audience: **g,l,u,f.** *Choice, 2004.*

Schneider, Carl E. (Editor) **KF3827.E87L39 2000**
Law at the End of Life: The Supreme Court and Assisted Suicide. Trade Cloth. University of Michigan Press. Chicago, IL. 2000. 376p. ISBN:0-472-11157-4, ISBN13: 978-0-472-11157-2. Dewey:344.73/04197. LCCN:00-034388.
Audience: **u,f.** *Choice, 2001.*

Schultz, David **KF8742.A35S54 2005**
The Encyclopedia of the Supreme Court. Trade Cloth. Facts On File, Inc. New York, NY. 2005. 576p. Facts on File Library of American History ISBN:0-8160-5086-4, ISBN13: 978-0-8160-5086-4. Dewey:347.73/26/03. LCCN:2004-013174.
Audience: **g,l,u,f.** *Choice, 2005.*

Schwartz, Bernard **KF228.B34S39 1988**
Behind Bakke: Affirmative Action and the Supreme Court. Cloth Text. New York University Press. New York, NY. 1988. 208p. ISBN:0-8147-7878-X, ISBN13: 978-0-8147-7878-4. Dewey:347.73/0798. LCCN:87-028086.
Audience: **g,l,u,f.** *Choice, 1988.*

Schwartz, Bernard (Editor) **KF4541.B855 1998**
The Burger Court: Counter-Revolution or Confirmation? Trade Cloth. Oxford University Press, Inc. New York, NY. 1998. 328p. ISBN:0-19-512259-3, ISBN13: 978-0-19-512259-6. Dewey:347.7/326. LCCN:97-051416.
Audience: **u,f.** *Choice, 1999.*

Schwartz, Bernard **KF8742.S323 1996**
Decision: How the Supreme Court Decides Cases. Trade Cloth. Oxford University Press, Inc. New York, NY. 1996. 288p. ISBN:0-19-509859-5, ISBN13: 978-0-19-509859-4. Dewey:347.3/0735/2. LCCN:95-016119.
Audience: **g,l,u,f.** *Choice, 1996.*

Schwartz, Bernard **KF8742.S39 1993**
A History of the Supreme Court. Trade Cloth. Oxford University Press, Inc. New York, NY. 1993. 480p. ISBN:0-19-508099-8, ISBN13: 978-0-19-508099-5. Dewey:347.732609. LCCN:92-044097.
Audience: **g,l,u,f.**

Schwartz, Herman (Editor) **KF8742**
The Rehnquist Court: Judicial Activism on the Right. Trade Cloth. DIANE Publishing Company. Collingdale, PA. 2005. 276p. ISBN:0-7567-9671-7, ISBN13: 978-0-7567-9671-6. Dewey:347.73/2635.
Audience: **u,f.** *Choice, 2003.*

Schwartz, Herman (Author, Editor, Introduction by) **KF8742.A5R44 2002**
The Rehnquist Court: Judicial Activism on the Right. Cloth over Boards. Farrar, Straus & Giroux. New York, NY. 2002. 288p. ISBN:0-8090-8073-7, ISBN13: 978-0-8090-8073-1. Dewey:347.73/2635. LCCN:2002-068670.
Audience: **g,l,u,f.** *Choice, 2003.*

Semonche, John E. **KF8742.S444 1998**
Keeping the Faith: A Cultural History of the U. S. Supreme Court. Trade Cloth. Rowman & Littlefield Publishers, Inc. Lanham, MD. 1998. 499p. ISBN:0-8476-8985-9, ISBN13: 978-0-8476-8985-9. Dewey:347.73/26. LCCN:97-032481.
Audience: **g.** *Choice, 1998.*

Sepinuck, Stephen L. & Treuthart, Mary P. **KD7540.L48 1999**
The Conscience of the Court: Selected Opinions of Justice William J. Brennan, Jr. on Freedom and Equality. Trade Cloth. Southern Illinois University Press. Carbondale, IL. 1999. 304p. ISBN:0-8093-2234-X, ISBN13: 978-0-8093-2234-3. Dewey:345.42/075. LCCN:99-012923.
Audience: **u,f.** *Choice, 2000.*

Shaw, Stephen K. (Editor), et al. **KF8742.F73 2003**
Franklin D. Roosevelt and the Transformation of the Supreme Court. William D. Pederson & Frank J. Williams (Editors). Trade Cloth. M. E. Sharpe Inc. Armonk, NY. 2004. 280p. Library of Franklin D. Roosevelt Studies, Vol. 3 ISBN:0-7656-1032-9, ISBN13: 978-0-7656-1032-4. Dewey:347.73/26/09. LCCN:2002-066944.
Audience: **u,f.** *Choice, 2004.*

Sheffer, Martin S. **KF5060**
The Judicial Development of Presidential War Powers. Trade Cloth. Greenwood Publishing Group, Inc. Portsmouth, NH. 1999. 248p. ISBN:0-275-96435-3, ISBN13: 978-0-275-96435-1. Dewey:342.73/062. LCCN:98-038287.
Audience: **u,f.** *Choice, 2000.*

Shipan, Charles R. **KF4575.S54 1997**
Designing Judicial Review: Interest Groups, Congress and Communications Policy. Trade Cloth. University of Michigan Press. Chicago, IL. 1997. 192p. ISBN:0-472-10703-8, ISBN13: 978-0-472-10703-2. Dewey:347.73/12. LCCN:97-004658.
Audience: **u,f.** *Choice, 1998.*

Simon, James F. **KF8742.S55 1995**
The Center Holds: The Power Struggle Inside the Rehnquist Court. Trade Cloth. Simon & Schuster. New York, NY. 1995. 336p. ISBN:0-684-80293-7, ISBN13: 978-0-684-80293-0. Dewey:347.73/26. LCCN:95-011729.
Audience: **g,l,u,f.**

Simon, Paul **KF8776.S56 1992**
Advice and Consent: Clarence Thomas, Robert Bork and the Intriguing History of the Supreme Court's Nomination Battles. Trade Cloth. National Press Books. Washington, DC. 1992. 328p. ISBN:0-915765-98-5, ISBN13: 978-0-915765-98-0. Dewey:347.73/14 347.30714. LCCN:92-016107.
Audience: **g,u,f.**

Smith, Christopher E. **KF8745**
Justice Antonin Scalia and the Supreme Court's Conservative Moment. Trade Cloth. Greenwood Publishing Group, Inc. Portsmouth, NH. 1993. 160p. ISBN:0-275-94705-X, ISBN13: 978-0-275-94705-7. Dewey:347.30735. LCCN:93-025057.
Audience: **g,u,f.** *Choice, 1994.*

Smith, Christopher E. **KF9225.S64 1997**
The Rehnquist Court and Criminal Punishment. Cloth Text. Garland Publishing, Inc. New York, NY. 1997. 176p. Current Issues in Criminal Justice Ser., No. 21 ISBN:0-8153-2573-8, ISBN13: 978-0-8153-2573-4. Dewey:345.73/077. LCCN:97-010778.
Audience: **u,f.** *Choice, 1998.*

Spaeth, Harold J. & Segal, Jeffrey A. **KF8748 .S545 2001**
Majority Rule or Minority Will: Adherence to Precedent on the U. S. Supreme Court. Cloth Text. Cambridge University Press. New York, NY. 1999. 378p. ISBN:0-521-62424-X, ISBN13: 978-0-521-62424-4. Dewey:347.7/326/3. LCCN:98-035793.
Audience: **u,f.** *Choice, 1999.*

Spann, Girardeau A. **KF4757**
Race Against the Court: The Supreme Court and Minorities in Contemporary America. Trade Cloth. New York University Press. New York, NY. 1993. 272p. ISBN:0-8147-7963-8, ISBN13: 978-0-8147-7963-7. Dewey:347.302873. LCCN:92-031343.
Audience: **u,f.** *Choice, 1993.*

Starr, Kenneth W. **KF8748.S815 2002**
First among Equals: The Supreme Court in American Life. Trade Cloth. Warner Books, Inc. New York, NY. 2002. 352p. ISBN:0-446-52756-4, ISBN13: 978-0-446-52756-9. Dewey:347.73/26. LCCN:2002-016896.
Audience: **g,l,u,f.**

Steamer, Robert J. **KF8744.S74 1986**
Chief Justice: Leadership and the Supreme Court. Trade Cloth. University of South Carolina Press. Columbia, SC. 1986. 288p. ISBN:0-87249-482-9, ISBN13: 978-0-87249-482-4. Dewey:347.73/2634/09. LCCN:86-004331.
Audience: **u,f.** *Choice, 1986.*

Stearns, Maxwell L. **KF8742.S745 2000**
Constitutional Process: A Social Choice Analysis of Supreme Court Decision Making. Trade Cloth. University of Michigan Press. Chicago, IL. 2000. 448p. ISBN:0-472-11130-2, ISBN13: 978-0-472-11130-5. Dewey:347.73/26. LCCN:00-031716.
Audience: **u,f.** *Choice, 2001.*

Stephenson, D. Grier **KF8742.S74 1999**
Campaigns and the Court: The U. S. Supreme Court in Presidential Elections. Trade Cloth. Columbia University Press. New York, NY. 1999. 380p. Power, Conflict, and Democracy Ser. ISBN:0-231-10034-5, ISBN13: 978-0-231-10034-2. Dewey:347.73/2635. LCCN:98-037351.
Audience: **u,f.** *Choice, 1999.*

Stevens, Richard G. & Franck, Matthew J. (Editors) **KF8742.S58 1999**
Sober as a Judge: The Supreme Court and Republican Liberty. Trade Cloth. Lexington Books. Lanham, MD. 1999. 344p. ISBN:0-7391-0010-6, ISBN13: 978-0-7391-0010-3. Dewey:347.73/2634. LCCN:99-029370.
Audience: **u,f.** *Choice, 2000.*

Sunstein, Cass R. **KF8748.S875 1999**
One Case at a Time: Judicial Minimalism on the Supreme Court. Trade Cloth. Harvard University Press. Cambridge, MA. 1999. 304p. ISBN:0-674-63790-9, ISBN13: 978-0-674-63790-0. Dewey:347.73/26. LCCN:98-036954.
Audience: **u,f.**

Thomas, Andrew Peyton **KF8745.T48T48 2002**
Clarence Thomas: A Biography. Trade Cloth. Encounter Books. New York, NY. 2002. 661p. ISBN:1-893554-36-8, ISBN13: 978-1-893554-36-8. Dewey:347.73/2634 B. LCCN:2001-040501.
Audience: **g,l,u,f.**

Tucker, David **KF8748.T83 1995**
The Rehnquist Court and Civil Rights. Trade Cloth. Ashgate Publishing, Ltd. Aldershot, 1995. 256p. Applied Legal Philosophy Ser. ISBN:1-85521-310-9, ISBN13: 978-1-85521-310-4. Dewey:342.73/085. LCCN:94-024128.
Audience: **u,f.** *Choice, 1995.*

Tushnet, Mark **KF8742.T87 2005**
A Court Divided: The Rehnquist Court and the Future of Constitutional Law. Trade Cloth. W. W. Norton & Company, Inc. New York, NY. 2005. 416p. ISBN:0-393-05868-9, ISBN13: 978-0-393-05868-0. Dewey:347.73/26. LCCN:2004-013786.
Audience: **g,l,u,f.**

Vestal, Theodore M. **KF8742**
The Eisenhower Court and Civil Liberties. Trade Cloth. Greenwood Publishing Group, Inc. Portsmouth, NH. 2002. 360p. ISBN:0-275-97284-4, ISBN13: 978-0-275-97284-4. Dewey:342.73/085. LCCN:2001-051175.
Audience: **u,f.** *Choice, 2002.*

Ward, Artemus **KF8742.W368 2003**
Deciding to Leave: The Politics of Retirement from the United States Supreme Court. Cloth Text. State University of New York Press. Albany, NY. 2003. 336p. SUNY Series in American Constitutionalism ISBN:0-7914-5651-X, ISBN13: 978-0-7914-5651-4. Dewey:347.73/2634. LCCN:2002-030977.
Audience: **u,f.** *Choice, 2003.*

White, G. Edward **KF8745.H6W473 2005**
Oliver Wendell Holmes. Ed. 2. Trade Cloth. Oxford University Press, Inc. New York, NY. 2006. 172p. Lives and Legacies Ser. ISBN:0-19-530536-1, ISBN13: 978-0-19-530536-4. Dewey:347.73/2634 B. LCCN:2005-020771.
Audience: **g,l,u,f.**

Wilkinson, Charles F. **KF8205.W53 1987**
American Indians, Time and the Law: Historical Rights at the Bar of the Supreme Court. Trade Cloth. Yale University Press. Cumberland, RI. 1987. 256p. ISBN:0-300-03589-6, ISBN13: 978-0-300-03589-6. Dewey:342.73/0872. LCCN:86-009164.
Audience: **u,f.** *Choice, 1987.*

Yarbrough, Tinsley E. **KF8745.S68Y37 2005**
David Hackett Souter: Traditional Republican on the Rehnquist Court. Trade Cloth. Oxford University Press, Inc. New York, NY. 2005. 336p. ISBN:0-19-515933-0, ISBN13: 978-0-19-515933-2. Dewey:347.73/2634 B. LCCN:2005-002395.
Audience: **g,l,u,f.** *Choice, 2006.*

Yarbrough, Tinsley E. **KF8742.Y37 2000**
The Rehnquist Court and the Constitution. Trade Cloth. Oxford University Press, Inc. New York, NY. 2000. 320p. ISBN:0-19-510346-7, ISBN13: 978-0-19-510346-5. Dewey:347.73/26. LCCN:99-018538.
Audience: **g.** *Choice, 2000.*

Yates, Jeff **KF8742.Y38 2002**
Popular Justice: Presidential Prestige and Executive Success in the Supreme Court. Cloth Text. State University of New York Press. Albany, NY. 2002. xii, 131p. ISBN:0-7914-5447-9,

ISBN13: 978-0-7914-5447-3. Dewey:347.73/26. LCCN:2001-049807.
Audience: **u,f.** *Choice, 2003.*

American Government and Politics > Federal Government > Judicial Branch > Judicial Activism

Carrese, Paul O. **K2146.C375 2003**
The Cloaking of Power: Montesquieu, Blackstone, and the Rise of Judicial Activism. Trade Cloth. University of Chicago Press. Chicago, IL. 2003. 349p. ISBN:0-226-09482-0, ISBN13: 978-0-226-09482-3. Dewey:340/.11. LCCN:2002-152313.
Audience: **u,f.** *Choice, 2004.*

Geyh, Charles Gardner **KF5130.G49 2006**
When Courts and Congress Collide: The Struggle for Control of America's Judicial System. Trade Cloth. University of Michigan Press. Chicago, IL. 2006. 344p. ISBN:0-472-09922-1, ISBN13: 978-0-472-09922-1. Dewey:347.73/12. LCCN:2005-031392.
Audience: **u,f.**

Leishman, Rory **KE8200**
Against Judicial Activism: The Decline of Freedom and Democracy in Canada. Trade Cloth. McGill-Queen's University Press. Montreal, PQ. 2006. 320p. ISBN:0-7735-3054-1, ISBN13: 978-0-7735-3054-6. Dewey:347.71/035.
Audience: **u,f.**

Lott, John R. **KF8776.L68 2006**
Confirmation Trials: Causes and Consequences of Judicial Selection Battles. Trade Cloth. American Enterprise Institute for Public Policy Research. Washington, DC. 2006. ISBN:0-8447-4245-7, ISBN13: 978-0-8447-4245-8. Dewey:347.73/14. LCCN:2006-001688.
Audience: **u,f.**

Owens, Lori J. **KF8742.O94 2006**
Original Intent and the Struggle for the Supreme Court: The Politics of Judicial Appointments. Trade Cloth. Edwin Mellen Press, The. Lewiston, NY. 2006. 312p. ISBN:0-7734-5852-2, ISBN13: 978-0-7734-5852-9. Dewey:347.73/2634. LCCN:2006-041861.
Audience: **u,f.**

Pickering, Charles W. Sr. **KF8776.P53 2006**
Supreme Chaos: The Politics of Judicial Confirmation and the Culture War. Ed Meese (Foreword by). Trade Cloth. Stroud & Hall Publishing. Atlanta, GA. 2006. 240p. ISBN:0-9745376-5-9, ISBN13: 978-0-9745376-5-8. Dewey:347.73/14. LCCN:2005-035096.
Audience: **g,l,u,f.**

Powers, Stephen & Rothman, Stanley **KF5130**
The Least Dangerous Branch?: Consequences of Judicial Activism. Smith College, Center for the Study of Social and Political Change Staff (Contribution by). Trade Cloth. Greenwood Publishing Group, Inc. Portsmouth, NH. 2002. 232p. ISBN:0-275-97536-3, ISBN13: 978-0-275-97536-4. Dewey:347.73/1. LCCN:2002-025311.
Audience: **u,f.** *Choice, 2003.*

Roosevelt, Kermit III **KF8742.R65 2006**
The Myth of Judicial Activism: Making Sense of Supreme Court Decisions. Cloth over Boards. Yale University Press. Cumberland, RI. 2006. 272p. ISBN:0-300-11468-0, ISBN13: 978-0-300-11468-3. Dewey:347.73/26. LCCN:2006-013002.
Audience: **u,f.**

Schwartz, Herman (Editor) **KF8742**
The Rehnquist Court: Judicial Activism on the Right. Trade Cloth. DIANE Publishing Company. Collingdale, PA. 2005. 276p. ISBN:0-7567-9671-7, ISBN13: 978-0-7567-9671-6. Dewey:347.73/2635.
Audience: **u,f.** *Choice, 2003.*

Weaver, Jace **KF373.B545W43 1993**
Then to the Rock Let Me Fly: Luther Bohanon and Judicial Activism. Robert H. Henry (Foreword by). Trade Cloth. University of Oklahoma Press. Norman, OK. 1993. 212p. ISBN:0-8061-2554-3, ISBN13: 978-0-8061-2554-1. Dewey:347.30732234. LCCN:93-002441.
Audience: **u,f.** *Choice, 1994.*

American Government and Politics > State Government

Hogan, Sean O. **KF8735**
The Judicial Branch of State Government: People, Process, and Politics. Library Binding. ABC-CLIO, Inc. Santa Barbara, CA. 2006. ISBN:1-85109-751-1, ISBN13: 978-1-85109-751-7. Dewey:347.73/3. LCCN:2006-018461.
Audience: **g,l,u.**

Rosenthal, Alan **JK2494.R67 1990**
Governors and Legislatures: Contending Powers. Trade Cloth. Congressional Quarterly, Inc. Washington, DC. 1990. 223p. ISBN:0-87187-545-4, ISBN13: 978-0-87187-545-7. Dewey:320.473. LCCN:90-001356.
Audience: **u,f.** *Choice, 1990.*

American Government and Politics > State Government > Individual States

Flynt, Wayne **F326.F754 2004**
Alabama in the Twentieth Century. Trade Cloth. University of Alabama Press. Tuscaloosa, AL. 2004. 624p. The Modern South Ser. ISBN:0-8173-1430-X, ISBN13: 978-0-8173-1430-9. Dewey:976.1/063. LCCN:2004-002841.
Audience: **g,l,u,f.** *Choice, 2005.*

Grose, Philip Jr. **F275.42.M35G78 2006**
South Carolina at the Brink. Trade Cloth. University of South Carolina Press. Columbia, SC. 2006. 408p. ISBN:1-57003-624-1, ISBN13: 978-1-57003-624-8. Dewey:975.7/043092 B. LCCN:2006-003515.
Audience: **u,f.**

Grunwald, Michael **F317.E9G78 2005**
The Swamp: The Everglades, Florida, and the Politics of Paradise. Trade Cloth. Simon & Schuster. New York, NY. 2006. 464p. ISBN:0-7432-5105-9, ISBN13: 978-0-7432-5105-1. Dewey:975.9/39. LCCN:2005-056329.
Audience: **g,l,u,f.**

McKinney, Gordon B. **E664.V2M34 2004**
Zeb Vance: North Carolina's Civil War Governor and Gilded Age Political Leader. Trade Cloth. University of North Carolina Press. Chapel Hill, NC. 2004. 528p. ISBN:0-8078-2865-3, ISBN13: 978-0-8078-2865-6. Dewey:975.6/03 B. LCCN:2003-027749.
Audience: **u,f.** *Choice, 2005.*

Munroe, John A. **F164.5.M86 2004**
The Philadelawareans, and Other Essays Relating to Delaware. Trade Cloth. University of Delaware Press. Newark, DE. 2004. 312p. Cultural Studies of Delaware and the Eastern Shore ISBN:0-87413-872-8, ISBN13: 978-0-87413-872-6. Dewey:975.1. LCCN:2003-027281.
Audience: **u,f.**

Phillips, George Harwood **E78.C15P445 2004**
Bringing Them under Subjection: California's Tejon Indian Reservation and Beyond, 1852-1864. Trade Cloth. University of Nebraska Press. Lincoln, NE. 2004. 384p. ISBN:0-8032-3736-7, ISBN13: 978-0-8032-3736-0. Dewey:979.4004/97. LCCN:2003-059620.
Audience: **u,f.** *Choice, 2005.*

Silbey, Joel H. **F390.S558 2005**
Storm over Texas: The Annexation Controversy and the Road to Civil War. Trade Cloth. Oxford University Press, Inc. New York, NY. 2005. 256p. Pivotal Moments in American History Ser. ISBN:0-19-513944-5, ISBN13: 978-0-19-513944-0. Dewey:976.4/04. LCCN:2005-040636.
Audience: **f.**

Sublett, Michael D. **JS451.I35S83 2004**
Township: Diffusion and Persistence of Grassroots Government in Illinois, 1850-2000. Trade Cloth. Peter Lang Publishing, Inc. New York, NY. 2004. xviii, 398p. ISBN:0-8204-7055-4, ISBN13: 978-0-8204-7055-9. Dewey:320.8/3. LCCN:2003-025252.
Audience: **u,f.**

Ward, Robert David & Rogers, William Warren **HV9475.A2W37 2003**
Alabama's Response to the Penitentiary Movement, 1829-1865. Trade Cloth. University Press of Florida. Gainesville, FL. 2003. 192p. ISBN:0-8130-2663-6, ISBN13: 978-0-8130-2663-3. Dewey:365/.9761/09034. LCCN:2003-057915.
Audience: **u,f.** *Choice, 2004.*

American Government and Politics > Local Government > Counties. Metropolitan Areas

Agranoff, Robert & McGuire, Michael **JS356.A37 2003**
Collaborative Public Management: New Strategies for Local Governments. Trade Cloth, Trade Paper. Georgetown University Press. Washington, DC. 2004. 232p. American Governance and Public Policy Ser. ISBN:1-58901-018-3, ISBN13: 978-1-58901-018-5. Dewey:352.14/0973. LCCN:2002-014315.
Audience: **u,f.** *Choice, 2003.*

Benjamin, Gerald & Nathan, Richard P. **JS1230**
Regionalism and Realism: A Study of Government in the New York Metropolitan Area. Trade Cloth. Brookings Institution Press. Washington, DC. 2001. 304p. ISBN:0-8157-0088-1, ISBN13: 978-0-8157-0088-3. Dewey:320.8097471.
Audience: **u,f.** *Choice, 2002.*

Collier, Christopher **F99.C65 2003**
All Politics Is Local: Family, Friends, and Provincial Interests in the Creation of the Constitution. Library Binding. University Press of New England. Lebanon, NH. 2003. 244.p. ISBN:1-58465-290-X, ISBN13: 978-1-58465-290-8. Dewey:973.3/18. LCCN:2003-016930.
Audience: **l,u,f.** *Choice, 2004.*

Dilworth, Richardson **HT334.U5D55 2004**
The Urban Origins of Suburban Autonomy. Trade Cloth. Harvard University Press. Cambridge, MA. 2005. 280p. ISBN:0-674-01531-2, ISBN13: 978-0-674-01531-9. Dewey:307.76/4/0973. LCCN:2004-054250.
Audience: **u,f.** *Choice, 2005.*

Dunn, Mark R. & Dunn, Mary W. **E180.D86 2003**
United States Counties. Cloth Text. McFarland & Company, Incorporated Publishers. Jefferson, NC. 2003. 472p. ISBN:0-7864-1515-0, ISBN13: 978-0-7864-1515-1. Dewey:917.3/003. LCCN:2003-014379.
Audience: **g,l,u.** *Choice, 2004.*

Harris, Michael **JK2443.I56 2003**
Innovation and Entrepreneurship in State and Local Government. Rhonda Kinney (Editor). Trade Cloth. Lexington Books. Lanham, MD. 2003. 212p. Studies in Public Policy Ser. ISBN:0-7391-0705-4, ISBN13: 978-0-7391-0705-8. Dewey:352.3/67. LCCN:2003-011716.
Audience: **u,f.**

Leland, Suzanne M. & Thurmaier, Kurt M. **JS422.C37 2004**
Case Studies of City-County Consolidation: Reshaping the Local Government Landscape. Trade Cloth. M. E. Sharpe Inc. Armonk, NY. 2004. 352p. Reshaping the Local Government Landscape Ser. ISBN:0-7656-0943-6, ISBN13: 978-0-7656-0943-4. Dewey:320.8/3/0973. LCCN:2003-024080.
Audience: **u,f.** *Choice, 2005.*

Luton, Larry S. **HD4484.W2L88 1996**
The Politics of Garbage: A Community Perspective on Solid Waste Policy Making. Cloth Text. University of Pittsburgh Press. Pittsburgh, PA. 1997. 272p. Pitt Series in Policy and Institutional ISBN:0-8229-3946-0, ISBN13: 978-0-8229-3946-7. Dewey:363.72/88. LCCN:96-010050.
Audience: **u,f.** *Choice, 1997.*

Lyons, W. E., et al. **JS323.L97 1992**
The Politics of Dissatisfaction: Citizens, Services and Urban Institutions. David Lowery & Ruth Hoogland DeHoog (Authors), Kenneth S. Meier (Foreword by). Cloth Text. M. E. Sharpe Inc. Armonk, NY. 1992. 248p. Bureaucracies, Public Administration, and Public Policy Ser. ISBN:0-87332-898-1, ISBN13: 978-0-87332-898-2. Dewey:321.80973. LCCN:91-035287.
Audience: **l,u,f.** *Choice, 1993.*

National Research Council Staff **JS422.N39 1999**
Governance and Opportunity in Metropolitan America: Governmental Arrangements and Individual Life Chances in Urban America. Alan Altshuler (Editor). Trade Cloth. National Academies Press. Washington, DC. 1999. ix, 347p.

ISBN:0-309-06553-4, ISBN13: 978-0-309-06553-5. Dewey:352.14/0973. LCCN:99-006607.
Audience: **l,u,f.** *Choice, 2000.*

Owen, C. James & York, Willbern **JS943.A8O94 1985**
Governing Metropolitan Indianapolis. Trade Cloth. University of California Press. Berkeley, CA. 1985. Lane Studies in Regional Government, No. 6 ISBN:0-520-05147-5, ISBN13: 978-0-520-05147-8. Dewey:320.8/09772/52. LCCN:85-002776.
Audience: **u,f.** *Choice, 1986.*

Persky, Joseph & Wiewel, Wim **HC108.C4P47 2000**
When Corporations Leave Town: The Costs and Benefits of Metropolitan Job Sprawl. Trade Cloth. Wayne State University Press. Detroit, MI. 2000. 192p. ISBN:0-8143-2907-1, ISBN13: 978-0-8143-2907-8. Dewey:338.6/042/0977311. LCCN:00-009540.
Audience: **u,f.** *Choice, 2001.*

Schick, Allen **HJ2051.S33 1990**
The Capacity to Budget. Trade Cloth. Urban Institute Press. Washington, DC. 1990. 244p. ISBN:0-87766-438-2, ISBN13: 978-0-87766-438-3. Dewey:336.73. LCCN:89-025003.
Audience: **u,f.** *Choice, 1991.*

Schneider, Mark **HJ9145.S36 1989**
The Competitive City: The Political Economy of Suburbia. Trade Cloth. University of Pittsburgh Press. Pittsburgh, PA. 1989. 261p. Series in Policy and Institutional Studies ISBN:0-8229-3610-0, ISBN13: 978-0-8229-3610-7. Dewey:363/.0973. LCCN:89-030015.
Audience: **l,u,f.** *Choice, 1990.*

Sellers, Jeffrey M. **JS241 .S45 2002**
Governing from Below: Urban Regions and the Global Economy. Cloth Text. Cambridge University Press. New York, NY. 2002. 420p. Studies in Comparative Politics ISBN:0-521-65153-0, ISBN13: 978-0-521-65153-0. Dewey:330.9173/2. LCCN:2001-022306.
Audience: **u,f.** *Choice, 2003, 2002.*

Stephens, G. Ross & Wikstrom, Nelson **JS422.S74 2000**
Metropolitan Government and Governance: Theoretical Perspectives, Empirical Analysis, and the Future. Cloth Text. Oxford University Press, Inc. New York, NY. 1999. 256p. ISBN:0-19-511297-0, ISBN13: 978-0-19-511297-9. Dewey:320.8/5. LCCN:98-036766.
Audience: **u,f.** *Choice, 2000.*

American Government and Politics > Local Government > Cities

Agranoff, Robert & McGuire, Michael **JS356.A37 2003**
Collaborative Public Management: New Strategies for Local Governments. Trade Cloth, Trade Paper. Georgetown University Press. Washington, DC. 2004. 232p. American Governance and Public Policy Ser. ISBN:1-58901-018-3, ISBN13: 978-1-58901-018-5. Dewey:352.14/0973. LCCN:2002-014315.
Audience: **u,f.** *Choice, 2003.*

Bowers, James R. & Rich, Wilbur C. (Editors) **JS356.G68 2000**
Governing Middle-Sized Cities: Studies in Mayoral Leadership. Trade Cloth. Lynne Rienner Publishers, Inc. Boulder, CO. 2000. xi, 252p. ISBN:1-55587-895-4, ISBN13: 978-1-55587-895-5. Dewey:352.23/216/0973. LCCN:99-056088.
Audience: **u,f.** *Choice, 2000.*

Clark, Gordon L. **HN59.2**
Judges and the Cities: Interpreting Local Autonomy. Trade Cloth. University of Chicago Press. Chicago, IL. 1985. 264p. ISBN:0-226-10753-1, ISBN13: 978-0-226-10753-0. Dewey:306/.0973. LCCN:85-001018.
Audience: **u,f.** *Choice, 1986.*

Collier, Christopher **F99.C65 2003**
All Politics Is Local: Family, Friends, and Provincial Interests in the Creation of the Constitution. Library Binding. University Press of New England. Lebanon, NH. 2003. 244.p. ISBN:1-58465-290-X, ISBN13: 978-1-58465-290-8. Dewey:973.3/18. LCCN:2003-016930.
Audience: **l,u,f.** *Choice, 2004.*

Crooks, James B. **F319.J1C765 2004**
Jacksonville: The Consolidation Story, from Civil Rights to the Jaguars. Trade Cloth. University Press of Florida. Gainesville, FL. 2004. 296p. The Florida History and Culture Ser. ISBN:0-8130-2708-X, ISBN13: 978-0-8130-2708-1. Dewey:975.9/12043. LCCN:2003-066587.
Audience: **u,f.** *Choice, 2004.*

De La Torre, Miguel A. **F319.M6 D4 2003**
La Lucha for Cuba: Religion and Politics on the Streets of Miami. Trade Cloth. University of California Press. Berkeley, CA. 2003. 200p. ISBN:0-520-23526-6, ISBN13: 978-0-520-23526-7. Dewey:305.868/72910759381. LCCN:2002-015443.
Audience: **u,f.** *Choice, 2004.*

Elazar, Daniel J., et al. **JS434**
Opening Cybernetic Frontier: Cities of the Prairie. Joseph R. Marbach, Stephen L. Schechter, Rozanne Rothman, Maren Allan Stein & Karl Nollenberger (Authors). Trade Cloth. Transaction Publishers. Somerset, NJ. 2004. 390p. ISBN:0-7658-0201-5, ISBN13: 978-0-7658-0201-9. Dewey:307.76/0977. LCCN:2003-071116.
Audience: **u,f.** *Choice, 2005.*

Elkind, Sarah S. **HD4464.B67E45 1998**
Bay Cities and Water Politics: The Battle for Resources in Boston and Oakland. Trade Cloth. University Press of Kansas. Lawrence, KS. 1998. viii, 246p. Development of Western Resources Ser. ISBN:0-7006-0907-5, ISBN13: 978-0-7006-0907-9. Dewey:363.6/1/0974461. LCCN:96-012351.
Audience: **l,u,f.** *Choice, 1999.*

Healey, Patsy (Editor), et al. **HT107.M35 1995**
Managing Cities: The New Urban Context. Stuart Cameron, Simin Davoudi, Stephen Graham & Ali Madani-Pour (Editors). Trade Cloth. John Wiley & Sons, Inc. Hoboken, NJ. 1995. 332p. ISBN:0-471-94922-1, ISBN13: 978-0-471-94922-0. Dewey:307.76. LCCN:94-040240.
Audience: **l,u,f.** *Choice, 1995.*

Henig, Jeffrey R. & Rich, Wilbur C. (Editors) **LC5131.M39 2004**
Mayors in the Middle: Politics, Race, and Mayoral Control of Urban Schools. Trade Cloth. Princeton University Press.

Princeton, NJ. 2003. 280p. ISBN:0-691-11506-0, ISBN13: 978-0-691-11506-1. Dewey:370/.9173/2. LCCN:2003-054450.
Audience: **u,f.** *Choice, 2004.*

Imbroscio, David L. **HT123.I43 1997**
Reconstructing City Politics: Alternative Economic Development and Urban Regimes. Trade Paper. SAGE Publications, Inc. Thousand Oaks, CA. 1997. 232p. Cities and Planning Ser., Vol. 1 ISBN:0-7619-0613-4, ISBN13: 978-0-7619-0613-1. Dewey:307.76/0973. LCCN:96-035645.
Audience: **u,f.** *Choice, 1997.*

Isin, Engin F. **JS67.D45 2000**
Democracy, Citizenship and the Global City: Rights, Democracy and Place. Paper over Boards. Routledge. New York, NY. 2000. 336p. Innis Centenary Ser. ISBN:0-415-21667-2, ISBN13: 978-0-415-21667-8. Dewey:321.8. LCCN:00-025432.
Audience: **l,u,f.** *Choice, 2001.*

Jones-Correa, Michael (Editor) **JS323.G59 2001**
Governing American Cities: Inter-Ethnic Coalitions, Competition, and Conflict. Trade Cloth. Russell Sage Foundation. New York, NY. 2001. 272p. ISBN:0-87154-415-6, ISBN13: 978-0-87154-415-5. Dewey:320.8/5/0973. LCCN:2001-041782.
Audience: **u,f.** *Choice, 2002.*

Kaufmann, Karen M. **JS395.K38 2004**
The Urban Voter: Group Conflict and Mayoral Voting Behavior in American Cities. Trade Cloth. University of Michigan Press. Chicago, IL. 2004. 256p. The Politics of Race and Ethnicity Ser. ISBN:0-472-09857-8, ISBN13: 978-0-472-09857-6. Dewey:324.973/092/091732. LCCN:2003-016346.
Audience: **u,f.** *Choice, 2005.*

Ladd, Helen F. & Yinger, John M. **HJ9145.L32 1989**
America's Ailing Cities: Fiscal Health and the Design of Urban Policy. Trade Cloth. Johns Hopkins University Press. Baltimore, MD. 1989. 368p. ISBN:0-8018-3767-7, ISBN13: 978-0-8018-3767-8. Dewey:336/.014/73. LCCN:88-013653.
Audience: **l,u,f.** *Choice, 1989.*

Leland, Suzanne M. & Thurmaier, Kurt M. **JS422.C37 2004**
Case Studies of City-County Consolidation: Reshaping the Local Government Landscape. Trade Cloth. M. E. Sharpe Inc. Armonk, NY. 2004. 352p. Reshaping the Local Government Landscape Ser. ISBN:0-7656-0943-6, ISBN13: 978-0-7656-0943-4. Dewey:320.8/3/0973. LCCN:2003-024080.
Audience: **u,f.** *Choice, 2005.*

Logan, Michael F. **HT371.L64 1995**
Fighting Sprawl and City Hall: Resistance to Urban Growth in the Southwest. Trade Cloth. University of Arizona Press. Tucson, AZ. 1995. 223p. ISBN:0-8165-1512-3, ISBN13: 978-0-8165-1512-7. Dewey:307.1/716/09791776. LCCN:95-005590.
Audience: **u,f.** *Choice, 1996.*

Mudd, John **JS1228.M83 1984**
Neighborhood Services: Making Big Cities Work. Trade Cloth. Yale University Press. Cumberland, RI. 1985. 256p. ISBN:0-300-02657-9, ISBN13: 978-0-300-02657-3. Dewey:352/.000473/097471. LCCN:84-020975.
Audience: **u,f.** *Choice, 1985.*

Pagano, Michael A. & Moore, Richard **HJ9145.P34 1985**
Cities and Fiscal Choices: A New Model of Urban Public Investment. Trade Cloth. Duke University Press. Durham, NC. 1985. xii, 166p. Duke Press Policy Studies ISBN:0-8223-0653-0, ISBN13: 978-0-8223-0653-5. Dewey:336.02/73. LCCN:85-016211.
Audience: **l,u,f.** *Choice, 1986.*

Pammer, William J. Jr. **HJ9145**
Managing Fiscal Strain in Major American Cities: Understanding Retrenchment in the Public Sector, 247. Trade Cloth. Greenwood Publishing Group, Inc. Portsmouth, NH. 1990. 151p. Contributions in Political Science Ser., No. 247 ISBN:0-313-26656-5, ISBN13: 978-0-313-26656-0. Dewey:352.1/0973. LCCN:89-017073.
Audience: **u,f.** *Choice, 1990.*

Sonenshein, Raphael **JS1003.A2S66 2004**
The City at Stake: Secession, Reform, and the Battle for Los Angeles. Trade Cloth. Princeton University Press. Princeton, NJ. 2004. 328p. ISBN:0-691-11590-7, ISBN13: 978-0-691-11590-0. Dewey:320.9794/94. LCCN:2004-044253.
Audience: **f.** *Choice, 2005.*

Squires, Gregory D., et al. **HN80.C5C54 1987**
Chicago: Race, Class, and the Response to Urban Decline. Larry Bennett, Kathleen McCourt & Phillip Nyden (Authors). Trade Cloth. Temple University Press. Philadelphia, PA. 1987. 248p. Comparative American Cities Ser. ISBN:0-87722-487-0, ISBN13: 978-0-87722-487-7. Dewey:306/.09773/11. LCCN:87-001876.
Audience: **u,f.** *Choice, 1988.*

Teaford, Jon C. **JS411.T43 1997**
Post-Suburbia: Government and Politics in the Edge Cities. Trade Cloth. Johns Hopkins University Press. Baltimore, MD. 1996. 224p. ISBN:0-8018-5450-4, ISBN13: 978-0-8018-5450-7. Dewey:320.8/0973. LCCN:96-024378.
Audience: **g,u,f.** *Choice, 1997.*

Vogel, Ronald K. (Editor) **HT110**
Handbook of Research on Urban Politics and Policy in the United States, Vol. 28, no. 13. Cloth Text. Greenwood Publishing Group, Inc. Portsmouth, NH. 1997. 464p. ISBN:0-313-29166-7, ISBN13: 978-0-313-29166-1. Dewey:307.76/0973. LCCN:96-005786.
Audience: **l,u,f.** *Choice, 1997.*

Waste, Robert J. **JS341**
Power and Pluralism in American Cities: Researching the Urban Laboratory. Trade Cloth. Greenwood Publishing Group, Inc. Portsmouth, NH. 1987. 192p. Contributions in Political Science Ser., No. 165 ISBN:0-313-25016-2, ISBN13: 978-0-313-25016-3. Dewey:320.8/0973. LCCN:86-019381.
Audience: **u,f.** *Choice, 1987.*

Willem, Van Vliet (Editor) **HT65.C57 2001**
Cities in a Globalizing World: Global Report on Human Settlements. Trade Cloth. Earthscan/James & James. London, 2001. 350p. ISBN:1-85383-805-5, ISBN13: 978-1-85383-805-7. Dewey:307.76. LCCN:2001-002401.
Audience: **l,u,f.** *Choice, 2002.*

American Government and Politics > Public Administration

Baker, Randall (Editor) **JF1501**
Transitions from Authoritarianism: The Role of the Bureaucracy. Trade Cloth. Greenwood Publishing Group, Inc. Portsmouth, NH. 2001. 320p. ISBN:0-275-96458-2, ISBN13: 978-0-275-96458-0. Dewey:320.947. LCCN:2001-034582.
Audience: **u,f.** *Choice, 2003.*

Box, Richard C. **JF1351.B648 2004**
Critical Social Theory in Public Administration. Trade Cloth. M. E. Sharpe Inc. Armonk, NY. 2005. 176p. ISBN:0-7656-1554-1, ISBN13: 978-0-7656-1554-1. Dewey:351/.01/1. LCCN:2004-005154.
Audience: **u,f.** *Choice, 2005.*

Bresser-Pereira, Luiz Carlos **JC325**
Democracy and Public Management Reform: Building the Republican State. Trade Cloth. Oxford University Press, Inc. New York, NY. 2004. 328p. ISBN:0-19-926118-0, ISBN13: 978-0-19-926118-5. Dewey:351. LCCN:2005-295720.
Audience: **u,f.** *Choice, 2006.*

Denhardt, Janet Vinzant & Denhardt, Robert B. **JF1351.D4495 2002**
The New Public Service: Serving, Not Steering. Trade Cloth. M. E. Sharpe Inc. Armonk, NY. 2003. 216p. ISBN:0-7656-0845-6, ISBN13: 978-0-7656-0845-1. Dewey:351. LCCN:2002-066974.
Audience: **g,l,u,f.** *Choice, 2003.*

Denhardt, Robert B. **JF1351**
The Pursuit of Significance: Strategies for Managerial Success in Public Organizations. Paper Text. Waveland Press, Inc. Prospect Heights, IL. 2000. 300p. ISBN:1-57766-114-1, ISBN13: 978-1-57766-114-6. Dewey:350.
Audience: **g,u,f.**

Downs, Anthony **JF1351.D65**
An Economic Theory of Democracy. Trade Paper. Books on Demand. Ann Arbor, MI. 322p. ISBN:0-598-84640-9, ISBN13: 978-0-598-84640-2. Dewey:351. LCCN:57-010571.
Audience: **u,f.** ***E***

Downs, Anthony **JF1351**
Inside Bureaucracy. Paper Text. Waveland Press, Inc. Prospect Heights, IL. 1994. 292p. ISBN:0-88133-778-1, ISBN13: 978-0-88133-778-5. Dewey:301.18.
Audience: **g,l,u,f.** ***E***

Frederickson, H. George & Smith, Kevin B. **JF1351.F734 2003**
Public Administration Theory Primer. Trade Paper. Westview Press. Boulder, CO. 2003. 288p. ISBN:0-8133-9804-5, ISBN13: 978-0-8133-9804-4. Dewey:351/.01. LCCN:2003-001691.
Audience: **l,u.** *Choice, 2003.*

Fry, Brian R. **JF1341.F78 1989**
Mastering Public Administration: From Max Weber to Dwight Waldo. Paper Text. CQ Press. Washington, DC. 1989. 272p. Public Administration and Public Policy Ser. ISBN:0-934540-56-X, ISBN13: 978-0-934540-56-8. Dewey:352. LCCN:89-000624.
Audience: **l,u.** *Choice, 1990.*

Holden, Matthew Jr. **JF1351.H65 1996**
Continuity and Disruption: Essays in Public Administration. Cloth Text. University of Pittsburgh Press. Pittsburgh, PA. 1996. 291p. Series in Policy and Institutional Studies ISBN:0-8229-3885-5, ISBN13: 978-0-8229-3885-9. Dewey:350. LCCN:95-016081.
Audience: **l,u,f.** *Choice, 1997.*

Lilleker, Darren G. & Lees-Marshment, Jennifer (Editors) **JF112.C3**
Political Marketing: A Comparative Perspective. Trade Paper, Perfect. Manchester University Press. Manchester, 2005. 256p. ISBN:0-7190-6871-1, ISBN13: 978-0-7190-6871-3. Dewey:324.7. LCCN:2005-282341.
Audience: **u,f.** *Choice, 2006.*

Lynn, Laurence E. Jr. **JF1338.A3U56 1996**
Public Management As Art, Science, and Profession. Paper Text. CQ Press. Washington, DC. 1996. 208p. Public Administration and Public Policy Ser. ISBN:1-56643-034-8, ISBN13: 978-1-56643-034-0. Dewey:350. LCCN:95-041793.
Audience: **g,l,u.** *Choice, 1996.*

Moore, Mark H. **JF1525.E8M66 1995**
Creating Public Value: Strategic Management in Government. Trade Cloth. Harvard University Press. Cambridge, MA. 1995. 416p. ISBN:0-674-17557-3, ISBN13: 978-0-674-17557-0. Dewey:351.7/3. LCCN:95-018074.
Audience: **u,f.** *Choice, 1996.*

Peters, B. Guy & Pierre, Jon (Editors) **JF1351**
Handbook of Public Administration. Trade Cloth. SAGE Publications, Inc. Thousand Oaks, CA. 2003. 640p. ISBN:0-7619-7224-2, ISBN13: 978-0-7619-7224-2. Dewey:351. LCCN:2002-109398.
Audience: **g,l,u,f.** *Choice, 2004.*

Philanthropic Research, Inc., **HV89**
GuideStar.org.
http://www.guidestar.org/
Audience: **g,l,u,f.**

Rice, Mitchell F. **JF1658.D58 2004**
Diversity and Public Administration: Theory, Issues, and Perspectives. Trade Cloth. M. E. Sharpe Inc. Armonk, NY. 2005. 264p. ISBN:0-7656-1431-6, ISBN13: 978-0-7656-1431-5. Dewey:352.6/08. LCCN:2004-002827.
Audience: **l,u,f.** *Choice, 2005.*

Silberman, Bernard S. **JF1341.S55 1993**
Cages of Reason: The Rise of the Rational State in France, Japan, the United States, and Great Britain. Trade Paper. University of Chicago Press. Chicago, IL. 1993. 495p. ISBN:0-226-75737-4, ISBN13: 978-0-226-75737-7. Dewey:351.0009. LCCN:92-031653.
Audience: **l,u,f.** *Choice, 1994.*

American Government and Politics > Public Administration > Civil Service

Beito, David T. (Editor), et al. **JS78.V6 2002**
The Voluntary City: Choice, Community, and Civil Society. Deborah Gordon & Alexander Tabarrok (Editors). Trade Cloth.

University of Michigan Press. Chicago, IL. 2002. 480p. Economics, Cognition and Society Ser. ISBN:0-472-11240-6, ISBN13: 978-0-472-11240-1. Dewey:307.76. LCCN:2001-006444.
Audience: **u,f.** *Choice, 2003.*

Denhardt, Janet Vinzant & Denhardt, Robert B. **JF1351.D4495 2002**
The New Public Service: Serving, Not Steering. Trade Cloth. M. E. Sharpe Inc. Armonk, NY. 2003. 216p. ISBN:0-7656-0845-6, ISBN13: 978-0-7656-0845-1. Dewey:351. LCCN:2002-066974.
Audience: **g,l,u,f.** *Choice, 2003.*

Farazmand, Ali (Editor) **JF1501.M63 1997**
Modern Systems of Government: Exploring the Role of Bureaucrats and Politicians. Trade Paper. SAGE Publications, Inc. Thousand Oaks, CA. 1997. 336p. ISBN:0-7619-0609-6, ISBN13: 978-0-7619-0609-4. Dewey:350. LCCN:96-051224.
Audience: **u,f.** *Choice, 1997.*

Herman, Michael **JF1525.I6 H47 1996**
Intelligence Power in Peace and War. Trade Cloth. Cambridge University Press. New York, NY. 1996. 436p. ISBN:0-521-56231-7, ISBN13: 978-0-521-56231-7. Dewey:327.1/2. LCCN:95-048112.
Audience: **u,f.** *Choice, 1997.*

Light, Paul Charles **JK411.L54 1997**
The Tides of Reform: Making Government Work, 1945-1995. Cloth over Boards. Yale University Press. Cumberland, RI. 1997. 304p. ISBN:0-300-06987-1, ISBN13: 978-0-300-06987-7. Dewey:353.09. LCCN:96-038557.
Audience: **u,f.** *Choice, 1997.*

Moore, Mark H. **JF1525.E8M66 1995**
Creating Public Value: Strategic Management in Government. Trade Cloth. Harvard University Press. Cambridge, MA. 1995. 416p. ISBN:0-674-17557-3, ISBN13: 978-0-674-17557-0. Dewey:351.7/3. LCCN:95-018074.
Audience: **u,f.** *Choice, 1996.*

Pitz, Mary E. **JK716.P58 1994**
Careers in Government. Trade Cloth. McGraw-Hill/Contemporary. Lincolnwood, IL. 1995. 160p. VGM Professional Careers Ser. ISBN:0-8442-4194-6, ISBN13: 978-0-8442-4194-4. Dewey:351.73/023. LCCN:93-047955.
Audience: **g,l,u.**

Riccucci, Norma M. **JK723.E9R53 1995**
Unsung Heroes: Federal Execucrats Making a Difference. Trade Cloth. Georgetown University Press. Washington, DC. 1995. 266p. ISBN:0-87840-592-5, ISBN13: 978-0-87840-592-3. Dewey:331.7/95/092273. LCCN:95-007073.
Audience: **g,l,u.** *Choice, 1996.*

Rohr, John A. **K3440.R64 2002**
Civil Servants and Their Constitutions. Trade Cloth. University Press of Kansas. Lawrence, KS. 2002. 216p. Studies in Government and Public Policy ISBN:0-7006-1162-2, ISBN13: 978-0-7006-1162-1. Dewey:342/.068. LCCN:2001-006343.
Audience: **u,f.** *Choice, 2002.*

Rung, Margaret C. **JK765.R86 2002**
Servants of the State: Managing Diversity and Democracy in the Federal Workforce, 1933-1953. Trade Cloth. University of Georgia Press. Athens, GA. 2002. 312p. ISBN:0-8203-2362-4, ISBN13: 978-0-8203-2362-6. Dewey:352.6/0973. LCCN:2001-008552.
Audience: **u,f.** *Choice, 2003.*

Van Wart, Montgomery **JF1525.L4V35 2005**
The Dynamics of Leadership: Theory and Practice. Trade Cloth. M. E. Sharpe Inc. Armonk, NY. 2005. 520p. ISBN:0-7656-0901-0, ISBN13: 978-0-7656-0901-4. Dewey:352.3/9. LCCN:2004-017454.
Audience: **u,f.** *Choice, 2005.*

Waterman, Richard W., et al. **JF1501.W37 2004**
Bureaucrats, Politics, and the Environment. Amelia A. Rouse & Robert Wright (Authors). Trade Paper. University of Pittsburgh Press. Pittsburgh, PA. 2004. 160p. ISBN:0-8229-5829-5, ISBN13: 978-0-8229-5829-1. Dewey:351/.01. LCCN:2003-015505.
Audience: **l,u,f.** *Choice, 2005.*

White, Richard D. **E757.W575 2003**
Roosevelt the Reformer: Theodore Roosevelt As Civil Service Commissioner, 1889-1895. Trade Cloth. University of Alabama Press. Tuscaloosa, AL. 2003. 272p. ISBN:0-8173-1361-3, ISBN13: 978-0-8173-1361-6. Dewey:352.6/3/092 B. LCCN:2003-005508.
Audience: **u,f.** *Choice, 2004.*

Wilson, H. T. **JF1601.W55 2001**
Bureaucratic Representation: Civil Servants and the Future of Capitalist Democracies. Trade Cloth. Brill Academic Publishers. Leiden, 2001. 230p. International Comparative Social Studies, Vol. 1 ISBN:90-04-12194-3, ISBN13: 978-90-04-12194-2. Dewey:351. LCCN:2001-025260.
Audience: **u,f.** *Choice, 2002.*

American Government and Politics > Public Administration > E-government

ZA5075
☐ FirstGov.gov: The U.S. Government's Official Web Portal. http://www.firstgov.gov/
Audience: **g,l,u,f.**

Abramson, Mark A. & Morin, Therese L. **JK468.A8**
E-Government 2003. Book, Other. Rowman & Littlefield Publishers, Inc. Lanham, MD. 2002. 416p. The Pricewaterhouse-Coopers Endowment Series on the Business of Government ISBN:0-7425-2796-4, ISBN13: 978-0-7425-2796-6. Dewey:350.
Audience: **g,l,u,f.**

Blackstone, Erwin A., et al. **JK468.A8I56 2005**
Innovations in E-Government: The Thoughts of Governors and Mayors. Michael Bognanno & Simon Hakim (Authors). Trade Cloth. Rowman & Littlefield Publishers, Inc. Lanham, MD. 2005. 312p. ISBN:0-7425-4912-7, ISBN13: 978-0-7425-4912-8. Dewey:352.3/8213/02854678. LCCN:2005-009263.
Audience: **g,l,u,f.**

Curtain, Gregory G. (Editor), et al. **JF1525.A8W674 2004**
The World of E-Government. Michael H. Sommer & Veronika Vis-Sommer (Editors). Cloth Text. Haworth Press, Incorporated,

The. Binghamton, NY. 2003. 254p. A Monograph Published Simultaneously As the Journal of Political Marketing Ser. ISBN:0-7890-2305-9, ISBN13: 978-0-7890-2305-6. Dewey:352.3/8/02854678. LCCN:2003-015574.
Audience: **g,l,u,f.**

United Nations, Department of Economic and Social Affairs Staff **JF1525.A8W68 2003**
World Public Sector Report 2003: E-Government at the Crossroads. Trade Paper. United Nations Publications. New York, NY. 2003. 256p. ISBN:92-1-123150-7, ISBN13: 978-92-1-123150-2. Dewey:384.33. LCCN:2004-299333.
Audience: **g,l,u,f.**

American Government and Politics > Citizenship

Boyte, Harry Chatten **JK1764.B697 2004**
Everyday Politics: The Power of Public Work. Trade Cloth. University of Pennsylvania Press. Philadelphia, PA. 2004. 264p. ISBN:0-8122-3814-1, ISBN13: 978-0-8122-3814-3. Dewey:306.2/0973. LCCN:2004-041297.
Audience: **l,u,f.** *Choice, 2005.*

Croteau, David **JK1764.C76 1995**
Politics and the Class Divide: Working People and the Middle Class Left. Paper Text. Temple University Press. Philadelphia, PA. 1994. 320p. Labor and Social Change Ser. ISBN:1-56639-255-1, ISBN13: 978-1-56639-255-6. Dewey:323/.042/0973. LCCN:94-037907.
Audience: **l,u,f.**

Ellis, Richard J. **JK1759.E37 2004**
To the Flag: The History of the Pledge of Allegiance. Trade Cloth. University Press of Kansas. Lawrence, KS. 2005. 312p. ISBN:0-7006-1372-2, ISBN13: 978-0-7006-1372-4. Dewey:323.6/5/0973. LCCN:2004-023110.
Audience: **g,l,u,f.** *Choice, 2006.*

Fullinwider, Robert K. (Editor) **JK1764.C5267 1999**
Civil Society, Democracy and Civic Renewal. Book, Other. Rowman & Littlefield Publishers, Inc. Lanham, MD. 1999. 442p. ISBN:0-8476-9355-4, ISBN13: 978-0-8476-9355-9. Dewey:301/.0973. LCCN:98-048272.
Audience: **l,u,f.**

Kymlicka, Will **JF1061.K96 1996**
[e] Multicultural Citizenship: A Liberal Theory of Minority Rights. E-Book. NetLibrary, Inc. Boulder, CO. 1996. ISBN:0-585-42845-X, ISBN13: 978-0-585-42845-1. Dewey:323.1/1.
Audience: **l,u,f.** *Choice, 1996.*

Macedo, Stephen **JK1764.M33 2005**
Democracy at Risk: How Political Choices Undermine Citizen Participation, and What We Can Do about It. Perfect, Paper over Boards, Dust Jacket. Brookings Institution Press. Washington, DC. 2005. 228p. ISBN:0-8157-5404-3, ISBN13: 978-0-8157-5404-6. Dewey:323/.042/0973. LCCN:2005-012395.
Audience: **l,u,f.** *Choice, 2006.*

Nie, Norman H., et al. **JK1764.N54 1996**
Education and Democratic Citizenship in America. Jane Junn & Kenneth Stehlik-Barry (Authors). Trade Paper. University of Chicago Press. Chicago, IL. 1996. 290p. ISBN:0-226-58389-9, ISBN13: 978-0-226-58389-1. Dewey:306.2. LCCN:95-026657.
Audience: **g,l,u,f.** *Choice, 1997.*

Rosenstone, Steven J. & Hansen, John Mark **JK1764**
Mobilization, Participation and Democracy in America. Trade Paper. Longman Publishing Group. White Plains, NY. 2002. 368p. Classic Ser. ISBN:0-321-12186-4, ISBN13: 978-0-321-12186-8. Dewey:323.042.
Audience: **l,u,f.**

Skocpol, Theda **JK1764.S544 2003**
Diminished Democracy: From Membership to Management in American Civic Life. Trade Cloth. University of Oklahoma Press. Norman, OK. 2003. 384p. The Julian J. Rothbaum Distinguished Lecture Ser., Vol. 8 ISBN:0-8061-3532-8, ISBN13: 978-0-8061-3532-8. Dewey:306.2/0973. LCCN:2002-029138.
Audience: **g,l,u,f.**

Skocpol, Theda & Fiorina, Morris (Editors) **JK1764.C5266 1999**
Civic Engagement in American Democracy. Trade Paper. Brookings Institution Press. Washington, DC. 1999. 528p. ISBN:0-8157-2810-7, ISBN13: 978-0-8157-2810-8. Dewey:323/.042/0973. LCCN:99-006407.
Audience: **g,l,u,f.** *Choice, 2000.*

American Government and Politics > Campaigns and Elections

Alice McGillivray, Richard Scammon, and Rhodes Cook **JK1967**
America Votes 26: 2003-2004, Election Returns by State. CQ Press. 2005. America Votes ISBN:1-56802-974-8, ISBN13: 978-1-56802-974-0.
Audience: **g,l,u,f.**

American National Election Studies **JF1001**
□ American National Elections Studies (ANES). http://www.electionstudies.org/
Audience: **u,f.**

Binning, William C., et al. **JK9**
Encyclopedia of American Parties, Campaigns and Elections. Larry E. Esterly & Paul A. Sracic (Authors). Cloth Text. Greenwood Publishing Group, Inc. Portsmouth, NH. 1999. 480p. ISBN:0-313-30312-6, ISBN13: 978-0-313-30312-8. Dewey:324/.0973/03. LCCN:98-046810.
Audience: **g,l,u,f.** *Choice, 2000.*

C. Q. Press Staff **JK1976**
Guide to U. S. Elections. Ed. 5. Trade Cloth. CQ Press. Washington, DC. 2005. 1,101p. ISBN:1-56802-981-0, ISBN13: 978-1-56802-981-8. Dewey:324.973.
Audience: **g,l,u,f.**

Eagleton Institute of Politics, Rutgers University **HQ1236.5.U6**
□ Center for American Women and Politics. http://www.rci.rutgers.edu/~cawp/index.html
Audience: **l,u,f.**

Federal Election Commission **JK1991**
Federal Election Commission. http://www.fec.gov/
Audience: **g,l,u,f.**

Ford, Gerald, et al. **JK1965**
To Assure Pride and Confidence in the Electoral Process: Report of the National Commission on Federal Election Reform. Jimmy Carter, Robert H. Michell & Lloyd N. Cutler (Authors). Trade Paper. Brookings Institution Press. Washington, DC. 2002. 400p. ISBN:0-8157-0631-6, ISBN13: 978-0-8157-0631-1. Dewey:324.6/5/0973. LCCN:2002-020054.
Audience: **g,l,u,f.** *Choice, 2003.*

Herrnson, Paul (Editor), et al. **JK2265.G84 2005**
Guide to Political Campaigns in America. Colton Campbell, Marni Ezra & Stephen K. Medvic (Editors). Perfect, Paper over Boards. CQ Press. Washington, DC. 2005. 457p. ISBN:1-56802-876-8, ISBN13: 978-1-56802-876-7. Dewey:324.7/0973. LCCN:2005-018123.
Audience: **g,l,u,f.** *Choice, 2006.*

Maisel, Louis S. (Editor) **JK2261.P633 1991**
Political Parties and Elections in the United States: An Encyclopedia, Set. Paper over Boards. Garland Publishing, Inc. New York, NY. 1991. 1367p. ISBN:0-8240-7975-2, ISBN13: 978-0-8240-7975-8. Dewey:324.273/03. LCCN:91-006940.
Audience: **g,l,u,f.** *Choice, 1991.*

Richardson, Glenn W. Jr. **JK2281.R53 2002**
Pulp Politics: How Political Advertising Tells the Stories of American Politics. Book, Other. Rowman & Littlefield Publishers, Inc. Lanham, MD. 2002. 192p. ISBN:0-7425-0100-0, ISBN13: 978-0-7425-0100-3. Dewey:324.7/3/0973. LCCN:2002-010309.
Audience: **g,l,u,f.** *Choice, 2003.*

Rusk, Jerrold G. **JK1967.R87 2001**
A Statistical History of the American Electorate. Trade Paper. CQ Press. Washington, DC. 2001. 450p. ISBN:1-56802-363-4, ISBN13: 978-1-56802-363-2. Dewey:324.973. LCCN:00-067453.
Audience: **g,l,u,f.** *Choice, 2002.*

Shafer, Byron E. (Editor) **JK2261.E475 1991**
The End of Realignment?: Interpreting American Electoral Eras. Trade Paper. University of Wisconsin Press. Chicago, IL. 1991. 200p. ISBN:0-299-12974-8, ISBN13: 978-0-299-12974-3. Dewey:324.973. LCCN:91-007505.
Audience: **l,u,f.** *Choice, 1992.*

American Government and Politics > Campaigns and Elections > Electoral System

Beyle, Thad L. (Editor) **JK2447.G82 1989**
Gubernatorial Transitions: The 1983 and 1984 Elections. Barry Van Lare (Preface by). Cloth Text. Duke University Press. Durham, NC. 1988. x, 384p. ISBN:0-8223-0858-4, ISBN13: 978-0-8223-0858-4. Dewey:353.9/134. LCCN:88-014711.
Audience: **l,u,f.** *Choice, 1989.*

Boatright, Robert G. **JK1976.B57 2004**
Expressive Politics: Issue Strategies of Congressional Challengers. Trade Cloth. Ohio State University Press. Columbus, OH. 2004. xxiii, 253p. ISBN:0-8142-9044-2, ISBN13: 978-0-8142-9044-6. Dewey:823/.912. LCCN:2004-003369.
Audience: **g,l,u.** *Choice, 2005.*

Brady, David W., et al. **JK1965.C578 2000**
Continuity and Change in House Elections. John F. Cogan & Morris P. Fiorina (Authors). Trade Paper. Stanford University Press. Palo Alto, CA. 2000. xv, 297p. ISBN:0-8047-3739-8, ISBN13: 978-0-8047-3739-5. Dewey:324.973/0929. LCCN:00-039488.
Audience: **g,l,u.** *Choice, 2001.*

Burbank, Garin **JK2391**
When Farmers Voted Red: The Gospel of Socialism in the Oklahoma Countryside, 1910-1924. Trade Cloth. Greenwood Publishing Group, Inc. Portsmouth, NH. 1977. 225p. Contributions in American History Ser., No. 53 ISBN:0-8371-8903-9, ISBN13: 978-0-8371-8903-1. Dewey:335/.009766. LCCN:76-005259.
Audience: **u,f.**

Burnham, Walter Dean **JK1965.B85**
Critical Elections and the Mainsprings of American Politics. Trade Cloth. Norton. Farnborough, 1970. xii, 210p. ISBN:0-393-09962-8, ISBN13: 978-0-393-09962-1. Dewey:324/.73. LCCN:70-117450.
Audience: **l,u,f.**

C. Q. Press Staff **JK1976**
Guide to U. S. Elections. Ed. 5. Trade Cloth. CQ Press. Washington, DC. 2005. 1,101p. ISBN:1-56802-981-0, ISBN13: 978-1-56802-981-8. Dewey:324.973.
Audience: **g,l,u,f.**

Campbell, Angus, et al. **JK1976**
The American Voter. Philip E. Converse, Warren E. Miller & Donald E. Stokes (Authors). Trade Paper. University of Chicago Press. Chicago, IL. 1980. 576p. Midway Reprint Ser. ISBN:0-226-09254-2, ISBN13: 978-0-226-09254-6. Dewey:324.2. LCCN:76-021115.
Audience: **g,l,u.**

Dudley, Robert L. & Gitelson, Alan R. **JK1976.D83 2002**
American Elections: The Rules Matter. Trade Paper. Longman Publishing Group. White Plains, NY. 2001. 176p. ISBN:0-321-08684-8, ISBN13: 978-0-321-08684-6. Dewey:324.6/3/0973. LCCN:2001-038522.
Audience: **g,l,u,f.**

Dwyre, Diana & Farrar-Myers, Victoria **JK1991.D99 2001**
Legislative Labyrinth: Congress and Campaign Finance Reform. Trade Paper. CQ Press. Washington, DC. 2000. xii, 291p. ISBN:1-56802-568-8, ISBN13: 978-1-56802-568-1. Dewey:324.7/8/0973. LCCN:00-046830.
Audience: **l,u,f.** *Choice, 2001.*

Ford, Gerald, et al. **JK1965**
To Assure Pride and Confidence in the Electoral Process: Report of the National Commission on Federal Election Reform. Jimmy Carter, Robert H. Michell & Lloyd N. Cutler (Authors). Trade Paper. Brookings Institution Press. Washington, DC. 2002. 400p.

ISBN:0-8157-0631-6, ISBN13: 978-0-8157-0631-1. Dewey:324.6/5/0973. LCCN:2002-020054.
Audience: **g,l,u,f.** *Choice, 2003.*

Herrnson, Paul S. **JK1976.H47 2004**
Congressional Elections: Campaigning at Home and in Washington. Ed. 4. Trade Paper. CQ Press. Washington, DC. 2003. 331p. ISBN:1-56802-826-1, ISBN13: 978-1-56802-826-2. Dewey:324.973/0931. LCCN:2003-017650.
Audience: **g,l,u,f.** *Choice, 1995.*

Herrnson, Paul S. **JK1976.H473 2001**
Playing Hardball: Campaigning for the U. S. Congress. Trade Paper. Prentice Hall PTR. Upper Saddle River, NJ. 2000. 160p. Real Politics in America Ser. ISBN:0-13-027133-0, ISBN13: 978-0-13-027133-4. Dewey:324.7/0973. LCCN:00-061979.
Audience: **g,l,u,f.**

Jacobson, Gary C. **JK1976.J27 2004**
The Politics of Congressional Elections. Ed. 6. Trade Paper. Longman Publishing. Boston, MA. 2003. 296p. Longman Classics in Political Science Ser. ISBN:0-321-10040-9, ISBN13: 978-0-321-10040-5. Dewey:324.973. LCCN:2003-060922.
Audience: **g,l,u,f.**

Kornbluh, Mark Lawrence **JK1965.K67 2000**
Why America Stopped Voting: The Decline of Participatory Democracy and the Emergence of Modern A. Trade Cloth. New York University Press. New York, NY. 1999. 352p. American Social Experience Ser. ISBN:0-8147-4708-6, ISBN13: 978-0-8147-4708-7. Dewey:324.973. LCCN:99-006956.
Audience: **g,l,u,f.** *Choice, 2000.*

Mann, Thomas E. **JK1976.M355**
Unsafe at Any Margin: Interpreting Congressional Elections. Trade Paper. Books on Demand. Ann Arbor, MI. 124p. AEI Studies, Vol. 220 ISBN:0-598-09291-9, ISBN13: 978-0-598-09291-5. Dewey:324.973. LCCN:78-020335.
Audience: **u,f.**

Mayer, William G. & Busch, Andrew E. **JK2071.M39 2003**
The Front-Loading Problem in Presidential Nominations. Trade Paper. Brookings Institution Press. Washington, DC. 2003. 288p. ISBN:0-8157-5519-8, ISBN13: 978-0-8157-5519-7. Dewey:324.273/154. LCCN:2003-019912.
Audience: **u,f.**

National Association of Secretaries of State (NASS)
State Election Laws & Administration Issues. http://www.nass.org/electioninfo/laws&admin.htm
Audience: **g,l,u,f.**

Nimmo, Dan D. **JK1976.N5 2001**
The Political Persuaders: The Techniques of Modern Election Campaigns. Ed. 2. Trade Paper. Transaction Publishers. Somerset, NJ. 2001. 246p. Classics in Communication and Mass Culture Ser. ISBN:0-7658-0613-4, ISBN13: 978-0-7658-0613-0. Dewey:324.7. LCCN:99-013923.
Audience: **l,u,f.**

Patterson, Thomas E. **JK1965**
The Vanishing Voter: Public Involvement in an Age of Uncertainty. Trade Paper. Knopf Publishing Group. New York, NY. 2003. 288p. ISBN:0-375-71379-4, ISBN13: 978-0-375-71379-8. Dewey:324.6/5/0973.
Audience: **g,l,u.** *Choice, 2003.*

Piven, Frances Fox & Cloward, Richard A. **JK1987.P58 2000**
Why Americans Still Don't Vote: And Why Politicians Want It That Way. Trade Paper. Beacon Press. Boston, MA. 2000. 296p. ISBN:0-8070-0449-9, ISBN13: 978-0-8070-0449-4. Dewey:324.973. LCCN:00-039770.
Audience: **g,l,u.** *Choice, 2001.*

Rosenof, Theodore **JK1967.R66 2003**
Realignment: The Theory That Changed the Way We Think about American Politics. Trade Paper. Rowman & Littlefield Publishers, Inc. Lanham, MD. 2003. 248p. ISBN:0-7425-3105-8, ISBN13: 978-0-7425-3105-5. Dewey:324.973/001. LCCN:2002-153094.
Audience: **u,f.** *Choice, 2004.*

Rusk, Jerrold G. **JK1967.R87 2001**
A Statistical History of the American Electorate. Trade Paper. CQ Press. Washington, DC. 2001. 450p. ISBN:1-56802-363-4, ISBN13: 978-1-56802-363-2. Dewey:324.973. LCCN:00-067453.
Audience: **g,l,u,f.** *Choice, 2002.*

Sabato, Larry J. **JK1968 2002.M53 2003**
Midterm Madness: The Elections of 2002. Book, Other. Rowman & Littlefield Publishers, Inc. Lanham, MD. 2003. 296p. Center for Politics Ser. ISBN:0-7425-2685-2, ISBN13: 978-0-7425-2685-3. Dewey:324.973/0931. LCCN:2003-001964.
Audience: **g,l,u.** *Choice, 2003.*

Sanders, Randy **JK1965.S26 2002**
Mighty Peculiar Elections: The New South Gubernatorial Campaigns of 1970 and the Changing Politics of Race. Trade Cloth. University Press of Florida. Gainesville, FL. 2002. xii, 218p. ISBN:0-8130-2565-6, ISBN13: 978-0-8130-2565-0. Dewey:324.975/043. LCCN:2002-027135.
Audience: **u,f.** *Choice, 2003.*

Scala, Dante J. **JK2075.N42S33 2003**
Stormy Weather: The New Hampshire Primary and Presidential Politics. Cloth over Boards. Palgrave Macmillan. New York, NY. 2003. 224p. ISBN:0-312-29622-3, ISBN13: 978-0-312-29622-3. Dewey:324.273/0154/09742. LCCN:2003-062319.
Audience: **l,u,f.** *Choice, 2004.*

Scammon, Richard M. **JK1967**
America Votes: A Handbook of Contemporary American Election Statistics, Vol. 24. Trade Cloth. CQ Press. Washington, DC. 2001. 500p. ISBN:1-56802-600-5, ISBN13: 978-1-56802-600-8. Dewey:324.973.
Audience: **g,l,u,f.**

Schier, Steven E. **JK1976.S36 2003**
You Call This an Election?: America's Peculiar Democracy. Trade Cloth. Georgetown University Press. Washington, DC. 2003. 176p. ISBN:0-87840-895-9, ISBN13: 978-0-87840-895-5. Dewey:324.6/2/0973. LCCN:2002-013812.
Audience: **g,l.** *Choice, 2003.*

Semetko, Holli A., et al. **JK1976.F67 1991**
The Formation of Campaign Agendas: A Comparative Analysis of Party and Media Roles in Recent American and British Elections. Jay G. Blumler & Michael Gurevitch (Authors). Cloth

Text. Lawrence Erlbaum Associates, Inc. Mahwah, NJ. 1990. 216p. ISBN:0-8058-0656-3, ISBN13: 978-0-8058-0656-4. Dewey:324.7/0973. LCCN:90-040152.
Audience: **l,u,f.** *Choice, 1991.*

Shade, William Gerald (Editor), et al. **JK1965.A57 2002**
American Presidential Campaigns and Elections: A Reference Guide, Set. Rob Campbell, Ballard C. Campbell & Craig R. Coenen (Editors). Library Binding, Trade Cloth. M. E. Sharpe Inc. Armonk, NY. 2003. 1328p. ISBN:0-7656-8042-4, ISBN13: 978-0-7656-8042-6. Dewey:324.973. LCCN:2002-021185.
Audience: **g,l,u,f.** *Choice, 2003.*

Sidlow, Edward I. **JK1343.I3S53 2004**
Challenging the Incumbent: An Underdog's Undertaking. Trade Paper. CQ Press. Washington, DC. 2003. 150p. ISBN:1-56802-820-2, ISBN13: 978-1-56802-820-0. Dewey:324.9773/2044. LCCN:2003-014504.
Audience: **g,l,u,f.**

Squire, Peverill & Hamm, Keith E. **JK2488.S69 2005**
101 Chambers: Congress, State Legislatures, and the Future of Legislative Studies. Trade Cloth. Ohio State University Press. Columbus, OH. 2005. x, 209p. ISBN:0-8142-0938-6, ISBN13: 978-0-8142-0938-7. Dewey:328.73. LCCN:2004-023577.
Audience: **u,f.** *Choice, 2005.*

Ware, Alan **JK2071.W37 2002**
The American Direct Primary: Party Institutionalization and Transformation in the American North. Trade Cloth. Cambridge University Press. New York, NY. 2002. 286p. ISBN:0-521-81492-8, ISBN13: 978-0-521-81492-8. Dewey:324.273/0154. LCCN:2002-073481.
Audience: **l,u,f.** *Choice, 2003.*

Watson, Robert P. **JK1976.C645 2004**
Counting Votes: Lessons from the 2000 Presidential Election in Florida. Trade Cloth. University Press of Florida. Gainesville, FL. 2004. 336p. ISBN:0-8130-2714-4, ISBN13: 978-0-8130-2714-2. Dewey:324.973. LCCN:2004-043737.
Audience: **g,l,u,f.** *Choice, 2005.*

Wattenberg, Martin P. **JK2261.W38 1991**
The Rise of Candidate-Centered Politics: Presidential Elections of the 1980s. Trade Cloth. Harvard University Press. Cambridge, MA. 1991. 198p. ISBN:0-674-77130-3, ISBN13: 978-0-674-77130-7. Dewey:324.973/092. LCCN:90-036471.
Audience: **l,u,f.** *Choice, 1991.*

Westlye, Mark C. **JK1965.W47**
Senate Elections and Campaign Intensity. Trade Paper. Books on Demand. Ann Arbor, MI. 276p. ISBN:0-608-06715-6, ISBN13: 978-0-608-06715-5. Dewey:324.7/0973. LCCN:90-046421.
Audience: **l,u,f.** *Choice, 1992.*

Whillock, Rita K. **JK1976**
Political Empiricism: Communication Strategies in State and Regional Elections. Trade Cloth. Greenwood Publishing Group, Inc. Portsmouth, NH. 1991. 272p. Praeger Series in Political Communication ISBN:0-275-93554-X, ISBN13: 978-0-275-93554-2. Dewey:324.7/0973. LCCN:91-019412.
Audience: **u,f.** *Choice, 1992.*

American Government and Politics > Campaigns and Elections > Political Parties

Black, Earl & Black, Merle **JK2295.A13B583 1992**
The Vital South: How Presidents Are Elected. Trade Cloth. Harvard University Press. Cambridge, MA. 1992. 416p. ISBN:0-674-94130-6, ISBN13: 978-0-674-94130-4. Dewey:324.975. LCCN:91-026725.
Audience: **l,u,f.** *Choice, 1992.*

Boix, Carles **JF2011 .B65 1998**
Political Parties, Growth and Equality: Conservative and Social Democratic Economic Strategies in the World Economy. Trade Paper. Cambridge University Press. New York, NY. 1998. 295p. Studies in Comparative Politics ISBN:0-521-58595-3, ISBN13: 978-0-521-58595-8. Dewey:324.2. LCCN:97-027896.
Audience: **u,f.** *Choice, 1999.*

Burden, Barry C. & Kimball, David C. **JK2271.B9155 2002**
Why Americans Split Their Tickets: Campaigns, Competition, and Divided Government. Trade Cloth. University of Michigan Press. Chicago, IL. 2002. 216p. ISBN:0-472-11286-4, ISBN13: 978-0-472-11286-9. Dewey:324.973. LCCN:2002-005413.
Audience: **u,f.** *Choice, 2003.*

Burns, Nancy, et al. **JK1764.B87 2001**
The Private Roots of Public Action: Gender, Equality, and Political Participation. Kay Lehman Schlozman & Sidney Verba (Authors). Trade Paper. Harvard University Press. Cambridge, MA. 2001. 480p. ISBN:0-674-00660-7, ISBN13: 978-0-674-00660-7. Dewey:323/.042/0973. LCCN:2001-024928.
Audience: **l,u,f.** *Choice, 2002.*

Fenno, Richard F. Jr. **JK2281**
Senators on the Campaign Trail: The Politics of Representation. Trade Paper. University of Oklahoma Press. Norman, OK. 1998. 448p. Julian J. Rothbaum Distinguished Lecture Ser., Vol. 6 ISBN:0-8061-3062-8, ISBN13: 978-0-8061-3062-0. Dewey:324.7/0973.
Audience: **g,l,u,f.** *Choice, 1996.*

Friedenberg, Robert V. **JK2281**
Communication Consultants in Political Campaigns: Ballot Box Warriors. Paper Text. Greenwood Publishing Group, Inc. Portsmouth, NH. 1997. 240p. Praeger Series in Political Communication ISBN:0-275-95207-X, ISBN13: 978-0-275-95207-5. Dewey:659.2/9324/0973. LCCN:97-014471.
Audience: **l,u,f.** *Choice, 1998.*

Gaddie, Ronald Keith **JK2281.G33 2003**
Born to Run: Origins of the Political Career. Trade Paper. Rowman & Littlefield Publishers, Inc. Lanham, MD. 2003. 240p. Campaigning American Style Ser. ISBN:0-7425-1928-7,

ISBN13: 978-0-7425-1928-2. Dewey:324.7/0973.
LCCN:2003-013487.
Audience: **l,u,f.** *Choice, 2004.*

Gimpel, James & Schuknecht, Jason **JK2261**
Patchwork Nation: Sectionalism and Political Change in American Politics. Trade Paper. University of Michigan Press. Chicago, IL. 2004. 488p. ISBN:0-472-03030-2, ISBN13: 978-0-472-03030-9. Dewey:324.973/092. LCCN:2002-156536.
Audience: **u,f.**

Goldman, Ralph M. **JK2263 1990**
The National Party Chairmen and Committees: Factionalism at the Top. Cloth Text. M. E. Sharpe Inc. Armonk, NY. 1990. 672p. ISBN:0-87332-636-9, ISBN13: 978-0-87332-636-0. Dewey:324.273/09. LCCN:89-070272.
Audience: **l,u,f.** *Choice, 1991.*

Green, John C. & Herrnson, Paul S. (Editors) **JK2261.R47 2002**
Responsible Partisanship?: The Evolution of American Political Parties since 1950. Trade Paper. University Press of Kansas. Lawrence, KS. 2003. xii, 252p. Studies in Government and Public Policy ISBN:0-7006-1217-3, ISBN13: 978-0-7006-1217-8. Dewey:324.273/09/045. LCCN:2002-009286.
Audience: **l,u,f.** *Choice, 2003.*

James, Scott C. **JK2316 .J36 2000**
Presidents, Parties, and the State: A Party System Perspective on Democratic Regulatory Choice, 1884-1936. Trade Cloth. Cambridge University Press. New York, NY. 2000. 318p. ISBN:0-521-66277-X, ISBN13: 978-0-521-66277-2. Dewey:324.2736/09/034. LCCN:99-037782.
Audience: **u,f.** *Choice, 2001.*

Kahn, Kim Fridkin & Kenney, Patrick J. **JK2281.K24 1999**
The Spectacle of U. S. Senate Campaigns. Trade Paper. Princeton University Press. Princeton, NJ. 1999. 292p. ISBN:0-691-00505-2, ISBN13: 978-0-691-00505-8. Dewey:324.7/0973. LCCN:98-032011.
Audience: **l,u,f.** *Choice, 2000.*

Kohl, Lawrence F. **JK2261**
The Politics of Individualism: Parties and the American Character in the Jacksonian Era. Trade Paper. Oxford University Press, Inc. New York, NY. 1991. 288p. ISBN:0-19-506781-9, ISBN13: 978-0-19-506781-1. Dewey:324.273/09.
Audience: **u,f.** *Choice, 1989.*

Kymlicka, Will **JF1061.K96 1996**
e Multicultural Citizenship: A Liberal Theory of Minority Rights. E-Book. NetLibrary, Inc. Boulder, CO. 1996. ISBN:0-585-42845-X, ISBN13: 978-0-585-42845-1. Dewey:323.1/1.
Audience: **l,u,f.** *Choice, 1996.*

Lublin, David **JK2356.L89 2004**
The Republican South: Democratization and Partisan Change. Trade Cloth. Princeton University Press. Princeton, NJ. 2004. 272p. ISBN:0-691-05041-4, ISBN13: 978-0-691-05041-6. Dewey:324.2734/0975. LCCN:2004-041468.
Audience: **l,u,f.** *Choice, 2004.*

Maisel, L. Sandy (Editor) **JK2261.P29 1998**
The Parties Respond: Changes in American Parties and Campaigns. Ed. 3. Trade Paper. Westview Press. Boulder, CO. 1997. 432p. Transforming American Politics Ser. ISBN:0-8133-9960-2, ISBN13: 978-0-8133-9960-7. Dewey:324.273. LCCN:97-032510.
Audience: **l,u.** *Choice, 2003.*

Maisel, Louis S. (Editor) **JK2261.P633 1991**
Political Parties and Elections in the United States: An Encyclopedia, Set. Paper over Boards. Garland Publishing, Inc. New York, NY. 1991. 1367p. ISBN:0-8240-7975-2, ISBN13: 978-0-8240-7975-8. Dewey:324.273/03. LCCN:91-006940.
Audience: **g,l,u,f.** *Choice, 1991.*

Mayer, William G. **JK2316.M29 1996**
Divided Democrats: Ideological Unity, Party Reform, and Presidential Elections. Trade Paper. Westview Press. Boulder, CO. 1996. 240p. Transforming American Politics Ser. ISBN:0-8133-2680-X, ISBN13: 978-0-8133-2680-1. Dewey:324.2/73/06. LCCN:96-008135.
Audience: **l,u,f.** *Choice, 1997.*

Mayhew, David **JK2261**
Divided We Govern: Party Control, Lawmaking, and Investigations, 1946-2002. Ed. 2. Trade Paper. Yale University Press. Cumberland, RI. 2005. 288p. ISBN:0-300-10288-7, ISBN13: 978-0-300-10288-8. Dewey:328.73077.
Audience: **l,u,f.**

Mayhew, David R. **JK2261.M364 2004**
Electoral Realignments: A Critique of an American Genre. Trade Paper. Yale University Press. Cumberland, RI. 2004. 192p. The Institution for Social and Policy St Ser. ISBN:0-300-09365-9, ISBN13: 978-0-300-09365-0. Dewey:324/.0973.
Audience: **u,f.** *Choice, 2003.*

McCaffery, Peter **JK2359.P53.M33 1993**
When Bosses Ruled Philadelphia: The Emergence of the Republican Machine, 1867-1933. Trade Cloth. Pennsylvania State University Press. University Park, PA. 1993. 304p. ISBN:0-271-00923-3, ISBN13: 978-0-271-00923-0. Dewey:324.2748/1104. LCCN:92-042467.
Audience: **l,u,f.** *Choice, 1994.*

Morreale, Joanne **JK2281**
The Presidential Campaign Film: A Critical History. Paper Text. Greenwood Publishing Group, Inc. Portsmouth, NH. 1996. 224p. ISBN:0-275-95580-X, ISBN13: 978-0-275-95580-9. Dewey:324.730973. LCCN:93-020129.
Audience: **l,u,f.** *Choice, 1994.*

Shafer, Byron E. **JK2255.S49 1988**
Bifurcated Politics: Evolution and Reform in the National Party Convention. Trade Cloth. Harvard University Press. Cambridge, MA. 1988. 416p. Russell Sage Foundation Study Ser. ISBN:0-674-07256-1, ISBN13: 978-0-674-07256-5. Dewey:324.5/6/0973. LCCN:87-033493.
Audience: **l,u,f.** *Choice, 1988.*

Steed, Robert P. (Editor), et al. **JK2295.A13S66 1997**
Southern Parties and Elections: Studies in Regional Political Change. Laurence W. Moreland & Tod A. Baker (Editors). Trade Cloth. University of Alabama Press. Tuscaloosa, AL.

1997. 240p. ISBN:0-8173-0862-8, ISBN13: 978-0-8173-0862-9. Dewey:324.275. LCCN:96-035563.
Audience: **u,f.** *Choice, 1998.*

Stonecash, Jeffrey M. **JK2261.S86 2000**
Class and Party in American Politics. Trade Paper. Westview Press. Boulder, CO. 2000. 208p. Transforming American Politics Ser. ISBN:0-8133-9756-1, ISBN13: 978-0-8133-9756-6. Dewey:324.273/09/045. LCCN:00-027528.
Audience: **l,u,f.** *Choice, 2001.*

Stonecash, Jeffrey M. **JK2261.S863 2006**
Political Parties Matter: Realignment and the Return of Partisan Voting. Paper Text. Lynne Rienner Publishers, Inc. Boulder, CO. 2005. 175p. ISBN:1-58826-394-0, ISBN13: 978-1-58826-394-0. Dewey:324.273. LCCN:2005-018291.
Audience: **l,u,f.** *Choice, 2006.*

Stonecash, Jeffrey M. & McGuire, Mary P. **JK2295.N6S76 2002**
The Emergence of State Government: Parties and New Jersey Politics, 1950-1999. Trade Cloth. Fairleigh Dickinson University Press. Cranbury, NJ. 2003. 304p. ISBN:0-8386-3953-4, ISBN13: 978-0-8386-3953-5. Dewey:320.9749/09/045. LCCN:2002-190213.
Audience: **l,u,f.** *Choice, 2003.*

Voss-Hubbard, Mark **JK2341.A6V67 2002**
Beyond Party: Cultures of Antipartisanship in Northern Politics Before the Civil War. Trade Cloth. Johns Hopkins University Press. Baltimore, MD. 2002. 280p. Reconfiguring American Political History Ser. ISBN:0-8018-6940-4, ISBN13: 978-0-8018-6940-2. Dewey:324.2732. LCCN:2001-006623.
Audience: **u,f.** *Choice, 2004.*

Watson, Robert P. & Campbell, Colton C. (Editors) **JK2281.C354 2003**
Campaigns and Elections: Issues, Concepts, Cases. Paper Text. Lynne Rienner Publishers, Inc. Boulder, CO. 2003. 300p. ISBN:1-58826-144-1, ISBN13: 978-1-58826-144-1. Dewey:324.973. LCCN:2002-068270.
Audience: **l,u.** *Choice, 2003.*

White, John Kenneth & Shea, Daniel M. **JK2261**
New Party Politics: From Jefferson and Hamilton to the Information Age. Ed. 2. Paper Text. Thomson Wadsworth. Belmont, CA. 2003. 400p. ISBN:0-534-56023-7, ISBN13: 978-0-534-56023-2. Dewey:324.273. LCCN:2003-103163.
Audience: **l,u,f.**

American Government and Politics > Campaigns and Elections > Political Parties > History

Aldrich, John H. **JK2261.A46 1995**
Why Parties?: The Origin and Transformation of Political Parties in America. Trade Paper. University of Chicago Press. Chicago, IL. 1995. 355p. American Politics and Political Economy Ser. ISBN:0-226-01272-7, ISBN13: 978-0-226-01272-8. Dewey:324.2/73/09. LCCN:94-036879.
Audience: **l,u.** *Choice, 1995.*

Green, John C. & Herrnson, Paul S. (Editors) **JK2261.R47 2002**
Responsible Partisanship?: The Evolution of American Political Parties since 1950. Trade Paper. University Press of Kansas. Lawrence, KS. 2003. xii, 252p. Studies in Government and Public Policy ISBN:0-7006-1217-3, ISBN13: 978-0-7006-1217-8. Dewey:324.273/09/045. LCCN:2002-009286.
Audience: **l,u,f.** *Choice, 2003.*

James, Scott C. **JK2316 .J36 2000**
Presidents, Parties, and the State: A Party System Perspective on Democratic Regulatory Choice, 1884-1936. Trade Cloth. Cambridge University Press. New York, NY. 2000. 318p. ISBN:0-521-66277-X, ISBN13: 978-0-521-66277-2. Dewey:324.2736/09/034. LCCN:99-037782.
Audience: **u,f.** *Choice, 2001.*

Kohl, Lawrence F. **JK2261**
The Politics of Individualism: Parties and the American Character in the Jacksonian Era. Trade Paper. Oxford University Press, Inc. New York, NY. 1991. 288p. ISBN:0-19-506781-9, ISBN13: 978-0-19-506781-1. Dewey:324.273/09.
Audience: **u,f.** *Choice, 1989.*

Mayhew, David **JK2261**
Divided We Govern: Party Control, Lawmaking, and Investigations, 1946-2002. Ed. 2. Trade Paper. Yale University Press. Cumberland, RI. 2005. 288p. ISBN:0-300-10288-7, ISBN13: 978-0-300-10288-8. Dewey:328.73077.
Audience: **l,u,f.**

McCaffery, Peter **JK2359.P53.M33 1993**
When Bosses Ruled Philadelphia: The Emergence of the Republican Machine, 1867-1933. Trade Cloth. Pennsylvania State University Press. University Park, PA. 1993. 304p. ISBN:0-271-00923-3, ISBN13: 978-0-271-00923-0. Dewey:324.2748/1104. LCCN:92-042467.
Audience: **l,u,f.** *Choice, 1994.*

McGerr, Michael E. **E661.M415 2003**
A Fierce Discontent: The Rise and Fall of the Progressive Movement in America, 1870-1920. Trade Cloth. Simon & Schuster. New York, NY. 2003. 416p. ISBN:0-684-85975-0, ISBN13: 978-0-684-85975-0. Dewey:324.2732/7. LCCN:2003-048499.
Audience: **u.** *Choice, 2004.*

Naison, Mark **JK2391.C53**
Communists in Harlem During the Depression. Trade Paper. University of Illinois Press. Champaign, IL. 2004. 378p. ISBN:0-252-07271-5, ISBN13: 978-0-252-07271-0. Dewey:324.27375097471. LCCN:2005-272203.
Audience: **l,u,f.** B

Shafer, Byron E. (Editor) **JK2261.E475 1991**
The End of Realignment?: Interpreting American Electoral Eras. Trade Paper. University of Wisconsin Press. Chicago, IL. 1991. 200p. ISBN:0-299-12974-8, ISBN13: 978-0-299-12974-3. Dewey:324.973. LCCN:91-007505.
Audience: **l,u,f.** *Choice, 1992.*

Stonecash, Jeffrey M. & McGuire, Mary P. **JK2295.N6S76 2002**
The Emergence of State Government: Parties and New Jersey Politics, 1950-1999. Trade Cloth. Fairleigh Dickinson University Press. Cranbury, NJ. 2003. 304p. ISBN:0-8386-3953-4, ISBN13:

978-0-8386-3953-5. Dewey:320.9749/09/045. LCCN:2002-190213.
Audience: **l,u,f.** *Choice, 2003.*

Voss-Hubbard, Mark **JK2341.A6V67 2002**
Beyond Party: Cultures of Antipartisanship in Northern Politics Before the Civil War. Trade Cloth. Johns Hopkins University Press. Baltimore, MD. 2002. 280p. Reconfiguring American Political History Ser. ISBN:0-8018-6940-4, ISBN13: 978-0-8018-6940-2. Dewey:324.2732. LCCN:2001-006623.
Audience: **u,f.** *Choice, 2004.*

Ware, Alan **JK2316.W373 2006**
The Democratic Party Heads North. 1877-1962. Trade Paper. Cambridge University Press. New York, NY. 2006. 160p. ISBN:0-521-67500-6, ISBN13: 978-0-521-67500-0. Dewey:324.2736/09. LCCN:2005-018254.
Audience: **u,f.** *Choice, 2006.*

White, John Kenneth & Shea, Daniel M. **JK2261**
New Party Politics: From Jefferson and Hamilton to the Information Age. Ed. 2. Paper Text. Thomson Wadsworth. Belmont, CA. 2003. 400p. ISBN:0-534-56023-7, ISBN13: 978-0-534-56023-2. Dewey:324.273. LCCN:2003-103163.
Audience: **l,u,f.**

American Government and Politics > Campaigns and Elections > Political Parties > Democrats

Camejo, Peter, et al. **JK2317 1959**
The Lesser Evil?: Debates on the Democratic Party and Independent Working-Class Politics. Michael Harrington, Jack Barnes, Stanley Aronowitz, George Breitman & Carl Haessler (Authors). Trade Paper. Pathfinder Press. New York, NY. 1978. 147p. ISBN:0-87348-518-1, ISBN13: 978-0-87348-518-0. Dewey:324.2736/09. LCCN:77-085124.
Audience: **g,l,u,f.**

Democratic National Committee
□ The Democratic Party.
http://www.democrats.org/index.html
Audience: **g,l,u,f.**

Mayer, William G. **JK2316.M29 1996**
Divided Democrats: Ideological Unity, Party Reform, and Presidential Elections. Trade Paper. Westview Press. Boulder, CO. 1996. 240p. Transforming American Politics Ser. ISBN:0-8133-2680-X, ISBN13: 978-0-8133-2680-1. Dewey:324.2/73/06. LCCN:96-008135.
Audience: **l,u,f.** *Choice, 1997.*

Ware, Alan **JK2316.W373 2006**
The Democratic Party Heads North. 1877-1962. Trade Paper. Cambridge University Press. New York, NY. 2006. 160p. ISBN:0-521-67500-6, ISBN13: 978-0-521-67500-0. Dewey:324.2736/09. LCCN:2005-018254.
Audience: **u,f.** *Choice, 2006.*

American Government and Politics > Campaigns and Elections > Political Parties > Republicans

Hacker, Jacob & Pierson, Paul **JK2356.H155 2005**
Off Center: The Republican Revolution and the Erosion of American Democracy. Cloth over Boards. Yale University Press. Cumberland, RI. 2005. 272p. ISBN:0-300-10870-2, ISBN13: 978-0-300-10870-5. Dewey:324.2734/09/0511. LCCN:2005-015114.
Audience: **g,l,u,f.** *Choice, 2006.*

Lublin, David **JK2356.L89 2004**
The Republican South: Democratization and Partisan Change. Trade Cloth. Princeton University Press. Princeton, NJ. 2004. 272p. ISBN:0-691-05041-4, ISBN13: 978-0-691-05041-6. Dewey:324.2734/0975. LCCN:2004-041468.
Audience: **l,u,f.** *Choice, 2004.*

McCaffery, Peter **JK2359.P53.M33 1993**
When Bosses Ruled Philadelphia: The Emergence of the Republican Machine, 1867-1933. Trade Cloth. Pennsylvania State University Press. University Park, PA. 1993. 304p. ISBN:0-271-00923-3, ISBN13: 978-0-271-00923-0. Dewey:324.2748/1104. LCCN:92-042467.
Audience: **l,u,f.** *Choice, 1994.*

Republican National Committee
□ Republican National Committee.
http://www.rnc.org/
Audience: **g,l,u,f.**

American Government and Politics > Campaigns and Elections > Political Parties > Political Ideologies and Movements

Goldman, Emma **HX843.7.G65 E427**
Emma Goldman: A Documentary History of the American Years. Candace Falk, Barry Pateman & Jessica M. Moran (Editors). Trade Cloth. University of California Press. Berkeley, CA. 2003. 696p. Emma Goldman Ser., :A Documentary History of the American Years Ser. ISBN:0-520-08670-8, ISBN13: 978-0-520-08670-8. Dewey:335/.83/092 B. LCCN:2002-028943.
Audience: **g,l,u,f.** *Choice, 2003.*

Kelley, Robin D. **HX91.A2K45 1990**
Hammer and Hoe: Alabama Communists During the Great Depression. Trade Paper. University of North Carolina Press. Chapel Hill, NC. 1990. 392p. Fred W. Morrison Series in Southern Studies ISBN:0-8078-4288-5, ISBN13: 978-0-8078-4288-1. Dewey:324.2761/075/09042. LCCN:90-050018.
Audience: **g,l,u,f.** *Choice, 1991.*

Labaree, Leonard W. **E188**
Conservatism in Early American History. Trade Paper. Cornell University Press. Ithaca, NY. 1959. 182p. ISBN:0-8014-9008-1, ISBN13: 978-0-8014-9008-8. Dewey:320.520973.
Audience: **u,f.**

Lipset, Seymour Martin & Marks, Gary **HX83.L55 2000**
It Didn't Happen Here: Why Socialism Failed in the United States. Trade Cloth. W. W. Norton & Company, Inc. New York, NY. 2000. 384p. ISBN:0-393-04098-4, ISBN13: 978-0-393-04098-2. Dewey:335/.00973. LCCN:00-021489.
Audience: **g,l,u,f.** *Choice, 2000.*

Rosemont, Franklin & Radcliffe, Charles **HX843.D36 2004**
Dancin' in the Streets!: Anarchists, IWWs, Surrealists, Situationists and Provos in the 1960s As Recorded in the Pages of the Rebel Worker and Heatwave. Trade Paper. Charles H. Kerr Publishing Company. Chicago, IL. 2005. 450p. The Sixties Ser., Vol. 3 ISBN:0-88286-301-0, ISBN13: 978-0-88286-301-6. Dewey:335/.83/097309046. LCCN:2004-056799.
Audience: **g,l,u,f.** *Choice, 2005.*

Schwarzmantel, J. J. **JA83.S367 1998**
The Age of Ideology: Political Ideologies from the American Revolution to Postmodern Times. Trade Cloth. New York University Press. New York, NY. 1998. 304p. ISBN:0-8147-8095-4, ISBN13: 978-0-8147-8095-4. Dewey:320.5. LCCN:97-025893.
Audience: **u,f.** *Choice, 1999.*

Solomon, Mark **HX83.S665 1998**
The Cry Was Unity: Communists and African Americans, 1917-1936. Trade Paper. University Press of Mississippi. Jackson, MS. 1998. 400p. ISBN:1-57806-095-8, ISBN13: 978-1-57806-095-5. Dewey:335.43/089/96073. LCCN:98-016013.
Audience: **l,u,f.** *Choice, 1999.*

American Government and Politics > Campaigns and Elections > Political Parties > Local Politics

Naison, Mark **JK2391.C53**
Communists in Harlem During the Depression. Trade Paper. University of Illinois Press. Champaign, IL. 2004. 378p. ISBN:0-252-07271-5, ISBN13: 978-0-252-07271-0. Dewey:324.27375097471. LCCN:2005-272203.
Audience: **l,u,f.** B

Steed, Robert P. (Editor), et al. **JK2295.A13S66 1997**
Southern Parties and Elections: Studies in Regional Political Change. Laurence W. Moreland & Tod A. Baker (Editors). Trade Cloth. University of Alabama Press. Tuscaloosa, AL. 1997. 240p. ISBN:0-8173-0862-8, ISBN13: 978-0-8173-0862-9. Dewey:324.275. LCCN:96-035563.
Audience: **u,f.** *Choice, 1998.*

Stonecash, Jeffrey M. & McGuire, Mary P. **JK2295.N6S76 2002**
The Emergence of State Government: Parties and New Jersey Politics, 1950-1999. Trade Cloth. Fairleigh Dickinson University Press. Cranbury, NJ. 2003. 304p. ISBN:0-8386-3953-4, ISBN13: 978-0-8386-3953-5. Dewey:320.9749/09/045. LCCN:2002-190213.
Audience: **l,u,f.** *Choice, 2003.*

American Government and Politics > Campaigns and Elections > Political Participation

Armstrong, Jerome & Moulitsas Zúniga, Markos **JK1764.A76 2005**
Crashing the Gate: Netroots, Grassroots, and the Rise of People-Powered Politics. Trade Cloth. Chelsea Green Publishing. White River Junction, VT. 2006. 216p. ISBN:1-931498-99-7, ISBN13: 978-1-931498-99-9. Dewey:324.70973. LCCN:2005-036402.
Audience: **g,l,u,f.** *Choice, 2006.*

Barber, Benjamin R. **JK1726 .B27 1998**
A Passion for Democracy: American Essays. Trade Paper. Princeton University Press. Princeton, NJ. 2000. 306p. ISBN:0-691-05024-4, ISBN13: 978-0-691-05024-9. Dewey:320.473.
Audience: **g,l,u,f.** *Choice, 1999.*

Cobb, Roger W. & Elder, Charles D. **JK1764.C54**
Participation in American Politics: The Dynamics of Agenda Building. Ed. 2. Trade Paper. Books on Demand. Ann Arbor, MI. 210p. ISBN:0-8357-8259-X, ISBN13: 978-0-8357-8259-3. Dewey:323.0420973. LCCN:83-048051.
Audience: **l,u,f.**

Cooney, Robert P. J. Jr. **JK1896.C65 2005**
Winning the Vote: The Triumph of the American Woman Suffrage Movement. Cloth Text. American Graphic Press. Santa Cruz, CA. 2005. 496p. ISBN:0-9770095-0-5, ISBN13: 978-0-9770095-0-3. Dewey:324.6/230973. LCCN:2005-904560.
Audience: **g,l,u,f.** *Choice, 2006.*

Davidson, Chandler **JK1929.A2Q54 1994**
Quiet Revolution in the South: The Impact of the Voting Rights Act, 1965-1990. Bernard N. Grofman (Editor). Trade Paper. Princeton University Press. Princeton, NJ. 1994. 516p. ISBN:0-691-02108-2, ISBN13: 978-0-691-02108-9. Dewey:324.6/2/08996073075. LCCN:93-038961.
Audience: **l,u,f.** *Choice, 1994.*

Ehrenhalt, Alan **JK1717.E36 1991**
United States of Ambition: Politicians, Power, and the Pursuit of Office. Trade Cloth. Random House, Inc. New York, NY. 1991. vii, 309p. ISBN:0-8129-1894-0, ISBN13: 978-0-8129-1894-6. Dewey:324/.0973. LCCN:90-046243.
Audience: **g,l,u,f.** *Choice, 1991.*

Hibbing, John R. & Theiss-Morse, Elizabeth **JK1764**
e Stealth Democracy: Americans' Beliefs about How Government Should Work. James H. Kuklinski & Dennis Chong (Contribution by). E-Book. Cambridge University Press. New York, NY. 2005. Cambridge Studies in Public Opinion and Political Psychology Ser. ISBN:0-511-02984-5, ISBN13: 978-0-511-02984-4. Dewey:323/.042/0973.
Audience: **g,l,u,f.** *Choice, 2003.*

Karvonen, Lauri (Editor), et al. **JF2051.P296 2000**
Party Systems and Voter Alignments Revisited. Ed. 2. Stein Kuhnle & Seymour Martin Lipset (Editors). Paper over Boards. Routledge. New York, NY. 2000. 336p. Advances in

International Relations and Politics Ser. ISBN:0-415-23720-3, ISBN13: 978-0-415-23720-8. Dewey:324.9. LCCN:00-029115.
Audience: **l,u.** *Choice, 2001.*

Keiser, Richard A. JK1764.K45 1997
Subordination or Empowerment?: African-American Leadership and the Struggle for Urban Political Power. Trade Cloth. Oxford University Press, Inc. New York, NY. 1997. 254p. ISBN:0-19-507569-2, ISBN13: 978-0-19-507569-4. Dewey:303.3/089/96073. LCCN:96-041161.
Audience: **l,u,f.** *Choice, 1998.*

Kousser, J. Morgan JK1924.K68 1999
Colorblind Injustice: Minority Voting Rights and the Undoing of the Second Reconstruction. Trade Paper. University of North Carolina Press. Chapel Hill, NC. 1999. 608p. ISBN:0-8078-4738-0, ISBN13: 978-0-8078-4738-1. Dewey:328.750734. LCCN:98-016693.
Audience: **l,u,f.**

Morone, James A. JK1764.M67 1998
The Democratic Wish: Popular Participation and the Limits of American Government. Ed. 2. Trade Paper. Yale University Press. Cumberland, RI. 1998. 416p. ISBN:0-300-07465-4, ISBN13: 978-0-300-07465-9. Dewey:323/.042/0973. LCCN:97-080178.
Audience: **l,u,f.**

Osterman, Paul JK1764.O85 2002
Gathering Power: The Future of Progressive Politics in America. Trade Cloth. Beacon Press. Boston, MA. 2003. 256p. ISBN:0-8070-4338-9, ISBN13: 978-0-8070-4338-7. Dewey:322.4/0973. LCCN:2002-006811.
Audience: **g,l,u,f.** *Choice, 2003.*

Parker, Frank R. E185.93.M6P37 1990
Black Votes Count: Political Empowerment in Mississippi after 1965. Trade Paper. University of North Carolina Press. Chapel Hill, NC. 1990. 272p. ISBN:0-8078-4274-5, ISBN13: 978-0-8078-4274-4. Dewey:323.1/1960730762. LCCN:89-039074.
Audience: **l,u,f.** *Choice, 1991.*

Patterson, Thomas E. JK1965
The Vanishing Voter: Public Involvement in an Age of Uncertainty. Trade Paper. Knopf Publishing Group. New York, NY. 2003. 288p. ISBN:0-375-71379-4, ISBN13: 978-0-375-71379-8. Dewey:324.6/5/0973.
Audience: **g,l,u.** *Choice, 2003.*

Pomper, Gerald M. & Weiner, Marc D. (Editors) JK1726.F88 2003
The Future of American Democratic Politics: Principles and Practices. Trade Paper. Rutgers University Press. Piscataway, NJ. 2003. 296p. ISBN:0-8135-3298-1, ISBN13: 978-0-8135-3298-1. Dewey:320.973. LCCN:2002-037013.
Audience: **l,u,f.** *Choice, 2004.*

Rusk, Jerrold G. JK1967.R87 2001
A Statistical History of the American Electorate. Trade Paper. CQ Press. Washington, DC. 2001. 450p. ISBN:1-56802-363-4, ISBN13: 978-1-56802-363-2. Dewey:324.973. LCCN:00-067453.
Audience: **g,l,u,f.** *Choice, 2002.*

Sandel, Michael J. JK1726.S325 1996
Democracy's Discontent: America in Search of a Public Philosophy. Trade Cloth. Harvard University Press. Cambridge, MA. 1996. 432p. ISBN:0-674-19744-5, ISBN13: 978-0-674-19744-2. Dewey:320.9/73. LCCN:95-046825.
Audience: **u,f.**

Skocpol, Theda JK1764.S544 2003
Diminished Democracy: From Membership to Management in American Civic Life. Trade Cloth. University of Oklahoma Press. Norman, OK. 2003. 384p. The Julian J. Rothbaum Distinguished Lecture Ser., Vol. 8 ISBN:0-8061-3532-8, ISBN13: 978-0-8061-3532-8. Dewey:306.2/0973. LCCN:2002-029138.
Audience: **g,l,u,f.**

Skocpol, Theda & Fiorina, Morris (Editors) JK1764.C5266 1999
Civic Engagement in American Democracy. Trade Paper. Brookings Institution Press. Washington, DC. 1999. 528p. ISBN:0-8157-2809-3, ISBN13: 978-0-8157-2809-2. Dewey:323/.042/0973. LCCN:99-006407.
Audience: **g,l,u,f.** *Choice, 2000.*

Stonecash, Jeffrey M. JK2261.S863 2006
Political Parties Matter: Realignment and the Return of Partisan Voting. Paper Text. Lynne Rienner Publishers, Inc. Boulder, CO. 2005. 175p. ISBN:1-58826-394-0, ISBN13: 978-1-58826-394-0. Dewey:324.273. LCCN:2005-018291.
Audience: **l,u,f.** *Choice, 2006.*

Verba, Sidney & Nie, Norman H. JK1764.V467 1987
Participation in America: Political Democracy and Social Equality. Trade Paper. University of Chicago Press. Chicago, IL. 2004. 452p. ISBN:0-226-85296-2, ISBN13: 978-0-226-85296-6. Dewey:323/.042/0973. LCCN:87-010825.
Audience: **g,l,u,f.** B

Walters, Ronald W. JK1924.W34 1988
Black Presidential Politics in America: A Strategic Approach. Paper Text. State University of New York Press. Albany, NY. 1987. 255p. SUNY Series in Afro-American Studies ISBN:0-88706-547-3, ISBN13: 978-0-88706-547-7. Dewey:324.6/2/08996073. LCCN:86-030160.
Audience: **l,u,f.** *Choice, 1988.*

Walters, Ronald W. JK1924.W343 2005
Freedom Is Not Enough: Black Voters, Black Candidates, and American Presidential Politics. Trade Cloth. Rowman & Littlefield Publishers, Inc. Lanham, MD. 2005. 256p. American Political Challenges Ser. ISBN:0-7425-3837-0, ISBN13: 978-0-7425-3837-5. Dewey:324.6/2/08996073. LCCN:2005-008343.
Audience: **g,l,u,f.** *Choice, 2006.*

American Government and Politics > Campaigns and Elections > Presidential Elections

Alice McGillivray, Richard Scammon, and Rhodes Cook JK524.A73 1994
America at the Polls 1920-1956: Harding to Eisenhower'A Handbook of American Presidential Election Statistics. CQ

Press. 1999. America at the Polls ISBN:1-56802-058-9, ISBN13: 978-1-56802-058-7.
Audience: **l,u,f.**

Black, Earl & Black, Merle **JK2295.A13B583 1992**
The Vital South: How Presidents Are Elected. Trade Cloth. Harvard University Press. Cambridge, MA. 1992. 416p. ISBN:0-674-94130-6, ISBN13: 978-0-674-94130-4. Dewey:324.975. LCCN:91-026725.
Audience: **l,u,f.** *Choice, 1992.*

Burnham, W. Dean **JK524 .B8 1976**
Presidential Ballots, 1836-1892. Trade Cloth. Ayer Company Publishers, Inc. Manchester, NH. 1976. America in Two Centuries Ser. ISBN:0-405-07678-9, ISBN13: 978-0-405-07678-7. Dewey:329/.023/73. LCCN:75-022806.
Audience: **g,l,u,f.**

C. Q. Press Staff **E176.1**
Presidential Elections 1789-2004. Trade Paper. CQ Press. Washington, DC. 2005. 320p. ISBN:1-56802-983-7, ISBN13: 978-1-56802-983-2. Dewey:324.973.
Audience: **g,l,u,f.**

Geospatial & Statistical Data Center, University of Virginia Library **29622**
US Presidential Election Maps: 1860-1996.
http://fisher.lib.virginia.edu/collections/stats/elections/maps/
Audience: **g,l,u,f.**

Hohenberg, John **E884.H64 1994**
The Bill Clinton Story: Winning the Presidency. Trade Cloth. Syracuse University Press. Syracuse, NY. 1994. 296p. ISBN:0-8156-0284-7, ISBN13: 978-0-8156-0284-2. Dewey:324.9730928. LCCN:93-047406.
Audience: **g,l,u,f.**

McGillivray, Alice V., et al. **JK524.A73 2005**
America at the Polls 1960-2004: Kennedy to George W. Bush - A Handbook of American Presidential Election Statistics, Vol. 2. Richard M. Scammon & Rhodes Cook (Authors). Trade Cloth. CQ Press. Washington, DC. 2005. 1,184p. ISBN:1-56802-977-2, ISBN13: 978-1-56802-977-1. Dewey:324.97309021.
Audience: **g,l,u,f.**

National Archives and Records Administration (NARA) **CD3023**
NARA: U.S. Electoral College.
http://www.archives.gov/federal-register/electoral-college/index.html
Audience: **g,l,u,f.**

Roberts, Robert North & Hammond, Scott J. **E176**
Encyclopedia of Presidential Campaigns, Slogans, Issues, and Platforms. Cloth Text. Greenwood Publishing Group, Inc. Portsmouth, NH. 2004. 432p. ISBN:0-313-31973-1, ISBN13: 978-0-313-31973-0. Dewey:324.973/003. LCCN:2003-059538.
Audience: **g,l,u,f.** *Choice, 2004.*

Schroeder, Alan **JF2112.D43S37 2000**
Presidential Debates: Forty Years of High-Risk TV. Trade Cloth. Columbia University Press. New York, NY. 2000. 280p. ISBN:0-231-11400-1, ISBN13: 978-0-231-11400-4. Dewey:324.7/3/0973. LCCN:00-035831.
Audience: **g,l,u,f.** *Choice, 2001.*

Shade, William Gerald (Editor), et al. **JK1965.A57 2002**
American Presidential Campaigns and Elections: A Reference Guide, Set. Rob Campbell, Ballard C. Campbell & Craig R. Coenen (Editors). Library Binding, Trade Cloth. M. E. Sharpe Inc. Armonk, NY. 2003. 1328p. ISBN:0-7656-8042-4, ISBN13: 978-0-7656-8042-6. Dewey:324.973. LCCN:2002-021185.
Audience: **g,l,u,f.** *Choice, 2003.*

Thomas, G. Scott **JK524**
The Pursuit of the White House: A Handbook of Presidential Election Statistics and History. Cloth Text. Greenwood Publishing Group, Inc. Portsmouth, NH. 1987. 501p. ISBN:0-313-25795-7, ISBN13: 978-0-313-25795-7. Dewey:324.973/0021. LCCN:87-011968.
Audience: **g,l,u,f.** *Choice, 1988.*

Walters, Ronald W. **JK1924.W34 1988**
Black Presidential Politics in America: A Strategic Approach. E-Book. NetLibrary, Inc. Boulder, CO. 1988. ISBN:0-585-09216-8, ISBN13: 978-0-585-09216-4. Dewey:324.6/2/08996073.
Audience: **l,u,f.** *Choice, 1988.*

Walters, Ronald W. **JK1924.W34 1988**
Black Presidential Politics in America: A Strategic Approach. Paper Text. State University of New York Press. Albany, NY. 1987. 255p. SUNY Series in Afro-American Studies ISBN:0-88706-547-3, ISBN13: 978-0-88706-547-7. Dewey:324.6/2/08996073. LCCN:86-030160.
Audience: **l,u,f.** *Choice, 1988.*

Wattenberg, Martin P. **JK2261.W38 1991**
The Rise of Candidate-Centered Politics: Presidential Elections of the 1980s. Trade Cloth. Harvard University Press. Cambridge, MA. 1991. 198p. ISBN:0-674-77130-3, ISBN13: 978-0-674-77130-7. Dewey:324.973/092. LCCN:90-036471.
Audience: **l,u,f.** *Choice, 1991.*

American Government and Politics > Campaigns and Elections > Presidential Elections > Primaries and Caucuses

Bartels, Larry M. **JK522.B37 1988**
Presidential Primaries and the Dynamics of Public Choice. Trade Paper. Princeton University Press. Princeton, NJ. 1988. 400p. ISBN:0-691-02283-6, ISBN13: 978-0-691-02283-3. Dewey:324.54. LCCN:87-038187.
Audience: **u,f.** *Choice, 1988.*

Burnham, W. Dean **JK524 .B8 1976**
Presidential Ballots, 1836-1892. Trade Cloth. Ayer Company Publishers, Inc. Manchester, NH. 1976. America in Two Centuries Ser. ISBN:0-405-07678-9, ISBN13: 978-0-405-07678-7. Dewey:329/.023/73. LCCN:75-022806.
Audience: **g,l,u,f.**

National Archives and Records Administration (NARA) **CD3023**
NARA: U.S. Electoral College.
http://www.archives.gov/federal-register/electoral-college/index.html
Audience: **g,l,u,f.**

American Government and Politics > Campaigns and Elections > Congressional Elections

Clerk of the U.S. House of Representatives
Congressional Election Statistics 1920 - 2004.
http://clerk.house.gov/members/electionInfo/elections.html
Audience: **g,l,u,f.**

Congressional Quarterly, Inc. Staff **JK1967.C64 1998**
Congressional Elections, 1946-1996. Cloth Text. Congressional Quarterly, Inc. Washington, DC. 1997. 375p. ISBN:1-56802-248-4, ISBN13: 978-1-56802-248-2. Dewey:324.973/092. LCCN:97-035242.
Audience: **g,l,u,f.**

CQ Editors **JK1341.C65 2003**
Congressional Districts in the 2000s: A Portrait of America. Trade Cloth. CQ Press. Washington, DC. 2003. 1,200p. ISBN:1-56802-849-0, ISBN13: 978-1-56802-849-1. Dewey:328.73/07345/090511. LCCN:2003-065430.
Audience: **g,l,u,f.** *Choice, 2004.*

Dubin, Michael J. **JK1967.D77 1998**
United States Congressional Elections, 1788-1997: The Official Results of the Elections of the 1st Through 105th Congresses. Cloth Text. McFarland & Company, Incorporated Publishers. Jefferson, NC. 1998. 1035p. ISBN:0-7864-0283-0, ISBN13: 978-0-7864-0283-0. Dewey:324.973. LCCN:96-9841.
Audience: **g,l,u,f.** *Choice, 1998.*

Fenno, Richard F. Jr. **JK2281**
Senators on the Campaign Trail: The Politics of Representation. Trade Paper. University of Oklahoma Press. Norman, OK. 1998. 448p. Julian J. Rothbaum Distinguished Lecture Ser., Vol. 6 ISBN:0-8061-3062-8, ISBN13: 978-0-8061-3062-0. Dewey:324.7/0973.
Audience: **g,l,u,f.** *Choice, 1996.*

Jacobson, Gary C. **JK1991.J32**
Money in Congressional Elections. Trade Paper. Books on Demand. Ann Arbor, MI. 271p. ISBN:0-7837-5308-X, ISBN13: 978-0-7837-5308-9. Dewey:324.7/8/0973. LCCN:79-020669.
Audience: **g,l,u,f.** B

Kahn, Kim Fridkin & Kenney, Patrick J. **JK2281.K24 1999**
The Spectacle of U. S. Senate Campaigns. Trade Paper. Princeton University Press. Princeton, NJ. 1999. 292p. ISBN:0-691-00505-2, ISBN13: 978-0-691-00505-8. Dewey:324.7/0973. LCCN:98-032011.
Audience: **l,u,f.** *Choice, 2000.*

Westlye, Mark C. **JK1965.W47**
Senate Elections and Campaign Intensity. Trade Paper. Books on Demand. Ann Arbor, MI. 276p. ISBN:0-608-06715-6, ISBN13: 978-0-608-06715-5. Dewey:324.7/0973. LCCN:90-046421.
Audience: **l,u,f.** *Choice, 1992.*

American Government and Politics > Campaigns and Elections > Gubernatorial Elections

Beyle, Thad L. (Editor) **JK2447.G82 1989**
Gubernatorial Transitions: The 1983 and 1984 Elections. Barry Van Lare (Preface by). Cloth Text. Duke University Press. Durham, NC. 1988. x, 384p. ISBN:0-8223-0858-4, ISBN13: 978-0-8223-0858-4. Dewey:353.9/134. LCCN:88-014711.
Audience: **l,u,f.** *Choice, 1989.*

Congressional Quarterly, Inc. Staff **JK2447.G76 1998**
Gubernatorial Elections, 1787-1997. Paper Text. Congressional Quarterly, Inc. Washington, DC. 1998. 183p. ISBN:1-56802-396-0, ISBN13: 978-1-56802-396-0. Dewey:324.973. LCCN:97-050560.
Audience: **g,l,u,f.**

Glashan, Roy (Compiled by) **JK2447**
American Governors and Gubernatorial Elections, 1775-1978. Cloth Text. Greenwood Publishing Group, Inc. Portsmouth, NH. 1979. 384p. ISBN:0-313-28134-3, ISBN13: 978-0-313-28134-1. Dewey:352.232131. LCCN:79-015021.
Audience: **g,l,u,f.**

Mullaney, Marie M. (Compiled by) **JK2447**
American Governors and Gubernatorial Elections, 1979-1987. Cloth Text. Greenwood Publishing Group, Inc. Portsmouth, NH. 1988. 104p. ISBN:0-313-28092-4, ISBN13: 978-0-313-28092-4. Dewey:352.232131. LCCN:88-013248.
Audience: **g,l,u,f.**

American Government and Politics > Campaigns and Elections > Campaign Finance

Center for Responsive Politics **JK1968**
OpenSecrets.org.
http://www.opensecrets.org/index.asp
Audience: **g,l,u,f.**

Federal Election Commission
Federal Election Commission Campaign Finance Reports and Data.
http://www.fec.gov/disclosure.shtml
Audience: **g,l,u,f.**

Grossman, Mark (Editor) **JK2249.G767 2003**
Political Corruption in America: An Encyclopedia of Scandals, Power, and Greed. Library Binding. ABC-CLIO, Inc. Santa

Barbara, CA. 2003. 400p. ISBN:1-57607-060-3, ISBN13: 978-1-57607-060-4. Dewey:973/.03. LCCN:2003-013127.
Audience: **g,l.** *Choice, 2004.*

Haggard, William **PR6015.I3**
The Money Men. Trade Cloth. Amereon, Ltd. Mattituck, NY. ISBN:0-88411-679-4, ISBN13: 978-0-88411-679-0. Dewey:823/.914.
Audience: **g,l,u,f.**

Institute on Money in State Politics **JK1991**
□ Follow the Money.
http://www.followthemoney.org/
Audience: **g,l,u,f.**

Investigative Reporters and Editors, Missouri School of Journalism
□ Campaign Finance Information Center.
http://www.campaignfinance.org/
Audience: **g,l,u,f.**

Jacobson, Gary C. **JK1991.J32**
Money in Congressional Elections. Trade Paper. Books on Demand. Ann Arbor, MI. 271p. ISBN:0-7837-5308-X, ISBN13: 978-0-7837-5308-9. Dewey:324.7/8/0973. LCCN:79-020669.
Audience: **g,l,u,f.** B

American Government and Politics > Campaigns and Elections > Campaign Management

Mauser, Gary A. **JF2112**
Political Marketing: An Approach to Campaign Strategy. Steven E. Permut (Editor). Trade Cloth. Greenwood Publishing Group, Inc. Portsmouth, NH. 1983. 304p. Praeger Series in Public and Nonprofit Sector Marketing ISBN:0-275-91721-5, ISBN13: 978-0-275-91721-0. Dewey:324.7. LCCN:82-025973.
Audience: **g,l,u,f.** B

Sabato, Larry J. **JK2281.S2**
The Rise of Political Consultants. Trade Cloth. Basic Books. New York, NY. 1981. 288p. ISBN:0-465-07040-X, ISBN13: 978-0-465-07040-4. Dewey:324.7/0973. LCCN:81-066104.
Audience: **g,l,u,f.** B

Semetko, Holli A., et al. **JK1976.F67 1991**
The Formation of Campaign Agendas: A Comparative Analysis of Party and Media Roles in Recent American and British Elections. Jay G. Blumler & Michael Gurevitch (Authors). Cloth Text. Lawrence Erlbaum Associates, Inc. Mahwah, NJ. 1990. 216p. ISBN:0-8058-0656-3, ISBN13: 978-0-8058-0656-4. Dewey:324.7/0973. LCCN:90-040152.
Audience: **l,u,f.** *Choice, 1991.*

Thurber, James A. & Nelson, Candice J. (Editors) **JK2281.C323 2000**
Campaign Warriors: Political Consultants in Elections. Trade Paper. Brookings Institution Press. Washington, DC. 2000. 216p. ISBN:0-8157-8453-8, ISBN13: 978-0-8157-8453-1. Dewey:324.7/0973. LCCN:99-050915.
Audience: **g,l,u,f.** *Choice, 2001.*

Whillock, Rita K. **JK1976**
Political Empiricism: Communication Strategies in State and Regional Elections. Trade Cloth. Greenwood Publishing Group, Inc. Portsmouth, NH. 1991. 272p. Praeger Series in Political Communication ISBN:0-275-93554-X, ISBN13: 978-0-275-93554-2. Dewey:324.7/0973. LCCN:91-019412.
Audience: **u,f.** *Choice, 1992.*

American Government and Politics > Mass Media and Politics

Denton, Robert E. Jr. (Editor) **JK526**
The 2000 Presidential Campaign: A Communication Perspective. Paper Text. Greenwood Publishing Group, Inc. Portsmouth, NH. 2002. 304p. Praeger Series in Political Communication ISBN:0-275-97120-1, ISBN13: 978-0-275-97120-5. Dewey:324.973/0929. LCCN:2001-059151.
Audience: **l,u,f.** *Choice, 2003.*

Entman, Robert M. **PN4888.P6**
Democracy Without Citizens: Media and the Decay of American Politics. Paper Text. Oxford University Press, Inc. New York, NY. 1990. 256p. ISBN:0-19-506576-X, ISBN13: 978-0-19-506576-3. Dewey:070/.973.
Audience: **l,u.** *Choice, 1989.*

Farnsworth, Stephen J. & Lichter, S. Robert **E176.1.F228 2005**
The Mediated Presidency: Television News and Presidential Governance. Trade Cloth. Rowman & Littlefield Publishers, Inc. Lanham, MD. 2005. 236p. ISBN:0-7425-3677-7, ISBN13: 978-0-7425-3677-7. Dewey:070.449320973. LCCN:2005-008333.
Audience: **l,u,f.** *Choice, 2006.*

Kaplan, E. Ann **PN1995.9.T46K37 2005**
Trauma Culture: The Politics of Terror and Loss in Media and Literature. Trade Cloth. Rutgers University Press. Piscataway, NJ. 2005. 224p. ISBN:0-8135-3590-5, ISBN13: 978-0-8135-3590-6. Dewey:791.43/6552. LCCN:2004-023482.
Audience: **u,f.** *Choice, 2006.*

McChesney, Robert Waterman & Scott, Ben **PN4738.O94 2004**
Our Unfree Press: 100 Years of Radical Media Criticism. Trade Cloth. New Press, The. New York, NY. 2004. vi, 438p. ISBN:1-56584-917-5, ISBN13: 978-1-56584-917-4. Dewey:323.44/5/0973. LCCN:2003-061542.
Audience: **g,l,u,f.**

Moy, Patricia & Pfau, Michael **P95**
With Malice Toward All?: The Media and Public Confidence in Democratic Institutions. Paper Text. Greenwood Publishing Group, Inc. Portsmouth, NH. 2000. 240p. Series in Political Communication ISBN:0-275-96434-5, ISBN13: 978-0-275-96434-4. Dewey:302.23/0973. LCCN:99-046408.
Audience: **g,l,u,f.** *Choice, 2000.*

Nacos, Brigitte Lebens **PN4784.T45N35 2002**
Mass-Mediated Terrorism: The Central Role of the Media in Terrorism and Counterterrorism. Book, Other. Rowman & Littlefield Publishers, Inc. Lanham, MD. 2002. 208p. ISBN:0-7425-1082-4, ISBN13: 978-0-7425-1082-1. Dewey:070.4/49303625/0973. LCCN:2002-003675.
Audience: **u,f.** *Choice, 2003.*

Paletz, David L. & Schmid, Alex P. (Editors) **P96.T47T48 1992**
Terrorism and the Media. Trade Paper. SAGE Publications, Inc. Thousand Oaks, CA. 1992. 250p. ISBN:0-8039-4483-7, ISBN13: 978-0-8039-4483-1. Dewey:303.6/25. LCCN:92-003738.
Audience: **u,f.** *Choice, 1992.*

Schultz, Jeffrey **JA71**
Encyclopedia of Media and Politics in America. Trade Cloth. CQ Press. Washington, DC. 2005. 400p. ISBN:1-56802-835-0, ISBN13: 978-1-56802-835-4. Dewey:320.
Audience: **g,l,u,f.**

Semetko, Holli A., et al. **JK1976.F67 1991**
The Formation of Campaign Agendas: A Comparative Analysis of Party and Media Roles in Recent American and British Elections. Jay G. Blumler & Michael Gurevitch (Authors). Cloth Text. Lawrence Erlbaum Associates, Inc. Mahwah, NJ. 1990. 216p. ISBN:0-8058-0656-3, ISBN13: 978-0-8058-0656-4. Dewey:324.7/0973. LCCN:90-040152.
Audience: **l,u,f.** *Choice, 1991.*

Whillock, Rita K. **JK1976**
Political Empiricism: Communication Strategies in State and Regional Elections. Trade Cloth. Greenwood Publishing Group, Inc. Portsmouth, NH. 1991. 272p. Praeger Series in Political Communication ISBN:0-275-93554-X, ISBN13: 978-0-275-93554-2. Dewey:324.7/0973. LCCN:91-019412.
Audience: **u,f.** *Choice, 1992.*

American Government and Politics > Public Policy

Rostow, W. W. **D843.R656 2003**
Concept and Controversy: Sixty Years of Taking Ideas to Market. Trade Cloth. University of Texas Press. Austin, TX. 2003. 484p. ISBN:0-292-77124-X, ISBN13: 978-0-292-77124-6. Dewey:327.73/009/045. LCCN:2002-015038.
Audience: **u,f.** *Choice, 2004.*

American Government and Politics > Public Policy > Public Opinion

HM261
PollingReport.com.
http://www.pollingreport.com/
Audience: **g,l,u,f.**

HN59.2
Public Agenda.
http://www.publicagenda.org/
Audience: **g,l,u,f.**

Alvarez, R. Michael & Brehm, John **HM1236.A46 2002**
Hard Choices, Easy Answers: Values, Information, and American Public Opinion. Trade Paper. Princeton University Press. Princeton, NJ. 2002. 264p. ISBN:0-691-09635-X, ISBN13: 978-0-691-09635-3. Dewey:303.3/8/0973. LCCN:2001-050023.
Audience: **u,f.** *Choice, 2003.*

Baum, Matthew A. **PN4888.T4B34 2005**
Soft News Goes to War: Public Opinion and American Foreign Policy in the New Media Age. Trade Paper, Perfect. Princeton University Press. Princeton, NJ. 2005. 344p. ISBN:0-691-12377-2, ISBN13: 978-0-691-12377-6. Dewey:070.1950973.
Audience: **u,f.** *Choice, 2004.*

Berinsky, Adam J. **HN90.P8B47 2005**
Silent Voices: Public Opinion and Political Participation in America. Trade Paper. Princeton University Press. Princeton, NJ. 2005. 240p. ISBN:0-691-12378-0, ISBN13: 978-0-691-12378-3. Dewey:303.3/8.
Audience: **l,u,f.** *Choice, 2004.*

Hutchings, Vincent L. **JK1764.H883 2005**
Public Opinion and Democratic Accountability: How Citizens Learn about Politics. Trade Paper. Princeton University Press. Princeton, NJ. 2005. 192p. ISBN:0-691-12379-9, ISBN13: 978-0-691-12379-0. Dewey:323/.042/0973.
Audience: **l,u,f.** *Choice, 2004.*

Weissberg, Robert **HV91.W4659 2002**
Polling, Policy, and Public Opinion: The Case Against Heeding the Voice of the People. Cloth over Boards. Palgrave Macmillan. New York, NY. 2002. 288p. ISBN:0-312-29495-6, ISBN13: 978-0-312-29495-3. Dewey:361.6/0973. LCCN:2002-068427.
Audience: **g,l,u,f.**

American Government and Politics > Public Policy > Special Interest Groups

Browne, William P. **JK1118.B76 1998**
Groups, Interests, and U. S. Public Policy. Trade Cloth. Georgetown University Press. Washington, DC. 1998. 276p. ISBN:0-87840-681-6, ISBN13: 978-0-87840-681-4. Dewey:324/.4/0973. LCCN:97-041520.
Audience: **l,u,f.** *Choice, 1998.*

Center for Responsive Politics **JK1968**
opensecrets.org.
http://www.opensecrets.org/
Audience: **g,l,u,f.**

CQ Press Editors **JK1118.P78 2004**
Public Interest Group Profiles 2004-2005. Ed. 11. Trade Cloth. CQ Press. Washington, DC. 2004. 800p. ISBN:1-56802-886-5, ISBN13: 978-1-56802-886-6. Dewey:322.4/3/02573. LCCN:2004-017668.
Audience: **g,l,u,f.**

CQ Press Staff (Editor) **AE5**
The Almanac of Federal PACs: 2006-2007. Trade Paper. CQ Press. Washington, DC. 2006. ISBN:1-933116-37-4, ISBN13: 978-1-933116-37-2. Dewey:031.
Audience: **g,l,u,f.**

Kleidman, Robert **JX1961.U6K55 1993**
Organizing for Peace: Neutrality, the Test Ban, and the Freeze. Trade Cloth. Syracuse University Press. Syracuse, NY. 1993. 272p. Syracuse Studies on Peace and Conflict Resolution ISBN:0-8156-2573-1, ISBN13: 978-0-8156-2573-5. Dewey:327.1/72. LCCN:92-040181.
Audience: **l,u,f.** *Choice, 1994.*

National Institute for Research Advancement **Q180.A1**
NIRA's World Directory of Think Tanks.
http://www.nira.go.jp/ice/index.html
Audience: **g,l,u,f.**

West, John G. Jr. & Maclean, Iain **BL2525.E52 1999**
Encyclopedia of Religion in American Politics. Jeffrey D. Schultz (Editor), Helen Thomas (Foreword by). Cloth Text. Greenwood Publishing Group, Inc. Portsmouth, NH. 1998. 424p. The American Political Landscape Ser., Vol. 2 ISBN:1-57356-130-4, ISBN13: 978-1-57356-130-3. Dewey:322/.1/097303. LCCN:98-047223.
Audience: **g,l,u,f.** *Choice, 1999.*

American Government and Politics > Foreign Policy

Aruri, Naseer Hasan **DS119.76.A773 2003**
Dishonest Broker: America's Role in Israel and Palestine. Ed. 2. Trade Paper. South End Press. Cambridge, MA. 2003. 248p. ISBN:0-89608-687-9, ISBN13: 978-0-89608-687-6. Dewey:327.73054/09/045. LCCN:2002-042886.
Audience: **g,l,u,f.**

Boyle, Peter G. **DA566.9.E28A4 2005**
The Eden-Eisenhower Correspondence, 1955-1957. Trade Cloth. University of North Carolina Press. Chapel Hill, NC. 2005. 272p. ISBN:0-8078-2935-8, ISBN13: 978-0-8078-2935-6. Dewey:327.41073/09/045. LCCN:2004-027158.
Audience: **u,f.**

Brune, Lester H. & Burns, Richard Dean **E183.7.B745 2002**
Chronological History of U. S. Foreign Relations, Set. Ed. 2. Paper over Boards. Routledge. New York, NY. 2002. 1488p. ISBN:0-415-93914-3, ISBN13: 978-0-415-93914-0. Dewey:327.73/002/02. LCCN:2002-023693.
Audience: **g,l,u,f.**

Ferguson, Niall **JZ1480.F47 2004**
Colossus: The Price of America's Empire. Trade Cloth. Penguin Group (USA) Inc. New York, NY. 2004. 400p. ISBN:1-59420-013-0, ISBN13: 978-1-59420-013-7. Dewey:327.73. LCCN:2003-070693.
Audience: **g,u,f.** *Choice, 2004.*

Ikenberry, G. John **JZ1480.A96 2005**
American Foreign Policy: Theoretical Essays. Ed. 5. Trade Paper. Longman Publishing Group. White Plains, NY. 2004. 608p. ISBN:0-321-15973-X, ISBN13: 978-0-321-15973-1. Dewey:327.73. LCCN:2004-009409.
Audience: **l,u.**

Kissinger, Henry A. & Summers, Lawrence H. **D1065.U5R44 2004**
Renewing the Atlantic Partnership: Independent Task Force Report. Charles A. Kupchan (Contribution by). Trade Paper. Council on Foreign Relations. New York, NY. 2004. 52p. Task Force Report (Council on Foreign Relations) Ser. ISBN:0-87609-342-X, ISBN13: 978-0-87609-342-9. Dewey:327.4073. LCCN:2004-561120.
Audience: **g,l,u,f.**

Kitfield, James **E902.K58 2005**
War and Destiny: How the Bush Revolution in Foreign and Military Affairs Redefined American Power. Saddle Stitched, Cloth over Boards. Potomac Books, Inc. Dulles, VA. 2005. 386p. ISBN:1-57488-959-1, ISBN13: 978-1-57488-959-8. Dewey:327.73/009/0511. LCCN:2005-003860.
Audience: **l,u,f.** *Choice, 2005.*

Lindsay, James & Daalder, Ivo **E902.D23 2003**
America Unbound: The Bush Revolution in Foreign Policy. Trade Cloth. Brookings Institution Press. Washington, DC. 2003. 246p. ISBN:0-8157-1688-5, ISBN13: 978-0-8157-1688-4. Dewey:327.73. LCCN:2003-016767.
Audience: **u,f.** *Choice, 2004.*

Mead, Walter Russell **JZ1480.M43 2005**
Power, Terror, Peace, and War: America's Grand Strategy in a World at Risk. Trade Paper, Perfect. Knopf Publishing Group. New York, NY. 2005. 256p. ISBN:1-4000-7703-6, ISBN13: 978-1-4000-7703-8. Dewey:327.73. LCCN:2005-278044.
Audience: **l,u,f.** *Choice, 2005.*

Simons, Geoff **DS79.75**
Future Iraq: US Policy in Reshaping the Middle East. Trade Paper. Saqi Books. London, 2006. 400p. ISBN:0-86356-132-2, ISBN13: 978-0-86356-132-0. Dewey:956.7044/3. LCCN:2004-557635.
Audience: **g,l,u,f.**

Spanier, John W. & Hook, Steven W. **E744.S8 2000**
American Foreign Policy since World War II. Ed. 15. Trade Paper. CQ Press. Washington, DC. 2000. xvi, 424p. ISBN:1-56802-578-5, ISBN13: 978-1-56802-578-0. Dewey:327.73/009/045. LCCN:00-040384.
Audience: **l,u,f.**

Stathis, Stephen W. **KF68.S73 2003**
Landmark Legislation, 1774-2002: Major U. S. Acts and Treaties. Trade Cloth. CQ Press. Washington, DC. 2003. 426p. ISBN:1-56802-781-8, ISBN13: 978-1-56802-781-4. Dewey:348.73/2. LCCN:2003-003531.
Audience: **g,l,u,f.** *Choice, 2004.*

Staudt, Kathleen & Coronado, Irasema **HM671.S73 2002**
Fronteras No Mas: Toward Social Justice at the U. S. - Mexico Border. Trade Paper. Palgrave Macmillan. New York, NY. 2002. 224p. ISBN:0-312-29547-2, ISBN13: 978-0-312-29547-9. Dewey:303.3/72/09721. LCCN:2002-068413.
Audience: **g,l.** *Choice, 2003.*

Stearns, Monteagle **E840.S724**
Talking to Strangers: Improving American Diplomacy at Home and Abroad. Trade Paper. Princeton University Press. Princeton, NJ. 1999. 230p. ISBN:0-691-00745-4, ISBN13: 978-0-691-00745-8. Dewey:327.73.
Audience: **g,u,f.** *Choice, 1996.*

Strong, Robert A. **E872.S79 2000**
Working in the World: Jimmy Carter and the Making of American Foreign Policy. Cloth Text. Louisiana State University Press. Baton Rouge, LA. 2000. 304p. Miller Center Series on the American Presidency ISBN:0-8071-2445-1, ISBN13: 978-0-8071-2445-1. Dewey:973.926/092. LCCN:99-016464.
Audience: **g,l,u,f.** *Choice, 2000.*

Thomson Gale Staff (Contribution by) **E183.7.E52 2002**
Encyclopedia of American Foreign Policy, Set. Ed. 2. Trade Cloth. Thomson Gale. Farmington Hills, MI. 2001. 1500p. ISBN:0-684-80657-6, ISBN13: 978-0-684-80657-0. Dewey:327.73/003. LCCN:2001-049800.
Audience: **g,l,u,f.** *Choice, 2002.*

Tucker, Nancy B. **E183.8.C5T835 2001**
China Confidential: American Diplomats and Sino-American Relations, 1945-1996. Trade Cloth. Columbia University Press. New York, NY. 2000. 638p. ISBN:0-231-10630-0, ISBN13: 978-0-231-10630-6. Dewey:327.73051. LCCN:00-040445.
Audience: **u,f.** *Choice, 2001.*

U.S. Department of State **JX1407**
Foreign Relations of the United States. http://www.state.gov/r/pa/ho/frus/
Audience: **g,l,u,f.**

U.S. Department of State **JX1407**
Foreign Relations of the United States. http://digicoll.library.wisc.edu/FRUS/ University of Wisconsin.
Audience: **g,l,u,f.**

American Government and Politics > Foreign Policy > Military

Clark, Wesley K. **E902**
Winning Modern Wars: Iraq, Terrorism, and the American Empire. Trade Cloth. PublicAffairs. New York, NY. 2003. 240p. ISBN:1-58648-218-1, ISBN13: 978-1-58648-218-3. Dewey:956.7044/34. LCCN:2003-062342.
Audience: **g,l,u,f.** *Choice, 2004.*

Eisenstadt, Michael (Editor) **DS70.96.G7B75 2003**
The British Experience in Iraq: Lessons for U.S. Policymakers. Washington Institute for Near East Policy Staff (Contribution by). Trade Paper. Washington Institute for Near East Policy, The. Washington, DC. 2003. 84p. ISBN:0-944029-84-1, ISBN13: 978-0-944029-84-8. Dewey:327.410567/09/04. LCCN:2003-004627.
Audience: **l,u.**

Feaver, Peter & Gelpi, Christopher **JK330.F434 2004**
Choosing Your Battles: American Civil-Military Relations and the Use of Force. Trade Cloth. Princeton University Press. Princeton, NJ. 2003. 256p. ISBN:0-691-11584-2, ISBN13: 978-0-691-11584-9. Dewey:322/.5/0973. LCCN:2003-043344.
Audience: **u,f.** *Choice, 2004.*

Feaver, Peter & Kohn, Richard (Editors) **UA23.S5269 2001**
Soldiers and Civilians: The Civil-Military Gap and American National Security. Trade Paper. MIT Press. Cambridge, MA. 2001. 550p. BCSIA Studies in International Security ISBN:0-262-56142-5, ISBN13: 978-0-262-56142-6. Dewey:306.2/7/0973. LCCN:2001-042558.
Audience: **u,f.** *Choice, 2002.*

Greider, William **HC110.D4G74 1998**
Fortress America: The American Military and the Consequences of Peace. Trade Cloth. PublicAffairs. New York, NY. 1998. 224p. ISBN:1-891620-09-6, ISBN13: 978-1-891620-09-6. Dewey:330.973/0929. LCCN:98-030426.
Audience: **g,l,u,f.**

Harclerode, Peter **U262**
Fighting Dirty: The Inside Story of Covert Operations from Ho Chi Minh to Osama Bin Laden. Trade Cloth. DIANE Publishing Company. Collingdale, PA. 2005. 625p. ISBN:0-7567-8675-4, ISBN13: 978-0-7567-8675-5. Dewey:356.1/6.
Audience: **g,l,u,f.** *Choice, 2002.*

Marullo, Sam **E840.M37 1993**
Ending the Cold War at Home: From Militarism to a More Peaceful World Order. Trade Cloth. Lexington Books. Lanham, MD. 1994. 74p. Lexington Book Series on Social Issues ISBN:0-669-24231-4, ISBN13: 978-0-669-24231-7. Dewey:327.73/009/045. LCCN:93-029852.
Audience: **g,l,u.**

National Academy of Sciences Staff **UA23.N227 1997**
The Future of U. S. Nuclear Weapons Policy. Trade Paper. National Academies Press. Washington, DC. 1997. 100p. ISBN:0-309-06367-1, ISBN13: 978-0-309-06367-8. Dewey:355.02/17/0973. LCCN:97-068120.
Audience: **u,f.**

Record, Jeffrey **DS79.76.R43 2004**
Dark Victory: America's Second War Against Iraq. Trade Cloth. Naval Institute Press. Annapolis, MD. 2004. 224p. ISBN:1-59114-711-5, ISBN13: 978-1-59114-711-4. Dewey:956.7044/3. LCCN:2003-026154.
Audience: **u,f.** *Choice, 2004.*

Stoler, Mark A. **D769.1.S76 2000**
Allies and Adversaries: The Joint Chiefs of Staff, the Grand Alliance and U. S. Strategy in World War II. Trade Cloth. University of North Carolina Press. Chapel Hill, NC. 2000. 408p. ISBN:0-8078-2557-3, ISBN13: 978-0-8078-2557-0. Dewey:940.54/012. LCCN:00-032589.
Audience: **u,f.** *Choice, 2001.*

American Government and Politics > Foreign Policy > Security

National Security Archive Documents. http://www.gwu.edu/~nsarchiv/NSAEBB/index.html George Washington University.
Audience: **g,l,u,f.**

Baer, Martha, et al. **HV6432.S23 2005**
Safe: The Race to Protect Ourselves in a Newly Dangerous World. Katrina Heron, Oliver Morton & Evan Ratliff (Authors). Trade Cloth. HarperCollins Publishers. New York, NY. 2005. 416p. ISBN:0-06-057715-0, ISBN13: 978-0-06-057715-5. Dewey:363.32. LCCN:2004-053935.
Audience: **g,l,u.** *Choice, 2005.*

Brasch, Walter M. **JC599.U5B67 2005**
America's Unpatriot Acts: The Federal Government's Violation of Constitutional and Civil Rights. Trade Paper. Peter Lang Publishing, Inc. New York, NY. 2005. xvi;231p. ISBN:0-8204-7608-0, ISBN13: 978-0-8204-7608-7. Dewey:973.931. LCCN:2004-018808.
Audience: **g,l,u.** *Choice, 2006.*

Cordesman, Anthony **DS79.76.C677 2004**
The War after the War. Paper Text. Center for Strategic & International Studies. Washington, DC. 2004. xix, 73p. CSIS Significant Issues Ser., 26 ISBN:0-89206-450-1, ISBN13: 978-0-89206-450-2. Dewey:327.730567/09/0511. LCCN:2004-011306.
Audience: **u,f.**

Greenberg, Karen J. (Editor) **HV6432.5.Q2Q34 2005**
The Torture Debate in America. Trade Cloth. Cambridge University Press. New York, NY. 2005. 432p. ISBN:0-521-85792-9, ISBN13: 978-0-521-85792-5. Dewey:303.6/25. LCCN:2005-019855.
Audience: **l,u,f.**

Johnson, Loch & Inderfurth, Karl F. (Editors) **UA23.15.F38 2003**
Fateful Decisions: Inside the National Security Council. Cloth Text. Oxford University Press, Inc. New York, NY. 2004. 400p. ISBN:0-19-515965-9, ISBN13: 978-0-19-515965-3. Dewey:355/.033073. LCCN:2003-053585.
Audience: **l,u,f.**

Kissinger, Henry A. & Summers, Lawrence H. **D1065.U5R44 2004**
Renewing the Atlantic Partnership: Independent Task Force Report. Charles A. Kupchan (Contribution by). Trade Paper. Council on Foreign Relations. New York, NY. 2004. 52p. Task Force Report (Council on Foreign Relations) Ser. ISBN:0-87609-342-X, ISBN13: 978-0-87609-342-9. Dewey:327.4073. LCCN:2004-561120.
Audience: **g,l,u,f.**

Krepon, Michael & Caldwell, Dan (Editors) **JX1974.P6238 1991**
The Politics of Arms Control Treaty Ratification. Cloth over Boards. Palgrave Macmillan. New York, NY. 1992. 494p. A Henry L. Stimson Center Bk. ISBN:0-312-06604-X, ISBN13: 978-0-312-06604-8. Dewey:341.3/7/0941. LCCN:91-034787.
Audience: **g,l,u,f.** *Choice, 1992.*

Lyon, David **HN59.2.L96 2003**
Surveillance after September 11. Trade Paper. Blackwell Publishing, Inc. Malden, MA. 2003. 208p. Themes for the 21st Century Ser. ISBN:0-7456-3181-9, ISBN13: 978-0-7456-3181-3. Dewey:303.3/3. LCCN:2003-001340.
Audience: **u,f.** *Choice, 2004.*

McCoy, Alfred **HV8599.U6M33 2006**
A Question of Torture: CIA Interrogation, from the Cold War to the War on Terror. Cloth over Boards. Henry Holt & Company. New York, NY. 2006. 304p. The American Empire Project Ser. ISBN:0-8050-8041-4, ISBN13: 978-0-8050-8041-4. Dewey:323.4/9. LCCN:2005-051124.
Audience: **g,l,u,f.**

McNamara, Robert S. & Blight, James G. **JZ5538.M36 2001**
Wilson's Ghost: Reducing the Risk of Conflict, Killing, and Catastrophe in the 21st Century. Trade Cloth. PublicAffairs. New York, NY. 2001. 288p. ISBN:1-891620-89-4, ISBN13: 978-1-891620-89-8. Dewey:327.1/7. LCCN:2001-019182.
Audience: **g,l,u,f.** *Choice, 2001.*

Soderberg, Nancy **UA23.S52626 2005**
The Superpower Myth: The Use and Misuse of American Might. Bill Clinton (Foreword by). Trade Cloth. John Wiley & Sons, Inc. Hoboken, NJ. 2005. 416p. ISBN:0-471-65683-6, ISBN13: 978-0-471-65683-8. Dewey:355/.033073. LCCN:2004-017099.
Audience: **g,l,u,f.**

Talbott, Strobe **JX1974.76.T34 1984**
Deadly Gambits: The Reagan Administration and the Stalemate in Nuclear Arms Control. Trade Cloth. Alfred A. Knopf Inc. New York, NY. 1984. 353p. ISBN:0-394-53637-1, ISBN13: 978-0-394-53637-8. Dewey:327.1/74. LCCN:84-047781.
Audience: **g,l,u,f.** B

Turner, Stansfield **JK468.I6T868 2005**
Burn Before Reading: Presidents, CIA Directors, and Secret Intelligence. Trade Cloth. Hyperion Press. New York, NY. 2005. 320p. ISBN:0-7868-6782-5, ISBN13: 978-0-7868-6782-0. Dewey:327.1273/09. LCCN:2005-046264.
Audience: **g,l,u,f.**

Watson, Cynthia A. **UA23.W36397 2002**
US National Security: A Reference Handbook. Library Binding. ABC-CLIO, Inc. Santa Barbara, CA. 2002. 357p. Contemporary World Issues Ser. ISBN:1-57607-598-2, ISBN13: 978-1-57607-598-2. Dewey:355/.033073. LCCN:2002-006366.
Audience: **l,u,f.** *Choice, 2003.*

Wilson, Joseph **JK468.E7W55 2004**
The Politics of Truth: Inside the Lies That Led to War and Betrayed My Wife's CIA Identity, A Diplomat's Memoir. Trade Cloth. Avalon Publishing Group. New York, NY. 2004. 528p. ISBN:0-7867-1378-X, ISBN13: 978-0-7867-1378-3. Dewey:327.73/0092 B. LCCN:2004-045897.
Audience: **g,l,u,f.**

American Government and Politics > Foreign Policy > Security > Terrorism

Ahmed, Nafeez Mosaddeq **DS79.76.A37 2003**
Behind the War on Terror: Western Secret Strategy and the Struggle for Iraq. Trade Paper. New Society Publishers, Ltd. Gabriola Island, BC. 2003. 368p. ISBN:0-86571-506-8, ISBN13: 978-0-86571-506-6. Dewey:956.7044/31. LCCN:2004-444998.
Audience: **g,l,u.**

Benjamin, Daniel & Simon, Steven **HV6432.7.B425 2005**
The Next Attack: The Failure of the War on Terror and a Strategy for Getting It Right. Cloth over Boards, Saddle Stitched, Dust Jacket. Henry Holt & Company. New York, NY. 2005. 352p. ISBN:0-8050-7941-6, ISBN13: 978-0-8050-7941-8. Dewey:973.931. LCCN:2005-051444.
Audience: **g,l,u,f.**

Berman, Paul **HV6431.B4794 2003**
Terror and Liberalism. Trade Cloth. W. W. Norton & Company, Inc. New York, NY. 2003. 128p. ISBN:0-393-05775-5, ISBN13: 978-0-393-05775-1. Dewey:303.6/25. LCCN:2002-156445.
Audience: **g,l,u.** *Choice, 2003.*

Brasch, Walter M. **JC599.U5B67 2005**
America's Unpatriot Acts: The Federal Government's Violation of Constitutional and Civil Rights. Trade Paper. Peter Lang Publishing, Inc. New York, NY. 2005. xvi;231p. ISBN:0-8204-7608-0, ISBN13: 978-0-8204-7608-7. Dewey:973.931. LCCN:2004-018808.
Audience: **g,l,u.** *Choice, 2006.*

Clark, Wesley K. **E902**
Winning Modern Wars: Iraq, Terrorism, and the American Empire. Trade Cloth. PublicAffairs. New York, NY. 2003. 240p. ISBN:1-58648-218-1, ISBN13: 978-1-58648-218-3. Dewey:956.7044/34. LCCN:2003-062342.
Audience: **g,l,u,f.** *Choice, 2004.*

Clarke, Richard A. **HV6432**
Against All Enemies: Inside America's War on Terror. Trade Cloth. Simon & Schuster. New York, NY. 2004. 320p. ISBN:0-7432-6024-4, ISBN13: 978-0-7432-6024-4. Dewey:973.931. LCCN:2004-273844.
Audience: **g,l,u,f.**

Cohen, David B. & Wells, John W. (Editors) **JC599.U5A4985 2004**
American National Security and Civil Liberties in an Era of Terrorism. Cloth over Boards. Palgrave Macmillan. New York, NY. 2004. 240p. ISBN:1-4039-6199-9, ISBN13: 978-1-4039-6199-0. Dewey:323/.0973. LCCN:2003-065607.
Audience: **u,f.** *Choice, 2005.*

Cohen-Tanugi, Laurent **D1065.U5C573 2003**
An Alliance at Risk: The United States and Europe since September 11. George A. Holoch (Translator). Trade Cloth. Johns Hopkins University Press. Baltimore, MD. 2003. 168p. ISBN:0-8018-7841-1, ISBN13: 978-0-8018-7841-1. Dewey:327/.094. LCCN:2003-010632.
Audience: **g,l,u,f.** *Choice, 2004.*

Cole, David **KF4850.C65 2006**
Terrorism and the Constitution: Sacrificing Civil Liberties in the Name of National Security. Ed. 3. Trade Paper. New Press, The. New York, NY. 2006. 256p. ISBN:1-56584-939-6, ISBN13: 978-1-56584-939-6. Dewey:343.7301. LCCN:2006-273542.
Audience: **g.** *Choice, 2003.*

Crotty, William J. (Editor) **E902.P65 2004**
The Politics of Terror: The U. S. Response to 9/11. Trade Cloth. Northeastern University Press. Boston, MA. 2003. 256p. The Northeastern Series on Democratization and Political Development ISBN:1-55553-577-1, ISBN13: 978-1-55553-577-3. Dewey:973.931. LCCN:2003-010692.
Audience: **u,f.** *Choice, 2004.*

Dadge, David **PN4745.D33 2004**
Casualty of War: The Bush Administration's Assault on a Free Press. Trade Cloth. Prometheus Books, Publishers. Amherst, NY. 2004. 350p. ISBN:1-59102-147-2, ISBN13: 978-1-59102-147-6. Dewey:323.44/5/0973. LCCN:2003-023766.
Audience: **g,l,u,f.** *Choice, 2004.*

Dando, Malcolm R. **KZ5825.3.D36 2002**
Preventing Biological Warfare: The Failure of American Leadership. Cloth over Boards. Palgrave Macmillan. New York, NY. 2002. 244p. Global Issues Ser. ISBN:0-333-79309-9, ISBN13: 978-0-333-79309-1. Dewey:341.7/35. LCCN:2001-057534.
Audience: **g,l,u,f.** *Choice, 2003.*

Dudziak, Mary L. (Editor) **HV6432.7.S45 2003**
September 11 in History: A Watershed Moment? Trade Cloth. Duke University Press. Durham, NC. 2003. 248p. American Encounters/Global Interactions Ser. ISBN:0-8223-3229-9, ISBN13: 978-0-8223-3229-9. Dewey:973.931. LCCN:2003-010840.
Audience: **g,l,u,f.** *Choice, 2004.*

Etzioni, Amitai & Marsh, Jason H. **HV6432.E88 2003**
Rights vs. Public Safety after 9/11: America in the Age of Terrorism. Book, Other. Rowman & Littlefield Publishers, Inc. Lanham, MD. 2003. 200p. Rights and Responsibilities, :Communitarian Perspectives Ser. ISBN:0-7425-2754-9, ISBN13: 978-0-7425-2754-6. Dewey:363.3/2/0973. LCCN:2002-012832.
Audience: **g,l,u.** *Choice, 2003.*

Falk, Richard A. **HV6432.F34 2002**
The Great Terror War. Trade Cloth. Interlink Publishing Group, Inc. Northampton, MA. 2004. 256p. Bestselling History and Politics Ser. ISBN:1-56656-460-3, ISBN13: 978-1-56656-460-1. Dewey:973.931. LCCN:2002-008389.
Audience: **g,l,u.** *Choice, 2003.*

Gardner, Hall **JZ1480.G367 2005**
American Global Strategy and the 'War on Terrorism'. Trade Cloth. Ashgate Publishing, Ltd. Aldershot, 2005. 240p. ISBN:0-7546-4512-6, ISBN13: 978-0-7546-4512-2. Dewey:327.73/009/0511. LCCN:2005-013076.
Audience: **g,l,u.** *Choice, 2006.*

Goldstein, Joshua S. **HV6432.G64 2004**
The Real Price of War: How You Pay for the War on Terror. Trade Cloth. New York University Press. New York, NY. 2004. 239p. ISBN:0-8147-3161-9, ISBN13: 978-0-8147-3161-1. Dewey:973.931. LCCN:2004-008513.
Audience: **g,l,u,f.**

Henderson, Harry **HV6432.H46 2003**
Terrorist Challenge to America. Trade Cloth. Facts On File, Inc. New York, NY. 2003. 320p. Library in a Book ISBN:0-8160-4975-0, ISBN13: 978-0-8160-4975-2. Dewey:363.3/2/0973. LCCN:2002-014585.
Audience: **g,l,u.** *Choice, 2003.*

Hentoff, Nat **JC599.U45H46 2003**
The War on the Bill of Rights: And the Gathering Resistance. Trade Cloth. Seven Stories Press. New York, NY. 2003. 176p. ISBN:1-58322-621-4, ISBN13: 978-1-58322-621-6. Dewey:323.4/9/0973. LCCN:2003-014162.
Audience: **g,l,u.**

Hess, Stephen & Kalb, Marvin (Editors) **PN4784.T45M38 2003**
The Media and the War on Terrorism. Trade Paper. Brookings Institution Press. Washington, DC. 2003. 320p. ISBN:0-8157-3581-2, ISBN13: 978-0-8157-3581-6. Dewey:070.4/49303625. LCCN:2003-007527.
Audience: **u,f.**

Hewitt, Christopher **HN90**
Political Violence and Terrorism in Modern America: A Chronology. Book, Other. Greenwood Publishing Group, Inc. Portsmouth, NH. 2005. 199p. ISBN:0-313-33418-8, ISBN13: 978-0-313-33418-4. Dewey:303.6/2/097309045. LCCN:2005-018671.
Audience: **g,l,u.** *Choice, 2006.*

Heymann, Philip B. **HV6432.H494 2003**
Terrorism, Freedom, and Security: Winning Without War. Trade Cloth. MIT Press. Cambridge, MA. 2003. 228p. BCSIA Studies

in International Security Ser. ISBN:0-262-08327-2, ISBN13: 978-0-262-08327-0. Dewey:363.3/2/0973. LCCN:2003-051126.
Audience: **g,l,u,f.** *Choice, 2004.*

Hoge, James F. Jr. & Rose, Gideon (Editors) **HV6432.H69**
How Did This Happen?: Terrorism and the New War. Trade Cloth. DIANE Publishing Company. Collingdale, PA. 2005. 324p. ISBN:0-7567-9196-0, ISBN13: 978-0-7567-9196-4. Dewey:973.931.
Audience: **g,l,u.** *Choice, 2002.*

Howard, Russell & Sawyer, Reid **HV6431**
Terrorism and Counter-Terrorism: Understanding the New Security Environment, Readings and Interpretations. Trade Paper. McGraw-Hill Higher Education. Burr Ridge, IL. 2002. 656p. Textbook ISBN:0-07-283778-0, ISBN13: 978-0-07-283778-0. Dewey:363.32/0973. LCCN:2002-106286.
Audience: **u,f.** *Choice, 2003.*

Howitt, Arnold M. & Pangi, Robyn L. (Editors) **HV6432**
Countering Terrorism: Dimensions of Preparedness. Trade Cloth. MIT Press. Cambridge, MA. 2003. 352p. BCSIA Studies in International Security Ser. ISBN:0-262-08324-8, ISBN13: 978-0-262-08324-9. Dewey:363.320973. LCCN:2003-109413.
Audience: **u,f.** *Choice, 2004.*

Ivie, Robert L. **HV6432.I94**
Democracy and America's War on Terror. Trade Paper. University of Alabama Press. Tuscaloosa, AL. 2006. 264p. Albma Rhetoric Cult and Soc Crit Ser. ISBN:0-8173-5338-0, ISBN13: 978-0-8173-5338-4. Dewey:973.931.
Audience: **l,u,f.** *Choice, 2005.*

Judt, Tony **HV6431.S765 2002**
Striking Terror: America's New War. Robert B. Silvers & Barbara Epstein (Editors). Trade Paper. New York Review of Books, Incorporated, The. New York, NY. 2002. 372p. ISBN:1-59017-012-1, ISBN13: 978-1-59017-012-0. Dewey:363.3/2. LCCN:2001-008628.
Audience: **g,l,u,f.** *Choice, 2003.*

Kean, Thomas H. & Hamilton, Lee **HV6432.7.N39 2004**
The 9/11 Commission Report: Final Report of the National Commission on Terrorist Attacks upon the United States. National Commission on Terrorist Attacks Staff (Contribution by). Trade Paper. United States Government Printing Office. Washington, DC. 2004. 567p. ISBN:0-16-072304-3, ISBN13: 978-0-16-072304-9. Dewey:973.931. LCCN:2004-356401.
Audience: **g,l,u,f.**

Kitfield, James **E902.K58 2005**
War and Destiny: How the Bush Revolution in Foreign and Military Affairs Redefined American Power. Saddle Stitched, Cloth over Boards. Potomac Books, Inc. Dulles, VA. 2005. 386p. ISBN:1-57488-959-1, ISBN13: 978-1-57488-959-8. Dewey:327.73/009/0511. LCCN:2005-003860.
Audience: **l,u,f.** *Choice, 2005.*

Lansford, Tom **D860.L355 2002**
All for One: Terrorism, NATO and the United States. Trade Cloth. Ashgate Publishing, Ltd. Aldershot, 2002. 222p. ISBN:0-7546-3045-5, ISBN13: 978-0-7546-3045-6. Dewey:973.931. LCCN:2002-024893.
Audience: **l,u,f.** *Choice, 2003.*

Lawson Mack, Raneta & Kelly, Michael J. **KF4765.M23 2004**
Equal Justice in the Balance: America's Legal Responses to the Emerging Terrorist Threat. Janet Reno (Foreword by), Michael Ratner (Afterword by). Trade Cloth. University of Michigan Press. Chicago, IL. 2004. 320p. ISBN:0-472-11394-1, ISBN13: 978-0-472-11394-1. Dewey:342.7308/5. LCCN:2003-027630.
Audience: **u,f.** *Choice, 2005.*

Leone, Richard C. & Anrig, Gregory **JC599.U5W313 2003**
The War on Our Freedoms: Civil Liberties in an Age of Terrorism. Trade Paper. PublicAffairs. New York, NY. 2003. 336p. ISBN:1-58648-210-6, ISBN13: 978-1-58648-210-7. Dewey:323/.0973. LCCN:2003-046681.
Audience: **g,l,u,f.** *Choice, 2004.*

Leverett, Flynt (Editor) **DS63.2.U5R58 2005**
The Road Ahead: Middle East Policy in the Bush Administration's Second Term. Trade Paper, Perfect. Brookings Institution Press. Washington, DC. 2005. 107p. ISBN:0-8157-5205-9, ISBN13: 978-0-8157-5205-9. Dewey:327.73056. LCCN:2005-351711.
Audience: **u,f.**

Levitt, Geoffrey M. **HV6431**
The Western Response to State-Supported Terrorism. Trade Cloth. Greenwood Publishing Group, Inc. Portsmouth, NH. 1988. 156p. The Washington Papers, No. 134 ISBN:0-275-93021-1, ISBN13: 978-0-275-93021-9. Dewey:363.3/2. LCCN:88-009859.
Audience: **l,u.** *Choice, 1989.*

Levitt, Matthew **HV6432.L48 2002**
Targeting Terror: U.S. Policy Toward Middle Eastern State Sponsors and Terrorist Organizations, Post-September 11. Trade Paper. Washington Institute for Near East Policy, The. Washington, DC. 2002. 141p. ISBN:0-944029-81-7, ISBN13: 978-0-944029-81-7. Dewey:363.3/2/0973. LCCN:2002-014053.
Audience: **l,u,f.** *Choice, 2003.*

Lincoln, Bruce **BL65.T47L56 2002**
Holy Terrors: Thinking about Religion after September 11. Trade Cloth. University of Chicago Press. Chicago, IL. 2002. 185p. ISBN:0-226-48192-1, ISBN13: 978-0-226-48192-0. Dewey:291.1/787. LCCN:2002-007099.
Audience: **g,l,u.** *Choice, 2003.*

Malveaux, Julianne & Green, Reginna A. (Editors) **HV6432.7.P37 2002**
The Paradox of Loyalty: An African American Response to the War on Terrorism. Trade Cloth. Third World Press. Chicago, IL. 2002. 240p. ISBN:0-88378-243-X, ISBN13: 978-0-88378-243-9. Dewey:973.931. LCCN:2002-073285.
Audience: **g,l,u,f.** *Choice, 2003.*

Mead, Walter Russell **JZ1480.M43 2004**
Power, Terror, Peace, and War: America's Grand Strategy in a World at Risk. Trade Cloth. Alfred A. Knopf Inc. New York, NY. 2004. 240p. ISBN:1-4000-4237-2, ISBN13: 978-1-4000-4237-1. Dewey:327.73. LCCN:2003-067277.
Audience: **l,u,f.** *Choice, 2005.*

Mockaitis, Thomas R. & Rich, Paul **HV6431.G728 2003**
Grand Strategy in the War Against Terrorism. B. Bundgaard Rasmussen & Annette Rathje (Editors). Trade Paper. Routledge.

New York, NY. 2003. 160p. ISBN:0-7146-8268-3, ISBN13: 978-0-7146-8268-6. Dewey:973.931. LCCN:2003-016417.
Audience: **l,u,f.** *Choice, 2004.*

Naftali, Timothy **HV6432.N34 2005**
Blind Spot: The Secret History of American Counterterrorism. Perfect, Paper over Boards, Dust Jacket. Basic Books. New York, NY. 2005. 399p. ISBN:0-465-09281-0, ISBN13: 978-0-465-09281-9. Dewey:363.32/0973. LCCN:2005-003248.
Audience: **g,l,u.** *Choice, 2005.*

O'Sullivan, Meghan L. **HF1413.5.O78 2003**
Shrewd Sanctions: Economic Statecraft in An Age of Global Terrorism. Trade Cloth. Brookings Institution Press. Washington, DC. 2002. 336p. ISBN:0-8157-0602-2, ISBN13: 978-0-8157-0602-1. Dewey:327.1/17. LCCN:2002-151487.
Audience: **u,f.** *Choice, 2003.*

Peterson, Kate Dempsey & Burns, Vincent **HV6432**
Terrorism: A Documentary and Reference Guide. Cloth Text. Greenwood Publishing Group, Inc. Portsmouth, NH. 2005. 336p. ISBN:0-313-33213-4, ISBN13: 978-0-313-33213-5. Dewey:303.6/25/0973. LCCN:2005-003390.
Audience: **l,u.** *Choice, 2005.*

Pillar, Paul R. **HV6431.P56 2003**
Terrorism and U. S. Foreign Policy. Trade Paper. Brookings Institution Press. Washington, DC. 2003. 272p. ISBN:0-8157-7077-4, ISBN13: 978-0-8157-7077-0. Dewey:327.73. LCCN:2004-556265.
Audience: **u,f.** *Choice, 2001.*

Piszkiewicz, Dennis **HV6432**
Terrorism's War with America: A History. Trade Cloth. Greenwood Publishing Group, Inc. Portsmouth, NH. 2003. 224p. ISBN:0-275-97952-0, ISBN13: 978-0-275-97952-2. Dewey:303.6/25/0973. LCCN:2003-042940.
Audience: **g,l,u.** *Choice, 2004.*

Preble, Christopher A. **DS79.76.E95 2004**
Exiting Iraq: Why the U. S. Must End the Military Occupation and Renew the War Against Al Qaeda. Cato Institute Staff (Contribution by). Trade Paper. Cato Institute. Washington, DC. 2004. 98p. ISBN:1-930865-64-3, ISBN13: 978-1-930865-64-8. Dewey:956.7044/31. LCCN:2004-051876.
Audience: **l,u,f.**

Sidel, Mark **HV6432.S547 2004**
More Secure, Less Free?: Antiterrorism Policy and Civil Liberties after September 11. Trade Cloth. University of Michigan Press. Chicago, IL. 2004. 216p. ISBN:0-472-11428-X, ISBN13: 978-0-472-11428-3. Dewey:363.32/0973. LCCN:2004-017532.
Audience: **l,u,f.** *Choice, 2005.*

Smith, Brent L. **HV6432.S63 1994**
Terrorism in America: Pipe Bombs and Pipe Dreams. Cloth Text. State University of New York Press. Albany, NY. 1994. 256p. Series in New Directions in Crime and Justice Studies ISBN:0-7914-1759-X, ISBN13: 978-0-7914-1759-1. Dewey:303.6/25/0973. LCCN:93-006941.
Audience: **u.** *Choice, 1994.*

Stone, Geoffrey **JC591.S76 2004**
Perilous Times: Free Speech in Wartime from the Sedition Act of 1798 to the War on Terrorism. Trade Cloth. W. W. Norton & Company, Inc. New York, NY. 2004. 800p. ISBN:0-393-05880-8, ISBN13: 978-0-393-05880-2. Dewey:323.44/3/0973. LCCN:2004-017871.
Audience: **l,u,f.** *Choice, 2005.*

U.S. Navy. Dudley Knox Library. Naval Postgraduate School **HV6431**
☐ Terrorism.
http://library.nps.navy.mil/home/terrorism.htm
U.S. Navy.
Audience: **g,l,u,f.**

Weiss, Thomas George, et al. **HV6432.W38 2004**
Wars on Terrorism and Iraq: Human Rights, Unilateralism, and U.S. Foreign Policy. Margaret E. Crahan & John Goering (Authors). Trade Paper. Routledge. New York, NY. 2004. 272p. ISBN:0-415-70063-9, ISBN13: 978-0-415-70063-4. Dewey:973.931. LCCN:2003-021057.
Audience: **u,f.**

Winkler, Carol K. **HV6432.W56 2005**
In the Name of Terrorism: Presidents on Political Violence in the Post-World War II Era. Perfect, Paper over Boards. State University of New York Press. Albany, NY. 2005. 260p. SUNY Series in the Trajectory of Terror ISBN:0-7914-6617-5, ISBN13: 978-0-7914-6617-9. Dewey:303.6/25/0973. LCCN:2005-000072.
Audience: **g,l,u.**

Woodward, Bob **E903.3 .W66 2003**
Bush at War: Inside the Bush White House. Trade Cloth. Thorndike Press. Waterville, ME. 2003. 577p. ISBN:0-7862-5264-2, ISBN13: 978-0-7862-5264-0. Dewey:973.931. LCCN:2003-040657.
Audience: **g,l,u,f.**

Zunes, Stephen **HV6433.M628**
Tinderbox: U. S. Foreign Policy and the Roots of Terrorism. Trade Cloth. Common Courage Press. Monroe, ME. 2002. 332p. ISBN:1-56751-227-5, ISBN13: 978-1-56751-227-4. Dewey:956.04.
Audience: **u,f.** *Choice, 2003.*

American Government and Politics > Foreign Policy > Diplomacy

Aruri, Naseer Hasan **DS119.76.A773 2003**
Dishonest Broker: America's Role in Israel and Palestine. Ed. 2. Trade Paper. South End Press. Cambridge, MA. 2003. 248p. ISBN:0-89608-687-9, ISBN13: 978-0-89608-687-6. Dewey:327.73054/09/045. LCCN:2002-042886.
Audience: **g,l,u,f.**

Berwanger, Eugene H. **E469.B54 1994**
The British Foreign Service and the American Civil War. Library Binding. University Press of Kentucky. Lexington, KY. 1994. 216p. ISBN:0-8131-1876-X, ISBN13: 978-0-8131-1876-5. Dewey:973.7/21. LCCN:94-006468.
Audience: **u,f.** *Choice, 1995.*

Buhite, Russell D. **D734.C7**
Decisions at Yalta: An Appraisal of Summit Diplomacy. Trade Cloth. Rowman & Littlefield Publishers, Inc. Lanham, MD. 1986. 176p. ISBN:0-8420-2256-2, ISBN13: 978-0-8420-2256-9. Dewey:940.53/4. LCCN:86-013779.
Audience: **l,u.** *Choice, 1987.*

Crapol, Edward P. (Editor) **E183.7**
Women and American Foreign Policy: Lobbyists, Critics, and Insiders. Ed. 2. Book, Other. Rowman & Littlefield Publishers, Inc. Lanham, MD. 1992. 200p. America in the Modern World Ser. ISBN:0-8420-2431-X, ISBN13: 978-0-8420-2431-0. Dewey:327.73/0088042. LCCN:91-046045.
Audience: **l,u,f.** *Choice, 1987.*

Sigal, Leon V. **JZ5675**
Disarming Strangers: Nuclear Diplomacy with North Korea. Trade Paper. Princeton University Press. Princeton, NJ. 1999. 336p. Princeton Studies in International History and Politics ISBN:0-691-01006-4, ISBN13: 978-0-691-01006-9. Dewey:327.1/747. LCCN:97-024502.
Audience: **u,f.** *Choice, 1998.*

Stearns, Monteagle **E840.S724**
Talking to Strangers: Improving American Diplomacy at Home and Abroad. Trade Paper. Princeton University Press. Princeton, NJ. 1999. 230p. ISBN:0-691-00745-4, ISBN13: 978-0-691-00745-8. Dewey:327.73.
Audience: **g,u,f.** *Choice, 1996.*

Stein, Kenneth W. **DS119.7.S6749 1999**
Heroic Diplomacy: Sadat, Kissinger, Carter, Begin and the Quest for Arab-Israeli Peace. Trade Paper. Routledge. New York, NY. 1999. 352p. ISBN:0-415-92155-4, ISBN13: 978-0-415-92155-8. Dewey:956.04. LCCN:98-049359.
Audience: **u,f.** *Choice, 2000.*

Tucker, Nancy B. **E183.8.C5T835 2001**
China Confidential: American Diplomats and Sino-American Relations, 1945-1996. Trade Cloth. Columbia University Press. New York, NY. 2000. 638p. ISBN:0-231-10630-0, ISBN13: 978-0-231-10630-6. Dewey:327.73051. LCCN:00-040445.
Audience: **u,f.** *Choice, 2001.*

U.S. Department of State **JX1407**
☐ Foreign Relations of the United States.
http://www.state.gov/r/pa/ho/frus/
Audience: **g,l,u,f.**

U.S. Department of State **JX1407**
☐ Foreign Relations of the United States.
http://digicoll.library.wisc.edu/FRUS/
University of Wisconsin.
Audience: **g,l,u,f.**

American Government and Politics > Environmental Policy

Caldwell, Lynton K. **HC79.E5 C333**
Environment As a Focus for Public Policy. Robert V. Bartlett & James N. Gladden (Editors). Trade Cloth. Texas A&M University Press. College Station, TX. 1995. 368p. ISBN:0-89096-643-5, ISBN13: 978-0-89096-643-3. Dewey:363.7. LCCN:94-037751.
Audience: **u,f.** *Choice, 1995.*

Dewey, Scott Hamilton **TD883.2.D48 2000**
Don't Breathe the Air: Air Pollution and U. S. Environmental Politics, 1945-1970. Trade Cloth. Texas A&M University Press. College Station, TX. 2000. 321p. Environmental History Ser., Vol. 16 ISBN:0-89096-914-0, ISBN13: 978-0-89096-914-4. Dewey:363.739/2/0973. LCCN:99-088267.
Audience: **g,l,u,f.** *Choice, 2001.*

Flippen, J. Brooks **GE180.F55 2000**
Nixon and the Environment. Trade Cloth. University of New Mexico Press. Albuquerque, NM. 2000. 308p. ISBN:0-8263-1993-9, ISBN13: 978-0-8263-1993-7. Dewey:363.7/056/097309047. LCCN:00-008607.
Audience: **u,f.** *Choice, 2001.*

Hays, Samuel P. **GE180.H392 2000**
A History of Environmental Politics. Trade Cloth. University of Pittsburgh Press. Pittsburgh, PA. 2000. ix, 256p. ISBN:0-8229-4128-7, ISBN13: 978-0-8229-4128-6. Dewey:363.7/05/0973. LCCN:00-009651.
Audience: **l,u,f.** *Choice, 2001.*

Lester, James P., et al. **GE180**
Environmental Injustice in the U. S.: Myth and Realities. David Allen & Kelly Hill (Authors). Trade Paper. Westview Press. Boulder, CO. 2000. 232p. ISBN:0-8133-3819-0, ISBN13: 978-0-8133-3819-4. Dewey:363.7/05/793. LCCN:00-043787.
Audience: **l,u,f.** *Choice, 2001.*

Mooney, Chris **Q127.U6**
The Republican War on Science. Trade Paper. Basic Books. New York, NY. 2006. 376p. ISBN:0-465-04676-2, ISBN13: 978-0-465-04676-8. Dewey:509/.73.
Audience: **g,l,u,f.** *Choice, 2006.*

Neimark, Peninah Rhodes & Mott, Peter (Editors) **GE197**
The Environmental Debate: A Documentary History. Cloth Text. Greenwood Publishing Group, Inc. Portsmouth, NH. 1999. 352p. Primary Documents in American History and Contemporary Issues Ser. ISBN:0-313-30020-8, ISBN13: 978-0-313-30020-2. Dewey:363.7/05/0973. LCCN:99-017844.
Audience: **l,u,f.** *Choice, 2000.*

Susskind, Lawrence E., et al. **GE180.S855 2001**
Better Environmental Policy Studies: How to Design and Conduct More Effective Analysis. Ravi K. Jain & Andrew O. Martyniuk (Authors). Trade Cloth. Island Press. Washington, DC. 2001. 256p. ISBN:1-55963-870-2, ISBN13: 978-1-55963-870-8. Dewey:363.7/056/0973. LCCN:2001-003712.
Audience: **u,f.** *Choice, 2002.*

Wilkinson, Todd **GE180.W55 1998**
Science under Siege: The Politicians' War on Nature and Truth. David Brower (Foreword by), Jim Baca (Introduction by). Trade Cloth. Johnson Books. Boulder, CO. 1998. 414p. ISBN:1-55566-210-2, ISBN13: 978-1-55566-210-3. Dewey:363.7. LCCN:98-012458.
Audience: **g,l,u,f.** *Choice, 1998.*

American Government and Politics > Economic Policy

Carroll, Richard J. **HC106.82.C37 2000**
CQ's Desk Reference on the Economy: Over 600 Answers to Questions That Will Help You Understand News, Trends and Issues. Trade Paper. CQ Press. Washington, DC. 2000. x, 342p. Desk Reference Ser. ISBN:1-56802-525-4, ISBN13: 978-1-56802-525-4. Dewey:330.973. LCCN:00-036016.
Audience: **g,l,u,f.**

Destler, I. M. **HF1455.D48 2005**
American Trade Politics. Ed. 4. Trade Paper, Perfect. Institute for International Economics. Washington, DC. 2005. 373p. ISBN:0-88132-382-9, ISBN13: 978-0-88132-382-5. Dewey:382/.3/0973. LCCN:2005-043367.
Audience: **g,l,u,f.** *Choice, 2005.*

Porter, Glenn **HC103.E52**
Encyclopedia of American Economic History, Set. Trade Cloth. Thomson Gale. Farmington Hills, MI. 1980. 1232p. Encyclopedia of American Economic History 3v St LC Ser., Vol. 1 ISBN:0-684-16271-7, ISBN13: 978-0-684-16271-3. Dewey:330.9/73. LCCN:79-004946.
Audience: **l,u,f.**

Shick, Allen & Lostracco, Felix **HJ2051.S3424 2000**
The Federal Budget: Politics, Policy, Process. Trade Cloth. Brookings Institution Press. Washington, DC. 2000. x, 307p. ISBN:0-8157-7726-4, ISBN13: 978-0-8157-7726-7. Dewey:352.4/8/0973. LCCN:99-050857.
Audience: **u,f.** *Choice, 2000.*

American Government and Politics > Social Policy

Huff, C. Ronald, et al. **KF9756.H84 1996**
Convicted but Innocent: Wrongful Conviction and Public Policy. Arye Rattner & Edward Sagarin (Authors), Simon Dinitz (Foreword by). Trade Cloth. SAGE Publications, Inc. Thousand Oaks, CA. 1996. 204p. ISBN:0-8039-5952-4, ISBN13: 978-0-8039-5952-1. Dewey:342.7/12. LCCN:95-041748.
Audience: **g,l,u,f.** *Choice, 1996.*

Sharp, Elaine B. **HN57.S49 1999**
The Sometime Connection: Public Opinion and Social Policy. Cloth Text. State University of New York Press. Albany, NY. 1999. 256p. SUNY Series in Urban Public Policy ISBN:0-7914-4295-0, ISBN13: 978-0-7914-4295-1. Dewey:361.6/1/0973. LCCN:98-053599.
Audience: **l,u,f.** *Choice, 2000.*

Sidney, Mara S. **HD7288.76.U5S53 2003**
Unfair Housing: How National Policy Shapes Community Action. Trade Cloth. University Press of Kansas. Lawrence, KS. 2003. xiv, 186p. Studies in Government and Public Policy ISBN:0-7006-1275-0, ISBN13: 978-0-7006-1275-8. Dewey:363.5/5/0973. LCCN:2003-008802.
Audience: **l,u,f.** *Choice, 2004.*

Williams, Walter **HN60.W55 1998**
Honest Numbers and Democracy: Social Policy Analysis in the White House, Congress, and the Federal Agencies. Book, Other. Georgetown University Press. Washington, DC. 1998. 336p. ISBN:0-87840-684-0, ISBN13: 978-0-87840-684-5. Dewey:306/.0973. LCCN:97-037972.
Audience: **g,l,u,f.** *Choice, 1998.*

American Government and Politics > Political Issues > Censorship and Politics

Stone, Geoffrey **JC591.S76 2004**
Perilous Times: Free Speech in Wartime from the Sedition Act of 1798 to the War on Terrorism. Trade Cloth. W. W. Norton & Company, Inc. New York, NY. 2004. 800p. ISBN:0-393-05880-8, ISBN13: 978-0-393-05880-2. Dewey:323.44/3/0973. LCCN:2004-017871.
Audience: **l,u,f.** *Choice, 2005.*

American Government and Politics > Political Issues > Crime and Politics

Marion, Nancy E. **HV7921**
A History of Federal Crime Control Initiatives, 1960-1993. Trade Cloth. Greenwood Publishing Group, Inc. Portsmouth, NH. 1994. 288p. Criminology and Crime Control Policy Ser. ISBN:0-275-94649-5, ISBN13: 978-0-275-94649-4. Dewey:364.973. LCCN:93-048214.
Audience: **u,f.** *Choice, 1994.*

Windlesham, Lord **HV9950.W56 1998**
Politics, Punishment and Populism. Cloth Text. Oxford University Press, Inc. New York, NY. 1998. 288p. Studies in Crime and Public Policy ISBN:0-19-511530-9, ISBN13: 978-0-19-511530-7. Dewey:364.9/73. LCCN:97-051415.
Audience: **g,l,u,f.** *Choice, 1999.*

American Government and Politics > Political Issues > Crime and Politics > Capital Punishment

Acker, James R. (Editor), et al. **HV8699.U5A746 1998**
America's Experiment with Capital Punishment: Reflections on the Past, Present, and Future of the Ultimate Penal Sanction. Robert M. Bohm & Charles S. Lanier (Editors). Trade Paper. Carolina Academic Press. Durham, NC. 1998. 592p. ISBN:0-89089-651-8, ISBN13: 978-0-89089-651-8. Dewey:364.66/0973. LCCN:97-039985.
Audience: **l,u.**

Bedau, Hugo Adam & Cassell, Paul G. (Editors) **HV8699.U5D635 2004**
Debating the Death Penalty: Should America Have Capital Punishment? The Experts on Both Sides Make Their Best Case. Trade Cloth. Oxford University Press, Inc. New York, NY. 2004. 256p. ISBN:0-19-516983-2, ISBN13: 978-0-19-516983-6. Dewey:364.66/0973. LCCN:2003-049868.
Audience: **g,l,u.** *Choice, 2004.*

Marquart, James W., et al. **HV8699.U5.M35 1994**
The Rope, the Chair and the Needle: Capital Punishment in Texas, 1923-1990. Sheldon Ekland-Olson & Jonathan R. Sorensen (Authors). Trade Cloth. University of Texas Press. Austin, TX. 1994. 328p. ISBN:0-292-75158-3, ISBN13: 978-0-292-75158-3. Dewey:364.6/6/097640904. LCCN:93-015717.
Audience: **u,f.** *Choice, 1995.*

Martinez, J. Michael (Editor), et al. **HV8694.L475 2002**
Leviathan's Choice: Capital Punishment in the Twenty-First Century. William D. Richardson & D. Brandon Hornsby (Editors). Book, Other. Rowman & Littlefield Publishers, Inc.

Lanham, MD. 2002. 440p. ISBN:0-8476-9730-4, ISBN13: 978-0-8476-9730-4. Dewey:364.66. LCCN:2002-005055.
Audience: **g,l,u.** *Choice, 2003.*

Vila, Bryan & Morris, Cynthia (Editors) **HV8699**
Capital Punishment in the United States: A Documentary History. Cloth Text. Greenwood Publishing Group, Inc. Portsmouth, NH. 1997. 384p. Primary Documents in American History and Contemporary Issues Ser. ISBN:0-313-29942-0, ISBN13: 978-0-313-29942-1. Dewey:364.66/0973. LCCN:96-051137.
Audience: **g,l,u,f.**

American Government and Politics > Political Issues > Crime and Politics > Drug Policy

Belenko, Steven R. **HV5810**
Crack and the Evolution of Anti-Drug Policy. Trade Cloth. Greenwood Publishing Group, Inc. Portsmouth, NH. 1993. 216p. Contributions in Criminology and Penology Ser., No. 42 ISBN:0-313-28030-4, ISBN13: 978-0-313-28030-6. Dewey:362.29870973. LCCN:93-009312.
Audience: **g,l,u,f.** *Choice, 1994.*

Bertram, Eva, et al. **HV5825.D7778 1996**
Drug War Politics: The Price of Denial. Morris J. Blachman, Kenneth Sharpe & Peter Andreas (Authors). Trade Cloth. University of California Press. Berkeley, CA. 1996. 349p. ISBN:0-520-20309-7, ISBN13: 978-0-520-20309-9. Dewey:363.4/5/0973. LCCN:95-019168.
Audience: **g,l,u,f.** *Choice, 1997.*

Gerber, Rudolph J. **HV5822**
Legalizing Marijuana: Drug Policy Reform and Prohibition Politics. Trade Cloth. Greenwood Publishing Group, Inc. Portsmouth, NH. 2004. 208p. ISBN:0-275-97448-0, ISBN13: 978-0-275-97448-0. Dewey:364.1/77. LCCN:2003-068715.
Audience: **l,u.** *Choice, 2005.*

Musto, David F. & Korsmeyer, Pamela **HV5825.M845 2002**
The Quest for Drug Control: Politics and Federal Policy in a Period of Increasing Substance Abuse, 1963-1981. Cloth over Boards. Yale University Press. Cumberland, RI. 2002. 338p. ISBN:0-300-09036-6, ISBN13: 978-0-300-09036-9. Dewey:362.29/156/097309045. LCCN:2002-016702.
Audience: **u,f.** *Choice, 2003.*

Walker, Samuel **HV9950.W35 2006**
Sense and Nonsense about Crime and Drugs: A Policy Guide. Ed. 6. Paper Text. Thomson Wadsworth. Belmont, CA. 2005. 360p. ISBN:0-534-61654-2, ISBN13: 978-0-534-61654-0. Dewey:364.4/04560973. LCCN:2005-928204.
Audience: **l,u.**

American Government and Politics > Political Issues > Crime and Politics > Hate Crimes

Altschiller, Donald **HV6773.52.A47 2005**
Hate Crimes: A Reference Handbook. Ed. 2. Mildred Vasan (Editor). Library Binding. ABC-CLIO, Inc. Santa Barbara, CA. 2005. 391p. Contemporary World Issues Ser. ISBN:1-85109-624-8, ISBN13: 978-1-85109-624-4. Dewey:364.15. LCCN:2005-007151.
Audience: **l,u.** *Choice, 2006, 2000.*

Berrill, Kevin T. (Author, Editor) **HV6250.4.H66H38 1992**
Hate Crimes: Confronting Violence Against Lesbians and Gay Men. Gregory M. Herek (Editor). Trade Paper. SAGE Publications, Inc. Thousand Oaks, CA. 1991. 328p. ISBN:0-8039-4542-6, ISBN13: 978-0-8039-4542-5. Dewey:364.15508664. LCCN:91-034912.
Audience: **l,u,f.** *Choice, 1992.*

Hutchinson, Earl O. **HV9950.H87 1996**
Betrayed: A History of Presidential Failure to Protect Black Lives. Trade Paper. Westview Press. Boulder, CO. 1996. 272p. ISBN:0-8133-2465-3, ISBN13: 978-0-8133-2465-4. Dewey:323.1/1/96073. LCCN:95-052170.
Audience: **g,l,u.** *Choice, 1996.*

Jacobs, James B. & Potter, Kimberly **KF9345**
Hate Crimes: Criminal Law and Identity Politics. Trade Paper. Oxford University Press, Inc. New York, NY. 2000. 222p. Studies in Crime and Public Policy ISBN:0-19-514054-0, ISBN13: 978-0-19-514054-5. Dewey:345.73/025.
Audience: **g.**

Lawrence, Frederick M. **KF9345**
Punishing Hate: Bias Crimes under American Law. Trade Paper. Harvard University Press. Cambridge, MA. 2002. 282p. ISBN:0-674-00972-X, ISBN13: 978-0-674-00972-1. Dewey:345.73/025.
Audience: **g,l,u.** *Choice, 1999.*

American Government and Politics > Political Issues > Gender and Politics

Cooney, Robert P. J. Jr. **JK1896.C65 2005**
Winning the Vote: The Triumph of the American Woman Suffrage Movement. Cloth Text. American Graphic Press. Santa Cruz, CA. 2005. 496p. ISBN:0-9770095-0-5, ISBN13: 978-0-9770095-0-3. Dewey:324.6/230973. LCCN:2005-904560.
Audience: **g,l,u,f.** *Choice, 2006.*

Crapol, Edward P. (Editor) **E183.7**
Women and American Foreign Policy: Lobbyists, Critics, and Insiders. Ed. 2. Book, Other. Rowman & Littlefield Publishers, Inc. Lanham, MD. 1992. 200p. America in the Modern World Ser. ISBN:0-8420-2431-X, ISBN13: 978-0-8420-2431-0. Dewey:327.73/0088042. LCCN:91-046045.
Audience: **l,u,f.** *Choice, 1987.*

Eagleton Institute of Politics, Rutgers University **HQ1236.5.U6**
☐ Center for American Women and Politics. http://www.rci.rutgers.edu/~cawp/index.html
Audience: **l,u,f.**

Green, Elna C. **JK1896.G695 1997**
Southern Strategies: Southern Women and the Woman Suffrage Question. Trade Paper. University of North Carolina Press. Chapel Hill, NC. 1997. 312p. ISBN:0-8078-4641-4, ISBN13: 978-0-8078-4641-4. Dewey:324.6/23/0975. LCCN:96-036992.
Audience: **l,u,f.** *Choice, 1997.*

Roberts, Cokie **E176.R63 2004**
Founding Mothers: The Women Who Raised Our Nation. Trade Cloth. HarperCollins Publishers. New York, NY. 2004. 384p. ISBN:0-06-009025-1, ISBN13: 978-0-06-009025-8. Dewey:973.3/092/2 B. LCCN:2004-042873.
Audience: **g,l,u,f.**

Roosevelt, Eleanor & Black, Allida M. **E807.1.R48A3 1999**
Courage in a Dangerous World: The Political Writings of Eleanor Roosevelt. Trade Cloth. Columbia University Press. New York, NY. 1999. 360p. ISBN:0-231-11180-0, ISBN13: 978-0-231-11180-5. Dewey:973.917/092. LCCN:98-033807.
Audience: **g,u,f.** *Choice, 1999.*

Stuhler, Barbara **JK1881**
For the Public Record: A Documentary History of the League of Women Voters. Trade Cloth. Greenwood Publishing Group, Inc. Portsmouth, NH. 2000. 360p. Contributions in American Studies, No. 108 ISBN:0-313-25316-1, ISBN13: 978-0-313-25316-4. Dewey:324.6/23/0973. LCCN:99-022094.
Audience: **g,l,u,f.** *Choice, 2000.*

van Assendelft, Laura **HQ1236.5.U6E53 1998**
Encyclopedia of Women in American Politics. Jeffrey D. Schultz (Editor), Helen Thomas (Foreword by). Cloth Text. Greenwood Publishing Group, Inc. Portsmouth, NH. 1998. 384p. The American Political Landscape Ser., No. 1 ISBN:1-57356-131-2, ISBN13: 978-1-57356-131-0. Dewey:320/.082. LCCN:98-036327.
Audience: **g,l,u,f.** *Choice, 1999.*

American Government and Politics > Political Issues > Gender and Politics > Abortion. Reproduction

Blanchard, Dallas A. & Prewitt, Terry J. **HQ767.25.B53 1993**
Religious Violence and Abortion: The Gideon Project. Trade Cloth. University Press of Florida. Gainesville, FL. 1993. 368p. ISBN:0-8130-1193-0, ISBN13: 978-0-8130-1193-6. Dewey:363.4/6/0975999. LCCN:92-039693.
Audience: **l,u,f.** *Choice, 1993.*

Craig, Barbara H. & O'Brien, David M. **HQ767.5.U5.C73 1993**
Abortion and American Politics. Trade Cloth. Seven Bridges Press, LLC. New York, NY. 1993. 398p. American Politics Ser. ISBN:0-934540-88-8, ISBN13: 978-0-934540-88-9. Dewey:363.4/6/0973. LCCN:92-041395.
Audience: **l,u,f.** *Choice, 1993.*

Dixon-Mueller, Ruth **HQ767.D59 2002**
Abortion and Common Sense. Trade Paper. Xlibris Corporation. Philadelphia, PA. 2002. 298p. ISBN:1-4010-5954-6, ISBN13: 978-1-4010-5954-5. Dewey:363.46. LCCN:2002-092236.
Audience: **l,u.** *Choice, 2003.*

Gordon, Linda **HQ766.5.U5G66 2002**
The Moral Property of Women: A History of Birth Control Politics in America. Ed. 3. Trade Cloth. University of Illinois Press. Champaign, IL. 2002. 464p. ISBN:0-252-02764-7, ISBN13: 978-0-252-02764-2. Dewey:363.9/6/0973. LCCN:2002-001551.
Audience: **l,u,f.** *Choice, 2003.*

Gordon, Linda **HQ766.5.U5.G67**
Woman's Body, Woman's Right: A Social History of Birth Control in America. Trade Cloth. Penguin Group (USA) Inc. New York, NY. 1976. xviii, 479p. ISBN:0-670-77817-6, ISBN13: 978-0-670-77817-1. Dewey:301.32/1. LCCN:76-022691.
Audience: **l,u,f.** B

Irvine, Janice M. **HQ57.5.A3 I78 2002**
Talk about Sex: The Battle over Sex Education in the United States. Trade Cloth. University of California Press. Berkeley, CA. 2002. 294p. ISBN:0-520-23503-7, ISBN13: 978-0-520-23503-8. Dewey:613.9/07/073. LCCN:2001-058500.
Audience: **g,l,u,f.** *Choice, 2003.*

Schroedel, Jean Reith **KF481.S37 2000**
Is the Fetus a Person?: A Comparison of Policies Across the Fifty States. Trade Cloth. Cornell University Press. Ithaca, NY. 2000. 256p. ISBN:0-8014-3707-5, ISBN13: 978-0-8014-3707-6. Dewey:342.73/085. LCCN:00-025087.
Audience: **g,l,u,f.** *Choice, 2001.*

American Government and Politics > Political Issues > Gender and Politics > Gay, Lesbian, Bisexual, Transgendered

Belkin, Aaron & Bateman, Geoffrey (Editors) **UB418.G38D65 2003**
Don't Ask, Don't Tell: Debating the Gay Ban in the U. S. Military. Paper Text. Lynne Rienner Publishers, Inc. Boulder, CO. 2003. 190p. ISBN:1-58826-146-8, ISBN13: 978-1-58826-146-5. Dewey:355/.0086/640973. LCCN:2002-031836.
Audience: **g,l,u,f.**

D'Emilio, John **HQ76.8.U5D454 2002**
The World Turned: Essays on Gay History, Politics, and Culture. Trade Cloth. Duke University Press. Durham, NC. 2002. 328p. ISBN:0-8223-2930-1, ISBN13: 978-0-8223-2930-5. Dewey:305.9/0664/0973. LCCN:2002-001674.
Audience: **g,l.**

D'Emilio, John (Editor), et al. **HQ76.8.U5C74 2000**
Creating Change: Public Policy, Civil Rights and Sexuality. William B. Turner & Urvashi Vaid (Editors). Cloth over Boards. St. Martin's Press. Gordonville, VA. 2000. 528p. ISBN:0-312-24375-8, ISBN13: 978-0-312-24375-3. Dewey:305.9/0664/0973. LCCN:00-031718.
Audience: **g,l.**

Goldberg-Hiller, Jonathan **HQ1034**
The Limits to Union: Same-Sex Marriage and the Politics of Civil Rights. Trade Paper. University of Michigan Press. Chicago, IL. 2004. 304p. Law, Meaning, and Violence Ser. ISBN:0-472-03049-3, ISBN13: 978-0-472-03049-1. Dewey:306.84/8.
Audience: **l,u.** *Choice, 2003, 2002.*

Riggle, Ellen D. & Tadlock, Barry L. (Editors) **HQ76.3.U5**
Gays and Lesbians in the Democratic Process: Public Policy, Public Opinion and Political Representation. Trade Paper. Columbia University Press. New York, NY. 1999. 384p. Power,

Conflict, and Democracy Ser. ISBN:0-231-11585-7, ISBN13: 978-0-231-11585-8. Dewey:305.9/0664.
Audience: **l,u,f.** *Choice, 2000.*

Rimmerman, Craig A. **HQ76.8.U5R56 2002**
From Identity to Politics: The Lesbian and Gay Movements in the United States. Paper Text. Temple University Press. Philadelphia, PA. 2002. 272p. Queer Politics, Queer Theories Ser. ISBN:1-56639-905-X, ISBN13: 978-1-56639-905-0. Dewey:305.9/0664. LCCN:2001-027644.
Audience: **l,u,f.** *Choice, 2002.*

Robinson, Paul **HQ76.85.R63 2005**
Queer Wars: The New Gay Right and Its Critics. Trade Cloth. University of Chicago Press. Chicago, IL. 2005. 192p. ISBN:0-226-72200-7, ISBN13: 978-0-226-72200-9. Dewey:306.76/6. LCCN:2004-005111.
Audience: **u,f.** *Choice, 2005.*

Smith, Raymond A. & Haider-Markel, Donald P. **HQ76.3.U5S59 2002**
[e] Gay and Lesbian Americans and Political Participation: A Reference Handbook. E-Book. ABC-CLIO, Inc. Santa Barbara, CA. 2003. Political Participation in America Ser. ISBN:1-57607-731-4, ISBN13: 978-1-57607-731-3. Dewey:305.9/0664/0973.
Audience: **g.** *Choice, 2003.*

Stein, Arlene **HQ76.8.U5**
The Stranger Next Door: The Story of a Small Community's Battle over Sex, Faith, and Civil Rights. Trade Paper. Beacon Press. Boston, MA. 2002. 280p. ISBN:0-8070-7953-7, ISBN13: 978-0-8070-7953-9. Dewey:305.9/0664/09795.
Audience: **g,l.** *Choice, 2001.*

Strasser, Mark P. **KF539**
The Challenge of Same-Sex Marriage: Federalist Principles and Constitutional Protections. Trade Cloth. Greenwood Publishing Group, Inc. Portsmouth, NH. 1999. 272p. ISBN:0-275-96624-0, ISBN13: 978-0-275-96624-9. Dewey:346.7301/6. LCCN:99-021589.
Audience: **u,f.**

Sullivan, Andrew (Editor) **HQ1033.S26**
For Better or Worse?: Same Sex Marriages, Pro and Con: A Reader. Trade Paper. Knopf Publishing Group. New York, NY. 1997. ISBN:0-614-28079-6, ISBN13: 978-0-614-28079-1. Dewey:306.84/8.
Audience: **g,l.**

Weeks, Jeffrey **HQ18.G7W43 1989**
Sex, Politics and Society: The Regulation of Sexuality since 1800. Ed. 2. Trade Paper. Pearson Education. Boston, MA. 1989. 336p. Themes in British Social History Ser. ISBN:0-582-02383-1, ISBN13: 978-0-582-02383-3. Dewey:306.7/0941. LCCN:88-013197.
Audience: **l,u,f.**

American Government and Politics > Political Issues > Immigration and Politics

Azuma, Eiichiro **F596.3.J3A98 2005**
Between Two Empires: Race, History, and Transnationalism in Japanese America. Trade Cloth. Oxford University Press, Inc. New York, NY. 2005. 320p. ISBN:0-19-515940-3, ISBN13: 978-0-19-515940-0. Dewey:973/.04956. LCCN:2004-050145.
Audience: **l,u,f.** *Choice, 2006.*

Bakken, Gordon Morris & Kindell, Alexandra (Editors) **HB1965.E53 2006**
Encyclopedia of Immigration and Migration in the American West. Trade Cloth. SAGE Publications, Inc. Thousand Oaks, CA. 2006. 1000p. ISBN:1-4129-0550-8, ISBN13: 978-1-4129-0550-3. Dewey:304.8/78003. LCCN:2005-025714.
Audience: **l,u.** *Choice, 2006.*

Calavita, Kitty **JV6493.C35 1992**
Inside the State: The Bracero Program, Illegal Immigrants, and the INS. Cloth Text. Routledge. New York, NY. 1992. 256p. After the Law Ser. ISBN:0-415-90537-0, ISBN13: 978-0-415-90537-4. Dewey:353.00817. LCCN:92-012340.
Audience: **u,f.**

Daniels, Roger **JV6483.D36 2003**
Guarding the Golden Door: American Immigration Policy and Immigrants since 1882. Cloth over Boards. Farrar, Straus & Giroux. New York, NY. 2004. 344p. ISBN:0-8090-5343-8, ISBN13: 978-0-8090-5343-8. Dewey:325.73. LCCN:2003-007714.
Audience: **g,l,u,f.** *Choice, 2004.*

Daniels, Roger **D769.8.A6**
The Politics of Prejudice: The Anti-Japanese Movement in California and the Struggle for Japanese Exclusion. Ed. 2. Trade Paper. University of California Press. Berkeley, CA. 1999. 182p. ISBN:0-520-21950-3, ISBN13: 978-0-520-21950-2. Dewey:323.1195607.
Audience: **u,f.** [BCL3]

Graham, Hugh Davis **JV6483.G73 2002**
Collision Course: The Strange Convergence of Affirmative Action and Immigration Policy in America. Trade Cloth. Oxford University Press, Inc. New York, NY. 2002. 256p. ISBN:0-19-514318-3, ISBN13: 978-0-19-514318-8. Dewey:325.73. LCCN:2001-037476.
Audience: **u,f.**

Grasmuck, Sherri & Pessar, Patricia R. **JV7395.G7 1991**
Between Two Islands: Dominican International Migration. Trade Cloth. University of California Press. Berkeley, CA. 1991. 280p. ISBN:0-520-07149-2, ISBN13: 978-0-520-07149-0. Dewey:304.8/097293. LCCN:90-050924.
Audience: **u,f.** *Choice, 1992.*

Haines, David W. (Editor) **HV640**
Refugees in America in the 1990s: A Reference Handbook. Cloth Text. Greenwood Publishing Group, Inc. Portsmouth, NH. 1996. 480p. ISBN:0-313-29344-9, ISBN13: 978-0-313-29344-3. Dewey:362.87/0973. LCCN:95-050902.
Audience: **l,u.** *Choice, 1997.*

Hamermesh, Daniel S. & Bean, Frank D. (Editors) **JV6471.H45 1998**
Help or Hindrance?: The Economic Implications of Immigration for African Americans. Trade Cloth. Russell Sage Foundation. New York, NY. 1998. 396p. ISBN:0-87154-387-7, ISBN13: 978-0-87154-387-5. Dewey:331.6/396073. LCCN:97-046611.
Audience: **u,f.** *Choice, 1999.*

Handlin, Oscar **JV6450**
The Uprooted: The Epic Story of the Great Migrations That Made the American People. Ed. 2. Book, Other. University of Pennsylvania Press. Philadelphia, PA. 2002. 344p. ISBN:0-8122-1788-8, ISBN13: 978-0-8122-1788-9. Dewey:304.8/73. LCCN:2001-048096.
Audience: **u,f.**

Hatamiya, Leslie T. **D769.8.A6H38**
Righting a Wrong: Japanese Americans and the Passage of the Civil Liberties Act of 1988. Trade Paper. Stanford University Press. Palo Alto, CA. 1994. 283p. Asian America ISBN:0-8047-2366-4, ISBN13: 978-0-8047-2366-4. Dewey:940.53/1503956073. LCCN:92-040402.
Audience: **g,l,u,f.** *Choice, 1994.*

Hein, Jeremy **HV640.5.I5H44 1995**
From Migrants to Ethnic Minorities: The Settlement of Refugees from Vietnam, Laos, and Cambodia in the United States. Trade Cloth. Thomson Gale. Farmington Hills, MI. 1995. 193p. Twayne's Immigrant Heritage of America Ser. ISBN:0-8057-8432-2, ISBN13: 978-0-8057-8432-9. Dewey:362.87/089/959. LCCN:94-041960.
Audience: **g,l,u,f.** *Choice, 1995.*

Hing, Bill Ong **JV6483.H56 2004**
Defining America Through Immigration Policy. Trade Cloth. Temple University Press. Philadelphia, PA. 2004. 376p. Mapping Racisms Ser. ISBN:1-59213-232-4, ISBN13: 978-1-59213-232-4. Dewey:325.73. LCCN:2003-053949.
Audience: **g,l,u,f.** *Choice, 2004.*

Jacobson, Matthew F. **E184.E95J33 1998**
Whiteness of a Different Color: European Immigrants and the Alchemy of Race. Trade Cloth. Harvard University Press. Cambridge, MA. 1998. 352p. ISBN:0-674-06371-6, ISBN13: 978-0-674-06371-6. Dewey:305.8/00973. LCCN:98-015754.
Audience: **l,u,f.**

Jacobson, Matthew Frye **E178.1**
Barbarian Virtues: The United States Encounters Foreign Peoples at Home and Abroad, 1876-1917. Trade Paper. Farrar, Straus & Giroux. New York, NY. 2001. 336p. ISBN:0-8090-1628-1, ISBN13: 978-0-8090-1628-0. Dewey:973.
Audience: **l,u,f.** *Choice, 2000.*

Jacoby, Tamar **JV6450**
Reinventing the Melting Pot: The New Immigrants and What It Means to Be American. Trade Paper. Basic Books. New York, NY. 2004. 352p. ISBN:0-465-03635-X, ISBN13: 978-0-465-03635-6. Dewey:304.8/73.
Audience: **g,l,u,f.** *Choice, 2004.*

Massey, Douglas S., et al. **JV6483.M33 2002**
Beyond Smoke and Mirrors: Mexican Immigration in an Era of Free Trade. Jorge Durand & Nolan J. Malone (Authors). Trade Cloth. Russell Sage Foundation. New York, NY. 2002. ix, 199p. ISBN:0-87154-589-6, ISBN13: 978-0-87154-589-3. Dewey:325/.272073. LCCN:2001-055712.
Audience: **u,f.** *Choice, 2002.*

Muller, Thomas **JV6471.M85 1993**
Immigrants and the American City. Trade Cloth. New York University Press. New York, NY. 1993. 600p. ISBN:0-8147-5479-1, ISBN13: 978-0-8147-5479-5. Dewey:304.873. LCCN:92-008934.
Audience: **u,f.** *Choice, 1993.*

Ngai, Mae M. **KF4800.N485 2005**
Impossible Subjects: Illegal Aliens and the Making of Modern America. Trade Paper. Princeton University Press. Princeton, NJ. 2005. 400p. Politics and Society in Twentieth Century America Ser. ISBN:0-691-12429-9, ISBN13: 978-0-691-12429-2. Dewey:342.73/083.
Audience: **l,u,f.** *Choice, 2004.*

Nugent, Walter **JV6465.N84 1992**
Crossings: The Great Transatlantic Migrations, 1870-1914. Cloth Text. Indiana University Press. Bloomington, IN. 1992. 256p. ISBN:0-253-34140-X, ISBN13: 978-0-253-34140-2. Dewey:304.8/094. LCCN:92-007156.
Audience: **g,l,u,f.** *Choice, 1993.*

Ostergren, Robert C. **JV6749.I83O88 1988**
A Community Transplanted: The Trans-Atlantic Experience of a Swedish Immigrant Settlement in the Upper Middle West, 1835-1915. Trade Cloth. University of Wisconsin Press. Chicago, IL. 1988. 416p. ISBN:0-299-11320-5, ISBN13: 978-0-299-11320-9. Dewey:325/.2485/0977664. LCCN:88-000211.
Audience: **g,l,u,f.** *Choice, 1988.*

Portes, Alejandro & Bach, Robert L. **E184.C97**
Latin Journey: Cuban and Mexican Immigrants in the United States. Trade Cloth. University of California Press. Berkeley, CA. 1985. 432p. ISBN:0-520-05004-5, ISBN13: 978-0-520-05004-4. Dewey:305.8/687291/073. LCCN:83-009292.
Audience: **l,u.**

Ramakrishnan, S. Karthick **JV6477.R35 2005**
Democracy in Immigrant America: Demographics and Political Participation. Trade Cloth. Stanford University Press. Palo Alto, CA. 2005. 240p. ISBN:0-8047-5044-0, ISBN13: 978-0-8047-5044-8. Dewey:323/.042/0869120973. LCCN:2004-009114.
Audience: **u,f.** *Choice, 2005.*

Ramirez, Bruno & Otis, Yves **E183.8.C2R32 2001**
Crossing the 49th Parallel: Migration from Canada to the United States, 1900-1930. Book, Other. Cornell University Press. Ithaca, NY. 2001. 272p. ISBN:0-8014-3288-X, ISBN13: 978-0-8014-3288-0. Dewey:973/.0411. LCCN:00-011450.
Audience: **u,f.** *Choice, 2001.*

Roediger, David R. **E184.A1**
Working Toward Whiteness: How America's Immigrants Became White - The Strange Journey from Ellis Island to the Suburbs. Trade Paper. Basic Books. New York, NY. 2006. 352p. ISBN:0-465-07074-4, ISBN13: 978-0-465-07074-9.
Audience: **g,l,u,f.** *Choice, 2006.*

Shain, Yossi **E184.A1 S565 1999**
Marketing the American Creed Abroad: Diasporas in the U. S. and Their Homelands. Trade Paper. Cambridge University Press. New York, NY. 1999. 312p. ISBN:0-521-64531-X, ISBN13: 978-0-521-64531-7. Dewey:323/.042/08691. LCCN:98-011676.
Audience: **u,f.** *Choice, 1999.*

Weir, Margaret (Editor), et al. **HN65.P635 1988**
The Politics of Social Policy in the United States. Ann S. Orloff & Theda Skocpol (Editors). Trade Cloth. Princeton University

Press. Princeton, NJ. 1988. 500p. Studies from the Project on the Federal Social Role ISBN:0-691-09436-5, ISBN13: 978-0-691-09436-6. Dewey:361.6/1/0973. LCCN:87-025702.
Audience: **u,f.** *Choice, 1988.*

American Government and Politics > Political Issues > Labor and Politics

Nissen, Bruce (Editor) **HD6483.U66 2002**
Unions in a Globalized Environment: Changing Borders, Organizational Boundaries, and Social Roles. Cloth Text. M. E. Sharpe Inc. Armonk, NY. 2002. 296p. ISBN:0-7656-0869-3, ISBN13: 978-0-7656-0869-7. Dewey:331.88/091. LCCN:2001-049525.
Audience: **u,f.** *Choice, 2003, 2002.*

American Government and Politics > Political Issues > Political Protest

Hentoff, Nat **JC599.U45H46 2003**
The War on the Bill of Rights: And the Gathering Resistance. Trade Cloth. Seven Stories Press. New York, NY. 2003. 176p. ISBN:1-58322-621-4, ISBN13: 978-1-58322-621-6. Dewey:323.4/9/0973. LCCN:2003-014162.
Audience: **g,l,u.**

Newman, Richard (Editor), et al. **E184.6.P36 2001**
Pamphlets of Protest: An Anthology of Early African-American Protest Literature, 1790-1860. Patrick Rael & Phillip Lapsansky (Editors). Paper over Boards. Routledge. New York, NY. 2000. 320p. ISBN:0-415-92443-X, ISBN13: 978-0-415-92443-6. Dewey:323.1/196073. LCCN:00-038254.
Audience: **g,l,u,f.** *Choice, 2001.*

Phillips, Kevin **JK2249.P48 1994**
The Arrogant Capital: Washington, Wall Street, and the Frustrations of American Politics. Trade Cloth. Little Brown & Company. New York, NY. 1994. xviii, 231p. ISBN:0-316-70618-3, ISBN13: 978-0-316-70618-6. Dewey:320.973. LCCN:94-010035.
Audience: **g,l,u,f.**

Wittner, Lawrence S. **JX1961.U6**
Rebels Against War: The American Peace Movement, 1933-1983. Trade Paper. Temple University Press. Philadelphia, PA. 1984. 384p. ISBN:0-87722-342-4, ISBN13: 978-0-87722-342-9. Dewey:327.1/72/0973. LCCN:83-027523.
Audience: **g,l,u.** B

American Government and Politics > Political Issues > Privacy. Cybersecurity

Brasch, Walter M. **JC599.U5B67 2005**
America's Unpatriot Acts: The Federal Government's Violation of Constitutional and Civil Rights. Trade Paper. Peter Lang Publishing, Inc. New York, NY. 2005. xvi;231p. ISBN:0-8204-7608-0, ISBN13: 978-0-8204-7608-7. Dewey:973.931. LCCN:2004-018808.
Audience: **g,l,u.** *Choice, 2006.*

Cohen, David B. & Wells, John W. (Editors) **JC599.U5A4985 2004**
American National Security and Civil Liberties in an Era of Terrorism. Cloth over Boards. Palgrave Macmillan. New York, NY. 2004. 240p. ISBN:1-4039-6199-9, ISBN13: 978-1-4039-6199-0. Dewey:323/.0973. LCCN:2003-065607.
Audience: **u,f.** *Choice, 2005.*

Cole, David **KF4850.C65 2006**
Terrorism and the Constitution: Sacrificing Civil Liberties in the Name of National Security. Ed. 3. Trade Paper. New Press, The. New York, NY. 2006. 256p. ISBN:1-56584-939-6, ISBN13: 978-1-56584-939-6. Dewey:343.7301. LCCN:2006-273542.
Audience: **g.** *Choice, 2003.*

Etzioni, Amitai & Marsh, Jason H. **HV6432.E88 2003**
Rights vs. Public Safety after 9/11: America in the Age of Terrorism. Book, Other. Rowman & Littlefield Publishers, Inc. Lanham, MD. 2003. 200p. Rights and Responsibilities, :Communitarian Perspectives Ser. ISBN:0-7425-2754-9, ISBN13: 978-0-7425-2754-6. Dewey:363.3/2/0973. LCCN:2002-012832.
Audience: **g,l,u.** *Choice, 2003.*

Leone, Richard C. & Anrig, Gregory **JC599.U5W313 2003**
The War on Our Freedoms: Civil Liberties in an Age of Terrorism. Trade Paper. PublicAffairs. New York, NY. 2003. 336p. ISBN:1-58648-210-6, ISBN13: 978-1-58648-210-7. Dewey:323/.0973. LCCN:2003-046681.
Audience: **g,l,u,f.** *Choice, 2004.*

Lyon, David **HN59.2.L96 2003**
Surveillance after September 11. Trade Paper. Blackwell Publishing, Inc. Malden, MA. 2003. 208p. Themes for the 21st Century Ser. ISBN:0-7456-3181-9, ISBN13: 978-0-7456-3181-3. Dewey:303.3/3. LCCN:2003-001340.
Audience: **u,f.** *Choice, 2004.*

Sidel, Mark **HV6432.S547 2004**
More Secure, Less Free?: Antiterrorism Policy and Civil Liberties after September 11. Trade Cloth. University of Michigan Press. Chicago, IL. 2004. 216p. ISBN:0-472-11428-X, ISBN13: 978-0-472-11428-3. Dewey:363.32/0973. LCCN:2004-017532.
Audience: **l,u,f.** *Choice, 2005.*

American Government and Politics > Political Issues > Race, Ethnicity, and Politics

Azuma, Eiichiro **F596.3.J3A98 2005**
Between Two Empires: Race, History, and Transnationalism in Japanese America. Trade Cloth. Oxford University Press, Inc. New York, NY. 2005. 320p. ISBN:0-19-515940-3, ISBN13: 978-0-19-515940-0. Dewey:973/.04956. LCCN:2004-050145.
Audience: **l,u,f.** *Choice, 2006.*

Brown, Dee **E81.B75 2001**
Bury My Heart at Wounded Knee: An Indian History of the American West. Ed. 30. Cloth over Boards. Henry Holt & Company. New York, NY. 2001. 512p. ISBN:0-8050-6634-9, ISBN13: 978-0-8050-6634-0. Dewey:970.5. LCCN:00-040958.
Audience: **g,u,f.**

Davidson, Chandler **JK1929.A2Q54 1994**
Quiet Revolution in the South: The Impact of the Voting Rights Act, 1965-1990. Bernard N. Grofman (Editor). Trade Paper. Princeton University Press. Princeton, NJ. 1994. 516p. ISBN:0-691-02108-2, ISBN13: 978-0-691-02108-9. Dewey:324.6/2/08996073075. LCCN:93-038961.
Audience: **l,u,f.** *Choice, 1994.*

Hadjor, Kofi B. **E185.615.H235 1995**
Another America: The Politics of Race and Blame. Trade Cloth. South End Press. Cambridge, MA. 1995. 219p. African-American Studies ISBN:0-89608-516-3, ISBN13: 978-0-89608-516-9. Dewey:305.896/073. LCCN:95-034269.
Audience: **l,u,f.**

Heumann, Milton & Cassak, Lance **HV8141.C37 2003**
Good Cop, Bad Cop: Racial Profiling and Competing Views of Justice. Trade Paper. Peter Lang Publishing, Inc. New York, NY. 2003. ix, 246p. Studies in Crime and Punishment Ser. ISBN:0-8204-5829-5, ISBN13: 978-0-8204-5829-8. Dewey:363.2/3/08900973. LCCN:2003-002788.
Audience: **l,u.** *Choice, 2004.*

Keiser, Richard A. **JK1764.K45 1997**
Subordination or Empowerment?: African-American Leadership and the Struggle for Urban Political Power. Trade Cloth. Oxford University Press, Inc. New York, NY. 1997. 254p. ISBN:0-19-507569-2, ISBN13: 978-0-19-507569-4. Dewey:303.3/089/96073. LCCN:96-041161.
Audience: **l,u,f.** *Choice, 1998.*

Kousser, J. Morgan **JK1924.K68 1999**
Colorblind Injustice: Minority Voting Rights and the Undoing of the Second Reconstruction. Trade Paper. University of North Carolina Press. Chapel Hill, NC. 1999. 608p. ISBN:0-8078-4738-0, ISBN13: 978-0-8078-4738-1. Dewey:328.750734. LCCN:98-016693.
Audience: **l,u,f.**

Kymlicka, Will **JF1061.K96 1996**
[e] Multicultural Citizenship: A Liberal Theory of Minority Rights. E-Book. NetLibrary, Inc. Boulder, CO. 1996. ISBN:0-585-42845-X, ISBN13: 978-0-585-42845-1. Dewey:323.1/1.
Audience: **l,u,f.** *Choice, 1996.*

Marable, Manning **E185.615.M2784 1997**
Black Liberation in Conservative America. Trade Cloth. South End Press. Cambridge, MA. 1997. 285p. African-American Studies ISBN:0-89608-560-0, ISBN13: 978-0-89608-560-2. Dewey:973/.0496073. LCCN:96-048679.
Audience: **g,l,u.** *Choice, 1997.*

Marable, Manning **E185.615.M283 2002**
The Great Wells of Democracy: The Meaning of Race in American Life. Trade Cloth. Basic Books. New York, NY. 2002. 384p. ISBN:0-465-04393-3, ISBN13: 978-0-465-04393-4. Dewey:323.1/196073. LCCN:2002-015848.
Audience: **g,l,u.**

Parker, Frank R. **E185.93.M6P37 1990**
Black Votes Count: Political Empowerment in Mississippi after 1965. Trade Paper. University of North Carolina Press. Chapel Hill, NC. 1990. 272p. ISBN:0-8078-4274-5, ISBN13: 978-0-8078-4274-4. Dewey:323.1/1960730762. LCCN:89-039074.
Audience: **l,u,f.** *Choice, 1991.*

Perman, Michael **JK1929.A2P47 2001**
Struggle for Mastery: Disfranchisement in the South, 1888-1908. Trade Paper. University of North Carolina Press. Chapel Hill, NC. 2001. 416p. Fred W. Morrison Series in Southern Studies ISBN:0-8078-4909-X, ISBN13: 978-0-8078-4909-5. Dewey:324.6/2/097509034. LCCN:00-041773.
Audience: **l,u,f.** *Choice, 2001.*

Prucha, Francis P. **JX235.9**
American Indian Treaties: The History of a Political Anomaly. Trade Paper. University of California Press. Berkeley, CA. 1997. 578p. ISBN:0-520-20895-1, ISBN13: 978-0-520-20895-7. Dewey:341/.026673. LCCN:93-036297.
Audience: **g,l,u,f.** *Choice, 1995.*

Robinson, Dean E. **E185.61 .R679 2001**
Black Nationalism in American Politics and Thought. Cloth Text. Cambridge University Press. New York, NY. 2001. 182p. ISBN:0-521-62326-X, ISBN13: 978-0-521-62326-1. Dewey:320.5408996073. LCCN:00-031277.
Audience: **l,u,f.** *Choice, 2002.*

Robinson, Jo Ann Ooiman (Editor) **JC599**
Affirmative Action: A Documentary History. Cloth Text. Greenwood Publishing Group, Inc. Portsmouth, NH. 2001. 464p. Primary Documents in American History and Contemporary Issues Ser. ISBN:0-313-30169-7, ISBN13: 978-0-313-30169-8. Dewey:331.13/3/0973. LCCN:00-049508.
Audience: **g,l,u,f.**

Savage, Barbara D. **E185.61.S32 1999**
Broadcasting Freedom: Radio War and the Politics of Race, 1938-1948. Trade Cloth. University of North Carolina Press. Chapel Hill, NC. 1999. 408p. John Hope Franklin Series in African American History and Cult Ser. ISBN:0-8078-2477-1, ISBN13: 978-0-8078-2477-1. Dewey:305.8/00973. LCCN:98-048030.
Audience: **u,f.** *Choice, 1999.*

Schultz, Jeffrey D. (Editor), et al. **E184.A1E574 2000**
Encyclopedia of Minorities in American Politics, Set. Kerry L. Haynie, Anne Merline McCulloch & Andrew L. Aoki (Editors), Helen Thomas (Foreword by). Cloth Text. Greenwood Publishing Group, Inc. Portsmouth, NH. 1999. 800p. The American Political Landscape Ser. ISBN:1-57356-129-0, ISBN13: 978-1-57356-129-7. Dewey:305.8/00973/03. LCCN:99-043451.
Audience: **g,l,u,f.** *Choice, 2000.*

Symposium on Science, Reason, and Modern Democracy S **JK1726.M77 1998**
Multiculturalism and American Democracy. Arthur M. Melzer, Jerry Weinberger & M. Richard Zinman (Editors). Trade Paper. University Press of Kansas. Lawrence, KS. 1998. viii, 238p. ISBN:0-7006-0882-6, ISBN13: 978-0-7006-0882-9. Dewey:305.8/00973. LCCN:97-045707.
Audience: **l,u,f.** *Choice, 1998.*

Walters, Ronald W. **JK1924.W34 1988**
[e] Black Presidential Politics in America: A Strategic Approach. E-Book. NetLibrary, Inc. Boulder, CO. 1988. ISBN:0-585-09216-8, ISBN13: 978-0-585-09216-4. Dewey:324.6/2/08996073.
Audience: **l,u,f.** *Choice, 1988.*

Walton, Hanes **E185.615.W315 1997**
African American Power and Politics: The Political Context Variable. Trade Cloth. Columbia University Press. New York, NY. 1997. 544p. Power, Conflict, and Democracy Ser. ISBN:0-231-10418-9, ISBN13: 978-0-231-10418-0. Dewey:323.1/196073. LCCN:96-035063.
Audience: **u,f.** *Choice, 1998.*

Williams, Robert A. Jr. **E93.W755 1997**
Linking Arms Together: American Indian Treaty Visions of Law and Peace, 1600-1800. Trade Cloth. Oxford University Press, Inc. New York, NY. 1997. 202p. ISBN:0-19-506591-3, ISBN13: 978-0-19-506591-6. Dewey:342.7/3/0872. LCCN:96-023095.
Audience: **u,f.** *Choice, 1997.*

Comparative Government

HC59
☐ United Nations Common Database.
http://unstats.un.org/unsd/cdb/cdb_help/cdb_quick_start.asp
United Nations.
Audience: **g,l,u,f.**

JF37
Worldwide Government Directory: With International Organizations. Ed. 23. Trade Cloth. C Q Staff Directories, Inc. Washington, DC. 2005. 1,550p. ISBN:0-87289-235-2, ISBN13: 978-0-87289-235-4. Dewey:909.
Audience: **g,l,u,f.**

Banks, Arthur S. (Editor), et al. **D860**
Political Handbook of the World 2005. Thomas C. Muller & William R. Overstreet (Editors). Trade Cloth. CQ Press. Washington, DC. 2005. 1,632p. ISBN:1-56802-952-7, ISBN13: 978-1-56802-952-8. Dewey:320.9.
Audience: **l,u.** *Choice, 2006.*

Finer, Herman **JF51 .F52 1970**
Theory and Practice of Modern Government. Trade Cloth. Greenwood Publishing Group, Inc. Portsmouth, NH. 1971. 978p. ISBN:0-8371-1989-8, ISBN13: 978-0-8371-1989-2. Dewey:320. LCCN:69-013895.
Audience: **l,u.** B

Friedrich, Carl J. **JF51**
Limited Government: A Comparison. Trade Cloth. Prentice-Hall. Upper Saddle, NJ. 1974. 176p. Contemporary Comparative Politics Ser. ISBN:0-13-537167-8, ISBN13: 978-0-13-537167-1. Dewey:320.3. LCCN:74-000802.
Audience: **l,u.** B

Library of Congress **JA1**
☐ Library of Congress Country Studies.
http://lcweb2.loc.gov/frd/cs/cshome.html
Audience: **g,l,u.**

Sartori, Giovanni **JF51.S29 1997**
Comparative Constitutional Engineering: An Inquiry into Structures, Incentives, and Outcomes. Ed. 2. Trade Paper. New York University Press. New York, NY. 1997. 229p. ISBN:0-8147-8063-6, ISBN13: 978-0-8147-8063-3. Dewey:320.445. LCCN:96-026403.
Audience: **u,f.** *Choice, 1995.*

Uphoff, Norman T. & Ilchman, Warren F. (Editors) **JF60.U64**
The Political Economy of Development: Theoretical and Empirical Contributions. Trade Cloth. University of California Press. Berkeley, CA. 1972. xi, 506p. ISBN:0-520-02062-6, ISBN13: 978-0-520-02062-7. Dewey:320.9/172/4. LCCN:77-161999.
Audience: **u,f.** B

Wolpin, Miles D. **JF60.W63**
Militarism and Social Revolution in the Third World. Book, Other. Rowman & Littlefield Publishers, Inc. Lanham, MD. 1982. 272p. ISBN:0-86598-021-7, ISBN13: 978-0-86598-021-1. Dewey:322/.5/091724. LCCN:81-065014.
Audience: **u,f.** B

Young, Crawford **JF60**
The Politics of Cultural Pluralism. Trade Cloth. University of Wisconsin Press. Chicago, IL. 1976. 574p. ISBN:0-299-06740-8, ISBN13: 978-0-299-06740-3. Dewey:320.9/172/4. LCCN:74-027318.
Audience: **u,f.** B

Comparative Government > Constitutional History. General

Krejci, Oskar **JN2228.K659 1995**
History of Elections in Bohemia and Moravia. Trade Cloth. Eastern European Monographs. Bradenton, FL. 1995. 425p. ISBN:0-88033-330-8, ISBN13: 978-0-88033-330-6. Dewey:324.6. LCCN:95-061359.
Audience: **l,u,f.**

Maddex, Robert L. **K3165.M33 2001**
Constitutions of the World. Ed. 2. Trade Cloth. CQ Press. Washington, DC. 2001. 440p. ISBN:1-56802-682-X, ISBN13: 978-1-56802-682-4. Dewey:342/.029. LCCN:2001-280083.
Audience: **u,f.**

Comparative Government > Organs and Functions of Government

Baldwin, Nicholas & Shell, Donald (Editors) **JF541.S39 2001**
Second Chambers. Paper over Boards. Taylor & Francis Group. Abingdon, 2001. 200p. The Library of Legislative Studies ISBN:0-7146-5144-3, ISBN13: 978-0-7146-5144-6. Dewey:328.3/1. LCCN:2001-003645.
Audience: **l,u.** *Choice, 2002.*

Bentham, Jeremy **JF511 .B5 1952**
Bentham's Handbook of Political Fallacies. Harold A. Larrabee (Editor). Library Binding. Hippocrene Books, Inc. New York, NY. 1980. xxxii, 269p. ISBN:0-374-90580-0, ISBN13: 978-0-374-90580-4. Dewey:328.
Audience: **l,u,f.** B

Browne, Eric C. & Dreijmanis, John (Editors) **JN12**
Government Coalitions in Western Democracies. Cloth Text. Longman Publishing Group. White Plains, NY. 1982. 384p. Professional Studies Ser. ISBN:0-582-28218-7, ISBN13: 978-0-582-28218-6. Dewey:321.8/043. LCCN:81-008241.
Audience: **l,u.** B

Butler, David & Ranney, Austin (Editors) **JF491.R393 1994**
Referendums Around the World: The Growing Use of Direct Democracy. Trade Cloth. American Enterprise Institute for Public Policy Research. Washington, DC. 1994. 318p. ISBN:0-8447-3852-2, ISBN13: 978-0-8447-3852-9. Dewey:328.2/3. LCCN:94-013296.
Audience: **u,f.**

Cohen, Eliot A. **JF195.C65 2003**
Supreme Command: Soldiers, Statesmen, and Leadership in Wartime. Trade Paper. Knopf Publishing Group. New York, NY. 2003. 320p. ISBN:1-4000-3404-3, ISBN13: 978-1-4000-3404-8. Dewey:322/.5. LCCN:2003-044398.
Audience: **g,l.** *Choice, 2003.*

Dahl, Robert A. (Editor) **JF518**
Regimes and Oppositions. Trade Cloth. Yale University Press. Cumberland, RI. 1973. 41p. ISBN:0-300-01390-6, ISBN13: 978-0-300-01390-0. Dewey:321.8. LCCN:79-151571.
Audience: **u,f.**

Dahl, Robert Alan **JF518.D32**
Polyarchy: Participation and Opposition. Trade Cloth. Yale University Press. Cumberland, RI. 2004. 257p. ISBN:0-300-01391-4, ISBN13: 978-0-300-01391-7. Dewey:321.8. LCCN:70-140524.
Audience: **u,f.**

de Mesquita, Bruce Bueno, et al. **JF285.L64 2004**
The Logic of Political Survival. Alastair Smith, Randolph M. Siverson & James D. Morrow (Authors). Trade Cloth. MIT Press. Cambridge, MA. 2003. 480p. ISBN:0-262-02546-9, ISBN13: 978-0-262-02546-1. Dewey:320/.01/1. LCCN:2003-045943.
Audience: **u,f.** *Choice, 2004.*

Finer, S. E. **JF195.C5F56 2002**
The Man on Horseback: The Role of the Military in Politics. Jay Stanley (Introduction by). Trade Paper. Transaction Publishers. Somerset, NJ. 2002. 268p. ISBN:0-7658-0922-2, ISBN13: 978-0-7658-0922-3. Dewey:322/.5/0904. LCCN:2002-020276.
Audience: **l,u,f.**

Hayes, Michael T. **JF529**
Lobbyists and Legislators: A Theory of Political Markets. Trade Paper. Rutgers University Press. Piscataway, NJ. 1984. 208p. ISBN:0-8135-1043-0, ISBN13: 978-0-8135-1043-9. Dewey:328/.38.
Audience: **u,f.**

Kopecky, Petr **JN2223.K668 2001**
Parliaments in the Czech and Slovak Republics: Party Competition and Parliamentary Institutionalization. Trade Cloth. Ashgate Publishing, Ltd. Aldershot, 2001. 262p. ISBN:0-7546-1644-4, ISBN13: 978-0-7546-1644-3. Dewey:328.4371. LCCN:2001-086239.
Audience: **u,f.**

Kurian, George Thomas, et al. **JF511.W67 1998**
The World Encyclopedia of Parliaments and Legislatures, Set. Lawrence D. Longley, International Political Science Association Staff & Commonwealth Parliamentary Association Staff (Authors). Trade Cloth. CQ Press. Washington, DC. 1997. 916p. ISBN:0-87187-987-5, ISBN13: 978-0-87187-987-5. Dewey:328/.03. LCCN:97-030226.
Audience: **l,u.** *Choice, 1998.*

Norton, Philip (Editor) **JF511.L37 1990**
Legislatures. Trade Cloth. Oxford University Press, Inc. New York, NY. 1990. 352p. Oxford Readings in Politics and Government Ser. ISBN:0-19-827582-X, ISBN13: 978-0-19-827582-4. Dewey:328.3. LCCN:89-022989.
Audience: **l,u.**

Olson, David M. **JF501.O47 1994**
Democratic Legislative Institutions: A Comparative View. Cloth Text. M. E. Sharpe Inc. Armonk, NY. 1994. 200p. Comparative Politics Ser. ISBN:1-56324-314-8, ISBN13: 978-1-56324-314-1. Dewey:321.8. LCCN:94-018913.
Audience: **l,u.**

Ornstein, Norman J. (Editor) **JF511.R63**
Role of the Legislature in Western Democracies. Trade Cloth. American Enterprise Institute for Public Policy Research. Washington, DC. 1981. 192p. ISBN:0-8447-2214-6, ISBN13: 978-0-8447-2214-6. Dewey:328/.3. LCCN:81-007923.
Audience: **l,u,f.**

Robert, Henry M. & Evans, William J. (Editors) **JF515.R692**
Robert's Rules of Order. Ed. 9. Trade Cloth. HarperCollins Publishers. New York, NY. 2000. 802p. ISBN:0-06-275002-X, ISBN13: 978-0-06-275002-0. Dewey:060.42.
Audience: **g,l,u,f.**

Rose, Richard & Suleiman, Ezra N. (Editors) **JF51.P68**
Presidents and Prime Mininsters. Trade Paper. American Enterprise Institute for Public Policy Research. Washington, DC. 1980. 347p. ISBN:0-8447-3386-5, ISBN13: 978-0-8447-3386-9. Dewey:351.003/13. LCCN:80-017898.
Audience: **g,l,u,f.**

Rossiter, Clinton Lawrence **JF256.R6 2002**
Constitutional Dictatorship: Crisis Government in the Modern Democracies. Trade Paper. Transaction Publishers. Somerset, NJ. 2002. 330p. ISBN:0-7658-0975-3, ISBN13: 978-0-7658-0975-9. Dewey:321.8. LCCN:2002-070330.
Audience: **u,f.**

Silbey, Joel H. (Editor) **JF501.E53 1994**
Encyclopedia of the American Legislative System, Set. Trade Cloth. Thomson Gale. Farmington Hills, MI. 1994. 1738p. ISBN:0-684-19243-8, ISBN13: 978-0-684-19243-7. Dewey:328.73/003. LCCN:93-035874.
Audience: **g,l,u,f.** *Choice, 1994.*

Tsebelis, George **JF51.T745 2002**
Veto Players: How Political Institutions Work. Trade Cloth. Princeton University Press. Princeton, NJ. 2002. 320p. ISBN:0-691-09988-X, ISBN13: 978-0-691-09988-0. Dewey:320.3. LCCN:2002-074909.
Audience: **u,f.**

Turner, Barry (Editor) **JA51.S7 2005**
The Statesman's Yearbook: The Politics, Cultures and Economies of the World. Ed. 142. Saddle Stitched, Cloth over Boards, Dust Jacket. Palgrave Macmillan. New York, NY. 2005.

2112p. ISBN:1-4039-1482-6, ISBN13: 978-1-4039-1482-8. Dewey:909.8305.
Audience: **g,l,u,f.**

Vile, M. J. **JF229.V5 1998**
Constitutionalism and the Separation of Powers. Ed. 2. Trade Cloth. Liberty Fund, Inc. Indianapolis, IN. 1998. 467p. ISBN:0-86597-174-9, ISBN13: 978-0-86597-174-5. Dewey:320.473/04. LCCN:97-029369.
Audience: **u,f.**

Whitmore, Sarah **JN6637.W56 2004**
State Building in Ukraine: The Ukrainian Parliament, 1990-2003. Paper over Boards. Routledge. New York, NY. 2004. 240p. BASEES/RoutledgeCurzon Series on Russian and East European Studies, Vol. 10 ISBN:0-415-33195-1, ISBN13: 978-0-415-33195-1. Dewey:328.477. LCCN:2003-023941.
Audience: **l,u,f.**

Comparative Government > Political Rights and Representation

Amy, Douglas J. **JF1075.U6A49 2002**
[e] Real Choices/new Voices: How Proportional Representation Elections Could Revitalize American Democracy. Ed. 2. E-Book. Columbia University Press. New York, NY. ISBN:0-231-50075-0, ISBN13: 978-0-231-50075-3. Dewey:328.73/07347.
Audience: **g,l,u.**

Benhabib, Seyla **JF799.B44 2004**
The Rights of Others: Aliens, Residents and Citizens. Trade Cloth. Cambridge University Press. New York, NY. 2004. 264p. The John Robert Seeley Lectures, Vol. 5 ISBN:0-521-83134-2, ISBN13: 978-0-521-83134-5. Dewey:323.3/291. LCCN:2004-045665.
Audience: **l,u,f.**

Gallagher, Michael & Mitchell, Paul (Editors) **JF1001**
The Politics of Electoral Systems: A Handbook. Trade Cloth. Oxford University Press, Inc. New York, NY. 2006. 688p. ISBN:0-19-925756-6, ISBN13: 978-0-19-925756-0. Dewey:324.63. LCCN:2005-296344.
Audience: **l,u,f.**

Grofman, Bernard N. & Lijphart, Arend (Editors) **JF1001.E395 1986**
[e] Electoral Laws and Their Political Consequences. E-Book. Algora Publishing. New York, NY. 2003. ISBN:0-87586-267-5, ISBN13: 978-0-87586-267-5. Dewey:324.6.
Audience: **u,f.**

Ingram, David **JF1061.I54 2000**
Group Rights: Reconciling Equality and Difference. Trade Paper. University Press of Kansas. Lawrence, KS. 2000. x, 326p. ISBN:0-7006-1007-3, ISBN13: 978-0-7006-1007-5. Dewey:323.1/73. LCCN:99-053552.
Audience: **u,f.** *Choice, 2000.*

Lijphart, Arend & Grofman, Bernard N. (Editors) **JF1051**
Choosing an Electoral System: Issues and Alternatives. Trade Cloth. Greenwood Publishing Group, Inc. Portsmouth, NH. 1984. 273p. American Political Parties and Elections Ser. ISBN:0-275-91216-7, ISBN13: 978-0-275-91216-1. Dewey:324.6/3. LCCN:84-018283.
Audience: **l,u,f.**

Mueller, Dennis C. **JF1001.M78 2002**
Public Choice III. Ed. 3. Cloth Text. Cambridge University Press. New York, NY. 2003. 788p. ISBN:0-521-81546-0, ISBN13: 978-0-521-81546-8. Dewey:320. LCCN:2002-022287.
Audience: **u,f.** *Choice, 2003.*

Pinkney, Robert **JQ3036.P56 1997**
Democracy and Dictatorship in Ghana and Tanzania. Ed. 1. Trade Cloth. Palgrave Macmillan. New York, NY. 1997. 208p. ISBN:0-312-17518-3, ISBN13: 978-0-312-17518-4. Dewey:321.8/09667. LCCN:97-009157.
Audience: **l,u,f.** *Choice, 1998.*

Pitkin, Hanna F. **JF1051**
The Concept of Representation. Trade Cloth. University of California Press. Berkeley, CA. 1967. 329p. ISBN:0-520-02156-8, ISBN13: 978-0-520-02156-3. Dewey:328.3/34. LCCN:67-025052.
Audience: **u,f.** [BCL3]

Preuss, Ulrich K. **JF1051.P7213 1995**
Constitutional Revolution: The Link Between Constitutionalism and Progress. Deborah L. Schneider (Translator). Trade Cloth. Brill Academic Publishers, Inc. Boston, MA. 1995. 136p. ISBN:0-391-03853-2, ISBN13: 978-0-391-03853-0. Dewey:323/.042. LCCN:94-037939.
Audience: **g,l,u.** *Choice, 1996.*

Rehfeld, Andrew **JF1051.R44 2005**
The Concept of Constituency: Political Representation, Democratic Legitimacy, and Institutional Design. Cloth Text. Cambridge University Press. New York, NY. 2005. 280p. ISBN:0-521-84984-5, ISBN13: 978-0-521-84984-5. Dewey:321.8. LCCN:2004-019645.
Audience: **u,f.**

Strom, Kaare (Editor), et al. **JF1051**
Delegation and Accountability in Parliamentary Democracies. Wolfgang C. Muller & Torbjorn Bergman (Editors). Trade Cloth. Oxford University Press, Inc. New York, NY. 2004. 784p. Comparative Politics Ser. ISBN:0-19-829784-X, ISBN13: 978-0-19-829784-0. Dewey:321.809409045. LCCN:2004-297885.
Audience: **u,f.**

Wattenberg, Martin P. & Shugart, Matthew Soberg **JF1071.M59 2001**
Mixed-Member Electoral Systems: The Best of Both Worlds? Cloth Text. Oxford University Press, Inc. New York, NY. 2001. 680p. Comparative Politics Ser. ISBN:0-19-924079-5, ISBN13: 978-0-19-924079-1. Dewey:324.6/3. LCCN:00-044597.
Audience: **u,f.**

Young, Crawford **JF60**
The Politics of Cultural Pluralism. Trade Paper. University of Wisconsin Press. Chicago, IL. 1979. 574p. ISBN:0-299-06744-0, ISBN13: 978-0-299-06744-1. Dewey:320.9/172/4. LCCN:74-027318.
Audience: **u,f.** [BCL3]

Comparative Government > Political Participation

Birch, Sarah **JN6639.A5B57 2000**
Elections and Democratization in Ukraine. Cloth over Boards. Palgrave Macmillan. New York, NY. 2000. 226p. ISBN:0-312-23457-0, ISBN13: 978-0-312-23457-7. Dewey:324.9477086. LCCN:00-024439.
Audience: **l,u,f.** *Choice, 2001.*

Bogdanor, Vernon & Butler, David (Editors) **JF1001**
Democracy and Elections: Electoral Systems and Their Political Consequences. Trade Cloth. Cambridge University Press. New York, NY. 1983. 280p. ISBN:0-521-25295-4, ISBN13: 978-0-521-25295-9. Dewey:324.6/3. LCCN:82-025300.
Audience: **u,f.** B

Colomer, Josep (Editor) **JF1001.H26 2004**
Handbook of Electoral System Choice. Cloth over Boards. Palgrave Macmillan. New York, NY. 2004. 592p. ISBN:1-4039-0454-5, ISBN13: 978-1-4039-0454-6. Dewey:324.6/3. LCCN:2003-062675.
Audience: **l,u,f.**

Cox, Gary W. **JF1001 .C69 1997**
Making Votes Count: Strategic Coordination in the World's Electoral Systems. Randall L. Calvert & Thrainn Eggertsson (Contribution by). Cloth Text. Cambridge University Press. New York, NY. 1997. 356p. Political Economy of Institutions and Decisions Ser. ISBN:0-521-58516-3, ISBN13: 978-0-521-58516-3. Dewey:324.6/015/193. LCCN:96-036254.
Audience: **l,u,f.** *Choice, 1998.*

Franklin, Mark N. **JF1001.F729 2004**
Voter Turnout and the Dynamics of Electoral Competition in Established Democracies since 1945. Diana Evans, Michael Fotos, Wolfgang Hirczy de Mino, Michael Marsh, Bernard Wessels & Cees Van der Eijk (As told tos). Cloth Text. Cambridge University Press. New York, NY. 2004. 294p. ISBN:0-521-83364-7, ISBN13: 978-0-521-83364-6. Dewey:324.9/045. LCCN:2003-055054.
Audience: **u,f.**

Ginsborg, Paul **HN18.3**
The Politics of Everyday Life: Making Choices, Changing Lives. Cloth over Boards. Yale University Press. Cumberland, RI. 2005. 224p. ISBN:0-300-10748-X, ISBN13: 978-0-300-10748-7. Dewey:306.209/0511. LCCN:2005-925106.
Audience: **g,l,u.** *Choice, 2006.*

Gosnell, Harold F. **JF831 .G6 1977**
Democracy, the Threshold of Freedom. Library Binding. Greenwood Publishing Group, Inc. Portsmouth, NH. 1977. ISBN:0-8371-9509-8, ISBN13: 978-0-8371-9509-4. Dewey:324. LCCN:77-001256.
Audience: **g,l,u.**

Harrop, Martin & Miller, William L. (Editors) **JF1001 .H37**
Elections and Voters: A Comparative Introduction. Trade Paper. Ivan R. Dee Publisher. Blue Ridge Summit, PA. 1987. 304p. ISBN:0-941533-84-0, ISBN13: 978-0-941533-84-3. Dewey:324.9.
Audience: **l,u.**

Heater, Derek **JF801**
Citizenship: The Civic Ideal in World History, Politics and Education. Ed. 3. Cloth over Boards. Manchester University Press. Manchester, 2004. 384p. ISBN:0-7190-6840-1, ISBN13: 978-0-7190-6840-9. Dewey:323.6. LCCN:2004-276607.
Audience: **l,u,f.**

Krejci, Oskar **JN2228.K659 1995**
History of Elections in Bohemia and Moravia. Trade Cloth. Eastern European Monographs. Bradenton, FL. 1995. 425p. ISBN:0-88033-330-8, ISBN13: 978-0-88033-330-6. Dewey:324.6. LCCN:95-061359.
Audience: **l,u,f.**

Lakeman, Enid **HE9788 .S64 1974**
How Democracies Vote. Trade Cloth. Faber & Faber, Ltd. London, 1982. ISBN:0-571-09690-5, ISBN13: 978-0-571-09690-9. Dewey:387.7/44. LCCN:74-193787.
Audience: **u,f.**

Lilleker, Darren G. & Lees-Marshment, Jennifer (Editors) **JF112.C3**
Political Marketing: A Comparative Perspective. Cloth over Boards. Manchester University Press. Manchester, 2005. 256p. ISBN:0-7190-6870-3, ISBN13: 978-0-7190-6870-6. Dewey:324.7. LCCN:2005-282341.
Audience: **l,u,f.** *Choice, 2006.*

Mackie, Thomas T. & Rohds, Richard **JF1001.M17 1991**
The International Almanac of Electoral History. Ed. 3. Trade Cloth. Congressional Quarterly, Inc. Washington, DC. 1991. 511p. ISBN:0-87187-575-6, ISBN13: 978-0-87187-575-4. Dewey:324.9171/3/0212. LCCN:89-013992.
Audience: **l,u,f.**

Norris, Pippa **JF799.N67 2002**
Democratic Phoenix: Reinventing Political Activism. Trade Cloth. Cambridge University Press. New York, NY. 2002. 304p. ISBN:0-521-81177-5, ISBN13: 978-0-521-81177-4. Dewey:323/.042. LCCN:2002-020164.
Audience: **u,f.** *Choice, 2003.*

Norris, Pippa **JF1001.N67 2004**
Electoral Engineering: Voting Rules and Political Behavior. Trade Cloth. Cambridge University Press. New York, NY. 2004. 390p. ISBN:0-521-82977-1, ISBN13: 978-0-521-82977-9. Dewey:324.6/3. LCCN:2003-055179.
Audience: **u,f.** *Choice, 2004.*

Powell, G. Bingham **JF1001.P674 2000**
Elections as Instruments of Democracy: Majoritarian and Proportional Visions. Trade Paper. Yale University Press. Cumberland, RI. 2000. 312p. The Renaissance in Europe Ser., :A Cultural Enquiry ISBN:0-300-08016-6, ISBN13: 978-0-300-08016-2. Dewey:321.8. LCCN:99-059159.
Audience: **u,f.** *Choice, 2000.*

Powell, G. Bingham Jr. **JC423**
Contemporary Democracies: Participation, Stability and Violence. Trade Cloth. Harvard University Press. Cambridge, MA. 1982. 294p. ISBN:0-674-16686-8, ISBN13: 978-0-674-16686-8. Dewey:321.8. LCCN:82-002890.
Audience: **u,f.**

Reeve, Andrew & Ware, Alan **JF1001.R38 1992**
Electoral Systems: A Theoretical and Comparative Introduction.

Children's Board Books. Routledge. New York, NY. 1991. 272p. Theory and Practice in British Politics Ser. ISBN:0-415-01204-X, ISBN13: 978-0-415-01204-1. Dewey:324.6. LCCN:91-010688.

Audience: **l,u.**

Riesenberg, Peter N. **JF801.R54 1992**
Ⓔ Citizenship in the Western Tradition: Plato to Rousseau. E-Book. University of North Carolina Press. Chapel Hill, NC. 1992. ISBN:0-8078-6412-9, ISBN13: 978-0-8078-6412-8. Dewey:323.6/09.

Audience: **g,l,u.** *Choice, 1993.*

Rose, Richard & Munro, Neil **JN6699.A5 R665 2002**
Elections Without Order: Russia's Challenge to Vladimir Putin. Cloth Text. Cambridge University Press. New York, NY. 2002. 272p. ISBN:0-521-81609-2, ISBN13: 978-0-521-81609-0. Dewey:324/.0947. LCCN:2002-022950.

Audience: **l,u,f.** *Choice, 2003.*

Sisk, Timothy D. & Reynolds, Andrew **JQ1879.A5E43 1998**
Elections and Conflict Management in Africa. Book, Other. United States Institute of Peace Press (USIP Press). Washington, DC. 1998. 192p. ISBN:1-878379-79-8, ISBN13: 978-1-878379-79-5. Dewey:324.96. LCCN:98-016504.

Audience: **g,l,u,f.**

Taagepera, Rein & Shugart, Matthew **JF1001.T33 1989**
Seats and Votes: The Effects and Determinants of Electoral Systems. Cloth over Boards. Yale University Press. Cumberland, RI. 1989. 288p. ISBN:0-300-04319-8, ISBN13: 978-0-300-04319-8. Dewey:324.6. LCCN:88-026088.

Audience: **u,f.** *Choice, 1990.*

Trent, Judith S. & Friedenberg, Robert V. **JF1001.T73 2004**
Political Campaign Communication: Philosophy and Practice. Ed. 5. Book, Other. Rowman & Littlefield Publishers, Inc. Lanham, MD. 2003. 424p. Communication, Media, and Politics Ser. ISBN:0-7425-2967-3, ISBN13: 978-0-7425-2967-0. Dewey:324.7. LCCN:2003-018144.

Audience: **g,l,u,f.**

Verba, Sidney, et al. **JF2011.V46 1987**
Participation and Political Equality: A Seven-Nation Comparison. Norman H. Nie & Jae-on Kim (Authors). Trade Paper. University of Chicago Press. Chicago, IL. 1987. 416p. ISBN:0-226-85298-9, ISBN13: 978-0-226-85298-0. Dewey:323/.042. LCCN:87-010781.

Audience: **l,u,f.**

Wyman, Matthew, et al. **JN6699.A5E438 1998**
Elections and Voters in Post-Communist Russia. Stephen White & Sarah Oates (Authors). Trade Cloth. Edward Elgar Publishing, Inc. Northampton, MA. 1998. 304p. Studies of Communism in Transition ISBN:1-85898-743-1, ISBN13: 978-1-85898-743-9. Dewey:324.947/086. LCCN:98-027696.

Audience: **l,u,f.** *Choice, 1999.*

Comparative Government > Political Parties

Ahmad, Abdel Ghaffar Muhammad **DT31**
African Political Parties: Evolution, Institutionalisation and Governance. M. A. Mohamed Salih (Editor). Trade Cloth. Pluto Press. London, 2003. 392p. Ossrea Ser. ISBN:0-7453-2038-4, ISBN13: 978-0-7453-2038-0. Dewey:324.2096. LCCN:2003-270640.

Audience: **g,l,u,f.** *Choice, 2004.*

Aldrich, John H. **JK2261.A46 1995**
Why Parties?: The Origin and Transformation of Political Parties in America. Trade Paper. University of Chicago Press. Chicago, IL. 1995. 355p. American Politics and Political Economy Ser. ISBN:0-226-01272-7, ISBN13: 978-0-226-01272-8. Dewey:324.2/73/09. LCCN:94-036879.

Audience: **l,u.** *Choice, 1995.*

Arter, David **JN6615.A58A78 1996**
Parties and Democracy in the Post-Soviet Republics: The Case of Estonia. Trade Cloth. Ashgate Publishing, Ltd. Aldershot, 1996. 302p. ISBN:1-85521-466-0, ISBN13: 978-1-85521-466-8. Dewey:320.9/4741. LCCN:96-014975.

Audience: **l,u,f.** *Choice, 1997.*

Boix, Carles **JF2011 .B65 1998**
Political Parties, Growth and Equality: Conservative and Social Democratic Economic Strategies in the World Economy. Trade Paper. Cambridge University Press. New York, NY. 1998. 295p. Studies in Comparative Politics ISBN:0-521-58595-3, ISBN13: 978-0-521-58595-8. Dewey:324.2. LCCN:97-027896.

Audience: **u,f.** *Choice, 1999.*

Chhibber, Pradeep K. & Kollman, Ken **JF2011.C53 2004**
The Formation of National Party Systems: Federalism and Party Competition in Canada, Great Britain, India, and the United States. Trade Cloth. Princeton University Press. Princeton, NJ. 2004. 272p. ISBN:0-691-11931-7, ISBN13: 978-0-691-11931-1. Dewey:324.2. LCCN:2003-064676.

Audience: **l,u.** *Choice, 2005.*

Cox, Gary W. **JF1001 .C69 1997**
Making Votes Count: Strategic Coordination in the World's Electoral Systems. Randall L. Calvert & Thrainn Eggertsson (Contribution by). Cloth Text. Cambridge University Press. New York, NY. 1997. 356p. Political Economy of Institutions and Decisions Ser. ISBN:0-521-58516-3, ISBN13: 978-0-521-58516-3. Dewey:324.6/015/193. LCCN:96-036254.

Audience: **l,u,f.** *Choice, 1998.*

Dalton, Russell J. **JF2011.D34 2006**
Citizen Politics: Public Opinion and Political Parties in Advanced Industrial Democracies. Ed. 4. Trade Paper. CQ Press. Washington, DC. 2005. 311p. ISBN:1-56802-999-3, ISBN13: 978-1-56802-999-3. Dewey:323/.042. LCCN:2005-016096.

Audience: **l,u,f.**

Duverger, Maurice **JF2051.D883 1969**
Political Parties: Their Organization and Activity in the Modern State. Ed. 3. Barbara North & Robert North (Translators), D. W. Brogan (Foreword by). Trade Paper. Routledge. New York, NY. 1964. xxxvii, 439p. ISBN:0-416-68320-7, ISBN13: 978-0-416-68320-2. Dewey:329/.02. LCCN:70-027893.
Audience: **u,f.**

Gill, Graeme J. & Pitty, Roderic **JN6598.K7.G5237 1997**
Power in the Party: The Organization of Power and Central-Republican Relations in the CPSU. Trade Cloth. Bow Historical Books. New Providence, NJ. 1997. 240p. ISBN:0-333-66656-9, ISBN13: 978-0-333-66656-2. Dewey:947/.085. LCCN:96-034345.
Audience: **l,u,f.**

Goldstone, Jack A. (Editor) **JF2011.S73 2003**
States, Parties, and Social Movements. Sidney Tarrow (Contribution by). Trade Cloth. Cambridge University Press. New York, NY. 2003. 312p. Cambridge Studies in Contentious Politics ISBN:0-521-81679-3, ISBN13: 978-0-521-81679-3. Dewey:303.48/4. LCCN:2002-067649.
Audience: **l,u,f.** *Choice, 2004.*

Hug, Simon **JF2051.H83 2001**
Altering Party Systems: Strategic Behavior and the Emergence of New Political Parties in Western Democracies. Trade Cloth. University of Michigan Press. Chicago, IL. 2001. 216p. Interests, Identities, and Institutions in Comparative Politics Ser. ISBN:0-472-11184-1, ISBN13: 978-0-472-11184-8. Dewey:324.2/09171/3. LCCN:2001-018111.
Audience: **u,f.** *Choice, 2002.*

James, Scott C. **JK2316 .J36 2000**
Presidents, Parties, and the State: A Party System Perspective on Democratic Regulatory Choice, 1884-1936. Trade Cloth. Cambridge University Press. New York, NY. 2000. 318p. ISBN:0-521-66277-X, ISBN13: 978-0-521-66277-2. Dewey:324.2736/09/034. LCCN:99-037782.
Audience: **u,f.** *Choice, 2001.*

Karvonen, Lauri (Editor), et al. **JF2051.P296 2000**
Party Systems and Voter Alignments Revisited. Ed. 2. Stein Kuhnle & Seymour Martin Lipset (Editors). Paper over Boards. Routledge. New York, NY. 2000. 336p. Advances in International Relations and Politics Ser. ISBN:0-415-23720-3, ISBN13: 978-0-415-23720-8. Dewey:324.9. LCCN:00-029115.
Audience: **l,u.** *Choice, 2001.*

Katz, Richard S. **JF2051.K33**
A Theory of Parties and Electoral Systems. Trade Paper. Books on Demand. Ann Arbor, MI. 1980. 167p. ISBN:0-608-03705-2, ISBN13: 978-0-608-03705-9. Dewey:324. LCCN:80-008019.
Audience: **l,u.**

Klingemann, Hans-Dieter, et al. **JF2011.K55 1994**
Parties, Policies, and Democracy. Richard I. Hofferbert & Ian Budge (Authors), Hans Keman (Contribution by). Trade Paper. Westview Press. Boulder, CO. 1994. 318p. Theoretical Lenses on Public Policy Ser. ISBN:0-8133-2069-0, ISBN13: 978-0-8133-2069-4. Dewey:324.2. LCCN:94-021322.
Audience: **l,u,f.**

Kousser, J. Morgan **JK1924.K68 1999**
Colorblind Injustice: Minority Voting Rights and the Undoing of the Second Reconstruction. Trade Paper. University of North Carolina Press. Chapel Hill, NC. 1999. 608p. ISBN:0-8078-4738-0, ISBN13: 978-0-8078-4738-1. Dewey:328.750734. LCCN:98-016693.
Audience: **l,u,f.**

Kymlicka, Will **JF1061.K96 1996**
Multicultural Citizenship: A Liberal Theory of Minority Rights. E-Book. NetLibrary, Inc. Boulder, CO. 1996. ISBN:0-585-42845-X, ISBN13: 978-0-585-42845-1. Dewey:323.1/1.
Audience: **l,u,f.** *Choice, 1996.*

Morone, James A. **JK1764.M67 1998**
The Democratic Wish: Popular Participation and the Limits of American Government. Ed. 2. Trade Paper. Yale University Press. Cumberland, RI. 1998. 416p. ISBN:0-300-07465-4, ISBN13: 978-0-300-07465-9. Dewey:323/.042/0973. LCCN:97-080178.
Audience: **l,u,f.**

Parker, Frank R. **E185.93.M6P37 1990**
Black Votes Count: Political Empowerment in Mississippi after 1965. Trade Paper. University of North Carolina Press. Chapel Hill, NC. 1990. 272p. ISBN:0-8078-4274-5, ISBN13: 978-0-8078-4274-4. Dewey:323.1/1960730762. LCCN:89-039074.
Audience: **l,u,f.** *Choice, 1991.*

Pelinka, Anton & Plasser, Fritz (Editors) **JN2030.A97 1989**
The Austrian Party System. Paper Text. Westview Press. Boulder, CO. 1989. 458p. ISBN:0-8133-7755-2, ISBN13: 978-0-8133-7755-1. Dewey:324.2436. LCCN:89-032835.
Audience: **l,u,f.** *Choice, 1990.*

Sartori, Giovanni **JF2051**
Parties and Party Systems: A Framework for Analysis, Vol. 2. Paper Text. Cambridge University Press. New York, NY. 1976. 383p. ISBN:0-521-29106-2, ISBN13: 978-0-521-29106-4. Dewey:324.2. LCCN:76-004756.
Audience: **l,u,f.**

Stokes, Gale **JN9659.A45S86 1990**
Politics As Development: The Emergence of Political Parties in Nineteenth-Century Serbia. Cloth Text. Duke University Press. Durham, NC. 1990. 416p. ISBN:0-8223-1016-3, ISBN13: 978-0-8223-1016-7. Dewey:324.2497/1/009. LCCN:89-039903.
Audience: **u,f.** *Choice, 1991.*

Szczerbiak, Aleksander Andrzej **JN6769.A45S78 2001**
Poles Together?: The Emergence and Development of Political Parties in Post-Communist Poland. Trade Cloth. Central European University Press. Herndon, VA. 2002. 280p. ISBN:963-9241-23-7, ISBN13: 978-963-9241-23-7. Dewey:324.2438. LCCN:2001-056169.
Audience: **l,u,f.** *Choice, 2003.*

Tworzecki, Hubert **JN6769.A45T94 1996**
Parties and Politics in Post 1989 Poland. Trade Paper. Westview Press. Boulder, CO. 1996. 219p. ISBN:0-8133-8977-1, ISBN13: 978-0-8133-8977-6. Dewey:320.9/438. LCCN:96-016625.
Audience: **l,u,f.** *Choice, 1996.*

Verba, Sidney & Nie, Norman H. **JK1764.V467 1987**
Participation in America: Political Democracy and Social Equality. Trade Paper. University of Chicago Press. Chicago, IL. 2004. 452p. ISBN:0-226-85296-2, ISBN13: 978-0-226-85296-6. Dewey:323/.042/0973. LCCN:87-010825.
Audience: **g,l,u,f.** B

Verba, Sidney, et al. **JF2011.V46 1987**
Participation and Political Equality: A Seven-Nation Comparison. Norman H. Nie & Jae-on Kim (Authors). Trade Paper. University of Chicago Press. Chicago, IL. 1987. 416p. ISBN:0-226-85298-9, ISBN13: 978-0-226-85298-0. Dewey:323/.042. LCCN:87-010781.
Audience: **l,u,f.**

Comparative Government > Public Administration

Box, Richard C. **JF1351.B648 2004**
Critical Social Theory in Public Administration. Trade Cloth. M. E. Sharpe Inc. Armonk, NY. 2005. 176p. ISBN:0-7656-1554-1, ISBN13: 978-0-7656-1554-1. Dewey:351/.01/1. LCCN:2004-005154.
Audience: **u,f.** *Choice, 2005.*

Boyle, Richard & Lemaire, Donald (Editors) **JF1351.B83 1998**
Building Effective Evaluation Capacity: Lessons from Practice. Trade Cloth. Transaction Publishers. Somerset, NJ. 1999. 202p. Comparative Policy Analysis Ser. ISBN:1-56000-396-0, ISBN13: 978-1-56000-396-0. Dewey:352.3/0973. LCCN:98-040492.
Audience: **u,f.** *Choice, 1999.*

Denhardt, Janet Vinzant & Denhardt, Robert B. **JF1351.D4495 2002**
The New Public Service: Serving, Not Steering. Trade Cloth. M. E. Sharpe Inc. Armonk, NY. 2003. 216p. ISBN:0-7656-0845-6, ISBN13: 978-0-7656-0845-1. Dewey:351. LCCN:2002-066974.
Audience: **g,l,u,f.** *Choice, 2003.*

Denhardt, Robert B. **JF1351**
The Pursuit of Significance: Strategies for Managerial Success in Public Organizations. Paper Text. Waveland Press, Inc. Prospect Heights, IL. 2000. 300p. ISBN:1-57766-114-1, ISBN13: 978-1-57766-114-6. Dewey:350.
Audience: **g,u,f.**

Downs, Anthony **JF1351.D65**
An Economic Theory of Democracy. Trade Paper. Books on Demand. Ann Arbor, MI. 322p. ISBN:0-598-84640-9, ISBN13: 978-0-598-84640-2. Dewey:351. LCCN:57-010571.
Audience: **u,f.** B

Downs, Anthony **JF1351**
Inside Bureaucracy. Paper Text. Waveland Press, Inc. Prospect Heights, IL. 1994. 292p. ISBN:0-88133-778-1, ISBN13: 978-0-88133-778-5. Dewey:301.18.
Audience: **g,l,u,f.** B

Frederickson, H. George & Smith, Kevin B. **JF1351.F734 2003**
Public Administration Theory Primer. Trade Paper. Westview Press. Boulder, CO. 2003. 288p. ISBN:0-8133-9804-5, ISBN13: 978-0-8133-9804-4. Dewey:351/.01. LCCN:2003-001691.
Audience: **l,u.** *Choice, 2003.*

Fry, Brian R. **JF1341.F78 1989**
Mastering Public Administration: From Max Weber to Dwight Waldo. Paper Text. CQ Press. Washington, DC. 1989. 272p. Public Administration and Public Policy Ser. ISBN:0-934540-56-X, ISBN13: 978-0-934540-56-8. Dewey:352. LCCN:89-000624.
Audience: **l,u.** *Choice, 1990.*

Heidenheimer, Arnold J. & Johnston, Michael (Editors) **JF1525.C66P65 2002**
Political Corruption. Ed. 3. Trade Paper. Transaction Publishers. Somerset, NJ. 2001. 850p. ISBN:0-7658-0761-0, ISBN13: 978-0-7658-0761-8. Dewey:364.1/323. LCCN:2001-041596.
Audience: **l,u,f.**

Herman, Michael **JF1525.I6 H47 1996**
Intelligence Power in Peace and War. Trade Cloth. Cambridge University Press. New York, NY. 1996. 436p. ISBN:0-521-56231-7, ISBN13: 978-0-521-56231-7. Dewey:327.1/2. LCCN:95-048112.
Audience: **u,f.** *Choice, 1997.*

Holden, Matthew Jr. **JF1351.H65 1996**
Continuity and Disruption: Essays in Public Administration. Cloth Text. University of Pittsburgh Press. Pittsburgh, PA. 1996. 291p. Series in Policy and Institutional Studies ISBN:0-8229-3885-5, ISBN13: 978-0-8229-3885-9. Dewey:350. LCCN:95-016081.
Audience: **l,u,f.** *Choice, 1997.*

Ingraham, Patricia W. & Lynn, Laurence E. (Editors) **JF1338.A2A78 2004**
The Art of Governance: Analyzing Management and Administration. Book, Other. Georgetown University Press. Washington, DC. 2004. 240p. ISBN:1-58901-034-5, ISBN13: 978-1-58901-034-5. Dewey:351. LCCN:2004-005617.
Audience: **u,f.** *Choice, 2005.*

Lynn, Laurence E. Jr. **JF1338.A3U56 1996**
Public Management As Art, Science, and Profession. Paper Text. CQ Press. Washington, DC. 1996. 208p. Public Administration and Public Policy Ser. ISBN:1-56643-034-8, ISBN13: 978-1-56643-034-0. Dewey:350. LCCN:95-041793.
Audience: **g,l,u.** *Choice, 1996.*

Peters, B. Guy & Pierre, Jon (Editors) **JF1351**
Handbook of Public Administration. Trade Cloth. SAGE Publications, Inc. Thousand Oaks, CA. 2003. 640p. ISBN:0-7619-7224-2, ISBN13: 978-0-7619-7224-2. Dewey:351. LCCN:2002-109398.
Audience: **g,l,u,f.** *Choice, 2004.*

Pierre, Jon & Peters, B. Guy **JF1351.P54 2005**
Governing Complex Societies: Trajectories and Scenarios. Saddle Stitched, Cloth over Boards, Dust Jacket. Palgrave Macmillan. New York, NY. 2005. 168p. ISBN:1-4039-4660-4, ISBN13: 978-1-4039-4660-7. Dewey:351/.01. LCCN:2004-060144.
Audience: **u,f.** *Choice, 2006.*

Rice, Mitchell F. **JF1658.D58 2004**
Diversity and Public Administration: Theory, Issues, and Perspectives. Trade Cloth. M. E. Sharpe Inc. Armonk, NY. 2005. 264p. ISBN:0-7656-1431-6, ISBN13: 978-0-7656-1431-5. Dewey:352.6/08. LCCN:2004-002827.
Audience: **l,u,f.** *Choice, 2005.*

Silberman, Bernard S. **JF1341.S55 1993**
Cages of Reason: The Rise of the Rational State in France, Japan, the United States, and Great Britain. Trade Paper. University of Chicago Press. Chicago, IL. 1993. 495p. ISBN:0-226-75737-4, ISBN13: 978-0-226-75737-7. Dewey:351.0009. LCCN:92-031653.
Audience: **l,u,f.** *Choice, 1994.*

Suleiman, Ezra **JF1525.O73S88 2005**
Dismantling Democratic States. Trade Paper. Princeton University Press. Princeton, NJ. 2005. 344p. ISBN:0-691-12251-2, ISBN13: 978-0-691-12251-9. Dewey:321.8.
Audience: **l,u,f.**

Comparative Government > Local Government > Canada

Ewing, Kenneth D. **KE4646.E96 1992**
Money, Politics, and Law: A Study of Electoral Campaign Finance Reform in Canada. Trade Cloth. Oxford University Press, Inc. New York, NY. 1992. 272p. ISBN:0-19-825738-4, ISBN13: 978-0-19-825738-7. Dewey:347.10278. LCCN:91-047935.
Audience: **u,f.** *Choice, 1993.*

Handler, Richard **F1053.2.H36 1988**
Nationalism and the Politics of Culture in Quebec. Cloth Text. University of Wisconsin Press. Chicago, IL. 1988. 240p. New Directions in Anthropological Writing Ser. ISBN:0-299-11510-0, ISBN13: 978-0-299-11510-4. Dewey:306.4/09714. LCCN:87-040362.
Audience: **u,f.** *Choice, 1988.*

Hero, Alfred O. Jr. & Balthazar, Louis **E183.8.C2H37 1988**
Contemporary Quebec and the United States, 1960-1985. Trade Cloth. University Press of America, Inc. Lanham, MD. 1988. 548p. ISBN:0-8191-6876-9, ISBN13: 978-0-8191-6876-4. Dewey:303.4/8273/0714. LCCN:87-035996.
Audience: **l,u,f.** *Choice, 1989.*

Lemco, Jonathan **JL246.S8L45 1994**
Turmoil in the Peacable Kingdom: The Quebec Sovereignty Movement and Its Implications for Canada and the U. S. Cloth Text. University of Toronto Press. Toronto, ON. 1994. 266p. ISBN:0-8020-0532-2, ISBN13: 978-0-8020-0532-8. Dewey:971.4/04. LCCN:95-166253.
Audience: **u,f.** *Choice, 1995.*

McAllister, Mary Louise **JS1708**
Governing Ourselves?: The Politics of Canadian Communities. Trade Cloth. University of British Columbia Press. Vancouver, BC. 2004. 352p. ISBN:0-7748-1062-9, ISBN13: 978-0-7748-1062-3. Dewey:320.8/5/0971. LCCN:2004-463309.
Audience: **g,l,u.** *Choice, 2005.*

Stevenson, Garth **F1055.E53S84 1999**
Community Besieged: The Anglophone Minority and the Politics of Quebec. Trade Cloth. McGill-Queen's University Press. Montreal, PQ. 1999. x, 363p. ISBN:0-7735-1839-8, ISBN13: 978-0-7735-1839-1. Dewey:971.4/004112. LCCN:00-699740.
Audience: **u,f.** *Choice, 2000.*

Taucar, Christopher Edward **JL27.T395 2000**
Canadian Federalism and Quebec Sovereignty. Trade Cloth. Peter Lang Publishing, Inc. New York, NY. 2000. 256p. American University Studies, Vol. 47:Political Science ISBN:0-8204-4952-0, ISBN13: 978-0-8204-4952-4. Dewey:320.471/049. LCCN:00-020960.
Audience: **u,f.** *Choice, 2001.*

Taylor, Alan **E99.I7T299 2006**
The Divided Ground: Indians, Settlers, and the Northern Borderland of the American Revolution. Trade Cloth. Alfred A. Knopf Inc. New York, NY. 2006. 560p. ISBN:0-679-45471-3, ISBN13: 978-0-679-45471-7. Dewey:974.7004/9755. LCCN:2005-043582.
Audience: **g,l,u,f.** *Choice, 2006.*

Verney, Jack **UA703.Z9 C378 1991**
The Good Regiment: The Carignan-Salihres Regiment in Canada, 1665-1668. Trade Cloth. McGill-Queen's University Press. Montreal, PQ. 1991. 240p. ISBN:0-7735-0813-9, ISBN13: 978-0-7735-0813-2. Dewey:356.1660944. LCCN:92-222655.
Audience: **u,f.** *Choice, 1991.*

Vigod, Bernard L. **F1053.T37 V54 1986**
Quebec Before Duplessis: The Political Career of Louis-Alexandre Taschereau. Trade Cloth. McGill-Queen's University Press. Montreal, PQ. 1986. 328p. ISBN:0-7735-0588-1, ISBN13: 978-0-7735-0588-9. Dewey:971.4/03/0924. LCCN:86-173610.
Audience: **u,f.** *Choice, 1986.*

Young, Robert (Editor) **JL27.S77 1999**
Stretching the Federation: The Art of the State in Canada. Trade Cloth. Queen's University, Institute of Intergovernmental Relations. Kingston, ON. 1999. xiv, 255p. ISBN:0-88911-777-2, ISBN13: 978-0-88911-777-8. Dewey:320.471/049. LCCN:00-363852.
Audience: **u,f.** *Choice, 2000.*

Comparative Government > Local Government > Europe

HN643.5
Romania. Trade Cloth. Council of Europe. Strasbourg, 1999. Structure and Operation of Local and Regional Democracy Ser. ISBN:92-871-3949-0, ISBN13: 978-92-871-3949-8. Dewey:306/.09498.
Audience: **u,f.** *Choice, 1985.*

Beevor, Antony & Cooper, Artemis **DC737.B38 1994**
Paris after the Liberation, 1944-1949. Trade Cloth. Doubleday Canada, Ltd. Toronto, ON. 1994. 496p. ISBN:0-385-47195-5, ISBN13: 978-0-385-47195-4. Dewey:944/.361082. LCCN:94-008799.
Audience: **g,l,u,f.**

Bennett, Robert J. (Editor) **JS3000.2**
Local Government in the New Europe. Cloth Text. John Wiley & Sons, Inc. Hoboken, NJ. 309p. ISBN:0-470-22033-3, ISBN13: 978-0-470-22033-7. Dewey:352.04. LCCN:93-014612.
Audience: **g,u,f.** *Choice, 1994.*

Fletcher, Anthony **DA375.F57 1986**
Reform in the Provinces: The Government of Stuart England. Trade Cloth. Yale University Press. Cumberland, RI. 1986. 386p. ISBN:0-300-03673-6, ISBN13: 978-0-300-03673-2. Dewey:941.06. LCCN:86-001684.
Audience: **u,f.** *Choice, 1987.*

Ladd, Brian **HT169.G32B4127 1997**
The Ghosts of Berlin: Confronting German History in the Urban Landscape. Trade Cloth. University of Chicago Press. Chicago, IL. 1997. 282p. ISBN:0-226-46761-9, ISBN13: 978-0-226-46761-0. Dewey:307.121. LCCN:96-028562.
Audience: **g,l,u,f.**

Leach, Richard H., et al. **JS3095 1990**
Local Government and Thatcherism. H. Butcher, I. G. Law & Maurice Mullard (Authors). Cloth Text. Routledge. New York, NY. 1990. 240p. ISBN:0-415-03211-3, ISBN13: 978-0-415-03211-7. Dewey:352.041. LCCN:89-010907.
Audience: **u,f.** *Choice, 1990.*

Linehan, Thomas P. **DA685.E1L56 1996**
East London for Mosley: The Membership and Branches of the British Union of Fascists in East London and South-West Essex, 1933-40. Cloth Text. Taylor & Francis Group. Abingdon, 1996. 336p. ISBN:0-7146-4568-0, ISBN13: 978-0-7146-4568-1. Dewey:320.94267. LCCN:96-018660.
Audience: **u,f.** *Choice, 1997.*

Miller, William L. (Editor), et al. **JN96.A56C655 2001**
A Culture of Corruption?: Coping with Government in Post-Communist Europe. Ase B. Grodeland & Tatyana Y. Koshechkina (Editors). Trade Cloth. Central European University Press. Herndon, VA. 2000. 384p. ISBN:963-9116-98-X, ISBN13: 978-963-9116-98-6. Dewey:616.85/8. LCCN:00-065592.
Audience: **u,f.** *Choice, 2002.*

Newton, Michael T. **JN8210 .N48 1997**
Institutions of Modern Spain: A Political and Economic Guide. Ed. 2. Peter J. Donaghy (As told to). Cloth Text. Cambridge University Press. New York, NY. 1997. 407p. ISBN:0-521-57348-3, ISBN13: 978-0-521-57348-1. Dewey:306.2/0946. LCCN:96-002353.
Audience: **l,u.** *Choice, 1997.*

O'Neill, Kathleen **JL1859.5.D42O54 2005**
Decentralizing the State: Elections, Parties, and Local Power in the Andes. Cloth Text. Cambridge University Press. New York, NY. 2005. 286p. ISBN:0-521-84694-3, ISBN13: 978-0-521-84694-3. Dewey:320.8/098. LCCN:2004-024335.
Audience: **u,f.** *Choice, 2005.*

Page, Edward C. & Goldsmith, Michael J. (Editors) **JS3000.3.A3.C36 1987**
Central and Local Government Relations: A Comparative Analysis of West European Unitary States. Cloth Text. SAGE Publications, Inc. Thousand Oaks, CA. 1987. 192p. Modern Politics Ser., Vol. 13 ISBN:0-8039-8071-X, ISBN13: 978-0-8039-8071-6. Dewey:352.04. LCCN:87-061112.
Audience: **u,f.** *Choice, 1988.*

Reddaway, Peter **JN6693.5.S8D86 2003**
Dynamics of Russian Politics: Putin's Federal-Regional Reforms. Robert W. Orttung (Editor). Book, Other. Rowman & Littlefield Publishers, Inc. Lanham, MD. 2003. 304p. ISBN:0-7425-2644-5, ISBN13: 978-0-7425-2644-0. Dewey:320.447/049. LCCN:2003-011934.
Audience: **u,f.** *Choice, 2006, 2005.*

Temple, Michael **JS3137.T46 2000**
How Britain Works: From Ideology to Output Politics. Trade Cloth. St. Martin's Press. Gordonville, VA. 2000. xi, 228p. ISBN:0-333-73885-3, ISBN13: 978-0-333-73885-6. Dewey:320.8/0941. LCCN:00-036913.
Audience: **u,f.** *Choice, 2001.*

Comparative Government > Colonies and Colonization

Newbury, Catharine **JQ3567.A2N48 1988**
The Cohesion of Oppression: Clientship and Ethnicity in Rwanda, 1860-1960. Trade Cloth. Columbia University Press. New York, NY. 1989. 322p. ISBN:0-231-06256-7, ISBN13: 978-0-231-06256-5. Dewey:306/.2/0967571. LCCN:88-007349.
Audience: **l,u,f.** *Choice, 1989.*

Reid, Richard J. **JQ2951.A99B847 2002**
Political Power in Pre-Colonial Buganda: Economy, Society and Welfare in the Nineteenth Century. Trade Paper. Ohio University Press. Athens, OH. 2003. 288p. Eastern African Studies ISBN:0-8214-1478-X, ISBN13: 978-0-8214-1478-1. Dewey:967.61. LCCN:2002-074343.
Audience: **u,f.** *Choice, 2003.*

Werbner, Richard P. & Ranger, Terence (Editors) **JQ1879.A15P69 1996**
Postcolonial Identities in Africa. Trade Paper. Zed Books, Ltd. London, 1996. 304p. Postcolonial Encounters Ser. ISBN:1-85649-416-0, ISBN13: 978-1-85649-416-8. Dewey:960.3/29. LCCN:96-008379.
Audience: **g,l,u,f.**

Comparative Government > Colonies and Colonization > History

Ahmida, Ali Abdullatif **DT233 .A38 1994**
The Making of Modern Libya: State Formation, Colonization, and Resistance, 1830-1932. Paper Text. State University of New York Press. Albany, NY. 1994. 222p. SUNY Series in the Social and Economic History of the Middle East ISBN:0-7914-1762-X, ISBN13: 978-0-7914-1762-1. Dewey:961.2/02. LCCN:93-018526.
Audience: **u,f.** *Choice, 1994.*

Birmingham, David **JV125.B57 2000**
Trade and Empire in the Atlantic, 1400-1600. Trade Paper. Routledge. New York, NY. 2000. 112p. Introduction to History Ser. ISBN:0-415-23206-6, ISBN13: 978-0-415-23206-7. Dewey:325.32091821. LCCN:99-058424.
Audience: **l,u,f.** *Choice, 2001.*

Gifford, Prosser & Louis, William Roger **DT30.5.D42 1988**
Decolonization and African Independence: The Transfers of Power 1960-1980. Trade Cloth. Yale University Press. Cumberland, RI. 1988. 736p. ISBN:0-300-04070-9, ISBN13: 978-0-300-04070-8. Dewey:960/.32. LCCN:87-014756.
Audience: **g,l,u,f.** *Choice, 1989.*

Gifford, Prosser & Louis, William Roger **DT30**
The Transfer in Power of Africa: Decolonization, 1940-1960. Trade Paper. Yale University Press. Cumberland, RI. 1988. 656p. ISBN:0-300-04348-1, ISBN13: 978-0-300-04348-8. Dewey:960/.324. LCCN:81-001931.
Audience: **g,l,u,f.**

Hargreaves, John D. **DT29.H37 1996**
Decolonization in Africa. Ed. 2. Trade Paper. Pearson Education. Boston, MA. 2002. 320p. The Postwar World Ser. ISBN:0-582-24917-1, ISBN13: 978-0-582-24917-2. Dewey:960.3/2. LCCN:95-041858.
Audience: **g,l,u,f.** *Choice, 1989.*

Muldoon, James **F1411.S6973M85 1994**
The Americas in the Spanish World Order: The Justification for Conquest in the Seventeenth Century. Trade Cloth. University of Pennsylvania Press. Philadelphia, PA. 1994. 256p. ISBN:0-8122-3245-3, ISBN13: 978-0-8122-3245-5. Dewey:325/.346098/09032. LCCN:93-050529.
Audience: **u,f.** *Choice, 1995.*

Olson, James S. (Editor) **D217**
Historical Dictionary of European Imperialism. Ross Marlay, William Ratliff, Joseph M. Rowe & Robert M. Shadle (Contribution by). Cloth Text. Greenwood Publishing Group, Inc. Portsmouth, NH. 1991. 804p. ISBN:0-313-26257-8, ISBN13: 978-0-313-26257-9. Dewey:903. LCCN:90-038413.
Audience: **l,u,f.** *Choice, 1992.*

Osterhammel, Jürgen **JV51.O8713 2004**
Colonialism: A Theoretical Overview. Ed. 2. Shelley Frisch (Translator), Robert Tignor (Introduction by). Trade Cloth. Markus Wiener Publishers, Inc. Princeton, NJ. 2005. 200p. ISBN:1-55876-339-2, ISBN13: 978-1-55876-339-5. Dewey:325/.3. LCCN:2004-059632.
Audience: **u,f.**

Pakenham, Thomas **DT28**
Scramble for Africa... Trade Paper. HarperCollins Publishers. New York, NY. 1992. 800p. ISBN:0-380-71999-1, ISBN13: 978-0-380-71999-0. Dewey:325.3409609041. LCCN:91-052681.
Audience: **g,l.**

Rodríguez O, Jaime E. **F1412 .R68213 1998**
The Independence of Spanish America. Alan Knight (Contribution by). Cloth Text. Cambridge University Press. New York, NY. 1998. 292p. Latin American Studies, No. 84 ISBN:0-521-62298-0, ISBN13: 978-0-521-62298-1. Dewey:980/.02. LCCN:97-036310.
Audience: **l,u,f.** *Choice, 1998.*

Springhall, John **DS33.1**
Decolonization since 1945: Collapse of European Overseas Empires. Trade Paper. Palgrave Macmillan. New York, NY. 2001. 268p. ISBN:0-333-74600-7, ISBN13: 978-0-333-74600-4. Dewey:325.3409045.
Audience: **l,u.** *Choice, 2001.*

Wesseling, H. L. **D539**
Imperialism and Colonialism: Essays on the History of European Expansion. Book, Other. Greenwood Publishing Group, Inc. Portsmouth, NH. 1997. 224p. Contributions in Comparative Colonial Studies, Vol. 32 ISBN:0-313-30431-9, ISBN13: 978-0-313-30431-6. Dewey:325/.32/091821. LCCN:96-053847.
Audience: **u,f.**

Wesseling, H. L. **DT28**
Divide and Rule: The Partition of Africa, 1880-1914. Arnold J. Pomerans (Translator). Paper Text. Greenwood Publishing Group, Inc. Portsmouth, NH. 1996. 464p. ISBN:0-275-95138-3, ISBN13: 978-0-275-95138-2. Dewey:960.3/12. LCCN:95-038253.
Audience: **g,l,u,f.** *Choice, 1996.*

Comparative Government > Colonies and Colonization > History > Great Britain

Boyce, D. George **DA16.B64 1999**
Decolonisation and the British Empire, 1775-1997. Cloth over Boards. Palgrave Macmillan. New York, NY. 1999. 329p. ISBN:0-312-22325-0, ISBN13: 978-0-312-22325-0. Dewey:941. LCCN:99-012192.
Audience: **u,f.** *Choice, 2000.*

Cain, Peter & Hopkins, Tony **JV1011.C17 2001**
British Imperialism: 1688-2000. Ed. 2. Trade Paper. Longman Publishing. Boston, MA. 2001. 768p. ISBN:0-582-47286-5, ISBN13: 978-0-582-47286-0. Dewey:325/.341. LCCN:2001-029981.
Audience: **u,f.**

Hintjens, Helen M. **JV151.H55 1995**
Alternatives to Independence: Explorations in Post-Colonial Relations. Trade Cloth. Ashgate Publishing, Ltd. Aldershot, 1995. 240p. ISBN:1-85521-069-X, ISBN13: 978-1-85521-069-1. Dewey:325/.3144/09045. LCCN:95-019402.
Audience: **u,f.**

Mehta, Uday Singh **JC574.2.G7M44 1999**
Liberalism and Empire: A Study in Nineteenth-Century British Liberal Thought. Trade Paper. University of Chicago Press. Chicago, IL. 1999. 245p. ISBN:0-226-51882-5, ISBN13: 978-0-226-51882-4. Dewey:320.5/13/0941. LCCN:98-040812.
Audience: **l,u,f.**

Scott, H. M. **DA510.S26 1990**
British Foreign Policy in the Age of the American Revolution. Trade Cloth. Oxford University Press, Inc. New York, NY. 1991. 392p. ISBN:0-19-820195-8, ISBN13: 978-0-19-820195-3. Dewey:327.41/009/033. LCCN:90-006886.
Audience: **u,f.** *Choice, 1991.*

Comparative Government > Colonies and Colonization > History > France

Aldrich, Richard J. **DU50.A39 1993**
France and the South Pacific since, 1940. Trade Cloth. University of Hawaii Press. Honolulu, HI. 1993. 440p. ISBN:0-8248-1558-0, ISBN13: 978-0-8248-1558-5. Dewey:996.2. LCCN:93-006783.
Audience: **g,l,u,f.** *Choice, 1994.*

Aldrich, Robert **DU50.A4 1990**
The French Presence in the South Pacific, 1842-1940. Cloth Text. University of Hawaii Press. Honolulu, HI. 1989. 400p. ISBN:0-8248-1268-9, ISBN13: 978-0-8248-1268-3. Dewey:327.4401823. LCCN:89-004904.
Audience: **g,l,u,f.**

Betts, Raymond F. **JV1835.B48 2005**
Assimilation and Association in French Colonial Theory, 1890-1914. Trade Paper. University of Nebraska Press. Lincoln, NE. 2005. 238p. ISBN:0-8032-6247-7, ISBN13: 978-0-8032-6247-8. Dewey:325/.344. LCCN:2005-012402.
Audience: **u,f.**

Chafer, Tony **DT352.5.C48 2002**
The End of Empire in French West Africa: France's Successful Decolonization? Cloth over Boards. Berg Publishers. Oxford, 2002. 256p. ISBN:1-85973-552-5, ISBN13: 978-1-85973-552-7. Dewey:960/.917541. LCCN:2002-001531.
Audience: **u,f.** *Choice, 2003.*

Clayton, Anthony **JV1818**
The Wars of French Decolonization: Modern Wars in Perspective. Ed. 1. Trade Cloth. Longman Publishing Group. White Plains, NY. 1994. 256p. Modern Wars in Perspective Ser. ISBN:0-582-09802-5, ISBN13: 978-0-582-09802-2. Dewey:325/.344/0904. LCCN:93-029506.
Audience: **g,l,u.**

Hargreaves, John D. **DT29.H37 1996**
Decolonization in Africa. Ed. 2. Trade Paper. Pearson Education. Boston, MA. 2002. 320p. The Postwar World Ser. ISBN:0-582-24917-1, ISBN13: 978-0-582-24917-2. Dewey:960.3/2. LCCN:95-041858.
Audience: **g,l,u,f.** *Choice, 1989.*

Hintjens, Helen M. **JV151.H55 1995**
Alternatives to Independence: Explorations in Post-Colonial Relations. Trade Cloth. Ashgate Publishing, Ltd. Aldershot, 1995. 240p. ISBN:1-85521-069-X, ISBN13: 978-1-85521-069-1. Dewey:325/.3144/09045. LCCN:95-019402.
Audience: **u,f.**

Horne, Alistair **DT295.H64 2006**
A Savage War of Peace: Algeria 1954-1962. Trade Paper. New York Review of Books, Incorporated, The. New York, NY. 2006. 600p. New York Review Books Classics ISBN:1-59017-218-3, ISBN13: 978-1-59017-218-6. Dewey:965/.046. LCCN:2006-003506.
Audience: **g,u,f.**

Naylor, Phillip C. **DT287.5.F8N39 2000**
France and Algeria: A History of Decolonization and Transformation. Trade Cloth. University Press of Florida. Gainesville, FL. 2000. xviii, 457p. ISBN:0-8130-1801-3, ISBN13: 978-0-8130-1801-0. Dewey:965/.04. LCCN:00-048884.
Audience: **l,u.** *Choice, 2001.*

Comparative Government > Colonies and Colonization > History > Germany

Friedrichsmeyer, Sara (Editor), et al. **NX550.A1I53 1998**
The Imperialist Imagination: German Colonialism and Its Legacy. Sara Lennox & Susanne Zantop (Editors). Trade Paper. University of Michigan Press. Chicago, IL. 1999. 376p. Social History, Popular Culture, and Politics in Germany Ser. ISBN:0-472-06682-X, ISBN13: 978-0-472-06682-7. Dewey:325/.343. LCCN:98-025522.
Audience: **u,f.**

Smith, Woodruff D. **JV2011.S63**
The German Colonial Empire. Trade Cloth. University of North Carolina Press. Chapel Hill, NC. 1978. xiv, 274p. ISBN:0-8078-1322-2, ISBN13: 978-0-8078-1322-5. Dewey:325/.343. LCCN:77-018155.
Audience: **l,u,f.**

Comparative Government > Colonies and Colonization > History > Other Colonizing Nations

MacQueen, Norrie **DT36.5.M33 1997**
The Decolonization of Portuguese Africa: Metropolitan Revolution and the Dissolution of Empire. Paper Text. Longman Publishing Group. White Plains, NY. 1997. 266p. ISBN:0-582-25993-2, ISBN13: 978-0-582-25993-5. Dewey:960/.097569. LCCN:96-034685.
Audience: **u,f.** *Choice, 1997.*

Newbury, Catharine **JQ3567.A2N48 1988**
The Cohesion of Oppression: Clientship and Ethnicity in Rwanda, 1860-1960. Trade Cloth. Columbia University Press. New York, NY. 1989. 322p. ISBN:0-231-06256-7, ISBN13: 978-0-231-06256-5. Dewey:306/.2/0967571. LCCN:88-007349.
Audience: **l,u,f.** *Choice, 1989.*

Comparative Government > Democratization

Adams, Francis **JL966**
Deepening Democracy: Global Governance and Political Reform in Latin America. Trade Cloth. Greenwood Publishing Group, Inc. Portsmouth, NH. 2003. 184p. ISBN:0-275-97038-8, ISBN13: 978-0-275-97038-3. Dewey:320.98. LCCN:2002-030723.
Audience: **u,f.** *Choice, 2004.*

Arter, David **JN6615.A58A78 1996**
Parties and Democracy in the Post-Soviet Republics: The Case of Estonia. Trade Cloth. Ashgate Publishing, Ltd. Aldershot, 1996. 302p. ISBN:1-85521-466-0, ISBN13: 978-1-85521-466-8. Dewey:320.9/4741. LCCN:96-014975.
Audience: **l,u,f.** *Choice, 1997.*

Birch, Sarah **JN6639.A5B57 2000**
Elections and Democratization in Ukraine. Cloth over Boards. Palgrave Macmillan. New York, NY. 2000. 226p. ISBN:0-312-23457-0, ISBN13: 978-0-312-23457-7. Dewey:324.9477086. LCCN:00-024439.
Audience: **l,u,f.** *Choice, 2001.*

Bratton, Michael & Walle, Nicholas van de **JQ1879.A15 B73 1997**
Democratic Experiments in Africa: Regime Transitions in Comparative Perspective. Robert H. Bates, Ellen Comisso, Peter Hall, Peter Lange, Joel Migdal & Helen Milner (Contribution by). Trade Paper. Cambridge University Press. New York, NY. 1997. 329p. Studies in Comparative Politics ISBN:0-521-55612-0, ISBN13: 978-0-521-55612-5. Dewey:321.8/0967. LCCN:96-034865.
Audience: **l,u,f.** *Choice, 1998.*

Carothers, Thomas **JN9636.C35 1996**
Assessing Democracy Assistance: The Case of Romania. Trade Paper. Carnegie Endowment for International Peace.

Washington, DC. 1996. 144p. ISBN:0-87003-102-3, ISBN13: 978-0-87003-102-1. Dewey:320.9498/09/049. LCCN:95-050999.
Audience: **l,u,f.**

Chesterman, Simon **JZ6374**
You, the People: The United Nations, Transitional Administration, and State-Building. Trade Paper, Perfect. Oxford University Press, Inc. New York, NY. 2005. 316p. ISBN:0-19-928400-8, ISBN13: 978-0-19-928400-9. Dewey:341.584. LCCN:2004-300664.
Audience: **u,f.**

Conteh-Morgan, Earl **JQ1879**
Democratization in Africa: The Theory and Dynamics of Political Transitions. Trade Cloth. Greenwood Publishing Group, Inc. Portsmouth, NH. 1997. 208p. ISBN:0-275-95780-2, ISBN13: 978-0-275-95780-3. Dewey:320.967/09/045. LCCN:96-033193.
Audience: **l,u.** *Choice, 1997.*

Dawisha, Karen & Parrott, Bruce (Editor, Contribution by) **JN6690 .D46 1997**
Democratic Changes and Authoritarian Reactions in Russia, Ukraine, Belarus and Moldova. Trade Paper. Cambridge University Press. New York, NY. 1997. 404p. Democratization and Authoritarianism in Post-Communist Societies Ser., Vol. 3 ISBN:0-521-59732-3, ISBN13: 978-0-521-59732-6. Dewey:320.9/47. LCCN:96-046494.
Audience: **l,u,f.** *Choice, 1998.*

Ihonvbere, Julius Omozuanvbo & Mbaku, John Mukum (Editors) **JQ1879**
Political Liberalization and Democratization in Africa: Lessons from Country Experiences. Trade Cloth. Greenwood Publishing Group, Inc. Portsmouth, NH. 2003. 400p. ISBN:0-275-97506-1, ISBN13: 978-0-275-97506-7. Dewey:320.967. LCCN:2003-052897.
Audience: **l,u,f.** *Choice, 2004.*

Jacoby, Wade **HC240.25.E852**
The Enlargement of the European Union and NATO: Ordering from the Menu in Central Europe. Trade Paper. Cambridge University Press. New York, NY. 2006. 302p. ISBN:0-521-68208-8, ISBN13: 978-0-521-68208-4. Dewey:341.242/2/0943.
Audience: **u,f.** *Choice, 2005.*

King, Stephen J. **JQ3336.K56 2003**
Liberalization Against Democracy: The Local Politics of Economic Reform in Tunisia. Trade Cloth. Indiana University Press. Bloomington, IN. 2003. 168p. Indiana Series in Middle East Studies ISBN:0-253-21583-8, ISBN13: 978-0-253-21583-3. Dewey:320.9611. LCCN:2002-014600.
Audience: **l,u,f.** *Choice, 2004.*

Kuzio, Taras & D'Anieri, Paul J. (Editors) **JN6635**
Dilemmas of State-Led Nation Building in Ukraine. Trade Cloth. Greenwood Publishing Group, Inc. Portsmouth, NH. 2002. 224p. ISBN:0-275-97786-2, ISBN13: 978-0-275-97786-3. Dewey:320.9477. LCCN:2002-068612.
Audience: **l,u,f.** *Choice, 2003.*

Mbaku, John Mukum & Ihonvbere, Julius Omozuanvbo (Editors) **JQ1879**
The Transition to Democratic Governance in Africa: The Continuing Struggle. Trade Cloth. Greenwood Publishing Group, Inc. Portsmouth, NH. 2003. 472p. ISBN:0-275-97505-3, ISBN13: 978-0-275-97505-0. Dewey:320.96. LCCN:2002-190905.
Audience: **l,u,f.** *Choice, 2004.*

Mbaku, John M. & Ihonvbere, Julius O. (Editors) **JQ1875.M83 1995**
Multiparty Democracy and Political Change: Constraints to Democratization in Africa. Trade Cloth. Ashgate Publishing, Ltd. Aldershot, 1998. 354p. ISBN:1-84014-379-7, ISBN13: 978-1-84014-379-9. Dewey:320.96/09/049. LCCN:97-077172.
Audience: **l,u,f.**

Melone, Albert P. **JN9607.M45 1998**
Creating Parliamentary Government: The Transition to Democracy in Bulgaria. Paper Text. Ohio State University Press. Columbus, OH. 1998. 350p. Parliaments and Legislatures Ser. ISBN:0-8142-0770-7, ISBN13: 978-0-8142-0770-3. Dewey:320.9499/09/049. LCCN:98-016298.
Audience: **l,u,f.** *Choice, 1999.*

Monga, Celestin **JQ1879.A15M6613 1996**
The Anthropology of Anger: Civil Society and Democracy in Africa. Trade Cloth. Lynne Rienner Publishers, Inc. Boulder, CO. 1996. 219p. ISBN:1-55587-644-7, ISBN13: 978-1-55587-644-9. Dewey:347.73/5. LCCN:96-007588.
Audience: **l,u,f.** *Choice, 1997.*

Petro, Nicolai N. **JN6581.P47 1995**
The Rebirth of Russian Democracy: An Interpretation of Political Culture. Trade Cloth. Harvard University Press. Cambridge, MA. 1998. 240p. ISBN:0-674-75001-2, ISBN13: 978-0-674-75001-2. Dewey:306.2/0947. LCCN:94-045431.
Audience: **l,u,f.** *Choice, 1996.*

Quigley, Kevin F. F. **HC244.Q35 1997**
For Democracy's Sake: Foundations and Democracy Assistance in Central Europe. Trade Paper. Woodrow Wilson Center Press. Washington, DC. 1997. 189p. ISBN:0-943875-81-1, ISBN13: 978-0-943875-81-1. Dewey:338.91/0943. LCCN:97-001541.
Audience: **u,f.** *Choice, 1997.*

Schaffer, Frederic C. **JQ3396.A91**
Democracy in Translation: Understanding Politics in an Unfamiliar Culture. Trade Paper. Cornell University Press. Ithaca, NY. 2000. 192p. Wilder House Series in Politics, History, and Culture Ser. ISBN:0-8014-8691-2, ISBN13: 978-0-8014-8691-3. Dewey:320.9663.
Audience: **l,u,f.**

Staar, Richard F. (Editor) **JN6766.T73 1993**
Transition to Democracy in Poland. Trade Cloth. Palgrave Macmillan. New York, NY. 1993. 288p. ISBN:0-312-10000-0, ISBN13: 978-0-312-10000-1. Dewey:320.9/438/09049. LCCN:93-026014.
Audience: **l,u,f.** *Choice, 1994.*

Tulchin, Joseph S. & Selee, Andrew D. **JQ1875.A55D423 2004**
Decentralization, Democratic Governance, and Civil Society in Comparative Perspective: Africa, Asia, and Latin America. Philip Oxhorn (Editor). Trade Cloth. Johns Hopkins University Press. Baltimore, MD. 2004. 368p. ISBN:0-8018-7919-1, ISBN13: 978-0-8018-7919-7. Dewey:320.8. LCCN:2004-001537.
Audience: **l,u,f.** *Choice, 2005.*

United Nations Development Programme Staff **HD75.H8 2002**
Human Development Report 2002: Deepening Democracy in a Fragmented World. Paper Text. Oxford University Press, Inc. New York, NY. 2002. 260p. ISBN:0-19-521915-5, ISBN13: 978-0-19-521915-9. Dewey:338.9/005.
Audience: **g,l,u,f.**

United Nations Staff **JX1977.2.C18U55 1995**
The United Nations and Cambodia, 1991-1995. Boutros Boutros-Ghali (Introduction by). Trade Cloth. United Nations Publications. New York, NY. 1995. 360p. Blue Bks., Vol. II ISBN:92-1-100548-5, ISBN13: 978-92-1-100548-6. Dewey:341.23596. LCCN:95-154041.
Audience: **l,u,f.** *Choice, 1996.*

Volpi, Frederic **JQ3231.V65 2002**
Islam and Democracy: The Failure of Dialogue in Algeria. Trade Paper. Pluto Press. London, 2002. 184p. ISBN:0-7453-1976-9, ISBN13: 978-0-7453-1976-6. Dewey:965.05/3. LCCN:2002-005040.
Audience: **u,f.** *Choice, 2003.*

Whitmore, Sarah **JN6637.W56 2004**
State Building in Ukraine: The Ukrainian Parliament, 1990-2003. Paper over Boards. Routledge. New York, NY. 2004. 240p. BASEES/RoutledgeCurzon Series on Russian and East European Studies, Vol. 10 ISBN:0-415-33195-1, ISBN13: 978-0-415-33195-1. Dewey:328.477. LCCN:2003-023941.
Audience: **l,u,f.**

Comparative Government > North America

Lipset, Seymour Martin **E183.8.C2**
Continental Divide: The Values and Institutions of the United States and Canada. Trade Paper. Routledge. New York, NY. 1990. 352p. ISBN:0-415-90385-8, ISBN13: 978-0-415-90385-1. Dewey:303.48/273071. LCCN:89-048660.
Audience: **u,f.** *Choice, 1990.*

Comparative Government > North America > Canada

Atkinson, Michael M. & Chandler, Marsha A. (Editors) **JL65**
The Politics of Canadian Public Policy. Trade Cloth. University of Toronto Press. Toronto, ON. 1983. 296p. ISBN:0-8020-2485-8, ISBN13: 978-0-8020-2485-5. Dewey:320.971. LCCN:83-171573.
Audience: **u,f.** BCL3

Bakvis, Herman & Chandler, William M. (Editors) **JL27**
Federalism and the Role of the State. Cloth Text. University of Toronto Press. Toronto, ON. 1987. viii, 328p. ISBN:0-8020-2599-4, ISBN13: 978-0-8020-2599-9. Dewey:321.02.
Audience: **u,f.**

Bickerton, James & Gagnon, Alain-G **JL65.C38 2004**
Canadian Politics. Ed. 4. Trade Paper. Broadview Press. Peterborough, ON. 2004. 512p. ISBN:1-55111-595-6, ISBN13: 978-1-55111-595-5. Dewey:320.971. LCCN:2005-270177.
Audience: **l,u.**

Black, Edwin R. **JL27**
Divided Loyalties: Canadian Concepts of Federalism. Trade Cloth. University of Toronto Press. Toronto, ON. 1975. 264p. ISBN:0-7735-0230-0, ISBN13: 978-0-7735-0230-7. Dewey:321/.02/0971. LCCN:75-319658.
Audience: **u,f.** BCL3

Canada **JL15**
Web: Government of Canada, Gouvernement du Canada. http://canada.gc.ca
Audience: **g,l,u,f.**

Cook, Curtis (Editor) **JL65 1994**
Constitutional Predicament: Canada after the Referendum of 1992. Trade Cloth. McGill-Queen's University Press. Montreal, PQ. 1994. 304p. ISBN:0-7735-1192-X, ISBN13: 978-0-7735-1192-7. Dewey:320.971/09/049. LCCN:94-231392.
Audience: **u,f.** *Choice, 1995.*

Courtney, John C. **JL193.C598 2004**
Elections. Trade Cloth. University of British Columbia Press. Vancouver, BC. 2005. 224p. ISBN:0-7748-0917-5, ISBN13: 978-0-7748-0917-7. Dewey:321.8/043/0971. LCCN:2004-426307.
Audience: **g,l,u,f.** *Choice, 2005.*

Eagles, Munroe (Editor), et al. **JL167.A56 1995**
The Almanac of Canadian Politics. Ed. 2. James P. Bickerton, Alain-G Gagnon & Patrick J. Smith (Editors). Cloth Text. Oxford University Press, Inc. New York, NY. 1996. 784p. ISBN:0-19-541140-4, ISBN13: 978-0-19-541140-9. Dewey:320.9/71. LCCN:96-122072.
Audience: **g,l,u,f.** *Choice, 1996.*

Gerin-Lajoie, Paul **KZ0105.G47**
Constitutional Amendment in Canada. Trade Paper. Books on Demand. Ann Arbor, MI. 384p. Canadian Government Ser., Vol. 3 ISBN:0-598-18518-6, ISBN13: 978-0-598-18518-1. Dewey:342.7103.
Audience: **u,f.**

Gidengil, Elisabeth **JL186.5**
Citizens. Trade Cloth. University of British Columbia Press. Vancouver, BC. 2005. 224p. Canadian Democratic Audit Ser. ISBN:0-7748-0919-1, ISBN13: 978-0-7748-0919-1. Dewey:323/.042/0971. LCCN:2004-445868.
Audience: **u,f.**

Kornberg, Allan & Clarke, Harold D. **JL27.P64 1983**
Political Support in Canada: The Crisis Years. Cloth Text. Duke University Press. Durham, NC. 1983. xvi, 463p. ISBN:0-8223-0546-1, ISBN13: 978-0-8223-0546-0. Dewey:320.971. LCCN:83-011567.
Audience: **u,f.** BCL3

Lipset, Seymour Martin **E183.8.C2**
Continental Divide: The Values and Institutions of the United States and Canada. Trade Paper. Routledge. New York, NY.

1990. 352p. ISBN:0-415-90385-8, ISBN13: 978-0-415-90385-1. Dewey:303.48/273071. LCCN:89-048660.
Audience: **u,f.** *Choice, 1990.*

Martin, Chester **JL15 .M3 1975**
Empire and Commonwealth. Trade Cloth. Greenwood Publishing Group, Inc. Portsmouth, NH. 1975. 385p. ISBN:0-8371-7626-3, ISBN13: 978-0-8371-7626-0. Dewey:320.9/71. LCCN:74-009227.
Audience: **u,f.**

McAllister, Mary Louise **JS1708**
Governing Ourselves?: The Politics of Canadian Communities. Trade Cloth. University of British Columbia Press. Vancouver, BC. 2004. 352p. ISBN:0-7748-1062-9, ISBN13: 978-0-7748-1062-3. Dewey:320.8/5/0971. LCCN:2004-463309.
Audience: **g,l,u.** *Choice, 2005.*

Meisel, John **JL193 .M45 1975**
Working Papers on Canadian Politics. Ed. 2. Trade Paper. McGill-Queen's University Press. Montreal, PQ. 1975. ISBN:0-7735-0245-9, ISBN13: 978-0-7735-0245-1. Dewey:329/.00971. LCCN:75-329798.
Audience: **l,u,f.** B

Monahan, Patrick J. **KE4270.M66 1991**
Meech Lake: The Inside Story. Ian Scott (Introduction by). Paper Text. University of Toronto Press. Toronto, ON. 1991. 540p. ISBN:0-8020-6896-0, ISBN13: 978-0-8020-6896-5. Dewey:347.102. LCCN:92-129235.
Audience: **l,u,f.** *Choice, 1992.*

Murphy, Michael (Editor) **E92 .C36**
Canada: the State of the Federation: Reconfiguring Aboriginal-State Relations. Trade Cloth. McGill-Queen's University Press. Montreal, PQ. 2005. 400p. ISBN:1-55339-011-3, ISBN13: 978-1-55339-011-4. Dewey:323.1197071.
Audience: **g,l,u.**

Savoie, Donald J. **JL75.S28 1999**
Governing from the Centre: The Concentration of Power in Canadian Politics. Trade Cloth. University of Toronto Press. Toronto, ON. 1999. 836p. ISBN:0-8020-4476-X, ISBN13: 978-0-8020-4476-1. Dewey:351.71. LCCN:00-551128.
Audience: **u,f.** *Choice, 2000.*

Schwartz, Mildred A. **JL27.S36**
Politics and Territory: The Sociology of Regional Persistence in Canada. Trade Cloth. McGill-Queen's University Press. Montreal, PQ. 1974. 360p. ISBN:0-7735-0166-5, ISBN13: 978-0-7735-0166-9. Dewey:301.5/92. LCCN:73-079502.
Audience: **u,f.** B

Simeon, Richard **JL27**
Federal-Provincial Diplomacy. Book, Other. University of Toronto Press. Toronto, ON. 2006. 380p. ISBN:0-8020-9411-2, ISBN13: 978-0-8020-9411-7. Dewey:320.471/049.
Audience: **u,f.**

Smith, Jennifer **JL27.S645 2004**
Federalism. Trade Cloth. University of British Columbia Press. Vancouver, BC. 2005. 208p. Canadian Democratic Audit Ser. ISBN:0-7748-1060-2, ISBN13: 978-0-7748-1060-9. Dewey:320.471. LCCN:2005-360633.
Audience: **u,f.**

Soroka, Stuart Neil **P96.P832C217 2002**
Agenda-Setting Dynamics in Canada. Trade Paper. University of British Columbia Press. Vancouver, BC. 2003. 160p. ISBN:0-7748-0959-0, ISBN13: 978-0-7748-0959-7. Dewey:302.23/0971/09048. LCCN:2003-427470.
Audience: **u,f.** *Choice, 2003.*

Stevenson, Garth **JL27.S73 2004**
Unfulfilled Union: Canadian Federalism and National Unity. Ed. 4. Trade Paper. McGill-Queen's University Press. Montreal, PQ. 2004. 336p. ISBN:0-7735-2744-3, ISBN13: 978-0-7735-2744-7. Dewey:320.471. LCCN:2004-484716.
Audience: **l,u.** B

Taylor, Charles **JL27.T39 1993**
Reconciling the Solitudes: Essays on Canadian Federalism and Nationalism. Trade Cloth. McGill-Queen's University Press. Montreal, PQ. 1993. 192p. ISBN:0-7735-1105-9, ISBN13: 978-0-7735-1105-7. Dewey:971.064. LCCN:94-160860.
Audience: **u,f.** *Choice, 1993.*

Thomas, David (Editor) **HC115**
Canada and the United States: Differences That Count. Trade Paper. Broadview Press. Peterborough, ON. 1993. 420p. ISBN:1-55111-018-0, ISBN13: 978-1-55111-018-9. Dewey:971.064/7.
Audience: **l,u.**

Waite, P. B. **JL55**
The Confederation Debates in the Province of Canada 1865. Ed. 2. Trade Cloth. McGill-Queen's University Press. Montreal, PQ. 2006. 200p. ISBN:0-7735-3092-4, ISBN13: 978-0-7735-3092-8. Dewey:342.71024.
Audience: **l,u,f.**

Weaver, R. Kent (Editor) **JL27.C58 1992**
The Collapse of Canada? Trade Paper. Brookings Institution Press. Washington, DC. 1992. 200p. ISBN:0-8157-9253-0, ISBN13: 978-0-8157-9253-6. Dewey:321.020971. LCCN:91-048027.
Audience: **g,l,u,f.** *Choice, 1992.*

Whittington, Michael & Williams, Glen (Editors) **JL65.C39 2000**
Canadian Politics in the 21st Century. Ed. 5. Cloth Text. Nelson Thomson Learning. Scarborough, ON. 2000. ix, 432p. ISBN:0-17-616676-9, ISBN13: 978-0-17-616676-2. Dewey:971.064. LCCN:00-693509.
Audience: **l,u.**

Comparative Government > North America > Canada > Branches of Government

Canada **JL198**
Government of Canada: Provinces and Territories. http://www.canada.gc.ca/othergov/prov_e.html
Audience: **g,l,u,f.**

Dawson, Robert M. **JL15**
The Government of Canada. Ed. 5. Norman Ward (Revised by). Cloth Text. University of Toronto Press. Toronto, ON. 1970. Canadian Government Ser. ISBN:0-8020-2046-1, ISBN13: 978-0-8020-2046-8. Dewey:342/.71. LCCN:63-005198.
Audience: **l,u.**

Docherty, David **JL136 .D62 2005**
Legislatures. Trade Cloth. University of British Columbia Press. Vancouver, BC. 2005. 240p. Canadian Democratic Audit Ser. ISBN:0-7748-1064-5, ISBN13: 978-0-7748-1064-7. Dewey:328.71.
Audience: **g,l,u,f.**

Hawkes, David C. (Editor) **E78.C2**
Aboriginal Peoples and Government Responsibility: Exploring Federal and Provincial Roles, No. 12. Trade Paper. McGill-Queen's University Press. Montreal, PQ. 369p. ISBN:0-88629-090-2, ISBN13: 978-0-88629-090-0. Dewey:323.1/197071.
Audience: **u,f.**

Hockin, Thomas A. **JL99.H62 1977**
Apex of Power: The Prime Minister and Political Leadership in Canada. Trade Cloth. Prentice Hall Canada. Scarborough, ON. 1977. xv, 359p. ISBN:0-13-038653-7, ISBN13: 978-0-13-038653-3. Dewey:320.9/71/06. LCCN:77-373755.
Audience: **l,u.** B

Hodgetts, J. E., et al. **JL108**
The Biography of an Institution: The Civil Service Commission of Canada, 1908-1967. William B. McCloskey Jr., Reginald Whitaker & V. Seymour Wilson (Authors). Trade Cloth. McGill-Queen's University Press. Montreal, PQ. 1972. 540p. Canadian Public Administration Ser. ISBN:0-7735-0140-1, ISBN13: 978-0-7735-0140-9. Dewey:354/.71/001. LCCN:72-087185.
Audience: **u,f.** B

Hodgetts, John Edwin **JL0108.H62**
The Canadian Public Service: A Physiology of Government, 1867-1970. Trade Paper. Books on Demand. Ann Arbor, MI. 386p. Studies in the Structure of Power, Vol. 7 ISBN:0-598-16016-7, ISBN13: 978-0-598-16016-4. Dewey:354/.71/04. LCCN:72-090738.
Audience: **u,f.**

Macintosh, Donald, et al. **GV585**
Sport and Politics in Canada: Federal Government Involvement since 1961. Tom Bedecki & C. E. S. Franks (Authors). Cloth Text. McGill-Queen's University Press. Montreal, PQ. 1987. 224p. ISBN:0-7735-0609-8, ISBN13: 978-0-7735-0609-1. Dewey:796.0971. LCCN:88-156546.
Audience: **l,u,f.**

Savoie, Donald J. **JL75.S27 2003**
Breaking the Bargain: Public Servants, Ministers and Parliament. Cloth over Boards. University of Toronto Press. Toronto, ON. 2003. 336p. ISBN:0-8020-8810-4, ISBN13: 978-0-8020-8810-9. Dewey:352.3/5/0971. LCCN:2004-272536.
Audience: **g,l,u,f.** *Choice, 2004.*

Smith, David E. **JL15**
The Republican Option in Canada: Past and Present. Trade Cloth. University of Toronto Press. Toronto, ON. 1999. 694p. ISBN:0-8020-4469-7, ISBN13: 978-0-8020-4469-3. Dewey:320.971.
Audience: **u,f.** *Choice, 2000.*

White, Graham **JL27**
Cabinets and First Ministers. Trade Cloth. University of British Columbia Press. Vancouver, BC. 2005. 208p. ISBN:0-7748-1158-7, ISBN13: 978-0-7748-1158-3. Dewey:321.8/043/0971. LCCN:2005-432996.
Audience: **u,f.**

Comparative Government > North America > Canada > Political Parties

Alexander, Robert J. (Contribution by) **JL195**
Political Parties of the Americas: Canada, Latin America, and the West Indies. Cloth Text. Greenwood Publishing Group, Inc. Portsmouth, NH. 1982. 1274p. The Greenwood Historical Encyclopedia of the World's Political Parties Ser. ISBN:0-313-21474-3, ISBN13: 978-0-313-21474-5. Dewey:324.2/098. LCCN:81-006952.
Audience: **g,l,u,f.** B

Ameringer, Charles D. (Editor) **JL195**
Political Parties of the Americas, 1980s to 1990s: Canada, Latin America, and the West Indies. Cloth Text. Greenwood Publishing Group, Inc. Portsmouth, NH. 1992. 696p. ISBN:0-313-27418-5, ISBN13: 978-0-313-27418-3. Dewey:324.27. LCCN:92-003032.
Audience: **g,l,u,f.** *Choice, 1993.*

Carty, R. Kenneth (Editor) **JL195**
Canadian Political Party Systems. Trade Paper. Broadview Press. Peterborough, ON. 1992. 376p. ISBN:0-921149-90-5, ISBN13: 978-0-921149-90-3. Dewey:324.271.
Audience: **l,u.**

Courtney, John C. **JL99.C68 1995**
Do Conventions Matter?: Choosing National Party Leaders in Canada. Trade Paper. McGill-Queen's University Press. Montreal, PQ. 1995. 432p. ISBN:0-7735-1358-2, ISBN13: 978-0-7735-1358-7. Dewey:324.5/6/0971. LCCN:96-153762.
Audience: **l,u.**

Cross, William P. **JL195.C76 2004**
Political Parties. Trade Cloth. University of British Columbia Press. Vancouver, BC. 2005. 218p. Canadian Democratic Audit Ser. ISBN:0-7748-0940-X, ISBN13: 978-0-7748-0940-5. Dewey:324.271. LCCN:2004-541324.
Audience: **g,l,u,f.** *Choice, 2005.*

English, John **JL197.P67E53 1993**
The Decline of Politics: The Conservatives and the Party System, 1901-1920. Paper Text. University of Toronto Press. Toronto, ON. 1993. 400p. Reprints in Canadian History Ser. ISBN:0-8020-6956-8, ISBN13: 978-0-8020-6956-6. Dewey:324.27104. LCCN:94-108588.
Audience: **u,f.**

Granatstein, Jack L. **JL197.P67**
Politics of Survival: The Conservative Party of Canada 1939-1945. Trade Cloth. University of Toronto Press. Toronto, ON. 1967. ISBN:0-8020-5192-8, ISBN13: 978-0-8020-5192-9. Dewey:320.9/71. LCCN:68-072926.
Audience: **u,f.**

Lipset, Seymour Martin **JL197.C6**
Agrarian Socialism: The Cooperative Commonwealth Federation in Saskatchewan: A Study in Political Sociology. Trade Paper. University of California Press. Berkeley, CA. 1971. ISBN:0-520-02056-1, ISBN13: 978-0-520-02056-6. Dewey:329.9/7.124.
Audience: **u,f.**

Perlin, George C. **JL197.P67.P47**
The Tory Syndrome: Leadership Politics in the Progressive Conservative Party. Trade Cloth. McGill-Queen's University Press. Montreal, PQ. 1982. 262p. ISBN:0-7735-0350-1, ISBN13: 978-0-7735-0350-2. Dewey:324.27104. LCCN:80-474879.
Audience: **u,f.**

Robin, M. **JL195 .R6 1978**
Canadian Provincial Politics. Ed. 2. Trade Paper. Prentice Hall PTR. Upper Saddle River, NJ. 1978. ISBN:0-13-113233-4, ISBN13: 978-0-13-113233-7. Dewey:329/.00971. LCCN:79-305629.
Audience: **l,u.**

Thorburn, Hugh **JL195 .P37 1991**
Party Politics in Canada. Ed. 6. Paper Text. Prentice Hall PTR. Upper Saddle River, NJ. 1991. ISBN:0-13-650847-2, ISBN13: 978-0-13-650847-2. Dewey:324.271. LCCN:92-214946.
Audience: **u,f.**

Thorburn, Hugh G. **JL195**
Party Politics in Canada. Ed. 8. Pearson Education Canada. 2001. ISBN:0-13-020920-1, ISBN13: 978-0-13-020920-7.
Audience: **u,f.**

Whitaker, Reginald **JL0197.L5W48**
The Government Party: Organizing and Financing the Liberal Party of Canada, 1930-58. Trade Paper. Books on Demand. Ann Arbor, MI. 531p. Canadian Government Ser., No. 20 ISBN:0-608-16385-6, ISBN13: 978-0-608-16385-7. Dewey:324.27106. LCCN:78-301195.
Audience: **u,f.**

Young, Walter D. **JL197.C6.Y6**
The Anatomy of a Party: The National CCF, 1932-1961. Trade Cloth. University of Toronto Press. Toronto, ON. 1969. 328p. ISBN:0-8020-5221-5, ISBN13: 978-0-8020-5221-6. Dewey:329.9/71. LCCN:73-460705.
Audience: **u,f.**

Comparative Government > North America > Canada > Provincial Politics

Beck, J. Murray **JL304.B4**
Government of Nova Scotia. Trade Cloth. University of Toronto Press. Toronto, ON. 1957. xii, 372p. ISBN:0-8020-7001-9, ISBN13: 978-0-8020-7001-2. Dewey:354.7196. LCCN:58-000542.
Audience: **l,u.**

Brownsey, Keith & Howlett, Michael (Editors) **JL198.P78 2001**
The Provincial State: Politics in Canada's Provinces and Territories. Trade Paper. Broadview Press. Peterborough, ON. 2000. 494p. ISBN:1-55111-368-6, ISBN13: 978-1-55111-368-5. Dewey:971.06. LCCN:2001-334700.
Audience: **l,u.** *Choice, 2001.*

Cameron, Kirk & White, Graham **JL495.A58C36 1995**
Northern Governments in Transition: Political and Constitutional Development in the Yukon, Nunavut and the Western Northwest Territories. Trade Paper. Institute for Research on Public Policy. 1995. 152p. ISBN:0-88645-177-9, ISBN13: 978-0-88645-177-6. Dewey:306.2/089/9710719. LCCN:96-111285.
Audience: **u.**

Carty, Ken (Editor) **F1088.P65 1996**
Politics, Policy, and Government in British Columbia. Trade Cloth. University of Washington Press. Seattle, WA. 1996. 396p. ISBN:0-7748-0582-X, ISBN13: 978-0-7748-0582-7. Dewey:971.1/04. LCCN:96-221740.
Audience: **u,f.**

Dickinson, John Alexander & Young, Brian **F1052**
A Short History of Quebec. Ed. 3. Cloth Text. McGill-Queen's University Press. Montreal, PQ. 2002. 400p. ISBN:0-7735-2393-6, ISBN13: 978-0-7735-2393-7. Dewey:971.4. LCCN:2003-269861.
Audience: **g,l,u,f.**

Donnelly, M. S. **JL500.M3**
The Government of Manitoba. Trade Cloth. University of Toronto Press. Toronto, ON. 1963. ISBN:0-8020-7063-9, ISBN13: 978-0-8020-7063-0. Dewey:354.71. LCCN:63-023544.
Audience: **u.**

Dunn, Chris **JL198.P745 1996**
Provinces: Canadian Provincial Politics. Trade Paper. Broadview Press. Peterborough, ON. 1996. 532p. ISBN:1-55111-090-3, ISBN13: 978-1-55111-090-5. Dewey:320.971. LCCN:97-127785.
Audience: **l,u.**

Dyck, Perry Rand **JL198 .D93 1996**
Provincial Politics in Canada: Towards the Turn of the Century. Ed. 3. Trade Paper. Prentice Hall PTR. Upper Saddle River, NJ. 1996. 692p. ISBN:0-13-443391-2, ISBN13: 978-0-13-443391-2. Dewey:320.971.
Audience: **l,u.**

Feldman, Elliot J. & Nevitte, Neil (Editors) **JL27.F87 1985**
The Future of North America: Canada, the United States and Quebec Nationalism. Trade Cloth. University Press of America, Inc. Lanham, MD. 1979. 370p. Harvard Studies in International Affairs, No. 42 ISBN:0-8191-4057-0, ISBN13: 978-0-8191-4057-9. Dewey:321.02/0971. LCCN:84-029184.
Audience: **g,l,u,f.**

Kornberg, Allan **JL198.K67 1982**
Representative Democracy in the Canadian Provinces. Trade Cloth. Prentice Hall Canada. Scarborough, ON. 1982. xii, 292p. ISBN:0-13-773754-8, ISBN13: 978-0-13-773754-3. Dewey:320.971. LCCN:82-188852.
Audience: **l,u.**

Lachapelle, Guy, et al. **JL250**
The Quebec Democracy: Structures, Processes and Policies. Gerald Bernier, Daniel Salee & Luc Bernier (Authors). Paper Text. McGraw-Hill Companies, The. New York, NY. 1993. ISBN:0-07-551394-3, ISBN13: 978-0-07-551394-0. Dewey:320.9714.
Audience: **l,u.**

Lemco, Jonathan **JL246.S8L45 1994**
Turmoil in the Peacable Kingdom: The Quebec Sovereignty Movement and Its Implications for Canada and the U. S. Cloth Text. University of Toronto Press. Toronto, ON. 1994. 266p. ISBN:0-8020-0532-2, ISBN13: 978-0-8020-0532-8. Dewey:971.4/04. LCCN:95-166253.
Audience: **u,f.** *Choice, 1995.*

Lingard, C. Cecil **JL462**
Territorial Government in Canada: The Autonomy Question in the Old North-West Territories. Trade Cloth. University of Toronto Press. Toronto, ON. 1980. Scholarly Reprint Ser. ISBN:0-8020-7095-7, ISBN13: 978-0-8020-7095-1. Dewey:342.7192.
Audience: **u,f.**

MacKinnon, Frank **JL382**
The Government of Prince Edward Island. Paper Text. Textbook Publishers. Temecula, CA. 2003. xii, 385p. ISBN:0-7581-1478-8, ISBN13: 978-0-7581-1478-5. Dewey:354.7197.
Audience: **l.** B

Macpherson, C. B. **JL500.A8 M3**
Democracy in Alberta: Social Credit and the Party System. Ed. 2. Trade Paper. University of Toronto Press. Toronto, ON. 1953. 369p. Social Credit in Alberta Ser. ISBN:0-8020-6009-9, ISBN13: 978-0-8020-6009-9. Dewey:332.56. LCCN:54-004046.
Audience: **u,f.**

McWhinney, Edward **JL65 1979.M32**
Quebec and the Constitution: Nineteen Sixty to Nineteen Seventy-Eight. Trade Cloth. University of Toronto Press. Toronto, ON. 1979. xvi, 170p. ISBN:0-8020-5456-0, ISBN13: 978-0-8020-5456-2. Dewey:342.71/05. LCCN:79-316335.
Audience: **u,f.** B

Quinn, Herbert F. **JL259.A58.Q56 1979**
The Union Nationale: Quebec Nationalism from Duplessis to Levesque. Trade Cloth. University of Toronto Press. Toronto, ON. 1980. xiii, 342p. ISBN:0-8020-2318-5, ISBN13: 978-0-8020-2318-6. Dewey:324.2714/093. LCCN:80-472454.
Audience: **u,f.** B

Saywell, John T. **JL259.A56.S28**
The Rise of the Parti Quebecois 1967-76. Trade Cloth. University of Toronto Press. Toronto, ON. 1977. 174p. ISBN:0-8020-2275-8, ISBN13: 978-0-8020-2275-2. Dewey:329.9/714. LCCN:77-372992.
Audience: **u,f.** B

Schindeler, Fred F. **JL263**
Responsible Government in Ontario. Trade Paper. University of Toronto Press. Toronto, ON. 1969. ISBN:0-8020-6189-3, ISBN13: 978-0-8020-6189-8. Dewey:320.9/713. LCCN:70-390334.
Audience: **u,f.**

Smith, David E. **JL319.A54.S6 1975**
Prairie Liberalism: The Liberal Party in Saskatchewan, 1905-1971. Trade Cloth. University of Toronto Press. Toronto, ON. 1975. x, 352p. ISBN:0-8020-5313-0, ISBN13: 978-0-8020-5313-8. Dewey:329.9/7124. LCCN:74-078676.
Audience: **u,f.** B

Thomas, Lewis H. **JL462 .T5 1978**
The Struggle for Responsible Government in the North-West Territories 1870-97. Ed. 2. Trade Cloth. University of Toronto Press. Toronto, ON. 1978. ISBN:0-8020-2287-1, ISBN13: 978-0-8020-2287-5. Dewey:320.9/719/02. LCCN:78-323901.
Audience: **u,f.**

Thorburn, Hugh G. **JL350**
Politics in New Brunswick. Ed. 1961. Trade Cloth. University of Toronto Press. Toronto, ON. 1981. ISBN:0-8020-7057-4, ISBN13: 978-0-8020-7057-9. Dewey:354.715. LCCN:63-025108.
Audience: **l,u.** B

Comparative Government > North America > Canada > Elections. Political Participation

Barney, Darin **JL186.5B37 2005**
Communication Technology. Trade Cloth. University of British Columbia Press. Vancouver, BC. 2005. 224p. Canadian Democratic Audit Ser., Vol. 8 ISBN:0-7748-1182-X, ISBN13: 978-0-7748-1182-8. Dewey:321.8/0971. LCCN:2005-432993.
Audience: **l,u,f.**

Carbert, Louise I. **HQ1459.O57C37 1995**
Agrarian Feminism: The Politics of Ontario Farm Women. Trade Cloth. University of Toronto Press. Toronto, ON. 1995. 530p. ISBN:0-8020-2931-0, ISBN13: 978-0-8020-2931-7. Dewey:305.4/09713. LCCN:95-178422.
Audience: **u,f.** *Choice, 1996.*

Clarke, Harold D.; **JL193**
Jenson, Jane; LeDuc, Lawrence; Pammett, Jon H.
Absent Mandate: Canadian Electoral Politics in an Era of Restructuring. Ed. 3. Gage Educational Publishing Company. 1996. ISBN:0-7715-5116-9, ISBN13: 978-0-7715-5116-1.
Audience: **u.**

Cleverdon, Catherine Lyle **JL192.C6 1974**
The Woman Suffrage Movement in Canada. Trade Cloth. University of Toronto Press. Toronto, ON. 1974. ISBN:0-8020-2108-5, ISBN13: 978-0-8020-2108-3. Dewey:324/.3/0971. LCCN:73-082587.
Audience: **u,f.** B

Feigert, Frank **F1413 .L66 1989**
Canada Votes, 1935-1989. Cloth Text. Duke University Press. Durham, NC. 1989. 352p. ISBN:0-8223-0894-0, ISBN13: 978-0-8223-0894-2. Dewey:980/.03. LCCN:88-026741.
Audience: **u,f.**

Johnston, Richard, et al. **JL193.L48 1992**
Letting the People Decide: The Dynamics of a Canadian Election. Andre Blais, Henry E. Brady & Jean Crete (Authors). Trade Cloth. Stanford University Press. Palo Alto, CA. 1992. 288p. ISBN:0-8047-2077-0, ISBN13: 978-0-8047-2077-9. Dewey:324.971/0647. LCCN:91-068213.
Audience: **u,f.** *Choice, 1993.*

Penniman, Howard R. (Editor) **JL193.C344 1988**
Canada at the Polls, 1984: A Study of the Federal General Elections. Cloth Text. Duke University Press. Durham, NC.

1988. xiii, 218p. At the Polls Ser. ISBN:0-8223-0805-3, ISBN13: 978-0-8223-0805-8. Dewey:324.971/0645. LCCN:87-027252.
Audience: **l,u,f.** *Choice, 1988.*

Presthus, R. **JL148.5**
Elite Accommodation in Canadian Politics. Trade Cloth. Cambridge University Press. New York, NY. 1973. 384p. ISBN:0-521-08695-7, ISBN13: 978-0-521-08695-0. Dewey:322.4/3/0971. LCCN:72-083598.
Audience: **u,f.** B

Young, Lisa & Everitt, Joanna **JL148.5**
Advocacy Groups. Trade Cloth. University of British Columbia Press. Vancouver, BC. 2005. 188p. Canadian Democratic Audit Ser. ISBN:0-7748-1110-2, ISBN13: 978-0-7748-1110-1. Dewey:322.4/3/0971.
Audience: **u,f.**

Comparative Government > North America > United States (See Also American Politics)

Bukovansky, Mlada **JC327.B764 2002**
Legitimacy and Power Politics: The American and French Revolutions in International Political Culture. Trade Cloth. Princeton University Press. Princeton, NJ. 2002. 272p. Princeton Studies in International History and Politics ISBN:0-691-07434-8, ISBN13: 978-0-691-07434-4. Dewey:306.2/0944/09033. LCCN:2001-055407.
Audience: **l,u,f.** *Choice, 2003.*

Lipset, Seymour Martin **E183.8.C2**
Continental Divide: The Values and Institutions of the United States and Canada. Trade Paper. Routledge. New York, NY. 1990. 352p. ISBN:0-415-90385-8, ISBN13: 978-0-415-90385-1. Dewey:303.48/273071. LCCN:89-048660.
Audience: **u,f.** *Choice, 1990.*

Comparative Government > Latin America

Z1601
☐ Handbook of Latin American Studies (HLAS). http://lcweb2.loc.gov/hlas/
Audience: **u,f.**

F1408
☐ LANIC (Latin American Network Information Center). http://lanic.utexas.edu/
Audience: **l,u,f.**

JL951
☐ Political Database of the Americas. http://www.georgetown.edu/pdba/
Audience: **u,f.**

Aguero, Felipe & Stark, Jeffrey (Editors) **JL966.F38 1998**
Fault Lines of Democracy in Post-Transition Latin America. Trade Paper. University of Miami, North/South Center Press. Coral Gables, FL. 1998. 407p. ISBN:1-57454-046-7, ISBN13: 978-1-57454-046-8. Dewey:320.98/09/048. LCCN:98-042225.
Audience: **l,u,f.** *Choice, 1999.*

Alves, Maria H. **F2538.25.A48 1985**
State and Opposition in Military Brazil. Trade Cloth. University of Texas Press. Austin, TX. 1985. 368p. Latin American Monographs, No. 63 ISBN:0-292-77598-9, ISBN13: 978-0-292-77598-5. Dewey:320.981. LCCN:84-013151.
Audience: **u,f.** *Choice, 1986.*

Arriagada, Genaro **F3100.A73413 1988**
Pinochet: The Politics of Power. Trade Cloth. Routledge. New York, NY. 1988. 224p. ISBN:0-04-497061-7, ISBN13: 978-0-04-497061-3. Dewey:983/.0647. LCCN:88-001907.
Audience: **u,f.** *Choice, 1989.*

Calvert, Peter (Editor) **F1424**
A Political and Economic Dictionary of Latin America. Paper over Boards. Taylor & Francis Group. Abingdon, 2004. 336p. Political and Economic Dictionaries Ser. ISBN:1-85743-211-8, ISBN13: 978-1-85743-211-4. Dewey:320.9803. LCCN:2004-559188.
Audience: **l,u,f.**

Cameron, Maxwell A. **JL3481.C36 1994**
Democracy and Authoritarianism in Peru: Political Coalitions and Social Change. Cloth over Boards. Palgrave Macmillan. New York, NY. 1994. 240p. ISBN:0-312-12153-9, ISBN13: 978-0-312-12153-2. Dewey:320.985. LCCN:94-009119.
Audience: **u,f.** *Choice, 1995.*

Centeno, Miguel Angel **F1410.5.C46 2002**
Blood and Debt: War and the Nation-State in Latin America. Trade Cloth. Pennsylvania State University Press. University Park, PA. 2002. 344p. ISBN:0-271-02165-9, ISBN13: 978-0-271-02165-2. Dewey:303.6/6/098. LCCN:2001-036764.
Audience: **u,f.** *Choice, 2003.*

Cleary, Edward L. & Steigenga, Timothy J. **BL2540.R47 2004**
Resurgent Voice in Latin America: Indigenous Peoples, Political Mobilization, and Religious Change. Trade Paper. Rutgers University Press. Piscataway, NJ. 2004. 304p. ISBN:0-8135-3461-5, ISBN13: 978-0-8135-3461-9. Dewey:306.6/098. LCCN:2004-000300.
Audience: **u,f.** *Choice, 2005.*

Farcau, Bruce W. **JL956**
The Transition to Democracy in Latin America: The Role of the Military. Trade Cloth. Greenwood Publishing Group, Inc. Portsmouth, NH. 1996. 200p. ISBN:0-275-95636-9, ISBN13: 978-0-275-95636-3. Dewey:322/.5/098. LCCN:96-005538.
Audience: **u,f.** *Choice, 1997.*

Francis, J. Michael & Kaufman, Will (Editors) **E18.75.I24 2005**
Iberia and the Americas: Culture, Politics, and History. Library Binding. ABC-CLIO, Inc. Santa Barbara, CA. 2005. 800p. Transatlantic Relations Ser. ISBN:1-85109-421-0, ISBN13: 978-1-85109-421-9. Dewey:303.48/2181204603. LCCN:2005-025407.
Audience: **g,l.**

Gillespie, Charles Guy **JL3698.A1 G5 1991**
Negotiating Democracy: Politicians and Generals in Uruguay. Alan Knight (Contribution by). Trade Paper. Cambridge University Press. New York, NY. 2006. 282p. Cambridge Latin

American Studies ISBN:0-521-02563-X, ISBN13: 978-0-521-02563-8. Dewey:320.9895.
Audience: **u,f.** *Choice, 1992.*

Hunter, Wendy **JL2420.C58H86 1997**
Eroding Military Influence in Brazil: Politicians Against Soldiers. Trade Paper. University of North Carolina Press. Chapel Hill, NC. 1997. 260p. ISBN:0-8078-4620-1, ISBN13: 978-0-8078-4620-9. Dewey:320.981. LCCN:96-022285.
Audience: **u,f.** *Choice, 1997.*

Kapiszewski, Diana & Kazan, Alexander (Editors) **F1410**
Encyclopedia of Latin American Politics. Cloth Text. Greenwood Publishing Group, Inc. Portsmouth, NH. 2002. 384p. ISBN:1-57356-306-4, ISBN13: 978-1-57356-306-2. Dewey:320.98/03. LCCN:2001-036182.
Audience: **l,u,f.** *Choice, 2002.*

Kryzanek, Michael J. & Wiarda, Howard J. **F1938**
The Politics of External Influence in the Dominican Republic. Trade Cloth. Greenwood Publishing Group, Inc. Portsmouth, NH. 1988. 199p. Politics in Latin America Ser. ISBN:0-275-92992-2, ISBN13: 978-0-275-92992-3. Dewey:972.93/054. LCCN:87-038484.
Audience: **u,f.** *Choice, 1989.*

Lewis, Paul H. **F2849**
Guerrillas and Generals: The "Dirty War" in Argentina. Trade Cloth. Greenwood Publishing Group, Inc. Portsmouth, NH. 2001. 280p. ISBN:0-275-97359-X, ISBN13: 978-0-275-97359-9. Dewey:982.06. LCCN:2001-021650.
Audience: **u,f.** *Choice, 2002.*

Loveman, Brian **JL952.L68 1993**
The Constitution of Tyranny: Regimes of Exception in Spanish America. Cloth Text. University of Pittsburgh Press. Pittsburgh, PA. 1994. 496p. Latin American Ser. ISBN:0-8229-3766-2, ISBN13: 978-0-8229-3766-1. Dewey:351.003/22/09809034. LCCN:93-028177.
Audience: **u,f.** *Choice, 1994.*

Loveman, Brian **JL956.C58L68 1999**
For la Patria: Politics and the Armed Forces in Latin America. Book, Other. Rowman & Littlefield Publishers, Inc. Lanham, MD. 1999. 333p. Latin American Silhouettes Ser. ISBN:0-8420-2772-6, ISBN13: 978-0-8420-2772-4. Dewey:322/.5/098. LCCN:98-007793.
Audience: **u,f.** *Choice, 1999.*

Lynch, John **JL950**
Spanish Colonial Administration, 1782-1810: The Intendant System in the Viceroyalty of the Rio De la Plata, 5. Trade Cloth. Greenwood Publishing Group, Inc. Portsmouth, NH. 1969. 335p. University of London. Historical Studies ISBN:0-8371-0546-3, ISBN13: 978-0-8371-0546-8. Dewey:325.3/1/0946. LCCN:69-013979.
Audience: **u,f.** B

Norden, Deborah L. **F2849.2.N67 1996**
Military Rebellion in Argentina: Between Coups and Consolidation. Cloth Text. University of Nebraska Press. Lincoln, NE. 1996. 240p. ISBN:0-8032-3339-6, ISBN13: 978-0-8032-3339-3. Dewey:322/.5/098209045. LCCN:95-032285.
Audience: **u,f.** *Choice, 1996.*

Parry, J. H. **JL1200**
The Audiencia of New Galicia in the Sixteeenth Century: A Study in Spanish Colonial Government. Trade Cloth. Greenwood Publishing Group, Inc. Portsmouth, NH. 1985. 205p. ISBN:0-313-24957-1, ISBN13: 978-0-313-24957-0. Dewey:972/.3. LCCN:85-010039.
Audience: **u,f.**

Pion-Berlin, David **F2849.2.P565 1997**
Through Corridors of Power: Institutions and Civil-Military Relations in Argentina. Trade Cloth. Pennsylvania State University Press. University Park, PA. 1997. 264p. ISBN:0-271-01705-8, ISBN13: 978-0-271-01705-1. Dewey:322/.5/098209048. LCCN:96-048046.
Audience: **u,f.**

Potash, Robert A. **UA613**
The Army and Politics in Argentina, 1928-1945: Yrigoyen to Peron. Trade Cloth. Stanford University Press. Palo Alto, CA. 1969. xiv, 314p. ISBN:0-8047-0683-2, ISBN13: 978-0-8047-0683-4. Dewey:320.9/82. LCCN:69-013182.
Audience: **u,f.**

Potash, Robert A. **UA613**
The Army and Politics in Argentina, 1945-1962: Peron to Frondizi. Trade Cloth. Stanford University Press. Palo Alto, CA. 1980. xiv, 418p. ISBN:0-8047-1056-2, ISBN13: 978-0-8047-1056-5. Dewey:320.9/82. LCCN:79-064220.
Audience: **u,f.** B

Potash, Robert A. **UA613 .P67**
The Army and Politics in Argentina, 1962-1973: From Frondizi's Fall to the Peronist Restoration. Trade Cloth. Stanford University Press. Palo Alto, CA. 1996. 592p. ISBN:0-8047-2414-8, ISBN13: 978-0-8047-2414-2. Dewey:320.9/82. LCCN:69-013182.
Audience: **u,f.** *Choice, 1996.*

Przeworski, Adam **HC244 .P8 1991**
Democracy and the Market: Political and Economic Reforms in Eastern Europe and Latin America. Jon Elster & Gudmund Hernes (Contribution by). Trade Paper. Cambridge University Press. New York, NY. 1991. 224p. Studies in Rationality and Social Change ISBN:0-521-42335-X, ISBN13: 978-0-521-42335-9. Dewey:338.947. LCCN:91-007524.
Audience: **u,f.** *Choice, 1992.*

Rochlin, James F. **F1414.2.R55 2002**
Vanguard Revolutionaries in Latin America: Peru, Colombia, Mexico. Library Binding. Lynne Rienner Publishers, Inc. Boulder, CO. 2002. 300p. ISBN:1-55587-984-5, ISBN13: 978-1-55587-984-6. Dewey:980.3/3. LCCN:2002-075198.
Audience: **u,f.** *Choice, 2003.*

Romero, Jose L. **JL2011 .R613**
A History of Argentine Political Thought. Thomas F. McGann (Translator). Trade Cloth. Stanford University Press. Palo Alto, CA. 1963. xvii, 270p. ISBN:0-8047-0108-3, ISBN13: 978-0-8047-0108-2. Dewey:342.82.
Audience: **l,u,f.**

Rouquie, Alain **JL956.C58R6813 1987**
The Military and the State in Latin America. Paul E. Sigmund (Translator). Trade Cloth. University of California Press. Berkeley, CA. 1987. 520p. ISBN:0-520-05559-4, ISBN13: 978-0-520-05559-9. Dewey:322/.5/098. LCCN:86-014666.
Audience: **u,f.** *Choice, 1988.*

Rudolph, James D. **F3448**
Peru: The Evolution of a Crisis. Trade Cloth. Greenwood Publishing Group, Inc. Portsmouth, NH. 1992. 192p. Politics in Latin America Ser. ISBN:0-275-94146-9, ISBN13: 978-0-275-94146-8. Dewey:985.063. LCCN:91-023655.
Audience: **u,f.**

Silva, Patricio (Editor) **JL1856.C58S65 2001**
The Soldier and the State in South America: Essays in Civil-Military Relations. Cloth over Boards. Palgrave Macmillan. New York, NY. 2001. 224p. Latin American Studies ISBN:0-333-93093-2, ISBN13: 978-0-333-93093-9. Dewey:322.5098. LCCN:00-048354.
Audience: **u,f.** *Choice, 2001.*

Smith, Peter H. **JL966.S6 2005**
Democracy in Latin America: Political Change in Comparative Perspective. Paper Text. Oxford University Press, Inc. New York, NY. 2005. 412p. ISBN:0-19-515759-1, ISBN13: 978-0-19-515759-8. Dewey:320.98. LCCN:2004-056096.
Audience: **l,u.**

Stepan, Alfred **F2538.25.S79 1988**
Rethinking Military Politics: Brazil and the Southern Cone. Trade Paper. Princeton University Press. Princeton, NJ. 1988. 192p. ISBN:0-691-02274-7, ISBN13: 978-0-691-02274-1. Dewey:322/.5/0981. LCCN:87-045537.
Audience: **u,f.** *Choice, 1988.*

Taylor, Philip Bates **JA37**
Government and Politics of Uruguay. Paper Text. Textbook Publishers. Temecula, CA. 2003. 285p. ISBN:0-7581-3052-X, ISBN13: 978-0-7581-3052-5. Dewey:989.505.
Audience: **l,u.**

Tulchin, Joseph S. **F3448.2.P4735 1994**
Peru in Crisis: Dictatorship or Democracy? Paper Text. Lynne Rienner Publishers, Inc. Boulder, CO. 1994. 200p. Woodrow Wilson Center Current Studies on Latin America ISBN:1-55587-543-2, ISBN13: 978-1-55587-543-5. Dewey:320.985. LCCN:94-014646.
Audience: **u,f.** *Choice, 1995.*

Waisman, Carlos H. & Peralta-Ramos, Monica (Editors) **F2849.2.F69 1987**
From Military Rule to Liberal Democracy in Argentina. Paper Text. Westview Press. Boulder, CO. 1986. 192p. ISBN:0-8133-7101-5, ISBN13: 978-0-8133-7101-6. Dewey:982/.06. LCCN:86-004068.
Audience: **u,f.** *Choice, 1987.*

Weeks, Gregory **F3100.W43 2003**
The Military and Politics in Postauthoritarian Chile. Trade Cloth. University of Alabama Press. Tuscaloosa, AL. 2003. 248p. ISBN:0-8173-1177-7, ISBN13: 978-0-8173-1177-3. Dewey:320.983/09/049. LCCN:2003-000561.
Audience: **u,f.** *Choice, 2004.*

Wiarda, Howard J. **JL960 .W5 1978**
Critical Elections and Critical Coups: State, Society and the Military in the Processes of Latin American Development. Trade Paper. Ohio University Press. Athens, OH. 1979. Papers in International Studies: Latin America Ser., No. 5 ISBN:0-89680-082-2, ISBN13: 978-0-89680-082-3. Dewey:322/.5/098. LCCN:79-004433.
Audience: **u,f.**

Wiarda, Howard J. & Kline, Harvey F. **F1410.L39 2006**
Latin American Politics and Development. Ed. 6. Trade Paper. Westview Press. Boulder, CO. 2006. 624p. ISBN:0-8133-4327-5, ISBN13: 978-0-8133-4327-3. Dewey:980. LCCN:2006-003512.
Audience: **l,u.**

Williams, Philip J. & Walter, Knut **JL1566.C58W54 1997**
Militarization and Demilitarization in El Salvador's Transition to Democracy. Trade Paper. University of Pittsburgh Press. Pittsburgh, PA. 1998. 260p. Pitt Latin American Ser. ISBN:0-8229-5646-2, ISBN13: 978-0-8229-5646-4. Dewey:322/.5/097284. LCCN:97-004920.
Audience: **u,f.**

Zagorski, Paul W. **JL1856.C58Z34 1992**
Democracy vs. National Security: Civil-Military Relations in Latin America. Library Binding. Lynne Rienner Publishers, Inc. Boulder, CO. 1991. 220p. ISBN:1-55587-300-6, ISBN13: 978-1-55587-300-4. Dewey:322/.5/098. LCCN:91-026176.
Audience: **l,u,f.** *Choice, 1992.*

Comparative Government > Latin America > Mexico

Bruhn, Kathleen **JL1298.A1B78 1997**
Taking on Goliath: Party Formation, Party System Change, and Democratization in Mexico. Trade Paper. Pennsylvania State University Press. University Park, PA. 1996. 520p. ISBN:0-271-01587-X, ISBN13: 978-0-271-01587-3. Dewey:324/.0972/09049. LCCN:95-047061.
Audience: **u,f.** *Choice, 1997.*

Hodges, Donald C. & Gandy, Ross **F1234.H7975 2002**
Mexico, the End of the Revolution. Paper Text. Greenwood Publishing Group, Inc. Portsmouth, NH. 2001. 224p. ISBN:0-275-97333-6, ISBN13: 978-0-275-97333-9. Dewey:972.08/2. LCCN:2001-034623.
Audience: **g,l,u,f.** *Choice, 2002.*

Needler, Martin C. **JL1281.N43 1982**
Mexican Politics: The Containment of Conflict. Trade Cloth. Bow Historical Books. New Providence, NJ. 1982. xi, 157p. ISBN:0-03-062041-4, ISBN13: 978-0-03-062041-6. Dewey:972.08/3. LCCN:82-005376.
Audience: **l,u,f.**

Randall, Laura (Editor) **HC135.C44 2005**
Changing Structure of Mexico: Political, Social, and Economic Prospects. Ed. 2. Cloth Text. M. E. Sharpe Inc. Armonk, NY. 2006. 512p. Columbia University Seminar Ser. ISBN:0-7656-1404-9, ISBN13: 978-0-7656-1404-9. Dewey:972.08/4. LCCN:2004-029098.
Audience: **u,f.**

Rochlin, James F. **JL1281.R6 1997**
Redefining Mexican "Security": Society, State, and Region under NAFTA. Trade Cloth. Lynne Rienner Publishers, Inc. Boulder, CO. 1997. 217p. ISBN:1-55587-569-6, ISBN13: 978-1-55587-569-5. Dewey:972.08/36. LCCN:97-013585.
Audience: **u,f.** *Choice, 1998.*

Russell, Philip **F1236.R88 1994**
Mexico under Salinas. Paper Text. Mexico Resource Center. Austin, TX. 1994. x, 486p. ISBN:0-9639223-0-0, ISBN13: 978-0-9639223-0-4. Dewey:327.72. LCCN:93-081213.
Audience: **g,l,u.** *Choice, 1994.*

Ugalde, Luis Carlos **JL1265.U38 2000**
The Mexican Congress: Old Player, New Power. Armand B. Peschard-Sverdrup (Foreword by). Paper Text. Center for Strategic & International Studies. Washington, DC. 2000. 203p. CSIS Significant Issues Ser., No. 22 ISBN:0-89206-382-3, ISBN13: 978-0-89206-382-6. Dewey:328.72/072. LCCN:00-011772.
Audience: **u,f.** *Choice, 2001.*

Comparative Government > Europe > Italy

Ferraresi, Franco **DG577.5.F4713 1996**
Threats to Democracy: The Radical Right in Italy after the War. Cloth Text. Princeton University Press. Princeton, NJ. 1996. 296p. ISBN:0-691-04499-6, ISBN13: 978-0-691-04499-6. Dewey:320.5/33/094509045. LCCN:96-004738.
Audience: **u,f.** *Choice, 1997.*

Ginsborg, Paul **JN5451**
A History of Contemporary Italy: Society and Politics, 1943-1988. Trade Paper. Palgrave Macmillan. New York, NY. 2003. 592p. ISBN:1-4039-6153-0, ISBN13: 978-1-4039-6153-2. Dewey:945/.0928.
Audience: **u,f.**

Guiat, Cyrille **JN3007.C6G83 2002**
Contrasting the French and Italian Communist Parties: Comrades and Culture. B. Bundgaard Rasmussen & Annette Rathje (Editors). Paper over Boards. Taylor & Francis Group. Abingdon, 2003. 210p. Cass Series on Totalitarian Movements and Political Religions ISBN:0-7146-5332-2, ISBN13: 978-0-7146-5332-7. Dewey:324.244/075. LCCN:2002-026784.
Audience: **u,f.** *Choice, 2004.*

Gundle, Stephen & Parker, Simon (Editors) **JN5451.N45 1996**
The New Italian Republic: From the Fall of the Berlin Wall to Berlusconi. Paper over Boards. Routledge. New York, NY. 1996. 352p. ISBN:0-415-12161-2, ISBN13: 978-0-415-12161-3. Dewey:320.9/45. LCCN:95-020748.
Audience: **g,l,u,f.** *Choice, 1996.*

Hine, David **JN5451.H56 1993**
Governing Italy: The Politics of Bargained Pluralism. Paper Text. Oxford University Press, Inc. New York, NY. 1993. 396p. ISBN:0-19-876171-6, ISBN13: 978-0-19-876171-6. Dewey:320.945. LCCN:92-030854.
Audience: **l,u.** *Choice, 1994.*

Kertzer, David I. **JN5451**
Politics and Symbols: The Italian Communist Party and the Fall of Communism. Trade Paper. Yale University Press. Cumberland, RI. 1998. 224p. ISBN:0-300-07724-6, ISBN13: 978-0-300-07724-7. Dewey:320.9/45.
Audience: **g,l,u,f.** *Choice, 1997.*

LaPalombara, Joseph **JN5451.L36 1987**
Democracy, Italian Style. Trade Cloth. Yale University Press. Cumberland, RI. 1987. 320p. ISBN:0-300-03913-1, ISBN13: 978-0-300-03913-9. Dewey:320.945. LCCN:87-006124.
Audience: **g,l,u,f.** *Choice, 1988.*

Putnam, Robert D. **JN5477.R35.P866 1993**
Making Democracy Work: Civic Traditions in Modern Italy. Cloth Text. Princeton University Press. Princeton, NJ. 1992. 288p. ISBN:0-691-07889-0, ISBN13: 978-0-691-07889-2. Dewey:306.2/0945/09045. LCCN:92-018377.
Audience: **f.** *Choice, 1993.*

Sassoon, Donald **DG577.5.S28 1997**
Contemporary Italy: Politics, Economy and Society Since 1945. Ed. 2. Trade Paper. Addison-Wesley Longman, Inc. Boston, MA. 1997. 336p. ISBN:0-582-21428-9, ISBN13: 978-0-582-21428-6. Dewey:945/.092. LCCN:97-019610.
Audience: **l,u,f.**

Tarrow, Sidney **JN5451.T37 1989**
Democracy and Disorder: Protest and Politics in Italy, 1965-1975. Trade Cloth. Oxford University Press, Inc. New York, NY. 1989. 416p. ISBN:0-19-827561-7, ISBN13: 978-0-19-827561-9. Dewey:322.4/0945. LCCN:88-026040.
Audience: **u,f.** *Choice, 1990.*

Comparative Government > Europe > Scandinavia

Engman, Max & Kirby, David (Editors) **DL1032.F56 1989**
Finland: People, Nation State. Trade Cloth. Indiana University Press. Bloomington, IN. 1989. 272p. ISBN:0-253-32067-4, ISBN13: 978-0-253-32067-4. Dewey:948.97. LCCN:88-033057.
Audience: **g,l,u.** *Choice, 1990.*

Heidar, Knut **JN7461**
Norway: Elites on Trial. Westview Press. 2001. ISBN:0-8133-3200-1, ISBN13: 978-0-8133-3200-0.
Audience: **g,l.**

Huber, Evelyne & Stephens, John D. **JC479.H83 2001**
Development and Crisis of the Welfare State: Parties and Policies in Global Markets. Trade Cloth. University of Chicago Press. Chicago, IL. 2001. 368p. ISBN:0-226-35646-9, ISBN13: 978-0-226-35646-4. Dewey:361.6/5. LCCN:00-012178.
Audience: **u,f.** *Choice, 2002.*

Miller, Kenneth E. **HC355.M55 1991**
Denmark: A Troubled Welfare State. Trade Paper. Westview Press. Boulder, CO. 1991. 224p. ISBN:0-8133-0834-8, ISBN13: 978-0-8133-0834-0. Dewey:361.6/5/09489. LCCN:90-020803.
Audience: **l,u.**

Shaffer, William R. **JN7543.S53 1998**
Parties and Parliaments: Political Change in Norway. Cloth Text. Ohio State University Press. Columbus, OH. 1998. 302p. Parliaments and Legislatures Ser. ISBN:0-8142-0787-1, ISBN13: 978-0-8142-0787-1. Dewey:328.481. LCCN:98-023025.
Audience: **u,f.** *Choice, 1999.*

Timonen, Virpi **HV315.5.T56 2003**
Restructuring the Welfare State: Globalisation and Social Policy Reform in Finland and Sweden. Trade Cloth. Edward Elgar Publishing, Inc. Northampton, MA. 2003. 232p. Globalization

and Welfare Ser. ISBN:1-84376-124-6, ISBN13: 978-1-84376-124-2. Dewey:361.6/5/094897. LCCN:2002-037928.

Audience: **u,f.**

Comparative Government > Europe > Switzerland

Kobach, Kris W. **JF493.S94.K6 1993**
Referendum: Direct Democracy in Switzerland. Trade Cloth. Ashgate Publishing, Ltd. Aldershot, 1993. 282p. ISBN:1-85521-397-4, ISBN13: 978-1-85521-397-5. Dewey:328.2494. LCCN:93-022657.

Audience: **u,f.** *Choice, 1994.*

Comparative Government > Europe > Austria. Hungary

Bozoki, Andras (Editor), et al. **JN2067.R68 2002**
The Roundtable Talks of 1989: The Genesis of Hungarian Democracy. Marta Elbert, Melinda Kalmar, Bela Revesz, Erzsebet Ripp & Zoltan Ripp (Editors). Trade Cloth. Central European University Press. Herndon, VA. 2002. 520p. ISBN:963-9241-21-0, ISBN13: 978-963-9241-21-3. Dewey:320.9439. LCCN:2002-000046.

Audience: **l,u.**

Bozoki, Andras (Editor), et al. **JN2067.P67 1992**
Post-Communist Transition: Emerging Pluralism in Hungary. Andras Koroseny & George Schopflin (Editors). Trade Cloth. Palgrave Macmillan. New York, NY. 1992. 208p. ISBN:0-312-08092-1, ISBN13: 978-0-312-08092-1. Dewey:321.0909439. LCCN:92-006508.

Audience: **l,u,f.**

Bugajski, Janusz **JN96.A979B84 2002**
Political Parties of Eastern Europe: A Guide to Politics in the Post-Communist Era. Trade Cloth. M. E. Sharpe Inc. Armonk, NY. 2003. 1118p. ISBN:1-56324-676-7, ISBN13: 978-1-56324-676-0. Dewey:320.947/09/049. LCCN:2001-032823.

Audience: **g,l,u,f.** *Choice, 2003, 2002.*

Center for Russian, East European and Asian Studies, University of Texas at Austin **DK510.23**
REENIC: Russian and East European Network Information Center.
http://reenic.utexas.edu/reenic/index.html

Audience: **u,f.**

Korosenyi, Andras **JN2067.K6813 1999**
Government and Politics in Hungary. Trade Cloth. Central European University Press. Herndon, VA. 1999. xxi, 330p. ISBN:963-9116-61-0, ISBN13: 978-963-9116-61-0. Dewey:320.9439. LCCN:00-060344.

Audience: **g,l,u.** *Choice, 2001.*

Korosenyi, Andras **JN2067.K6813 1999**
Government and Politics in Hungary. Trade Cloth. Central European University Press. Herndon, VA. 2000. 330p. ISBN:963-9116-76-9, ISBN13: 978-963-9116-76-4. Dewey:320.9439. LCCN:00-060344.

Audience: **l,u.** *Choice, 2001.*

O'Neil, Patrick **JN2191.S92O646 1998**
Revolution from Within: The Hungarian Socialist Workers' Party and the Collapse of Communism. Trade Cloth. Edward Elgar Publishing, Inc. Northampton, MA. 1998. 288p. Studies of Communism in Transition ISBN:1-85898-766-0, ISBN13: 978-1-85898-766-8. Dewey:324.2439/074/09048. LCCN:97-035438.

Audience: **l,u,f.** *Choice, 1998.*

Pelinka, Anton **JN2026.P44 1998**
Austria: Out of the Shadow of the Past. Trade Paper. Westview Press. Boulder, CO. 1998. 272p. Nations of the Modern World Ser. ISBN:0-8133-2918-3, ISBN13: 978-0-8133-2918-5. Dewey:306.2/09436. LCCN:98-022740.

Audience: **l,u,f.** *Choice, 1999.*

Pelinka, Anton & Plasser, Fritz (Editors) **JN2030.A97 1989**
The Austrian Party System. Paper Text. Westview Press. Boulder, CO. 1989. 458p. ISBN:0-8133-7755-2, ISBN13: 978-0-8133-7755-1. Dewey:324.2436. LCCN:89-032835.

Audience: **l,u,f.** *Choice, 1990.*

Strong, George V. **JN2012.3.S85 1998**
Seedtime for Fascism: The Disintegration of Austrian Political Culture, 1867-1918. Cloth Text. M. E. Sharpe Inc. Armonk, NY. 1998. 224p. ISBN:0-7656-0189-3, ISBN13: 978-0-7656-0189-6. Dewey:306.2/09436/09034. LCCN:97-030245.

Audience: **l,u,f.** *Choice, 1998.*

Sully, Melanie A. **JN2031.F73 S85 1997**
The Haider Phenomenon. Trade Cloth. Eastern European Monographs. Bradenton, FL. 1997. 225p. ISBN:0-88033-381-2, ISBN13: 978-0-88033-381-8. Dewey:943.6053092. LCCN:97-061667.

Audience: **u,f.** *Choice, 1998.*

Tökés, Rudolf L. **JN2066 .T58 1996**
Hungary's Negotiated Revolution: Economic Reform, Social Change and Political Succession. Trade Cloth. Cambridge University Press. New York, NY. 1996. 571p. Cambridge Russian, Soviet and Post-Soviet Studies, No. 101 ISBN:0-521-57044-1, ISBN13: 978-0-521-57044-2. Dewey:943.9/053. LCCN:95-048155.

Audience: **l,u,f.** *Choice, 1997.*

Wodak, Ruth & Pelinka, Anton (Editors) **JN2031.F73H355 2001**
The Haider Phenomenon in Austria. Trade Cloth. Transaction Publishers. Somerset, NJ. 2001. xxvii, 264p. ISBN:0-7658-0116-7, ISBN13: 978-0-7658-0116-6. Dewey:324.2436/038. LCCN:2001-034722.

Audience: **l,u,f.** *Choice, 2003.*

Wodak, Ruth & Pelinka, Anton (Editors) **JN2031.F73**
The Haider Phenomenon in Austria. Trade Cloth. Transaction Publishers. Somerset, NJ. 2002. 264p. ISBN:0-7658-0117-5, ISBN13: 978-0-7658-0117-3. Dewey:324.2436/038. LCCN:2001-034722.

Audience: **l,u,f.** *Choice, 2003.*

Comparative Government > Europe > Czech Republic

Bugajski, Janusz **JN96.A979B84 2002**
Political Parties of Eastern Europe: A Guide to Politics in the Post-Communist Era. Trade Cloth. M. E. Sharpe Inc. Armonk, NY. 2003. 1118p. ISBN:1-56324-676-7, ISBN13: 978-1-56324-676-0. Dewey:320.947/09/049. LCCN:2001-032823.
Audience: **g,l,u,f.** *Choice, 2003, 2002.*

Center for Russian, **DK510.23**
East European and Asian Studies, University of Texas at Austin
☐ REENIC: Russian and East European Network Information Center.
http://reenic.utexas.edu/reenic/index.html
Audience: **u,f.**

Kopecky, Petr **JN2223.K668 2001**
Parliaments in the Czech and Slovak Republics: Party Competition and Parliamentary Institutionalization. Trade Cloth. Ashgate Publishing, Ltd. Aldershot, 2001. 262p. ISBN:0-7546-1644-4, ISBN13: 978-0-7546-1644-3. Dewey:328.4371. LCCN:2001-086239.
Audience: **u,f.**

Krejci, Oskar **JN2228.K659 1995**
History of Elections in Bohemia and Moravia. Trade Cloth. Eastern European Monographs. Bradenton, FL. 1995. 425p. ISBN:0-88033-330-8, ISBN13: 978-0-88033-330-6. Dewey:324.6. LCCN:95-061359.
Audience: **l,u,f.**

Okey, Robin **DJK50**
The Demise of Communist East Europe: 1989 in Context. Trade Paper. Oxford University Press, Inc. New York, NY. 2004. 240p. A Hodder Arnold Publication ISBN:0-340-74057-4, ISBN13: 978-0-340-74057-6. Dewey:947/.0009045. LCCN:2005-272438.
Audience: **g,l,u,f.** *Choice, 2005.*

Saxonberg, Steven **HX240.7.A6**
Fall: A Comparative Study of the End of Communism in Czechoslovakia, East Germany, Hungary and Poland. Cloth Text. Gordon & Breach Publishing Group. New York, NY. 2000. 452p. International Studies in Global Change ISBN:90-5823-097-X, ISBN13: 978-90-5823-097-3. Dewey:320.532.
Audience: **g,l,u,f.** *Choice, 2001.*

Comparative Government > Europe > Poland

Bugajski, Janusz **JN96.A979B84 2002**
Political Parties of Eastern Europe: A Guide to Politics in the Post-Communist Era. Trade Cloth. M. E. Sharpe Inc. Armonk, NY. 2003. 1118p. ISBN:1-56324-676-7, ISBN13: 978-1-56324-676-0. Dewey:320.947/09/049. LCCN:2001-032823.
Audience: **g,l,u,f.** *Choice, 2003, 2002.*

Center for Russian, **DK510.23**
East European and Asian Studies, University of Texas at Austin
☐ REENIC: Russian and East European Network Information Center.
http://reenic.utexas.edu/reenic/index.html
Audience: **u,f.**

Cordell, Karl & **JN6760.P654 2000**
Antoszewski, Andrzej (Editors)
Poland and the European Union. Paper over Boards. Routledge. New York, NY. 2000. 224p. Studies of Societies in Transition, Vol. 15 ISBN:0-415-23885-4, ISBN13: 978-0-415-23885-4. Dewey:327.43804. LCCN:00-020055.
Audience: **u,f.** *Choice, 2001.*

Kaminski, Bartlomiej **HX315.7.A6K36 1991**
The Collapse of State Socialism: The Case of Poland. Trade Paper. Princeton University Press. Princeton, NJ. 1991. 252p. ISBN:0-691-02335-2, ISBN13: 978-0-691-02335-9. Dewey:335.43/09438. LCCN:90-021737.
Audience: **l,u,f.** *Choice, 1992.*

Millard, F. **JN6766.M55 1999**
Polish Politics and Society. Paper over Boards. Routledge. New York, NY. 1999. 248p. Routledge Studies of Societies in Transition Ser. ISBN:0-415-15903-2, ISBN13: 978-0-415-15903-6. Dewey:306.2/09438/09049. LCCN:99-012745.
Audience: **l,u,f.** *Choice, 2000.*

Okey, Robin **DJK50**
The Demise of Communist East Europe: 1989 in Context. Trade Paper. Oxford University Press, Inc. New York, NY. 2004. 240p. A Hodder Arnold Publication ISBN:0-340-74057-4, ISBN13: 978-0-340-74057-6. Dewey:947/.0009045. LCCN:2005-272438.
Audience: **g,l,u,f.** *Choice, 2005.*

Paczkowski, Andrzej **DK4400**
The Spring Will Be Ours: Poland and the Poles from Occupation to Freedom. Jane Cave (Translator). Trade Cloth. Pennsylvania State University Press. University Park, PA. 2003. 600p. ISBN:0-271-02308-2, ISBN13: 978-0-271-02308-3. Dewey:943.805. LCCN:2003-022446.
Audience: **l,u,f.** *Choice, 2004.*

Sanford, George **JN6760**
Democratic Government in Poland: Constitutional Politics since 1989. Cloth over Boards. Palgrave Macmillan. New York, NY. 2002. 280p. ISBN:0-333-77475-2, ISBN13: 978-0-333-77475-5. Dewey:320.9438. LCCN:2002-020059.
Audience: **l,u,f.** *Choice, 2003.*

Saxonberg, Steven **HX240.7.A6**
Fall: A Comparative Study of the End of Communism in Czechoslovakia, East Germany, Hungary and Poland. Cloth Text. Gordon & Breach Publishing Group. New York, NY. 2000. 452p. International Studies in Global Change ISBN:90-5823-097-X, ISBN13: 978-90-5823-097-3. Dewey:320.532.
Audience: **g,l,u,f.** *Choice, 2001.*

Staar, Richard F. **JN6766.T73 1993**
(Editor)
Transition to Democracy in Poland. Trade Cloth. Palgrave Macmillan. New York, NY. 1993. 288p. ISBN:0-312-10000-0, ISBN13: 978-0-312-10000-1. Dewey:320.9/438/09049. LCCN:93-026014.
Audience: **l,u,f.** *Choice, 1994.*

Szczerbiak, Aleksander Andrzej **JN6769.A45S78 2001**
Poles Together?: The Emergence and Development of Political Parties in Post-Communist Poland. Trade Cloth. Central European University Press. Herndon, VA. 2002. 280p. ISBN:963-9241-23-7, ISBN13: 978-963-9241-23-7. Dewey:324.2438. LCCN:2001-056169.
Audience: **l,u,f.** *Choice, 2003.*

Taras, Ray & Castle, Marjorie **JN6766.C37 2002**
Democracy in Poland. Ed. 2. Trade Paper. Westview Press. Boulder, CO. 2002. 312p. ISBN:0-8133-3935-9, ISBN13: 978-0-8133-3935-1. Dewey:320.9438. LCCN:2002-002968.
Audience: **g,l,u,f.**

Tworzecki, Hubert **JN6769.A45T94 1996**
Parties and Politics in Post 1989 Poland. Trade Paper. Westview Press. Boulder, CO. 1996. 219p. ISBN:0-8133-8977-1, ISBN13: 978-0-8133-8977-6. Dewey:320.9/438. LCCN:96-016625.
Audience: **l,u,f.** *Choice, 1996.*

Comparative Government > Europe > Greece

Clogg, Richard **JN5185.A1.C56 1987**
Parties and Elections in Greece: The Search for Legitimacy. Cloth Text. Duke University Press. Durham, NC. 1988. xvii, 268p. ISBN:0-8223-0794-4, ISBN13: 978-0-8223-0794-5. Dewey:320.9495. LCCN:87-030376.
Audience: **g,u,f.** *Choice, 1988.*

Comparative Government > Europe > Soviet Union. Russia. Former Soviet Republics

Anderson, Richard, et al. **JN6531.P67 2001**
Postcommunism and the Theory of Democracy. M. Steven Fish, Stephen E. Hanson & Philip G. Roeder (Authors). Trade Paper. Princeton University Press. Princeton, NJ. 2001. 216p. ISBN:0-691-08917-5, ISBN13: 978-0-691-08917-1. Dewey:320.947. LCCN:2001-032107.
Audience: **g,l,u.** *Choice, 2002.*

Arter, David **JN6615.A58A78 1996**
Parties and Democracy in the Post-Soviet Republics: The Case of Estonia. Trade Cloth. Ashgate Publishing, Ltd. Aldershot, 1996. 302p. ISBN:1-85521-466-0, ISBN13: 978-1-85521-466-8. Dewey:320.9/4741. LCCN:96-014975.
Audience: **l,u,f.** *Choice, 1997.*

Balmaceda, Margarita Mercedes **JZ1624.O5 2000**
On the Edge: Ukrainian-Central European-Russian Security Triangle. E-Book. NetLibrary, Inc. Boulder, CO. 2000. ISBN:0-585-45768-9, ISBN13: 978-0-585-45768-0. Dewey:327/.0947.
Audience: **u,f.**

Betz, David **JN6693.5.C58B47 2004**
Civil-Military Relations in Russia and Eastern Europe. Paper over Boards. Routledge. New York, NY. 2004. 216p. RoutledgeCurzon Contemporary Russia and Eastern Europe Ser., Vol. 2 ISBN:0-415-32477-7, ISBN13: 978-0-415-32477-9. Dewey:322/.5/0947. LCCN:2003-020540.
Audience: **l,u,f.**

Birch, Sarah **JN6639.A5B57 2000**
Elections and Democratization in Ukraine. Cloth over Boards. Palgrave Macmillan. New York, NY. 2000. 226p. ISBN:0-312-23457-0, ISBN13: 978-0-312-23457-7. Dewey:324.9477086. LCCN:00-024439.
Audience: **l,u,f.** *Choice, 2001.*

Brown, Archie (Editor) **JN6695.C66 2001**
Contemporary Russian Politics: A Reader. Paper Text. Oxford University Press, Inc. New York, NY. 2001. 574p. ISBN:0-19-829999-0, ISBN13: 978-0-19-829999-8. Dewey:320.947. LCCN:2001-033919.
Audience: **l,u,f.**

Bugajski, Janusz **JN96.A979B84 2002**
Political Parties of Eastern Europe: A Guide to Politics in the Post-Communist Era. Trade Cloth. M. E. Sharpe Inc. Armonk, NY. 2003. 1118p. ISBN:1-56324-676-7, ISBN13: 978-1-56324-676-0. Dewey:320.947/09/049. LCCN:2001-032823.
Audience: **g,l,u,f.** *Choice, 2003, 2002.*

Center for Russian, East European and Asian Studies, University of Texas at Austin **DK510.23**
REENIC: Russian and East European Network Information Center.
http://reenic.utexas.edu/reenic/index.html
Audience: **u,f.**

D'Anieri, Paul, et al. **JN6635.D36 1999**
Politics and Society in Ukraine. Robert Kravchuk & Taras Kuzio (Authors). Trade Paper. Westview Press. Boulder, CO. 1999. 352p. Westview Series on the Post-Soviet Republics ISBN:0-8133-3538-8, ISBN13: 978-0-8133-3538-4. Dewey:306.2/09477/09049. LCCN:99-030503.
Audience: **g,l,u,f.** *Choice, 2000.*

Dawisha, Karen & Parrott, Bruce (Editor, Contribution by) **JN6690 .D46 1997**
Democratic Changes and Authoritarian Reactions in Russia, Ukraine, Belarus and Moldova. Trade Paper. Cambridge University Press. New York, NY. 1997. 404p. Democratization and Authoritarianism in Post-Communist Societies Ser., Vol. 3 ISBN:0-521-59732-3, ISBN13: 978-0-521-59732-6. Dewey:320.9/47. LCCN:96-046494.
Audience: **l,u,f.** *Choice, 1998.*

Fish, M. Steven **JN6695.F57 2005**
Democracy Derailed in Russia: The Failure of Open Politics. Robert H. Bates, Ellen Comisso, Peter Hall, Peter Lange, Joel Migdal & Helen Milner (Contribution by). Cloth Text. Cambridge University Press. New York, NY. 2005. 334p. Cambridge Studies in Comparative Politics ISBN:0-521-85361-3, ISBN13: 978-0-521-85361-3. Dewey:320.947. LCCN:2004-029359.
Audience: **l,u,f.** *Choice, 2006.*

Gill, Graeme J. & Pitty, Roderic **JN6598.K7.G5237 1997**
Power in the Party: The Organization of Power and Central-Republican Relations in the CPSU. Trade Cloth. Bow Historical Books. New Providence, NJ. 1997. 240p.

ISBN:0-333-66656-9, ISBN13: 978-0-333-66656-2.
Dewey:947/.085. LCCN:96-034345.
Audience: **l,u,f.**

Hough, Jerry F. **JN6500.H68 1997**
Democratization and Revolution in the U. S. S. R., 1985-91. Trade Paper. Brookings Institution Press. Washington, DC. 1997. 442p. ISBN:0-8157-3749-1, ISBN13: 978-0-8157-3749-0. Dewey:947.08. LCCN:96-044483.
Audience: **g,l,u,f.** *Choice, 1998.*

Kelley, Donald R. **JN6531.A33 2003**
After Communism: Perspectives on Democracy. Trade Paper. University of Arkansas Press. Fayetteville, AR. 2003. 300p. The Fulbright Institute Series on International Affairs, Vol. 1 ISBN:1-55728-746-5, ISBN13: 978-1-55728-746-5. Dewey:320.947. LCCN:2003-000202.
Audience: **l,u,f.** *Choice, 2004.*

Kolsto, Pal **JN6581.K65 2000**
Political Construction Sites: Nation Building in Russia and the Post-Soviet States. Trade Paper. Westview Press. Boulder, CO. 2000. 320p. ISBN:0-8133-3752-6, ISBN13: 978-0-8133-3752-4. Dewey:320.947. LCCN:99-059717.
Audience: **l,u.** *Choice, 2000.*

Kuzio, Taras **JN6630.K89 1997**
Ukraine under Kuchma: Political Reform, Economic Transformation, and Security in Independent Ukraine. Cloth over Boards. Palgrave Macmillan. New York, NY. 1997. 312p. Studies in Russian and East European History and Society ISBN:0-312-17625-2, ISBN13: 978-0-312-17625-9. Dewey:324.9477/086. LCCN:97-015184.
Audience: **l,u,f.** *Choice, 1998.*

Kuzio, Taras & D'Anieri, Paul J. (Editors) **JN6635**
Dilemmas of State-Led Nation Building in Ukraine. Trade Cloth. Greenwood Publishing Group, Inc. Portsmouth, NH. 2002. 224p. ISBN:0-275-97786-2, ISBN13: 978-0-275-97786-3. Dewey:320.9477. LCCN:2002-068612.
Audience: **l,u,f.** *Choice, 2003.*

Malia, Martin E. **HX311.5**
The Soviet Tragedy: A History of Socialism in Russia 1917-1991. Trade Paper. Simon & Schuster. New York, NY. 1995. 592p. ISBN:0-684-82313-6, ISBN13: 978-0-684-82313-3. Dewey:321.9/2/09470904. LCCN:93-050128.
Audience: **l,u,f.**

Mawdsley, Evan & White, Stephen **JN6549.E9M39 2000**
The Soviet Elite from Lenin to Gorbachev: The Central Committee and Its Members, 1917-1991. Trade Cloth. Oxford University Press, Inc. New York, NY. 2000. 348p. ISBN:0-19-829738-6, ISBN13: 978-0-19-829738-3. Dewey:324.247/075/0922. LCCN:99-053199.
Audience: **u,f.** *Choice, 2001.*

Millar, James R. (Editor) **JN6598.K7.C73 1992**
Cracks in the Monolith: Party Power in the Brezhnev Era. Cloth Text. M. E. Sharpe Inc. Armonk, NY. 1992. 256p. Contemporary Soviet - Post Soviet Politics Ser. ISBN:0-87332-885-X, ISBN13: 978-0-87332-885-2. Dewey:324.247/075. LCCN:92-009300.
Audience: **u,f.** *Choice, 1993.*

Moran, John P. **JN6693**
From Garrison State to Nation-State: Political Power and the Russian Military under Gorbachev and Yeltsin. Trade Cloth. Greenwood Publishing Group, Inc. Portsmouth, NH. 2002. 248p. ISBN:0-275-97217-8, ISBN13: 978-0-275-97217-2. Dewey:322/.5/094709048. LCCN:2001-057733.
Audience: **l,u,f.** *Choice, 2003.*

Orttung, Robert W. & Reddaway, Peter (Editors) **JN6693.5.S8D86 2003**
Dynamics of Russian Politics: Putin's Federal-Regional Reforms. Book, Other. Rowman & Littlefield Publishers, Inc. Lanham, MD. 2003. 304p. ISBN:0-7425-2643-7, ISBN13: 978-0-7425-2643-3. Dewey:320.447/049. LCCN:2003-011934.
Audience: **l,u,f.** *Choice, 2006, 2005.*

Ozinga, James R., et al. **JN6598.K7L627 1992**
The Rise and Fall of the Soviet Politburo. John Lowenhardt & Erik van Ree (Authors). Trade Cloth. Palgrave Macmillan. New York, NY. 1992. 264p. ISBN:0-312-04784-3, ISBN13: 978-0-312-04784-9. Dewey:324.247/075. LCCN:91-029623.
Audience: **l,u.** *Choice, 1992.*

Pascal, Elizabeth **JN6693**
Defining Russian Federalism. Trade Cloth. Greenwood Publishing Group, Inc. Portsmouth, NH. 2003. 224p. ISBN:0-275-97938-5, ISBN13: 978-0-275-97938-6. Dewey:320.447/049. LCCN:2003-042925.
Audience: **u,f.** *Choice, 2004.*

Petro, Nicolai N. **JN6581.P47 1995**
The Rebirth of Russian Democracy: An Interpretation of Political Culture. Trade Cloth. Harvard University Press. Cambridge, MA. 1998. 240p. ISBN:0-674-75001-2, ISBN13: 978-0-674-75001-2. Dewey:306.2/0947. LCCN:94-045431.
Audience: **l,u,f.** *Choice, 1996.*

Primakov, Yevgeny **DK510.763.P744 2004**
Russian Crossroads: Toward the New Millennium. Felix Rosenthal (Translator). Cloth over Boards. Yale University Press. Cumberland, RI. 2004. 352p. ISBN:0-300-09792-1, ISBN13: 978-0-300-09792-4. Dewey:947.086. LCCN:2004-008354.
Audience: **u,f.** *Choice, 2005.*

Reddaway, Peter **JN6693.5.S8D86 2003**
Dynamics of Russian Politics: Putin's Federal-Regional Reforms. Robert W. Orttung (Editor). Book, Other. Rowman & Littlefield Publishers, Inc. Lanham, MD. 2003. 304p. ISBN:0-7425-2644-5, ISBN13: 978-0-7425-2644-0. Dewey:320.447/049. LCCN:2003-011934.
Audience: **u,f.** *Choice, 2006, 2005.*

Remington, Thomas F. **JN6695.R46 2002**
Politics in Russia. Ed. 2. Paper Text. Longman Publishing Group. White Plains, NY. 2001. 304p. Comparative Politics Ser. ISBN:0-321-08557-4, ISBN13: 978-0-321-08557-3. Dewey:320.947. LCCN:00-140208.
Audience: **g,l,u,f.**

Remington, Thomas F. **JN6581.R46**
The Truth of Authority: Ideology and Communication in the Soviet Union. Trade Paper. Books on Demand. Ann Arbor, MI. 271p. Series in Russian and East European Studies, Vol. 9 ISBN:0-608-22074-4, ISBN13: 978-0-608-22074-1. Dewey:303.3/2/0947. LCCN:88-004745.
Audience: **l,u,f.** *Choice, 1989.*

Rose, Richard & Munro, Neil **JN6699.A5 R665 2002**
Elections Without Order: Russia's Challenge to Vladimir Putin. Cloth Text. Cambridge University Press. New York, NY. 2002. 272p. ISBN:0-521-81609-2, ISBN13: 978-0-521-81609-0. Dewey:324/.0947. LCCN:2002-022950.
Audience: **l,u,f.** *Choice, 2003.*

Rumer, Boris (Editor) **JQ1080.C44 2005**
Central Asia at the End of the Transition. Perfect, Paper over Boards. M. E. Sharpe Inc. Armonk, NY. 2005. 449p. ISBN:0-7656-1575-4, ISBN13: 978-0-7656-1575-6. Dewey:958.043. LCCN:2004-028503.
Audience: **l,u,f.** *Choice, 2006.*

Taylor, Brian D. **JN6520.C58T39 2002**
Politics and the Russian Army: Civil-Military Relations, 1689-2000. Trade Paper. Cambridge University Press. New York, NY. 2003. 374p. ISBN:0-521-01694-0, ISBN13: 978-0-521-01694-0. Dewey:322.50947. LCCN:2002-067688.
Audience: **g,l,u,f.**

Tismaneanu, Vladimir (Editor) **JN6581.P625 1995**
The International Politics of Eurasia: Political Culture and Civil Society in Russia and the New States of Eurasia. Cloth Text. M. E. Sharpe Inc. Armonk, NY. 1995. 400p. International Politics of Eurasia Ser. ISBN:1-56324-364-4, ISBN13: 978-1-56324-364-6. Dewey:306.2/0947/09049. LCCN:95-016492.
Audience: **l,u,f.** *Choice, 1996.*

Troxel, Tiffany A. **JN6697.8.T76 2002**
Parliamentary Power in Russia, 1994-2001: A New Era. Cloth over Boards. Palgrave Macmillan. New York, NY. 2003. 272p. St. Antony's Ser. ISBN:0-333-99283-0, ISBN13: 978-0-333-99283-8. Dewey:328.47. LCCN:2002-028746.
Audience: **l,u,f.** *Choice, 2003.*

Urban, Joan Barth & Solovei, Valerii D. **JN6699.A8K638 1997**
Russia's Communists at the Crossroads. Trade Paper. Westview Press. Boulder, CO. 1997. 224p. ISBN:0-8133-2931-0, ISBN13: 978-0-8133-2931-4. Dewey:324.247/075. LCCN:96-053174.
Audience: **l,u,f.** *Choice, 1997.*

White, Stephen, et al. **JN6649.A15P67 2004**
Postcommunist Belarus. Elena A. Korosteleva & John Lowenhardt (Authors). Book, Other. Rowman & Littlefield Publishers, Inc. Lanham, MD. 2004. 208p. ISBN:0-7425-3555-X, ISBN13: 978-0-7425-3555-8. Dewey:306.2/09478. LCCN:2004-021899.
Audience: **l,u,f.** *Choice, 2006.*

White, Stephen, et al. **JN6699.A5W48 1997**
How Russia Votes. Richard Rose & Ian McAllister (Authors). Paper Text. CQ Press. Washington, DC. 1997. 352p. Comparative Politics and the International Political Economy Ser. ISBN:1-56643-037-2, ISBN13: 978-1-56643-037-1. Dewey:324.6/0947/0904. LCCN:96-042449.
Audience: **g,l,u,f.**

Whitmore, Sarah **JN6637.W56 2004**
State Building in Ukraine: The Ukrainian Parliament, 1990-2003. Paper over Boards. Routledge. New York, NY. 2004. 240p. BASEES/RoutledgeCurzon Series on Russian and East European Studies, Vol. 10 ISBN:0-415-33195-1, ISBN13: 978-0-415-33195-1. Dewey:328.477. LCCN:2003-023941.
Audience: **l,u,f.**

Whittaker, Cynthia H. **JN6540.W475 2003**
Russian Monarchy: Eighteenth-Century Rulers and Writers in Political Dialogue. Trade Cloth. Northern Illinois University Press. DeKalb, IL. 2003. 320p. ISBN:0-87580-308-3, ISBN13: 978-0-87580-308-1. Dewey:320.947/09/033. LCCN:2002-040951.
Audience: **u,f.** *Choice, 2004.*

Willerton, John P. **JN6549.E9 W55 1992**
Patronage and Politics in the U. S. S. R. Trade Cloth. Cambridge University Press. New York, NY. 1991. 321p. Cambridge Russian, Soviet and Post-Soviet Studies, No. 82 ISBN:0-521-39288-8, ISBN13: 978-0-521-39288-4. Dewey:324.2/04. LCCN:91-000057.
Audience: **g,l,u,f.**

Wilson, Andrew **JN6581.W47 2005**
Virtual Politics: Faking Democracy in the Post-Soviet World. Cloth over Boards. Yale University Press. Cumberland, RI. 2005. 352p. ISBN:0-300-09545-7, ISBN13: 978-0-300-09545-6. Dewey:320.947. LCCN:2004-029345.
Audience: **l,u,f.** *Choice, 2005.*

Wyman, Matthew, et al. **JN6699.A5E438 1998**
Elections and Voters in Post-Communist Russia. Stephen White & Sarah Oates (Authors). Trade Cloth. Edward Elgar Publishing, Inc. Northampton, MA. 1998. 304p. Studies of Communism in Transition ISBN:1-85898-743-1, ISBN13: 978-1-85898-743-9. Dewey:324.947/086. LCCN:98-027696.
Audience: **l,u,f.** *Choice, 1999.*

Zielonka, Jan **JN6699.A15P6525 2005**
Political Culture and Post-Communism. Stephen Whitefield (Editor). Cloth over Boards. Palgrave Macmillan. New York, NY. 2005. 272p. St. Antony's Ser. ISBN:1-4039-4520-9, ISBN13: 978-1-4039-4520-4. Dewey:306.2/0947/09049. LCCN:2005-049048.
Audience: **l,u,f.**

Comparative Government > Europe > Soviet Union. Russia. Former Soviet Republics > Communist Party

Gill, Graeme J. & Pitty, Roderic **JN6598.K7.G5237 1997**
Power in the Party: The Organization of Power and Central-Republican Relations in the CPSU. Trade Cloth. Bow Historical Books. New Providence, NJ. 1997. 240p. ISBN:0-333-66656-9, ISBN13: 978-0-333-66656-2. Dewey:947/.085. LCCN:96-034345.
Audience: **l,u,f.**

Millar, James R. (Editor) **JN6598.K7.C73 1992**
Cracks in the Monolith: Party Power in the Brezhnev Era. Cloth Text. M. E. Sharpe Inc. Armonk, NY. 1992. 256p. Contemporary Soviet - Post Soviet Politics Ser. ISBN:0-87332-885-X, ISBN13: 978-0-87332-885-2. Dewey:324.247/075. LCCN:92-009300.
Audience: **u,f.** *Choice, 1993.*

Ozinga, James R., et al. **JN6598.K7L627 1992**
The Rise and Fall of the Soviet Politburo. John Lowenhardt & Erik van Ree (Authors). Trade Cloth. Palgrave Macmillan. New York, NY. 1992. 264p. ISBN:0-312-04784-3, ISBN13: 978-0-312-04784-9. Dewey:324.247/075. LCCN:91-029623.
Audience: **l,u.** *Choice, 1992.*

Urban, Joan Barth & Solovei, Valerii D. **JN6699.A8K638 1997**
Russia's Communists at the Crossroads. Trade Paper. Westview Press. Boulder, CO. 1997. 224p. ISBN:0-8133-2931-0, ISBN13: 978-0-8133-2931-4. Dewey:324.247/075. LCCN:96-053174.
Audience: **l,u,f.** *Choice, 1997.*

Comparative Government > Europe > Balkan States. Bulgaria. Romania. Yugoslavia

Biberaj, Elez **JN9689.A15**
Albania in Transition: The Rocky Road to Democracy. Trade Paper. Westview Press. Boulder, CO. 1999. 400p. Nations of the Modern World Ser., :Europe ISBN:0-8133-3688-0, ISBN13: 978-0-8133-3688-6. Dewey:320.94965/09/049.
Audience: **l,u,f.** *Choice, 1999.*

Bugajski, Janusz **JN96.A979B84 2002**
Political Parties of Eastern Europe: A Guide to Politics in the Post-Communist Era. Trade Cloth. M. E. Sharpe Inc. Armonk, NY. 2003. 1118p. ISBN:1-56324-676-7, ISBN13: 978-1-56324-676-0. Dewey:320.947/09/049. LCCN:2001-032823.
Audience: **g,l,u,f.** *Choice, 2003, 2002.*

Carey, Henry F. (Editor) **JN9630.R665 2003**
Romania since 1989: Politics, Economics, and Society. Book, Other. Lexington Books. Lanham, MD. 2004. 664p. ISBN:0-7391-0592-2, ISBN13: 978-0-7391-0592-4. Dewey:320.9498. LCCN:2003-014082.
Audience: **g,l,u,f.** *Choice, 2005.*

Carothers, Thomas **JN9636.C35 1996**
Assessing Democracy Assistance: The Case of Romania. Trade Paper. Carnegie Endowment for International Peace. Washington, DC. 1996. 144p. ISBN:0-87003-102-3, ISBN13: 978-0-87003-102-1. Dewey:320.9498/09/049. LCCN:95-050999.
Audience: **l,u,f.**

Center for Russian, East European and Asian Studies, University of Texas at Austin **DK510.23**
☐ REENIC: Russian and East European Network Information Center.
http://reenic.utexas.edu/reenic/index.html
Audience: **u,f.**

Gilberg, Trond **HX550.N3G53 1990**
Nationalism and Communism in Romania: The Rise and Fall of Ceausescu's Personal Dictatorship. Cloth Text. Westview Press. Boulder, CO. 1990. 289p. Special Studies on the Soviet Union and Eastern Europe ISBN:0-8133-7497-9, ISBN13: 978-0-8133-7497-0. Dewey:306.2/09498. LCCN:89-025056.
Audience: **u,f.** *Choice, 1991.*

Lavinia, Stan (Editor) **JN9620.R66 1997**
Romania in Transition. Trade Cloth. Ashgate Publishing, Ltd. Aldershot, 1997. 238p. ISBN:1-85521-886-0, ISBN13: 978-1-85521-886-4. Dewey:320.9/498. LCCN:96-036537.
Audience: **l,u,f.**

Malesevic, Sinisa **JN9670.M35 2002**
Ideology, Legitimacy and the New State: Yugoslavia, Serbia and Croatia. Paper over Boards. Taylor & Francis Group. Abingdon, 2002. 352p. Cass Series on Nationalism and Ethnicity, Vol. 4 ISBN:0-7146-5215-6, ISBN13: 978-0-7146-5215-3. Dewey:320.9497. LCCN:2002-020215.
Audience: **l,u,f.** *Choice, 2003.*

Melone, Albert P. **JN9607.M45 1998**
Creating Parliamentary Government: The Transition to Democracy in Bulgaria. Cloth Text. Ohio State University Press. Columbus, OH. 1998. 350p. Parliaments and Legislatures Ser. ISBN:0-8142-0769-3, ISBN13: 978-0-8142-0769-7. Dewey:320.9499/09/049. LCCN:98-016298.
Audience: **u,f.** *Choice, 1999.*

Melone, Albert P. **JN9607.M45 1998**
Creating Parliamentary Government: The Transition to Democracy in Bulgaria. Paper Text. Ohio State University Press. Columbus, OH. 1998. 350p. Parliaments and Legislatures Ser. ISBN:0-8142-0770-7, ISBN13: 978-0-8142-0770-3. Dewey:320.9499/09/049. LCCN:98-016298.
Audience: **l,u,f.** *Choice, 1999.*

Okey, Robin **DJK50**
The Demise of Communist East Europe: 1989 in Context. Trade Paper. Oxford University Press, Inc. New York, NY. 2004. 240p. A Hodder Arnold Publication ISBN:0-340-74057-4, ISBN13: 978-0-340-74057-6. Dewey:947/.0009045. LCCN:2005-272438.
Audience: **g,l,u,f.** *Choice, 2005.*

Saxonberg, Steven **HX240.7.A6**
Fall: A Comparative Study of the End of Communism in Czechoslovakia, East Germany, Hungary and Poland. Cloth Text. Gordon & Breach Publishing Group. New York, NY. 2000. 452p. International Studies in Global Change ISBN:90-5823-097-X, ISBN13: 978-90-5823-097-3. Dewey:320.532.
Audience: **g,l,u,f.** *Choice, 2001.*

Stokes, Gale **JN9659.A45S86 1990**
Politics As Development: The Emergence of Political Parties in Nineteenth-Century Serbia. Cloth Text. Duke University Press. Durham, NC. 1990. 416p. ISBN:0-8223-1016-3, ISBN13: 978-0-8223-1016-7. Dewey:324.2497/1/009. LCCN:89-039903.
Audience: **u,f.** *Choice, 1991.*

Tismaneanu, Vladimir **JN9639.A53 T57 2003**
Stalinism for All Seasons: A Political History of Romanian Communism. Trade Cloth. University of California Press. Berkeley, CA. 2003. 400p. Societies and Culture in East-Central Europe Ser., Vol. 11 ISBN:0-520-23747-1, ISBN13: 978-0-520-23747-6. Dewey:324.2498/075. LCCN:2002-154941.
Audience: **g,l,u,f.** *Choice, 2004.*

Comparative Government > Europe > Netherlands. Belgium

Fitzmaurice, John **JN6165.F57 1996**
The Politics of Belgium: A Unique Federalism. Trade Paper. Westview Press. Boulder, CO. 1996. 304p. ISBN:0-8133-2387-8,

ISBN13: 978-0-8133-2387-9. Dewey:320.4/493. LCCN:95-009001.
Audience: **g,l,u,f.**

Gladdish, Ken **JN5801.G53 1991**
Governing from the Center: Politics and Policy-Making in the Netherlands. Library Binding. Northern Illinois University Press. DeKalb, IL. 1991. 191p. ISBN:0-87580-162-5, ISBN13: 978-0-87580-162-9. Dewey:320.9492. LCCN:90-021363.
Audience: **l,u,f.** *Choice, 1991.*

Comparative Government > Europe > General

D843
Europa World Year Book 2005. Ed. 46. Paper over Boards. Routledge. New York, NY. 2005. 4900p. ISBN:1-85743-306-8, ISBN13: 978-1-85743-306-7. Dewey:909.82905.
Audience: **l,u,f.**

HA1107
☐ Europe in Figures—Eurostat Yearbook 2005. http://epp.eurostat.cec.eu.int/portal/page?_pageid=1334,49092079,1334_49092702&_dad=portal&_schema=PORTAL
Office for Official Publications of the European Union.
Audience: **g,l,u,f.**

Aberbach, Joel D., et al. **JF51**
Bureaucrats and Politicians in Western Democracies. Robert D. Putnam & Bert A. Rockman (Authors). Trade Cloth. Harvard University Press. Cambridge, MA. 1981. 322p. ISBN:0-674-08625-2, ISBN13: 978-0-674-08625-8. Dewey:351.007/2. LCCN:81-002899.
Audience: **l,u,f.**

Babuscio, Jack & Dunn, Richard M. **JN9.B3 1984**
European Political Facts, 1648-1789. Trade Cloth. Facts On File, Inc. New York, NY. 1984. 440p. ISBN:0-87196-992-0, ISBN13: 978-0-87196-992-7. Dewey:940.2/5. LCCN:83-025390.
Audience: **g,l,u.**

Bartolini, Stefano **D2009**
Restructuring Europe: Centre Formation, System Building, and Political Structuring between the Nation State and the European Union. Trade Cloth. Oxford University Press, Inc. New York, NY. 2005. 448p. ISBN:0-19-928643-4, ISBN13: 978-0-19-928643-0. Dewey:341.242/2. LCCN:2005-020572.
Audience: **u,f.**

Betz, Hans-Georg **JN94.A979B48 1994**
Radical Right-Wing Populism in Western Europe. Cloth over Boards. Palgrave Macmillan. New York, NY. 1994. 288p. ISBN:0-312-08390-4, ISBN13: 978-0-312-08390-8. Dewey:324.94/0559. LCCN:94-006696.
Audience: **g,l,u.**

Blondel, Jean & Thiebault, J. L. (Editors) **JN94.A63P76 1991**
Profession of Government Minister in Western Europe. Cloth Text. Palgrave Macmillan. New York, NY. 1991. 220p. ISBN:0-312-05373-8, ISBN13: 978-0-312-05373-4. Dewey:351.007/4/094. LCCN:90-008935.
Audience: **u,f.** *Choice, 1991.*

Carstairs, Andrew M. **JN94.A95**
Short History of Electoral Systems in Western Europe. Cloth Text. Routledge. New York, NY. 1980. 256p. ISBN:0-04-324006-2, ISBN13: 978-0-04-324006-9. Dewey:324.6/3/094. LCCN:80-040547.
Audience: **l,u.**

Cook, Chris & Paxton, John (Editors) **JN12.C643 2001**
European Political Facts of the 20th Century. Ed. 5. Cloth over Boards. Palgrave Macmillan. New York, NY. 2001. 493p. ISBN:0-333-79203-3, ISBN13: 978-0-333-79203-2. Dewey:320.94/02/02. LCCN:00-055686.
Audience: **l,u.** *Choice, 2001.*

Daalder, Hans & Mair, Peter (Editors) **JN94.A979**
Western European Party Systems: Continuity and Change. Trade Paper. SAGE Publications, Inc. Thousand Oaks, CA. 1985. 482p. ISBN:0-8039-9702-7, ISBN13: 978-0-8039-9702-8. Dewey:324.24.
Audience: **u,f.**

Flanz, Gisbert H. **KJC5144.W65 F52 1983**
Comparative Women's Rights and Political Participation in Europe. Trade Paper. Transnational Publishers, Inc. Ardsley, NY. 1983. 544p. Comparative Women's Rights Ser. ISBN:0-941320-02-2, ISBN13: 978-0-941320-02-3. Dewey:346.401/34 344.06134. LCCN:82-019317.
Audience: **u,f.**

Givens, Terri E. **JN45.G57 2005**
Voting Radical Right in Western Europe. Cloth Text. Cambridge University Press. New York, NY. 2005. 188p. ISBN:0-521-85134-3, ISBN13: 978-0-521-85134-3. Dewey:324.2/13/094. LCCN:2005-000122.
Audience: **u,f.** *Choice, 2006.*

Grzymala-Busse, Anna **JN96.A979 G79 2002**
Redeeming the Communist Past: The Regeneration of Communist Parties in East Central Europe. Robert H. Bates, Ellen Comisso, Peter Hall, Peter Lange, Joel Samuel Migdal & Helen V. Milner (Contribution by). Cloth Text. Cambridge University Press. New York, NY. 2002. 360p. Studies in Comparative Politics ISBN:0-521-80669-0, ISBN13: 978-0-521-80669-5. Dewey:324.21750943. LCCN:2001-025947.
Audience: **u,f.** *Choice, 2002.*

Ireland, Patrick **JV7590.I74 2004**
Becoming Europe: Immigration, Integration, and the Welfare State. Trade Cloth. University of Pittsburgh Press. Pittsburgh, PA. 2004. 288p. ISBN:0-8229-5845-7, ISBN13: 978-0-8229-5845-1. Dewey:325.4. LCCN:2004-011316.
Audience: **u,f.** *Choice, 2005.*

Kalyvas, Stathis N. **JN94.A979K35 1996**
The Rise of Christian Democracy in Europe. Book, Other. Cornell University Press. Ithaca, NY. 1996. 344p. The Wilder House Series in Politics, History, and Culture

ISBN:0-8014-3241-3, ISBN13: 978-0-8014-3241-5. Dewey:324.2/182/094. LCCN:96-005600.
Audience: **u,f.** *Choice, 1997.*

Mair, Peter (Editor) **JN94.A979W45 1990**
The West European Party System. Paper Text. Oxford University Press, Inc. New York, NY. 1990. 376p. Oxford Readings in Politics and Government Ser. ISBN:0-19-827583-8, ISBN13: 978-0-19-827583-1. Dewey:324.24. LCCN:89-027449.
Audience: **l,u.**

Merkl, Peter H. (Editor) **JN94.A979**
Western European Party Systems: Trends and Prospects. Trade Cloth. Simon & Schuster. New York, NY. 1980. xi, 676p. ISBN:0-02-920060-1, ISBN13: 978-0-02-920060-5. Dewey:324.24. LCCN:78-022783.
Audience: **l,u,f.**

Moch, Leslie Page **JV7590.M63 2003**
Moving Europeans: Migration in Western Europe since 1650. Ed. 2. Trade Paper. Indiana University Press. Bloomington, IN. 2003. 336p. Interdisciplinary Studies in History ISBN:0-253-21595-1, ISBN13: 978-0-253-21595-6. Dewey:304.8/094. LCCN:2002-151588.
Audience: **u,f.** *Choice, 2004, 1993.*

O'Neill, Michael **JA75.8.O64 1997**
Green Parties and Political Change in Contemporary Europe: New Politics, Old Predicaments. Trade Cloth. Ashgate Publishing, Ltd. Aldershot, 1997. 544p. ISBN:1-85521-786-4, ISBN13: 978-1-85521-786-7. Dewey:324.2/187/094. LCCN:97-025958.
Audience: **u,f.** *Choice, 1998.*

Tilly, Charles **JN94.A2T54 1990**
Coercion, Capital, and European States, AD 990-1990. Cloth Text. Blackwell Publishing, Inc. Malden, MA. 1990. 288p. ISBN:1-55786-067-X, ISBN13: 978-1-55786-067-5. Dewey:940. LCCN:89-017730.
Audience: **u,f.** *Choice, 1990.*

Tilly, Charles (Editor) **JN94.A2.F67**
The Formation of National States in Western Europe. Committee on Comparative Politics & Gabriel Ardant (Contribution by). Trade Cloth. Princeton University Press. Princeton, NJ. 1975. "xiv, 711"p. Studies in Political Development Ser., Vol. 8 ISBN:0-691-05219-0, ISBN13: 978-0-691-05219-9. Dewey:320.1/094. LCCN:74-020941.
Audience: **u,f.**

Comparative Government > Europe > European Union

Barbour, Philippe **D1060.E8685 2002**
The European Union Handbook. Ed. 2. Trade Cloth. Fitzroy Dearborn Publishers, Inc. Chicago, IL. 2002. 360p. Regional Handbooks of Economic Development Ser., :Prospects onto the 21st Century ISBN:1-57958-223-0, ISBN13: 978-1-57958-223-4. Dewey:341.242/2. LCCN:2002-727715.
Audience: **g,l,u.**

Barnes, Pamela M. & Barnes, Ian G. **GE190.E85B37 1999**
Environmental Policy in the European Union. Trade Cloth. Edward Elgar Publishing, Inc. Northampton, MA. 1999. 360p. ISBN:1-85898-339-8, ISBN13: 978-1-85898-339-4. Dewey:363.7/0094. LCCN:99-015403.
Audience: **l,u,f.** *Choice, 2000.*

Bellamy, Richard & Warleigh, Alex (Editors) **JN40**
Citizenship and Governance in the European Union. Trade Paper. Continuum International Publishing Group, Ltd. London, 2005. 256p. ISBN:0-8264-7919-7, ISBN13: 978-0-8264-7919-8. Dewey:323.6/094.
Audience: **u.** *Choice, 2002.*

Booker, Christopher & North, Richard **JN94.A2**
The Great Deception: The Secret History of the European Union. Trade Cloth. Continuum International Publishing Group, Ltd. London, 2003. 456p. ISBN:0-8264-7105-6, ISBN13: 978-0-8264-7105-5. Dewey:341.242/2. LCCN:2004-298035.
Audience: **u,f.** *Choice, 2004.*

Caporaso, James A. **JN30.C38 2000**
European Union: Dilemmas of Regional Integration. Trade Paper. Westview Press. Boulder, CO. 2000. 166p. Dilemmas in World Politics Ser. ISBN:0-8133-2583-8, ISBN13: 978-0-8133-2583-5. Dewey:341.242/2. LCCN:00-023372.
Audience: **g,l,u,f.** *Choice, 2001.*

Carkoglu, Ali & Rubin, Barry (Editors) **DR479.E85T87 2003**
Turkey and the European Union: Domestic Politics, Economic Integration and International Dynamics. Trade Paper. Taylor & Francis Group. Abingdon, 2003. 200p. ISBN:0-7146-8335-3, ISBN13: 978-0-7146-8335-5. Dewey:327.56104. LCCN:2002-154406.
Audience: **u,f.** *Choice, 2004.*

Cordell, Karl & Antoszewski, Andrzej (Editors) **JN6760.P654 2000**
Poland and the European Union. Paper over Boards. Routledge. New York, NY. 2000. 224p. Studies of Societies in Transition, Vol. 15 ISBN:0-415-23885-4, ISBN13: 978-0-415-23885-4. Dewey:327.43804. LCCN:00-020055.
Audience: **u,f.** *Choice, 2001.*

Diez, Thomas (Editor) **D1065.C94E87 2002**
The European Union and the Cyprus Conflict: Modern Conflict, Postmodern Union. Cloth over Boards. Manchester University Press. Manchester, 2002. 256p. Europe in Change Ser. ISBN:0-7190-6079-6, ISBN13: 978-0-7190-6079-3. Dewey:956.9304. LCCN:2002-020741.
Audience: **u,f.** *Choice, 2003.*

Dinan, Desmond (Editor) **JN30.E52 2000**
Encyclopedia of the European Union. Trade Paper. Lynne Rienner Publishers, Inc. Boulder, CO. 2000. viii, 566p. ISBN:1-55587-926-8, ISBN13: 978-1-55587-926-6. Dewey:341.2/422/03. LCCN:99-086544.
Audience: **l,u,f.** *Choice, 1999.*

Dinan, Desmond **HC241.2.D476 2005**
Ever Closer Union: An Introduction to European Integration. Ed. 3. Library Binding. Lynne Rienner Publishers, Inc. Boulder, CO. 2005. 625p. ISBN:1-58826-234-0, ISBN13: 978-1-58826-234-9. Dewey:337.1/42. LCCN:2005-010768.
Audience: **l,u,f.** *Choice, 1999.*

European Union **JN30**
☐ Europa: Gateway to the European Union.
http://europa.eu.int/index_en.htm
Audience: **g,l,u,f.**

European Union - Delegation of the European Commission to the United States **JN30**
☐ European Union—A Guide for Americans.
http://www.eurunion.org/infores/euguide/euguide.htm
European Union - Delegation of the European Commission to the United States.
Audience: **g,l,u,f.**

Greenwood, Justin **JN36.G74 1997**
Representing Interests in the European Union. Cloth over Boards. Palgrave Macmillan. New York, NY. 1997. 312p. European Union Ser. ISBN:0-312-17288-5, ISBN13: 978-0-312-17288-6. Dewey:322.4/3/094. LCCN:96-036917.
Audience: **u,f.** *Choice, 1998.*

Hayward, Jack Ernest Shalom (Editor), et al. **JN30.G6784 2003**
Governing Europe. Anand Menon & Jack Hayward (Editors). Trade Paper. Oxford University Press, Inc. New York, NY. 2003. 514p. ISBN:0-19-925015-4, ISBN13: 978-0-19-925015-8. Dewey:320.94. LCCN:2002-038197.
Audience: **u,f.** *Choice, 2004.*

Hix, Simon **JN30.H5 2005**
The Political System of the European Union. Ed. 2. Cloth over Boards. Palgrave Macmillan. New York, NY. 2005. 448p. The European Union Ser. ISBN:0-333-96181-1, ISBN13: 978-0-333-96181-0. Dewey:341.242/2. LCCN:2004-056955.
Audience: **g,l,u,f.** *Choice, 2000.*

Hix, Simon & Lord, Christopher **JN50.H59 1997**
Political Parties in the European Union. Trade Cloth. Palgrave Macmillan. New York, NY. 1997. 272p. European Union Ser. ISBN:0-312-17291-5, ISBN13: 978-0-312-17291-6. Dewey:324.2/4. LCCN:96-040842.
Audience: **u,f.**

Holland, Martin **JN15.H665 1994**
European Community Integration: From Community to Unity. Trade Paper. St. Martin's Press. Gordonville, VA. 1994. 258p. ISBN:1-85567-241-3, ISBN13: 978-1-85567-241-3. Dewey:341.2422. LCCN:94-238944.
Audience: **u,f.**

Jacoby, Wade **JN96.A58J33 2004**
The Enlargement of the European Union and NATO: Ordering from the Menu in Central Europe. Trade Cloth. Cambridge University Press. New York, NY. 2004. 300p. ISBN:0-521-83359-0, ISBN13: 978-0-521-83359-2. Dewey:341.242/2/0943. LCCN:2003-069727.
Audience: **g,l,u,f.** *Choice, 2005.*

Leach, Rodney **JN30**
Europe: A Concise Encyclopedia of the European Union from Aachen to Zollverein. Ed. 4. Trade Cloth. Profile Books Ltd. London, 2000. 288p. ISBN:1-86197-280-6, ISBN13: 978-1-86197-280-4. Dewey:341.2/422.
Audience: **l,u.**

Magone, Jose M. **HC240**
The Politics of Southern Europe: Integration into the European Union. Trade Cloth. Greenwood Publishing Group, Inc. Portsmouth, NH. 2003. 352p. ISBN:0-275-97787-0, ISBN13: 978-0-275-97787-0. Dewey:320.94. LCCN:2002-070955.
Audience: **u,f.** *Choice, 2004.*

Moussis, Nicholas **HC240.M754 1998**
Handbook of European Union. Ed. 5. Trade Paper. Euroconfidential. Genval, 1998. 360p. The Euroconfidential Collection ISBN:2-930119-20-9, ISBN13: 978-2-930119-20-5. Dewey:337.1/42. LCCN:99-461790.
Audience: **g,l,u,f.**

Newman, Michael **JN30.N49 1996**
Democracy, Sovereignty and the European Community. Trade Cloth. Palgrave Macmillan. New York, NY. 1996. 224p. ISBN:0-312-15860-2, ISBN13: 978-0-312-15860-6. Dewey:341.24/2. LCCN:95-026282.
Audience: **l,u.** *Choice, 1997.*

Phinnemore, David & McGowan, Lee **KJE6415**
A Dictionary of the European Union. Ed. 2. Paper over Boards. Taylor & Francis Group. Abingdon, 2004. 432p. ISBN:1-85743-260-6, ISBN13: 978-1-85743-260-2. Dewey:341.242/2/03. LCCN:2004-555399.
Audience: **g,l,u,f.**

Ramsay, Anne Fla (Editor) **HC240.E748 2000**
Eurojargon: A Dictionary of the European Union. Ed. 6. Cloth Text. Fitzroy Dearborn Publishers, Inc. Chicago, IL. 2000. 260p. ISBN:1-57958-274-5, ISBN13: 978-1-57958-274-6. Dewey:341.242/2/03. LCCN:2002-276081.
Audience: **g,l,u,f.** *Choice, 2001.*

Scully, Roger **JN36**
Becoming Europeans?: Attitudes, Behaviour, and Socialization in the European Parliament. Trade Cloth. Oxford University Press, Inc. New York, NY. 2005. 184p. ISBN:0-19-928432-6, ISBN13: 978-0-19-928432-0. Dewey:328.4. LCCN:2005-018739.
Audience: **u,f.**

Sedelmeier, Ulrich & Schimmelfennig, Frank (Editors) **JN30.P6533 2005**
The Politics of European Union Enlargement: Theoretical Approaches. Paper over Boards. Routledge. New York, NY. 2005. XIV, 306p. Routledge Advances in European Politics Ser., Vol. 30 ISBN:0-415-36129-X, ISBN13: 978-0-415-36129-3. Dewey:341.242/2. LCCN:2004-028648.
Audience: **u,f.**

Siedentop, Larry **JN30.S47 2001**
Democracy in Europe. Trade Paper. Columbia University Press. New York, NY. 2002. 272p. ISBN:0-231-12377-9, ISBN13: 978-0-231-12377-8. Dewey:320.94. LCCN:00-065576.
Audience: **g,l,u,f.** *Choice, 2001.*

Smith, Hazel **D1060.S58 2002**
European Union Foreign Policy: What It Is and What It Does. Trade Cloth. Pluto Press. London, 2002. 312p. ISBN:0-7453-1870-3, ISBN13: 978-0-7453-1870-7. Dewey:341.7/094. LCCN:2001-005310.
Audience: **u,f.** *Choice, 2003.*

Van Gerven, Walter **D2009.G475 2005**
The European Union: A Polity of States and Peoples. Trade Paper. Stanford University Press. Palo Alto, CA. 2005. xvii, 397p. ISBN:0-8047-5064-5, ISBN13: 978-0-8047-5064-6. Dewey:341.242/2. LCCN:2004-026677.
Audience: **u,f.** *Choice, 2006.*

Wurzel, Rudiger K. **GE190.G7W87 2002**
Environmental Policy-Making in Britain, Germany and the European Union: The Europeanisation of Air and Water Pollution Control. Cloth over Boards. Manchester University Press. Manchester, 2002. 304p. Issues in Environmental Politics Ser. ISBN:0-7190-5997-6, ISBN13: 978-0-7190-5997-1. Dewey:363.7/0094. LCCN:2002-072532.
Audience: **u,f.** *Choice, 2003.*

Comparative Government > Europe > United Kingdom

Bagehot, Walter **KD3934**
The English Constitution. Miles Taylor (Editor). Trade Paper. Oxford University Press, Inc. New York, NY. 2001. 254p. Oxford World's Classics Ser. ISBN:0-19-283975-6, ISBN13: 978-0-19-283975-6. Dewey:342.4/2/029.
Audience: **l,u,f.**

United Kingdom. Central Office of Information. **KD4882.Z9**
DirectGov.
http://www.direct.gov.uk
United Kingdom. Central Office of Information..
Audience: **g,l,u,f.**

United Kingdom. Office for National Statistics **HA1134**
National Statistics Online.
http://www.statistics.gov.uk
United Kingdom. Office for National Statistics.
Audience: **g,l,u,f.**

United Kingdom. Prime Minister. **DA687.D7 S35**
10 Downing Street.
http://www.number-10.gov.uk
United Kingdom. Prime Minister..
Audience: **g,l,u,f.**

Comparative Government > Europe > United Kingdom > By Period

Bartley, Paula **JN979.P28B37 2002**
Emmeline Pankhurst. Trade Paper. Routledge. New York, NY. 2003. 304p. Historical Biographies Ser. ISBN:0-415-20651-0, ISBN13: 978-0-415-20651-8. Dewey:324.6/23/092 B. LCCN:2002-068319.
Audience: **g,l,u.**

Cox, Gary W. **JN1120.C69 2005**
The Efficient Secret: The Cabinet and the Development of Political Parties in Victorian England. Randall Calvert & Thrainn Eggertsson (Contribution by). Trade Paper. Cambridge University Press. New York, NY. 2005. 201p. Political Economy of Institutions and Decisions Ser. ISBN:0-521-01901-X, ISBN13: 978-0-521-01901-9. Dewey:324.241/009. LCCN:2006-273368.
Audience: **u,f.** *Choice, 1987.*

Fishman, Nina **JN1129.C62F57 1995**
The British Communist Party and the Trade Unions, 1933-45. Trade Cloth. Ashgate Publishing, Ltd. Aldershot, 1995. 394p. ISBN:1-85928-116-8, ISBN13: 978-1-85928-116-1. Dewey:324.241/0975. LCCN:94-005837.
Audience: **u,f.** *Choice, 1995.*

Gullace, Nicoletta F. **JN906.G85 2004**
The Blood of Our Sons: Men, Women, and the Renegotiation of British Citizenship During the Great War. Trade Paper. Palgrave Macmillan. New York, NY. 2004. 308p. ISBN:1-4039-6710-5, ISBN13: 978-1-4039-6710-7. Dewey:940.3/1/0941.
Audience: **g,l,u,f.** *Choice, 2003.*

O'Gorman, Frank **JN951.O46 1989**
Voters, Patrons, and Parties: The Unreformed Electorate of Hanoverian England 1734-1832. Trade Cloth. Oxford University Press, Inc. New York, NY. 1989. 460p. ISBN:0-19-820056-0, ISBN13: 978-0-19-820056-7. Dewey:324.241/009. LCCN:88-030304.
Audience: **g,l,u,f.** *Choice, 1990.*

Pankhurst, E. Sylvia **JN979.P3 1970**
The Suffragette; the History of the Women's Militant Suffrage Movement, 1905-1910. Trade Cloth. Sourcebook Project, The. Glen Arm, MD. 1970. 517p. ISBN:0-87681-087-3, ISBN13: 978-0-87681-087-3. Dewey:324/.3/0942. LCCN:70-133998.
Audience: **g,l,u,f.**

Pankhurst, Emmeline **JN979**
My Own Story. Trade Cloth. Greenwood Publishing Group, Inc. Portsmouth, NH. 1985. 364p. ISBN:0-313-24926-1, ISBN13: 978-0-313-24926-6. Dewey:324.6/23/0924 B. LCCN:85-000952.
Audience: **g,l,u,f.**

Pugh, Martin **HQ1597.P84 2000**
Women and the Women's Movement in Britain 1914-1999. Cloth over Boards. Palgrave Macmillan. New York, NY. 2000. 401p. ISBN:0-312-23491-0, ISBN13: 978-0-312-23491-1. Dewey:305.4/2/0941. LCCN:00-026942.
Audience: **g,l,u,f.**

Saville, John **HD8396.S28 1987**
1848: The British State and the Chartist Movement. Trade Cloth. Cambridge University Press. New York, NY. 1987. 319p. ISBN:0-521-33341-5, ISBN13: 978-0-521-33341-2. Dewey:322.209. LCCN:86-029975.
Audience: **u,f.** *Choice, 1988.*

Searle, G. R. **JN1129.L45S43 1992**
The Liberal Party: Triumph and Disintegration, 1886-1929. Cloth Text. Palgrave Macmillan. New York, NY. 1992. 180p. British History in Perspective Ser. ISBN:0-312-08039-5,

ISBN13: 978-0-312-08039-6. Dewey:324.24106/09.
LCCN:92-002604.
Audience: **g,l,u,f.** *Choice, 1993.*

Comparative Government > Europe > United Kingdom > Commonwealth of Nations

Adamson, David **DA16.A44 1989**
The Last Empire: Britain and the Commonwealth. Cloth Text. I. B. Tauris & Company, Ltd. London, 1990. 224p.
ISBN:1-85043-152-3, ISBN13: 978-1-85043-152-7.
Dewey:909/.09712410828. LCCN:90-191643.
Audience: **g,l,u.** *Choice, 1990.*

Brown, Judith M. & Louis, Roger (Editors) **DA18**
The Oxford History of the British Empire: The Twentieth Century. Trade Cloth. Oxford University Press, Inc. New York, NY. 1999. 800p. Oxford History of the British Empire Ser., Vol. IV ISBN:0-19-820564-3, ISBN13: 978-0-19-820564-7.
Dewey:325.3/41/0904.
Audience: **u,f.** *Choice, 2000.*

Butler, David E. & Low, D. A. (Editors) **JF251.S87 1990**
Sovereigns and Surrogates: Constitutional Heads of State in the Commonwealth. Cloth Text. Palgrave Macmillan. New York, NY. 1991. 200p. ISBN:0-312-05710-5, ISBN13: 978-0-312-05710-7. Dewey:351.003/12. LCCN:90-009125.
Audience: **u,f.** *Choice, 1991.*

Canny, Nicholas (Editor) **DA16**
The Oxford History of the British Empire: The Origins of Empire: British Overseas Enterprise to the Close of the Seventeenth Century. Trade Cloth. Oxford University Press, Inc. New York, NY. 1998. 554p. Oxford History of the British Empire Ser. ISBN:0-19-820562-7, ISBN13: 978-0-19-820562-3.
Dewey:325.3/41.
Audience: **u,f.**

Commonwealth Secretariat **JN248**
☐ Commonwealth Secretariat.
http://www.thecommonwealth.org
Commonwealth Secretariat.
Audience: **g,l,u,f.**

Karatani, Rieko **KD4050.K37 2002**
Defining British Citizenship: Empire Commonwealth and Modern Britain. Irina Filatova & Valentin Gorodnov (Editors). Paper over Boards. Taylor & Francis Group. Abingdon, 2003. 256p. British Politics and Society Ser. ISBN:0-7146-5336-5, ISBN13: 978-0-7146-5336-5. Dewey:342.41/083.
LCCN:2002-026783.
Audience: **u,f.** *Choice, 2003.*

Marshall, P. J. & Low, Alaine (Editors) **DA16**
The Oxford History of the British Empire: The Eighteenth Century. Trade Cloth. Oxford University Press, Inc. New York, NY. 1998. 662p. Oxford History of the British Empire Ser. ISBN:0-19-820563-5, ISBN13: 978-0-19-820563-0.
Dewey:325.3/41.
Audience: **u,f.**

Martin, Chester **JL15 .M3 1975**
Empire and Commonwealth. Trade Cloth. Greenwood Publishing Group, Inc. Portsmouth, NH. 1975. 385p.
ISBN:0-8371-7626-3, ISBN13: 978-0-8371-7626-0.
Dewey:320.9/71. LCCN:74-009227.
Audience: **u,f.**

Porter, Andrew **JV1017**
The Oxford History of the British Empire: The Nineteenth Century. Trade Cloth. Oxford University Press, Inc. New York, NY. 1999. 796p. Oxford History of the British Empire Ser., Vol. 3 ISBN:0-19-820565-1, ISBN13: 978-0-19-820565-4.
Dewey:325.3/41/09034.
Audience: **u,f.**

Comparative Government > Europe > United Kingdom > Executive

Barberis, Peter **JN425.B37 1996**
The Elite of the Elite: Permanent Secretaries in the British Higher Civil Service. Trade Cloth. Ashgate Publishing, Ltd. Aldershot, 1996. 302p. ISBN:1-85521-479-2, ISBN13: 978-1-85521-479-8. Dewey:354.410023. LCCN:95-034896.
Audience: **u,f.** *Choice, 1996.*

Foley, Michael **DA591.B56**
The British Presidency: Tony Blair and the Politics of Public Leadership. Trade Paper. Manchester University Press. Manchester, 2001. 320p. ISBN:0-7190-5016-2, ISBN13: 978-0-7190-5016-9. Dewey:321.8/043/0941/09049.
Audience: **u,f.**

Riddell, Peter **DA589.7.R53 1990**
The Thatcher Decade: Britain in the 1980s. Cloth Text. Blackwell Publishing, Inc. Malden, MA. 1990. 224p.
ISBN:0-631-16274-7, ISBN13: 978-0-631-16274-2.
Dewey:941.085/8. LCCN:89-031770.
Audience: **u,f.** *Choice, 1990.*

Seldon, Anthony (Editor) **JN1129.L32 B58 2001**
The Blair Effect: The Blair Government, 1997-2001. Trade Paper. Little, Brown Book Group Ltd. London, 2002. 352p.
ISBN:0-316-85636-3, ISBN13: 978-0-316-85636-2.
Dewey:320.9/41/09049. LCCN:2001-409464.
Audience: **g,l,u,f.** *Choice, 2002.*

Seldon, Anthony & Kavanagh, Dennis (Editors) **DA592**
The Blair Effect, 2001-5: A Wasted Term? Cloth Text. Cambridge University Press. New York, NY. 2005. 496p.
ISBN:0-521-86142-X, ISBN13: 978-0-521-86142-7.
Dewey:320.94109051. LCCN:2006-295746.
Audience: **g,l,u,f.** *Choice, 2006.*

United Kingdom. Prime Minister. **DA687.D7 S35**
☐ 10 Downing Street.
http://www.number-10.gov.uk
United Kingdom. Prime Minister..
Audience: **g,l,u,f.**

Comparative Government > Europe > United Kingdom > Parliament

Crewe, Emma **JN621**
Lords of Parliament: Manners, Rituals and Politics. Cloth over Boards. Manchester University Press. Manchester, 2005. 288p. ISBN:0-7190-7206-9, ISBN13: 978-0-7190-7206-2. Dewey:328.41. LCCN:2006-272286.
Audience: **l,u,f.**

Radice, Lisanne **JN677.R33 1987**
Member of Parliament: The Job of a Backbencher. Cloth Text. Palgrave Macmillan. New York, NY. 1988. 300p. ISBN:0-312-00766-3, ISBN13: 978-0-312-00766-9. Dewey:328.41/0731. LCCN:87-004483.
Audience: **l,u,f.** *Choice, 1988.*

Riddell, Peter **JN550.R53 2000**
Parliament under Blair. Trade Paper. Politico's Publishing Ltd. Tunbridge Wells, 2000. 0p. ISBN:1-902301-60-9, ISBN13: 978-1-902301-60-0. Dewey:328.41. LCCN:2001-339058.
Audience: **u,f.** *Choice, 2001.*

Comparative Government > Europe > United Kingdom > Elections

Blackburn, Robert **JN961.B58 1995**
The Electoral System in Britain. Cloth Text. Palgrave Macmillan. New York, NY. 1995. xiv, 487p. ISBN:0-312-12391-4, ISBN13: 978-0-312-12391-8. Dewey:324.6/3/0941. LCCN:94-022533.
Audience: **l,u,f.** *Choice, 1996.*

Butler, David (Editor) **JN956**
The British General Elections, 1945-1992, Set. Cloth over Boards. Palgrave Macmillan. New York, NY. 1999. 5435p. ISBN:0-333-77863-4, ISBN13: 978-0-333-77863-0. Dewey:324.9/41/085.
Audience: **g,l,u,f.**

Butler, David & Stokes, Donald E. **JN956 .B87**
Political Change in Britain, 1963-1970. Trade Cloth. Inter-University Consortium for Political & Social Research. Ann Arbor, MI. 1972. ISBN:0-89138-055-8, ISBN13: 978-0-89138-055-9. Dewey:301.5/92/0941.
Audience: **u,f.**

Crewe, Ivor, et al. **JN956 .C74 1995**
The British Electorate, 1963-1992: A Compendium of Data from the British Election Studies. Ed. 2. Anthony Fox & Neil Day (Authors). Trade Cloth. Cambridge University Press. New York, NY. 1995. 511p. ISBN:0-521-49646-2, ISBN13: 978-0-521-49646-9. Dewey:324.9/41/085. LCCN:95-017547.
Audience: **u,f.** *Choice, 1996.*

Heath, Anthony **JN956.U53 1990**
Understanding Political Change: The British Voter 1964-1987. Trade Cloth. Elsevier Science & Technology Books. Saint Louis, MO. 1991. 335p. ISBN:0-08-037255-4, ISBN13: 978-0-08-037255-6. Dewey:324.941/085. LCCN:90-048282.
Audience: **u,f.**

O'Gorman, Frank **JN951.O46 1989**
Voters, Patrons, and Parties: The Unreformed Electorate of Hanoverian England 1734-1832. Trade Cloth. Oxford University Press, Inc. New York, NY. 1989. 460p. ISBN:0-19-820056-0, ISBN13: 978-0-19-820056-7. Dewey:324.241/009. LCCN:88-030304.
Audience: **g,l,u,f.** *Choice, 1990.*

Pankhurst, Emmeline **JN979**
My Own Story. Trade Cloth. Greenwood Publishing Group, Inc. Portsmouth, NH. 1985. 364p. ISBN:0-313-24926-1, ISBN13: 978-0-313-24926-6. Dewey:324.6/23/0924 B. LCCN:85-000952.
Audience: **g,l,u,f.**

Comparative Government > Europe > United Kingdom > Political Parties

Blake, Robert **JN1129.C7 B54 1985**
The Conservative Party from Peel to Thatcher. Fontana. 1985. ISBN:0-00-686003-6, ISBN13: 978-0-00-686003-7.
Audience: **l,u,f.**

Crewe, Ivor & King, Anthony **JN1129.S58C74 1995**
SDP: The Birth, Life, and Death of the Social Democratic Party. Trade Cloth. Oxford University Press, Inc. New York, NY. 1996. 636p. ISBN:0-19-828050-5, ISBN13: 978-0-19-828050-7. Dewey:324.241/0972. LCCN:96-124555.
Audience: **l,u.** *Choice, 1996.*

Cronin, James E. **JN1129.L32**
New Labour's Pasts: The Labour Party and Its Discontents. Cloth Text. Longman Publishing Group. White Plains, NY. 2004. 512p. ISBN:0-582-43827-6, ISBN13: 978-0-582-43827-9. Dewey:324.24107. LCCN:2003-070662.
Audience: **g,l,u,f.** *Choice, 2006.*

Fishman, Nina **JN1129.C62F57 1995**
The British Communist Party and the Trade Unions, 1933-45. Trade Cloth. Ashgate Publishing, Ltd. Aldershot, 1995. 394p. ISBN:1-85928-116-8, ISBN13: 978-1-85928-116-1. Dewey:324.241/0975. LCCN:94-005837.
Audience: **u,f.** *Choice, 1995.*

Messina, Anthony M. **DA125.A1M47 1989**
Race and Party Competition in Britain. Trade Cloth. Oxford University Press, Inc. New York, NY. 1989. 216p. ISBN:0-19-827534-X, ISBN13: 978-0-19-827534-3. Dewey:320.5/6/0941. LCCN:89-030047.
Audience: **u,f.** *Choice, 1990.*

Pelling, Henry & Reid, Alastair J. **JN1129**
A Short History of the Labour Party. Ed. 12. Trade Paper, Perfect. Palgrave Macmillan. New York, NY. 2005. 224p. ISBN:1-4039-9313-0, ISBN13: 978-1-4039-9313-7. Dewey:324.24107. LCCN:2005-046933.
Audience: **g,l.**

Rosen, Greg **PR1322**
Old Labour to New: The Dreams That Inspired, the Battles That Divided. Trade Cloth. Politico's Publishing Ltd. Tunbridge Wells, 2005. 400p. ISBN:1-84275-045-3, ISBN13: 978-1-84275-045-2. Dewey:324.2/4107.
Audience: **g,l,u,f.**

Searle, G. R. **JN1129.L45S43 1992**
The Liberal Party: Triumph and Disintegration, 1886-1929. Cloth Text. Palgrave Macmillan. New York, NY. 1992. 180p. British History in Perspective Ser. ISBN:0-312-08039-5, ISBN13: 978-0-312-08039-6. Dewey:324.24106/09. LCCN:92-002604.
Audience: **g,l,u,f.** *Choice, 1993.*

Seldon, Anthony & Ball, Stuart (Editors) **JN1129.C7C5745 1994**
Conservative Century: The Conservative Party since 1900. Trade Cloth. Oxford University Press, Inc. New York, NY. 1994. 896p. ISBN:0-19-820238-5, ISBN13: 978-0-19-820238-7. Dewey:324.24104/09/04. LCCN:94-001875.
Audience: **g,l,u,f.** *Choice, 1995.*

Shaw, Eric **JN1129.L32S457 1994**
The Labour Party since 1979: Crisis and Transformation. Paper over Boards. Routledge. New York, NY. 1994. 280p. ISBN:0-415-05614-4, ISBN13: 978-0-415-05614-4. Dewey:324.24107/09/048. LCCN:94-008635.
Audience: **l,u,f.**

Sherman, Alfred **DA589.7.S52 2005**
Paradoxes of Power: Reflections on the Thatcher Interlude. Trade Cloth. Imprint Academic. Exeter, 2005. 184p. ISBN:1-84540-014-3, ISBN13: 978-1-84540-014-9. Dewey:941.082. LCCN:2004-117682.
Audience: **g,l.**

Tivey, L. J. (Editor) **JN1121.P38 1989**
Party Ideology in Britian. Trade Cloth. Routledge. New York, NY. 1989. 240p. ISBN:0-415-02307-6, ISBN13: 978-0-415-02307-8. Dewey:324.2/3/0941. LCCN:89-031074.
Audience: **g,l,u,f.** *Choice, 1990.*

Comparative Government > Europe > United Kingdom > England

Greenleaf, W. H. **DA566**
The British Political Tradition, Set. Paper over Boards. Routledge. New York, NY. 2003. 2000p. ISBN:0-415-30299-4, ISBN13: 978-0-415-30299-9. Dewey:320.0941. LCCN:82-018871.
Audience: **u,f.**

Comparative Government > Europe > United Kingdom > Scotland

Brown, Alice, et al. **JN1213.B76 1996**
Politics and Society in Scotland. David McCrone & Lindsay Paterson (Authors). Cloth over Boards. Palgrave Macmillan. New York, NY. 1996. 272p. ISBN:0-312-16040-2, ISBN13: 978-0-312-16040-1. Dewey:320.9/411. LCCN:96-017552.
Audience: **l,u.** *Choice, 1996.*

Keating, Michael **JN1263**
The Government of Scotland: Public Policy Making after Devolution. Trade Paper, Perfect. Edinburgh University Press. Edinburgh, 2005. 256p. ISBN:0-7486-1822-8, ISBN13: 978-0-7486-1822-4. Dewey:328.411.
Audience: **g,l,u.**

Comparative Government > Europe > United Kingdom > Wales

Davies, Charlotte A. **DA722**
Welsh Nationalism in the Twentieth Century: The Ethnic Option and the Modern State. Book, Other. Greenwood Publishing Group, Inc. Portsmouth, NH. 1989. 153p. ISBN:0-275-93116-1, ISBN13: 978-0-275-93116-2. Dewey:942.9/0858. LCCN:88-028832.
Audience: **l,u,f.**

Comparative Government > Europe > United Kingdom > Northern Ireland

Bruce, Steve **DA990.U46B678 1992**
The Red Hand: Protestant Paramilitaries in Northern Ireland. Trade Cloth. Oxford University Press, Inc. New York, NY. 1992. 336p. ISBN:0-19-215961-5, ISBN13: 978-0-19-215961-8. Dewey:941.60824. LCCN:91-046663.
Audience: **u,f.** *Choice, 1993.*

Bruce, William, et al. **DA995.B5**
Belfast Politics. Henry Joy & John Bew (Authors). Trade Paper. University College Dublin Press. Dublin, 2005. 225p. ISBN:1-904558-21-6, ISBN13: 978-1-904558-21-7. Dewey:320.9/4167.
Audience: **g,l,u,f.**

McCarry, John & O'Leary, Brendan (Editors) **DA990.U46F87 1990**
The Future of Northern Ireland. Arend Lijphart (Foreword by). Trade Cloth. Oxford University Press, Inc. New York, NY. 1991. 400p. ISBN:0-19-827329-0, ISBN13: 978-0-19-827329-5. Dewey:941.50824. LCCN:90-036853.
Audience: **u,f.** *Choice, 1991.*

Mitchell, Paul & Wilford, Rick (Editors) **JN1572.A58P65 1999**
Politics in Northern Ireland. Trade Paper. Westview Press. Boulder, CO. 1998. 352p. Studies in Irish Politics ISBN:0-8133-3528-0, ISBN13: 978-0-8133-3528-5. Dewey:320.9416. LCCN:98-027569.
Audience: **l.** *Choice, 1999.*

Ruane, Joseph & Todd, Jennifer **DA990.U46 R83 1996**
The Dynamics of Conflict in Northern Ireland: Power, Conflict and Emancipation. Trade Paper. Cambridge University Press. New York, NY. 1996. 381p. ISBN:0-521-56879-X, ISBN13: 978-0-521-56879-1. Dewey:941.6/082. LCCN:95-052013.
Audience: **f.** *Choice, 1997.*

Comparative Government > Europe > Ireland

Chubb, Basil **JN1415**
The Government and Politics of Ireland. Ed. 3. Trade Paper. Addison-Wesley Longman, Inc. Boston, MA. 1995. 360p. ISBN:0-582-08624-8, ISBN13: 978-0-582-08624-1. Dewey:320.9417.
Audience: **l,u.**

Coakley, John & Gallagher, Michael (Editors) **JN1415.P65 2004**
Politics in the Republic of Ireland. Ed. 4. Paper over Boards. Routledge. New York, NY. 2004. 528p. ISBN:0-415-28066-4, ISBN13: 978-0-415-28066-2. Dewey:320.9417. LCCN:2004-006824.
Audience: **l,u.**

Sinnott, Richard **JN1541.S57 1995**
Irish Voters Decide: Voting Behaviour in the Republic of Ireland. Cloth Text. Manchester University Press. Manchester, 1995. 250p. ISBN:0-7190-4037-X, ISBN13: 978-0-7190-4037-5. Dewey:324.9417/082. LCCN:93-049042.
Audience: **u,f.**

Comparative Government > Europe > Spain. Portugal

Balcells, Albert **DP302.C67B3513 1995**
Catalan Nationalism: Past and Present. Geoffrey J. Walker (Editor, Introduction by). Cloth over Boards. Palgrave Macmillan. New York, NY. 1995. 248p. ISBN:0-312-12611-5, ISBN13: 978-0-312-12611-7. Dewey:320.5/4/0946. LCCN:94-047389.
Audience: **g,l,u.** *Choice, 1996.*

Gunther, Richard, et al. **JN8341.G86 2004**
Democracy in Modern Spain. Jose R. Montero & Joan Botella (Authors). Cloth over Boards. Yale University Press. Cumberland, RI. 2004. 496p. ISBN:0-300-10152-X, ISBN13: 978-0-300-10152-2. Dewey:320.946. LCCN:2003-067231.
Audience: **u,f.** *Choice, 2005.*

Gunther, Richard, et al. **JN8203**
Spain after Franco: The Making of a Competitive Party System. Giacomo Sani & Goldie Shabad (Authors). Trade Cloth. University of California Press. Berkeley, CA. 1985. 416p. ISBN:0-520-06384-8, ISBN13: 978-0-520-06384-6. Dewey:320.946. LCCN:84-016172.
Audience: **u,f.**

Heywood, Paul **JN8111.H49 1995**
The Government and Politics of Spain. Trade Cloth. Palgrave Macmillan. New York, NY. 1995. 344p. ISBN:0-312-15796-7, ISBN13: 978-0-312-15796-8. Dewey:320.446. LCCN:95-024441.
Audience: **l,u.** *Choice, 1996.*

Maxwell, Kenneth **DP681 .M39 1995**
The Making of Portuguese Democracy. Trade Paper. Cambridge University Press. New York, NY. 1997. 264p. ISBN:0-521-58596-1, ISBN13: 978-0-521-58596-5. Dewey:946.9/044.
Audience: **g,l,u,f.**

McDonough, Peter, et al. **JN8210.M39 1998**
The Cultural Dynamics of Democratization in Spain. Samuel H. Barnes & Antonio L. Pina (Authors). Book, Other. Cornell University Press. Ithaca, NY. 1998. 288p. ISBN:0-8014-3516-1, ISBN13: 978-0-8014-3516-4. Dewey:306.2/0946/09048. LCCN:98-015273.
Audience: **u,f.** *Choice, 1999.*

Newton, Michael T. **JN8210 .N48 1997**
Institutions of Modern Spain: A Political and Economic Guide. Ed. 2. Peter J. Donaghy (As told to). Cloth Text. Cambridge University Press. New York, NY. 1997. 407p. ISBN:0-521-57348-3, ISBN13: 978-0-521-57348-1. Dewey:306.2/0946. LCCN:96-002353.
Audience: **l,u.** *Choice, 1997.*

Payne, Stanley G. **DP270.P365 2000**
The Franco Regime, 1936-1975. Trade Paper. Sterling Publishing Co., Inc. New York, NY. 2000. 704p. Phoenix Press Ser. ISBN:1-84212-046-8, ISBN13: 978-1-84212-046-0. Dewey:946.081. LCCN:00-690729.
Audience: **g,u,f.** *Choice, 1988.*

Sullivan, J. L. **DP302.B48**
ETA and Basque Nationalism: The Fight for Euskadi, 1890-1986. Library Binding. Routledge. New York, NY. 1988. 256p. ISBN:0-415-00366-0, ISBN13: 978-0-415-00366-7. Dewey:322.4/2/09466. LCCN:88-004405.
Audience: **u,f.** *Choice, 1988.*

Comparative Government > Europe > France

Brubaker, Rogers **JN2919.B78 1992**
Citizenship and Nationhood in France and Germany. Trade Paper. Harvard University Press. Cambridge, MA. 1998. 288p. ISBN:0-674-13178-9, ISBN13: 978-0-674-13178-1. Dewey:323.6/0943. LCCN:91-042897.
Audience: **g,l,u,f.** *Choice, 1993.*

Bukovansky, Mlada **JC327.B764 2002**
Legitimacy and Power Politics: The American and French Revolutions in International Political Culture. Trade Cloth. Princeton University Press. Princeton, NJ. 2002. 272p. Princeton Studies in International History and Politics ISBN:0-691-07434-8, ISBN13: 978-0-691-07434-4. Dewey:306.2/0944/09033. LCCN:2001-055407.
Audience: **l,u,f.** *Choice, 2003.*

Crook, Malcolm **JN2959 .C76 1996**
Elections in the French Revolution: An Apprenticeship in Democracy, 1789-1799. Trade Cloth. Cambridge University Press. New York, NY. 1996. 235p. ISBN:0-521-45191-4, ISBN13: 978-0-521-45191-8. Dewey:324.6/0944. LCCN:95-017894.
Audience: **u,f.** *Choice, 1997.*

Ehrmann, Henry Walter & Schain, Martin A. **JN2594.2**
Politics in France. Ed. 5. Trade Paper. Addison-Wesley Educational Publishers, Inc. Boston, MA. 1997. 446p. ISBN:0-673-52112-5, ISBN13: 978-0-673-52112-5. Dewey:320.944.
Audience: **l,u.**

Kolodziej, Edward A. **HD9743.F82K64 1987**
Making and Marketing Arms. Cloth Text. Princeton University Press. Princeton, NJ. 1987. 480p. ISBN:0-691-07734-7, ISBN13: 978-0-691-07734-5. Dewey:338.4/76234/0944. LCCN:86-030567.
Audience: **u,f.** *Choice, 1988.*

Lebovics, Herman **JN2610.R4L42 2004**
Bringing the Empire Back Home: France in the Global Age. Trade Cloth. Duke University Press. Durham, NC. 2004. 240p. Radical Perspectives Ser. ISBN:0-8223-3260-4, ISBN13: 978-0-8223-3260-2. Dewey:306/.0944. LCCN:2003-025001.
Audience: **g,l,u,f.** *Choice, 2005.*

Lewis-Beck, Michael S. (Editor) **JN2594.2.H69 1999**
How France Votes. Paper Text. CQ Press. Washington, DC. 1999. xi, 292p. Comparative Politics and the International Political Economy Ser. ISBN:1-56643-069-0, ISBN13: 978-1-56643-069-2. Dewey:324.944. LCCN:98-058099.
Audience: **u,f.** *Choice, 2000.*

Ross, George M. (Editor), et al. **DC423**
The Mitterrand Experiment: Continuity and Change in Modern France. Stanley Hoffmann & Sylvia Malzacher (Editors). Trade Cloth. Oxford University Press, Inc. New York, NY. 1987. 384p. Europe and the International Order Ser. ISBN:0-19-520608-8, ISBN13: 978-0-19-520608-1. Dewey:944.083/8.
Audience: **u,f.** *Choice, 1988.*

Wright, Vincent **JN2594.W74 2001**
The Government and Politics of France. Ed. 4. Trade Paper. Routledge. New York, NY. 2001. 480p. ISBN:0-415-10770-9, ISBN13: 978-0-415-10770-9. Dewey:320.9/44/082. LCCN:00-065333.
Audience: **l,u.**

Comparative Government > Europe > France > Political Parties

Frears, John R. **JN2997.F73 1991**
Parties and Voters in France. Cloth Text. Palgrave Macmillan. New York, NY. 1991. 208p. ISBN:0-312-06028-9, ISBN13: 978-0-312-06028-2. Dewey:324.244. LCCN:90-022794.
Audience: **l,u.** *Choice, 1991.*

Guiat, Cyrille **JN3007.C6G83 2002**
Contrasting the French and Italian Communist Parties: Comrades and Culture. B. Bundgaard Rasmussen & Annette Rathje (Editors). Paper over Boards. Taylor & Francis Group. Abingdon, 2003. 210p. Cass Series on Totalitarian Movements and Political Religions ISBN:0-7146-5332-2, ISBN13: 978-0-7146-5332-7. Dewey:324.244/075. LCCN:2002-026784.
Audience: **u,f.** *Choice, 2004.*

Knapp, Andrew **JN2997.K58 2004**
Parties and the Party System in France: A Disconnected Democracy? Cloth over Boards. Palgrave Macmillan. New York, NY. 2004. 272p. French Politics, Society and Culture Ser. ISBN:0-333-92083-X, ISBN13: 978-0-333-92083-1. Dewey:324.244009045. LCCN:2003-063274.
Audience: **l,u,f.** *Choice, 2005.*

Comparative Government > Europe > Germany

Anderson, Eugene N. **JN4451 .A54**
The Social and Political Conflict in Prussia, 1858-1864. Paper Text. Textbook Publishers. Temecula, CA. 2003. x, 445p. ISBN:0-7581-3159-3, ISBN13: 978-0-7581-3159-1. Dewey:943/.07.
Audience: **l,u.**

Brubaker, Rogers **JN2919.B78 1992**
Citizenship and Nationhood in France and Germany. Trade Paper. Harvard University Press. Cambridge, MA. 1998. 288p. ISBN:0-674-13178-9, ISBN13: 978-0-674-13178-1. Dewey:323.6/0943. LCCN:91-042897.
Audience: **g,l,u,f.** *Choice, 1993.*

Cary, Noel D. **JN3933.C37 1996**
The Path to Christian Democracy: German Catholics and the Party System from Windthorst to Adenauer. Trade Cloth. Harvard University Press. Cambridge, MA. 1996. 368p. ISBN:0-674-65783-7, ISBN13: 978-0-674-65783-0. Dewey:324.218209430904. LCCN:95-040145.
Audience: **g,l,u,f.** *Choice, 1997.*

Childers, Thomas **83-5924**
The Nazi Voter: The Social Foundations of Fascism in Germany, 1919-1933. Trade Paper. University of North Carolina Press. Chapel Hill, NC. 1985. 383p. ISBN:0-8078-4147-1, ISBN13: 978-0-8078-4147-1. Dewey:324.943/085. LCCN:83-005924.
Audience: **g,l,u.**

Dennis, J. M. & Dennis, Mike **DD286.4.D46 2000**
Rise and Fall of the German Democratic Republic 1945-1990. Trade Paper. Longman Publishing. Boston, MA. 2000. 352p. ISBN:0-582-24562-1, ISBN13: 978-0-582-24562-4. Dewey:943/.1087. LCCN:00-045311.
Audience: **g,l,u.** *Choice, 2001.*

Jacoby, Wade **JN3971.A58**
Imitation and Politics: Redesigning Modern Germany. Trade Paper. Cornell University Press. Ithaca, NY. 2001. 240p. ISBN:0-8014-8769-2, ISBN13: 978-0-8014-8769-9. Dewey:306.2/0943/09049.
Audience: **u,f.**

Jarausch, Konrad H. **DD290.25.J37 1994**
The Rush to German Unity. Trade Cloth. Oxford University Press, Inc. New York, NY. 1994. 304p. ISBN:0-19-507275-8, ISBN13: 978-0-19-507275-4. Dewey:943.087. LCCN:93-000625.
Audience: **g,l,u,f.** *Choice, 1994.*

Kater, Michael H. **JN3946.N36.K37 1983**
The Nazi Party: A Social Profile of Members and Leaders, 1919-1945. Trade Cloth. Harvard University Press. Cambridge, MA. 1983. 432p. ISBN:0-674-60655-8, ISBN13: 978-0-674-60655-5. Dewey:324.243/038. LCCN:82-015814.
Audience: **g,l,u,f.**

Katzenstein, Peter J. **DD258.75.K37 1987**
Policy and Politics in West Germany: A Semisovereign State. Trade Paper. Temple University Press. Philadelphia, PA. 1987. 464p. Policy and Politics in Industrial States Ser. ISBN:0-87722-264-9, ISBN13: 978-0-87722-264-4. Dewey:320.943. LCCN:87-001909.
Audience: **u,f.** *Choice, 1987.*

Kvistad, Gregg **JN3770.K83 1999**
The Rise and Demise of German Statism: Loyalty and Political Membership. Trade Cloth. Berghahn Books, Inc. New York, NY. 1999. 256p. ISBN:1-57181-161-3, ISBN13: 978-1-57181-161-5. Dewey:324.2/43. LCCN:98-041129.
Audience: **u,f.** *Choice, 1999.*

Levy, Richard S. **JN3931**
The Downfall of the Anti-Semitic Political Parties in Imperial Germany. Trade Cloth. Yale University Press. Cumberland, RI.

1975. 336p. Historical Publications, No. 106
ISBN:0-300-01803-7, ISBN13: 978-0-300-01803-5.
Dewey:329.9/43. LCCN:74-020083.
Audience: **u,f.**

Mayer, Margit & Ely, John **JN3971.A98G723293**
The German Greens: Paradox Between Movement and Party. Trade Cloth. Temple University Press. Philadelphia, PA. 1998. 352p. ISBN:1-56639-515-1, ISBN13: 978-1-56639-515-1. Dewey:324.243/08. LCCN:96-003065.
Audience: **u,f.** *Choice, 1998.*

McAdams, A. James **DD257.25**
Germany Divided: From the Wall to Reunification. Trade Paper. Princeton University Press. Princeton, NJ. 1994. 286p. Princeton Studies in International History and Politics
ISBN:0-691-00108-1, ISBN13: 978-0-691-00108-1. Dewey:943.087. LCCN:92-015654.
Audience: **g,l,u,f.** *Choice, 1993.*

Olivo, Christiane **JN3971.A91O45 2001**
Creating a Democratic Civil Society in Eastern Germany: The Case of the Citizen Movements and Alliance 90. Cloth over Boards. Palgrave Macmillan. New York, NY. 2001. 304p. ISBN:0-312-23401-5, ISBN13: 978-0-312-23401-0. Dewey:300.943/1. LCCN:00-068198.
Audience: **g,l,u,f.** *Choice, 2002.*

Rogers, Daniel E. **JN3971.A979**
Politics after Hitler: The Western Allies and the German Party System. Trade Cloth. New York University Press. New York, NY. 1995. 224p. ISBN:0-8147-7164-5, ISBN13: 978-0-8147-7164-8. Dewey:324.243/009/045.
Audience: **u,f.** *Choice, 1996.*

Rohrschneider, Robert **JN3971.A91R655 1999**
Learning Democracy: Democratic and Economic Values in Unified Germany. Trade Cloth. Oxford University Press, Inc. New York, NY. 1999. 326p. Comparative Politics Ser. ISBN:0-19-829517-0, ISBN13: 978-0-19-829517-4. Dewey:320.943/09/049. LCCN:98-054769.
Audience: **u,f.** *Choice, 2000.*

Schorske, Carl E. **JN3971.A98**
German Social Democracy, 1905-1917: The Development of the Great Schism. Trade Paper. Harvard University Press. Cambridge, MA. 1983. 374p. Historical Studies, No. 65
ISBN:0-674-35125-8, ISBN13: 978-0-674-35125-7. Dewey:324.243072.
Audience: **u,f.**

Thomas, Nick **HM881**
Protest Movements in 1960s West Germany: A Social History of Dissent and Democracy. Cloth over Boards. Berg Publishers. Oxford, 2003. 288p. ISBN:1-85973-645-9, ISBN13: 978-1-85973-645-6. Dewey:303.48/4/0943. LCCN:2002-151465.
Audience: **g,l,u,f.** *Choice, 2003.*

Yoder, Jennifer A. **JN3971.A58Y63 1999**
From East Germans to Germans?: The New Postcommunist Elites. Trade Cloth. Duke University Press. Durham, NC. 1999. 320p. ISBN:0-8223-2351-6, ISBN13: 978-0-8223-2351-8. Dewey:943/.10879. LCCN:99-025935.
Audience: **u,f.** *Choice, 2000.*

Young, Brigitte **HQ1623**
Triumph of the Fatherland: German Unification and the Marginalization of Women. Trade Cloth. University of Michigan Press. Chicago, IL. 1999. 296p. Social History, Popular Culture, and Politics in Germany Ser. ISBN:0-472-10948-0, ISBN13: 978-0-472-10948-7. Dewey:305.42/0943. LCCN:98-040080.
Audience: **g,l,u,f.** *Choice, 2000.*

Comparative Government > Europe > Germany > Prussia

Anderson, Eugene N. **JN4451 .A54**
The Social and Political Conflict in Prussia, 1858-1864. Paper Text. Textbook Publishers. Temecula, CA. 2003. x, 445p. ISBN:0-7581-3159-3, ISBN13: 978-0-7581-3159-1. Dewey:943/.07.
Audience: **l,u.**

Comparative Government > Africa

☐ Africa South of the Sahara: African Politics and Government. http://www-sul.stanford.edu/depts/ssrg/africa/poli1.html
Audience: **g,l,u,f.**

Ahmad, Abdel Ghaffar Muhammad **DT31**
African Political Parties: Evolution, Institutionalisation and Governance. M. A. Mohamed Salih (Editor). Trade Cloth. Pluto Press. London, 2003. 392p. Ossrea Ser. ISBN:0-7453-2038-4, ISBN13: 978-0-7453-2038-0. Dewey:324.2096. LCCN:2003-270640.
Audience: **g,l,u,f.** *Choice, 2004.*

Apter, David E. **JQ2951.A99B843 1997**
The Political Kingdom in Uganda: A Study in Bureaucratic Nationalism. Ed. 3. Trade Paper. Irish Academic Press. Dublin, 1997. 592p. ISBN:0-7146-4234-7, ISBN13: 978-0-7146-4234-5. Dewey:306.2/09676. LCCN:97-013495.
Audience: **u,f.** *Choice, 1998.*

Apter, David E. & Rosberg, Carl G. **JQ1879.A15 P62 1994**
Political Development and the New Realism in Sub-Saharan Africa. Paper Text. University Press of Virginia. Charlottesville, VA. 1994. 339p. ISBN:0-8139-1480-9, ISBN13: 978-0-8139-1480-0. Dewey:306.20967. LCCN:93-002428.
Audience: **l,u,f.** *Choice, 1994.*

Bauer, Gretchen & Taylor, Scott D. **JQ2720.A58B38 2005**
Politics in Southern Africa: State and Society in Transition. Trade Cloth. Lynne Rienner Publishers, Inc. Boulder, CO. 2005. 400p. ISBN:1-58826-332-0, ISBN13: 978-1-58826-332-2. Dewey:320.968. LCCN:2004-024451.
Audience: **g,l,u,f.** *Choice, 2005.*

Bay, Edna G. **JQ3376.A91B39 1998**
Wives of the Leopard: Gender, Politics, and Culture in the Kingdom of Dahomey. Cloth Text. University Press of Virginia. Charlottesville, VA. 1998. 392p. ISBN:0-8139-1791-3, ISBN13: 978-0-8139-1791-7. Dewey:320/.082/096683. LCCN:97-045943.
Audience: **l,u,f.** *Choice, 2000.*

Bayart, Jean-Francois, et al. **JQ1875.A55C63513**
The Criminalization of the State in Africa. Stephen Ellis & Beatrice Hibou (Authors). Trade Cloth. Indiana University Press. Bloomington, IN. 1999. xviii, 126p. African Issues Ser. ISBN:0-253-33524-8, ISBN13: 978-0-253-33524-1. Dewey:364.1/323/096. LCCN:98-038856.
Audience: **u,f.**

Bayart, Jean-Francois **JQ1879.A15.B3**
The State in Africa: The Politics of the Belly. Chris Harrison, Elizabeth Harrison & Mary Harper (Translators). Cloth Text. Longman Publishing Group. White Plains, NY. 1992. 400p. ISBN:0-582-06422-8, ISBN13: 978-0-582-06422-5. Dewey:967.032. LCCN:92-028666.
Audience: **l,u,f.**

Bratton, Michael & Walle, Nicholas van de **JQ1879.A15 B73 1997**
Democratic Experiments in Africa: Regime Transitions in Comparative Perspective. Robert H. Bates, Ellen Comisso, Peter Hall, Peter Lange, Joel Migdal & Helen Milner (Contribution by). Trade Paper. Cambridge University Press. New York, NY. 1997. 329p. Studies in Comparative Politics ISBN:0-521-55612-0, ISBN13: 978-0-521-55612-5. Dewey:321.8/0967. LCCN:96-034865.
Audience: **l,u,f.** *Choice, 1998.*

Chabal, Patrick **JQ1872.C48 1994**
Power in Africa: An Essay in Political Interpretation. Trade Paper. Palgrave Macmillan. New York, NY. 1993. 321p. ISBN:0-312-09954-1, ISBN13: 978-0-312-09954-1. Dewey:320.96. LCCN:93-032786.
Audience: **u,f.** *Choice, 1992.*

Chabal, Patrick & Daloz, Jean-Pascal **JQ1875.C5 1999**
Africa Works: The Political Instrumentalisation of Disorder. Cloth Text. Indiana University Press. Bloomington, IN. 1999. xxi, 170p. African Issues Ser. ISBN:0-253-33525-6, ISBN13: 978-0-253-33525-8. Dewey:306.2/0967. LCCN:98-038855.
Audience: **u,f.** *Choice, 1999.*

Chikulo, Bornwell C. & Hope, Kempe Ronald (Editors) **JQ1875.A55C6364 1999**
Corruption and Development in Africa: Lessons from Country Case-Studies. Cloth over Boards. Palgrave Macmillan. New York, NY. 1999. 332p. ISBN:0-312-22387-0, ISBN13: 978-0-312-22387-8. Dewey:364.1/323/096. LCCN:99-018543.
Audience: **l,u.** *Choice, 2000.*

Columbia University Libraries
☐ African Studies: Human Rights and Governance in Africa. http://www.columbia.edu/cu/lweb/indiv/africa/cuvl/IORights.html
Audience: **g,l,u,f.**

Conteh-Morgan, Earl **JQ1879**
Democratization in Africa: The Theory and Dynamics of Political Transitions. Trade Cloth. Greenwood Publishing Group, Inc. Portsmouth, NH. 1997. 208p. ISBN:0-275-95780-2, ISBN13: 978-0-275-95780-3. Dewey:320.967/09/045. LCCN:96-033193.
Audience: **l,u.** *Choice, 1997.*

Englund, Harri (Editor) **JQ2941.A58D45 2002**
A Democracy of Chameleons: Politics and Culture in the New Malawi. Trade Paper. Nordic Africa Institute, The. Uppsala, 2002. 28p. ISBN:91-7106-499-0, ISBN13: 978-91-7106-499-8. Dewey:968.97042. LCCN:2003-502617.
Audience: **l,u,f.** *Choice, 2003.*

Ergas, Zaki (Editor) **JQ1872.A35 1987**
The African State in Transition. Cloth Text. Palgrave Macmillan. New York, NY. 1987. 320p. ISBN:0-312-00768-X, ISBN13: 978-0-312-00768-3. Dewey:320.96. LCCN:87-004727.
Audience: **l,u,f.**

Grant, J. Andrew & Soderbaum, Fredrik (Editors) **DT30.5**
The New Regionalism in Africa. Trade Cloth. Ashgate Publishing, Ltd. Aldershot, 2003. 266p. The International Political Economy of New Regionalisms Ser. ISBN:0-7546-3262-8, ISBN13: 978-0-7546-3262-7. Dewey:327.6. LCCN:2003-056050.
Audience: **l,u,f.**

Herbst, Jeffrey Ira **JQ1875.H47 2000**
States and Power in Africa: Comparative Lessons in Authority and Control. Trade Paper. Princeton University Press. Princeton, NJ. 2000. 290p. Princeton Studies in International History and Politics ISBN:0-691-01028-5, ISBN13: 978-0-691-01028-1. Dewey:303.3/096. LCCN:99-041736.
Audience: **l,u,f.** *Choice, 2000.*

Ihonvbere, Julius Omozuanvbo & Mbaku, John Mukum (Editors) **JQ1879**
Political Liberalization and Democratization in Africa: Lessons from Country Experiences. Trade Cloth. Greenwood Publishing Group, Inc. Portsmouth, NH. 2003. 400p. ISBN:0-275-97506-1, ISBN13: 978-0-275-97506-7. Dewey:320.967. LCCN:2003-052897.
Audience: **l,u,f.** *Choice, 2004.*

Joseph, Richard **JQ1879.A15S84 1999**
State, Conflict and Democracy in Africa. Trade Cloth. Lynne Rienner Publishers, Inc. Boulder, CO. 1999. 532p. ISBN:1-55587-533-5, ISBN13: 978-1-55587-533-6. Dewey:320.96/09/045. LCCN:98-006153.
Audience: **l,u,f.** *Choice, 1999.*

Joseph, Richard (Editor) **JQ1879.A15S84 1998**
State, Conflict, and Democracy in Africa. Library Binding. Lynne Rienner Publishers, Inc. Boulder, CO. 1998. 527p. ISBN:1-55587-799-0, ISBN13: 978-1-55587-799-6. Dewey:320.96/09/045. LCCN:98-006153.
Audience: **l,u,f.** *Choice, 1999.*

Kandeh, Jimmy D. **JQ2998.A38C584 2004**
Coups from Below: Armed Subalterns and State Power in West Africa. Cloth over Boards. Palgrave Macmillan. New York, NY. 2004. 272p. ISBN:1-4039-6715-6, ISBN13: 978-1-4039-6715-2. Dewey:332/.5/0966. LCCN:2004-049755.
Audience: **u,f.** *Choice, 2006.*

Kassem, Maye **JQ3881.K37 2004**
Egyptian Politics: The Dynamics of Authoritarian Rule. Paper Text. Lynne Rienner Publishers, Inc. Boulder, CO. 2004. 230p. ISBN:1-58826-247-2, ISBN13: 978-1-58826-247-9. Dewey:320.962. LCCN:2003-060297.
Audience: **l,u,f.** *Choice, 2005.*

King, Stephen J. **JQ3336.K56 2003**
Liberalization Against Democracy: The Local Politics of Economic Reform in Tunisia. Trade Cloth. Indiana University

Press. Bloomington, IN. 2003. 168p. Indiana Series in Middle East Studies ISBN:0-253-21583-8, ISBN13: 978-0-253-21583-3. Dewey:320.9611. LCCN:2002-014600.
Audience: **l,u,f.** *Choice, 2004.*

Le Vine, Victor T. **JQ3360.L425 2004**
Politics in Francophone Africa. Library Binding. Lynne Rienner Publishers, Inc. Boulder, CO. 2004. 425p. ISBN:1-58826-249-9, ISBN13: 978-1-58826-249-3. Dewey:320.966/0917/541. LCCN:2004-001833.
Audience: **g,l,u,f.** *Choice, 2005.*

Library of Congress **DK510**
☐ Library of Congress Country Studies: Africa. http://lcweb2.loc.gov/frd/cs/continent_africa.html
Audience: **g,l,u,f.**

Mbaku, John M. **JQ1870**
Institutions and Reform in Africa: The Public Choice Perspective. Trade Cloth. Greenwood Publishing Group, Inc. Portsmouth, NH. 1997. 304p. ISBN:0-275-95879-5, ISBN13: 978-0-275-95879-4. Dewey:320.96/09/045. LCCN:96-052631.
Audience: **u,f.**

Mbaku, John Mukum **JQ1875.A55C639 2000**
Bureaucratic and Political Corruption in Africa: The Public Choice Perspective. Trade Paper. Krieger Publishing Company. Melbourne, FL. 2000. xvii, 222p. ISBN:1-57524-120-X, ISBN13: 978-1-57524-120-3. Dewey:364.1/323/096. LCCN:99-032677.
Audience: **u,f.** *Choice, 2000.*

Mbaku, John Mukum **JQ1879**
& Ihonvbere, Julius Omozuanvbo (Editors)
The Transition to Democratic Governance in Africa: The Continuing Struggle. Trade Cloth. Greenwood Publishing Group, Inc. Portsmouth, NH. 2003. 472p. ISBN:0-275-97505-3, ISBN13: 978-0-275-97505-0. Dewey:320.96. LCCN:2002-190905.
Audience: **l,u,f.** *Choice, 2004.*

Mbaku, John M. & **JQ1875.M83 1995**
Ihonvbere, Julius O. (Editors)
Multiparty Democracy and Political Change: Constraints to Democratization in Africa. Trade Cloth. Ashgate Publishing, Ltd. Aldershot, 1998. 354p. ISBN:1-84014-379-7, ISBN13: 978-1-84014-379-9. Dewey:320.96/09/049. LCCN:97-077172.
Audience: **l,u,f.**

Monga, Celestin **JQ1879.A15M6613 1996**
The Anthropology of Anger: Civil Society and Democracy in Africa. Trade Cloth. Lynne Rienner Publishers, Inc. Boulder, CO. 1996. 219p. ISBN:1-55587-644-7, ISBN13: 978-1-55587-644-9. Dewey:347.73/5. LCCN:96-007588.
Audience: **l,u,f.** *Choice, 1997.*

Newbury, Catharine **JQ3567.A2N48 1988**
The Cohesion of Oppression: Clientship and Ethnicity in Rwanda, 1860-1960. Trade Cloth. Columbia University Press. New York, NY. 1989. 322p. ISBN:0-231-06256-7, ISBN13: 978-0-231-06256-5. Dewey:306/.2/0967571. LCCN:88-007349.
Audience: **l,u,f.** *Choice, 1989.*

Nohlen, Dieter (Editor), **JQ1879.A55E44 1999**
et al.
Elections in Africa: A Data Handbook. Berhard Thibaut & Michael Krennerich (Editors). Trade Cloth. Oxford University Press, Inc. New York, NY. 1999. 1,000p. ISBN:0-19-829645-2, ISBN13: 978-0-19-829645-4. Dewey:324.96/032/021. LCCN:99-015993.
Audience: **g,l,u,f.** *Choice, 2000.*

Ottaway, Marina **JQ3766**
(Editor)
The Political Economy of Ethiopia. Trade Cloth. Greenwood Publishing Group, Inc. Portsmouth, NH. 1990. 264p. SAIS Studies of Africa ISBN:0-275-93472-1, ISBN13: 978-0-275-93472-9. Dewey:320.963/09045. LCCN:89-077108.
Audience: **l,u,f.** *Choice, 1991.*

Pateman, Roy & Gros, **JQ3529.A15C36 2003**
Jean-Germain
Cameroon: Politics and Society in Critical Perspectives. Trade Paper. University Press of America, Inc. Lanham, MD. 2003. 262p. ISBN:0-7618-2591-6, ISBN13: 978-0-7618-2591-3. Dewey:320.96711. LCCN:2003-053321.
Audience: **l,u,f.** *Choice, 2004.*

Pausewang, Siegfried **JQ3766.E84 2003**
(Editor), et al.
Ethiopia since the DERG: A Decade of Democratic Pretension and Performance. Kjetil Tronvoll & Lovise Aalen (Editors). Trade Paper. Zed Books, Ltd. London, 2003. 272p. ISBN:1-84277-177-9, ISBN13: 978-1-84277-177-8. Dewey:320.963. LCCN:2002-031133.
Audience: **u,f.** *Choice, 2003.*

Pinkney, Robert **JQ3036.P56 1997**
Democracy and Dictatorship in Ghana and Tanzania. Ed. 1. Trade Cloth. Palgrave Macmillan. New York, NY. 1997. 208p. ISBN:0-312-17518-3, ISBN13: 978-0-312-17518-4. Dewey:321.8/09667. LCCN:97-009157.
Audience: **l,u,f.** *Choice, 1998.*

Posner, Daniel N. **JQ2831.P67 2004**
Institutions and Ethnic Politics in Africa. Randall Calvert & Thrainn Eggertsson (Contribution by). Trade Paper. Cambridge University Press. New York, NY. 2005. 358p. Political Economy of Institutions and Decisions Ser. ISBN:0-521-54179-4, ISBN13: 978-0-521-54179-4. Dewey:324/.089/0096894. LCCN:2004-045197.
Audience: **l,u,f.** *Choice, 2005.*

Posner, Daniel N. **JQ2831.P67 2004**
Institutions and Ethnic Politics in Africa. Randall Calvert & Thrainn Eggertsson (Contribution by). Cloth Text. Cambridge University Press. New York, NY. 2005. 358p. Political Economy of Institutions and Decisions Ser. ISBN:0-521-83398-1, ISBN13: 978-0-521-83398-1. Dewey:324/.089/0096894. LCCN:2004-045197.
Audience: **l,u,f.** *Choice, 2005.*

Reid, Richard J. **JQ2951.A99B847 2002**
Political Power in Pre-Colonial Buganda: Economy, Society and Welfare in the Nineteenth Century. Trade Paper. Ohio University Press. Athens, OH. 2003. 288p. Eastern African Studies ISBN:0-8214-1478-X, ISBN13: 978-0-8214-1478-1. Dewey:967.61. LCCN:2002-074343.
Audience: **u,f.** *Choice, 2003.*

Reno, William **JQ3121.A56C6 1995**
Corruption and State Politics in Sierra Leone. Cloth Text. Cambridge University Press. New York, NY. 1995. 242p. African Studies, 83 ISBN:0-521-47179-6, ISBN13: 978-0-521-47179-4. Dewey:320.9664/09/04. LCCN:94-012865.
Audience: **u,f.** *Choice, 1996.*

Rupesinghe, Kumar **JQ2951.A2C66 1989**
Conflict Resolution in Uganda. Trade Cloth. Ohio University Press. Athens, OH. 1989. 316p. ISBN:0-8214-0929-8, ISBN13: 978-0-8214-0929-9. Dewey:967.6/104. LCCN:89-030799.
Audience: **l,u,f.** *Choice, 1990.*

Salih, Mohamed Abdel Rahim M. **JQ1879.A15.S25 2001**
African Democracies and African Politics. Trade Paper. Pluto Press. London, 2001. 224p. Human Security in the Global Economy Ser. ISBN:0-7453-1724-3, ISBN13: 978-0-7453-1724-3. Dewey:320.96. LCCN:00-012647.
Audience: **g,l,u.** *Choice, 2002.*

Schaffer, Frederic C. **JQ3396.A91**
Democracy in Translation: Understanding Politics in an Unfamiliar Culture. Trade Paper. Cornell University Press. Ithaca, NY. 2000. 192p. Wilder House Series in Politics, History, and Culture Ser. ISBN:0-8014-8691-2, ISBN13: 978-0-8014-8691-3. Dewey:320.9663.
Audience: **l,u,f.**

Schatzberg, Michael G. **JQ1879.A15S32 2001**
[e] Political Legitimacy in Middle Africa: Father, Family, Food. E-Book. Indiana University Press. Bloomington, IN. 2001. xi, 292p. ISBN:0-253-33992-8, ISBN13: 978-0-253-33992-8. Dewey:306.2/0967. LCCN:2001-002060.
Audience: **l,u,f.** *Choice, 2002.*

Sisk, Timothy D. & Reynolds, Andrew **JQ1879.A5E43 1998**
Elections and Conflict Management in Africa. Book, Other. United States Institute of Peace Press (USIP Press). Washington, DC. 1998. 192p. ISBN:1-878379-79-8, ISBN13: 978-1-878379-79-5. Dewey:324.96. LCCN:98-016504.
Audience: **g,l,u,f.**

Takougang, Joseph & Krieger, Milton **JQ3525 .T35**
African State and Society in the 1990s: Cameroon's Political Crossroads. Trade Paper. Westview Press. Boulder, CO. 2000. 284p. ISBN:0-8133-3895-6, ISBN13: 978-0-8133-3895-8. Dewey:320.96711.
Audience: **l,u,f.**

Tettey, Wisdom (Editor), et al. **JQ3036.C75 2003**
Critical Perspectives in Politics and Socio-Economic Development in Ghana. Korbla P. Puplampu & Bruce J. Berman (Editors). Trade Paper. Brill Academic Publishers. Leiden, 2003. xxii, 458p. African Social Studies, Vol. 6 ISBN:90-04-13013-6, ISBN13: 978-90-04-13013-5. Dewey:320.9667. LCCN:2003-041896.
Audience: **l,u.** *Choice, 2004.*

Tordoff, William **JQ1875.T67 2002**
Government and Politics in Africa. Ed. 4. Trade Paper. Indiana University Press. Bloomington, IN. 2002. xviii, 326p. ISBN:0-253-21545-5, ISBN13: 978-0-253-21545-1. Dewey:320.96. LCCN:2002-068682.
Audience: **g,l.** B

Tulchin, Joseph S. & Selee, Andrew D. **JQ1875.A55D423 2004**
Decentralization, Democratic Governance, and Civil Society in Comparative Perspective: Africa, Asia, and Latin America. Philip Oxhorn (Editor). Trade Cloth. Johns Hopkins University Press. Baltimore, MD. 2004. 368p. ISBN:0-8018-7919-1, ISBN13: 978-0-8018-7919-7. Dewey:320.8. LCCN:2004-001537.
Audience: **l,u,f.** *Choice, 2005.*

Volpi, Frederic **JQ3231.V65 2002**
Islam and Democracy: The Failure of Dialogue in Algeria. Trade Paper. Pluto Press. London, 2002. 184p. ISBN:0-7453-1976-9, ISBN13: 978-0-7453-1976-6. Dewey:965.05/3. LCCN:2002-005040.
Audience: **u,f.** *Choice, 2003.*

Werbner, Richard P. & Ranger, Terence (Editors) **JQ1879.A15P69 1996**
Postcolonial Identities in Africa. Trade Paper. Zed Books, Ltd. London, 1996. 304p. Postcolonial Encounters Ser. ISBN:1-85649-416-0, ISBN13: 978-1-85649-416-8. Dewey:960.3/29. LCCN:96-008379.
Audience: **g,l,u,f.**

Zartman, I. William (Editor) **JQ1879.A15C647 1995**
Collapsed States: The Disintegration and Restoration of Legitimate Authority. Paper Text. Lynne Rienner Publishers, Inc. Boulder, CO. 1995. 330p. SAIS African Studies Library ISBN:1-55587-560-2, ISBN13: 978-1-55587-560-2. Dewey:320.96/09/045. LCCN:94-025734.
Audience: **l,u,f.** *Choice, 1995.*

Comparative Government > Africa > South Africa

Bauer, Gretchen & Taylor, Scott D. **JQ2720.A58B38 2005**
Politics in Southern Africa: State and Society in Transition. Trade Cloth. Lynne Rienner Publishers, Inc. Boulder, CO. 2005. 400p. ISBN:1-58826-332-0, ISBN13: 978-1-58826-332-2. Dewey:320.968. LCCN:2004-024451.
Audience: **g,l,u,f.** *Choice, 2005.*

Ellis, Stephen & Mabandla, Oyama **JQ1998.C64E45 1991**
Comrades Against Apartheid: The ANC and the South African Communist Party in Exile, 1966-1990. Trade Cloth. Indiana University Press. Bloomington, IN. 1992. 228p. ISBN:0-253-31838-6, ISBN13: 978-0-253-31838-1. Dewey:324.268/083. LCCN:91-018439.
Audience: **l,u,f.** *Choice, 1992.*

Holland, Heidi **JQ1998.A4H65 1990**
The Struggle: A History of the African National Congress. Trade Cloth. George Braziller Inc. New York, NY. 1970. 256p. ISBN:0-8076-1238-3, ISBN13: 978-0-8076-1238-5. Dewey:324.268/083. LCCN:89-070782.
Audience: **g,l,u,f.** *Choice, 1990.*

Human Rights Watch Staff **JC571.S63 1995**
Slaughter among Neighbors: Political Origins of Communal Violence. Trade Cloth. Yale University Press. Cumberland, RI. 1995. 192p. ISBN:0-300-06496-9, ISBN13: 978-0-300-06496-4. Dewey:323.1/1. LCCN:95-023132.
Audience: **l,u,f.** *Choice, 1996.*

Johnson, R. W. **JQ1994.L38 1996**
Launching Democracy in South Africa: The First Open Election, April 1994. Lawrence Schlemmer (Editor). Cloth over Boards.

Yale University Press. Cumberland, RI. 1996. 426p. ISBN:0-300-06391-1, ISBN13: 978-0-300-06391-2. Dewey:324.9/68/064. LCCN:95-006564.
Audience: **g,l,u,f.** *Choice, 1996.*

Jung, Courtney Elizabeth **JQ1981.J85 2000**
Then I Was Black: South African Political Identitites in Transition. Cloth over Boards. Yale University Press. Cumberland, RI. 2000. 304p. The Renaissance in Europe Ser., :A Cultural Enquiry ISBN:0-300-08013-1, ISBN13: 978-0-300-08013-1. Dewey:305.896/8. LCCN:99-059628.
Audience: **g,l,u,f.** *Choice, 2001.*

Meli, Francis **JQ1998.A4M45 1989**
South Africa Belongs to Us: A History of the ANC. Trade Paper. Indiana University Press. Bloomington, IN. 1989. 290p. ISBN:0-253-28591-7, ISBN13: 978-0-253-28591-1. Dewey:322.4/2/0968. LCCN:88-039946.
Audience: **g,l,u,f.** *Choice, 1990.*

Motala, Ziyad **JQ1872.M69 1994**
Constitutional Options for A Democratic South Africa: A Comparative Perspective. Trade Cloth. Howard University Press. Washington, DC. 1994. vii, 276p. ISBN:0-88258-187-2, ISBN13: 978-0-88258-187-3. Dewey:342.68. LCCN:94-006680.
Audience: **u,f.** *Choice, 1995.*

Schrire, Robert A. (Editor) **JQ1941.M35 1994**
Malan to de Klerk: Leadership in the Apartheid State. Trade Cloth. Palgrave Macmillan. New York, NY. 1994. viii, 312p. ISBN:0-312-10219-4, ISBN13: 978-0-312-10219-7. Dewey:354.6803/13. LCCN:93-025824.
Audience: **l,u,f.** *Choice, 1994.*

Sisk, Timothy D. **JQ1911.S57 1995**
Democratization in South Africa: The Elusive Social Contract. Trade Cloth. Princeton University Press. Princeton, NJ. 1994. 365p. ISBN:0-691-03622-5, ISBN13: 978-0-691-03622-9. Dewey:321.8/0968. LCCN:94-016987.
Audience: **l,u,f.** *Choice, 1995.*

Wood, Elisabeth Jean **JQ1981 .W66 2000**
Forging Democracy from Below: Insurgent Transitions in South Africa and el Salvador. Robert H. Bates, Ellen Comisso, Peter Hall, Peter Lange, Joel Migdal & Helen Milner (Contribution by). Trade Paper. Cambridge University Press. New York, NY. 2000. 272p. Studies in Comparative Politics ISBN:0-521-78887-0, ISBN13: 978-0-521-78887-8. Dewey:320.968. LCCN:00-023018.
Audience: **l,u,f.** *Choice, 2001.*

Comparative Government > Middle East

Alexander, Yonah **JQ1830.A98H373 2002**
Palestinian Religious Terrorism: Hamas and Islamic Jihad. Trade Paper. Transnational Publishers, Inc. Ardsley, NY. 2002. 426p. ISBN:1-57105-247-X, ISBN13: 978-1-57105-247-6. Dewey:322.4/2/095694. LCCN:2002-190388.
Audience: **l,u,f.** *Choice, 2003.*

Carapico, Sheila **JQ1842.A91 C37 1998**
Civil Society in the Yemen: The Political Economy of Activism in Modern Arabia. Julia A. Clancy-Smith, Israel Gershoni, Roger Owen, Yezid Sayigh, Charles Tripp & Judith E. Tucker (Contribution by). Trade Cloth. Cambridge University Press. New York, NY. 1998. 272p. Middle East Studies, No. 9 ISBN:0-521-59098-1, ISBN13: 978-0-521-59098-3. Dewey:306.2. LCCN:97-023259.
Audience: **l,u,f.** *Choice, 1998.*

Findley, Carter V. **JQ1806.Z1**
Bureaucratic Reform in the Ottoman Empire: The Sublime Porte, 1789-1922. Trade Cloth. Princeton University Press. Princeton, NJ. 1980. 496p. Near East Studies ISBN:0-691-05288-3, ISBN13: 978-0-691-05288-5. Dewey:354/.496. LCCN:79-083987.
Audience: **u,f.** B

Findley, Carter V. **JQ1806.Z1F56**
Ottoman Civil Officialdom: A Social History. Trade Paper. Books on Demand. Ann Arbor, MI. 423p. ISBN:0-608-06371-1, ISBN13: 978-0-608-06371-3. Dewey:354.561006. LCCN:88-017810.
Audience: **l,u,f.** *Choice, 1990.*

Ghanem, As'ad **JQ1830**
The Palestinian regime: a partial democracy. Sussex Academic. 2001. ISBN:1-902210-68-9, ISBN13: 978-1-902210-68-1.
Audience: **l,u,f.**

Hanf, Theodor **DS87.H33913 1993**
Co-Existence in Wartime Lebanon: Death of a State and Birth of a Nation. Cloth over Boards. I. B. Tauris & Company, Ltd. London, 1994. 512p. ISBN:1-85043-651-7, ISBN13: 978-1-85043-651-5. Dewey:956.92044. LCCN:94-168271.
Audience: **l,u,f.** *Choice, 1994.*

Heydemann, Steven (Editor) **JQ1850.A91N48 2004**
Networks of Privilege in the Middle East: The Politics of Economic Reform Revisited. Cloth over Boards. Palgrave Macmillan. New York, NY. 2004. 352p. ISBN:1-4039-6352-5, ISBN13: 978-1-4039-6352-9. Dewey:330.956. LCCN:2004-044257.
Audience: **u,f.** *Choice, 2005.*

Ismael, Tareq Y. **JQ1758.A58I86 2001**
Middle East Politics Today: Government and Civil Society. Trade Cloth. University Press of Florida. Gainesville, FL. 2001. 528p. ISBN:0-8130-2098-0, ISBN13: 978-0-8130-2098-3. Dewey:320.3/0956. LCCN:2001-034075.
Audience: **l,u,f.** *Choice, 2002.*

Kedourie, Elie **DS62.4.K4 2004**
The Chatham House Version: And Other Middle Eastern Studies. Ed. 3. Trade Paper. Ivan R. Dee Publisher. Blue Ridge Summit, PA. 2004. 512p. ISBN:1-56663-561-6, ISBN13: 978-1-56663-561-5. Dewey:956.04. LCCN:2003-064633.
Audience: **l,u,f.**

Kostiner, Joseph (Editor) **JQ1758.A58M53 2000**
Middle East Monarchies: The Challenge of Modernity. Library Binding. Lynne Rienner Publishers, Inc. Boulder, CO. 2000. vii, 344p. ISBN:1-55587-862-8, ISBN13: 978-1-55587-862-7. Dewey:321/.6/0956. LCCN:99-051384.
Audience: **l,u,f.** *Choice, 2001.*

Lewis, Bernard **DS44.L48 2004**
From Babel to Dragomans: Interpreting the Middle East. Trade Cloth. Oxford University Press, Inc. New York, NY. 2004. 456p.

ISBN:0-19-517336-8, ISBN13: 978-0-19-517336-9. Dewey:956. LCCN:2004-041542.

Audience: **l,u,f.**

Lust-Okar, Ellen **JQ1850.A792O65 2005**
Structuring Conflict in the Arab World: Incumbents, Opponents and Institutions. Trade Cloth. Cambridge University Press. New York, NY. 2005. 296p. ISBN:0-521-83818-5, ISBN13: 978-0-521-83818-4. Dewey:320.917/4927. LCCN:2004-051803.
Audience: **l,u,f.** *Choice, 2005.*

Nasr, Seyyed Vali Reza **JQ559.A54N37 1994**
The Vanguard of Islamic Revolution: The Jamaat-I Islami of Pakistan. Trade Paper. University of California Press. Berkeley, CA. 1994. xxii, 301p. Comparative Studies on Muslim Societies, No. 19 ISBN:0-520-08369-5, ISBN13: 978-0-520-08369-1. Dewey:324.25491/082. LCCN:93-005403.
Audience: **l,u,f.** *Choice, 1995.*

Ottaway, Marina & Carothers, Thomas (Editors) **JQ1758.A91U53 2005**
Uncharted Journey: Promoting Democracy in the Middle East. Trade Cloth. Carnegie Endowment for International Peace. Washington, DC. 2005. 256p. Global Policy Books ISBN:0-87003-212-7, ISBN13: 978-0-87003-212-7. Dewey:320.956. LCCN:2004-024551.
Audience: **g,l,u,f.** *Choice, 2006.*

Reich, Bernard **JQ1758**
Handbook of Political Science Research on the Middle East and North Africa. Cloth Text. Greenwood Publishing Group, Inc. Portsmouth, NH. 1998. 400p. ISBN:0-313-27372-3, ISBN13: 978-0-313-27372-8. Dewey:956/.007/2. LCCN:97-037549.
Audience: **g,l,u,f.** *Choice, 1998.*

Rubin, Barry **JQ1758.A91R83 2006**
The Long War for Freedom: The Arab Struggle for Democracy in the Middle East. Trade Cloth. John Wiley & Sons, Inc. Hoboken, NJ. 2005. 304p. ISBN:0-471-73901-4, ISBN13: 978-0-471-73901-2. Dewey:320.956. LCCN:2005-020231.
Audience: **g,l,u,f.** *Choice, 2006.*

Sadiki, Larbi **JQ1850.A91S235 2001**
The Search for Arab Democracy: Discourses and Counter-Discourses. Trade Cloth. Columbia University Press. New York, NY. 2004. 457p. ISBN:0-231-12580-1, ISBN13: 978-0-231-12580-2. Dewey:321.8/0917/4927. LCCN:2001-042519.
Audience: **l,u,f.** *Choice, 2005.*

The Center for Middle Eastern Studies at the University of Texas at Austin
MENIC: The Middle East Information Center - Countries & Regions.
http://menic.utexas.edu/menic/Countries_and_Regions/
Audience: **g,l,u,f.**

United Nations Development Programme Staff & Arab Fund for Economic and Social Development Staff **HN766.A8**
Arab Human Development Report 2004: Towards Freedom in the Arab World. Trade Paper. United Nations Publications. New York, NY. 2005. 247p. ISBN:92-1-126165-1, ISBN13: 978-92-1-126165-3. Dewey:306.09174927.
Audience: **g,l,u,f.**

Comparative Government > Middle East > Israel

Arian, Asher & Shamir, Michal (Editors) **JQ1825.P365E448 1995**
The Elections in Israel 1992. Cloth Text. State University of New York Press. Albany, NY. 1994. 326p. SUNY Series in Israeli Studies ISBN:0-7914-2175-9, ISBN13: 978-0-7914-2175-8. Dewey:324.95694/054. LCCN:93-049761.
Audience: **g,l,u,f.** *Choice, 1995.*

Drezon-Tepler, Marcia **JQ1825.P359D74 1990**
Interest Groups and Political Change in Israel. E-Book. NetLibrary, Inc. Boulder, CO. 1990. ISBN:0-585-06322-2, ISBN13: 978-0-585-06322-5. Dewey:322.4/3/095694.
Audience: **g,l,u,f.** *Choice, 1991.*

Horowitz, Dan & Lissak, Moshe **JQ1825.P3H68 1989**
Trouble in Utopia: The Overburdened Polity of Israel. Paper Text. State University of New York Press. Albany, NY. 1989. 357p. SUNY Series in Israeli Studies ISBN:0-7914-0114-6, ISBN13: 978-0-7914-0114-9. Dewey:306/.2/095694. LCCN:88-037557.
Audience: **l,u,f.** *Choice, 1990.*

Inbar, Efraim **JQ1825.P373A952 1991**
War and Peace in Israeli Politics: Labor Party Positions on National Security. Library Binding. Lynne Rienner Publishers, Inc. Boulder, CO. 1991. 180p. ISBN:1-55587-236-0, ISBN13: 978-1-55587-236-6. Dewey:324.25694/074. LCCN:90-043019.
Audience: **l,u,f.** *Choice, 1991.*

Lehman-Wilzig, Sam N. **JQ1825.P359L44 1990**
Stiff-Necked People, Bottle-Necked System: The Evolution and Roots of Israeli Public Protest, 1949-1986. Trade Cloth. Indiana University Press. Bloomington, IN. 1991. 224p. Jewish Political and Social Studies ISBN:0-253-33293-1, ISBN13: 978-0-253-33293-6. Dewey:323/.042/095694. LCCN:89-045858.
Audience: **l,u,f.** *Choice, 1991.*

Mahler, Gregory S. **JQ1825.P3A176 1990**
Israel after Begin. E-Book. NetLibrary, Inc. Boulder, CO. 1990. ISBN:0-585-05507-6, ISBN13: 978-0-585-05507-7. Dewey:956.9405/4.
Audience: **l,u,f.** *Choice, 1991.*

Medding, Peter Y. **JQ1825.P3A443 1990**
The Founding of Israeli Democracy, 1948-1967. Trade Cloth. Oxford University Press, Inc. New York, NY. 1990. 262p. ISBN:0-19-505648-5, ISBN13: 978-0-19-505648-8. Dewey:320.95694. LCCN:89-032699.
Audience: **g,l,u,f.** *Choice, 1991.*

Reich, Bernard & Kieval, Gershon R. (Editors) **JQ1825**
Israeli Politics in the 1990s: Key Domestic and Foreign Policy Factors. Trade Cloth. Greenwood Publishing Group, Inc. Portsmouth, NH. 1991. 208p. Contributions in Political Science Ser., No. 285 ISBN:0-313-27349-9, ISBN13: 978-0-313-27349-0. Dewey:956.9405/4. LCCN:91-003956.
Audience: **l,u,f.** *Choice, 1992.*

Sharkansky, Ira **JQ1830.A56S53 1997**
Policy Making in Israel: Routines for Simple Problems and Coping with the Complex. Trade Paper. University of Pittsburgh Press. Pittsburgh, PA. 1997. 220p. Pitt Series in Policy and

Institutional Studies ISBN:0-8229-5633-0, ISBN13: 978-0-8229-5633-4. Dewey:320/.6/095694. LCCN:97-004756.
Audience: **l,u,f.** *Choice, 1998.*

Comparative Government > Middle East > Jordan. Lebanon. Syria

George, Alan **JQ1826.A58G46 2003**
Syria: Neither Bread nor Freedom. Trade Paper. Zed Books, Ltd. London, 2003. 192p. ISBN:1-84277-213-9, ISBN13: 978-1-84277-213-3. Dewey:956.9104/2. LCCN:2002-191071.
Audience: **g,l,u,f.** *Choice, 2004.*

Hamzeh, A.Nizar **JQ1828.A98H6245 2004**
In the Path of Hizbullah. Trade Cloth. Syracuse University Press. Syracuse, NY. 2004. 242p. Modern Intellectual and Political History of the Middle East Ser. ISBN:0-8156-3053-0, ISBN13: 978-0-8156-3053-1. Dewey:303.6/25/095692. LCCN:2004-021012.
Audience: **l,u,f.** *Choice, 2005.*

Hanf, Theodor **DS87.H33913 1993**
Co-Existence in Wartime Lebanon: Death of a State and Birth of a Nation. Cloth over Boards. I. B. Tauris & Company, Ltd. London, 1994. 512p. ISBN:1-85043-651-7, ISBN13: 978-1-85043-651-5. Dewey:956.92044. LCCN:94-168271.
Audience: **l,u,f.** *Choice, 1994.*

Richani, Nazih **JQ1828.A98H597 1998**
Dilemmas of Democracy and Political Parties in Sectarian Societies: The Case of the PSP in Lebanon. Cloth over Boards. Palgrave Macmillan. New York, NY. 1998. 234p. ISBN:0-312-17450-0, ISBN13: 978-0-312-17450-7. Dewey:324.25692/072. LCCN:97-030288.
Audience: **u,f.** *Choice, 1999.*

Comparative Government > Middle East > Iran. Iraq. Turkey

Afary, Janet **JQ1782.A35 1996**
The Iranian Constitutional Revolution, 1906-1911: Grassroots Democracy, Social Democracy, and the Origins of Feminism. Trade Cloth. Columbia University Press. New York, NY. 1996. 448p. History and Society of the Modern Middle East Ser. ISBN:0-231-10350-6, ISBN13: 978-0-231-10350-3. Dewey:320.955. LCCN:95-050433.
Audience: **l,u,f.** *Choice, 1997.*

Baktiari, Bahman **JQ1787.7.B35 1996**
Parliamentary Politics in Revolutionary Iran: The Institutionalization of Factional Politics. Trade Cloth. University Press of Florida. Gainesville, FL. 1996. 312p. ISBN:0-8130-1461-1, ISBN13: 978-0-8130-1461-6. Dewey:328.55/07. LCCN:96-005638.
Audience: **l,u,f.** *Choice, 1997.*

Balim, Cigdem (Editor) **JQ1809.A15T863 1995**
Turkey: Political, Social and Economic Challenges in the 1990s. Trade Cloth. Brill Academic Publishers, Inc. Boston, MA. 1995. 280p. Social, Economic, and Political Studies of the Middle East, No. 53 ISBN:90-04-10283-3, ISBN13: 978-90-04-10283-5. Dewey:956.103/8. LCCN:95-012128.
Audience: **l,u.** *Choice, 1996.*

Farazmand, Ali **JQ1786**
The State, Bureaucracy, and Revolution in Modern Iran: Agrarian Reforms and Regime Politics. Trade Cloth. Greenwood Publishing Group, Inc. Portsmouth, NH. 1989. 303p. ISBN:0-275-92855-1, ISBN13: 978-0-275-92855-1. Dewey:333.3/1/55. LCCN:88-029268.
Audience: **u,f.** *Choice, 1990.*

Ozbudun, Ergun **JQ1805.A7O92 2000**
Contemporary Turkish Politics: Challenges to Democratic Consolidation. Trade Cloth. Lynne Rienner Publishers, Inc. Boulder, CO. 1999. ix, 171p. ISBN:1-55587-735-4, ISBN13: 978-1-55587-735-4. Dewey:320.9561/09/045. LCCN:99-038717.
Audience: **l,u.** *Choice, 2000.*

Rubin, Barry M. & Heper, Metin (Editors) **JQ1809.A795P654 2002**
Political Parties in Turkey. Paper over Boards. Taylor & Francis Group. Abingdon, 2002. 160p. ISBN:0-7146-5274-1, ISBN13: 978-0-7146-5274-0. Dewey:324.2561. LCCN:2001-007614.
Audience: **g,l,u,f.** *Choice, 2003.*

Saban Center for Middle East Policy, Brookings Institute **DS79.76**
☐ Iraq Index.
http://www.brookings.edu/iraqindex
Audience: **l,u,f.**

Sayari, Sabri & Esmer, Yilmaz (Editors) **JQ1809.A795P67 2002**
Politics, Parties and Elections in Turkey. Library Binding. Lynne Rienner Publishers, Inc. Boulder, CO. 2002. 270p. ISBN:1-58826-022-4, ISBN13: 978-1-58826-022-2. Dewey:324.9561. LCCN:2001-058461.
Audience: **l,u,f.** *Choice, 2002.*

Comparative Government > Asia

Alagappa, Muthiah **JQ36.C58 2004**
Civil Society and Political Change in Asia: Expanding and Contracting Democratic Space. Trade Paper. Stanford University Press. Palo Alto, CA. 2004. 552p. ISBN:0-8047-5097-1, ISBN13: 978-0-8047-5097-4. Dewey:300/.95. LCCN:2004-013177.
Audience: **l,u,f.**

Alagappa, Muthiah (Editor) **JQ26.C64 2001**
Coercion and Governance: The Declining Political Role of the Military in Asia. Trade Cloth. Stanford University Press. Palo Alto, CA. 2001. 584p. ISBN:0-8047-4226-X, ISBN13: 978-0-8047-4226-9. Dewey:322/.5/095. LCCN:2001-020988.
Audience: **l,u,f.** *Choice, 2002.*

Charlton, Sue **JQ24.C48 2004**
Comparing Asian Politics: India, China, and Japan. Ed. 2. Trade Paper. Westview Press. Boulder, CO. 2004. 352p. ISBN:0-8133-4204-X, ISBN13: 978-0-8133-4204-7. Dewey:320.3/095. LCCN:2003-020205.
Audience: **l,u.**

De Bary, William Theodore **JQ36.D43 2004**
Nobility and Civility: Asian Ideals of Leadership and the Common Good. Trade Cloth. Harvard University Press.

Cambridge, MA. 2004. 272p. ISBN:0-674-01557-6, ISBN13: 978-0-674-01557-9. Dewey:303.3/4/095. LCCN:2004-042212.
Audience: **l,u,f.** *Choice, 2005.*

Comparative Government > Asia > South Asia

Chadda, Maya **JQ98.A91C46 2000**
Building Democracy in South Asia: India, Nepal, Pakistan. Library Binding. Lynne Rienner Publishers, Inc. Boulder, CO. 2000. xv, 248p. ISBN:1-55587-748-6, ISBN13: 978-1-55587-748-4. Dewey:320.454. LCCN:99-089666.
Audience: **l,u,f.** *Choice, 2001.*

Haqqani, Husain **JQ629.A38C585 2005**
Pakistan: Between Mosque and Military. Carnegie Endowment for International Peace Staff (Contribution by). Book, Other. Carnegie Endowment for International Peace. Washington, DC. 2005. xi, 397p. ISBN:0-87003-223-2, ISBN13: 978-0-87003-223-3. Dewey:322/.5/09549. LCCN:2005-012396.
Audience: **l,u,f.** *Choice, 2006.*

Kukreja, Veena **JQ546.C58K85 1991**
Civil-Military Relations in South Asia: Pakistan, Bangladesh and India. Trade Cloth. SAGE Publications, Inc. Thousand Oaks, CA. 1992. 306p. ISBN:0-8039-9699-3, ISBN13: 978-0-8039-9699-1. Dewey:322.50954. LCCN:91-015168.
Audience: **l,u,f.** *Choice, 1992.*

Lawoti, Mahendra **JQ628.A91L38 2004**
Towards a Democratic Nepal: Inclusive Political Institutions for a Multicultural Society. Cloth Text. SAGE Publications India Pvt, Ltd. New Delhi, 2005. 345p. ISBN:0-7619-3318-2, ISBN13: 978-0-7619-3318-2. Dewey:320.95496. LCCN:2004-021320.
Audience: **l,u,f.** *Choice, 2005.*

Maung, Mya **JQ442**
Totalitarianism in Burma: prospects for economic development. Paragon House. 1992. ISBN:1-55778-553-8, ISBN13: 978-1-55778-553-4.
Audience: **g,u,f.**

Nasr, Seyyed Vali Reza **JQ559.A54N37 1994**
The Vanguard of Islamic Revolution: The Jamaat-I Islami of Pakistan. Trade Paper. University of California Press. Berkeley, CA. 1994. xxii, 301p. Comparative Studies on Muslim Societies, No. 19 ISBN:0-520-08369-5, ISBN13: 978-0-520-08369-1. Dewey:324.25491/082. LCCN:93-005403.
Audience: **l,u,f.** *Choice, 1995.*

Comparative Government > Asia > South Asia > India

Aloysius, G. **DS463.A565 1997**
Nationalism Without a Nation in India. Trade Cloth. Oxford University Press, Inc. New York, NY. 1998. 280p. ISBN:0-19-564104-3, ISBN13: 978-0-19-564104-2. Dewey:322.4/2/0954. LCCN:97-903271.
Audience: **g,u,f.**

Bartlett, Beatrice S. **JQ1508.B37 1991**
Monarchs and Ministers: The Grand Council in Mid-Ch'ing China, 1723-1820. Trade Cloth. University of California Press. Berkeley, CA. 1990. 417p. ISBN:0-520-06591-3, ISBN13: 978-0-520-06591-8. Dewey:354.5104/09/033. LCCN:90-011068.
Audience: **u,f.** *Choice, 1992.*

Chadda, Maya **JQ98.A91C46 2000**
Building Democracy in South Asia: India, Nepal, Pakistan. Library Binding. Lynne Rienner Publishers, Inc. Boulder, CO. 2000. xv, 248p. ISBN:1-55587-748-6, ISBN13: 978-1-55587-748-4. Dewey:320.454. LCCN:99-089666.
Audience: **l,u,f.** *Choice, 2001.*

Chhibber, Pradeep K. **JQ298.A1 C48 1999**
Democracy without Associations: Transformation of the Party System and Social Cleavages in India. Trade Cloth. University of Michigan Press. Chicago, IL. 1999. 304p. Interests, Identities, and Institutions in Comparative Politics Ser. ISBN:0-472-10962-6, ISBN13: 978-0-472-10962-3. Dewey:324.253. LCCN:98-025511.
Audience: **u,f.** *Choice, 2000.*

Datta, Prabhat K. **JQ211.D387 1997**
India's Democracy: New Challenges. Trade Cloth. Kanishka Publishing House. New Delhi, 1997. ISBN:81-7391-193-2, ISBN13: 978-81-7391-193-4. Dewey:320.954/09/045. LCCN:97-905323.
Audience: **l,u.**

Graham, Bruce **JQ298.B5G73 1990**
Hindu Nationalism and Indian Politics: The Origins and Development of the Bharatiya Jana Sangh. Trade Cloth. Cambridge University Press. New York, NY. 1990. 295p. South Asian Studies, No. 47 ISBN:0-521-38348-X, ISBN13: 978-0-521-38348-6. Dewey:324.254/083/09. LCCN:89-038036.
Audience: **l,u,f.** *Choice, 1991.*

Haqqani, Husain **JQ629.A38C585 2005**
Pakistan: Between Mosque and Military. Carnegie Endowment for International Peace Staff (Contribution by). Book, Other. Carnegie Endowment for International Peace. Washington, DC. 2005. xi, 397p. ISBN:0-87003-223-2, ISBN13: 978-0-87003-223-3. Dewey:322/.5/09549. LCCN:2005-012396.
Audience: **l,u,f.** *Choice, 2006.*

Hardgrave, Robert L. Jr. & Kochanek, Stanley A. **JQ231.H37 2000**
India: Government and Politics in a Developing Nation. Ed. 6. Paper Text. Thomson Wadsworth. Belmont, CA. 1999. 536p. ISBN:0-15-507894-1, ISBN13: 978-0-15-507894-9. Dewey:320.9/54/05. LCCN:99-064644.
Audience: **g,l,u.**

Jenkins, Rob **HC435.2**
Democratic Politics and Economic Reform in India. Jan Breman, G. P. Hawthorn, Ayesha Jalal, Patricia Jeffery, Atul Kohli & Dharma Kumar (Contribution by). Trade Paper. Cambridge University Press. New York, NY. 2000. 260p. Contemporary South Asia Ser., No. 5 ISBN:0-521-65987-6, ISBN13: 978-0-521-65987-1. Dewey:338.954/009/049.
Audience: **l,u,f.** *Choice, 2000.*

Kohli, Atul (Editor) **JQ0281.I53**
India's Democracy: An Analysis of Changing State-Society Relations. Pranab Bardhan (Contribution by), John P. Lewis (Foreword by). Trade Paper. Books on Demand. Ann Arbor, MI. 1990. 365p. ISBN:0-608-07652-X, ISBN13: 978-0-608-07652-2. Dewey:320.954. LCCN:90-222836.
Audience: **l,u,f.** *Choice, 1988.*

Kukreja, Veena **JQ546.C58K85 1991**
Civil-Military Relations in South Asia: Pakistan, Bangladesh and India. Trade Cloth. SAGE Publications, Inc. Thousand Oaks, CA. 1992. 306p. ISBN:0-8039-9699-3, ISBN13: 978-0-8039-9699-1. Dewey:322.50954. LCCN:91-015168.
Audience: **l,u,f.** *Choice, 1992.*

Malik, Yogendra K. & Singh, V. B **JQ298.B55M35 1994**
Hindu Nationalists in India: The Rise of the Bharatiya Janata Party. Trade Paper. Westview Press. Boulder, CO. 1994. x, 262p. ISBN:0-8133-8810-4, ISBN13: 978-0-8133-8810-6. Dewey:324.254/083. LCCN:94-023352.
Audience: **l,u,f.** *Choice, 1995.*

Rao, M. Govinda & Singh, Nirvikar **JQ220.S8G68 2005**
Political Economy of Indian Federalism. Trade Cloth. Oxford University Press, Inc. New York, NY. 2005. 432p. ISBN:0-19-567017-5, ISBN13: 978-0-19-567017-2. Dewey:330.954. LCCN:2005-281111.
Audience: **u,f.** *Choice, 2005.*

Thakurta, Paranjoy Guha & Raghuraman, Shankar **JQ298.A1T43 2004**
A Time of Coalitions: Divided We Stand. Trade Paper. SAGE Publications, Inc. Thousand Oaks, CA. 2004. 408p. ISBN:0-7619-3237-2, ISBN13: 978-0-7619-3237-6. Dewey:324.254. LCCN:2004-003260.
Audience: **l,u,f.** *Choice, 2005.*

Thomas, Raju G. C. **JQ281.T56 1996**
Democracy, Security, and Development in India. Cloth over Boards. Palgrave Macmillan. New York, NY. 1996. 170p. ISBN:0-312-06607-4, ISBN13: 978-0-312-06607-9. Dewey:320.954. LCCN:95-026193.
Audience: **g,l,u,f.** *Choice, 1996.*

Vanaik, Achin **JQ281.V34 1990**
Painful Transition: Bourgeois Democracy in India. Trade Paper. Analytical Psychology Club of San Francisco, Inc. San Francisco, CA. 1990. 302p. ISBN:0-86091-504-2, ISBN13: 978-0-86091-504-1. Dewey:954.05/2. LCCN:90-037486.
Audience: **l,u,f.** *Choice, 1991.*

Vora, Rajendra & Palshikar, Suhas (Editors) **JQ281.I515 2003**
Indian Democracy: Meanings and Practices. Trade Cloth. SAGE Publications, Inc. Thousand Oaks, CA. 2004. 428p. ISBN:0-7619-9790-3, ISBN13: 978-0-7619-9790-0. Dewey:320.954. LCCN:2003-005711.
Audience: **l,u,f.** *Choice, 2005.*

Wilkinson, Steven **JQ292.W55 2004**
Votes and Violence: Electoral Competition and Ethnic Riots in India. Peter Lange, Robert H. Bates, Ellen Comisso, Peter Hall, Joel Migdal & Helen Milner (Contribution by). Trade Cloth. Cambridge University Press. New York, NY. 2004. 310p. Cambridge Studies in Comparative Politics Ser. ISBN:0-521-82916-X, ISBN13: 978-0-521-82916-8. Dewey:303.6/2/08900954. LCCN:2003-068721.
Audience: **l,u,f.** *Choice, 2005.*

Comparative Government > Asia > East Asia

Alagappa, Muthiah (Editor) **JQ1538**
Taiwan's Presidential Politics: Democratization and Cross-Strait Relations in the Twenty- First Century. Paper Text. M. E. Sharpe Inc. Armonk, NY. 2001. 326p. Taiwan in the Modern World Ser. ISBN:0-7656-0834-0, ISBN13: 978-0-7656-0834-5. Dewey:320.951249. LCCN:2001-049155.
Audience: **u,f.** *Choice, 2002.*

Dittmer, Lowell (Editor), et al. **JQ1499.A58 I54 2000**
Informal Politics in East Asia. Haruhiro Fukui & Peter N. S. Lee (Editors). Cloth Text. Cambridge University Press. New York, NY. 2000. 342p. ISBN:0-521-64232-9, ISBN13: 978-0-521-64232-3. Dewey:306.2/095. LCCN:99-040245.
Audience: **l,u,f.** *Choice, 2001.*

Marsh, Ian **JQ1499.A91D446 1999**
Democracy, Governance and Economic Performance: East and Southeast Asia. Trade Paper. United Nations Publications. New York, NY. 2005. 392p. The Changing Nature of Democracy Ser. ISBN:92-808-1039-1, ISBN13: 978-92-808-1039-4. Dewey:338.95. LCCN:99-050732.
Audience: **l,u,f.** *Choice, 2000.*

Moody, Peter R. Jr. **JQ1536**
Political Change on Taiwan: A Study of Ruling Party Adaptability. Trade Cloth. Greenwood Publishing Group, Inc. Portsmouth, NH. 1991. 224p. ISBN:0-275-94035-7, ISBN13: 978-0-275-94035-5. Dewey:951.249/058. LCCN:91-015311.
Audience: **l,u,f.** *Choice, 1992.*

Pempel, T. J. (Editor) **JQ1499.A38R46 2004**
Remapping East Asia. Trade Paper. Cornell University Press. Ithaca, NY. 2004. 334p. Cornell Studies in Political Economy ISBN:0-8014-8909-1, ISBN13: 978-0-8014-8909-9. Dewey:337.5. LCCN:2004-015299.
Audience: **l,u,f.**

So, Alvin Y. **JQ1539.5.A91S65 1999**
Hong Kong's Embattled Democracy: A Societal Analysis. Trade Cloth. Johns Hopkins University Press. Baltimore, MD. 1999. 328p. ISBN:0-8018-6145-4, ISBN13: 978-0-8018-6145-1. Dewey:320.95125/09/049. LCCN:99-025083.
Audience: **l,u,f.** *Choice, 2000.*

Weller, Robert P. **JQ1516.W45 2001**
Alternate Civilities: Democracy and Culture in China and Taiwan. Trade Paper. Westview Press. Boulder, CO. 2001. 188p. ISBN:0-8133-3931-6, ISBN13: 978-0-8133-3931-3. Dewey:306.2/0951. LCCN:2001-017938.
Audience: **l,u,f.**

Zhang, Yumei **JQ1499.A792P5395**
Pacific Asia. Paper over Boards. Routledge. New York, NY. 2003. 208p. The Making of the Contemporary World Ser.

ISBN:0-415-18488-6, ISBN13: 978-0-415-18488-5. Dewey:320.95. LCCN:2002-011675.
Audience: **g,l,u.** *Choice, 2004.*

Comparative Government > Asia > East Asia > China

Bachman, David **JQ1508 .B28 1991**
Bureaucracy, Economy, and Leadership in China: The Institutional Origins of the Great Leap Forward. Cloth Text. Cambridge University Press. New York, NY. 1991. 284p. ISBN:0-521-40275-1, ISBN13: 978-0-521-40275-0. Dewey:338.95/009/045. LCCN:90-049810.
Audience: **u,f.** *Choice, 1992.*

Bartlett, Beatrice S. **JQ1508.B37 1991**
Monarchs and Ministers: The Grand Council in Mid-Ch'ing China, 1723-1820. Trade Cloth. University of California Press. Berkeley, CA. 1990. 417p. ISBN:0-520-06591-3, ISBN13: 978-0-520-06591-8. Dewey:354.5104/09/033. LCCN:90-011068.
Audience: **u,f.** *Choice, 1992.*

Chen, An **JQ1510.C483 1999**
Restructing Political Power in China: Alliances and Opposition, 1978-1998. Trade Cloth. Lynne Rienner Publishers, Inc. Boulder, CO. 1999. 280p. ISBN:1-55587-842-3, ISBN13: 978-1-55587-842-9. Dewey:320.951/09/048. LCCN:99-011103.
Audience: **u,f.** *Choice, 2000.*

Chen, Jie **JQ1516.C435 2004**
Popular Political Support in Urban China. Trade Cloth. Woodrow Wilson Center Press. Washington, DC. 2003. 336p. ISBN:0-8047-4959-0, ISBN13: 978-0-8047-4959-6. Dewey:306.2/0951. LCCN:2003-014594.
Audience: **l,u,f.** *Choice, 2004.*

Ch'i, Hsi-sheng **JQ1519.A5C475356**
Politics of Disillusionment: The Chinese Communist Party under Deng Xiaoping, 1978-1989. Cloth Text. M. E. Sharpe Inc. Armonk, NY. 1991. 352p. Studies on Contemporary China ISBN:0-87332-689-X, ISBN13: 978-0-87332-689-6. Dewey:324.251/075/09048. LCCN:90-020867.
Audience: **l,u,f.** *Choice, 1991.*

de Bary, Wm. Theodore (Translator) **JQ1508.H7883**
Waiting for the Dawn: A Plan for the Prince. Trade Paper. Columbia University Press. New York, NY. 1994. 340p. ISBN:0-231-08097-2, ISBN13: 978-0-231-08097-2. Dewey:321/.6/0951.
Audience: **g,u,f.**

Dickson, Bruce J. **JQ1519.A5D53 2003**
Red Capitalists in China: The Party, Private Entrepreneurs, and Prospects for Political Change. William Kirby (Contribution by). Trade Paper. Cambridge University Press. New York, NY. 2003. 198p. Cambridge Modern China Ser. ISBN:0-521-52143-2, ISBN13: 978-0-521-52143-7. Dewey:324.251/075. LCCN:2002-067069.
Audience: **l,u,f.** *Choice, 2003.*

Dreyer, June Teufel **JQ1510.D74 2004**
China's Political System: Modernization and Tradition. Ed. 5. Trade Paper, Perfect. Longman Publishing. Boston, MA. 2005. 347p. ISBN:0-321-35510-5, ISBN13: 978-0-321-35510-2. Dewey:320.451. LCCN:2005-048663.
Audience: **g,l,u,f.** *Choice, 1993.*

Fewsmith, Joseph **JQ1510 .F48 2001**
China since Tiananmen: The Politics of Transition. William Kirby (Contribution by). Trade Paper. Cambridge University Press. New York, NY. 2001. 332p. Modern China Ser. ISBN:0-521-00105-6, ISBN13: 978-0-521-00105-2. Dewey:951.059. LCCN:2001-018436.
Audience: **l,u,f.** *Choice, 2002.*

Finkelstein, David M. & Kivlehan, Maryanne (Editors) **JQ1516.C4527 2002**
China's Leadership in the Twenty-first Century: The Rise of the Fourth Generation. Trade Cloth. M. E. Sharpe Inc. Armonk, NY. 2002. 312p. ISBN:0-7656-1115-5, ISBN13: 978-0-7656-1115-4. Dewey:320.951. LCCN:2002-029410.
Audience: **l,u,f.** *Choice, 2003.*

Friedman, Edward (Editor, Contribution by) **JQ1516.W48 2000**
What If China Doesn't Democratize?: Implications for War and Peace. Barrett L. McCormick (Editor, Introduction by), Andrew Nathan (Preface by), Suisheng Zhao, Jianwei Wang, Minxin Pei, Samuel Kim, June Teufel Dreyer, David Bachman, Harvey Nelsen, Su Shaozhi & Michael Sullivan (Contribution by). Cloth Text. M. E. Sharpe Inc. Armonk, NY. 2000. 376p. Asia and the Pacific Ser. ISBN:0-7656-0567-8, ISBN13: 978-0-7656-0567-2. Dewey:320.951. LCCN:00-020162.
Audience: **l,u,f.** *Choice, 2001.*

Fung, Edmund S. K. **JQ1516 .F86 2000**
In Search of Chinese Democracy: Civil Opposition in Nationalist China, 1929-1949. William Kirby (Contribution by). Cloth Text. Cambridge University Press. New York, NY. 2000. 426p. Modern China Ser. ISBN:0-521-77124-2, ISBN13: 978-0-521-77124-5. Dewey:320.951/09/043. LCCN:99-036625.
Audience: **l,u,f.** *Choice, 2001.*

Fung, Edmund S. K. **JQ1516 .F86 2000**
In Search of Chinese Democracy: Civil Opposition in Nationalist China, 1929-1949. William Kirby (Contribution by). Trade Paper. Cambridge University Press. New York, NY. 2006. 425p. Cambridge Modern China Ser. ISBN:0-521-02581-8, ISBN13: 978-0-521-02581-2. Dewey:320.951/09/043.
Audience: **l,u,f.** *Choice, 2001.*

Goldman, Merle **JQ1516.G63 2005**
From Comrade to Citizen: The Struggle for Political Rights in China. Trade Cloth. Harvard University Press. Cambridge, MA. 2005. 304p. ISBN:0-674-01890-7, ISBN13: 978-0-674-01890-7. Dewey:320.651. LCCN:2005-040287.
Audience: **g,l,u,f.** *Choice, 2006.*

Goldman, Merle & Perry, Elizabeth J. (Editors) **JQ1517.A2C53 2002**
Changing Meanings of Citizenship in Modern China. Trade Cloth. Harvard University Press. Cambridge, MA. 2002. 480p. Contemporary China Ser., Vol. 13 ISBN:0-674-00766-2, ISBN13: 978-0-674-00766-6. Dewey:323.6/0951. LCCN:2001-059351.
Audience: **l,u,f.** *Choice, 2003.*

Goldstein, Avery N. **JQ1516.G65 1991**
From Bandwagon to Balance-of-Power Politics: Structural Constraints and Politics in China, 1949-1978. Trade Cloth. Stanford University Press. Palo Alto, CA. 1991. 376p. ISBN:0-8047-1850-4, ISBN13: 978-0-8047-1850-9. Dewey:951.05. LCCN:90-037483.
Audience: **u,f.** *Choice, 1991.*

Henry Yuhuai He **JQ1501.A25H4 2001**
Dictionary of the Political Thought of the People's Republic of China. M.E. Sharpe. 2000. ISBN:0-7656-0569-4, ISBN13: 978-0-7656-0569-6.
Audience: **g,l,u,f.**

Hong Yung Lee **JQ1519.A5L35 1991**
From Revolutionary Cadres to Party Technocrats in Socialist China. Trade Cloth. University of California Press. Berkeley, CA. 1990. 437p. Center for Chinese Studies, UC Berkeley Ser. ISBN:0-520-06679-0, ISBN13: 978-0-520-06679-3. Dewey:324.251/075/09. LCCN:90-030762.
Audience: **l,u,f.** *Choice, 1991.*

Howell, Jude **JQ1510.G68 2003**
Governance in China. Book, Other. Rowman & Littlefield Publishers, Inc. Lanham, MD. 2003. 304p. ISBN:0-7425-1988-0, ISBN13: 978-0-7425-1988-6. Dewey:320.951. LCCN:2003-008631.
Audience: **g,l,u.** *Choice, 2004.*

Johnson, Ian **JQ1516.J64 2004**
Wild Grass: Three Stories of Change in Modern China. Trade Cloth. Knopf Publishing Group. New York, NY. 2004. 336p. ISBN:0-375-42186-6, ISBN13: 978-0-375-42186-0. Dewey:323/.04/0951. LCCN:2003-058082.
Audience: **l,u,f.**

Kent, Ann **JC599.C6K46 1993**
Between Freedom and Subsistence: China and Human Rights. Paper Text. Oxford University Press, Inc. New York, NY. 1995. 308p. ISBN:0-19-585521-3, ISBN13: 978-0-19-585521-0. Dewey:323.490951. LCCN:92-019756.
Audience: **g,l,u,f.**

Kuhn, Philip A. & Brook, Timothy (Editors) **JQ1508.M56 1989**
National Polity and Local Power: The Transformation of Late Imperial China. Trade Cloth. Harvard University Press. Cambridge, MA. 1990. 316p. Harvard-Yenching Institute Monographs, No. 27 ISBN:0-674-60225-0, ISBN13: 978-0-674-60225-0. Dewey:320.8/0951. LCCN:87-036474.
Audience: **u,f.** *Choice, 1990.*

Lieberthal, Kenneth & Dickson, Bruce **JQ1519.A5L474 1989**
A Research Guide to Central Party and Government Meetings in China, 1949-1986. Ed. 2. Cloth Text. M. E. Sharpe Inc. Armonk, NY. 1989. 392p. ISBN:0-87332-492-7, ISBN13: 978-0-87332-492-2. Dewey:324.251/075. LCCN:88-018527.
Audience: **u,f.** *Choice, 1989.*

Liu, Xiaoyuan **JQ1506.M5**
Frontier Passages: Ethnopolitics and the Rise of Chinese Communism, 1921-1945. Trade Cloth. Stanford University Press. Palo Alto, CA. 2003. 252p. ISBN:0-8047-4960-4, ISBN13: 978-0-8047-4960-2. Dewey:323.1/51/09042. LCCN:2003-016314.
Audience: **l,u,f.** *Choice, 2004.*

Lu, Xiaobo **JQ1509.5.C6L8 2000**
Cadres and Corruption: The Organizational Involution of the Chinese Communist Party. Trade Cloth. Stanford University Press. Palo Alto, CA. 2000. xviii, 368p. Studies of the East Asian Institute, Columbia University ISBN:0-8047-3958-7, ISBN13: 978-0-8047-3958-0. Dewey:324.251/075. LCCN:00-027396.
Audience: **l,u,f.** *Choice, 2001.*

Manion, Melanie **JQ1509.5.C6M36 2004**
Corruption by Design: Building Clean Government in Mainland China and Hong Kong. Trade Cloth. Harvard University Press. Cambridge, MA. 2004. 296p. ISBN:0-674-01486-3, ISBN13: 978-0-674-01486-2. Dewey:364.1/323/0951. LCCN:2004-047348.
Audience: **l,u,f.** *Choice, 2005.*

O'Brien, Kevin J. **JQ1513 .O27 1990**
Reform Without Liberalization: China's National People's Congress and the Politics of Institutional Change. Trade Cloth. Cambridge University Press. New York, NY. 1990. 277p. ISBN:0-521-38086-3, ISBN13: 978-0-521-38086-7. Dewey:328.51/072. LCCN:90-001911.
Audience: **l,u,f.** *Choice, 1991.*

Qing, Dai **JQ1519.A5T16213 1993**
Wang Shiwei and "Wild Lilies": Rectification and Purges in the Chinese Communist Party, 1942-1944. David E. Apter & Timothy Cheek (Editors), Nancy Liu & Lawrence R. Sullivan (Translators). Paper Text. M. E. Sharpe Inc. Armonk, NY. 1994. 224p. ISBN:1-56324-256-7, ISBN13: 978-1-56324-256-4. Dewey:324.251/075. LCCN:93-034022.
Audience: **l,u,f.** *Choice, 1994.*

Rossabi, Morris **JQ1506.M5G68 2005**
Governing China's Multiethnic Frontiers. Trade Cloth. University of Washington Press. Seattle, WA. 2005. 304p. ISBN:0-295-98412-0, ISBN13: 978-0-295-98412-4. Dewey:323.151.
Audience: **l,u,f.** *Choice, 2004.*

Shi, Tianjian **JQ1516.S53 1997**
Political Participation in Beijing. Trade Cloth. Harvard University Press. Cambridge, MA. 1997. 352p. ISBN:0-674-68640-3, ISBN13: 978-0-674-68640-3. Dewey:323/.04/0951. LCCN:96-053018.
Audience: **g,l,u,f.** *Choice, 1998.*

Shue, Vivienne **DS777.55**
The Reach of the State: Sketches of the Chinese Body Politic. Trade Paper. Stanford University Press. Palo Alto, CA. 1988. 189p. ISBN:0-8047-1804-0, ISBN13: 978-0-8047-1804-2. Dewey:951.05. LCCN:87-027447.
Audience: **l,u,f.** *Choice, 1988.*

Sun, Yan **JQ1509.5.C6S88 2004**
Corruption and Market in Contemporary China. Book, Other. Cornell University Press. Ithaca, NY. 2004. 272p. ISBN:0-8014-8942-3, ISBN13: 978-0-8014-8942-6. Dewey:364.1/323/0951. LCCN:2004-007180.
Audience: **l,u,f.** *Choice, 2005.*

Unger, Jonathan (Editor) **JQ1510.N376 2002**
The Nature of Chinese Politics: From Mao to Jiang. Trade Cloth. M. E. Sharpe Inc. Armonk, NY. 2002. 350p. Contemporary China Papers, Australian National University Ser. ISBN:0-7656-0847-2, ISBN13: 978-0-7656-0847-5. Dewey:320.951/09/045. LCCN:2002-066510.
Audience: **l,u.** *Choice, 2003.*

Weller, Robert P. **JQ1516.W45 2001**
Alternate Civilities: Democracy and Culture in China and Taiwan. Trade Paper. Westview Press. Boulder, CO. 2001. 188p. ISBN:0-8133-3931-6, ISBN13: 978-0-8133-3931-3. Dewey:306.2/0951. LCCN:2001-017938.
Audience: **l,u,f.**

Zhao, Suisheng **JQ1516.C4525 2000**
China and Democracy: Reconsidering Prospects for a Democratic China. Paper over Boards. Routledge. New York, NY. 2000. 272p. ISBN:0-415-92693-9, ISBN13: 978-0-415-92693-5. Dewey:320.951. LCCN:00-032310.
Audience: **g,l,u,f.** *Choice, 2001.*

Zhao, Suisheng **JQ1522.Z43 1996**
Power by Design: Constitution-Making in Nationalist China. Trade Cloth. University of Hawaii Press. Honolulu, HI. 1996. 232p. ISBN:0-8248-1721-4, ISBN13: 978-0-8248-1721-3. Dewey:320.951/09/041. LCCN:95-023127.
Audience: **l,u,f.** *Choice, 1996.*

Zheng, Shiping **JQ1519.A5 Z49 1997**
Party vs. State in Post-1949 China: The Institutional Dilemma. William Kirby (Contribution by). Trade Cloth. Cambridge University Press. New York, NY. 1997. 310p. Modern China Ser. ISBN:0-521-58205-9, ISBN13: 978-0-521-58205-6. Dewey:320.9/51/09045. LCCN:96-050078.
Audience: **l,u,f.** *Choice, 1998.*

Comparative Government > Asia > East Asia > Korea

Bedeski, Robert E. **HG5772.B74 1994**
The Transformation of South Korea: Reform and Reconstitution in the Sixth Republic under Roe Tae Woo, 1987-1992. Trade Paper. Routledge. New York, NY. 1994. 208p. ISBN:0-415-10604-4, ISBN13: 978-0-415-10604-7. Dewey:951.95043. LCCN:93-030537.
Audience: **l,u,f.** *Choice, 1995.*

Duncan, John B. **JQ1725.A7D86 2000**
The Origins of the Chosfon Dynasty. Trade Cloth. University of Washington Press. Seattle, WA. 2000. xii, 395p. Korean Studies of the Henry M. Jackson School of International Studies ISBN:0-295-97985-2, ISBN13: 978-0-295-97985-4. Dewey:951.9/02. LCCN:00-029876.
Audience: **l,u,f.** *Choice, 2001.*

Hahm, Sung D. & Plein, L. Christopher **JQ1725.H345 1997**
After Development: The Transformation of the Korean Presidency and Bureaucracy. Trade Cloth. Georgetown University Press. Washington, DC. 1997. 224p. ISBN:0-87840-639-5, ISBN13: 978-0-87840-639-5. Dewey:352.23/095195. LCCN:96-047406.
Audience: **l,u,f.** *Choice, 1998.*

Kang, David C. **JQ1725.A55 K36 2002**
Crony Capitalism: Corruption and Development in South Korea and the Philippines. Robert H. Bates, Ellen Comisso, Peter Hall, Peter Lange, Joel Migdal & Helen Milner (Contribution by). Trade Paper. Cambridge University Press. New York, NY. 2002. 220p. Studies in Comparative Politics ISBN:0-521-00408-X, ISBN13: 978-0-521-00408-4. Dewey:320.95195. LCCN:2001-025806.
Audience: **l,u,f.** *Choice, 2003.*

Kang, David C. **JQ1729.A15**
(e) Crony Capitalism: Corruption and Development in South Korea and the Philippines. Peter Lange, Robert H. Bates, Ellen Comisso, Peter Hall, Joel Migdal & Helen Milner (Contribution by). E-Book. Cambridge University Press. New York, NY. 2005. Cambridge Studies in Comparative Politics Ser. ISBN:0-511-02926-8, ISBN13: 978-0-511-02926-4. Dewey:320.95195.
Audience: **l,u,f.** *Choice, 2003.*

Kim, Sunhyuk **JQ1729.A15S58 2000**
The Politics of Democratization in Korea: The Role of Civil Society. Trade Paper. University of Pittsburgh Press. Pittsburgh, PA. 2000. xiv, 183p. Political Science Ser. ISBN:0-8229-5736-1, ISBN13: 978-0-8229-5736-2. Dewey:320.95195. LCCN:00-010611.
Audience: **l,u,f.** *Choice, 2001.*

Shin, Doh C. **JQ1729.A15 S55 1999**
Mass Politics and Culture in Democratizing Korea. Trade Paper. Cambridge University Press. New York, NY. 1999. 372p. Cambridge Asia-Pacific Studies ISBN:0-521-65823-3, ISBN13: 978-0-521-65823-2. Dewey:320.95195. LCCN:98-049357.
Audience: **l,u.** *Choice, 2000.*

Comparative Government > Asia > East Asia > Japan

Bowen, Roger W. **JQ1681.B684 2002**
Japan's Dysfunctional Democracy: The Liberal Democractic Party and Structural Corruption. Trade Cloth. M. E. Sharpe Inc. Armonk, NY. 2003. 152p. ISBN:0-7656-1102-3, ISBN13: 978-0-7656-1102-4. Dewey:320.952. LCCN:2002-030892.
Audience: **l,u,f.** *Choice, 2003.*

Boyd, J. Patrick & Samuels, Richard J. **KNX2064.51947.Z8**
Nine Lives?: The Politics of Constitutional Reform in Japan. Perfect. East-West Center Washington. Washington, DC. 2005. 84p. Policy Studies, 19 ISBN:1-932728-36-8, ISBN13: 978-1-932728-36-1. LCCN:2005-284489.
Audience: **u,f.**

Curtis, Gerald L. **JQ1631.C87 1999**
The Logic of Japanese Politics: Leaders, Institutions and the Limits of Change. Trade Paper. Columbia University Press. New York, NY. 2000. 336p. Studies of the East Asian Institute ISBN:0-231-10843-5, ISBN13: 978-0-231-10843-0. Dewey:320.952/09/049. LCCN:99-019910.
Audience: **l,u,f.**

Curtis, Gerald L. (Editor) **JQ1631**
Politicians and Policymaking in Japan. Trade Paper. Japan Center for International Exchange. Tokyo, 2002. 200p. ISBN:4-88907-062-1, ISBN13: 978-4-88907-062-0. Dewey:320.952.
Audience: **l,u.** *Choice, 2003.*

Ishida, Takeshi & Krauss, Ellis S. (Editors) **JQ1681.D45 1989**
Democracy in Japan. Trade Paper. University of Pittsburgh Press. Pittsburgh, PA. 1989. 364p. Series in Policy and Institutional Studies ISBN:0-8229-5414-1, ISBN13: 978-0-8229-5414-9. Dewey:306/.2/0952. LCCN:88-028057.
Audience: **g,l,u.** *Choice, 1990.*

Kohno, Masaru **JQ1698.A1K64 1997**
Japan's Postwar Party Politics. Cloth Text. Princeton University Press. Princeton, NJ. 1997. 172p. ISBN:0-691-02629-7, ISBN13: 978-0-691-02629-9. Dewey:324.252. LCCN:96-026393.
Audience: **l,u,f.** *Choice, 1997.*

Kuroda, Yasumasa **JQ1654.K87 2005**
The Core of Japanese Democracy: Latent Interparty Politics. Cloth over Boards. Palgrave Macmillan. New York, NY. 2005. 272p. ISBN:1-4039-6901-9, ISBN13: 978-1-4039-6901-9. Dewey:320.952. LCCN:2004-061824.
Audience: **l,u,f.** *Choice, 2006.*

Ruoff, Kenneth J. **JQ1640.R86 2001**
The People's Emperor: Democracy and the Japanese Monarchy, 1945-1995. Trade Cloth. Harvard University Press. Cambridge, MA. 2002. 360p. Harvard East Asian Monographs, Vol. 211 ISBN:0-674-00840-5, ISBN13: 978-0-674-00840-3. Dewey:952.04. LCCN:2001-039392.
Audience: **l,u,f.** *Choice, 2002.*

Samuels, Richard J. **JN5345.S25 2005**
Machiavelli's Children: Leaders and Their Legacies in Italy and Japan. Book, Other. Cornell University Press. Ithaca, NY. 2005. 480p. ISBN:0-8014-8982-2, ISBN13: 978-0-8014-8982-2. Dewey:303.34094509034.
Audience: **l,u,f.** *Choice, 2003.*

Scheiner, Ethan **JQ1681.S34 2006**
Democracy Without Competition in Japan: Opposition Failure in a One-Party Dominant State. Trade Paper, Perfect. Cambridge University Press. New York, NY. 2005. 286p. ISBN:0-521-60969-0, ISBN13: 978-0-521-60969-2. Dewey:324.252. LCCN:2004-030868.
Audience: **l,u,f.** *Choice, 2006.*

Takeda, Kiyoko **JQ1641.T33413 1988**
The Dual-Image of the Japanese Emperor. Trade Cloth. New York University Press. New York, NY. 1988. 208p. ISBN:0-8147-8178-0, ISBN13: 978-0-8147-8178-4. Dewey:354.5203/12. LCCN:88-017243.
Audience: **l,u,f.** *Choice, 1989.*

Van Wolferen, Karel **JQ1681.W65 1990**
The Enigma of Japanese Power: People and Politics in a Stateless Nation. UK-Trade Paper. Knopf Publishing Group. New York, NY. 1990. 524p. ISBN:0-679-72802-3, ISBN13: 978-0-679-72802-3. Dewey:306.2/0952. LCCN:89-040552.
Audience: **l,u,f.**

Zhao, Quansheng **JQ1681**
Japanese Policymaking -: The Politics Behind Politics, Informal Mechanisms and the Making of China Policy. Trade Cloth. Greenwood Publishing Group, Inc. Portsmouth, NH. 1993. 256p. ISBN:0-275-94449-2, ISBN13: 978-0-275-94449-0. Dewey:306.2/0952. LCCN:92-020052.
Audience: **l,u,f.** *Choice, 1993.*

Comparative Government > Asia > Southeast Asia

Kingsbury, Damien **JQ750.A58K56 2001**
South-East Asia: A Political Profile. Trade Paper. Oxford University Press, Inc. New York, NY. 2001. 464p. ISBN:0-19-551003-8, ISBN13: 978-0-19-551003-4. Dewey:320.959. LCCN:2001-273240.
Audience: **g,l,u.** *Choice, 2002.*

Marsh, Ian **JQ1499.A91D446 1999**
Democracy, Governance and Economic Performance: East and Southeast Asia. Trade Paper. United Nations Publications. New York, NY. 2005. 392p. The Changing Nature of Democracy Ser. ISBN:92-808-1039-1, ISBN13: 978-92-808-1039-4. Dewey:338.95. LCCN:99-050732.
Audience: **l,u,f.** *Choice, 2000.*

Zhang, Yumei **JQ1499.A792P5395**
Pacific Asia. Paper over Boards. Routledge. New York, NY. 2003. 208p. The Making of the Contemporary World Ser. ISBN:0-415-18488-6, ISBN13: 978-0-415-18488-5. Dewey:320.95. LCCN:2002-011675.
Audience: **g,l,u.** *Choice, 2004.*

Comparative Government > Asia > Southeast Asia > Vietnam

Abuza, Zachary **JQ898.D293A25 2001**
Renovating Politics in Contemporary Vietnam. Cloth Text. Lynne Rienner Publishers, Inc. Boulder, CO. 2001. v, 273p. ISBN:1-55587-961-6, ISBN13: 978-1-55587-961-7. Dewey:320.9597. LCCN:00-066502.
Audience: **l,u,f.** *Choice, 2002.*

Thayer, Carlyle A. **DS556.9**
War by Other Means: National Liberation and Revolution. Trade Cloth. Routledge. New York, NY. 1989. 282p. ISBN:0-04-820045-X, ISBN13: 978-0-04-820045-7. Dewey:959.7042. LCCN:89-083595.
Audience: **l,u,f.** *Choice, 1990.*

Comparative Government > Asia > Southeast Asia > Thailand

Ockey, James **JQ1749.A15O25 2004**
Making Democracy: Leadership, Class, Gender, and Political Participation in Thailand. Trade Cloth. University of Hawaii Press. Honolulu, HI. 2004. 264p. ISBN:0-8248-2781-3, ISBN13: 978-0-8248-2781-6. Dewey:320.9593. LCCN:2004-003471.
Audience: **l,u,f.** *Choice, 2005.*

Comparative Government > Asia > Southeast Asia > Hong Kong. Malaysia. Singapore. Indonesia

Crouch, Harold **JQ712.C76 1996**
Government and Society in Malaysia. Book, Other. Cornell University Press. Ithaca, NY. 1996. 280p. Asia East by South Ser. ISBN:0-8014-3218-9, ISBN13: 978-0-8014-3218-7. Dewey:306.2/09595. LCCN:95-045155.
Audience: **g,l,u.** *Choice, 1996.*

Emmerson, Donald K. (Editor) **JQ770.I57 1999**
Indonesia Beyond Suharto: Polity Economy Society Transition. Trade Cloth. M. E. Sharpe Inc. Armonk, NY. 1999. 395p. Asia and the Pacific Ser. ISBN:1-56324-890-5, ISBN13: 978-1-56324-890-0. Dewey:320.9598/09/045. LCCN:99-023949.
Audience: **l,u,f.** *Choice, 2000.*

Honna, Jun **JQ766.C58H663 2003**
Military Politics and Democratization in Indonesia. Paper over Boards. Routledge. New York, NY. 2003. 320p.

RoutledgeCurzon Research on Southeast Asia Ser. ISBN:0-415-27228-9, ISBN13: 978-0-415-27228-5. Dewey:322/.5/09598. LCCN:2002-068242.
Audience: **l,u,f.** *Choice, 2004.*

Rodan **JQ745.S5**
Singapore Changes Guard. Cloth Text. Addison-Wesley Longman, Ltd. Harlow, 232p. ISBN:0-582-87610-9, ISBN13: 978-0-582-87610-1. Dewey:959.5705C.
Audience: **u,f.**

Suryadinata, Leo **JQ779.A576S87 1989**
Military Ascendancy and Political Culture: A Study of Indonesia's Golkar. Trade Paper. Ohio University Press. Athens, OH. 1989. 235p. Monographs in International Studies, No. 85 ISBN:0-89680-154-3, ISBN13: 978-0-89680-154-7. Dewey:322/.5/09598. LCCN:89-003083.
Audience: **l,u,f.** *Choice, 1990.*

Comparative Government > Asia > Central Asia

DK851
A Country Study: Kazakhstan. http://lcweb2.loc.gov/frd/cs/kztoc.html Library of Congress.
Audience: **g,l,u,f.**

DT215
A Country Study: Kyrgyzstan. http://lcweb2.loc.gov/frd/cs/kgtoc.html
Audience: **g,l,u,f.**

DS798
A Country Study: Mongolia. http://lcweb2.loc.gov/frd/cs/mntoc.html Library of Congress.
Audience: **g,l,u,f.**

DK851
A Country Study: Tajikistan. http://lcweb2.loc.gov/frd/cs/tjtoc.html Library of Congress.
Audience: **g,l,u,f.**

DK502
A Country Study: Turkmenistan. http://lcweb2.loc.gov/frd/cs/tmtoc.html
Audience: **g,l,u,f.**

DK851
A Country Study: Uzbekistan. http://lcweb2.loc.gov/frd/cs/uztoc.html LIbrary of Congress.
Audience: **g,l,u,f.**

Allsen, Thomas T. **DS740.5.I7 A45 2001**
Culture and Conquest in Mongol Eurasia. David Morgan (Contribution by). Trade Paper. Cambridge University Press. New York, NY. 2004. 261p. Cambridge Studies in Islamic Civilization Ser. ISBN:0-521-60270-X, ISBN13: 978-0-521-60270-9. Dewey:303.4825505109022.
Audience: **u.** *Choice, 2003, 2002.*

Barfield, Thomas J. **DS329.4.B37 1989**
The Perilous Frontier: Nomadic Empires and China. Cloth Text. Blackwell Publishing, Inc. Malden, MA. 1989. 300p. ISBN:1-55786-043-2, ISBN13: 978-1-55786-043-9. Dewey:958. LCCN:88-007746.
Audience: **u,f.** *Choice, 1990.*

Bertsch, Gary K. (Editor) **DK509.C76 2000**
Crossroads and Conflict: Security and Foreign Policy in the Caucasus and Central Asia. Paper over Boards. Routledge. New York, NY. 1999. 328p. ISBN:0-415-92273-9, ISBN13: 978-0-415-92273-9. Dewey:327.475. LCCN:99-020477.
Audience: **u,f.** *Choice, 2000.*

Dawisha, Karen & Parrott, Bruce (Editors) **DK859.5 .C66 1997**
Conflict, Cleavage, and Change in Central Asia and the Caucasus. Cloth Text. Cambridge University Press. New York, NY. 1997. 441p. Democratization and Authoritarianism in Post-Communist Societies Ser., Vol. 4 ISBN:0-521-59246-1, ISBN13: 978-0-521-59246-8. Dewey:320.958/09/049. LCCN:96-052478.
Audience: **u,f.** *Choice, 1998.*

Endicott-West, E., et al. **HC412.M58 1991**
The Modernization of Inner Asia. E. Naby, A. Waldron, Cyril E. Black, Daniel Matuszewski & Louis Dupree (Authors). Cloth Text. M. E. Sharpe Inc. Armonk, NY. 1991. 424p. ISBN:0-87332-778-0, ISBN13: 978-0-87332-778-7. Dewey:338.958. LCCN:90-023385.
Audience: **u,f.** *Choice, 1992.*

Jones Luong, Pauline **HN670.22.A8T73 2003**
The Transformation of Central Asia: States and Societies from Soviet Rule to Independence. Book, Other. Cornell University Press. Ithaca, NY. 2003. 400p. ISBN:0-8014-4151-X, ISBN13: 978-0-8014-4151-6. Dewey:306/.0958. LCCN:2003-011825.
Audience: **u,f.** *Choice, 2004.*

Mekenkamp, Monique (Editor), et al. **JZ5597.S43 2002**
Searching for Peace in Central and South Asia: An Overview of Conflict Prevention and Peacebuilding Activities. Paul Van Tongeren & Hans van de Veen (Editors). Library Binding. Lynne Rienner Publishers, Inc. Boulder, CO. 2002. xiv, 640p. European Centre for Conflict Prevention Ser. ISBN:1-58826-096-8, ISBN13: 978-1-58826-096-3. Dewey:327.1/72. LCCN:2002-017882.
Audience: **u,f.** *Choice, 2003.*

Meyer, Karl E. & Brysac, Shareen Blair **DS329.4**
Tournament of Shadows: The Great Game and the Race for Empire in Central Asia. Trade Paper. Basic Books. New York, NY. 2000. 672p. ISBN:1-58243-106-X, ISBN13: 978-1-58243-106-2. Dewey:958.
Audience: **g,l,u.**

Rhoads, Edward J. M. **DS761.2.R49 2000**
Manchus and Han: Ethnic Relations and Political Power in Late Qing and Early Republican China, 1861-1928. Trade Cloth. University of Washington Press. Seattle, WA. 2000. x, 394p. Studies on Ethnic Groups in China ISBN:0-295-97938-0, ISBN13: 978-0-295-97938-0. Dewey:951/.035. LCCN:00-008470.
Audience: **u,f.** *Choice, 2001.*

Rumer, Boris (Editor) **JQ1080.C44 2005**
Central Asia at the End of the Transition. Perfect, Paper over Boards. M. E. Sharpe Inc. Armonk, NY. 2005. 449p. ISBN:0-7656-1575-4, ISBN13: 978-0-7656-1575-6. Dewey:958.043. LCCN:2004-028503.
Audience: **l,u,f.** *Choice, 2006.*

Comparative Government > Australia. New Zealand. Pacific Ocean Islands

Aimer, Peter & Mulgan, Richard **JQ5831.M85 2004**
Politics in New Zealand. Ed. 3. Trade Paper. Auckland University Press. Auckland, 2004. 332p. ISBN:1-86940-318-5, ISBN13: 978-1-86940-318-8. Dewey:320.493. LCCN:2004-445708.
Audience: **u,f.**

Attwood, Bain & Markus, Andrew (Editors) **GN666.S85 1999**
The Struggle for Aboriginal Rights: A Documentary History. Trade Paper. Allen & Unwin Pty., Ltd. Crows Nest, NSW. 1998. 400p. ISBN:1-86448-584-1, ISBN13: 978-1-86448-584-4. Dewey:323.119915. LCCN:00-303975.
Audience: **l,u,f.** *Choice, 2000.*

Hamer, David **DU420.22.H35 1988**
The New Zealand Liberals: The Years of Power, 1891-1912. Trade Cloth. Oxford University Press, Inc. New York, NY. 1988. 432p. ISBN:1-86940-014-3, ISBN13: 978-1-86940-014-9. Dewey:324.2931/06/09. LCCN:88-192276.
Audience: **u,f.** *Choice, 1989.*

Lawson, Stephanie **JC423 .L373 1996**
Tradition versus Democracy in the South Pacific: Fiji, Tonga and Western Samoa. John Ravenhill, James Cotton, Donald Denoon, Mark Elvin, Hal Hill, Anothy Low, Ron May, Anthony Milner & Tessa Morris-Suzuki (Contribution by). Trade Cloth. Cambridge University Press. New York, NY. 1996. 240p. Asia-Pacific Studies, No. 2 ISBN:0-521-49638-1, ISBN13: 978-0-521-49638-4. Dewey:320.9/961. LCCN:95-032415.
Audience: **g,l,u,f.** *Choice, 1996.*

McMinn, Winston G. **JQ4020.S8M35 1994**
Nationalism and Federalism in Australia. Paper Text. Oxford University Press, Inc. New York, NY. 1995. 324p. ISBN:0-19-553667-3, ISBN13: 978-0-19-553667-6. Dewey:320.994. LCCN:95-107132.
Audience: **u,f.** *Choice, 1995.*

Moon, Jeremy; Sharman, Campbell **JQ4031**
☐ Australian Government and Politics Database. http://elections.uwa.edu.au
Moon, Jeremy (Project Coordinator) ; Sharman, Campbell (Project Coordinator). University of Western Australia.
Audience: **l,u,f.**

Sharman, Campbell & Moon, Jeremy (Editors) **JQ4031**
Australian Politics and Government: The Commonwealth, States and Territories. Cloth Text. Cambridge University Press. New York, NY. 2003. 336p. ISBN:0-521-82507-5, ISBN13: 978-0-521-82507-8. Dewey:320.494/049. LCCN:2003-446241.
Audience: **u,f.** *Choice, 2004.*

Warhurst, John & MacKerras, Malcolm (Editors) **JQ4031.C65 2002**
Constitutional Politics: The Republic Referendum and the Future. Trade Paper. University of Queensland Press. Saint Lucia, QLD. 2002. 320p. UQP Australian Studies ISBN:0-7022-3341-2, ISBN13: 978-0-7022-3341-8. Dewey:342.9402/9. LCCN:2003-283381.
Audience: **l,u.**

International Relations. Transnational Relations

D860
☐ CIAO (Columbia International Affairs Online). http://www.ciaonet.org/
Columbia University.
Audience: **l,u,f.**

Amstutz, Mark R. **JC571.A48 2004**
The Healing of Nations: The Promise and Limits of Political Forgiveness. Book, Other. Rowman & Littlefield Publishers, Inc. Lanham, MD. 2004. 296p. ISBN:0-7425-3581-9, ISBN13: 978-0-7425-3581-7. Dewey:323.4/9. LCCN:2004-001064.
Audience: **l,u,f.** *Choice, 2005.*

Bronner, Stephen Eric **JZ1318.P53 2005**
Planetary Politics: Human Rights, Terror, and Global Society. Book, Other. Rowman & Littlefield Publishers, Inc. Lanham, MD. 2005. 248p. ISBN:0-7425-4198-3, ISBN13: 978-0-7425-4198-6. Dewey:327. LCCN:2004-017766.
Audience: **l,u,f.**

Franda, Marcus **JZ1254.F73 2002**
Launching into Cyberspace: Internet Development and Politics in Five World Regions. Trade Paper. Lynne Rienner Publishers, Inc. Boulder, CO. 2001. 280p. Ipolitics Ser. ISBN:1-58826-037-2, ISBN13: 978-1-58826-037-6. Dewey:327/.0285/4678. LCCN:2001-031627.
Audience: **l,u,f.** *Choice, 2002.*

Holsti, Kalevi J. **JZ1310.H65 2004**
Taming the Sovereigns: Institutional Change in International Politics. Thomas Biersteker, Chris Brown, Phil Cerny, Joseph Grieco, A. J. R. Groom & Steve Smith (Contribution by). Cloth Text. Cambridge University Press. New York, NY. 2004. 372p. Cambridge Studies in International Relations Ser., Vol. 94 ISBN:0-521-83403-1, ISBN13: 978-0-521-83403-2. Dewey:327.1/01. LCCN:2003-047255.
Audience: **l,u,f.** *Choice, 2004.*

Katzenstein, Peter J. (Editor), et al. **JZ1242.E98 1999**
Exploration and Contestation in the Study of World Politics: A Special Issue of International Organization. Robert O. Keohane & Stephen D. Krasner (Editors). Trade Paper. MIT Press. Cambridge, MA. 1999. 432p. International Organization Reader Ser. ISBN:0-262-61144-9, ISBN13: 978-0-262-61144-2. Dewey:327.1/01. LCCN:98-050302.
Audience: **u,f.**

Kydd, Andrew **JZ1305.K93 2005**
Trust and Mistrust in International Relations. Trade Cloth. Princeton University Press. Princeton, NJ. 2005. 288p. ISBN:0-691-12170-2, ISBN13: 978-0-691-12170-3. Dewey:327.1/01. LCCN:2004-022495.
Audience: **l,u,f.** *Choice, 2006.*

Lake, David A. & Powell, Robert (Editors) **JZ1305.S765 1999**
Strategic Choice and International Relations. Trade Paper. Princeton University Press. Princeton, NJ. 1999. 280p. ISBN:0-691-02697-1, ISBN13: 978-0-691-02697-8. Dewey:327.1/01. LCCN:99-012215.
Audience: **l,u,f.**

Lieber, Robert J. **JZ1242.L53 2001**
No Common Power: Understanding International Relations. Ed. 4. Trade Paper. Prentice Hall PTR. Upper Saddle River, NJ. 2000. 398p. ISBN:0-13-011504-5, ISBN13: 978-0-13-011504-1. Dewey:327. LCCN:00-025982.
Audience: **l,u.**

Long, David & Schmidt, Brian C. (Editors) **JZ1308.I46 2005**
Imperialism and Internationalism in the Discipline of International Relations. Perfect, Paper over Boards. State University of New York Press. Albany, NY. 2005. 212p. SUNY Series in Global Politics ISBN:0-7914-6323-0, ISBN13: 978-0-7914-6323-9. Dewey:325/.32. LCCN:2004-029289.
Audience: **l,u,f.** *Choice, 2006.*

Mingst, Karen A. & Snyder, Jack L. **JZ1305.E85 2004**
Essential Readings in World Politics. Ed. 2. Trade Paper. W. W. Norton & Company, Inc. New York, NY. 2004. ix, 483p. The Norton Series in World Politics ISBN:0-393-92406-8, ISBN13: 978-0-393-92406-0. Dewey:327. LCCN:2004-041541.
Audience: **l,u.**

Powell, Robert **JZ1242.P68 1999**
In the Shadow of Power: States and Strategies in International Politics. Trade Paper. Princeton University Press. Princeton, NJ. 1999. 318p. ISBN:0-691-00457-9, ISBN13: 978-0-691-00457-0. Dewey:327.1/01. LCCN:99-012207.
Audience: **l,u,f.** *Choice, 2000.*

Rawls, John **JZ1242.R39 1999**
The Law of Peoples. Trade Cloth. Harvard University Press. Cambridge, MA. 1999. 210p. ISBN:0-674-00079-X, ISBN13: 978-0-674-00079-7. Dewey:320.51. LCCN:99-034785.
Audience: **l,u,f.**

Ruggie, John G. **JZ1305.R84 1998**
Constructing the World Polity: Essays on International Institutionalization. Trade Paper. Routledge. New York, NY. 1998. 336p. New International Relations Ser. ISBN:0-415-09991-9, ISBN13: 978-0-415-09991-2. Dewey:327.1/01. LCCN:98-192711.
Audience: **l,u,f.**

Tarrow, Sidney (Author, Contribution by) **JZ1308.T377 2005**
The New Transnational Activism. Douglas McAdam & Charles Tilly (Contribution by). Trade Paper. Cambridge University Press. New York, NY. 2005. 276p. Cambridge Studies in Contentious Politics Ser. ISBN:0-521-61677-8, ISBN13: 978-0-521-61677-5. Dewey:303.48/2. LCCN:2005-000307.
Audience: **g,l,u,f.** *Choice, 2006.*

Turner, Barry (Editor) **JA51.S7 2005**
The Statesman's Yearbook: The Politics, Cultures and Economies of the World. Ed. 142. Saddle Stitched, Cloth over Boards, Dust Jacket. Palgrave Macmillan. New York, NY. 2005. 2112p. ISBN:1-4039-1482-6, ISBN13: 978-1-4039-1482-8. Dewey:909.8305.
Audience: **g,l,u,f.**

Waltz, Kenneth N. **JX1395**
Theory of International Politics. Trade Cloth. Addison-Wesley Longman, Inc. Boston, MA. 1979. 251p. Addison-Wesley Series in Political Science Ser. ISBN:0-201-08349-3, ISBN13: 978-0-201-08349-1. Dewey:327.1/01. LCCN:78-062549.
Audience: **g,l,u,f.**

International Relations. Transnational Relations > Theory. Study and Teaching

D31
Correlates of War (COW) Project.
http://www.correlatesofwar.org/
Audience: **u,f.**

HC59
United Nations Common Database.
http://unstats.un.org/unsd/cdb/cdb_help/cdb_quick_start.asp
United Nations.
Audience: **g,l,u,f.**

Art, Robert J. & Jervis, Robert **JZ1242.I574 2005**
International Politics: Enduring Concepts and Contemporary Issues. Ed. 7. Trade Paper. Pearson Education. Boston, MA. 2004. 608p. ISBN:0-321-20947-8, ISBN13: 978-0-321-20947-4. Dewey:327.1. LCCN:2004-006652.
Audience: **g,l,u.**

Axelrod, Robert **HM 131 A89**
The Evolution of Cooperation. Trade Paper. Basic Books. New York, NY. 2006. 272p. ISBN:0-465-00564-0, ISBN13: 978-0-465-00564-2. Dewey:302/.14.
Audience: **g,l,u,f.**

Bueno de Mesquita, Bruce **JZ1242.B84 2006**
Principles of International Politics: People's Powers, Preferences, and Perceptions. Ed. 3. Trade Paper. CQ Press. Washington, DC. 2005. 659p. ISBN:1-933116-11-0, ISBN13: 978-1-933116-11-2. Dewey:327.1/01. LCCN:2005-020664.
Audience: **l,u.**

Bull, Hedley **JX1954 .B79 1995**
The Anarchical Society: A Study of Order in World Politics. Ed. 3. Andrew Hurrell & Stanley Hoffman (Foreword by). Trade Cloth. Columbia University Press. New York, NY. 2002. 368p. ISBN:0-231-12762-6, ISBN13: 978-0-231-12762-2. Dewey:327.
Audience: **u,f.**

Bull, Hedley (Editor), et al. **JC251.M6**
Hugo Grotius and International Relations. Benedict Kingsbury & Adam Roberts (Editors). Trade Paper. Oxford University Press, Inc. New York, NY. 1992. 346p. ISBN:0-19-827771-7, ISBN13: 978-0-19-827771-2. Dewey:327/.092.
Audience: **l,u,f.** *Choice, 1991.*

Davis, James W. **JZ1253.D38 2003**
Threats and Promises: The Pursuit of International Influence. Trade Paper. Johns Hopkins University Press. Baltimore, MD.

2003. 240p. ISBN:0-8018-7736-9, ISBN13: 978-0-8018-7736-0. Dewey:327.1/01.
Audience: **u,f.** *Choice, 2001.*

Etzioni, Amitai **JZ1480.E89 2004**
From Empire to Community: A New Approach to International Relations. Cloth over Boards. Palgrave Macmillan. New York, NY. 2004. 272p. ISBN:1-4039-6535-8, ISBN13: 978-1-4039-6535-6. Dewey:327.73. LCCN:2003-064013.
Audience: **g,l,u.** *Choice, 2005.*

Evans, Graham & Newnham, Richard **JZ1161.E94 1998**
The Penguin Dictionary of International Relations. Trade Paper. Penguin Group (USA) Inc. New York, NY. 1999. 640p. Penguin Reference Bks. ISBN:0-14-051397-3, ISBN13: 978-0-14-051397-4. Dewey:327/.03. LCCN:99-199845.
Audience: **g,l,u.** *Choice, 1999.*

Falk, Richard A. **BL65.I55**
Religion and Humane Global Governance. Cloth over Boards. Palgrave Macmillan. New York, NY. 2001. 208p. ISBN:0-312-23337-X, ISBN13: 978-0-312-23337-2. Dewey:291.1/787. LCCN:00-068845.
Audience: **u,f.** *Choice, 2002.*

Foot, Rosemary (Editor), et al. **JZ1308.O73 2003**
Order and Justice in International Relations. John Lewis Gaddis & Andrew Hurrell (Editors). Trade Paper. Oxford University Press, Inc. New York, NY. 2003. 328p. ISBN:0-19-925119-3, ISBN13: 978-0-19-925119-3. Dewey:327.1/01. LCCN:2002-028264.
Audience: **g,l,u.**

Friedrichs, Jorg **JZ1237.F75 2004**
European Approaches to International Relations Theory: A House with Many Mansions. Paper over Boards. Routledge. New York, NY. 2004. 224p. The New International Relations Ser. ISBN:0-415-33265-6, ISBN13: 978-0-415-33265-1. Dewey:327.1/01. LCCN:2003-024477.
Audience: **l,u.**

Geldenhuys, Deon **D860.G485 2004**
Deviant Conduct in World Politics. Trade Cloth. Palgrave Macmillan. New York, NY. 2004. 448p. ISBN:1-4039-3247-6, ISBN13: 978-1-4039-3247-1. Dewey:909.83. LCCN:2003-066189.
Audience: **l,u.** *Choice, 2005.*

Grieco, Joseph M. & Ikenberry, G. John **HF1359.G73 2002**
State Power and World Markets: The International Political Economy. Trade Paper. W. W. Norton & Company, Inc. New York, NY. 2002. 384p. ISBN:0-393-97419-7, ISBN13: 978-0-393-97419-5. Dewey:337. LCCN:2002-025505.
Audience: **u.**

Griffiths, Martin (Editor) **JX1226**
Encyclopedia of International Relations and Global Politics. Paper over Boards. Routledge. New York, NY. 2005. XVIII, 918p. ISBN:0-415-31160-8, ISBN13: 978-0-415-31160-1. Dewey:327.03.
Audience: **g,l,u,f.** *Choice, 2006.*

Griffiths, Martin & O'Callaghan, Terry **JZ1160.G75 2002**
International Relations: The Key Concepts. Cloth Text. Routledge. New York, NY. 2001. 384p. Key Guides ISBN:0-415-22882-4, ISBN13: 978-0-415-22882-4. Dewey:327/.03. LCCN:2001-038715.
Audience: **g,l,u.**

Haas, Ernst B. **JX1395 .H2**
Dynamics of International Relations. Paper Text. Textbook Publishers. Temecula, CA. 2003. 557p. ISBN:0-7581-8576-6, ISBN13: 978-0-7581-8576-1. Dewey:327.
Audience: **l,u.**

Ikenberry, G. John **JZ1480.A96 2005**
American Foreign Policy: Theoretical Essays. Ed. 5. Trade Paper. Longman Publishing Group. White Plains, NY. 2004. 608p. ISBN:0-321-15973-X, ISBN13: 978-0-321-15973-1. Dewey:327.73. LCCN:2004-009409.
Audience: **l,u.**

Kadera, Kelly M. **JZ1310.K33 2001**
The Power-Conflict Story: A Dynamic Model of Interstate Rivalry. Trade Cloth. University of Michigan Press. Chicago, IL. 2001. 208p. ISBN:0-472-11191-4, ISBN13: 978-0-472-11191-6. Dewey:327.1/01. LCCN:00-051173.
Audience: **u,f.** *Choice, 2002.*

Keohane, Robert O. **HF1359**
After Hegemony: Cooperation and Discord in the World Political Economy. Trade Paper. Princeton University Press. Princeton, NJ. 2005. 312p. ISBN:0-691-12248-2, ISBN13: 978-0-691-12248-9. Dewey:337. LCCN:2004-116492.
Audience: **u,f.** B

Keohane, Robert O. & Nye, Joseph S. **JX1395 .K428 2001**
Power and Interdependence. Ed. 3. Trade Paper. Longman Publishing. Boston, MA. 2000. 352p. ISBN:0-321-04857-1, ISBN13: 978-0-321-04857-8. Dewey:327. LCCN:00-018354.
Audience: **l,u.**

LeBow, Richard Ned **UA10.5.L43 2003**
The Tragic Vision of Politics: Ethics, Interests and Orders. Cloth Text. Cambridge University Press. New York, NY. 2003. 424p. ISBN:0-521-82753-1, ISBN13: 978-0-521-82753-9. Dewey:172/.4. LCCN:2002-041445.
Audience: **u,f.** *Choice, 2004.*

Morgenthau, Hans J. **JX1391.M6 1978**
Politics among Nations: The Struggle for Power and Peace. Ed. 5. Trade Cloth. Alfred A. Knopf Inc. New York, NY. 1978. ISBN:0-394-50085-7, ISBN13: 978-0-394-50085-0. Dewey:327. LCCN:77-026277.
Audience: **f.** B

Morgenthau, Hans J., et al. **JZ1242.M68 2005**
Politics among Nations. Ed. 7. David Clinton & Kenneth W. Thompson (Authors). Paper Text. McGraw-Hill Higher Education. Burr Ridge, IL. 2005. 752p. ISBN:0-07-289539-X, ISBN13: 978-0-07-289539-1. Dewey:327. LCCN:2005-041520.
Audience: **l,u.**

Nye, Joseph S. **JZ1305.N94 2005**
Understanding International Conflicts: An Introduction to Theory and History. Ed. 5. Trade Paper. Pearson Education. Boston,

MA. 2004. 288p. Longman Classics in Political Science Ser. ISBN:0-321-20945-1, ISBN13: 978-0-321-20945-0. Dewey:327/.09/04. LCCN:2004-009190.
Audience: **l,u.**

Smith, Michael J. **JX1291**
Realist Thought from Weber to Kissinger. Paper Text. Louisiana State University Press. Baton Rouge, LA. 1990. 304p. Political Traditions in Foreign Policy Ser. ISBN:0-8071-1632-7, ISBN13: 978-0-8071-1632-6. Dewey:327/.072. LCCN:86-015180.
Audience: **l,u,f.** *Choice, 1987.*

Sprinz, Detlef F. & Wolinsky-Nahmias, Yael (Editors) **JZ1234.M63 2004**
Models, Numbers, and Cases: Methods for Studying International Relations. Trade Cloth. University of Michigan Press. Chicago, IL. 2004. 424p. ISBN:0-472-09861-6, ISBN13: 978-0-472-09861-3. Dewey:327/.072. LCCN:2003-021557.
Audience: **u,f.**

Strachan, Hew **U43.E95**
European Armies and the Conduct of War. Trade Paper. Routledge. New York, NY. 1988. 240p. ISBN:0-415-07863-6, ISBN13: 978-0-415-07863-4. Dewey:355/.02/094.
Audience: **l,u,f.**

Sullivan, Michael P. **JZ1242.S85 2001**
Theories of International Relations: Transition vs. Persistence. Cloth over Boards. Palgrave Macmillan. New York, NY. 2001. 336p. ISBN:0-312-23074-5, ISBN13: 978-0-312-23074-6. Dewey:327.1/01. LCCN:00-068844.
Audience: **u.** *Choice, 2002.*

Tunkin, G. I. **JX1245.T8113 1974**
Theory of International Law. William Elliott Butler (Translator). Trade Cloth. Harvard University Press. Cambridge, MA. 1974. 480p. ISBN:0-674-88001-3, ISBN13: 978-0-674-88001-6. Dewey:341/.01. LCCN:73-092258.
Audience: **g,l,u.**

Valls, Andrew **JZ1306.E88 2000**
Ethics in International Affairs: Theories and Cases. Virginia Held (Foreword by). Trade Paper. Rowman & Littlefield Publishers, Inc. Lanham, MD. 2000. xx, 241p. ISBN:0-8476-9157-8, ISBN13: 978-0-8476-9157-9. Dewey:172/.4. LCCN:99-057384.
Audience: **g,l,u.** *Choice, 2000.*

Waltz, Kenneth N. **JZ1305**
Theory of International Politics. Paper Text. McGraw-Hill Higher Education. Burr Ridge, IL. 1979. 250p. ISBN:0-07-554852-6, ISBN13: 978-0-07-554852-2. Dewey:327.1/01.
Audience: **l,u.**

Wapner, Paul & Falk, Richard A. **JZ1242.P75 2000**
Principled World Politics: The Challenge of Normative International Relations at the Millennium. Lester E. Ruiz (Editor). Book, Other. Rowman & Littlefield Publishers, Inc. Lanham, MD. 2000. 416p. ISBN:0-7425-0065-9, ISBN13: 978-0-7425-0065-5. Dewey:327.1/01. LCCN:99-053985.
Audience: **u,f.** *Choice, 2000.*

Waters, Neil L. **D16.25.B5 2000**
Beyond the Area Studies Wars: Toward a New International Studies. Perfect. Wesleyan University Press. Middletown, CT. 2000. 256p. The Middlebury Bicentennial Series in International Studies ISBN:1-58465-074-5, ISBN13: 978-1-58465-074-4. Dewey:907/.2. LCCN:00-009483.
Audience: **u,f.** *Choice, 2001.*

Weart, Spencer R. **JC421.W43 1998**
Never at War: Why Democracies Will Not Fight One Another. Cloth over Boards. Yale University Press. Cumberland, RI. 1998. 430p. ISBN:0-300-07017-9, ISBN13: 978-0-300-07017-0. Dewey:327.1/7. LCCN:98-002664.
Audience: **g,l,u,f.** *Choice, 1999.*

Weigall, David **JZ1161.W45 2002**
International Relations: A Concise Companion. Paper Text. Oxford University Press, Inc. New York, NY. 2003. 224p. A Hodder Arnold Publication ISBN:0-340-76333-7, ISBN13: 978-0-340-76333-9. Dewey:327. LCCN:2003-545413.
Audience: **g,l,u,f.**

Wendt, Alexander **JZ1251 .W46 1999**
Social Theory of International Politics. Thomas Biersteker, Chris Brown & Phil Cerny (Contribution by). Cloth Text. Cambridge University Press. New York, NY. 1999. 449p. Studies in International Relations, No. 67 ISBN:0-521-46557-5, ISBN13: 978-0-521-46557-1. Dewey:327. LCCN:98-048329.
Audience: **l,u,f.** *Choice, 2000.*

International Relations. Transnational Relations > History

KZ233.U55
The Cumulated Index to the U. S. Department of State Papers Relating to the Foreign Relations of the United States, 1939-1945, Set. Library Binding. Kraus International Publications. Hackensack, NJ. 1981. ISBN:0-527-20744-6, ISBN13: 978-0-527-20744-1. Dewey:327.73. LCCN:81-160874.
Audience: **l,u,f.**

Addington, Larry H. **D214**
The Patterns of War since the Eighteenth Century. Paper Text. DIANE Publishing Company. Collingdale, PA. 1999. 318p. ISBN:0-7881-6088-5, ISBN13: 978-0-7881-6088-2. Dewey:355/.02/0903.
Audience: **l,u.**

Boyle, Francis A. **KZ1242.B69 1999**
Foundations of World Order: The Legalist Approach to International Relations, 1898-1921. Trade Cloth. Duke University Press. Durham, NC. 1999. 264p. ISBN:0-8223-2327-3, ISBN13: 978-0-8223-2327-3. Dewey:341/.09. LCCN:98-032014.
Audience: **u,f.** *Choice, 2000.*

Brune, Lester H. & Burns, Richard Dean **E183.7.B745 2002**
Chronological History of U. S. Foreign Relations, Set. Ed. 2. Paper over Boards. Routledge. New York, NY. 2002. 1488p. ISBN:0-415-93914-3, ISBN13: 978-0-415-93914-0. Dewey:327.73/002/02. LCCN:2002-023693.
Audience: **g,l,u,f.**

Diamond, Jared M. **HM206.D48 2005**
Guns, Germs, and Steel: The Fates of Human Societies. Trade Cloth. W. W. Norton & Company, Inc. New York, NY. 2005. 512p. ISBN:0-393-06131-0, ISBN13: 978-0-393-06131-4. Dewey:303.4. LCCN:2005-284261.
Audience: **g,l,u,f.** *Choice, 1997.*

Gaddis, John Lewis **D843.G22 2005**
The Cold War: A New History. Trade Cloth. Penguin Group (USA) Inc. New York, NY. 2005. 352p. ISBN:1-59420-062-9, ISBN13: 978-1-59420-062-5. Dewey:909.82/5. LCCN:2005-053406.
Audience: **g,l,u,f.** *Choice, 2006.*

Garton Ash, Timothy **D860.G29 2004**
Free World: America, Europe, and the Surprising Future of the West. Trade Cloth. Random House Adult Trade Publishing Group. New York, NY. 2004. 304p. ISBN:1-4000-6219-5, ISBN13: 978-1-4000-6219-5. Dewey:909.09821083. LCCN:2004-053862.
Audience: **g,l,u,f.** *Choice, 2005.*

Griffiths, Martin **JZ1305.G75 1999**
Fifty Key Thinkers in International Relations. Trade Paper. Routledge. New York, NY. 2000. 296p. Key Guides ISBN:0-415-16228-9, ISBN13: 978-0-415-16228-9. Dewey:327.1/01. LCCN:00-269065.
Audience: **l,u.**

Herwig, Holger H. & Bercuson, David J. **D753; D750**
One Christmas in Washington: The Secret Meeting Between Roosevelt and Churchill That Changed the World. Perfect, Paper over Boards, Dust Jacket. Overlook Press, The. New York, NY. 2005. 320p. ISBN:1-58567-403-6, ISBN13: 978-1-58567-403-9. Dewey:940.53/2241.
Audience: **g,l,u.**

Hewitt, Christopher & Cheetham, Tom **HM716.H48 2000**
Encyclopedia of Modern Separatist Movements. Library Binding. ABC-CLIO, Inc. Santa Barbara, CA. 2000. 0300p. ISBN:1-57607-007-7, ISBN13: 978-1-57607-007-9. Dewey:322.4/2/03. LCCN:00-024975.
Audience: **g,l,u.** *Choice, 2000.*

Hill, Christopher **JZ1253.H55 2002**
The Changing Politics of Foreign Policy. Cloth over Boards. Palgrave Macmillan. New York, NY. 2003. 416p. ISBN:0-333-75421-2, ISBN13: 978-0-333-75421-4. Dewey:327.1. LCCN:2002-075289.
Audience: **l,u,f.**

Jentleson, Bruce W. & Paterson, Thomas G. (Editors) **E183.7.E53 1997**
Encyclopedia of U. S. Foreign Relations, Set. Trade Cloth. Oxford University Press, Inc. New York, NY. 1997. 1861p. ISBN:0-19-511055-2, ISBN13: 978-0-19-511055-5. Dewey:327.73. LCCN:96-008159.
Audience: **g,l,u,f.** *Choice, 1997.*

Keylor, William R. **D840.K42 2003**
A World of Nations: The International Order since 1945. Cloth Text. Oxford University Press, Inc. New York, NY. 2002. 464p. ISBN:0-19-510601-6, ISBN13: 978-0-19-510601-5. Dewey:327/.09/045. LCCN:2002-025239.
Audience: **l,u.**

Thompson, William R. **D217.G74 1999**
Great Power Rivalries. Cloth Text. University of South Carolina Press. Columbia, SC. 1999. 352p. Studies in International Relations ISBN:1-57003-279-3, ISBN13: 978-1-57003-279-0. Dewey:327. LCCN:98-040228.
Audience: **l,u.**

Thomson Gale Staff (Contribution by) **E183.7.E52 2002**
Encyclopedia of American Foreign Policy, Set. Ed. 2. Trade Cloth. Thomson Gale. Farmington Hills, MI. 2001. 1500p. ISBN:0-684-80657-6, ISBN13: 978-0-684-80657-0. Dewey:327.73/003. LCCN:2001-049800.
Audience: **g,l,u,f.** *Choice, 2002.*

Watt, Donald Cameron **JX1403 .W3**
Documents on the Suez Crisis, 26 July to 6 November 1956. Paper Text. Textbook Publishers. Temecula, CA. 2003. 88p. ISBN:0-7581-4490-3, ISBN13: 978-0-7581-4490-4. Dewey:386.43.
Audience: **l,u,f.**

Wawro, Geoffrey **D361.W38 2000**
Warfare and Society in Europe, 1792-1914. Trade Paper. Routledge. New York, NY. 2000. 256p. Warfare and History Ser. ISBN:0-415-21445-9, ISBN13: 978-0-415-21445-2. Dewey:355/.0094/09034. LCCN:99-041813.
Audience: **l,u.**

Wright, Quincy **JX1952 .W72**
Problems of Stability and Progress in International Relations. Paper Text. Textbook Publishers. Temecula, CA. 2003. xii, 378p. ISBN:0-7581-2644-1, ISBN13: 978-0-7581-2644-3. Dewey:341.2.
Audience: **g,l,u.** B

International Relations. Transnational Relations > International Organization

Brinton, Clarence C. **JX1938**
From Many, One: The Process of Political Integration. Trade Cloth. Greenwood Publishing Group, Inc. Portsmouth, NH. 1971. 126p. ISBN:0-8371-5964-4, ISBN13: 978-0-8371-5964-5. Dewey:321/.04. LCCN:70-143309.
Audience: **l,u,f.** B

Bull, Hedley **JX1954 .B79 1995**
The Anarchical Society: A Study of Order in World Politics. Ed. 3. Andrew Hurrell & Stanley Hoffman (Foreword by). Trade Cloth. Columbia University Press. New York, NY. 2002. 368p. ISBN:0-231-12762-6, ISBN13: 978-0-231-12762-2. Dewey:327.
Audience: **u,f.** B

Caplan, Richard **JZ6374.C37 2005**
International Governance of War-Torn Territories: Rule and Reconstruction. Trade Cloth. Oxford University Press, Inc. New York, NY. 2005. 304p. ISBN:0-19-926345-0, ISBN13: 978-0-19-926345-5. Dewey:341.5/84. LCCN:2004-024297.
Audience: **l,u.**

Claude, Inis L. Jr. **JX1954 .C54 1971**
Swords into Plowshares: The Problems and Progress of International Organization. Ed. 4. Trade Cloth. Random House, Inc. New York, NY. 1971. "xii, 514"p. ISBN:0-394-31003-9, ISBN13: 978-0-394-31003-9. Dewey:341/.2. LCCN:70-122480.
Audience: **g,l,u.** B

Etzioni, Amitai **JZ1480.E89 2004**
From Empire to Community: A New Approach to International Relations. Cloth over Boards. Palgrave Macmillan. New York, NY. 2004. 272p. ISBN:1-4039-6535-8, ISBN13: 978-1-4039-6535-6. Dewey:327.73. LCCN:2003-064013.
Audience: **g,l,u.** *Choice, 2005.*

Etzioni, Amitai **JZ5566.E88 2001**
Political Unification Revisited: On Building Supranational Communities. Ed. 2. Trade Paper. Lexington Books. Lanham, MD. 2001. 412p. ISBN:0-7391-0273-7, ISBN13: 978-0-7391-0273-2. Dewey:327.1. LCCN:2001-029635.
Audience: **u,f.** *Choice, 2002.*

Haas, Ernst B. **HD6475.A1H17**
Beyond the Nation-State: Functionalism and International Organization. Trade Paper. Books on Demand. Ann Arbor, MI. 607p. ISBN:0-608-09118-9, ISBN13: 978-0-608-09118-1. Dewey:341.11. LCCN:64-021999.
Audience: **u,f.**

Haas, Ernst B. **JX1995.H24**
When Knowledge Is Power: Three Models of Change in International Organizations. Trade Paper. University of California Press. Berkeley, CA. 1991. 278p. Studies in International Political Economy, Vol. 22 ISBN:0-520-07402-5, ISBN13: 978-0-520-07402-6. Dewey:341.2.
Audience: **l,u,f.** *Choice, 1990.*

Jordan, Robert S., et al. **JZ4850**
International Organizations: A Comparative Approach to the Management of Cooperation. Ed. 4. Clive P. Archer, Gregory Granger & Kerry Ordes (Authors). Paper Text. Greenwood Publishing Group, Inc. Portsmouth, NH. 2001. 304p. ISBN:0-275-96550-3, ISBN13: 978-0-275-96550-1. Dewey:341.2. LCCN:00-052844.
Audience: **l,u.**

Katzenstein, Peter J. (Editor), et al. **JZ1242.E98 1999**
Exploration and Contestation in the Study of World Politics: A Special Issue of International Organization. Robert O. Keohane & Stephen D. Krasner (Editors). Trade Paper. MIT Press. Cambridge, MA. 1999. 432p. International Organization Reader Ser. ISBN:0-262-61144-9, ISBN13: 978-0-262-61144-2. Dewey:327.1/01. LCCN:98-050302.
Audience: **u,f.**

Mangone, Gerard J. **JX1954**
The Idea and Practice of World Government. Trade Cloth. Greenwood Publishing Group, Inc. Portsmouth, NH. 1975. 278p. ISBN:0-8371-7453-8, ISBN13: 978-0-8371-7453-2. Dewey:321.04. LCCN:74-003620.
Audience: **l,u.**

Muldoon, James P. Jr. **JZ5566.M85 2003**
The Architecture of Global Governance: An Introduction to the Study of International Organizations. Trade Paper. Westview Press. Boulder, CO. 2003. 336p. ISBN:0-8133-6844-8, ISBN13: 978-0-8133-6844-3. Dewey:341.2. LCCN:2003-006403.
Audience: **l,u.** *Choice, 2004.*

Russett, Bruce M. **JX1979 .R8 1975**
International Regions and the International System: A Study in Political Ecology. Trade Cloth. Greenwood Publishing Group, Inc. Portsmouth, NH. 1975. 252p. ISBN:0-8371-7191-1, ISBN13: 978-0-8371-7191-3. Dewey:341.24. LCCN:73-016608.
Audience: **u,f.**

Todorov, Tzvetan **D860**
The New World Disorder. Trade Cloth. Polity Press. Cambridge, 2004. 120p. ISBN:0-7456-3368-4, ISBN13: 978-0-7456-3368-8. Dewey:909.82/9. LCCN:2005-298466.
Audience: **l,u.**

Trachtenberg, Marc **D1058.T718 1999**
A Constructed Peace: The Making of the European Settlement, 1945-1963. Trade Paper. Princeton University Press. Princeton, NJ. 1999. 440p. Princeton Studies in International History and Politics ISBN:0-691-00273-8, ISBN13: 978-0-691-00273-6. Dewey:327/.094/09045. LCCN:98-034874.
Audience: **u,f.** *Choice, 1999.*

International Relations. Transnational Relations > International Organization > International Treaties

Beilin, Yossi **DS119.76**
The Path to Geneva: The Quest for a Permanent Agreement, 1996-2003. Trade Cloth. Akashic Books. New York, NY. 2004. 300p. ISBN:0-9719206-3-X, ISBN13: 978-0-9719206-3-7. Dewey:956.05/3. LCCN:2003-116635.
Audience: **g,u,f.** *Choice, 2005.*

Chill, Emanuel **KZ184.2.I8 2001**
Major Peace Treaties of Modern History, 1648-2001. Fred L. Israel (Editor). Trade Cloth. Facts On File, Inc. New York, NY. 2001. v. 2-5p. ISBN:0-7910-6659-2, ISBN13: 978-0-7910-6659-1. Dewey:341.7/3/0265. LCCN:2001-053697.
Audience: **g,l,u.** *Choice, 2002.*

Dyson, Kenneth & Featherstone, Kevin **HG925.D97 1999**
The Road to Maastricht: Negotiating Economic and Monetary Union. Trade Paper. Oxford University Press, Inc. New York, NY. 2000. 884p. ISBN:0-19-829638-X, ISBN13: 978-0-19-829638-6. Dewey:332.4/566/094. LCCN:99-025739.
Audience: **u,f.** *Choice, 2000.*

Grenville, J. A. S. **JX171.G736 1987**
Major International Treaties, 1914-1945: A History and Guide with Texts. Library Binding. Routledge. New York, NY. 1988. 300p. ISBN:0-416-08092-8, ISBN13: 978-0-416-08092-6. Dewey:341/.026. LCCN:87-014091.
Audience: **g,l,u.**

Hall, Timothy L. & Moose, Christian J. (Editors) **KF385.A4U152 2003**
US Laws, Acts, and Treaties, Volume 1: 1776-1928. Library Binding. Salem Press, Inc. Hackensack, NJ. 2003. Magill's Choice Ser. ISBN:1-58765-099-1, ISBN13: 978-1-58765-099-4. Dewey:348.73/2. LCCN:2002-156063.
Audience: **g,l,u.**

Hall, Timothy L. & Moose, Christian J. (Editors) **KF385.A4U152 2003**
US Laws, Acts, and Treaties, Volume 2: 1929-1970. Laminated. Salem Press, Inc. Hackensack, NJ. 2003. Magill's Choice Ser. ISBN:1-58765-100-9, ISBN13: 978-1-58765-100-7. Dewey:348.73/2. LCCN:2002-156063.
Audience: **g,l,u.**

Hall, Timothy L. & Moose, Christian J. (Editors) **KF385.A4U152 2003**
US Laws, Acts, and Treaties, Volume 3: 1970-2002. Trade Cloth. Salem Press, Inc. Hackensack, NJ. 2003. Magill's Choice Ser. ISBN:1-58765-101-7, ISBN13: 978-1-58765-101-4. Dewey:348.73/2. LCCN:2002-156063.
Audience: **g,l,u.**

Havard, Gilles **E92.H39 2001**
The Great Peace of Montreal of 1701: French-Native Diplomacy in the Seventeenth Century. Phyllis Aronoff & Howard Scott (Translators). Trade Cloth. McGill-Queen's University Press. Montreal, PQ. 2001. xi, 308p. ISBN:0-7735-2209-3, ISBN13: 978-0-7735-2209-1. Dewey:971.01/8. LCCN:2002-489834.
Audience: **u,f.** *Choice, 2002.*

Hoffman, Ronald & Albert, Peter J. (Editors) **E249.P42 1986**
Peace and the Peacemakers: The Treaty of 1783. Cloth Text. University Press of Virginia. Charlottesville, VA. 1986. xvi, 263p. U. S. Capitol Historical Society, Perspectives on the American Revolution Ser. ISBN:0-8139-1071-4, ISBN13: 978-0-8139-1071-0. Dewey:973.3/17. LCCN:85-010618.
Audience: **l,u.** *Choice, 1986.*

Krepon, Michael & Caldwell, Dan (Editors) **JX1974.P6238 1991**
The Politics of Arms Control Treaty Ratification. Cloth over Boards. Palgrave Macmillan. New York, NY. 1992. 494p. A Henry L. Stimson Center Bk. ISBN:0-312-06604-X, ISBN13: 978-0-312-06604-8. Dewey:341.3/7/0941. LCCN:91-034787.
Audience: **g,l,u,f.** *Choice, 1992.*

MacMillan, Margaret **D644.M32 2002**
Paris 1919: Six Months That Changed the World. Richard Holbrooke (Foreword by). Trade Cloth. Random House Adult Trade Publishing Group. New York, NY. 2002. 608p. ISBN:0-375-50826-0, ISBN13: 978-0-375-50826-4. Dewey:940.3/141. LCCN:2002-023707.
Audience: **g,l,u.** *Choice, 2003.*

Masyny, Vojtech & Byrne, Malcolm (Editors) **UA646.8C37 2005**
A Cardboard Castle?: An Inside History of the Warsaw Pact, 1955-1991. Trade Cloth. Central European University Press. Herndon, VA. 2005. 800p. National Security Archive Cold War Readers Ser. ISBN:963-7326-08-1, ISBN13: 978-963-7326-08-0. Dewey:355/.031/0947. LCCN:2005-002291.
Audience: **u,f.** *Choice, 2005.*

Mattox, Gale A. & Rachwald, Arthur R. (Editors) **UA646.3.E53 2001**
Enlarging NATO: The National Debates. Trade Cloth. Lynne Rienner Publishers, Inc. Boulder, CO. 2001. 300p. ISBN:1-55587-908-X, ISBN13: 978-1-55587-908-2. Dewey:355/.031091821. LCCN:2001-019005.
Audience: **g,l,u,f.** *Choice, 2002.*

Said, Edward W. **DS119.76.S245 2000**
The End of the Peace Process: Oslo and After. Trade Cloth. Knopf Publishing Group. New York, NY. 2000. 368p. ISBN:0-375-40930-0, ISBN13: 978-0-375-40930-1. Dewey:956/.053. LCCN:99-044765.
Audience: **g,l,u,f.**

Sampson, Gary P. & Woolcock, Stephen (Editor, Contribution by) **HF1418.5.R4438 2003**
Regionalism, Multilateralism, and Economic Integration: The Recent Experience. Luk Van Langenhoven, Brigid Gavin, Magnus Feldman, Joakim Reiter & Tomas Baert (Contribution by). Trade Paper. United Nations Publications. New York, NY. 2005. 384p. ISBN:92-808-1083-9, ISBN13: 978-92-808-1083-7. Dewey:382/.9. LCCN:2003-010733.
Audience: **u,f.** *Choice, 2004.*

Stathis, Stephen W. **KF68.S73 2003**
Landmark Legislation, 1774-2002: Major U. S. Acts and Treaties. Trade Cloth. CQ Press. Washington, DC. 2003. 426p. ISBN:1-56802-781-8, ISBN13: 978-1-56802-781-4. Dewey:348.73/2. LCCN:2003-003531.
Audience: **g,l,u,f.** *Choice, 2004.*

Wilson, William W. **HD9005.K66 2002**
Agricultural Trade under CUSTA. Won W. Koo (Editor). Trade Cloth. Nova Science Publishers, Inc. Hauppauge, NY. 2002. 355p. ISBN:1-59033-192-3, ISBN13: 978-1-59033-192-7. Dewey:382/.41/0973. LCCN:2001-059618.
Audience: **u,f.** *Choice, 2003, 2002.*

International Relations. Transnational Relations > International Organization > Intergovernmental Organizations. IGOs

Caufield, Catherine **HC60.C345 1996**
Masters of Illusion: The World Bank and the Poverty of Nations. Trade Cloth. Henry Holt & Company. New York, NY. 1997. 448p. ISBN:0-8050-2875-7, ISBN13: 978-0-8050-2875-1. Dewey:332.1/532/09. LCCN:96-016804.
Audience: **u,f.** *Choice, 1997.*

Endres, Anthony M. & Fleming, Grant A. **HD87 .E53 2002**
International Organizations and the Analysis of Economic Policy, 1919-1950. Craufurd D. Goodwin (Contribution by). Trade Paper. Cambridge University Press. New York, NY. 2005. 304p. Historical Perspectives on Modern Economics Ser. ISBN:0-521-02241-X, ISBN13: 978-0-521-02241-5. Dewey:338.9009041.
Audience: **u,f.**

Foot, Rosemary (Editor), et al. **JZ1480.U813 2003**
U.S. Hegemony and International Organizations. S. Neil MacFarlane & Michael Mastanduno (Editors). Trade Paper. Oxford University Press, Inc. New York, NY. 2003. 310p. ISBN:0-19-926143-1, ISBN13: 978-0-19-926143-7. Dewey:341.2. LCCN:2002-035570.
Audience: **u,f.**

Hajnal, Peter I. (Editor) **Z672**
International Information: Doc, Pub and Electronic Information of International Organizations. Ed. 2. Trade Cloth. Libraries Unlimited, Inc. Westport, CT. 2001. 402p. ISBN:1-56308-808-8, ISBN13: 978-1-56308-808-7. Dewey:020.621. LCCN:97-023470.
Audience: **g,l,u,f.**

Hajnal, Peter I. **HF1359.H34 1999**
The G7/G8 System: Evolution, Role and Documentation. Sian Meikle (Contribution by). Trade Cloth. Ashgate Publishing, Ltd. Aldershot, 1999. 202p. The Group of Eight and Global Governance Ser. ISBN:1-84014-776-8, ISBN13: 978-1-84014-776-6. Dewey:337.1. LCCN:99-072597.
Audience: **u,f.**

Harris, Gordon (Compiled by) **Z3504.O743H37 1994**
Organization of African Unity: An Annotated Bibliography. Trade Cloth. Transaction Publishers. Somerset, NJ. 1994. 139p. International Organizations Ser., Vol. 7 ISBN:1-56000-153-4,

ISBN13: 978-1-56000-153-9. Dewey:016.34124/9. LCCN:93-042579.
Audience: **l,u,f.** *Choice, 1994.*

Lansford, Tom **D860.L355 2002**
All for One: Terrorism, NATO and the United States. Trade Cloth. Ashgate Publishing, Ltd. Aldershot, 2002. 222p. ISBN:0-7546-3045-5, ISBN13: 978-0-7546-3045-6. Dewey:973.931. LCCN:2002-024893.
Audience: **l,u,f.** *Choice, 2003.*

Sheinin, David **F1402.S5 1995**
The Organization of American States, Vol. 11. Trade Cloth. Transaction Publishers. Somerset, NJ. 1995. 209p. International Organizations Ser. ISBN:1-56000-243-3, ISBN13: 978-1-56000-243-7. Dewey:341.24/5. LCCN:95-000698.
Audience: **u,f.** *Choice, 1996.*

Sloan, Elinor C. **U42 .S58 2002**
The Revolution in Military Affairs: Implications for Canada and NATO. Raoul-Dandurand Chair of Strategic and Diplomatic Studies Staff & Universite du Quebec a Montreal, Centre d'etudes des Politiques Etrangeres et de Securite Staff (Contribution by). Trade Cloth. McGill-Queen's University Press. Montreal, PQ. 2002. 192p. ISBN:0-7735-2363-4, ISBN13: 978-0-7735-2363-0. Dewey:355/.0330049.
Audience: **u,f.** *Choice, 2003, 2002.*

Walraven, Klaas van **DT30.5.W36 1999**
Dreams of Power: The Role of the Organization of African Unity in the Politics of Africa, 1963-1993. Trade Paper. Ashgate Publishing, Ltd. Aldershot, 2000. 496p. ISBN:1-85628-916-8, ISBN13: 978-1-85628-916-0. Dewey:320.54/9/096. LCCN:00-269376.
Audience: **u,f.**

International Relations. Transnational Relations > International Organization > Intergovernmental Organizations. IGOs > League of Nations

Burton, David Henry **E762.B88 2003**
Taft, Wilson, and World Order. Trade Paper. Fairleigh Dickinson University Press. Cranbury, NJ. 2003. 144p. ISBN:0-8386-3969-0, ISBN13: 978-0-8386-3969-6. Dewey:973.91/2/092. LCCN:2002-071287.
Audience: **u,f.**

Callahan, Michael D. **JZ4871.5.C35 1999**
Mandates and Empire: The League of Nations and Africa, 1914-1931. Trade Cloth. Sussex Academic Press. Eastbourne, 1999. 336p. ISBN:1-902210-23-9, ISBN13: 978-1-902210-23-0. Dewey:341.27/096/09042. LCCN:99-020795.
Audience: **u,f.** *Choice, 2000.*

Callahan, Michael D. **DT29.C35 2004**
A Sacred Trust: The League of Nations and Africa, 1929-1946. Trade Cloth. Sussex Academic Press. Eastbourne, 2004. 308p. ISBN:1-84519-016-5, ISBN13: 978-1-84519-016-3. Dewey:960.3/16. LCCN:2004-007294.
Audience: **u,f.** *Choice, 2005.*

Cooper, John Milton Jr. **E768.C66 2001**
Breaking the Heart of the World: Woodrow Wilson and the Fight for the League of Nations. Trade Cloth. Cambridge University Press. New York, NY. 2001. 464p. ISBN:0-521-80786-7, ISBN13: 978-0-521-80786-9. Dewey:973.91/3. LCCN:2001-025489.
Audience: **u,f.** *Choice, 2002.*

Fleming, Denna F. **JX1975.5.U5 F6**
United States and World Organization, 1920-1933. Trade Cloth. A M S Press, Inc. New York, NY. ISBN:0-404-02435-1, ISBN13: 978-0-404-02435-2. Dewey:341.1. LCCN:70-168040.
Audience: **l,u.**

Greaves, Harold R. **JX1975 .G675 1979**
The League Committees and World Order. Trade Cloth. A M S Press, Inc. New York, NY. ISBN:0-404-15336-4, ISBN13: 978-0-404-15336-6. Dewey:341.22. LCCN:76-029430.
Audience: **u,f.**

Haigh, R. H., et al. **DK266.H246 1986**
Soviet Foreign Policy, the League of Nations and Europe, 1917-1939. D. S. Morris & A. R. Peters (Authors). Trade Cloth. Rowman & Littlefield Publishers, Inc. Lanham, MD. 1986. 224p. ISBN:0-389-20611-3, ISBN13: 978-0-389-20611-8. Dewey:327.47. LCCN:85-030630.
Audience: **u,f.** *Choice, 1986.*

Henig, Ruth **D643.A7H43 1995**
Versailles and After, 1919-1933. Ed. 2. Trade Paper. Routledge. New York, NY. 1995. 96p. Lancaster Pamphlets Ser. ISBN:0-415-12710-6, ISBN13: 978-0-415-12710-3. Dewey:940.3/142. LCCN:94-041756.
Audience: **l,u.**

Joyce, James Avery **JX1975**
Broken Star: The Story of the League of Nations (1919-1939). Trade Cloth. Christopher Davies Publishers, Ltd. Swansea, 1978. 231p. ISBN:0-7154-0419-9, ISBN13: 978-0-7154-0419-5. Dewey:341.22. LCCN:79-300195.
Audience: **l,u.**

Knock, Thomas J **E767.1.K56 1992**
To End All Wars: Woodrow Wilson and the Quest for a New World Order. Oxford University Press, Inc. 1992. ISBN:0-19-507501-3, ISBN13: 978-0-19-507501-4.
Audience: **u,f.**

Lansing, Robert Jr. **D644.L3**
The Peace Negotiations. Trade Paper. 1st World Publishing, Inc. Fairfield, IA. 2005. 344p. ISBN:1-4218-0184-1, ISBN13: 978-1-4218-0184-1. Dewey:940.3/142. LCCN:2004195350.
Audience: **g,l,u.**

Lawrence, T. J. **JZ4871.L39 2005**
The Society of Nations: Its Past, Present, and Possible Future. Trade Cloth. Lawbook Exchange, Limited, The. Clark, NJ. 2005. 208p. ISBN:1-58477-562-9, ISBN13: 978-1-58477-562-1. Dewey:341.22. LCCN:2004-057780.
Audience: **u,f.**

Miller, David H. **JZ4872.M55 2002**
The Drafting of the Covenant. Library Binding. William S. Hein & Company, Inc. Buffalo, NY. 2002. ISBN:1-57588-727-4, ISBN13: 978-1-57588-727-2. Dewey:341.22/2. LCCN:2002-068824.
Audience: **l,u,f.**

Northedge, F. S. **JX1975.N78 1986**
The League of Nations: Its Life and Times, 1920-1946. Cloth Text. Holmes & Meier Publishers, Inc. Teaneck, NJ. 1986. 350p.

ISBN:0-8419-1065-0, ISBN13: 978-0-8419-1065-2. Dewey:341.22/09. LCCN:85-021989.
Audience: **u,f.** *Choice, 1986.*

Ranshofen-Wertheimer, E. F. **JX1975**
The International Secretariat: A Great Experiment in International Administration. Trade Cloth. Periodicals Service Company. Germantown, NY. 1969. Studies in the Administration of International Law and Organization ISBN:0-527-00881-8, ISBN13: 978-0-527-00881-9. Dewey:341.127.
Audience: **u,f.**

Taft, William Howard **E660.T11 2001 VOL.7**
The Collected Works of William Howard Taft: Taft Papers on League of Nations. Frank X. Gerrity (Editor). Trade Cloth. Ohio University Press. Athens, OH. 2004. 288p. Collected Works W H Taft Ser. ISBN:0-8214-1518-2, ISBN13: 978-0-8214-1518-4. Dewey:352.23/8/097309041 s. LCCN:2003-017871.
Audience: **g,l,u,f.**

Walters, F. P. **JX1975 .W28**
A History of the League of Nations. Paper Text. Textbook Publishers. Temecula, CA. 2003. xv, 833p. ISBN:0-7581-6912-4, ISBN13: 978-0-7581-6912-9. Dewey:341.22/09.
Audience: **l,u.** B

International Relations. Transnational Relations > International Organization > Intergovernmental Organizations. IGOs > United Nations

JZ5005
☐ American Model United Nations International (collegiate). http://www.amun.org//modelun/index.asp
Audience: **g,l,u.**

JF1001
The United Nations and Electoral Assistance. Trade Paper. United Nations Publications. New York, NY. 1996. The United Nations Blue Bks. ISBN:92-1-100601-5, ISBN13: 978-92-1-100601-8. Dewey:324.9.
Audience: **g,l,u.**

JX1977.2.H2
The United Nations and Haiti. Trade Paper. United Nations Publications. New York, NY. 1996. The United Nations Blue Bks. ISBN:92-1-100606-6, ISBN13: 978-92-1-100606-3. Dewey:341.23.
Audience: **g,l,u.**

HQ1236U5 1995
The United Nations and the Advancement of Women, 1945-1995. Trade Cloth. United Nations Publications. New York, NY. 1995. 689p. The United Nations Blue Bks., Vol. VI ISBN:92-1-100567-1, ISBN13: 978-92-1-100567-7. Dewey:305.42/09. LCCN:95-213673.
Audience: **g,l,u.** *Choice, 1996.*

JA51
Yearbook of the United Nations Collection on CD-ROM 1946-2002: Network Version. CD-ROM. United Nations Publications. New York, NY. 2002. ISBN:92-1-100951-0, ISBN13: 978-92-1-100951-4. Dewey:320.
Audience: **l,u,f.**

Alger, Chadwick F. (Editor) **JZ4984.5.F88 1998**
The Future of the United Nations System: Potential for the Twenty-First Century. Trade Paper. United Nations University Press. Tokyo, 1998. 400p. ISBN:92-808-0973-3, ISBN13: 978-92-808-0973-2. Dewey:341.23/1. LCCN:98-008997.
Audience: **l,u.** *Choice, 1999.*

Annan, Kofi A. (Foreword by) **JX1977.A37 B3**
Basic Facts about the United Nations. Paper Text. DIANE Publishing Company. Collingdale, PA. 2005. 359p. ISBN:0-7567-4651-5, ISBN13: 978-0-7567-4651-3. Dewey:341.23/05.
Audience: **g,l,u.**

Baehr, Peter R. & Gordenker, Leon **JZ4984.5.B34 2005**
The United Nations: Reality and Ideal. Ed. 4. Mixed Media, Trade Paper, Trade Cloth. Palgrave Macmillan. New York, NY. 2006. 208p. ISBN:1-4039-4905-0, ISBN13: 978-1-4039-4905-9. Dewey:341.23. LCCN:2005-046333.
Audience: **g,l,u.**

Baehr, Peter R. & Gordenker, Leon **JZ4984.5 .B34 1999**
The United Nations at the End of the 1990's. Ed. 3. Trade Paper. Palgrave Macmillan. New York, NY. 1999. 221p. ISBN:0-312-22017-0, ISBN13: 978-0-312-22017-4. Dewey:341.23. LCCN:98-042264.
Audience: **g,l,u.**

Bailey, Sydney D. **JX1977.A362 B34 1978**
The Secretariat of the United Nations. Trade Cloth. Greenwood Publishing Group, Inc. Portsmouth, NH. 1978. 132p. Carnegie Endowment for International Peace, United Nations Studies, No. 11 ISBN:0-313-20338-5, ISBN13: 978-0-313-20338-1. Dewey:341.23/2. LCCN:78-002880.
Audience: **g,l,u,f.**

Baratta, Joseph P. (Compiled by) **JX1977.B284 1995**
United Nations System: An Annotated Bibliography. Trade Cloth. Transaction Publishers. Somerset, NJ. 1995. 511p. International Organizations Ser., Vol. 10 ISBN:1-56000-216-6, ISBN13: 978-1-56000-216-1. Dewey:341.23. LCCN:94-041759.
Audience: **l,u,f.** *Choice, 1996.*

Barnett, Michael N. **DT450.435.B38 2002**
Eyewitness to a Genocide: The United Nations and Rwanda. Trade Cloth. Cornell University Press. Ithaca, NY. 2002. 240p. ISBN:0-8014-3883-7, ISBN13: 978-0-8014-3883-7. Dewey:967.57104. LCCN:2001-005561.
Audience: **l,u,f.** *Choice, 2002.*

Bennett, A. LeRoy **JX1976.B395 1995**
Historical Dictionary of the United Nations. Trade Cloth. Scarecrow Press, Inc. Lanham, MD. 1995. 290p. International Organizations Ser., No. 8 ISBN:0-8108-2992-4, ISBN13: 978-0-8108-2992-3. Dewey:341.23. LCCN:95-001505.
Audience: **g,l,u,f.**

Berkes, Ross N. **JX1977.2.I47**
The Diplomacy of India: Indian Foreign Policy in the United Nations,. Paper Text. Textbook Publishers. Temecula, CA. 2003. 221p. ISBN:0-7581-3441-X, ISBN13: 978-0-7581-3441-7. Dewey:341.139.
Audience: **g,l,u.**

Berthelot, Yves (Editor) **HD82.U57 2003**
Unity and Diversity in Development Ideas: Perspectives from the U. N. Regional Commissions. Trade Paper. Indiana University Press. Bloomington, IN. 2003. 408p. United Nations Intellectual History Project Ser., Vol. 2 ISBN:0-253-21638-9, ISBN13: 978-0-253-21638-0. Dewey:341.7/59. LCCN:2003-009550.
Audience: **l,u.**

Boudreau, Thomas E. **JX1977**
Sheathing the Sword: The U. N. Secretary-General and the Prevention of Internation Conflict. Trade Cloth. Greenwood Publishing Group, Inc. Portsmouth, NH. 1991. 208p. Contributions in Political Science Ser., No. 273 ISBN:0-313-26109-1, ISBN13: 978-0-313-26109-1. Dewey:327.1/7. LCCN:90-047520.
Audience: **l,u.** *Choice, 1991.*

Boulden, Jane & Weiss, Thomas George **HV6431.T4635 2004**
Terrorism and the UN: Before and after September 11. Trade Cloth. Indiana University Press. Bloomington, IN. 2004. 248p. ISBN:0-253-21662-1, ISBN13: 978-0-253-21662-5. Dewey:345/.02. LCCN:2003-020232.
Audience: **g,l,u,f.** *Choice, 2004.*

Bourantonis, Dimitris & Wiener, Jarrod (Editors) **JX1977**
The United Nations in the New World Order: The World Organization at Fifty. Trade Paper. Palgrave Macmillan. New York, NY. 1996. 235p. ISBN:0-312-16118-2, ISBN13: 978-0-312-16118-7. Dewey:341.23.
Audience: **g,l,u.**

Boutros-Ghali, Boutros (Introduction by) **JX1977.2.M85U55 1995**
The United Nations and Mozambique, 1992-1995. Trade Cloth. United Nations Publications. New York, NY. 1996. 321p. Blue Bks., Vol. V ISBN:92-1-100559-0, ISBN13: 978-92-1-100559-2. Dewey:341.23679. LCCN:95-192058.
Audience: **g,l,u.** *Choice, 1996.*

Bowles, Newton **JZ4984.5**
The Diplomacy of Hope: The United Nations since the Cold War. Trade Paper. I. B. Tauris & Company, Ltd. London, 2004. 205p. ISBN:1-85043-458-1, ISBN13: 978-1-85043-458-0. Dewey:341.23. LCCN:2005-271271.
Audience: **g,l.** *Choice, 2005.*

Burgess, Stephen **JZ4984.5.B87 2001**
The United Nations under Boutros Boutros-Ghali, 1992-1997. Trade Cloth. Scarecrow Press, Inc. Lanham, MD. 2001. 250p. Partners for Peace Ser., Vol. 6 ISBN:0-8108-3703-X, ISBN13: 978-0-8108-3703-4. Dewey:341.23/09/049. LCCN:2001-049238.
Audience: **g,l,u.**

Carpenter, Ted G. **JX1977.D43 1997**
Delusions of Grandeur: The United Nations and Global Intervention. Trade Cloth. Cato Institute. Washington, DC. 1997. 184p. ISBN:1-882577-49-3, ISBN13: 978-1-882577-49-1. Dewey:341.5/84. LCCN:97-016247.
Audience: **u,f.** *Choice, 1998.*

Coulon, Jocelyn **JZ6374.C6813 1998**
Soldiers of Diplomacy (Les Casques Bleus): The United Nations, Peacekeeping and the New World Order. Phyllis Aronoff & Howard Scott (Translators). Trade Cloth. University of Toronto Press. Toronto, ON. 1998. 526p. ISBN:0-8020-0899-2, ISBN13: 978-0-8020-0899-2. Dewey:341.5/23. LCCN:98-229699.
Audience: **g,l,u,f.** *Choice, 1999.*

Dobbins, James, et al. **JZ4984.5.U534 2005**
The UN's Role in Nation-Building: From the Congo to Iraq. Keith Crane & Seth G. Jones (Authors). Trade Paper. RAND Corporation, The. Santa Monica, CA. 2005. 344p. ISBN:0-8330-3589-4, ISBN13: 978-0-8330-3589-9. Dewey:341.5/84. LCCN:2004-027669.
Audience: **l,u,f.** *Choice, 2006.*

Durch, William J. **JX1981.P7U197 1996**
The United Nations Peacekeeper of American Policies and Uncivilizations. Cloth over Boards. Palgrave Macmillan. New York, NY. 1996. 416p. A Henry L. Stimson Center Bk. ISBN:0-312-12930-0, ISBN13: 978-0-312-12930-9. Dewey:341.5/8. LCCN:96-034880.
Audience: **u,f.** *Choice, 1997.*

Emmerij, Louis, et al. **JZ4986.E47 2001**
[e] Ahead of the Curve?: U. N. Ideas and Global Challenges. Richard Jolly & Thomas George Weiss (Authors), Kofi A. Annan (Foreword by). E-Book. Indiana University Press. Bloomington, IN. 2001. xvii, 257p. United Nations Intellectual History Ser. ISBN:0-253-33950-2, ISBN13: 978-0-253-33950-8. Dewey:341.23. LCCN:00-054098.
Audience: **u,f.** *Choice, 2002.*

Finger, Seymour M. & Saltzman, Arnold A. **JX1977**
Bending with the Winds: Kurt Waldheim and the United Nations. Trade Cloth. Greenwood Publishing Group, Inc. Portsmouth, NH. 1990. 144p. ISBN:0-275-93701-1, ISBN13: 978-0-275-93701-0. Dewey:341.23/24/092. LCCN:90-037861.
Audience: **l,u.** *Choice, 1991.*

Forsythe, David, et al. **JZ4984.5**
The United Nations and Changing World Politics. Ed. 4. Thomas Weiss & Roger Coate (Authors). Trade Paper. Westview Press. Boulder, CO. 2004. 448p. ISBN:0-8133-4206-6, ISBN13: 978-0-8133-4206-1. Dewey:341.23/1.
Audience: **g,l,u.**

Franck, Thomas M. **JX1977.F694 1985**
Nation Against Nation: What Happened to the U. N. Dream and What the U. S. Can Do about It. Cloth Text. Oxford University Press, Inc. New York, NY. 1985. 334p. ISBN:0-19-503587-9, ISBN13: 978-0-19-503587-2. Dewey:341.23. LCCN:84-025393.
Audience: **g,l,u.** *Choice, 1985.*

Gordenker, Leon **JZ5008.G67 2005**
The UN Secretary General and Secretariat. Trade Paper. Routledge. New York, NY. 2005. XVIII, 118p. ISBN:0-415-34379-8, ISBN13: 978-0-415-34379-4. Dewey:352.11/3. LCCN:2004-028078.
Audience: **g,l,u.**

Gorman, Robert F. **KZ4968**
Great Debates at the United Nations: An Encyclopedia of Fifty Key Issues, 1945-2000. Cloth Text. Greenwood Publishing Group, Inc. Portsmouth, NH. 2001. 496p. ISBN:0-313-31386-5, ISBN13: 978-0-313-31386-8. Dewey:341.23. LCCN:00-057652.
Audience: **g,l,u.** *Choice, 2001.*

Groom, A. J. R. **JZ5005.U527 2000**
The United Nations at the Millennium. Trade Paper. Continuum International Publishing Group, Ltd. London, 2000. 224p.

ISBN:0-8264-4778-3, ISBN13: 978-0-8264-4778-4. Dewey:341.23. LCCN:00-059037.
Audience: **g,l,u.**

Haas, Michael E. **DS918.8.H33 2000**
In the Devil's Shadow: U. N. Special Operations During the Korean War. Trade Cloth. Naval Institute Press. Annapolis, MD. 2000. 272p. Naval Institute Special Warfare Ser. ISBN:1-55750-344-3, ISBN13: 978-1-55750-344-2. Dewey:951.904/24. LCCN:99-042004.
Audience: **g,l,u.**

Heller, Peter B. **D839.7.H3H37 2001**
The United Nations under Dag Hammarskjold, 1953-1961. Trade Cloth. Scarecrow Press, Inc. Lanham, MD. 2001. 320p. Partners for Peace Ser., Vol. 2 ISBN:0-8108-3699-8, ISBN13: 978-0-8108-3699-0. Dewey:341.23/09/045. LCCN:2001-020652.
Audience: **g,l,u.**

Jain, Devaki **HQ1240.J35 2005**
Women, Development, and the UN: A Sixty-Year Quest for Equality and Justice. Amartya K. Sen (Foreword by). Saddle Stitched, Cloth over Boards. Indiana University Press. Bloomington, IN. 2005. 230p. United Nations Intellectual History Project Ser. ISBN:0-253-34697-5, ISBN13: 978-0-253-34697-1. Dewey:305.42/09172/4. LCCN:2005-003698.
Audience: **l,u.** *Choice, 2006.*

Jolly, Richard **HD82.U18 2004**
[e] UN Contributions to Development Thinking and Practice. E-Book. Indiana University Press. Bloomington, IN. 2004. 320p. United Nations Intellectual History Project Ser. ISBN:0-253-34407-7, ISBN13: 978-0-253-34407-6. Dewey:338.9. LCCN:2003-026468.
Audience: **u,f.** *Choice, 2005.*

Joyner, Christopher C. (Editor) **KZ4993 .U55 1997**
The United Nations and International Law. Ed. 2. Trade Paper. Cambridge University Press. New York, NY. 1997. 500p. ISBN:0-521-58659-3, ISBN13: 978-0-521-58659-7. Dewey:341.2/3. LCCN:96-043488.
Audience: **u.** *Choice, 1998.*

Kapteyn & Koojmans **KZ4850 .I58**
International Organization and Integration, Vols. 1a & 1b. Trade Cloth. Kluwer Law International. Alphen a/d Rijn, 1998. 1712p. ISBN:0-7923-1972-9, ISBN13: 978-0-7923-1972-6. Dewey:341.2.
Audience: **u,f.**

Knight, W. Andy (Editor) **JX1963**
Adapting the United Nations to a Postmodern Era: Lessons Learned. Ed. 2. Trade Paper, Perfect. Palgrave Macmillan. New York, NY. 2005. 272p. Global Issues Ser. ISBN:1-4039-1715-9, ISBN13: 978-1-4039-1715-7. Dewey:341.23.
Audience: **g,l,u.**

Knight, W. Andy **JZ4984.5.K58 2000**
A Changing United Nations: Multilateral Evolution and the Quest for Global Governance. Trade Cloth. St. Martin's Press. Gordonville, VA. 2000. ISBN:0-312-23723-5, ISBN13: 978-0-312-23723-3. Dewey:341.23. LCCN:00-033356.
Audience: **l,u.**

Loescher, Gil **HV640.3.L64 2001**
The UNHCR and World Politics: A Perilous Path. Trade Paper. Oxford University Press, Inc. New York, NY. 2001. 446p. ISBN:0-19-924691-2, ISBN13: 978-0-19-924691-5. Dewey:362.87/56. LCCN:2001-021839.
Audience: **l,u.**

Malone, David M. (Editor) **JZ5006.5.U545 2004**
The UN Security Council: From the Cold War to the 21st Century. Library Binding. Lynne Rienner Publishers, Inc. Boulder, CO. 2004. 800p. A Project of the International Peace Academy Ser. ISBN:1-58826-215-4, ISBN13: 978-1-58826-215-8. Dewey:341.23/23. LCCN:2003-058572.
Audience: **l,u.**

Meisler, Stanley **JX1977.M442**
United Nations: The First Fifty Years. Trade Paper. Grove/Atlantic, Inc. New York, NY. 1997. 416p. ISBN:0-87113-656-2, ISBN13: 978-0-87113-656-5. Dewey:341.23.
Audience: **g,l,u.**

Mingst, Karen A. & Karns, Margaret P. **JZ5005.M56 2000**
The United Nations in the Post-Cold War Era. Ed. 2. Trade Paper. Westview Press. Boulder, CO. 1999. 288p. Dilemmas in World Politics Ser. ISBN:0-8133-6847-2, ISBN13: 978-0-8133-6847-4. Dewey:341.23. LCCN:99-048946.
Audience: **l,u.** *Choice, 1996.*

Moore, John A. Jr. & Pubantz, Jerry **E840.M586 1999**
To Create a New World? American Presidents and the United Nations. Trade Paper. Peter Lang Publishing, Inc. New York, NY. 1999. xi, 378p. ISBN:0-8204-3935-5, ISBN13: 978-0-8204-3935-8. Dewey:327.73. LCCN:98-053628.
Audience: **g,l,u,f.** *Choice, 2000.*

Moore, John Allphin & Pubantz, Jerry **KZ4968.M66 2002**
Encyclopedia of the United Nations. Trade Cloth. Facts On File, Inc. New York, NY. 2002. 512p. ISBN:0-8160-4417-1, ISBN13: 978-0-8160-4417-7. Dewey:341.23/03. LCCN:2002-072222.
Audience: **g,l,u,f.** *Choice, 2003.*

Moskos, Charles C. Jr. **JX1981.P7**
Peace Soldiers: The Sociology of a United Nations Military Force. Library Binding. University of Chicago Press. Chicago, IL. 1992. xi, 171p. ISBN:0-226-54225-4, ISBN13: 978-0-226-54225-6. Dewey:306/.27. LCCN:75-005070.
Audience: **l,u.**

Muller, Robert & Roche, Douglas **JX1977.M78 1995**
Safe Passage into the Twenty-First Century: The United Nations' Quest for Peace, Equality, Justice and Development. Trade Paper. Continuum International Publishing Group, Ltd. London, 1995. 146p. ISBN:0-8264-0866-4, ISBN13: 978-0-8264-0866-2. Dewey:341.23. LCCN:58-014432.
Audience: **l,u,f.**

New Zealand, Ministry of Foreign Affairs **JX1977.2.N5**
United Nations Handbook. Ministry of Foreign Affairs. 2005.
Audience: **g,l,u,f.**

Nicholas, H. G. **JX1977**
The United Nations As a Political Institution. Ed. 5. Paper Text. Oxford University Press, Inc. New York, NY. 1975. 272p. ISBN:0-19-519826-3, ISBN13: 978-0-19-519826-3. Dewey:341.23.
Audience: **l,u.**

Osmanczyk, Edmund Jan & Mango, Anthony (Editors) **JZ4986**
Encyclopedia of the United Nations: And International Agreements, Set. Ed. 3. Kofi A. Annan (Foreword by). Paper over Boards. Routledge. New York, NY. 2002. 3500p. ISBN:0-415-93920-8, ISBN13: 978-0-415-93920-1. Dewey:341.23/03. LCCN:2002-010761.
Audience: **l,u,f.** *Choice, 2003.*

Perez de Cuellar, Javier **D839.7.P47A3 1997**
Pilgrimage for Peace: A Secretary General's Memoir. Cloth over Boards. Palgrave Macmillan. New York, NY. 1997. 544p. ISBN:0-312-16486-6, ISBN13: 978-0-312-16486-7. Dewey:352.1/13/092. LCCN:97-009798.
Audience: **g,l,u.**

Riggs, Robert Edwon **JX1977**
Politics in the United Nations: A Study of United States Influence in the General Assembly. Paper Text. Textbook Publishers. Temecula, CA. 2003. vi, 208p. ISBN:0-7581-2233-0, ISBN13: 978-0-7581-2233-9. Dewey:341.23/73.
Audience: **g,l,u.**

Righter, Rosemary **JX1977**
Utopia Lost: The United Nations and World Order. Trade Paper. Century Foundation, The. New York, NY. 1995. 421p. ISBN:0-87078-359-9, ISBN13: 978-0-87078-359-3. Dewey:341.23/1. LCCN:94-033886.
Audience: **g,l,u.** *Choice, 1995.*

Roberts, Adam & Kingsbury, Benedict (Editors) **JX1977.U42587 1993**
United Nations, Divided World: The U. N.'s Roles in International Relations. Ed. 2. Paper Text. Oxford University Press, Inc. New York, NY. 1994. 606p. ISBN:0-19-827926-4, ISBN13: 978-0-19-827926-6. Dewey:341.23. LCCN:93-002566.
Audience: **u,f.** *Choice, 1989.*

Schlesinger, Stephen **JZ4986.S358 2003**
Act of Creation: The Founding of the United Nations. Trade Cloth. Westview Press. Boulder, CO. 2003. 392p. ISBN:0-8133-3324-5, ISBN13: 978-0-8133-3324-3. Dewey:341.23/09/044. LCCN:2003-014600.
Audience: **l,u.** *Choice, 2004.*

Sohn, Louis B. & Clark, Grenville **JX1977**
Introduction to World Peace Through World Law. Trade Paper. World Without War Council. Berkeley, CA. 1984. 112p. Modern Classics of Peace Ser. ISBN:0-912018-18-6, ISBN13: 978-0-912018-18-8. Dewey:341.132.
Audience: **g,l,u.**

Stevenson, Adlai E. **JX1977**
Looking Outward: Years of Crisis at the United Nations. Robert L. Schiffer, Selma Schiffer & John F. Kennedy (Editors). Trade Cloth. Greenwood Publishing Group, Inc. Portsmouth, NH. 1984. 295p. ISBN:0-313-24529-0, ISBN13: 978-0-313-24529-9. Dewey:341.23/73. LCCN:84-006708.
Audience: **g,l,u.**

Stoessinger, John George **JX1977.2.U5.S8 1977**
The United Nations and the Superpowers: China, Russia and America. Trade Cloth. Random House, Inc. New York, NY. 1977. xxv, 245p. ISBN:0-394-31269-4, ISBN13: 978-0-394-31269-9. Dewey:341.23. LCCN:76-048733.
Audience: **l,u.**

Thakur, Ramesh (Editor) **JZ4986.P37 1998**
Past Imperfect, Future Uncertain: The United Nations at Fifty. Cloth over Boards. Palgrave Macmillan. New York, NY. 1998. 295p. ISBN:0-312-21246-1, ISBN13: 978-0-312-21246-9. Dewey:341.23. LCCN:97-040993.
Audience: **g,l,u.** *Choice, 1998.*

United Nations **KZ4991.A12**
Charter of the United Nations and Statute of the International Court of Justice.
http://www.icj-cij.org/icjwww/ibasicdocuments.htm
United Nations. International Court of Justice..
Audience: **g,l,u,f.**

United Nations **JX1977.A1**
UN Documentation Centre.
http://www.un.org/documents/
United Nations.
Audience: **g,l,u,f.**

United Nations **JZ5005**
Main Bodies [of the United Nations].
http://www.un.org/aboutun/mainbodies.htm
Audience: **g,l,u,f.**

United Nations **JZ5005**
UN Millennium Development Goals.
http://www.un.org/millenniumgoals/index.asp
Audience: **g,l,u,f.**

United Nations Conference on International Organization Staff **JX1976**
Charter of the United Nations: Report to the President on the Results of the San Francisco Conference. Trade Cloth. Greenwood Publishing Group, Inc. Portsmouth, NH. 1969. 266p. United States Department of State. Publication 2349 Ser. ISBN:0-8371-2467-0, ISBN13: 978-0-8371-2467-4. Dewey:341.13/2. LCCN:73-094623.
Audience: **u,f.**

United Nations Staff **DT1757.U54 1994**
The United Nations and Apartheid, 1948-1994. Trade Cloth. United Nations Publications. New York, NY. 1994. 565p. Blue Bks., Vol. I ISBN:92-1-100546-9, ISBN13: 978-92-1-100546-2. Dewey:305.8/00968. LCCN:95-123119.
Audience: **l,u,f.** *Choice, 1995.*

United Nations Staff **JX1974.73.U53 1995**
The United Nations and Nuclear Non-Proliferation. Trade Cloth. United Nations Publications. New York, NY. 1995. 200p. Blue Bks., Vol. III ISBN:92-1-100557-4, ISBN13: 978-92-1-100557-8. Dewey:341.7/34. LCCN:95-152663.
Audience: **g,l,u.**

United Nations Staff **JZ4947**
Yearbook of the United Nations 2003, Vol. 57. Trade Cloth. United Nations Publications. New York, NY. 2005. 1630p.

ISBN:92-1-100905-7, ISBN13: 978-92-1-100905-7.
Dewey:341.23.
Audience: **l,u,f.**

United Nations Staff **JX1977.2.C18U55 1995**
The United Nations and Cambodia, 1991-1995. Boutros Boutros-Ghali (Introduction by). Trade Cloth. United Nations Publications. New York, NY. 1995. 360p. Blue Bks., Vol. II ISBN:92-1-100548-5, ISBN13: 978-92-1-100548-6.
Dewey:341.23596. LCCN:95-154041.
Audience: **l,u,f.** *Choice, 1996.*

United Nations Staff **JX1977.2.S2U54 1995**
The United Nations and El Salvador, 1990-1995. Boutros Boutros-Ghali (Introduction by). Trade Cloth. United Nations Publications. New York, NY. 1996. 611p. Blue Bks., Vol. IV ISBN:92-1-100552-3, ISBN13: 978-92-1-100552-3.
Dewey:341.237284. LCCN:95-152667.
Audience: **g,l,u.** *Choice, 1996.*

Ward, Michael **HA36.W37 2004**
Quantifying the World: United Nations Ideas and Statistics. E-Book. Indiana University Press. Bloomington, IN. 2004. xx, 329p. United Nations Intellectual History Project Ser., Vol. 3 ISBN:0-253-34397-6, ISBN13: 978-0-253-34397-0.
Dewey:001.4/06/01. LCCN:2003-023831.
Audience: **l,u.** *Choice, 2004.*

Weiss, Thomas G., et al. **JZ4984.5.U532 2005**
UN Voices: The Struggle for Development and Social Justice. Tatiana Carayannis, Louis Emmerij & Richard Jolly (Authors). Trade Paper, Perfect. Indiana University Press. Bloomington, IN. 2005. 520p. United Nations Intellectual History Project Ser. ISBN:0-253-21788-1, ISBN13: 978-0-253-21788-2.
Dewey:341.23/09. LCCN:2005-000230.
Audience: **g,l,u.** *Choice, 2006.*

Ziring, Lawrence, et al. **JZ4984.5.Z57 2005**
The United Nations: International Organization and World Politics. Ed. 4. Robert E. Riggs & Jack A. Plano (Authors). Paper Text. Thomson Wadsworth. Belmont, CA. 2004. 600p. ISBN:0-534-63186-X, ISBN13: 978-0-534-63186-4.
Dewey:341.23. LCCN:2004-101398.
Audience: **l,u.**

International Relations. Transnational Relations > International Organization > Intergovernmental Organizations. IGOs > European Union

KJE4445
A Constitution for Europe.
http://europa.eu.int/constitution/index_en.htm
Audience: **g,l,u,f.**

JN30
EU at a Glance.
http://europa.eu.int/abc/index_en.htm
Audience: **g,l,u,f.**

HA1107
Europe in Figures—Eurostat Yearbook 2005.
http://epp.eurostat.cec.eu.int/portal/page?_pageid=1334,49092079,1334_49092702&_dad=portal&_schema=PORTAL
Office for Official Publications of the European Union.
Audience: **g,l,u,f.**

JX131
Treaties.
http://europa.eu.int/eur-lex/lex/en/treaties/index.htm
Audience: **g,u,f.**

Andersen, Svein S. & Eliassen, Kjell A. (Editors) **H97**
Making Policy in Europe. Ed. 2. Paper Text. SAGE Publications, Ltd. London, 2001. 304p. Eu Politics Ser. ISBN:0-7619-6751-6, ISBN13: 978-0-7619-6751-4.
Dewey:320/.6. LCCN:00-135055.
Audience: **l,u.**

Bainbridge, Timothy **HC240.B35 2002**
Penguin Companion to European Union. Ed. 3. Penguin Books. 2003. ISBN:0-14-100769-9, ISBN13: 978-0-14-100769-4.
Audience: **g,l,u,f.**

Barbour, Philippe **D1060.E8685 2002**
The European Union Handbook. Ed. 2. Trade Cloth. Fitzroy Dearborn Publishers, Inc. Chicago, IL. 2002. 360p. Regional Handbooks of Economic Development Ser., :Prospects onto the 21st Century ISBN:1-57958-223-0, ISBN13: 978-1-57958-223-4.
Dewey:341.242/2. LCCN:2002-727715.
Audience: **g,l,u.**

Bellamy, Richard & Warleigh, Alex (Editors) **JN40**
Citizenship and Governance in the European Union. Trade Paper. Continuum International Publishing Group, Ltd. London, 2005. 256p. ISBN:0-8264-7919-7, ISBN13: 978-0-8264-7919-8.
Dewey:323.6/094.
Audience: **u.** *Choice, 2002.*

Blankart, Charles Beat & Mueller, Dennis C. (Editors) **KJE4445.C658 2004**
A Constitution for the European Union. Trade Cloth. MIT Press. Cambridge, MA. 2004. 280p. CESifo Seminar Ser. ISBN:0-262-02566-3, ISBN13: 978-0-262-02566-9.
Dewey:342.402. LCCN:2004-042787.
Audience: **u,f.** *Choice, 2005.*

Booker, Christopher & North, Richard **JN94.A2**
The Great Deception: The Secret History of the European Union. Trade Cloth. Continuum International Publishing Group, Ltd. London, 2003. 456p. ISBN:0-8264-7105-6, ISBN13: 978-0-8264-7105-5. Dewey:341.242/2. LCCN:2004-298035.
Audience: **u,f.** *Choice, 2004.*

Brown, Brendan **HG3942.B76 2004**
Euro on Trial: To Reform or Split Up? Cloth over Boards. Palgrave Macmillan. New York, NY. 2004. 192p. ISBN:1-4039-1284-X, ISBN13: 978-1-4039-1284-8.
Dewey:332.4/94. LCCN:2003-066470.
Audience: **g,l,u,f.** *Choice, 2004.*

Carkoglu, Ali & Rubin, Barry (Editors) **DR479.E85T87 2003**
Turkey and the European Union: Domestic Politics, Economic Integration and International Dynamics. Trade Paper. Taylor & Francis Group. Abingdon, 2003. 200p. ISBN:0-7146-8335-3,

ISBN13: 978-0-7146-8335-5. Dewey:327.56104. LCCN:2002-154406.
Audience: **u,f.** *Choice, 2004.*

Collins, Ray & Green, Pauline **JQ1811**
Embracing Cyprus: The Path to Unity in the New Europe. Cloth over Boards. I. B. Tauris & Company, Ltd. London, 2003. 150p. ISBN:1-86064-840-1, ISBN13: 978-1-86064-840-3. Dewey:337.1/42/095693. LCCN:2003-481440.
Audience: **l,u.**

Diez, Thomas (Editor) **D1065.C94E87 2002**
The European Union and the Cyprus Conflict: Modern Conflict, Postmodern Union. Cloth over Boards. Manchester University Press. Manchester, 2002. 256p. Europe in Change Ser. ISBN:0-7190-6079-6, ISBN13: 978-0-7190-6079-3. Dewey:956.9304. LCCN:2002-020741.
Audience: **u,f.** *Choice, 2003.*

Dinan, Desmond (Editor) **JN30.E52 2000**
Encyclopedia of the European Union. Trade Paper. Lynne Rienner Publishers, Inc. Boulder, CO. 2000. viii, 566p. ISBN:1-55587-926-8, ISBN13: 978-1-55587-926-6. Dewey:341.2/422/03. LCCN:99-086544.
Audience: **l,u,f.** *Choice, 1999.*

Dinan, Desmond **HC241.2.D476 2005**
Ever Closer Union: An Introduction to European Integration. Ed. 3. Library Binding. Lynne Rienner Publishers, Inc. Boulder, CO. 2005. 625p. ISBN:1-58826-234-0, ISBN13: 978-1-58826-234-9. Dewey:337.1/42. LCCN:2005-010768.
Audience: **l,u,f.** *Choice, 1999.*

Dyson, Kenneth & Featherstone, Kevin **HG925.D97 1999**
The Road to Maastricht: Negotiating Economic and Monetary Union. Trade Paper. Oxford University Press, Inc. New York, NY. 2000. 884p. ISBN:0-19-829638-X, ISBN13: 978-0-19-829638-6. Dewey:332.4/566/094. LCCN:99-025739.
Audience: **u,f.** *Choice, 2000.*

European Commission **HN380.5.Z9**
☐ Eurobarometer.
http://europa.eu.int/comm/public_opinion/index_en.htm
Audience: **g,l,u,f.**

European Union **JN30**
☐ Europa—Gateway to the European Union.
http://europa.eu.int/index_en.htm
Audience: **g,l,u,f.**

European Union - Delegation of the European Commission to the United States **JN30**
☐ European Union—A Guide for Americans.
http://www.eurunion.org/infores/euguide/euguide.htm
European Union - Delegation of the European Commission to the United States.
Audience: **g,l,u,f.**

Giauque, Jeffrey Glen **D843.G4478 2002**
Grand Designs and Visions of Unity: The Atlantic Powers and the Reorganization of Western Europe, 1955-1963. Trade Cloth. University of North Carolina Press. Chapel Hill, NC. 2002. 344p. The New Cold War History Ser. ISBN:0-8078-2679-0, ISBN13: 978-0-8078-2679-9. Dewey:327/.094/09045. LCCN:2001-047647.
Audience: **l,u,f.** *Choice, 2003, 2002.*

Haas, Ernst B. **JN15.H215 2003**
The Uniting of Europe: Political, Social, and Economical Forces, 1950-1957. Trade Cloth. University of Notre Dame Press. Notre Dame, IN. 2004. 568p. Contemporary European Politics and Society Ser. ISBN:0-268-04346-9, ISBN13: 978-0-268-04346-9. Dewey:341.24/2. LCCN:2003-070256.
Audience: **u,f.**

Hayward, Jack Ernest Shalom (Editor), et al. **JN30.G6784 2003**
Governing Europe. Anand Menon & Jack Hayward (Editors). Trade Paper. Oxford University Press, Inc. New York, NY. 2003. 514p. ISBN:0-19-925015-4, ISBN13: 978-0-19-925015-8. Dewey:320.94. LCCN:2002-038197.
Audience: **u,f.** *Choice, 2004.*

Hix, Simon **JN30.H5 2005**
The Political System of the European Union. Ed. 2. Cloth over Boards. Palgrave Macmillan. New York, NY. 2005. 448p. The European Union Ser. ISBN:0-333-96181-1, ISBN13: 978-0-333-96181-0. Dewey:341.242/2. LCCN:2004-056955.
Audience: **g,l,u,f.** *Choice, 2000.*

Jacoby, Wade **JN96.A58J33 2004**
The Enlargement of the European Union and NATO: Ordering from the Menu in Central Europe. Trade Cloth. Cambridge University Press. New York, NY. 2004. 300p. ISBN:0-521-83359-0, ISBN13: 978-0-521-83359-2. Dewey:341.242/2/0943. LCCN:2003-069727.
Audience: **g,l,u,f.** *Choice, 2005.*

Kagan, Robert **D1065.U5K26 2003**
Of Paradise and Power: America and Europe in the New World Order. Trade Cloth. Knopf Publishing Group. New York, NY. 2003. 112p. ISBN:1-4000-4093-0, ISBN13: 978-1-4000-4093-3. Dewey:327.7304/09/0511. LCCN:2002-038549.
Audience: **g,l,u,f.**

Kelemen, R. Daniel **GE170.K45 2004**
The Rules of Federalism: Institutions and Regulatory Politics in the EU and Beyond. Trade Cloth. Harvard University Press. Cambridge, MA. 2004. 256p. ISBN:0-674-01309-3, ISBN13: 978-0-674-01309-4. Dewey:363.7/056/094. LCCN:2003-056904.
Audience: **u,f.** *Choice, 2004.*

Lahav, Gallya **JV7590.L34 2003**
Immigration and Politics in the New Europe: Reinventing Borders. Johan P. Olsen & Andreas Fellésdal (Contribution by). Trade Paper. Cambridge University Press. New York, NY. 2004. 334p. Themes in European Governance Ser. ISBN:0-521-53530-1, ISBN13: 978-0-521-53530-4. Dewey:325.4. LCCN:2003-046131.
Audience: **u,f.** *Choice, 2005.*

Leach, Rodney **JN30**
Europe: A Concise Encyclopedia of the European Union from Aachen to Zollverein. Ed. 4. Trade Cloth. Profile Books Ltd. London, 2000. 288p. ISBN:1-86197-280-6, ISBN13: 978-1-86197-280-4. Dewey:341.2/422.
Audience: **l,u.**

Leonard, R.L. (Richard Lawrence) **HC240**
Economist Guide to the European Union. Profile Books. 2005. ISBN:1-86197-930-4, ISBN13: 978-1-86197-930-8.
Audience: **g,l,u.**

Lieven, Anatol & Trenin, Dmitri (Editors) **HC240.25.E852A43**
Ambivalent Neighbors: The EU, NATO and the Price of Membership. Trade Cloth. Carnegie Endowment for International Peace. Washington, DC. 2003. 352p. ISBN:0-87003-200-3, ISBN13: 978-0-87003-200-4. Dewey:341.242/2. LCCN:2002-013915.
Audience: **g,u,f.** *Choice, 2004.*

Lundestad, Geir **D1065.U5L86 1998**
Empire by Integration: The United States and European Integration, 1945-1997. Cloth Text. Oxford University Press, Inc. New York, NY. 1998. 216p. ISBN:0-19-878212-8, ISBN13: 978-0-19-878212-4. Dewey:327.7304. LCCN:97-022509.
Audience: **u,f.**

Magone, Jose M. **HC240**
The Politics of Southern Europe: Integration into the European Union. Trade Cloth. Greenwood Publishing Group, Inc. Portsmouth, NH. 2003. 352p. ISBN:0-275-97787-0, ISBN13: 978-0-275-97787-0. Dewey:320.94. LCCN:2002-070955.
Audience: **u,f.** *Choice, 2004.*

Moussis, Nicholas **HC240.M754 1998**
Handbook of European Union. Ed. 5. Trade Paper. Euroconfidential. Genval, 1998. 360p. The Euroconfidential Collection ISBN:2-930119-20-9, ISBN13: 978-2-930119-20-5. Dewey:337.1/42. LCCN:99-461790.
Audience: **g,l,u,f.**

Muftuler-Bac, Meltem **D1065.T8M84 1997**
Turkey's Relations with a Changing Europe. Trade Paper. Manchester University Press. Manchester, 1996. 133p. Europe in Change Ser. ISBN:0-7190-4234-8, ISBN13: 978-0-7190-4234-8. Dewey:327.56104. LCCN:96-003411.
Audience: **g,l,u,f.** *Choice, 1997.*

Parsons, Craig **JN30.P38 2003**
A Certain Idea of Europe. Trade Cloth. Cornell University Press. Ithaca, NY. 2003. 272p. Cornell Studies in Political Economy ISBN:0-8014-4086-6, ISBN13: 978-0-8014-4086-1. Dewey:341.242/2. LCCN:2003-002363.
Audience: **g,u,f.** *Choice, 2004.*

Phinnemore, David & McGowan, Lee **KJE6415**
A Dictionary of the European Union. Ed. 2. Paper over Boards. Taylor & Francis Group. Abingdon, 2004. 432p. ISBN:1-85743-260-6, ISBN13: 978-1-85743-260-2. Dewey:341.242/2/03. LCCN:2004-555399.
Audience: **g,l,u,f.**

Poole, Peter A. **HC240**
Europe Unites: The E. U.'s Eastern Enlargement. Trade Cloth. Greenwood Publishing Group, Inc. Portsmouth, NH. 2003. 232p. ISBN:0-275-97704-8, ISBN13: 978-0-275-97704-7. Dewey:341.242/2/0947. LCCN:2002-193022.
Audience: **g,l,u,f.** *Choice, 2004.*

Ramsay, Anne Fla (Editor) **HC240.E748 2000**
Eurojargon: A Dictionary of the European Union. Ed. 6. Cloth Text. Fitzroy Dearborn Publishers, Inc. Chicago, IL. 2000. 260p. ISBN:1-57958-274-5, ISBN13: 978-1-57958-274-6. Dewey:341.242/2/03. LCCN:2002-276081.
Audience: **g,l,u,f.** *Choice, 2001.*

Reid, T. R. **D1060.R46 2004**
The United States of Europe: The New Superpower and the End of American Supremacy. Trade Cloth. Penguin Group (USA) Inc. New York, NY. 2004. 320p. ISBN:1-59420-033-5, ISBN13: 978-1-59420-033-5. Dewey:327.7304/09/045. LCCN:2004-044784.
Audience: **g,l,u.** *Choice, 2005.*

Ruane, Kevin **UA646.R896 2000**
The Rise and Fall of the European Defence Community: Anglo-American Relations and the Crises of European Defence, 1950-55. Cloth over Boards. Palgrave Macmillan. New York, NY. 2000. 264p. Cold War History Ser. ISBN:0-312-23482-1, ISBN13: 978-0-312-23482-9. Dewey:355.031091821. LCCN:00-027836.
Audience: **l,u,f.** *Choice, 2001.*

Salmon, Trevor C. & Shepherd, Alistair J. K. **UA646.S24 2003**
Toward a European Army: Military Power in the Making? Library Binding. Lynne Rienner Publishers, Inc. Boulder, CO. 2003. 200p. ISBN:1-58826-236-7, ISBN13: 978-1-58826-236-3. Dewey:355/.03354. LCCN:2003-046725.
Audience: **g,l,u,f.** *Choice, 2004.*

Siedentop, Larry **JN30.S47 2001**
Democracy in Europe. Trade Paper. Columbia University Press. New York, NY. 2002. 272p. ISBN:0-231-12377-9, ISBN13: 978-0-231-12377-8. Dewey:320.94. LCCN:00-065576.
Audience: **g,l,u,f.** *Choice, 2001.*

Smith, Hazel **D1060.S58 2002**
European Union Foreign Policy: What It Is and What It Does. Trade Cloth. Pluto Press. London, 2002. 312p. ISBN:0-7453-1870-3, ISBN13: 978-0-7453-1870-7. Dewey:341.7/094. LCCN:2001-005310.
Audience: **u,f.** *Choice, 2003.*

Smith, Michael E. **D860.S65 2003**
Europe's Foreign and Security Policy: The Institutionalization of Cooperation. Andreas Fllesdal (Contribution by). Trade Paper. Cambridge University Press. New York, NY. 2003. 308p. Themes in European Governance Ser. ISBN:0-521-53861-0, ISBN13: 978-0-521-53861-9. Dewey:327/.094. LCCN:2003-048990.
Audience: **u,f.** *Choice, 2004.*

Tibor, Palankai **HC240.E286 2003**
Economics of European Integration. Trade Paper. Akademiai Kiado. Budapest, 2003. 460p. ISBN:963-05-7990-1, ISBN13: 978-963-05-7990-2. Dewey:337.1/42. LCCN:2004-393278.
Audience: **u,f.** *Choice, 2003.*

Torbiorn, Kjell M. **JN12.T58 2003**
Destination Europe: The Political and Economic Growth of a Continent. Cloth over Boards. Manchester University Press. Manchester, 2004. 328p. ISBN:0-7190-6572-0, ISBN13: 978-0-7190-6572-9. Dewey:940.55. LCCN:2003-065142.
Audience: **l,u,f.** *Choice, 2004.*

Van Gerven, Walter **D2009.G475 2005**
The European Union: A Polity of States and Peoples. Trade Paper. Stanford University Press. Palo Alto, CA. 2005. xvii,

397p. ISBN:0-8047-5064-5, ISBN13: 978-0-8047-5064-6. Dewey:341.242/2. LCCN:2004-026677.
Audience: **u,f.** *Choice, 2006.*

Weiler, Joseph H. & Wind, Marlene (Editors) **KJE947**
European Constitutionalism Beyond the State. Trade Paper. Cambridge University Press. New York, NY. 2003. 252p. ISBN:0-521-79671-7, ISBN13: 978-0-521-79671-2. Dewey:341.2422. LCCN:2004-555379.
Audience: **u,f.** *Choice, 2004.*

International Relations. Transnational Relations > International Organization > Intergovernmental Organizations. IGOs > NATO

Asmus, Ronald D. **UA646.3A82 2002**
Opening NATO's Door: How the Alliance Remade Itself for a New Era. Trade Cloth. Columbia University Press. New York, NY. 2002. 415p. ISBN:0-231-12776-6, ISBN13: 978-0-231-12776-9. Dewey:355/.031091821. LCCN:2002-073637.
Audience: **g,l,u.**

Barany, Zoltan **UA646.8.B37 2003**
The Future of NATO Expansion: Four Case Studies. Cloth Text. Cambridge University Press. New York, NY. 2003. 278p. ISBN:0-521-82169-X, ISBN13: 978-0-521-82169-8. Dewey:355/.031/091821. LCCN:2002-035086.
Audience: **u,f.** *Choice, 2004.*

Carpenter, Ted Galen (Editor) **UA646.3.N24252 2001**
NATO Enters the 21st Century. Trade Paper. Taylor & Francis Group. Abingdon, 2000. 200p. ISBN:0-7146-8109-1, ISBN13: 978-0-7146-8109-2. Dewey:355/.031091821/0905. LCCN:00-063920.
Audience: **g,l,u.** *Choice, 2001.*

Clemens, Clay (Editor) **UA646.3.N229 1997**
NATO and the Quest for Post-Cold War Security. Cloth over Boards. Palgrave Macmillan. New York, NY. 1997. 232p. ISBN:0-312-17603-1, ISBN13: 978-0-312-17603-7. Dewey:355/.031/091821. LCCN:97-003274.
Audience: **g,l,u,f.** *Choice, 1998.*

David, Charles-Philippe & Levesque, Jacques (Editors) **JZ5930 .F88 1999**
The Future of NATO: Enlargement, Russia and European Security. Trade Paper. McGill-Queen's University Press. Montreal, PQ. 1999. 261p. ISBN:0-7735-1872-X, ISBN13: 978-0-7735-1872-8. Dewey:355/.031/091821. LCCN:2001-431352.
Audience: **u.** *Choice, 2000.*

Duffield, John S. **UA646.3.D817 1995**
Power Rules: The Evolution of NATO's Conventional Force Posture. Trade Cloth. Stanford University Press. Palo Alto, CA. 1995. xi, 386p. ISBN:0-8047-2396-6, ISBN13: 978-0-8047-2396-1. Dewey:355/.031/091821. LCCN:94-025006.
Audience: **l,u.** *Choice, 1995.*

Heuser, Beatrice **UA646.H48 1997**
NATO, Britain, France, and the FRG: Nuclear Strategies and Forces for Europe, 1949-2000. Cloth over Boards. Palgrave Macmillan. New York, NY. 1997. 276p. ISBN:0-312-17498-5, ISBN13: 978-0-312-17498-9. Dewey:355.02/17/094. LCCN:97-001895.
Audience: **l,u,f.** *Choice, 1998.*

Krupnick, Charles **UA646.8.A445 2002**
Almost NATO: Partner and Players in Central and Eastern European Security. Book, Other. Rowman & Littlefield Publishers, Inc. Lanham, MD. 2003. 360p. New International Relations of Europe Ser. ISBN:0-7425-2458-2, ISBN13: 978-0-7425-2458-3. Dewey:355/.031091821. LCCN:2002-034781.
Audience: **u,f.** *Choice, 2003.*

Mattox, Gale A. & Rachwald, Arthur R. (Editors) **UA646.3.E53 2001**
Enlarging NATO: The National Debates. Trade Cloth. Lynne Rienner Publishers, Inc. Boulder, CO. 2001. 300p. ISBN:1-55587-908-X, ISBN13: 978-1-55587-908-2. Dewey:355/.031091821. LCCN:2001-019005.
Audience: **g,l,u,f.** *Choice, 2002.*

Michta, Andrew A. **DAW1051.A47 1999**
America's New Allies: Poland, Hungary, and the Czech Republic in NATO. Trade Paper. University of Washington Press. Seattle, WA. 1999. 250p. ISBN:0-295-97906-2, ISBN13: 978-0-295-97906-9. Dewey:355/.031091821. LCCN:99-035704.
Audience: **l,u.** *Choice, 2000.*

Papacosma, S. Victor & Heiss, Mary A. (Editors) **UA646.3.N2437 1995**
NATO in the Post-Cold War Era: Does It Have a Future? Cloth over Boards. Palgrave Macmillan. New York, NY. 1995. 384p. ISBN:0-312-12130-X, ISBN13: 978-0-312-12130-3. Dewey:355/.031/091821. LCCN:95-035559.
Audience: **l,u,f.**

Rauchhaus, Robert W. (Editor) **UA646.5.E85E97 2001**
Explaining NATO Enlargement. Cloth Text. Taylor & Francis Group. Abingdon, 2000. 232p. ISBN:0-7146-5127-3, ISBN13: 978-0-7146-5127-9. Dewey:355/.031091821. LCCN:00-047498.
Audience: **l,u,f.**

Schmidt, Gustav (Editor) **UA646.3.H56 2001**
A History of NATO: The First Fifty Years, Set. Cloth over Boards. Palgrave Macmillan. New York, NY. 2001. 1433p. ISBN:0-333-96277-X, ISBN13: 978-0-333-96277-0. Dewey:355/.031091821. LCCN:2001-032752.
Audience: **g,l,u,f.** *Choice, 2002.*

Smith, Mark **D1065.E85S65 2000**
e NATO Enlargement During the Cold War: Strategy and System in the Western Alliance. E-Book. Palgrave Macmillan. New York, NY. 2000. x, 207p. Cold War History Ser. ISBN:0-333-91818-5, ISBN13: 978-0-333-91818-0. Dewey:355/.031091821. LCCN:00-033352.
Audience: **l,u,f.** *Choice, 2001.*

Yost, David S. **UA646.3.Y674 1998**
NATO Transformed: The Alliance's New Roles in International Security. Trade Paper. United States Institute of Peace Press (USIP Press). Washington, DC. 1998. 432p.

ISBN:1-878379-81-X, ISBN13: 978-1-878379-81-8. Dewey:355/.031091821. LCCN:98-040939.
Audience: **l,u.** *Choice, 1999.*

International Relations. Transnational Relations > International Organization > Non-governmental Organizations. NGOs

Adams, Francis **JL966**
Deepening Democracy: Global Governance and Political Reform in Latin America. Trade Cloth. Greenwood Publishing Group, Inc. Portsmouth, NH. 2003. 184p. ISBN:0-275-97038-8, ISBN13: 978-0-275-97038-3. Dewey:320.98. LCCN:2002-030723.
Audience: **u,f.** *Choice, 2004.*

Gidron, Benjamin (Editor), et al. **JZ6045.R47 2002**
Mobilizing for Peace: Conflict Resolution in Northern Ireland, Israel/Palestine, and South Africa. Stanley Nider Katz & Yeheskel Hasenfeld (Editors). Trade Cloth. Oxford University Press, Inc. New York, NY. 2002. 304p. ISBN:0-19-512592-4, ISBN13: 978-0-19-512592-4. Dewey:303.6/9. LCCN:2001-050017.
Audience: **u.** *Choice, 2003.*

Gunter, Michael M. **JZ4841.G86 2004**
Building the Next Ark: How NGOs Work to Protect Biodiversity. Trade Cloth. University Press of New England. Lebanon, NH. 2005. xvii, 252p. ISBN:1-58465-383-3, ISBN13: 978-1-58465-383-7. Dewey:333.95/16. LCCN:2004-013580.
Audience: **l,u.** *Choice, 2005.*

Hajnal, Peter I. (Editor) **JC337.C564 2002**
Civil Society in the Information Age. Trade Cloth. Ashgate Publishing, Ltd. Aldershot, 2002. 312p. ISBN:0-7546-1838-2, ISBN13: 978-0-7546-1838-6. Dewey:300. LCCN:2002-074453.
Audience: **u,f.**

Hirata, Keiko **JQ1681.H575 2002**
Civil Society in Japan: The Growing Role of NGOs in Tokyo's Aid and Development Policy. Cloth over Boards. Palgrave Macmillan. New York, NY. 2002. 272p. ISBN:0-312-23936-X, ISBN13: 978-0-312-23936-7. Dewey:338.91/52. LCCN:2002-023881.
Audience: **u,f.** *Choice, 2003.*

Howard, Marc Morje **JC599.E92H68 2002**
The Weakness of Civil Society in Post-Communist Europe. Cloth Text. Cambridge University Press. New York, NY. 2003. 220p. ISBN:0-521-81223-2, ISBN13: 978-0-521-81223-8. Dewey:300/.947. LCCN:2002-024638.
Audience: **l,u,f.** *Choice, 2003.*

Iriye, Akira **JZ4841 .I75 2002**
Global Community: The Role of International Organizations in the Making of the Contemporary World. Trade Cloth. University of California Press. Berkeley, CA. 2002. 256p. ISBN:0-520-23127-9, ISBN13: 978-0-520-23127-6. Dewey:327/.06. LCCN:2001-004247.
Audience: **l,u,f.** *Choice, 2003.*

Josselin, Daphne & Wallace, William (Editors) **JZ1305.N66 2001**
Non-State Actors in World Politics. Trade Paper. Palgrave Macmillan. New York, NY. 2002. 308p. ISBN:0-333-96814-X, ISBN13: 978-0-333-96814-7. Dewey:327. LCCN:2001-033120.
Audience: **g,l,u.**

Keck, Margaret E. & Sikkink, Kathryn **JF529.K43 1998**
Activists Beyond Borders: Advocacy Networks in International Politics. Trade Paper. Cornell University Press. Ithaca, NY. 1998. 240p. ISBN:0-8014-8456-1, ISBN13: 978-0-8014-8456-8. Dewey:322.4/3. LCCN:97-033165.
Audience: **l,u,f.** *Choice, 1998.*

Quigley, Kevin F. F. **HC244.Q35 1997**
For Democracy's Sake: Foundations and Democracy Assistance in Central Europe. Trade Paper. Woodrow Wilson Center Press. Washington, DC. 1997. 189p. ISBN:0-943875-81-1, ISBN13: 978-0-943875-81-1. Dewey:338.91/0943. LCCN:97-001541.
Audience: **u,f.** *Choice, 1997.*

Smith, Jackie & Johnston, Hank **HN17.5.G58 2002**
Globalization and Resistance: Transnational Dimensions of Social Movements. Book, Other. Rowman & Littlefield Publishers, Inc. Lanham, MD. 2002. 264p. ISBN:0-7425-1989-9, ISBN13: 978-0-7425-1989-3. Dewey:303.48/4. LCCN:2002-069691.
Audience: **l,u.**

Staudt, Kathleen & Coronado, Irasema **HM671.S73 2002**
Fronteras No Mas: Toward Social Justice at the U. S. - Mexico Border. Trade Paper. Palgrave Macmillan. New York, NY. 2002. 224p. ISBN:0-312-29547-2, ISBN13: 978-0-312-29547-9. Dewey:303.3/72/09721. LCCN:2002-068413.
Audience: **g,l.** *Choice, 2003.*

Suter, Keith **JZ1318**
Global Order and Global Disorder: Globalization and the Nation-State. Trade Cloth. Greenwood Publishing Group, Inc. Portsmouth, NH. 2003. 216p. ISBN:0-275-97388-3, ISBN13: 978-0-275-97388-9. Dewey:327.1. LCCN:2002-070863.
Audience: **l,u.** *Choice, 2004.*

Welch, Claude E. **JC599.A36W45 1995**
Protecting Human Rights in Africa: Roles and Strategies of Non-Governmental Organizations. Trade Cloth. University of Pennsylvania Press. Philadelphia, PA. 1995. 360p. Pennsylvania Studies in Human Rights ISBN:0-8122-3330-1, ISBN13: 978-0-8122-3330-8. Dewey:323/.096. LCCN:95-030107.
Audience: **l,u.** *Choice, 1996.*

Woods, Lawrence T. **HF1642.55 .W66 1993**
Asia-Pacific Diplomacy: The Nongovernmental Approach to Regional Economic Cooperation. Trade Cloth. University of British Columbia Press. Vancouver, BC. 1993. 268p. ISBN:0-7748-0440-8, ISBN13: 978-0-7748-0440-0. Dewey:337.11823. LCCN:94-127305.
Audience: **l,u,f.** *Choice, 1994.*

International Relations. Transnational Relations > By Country, Territory, or Region

Al-Saud, Faisal Bin Salman **U162**
Iran, Saudi Arabia and the Gulf: Power Politics in Transition.

Cloth over Boards. I. B. Tauris & Company, Ltd. London, 2004. 200p. ISBN:1-86064-881-9, ISBN13: 978-1-86064-881-6. Dewey:327.5/38055. LCCN:2004-302041.
Audience: **g,l,u.**

Aruri, Naseer Hasan **DS119.76.A773 2003**
Dishonest Broker: America's Role in Israel and Palestine. Ed. 2. Trade Paper. South End Press. Cambridge, MA. 2003. 248p. ISBN:0-89608-687-9, ISBN13: 978-0-89608-687-6. Dewey:327.73054/09/045. LCCN:2002-042886.
Audience: **g,l,u,f.**

Bekes, Csaba & Byrne, Malcom (Editors) **DB956.7.A15 2002**
The 1956 Hungarian Revolution: A History in Documents. Janos Rainer (Engineer). Trade Cloth. Central European University Press. Herndon, VA. 2002. 600p. National Security Archive Cold War Readers Ser. ISBN:963-9241-48-2, ISBN13: 978-963-9241-48-0. Dewey:943.905/2. LCCN:2002-007516.
Audience: **u,f.**

Byrne, Malcom & Ostermann, Christian F. (Editors) **DD286.2.U67 2001**
Uprising in East Germany 1953: The Cold War, the German Question and the First Major Upheavel Behind the Iron Curtain. Trade Cloth. Central European University Press. Herndon, VA. 2003. 492p. National Security Archive Cold War Readers Ser. ISBN:963-9241-17-2, ISBN13: 978-963-9241-17-6. Dewey:943/.10875. LCCN:2001-047177.
Audience: **u,f.**

Cooley, John K. **DS119.8**
Alliance Against Babylon: The US, Israel and Iraq. Trade Cloth. Pluto Press. London, 2005. 278p. ISBN:0-7453-2282-4, ISBN13: 978-0-7453-2282-7. Dewey:956.704/3. LCCN:2005-276712.
Audience: **g,l,u.** *Choice, 2005.*

Curry, Anne **DC96.C87 2003**
The Hundred Years War. Ed. 2. Cloth over Boards. Palgrave Macmillan. New York, NY. 2003. 240p. British History in Perspective Ser. ISBN:1-4039-0816-8, ISBN13: 978-1-4039-0816-2. Dewey:944/.025. LCCN:2003-040483.
Audience: **g,l,u,f.** *Choice, 1993.*

Dent, David W. **F1418**
Historical Dictionary of U. S. -Latin American Relations. Cloth Text. Greenwood Publishing Group, Inc. Portsmouth, NH. 2005. 568p. ISBN:0-313-32196-5, ISBN13: 978-0-313-32196-2. Dewey:327.7308/09/03. LCCN:2005-007698.
Audience: **g,l,u,f.** *Choice, 2006.*

Dukes, Paul **E183.8.S65D85 2004**
The USA in the Making of the USSR: The Washington Conference, 1921-1922, and "Uninvited Russia". Paper over Boards. Routledge. New York, NY. 2004. 168p. RoutledgeCurzon Studies on the History of Russia and Eastern Europe, Vol. 2 ISBN:0-415-32930-2, ISBN13: 978-0-415-32930-9. Dewey:327.1/09/041. LCCN:2004-002710.
Audience: **l,u,f.**

Dunn, Kevin C. & Shaw, Timothy M. (Editors) **JZ1773.A92 2001**
Africa's Challenge to International Relations Theory. Cloth over Boards. Palgrave Macmillan. New York, NY. 2001. 264p. International Political Economy Ser. ISBN:0-333-91828-2, ISBN13: 978-0-333-91828-9. Dewey:327/.096. LCCN:00-048334.
Audience: **u,f.**

Faroqhi, Suraiya **DR486**
The Ottoman Empire and the World Around It. Cloth over Boards. I. B. Tauris & Company, Ltd. London, 2005. 304p. Library of Ottoman Studies ISBN:1-85043-715-7, ISBN13: 978-1-85043-715-4. Dewey:956.1/015. LCCN:2005-297308.
Audience: **g,l,u,f.** *Choice, 2005.*

Hansen, Birthe & Heurlin, Bertel (Editors) **JZ1628.B35 1998**
The Baltic States in World Politics. Trade Paper. Palgrave Macmillan. New York, NY. 1998. 188p. ISBN:0-312-21527-4, ISBN13: 978-0-312-21527-9. Dewey:320.9/479. LCCN:98-016502.
Audience: **l,u,f.** *Choice, 1999.*

Harbour, Frances V. **JZ1480.H37 1999**
Thinking about International Ethics: Moral Theory and Cases from American Foreign Policy. Trade Paper. Westview Press. Boulder, CO. 1998. 224p. ISBN:0-8133-2847-0, ISBN13: 978-0-8133-2847-8. Dewey:172.4/0973. LCCN:98-026744.
Audience: **l,u,f.**

✓ **Hehir, Bryan, et al.** **JZ1480.L53 2004**
Liberty and Power: A Dialogue on Religion and U. S. Foreign Policy in an Unjust World. Michael Walzer, Charles Krauthammer, Louise Richardson & Shibley Telhami (Authors). Trade Paper. Brookings Institution Press. Washington, DC. 2004. 119p. The Pew Forum Dialogues on Religion and Public Life Ser. ISBN:0-8157-3545-6, ISBN13: 978-0-8157-3545-8. Dewey:205/.624. LCCN:2004-019511.
Audience: **l,u,f.**

Jazbec, Milan **JZ1570.J39 2001**
The Diplomacies of New Small States: The Case of Slovenia with Some Comparison from the Baltics. Trade Cloth. Ashgate Publishing, Ltd. Aldershot, 2001. x, 238p. ISBN:0-7546-1706-8, ISBN13: 978-0-7546-1706-8. Dewey:327.4973. LCCN:00-054301.
Audience: **l,u,f.**

Kagan, Robert **D1065.U5K26 2003**
Of Paradise and Power: America and Europe in the New World Order. Trade Cloth. Knopf Publishing Group. New York, NY. 2003. 112p. ISBN:1-4000-4093-0, ISBN13: 978-1-4000-4093-3. Dewey:327.7304/09/0511. LCCN:2002-038549.
Audience: **g,l,u,f.**

Khalidi, Rashid **DS63.2.U5K49 2004**
Resurrecting Empire: Western Footprints and America's Perilous Path in the Middle East. Trade Cloth. Beacon Press. Boston, MA. 2004. 192p. ISBN:0-8070-0234-8, ISBN13: 978-0-8070-0234-6. Dewey:303.48/273056. LCCN:2003-023161.
Audience: **g,l,u,f.**

Lieber, Robert J. **JZ1480.E16 2002**
Eagle Rules?: Foreign Policy and American Primacy in the Twenty-First Century. Trade Paper. Prentice Hall PTR. Upper Saddle River, NJ. 2001. 366p. ISBN:0-13-090987-4, ISBN13: 978-0-13-090987-9. Dewey:327.73. LCCN:2001-019903.
Audience: **g,l.** *Choice, 2002.*

Lundestad, Geir **D1065.U5L86 1998**
Empire by Integration: The United States and European Integration, 1945-1997. Cloth Text. Oxford University Press, Inc. New York, NY. 1998. 216p. ISBN:0-19-878212-8, ISBN13: 978-0-19-878212-4. Dewey:327.7304. LCCN:97-022509.
Audience: **u,f.**

McDermott, Rose **JZ1480.M35 1998**
Risk Taking in International Politics: Prospect Theory in American Foreign Policy. Trade Cloth. University of Michigan Press. Chicago, IL. 1998. 256p. ISBN:0-472-10867-0, ISBN13: 978-0-472-10867-1. Dewey:327.73/001/9. LCCN:97-021113.
Audience: **u,f.**

Meyer, Karl E. **DS329.4.M46 2003**
The Dust of Empire: The Race for Mastery in the Asian Heartland. Trade Cloth. PublicAffairs. New York, NY. 2003. 272p. ISBN:1-58648-048-0, ISBN13: 978-1-58648-048-6. Dewey:958. LCCN:2002-037186.
Audience: **g,l,u,f.**

Mowle, Thomas **D2009.M68 2004**
Allies at Odds?: The United States and the European Union. Cloth over Boards. Palgrave Macmillan. New York, NY. 2004. 240p. ISBN:1-4039-6650-8, ISBN13: 978-1-4039-6650-6. Dewey:327.7304/09/0511. LCCN:2004-041596.
Audience: **l,u,f.** *Choice, 2005.*

Patten, Chris **D863.3.P37 2006**
Cousins and Strangers: America, Britain, and Europe in a New Century. Cloth over Boards. Henry Holt & Company. New York, NY. 2006. 320p. ISBN:0-8050-7788-X, ISBN13: 978-0-8050-7788-9. Dewey:327.1/7/09182109051. LCCN:2005-053825.
Audience: **g,l,u,f.**

Saikal, Amin **DS63.2.U5S2335 2003**
Islam and the West: Conflict or Cooperation? Cloth over Boards. Palgrave Macmillan. New York, NY. 2003. 176p. ISBN:1-4039-0357-3, ISBN13: 978-1-4039-0357-0. Dewey:327.73017/671/090511. LCCN:2003-040518.
Audience: **u,f.** *Choice, 2004.*

Stein, Kenneth W. **DS119.7.S6749 1999**
Heroic Diplomacy: Sadat, Kissinger, Carter, Begin and the Quest for Arab-Israeli Peace. Trade Paper. Routledge. New York, NY. 1999. 352p. ISBN:0-415-92155-4, ISBN13: 978-0-415-92155-8. Dewey:956.04. LCCN:98-049359.
Audience: **u,f.** *Choice, 2000.*

International Relations. Transnational Relations > By Country, Territory, or Region > United States (See Also American Politics > Foreign Policy)

City College of New York Library **DS79.76**
Government Views of Iraq.
http://www.ccny.cuny.edu/library/Divisions/Government/Iraqbib.html
Audience: **g,l,u,f.**

Haass, Richard N. & O'Sullivan, Meghan L. (Editors) **JZ1480.H66 2000**
Honey and Vinegar: Incentives, Sanctions and Foreign Policies. Trade Paper. Brookings Institution Press. Washington, DC. 2000. xii, 211p. ISBN:0-8157-3355-0, ISBN13: 978-0-8157-3355-3. Dewey:327.73. LCCN:00-008815.
Audience: **g,l,u,f.** *Choice, 2001.*

Hehir, Bryan, et al. **JZ1480.L53 2004**
Liberty and Power: A Dialogue on Religion and U. S. Foreign Policy in an Unjust World. Michael Walzer, Charles Krauthammer, Louise Richardson & Shibley Telhami (Authors). Trade Paper. Brookings Institution Press. Washington, DC. 2004. 119p. The Pew Forum Dialogues on Religion and Public Life Ser. ISBN:0-8157-3545-6, ISBN13: 978-0-8157-3545-8. Dewey:205/.624. LCCN:2004-019511.
Audience: **l,u,f.**

Kupchan, Charles **JZ1480.K87 2002**
The End of the American Era: U. S. Foreign Policy and the Geopolitics of the Twenty-First Century. Trade Paper. Knopf Publishing Group. New York, NY. 2003. 416p. ISBN:0-375-72659-4, ISBN13: 978-0-375-72659-0. Dewey:327.73. LCCN:2002-018443.
Audience: **l,u,f.** *Choice, 2003.*

Lieber, Robert J. **JZ1480.E16 2002**
Eagle Rules?: Foreign Policy and American Primacy in the Twenty-First Century. Trade Paper. Prentice Hall PTR. Upper Saddle River, NJ. 2001. 366p. ISBN:0-13-090987-4, ISBN13: 978-0-13-090987-9. Dewey:327.73. LCCN:2001-019903.
Audience: **g,l.** *Choice, 2002.*

Malik, Yogendra K. **E183.8.I4I52 2002**
India and the United States in a Changing World. Ashok Kapur, Harold Gould & Arthur G. Rubinoff (Editors). Trade Cloth. SAGE Publications, Inc. Thousand Oaks, CA. 2002. 560p. ISBN:0-7619-9592-7, ISBN13: 978-0-7619-9592-0. Dewey:327.54073. LCCN:2001-059021.
Audience: **u,f.**

Malone, David M. & Khong, Yuen Koong (Editors) **JZ1480.U544 2003**
Unilateralism and U. S. Foreign Policy: International Perspectives. Library Binding. Lynne Rienner Publishers, Inc. Boulder, CO. 2003. 460p. Center on International Cooperation Studies in Multilateralism ISBN:1-58826-143-3, ISBN13: 978-1-58826-143-4. Dewey:327.73. LCCN:2002-073986.
Audience: **u,f.** *Choice, 2003.*

McDermott, Rose **JZ1480.M35 1998**
Risk Taking in International Politics: Prospect Theory in American Foreign Policy. Trade Cloth. University of Michigan Press. Chicago, IL. 1998. 256p. ISBN:0-472-10867-0, ISBN13: 978-0-472-10867-1. Dewey:327.73/001/9. LCCN:97-021113.
Audience: **u,f.**

Mead, Walter Russell **JZ1480.M43 2004**
Power, Terror, Peace, and War: America's Grand Strategy in a World at Risk. Trade Cloth. Alfred A. Knopf Inc. New York, NY. 2004. 240p. ISBN:1-4000-4237-2, ISBN13: 978-1-4000-4237-1. Dewey:327.73. LCCN:2003-067277.
Audience: **l,u,f.** *Choice, 2005.*

Schlesinger, Arthur M. Jr. **JZ1480.S35 2004**
War and the American Presidency. Trade Cloth. W. W. Norton & Company, Inc. New York, NY. 2004. 224p. ISBN:0-393-06002-0, ISBN13: 978-0-393-06002-7. Dewey:327.1/6/0973. LCCN:2004-009872.
Audience: **g,l,u,f.** *Choice, 2005.*

U.S. Department of State **JX1407**
Foreign Relations of the United States.
http://www.state.gov/r/pa/ho/frus/
Audience: **g,l,u,f.**

U.S. Department of State **JX1407**
Foreign Relations of the United States.
http://digicoll.library.wisc.edu/FRUS/
University of Wisconsin.
Audience: **g,l,u,f.**

International Relations. Transnational Relations > By Country, Territory, or Region > Other Countries (See Also Comparative Politics)

AbuKhalil, Asad **DS228.U6**
The Battle for Saudi Arabia: Royalty, Fundamentalism, and Global Power. Trade Paper. Seven Stories Press. New York, NY. 2003. 176p. An Open Media Book Ser. ISBN:1-58322-610-9, ISBN13: 978-1-58322-610-0. Dewey:327.5/380/73.
Audience: **g,l,u,f.**

Arnaldi, Girolamo **DG473.A7613 2005**
Italy and Its Invaders. Antony Shugaar (Translator). Trade Cloth. Harvard University Press. Cambridge, MA. 2005. 240p. ISBN:0-674-01870-2, ISBN13: 978-0-674-01870-9. Dewey:945. LCCN:2005-050770.
Audience: **l,u.** *Choice, 2006.*

Bell, P. M. **DC59.8.G7B45 1996**
France and Britain 1900-1940. Ed. 1. Cloth Text. Longman Publishing Group. White Plains, NY. 1996. 256p. ISBN:0-582-22954-5, ISBN13: 978-0-582-22954-9. Dewey:327.4/1/044. LCCN:95-041012.
Audience: **g,l,u,f.**

Bell, P. M. **DA589.8.B45 1997**
France and Britain, 1940-1994: The Long Separation. Trade Paper. Longman Publishing Group. White Plains, NY. 1997. 328p. ISBN:0-582-28920-3, ISBN13: 978-0-582-28920-8. Dewey:327.41044. LCCN:96-043210.
Audience: **g,l,u,f.** *Choice, 1997.*

Beschloss, Michael R. & Talbott, Strobe **E183.8.S65B4685**
At the Highest Levels: The Inside Story of the End of the Cold War. Trade Paper. Little Brown & Company. New York, NY. 1994. 521p. ISBN:0-316-09282-7, ISBN13: 978-0-316-09282-1. Dewey:327.73. LCCN:92-036336.
Audience: **g,l,u.**

Bozo, Frederic **UA646.5.F7B6913 2001**
Two Strategies for Europe: De Gaulle, the United States and the Atlantic Alliance. Susan Emanuel (Translator). Book, Other. Rowman & Littlefield Publishers, Inc. Lanham, MD. 2000. 304p. ISBN:0-8476-9530-1, ISBN13: 978-0-8476-9530-0. Dewey:355/.031091821. LCCN:00-040301.
Audience: **g,l,u.** *Choice, 2001.*

Cogan, Charles **JZ6045.C64 2003**
French Negotiating Behavior: Dealing with la Grande Nation. Trade Cloth. United States Institute of Peace Press (USIP Press). Washington, DC. 2004. 364p. ISBN:1-929223-53-6, ISBN13: 978-1-929223-53-4. Dewey:327.2/0944. LCCN:2003-061296.
Audience: **g,l,u,f.** *Choice, 2004.*

Cohen, Stephen Philip **DS376.9.C63 2004**
The Idea of Pakistan. Trade Cloth. Brookings Institution Press. Washington, DC. 2004. 382p. ISBN:0-8157-1502-1, ISBN13: 978-0-8157-1502-3. Dewey:954.91. LCCN:2004-016553.
Audience: **l,u,f.** *Choice, 2005.*

Collins, Alan **UA830**
The Security Dilemmas of Southeast Asia. Trade Cloth. Institute of Southeast Asian Studies. Pasir Panjang, 2001. 256p. ISBN:981-230-108-9, ISBN13: 978-981-230-108-6. Dewey:355/.033059.
Audience: **g,l,u,f.** *Choice, 2001.*

Cull, Nicholas J. **D810.P6**
Selling War: The British Propaganda Campaign Against American Neutrality in World War II. Trade Paper. Oxford University Press, Inc. New York, NY. 1996. 292p. ISBN:0-19-511150-8, ISBN13: 978-0-19-511150-7. Dewey:940.54/88.
Audience: **u,f.** *Choice, 1995.*

Curry, Anne **DC96.C87 2003**
The Hundred Years War. Ed. 2. Cloth over Boards. Palgrave Macmillan. New York, NY. 2003. 240p. British History in Perspective Ser. ISBN:1-4039-0816-8, ISBN13: 978-1-4039-0816-2. Dewey:944/.025. LCCN:2003-040483.
Audience: **g,l,u,f.** *Choice, 1993.*

Dickie, John **JX1784**
The New Mandarins: How British Foreign Policy Works. Saddle Stitched, Cloth over Boards, Dust Jacket. I. B. Tauris & Company, Ltd. London, 2004. 256p. ISBN:1-86064-978-5, ISBN13: 978-1-86064-978-3. Dewey:327.4/1.
Audience: **u,f.** *Choice, 2005.*

Dodge, Toby **DS70.96.G7D633**
Inventing Iraq: The Failure of Nation-Building and a History Denied. Trade Cloth. Columbia University Press. New York, NY. 2003. 288p. ISBN:0-231-13166-6, ISBN13: 978-0-231-13166-7. Dewey:956.704/1. LCCN:2003-051453.
Audience: **l,u,f.** *Choice, 2004.*

Dunn, Kevin C. & Shaw, Timothy M. (Editors) **JZ1773.A92 2001**
Africa's Challenge to International Relations Theory. Cloth over Boards. Palgrave Macmillan. New York, NY. 2001. 264p. International Political Economy Ser. ISBN:0-333-91828-2, ISBN13: 978-0-333-91828-9. Dewey:327/.096. LCCN:00-048334.
Audience: **u,f.**

Eisenstadt, Michael (Editor) **DS70.96.G7B75 2003**
The British Experience in Iraq: Lessons for U.S. Policymakers. Washington Institute for Near East Policy Staff (Contribution by). Trade Paper. Washington Institute for Near East Policy, The. Washington, DC. 2003. 84p. ISBN:0-944029-84-1, ISBN13: 978-0-944029-84-8. Dewey:327.410567/09/04. LCCN:2003-004627.
Audience: **l,u.**

Gilbert, Martin **DA566.9.C5G4445 2005**
Churchill and America. Trade Cloth. Simon & Schuster. New York, NY. 2005. 528p. ISBN:0-7432-5992-0, ISBN13: 978-0-7432-5992-7. Dewey:941.084/092. LCCN:2005-049412.
Audience: **g,l,u.**

Hansen, Birthe & Heurlin, Bertel (Editors) **JZ1628.B35 1998**
The Baltic States in World Politics. Trade Paper. Palgrave Macmillan. New York, NY. 1998. 188p. ISBN:0-312-21527-4, ISBN13: 978-0-312-21527-9. Dewey:320.9/479. LCCN:98-016502.
Audience: **l,u,f.** *Choice, 1999.*

Harbour, Frances V. **JZ1480.H37 1999**
Thinking about International Ethics: Moral Theory and Cases from American Foreign Policy. Trade Paper. Westview Press. Boulder, CO. 1998. 224p. ISBN:0-8133-2847-0, ISBN13: 978-0-8133-2847-8. Dewey:172.4/0973. LCCN:98-026744.
Audience: **l,u,f.**

Jazbec, Milan **JZ1570.J39 2001**
The Diplomacies of New Small States: The Case of Slovenia with Some Comparison from the Baltics. Trade Cloth. Ashgate Publishing, Ltd. Aldershot, 2001. x, 238p. ISBN:0-7546-1706-8, ISBN13: 978-0-7546-1706-8. Dewey:327.4973. LCCN:00-054301.
Audience: **l,u,f.**

Kux, Dennis **E183.8.P18K89 2001**
The U. S. and Pakistan, 1947-2000: Disenchanted Allies. Trade Paper. Johns Hopkins University Press. Baltimore, MD. 2001. 496p. ISBN:0-8018-6572-7, ISBN13: 978-0-8018-6572-5. Dewey:327.7305491/09/045. LCCN:00-013260.
Audience: **l,u,f.** *Choice, 2002.*

Legault, Albert & Fortmann, Michel **JX1974.L55513 1992**
A Diplomacy of Hope: Canada and Disarmament, 1945-1988. Trade Paper. McGill-Queen's University Press. Montreal, PQ. 1992. 696p. ISBN:0-7735-0955-0, ISBN13: 978-0-7735-0955-9. Dewey:327.1/74/097109045. LCCN:94-149283.
Audience: **u,f.** *Choice, 1993.*

Levitt, Joseph **JX1974.7.L355 1993**
Pearson and Canada's Role in Nuclear Disarmament and Arms Control Negotiations, 1945-1957. Trade Cloth. McGill-Queen's University Press. Montreal, PQ. 1993. 344p. ISBN:0-7735-0905-4, ISBN13: 978-0-7735-0905-4. Dewey:327.1/74. LCCN:94-149837.
Audience: **u,f.** *Choice, 1993.*

Malik, Yogendra K. **E183.8.I4I52 2002**
India and the United States in a Changing World. Ashok Kapur, Harold Gould & Arthur G. Rubinoff (Editors). Trade Cloth. SAGE Publications, Inc. Thousand Oaks, CA. 2002. 560p. ISBN:0-7619-9592-7, ISBN13: 978-0-7619-9592-0. Dewey:327.54073. LCCN:2001-059021.
Audience: **u,f.**

Masterson, William H. **E183.8.G7M35**
Tories and Democrats: British Diplomats in Pre-Jacksonian America. Trade Paper. Texas A&M University Press. College Station, TX. 2000. 328p. ISBN:1-58544-078-7, ISBN13: 978-1-58544-078-8. Dewey:327.41073. LCCN:85-040046.
Audience: **l,u,f.** *Choice, 1986.*

Motyl, Alexander (Editor), et al. **DK510.764.T73 2004**
Russia's Engagement with the West. Blair Ruble & Lilia Shevtsova (Editors). Cloth Text. M. E. Sharpe Inc. Armonk, NY. 2004. 328p. ISBN:0-7656-1441-3, ISBN13: 978-0-7656-1441-4. Dewey:327.4704/09/0511. LCCN:2004-005787.
Audience: **u,f.** *Choice, 2005.*

Norris, John **DR2087**
Collision Course: NATO, Russia, and Kosovo. Trade Cloth. Greenwood Publishing Group, Inc. Portsmouth, NH. 2005. 360p. ISBN:0-275-98753-1, ISBN13: 978-0-275-98753-4. Dewey:949.703. LCCN:2005-002147.
Audience: **g,u.** *Choice, 2006.*

Poo, Mu-chou **DS71.P63 2005**
Enemies of Civilization: Attitudes Toward Foreigners in Ancient Mesopotamia, Egypt, and China. Cloth Text. State University of New York Press. Albany, NY. 2005. 224p. SUNY Series in Chinese Philosophy and Culture ISBN:0-7914-6363-X, ISBN13: 978-0-7914-6363-5. Dewey:327.3/009. LCCN:2004-045401.
Audience: **u,f.** *Choice, 2005.*

Sigal, Leon V. **JZ5675**
Disarming Strangers: Nuclear Diplomacy with North Korea. Trade Paper. Princeton University Press. Princeton, NJ. 1999. 336p. Princeton Studies in International History and Politics ISBN:0-691-01006-4, ISBN13: 978-0-691-01006-9. Dewey:327.1/747. LCCN:97-024502.
Audience: **u,f.** *Choice, 1998.*

Snyder, Scott **DS935.65.S69 1999**
Negotiating on the Edge: North Korean Negotiating Behavior. Trade Cloth. United States Institute of Peace Press (USIP Press). Washington, DC. 1999. 236p. ISBN:1-878379-95-X, ISBN13: 978-1-878379-95-5. Dewey:327.5193. LCCN:99-048064.
Audience: **g,l,u,f.** *Choice, 2000.*

Talbott, Strobe **E183.8.I4T35 2004**
Engaging India: Diplomacy, Democracy, and the Bomb. Trade Cloth. Brookings Institution Press. Washington, DC. 2004. 268p. ISBN:0-8157-8300-0, ISBN13: 978-0-8157-8300-8. Dewey:327.73054/09/049. LCCN:2004-012803.
Audience: **u,f.** *Choice, 2005.*

Tucker, Nancy B. **E183.8.C5T835 2001**
China Confidential: American Diplomats and Sino-American Relations, 1945-1996. Trade Cloth. Columbia University Press. New York, NY. 2000. 638p. ISBN:0-231-10630-0, ISBN13: 978-0-231-10630-6. Dewey:327.73051. LCCN:00-040445.
Audience: **u,f.** *Choice, 2001.*

Wilson, William W. **HD9005.K66 2002**
Agricultural Trade under CUSTA. Won W. Koo (Editor). Trade Cloth. Nova Science Publishers, Inc. Hauppauge, NY. 2002. 355p. ISBN:1-59033-192-3, ISBN13: 978-1-59033-192-7. Dewey:382/.41/0973. LCCN:2001-059618.
Audience: **u,f.** *Choice, 2003, 2002.*

International Relations. Transnational Relations > Diplomacy

Art, Robert J. & Cronin, Patrick M. (Editors) **JZ1480.U553 2003**
The United States and Coercive Diplomacy. Trade Cloth. United States Institute of Peace Press (USIP Press). Washington, DC.

2003. 464p. ISBN:1-929223-45-5, ISBN13: 978-1-929223-45-9. Dewey:327.73/009/049. LCCN:2003-041666.
Audience: **g,l,u.** *Choice, 2004.*

Barston, R. **JZ1405.B37 2006**
Modern Diplomacy. Ed. 3. Trade Paper. Longman Publishing. Boston, MA. 2006. 408p. ISBN:1-4058-1201-X, ISBN13: 978-1-4058-1201-6. Dewey:327.2. LCCN:2006-040998.
Audience: **l,u.**

Berridge, G. R. **JZ1305**
Diplomacy: Theory and Practice. Ed. 3. Trade Paper, Perfect. Palgrave Macmillan. New York, NY. 2005. 240p. ISBN:1-4039-9311-4, ISBN13: 978-1-4039-9311-3. Dewey:327.2. LCCN:2005-043765.
Audience: **l,u.**

Berridge, G. R. (Editor), et al. **JZ1305.D57 2001**
Diplomatic Theory from Machiavelli to Kissinger. Maurice Keens-Soper & T. G. Otte (Editors). Trade Paper. Palgrave Macmillan. New York, NY. 2001. 226p. Studies in Diplomacy ISBN:0-333-75366-6, ISBN13: 978-0-333-75366-8. Dewey:327.1/01. LCCN:00-048350.
Audience: **l,u.** *Choice, 2002.*

Beschloss, Michael R. & Talbott, Strobe **E183.8.S65B4685**
At the Highest Levels: The Inside Story of the End of the Cold War. Trade Paper. Little Brown & Company. New York, NY. 1994. 521p. ISBN:0-316-09282-7, ISBN13: 978-0-316-09282-1. Dewey:327.73. LCCN:92-036336.
Audience: **g,l,u.**

Black, Jeremy **DA28.35.H36**
British Diplomats and Diplomacy, 1660-1800. Trade Cloth. University of Exeter Press. Exeter, 2001. 256p. ISBN:0-85989-613-7, ISBN13: 978-0-85989-613-9. Dewey:327.4/1/009033.
Audience: **u,f.** *Choice, 2002.*

Cogan, Charles **JZ6045.C64 2003**
French Negotiating Behavior: Dealing with la Grande Nation. Trade Cloth. United States Institute of Peace Press (USIP Press). Washington, DC. 2004. 364p. ISBN:1-929223-53-6, ISBN13: 978-1-929223-53-4. Dewey:327.2/0944. LCCN:2003-061296.
Audience: **g,l,u,f.** *Choice, 2004.*

Cohen, Stephen Philip **DS376.9.C63 2004**
The Idea of Pakistan. Trade Cloth. Brookings Institution Press. Washington, DC. 2004. 382p. ISBN:0-8157-1502-1, ISBN13: 978-0-8157-1502-3. Dewey:954.91. LCCN:2004-016553.
Audience: **l,u,f.** *Choice, 2005.*

Crocker, Chester A., et al. **JZ5599.C76 2004**
Taming Intractable Conflicts: Mediation in the Hardest Cases. Fen Osler Hampson & Pamela R. Aall (Authors). Trade Cloth. United States Institute of Peace Press (USIP Press). Washington, DC. 2004. 224p. ISBN:1-929223-56-0, ISBN13: 978-1-929223-56-5. Dewey:327.1/7. LCCN:2004-043385.
Audience: **g,l,u.** *Choice, 2005.*

Davis, Calvin D. **JX1916.D32 1976**
The United States and the Second Hague Peace Conference: American Diplomacy and International Organization, 1899-1914. Cloth Text. Duke University Press. Durham, NC. 1976. ix, 398p. ISBN:0-8223-0346-9, ISBN13: 978-0-8223-0346-6. Dewey:341.5. LCCN:75-017353.
Audience: **u,f.** B

Dickie, John **JX1784**
The New Mandarins: How British Foreign Policy Works. Saddle Stitched, Cloth over Boards, Dust Jacket. I. B. Tauris & Company, Ltd. London, 2004. 256p. ISBN:1-86064-978-5, ISBN13: 978-1-86064-978-3. Dewey:327.4/1.
Audience: **u,f.** *Choice, 2005.*

Eban, Abba **JZ1305.E22 1998**
Diplomacy for a Next Century. Cloth over Boards. Yale University Press. Cumberland, RI. 1998. 200p. Castle Lectures Ser. ISBN:0-300-07287-2, ISBN13: 978-0-300-07287-7. Dewey:327. LCCN:97-039250.
Audience: **g,l,u.** *Choice, 1998.*

Gaddis, John Lewis (Editor), et al. **JZ5665.C65 1999**
Cold War Statesmen Confront the Bomb: Nuclear Diplomacy since 1945. Philip H. Gordon, Ernest R. May & Jonathan Rosenberg (Editors). Cloth Text. Oxford University Press, Inc. New York, NY. 1999. 408p. ISBN:0-19-829468-9, ISBN13: 978-0-19-829468-9. Dewey:327.47073/09045. LCCN:98-049340.
Audience: **u,f.** *Choice, 1999.*

Haigh, R. H., et al. **DK266.H246 1986**
Soviet Foreign Policy, the League of Nations and Europe, 1917-1939. D. S. Morris & A. R. Peters (Authors). Trade Cloth. Rowman & Littlefield Publishers, Inc. Lanham, MD. 1986. 224p. ISBN:0-389-20611-3, ISBN13: 978-0-389-20611-8. Dewey:327.47. LCCN:85-030630.
Audience: **u,f.** *Choice, 1986.*

Kissinger, Henry A. **E744**
Diplomacy. Paper Text. DIANE Publishing Company. Collingdale, PA. 1998. 912p. ISBN:0-7881-5690-X, ISBN13: 978-0-7881-5690-8. Dewey:327.7/3.
Audience: **g,l,u,f.**

Kremenyuk, Victor A. (Editor) **JZ6045.I58 2002**
International Negotiation: Analysis, Approaches, Issues. Ed. 2. Trade Paper. John Wiley & Sons, Inc. Hoboken, NJ. 2002. 592p. ISBN:0-7879-5886-7, ISBN13: 978-0-7879-5886-2. Dewey:327.1/7. LCCN:2001-003468.
Audience: **l,u.** *Choice, 1991.*

Larres, Klaus **DA588.L364 2002**
Churchill's Cold War: The Politics of Personal Diplomacy. Cloth over Boards. Yale University Press. Cumberland, RI. 2002. 608p. ISBN:0-300-09438-8, ISBN13: 978-0-300-09438-1. Dewey:327.41/0092. LCCN:2002-000830.
Audience: **g,l,u.**

Masterson, William H. **E183.8.G7M35**
Tories and Democrats: British Diplomats in Pre-Jacksonian America. Trade Paper. Texas A&M University Press. College Station, TX. 2000. 328p. ISBN:1-58544-078-7, ISBN13: 978-1-58544-078-8. Dewey:327.41073. LCCN:85-040046.
Audience: **l,u,f.** *Choice, 1986.*

Meyer, Christopher **DA566.9**
DC Confidential: The Controversial Memoirs of Britain's Ambassador at the Time of 9/11 and the Iraq War. Trade Cloth. Weidenfeld & Nicolson, Ltd. London, 2006. 288p.

ISBN:0-297-85114-4, ISBN13: 978-0-297-85114-1. Dewey:327.410092.
Audience: **g,l,u.**

Oppenheim, Felix E. **JX1255.O66 1991**
The Place of Morality in Foreign Policy. Trade Cloth. Simon & Schuster. New York, NY. 1991. 128p. Issues in World Politics Ser. ISBN:0-669-21450-7, ISBN13: 978-0-669-21450-5. Dewey:172/.4. LCCN:90-025426.
Audience: **l,u.**

Rock, Stephen R. **JZ5599.R63 2000**
Appeasement in International Politics. Trade Cloth. University Press of Kentucky. Lexington, KY. 2000. 237p. ISBN:0-8131-2160-4, ISBN13: 978-0-8131-2160-4. Dewey:327.1/1. LCCN:99-087216.
Audience: **u,f.** *Choice, 2001.*

Snyder, Scott **DS935.65.S69 1999**
Negotiating on the Edge: North Korean Negotiating Behavior. Trade Cloth. United States Institute of Peace Press (USIP Press). Washington, DC. 1999. 236p. ISBN:1-878379-95-X, ISBN13: 978-1-878379-95-5. Dewey:327.5193. LCCN:99-048064.
Audience: **g,l,u,f.** *Choice, 2000.*

Starkey, Brigid, et al. **JZ6045.S73 2005**
Negotiating a Complex World: An Introduction to International Negotiation. Ed. 2. Mark A. Boyer & Jonathan Wilkenfeld (Authors). Book, Other. Rowman & Littlefield Publishers, Inc. Lanham, MD. 2005. 192p. New Millennium Books in International Studies ISBN:0-7425-3576-2, ISBN13: 978-0-7425-3576-3. Dewey:327.1/7. LCCN:2004-018463.
Audience: **l,u.** *Choice, 2000.*

Stein, Kenneth W. **DS119.7.S6749 1999**
Heroic Diplomacy: Sadat, Kissinger, Carter, Begin and the Quest for Arab-Israeli Peace. Paper over Boards. Routledge. New York, NY. 1999. 352p. ISBN:0-415-92154-6, ISBN13: 978-0-415-92154-1. Dewey:956.04. LCCN:98-049359.
Audience: **u.** *Choice, 2000.*

Talbott, Strobe **E183.8.I4T35 2004**
Engaging India: Diplomacy, Democracy, and the Bomb. Trade Cloth. Brookings Institution Press. Washington, DC. 2004. 268p. ISBN:0-8157-8300-0, ISBN13: 978-0-8157-8300-8. Dewey:327.73054/09/049. LCCN:2004-012803.
Audience: **u,f.** *Choice, 2005.*

Talbott, Strobe **E183.8.R9T27**
The Russia Hand: A Memoir of Presidential Diplomacy. Book, Other. Random House Adult Trade Publishing Group. New York, NY. 2003. 512p. ISBN:0-8129-6846-8, ISBN13: 978-0-8129-6846-0. Dewey:327.73047.
Audience: **g,l,u.** *Choice, 2003.*

Watkins, Michael & Rosegrant, Susan **JZ6045.W38 2001**
Breakthrough International Negotiation: How Great Negotiators Transformed the World's Toughest Post-Cold War Conflicts. Shimon Perez (Foreword by). Trade Cloth. John Wiley & Sons, Inc. Hoboken, NJ. 2001. 368p. ISBN:0-7879-5743-7, ISBN13: 978-0-7879-5743-8. Dewey:327.1/7. LCCN:2001-038577.
Audience: **g,l,u.**

Zartman, I. William & Rubin, Jeffrey Z. (Editors) **JZ6045.P69 2000**
Power and Negotiation. Trade Cloth. University of Michigan Press. Chicago, IL. 2000. 328p. ISBN:0-472-11079-9, ISBN13: 978-0-472-11079-7. Dewey:327.1/7. LCCN:99-043531.
Audience: **u,f.** *Choice, 2001.*

International Relations. Transnational Relations > War and Peace

Addington, Larry H. **D214**
The Patterns of War since the Eighteenth Century. Paper Text. DIANE Publishing Company. Collingdale, PA. 1999. 318p. ISBN:0-7881-6088-5, ISBN13: 978-0-7881-6088-2. Dewey:355/.02/0903.
Audience: **l,u.**

Ben-Ami, Shlomo **DS119.7.B3826 2005**
Scars of War, Wounds of Peace: The Israeli-Arab Tragedy. Trade Cloth. Oxford University Press, Inc. New York, NY. 2006. 368p. ISBN:0-19-518158-1, ISBN13: 978-0-19-518158-6. Dewey:956.9405. LCCN:2005-025383.
Audience: **g,l,u,f.**

Boutros-Ghali, Boutros (Introduction by) **JX1977.2.M85U55 1995**
The United Nations and Mozambique, 1992-1995. Trade Cloth. United Nations Publications. New York, NY. 1996. 321p. Blue Bks., Vol. V ISBN:92-1-100559-0, ISBN13: 978-92-1-100559-2. Dewey:341.23679. LCCN:95-192058.
Audience: **g,l,u.** *Choice, 1996.*

Brown, Dee **E81.B75 2001**
Bury My Heart at Wounded Knee: An Indian History of the American West. Ed. 30. Cloth over Boards. Henry Holt & Company. New York, NY. 2001. 512p. ISBN:0-8050-6634-9, ISBN13: 978-0-8050-6634-0. Dewey:970.5. LCCN:00-040958.
Audience: **g,u,f.**

Bueno de Mesquita, Bruce & Lalman, David **JX1391.B83**
War and Reason: Domestic and International Imperatives. Trade Paper. Yale University Press. Cumberland, RI. 1994. 336p. ISBN:0-300-05922-1, ISBN13: 978-0-300-05922-9. Dewey:327.1.
Audience: **l,u,f.** *Choice, 1992.*

Byers, Michael **KZ6385.B94 2006**
War Law: Understanding International Law and Armed Conflict. Trade Cloth. Grove/Atlantic, Inc. New York, NY. 2006. 224p. ISBN:0-8021-1809-7, ISBN13: 978-0-8021-1809-7. Dewey:341.6. LCCN:2005-045641.
Audience: **g,u.**

Cordesman, Anthony **DS79.76.C677 2004**
The War after the War. Paper Text. Center for Strategic & International Studies. Washington, DC. 2004. xix, 73p. CSIS Significant Issues Ser., 26 ISBN:0-89206-450-1, ISBN13: 978-0-89206-450-2. Dewey:327.730567/09/0511. LCCN:2004-011306.
Audience: **u,f.**

Cull, Nicholas J. **D810.P6**
Selling War: The British Propaganda Campaign Against American Neutrality in World War II. Trade Paper. Oxford University Press, Inc. New York, NY. 1996. 292p. ISBN:0-19-511150-8, ISBN13: 978-0-19-511150-7. Dewey:940.54/88.
Audience: **u,f.** *Choice, 1995.*

Curry, Anne **DC96.C87 2003**
The Hundred Years War. Ed. 2. Cloth over Boards. Palgrave Macmillan. New York, NY. 2003. 240p. British History in Perspective Ser. ISBN:1-4039-0816-8, ISBN13: 978-1-4039-0816-2. Dewey:944/.025. LCCN:2003-040483.
Audience: **g,l,u,f.** *Choice, 1993.*

Curti, Merle E. **JX1961.U6 C83**
Peace or War: The American Struggle, 1636-1936. Library Binding. Jerome S. Ozer Publisher, Inc. Englewood, NJ. 1972. 374p. Peace Movement in America Ser. ISBN:0-89198-064-4, ISBN13: 978-0-89198-064-3. Dewey:327/.172. LCCN:70-143428.
Audience: **l,u.**

Diamond, Larry & Diamond, Larry Jay **DS79.76.D53 2005**
Squandered Victory: The American Occupation and Bungled Effort to Bring Democracy to Iraq. Trade Cloth. Henry Holt & Company. New York, NY. 2005. 384p. ISBN:0-8050-7868-1, ISBN13: 978-0-8050-7868-8. Dewey:956.7044/3. LCCN:2005-043074.
Audience: **u,f.**

Dickinson, G. Lowes **U21**
Causes of International War. Trade Cloth. Greenwood Publishing Group, Inc. Portsmouth, NH. 1984. 110p. ISBN:0-313-24565-7, ISBN13: 978-0-313-24565-7. Dewey:355/.027. LCCN:84-012797.
Audience: **l,u.**

Frank, Jerome D. **JX1255.F7**
Sanity and Survival in the Nuclear Age: Psychological Aspects of War and Peace. Trade Paper. University Press of America, Inc. Lanham, MD. 1987. 346p. ISBN:0-8191-6744-4, ISBN13: 978-0-8191-6744-6. Dewey:327/.01/9.
Audience: **g,l,u.**

Gaddis, John Lewis (Editor), et al. **JZ5665.C65 1999**
Cold War Statesmen Confront the Bomb: Nuclear Diplomacy since 1945. Philip H. Gordon, Ernest R. May & Jonathan Rosenberg (Editors). Cloth Text. Oxford University Press, Inc. New York, NY. 1999. 408p. ISBN:0-19-829468-9, ISBN13: 978-0-19-829468-9. Dewey:327.47073/09045. LCCN:98-049340.
Audience: **u,f.** *Choice, 1999.*

Hasegawa, Tsuyoshi **D813.J3H37 2005**
Racing the Enemy: Stalin, Truman, and the Surrender of Japan. Trade Cloth. Harvard University Press. Cambridge, MA. 2005. 432p. ISBN:0-674-01693-9, ISBN13: 978-0-674-01693-4. Dewey:940.53/2452. LCCN:2004-059786.
Audience: **g,l,u,f.** *Choice, 2006.*

Hastings, Max **D743.H36 2004**
Armageddon: The Battle for Germany, 1944-1945. Trade Cloth. Alfred A. Knopf Inc. New York, NY. 2004. 640p. ISBN:0-375-41433-9, ISBN13: 978-0-375-41433-6. Dewey:940.54/21. LCCN:2004-046468.
Audience: **g,l,u,f.** *Choice, 2005.*

Hironaka, Ann **JZ6385.H57 2005**
Neverending Wars: The International Community, Weak States, and the Perpetuation of Civil War. Trade Cloth. Harvard University Press. Cambridge, MA. 2005. 204p. ISBN:0-674-01532-0, ISBN13: 978-0-674-01532-6. Dewey:303.6/4/091724. LCCN:2004-052600.
Audience: **l,u,f.** *Choice, 2005.*

Howard, Michael Eliot **CB481.H68 2000**
The Invention of Peace: Reflections on War and International Order. Cloth over Boards. Yale University Press. Cumberland, RI. 2001. 128p. ISBN:0-300-08866-3, ISBN13: 978-0-300-08866-3. Dewey:327.1/72. LCCN:00-043599.
Audience: **u,f.**

Kadera, Kelly M. **JZ1310.K33 2001**
The Power-Conflict Story: A Dynamic Model of Interstate Rivalry. Trade Cloth. University of Michigan Press. Chicago, IL. 2001. 208p. ISBN:0-472-11191-4, ISBN13: 978-0-472-11191-6. Dewey:327.1/01. LCCN:00-051173.
Audience: **u,f.** *Choice, 2002.*

Knights, Michael Andrew **DS79.755**
Cradle of Conflict: Iraq and the Birth of the Modern U. S. Military. Perfect, Paper over Boards, Dust Jacket. Naval Institute Press. Annapolis, MD. 2005. 462p. ISBN:1-59114-444-2, ISBN13: 978-1-59114-444-1. Dewey:956.7044/24/0973. LCCN:2005-021002.
Audience: **g,u,f.**

Moss, Norman **D755.2.M67 2003**
Nineteen Weeks: America, Britain, and the Fateful Summer of 1940. Trade Cloth. Houghton Mifflin Company Trade & Reference Division. Boston, MA. 2003. 416p. ISBN:0-618-10471-2, ISBN13: 978-0-618-10471-0. Dewey:940.53. LCCN:2002-192159.
Audience: **g,u,f.** *Choice, 2004.*

Nachmani, Amikam **DF849**
International Intervention in the Greek Civil War: The United Nations Special Committee on the Balkans, 1947-1952. Trade Cloth. Greenwood Publishing Group, Inc. Portsmouth, NH. 1990. 216p. ISBN:0-275-93367-9, ISBN13: 978-0-275-93367-8. Dewey:949.507/4. LCCN:89-026544.
Audience: **g,l,u.** *Choice, 1991.*

Rotberg, Robert I. & Rabb, Theodore K. (Editors) **U21.2.O72 1989**
The Origin and Prevention of Major Wars. John F. Guilmartin, Myron P. Gutmann, Jeffrey L. Hughes, Robert Jervis, Jack S. Levy, Charles S. Maier, Joseph S. Nye, George H. Quester, Gunther E. Rothenberg, Scott D. Sagan, Kenneth N. Waltz, Samuel R. Williamson, Bruce Bueno de Mesquita & Robert Gilpin (Contribution by). Trade Paper. Cambridge University Press. New York, NY. 1989. 360p. Studies in Interdisciplinary History ISBN:0-521-37955-5, ISBN13: 978-0-521-37955-7. Dewey:355/.02. LCCN:88-030223.
Audience: **u,f.** *Choice, 1989.*

Shawcross, William **DS79.76.S53 2004**
Allies: The U. S. Britain, and Europe in the Aftermath of the Iraq War. Trade Cloth. PublicAffairs. New York, NY. 2003. 272p. ISBN:1-58648-216-5, ISBN13: 978-1-58648-216-9. Dewey:956.7044/3. LCCN:2003-064786.
Audience: **g,u,f.**

Strachan, Hew **U43.E95**
European Armies and the Conduct of War. Trade Paper. Routledge. New York, NY. 1988. 240p. ISBN:0-415-07863-6, ISBN13: 978-0-415-07863-4. Dewey:355/.02/094.
Audience: **l,u,f.**

Trachtenberg, Marc **D1058.T718 1999**
A Constructed Peace: The Making of the European Settlement, 1945-1963. Trade Paper. Princeton University Press. Princeton,

NJ. 1999. 440p. Princeton Studies in International History and Politics ISBN:0-691-00273-8, ISBN13: 978-0-691-00273-6. Dewey:327/.094/09045. LCCN:98-034874.
Audience: **u,f.** *Choice, 1999.*

Wawro, Geoffrey **D361.W38 2000**
Warfare and Society in Europe, 1792-1914. Trade Paper. Routledge. New York, NY. 2000. 256p. Warfare and History Ser. ISBN:0-415-21445-9, ISBN13: 978-0-415-21445-2. Dewey:355/.0094/09034. LCCN:99-041813.
Audience: **l,u.**

Weart, Spencer R. **JC421.W43 1998**
Never at War: Why Democracies Will Not Fight One Another. Cloth over Boards. Yale University Press. Cumberland, RI. 1998. 430p. ISBN:0-300-07017-9, ISBN13: 978-0-300-07017-0. Dewey:327.1/7. LCCN:98-002664.
Audience: **g,l,u,f.** *Choice, 1999.*

Weisburd, A. Mark **KZ6368.W45 1997**
Use of Force: The Practice of States, 1945-1991. Trade Paper. Pennsylvania State University Press. University Park, PA. 1997. 566p. ISBN:0-271-01680-9, ISBN13: 978-0-271-01680-1. Dewey:341.5/84. LCCN:96-044645.
Audience: **g,l,u,f.** *Choice, 1998.*

Wilson, Joseph **JK468.E7W55 2004**
The Politics of Truth: Inside the Lies That Led to War and Betrayed My Wife's CIA Identity, A Diplomat's Memoir. Trade Cloth. Avalon Publishing Group. New York, NY. 2004. 528p. ISBN:0-7867-1378-X, ISBN13: 978-0-7867-1378-3. Dewey:327.73/0092 B. LCCN:2004-045897.
Audience: **g,l,u,f.**

International Relations. Transnational Relations > War and Peace > Peacekeeping. Dispute Settlement

JX1977.2.H2
The United Nations and Haiti. Trade Paper. United Nations Publications. New York, NY. 1996. The United Nations Blue Bks. ISBN:92-1-100606-6, ISBN13: 978-92-1-100606-3. Dewey:341.23.
Audience: **g,l,u.**

Bellamy, Alex J. & Williams, Paul **JZ6374**
Peace Operations and Global Order. Paper over Boards. Routledge. New York, NY. 2005. VIII, 234p. Cass Series on Peacekeeping Ser. ISBN:0-7146-5595-3, ISBN13: 978-0-7146-5595-6. Dewey:327.1/27.
Audience: **g,l,u,f.**

Ben-Ami, Shlomo **DS119.7.B3826 2005**
Scars of War, Wounds of Peace: The Israeli-Arab Tragedy. Trade Cloth. Oxford University Press, Inc. New York, NY. 2006. 368p. ISBN:0-19-518158-1, ISBN13: 978-0-19-518158-6. Dewey:956.9405. LCCN:2005-025383.
Audience: **g,l,u,f.**

Bentsur, Eytan **DS119**
Making Peace: A First Hand Account of the Arab-Israeli Peace Process. Book, Other. Greenwood Publishing Group, Inc. Portsmouth, NH. 2000. 288p. ISBN:0-275-96876-6, ISBN13: 978-0-275-96876-2. Dewey:956.05/3. LCCN:00-032383.
Audience: **l,u.** *Choice, 2001.*

Boudreau, Thomas E. **JX1977**
Sheathing the Sword: The U. N. Secretary-General and the Prevention of Internation Conflict. Trade Cloth. Greenwood Publishing Group, Inc. Portsmouth, NH. 1991. 208p. Contributions in Political Science Ser., No. 273 ISBN:0-313-26109-1, ISBN13: 978-0-313-26109-1. Dewey:327.1/7. LCCN:90-047520.
Audience: **l,u.** *Choice, 1991.*

Boulden, Jane **KZ6376**
Peace Enforcement: The United Nations Experience in Congo, Somalia and Bosnia. Trade Cloth. Greenwood Publishing Group, Inc. Portsmouth, NH. 2001. 176p. ISBN:0-275-96906-1, ISBN13: 978-0-275-96906-6. Dewey:327.1/72. LCCN:00-064952.
Audience: **g,l,u.** *Choice, 2001.*

Boutros-Ghali, Boutros (Introduction by) **JX1977.2.M85U55 1995**
The United Nations and Mozambique, 1992-1995. Trade Cloth. United Nations Publications. New York, NY. 1996. 321p. Blue Bks., Vol. V ISBN:92-1-100559-0, ISBN13: 978-92-1-100559-2. Dewey:341.23679. LCCN:95-192058.
Audience: **g,l,u.** *Choice, 1996.*

Brock, Peter & Young, Nigel **JZ5560.B76 1999**
Pacifism in the Twentieth Century: A Survey from Antiquity to the Outset of the Twentieth Century. Trade Paper. Syracuse University Press. Syracuse, NY. 2004. liv, 436p. Peace and Conflict Resolution Studies ISBN:0-8156-8125-9, ISBN13: 978-0-8156-8125-0. Dewey:327.1/72/0904. LCCN:99-201765.
Audience: **l,u,f.** *Choice, 1999.*

Cordesman, Anthony **DS79.76.C677 2004**
The War after the War. Paper Text. Center for Strategic & International Studies. Washington, DC. 2004. xix, 73p. CSIS Significant Issues Ser., 26 ISBN:0-89206-450-1, ISBN13: 978-0-89206-450-2. Dewey:327.730567/09/0511. LCCN:2004-011306.
Audience: **u,f.**

Coulon, Jocelyn **JZ6374.C6813 1998**
Soldiers of Diplomacy (Les Casques Bleus): The United Nations, Peacekeeping and the New World Order. Phyllis Aronoff & Howard Scott (Translators). Trade Cloth. University of Toronto Press. Toronto, ON. 1998. 526p. ISBN:0-8020-0899-2, ISBN13: 978-0-8020-0899-2. Dewey:341.5/23. LCCN:98-229699.
Audience: **g,l,u,f.** *Choice, 1999.*

Curti, Merle E. **JX1961.U6 C83**
Peace or War: The American Struggle, 1636-1936. Library Binding. Jerome S. Ozer Publisher, Inc. Englewood, NJ. 1972. 374p. Peace Movement in America Ser. ISBN:0-89198-064-4, ISBN13: 978-0-89198-064-3. Dewey:327/.172. LCCN:70-143428.
Audience: **l,u.**

Darby, John **JZ6010.D37 2001**
The Effects of Violence on Peace Processes. Trade Paper. United States Institute of Peace Press (USIP Press). Washington, DC. 2001. 144p. ISBN:1-929223-31-5, ISBN13: 978-1-929223-31-2. Dewey:327.1/72. LCCN:2001-039760.
Audience: **g,l,u,f.** *Choice, 2002.*

Davis, Calvin D. **JX1916.D32 1976**
The United States and the Second Hague Peace Conference: American Diplomacy and International Organization, 1899-1914.

Cloth Text. Duke University Press. Durham, NC. 1976. ix, 398p. ISBN:0-8223-0346-9, ISBN13: 978-0-8223-0346-6. Dewey:341.5. LCCN:75-017353.
Audience: **u,f.**

DeBenedetti, Charles **JX1961.U6**
The Peace Reform in American History. Trade Cloth. Indiana University Press. Bloomington, IN. 1980. 264p. ISBN:0-253-13095-6, ISBN13: 978-0-253-13095-2. Dewey:327/.172/0973. LCCN:79-002173.
Audience: **l,u,f.**

Dickinson, G. Lowes **U21**
Causes of International War. Trade Cloth. Greenwood Publishing Group, Inc. Portsmouth, NH. 1984. 110p. ISBN:0-313-24565-7, ISBN13: 978-0-313-24565-7. Dewey:355/.027. LCCN:84-012797.
Audience: **l,u.**

Durch, William J. (Editor) **JX1981.P7E92 1993**
The Evolution of U. N. Peacekeeping: Case Studies and Comparative Analysis. Cloth over Boards. Palgrave Macmillan. New York, NY. 1993. 544p. ISBN:0-312-06600-7, ISBN13: 978-0-312-06600-0. Dewey:341.5/8. LCCN:92-036820.
Audience: **u,f.** *Choice, 1993.*

Enderlin, Charles **DS119.76.E5913 2003**
Shattered Dreams: The Failure of the Peace Process in the Middle East, 1995-2002. Susan Fairfield (Translator). Trade Cloth. Other Press, LLC. New York, NY. 2006. 480p. ISBN:1-59051-060-7, ISBN13: 978-1-59051-060-5. Dewey:956.05/3. LCCN:2002-032173.
Audience: **g,l,u.**

Frank, Jerome D. **JX1255.F7**
Sanity and Survival in the Nuclear Age: Psychological Aspects of War and Peace. Trade Paper. University Press of America, Inc. Lanham, MD. 1987. 346p. ISBN:0-8191-6744-4, ISBN13: 978-0-8191-6744-6. Dewey:327/.01/9.
Audience: **g,l,u.**

Gelpi, Christopher **JZ5595.5.G45 2003**
The Power of Legitimacy: Assessing the Role of Norms in Crisis Bargaining. Trade Cloth. Princeton University Press. Princeton, NJ. 2002. 232p. ISBN:0-691-09248-6, ISBN13: 978-0-691-09248-5. Dewey:327.1/7. LCCN:2002-023129.
Audience: **u,f.**

Gidron, Benjamin (Editor), et al. **JZ6045.R47 2002**
Mobilizing for Peace: Conflict Resolution in Northern Ireland, Israel/Palestine, and South Africa. Stanley Nider Katz & Yeheskel Hasenfeld (Editors). Trade Cloth. Oxford University Press, Inc. New York, NY. 2002. 304p. ISBN:0-19-512592-4, ISBN13: 978-0-19-512592-4. Dewey:303.6/9. LCCN:2001-050017.
Audience: **u.** *Choice, 2003.*

Goemans, Hein **D613.G62 2000**
War and Punishment: The Causes of War Termination and the First World War. Cloth Text. Princeton University Press. Princeton, NJ. 2000. 296p. Princeton Studies in International History and Politics ISBN:0-691-04943-2, ISBN13: 978-0-691-04943-4. Dewey:940.4/39. LCCN:00-036693.
Audience: **l,u,f.** *Choice, 2001.*

Heininger, Janet **JX1981.P7H45 1994**
Peacekeeping in Transition: The United Nations in Cambodia. Trade Paper. Century Foundation, The. New York, NY. 1994. 183p. ISBN:0-87078-362-9, ISBN13: 978-0-87078-362-3. Dewey:341.5/8. LCCN:94-031673.
Audience: **g,l,u.** *Choice, 1995.*

Helmick, Raymond G. **DS119.76.H455 2004**
Negotiating Outside the Law: Why Camp David Failed. Jesse Jackson (Introduction by). Trade Cloth. Pluto Press. London, 2004. 336p. ISBN:0-7453-2219-0, ISBN13: 978-0-7453-2219-3. Dewey:956.9405/4. LCCN:2004-010077.
Audience: **g,l,u,f.**

Herz, Monica & Nogueira, Joao Pontes **F3738.2.H479 2002**
Ecuador vs. Peru: Peacemaking Amid Rivalry. Paper Text. Lynne Rienner Publishers, Inc. Boulder, CO. 2002. 120p. International Peace Academy Ser. ISBN:1-58826-075-5, ISBN13: 978-1-58826-075-8. Dewey:986.607/4. LCCN:2002-017809.
Audience: **l,u,f.** *Choice, 2002.*

Hill, Stephen M. & Malik, Shahin P. (Editors) **JX1981.P7H55 1996**
Peacekeeping and the United Nations. Trade Paper. Ashgate Publishing, Ltd. Aldershot, 1996. 256p. Issues in International Security Ser. ISBN:1-85521-613-2, ISBN13: 978-1-85521-613-6. Dewey:327.1/72. LCCN:96-019228.
Audience: **u,f.** *Choice, 1997.*

Hinsley, Francis H. **JX1944.H5 1967**
Power and the Pursuit of Peace: Theory and Practice in the History of Relations Between States. Trade Paper. Cambridge University Press. New York, NY. 1967. 424p. ISBN:0-521-09448-8, ISBN13: 978-0-521-09448-1. Dewey:341.1. LCCN:68-092375.
Audience: **l,u.**

Howard, Michael Eliot **CB481.H68 2000**
The Invention of Peace: Reflections on War and International Order. Cloth over Boards. Yale University Press. Cumberland, RI. 2001. 128p. ISBN:0-300-08866-3, ISBN13: 978-0-300-08866-3. Dewey:327.1/72. LCCN:00-043599.
Audience: **u,f.**

Hume, Cameron R. **JX1977.2.I7H85 1994**
The United Nations, Iran and Iraq: How Peacemaking Changed. Trade Cloth. Indiana University Press. Bloomington, IN. 1994. 292p. ISBN:0-253-32874-8, ISBN13: 978-0-253-32874-8. Dewey:341.5/2. LCCN:93-026951.
Audience: **u,f.** *Choice, 1994.*

Kant, Immanuel **KZ2322.A3Z8613 2003**
To Perpetual Peace. Ted Humphrey (Translator). Trade Cloth. Hackett Publishing Company, Inc. Indianapolis, IN. 2003. 50p. ISBN:0-87220-692-0, ISBN13: 978-0-87220-692-2. Dewey:341.7/3. LCCN:2003-047180.
Audience: **g,u,f.**

MacQueen, Norrie **JZ6373**
United Nations Peacekeeping in Africa Since 1960. Trade Paper. Longman Publishing. Boston, MA. 2002. 328p. ISBN:0-582-38253-X, ISBN13: 978-0-582-38253-4. Dewey:355.3/57/096.
Audience: **g,l,u.** *Choice, 2003.*

Maoz, Zeev **JZ1234.M85 2004**
Multiple Paths to Knowledge in International Relations: Methodology in the Study of Conflict Management and Conflict Resolution. Trade Cloth. Lexington Books. Lanham, MD. 2004. 416p. Innovations in the Study of World Politics Ser. ISBN:0-7391-0671-6, ISBN13: 978-0-7391-0671-6. Dewey:327.1/6/072. LCCN:2003-065895.
Audience: **u.**

Mays, Terry M. **JZ6374.M38 2004**
Historical Dictionary of Multinational Peacekeeping. Ed. 2. Trade Cloth. Scarecrow Press, Inc. Lanham, MD. 2003. 384p. Historical Dictionaries of International Organizations Ser. ISBN:0-8108-4874-0, ISBN13: 978-0-8108-4874-0. Dewey:341.5/84. LCCN:2003-013056.
Audience: **g,l,u,f.** *Choice, 2004, 1997.*

Mazurana, Dyan E., et al. **JZ6405.W66G45 2004**
Gender, Conflict, and Peacekeeping. Angela Raven-Roberts & Jane L. Parpart (Authors). Book, Other. Rowman & Littlefield Publishers, Inc. Lanham, MD. 2005. 320p. War and Peace Library ISBN:0-7425-3632-7, ISBN13: 978-0-7425-3632-6. Dewey:303.6/9. LCCN:2004-017767.
Audience: **l,u,f.** *Choice, 2006.*

McCarthy, Ronald & Sharp, Gene **Z7164.P19M33 1997**
Nonviolent Action: A Research Guide. Library Binding. Garland Publishing, Inc. New York, NY. 1997. 760p. History Reference Ser. ISBN:0-8153-1577-5, ISBN13: 978-0-8153-1577-3. Dewey:016.3036/1. LCCN:97-025316.
Audience: **g,l,u,f.** *Choice, 1998.*

Mekenkamp, Monique (Editor), et al. **JZ5597.S43 2002**
Searching for Peace in Central and South Asia: An Overview of Conflict Prevention and Peacebuilding Activities. Paul Van Tongeren & Hans van de Veen (Editors). Library Binding. Lynne Rienner Publishers, Inc. Boulder, CO. 2002. xiv, 640p. European Centre for Conflict Prevention Ser. ISBN:1-58826-096-8, ISBN13: 978-1-58826-096-3. Dewey:327.1/72. LCCN:2002-017882.
Audience: **u,f.** *Choice, 2003.*

Moskos, Charles C. Jr. **JX1981.P7**
Peace Soldiers: The Sociology of a United Nations Military Force. Library Binding. University of Chicago Press. Chicago, IL. 1992. xi, 171p. ISBN:0-226-54225-4, ISBN13: 978-0-226-54225-6. Dewey:306/.27. LCCN:75-005070.
Audience: **l,u.** B

Nachmani, Amikam **DF849**
International Intervention in the Greek Civil War: The United Nations Special Committee on the Balkans, 1947-1952. Trade Cloth. Greenwood Publishing Group, Inc. Portsmouth, NH. 1990. 216p. ISBN:0-275-93367-9, ISBN13: 978-0-275-93367-8. Dewey:949.507/4. LCCN:89-026544.
Audience: **g,l,u.** *Choice, 1991.*

Perez de Cuellar, Javier **D839.7.P47A3 1997**
Pilgrimage for Peace: A Secretary General's Memoir. Cloth over Boards. Palgrave Macmillan. New York, NY. 1997. 544p. ISBN:0-312-16486-6, ISBN13: 978-0-312-16486-7. Dewey:352.1/13/092. LCCN:97-009798.
Audience: **g,l,u.**

Rabinovich, Itamar **DS119.8.S95R33**
The Brink of Peace: The Israeli-Syrian Negotiations. Trade Paper. Princeton University Press. Princeton, NJ. 1999. 302p. ISBN:0-691-01023-4, ISBN13: 978-0-691-01023-6. Dewey:327.56940569. LCCN:98-014418.
Audience: **g,l,u,f.** *Choice, 1999.*

Ross, Dennis B. **DS119.76.R68 2004**
The Missing Peace: The Inside Story of the Fight for Middle East Peace. Cloth over Boards. Farrar, Straus & Giroux. New York, NY. 2004. 872p. ISBN:0-374-19973-6, ISBN13: 978-0-374-19973-9. Dewey:956.05/3. LCCN:2003-027827.
Audience: **l,u,f.**

Said, Edward W. **DS119.76.S245 2001**
The End of the Peace Process: Oslo and After. Trade Paper. Knopf Publishing Group. New York, NY. 2001. 432p. Vintage Bks. ISBN:0-375-72574-1, ISBN13: 978-0-375-72574-6. Dewey:956/.053. LCCN:2001-271107.
Audience: **g,l,u,f.**

Sharp, Alan **D644.S478 1991**
The Versailles Settlement: Peacemaking in Paris, 1919. Cloth Text. Palgrave Macmillan. New York, NY. 1991. 248p. The Making of the 20th Century Ser. ISBN:0-312-06049-1, ISBN13: 978-0-312-06049-7. Dewey:940.3/142. LCCN:90-022402.
Audience: **g,l,u.** *Choice, 1992.*

Sharp, Gene **HM1281.S53 2005**
Waging Nonviolent Struggle: 20th Century Practice and 21st Century Potential. Joshua Paulson, Christopher Miller & Hardy Merriman (Contribution by). Trade Cloth. Porter Sargent Publishers, Inc. Boston, MA. 2005. 640p. ISBN:0-87558-161-7, ISBN13: 978-0-87558-161-3. Dewey:303.6/1. LCCN:2004-027014.
Audience: **g,l,u,f.**

Stein, Kenneth W. **DS119.7.S6749 1999**
Heroic Diplomacy: Sadat, Kissinger, Carter, Begin and the Quest for Arab-Israeli Peace. Trade Paper. Routledge. New York, NY. 1999. 352p. ISBN:0-415-92155-4, ISBN13: 978-0-415-92155-8. Dewey:956.04. LCCN:98-049359.
Audience: **u,f.** *Choice, 2000.*

Stein, Kenneth W. **DS119.7.S6749 1999**
Heroic Diplomacy: Sadat, Kissinger, Carter, Begin and the Quest for Arab-Israeli Peace. Paper over Boards. Routledge. New York, NY. 1999. 352p. ISBN:0-415-92154-6, ISBN13: 978-0-415-92154-1. Dewey:956.04. LCCN:98-049359.
Audience: **u.** *Choice, 2000.*

Tilley, Virginia Q. **DS119.7.T495 2005**
The One-State Solution: A Breakthrough for Peace in the Israeli-Palestinian Deadlock. Trade Cloth. University of Michigan Press. Chicago, IL. 2005. 288p. ISBN:0-472-11513-8, ISBN13: 978-0-472-11513-6. Dewey:956.9405/4. LCCN:2005-002497.
Audience: **u,f.**

Touval, Saadia **DR1313.7.D58T678**
Mediation in the Yugoslav Wars: The Critical Years, 1990-95. Cloth over Boards. Palgrave Macmillan. New York, NY. 2002. 227p. Advances in Political Science Ser. ISBN:0-333-96503-5, ISBN13: 978-0-333-96503-0. Dewey:949.703. LCCN:2001-034804.
Audience: **l,u,f.** *Choice, 2003, 2002.*

United Nations Staff **JX1977.2.S2U54 1995**
The United Nations and El Salvador, 1990-1995. Boutros Boutros-Ghali (Introduction by). Trade Cloth. United Nations Publications. New York, NY. 1996. 611p. Blue Bks., Vol. IV ISBN:92-1-100552-3, ISBN13: 978-92-1-100552-3. Dewey:341.237284. LCCN:95-152667.
Audience: **g,l,u.** *Choice, 1996.*

Veblen, Thorstein **JX1952.V38**
An Inquiry into the Nature of Peace and the Terms of its Perpetuation. Trade Paper. Kessinger Publishing, LLC. Whitefish, MT. 2004. ISBN:1-4179-1630-3, ISBN13: 978-1-4179-1630-6. Dewey:341.1.
Audience: **l,u,f.**

Walter, Barbara F. **U240.W35 2002**
Committing to Peace: The Successful Settlement of Civil Wars. Trade Cloth. Princeton University Press. Princeton, NJ. 2002. 150p. ISBN:0-691-08930-2, ISBN13: 978-0-691-08930-0. Dewey:303.6/4. LCCN:2001-036379.
Audience: **u,f.** *Choice, 2002.*

Weart, Spencer R. **JC421.W43 1998**
Never at War: Why Democracies Will Not Fight One Another. Cloth over Boards. Yale University Press. Cumberland, RI. 1998. 430p. ISBN:0-300-07017-9, ISBN13: 978-0-300-07017-0. Dewey:327.1/7. LCCN:98-002664.
Audience: **g,l,u,f.** *Choice, 1999.*

Weisburd, A. Mark **KZ6368.W45 1997**
Use of Force: The Practice of States, 1945-1991. Trade Paper. Pennsylvania State University Press. University Park, PA. 1997. 566p. ISBN:0-271-01680-9, ISBN13: 978-0-271-01680-1. Dewey:341.5/84. LCCN:96-044645.
Audience: **g,l,u,f.** *Choice, 1998.*

Wittner, Lawrence S. **JX1961.U6**
Rebels Against War: The American Peace Movement, 1933-1983. Trade Paper. Temple University Press. Philadelphia, PA. 1984. 384p. ISBN:0-87722-342-4, ISBN13: 978-0-87722-342-9. Dewey:327.1/72/0973. LCCN:83-027523.
Audience: **g,l,u.**

International Relations. Transnational Relations > War and Peace > War Crimes

Adelman, Howard & Suhrke, Astri (Editors) **DT449.R97**
The Path of a Genocide: The Rwanda Crisis from Uganda to Zaire. Trade Paper. Transaction Publishers. Somerset, NJ. 2000. 414p. ISBN:0-7658-0768-8, ISBN13: 978-0-7658-0768-7. Dewey:320.9/67571.
Audience: **u,f.** *Choice, 2000.*

Akcam, Taner **DS195.5.A417 2004**
From Empire to Republic: Turkish Nationalism and the Armenian Genocide. Cloth over Boards. Zed Books, Ltd. London, 2004. 288p. ISBN:1-84277-526-X, ISBN13: 978-1-84277-526-4. Dewey:956.6/2023. LCCN:2004-043631.
Audience: **u,f.** *Choice, 2004.*

Allen, Beverly **HV6569.B54A45 1996**
Rape Warfare: The Hidden Genocide in Bosnia-Herzegovina and Croatia. Trade Cloth. University of Minnesota Press. Minneapolis, MN. 1996. 208p. ISBN:0-8166-2818-1, ISBN13: 978-0-8166-2818-6. Dewey:364.1/532/0949742. LCCN:95-025576.
Audience: **u,f.**

Alvarez, Alex **HV6322.7.A58 2001**
[e] Governments, Citizens and Genocide: A Comparative and Interdisciplinary Analysis. E-Book. Indiana University Press. Bloomington, IN. 2001. x, 224p. ISBN:0-253-33849-2, ISBN13: 978-0-253-33849-5. Dewey:304.6/63. LCCN:00-057501.
Audience: **u,f.** *Choice, 2001.*

Auron, Yair **DS195.5.A96 2003**
The Banality of Denial: Israel and the Armenian Genocide. Trade Cloth. Transaction Publishers. Somerset, NJ. 2003. 338p. ISBN:0-7658-0191-4, ISBN13: 978-0-7658-0191-3. Dewey:956.6/2015. LCCN:2002-040933.
Audience: **u,f.** *Choice, 2003.*

Balakian, Peter **DS195.5**
The Burning Tigris: The Armenian Genocide and America's Response. Trade Paper. HarperCollins Publishers. New York, NY. 2004. 528p. ISBN:0-06-055870-9, ISBN13: 978-0-06-055870-3. Dewey:956.6/2015. LCCN:2003-044986.
Audience: **g,l,u,f.**

Barnett, Michael N. **DT450.435.B38 2002**
Eyewitness to a Genocide: The United Nations and Rwanda. Trade Cloth. Cornell University Press. Ithaca, NY. 2002. 240p. ISBN:0-8014-3883-7, ISBN13: 978-0-8014-3883-7. Dewey:967.57104. LCCN:2001-005561.
Audience: **l,u,f.** *Choice, 2002.*

Bartov, Omer **D804.348.B37**
Mirrors of Destruction: War, Genocide, and Modern Identity. Trade Paper. Oxford University Press, Inc. New York, NY. 2002. 312p. ISBN:0-19-515184-4, ISBN13: 978-0-19-515184-8. Dewey:940.5.
Audience: **u,f.** *Choice, 2001.*

Bergen, Doris L. **DD256.5B3916 2002**
War and Genocide: A Concise History of the Holocaust. Trade Cloth. Rowman & Littlefield Publishers, Inc. Lanham, MD. 2002. 280p. Critical Issues in History Ser. ISBN:0-8476-9630-8, ISBN13: 978-0-8476-9630-7. Dewey:943.086. LCCN:2002-008963.
Audience: **g,l,u,f.** *Choice, 2003.*

Bloxham, Donald **DS195.5**
Great Game of Genocide: Imperialism, Nationalism, and the Destruction of the Ottoman Armenians. Trade Cloth. Oxford University Press, Inc. New York, NY. 2005. 340p. ISBN:0-19-927356-1, ISBN13: 978-0-19-927356-0. Dewey:956.6/20154. LCCN:2005-299404.
Audience: **u,f.** *Choice, 2005.*

Campbell, Kenneth J. **HV6322.7.C35 2001**
Genocide and the Global Village. Ed. 2. Trade Cloth. Palgrave Macmillan. New York, NY. 2001. 256p. ISBN:0-312-21890-7, ISBN13: 978-0-312-21890-4. Dewey:364.1/51. LCCN:2001-021892.
Audience: **u,f.** *Choice, 2002.*

Chalk, Frank & Jonassohn, Kurt **HV6322.7.C44 1990**
The History and Sociology of Genocide: Analyses and Case Studies. Trade Paper. Yale University Press. Cumberland, RI.

1990. 480p. ISBN:0-300-04446-1, ISBN13: 978-0-300-04446-1. Dewey:304.6/63. LCCN:89-027381.
Audience: **u,f.** *Choice, 1991.*

Charney, Israel W. (Editor) **Z7164.G45.G45**
The Widening Circle of Genocide. Trade Cloth. Transaction Publishers. Somerset, NJ. 1994. 375p. Genocide Ser., Vol. 3 ISBN:1-56000-172-0, ISBN13: 978-1-56000-172-0. Dewey:016.364/51. LCCN:93-046257.
Audience: **u,f.** *Choice, 1995.*

Cigar, Norman **DR1313**
Genocide in Bosnia: The Policy of "Ethnic Cleansing". Trade Paper. Texas A&M University Press. College Station, TX. 2000. 264p. Eastern European Studies, Vol. 1 ISBN:1-58544-004-3, ISBN13: 978-1-58544-004-7. Dewey:949.702/4. LCCN:94-032948.
Audience: **u,f.** *Choice, 1995.*

Clark, Ramsey **DS79.736 .C54**
The Fire This Time: U. S. War Crimes in the Gulf. Trade Paper. International Action Center. New York, NY. 2005. 380p. ISBN:0-9656916-8-3, ISBN13: 978-0-9656916-8-0. Dewey:956.704/3.
Audience: **g,u,f.**

Cushman, Thomas & Mestrovic, Stjepan G. (Editors) **DR1313.T485 1996**
This Time We Knew: Western Responses to Genocide in Bosnia. Trade Cloth. New York University Press. New York, NY. 1996. 296p. ISBN:0-8147-1534-6, ISBN13: 978-0-8147-1534-5. Dewey:949.702/4. LCCN:96-010071.
Audience: **u,f.** *Choice, 1997.*

Dadrian, Vahakn N. **DS195.5.D337 2003**
Warrant for Genocide: Key Elements of Turko-Armenian Conflict. Trade Paper. Transaction Publishers. Somerset, NJ. 2003. 214p. ISBN:0-7658-0559-6, ISBN13: 978-0-7658-0559-1. Dewey:956.6/2015. LCCN:2003-277715.
Audience: **u,f.** *Choice, 1999.*

Destexhe, Alain **DT450.435.D4713 1995**
Rwanda and Genocide in the Twentieth Century. Alison Marschner (Translator), William Shawcross (Foreword by). Trade Cloth. New York University Press. New York, NY. 1995. 360p. ISBN:0-8147-1873-6, ISBN13: 978-0-8147-1873-5. Dewey:967.57104. LCCN:95-017419.
Audience: **u,f.**

Dobkowski, Michael N. & Wallimann, Isidor (Editors) **Z7164.G45D63 1992**
Genocide in Our Time: An Annotated Bibliography with Analytical Introductions. Trade Paper. Pierian Press. Ann Arbor, MI. 1992. 200p. Resources on Contemporary Issues Ser., No. 6 ISBN:0-87650-280-X, ISBN13: 978-0-87650-280-8. Dewey:016.3641/51. LCCN:93-215834.
Audience: **g,l,u,f.** *Choice, 1993.*

El Bushra, Judy & Gardner, Judith (Editors) **HQ1795.S66 2004**
Somalia—The Untold Story: The War Through the Eyes of Somali Women. Trade Cloth. Pluto Press. London, 2004. 272p. ISBN:0-7453-2209-3, ISBN13: 978-0-7453-2209-4. Dewey:305.4/096773. LCCN:2003-020195.
Audience: **g,l,u,f.** *Choice, 2004.*

Etcheson, Craig **DS554**
After the Killing Fields: Lessons from the Cambodian Genocide. Trade Cloth. Greenwood Publishing Group, Inc. Portsmouth, NH. 2005. 272p. ISBN:0-275-98513-X, ISBN13: 978-0-275-98513-4. Dewey:959.604. LCCN:2004-022487.
Audience: **u,f.** *Choice, 2006.*

Friedlander, Henry **94-40941 [DD]**
The Origins of Nazi Genocide: From Euthanasia to the Final Solution. Trade Paper. University of North Carolina Press. Chapel Hill, NC. 1997. 448p. ISBN:0-8078-4675-9, ISBN13: 978-0-8078-4675-9. Dewey:943/.086. LCCN:94-040941.
Audience: **g,l,u,f.** *Choice, 1996.*

Gellately, Robert & Kiernan, Ben (Editors) **HV6322.7.S654 2003**
The Specter of Genocide: Mass Murder in Historical Perspective. Trade Cloth. Cambridge University Press. New York, NY. 2003. 406p. ISBN:0-521-82063-4, ISBN13: 978-0-521-82063-9. Dewey:304.6/63/09. LCCN:2002-031553.
Audience: **u,f.** *Choice, 2004.*

Glover, Jonathan **D204.G56 2000**
Humanity: A Moral History of the Twentieth Century. Cloth over Boards. Yale University Press. Cumberland, RI. 2000. 480p. ISBN:0-300-08700-4, ISBN13: 978-0-300-08700-0. Dewey:909.82. LCCN:00-036500.
Audience: **g,u,f.**

Gutman, Roy & Rieff, David (Editors) **K5301.C75 1999**
Crimes of War: What the Public Should Know. Trade Paper. W. W. Norton & Company, Inc. New York, NY. 1999. 400p. ISBN:0-393-31914-8, ISBN13: 978-0-393-31914-9. Dewey:341.6/9. LCCN:98-035643.
Audience: **g,l,u,f.** *Choice, 1999.*

Heidenrich, John G. **HV6322**
How to Prevent Genocide: A Guide for Policymakers, Scholars, and the Concerned Citizen. Trade Cloth. Greenwood Publishing Group, Inc. Portsmouth, NH. 2001. 296p. ISBN:0-275-96987-8, ISBN13: 978-0-275-96987-5. Dewey:179.7. LCCN:00-064962.
Audience: **u,f.** *Choice, 2002.*

Jefremovas, Villia **HD8795.J44 2002**
Brickyards to Graveyards: From Production to Genocide in Rwanda. Paper Text. State University of New York Press. Albany, NY. 2002. xi, 162p. SUNY Series in Anthropology of Work ISBN:0-7914-5488-6, ISBN13: 978-0-7914-5488-6. Dewey:338.4/766673/0967571. LCCN:2002-070716.
Audience: **u,f.** *Choice, 2003.*

Jones, Adam (Editor) **HV6322.7.G458 2004**
Genocide, War Crimes and the West: History and Complicity. Trade Paper. Zed Books, Ltd. London, 2004. 400p. ISBN:1-84277-191-4, ISBN13: 978-1-84277-191-4. LCCN:2003-047914.
Audience: **u,f.** *Choice, 2005.*

Kiernan, Ben **DS554.8**
The Pol Pot Regime: Race, Power, and Genocide in Cambodia under the Khmer Rouge, 1975-79. Ed. 2. Trade Paper. Yale University Press. Cumberland, RI. 2002. 528p. ISBN:0-300-09649-6, ISBN13: 978-0-300-09649-1. Dewey:959.6/04.
Audience: **g,u,f.** *Choice, 1997.*

Kiernan, Ben (Introduction by) **DS554.8.G45 1993**
Genocide and Democracy in Cambodia: The Khmer Rouge, the U. N. and the International Community. George Andreopolos (Preface by). Trade Paper. Yale University Southeast Asia Studies. New Haven, CT. 1993. Monograph Ser. - Yale University Southeast Asia Studies, No. 41 ISBN:0-685-70431-9, ISBN13: 978-0-685-70431-8. Dewey:304.6/63/09596. LCCN:93-060073.
Audience: **u,f.** *Choice, 1994.*

Lemarchand, Reni **DT450.64 .L46 1994**
Burundi: Ethnic Conflict and Genocide. Lee H. Hamilton (Contribution by). Trade Paper. Cambridge University Press. New York, NY. 1996. 232p. Woodrow Wilson Center Press Ser. ISBN:0-521-56623-1, ISBN13: 978-0-521-56623-0. Dewey:323.1/67572. LCCN:96-233050.
Audience: **u,f.** *Choice, 1994.*

Lifton, Robert J. **R853**
The Nazi Doctors: Medical Killing and the Psychology of Genocide. Trade Paper. Basic Books. New York, NY. 1988. 576p. ISBN:0-465-04905-2, ISBN13: 978-0-465-04905-9. Dewey:940.54/05. LCCN:85-073874.
Audience: **g,u,f.** *Choice, 1987.*

Lohr, Eric **DK34.R9L64 2003**
Nationalizing the Russian Empire: The Campaign Against Enemy Aliens During World War I. Trade Cloth. Harvard University Press. Cambridge, MA. 2003. 256p. Russian Research Center Studies, Vol. 94 ISBN:0-674-01041-8, ISBN13: 978-0-674-01041-3. Dewey:940.3/086/91. LCCN:2002-191913.
Audience: **u,f.** *Choice, 2004.*

Mandel, Maud **DS135.F83M364 2003**
In the Aftermath of Genocide: Armenians and Jews in Twentieth Century France. Trade Cloth. Duke University Press. Durham, NC. 2003. 352p. ISBN:0-8223-3134-9, ISBN13: 978-0-8223-3134-6. Dewey:305.891/992044/0904. LCCN:2003-000437.
Audience: **u,f.** *Choice, 2004.*

Maogoto, Jackson Nyamuya **K5301.M36 2004**
War Crimes and Realpolitik: International Justice from World War I to the 21st Century. Library Binding. Lynne Rienner Publishers, Inc. Boulder, CO. 2004. 260p. ISBN:1-58826-276-6, ISBN13: 978-1-58826-276-9. Dewey:341.6/9/09. LCCN:2003-023330.
Audience: **u,f.** *Choice, 2005.*

Melson, Robert **DS195.5.M45**
Revolution and Genocide: On the Origins of the Armenian Genocide and the Holocaust. Trade Paper. University of Chicago Press. Chicago, IL. 1996. 386p. ISBN:0-226-51991-0, ISBN13: 978-0-226-51991-3. Dewey:956.6015.
Audience: **u,f.** *Choice, 1993.*

Melvern, Linda **DT450.435.M423 2004**
Conspiracy to Murder: The Rwanda Genocide. Trade Cloth. Verso Books. London, 2004. 256p. ISBN:1-85984-588-6, ISBN13: 978-1-85984-588-2. Dewey:967.57104/31. LCCN:2004-000822.
Audience: **l,u,f.** *Choice, 2004.*

Neier, Aryeh **K5301.N45 1998**
War Crimes: Brutality, Genocide, Terror, and the Struggle for Justice. Trade Cloth. Crown Publishing Group. New York, NY. 1998. 288p. ISBN:0-8129-2381-2, ISBN13: 978-0-8129-2381-0. Dewey:341.6/9. LCCN:98-005783.
Audience: **g,l,u,f.** *Choice, 1999.*

Odom, Thomas P. **DT450.435.O34 2005**
Journey into Darkness: Genocide in Rwanda. Dennis J. Reimer (Foreword by). Trade Cloth. Texas A&M University Press. College Station, TX. 2005. 320p. Texas a & M University Military History Ser., Vol. 100 ISBN:1-58544-427-8, ISBN13: 978-1-58544-427-4. Dewey:967.57104/31. LCCN:2004-028031.
Audience: **g,l,u,f.** *Choice, 2006.*

Prunier, Gerard **DT159.6.D27P78 2005**
Darfur: The Ambiguous Genocide. Saddle Stitched, Cloth over Boards, Dust Jacket. Cornell University Press. Ithaca, NY. 2005. 312p. Crises in World Politics Ser. ISBN:0-8014-4450-0, ISBN13: 978-0-8014-4450-0. Dewey:962.7. LCCN:2005-048490.
Audience: **g,l,u,f.** *Choice, 2006.*

Prunier, Gérard **DT450.435**
The Rwanda Crisis: History of a Genocide. Trade Paper. Columbia University Press. New York, NY. 1997. 389p. ISBN:0-231-10409-X, ISBN13: 978-0-231-10409-8. Dewey:364.1/51/0967571.
Audience: **g,l,u,f.**

Rittner, Carol Ann (Editor), et al. **HV6322.7.W545 2002**
Will Genocide Ever End? John K. Roth & James M. Smith (Editors). Trade Paper. Paragon House Publishers. Saint Paul, MN. 2002. 272p. ISBN:1-55778-819-7, ISBN13: 978-1-55778-819-1. Dewey:364.15/1. LCCN:2002-007312.
Audience: **g,l,u,f.** *Choice, 2003.*

Rittner, Carol (Author, Editor), et al. **DT450.435.G474 2004**
Genocide in Rwanda: Complicity of the Churches. John K. Roth & Wendy Whitworth (Author, Editors). Trade Paper. Paragon House Publishers. Saint Paul, MN. 2004. 332p. ISBN:1-55778-837-5, ISBN13: 978-1-55778-837-5. Dewey:261.8/33151/0967571. LCCN:2004-014772.
Audience: **u,f.** *Choice, 2005.*

Schabas, William A. **K5302 .S32 2000**
Genocide in International Law: The Crimes of Crimes. Trade Paper. Cambridge University Press. New York, NY. 2000. 640p. ISBN:0-521-78790-4, ISBN13: 978-0-521-78790-1. Dewey:341.778. LCCN:99-087924.
Audience: **u,f.** *Choice, 2001.*

Secher, Reynald **DC218.S43313 2003**
A French Genocide: The Vendee. George Holoch (Translator). Trade Cloth. University of Notre Dame Press. Notre Dame, IN. 2003. 304p. ISBN:0-268-02865-6, ISBN13: 978-0-268-02865-7. Dewey:944.6/104. LCCN:2003-047333.
Audience: **u,f.** *Choice, 2004.*

Shaw, Martin **U21.2.S523 2003**
War and Genocide: Organized Killing in Modern Society. Trade Paper. Polity Press. Cambridge, 2003. 272p. ISBN:0-7456-1907-X, ISBN13: 978-0-7456-1907-1. Dewey:304.6/63. LCCN:2002-151767.
Audience: **u,f.** *Choice, 2004.*

Shelton, Dinah **HV6322.7.E532 2004**
Encyclopedia of Genocide and Crimes Against Humanity. Trade Cloth. Thomson Gale. Farmington Hills, MI. 2004. xxxvi,

1458p. ISBN:0-02-865847-7, ISBN13: 978-0-02-865847-6. Dewey:304.6/63/03. LCCN:2004-006587.
Audience: **g,l,u,f.** *Choice, 2005.*

Stover, Eric **KZ1203.A2S76 2005**
The Witnesses: War Crimes and the Promise of Justice in the Hague. Trade Cloth. University of Pennsylvania Press. Philadelphia, PA. 2005. 230p. ISBN:0-8122-3890-7, ISBN13: 978-0-8122-3890-7. Dewey:341.6/9/0268. LCCN:2005-041607.
Audience: **u,f.** *Choice, 2006.*

Twagilimana, Aimable **DT450.435.D44 2003**
The Debris of Ham: Ethnicity, Regionalism, and the 1994 Rwandan Genocide. Trade Paper. University Press of America, Inc. Lanham, MD. 2003. 250p. ISBN:0-7618-2585-1, ISBN13: 978-0-7618-2585-2. Dewey:967.57104. LCCN:2003-053331.
Audience: **u,f.** *Choice, 2004.*

Valentino, Benjamin A. **HV6322.7.V35 2004**
Final Solutions: Mass Killing and Genocide in the 20th Century. Trade Cloth. Cornell University Press. Ithaca, NY. 2005. 336p. Cornell Studies in Security Affairs Ser. ISBN:0-8014-3965-5, ISBN13: 978-0-8014-3965-0. Dewey:364.15/1/0904. LCCN:2003-019941.
Audience: **l,u,f.** *Choice, 2004.*

Waller, James **HV6322.7W35 2005**
Becoming Evil: How Ordinary People Commit Genocide and Mass Killing. Trade Paper. Oxford University Press, Inc. New York, NY. 2005. 336p. ISBN:0-19-518949-3, ISBN13: 978-0-19-518949-0. Dewey:364.15/1019.
Audience: **u,f.**

Wallimann, Isidor & Dobkowski, Michael N. (Editors) **D445**
Genocide and the Modern Age: Etiology and Case Studies of Mass Death, 3. Trade Cloth. Greenwood Publishing Group, Inc. Portsmouth, NH. 1987. 340p. Contributions to the Study of World History Ser. ISBN:0-313-24198-8, ISBN13: 978-0-313-24198-7. Dewey:304.6/63. LCCN:86-009978.
Audience: **u,f.** *Choice, 1987.*

Waugh, Colin M. **DT450.437.K34W38**
Paul Kagame and Rwanda: Power, Genocide and the Rwandan Patriotic Front. Paper Text. McFarland & Company, Incorporated Publishers. Jefferson, NC. 2004. 364p. ISBN:0-7864-1941-5, ISBN13: 978-0-7864-1941-8. Dewey:967.57104/31/092. LCCN:2004-017525.
Audience: **l,u,f.** *Choice, 2005.*

Zawati, Hilmi M. & Mahmoud, Ibtisam M. **K5302.A12Z39 2005**
A Selected Socio-Legal Bibliography on Ethnic Cleansing, Wartime Rape, and Genocide in the Former Yugoslavia and Rwanda. Trade Cloth. Edwin Mellen Press, The. Lewiston, NY. 2004. 612p. ISBN:0-7734-6260-0, ISBN13: 978-0-7734-6260-1. Dewey:016.3416/9/09049. LCCN:2004-056876.
Audience: **l,u,f.** *Choice, 2005.*

Zuccotti, Susan **DS135.I8Z87 2000**
Under His Very Windows: The Vatican and the Holocaust in Italy. Cloth over Boards. Yale University Press. Cumberland, RI. 2000. 420p. ISBN:0-300-08487-0, ISBN13: 978-0-300-08487-0. Dewey:940.53/18/0945. LCCN:00-043307.
Audience: **g,u,f.** *Choice, 2001.*

International Relations. Transnational Relations > International Security

Art, Robert J. & Waltz, Kenneth N. **JZ1310.U83 2003**
The Use of Force: Military Power and International Politics. Ed. 6. Book, Other. Rowman & Littlefield Publishers, Inc. Lanham, MD. 2003. 512p. ISBN:0-7425-2556-2, ISBN13: 978-0-7425-2556-6. Dewey:327.1/17. LCCN:2003-046650.
Audience: **u,f.**

Chernoff, Fred (Editor) **UA646.3.C494 1995**
After Bipolarity: The Vanishing Threat, Theories of Cooperation and the Future of the Atlantic Alliance. Trade Cloth. University of Michigan Press. Chicago, IL. 1995. 320p. ISBN:0-472-10550-7, ISBN13: 978-0-472-10550-2. Dewey:355/.031091821. LCCN:94-033094.
Audience: **u,f.** *Choice, 1995.*

Duffield, John S. **UA646.3.D817 1995**
Power Rules: The Evolution of NATO's Conventional Force Posture. Trade Cloth. Stanford University Press. Palo Alto, CA. 1995. xi, 386p. ISBN:0-8047-2396-6, ISBN13: 978-0-8047-2396-1. Dewey:355/.031/091821. LCCN:94-025006.
Audience: **l,u.** *Choice, 1995.*

Giauque, Jeffrey Glen **D843.G4478 2002**
Grand Designs and Visions of Unity: The Atlantic Powers and the Reorganization of Western Europe, 1955-1963. Trade Cloth. University of North Carolina Press. Chapel Hill, NC. 2002. 344p. The New Cold War History Ser. ISBN:0-8078-2679-0, ISBN13: 978-0-8078-2679-9. Dewey:327/.094/09045. LCCN:2001-047647.
Audience: **l,u,f.** *Choice, 2003, 2002.*

Heuser, Beatrice **UA646.H48 1997**
NATO, Britain, France, and the FRG: Nuclear Strategies and Forces for Europe, 1949-2000. Cloth over Boards. Palgrave Macmillan. New York, NY. 1997. 276p. ISBN:0-312-17498-5, ISBN13: 978-0-312-17498-9. Dewey:355.02/17/094. LCCN:97-001895.
Audience: **l,u,f.** *Choice, 1998.*

Hilderbrand, Robert C. **89-28392**
Dumbarton Oaks: The Origins of the United Nations and the Search for Postwar Security. Trade Paper. University of North Carolina Press. Chapel Hill, NC. 2001. 332p. ISBN:0-8078-4950-2, ISBN13: 978-0-8078-4950-7. Dewey:341.230. LCCN:89-028392.
Audience: **l,u,f.** *Choice, 1991.*

Kinzer, Stephen **DS318.K49 2003**
All the Shah's Men: An American Coup and the Roots of Middle East Terror. Trade Cloth. John Wiley & Sons, Inc. Hoboken, NJ. 2003. 272p. ISBN:0-471-26517-9, ISBN13: 978-0-471-26517-7. Dewey:955.05/3. LCCN:2003-009968.
Audience: **g,l,u,f.** *Choice, 2004.*

Krupnick, Charles **UA646.8.A445 2002**
Almost NATO: Partner and Players in Central and Eastern European Security. Book, Other. Rowman & Littlefield Publishers, Inc. Lanham, MD. 2003. 360p. New International Relations of Europe Ser. ISBN:0-7425-2458-2, ISBN13: 978-0-7425-2458-3. Dewey:355/.031091821. LCCN:2002-034781.
Audience: **u,f.** *Choice, 2003.*

McGoldrick, Dominic **K5256**
From '9-11' to the 'Iraq War 2003': International Law in an Age of Complexity. Trade Paper. Hart Publishing Ltd. Oxford, 2004. 396p. ISBN:1-84113-496-1, ISBN13: 978-1-84113-496-3. Dewey:345/.0235. LCCN:2004-301382.
Audience: **l,u.**

Myers, David B. **UA23.M95 1990**
New Soviet Thinking and U. S. Nuclear Policy. Trade Cloth. Temple University Press. Philadelphia, PA. 1990. 304p. ISBN:0-87722-710-1, ISBN13: 978-0-87722-710-6. Dewey:355/.033573. LCCN:90-010863.
Audience: **u,f.** *Choice, 1991.*

Ruane, Kevin **UA646.R896 2000**
The Rise and Fall of the European Defence Community: Anglo-American Relations and the Crises of European Defence, 1950-55. Cloth over Boards. Palgrave Macmillan. New York, NY. 2000. 264p. Cold War History Ser. ISBN:0-312-23482-1, ISBN13: 978-0-312-23482-9. Dewey:355.031091821. LCCN:00-027836.
Audience: **l,u,f.** *Choice, 2001.*

Sloan, Elinor C. **U42 .S58 2002**
The Revolution in Military Affairs: Implications for Canada and NATO. Raoul-Dandurand Chair of Strategic and Diplomatic Studies Staff & Universite du Quebec a Montreal, Centre d'etudes des Politiques Etrangeres et de Securite Staff (Contribution by). Trade Cloth. McGill-Queen's University Press. Montreal, PQ. 2002. 192p. ISBN:0-7735-2363-4, ISBN13: 978-0-7735-2363-0. Dewey:355/.0330049.
Audience: **u,f.** *Choice, 2003, 2002.*

United Nations Staff **HV5801**
World Drug Report 2005, Set. Trade Paper. United Nations Publications. New York, NY. 2005. 397p. ISBN:92-1-148203-8, ISBN13: 978-92-1-148203-4. Dewey:362.29/2.
Audience: **u,f.**

Yost, David S. **UA646.3.Y674 1998**
NATO Transformed: The Alliance's New Roles in International Security. Trade Paper. United States Institute of Peace Press (USIP Press). Washington, DC. 1998. 432p. ISBN:1-878379-81-X, ISBN13: 978-1-878379-81-8. Dewey:355/.031091821. LCCN:98-040939.
Audience: **l,u.** *Choice, 1999.*

International Relations. Transnational Relations > International Security > Disarmament

Barnaby, Frank & Huisken, Ronald (Editors) **UF500**
Arms Uncontrolled. Trade Cloth. Harvard University Press. Cambridge, MA. 1975. 269p. Stockholm International Peace Research Institute Ser. ISBN:0-674-04655-2, ISBN13: 978-0-674-04655-9. Dewey:355.8/2. LCCN:75-002815.
Audience: **g,l,u,f.** B

Beker, Avi **JX1974**
Disarmament Without Order: The Politics of Disarmament at the United Nations. Trade Cloth. Greenwood Publishing Group, Inc. Portsmouth, NH. 1985. 212p. Contributions in Political Science Ser., No.118 ISBN:0-313-24362-X, ISBN13: 978-0-313-24362-2. Dewey:341.7/33. LCCN:84-006722.
Audience: **l,u,f.** B *Choice, 1985.*

Bidwai, Praful & Vanaik, Achin **JZ5675.B53 1999**
New Nukes: India, Pakistan and Global Nuclear Disarmament. Arundhati Roy (Introduction by). Trade Cloth. Interlink Publishing Group, Inc. Northampton, MA. 2004. 320p. Bestselling History and Politics Ser. ISBN:1-56656-317-8, ISBN13: 978-1-56656-317-8. Dewey:327.1/747/0954. LCCN:99-023965.
Audience: **g,l,u,f.** *Choice, 2000.*

Blix, Hans **U793.B58 2004**
Disarming Iraq. Trade Cloth. Knopf Publishing Group. New York, NY. 2004. 304p. ISBN:0-375-42302-8, ISBN13: 978-0-375-42302-4. Dewey:956.7044/3. LCCN:2004-040028.
Audience: **g,l,u,f.**

Bourantonis, Dimitris **JX1974.7.B655 1993**
The United Nations and the Quest for Nuclear Disarmament. Trade Cloth. Ashgate Publishing, Ltd. Aldershot, 1993. 224p. ISBN:1-85521-344-3, ISBN13: 978-1-85521-344-9. Dewey:327.174. LCCN:93-020001.
Audience: **g,l,u,f.** *Choice, 1994.*

Bull, Hedley **JX1974; KZ5624**
The Control of the Arms Race: Disarmament and Arms Control in the Missile Age,. Paper Text. Textbook Publishers. Temecula, CA. 2003. 215p. ISBN:0-7581-6150-6, ISBN13: 978-0-7581-6150-5. Dewey:341.67.
Audience: **g,l,u,f.**

Burns, Richard D. (Introduction by) **JX1974.E57 1993**
Encyclopedia of Arms Control and Disarmament, Set. Trade Cloth. Thomson Gale. Farmington Hills, MI. 1993. 1692p. ISBN:0-684-19281-0, ISBN13: 978-0-684-19281-9. Dewey:327.174. LCCN:92-036167.
Audience: **g,l,u.** *Choice, 1993.*

Butler, Richard **DS79.755.B88 2000**
The Greatest Threat: Iraq, Weapons of Mass Destruction, and the Crisis of Global Security. Trade Cloth. PublicAffairs. New York, NY. 2000. 288p. ISBN:1-891620-53-3, ISBN13: 978-1-891620-53-9. Dewey:327.1/745/09567. LCCN:00-029098.
Audience: **g,l,u,f.** *Choice, 2001, 2000.*

Campbell, Kurt M. (Editor), et al. **JZ5675.N848 2004**
The Nuclear Tipping Point: Why States Reconsider Their Nuclear Choices. Robert Einhorn & Mitchell Reiss (Editors), Leon S. fuerth, Ellen Laipson, Thomas W. Lippman, Jenifer Mackby, Derek Mitchell & Joseph F. Pilat (Contribution by). Trade Cloth. Brookings Institution Press. Washington, DC. 2004. 367p. ISBN:0-8157-1330-4, ISBN13: 978-0-8157-1330-2. Dewey:327.1/747. LCCN:2004-010941.
Audience: **l,u,f.**

Cirincione, Joseph, et al. **U793.C57 2005**
Deadly Arsenals: Nuclear, Biological and Chemical Threats. Ed. 2. Jon B. Wolfsthal & Miriam Rajkumar Rajkumar (Authors). Trade Paper, Perfect. Carnegie Endowment for International Peace. Washington, DC. 2005. 490p. ISBN:0-87003-216-X, ISBN13: 978-0-87003-216-5. Dewey:327.1/74. LCCN:2005-012915.
Audience: **l,u,f.**

Cole, Leonard A. **JX1974.7**
The Eleventh Plague: The Politics of Biological and Chemical Warfare. Trade Paper. DIANE Publishing Company. Collingdale,

PA. 2003. ISBN:0-7567-6533-1, ISBN13: 978-0-7567-6533-0. Dewey:327.1/74.
Audience: **g,l,u,f.** *Choice, 1997.*

Deaver, Michael V. **JZ1682**
Disarming Iraq: Monitoring Power and Resistance. Trade Cloth. Greenwood Publishing Group, Inc. Portsmouth, NH. 2001. 168p. ISBN:0-275-97261-5, ISBN13: 978-0-275-97261-5. Dewey:341.7/33/09567. LCCN:00-049161.
Audience: **u,f.** *Choice, 2002.*

Dukes, Paul **E183.8.S65D85 2004**
The USA in the Making of the USSR: The Washington Conference, 1921-1922, and "Uninvited Russia". Paper over Boards. Routledge. New York, NY. 2004. 168p. RoutledgeCurzon Studies on the History of Russia and Eastern Europe, Vol. 2 ISBN:0-415-32930-2, ISBN13: 978-0-415-32930-9. Dewey:327.1/09/041. LCCN:2004-002710.
Audience: **l,u,f.**

Dyson **JX1974.7**
Weapons and Hope: International Edition. Trade Cloth. HarperCollins Publishers. New York, NY. 1984. viii, 340p. ISBN:0-06-337037-9, ISBN13: 978-0-06-337037-1. Dewey:327.1/74. LCCN:83-048343.
Audience: **g,l,u,f.**

Evangelista, Matthew **D860**
Unarmed Forces: The Transnational Movement to End the Cold War. Trade Paper. Cornell University Press. Ithaca, NY. 2002. 416p. ISBN:0-8014-8784-6, ISBN13: 978-0-8014-8784-2. Dewey:327.1/74/09045.
Audience: **u,f.** *Choice, 2000.*

Finnis, John, et al. **U22**
Nuclear Deterrence, Morality and Realism. Joseph M. Boyle & Germain Grisez (Authors). Trade Paper. Oxford University Press, Inc. New York, NY. 1988. 444p. ISBN:0-19-824791-5, ISBN13: 978-0-19-824791-3. Dewey:172/.42. LCCN:86-023804.
Audience: **u,f.** *Choice, 1988.*

Gleditsch, Nils P. (Compiled by), et al. **Z6464.Z9M33**
Making Peace Pay: A Bibliography on Disarmament and Conversion. Goran Lindgren, Naima Mouhleb, Sjoerd Smith & Indra de Soysa (Compiled by). Cloth Text. Regina Books. Claremont, CA. 2000. 280p. The New War/Peace Bibliography Ser., Vol. 3 ISBN:1-930053-03-7, ISBN13: 978-1-930053-03-8. Dewey:016.3384/76234. LCCN:00-059089.
Audience: **l,u.** *Choice, 2001.*

Goldblat, Jozef **KZ5624.G654 2002**
Arms Control: The New Guide to Negotiations and Agreements with New Supplement. Ed. 2. Trade Paper. SAGE Publications, Inc. Thousand Oaks, CA. 2002. 396p. International Peace Research Institute, Oslo (PRIO) Ser. ISBN:0-7619-4016-2, ISBN13: 978-0-7619-4016-6. Dewey:341.7/3. LCCN:2002-102784.
Audience: **u,f.**

Jervis, Robert **U263.J47 1989**
The Meaning of the Nuclear Revolution: Statecraft and the Prospect of Armageddon. Book, Other. Cornell University Press. Ithaca, NY. 1990. 272p. Cornell Studies in Security Affairs ISBN:0-8014-9565-2, ISBN13: 978-0-8014-9565-6. Dewey:355/.0217. LCCN:88-043443.
Audience: **u,f.** *Choice, 1990.*

Krasno, Jean E. & Sutterlin, James S. **UG447**
The United Nations and Iraq: Defanging the Viper. Paper Text. Greenwood Publishing Group, Inc. Portsmouth, NH. 2003. 264p. ISBN:0-275-97839-7, ISBN13: 978-0-275-97839-6. Dewey:341.7/35/09567. LCCN:2002-068627.
Audience: **u,f.** *Choice, 2004.*

Larsen, Jeffrey Arthur & Smith, James M. **JZ5645.L38 2005**
Historical Dictionary of Arms Control and Disarmament. Trade Cloth. Scarecrow Press, Inc. Lanham, MD. 2005. 424p. Historical Dictionaries of War, Revolution, and Civil Unrest Ser., No. 28 ISBN:0-8108-5060-5, ISBN13: 978-0-8108-5060-6. Dewey:327.1/74/03. LCCN:2004-025199.
Audience: **g,l,u,f.** *Choice, 2005.*

Legault, Albert & Fortmann, Michel **JX1974.L55513 1992**
A Diplomacy of Hope: Canada and Disarmament, 1945-1988. Trade Paper. McGill-Queen's University Press. Montreal, PQ. 1992. 696p. ISBN:0-7735-0955-0, ISBN13: 978-0-7735-0955-9. Dewey:327.1/74/097109045. LCCN:94-149283.
Audience: **u,f.** *Choice, 1993.*

Levitt, Joseph **JX1974.7.L355 1993**
Pearson and Canada's Role in Nuclear Disarmament and Arms Control Negotiations, 1945-1957. Trade Cloth. McGill-Queen's University Press. Montreal, PQ. 1993. 344p. ISBN:0-7735-0905-4, ISBN13: 978-0-7735-0905-4. Dewey:327.1/74. LCCN:94-149837.
Audience: **u,f.** *Choice, 1993.*

National Academy of Sciences Staff **JX1974.7.R49 1988**
Reykjavik and Beyond: Deep Reductions in Strategic Nuclear Arsenals and the Future Direction of Arms Control. Paper Text. National Academies Press. Washington, DC. 1988. 80p. ISBN:0-309-03799-9, ISBN13: 978-0-309-03799-0. Dewey:327.1/74. LCCN:87-030193.
Audience: **u,f.**

Reiss, Mitchell **U264.R45 1995**
Bridled Ambition: Why Countries Constrain Their Nuclear Capabilities. Trade Paper. Woodrow Wilson Center Press. Washington, DC. 1995. 356p. ISBN:0-943875-71-4, ISBN13: 978-0-943875-71-2. Dewey:355.02/17. LCCN:95-002646.
Audience: **l,u,f.** *Choice, 1995.*

Russell, Bertrand **JX1974.7**
Has Man a Future? Trade Cloth. Spokesman Books. Nottingham, 2001. 154p. ISBN:0-85124-638-9, ISBN13: 978-0-85124-638-3. Dewey:327.1/74.
Audience: **g,l,u,f.**

Russell, Bertrand Arthur **JZ5538.R87 2001**
Commonsense and Nuclear Warfare. Trade Paper. Routledge. New York, NY. 2001. 240p. ISBN:0-415-24995-3, ISBN13: 978-0-415-24995-9. Dewey:327.1/72. LCCN:00-069683.
Audience: **l,u.**

Schell, Jonathan **UF767.S2365 2000**
The Fate of the Earth and the Abolition. Trade Paper. Stanford University Press. Palo Alto, CA. 1999. 458p. Stanford Nuclear Age Ser. ISBN:0-8047-3702-9, ISBN13: 978-0-8047-3702-9. Dewey:355.02/17. LCCN:99-067025.
Audience: **g,l,u,f.**

Schell, Jonathan **KZ5665.S2365 2003**
Unfinished Twentieth Century: The Crisis of Arms Control. Trade Paper. Verso Books. London, 2001. 144p. ISBN:1-85984-493-6, ISBN13: 978-1-85984-493-9. Dewey:327.1/747.
Audience: **u,f.**

Sigal, Leon V. **JZ5675**
Disarming Strangers: Nuclear Diplomacy with North Korea. Trade Paper. Princeton University Press. Princeton, NJ. 1999. 336p. Princeton Studies in International History and Politics ISBN:0-691-01006-4, ISBN13: 978-0-691-01006-9. Dewey:327.1/747. LCCN:97-024502.
Audience: **u,f.** *Choice, 1998.*

Stanford Arms Control Group Staff **JX1974.I55 1984**
International Arms Control: Issues and Agreements. Ed. 2. Coit D. Blacker & Gloria Duffy (Editors). Trade Paper. Stanford University Press. Palo Alto, CA. 1984. 516p. ISIS Studies in International Policy, Vol. 1 ISBN:0-8047-1222-0, ISBN13: 978-0-8047-1222-4. Dewey:327.1/74. LCCN:83-040091.
Audience: **l,u.**

Talbott, Strobe **JX1974.76.T34 1984**
Deadly Gambits: The Reagan Administration and the Stalemate in Nuclear Arms Control. Trade Cloth. Alfred A. Knopf Inc. New York, NY. 1984. 353p. ISBN:0-394-53637-1, ISBN13: 978-0-394-53637-8. Dewey:327.1/74. LCCN:84-047781.
Audience: **g,l,u,f.** B

Towle, Philip **JZ5625.T69 1997**
Enforced Disarmament: From the Napoleonic Campaigns to the Gulf War. Trade Cloth. Oxford University Press, Inc. New York, NY. 1997. 276p. ISBN:0-19-820636-4, ISBN13: 978-0-19-820636-1. Dewey:327.1/74/09. LCCN:97-188749.
Audience: **u,f.** *Choice, 1998.*

Tulliu, Steve & Schmalberger, Thomas **KZ5624**
Coming to Terms with Security: A Lexicon for Arms Control, Disarmament and Confidence-Building. Trade Cloth. United Nations Institute for Disarmament Research. Geneva 10, 2005. 520p. UNIDIR Ser., Vol. 2003/22 ISBN:92-9045-152-1, ISBN13: 978-92-9045-152-5. Dewey:327.1/74/03.
Audience: **l,u,f.**

United Nations **JZ5588**
United Nations Disarmament Yearbook 2004. United Nations. Department for Disarmament Affairs. 2005. ISBN:92-1-142251-5, ISBN13: 978-92-1-142251-1.
Audience: **g,l,u,f.**

United Nations Staff **JX1974.73.U53 1995**
The United Nations and Nuclear Non-Proliferation. Trade Cloth. United Nations Publications. New York, NY. 1995. 200p. Blue Bks., Vol. III ISBN:92-1-100557-4, ISBN13: 978-92-1-100557-8. Dewey:341.7/34. LCCN:95-152663.
Audience: **g,l,u.**

Wittner, Lawrence S. **JX1974.7.W575**
The Struggle Against the Bomb: One World or None: A History of the World Nuclear Disarmament Movement Through 1953. Trade Paper. Stanford University Press. Palo Alto, CA. 1995. 488p. Stanford Nuclear Age Ser., Vol. 1 ISBN:0-8047-2528-4, ISBN13: 978-0-8047-2528-6. Dewey:327.1/74/09.
Audience: **g,l,u.**

Wittner, Lawrence S. **JX1974.7.W575 1993**
The Struggle Against the Bomb: Resisting the Bomb: A History of the World Nuclear Disarmament Movement, 1954-1970. Trade Cloth. Stanford University Press. Palo Alto, CA. 1997. 732p. ISBN:0-8047-2918-2, ISBN13: 978-0-8047-2918-5. Dewey:327.1/747/09. LCCN:92-028026.
Audience: **g,l,u.** *Choice, 1998.*

Wittner, Lawrence S. **JX1974.7.W575 1993**
Toward Nuclear Abolition: A History of the World Nuclear Disarmament Movement, 1971-Present. Trade Cloth. Stanford University Press. Palo Alto, CA. 2003. 688p. ISBN:0-8047-4861-6, ISBN13: 978-0-8047-4861-2. Dewey:327.17409. LCCN:92-028026.
Audience: **g,l,u.**

Wright, Susan (Editor) **UG447.8.B5645 2002**
Biological Warfare and Disarmament: New Problems/New Perspectives. Book, Other. Rowman & Littlefield Publishers, Inc. Lanham, MD. 2002. 448p. War and Peace Library ISBN:0-7425-2468-X, ISBN13: 978-0-7425-2468-2. Dewey:327.1/745. LCCN:2002-009704.
Audience: **g,l,u,f.** *Choice, 2003.*

Zagare, Frank C. **JX1291.Z34 1987**
The Dynamics of Deterrence. Trade Cloth. University of Chicago Press. Chicago, IL. 1986. 208p. ISBN:0-226-97763-3, ISBN13: 978-0-226-97763-8. Dewey:327/.072. LCCN:86-007037.
Audience: **l,u,f.** *Choice, 1987.*

International Relations. Transnational Relations > International Security > Terrorism

Abuza, Zachary **HV6433.A785A28 2003**
Militant Islam in Southeast Asia: Crucible of Terror. Library Binding. Lynne Rienner Publishers, Inc. Boulder, CO. 2003. 260p. ISBN:1-58826-212-X, ISBN13: 978-1-58826-212-7. Dewey:303.6/25/0959. LCCN:2003-047046.
Audience: **u,f.** *Choice, 2004.*

Anderson, Sean K. & Sloan, Stephen **HV6431.A537 2002**
Historical Dictionary of Terrorism. Ed. 2. Trade Cloth. Scarecrow Press, Inc. Lanham, MD. 2002. 624p. Historical Dictionaries of Religions, Philosophies, and Movements Ser., No. 41: ISBN:0-8108-4101-0, ISBN13: 978-0-8108-4101-7. Dewey:909. LCCN:2001-049656.
Audience: **g,l,u,f.** *Choice, 2002.*

Bell, J. Bowyer **HV6431.B425 2003**
Murder on the Nile, the World Trade Center and Global Terror. Trade Cloth, Prepack. Encounter Books. New York, NY. 2002. 206p. Ser. ISBN:1-893554-63-5, ISBN13: 978-1-893554-63-4. Dewey:303.6/25/0962. LCCN:2002-040885.
Audience: **g,l,u,f.** *Choice, 2003.*

Berman, Paul **HV6431.B4794 2003**
Terror and Liberalism. Trade Cloth. W. W. Norton & Company, Inc. New York, NY. 2003. 128p. ISBN:0-393-05775-5, ISBN13: 978-0-393-05775-1. Dewey:303.6/25. LCCN:2002-156445.
Audience: **g,l,u.** *Choice, 2003.*

Bin Laden, Osama **HV6430.B55**
Messages to the World: The Statements of Osama Bin Laden. James Howarth (Translator). Trade Paper, Perfect. Verso Books. London, 2005. 292p. ISBN:1-84467-045-7, ISBN13: 978-1-84467-045-1. Dewey:958.104/6092. LCCN:2005-027355.
Audience: **g,l,u,f.**

Bloom, Mia **HV6431.B576 2005**
Dying to Kill: The Allure of Suicide Terror. Trade Cloth. Columbia University Press. New York, NY. 2005. 280p. ISBN:0-231-13320-0, ISBN13: 978-0-231-13320-3. Dewey:303.6/25. LCCN:2004-063474.
Audience: **u,f.**

Booth, Ken & Dunne, Timothy (Editors) **HV6431.W635 2002**
Worlds in Collision: Terror and the Future of Global Order. Cloth over Boards. Palgrave Macmillan. New York, NY. 2002. 386p. ISBN:0-333-99804-9, ISBN13: 978-0-333-99804-5. Dewey:303.6/25. LCCN:2002-019596.
Audience: **u,f.** *Choice, 2003.*

Boulden, Jane & Weiss, Thomas George **HV6431.T4635 2004**
Terrorism and the UN: Before and after September 11. Trade Cloth. Indiana University Press. Bloomington, IN. 2004. 248p. ISBN:0-253-21662-1, ISBN13: 978-0-253-21662-5. Dewey:345/.02. LCCN:2003-020232.
Audience: **g,l,u,f.** *Choice, 2004.*

Bronner, Stephen Eric **JZ1318.P53 2005**
Planetary Politics: Human Rights, Terror, and Global Society. Book, Other. Rowman & Littlefield Publishers, Inc. Lanham, MD. 2005. 248p. ISBN:0-7425-4198-3, ISBN13: 978-0-7425-4198-6. Dewey:327. LCCN:2004-017766.
Audience: **l,u,f.**

Byman, Daniel **HV6431.B96 2005**
Deadly Connections: States that Sponsor Terrorism. Cloth Text. Cambridge University Press. New York, NY. 2005. 380p. ISBN:0-521-83973-4, ISBN13: 978-0-521-83973-0. Dewey:327.1/17. LCCN:2005-047002.
Audience: **l,u,f.** *Choice, 2006.*

Carlton, David **HV6431.C365 2005**
The West's Road to 9/11: Resisting, Appeasing, and Encouraging Terrorism since 1970. Cloth over Boards. Palgrave Macmillan. New York, NY. 2006. 272p. ISBN:1-4039-9608-3, ISBN13: 978-1-4039-9608-4. Dewey:303.6/25/09045. LCCN:2005-047614.
Audience: **u,f.** *Choice, 2006.*

Chalk, Peter & Rosenau, William **HV6431.C443 2004**
Confronting the Enemy Within: Security Intelligence, the Police, and Counterterrorism in Four Democracies. Trade Cloth. RAND Corporation, The. Santa Monica, CA. 2004. 88p. ISBN:0-8330-3513-4, ISBN13: 978-0-8330-3513-4. Dewey:363.32. LCCN:2003-024359.
Audience: **u,f.**

Chasdi, Richard J. **HV6433.M5C534 2002**
Tapestry of Terror: A Portrait of Middle East Terrorism, 1994-1999. Trade Cloth. Lexington Books. Lanham, MD. 2002. 536p. ISBN:0-7391-0354-7, ISBN13: 978-0-7391-0354-8. Dewey:303.6/25/095609049. LCCN:2002-066052.
Audience: **u,f.** *Choice, 2003.*

Chasdi, Richard J. **HV6433.M5C53 1999**
Serenade of Suffering: A Portrait of Middle East Terrorism, 1968-1993. Michael Stohl (Foreword by). Trade Cloth. Lexington Books. Lanham, MD. 1999. 288p. ISBN:0-7391-0057-2, ISBN13: 978-0-7391-0057-8. Dewey:303.6/25/0956. LCCN:98-052753.
Audience: **u,f.** *Choice, 2000.*

Chomsky, Noam **HV6431.C47 2002**
Pirates and Emperors, Old and New: International Terrorism in the Real World. Trade Cloth. South End Press. Cambridge, MA. 2003. 224p. ISBN:0-89608-686-0, ISBN13: 978-0-89608-686-9. Dewey:956.04. LCCN:2002-110014.
Audience: **g,l,u,f.**

Courtois, Stéphane, et al. **HX44.L59 1999**
The Black Book of Communism: Crimes, Terror, Repression. Nicolas Werth, Jean-Louis Panné, Andrzej Paczkowski, Karel Bartosek & Jean-Louis Margolin (Authors), Jonathan Murphy & Mark Kramer (Translators), Martin Malia (Foreword by). Trade Cloth. Harvard University Press. Cambridge, MA. 1999. 912p. ISBN:0-674-07608-7, ISBN13: 978-0-674-07608-2. Dewey:320.53/2. LCCN:99-029759.
Audience: **g,l,u,f.**

Crotty, William (Editor) **JC423.D46 2005**
Democratic Development and Political Terrorism: The Global Perspective. Trade Cloth. Northeastern University Press. Boston, MA. 2004. 544p. Northeastern Series on Democratization and Political Development ISBN:1-55553-625-5, ISBN13: 978-1-55553-625-1. Dewey:303.6/25. LCCN:2004-009740.
Audience: **l,u,f.** *Choice, 2005.*

Dershowitz, Alan M. **HV6431.D473 2002**
Why Terrorism Works: Understanding the Threat, Responding to the Challenge. Cloth over Boards. Yale University Press. Cumberland, RI. 2002. 288p. ISBN:0-300-09766-2, ISBN13: 978-0-300-09766-5. Dewey:303.6/25. LCCN:2002-006387.
Audience: **g,l,u.** *Choice, 2003.*

Devji, Faisal **HV6431.D48 2005**
Landscapes of the Jihad: Militancy, Morality, Modernity. Saddle Stitched, Cloth over Boards, Dust Jacket. Cornell University Press. Ithaca, NY. 2005. 184p. Crises in World Politics Ser. ISBN:0-8014-4437-3, ISBN13: 978-0-8014-4437-1. Dewey:303.6/25. LCCN:2005-049397.
Audience: **g,l,u,f.** *Choice, 2006.*

Drury, Shadia B. **BT736.15.D78 2004**
Terror and Civilization: Christianity, Politics, and the Western Psyche. Cloth over Boards. Palgrave Macmillan. New York, NY. 2004. 228p. ISBN:1-4039-6404-1, ISBN13: 978-1-4039-6404-5. Dewey:261.7. LCCN:2003-050572.
Audience: **u,f.** *Choice, 2004.*

Esposito, John L. **HV6431**
Unholy War: Terror in the Name of Islam. Trade Paper. Oxford University Press, Inc. New York, NY. 2003. 210p. ISBN:0-19-516886-0, ISBN13: 978-0-19-516886-0. Dewey:322.4/2/0882971.
Audience: **g,l,u,f.** *Choice, 2003, 2002.*

Ferguson, Charles D., et al. **HV6431.F43 2005**
The Four Faces of Nuclear Terrorism. William C. Potter & Amy Sands (Authors). Trade Paper. Routledge. New York, NY. 2005. 392p. ISBN:0-415-95244-1, ISBN13: 978-0-415-95244-6. Dewey:363.32. LCCN:2005-005277.
Audience: **u,f.**

Freeman, Michael **JC571**
Freedom or Security: The Consequences for Democracies Using Emergency Powers to Fight Terror. Trade Cloth. Greenwood Publishing Group, Inc. Portsmouth, NH. 2003. 232p. ISBN:0-275-97913-X, ISBN13: 978-0-275-97913-3. Dewey:323.44. LCCN:2002-029884.
Audience: **l,u.** *Choice, 2004.*

Frey, Bruno S. **HV6431.F724 2004**
Dealing with Terrorism. Trade Cloth. Edward Elgar Publishing, Inc. Northampton, MA. 2004. 200p. ISBN:1-84376-828-3, ISBN13: 978-1-84376-828-9. Dewey:363.32. LCCN:2004-046961.
Audience: **u,f.** *Choice, 2005.*

Graham, Stephen (Editor) **HT119.C573 2004**
Cities, War, and Terrorism: Towards an Urban Geopolitics. Trade Paper. Blackwell Publishing, Inc. Malden, MA. 2004. 416p. Studies in Urban and Social Change ISBN:1-4051-1575-0, ISBN13: 978-1-4051-1575-9. Dewey:307.76. LCCN:2004-004244.
Audience: **l,u,f.** *Choice, 2005.*

Greenberg, Karen J. (Editor) **HV6432.5Q2**
Al Qaeda Now: Understanding Today's Terrorists. Trade Cloth. Cambridge University Press. New York, NY. 2005. 282p. ISBN:0-521-85911-5, ISBN13: 978-0-521-85911-0. Dewey:303.6/25. LCCN:2005-019855.
Audience: **g,l,u,f.**

Habeck, Mary **BP190.5.T47H33 2006**
Knowing the Enemy: Jihadist Ideology and the War on Terror. Cloth over Boards. Yale University Press. Cumberland, RI. 2006. 256p. ISBN:0-300-11306-4, ISBN13: 978-0-300-11306-8. Dewey:297.2/72. LCCN:2005-015210.
Audience: **g,l,u,f.**

Harclerode, Peter **U262**
Fighting Dirty: The Inside Story of Covert Operations from Ho Chi Minh to Osama Bin Laden. Trade Paper. Cassell P L C. London, 2003. 640p. Cassell Military Paperbacks Ser. ISBN:0-304-36468-1, ISBN13: 978-0-304-36468-8. Dewey:356.1/6.
Audience: **g,l,u,f.** *Choice, 2002.*

Held, David **E895**
Global Covenant: The Social Democratic Alternative to the Washington Consensus. Trade Cloth. Polity Press. Cambridge, 2004. 216p. ISBN:0-7456-3352-8, ISBN13: 978-0-7456-3352-7. Dewey:303.6/25.
Audience: **l,u.** *Choice, 2005.*

Herbst, Philip **HV6431**
Talking Terrorism: A Dictionary of the Loaded Language of Political Violence. Cloth Text. Greenwood Publishing Group, Inc. Portsmouth, NH. 2003. 240p. ISBN:0-313-32486-7, ISBN13: 978-0-313-32486-4. Dewey:303.6/03. LCCN:2003-044071.
Audience: **g,l,u,f.** *Choice, 2004.*

Hersh, Seymour M. **DS79.76.H465 2004**
Chain of Command: The Road from 9/11 to Abu Ghraib. Trade Cloth. HarperCollins Publishers. New York, NY. 2004. 416p. ISBN:0-06-019591-6, ISBN13: 978-0-06-019591-5. Dewey:956.7044/37. LCCN:2004-541382.
Audience: **g,u,f.**

Heymann, Philip B. **HV6432.H494 2003**
Terrorism, Freedom, and Security: Winning Without War. Trade Cloth. MIT Press. Cambridge, MA. 2003. 228p. BCSIA Studies in International Security Ser. ISBN:0-262-08327-2, ISBN13: 978-0-262-08327-0. Dewey:363.3/2/0973. LCCN:2003-051126.
Audience: **g,l,u,f.** *Choice, 2004.*

Hoffman, Bruce **HV6431.H626 2006**
Inside Terrorism. Trade Cloth. Columbia University Press. New York, NY. 2006. 512p. ISBN:0-231-51046-2, ISBN13: 978-0-231-51046-2. Dewey:363.325. LCCN:2005-033841.
Audience: **l,u,f.** *Choice, 1999.*

Holden, Robert H. **HN125.2.V5H65 2003**
Armies Without Nations: Public Violence and State Formation in Central America, 1821-1960. Trade Cloth. Oxford University Press, Inc. New York, NY. 2004. 352p. ISBN:0-19-516120-3, ISBN13: 978-0-19-516120-5. Dewey:303.6/09728. LCCN:2003-053090.
Audience: **u,f.** *Choice, 2004.*

Ignatieff, Michael **JA79.I36 2004**
The Lesser Evil: Political Ethics in an Age of Terror. Cloth Text. Princeton University Press. Princeton, NJ. 2004. 232p. The Gifford Lectures ISBN:0-691-11751-9, ISBN13: 978-0-691-11751-5. Dewey:172.4. LCCN:2003-107023.
Audience: **g,l,u,f.** *Choice, 2005.*

Jacquard, Roland **HV6430.B55J3313 2002**
In the Name of Osama Bin Laden: Global Terrorism and the Bin Laden Brotherhood. Trade Cloth. Duke University Press. Durham, NC. 2002. 320p. ISBN:0-8223-2977-8, ISBN13: 978-0-8223-2977-0. Dewey:958.104/6/092. LCCN:2001-008513.
Audience: **g,l,u,f.** *Choice, 2002.*

Jenkins, Philip **HV6431.J46 2002**
Images of Terror: What We Can and Can't Know about Terrorism. Trade Cloth. Aldine Transaction. Somerset, NJ. 2003. 227p. Social Problems and Social Issues Ser. ISBN:0-202-30678-X, ISBN13: 978-0-202-30678-0. Dewey:303.6/25. LCCN:2002-013178.
Audience: **g,l,u,f.** *Choice, 2003.*

Kassimeris, George **HV6433.G72E635 2001**
Europe's Last Red Terrorists: The Revolutionary Organization 17 November. Trade Cloth. New York University Press. New York, NY. 2001. 288p. ISBN:0-8147-4756-6, ISBN13: 978-0-8147-4756-8. Dewey:303.62509495. LCCN:00-066432.
Audience: **u,f.** *Choice, 2002.*

Kean, Thomas H. & Hamilton, Lee **HV6432.7.N39 2004**
The 9/11 Commission Report: Final Report of the National Commission on Terrorist Attacks upon the United States. National Commission on Terrorist Attacks Staff (Contribution by). Trade Paper. United States Government Printing Office. Washington, DC. 2004. 567p. ISBN:0-16-072304-3, ISBN13: 978-0-16-072304-9. Dewey:973.931. LCCN:2004-356401.
Audience: **g,l,u,f.**

Kronenwetter, Michael **HV6431**
Terrorism: A Guide to Events and Documents. Cloth Text. Greenwood Publishing Group, Inc. Portsmouth, NH. 2004. 312p. ISBN:0-313-32578-2, ISBN13: 978-0-313-32578-6. Dewey:303.6/25. LCCN:2004-006619.
Audience: **g,l,u,f.** *Choice, 2004.*

Lansford, Tom **D860.L355 2002**
All for One: Terrorism, NATO and the United States. Trade Cloth. Ashgate Publishing, Ltd. Aldershot, 2002. 222p. ISBN:0-7546-3045-5, ISBN13: 978-0-7546-3045-6. Dewey:973.931. LCCN:2002-024893.
Audience: **l,u,f.** *Choice, 2003.*

Laqueur, Walter **HV6431**
The Age of Terrorism. Trade Paper. Little Brown & Company. New York, NY. 1988. ISBN:0-316-51479-9, ISBN13: 978-0-316-51479-8. Dewey:322.4/2.
Audience: **g,l,u,f.** *Choice, 1987.*

Laqueur, Walter **HV6431.L366 2002**
No End to War: Terrorism in the 21st Century. Trade Cloth. Continuum International Publishing Group, Ltd. London, 2003. 304p. ISBN:0-8264-1435-4, ISBN13: 978-0-8264-1435-9. Dewey:303.6/25. LCCN:2002-151954.
Audience: **g,l,u,f.** *Choice, 2003.*

Leeman, Richard W. **JK468**
The Rhetoric of Terrorism and Counterterrorism. Trade Cloth. Greenwood Publishing Group, Inc. Portsmouth, NH. 1991. 232p. Contributions to the Study of Mass Media and Communications Ser., No. 29 ISBN:0-313-27587-4, ISBN13: 978-0-313-27587-6. Dewey:363.3/2. LCCN:90-047522.
Audience: **l,u.** *Choice, 1991.*

Leone, Richard C. & Anrig, Gregory **JC599.U5W313 2003**
The War on Our Freedoms: Civil Liberties in an Age of Terrorism. Trade Paper. PublicAffairs. New York, NY. 2003. 336p. ISBN:1-58648-210-6, ISBN13: 978-1-58648-210-7. Dewey:323/.0973. LCCN:2003-046681.
Audience: **g,l,u,f.** *Choice, 2004.*

Lincoln, Bruce **BL65.T47L56 2002**
Holy Terrors: Thinking about Religion after September 11. Trade Cloth. University of Chicago Press. Chicago, IL. 2002. 185p. ISBN:0-226-48192-1, ISBN13: 978-0-226-48192-0. Dewey:291.1/787. LCCN:2002-007099.
Audience: **g,l,u.** *Choice, 2003.*

Lutz, James M. & Lutz, Brenda J. **HV6431.L87 2005**
Terrorism: Origins and Evolution. Cloth over Boards. Palgrave Macmillan. New York, NY. 2005. 240p. ISBN:1-4039-6646-X, ISBN13: 978-1-4039-6646-9. Dewey:303.6/25. LCCN:2005-042972.
Audience: **u,f.**

Mann, Michael **HV6322.M36 2004**
The Dark Side of Democracy: Explaining Ethnic Cleansing. Trade Paper. Cambridge University Press. New York, NY. 2004. 584p. ISBN:0-521-53854-8, ISBN13: 978-0-521-53854-1. Dewey:304.6/63. LCCN:2004-045626.
Audience: **u,f.** *Choice, 2005.*

Mannes, Aaron **HV6433.M5M35 2004**
Profiles in Terror: The Guide to Middle East Terrorist Organizations. Trade Cloth. Rowman & Littlefield Publishers, Inc. Lanham, MD. 2004. 392p. ISBN:0-7425-3525-8, ISBN13: 978-0-7425-3525-1. Dewey:363.3250956. LCCN:2004-014124.
Audience: **u,f.** *Choice, 2005.*

Marchak, M. Patricia & Marchak, William **HV6433.A7M37 1999**
God's Assassins: State Terrorism in Argentina in the 1970s. Trade Cloth. McGill-Queen's University Press. Montreal, PQ. 1999. 393p. ISBN:0-7735-2013-9, ISBN13: 978-0-7735-2013-4. Dewey:982.06/4. LCCN:2001-269614.
Audience: **l,u,f.** *Choice, 2000.*

Maxwell, Bruce **HV6431.T4594 2003**
Terrorism: A Documentary History. Trade Cloth. CQ Press. Washington, DC. 2002. 512p. ISBN:1-56802-767-2, ISBN13: 978-1-56802-767-8. Dewey:303.6/25/09045. LCCN:2002-151050.
Audience: **l,u,f.** *Choice, 2003.*

McGoldrick, Dominic **K5256**
From '9-11' to the 'Iraq War 2003': International Law in an Age of Complexity. Trade Paper. Hart Publishing Ltd. Oxford, 2004. 396p. ISBN:1-84113-496-1, ISBN13: 978-1-84113-496-3. Dewey:345/.0235. LCCN:2004-301382.
Audience: **l,u.**

McSherry, J. Patrice **HV6433.L32O64 2005**
Predatory States: Operation Condor and Covert War in Latin America. Book, Other. Rowman & Littlefield Publishers, Inc. Lanham, MD. 2005. 336p. ISBN:0-7425-3687-4, ISBN13: 978-0-7425-3687-6. Dewey:980.03/3. LCCN:2004-029817.
Audience: **u,f.** *Choice, 2006.*

Mockaitis, Thomas R. & Rich, Paul **HV6431.G728 2003**
Grand Strategy in the War Against Terrorism. B. Bundgaard Rasmussen & Annette Rathje (Editors). Trade Paper. Routledge. New York, NY. 2003. 160p. ISBN:0-7146-8268-3, ISBN13: 978-0-7146-8268-6. Dewey:973.931. LCCN:2003-016417.
Audience: **l,u,f.** *Choice, 2004.*

Moghaddam, Fathali M. & Marsella, Anthony J. (Editors) **HV6431.U35 2003**
Understanding Terrorism: Psychosocial Roots, Consequences, and Interventions. Trade Cloth. American Psychological Association. Washington, DC. 2003. 328p. ISBN:1-59147-032-3, ISBN13: 978-1-59147-032-8. Dewey:303.6/25. LCCN:2003-009643.
Audience: **u,f.** *Choice, 2004.*

Moreno, Jonathan D. (Editor) **R725.5.I5 2004**
In the Wake of Terror: Medicine and Morality in a Time of Crisis. Ford Rowan (Foreword by). Trade Paper. MIT Press. Cambridge, MA. 2004. 264p. Basic Bioethics Ser. ISBN:0-262-63302-7, ISBN13: 978-0-262-63302-4. Dewey:174/.2. LCCN:2002-043132.
Audience: **g,l,u,f.** *Choice, 2003.*

Napoleoni, Loretta **HV6431.N3654 2005**
Terror Incorporated: Tracing the Dollars Behind the Terror Networks. Greg Palast (Foreword by). Trade Paper, Perfect. Seven Stories Press. New York, NY. 2005. 336p. ISBN:1-58322-673-7, ISBN13: 978-1-58322-673-5. Dewey:303.6/25. LCCN:2004-024807.
Audience: **g,l,u,f.**

Nassar, Jamal R. **HV6431.N38 2004**
Globalization and Terrorism: The Migration of Dreams and Nightmares. Book, Other. Rowman & Littlefield Publishers, Inc. Lanham, MD. 2004. 160p. Globalization Ser. ISBN:0-7425-2503-1, ISBN13: 978-0-7425-2503-0. Dewey:303.6/25. LCCN:2004-006795.
Audience: **u,f.** *Choice, 2005.*

Oliver, Anne Marie & Steinberg, Paul **HV6433.G39O55 2004**
The Road to Martyrs' Square: A Journey into the World of the Suicide Bomber. Trade Cloth. Oxford University Press, Inc. New York, NY. 2005. 237p. ISBN:0-19-511600-3, ISBN13: 978-0-19-511600-7. Dewey:956.9405/4. LCCN:2004-008861.
Audience: **g,l,u.**

O'Neill, Bard E. **U240.O54 2005**
Insurgency and Terrorism: Inside Modern Revolutionary Warfare. Ed. 2. Trade Cloth. Potomac Books, Inc. Dulles, VA. 2005. 216p. ISBN:1-57488-172-8, ISBN13: 978-1-57488-172-1. Dewey:355.02/18. LCCN:2005-001243.
Audience: **u,f.** *Choice, 1991.*

Paletz, David L. & Schmid, Alex P. (Editors) **P96.T47T48 1992**
Terrorism and the Media. Trade Paper. SAGE Publications, Inc. Thousand Oaks, CA. 1992. 250p. ISBN:0-8039-4483-7, ISBN13: 978-0-8039-4483-1. Dewey:303.6/25. LCCN:92-003738.
Audience: **u,f.** *Choice, 1992.*

Pearlstein, Richard M. **HV6431.P43 1991**
The Mind of the Political Terrorist. Trade Cloth. Rowman & Littlefield Publishers, Inc. Lanham, MD. 1991. 237p. ISBN:0-8420-2345-3, ISBN13: 978-0-8420-2345-0. Dewey:303.6/25. LCCN:90-009134.
Audience: **u.** *Choice, 1992.*

Peimani, Hooman **DS371**
Falling Terrorism and Rising Conflicts: The Afghan Contribution to Polarization and Confrontation in West and South Asia. Book, Other. Greenwood Publishing Group, Inc. Portsmouth, NH. 2003. 160p. ISBN:0-275-97857-5, ISBN13: 978-0-275-97857-0. Dewey:958.104/6. LCCN:2003-048221.
Audience: **l,u,f.**

Pellicani, Luciano **HM876**
Revolutionary Apocalypse: Ideological Roots of Terrorism. Trade Cloth. Greenwood Publishing Group, Inc. Portsmouth, NH. 2003. 320p. ISBN:0-275-98145-2, ISBN13: 978-0-275-98145-7. Dewey:303.6/4. LCCN:2003-045761.
Audience: **l,u.** *Choice, 2004.*

Peterson, Kate Dempsey & Burns, Vincent **HV6432**
Terrorism: A Documentary and Reference Guide. Cloth Text. Greenwood Publishing Group, Inc. Portsmouth, NH. 2005. 336p. ISBN:0-313-33213-4, ISBN13: 978-0-313-33213-5. Dewey:303.6/25/0973. LCCN:2005-003390.
Audience: **l,u.** *Choice, 2005.*

Pipes, Richard **DK236.D44P57 2003**
The Degaev Affair: Terror and Treason in Tsarist Russia. Cloth over Boards. Yale University Press. Cumberland, RI. 2003. 176p. ISBN:0-300-09848-0, ISBN13: 978-0-300-09848-8. Dewey:322.42092. LCCN:2002-010803.
Audience: **g,l,u.** *Choice, 2003.*

Primakov, Yevgeny M. **HV6431.P74 2004**
A World Challenged: Fighting Terrorism in the Twenty-First Century. Trade Cloth. Brookings Institution Press. Washington, DC. 2003. 144p. ISBN:0-8157-7194-0, ISBN13: 978-0-8157-7194-4. Dewey:363.32. LCCN:2003-023943.
Audience: **l,u,f.**

Primoratz, Igor (Editor) **HV6431.T499 2004**
Terrorism: The Philosophical Issues. Cloth over Boards. Palgrave Macmillan. New York, NY. 2005. 272p. ISBN:1-4039-1816-3, ISBN13: 978-1-4039-1816-1. Dewey:303.6/25/01. LCCN:2004-050424.
Audience: **u,f.** *Choice, 2005.*

Qureshi, Emran & Sells, Michael Anthony (Editors) **D860.N389 2003**
The New Crusades: Constructing the Muslim Enemy. Trade Cloth. Columbia University Press. New York, NY. 2003. 400p. ISBN:0-231-12666-2, ISBN13: 978-0-231-12666-3. Dewey:327.4017/671/09045. LCCN:2003-043768.
Audience: **u,f.** *Choice, 2004.*

Randal, Jonathan **HV6430.B55R36 2004**
Osama: The Making of a Terrorist. Trade Cloth. Knopf Publishing Group. New York, NY. 2004. 352p. ISBN:0-375-40901-7, ISBN13: 978-0-375-40901-1. Dewey:958.104/6092 B. LCCN:2004-046522.
Audience: **g,l,u,f.**

Rees, Martin **CB161.R38 2004**
Our Final Hour: A Scientist's Warning: How Terror, Error, and Environmental Disaster Threaten Humankind's Future in This Century - On Earth and Beyond. Trade Paper. Basic Books. New York, NY. 2004. 240p. ISBN:0-465-06863-4, ISBN13: 978-0-465-06863-0. Dewey:303.49/09/05. LCCN:2004-556001.
Audience: **g,l,u,f.** *Choice, 2003.*

Rehman, Javaid **KBP144**
Islamic State Practices, International Law and the Threat from Terrorism: A Critique of the 'Clash of Civilizations' in the New World Order. Trade Cloth. Hart Publishing Ltd. Oxford, 2005. 280p. ISBN:1-84113-501-1, ISBN13: 978-1-84113-501-4. Dewey:341.091767. LCCN:2005-301399.
Audience: **u,f.**

Reich, Walter (Editor) **HV6431.O74 1998**
Origins of Terrorism: Psychologies, Ideologies, Theologies, States of Mind. Walter Laquer (Foreword by). Trade Paper. Woodrow Wilson Center Press. Washington, DC. 1998. 304p. ISBN:0-943875-89-7, ISBN13: 978-0-943875-89-7. Dewey:303.6/25. LCCN:98-024652.
Audience: **g,l,u,f.** *Choice, 1991.*

Roach, Kent **HV6433**
September 11: Consequences for Canada. Trade Paper. McGill-Queen's University Press. Montreal, PQ. 2003. 208p. ISBN:0-7735-2585-8, ISBN13: 978-0-7735-2585-6. Dewey:971.064/8. LCCN:2004-445610.
Audience: **g,l,u,f.** *Choice, 2003.*

Schmid, Alex Peter & Jongman, A. J. **HV6431.S349 2005**
Political Terrorism: A New Guide to Actors, Authors, Concepts, Data Bases, Theories, and Literature. Ed. 2. Trade Paper. Transaction Publishers. Somerset, NJ. 2005. 700p. ISBN:1-4128-0469-8, ISBN13: 978-1-4128-0469-1. Dewey:303.6/25. LCCN:2004-062019.
Audience: **l,u,f.**

Shanty, Frank G. (Editor), et al. **HV6431.E53 2003**
Encyclopedia of World Terrorism, 1996-2002 and Encyclopedia of World Terrorism, Documents, Set. Raymond Picquet & John Lalla (Editors). Library Binding, Trade Cloth. M. E. Sharpe Inc.

Armonk, NY. 2003. 1200p. ISBN:1-56324-807-7, ISBN13: 978-1-56324-807-8. Dewey:303.6/25. LCCN:2002-075983.
Audience: **g,l,u,f.** *Choice, 2004.*

Smith, Paul J. (Editor) **HV6433.A785T47 2004**
Terrorism and Violence in Southeast Asia: Transnational Challenges to States and Regional Stability. Cloth Text. M. E. Sharpe Inc. Armonk, NY. 2004. 288p. ISBN:0-7656-1433-2, ISBN13: 978-0-7656-1433-9. Dewey:303.6/25/0959. LCCN:2004-007994.
Audience: **u,f.** *Choice, 2005.*

Stern, Jessica **BL65.T47S74 2003**
Terror in the Name of God: Why Religious Militants Kill. Trade Cloth. HarperCollins Publishers. New York, NY. 2003. 400p. ISBN:0-06-050532-X, ISBN13: 978-0-06-050532-5. Dewey:303.6/25. LCCN:2003-048508.
Audience: **g,l,u.**

Stohl, Michael (Editor) **HV6431.P64 1988**
The Politics of Terrorism. Ed. 3. Paper over Boards. Marcel Dekker Inc. New York, NY. 1988. 622p. Public Administration and Public Policy Ser., Vol. 33:A Comprehensive Publication Program ISBN:0-8247-7814-6, ISBN13: 978-0-8247-7814-9. Dewey:322.4/2. LCCN:87-027578.
Audience: **g,l,u.**

Stout, Chris E. **HV6431.P798 2002**
[Ebook] The Psychology of Terrorism. E-Book. Greenwood Publishing Group, Inc. Portsmouth, NH. ISBN:0-313-01563-5, ISBN13: 978-0-313-01563-2. Dewey:303.6/25.
Audience: **l,u.** *Choice, 2003.*

Talbott, Strobe & Chanda, Nayan (Editors) **HV6432.A43**
The Age of Terror: America and the World after September 11. Trade Cloth. DIANE Publishing Company. Collingdale, PA. 2003. 232p. ISBN:0-7567-6831-4, ISBN13: 978-0-7567-6831-7. Dewey:973.931.
Audience: **g,l,u,f.** *Choice, 2002.*

Thackrah, J. R. **HV6431**
Dictionary of Terrorism. Ed. 2. Trade Paper. Routledge. New York, NY. 2003. 336p. ISBN:0-415-29821-0, ISBN13: 978-0-415-29821-6. Dewey:303.6/25/03. LCCN:2003-011680.
Audience: **l,u,f.**

United Nations **HV6431**
[Web] Conventions Against Terrorism.
http://www.unodc.org/unodc/terrorism_conventions.html
United Nations. Office on Drugs and Crime.
Audience: **g,l,u,f.**

Wardlaw, Grant **HV6431.W365 1989**
Political Terrorism: Theory, Tactics and Counter-Measures. Ed. 2. Trade Cloth. Cambridge University Press. New York, NY. 1989. 264p. ISBN:0-521-36296-2, ISBN13: 978-0-521-36296-2. Dewey:322.42. LCCN:88-020362.
Audience: **u,f.**

Webel, Charles **HV6431.W42 2004**
Terror, Terrorism, and the Human Condition. Cloth over Boards. Palgrave Macmillan. New York, NY. 2004. 176p. ISBN:1-4039-6161-1, ISBN13: 978-1-4039-6161-7. Dewey:303.6/25. LCCN:2004-049006.
Audience: **u,f.** *Choice, 2005.*

Weinberg, Leonard **HV6431**
Global Terrorism: A Beginner's Guide. Trade Paper. Oneworld Publications. Oxford, 2005. 192p. ISBN:1-85168-358-5, ISBN13: 978-1-85168-358-1. Dewey:303.625.
Audience: **g,l,u.** *Choice, 2005.*

Wilkinson, Paul **HV6431.W564 2001**
Terrorism vs. Democracy: The Liberal State Response. Trade Paper. Routledge. New York, NY. 2000. 272p. Political Violence Ser., Vol. 9 ISBN:0-7146-8165-2, ISBN13: 978-0-7146-8165-8. Dewey:363.3/2. LCCN:00-047530.
Audience: **l,u,f.** *Choice, 2001.*

Williams, Paul L. O.P. **HV6433.M52Q35 2002**
Al-Qaeda: Brotherhood of Terror. Trade Paper. Penguin Group (USA) Inc. New York, NY. 2002. 240p. ISBN:0-02-864352-6, ISBN13: 978-0-02-864352-6. Dewey:303.6/25. LCCN:2001-099421.
Audience: **g,l,u.** *Choice, 2003.*

Wilshire, Bruce **HV6322.7.W55 2004**
Get 'Em All! Kill 'Em!: Genocide, Terrorism, Righteous Communities. Trade Cloth. Lexington Books. Lanham, MD. 2004. 232p. ISBN:0-7391-0873-5, ISBN13: 978-0-7391-0873-4. Dewey:304.6/63. LCCN:2004-016986.
Audience: **u,f.** *Choice, 2005.*

International Relations. Transnational Relations > Globalization

HQ1154
Women Go Global. CD-ROM. United Nations Publications. New York, NY. 2005. ISBN:92-1-130211-0, ISBN13: 978-92-1-130211-0. Dewey:305.42.
Audience: **g,l,u,f.**

Brawley, Mark R. **JZ1318.B73 2003**
The Politics of Globalization: Gaining Perspective, Assessing Consequences. Trade Paper. Broadview Press. Peterborough, ON. 2003. 223p. ISBN:1-55111-280-9, ISBN13: 978-1-55111-280-0. Dewey:327.1. LCCN:2003-446462.
Audience: **l,u.**

CQ Press Staff (Contribution by) **JZ1242.W67 2002**
World at Risk: A Global Issues Sourcebook. Trade Cloth. CQ Press. Washington, DC. 2002. 704p. ISBN:1-56802-707-9, ISBN13: 978-1-56802-707-4. Dewey:300. LCCN:2001-008737.
Audience: **g,l,u.** *Choice, 2002.*

Department of Economic and Social Affairs Staff **HQ796.W63846 2004**
World Youth Report 2003: The Global Situation of Young People. Trade Paper. United Nations Publications. New York, NY. 2003. 426p. ISBN:92-1-130228-5, ISBN13: 978-92-1-130228-8. Dewey:305.235. LCCN:2004-302887.
Audience: **g,l,u,f.** *Choice, 2005.*

Dobkowski, Michael N. & Wallimann, Isidor (Editors) **HB199.C635 1998**
The Coming Age of Scarcity: Preventing Mass Death and Genocide in the Twenty-First Century. Trade Cloth. Syracuse University Press. Syracuse, NY. 1997. 384p. Peace and Conflict Resolution Ser. ISBN:0-8156-2744-0, ISBN13: 978-0-8156-2744-9. Dewey:333.7. LCCN:97-018715.
Audience: **l,u,f.** *Choice, 1998.*

Hall, Rodney Bruce & Biersteker, Thomas J. (Editors) **K250.E46 2002**
The Emergence of Private Authority in Global Governance. Chris Brown, Thomas Biersteker, Phil Cerny, Joseph Grieco, A. J. R. Groom, Richard Higgott, G. John Ikenberry, Caroline Kennedy-Pipe, Steve Lamy & Steve Smith (Contribution by). Trade Paper. Cambridge University Press. New York, NY. 2002. 272p. Cambridge Studies in International Relations, Vol. 85 ISBN:0-521-52337-0, ISBN13: 978-0-521-52337-0. Dewey:340/.115. LCCN:2002-023443.
Audience: **u,f.**

Held, David & McGrew, Anthony G. (Editors) **JZ1318.G56 2003**
The Global Transformations Reader: An Introduction to the Globalization Debate. Ed. 2. Trade Paper. Polity Press. Cambridge, 2003. 624p. ISBN:0-7456-3135-5, ISBN13: 978-0-7456-3135-6. Dewey:303.48/2. LCCN:2002-152351.
Audience: **g,l,u.**

Hirata, Keiko **JQ1681.H575 2002**
Civil Society in Japan: The Growing Role of NGOs in Tokyo's Aid and Development Policy. Cloth over Boards. Palgrave Macmillan. New York, NY. 2002. 272p. ISBN:0-312-23936-X, ISBN13: 978-0-312-23936-7. Dewey:338.91/52. LCCN:2002-023881.
Audience: **u,f.** *Choice, 2003.*

J Kirton, John & I Hajnal, Peter **HC79.E5**
Sustainability Civil Society and International Governance: Local North American and Global Perspectives. Trade Cloth. Ashgate Publishing, Ltd. Aldershot, 2006. 422p. ISBN:0-7546-3884-7, ISBN13: 978-0-7546-3884-1. Dewey:338.927. LCCN:2006-921289.
Audience: **g,l,u.**

Keohane, Robert O. **D2009.K46 2002**
Power and Governance in a Partially Globalized World. Trade Paper. Routledge. New York, NY. 2002. 312p. ISBN:0-415-28819-3, ISBN13: 978-0-415-28819-4. Dewey:327.1/01. LCCN:2002-068317.
Audience: **l,u.**

Nassar, Jamal R. **HV6431.N38 2004**
Globalization and Terrorism: The Migration of Dreams and Nightmares. Book, Other. Rowman & Littlefield Publishers, Inc. Lanham, MD. 2004. 160p. Globalization Ser. ISBN:0-7425-2504-X, ISBN13: 978-0-7425-2504-7. Dewey:303.6/25. LCCN:2004-006795.
Audience: **g,l,u,f.** *Choice, 2005.*

Smith, Jackie & Johnston, Hank **HN17.5.G58 2002**
Globalization and Resistance: Transnational Dimensions of Social Movements. Book, Other. Rowman & Littlefield Publishers, Inc. Lanham, MD. 2002. 264p. ISBN:0-7425-1989-9, ISBN13: 978-0-7425-1989-3. Dewey:303.48/4. LCCN:2002-069691.
Audience: **l,u.**

Suter, Keith **JZ1318**
Global Order and Global Disorder: Globalization and the Nation-State. Trade Cloth. Greenwood Publishing Group, Inc. Portsmouth, NH. 2003. 216p. ISBN:0-275-97388-3, ISBN13: 978-0-275-97388-9. Dewey:327.1. LCCN:2002-070863.
Audience: **l,u.** *Choice, 2004.*

United Nations **HM821**
State of World Population 2005: The Promise of Equality, Gender Equity, Reproductive Health and the Millennium Development Goals. United Nations Population Fund (UNFPA). 2005. ISBN:0-89714-750-2, ISBN13: 978-0-89714-750-7.
Audience: **g,l,u,f.**

United Nations **HQ796**
World Youth Report 2005: Young People Today, and in 2015. United Nations. Department of Economic and Social Affairs. 2005. ISBN:92-1-130244-7, ISBN13: 978-92-1-130244-8.
Audience: **g,l,u,f.**

United Nations, Department of Economic and Social Affairs, Population Division Staff **HB885**
World Population Monitoring, 2003: Population, Education and Development. Trade Paper. United Nations Publications. New York, NY. 2005. 204p. ISBN:92-1-151383-9, ISBN13: 978-92-1-151383-7. Dewey:304.6.
Audience: **g,l,u,f.**

United Nations: Human Settlements Programme **HT151**
The State of the World's Cities 2004/2005: Globalization and Urban Culture. Trade Paper. United Nations Publications. New York, NY. 2005. 216p. ISBN:92-1-131705-3, ISBN13: 978-92-1-131705-3. Dewey:307.76.
Audience: **l,u,f.**

Weinstein, Michael M. **HF1379.G594 2005**
Globalization: What's New. Trade Cloth. Edinburgh University Press. Edinburgh, 2005. 296p. ISBN:0-231-13458-4, ISBN13: 978-0-231-13458-3. Dewey:337. LCCN:2004-058290.
Audience: **u,f.** *Choice, 2005.*

International Relations. Transnational Relations > Globalization > Economic Development. Trade

Aaronson, Susan Ariel **HF1713.A15 2001**
Taking Trade to the Streets: The Lost History of Public Efforts to Shape Globalization. Trade Cloth. University of Michigan Press. Chicago, IL. 2001. 248p. ISBN:0-472-11212-0, ISBN13: 978-0-472-11212-8. Dewey:382. LCCN:2001-027049.
Audience: **l,u.** *Choice, 2002.*

Berthelot, Yves (Editor) **HD82.U57 2003**
Unity and Diversity in Development Ideas: Perspectives from the U. N. Regional Commissions. Trade Paper. Indiana University Press. Bloomington, IN. 2003. 408p. United Nations Intellectual History Project Ser., Vol. 2 ISBN:0-253-21638-9, ISBN13: 978-0-253-21638-0. Dewey:341.7/59. LCCN:2003-009550.
Audience: **l,u.**

Bhagwati, Jagdish N. **HF1359.B499 2004**
In Defense of Globalization. Trade Cloth. Oxford University Press, Inc. New York, NY. 2004. 320p. ISBN:0-19-517025-3, ISBN13: 978-0-19-517025-2. Dewey:337. LCCN:2003-023641.
Audience: **g,l,u,f.** *Choice, 2004.*

Bhagwati, Jagdish N. **HF1455.B48 2000**
The Wind of the Hundred Days: How Washington Mismanaged Globalization. Trade Cloth. MIT Press. Cambridge, MA. 2000.

397p. ISBN:0-262-02495-0, ISBN13: 978-0-262-02495-2. Dewey:337.73. LCCN:00-064596.
Audience: **g,l,u,f.** *Choice, 2001.*

Blyth, Mark **JC574.2.U6B59 2002**
Great Transformations: Economic Ideas and Institutional Change in the Twentieth Century. Trade Paper. Cambridge University Press. New York, NY. 2002. 296p. ISBN:0-521-01052-7, ISBN13: 978-0-521-01052-8. Dewey:320.51309485. LCCN:2002-067685.
Audience: **l,u,f.** *Choice, 2003.*

Chikulo, Bornwell C. & Hope, Kempe Ronald (Editors) **JQ1875.A55C6364 1999**
Corruption and Development in Africa: Lessons from Country Case-Studies. Cloth over Boards. Palgrave Macmillan. New York, NY. 1999. 332p. ISBN:0-312-22387-0, ISBN13: 978-0-312-22387-8. Dewey:364.1/323/096. LCCN:99-018543.
Audience: **l,u.** *Choice, 2000.*

Conybeare, John A. C. **HD9710.A2C65 2003**
Merging Traffic: The Consolidation of the International Automobile Industry. Book, Other. Rowman & Littlefield Publishers, Inc. Lanham, MD. 2003. 192p. ISBN:0-7425-2828-6, ISBN13: 978-0-7425-2828-4. Dewey:338.8/3629222. LCCN:2003-007758.
Audience: **u,f.** *Choice, 2004.*

Das, Dilip K. **HF1379.D373 2003**
The Economic Dimensions of Globalization. Cloth over Boards. Palgrave Macmillan. New York, NY. 2004. 240p. ISBN:1-4039-1895-3, ISBN13: 978-1-4039-1895-6. Dewey:337. LCCN:2003-053277.
Audience: **u,f.** *Choice, 2004.*

Das, Dilip K. **HF1713.D343 2001**
Global Trading System at Crossroads: A Post-Seattle Perspective. Paper over Boards. Routledge. New York, NY. 2001. 192p. Studies in the Modern World Economy, Vol. 33 ISBN:0-415-26015-9, ISBN13: 978-0-415-26015-2. Dewey:382. LCCN:2001-019316.
Audience: **u,f.** *Choice, 2002.*

Dowlah, Caf **HF2580**
Backwaters of Global Prosperity: How Forces of Globalization and GATT/WTO Trade Regimes Contribute to the Marginalization of the World's Poorest Nations. Trade Cloth. Greenwood Publishing Group, Inc. Portsmouth, NH. 2004. 220p. ISBN:0-275-98043-X, ISBN13: 978-0-275-98043-6. Dewey:382/.09172/4. LCCN:2004-011890.
Audience: **l,u.** *Choice, 2005.*

Economic Commission for Africa **HC800.A1**
Economic Report on Africa 2004: Unlocking Africa's Trade Potential. Trade Paper. United Nations Publications. New York, NY. 2004. 228p. ISBN:92-1-125094-3, ISBN13: 978-92-1-125094-7. Dewey:338.96.
Audience: **g,l,u,f.**

Frieden, Jeffry A. **HF1359.F735 2006**
Global Capitalism: Its Fall and Rise in the Twentieth Century. Trade Cloth. W. W. Norton & Company, Inc. New York, NY. 2006. 448p. ISBN:0-393-05808-5, ISBN13: 978-0-393-05808-6. Dewey:337/.09/04. LCCN:2005-024357.
Audience: **l,u,f.**

Greider, William
One World, Ready or Not: The Manic Logic of Global Capitalism. Trade Paper. Simon & Schuster. New York, NY. 1998. 528p. ISBN:0-684-83554-1, ISBN13: 978-0-684-83554-9. Dewey:330.1.
Audience: **g,l,u.**

Hartman, Laura P. (Editor), et al. **HF5549**
Rising above Sweatshops: Innovative Approaches to Global Labor Challenges. Denis G. Arnold & Richard E. Wokutch (Editors). Trade Cloth. Greenwood Publishing Group, Inc. Portsmouth, NH. 2003. 440p. ISBN:1-56720-618-2, ISBN13: 978-1-56720-618-0. Dewey:658.3/009172/4. LCCN:2003-052901.
Audience: **l,u,f.** *Choice, 2004.*

Herman, Barry & United Nations Staff **HG3881.G57535 1999**
Global Financial Turmoil and Reform: A United Nations Perspective. Trade Paper. United Nations University Press. Tokyo, 2004. 472p. Unu Policy Perspectives Ser. ISBN:92-808-1032-4, ISBN13: 978-92-808-1032-5. Dewey:332/.042. LCCN:99-006223.
Audience: **l,u,f.** *Choice, 1999.*

Irwin, Douglas A. **HF1411**
Against the Tide: An Intellectual History of Free Trade. Trade Paper. Princeton University Press. Princeton, NJ. 1997. 278p. ISBN:0-691-05896-2, ISBN13: 978-0-691-05896-2. Dewey:382.7/1/09.
Audience: **u,f.** *Choice, 1996.*

Irwin, Douglas A. **HF1756.I68 2002**
Free Trade under Fire. Cloth Text. Princeton University Press. Princeton, NJ. 2002. 288p. ISBN:0-691-08843-8, ISBN13: 978-0-691-08843-3. Dewey:382/.71. LCCN:2001-043159.
Audience: **g,l,u,f.** *Choice, 2003.*

James, Harold **HF1359.J36 2001**
The End of Globalization: Lessons from the Great Depression. Trade Cloth. Harvard University Press. Cambridge, MA. 2001. 272p. ISBN:0-674-00474-4, ISBN13: 978-0-674-00474-0. Dewey:337. LCCN:00-054157.
Audience: **g,l,u,f.** *Choice, 2001.*

Jolly, Richard **HD82.U18 2004**
[e] UN Contributions to Development Thinking and Practice. E-Book. Indiana University Press. Bloomington, IN. 2004. 320p. United Nations Intellectual History Project Ser. ISBN:0-253-34407-7, ISBN13: 978-0-253-34407-6. Dewey:338.9. LCCN:2003-026468.
Audience: **u,f.** *Choice, 2005.*

Jones, Kent Albert & Jones, Kent **HF1385.J67 2003**
Who's Afraid of the WTO? Trade Cloth. Oxford University Press, Inc. New York, NY. 2004. 248p. ISBN:0-19-516616-7, ISBN13: 978-0-19-516616-3. Dewey:382/.92. LCCN:2003-048292.
Audience: **g,l,u,f.** *Choice, 2004.*

Keohane, Robert O. **HF1359**
After Hegemony: Cooperation and Discord in the World Political Economy. Trade Paper. Princeton University Press. Princeton, NJ. 2005. 312p. ISBN:0-691-12248-2, ISBN13: 978-0-691-12248-9. Dewey:337. LCCN:2004-116492.
Audience: **u,f.** B

Kiggundu, Moses N. **HF1413**
Managing Globalization in Developing Countries and Transition Economies: Building Capacities for a Changing World. Trade Cloth. Greenwood Publishing Group, Inc. Portsmouth, NH. 2002. 360p. ISBN:1-56720-615-8, ISBN13: 978-1-56720-615-9. Dewey:337/.09172/4. LCCN:2002-069694.
Audience: **g,l,u,f.** *Choice, 2003.*

Kohli, Atul, et al. **HC59.7.S7585 2003**
State, Markets, and Just Growth: Development in the Twenty-First Century. Chung-In Moon & George Sorensen (Authors). Trade Paper. United Nations Publications. New York, NY. 2005. 312p. The United Nations in the Twenty-First Century Ser. ISBN:92-808-1076-6, ISBN13: 978-92-808-1076-9. Dewey:330.9172/4. LCCN:2002-154101.
Audience: **l,u,f.** *Choice, 2003.*

Kuttner, Robert **HC106.8**
The End of Laissez-Faire: National Purpose and the Global Economy after the Cold War. Book, Other. University of Pennsylvania Press. Philadelphia, PA. 1992. 320p. ISBN:0-8122-1401-3, ISBN13: 978-0-8122-1401-7. Dewey:338.973/009/048. LCCN:90-005174.
Audience: **l,u.**

Lynn, Barry C. **HD2755.5.L96 2005**
End of the Line: The Rise and Coming Fall of the Global Corporation. Trade Cloth. Doubleday Publishing. New York, NY. 2005. 320p. ISBN:0-385-51024-1, ISBN13: 978-0-385-51024-0. Dewey:338.8/8. LCCN:2005-045573.
Audience: **l,u,f.** *Choice, 2006.*

Moore, Mike **HF1713**
A World Without Walls: Freedom, Development, Free Trade and Global Governance. Trade Cloth. Cambridge University Press. New York, NY. 2003. 304p. ISBN:0-521-82701-9, ISBN13: 978-0-521-82701-0. Dewey:382.71. LCCN:2003-271755.
Audience: **u,f.** *Choice, 2003.*

Nissen, Bruce (Editor) **HD6483.U66 2002**
Unions in a Globalized Environment: Changing Borders, Organizational Boundaries, and Social Roles. Cloth Text. M. E. Sharpe Inc. Armonk, NY. 2002. 296p. ISBN:0-7656-0869-3, ISBN13: 978-0-7656-0869-7. Dewey:331.88/091. LCCN:2001-049525.
Audience: **u,f.** *Choice, 2003, 2002.*

Porter, Michael E. **HD3611.P654 1998**
The Competitive Advantage of Nations. Trade Cloth. Simon & Schuster. New York, NY. 1998. 896p. ISBN:0-684-84147-9, ISBN13: 978-0-684-84147-2. Dewey:338.6/048. LCCN:98-009584.
Audience: **g,u,f.**

Prahalad, C. K. **HD2755.5**
The Fortune at the Bottom of the Pyramid: Eradicating Poverty Through Profits. Trade Paper. Wharton School Publishing. Upper Saddle River, NJ. 2006. 304p. ISBN:0-13-187729-1, ISBN13: 978-0-13-187729-0. Dewey:338.8/881724. LCCN:2005-931851.
Audience: **l,u,f.** *Choice, 2005.*

Rosen, Ellen Israel **HD9940.U4 R666 2002**
Making Sweatshops: The Globalization of the U. S. Apparel Industry. Trade Paper. University of California Press. Berkeley, CA. 2002. 334p. ISBN:0-520-23337-9, ISBN13: 978-0-520-23337-9. Dewey:338.4/7687/0973. LCCN:2001-005493.
Audience: **l,u,f.** *Choice, 2003.*

Runge, C. Ford, et al. **HD9000.6.E53 2003**
Ending Hunger in Our Lifetime: Food Security and Globalization. Philip G. Pardey, Mark W. Rosegrant & Benjamin Senauer (Authors). Trade Paper. International Food Policy Research Institute. Washington, DC. 2003. 312p. ISBN:0-8018-7726-1, ISBN13: 978-0-8018-7726-1. Dewey:338.1/9. LCCN:2003-044709.
Audience: **g,l,u,f.** *Choice, 2004.*

Sampson, Gary P. & Woolcock, Stephen (Editor, Contribution by) **HF1418.5.R4438 2003**
Regionalism, Multilateralism, and Economic Integration: The Recent Experience. Luk Van Langenhoven, Brigid Gavin, Magnus Feldman, Joakim Reiter & Tomas Baert (Contribution by). Trade Paper. United Nations Publications. New York, NY. 2005. 384p. ISBN:92-808-1083-9, ISBN13: 978-92-808-1083-7. Dewey:382/.9. LCCN:2003-010733.
Audience: **u,f.** *Choice, 2004.*

Soros, George **HF1359.S65 2002**
George Soros on Globalization. Trade Cloth. PublicAffairs. New York, NY. 2002. 208p. ISBN:1-58648-125-8, ISBN13: 978-1-58648-125-4. Dewey:337. LCCN:2001-058868.
Audience: **g,l,u,f.** *Choice, 2002.*

Steger, Manfred B. **HF1379.S738 2002**
Globalism: The New Market Ideology. Book, Other. Rowman & Littlefield Publishers, Inc. Lanham, MD. 2001. 224p. ISBN:0-7425-0072-1, ISBN13: 978-0-7425-0072-3. Dewey:337. LCCN:2001-041702.
Audience: **l,u,f.** *Choice, 2002.*

Stiglitz, Joseph E. **HF1418.5.S75 2002**
Globalization and Its Discontents. Trade Cloth. W. W. Norton & Company, Inc. New York, NY. 2003. 192p. ISBN:0-393-05124-2, ISBN13: 978-0-393-05124-7. Dewey:337. LCCN:2002-023148.
Audience: **g,l,u,f.** *Choice, 2002.*

Stiglitz, Joseph E. & Charlton, Andrew **HF1413.S85 2005**
Fair Trade for All: How Trade Can Promote Development. Trade Cloth. Oxford University Press, Inc. New York, NY. 2006. 352p. The Initiative for Policy Dialogue Ser. ISBN:0-19-929090-3, ISBN13: 978-0-19-929090-1. Dewey:382/.3. LCCN:2005-027734.
Audience: **l,u.**

The World Bank **HD82**
World Development Report 2005: Investment Climate, Growth and Poverty. Ed. 2005. Paper Text. World Bank Publications. Washington, DC. 2004. 288p. A World Bank Publication ISBN:0-8213-5682-8, ISBN13: 978-0-8213-5682-1. Dewey:338.9/109051. LCCN:2004-304824.
Audience: **g,l,u,f.**

Toye, J. F. J. & Toye, Richard **JZ4972.T69 2004**
The UN and Global Political Economy: Trade, Finance, and Development. Trade Cloth. Indiana University Press. Bloomington, IN. 2004. 344p. United Nations Intellectual History Project Ser. ISBN:0-253-34411-5, ISBN13: 978-0-253-34411-3. Dewey:337. LCCN:2003-025353.
Audience: **g,l,u,f.** *Choice, 2004.*

United Nations **HF1428**
Trade and Development Report 2005: New Features of Global Interdependence. United Nations. United Nations Conference on Trade and Development. 2005. ISBN:92-1-112673-8, ISBN13: 978-92-1-112673-0.
Audience: **u,f.**

United Nations **HC59**
World Economic and Social Survey 2005: Financing for Development. United Nations. Department of Economic and Social Affairs. 2005. ISBN:92-1-109149-7, ISBN13: 978-92-1-109149-6.
Audience: **u,f.**

United Nations **HF1352**
World Economic Situation and Prospects 2005. United Nations. Department of Economic and Social Affairs. 2005. ISBN:92-1-109148-9, ISBN13: 978-92-1-109148-9.
Audience: **u,f.**

United Nations (UN) **HC59.15**
World Economic and Social Survey: 2004 Supplement: World Economic Situation and Prospects. Trade Paper. United Nations Publications. New York, NY. 2004. 82p. ISBN:92-1-109146-2, ISBN13: 978-92-1-109146-5. Dewey:330.9.
Audience: **g,l,u,f.**

United Nations **HC59.7.L328**
Conference on Trade and Development
The Least Developed Countries Report. Trade Paper. United Nations Publications. New York, NY. 2004. 378p. ISBN:92-1-112581-2, ISBN13: 978-92-1-112581-8. Dewey:330.9172/4.
Audience: **l,u,f.**

United Nations **HD72**
Development Programme Staff
Human Development Report 2005: International Cooperation at a Crossroads: Aid, Trade and Security in an Unequal World. Trade Paper. Oxford University Press, Inc. New York, NY. 2005. 388p. ISBN:0-19-530511-6, ISBN13: 978-0-19-530511-1. Dewey:338.9.
Audience: **g,l,u,f.** *Choice, 2006.*

United Nations, Dept. of **HM651.U53 2005**
Economic and Social Affairs Staff (Contribution by)
World Economic and Social Survey 2004: Trends and Policies in the World Economy. Trade Paper. United Nations Publications. New York, NY. 2004. 186p. ISBN:92-1-109145-4, ISBN13: 978-92-1-109145-8. Dewey:306.4/20905102. LCCN:2005-416785.
Audience: **g,l,u,f.**

Wichterich, Christa **HD6053.W44713 2000**
The Globalized Woman: Reports from a Future of Inequality. Patrick Camiller (Translator). Cloth over Boards. Zed Books, Ltd. London, 2000. 224p. ISBN:1-85649-740-2, ISBN13: 978-1-85649-740-4. Dewey:331.4. LCCN:99-056211.
Audience: **l,u,f.**

Wilson, William W. **HD9005.K66 2002**
Agricultural Trade under CUSTA. Won W. Koo (Editor). Trade Cloth. Nova Science Publishers, Inc. Hauppauge, NY. 2002. 355p. ISBN:1-59033-192-3, ISBN13: 978-1-59033-192-7. Dewey:382/.41/0973. LCCN:2001-059618.
Audience: **u,f.** *Choice, 2003, 2002.*

Wolf, Martin **HF1359.W6534 2004**
Why Globalization Works. Cloth over Boards. Yale University Press. Cumberland, RI. 2004. 416p. ISBN:0-300-10252-6, ISBN13: 978-0-300-10252-9. Dewey:337. LCCN:2004-000475.
Audience: **g,l,u,f.** *Choice, 2004.*

International Relations. Transnational Relations > Globalization > Environmental Development

Andersen, Stephen O. & **QC879.7.A53 2002**
Sarma, K. Madhava
Protecting the Ozone Layer: The United Nations History. Lani Sinclair (Editor). Trade Cloth. Earthscan/James & James. London, 2005. 548p. ISBN:1-85383-905-1, ISBN13: 978-1-85383-905-4. Dewey:363.738/75526. LCCN:2002-005805.
Audience: **g,l,u,f.** *Choice, 2003.*

Barry, John & **GE170.I55 2001**
Frankland, E. Gene (Editors)
International Encyclopedia of Environmental Politics. Paper over Boards. Routledge. New York, NY. 2001. 544p. ISBN:0-415-20285-X, ISBN13: 978-0-415-20285-5. Dewey:363.7/056. LCCN:2001-019754.
Audience: **g,l,f.** *Choice, 2002.*

Chasek, Pamela S. **HC79.E5G5927 2000**
The Global Environment in the Twenty-First Century: Prospects for International Cooperation. Book, Other. United Nations Publications. New York, NY. 2005. 476p. The United Nations System in the Twenty-First Century Ser. ISBN:92-808-1029-4, ISBN13: 978-92-808-1029-5. Dewey:363.7/0526. LCCN:99-050800.
Audience: **g,l,u.** *Choice, 2000.*

Clapp, Jennifer & **HC79.E5C557 2005**
Dauvergne, Peter
Paths to a Green World: The Political Economy of the Global Environment. Trade Cloth. MIT Press. Cambridge, MA. 2005. 336p. ISBN:0-262-03329-1, ISBN13: 978-0-262-03329-9. Dewey:333.7. LCCN:2004-059256.
Audience: **g,l,u,f.** *Choice, 2005.*

Gunter, Michael M. **JZ4841.G86 2004**
Building the Next Ark: How NGOs Work to Protect Biodiversity. Trade Cloth. University Press of New England. Lebanon, NH. 2005. xvii, 252p. ISBN:1-58465-383-3, ISBN13: 978-1-58465-383-7. Dewey:333.95/16. LCCN:2004-013580.
Audience: **l,u.** *Choice, 2005.*

Keohane, Robert O. & **HD75.6.I573 1996**
Levy, Marc A. (Editors)
Institutions for Environmental Aid: Pitfalls and Promise. Trade Paper. MIT Press. Cambridge, MA. 1996. 480p. Global Environmental Accord Ser. ISBN:0-262-61120-1, ISBN13: 978-0-262-61120-6. Dewey:363.7. LCCN:96-002486.
Audience: **u,f.** *Choice, 1997.*

Miller, Clark & **GE300.C48 2001**
Edwards, Paul N. (Editors)
Changing the Atmosphere: Expert Knowledge and Environmental Governance. Trade Cloth. MIT Press. Cambridge, MA. 2001. 375p. Politics, Science and the Environment Ser. ISBN:0-262-13387-3, ISBN13: 978-0-262-13387-6. Dewey:551.6. LCCN:00-069548.
Audience: **u,f.** *Choice, 2002.*

Paehlke, Robert **JC423.P222 2003**
Democracy's Dilemma: Environment, Social Equity, and the Global Economy. Trade Cloth. MIT Press. Cambridge, MA. 2003. 316p. ISBN:0-262-16215-6, ISBN13: 978-0-262-16215-9. Dewey:306.2. LCCN:2002-038071.
Audience: **l,u,f.** *Choice, 2003.*

Rees, Martin **CB161.R38 2004**
Our Final Hour: A Scientist's Warning: How Terror, Error, and Environmental Disaster Threaten Humankind's Future in This Century - On Earth and Beyond. Trade Paper. Basic Books. New York, NY. 2004. 240p. ISBN:0-465-06863-4, ISBN13: 978-0-465-06863-0. Dewey:303.49/09/05. LCCN:2004-556001.
Audience: **g,l,u,f.** *Choice, 2003.*

Smil, Vaclav **HD9502.A2S543 2003**
Energy at the Crossroads: Global Perspectives and Uncertainties. Trade Cloth. MIT Press. Cambridge, MA. 2003. 448p. ISBN:0-262-19492-9, ISBN13: 978-0-262-19492-1. Dewey:333.79. LCCN:2002-045222.
Audience: **l,u,f.** *Choice, 2004.*

Speth, James Gustave (Editor) **GE170.W674 2003**
Worlds Apart: Globalization and the Environment. Cloth Text. Island Press. Washington, DC. 2003. 192p. ISBN:1-55963-998-9, ISBN13: 978-1-55963-998-9. Dewey:363.7/05. LCCN:2003-001904.
Audience: **g,l,u.** *Choice, 2004.*

United Nations Staff **TC405**
Water for People, Water for Life: The United Nations World Water Development Report. Trade Cloth. UNESCO Publishing. Paris, 2003. xxiii + 576p. ISBN:92-3-103881-8, ISBN13: 978-92-3-103881-5. Dewey:363.6/1.
Audience: **g,l,u,f.** *Choice, 2004.*

International Relations. Transnational Relations > Migration

HV640
Forced Migration Online. http://www.forcedmigration.org/ Refugee Studies Centre.
Audience: **g,l,u,f.**

Department of Economic and Social Affairs Staff (Editor) **JV6035**
World Economic and Social Survey, 2004: International Migration. Trade Paper. United Nations Publications. New York, NY. 2005. 272p. ISBN:92-1-109147-0, ISBN13: 978-92-1-109147-2. Dewey:304.8.
Audience: **g,l,u,f.**

Global IDP Survey Staff (Contribution by) **HV640.I516 2002**
Internally Displaced People: A Global Survey. Ed. 2. Trade Cloth. Earthscan Canada. Toronto, ON. 2002. 256p. ISBN:1-85383-953-1, ISBN13: 978-1-85383-953-5. Dewey:325/.21. LCCN:2002-012951.
Audience: **l,u,f.** *Choice, 2003.*

Gorman, Robert F. **HV640.G66 2000**
Historical Dictionary of Refugee and Disaster Relief Organizations. Ed. 2. Trade Cloth. Scarecrow Press, Inc. Lanham, MD. 2000. 416p. Historical Dictionaries of International Organizations Ser. ISBN:0-8108-3774-9, ISBN13: 978-0-8108-3774-4. Dewey:362.87/8/025. LCCN:00-024789.
Audience: **g,l,u,f.** *Choice, 2001, 1995.*

Hansen, Marcus L. **JV6450**
The Atlantic Migration, 1607-1860. Arthur M. Schlesinger Jr. (Foreword by). Trade Paper. Simon Publications, Inc. 2001. 392p. ISBN:1-931313-29-6, ISBN13: 978-1-931313-29-2. Dewey:325.73. LCCN:40-006920.
Audience: **g,l,u,f.**

Hawkins, Freda **JV7225**
Critical Years in Immigration: Canada and Australia Compared, Vol. 2. Ed. 2. Trade Paper. McGill-Queen's University Press. Montreal, PQ. 1991. 408p. McGill-Queen's Studies in Ethnic History ISBN:0-7735-0852-X, ISBN13: 978-0-7735-0852-1. Dewey:325.71.
Audience: **u,f.** *Choice, 1989.*

Helton, Arthur C. **JV6346.H44 2002**
The Price of Indifference: Refugees and Humanitarian Action in the New Century. Trade Cloth. Oxford University Press, Inc. New York, NY. 2002. 328p. ISBN:0-19-925030-8, ISBN13: 978-0-19-925030-1. Dewey:362.87/56. LCCN:2001-058067.
Audience: **l,u,f.**

Hofstetter, Eleanore O. **Z7164**
Women in Global Migration, 1945-2000: A Comprehensive Multidisciplinary Bibliography. Book, Other. Greenwood Publishing Group, Inc. Portsmouth, NH. 2001. 552p. Bibliographies and Indexes in Women's Studies, Vol. 30 ISBN:0-313-31810-7, ISBN13: 978-0-313-31810-8. Dewey:016.3048/082/09045. LCCN:00-068174.
Audience: **l,u,f.** *Choice, 2001.*

IDC: Internal Displacement Monitoring Centre
Internal Displacement: A Global Overview of Trends and Developments in 2005. http://www.internal-displacement.org/8025708F004CFA06/(httpPublications)/07E155A5F6DA0DA6C1257138004691BD?OpenDocument
Audience: **l,u,f.**

International Organization for Migration Staff (Contribution by) **HB1952**
World Migration, 2005: Costs and Benefits of International Migration. Trade Paper. International Organization for Migration (IOM). Washington, DC. 2005. 494p. IOM World Migration Report Ser., Vol. 3 ISBN:92-9068-209-4, ISBN13: 978-92-9068-209-7. Dewey:304.8.
Audience: **l,u,f.**

Karatani, Rieko **KD4050.K37 2002**
Defining British Citizenship: Empire Commonwealth and Modern Britain. Irina Filatova & Valentin Gorodnov (Editors). Paper over Boards. Taylor & Francis Group. Abingdon, 2003. 256p. British Politics and Society Ser. ISBN:0-7146-5336-5, ISBN13: 978-0-7146-5336-5. Dewey:342.41/083. LCCN:2002-026783.
Audience: **u,f.** *Choice, 2003.*

Kraut, Alan M. **JV6450.K7 2001**
The Huddled Masses: The Immigrant in American Society, 1880-1921. Ed. 2. Abraham S. Eisenstadt & John H. Franklin (Editors). Trade Cloth. Harlan Davidson Inc. Wheeling, IL. 2003. 267p. The American History Ser. ISBN:0-88295-934-4,

ISBN13: 978-0-88295-934-4. Dewey:304.8/73/009034. LCCN:00-047505.

Audience: **l,u,f.**

Kushner, Tony & Knox, Katharine **HV640.K58 1999**
Refugees in an Age of Genocide: Global, National and Local Perspectives During the Twentieth Century. Hermann Ouseley (Foreword by). Paper over Boards. Taylor & Francis Group. Abingdon, 1999. 544p. ISBN:0-7146-4783-7, ISBN13: 978-0-7146-4783-8. Dewey:362.87/09/04. LCCN:99-012037.

Audience: **g,l,u,f.** *Choice, 2000.*

Lahav, Gallya **JV7590.L34 2003**
Immigration and Politics in the New Europe: Reinventing Borders. Johan P. Olsen & Andreas Fellésdal (Contribution by). Trade Paper. Cambridge University Press. New York, NY. 2004. 334p. Themes in European Governance Ser. ISBN:0-521-53530-1, ISBN13: 978-0-521-53530-4. Dewey:325.4. LCCN:2003-046131.

Audience: **u,f.** *Choice, 2005.*

Sherman, A. J. **JV7685.J46S55 1994**
Island Refuge: Britain and Refugees from the Third Reich, 1933-1939. Ed. 2. Trade Paper. Taylor & Francis Group. Abingdon, 1994. 304p. ISBN:0-7146-4573-7, ISBN13: 978-0-7146-4573-5. Dewey:940.53/159/0941. LCCN:94-018209.

Audience: **u,f.**

Tastsoglou, Evangelia & Dobrowolsky, Alexandra (Editors) **JV6347**
Women, Migration and Citizenship: Making Local, National and Transnational Connections. Trade Cloth. Ashgate Publishing, Ltd. Aldershot, 2006. 272p. Gender in a Global/Local World Ser. ISBN:0-7546-4379-4, ISBN13: 978-0-7546-4379-1. Dewey:305.48/96914090511. LCCN:2005-034910.

Audience: **l,u,f.**

Taylor, Philip A. M. **JV6450.T37 1971**
The Distant Magnet; European Emigration to the U. S. A. Trade Cloth. Harper & Row Ltd. London, 1971. xvi, 326p. ISBN:0-06-136058-9, ISBN13: 978-0-06-136058-9. Dewey:325.2/4/0973. LCCN:70-162288.

Audience: **l,u,f.**

UN Office for the Coordination of Humanitarian Affairs (UNOCHA)
☐ Relief Web: Policy and Issues.
http://www.reliefweb.int/rw/lib.nsf/doc207?OpenForm&query=3

Audience: **g,l,u,f.**

International Relations. Transnational Relations > Global Health

HD2769
☐ Doctors Without Borders/ Medecins Sans Frontieres.
http://www.doctorswithoutborders.org/home.cfm

Audience: **g,l,u,f.**

HQ792.2
The State of the World's Children 2004: Girls, Education and Development. Trade Cloth. UNICEF (United Nations Children's Fund). New York, NY. 2004. 156p. The State of the World's Children Ser., Vol. 2004 ISBN:92-806-3826-2, ISBN13: 978-92-806-3826-4. Dewey:339.5.

Audience: **g,l,u,f.**

Center for HIV Information
☐ HIV InSite: HIV Policy.
http://hivinsite.ucsf.edu/InSite?page=kb-08

Audience: **g,l,u,f.**

Daulaire, Nils (Editor), et al. **RA441.G5685 2005**
Global Health Leadership and Management. Robert E. Black, William H. Foege & Clarence E. Pearson (Editors), David Rockefeller (Foreword by). Trade Cloth. John Wiley & Sons, Inc. Hoboken, NJ. 2005. 288p. J-B Public Health/Health Services Text Ser. ISBN:0-7879-7153-7, ISBN13: 978-0-7879-7153-3. Dewey:362.1. LCCN:2005-003187.

Audience: **u,f.**

Department of Economic and Social Affairs, Population Division Staff **HB849.53.W669 2004**
World Population to 2300. Trade Paper. United Nations Publications. New York, NY. 2005. 251p. ISBN:92-1-151401-0, ISBN13: 978-92-1-151401-8. Dewey:304.6. LCCN:2005-276782.

Audience: **g,l,u,f.**

Fordham, Graham (Editor) **DA990.U46P395 2002**
A New Look at Thai AIDS: Perspectives from the Margin. Trade Cloth. Berghahn Books, Inc. New York, NY. 2004. 338p. Fertility, Reproduction, and Sexuality Ser., Vol. 4 ISBN:1-57181-519-8, ISBN13: 978-1-57181-519-4. Dewey:614.5/99392/09593. LCCN:2004-053831.

Audience: **u,f.** *Choice, 2005.*

Garrett, Laurie **RA411.G37 2000**
Betrayal of Trust: The Collapse of Global Public Health. Trade Paper. Hyperion Press. New York, NY. 2001. 768p. ISBN:0-7868-8440-1, ISBN13: 978-0-7868-8440-7. Dewey:362.1.

Audience: **g,l,u,f.**

Joint United Nations Programme on HIV/AIDS **RA643.8**
Report on the global AIDS epidemic : 4th global report. UNAIDS. 2004. ISBN:92-9173-355-5, ISBN13: 978-92-9173-355-2.

Audience: **g,l,u,f.**

Kemp, Charles & Rasbridge, Lance **RA418.5.T73K45 2004**
Refugee and Immigrant Health: A Handbook for Health Professionals. Trade Cloth. Cambridge University Press. New York, NY. 2004. 394p. ISBN:0-521-82859-7, ISBN13: 978-0-521-82859-8. Dewey:362.1. LCCN:2003-069744.

Audience: **u,f.**

Marks, Stephen P. **K3570**
Health and Human Rights: Basic International Documents. Trade Paper. Harvard University Press. Cambridge, MA. 2005. 300p. Harvard Series on Health and Human Rights Ser. ISBN:0-674-01809-5, ISBN13: 978-0-674-01809-9. Dewey:341.48.

Audience: **l,u,f.**

Moreno, Jonathan D. (Editor) **R725.5.I5 2003**
In the Wake of Terror: Medicine and Morality in a Time of Crisis. Ford Rowan (Foreword by). Trade Cloth. MIT Press. Cambridge, MA. 2003. 257p. Basic Bioethics Ser. ISBN:0-262-13428-4, ISBN13: 978-0-262-13428-6. Dewey:174/.2. LCCN:2002-043132.
Audience: **l,u,f.** *Choice, 2003.*

Petchesky, Rosalind P. **RA778.P476 2003**
Global Prescriptions: Gendering Health and Human Rights. Cloth over Boards. Zed Books, Ltd. London, 2003. 320p. ISBN:1-84277-004-7, ISBN13: 978-1-84277-004-7. Dewey:362.1/082. LCCN:2002-191072.
Audience: **l,u,f.** *Choice, 2004.*

Twigg, Judyth L. **RA644.A25**
HIV/AIDS in Russia and Eurasia, Vol. 1. Strobe Talbott (Foreword by). Cloth over Boards. Palgrave Macmillan. New York, NY. 2006. 240p. ISBN:1-4039-7057-2, ISBN13: 978-1-4039-7057-2. Dewey:362.196/979200947. LCCN:2006-044763.
Audience: **l,u,f.**

UN Office for the Coordination of Humanitarian Affairs (UNOCHA)
☐ Relief Web: Policy and Issues.
http://www.reliefweb.int/rw/lib.nsf/doc207?OpenForm&query=3
Audience: **g,l,u,f.**

UNAIDS/WHO **RC607.A26**
☐ AIDS Epidemic Update: December 2005.
http://www.unaids.org/epi/2005/doc/report_pdf.asp
Audience: **g,l,u,f.**

United Nations **HB883.5**
World Population Policies 2003. United Nations. Department of Economic and Social Affairs. 2003. ISBN:92-1-151393-6, ISBN13: 978-92-1-151393-6.
Audience: **g,l,u,f.**

United Nations Association Staff **HB884**
State of World Population 2004: The Cairo Consensus at Ten; Population, Reproductive Health and the Global Effort to End Poverty. Trade Paper. United Nations Publications. New York, NY. 2004. 115p. ISBN:0-89714-720-0, ISBN13: 978-0-89714-720-0. Dewey:363.9091724.
Audience: **g,l,u,f.**

Watstein, Sarah & Stratton, Stephen E. **RC606.6.W385 2003**
The Encyclopedia of HIV and AIDS. Ed. 2. Trade Cloth. Facts On File, Inc. New York, NY. 2003. 672p. The Facts on File Library of Health and Living ISBN:0-8160-4808-8, ISBN13: 978-0-8160-4808-3. Dewey:616.97/92/003. LCCN:2002-035220.
Audience: **g,l,u,f.** *Choice, 2004.*

World Health Organization **RA8**
☐ World Health Report.
http://www.who.int/whr/en/
Audience: **g,l,u,f.**

World Health Organization **RA8.A3**
☐ World Health Report 2006: Working Together for Health.
http://www.who.int/whr/2006/en/index.html
World Health Organization.
Audience: **g,l,u,f.**

International Relations. Transnational Relations > Human Rights

Amnesty International
☐ Amnesty International Library.
http://web.amnesty.org/library/engindex
Audience: **g,l,u,f.**

Benhabib, Seyla **JF799.B44 2004**
The Rights of Others: Aliens, Residents and Citizens. Trade Cloth. Cambridge University Press. New York, NY. 2004. 264p. The John Robert Seeley Lectures, Vol. 5 ISBN:0-521-83134-2, ISBN13: 978-0-521-83134-5. Dewey:323.3/291. LCCN:2004-045665.
Audience: **l,u,f.**

Bronner, Stephen Eric **JZ1318.P53 2005**
Planetary Politics: Human Rights, Terror, and Global Society. Book, Other. Rowman & Littlefield Publishers, Inc. Lanham, MD. 2005. 248p. ISBN:0-7425-4198-3, ISBN13: 978-0-7425-4198-6. Dewey:327. LCCN:2004-017766.
Audience: **l,u,f.**

Conde, H. Victor **K3239.6.C66 2004**
A Handbook of International Human Rights Terminology. Ed. 2. Cloth Text. University of Nebraska Press. Lincoln, NE. 2004. 536p. Human Rights in International Perspective Ser., Vol. 8 ISBN:0-8032-1534-7, ISBN13: 978-0-8032-1534-4. Dewey:341.4/8/03. LCCN:2003-067182.
Audience: **l,u,f.** *Choice, 2000.*

Edmundson, William A. **JC571.E42 2004**
An Introduction to Rights. Cloth Text. Cambridge University Press. New York, NY. 2004. 240p. Cambridge Introductions to Philosophy and Law Ser. ISBN:0-521-80398-5, ISBN13: 978-0-521-80398-4. Dewey:323. LCCN:2003-059594.
Audience: **g,l,u.** *Choice, 2005.*

Foot, Rosemary **K3240.F66 2000**
Rights Beyond Borders: The Global Community and the Struggle over Human Rights in China. Trade Paper. Oxford University Press, Inc. New York, NY. 2001. 308p. ISBN:0-19-829776-9, ISBN13: 978-0-19-829776-5. Dewey:341.4/81. LCCN:00-031352.
Audience: **u,f.** *Choice, 2001.*

Forsythe, David P. & McMahon, Patrice C. (Editors) **JC571.H76876 2003**
Human Rights and Diversity: Area Studies Revisited. Trade Cloth. University of Nebraska Press. Lincoln, NE. 2004. 480p. Human Rights in International Perspective Ser., Vol. 7 ISBN:0-8032-2020-0, ISBN13: 978-0-8032-2020-1. Dewey:323. LCCN:2002-156584.
Audience: **u,f.** *Choice, 2004.*

Hanson, Carol R., et al. **K3240.4.H847 1999**
Human Rights: The Essential Reference. Ralph Wilde & Carol Devine (Authors), Hilary Poole (Editor). Cloth Text. Greenwood Publishing Group, Inc. Portsmouth, NH. 1999. 304p. ISBN:1-57356-205-X, ISBN13: 978-1-57356-205-8. Dewey:323. LCCN:99-024395.
Audience: **g.** *Choice, 1999.*

Holzgrefe, J. L. (Author, Editor) **KZ6369**
Humanitarian Intervention: Ethical, Legal and Political Dilemmas. Robert O. Keohane (Editor). Cloth Text. Cambridge

University Press. New York, NY. 2003. 362p. ISBN:0-521-82198-3, ISBN13: 978-0-521-82198-8. Dewey:341.5/84. LCCN:2003-269355.
Audience: **u,f.** *Choice, 2004.*

Horowitz, Shale Asher & Schnabel, Albrecht **JC571.H86 2004**
Human Rights and Societies in Transition: Causes, Consequences, Responses. Trade Paper. United Nations University Press. Tokyo, 2004. 466p. ISBN:92-808-1092-8, ISBN13: 978-92-808-1092-9. Dewey:323. LCCN:2004-004113.
Audience: **u,f.**

Human Rights Watch **JC571**
☐ Human Rights Watch Publications.
http://www.hrw.org/doc/?t=pubs
Audience: **g,l,u,f.**

Loescher, Gil **HV640.3.L64 2001**
The UNHCR and World Politics: A Perilous Path. Trade Paper. Oxford University Press, Inc. New York, NY. 2001. 446p. ISBN:0-19-924691-2, ISBN13: 978-0-19-924691-5. Dewey:362.87/56. LCCN:2001-021839.
Audience: **l,u.**

Marks, Stephen P. **K3570**
Health and Human Rights: Basic International Documents. Trade Paper. Harvard University Press. Cambridge, MA. 2005. 300p. Harvard Series on Health and Human Rights Ser. ISBN:0-674-01809-5, ISBN13: 978-0-674-01809-9. Dewey:341.48.
Audience: **l,u,f.**

Talbott, William **JC571.T1445 2005**
Which Rights Should Be Universal? Trade Cloth. Oxford University Press, Inc. New York, NY. 2005. 232p. ISBN:0-19-517347-3, ISBN13: 978-0-19-517347-5. Dewey:323/.01. LCCN:2004-052064.
Audience: **g,l,u.** *Choice, 2005.*

U.S. Department of State
☐ Country Reports on Human Rights Practices.
http://www.state.gov/g/drl/hr/c1470.htm
Audience: **g,l,u,f.**

UN Office for the Coordination of Humanitarian Affairs (UNOCHA)
☐ Relief Web: Policy and Issues.
http://www.reliefweb.int/rw/lib.nsf/doc207?OpenForm&query=3
Audience: **g,l,u,f.**

UNICEF Staff **HQ792.2**
State of the World's Children 2005: Childhood under Threat. Trade Paper. UNICEF (United Nations Children's Fund). New York, NY. 2005. 158p. ISBN:92-806-3817-3, ISBN13: 978-92-806-3817-2. Dewey:305.2308694.
Audience: **g,l,u,f.**

UNICEF **RA422**
The State of the World's Children 2006: Excluded and Invisible. Patricia Moccia (Editor). Trade Paper. UNICEF (United Nations Children's Fund). New York, NY. 2005. 150p. The State of the World's Children Ser. ISBN:92-806-3916-1, ISBN13: 978-92-806-3916-2. Dewey:614.
Audience: **g,l,u,f.**

United Nations. OHCHR **JC571**
☐ Office of the United Nations High Commissioner for Human Rights Documents.
http://www.ohchr.org/english/docsearch.htm
Audience: **g,l,u,f.**

University of Minnesota Human Rights Center **JC571**
☐ University of Minnesota Human Rights Library.
http://www1.umn.edu/humanrts/
Audience: **g,l,u,f.**

Welch, Claude E. **JC599.A36W45 1995**
Protecting Human Rights in Africa: Roles and Strategies of Non-Governmental Organizations. Trade Cloth. University of Pennsylvania Press. Philadelphia, PA. 1995. 360p. Pennsylvania Studies in Human Rights ISBN:0-8122-3330-1, ISBN13: 978-0-8122-3330-8. Dewey:323/.096. LCCN:95-030107.
Audience: **l,u.** *Choice, 1996.*

Wronka, Joseph **JC571.W96 1998**
Human Rights and Social Policy in the 21st Century: A History of the Idea of Human Rights and Comparison of the United Nations Universal Declaration of Human Rights with United States Federal and State Constitutions. Trade Cloth. University Press of America, Inc. Lanham, MD. 1998. 336p. ISBN:0-7618-1010-2, ISBN13: 978-0-7618-1010-0. Dewey:323/.09. LCCN:97-046436.
Audience: **l,u,f.**

International Relations. Transnational Relations > Humanitarian Assistance

Berry, Nicholas O. **HV568.B47 1997**
War and the Red Cross: The Unspoken Mission. Trade Cloth. Palgrave Macmillan. New York, NY. 1997. 180p. ISBN:0-312-16517-X, ISBN13: 978-0-312-16517-8. Dewey:327.1/72. LCCN:96-048926.
Audience: **g,l,u,f.** *Choice, 1998.*

Bhatia, Michael V. **JZ6368.B48 2003**
War and Intervention: A Global Survey of Peace Operations. Trade Cloth. Kumarian Press, Inc. Bloomfield, CT. 2003. 240p. ISBN:1-56549-165-3, ISBN13: 978-1-56549-165-6. Dewey:341.5. LCCN:2002-156660.
Audience: **g,l,u,f.** *Choice, 2004.*

Gorman, Robert F. & Mihalkanin, Edward S. **JC571.G655 1997**
Historical Dictionary of Human Rights and Humanitarian Organizations. Trade Cloth. Scarecrow Press, Inc. Lanham, MD. 1997. 336p. Historical Dictionaries of International Organizations Ser., No. 12 ISBN:0-8108-3263-1, ISBN13: 978-0-8108-3263-3. Dewey:323/.025. LCCN:96-036583.
Audience: **g,l,u,f.** *Choice, 1997.*

Helton, Arthur C. **JV6346.H44 2002**
The Price of Indifference: Refugees and Humanitarian Action in the New Century. Trade Cloth. Oxford University Press, Inc. New York, NY. 2002. 328p. ISBN:0-19-925030-8, ISBN13: 978-0-19-925030-1. Dewey:362.87/56. LCCN:2001-058067.
Audience: **l,u,f.**

Holzgrefe, J. L. (Author, Editor) **KZ6369**
Humanitarian Intervention: Ethical, Legal and Political Dilemmas. Robert O. Keohane (Editor). Cloth Text. Cambridge University Press. New York, NY. 2003. 362p. ISBN:0-521-82198-3, ISBN13: 978-0-521-82198-8. Dewey:341.5/84. LCCN:2003-269355.
Audience: **u,f.** *Choice, 2004.*

Maynard, Kimberly A. **HV553.M39 1999**
Healing Communities in Conflict: International Assistance in Complex Emergencies. Trade Paper. Columbia University Press. New York, NY. 2002. 280p. ISBN:0-231-11279-3, ISBN13: 978-0-231-11279-6. Dewey:362.8/7526. LCCN:98-046125.
Audience: **l,u,f.** *Choice, 1999.*

Rieff, David **HV639.R54 2003**
A Bed for the Night: Humanitarianism in Crisis. Trade Paper. Simon & Schuster. New York, NY. 2003. 400p. ISBN:0-7432-5211-X, ISBN13: 978-0-7432-5211-9. Dewey:361.2/6. LCCN:2003-283640.
Audience: **g,l,u.**

UN Office for the Coordination of Humanitarian Affairs (UNOCHA)
Relief Web: Policy and Issues.
http://www.reliefweb.int/rw/lib.nsf/doc207?OpenForm&query=3
Audience: **g,l,u,f.**

Welsh, Jennifer M. (Editor) **JZ6369**
Humanitarian Intervention and International Relations. Trade Paper. Oxford University Press, Inc. New York, NY. 2006. 244p. ISBN:0-19-929162-4, ISBN13: 978-0-19-929162-5. Dewey:341.5/84.
Audience: **u,f.**

Wheeler, Nicholas J. **JZ6374**
Saving Strangers: Humanitarian Intervention in International Society. Trade Paper. Oxford University Press, Inc. New York, NY. 2003. 352p. ISBN:0-19-925310-2, ISBN13: 978-0-19-925310-4. Dewey:341.5/84. LCCN:00-037484.
Audience: **l,u,f.**

SOCIOLOGY

This section represents titles approrpiate to the undergraduate study of sociolgy, with some minimal provision for a pre-social work curriculum.

An effort was made to avoid out-of-print sources. Several items from BCL3 were out of print and other titles were clearly dated and were not forwarded to this list.

For new materials added to this section, an attempt was made to cover areas around the world so the list showed an international approach to the subject; much more material seems available on different parts of the world, especial Africa and Asia, which received minimal coverage in BCL3.

Many topics traditionally classified under sociology (e.g. gender, criminology) are treated in separate sections in RCL. Coverage of these topics in this section reflects the extent to which those topics remain a part of the undergraduate sociology curriculum per se.

— Stephen Stratton

HM403
☐ Annual Review of Sociology.
http://arjournals.annualreviews.org/loi/soc
Annual Reviews.
Audience: **u,f.**

HM403
☐ SOCindex.
http://search.epnet.com/login.asp?profile=web&defaultdb=snh
Ebsco Publishing.
Audience: **l,u,f.**

HM403
☐ Sociological Abstracts.
http://www.csa.com/factsheets/socioabs-set-c.php
Cambridge Scientific Abstracts.
Audience: **l,u,f.**

Julian Dierkes **HM571**
☐ SocioLog : Julian Dierkes' Comprehensive Guide to Sociology On-line.
http://www.sociolog.com/
Julian Dierkes.
Audience: **l,u,f.**

University of Surrey **H61.95**
☐ SOSIG : Sociology.
http://sosig.esrc.bris.ac.uk/sociology/
Social Science Information Gateway (Project) ; Economic and Social Research Council (Great Britain) ; Joint Information Systems Committee. ; University of Bristol.; Institute of Learning and Research Technology.
Audience: **l,u,f.**

Principles

Bottomore, Tom **HM22**
Frankfurt School. Ed. 2. Paper over Boards. Routledge. New York, NY. 2003. 96p. Key Sociologists Ser. ISBN:0-415-28538-0, ISBN13: 978-0-415-28538-4. Dewey:300.1.
Audience: **u,f.**

Hughes, Michael & Kroehler, Carolyn J. **HM585 .H84**
Sociology: The Core, with PowerWeb. Ed. 7. Trade Paper. McGraw-Hill Higher Education. Burr Ridge, IL. 2004. 560p. ISBN:0-07-299636-6, ISBN13: 978-0-07-299636-4. Dewey:301.
Audience: **l,u.**

Lemert, Charles **HM585.S66235 2004**
Social Theory: The Multicultural and Classic Readings. Ed. 3. Trade Paper. Westview Press. Boulder, CO. 2004. 704p. ISBN:0-8133-4217-1, ISBN13: 978-0-8133-4217-7. Dewey:301. LCCN:2004-043058.
Audience: **l,u.**

Parsons, Talcott & Turner, Bryan S. **HM585.P372 1999**
The Talcott Parsons Reader. Trade Cloth. Blackwell Publishing, Inc. Malden, MA. 1999. 368p. Reader Ser. ISBN:1-55786-543-4, ISBN13: 978-1-55786-543-4. Dewey:301. LCCN:99-025740.
Audience: **l,u,f.**

Ridener, Larry E. **HM478**
☐ Dead Sociologists' Society.
http://www2.pfeiffer.edu/~lridener/DSS/DEADSOC.HTML
Larry E. Ridener ; Radford University.
Audience: **g,l.**

Smelser, Neil J. **HM51.S634 1995**
Sociology. Ed. 5. Trade Paper. Prentice Hall PTR. Upper Saddle River, NJ. 1994. 464p. ISBN:0-13-063835-8, ISBN13: 978-0-13-063835-9. Dewey:301. LCCN:94-018607.
Audience: **l.** *Choice, 1995.*

Principles > Teaching/Communicating

Campbell, Frederick L. (Editor), et al. **HM45.T37 1985**
Teaching Sociology: The Quest for Excellence. Hubert M. Blalock Jr. & Reece McGee (Editors). Book, Other. Rowman & Littlefield Publishers, Inc. Lanham, MD. 2006. 256p. ISBN:0-8304-1097-X, ISBN13: 978-0-8304-1097-2. Dewey:301/.07. LCCN:84-001107.
Audience: **u,f.**

Du Bois, William & Wright, R. Dean **HN29.5.D8 2001**
Applying Sociology: Making a Better World. Allyn and Bacon Editorial Staff (Editor). Trade Paper. Allyn & Bacon, Inc. Boston, MA. 2000. 272p. ISBN:0-205-30616-0, ISBN13: 978-0-205-30616-9. Dewey:301. LCCN:00-044769.
Audience: **l,u,f.**

Glassner, Barry & Hertz, Rosanna (Editors) **HM578.N7O97 2003**
Our Studies, Ourselves: Sociologists' Lives and Work. Trade Cloth. Oxford University Press, Inc. New York, NY. 2003. 296p. ISBN:0-19-514661-1, ISBN13: 978-0-19-514661-5. Dewey:301/.07/207. LCCN:2002-151655.
Audience: **u,f.** *Choice, 2004.*

Langton, Phyllis & Kammerer, Dianne **HN29.5.L36 2004**
Practicing Sociology in the Community: A Student's Guide. Trade Paper. Prentice Hall PTR. Upper Saddle River, NJ. 2004. 168p. ISBN:0-13-042019-0, ISBN13: 978-0-13-042019-0. Dewey:301. LCCN:2004-014152.
Audience: **l,u,f.**

Mullins **H91**
Guide to Writing and Publishing in the Social and Behavioral Sciences Cloth. Ed. 99. Trade Cloth. John Wiley & Sons, Inc. Hoboken, NJ. 1977. 431p. ISBN:0-471-62420-9, ISBN13: 978-0-471-62420-2. Dewey:808/.0663021. LCCN:77-001153.
Audience: **g,l,u.** B

Ostrow, James (Editor), et al. **HM45.C84 1999**
Cultivating the Sociological Imagination: Concepts and Models for Service-Learning in Sociology. Garry Hesser & Sandra Enos (Editors). Perfect. American Association for Higher Education. Washington, DC. 1999. 244p. AAHE's Series on Service-Learning in the Disciplines, Vol. 15 ISBN:1-56377-017-2, ISBN13: 978-1-56377-017-3. Dewey:301/.071/1. LCCN:2001-269338.
Audience: **u,f.**

Ruggiero, Vincent R. **HM45.R84 1996**
A Guide to Sociological Thinking. Trade Cloth. SAGE Publications, Inc. Thousand Oaks, CA. 1995. 150p. ISBN:0-8039-5741-6, ISBN13: 978-0-8039-5741-1. Dewey:302. LCCN:95-039046.
Audience: **g,l.**

Social Science Research and Instructional Council, California State University. **H61.95**
Teaching Resources Depository (TRD).
http://www.ssric.org/trd
California State University. Social Science Research and Instructional Council (SSRIC)..
Audience: **l,u,f.**

Principles > Dictionaries and Encyclopedias

HQ772
Gale Encyclopedia of Childhood and Adolescence. Ed. 2. Trade Cloth. Thomson Gale. Farmington Hills, MI. 2005. ISBN:0-7876-3640-1, ISBN13: 978-0-7876-3640-1. Dewey:305.231/03.
Audience: **g,l.**

HA202
Historical Statistics of the United States.
http://hsus.cambridge.org/
Cambridge University Press.
Audience: **g,l,u,f.**

Alcock, Peter (Editor), et al. **HN17.5.B57 2002**
Blackwell Dictionary of Social Policy. Angus Erskine & Margaret May (Editors). Trade Paper. Blackwell Publishing, Inc. Malden, MA. 2002. 304p. ISBN:0-631-21847-5, ISBN13: 978-0-631-21847-0. Dewey:361.6103. LCCN:2002-066642.
Audience: **g,l.** *Choice, 2003.*

Andermahr, Sonya, et al. **HQ1190.A53 1997**
A Glossary of Feminist Theory. Terry Lovell & Carol Wolkowitz (Authors). Cloth Text. Oxford University Press, Inc. New York, NY. 1997. 356p. An Arnold Publication Ser. ISBN:0-340-59662-7, ISBN13: 978-0-340-59662-3. Dewey:305.42/01. LCCN:97-003800.
Audience: **g,l.**

Anderson, James F., et al. **HV7411 .C74 2002**
Criminal Justice and Criminology: Concepts and Terms. Nancie Mangels, Adam Langsam & Laronistine Dyson (Authors). Trade Paper. University Press of America, Inc. Lanham, MD. 2002. 374p. ISBN:0-7618-2224-0, ISBN13: 978-0-7618-2224-0. Dewey:364.03.
Audience: **g,l.** *Choice, 2002.*

Anderson, Margo J. (Editor) **HA37.U55E53 2000**
Encyclopedia of the U. S. Census. Trade Cloth. CQ Press. Washington, DC. 2000. 424p. ISBN:1-56802-428-2, ISBN13: 978-1-56802-428-8. Dewey:304.6/07/23. LCCN:00-030522.
Audience: **g,l,u,f.** *Choice, 2001.*

Armstrong, Gordon M. **HV6789**
Crime and the Justice System in America: An Encyclopedia. Frank M. Schmalleger (Editor). Cloth Text. Greenwood Publishing Group, Inc. Portsmouth, NH. 1997. 312p. ISBN:0-313-29409-7, ISBN13: 978-0-313-29409-9. Dewey:364/.0973. LCCN:96-010748.
Audience: **g,l.** *Choice, 1998.*

Baer, Judith A. (Editor) **HQ766**
Historical and Multicultural Encyclopedia of Women's Reproductive Rights in the United States. Cloth Text. Greenwood Publishing Group, Inc. Portsmouth, NH. 2002. 272p. ISBN:0-313-30644-3, ISBN13: 978-0-313-30644-0. Dewey:363.9/6/097303. LCCN:2001-037781.
Audience: **g,l.** *Choice, 2002.*

Bailey, William G. (Editor) **HV7901.E53 1995**
Encyclopedia of Police Science. Ed. 2. Library Binding. Garland Publishing, Inc. New York, NY. 1995. 888p. Reference Library of the Humanities, Vol. 1729 ISBN:0-8153-1331-4, ISBN13: 978-0-8153-1331-1. Dewey:363.2/03. LCCN:94-046828.
Audience: **g,l,u.** *Choice, 1995.*

Balter, Lawrence & McCall, Robert B. **HQ755.8.P3783 2000**
Parenthood in America: An Encyclopedia. E-Book. ABC-CLIO, Inc. Santa Barbara, CA. 2002. xxxiii, 745p. The American Family Ser. ISBN:1-57607-387-4, ISBN13: 978-1-57607-387-2. Dewey:306.85. LCCN:00-011782.
Audience: **g,l.** *Choice, 2001.*

Bardis, Panos D. **HM17**
Dictionary of Quotations in Sociology. Cloth Text. Greenwood Publishing Group, Inc. Portsmouth, NH. 1985. 356p. ISBN:0-313-23778-6, ISBN13: 978-0-313-23778-2. Dewey:301/.03/21. LCCN:85-000943.
Audience: **g,l,u,f.**

Barker, Chris **HM623**
The SAGE Dictionary of Cultural Studies. Paper Text. SAGE Publications, Inc. Thousand Oaks, CA. 2004. 240p. ISBN:0-7619-7341-9, ISBN13: 978-0-7619-7341-6. Dewey:306/.03. LCCN:2003-115420.
Audience: **g,l,u,f.**

Borgatta, Edgar F. & Montgomery, Rhonda J. V. (Editors) **HM425.E5 2000**
Encyclopedia of Sociology, Set. Ed. 2. Trade Cloth. Thomson Gale. Farmington Hills, MI. 2000. xxxix, 3481p. ISBN:0-02-864853-6, ISBN13: 978-0-02-864853-8. Dewey:301/.03. LCCN:00-028402.
Audience: **g,l,u,f.** *Choice, 2001, 1992.*

Boudon, Raymond & Bourricaud, Francois **HM17.B6813 1989**
A Critical Dictionary of Sociology. Peter Hamilton (Translator, Selected by). Trade Cloth. University of Chicago Press. Chicago, IL. 1990. 452p. ISBN:0-226-06728-9, ISBN13: 978-0-226-06728-5. Dewey:301/.03. LCCN:89-004868.
Audience: **g,l,u,f.**

Brooker, Peter **HM101.B775 2003**
A Glossary of Cultural Theory. Ed. 2. Trade Paper. Oxford University Press, Inc. New York, NY. 2003. 312p. An Arnold Publication ISBN:0-340-80701-6, ISBN13: 978-0-340-80701-9. Dewey:306.014.
Audience: **g,l.**

Bryant, Clifton D. (Editor) **HV6017.E53 2001**
Encyclopedia of Criminology and Deviant Behaviour, Set. Paper over Boards. Brunner-Routledge. Philadelphia, PA. 2000. 3000p. ISBN:1-56032-772-3, ISBN13: 978-1-56032-772-1. Dewey:364/.03. LCCN:00-058558.
Audience: **g,l,u,f.**

Calhoun, Craig (Editor) **H41.D53 2001**
Dictionary of the Social Sciences. Trade Cloth. Oxford University Press, Inc. New York, NY. 2002. 582p. ISBN:0-19-512371-9, ISBN13: 978-0-19-512371-5. Dewey:300/.3. LCCN:00-068151.
Audience: **g,l,u.** *Choice, 2002.*

Cayton, Mary K. (Editor), et al. **HN57.E58 1993**
Encyclopedia of American Social History, Set. Elliot J. Gorn & Peter W. Williams (Editors). Trade Cloth. Thomson Gale. Farmington Hills, MI. 1993. 2653p. ISBN:0-684-19246-2, ISBN13: 978-0-684-19246-8. Dewey:301/.0973. LCCN:92-010577.
Audience: **g,l.** *Choice, 1993.*

Champion, Dean John **HV6017**
The American Dictionary of Criminal Justice: Key Terms and Major Court Cases. Ed. 3. Trade Cloth. Scarecrow Press, Inc. Lanham, MD. 2004. 456p. ISBN:0-8108-5406-6, ISBN13: 978-0-8108-5406-2. Dewey:364/.03. LCCN:2004-042836.
Audience: **g,l.**

Cockerham, William C. & Ritchey, Ferris J. **RA418**
Dictionary of Medical Sociology. Cloth Text. Greenwood Publishing Group, Inc. Portsmouth, NH. 1997. 200p. ISBN:0-313-29269-8, ISBN13: 978-0-313-29269-9. Dewey:306.4/61/03. LCCN:96-036575.
Audience: **g,l,u.** *Choice, 1997.*

Deutsch, Eliot, et al. **HM435.C53 2002**
Classical Sociological Theory. Ron Bontekoe, James Moody, Steven Pfaff, Kathryn E. Schmidt & Indermohan Virk (Authors). Trade Cloth. Blackwell Publishing, Inc. Malden, MA. 2002. 456p. Readers in Sociology Ser., Vol. 9 ISBN:0-631-21347-3, ISBN13: 978-0-631-21347-5. Dewey:301/.01. LCCN:2001-043998.
Audience: **g,l.**

Douglas, Ian (Editor) **GE10**
Encyclopedia of Global Environmental Change, Causes and Consequences of Global Environmental Change, Vol. 3. Trade Cloth. John Wiley & Sons, Inc. Hoboken, NJ. 2003. 688p. ISBN:0-470-85362-X, ISBN13: 978-0-470-85362-7. Dewey:363.7003.
Audience: **g,l,u,f.**

Dressler, Joshua (Editor) **HV6017.E52 2002**
Encyclopedia of Crime and Justice, Set. Ed. 2. Thomson Gale Staff (Contribution by). Trade Cloth. Thomson Gale. Farmington Hills, MI. 2001. 1780p. ISBN:0-02-865319-X, ISBN13: 978-0-02-865319-8. Dewey:364/.03. LCCN:2001-042707.
Audience: **g,l,u.** *Choice, 2002.*

Eadie, Jo **HQ23**
Sexuality: A Glossary. Trade Paper. Oxford University Press, Inc. New York, NY. 2004. 304p. A Hodder Arnold Publication ISBN:0-340-80676-1, ISBN13: 978-0-340-80676-0. Dewey:306.7/03. LCCN:2004-484958.
Audience: **g,l.**

Edwards, Richard L. (Editor) **HV35**
Encyclopedia of Social Work. Ed. 19. Trade Cloth. National Association of Social Workers/N A S W Press. Washington, DC. 1995. 4646p. ISBN:0-87101-255-3, ISBN13: 978-0-87101-255-5. Dewey:361.303.
Audience: **u,f.** *Choice, 1995.*

Edwards, Richard L. (Editor) **HV35**
Encyclopedia of Social Work, 1997 Supplement. Ed. 19. Trade Paper. National Association of Social Workers/N A S W Press. Washington, DC. 1997. 428p. ISBN:0-87101-277-4, ISBN13: 978-0-87101-277-7. Dewey:361.303.
Audience: **u,f.**

Elliott, Anthony & Ray, Larry (Editors) **H61.K473 2002**
Key Contemporary Social Theorists. Trade Paper. Blackwell Publishing, Inc. Malden, MA. 2002. 336p. ISBN:0-631-21972-2, ISBN13: 978-0-631-21972-9. Dewey:300/.1. LCCN:2001-007499.
Audience: **g,l,u,f.** *Choice, 2003.*

English, Richard A. (Editor) **HV91**
Encyclopedia of Social Work: Supplement 2003. Ed. 19. Trade Paper. National Association of Social Workers/N A S W Press. Washington, DC. 2003. 236p. ISBN:0-87101-353-3, ISBN13: 978-0-87101-353-8. Dewey:361.3/0973.
Audience: **u,f.**

Evans, Glen & Farberow, Norman L. **HV6545.E87 2003**
The Encyclopedia of Suicide. Ed. 2. Trade Cloth. Facts On File, Inc. New York, NY. 2003. 368p. Library of Health and Living Ser. ISBN:0-8160-4525-9, ISBN13: 978-0-8160-4525-9. Dewey:362.2/8/03. LCCN:2002-027166.
Audience: **g,l,u.** *Choice, 2003.*

Francoeur, Robert T. (Editor), et al. **HQ21.I68 2003**
The Continuum Complete International Encyclopedia of Sexuality. Raymond J. Noonan & Martha Cornog (Editors). Trade Cloth. Continuum International Publishing Group, Ltd. London, 2003. 1450p. ISBN:0-8264-1488-5, ISBN13: 978-0-8264-1488-5. Dewey:306.7/03. LCCN:2003-006391.
Audience: **g,l,u,f.** *Choice, 2004.*

Johnson, Allan G. **HM425.J64 2000**
The Blackwell Dictionary of Sociology: A User's Guide to Sociological Language. Ed. 2. Book, Other. Blackwell Publishing, Inc. Malden, MA. 2000. 432p. ISBN:0-631-21680-4, ISBN13: 978-0-631-21680-3. Dewey:301/.03. LCCN:99-049053.
Audience: **g,l,u.** *Choice, 2000.*

Kausler, Donald H. & Kausler, Barry C. **HQ1064.U5K39 2001**
The Graying of America: An Encyclopedia of Aging, Health, Mind and Behavior. Ed. 2. Trade Cloth. University of Illinois Press. Champaign, IL. 2001. 496p. ISBN:0-252-02635-7, ISBN13: 978-0-252-02635-5. Dewey:305.26/03. LCCN:00-011202.
Audience: **g,l.** *Choice, 2001, 1997.*

Kempf-Leonard, Kimberly (Editor-In-Chief) **H62**
Encyclopedia of Social Measurement, Set. Trade Cloth. Elsevier Science & Technology Books. Saint Louis, MO. 2004. 3000p. ISBN:0-12-443890-3, ISBN13: 978-0-12-443890-3. Dewey:300.7/2.
Audience: **u,f.** *Choice, 2005.*

Kimmel, Michael (Editor) **HM585.C59 2007**
Classical Social Theory. Ed. 2. Trade Paper. Oxford University Press, Inc. New York, NY. 2006. 464p. ISBN:0-19-518785-7, ISBN13: 978-0-19-518785-4. Dewey:301. LCCN:2006-040136.
Audience: **g,l.**

Kushner, Harvey W. **HV6431.K883 2003**
Encyclopedia of Terrorism. Trade Cloth. SAGE Publications, Inc. Thousand Oaks, CA. 2002. 552p. ISBN:0-7619-2408-6, ISBN13: 978-0-7619-2408-1. Dewey:303.6/25/03. LCCN:2002-015938.
Audience: **g,l,u.** *Choice, 2003.*

Levinson, David (Editor) **HV4493**
Encyclopedia of Homelessness. Trade Cloth. SAGE Publications, Inc. Thousand Oaks, CA. 2004. 928p. ISBN:0-7619-2751-4, ISBN13: 978-0-7619-2751-8. Dewey:362.5/0973/03. LCCN:2004-009279.
Audience: **g,l,u.** *Choice, 2005.*

Macmillan Library Reference Staff **HV5804.E53 2001**
Encyclopedia of Drugs, Alcohol and Addictive Behavior, Set. Ed. 2. Trade Cloth. Thomson Gale. Farmington Hills, MI. 2000. lx, 1863p. ISBN:0-02-865541-9, ISBN13: 978-0-02-865541-3. Dewey:362.29/03. LCCN:00-046068.
Audience: **g,l,u,f.** *Choice, 2001.*

Macmillan Library Reference Staff **HQ1073.M33 2002**
Macmillan Encyclopedia of Death and Dying, Set. Trade Cloth. Thomson Gale. Farmington Hills, MI. 2002. 1000p. ISBN:0-02-865689-X, ISBN13: 978-0-02-865689-2. Dewey:306.9. LCCN:2002-005809.
Audience: **g,l,u,f.** *Choice, 2003.*

Miller, J. Mitchell & Wright, Richard A. Jr. (Editors) **HV6017.E5295 2005**
Encyclopedia of Criminology. Ed. 3. Library Binding. Routledge. New York, NY. 2005. 1904p. ISBN:1-57958-387-3, ISBN13: 978-1-57958-387-3. Dewey:364/.03. LCCN:2004-004861.
Audience: **g,l,u,f.** *Choice, 2005.*

Morris, James M. & Kross, Andrea L. **HX806.M626 2004**
Historical Dictionary of Utopianism. Trade Cloth. Scarecrow Press, Inc. Lanham, MD. 2004. 432p. Historical Dictionaries of Religions, Philosophies, and Movements Ser., No. 51 ISBN:0-8108-4912-7, ISBN13: 978-0-8108-4912-9. Dewey:335/.02/03. LCCN:2003-023551.
Audience: **g,l,u.** *Choice, 2004.*

Ness, Immanuel (Editor) **HN57.E594 2004**
Encyclopedia of American Social Movements. Library Binding, Trade Cloth. M. E. Sharpe Inc. Armonk, NY. 2004. 1,864p. ISBN:0-7656-8045-9, ISBN13: 978-0-7656-8045-7. Dewey:303.48/4/097303. LCCN:2002-042613.
Audience: **g,l,u,f.** *Choice, 2005.*

Ness, Immanuel & Ciment, James **HB871.N43 1999**
The Encyclopedia of Global Population and Demographics, Two-Vol. Set. CD-ROM, Library Binding, Trade Cloth. M. E. Sharpe Inc. Armonk, NY. 1998. 984p. ISBN:1-56324-710-0, ISBN13: 978-1-56324-710-1. Dewey:304.6/03. LCCN:98-046436.
Audience: **g,l,u,f.** *Choice, 1999.*

Petersen, William & Petersen, Renee **HB849**
Dictionary of Demography: Terms, Concepts, and Institutions. Cloth Text. Greenwood Publishing Group, Inc. Portsmouth, NH. 1986. 1772p. ISBN:0-313-24134-1, ISBN13: 978-0-313-24134-5. Dewey:304.6/03/21. LCCN:83-012571.
Audience: **g,l,u,f.**

Restivo, Sal P. **HM846.S43 2005**
Science, Technology, and Society: An Encyclopedia. Trade Cloth. Oxford University Press, Inc. New York, NY. 2005. 726p. ISBN:0-19-514193-8, ISBN13: 978-0-19-514193-1. Dewey:306.4/5. LCCN:2004-031121.
Audience: **g,l,u,f.** *Choice, 2005.*

Ritzer, George (Editor) **HM425.E47 2004**
Encyclopedia of Social Theory. Trade Cloth. SAGE Publications, Inc. Thousand Oaks, CA. 2004. 1056p. ISBN:0-7619-2611-9, ISBN13: 978-0-7619-2611-5. Dewey:301/.01. LCCN:2004-003251.
Audience: **g,l,u,f.** *Choice, 2005.*

Siegel, Jay A. (Editor), et al. **HV8073.E517 2000**
Encyclopedia of Forensic Sciences, Set. Pekka J. Saukko & Geoffrey C. Knupfer (Editors). Trade Cloth. Elsevier Science & Technology Books. Saint Louis, MO. 2000. 1440p. ISBN:0-12-227215-3, ISBN13: 978-0-12-227215-8. Dewey:363.2503. LCCN:99-067362.
Audience: **g,l,u,f.** *Choice, 2001.*

Sifakis, Carl **HV9471.S54 2002**
The Encyclopedia of American Prisons. Trade Cloth. Facts On File, Inc. New York, NY. 2002. 336p. Facts on File Crime Library ISBN:0-8160-4511-9, ISBN13: 978-0-8160-4511-2. Dewey:365.973. LCCN:2002-022675.
Audience: **g,l.** *Choice, 2003.*

Smelser, Neil J. & Baltes, Paul B. **H41.I58 2001**
International Encyclopedia of Social and Behavioral Sciences. Trade Cloth. Elsevier Science & Technology Books. Saint Louis, MO. 2001. 17500p. ISBN:0-08-043076-7, ISBN13: 978-0-08-043076-8. Dewey:300/.3. LCCN:2001-044791.
Audience: **g,l,u,f.** *Choice, 2002.*

Swatos, William H. **BL60.E53 1998**
Encyclopedia of Religion and Society. Trade Cloth. AltaMira Press. Walnut Creek, CA. 1998. 604p. ISBN:0-7619-8956-0, ISBN13: 978-0-7619-8956-1. Dewey:306.6/03. LCCN:97-033724.
Audience: **g,l.**

Thompson, Kenneth **HM17.T56 1996**
Key Quotations in Sociology. Trade Paper. Routledge. New York, NY. 1996. 224p. ISBN:0-415-05761-2, ISBN13: 978-0-415-05761-5. Dewey:301. LCCN:95-019335.
Audience: **g,l,u,f.**

Tierney, Helen (Editor) **HQ1115**
Women's Studies Encyclopedia. Cloth Text. Greenwood Publishing Group, Inc. Portsmouth, NH. 1999. 1640p. ISBN:0-313-29620-0, ISBN13: 978-0-313-29620-8. Dewey:305.403. LCCN:98-014236.
Audience: **g,l,u,f.** *Choice, 2000.*

Timmerman, Peter (Editor) **GE10**
Encyclopedia of Global Environmental Change, Social and Economic Dimensions of Global Environmental Change, Vol. 5. Trade Cloth. John Wiley & Sons, Inc. Hoboken, NJ. 2003. 688p. ISBN:0-470-85364-6, ISBN13: 978-0-470-85364-1. Dewey:363.7003.
Audience: **g,l,u,f.**

Turpin, Jennifer (Editor) **HM886.E53 1999**
Encyclopedia of Violence, Peace and Conflict, Set. Lester R. Kurtz (Editor-In-Chief). Trade Cloth. Elsevier Science & Technology Books. Saint Louis, MO. 1999. 2598p. ISBN:0-12-227010-X, ISBN13: 978-0-12-227010-9. Dewey:303.6/03. LCCN:99-060408.
Audience: **g,l,u,f.** *Choice, 2000.*

U.S. Census Bureau **HA202**
Statistical Abstract of the United States. http://www.census.gov/statab/www/
Audience: **g,l,u,f.**

Vogt, W. Paul **HA17.V64 2005**
Dictionary of Statistics and Methodology: A Nontechnical Guide for the Social Sciences. Ed. 3. Cloth Text. SAGE Publications, Inc. Thousand Oaks, CA. 2005. 376p. ISBN:0-7619-8854-8, ISBN13: 978-0-7619-8854-0. Dewey:300/.1/5195. LCCN:2004-027624.
Audience: **g,l,u,f.** *Choice, 2005.*

Walter, Lynn & Desai, Manisha (Editors) **HQ1726.G74 2003**
The Greenwood Encyclopedia of Women's Issues Worldwide. Trade Cloth. Greenwood Publishing Group, Inc. Portsmouth, NH. 2003. 380p. ISBN:0-313-32087-X, ISBN13: 978-0-313-32087-3. Dewey:305.42/095. LCCN:2003-048525.
Audience: **g,l,u,f.** *Choice, 2004.*

Worell, Judith (Editor) **HQ1115.E43 2001**
Encyclopedia of Women and Gender: Sex Similarities and Differences and the Impact of Society on Gender, Vol. 1. Trade Cloth. Elsevier Science & Technology Books. Saint Louis, MO. 2001. xvii, 1256p. ISBN:0-12-227246-3, ISBN13: 978-0-12-227246-2. Dewey:305.4/03. LCCN:2001-088812.
Audience: **g,l,u,f.**

Worell, Judith (Editor) **HQ1115.E43 2001**
Encyclopedia of Women and Gender: Sex Similarities and Differences and the Impact of Society on Gender, Vol. 2. Trade Cloth. Elsevier Science & Technology Books. Saint Louis, MO. 2001. xvii, 1256p. ISBN:0-12-227247-1, ISBN13: 978-0-12-227247-9. Dewey:305.4/03. LCCN:2001-088812.
Audience: **g,l,u,f.**

Principles > Theories

Alexander, Jeffrey C. **HM24.A465 1982**
Theoretical Logic in Sociology. Trade Cloth. University of California Press. Berkeley, CA. 1982. ISBN:0-520-03062-1, ISBN13: 978-0-520-03062-6. Dewey:301. LCCN:75-017305.
Audience: **l,u,f.** B

Bell, Daniel **HM24.B386**
The Winding Passage: Essays and Sociological Journeys, 1960-1980. Trade Cloth. University Press of America, Inc. Lanham, MD. 1984. 394p. ISBN:0-8191-4142-9, ISBN13: 978-0-8191-4142-2. Dewey:301.
Audience: **l,u,f.** B

Berger, Peter L. **HM51 .B45**
Invitation to Sociology: A Humanistic Perspective. Trade Paper. Doubleday Publishing. New York, NY. 1963. 208p. ISBN:0-385-06529-9, ISBN13: 978-0-385-06529-0. Dewey:301. LCCN:63-008758.
Audience: **l,u.** B

Caccamo, Rita **HN80.M85**
Back to Middletown: Three Generations of Sociological Reflections. Trade Paper. Stanford University Press. Palo Alto, CA. 2001. 176p. ISBN:0-8047-3846-7, ISBN13: 978-0-8047-3846-0. Dewey:306/.09772/65. LCCN:99-016822.
Audience: **l,u,f.**

Comte, Auguste **HM0055.C72**
Early Essays on Social Philosophy. Henry Dix Hutton (Translator). Trade Paper. Books on Demand. Ann Arbor, MI. 358p. ISBN:0-598-89967-7, ISBN13: 978-0-598-89967-5. Dewey:194.8. LCCN:12-016153.
Audience: **l,u,f.**

Coser, Lewis A. & Rosenberg, B. (Editors) **HM51**
Sociological Theory: A Book of Readings. Ed. 5. Paper Text. Waveland Press, Inc. Prospect Heights, IL. 1989. 603p. ISBN:0-88133-457-X, ISBN13: 978-0-88133-457-9. Dewey:301.08.
Audience: **l,u.**

Dahrendorf, Ralf **HM51 .D25**
Essays in the Theory of Society. Trade Cloth. Stanford University Press. Palo Alto, CA. 1968. x, 300p. ISBN:0-8047-0286-1, ISBN13: 978-0-8047-0286-7. Dewey:301. LCCN:67-026526.
Audience: **l,u,f.** B

Ekeh, Peter P. **HM24.E37**
Social Exchange Theory: The Two Traditions. Trade Cloth. Harvard University Press. Cambridge, MA. 1974. 252p. ISBN:0-674-81201-8, ISBN13: 978-0-674-81201-7. Dewey:301/.01. LCCN:74-079403.
Audience: **l,u,f.** B

Game, Ann **HM24**
Undoing the Social: Towards a Deconstructive Sociology. Cloth Text. University of Toronto Press. Toronto, ON. 1991. 224p. ISBN:0-8020-5970-8, ISBN13: 978-0-8020-5970-3. Dewey:301.
Audience: **u,f.** *Choice, 1992.*

Gane, Mike J. **HM22**
French Social Theory. Cloth Text. SAGE Publications, Inc. Thousand Oaks, CA. 2003. 208p. Theory, Culture and Society Ser. ISBN:0-7619-6830-X, ISBN13: 978-0-7619-6830-6. Dewey:301/.01. LCCN:2002-108285.
Audience: **u,f.** *Choice, 2003.*

Gellner, Ernest **HM26**
Relativism and the Social Sciences. Trade Paper. Cambridge University Press. New York, NY. 1987. 212p. ISBN:0-521-33798-4, ISBN13: 978-0-521-33798-4. Dewey:300.1.
Audience: **l,u,f.** *Choice, 1986.*

Giddens, Anthony **HM19**
Capitalism and Modern Social Theory: An Analysis of the Writings of Marx, Durkheim and Max Weber. Trade Paper. Cambridge University Press. New York, NY. 1973. 280p. ISBN:0-521-09785-1, ISBN13: 978-0-521-09785-7. Dewey:301. LCCN:70-161291.
Audience: **u,f.** B

Giddens, Anthony **HM24**
The Constitution of Society: Outline of the Theory of Structuration. Trade Paper. University of California Press.

Berkeley, CA. 1986. 417p. ISBN:0-520-05728-7, ISBN13: 978-0-520-05728-9. Dewey:301. LCCN:84-040290.
Audience: **u,f.** B

Halfpenny, Peter **HM24**
Positivism and Sociology: Explaining Social Life. Trade Cloth. Ashgate Publishing, Ltd. Aldershot, 1992. 144p. Modern Revivals in Sociology Ser. ISBN:0-7512-0059-X, ISBN13: 978-0-7512-0059-1. Dewey:301/.01.
Audience: **l,u,f.** B

Lefebvre, Henri **BD431.L36513 1991**
Critique of Everyday Life, Vol. 1. Trade Cloth. Verso Books. London, 2003. 192p. ISBN:0-86091-340-6, ISBN13: 978-0-86091-340-5. Dewey:194. LCCN:91-020747.
Audience: **u,f.** *Choice, 1992.*

Lengermann, Patricia Madoo & Niebrugge-Brantley, Jill **HM19.W595 1998**
The Women Founders: Sociology and Social Theory, 1830-1930, A Text with Readings. Paper Text. McGraw-Hill Higher Education. Burr Ridge, IL. 1997. 336p. ISBN:0-07-037169-5, ISBN13: 978-0-07-037169-9. Dewey:305.43/309. LCCN:97-041765.
Audience: **g,l,u.**

Martindale, Don **HM1**
The Nature and Types of Sociological Theory. Ed. 2. Houghton Mifflin. 1981. ISBN:0-395-29732-X, ISBN13: 978-0-395-29732-2.
Audience: **l,u.**

Merton, Robert K. **HM24.M472**
Sociological Ambivalence and Other Essays. Trade Paper. Simon & Schuster. New York, NY. 1976. 287p. ISBN:0-02-921120-4, ISBN13: 978-0-02-921120-5. Dewey:301. LCCN:76-001033.
Audience: **u,f.** B

Morrow, Raymond A. & Brown, David D. **HM24.M622 1994**
Critical Theory and Methodology, Vol. 3. Trade Paper. SAGE Publications, Inc. Thousand Oaks, CA. 1994. 390p. Contemporary Social Theory Ser., Vol. 3 ISBN:0-8039-4683-X, ISBN13: 978-0-8039-4683-5. Dewey:301/.01. LCCN:94-010888.
Audience: **l,u.**

Mouzelis, Nicos **HM24.M685 1995**
Sociological Theory: What Went Wrong?: Diagnosis and Remedies. Paper over Boards. Routledge. New York, NY. 1995. 232p. ISBN:0-415-12720-3, ISBN13: 978-0-415-12720-2. Dewey:301. LCCN:94-044296.
Audience: **l,u,f.** *Choice, 1996.*

Murphy, Raymond **HM206.M95**
Sociology and Nature: Social Action in Context. Trade Paper. Westview Press. Boulder, CO. 1998. 336p. ISBN:0-8133-6661-5, ISBN13: 978-0-8133-6661-6. Dewey:304.2.
Audience: **l,u.** *Choice, 1998.*

Nisbet, Robert A. **HM445.N53 2002**
Sociology as an Art Form. Ed. 2. Trade Paper. Transaction Publishers. Somerset, NJ. 2001. 145p. ISBN:0-7658-0756-4, ISBN13: 978-0-7658-0756-4. Dewey:301/.09. LCCN:00-064814.
Audience: **l,u,f.**

Park, Robert Ezra & Burgess, Ernest W. **HM51.P3 1969B**
Introduction to the Science of Sociology. Library Binding. Greenwood Publishing Group, Inc. Portsmouth, NH. 1985. ISBN:0-8371-2356-9, ISBN13: 978-0-8371-2356-1. Dewey:301.
Audience: **g,l.** B

Parsons, Talcott **HM15 .P3**
Essays in Sociological Theory. Trade Paper. Simon & Schuster. New York, NY. 1964. 460p. ISBN:0-02-924030-1, ISBN13: 978-0-02-924030-4. Dewey:301.
Audience: **l,u.** B

Parsons, Talcott **HM51.P37**
Sociological Theory and Modern Society. Trade Cloth. Simon & Schuster. New York, NY. 1967. ISBN:0-02-924200-2, ISBN13: 978-0-02-924200-1. Dewey:301. LCCN:67-012517.
Audience: **u,f.** B

Ritzer, George (Editor) **HM425.E47 2004**
Encyclopedia of Social Theory. Trade Cloth. SAGE Publications, Inc. Thousand Oaks, CA. 2004. 1056p. ISBN:0-7619-2611-9, ISBN13: 978-0-7619-2611-5. Dewey:301/.01. LCCN:2004-003251.
Audience: **g,l,u,f.** *Choice, 2005.*

Sherman, Lawrence W. (Editor) **H61**
Misleading Evidence and Evidence-Led Policy: Making Social Science More Experimental. Trade Cloth. SAGE Publications, Inc. Thousand Oaks, CA. 2003. 236p. The ANNALS of the American Academy of Political and Social Science Ser. ISBN:0-7619-2857-X, ISBN13: 978-0-7619-2857-7. Dewey:300.72.
Audience: **l,u,f.**

Sorokin, Pitirim A. **HM51 .S674 1979**
Sociological Theories of Today. Lewis A. Coser & Walter W. Powell (Editors). Library Binding. Ayer Company Publishers, Inc. Manchester, NH. 1980. Perennial Works in Sociology ISBN:0-405-12121-0, ISBN13: 978-0-405-12121-0. Dewey:301/.01. LCCN:79-007022.
Audience: **g,l.**

Strasser, Hermann **HM1**
The Normative Structure of Sociology : Conservative and Emancipatory Themes in Social Thought. Routledge & K. Paul. 1976. ISBN:0-7100-8166-9, ISBN13: 978-0-7100-8166-7.
Audience: **u,f.**

Wallerstein, Immanuel **HD78.W35 2001**
Unthinking Social Science: The Limits of Nineteenth-Century Paradigms. Ed. 2. Library Binding. Temple University Press. Philadelphia, PA. 2001. xii, 286p. ISBN:1-56639-898-3, ISBN13: 978-1-56639-898-5. Dewey:330/.09/03. LCCN:00-069053.
Audience: **l,u,f.**

Principles > Theories > Marx

Feagin, Joe R. **S**
Liberation Sociology. Hernán Vera. Westview Press. 2001. ISBN:0-8133-3323-7, ISBN13: 978-0-8133-3323-6.
Audience: **g,l,f.**

Lefebvre, Henri **HX542**
The Sociology of Marx. Trade Paper. Columbia University Press. New York, NY. 1982. 214p. ISBN:0-231-05581-1,

ISBN13: 978-0-231-05581-9. Dewey:335.43/8/301. LCCN:82-009539.
Audience: **g,l,u,f.**

Marx, Karl **HX39.5 .B621**
Karl Marx Selected Writings in Sociology and Social Philosophy. Paper Text. McGraw-Hill Higher Education. Burr Ridge, IL. 1964. 267p. ISBN:0-07-040672-3, ISBN13: 978-0-07-040672-8. Dewey:335.4. LCCN:64-005474.
Audience: **l,u,f.**

Marx, Karl **HM101**
Karl Marx on Society and Social Change: With Selections by Friedrich Engels. Neil J. Smelser (Editor). Trade Paper. University of Chicago Press. Chicago, IL. 1975. 248p. The Heritage of Sociology Ser., :Midway Reprint ISBN:0-226-50918-4, ISBN13: 978-0-226-50918-1. Dewey:303.4. LCCN:73-078669.
Audience: **l,u,f.**

Principles > Theories > Weber

Eliaeson, Sven **HM511.E43 2002**
Max Weber's Methodologies: Interpretation and Critique. Trade Paper. Polity Press. Cambridge, 2002. 240p. ISBN:0-7456-1813-8, ISBN13: 978-0-7456-1813-5. Dewey:301/.01. LCCN:2002-001669.
Audience: **u,f.** *Choice, 2003.*

Gerth, H. H. & Mills, C. Wright (Editor, Translator, Introduction by) **H33**
From Max Weber: Essays in Sociology. Paper over Boards. Routledge. New York, NY. 2003. 504p. International Library of Sociology Ser. ISBN:0-415-17503-8, ISBN13: 978-0-415-17503-6. Dewey:301.
Audience: **l,u,f.**

Honigsheim, Paul **H59.W4H65 2000**
The Unknown Max Weber. Alan Sica (Editor, Introduction by). Trade Cloth. Transaction Publishers. Somerset, NJ. 2000. 290p. ISBN:0-7658-0015-2, ISBN13: 978-0-7658-0015-2. Dewey:300. LCCN:00-034405.
Audience: **u,f.** *Choice, 2001.*

Kalberg, Stephen **HM22.G32W435 1994**
Max Weber's Comparative-Historical Sociology. Trade Paper. University of Chicago Press. Chicago, IL. 1994. 240p. ISBN:0-226-42303-4, ISBN13: 978-0-226-42303-6. Dewey:301/.0943. LCCN:93-010012.
Audience: **l,u,f.**

Ringer, Fritz K. **H59.W4**
Max Weber's Methodology: The Unification of the Cultural and Social Sciences. Trade Paper. Harvard University Press. Cambridge, MA. 2000. 208p. ISBN:0-674-00183-4, ISBN13: 978-0-674-00183-1. Dewey:300.
Audience: **u,f.** *Choice, 1998.*

Swedberg, Richard **HM35.S95**
Max Weber and the Idea of Economic Sociology. Trade Paper. Princeton University Press. Princeton, NJ. 2000. 328p. ISBN:0-691-07013-X, ISBN13: 978-0-691-07013-1. Dewey:306.3. LCCN:98-005129.
Audience: **u,f.** *Choice, 1999.*

Weber, Max **BX8009**
Protestantism and the Rise of Capitalism. Trade Paper. Kessinger Publishing, LLC. Whitefish, MT. 2004. ISBN:1-4191-4330-1, ISBN13: 978-1-4191-4330-4. Dewey:284.
Audience: **l,u,f.**

Weber, Max **HM35.W42 1999**
Essays in Economic Sociology. Richard Swedberg (Editor). Trade Cloth. Princeton University Press. Princeton, NJ. 1999. 322p. ISBN:0-691-00906-6, ISBN13: 978-0-691-00906-3. Dewey:306.3. LCCN:99-017413.
Audience: **l,u,f.**

Principles > Theories > Durkheim

Gane, Mike **HM24.G287 1988**
On Durkheim's Rules of Sociological Method. Trade Cloth. Routledge. New York, NY. 1989. 224p. ISBN:0-415-00251-6, ISBN13: 978-0-415-00251-6. Dewey:301/.092/4. LCCN:87-023556.
Audience: **l,u,f.** *Choice, 1988.*

Hall, Robert T. **BJ319**
Emile Durkheim: Ethics and the Sociology of Morals. Trade Cloth. Greenwood Publishing Group, Inc. Portsmouth, NH. 1987. 248p. Contributions in Sociology Ser. ISBN:0-313-25847-3, ISBN13: 978-0-313-25847-3. Dewey:303.3/72. LCCN:87-010713.
Audience: **u,f.** *Choice, 1988.*

Lamanna, Mary Ann **HQ518.L35 2002**
Emile Durkheim on the Family. Trade Paper. SAGE Publications, Inc. Thousand Oaks, CA. 2001. 288p. Understanding Families Ser., Vol. 20 ISBN:0-7619-1207-X, ISBN13: 978-0-7619-1207-1. Dewey:306.85. LCCN:2001-002980.
Audience: **l,u.** *Choice, 2002.*

Principles > Theories > Other

Collins, Randall **HM2**
Conflict Sociology : Toward an Explanatory Science. Academic Press. 1975. ISBN:0-12-181350-9, ISBN13: 978-0-12-181350-5.
Audience: **u,f.**

Eisenstadt, Samuel N. **HM24.E36 1995**
Power, Trust, and Meaning: Essays in Sociological Theory and Analysis. Trade Cloth. University of Chicago Press. Chicago, IL. 1995. 414p. ISBN:0-226-19555-4, ISBN13: 978-0-226-19555-1. Dewey:301/.01. LCCN:94-038879.
Audience: **l,u,f.**

Gilman, Charlotte Perkins **HM665**
Social Ethics: Sociology and the Future of Society. Michael R. Hill & Mary Jo Deegan (Editors). Trade Cloth. Greenwood Publishing Group, Inc. Portsmouth, NH. 2004. 200p. ISBN:0-275-97886-9, ISBN13: 978-0-275-97886-0. Dewey:303.3/72. LCCN:2003-053021.
Audience: **l,u,f.** *Choice, 2005.*

Mills, C. Wright **H61.M5 2000**
The Sociological Imagination. Ed. 40. Todd Gitlin (Afterword by). Trade Cloth. Oxford University Press, Inc. New York, NY. 2000. 256p. ISBN:0-19-513373-0, ISBN13: 978-0-19-513373-8. Dewey:301. LCCN:99-016199.
Audience: **l,u,f.** B

Rosenau, Pauline Marie **HM73.R59 1991**
Post-Modernism and the Social Sciences: Insights, Inroads, and Intrusions. Trade Paper. Princeton University Press. Princeton, NJ. 1991. 248p. ISBN:0-691-02347-6, ISBN13: 978-0-691-02347-2. Dewey:300/.1. LCCN:91-019258.
Audience: **u,f.** *Choice, 1992.*

Scott, John **HM24.S3775 1995**
Sociological Theory: Contemporary Debates. Trade Cloth. Edward Elgar Publishing, Inc. Northampton, MA. 1995. 320p. ISBN:1-85278-418-0, ISBN13: 978-1-85278-418-8. Dewey:301/.01. LCCN:94-040622.
Audience: **g,l.** *Choice, 1995.*

Strauss, Anselm L. **HM24.S773 1993**
Continual Permutations of Action. Trade Cloth. Aldine Transaction. Somerset, NJ. 1993. 280p. Communication and Social Order Ser. ISBN:0-202-30471-X, ISBN13: 978-0-202-30471-7. Dewey:302. LCCN:93-004075.
Audience: **u,f.** *Choice, 1994.*

Swartz, David **HM22.F8B773 1997**
Culture and Power: The Sociology of Pierre Bourdieu. Trade Paper. University of Chicago Press. Chicago, IL. 1998. 342p. ISBN:0-226-78595-5, ISBN13: 978-0-226-78595-0. Dewey:301/.0944. LCCN:97-007479.
Audience: **u,f.** *Choice, 1998.*

Principles > History of Sociology

Aron, Raymond **HM19 .A6913 1998**
Main Currents in Sociological Thought: Durkheim, Pareto, Weber. Daniel J. Mahoney & Brian C. Anderson (Introduction by). Trade Paper. Transaction Publishers. Somerset, NJ. 1998. 346p. ISBN:0-7658-0436-0, ISBN13: 978-0-7658-0436-5. Dewey:301/.09. LCCN:97-030354.
Audience: **l,u.**

Aron, Raymond **HM19.A6913 1998**
Main Currents in Sociological Thought: Montesquieu, Comte, Marx, Tocqueville, and the Sociologists and the Revolution of 1848. Daniel J. Mahoney & Brian C. Anderson (Introduction by), Pierre Manent (Foreword by). Trade Paper. Transaction Publishers. Somerset, NJ. 1998. 354p. ISBN:0-7658-0401-8, ISBN13: 978-0-7658-0401-3. Dewey:301/.09. LCCN:97-030354.
Audience: **l,u.**

Bendix, Reinhard **HM51.B394 1988**
Embattled Reason: Essays on Social Knowledge, Vol. 2. Ed. 2. Trade Cloth. Transaction Publishers. Somerset, NJ. 1989. 480p. ISBN:0-88738-197-9, ISBN13: 978-0-88738-197-3. Dewey:301. LCCN:86-024892.
Audience: **l,u,f.** B

Bendix, Reinhard **HM51.B394 1988**
Embattled Reason, Vol. 1. Ed. 2. Trade Cloth. Transaction Publishers. Somerset, NJ. 1987. 324p. ISBN:0-88738-110-3, ISBN13: 978-0-88738-110-2. Dewey:301. LCCN:86-024892.
Audience: **l,u,f.**

Blumer, Herbert **HM499.B58 2003**
George Herbert Mead and Human Conduct. Thomas J. Morrione (Editor). Trade Cloth. AltaMira Press. Walnut Creek, CA. 2003. 218p. ISBN:0-7591-0467-0, ISBN13: 978-0-7591-0467-9. Dewey:496. LCCN:2003-012181.
Audience: **l,u,f.** *Choice, 2004.*

Burke, Peter **HM551.B85 2005**
History and Social Theory. Ed. 2. Trade Cloth. Cornell University Press. Ithaca, NY. 2005. 208p. ISBN:0-8014-4453-5, ISBN13: 978-0-8014-4453-1. Dewey:306/.09. LCCN:2005-049684.
Audience: **l,u,f.** *Choice, 1993.*

Clark, Mary E. **GN281.C515 2002**
In Search of Human Nature: The Decline and Revival of Darwinism in American Social Thought. Trade Paper. Routledge. New York, NY. 2002. 576p. ISBN:0-415-28660-3, ISBN13: 978-0-415-28660-2. Dewey:599.93/8. LCCN:2002-075108.
Audience: **u,f.** *Choice, 2003.*

Coser, Lewis A. **GN20**
Masters of Sociological Thought: Ideas in Historical and Social Context. Ed. 2. Paper Text. Waveland Press, Inc. Prospect Heights, IL. 2003. 611p. ISBN:1-57766-307-1, ISBN13: 978-1-57766-307-2. Dewey:301/.092/2.
Audience: **l,u,f.** B

Duby, Georges **HN11.D78 1977**
The Chivalrous Society. Cynthia Postan (Translator). Trade Cloth. University of California Press. Berkeley, CA. 1978. 254p. ISBN:0-520-02813-9, ISBN13: 978-0-520-02813-5. Dewey:309.1/4/01. LCCN:74-081431.
Audience: **u,f.** B

Durkheim, Emile **JC179.M8 D83**
Montesquieu and Rousseau: Forerunners of Sociology. Paper Text. Textbook Publishers. Temecula, CA. 2003. xvi, 155p. ISBN:0-7581-2068-0, ISBN13: 978-0-7581-2068-7. Dewey:301.
Audience: **u,f.** B

Fine, Gary Alan (Editor) **HM47.U62C47 1995**
A Second Chicago School?: The Development of a Postwar American Sociology. Trade Cloth. University of Chicago Press. Chicago, IL. 1995. 436p. ISBN:0-226-24938-7, ISBN13: 978-0-226-24938-4. Dewey:301/.0973. LCCN:94-046877.
Audience: **u,f.**

Friedman, Susan W. **D15.B596 F75 1996**
Marc Bloch, Sociology and Geography: Encountering Changing Disciplines. Alan R. H. Baker, Richard Dennis & Deryck Holdworth (Contribution by). Trade Paper. Cambridge University Press. New York, NY. 2004. 272p. Cambridge Studies in Historical Geography Ser., Vol. 24 ISBN:0-521-61215-2, ISBN13: 978-0-521-61215-9. Dewey:304.2/3. LCCN:2005-275533.
Audience: **u,f.** *Choice, 1997.*

Gouldner, Alvin Ward **S**
The Coming Crisis of Western Sociology. Basic Books. 1970. ISBN:0-465-01278-7, ISBN13: 978-0-465-01278-7.
Audience: **l,u,f.**

Grenfell, Michael **HM479.B68G73 2004**
Pierre Bourdieu: Agent Provocateur. Trade Paper. Continuum International Publishing Group, Ltd. London, 2005. 240p. ISBN:0-8264-6709-1, ISBN13: 978-0-8264-6709-6. Dewey:301/.092 B. LCCN:2004-055282.
Audience: **u,f.** *Choice, 2005.*

Grimes, Michael D. & Morris, Joan M. **HM22**
Caught in the Middle: Contradictions in the Lives of Sociologists from Working Class Backgrounds. Trade Cloth. Greenwood Publishing Group, Inc. Portsmouth, NH. 1997. 248p.

ISBN:0-275-95711-X, ISBN13: 978-0-275-95711-7. Dewey:301/.092/2. LCCN:97-005586.
Audience: **u,f.** *Choice, 1998.*

Hofstadter, Richard **HM22.U5H6 1959**
Social Darwinism in American Thought. Trade Cloth. George Braziller Inc. New York, NY. 1959. ISBN:0-8076-0079-2, ISBN13: 978-0-8076-0079-5. Dewey:301/.0973. LCCN:59-009543.
Audience: **f.** B

Hughes, John, et al. **HM24**
Understanding Classical Sociology: Marx, Weber, Durkheim. Ed. 2. Wes Sharrock & Peter J. Martin (Authors). Cloth Text. SAGE Publications, Inc. Thousand Oaks, CA. 2003. 246p. ISBN:0-7619-5466-X, ISBN13: 978-0-7619-5466-8. Dewey:301. LCCN:2002-116688.
Audience: **g,l.**

Keen, Mike Forrest **HM477.U6**
Stalking Sociologists: J. Edgar Hoover's FBI Surveillance of American Sociology. Trade Paper. Transaction Publishers. Somerset, NJ. 2003. 254p. ISBN:0-7658-0563-4, ISBN13: 978-0-7658-0563-8. Dewey:301/.0973/0904. LCCN:2003-065011.
Audience: **g,l,u,f.**

Keen, Mike Forrest & Mucha, Janusz L. (Editors) **HM47**
Eastern Europe in Transformation: The Impact on Sociology. Trade Cloth. Greenwood Publishing Group, Inc. Portsmouth, NH. 1994. 224p. Contributions in Sociology Ser., Vol. 109 ISBN:0-313-28375-3, ISBN13: 978-0-313-28375-8. Dewey:301/.0947. LCCN:93-044515.
Audience: **u,f.** *Choice, 1995.*

Ladner, Joyce A. (Editor) **E185.86.L331 1998**
The Death of White Sociology. Trade Paper. Black Classic Press. Baltimore, MD. 1998. 500p. ISBN:1-57478-007-7, ISBN13: 978-1-57478-007-9. Dewey:309.173092. LCCN:97-073660.
Audience: **l,u,f.**

Lemert, Charles **HM479.D87**
Durkheim's Ghosts: Cultural Logics and Social Things. Trade Cloth. Cambridge University Press. New York, NY. 2006. 304p. ISBN:0-521-84266-2, ISBN13: 978-0-521-84266-2. Dewey:301.092. LCCN:2006-276424.
Audience: **u,f.**

Lemert, Charles C. **HM435.L46 2005**
Social Things: An Introduction to the Sociological Life. Ed. 3. Book, Other. Rowman & Littlefield Publishers, Inc. Lanham, MD. 2005. 248p. ISBN:0-7425-3548-7, ISBN13: 978-0-7425-3548-0. Dewey:301. LCCN:2005-008612.
Audience: **g,l.**

McCarthy, George E. **HM435.M33 2003**
Classical Horizons: The Origins of Sociology in Ancient Greece. Paper Text. State University of New York Press. Albany, NY. 2002. viii, 202p. ISBN:0-7914-5564-5, ISBN13: 978-0-7914-5564-7. Dewey:301/.09. LCCN:2002-020078.
Audience: **l,u.** *Choice, 2003.*

McDonald, Lynn **H51.M4 1993**
The Early Origins of the Social Sciences. Trade Cloth. McGill-Queen's University Press. Montreal, PQ. 1993. 408p. ISBN:0-7735-1124-5, ISBN13: 978-0-7735-1124-8. Dewey:300/.9. LCCN:95-122422.
Audience: **l,u,f.** *Choice, 1994.*

Nisbet, Robert A. **HM19 .N5 1993**
The Sociological Tradition. Trade Paper. Transaction Publishers. Somerset, NJ. 1993. 349p. ISBN:1-56000-667-6, ISBN13: 978-1-56000-667-1. Dewey:301/.09. LCCN:92-035189.
Audience: **l,u.**

Parsons, Talcott (Editor) **HM15 .P33**
Theories of Society, Vol. 1. Trade Cloth. Simon & Schuster. New York, NY. 1965. 1479p. ISBN:0-02-924450-1, ISBN13: 978-0-02-924450-0. Dewey:301. LCCN:61-009171.
Audience: **l,u,f.**

Platt, Anthony M. **HM22.U6F736 1991**
E. Franklin Frazier Reconsidered. Cloth Text. Rutgers University Press. Piscataway, NJ. 1991. 310p. ISBN:0-8135-1631-5, ISBN13: 978-0-8135-1631-8. Dewey:301/.092 B. LCCN:90-036223.
Audience: **u,f.** *Choice, 1991.*

Ritzer, George **HM2**
Sociology : A Mulitple Paradigm Science. Ed. 2. Allyn and Bacon. 1980. ISBN:0-205-07073-6, ISBN13: 978-0-205-07073-2.
Audience: **l,u.**

Sanford, Nevitt & Comstock, Craig **HM216 .S273**
Sanctions for Evil: Sources of Social Destructiveness. Trade Cloth. John Wiley & Sons, Inc. Hoboken, NJ. 1971. Social and Behavioral Science Ser. ISBN:0-87589-077-6, ISBN13: 978-0-87589-077-7. Dewey:301.2. LCCN:79-129769.
Audience: **u,f.**

Sorokin, Pitirim A. **HM51 .S67 1976**
Fads and Foibles in Modern Sociology and Related Sciences. Trade Cloth. Greenwood Publishing Group, Inc. Portsmouth, NH. 1976. 357p. ISBN:0-8371-8733-8, ISBN13: 978-0-8371-8733-4. Dewey:301. LCCN:76-000154.
Audience: **l,u.**

Sorokin, Pitirim A. **HM101 .S763**
Society, Culture and Personality: Their Structure and Dynamics. Trade Cloth. Cooper Square Publishers, Inc. New York, NY. 1962. ISBN:0-8154-0210-4, ISBN13: 978-0-8154-0210-7. Dewey:301. LCCN:62-019527.
Audience: **u,f.** B

Sorokin, Pitirim A. **HM61.S673 1998**
On the Practice of Sociology. Barry V. Johnston (Editor). Trade Cloth. University of Chicago Press. Chicago, IL. 1998. 336p. The Heritage of Sociology Ser., :Midway Reprint ISBN:0-226-76828-7, ISBN13: 978-0-226-76828-1. Dewey:301. LCCN:97-032778.
Audience: **l,u,f.** *Choice, 1998.*

Spencer, Herbert **HM51**
The Principles of Sociology, Vol. 1. Trade Paper. University Press of the Pacific. Miami, FL. 2004. 456p. ISBN:1-4102-1184-3, ISBN13: 978-1-4102-1184-2. Dewey:301.
Audience: **l,u,f.**

Spencer, Herbert **HM51**
The Principles of Sociology, Vol. 4. Trade Paper. University Press of the Pacific. Miami, FL. 2004. 448p. ISBN:1-4102-1187-8, ISBN13: 978-1-4102-1187-3. Dewey:301.
Audience: **l,u,f.**

Spencer, Herbert **HM51**
The Principles of Sociology, Vol. 2. Trade Paper. University Press of the Pacific. Miami, FL. 2004. 444p. ISBN:1-4102-1185-1, ISBN13: 978-1-4102-1185-9. Dewey:301.
Audience: **l,u,f.**

Spencer, Herbert **HM51**
The Principles of Sociology, Vol. 3. Trade Paper. University Press of the Pacific. Miami, FL. 2004. 460p. ISBN:1-4102-1186-X, ISBN13: 978-1-4102-1186-6. Dewey:301.
Audience: **l,u,f.**

Spencer, Herbert **HM51**
Social statics; or, the conditions essential to human happiness specified, and the first of them developed. by Herbert Spencer ... with a notice of the author and a steel Portrait. Trade Cloth. Scholarly Publishing Office, University of Michigan Library. Ann Arbor, MI. 2004. ISBN:1-4181-3460-0, ISBN13: 978-1-4181-3460-0. Dewey:300.
Audience: **u,f.**

Spencer, Herbert **HM51.S75**
The Study of Sociology. Trade Paper. University Press of the Pacific. Miami, FL. 2002. 428p. ISBN:0-89875-863-7, ISBN13: 978-0-89875-863-4. Dewey:302.
Audience: **l,u,f.**

Thomas, William I. **HM24.T55**
W. I. Thomas on Social Organization and Social Personality. Morris Janowitz (Editor). Trade Cloth. University of Chicago Press. Chicago, IL. 1966. ISBN:0-226-79680-9, ISBN13: 978-0-226-79680-2. Dewey:301. LCCN:66-023701.
Audience: **u,f.**

Tilly, Charles **HN13.T54**
As Sociology Meets History. Trade Cloth. Elsevier Science & Technology Books. Saint Louis, MO. 1981. xiii, 237p. Studies in Social Discontinuity Ser. ISBN:0-12-691280-7, ISBN13: 978-0-12-691280-7. Dewey:907/.2. LCCN:81-012728.
Audience: **u,f.** B

Turner, Jonathan H. **HM585.T89 2002**
The Structure of Sociological Theory. Ed. 7. Cloth Text. Thomson Wadsworth. Belmont, CA. 2002. 560p. ISBN:0-534-53599-2, ISBN13: 978-0-534-53599-5. Dewey:301. LCCN:2001-056807.
Audience: **l,u.** B

Turner, Stephen & Sica, Alan (Editors) **HM478.D58 2005**
The Disobedient Generation: Social Theorists in the Sixties. Trade Cloth. University of Chicago Press. Chicago, IL. 2006. 336p. ISBN:0-226-75624-6, ISBN13: 978-0-226-75624-0. Dewey:301/.092/2 B. LCCN:2005-008511.
Audience: **u,f.**

Van den Berghe, Pierre L. **HM51 .V33 1978**
Man in Society: A Biosocial View. Trade Cloth. Greenwood Publishing Group, Inc. Portsmouth, NH. 1981. 349p. ISBN:0-444-99051-8, ISBN13: 978-0-444-99051-8. Dewey:301. LCCN:78-001393.
Audience: **u,f.**

Ward, Lester F. **HM51.W28**
Dynamic Sociology. D. W. Noble (Introduction by). Trade Cloth. Johnson Reprint Corporation. New York, NY. American Studies ISBN:0-384-65763-X, ISBN13: 978-0-384-65763-2. Dewey:301.
Audience: **u,f.**

Weinberg, Elizabeth Ann **HM477.S65W45 2004**
Sociology in the Soviet Union and Beyond: Social Enquiry and Social Change. Trade Cloth. Ashgate Publishing, Ltd. Aldershot, 2004. 216p. ISBN:0-7546-3817-0, ISBN13: 978-0-7546-3817-9. Dewey:301/.0947. LCCN:2003-063799.
Audience: **u,f.**

Wilson, Raymond Jackson **HM22.U5.W54**
In Quest of Community. Ed. 99. Cloth Text. John Wiley & Sons, Inc. Hoboken, NJ. 1968. 177p. ISBN:0-471-94960-4, ISBN13: 978-0-471-94960-2. Dewey:301/.0973. LCCN:68-030924.
Audience: **u,f.**

Principles > History of Sociology > By Country or Region

Aron, Raymond **HM22.G2 A713 1979**
German Sociology. Lewis A. Coser & Walter W. Powell (Editors), Mary Bottomore & Thomas B. Bottomore (Translators). Library Binding. Ayer Company Publishers, Inc. Manchester, NH. 1980. Perennial Works in Sociology ISBN:0-405-12083-4, ISBN13: 978-0-405-12083-1. Dewey:301/.0943. LCCN:79-006983.
Audience: **u,f.** B

Bendix, Reinhard **HM22.G3W42 1998**
Max Weber: An Intellectual Portrait. Paper over Boards. Routledge. New York, NY. 1998. 492p. Max Weber Classic Monographs ISBN:0-415-17453-8, ISBN13: 978-0-415-17453-4. Dewey:301/.092. LCCN:98-026542.
Audience: **u,f.** B

Comte, Auguste **HM55.C76 2001**
System of Positive Polity 1875-1877, Set. John Henry Bridges (Translator). Trade Cloth. Continuum International Publishing Group, Ltd. London, 2002. 2496p. ISBN:1-85506-936-9, ISBN13: 978-1-85506-936-7. Dewey:194.
Audience: **u,f.** B

Davis, Harold Eugene **HM22.S76**
Latin American Social Thought. University Press of Washington, D.C.. 1961.
Audience: **l,u,f.**

Durkheim, Emile **HM22.F8**
On Morality and Society: Selected Writings. Robert N. Bellah (Editor). Trade Paper. University of Chicago Press. Chicago, IL. 1975. 300p. The Heritage of Sociology Ser., :Midway Reprint ISBN:0-226-17336-4, ISBN13: 978-0-226-17336-8. Dewey:301/.092/4. LCCN:73-076594.
Audience: **l,u,f.** B

Durkheim, Emile & Giddens, Anthony **HM22.F8D875 1972**
Emile Durkheim: Selected Writings. Trade Paper. Cambridge University Press. New York, NY. 1972. 282p. ISBN:0-521-09712-6, ISBN13: 978-0-521-09712-3. Dewey:301.
Audience: **l,u,f.**

Durkheim, Emile **HM24**
Sociology and Philosophy. D. F. Pocock (Translator). Trade Cloth. Simon & Schuster. New York, NY. 1953. 97p. ISBN:0-02-908570-5, ISBN13: 978-0-02-908570-7. Dewey:301/.01. LCCN:54-002835.
Audience: **l,u.**

Giddens, Anthony **HM22.F8.D82 1979**
Emile Durkheim. Trade Cloth. Penguin Group (USA) Inc. New York, NY. 1979. 132p. ISBN:0-670-29283-4, ISBN13: 978-0-670-29283-7. Dewey:301/.092/4. LCCN:78-026657.
Audience: **g,l,u,f.**

Hofstadter, Richard **HM22.U5H6 1992**
Social Darwinism in American Thought. Eric Foner (Introduction by). Trade Paper. Beacon Press. Boston, MA. 1992. 288p. ISBN:0-8070-5503-4, ISBN13: 978-0-8070-5503-8. Dewey:301/.0973. LCCN:91-045525.
Audience: **f.**

Horowitz, Irving L. **HM22.F8**
C. Wright Mills: An American Utopian. Trade Paper. Simon & Schuster. New York, NY. 1985. 352p. ISBN:0-02-915010-8, ISBN13: 978-0-02-915010-8. Dewey:301/.092/4.
Audience: **g,l,u,f.**

Kenneth Thompson **HM22.F8**
Auguste Comte : The Foundation of Sociology. Wiley. 1975. ISBN:0-470-85988-1, ISBN13: 978-0-470-85988-9.
Audience: **l,u,f.**

Kilminster, Richard **HX542**
Praxis and Method: A Sociological Dialogue with Lukacs, Gramsci and the Early Frankfurt School. Trade Cloth. Routledge. New York, NY. 1979. xi, 334p. International Library of Sociology ISBN:0-7100-0094-4, ISBN13: 978-0-7100-0094-1. Dewey:301. LCCN:79-040376.
Audience: **u,f.**

Lazarsfeld, Patricia K. (Editor) **HM51**
The Varied Sociology of Paul F. Lazarsfeld. James Coleman (Introduction by). Trade Cloth. Eastern European Monographs. Bradenton, FL. 1982. 417p. ISBN:0-231-05122-0, ISBN13: 978-0-231-05122-4. Dewey:301. LCCN:81-024205.
Audience: **u,f.**

Le Play, Frederic **HM51**
Frederic Le Play on Family, Work, and Social Change. University of Chicago Press. 1982. ISBN:0-226-47266-3, ISBN13: 978-0-226-47266-9.
Audience: **l,u,f.**

Lemert, Charles C. **HM24**
Sociology and the Twilight of Man: Homocentrism and Discourse in Sociological Theory. Trade Paper. Southern Illinois University Press. Carbondale, IL. 1980. 276p. ISBN:0-8093-0975-0, ISBN13: 978-0-8093-0975-7. Dewey:301/.01. LCCN:78-017146.
Audience: **l,u,f.**

Mannheim, Karl **HM24 .M2613 1985**
Ideology and Utopia: An Introduction to the Sociology of Knowledge. Trade Paper. Harcourt Trade Publishers. New York, NY. 1955. 384p. ISBN:0-15-643955-7, ISBN13: 978-0-15-643955-8. Dewey:301. LCCN:85-005841.
Audience: **l,u.**

Marcuse, Herbert **HM22.G3H43 1999**
Reason and Revolution. Ed. 10. Trade Cloth. Prometheus Books, Publishers. Amherst, NY. 1999. 440p. ISBN:1-57392-718-X, ISBN13: 978-1-57392-718-5. Dewey:301. LCCN:99-013602.
Audience: **u,f.**

Matthews, Fred H. **HM0022.U6.P3**
The Quest for an American Sociology: Robert E. Park and the Chicago School. Trade Paper. Books on Demand. Ann Arbor, MI. 288p. ISBN:0-7837-1029-1, ISBN13: 978-0-7837-1029-7. Dewey:301/.092/4. LCCN:77-373940.
Audience: **l,u,f.**

Meeks, Brian ; Lindahl, Folke **JL60**
New Caribbean Thought : A Reader. University of the West Indies Press. 2001. ISBN:976-640-103-9, ISBN13: 978-976-640-103-0.
Audience: **l,u,f.**

Nisbet, Robert A. **HM22.F8 D86 1976**
Emile Durkheim. Trade Cloth. Greenwood Publishing Group, Inc. Portsmouth, NH. 1976. 179p. ISBN:0-8371-8626-9, ISBN13: 978-0-8371-8626-9. Dewey:301/.01. LCCN:75-036358.
Audience: **u,f.**

Pareto, Vilfredo **HM59.P25**
Mind and Society, Vol. 3. Trade Paper. Kessinger Publishing, LLC. Whitefish, MT. 2003. ISBN:0-7661-5149-2, ISBN13: 978-0-7661-5149-9. Dewey:301.
Audience: **u,f.**

Pareto, Vilfredo **HM59.P25**
Mind and Society, Vol. 1. Trade Paper. Kessinger Publishing, LLC. Whitefish, MT. 2003. ISBN:0-7661-5147-6, ISBN13: 978-0-7661-5147-5. Dewey:301.
Audience: **u,f.**

Pareto, Vilfredo **HM59**
Mind and Society, Vol. 4. Trade Paper. Kessinger Publishing, LLC. Whitefish, MT. 2003. ISBN:0-7661-5150-6, ISBN13: 978-0-7661-5150-5. Dewey:301.
Audience: **u,f.**

Pareto, Vilfredo **HM59.P25**
Mind and Society, Vol. 2. Trade Paper. Kessinger Publishing, LLC. Whitefish, MT. 2003. ISBN:0-7661-5148-4, ISBN13: 978-0-7661-5148-2. Dewey:301.
Audience: **u,f.**

Pareto, Vilfredo **HM59 .P1813 1976**
Sociological Writings. S. E. Finer (Editor), Derick Mirfin (Illustrator). Trade Cloth. Rowman & Littlefield Publishers, Inc. Lanham, MD. 1976. 335p. ISBN:0-87471-855-4, ISBN13: 978-0-87471-855-3. Dewey:301/.044. LCCN:76-150502.
Audience: **l,u.**

Schutte, Ofelia **F1414 .S36 1993**
Cultural Identity and Social Liberation in Latin American Thought. Paper Text. State University of New York Press. Albany, NY. 1993. 313p. Series in Latin American and Iberian Thought and Culture ISBN:0-7914-1318-7, ISBN13: 978-0-7914-1318-0. Dewey:980.03/3. LCCN:92-000752.
Audience: **g,l,u,f.** *Choice, 1993.*

Schutz, Alfred **B829.5**
Alfred Schutz on Phenomenology and Social Relations: Selected Writings. Helmut R. Wagner (Introduction by). Trade Cloth.

University of Chicago Press. Chicago, IL. 1970. vii, 327p. ISBN:0-226-74152-4, ISBN13: 978-0-226-74152-9. Dewey:301/.045. LCCN:73-102072.
Audience: **u,f.**

Schutz, Alfred **HM57**
Phenomenology of the Social World. George Walsh & Fredrick Lehnert (Translators). Trade Paper. Northwestern University Press. Evanston, IL. 1967. 255p. Studies in Phenomenology and Existential Philosophy ISBN:0-8101-0390-7, ISBN13: 978-0-8101-0390-0. Dewey:301.01.
Audience: **l,u,f.** B

Seidman, Steven **HM22.E9**
Liberalism and the Origins of European Social Theory. Trade Paper. University of California Press. Berkeley, CA. 1984. 416p. ISBN:0-520-04986-1, ISBN13: 978-0-520-04986-4. Dewey:301/.094. LCCN:82-021802.
Audience: **u,f.** B

Simmel, Georg & Wolff, Kurt H. **HM57.S482**
The Sociology of Georg Simmel. Trade Cloth. John Wiley & Sons, Inc. Hoboken, NJ. ISBN:0-02-928910-6, ISBN13: 978-0-02-928910-5. Dewey:301/.01.
Audience: **l,u,f.**

Sumner, William Graham. **HM22.G8.S78**
Social Darwinism : Selected Essays. Prentice-Hall. 1963. ISBN:0-19-821873-7, ISBN13: 978-0-19-821873-9.
Audience: **l,u,f.**

Tonnies, Ferdinand **HM706.T61613 2002**
Community and Society. Trade Paper. Dover Publications, Inc. Mineola, NY. 2002. 304p. ISBN:0-486-42497-9, ISBN13: 978-0-486-42497-2. Dewey:301. LCCN:2002-073903.
Audience: **l,u.**

Turner, Bryan S. **HM22.G3W4586 1996**
For Weber: Essays on the Sociology of Fate. Ed. 2. Cloth Text. SAGE Publications, Ltd. London, 1996. 448p. Theory, Culture and Society Ser. ISBN:0-8039-7633-X, ISBN13: 978-0-8039-7633-7. Dewey:301/.01. LCCN:95-072464.
Audience: **l,u,f.**

Wagner, Helmut R. **HM22.G3S299**
Alfred Schutz: An Intellectual Biography. Trade Cloth. University of Chicago Press. Chicago, IL. 1993. xiv, 358p. The Heritage of Sociology Ser., :Midway Reprint ISBN:0-226-86936-9, ISBN13: 978-0-226-86936-0. Dewey:301/.092/4. LCCN:82-013630.
Audience: **u,f.** B

Ward, Lester F. & Gerver, Israel (Introduction by) **HM22.U6 W13 1976**
Lester Frank Ward: Selections from His Work. Library Binding. Greenwood Publishing Group, Inc. Portsmouth, NH. 1976. 91p. ISBN:0-8371-9010-X, ISBN13: 978-0-8371-9010-5. Dewey:301. LCCN:76-023119.
Audience: **u,f.**

Wiltshire, David **HM22.G8.S78**
The Social and Political Thought of Herbert Spencer. Oxford University Press. 1978. ISBN:0-19-821873-7, ISBN13: 978-0-19-821873-9.
Audience: **l,u,f.**

Research Methods

Bechhofer, Frank & Paterson, Lindsay **H61.B425 2000**
Principles of Research Design in Social Sciences. Paper over Boards. Routledge. New York, NY. 2000. 192p. Social Research Today Ser. ISBN:0-415-21442-4, ISBN13: 978-0-415-21442-1. Dewey:300/.7/2. LCCN:99-044348.
Audience: **l,u,f.** *Choice, 2001.*

Brewer, John & Hunter, Albert **H62.B658 2006**
Multimethod Research: Synthesizing Styles. Ed. 2. Paper Text. SAGE Publications, Inc. Thousand Oaks, CA. 2005. 240p. ISBN:0-7619-8861-0, ISBN13: 978-0-7619-8861-8. Dewey:300.72. LCCN:2005-008156.
Audience: **u,f.**

Durkheim, Emile **HM24**
The Rules of Sociological Method. Trade Paper. Simon & Schuster. New York, NY. 1982. 272p. ISBN:0-02-907940-3, ISBN13: 978-0-02-907940-9. Dewey:301/.01/8. LCCN:82-008492.
Audience: **l,u,f.** B

Giddens, Anthony **HM24.G447 1993**
New Rules of Sociological Method. Ed. 2. Trade Cloth. Stanford University Press. Palo Alto, CA. 1993. 200p. ISBN:0-8047-2225-0, ISBN13: 978-0-8047-2225-4. Dewey:301/.01. LCCN:93-083809.
Audience: **l,u,f.**

Krueger, Richard A. & Casey, Mary Anne **H61.28.K78 2000**
Focus Groups: A Practical Guide for Applied Research. Ed. 3. Cloth Text. SAGE Publications, Inc. Thousand Oaks, CA. 2000. 320p. ISBN:0-7619-2070-6, ISBN13: 978-0-7619-2070-0. Dewey:361.6/1/068. LCCN:00-008040.
Audience: **u,f.**

Lewis-Beck, Michael S. (Editor), et al. **H62.L456 2004**
The SAGE Encyclopedia of Social Science Research Methods. Alan E. Bryman & Tim Futing Liao (Editors). Trade Cloth. SAGE Publications, Inc. Thousand Oaks, CA. 2003. 1528p. ISBN:0-7619-2363-2, ISBN13: 978-0-7619-2363-3. Dewey:300/.72. LCCN:2003-015882.
Audience: **g.** *Choice, 2004.*

Lipsey, Mark W. **HV29.L57 1990**
Design Sensitivity: Statistical Power for Experimental Research. Paper Text. SAGE Publications, Inc. Thousand Oaks, CA. 1989. 208p. ISBN:0-8039-3063-1, ISBN13: 978-0-8039-3063-6. Dewey:362.3/072. LCCN:89-037647.
Audience: **u,f.**

Menard, Scott **H62.M39 2002**
Longitudinal Research. Ed. 2. Paper Text. SAGE Publications, Inc. Thousand Oaks, CA. 2002. 104p. Sage University Papers, Nos. 07-76 ISBN:0-7619-2209-1, ISBN13: 978-0-7619-2209-4. Dewey:300/.7/2. LCCN:2002-005572.
Audience: **l,u,f.**

Miller, Delbert C. & Salkind, Neil J. **H62.M44 2002**
Handbook of Research Design and Social Measurement. Ed. 6.

Cloth Text. SAGE Publications, Inc. Thousand Oaks, CA. 2002. 808p. ISBN:0-7619-2045-5, ISBN13: 978-0-7619-2045-8. Dewey:300/.72. LCCN:2001-006672.
Audience: **g,l.**

Miller, P. M. & Wilson, M. J. **H61**
A Dictionary of Social Science Methods. Trade Paper. John Wiley & Sons, Inc. Hoboken, NJ. 1983. 134p. ISBN:0-471-90036-2, ISBN13: 978-0-471-90036-8. Dewey:300/.1/8. LCCN:82-013681.
Audience: **g.**

Morgan, David L. **H61.28.M67 1997**
Focus Groups as Qualitative Research. Ed. 2. Paper Text. SAGE Publications, Inc. Thousand Oaks, CA. 1996. 88p. Qualitative Research Methods Ser., Vol. 16 ISBN:0-7619-0343-7, ISBN13: 978-0-7619-0343-7. Dewey:300/.723. LCCN:96-025389.
Audience: **l,f.**

Prior, Lindsay **H62**
Using Documents in Social Research. Cloth Text. SAGE Publications, Ltd. London, 2003. 196p. Introducing Qualitative Methods Ser. ISBN:0-7619-5746-4, ISBN13: 978-0-7619-5746-1. Dewey:300.7/2.
Audience: **l,u,f.**

Romm, Norma R. A. **H62.R644 2001**
Accountability in Social Research: Issues and Debates. Trade Cloth. Springer. New York, NY. 2001. 326p. ISBN:0-306-46564-7, ISBN13: 978-0-306-46564-2. Dewey:300/.7/2. LCCN:2001-018618.
Audience: **u,f.**

Stanfield, John H. II & Dennis, Rutledge M. (Editors) **GN496.R33 1993**
Race and Ethnicity in Research Methods. Trade Cloth. SAGE Publications, Inc. Thousand Oaks, CA. 1993. 320p. Focus Editions Ser., Vol. 157 ISBN:0-8039-5006-3, ISBN13: 978-0-8039-5006-1. Dewey:305.80072. LCCN:93-009489.
Audience: **l,u,f.**

Stewart, David & Shamdasani, Prem N. **H61.28.S74 1990**
Focus Groups: Theory and Practice. Cloth Text. SAGE Publications, Inc. Thousand Oaks, CA. 1990. 160p. Applied Social Research Methods Ser., Vol. 20 ISBN:0-8039-3389-4, ISBN13: 978-0-8039-3389-7. Dewey:300/.723. LCCN:90-008235.
Audience: **l,u,f.**

Treviano, A. Javier (Editor) **HM477.U6T35 2001**
Talcott Parsons Today: His Theory and Legacy in Contemporary Sociology. Book, Other. Rowman & Littlefield Publishers, Inc. Lanham, MD. 2001. 320p. ISBN:0-7425-0957-5, ISBN13: 978-0-7425-0957-3. Dewey:301/.0973. LCCN:2001-019742.
Audience: **l,u,f.** *Choice, 2002.*

Wolcott, Harry F. **T11.W65 2001**
Writing up Qualitative Research. Ed. 2. Paper Text. SAGE Publications, Inc. Thousand Oaks, CA. 2001. 208p. ISBN:0-7619-2429-9, ISBN13: 978-0-7619-2429-6. Dewey:808/.0666. LCCN:2001-000094.
Audience: **l,u.**

Research Methods > Models

Becker, Howard S. **H91.B38 1998**
Tricks of the Trade: How to Think about Your Research While You're Doing It. Trade Paper. University of Chicago Press. Chicago, IL. 1998. 239p. Chicago Guides to Writing, Editing, and Publishing ISBN:0-226-04124-7, ISBN13: 978-0-226-04124-7. Dewey:300/.72. LCCN:97-019618.
Audience: **l,u,f.**

Blalock, H. M. Jr. (Editor) **H61.25.C38 1985**
Causal Models in the Social Sciences. Ed. 2. Trade Cloth. Aldine Transaction. Somerset, NJ. 1985. 448p. ISBN:0-202-30313-6, ISBN13: 978-0-202-30313-0. Dewey:300/.724. LCCN:84-024258.
Audience: **u,f.**

Eichler, Magrit **H62.E453 1988**
Nonsexist Research Methods: A Practical Guide. Trade Cloth. Routledge. New York, NY. 1987. 144p. ISBN:0-04-497044-7, ISBN13: 978-0-04-497044-6. Dewey:300/.72. LCCN:87-011477.
Audience: **l,u,f.** *Choice, 1988.*

Gracitua-Mario, Estanislao & Wodon, Quentin (Editors) **HC130.P6M43 2001**
Measurement and Meaning: Combining Quantitative and Qualitative Methods for the Analysis of Poverty and Social Exclusion in Latin America. Trade Paper. World Bank Publications. Washington, DC. 2001. 96p. World Bank Technical Papers, No. 518 ISBN:0-8213-5054-4, ISBN13: 978-0-8213-5054-6. Dewey:339.4/6/098. LCCN:2002-328311.
Audience: **u,f.**

Lipsey, Mark W. & Wilson, David B. **HA29.L83153 2000**
Practical Meta-Analysis. Cloth Text. SAGE Publications, Inc. Thousand Oaks, CA. 2000. 264p. Applied Social Research Methods Ser., Vol. 49 ISBN:0-7619-2167-2, ISBN13: 978-0-7619-2167-7. Dewey:300/.7/2. LCCN:00-035379.
Audience: **f.**

Marshall, Catherine & Rossman, Gretchen B. **H62.M277 2006**
Designing Qualitative Research. Ed. 4. Cloth Text. SAGE Publications, Inc. Thousand Oaks, CA. 2006. 280p. ISBN:1-4129-2488-X, ISBN13: 978-1-4129-2488-7. Dewey:300.72. LCCN:2005-026958.
Audience: **u,f.** *Choice, 1989.*

Morgan, Mary S. & Morrison, Margaret (Editors) **Q158.5 .M63 1999**
Models As Mediators: Perspectives on Natural and Social Science. Trade Cloth. Cambridge University Press. New York, NY. 1999. 416p. Ideas in Context Ser., No. 52 ISBN:0-521-65097-6, ISBN13: 978-0-521-65097-7. Dewey:510/.1/5118. LCCN:98-041630.
Audience: **u,f.**

Prus, Robert **HM291.P727 1996**
Symbolic Interaction and Ethnographic Research: Intersubjectivity and the Study of Human Lived Experience. Paper Text. State University of New York Press. Albany, NY. 1995. 301p. ISBN:0-7914-2702-1, ISBN13: 978-0-7914-2702-6. Dewey:302. LCCN:94-049571.
Audience: **u,f.** *Choice, 1996.*

Reinhartz, Shulamit **HQ1180.R45 1991**
Social Research Methods, Feminist Perspectives. Paper Text. PPI-UK. Oxford, 1993. Athene Ser. ISBN:0-08-032793-1, ISBN13: 978-0-08-032793-8. Dewey:305.42/072. LCCN:90-048178.
Audience: **u,f.**

Reinharz, Shulamit & Davidman, Lynn **HQ1180.R448 1992**
Feminist Methods in Social Research. Trade Paper. Oxford University Press, Inc. New York, NY. 1992. 422p. ISBN:0-19-507386-X, ISBN13: 978-0-19-507386-7. Dewey:301/.072. LCCN:91-027838.
Audience: **l,u,f.** *Choice, 1992.*

Risjord, Mark W. **H61.R569 2000**
Woodcutters and Witchcraft: Rationality and Interpretive Change in the Social Sciences. Cloth Text. State University of New York Press. Albany, NY. 2000. ix, 201p. ISBN:0-7914-4511-9, ISBN13: 978-0-7914-4511-2. Dewey:302.5/42. LCCN:99-042500.
Audience: **u,f.**

Strauss, Anselm L. & Corbin, Juliet M. **HA29.S823 1998**
Basics of Qualitative Research: Techniques and Procedures for Developing Grounded Theory. Ed. 2. Paper Text. SAGE Publications, Inc. Thousand Oaks, CA. 1998. 336p. ISBN:0-8039-5940-0, ISBN13: 978-0-8039-5940-8. Dewey:300/.7/2. LCCN:98-025369.
Audience: **l,u,f.**

Thomas, William I. & Volkart, Edmund H. **HM51 .T58 1981**
Social Behavior and Personality: Contributions of W. I. Thomas to Theory and Social Research. Donald Young (Foreword by). Trade Cloth. Greenwood Publishing Group, Inc. Portsmouth, NH. 1981. 338p. ISBN:0-313-22778-0, ISBN13: 978-0-313-22778-3. Dewey:301. LCCN:80-029595.
Audience: **u,f.**

Tindale, R. S., et al. **HM133.T47 1998**
Theory and Research on Small Groups. L. Heath, J Edwards, E. J. Posavac, F. B. Bryant, J. Myers, Y. Suarez-Balcazar & E. Henderson-King (Authors). Trade Cloth. Basic Books. New York, NY. 1998. 270p. Social Psychological Applications to Social Issues Ser., Vol. 4 ISBN:0-306-45679-6, ISBN13: 978-0-306-45679-4. Dewey:302.3/4. LCCN:97-040977.
Audience: **l,u,f.** *Choice, 1998.*

Yin, Robert K. **H62.Y56 2002**
Case Study Research: Design and Methods. Ed. 3. Cloth Text. SAGE Publications, Inc. Thousand Oaks, CA. 2002. 200p. ASRM Ser., Vol. 5 ISBN:0-7619-2552-X, ISBN13: 978-0-7619-2552-1. Dewey:300/.7/22. LCCN:2002-152696.
Audience: **u,f.**

Research Methods > Models > Ethnomethodology

Francis, David & Hester, Stephen **HM481**
An Invitation to Ethnomethodology: Language, Society and Interaction. Cloth Text. SAGE Publications, Inc. Thousand Oaks, CA. 2004. 232p. ISBN:0-7619-6641-2, ISBN13: 978-0-7619-6641-8. Dewey:305.8/001. LCCN:2003-103982.
Audience: **u,f.**

Garfinkel, Harold **HM24 .G3 1984**
Studies in Ethnomethodology. Ed. 2. Trade Paper. Polity Press. Cambridge, 1985. 304p. Polity Press Bks. ISBN:0-7456-0005-0, ISBN13: 978-0-7456-0005-5. Dewey:305.8. LCCN:85-213630.
Audience: **u,f.** B

Garfinkel, Harold **HM481.G37 2002**
Ethnomethodology's Program: Working Out Durkheim's Aphorism. Anne W. Rawls (Editor). Book, Other. Rowman & Littlefield Publishers, Inc. Lanham, MD. 2002. 320p. Legacies of Social Thought Ser. ISBN:0-7425-1641-5, ISBN13: 978-0-7425-1641-0. Dewey:306.01. LCCN:2001-058749.
Audience: **u,f.**

Heritage, John **HM24.H485 1984**
Garfinkel and Ethnomethodology. Trade Paper. Blackwell Publishing, Inc. Malden, MA. 1993. 344p. ISBN:0-7456-0061-1, ISBN13: 978-0-7456-0061-1. Dewey:306/.072. LCCN:84-020615.
Audience: **u,f.** *Choice, 1986.*

Hilbert, Richard A. **91-47747**
The Classical Roots of Ethnomethodology: Durkheim, Weber, and Garfinkel. Randall Collins (Foreword by). Trade Paper. University of North Carolina Press. Chapel Hill, NC. 2001. 278p. ISBN:0-8078-4952-9, ISBN13: 978-0-8078-4952-1. Dewey:301/.01. LCCN:91-047747.
Audience: **u,f.** *Choice, 1993.*

Rogers, Mary F. **HM2**
Sociology, Ethnomethodology, and Experience : A Phenomenological Critique. Cambridge University Press. 1983. ISBN:0-521-25389-6, ISBN13: 978-0-521-25389-5.
Audience: **u,f.**

Research Methods > Models > Rational Choice

Archer, Margaret S. & Tritter, Jonathon Q. (Editors) **HM495.R37 2001**
Rational Choice Theory: Resisting Colonisation. Paper over Boards. Routledge. New York, NY. 2001. 272p. Critical Realism Ser. ISBN:0-415-24271-1, ISBN13: 978-0-415-24271-4. Dewey:301/.01. LCCN:00-059244.
Audience: **l,u,f.**

Gould, Roger V. (Editor) **HM487.R38 2001**
The Rational Choice Controversy in Historical Sociology. Trade Cloth. University of Chicago Press. Chicago, IL. 2006. 264p. ISBN:0-226-30564-3, ISBN13: 978-0-226-30564-6. Dewey:306/.09. LCCN:00-069064.
Audience: **u,f.**

Research Methods > Models > Game Theory

Hargreaves Heap, Shaun & Varoufakis, Yanis **H61.25.H4 2004**
Game Theory: A Critical Introduction. Ed. 2. Paper over Boards. Routledge. New York, NY. 2004. 384p. ISBN:0-415-25094-3, ISBN13: 978-0-415-25094-8. Dewey:519.3. LCCN:2003-058677.
Audience: **l,u,f.**

Shubik, Martin **H61.25**
Game Theory in the Social Sciences: Concepts and Solutions. Trade Cloth. MIT Press. Cambridge, MA. 1982. 514p. ISBN:0-262-19195-4, ISBN13: 978-0-262-19195-1. Dewey:300/.1/5193. LCCN:82-000063.
Audience: **l,u,f.** *B*

Research Methods > Models > Other

Young, Copeland H., et al. **H62.Y667 1991**
Inventory of Longitudinal Studies in the Social Sciences. Kristen L. Savola & Erin Phelps (Authors). Trade Cloth. SAGE Publications, Inc. Thousand Oaks, CA. 1991. 568p. ISBN:0-8039-4315-6, ISBN13: 978-0-8039-4315-5. Dewey:300. LCCN:91-011195.
Audience: **u,f.** *Choice, 1992.*

Research Methods > Statistical Methods

H61.3
☐ Inter-university Consortium for Political and Social Research (ICPSR).
http://www.icpsr.umich.edu/
University of Michigan.
Audience: **u,f.**

Best, Joel **HM535 .B474 2004**
More Damned Lies and Statistics: How Numbers Confuse Public Issues. Trade Cloth. University of California Press. Berkeley, CA. 2004. 222p. ISBN:0-520-23830-3, ISBN13: 978-0-520-23830-5. Dewey:303.3/8. LCCN:2003-028076.
Audience: **g,l.** *Choice, 2005.*

Blalock, Hubert M. **H0061.B4823**
Conceptualization and Measurement in the Social Sciences. Trade Paper. Books on Demand. Ann Arbor, MI. 285p. ISBN:0-608-01116-9, ISBN13: 978-0-608-01116-5. Dewey:300/.724. LCCN:81-023269.
Audience: **l,u.**

Clare, Judith & Hamilton, Helen **PN146**
Writing Research: Transforming Data into Text. Trade Paper. Elsevier - Health Sciences Division. Philadelphia, PA. 2003. 240p. ISBN:0-443-07182-9, ISBN13: 978-0-443-07182-9. Dewey:808/.066/0014.
Audience: **l,u,f.**

Hunter, John E. & Schmidt, Frank L. **HA29.H847 2004**
Methods of Meta-Analysis: Correcting Error and Bias in Research Findings. Ed. 2. Trade Cloth. SAGE Publications, Inc. Thousand Oaks, CA. 2004. 612p. ISBN:0-7619-2697-6, ISBN13: 978-0-7619-2697-9. Dewey:300/.72. LCCN:2003-026057.
Audience: **u,f.**

Lee, Thomas W. **HM131.L386 1998**
Using Qualitative Methods in Organizational Research. Trade Paper. SAGE Publications, Inc. Thousand Oaks, CA. 1998. 208p. Organizational Research Methods Ser. ISBN:0-7619-0807-2, ISBN13: 978-0-7619-0807-4. Dewey:302.3/5/072. LCCN:98-009083.
Audience: **l,u.**

Long, J. Scott **HA29.C7325 1988**
Common Problems - Proper Solutions: Avoiding Error in Quantitative Research. Trade Cloth. SAGE Publications, Inc. Thousand Oaks, CA. 1988. 336p. Focus Editions Ser., Vol. 94 ISBN:0-8039-2806-8, ISBN13: 978-0-8039-2806-0. Dewey:300/.72. LCCN:87-020625.
Audience: **u,f.**

Lorr, Maurice **HA31.3.L67 1983**
Cluster Analysis for Social Scientists. Trade Cloth. John Wiley & Sons, Inc. Hoboken, NJ. 1983. xvi, 233p. ISBN:0-87589-566-2, ISBN13: 978-0-87589-566-6. Dewey:519.5/3. LCCN:82-049283.
Audience: **u,f.** *B*

McDonald, Roderick P. **BF39.M175 1999**
Test Theory: A Unified Treatment. Cloth over Boards. Lawrence Erlbaum Associates, Inc. Mahwah, NJ. 1999. 504p. ISBN:0-8058-3075-8, ISBN13: 978-0-8058-3075-0. Dewey:150/.28/7. LCCN:99-024196.
Audience: **u,f.**

Schulze, Ralf **R853.M48**
Meta-Analysis, a Comparison of Approaches. Perfect. Hogrefe & Huber Publishers. Cambridge, MA. 2004. 256p. ISBN:0-88937-280-2, ISBN13: 978-0-88937-280-1. Dewey:300/.72/7. LCCN:2003-116468.
Audience: **u,f.**

Schwandt, Thomas A. **H61.S4435 2001**
Dictionary of Qualitative Inquiry. Ed. 2. Paper Text. SAGE Publications, Inc. Thousand Oaks, CA. 2001. 320p. ISBN:0-7619-2166-4, ISBN13: 978-0-7619-2166-0. Dewey:300/.7/2. LCCN:00-012062.
Audience: **g.** *Choice, 2001.*

Sociometrics **HN59.2**
☐ Social Science Electronic Data Library.
http://www.socio.com/edl.htm
Sociometrics; Thomson-Gale.
Audience: **u,f.**

Research Methods > Statistical Methods > Computer Methods

Altman, Micah, et al. **QA276.4.A398 2004**
Numerical Issues in Statistical Computing for the Social Scientist. Jeff Gill & Michael P. McDonald (Authors). Trade Cloth. John Wiley & Sons, Inc. Hoboken, NJ. 2003. 323p. Wiley Series in Probability and Statistics ISBN:0-471-23633-0, ISBN13: 978-0-471-23633-7. Dewey:519.5. LCCN:2003-053470.
Audience: **u,f.** *Choice, 2004.*

Antonius, Rachad **HA32.A68 2003**
Interpreting Quantitative Data with SPSS. Cloth Text. SAGE Publications, Ltd. London, 2003. 306p. ISBN:0-7619-7398-2, ISBN13: 978-0-7619-7398-0. Dewey:300/.7/27. LCCN:2002-102782.
Audience: **l,u,f.** *Choice, 2003.*

Kaufman, Leonard & Rousseeuw, Peter J. **QA278**
Finding Groups in Data: An Introduction to Cluster Analysis. Ed. 2. Trade Paper. John Wiley & Sons, Inc. Hoboken, NJ.

2005. 368p. Wiley Series in Probability and Statistics Ser. ISBN:0-471-73578-7, ISBN13: 978-0-471-73578-6. Dewey:519.5/3. LCCN:2005-278659.
Audience: **u,f.** *Choice, 1991.*

Lawal, H. Bayo **QA278.L384 2003**
Categorical Data Analysis with SAS and SPSS Applications. Cloth over Boards. Lawrence Erlbaum Associates, Inc. Mahwah, NJ. 2003. 568p. The Inquiry and Pedagogy Across Diverse Contexts Ser. ISBN:0-8058-4605-0, ISBN13: 978-0-8058-4605-8. Dewey:519.5/3. LCCN:2003-044361.
Audience: **u,f.** *Choice, 2004.*

Maier, Mark H. **HA29.M236 1999**
The Data Game: Controversies in Social Science Statistics. Ed. 3. Cloth Text. M. E. Sharpe Inc. Armonk, NY. 1999. 350p. ISBN:0-7656-0375-6, ISBN13: 978-0-7656-0375-3. Dewey:300/.1/5195. LCCN:98-055371.
Audience: **u,f.** *Choice, 1991.*

Miles, Matthew B. & Huberman, A. Michael (Editors) **H62.Q3564 2002**
The Qualitative Researcher's Companion. Cloth Text. SAGE Publications, Inc. Thousand Oaks, CA. 2002. 424p. ISBN:0-7619-1190-1, ISBN13: 978-0-7619-1190-6. Dewey:001.4/2. LCCN:2001-008003.
Audience: **g,u,f.**

Research Methods > Statistical Methods > Simulation

Cubitt, Sean **HM585.C82 2001**
Simulation and Social Theory. Cloth Text. SAGE Publications, Inc. Thousand Oaks, CA. 2001. 192p. Theory, Culture and Society Ser. ISBN:0-7619-6109-7, ISBN13: 978-0-7619-6109-3. Dewey:301/.01. LCCN:2001-274342.
Audience: **u,f.**

Szmatka, Jacek (Editor), et al. **HM716**
The Growth of Social Knowledge: Theory, Simulation, and Empirical Research in Group Processes. Michael J. Lovaglia & Kinga Wysienska (Editors). Trade Cloth. Greenwood Publishing Group, Inc. Portsmouth, NH. 2002. 312p. ISBN:0-275-97213-5, ISBN13: 978-0-275-97213-4. Dewey:305/.07/2. LCCN:2001-058046.
Audience: **l,u,f.**

Research Methods > Frameworks/Methodology

Ball, Michael S. & Smith, Gregory W. **H62.B288 1992**
Analyzing Visual Data. Trade Paper. SAGE Publications, Inc. Thousand Oaks, CA. 1992. 88p. Qualitative Research Methods Ser., Vol. 24 ISBN:0-8039-3435-1, ISBN13: 978-0-8039-3435-1. Dewey:300.72. LCCN:92-007984.
Audience: **u,f.**

Brewer, John D. **HN398.N6B74 2003**
C. Wright Mills and the Ending of Violence. Cloth over Boards. Palgrave Macmillan. New York, NY. 2003. 224p. ISBN:0-333-80180-6, ISBN13: 978-0-333-80180-2. Dewey:303.6/09416. LCCN:2003-048276.
Audience: **u,f.** *Choice, 2004.*

Harding, Sandra (Editor) **H61.F38 1987**
Feminism and Methodology: Social Science Issues. Trade Cloth. Indiana University Press. Bloomington, IN. 1988. 204p. ISBN:0-253-32243-X, ISBN13: 978-0-253-32243-2. Dewey:300. LCCN:86-043050.
Audience: **u,f.**

Hill, Michael R. & Hoecker-Drysdale, Susan (Editors) **HM477.G7H37 2001**
Harriet Martineau: Theoretical and Methodological Perspectives. Helena Z. Lopate (Foreword by). Paper over Boards. Garland Publishing, Inc. New York, NY. 2001. 234p. Women and Sociological Theory Ser. ISBN:0-8153-3451-6, ISBN13: 978-0-8153-3451-4. Dewey:301/.092. LCCN:2001-019121.
Audience: **u,f.** *Choice, 2002.*

Jorgensen, Danny L. **H62.J625 1989**
Participant Observation: A Methodology for Human Studies. Paper Text. SAGE Publications, Inc. Thousand Oaks, CA. 1989. 136p. Applied Social Research Methods Ser., Vol. 15 ISBN:0-8039-2877-7, ISBN13: 978-0-8039-2877-0. Dewey:300/.72. LCCN:88-026510.
Audience: **l,u,f.**

Shadish, William R., et al. **H97**
Foundations of Program Evaluation: Theories of Practice. Thomas Cook & Laura C. Leviton (Authors). Trade Paper. SAGE Publications, Inc. Thousand Oaks, CA. 1990. 536p. ISBN:0-8039-5301-1, ISBN13: 978-0-8039-5301-7. Dewey:361.61.
Audience: **u,f.**

Research Methods > Frameworks/Methodology > Field Work

Feldman, Martha S., et al. **H62.F3915 2002**
Gaining Access: A Practical and Theoretical Guide for Qualitative Researchers. Jeannine Bell & Michele Tracy Berger (Authors). Trade Paper, Perfect. AltaMira Press. Walnut Creek, CA. 2003. 173p. ISBN:0-7591-0216-3, ISBN13: 978-0-7591-0216-3. Dewey:300.72. LCCN:2002-014164.
Audience: **u,f.** *Choice, 2003.*

Jackson, Bruce **GR45.5.J33 1987**
Fieldwork. Trade Paper. University of Illinois Press. Champaign, IL. 1987. 328p. ISBN:0-252-01372-7, ISBN13: 978-0-252-01372-0. Dewey:390/.072. LCCN:86-016010.
Audience: **l,u,f.** *Choice, 1987.*

Lee-Treweek, Geraldine & Linkogle, Stephanie **H62.L419 2000**
Danger in the Field: Ethics and Risk in Social Research. Paper over Boards. Routledge. New York, NY. 2000. 224p. ISBN:0-415-19321-4, ISBN13: 978-0-415-19321-4. Dewey:300/.7/2. LCCN:00-035278.
Audience: **l,u,f.** *Choice, 2001.*

Punch, Maurice **H0062.P94**
The Politics and Ethics of Fieldwork. Trade Paper. Books on Demand. Ann Arbor, MI. 96p. Qualitative Research Methods Ser., Vol. 3 ISBN:0-598-05703-X, ISBN13: 978-0-598-05703-7. Dewey:300/.72. LCCN:85-062291.
Audience: **l,u,f.**

Rubin, Herbert J. & Rubin, Irene **H62.R737 2005**
Qualitative Interviewing: The Art of Hearing Data. Ed. 2. Cloth Text. SAGE Publications, Inc. Thousand Oaks, CA. 2004. 304p. ISBN:0-7619-2074-9, ISBN13: 978-0-7619-2074-8. Dewey:001.4/33. LCCN:2004-005677.
Audience: **l,u,f.**

Research Methods > Frameworks/Methodology > Social Surveys

Arksey, Hilary & Knight, Peter **H61.28.A75 1999**
Interviewing for Social Scientists: An Introductory Resource with Examples. Cloth Text. SAGE Publications, Ltd. London, 1999. 224p. ISBN:0-7619-5869-X, ISBN13: 978-0-7619-5869-7. Dewey:300/.7/23. LCCN:99-072817.
Audience: **l,u,f.**

Briggs, Charles L. **H61**
Learning How to Ask: A Sociolinguistic Appraisal of the Role of the Interview in Social Science Research. Judith Irvine, Bambi Schieffelin, Marjorie H. Goodwin, Joel Kuipers, Don Kulick, John Lucy, Elinor Ochs & Michael Silverstein (Contribution by). Trade Paper. Cambridge University Press. New York, NY. 1986. 175p. Cambridge Studies in the Social and Cultural Foundations of Language, No. 1 ISBN:0-521-31113-6, ISBN13: 978-0-521-31113-7. Dewey:300/.723. LCCN:85-029153.
Audience: **u,f.** *Choice, 1987.*

Fowler, Floyd J. Jr. & Mangione, Thomas W. **H61.28.F68 1990**
Standardized Survey Interviewing: Minimizing Interviewer-Related Error. Paper Text. SAGE Publications, Inc. Thousand Oaks, CA. 1989. 152p. Applied Social Research Methods Ser., Vol. 18 ISBN:0-8039-3093-3, ISBN13: 978-0-8039-3093-3. Dewey:300/.723. LCCN:89-010514.
Audience: **u,f.**

Groves, Robert M. (Editor), et al. **H91**
Telephone Survey Methodology. Paul P. Biemer, Lars E. Lyberg, James T. Massey, William L. Nicholls & Joseph Waksberg (Editors). Trade Paper. John Wiley & Sons, Inc. Hoboken, NJ. 2001. 608p. Wiley Series in Survey Methodology Ser., Vol. 328 ISBN:0-471-20956-2, ISBN13: 978-0-471-20956-0. Dewey:001.4/33.
Audience: **l,u,f.**

Houtkoop-Steenstra, Hanneke **HM526 .H68 2000**
Interaction and the Standardized Survey Interview: The Living Questionnaire. Trade Cloth. Cambridge University Press. New York, NY. 2000. 224p. ISBN:0-521-66202-8, ISBN13: 978-0-521-66202-4. Dewey:001.433. LCCN:99-042112.
Audience: **l,u,f.**

Leon, Joseph J. Sr., et al. **H62**
Survey Research: In-Person, Mail, Telephone and Web Methods. Wayne C. Brown Sr., Libby O. Ruch Sr. & Thomas E. Johnson Sr. (Authors). Spiral. Streamline Surveys, Inc. Honolulu, HI. 2003. 186p. ISBN:0-9668165-1-X, ISBN13: 978-0-9668165-1-8. Dewey:300.72.
Audience: **l,u,f.**

Mishler, Elliot G. **HN29**
Research Interviewing: Context and Narrative. Trade Paper. Harvard University Press. Cambridge, MA. 1991. 206p. ISBN:0-674-76461-7, ISBN13: 978-0-674-76461-3. Dewey:300.72.
Audience: **l,u,f.**

Rea, Louis M. & Parker, Richard A. **HA31.2.R43 2005**
Designing and Conducting Survey Research: A Comprehensive Guide. Ed. 3. Trade Cloth. John Wiley & Sons, Inc. Hoboken, NJ. 2005. 304p. ISBN:0-7879-7546-X, ISBN13: 978-0-7879-7546-3. Dewey:300/.72/3. LCCN:2005-017233.
Audience: **l,u,f.**

Schuman, Howard & Presser, Stanley **HN29.S338 1996**
Questions and Answers in Attitude Surveys: Experiments on Question Form, Wording, and Context. Trade Paper. SAGE Publications, Inc. Thousand Oaks, CA. 1996. 392p. ISBN:0-7619-0359-3, ISBN13: 978-0-7619-0359-8. Dewey:001.4/222. LCCN:95-048479.
Audience: **u,f.**

Research Methods > Frameworks/Methodology > Other

Chen, Shing-Ling & Hall, G. Jon **HM571.O55 2002**
Online Social Research: Methods, Issues and Ethics. Trade Cloth. Peter Lang Publishing, Inc. New York, NY. 2003. 288p. Digital Formations Ser., Vol. 7 ISBN:0-8204-6101-6, ISBN13: 978-0-8204-6101-4. Dewey:301/.0285678. LCCN:2002-025388.
Audience: **l,u,f.**

Fox, James A. & Tracy, Paul E. **HN29.F69 1986**
Randomized Response: A Method for Sensitive Surveys. Trade Paper. SAGE Publications, Inc. Thousand Oaks, CA. 1986. 80p. Quantitative Applications in the Social Sciences Ser., Vol. 58 ISBN:0-8039-2309-0, ISBN13: 978-0-8039-2309-6. Dewey:301/.0723. LCCN:85-063713.
Audience: **u,f.**

Social Psychology

Ball, Philip **HM585.B35 2004**
Critical Mass: How One Thing Leads to Another. Cloth over Boards. Farrar, Straus & Giroux. New York, NY. 2004. 528p. ISBN:0-374-28125-4, ISBN13: 978-0-374-28125-0. Dewey:301. LCCN:2003-064178.
Audience: **g,l.** *Choice, 2004.*

Gilbert, Daniel T. (Editor), et al. **HM251.H224 1998**
The Handbook of Social Psychology, Set. Ed. 4. Susan T. Fiske & Gardner Lindzey (Editors). Trade Cloth. Oxford University Press, Inc. New York, NY. 1998. 1,984p. ISBN:0-19-521376-9, ISBN13: 978-0-19-521376-8. Dewey:302. LCCN:97-005436.
Audience: **g,l,u.**

Homans, George C., et al. **HM133.H577 1992**
The Human Group. A. Paul Hare & Richard B. Polley (Authors). Trade Paper. Transaction Publishers. Somerset, NJ. 2001. 545p. ISBN:1-56000-572-6, ISBN13: 978-1-56000-572-8. Dewey:302.3. LCCN:91-019944.
Audience: **u,f.**

Parsons, Talcott & Shils, Edward A. **HM484.T68 2001**
Toward a General Theory of Action. Neil J. Smelser (Introduction by). Trade Paper. Transaction Publishers. Somerset, NJ. 2001. 265p. Social Science Classics Ser. ISBN:0-7658-0718-1, ISBN13: 978-0-7658-0718-2. Dewey:301. LCCN:00-055200.
Audience: **u,f.**

Rebach, Howard M. & Bruhn, John G. (Editors) **HM585.H35 2001**
Handbook of Clinical Sociology. Ed. 2. Trade Cloth. Springer. New York, NY. 2001. 436p. Clinical Sociology Ser. ISBN:0-306-46512-4, ISBN13: 978-0-306-46512-3. Dewey:301. LCCN:2001-029650.
Audience: **g,l,u.**

Sherif, Muzafer **HM251 .S55**
Psychology of Social Norms. Library Binding. Hippocrene Books, Inc. New York, NY. 1965. ISBN:0-374-97353-9, ISBN13: 978-0-374-97353-7. Dewey:301.152.
Audience: **u,f.**

Sherif, Muzafer & Brannigan, Augustine **HM1033.S49 2005**
Social Interaction: Process and Products. Trade Paper. Aldine Transaction. Somerset, NJ. 2005. 528p. ISBN:0-202-30788-3, ISBN13: 978-0-202-30788-6. Dewey:302. LCCN:2005-053648.
Audience: **l,u.**

Smelser, Neil J. **HM251 .S628**
Theory of Collective Behavior. Trade Paper. Simon & Schuster. New York, NY. 1972. ISBN:0-02-929400-2, ISBN13: 978-0-02-929400-0. Dewey:301.15. LCCN:62-015350.
Audience: **u,f.**

Turner, Bryan (Introduction by) **HM585.M34513 1997**
Essays on Sociology and Social Psychology. Library Binding. Routledge. New York, NY. 1998. viii, 319p. Karl Mannheim Ser., Vol. 6:Collected Works ISBN:0-415-13676-8, ISBN13: 978-0-415-13676-1. Dewey:302.
Audience: **l,u.**

Social Psychology > History

Blumer, Herbert **HM499.B58 2003**
George Herbert Mead and Human Conduct. Thomas J. Morrione (Editor). Trade Cloth. AltaMira Press. Walnut Creek, CA. 2003. 218p. ISBN:0-7591-0467-0, ISBN13: 978-0-7591-0467-9. Dewey:496. LCCN:2003-012181.
Audience: **l,u,f.** *Choice, 2004.*

Zaretsky, Eli **BF175**
Secrets of the Soul: A Social and Cultural History of Psychoanalysis. Trade Paper. Knopf Publishing Group. New York, NY. 2005. 448p. ISBN:1-4000-7923-3, ISBN13: 978-1-4000-7923-0. Dewey:150.19/5/09.
Audience: **l,u,f.** *Choice, 2004.*

Social Psychology > Theory

Aronson, Elliot & Meyers, David G. **HM251.A79**
Psychology, in Modules, Critical Thinking Companion and PsychInquiry. Ed. 7. Susan Brennan (Editor). Quantity Pack. Worth Publishers, Inc. New York, NY. 2005. 528p. ISBN:0-7167-2624-6, ISBN13: 978-0-7167-2624-1. Dewey:150.
Audience: **g,l.**

Bales, Robert Freed **HM133.B34**
Personality and Interpersonal Behavior. Trade Cloth. Bow Historical Books. New Providence, NJ. 1969. xiv, 561p. ISBN:0-03-080450-7, ISBN13: 978-0-03-080450-2. Dewey:301.1. LCCN:71-084682.
Audience: **l,u,f.**

Brown, Rupert **HM131.B726 2000**
Group Processes: Dynamics Within and Between Groups. Ed. 2. Trade Paper. Blackwell Publishing, Inc. Malden, MA. 2000. 448p. ISBN:0-631-18496-1, ISBN13: 978-0-631-18496-6. Dewey:302.3. LCCN:99-037854.
Audience: **l,u,f.** *Choice, 1989.*

Cooley, Charles Horton **HM251 .C8 1983**
Human Nature and the Social Order. Philip Rieff (Introduction by). Trade Paper. Transaction Publishers. Somerset, NJ. 1991. 457p. Social Science Classics Ser. ISBN:0-87855-918-3, ISBN13: 978-0-87855-918-3. Dewey:302.5. LCCN:82-011002.
Audience: **l,u,f.**

Gilligan, Carol **HQ1206.G58 1993**
In a Different Voice: Psychological Theory and Women's Development. Trade Paper. Harvard University Press. Cambridge, MA. 1993. 216p. ISBN:0-674-44544-9, ISBN13: 978-0-674-44544-4. Dewey:305.4/2. LCCN:81-013478.
Audience: **g,l,u,f.**

Lofland, John Jr. **HM132**
Doing Social Life: The Qualitative Study of Human Interaction in Natural Settings. Trade Cloth. John Wiley & Sons, Inc. Hoboken, NJ. 1976. 328p. ISBN:0-471-01563-6, ISBN13: 978-0-471-01563-5. Dewey:302. LCCN:76-025077.
Audience: **u,f.**

Social Psychology > Perception

Anderson, Elijah **HM736.A53 2003**
A Place on the Corner. Ed. 2. Trade Paper. University of Chicago Press. Chicago, IL. 2003. 288p. Fieldwork Encounters and Discoveries Ser. ISBN:0-226-01959-4, ISBN13: 978-0-226-01959-8. Dewey:302.3/4. LCCN:2003-048351.
Audience: **g,l,u,f.**

Cicourel, Aaron V. **HM291 .C56 1974**
Cognitive Sociology. Trade Cloth. Simon & Schuster. New York, NY. 1974. ISBN:0-02-905440-0, ISBN13: 978-0-02-905440-6. Dewey:301.2/1. LCCN:73-018771.
Audience: **l,u.**

Wyer, Robert S. Jr. & Srull, Thomas K. (Editors) **HM132 .H333 1994**
Handbook of Social Cognition, Set. Ed. 2. Trade Cloth. Lawrence Erlbaum Associates, Inc. Mahwah, NJ. 1994. 488p. ISBN:0-8058-1057-9, ISBN13: 978-0-8058-1057-8. Dewey:302/.12. LCCN:93-029484.
Audience: **l,u.**

Social Psychology > Perception > Self Concept

Douglas, Jack D. **HV6545.D6**
The Social Meanings of Suicide. Trade Paper. Books on Demand. Ann Arbor, MI. 1973. 412p. ISBN:0-7837-8166-0, ISBN13: 978-0-7837-8166-2. Dewey:301.1. LCCN:67-014408.
Audience: **g,l,u,f.**

Durkheim, Emile **HV6545**
Suicide: A Study in Sociology. George Simpson (Author, Editor), John A. Spaulding (Author). Trade Paper. Simon & Schuster. New York, NY. 1997. 416p. ISBN:0-684-83632-7, ISBN13: 978-0-684-83632-4. Dewey:362.2/8.
Audience: **u,f.**

Eakin, Paul J. **CT25.E25 1999**
How Our Lives Become Stories: Making Selves. Book, Other. Cornell University Press. Ithaca, NY. 1999. 224p. ISBN:0-8014-8598-3, ISBN13: 978-0-8014-8598-5. Dewey:808/.06692. LCCN:99-028793.
Audience: **l,u.** *Choice, 2000.*

Hewstone, Miles **BF697.5.S43S429 2003**
Self and Social Identity. Marilynn B. Brewer (Editor). Trade Paper. Blackwell Publishing, Inc. Malden, MA. 2004. 352p. Perspectives on Social Psychology Ser. ISBN:1-4051-1069-4, ISBN13: 978-1-4051-1069-3. Dewey:302/.1. LCCN:2003-004955.
Audience: **l,u,f.** *Choice, 2004.*

Mead, George Herbert **HM251**
The Individual and the Social Self: Unpublished Work of George Herbert Mead. David L. Miller (Editor). Library Binding. University of Chicago Press. Chicago, IL. 1992. 232p. Chicago Original Paperback Ser. ISBN:0-226-51673-3, ISBN13: 978-0-226-51673-8. Dewey:302. LCCN:82-004885.
Audience: **l,u,f.**

Mead, George Herbert **HM251**
Mind, Self, and Society: From the Standpoint of a Social Behaviorist. Charles W. Morris (Editor). Trade Paper. University of Chicago Press. Chicago, IL. 1967. 440p. ISBN:0-226-51668-7, ISBN13: 978-0-226-51668-4. Dewey:302.
Audience: **u,f.**

Modell, Arnold H. **BF697.5.S43M63 1993**
The Private Self. Trade Cloth. Harvard University Press. Cambridge, MA. 1993. 262p. ISBN:0-674-70752-4, ISBN13: 978-0-674-70752-8. Dewey:155.2. LCCN:93-014974.
Audience: **u.** *Choice, 1994.*

Offer, D., et al. **BF724.3.S35T44 1988**
The Teenage World: Adolescents' Self-Image in Ten Countries. E. Ostrov, K. I. Howard & R. Atkinson (Authors). Trade Cloth. Springer. New York, NY. 1988. 288p. ISBN:0-306-42747-8, ISBN13: 978-0-306-42747-3. Dewey:155.5. LCCN:88-004127.
Audience: **l,u,f.** *Choice, 1988.*

Rosen, Bernard Carl **HQ799**
Masks and Mirrors: Generation X and the Chameleon Personality. Trade Cloth. Greenwood Publishing Group, Inc. Portsmouth, NH. 2001. 208p. ISBN:0-275-97325-5, ISBN13: 978-0-275-97325-4. Dewey:305.242/0973. LCCN:00-069863.
Audience: **l,u,f.** *Choice, 2002.*

Rosenberger, Nancy R. (Editor) **BF697.5S43J36 1994**
Japanese Sense of Self. Naomi Quinn, Daniel Fessler, Allen W. Johnson, Takie Sugiyama Lebra, John Lucy, Claudia Strauss & Harriet Whitehead (Contribution by). Trade Paper. Cambridge University Press. New York, NY. 1994. 188p. Publications of the Society for Psychological Anthropology ISBN:0-521-46637-7, ISBN13: 978-0-521-46637-0. Dewey:155.8/952.
Audience: **l,u,f.** *Choice, 1993.*

Stephens, G. Lynn & Graham, George **RC553.A84S74 2000**
When Self-Consciousness Breaks: Alien Voices and Inserted Thoughts. Trade Cloth. MIT Press. Cambridge, MA. 2000. 212p. Philosophical Psychopathology Ser. ISBN:0-262-19437-6, ISBN13: 978-0-262-19437-2. Dewey:154.4. LCCN:00-026720.
Audience: **u,f.** *Choice, 2001.*

Williams, John E. & Best, Deborah L. **HQ1075.W53 1990**
Sex and Psyche: Gender and Self Viewed Cross-Culturally. Trade Cloth. SAGE Publications, Inc. Thousand Oaks, CA. 1990. 214p. Cross-Cultural Research and Methodology Ser., Vol. 13 ISBN:0-8039-3769-5, ISBN13: 978-0-8039-3769-7. Dewey:305.3. LCCN:90-031839.
Audience: **u,f.** *Choice, 1990.*

Social Psychology > Perception > Social Identity

Appiah, Anthony **BJ1031.A64 2005**
The Ethics of Identity. Trade Cloth. Princeton University Press. Princeton, NJ. 2004. 400p. ISBN:0-691-12036-6, ISBN13: 978-0-691-12036-2. Dewey:170. LCCN:2004-044535.
Audience: **g,l,u,f.** *Choice, 2005.*

Aronowitz, Stanley **HN90.S6A76 1991**
The Politics of Identity: Class, Culture, Social Movements. UK-B Format Paperback. Routledge. New York, NY. 1992. 288p. ISBN:0-415-90437-4, ISBN13: 978-0-415-90437-7. Dewey:305.50973. LCCN:91-040561.
Audience: **l,u,f.**

Boissevain **HM291 .B634**
Friends of Friends. Trade Cloth. Blackwell Publishing, Inc. Malden, MA. ISBN:0-631-14970-8, ISBN13: 978-0-631-14970-5. Dewey:301.11. LCCN:74-165419.
Audience: **l,u,f.**

Cooley, Charles Horton **HM251 .C8 1983**
Human Nature and the Social Order. Philip Rieff (Introduction by). Trade Paper. Transaction Publishers. Somerset, NJ. 1991. 457p. Social Science Classics Ser. ISBN:0-87855-918-3, ISBN13: 978-0-87855-918-3. Dewey:302.5. LCCN:82-011002.
Audience: **l,u,f.**

Cooley, Charles Horton **HM251 .C85 1983**
Social Organization: A Study of the Larger Mind. Philip Rieff (Introduction by). Trade Paper. Transaction Publishers. Somerset, NJ. 1983. 457p. Social Science Classics Ser. ISBN:0-87855-824-1, ISBN13: 978-0-87855-824-7. Dewey:301. LCCN:80-015746.
Audience: **l,u,f.**

Goffman, Erving **HM291 .G6**
The Presentation of Self in Everyday Life. Trade Cloth. Peter Smith Publisher, Inc. Magnolia, MA. 1999. ISBN:0-8446-7017-0, ISBN13: 978-0-8446-7017-1. Dewey:301.15.
Audience: **l,u.** *B*

Howe, Daniel W. **E169.1.H76 1997**
Making the American Self: Jonathan Edwards to Abraham Lincoln. Trade Cloth. Harvard University Press. Cambridge, MA. 1997. 348p. Studies in Cultural History ISBN:0-674-16555-1, ISBN13: 978-0-674-16555-7. Dewey:973. LCCN:96-034982.
Audience: **g,l,u,f.** *Choice, 1997.*

Joseph, John E. **P107.J67 2004**
Language and Identity: National, Ethnic, Religious. Cloth over Boards. Palgrave Macmillan. New York, NY. 2004. 288p. ISBN:0-333-99752-2, ISBN13: 978-0-333-99752-9. Dewey:400. LCCN:2004-043621.
Audience: **l,u,f.** *Choice, 2005.*

Pappano, Laura **BF575.L7P36 2001**
The Connection Gap: Why Americans Feel So Alone. Trade Cloth. Rutgers University Press. Piscataway, NJ. 2001. 224p. ISBN:0-8135-2979-4, ISBN13: 978-0-8135-2979-0. Dewey:155.9/2. LCCN:00-068349.
Audience: **g.** *Choice, 2002.*

Social Psychology > Perception > Stereotypes

Bar-Tal, Daniel (Editor), et al. **BF323.S63S74 1989**
Stereotyping and Prejudice. C. T. Graumann, Arie W. Kruglanski & Wolfgang Stroebe (Editors). Cloth Text. Springer. New York, NY. 1989. 273p. Social Psychology Ser. ISBN:0-387-96883-0, ISBN13: 978-0-387-96883-4. Dewey:305. LCCN:88-038198.
Audience: **l,u,f.** *Choice, 1989.*

Helmreich, William B. **HM291**
The Things They Say Behind Your Back: Stereotypes and the Myths Behind Them. Trade Paper. Transaction Publishers. Somerset, NJ. 1983. 276p. ISBN:0-87855-953-1, ISBN13: 978-0-87855-953-4. Dewey:303.3/85. LCCN:83-009149.
Audience: **l,u,f.**

Leyens, Jacques-Philippe, et al. **HM132.L49 1994**
Stereotypes and Social Cognition. Vincent Y. A. Yzerbyt & Georges Schadron (Authors). Cloth Text. SAGE Publications, Ltd. London, 1994. 256p. ISBN:0-8039-8583-5, ISBN13: 978-0-8039-8583-4. Dewey:302/.12. LCCN:94-067832.
Audience: **l,u,f.** *Choice, 1995.*

Schneider, David J. **BF323.S63S36 2003**
The Psychology of Stereotyping. Cloth over Boards. Guilford Publications, Inc. New York, NY. 2003. 704p. Distinguished Contributions in Psychology Ser. ISBN:1-57230-929-6, ISBN13: 978-1-57230-929-6. Dewey:303.3/85. LCCN:2003-008819.
Audience: **l,u,f.** *Choice, 2004.*

Social Psychology > Perception > Emotions

Brody, Leslie **RC455.4.E46B76 1999**
Gender, Emotion, and the Family. Trade Cloth. Harvard University Press. Cambridge, MA. 1999. 368p. ISBN:0-674-34186-4, ISBN13: 978-0-674-34186-9. Dewey:152.4. LCCN:98-032351.
Audience: **l,u,f.** *Choice, 1999.*

Collins, Randall **HM1111**
Interaction Ritual Chains. Trade Paper. Princeton University Press. Princeton, NJ. 2005. 464p. Princeton Studies in Cultural Sociology Ser. ISBN:0-691-12389-6, ISBN13: 978-0-691-12389-9. Dewey:302.
Audience: **u,f.** *Choice, 2004.*

Fischer, Agneta H. (Editor) **BF591 .G45 2000**
Gender and Emotion: Social Psychological Perspectives. Keith Oatley & Antony Manstead (Contribution by). Cloth Text. Cambridge University Press. New York, NY. 2000. 344p. Studies in Emotion and Social Interaction ISBN:0-521-63015-0, ISBN13: 978-0-521-63015-3. Dewey:155.3/3. LCCN:99-029140.
Audience: **l,u.** *Choice, 2000.*

Forgas, Joseph P. (Editor) **BF531 .F44 1999**
Feeling and Thinking: The Role of Affect in Social Cognition. Antony Manstead & Keith Oatley (Contribution by). Trade Cloth. Cambridge University Press. New York, NY. 1999. 438p. Studies in Emotion and Social Interaction ISBN:0-521-64223-X, ISBN13: 978-0-521-64223-1. Dewey:152.4. LCCN:99-018219.
Audience: **u,f.** *Choice, 2000.*

Gordon, Suzanne **HM132**
Lonely in America. Trade Paper. Simon & Schuster. New York, NY. 1977. ISBN:0-671-22754-8, ISBN13: 978-0-671-22754-8. Dewey:301.11/3.
Audience: **g,l,u.** *B*

King, Debra & Flam, Helena **HM881**
Emotions and Social Movements. Paper over Boards. Routledge. New York, NY. 2005. 208p. Routledge Advances in Sociology Ser. ISBN:0-415-36316-0, ISBN13: 978-0-415-36316-7. Dewey:303.4/84.
Audience: **l,u,f.**

Siegel, Marc **HM1033.S525 2005**
False Alarm: The Truth about the Epidemic of Fear. Trade Cloth. John Wiley & Sons, Inc. Hoboken, NJ. 2005. 256p. ISBN:0-471-67869-4, ISBN13: 978-0-471-67869-4. Dewey:302/.17. LCCN:2004-022952.
Audience: **g,l.**

Sorokin, Pitirim Aleksandrovich **BJ1474.S69 2002**
The Ways and Power of Love: Types, Factors, and Techniques of Moral Transformation. Stephen G. Post (Introduction by). Trade Cloth. Templeton Foundation Press. Radnor, PA. 2002. 584p. ISBN:1-890151-86-6, ISBN13: 978-1-890151-86-7. Dewey:171/.8. LCCN:2001-058134.
Audience: **l,u,f.** *Choice, 2003, 2002.*

Stivers, Richard **HM851.S75 2004**
Shades of Loneliness: Pathologies of a Technological Society. Book, Other. Rowman & Littlefield Publishers, Inc. Lanham, MD. 2004. 208p. New Social Formations Ser. ISBN:0-7425-3003-5, ISBN13: 978-0-7425-3003-4. Dewey:303.48/33. LCCN:2003-020758.
Audience: **u,f.**

Vygotsky, L. S. **BF121.V9413 1987**
The Collected Works of L. S. Vygotsky: Problems of General Psychology, Including the Volume "Thinking and Speech". Trade Cloth. Basic Books. New York, NY. 1988. 406p. Cognition and Language Ser. ISBN:0-306-42441-X, ISBN13: 978-0-306-42441-0. Dewey:150. LCCN:87-007219.
Audience: **l,u.**

Warhol, Robyn R. **PN56.5.W64W375 2002**
Having a Good Cry: Effeminate Feelings and Pop-Culture Forms. Trade Cloth. Ohio State University Press. Columbus, OH. 2002. xx, 148p. The Theory and Interpretation of Narrative Ser. ISBN:0-8142-0928-9, ISBN13: 978-0-8142-0928-8. Dewey:809/.89287. LCCN:2002-013495.
Audience: **l,u,f.** *Choice, 2003.*

Social Psychology > Influence

Lewin, Kurt **HM251.L474**
Resolving Social Conflicts: Selected Papers on Group Dynamics. Lewin, Gertrud Weiss (Editor); Allport, Gordon W. (Translator). Harper. 1948.
Audience: **l,u,f.**

Linton, Ralph **BF637.F67**
The Cultural Background of Personality. Library Binding. Greenwood Publishing Group, Inc. Portsmouth, NH. 1981. 157p. ISBN:0-313-22783-7, ISBN13: 978-0-313-22783-7. Dewey:155.9/2. LCCN:80-029240.
Audience: **u,f.** B

Sztompka, Piotr **HM1181 .S97 1999**
Trust: A Sociological Theory. Jeffrey C. Alexander & Steven Seidman (Contribution by). Trade Paper. Cambridge University Press. New York, NY. 2000. 226p. Cultural Social Studies ISBN:0-521-59850-8, ISBN13: 978-0-521-59850-7. Dewey:na. LCCN:00-266562.
Audience: **l,u.**

Social Psychology > Influence > Persuasion

Bales, Robert F. **HM291**
Interaction Process Analysis. Paper Text. University of Chicago Press. Chicago, IL. 1976. Midway Reprint Ser. ISBN:0-226-03618-9, ISBN13: 978-0-226-03618-2. Dewey:301.15.
Audience: **l,u,f.**

Blumer, Herbert **HM291**
Symbolic Interactionism: Perspective and Method. Trade Cloth. University of California Press. Berkeley, CA. 1986. ISBN:0-520-05675-2, ISBN13: 978-0-520-05675-6. Dewey:302.
Audience: **u,f.** B

Gouldner, Alvin W. **HM141**
Studies in Leadership. Arthur P. Brief (Editor). Library Binding. Garland Publishing, Inc. New York, NY. 1987. 736p. Continuity in Administrative Science and Ancestral Books in the Management of Organizations ISBN:0-8240-8230-3, ISBN13: 978-0-8240-8230-7. Dewey:303.3/4. LCCN:86-027053.
Audience: **l,u,f.**

Milgram, Stanley **HM1251.M53 2004**
Obedience to Authority: An Experimental View. Trade Paper. HarperCollins Publishers. New York, NY. 2004. 256p. Perennial Classics Ser. ISBN:0-06-073728-X, ISBN13: 978-0-06-073728-3. Dewey:303.3/6. LCCN:2004-051001.
Audience: **u,f.** B

Sennett, Richard **HM271**
Authority. Trade Paper. W. W. Norton & Company, Inc. New York, NY. 1993. 224p. ISBN:0-393-31027-2, ISBN13: 978-0-393-31027-6. Dewey:303.3/6.
Audience: **l,u,f.** B

Social Psychology > Influence > Conformity

Hogan, Patrick Colm **HM1246.H64 2001**
The Culture of Conformism: Understanding Social Consent. Trade Cloth. Duke University Press. Durham, NC. 2001. 200p. ISBN:0-8223-2705-8, ISBN13: 978-0-8223-2705-9. Dewey:303.3/2. LCCN:00-045184.
Audience: **l,u,f.**

Kohn, Melvin L. **HQ734**
Class and Conformity: A Study in Values. Ed. 2. Trade Paper. University of Chicago Press. Chicago, IL. 1989. 376p. Midway Reprint Ser. ISBN:0-226-45026-0, ISBN13: 978-0-226-45026-1. Dewey:301.42/7. LCCN:77-085194.
Audience: **l,u,f.**

Potter, David M. **E169.1 .P599**
Freedom and Its Limitations in American Life. Don E. Fehrenbacher (Editor). Trade Paper. Stanford University Press. Palo Alto, CA. 1976. xiv, 90p. ISBN:0-8047-1009-0, ISBN13: 978-0-8047-1009-1. Dewey:973. LCCN:76-017786.
Audience: **l,u,f.**

Sunstein, Cass R. **JC328.3.S93 2005**
Why Societies Need Dissent. Trade Paper. Harvard University Press. Cambridge, MA. 2005. 256p. Oliver Wendell Holmes Lectures ISBN:0-674-01768-4, ISBN13: 978-0-674-01768-9. Dewey:303.48/4.
Audience: **l,u,f.** *Choice, 2004.*

Social Psychology > Influence > Deviance

Becker, Howard S. **HM291**
Outsiders. Trade Cloth. Simon & Schuster. New York, NY. 1997. 224p. ISBN:0-684-83635-1, ISBN13: 978-0-684-83635-5. Dewey:302.5/42.
Audience: **g,l,u,f.**

Clinard, Marshall B. & Meier, Robert F. **HM811.C58 2004**
Sociology of Deviant Behavior. Ed. 12. Cloth Text. Thomson

Wadsworth. Belmont, CA. 2003. 704p. ISBN:0-534-61947-9, ISBN13: 978-0-534-61947-3. Dewey:302.5/42/0973. LCCN:2003-101956.
Audience: **u,f.** BCL3

Hendershott, Anne B. **HM811.H46 2002**
The Politics of Deviance. Trade Cloth. Encounter Books. New York, NY. 2005. 194p. Ser. ISBN:1-893554-47-3, ISBN13: 978-1-893554-47-4. Dewey:302.5/42. LCCN:2002-017915.
Audience: **u,f.** *Choice, 2003.*

Lofland, John **HM811.L6 2002**
Deviance and Identity. Paper Text. Eliot Werner Publications, Inc. Clinton Corners, NY. 2002. 362p. Foundations of Sociology Ser. ISBN:0-9712427-9-8, ISBN13: 978-0-9712427-9-1. Dewey:302.5/42. LCCN:2002-102713.
Audience: **u,f.**

Social Psychology > Influence > Media/Communication

Habermas, Jurgen **HM106.H313**
Communication and the Evolution of Society. Thomas McCarthy (Translator). Trade Cloth. Beacon Press. Boston, MA. 1979. 234p. ISBN:0-8070-1512-1, ISBN13: 978-0-8070-1512-4. Dewey:301.14. LCCN:77-088324.
Audience: **g,l.** BCL3

Hall, Edward T. **P40**
Beyond Culture. Trade Cloth. Peter Smith Publisher, Inc. Magnolia, MA. 1992. ISBN:0-8446-6551-7, ISBN13: 978-0-8446-6551-1. Dewey:301.2/1.
Audience: **u,f.** BCL3

Hoggart, Richard **HM1206**
Mass Media in a Mass Society: Myth and Reality. Trade Paper. Continuum International Publishing Group, Ltd. London, 2005. 224p. ISBN:0-8264-7626-0, ISBN13: 978-0-8264-7626-5. Dewey:306/.0941.
Audience: **l,u,f.** *Choice, 2004.*

Peters, John Durham & Simonson, Peter **HM1206.M36 2004**
Mass Communication and American Social Thought: Key Texts, 1919-1968. Book, Other. Rowman & Littlefield Publishers, Inc. Lanham, MD. 2004. 552p. Critical Media Studies, :Institutions, Politics, and Culture Ser. ISBN:0-7425-2838-3, ISBN13: 978-0-7425-2838-3. Dewey:302.23. LCCN:2004-002451.
Audience: **g,l,u,f.** *Choice, 2005.*

Turow, Joseph **P90.T87 1997**
Media Systems in Society: Understanding Industries, Strategies, and Power. Ed. 2. Trade Paper. Allyn & Bacon, Inc. Boston, MA. 1996. 320p. ISBN:0-8013-1704-5, ISBN13: 978-0-8013-1704-0. Dewey:302.23. LCCN:96-008986.
Audience: **l,u,f.**

Social Psychology > Influence > Media/Communication > Propaganda

Ellul, Jacques **HM263 .E413 1973**
Propaganda: The Formation of Men's Attitudes. Trade Cloth. Knopf Publishing Group. New York, NY. 1973. 352p. ISBN:0-394-71874-7, ISBN13: 978-0-394-71874-3. Dewey:301.15/4. LCCN:72-008053.
Audience: **u,f.**

Hacker, Kenneth L. **JK524.P664 2004**
Presidential Candidate Images. Book, Other. Rowman & Littlefield Publishers, Inc. Lanham, MD. 2004. 288p. Communication, Media, and Politics Ser. ISBN:0-7425-3664-5, ISBN13: 978-0-7425-3664-7. Dewey:324.7/3/0973. LCCN:2004-008428.
Audience: **l,u,f.** *Choice, 2005.*

Huxley, Aldous **PR6015**
Brave New World Revisited. UK-B Format Paperback. Knopf Publishing Group. New York, NY. 2004. 208p. ISBN:0-09-945823-3, ISBN13: 978-0-09-945823-4. Dewey:823/.912.
Audience: **g,l,u,f.** BCL3

Lasswell, Harold D. (Editor) **HM258.P74**
Propaganda and Communication in World History: The Symbolic Instrument in Early Times, Vol. 1. Cloth Text. University of Hawaii Press. Honolulu, HI. 1979. Propaganda and Communication in World History Ser. ISBN:0-8248-0496-1, ISBN13: 978-0-8248-0496-1. Dewey:301.14. LCCN:78-023964.
Audience: **u,f.** BCL3

Lasswell, Harold D. (Editor), et al. **HM258 .P74 VOL. 2**
Propaganda and Communication in World History: Emergence of Public Opinion in the West, Vol. 2. Daniel Lerner & Hans Speier (Editors). Cloth Text. University of Hawaii Press. Honolulu, HI. 1979. Propaganda and Communication in World History Ser. ISBN:0-8248-0504-6, ISBN13: 978-0-8248-0504-3. Dewey:301.14. LCCN:79-018790.
Audience: **u,f.**

Lasswell, Harold D. (Editor), et al. **HM258 .P74 VOL. 3**
Propaganda and Communication in World History: A Pluralizing World in Formation, Vol. 3. Daniel Lerner & Hans Speier (Editors). Cloth Text. University of Hawaii Press. Honolulu, HI. 1980. Propaganda and Communication in World History Ser. ISBN:0-8248-0507-0, ISBN13: 978-0-8248-0507-4. Dewey:301.14. LCCN:79-021108.
Audience: **u,f.**

Social Psychology > Influence > Media/Communication > Advertising

Kitch, Carolyn **P94.5.W652U655 2001**
The Girl on the Magazine Cover: The Origins of Visual Stereotypes in American Mass Media. Trade Paper. University of North Carolina Press. Chapel Hill, NC. 2001. 272p. ISBN:0-8078-4978-2, ISBN13: 978-0-8078-4978-1. Dewey:302.23/082/0973. LCCN:2001-027415.
Audience: **l,u,f.** *Choice, 2002.*

McAllister, Matthew P. **HF5813.U6M327 1996**
The Commercialization of American Culture: New Advertising, Control and Democracy. Trade Cloth. SAGE Publications, Inc. Thousand Oaks, CA. 1995. 292p. ISBN:0-8039-5379-8, ISBN13: 978-0-8039-5379-6. Dewey:659. LCCN:95-035569.
Audience: **l,u,f.** *Choice, 1996.*

Social Psychology > Influence > Media/Communication > Public Opinion/Social Surveys

Polling the Nations.
http://www.orspub.com/
ORS Publishing.
Audience: **l,u.**

Backstrom, Charles H. & Hursh-Cesar, Gerald D. **HM261**
Survey Research. Ed. 2. Trade Paper. Prentice Hall PTR. Upper Saddle River, NJ. 1998. 436p. ISBN:0-02-305080-2, ISBN13: 978-0-02-305080-0. Dewey:320.018. LCCN:81-001738.
Audience: **l,u,f.**

Gallup, George H. **HN90.P8 G3**
The Gallup Poll: Public Opinion, 1935-1971, Set. Trade Cloth. Greenwood Publishing Group, Inc. Portsmouth, NH. 1977. 1900p. Documentary Reference Collections ISBN:0-313-20129-3, ISBN13: 978-0-313-20129-5. Dewey:301.15/43/32900973.
Audience: **u,f.**

Lippmann, Walter **HM261.L75 2004**
Public Opinion. Trade Paper. Dover Publications, Inc. Mineola, NY. 2004. 240p. ISBN:0-486-43703-5, ISBN13: 978-0-486-43703-3. Dewey:303.3/8. LCCN:2004-050241.
Audience: **g,l,u,f.**

McCombs, Maxwell **PN4888.S6**
Setting the Agenda: The Mass Media and Public Opinion. Trade Cloth. Polity Press. Cambridge, 2004. 198p. ISBN:0-7456-2312-3, ISBN13: 978-0-7456-2312-2. Dewey:302.23. LCCN:2005-274771.
Audience: **l,u,f.** *Choice, 2005.*

Wolfe, Alan **HT690.U6W65 1998**
One Nation, after All: What Middle-Class Americans Really Think about God, Country, Family, Racism, Welfare, Immigration, Homosexuality, Work, the Right, the Left and Each Other. Trade Paper. Penguin Group (USA) Inc. New York, NY. 1999. 368p. ISBN:0-14-027572-X, ISBN13: 978-0-14-027572-8. Dewey:305.5/5/0973. LCCN:97-036925.
Audience: **g.**

Social Psychology > Interaction

Goffman, Erving **HM291 .G59 1982**
Interaction Ritual: Essays in Face-to-Face Behavior. Trade Paper. Knopf Publishing Group. New York, NY. 1982. 288p. ISBN:0-394-70631-5, ISBN13: 978-0-394-70631-3. Dewey:302. LCCN:81-014000.
Audience: **l,u,f.**

Rawlins, William K. **HM132.5.R38 1991**
Friendship Matters: Communication, Dialectics, and the Life Course. Trade Cloth. Aldine Transaction. Somerset, NJ. 1992. 307p. Communication and Social Order Ser. ISBN:0-202-30403-5, ISBN13: 978-0-202-30403-8. Dewey:302.3/4. LCCN:91-030676.
Audience: **u,f.** *Choice, 1992.*

Schur, Edwin M. **HM291**
Labeling Deviant Behavior: Its Sociological Implications. Paper Text. HarperCollins Publishers. New York, NY. 1971. xi, 177p. Demearath Ser. ISBN:0-06-045812-7, ISBN13: 978-0-06-045812-6. Dewey:301.6/2. LCCN:75-168359.
Audience: **u,f.** B

Walton, John **HN79.C22**
Western Times and Water Wars: State, Culture, and Rebellion in California. Trade Paper. University of California Press. Berkeley, CA. 1993. 388p. ISBN:0-520-08453-5, ISBN13: 978-0-520-08453-7. Dewey:303.4/84/0979494.
Audience: **g,l,u,f.** *Choice, 1992.*

Social Psychology > Interaction > Leadership

Brown, Marvin T. **HD60.B766 2005**
Corporate Integrity: Rethinking Organizational Ethics and Leadership. Trade Cloth. Cambridge University Press. New York, NY. 2005. 284p. ISBN:0-521-84481-9, ISBN13: 978-0-521-84481-9. Dewey:174/.4. LCCN:2004-057062.
Audience: **l,u,f.** *Choice, 2006.*

Ciulla, Joanne B. (Editor) **HF5387**
Ethics, the Heart of Leadership. Ed. 2. Trade Cloth. Greenwood Publishing Group, Inc. Portsmouth, NH. 2004. 224p. ISBN:0-275-98248-3, ISBN13: 978-0-275-98248-5. Dewey:174/.4. LCCN:2004-009602.
Audience: **g,l,u.** *Choice, 1998.*

Gardner, John W. **HM141**
On Leadership. Trade Paper. Simon & Schuster. New York, NY. 1993. 220p. ISBN:0-02-911312-1, ISBN13: 978-0-02-911312-7. Dewey:303.3/4. LCCN:89-016894.
Audience: **g,l,u,f.** *Choice, 1990.*

Kellerman, Barbara **HD57.7.K47 2004**
Bad Leadership: What It Is, How It Happens, Why It Matters. Trade Paper. Harvard Business School Press. Boston, MA. 2004. 256p. Leadership for the Common Good Ser. ISBN:1-59139-166-0, ISBN13: 978-1-59139-166-1. Dewey:658.4/092. LCCN:2004-014041.
Audience: **l,u.** *Choice, 2005.*

Lombardi, Vince **HD57.7**
What It Takes to Be #1: Vince Lombardi on Leadership. Trade Cloth. McGraw-Hill Companies, The. New York, NY. 2003.

278p. ISBN:0-07-142036-3, ISBN13: 978-0-07-142036-5. Dewey:658.4/092.
Audience: **g,l,u,f.**

Post, Jerrold M. **JC330.3.P68 2004**
Leaders and Their Followers in a Dangerous World: The Psychology of Political Behavior. Alexander George (Foreword by). Trade Cloth. Cornell University Press. Ithaca, NY. 2004. 320p. Psychoanalysis and Social Theory Ser. ISBN:0-8014-4169-2, ISBN13: 978-0-8014-4169-1. Dewey:320/.01/9. LCCN:2003-021237.
Audience: **l,u,f.** *Choice, 2005.*

Rubenzer, Steven J. & Faschingbauer, Thomas R. **E176.1.R89 2004**
Personality, Character, and Leadership in the White House: Psychologists Assess the Presidents. Trade Cloth. Potomac Books, Inc. Dulles, VA. 2004. 432p. ISBN:1-57488-815-3, ISBN13: 978-1-57488-815-7. Dewey:973/.09/9. LCCN:2004-008632.
Audience: **l,u.** *Choice, 2005.*

Sims, Ronald R. & Quatro, Scott A. (Editors) **HD57.7.L4355 2004**
Leadership: Succeeding in the Private, Public, and Not-For-Profit Sectors. Trade Paper. M. E. Sharpe Inc. Armonk, NY. 2005. 448p. ISBN:0-7656-1430-8, ISBN13: 978-0-7656-1430-8. Dewey:658.4/092. LCCN:2004-009101.
Audience: **l,u.** *Choice, 2005.*

Van Wart, Montgomery **JF1525.L4V35 2005**
The Dynamics of Leadership: Theory and Practice. Trade Cloth. M. E. Sharpe Inc. Armonk, NY. 2005. 520p. ISBN:0-7656-0901-0, ISBN13: 978-0-7656-0901-4. Dewey:352.3/9. LCCN:2004-017454.
Audience: **u,f.** *Choice, 2005.*

Social Psychology > Interaction > Conflict

Fisher, R. J. **HM131.F525 1990**
The Social Psychology of Intergroup and International Conflict Resolution. Cloth Text. Springer. New York, NY. 1989. 277p. Social Psychology Ser. ISBN:0-387-97073-8, ISBN13: 978-0-387-97073-8. Dewey:303.6/9. LCCN:89-035512.
Audience: **l,u,f.** *Choice, 1990.*

Gelfand, Michele J. & Brett, Jeanne M. **BF637.N4H365 2004**
The Handbook of Negotiation: Theoretical Advances and Cross-Cultural Perspectives. Trade Cloth. Stanford University Press. Palo Alto, CA. 2004. 480p. ISBN:0-8047-4586-2, ISBN13: 978-0-8047-4586-4. Dewey:302.3. LCCN:2003-025169.
Audience: **g,l,u,f.** *Choice, 2005.*

Miller, Arthur G. (Editor) **HM1116.S63 2004**
The Social Psychology of Good and Evil. Trade Paper. Guilford Publications, Inc. New York, NY. 2005. 498p. ISBN:1-59385-194-4, ISBN13: 978-1-59385-194-1. Dewey:303.3/72.
Audience: **g,l,u,f.** *Choice, 2004.*

Perelman, Michael **HM221.P44 1998**
Class Warfare in the Information Age. Cloth over Boards. Palgrave Macmillan. New York, NY. 1998. 160p. ISBN:0-312-17758-5, ISBN13: 978-0-312-17758-4. Dewey:305.5. LCCN:97-053280.
Audience: **l,u,f.** *Choice, 1999.*

Social Psychology > Interaction > Conflict > Aggression

del Mar, David Peterson **HM886.P474 2002**
Beaten Down: A History of Interpersonal Violence in the West. Trade Cloth. University of Washington Press. Seattle, WA. 2002. 312p. ISBN:0-295-98260-8, ISBN13: 978-0-295-98260-1. Dewey:303.6/0978. LCCN:2002-072684.
Audience: **l,u,f.** *Choice, 2003.*

Social Psychology > Interaction > Conflict > Prejudice

Chin, Jean Lau (Editor) **BF575**
The Psychology of Prejudice and Discrimination. Cloth Text. Greenwood Publishing Group, Inc. Portsmouth, NH. 2004. 1,000p. Race and Ethnicity in Psychology Ser. ISBN:0-275-98234-3, ISBN13: 978-0-275-98234-8. Dewey:303.3/85/0973. LCCN:2004-042289.
Audience: **l,u.** *Choice, 2005.*

Lott, Bernice & Maluso, Diane (Editors) **BF575.P9S64 1995**
The Social Psychology of Interpersonal Discrimination. Cloth over Boards. Guilford Publications, Inc. New York, NY. 1995. 232p. ISBN:1-57230-021-3, ISBN13: 978-1-57230-021-7. Dewey:303.3/85. LCCN:95-002851.
Audience: **l,u,f.** *Choice, 1996.*

Ruscher, Janet B. **BF575.P9R87 2001**
Prejudiced Communication: A Social Psychological Perspective. Cloth over Boards. Guilford Publications, Inc. New York, NY. 2001. 240p. ISBN:1-57230-638-6, ISBN13: 978-1-57230-638-7. Dewey:303.3/85. LCCN:00-054356.
Audience: **u,f.** *Choice, 2001.*

Waller, James **E184.A1W216 2000**
Prejudice Across America. Trade Cloth. University Press of Mississippi. Jackson, MS. 2000. xxvi, 310p. ISBN:1-57806-269-1, ISBN13: 978-1-57806-269-0. Dewey:305.8/00973. LCCN:00-035195.
Audience: **g,l,u,f.** *Choice, 2001.*

Social Psychology > Interaction > Conflict > Stress

Cooper, Cary L. & Dewe, Philip **BF575.S75C646 2004**
Stress: A Brief History. Trade Cloth. Blackwell Publishing, Inc. Malden, MA. 2004. 160p. Blackwell Brief Histories of Psychology Ser., Vol. 1 ISBN:1-4051-0744-8, ISBN13: 978-1-4051-0744-0. Dewey:155.9/042/09. LCCN:2003-023501.
Audience: **g,l,u,f.** *Choice, 2004.*

Fullerton, Carol S. & Ursano, Robert J. (Editors) **RC552.P67P666 1997**
Posttraumatic Stress Disorder: Acute and Long-Term Responses to Trauma and Disaster. Cloth Text. American Psychiatric Publishing, Inc. Arlington, VA. 1997. 256p. Progress in Psychiatry Ser., Vol. 51 ISBN:0-88048-751-8, ISBN13: 978-0-88048-751-1. Dewey:616.85/21. LCCN:96-024027.
Audience: **l,u,f.** *Choice, 1997.*

Linsky, Arnold, et al. **HN90.V5**
Stress, Culture, and Aggression. Ronet Bachman & Murray Straus (Authors). Trade Paper. Yale University Press. Cumberland, RI. 2004. 208p. ISBN:0-300-10209-7, ISBN13: 978-0-300-10209-3. Dewey:303.6.
Audience: **l,u,f.**

Mirowsky, John & Ross, Catherine E. **RC455.4.S87M57 2002**
Social Causes of Psychological Distress. Ed. 2. Trade Cloth. Aldine Transaction. Somerset, NJ. 2003. 320p. Social Institutions and Social Change Ser. ISBN:0-202-30708-5, ISBN13: 978-0-202-30708-4. Dewey:155.9/042. LCCN:2002-011167.
Audience: **l,u,f.** *Choice, 1990.*

Moos, Rudolf H. **BF335.C59 1986**
Coping with Life Crises: An Integrated Approach. Trade Cloth. Basic Books. New York, NY. 1986. 444p. Stress and Coping Ser. ISBN:0-306-42133-X, ISBN13: 978-0-306-42133-4. Dewey:155. LCCN:85-028149.
Audience: **l,u.** *Choice, 1986.*

Wong, Paul T. P. & Wong, Lilian C. J. (Editors) **BF335.H36 2006**
e Handbook of Multicultural Perspectives on Stress and Coping. E-Book. Springer. New York, NY. 2006. 636p. ISBN:0-387-26238-5, ISBN13: 978-0-387-26238-3. Dewey:362.196/98. LCCN:2005-927415.
Audience: **l,u.**

Zautra, Alex J. **R726.7.Z38 2003**
Emotions, Stress, and Health. Trade Cloth. Oxford University Press, Inc. New York, NY. 2003. 326p. ISBN:0-19-513359-5, ISBN13: 978-0-19-513359-2. Dewey:616/.001/9. LCCN:2002-001456.
Audience: **l,u.** *Choice, 2003.*

Social History

Burke, Peter **HM551.B85 2005**
History and Social Theory. Ed. 2. Trade Cloth. Cornell University Press. Ithaca, NY. 2005. 208p. ISBN:0-8014-4453-5, ISBN13: 978-0-8014-4453-1. Dewey:306/.09. LCCN:2005-049684.
Audience: **l,u,f.** *Choice, 1993.*

Merton, Robert K. **HM5**
Social Theory and Social Structure. Free Press. 1968. ISBN:0-02-921130-1, ISBN13: 978-0-02-921130-4.
Audience: **g,l.**

Stearns, Peter (Editor) **HN373.E63 2001**
Encyclopedia of European Social History: From 1350 to 2000, Set. Trade Cloth. Thomson Gale. Farmington Hills, MI. 1905. 3186p. ISBN:0-684-80582-0, ISBN13: 978-0-684-80582-5. Dewey:306/.094/03. LCCN:00-046376.
Audience: **g,l,u.** *Choice, 2001.*

Social History > Culture

Arato, Andrew & Gebhardt, Eike (Editors) **HM24**
The Essential Frankfurt School Reader. Trade Paper. Continuum International Publishing Group, Ltd. London, 1982. 576p. Essential Frankfurt School Reader Ser., Vol. 1 ISBN:0-8264-0194-5, ISBN13: 978-0-8264-0194-6. Dewey:301/.01. LCCN:82-008063.
Audience: **l,u.**

Barr, Andrew **HV5292**
Drink: A Social History of America. Trade Paper. DIANE Publishing Company. Collingdale, PA. 2002. 466p. ISBN:0-7567-5321-X, ISBN13: 978-0-7567-5321-4. Dewey:394.1/3/0973.
Audience: **g,l,u.** *Choice, 1999.*

Bauman, Zygmunt **HM101.B285 1999**
Culture as Praxis. Cloth Text. SAGE Publications, Ltd. London, 1999. 208p. Theory, Culture and Society Ser. ISBN:0-7619-5988-2, ISBN13: 978-0-7619-5988-5. Dewey:306. LCCN:98-075101.
Audience: **u,f.**

Bayart, Jean-Francois **HM753.B38513 2005**
The Illusion of Cultural Identity. Steven Rendall, Janet Roitman, Cynthia Schoch & Jonathan Derrick (Translators). Trade Cloth. University of Chicago Press. Chicago, IL. 2005. 296p. ISBN:0-226-03961-7, ISBN13: 978-0-226-03961-9. Dewey:305.8/009. LCCN:2005-006370.
Audience: **u,f.** *Choice, 2006.*

Bragg, Lois (Editor) **HV2545.D43 2001**
Deaf World: A Historical Reader and Primary Sourcebook. Trade Cloth. New York University Press. New York, NY. 2001. 430p. ISBN:0-8147-9852-7, ISBN13: 978-0-8147-9852-2. Dewey:305.9/08162. LCCN:00-058727.
Audience: **g,l.**

Burch, Susan **HV2530.B87 2004**
Signs of Resistance: American Deaf Cultural History,1900 to 1942. Trade Paper. New York University Press. New York, NY. 2004. 240p. ISBN:0-8147-9894-2, ISBN13: 978-0-8147-9894-2. Dewey:305.9/082/0973/09041. LCCN:2002-007720.
Audience: **g,l,u,f.**

Chambers, Deborah, et al. **HM101**
The Practice of Cultural Studies: A Guide to the Practice and Politics of Cultural Studies. Richard Johnson, Estella Tincknell & Parvati Raghuram (Authors). Cloth Text. SAGE Publications, Inc. Thousand Oaks, CA. 2004. 312p. ISBN:0-7619-6099-6, ISBN13: 978-0-7619-6099-7. Dewey:306. LCCN:2004-556038.
Audience: **l,u.**

Duis, Perry R. **HV5201.S6D84 1999**
Saloon: Public Drinking in Chicago and Boston, 1880-1920. Trade Paper. University of Illinois Press. Champaign, IL. 1998. 416p. ISBN:0-252-06781-9, ISBN13: 978-0-252-06781-5. Dewey:647.9573. LCCN:00-267506.
Audience: **u.**

Friedland, Roger & Mohr, John W. (Editors) **HM623.M38 2004**
Matters of Culture: Cultural Sociology in Practice. Jeffrey C. Alexander & Steven Seidman (Contribution by). Cloth Text. Cambridge University Press. New York, NY. 2004. 424p.

Cambridge Cultural Social Studies ISBN:0-521-79162-6, ISBN13: 978-0-521-79162-5. Dewey:306/.071. LCCN:2003-055748.

Audience: **l,u.**

Gellner, Ernest **B1626.G441G76 2003**
Cause and Meaning in the Social Sciences. Paper over Boards. Routledge. New York, NY. 2003. 240p. Ernest Gellner Ser., Vol. 1:Selected Philosophical Themes ISBN:0-415-30296-X, ISBN13: 978-0-415-30296-8. Dewey:300.1. LCCN:2002-036919.
Audience: **l,u.**

Huntington, Samuel P. & Harrison, Lawrence E. (Editors) **HM681.C85 2000**
Culture Matters: How Values Shape Human Progress. Trade Cloth. Basic Books. New York, NY. 2000. 384p. ISBN:0-465-03175-7, ISBN13: 978-0-465-03175-7. Dewey:306. LCCN:00-022951.
Audience: **g,l,u.**

Lender, Mark Edward & Martin, James K. **HV5292.L4 1987**
Drinking in America: A History. Trade Paper. Simon & Schuster. New York, NY. 1987. 256p. ISBN:0-02-918570-X, ISBN13: 978-0-02-918570-4. Dewey:394.1/3/0973. LCCN:86-032885.
Audience: **g,l.**

Malinowski, Bronislaw **HM101 .M24 1976**
Freedom and Civilization. Valetta Malinowska (Preface by). Trade Cloth. Greenwood Publishing Group, Inc. Portsmouth, NH. 1977. 338p. ISBN:0-8371-9277-3, ISBN13: 978-0-8371-9277-2. Dewey:301.2. LCCN:76-040226.
Audience: **u,f.** B

Marcuse, Herbert **HM101.M268 1991**
One-Dimensional Man: Studies in the Ideology of Advanced Industrial Society. Douglas Kellner (Introduction by). Trade Paper. Beacon Press. Boston, MA. 1991. 320p. ISBN:0-8070-1417-6, ISBN13: 978-0-8070-1417-2. Dewey:301. LCCN:91-018246.
Audience: **u,f.** B

Mead, Robert Douglas (Author, Illustrator) **HM101.M38 1978**
Culture and Commitment: The New Relationships Between the Generations in the 1970s. Cloth Text. Columbia University Press. New York, NY. 1978. xx, 178p. ISBN:0-231-04632-4, ISBN13: 978-0-231-04632-9. Dewey:301.2. LCCN:78-014589.
Audience: **u,f.** B

Nisbet, Robert A. **HM101.N574 1994**
History of the Idea of Progress. Ed. 2. Trade Paper. Transaction Publishers. Somerset, NJ. 1994. 370p. ISBN:1-56000-713-3, ISBN13: 978-1-56000-713-5. Dewey:303.44/09. LCCN:93-028738.
Audience: **u,f.** B

Padden, Carol & Humphries, Tom **HV2545.P33 1988**
Deaf in America: Voices from a Culture. Trade Paper. Harvard University Press. Cambridge, MA. 1990. 144p. ISBN:0-674-19424-1, ISBN13: 978-0-674-19424-3. Dewey:362.4/2/0973. LCCN:88-011769.
Audience: **g,l,u,f.**

Semmes, Clovis E. **E185**
Cultural Hegemony and African American Development. Trade Cloth. Greenwood Publishing Group, Inc. Portsmouth, NH. 1992. 288p. ISBN:0-275-93923-5, ISBN13: 978-0-275-93923-6. Dewey:305.896/073. LCCN:92-016205.
Audience: **u,f.** *Choice, 1993.*

Sorokin, Pitirim A. **HM101.S7512**
Social and Cultural Dynamics. Trade Cloth. Porter Sargent Publishers, Inc. Boston, MA. 1985. 720p. Extending Horizons Ser. ISBN:0-87558-029-7, ISBN13: 978-0-87558-029-6. Dewey:901.9. LCCN:57-014120.
Audience: **l,u.**

Sorokin, Pitirim A. **HM61.S6 1959**
Social and Cultural Mobility. Trade Cloth. Simon & Schuster. New York, NY. 1959. ISBN:0-02-930270-6, ISBN13: 978-0-02-930270-5. Dewey:301.44. LCCN:59-013122.
Audience: **g,l,u,f.** B

Social History > Culture > By Country or Region

HN490.V5.V56
Violence and Civil Disorder in Italian Cities, 1200-1500. Trade Cloth. University of California Press. Berkeley, CA. 1972. viii, 353p. ISBN:0-520-01906-7, ISBN13: 978-0-520-01906-5. Dewey:309.1/45. LCCN:71-145791.
Audience: **l,u,f.** B

Agbasiere, Joseph Therese & Ardener, Shirley **DT515.45.I33A35 2000**
Women in Igbo Life and Thought. Trade Paper. Routledge. New York, NY. 2000. 224p. ISBN:0-415-22704-6, ISBN13: 978-0-415-22704-9. Dewey:305.48/896332. LCCN:99-040300.
Audience: **u,f.** *Choice, 2001.*

Allen, Catherine J. **F2230.2.K4.A45 1988**
The Hold Life Has: Coca and Cultural Identity in an Andean Community. Book, Other. Smithsonian Institution Press. Washington, DC. 1988. 352p. Series in Ethnographic Inquiry ISBN:0-87474-255-2, ISBN13: 978-0-87474-255-8. Dewey:305.898/323. LCCN:88-003965.
Audience: **u,f.** *Choice, 1989.*

Allen, Robert L. & Allen, Pamela P. **HN57**
Reluctant Reformers: The Impact of Racism on American Social Reform Movements. Trade Paper. Doubleday Publishing. New York, NY. 1975. 360p. ISBN:0-385-03996-4, ISBN13: 978-0-385-03996-3. Dewey:301.2420973.
Audience: **l,u,f.**

Artibise, A. F. **HN110.W5**
Winnipeg: A Social History of Urban Growth, 1874-1914. Trade Cloth. McGill-Queen's University Press. Montreal, PQ. 1975. 400p. ISBN:0-7735-0202-5, ISBN13: 978-0-7735-0202-4. Dewey:309.1/7127/402. LCCN:75-325419.
Audience: **u,f.** B

Baer, Gabriel **HN656.A8**
Fellah and Townsman in the Middle East: Studies in Social History. Trade Paper. Taylor & Francis Group. Abingdon, 1982. 330p. ISBN:0-7146-3126-4, ISBN13: 978-0-7146-3126-4. Dewey:956. LCCN:82-183738.
Audience: **u,f.** B

Barber, Bernard & Barber, Elinor G. **HN380.Z9 S635 1977**
European Social Class: Stability and Change. Trade Cloth.

Greenwood Publishing Group, Inc. Portsmouth, NH. 1978. 145p. Main Themes in European History ISBN:0-8371-9860-7, ISBN13: 978-0-8371-9860-6. Dewey:301.44/094. LCCN:77-013508.
Audience: **u,f.**

Barrett, Stanley R. **HN800.N5.B35**
Two Villages on Stilts; Economic and Family Change in Nigeria. Trade Cloth. Chandler Publishing Company. New York, NY. 1974. xi, 115p. ISBN:0-8102-0475-4, ISBN13: 978-0-8102-0475-1. Dewey:301.42/3/09669. LCCN:73-019765.
Audience: **l,u,f.**

Barz, Gregory F. **ML3920.B25 2005**
Singing for Life: HIV/AIDS and Music in Uganda. Jim Wooten (Foreword by). Paper over Boards. Routledge. New York, NY. 2005. 280p. ISBN:0-415-97289-2, ISBN13: 978-0-415-97289-5. Dewey:362.196/9792/0096761. LCCN:2005-013959.
Audience: **u,f.**

Bell, Daniel **HN58.B424 2000**
The End of Ideology: On the Exhaustion of Political Ideas in the Fifties, with the Resumption of History in the New Century. Ed. 2. Trade Paper. Harvard University Press. Cambridge, MA. 2000. 540p. ISBN:0-674-00426-4, ISBN13: 978-0-674-00426-9. Dewey:306/.0973. LCCN:00-057523.
Audience: **u,f.**

Bell, Peter D. **HD1492.H8**
Peasants in Socialist Transition: Life in a Collectivized Hungarian Village. Trade Cloth. University of California Press. Berkeley, CA. 1984. 320p. ISBN:0-520-04157-7, ISBN13: 978-0-520-04157-8. Dewey:334/.683/09439. LCCN:80-025126.
Audience: **u,f.**

Bianchi, Robert S. **DT159**
Daily Life of the Nubians. Cloth Text. Greenwood Publishing Group, Inc. Portsmouth, NH. 2004. 312p. The Greenwood Press Daily Life Through History Ser. ISBN:0-313-32501-4, ISBN13: 978-0-313-32501-4. Dewey:939/.78. LCCN:2004-013208.
Audience: **g,l,u,f.** *Choice, 2005.*

Bigalike, Terence **DS632.T7**
Tana Toraja: A Social History of an Indonesian People. Trade Cloth. Singapore University Press Proprietary, Ltd. Singapore, 2005. 416p. ISBN:9971-69-318-6, ISBN13: 978-9971-69-318-3. Dewey:306.089/9922.
Audience: **u,f.**

Blum, Jerome **HN373**
The End of the Old Order in Rural Europe. Trade Cloth. Princeton University Press. Princeton, NJ. 1978. 528p. ISBN:0-691-05266-2, ISBN13: 978-0-691-05266-3. Dewey:309.1/4/02. LCCN:77-085530.
Audience: **l,u,f.**

Blythe, Ronald **DA670.S9**
Akenfield: Portrait of an English Village. Trade Paper. Akadine Press, The. Pleasantville, NY. 2001. 287p. ISBN:1-58579-009-5, ISBN13: 978-1-58579-009-8. Dewey:630.11/4264.
Audience: **l,u,f.**

Browne, Ray B. & Ambrosetti, Ronald J. (Editors) **E169.C746 1993**
Continuities in Popular Culture: The Present in the Past and the Past in the Present and Future. Trade Cloth. University of Wisconsin Press. Chicago, IL. 1993. 268p. ISBN:0-87972-592-3, ISBN13: 978-0-87972-592-1. Dewey:306/.0973. LCCN:93-070931.
Audience: **l,u.**

Cepede, M. & Abensour, E. S. **HN380.A4C4**
Rural Problems in the Alpine Region: An International Study. Trade Paper. Bernan Associates. Lanham, MD. 1961. 201p. ISBN:92-5-101667-4, ISBN13: 978-92-5-101667-1. Dewey:309.14947.
Audience: **f.**

Chan, Anita, et al. **HN733.5.C423 1992**
Chen Village under Mao and Deng: The Recent History of a Peasant Community in Mao's China. Ed. 2. Richard Madsen & Jonathan Unger (Authors). Trade Paper. University of California Press. Berkeley, CA. 1992. 354p. ISBN:0-520-08109-9, ISBN13: 978-0-520-08109-3. Dewey:307.720951. LCCN:92-014342.
Audience: **g,l,u,f.**

Chang, Chung-Li **HN673**
Chinese Gentry: Studies on Their Role in 19th-Century Chinese Society. F. Michael (Introduction by). Trade Cloth. University of Washington Press. Seattle, WA. 1967. 272p. Washington Paperbacks on Russia and Asia Ser., No. 4 ISBN:0-295-73743-3, ISBN13: 978-0-295-73743-0. Dewey:301.44. LCCN:55-006738.
Audience: **u,f.**

Ch'u, T'ung-tsu **HN673**
Han Social Structure. Jack L. Dull (Editor). Trade Cloth. University of Washington Press. Seattle, WA. 1972. 570p. Han Dynasty China Ser., Vol. 1 ISBN:0-295-95068-4, ISBN13: 978-0-295-95068-6. Dewey:309.1/31. LCCN:69-014206.
Audience: **u,f.**

Collins, E. J. T. (Editor) **HD1930.E5**
The Agrarian History of England and Wales, 1850-1914, Set. Joan Thirsk (Foreword by). Trade Cloth. Cambridge University Press. New York, NY. 2000. 2336p. Agrarian History of England and Wales Ser., Vol. 7 ISBN:0-521-66214-1, ISBN13: 978-0-521-66214-7. Dewey:338.1/0942.
Audience: **u,f.** *Choice, 2002.*

Cutileiro, José **HD2027**
A Portuguese Rural Society. Trade Cloth. Oxford University Press, Inc. New York, NY. 1971. xvii, 314p. ISBN:0-19-823173-3, ISBN13: 978-0-19-823173-8. Dewey:301.29/469/5. LCCN:79-881336.
Audience: **u,f.**

Dahrendorf, Ralf **HN445**
Society and Democracy in Germany. Trade Cloth. Ashgate Publishing, Ltd. Aldershot, 1993. 496p. Modern Revivals in Sociology Ser. ISBN:0-7512-0117-0, ISBN13: 978-0-7512-0117-8. Dewey:309.1/43.
Audience: **l,u.**

Davis, Allison, et al. **HN79.A2**
Deep South: A Social Anthropological Study of Caste and Class. Burleigh B. Gardner & Mary R. Gardner (Authors), Claudia Mitchell-Kernan (Foreword by). Trade Cloth. C A A S Publications. Los Angeles, CA. 1988. 567p. CAAS Community Classics Ser., Vol. 1 ISBN:0-934934-26-6, ISBN13: 978-0-934934-26-8. Dewey:975.0049607. LCCN:41-023645.
Audience: **l,u,f.**

de Boulay, Juliet **HN650.5.Z9**
Portrait of a Greek Mountain Village. Ed. 3. Mass Market. Cosmos Publishing Company, Inc. River Vale, NJ. 1994. 292p. ISBN:960-7120-05-1, ISBN13: 978-960-7120-05-2. Dewey:914.95.
Audience: **l,u.**

De Vos, George A. **HN723.5.D48**
Socialization for Achievement: Essays on the Cultural Psychology of the Japanese. Trade Cloth. University of California Press. Berkeley, CA. 1973. 613p. Center for Japanese Studies, UC Berkeley, No. 7 ISBN:0-520-01827-3, ISBN13: 978-0-520-01827-3. Dewey:301.15/7/0952. LCCN:78-132420.
Audience: **u,f.**

Deliege, Robert **DS422.C3**
The Untouchables of India. Nora Scott (Translator). Cloth over Boards. Berg Publishers. Oxford, 1999. 288p. Global Issues Ser. ISBN:1-85973-209-7, ISBN13: 978-1-85973-209-0. Dewey:305.5/68.
Audience: **l,u.** *Choice, 2000.*

Demos, John **E162.D46 2004**
Circles and Lines: The Shape of Life in Early America. Trade Cloth. Harvard University Press. Cambridge, MA. 2004. 112p. The William E. Massey Sr. Lectures in the History of American Civilization Ser., Vol. 2002 ISBN:0-674-01324-7, ISBN13: 978-0-674-01324-7. Dewey:973. LCCN:2003-056917.
Audience: **l,u,f.**

Diop, Cheikh Anta **DT61**
The African Origin of Civilization: Myth or Reality. Mercer Cook (Editor, Translator). Trade Paper. Chicago Review Press, Inc. Chicago, IL. 1989. 317p. ISBN:1-55652-072-7, ISBN13: 978-1-55652-072-3. Dewey:932.01. LCCN:73-081746.
Audience: **g,l,u,f.**

Domhoff, G. William **HN90.E4D652 2005**
Who Rules America? Power, Politics, and Social Change. Ed. 5. Paper Text. McGraw-Hill Higher Education. Burr Ridge, IL. 2005. 288p. ISBN:0-07-287625-5, ISBN13: 978-0-07-287625-3. Dewey:305.5/2/0973. LCCN:2005-041604.
Audience: **l,u,f.**

Dupeux, Georges **HN425**
French Society, Seventeen Eighty-Nine to Nineteen Seventy. Peter Wait (Translator). Trade Cloth. Routledge. New York, NY. 1976. 294p. ISBN:0-416-65250-6, ISBN13: 978-0-416-65250-5. Dewey:944.04. LCCN:75-046320.
Audience: **u,f.**

Dyer, Christopher **HC254**
Making a Living in the Middle Ages: The People of Britain 850-1520. Trade Paper. Yale University Press. Cumberland, RI. 2003. 424p. The New Economic History of Britain Seri Ser. ISBN:0-300-10191-0, ISBN13: 978-0-300-10191-1. Dewey:330.941/03.
Audience: **g,l,u,f.** *Choice, 2002.*

Fakhouri, Hani **HN786.K33**
Kafr El-Elow: Continuity and Change in an Egyptian Community. Ed. 2. Paper Text. Waveland Press, Inc. Prospect Heights, IL. 1987. 164p. ISBN:0-88133-285-2, ISBN13: 978-0-88133-285-8. Dewey:306.096216.
Audience: **u,f.**

Falola, Toyin Omoyeni **E184.N55F35**
A Mouth Sweeter Than Salt: An African Memoir. Trade Paper. University of Michigan Press. Chicago, IL. 2005. 288p. ISBN:0-472-03132-5, ISBN13: 978-0-472-03132-0. Dewey:966.928051092.
Audience: **g,l.** *Choice, 2005.*

Fish, John H. **HN80.C5 F58**
Black Power-White Control: The Struggle of the Woodlawn Organization in Chicago. Trade Cloth. Princeton University Press. Princeton, NJ. 1973. 360p. Studies in Religion and Society, Center for the Scientific Study of Religion ISBN:0-691-09358-X, ISBN13: 978-0-691-09358-1. Dewey:322.4/4/0977311. LCCN:72-005379.
Audience: **u,f.**

Fitchen, Janet M. **HN79.N4F58 1991**
Endangered Spaces, Enduring Places: Change, Identity, and Survival in Rural America. Trade Paper. Westview Press. Boulder, CO. 1991. 314p. ISBN:0-8133-1115-2, ISBN13: 978-0-8133-1115-9. Dewey:307.72/0973. LCCN:90-019908.
Audience: **u,f.** *Choice, 1992.*

Foster, George McClelland **HN120.T95.F6 1979**
Tzintzuntzan: Mexican Peasants in a Changing World. Trade Cloth. Elsevier. New York, NY. 1979. 392p. ISBN:0-444-99069-0, ISBN13: 978-0-444-99069-3. Dewey:309.1/72/3. LCCN:79-009496.
Audience: **g,l,u,f.**

Fredericks, Marcel, et al. **RA418.3.G95S63 1986**
Society and Health in Guyana: The Sociology of Health Care in a Developing Nation. John Lennon, Paul Mundy & Janet Fredericks (Authors). Library Binding. Carolina Academic Press. Durham, NC. 1986. 189p. ISBN:0-89089-295-4, ISBN13: 978-0-89089-295-4. Dewey:362.1/0988/1. LCCN:84-070752.
Audience: **u,f.** *Choice, 1986.*

Frolic, B. Michael **HN737 .M36**
Mao's People: Sixteen Portraits of Life in Revolutionary China. Trade Paper. Harvard University Press. Cambridge, MA. 1980. 278p. ISBN:0-674-54845-0, ISBN13: 978-0-674-54845-9. Dewey:309.1/51/05.
Audience: **g,l,u,f.**

Fuchs, Lawrence H. **DU625 .F84 1992**
Hawaii Pono: An Ethnic and Political History. Trade Paper. Bess Press, Inc. Honolulu, HI. 1993. 528p. ISBN:1-880188-48-1, ISBN13: 978-1-880188-48-4. Dewey:996.9. LCCN:92-075297.
Audience: **g,l,u.**

Gans, Herbert J. **HN80.W497 G36 1982**
The Levittowners: Ways of Life and Politics in a New Suburban Community. Trade Paper. Columbia University Press. New York, NY. 1982. 474p. ISBN:0-231-05571-4, ISBN13: 978-0-231-05571-0. Dewey:307.7/6/0973. LCCN:82-004375.
Audience: **l,u,f.**

Gans, Herbert J. **HN80.B7G2 1982**
The Urban Villagers. Ed. 2. Trade Cloth. Simon & Schuster. New York, NY. 1982. 456p. ISBN:0-02-911250-8, ISBN13: 978-0-02-911250-2. Dewey:305.8/51/073. LCCN:82-008577.
Audience: **l,u,f.**

Gavron, Daniel **HX742.2.A3G39 2000**
The Kibbutz: Awakening from Utopia. Trade Cloth. Rowman & Littlefield Publishers, Inc. Lanham, MD. 2000. 320p. ISBN:0-8476-9526-3, ISBN13: 978-0-8476-9526-3. Dewey:307.77/6/09. LCCN:99-058411.
Audience: **l,u,f.**

Geertz, Clifford **HN710**
The Social History of an Indonesian Town. Trade Cloth. Greenwood Publishing Group, Inc. Portsmouth, NH. 1975. 227p. ISBN:0-8371-8431-2, ISBN13: 978-0-8371-8431-9. Dewey:309.1/598/2. LCCN:75-029282.
Audience: **u,f.** B

Gerber, Haim **HN656.G47 1987**
The Social Origins of the Modern Middle East. Library Binding. Lynne Rienner Publishers, Inc. Boulder, CO. 1987. 224p. ISBN:0-931477-63-8, ISBN13: 978-0-931477-63-8. Dewey:956. LCCN:86-021925.
Audience: **l,u,f.** B *Choice, 1987.*

Gies, Frances & Gies, Joseph **CB353.G38**
Life in a Medieval City. Trade Paper. HarperCollins Publishers. New York, NY. 1981. 288p. ISBN:0-06-090880-7, ISBN13: 978-0-06-090880-5. Dewey:940.1. LCCN:74-013058.
Audience: **g.**

Gilmore, David D. **HN590.F8**
The People of the Plain: Class and Community in Lower Andalusia. Trade Cloth. Columbia University Press. New York, NY. 1980. 247p. ISBN:0-231-04754-1, ISBN13: 978-0-231-04754-8. Dewey:309.1/46/354. LCCN:79-020048.
Audience: **u.** B

Glass, D. V. (Editor) **HN90.S65**
Social Mobility in Britain. Paper over Boards. Routledge. New York, NY. 2003. 420p. International Library of Sociology Ser., Vol. 114 ISBN:0-415-17634-4, ISBN13: 978-0-415-17634-7. Dewey:305.5/13/0941.
Audience: **u,f.**

Gomez-Moriana, Antonio & Duran-Cogan, Mercedes (Editors) **HN110.5**
National Identities and Socio-Political Changes in Latin America. Cloth Text. Garland Publishing, Inc. New York, NY. 2001. 400p. Hispanic Issues Ser. ISBN:0-8153-3061-8, ISBN13: 978-0-8153-3061-5. Dewey:306.09805. LCCN:00-065298.
Audience: **l,u,f.**

Gould, Harold A. **HT720.G68 1987**
The Hindu Caste System: The Sacralization of a Social Order. Trade Cloth. Chanakya Publications. 1987. 200p. ISBN:81-7001-023-3, ISBN13: 978-81-7001-023-4. Dewey:305.5/122/0954. LCCN:87-900331.
Audience: **l,u.**

Hane, Mikiso **HN723.H36 2003**
Peasants, Rebels, Women, and Outcastes: The Underside of Modern Japan. Ed. 2. Book, Other. Rowman & Littlefield Publishers, Inc. Lanham, MD. 2003. 368p. ISBN:0-7425-2525-2, ISBN13: 978-0-7425-2525-2. Dewey:306/.0952. LCCN:2002-151950.
Audience: **u,f.**

Hansen, Karen T. **GN657.R4H36 1996**
Keeping House in Lusaka. Trade Cloth. Columbia University Press. New York, NY. 1996. 256p. ISBN:0-231-08142-1, ISBN13: 978-0-231-08142-9. Dewey:307.76/096894. LCCN:96-021351.
Audience: **u.** *Choice, 1997.*

Harrington, Michael **HN58.H245 1981**
The Next America: The Decline and Rise of the United States. Bob Adelman (Photographer). Trade Cloth. Henry Holt & Company. New York, NY. 1981. 160p. ISBN:0-03-057468-4, ISBN13: 978-0-03-057468-9. Dewey:973.92. LCCN:81-001086.
Audience: **g,l,u.** B

Harrison, J. F. **HN398.E5H37 1984**
The English Common People: A Social History from the Norman Conquest to the Present. Trade Cloth. Barnes & Noble Books-Imports. Lanham, MD. 1984. 446p. ISBN:0-389-20470-6, ISBN13: 978-0-389-20470-1. Dewey:306/.0942. LCCN:84-000437.
Audience: **l,u.** B

Hlophe, Stephen S. **HN835.Z9.S65**
Class Ethnicity and Politics in Liberia: A Class Analysis of Power Struggles in the Tubman and Tolbert Administrations from 1944-1975. Trade Paper. University Press of America, Inc. Lanham, MD. 1979. 336p. ISBN:0-8191-0721-2, ISBN13: 978-0-8191-0721-3. Dewey:306/.2/096662. LCCN:79-063261.
Audience: **u,f.** B

Hobsbawm, E. J. **HN385.H57.H6 1974**
Labour's Turning Point, 1880-1900: Extracts from Contemporary Sources. Trade Cloth. Fairleigh Dickinson University Press. Cranbury, NJ. 1974. xxvi, 166p. ISBN:0-8386-1542-2, ISBN13: 978-0-8386-1542-3. Dewey:331.88/0941. LCCN:74-000498.
Audience: **l,u,f.** B

Hollander, Gayle D. **HM263**
Soviet Political Indoctrination: Developments in Mass Media and Propaganda Since Stalin. Trade Cloth. Irvington Publishers. New York, NY. 1972. xviii, 245p. Special Studies in International Politics and Government ISBN:0-275-28202-3, ISBN13: 978-0-275-28202-8. Dewey:301.15/4/0947. LCCN:70-163927.
Audience: **u,f.**

Holmes, Richard **HN0080.B45H6**
Communities in Transition: Bedford and Lincoln, Massachusetts, 1729-1850. Robert Berkhofer (Editor). Trade Paper. Books on Demand. Ann Arbor, MI. 1980. 223p. Studies in American History and Culture, Vol. 16 ISBN:0-8357-1098-X, ISBN13: 978-0-8357-1098-5. Dewey:307.7/2/097444. LCCN:80-018459.
Audience: **l,u,f.** B

Hopkins, Nicholas S. & Ibrahim, Saad Eddin (Contribution by) **HN766.A8A7 1997**
Arab Society: Class, Gender, Power, and Development. Ed. 3. Trade Paper. American University in Cairo Press. New York, NY. 1998. 600p. ISBN:977-424-404-4, ISBN13: 978-977-424-404-9. Dewey:306/.0917/4927. LCCN:98-149923.
Audience: **l,u,f.**

Horowitz, Irving L. (Editor) **HN110.5.A8**
Masses in Latin America. Trade Cloth. Oxford University Press, Inc. New York, NY. 1970. ISBN:0-19-500795-6, ISBN13: 978-0-19-500795-4. Dewey:309.1/8. LCCN:73-083045.
Audience: **l,u,f.** B

Hunter, Susan **RA643.86.A78H86 2004**
AIDS in Asia: A Continent in Peril. Cloth over Boards. Palgrave Macmillan. New York, NY. 2005. 304p. ISBN:1-4039-6774-1, ISBN13: 978-1-4039-6774-9. Dewey:362.196/9792/0095. LCCN:2004-053467.
Audience: **g,l,u,f.** *Choice, 2005.*

Janowitz, Morris **HN57 .J2479**
The Last Half-Century: Societal Change and Politics in America. Trade Paper. University of Chicago Press. Chicago, IL. 1984. 598p. ISBN:0-226-39307-0, ISBN13: 978-0-226-39307-0. Dewey:301.15/0973. LCCN:78-017715.
Audience: **u,f.** B

Kidder, Tracy **F74.N86K53 1999**
Home Town. Trade Cloth. Random House, Inc. New York, NY. 1999. 344p. ISBN:0-679-45588-4, ISBN13: 978-0-679-45588-2. Dewey:974.4/23. LCCN:99-013614.
Audience: **g,l.**

Klass, Morton **HN690.B4K53 1996**
From Field to Factory: Community Structure and Industrialization in West Bengal. Trade Paper. University Press of America, Inc. Lanham, MD. 1996. 272p. ISBN:0-7618-0420-X, ISBN13: 978-0-7618-0420-8. Dewey:307.72/095414. LCCN:96-022806.
Audience: **u,f.** B

Lasch, Christopher **HN65**
The Culture of Narcissism: American Life in an Age of Diminishing Expectations. Trade Paper. W. W. Norton & Company, Inc. New York, NY. 1991. 302p. ISBN:0-393-30738-7, ISBN13: 978-0-393-30738-2. Dewey:973.927.
Audience: **l,u.** B

Laslett, Peter **HN385.L35 1984**
The World We Have Lost. Ed. 3. Paper Text. Simon & Schuster. New York, NY. 1986. ISBN:0-684-18079-0, ISBN13: 978-0-684-18079-3. Dewey:309.1/42. LCCN:84-001242.
Audience: **l,u,f.**

Latin American Network Information Center (LANIC) **HM582.L8**
☐ Sociology in Latin America.
http://lanic.utexas.edu/la/region/sociology/
Latin American Network Information Center (LANIC).
Audience: **l,u.**

Lee, Martin A. & Shlain, Bruce **HV5822.L9L44 1985**
Acid Dreams: The CIA, LSD and the Sixties Rebellion. Trade Cloth. Grove/Atlantic, Inc. New York, NY. 1986. 343p. History and Sociology Ser. ISBN:0-394-55013-7, ISBN13: 978-0-394-55013-8. Dewey:306/.1. LCCN:85-017704.
Audience: **u,f.** *Choice, 1987.*

Lewis, Oscar **HN0683.L4**
Village Life in Northern India. Trade Paper. Books on Demand. Ann Arbor, MI. 400p. ISBN:0-598-00120-4, ISBN13: 978-0-598-00120-7. Dewey:307.76/0954. LCCN:57-006953.
Audience: **l,u,f.**

Lewis, P. S. **HN425**
Later Medieval France: The Polity. Cloth Text. Palgrave Macmillan. New York, NY. 1969. ISBN:0-312-47250-1, ISBN13: 978-0-312-47250-4. Dewey:309.1/44.
Audience: **u,f.** B

Liebow, Elliot **E185.93.D6L5 2003**
Tally's Corner: A Study of Negro Streetcorner Men. Ed. 2. Book, Other. Rowman & Littlefield Publishers, Inc. Lanham, MD. 2003. 224p. Legacies of Social Thought Ser. ISBN:0-7425-2895-2, ISBN13: 978-0-7425-2895-6. Dewey:305.896/0730753. LCCN:2003-008589.
Audience: **u,f.**

Lomnitz, Larissa Adler de **HN120.M45.L6513**
Networks and Marginality: Life in a Mexican Shantytown. Trade Cloth. Elsevier Science & Technology Books. Saint Louis, MO. 1977. xvi, 230p. ISBN:0-12-456450-X, ISBN13: 978-0-12-456450-3. Dewey:305.5/6. LCCN:76-055974.
Audience: **l,u,f.** B

Long, Ngo Vinh **HD1536.I8**
Before the Revolution: The Vietnamese Peasants under the French. Trade Paper. Columbia University Press. New York, NY. 1991. 292p. A Morningside Book Ser. ISBN:0-231-07679-7, ISBN13: 978-0-231-07679-1. Dewey:305.5/63.
Audience: **l,u.** B

Lowenthal, David ; Comitos, Lambros **HN19.5**
Consequences of Class and Color: West Indian Perspectives. Anchor Press. 1973. ISBN:0-385-04402-X, ISBN13: 978-0-385-04402-8.
Audience: **l,u.**

Lynd, Helen M. **HN385.L9 1984**
England in the Eighteen-Eighties: Toward a Social Basis for Freedom. Gerald M. Pomper (Introduction by). Trade Cloth. Transaction Publishers. Somerset, NJ. 1984. 526p. ISBN:0-88738-004-2, ISBN13: 978-0-88738-004-4. Dewey:306/.0942. LCCN:84-000194.
Audience: **u,f.**

Lynd, Robert S. & Lynd, Helen M. **HN57**
Middletown: A Study in Modern American Culture. Trade Paper. Harcourt Trade Publishers. New York, NY. 1959. 564p. ISBN:0-15-659550-8, ISBN13: 978-0-15-659550-6. Dewey:973.91.
Audience: **g,l.**

Lynd, Robert S. & Lynd, Helen M. **HN57 .L84 1982**
Middletown in Transition: A Study in Cultural Conflicts. Trade Paper. Harcourt Trade Publishers. New York, NY. 1982. 624p. Harvest Book Ser. ISBN:0-15-659551-6, ISBN13: 978-0-15-659551-3. Dewey:973.91. LCCN:37-027243.
Audience: **g,l.**

Maira, Sunaina **F128.9.E2M35 2002**
Desis in the House: Indian American Youth Culture in New York City. Library Binding. Temple University Press. Philadelphia, PA. 2002. 256p. Asian American History and Culture Ser. ISBN:1-56639-926-2, ISBN13: 978-1-56639-926-5. Dewey:305.89140747. LCCN:2001-034071.
Audience: **l,u.** *Choice, 2003, 2002.*

Marsh, David C. **HB3585**
The Changing Social Structure of England and Wales 1871-1961. Paper over Boards. Routledge. New York, NY. 2003. 288p. International Library of Sociology Ser., Vol. 100 ISBN:0-415-17616-6, ISBN13: 978-0-415-17616-3. Dewey:304.6/0942.
Audience: **u,f.** B

Marwick, Arthur **HN385.5**
British Society since 1945. Ed. 3. Trade Paper. Penguin Books, Ltd. London, 1996. 528p. ISBN:0-14-024939-7, ISBN13: 978-0-14-024939-2. Dewey:306/.0941.
Audience: **l,u.**

Matejko, Alexander J. **HN539.5.S6.M38**
Social Change and Stratification in Eastern Europe: An Interpretive Analysis of Poland and Her Neighbors. Trade Cloth. Greenwood Publishing Group, Inc. Portsmouth, NH. 1974. xxv, 272p. ISBN:0-275-09570-3, ISBN13: 978-0-275-09570-3. Dewey:301.44/09438. LCCN:74-009424.
Audience: **u,f.**

Matthews, Mervyn **HN530.Z9E4**
Privilege in the Soviet Union. Cloth Text. Routledge. New York, NY. 1978. 197p. ISBN:0-04-323020-2, ISBN13: 978-0-04-323020-6. Dewey:301.44/92. LCCN:78-315486.
Audience: **l,u.**

McCoy, Alfred W. & De Jesus, Ed. C. (Editors) **HN713**
Philippine Social History: Global Trade and Local Transformations. Paper Text. University of Hawaii Press. Honolulu, HI. 1982. 488p. ISBN:0-8248-0803-7, ISBN13: 978-0-8248-0803-7. Dewey:959.9.
Audience: **u,f.**

Mendras, Henri **HN425.5**
The Vanishing Peasant: Innovation and Change in French Agriculture. Jean Lerner (Translator), Daniel Lerner (Introduction by). Trade Cloth. MIT Press. Cambridge, MA. 1971. xiii, 289p. ISBN:0-262-13065-3, ISBN13: 978-0-262-13065-3. Dewey:301.3/5/0944. LCCN:79-118349.
Audience: **u,f.**

Merriman, John (Editor) **HN380.Z9 S6385 1979**
Consciousness and Class Experience in 19th Century Europe. Trade Cloth. Holmes & Meier Publishers, Inc. Teaneck, NJ. 1979. 261p. ISBN:0-8419-0444-8, ISBN13: 978-0-8419-0444-6. Dewey:301.44/094. LCCN:79-016032.
Audience: **l,u.**

Mingay, G. E. **HN385 .M5**
English Landed Society in the Eighteenth Century. Trade Cloth. University of Toronto Press. Toronto, ON. 1963. ISBN:0-8020-1239-6, ISBN13: 978-0-8020-1239-5. Dewey:333.30942. LCCN:63-025746.
Audience: **u,f.**

Nakane, Chie **HN723**
Japanese Society. Trade Cloth. University of California Press. Berkeley, CA. 1972. 188p. Center for Japanese and Korean Studies, UC Berkeley, No. 4 ISBN:0-520-02154-1, ISBN13: 978-0-520-02154-9. Dewey:301.44/0952. LCCN:71-100021.
Audience: **g,l,u,f.**

Nye, Robert A. **HN440.P8**
Crime, Madness and Politics in Modern France: The Medical Concept of National Decline. Trade Cloth. Princeton University Press. Princeton, NJ. 1984. 384p. ISBN:0-691-05414-2, ISBN13: 978-0-691-05414-8. Dewey:302.5/42/0944. LCCN:83-043087.
Audience: **u,f.**

Orlans, Harold **HN398.S8.O7 1971**
Stevenage: A Sociological Study of a New Town. Library Binding. Greenwood Publishing Group, Inc. Portsmouth, NH. 1971. 313p. ISBN:0-8371-5758-7, ISBN13: 978-0-8371-5758-0. Dewey:309.1/425/8. LCCN:71-139142.
Audience: **u,f.**

Panikkar, Kavalam N. **DS422.C64 C65 1991**
Communalism in India: History, Politics and Culture. Trade Cloth. Manohar Publications. New Delhi, 1991. ISBN:81-85425-51-5, ISBN13: 978-81-85425-51-1. Dewey:322.420954. LCCN:91-907612.
Audience: **l,u.**

Pasternak, Burton **HN680.5.T3 P37**
Kinship and Community in Two Chinese Villages. Trade Cloth. Stanford University Press. Palo Alto, CA. 1972. 192p. ISBN:0-8047-0823-1, ISBN13: 978-0-8047-0823-4. Dewey:309.1/51/249. LCCN:72-078870.
Audience: **l,u,f.**

Pastore, Jose & Haller, Archibald O. **HN290.Z9S65**
Inequality and Social Mobility in Brazil. Cloth Text. University of Wisconsin Press. Chicago, IL. 1982. 240p. ISBN:0-299-08830-8, ISBN13: 978-0-299-08830-9. Dewey:305.5/13/0981. LCCN:81-069826.
Audience: **l,u,f.**

Penningroth, Dylan C. **E185.8.P39 2003**
The Claims of Kinfolk: African American Property and Community in the Nineteenth-Century South. Trade Cloth. University of North Carolina Press. Chapel Hill, NC. 2003. 304p. The John Hope Franklin Series in African American History and Culture ISBN:0-8078-2797-5, ISBN13: 978-0-8078-2797-0. Dewey:333.33/5/08996073075. LCCN:2003-000212.
Audience: **u,f.** *Choice, 2004.*

Perinbam, B. Marie **DT551.45.M36P47 1997**
Family Identity and the State in the Bamako Kafu, c. 1800-c.1900. Trade Paper. Westview Press. Boulder, CO. 1996. 352p. African States and Societies in History Ser. ISBN:0-8133-3080-7, ISBN13: 978-0-8133-3080-8. Dewey:305.8/9634. LCCN:96-035478.
Audience: **l,u.** *Choice, 1997.*

Pierce, T. Jones **HN398.W26.J63 1972**
Medieval Welsh Society: Selected Essays. J. Beverley Smith (Editor). Cloth Text. Lawrence Verry Inc. Mystic, CT. 1973. 452p. ISBN:0-7083-0447-8, ISBN13: 978-0-7083-0447-1. Dewey:309.1/429. LCCN:73-164114.
Audience: **l,u.**

Pitt-Rivers, Julian Alfred ; Abu Zayd, Ahmad **HN380.M4 P5 1977**
Mediterranean Countrymen : Essays in the Social Anthropology of the Mediterranean. Greenwood Press. 1977. ISBN:0-8371-9526-8, ISBN13: 978-0-8371-9526-1.
Audience: **l,u.**

Pleck, Elizabeth H. **GT4986.A1P54 2000**
Celebrating the Family: Ethnicity, Consumer Culture, and Family Rituals. Trade Cloth. Harvard University Press. Cambridge, MA. 2000. 338p. ISBN:0-674-00230-X, ISBN13: 978-0-674-00230-2. Dewey:394.26973. LCCN:99-045200.
Audience: **l,u,f.** *Choice, 2001.*

Polsky, Ned **HN57.P57 1998**
Hustlers, Beats and Others. Trade Paper. Globe Pequot Press, The. Guilford, CT. 1998. 288p. ISBN:1-55821-404-6, ISBN13: 978-1-55821-404-0. Dewey:302.5/420973. LCCN:97-043059.
Audience: **l,u,f.** *B*

Porter, John **HN103.5 .P6 1968**
The Vertical Mosaic: An Analysis of Social Class and Power in Canada. Trade Paper. University of Toronto Press. Toronto, ON. 1965. 626p. ISBN:0-8020-6055-2, ISBN13: 978-0-8020-6055-6. Dewey:301.44/0971. LCCN:78-418980.
Audience: **u,f.**

Porter, Roy
A Social History of Madness: The World Through the Eyes of the Insane. Grove. 1988. ISBN:1-55584-185-6, ISBN13: 978-1-55584-185-0.
Audience: **g,l,u.**

Putnam, Robert D. **HN65.P878 2000**
Bowling Alone: The Collapse and Revival of American Community. Trade Cloth. Simon & Schuster. New York, NY. 2000. 544p. ISBN:0-684-83283-6, ISBN13: 978-0-684-83283-8. Dewey:306/.0973. LCCN:00-027278.
Audience: **g,l,u,f.** *Choice, 2000.*

Roberts, R. **HN398.S2**
The Classic Slum: Salford Life in the First Quarter of the Century. Trade Cloth. Manchester University Press. Manchester, 1978. 218p. ISBN:0-7190-0453-5, ISBN13: 978-0-7190-0453-7. Dewey:914.27/2. LCCN:74-855642.
Audience: **u,f.** *B*

Root, Maria P. (Editor) **E184.F4F385 1997**
Filipino Americans: Transformation and Identity. Trade Cloth. SAGE Publications, Inc. Thousand Oaks, CA. 1997. 368p. ISBN:0-7619-0578-2, ISBN13: 978-0-7619-0578-3. Dewey:973/.049921. LCCN:97-004591.
Audience: **l.** *Choice, 1997.*

Rubin, Lillian B. **HQ536 .R8 1992**
Worlds of Pain: Life in the Working-Class Family. Trade Paper. Basic Books. New York, NY. 1992. 320p. ISBN:0-465-09248-9, ISBN13: 978-0-465-09248-2. Dewey:305.5/62. LCCN:92-052719.
Audience: **l,u.**

Rude, George **HN373.R83 1985**
Europe in the 18th Century: Aristocracy and the Bourgeois Challenge. Trade Paper. Harvard University Press. Cambridge, MA. 1985. 292p. ISBN:0-674-26921-7, ISBN13: 978-0-674-26921-7. Dewey:940.2/53. LCCN:84-019735.
Audience: **u,f.**

Rude, George **HN438.P3.R8 1971**
Paris and London in Eighteenth Century. Trade Cloth. Penguin Group (USA) Inc. New York, NY. 1971. 350p. ISBN:0-670-53832-9, ISBN13: 978-0-670-53832-4. Dewey:301.6/332/09421. LCCN:73-148267.
Audience: **u.** *B*

Ruggiero, Kristin Hoffman **F3011.C653R83 1988**
And Here the World Ends: The Life of an Argentine Village. Trade Cloth. Stanford University Press. Palo Alto, CA. 1988. 248p. ISBN:0-8047-1379-0, ISBN13: 978-0-8047-1379-5. Dewey:982/.76. LCCN:87-020311.
Audience: **l,u.** *Choice, 1988.*

Ryan, William **HN65.R9 1976**
Blaming the Victim. Trade Cloth. Random House, Inc. New York, NY. 1976. xv, 351p. ISBN:0-394-71762-7, ISBN13: 978-0-394-71762-3. Dewey:309.1/73/0924. LCCN:76-378867.
Audience: **g,l,u.** *B*

Sagarra, Eda **HN445.S23**
A Social History of Germany 1648-1914. Trade Paper. Transaction Publishers. Somerset, NJ. 2002. 485p. ISBN:0-7658-0982-6, ISBN13: 978-0-7658-0982-7. Dewey:306.0943. LCCN:2002-075017.
Audience: **l,u.** *B*

Sandage, Scott A. **HN90.M6S25 2006**
Born Losers: A History of Failure in America. Trade Paper. Harvard University Press. Cambridge, MA. 2006. 384p. ISBN:0-674-02107-X, ISBN13: 978-0-674-02107-5. Dewey:303.3/72/097309034.
Audience: **g,l,u,f.** *Choice, 2005.*

Schivelbusch, Wolfgang **U21.2**
The Culture of Defeat: On National Trauma, Mourning, and Recovery. Jefferson Chase (Translator). Trade Paper. Picador. New York, NY. 2004. 416p. ISBN:0-312-42319-5, ISBN13: 978-0-312-42319-3. Dewey:303.6/6.
Audience: **l,u.**

Schmid, Carol L. **HN603.5**
Conflict and Consensus in Switzerland. Trade Cloth. University of California Press. Berkeley, CA. 1981. x, 198p. ISBN:0-520-04079-1, ISBN13: 978-0-520-04079-3. Dewey:305.8/009494. LCCN:80-018458.
Audience: **l,u.** *B*

Schwartz, Marie Jenkins **E443.S39 2000**
Born in Bondage: Growing up Enslaved in the Antebellum South. Trade Cloth. Harvard University Press. Cambridge, MA. 2000. 288p. Ser. ISBN:0-674-00162-1, ISBN13: 978-0-674-00162-6. Dewey:306.3/62/083/0975. LCCN:99-087747.
Audience: **l,u.** *Choice, 2000.*

Scobie, James R. **HN270.B8.S3**
Buenos Aires: Plaza to Suburb Eighteen Seventy to Nineteen Ten. Cloth Text. Oxford University Press, Inc. New York, NY. 1978. xvii, 323p. ISBN:0-19-501821-4, ISBN13: 978-0-19-501821-9. Dewey:309.1/82/1. LCCN:74-079629.
Audience: **u.** *B*

Scott, Hilda **HN577.S36**
Sweden's Right to Be Human : Sex-Role Equality: The Goal and the Reality. Trade Cloth. M. E. Sharpe Inc. Armonk, NY. 1982. 240p. ISBN:0-87332-182-0, ISBN13: 978-0-87332-182-2. Dewey:362.8/356/09485. LCCN:81-005239.
Audience: **l,u,f.** *B*

Sewell, William H. Jr. **HN438.M35S48 1985**
Structure and Mobility: The Men and Women of Marseille, 1820-1870. Cloth Text. Cambridge University Press. New York, NY. 1985. 416p. ISBN:0-521-26237-2, ISBN13: 978-0-521-26237-8. Dewey:305/.0944/912. LCCN:84-005860.
Audience: **u,f.** *B* *Choice, 1985.*

Sharma, Kanhayalal L. **HN690.Z9S6438 1997**
Social Stratification in India: Issues and Themes. Trade Cloth. SAGE Publications, Inc. Thousand Oaks, CA. 1997. 220p.

ISBN:0-8039-9362-5, ISBN13: 978-0-8039-9362-4. Dewey:305.5/0954. LCCN:97-003382.
Audience: **l,u.** *Choice, 1998.*

Sharpe, J. A. **DA300.S5 1987**
Early-Modern England: A Social History, 1550-1760. Trade Cloth. Hodder Education. London, 1988. 388p. ISBN:0-7131-6512-X, ISBN13: 978-0-7131-6512-8. Dewey:942. LCCN:88-116340.
Audience: **l,u.**

Shoshani, Jesheskel, et al. **NK5989**
Elephant: The Animal and Its Ivory in African Culture. Mary Jo Arnoldi & Donald J. Cosentino (Authors), Doran H. Ross (Editor). Trade Paper. University of California Los Angeles, Fowler Museum of Cultural History. Los Angeles, CA. 1992. 424p. ISBN:0-930741-26-9, ISBN13: 978-0-930741-26-6. Dewey:730/.096/07479494. LCCN:92-073840.
Audience: **g,l,u.** *Choice, 1995.*

Singh, K. S. (Editor) **DS422.C3**
The Scheduled Castes. Trade Cloth. Oxford University Press, Inc. New York, NY. 1994. 1400p. People of India Ser., Vol. II ISBN:0-19-563254-0, ISBN13: 978-0-19-563254-5. Dewey:305.51220954.
Audience: **u,f.** *Choice, 1994.*

Slater, Candace **F2546 .S67 2002**
Entangled Edens: Visions of the Amazon. Trade Cloth. University of California Press. Berkeley, CA. 2001. 332p. ISBN:0-520-22641-0, ISBN13: 978-0-520-22641-8. Dewey:981. LCCN:2001-035866.
Audience: **l,u.**

Slayton, Robert A. **HN80.C5**
Back of the Yards: The Making of a Local Democracy. Trade Paper. University of Chicago Press. Chicago, IL. 1988. 291p. ISBN:0-226-76199-1, ISBN13: 978-0-226-76199-2. Dewey:307/.14/0977311. LCCN:85-016518.
Audience: **l,u,f.** B *Choice, 1986.*

Smith, Robert J. **HN730.S534**
Kurusu: The Price of Progress in a Japanese Village, 1951-1975. Trade Paper. Stanford University Press. Palo Alto, CA. 1978. xviii, 270p. ISBN:0-8047-1060-0, ISBN13: 978-0-8047-1060-2. Dewey:301.29/52/3. LCCN:77-079999.
Audience: **u,f.** B

Stearns, Peter (Editor) **HN373.E63 2001**
Encyclopedia of European Social History: From 1350 to 2000, Set. Trade Cloth. Thomson Gale. Farmington Hills, MI. 1905. 3186p. ISBN:0-684-80582-0, ISBN13: 978-0-684-80582-5. Dewey:306/.094/03. LCCN:00-046376.
Audience: **g,l,u.** *Choice, 2001.*

Stevenson, Thomas B. **HN664.A8S73 1985**
Social Change in a Yemeni Highlands Town. Trade Cloth. University of Utah Press. Salt Lake City, UT. 1985. 232p. ISBN:0-87480-112-5, ISBN13: 978-0-87480-112-5. Dewey:306/.0953/32. LCCN:85-005322.
Audience: **l,u,f.** B *Choice, 1986.*

Story, Ronald **HN80.B7.S76**
The Forging of an Aristocracy. Trade Cloth. Wesleyan University Press. Middletown, CT. 1980. 356p. ISBN:0-8195-5044-2, ISBN13: 978-0-8195-5044-6. Dewey:305.5/2/09. LCCN:80-000460.
Audience: **u,f.** B

Suttles, Gerald D. **HN80.C5**
The Social Order of the Slum: Ethnicity and Territory in the Inner City. Trade Paper. University of Chicago Press. Chicago, IL. 1970. 266p. Studies of Urban Society ISBN:0-226-78192-5, ISBN13: 978-0-226-78192-1. Dewey:301.364.
Audience: **l,u,f.** B

Takaki, Ronald T. **E184.A1.T335 1993**
A Different Mirror: A History of Multicultural America. Trade Cloth. Little Brown & Company. New York, NY. 1993. 508p. ISBN:0-316-83112-3, ISBN13: 978-0-316-83112-3. Dewey:973/.04. LCCN:92-033491.
Audience: **g,l,u.** *Choice, 1993.*

Thernstrom, Stephan A. **HN80.B7**
The Other Bostonians: Poverty and Progress in the American Metropolis, 1880-1970. Trade Paper. iUniverse, Inc. Lincoln, NE. 1999. 368p. ISBN:1-58348-443-4, ISBN13: 978-1-58348-443-2. Dewey:301.4/009744/61. LCCN:99-090958.
Audience: **l,u,f.** B

Thomsen, Moritz **HC60.5**
Living Poor: A Peace Corps Chronicle. Trade Cloth. University of Washington Press. Seattle, WA. 2003. 280p. ISBN:0-295-96928-8, ISBN13: 978-0-295-96928-2. Dewey:361.60986.
Audience: **g,l.**

Tilly, Charles, et al. **HN425.T54**
The Rebellious Century: 1830-1930. Louise Tilly & Richard Tilly (Authors). Trade Cloth. Harvard University Press. Cambridge, MA. 1975. xi, 354p. ISBN:0-674-74955-3, ISBN13: 978-0-674-74955-9. Dewey:309.1/4/028. LCCN:74-016802.
Audience: **l,u.** B

Tsurumi, Kazuko **HN723 .T75**
Social Change and the Individual: Japan Before and After Defeat in World War II. Trade Cloth. Princeton University Press. Princeton, NJ. 1970. 456p. ISBN:0-691-09347-4, ISBN13: 978-0-691-09347-5. Dewey:309.1/52. LCCN:69-018073.
Audience: **l,u.** B

Tuden, Arthur & Plotnicov, Leonard **HN773**
Social Stratification in Africa. Trade Cloth. Simon & Schuster. New York, NY. 1970. viii, 392p. ISBN:0-02-932780-6, ISBN13: 978-0-02-932780-7. Dewey:301.44/096. LCCN:78-091223.
Audience: **l,u,f.**

Tumin, Melvin M. & Feldman, Arnold S. **QM23.2**
Social Class and Social Change in Puerto Rico. Trade Cloth. Irvington Publishers. New York, NY. 1971. ISBN:0-672-61375-1, ISBN13: 978-0-672-61375-3. Dewey:611. LCCN:70-145756.
Audience: **l,u,f.** B

Turner, Jonathan H. **HN65 .T87 1976**
American Society: Problems of Structure. Ed. 2. Paper Text. Addison-Wesley Educational Publishers, Inc. Boston, MA. 1976. 320p. ISBN:0-06-046706-1, ISBN13: 978-0-06-046706-7. Dewey:309.1/73/092. LCCN:76-002714.
Audience: **u,f.** B

Van Hoorn, Judith L., et al. **HQ799.H8A35 2000**
Adolescent Development and Rapid Social Change: Perspectives from Eastern Europe. Akos Komlosi, Elzbieta Suchar & Doreen

A. Samelson (Authors). Cloth Text. State University of New York Press. Albany, NY. 2000. x, 309p. ISBN:0-7914-4473-2, ISBN13: 978-0-7914-4473-3. Dewey:305.235/09439. LCCN:99-039700.
Audience: **l,u.**

Volavka, Zdenka **CR920.N94V65 1998**
Crown and Ritual: The Royal Insignia of Ngoyo. Wendy A. Thomas (Editor), Colleen E. Kriger (Introduction by). Trade Cloth. University of Toronto Press. Toronto, ON. 1998. 836p. ISBN:0-8020-4227-9, ISBN13: 978-0-8020-4227-9. Dewey:967.51. LCCN:99-218554.
Audience: **u,f.** *Choice, 1999.*

Warner, Lloyd W. & Low, V. O. **HN57 .W34**
Yankee City. Trade Cloth. Yale University Press. Cumberland, RI. 1963. 448p. ISBN:0-300-01026-5, ISBN13: 978-0-300-01026-8. Dewey:301.36. LCCN:63-007588.
Audience: **l,u.**

Warner, William L. **HN57 .W3 1976**
Democracy in Jonesville: A Study in Quality and Inequality. Library Binding. Greenwood Publishing Group, Inc. Portsmouth, NH. 1976. 313p. ISBN:0-8371-8741-9, ISBN13: 978-0-8371-8741-9. Dewey:309.1/73. LCCN:76-002034.
Audience: **l,u.**

Watson, J. Wreford **HN57.W352**
Social Geography of the United States. Trade Cloth. Longman Publishing Group. White Plains, NY. 1979. 290p. ISBN:0-582-48196-1, ISBN13: 978-0-582-48196-1. Dewey:309.1/73. LCCN:77-030747.
Audience: **g,l,u,f.** B

Watts, Sheldon J. **HN373.W37 1984**
Social History of Western Europe, 1450-1720: Tensions and Solidarities Amongst the Rural People. Trade Paper. Hutchinson University Library. Cheltenham, 1984. 336p. ISBN:0-09-156081-0, ISBN13: 978-0-09-156081-2. Dewey:306/.094. LCCN:84-159439.
Audience: **l,u.** B

Wolf, Stephanie G. **HN80.G46 W6**
Urban Village: Population, Community, and Family Structure in Germantown, Pennsylvania, 1683-1800. Trade Paper. Princeton University Press. Princeton, NJ. 1980. 374p. ISBN:0-691-00590-7, ISBN13: 978-0-691-00590-4. Dewey:301.36. LCCN:76-003025.
Audience: **l,u,f.**

Woodhull, Victoria C. **HN64.M393 1974**
The Victoria Woodhull Reader. Madeleine B. Stern (Editor). Trade Cloth. M & S Press. Providence, RI. 1974. 650p. ISBN:0-87730-009-7, ISBN13: 978-0-87730-009-0. Dewey:309.1/73/08. LCCN:74-193236.
Audience: **l,u.** B

Yang, Ch'ing-k'un **HN733**
A Chinese Village in Early Communist Transition. Trade Cloth. Greenwood Publishing Group, Inc. Portsmouth, NH. 1984. 284p. ISBN:0-313-24456-1, ISBN13: 978-0-313-24456-8. Dewey:307.7/62/0951. LCCN:84-006618.
Audience: **u,f.**

Zonabend, Francoise **DC801.M6693Z6613**
The Enduring Memory: Time and History in a French Village. Anthony Forster (Translator). Trade Cloth. Manchester University Press. Manchester, 1988. 230p. ISBN:0-7190-1781-5, ISBN13: 978-0-7190-1781-0. Dewey:944/.42. LCCN:85-002987.
Audience: **u,f.** *Choice, 1986.*

Zureik, Elia & Nakhleh, Khalil **HN660.A8.S63 1980**
The Sociology of the Palestinians. Cloth Text. Palgrave Macmillan. New York, NY. 1980. 238p. ISBN:0-312-74073-5, ISBN13: 978-0-312-74073-3. Dewey:301.45/19/275694. LCCN:79-012706.
Audience: **l,u,f.** B

Social History > Culture > Kinship

Coster, Will **HQ615.C67 2001**
Family and Kinship in England, 1450-1800. Trade Paper. Pearson Education. Boston, MA. 2001. 176p. Seminar Studies in History Ser. ISBN:0-582-35717-9, ISBN13: 978-0-582-35717-4. Dewey:306.85/0942. LCCN:2001-050511.
Audience: **l,u.**

Harrell, Stevan **GN487**
Human Families. Trade Paper. Westview Press. Boulder, CO. 1998. 624p. Social Change in Global Perspective Ser. ISBN:0-8133-3622-8, ISBN13: 978-0-8133-3622-0. Dewey:306.8/3.
Audience: **g,l,u,f.** *Choice, 1997.*

Volkman, Toby Alice (Editor) **HV875.5.C86 2005**
Cultures of Transnational Adoption. Trade Cloth. Duke University Press. Durham, NC. 2005. 232p. ISBN:0-8223-3576-X, ISBN13: 978-0-8223-3576-4. Dewey:362.734. LCCN:2004-026187.
Audience: **l,u.**

Social History > Culture > Cohesion/Integration

Brueggemann, Brenda Jo **HV2380.B69 1999**
Lend Me Your Ear: Rhetorical Constructions of Deafness. Trade Cloth. Gallaudet University Press. Washington, DC. 1999. 375p. ISBN:1-56368-079-3, ISBN13: 978-1-56368-079-3. Dewey:362.4/2. LCCN:99-020807.
Audience: **u,f.**

Hirszowicz, Maria **JC474.H495 1985**
Coercion and Control in Communist Society: The Visible Hand in a Command Economy. Cloth Text. Palgrave Macmillan. New York, NY. 1986. 233p. ISBN:0-312-14639-6, ISBN13: 978-0-312-14639-9. Dewey:321.9/2. LCCN:85-014538.
Audience: **l,u.** *Choice, 1986.*

Jones, Jacqueline **HC110.P6**
The Dispossessed: America's Underclasses from the Civil War to the Present. Trade Cloth. Basic Books. New York, NY. 1993. 448p. ISBN:0-465-01674-X, ISBN13: 978-0-465-01674-7. Dewey:305.5/69/0973. LCCN:91-037289.
Audience: **l,u.** *Choice, 1992.*

Khazanov, Anatoly M. **GN387.K4513 1994**
Nomads and the Outside World. Ed. 2. Julia Crookenden (Translator), Ernest Gellner (Foreword by). Trade Paper.

University of Wisconsin Press. Chicago, IL. 1994. 442p. ISBN:0-299-14284-1, ISBN13: 978-0-299-14284-1. Dewey:305.8. LCCN:93-041133.
Audience: **u,f.**

Melley, Timothy (Contribution by) **PS374.C594M45 2000**
Empire of Conspiracy: The Culture of Paranoia in Postwar America. Book, Other. Cornell University Press. Ithaca, NY. 1999. 264p. ISBN:0-8014-3668-0, ISBN13: 978-0-8014-3668-0. Dewey:813/.5409358. LCCN:99-041667.
Audience: **g,l,u,f.** *Choice, 2000.*

Padden, Carol A. & Humphries, Tom L. **HV2545.P35 2005**
Inside Deaf Culture. Trade Cloth. Harvard University Press. Cambridge, MA. 2005. 224p. ISBN:0-674-01506-1, ISBN13: 978-0-674-01506-7. Dewey:305.9/082/0973. LCCN:2004-051135.
Audience: **l,u.** *Choice, 2005.*

Snider, Bruce C. (Editor), et al. **HV2359.I487 1989**
The Deaf Way: Perspectives from the International Conference on Deaf Culture. Carol J. Erting, Robert C. Johnson & Dorothy L. Smith (Editors). Trade Cloth. Gallaudet University Press. Washington, DC. 1994. 907p. ISBN:1-56368-026-2, ISBN13: 978-1-56368-026-7. Dewey:305.9/08162. LCCN:94-017860.
Audience: **g,l,u,f.** *Choice, 1995.*

Wood, Peter **E184.A1W715 2002**
Diversity: A Biography of a Concept. Trade Cloth. Encounter Books. New York, NY. 2005. 351p. Ser. ISBN:1-893554-62-7, ISBN13: 978-1-893554-62-7. Dewey:305.8/00973. LCCN:2002-029992.
Audience: **l,u,f.** *Choice, 2003.*

Social History > Culture > Social Representations

Burnham, John C. **HN57.B87**
Bad Habits: Drinking, Smoking, Taking Drugs, Gambling, Sexual Misbehavior and Swearing in American History. Trade Paper. New York University Press. New York, NY. 1994. 353p. American Social Experience Ser., Vol. 28 ISBN:0-8147-1224-X, ISBN13: 978-0-8147-1224-5. Dewey:306.0973.
Audience: **g,l,u,f.** *Choice, 1993.*

Harkins, Anthony **E184.M83H37 2003**
Hillbilly: A Cultural History of an American Icon. Trade Cloth. Oxford University Press, Inc. New York, NY. 2003. 336p. ISBN:0-19-514631-X, ISBN13: 978-0-19-514631-8. Dewey:975/.00943. LCCN:2003-041974.
Audience: **g,l,u.** *Choice, 2004.*

Ifekwunigwe, Jayne O. **HT1523.I36 1999**
Scattered Be-Longings: Cultural Paradoxes of Race, Nation and Gender. Paper over Boards. Routledge. New York, NY. 1999. 240p. ISBN:0-415-17095-8, ISBN13: 978-0-415-17095-6. Dewey:305.8. LCCN:98-020493.
Audience: **l,u,f.**

Venuti, Lawrence **P306.2.V45 1998**
The Scandals of Translation: Towards an Ethics of Difference. Paper over Boards. Routledge. New York, NY. 1998. 224p. ISBN:0-415-16929-1, ISBN13: 978-0-415-16929-5. Dewey:418/.02. LCCN:98-009530.
Audience: **l,u.** *Choice, 1999.*

Social History > Culture > Counterculture

Baritz, Loren (Editor) **JK274**
American Left: Radical Political Thought in the Twentieth Century. Cloth Text. Basic Books. New York, NY. 1971. 264p. ISBN:0-465-00145-9, ISBN13: 978-0-465-00145-3. Dewey:320.9/73.
Audience: **u,f.** B

McKay, George
Senseless Acts of Beauty: Cultures of Resistence since the Sixties. Trade Paper. Analytical Psychology Club of San Francisco, Inc. San Francisco, CA. 1996. 224p. ISBN:1-85984-028-0, ISBN13: 978-1-85984-028-3. Dewey:306.1/0941.
Audience: **g,l,u.**

Muggleton, David **HM646.M84**
Inside Subculture: The Postmodern Meaning of Style. Trade Paper. Berg Publishers. Oxford, 2002. 224p. Dress, Body, Culture Ser. ISBN:1-85973-352-2, ISBN13: 978-1-85973-352-3. Dewey:306.1.
Audience: **l,u.** *Choice, 2001.*

Palmer, Bryan D. **HM646.P35 2000**
Cultures of Darkness: Night Travels in the Histories of Transgression. Trade Cloth. Monthly Review Press. New York, NY. 2000. 69p. ISBN:1-58367-026-2, ISBN13: 978-1-58367-026-2. Dewey:306/.1. LCCN:00-045086.
Audience: **u,f.** *Choice, 2001.*

Thomas, Douglas **QA76.9.M65T456 2002**
Hacker Culture. Book, Other. University of Minnesota Press. Minneapolis, MN. 2002. 266p. ISBN:0-8166-3345-2, ISBN13: 978-0-8166-3345-6. Dewey:306.1. LCCN:2001-005377.
Audience: **g,l,u,f.** *Choice, 2002.*

Toth, Jennifer **HV4506.N6 T68**
The Mole People: Life in the Tunnels Beneath New York City. Trade Paper. Chicago Review Press, Inc. Chicago, IL. 1995. 280p. ISBN:1-55652-241-X, ISBN13: 978-1-55652-241-3. Dewey:305.5/69. LCCN:93-023912.
Audience: **g,l,u.**

Social History > Things

Burnham, John C. **HN57.B87**
Bad Habits: Drinking, Smoking, Taking Drugs, Gambling, Sexual Misbehavior and Swearing in American History. Trade Paper. New York University Press. New York, NY. 1994. 353p. American Social Experience Ser., Vol. 28 ISBN:0-8147-1224-X, ISBN13: 978-0-8147-1224-5. Dewey:306.0973.
Audience: **g,l,u,f.** *Choice, 1993.*

Burns, Eric **GT2880**
The Spirits of America: A Social History of Alcohol. Trade Paper. Temple University Press. Philadelphia, PA. 2004. 352p. ISBN:1-59213-269-3, ISBN13: 978-1-59213-269-0. Dewey:394.1/3/0973.
Audience: **g.** *Choice, 2004.*

Schivelbusch, Wolfgang **GT2880 .S3613 1993**
Tastes of Paradise: A Social History of Spices, Stimulants, and Intoxicants. David Jacobson (Translator). Trade Paper. Knopf Publishing Group. New York, NY. 1993. 256p. ISBN:0-679-74438-X, ISBN13: 978-0-679-74438-2. Dewey:394.1/2. LCCN:92-050603.
Audience: **g,l,u,f.**

Shoshani, Jesheskel, et al. **NK5989**
Elephant: The Animal and Its Ivory in African Culture. Mary Jo Arnoldi & Donald J. Cosentino (Authors), Doran H. Ross (Editor). Trade Paper. University of California Los Angeles, Fowler Museum of Cultural History. Los Angeles, CA. 1992. 424p. ISBN:0-930741-26-9, ISBN13: 978-0-930741-26-6. Dewey:730/.096/07479494. LCCN:92-073840.
Audience: **g,l,u.** *Choice, 1995.*

Standage, Tom **GT2880.S83 2005**
A History of the World in Six Glasses. Cloth over Boards. Walker & Company. New York, NY. 2005. 240p. ISBN:0-8027-1447-1, ISBN13: 978-0-8027-1447-3. Dewey:394.1/2. LCCN:2004-061209.
Audience: **g,l,u.** *Choice, 2005.*

Social History > Mass Phenomena > Social Movements

Aronowitz, Stanley **HN90.S6A75 2003**
How Class Works: Power and Social Movement. Cloth over Boards. Yale University Press. Cumberland, RI. 2003. 272p. ISBN:0-300-09859-6, ISBN13: 978-0-300-09859-4. Dewey:305.5. LCCN:2002-151179.
Audience: **l,u.** *Choice, 2004.*

Cantril, Hadley **HM881.C36 2001**
The Psychology of Social Movements. Albert H. Cantril (Introduction by). Trade Cloth. Transaction Publishers. Somerset, NJ. 2002. 275p. ISBN:0-7658-0089-6, ISBN13: 978-0-7658-0089-3. Dewey:303.48/4. LCCN:2001-044349.
Audience: **l,u,f.** B

Fendrich, James Max **E185.96**
Ideal Citizens: The Legacy of the Civil Rights Movement. Paper Text. State University of New York Press. Albany, NY. 1993. 226p. SUNY Series in Afro-American Studies ISBN:0-7914-1324-1, ISBN13: 978-0-7914-1324-1. Dewey:323/.092/273. LCCN:92-002538.
Audience: **g,l,u.** *Choice, 1993.*

Gamson, William A. **HN64.G23 1990**
The Strategy of Social Protest. Ed. 2. Trade Paper. Thomson Wadsworth. Belmont, CA. 1989. 357p. ISBN:0-534-12078-4, ISBN13: 978-0-534-12078-8. Dewey:303.48/4. LCCN:89-034947.
Audience: **l,u.** B

Hoffer, Eric **HM716.H63 2002**
The True Believer: Thoughts on the Nature of Mass Movements. Trade Paper. HarperCollins Publishers. New York, NY. 2002. 192p. Perennial Classics Ser. ISBN:0-06-050591-5, ISBN13: 978-0-06-050591-2. Dewey:303.48/4. LCCN:2002-072255.
Audience: **u,f.** B

Kent, Stephen **HN59.K44 2001**
From Slogans to Mantras: Social Protest and Religious Conversion in the Late Vietnam Era. Trade Cloth. Syracuse University Press. Syracuse, NY. 2004. 224p. Religion and Politics Ser. ISBN:0-8156-2923-0, ISBN13: 978-0-8156-2923-8. Dewey:303.48/4/0973. LCCN:2001-042998.
Audience: **l,u.** *Choice, 2002.*

Larana, Enrique **HN17.5.N4855 1994**
(Editor), et al.
New Social Movements: From Ideology to Identity. Hank Johnston & Joseph R. Gusfield (Editors). Cloth Text. Temple University Press. Philadelphia, PA. 1994. 384p. ISBN:1-56639-186-5, ISBN13: 978-1-56639-186-3. Dewey:303.48/4. LCCN:93-037495.
Audience: **u,f.** *Choice, 1995.*

Reed, T.V. **HM881**
☐ Social Movements and Culture : A Resource Site. http://www.wsu.edu:8080/~amerstu/smc/smcframe.html T.V. Reed.
Audience: **g.**

Rude, George **HM281.R8 1995**
Ideology and Popular Protest. Harvey J. Kaye (Foreword by). Trade Cloth. University of North Carolina Press. Chapel Hill, NC. 1995. 198p. ISBN:0-8078-4514-0, ISBN13: 978-0-8078-4514-1. Dewey:303.6/4. LCCN:94-032657.
Audience: **l,u.** B

Snow, David A. **HM881**
(Editor), et al.
The Blackwell Companion to Social Movements. Sarah A. Soule & Hanspeter Kriesi (Editors). Trade Cloth. Blackwell Publishing, Inc. Malden, MA. 2004. 776p. Blackwell Companions to Sociology Ser. ISBN:0-631-22669-9, ISBN13: 978-0-631-22669-7. Dewey:303.48/4. LCCN:2003-020377.
Audience: **g,l.** *Choice, 2004.*

Social History > Mass Phenomena > Social Movements > By Country or Region

Anderson, Bonnie S. **HQ1154.A6856 2000**
Joyous Greetings: The First International Women's Movement, 1830-1860. Trade Cloth. Oxford University Press, Inc. New York, NY. 2000. 314p. ISBN:0-19-512623-8, ISBN13: 978-0-19-512623-5. Dewey:305.42/09/034. LCCN:99-014778.
Audience: **u,f.** *Choice, 2000.*

Baldez, Lisa **HQ1236.5.C5 B35 2002**
Why Women Protest: Women's Movements in Chile. Cloth Text. Cambridge University Press. New York, NY. 2002. 254p. Cambridge Studies in Comparative Politics ISBN:0-521-81150-3, ISBN13: 978-0-521-81150-7. Dewey:305.420983. LCCN:2001-052842.
Audience: **l,u,f.** *Choice, 2003.*

Burgmann, Verity **HN843.5.B88 2003**
Power, Profit and Protest: Australian Social Movements and Globalisation. Trade Paper. Allen & Unwin Pty., Ltd. Crows Nest, NSW. 2003. 400p. ISBN:1-74114-016-1, ISBN13: 978-1-74114-016-3. Dewey:303.48/4/0994. LCCN:2003-446236.
Audience: **l,u.**

Carter, David **HQ76.3.U5**
Stonewall: The Riots That Sparked the Gay Revolution. Trade Paper, Perfect. St. Martin's Press. Gordonville, VA. 2005. 352p.

ISBN:0-312-34269-1, ISBN13: 978-0-312-34269-2. Dewey:306.76/6/0973.
Audience: **g.** *Choice, 2005.*

Downs, Laura Lee **LC5771.F8D69 2002**
Childhood in the Promised Land: Working-Class Movements and the Colonies de Vacances in France, 1880-1960. Trade Paper. Duke University Press. Durham, NC. 2002. 424p. ISBN:0-8223-2944-1, ISBN13: 978-0-8223-2944-2. Dewey:371.826/23/0944. LCCN:2002-005513.
Audience: **l,u.** *Choice, 2003.*

Edmonds, Ennis Barrington **BL2532.R37E36 2002**
Rastafari: From Outcasts to Culture Bearers. Trade Cloth. Oxford University Press, Inc. New York, NY. 2002. 208p. ISBN:0-19-513376-5, ISBN13: 978-0-19-513376-9. Dewey:299/.676. LCCN:2002-074897.
Audience: **l,u.** *Choice, 2003.*

Eymann, Marcia & Wollenberg, Charles **F866.2 .W48 2004**
What's Going On?: California and the Vietnam Era. Oakland Museum of California Staff (Contribution by). Trade Paper. University of California Press. Berkeley, CA. 2004. 240p. ISBN:0-520-24244-0, ISBN13: 978-0-520-24244-9. Dewey:959.704. LCCN:2004-006308.
Audience: **l,u.** *Choice, 2005.*

Foweraker, Joe & Craig, Ann L. (Editors) **JL1281.P67 1990**
Popular Movements and Political Change in Mexico. Library Binding. Lynne Rienner Publishers, Inc. Boulder, CO. 1990. 312p. ISBN:1-55587-211-5, ISBN13: 978-1-55587-211-3. Dewey:323.3/0972. LCCN:90-034593.
Audience: **l,u.** *Choice, 1991.*

Goldstone, Jack A. (Editor) **JF2011.S73 2003**
States, Parties, and Social Movements. Sidney Tarrow (Contribution by). Trade Paper. Cambridge University Press. New York, NY. 2003. 312p. Cambridge Studies in Contentious Politics ISBN:0-521-01699-1, ISBN13: 978-0-521-01699-5. Dewey:303.48/4. LCCN:2002-067649.
Audience: **l,u,f.** *Choice, 2004.*

Harvey, Neil **F1236.H37 1998**
The Chiapas Rebellion: The Struggle for Land and Democracy. Trade Cloth. Duke University Press. Durham, NC. 1998. 264p. ISBN:0-8223-2209-9, ISBN13: 978-0-8223-2209-2. Dewey:972/.750835. LCCN:98-016066.
Audience: **l,u,f.** *Choice, 1999.*

Jebens, Holger (Editor) **GN472.75.C37 2004**
Cargo, Cult, and Culture Critique. Trade Cloth. University of Hawaii Press. Honolulu, HI. 2004. 336p. ISBN:0-8248-2814-3, ISBN13: 978-0-8248-2814-1. Dewey:306.6/99925. LCCN:2004-003470.
Audience: **l,u,f.** *Choice, 2005.*

Kellogg, Michael **DD78.R87K45 2004**
The Russian Roots of Nazism: White Émigrés and the Making of National Socialism, 1917-1945. Peter Baldwin, Christopher Clark, James B. Collins, Lyndal Roper & Mia Rodr¡guez-Salgado (Contribution by). Trade Cloth. Cambridge University Press. New York, NY. 2005. 344p. New Studies in European History Ser. ISBN:0-521-84512-2, ISBN13: 978-0-521-84512-0. Dewey:320.53/3/094309041. LCCN:2004-051101.
Audience: **u,f.** *Choice, 2005.*

Kelly, Christine **HM881.K45 2001**
Tangled up in Red, White and Blue: New Social Movements in America. Book, Other. Rowman & Littlefield Publishers, Inc. Lanham, MD. 2001. 216p. ISBN:0-7425-0813-7, ISBN13: 978-0-7425-0813-2. Dewey:303.48/4/0973. LCCN:00-057587.
Audience: **l,u,f.** *Choice, 2001.*

Lent, Adam **HN385.5.L46 2001**
British Social Movements since 1945: Sex, Colour, Peace and Power. Cloth over Boards. Palgrave Macmillan. New York, NY. 2002. 268p. Contemporary History in Context Ser. ISBN:0-333-72009-1, ISBN13: 978-0-333-72009-7. Dewey:303.48/4/09. LCCN:2001-035823.
Audience: **l,u.** *Choice, 2002.*

Mamdani, Mahmood, et al. **HN773+**
African Studies in Social Movements and Democracy. Ernest Wamba-dia-Wamba & Codesria Staff (Authors). Cloth Text. Codesria (Conseil pour le Developpement de la Recherche Economique et Sociale en Afrique). Dakar, 2000. 626p. ISBN:2-86978-051-6, ISBN13: 978-2-86978-051-4. Dewey:303.484096. LCCN:99-889758.
Audience: **l,u,f.**

Newton, Judith Lowder **HQ1090.3.N493 2004**
From Panthers to Promise Keepers: Rethinking the Men's Movement. Book, Other. Rowman & Littlefield Publishers, Inc. Lanham, MD. 2004. 304p. New Social Formations Ser. ISBN:0-8476-9129-2, ISBN13: 978-0-8476-9129-6. Dewey:305.32/0973. LCCN:2004-013004.
Audience: **l,u.** *Choice, 2005.*

Polletta, Francesca **HN57**
Freedom Is an Endless Meeting: Democracy in American Social Movements. Trade Paper. University of Chicago Press. Chicago, IL. 2004. 294p. ISBN:0-226-67449-5, ISBN13: 978-0-226-67449-0. Dewey:303.48/4/0973.
Audience: **l,u.** *Choice, 2003.*

Sawyer, Suzana **F3721.3.E25S29 2004**
Crude Chronicles: Indigenous Politics, Multinational Oil, and Neoliberalism in Ecuador. Trade Cloth, Pictures or Photographs. Duke University Press. Durham, NC. 2004. 280p. American Encounters/Global Interactions Ser. ISBN:0-8223-3283-3, ISBN13: 978-0-8223-3283-1. Dewey:986.607/400498. LCCN:2003-025004.
Audience: **u,f.** *Choice, 2005.*

Shah, Ghanshyam **HN683.5.S4448 2004**
Social Movements in India: A Review of the Literature. Ed. 2. Trade Paper. SAGE Publications, Inc. Thousand Oaks, CA. 2004. 281p. ISBN:0-7619-9834-9, ISBN13: 978-0-7619-9834-1. Dewey:303.48/4/0954. LCCN:2003-025405.
Audience: **l,u.** *Choice, 1991.*

Shin, Gi-Wook **DS916.55.S55 1996**
Peasant Protest and Social Change in Colonial Korea. Trade Cloth. University of Washington Press. Seattle, WA. 1996. 264p. Korean Studies of the Henry M. Jackson School of International Studies ISBN:0-295-97548-2, ISBN13: 978-0-295-97548-1. Dewey:951.9/03/08624. LCCN:96-031636.
Audience: **u,f.** *Choice, 1997.*

Starr, Amory **HD2755.5.S79 2000**
Naming the Enemy: Anti-Corporate Social Movements Confront Globalization. Cloth over Boards. Zed Books, Ltd. London, 2001. 320p. ISBN:1-85649-764-X, ISBN13: 978-1-85649-764-0. Dewey:303.484. LCCN:2002-391151.
Audience: **g,l,u.** *Choice, 2001.*

Thomas, Nick **HM881**
Protest Movements in 1960s West Germany: A Social History of Dissent and Democracy. Cloth over Boards. Berg Publishers. Oxford, 2003. 288p. ISBN:1-85973-645-9, ISBN13: 978-1-85973-645-6. Dewey:303.48/4/0943. LCCN:2002-151465.
Audience: **g,l,u,f.** *Choice, 2003.*

Tilly, Charles **HM881.T55 2004**
Social Movements, 1768-2004. Trade Paper. Paradigm Publishers. Boulder, CO. 2004. 194p. ISBN:1-59451-043-1, ISBN13: 978-1-59451-043-4. Dewey:303.484. LCCN:2003-025659.
Audience: **g,l,u.**

Warner, Tom **HQ76.8.C3W37 2002**
Never Going Back: A History of Queer Activism in Canada. Trade Cloth. University of Toronto Press. Toronto, ON. 2002. 480p. ISBN:0-8020-3608-2, ISBN13: 978-0-8020-3608-7. Dewey:305.9/0664/0971. LCCN:2002-726730.
Audience: **g,l,u.** *Choice, 2003.*

Wiktorowicz, Quintan (Editor) **HN766.A8I85 2003**
Ⓔ Islamic Activism: A Social Movement Theory Approach. E-Book. Indiana University Press. Bloomington, IN. 2004. 320p. Indiana Series in Middle East Studies ISBN:0-253-34281-3, ISBN13: 978-0-253-34281-2. Dewey:303.48/4/09174927. LCCN:2003-008458.
Audience: **u,f.** *Choice, 2004.*

Yamamoto, Mari **JZ5584.J3Y36 2004**
Grassroots Pacifism in Post-War Japan: The Rebirth of a Nation. Paper over Boards. Taylor & Francis Group. Philadelphia, PA. 2004. 320p. Sheffield Centre for Japanese Studies/RoutledgeCurzon Ser. ISBN:0-415-33581-7, ISBN13: 978-0-415-33581-2. Dewey:303.6/6. LCCN:2004-005189.
Audience: **l,u.**

Social History > Mass Phenomena > Pop Culture

Ashby, LeRoy **E169.1**
With Amusement for All: A History of American Popular Culture Since 1830. Trade Cloth. University Press of Kentucky. Lexington, KY. 2006. 640p. ISBN:0-8131-2397-6, ISBN13: 978-0-8131-2397-4. Dewey:306.4/80973. LCCN:2006-002558.
Audience: **g,l,u.**

Blau, Judith R. **NX180.S6**
The Shape of Culture: A Study of Contemporary Cultural Patterns in the United States. Ernest Q. Campbell (Contribution by). Trade Paper. Cambridge University Press. New York, NY. 1992. 219p. American Sociological Association Rose Monographs ISBN:0-521-43793-8, ISBN13: 978-0-521-43793-6. Dewey:700/.1/030973.
Audience: **l,u.** *Choice, 1991.*

Braunstein, Peter & Doyle, Michael William (Editors) **E839.4.I46 2001**
Imagine Nation: The American Counterculture of the 1960s and 1970s. Paper over Boards. Routledge. New York, NY. 2001. 408p. ISBN:0-415-93039-1, ISBN13: 978-0-415-93039-0. Dewey:306/.0973/0904. LCCN:2001-019648.
Audience: **l,u,f.** *Choice, 2003, 2002.*

Harris, Daniel **HQ76.2.U5H347 1997**
The Rise and Fall of Gay Culture. Trade Cloth. Hyperion Press. New York, NY. 1997. 278p. ISBN:0-7868-6165-7, ISBN13: 978-0-7868-6165-1. Dewey:305.38/96642. LCCN:96-047822.
Audience: **g,l,u,f.**

Hendershot, Cyndy **E743.5.H425 2003**
Anti-Communism and Popular Culture in Mid-Century America. Paper Text. McFarland & Company, Incorporated Publishers. Jefferson, NC. 2002. 183p. ISBN:0-7864-1440-5, ISBN13: 978-0-7864-1440-6. Dewey:306/.0973/09045. LCCN:2002-153824.
Audience: **l,u.** *Choice, 2003.*

Howland Kenney, William **ML3477.K46 1999**
Recorded Music in American Life: The Phonograph and Popular Memory, 1890-1945. Trade Cloth. Oxford University Press, Inc. New York, NY. 1999. 276p. ISBN:0-19-510046-8, ISBN13: 978-0-19-510046-4. Dewey:306.4/84. LCCN:98-008611.
Audience: **l,u.** *Choice, 2000.*

Mazur, Eric Michael & McCarthy, Kate **BL2525.G625 2000**
God in the Details: American Religion in Popular Culture. Paper over Boards. Routledge. New York, NY. 2000. 352p. ISBN:0-415-92563-0, ISBN13: 978-0-415-92563-1. Dewey:306/.0973. LCCN:00-035309.
Audience: **g,l,u.** *Choice, 2001.*

Negron-Muntaner, Frances **E169.12**
Boricua Pop: Puerto Ricans and American Culture from West Side Story to Jennifer Lopez. Trade Cloth. New York University Press. New York, NY. 2004. 368p. Sexual Cultures Ser. ISBN:0-8147-5817-7, ISBN13: 978-0-8147-5817-5. Dewey:305.868/7295073. LCCN:2003-025217.
Audience: **u,f.** *Choice, 2004.*

Rheingold, Howard **HM846.R54 2002**
Smart Mobs: The Next Social Revolution: Transforming Cultures and Communities in the Age of Instant Access. Trade Cloth. Basic Books. New York, NY. 2002. 288p. ISBN:0-7382-0608-3, ISBN13: 978-0-7382-0608-0. Dewey:303.4/833. LCCN:2002-112392.
Audience: **l,u,f.** *Choice, 2003.*

Shaw, Lisa & Dennison, Stephanie **F1414.2.S495 2005**
Ⓔ Pop Culture Latin America!: Media, Arts, and Lifestyle. E-Book. ABC-CLIO, Inc. Santa Barbara, CA. 2005. xii, 404p. Popular Culture Ser. ISBN:1-85109-509-8, ISBN13: 978-1-85109-509-4. Dewey:306/.098/09045. LCCN:2004-024669.
Audience: **g,l.** *Choice, 2005.*

Sternheimer, Karen **HQ799.2.M35S84 2003**
Its Not the Media: The Truth about Pop Culture's Influence on Children. Trade Cloth. Westview Press. Boulder, CO. 2003.

288p. ISBN:0-8133-4138-8, ISBN13: 978-0-8133-4138-5. Dewey:302.23/0835. LCCN:2003-014599.
Audience: **g,l,u,f.** *Choice, 2004.*

Social History > Mass Phenomena > Collective Behavior

Gilbert, Margaret **HM24**
On Social Facts. Cloth Text. Princeton University Press. Princeton, NJ. 1992. 536p. ISBN:0-691-07401-1, ISBN13: 978-0-691-07401-6. Dewey:301/.01. LCCN:91-038727.
Audience: **l,u.** *Choice, 1990.*

Hogg, Michael & Abrams, Dominic **HM131.H594 1988**
Social Identifications: A Social Psychology of Intergroup Relations and Group Processes. UK-B Format Paperback. Routledge. New York, NY. 1990. 288p. ISBN:0-415-00695-3, ISBN13: 978-0-415-00695-8. Dewey:302.3. LCCN:87-030779.
Audience: **l,u.** *Choice, 1988.*

Le Bon, Gustave **HM281**
The Crowd: A Study of the Popular Mind. Cloth Text. Amereon, Ltd. Mattituck, NY. 2004. ISBN:0-8488-2691-4, ISBN13: 978-0-8488-2691-8. Dewey:302.3/3.
Audience: **g,l,u.**

May, Larry **HM216.M315 1987**
The Morality of Groups: Collective Responsibility, Group-Based Harm and Corporate Rights. Cloth Text. University of Notre Dame Press. Notre Dame, IN. 1989. 216p. Soundings: A Series in Ethics, Economics and Business, Vol. 1 ISBN:0-268-01366-7, ISBN13: 978-0-268-01366-0. Dewey:302.3. LCCN:87-040350.
Audience: **l,u,f.** *Choice, 1988.*

Park, Robert Ezra **HM51**
The Crowd and the Public: And Other Essays. Henry Elsner Jr. (Editor), Charlotte Elsner (Translator). Library Binding. University of Chicago Press. Chicago, IL. 1994. 184p. The Heritage of Sociology Ser., :Midway Reprint ISBN:0-226-64609-2, ISBN13: 978-0-226-64609-1. Dewey:301. LCCN:78-189361.
Audience: **l,u.** *B*

Rude, George **HM871**
Crowd in History. Ed. 2. Trade Paper. Serif. London, 2005. 288p. ISBN:1-897959-47-8, ISBN13: 978-1-897959-47-3. Dewey:302.33.
Audience: **l,u.**

Rude, George **HM281**
Ideology and Popular Protest. Trade Paper. Lawrence & Wishart, Ltd. London, 1980. 176p. ISBN:0-85315-514-3, ISBN13: 978-0-85315-514-0. Dewey:303.6/4.
Audience: **l,u,f.** *B*

Tarrow, Sidney **HM291 .T353 1998**
Power in Movement: Social Movements, Collective Action and Politics. Ed. 2. Cloth Text. Cambridge University Press. New York, NY. 1998. 287p. Studies in Comparative Politics ISBN:0-521-62072-4, ISBN13: 978-0-521-62072-7. Dewey:303.48/4/09. LCCN:97-035137.
Audience: **l,u.** *Choice, 1995.*

van Ginneken, Jaap **HM1236.G556 2002**
Collective Behavior and Public Opinion: Rapid Shifts in Opinion and Communication. Cloth over Boards. Lawrence Erlbaum Associates, Inc. Mahwah, NJ. 2003. 312p. The European Institute for the Media Ser. ISBN:0-8058-4386-8, ISBN13: 978-0-8058-4386-6. Dewey:303.3/8. LCCN:2002-019731.
Audience: **u,f.** *Choice, 2003.*

Wright, Sam **HM281**
Crowds and Riots: A Study in Social Organization. Trade Cloth. SAGE Publications, Inc. Thousand Oaks, CA. 1978. 207p. Sociological Observations Ser., No. 4 ISBN:0-8039-0995-0, ISBN13: 978-0-8039-0995-3. Dewey:302.3/3. LCCN:78-000626.
Audience: **l,u.**

Social History > Mass Phenomena > Collective Behavior > Riots

Ablemann, Nancy & Lie, John **F869.L89K616 1995**
Blue Dreams: Korean Americans and the Los Angeles Riots. Trade Cloth. Harvard University Press. Cambridge, MA. 1995. 288p. ISBN:0-674-07704-0, ISBN13: 978-0-674-07704-1. Dewey:979.4/94004957. LCCN:94-023034.
Audience: **g,l,u.** *Choice, 1995.*

Baldassare, Mark (Editor) **F869.L89N4 1994**
The Los Angeles Riots. Trade Paper. Westview Press. Boulder, CO. 1994. 255p. Urban Policy Challenges Ser. ISBN:0-8133-2391-6, ISBN13: 978-0-8133-2391-6. Dewey:979.4/94. LCCN:94-032452.
Audience: **g.** *Choice, 1995.*

Horowitz, Donald L. **HV6474 .H67 2001**
The Deadly Ethnic Riot. Trade Cloth. University of California Press. Berkeley, CA. 2001. 608p. ISBN:0-520-22447-7, ISBN13: 978-0-520-22447-6. Dewey:303.6/23. LCCN:99-086512.
Audience: **g,l,u.** *Choice, 2001.*

Klein, Philip S. & Hoogenboom, Ari **GT4803.C76 2002**
Riot and Revelry in Early America. Ed. 2. William Pencak, Matthew Dennis & Simon P. Newman (Editors). Trade Cloth. Pennsylvania State University Press. University Park, PA. 2002. 633p. ISBN:0-271-02141-1, ISBN13: 978-0-271-02141-6. Dewey:394.26973. LCCN:2001-036462.
Audience: **u,f.** *Choice, 2002.*

Schecter, Barnet **F128.44.S33 2005**
The Devil's Own Work: The Civil War Draft Riots and the Fight to Reconstruct America. Cloth over Boards. Walker & Company. New York, NY. 2005. 448p. ISBN:0-8027-1439-0, ISBN13: 978-0-8027-1439-8. Dewey:974.7/103. LCCN:2005-018089.
Audience: **u,f.**

Tager, Jack **HV6483.B6T34 2001**
Boston Riots: Three Centuries of Social Violence. Trade Cloth. Northeastern University Press. Boston, MA. 2000. xi, 289p. ISBN:1-55553-461-9, ISBN13: 978-1-55553-461-5. Dewey:303.6/23/0974461. LCCN:00-041816.
Audience: **u,f.** *Choice, 2001.*

Tambiah, Stanley J. **HV6485.S64T35 1996**
Leveling Crowds: Ethno-Nationalist Conflicts and Collective Violence in South Asia. Trade Cloth. University of California Press. Berkeley, CA. 1997. 417p. Comparative Studies in

Religion and Society, Vol. 10 ISBN:0-520-20002-0, ISBN13: 978-0-520-20002-9. Dewey:303.6/23/0954. LCCN:95-048114.
Audience: **l,u.** *Choice, 1997.*

Social History > Mass Phenomena > Collective Behavior > Hysteria

Bartholomew, Robert E. **HM1033.B37 2001**
Little Green Men, Meowing Nuns and Head-Hunting Panics: A Study of Mass Psychogenic Illnesses and Social Delusion. Paper Text. McFarland & Company, Incorporated Publishers. Jefferson, NC. 2001. 303p. ISBN:0-7864-0997-5, ISBN13: 978-0-7864-0997-6. Dewey:302/.17. LCCN:2001-018029.
Audience: **u,f.**

Blackman, Lisa & Walkerdine, Valerie **P96.P75B58 2001**
Mass Hysteria: Critical Psychology and Media Studies. Cloth over Boards. Palgrave Macmillan. New York, NY. 2001. 226p. ISBN:0-333-64781-5, ISBN13: 978-0-333-64781-3. Dewey:302.2/3/019. LCCN:00-059180.
Audience: **g,l,u,f.**

Micklem, Niel **RC532.M54 1996**
The Nature of Hysteria. Paper over Boards. Routledge. New York, NY. 1995. 144p. ISBN:0-415-12186-8, ISBN13: 978-0-415-12186-6. Dewey:616.85/24. LCCN:95-018320.
Audience: **g,l,u,f.** *Choice, 1997.*

Murray, Robert K. **E743.5**
Red Scare: A Study in National Hysteria, 1919-1920. Paper Text. McGraw-Hill Companies, The. New York, NY. 1955. ISBN:0-07-044075-1, ISBN13: 978-0-07-044075-3. Dewey:973.913.
Audience: **g,l,u.**

Ofshe, Richard & Watters, Ethan **RC480.5**
Making Monsters: False Memories, Psychotherapy, and Sexual Hysteria. Cloth Text. DIANE Publishing Company. Collingdale, PA. 1998. 340p. ISBN:0-7881-5931-3, ISBN13: 978-0-7881-5931-2. Dewey:616.8/914.
Audience: **l,u,f.** *Choice, 1995.*

Showalter, Elaine **RC532**
Hystories: Hysterical Epidemics and Modern Media. Trade Paper. Columbia University Press. New York, NY. 1998. 224p. ISBN:0-231-10459-6, ISBN13: 978-0-231-10459-3. Dewey:616.85/24.
Audience: **l,u.**

Social History > Mass Phenomena > Collective Behavior > Gangs

Asbury, Herbert **HV6439.U7N4 2003**
The Gangs of New York: An Informal History of the Underworld. Trade Cloth. Thomson Gale. Farmington Hills, MI. 2003. 353p. ISBN:1-58724-463-2, ISBN13: 978-1-58724-463-6. Dewey:364.1/06/097471. LCCN:2003-049677.
Audience: **g,l.**

Covey, Herbert C. **HV6437.C68 2003**
Street Gangs Throughout the World. Paper Text. Charles C. Thomas Publisher, Ltd. Springfield, IL. 2003. 280p. ISBN:0-398-07429-1, ISBN13: 978-0-398-07429-6. Dewey:364.1/06/6. LCCN:2003-050397.
Audience: **g,l.**

Esbensen, Finn-Aage (Editor), et al. **HV6439.U5 E73 2004**
American Youth Gangs at the Millennium. Stephen G. Tibbetts & Larry Gaines (Editors). Paper Text. Waveland Press, Inc. Prospect Heights, IL. 2004. 389p. ISBN:1-57766-324-1, ISBN13: 978-1-57766-324-9. Dewey:364.1/06/60973. LCCN:2004-301008.
Audience: **l,u,f.** *Choice, 2004.*

Fleisher, Mark S. **HV9106.K2F54 1998**
Dead End Kids: Gang Girls and the Boys They Know. Trade Cloth. University of Wisconsin Press. Chicago, IL. 2000. 336p. ISBN:0-299-15880-2, ISBN13: 978-0-299-15880-4. Dewey:364.36/082/09778411. LCCN:98-015537.
Audience: **l,u,f.** *Choice, 1999.*

Jankowski, Martin S. **HV6439.U5J36 1991**
Islands in the Street: Gangs and American Urban Society. Trade Paper. University of California Press. Berkeley, CA. 1992. 396p. ISBN:0-520-07434-3, ISBN13: 978-0-520-07434-7. Dewey:364.1/06/0973.
Audience: **l,u.** *Choice, 1991.*

Kontos, Louis (Editor), et al. **HV6439.U5G3597 2003**
Gangs and Society: Alternative Perspectives. David Brotherton & Luis Barrios (Editors). Trade Cloth. Columbia University Press. New York, NY. 2003. 352p. ISBN:0-231-12140-7, ISBN13: 978-0-231-12140-8. Dewey:302.3/4. LCCN:2002-035038.
Audience: **g,l,u,f.** *Choice, 2004.*

Phillips, Susan **GT3913.13.C2P55 1999**
Wallbangin': Graffiti and Gangs in L. A. Trade Paper. University of Chicago Press. Chicago, IL. 1999. 414p. ISBN:0-226-66772-3, ISBN13: 978-0-226-66772-0. Dewey:364.1/06/60979494. LCCN:98-031899.
Audience: **g,l,u.**

Rodriguez, Luis J. **HV6439.U7 L77**
Always Running: Gang Days in L. A. Library Binding. Sagebrush Education Resources. Caledonia, MN. 1994. ISBN:0-613-01323-9, ISBN13: 978-0-613-01323-9. Dewey:364.1/092 B.
Audience: **g,l.**

Shakur, Sanyika **HV6439.U7L774 1993**
Monster: The Autobiography of an L. A. Gang Member. Trade Paper. Grove/Atlantic, Inc. New York, NY. 2004. 400p. ISBN:0-8021-4144-7, ISBN13: 978-0-8021-4144-6. Dewey:364.1/06/092. LCCN:93-014948.
Audience: **g,l.**

Vigil, James Diego **HV6439.U7L788 2002**
A Rainbow of Gangs: Street Cultures in the Mega-City. Trade Cloth. University of Texas Press. Austin, TX. 2002. 224p. ISBN:0-292-78748-0, ISBN13: 978-0-292-78748-3. Dewey:364.1/06/60979494. LCCN:2002-001063.
Audience: **l,u.** *Choice, 2003.*

Social History > Mass Phenomena > Collective Behavior > Genocide

Dallaire, Romeo & Beardsley, Brent **DT450.435**
Shake Hands with the Devil: The Failure of Humanity in Rwanda. Trade Paper. Random House of Canada, Ltd. Mississauga, ON. 2004. 592p. ISBN:0-679-31172-6, ISBN13: 978-0-679-31172-0. Dewey:967.57104/31/092 B.
Audience: **g,l,u.**

Gourevitch, Philip **DT450.435.G68 1999**
We Wish to Inform You That Tomorrow We Will Be Killed with Our Families: Stories from Rwanda. Trade Paper. Picador. New York, NY. 1999. 368p. ISBN:0-312-24335-9, ISBN13: 978-0-312-24335-7. Dewey:364.15/1/0967571. LCCN:2004-559125.
Audience: **g,l,u,f.** *Choice, 1999.*

Mann, Michael **HV6322.M36 2004**
The Dark Side of Democracy: Explaining Ethnic Cleansing. Cloth Text. Cambridge University Press. New York, NY. 2004. 590p. ISBN:0-521-83130-X, ISBN13: 978-0-521-83130-7. Dewey:304.6/63. LCCN:2004-045626.
Audience: **g,l,u,f.** *Choice, 2005.*

Odom, Thomas P. **DT450.435.O34 2005**
Journey into Darkness: Genocide in Rwanda. Dennis J. Reimer (Foreword by). Trade Cloth. Texas A&M University Press. College Station, TX. 2005. 320p. Texas a & M University Military History Ser., Vol. 100 ISBN:1-58544-427-8, ISBN13: 978-1-58544-427-4. Dewey:967.57104/31. LCCN:2004-028031.
Audience: **g,l,u,f.** *Choice, 2006.*

Power, Samantha **HV6322.7.P69 2003**
"A Problem from Hell": America and the Age of Genocide. Trade Paper. HarperCollins Publishers. New York, NY. 2003. 656p. ISBN:0-06-054164-4, ISBN13: 978-0-06-054164-4. Dewey:304.6/63/09. LCCN:2003-043341.
Audience: **l,u,f.**

Staub, Ervin **HV6322.7**
The Roots of Evil: The Origins of Genocide and Other Group Violence. Trade Paper. Cambridge University Press. New York, NY. 1992. 352p. ISBN:0-521-42214-0, ISBN13: 978-0-521-42214-7. Dewey:364.1/51.
Audience: **l,u,f.**

Valentino, Benjamin A. **HV6322.7.V35 2004**
Final Solutions: Mass Killing and Genocide in the 20th Century. Trade Cloth. Cornell University Press. Ithaca, NY. 2005. 336p. Cornell Studies in Security Affairs Ser. ISBN:0-8014-3965-5, ISBN13: 978-0-8014-3965-0. Dewey:364.15/1/0904. LCCN:2003-019941.
Audience: **l,u,f.** *Choice, 2004.*

Weitz, Eric D. **HV6322.7.W45 2003**
A Century of Genocide: Utopias of Race and Nation. Cloth Text. Princeton University Press. Princeton, NJ. 2003. 368p. ISBN:0-691-00913-9, ISBN13: 978-0-691-00913-1. Dewey:364.15/1/0904. LCCN:2002-030264.
Audience: **l,u.** *Choice, 2003.*

Social History > Mass Phenomena > Sports

Cosgrave, James F. (Editor) **HV6710.S65 2006**
The Sociology of Risk and Gambling Reader. Cloth Text. Routledge. New York, NY. 2006. 384p. ISBN:0-415-95221-2, ISBN13: 978-0-415-95221-7. Dewey:306.4/82. LCCN:2005-035574.
Audience: **l,u.**

Davies, Richard O. & Abram, Richard G. **GV717.D38 2001**
Betting the Line: Sports Wagering in American Life. Trade Cloth. Ohio State University Press. Columbus, OH. 2001. 208p. ISBN:0-8142-0880-0, ISBN13: 978-0-8142-0880-9. Dewey:796. LCCN:2001-000771.
Audience: **l,u.** *Choice, 2002.*

Dunning, Eric (Editor), et al. **GV943.9.F35F53 2002**
Fighting Fans: Football Hooliganism as a World Phenomenon. Patrick Murphy, Ivan Waddington & Antonio E. Astrinakis (Editors). Trade Cloth. University College Dublin Press. Dublin, 2002. 27p. ISBN:1-900621-73-8, ISBN13: 978-1-900621-73-1. Dewey:306.4/83. LCCN:2003-464716.
Audience: **u.** *Choice, 2003.*

Fair, John D. **GV545.52.H64F35 1999**
Muscletown USA: Bob Hoffman and the Manly Culture of York Barbell. Trade Cloth. Pennsylvania State University Press. University Park, PA. 1999. 804p. ISBN:0-271-01854-2, ISBN13: 978-0-271-01854-6. Dewey:338.7/6887641/092 B. LCCN:98-039333.
Audience: **l,u,f.**

Feezell, Randolph **GV706.3.F44 2004**
Sport, Play, and Ethical Reflection. Trade Cloth. University of Illinois Press. Champaign, IL. 2004. 192p. ISBN:0-252-02955-0, ISBN13: 978-0-252-02955-4. Dewey:175. LCCN:2004-002534.
Audience: **l,u.** *Choice, 2005.*

French, Peter A. **GV361.F64 2004**
Ethics and College Sports: Ethics, Sports, and the University. Book, Other. Rowman & Littlefield Publishers, Inc. Lanham, MD. 2004. 208p. Issues in Academic Ethics Ser. ISBN:0-7425-1273-8, ISBN13: 978-0-7425-1273-3. Dewey:796.04/3/0973. LCCN:2004-004349.
Audience: **g,l,u,f.** *Choice, 2005.*

Giulianotti, Richard (Editor) **GV706.5.S69424 2004**
Sport and Modern Social Theorists: Theorizing Homo Ludens. Cloth over Boards. Palgrave Macmillan. New York, NY. 2004. 264p. ISBN:0-333-80078-8, ISBN13: 978-0-333-80078-2. Dewey:306.4/83. LCCN:2004-050021.
Audience: **u,f.** *Choice, 2005.*

Guttmann, Allen **GV571.G88 2004**
Sports: The First Five Millenia. Trade Cloth. University of Massachusetts Press. Amherst, MA. 2004. 448p.

ISBN:1-55849-470-7, ISBN13: 978-1-55849-470-1. Dewey:796/.09. LCCN:2004-013506.
Audience: **g,l.** *Choice, 2005.*

Hartmann-Tews, Ilse **GV709.S66 2003**
Sport and Women: Social Issues in International Perspective. Gertrud Pfister (Editor). Paper over Boards. Routledge. New York, NY. 2002. 304p. ISBN:0-415-24627-X, ISBN13: 978-0-415-24627-9. Dewey:796/.082. LCCN:2002-073982.
Audience: **g,l,u,f.** *Choice, 2003.*

Jay, Kathryn **GV706.5.J39 2004**
More Than Just a Game: Sports in American Life since 1945. Trade Cloth. Kegan Paul International, Ltd. London, 2004. 304p. Columbia Histories of Modern American Life Ser. ISBN:0-231-12534-8, ISBN13: 978-0-231-12534-5. Dewey:796.357/0973/09045. LCCN:2004-044498.
Audience: **g,l,u,f.** *Choice, 2005.*

Mangan, J. A. & Da Costa, Lamartine P. (Editors) **GV586.S66 2001**
Sport in Latin American Society: Past and Present. Paper over Boards. Taylor & Francis Group. Philadelphia, PA. 2001. 224p. International Journal of the History of Sport Ser. ISBN:0-7146-5126-5, ISBN13: 978-0-7146-5126-2. Dewey:306.4/83/098. LCCN:2001-004347.
Audience: **l,u.** *Choice, 2002.*

Moss, Richard J. **GV979.S63M67 2001**
Golf and the American Country Club. Trade Cloth. University of Illinois Press. Champaign, IL. 2001. 232p. Sport and Society Ser. ISBN:0-252-02642-X, ISBN13: 978-0-252-02642-3. Dewey:796.352/06/873. LCCN:00-010832.
Audience: **g,l,u.** *Choice, 2001.*

Toma, J. D. **GV959.5.T66 2003**
Football U.: Spectator Sports in the Life of the American University. Trade Cloth. University of Michigan Press. Chicago, IL. 2003. 220p. ISBN:0-472-11299-6, ISBN13: 978-0-472-11299-9. Dewey:796.332/63/0973. LCCN:2002-153617.
Audience: **g,l,u.** *Choice, 2004.*

Williams, Peter **GV706.5.W54 1994**
The Sports Immortals: Deifying the American Athlete. Trade Paper. University of Wisconsin Press. Chicago, IL. 1994. 161p. Sports and Culture Ser. ISBN:0-87972-670-9, ISBN13: 978-0-87972-670-6. Dewey:306.483. LCCN:94-078929.
Audience: **l,u.** *Choice, 1995.*

Wilson, John **GV706.5.W55 1994**
Playing by the Rules: Sport, Society, and the State. Cloth Text. Wayne State University Press. Detroit, MI. 1994. 430p. ISBN:0-8143-2107-0, ISBN13: 978-0-8143-2107-2. Dewey:306.4/83/0973. LCCN:93-019671.
Audience: **u,f.** *Choice, 1994.*

Social History > Mass Phenomena > Leisure/Tourism

Cross, Gary **GV14.45.C76 1990**
A Social History of Leisure Since 1600. Trade Cloth. Venture Publishing, Inc. State College, PA. 1990. 297p. ISBN:0-910251-35-5, ISBN13: 978-0-910251-35-8. Dewey:306.4812. LCCN:90-070208.
Audience: **g,l,u,f.** *Choice, 1991.*

Grover, Kathryn (Editor) **GV53.H28 1992**
Hard at Play: Leisure in America, 1840-1940. Cloth Text. University of Massachusetts Press. Amherst, MA. 1992. 272p. ISBN:0-87023-792-6, ISBN13: 978-0-87023-792-8. Dewey:790/.01/350973. LCCN:91-039908.
Audience: **l,u.** *Choice, 1993.*

Harris, David E. **GV14.5**
Key Concepts in Leisure Studies. Cloth Text. SAGE Publications, Inc. Thousand Oaks, CA. 2005. 288p. SAGE Key Concepts Ser. ISBN:0-7619-7057-6, ISBN13: 978-0-7619-7057-6. Dewey:790.1. LCCN:2005-295466.
Audience: **g,l,u.** *Choice, 2005.*

Johannis, Theodore B. & Bull, Neil (Editors) **HD4904.7**
Sociology of Leisure. Trade Paper. SAGE Publications, Inc. Thousand Oaks, CA. 1975. 135p. Sage Contemporary Social Science Issues, No. 1 ISBN:0-8039-0318-9, ISBN13: 978-0-8039-0318-0. Dewey:301.5/7/0973. LCCN:73-087853.
Audience: **l,u.**

Koshar, Rudy (Editor) **GV73.H57 2002**
Histories of Leisure. Trade Paper. Berg Publishers. Oxford, 2002. 352p. Leisure, Consumption and Culture Ser. ISBN:1-85973-525-8, ISBN13: 978-1-85973-525-1. Dewey:306.4/812. LCCN:2002-000202.
Audience: **l,u.** *Choice, 2003.*

Organizations

Coleman, James S. **HM131.C7419 1982**
The Asymmetric Society. Trade Cloth. Syracuse University Press. Syracuse, NY. 1982. 192p. Frank W. Abrams Lectures ISBN:0-8156-0172-7, ISBN13: 978-0-8156-0172-2. Dewey:305. LCCN:81-023255.
Audience: **l,u,f.** B

Etzioni, Amitai **HM131**
A Comparative Analysis of Complex Organizations. Trade Cloth. Simon & Schuster. New York, NY. 1975. xxiv, 584p. ISBN:0-02-909650-2, ISBN13: 978-0-02-909650-5. Dewey:302.3/5. LCCN:74-021488.
Audience: **u,f.**

Katz, Daniel & Kahn, Robert L. **HD58.7**
The Social Psychology of Organizations. Ed. 2. Trade Cloth. John Wiley & Sons, Inc. Hoboken, NJ. 1978. 848p. ISBN:0-471-02355-8, ISBN13: 978-0-471-02355-5. Dewey:302.3/5. LCCN:77-018764.
Audience: **g,l.** B

Parsons, Talcott **HM131 .P33**
Structure and Process in Modern Societies. Trade Cloth. Simon & Schuster. New York, NY. 1960. ISBN:0-02-924340-8, ISBN13: 978-0-02-924340-4. Dewey:301.4.
Audience: **u,f.** B

Scott, W. Richard **HM786.S3845 2001**
Institutions and Organizations. Ed. 2. Trade Cloth. SAGE Publications, Inc. Thousand Oaks, CA. 2000. 280p. Foundations for Organizational Science Ser. ISBN:0-7619-2000-5, ISBN13: 978-0-7619-2000-7. Dewey:302.3/5. LCCN:00-011072.
Audience: **g,l.**

Sherif, Muzafer **HM131 .S45**
Groups in Harmony and Tension: An Integration of Studies on Intergroup Relations. Paper Text. Textbook Publishers. Temecula, CA. 2003. xiii, 316p. ISBN:0-7581-7451-9, ISBN13: 978-0-7581-7451-2. Dewey:301.15.
Audience: **u,f.**

Organizations > Work

Blau, Peter Michael & Scott, W. Richard **HD31.B53 2004**
Formal Organizations: A Comparative Approach. Trade Paper. Stanford University Press. Palo Alto, CA. 2003. 344p. Stanford Business Classics Ser. ISBN:0-8047-4890-X, ISBN13: 978-0-8047-4890-2. Dewey:302.3/5. LCCN:2003-015350.
Audience: **l,u.**

Caplow, Theodore **HM211 .C3 1978**
The Sociology of Work. Trade Cloth. Greenwood Publishing Group, Inc. Portsmouth, NH. 1978. 330p. ISBN:0-313-20111-0, ISBN13: 978-0-313-20111-0. Dewey:301.5/5. LCCN:77-018112.
Audience: **l,u.**

Doeringer, Peter B. & Piore, Michael J. **HD5724.D588 1985**
Internal Labor Markets and Manpower Analysis. Cloth Text. M. E. Sharpe Inc. Armonk, NY. 1985. 248p. ISBN:0-87332-351-3, ISBN13: 978-0-87332-351-2. Dewey:331.12/0973. LCCN:85-002063.
Audience: **u,f.**

Harper, Doug & Lawson, Helene (Editors) **HD6955.C86 2003**
Cultural Study of Work. Book, Other. Rowman & Littlefield Publishers, Inc. Lanham, MD. 2003. 504p. ISBN:0-7425-1917-1, ISBN13: 978-0-7425-1917-6. Dewey:306.3/6. LCCN:2003-009704.
Audience: **l,u.** *Choice, 2004.*

Petzinger, Thomas Jr. **HD31 .P394**
The New Pioneers: The Men and Women Who are Transforming the Workplace and Market Place. Trade Cloth. DIANE Publishing Company. Collingdale, PA. 2005. 302p. ISBN:0-7567-9522-2, ISBN13: 978-0-7567-9522-1. Dewey:658.
Audience: **g,l,u,f.**

Sennett, Richard **HD8072.5.S46 1998**
The Corrosion of Character: The Personal Consequences of Work in the New Capitalism. Trade Cloth. W. W. Norton & Company, Inc. New York, NY. 1998. 192p. ISBN:0-393-04678-8, ISBN13: 978-0-393-04678-6. Dewey:305.5/62. LCCN:98-017106.
Audience: **l,u.** *Choice, 1999.*

Terkel, Studs **HD8072.T4**
Working: People Talk about What They Do All Day and How They Feel about What They Do. Adam Cohen (Foreword by). Trade Paper. New Press, The. New York, NY. 1997. 640p. ISBN:1-56584-342-8, ISBN13: 978-1-56584-342-4. Dewey:331.2/0973/09047. LCCN:73-018037.
Audience: **g,l,u,f.**

Organizations > Work > Workplace

Perrow, Charles **HM131.P383**
Organizational Analysis: A Sociological View. Wadsworth Pub. Co.. 1970. Behavioral Science in Industry Series
Audience: **l,u.**

Organizations > Military

UB416
Center for the Study of Sexual Minorities in the Military. http://www.gaymilitary.ucsb.edu/
Audience: **g,l,u,f.**

Ambrose, Stephen E. & Barber, James A. Jr. (Editors) **UA25 .A68**
The Military and American Society. Trade Cloth. Simon & Schuster. New York, NY. 1973. ISBN:0-02-900550-7, ISBN13: 978-0-02-900550-7. Dewey:301.5/93/0973. LCCN:77-163236.
Audience: **l,u,f.**

Buckley, Gail Lumet **E185.63.B93 2002**
American Patriots: The Story of Blacks in the Military from the Revolution to Desert Storm. David Halberstam (Foreword by). Book, Other. Knopf Publishing Group. New York, NY. 2002. 608p. ISBN:0-375-76009-1, ISBN13: 978-0-375-76009-9. Dewey:355/.008996/73. LCCN:2002-069924.
Audience: **g,l.** *Choice, 2002.*

Caforio, Giuseppe (Editor) **U21.5.H368 2003**
Handbook of the Sociology of the Military. Trade Cloth. Springer. New York, NY. 2003. 496p. Handbooks of Sociology and Social Research ISBN:0-306-47295-3, ISBN13: 978-0-306-47295-4. Dewey:306.2/7. LCCN:2002-028692.
Audience: **u,f.** *Choice, 2003.*

Herbert, Melissa S. **UB418.W65H47**
Camouflage Isn't Only for Combat: Gender, Sexuality, and Women in the Military. Trade Paper. New York University Press. New York, NY. 2000. 208p. ISBN:0-8147-3548-7, ISBN13: 978-0-8147-3548-0. Dewey:355.0082. LCCN:97-045414.
Audience: **u,f.** *Choice, 1999.*

Johnson, John J. **F1410 .J7**
The Military and Society in Latin America. Trade Cloth. Stanford University Press. Palo Alto, CA. 1964. x, 308p. ISBN:0-8047-0198-9, ISBN13: 978-0-8047-0198-3. Dewey:980.
Audience: **l,u,f.**

Karsten, Peter **U21.5 .K37**
Soldiers and Society: The Effects of Military Service and War on American Life. Trade Cloth. Greenwood Publishing Group, Inc. Portsmouth, NH. 1978. 339p. Grass Roots Perspectives on American History Ser., No. 1 ISBN:0-313-20056-4, ISBN13: 978-0-313-20056-4. Dewey:301.5/93/0973. LCCN:77-087972.
Audience: **u,f.**

Katzenstein, Mary F. & Reppy, Judith (Editors) **UB417.B48 1999**
Beyond Zero Tolerance: Discrimination in Military Culture. Book, Other. Rowman & Littlefield Publishers, Inc. Lanham, MD. 1999. 308p. ISBN:0-8476-9315-5, ISBN13: 978-0-8476-9315-3. Dewey:355/.0089/00973. LCCN:98-041935.
Audience: **g,l,u,f.**

Leckie, William H. **357/.1/0973**
The Buffalo Soldiers: A Narrative of the Negro Cavalry in the West. Trade Paper. University of Oklahoma Press. Norman, OK. 1975. 304p. ISBN:0-8061-1244-1, ISBN13: 978-0-8061-1244-2. Dewey:357/.1/0973. LCCN:67-015571.
Audience: **g,l.**

Southern, Pat **U35.S625 2006**
The Roman Army: A Social and Institutional History. Bruce Vandervort (Editor). Library Binding. ABC-CLIO, Inc. Santa Barbara, CA. 2006. x, 383p. ISBN:1-85109-730-9, ISBN13: 978-1-85109-730-2. Dewey:355.00937. LCCN:2005-030389.
Audience: **u,f.**

Organizations > Bureaucracy

Herzfeld, Michael **HM141.H47 1993**
The Social Production of Indifference: Exploring the Symbolic Roots of Western Bureaucracy. Trade Paper. University of Chicago Press. Chicago, IL. 1993. 207p. ISBN:0-226-32908-9, ISBN13: 978-0-226-32908-6. Dewey:302.35. LCCN:93-001674.
Audience: **u,f.** *Choice, 1992.*

Rose, Arnold M. (Editor) **HN15 .R59**
Institutions of Advanced Societies. Trade Cloth. University of Minnesota Press. Minneapolis, MN. 1958. ISBN:0-8166-0168-2, ISBN13: 978-0-8166-0168-4. Dewey:301.1536 301.2. LCCN:57-011006.
Audience: **u,f.**

Turner, Jonathan H. **HM826.T87 2003**
Human Institutions: A Theory of Societal Evolution. Book, Other. Rowman & Littlefield Publishers, Inc. Lanham, MD. 2003. 328p. ISBN:0-7425-2558-9, ISBN13: 978-0-7425-2558-0. Dewey:306. LCCN:2002-151047.
Audience: **u,f.** *Choice, 2004.*

Organizations > Sociology of Business

Ali, Abbas J. **HD2916.5**
Islamic Perspectives on Management and Organization. Trade Cloth. Edward Elgar Publishing, Inc. Northampton, MA. 2005. 272p. New Horizons in Management Ser. ISBN:1-84376-766-X, ISBN13: 978-1-84376-766-4. Dewey:658/.00917/67. LCCN:2004-063491.
Audience: **u,f.**

Arendt, Hannah **HM211.A7 1998**
The Human Condition. Ed. 2. Margaret Canovan (Introduction by). Trade Cloth. University of Chicago Press. Chicago, IL. 1998. 370p. ISBN:0-226-02599-3, ISBN13: 978-0-226-02599-5. Dewey:301. LCCN:98-017015.
Audience: **g,l.** B

Blau, Peter M. (Editor) **HD58.7**
On the Nature of Organizations. Trade Cloth. Krieger Publishing Company. Melbourne, FL. 1983. 368p. ISBN:0-89874-463-6, ISBN13: 978-0-89874-463-7. Dewey:302.3/5. LCCN:81-019330.
Audience: **g,l,f.** B

Blumberg, Paul **HM146.B59**
Inequality in an Age of Decline. Trade Cloth. Oxford University Press, Inc. New York, NY. 1980. xv, 290p. ISBN:0-19-502804-X, ISBN13: 978-0-19-502804-1. Dewey:305.5. LCCN:80-016047.
Audience: **u,f.** B

Davis, Gerald (Editor), et al. **HM881.S6293 2005**
Social Movements and Organization Theory. W. Richard Scott, Mayer Zald, Gerald F. Davis, Mayer N. Zald & Doug McAdam (Editors), Douglas McAdam, Sidney Tarrow & Charles Tilly (Contribution by). Trade Paper. Cambridge University Press. New York, NY. 2005. 452p. Cambridge Studies in Contentious Politics Ser. ISBN:0-521-54836-5, ISBN13: 978-0-521-54836-6. Dewey:303.48/4. LCCN:2004-051186.
Audience: **u,f.** *Choice, 2006.*

Festinger, Leon **HM0251.F4**
Social Pressures in Informal Groups: A Study of Human Factors in Housing. Trade Cloth. Stanford University Press. Palo Alto, CA. 1950. x, 197p. ISBN:0-8047-0173-3, ISBN13: 978-0-8047-0173-0. Dewey:300.
Audience: **u,f.**

Hofstede, Geert **GN502.H628 2001**
Culture's Consequences: Comparing Values, Behaviors, Institutions and Organizations Across Nations. Ed. 2. Cloth Text. SAGE Publications, Inc. Thousand Oaks, CA. 2001. 616p. ISBN:0-8039-7323-3, ISBN13: 978-0-8039-7323-7. Dewey:155.8/9. LCCN:00-010498.
Audience: **l,u.**

Mowshowitz, Abbe **HM851**
Virtual Organization: Toward a Theory of Societal Transformation Stimulated by Information Technology. Murray Turoff (Foreword by). Trade Cloth. Greenwood Publishing Group, Inc. Portsmouth, NH. 2002. 280p. ISBN:1-56720-501-1, ISBN13: 978-1-56720-501-5. Dewey:303.48/33. LCCN:2001-051097.
Audience: **l,u,f.** *Choice, 2003, 2002.*

Smelser, Neil J. & Swedberg, Richard (Editors) **HM548.H25 2005**
The Handbook of Economic Sociology. Ed. 2. Trade Paper. Princeton University Press. Princeton, NJ. 2005. 748p. ISBN:0-691-12126-5, ISBN13: 978-0-691-12126-0. Dewey:306.3. LCCN:2004-050524.
Audience: **l,u,f.** *Choice, 1995.*

Stinchcombe, Arthur L. **HM3**
Economic Sociology. Academic Press. 1983. ISBN:0-12-671380-4, ISBN13: 978-0-12-671380-0.
Audience: **l,u.**

Weber, Max M. **HM211**
Economy and Society. Guenther Roth & Claus Wittich (Editors). Trade Paper. University of California Press. Berkeley, CA. 1978. 2p. ISBN:0-520-03500-3, ISBN13: 978-0-520-03500-3. Dewey:330. LCCN:74-081443.
Audience: **l,u,f.**

Zelizer, Viviana A. **HG221.Z45 1997**
The Social Meaning of Money: Pin Money, Paychecks, Poor Relief, and Other Currencies. Trade Paper. Princeton University Press. Princeton, NJ. 1997. 300p. ISBN:0-691-04821-5, ISBN13: 978-0-691-04821-5. Dewey:332.4. LCCN:97-019216.
Audience: **l,u,f.**

978-0-300-10024-2. Dewey:200/.973/09045.
LCCN:2003-005802.
Audience: **g,l,u,f.** *Choice, 2004.*

Plekon, Michael **BX1407.P63A46 2004**
Tradition Alive: On the Church and the Christian Life in Our Time. Book, Other. Rowman & Littlefield Publishers, Inc. Lanham, MD. 2003. 320p. American Catholics in the Public Square Ser., Vol. 1 ISBN:0-7425-3159-7, ISBN13: 978-0-7425-3159-8. Dewey:261.8/088/22. LCCN:2003-013285.
Audience: **u,f.** *Choice, 2004.*

Rieser, Andrew Chamberlin **LC6551.R54 2003**
The Chautauqua Moment: Protestants, Progressives, and the Culture of Modern Liberalism, 1874-1920. Trade Cloth. Eastern European Monographs. Bradenton, FL. 2003. 416p. ISBN:0-231-12642-5, ISBN13: 978-0-231-12642-7. Dewey:374/.973. LCCN:2003-046004.
Audience: **u,f.** *Choice, 2004.*

Smith, Christian **BT83.57.S64 1991**
The Emergence of Liberation Theology: Radical Religion and Social Movement Theory. Trade Cloth. University of Chicago Press. Chicago, IL. 1991. 314p. ISBN:0-226-76409-5, ISBN13: 978-0-226-76409-2. Dewey:306.6/3028. LCCN:90-026575.
Audience: **u,f.** *Choice, 1992.*

Steinfels, Margaret O'Brien **BX1406.3.A485 2004**
American Catholics, American Culture: Tradition and Resistance. Book, Other. Rowman & Littlefield Publishers, Inc. Lanham, MD. 2004. 224p. American Catholics in the Public Square Ser., Vol. 2 ISBN:0-7425-3160-0, ISBN13: 978-0-7425-3160-4. Dewey:261.8/088/282. LCCN:2003-019713.
Audience: **l,u,f.**

Weber, Max M. **BR115.C3W413 2003**
The Protestant Ethic and the Spirit of Capitalism. Talcott Parsons (Translator). Trade Paper. Dover Publications, Inc. Mineola, NY. 2003. 320p. American Indians Ser. ISBN:0-486-42703-X, ISBN13: 978-0-486-42703-4. Dewey:306.6. LCCN:2002-041124.
Audience: **l,u,f.** *Choice, 2002.*

Wimbush, Vincent L. & Rodman, Rosemary C. (Editors) **BR563.N4A38 2000**
African Americans and the Bible: Sacred Texts and Social Textures. Trade Cloth. Continuum International Publishing Group, Ltd. London, 2000. 750p. ISBN:0-8264-1293-9, ISBN13: 978-0-8264-1293-5. Dewey:220/.089/96073. LCCN:00-030520.
Audience: **u,f.**

Sociology of Religion > Islam

Berkey, Jonathan P. **BP63.A35B47 2002**
The Formation of Islam: Religion and Society in the near East, 600-1800. Patricia Crone (Contribution by). Cloth Text. Cambridge University Press. New York, NY. 2002. 302p. Themes in Islamic History Ser., Vol. 2 ISBN:0-521-58214-8, ISBN13: 978-0-521-58214-8. Dewey:297/.09. LCCN:2002-031470.
Audience: **l,u,f.** *Choice, 2003.*

Bukhari, Zahid Hussain **E184.M88M87 2004**
Muslims' Place in the American Public Square: Hopes, Fears, and Aspirations. Trade Cloth. AltaMira Press. Walnut Creek, CA. 2004. 440p. ISBN:0-7591-0612-6, ISBN13: 978-0-7591-0612-3. Dewey:305.6/97/0973. LCCN:2003-021528.
Audience: **l,u,f.** *Choice, 2005.*

Heyneman, Stephen P. (Editor) **BP173.25I738 2004**
Islam and Social Policy. Trade Cloth. Vanderbilt University Press. Nashville, TN. 2004. 232p. ISBN:0-8265-1446-4, ISBN13: 978-0-8265-1446-2. Dewey:297.2/7. LCCN:2003-017648.
Audience: **l,u.**

Shariati, Ali **BP173.25 .S52**
On the Sociology of Islam. Ed. 3. Hamid Algar (Translator). Trade Cloth. Mizan Press. Oneonta, NY. 1980. ISBN:0-933782-01-2, ISBN13: 978-0-933782-01-3. Dewey:297/.197/8. LCCN:79-083552.
Audience: **l,u,f.**

Sociology of Religion > Other Religions

Dawson, Lorne L. **BP603.D39**
Comprehending Cults: The Sociology of New Religious Movements. Ed. 2. Trade Paper. Oxford University Press, Inc. New York, NY. 2006. 272p. ISBN:0-19-542009-8, ISBN13: 978-0-19-542009-8. Dewey:306.6.
Audience: **g,l,u,f.** *Choice, 1999.*

Deloria, Vine Jr. **BL2776.D44 2003**
God Is Red: A Native View of Religion. Ed. 30. Trade Paper. Fulcrum Publishing. Golden, CO. 2003. 352p. ISBN:1-55591-498-5, ISBN13: 978-1-55591-498-1. LCCN:2003-006477.
Audience: **g,l,u,f.**

Fishman, Sylvia Barack **HQ1031.F56 2004**
Double or Nothing?: Jewish Families and Mixed Marriage. Trade Cloth. University Press of New England. Lebanon, NH. 2004. 256p. Brandeis Series on Jewish Women ISBN:1-58465-206-3, ISBN13: 978-1-58465-206-9. Dewey:306.84/3/0973. LCCN:2003-021956.
Audience: **u,f.** *Choice, 2004.*

Foster, Lawrence **HX654 .F67 1984**
Religion and Sexuality: The Shakers, the Mormons and the Oneida Community. Trade Paper. University of Illinois Press. Champaign, IL. 1984. 384p. ISBN:0-252-01119-8, ISBN13: 978-0-252-01119-1. Dewey:0252011198. LCCN:83-018315.
Audience: **u,f.**

Gellner, David N. **BQ4570.S6**
The Anthropology of Buddhism and Hinduism: Weberian Themes. Trade Paper. Oxford University Press, Inc. New York, NY. 2003. 416p. ISBN:0-19-566611-9, ISBN13: 978-0-19-566611-3. Dewey:306.6/943.
Audience: **u,f.** *Choice, 2001.*

Goldscheider, Calvin & Neusner, Jacob **BM157.S62 1990**
Social Foundations of Judiasm. Paper Text. Prentice Hall PTR. Upper Saddle River, NJ. 1989. 272p. ISBN:0-13-818683-9, ISBN13: 978-0-13-818683-8. Dewey:296.3/87. LCCN:89-016274.
Audience: **l,u,f.**

Gonzalez-Wippler, Migene **BL2532.S3G674 1994**
Santeria: The Religion. Ed. 2. Llewellyn Publications. 2002. Llewellyn's World Religion and Magic ISBN:1-56718-329-8, ISBN13: 978-1-56718-329-0.
Audience: **g,l,u.**

Gordis, Robert **BM0538.S7G6**
The Root and the Branch, Judaism and the Free Society. Trade Paper. Books on Demand. Ann Arbor, MI. 254p. ISBN:0-608-09314-9, ISBN13: 978-0-608-09314-7. Dewey:296.38. LCCN:62-017133.
Audience: **u,f.**

Marty, Martin E. & Appleby, R. Scott (Editors) **BL238.F83 1991 VOL.5**
Fundamentalisms Comprehended. Trade Cloth. University of Chicago Press. Chicago, IL. 1995. 528p. Fundamentalism Project Ser., Vol. 5 ISBN:0-226-50887-0, ISBN13: 978-0-226-50887-0. Dewey:291/.09/04 s. LCCN:94-045338.
Audience: **l,u,f.** *Choice, 1996.*

Sharot, Stephen **BL60.S529 2001**
A Comparative Sociology of World Religions: Virtuosi, Priests, and Popular Religion. Trade Cloth. New York University Press. New York, NY. 2001. 352p. ISBN:0-8147-9804-7, ISBN13: 978-0-8147-9804-1. Dewey:306.6. LCCN:2001-000737.
Audience: **l,u,f.**

Weber, Max **BL2001**
Religion of India: The Sociology of Hinduism and Buddhism. Trade Paper. Munshiram Manoharial Publishers Private, Ltd. New Delhi, 1992. 397p. ISBN:81-215-0571-2, ISBN13: 978-81-215-0571-0. Dewey:294.
Audience: **l,u,f.** B

Stratification/Differentiation > Social Stratification

Bluestone, Barry **HD5708.55.U6**
The Deindustrialization of America : Plant Closings, Community Abandonment, and the Dismantling of Basic Industry. Harrison, Bennett. Basic Books. 1982. ISBN:0-465-01590-5, ISBN13: 978-0-465-01590-0.
Audience: **l,u.**

Bluestone, Barry & Harrison, Bennett **HC110.I5B539 2000**
Growing Prosperity: The Battle for Growth with Equity in the Twenty-First Century. Trade Paper. Houghton Mifflin Company Trade & Reference Division. Boston, MA. 2000. 352p. Century Foundation/Twentieth Century Fund Report Ser. ISBN:0-395-82286-6, ISBN13: 978-0-395-82286-9. Dewey:339.2/0973. LCCN:99-046647.
Audience: **u,f.** *Choice, 2000.*

Crompton, Rosemary & Mann, Michael **HQ1075.5.G7G46 1986**
Gender and Stratification. Trade Paper. Blackwell Publishing, Inc. Malden, MA. 1986. 304p. ISBN:0-7456-0168-5, ISBN13: 978-0-7456-0168-7. Dewey:305.3. LCCN:85-028342.
Audience: **l,u,f.** *Choice, 1987.*

Duncan, Greg J. **HD6983.D85**
Years of Poverty, Years of Plenty. Cloth Text. University of Michigan Press. Chicago, IL. 1984. 200p. ISBN:0-472-00702-5, ISBN13: 978-0-472-00702-8. Dewey:339.4/1/0973.
Audience: **l,u.**

Durkheim, Emile & Coser, Lewis A. **HD6955**
The Division of Labor in Society. Trade Paper. Simon & Schuster. New York, NY. 1997. 416p. ISBN:0-684-83638-6, ISBN13: 978-0-684-83638-6. Dewey:306.3/6.
Audience: **l.** B

Graetz, Michael J. & Mashaw, Jerry L. **HD7125.G69 1999**
True Security: Rethinking American Social Insurance. Cloth over Boards. Yale University Press. Cumberland, RI. 1999. 384p. Yale ISPS Ser. ISBN:0-300-08150-2, ISBN13: 978-0-300-08150-3. Dewey:368.4/3/00973. LCCN:99-030910.
Audience: **l,u.** *Choice, 2000.*

Grusky, David B. (Editor) **HM821.S65 2001**
Social Stratification, Class, Race, and Gender in Sociological Perspective. Ed. 2. Trade Paper. Westview Press. Boulder, CO. 2000. 928p. ISBN:0-8133-6654-2, ISBN13: 978-0-8133-6654-8. Dewey:305. LCCN:2001-265806.
Audience: **l,u.**

Jencks, Christopher **HN59.2**
Rethinking Social Policy: Race, Poverty, and the Underclass. Trade Paper. HarperCollins Publishers. New York, NY. 1993. 288p. ISBN:0-06-097534-2, ISBN13: 978-0-06-097534-0. Dewey:361.6/1/0973. LCCN:92-053407.
Audience: **l,u.**

Lenski, Gerhard E. **HT609**
Power and Privilege: A Theory of Social Stratification. Trade Cloth. University of North Carolina Press. Chapel Hill, NC. 1984. 525p. ISBN:0-8078-4119-6, ISBN13: 978-0-8078-4119-8. Dewey:305. LCCN:83-026049.
Audience: **u,f.**

Lipset, Seymour Martin & Bendix, Reinhard **HT609.L52 1991**
Social Mobility in Industrial Society. Trade Paper. Transaction Publishers. Somerset, NJ. 1991. 332p. ISBN:1-56000-606-4, ISBN13: 978-1-56000-606-0. Dewey:305.5/13. LCCN:91-012490.
Audience: **l,u,f.** B

Takahashi, Lois **HM136.T25 1998**
Homelessness, AIDS, and Stigmatization: The NIMBY Syndrome in the United States at the End of the Twentieth Century. Trade Cloth. Oxford University Press, Inc. New York, NY. 1999. 286p. Oxford Geographical and Environmental Studies ISBN:0-19-823362-0, ISBN13: 978-0-19-823362-6. Dewey:361.6/1/0973. LCCN:98-023022.
Audience: **u,f.**

Stratification/Differentiation > Social Stratification > Castes

Bayly, Susan **DS436 .N47 1999 PT.**
Caste, Society and Politics in India from the Eighteenth Century to the Modern Age. C. A. Bayly, Gordon Johnson & John F.

Richards (Contribution by). Cloth Text. Cambridge University Press. New York, NY. 1999. 440p. History of India Ser., Vol. IV:3 ISBN:0-521-26434-0, ISBN13: 978-0-521-26434-1. Dewey:305.5/122/0954. LCCN:98-038434.
Audience: **u,f.** *Choice, 2000.*

Blum, Jerome **HT807**
Lord and Peasant in Russia: From the 9th to the 19th Century. Trade Paper. Princeton University Press. Princeton, NJ. 1971. 688p. ISBN:0-691-00764-0, ISBN13: 978-0-691-00764-9. Dewey:947.
Audience: **u,f.**

Dumont, Louis **HT720.D813 1970**
Homo Hierarchicus; an Essay on the Caste System. Trade Cloth. University of Chicago Press. Chicago, IL. 1970. xxi, 386p. ISBN:0-226-16959-6, ISBN13: 978-0-226-16959-0. Dewey:301.44/0954. LCCN:77-123751.
Audience: **u,f.**

Prashad, Vijay **DS422.C3**
Untouchable Freedom: A Social History of a Dalit Community. Paper Text. Oxford University Press, Inc. New York, NY. 2001. 186p. ISBN:0-19-565848-5, ISBN13: 978-0-19-565848-4. Dewey:305.5/68.
Audience: **u,f.** *Choice, 2001.*

Quigley, Declan **GN491.4.Q54 1993**
The Interpretation of Caste. Trade Cloth. Oxford University Press, Inc. New York, NY. 1993. 200p. Oxford Studies in Social and Cultural Anthropology - Cultural Forms ISBN:0-19-827882-9, ISBN13: 978-0-19-827882-5. Dewey:305.5/122/0954. LCCN:92-027757.
Audience: **u,f.** *Choice, 1994.*

Sharma, Arvind **HM683.S52 2005**
Reservation and Affirmative Action: Models of Social Integration in India and the United States. Cloth Text. SAGE Publications India Pvt, Ltd. New Delhi, 2005. 200p. ISBN:0-7619-3380-8, ISBN13: 978-0-7619-3380-9. Dewey:305/.0954. LCCN:2005-008608.
Audience: **u,f.**

Weiner, Mark S. **KF4757**
Black Trials: Citizenship from the Beginnings of Slavery to the End of Caste. Trade Paper. Knopf Publishing Group. New York, NY. 2006. 448p. ISBN:0-375-70884-7, ISBN13: 978-0-375-70884-8. Dewey:342.7308/73.
Audience: **u,f.** *Choice, 2005.*

Stratification/Differentiation > Social Stratification > Classes

Anderson, Elijah **F158.9.N4A52 1999**
Code of the Streets: Decency, Violence and the Moral Life of the Inner City. Trade Cloth. W. W. Norton & Company, Inc. New York, NY. 1999. 224p. ISBN:0-393-04023-2, ISBN13: 978-0-393-04023-4. Dewey:303.330896073074811. LCCN:98-036800.
Audience: **l,u,f.** *Choice, 1999.*

Barber, Bernard & Barber, Elinor G. **HN380.Z9 S635 1977**
European Social Class: Stability and Change. Trade Cloth. Greenwood Publishing Group, Inc. Portsmouth, NH. 1978. 145p. Main Themes in European History ISBN:0-8371-9860-7, ISBN13: 978-0-8371-9860-6. Dewey:301.44/094. LCCN:77-013508.
Audience: **u,f.** ℬ

Barber, Elinor G. **HT690.F8**
Bourgeoisie in Eighteenth Century France. Trade Cloth. Princeton University Press. Princeton, NJ. 1955. ISBN:0-691-09309-1, ISBN13: 978-0-691-09309-3. Dewey:323.32.
Audience: **u,f.**

Bendix, Reinhard & Lipset, Seymour Martin (Editors) **HT605 .B4 1966**
Class, Status and Power: A Reader in Social Stratification. Trade Cloth. Simon & Schuster. New York, NY. 1966. ISBN:0-02-902630-X, ISBN13: 978-0-02-902630-4. Dewey:323.3. LCCN:65-023025.
Audience: **l,u.**

Bettie, Julie **HQ798 .B425 2003**
Women Without Class: Girls, Race and Identity. Trade Paper. University of California Press. Berkeley, CA. 2003. 260p. ISBN:0-520-23542-8, ISBN13: 978-0-520-23542-7. Dewey:305.235. LCCN:2001-007757.
Audience: **l,u.** *Choice, 2003.*

Chafetz, Janet S. **HQ1206.C395**
Gender Equity: An Integrated Theory of Stability and Change. Trade Paper. Books on Demand. Ann Arbor, MI. 1990. 256p. Sage Library of Social Research, Vol. 176 ISBN:0-608-04304-4, ISBN13: 978-0-608-04304-3. Dewey:305.3. LCCN:89-010720.
Audience: **u.** *Choice, 1990.*

Charles, Maria & Grusky, David B. **HD6053**
Occupational Ghettos: The Worldwide Segregation of Women and Men. Trade Cloth. Stanford University Press. Palo Alto, CA. 2004. 400p. Studies in Social Inequality ISBN:0-8047-3634-0, ISBN13: 978-0-8047-3634-3. Dewey:306.3/615. LCCN:2003-023988.
Audience: **l,u.** *Choice, 2005.*

Chase-Dunn, Christopher **HC59.C51424 1998**
Global Formation: Structures of the World Economy. Ed. 2. Trade Cloth. Rowman & Littlefield Publishers, Inc. Lanham, MD. 1998. 500p. ISBN:0-8476-9101-2, ISBN13: 978-0-8476-9101-2. Dewey:330.12/2. LCCN:98-008613.
Audience: **l,u.**

Cose, Ellis **E185.86**
The Rage of a Privileged Class: Why Do Prosperous Blacks Still Have the Blues? Trade Paper. HarperCollins Publishers. New York, NY. 1995. 208p. ISBN:0-06-092594-9, ISBN13: 978-0-06-092594-9. Dewey:305.896/073. LCCN:93-033202.
Audience: **g,l,u.**

Cott, Nancy F. **HQ1420.C67 1987**
The Grounding of Modern Feminism. Cloth over Boards. Yale University Press. Cumberland, RI. 1987. 378p. ISBN:0-300-03892-5, ISBN13: 978-0-300-03892-7. Dewey:305.4/2/0973/0904. LCCN:87-010642.
Audience: **l,u.** *Choice, 1988.*

Currie, Elliott **HQ796**
The Road to Whatever: Middle-Class Culture and the Crisis of Adolescence. Trade Paper. Henry Holt & Company. New York,

NY. 2005. 320p. ISBN:0-8050-8000-7, ISBN13: 978-0-8050-8000-1. Dewey:305.235/086/920973.
Audience: **g,l,u,f.** *Choice, 2005.*

Dahrendorf, Ralf **HT609**
Class and Class Conflict in Industrial Society. Trade Paper. Stanford University Press. Palo Alto, CA. 1959. 352p. ISBN:0-8047-0561-5, ISBN13: 978-0-8047-0561-5. Dewey:301.44.
Audience: **u,f.** B

Davidson, Douglas V. **E185.86.D377 2000**
Ethcaste: PanAfrican Communalism and the Black Middleclass. Trade Cloth. University Press of America, Inc. Lanham, MD. 2001. 256p. ISBN:0-7618-1915-0, ISBN13: 978-0-7618-1915-8. Dewey:305.896073. LCCN:00-048909.
Audience: **u,f.**

Dye, Thomas R. **HN90.E4D93 2002**
Who's Running America?: The Bush Restoration. Ed. 7. Trade Paper. Prentice Hall PTR. Upper Saddle River, NJ. 2001. 220p. ISBN:0-13-097462-5, ISBN13: 978-0-13-097462-4. Dewey:305.5/2/0973. LCCN:2001-054896.
Audience: **g.**

Edin, Kathryn & Kefalas, Maria **HQ759.45 .E35 2005**
Promises I Can Keep: Why Poor Women Put Motherhood Before Marriage. Trade Cloth. University of California Press. Berkeley, CA. 2005. 312p. ISBN:0-520-24113-4, ISBN13: 978-0-520-24113-8. Dewey:306.8560974811. LCCN:2004-022032.
Audience: **l,u,f.** *Choice, 2006.*

England, Paula & Farkas, George **HQ536.E54 1986**
Households, Employment and Gender: A Social, Economic and Demographic View. Trade Paper. Aldine Transaction. Somerset, NJ. 1986. 237p. Social Institutions and Social Change Ser. ISBN:0-202-30323-3, ISBN13: 978-0-202-30323-9. Dewey:304.6. LCCN:85-018628.
Audience: **u,f.** B *Choice, 1986.*

Firestone, Shulamith **HQ1190**
The Dialectic of Sex: The Case for Feminist Revolution. Trade Paper. Farrar, Straus & Giroux. New York, NY. 2003. 240p. ISBN:0-374-52787-3, ISBN13: 978-0-374-52787-7. Dewey:301.41/2.
Audience: **u,f.**

Giddens, Anthony **HT609 .G47 1975**
The Class Structure of the Advanced Societies. Mass Market. HarperCollins Publishers. New York, NY. 1975. ISBN:0-06-131845-0, ISBN13: 978-0-06-131845-0. Dewey:305.5. LCCN:74-007825.
Audience: **u,f.** B

Gilbert, Dennis **HN90.S6G54 2003**
The American Class Structure in an Age of Growing Inequality: A New Synthesis. Ed. 6. Paper Text. Thomson Wadsworth. Belmont, CA. 2002. 336p. ISBN:0-534-54110-0, ISBN13: 978-0-534-54110-1. Dewey:305.5/0973. LCCN:2002-109710.
Audience: **l,u,f.**

Halttunen, Karen **HT690.U6**
Confidence Men and Painted Women: Study of Middle Class Culture in America, 1830-70. Trade Cloth. Yale University Press. Cumberland, RI. 1982. 280p. ISBN:0-300-02835-0, ISBN13: 978-0-300-02835-5. Dewey:305.5/5/0973. LCCN:82-008336.
Audience: **l,u,f.** B

Hauser, Robert Mason **HN90.S65.H38**
The Process of Stratification. Trade Cloth. Elsevier Science & Technology Books. Saint Louis, MO. 1977. xxviii, 372p. ISBN:0-12-333050-5, ISBN13: 978-0-12-333050-5. Dewey:301.44/044/0973. LCCN:76-019487.
Audience: **u,f.** B

Horton, Mark & Middleton, John **DT429.5.S94H67 2000**
The Swahili. Trade Cloth. Blackwell Publishing, Inc. Malden, MA. 2001. 288p. The Peoples of Africa Ser. ISBN:0-631-18919-X, ISBN13: 978-0-631-18919-0. Dewey:967.6004/96392. LCCN:00-009633.
Audience: **u,f.** *Choice, 2001.*

Jernegan, Marcus W. **HN90.S6 J47 1980**
Laboring and Dependent Classes in Colonial America, 1607-1783. Trade Cloth. Greenwood Publishing Group, Inc. Portsmouth, NH. 1980. 256p. American Classics Ser. ISBN:0-313-22399-8, ISBN13: 978-0-313-22399-0. Dewey:305.5/6. LCCN:80-011342.
Audience: **u,f.**

Keller, Suzanne **HM141.K4 1991**
Beyond the Ruling Class: Strategic Elites in Modern Society. Trade Paper. Transaction Publishers. Somerset, NJ. 1991. 354p. ISBN:1-56000-550-5, ISBN13: 978-1-56000-550-6. Dewey:305.5/2. LCCN:91-006453.
Audience: **u,f.**

Kimmel, Michael S. & Ferber, Abby L. **HN90.S6P75 2003**
Privilege: A Reader. Trade Paper. Westview Press. Boulder, CO. 2003. 432p. ISBN:0-8133-4056-X, ISBN13: 978-0-8133-4056-2. Dewey:305.5. LCCN:2002-015756.
Audience: **l,u.**

Kohn, Melvin L. **HQ734**
Class and Conformity: A Study in Values. Ed. 2. Trade Paper. University of Chicago Press. Chicago, IL. 1989. 376p. Midway Reprint Ser. ISBN:0-226-45026-0, ISBN13: 978-0-226-45026-1. Dewey:301.42/7. LCCN:77-085194.
Audience: **l,u,f.**

Marwick, Arthur **HN90.S6.M35**
Class: Image and Reality in Britain, France and the U. S. A. since 1930. Trade Cloth. Oxford University Press, Inc. New York, NY. 1980. 416p. ISBN:0-19-520203-1, ISBN13: 978-0-19-520203-8. Dewey:305.5/0941. LCCN:80-135297.
Audience: **l,u,f.** B

Mills, C. Wright & Jacoby, Russell **HT690.U6M5 2002**
White Collar: The American Middle Classes. Ed. 2. Trade Paper. Oxford University Press, Inc. New York, NY. 2002. 414p. ISBN:0-19-515708-7, ISBN13: 978-0-19-515708-6. Dewey:305.5/5/0973. LCCN:2002-070042.
Audience: **g.** B

Mills, C. Wright **HN90.P6M55 1999**
Power Elite. Ed. 2. Alan Wolfe (Foreword by). Trade Paper. Oxford University Press, Inc. New York, NY. 2000. 448p.

ISBN:0-19-513354-4, ISBN13: 978-0-19-513354-7. Dewey:303.3/0973. LCCN:99-016200.
Audience: **g,l,u,f.**

Moen, Phyllis (Editor), et al. **HN90.S6N37 1999**
A Nation Divided: Diversity, Inequality and Community in American Society. Donna Dempster-McClain & Henry A. Walker (Editors). Book, Other. Cornell University Press. Ithaca, NY. 1999. 360p. ISBN:0-8014-8588-6, ISBN13: 978-0-8014-8588-6. Dewey:305.5/0973. LCCN:99-015783.
Audience: **g,l,u,f.**

Moore, Wilbert E. **HT687.M63**
The Professions: Roles and Rules. Trade Cloth. Russell Sage Foundation. New York, NY. 1970. 316p. ISBN:0-87154-604-3, ISBN13: 978-0-87154-604-3. Dewey:331.7/1. LCCN:78-104184.
Audience: **u,f.**

Newman, Katherine S. **HN90.S65 N48 1999**
Falling from Grace: Downward Mobility in the Age of Affluence. Trade Paper. University of California Press. Berkeley, CA. 1999. 344p. ISBN:0-520-21842-6, ISBN13: 978-0-520-21842-0. Dewey:305.5/13/0973. LCCN:98-038119.
Audience: **l,u.**

Pattillo-McCoy, Mary **F548.9.N4P38 1999**
Black Picket Fences: Privilege and Peril among the Black Middle Class. Trade Cloth. University of Chicago Press. Chicago, IL. 1999. 283p. ISBN:0-226-64928-8, ISBN13: 978-0-226-64928-3. Dewey:305.896/073077311. LCCN:99-018913.
Audience: **l,u,f.** *Choice, 2000.*

Perrucci, Robert & Wysong, Earl **HN90.S6P47 2002**
The New Class Society: Goodbye American Dream? Ed. 2. Book, Other. Rowman & Littlefield Publishers, Inc. Lanham, MD. 2002. 256p. ISBN:0-7425-1938-4, ISBN13: 978-0-7425-1938-1. Dewey:305.5/0973. LCCN:2002-001368.
Audience: **g,l,u.** *Choice, 2003.*

Reskin, Barbara F. & Roos, Patricia A. **HD6060.65.U5R473**
Job Queues, Gender Queues: Explaining Women's Inroads into Male Occupations. Trade Cloth. Temple University Press. Philadelphia, PA. 1990. 368p. Women in the Political Economy Ser. ISBN:0-87722-743-8, ISBN13: 978-0-87722-743-4. Dewey:306.3/615/0973. LCCN:90-031544.
Audience: **u,f.** *Choice, 1991.*

Shibutani, Tamotsu ; Kwan, Kian M. **HM107.S5**
Ethnic Stratification: A Comparative Approach. Billigmeier, Robert H.. Macmillan. 1965.
Audience: **u,f.**

Thompson, E. P. **HD8389**
The Making of the English Working Class. Trade Cloth. Peter Smith Publisher, Inc. Magnolia, MA. 1999. ISBN:0-8446-6993-8, ISBN13: 978-0-8446-6993-9. Dewey:301.44/42/0942.
Audience: **l,u,f.**

Veblen, Thorstein B. **HB831.V4 1991**
The Theory of the Leisure Class. C. Wright Mills (Introduction by). Trade Paper. Transaction Publishers. Somerset, NJ. 1991. 282p. Reprints of Economic Classics Ser. ISBN:1-56000-562-9, ISBN13: 978-1-56000-562-9. Dewey:305.5. LCCN:91-023747.
Audience: **g,l,u,f.**

Vogel, Ezra F. **HT690.J3V6 1971**
Japan's New Middle Class; the Salary Man and His Family in a Tokyo Suburb. Ed. 2. E-Book. NetLibrary, Inc. Boulder, CO. 1971. ISBN:0-585-30062-3, ISBN13: 978-0-585-30062-7. Dewey:301.441.
Audience: **l,u,f.**

Warner, W. Lloyd **HT609**
What Social Class Is in America: The American Dream and Social Class. Paper Text. Irvington Publishers. New York, NY. 1993. Reprint Series in Sociology ISBN:0-8290-2654-1, ISBN13: 978-0-8290-2654-2. Dewey:305.5.
Audience: **l,u.**

Warner, W. Lloyd **HT609.W28 1960**
Social Class in America: A Manual of Procedure for the Measurement of Social Status. Meeker, Marchia; Eells, Kenneth. Harper. 1960. Harper Torchbooks, TB1013; The Academy library
Audience: **l,u.**

Warner, William L. & Lunt, Paul S. **HT123 .W24 1973**
The Social Life of a Modern Community. Trade Cloth. Greenwood Publishing Group, Inc. Portsmouth, NH. 1973. 460p. Yankee City Ser. ISBN:0-8371-6958-5, ISBN13: 978-0-8371-6958-3. Dewey:301.44. LCCN:73-008152.
Audience: **l,u,f.**

Weber, Max **HC21.W46 2002**
General Economic History. Trade Paper. Dover Publications, Inc. Mineola, NY. 2003. 432p. ISBN:0-486-42514-2, ISBN13: 978-0-486-42514-6. Dewey:330.9. LCCN:2002-031506.
Audience: **l,u,f.**

Weber, Max **BR115.E3**
The Protestant Ethic and the Spirit of Capitalism. E-Book. Digireads.com. Stilwell, KS. 2004. ISBN:1-4209-0973-8, ISBN13: 978-1-4209-0973-9. Dewey:261.8/5.
Audience: **l,u,f.**

Zunz, Olivier (Editor), et al. **HT690.E73S63 2002**
Social Contracts under Stress: The Middle Classes of America, Europe, and Japan at the Turn of the Century. Leonard J. Schoppa & Nobuhiro Hiwatari (Editors). Trade Cloth. Russell Sage Foundation. New York, NY. 2002. xii, 431p. ISBN:0-87154-997-2, ISBN13: 978-0-87154-997-6. Dewey:305.5/5/09049. LCCN:2001-055714.
Audience: **l,u,f.** *Choice, 2003.*

Stratification/Differentiation > Social Stratification > Classes > Hereditary

Baltzell, Edward Digby **F158.3.B3 1989**
Philadelphia Gentlemen: The Making of a National Upper Class. Trade Paper. Transaction Publishers. Somerset, NJ. 1989. 476p. ISBN:0-88738-789-6, ISBN13: 978-0-88738-789-0. Dewey:305.5/2/0974811. LCCN:89-004362.
Audience: **l,u,f.**

Baltzell, Edward Digby **HN90.S6 B35 1987**
The Protestant Establishment: Aristocracy and Caste in America. Trade Paper. Yale University Press. Cumberland, RI. 1987. 429p. ISBN:0-300-03818-6, ISBN13: 978-0-300-03818-7. Dewey:305.5/0973. LCCN:86-024678.
Audience: **l,u,f.**

Bourdieu, Pierre **DC33.7**
Distinction: A Social Critique of the Judgement of Taste. Richard Nice (Translator). Trade Paper. Harvard University Press. Cambridge, MA. 1984. 640p. ISBN:0-674-21277-0, ISBN13: 978-0-674-21277-0. Dewey:306/.0944. LCCN:84-000491.
Audience: **u,f.**

Butler, Lee **DS834.1.B88 2002**
Emperor and Aristocracy in Japan, 1467-1680: Resilience and Renewal. Trade Cloth. Harvard University Press. Cambridge, MA. 2002. 452p. Harvard East Asian Monographs, Vol. 209 ISBN:0-674-00851-0, ISBN13: 978-0-674-00851-9. Dewey:952/.02. LCCN:2002-024687.
Audience: **l,u,f.** *Choice, 2003.*

Domhoff, G. William **HS2725.S4.B774**
The Bohemian Grove and Other Retreats: A Study in Ruling-Class Cohesiveness. Trade Cloth. HarperCollins Publishers. New York, NY. 1974. xvi, 250p. ISBN:0-06-011048-1, ISBN13: 978-0-06-011048-2. Dewey:367/.973. LCCN:73-014253.
Audience: **u,f.** B

Elias, Norbert **HT647.E5313 1983**
The Court Society. Edmund Jephcott (Translator). Trade Cloth. Random House, Inc. New York, NY. 1983. 301p. ISBN:0-394-53282-1, ISBN13: 978-0-394-53282-0. Dewey:305.5/2. LCCN:83-004236.
Audience: **u,f.** B

Emmons, Terence **HT647.E6**
The Russian Landed Gentry and the Peasant Emancipation of 1861. Trade Paper. Books on Demand. Ann Arbor, MI. 496p. ISBN:0-608-12077-4, ISBN13: 978-0-608-12077-5. Dewey:323.3/0947. LCCN:68-029654.
Audience: **u,f.**

Girouard, Mark **DA115**
Life in the English Country House: A Social and Architectural History. Trade Paper. Yale University Press. Cumberland, RI. 1994. 352p. ISBN:0-300-05870-5, ISBN13: 978-0-300-05870-3. Dewey:728.80942. LCCN:78-009088.
Audience: **l,u.** B

Mingay, G. E. **HT657.M54 1976**
The Gentry: The Rise and Fall of a Ruling Class. Trade Cloth. Longman Publishing Group. White Plains, NY. 1976. xii, 216p. ISBN:0-582-48402-2, ISBN13: 978-0-582-48402-3. Dewey:929.7/2. LCCN:76-013576.
Audience: **u,f.** B

Phillips, Kevin **HC110.W4**
Wealth and Democracy: A Political History of the American Rich. UK-Trade Paper. Broadway Books. New York, NY. 2003. 496p. ISBN:0-7679-0534-2, ISBN13: 978-0-7679-0534-3. Dewey:305.5/234/0973.
Audience: **g,l.**

Stone, Lawrence **DA375**
An Open Elite?: England 1540-1880. Paper Text. Oxford University Press, Inc. New York, NY. 1984. 340p. ISBN:0-19-820607-0, ISBN13: 978-0-19-820607-1. Dewey:942/.06. LCCN:85-021597.
Audience: **l,u.**

Stratification/Differentiation > Social Stratification > Classes > Occupational

Aronowitz, Stanley **HD8072.A687 1992**
False Promises: The Shaping of American Working Class Consciousness. Cloth Text. Duke University Press. Durham, NC. 1991. 516p. ISBN:0-8223-1181-X, ISBN13: 978-0-8223-1181-2. Dewey:305.5/62/0973. LCCN:91-024168.
Audience: **u,f.**

Auletta, Ken **HV4045.A9 1999**
Underclass. Ed. 1. Trade Paper. Overlook Press, The. New York, NY. 1999. 348p. ISBN:0-87951-929-0, ISBN13: 978-0-87951-929-2. Dewey:362.5/0973. LCCN:98-047781.
Audience: **l,u.**

Bacon, David **HD8081.M6 B33 2004**
The Children of NAFTA: Labor Wars on the U. S.-Mexico Border. Trade Cloth. University of California Press. Berkeley, CA. 2004. 340p. ISBN:0-520-23778-1, ISBN13: 978-0-520-23778-0. Dewey:331.1/0972/1. LCCN:2003-015900.
Audience: **l,u,f.** *Choice, 2004.*

Blau, Peter M. & Duncan, Otis Dudley **HN90.S65 B53 1967**
The American Occupational Structure. Tyree, Andrea. Wiley. 1967.
Audience: **l,u.**

Hanna, Nelly **HT690.E3I5 2003**
In Praise of Books: A Cultural History of Cairo's Middle Class, Sixteenth to the Eighteenth Century. Trade Cloth. Syracuse University Press. Syracuse, NY. 2003. 224p. Middle East Studies Beyond Dominant Paradigms ISBN:0-8156-3012-3, ISBN13: 978-0-8156-3012-8. Dewey:305.5/5/0962. LCCN:2003-013954.
Audience: **l,u,f.**

Lipset, Seymour Martin & Bendix, Reinhard **HT609.L52 1991**
Social Mobility in Industrial Society. Trade Paper. Transaction Publishers. Somerset, NJ. 1991. 332p. ISBN:1-56000-606-4, ISBN13: 978-1-56000-606-0. Dewey:305.5/13. LCCN:91-012490.
Audience: **l,u,f.** B

Rose, Jonathan **Z1039.L3R67 2002**
The Intellectual Life of the British Working Classes. Trade Paper. Yale University Press. Cumberland, RI. 2003. 544p. ISBN:0-300-09808-1, ISBN13: 978-0-300-09808-2. Dewey:028/.9/0941.
Audience: **u,f.** *Choice, 2002.*

Shipler, David K. **HC110.P6S48 2004**
The Working Poor: Invisible in America. Trade Cloth. Alfred A. Knopf Inc. New York, NY. 2004. 336p. ISBN:0-375-40890-8, ISBN13: 978-0-375-40890-8. Dewey:305.5/69/0973. LCCN:2003-056191.
Audience: **g.** *Choice, 2004.*

Varano, Charles S. **HD5658.I52W48 1999**
Forced Choices: Class, Community, and Worker Ownership. Cloth Text. State University of New York Press. Albany, NY. 1999. 352p. SUNY Series in the Sociology of Work ISBN:0-7914-4181-4, ISBN13: 978-0-7914-4181-7. Dewey:338.7/669142/0975412. LCCN:98-031713.
Audience: **l,u,f.** *Choice, 1999.*

Vila, Pablo **HN120.C48C538 2005**
Border Identifications: Narratives of Religion, Gender, and Class on the U. S. -Mexico Border. Trade Cloth. University of Texas Press. Austin, TX. 2005. 312p. Inter-America Ser. ISBN:0-292-70291-4, ISBN13: 978-0-292-70291-2. Dewey:305/.0972/1. LCCN:2004-022257.
Audience: **u,f.**

Zweig, Michael **HD8066.Z84 2000**
The Working-Class Majority: America's Best-Kept Secret. Book, Other. Cornell University Press. Ithaca, NY. 2000. 208p. ISBN:0-8014-3637-0, ISBN13: 978-0-8014-3637-6. Dewey:305.5/62/0973. LCCN:00-268915.
Audience: **g,l,u,f.** *Choice, 2000.*

Stratification/Differentiation > Social Stratification > Slavery

E449

☐ Anti-Slavery Society.
http://www.anti-slaverysociety.addr.com/index.htm
Anti-Slavery Society.
Audience: **g.**

Davis, David B **HT861**
Slavery and Human Progress. Oxford University Press, Inc. 1984. ISBN:0-19-503439-2, ISBN13: 978-0-19-503439-4.
Audience: **g,l,u.** *B*

Foner, Eric **E449**
Nothing But Freedom: Emancipation and Its Legacy. Paper Text. Louisiana State University Press. Baton Rouge, LA. 1983. 142p. Walter Lynwood Fleming Lectures in South ISBN:0-8071-1189-9, ISBN13: 978-0-8071-1189-5. Dewey:326/.0973. LCCN:83-007906.
Audience: **l,u.** *B*

Koger, Larry (Compiled by) **E445.S7K64 1994**
Black Slaveowners: Free Black Slave Masters in South Carolina, 1790-1860. Trade Cloth. University of South Carolina Press. Columbia, SC. 1995. 300p. ISBN:1-57003-037-5, ISBN13: 978-1-57003-037-6. Dewey:975.7/00496073. LCCN:94-043848.
Audience: **u,f.** *Choice, 1986.*

Mason, John Edwin **HT1394.S6M37 2003**
Social Death and Resurrection: Slavery and Emancipation in South Africa. Trade Cloth. University Press of Virginia. Charlottesville, VA. 2003. 352p. Reconsiderations in Southern African History Ser. ISBN:0-8139-2178-3, ISBN13: 978-0-8139-2178-5. Dewey:306.3/62/0968. LCCN:2002-152295.
Audience: **l,f.**

Patterson, Orlando **E185.615.P353 1998**
Rituals of Blood: Consequences of Slavery in Two American Centuries. Trade Cloth. Basic Books. New York, NY. 1998. 330p. Civitas Ser. ISBN:1-887178-82-1, ISBN13: 978-1-887178-82-2. Dewey:305.8/00973. LCCN:98-047778.
Audience: **u,f.**

Patterson, Orlando **HT871**
Slavery and Social Death: A Comparative Study. Trade Cloth. Harvard University Press. Cambridge, MA. 1982. 528p. ISBN:0-674-81082-1, ISBN13: 978-0-674-81082-2. Dewey:306.3/62. LCCN:82-001072.
Audience: **l,u,f.** *B*

Patterson, Orlando **HT1096 .P3 1969**
Sociology of Slavery. Trade Cloth. Fairleigh Dickinson University Press. Cranbury, NJ. 1975. 310p. ISBN:0-8386-7469-0, ISBN13: 978-0-8386-7469-7. Dewey:301.45/22/097292. LCCN:70-084198.
Audience: **l,u.**

Rawley, James A. & Behrend, Stephen D. **HT985.R38 2005**
The Transatlantic Slave Trade: A History. Ed. 2. Trade Cloth. University of Nebraska Press. Lincoln, NE. 2005. 480p. ISBN:0-8032-3961-0, ISBN13: 978-0-8032-3961-6. Dewey:382/.44/09. LCCN:2004-028349.
Audience: **g.**

Westermann, W. L. **HT863.W4**
Slave Systems of Greek and Roman Antiquity. Trade Paper. American Philosophical Society. Canton, MA. 1984. 180p. Memoirs Ser., Vol. 40 ISBN:0-87169-040-3, ISBN13: 978-0-87169-040-1. Dewey:326.937. LCCN:54-009107.
Audience: **l,u.** *B*

Wilson, Carter A. **E184.A1W514 1996**
Racism: From Slavery to Advanced Capitalism. Trade Cloth. SAGE Publications, Inc. Thousand Oaks, CA. 1996. 288p. Race and Ethnic Relations Ser., Vol. 17 ISBN:0-8039-7336-5, ISBN13: 978-0-8039-7336-7. Dewey:305.8/009. LCCN:96-010053.
Audience: **l,u.**

Stratification/Differentiation > Social Stratification > Slavery > By Region

Bush, Barbara **HT1071.B87 1990**
Slave Women in Caribbean Society, 1650-1832. Trade Paper. Indiana University Press. Bloomington, IN. 1990. 198p. ISBN:0-253-21251-0, ISBN13: 978-0-253-21251-1. Dewey:305.5/67/082. LCCN:89-039563.
Audience: **l,u,f.** *Choice, 1990.*

Davis, Robert C. **HT1342.D38 2003**
Christian Slaves, Muslim Masters: White Slavery in the Mediterranean, the Barbary Coast and Italy, 1500-1800. Cloth over Boards. Palgrave Macmillan. New York, NY. 2003. 256p. Early Modern History Ser. ISBN:0-333-71966-2, ISBN13: 978-0-333-71966-4. Dewey:306.3/62/0945. LCCN:2002-192454.
Audience: **g,l,u.**

Donoghue, Eddie **HT1119.V6D66 2002**
Black Women/White Men: The Sexual Exploitation of Female Slaves in the Danish West Indies. Trade Paper. Africa World Press. Trenton, NJ. 2002. 240p. ISBN:0-86543-958-3, ISBN13: 978-0-86543-958-0. Dewey:305.48/9625/0972972. LCCN:2002-004842.
Audience: **l,u,f.**

Dunaway, Wilma A. **E443.D87 2002**
Slavery in the American Mountain South. Maurice Aymard, Jacques Revel & Immanuel Wallerstein (Contribution by). Cloth

Text. Cambridge University Press. New York, NY. 2003. 364p. Studies in Modern Capitalism ISBN:0-521-81275-5, ISBN13: 978-0-521-81275-7. Dewey:306.3/62/0974. LCCN:2002-071480.
Audience: **u,f.** *Choice, 2004.*

Hall, Gwendolyn M. **HT1081.H35 1996**
Social Control in Slave Plantation Societies: A Comparison of St. Domingue and Cuba. Trade Paper. Louisiana State University Press. Baton Rouge, LA. 1996. 166p. ISBN:0-8071-2083-9, ISBN13: 978-0-8071-2083-5. Dewey:306.3/62/097293. LCCN:95-050414.
Audience: **u.** B

Handler, Jerome S. & Lange, Fredrick W. **F2041**
Plantation Slavery in Barbados: An Archaeological and Historical Investigation. Trade Paper. iUniverse, Inc. Lincoln, NE. 2000. 388p. ISBN:1-58348-581-3, ISBN13: 978-1-58348-581-1. Dewey:972.98/1.
Audience: **u,f.** B

Hellie, Richard **HT1206.H44**
Slavery in Russia, 1450-1725. Trade Paper. Books on Demand. Ann Arbor, MI. 796p. ISBN:0-608-08814-5, ISBN13: 978-0-608-08814-3. Dewey:306/.3. LCCN:81-012954.
Audience: **u,f.**

Klein, Herbert S. **HT1052.5**
African Slavery in Latin America and the Caribbean. Paper Text. Oxford University Press, Inc. New York, NY. 1988. 338p. ISBN:0-19-503838-X, ISBN13: 978-0-19-503838-5. Dewey:306.3/62/098.
Audience: **l,u.**

Le Breton, Binka **HD4875.B8L4 2003**
Trapped: Modern-Day Slavery in the Brazilian Amazon. Desmond Tutu (Foreword by). Trade Cloth. Kumarian Press, Inc. Bloomfield, CT. 2003. 256p. ISBN:1-56549-156-4, ISBN13: 978-1-56549-156-4. Dewey:305.5/63. LCCN:2002-014319.
Audience: **g,l,u.**

Lovejoy, Paul E. **HT1321 .L68 2000**
Transformations in Slavery: A History of Slavery in Africa. Ed. 2. David Anderson, Carolyn Brown, Christopher Clapham, Michael Gomez, Patrick Manning, David Robinson & Leonardo A. Villalon (Contribution by). Cloth Text. Cambridge University Press. New York, NY. 2000. 352p. African Studies Ser., Vol. 36 ISBN:0-521-78012-8, ISBN13: 978-0-521-78012-4. Dewey:306.3/62/096. LCCN:99-059862.
Audience: **u,f.** B

Morrissey, Marietta **HT1071.M655 1989**
Slave Women in the New World: Gender Stratification in the Caribbean. Trade Cloth. University Press of Kansas. Lawrence, KS. 1989. xvi, 208p. Studies in Historical Social Change ISBN:0-7006-0394-8, ISBN13: 978-0-7006-0394-7. Dewey:305.4. LCCN:89-005454.
Audience: **u,f.** *Choice, 1989.*

Murray, David **HT1077**
Odious Commerce: Britain, Spain and the Abolition of the Cuban Slave Trade. Alan Knight (Contribution by). Trade Paper. Cambridge University Press. New York, NY. 2002. 437p. Cambridge Latin American Studies ISBN:0-521-52469-5, ISBN13: 978-0-521-52469-8. Dewey:380.1/44/097291.
Audience: **u,f.**

Palmer, Colin A. **HT1053.P35**
Slaves of the White God: Blacks in Mexico, 1570-1650. Trade Paper. Books on Demand. Ann Arbor, MI. 246p. ISBN:0-8357-8324-3, ISBN13: 978-0-8357-8324-8. Dewey:305.5/67/0972. LCCN:75-034054.
Audience: **l,u,f.** B

Temperley, Howard (Editor) **DT16.5.R48 2001**
After Slavery: Emancipation and Its Discontents. Trade Paper. Taylor & Francis Group. Abingdon, 2000. 320p. Studies in Slave and Post-Slave Societies and Cultures ISBN:0-7146-8079-6, ISBN13: 978-0-7146-8079-8. Dewey:981. LCCN:2001-028986.
Audience: **l,u,f.** *Choice, 2001.*

Turner, Mary **HT1096**
Slaves and Missionaries: The Disintegration of Jamaican Slave Society, 1787-1834. Trade Paper. University of the West Indies Press. Kingston, 1998. 236p. ISBN:976-640-045-8, ISBN13: 978-976-640-045-3. Dewey:261.8/34567/097292.
Audience: **u,f.** B

Willis, John R. (Editor) **HT1321**
Slaves and Slavery in Muslim Africa, Vol. 1. Cloth Text. Taylor & Francis Group. Abingdon, 1985. 267p. ISBN:0-7146-3142-6, ISBN13: 978-0-7146-3142-4. Dewey:306.3/62/096.
Audience: **l,u.** B *Choice, 1985.*

Willis, John R. (Editor) **HT1321.S56 1985**
Slaves and Slavery in Muslim Africa, Vol. 2. Cloth Text. Taylor & Francis Group. Abingdon, 1985. 198p. ISBN:0-7146-3201-5, ISBN13: 978-0-7146-3201-8. Dewey:306.3/62/096. LCCN:83-024313.
Audience: **l,u.** B *Choice, 1985.*

Stratification/Differentiation > Race

Blauner, Bob **E184.A1**
Racial Oppression in America. Harper & Row. 1972. ISBN:0-06-040771-9, ISBN13: 978-0-06-040771-1.
Audience: **g,l,u.**

Chase, Allan **HT1521**
The Legacy of Malthus: The Social Costs of the New Scientific Racism. Trade Paper. University of Illinois Press. Champaign, IL. 1980. 734p. ISBN:0-252-00790-5, ISBN13: 978-0-252-00790-3. Dewey:301.45/1042. LCCN:79-022799.
Audience: **l,u,f.**

Lamont, Michele (Editor) **E185.615.C85 1999**
The Cultural Territories of Race: Black and White Boundaries. Trade Cloth. University of Chicago Press. Chicago, IL. 1999. 436p. ISBN:0-226-46835-6, ISBN13: 978-0-226-46835-8. Dewey:305.800973. LCCN:98-048863.
Audience: **l,u,f.** *Choice, 2000.*

Lareau, Annette **HQ767.9 .L37 2003**
Unequal Childhood: The Importance of Social Class in Family Life. Trade Paper. University of California Press. Berkeley, CA. 2003. 416p. ISBN:0-520-23950-4, ISBN13: 978-0-520-23950-0. Dewey:305.23. LCCN:2002-154940.
Audience: **l,u,f.** *Choice, 2004.*

Montagu, Ashley **GN280.M59 1997**
Man's Most Dangerous Myth: The Fallacy of Race. Ed. 6. Trade Cloth. AltaMira Press. Walnut Creek, CA. 1998. 304p. ISBN:0-8039-4647-3, ISBN13: 978-0-8039-4647-7. Dewey:599.97. LCCN:97-021132.
Audience: **g.** B

Park, Robert Ezra **HT1521 .P3**
Race and Culture. Paper Text. Simon & Schuster. New York, NY. 1964. ISBN:0-02-923790-4, ISBN13: 978-0-02-923790-8. Dewey:572.081.
Audience: **l,u,f.**

Patterson, Orlando **E185.615.P35 1997**
The Ordeal of Integration: Progress and Resentment in America's "Racial" Crisis. Trade Cloth. Basic Books. New York, NY. 1997. 248p. ISBN:1-887178-61-9, ISBN13: 978-1-887178-61-7. Dewey:305.8/00973. LCCN:97-029254.
Audience: **u,f.**

Prucha, Francis P. **E93 .P9665 1985**
The Indians in American Society: From the Revolutionary War to the Present. Trade Cloth. University of California Press. Berkeley, CA. 1985. 127p. Quantum Bks., No. 29 ISBN:0-520-05503-9, ISBN13: 978-0-520-05503-2. Dewey:973/.0497. LCCN:85-001023.
Audience: **g,l,u.** *Choice, 1986.*

Van den Berghe, Pierre L. **HT1521**
The Ethnic Phenomenon. Trade Cloth. Greenwood Publishing Group, Inc. Portsmouth, NH. 1981. 301p. ISBN:0-444-01550-7, ISBN13: 978-0-444-01550-1. Dewey:305.8. LCCN:80-021092.
Audience: **l,u,f.** B

Wilson, Janet **HT1521**
Power, Racism and Privilege: Race Relations in Theoretical and Sociohistorical Perspectives. Trade Paper. Simon & Schuster. New York, NY. 1976. 240p. ISBN:0-02-935580-X, ISBN13: 978-0-02-935580-0. Dewey:305.8. LCCN:72-087160.
Audience: **u,f.**

Wu, Frank **E184.O6W84 2003**
Yellow: Race in America Beyond Black and White. Trade Paper. Basic Books. New York, NY. 2003. 416p. ISBN:0-465-00640-X, ISBN13: 978-0-465-00640-3. Dewey:305.8/95073.
Audience: **l,u,f.**

Stratification/Differentiation > Race > In America

Allen, Theodore W. **E184.A1**
The Invention of the White Race: The Origins of Racial Oppression in Anglo-America, Vol. II. Trade Cloth. Verso Books. London, 1997. 400p. ISBN:1-85984-981-4, ISBN13: 978-1-85984-981-1. Dewey:305.8/00973.
Audience: **l,u,f.**

Barrera, Mario **HD8081.M6**
Race and Class in the Southwest: A Theory of Racial Inequality. Paper Text. University of Notre Dame Press. Notre Dame, IN. 1980. 261p. ISBN:0-268-01601-1, ISBN13: 978-0-268-01601-2. Dewey:331.6/3/6872079. LCCN:78-062970.
Audience: **l,u.**

Bonilla-Silva, Eduardo **E184.A1B597 2003**
Racism Without Racists: Color-Blind Racism and the Persistence of Racial Inequality in the United States. Book, Other. Rowman & Littlefield Publishers, Inc. Lanham, MD. 2003. 224p. ISBN:0-7425-1632-6, ISBN13: 978-0-7425-1632-8. Dewey:305.8/00973. LCCN:2002-155381.
Audience: **l,u,f.** *Choice, 2004.*

Delgado, Richard **E185.615.D44 1996**
The Coming Race War?: And Other Apocalyptic Tales of America after Affirmative Action and Welfare. Andrew Hacker (Introduction by). Trade Cloth. New York University Press. New York, NY. 1996. 432p. ISBN:0-8147-1877-9, ISBN13: 978-0-8147-1877-3. Dewey:305.8/00973. LCCN:96-007801.
Audience: **g,l,u.** *Choice, 1997.*

Du Bois, W. E. B. **F158.9.N3 D8 1973**
The Philadelphia Negro: A Social Study. Trade Cloth. Kraus International Publications. Hackensack, NJ. 1973. 520p. ISBN:0-527-25320-0, ISBN13: 978-0-527-25320-2. Dewey:974.8/1100496073. LCCN:73-015644.
Audience: **l,u,f.**

Dyson, Michael Eric **E185.625.D969 2005**
The Michael Eric Dyson Reader. Trade Paper. Basic Books. New York, NY. 2004. 576p. ISBN:0-465-01771-1, ISBN13: 978-0-465-01771-3. Dewey:305.896/073. LCCN:2003-017294.
Audience: **l,u.** *Choice, 2004.*

Feagin, Joe R. & O'Brien, Eileen **E184.A1 F39**
White Men on Race: Power, Privilege, and the Shaping of Cultural Consciousness. Trade Paper. Beacon Press. Boston, MA. 2004. 288p. ISBN:0-8070-0983-0, ISBN13: 978-0-8070-0983-3. Dewey:305.800973. LCCN:2003-011632.
Audience: **g,l,u.**

Fernandez-Kelly, Maria P. **HD6073.T42 M63 1983**
For We are Sold, I and My People: Women and Industry in Mexico's Frontier. Paper Text. State University of New York Press. Albany, NY. 1984. 239p. SUNY Series in the Anthropology of Work ISBN:0-87395-718-0, ISBN13: 978-0-87395-718-2. Dewey:331.4/877/0097216. LCCN:82-019249.
Audience: **l,u,f.**

Franklin, Donna L. **E185.86.F68 1997**
Ensuring Inequality: The Structural Transformation of the African American Family. William Julius Wilson (Foreword by). Trade Cloth. Oxford University Press, Inc. New York, NY. 1997. 280p. ISBN:0-19-510078-6, ISBN13: 978-0-19-510078-5. Dewey:306.8/7/08996073. LCCN:96-007930.
Audience: **l,u.** *Choice, 1997.*

Genovese, Eugene D. **E185.6**
Roll, Jordan, Roll: The World the Slaves Made. Trade Cloth. Random House, Inc. New York, NY. 1974. xxii, 823p. ISBN:0-394-49131-9, ISBN13: 978-0-394-49131-8. Dewey:975/.00496073. LCCN:74-004760.
Audience: **g,l,u,f.** B

Giddings, Paula J. **E185.86.G49 1996**
When and Where I Enter: The Impact of Black Women on Race and Sex in America. Ed. 2. Trade Paper. HarperCollins Publishers. New York, NY. 1996. 416p. ISBN:0-688-14650-3, ISBN13: 978-0-688-14650-4. Dewey:305.4/8896073. LCCN:96-019349.
Audience: **g,l,u.**

Goldberg, David T. **HT1521.G55 1993**
Racist Culture: Philosophy and the Politics of Meaning. Trade Paper. Blackwell Publishing, Inc. Malden, MA. 1993. 328p. ISBN:0-631-18078-8, ISBN13: 978-0-631-18078-4. Dewey:305.8. LCCN:92-036107.
Audience: **u,f.** *Choice, 1994.*

Griffin, John Howard **E185.61.G8 2004**
Black Like Me. Studs Terkel (Foreword by), Robert Bonazzi (Afterword by). Trade Paper. Wings Press. San Antonio, TX. 2004. 239p. ISBN:0-930324-72-2, ISBN13: 978-0-930324-72-8. Dewey:975/.00496073. LCCN:2004-001549.
Audience: **g.** *Choice, 2005.*

Hacker, Andrew **E185.615.H23 2003**
Two Nations: Black and White, Separate, Hostile, Unequal. Trade Paper. Simon & Schuster. New York, NY. 2003. 288p. ISBN:0-7432-3824-9, ISBN13: 978-0-7432-3824-3. Dewey:305.8/00973. LCCN:2003-042565.
Audience: **g,l.** *Choice, 1992.*

Hare, Bruce R. (Editor) **E185.86.A195 2002**
2001 Race Odyssey: African Americans and Sociology. Trade Cloth. Syracuse University Press. Syracuse, NY. 2002. 440p. ISBN:0-8156-2938-9, ISBN13: 978-0-8156-2938-2. Dewey:305.896/073. LCCN:2002-009678.
Audience: **l,u,f.** *Choice, 2003.*

hooks, bell **E185.86**
Killing Rage: Ending Racism. Trade Paper. Henry Holt & Company. New York, NY. 1996. 288p. ISBN:0-8050-5027-2, ISBN13: 978-0-8050-5027-1. Dewey:305.8/96073. LCCN:95-006395.
Audience: **g,l,u.** *Choice, 1996.*

Massey, Douglas S. & Denton, Nancy A. **E185.61.M373 1993**
American Apartheid: Segregation and the Making of the Underclass. Trade Cloth. Harvard University Press. Cambridge, MA. 1993. 304p. ISBN:0-674-01820-6, ISBN13: 978-0-674-01820-4. Dewey:305.896073. LCCN:92-013889.
Audience: **l,u.** *Choice, 1993.*

Miller, Jerome G. **HV9950 .M55 1996**
Search and Destroy: African-American Males in the Criminal Justice System. Trade Cloth. Cambridge University Press. New York, NY. 1996. 344p. ISBN:0-521-46021-2, ISBN13: 978-0-521-46021-7. Dewey:364.3/496/073. LCCN:95-026128.
Audience: **g,l,u,f.** *Choice, 1996.*

Myrdal, Gunnar **E185.6.M95 1996**
An American Dilemma: The Negro Problem and Modern Democracy. Sissela Bok (Introduction by). Trade Paper. Transaction Publishers. Somerset, NJ. 1996. 936p. Black and African-American Studies ISBN:1-56000-857-1, ISBN13: 978-1-56000-857-6. Dewey:305.8/96073. LCCN:95-031355.
Audience: **l,u,f.** B

Myrdal, Gunner **E185.6 .M95 1975**
An American Dilemma. Trade Paper. Knopf Publishing Group. New York, NY. 1975. ISBN:0-394-73042-9, ISBN13: 978-0-394-73042-4. Dewey:301.45/19/6073. LCCN:74-018494.
Audience: **g,l,u,f.**

Nagel, Joane **E98.E85**
American Indian Ethnic Renewal: Red Power and the Resurgence of Identity and Culture. Trade Paper. Oxford University Press, Inc. New York, NY. 1997. 320p. ISBN:0-19-512063-9, ISBN13: 978-0-19-512063-9. Dewey:305.8/97.
Audience: **g,l,u,f.** *Choice, 1996.*

Oliver, Melvin L. & Shapiro, Thomas M. **HB835.O44 1995**
Black Wealth/White Wealth: A New Perspective on Racial Inequality. Paper over Boards. Routledge. New York, NY. 1995. 242p. ISBN:0-415-91375-6, ISBN13: 978-0-415-91375-1. Dewey:339.2/2/0973. LCCN:95-017000.
Audience: **l,u.**

Pattillo-McCoy, Mary **F548.9.N4P38 1999**
Black Picket Fences: Privilege and Peril among the Black Middle Class. Trade Cloth. University of Chicago Press. Chicago, IL. 1999. 283p. ISBN:0-226-64928-8, ISBN13: 978-0-226-64928-3. Dewey:305.896/073077311. LCCN:99-018913.
Audience: **l,u,f.** *Choice, 2000.*

Pulera, Dominic J. **E184.A1P85 2002**
Visible Differences: How Race Will Matter to Americans in the Twenty-First Century. Trade Cloth. Continuum International Publishing Group, Ltd. London, 2004. 416p. ISBN:0-8264-1407-9, ISBN13: 978-0-8264-1407-6. Dewey:305.8/00973. LCCN:2002-000377.
Audience: **l,u.** *Choice, 2003.*

Terkel, Studs **E184.A1T46 2005**
Race: How Blacks and Whites Think and Feel about the American Obsession. Trade Paper. New Press, The. New York, NY. 2005. 400p. ISBN:1-56584-989-2, ISBN13: 978-1-56584-989-1. Dewey:305.800973.
Audience: **g.**

Waldinger, Roger **F128.9.N3**
Still the Promised City?: African-Americans and New Immigrants in Postindustrial New York. Trade Paper. Harvard University Press. Cambridge, MA. 1999. 384p. ISBN:0-674-00072-2, ISBN13: 978-0-674-00072-8. Dewey:330.9/747/1/00896073.
Audience: **l,u,f.** *Choice, 1997.*

West, Cornel (Editor) **E185.615.W43 2001**
Race Matters. Trade Cloth. Beacon Press. Boston, MA. 2001. 144p. ISBN:0-8070-0972-5, ISBN13: 978-0-8070-0972-7. Dewey:305.8/00973. LCCN:2001-025310.
Audience: **g,l,u.**

Williams, Richard **E184.A1 W48 1990**
Hierarchical Structures and Social Value: The Creation of Black and Irish Identities in the United States. Trade Cloth. Cambridge University Press. New York, NY. 1990. 204p. ISBN:0-521-35147-2, ISBN13: 978-0-521-35147-8. Dewey:305.8/96073. LCCN:90-033316.
Audience: **u,f.** *Choice, 1991.*

Wilson, William Julius **E185.W73 1980**
The Declining Significance of Race: Blacks and Changing American Institutions. Ed. 2. Trade Paper. University of Chicago

Press. Chicago, IL. 1980. 251p. ISBN:0-226-90129-7, ISBN13: 978-0-226-90129-9. Dewey:305.8/00973. LCCN:80-018066.
Audience: **l,u,f.** *E*

Wu, Frank **E184.O6W84 2003**
Yellow: Race in America Beyond Black and White. Trade Paper. Basic Books. New York, NY. 2003. 416p. ISBN:0-465-00640-X, ISBN13: 978-0-465-00640-3. Dewey:305.8/95073.
Audience: **l,u,f.**

Stratification/Differentiation > Race > Elsewhere

Allen, Theodore W. **E185.A44 1994**
The Invention of the White Race: Racial Oppression and Social Control. Trade Cloth. Verso Books. London, 1994. 320p. Haymarket Ser., Vol. 1 ISBN:0-86091-480-1, ISBN13: 978-0-86091-480-8. Dewey:305.8/00973. LCCN:93-036787.
Audience: **l,u,f.** *Choice, 1994.*

Fenton, Steve **GN495.6.F46 2003**
Ethnicity. Trade Paper. Polity Press. Cambridge, 2003. 232p. ISBN:0-7456-2287-9, ISBN13: 978-0-7456-2287-3. Dewey:305.8. LCCN:2002-015375.
Audience: **l,u.** *Choice, 2003.*

Gracitua-Mario, Estanislao & Wodon, Quentin (Editors) **HC130.P6M43 2001**
Measurement and Meaning: Combining Quantitative and Qualitative Methods for the Analysis of Poverty and Social Exclusion in Latin America. Trade Paper. World Bank Publications. Washington, DC. 2001. 96p. World Bank Technical Papers, No. 518 ISBN:0-8213-5054-4, ISBN13: 978-0-8213-5054-6. Dewey:339.4/6/098. LCCN:2002-328311.
Audience: **u,f.**

Helleiner, Jane **DX217**
Irish Travellers: Racism and the Politics of Culture. Trade Paper. University of Toronto Press. Toronto, ON. 2003. 304p. Anthropological Horizons Ser. ISBN:0-8020-8628-4, ISBN13: 978-0-8020-8628-0. Dewey:305.9/0691.
Audience: **u,f.** *Choice, 2001.*

Mathabane, Mark **E185.97.M38 A3 1989**
Kaffir Boy in America: An Encounter with Apartheid. Children's Board Books. Simon & Schuster. New York, NY. 1989. 288p. ISBN:0-684-19043-5, ISBN13: 978-0-684-19043-3. Dewey:305.8/968/073. LCCN:89-004199.
Audience: **g.**

Truth and Reconcilation Commission of South Africa **DT1945**
Truth and Reconciliation: Commission of South Africa Report. Desmond Tutu (Foreword by). Cloth over Boards. Palgrave Macmillan. New York, NY. 2002. ISBN:0-312-23965-3, ISBN13: 978-0-312-23965-7. Dewey:323.4/9/0968.
Audience: **g,l,u,f.**

Van Dijk, Teun A. **HM291.D4962 1993**
Elite Discourse and Racism. Trade Paper. SAGE Publications, Inc. Thousand Oaks, CA. 1993. 336p. Race and Ethnic Relations Ser., Vol. 6 ISBN:0-8039-5071-3, ISBN13: 978-0-8039-5071-9. Dewey:305.8. LCCN:92-039455.
Audience: **u,f.** *Choice, 1993.*

Wade, Peter **GN564.L29W33 1997**
Race and Ethnicity in Latin America. Trade Cloth. Pluto Press. London, 1997. 160p. Critical Studies on Latin America ISBN:0-7453-0988-7, ISBN13: 978-0-7453-0988-0. Dewey:305.8/0098. LCCN:96-051820.
Audience: **l,u,f.**

Winant, Howard **HT1507**
The World Is a Ghetto: Race and Democracy since World War II. Trade Paper. Basic Books. New York, NY. 2002. 448p. ISBN:0-465-04341-0, ISBN13: 978-0-465-04341-5. Dewey:305.8/009.
Audience: **g,l,u,f.**

Family Life

Acock, Alan C. & Demo, David H. **HQ536.A225 1994**
Family Diversity and Well-Being. Trade Paper. SAGE Publications, Inc. Thousand Oaks, CA. 1994. 304p. Library of Social Research, Vol. 195 ISBN:0-8039-4267-2, ISBN13: 978-0-8039-4267-7. Dewey:306.85/0973. LCCN:94-011589.
Audience: **u,f.** *Choice, 1995.*

Barash, David P. & Lipton, Judith Eve **HQ806.B367 2001**
The Myth of Monogamy: Fidelity and Infidelity in Animals and People. Trade Cloth. W. H. Freeman & Company. New York, NY. 2001. 240p. ISBN:0-7167-4004-4, ISBN13: 978-0-7167-4004-9. Dewey:591.562. LCCN:2001-023209.
Audience: **l,u,f.** *Choice, 2001.*

Blumstein, Philip & Schwartz, Pepper **HQ734**
American Couples. Trade Paper. Simon & Schuster. New York, NY. 1985. ISBN:0-671-52353-8, ISBN13: 978-0-671-52353-4. Dewey:306.8.
Audience: **l,u.**

Croll, Elisabeth (Editor), et al. **HQ766.5.C6C452 1985**
China's One-Child Family Policy. Delia Davin & Penny Kane (Editors). Cloth Text. Palgrave Macmillan. New York, NY. 1985. 256p. ISBN:0-312-13356-1, ISBN13: 978-0-312-13356-6. Dewey:362.8/256/0951. LCCN:84-026756.
Audience: **u,f.** *E* *Choice, 1985.*

Demos, John Putnam **HQ536**
Past, Present, and Personal: The Family and the Life Course in American History. Trade Paper. Oxford University Press, Inc. New York, NY. 1988. 240p. ISBN:0-19-504766-4, ISBN13: 978-0-19-504766-0. Dewey:306.8/5/0973.
Audience: **u,f.** *Choice, 1987.*

Gauthier, Anne H. **HQ734.G34**
The State and the Family: A Comparative Analysis of Family Policies in Industrialized Countries. Trade Paper. Oxford University Press, Inc. New York, NY. 1999. 248p. ISBN:0-19-829499-9, ISBN13: 978-0-19-829499-3. Dewey:362.82.
Audience: **u,f.** *Choice, 1997.*

Hochschild, Arlie Russell **HD6955**
The Time Bind: When Work Becomes Home and Home Becomes Work. Trade Cloth. St. Martin's Press. Gordonville,

VA. 1997. ISBN:0-8050-5458-8, ISBN13: 978-0-8050-5458-3. Dewey:306.3/6.
Audience: **l,u,f.** *Choice, 1997.*

Kamerman, Sheila B. **HQ777.6.K35 1980**
Parenting in an Unresponsive Society: Managing Work and Family Life. Trade Cloth. Simon & Schuster. New York, NY. 1980. x, 196p. ISBN:0-02-916730-2, ISBN13: 978-0-02-916730-4. Dewey:306.8/7. LCCN:80-000641.
Audience: **l,u,f.** BCL3

Potuchek, Jean L. **HQ536.P668 1997**
Who Supports the Family: Gender and Breadwinning in Dual-Earner Marriages. Trade Cloth. Stanford University Press. Palo Alto, CA. 1997. 280p. ISBN:0-8047-2835-6, ISBN13: 978-0-8047-2835-5. Dewey:306.872. LCCN:96-034115.
Audience: **u,f.** *Choice, 1998.*

Scott, Jacqueline L. (Editor), et al. **HQ519.B53 2004**
The Blackwell Companion to the Sociology of Families. Judith Treas & Martin Richards (Editors). Trade Cloth. Blackwell Publishing, Inc. Malden, MA. 2003. 624p. Blackwell Companions to Sociology Ser., Vol. 9 ISBN:0-631-22158-1, ISBN13: 978-0-631-22158-6. Dewey:306.85/072. LCCN:2003-004166.
Audience: **g,l.** *Choice, 2004.*

Stacey, Judith **HQ536.15.S26 S73**
Brave New Families: Stories of Domestic Upheaval in Late-Twentieth-Century America. Trade Paper. University of California Press. Berkeley, CA. 1998. 352p. ISBN:0-520-21400-5, ISBN13: 978-0-520-21400-2. Dewey:306.85/09794/73. LCCN:97-049328.
Audience: **l,u.**

Visher, Emily B. & Visher, John S. **HQ777.7.V57**
Stepfamilies: A Guide to Working with Stepparents and Stepchildren. Jerry M. Lewis (Introduction by). Paper over Boards. Brunner-Routledge. Philadelphia, PA. 1979. 300p. ISBN:0-87630-190-1, ISBN13: 978-0-87630-190-6. Dewey:301.42/7. LCCN:78-025857.
Audience: **l,u.** BCL3

Waller, Willard W. **HM51**
Willard W. Waller on the Family, Education, and War: Selected Papers. William J. Goode, Frank F. Fustenberg & Larry R. Mitchell (Editors). Trade Cloth. University of Chicago Press. Chicago, IL. 1970. 376p. The Heritage of Sociology Ser., :Midway Reprint ISBN:0-226-87152-5, ISBN13: 978-0-226-87152-3. Dewey:301/.08. LCCN:70-132287.
Audience: **l,u,f.**

Family Life > By Country or Region

Aries, Philippe (Editor), et al. **GT2400.H5713 1987**
A History of Private Life: From Pagan Rome to Byzantium, Vol. 1. Georges Duby & Paul Veyne (Editors), Arthur Goldhammer (Translator). Trade Cloth. Harvard University Press. Cambridge, MA. 1987. 704p. History of Private Life Ser. ISBN:0-674-39975-7, ISBN13: 978-0-674-39975-4. Dewey:390/.009. LCCN:86-018286.
Audience: **l,u,f.** *Choice, 1987.*

Aris, Philippe A. **GT2400**
A History of Private Life: Riddles of Identity in Modern Times, Vol. 5. Georges Duby, Antoine Prost & Gerard Vincent (Editors), Arthur Goldhammer (Translator). Trade Cloth. Harvard University Press. Cambridge, MA. 1991. 656p. History of Private Life Ser. ISBN:0-674-39979-X, ISBN13: 978-0-674-39979-2. Dewey:909.09821. LCCN:86-018286.
Audience: **l,u,f.** *Choice, 1992.*

Bane, Mary Jo **HQ536.B3**
Here to Stay: American Families in the Twentieth Century. Cloth Text. Basic Books. New York, NY. 1976. 256p. ISBN:0-465-02927-2, ISBN13: 978-0-465-02927-3. Dewey:301.42/0973. LCCN:76-007674.
Audience: **l,u,f.** BCL3

Blood, Robert O. & Wolfe, Donald M. **HQ536 .B55 1978**
Husbands and Wives: The Dynamics of Married Living. Trade Cloth. Greenwood Publishing Group, Inc. Portsmouth, NH. 1978. 293p. ISBN:0-313-20453-5, ISBN13: 978-0-313-20453-1. Dewey:301.42. LCCN:78-005734.
Audience: **g,l.**

Calhoun, Arthur W. **HQ535 .C23 1973**
A Social History of the American Family from Colonial Times to the Present. Trade Cloth. Ayer Company Publishers, Inc. Manchester, NH. 1972. ISBN:0-405-03886-0, ISBN13: 978-0-405-03886-0. Dewey:301.42/0973. LCCN:73-005326.
Audience: **g,l,u.**

Caplow, Theodore, et al. **HQ535 .C25 1982**
Middletown Families: Fifty Years of Change and Continuity. Howard M. Bahr & Bruce A. Chadwick (Authors). Trade Cloth. University of Minnesota Press. Minneapolis, MN. 1985. 400p. ISBN:0-8166-1073-8, ISBN13: 978-0-8166-1073-0. Dewey:306.8. LCCN:81-014757.
Audience: **l,u,f.** BCL3

Censer, Jane T. **HQ555.N6**
North Carolina Planters and Their Children, 1800-1860. Cloth Text. Louisiana State University Press. Baton Rouge, LA. 1984. xxx, 191p. ISBN:0-8071-1135-X, ISBN13: 978-0-8071-1135-2. Dewey:306.8/5/09756. LCCN:83-019966.
Audience: **u,f.** BCL3

Chartier, Roger (Editor), et al. **CB245**
A History of Private Life: Passions of the Renaissance. Philippe Aries & Georges Duby (Editors), Arthur Goldhammer (Translator). Trade Cloth. Harvard University Press. Cambridge, MA. 1989. 655p. ISBN:0-674-39977-3, ISBN13: 978-0-674-39977-8. Dewey:909/.09821. LCCN:86-018286.
Audience: **g,l,u,f.** *Choice, 1989.*

Coontz, Stephanie **HQ535.C64 1988**
The Social Origins of Private Life: A History of American Families, 1600-1900. Cloth Text. Analytical Psychology Club of San Francisco, Inc. San Francisco, CA. 1988. 256p.

ISBN:0-86091-191-8, ISBN13: 978-0-86091-191-3. Dewey:306.8/5/0973. LCCN:88-017201.
Audience: **l,u,f.**

Demos, John Putnam **HQ557.P5D4 1999**
A Little Commonwealth: Family Life in Plymouth Colony. Ed. 2. Trade Cloth. Oxford University Press, Inc. New York, NY. 1999. 240p. ISBN:0-19-512889-3, ISBN13: 978-0-19-512889-5. Dewey:306.85/0974/82. LCCN:99-012551.
Audience: **u,f.**

Duby, Georges & Aries, Philippe (Editors) **CB245**
A History of Private Life: Revelations of the Medieval World, Vol. 2. Arthur Goldhammer (Translator). Trade Cloth. Harvard University Press. Cambridge, MA. 1988. 688p. History of Private Life Ser., Vol. 2 ISBN:0-674-39976-5, ISBN13: 978-0-674-39976-1. Dewey:909/.09821. LCCN:86-018286.
Audience: **l,u,f.**

Duby, Georges **HQ623**
The Knight, the Lady and the Priest: The Making of Modern Marriage in Medieval France. Barbara Bray (Translator). Trade Paper. University of Chicago Press. Chicago, IL. 1994. 332p. ISBN:0-226-16768-2, ISBN13: 978-0-226-16768-8. Dewey:306.8/1/0944. LCCN:93-027292.
Audience: **u,f.**

England, Paula & Farkas, George **HQ536.E54 1986**
Households, Employment and Gender: A Social, Economic and Demographic View. Trade Paper. Aldine Transaction. Somerset, NJ. 1986. 237p. Social Institutions and Social Change Ser. ISBN:0-202-30323-3, ISBN13: 978-0-202-30323-9. Dewey:304.6. LCCN:85-018628.
Audience: **u,f.** *Choice, 1986.*

Hage, Jerald & Powers, Charles **HM101**
Post Industrial Lives: Roles and Relationships in the 21st Century. Trade Cloth. SAGE Publications, Inc. Thousand Oaks, CA. 1992. 248p. ISBN:0-8039-4494-2, ISBN13: 978-0-8039-4494-7. Dewey:302. LCCN:92-010631.
Audience: **l,u.**

Hakim, Catherine **HQ613**
Models of the Family in Modern Societies: Ideals and Realities. Trade Paper. Ashgate Publishing, Ltd. Aldershot, 2004. 298p. ISBN:0-7546-4406-5, ISBN13: 978-0-7546-4406-4. Dewey:306.85.
Audience: **l,u.** *Choice, 2004.*

Hardy, Dennis **HX696.H28 2000**
Utopian Communities. Paper over Boards. Routledge. New York, NY. 2000. 320p. Studies in History, Planning, and the Environment ISBN:0-419-24660-6, ISBN13: 978-0-419-24660-2. Dewey:335/.1/0941. LCCN:00-039503.
Audience: **g,l,u.** *Choice, 2001.*

Jadhav, Narendra **HB126.I43J3313 2005**
Untouchables: My Family's Triumphant Journey Out of the Caste System in Modern India. Trade Cloth. Simon & Schuster. New York, NY. 2005. 320p. ISBN:0-7432-7079-7, ISBN13: 978-0-7432-7079-3. Dewey:305.5/688/092. LCCN:2005-044166.
Audience: **g.**

Jones, Gavin W. **DS523.4.M35J66 1994**
Marriage and Divorce in Islamic South-East Asia. Cloth Text. Oxford University Press, Inc. New York, NY. 1994. 376p. South-East Asian Social Science Monographs ISBN:967-65-3047-6, ISBN13: 978-967-65-3047-9. Dewey:306.81/0959/0917671. LCCN:93-038170.
Audience: **u,f.** *Choice, 1995.*

Kanter, Rosabeth Moss **H31.S67 NO. 9**
Work and Family in the United States: A Critical Review and Agenda for Research and Policy. Trade Paper. Russell Sage Foundation. New York, NY. 1977. 120p. Social Science Frontiers Ser. ISBN:0-87154-433-4, ISBN13: 978-0-87154-433-9. Dewey:300/.8. LCCN:76-046870.
Audience: **l,u,f.**

Kusserow, Adrie **HN80.N5K87 2004**
American Individualisms: Child Rearing and Social Class in Three Neighborhoods. Cloth over Boards. Palgrave Macmillan. New York, NY. 2004. 224p. Culture, Mind, and Society Ser. ISBN:1-4039-6481-5, ISBN13: 978-1-4039-6481-6. Dewey:305.5/09747/1. LCCN:2003-067551.
Audience: **u,f.** *Choice, 2005.*

Lewis, Oscar **HQ562 .L38**
Children of Sanchez. Trade Paper. Knopf Publishing Group. New York, NY. 1979. 544p. ISBN:0-394-70280-8, ISBN13: 978-0-394-70280-3. Dewey:309.172.
Audience: **g,l,u,f.**

Lewis, Oscar **HQ562 .L4**
Five Families: Mexican Case Studies in the Culture of Poverty. O. LaFarge (Foreword by). Trade Paper. Basic Books. New York, NY. 1975. 368p. ISBN:0-465-09705-7, ISBN13: 978-0-465-09705-0. Dewey:309.172. LCCN:59-010644.
Audience: **g,l,u.**

Mason, Mary Ann (Editor), et al. **HQ536.E88 1998**
The Evolving American Family: New Policies for a New Century. Arlene Skolnick & Stephen D. Sugarman (Editors). Paper Text. Oxford University Press, Inc. New York, NY. 1998. 272p. ISBN:0-19-510832-9, ISBN13: 978-0-19-510832-3. Dewey:306.85/0973. LCCN:97-007810.
Audience: **l,u.** *Choice, 1998.*

Mount, Ferdinand **HQ503**
The Subversive Family: An Alternative History of Love and Marriage. Trade Paper. Simon & Schuster. New York, NY. 1998. 296p. ISBN:0-684-86385-5, ISBN13: 978-0-684-86385-6. Dewey:306.8509. LCCN:92-030779.
Audience: **l,u,f.** *Choice, 1993.*

Muncy, Raymond Lee **HQ535**
Sex and Marriage in Utopian Communities : 19th Century America. Indiana University Press. 1973. ISBN:0-253-18064-3, ISBN13: 978-0-253-18064-3.
Audience: **g,l,u,f.**

Ouzgane, Lahoucine & Morrell, Robert (Editors) **HQ1090.7.A35A37 2004**
African Masculinities: Men in Africa from the Late Nineteenth Century to the Present. Cloth over Boards. Palgrave Macmillan. New York, NY. 2005. 320p. ISBN:1-4039-6587-0, ISBN13: 978-1-4039-6587-5. Dewey:305.31/096. LCCN:2004-054404.
Audience: **u,f.** *Choice, 2005.*

Parish, William L. & Whyte, Martin K. **HQ684**
Village and Family in Contemporary China. Trade Paper. University of Chicago Press. Chicago, IL. 1980. 436p. ISBN:0-226-64591-6, ISBN13: 978-0-226-64591-9. Dewey:951. LCCN:78-003411.
Audience: **u,f.** ℬ

Perrot, Michelle (Editor), et al. **GT2400 .H5713 1987**
A History of Private Life: From the Fires of Revolution to the Great War. Philippe Aries & Georges Duby (Editors), Arthur Goldhammer (Translator). Trade Cloth. Harvard University Press. Cambridge, MA. 1990. 744p. History of Private Life Ser., Vol. 4 ISBN:0-674-39978-1, ISBN13: 978-0-674-39978-5. Dewey:390.009.
Audience: **l,u,f.**

Pleck, Joseph H. **HQ0536.P59**
Working Wives, Working Husbands. Trade Paper. Books on Demand. Ann Arbor, MI. 1985. 168p. New Perspectives on Family Ser. ISBN:0-608-01525-3, ISBN13: 978-0-608-01525-5. Dewey:306.8/7. LCCN:85-011974.
Audience: **g,l,u,f.**

Richter, Linda & Morrell, Robert (Editors) **HQ756**
Baba: Men and Fatherhood in South Africa. Trade Paper. Human Sciences Research Council. Pretoria, 2006. 416p. ISBN:0-7969-2096-6, ISBN13: 978-0-7969-2096-6. Dewey:306.8742097.
Audience: **u,f.**

Ryan, Mary P. **HQ555.N7**
Cradle of the Middle Class: The Family in Oneida County, New York, 1790-1865. Robert Fogel & Stephan Thernstrom (Contribution by). Trade Paper. Cambridge University Press. New York, NY. 1983. 321p. Interdisciplinary Perspectives on Modern History Ser. ISBN:0-521-27403-6, ISBN13: 978-0-521-27403-6. Dewey:305.55. LCCN:80-018460.
Audience: **u,f.** ℬ

Scanzoni, John H. **HQ766.5.U5**
Sex Roles, Life Styles and Childbearing: Changing Patterns in Marriage and the Family. Trade Cloth. Simon & Schuster. New York, NY. 1975. xi, 259p. ISBN:0-02-927720-5, ISBN13: 978-0-02-927720-1. Dewey:301.42/6. LCCN:74-028939.
Audience: **l,u,f.** ℬ

Scanzoni, John H. **HQ0536.S337**
Shaping Tomorrow's Family: Theory and Policy for the 21st Century. Trade Paper. Books on Demand. Ann Arbor, MI. 272p. Sage Library of Social Research, Vol. 143 ISBN:0-598-10015-6, ISBN13: 978-0-598-10015-3. Dewey:173/.0973. LCCN:82-016876.
Audience: **u,f.** ℬ

Schneider, David M. **GN560.U6**
American Kinship: A Cultural Account. Ed. 2. Trade Paper. University of Chicago Press. Chicago, IL. 1980. 148p. ISBN:0-226-73930-9, ISBN13: 978-0-226-73930-4. Dewey:301.42/1/0973. LCCN:79-018185.
Audience: **l,u,f.** ℬ

Sennett, Richard **HQ536.S43 1984**
Families Against the City: Middle Class Homes of Industrial Chicago, 1872-1890. Trade Paper. Harvard University Press. Cambridge, MA. 1984. 270p. Joint Center for Urban Studies ISBN:0-674-29226-X, ISBN13: 978-0-674-29226-0. Dewey:305.5/5/0977311. LCCN:84-009046.
Audience: **l,u,f.** ℬ

Shanley, Mary L. **HQ536**
Making Babies, Making Families: What Matters Most in an Age of Reproductive Technologies, Surrogacy, Adoption, and Same-Sex and Unwed Parents' Rights. Trade Paper. Beacon Press. Boston, MA. 2002. 224p. ISBN:0-8070-4409-1, ISBN13: 978-0-8070-4409-4. Dewey:306.85/0973.
Audience: **g,l,u,f.**

Smith, Daniel B. **HQ555.C46**
Inside the Great House: Planter Family Life in Eighteenth-Century Chesapeake Society. Book, Other. Cornell University Press. Ithaca, NY. 1986. 306p. ISBN:0-8014-9380-3, ISBN13: 978-0-8014-9380-5. Dewey:306.8/5/0975518. LCCN:80-014557.
Audience: **u,f.** ℬ

Stacey, Judith **HQ684**
Patriarchy and Socialist Revolution in China. Trade Cloth. University of California Press. Berkeley, CA. 1983. 330p. ISBN:0-520-04825-3, ISBN13: 978-0-520-04825-6. Dewey:306.8/5/0951. LCCN:82-008482.
Audience: **u,f.** ℬ

Stone, Lawrence **HQ615**
Family, Sex and Marriage in England, Fifteen Hundred to Eighteen Hundred. Trade Paper. HarperCollins Publishers. New York, NY. 1980. ISBN:0-06-090735-5, ISBN13: 978-0-06-090735-8. Dewey:306.8.
Audience: **l,u.**

Yan, Yunxiang **HQ684.Z9.X539 2003**
Private Life under Changing Socialism: Love, Intimacy, and Family Change in a Chinese Village, 1949-1999. Cloth Text. Stanford University Press. Palo Alto, CA. 2003. 320p. ISBN:0-8047-3309-0, ISBN13: 978-0-8047-3309-0. Dewey:306.8/0951/84. LCCN:2002-013327.
Audience: **u,f.**

Family Life > Socialization

Johnson, Leanor Boulin & Staples, Robert **E185.86.S698 2004**
Black Families at the Crossroads: Challenges and Prospects. Trade Paper. John Wiley & Sons, Inc. Hoboken, NJ. 2004. 416p. ISBN:0-7879-7222-3, ISBN13: 978-0-7879-7222-6. Dewey:306.85/089/96073. LCCN:2004-010951.
Audience: **l,u.**

Pleck, Elizabeth H. **GT4986.A1P54 2000**
Celebrating the Family: Ethnicity, Consumer Culture, and Family Rituals. Trade Cloth. Harvard University Press. Cambridge, MA. 2000. 338p. ISBN:0-674-00230-X, ISBN13: 978-0-674-00230-2. Dewey:394.26973. LCCN:99-045200.
Audience: **l,u,f.** *Choice, 2001.*

Roschelle, Anne R. **HQ536.R65 1997**
No More Kin: Exploring Race, Class, and Gender in Family Networks. Trade Cloth. SAGE Publications, Inc. Thousand Oaks, CA. 1997. 253p. Understanding Families Ser., Vol. 8 ISBN:0-7619-0158-2, ISBN13: 978-0-7619-0158-7. Dewey:306.85/0973. LCCN:97-004677.
Audience: **u,f.** *Choice, 1997.*

White, James M. **HQ503.W69 1991**
Dynamics of Family Development: A Theoretical Perspective. Cloth over Boards. Guilford Publications, Inc. New York, NY. 1991. 254p. Perspectives on Marriage and the Family Ser. ISBN:0-89862-080-5, ISBN13: 978-0-89862-080-1. Dewey:306.85. LCCN:91-009053.
Audience: **l,u.** *Choice, 1991.*

Family Life > Childhood

Aries, Philippe **HQ792.F7A73 1962**
Centuries of Childhood: A Social History of Family Life. Trade Paper. Random House, Inc. New York, NY. 1965. 448p. ISBN:0-394-70286-7, ISBN13: 978-0-394-70286-5. LCCN:93-218907.
Audience: **l,u,f.**

Bettelheim, Bruno **HQ792.P3 B47**
The Children of the Dream. Trade Paper. Simon & Schuster. New York, NY. 2001. 380p. ISBN:0-7432-1795-0, ISBN13: 978-0-7432-1795-8. Dewey:155.41. LCCN:69-010505.
Audience: **u,f.** B

Bowlby, John **HQ782**
Secure Base: Parent-Child Attachment and Healthy Human Development. Trade Paper. Basic Books. New York, NY. 1990. 224p. ISBN:0-465-07597-5, ISBN13: 978-0-465-07597-3. Dewey:155.4/18.
Audience: **l,u,f.**

Bowlby, John, et al. **HQ772**
Child Care and the Growth of Love. Mary D. Salter Ainsworth & Margery Fry (Authors). Trade Paper. Penguin Group (USA) Inc. New York, NY. 1953. 256p. ISBN:0-14-020271-4, ISBN13: 978-0-14-020271-7. Dewey:305.231.
Audience: **u,f.** B

Brown, Harriet **HQ778.67.M33B76 1998**
The Good-Bye Window: A Year in the Life of a Day-Care Center. Trade Cloth. University of Wisconsin Press. Chicago, IL. 1998. 264p. ISBN:0-299-15870-5, ISBN13: 978-0-299-15870-5. Dewey:362.71/2/09775. LCCN:98-017528.
Audience: **g.** *Choice, 1999.*

Elkin **HQ783 .E43**
The Child and Society. Ed. 6. Paper Text. McGraw-Hill Companies, The. New York, NY. 2001. 352p. ISBN:0-07-232135-0, ISBN13: 978-0-07-232135-7. Dewey:303.3/2.
Audience: **l,u.**

Emery, Robert E. **RJ507.D59E44 1988**
Marriage, Divorce and Children's Adjustment. Trade Cloth. SAGE Publications, Inc. Thousand Oaks, CA. 1988. 160p. Developmental Clinical Psychology and Psychiatry Ser., Vol. 14 ISBN:0-8039-2780-0, ISBN13: 978-0-8039-2780-3. Dewey:155.4. LCCN:87-026502.
Audience: **l,u,f.** *Choice, 1989.*

Erikson, Erik H. **HQ767.9**
Childhood and Society. Trade Paper. W. W. Norton & Company, Inc. New York, NY. 1993. 446p. ISBN:0-393-31068-X, ISBN13: 978-0-393-31068-9. Dewey:305.2/3. LCCN:93-011229.
Audience: **g,l,u,f.** B

Freud, Anna & Burlingham, Dorothy T. **HQ784.W3 F7 1973**
War and Children. Philip R. Lehrman (Editor). Trade Cloth. Greenwood Publishing Group, Inc. Portsmouth, NH. 1973. 191p. ISBN:0-8371-6942-9, ISBN13: 978-0-8371-6942-2. Dewey:940.53/161. LCCN:73-007699.
Audience: **u,f.** B

Ginzberg, Eli (Editor) **HQ792.U5 G5 1972**
Values and Ideals of American Youth. John W. Gardner (Foreword by). Trade Cloth. Ayer Company Publishers, Inc. Manchester, NH. 1977. Essay Index Reprint Ser. ISBN:0-8369-7252-X, ISBN13: 978-0-8369-7252-8. Dewey:301.43/1/0973. LCCN:72-006798.
Audience: **u,f.** B

Mead, Margaret & Wolfenstein, Martha (Editors) **HQ768**
Childhood in Contemporary Cultures. Paper Text. University of Chicago Press. Chicago, IL. 1994. ISBN:0-226-51507-9, ISBN13: 978-0-226-51507-6. Dewey:392.3. LCCN:55-010248.
Audience: **l,u,f.** B

Pollock, Linda A. **HQ767.87 .P64 1983**
Forgotten Children: Parent-Child Relations from 1500 to 1900. Trade Paper. Cambridge University Press. New York, NY. 1983. 352p. ISBN:0-521-27133-9, ISBN13: 978-0-521-27133-2. Dewey:306.8/74/0941. LCCN:83-005315.
Audience: **l,u,f.** B

Smart, Carol, et al. **HQ777.5.S573 2001**
The Changing Experience of Childhood: Families and Divorce. Bren Neale & Amanda Wade (Authors). Trade Paper. Polity Press. Cambridge, 2001. 232p. ISBN:0-7456-2400-6, ISBN13: 978-0-7456-2400-6. Dewey:305.23. LCCN:2001-000148.
Audience: **l,u,f.** *Choice, 2002.*

Zelizer, Viviana A. **HQ792.U5Z45 1994**
Pricing the Priceless Child: The Changing Social Value of Children. Trade Paper. Princeton University Press. Princeton, NJ. 1994. 294p. ISBN:0-691-03459-1, ISBN13: 978-0-691-03459-1. Dewey:305.2/0973. LCCN:93-039140.
Audience: **l,u,f.** B *Choice, 1985.*

Family Life > Youth/Adolescence

Borkowski, John G., et al. **HQ759.4.I57 2001**
Interwoven Lives: Adolescent Mothers and Their Children. Thomas L. Whitman & Keri Weed (Authors). Cloth over Boards. Lawrence Erlbaum Associates, Inc. Mahwah, NJ. 2001. 280p. Research Monographs in Adolescence ISBN:0-8058-3127-4, ISBN13: 978-0-8058-3127-6. Dewey:306.874/3. LCCN:00-050286.
Audience: **u,f.** *Choice, 2001.*

Buchanan, Christy M., et al. **HQ777.5.B796 1996**
Adolescents after Divorce. Eleanor E. Maccoby & Sanford M. Dornbusch (Authors). Trade Cloth. Harvard University Press. Cambridge, MA. 1996. 352p. ISBN:0-674-00517-1, ISBN13: 978-0-674-00517-4. Dewey:306.8/74. LCCN:96-011882.
Audience: **l,u.** *Choice, 1997.*

Chambers-Schiller, Lee V. **HQ800.2**
Liberty, a Better Husband: Single Women in America: The Generations of 1780-1840. Trade Paper. Yale University Press.

Cumberland, RI. 1987. 292p. ISBN:0-300-03922-0, ISBN13: 978-0-300-03922-1. Dewey:305.4/890652. LCCN:84-003524.
Audience: **u,f.** BCL3

Friedenberg, Edgar Z. **HQ796**
The Vanishing Adolescent. David Riesman (Introduction by). Trade Cloth. Greenwood Publishing Group, Inc. Portsmouth, NH. 1985. 144p. ISBN:0-313-24920-2, ISBN13: 978-0-313-24920-4. Dewey:305.2/35. LCCN:85-000950.
Audience: **l,u.** BCL3

Furstenberg, Frank F. Jr. **HQ759.4 F87 1979**
Unplanned Parenthood: The Social Consequences of Teenage Childbearing. Trade Cloth. Simon & Schuster. New York, NY. 1979. ISBN:0-02-911030-0, ISBN13: 978-0-02-911030-0. Dewey:301.41/76/463. LCCN:76-008144.
Audience: **l,u,f.**

Gaines, Donna **HQ796.G25 1998**
Teenage Wasteland: Suburbia's Dead End Kids. Trade Paper. University of Chicago Press. Chicago, IL. 1998. 282p. ISBN:0-226-27872-7, ISBN13: 978-0-226-27872-8. Dewey:305.235/09749/21. LCCN:97-043544.
Audience: **g,l,u,f.**

Gillis, John R. **HQ796.G514 1981**
Youth and History: Tradition and Change in European Age Relations, 1770 to Present. Trade Paper. Elsevier Science & Technology Books. Saint Louis, MO. 1981. xiv, 250p. Studies in Social Discontinuity Ser. ISBN:0-12-785264-6, ISBN13: 978-0-12-785264-5. Dewey:305.2/3/09. LCCN:81-007919.
Audience: **u,f.** BCL3

Jenkins, Richard **HQ799.G72B44**
Lads, Citizens and Ordinary Kids: Working Class Youth Lifestyles in Belfast. Trade Paper. Routledge. New York, NY. 1983. 159p. Direct Editions Ser. ISBN:0-7100-9574-0, ISBN13: 978-0-7100-9574-9. Dewey:305.2/35/094167. LCCN:83-003339.
Audience: **l,u,f.** BCL3

Lipsitz, Joan **HQ796**
Growing up Forgotten. Trade Paper. Transaction Publishers. Somerset, NJ. 1980. 267p. ISBN:0-87855-792-X, ISBN13: 978-0-87855-792-9. Dewey:305.2/35/0973. LCCN:79-067002.
Audience: **l,u.**

Moran, Jeffrey P. **HQ27.5**
Teaching Sex: The Shaping of Adolescence in the 20th Century. Trade Cloth. Harvard University Press. Cambridge, MA. 2000. 304p. ISBN:0-674-00227-X, ISBN13: 978-0-674-00227-2. Dewey:613/.9/071/073. LCCN:99-054303.
Audience: **u,f.** *Choice, 2000.*

Odem, Mary E. **HQ27.5.O34 1995**
Delinquent Daughters: Protecting and Policing Adolescent Female Sexuality in the United States, 1885-1920. Trade Cloth. University of North Carolina Press. Chapel Hill, NC. 1995. 288p. Gender and American Culture Ser. ISBN:0-8078-2215-9, ISBN13: 978-0-8078-2215-9. Dewey:306.7/0835. LCCN:95-013185.
Audience: **u,f.** *Choice, 1996.*

Tallman, Irving (Editor), et al. **HQ783.T34 1983**
Adolescent Socialization in Cross-Cultural Perspective. Ramon Marotz-Braden & P. Pindas (Editors). Trade Cloth. Elsevier Science & Technology Books. Saint Louis, MO. 1983. xvii, 325p. Monograph Ser. ISBN:0-12-683180-7, ISBN13: 978-0-12-683180-1. Dewey:303.3/2. LCCN:83-002511.
Audience: **u,f.** BCL3

Weiner, Rex & Stillman, Deanne **HQ793.W26 1980**
Woodstock Census. Trade Paper. Ballantine Books. New York, NY. 1980. ISBN:0-449-90036-3, ISBN13: 978-0-449-90036-9. Dewey:305.235.
Audience: **l,u,f.**

Family Life > Adulthood

Andre, Rae **HQ0759.A5**
Homemakers, the Forgotten Workers. Trade Paper. Books on Demand. Ann Arbor, MI. 311p. ISBN:0-608-08042-X, ISBN13: 978-0-608-08042-0. Dewey:305.4/3. LCCN:80-021258.
Audience: **l,u,f.**

Chandrasekhar, Sripati **KD372.B7**
A Dirty Filthy Book: The Writings of Charles Knowlton and Annie Besant on Birth Control and Reproductive Physiology and an Account of the Bradlaugh-Besant Trial. Trade Cloth. University of California Press. Berkeley, CA. 1981. xi, 217p. ISBN:0-520-04168-2, ISBN13: 978-0-520-04168-4. Dewey:344.205/274. LCCN:80-015570.
Audience: **u,f.** BCL3

Chodorow, Nancy Julia **HQ759.C56 1999**
The Reproduction of Mothering: Psychoanalysis and the Sociology of Gender. Ed. 2. Trade Paper. University of California Press. Berkeley, CA. 1999. 284p. ISBN:0-520-22155-9, ISBN13: 978-0-520-22155-0. Dewey:306.874/3. LCCN:2001-266933.
Audience: **l,u,f.** BCL3

Coles, Robert **HQ759.64**
The Youngest Parents: Teenage Pregnancy As It Shapes Lives. Trade Paper. W. W. Norton & Company, Inc. New York, NY. 2000. 192p. ISBN:0-393-31996-2, ISBN13: 978-0-393-31996-5. Dewey:305.235. LCCN:96-047258.
Audience: **l,u.** *Choice, 1998.*

Cuca, Roberto & Pierce, Catherine S. **HQ766**
Experiments in Family Planning: Lessons from the Developing World. Trade Cloth. Johns Hopkins University Press. Baltimore, MD. 1978. 278p. World Bank Research Publications ISBN:0-8018-2013-8, ISBN13: 978-0-8018-2013-7. Dewey:363.9/6/091724. LCCN:77-016596.
Audience: **l,u.** BCL3

Daniels, Pamela & Weingarten, Kathy **HQ755.83**
Sooner or Later: The Timing of Parenthood in Adult Lives. Trade Paper. W. W. Norton & Company, Inc. New York, NY. 1983. 384p. ISBN:0-393-30132-X, ISBN13: 978-0-393-30132-8. Dewey:306.8/74. LCCN:81-011006.
Audience: **l,u.** BCL3

Harris, Marvin & Ross, Eric B. **GN33.5.H37 1987**
Death, Sex, and Fertility: Population Regulation in Pre-Industrial and Developing Societies. Cloth Text. Columbia University Press. New York, NY. 1987. 184p. ISBN:0-231-06270-2,

ISBN13: 978-0-231-06270-1. Dewey:304.6/32. LCCN:86-018401.
Audience: **u,f.** *Choice, 1987.*

Montagu, Ashley **BF710.M65 1981**
Growing Young. Cloth Text. McGraw-Hill Companies, The. New York, NY. 1983. ISBN:0-07-042841-7, ISBN13: 978-0-07-042841-6. Dewey:155. LCCN:81-008433.
Audience: **g,l,u.**

Rich, Adrienne **HQ759**
Of Woman Born: Motherhood as Experience and Institution. Trade Paper. W. W. Norton & Company, Inc. New York, NY. 1995. 352p. ISBN:0-393-31284-4, ISBN13: 978-0-393-31284-3. Dewey:306.8/743.
Audience: **g,l,u.**

Robinson, Bryan E. **HQ756.R635 1988**
Teenage Fathers. Trade Cloth. Simon & Schuster. New York, NY. 1987. 192p. ISBN:0-669-14586-6, ISBN13: 978-0-669-14586-1. Dewey:362.7/96. LCCN:86-045896.
Audience: **g,l,u.** *Choice, 1988.*

Family Life > Adulthood > Relationships

Bartholet, Elizabeth **HV875.55.B38 1999**
Family Bonds: Adoption, Infertility, and the New World of Child Production. Trade Paper. Beacon Press. Boston, MA. 1999. 286p. ISBN:0-8070-2803-7, ISBN13: 978-0-8070-2803-2. Dewey:362.73/4/0973. LCCN:99-026320.
Audience: **u,f.**

Carp, E. Wayne **HV875.55**
Family Matters: Secrecy and Disclosure in the History of Adoption. Trade Paper. Harvard University Press. Cambridge, MA. 2000. 320p. ISBN:0-674-00186-9, ISBN13: 978-0-674-00186-2. Dewey:362.73/4/0973.
Audience: **u,f.** *Choice, 1999.*

DeLamater, John & MacCorquodale, Patricia **HQ27**
Premarital Sexuality: Attitudes, Relationships, Behavior. Trade Cloth. University of Wisconsin Press. Chicago, IL. 1979. 314p. ISBN:0-299-07840-X, ISBN13: 978-0-299-07840-9. Dewey:301.41/75. LCCN:78-065019.
Audience: **g,l,u,f.**

Dordick, Gwendolyn A. **HV4506.N6D67 1997**
Something Left to Lose: Personal Relations and Survival Among New York's Homeless. Trade Cloth. Temple University Press. Philadelphia, PA. 1997. 224p. ISBN:1-56639-513-5, ISBN13: 978-1-56639-513-7. Dewey:305.5/69. LCCN:96-025094.
Audience: **u,f.** *Choice, 1997.*

Duncan, Greg J. **HD6983.D85**
Years of Poverty, Years of Plenty. Cloth Text. University of Michigan Press. Chicago, IL. 1984. 200p. ISBN:0-472-00702-5, ISBN13: 978-0-472-00702-8. Dewey:339.4/1/0973.
Audience: **l,u.**

Engels, Friedrich **HQ504**
The Origin of the Family, Private Property, and the State. Ernest Untermann (Translator). Trade Paper. University Press of the Pacific. Miami, FL. 2001. 220p. ISBN:0-89875-469-0, ISBN13: 978-0-89875-469-8. Dewey:321.1.
Audience: **g,l,u,f.**

Gardner, LeRoy **E185.62.G37 2000**
White/Black Race Mixing: An Essay on the Stereotypes and Realities of Interracial Marriage. Trade Paper. Paragon House Publishers. Saint Paul, MN. 2001. 180p. ISBN:1-55778-796-4, ISBN13: 978-1-55778-796-5. Dewey:306.84/6. LCCN:00-034659.
Audience: **l,u,f.**

Gilligan, Carol, et al. **HQ798.T39 1995**
Between Voice and Silence: Women and Girls, Race and Relationships. Jill M. Taylor & Amy M. Sullivan (Authors). Trade Cloth. Harvard University Press. Cambridge, MA. 1995. 267p. ISBN:0-674-06879-3, ISBN13: 978-0-674-06879-7. Dewey:305.23/5. LCCN:95-036209.
Audience: **u,f.** *Choice, 1996.*

Gilman, Charlotte Perkins **HQ734.G5 2002**
The Home: Its Work and Influence. Trade Cloth. AltaMira Press. Walnut Creek, CA. 2002. 368p. Classics in Gender Studies ISBN:0-7591-0305-4, ISBN13: 978-0-7591-0305-4. Dewey:640. LCCN:2002-066632.
Audience: **g,l,u,f.**

Herman, Judith L. **HQ71.H46 2000**
Father-Daughter Incest. Trade Paper. Harvard University Press. Cambridge, MA. 2000. 336p. ISBN:0-674-00270-9, ISBN13: 978-0-674-00270-8. Dewey:306.8/77. LCCN:99-059169.
Audience: **g,l,u.**

Laslett, Peter **HQ611**
Family Life and Illicit Love in Earlier Generations: Essays in Historical Sociology. Trade Cloth. Cambridge University Press. New York, NY. 1977. 320p. ISBN:0-521-21408-4, ISBN13: 978-0-521-21408-7. Dewey:301.42/1/094. LCCN:76-021010.
Audience: **l,u,f.**

MacCoby, Eleanor E. **BF692.2.M33 1998**
The Two Sexes: Growing up Apart, Coming Together. Trade Cloth. Harvard University Press. Cambridge, MA. 1999. 384p. The Family and Public Policy Ser. ISBN:0-674-91481-3, ISBN13: 978-0-674-91481-0. Dewey:155.3/3. LCCN:97-030594.
Audience: **l,u,f.** *Choice, 1998.*

Malinowski, Bronislaw **HQ504.M34 2001**
Sex and Repression in Savage Society. Ed. 2. Trade Paper. Routledge. New York, NY. 2001. 240p. Classics Ser. ISBN:0-415-25554-6, ISBN13: 978-0-415-25554-7. Dewey:306.7/09954/1. LCCN:2001-041225.
Audience: **l,u,f.**

Margolin, Leslie **HV43.M295 1997**
Under the Cover of Kindness: The Invention of Social Work. Trade Cloth. University Press of Virginia. Charlottesville, VA. 1997. 219p. Knowledge: Disciplinarity and Beyond Ser. ISBN:0-8139-1713-1, ISBN13: 978-0-8139-1713-9. Dewey:361.3/2. LCCN:96-047986.
Audience: **l,u,f.**

Moran, Rachel F. **HQ1031**
Interracial Intimacy: The Regulation of Race and Romance. Trade Paper. University of Chicago Press. Chicago, IL. 2003. 232p. ISBN:0-226-53663-7, ISBN13: 978-0-226-53663-7. Dewey:305.8/00973.
Audience: **u,f.** *Choice, 2002.*

Parsons, Talcott, et al. **HQ518**
Family Socialization and Interaction Process. Robert F. Bales, James Olds, Morris Zelditch & Philip E. Slater (Authors). Paper over Boards. Routledge. New York, NY. 2003. 440p. International Library of Sociology Ser., Vol. 127 ISBN:0-415-17647-6, ISBN13: 978-0-415-17647-7. Dewey:306.8/5.
Audience: **u,f.** B

Peterson, Nancy L. **HQ800.4.U6.P47 1981**
Our Lives for Ourselves: Women Who Have Never Married. Trade Cloth. Penguin Group (USA) Inc. New York, NY. 1981. 320p. ISBN:0-399-12476-4, ISBN13: 978-0-399-12476-1. Dewey:305.4/8. LCCN:80-023101.
Audience: **g.** B

Seccombe, Wally **HQ611**
A Millennium of Family Change: Feudalism to Capitalism in North Western Europe. Trade Paper. Analytical Psychology Club of San Francisco, Inc. San Francisco, CA. 1995. 304p. ISBN:1-85984-052-3, ISBN13: 978-1-85984-052-8. Dewey:306.85.
Audience: **l,u.**

Smith, George P. **HQ518**
Family Values and the New Society: Dilemmas of the 21st Century. Trade Cloth. Greenwood Publishing Group, Inc. Portsmouth, NH. 1998. 296p. ISBN:0-275-96221-0, ISBN13: 978-0-275-96221-0. Dewey:306.85. LCCN:97-043942.
Audience: **u,f.** *Choice, 1999.*

Staples, Robert **HQ800**
The World of Black Singles: Changing Patterns of Male-Female Relations. Trade Cloth. Greenwood Publishing Group, Inc. Portsmouth, NH. 1981. 259p. Contributions in Afro-American and African Studies Ser., No. 57 ISBN:0-313-22478-1, ISBN13: 978-0-313-22478-2. Dewey:305. LCCN:80-001025.
Audience: **l,u,f.** B

Vicinus, Martha **HQ800.2**
Independent Women: Work and Community for Single Women, 1850-1920. Trade Paper. University of Chicago Press. Chicago, IL. 1992. 412p. Women in Culture and Society Ser. ISBN:0-226-85568-6, ISBN13: 978-0-226-85568-4. Dewey:305.4/89/652/0942. LCCN:84-016158.
Audience: **u,f.** B *Choice, 1985.*

Walters, Suzanna D. **HQ759.W332**
Lives Together - Worlds Apart: Mothers and Daughters in Popular Culture. Trade Paper. University of California Press. Berkeley, CA. 1994. 310p. ISBN:0-520-08656-2, ISBN13: 978-0-520-08656-2. Dewey:306.8743. LCCN:91-032331.
Audience: **l,u,f.** *Choice, 1993.*

Wolf, Arthur P. & Durham, William H. **GN480.3.I53 2004**
Inbreeding, Incest, and the Incest Taboo: The State of Knowledge at the Turn of the Century. Trade Cloth. Stanford University Press. Palo Alto, CA. 2004. 288p. ISBN:0-8047-4596-X, ISBN13: 978-0-8047-4596-3. Dewey:306.877. LCCN:2004-003967.
Audience: **u,f.** *Choice, 2005.*

Zelizer, Viviana A. Rotman **HG179.Z45 2005**
The Purchase of Intimacy. Trade Cloth. Princeton University Press. Princeton, NJ. 2005. 232p. ISBN:0-691-12408-6, ISBN13: 978-0-691-12408-7. Dewey:332.024/01/0865. LCCN:2005-007983.
Audience: **g,l,u,f.**

Family Life > Adulthood > Relationships > Dating/Courtship

Brucker, Gene Adam **HQ806 .B78 2005**
Giovanni and Lusanna: Love and Marriage in Renaissance Florence. Ed. 2. Trade Paper, Perfect. University of California Press. Berkeley, CA. 2004. 156p. ISBN:0-520-24495-8, ISBN13: 978-0-520-24495-5. Dewey:306.81/0945/5109024. LCCN:2004-058860.
Audience: **u,f.**

Hamon, Raeann & Ingoldsby, Bron (Editors) **HQ801.M236 2003**
Mate Selection Across Cultures. Paper Text. SAGE Publications, Inc. Thousand Oaks, CA. 2003. 312p. ISBN:0-7619-2592-9, ISBN13: 978-0-7619-2592-7. Dewey:646.7/7. LCCN:2003-011938.
Audience: **u,f.** *Choice, 2004.*

Lewis, Thomas, et al. **BF575.L8 L49 2000**
A General Theory of Love. Fari Amini & Richard Lannon (Authors). Trade Paper. Knopf Publishing Group. New York, NY. 2001. 288p. ISBN:0-375-70922-3, ISBN13: 978-0-375-70922-7. Dewey:152.4/1. LCCN:99-049930.
Audience: **g,l.** *Choice, 2000.*

Rothman, Ellen K. **HQ801.R85 1987**
Hands and Hearts: A History of Courtship in America. Paper Text. Harvard University Press. Cambridge, MA. 1987. 384p. ISBN:0-674-37160-7, ISBN13: 978-0-674-37160-6. Dewey:306.7/34/0973. LCCN:86-019575.
Audience: **l,u.** B

Swidler, Ann **BF575.L8S92 2001**
Talk of Love: How Culture Matters. Trade Cloth. University of Chicago Press. Chicago, IL. 2000. 312p. ISBN:0-226-78690-0, ISBN13: 978-0-226-78690-2. Dewey:306.7. LCCN:00-060198.
Audience: **l,u.** *Choice, 2002.*

Wouters, Cas **BJ1854**
Sex and Manners: Female Emancipation in the West 1890 - 2000. Trade Cloth. SAGE Publications, Ltd. London, 2004. 200p. Theory, Culture and Society Ser. ISBN:0-8039-8369-7, ISBN13: 978-0-8039-8369-4. Dewey:392.4/09182/10904. LCCN:2005-295200.
Audience: **l,u,f.** *Choice, 2005.*

Family Life > Adulthood > Relationships > Marriage

Bernard, Jessie **HQ728**
The Future of Marriage. Ed. 2. Trade Paper. Yale University Press. Cumberland, RI. 1982. 384p. ISBN:0-300-02853-9, ISBN13: 978-0-300-02853-9. Dewey:306.8/1. LCCN:82-006991.
Audience: **l,u,f.**

Bernard, Jessie Shirley **HQ728 .B476**
Remarriage, a Study of Marriage. Paper Text. Textbook Publishers. Temecula, CA. 2003. 372p. ISBN:0-7581-4484-9, ISBN13: 978-0-7581-4484-3. Dewey:301.42/7.
Audience: **u,f.** B

Blumstein, Philip **HQ734.B659 1983**
American Couples: Money, Work, Sex. Trade Cloth. HarperCollins Publishers. New York, NY. 1983. 656p. ISBN:0-688-03772-0, ISBN13: 978-0-688-03772-7. Dewey:306.8/0973. LCCN:83-062066.
Audience: **l,u.**

Boswell, John **HQ76.3.E8**
Same-Sex Unions in Premodern Europe. UK-Trade Paper. Knopf Publishing Group. New York, NY. 1995. 464p. ISBN:0-679-75164-5, ISBN13: 978-0-679-75164-9. Dewey:306.76/6/094.
Audience: **g,l,u,f.** *Choice, 1994.*

Cott, Nancy F. **HQ536.C757 2000**
Public Vows: A History of Marriage and the Nation. Trade Cloth. Harvard University Press. Cambridge, MA. 2001. 304p. ISBN:0-674-00320-9, ISBN13: 978-0-674-00320-0. Dewey:306.8/0973. LCCN:00-031898.
Audience: **g,l,u,f.** *Choice, 2001.*

Crowley, Jocelyn Elise **HV741.C76 2003**
The Politics of Child Support in America. Trade Cloth. Cambridge University Press. New York, NY. 2003. 232p. ISBN:0-521-82460-5, ISBN13: 978-0-521-82460-6. Dewey:346.01/72/0973. LCCN:2002-045513.
Audience: **u,f.** *Choice, 2004.*

Goode, William J. **HQ728**
World Revolution and Family Patterns. Trade Paper. Simon & Schuster. New York, NY. 1970. xxv, 432p. ISBN:0-02-912460-3, ISBN13: 978-0-02-912460-4. Dewey:301.42/3. LCCN:63-013538.
Audience: **l,u,f.**

Hartog, Hendrik **KF510.H37 2000**
Man and Wife in America: A History. Trade Cloth. Harvard University Press. Cambridge, MA. 2000. 416p. ISBN:0-674-00262-8, ISBN13: 978-0-674-00262-3. Dewey:346.7301/63/09. LCCN:99-056466.
Audience: **g.** *Choice, 2000.*

Komarovsky, Mirra **HQ728.K57 1987**
Blue Collar Marriage. Ed. 2. Cloth over Boards. Yale University Press. Cumberland, RI. 1987. 416p. ISBN:0-300-03918-2, ISBN13: 978-0-300-03918-4. Dewey:306.8/7. LCCN:86-024658.
Audience: **l,u,f.**

Larossa, Ralph **HQ756.L37 1997**
The Modernization of Fatherhood: A Social and Political History. Trade Paper. University of Chicago Press. Chicago, IL. 1996. 295p. ISBN:0-226-46904-2, ISBN13: 978-0-226-46904-1. Dewey:306.874/2. LCCN:96-025634.
Audience: **l,u,f.** *Choice, 1997.*

McLanahan, Sara & Sandefur, Gary D. **HQ777.4.M39 1994**
Growing up with a Single Parent: What Hurts, What Helps. Trade Cloth. Harvard University Press. Cambridge, MA. 1994. 208p. ISBN:0-674-36407-4, ISBN13: 978-0-674-36407-3. Dewey:306.8/56/0973. LCCN:94-019995.
Audience: **g,l,u.** *Choice, 1995.*

National Center for Health Statistics Staff (Contribution by) **HB1125.C64 2002**
Cohabitation, Marriage, Divorce, and Remarriage in the United States. Trade Cloth. National Center for Health Statistics. Hyattsville, MD. 2002. vii, 93p. Vital and Health Statistics Ser., No. 22 ISBN:0-8406-0582-X, ISBN13: 978-0-8406-0582-5. Dewey:306.81/0973/09049. LCCN:2002-075369.
Audience: **u,f.**

Paul, Pamela **HQ536.P378 2003**
The Starter Marriage and the Future of Matrimony. Trade Paper. Random House Adult Trade Publishing Group. New York, NY. 2003. 320p. ISBN:0-8129-6676-7, ISBN13: 978-0-8129-6676-3. Dewey:306.81. LCCN:2002-026588.
Audience: **l,u.** *Choice, 2002.*

Rogers, Carl Ransom **HQ734.R69 1972**
Becoming Partners. Trade Paper. Dell Publishing. New York, NY. 1973. ISBN:0-385-28070-X, ISBN13: 978-0-385-28070-9. Dewey:301.42/2.
Audience: **g,l.**

Shorter, Edward **GN588**
The Making of the Modern Family. Trade Paper. Basic Books. New York, NY. 1977. 288p. ISBN:0-465-09722-7, ISBN13: 978-0-465-09722-7. Dewey:301.42/1/091812. LCCN:75-007266.
Audience: **l,u,f.**

Winch, Robert F. **HQ728 .W548**
Mate Selection: A Study of Complementary Needs. Library Binding. Irvington Publishers. New York, NY. Reprint Series in Sociology ISBN:0-697-00215-2, ISBN13: 978-0-697-00215-0. Dewey:392.4 301.425*.
Audience: **u,f.**

Family Life > Adulthood > Relationships > Divorce

Cherlin, Andrew J. **HQ535**
Marriage, Divorce, Remarriage. Trade Cloth. Harvard University Press. Cambridge, MA. 1981. 244p. Social Trends in the United States Ser. ISBN:0-674-55080-3, ISBN13: 978-0-674-55080-3. Dewey:306.80973. LCCN:81-002901.
Audience: **l,u,f.**

Chiriboga, David A. & Catron, Linda S. **HQ835.C2C45 1991**
Divorce: Crisis, Challenge or Relief? Cloth Text. New York University Press. New York, NY. 1991. 328p. ISBN:0-8147-1450-1, ISBN13: 978-0-8147-1450-8. Dewey:306.89. LCCN:90-022219.
Audience: **l,u,f.** *Choice, 1992.*

Epstein, Joseph **HQ834.E67**
Divorced in America: Marriage in an Age of Possibility. Trade Paper. Penguin Group (USA) Inc. New York, NY. 1975. ISBN:0-14-004016-1, ISBN13: 978-0-14-004016-6. Dewey:301.42/84/0973.
Audience: **g,l,u,f.**

Furstenberg, Frank F. Jr. & Cherlin, Andrew J. **HQ777.5.F87 1991**
Divided Families: What Happens to Children When Parents Part. Trade Cloth. Harvard University Press. Cambridge, MA. 1991. 152p. The Family and Public Policy Ser., No. 1 ISBN:0-674-65576-1, ISBN13: 978-0-674-65576-8. Dewey:306.8/9/0973. LCCN:90-048171.
Audience: **l,u,f.** *Choice, 1991.*

Goode, William J. **HQ814.G62 1993**
World Changes in Divorce Patterns. Cloth over Boards. Yale University Press. Cumberland, RI. 1993. 360p. ISBN:0-300-05537-4, ISBN13: 978-0-300-05537-5. Dewey:306.89. LCCN:92-044530.
Audience: **u,f.** *Choice, 1994.*

Mason, Mary A. **KF547.M37 1994**
From Father's Property to Children's Rights: The History of Child Custody in the United States. Trade Cloth. Columbia University Press. New York, NY. 1994. 256p. ISBN:0-231-08046-8, ISBN13: 978-0-231-08046-0. Dewey:346.7301/7. LCCN:93-034524.
Audience: **u,f.** *Choice, 1994.*

Phillips, Roderick **HQ811.P48 1988**
Putting Asunder: A History of Divorce in Western Society. Trade Cloth. Cambridge University Press. New York, NY. 1988. 672p. ISBN:0-521-32434-3, ISBN13: 978-0-521-32434-2. Dewey:306.8/9/09. LCCN:88-010867.
Audience: **l,u.** *Choice, 1989.*

Pryor, Jan & Rodgers, Bryan **HQ777.5.C428 2001**
Children in Changing Families: Life after Parental Seperation. Trade Paper. Blackwell Publishing, Inc. Malden, MA. 2001. 344p. Understanding Children's Worlds Ser. ISBN:0-631-21576-X, ISBN13: 978-0-631-21576-9. Dewey:306.874. LCCN:2001-043117.
Audience: **l,u,f.** *Choice, 2002.*

Family Life > Adulthood > Relationships > Re-marriage

Ganong, Lawrence H. & Coleman, Marilyn **HQ759.92.S7294 2004**
Stepfamily Relationships: Development, Dynamics, and Interventions. Trade Cloth. Springer. New York, NY. 2003. 284p. ISBN:0-306-47997-4, ISBN13: 978-0-306-47997-7. Dewey:306.874/7. LCCN:2003-060446.
Audience: **u,f.** *Choice, 2004.*

Family Life > Adulthood > Relationships > Marriage Alternatives

Berger, Bennett M. **HQ971.5.C2B47 2003**
The Survival of a Counterculture: Ideological Work and Everyday Life among Rural Communards. Trade Paper. Transaction Publishers. Somerset, NJ. 2003. 278p. ISBN:0-7658-0805-6, ISBN13: 978-0-7658-0805-9. Dewey:307.77/4. LCCN:2003-053341.
Audience: **u,f.**

Embry, Jessie L. **HQ988**
Mormon Polygamous Families: Life in the Principle. Trade Cloth. Greg Kofford Books, Inc. Draper, UT. 2006. 239p. ISBN:1-58958-098-2, ISBN13: 978-1-58958-098-5. Dewey:306.8/423.
Audience: **g,l,u,f.** *Choice, 1988.*

Garner, Abigail **HQ777.8.G37 2004**
Families Like Mine: Children of Gay Parents Tell It Like It Is. Trade Cloth. HarperCollins Publishers. New York, NY. 2004. 272p. ISBN:0-06-052757-9, ISBN13: 978-0-06-052757-0. Dewey:306.874/086/64. LCCN:2003-056975.
Audience: **g,l.**

Laslett, Peter (Editor), et al. **HQ998.B3**
Bastardy and Its Comparative History: Studies in the History of Illegitimacy and Martial Nonconformism. Karla Oosterveen & Richard M. Smith (Editors). Trade Cloth. Harvard University Press. Cambridge, MA. 1980. 446p. Studies in Social and Demographic History ISBN:0-674-06338-4, ISBN13: 978-0-674-06338-9. Dewey:306.7. LCCN:79-027692.
Audience: **u,f.** B

Metcalf, Bill **HQ971.5.C2**
Shared Visions, Shared Lives: Communal Living Around the Globe. Trade Paper. Findhorn Press. Forres, 1996. 192p. ISBN:1-899171-01-0, ISBN13: 978-1-899171-01-9. Dewey:307.7/74.
Audience: **l,u.**

Miller, Timothy **HQ971.M55 1999**
The 60's Communes: Hippies and Beyond. Trade Cloth. Syracuse University Press. Syracuse, NY. 1999. xxvi, 329p. ISBN:0-8156-2811-0, ISBN13: 978-0-8156-2811-8. Dewey:307.77/4/0973. LCCN:99-037768.
Audience: **l,u,f.** *Choice, 2000.*

Oved, Yaacov **HX653.O84 1988**
Two Hundred Years of American Communes. Hannah Lash (Translator). Trade Cloth. Transaction Publishers. Somerset, NJ. 1987. 516p. ISBN:0-88738-113-8, ISBN13: 978-0-88738-113-3. Dewey:335/.973. LCCN:87-005988.
Audience: **l,u,f.** *Choice, 1989.*

Van Wagoner, Richard S. **BX8641.V36 1989**
Mormon Polygamy: A History. Ed. 2. Trade Paper. Signature Books, LLC. Salt Lake City, UT. 1989. 267p. ISBN:0-941214-79-6, ISBN13: 978-0-941214-79-7. Dewey:289.3. LCCN:89-006222.
Audience: **g,l,u.**

Weston, Kath **HQ76.3.U5W48**
Families We Choose: Lesbians, Gays, Kinship. Ed. 2. Trade Paper. Columbia University Press. New York, NY. 1997. 288p. Between Men, Between Women Ser. ISBN:0-231-11093-6, ISBN13: 978-0-231-11093-8. Dewey:306.87. LCCN:90-049349.
Audience: **g,l,u,f.** *Choice, 1991.*

Zablocki, Benjamin D. **HQ971.Z3**
Alienation and Charisma: A Study of Contemporary American Communes. Trade Cloth. Simon & Schuster. New York, NY. 1980. xxiv, 455p. ISBN:0-02-935780-2, ISBN13: 978-0-02-935780-4. Dewey:307.7. LCCN:79-055938.
Audience: **u,f.** B

Family Life > Aging

Cherlin, Andrew J. & Furstenberg, Frank F. Jr. **HQ734**
The New American Grandparent: A Place in the Family, a Life Apart. Trade Paper. Harvard University Press. Cambridge, MA.

1992. 288p. ISBN:0-674-60838-0, ISBN13: 978-0-674-60838-2. Dewey:306.8/7. LCCN:92-013833.
Audience: **l,u.** *Choice, 1986.*

Lang, Frieder R. & Fingerman, Karen L. **HM1106.G76 2003**
Growing Together: Personal Relationships Across the Life Span. Mary Anne Fitzpatrick, Harry Reis & Anita Vangelista (Contribution by). Trade Cloth. Cambridge University Press. New York, NY. 2003. 430p. Advances in Personal Relationships Ser. ISBN:0-521-81310-7, ISBN13: 978-0-521-81310-5. Dewey:158.2. LCCN:2002-041683.
Audience: **u,f.** *Choice, 2004.*

Lopata, Helena Z. (Editor) **HQ1058.W53 1987**
Widows: North America. Paper Text. Duke University Press. Durham, NC. 1987. xii, 313p. ISBN:0-8223-0770-7, ISBN13: 978-0-8223-0770-9. Dewey:306.8/8. LCCN:87-005410.
Audience: **l,u,f.**

Lopata, Helena Z. (Editor) **HQ1058.W53 1987**
Widows, Vol. I: The Middle East, Asia, and the Pacific. Paper Text. Duke University Press. Durham, NC. 1987. xiii, 258p. ISBN:0-8223-0768-5, ISBN13: 978-0-8223-0768-6. Dewey:306.8/8. LCCN:87-005410.
Audience: **l,u,f.** *Choice, 1988.*

Lopata, Helena Z. **HQ1058 .L66**
Women As Widows: Support Systems. Trade Cloth. Elsevier. New York, NY. 1987. ISBN:0-318-82192-3, ISBN13: 978-0-318-82192-4. Dewey:301.42/86.
Audience: **l,u,f.**

Owen, Margaret **HQ1058.5.D4O94 1996**
A World of Widows. Trade Cloth. Zed Books, Ltd. London, 1996. 240p. ISBN:1-85649-419-5, ISBN13: 978-1-85649-419-9. Dewey:305.4/89654. LCCN:96-016270.
Audience: **l,u,f.** *Choice, 1997.*

Family Life > Aging > Middle Age

Binstock, Robert H. & George, Linda K. (Editors) **HQ1060**
Handbook of Aging and the Social Sciences. Ed. 6. Trade Paper. Elsevier Science & Technology Books. Saint Louis, MO. 2005. 544p. ISBN:0-12-088388-0, ISBN13: 978-0-12-088388-2. Dewey:305.26. LCCN:2005-029192.
Audience: **g,l,u.** *Choice, 2002.*

Farrell, Michael P. & Rosenberg, Stanley **HA1059**
Men at Midlife. Paper Text. Greenwood Publishing Group, Inc. Portsmouth, NH. 1981. 256p. ISBN:0-86569-062-6, ISBN13: 978-0-86569-062-2. Dewey:305.2/44/088041. LCCN:81-003624.
Audience: **g,l,u,f.**

Fontana, Andrea **HQ1061.F59**
The Last Frontier: The Social Meaning of Growing Old. Fred Davis (Preface by). Trade Paper. Books on Demand. Ann Arbor, MI. 1977. 215p. Sage Library of Social Research, Vol. 42 ISBN:0-608-01497-4, ISBN13: 978-0-608-01497-5. Dewey:301.43/5. LCCN:77-023186.
Audience: **l,u.**

Levinson, Daniel J. **BF692.5**
The Seasons of a Man's Life. UK-Trade Paper. Ballantine Books. New York, NY. 1986. 384p. ISBN:0-345-33901-0, ISBN13: 978-0-345-33901-0. Dewey:155.6/32.
Audience: **g.**

Levinson, Daniel J. & Levinson, Judy D. **HQ1206**
The Seasons of a Woman's Life. Trade Cloth. Alfred A. Knopf Inc. New York, NY. 1996. 438p. ISBN:0-614-09477-1, ISBN13: 978-0-614-09477-0. Dewey:155.6/33. LCCN:95-020893.
Audience: **g.**

Stub, Holger R. **HQ1061.S843 1982**
The Social Consequences of Long Life. Trade Paper. Charles C. Thomas Publisher, Ltd. Springfield, IL. 1982. 288p. ISBN:0-398-04723-5, ISBN13: 978-0-398-04723-8. Dewey:305.2/6. LCCN:82-005775.
Audience: **u,f.**

Willis, Sherry (Editor), et al. **BF724.6.L54 1999**
Life in the Middle: Psychological and Social Development in Middle Age. James D. Reid & James B. Reid (Editors). Trade Cloth. Elsevier Science & Technology Books. Saint Louis, MO. 1998. 304p. ISBN:0-12-757230-9, ISBN13: 978-0-12-757230-7. Dewey:155.6/6. LCCN:98-087563.
Audience: **l,u,f.** *Choice, 1999.*

Family Life > Aging > Seniors

Achenbaum, W. Andrew **HQ1064.U5A26**
Old Age in the New Land: The American Experience since 1790. Trade Paper. Books on Demand. Ann Arbor, MI. 251p. ISBN:0-8357-4333-0, ISBN13: 978-0-8357-4333-4. Dewey:301.43/5/0973. LCCN:77-028666.
Audience: **l,u.**

Bosworth, Barry & Burtless, Gary (Editors) **HQ1061.A4845 1998**
Aging Societies: The Global Dimension. Trade Cloth. Brookings Institution Press. Washington, DC. 1998. 236p. ISBN:0-8157-1026-7, ISBN13: 978-0-8157-1026-4. Dewey:305.26. LCCN:98-008944.
Audience: **l,u,f.**

Cole, Thomas R. **HQ1061**
The Journey of Life: A Cultural History of Aging in America. Trade Paper. Cambridge University Press. New York, NY. 1992. 298p. ISBN:0-521-44765-8, ISBN13: 978-0-521-44765-2. Dewey:305.2/6.
Audience: **l,u,f.** *Choice, 1992.*

Costa, Dora L. **HQ1063.2.U6C7 1998**
The Evolution of Retirement: An American Economic History, 1880-1990. Trade Cloth. University of Chicago Press. Chicago, IL. 1998. 248p. National Bureau of Economic Research Long Term Factors in Economic Development Ser. ISBN:0-226-11608-5, ISBN13: 978-0-226-11608-2. Dewey:306.3/8/0973. LCCN:97-029755.
Audience: **u,f.** *Choice, 1998.*

Freidenberg, Judith **HQ1064.U6N463 2000**
Growing Old in El Barrio. Trade Cloth. New York University Press. New York, NY. 2000. 320p. ISBN:0-8147-2702-6,

ISBN13: 978-0-8147-2702-7. Dewey:305.26/09747.
LCCN:00-056001.
Audience: **u,f.** *Choice, 2001.*

Golant, Stephen M. **HQ1064.U6I28 1984**
A Place to Grow Old: The Meaning of Environment in Old Age. Cloth Text. Columbia University Press. New York, NY. 1986. 420p. Studies of Social Gerontology and Aging ISBN:0-231-04840-8, ISBN13: 978-0-231-04840-8. Dewey:305.2/6. LCCN:84-005042.
Audience: **l,u,f.** B

Keith, Jennie **HQ1061**
Old People, New Lives: Community Creation in a Retirement Residence. Trade Paper. University of Chicago Press. Chicago, IL. 1982. 235p. ISBN:0-226-42965-2, ISBN13: 978-0-226-42965-6. Dewey:301.43/5. LCCN:76-008103.
Audience: **l,u.**

Smithers, Janice A. **HQ1063.S595 1985**
Determined Survivors: Community Life among the Urban Elderly. Paper Text. Rutgers University Press. Piscataway, NJ. 1985. 224p. ISBN:0-8135-1080-5, ISBN13: 978-0-8135-1080-4. Dewey:305.2/6/0979494. LCCN:84-017794.
Audience: **l,u,f.** B *Choice, 1985.*

Suzman, Richard M. (Editor), et al. **HQ1064.U5**
The Oldest Old. David P. Willis & Kenneth G. Manton (Editors). Trade Paper. Oxford University Press, Inc. New York, NY. 1995. 456p. ISBN:0-19-509757-2, ISBN13: 978-0-19-509757-3. Dewey:305.26/0973.
Audience: **l,u,f.** *Choice, 1993.*

Teski, Marea **HV1471.C38**
Living Together: An Ethnography of a Retirement Hotel. Trade Cloth. University Press of America, Inc. Lanham, MD. 1979. ISBN:0-8191-0769-7, ISBN13: 978-0-8191-0769-5. Dewey:352.9446098. LCCN:79-088268.
Audience: **l,u,f.** B

Unruh, David R. **HQ1061**
Invisible Lives: Social Worlds of the Aged. Anselm Strauss (Foreword by). Trade Cloth. SAGE Publications, Inc. Thousand Oaks, CA. 1983. 194p. Sociological Observations Ser., Vol. 14 ISBN:0-8039-1954-9, ISBN13: 978-0-8039-1954-9. Dewey:301.43/5. LCCN:82-023116.
Audience: **l,u,f.** B

Family Life > Death/Dying

Ariès, Philippe **HF5386**
Western Attitudes toward Death: From the Middle Ages to the Present. Patricia M. Ranum (Translator). Trade Paper. Johns Hopkins University Press. Baltimore, MD. 1975. 128p. Symposia in Comparative History Ser. ISBN:0-8018-1762-5, ISBN13: 978-0-8018-1762-5. Dewey:301.15/43/1285. LCCN:73-019340.
Audience: **l,u,f.** B

Cantor, Norman F. **RC172.C36 2001**
In the Wake of the Plague: The Black Death and the World It Made. Trade Cloth. Simon & Schuster. New York, NY. 2001. 256p. ISBN:0-684-85735-9, ISBN13: 978-0-684-85735-0. Dewey:614.5/732. LCCN:00-053555.
Audience: **l,u,f.** *Choice, 2001.*

Kubler-Ross, Elisabeth **BF789.D4K8 1997**
On Death and Dying. Trade Cloth. Simon & Schuster. New York, NY. 1997. 288p. Scribner Classics ISBN:0-684-84223-8, ISBN13: 978-0-684-84223-3. Dewey:306.9. LCCN:97-177294.
Audience: **g.** B

Rogers, Richard G., et al. **HB1335.R64 2000**
Living and Dying in the USA: Behavioral, Health, and Social Differentials of Adult Mortality. Robert A. Hummer & Charles B. Nam (Authors). Cloth Text. Elsevier Science & Technology Books. Saint Louis, MO. 1999. 354p. ISBN:0-12-593130-1, ISBN13: 978-0-12-593130-4. Dewey:304.6/4573. LCCN:99-061537.
Audience: **l,u,f.**

Family Life > Family Violence

Gelles, Richard J. (Editor) **HQ809.3.U5G448 1987**
Violent Home. Ed. 2. Trade Paper. SAGE Publications, Inc. Thousand Oaks, CA. 1987. 240p. Sage Library of Social Research, Vol. 13 ISBN:0-8039-3099-2, ISBN13: 978-0-8039-3099-5. Dewey:306.8/72. LCCN:73-094288.
Audience: **l,u.**

Gordon, Linda **HV6626.22.B67G67**
Heroes of Their Own Lives: The Politics and History of Family Violence: Boston, 1880-1960. Trade Paper. University of Illinois Press. Champaign, IL. 2002. 416p. ISBN:0-252-07079-8, ISBN13: 978-0-252-07079-2. Dewey:362.82/92/0974461. LCCN:2002-017124.
Audience: **u,f.**

Graham, Dee L., et al. **HV6250.4.W65G73 1994**
Loving to Survive: Sexual Terror, Men's Violence and Women's Lives. Edna I. Rawlings & Roberta K. Rigsby (Authors). Trade Cloth. New York University Press. New York, NY. 1994. 321p. Feminist Crosscurrents Ser. ISBN:0-8147-3058-2, ISBN13: 978-0-8147-3058-4. Dewey:362.82/92/0973. LCCN:94-003057.
Audience: **l,u,f.** *Choice, 1995.*

Hamon, Raeann & Ingoldsby, Bron (Editors) **HQ801.M236 2003**
Mate Selection Across Cultures. Paper Text. SAGE Publications, Inc. Thousand Oaks, CA. 2003. 312p. ISBN:0-7619-2592-9, ISBN13: 978-0-7619-2592-7. Dewey:646.7/7. LCCN:2003-011938.
Audience: **u,f.** *Choice, 2004.*

Johnson, Ida M. & Sigler, Robert T. **HV6558.J64 1997**
Forced Sexual Intercourse in Intimate Relationships. Trade Cloth. Ashgate Publishing, Ltd. Aldershot, 1997. 200p. ISBN:1-85521-917-4, ISBN13: 978-1-85521-917-5. Dewey:362.883. LCCN:96-048559.
Audience: **u,f.** *Choice, 1997.*

Pleck, Elizabeth Hafkin **HV6626.2.P58 2004**
Domestic Tyranny: The Making of Social Policy Against Family Violence from Colonial Times to the Present. Trade Cloth. University of Illinois Press. Champaign, IL. 2004. 320p. ISBN:0-252-02912-7, ISBN13: 978-0-252-02912-7. Dewey:362.82/92/0973. LCCN:2003-015318.
Audience: **l,u,f.**

Stacey, William A. & Shupe, Anson **HQ536**
The Family Secret: Domestic Violence in America. Trade Paper. Beacon Press. Boston, MA. 1984. 224p. ISBN:0-8070-4145-9, ISBN13: 978-0-8070-4145-1. Dewey:306.8/7/0973. LCCN:82-073965.
Audience: **g,l,u.** B

Straus, Murray A., et al. **HQ809.3.U5**
Behind Closed Doors: Violence in the American Family. Richard J. Gelles & Suzanne K. Steinmetz (Authors). Trade Paper. SAGE Publications, Inc. Thousand Oaks, CA. 1988. 312p. ISBN:0-8039-3292-8, ISBN13: 978-0-8039-3292-0. Dewey:306.87. LCCN:88-001975.
Audience: **l,u,f.**

Walker, Lenore E. **HV6626.2.W33 2000**
The Battered Woman Syndrome. Ed. 2. Trade Cloth. Springer Publishing Company, Inc. New York, NY. 1999. 304p. Springer Series, Focus on Women Ser. ISBN:0-8261-4322-9, ISBN13: 978-0-8261-4322-8. Dewey:362.82/92. LCCN:99-043559.
Audience: **g.**

Websdale, Neil **HV6250.4.W65.W453**
Rural Women Battering and the Justice System: An Ethnography. Trade Paper. SAGE Publications, Inc. Thousand Oaks, CA. 1997. 296p. Violence Against Women Ser. ISBN:0-7619-0852-8, ISBN13: 978-0-7619-0852-4. Dewey:364.15/553/09769. LCCN:2002-102784.
Audience: **u,f.**

Gender/Sexuality

Gauntlett, David **P96.S45G28 2002**
Media Gender and Identity: An Introduction. Paper over Boards. Routledge. New York, NY. 2002. 288p. ISBN:0-415-18959-4, ISBN13: 978-0-415-18959-0. Dewey:305.3. LCCN:2002-068076.
Audience: **l,u.**

Hirschfeld, Magnus **HQ77.H57 1991**
Transvestites: The Erotic Drive to Cross-Dress. Michael A. Lombardi-Nash (Translator), Vern L. Bullough (Foreword by). Trade Cloth. Prometheus Books, Publishers. Amherst, NY. 1991. 424p. ISBN:0-87975-665-9, ISBN13: 978-0-87975-665-9. Dewey:306.77. LCCN:90-024827.
Audience: **l,u,f.**

Gender/Sexuality > Gender Role

Andersen, Margaret **HQ1426.A6825 2005**
Thinking about Women: Sociological Perspectives on Sex and Gender. Ed. 7. Trade Paper. Allyn & Bacon, Inc. Boston, MA. 2005. 480p. ISBN:0-205-45647-2, ISBN13: 978-0-205-45647-5. Dewey:305.42/0973 2. LCCN:2005-046479.
Audience: **l,u,f.**

Barker-Benfield, G. J. **HQ1075.5.U6B37 2000**
Horrors of the Half-known Life: Male Attitudes Toward Women and Sexuality in 19th Century America. Ed. 2. UK-B Format Paperback. Routledge. New York, NY. 1999. 400p. ISBN:0-415-92500-2, ISBN13: 978-0-415-92500-6. Dewey:305.3/0973/09034. LCCN:99-040334.
Audience: **l,u,f.**

Beauvoir, Simone de **HQ1154**
The Second Sex. H. N. Pashley (Editor, Translator), Margaret Crosland (Introduction by). Trade Cloth. Alfred A. Knopf Inc. New York, NY. 1993. 848p. Everyman's Library ISBN:0-679-42016-9, ISBN13: 978-0-679-42016-3. Dewey:305.4/2. LCCN:92-054303.
Audience: **l,u,f.** B

Bourdieu, Pierre **HQ1075.B7213 2001**
Masculine Domination. Cloth Text. Stanford University Press. Palo Alto, CA. 152p. ISBN:0-8047-3818-1, ISBN13: 978-0-8047-3818-7. Dewey:305.3.
Audience: **u,f.**

Cole, Johnnetta B. & Guy-Sheftall, Beverly **E185.86.C58154 2003**
Gender Talk: The Struggle for Women's Equality in African American Communities. Trade Cloth. Ballantine Books. New York, NY. 2003. 336p. ISBN:0-345-45412-X, ISBN13: 978-0-345-45412-6. Dewey:305.48/896073. LCCN:2002-040875.
Audience: **g,l,u.** *Choice, 2003.*

Collins, Patricia Hill **E185.86.C58167 2004**
Black Sexual Politics: African Americans, Gender, and the New Racism. Paper over Boards. Routledge. New York, NY. 2004. 384p. ISBN:0-415-93099-5, ISBN13: 978-0-415-93099-4. Dewey:306.7/089/96073. LCCN:2003-022841.
Audience: **g,l,u,f.** *Choice, 2005.*

Connell, R. W. **HQ1075.C658 2002**
Gender. Trade Paper. Polity Press. Cambridge, 2002. 184p. Short Introductions Ser. ISBN:0-7456-2716-1, ISBN13: 978-0-7456-2716-8. Dewey:305.3/07/2. LCCN:2001-004496.
Audience: **g,l,u,f.**

Connell, R. W. **HQ1088**
Masculinities. Ed. 2. Trade Cloth. Polity Press. Cambridge, 2005. 352p. ISBN:0-7456-3426-5, ISBN13: 978-0-7456-3426-5. Dewey:305.3.
Audience: **l,u,f.**

Delamont, Sara **HQ1190.D44 2003**
Feminist Sociology. Cloth Text. SAGE Publications, Inc. Thousand Oaks, CA. 2003. 216p. BSA Sociological Horizons Ser. ISBN:0-7619-7254-4, ISBN13: 978-0-7619-7254-9. Dewey:305.42/0941. LCCN:2003-544689.
Audience: **l,u,f.**

Ferree, Myra Marx; Lorber, Judith; Hess, Beth B **HQ1190.R483 1998**
Revisioning Gender. Myra Marx Ferree (Editor) ; Judith Lorber (Editor) ; Beth B. Hess (Editor). Sage Publications, Inc. 2000. Gender Lens Ser. ISBN:0-7619-0617-7, ISBN13: 978-0-7619-0617-9.
Audience: **u,f.**

Firestone, Shulamith **HQ1154**
The Dialectic of Sex: The Case for Feminist Revolution. Trade Paper. HarperCollins Publishers. New York, NY. 2004. ISBN:0-688-06454-X, ISBN13: 978-0-688-06454-9. Dewey:301.41/2. LCCN:80-000438.
Audience: **u,f.**

Gauntlett, David **P96.S45G28 2002**
Media Gender and Identity: An Introduction. Trade Paper. Routledge. New York, NY. 2002. 288p. ISBN:0-415-18960-8, ISBN13: 978-0-415-18960-6. Dewey:305.3. LCCN:2002-068076.
Audience: **l,u.**

Hrdy, Sarah Blaffer **HQ759**
Mother Nature: Maternal Instincts and How They Shape the Human Species. UK-Trade Paper. Ballantine Books. New York, NY. 2000. 752p. ISBN:0-345-40893-4, ISBN13: 978-0-345-40893-8. Dewey:306.874/3.
Audience: **l,u,f.**

Hrdy, Sarah Blaffer **QL737.P9H79 1999**
The Woman That Never Evolved: With a New Preface and Bibliographical Updates. Trade Paper. Harvard University Press. Cambridge, MA. 1999. 304p. ISBN:0-674-95539-0, ISBN13: 978-0-674-95539-4. Dewey:599.8/138. LCCN:99-043596.
Audience: **l,u,f.**

Jaggar, Alison M. **HX546**
Feminist Politics and Human Nature. Trade Cloth. Rowman & Littlefield Publishers, Inc. Lanham, MD. 1983. 416p. Philosophy and Society Ser. ISBN:0-8476-7181-X, ISBN13: 978-0-8476-7181-6. Dewey:305.4/2. LCCN:83-003402.
Audience: **u,f.** B

Kimmel, Michael S. **HQ1075**
The Gendered Society: Identities, Behaviors, and Society. Ed. 2. Paper Text. Oxford University Press, Inc. New York, NY. 2005. ISBN:0-19-522145-1, ISBN13: 978-0-19-522145-9. Dewey:305.3.
Audience: **l,u,f.**

Lorde, Audre Geraldine **PS3562.O75S5 1984**
Sister Outsider: Essays and Speeches. Trade Cloth. Crossing Press, Incorporated, The. Berkeley, CA. 1984. 192p. Feminist Ser. ISBN:0-89594-141-4, ISBN13: 978-0-89594-141-1. Dewey:814/.54. LCCN:84-001844.
Audience: **g,l,u,f.**

Meyerowitz, Joanne **HQ77**
How Sex Changed: A History of Transsexuality in the United States. Trade Cloth. Harvard University Press. Cambridge, MA. 2002. 400p. ISBN:0-674-00925-8, ISBN13: 978-0-674-00925-7. Dewey:306.77. LCCN:2002-020536.
Audience: **g,l,u,f.** *Choice, 2003.*

Montagu, Ashley **HQ1206.M65 1999**
The Natural Superiority of Women. Ed. 5. Trade Cloth. AltaMira Press. Walnut Creek, CA. 1999. 300p. ISBN:0-7619-8981-1, ISBN13: 978-0-7619-8981-3. Dewey:305.4. LCCN:98-040173.
Audience: **g,l,u,f.**

Nagl-Docekal, Herta & Vester, Katharina **HQ1190.N34 2004**
Feminist Philosophy. Alison Jaggar (Foreword by). Trade Paper. Westview Press. Boulder, CO. 2004. 272p. Feminist Theory and Politics Ser. ISBN:0-8133-6571-6, ISBN13: 978-0-8133-6571-8. Dewey:305.42/01. LCCN:2003-023536.
Audience: **l,u,f.** *Choice, 2004.*

Oyewumi, Oyeronke (Editor) **HQ1075.5.A35A376**
African Gender Studies. Cloth over Boards. Palgrave Macmillan. New York, NY. 2005. 448p. ISBN:1-4039-6282-0, ISBN13: 978-1-4039-6282-9. Dewey:305.3/096. LCCN:2004-054696.
Audience: **l,u,f.**

Pease, Bob & Pringle, Keith (Editors) **HQ1090.D42 2001**
A Man's World?: Changing Men's Practices in a Globalized World. Cloth over Boards. Zed Books, Ltd. London, 2002. 304p. Global Masculinities Ser. ISBN:1-85649-911-1, ISBN13: 978-1-85649-911-8. Dewey:305.31. LCCN:2001-026236.
Audience: **l,u,f.** *Choice, 2003, 2002.*

Roughgarden, Joan **QH541.15.B56 R68**
Evolution's Rainbow: Diversity, Gender, and Sexuality in Nature and People. Trade Cloth. University of California Press. Berkeley, CA. 2004. 472p. ISBN:0-520-24073-1, ISBN13: 978-0-520-24073-5. Dewey:305.3. LCCN:2003-024512.
Audience: **g,l,u,f.** *Choice, 2004.*

Rudacille, Deborah **HQ77.95.U6R83 2005**
The Riddle of Gender: Science, Activism, and Transgender Rights. Trade Cloth. Knopf Publishing Group. New York, NY. 2005. 384p. ISBN:0-375-42162-9, ISBN13: 978-0-375-42162-4. Dewey:306.76/8. LCCN:2004-055297.
Audience: **u,f.** *Choice, 2006.*

Sanday, Peggy Reeves **HQ1075 .S26**
Female Power and Male Dominance: On the Origins of Sexual Inequality. Trade Paper. Cambridge University Press. New York, NY. 1981. 368p. ISBN:0-521-28075-3, ISBN13: 978-0-521-28075-4. Dewey:305.3/0880633. LCCN:80-018461.
Audience: **u,f.**

Smith, Dorothy E. **HQ1190**
The Conceptual Practices of Power: A Feminist Sociology of Knowledge. Cloth Text. Northeastern University Press. Boston, MA. 1990. 224p. Series in Feminist Theory ISBN:1-55553-072-9, ISBN13: 978-1-55553-072-3. Dewey:305.42/01.
Audience: **u,f.**

Wallace, Ruth A. (Editor) **HM13.F46 1989**
Feminism and Sociological Theory. Trade Paper. SAGE Publications, Inc. Thousand Oaks, CA. 1989. 216p. Key Issues in Sociological Theory Ser., Vol. 4 ISBN:0-8039-3398-3, ISBN13: 978-0-8039-3398-9. Dewey:301/.01. LCCN:89-010201.
Audience: **u,f.**

Wollstonecraft, Mary **HQ1596.W6 2003**
A Vindication of the Rights of Woman: With Strictures on Political and Moral Subjects. Trade Paper. Quiet Vision Publishing. Sandy, UT. 2004. ISBN:1-57646-811-9, ISBN13: 978-1-57646-811-1. Dewey:305.4094 Wol.
Audience: **u,f.**

Gender/Sexuality > Gender Role > Men

Adams, Rachel & Savran, David (Editors) **HQ1088.M377 2001**
The Masculinity Studies Reader. Trade Paper. Blackwell Publishing, Inc. Malden, MA. 2002. 432p. Keyworks in Cultural Studies, Vol. 5 ISBN:0-631-22660-5, ISBN13: 978-0-631-22660-4. Dewey:305.31. LCCN:2001-043229.
Audience: **g,l,u,f.**

Basso, Matthew (Editor), et al. **HQ1090.5.W4A37 2001**
Across the Great Divide: Cultures of Manhood in the American West. Laura McCall & Dee Garceau (Editors). Paper over Boards. Routledge. New York, NY. 2001. 304p. ISBN:0-415-92470-7, ISBN13: 978-0-415-92470-2. Dewey:305.31/0978. LCCN:00-042206.
Audience: **u,f.**

Bly, Robert **HQ1090.3.B59 2004**
Iron John: A Book about Men. Paper Text. Da Capo Press, Inc. Cambridge, MA. 2004. 288p. ISBN:0-306-81376-9, ISBN13: 978-0-306-81376-4. Dewey:305.31. LCCN:2004-056137.
Audience: **g,l.** *Choice, 1991.*

Coltrane, Scott **HQ503.C65**
Family Man: Fatherhood, Housework, and Gender Equity. Trade Paper. Oxford University Press, Inc. New York, NY. 1997. 304p. ISBN:0-19-511909-6, ISBN13: 978-0-19-511909-1. Dewey:306.85.
Audience: **l,u,f.** *Choice, 1996.*

Connell, R. W. **HQ1088 .C66 2005**
Masculinities. Ed. 2. Trade Paper. University of California Press. Berkeley, CA. 2005. 349p. ISBN:0-520-24698-5, ISBN13: 978-0-520-24698-0. Dewey:305.3. LCCN:2005-050590.
Audience: **g,l,u,f.**

Connor, Marlene K. **E185.86.C584 2003**
What Is Cool?: Understanding Black Manhood in America. Trade Paper. Agate Publishing, Inc. Evanston, IL. 2003. 210p. ISBN:0-9724562-3-6, ISBN13: 978-0-9724562-3-4. Dewey:305.38/896073. LCCN:2003-015996.
Audience: **g.**

Fine, Gary Alan **GV880.5**
With the Boys: Little League Baseball and Preadolescent Culture. Trade Paper. University of Chicago Press. Chicago, IL. 1987. 304p. ISBN:0-226-24937-9, ISBN13: 978-0-226-24937-7. Dewey:796.357/62. LCCN:86-016056.
Audience: **l,u.** *Choice, 1987.*

Gardiner, Judith Kegan **HQ1088.M375 2001**
Masculinity Studies and Feminist Theory. Trade Cloth. Columbia University Press. New York, NY. 2001. 336p. ISBN:0-231-12278-0, ISBN13: 978-0-231-12278-8. Dewey:305.31/07. LCCN:2001-047017.
Audience: **u,f.** *Choice, 2002.*

Kimmel, Michael S. **HQ1090.3.K552 2005**
The History of Men: Essays on the History of American and British Masculinities. Cloth Text. State University of New York Press. Albany, NY. 2005. 276p. ISBN:0-7914-6339-7, ISBN13: 978-0-7914-6339-0. Dewey:305.31/0973. LCCN:2004-060670.
Audience: **u,f.**

Kimmel, Michael S. **HQ1090.3.K553 2005**
Manhood in America. Ed. 2. Trade Paper. Oxford University Press, Inc. New York, NY. 2005. 352p. ISBN:0-19-518113-1, ISBN13: 978-0-19-518113-5. Dewey:305.31/0973. LCCN:2005-047346.
Audience: **g,l,u,f.**

McMahon, Anthony **HQ1090.3 .M383 1999**
Taking Care of Men: Sexual Politics in the Public Mind. Trade Cloth. Cambridge University Press. New York, NY. 1999. 240p. ISBN:0-521-58204-0, ISBN13: 978-0-521-58204-9. Dewey:305.31/0973. LCCN:99-025156.
Audience: **u,f.** *Choice, 2000.*

Messner, Michael A. **GV709**
Power at Play: Sports and the Problem of Masculinity. Trade Paper. Beacon Press. Boston, MA. 1995. 256p. ISBN:0-8070-4105-X, ISBN13: 978-0-8070-4105-5. Dewey:796/.0194.
Audience: **u,f.** *Choice, 1992.*

Messner, Michael A. **GV706.32.M47 2003**
Taking the Field: Women, Men and Sports. Trade Paper. University of Minnesota Press. Minneapolis, MN. 2002. 280p. Sport and Culture Ser., Vol. 4 ISBN:0-8166-3449-1, ISBN13: 978-0-8166-3449-1. Dewey:796/.082. LCCN:2001-008548.
Audience: **g,l,u,f.** *Choice, 2003.*

Rotundo, E. Anthony **HQ1090.3.R69 1993**
American Manhood: Transformations in Masculinity from the Revolution to the Modern Era. Trade Cloth. Basic Books. New York, NY. 1993. 400p. ISBN:0-465-01409-7, ISBN13: 978-0-465-01409-5. Dewey:305.32/0973. LCCN:92-053247.
Audience: **g,l,u,f.** *Choice, 1993.*

Sykes, Bryan **QH600.5.S98 2004**
Adam's Curse: A Future Without Men. Trade Cloth. W. W. Norton & Company, Inc. New York, NY. 2004. 320p. ISBN:0-393-05896-4, ISBN13: 978-0-393-05896-3. Dewey:305.3101576. LCCN:2004-003628.
Audience: **g,l,u,f.** *Choice, 2004.*

Tuana, Nancy (Editor), et al. **HQ1090.R455 2001**
Revealing Male Bodies. William Cowling, Maurice Hamington, Greg Johnson & Terrance MacMullan (Editors). Paper Text. Indiana University Press. Bloomington, IN. 2002. 352p. ISBN:0-253-21481-5, ISBN13: 978-0-253-21481-2. Dewey:305.31. LCCN:2001-004647.
Audience: **u,f.** *Choice, 2003.*

Gender/Sexuality > Gender Role > Women

Katzenstein, Mary F. **HQ1421.K27 1998**
Faithful and Fearless: Moving Feminist Protest Inside the Church and Military. Trade Cloth. Princeton University Press. Princeton, NJ. 1998. 284p. Princeton Studies in American

Politics ISBN:0-691-05852-0, ISBN13: 978-0-691-05852-8. Dewey:305.42/0973. LCCN:98-005516.
Audience: **l,u,f.** *Choice, 1999.*

Lorber, Judith **HQ1075.L667**
Paradoxes of Gender. Trade Paper. Yale University Press. Cumberland, RI. 1995. 435p. ISBN:0-300-06497-7, ISBN13: 978-0-300-06497-1. Dewey:305.3. LCCN:93-023459.
Audience: **l,u,f.** *Choice, 1994.*

Sigel, Roberta S. **HQ1075.5.U6S56 1996**
Ambition and Accommodation: How Women View Gender Relations. Trade Cloth. University of Chicago Press. Chicago, IL. 1996. 250p. ISBN:0-226-75695-5, ISBN13: 978-0-226-75695-0. Dewey:305.3. LCCN:95-039468.
Audience: **l,u,f.** *Choice, 1996.*

Gender/Sexuality > Gender Role > Transgender

Bloom, Amy **HQ77.95.U6**
Normal: Transexual CEOs, Crossdressing Cops and Hermaphrodites with Attitude. Trade Paper. Knopf Publishing Group. New York, NY. 2003. 176p. ISBN:1-4000-3244-X, ISBN13: 978-1-4000-3244-0. Dewey:306.77.
Audience: **g,l.**

Califia, Patrick **HQ77.9**
Sex Changes: Transgender Politics. Trade Cloth. Cleis Press. San Francisco, CA. 2003. 250p. ISBN:1-57344-164-3, ISBN13: 978-1-57344-164-3. Dewey:305.9/066.
Audience: **g,l.**

Dreger, Alice Domurat **RC883.D695 1998**
Hermaphrodites and the Medical Invention of Sex. Trade Cloth. Harvard University Press. Cambridge, MA. 1998. 286p. ISBN:0-674-08927-8, ISBN13: 978-0-674-08927-3. Dewey:616.694. LCCN:97-040487.
Audience: **l,u,f.** *Choice, 1998.*

Nanda, Serena **HQ449.N36 1998**
Neither Man nor Woman: The Hijras of India. Ed. 2. Paper Text. Thomson Wadsworth. Belmont, CA. 1998. 208p. Anthropology Ser. ISBN:0-534-50903-7, ISBN13: 978-0-534-50903-3. Dewey:305.3. LCCN:98-041187.
Audience: **l,u,f.** *Choice, 1990.*

Roscoe, Will (Editor) **E98.S48R67 1998**
Changing Ones: Third and Fourth Genders in Native North America. Trade Cloth. Palgrave Macmillan. New York, NY. 1998. 334p. ISBN:0-312-17539-6, ISBN13: 978-0-312-17539-9. Dewey:305.308997. LCCN:97-041762.
Audience: **g,l,u,f.** *Choice, 1998.*

Roughgarden, Joan **QH541.15.B56 R68**
Evolution's Rainbow: Diversity, Gender, and Sexuality in Nature and People. Trade Paper. University of California Press. Berkeley, CA. 2005. 474p. ISBN:0-520-24679-9, ISBN13: 978-0-520-24679-9. Dewey:305.3. LCCN:2003-024512.
Audience: **g,l,u,f.** *Choice, 2004.*

Gender/Sexuality > Gender Role > Gender Variant

Kulick, Don **HQ77.2.B7K85 1998**
Travesti: Sex, Gender, and Culture among Brazilian Transgendered Prostitutes. Trade Cloth. University of Chicago Press. Chicago, IL. 1998. 277p. Worlds of Desire Ser., :The Chicago Series on Sexuality, Gender, and Culture Ser. ISBN:0-226-46099-1, ISBN13: 978-0-226-46099-4. Dewey:306.77. LCCN:98-015319.
Audience: **u,f.** *Choice, 1999.*

Queen, Carol **HQ76.25.P66 1997**
PoMoSexuals: Challenging Assumptions about Gender and Sexuality. Schimel Queen (Editor). Trade Paper. Cleis Press. San Francisco, CA. 1997. 180p. ISBN:1-57344-074-4, ISBN13: 978-1-57344-074-5. Dewey:306.76/6. LCCN:97-037703.
Audience: **g,l,u.**

Gender/Sexuality > Sexuality

Allen, Peter Lewis **RA418**
The Wages of Sin: Sex and Disease, Past and Present. Trade Paper. University of Chicago Press. Chicago, IL. 2002. 226p. ISBN:0-226-01461-4, ISBN13: 978-0-226-01461-6. Dewey:306.4/61. LCCN:99-048603.
Audience: **l,u,f.** *Choice, 2000.*

Allyn, David **HQ18.U5A38 2000**
Make Love, Not War: The Sexual Revolution: an Unfettered History. Trade Cloth. Little Brown & Company. New York, NY. 2000. 400p. ISBN:0-316-03930-6, ISBN13: 978-0-316-03930-7. Dewey:306.70973. LCCN:99-033784.
Audience: **g.** *Choice, 2000.*

Altman, Dennis **HQ16.A38 2002**
Global Sex. Trade Paper. University of Chicago Press. Chicago, IL. 2002. 192p. ISBN:0-226-01605-6, ISBN13: 978-0-226-01605-4. Dewey:306.7.
Audience: **g,f.** *Choice, 2001.*

Archer, John & Lloyd, Barbara B. (Editors) **BF692.2 .A72 2002**
Sex and Gender. Ed. 2. Cloth Text. Cambridge University Press. New York, NY. 2002. 294p. ISBN:0-521-63230-7, ISBN13: 978-0-521-63230-0. Dewey:155.33. LCCN:2001-052482.
Audience: **l.** *Choice, 1986.*

Bancroft, John (Editor) **BF723.S4S47 2003**
Sexual Development in Childhood. Trade Cloth. Indiana University Press. Bloomington, IN. 2003. 456p. The Kinsey Institute Ser., Vol. 7 ISBN:0-253-34243-0, ISBN13: 978-0-253-34243-0. Dewey:306.7/083. LCCN:2003-001814.
Audience: **l,u,f.** *Choice, 2004.*

Bullough, Vern L. **HQ71**
Sexual Variance in Society and History. Library Binding. University of Chicago Press. Chicago, IL. 1980. xvii, 715p. ISBN:0-226-07995-3, ISBN13: 978-0-226-07995-0. Dewey:301.41/5/09. LCCN:79-026504.
Audience: **l,u,f.** B

Bullough, Vern L. & Brundage, James A. (Editors) **HQ12**
Sexual Practices and the Medieval Church. Trade Paper. Prometheus Books, Publishers. Amherst, NY. 1982. 301p.

ISBN:0-87975-268-8, ISBN13: 978-0-87975-268-2. Dewey:261.8/3577/0902. LCCN:80-085227.
Audience: **u,f.** *B*

Burstyn, Varda (Editor) **HQ471.W66 1985**
Women Against Censorship. Trade Paper. Salem House Publishers. Scranton, PA. 1985. 210p. ISBN:0-88894-455-1, ISBN13: 978-0-88894-455-9. Dewey:363.4/7. LCCN:85-098057.
Audience: **l,u,f.** *B* *Choice, 1985.*

Butler, Anne M. **HQ144**
Daughters of Joy, Sisters of Misery: Prostitutes in the American West, 1865-90. Trade Paper. University of Illinois Press. Champaign, IL. 1987. 232p. ISBN:0-252-01466-9, ISBN13: 978-0-252-01466-6. Dewey:306.7/42/0978. LCCN:84-000195.
Audience: **u,f.** *B* *Choice, 1985.*

Chafetz, Janet S. **HQ21.C449 1984**
Sex and Advantage: A Comparative, Macro-Structural Theory of Sex Stratification. Book, Other. Rowman & Littlefield Publishers, Inc. Lanham, MD. 1984. 142p. ISBN:0-86598-159-0, ISBN13: 978-0-86598-159-1. Dewey:305.4/2. LCCN:83-019077.
Audience: **u,f.** *B*

Crompton, Louis **HQ76.25.C76 2003**
Homosexuality and Civilization. Trade Cloth. Harvard University Press. Cambridge, MA. 2003. 648p. ISBN:0-674-01197-X, ISBN13: 978-0-674-01197-7. Dewey:306.76/6/09. LCCN:2003-045327.
Audience: **g,l,f.** *Choice, 2004.*

Daynes, Kathryn M. **BX8641.D39 2001**
More Wives Than One: Transformation of the Mormon Marriage System, 1840-1910. Trade Cloth. University of Illinois Press. Champaign, IL. 2001. 328p. ISBN:0-252-02681-0, ISBN13: 978-0-252-02681-2. Dewey:306.84/23/088283. LCCN:2001-000826.
Audience: **l,u,f.** *Choice, 2002.*

Dworkin, Andrea **HQ471**
Pornography: Men Possessing Women. Trade Paper. Penguin Group (USA) Inc. New York, NY. 1991. 336p. ISBN:0-452-26793-5, ISBN13: 978-0-452-26793-0. Dewey:363.4/7.
Audience: **l,u,f.** *B*

Ellis, Havelock **HQ21**
Studies in the Psychology of Sex: Sexual Selection in Man. Trade Paper. University Press of the Pacific. Miami, FL. 2001. 284p. ISBN:0-89875-584-0, ISBN13: 978-0-89875-584-8. Dewey:155.3.
Audience: **u,f.**

Ellis, Havelock **HQ21.E58**
Studies in the Psychology of Sex: The Evolution of Modesty - the Phenomena of Sexual Periodicity - Auto-Erotism. Trade Paper. University Press of the Pacific. Miami, FL. 2001. 292p. ISBN:0-89875-599-9, ISBN13: 978-0-89875-599-2. Dewey:155.3.
Audience: **u,f.**

Ellis, Havelock **HQ21**
Studies in the Psychology of Sex: Erotic Symbolism - the Mechanism of Detumescence - the Psychic State in Pregnancy. Trade Paper. University Press of the Pacific. Miami, FL. 2001. 296p. ISBN:0-89875-592-1, ISBN13: 978-0-89875-592-3. Dewey:155.3.
Audience: **u,f.**

Ellis, Havelock **HQ21**
Studies in the Psychology of Sex: Sexual Inversion. Ed. 2. Trade Paper. University Press of the Pacific. Miami, FL. 2001. 288p. ISBN:0-89875-601-4, ISBN13: 978-0-89875-601-2. Dewey:155.3.
Audience: **u,f.**

Ellis, Havelock **HQ21.E58**
Studies in the Psychology of Sex: Analysis of the Sexual Impulse - Love and Pain - the Sexual Impulse in Women. Trade Paper. University Press of the Pacific. Miami, FL. 2001. 280p. ISBN:0-89875-588-3, ISBN13: 978-0-89875-588-6. Dewey:155.3.
Audience: **u,f.**

Fausto-Sterling, Anne **HQ1075.F39 2000**
Sexing the Body: Gender Politics and the Construction of Sexuality. Trade Paper. Basic Books. New York, NY. 2000. 496p. ISBN:0-465-07714-5, ISBN13: 978-0-465-07714-4. Dewey:305.3. LCCN:00-703212.
Audience: **u,f.** *Choice, 2000.*

Firestone, Shulamith **HQ1190**
The Dialectic of Sex: The Case for Feminist Revolution. Trade Paper. Farrar, Straus & Giroux. New York, NY. 2003. 240p. ISBN:0-374-52787-3, ISBN13: 978-0-374-52787-7. Dewey:301.41/2.
Audience: **u,f.**

Flowers, R. Barri **HV1431**
Runaway Kids and Teenage Prostitution: America's Lost, Abandoned, and Sexually Exploited Children. Trade Cloth. Greenwood Publishing Group, Inc. Portsmouth, NH. 2001. 232p. Contributions in Criminology and Penology Ser., Vol. 54 ISBN:0-313-31492-6, ISBN13: 978-0-313-31492-6. Dewey:362.74. LCCN:00-069131.
Audience: **g,u.** *Choice, 2002.*

Foucault, Michel **HQ12.F6813 1980**
The History of Sexuality: The Use of Pleasure, Vol. 2. Trade Paper. Knopf Publishing Group. New York, NY. 1990. 304p. ISBN:0-394-75122-1, ISBN13: 978-0-394-75122-1. Dewey:306.7. LCCN:79-007460.
Audience: **u,f.**

Foucault, Michel **HQ12**
The History of Sexuality: The Care of the Self, Vol. 3. Trade Paper. Knopf Publishing Group. New York, NY. 1988. 288p. ISBN:0-394-74155-2, ISBN13: 978-0-394-74155-0. Dewey:306.7.
Audience: **u,f.**

Foucault, Michel **HQ16**
A History of Sexuality: An Introduction, Vol. 1. Trade Paper. Knopf Publishing Group. New York, NY. 1990. 176p. ISBN:0-679-72469-9, ISBN13: 978-0-679-72469-8. Dewey:306.7/091821. LCCN:79-007460.
Audience: **u,f.**

Francoeur, Robert T. (Editor), et al. **HQ21.I68 2003**
The Continuum Complete International Encyclopedia of Sexuality. Raymond J. Noonan & Martha Cornog (Editors). Trade Cloth. Continuum International Publishing Group, Ltd. London, 2003. 1450p. ISBN:0-8264-1488-5, ISBN13: 978-0-8264-1488-5. Dewey:306.7/03. LCCN:2003-006391.
Audience: **g,l,u,f.** *Choice, 2004.*

Freud, Sigmund **HQ21.F813 2000**
Three Essays on the Theory of Sexuality. Trade Paper. Basic Books. New York, NY. 2000. 192p. Basic Books Classics ISBN:0-465-09708-1, ISBN13: 978-0-465-09708-1. Dewey:306.7/01. LCCN:00-267325.
Audience: **g,l,u,f.** BCL3

Gubar, Susan & Hoff, Joan (Editors) **HQ471.F67 1989**
For Adult Users Only: The Dilemma of Violent Pornography. Trade Cloth. Indiana University Press. Bloomington, IN. 1989. 256p. Everywoman, :Studies in History, Literature and Culture ISBN:0-253-32365-7, ISBN13: 978-0-253-32365-1. Dewey:363.4/7/0973. LCCN:88-045499.
Audience: **l,u,f.** *Choice, 1989.*

Haggerty, George (Editor) **HQ75.13.G37 2000**
Gay Histories and Cultures. Trade Cloth. Garland Publishing, Inc. New York, NY. 1999. 800p. Special - Reference Ser. ISBN:0-8153-1880-4, ISBN13: 978-0-8153-1880-4. Dewey:306.76/6/03. LCCN:99-040905.
Audience: **g.** *Choice, 2000.*

Hirschfeld, Magnus **HQ76.25.H5813 2000**
The Homosexuality of Men and Women. Michael A. Lombardi-Nash (Translator), Vern L. Bullough (Introduction by). Trade Cloth. Prometheus Books, Publishers. Amherst, NY. 1999. 1200p. ISBN:1-57392-705-8, ISBN13: 978-1-57392-705-5. Dewey:306.76/6. LCCN:99-026829.
Audience: **l,u,f.** *Choice, 2001.*

Institute for Sex Research Staff, et al. **HQ29.S487 1998**
Sexual Behavior in the Human Female. Alfred C. Kinsey, Wardell B. Pomeroy, Clyde E. Martin & Paul H. Gebhard (Authors). Trade Cloth. Indiana University Press. Bloomington, IN. 1998. 872p. ISBN:0-253-33411-X, ISBN13: 978-0-253-33411-4. Dewey:306.7/082. LCCN:98-017888.
Audience: **g,l,u,f.**

Kinsey, Alfred C., et al. **HQ28.K55 1998**
Sexual Behavior in the Human Male. Wardell B. Pomeroy & Clyde E. Martin (Authors). Trade Cloth. Indiana University Press. Bloomington, IN. 1998. 830p. ISBN:0-253-33412-8, ISBN13: 978-0-253-33412-1. Dewey:306.7/081. LCCN:98-017912.
Audience: **g,l,u,f.** BCL3

Laumann, Edward O. (Editor), et al. **HQ18.U5S495 2004**
The Sexual Organization of the City. Stephen Ellingson, Jenna Mahay, Anthony Paik & Yoosik Youm (Editors). Trade Cloth. University of Chicago Press. Chicago, IL. 2004. 435p. ISBN:0-226-47031-8, ISBN13: 978-0-226-47031-3. Dewey:306.7/09773/11. LCCN:2003-017586.
Audience: **l,u,f.** *Choice, 2004.*

Laumann, Edward O., et al. **HQ18.U5**
The Social Organization of Sexuality: Sexual Practices in the United States. John H. Gagnon, Robert T. Michael & Stuart Michaels (Authors). Trade Paper. University of Chicago Press. Chicago, IL. 2000. 750p. ISBN:0-226-47020-2, ISBN13: 978-0-226-47020-7. Dewey:306.7/0973.
Audience: **l,u,f.** *Choice, 1995.*

Lederer, Laura (Editor) **HQ471**
Take Back the Night: Women on Pornography. Adrienne Rich (Afterword by). Trade Paper. HarperCollins Publishers. New York, NY. 1980. 352p. ISBN:0-688-08728-0, ISBN13: 978-0-688-08728-9. Dewey:363.4/7. LCCN:80-023701.
Audience: **g,l.** BCL3

Malamuth, Neil M. & Donnerstein, Edward **HQ471.P646 1984**
Pornography and Sexual Aggression. Trade Cloth. Elsevier Science & Technology Books. Saint Louis, MO. 1984. 333p. ISBN:0-12-466280-3, ISBN13: 978-0-12-466280-3. Dewey:363.4/7. LCCN:84-003086.
Audience: **l,u,f.** BCL3

Masters, William H., et al. **HQ21.M46157 1995**
Human Sexuality. Ed. 5. Virginia E. Johnson & Robert C. Kolodny (Authors). Cloth Text. Allyn & Bacon, Inc. Boston, MA. 1997. 769p. ISBN:0-673-46785-6, ISBN13: 978-0-673-46785-0. Dewey:306.7. LCCN:94-036210.
Audience: **g,l,u,f.** BCL3

Mead, Margaret **HQ21.M464 2001**
Male and Female: The Classic Study of the Sexes. Trade Paper. HarperCollins Publishers. New York, NY. 2001. 496p. ISBN:0-06-093496-4, ISBN13: 978-0-06-093496-5. Dewey:305.3. LCCN:2001-278683.
Audience: **l,u,f.**

Murray, Stephen O. **HQ76.3.N67M87 1996**
American Gay. Trade Cloth. University of Chicago Press. Chicago, IL. 1996. 345p. Worlds of Desire Ser. ISBN:0-226-55191-1, ISBN13: 978-0-226-55191-3. Dewey:306.76/6/097. LCCN:95-049388.
Audience: **u,f.** *Choice, 1996.*

Oosterhuis, Harry **HQ71.O57 2000**
Stepchildren of Nature: Krafft-Ebing, Psychiatry, and the Making of Sexual Identity. Trade Cloth. University of Chicago Press. Chicago, IL. 2000. 304p. Chicago Series on Sexuality, History and Society ISBN:0-226-63059-5, ISBN13: 978-0-226-63059-5. Dewey:616.85/83/009034. LCCN:00-023399.
Audience: **u,f.** *Choice, 2001.*

Renold, Emma **HQ784.S45R46 2005**
Girls, Boys and Junior Sexualities: Exploring Childrens' Gender and Sexual Relations in the Primary School. Paper over Boards. Routledge. New York, NY. 2005. 224p. ISBN:0-415-31496-8, ISBN13: 978-0-415-31496-1. Dewey:306.7/083/4. LCCN:2004-015900.
Audience: **l,u,f.**

Stengers, Jean & Van Neck, Anne **HQ447.S75 2001**
Masturbation: The History of a Great Terror. Kathryn A. Hoffmann (Translator). Cloth over Boards. Palgrave Macmillan. New York, NY. 2001. 240p. ISBN:0-312-22443-5, ISBN13: 978-0-312-22443-1. Dewey:306.77/2/09. LCCN:2001-019450.
Audience: **g.** *Choice, 2002.*

Strossen, Nadine **HQ472.U6S87 2000**
Defending Pornography. Ed. 2. Trade Paper. New York University Press. New York, NY. 2000. 384p. ISBN:0-8147-8149-7, ISBN13: 978-0-8147-8149-4. Dewey:363.4/7. LCCN:00-036067.
Audience: **g,l,u.**

Thomas, William I. **HQ21 .T5**
Sex and Society. Trade Cloth. AltaMira Press. Walnut Creek, CA. 2002. 300p. ISBN:0-7591-0390-9, ISBN13: 978-0-7591-0390-0. Dewey:301.41/7.
Audience: **l,u,f.**

Van Wagoner, Richard S. **BX8641.V36 1989**
Mormon Polygamy: A History. Ed. 2. Trade Paper. Signature Books, LLC. Salt Lake City, UT. 1989. 267p. ISBN:0-941214-79-6, ISBN13: 978-0-941214-79-7. Dewey:289.3. LCCN:89-006222.
Audience: **g,l,u.**

Vance, Carole S. **BV4817 .W413 1979**
Pleasure and Danger: Exploring Female Sexuality. Trade Paper. Routledge. New York, NY. 1990. xix, 169p. ISBN:0-7100-0248-3, ISBN13: 978-0-7100-0248-8. Dewey:248. LCCN:79-314678.
Audience: **l,u,f.**

Viney, Ethna **HQ1075.V55 1996**
Dancing to Different Tunes: Sexuality and Its Misconceptions. Trade Cloth. Blackstaff Press, The. 1997. 318p. ISBN:0-85640-570-1, ISBN13: 978-0-85640-570-9. Dewey:305.3. LCCN:97-102970.
Audience: **u,f.** *Choice, 1997.*

Von Krafft-Ebing, Richard **HQ71.K91213 1999**
Psychopathia Sexualis: A Clinical-Forensic Study. Brian King (Editor). Trade Paper. Bloat. Burbank, CA. 1998. xlv, 683p. ISBN:0-9650324-1-8, ISBN13: 978-0-9650324-1-4. Dewey:616.85/83. LCCN:00-265138.
Audience: **u,f.**

Walkowitz, Judith R. **HQ185.A5**
Prostitution and Victorian Society: Women, Class, and the State. Trade Paper. Cambridge University Press. New York, NY. 1982. 368p. ISBN:0-521-27064-2, ISBN13: 978-0-521-27064-9. Dewey:301.4154. LCCN:79-021050.
Audience: **u,f.**

Weeks, Jeffrey **HQ18.G7W43 1989**
Sex, Politics and Society: The Regulation of Sexuality since 1800. Ed. 2. Trade Paper. Pearson Education. Boston, MA. 1989. 336p. Themes in British Social History Ser. ISBN:0-582-02383-1, ISBN13: 978-0-582-02383-3. Dewey:306.7/0941. LCCN:88-013197.
Audience: **l,u,f.**

West, D. J. **HQ117**
Male Prostitution. Buz de Villiers (Contribution by). Trade Cloth. Haworth Press, Incorporated, The. Binghamton, NY. 1993. 358p. Gay and Lesbian Studies ISBN:1-56023-022-3, ISBN13: 978-1-56023-022-9. Dewey:306.74/3. LCCN:92-040327.
Audience: **l,u,f.** *Choice, 1993.*

Williams, Linda **HQ471.P59 2004**
Porn Studies. Trade Cloth. Duke University Press. Durham, NC. 2004. 520p. ISBN:0-8223-3300-7, ISBN13: 978-0-8223-3300-5. Dewey:363.4/7. LCCN:2003-025389.
Audience: **l,u,f.** *Choice, 2004.*

Wittig, Monique **HQ1190.W58 1992**
The Straight Mind and Other Essays. Trade Paper. Beacon Press. Boston, MA. 1992. 128p. ISBN:0-8070-7917-0, ISBN13: 978-0-8070-7917-1. Dewey:305.42. LCCN:91-018409.
Audience: **g,u,f.**

Wolfson, Nicholas **KF4772**
Hate Speech, Sex Speech, Free Speech. Trade Cloth. Greenwood Publishing Group, Inc. Portsmouth, NH. 1997. 184p. ISBN:0-275-95770-5, ISBN13: 978-0-275-95770-4. Dewey:342.73/0853. LCCN:96-044680.
Audience: **l,u,f.** *Choice, 1997.*

Zimmerman, Bonnie (Editor) **HQ75.5.L4395 2000**
Lesbian Histories and Cultures. Trade Cloth. Garland Publishing, Inc. New York, NY. 1999. 800p. Special - Reference Ser., Vol. 1 ISBN:0-8153-1920-7, ISBN13: 978-0-8153-1920-7. Dewey:306.76/63/03. LCCN:99-045010.
Audience: **g,l,u,f.** *Choice, 2000.*

Gender/Sexuality > Sexuality > Gay Males

Bullough, Vern L. **HQ76.25.B84**
Homosexuality: A History. Trade Paper. Penguin Group (USA) Inc. New York, NY. 1979. ISBN:0-452-00725-9, ISBN13: 978-0-452-00725-3. Dewey:306.7/6/09.
Audience: **g,l,u.**

D'Emilio, John **HQ76.8.U5**
Sexual Politics, Sexual Communities. Ed. 2. Trade Paper. University of Chicago Press. Chicago, IL. 1998. 286p. ISBN:0-226-14267-1, ISBN13: 978-0-226-14267-8. Dewey:305.9/0664. LCCN:98-024148.
Audience: **l,u,f.**

Dilley, Patrick **HQ76.2.U5D55 2002**
Queer Man on Campus: A History of Non-Heterosexual College Men 1945-2000. Paper over Boards. Routledge. New York, NY. 2002. 256p. ISBN:0-415-93336-6, ISBN13: 978-0-415-93336-0. Dewey:378.1/9826/642. LCCN:2002-031728.
Audience: **g,l,u.**

Downs, Alan **HQ76.D69 2005**
The Velvet Rage: Overcoming the Pain of Growing up Gay in a Straight Man's World. Trade Cloth. Da Capo Press, Inc. Cambridge, MA. 2005. 224p. ISBN:0-7382-1011-0, ISBN13: 978-0-7382-1011-7. Dewey:306.76620973. LCCN:2005-004606.
Audience: **g,l,u.**

Harry, Joseph & Devall, William B. **HQ76.3.U5**
The Social Organization of Gay Males. Trade Cloth. Greenwood Publishing Group, Inc. Portsmouth, NH. 1978. Praeger Special Studies ISBN:0-275-90296-X, ISBN13: 978-0-275-90296-4. Dewey:301.41/57/0973. LCCN:78-008381.
Audience: **u,f.**

Tejirian, Edward J. **HQ1090.T453 2000**
Male to Male: Sexual Feelings Across the Boundaries of Identity. Trade Cloth. Haworth Press, Incorporated, The. Binghamton, NY. 2000. xix, 382p. ISBN:1-56023-975-1, ISBN13: 978-1-56023-975-8. Dewey:305.31. LCCN:00-027137.
Audience: **u,f.**

Gender/Sexuality > Sexuality > Lesbians

Blackwood, Evelyn & Wieringa, Saskia **HQ75.5.F43 1999**
Female Desires: Same-Sex Relations and Transgender Practices Across Cultures. Trade Cloth. Columbia University Press. New York, NY. 1999. 352p. Between Men, Between Women Ser. ISBN:0-231-11260-2, ISBN13: 978-0-231-11260-4. Dewey:306.76/6. LCCN:98-037847.
Audience: **u,f.**

Boston Lesbian Psychologies Collective Staff (Editor) **HQ75.5.L445 1987**
Lesbian Psychologies: Explorations and Challenges. Trade Paper. University of Illinois Press. Champaign, IL. 1987. 384p. ISBN:0-252-01404-9, ISBN13: 978-0-252-01404-8. Dewey:306.7/663. LCCN:86-030736.
Audience: **l,u,f.** *Choice, 1988.*

Faderman, Lillian **HQ75.5.F33 1998**
Surpassing the Love of Men: Romantic Friendship and Love Between Women from the Renaissance to the Present. Trade Paper. HarperCollins Publishers. New York, NY. 1998. 496p. ISBN:0-688-13330-4, ISBN13: 978-0-688-13330-6. Dewey:306.76/63/09. LCCN:99-160164.
Audience: **g,l.** B

Kitzinger, Celia **HQ75.5.K58 1987**
The Social Construction of Lesbianism. Trade Cloth. SAGE Publications, Ltd. London, 1988. 240p. Inquiries in Social Construction Ser., Vol. 1 ISBN:0-8039-8116-3, ISBN13: 978-0-8039-8116-4. Dewey:306.7/663. LCCN:87-062029.
Audience: **u,f.** *Choice, 1988.*

Wilton, Tamsin **HQ29.W55 2004**
Sexual (Dis)Orientation: Gender, Sex, Desire and Self-Fashioning. Cloth over Boards. Palgrave Macmillan. New York, NY. 2004. 240p. ISBN:1-4039-0572-X, ISBN13: 978-1-4039-0572-7. Dewey:305.3. LCCN:2004-043790.
Audience: **u,f.**

Gender/Sexuality > Sexuality > Bisexuality

Haeberle, Erwin J. & Gindorf, Rolf (Editors) **HQ74.B575 1998**
Bisexualities: The Ideology and Practice of Sexual Contact with Both Males and Females. Trade Cloth. Continuum International Publishing Group, Ltd. London, 1997. 266p. ISBN:0-8264-0923-7, ISBN13: 978-0-8264-0923-2. Dewey:306.76/5. LCCN:96-040051.
Audience: **u,f.**

King, J. L. & Hunter, Karen **HQ74.2.U5K56 2004**
On the down Low: A Journey into the Lives of "Straight" Black Men Who Sleep with Men. Trade Paper. Broadway Books. New York, NY. 2005. 208p. ISBN:0-7679-1399-X, ISBN13: 978-0-7679-1399-7. Dewey:305.38/896073. LCCN:2003-056006.
Audience: **g,l.**

Rust, Paula C. **HQ75.6.U5R87 1995**
Bisexuality and the Challenge to Lesbian Politics: Sex, Loyalty, and Revolution. Trade Cloth. New York University Press. New York, NY. 1995. 387p. The Cutting Edge: Lesbian Life and Literature Ser. ISBN:0-8147-7444-X, ISBN13: 978-0-8147-7444-1. Dewey:305.48/9664. LCCN:95-031419.
Audience: **u,f.**

Storr, Merl **HQ74.B577 1999**
Bisexuality: A Critical Reader. Paper over Boards. Routledge. New York, NY. 1999. 256p. ISBN:0-415-16659-4, ISBN13: 978-0-415-16659-1. Dewey:306.76/5. LCCN:98-042140.
Audience: **g,u,f.**

Social Problems

Barak, Gregg **HN90.V5B37 2003**
Violence and Nonviolence: Pathways to Understanding. Cloth Text. SAGE Publications, Inc. Thousand Oaks, CA. 2003. 360p. ISBN:0-7619-2695-X, ISBN13: 978-0-7619-2695-5. Dewey:303.6. LCCN:2002-155653.
Audience: **g,l,u.**

Blau, Joel **HV4505**
The Visible Poor: Homelessness in the United States. Trade Cloth. Replica Books. Bridgewater, NJ. 2000. 247p. ISBN:0-7351-0316-X, ISBN13: 978-0-7351-0316-0. Dewey:362.5/0973.
Audience: **g,l,u.** *Choice, 1992.*

Dordick, Gwendolyn A. **HV4506.N6D67 1997**
Something Left to Lose: Personal Relations and Survival Among New York's Homeless. Trade Cloth. Temple University Press. Philadelphia, PA. 1997. 224p. ISBN:1-56639-513-5, ISBN13: 978-1-56639-513-7. Dewey:305.5/69. LCCN:96-025094.
Audience: **u,f.** *Choice, 1997.*

Etzioni, Amitai **HN65**
Social Problems. Paper Text. Prentice Hall PTR. Upper Saddle River, NJ. 1976. 192p. Foundations of Modern Sociology Ser. ISBN:0-13-817403-2, ISBN13: 978-0-13-817403-3. Dewey:309.1/73/092. LCCN:75-038703.
Audience: **g,l,u,f.** B

Huxley, Aldous **HN17.H84**
Ends and Means: An Inquiry into the Nature of Ideals and into the Methods Employed for Their Realization. Library Binding. Buccaneer Books, Inc. Cutchogue, NY. 1991. 396p. ISBN:0-89966-846-1, ISBN13: 978-0-89966-846-8. Dewey:301.
Audience: **l,u,f.** B

Jencks, Christopher **HV4505**
The Homeless. Trade Paper. Harvard University Press. Cambridge, MA. 1995. 176p. ISBN:0-674-40596-X, ISBN13: 978-0-674-40596-7. Dewey:362.5/0973. LCCN:93-046424.
Audience: **g,l,u,f.** *Choice, 1994.*

Morton, Margaret **HV4506.N6M67 1995**
The Tunnel: The Underground Homeless of New York City. Cloth over Boards. Yale University Press. Cumberland, RI. 1995. 160p. The Architecture of Despair Ser. ISBN:0-300-06538-8, ISBN13: 978-0-300-06538-1. Dewey:305.5/68/097471. LCCN:95-004894.
Audience: **l,u,f.**

Sinclair, Upton **HN5.C79 1996**
Cry for Justice: An Anthology of the Literature of Social Protest. Ed. 2. Trade Paper. Barricade Books, Inc. Fort Lee, NJ. 1996. 656p. ISBN:1-56980-069-3, ISBN13: 978-1-56980-069-0. Dewey:303.3/72. LCCN:95-051076.
Audience: **g,l.** B

Snow, David A. & Anderson, Leon **HV4505.S66**
Down on Their Luck: A Study of Homeless Street People. Trade Paper. University of California Press. Berkeley, CA. 1993. 406p. ISBN:0-520-07989-2, ISBN13: 978-0-520-07989-2. Dewey:362.50973. LCCN:91-043980.
Audience: **l,u,f.** *Choice, 1993.*

Vollmann, William T. **HM1116.V65 2004**
Rising Up and Rising Down: Some Thoughts on Violence, Freedom, and Urgent Means. Trade Cloth. HarperCollins Publishers. New York, NY. 2004. 752p. ISBN:0-06-054818-5, ISBN13: 978-0-06-054818-6. Dewey:303.6. LCCN:2004-053243.
Audience: **g,l,u,f.**

Whalen, Mollie **HV1445.W43 1996**
Counseling to End Violence Against Women: A Subversive Model. Trade Cloth. SAGE Publications, Inc. Thousand Oaks, CA. 1996. 184p. ISBN:0-8039-7379-9, ISBN13: 978-0-8039-7379-4. Dewey:361.3/23. LCCN:95-050177.
Audience: **l,u.** *Choice, 1996.*

Wright, James D., et al. **HV4505.W76 1998**
Beside the Golden Door: Policy, Politics, and the Homeless. Beth A. Rubin & Joel A. Devine (Authors). Trade Cloth. Aldine Transaction. Somerset, NJ. 1998. 238p. Social Institutions and Social Change Ser. ISBN:0-202-30613-5, ISBN13: 978-0-202-30613-1. Dewey:363.5/96942/0973. LCCN:97-052031.
Audience: **l,u,f.** *Choice, 1998.*

Social Problems > Gerontology

Angel, Ronald J. **HV1461 .A68**
Who Will Care for Us?: Aging and Long-Term Care in a Multicultural America. Trade Paper. New York University Press. New York, NY. 1999. 240p. ISBN:0-8147-0683-5, ISBN13: 978-0-8147-0683-1. Dewey:362.6.
Audience: **u,f.**

Bull, C. Neil **HQ1064.U5.A63457**
Aging in Rural America. Trade Cloth. SAGE Publications, Inc. Thousand Oaks, CA. 1993. 296p. Focus Editions Ser., Vol. 162 ISBN:0-8039-4885-9, ISBN13: 978-0-8039-4885-3. Dewey:305.26/0973. LCCN:93-025528.
Audience: **l,u.** *Choice, 1994.*

Schulz, Richard **HQ1061.E53 2006**
Encyclopedia of Aging. Ed. 4. Trade Cloth. Springer. New York, NY. 2006. ISBN:0-8261-4843-3, ISBN13: 978-0-8261-4843-8. Dewey:305.2603. LCCN:2006-003769.
Audience: **g,l,u.**

Social Problems > Criminology

HV6248.R57.M6413
I, Pierre Riviere, Having Slaughtered My Mother, My Sister, and My Brother. Trade Cloth. Pantheon Books. New York, NY. 1975. xiv, 288p. ISBN:0-394-49310-9, ISBN13: 978-0-394-49310-7. Dewey:364.1/523/0924. LCCN:74-026205.
Audience: **l,u,f.** B

Archer, Dane & Gartner, Rosemary **HV6241**
Violence and Crime in Cross-National Perspective. Trade Paper. Yale University Press. Cumberland, RI. 1987. 342p. ISBN:0-300-04023-7, ISBN13: 978-0-300-04023-4. Dewey:364.10904. LCCN:83-021700.
Audience: **u,f.** B

Berrill, Kevin T. (Author, Editor) **HV6250.4.H66H38 1992**
Hate Crimes: Confronting Violence Against Lesbians and Gay Men. Gregory M. Herek (Editor). Trade Paper. SAGE Publications, Inc. Thousand Oaks, CA. 1991. 328p. ISBN:0-8039-4542-6, ISBN13: 978-0-8039-4542-5. Dewey:364.15508664. LCCN:91-034912.
Audience: **l,u,f.** *Choice, 1992.*

Block, Alan A. **HV6446 .B57 1990**
Organizing Crime: Essays in Opposition. Trade Cloth. Springer. New York, NY. 1990. 254p. ISBN:0-7923-1033-0, ISBN13: 978-0-7923-1033-4. Dewey:364.1/06/0973. LCCN:90-019152.
Audience: **u,f.**

Blok, Anton **HV6453.I83**
The Mafia of a Sicilian Village, 1860-1960: A Study of Violent Peasant Entrepreneurs. Charles Tilly (Foreword by). Paper Text. Waveland Press, Inc. Prospect Heights, IL. 1988. 293p. ISBN:0-88133-325-5, ISBN13: 978-0-88133-325-1. Dewey:364.1/06/04582.
Audience: **l,u,f.** B

Brownmiller, Susan **HV6558**
Against Our Will: Men, Women and Rape. Trade Cloth. Martin Secker & Warburg, Ltd. London, 1975. 480p. ISBN:0-436-07108-8, ISBN13: 978-0-436-07108-9. Dewey:364.1/53.
Audience: **g,l.**

Cohen, Stanley **HV6028.C55 1988**
Against Criminology. Trade Cloth. Transaction Publishers. Somerset, NJ. 1988. 352p. ISBN:0-88738-153-7, ISBN13: 978-0-88738-153-9. Dewey:364. LCCN:87-016237.
Audience: **l,u,f.**

Davis, Angela **HV9471 .D38**
If They Come in the Morning: Voices of Resistance. Julian Bond (Foreword by). Trade Cloth. Okpaku Communications Corporation. New Rochelle, NY. 1971. 256p. ISBN:0-89388-022-1, ISBN13: 978-0-89388-022-4. Dewey:365/.45. LCCN:71-169154.
Audience: **l,u,f.** B

Dressler, Joshua (Editor) **HV6017.E52 2002**
Encyclopedia of Crime and Justice, Set. Ed. 2. Thomson Gale Staff (Contribution by). Trade Cloth. Thomson Gale. Farmington Hills, MI. 2001. 1780p. ISBN:0-02-865319-X, ISBN13: 978-0-02-865319-8. Dewey:364/.03. LCCN:2001-042707.
Audience: **g,l,u.** *Choice, 2002.*

Elias, Robert **HV8688**
Victims of the System: Crime Victims and Compensation in American Politics and Criminal Justice. Trade Cloth. Transaction Publishers. Somerset, NJ. 1984. 325p. ISBN:0-87855-470-X, ISBN13: 978-0-87855-470-6. Dewey:362.8/8. LCCN:83-000383.
Audience: **l,u.** B

Garland, David **HV9950.G36 2001**
The Culture of Control: Crime and Social Order in Contemporary Society. Trade Cloth. University of Chicago Press. Chicago, IL. 2001. 336p. ISBN:0-226-28383-6, ISBN13: 978-0-226-28383-8. Dewey:364.9/73. LCCN:00-051209.
Audience: **u,f.** *Choice, 2002.*

Hogg, Russell & Carrington, Kerry (Editors) **HV6019.C75 2002**
Critical Criminology: Issues, Debates, Challenges. Trade Cloth. Willan Publishing. Devon, 2002. 286p. ISBN:1-903240-69-7, ISBN13: 978-1-903240-69-4. Dewey:364. LCCN:2002-437456.
Audience: **l,u.** *Choice, 2003.*

Jones, Ann **HV6046.J66 1996**
Women Who Kill: With Previously Unpublished Material on the "Battered Women's Syndrome". Trade Paper. Beacon Press. Boston, MA. 1996. 464p. ISBN:0-8070-6775-X, ISBN13: 978-0-8070-6775-8. Dewey:364.1/523/082. LCCN:95-046961.
Audience: **l,u,f.**

Lombroso-Ferrero, Gina & Savitz, Leonard D. **HV6045.L83 1972**
Criminal Man: According to the Classification of Cesare Lombroso. Library Binding. Patterson Smith Publishing Corporation. Montclair, NJ. 1972. 395p. Criminology, Law Enforcement, and Social Problems Ser., No. 134 ISBN:0-87585-134-7, ISBN13: 978-0-87585-134-1. Dewey:364.1. LCCN:70-129338.
Audience: **u,f.** B

Pollak, Otto **HV6046**
The Criminality of Women. Trade Cloth. Greenwood Publishing Group, Inc. Portsmouth, NH. 1978. 180p. ISBN:0-8371-9869-0, ISBN13: 978-0-8371-9869-9. Dewey:364.3/74. LCCN:77-013959.
Audience: **l,u,f.** B

Radzinowicz, Leon **HV6025.R37**
Ideology and Crime: A Study of Crime in Its Social and Historical Context. Trade Cloth. Columbia University Press. New York, NY. 1966. James S. Carpentier Lecture Ser ISBN:0-231-02926-8, ISBN13: 978-0-231-02926-1. Dewey:364. LCCN:66-015724.
Audience: **l,u,f.**

Schechter, Susan **HV6250.4.W65**
Women and Male Violence: The Visions and Struggles of the Battered Women's Movement. Trade Cloth. South End Press. Cambridge, MA. 1982. 370p. Women's Studies ISBN:0-89608-160-5, ISBN13: 978-0-89608-160-4. Dewey:362.88. LCCN:82-061150.
Audience: **l,u,f.** B

Stanko, Elizabeth A. **HV6250.4.W65S73 1984**
Intimate Intrusions. Trade Paper. Routledge. New York, NY. 1986. x, 211p. ISBN:0-7102-0069-2, ISBN13: 978-0-7102-0069-3. Dewey:362.8/8. LCCN:84-009765.
Audience: **l,u,f.** B

Thomas, William I. **HV6046.T4 1969**
Unadjusted Girl, with Cases and Standpoint for Behavior Analysis. W. Dummer (Foreword by). Trade Cloth. Patterson Smith Publishing Corporation. Montclair, NJ. 1969. xvii, 261p. Criminology, Law Enforcement, and Social Problems Ser., No. 26 ISBN:0-87585-026-X, ISBN13: 978-0-87585-026-9. Dewey:364.36/4. LCCN:69-014951.
Audience: **u,f.** B

Thrasher, Frederic M. **HV6439.U52C57 2000**
The Gang: A Study of 1,313 Gangs in Chicago. Paper Text. New Chicago School Press, Inc. Peotone, IL. 2000. 239p. ISBN:0-9665155-5-2, ISBN13: 978-0-9665155-5-8. Dewey:364.1/06/60977311. LCCN:00-133629.
Audience: **u,f.** B

Watts, Meredith **HV9069.C76 1998**
Cross-Cultural Perspectives on Youth and Violence. Trade Cloth. Elsevier Science & Technology Books. Saint Louis, MO. 1998. 272p. Contemporary Studies in Sociology Ser., Vol. 18 ISBN:0-7623-0501-0, ISBN13: 978-0-7623-0501-8. Dewey:364.36/0973. LCCN:98-040313.
Audience: **l,u,f.**

Wells-Barnett, Ida B. **HV6457.W393 2002**
On Lynchings. Patricia Hill Collins (Introduction by). Trade Paper. Prometheus Books, Publishers. Amherst, NY. 2004. 202p. Classics in Black Studies ISBN:1-59102-008-5, ISBN13: 978-1-59102-008-0. Dewey:364.1/34. LCCN:2002-020554.
Audience: **g,l,u.**

Whyte, William F. **HV6446.W49 1993**
Street Corner Society: The Social Structure of an Italian Slum. Ed. 4. Trade Paper. University of Chicago Press. Chicago, IL. 1993. 418p. ISBN:0-226-89545-9, ISBN13: 978-0-226-89545-1. Dewey:302.340974461. LCCN:92-042262.
Audience: **l,u,f.**

Social Problems > Criminology > Prisons

Barnes, Harry E. **HV8497.B3 1972**
Story of Punishment: A Record of Man's Inhumanity to Man. Ed. 2. Trade Cloth. Patterson Smith Publishing Corporation. Montclair, NJ. 1972. xv, 292p. Criminology, Law Enforcement, and Social Problems Ser., No. 112 ISBN:0-87585-112-6, ISBN13: 978-0-87585-112-9. Dewey:364.6. LCCN:74-108229.
Audience: **g,l,u,f.** B

Christianson, Scott **HV9471**
With Liberty for Some: 500 Years of Imprisonment in America. Trade Paper. Northeastern University Press. Boston, MA. 2000. 416p. ISBN:1-55553-468-6, ISBN13: 978-1-55553-468-4. Dewey:365/.973. LCCN:98-023541.
Audience: **l,u,f.** *Choice, 1999.*

Foucault, Michel **HV8666.F6813 1995**
Discipline and Punish: The Birth of the Prison. Ed. 2. Trade Paper. Alfred A. Knopf Inc. New York, NY. 1995. 352p. ISBN:0-679-75255-2, ISBN13: 978-0-679-75255-4. Dewey:365.6/43. LCCN:95-203580.
Audience: **u,f.**

Ignatieff, Michael **HV9644.I36 1978**
A Just Measure of Pain: The Penitentiary in the Industrial Revolution, 1750-1850. Trade Cloth. Knopf Publishing Group. New York, NY. 1978. xiii, 257p. ISBN:0-394-41041-6, ISBN13: 978-0-394-41041-8. Dewey:365/.942. LCCN:78-051808.
Audience: **u,f.** B

Mauer, Marc **HV9950.M32 2006**
Race to Incarcerate. Sentencing Project (U.S.) Staff (Contribution by). Trade Paper. New Press, The. New York, NY. 2006. 256p. ISBN:1-59558-022-0, ISBN13: 978-1-59558-022-1. Dewey:364.6/0973. LCCN:2005-054376.
Audience: **g,l,u,f.**

Petersilia, Joan **HV9304**
When Prisoners Come Home: Parole and Prisoner Reentry. Trade Cloth. Oxford University Press, Inc. New York, NY. 2003. 288p. Studies in Crime and Public Policy ISBN:0-19-516086-X, ISBN13: 978-0-19-516086-4. Dewey:364.8/0973. LCCN:2002-011531.
Audience: **l,u,f.** *Choice, 2003.*

Pfeifer, Michael J. **HV6457.P44 2004**
Rough Justice: Lynching and American Society, 1874-1947. Trade Cloth. University of Illinois Press. Champaign, IL. 2004. 256p. ISBN:0-252-02917-8, ISBN13: 978-0-252-02917-2. Dewey:364.1/34. LCCN:2003-022987.
Audience: **l,u,f.** *Choice, 2005.*

Rude, George **HV8950.A8.R83**
Protest and Punishment: The Story of the Social and Political Protesters Transported to Australia, 1788-1868. Trade Cloth. Oxford University Press, Inc. New York, NY. 1978. 282p. ISBN:0-19-822430-3, ISBN13: 978-0-19-822430-3. Dewey:365/.3. LCCN:77-030539.
Audience: **u,f.** B

Solzhenitsyn, Aleksandr **HV9713.S6413 2002**
The Gulag Archipelago, 1918-1956. Trade Paper. HarperCollins Publishers. New York, NY. 2002. 512p. Perennial Classics Ser. ISBN:0-06-000776-1, ISBN13: 978-0-06-000776-8. Dewey:365/.45/0947. LCCN:2001-046504.
Audience: **g,l,u,f.**

Zimring, Franklin E. & Hawkins, Gordon **HV 9471.Z55 1997**
Incapacitation: Penal Confinement and the Restraint of Crime. Trade Paper. Oxford University Press, Inc. New York, NY. 1997. 202p. Studies in Crime and Public Policy ISBN:0-19-511583-X, ISBN13: 978-0-19-511583-3. Dewey:364.6.
Audience: **l,u,f.**

Social Problems > Criminology > Juvenile Delinquency

Alexander, Ruth M. **HV9105.N7A67 1995**
The Girl Problem: Female Sexual Delinquency in New York, 1900-1930. Book, Other. Cornell University Press. Ithaca, NY. 1995. 232p. ISBN:0-8014-2821-1, ISBN13: 978-0-8014-2821-0. Dewey:364.3/6/082. LCCN:94-047525.
Audience: **u,f.** *Choice, 1996.*

Donaldson, Greg **HN80.B87D66 1993**
The Ville: Cops and Kids in Urban America. Trade Cloth. Houghton Mifflin Company. New York, NY. 1993. 401p. ISBN:0-395-63315-X, ISBN13: 978-0-395-63315-1. Dewey:306/.097477/1. LCCN:93-026119.
Audience: **l,u,f.** *Choice, 1994.*

Hagedorn, John M. **HV6437**
Gangresearch.net.
http://www.gangresearch.net/
John M. Hagedorn.
Audience: **g,l,u,f.**

Laub, John H. & Sampson, Robert J. **HV9069.L28 2003**
Shared Beginnings, Divergent Lives: Delinquent Boys to Age 70. Trade Cloth. Harvard University Press. Cambridge, MA. 2003. 352p. ISBN:0-674-01191-0, ISBN13: 978-0-674-01191-5. Dewey:364.36/0973. LCCN:2003-050944.
Audience: **u,f.** *Choice, 2004.*

Muehlbauer, Gene **HV9104.M82 1983**
The Losers: Gang Delinquency in an American Suburb. Trade Cloth. Greenwood Publishing Group, Inc. Portsmouth, NH. 1983. xii, 138p. ISBN:0-03-060313-7, ISBN13: 978-0-03-060313-6. Dewey:364.3/6/0973. LCCN:82-025497.
Audience: **l,u,f.** B

Petersilia, Joan **HV9304**
When Prisoners Come Home: Parole and Prisoner Reentry. Trade Cloth. Oxford University Press, Inc. New York, NY. 2003. 288p. Studies in Crime and Public Policy ISBN:0-19-516086-X, ISBN13: 978-0-19-516086-4. Dewey:364.8/0973. LCCN:2002-011531.
Audience: **l,u,f.** *Choice, 2003.*

Richards, Pamela, et al. **HV9104.R52 1979**
Crime As Play: Delinquency in a Middle Class Suburb. Richard A. Berk & Brenda Forster (Authors). Trade Cloth. HarperCollins Publishers. New York, NY. 1979. 280p. ISBN:0-88410-798-1, ISBN13: 978-0-88410-798-9. Dewey:364.36. LCCN:79-012772.
Audience: **u,f.** B

Sato, Ikuya **HV6491.J3S29 1991**
Kamikaze Biker: Parody and Anomy in Affluent Japan. Gerald D. Suttles (Foreword by). Trade Cloth. University of Chicago Press. Chicago, IL. 1991. 296p. ISBN:0-226-73525-7, ISBN13: 978-0-226-73525-2. Dewey:364.1/06/0952. LCCN:90-048610.
Audience: **u,f.** *Choice, 1992.*

Tienda, Marta & Wilson, William Julius (Editors) **HQ796.Y5935 2002**
Youth in Cities: A Cross-National Perspective. Trade Cloth. Cambridge University Press. New York, NY. 2002. 302p. The Jacobs Foundation Series on Adolescence ISBN:0-521-80908-8, ISBN13: 978-0-521-80908-5. Dewey:305.235/09173/2. LCCN:2002-073750.
Audience: **l,u,f.**

Wolfgang, Marvin E., et al. **HV9106.P5**
Delinquency in a Birth Cohort. Robert M. Figlio & Thorsten D. Sellin (Authors), Norval Morris (Foreword by). Trade Paper. University of Chicago Press. Chicago, IL. 1987. 338p. Studies in Crime and Justice ISBN:0-226-90558-6, ISBN13: 978-0-226-90558-7. Dewey:364.36/09748/11. LCCN:75-187929.
Audience: **u,f.** B

Social Problems > Criminology > Victimology

Best, Joel **HV6789.B47 1998**
Random Violence: Worrying about New Crimes and New Victims. Trade Paper. University of California Press. Berkeley, CA. 1999. 260p. ISBN:0-520-21572-9, ISBN13: 978-0-520-21572-6. Dewey:364.973. LCCN:98-006234.
Audience: **l,u,f.** *Choice, 1999.*

Weed, Frank J. **HV6250.3.U5W44 1995**
Certainty of Justice: Reform in the Crime Victim Movement. Trade Cloth. Aldine Transaction. Somerset, NJ. 1995. 158p. Social Problems and Social Issues Ser. ISBN:0-202-30517-1, ISBN13: 978-0-202-30517-2. Dewey:362.88. LCCN:95-005658.
Audience: **u,f.** *Choice, 1996.*

Westervelt, Saundra D. **HV6250.25.W47 1999**
Shifting the Blame: How Victimization Became a Criminal Defense. Cloth Text. Rutgers University Press. Piscataway, NJ. 1999. 256p. ISBN:0-8135-2583-7, ISBN13: 978-0-8135-2583-9. Dewey:362.88. LCCN:98-015629.
Audience: **g,l,u,f.** *Choice, 1999.*

Social Problems > Criminology > Victimology > Restorative Justice

Acorn, Annalise E. **HV8688.A25 2004**
Compulsory Compassion: A Critique of Restorative Justice. Trade Cloth. University of British Columbia Press. Vancouver, BC. 2004. 224p. ISBN:0-7748-0942-6, ISBN13: 978-0-7748-0942-9. Dewey:345/.001. LCCN:2004-426310.
Audience: **l,u.** *Choice, 2004.*

Pavlich, George **HV6001-7220.5**
Governing Paradoxes of Restorative Justice. Trade Paper. Taylor & Francis Group. Abingdon, 2005. 300p. ISBN:1-904385-19-2, ISBN13: 978-1-904385-19-6. Dewey:364.6'8. LCCN:2006-271868.
Audience: **u,f.** *Choice, 2006.*

Strang, Heather **HV8688.S77 2004**
Repair or Revenge?: Victims and Restorative Justice. Trade Paper. Oxford University Press, Inc. New York, NY. 2004. 318p. Clarendon Studies in Criminology ISBN:0-19-927429-0, ISBN13: 978-0-19-927429-1. Dewey:344/.03288.
Audience: **u,f.**

Social Problems > Social Welfare Programs

Albelda, Randy Pearl & Withorn, Ann (Editors) **HV95.L73 2002**
Lost Ground: Welfare Reform, Poverty, and Beyond. Barbara Ehrenreich (Introduction by). Trade Cloth. South End Press. Cambridge, MA. 2002. 300p. Sociology Ser. ISBN:0-89608-659-3, ISBN13: 978-0-89608-659-3. Dewey:361.6/0973. LCCN:2002-021757.
Audience: **l,u,f.**

Bane, Mary J. & Ellwood, David T. **HV699.B36 1994**
Welfare Realities: From Rhetoric to Reform. Trade Cloth. Harvard University Press. Cambridge, MA. 1994. 238p. ISBN:0-674-94912-9, ISBN13: 978-0-674-94912-6. Dewey:362.5/82/0973. LCCN:93-045029.
Audience: **l,u,f.** *Choice, 1994.*

Berkowitz, Edward D. **HD7125.B38 1991**
America's Welfare State: From Roosevelt to Reagan. Trade Cloth. Johns Hopkins University Press. Baltimore, MD. 1991. 240p. The American Moment Ser. ISBN:0-8018-4127-5, ISBN13: 978-0-8018-4127-9. Dewey:361.973. LCCN:90-046424.
Audience: **l,u,f.** *Choice, 1991.*

Blank, Rebecca M. **HV95.B59 1996**
It Takes a Nation: A New Agenda for Fighting Poverty. Cloth Text. Princeton University Press. Princeton, NJ. 1996. 372p. ISBN:0-691-02675-0, ISBN13: 978-0-691-02675-6. Dewey:362.5/8/0973. LCCN:96-008671.
Audience: **l,u,f.** *Choice, 1998.*

Gans, Herbert J. **HV91**
War Against the Poor: The Underclass and Antipoverty Policy. Trade Paper. Basic Books. New York, NY. 1996. 208p. ISBN:0-465-01991-9, ISBN13: 978-0-465-01991-5. Dewey:362.58.
Audience: **g,l,u.**

Gordon, Linda **HV699**
Pitied but Not Entitled: Single Mothers and the History of Welfare. Trade Paper. Harvard University Press. Cambridge, MA. 1998. 448p. ISBN:0-674-66982-7, ISBN13: 978-0-674-66982-6. Dewey:362.8/294/8/0973.
Audience: **l,u.** *Choice, 1995.*

Gordon, Linda (Editor) **HV95.W66 1990**
Women, the State, and Welfare. Paper Text. University of Wisconsin Press. Chicago, IL. 1991. 328p. ISBN:0-299-12664-1, ISBN13: 978-0-299-12664-3. Dewey:362.83/0973. LCCN:90-050089.
Audience: **l,u,f.** *Choice, 1991.*

Herrick, John & Stuart, Paul H. (Editors) **HV12.E497 2005**
Encyclopedia of Social Welfare History in North America. Trade Cloth. SAGE Publications, Inc. Thousand Oaks, CA. 2004. 560p. ISBN:0-7619-2584-8, ISBN13: 978-0-7619-2584-2. Dewey:361.97/03. LCCN:2004-022284.
Audience: **g,l,u.** *Choice, 2005.*

Himmelfarb, Gertrude **HV4086.A3H55 1985**
The Idea of Poverty: England in the Early Industrial Age. Trade Paper. Knopf Publishing Group. New York, NY. 1985. 608p. ISBN:0-394-72607-3, ISBN13: 978-0-394-72607-6. Dewey:305.5/69/0941. LCCN:84-040005.
Audience: **u,f.** B

Kagan, Sharon L. & Neville, Peter **HV95.K278 1993**
Integrating Human Services: Understanding the Past to Shape the Future. Cloth over Boards. Yale University Press.

Cumberland, RI. 1994. 238p. ISBN:0-300-05871-3, ISBN13: 978-0-300-05871-0. Dewey:361.973. LCCN:93-031023.
Audience: **l,u,f.** *Choice, 1995.*

Mink, Gwendolyn **HV700.5.M56 1998**
Welfare's End. Book, Other. Cornell University Press. Ithaca, NY. 1998. 192p. ISBN:0-8014-3347-9, ISBN13: 978-0-8014-3347-4. Dewey:362.83/928/0973. LCCN:97-038838.
Audience: **l,u.** *Choice, 1998.*

Pringle, Keith **HQ1088.P75 1995**
Men, Masculinities and Social Welfare. Paper over Boards. Taylor & Francis Group. Abingdon, 1995. 224p. ISBN:1-85728-401-1, ISBN13: 978-1-85728-401-0. Dewey:305.32. LCCN:95-009566.
Audience: **u,f.** *Choice, 1996.*

Riis, Jacob A. **HV4046.N6 R584**
How the Other Half Lives. Trade Paper. Kessinger Publishing, LLC. Whitefish, MT. 2004. ISBN:1-4191-2476-5, ISBN13: 978-1-4191-2476-1. Dewey:305.56.
Audience: **g.**

Shah, Anwar **JF1525.P67M43 2005**
Public Services Delivery. World Bank Staff (Contribution by). Trade Paper, Perfect. World Bank Publications. Washington, DC. 2005. 26p. Public Sector, Governance, and Accountability Ser. ISBN:0-8213-6140-6, ISBN13: 978-0-8213-6140-5. Dewey:361.60684. LCCN:2005-043246.
Audience: **u,f.**

Tice, Karen W. **HV43.T43 1998**
Tales of Wayward Girls and Immoral Women: Case Records and the Professionalization of Social Work. Trade Paper. University of Illinois Press. Champaign, IL. 1998. 272p. ISBN:0-252-06698-7, ISBN13: 978-0-252-06698-6. Dewey:361.3/2. LCCN:97-033863.
Audience: **u,f.** *Choice, 1999.*

Towle, Charlotte **HV91.T6 1987**
Common Human Needs. Jacqueline Atkins (Introduction by). Trade Paper. National Association of Social Workers/N A S W Press. Washington, DC. 1987. 156p. ISBN:0-87101-154-9, ISBN13: 978-0-87101-154-1. Dewey:361. LCCN:87-022016.
Audience: **l,u.** B

Weber, Bruce A. (Editor), et al. **HC110.P6R855 2002**
Rural Dimensions of Welfare Reform: Welfare, Food Assistance, and Poverty in Rural America. Greg J. Duncan & Leslie A. Whitener (Editors). Trade Cloth. W. E. Upjohn Institute for Employment Research. Kalamazoo, MI. 2002. 500p. ISBN:0-88099-240-9, ISBN13: 978-0-88099-240-4. Dewey:361.6/8/091734. LCCN:2002-016815.
Audience: **u,f.** *Choice, 2003.*

Wuthnow, Robert **HV530.W885 2004**
Saving America?: Faith-Based Services and the Future of Civil Society. Trade Cloth. Princeton University Press. Princeton, NJ. 2004. 352p. ISBN:0-691-11926-0, ISBN13: 978-0-691-11926-7. Dewey:361.7/5/0973. LCCN:2003-066360.
Audience: **l,u,f.** *Choice, 2005.*

Social Problems > Social Welfare Programs > Child Welfare

Barrow, Christine (Editor) **HQ792.C37C48 2002**
Children's Rights: Caribbean Realities. Trade Paper. Ian Randle Publishers. Kingston, 2002. 416p. ISBN:976-637-060-5, ISBN13: 978-976-637-060-2. Dewey:305.230971. LCCN:2003-400971.
Audience: **u,f.**

Bensen, Robert (Editor) **E98.C89C55 2001**
Children of the Dragonfly: Native American Voices on Child Custody and Education. Carter Revard (Foreword by). Trade Cloth. University of Arizona Press. Tucson, AZ. 2001. 280p. ISBN:0-8165-2012-7, ISBN13: 978-0-8165-2012-1. Dewey:305.897. LCCN:00-011169.
Audience: **l,u.**

Billingsley, Andrew & Giovannoni, Jeanne M. **HV741 .B5**
Children of the Storm: Black Children and American Child Welfare. Paper Text. Harcourt College Publishers. Fort Worth, TX. 1972. 263p. ISBN:0-15-507271-4, ISBN13: 978-0-15-507271-8. Dewey:362.7. LCCN:72-075593.
Audience: **l,u.** B

Boswell, John **HV887.E8B67 1998**
The Kindness of Strangers: The Abandonment of Children in Western Europe from Late Antiquity to the Renaissance. Trade Paper. University of Chicago Press. Chicago, IL. 1998. 506p. ISBN:0-226-06712-2, ISBN13: 978-0-226-06712-4. Dewey:362.7/3/094. LCCN:98-019356.
Audience: **l,u,f.**

Chalcraft, Edwin L. & Collins, Cary C. **E97.65.N4C43 2004**
e Assimilation's Agent: My Life As a Superintendent in the Indian Boarding School System. E-Book. University of Nebraska Press. Lincoln, NE. 2004. lxvi, 360p. ISBN:0-8032-0435-3, ISBN13: 978-0-8032-0435-5. Dewey:371.2/011/092 B. LCCN:2004-000623.
Audience: **g,l,u.** *Choice, 2005.*

Coles, Robert **HV881 .C62**
Uprooted Children: The Early Life of Migrant Farm Workers. Trade Cloth. University of Pittsburgh Press. Pittsburgh, PA. 1970. 170p. Horace Mann Lecture Ser. ISBN:0-8229-3192-3, ISBN13: 978-0-8229-3192-8. Dewey:917.3/03/924. LCCN:70-098270.
Audience: **l,u,f.** B

Duncan, Greg J. & Chase-Lansdale, P. Lindsay (Editors) **HV741.F66 2002**
For Better and for Worse: Welfare Reform and the Well-Being of Children and Families. Trade Cloth. Russell Sage Foundation. New York, NY. 2002. 300p. ISBN:0-87154-245-5, ISBN13: 978-0-87154-245-8. Dewey:362.7/0973. LCCN:2001-041785.
Audience: **u,f.**

Fanshel, David & Shinn, Eugene B. **HV881**
Children in Foster Care: A Longitudinal Investigation. Cloth Text. Columbia University Press. New York, NY. 1978. 520p. Social Work and Social Issues Ser. ISBN:0-231-03576-4, ISBN13: 978-0-231-03576-7. Dewey:155.4/45/0973. LCCN:77-002872.
Audience: **l,u,f.** ℬ

Gustavsson, Nora S. & Segal, Elizabeth A. **HV741.G87 1994**
Critical Issues in Child Welfare. Trade Cloth. SAGE Publications, Inc. Thousand Oaks, CA. 1994. 230p. ISBN:0-8039-4504-3, ISBN13: 978-0-8039-4504-3. Dewey:362.7/0973. LCCN:93-046436.
Audience: **u,f.** *Choice, 1994.*

Harris, Kathleen M. **HQ759.4.H387 1997**
Teen Mothers and the Revolving Welfare Door. Frank F. Furstenberg Jr. (Foreword by). Trade Cloth. Temple University Press. Philadelphia, PA. 1996. 224p. Women in the Political Economy Ser. ISBN:1-56639-499-6, ISBN13: 978-1-56639-499-4. Dewey:306.874/3. LCCN:96-036157.
Audience: **l,u.** *Choice, 1997.*

Kalichman, Seth C. **HV8079.C46K35 1999**
Mandated Reporting of Suspected Child Abuse: Ethics, Law and Policy. Ed. 2. Cloth Text. American Psychological Association. Washington, DC. 1999. xiv, 235p. ISBN:1-55798-602-9, ISBN13: 978-1-55798-602-3. Dewey:363.25/95554. LCCN:99-028737.
Audience: **l,u,f.**

Lindsey, Duncan **HV741.L527 2003**
The Welfare of Children. Ed. 2. Trade Cloth. Oxford University Press, Inc. New York, NY. 2003. 472p. ISBN:0-19-513670-5, ISBN13: 978-0-19-513670-8. Dewey:362.7/0973. LCCN:2003-006097.
Audience: **l,u.** *Choice, 1995.*

Mallon, Gerald **HV1449.M35 1998**
We Don't Exactly Get the Welcome Wagon: The Experiences of Gay and Lesbian Adolescents in Child Welfare Systems. Cloth Text. Columbia University Press. New York, NY. 1998. 208p. ISBN:0-231-10454-5, ISBN13: 978-0-231-10454-8. Dewey:362.7/083. LCCN:97-045545.
Audience: **u,f.** *Choice, 1998.*

McLanahan, Sara S. (Editor), et al. **HQ536**
Future of Children: Marriage and Child Well-Being. Ron Haskins & Elisabeth Donahue (Editors). Trade Paper. Brookings Institution Press. Washington, DC. 2005. 200p. ISBN:0-8157-5561-9, ISBN13: 978-0-8157-5561-6. Dewey:305.23.
Audience: **l,u,f.**

National Clearinghouse on Child Abuse and Neglect Information **HV6626.5**
☐ National Clearinghouse on Child Abuse and Neglect Information.
http://nccanch.acf.hhs.gov/
United States Department of Health and Human Services, Administration for Children and Families, National Clearinghouse on Child Abuse and Neglect Information
Audience: **g.**

Penn, Helen **HQ792.2.P46 2005**
Unequal Childhoods: Young Children's Lives in Poor Countries. Perfect, Paper over Boards. Routledge. New York, NY. 2005. 240p. Contesting Early Childhood Ser. ISBN:0-415-32101-8, ISBN13: 978-0-415-32101-3. Dewey:305.23/09172/4. LCCN:2004-022286.
Audience: **l,u,f.**

Rainwater, Lee & Smeeding, Timothy M. **HV741.R33 2003**
Poor Kids in a Rich Country: America's Children in Comparative Perspective. Trade Cloth. Russell Sage Foundation. New York, NY. 2005. 280p. ISBN:0-87154-702-3, ISBN13: 978-0-87154-702-6. Dewey:362.7/086/9420973. LCCN:2003-047050.
Audience: **l,u,f.** *Choice, 2004.*

Talley, P. Forrest **RJ507.A29H36 2005**
Handbook for the Treatment of Abused and Neglected Children. Trade Paper, Perfect. Haworth Press, Incorporated, The. Binghamton, NY. 2005. 494p. Haworth Social Work Practice with Children and Families Ser. ISBN:0-7890-2678-3, ISBN13: 978-0-7890-2678-1. Dewey:362.76/86. LCCN:2004-028452.
Audience: **g,l,u.**

Wald, Michael S., et al. **HV742.C2W35 1988**
Protecting Abused and Neglected Children. J. M. Carlsmith & P. H. Leiderman (Authors), James Garbarino (Foreword by). Trade Cloth. Stanford University Press. Palo Alto, CA. 1988. 275p. ISBN:0-8047-1420-7, ISBN13: 978-0-8047-1420-4. Dewey:362.7/044. LCCN:87-010208.
Audience: **l,u,f.**

Social Problems > Social Welfare Programs > Medicare

Schoen, Johanna **HQ766.5.U5S36 2005**
Choice and Coercion: Birth Control, Sterilization, and Abortion in Public Health and Welfare. Trade Cloth. University of North Carolina Press. Chapel Hill, NC. 2005. 384p. Gender and American Culture Ser. ISBN:0-8078-2919-6, ISBN13: 978-0-8078-2919-6. Dewey:363.9/6/09756. LCCN:2004-017632.
Audience: **l,u,f.** *Choice, 2006.*

Scrambler, Graham **RA418.M344 2004**
Medical Sociology: Major Themes in Health and Social Welfare. Children's Board Books. Routledge. New York, NY. 2004. 432p. Major Themes in Health and Social Welfare Ser. ISBN:0-415-31782-7, ISBN13: 978-0-415-31782-5. Dewey:362.1. LCCN:2004-051009.
Audience: **l,u.**

Smith, David G. **RA412.3.S635 2002**
Entitlement Politics: Medicare and Medicaid, 1995-2001. Trade Cloth. Aldine Transaction. Somerset, NJ. 2002. 432p. Social Institutions and Social Change Ser. ISBN:0-202-30718-2, ISBN13: 978-0-202-30718-3. Dewey:368.4/26/00973. LCCN:2002-001111.
Audience: **l,u.** *Choice, 2003.*

Social Problems > Social Welfare Programs > Adult Care Services

DePastino, Todd **HV4504.D47 2003**
Citizen Hobo: How a Century of Homelessness Shaped America. Trade Cloth. University of Chicago Press. Chicago, IL. 2003. 350p. ISBN:0-226-14378-3, ISBN13: 978-0-226-14378-1. Dewey:305.5/68. LCCN:2002-154907.
Audience: **l,u,f.**

Vale, Lawrence J. **HD7288.78.U52M48**
From the Puritans to the Projects: Public Housing and Public Neighbors. Trade Cloth. Harvard University Press. Cambridge, MA. 2000. 482p. ISBN:0-674-00286-5, ISBN13: 978-0-674-00286-9. Dewey:363.5/85/0974461. LCCN:00-035084.
Audience: **u,f.** *Choice, 2001.*

Social Problems > Social Work Practice

HV40
☐ Social Work Abstracts.
http://www.ovid.com/site/catalog/DataBase/150.jsp?top=2&mid=3&bottom=7&subsection=10
National Association of Social Workers ; Wolters-Kluwer.
Audience: **l,u.**

Addams, Jane **HV4196.C4**
Twenty Years at Hull House. Trade Paper. Kessinger Publishing, LLC. Whitefish, MT. 2004. ISBN:1-4191-0008-4, ISBN13: 978-1-4191-0008-6. Dewey:331.85.
Audience: **g,l,u,f.** B

Alston, Margaret & Bowles, Wendy **HV11.A47 2003**
Research for Social Workers: An Introduction to Methods. Ed. 2. Trade Paper. Routledge. New York, NY. 2004. 352p. ISBN:0-415-30723-6, ISBN13: 978-0-415-30723-9. Dewey:361.3/072. LCCN:2002-036781.
Audience: **l,u.** *Choice, 2004.*

Bart, Pauline B. & O'Brien, Patricia H. **HV6558**
Stopping Rape: Successful Survival Strategies. Trade Cloth. Elsevier Science & Technology Books. Saint Louis, MO. 1985. 200p. Athene Ser. ISBN:0-08-032814-8, ISBN13: 978-0-08-032814-0. Dewey:364.1/532. LCCN:85-006589.
Audience: **g,l.** B

Bent-Goodley, Tricia B. (Editor) **HV3181.A374 2003**
African-American Social Workers and Social Policy. Trade Cloth. Haworth Press, Incorporated, The. Binghamton, NY. 2003. 211p. ISBN:0-7890-1621-4, ISBN13: 978-0-7890-1621-8. Dewey:362.84/96/073. LCCN:2002-027333.
Audience: **u,f.** *Choice, 2004.*

Bernstein, Nina **HV885.N5B46 2001**
The Lost Children of Wilder: The Epic Struggle to Change Foster Care. Trade Cloth. Knopf Publishing Group. New York, NY. 2001. 496p. ISBN:0-679-43979-X, ISBN13: 978-0-679-43979-0. Dewey:362.73/3/097471. LCCN:00-057456.
Audience: **g,l,u.** *Choice, 2002.*

Craig, Yvonne **HV245 .A6635 1998**
Advocacy, Counselling and Mediation in Casework: Processes of Empowerment. Trade Paper. Jessica Kingsley Ltd. London, 1998. 200p. ISBN:1-85302-564-X, ISBN13: 978-1-85302-564-8. Dewey:361.3/2/0941. LCCN:98-188762.
Audience: **u,f.**

Ehrenreich, John H. **HV95**
The Altruistic Imagination: A History of Social Work and Social Policy in the United States. Trade Cloth. Cornell University Press. Ithaca, NY. 1985. 304p. ISBN:0-8014-1764-3, ISBN13: 978-0-8014-1764-1. Dewey:361.3/0973. LCCN:84-045807.
Audience: **l,u,f.** B *Choice, 1985.*

Fanshel, David, et al. **HV881.F364 1990**
Foster Children in the Life Course Perspective: The Casey Family Program Experience. Stephen S. Finch & John F. Grundy (Authors). Trade Cloth. Columbia University Press. New York, NY. 1990. 352p. ISBN:0-231-07180-9, ISBN13: 978-0-231-07180-2. Dewey:362.7/33/0973. LCCN:90-035629.
Audience: **u.** *Choice, 1991.*

Fink, Arthur E. (Editor), et al. **HV0040.F45**
The Field of Social Work. Ed. 8. Jane H. Pfouts & Andrew W. Dobelstein (Editors). Trade Paper. Books on Demand. Ann Arbor, MI. 1985. 400p. ISBN:0-608-01493-1, ISBN13: 978-0-608-01493-7. Dewey:361.3. LCCN:84-018082.
Audience: **l,u.** B

Frost, Nick (Editor) **HV713**
Child Welfare: Major Themes in Health and Social Welfare. Library Binding. Routledge. New York, NY. 2004. 1632p. Major Themes in Health and Social Welfare Ser. ISBN:0-415-31253-1, ISBN13: 978-0-415-31253-0. Dewey:362.7. LCCN:2004-050801.
Audience: **l,u.**

Goldstein, Joseph, et al. **HV713**
Beyond the Best Interests of the Child. Anna Freud & Albert J. Solnit (Authors). Trade Cloth. Simon & Schuster. New York, NY. 1973. xiv, 170p. ISBN:0-02-912300-3, ISBN13: 978-0-02-912300-3. Dewey:342.4/32795. LCCN:73-009136.
Audience: **u,f.** B

Huxtable, Marion & Blyth, Eric (Editors) **LB3013.4.S732 2002**
School Social Work Worldwide. Trade Paper. National Association of Social Workers/N A S W Press. Washington, DC. 2002. 260p. ISBN:0-87101-348-7, ISBN13: 978-0-87101-348-4. Dewey:371.7. LCCN:2001-059090.
Audience: **l,u.**

Kadushin, Alfred & Harkness, Daniel **HV40.54**
Supervision in Social Work. Ed. 4. Trade Cloth. Columbia University Press. New York, NY. 2002. 501p. ISBN:0-231-12095-8, ISBN13: 978-0-231-12095-1. Dewey:361.3/2/0683.
Audience: **l,u,f.**

Kadushin, Alfred & Kadushin, Goldie **HV43.K26 1997**
The Social Work Interview: A Guide for Human Service Professionals. Ed. 4. Trade Cloth. Columbia University Press. New York, NY. 1997. 480p. ISBN:0-231-09658-5, ISBN13: 978-0-231-09658-4. Dewey:361.3/22. LCCN:96-038296.
Audience: **l,u.** B

Katz, Michael B. **HV91.K349 1986**
In the Shadow of the Poorhouse: A Social History of Welfare in America. Cloth Text. Basic Books. New York, NY. 1986. 544p. ISBN:0-465-03225-7, ISBN13: 978-0-465-03225-9. Dewey:362.5/8/0973. LCCN:85-073875.
Audience: **g,l,u.** BCL3 *Choice, 1987.*

Maluccio, Anthony N. (Editor), et al. **HV881.P74 1990**
Preparing Adolescents for Life After Foster Care: The Central Role of Foster Parents. Robin Krieger & Barbara A. Pine (Editors). Trade Paper. Child Welfare League of America, Inc. Washington, DC. 1990. xv, 225p. ISBN:0-87868-433-6, ISBN13: 978-0-87868-433-5. Dewey:362.7/33/0835. LCCN:90-035033.
Audience: **l,u.** *Choice, 1991.*

Margolin, Leslie **HV43.M295 1997**
Under the Cover of Kindness: The Invention of Social Work. Trade Cloth. University Press of Virginia. Charlottesville, VA. 1997. 219p. Knowledge: Disciplinarity and Beyond Ser. ISBN:0-8139-1713-1, ISBN13: 978-0-8139-1713-9. Dewey:361.3/2. LCCN:96-047986.
Audience: **l,u,f.**

Nelson, Gary M., et al. **HV91.F49 1995**
The Field of Adult Services: Social Work Practice and Administration. Ann C. Eller, Dennis W. Streets & Margaret L. Morse (Authors). Trade Paper. National Association of Social Workers/N A S W Press. Washington, DC. 1995. 406p. ISBN:0-87101-250-2, ISBN13: 978-0-87101-250-0. Dewey:361.3/0973. LCCN:95-009331.
Audience: **l,u.**

Padro, Fernando F. **HV51**
Statistical Handbook on the Social Safety Net. Cloth Text. Greenwood Publishing Group, Inc. Portsmouth, NH. 2004. 608p. Oryx Statistical Handbooks ISBN:1-57356-516-4, ISBN13: 978-1-57356-516-5. Dewey:025.06/361. LCCN:2004-043641.
Audience: **g.** *Choice, 2005.*

Patterson, James T. **HN59.P39 2000**
America's Struggle Against Poverty in the Twentieth Century. Ed. 4. Trade Paper. Harvard University Press. Cambridge, MA. 2000. 334p. ISBN:0-674-00434-5, ISBN13: 978-0-674-00434-4. Dewey:361.6/1/0973. LCCN:00-038277.
Audience: **g,l.** *Choice, 2001.*

Philleo, Joanne (Editor), et al. **HV5824.E85C84 1997**
Cultural Competence in Substance Abuse Prevention. Frances L. Brisbare & Leonard G. Spstein (Editors). Trade Paper. National Association of Social Workers/N A S W Press. Washington, DC. 1997. 184p. ISBN:0-87101-278-2, ISBN13: 978-0-87101-278-4. Dewey:362.29/17/08900973. LCCN:97-006111.
Audience: **l,u.**

Reamer, Frederic G. **HV41 .R4**
Ethical Dilemmas in Social Service: A Guide for Social Workers. Ed. 2. Trade Paper. Columbia University Press. New York, NY. 1993. 262p. ISBN:0-231-06969-3, ISBN13: 978-0-231-06969-4. Dewey:361.
Audience: **l,u,f.**

Reid, William J. **HV697.R35 1985**
Family Problem Solving. Trade Cloth. Columbia University Press. New York, NY. 1985. 343p. ISBN:0-231-06056-4, ISBN13: 978-0-231-06056-1. Dewey:362.8/253. LCCN:85-003833.
Audience: **l,u.** *Choice, 1986.*

Reisch, Michael & Andrews, Janice **HV91**
Road Not Taken: A History of Radical Social Work in the United States. UK-B Format Paperback. Brunner-Routledge. Philadelphia, PA. 2002. 296p. ISBN:0-415-93399-4, ISBN13: 978-0-415-93399-5. Dewey:361.32.
Audience: **l,u,f.**

Richmond, Mary E. **PS3507.A33Z52**
Social Diagnosis. Trade Cloth. Russell Sage Foundation. New York, NY. 1917. 512p. ISBN:0-87154-703-1, ISBN13: 978-0-87154-703-3. Dewey:928.1.
Audience: **u,f.**

Rosenfeld, Lawrence B. **HV553.W48 2003**
When Their World Falls Apart: Helping Families and Children Manage the Effects of Disasters. Trade Paper. National Association of Social Workers/N A S W Press. Washington, DC. 2003. 488p. ISBN:0-87101-358-4, ISBN13: 978-0-87101-358-3. Dewey:363.34/8. LCCN:2003-061078.
Audience: **l,u,f.**

Saari, Carolyn **HV43.S125 1991**
The Creation of Meaning in Clinical Social Work. Cloth over Boards. Guilford Publications, Inc. New York, NY. 1991. 216p. ISBN:0-89862-772-9, ISBN13: 978-0-89862-772-5. Dewey:361.3/2. LCCN:91-024651.
Audience: **l,u.** *Choice, 1992.*

Schwartz, Arthur, et al. **HV43**
Social Casework: A Behavioral Approach. Israel Goldiamond & Michael W. Howe (Authors). Trade Cloth. Columbia University Press. New York, NY. 1975. 315p. ISBN:0-231-03778-3, ISBN13: 978-0-231-03778-5. Dewey:361.3/2. LCCN:75-002298.
Audience: **l,u.** BCL3

Taylor, Samuel H. & Roberts, Robert E. **HV40**
Theory and Practice of Community Social Work. Trade Cloth. Columbia University Press. New York, NY. 1985. 442p. ISBN:0-231-05368-1, ISBN13: 978-0-231-05368-6. Dewey:361.8. LCCN:84-015628.
Audience: **l,u.** BCL3 *Choice, 1985.*

Tice, Karen W. **HV43.T43 1998**
Tales of Wayward Girls and Immoral Women: Case Records and the Professionalization of Social Work. Trade Cloth. University of Illinois Press. Champaign, IL. 1998. 272p. ISBN:0-252-02397-8, ISBN13: 978-0-252-02397-2. Dewey:361.3/2. LCCN:97-033863.
Audience: **u,f.** *Choice, 1999.*

Towle, Charlotte **HV91.T6 1987**
Common Human Needs. Jacqueline Atkins (Introduction by). Trade Paper. National Association of Social Workers/N A S W Press. Washington, DC. 1987. 156p. ISBN:0-87101-154-9, ISBN13: 978-0-87101-154-1. Dewey:361. LCCN:87-022016.
Audience: **l,u.** BCL3

Trattner, Walter I. (Editor) **HV27**
Biographical Dictionary of Social Welfare in America. Cloth Text. Greenwood Publishing Group, Inc. Portsmouth, NH. 1986.

911p. ISBN:0-313-23001-3, ISBN13: 978-0-313-23001-1. Dewey:361/.922 B. LCCN:85-009831.
Audience: **g.** *Choice, 1986.*

Walker, Lenore E. **HV6626.2.W33 2000**
The Battered Woman Syndrome. Ed. 2. Trade Cloth. Springer Publishing Company, Inc. New York, NY. 1999. 304p. Springer Series, Focus on Women Ser. ISBN:0-8261-4322-9, ISBN13: 978-0-8261-4322-8. Dewey:362.82/92. LCCN:99-043559.
Audience: **g.**

Weissman, Harold, et al. **HV41**
Agency-Based Social Work: Neglected Aspects of Clinical Practice. Irwin Epstein & Andrea Savage-Abramovitz (Authors). Paper Text. Temple University Press. Philadelphia, PA. 1983. 344p. ISBN:0-87722-330-0, ISBN13: 978-0-87722-330-6. Dewey:361/.0068. LCCN:83-009314.
Audience: **l,u.** B

Wozniak, Danielle **HV881.W68 2001**
They're All My Children: Foster Mothering in America. Trade Cloth. New York University Press. New York, NY. 2001. 356p. ISBN:0-8147-9346-0, ISBN13: 978-0-8147-9346-6. Dewey:362.73/3/0973. LCCN:2001-004428.
Audience: **l,u.** *Choice, 2002.*

Social Change

Janowitz, Morris **HN57 .J2479**
The Last Half-Century: Societal Change and Politics in America. Trade Paper. University of Chicago Press. Chicago, IL. 1984. 598p. ISBN:0-226-39307-0, ISBN13: 978-0-226-39307-0. Dewey:301.15/0973. LCCN:78-017715.
Audience: **u,f.** B

Sorel, Georges **CB155**
The Illusions of Progress. John Stanley & Charlotte Stanley (Translators). Trade Paper. University of California Press. Berkeley, CA. 1969. ISBN:0-520-02256-4, ISBN13: 978-0-520-02256-0. Dewey:301.2/45. LCCN:69-016511.
Audience: **l,u,f.** B

Social Change > Economics

Friedman, Monroe **HF5415.32.F75 1999**
Consumer Boycotts: Effecting Change Through the Marketplace and the Media. UK-B Format Paperback. Routledge. New York, NY. 1999. 304p. ISBN:0-415-92457-X, ISBN13: 978-0-415-92457-3. Dewey:381/.3. LCCN:99-018522.
Audience: **g,l,u.** *Choice, 2000.*

Lipper, Joanna **HQ759.4.L57 2003**
Growing up Fast. Cloth over Boards. Picador. New York, NY. 2003. 336p. ISBN:0-312-42222-9, ISBN13: 978-0-312-42222-6. Dewey:306.874/3. LCCN:2003-049862.
Audience: **g.**

Stoller, Paul **F128.9.A24S76 2002**
Money Has No Smell: The Africanization of New York City. Trade Cloth. University of Chicago Press. Chicago, IL. 2002. 232p. ISBN:0-226-77529-1, ISBN13: 978-0-226-77529-6. Dewey:305.896/607471. LCCN:2001-053384.
Audience: **l,u.**

Wallerstein, Immanuel **HC51.W29 2000**
The Essential Wallerstein. Trade Cloth. New Press, The. New York, NY. 2000. 496p. ISBN:1-56584-585-4, ISBN13: 978-1-56584-585-5. Dewey:330.1. LCCN:99-035781.
Audience: **g,l,u,f.**

Watkins, Evan **HM101.W278 1993**
Throwaways: Work Culture and Consumer Education. Trade Paper. Stanford University Press. Palo Alto, CA. 1993. 242p. ISBN:0-8047-2250-1, ISBN13: 978-0-8047-2250-6. Dewey:303.4. LCCN:93-019270.
Audience: **l,u.** *Choice, 1994.*

Wilson, William Julius **HV4045.W553 1996**
When Work Disappears: The World of the New Urban Poor. Trade Cloth. Alfred A. Knopf Inc. New York, NY. 1996. 352p. ISBN:0-394-57935-6, ISBN13: 978-0-394-57935-1. Dewey:362.5/0973/091732. LCCN:96-011803.
Audience: **l,u,f.** *Choice, 1997.*

Social Change > Development

Goldthorpe, J. E. **HN980**
The Sociology of the Third World: Disparity and Development. Ed. 2. Cloth Text. Cambridge University Press. New York, NY. 1984. 336p. ISBN:0-521-25303-9, ISBN13: 978-0-521-25303-1. Dewey:909/.097240828. LCCN:83-013506.
Audience: **l,u,f.** B

Sklair, Leslie **HD9734.M43M497 1989**
Assembling for Development: The Maquila Industry in Mexico and the United States. Trade Cloth. Routledge. New York, NY. 1989. 320p. ISBN:0-04-445278-0, ISBN13: 978-0-04-445278-2. Dewey:338.4/767/09721. LCCN:88-037613.
Audience: **u,f.** *Choice, 1993.*

Wallerstein, Immanuel **HN13.W35 2004**
World-Systems Analysis: An Introduction. Trade Paper. Duke University Press. Durham, NC. 2004. 170p. ISBN:0-8223-3442-9, ISBN13: 978-0-8223-3442-2. Dewey:303.4. LCCN:2004-003291.
Audience: **l,u,f.** *Choice, 2005.*

Walton, John **HN79.C22**
Western Times and Water Wars: State, Culture, and Rebellion in California. Trade Paper. University of California Press. Berkeley, CA. 1993. 388p. ISBN:0-520-08453-5, ISBN13: 978-0-520-08453-7. Dewey:303.4/84/0979494.
Audience: **g,l,u,f.** *Choice, 1992.*

Social Change > Development > Globalization

Adler, William M. **HD6068.2.U6**
Mollie's Job: A Story of Life and Work on the Global Assembly Line. Trade Paper. Simon & Schuster. New York, NY. 2001. 368p. ISBN:0-7432-0030-6, ISBN13: 978-0-7432-0030-1. Dewey:331.4/87.
Audience: **l,u.**

Heymann, Jody **HD4904.25.H478 2005**
Forgotten Families: Ending the Growing Crisis Confronting Children and Working Parents in the Global Economy. Trade Cloth. Oxford University Press, Inc. New York, NY. 2006. 328p.

ISBN:0-19-515659-5, ISBN13: 978-0-19-515659-1. Dewey:306.3/6. LCCN:2005-008503.
Audience: **u,f.** *Choice, 2006.*

Sklair, Leslie **HD2755.5**
Globalization: Capatalism and Its Alternatives. Ed. 3. Paper Text. Oxford University Press, Inc. New York, NY. 2002. 270p. ISBN:0-19-924744-7, ISBN13: 978-0-19-924744-8. Dewey:337. LCCN:2002-510705.
Audience: **l,u,f.**

Social Change > Revolution

Davies, James **HM283.D37 1997**
When Men Revolt and Why. Ed. 2. Trade Paper. Transaction Publishers. Somerset, NJ. 1997. 357p. ISBN:1-56000-939-X, ISBN13: 978-1-56000-939-9. Dewey:303.4/3. LCCN:96-038938.
Audience: **l,u,f.**

Eisenstadt, Samuel N. **HM281**
Revolution and the Transformation of Societies: A Comparative Study of Civilizations. Trade Cloth. Simon & Schuster. New York, NY. 1978. xvii, 348p. ISBN:0-02-909390-2, ISBN13: 978-0-02-909390-0. Dewey:303.6/4. LCCN:77-005203.
Audience: **l,u,f.**

Johnson, Chalmers A. **HM281**
Revolutionary Change. Ed. 2. Trade Paper. Stanford University Press. Palo Alto, CA. 1982. 232p. ISBN:0-8047-1145-3, ISBN13: 978-0-8047-1145-6. Dewey:303.6/4. LCCN:81-085448.
Audience: **l,u.** B

Sanderson, Stephen **JC491.S32 2005**
Revolutions: Worldwide Introduction to Political and Social Change. Library Binding. Paradigm Publishers. Boulder, CO. 2005. 234p. ISBN:1-59451-048-2, ISBN13: 978-1-59451-048-9. Dewey:303.6/4. LCCN:2005-004925.
Audience: **l,u.** *Choice, 2006.*

Skocpol, Theda **D299**
States and Social Revolutions: A Comparative Analysis of France, Russia and China. Trade Cloth. Cambridge University Press. New York, NY. 1979. 448p. ISBN:0-521-22439-X, ISBN13: 978-0-521-22439-0. Dewey:947.084/1. LCCN:78-014314.
Audience: **u,f.** B

Sorokin, Pitirim A. **HM281.S6**
The Sociology of Revolution. Trade Cloth. Howard Fertig Inc. New York, NY. 1967. ISBN:0-86527-184-4, ISBN13: 978-0-86527-184-5. Dewey:301.2.
Audience: **l,u,f.**

Social Change > Environmental Interactions

Diamond, Jared M. **HN13.D5 2005**
Collapse: How Societies Choose to Fail or Succeed. Trade Cloth. Penguin Group (USA) Inc. New York, NY. 2004. 592p. ISBN:0-670-03337-5, ISBN13: 978-0-670-03337-9. Dewey:304.2/8. LCCN:2004-057152.
Audience: **g,l,u,f.** *Choice, 2005.*

Dubos, Rene Jules **HM206.D87 1998**
So Human an Animal: How We Are Shaped by Surroundings and Events. Jill Cooper & David Mechanic (Introduction by). Trade Paper. Transaction Publishers. Somerset, NJ. 1998. 267p. ISBN:0-7658-0429-8, ISBN13: 978-0-7658-0429-7. Dewey:304.2. LCCN:98-011413.
Audience: **g,l,u,f.**

Dunlap, Riley E. & Michelson, William (Editors) **GE195.H35 2001**
Handbook of Environmental Sociology. Cloth Text. Greenwood Publishing Group, Inc. Portsmouth, NH. 2001. 616p. ISBN:0-313-26808-8, ISBN13: 978-0-313-26808-3. Dewey:304.2/8/097. LCCN:2001-023880.
Audience: **g.** *Choice, 2002.*

Montagu, Ashley **HM106 .M65**
On Being Human. Trade Cloth. Penguin Group (USA) Inc. New York, NY. ISBN:0-8015-5514-0, ISBN13: 978-0-8015-5514-5. Dewey:301.1.
Audience: **g,l,u,f.** B

Social Change > Environmental Interactions > Disasters

Aptekar, Lewis **HV551.2.A68 1994**
Environmental Disasters in Global Perspective. Trade Cloth. Macmillan Publishing Company, Inc. Old Tappan, NJ. 1993. 208p. Social Issues in Global Perspective Ser. ISBN:0-8161-7381-8, ISBN13: 978-0-8161-7381-5. Dewey:363.3/4. LCCN:93-012836.
Audience: **l,u,f.** *Choice, 1994.*

Erikson, Kai T. **HV 610 E74**
Everything in its Path: Destruction of Community in the Buffalo Creek Flood. Trade Paper. Simon & Schuster. New York, NY. 1978. 288p. ISBN:0-671-24067-6, ISBN13: 978-0-671-24067-7. Dewey:363. LCCN:76-026462.
Audience: **l,u,f.**

Erikson, Kai T. **HV555.U6E75 1994**
A New Species of Trouble: Exploration in Community, Disaster and Trauma. Trade Cloth. W. W. Norton & Company, Inc. New York, NY. 1994. 256p. ISBN:0-393-03594-8, ISBN13: 978-0-393-03594-0. Dewey:363.3480973. LCCN:93-024721.
Audience: **l,u,f.** *Choice, 1994.*

Vale, Lawrence J. & Campanella, Thomas J. **HT170.R46 2005**
The Resilient City: How Modern Cities Recover from Disaster. Trade Cloth. Oxford University Press, Inc. New York, NY. 2005. 390p. ISBN:0-19-517584-0, ISBN13: 978-0-19-517584-4. Dewey:307.3/416/09. LCCN:2004-049246.
Audience: **l,u,f.** *Choice, 2005.*

Social Change > Technology

Krug, Gary J. **P94.6**
Communication, Technology and Cultural Change. Cloth Text. SAGE Publications, Inc. Thousand Oaks, CA. 2005. 256p. ISBN:0-7619-7200-5, ISBN13: 978-0-7619-7200-6. Dewey:302.48/33. LCCN:2004-108291.
Audience: **l,u.**

Rogers, Everett M. **HM621.R57 2003**
Diffusion of Innovations. Ed. 5. Trade Paper. Simon & Schuster. New York, NY. 2003. 576p. ISBN:0-7432-2209-1, ISBN13: 978-0-7432-2209-9. Dewey:303.48/4. LCCN:2003-049022.
Audience: **l,u,f.**

Social Change > Technology > Industrial Society

Gershuny, Jonathan **HM548.G47 2000**
Changing Times: Work and Leisure in Postindustrial Society. Trade Cloth. Oxford University Press, Inc. New York, NY. 2001. 312p. ISBN:0-19-828787-9, ISBN13: 978-0-19-828787-2. Dewey:306.3/6. LCCN:00-032362.
Audience: **u,f.** *Choice, 2001.*

Marcuse, Herbert **HM101.M268 1991**
One-Dimensional Man: Studies in the Ideology of Advanced Industrial Society. Douglas Kellner (Introduction by). Trade Paper. Beacon Press. Boston, MA. 1991. 320p. ISBN:0-8070-1417-6, ISBN13: 978-0-8070-1417-2. Dewey:301. LCCN:91-018246.
Audience: **u,f.**

Roszak, Theodore **HN16 .R63**
Person/Planet: The Creative Disintegration of Industrial Society. Trade Paper. iUniverse, Inc. Lincoln, NE. 2003. 382p. ISBN:0-595-29747-1, ISBN13: 978-0-595-29747-4. Dewey:301.1.
Audience: **l,u,f.**

Social Change > Technology > Information Age

Castells, Manuel **HD79.I55C38 2001**
The Internet Galaxy: Reflections on the Internet, Business and Society. Trade Cloth. Oxford University Press, Inc. New York, NY. 2001. 304p. ISBN:0-19-924153-8, ISBN13: 978-0-19-924153-8. Dewey:303.48/33. LCCN:2001-036383.
Audience: **l,u,f.** *Choice, 2002.*

Cavalier, Robert J. (Editor) **TK5105.878.C38 2005**
The Impact of the Internet on Our Moral Lives. Cloth Text. State University of New York Press. Albany, NY. 2005. 264p. ISBN:0-7914-6345-1, ISBN13: 978-0-7914-6345-1. Dewey:303.48/33. LCCN:2004-045400.
Audience: **u,f.** *Choice, 2005.*

Cranor, Lorrie Faith & Wildman, Steven S. (Editors) **HC79.I55R47 2002**
Rethinking Rights and Regulations: Institutional Responses to New Communications Technologies. Trade Cloth. MIT Press. Cambridge, MA. 2003. 456p. Telecommunications Policy Research Conference Ser. ISBN:0-262-03314-3, ISBN13: 978-0-262-03314-5. Dewey:384. LCCN:2003-044504.
Audience: **u,f.**

Herman, Andrew & Swiss, Thomas (Editors) **HM621.W67 2000**
The World Wide Web and Contemporary Cultural Theory: Magic, Metaphor, Power. Paper over Boards. Routledge. New York, NY. 2000. 320p. ISBN:0-415-92501-0, ISBN13: 978-0-415-92501-3. Dewey:306.4/6. LCCN:00-044643.
Audience: **l,u,f.** *Choice, 2001.*

Himanen, Pekka **QA76.9.M65H56 2001**
The Hacker Ethic: And the Spirit of the Information Age. Trade Cloth. Random House, Inc. New York, NY. 2001. 256p. ISBN:0-375-50566-0, ISBN13: 978-0-375-50566-9. Dewey:303.4/833. LCCN:00-053354.
Audience: **g,l,u,f.** *Choice, 2001.*

Sunstein, Cass **HM851**
Republic. Com. Trade Paper. Princeton University Press. Princeton, NJ. 2002. 246p. ISBN:0-691-09589-2, ISBN13: 978-0-691-09589-9. Dewey:303.4833.
Audience: **g,l.**

Vaidhyanathan, Siva **HM851**
The Anarchist in the Library: How the Clash Between Freedom and Control Is Hacking the Real World and Crashing the System. Trade Cloth. Basic Books. New York, NY. 2004. 272p. ISBN:0-465-08984-4, ISBN13: 978-0-465-08984-0. Dewey:303.48/33. LCCN:2003-026089.
Audience: **l,u,f.** *Choice, 2005.*

Wark, McKenzie **HC79.I55W37 2004**
A Hacker Manifesto. Trade Cloth. Harvard University Press. Cambridge, MA. 2004. 208p. ISBN:0-674-01543-6, ISBN13: 978-0-674-01543-2. Dewey:303.48/33. LCCN:2004-047488.
Audience: **g,l,u,f.**

Webster, Juliet **HD6060.6.W43 1996**
Shaping Women's Work: Gender, Employment and Information Technology. Trade Cloth. Longman Publishing Group. White Plains, NY. 1996. 224p. Sociology Ser. ISBN:0-582-21810-1, ISBN13: 978-0-582-21810-9. Dewey:306.3/615. LCCN:96-000459.
Audience: **l,u,f.** *Choice, 1997.*

Sociology of Education

Barab, Sasha A. (Editor), et al. **LC5803.C65.D47 2003**
Designing for Virtual Communities in the Service of Learning. Rob Kling & James Gray (Editors). Trade Cloth. Cambridge University Press. New York, NY. 2004. 478p. Learning in Doing Ser., :Social, Cognitive and Computational Perspectives Ser. ISBN:0-521-81755-2, ISBN13: 978-0-521-81755-4. Dewey:371.3/58. LCCN:2003-051524.
Audience: **u,f.**

Bills, David B. **LC191.4.B53 2004**
Sociology of Education and Work. Trade Paper. Blackwell Publishing, Inc. Malden, MA. 2004. 264p. ISBN:0-631-22363-0, ISBN13: 978-0-631-22363-4. Dewey:306.43. LCCN:2003-024828.
Audience: **l,u.** *Choice, 2005.*

Freire, Paulo **LB880.F73P4313 2000**
Pedagogy of the Oppressed. Ed. 30. Trade Paper. Continuum International Publishing Group, Ltd. London, 2000. 192p. ISBN:0-8264-1276-9, ISBN13: 978-0-8264-1276-8. Dewey:379. LCCN:00-030304.
Audience: **u,f.**

Morrow, Raymond Allen & Torres, Carlos Alberto **LC196.M67 2002**
Reading Freire and Habermas: Critical Pedagogy and Transformative Social Change. Trade Cloth. Teachers College Press, Teachers College, Columbia University. New York, NY. 2002. 224p. ISBN:0-8077-4203-1, ISBN13: 978-0-8077-4203-7. Dewey:370.11/5. LCCN:2001-060375.
Audience: **u,f.** *Choice, 2002.*

Renninger, K. Ann & Shumar, Wesley **TK5105.83.B85 2002**
[e] Building Virtual Communities: Learning and Change in Cyberspace. E-Book. Cambridge University Press. New York, NY. ISBN:0-511-04090-3, ISBN13: 978-0-511-04090-0. Dewey:004.67.
Audience: **l,u,f.**

Renninger, K. Ann & Shumar, Wesley (Editors) **TK5105.83.B85 2002**
Building Virtual Communities: Learning and Change in Cyberspace. Trade Cloth. Cambridge University Press. New York, NY. 2002. 414p. Learning in Doing, :Social, Cognitive and Computational Perspectives Ser. ISBN:0-521-78075-6, ISBN13: 978-0-521-78075-9. Dewey:004.67. LCCN:2001-052485.
Audience: **l,u,f.**

Rury, John L. **LA205.R67 2002**
Education and Social Change: Themes in the History of American Schooling. Trade Paper. Lawrence Erlbaum Associates, Inc. Mahwah, NJ. 2002. 264p. Social Foundations in Education Ser. ISBN:0-8058-3339-0, ISBN13: 978-0-8058-3339-3. Dewey:370/.973. LCCN:2001-056913.
Audience: **l,u,f.** *Choice, 2002.*

Saha, Lawrence J. **LC191.I49 1997**
International Encyclopedia of Sociology of Education. Trade Cloth. Elsevier Science & Technology Books. Saint Louis, MO. 1997. 930p. Resources in Education Ser. ISBN:0-08-042990-4, ISBN13: 978-0-08-042990-8. Dewey:306.43/03. LCCN:97-024837.
Audience: **g,l,u.** *Choice, 1998.*

Turner, Bryan (Introduction by) **HM585.M34513 1997**
Essays on the Sociology of Knowledge. Paper over Boards. Routledge. New York, NY. 1998. 336p. Karl Mannheim Ser., Vol. 5:Collected Works ISBN:0-415-15083-3, ISBN13: 978-0-415-15083-5. Dewey:306.42.
Audience: **l,u,f.**

Wallerstein, Immanuel **H61.15.W35 2004**
The Uncertainties of Knowledge. Trade Cloth. Temple University Press. Philadelphia, PA. 2004. 224p. Politics, History, and Social Change Ser. ISBN:1-59213-242-1, ISBN13: 978-1-59213-242-3. Dewey:300/.1. LCCN:2003-061649.
Audience: **u,f.** *Choice, 2005.*

Sociology of Education > Public Schools

Bowles, Samuel **E**
Schooling in Capitalist America : Educational Reform and the Contradictions of Economic life. Gintis, Herbert. Basic Books. 1976. ISBN:0-465-07230-5, ISBN13: 978-0-465-07230-9.
Audience: **l,u,f.**

Taylor, Denny & Dorsey-Gaines, Catherine **LC5131.T39 1988**
Growing up Literate: Learning from Inner-City Families. Trade Paper. Heinemann. Portsmouth, NH. 1988. 256p. ISBN:0-435-08457-7, ISBN13: 978-0-435-08457-8. Dewey:370.19/346/0973. LCCN:87-35270.
Audience: **u,f.**

Zimmerman, Jonathan **LC191.4**
Whose America?: Culture Wars in the Public Schools. Trade Paper, Perfect. Harvard University Press. Cambridge, MA. 2005. 320p. ISBN:0-674-01860-5, ISBN13: 978-0-674-01860-0. Dewey:306.43/2/0973.
Audience: **g,l,u.** *Choice, 2003.*

Sociology of Education > Lifetime Learning

Coben, Diana **LC5225.S64C63 1998**
Radical Heroes: Gramsci, Freire and the Politics of Adult. Joe L. Kincheloe (Foreword by). Cloth Text. Garland Publishing, Inc. New York, NY. 1998. 280p. Studies in the History of Education, Vol. 6 ISBN:0-8153-1898-7, ISBN13: 978-0-8153-1898-9. Dewey:374/.01. LCCN:98-011116.
Audience: **u,f.**

Gordon, Edward E. & Gordon, Elaine H. **LC151**
Literacy in America: Historic Journey and Contemporary Solutions. Trade Cloth. Greenwood Publishing Group, Inc. Portsmouth, NH. 2002. 352p. ISBN:0-275-95524-9, ISBN13: 978-0-275-95524-3. Dewey:302.2/242. LCCN:2002-068609.
Audience: **l,u,f.** *Choice, 2003.*

Hooker, John **HM1211.H66 2004**
Working Across Cultures: A Professional's Guide to Cultural Understanding. Trade Cloth. Stanford University Press. Palo Alto, CA. 2003. 416p. ISBN:0-8047-4807-1, ISBN13: 978-0-8047-4807-0. Dewey:306. LCCN:2003-007573.
Audience: **g,l,u.** *Choice, 2004.*

Sociology of Education > Colleges and Universities

Bender, Thomas (Editor) **LA174**
The University and the City: From Medieval Origins to the Present. Paper Text. Oxford University Press, Inc. New York, NY. 1991. 328p. ISBN:0-19-506775-4, ISBN13: 978-0-19-506775-0. Dewey:378/.009. LCCN:88-001411.
Audience: **l,u,f.** *Choice, 1989.*

Mills, C. Wright **HM27.M5 1964**
Sociology and Pragmatism: The Higher Learning in America. Horowitz, Irving Louis (Editor). Paine-Whitman Publishers. 1964.
Audience: **l,u,f.**

Demography

HC59.L54
The Limits to Growth; A Report for the Club of Rome's Project on the Predicament of Mankind. Trade Cloth. Universe Books. Strathfield South, NSW. 1972. 205p. ISBN:0-87663-165-0, ISBN13: 978-0-87663-165-2. Dewey:330.9/04. LCCN:73-187907.
Audience: **l,u,f.**

JX1395
Statistical Yearbook, No. 44. CD-ROM, Book, Other. United Nations Publications. New York, NY. 2005. 900p. ISBN:92-1-161432-5, ISBN13: 978-92-1-161432-9. Dewey:327.
Audience: **g,l,u,f.**

Department for Economic and Social Affairs Statistics Division Staff (Editor) **HA17**
Demographic Yearbook 2001. Ed. 53. Trade Cloth. United Nations Publications. New York, NY. 2004. 749p. ISBN:92-1-051094-1, ISBN13: 978-92-1-051094-3. Dewey:304.6.
Audience: **g,l,u,f.**

Farley, Reynolds (Editor) **HC106.8.S7352 1995**
State of the Union: America in the 1990s: Economic Trends. Trade Cloth. Russell Sage Foundation. New York, NY. 1995. 375p. 1990 Census Research Ser., Vol. 1 ISBN:0-87154-240-4, ISBN13: 978-0-87154-240-3. Dewey:303.4/0973. LCCN:94-040284.
Audience: **l,u,f.** *Choice, 1995.*

Farley, Reynolds (Editor) **HC106.8.S7352 1995**
State of the Union: America in the 1990s: Social Trends. Trade Cloth. Russell Sage Foundation. New York, NY. 1995. 377p. 1990 Census Research Ser., Vol. 2 ISBN:0-87154-241-2, ISBN13: 978-0-87154-241-0. Dewey:303.4/0973. LCCN:94-040284.
Audience: **l,u,f.**

Hardin, Garrett **HQ766.7.H35 1993**
Living Within Limits: Ecology, Economics and Population Taboos. Cloth Text. Oxford University Press, Inc. New York, NY. 1993. 352p. ISBN:0-19-507811-X, ISBN13: 978-0-19-507811-4. Dewey:304.6/66. LCCN:92-024250.
Audience: **u,f.** *Choice, 1993.*

Malthus, Thomas. R. **HB861**
An Essay on the Principle of Population. Kessinger Publishing, LLC. 2004. ISBN:1-4191-0644-9, ISBN13: 978-1-4191-0644-6.
Audience: **g,l,u,f.**

Meadows, Dennis, et al. **HD75.6.M437 2004**
The Limits to Growth: The 30-Year Update. Jorgen Randers & Donella H. Meadows (Authors). Trade Cloth. Chelsea Green Publishing. White River Junction, VT. 2004. 352p. ISBN:1-931498-51-2, ISBN13: 978-1-931498-51-7. Dewey:330.9. LCCN:2004-000125.
Audience: **l,u,f.** *Choice, 2004.*

Skar, Sarah L **F2230.2.K4S58 1994**
Lives Together - Worlds Apart: Quechua Colonization in Jungle and City. Oxford University Press, Inc. 1994. ISBN:82-00-21957-7, ISBN13: 978-82-00-21957-6.
Audience: **u,f.**

Demography > Assimilation

Adams, David W. **E97.5.A35 1995**
Education for Extinction: American Indians and the Boarding School Experience, 1875-1928. Trade Cloth. University Press of Kansas. Lawrence, KS. 1997. 408p. ISBN:0-7006-0735-8, ISBN13: 978-0-7006-0735-8. Dewey:371.97/97. LCCN:95-007638.
Audience: **l,u.** *Choice, 1996.*

Caplan, Nathan, et al. **E184.I43.C37 1989**
The Boat People and Achievement in America: A Study of Economic and Educational Success. John K. Whitmore & Marcella Trautmann (Authors). Trade Cloth. University of Michigan Press. Chicago, IL. 1989. 256p. ISBN:0-472-09397-5, ISBN13: 978-0-472-09397-7. Dewey:306/.0899922. LCCN:89-030371.
Audience: **g,l,u,f.** *Choice, 1990.*

Hein, Jeremy **HV640.5.I5H44 1995**
From Migrants to Ethnic Minorities: The Settlement of Refugees from Vietnam, Laos, and Cambodia in the United States. Trade Cloth. Thomson Gale. Farmington Hills, MI. 1995. 193p. Twayne's Immigrant Heritage of America Ser. ISBN:0-8057-8432-2, ISBN13: 978-0-8057-8432-9. Dewey:362.87/089/959. LCCN:94-041960.
Audience: **g,l,u,f.** *Choice, 1995.*

Hing, Bill Ong **E184.A1H54 1997**
To Be an American: Cultural Pluralism and the Rhetoric of Assimilation. Trade Cloth. New York University Press. New York, NY. 1997. 304p. ISBN:0-8147-3523-1, ISBN13: 978-0-8147-3523-7. Dewey:305.8/00973. LCCN:96-035678.
Audience: **l,u,f.** *Choice, 1997.*

Read, Jen'nan Ghazal **E184.A65R43 2003**
Culture, Class, and Work among Arab-American Women. Library Binding. LFB Scholarly Publishing LLC. New York, NY. 2004. 166p. The New Americans, :Recent Immigration and American Society ISBN:1-59332-006-X, ISBN13: 978-1-59332-006-5. Dewey:331.4/089/927073. LCCN:2003-023712.
Audience: **u,f.**

Demography > Immigration

JV6008
International Organization for Migration (IOM). http://www.iom.int/
International Organization for Migration..
Audience: **g,l,u,f.**

Alarcon, Alicia **F870.C34M54 2004**
The Border Patrol Ate My Dust. Ethriam Cash Brammer (Translator). Trade Paper. Arte Publico Press. Houston, TX. 2004. 192p. ISBN:1-55885-432-0, ISBN13: 978-1-55885-432-1. Dewey:979.4/00468728. LCCN:2004-048530.
Audience: **g,l,u.**

Baily, Samuel L. **JV8131.B34 2004**
Immigrants in the Lands of Promise: Italians in Buenos Aires and New York City, 18701914. Trade Paper. Cornell University Press. Ithaca, NY. 2004. 336p. ISBN:0-8014-8882-6, ISBN13: 978-0-8014-8882-5. Dewey:305.8/5108212/09034.
Audience: **u,f.**

Baker, Jonathan & Aina, Tade Akin (Editors) **HB2121.A3 M53 1995**
The Migration Experience in Africa. Trade Cloth. Coronet Books. Philadelphia, PA. 1995. 353p. ISBN:91-7106-366-8, ISBN13: 978-91-7106-366-3. Dewey:304.80967. LCCN:95-233824.
Audience: **l,u,f.** *Choice, 1995.*

Barnes, Kenneth C. **DT634.B37 2004**
Journey of Hope: The Back to Africa Movement in Arkansas in the Late 1800s. Trade Paper. University of North Carolina Press. Chapel Hill, NC. 2004. 288p. John Hope Franklin Series in African American History and Culture ISBN:0-8078-5550-2, ISBN13: 978-0-8078-5550-8. Dewey:966.62/004960730767. LCCN:2003-027748.
Audience: **u,f.** *Choice, 2005.*

Bowden, Charles **HV5825.B692 2004**
Down by the River: Drugs, Money, Murder, and Family. Trade Paper. Simon & Schuster. New York, NY. 2003. 464p. ISBN:0-7432-4457-5, ISBN13: 978-0-7432-4457-2. Dewey:363.45/0972/1. LCCN:2002-070633.
Audience: **g,l,u,f.**

Caplan, Nathan, et al. **E184.I43.C37 1989**
The Boat People and Achievement in America: A Study of Economic and Educational Success. John K. Whitmore & Marcella Trautmann (Authors). Trade Cloth. University of Michigan Press. Chicago, IL. 1989. 256p. ISBN:0-472-09397-5, ISBN13: 978-0-472-09397-7. Dewey:306/.0899922. LCCN:89-030371.
Audience: **g,l,u,f.** *Choice, 1990.*

Clark, William A. V. **JV6465.C58 2003**
Immigrants and the American Dream: Remaking the Middle Class. Cloth over Boards. Guilford Publications, Inc. New York, NY. 2003. 254p. ISBN:1-57230-880-X, ISBN13: 978-1-57230-880-0. Dewey:973.92/086/91. LCCN:2003-004906.
Audience: **g,l,u.** *Choice, 2004.*

Clausen, Christopher **E169.12.C543 2000**
Faded Mosaic: The Emergence of Post-Cultural America. Book, Other. Ivan R. Dee Publisher. Blue Ridge Summit, PA. 2000. 224p. ISBN:1-56663-283-8, ISBN13: 978-1-56663-283-6. Dewey:306/.0973. LCCN:99-059433.
Audience: **u,f.**

Cook, Terrence E. **GN495**
Separation, Assimilation, or Accommodation: Contrasting Ethnic Minority Policies. Book, Other. Greenwood Publishing Group, Inc. Portsmouth, NH. 2003. 216p. ISBN:0-275-97825-7, ISBN13: 978-0-275-97825-9. Dewey:305.8. LCCN:2002-033384.
Audience: **u,f.** *Choice, 2004.*

Dow, Mark **JV6483.D69 2004**
American Gulag: Inside U. S. Immigration Prisons. Trade Cloth. University of California Press. Berkeley, CA. 2004. 385p. ISBN:0-520-23942-3, ISBN13: 978-0-520-23942-5. Dewey:365/.4. LCCN:2003-026179.
Audience: **l,u,f.** *Choice, 2004.*

Foner, Nancy (Editor) **JV6013.5.I55 2000**
Immigration Research for a New Century: Multidisciplinary Perspectives. Rumbaut, Ruben G. (Editor) ; Gold, Steven J. (Editor). Russell Sage Foundation. 2000. ISBN:0-87154-260-9, ISBN13: 978-0-87154-260-1.
Audience: **u,f.**

Fugita, Stephen S. & O'Brien, David J. **E184.J3**
Japanese American Ethnicity: The Persistence of Community. Paper Text. University of Washington Press. Seattle, WA. 1994. 218p. ISBN:0-295-97376-5, ISBN13: 978-0-295-97376-0. Dewey:305.895/6073. LCCN:90-256584.
Audience: **l,u,f.** *Choice, 1992.*

Gerber, David A. & Kraut, Alan M. (Editors) **JB6450**
American Immigration and Ethnicity: A Reader. Cloth over Boards. Palgrave Macmillan. New York, NY. 2005. 360p. ISBN:0-312-29349-6, ISBN13: 978-0-312-29349-9. Dewey:325.73. LCCN:2006-295464.
Audience: **g,l.**

Gutiérrez, David G. **E184.M5G86 1995**
Walls and Mirrors: Mexican Americans, Mexican Immigrants, and the Politics of Ethnicity. Trade Paper. University of California Press. Berkeley, CA. 1995. 334p. ISBN:0-520-20219-8, ISBN13: 978-0-520-20219-1. Dewey:323.1/168073. LCCN:94-001892.
Audience: **u,f.** *Choice, 1995.*

Heilman, Samuel C. **E184.J5H5345 1995**
Portrait of American Jews: The Last Half of the Twentieth Century. Trade Cloth. University of Washington Press. Seattle, WA. 1995. 208p. Samuel and Althea Stroum Lectures in Jewish Studies ISBN:0-295-97470-2, ISBN13: 978-0-295-97470-5. Dewey:305.892/4073. LCCN:95-013360.
Audience: **l,u,f.** *Choice, 1996.*

Hein, Jeremy **HV640.5.I5H44 1995**
From Migrants to Ethnic Minorities: The Settlement of Refugees from Vietnam, Laos, and Cambodia in the United States. Trade Cloth. Thomson Gale. Farmington Hills, MI. 1995. 193p. Twayne's Immigrant Heritage of America Ser. ISBN:0-8057-8432-2, ISBN13: 978-0-8057-8432-9. Dewey:362.87/089/959. LCCN:94-041960.
Audience: **g,l,u,f.** *Choice, 1995.*

International Organization for Migration (IOM) **GN387**
☐ International Organization for Migration (IOM). http://www.iom.int/
Audience: **g,l,u,f.**

Jacobsen, Knut A. & Pratap, Kumar P. **DS339.4.S67 2003**
South Asians in the Diaspora: Histories and Religious Traditions. Trade Cloth. Brill Academic Publishers. Leiden, 2004. xxiv, 520p. Studies in the History of Religions, Vol. 101 ISBN:90-04-12488-8, ISBN13: 978-90-04-12488-2. Dewey:909/.04914. LCCN:2003-065319.
Audience: **l,u,f.** *Choice, 2004.*

Jaffe, A. J. & Sperber, C. **E98.A84.J34 1992**
The First Immigrants from Asia: A Population History of the North American Indian. Trade Cloth. Basic Books. New York, NY. 1992. 358p. ISBN:0-306-43952-2, ISBN13: 978-0-306-43952-0. Dewey:970.00497. LCCN:92-013590.
Audience: **l,u,f.** *Choice, 1993.*

Kelley, Ninette & Trebilcock, Michael J. **JV7233.K45 1998**
The Making of the Mosaic: A History of Canadian Immigration Policy. Cloth over Boards. University of Toronto Press. Toronto,

ON. 1998. 704p. ISBN:0-8020-4323-2, ISBN13: 978-0-8020-4323-8. Dewey:325.71/09. LCCN:99-185777.
Audience: **l,u,f.** *Choice, 1999.*

Lawless, Richard (Editor) **JV7590**
Middle East and North African Immigrants in Europe: Current Impact; Local and National Responses. Trade Cloth. Routledge. New York, NY. 2005. 320p. ISBN:0-415-34830-7, ISBN13: 978-0-415-34830-0. Dewey:304.8/4056. LCCN:2004-061495.
Audience: **l,u,f.**

Ma, Laurence J. C. & Cartier, Carolyn L. **DS732.C5563 2002**
The Chinese Diaspora: Space, Place, Mobility and Identity. Book, Other. Rowman & Littlefield Publishers, Inc. Lanham, MD. 2003. 400p. Why of Where Ser. ISBN:0-7425-1755-1, ISBN13: 978-0-7425-1755-4. Dewey:909/.04951. LCCN:2002-151795.
Audience: **l,u,f.** *Choice, 2003.*

Martínez, Rubén **E184.AI**
The New Americans: Seven Families Journey to Another Country. Trade Paper. New Press, The. New York, NY. 2005. 264p. ISBN:1-56584-998-1, ISBN13: 978-1-56584-998-3. Dewey:304.873.
Audience: **g,l.**

Nugent, Walter **JV6465.N84 1992**
Crossings: The Great Transatlantic Migrations, 1870-1914. Cloth Text. Indiana University Press. Bloomington, IN. 1992. 256p. ISBN:0-253-34140-X, ISBN13: 978-0-253-34140-2. Dewey:304.8/094. LCCN:92-007156.
Audience: **g,l,u,f.** *Choice, 1993.*

Perlmann, Joel **E184.M5P427 2005**
Italians Then, Mexicans Now: Immigrant Origins and Second-Generation Progress, 1890 to 2000. Trade Cloth. Russell Sage Foundation. New York, NY. 2005. 208p. ISBN:0-87154-662-0, ISBN13: 978-0-87154-662-3. Dewey:330.973/0089/6872. LCCN:2005-048999.
Audience: **l,u,f.**

Urrea, Luis Alberto **JV6475.U77 2004**
The Devil's Highway: A True Story. Trade Cloth. Little Brown & Company. New York, NY. 2004. 256p. ISBN:0-316-74671-1, ISBN13: 978-0-316-74671-7. Dewey:304.8/73072. LCCN:2003-058930.
Audience: **g,l,u.**

Widdis, Randy William **E184.C2 W53 1998**
With Scarcely a Ripple: Anglo-Canadian Migration into the United States and Western Canada, 1880-1920. Trade Cloth. McGill-Queen's University Press. Montreal, PQ. 1998. 418p. ISBN:0-7735-1733-2, ISBN13: 978-0-7735-1733-2. Dewey:304.8/73071/089112. LCCN:00-340518.
Audience: **u,f.** *Choice, 1999.*

Wood, Andrew Grant **F787.O5 2004**
On the Border: Society and Culture Between the United States and Mexico. Book, Other. Rowman & Littlefield Publishers, Inc. Lanham, MD. 2004. 320p. Latin American Silhouettes Ser. ISBN:0-8420-5172-4, ISBN13: 978-0-8420-5172-9. Dewey:972/.1. LCCN:2003-023426.
Audience: **l,u,f.**

Demography > Immigration > Refugees

HV64.3

UNHCR : The UN Refugee Agency.
http://www.unhcr.ch/cgi-bin/texis/vtx/home
United Nations. Office of the United Nations High Commissioner for Refugees.
Audience: **g,l,u,f.**

Global IDP Survey Staff (Contribution by) **HV640.I516 2002**
Internally Displaced People: A Global Survey. Ed. 2. Trade Cloth. Earthscan Canada. Toronto, ON. 2002. 256p. ISBN:1-85383-953-1, ISBN13: 978-1-85383-953-5. Dewey:325/.21. LCCN:2002-012951.
Audience: **l,u,f.** *Choice, 2003.*

Moorehead, Caroline **HV640.M66 2005**
Human Cargo: A Journey among Refugees. Cloth over Boards. Henry Holt & Company. New York, NY. 2005. 352p. ISBN:0-8050-7443-0, ISBN13: 978-0-8050-7443-7. Dewey:305.9/06914. LCCN:2004-054239.
Audience: **g,l,u,f.**

United Nations High Commissioner for Refugees Staff **HV640.S677 2000**
The State of the World's Refugees 2000: Fifty Years of Humanitarian Action. Cloth Text. Oxford University Press, Inc. New York, NY. 2001. 352p. ISBN:0-19-924104-X, ISBN13: 978-0-19-924104-0. Dewey:362.87. LCCN:2001-274921.
Audience: **g,l,u.** *Choice, 2001.*

Van Hear, Nicholas **JV6032.V36 1998**
New Diasporas: The Mass Exodus, Dispersal and Regrouping of Migrant Communities. Trade Cloth. University of Washington Press. Seattle, WA. 1998. 298p. Global Diasporas Ser., Vol. 2: ISBN:0-295-97712-4, ISBN13: 978-0-295-97712-6. Dewey:304.8/09045. LCCN:98-012125.
Audience: **u,f.** *Choice, 1999.*

Zolberg, Aristide R., et al. **HV640.4.D44Z65 1992**
Escape from Violence: Conflict and the Refugee Crisis in the Developing World. Astri Suhrke & Sergio Aguayo (Authors). Trade Paper. Oxford University Press, Inc. New York, NY. 1992. 394p. ISBN:0-19-507916-7, ISBN13: 978-0-19-507916-6. Dewey:362.8/7/091724.
Audience: **u,f.** *Choice, 1990.*

Political Sociology

Habermas, Jürgen **HM24**
The Structural Transformation of the Public Sphere: An Inquiry into a Category of Bourgois Society. Thomas Burger (Translator). Trade Paper. MIT Press. Cambridge, MA. 1991. 333p. Studies in Contemporary German Social Thought ISBN:0-262-58108-6, ISBN13: 978-0-262-58108-0. Dewey:321.809.
Audience: **u,f.**

Kertzer, David I. **JA76**
Ritual, Politics and Power. Trade Paper. Yale University Press. Cumberland, RI. 1989. 235p. ISBN:0-300-04362-7, ISBN13: 978-0-300-04362-4. Dewey:306/.2.
Audience: **l,u,f.** *Choice, 1988.*

Mapel, David & Nardin, Terry **JZ1306.I58 1998**
International Society: Diverse Ethical Perspectives. Cloth Text. Princeton University Press. Princeton, NJ. 1998. 288p. Ethikon Series in Comparative Ethics ISBN:0-691-05771-0, ISBN13: 978-0-691-05771-2. Dewey:172/.4. LCCN:97-019756.
Audience: **u,f.** *Choice, 1998.*

Roberts, John & Crossley, Nick (Editors) **HM661**
After Habermas: New Perspectives on the Public Sphere. Trade Paper. Blackwell Publishing, Inc. Malden, MA. 2004. 192p. Sociological Review Monographs ISBN:1-4051-2365-6, ISBN13: 978-1-4051-2365-5. Dewey:303.3/8. LCCN:2004-302318.
Audience: **l,u,f.** *Choice, 2005.*

Political Sociology > War and Conflict

Aho, James **HM136.A324 1994**
This Thing of Darkness: A Sociology of the Enemy. Trade Cloth. University of Washington Press. Seattle, WA. 1994. 224p. ISBN:0-295-97355-2, ISBN13: 978-0-295-97355-5. Dewey:303.6. LCCN:94-012015.
Audience: **g.** *Choice, 1995.*

Bandura, Albert **BF575.A3**
Aggression: A Social Learning Analysis. Cloth Text. Prentice Hall PTR. Upper Saddle River, NJ. 1973. 368p. Social Learning Theory Ser. ISBN:0-13-020743-8, ISBN13: 978-0-13-020743-2. Dewey:302.5/4. LCCN:72-012990.
Audience: **u,f.** B

Coser, Lewis A. **HM136**
Functions of Social Conflict. Trade Paper. Simon & Schuster. New York, NY. 1964. 192p. ISBN:0-02-906810-X, ISBN13: 978-0-02-906810-6. Dewey:303.6. LCCN:56-006874.
Audience: **l,u,f.** B

Creighton, Colin & Shaw, Martin (Editors) **HM36.5 .S62 1987**
The Sociology of War and Peace. Paper Text. Sheridan House, Inc. Dobbs Ferry, NY. 1986. 256p. Explorations in Sociology Ser., No. 24 ISBN:0-911378-66-9, ISBN13: 978-0-911378-66-5. Dewey:303.6/6. LCCN:86-019915.
Audience: **l.** *Choice, 1987.*

Hale, John Rigby **U43.E95.H35 1985**
War and Society in Renaissance Europe, 1450-1620. Cloth Text. Palgrave Macmillan. New York, NY. 1985. 282p. ISBN:0-312-85603-2, ISBN13: 978-0-312-85603-8. Dewey:306/.27/094. LCCN:85-040404.
Audience: **u.** B *Choice, 1985.*

Hardin, Russell **HM131.H239 1995**
One for All: The Logic of Group Conflict. Cloth Text. Princeton University Press. Princeton, NJ. 1995. 276p. ISBN:0-691-04350-7, ISBN13: 978-0-691-04350-0. Dewey:305. LCCN:94-023626.
Audience: **l,u,f.** *Choice, 1995.*

Meyer, Leisa D. **UA565.W6M48 1996**
Creating G. I. Jane: Sexuality and Power in the Women's Army Corps During World War II. Trade Cloth. Columbia University Press. New York, NY. 1996. 288p. ISBN:0-231-10144-9, ISBN13: 978-0-231-10144-8. Dewey:940.54/0973/082. LCCN:96-013858.
Audience: **l,u.** *Choice, 1997.*

Meyer, Thomas **HM1211.M49 2001**
Identity Mania: Fundamentalism and the Politicization of Cultural Differences. Trade Cloth. Zed Books, Ltd. London, 2002. 144p. ISBN:1-84277-062-4, ISBN13: 978-1-84277-062-7. Dewey:306. LCCN:2001-045296.
Audience: **u,f.**

Roach, Colleen (Editor) **P91.C539 1993**
Communication and Culture in War and Peace. Trade Cloth. SAGE Publications, Inc. Thousand Oaks, CA. 1993. 276p. Communication and Human Values Ser., Vol. 11 ISBN:0-8039-5062-4, ISBN13: 978-0-8039-5062-7. Dewey:302.2. LCCN:92-035951.
Audience: **u,f.** *Choice, 1993.*

Simmel, Georg **B3329.S62**
The Conflict in Modern Culture and Other Essays. K. Peter Etzkorn (Translator). Trade Paper. Books on Demand. Ann Arbor, MI. 152p. ISBN:0-598-12101-3, ISBN13: 978-0-598-12101-1. Dewey:901.9. LCCN:67-025064.
Audience: **l,u,f.**

Political Sociology > War and Conflict > Peace

Brewer, John D. **HN398.N6B74 2003**
C. Wright Mills and the Ending of Violence. Cloth over Boards. Palgrave Macmillan. New York, NY. 2003. 224p. ISBN:0-333-80180-6, ISBN13: 978-0-333-80180-2. Dewey:303.6/09416. LCCN:2003-048276.
Audience: **u,f.** *Choice, 2004.*

Fry, Douglas P. **GN495.2.F79 2005**
The Human Potential for Peace: An Anthropological Challenge to Assumptions about War and Violence. Trade Cloth. Oxford University Press, Inc. New York, NY. 2005. 384p. ISBN:0-19-518177-8, ISBN13: 978-0-19-518177-7. Dewey:303.6. LCCN:2004-063133.
Audience: **u,f.**

Gandhi, Mahatma **HM1281.G35 2001**
Non-Violent Resistance. Trade Paper. Dover Publications, Inc. Mineola, NY. 2001. 416p. ISBN:0-486-41606-2, ISBN13: 978-0-486-41606-9. Dewey:322.4. LCCN:2001-017199.
Audience: **g,l,u,f.**

Lynd, Staughton & Lynd, Alice (Editors) **HM278.L9 1995**
Nonviolence in America: A Documentary History. Trade Cloth. Orbis Books. Maryknoll, NY. 1995. 600p. ISBN:1-57075-013-0, ISBN13: 978-1-57075-013-7. Dewey:303.6/1. LCCN:94-041973.
Audience: **g.** B

Schock, Kurt **HM1281.S36 2004**
Unarmed Insurrections. Trade Paper. University of Minnesota Press. Minneapolis, MN. 2004. 224p. ISBN:0-8166-4193-5, ISBN13: 978-0-8166-4193-2. Dewey:303.6/1. LCCN:2004-015059.
Audience: **g,l,u,f.**

Political Sociology > War and Conflict > Terrorism

Library of Congress Staff, et al. **HV 6431**
The Sociology and Psychology of Terrorism: Who Becomes a Terrorist and Why? Federal Research Division Staff & Rex A. Hudson (Authors). Trade Paper. University Press of the Pacific. Miami, FL. 2005. 192p. ISBN:1-4102-1277-7, ISBN13: 978-1-4102-1277-1. Dewey:303.6/25.
Audience: **g,l,u.**

Maharidge, Dale **HN59.2.M34 2003**
Homeland. Michael Williamson (Photographer). Trade Cloth. Seven Stories Press. New York, NY. 2004. 384p. ISBN:1-58322-627-3, ISBN13: 978-1-58322-627-8. Dewey:303.6/0973. LCCN:2004-003572.
Audience: **g.**

Moghaddam, Fathali M. & Marsella, Anthony J. (Editors) **HV6431.U35 2003**
Understanding Terrorism: Psychosocial Roots, Consequences, and Interventions. Trade Cloth. American Psychological Association. Washington, DC. 2003. 328p. ISBN:1-59147-032-3, ISBN13: 978-1-59147-032-8. Dewey:303.6/25. LCCN:2003-009643.
Audience: **u,f.** *Choice, 2004.*

Political Sociology > Political Systems

Adorno, Theodor W., et al. **HM271**
The Authoritarian Personality. Else Frenkel-Brunswick, Daniel J. Levinson & R. Nevitt Sanford (Authors). Trade Paper. W. W. Norton & Company, Inc. New York, NY. 1993. 520p. ISBN:0-393-31112-0, ISBN13: 978-0-393-31112-9. Dewey:303.3/6.
Audience: **u,f.**

Altemeyer, Bob **HV271**
Enemies of Freedom: Understanding Right-Wing Authoritarianism. Trade Cloth. John Wiley & Sons, Inc. Hoboken, NJ. 1988. 378p. Social and Behavioral Science Ser. ISBN:1-55542-097-4, ISBN13: 978-1-55542-097-0. Dewey:303.3/6. LCCN:88-042774.
Audience: **g,l,u.** *Choice, 1989.*

Laski, Harold J. **JC574.2.E85L37 1997**
The Rise of European Liberalism. John Stanley (Introduction by). Trade Paper. Transaction Publishers. Somerset, NJ. 1997. 287p. ISBN:1-56000-845-8, ISBN13: 978-1-56000-845-3. Dewey:320.5/1/094. LCCN:96-020337.
Audience: **u,f.**

Moore, Barrington Jr. **HN15.M775 1993**
Social Origins of Dictatorship and Democracy: Lord and Peasant in the Making of the Modern World. Edward Friedman (Introduction by, Preface by), James C. Scott (Preface by). Trade Paper. Beacon Press. Boston, MA. 1993. 592p. ISBN:0-8070-5073-3, ISBN13: 978-0-8070-5073-6. Dewey:301. LCCN:93-017802.
Audience: **l,u,f.** B

Political Sociology > Political Systems > Nationalism

Chalk, Frank & Jonassohn, Kurt **HV6322.7.C44 1990**
The History and Sociology of Genocide: Analyses and Case Studies. Cloth over Boards. Yale University Press. Cumberland, RI. 1990. 480p. ISBN:0-300-04445-3, ISBN13: 978-0-300-04445-4. Dewey:304.6/63. LCCN:89-027381.
Audience: **u,f.** *Choice, 1991.*

Fenton, Steve & May, Stephen **JC312.E84 2002**
Ethnonational Identities. Cloth over Boards. Palgrave Macmillan. New York, NY. 2003. 272p. ISBN:0-333-75012-8, ISBN13: 978-0-333-75012-4. Dewey:320.54. LCCN:2002-072839.
Audience: **u,f.**

Marvin, Carolyn & Ingle, David W. **JC346 .M27 1999**
Blood Sacrifice and the Nation: Totem Rituals and the American Flag. Jeffrey C. Alexander & Steven Seidman (Contribution by). Trade Paper. Cambridge University Press. New York, NY. 1999. 414p. Cultural Social Studies ISBN:0-521-62609-9, ISBN13: 978-0-521-62609-5. Dewey:306.2/0973. LCCN:97-025640.
Audience: **u,f.** *Choice, 2000.*

Paris, Erna **D804.3**
Long Shadows: Truth, Lies and History. Trade Paper. Bloomsbury Publishing. New York, NY. 2002. 496p. ISBN:1-58234-210-5, ISBN13: 978-1-58234-210-8. Dewey:940.53/18.
Audience: **g.** *Choice, 2002.*

Political Sociology > Political Systems > Democracy

Drucker, Peter F., et al. **HN57 .D78 1980**
Power and Democracy in America. Delbert C. Miller, Robert A. Dahl, William V. D'Antonio & Howard J. Ehrlich (Authors). Trade Cloth. Greenwood Publishing Group, Inc. Portsmouth, NH. 1980. 181p. ISBN:0-313-22319-X, ISBN13: 978-0-313-22319-8. Dewey:303.3/3. LCCN:79-028576.
Audience: **g,l,u,f.**

Habermas, Jürgen **K372.H3313 1996**
Between Facts and Norms: Contributions to a Discourse Theory of Law and Democracy. William Rehg (Translator). Trade Cloth. MIT Press. Cambridge, MA. 1996. 631p. Studies in Contemporary German Social Thought ISBN:0-262-08243-8, ISBN13: 978-0-262-08243-3. Dewey:340.1/15. LCCN:95-040229.
Audience: **u,f.** *Choice, 1997.*

Winant, Howard **HT1507**
The World Is a Ghetto: Race and Democracy since World War II. Trade Paper. Basic Books. New York, NY. 2002. 448p. ISBN:0-465-04341-0, ISBN13: 978-0-465-04341-5. Dewey:305.8/009.
Audience: **g,l,u,f.**

Political Sociology > Political Systems > Totalitarianism

Bramstedt, Ernest K. **HV7938**
Dictatorship and Political Police: International Library of Sociology C: Political Sociology. Paper over Boards. Routledge. New York, NY. 2003. 288p. International Library of Sociology Ser. ISBN:0-415-17542-9, ISBN13: 978-0-415-17542-5. Dewey:363.2.
Audience: **u,f.**

Fromm, Erich **JC585**
Escape from Freedom. Cloth Text. Harcourt College Publishers. Fort Worth, TX. 1993. ISBN:0-03-008455-5, ISBN13: 978-0-03-008455-3. Dewey:323.44.
Audience: **l,u.** B

Goodrick-Clarke, Nicholas **JC481.G567 2001**
Black Sun: Aryan Cults, Esoteric Nazism and the Politics of Identity. Trade Cloth. New York University Press. New York, NY. 2001. 378p. ISBN:0-8147-3124-4, ISBN13: 978-0-8147-3124-6. Dewey:320.53/3. LCCN:2001-004429.
Audience: **u,f.** *Choice, 2002.*

Larsen, Stein U;
Hagtvet, Bernt; Myklebust, Jan P
Who Were the Fascists?: Social Roots of European Fascism. Stein U. Larsen (Editor) ; Bernt Hagtvet (Editor) ; Jan P. Myklebust (Editor). Oxford University Press, Inc. 1985. A Scandinavian University Press Publication ISBN:82-00-05331-8, ISBN13: 978-82-00-05331-6.
Audience: **g,l,u,f.** B

Muhlberger, Detlef **D726.5.S65 1987**
(Editor)
The Social Basis of European Fascist Movements. Library Binding. Croom Helm, Ltd. London, 1987. 384p. ISBN:0-7099-3585-4, ISBN13: 978-0-7099-3585-8. Dewey:320.5/33/094. LCCN:87-014093.
Audience: **u,f.** *Choice, 1988.*

Political Sociology > Political Systems > Zionism

Susser, Bernard **B3213.B84**
Existence and Utopia: The Social and Political Thought of Martin Buber. Trade Cloth. Fairleigh Dickinson University Press. Cranbury, NJ. 1981. 240p. ISBN:0-8386-2292-5, ISBN13: 978-0-8386-2292-6. Dewey:301/.092/4. LCCN:78-075188.
Audience: **u,f.**

Political Sociology > Political Systems > Other

Etzioni, Amitai **HN90.C6E88 1993**
The Spirit of Community: Rights, Responsibilities, and the Communitarian Agenda. Trade Cloth. Crown Publishing Group. New York, NY. 1993. viii, 323p. ISBN:0-517-59277-0, ISBN13: 978-0-517-59277-9. Dewey:307.1/4/0973. LCCN:92-031527.
Audience: **u,f.** *Choice, 1993.*

Parekh, Bhikhu C. **HM1271**
Rethinking Multiculturalism: Cultural Diversity and Political Theory. Ed. 2. Cloth over Boards. Palgrave Macmillan. New York, NY. 2006. 432p. ISBN:1-4039-4452-0, ISBN13: 978-1-4039-4452-8. Dewey:305.8/001. LCCN:2005-053018.
Audience: **l,u,f.** *Choice, 2001.*

Political Sociology > Policy Studies

Blau, Judith R. & **JC571.B5516 2004**
Moncada, Alberto
Human Rights: Beyond the Liberal Vision. Book, Other. Rowman & Littlefield Publishers, Inc. Lanham, MD. 2005. 232p. ISBN:0-7425-4242-4, ISBN13: 978-0-7425-4242-6. Dewey:323. LCCN:2004-018266.
Audience: **g,l.**

Ferguson, Iain, et al. **HV31.F39 2002**
Rethinking Welfare: A Critical Perspective. Michael Lavalette & Gerry Mooney (Authors). Cloth Text. SAGE Publications, Inc. Thousand Oaks, CA. 2002. 212p. ISBN:0-7619-6417-7, ISBN13: 978-0-7619-6417-9. Dewey:361.65. LCCN:2001-135895.
Audience: **g.**

Giddens, Anthony **JC573.G53 1994**
Beyond Left and Right: The Future of Radical Politics. Trade Cloth. Stanford University Press. Palo Alto, CA. 1994. 280p. ISBN:0-8047-2450-4, ISBN13: 978-0-8047-2450-0. Dewey:320.5/3. LCCN:94-066194.
Audience: **g,l,u,f.** *Choice, 1995.*

Goodman, John C., **RA412.G66 2004**
et al.
Lives at Risk: Single-Payer National Health Insurance in Countries Around the World. Gerald L. Musgrave & Devon M. Herrick (Authors), National Center for Policy Analysis (U.S.) Staff (Contribution by). Book, Other. Rowman & Littlefield Publishers, Inc. Lanham, MD. 2004. 272p. ISBN:0-7425-4151-7, ISBN13: 978-0-7425-4151-1. Dewey:368.4/2. LCCN:2004-006468.
Audience: **u,f.** *Choice, 2005.*

Haussman, Melissa **HV767.5.U5H38 2005**
Abortion Politics in North America. Trade Cloth. Lynne Rienner Publishers, Inc. Boulder, CO. 2004. 210p. ISBN:1-58826-336-3, ISBN13: 978-1-58826-336-0. Dewey:363.46/097. LCCN:2004-026064.
Audience: **g.** *Choice, 2005.*

Lasch, Christopher **HN64 .L29**
The New Radicalism in America, 1889-1963: The Intellectual As a Social Type. Ed. 2. Trade Paper. W. W. Norton & Company, Inc. New York, NY. 1997. 384p. ISBN:0-393-31696-3, ISBN13: 978-0-393-31696-4. Dewey:305.5/52/0973. LCCN:86-001387.
Audience: **u,f.**

Lippmann, Walter **HN64.L53 1985**
Drift and Mastery. Trade Paper. University of Wisconsin Press. Chicago, IL. 1986. 186p. ISBN:0-299-10604-7, ISBN13: 978-0-299-10604-1. Dewey:306/.0973. LCCN:85-040764.
Audience: **l,u,f.**

Luker, Kristin **HQ767.5.U5**
Abortion and the Politics of Motherhood. Ed. 2. Trade Paper. University of California Press. Berkeley, CA. 2000. 324p.

California Series on Social Choice and Political Economy, Vol. 3 ISBN:0-520-22477-9, ISBN13: 978-0-520-22477-3. Dewey:363.4/6/0973.
Audience: **l,u,f.** *B*

Midgley, James (Contribution by), et al. **HN65.H345 2000**
The Handbook of Social Policy. Martin Tracy & Michelle Livermore (Contribution by). Trade Cloth. AltaMira Press. Walnut Creek, CA. 1999. xv, 550p. ISBN:0-7619-1562-1, ISBN13: 978-0-7619-1562-1. Dewey:361.6/1/0973. LCCN:99-006716.
Audience: **g,l,u.**

Mills, C. Wright **HM101 .M59**
Power, Politics and People: The Collected Essays of C. Wright Mills. Irving L. Horowitz (Editor). Trade Paper. Oxford University Press, Inc. New York, NY. 1967. 670p. ISBN:0-19-500752-2, ISBN13: 978-0-19-500752-7. Dewey:303.3.
Audience: **g,l,u,f.** *B*

Moynihan, Daniel P. **HN28.M69 1997**
Miles to Go: A Personal History of Social Policy. Trade Cloth. Harvard University Press. Cambridge, MA. 1996. 288p. ISBN:0-674-57440-0, ISBN13: 978-0-674-57440-3. Dewey:361.6/1. LCCN:96-008291.
Audience: **g.** *Choice, 1997.*

Schofield, Norman **JA77**
Architects of Political Change: Constitutional Quandaries and Social Choice Theory. Randall Calvert & Thrainn Eggertsson (Contribution by). Trade Cloth. Cambridge University Press. New York, NY. 2006. 336p. Political Economy of Institutions and Decisions Ser. ISBN:0-521-83202-0, ISBN13: 978-0-521-83202-1. Dewey:320.97301. LCCN:2006-004120.
Audience: **u,f.**

Skocpol, Theda **HV91.S56 1992**
Protecting Soldiers and Mothers: The Political Origins of Social Policy in the United States. Trade Cloth. Harvard University Press. Cambridge, MA. 1992. 736p. ISBN:0-674-71765-1, ISBN13: 978-0-674-71765-7. Dewey:361.9/73. LCCN:92-008062.
Audience: **l,u,f.** *Choice, 1993.*

Solinger, Rickie **HQ767.5.U5S73265**
Beggars and Choosers: How the Politics of Choice Shapes Adoption, Abortion, and Welfare in the United States. Cloth over Boards. Farrar, Straus & Giroux. New York, NY. 2001. 320p. ISBN:0-8090-9702-8, ISBN13: 978-0-8090-9702-9. Dewey:363.46. LCCN:2001-016652.
Audience: **l,u,f.** *Choice, 2002.*

Wright, James D., et al. **HV4505.W76 1998**
Beside the Golden Door: Policy, Politics and the Homeless. Beth A. Rubin & Joel A. Devine (Authors). Trade Paper. Aldine Transaction. Somerset, NJ. 1998. 238p. Social Institutions and Social Change Ser. ISBN:0-202-30614-3, ISBN13: 978-0-202-30614-8. Dewey:363.5/96942/0973. LCCN:97-052031.
Audience: **l,u,f.** *Choice, 1998.*

Political Sociology > Policy Studies > Planning/Forecasting

Bell, Daniel **HN17.5.B38 1999**
Coming of Post-Industrial Society: A Venture in Social Forecasting. Trade Paper. Basic Books. New York, NY. 1976. 616p. Harper Colophon Bks. ISBN:0-465-09713-8, ISBN13: 978-0-465-09713-5. Dewey:309.1/04. LCCN:99-462446.
Audience: **l,u,f.** *B*

Skocpol, Theda **HN65.S5635 2000**
The Missing Middle: Working Families and the Future of American Social Policy. Trade Cloth. W. W. Norton & Company, Inc. New York, NY. 2000. 256p. A Century Foundation Bk. ISBN:0-393-04822-5, ISBN13: 978-0-393-04822-3. Dewey:361.6/1/0973. LCCN:99-037842.
Audience: **g.** *Choice, 2000.*

Toffler, Alvin **HM101**
Future Shock. Library Binding. Sagebrush Education Resources. Caledonia, MN. 1971. ISBN:0-8085-0152-6, ISBN13: 978-0-8085-0152-7. Dewey:301.2/4.
Audience: **g.** *B*

Political Sociology > Policy Studies > Social Indicators

Fox, Karl A. **HN25**
Social Indicators and Social Theory: Elements of an Operational System. Ed. 99. Trade Cloth. John Wiley & Sons, Inc. Hoboken, NJ. 1974. 328p. Urban Research Ser. ISBN:0-471-27060-1, ISBN13: 978-0-471-27060-7. Dewey:300/.72. LCCN:74-016255.
Audience: **u,f.**

MacRae, Duncan Jr. **H97 .M33 1985**
Policy Indicators: Links Between Social Science and Public Debate. Trade Cloth. University of North Carolina Press. Chapel Hill, NC. 1985. 430p. Urban and Regional Policy and Development Studies ISBN:0-8078-1628-0, ISBN13: 978-0-8078-1628-8. Dewey:361.6/1. LCCN:84-017294.
Audience: **u,f.** *Choice, 1985.*

Political Sociology > Policy Studies > Ethics

Addams, Jane **HN64.A2 2002**
Democracy and Social Ethics. Charlene Haddock Seigfried (Introduction by). Trade Cloth. University of Illinois Press. Champaign, IL. 2001. 168p. ISBN:0-252-02710-8, ISBN13: 978-0-252-02710-9. Dewey:303.3/72/0973. LCCN:2001-002292.
Audience: **l,u.** *B*

Behrman, Greg **RA643.83.B44 2004**
The Invisible People: How the U. S. Has Slept Through the Global AIDS Pandemic, the Greatest Humanitarian Catastrophe of Our Time. Trade Cloth. Simon & Schuster. New York, NY.

2004. 368p. ISBN:0-7432-5755-3, ISBN13: 978-0-7432-5755-8. Dewey:362.196/9792/00973. LCCN:2004-040466.
Audience: **g,l,u.**

Etzioni, Amitai **HM216 .E85 1996**
The New Golden Rule: Community and Morality in a Democratic Society. Trade Paper. Basic Books. New York, NY. 1998. 336p. ISBN:0-465-04999-0, ISBN13: 978-0-465-04999-8. Dewey:320.5.
Audience: **g,l,u.**

Habermas, Jurgen **B3258.H322**
The Habermas Reader. William Outhwaite (Editor). Trade Cloth. Polity Press. Cambridge, 1996. 400p. ISBN:0-7456-1393-4, ISBN13: 978-0-7456-1393-2. Dewey:301/.01.
Audience: **l,u.**

Mappes, Thomas A. & Zembaty, Jane S. **HM216.M27 1997**
Social Ethics: Morality and Social Policy. Ed. 5. Trade Paper. McGraw-Hill Higher Education. Burr Ridge, IL. 1996. 544p. ISBN:0-07-040143-8, ISBN13: 978-0-07-040143-3. Dewey:170. LCCN:96-007924.
Audience: **l,u,f.**

Niebuhr, Reinhold **HM665.N5 2001**
Moral Man and Immoral Society: A Study in Ethics and Politics. Langdon B. Gilkey (Introduction by). Trade Cloth. Westminster John Knox Press. Louisville, KY. 2004. 320p. Library of Theological Ethics ISBN:0-664-22474-1, ISBN13: 978-0-664-22474-5. Dewey:301. LCCN:2003-267709.
Audience: **l,u,f.** B

Phillips, Derek L. **HM21**
Towards a Just Social Order. Princeton University Press. 1986. ISBN:0-691-09422-5, ISBN13: 978-0-691-09422-9.
Audience: **g,l,u,f.**

Sorokin, Pitirim A. & Lunden, Walter A. **HM216 .S59**
Power and Morality. Trade Cloth. Porter Sargent Publishers, Inc. Boston, MA. 1959. Extending Horizons Ser. ISBN:0-87558-032-7, ISBN13: 978-0-87558-032-6. Dewey:301.155.
Audience: **l,u.**

Sumner, William Graham **PN2285**
What Social Classes Owe to Each Other. Library Binding. Reprint Services Company. Temecula, CA. 1999. Notable American Authors Ser. ISBN:0-7812-8972-6, ISBN13: 978-0-7812-8972-6. Dewey:791.0922.
Audience: **g,l,u,f.** B

Szasz, Thomas **RC438.S92 1997**
The Manufacture of Madness: A Comparative Study of the Inquisition and the Mental Health Movement. Trade Paper. Syracuse University Press. Syracuse, NY. 1997. 426p. ISBN:0-8156-0461-0, ISBN13: 978-0-8156-0461-7. Dewey:616.89/009. LCCN:96-048784.
Audience: **l,u,f.**

Williams, Walter **HN60.W55 1998**
Honest Numbers and Democracy: Social Policy Analysis in the White House, Congress, and the Federal Agencies. Book, Other. Georgetown University Press. Washington, DC. 1998. 336p. ISBN:0-87840-684-0, ISBN13: 978-0-87840-684-5. Dewey:306/.0973. LCCN:97-037972.
Audience: **g,l,u,f.** *Choice, 1998.*

Community/Regional Studies

Bell, Colin & Newby, Howard **HM45**
Community Studies: An Introduction to the Sociology of the Local Community. Ed. 3. Paper Text. Routledge. New York, NY. 1979. Studies in Sociology ISBN:0-04-300032-0, ISBN13: 978-0-04-300032-8. Dewey:301.3/4/018.
Audience: **l.** B

Bender, Thomas **HN57 .B455**
Community and Social Change in America. Trade Cloth. Rutgers University Press. Piscataway, NJ. 1978. Sanford-Erpf Lectures ISBN:0-8135-0858-4, ISBN13: 978-0-8135-0858-0. Dewey:301.34/0973. LCCN:78-001677.
Audience: **g.**

Stoneall, Linda **HM131.S8257**
Country Life, City Life: Five Theories of Community. Trade Cloth. Greenwood Publishing Group, Inc. Portsmouth, NH. 1983. 336p. ISBN:0-275-91588-3, ISBN13: 978-0-275-91588-9. Dewey:307.
Audience: **g,l,u,f.** B

Velez-Ibanez, Carlos G. **F790.M5V45 1996**
Border Visions: Mexican Cultures of the Southwest United States. Trade Cloth. University of Arizona Press. Tucson, AZ. 1996. xii, 360p. ISBN:0-8165-1422-4, ISBN13: 978-0-8165-1422-9. Dewey:305.868/72073. LCCN:96-010100.
Audience: **l,u,f.** *Choice, 1997.*

Community/Regional Studies > Urban

Burgess, Ernest W. & Bogue, Donald J. (Editors) **HT108.B8**
Contributions to Urban Sociology. Library Binding. University of Chicago Press. Chicago, IL. 1964. ISBN:0-226-08055-2, ISBN13: 978-0-226-08055-0. Dewey:301.36082. LCCN:63-021309.
Audience: **l,u,f.** B

Duany, Andres, et al. **HT123**
Suburban Nation: The Rise of Sprawl and the Decline of the American Dream. Elizabeth Plater-Zyberk & Jeff Speck (Authors). Trade Paper. Farrar, Straus & Giroux. New York, NY. 2001. 320p. ISBN:0-86547-606-3, ISBN13: 978-0-86547-606-6. Dewey:307.76/0973.
Audience: **l,u,f.** *Choice, 2000.*

Fischer, Claude S. **HT111.F56**
To Dwell among Friends: Personal Networks in Town and City. Trade Paper. University of Chicago Press. Chicago, IL. 1982. 459p. ISBN:0-226-25138-1, ISBN13: 978-0-226-25138-7. Dewey:307. LCCN:81-011505.
Audience: **l,u,f.**

Garreau, Joel **HT334.U5G37 1991**
The Edge City: Life on the New Frontier. Trade Cloth. Doubleday Publishing. New York, NY. 1991. 560p. ISBN:0-385-26249-3, ISBN13: 978-0-385-26249-1. Dewey:307.76/0973. LCCN:91-010548.
Audience: **l,u,f.** *Choice, 1992.*

Groth, Paul **HD7288.U4G76 1994**
Living Downtown: The History of Residential Hotels in the United States. Trade Cloth. University of California Press. Berkeley, CA. 1994. 423p. ISBN:0-520-06876-9, ISBN13: 978-0-520-06876-6. Dewey:647.9473/01. LCCN:93-039896.
Audience: **g,l.** *Choice, 1995.*

Jargowsky, Paul A. **HN90.C6J37 1997**
Poverty and Place: Ghettos, Barrios, and the American City. Trade Cloth. Russell Sage Foundation. New York, NY. 1997. 304p. ISBN:0-87154-405-9, ISBN13: 978-0-87154-405-6. Dewey:307.336. LCCN:96-021097.
Audience: **l,u,f.** *Choice, 1997.*

Kunstler, James Howard **NA2542.35.K86 1993**
The Geography of Nowhere: The Rise and Decline of America's Man-Made Landscape. Trade Paper. Simon & Schuster. New York, NY. 1994. 304p. ISBN:0-671-88825-0, ISBN13: 978-0-671-88825-1. Dewey:720/.47. LCCN:93-020373.
Audience: **g.**

Lofland, Lyn H. **HT151.L6 1998**
The Public Realm: Exploring the City's Quintessential Social Territory. Trade Cloth. Aldine Transaction. Somerset, NJ. 1998. 305p. Communication and Social Order Ser. ISBN:0-202-30607-0, ISBN13: 978-0-202-30607-0. Dewey:307.76. LCCN:97-042290.
Audience: **u,f.** *Choice, 1998.*

Marshall, Alex **HT166.M259 2000**
How Cities Work: Suburbs, Sprawl, and the Roads Not Taken. Trade Cloth. University of Texas Press. Austin, TX. 2001. 288p. Constructs Ser. ISBN:0-292-75239-3, ISBN13: 978-0-292-75239-9. Dewey:307.76. LCCN:00-026691.
Audience: **l,u,f.** *Choice, 2001.*

Mingione, Enzo **HT153**
Social Conflict and the City. Paper Text. Blackwell Publishing, Inc. Malden, MA. 1986. 205p. ISBN:0-631-12716-X, ISBN13: 978-0-631-12716-1. Dewey:307.7/6.
Audience: **l,u,f.** B

Mumford, Lewis **HT111**
The City in History: Its Origins, Its Transformations and Its Prospects. Trade Paper. Harcourt Trade Publishers. New York, NY. 1968. 784p. ISBN:0-15-618035-9, ISBN13: 978-0-15-618035-1. Dewey:307.7. LCCN:61-007689.
Audience: **l,u,f.** B

Newman, Katherine S. **HV4045.N48 1999**
No Shame in My Game: The Working Poor in the Inner City. Trade Cloth. Alfred A. Knopf Inc. New York, NY. 1999. 416p. ISBN:0-375-40254-3, ISBN13: 978-0-375-40254-8. Dewey:362.5/0973/091732. LCCN:98-038244.
Audience: **l,u,f.** *Choice, 1999.*

Sugrue, Thomas J. **F574.D49N4835 2005**
The Origins of the Urban Crisis: Race and Inequality in Postwar Detroit. Ed. 2. I. R. A. Katznelson, Martin Shefter & Theda Skocpol (Editors). Trade Paper, Perfect. Princeton University Press. Princeton, NJ. 2005. 416p. Princeton Studies in American Politics ISBN:0-691-12186-9, ISBN13: 978-0-691-12186-4. Dewey:305.8/00977434. LCCN:2005-047695.
Audience: **l,u,f.** *Choice, 1997.*

Tracy, James D. (Editor) **UG405.2 .C58 2000**
City Walls: The Urban Enceinte in Global Perspective. Trade Cloth. Cambridge University Press. New York, NY. 2000. 752p. Studies in Comparative Early Modern History ISBN:0-521-65221-9, ISBN13: 978-0-521-65221-6. Dewey:623/.1. LCCN:99-045712.
Audience: **u,f.**

Wilson, William Julius **HV4045.W55 1987**
The Truly Disadvantaged: The Inner City, the Underclass, and Public Policy. Trade Cloth. University of Chicago Press. Chicago, IL. 1993. xii, 252p. ISBN:0-226-90130-0, ISBN13: 978-0-226-90130-5. Dewey:362.5/0973. LCCN:87-010822.
Audience: **l,u,f.** *Choice, 1988.*

Community/Regional Studies > Rural

Brown, David L. & Swanson, Louis E. (Editors) **HN59.2.C435 2003**
Challenges for Rural America in the 21st Century. Trade Cloth. Pennsylvania State University Press. University Park, PA. 2004. 330p. Rural Studies Series of the Rural Sociological Society ISBN:0-271-02241-8, ISBN13: 978-0-271-02241-3. Dewey:307.72/0973. LCCN:2003-009910.
Audience: **g,l,u,f.** *Choice, 2004.*

Bruegmann, Robert **HT371.B74 2005**
Sprawl: A Compact History. Trade Cloth. University of Chicago Press. Chicago, IL. 2005. 306p. ISBN:0-226-07690-3, ISBN13: 978-0-226-07690-4. Dewey:307.76. LCCN:2005-007591.
Audience: **g,l,u,f.**

Clarke, Colin **HD1531.M6C58 2000**
Class, Ethnicity, and Community in Southern Mexico: Oaxaca's Peasantries. Trade Cloth. Oxford University Press, Inc. New York, NY. 2001. 333p. Oxford Geographical and Environmental Studies ISBN:0-19-823387-6, ISBN13: 978-0-19-823387-9. Dewey:305.5/633/097274. LCCN:00-035696.
Audience: **u,f.**

Daniel, Pete **HM548**
Breaking the Land: The Transformation of Cotton, Tobacco, and Rice Cultures since 1880. Trade Paper. University of Illinois Press. Champaign, IL. 1986. 368p. ISBN:0-252-01391-3, ISBN13: 978-0-252-01391-1. Dewey:306/.3. LCCN:84-000197.
Audience: **l,u,f.** B *Choice, 1985.*

Donahue, Brian **HD1289.U6D66 1999**
Reclaiming the Commons: Community Farms and Forests in a New England Town. Wes Jackson (Foreword by). Cloth over Boards. Yale University Press. Cumberland, RI. 1999. 349p. Yale Agrarian Studies ISBN:0-300-07673-8, ISBN13: 978-0-300-07673-8. Dewey:333.2. LCCN:98-049122.
Audience: **u,f.** *Choice, 1999.*

Epstein, Scarlett, et al. **HN690.Z9C685376 1998**
Village Voices: Forty Years of Rural Transformation in South India. A. P. Suryanarayana & T. Thimmegowda (Authors). Trade Cloth. SAGE Publications, Inc. Thousand Oaks, CA. 1998. 244p. ISBN:0-7619-9265-0, ISBN13: 978-0-7619-9265-3. Dewey:303.4/0954. LCCN:98-024646.
Audience: **l,u,f.** *Choice, 1999.*

Fan, Jie, et al. **HN733.5.F35 2005**
Rural China. Thomas Heberer & Wolfgang Taubmann (Authors). Cloth Text. M. E. Sharpe Inc. Armonk, NY. 2005. 368p.

ISBN:0-7656-0818-9, ISBN13: 978-0-7656-0818-5. Dewey:306/.0951/091734. LCCN:2004-013795.
Audience: **l,u,f.**

Francis, Elizabeth **HN792.A8F73 2000**
Making a Living: Changing Livelihoods in Rural Africa. Trade Paper. Routledge. New York, NY. 2000. 232p. ISBN:0-415-14496-5, ISBN13: 978-0-415-14496-4. Dewey:307.72/096. LCCN:99-058782.
Audience: **l,u,f.**

Greenberg, James B. **E98.E85**
Blood Ties: Life and Violence in Rural Mexico. Trade Paper. University of Arizona Press. Tucson, AZ. 1993. 282p. ISBN:0-8165-1379-1, ISBN13: 978-0-8165-1379-6. Dewey:305.8/97. LCCN:88-029538.
Audience: **g,l,u,f.** *Choice, 1990.*

Grindle, Merilee S. **HN110.5.Z9C62665**
State and Countryside: Development Policy and Agrarian Politics in Latin America. Trade Cloth. Johns Hopkins University Press. Baltimore, MD. 1986. 272p. Studies in Development ISBN:0-8018-3278-0, ISBN13: 978-0-8018-3278-9. Dewey:307/.14/098. LCCN:85-008081.
Audience: **u,f.** *Choice, 1986.*

Grinker, Roy R. **DT650.E34G75 1994**
Houses in the Rain Forest: Ethnicity and Inequality among Farmers and Foragers in Central Africa. Trade Cloth. University of California Press. Berkeley, CA. 1994. 244p. ISBN:0-520-08357-1, ISBN13: 978-0-520-08357-8. Dewey:305.8/00967515. LCCN:93-036600.
Audience: **u,f.** *Choice, 1995.*

Holland, Barbara **F232.L8H65 1999**
Bingo Night at the Fire Hall: The Case for Cows, Orchards, Bake Sales and Fairs. Library Binding. Thomas T. Beeler Publisher. Rollinsford, NH. 1999. Large Print Ser. ISBN:1-57490-179-6, ISBN13: 978-1-57490-179-5. Dewey:975.5/28. LCCN:99-018704.
Audience: **l,u,f.**

Kotkin, Joel **HT111.K65 2005**
The City: A Global History. Trade Cloth. Random House, Inc. New York, NY. 2005. 256p. Modern Library Chronicles ISBN:0-679-60336-0, ISBN13: 978-0-679-60336-8. Dewey:307.76/09. LCCN:2004-058167.
Audience: **g,l,u,f.** *Choice, 2006.*

Madan, Vandana **HD2072.V55 2002**
The Village in India. Trade Cloth. Oxford University Press, Inc. New York, NY. 2002. 488p. Oxford in India Readings in Sociology and Social Anthropology Ser. ISBN:0-19-565820-5, ISBN13: 978-0-19-565820-0. Dewey:307.720954. LCCN:2002-512949.
Audience: **u,f.**

Newby, Howard (Author, Editor) **HT0421.154**
International Perspectives in Rural Sociology. Trade Paper. Books on Demand. Ann Arbor, MI. 230p. ISBN:0-598-14157-X, ISBN13: 978-0-598-14157-6. Dewey:307.72. LCCN:77-021274.
Audience: **l,u.**

Rydstrom, Helle **HQ792.V5R93 2003**
Embodying Morality: Growing up in Rural Northern Vietnam. Trade Cloth. University of Hawaii Press. Honolulu, HI. 2003. 256p. ISBN:0-8248-2524-1, ISBN13: 978-0-8248-2524-9. Dewey:305.23/09597/1734. LCCN:2002-075099.
Audience: **u,f.** *Choice, 2004.*

Sachs, Carolyn E. **HQ1240.S28 1996**
Gendered Fields: Rural Women, Agriculture, and Environment. Trade Paper. Westview Press. Boulder, CO. 1996. 224p. Rural Studies ISBN:0-8133-2520-X, ISBN13: 978-0-8133-2520-0. Dewey:338.9/0082. LCCN:95-043943.
Audience: **u,f.** *Choice, 1996.*

Vitebsky, Piers **DK759.E83V58 2005**
Reindeer People, Living with Animals and Spirits in Siberia. Piers Vitebsky. Houghton Mifflin Company Trade & Reference Division. 2005. ISBN:0-618-21188-8, ISBN13: 978-0-618-21188-3.
Audience: **g,l,u,f.**

Whetten, Nathan L. **HD325**
Rural Mexico. Manuel Gamio (Introduction by). Trade Cloth. University of Chicago Press. Chicago, IL. 1948. ISBN:0-226-89439-8, ISBN13: 978-0-226-89439-3. Dewey:323.354. LCCN:48-008023.
Audience: **l,u,f.**

Wild, Trevor **DA533**
Village England: A Social History of the Countryside. Cloth over Boards. I. B. Tauris & Company, Ltd. London, 2004. 224p. ISBN:1-86064-939-4, ISBN13: 978-1-86064-939-4. Dewey:942.009734. LCCN:2004-302333.
Audience: **l,u,f.** *Choice, 2005.*

Yan, Yunxiang **HQ684.Z9.X539 2003**
Private Life under Socialism: Love, Intimacy, and Family Change in a Chinese Village, 1949-1999. Trade Paper. Stanford University Press. Palo Alto, CA. 2003. 320p. ISBN:0-8047-4456-4, ISBN13: 978-0-8047-4456-0. Dewey:306.8/0951/84. LCCN:2002-013327.
Audience: **l,u,f.** *Choice, 2003.*

Community/Regional Studies > Electronic Communities

Chayko, Mary **HM1106.C488 2002**
Connecting: How We Form Social Bonds and Communities in the Internet Age. Paper Text. State University of New York Press. Albany, NY. 2002. 256p. ISBN:0-7914-5434-7, ISBN13: 978-0-7914-5434-3. Dewey:302. LCCN:2002-019099.
Audience: **l,u,f.** *Choice, 2003.*

Earnshaw, Rae A. (Editor), et al. **QA76.9.H85F76 2001**
Frontiers of Human-Centered Computing, Online Communities and Virtual Environments. R. A. Guedj, Andries Van Dam & J. A. Vince (Editors). Trade Cloth. Springer. New York, NY. 2001. XVI, 482p. ISBN:1-85233-238-7, ISBN13: 978-1-85233-238-9. Dewey:004/.01/9. LCCN:00-067967.
Audience: **l,u,f.**

Markoff, John **QA76.17.M37 2005**
What the Dormouse Said: How the Sixties Counterculture Shaped the Personal Computer Industry. Trade Cloth. Penguin Group (USA) Inc. New York, NY. 2005. 336p. ISBN:0-670-03382-0, ISBN13: 978-0-670-03382-9. Dewey:004.16. LCCN:2004-061181.
Audience: **l,u,f.** *Choice, 2005.*

Social Control

Bailey, Dennis **JC596.2.U5B35 2005**
The Open Society Paradox: Why the Twenty-First Century Calls for More Openness-Not Less. Trade Cloth. Potomac Books, Inc. Dulles, VA. 2004. 240p. ISBN:1-57488-916-8, ISBN13: 978-1-57488-916-1. Dewey:323.44/8/0973. LCCN:2004-010184.
Audience: **g,l,u,f.** *Choice, 2005.*

Caldeira, Teresa Pires Do Rio **HV6895.S3 C35 2000**
City of Walls: Crime, Segregation and Citizenship in São Paulo. Trade Paper. University of California Press. Berkeley, CA. 2001. 506p. ISBN:0-520-22143-5, ISBN13: 978-0-520-22143-7. Dewey:364.981/61. LCCN:00-028713.
Audience: **u,f.** *Choice, 2001.*

Garland, David **HV9960.G36 2002**
The Culture of Control: Crime and Social Order in Contemporary Society. Trade Paper. University of Chicago Press. Chicago, IL. 2002. 336p. ISBN:0-226-28384-4, ISBN13: 978-0-226-28384-5. Dewey:364.9/73.
Audience: **l,u,f.** *Choice, 2002.*

Gibbs, Jack P. **HM24.G4446 1989**
Control: Sociology's Central Notion. Trade Cloth. University of Illinois Press. Champaign, IL. 1989. 520p. ISBN:0-252-01590-8, ISBN13: 978-0-252-01590-8. Dewey:303.3/3. LCCN:88-026192.
Audience: **l,u,f.** *Choice, 1990.*

Harle, Vilho **HM271**
Ideas of Social Order in the Ancient World. Trade Cloth. Greenwood Publishing Group, Inc. Portsmouth, NH. 1998. 272p. Contributions in Political Science Ser., Vol. 383 ISBN:0-313-30582-X, ISBN13: 978-0-313-30582-5. Dewey:303.3/3/09. LCCN:97-033962.
Audience: **u,f.** *Choice, 1999.*

Migdal, Joel S. **JC131 .M54 2001**
State in Society: Studying How States and Societies Transform and Constitute One Another. Robert H. Bates, Ellen Comisso, Peter Hall, Peter Lange, Joel Samuel Migdal & Helen V. Milner (Contribution by). Cloth Text. Cambridge University Press. New York, NY. 2001. 304p. Studies in Comparative Politics ISBN:0-521-79286-X, ISBN13: 978-0-521-79286-8. Dewey:306.2. LCCN:2001-025468.
Audience: **u,f.**

Powell, Chris & Paton, George E. (Editors) **PN6149.S62H85 1988**
Humour in Society: Resistance and Control. Cloth Text. Palgrave Macmillan. New York, NY. 1988. 220p. ISBN:0-312-00933-X, ISBN13: 978-0-312-00933-5. Dewey:302.5. LCCN:87-023261.
Audience: **l,u,f.** *Choice, 1988.*

Roodenburg, Herman **HN373.S563 2004**
Social Control in Europe. Trade Cloth. Ohio State University Press. Columbus, OH. 2004. 456p. History of Crime and Criminal Justice Ser. ISBN:0-8142-0971-8, ISBN13: 978-0-8142-0971-4. Dewey:303.3/3/094. LCCN:2004-005763.
Audience: **u,f.** *Choice, 2005.*

Simmons, A. John **JA71**
On the Edge of Anarchy: Locke, Consent, and the Limits of Society. Paper Text. Princeton University Press. Princeton, NJ. 1995. 312p. ISBN:0-691-04483-X, ISBN13: 978-0-691-04483-5. Dewey:320/.01.
Audience: **u,f.** *Choice, 1994.*

Staples, William G. **HN57.S68 1991**
Castles of Our Conscience: Social Control and the American State, 1800-1985. Cloth Text. Rutgers University Press. Piscataway, NJ. 1991. 206p. ISBN:0-8135-1626-9, ISBN13: 978-0-8135-1626-4. Dewey:361.6/1/0973. LCCN:90-037620.
Audience: **l,u,f.** *Choice, 1991.*

Social Control > Power

Brandes, Stanley **GT4814.T95B7 1988**
Power and Persuasion: Fiestas and Social Control in Rural Mexico. Trade Cloth. University of Pennsylvania Press. Philadelphia, PA. 1988. 224p. ISBN:0-8122-8077-6, ISBN13: 978-0-8122-8077-7. Dewey:394.2/6972/37. LCCN:87-019205.
Audience: **u,f.** *Choice, 1988.*

Eckstein, Rick **HD9698.U52E25 1997**
Nuclear Power and Social Power. Library Binding. Temple University Press. Philadelphia, PA. 1996. 208p. ISBN:1-56639-485-6, ISBN13: 978-1-56639-485-7. Dewey:333.792/4. LCCN:96-023908.
Audience: **g,l,u.** *Choice, 1997.*

Galbraith, John Kenneth **HM271 .G27 1983**
The Anatomy of Power. Trade Cloth. Houghton Mifflin Company. New York, NY. 1983. 224p. ISBN:0-395-34400-X, ISBN13: 978-0-395-34400-2. Dewey:303.3. LCCN:83-012622.
Audience: **l,u,f.**

Social Control > Law

Bollier, David **KF2979.B64 2005**
Brand-Name Bullies: The Quest to Own and Control Culture. Trade Cloth. John Wiley & Sons, Inc. Hoboken, NJ. 2005. 320p. ISBN:0-471-67927-5, ISBN13: 978-0-471-67927-1. Dewey:346.7304/8. LCCN:2004-015801.
Audience: **g,l.**

Giacomello, Giampiero **HM851.G5 2005**
National Governments and Control of the Internet. Paper over Boards. Routledge. New York, NY. 2005. XVI, 208p. ISBN:0-415-33136-6, ISBN13: 978-0-415-33136-4. Dewey:303.48/33. LCCN:2004-016885.
Audience: **g,l,u,f.**

Mauer, Marc **HV9950.M32 2006**
Race to Incarcerate. Sentencing Project (U.S.) Staff (Contribution by). Trade Paper. New Press, The. New York, NY. 2006. 256p. ISBN:1-59558-022-0, ISBN13: 978-1-59558-022-1. Dewey:364.6/0973. LCCN:2005-054376.
Audience: **g,l,u,f.**

Miller, R. Robin & Browning, Sandra Lee **KF385.F67 2004**
For the Common Good: A Critical Examination of Law and Social Control. Trade Paper. Carolina Academic Press. Durham, NC. 2004. 376p. ISBN:0-89089-223-7, ISBN13: 978-0-89089-223-7. Dewey:340/.115. LCCN:2003-116522.
Audience: **l,u,f.** *Choice, 2004.*

Roberts, John & Crossley, Nick (Editors) **HM661**
After Habermas: New Perspectives on the Public Sphere. Trade Paper. Blackwell Publishing, Inc. Malden, MA. 2004. 192p. Sociological Review Monographs ISBN:1-4051-2365-6, ISBN13: 978-1-4051-2365-5. Dewey:303.3/8. LCCN:2004-302318.
Audience: **l,u,f.** *Choice, 2005.*

Roth, Rachel **KF481.R67 2000**
Making Women Pay: The Hidden Costs of Fetal Rights. Book, Other. Cornell University Press. Ithaca, NY. 1999. 264p. ISBN:0-8014-3607-9, ISBN13: 978-0-8014-3607-9. Dewey:342.73/085. LCCN:99-044982.
Audience: **g,l,u,f.** *Choice, 2000.*

Social Control > Police

Brewer, John D. **HV8272.A2B74 1994**
Black and Blue: Policing in South Africa. Trade Cloth. Oxford University Press, Inc. New York, NY. 1994. 390p. ISBN:0-19-827382-7, ISBN13: 978-0-19-827382-0. Dewey:363.2/0968. LCCN:93-040020.
Audience: **l,u,f.** *Choice, 1995.*

Escobar, Edward J. **HV8148.L55 E73 1999**
Race, Police, and the Making of a Political Identity: Mexican Americans and the Los Angeles Police Department, 1900-1945. Trade Cloth. University of California Press. Berkeley, CA. 1999. 372p. Latinos in American Society and Culture Ser., 7 ISBN:0-520-21334-3, ISBN13: 978-0-520-21334-0. Dewey:365/.9794/93. LCCN:98-023322.
Audience: **u,f.** *Choice, 2000.*

Rowe, Michael **HV8195**
Policing, Race and Racism. Les Johnston, Frank Leishman & Tim Newburn (Editors). Trade Paper. Willan Publishing. Devon, 2004. 192p. Policing and Society Ser. ISBN:1-84392-044-1, ISBN13: 978-1-84392-044-1. Dewey:363.208900941. LCCN:2004-302532.
Audience: **g,l,u.**

Weisburd, David, et al. **HV8141.A29 2001**
The Abuse of Police Authority: A National Study of Police Officers' Attitude. Rosann Greenspan, Edwin E. Hamilton, Kellie A. Bryant & Hubert Williams (Authors). Trade Paper. Police Foundation. Washington, DC. 2001. 210p. ISBN:1-884614-17-5, ISBN13: 978-1-884614-17-0. Dewey:363.2/0973. LCCN:2001-130311.
Audience: **g,l,u,f.**

Social Control > Police > Security

Herbert, Steven Kelly **HN90.C6H47 2006**
Citizens, Cops, and Power: Recognizing the Limits of Community. Trade Cloth. University of Chicago Press. Chicago, IL. 2006. 168p. ISBN:0-226-32730-2, ISBN13: 978-0-226-32730-3. Dewey:363.2/3/0973. LCCN:2005-021525.
Audience: **u,f.**

Health

Beardsley, Edward H. **RA413.5.U5**
A History of Neglect: Health Care for Southern Blacks and Mill Workers in the Twentieth-Century South. Trade Paper. University of Tennessee Press. Knoxville, TN. 1987. 400p. ISBN:0-87049-635-2, ISBN13: 978-0-87049-635-6. Dewey:362.1/0425. LCCN:86-024949.
Audience: **g,l,u.** *Choice, 1987.*

Bloom, Samuel William **RA418.3.U6B56 2002**
The Word as Scalpel: A History of Medical Sociology. Trade Cloth. Oxford University Press, Inc. New York, NY. 2002. 356p. ISBN:0-19-507232-4, ISBN13: 978-0-19-507232-7. Dewey:306.4/61/0973. LCCN:2001-037042.
Audience: **l,u,f.** *Choice, 2003.*

Friedman, Lester D. **RA440.5.C835 2004**
Cultural Sutures: Medicine and Media. Trade Cloth. Duke University Press. Durham, NC. 2004. 408p. ISBN:0-8223-3256-6, ISBN13: 978-0-8223-3256-5. Dewey:306.4/61. LCCN:2003-024988.
Audience: **l,u,f.** *Choice, 2005.*

Haiken, Elizabeth **RD119.H35 1997**
Venus Envy: A History of Cosmetic Surgery. Trade Cloth. Johns Hopkins University Press. Baltimore, MD. 1999. 384p. ISBN:0-8018-5763-5, ISBN13: 978-0-8018-5763-8. Dewey:617.9/5. LCCN:97-019823.
Audience: **g,l.** *Choice, 1998.*

Haller, John S. Jr. & Haller, Robin M. **HN90.M6.H34 1974**
The Physician and Sexuality in Victorian America. Trade Cloth. University of Illinois Press. Champaign, IL. 1974. 346p. ISBN:0-252-00207-5, ISBN13: 978-0-252-00207-6. Dewey:306.7/08/861. LCCN:73-002456.
Audience: **u,f.** B

Segrave, Kerry **RL89.S44 2006**
Suntanning in 20th Century America. Trade Paper, Perfect. McFarland & Company, Incorporated Publishers. Jefferson, NC. 2005. 216p. ISBN:0-7864-2394-3, ISBN13: 978-0-7864-2394-1. Dewey:613/.19309. LCCN:2005-025274.
Audience: **l,u.**

Weitz, Rose **RA418.3.U6W46 2004**
The Sociology of Health, Illness, and Health Care: A Critical Approach. Ed. 3. Cloth Text. Thomson Wadsworth. Belmont, CA. 2003. 504p. ISBN:0-534-61938-X, ISBN13: 978-0-534-61938-1. Dewey:306.4/61. LCCN:2003-101526.
Audience: **u,f.**

Health > Mental Health

Cohen, Stanley & Taylor, Laurie **BF575.E83C64 1992**
Escape Attempts: The Struggle of Resistance in Everyday Life. Ed. 2. Trade Paper. Routledge. New York, NY. 1992. 272p. ISBN:0-415-06500-3, ISBN13: 978-0-415-06500-9. Dewey:155.92. LCCN:92-005431.
Audience: **l,u,f.**

Fromm, Erich **HM271.F75 1990**
The Sane Society. Trade Paper. Henry Holt & Company. New York, NY. 1990. 384p. ISBN:0-8050-1402-0, ISBN13: 978-0-8050-1402-0. Dewey:306.3/42. LCCN:55-008006.
Audience: **g,l,u.**

Prior, Lindsay **RC455.P735 1993**
The Social Organization of Mental Illness, Vol. 1. Cloth Text. SAGE Publications, Ltd. London, 1993. 240p. ISBN:0-8039-8499-5, ISBN13: 978-0-8039-8499-8. Dewey:362.2. LCCN:93-084109.
Audience: **l,u,f.** *Choice, 1994.*

Prothrow-Stith, Deborah **HV6250.4.Y68**
Deadly Consequences. Trade Paper. HarperCollins Publishers. New York, NY. 1993. 288p. ISBN:0-06-092402-0, ISBN13: 978-0-06-092402-7. Dewey:364.36. LCCN:90-055938.
Audience: **g,l.**

Scheff, Thomas J. **HM291**
Microsociology: Discourse, Emotion, and Social Structure. Anthony Giddens (Foreword by). Trade Paper. University of Chicago Press. Chicago, IL. 1994. 232p. ISBN:0-226-73667-9, ISBN13: 978-0-226-73667-9. Dewey:302.
Audience: **u,f.**

Szasz, Thomas **RC451.4.S62S93 1994**
Cruel Compassion: Psychiatric Control of Society's Unwanted. Trade Cloth. John Wiley & Sons, Inc. Hoboken, NJ. 1994. 264p. ISBN:0-471-01012-X, ISBN13: 978-0-471-01012-8. Dewey:362.2. LCCN:93-031600.
Audience: **l,u,f.** *Choice, 1994.*

Health > Body

Beckman, Linda J. & Harvey, S. Marie (Editors) **HQ767.5.U5N45 1998**
The New Civil War: The Psychology, Culture and Politics of Abortion. Cloth Text. American Psychological Association. Washington, DC. 1998. 432p. Psychology of Women Bks., Div. 35 ISBN:1-55798-517-0, ISBN13: 978-1-55798-517-0. Dewey:363.46/0973. LCCN:98-003553.
Audience: **l,u,f.** *Choice, 1999.*

Black, Edwin **HQ755.5.U5B53 2004**
War Against the Weak: Eugenics and America's Campaign to Create a Master Race. Trade Paper. Avalon Publishing Group. New York, NY. 2004. 592p. ISBN:1-56858-321-4, ISBN13: 978-1-56858-321-1. Dewey:363.9/7.
Audience: **g,l,u,f.** *Choice, 2004.*

Boonin, David **HQ767.15.B66 2002**
A Defense of Abortion. Douglas MacLean (Contribution by). Trade Cloth. Cambridge University Press. New York, NY. 2002. 366p. Cambridge Studies in Philosophy and Public Policy ISBN:0-521-81701-3, ISBN13: 978-0-521-81701-1. Dewey:179.7/6. LCCN:2002-022282.
Audience: **g,l,u.** *Choice, 2003.*

Franks, Angela **HQ764**
Margaret Sanger's Eugenic Legacy: The Control of Female Fertility. Paper Text. McFarland & Company, Incorporated Publishers. Jefferson, NC. 2005. 359p. ISBN:0-7864-2011-1, ISBN13: 978-0-7864-2011-7. Dewey:363.9/2. LCCN:2004-029008.
Audience: **l,u,f.** *Choice, 2005.*

Gordon, Linda **HQ766.5.U5G66 2002**
The Moral Property of Women: A History of Birth Control Politics in America. Ed. 3. Trade Cloth. University of Illinois Press. Champaign, IL. 2002. 464p. ISBN:0-252-02764-7, ISBN13: 978-0-252-02764-2. Dewey:363.9/6/0973. LCCN:2002-001551.
Audience: **l,u,f.** *Choice, 2003.*

Gordon, Linda **HQ766.5.U5**
Woman's Body, Woman's Right: Birth Control in America. Trade Paper. Penguin Group (USA) Inc. New York, NY. 1990. 592p. ISBN:0-14-013127-2, ISBN13: 978-0-14-013127-7. Dewey:363.9/6/097309.
Audience: **g,l,u.**

Lowe, Donald M. **HN59.2.L69 1995**
The Body in Late-Capitalist U. S. A. Cloth Text. Duke University Press. Durham, NC. 1995. 224p. Post-Contemporary Interventions Ser. ISBN:0-8223-1660-9, ISBN13: 978-0-8223-1660-2. Dewey:306.4. LCCN:95-009237.
Audience: **l,u,f.** *Choice, 1996.*

Luker, Kristin **HQ766.5.U5**
Taking Chances: Abortion and the Decision Not to Contracept. Trade Cloth. University of California Press. Berkeley, CA. 1975. xii, 207p. ISBN:0-520-02872-4, ISBN13: 978-0-520-02872-2. Dewey:301.5. LCCN:74-022965.
Audience: **l,u,f.**

Rainwater, Lee **HQ766**
And the Poor Get Children: Sex, Contraception, and Family Planning in the Working Class. Trade Cloth. Greenwood Publishing Group, Inc. Portsmouth, NH. 1984. 202p. ISBN:0-313-24452-9, ISBN13: 978-0-313-24452-0. Dewey:304.6/6/0973. LCCN:84-012770.
Audience: **g,l,u,f.**

Tone, Andrea **HQ766.5.U5**
Devices and Desires: A History of Contraceptives in America. Trade Paper. Farrar, Straus & Giroux. New York, NY. 2002. 384p. ISBN:0-8090-3816-1, ISBN13: 978-0-8090-3816-9. Dewey:363.9/6/0973.
Audience: **g,u.** *Choice, 2002.*

Health > Compulsive Behaviors > Alcohol

Acker, Caroline J. & Tracy, Sarah W. (Editors) **HV5292.A393 2004**
Altering American Consciouness: Essays on the History of Alcohol and Drug Use in the United States, 1800-2000. Trade Cloth. University of Massachusetts Press. Amherst, MA. 2004. 448p. ISBN:1-55849-424-3, ISBN13: 978-1-55849-424-4. Dewey:362.29/0973/09034. LCCN:2003-013735.
Audience: **l,u,f.** *Choice, 2005.*

Barry, Kristen Lawton, et al. **RC564.5.A34B374 2001**
Alcohol Problems in Older Adults: Prevention and Management. David W. Oslin & Frederic C. Blow (Authors). Trade Paper. Springer Publishing Company, Inc. New York, NY. 2001. 152p. ISBN:0-8261-1403-2, ISBN13: 978-0-8261-1403-7. Dewey:618.97/6861. LCCN:00-052655.
Audience: **l,u.**

Deutsch, Charles **HV5132.D43**
Broken Bottles, Broken Dreams: Understanding and Helping the Children of Alcoholics. Trade Cloth. Bow Historical Books. New Providence, NJ. 1982. xiv, 213p. ISBN:0-8077-2664-8, ISBN13: 978-0-8077-2664-8. Dewey:362.8/28. LCCN:81-005729.
Audience: **g,l.** BCL3

Gusfield, Joseph R. **HV5292.G8 1986**
Symbolic Crusade: Status Politics and the American Temperance Movement. Ed. 2. Trade Paper. University of Illinois Press. Champaign, IL. 1986. 240p. ISBN:0-252-01312-3, ISBN13: 978-0-252-01312-6. Dewey:363.4/1/0973. LCCN:85-028858.
Audience: **u,f.** BCL3

Kurtz, Ernest **HV5278 .K85**
Not God: A History of Alcoholics Anonymous. Trade Paper. Hazelden Publishing & Educational Services. Center City, MN. 1998. 456p. ISBN:0-89486-065-8, ISBN13: 978-0-89486-065-2. Dewey:362.2/9286. LCCN:79-088264.
Audience: **g,l,u,f.** BCL3

MacAndrew, Craig & Edgerton, Robert B. **HV5035.M32 2003**
Drunken Comportment: A Social Explanation. Paper Text. Eliot Werner Publications, Inc. Clinton Corners, NY. 2003. 214p. Foundations of Anthropology Ser. ISBN:0-9719587-6-9, ISBN13: 978-0-9719587-6-0. Dewey:301.476861. LCCN:2002-113046.
Audience: **u,f.**

Marshall, Mac (Editor) **GT2884 .B44 1979**
Beliefs, Behaviors, and Alcoholic Beverages: A Cross-Cultural Survey. Trade Paper. University of Michigan Press. Chicago, IL. 1979. 504p. ISBN:0-472-08580-8, ISBN13: 978-0-472-08580-4. Dewey:394.1/3/08. LCCN:78-031552.
Audience: **l,u.**

Pyne, Hnin Hnin, et al. **HV5310.5.P96 2002**
Gender Dimensions of Alcohol Consumption and Alcohol-Related Problems in Latin America and the Caribbean. Mariam Claeson & Maria Correia (Authors). Trade Paper. World Bank Publications. Washington, DC. 2002. 48p. World Bank Discussion Papers, No. 433 ISBN:0-8213-5125-7, ISBN13: 978-0-8213-5125-3. Dewey:362.292/2/098. LCCN:2002-023455.
Audience: **l,u.**

Royce, James E. & Scratchley, David **RC565.R68 1996**
Alcoholism and Other Drug Problems. Trade Cloth. Simon & Schuster. New York, NY. 1996. 400p. ISBN:0-684-82314-4, ISBN13: 978-0-684-82314-0. Dewey:362.29/2. LCCN:95-044546.
Audience: **g,l.**

Rudgley, Richard **GT3020**
The Alchemy of Culture: Intoxicants in Society. Trade Cloth. DIANE Publishing Company. Collingdale, PA. 2001. ISBN:0-7881-9647-2, ISBN13: 978-0-7881-9647-8. Dewey:394.14.
Audience: **l,u,f.**

Tyrrell, Ian **HV5227.T97 1991**
Woman's World - Woman's Empire: The Woman's Christian Temperance Union in International Perspective, 1880-1930. Trade Cloth. University of North Carolina Press. Chapel Hill, NC. 1991. 400p. ISBN:0-8078-1950-6, ISBN13: 978-0-8078-1950-0. Dewey:322.4/4/0973. LCCN:90-043246.
Audience: **u,f.** *Choice, 1992.*

Health > Compulsive Behaviors > Drugs

Becker, Howard S. **HM291**
Outsiders. Trade Cloth. Simon & Schuster. New York, NY. 1997. 224p. ISBN:0-684-83635-1, ISBN13: 978-0-684-83635-5. Dewey:302.5/42.
Audience: **g,l,u,f.**

Bourgois, Philippe I. **HV5810.B68 2003**
In Search of Respect: Selling Crack in el Barrio. Ed. 2. Cloth Text. Cambridge University Press. New York, NY. 2002. 432p. Structural Analysis in the Social Sciences Ser. ISBN:0-521-81562-2, ISBN13: 978-0-521-81562-8. Dewey:363.4/5/097471. LCCN:2003-265509.
Audience: **g,l,u,f.** *Choice, 1996.*

Courtwright, David T. **HV5816.C648 2001**
Dark Paradise: A History of Opiate Addiction in America. Ed. 2. Trade Paper. Harvard University Press. Cambridge, MA. 2001. 352p. ISBN:0-674-00585-6, ISBN13: 978-0-674-00585-3. Dewey:362.29/3/0973. LCCN:2001-016547.
Audience: **g,l,u,f.**

Courtwright, David T. **HV4997.C68 2001**
Forces of Habit: Drugs and the Making of the Modern World. Trade Cloth. Harvard University Press. Cambridge, MA. 2001. 288p. ISBN:0-674-00458-2, ISBN13: 978-0-674-00458-0. Dewey:362.29. LCCN:00-061466.
Audience: **g,l,u,f.** *Choice, 2001.*

Furst, Peter T. **HV5822.H25.F87**
Hallucinogens and Culture. Botanical Museum of Howard University Staff (Illustrator). Paper Text. Chandler & Sharp Publishers, Inc. Novato, CA. 1976. 208p. Cross-Cultural Themes Ser. ISBN:0-88316-517-1, ISBN13: 978-0-88316-517-1. Dewey:301.2/2. LCCN:75-025442.
Audience: **l,u,f.** BCL3

Gfroerer, Joseph, et al. **HV5825 .N346**
National Household Survey on Drug Abuse: Population Estimates, 1996. Joseph Gustin, Sally Branson & Brenda K. Porter (Authors). Paper Text. DIANE Publishing Company. Collingdale, PA. 1998. 123p. ISBN:0-7881-7075-9, ISBN13: 978-0-7881-7075-1. Dewey:363.450973.
Audience: **u,f.**

Holland, Julie (Editor) **RM666.M35E373 2001**
Ecstasy: The Complete Guide - A Comprehensive Look at the Risks and Benefits of MDMA. Ralph Metzner, Douglas Rushkoff, Andrew Weil, Zalman Schachter & Rick Doblin (Contribution by). Trade Cloth. Inner Traditions International, Ltd. Rochester, VT. 2001. 464p. ISBN:0-89281-857-3, ISBN13: 978-0-89281-857-0. Dewey:615/.785. LCCN:2001-002945.
Audience: **g,l,u,f.** *Choice, 2002.*

Lanier, Doris **GT2898**
Absinthe, the Cocaine of the Nineteenth Century: A History of the Hallucinogenic Drug and Its Effect on Artists and Writers in Europe and the United States. Paper Text. McFarland & Company, Incorporated Publishers. Jefferson, NC. 2004. 195p. ISBN:0-7864-1967-9, ISBN13: 978-0-7864-1967-8. Dewey:394.13. LCCN:94-029166.
Audience: **g,l,u.**

Levin, Louis **RM316 .L4813 1998**
Phantastica: A Classic Survey on the Use and Abuse of Mind-Altering Plants. P. H. Wirth (Translator). Trade Cloth. Inner Traditions International, Ltd. Rochester, VT. 1998. 304p. ISBN:0-89281-783-6, ISBN13: 978-0-89281-783-2. Dewey:615/.78. LCCN:98-009484.
Audience: **g,l,u,f.**

MacCoun, Robert J. & Reuter, Peter **HV5825 .M225 2001**
Drug War Heresies: Learning from Other Vices, Times, and Places. Trade Cloth. Cambridge University Press. New York, NY. 2001. 496p. RAND Studies in Policy Analysis ISBN:0-521-57263-0, ISBN13: 978-0-521-57263-7. Dewey:364.1770973. LCCN:00-045451.
Audience: **l,u.** *Choice, 2002.*

Macmillan Library Reference Staff **HV5804.E53 2001**
Encyclopedia of Drugs, Alcohol and Addictive Behavior, Set. Ed. 2. Trade Cloth. Thomson Gale. Farmington Hills, MI. 2000. lx, 1863p. ISBN:0-02-865541-9, ISBN13: 978-0-02-865541-3. Dewey:362.29/03. LCCN:00-046068.
Audience: **g,l,u,f.** *Choice, 2001.*

Madge, Tim **HV5810**
White Mischief: A Cultural History of Cocaine. Trade Paper. DIANE Publishing Company. Collingdale, PA. 2005. 204p. ISBN:0-7567-9162-6, ISBN13: 978-0-7567-9162-9. Dewey:362.29/8.
Audience: **g,l.**

Peele, Stanton **RC564.P43 1995**
Diseasing of America: How We Allowed Recovery Zealots and the Treatment Industry to Convince Us We Are out of Control. Trade Paper. Lexington Books. Lanham, MD. 1995. 336p. ISBN:0-02-874014-9, ISBN13: 978-0-02-874014-0. Dewey:362.2/9/8. LCCN:95-006377.
Audience: **g,l,u,f.**

Reinarman, Craig & Levine, Harry G. **HV5810.C73 1997**
Crack in America: Demon Drugs and Social Justice. Trade Paper. University of California Press. Berkeley, CA. 1997. 406p. ISBN:0-520-20242-2, ISBN13: 978-0-520-20242-9. Dewey:362.29/8/0973. LCCN:96-047765.
Audience: **g,u.**

Shaw, Victor N. **HV4999**
Substance Use and Abuse: Sociological Perspectives. Trade Cloth. Greenwood Publishing Group, Inc. Portsmouth, NH. 2002. 288p. ISBN:0-275-97139-2, ISBN13: 978-0-275-97139-7. Dewey:362.29/1/0973. LCCN:2002-067938.
Audience: **l,u,f.** *Choice, 2003.*

Straussner, Shulamith Lala Ashenberg (Editor) **RC564**
Ethnocultural Factors in Substance Abuse Treatment. Trade Paper. Guilford Publications, Inc. New York, NY. 2002. 447p. ISBN:1-57230-885-0, ISBN13: 978-1-57230-885-5. Dewey:616.86/06.
Audience: **l,u,f.** *Choice, 2001.*

Torgoff, Martin **HV5825.T68 2004**
Can't Find My Way Home: America in the Great Stoned Age, 1945-2000. Trade Cloth. Simon & Schuster. New York, NY. 2004. 560p. ISBN:0-7432-3010-8, ISBN13: 978-0-7432-3010-0. Dewey:306/.1. LCCN:2004-042904.
Audience: **g,l,u,f.** *Choice, 2005.*

United States Department of Health and Human Services, Office of Applied Studies, Substance Abuse and Mental Health Services Administration (SAMHSA) **HV4999.2**
Substance Abuse and Mental Health Data Archive (SAMHDA).
http://www.icpsr.umich.edu/SAMHDA/
Inter-university Consortium for Political and Social Research.
Audience: **l,u,f.**

Walton, Stuart **GT2850**
Out of It: A Cultural History of Intoxication. Trade Cloth. DIANE Publishing Company. Collingdale, PA. 2005. 366p. ISBN:0-7567-8998-2, ISBN13: 978-0-7567-8998-5. Dewey:394.1.
Audience: **g,l,u.** *Choice, 2003.*

Health > Compulsive Behaviors > Gambling

Aasved, Mikal J. **HV6715.A37 2003**
The Sociology of Gambling. Cloth Text. Charles C. Thomas Publisher, Ltd. Springfield, IL. 2003. 458p. The Gambling Theory and Research Ser., Vol. 2 ISBN:0-398-07380-5, ISBN13: 978-0-398-07380-0. Dewey:306.4/82. LCCN:2002-040857.
Audience: **l,u,f.**

Custer, Robert L. & Milt, Harry **RC0569.5.G35**
When Luck Runs Out: Help for Compulsive Gamblers and Their Families. Trade Paper. Books on Demand. Ann Arbor, MI. 247p. ISBN:0-8357-3445-5, ISBN13: 978-0-8357-3445-5. Dewey:616.85/227. LCCN:84-026055.
Audience: **g,l,u.**

Longstreet, Stephen **G**
Win or Lose: A Social History of Gambling in America. Bobbs-Merrill. 1977. ISBN:0-672-52253-5, ISBN13: 978-0-672-52253-6.
Audience: **l,u.**

Thompson, William N. **GV1301.T47 2001**
Gambling in America: An Encyclopedia of History, Issues, and Society. Library Binding. ABC-CLIO, Inc. Santa Barbara, CA. 2001. 509p. ISBN:1-57607-159-6, ISBN13: 978-1-57607-159-5. Dewey:795/.0973. LCCN:2001-003493.
Audience: **g.** *Choice, 2002.*

Health > Compulsive Behaviors > Eating Issues

Gordon, Richard **RC552.E18G67 1999**
Eating Disorders: Anatomy of a Social Epidemic. Ed. 2. Book, Other. Blackwell Publishing, Inc. Malden, MA. 2000. 304p. ISBN:0-631-21495-X, ISBN13: 978-0-631-21495-3. Dewey:616.85/262. LCCN:99-016396.
Audience: **l,u,f.**

Hesse-Biber, Sharlene **BF697.5.B63H47**
Am I Thin Enough Yet?: The Cult of Thinness and the Commercialization of Identity. Paper Text. Oxford University Press, Inc. New York, NY. 1997. 200p. ISBN:0-19-511791-3, ISBN13: 978-0-19-511791-2. Dewey:306.4.
Audience: **g,l,u,f.** *Choice, 1996.*

Manton, Catherine **HQ1410**
Fed Up: Women and Food in America. Trade Cloth. Greenwood Publishing Group, Inc. Portsmouth, NH. 1999. 184p. ISBN:0-89789-448-0, ISBN13: 978-0-89789-448-7. Dewey:305.4/0973. LCCN:98-019215.
Audience: **l,u,f.** *Choice, 1999.*

Matossian, Mary K. **RA1422.M94 M38 1989**
Poisons of the Past: Molds, Epidemics, and History. Trade Paper. Yale University Press. Cumberland, RI. 1991. 208p. ISBN:0-300-05121-2, ISBN13: 978-0-300-05121-6. Dewey:614.4.
Audience: **l,u,f.** *Choice, 1990.*

Mennell, Stephen; **F**
Murcott, Anne Otterloo, Anneke H van
The Sociology of Food: Eating, Diet and Culture. International Sociological Association. Sage. 1992. ISBN:0-8039-8839-7, ISBN13: 978-0-8039-8839-2.
Audience: **l,u,f.**

Health > Health Care

Altman, Stuart H. **RA413.7.U53F88 1998**
(Editor), et al.
The Future U. S. Healthcare System: Who Will Care for the Poor and Uninsured? Uwe E. Reinhardt & Alexandra Shields (Editors). Paper Text. Health Administration Press. Chicago, IL. 1997. 426p. ISBN:1-56793-067-0, ISBN13: 978-1-56793-067-2. Dewey:362.1/086/9420973. LCCN:97-023221.
Audience: **g,l,u,f.**

Crellin, John K. **RM45.C74 2004**
A Social History of Medicines in the Twentieth Century: To Be Taken Three Times a Day. Trade Paper. Haworth Press, Incorporated, The. Binghamton, NY. 2004. 329p. ISBN:0-7890-1845-4, ISBN13: 978-0-7890-1845-8. Dewey:615/.1/0973. LCCN:2003-012397.
Audience: **l,u,f.** *Choice, 2004.*

Fadiman, Anne **RA418.5.T73**
The Spirit Catches You and You Fall Down: A Hmong Child, Her American Doctors, and the Collision of Two Cultures. Trade Paper. Farrar, Straus & Giroux. New York, NY. 1998. 352p. ISBN:0-374-52564-1, ISBN13: 978-0-374-52564-4. Dewey:306.461. LCCN:97-005175.
Audience: **g,l,u,f.**

Fox, Renee C. **RA418.F662 1989**
The Sociology of Medicine. Ed. 1. Trade Paper. Prentice Hall PTR. Upper Saddle River, NJ. 1998. 448p. Prentice Hall Foundations of Modern Sociology Ser. ISBN:0-13-820507-8, ISBN13: 978-0-13-820507-2. Dewey:362.1. LCCN:88-017957.
Audience: **g,l.** *Choice, 1989.*

Francome, Colin **HQ767.5.U5F718 1986**
Abortion Practice in Britain and the United States. Cloth Text. Routledge. New York, NY. 1986. 224p. ISBN:0-04-179003-0, ISBN13: 978-0-04-179003-0. Dewey:363.4/6/0941. LCCN:86-003632.
Audience: **l,u.** *Choice, 1987.*

Gerhardt, Uta **RA418.G44 1989**
Ideas about Illness: An Intellectual and Political History of Medical Sociology. Paper Text. New York University Press. New York, NY. 1981. 448p. ISBN:0-8147-3026-4, ISBN13: 978-0-8147-3026-3. Dewey:306/.46. LCCN:88-034512.
Audience: **u,f.** *Choice, 1990.*

Mack, Arien (Editor) **RA649.I5 1991**
In Time of Plague: The History and Social Consequences of Lethal Epidemic Disease. Trade Cloth. New York University Press. New York, NY. 1991. 272p. ISBN:0-8147-5467-8, ISBN13: 978-0-8147-5467-2. Dewey:306.4/61. LCCN:91-013750.
Audience: **l,u.** *Choice, 1992.*

Minkler, Meredith **RA427.8.C64 2005**
Community Organizing and Community Building for Health. Ed. 2. Trade Cloth. Rutgers University Press. Piscataway, NJ. 2004. xi, 489p. ISBN:0-8135-3473-9, ISBN13: 978-0-8135-3473-2. Dewey:362.1/2. LCCN:2004-000307.
Audience: **l,u.** *Choice, 1997.*

Riddle, John M. **RG136**
Eve's Herbs: A History of Contraception and Abortion in the West. Trade Paper. Harvard University Press. Cambridge, MA. 1999. 352p. ISBN:0-674-27026-6, ISBN13: 978-0-674-27026-8. Dewey:613.9/4. LCCN:96-040383.
Audience: **l,u,f.** *Choice, 1997.*

Health > Health Care > Illness

Farmer, Paul **RA418.5.P6 F37 1999**
Infections and Inequalities: The Modern Plagues. Trade Cloth. University of California Press. Berkeley, CA. 1999. 389p. ISBN:0-520-21544-3, ISBN13: 978-0-520-21544-3. Dewey:306.4/61. LCCN:98-023807.
Audience: **l,u,f.** *Choice, 2001.*

Sontag, Susan **RA644.A25S66 1989**
Illness As Metaphor and Aids and Its Metaphors. Cloth over Boards. Farrar, Straus & Giroux. New York, NY. 1989. 128p. ISBN:0-374-10257-0, ISBN13: 978-0-374-10257-9. LCCN:88-021173.
Audience: **g,l,u,f.**

Health > Health Care > Illness > Cancer

Kogevinas, Manolis; **RC262.S63 1997**
Pearce, Neil; Susser, Mervyn; Boffetta, P
Social Inequalities and Cancer. Manolis Kogevinas (Editor) ; Neil Pearce (Editor) ; Mervyn Susser (Editor) ; P. Boffetta (Editor). Oxford University Press, Inc. 1997. IARC Scientific Publications ISBN:92-832-2138-9, ISBN13: 978-92-832-2138-8.
Audience: **l,u,f.**

Patterson, James T. **RA645.C3**
The Dread Disease: Cancer and Modern American Culture. Trade Paper. Harvard University Press. Cambridge, MA. 1987. 416p. ISBN:0-674-21626-1, ISBN13: 978-0-674-21626-6. Dewey:362.1/96994/00973. LCCN:87-000160.
Audience: **g,l,u.** *Choice, 1988.*

Health > Health Care > Illness > AIDS

Bloor, Michael **RA644.A25B59 1995**
The Sociology of HIV Transmission. Cloth Text. SAGE Publications, Ltd. London, 1995. 176p. ISBN:0-8039-8749-8, ISBN13: 978-0-8039-8749-4. Dewey:362.1/969792. LCCN:95-068522.
Audience: **l,u,f.** *Choice, 1996.*

Green, Gill & Sobo, E. J. **RC606.6.G74 2000**
Endangered Self: Identity and Social Risk. Trade Paper. Taylor & Francis Group. Abingdon, 2000. 256p. Health, Risk and Society Ser. ISBN:1-85728-910-2, ISBN13: 978-1-85728-910-7. Dewey:362.1/69792. LCCN:00-710308.
Audience: **l,u.** *Choice, 2000.*

Kayal, Philip M. **HQ76.2.U5K39 1993**
Bearing Witness: Gay Men's Health Crisis and the Politics of AIDS. Trade Paper. Westview Press. Boulder, CO. 1993. 275p. ISBN:0-8133-1729-0, ISBN13: 978-0-8133-1729-8. Dewey:305.389664. LCCN:92-040293.
Audience: **g,l,f.** *Choice, 1994.*

Rosser, B. R. **HQ762**
Male Homosexual Behavior and the Effects of AIDS Education: A Study of Behavior and Safer Sex in New Zealand and South Australia. Trade Cloth. Greenwood Publishing Group, Inc. Portsmouth, NH. 1991. 264p. ISBN:0-275-93809-3, ISBN13: 978-0-275-93809-3. Dewey:306.7/08/6642. LCCN:91-004626.
Audience: **l,u,f.** *Choice, 1992.*

Triechler, Paula A. **RA644.A25T78 1999**
How to Have Theory in an Epidemic: Cultural Chronicles of AIDS. Trade Cloth. Duke University Press. Durham, NC. 1999. xi, 477p. ISBN:0-8223-2286-2, ISBN13: 978-0-8223-2286-3. Dewey:362.1/969792. LCCN:98-050855.
Audience: **u,f.** *Choice, 1999.*

Health > Health Care > Wellness

Marlatt, G. Alan (Editor) **RC564.H364 1998**
Harm Reduction: Pragmatic Strategies for Managing High-Risk Behaviors. Cloth over Boards. Guilford Publications, Inc. New York, NY. 1998. 390p. ISBN:1-57230-397-2, ISBN13: 978-1-57230-397-3. Dewey:616.86. LCCN:98-037938.
Audience: **u,f.** *Choice, 1999.*

SPORTS AND RECREATION

The academic integration of sport related topics has evolved since 1988. Instead of physical education departments, one might find departments of heath, physical education, and recreation; exercise science; or kinesiology. Undergraduate majors have a range of program names (e.g., physical education; health physical education; or health physical education and fitness, which include teaching and coaching concentrations). Athletic training includes sports medicine issues and some students in pre-med programs and biology majors also look for a possible sport option. Other programs include exercise physiology, kinesiology/exercise sciences, parks and recreation or parks recreation, leisure/fitness, sport/fitness administration and management, related areas business administration, health education, and landscaping/groundskeeping. There are some minors in sports studies that attract students. But, just as often, a sport-related course is offered another discipline (e.g., history, communications, or women's studies). Sport classes can include history of higher education, sport and society, literature and sport, and so forth. Issues related to sport can include ageism, ethnicity, race, gender, and homophobia.

The selection of subject categories for RCL reflects a combination and compromise of subject headings and course groupings. Textbooks have been included for faculty referral, and because there are times when they provide the best coverage of information on the subject.

The sport sciences are a new area within this category. These includes biomechanics, motor learning, and exercise science, with subcategories of sport nutrition, sport psychology, exercise training and physiology. Sports medicine include drugs (doping), injuries/rehabilitation, and athletic training, where overlap occurs in physical therapy and therapeutic recreation. The science of sports includes the engineering aspects of equipment as well as physics and mathematics of sport and sport equipment.

Other categories are arranged by general concepts. Business of sport incorporates politics, economics, and management and complements international sport contests and facilities and structure categories. Sport studies contains philosophy, history, literature, sociology, research, education, and religion. Recreation leisure, outdoor recreation, fitness and health and physical education & training overlap and complement but reflect a bit more focus on the topic. The minorities category was included to highlight the increased number of monographs that focus on history and experiences of "the other." Lastly, Sports A-Z includes the history, social and skills of a variety of sports.

There may be some minor philosophical disagreements between programs, but overall these categories should provide better access to the subject of sport and recreation. Websites and government documents are included to provide information not available in monograph format.

— Mila Su

Recreation and Leisure

HQ796.A1
☐ President's Council on Physical Fitness and Sports. http://fitness.gov/
Audience: **g,l,u,f.**

GV709
☐ Women's Sport Foundation (US). http://www.womenssportsfoundation.org/
Audience: **g,l,u,f.**

Carter, John M. **GV575**
Medieval Games: Sports and Recreations in Feudal Society, 30. Trade Cloth. Greenwood Publishing Group, Inc. Portsmouth, NH. 1992. 192p. Contributions to the Study of World History Ser., No. 30 ISBN:0-313-26743-X, ISBN13: 978-0-313-26743-7. Dewey:796/.094. LCCN:91-000785.
Audience: **g,l,u,f.** *Choice, 1992.*

Cotten, Doyice J. & Wolohan, John **KF3989.S64 2003**
Law for Recreation and Sport Managers. Ed. 3. Trade Paper. Kendall/Hunt Publishing Company. Dubuque, IA. 2003. 698p. ISBN:0-7872-9968-5, ISBN13: 978-0-7872-9968-2. Dewey:344.73/099. LCCN:2003-010664.
Audience: **l,u,f.**

Cross, Gary S. **GV53.E53 2004**
Encyclopedia of Recreation and Leisure in America. Trade Cloth. Thomson Gale. Farmington Hills, MI. 2004. 800p. The Scribner American Civilization Ser. ISBN:0-684-31265-4, ISBN13: 978-0-684-31265-1. Dewey:790/.0973/03. LCCN:2004-004617.
Audience: **l,u.** *Choice, 2005.*

Smith, Darren L. (Editor) **E160.S65 1992**
Parks Directory of the United States: A Guide to 4,000 National and State Parks, Recreational Areas, Historic Sites, Battlefields, Monuments, Forests, Preserves, Memorials, Seashores, and Other Designated Recreation Areas in the United States Administered by National and State Park Agencies. Library Binding. Omnigraphics, Inc. Detroit, MI. 1992. 360p. ISBN:1-55888-765-2, ISBN13: 978-1-55888-765-7. Dewey:917.3/0025. LCCN:91-045072.
Audience: **g,l,u.** *Choice, 1992.*

Recreation and Leisure > General

American College of Sports Medicine Staff (Contribution by) **RM725.A3 2002**
ACSM's Exercise Management for Persons with Chronic Diseases and Disabilities. Ed. 2. Trade Cloth. Human Kinetics Publishers. Champaign, IL. 2002. 384p. ISBN:0-7360-3872-8, ISBN13: 978-0-7360-3872-0. Dewey:615.8/24. LCCN:2002-006587.
Audience: **u,f.**

Austin, David R. (Editor), et al. **RM736.7**
Conceptual Foundations for Therapeutic Recreation. John Dattilo & Bryan P. McCormick (Editors). Cloth Text. Venture Publishing, Inc. State College, PA. 2002. 366p. ISBN:1-892132-30-3, ISBN13: 978-1-892132-30-7. Dewey:615.85101. LCCN:2002-104096.
Audience: **u,f.**

Butsch, Richard (Editor) **GV188.3.U6F67 1990**
For Fun and Profit: The Transformation of Leisure into Consumption. Trade Cloth. Temple University Press. Philadelphia, PA. 1990. 288p. Arts and Their Philosophies Ser. ISBN:0-87722-676-8, ISBN13: 978-0-87722-676-5. Dewey:338.4/77900135/0973. LCCN:89-027699.
Audience: **l,u.** *Choice, 1990.*

Carter, Marcia Jean & LeConey, Stephen P. **RM736.7**
Therapeutic Recreation Programs in the Community: An Inclusive Approach. Ed. 2. Trade Paper. Sagamore Publishing, L.L.C.. Champaign, IL. 2004. 217p. ISBN:1-57167-513-2, ISBN13: 978-1-57167-513-2. Dewey:790.196. LCCN:2004-101734.
Audience: **u,f.**

Currell, Susan **GV53.C79 2005**
The March of Spare Time: The Problem and Promise of Leisure in the Great Depression. Book, Other. University of Pennsylvania Press. Philadelphia, PA. 2005. 256p. ISBN:0-8122-3859-1, ISBN13: 978-0-8122-3859-4. Dewey:790.1/0973/09043. LCCN:2004-057246.
Audience: **l,u.** *Choice, 2005.*

DeGraaf, Kathy H., et al. **GV181.43 .D44**
Programming for Parks, Recreation, and Leisure Services. Debra J. Jordan & Donald G. DeGraaf (Authors). Cloth Text. Venture Publishing, Inc. State College, PA. 2005. ISBN:1-892132-51-6, ISBN13: 978-1-892132-51-2. Dewey:790.069.
Audience: **l,u.**

Elias, Norbert & Dunning, Eric **GV706.5**
The Quest for Excitement: Sport and Leisure in the Civilizing Process. Paper Text. Blackwell Publishing, Inc. Malden, MA. 1994. 314p. ISBN:0-631-19219-0, ISBN13: 978-0-631-19219-0. Dewey:306/.483.
Audience: **l,u.** *Choice, 1987.*

Fain, Gerald S. (Editor) **BJ1498**
Leisure and Ethics: Reflections on the Philosophy of Leisure, Vol. II. Paper Text. American Alliance for Health, Physical Education, Recreation & Dance. Oxon Hill, MD. 1995. 330p. ISBN:0-88314-850-1, ISBN13: 978-0-88314-850-1. Dewey:790.01.
Audience: **l,u.**

Fine, Aubrey H. & Fine, Nya M. **RJ53.R43F56 1996**
Therapeutic Recreation for Exceptional Children: Let Me in, I Want to Play. Ed. 2. Cloth Text. Charles C. Thomas Publisher, Ltd. Springfield, IL. 1996. 422p. ISBN:0-398-06661-2, ISBN13: 978-0-398-06661-1. Dewey:615.8/5153/0880816. LCCN:96-008263.
Audience: **g,l,u,f.** *Choice, 1989.*

freysinger Valeria J **GV14.45**
21st Century Leisure: Current Issues. Ed. 2. Venture. 2004. ISBN:1-892132-53-2, ISBN13: 978-1-892132-53-6.
Audience: **u,f.**

Gems, Gerald R. **GV584.5.C4G46 1997**
The Windy City Wars: Labor, Leisure, and Sport in the Making of Chicago. Trade Cloth. Scarecrow Press, Inc. Lanham, MD.

1997. 280p. American Sports History Ser., No. 8 ISBN:0-8108-3305-0, ISBN13: 978-0-8108-3305-0. Dewey:796/.09773/11. LCCN:97-012133.

Audience: **u,f.**

Giordano, Ralph G. **GV53**
Fun and Games in Twentieth-Century America: A Historical Guide to Leisure. Cloth Text. Greenwood Publishing Group, Inc. Portsmouth, NH. 2003. 328p. ISBN:0-313-32216-3, ISBN13: 978-0-313-32216-7. Dewey:790/.0973/0904. LCCN:2003-045533.

Audience: **g,l.** *Choice, 2004.*

Godbey, Geoffrey **GV174**
Leisure in Your Life: An Exploration. Ed. 6. Cloth Text. Venture Publishing, Inc. State College, PA. 2003. 417p. ISBN:1-892132-37-0, ISBN13: 978-1-892132-37-6. Dewey:790/.01/35.

Audience: **l,u.**

Grover, Kathryn (Editor) **GV53.H28 1992**
Hard at Play: Leisure in America, 1840-1940. Cloth Text. University of Massachusetts Press. Amherst, MA. 1992. 272p. ISBN:0-87023-792-6, ISBN13: 978-0-87023-792-8. Dewey:790/.01/350973. LCCN:91-039908.

Audience: **l,u.** *Choice, 1993.*

Harris, David E. **GV14.5**
Key Concepts in Leisure Studies. Cloth Text. SAGE Publications, Inc. Thousand Oaks, CA. 2005. 288p. SAGE Key Concepts Ser. ISBN:0-7619-7057-6, ISBN13: 978-0-7619-7057-6. Dewey:790.1. LCCN:2005-295466.

Audience: **g,l,u.** *Choice, 2005.*

Henderson, Karla A., et al. **GV183.B57 1996**
Both Gains and Gaps: Feminist Perspectives on Women's Leisure. M. Deborah Bialeschki, Susan M. Shaw & Valeria J. Freysinger (Authors). Trade Cloth. Venture Publishing, Inc. State College, PA. 1996. 357p. ISBN:0-910251-79-7, ISBN13: 978-0-910251-79-2. Dewey:790.1/94. LCCN:95-061907.

Audience: **u,f.**

Hughes, Bob **GV182.9.H84 2001**
Evolutionary Playwork and Reflective Analytic Practice. Trade Paper. Routledge. New York, NY. 2001. 320p. ISBN:0-415-25166-4, ISBN13: 978-0-415-25166-2. Dewey:155.4/18. LCCN:2001-018066.

Audience: **l,u.**

Jenkins, John & Pigram, John (Editors) **GV188**
Encyclopedia of Leisure and Outdoor Recreation. Paper over Boards. Routledge. New York, NY. 2004. 752p. ISBN:0-415-25226-1, ISBN13: 978-0-415-25226-3. Dewey:790/.03. LCCN:2003-058529.

Audience: **g,l,u,f.** *Choice, 2004.*

Koshar, Rudy (Editor) **GV73.H57 2002**
Histories of Leisure. Trade Paper. Berg Publishers. Oxford, 2002. 352p. Leisure, Consumption and Culture Ser. ISBN:1-85973-525-8, ISBN13: 978-1-85973-525-1. Dewey:306.4/812. LCCN:2002-000202.

Audience: **l,u.** *Choice, 2003.*

Kraus, Richard, et al. **GV160**
Introduction to Leisure Services: Career Perspectives. Elizabeth Barber & Ira Shapiro (Authors). Trade Paper. Sagamore Publishing, L.L.C.. Champaign, IL. 2001. 255p. ISBN:1-57167-482-9, ISBN13: 978-1-57167-482-1. Dewey:790.023. LCCN:00-107471.

Audience: **l,u.**

Lear, Roma **GV183.6**
Fun Without Fatigue. Ed. 2. Trade Paper. Elsevier - Health Sciences Division. Philadelphia, PA. 2001. 208p. ISBN:0-7506-2525-2, ISBN13: 978-0-7506-2525-8. Dewey:649.5/5/087.

Audience: **g,l,u,f.**

Leheny, David Richard **GV125.L43 2003**
The Rules of Play: National Identity and the Shaping of Japanese Leisure. Trade Cloth. Cornell University Press. Ithaca, NY. 2003. xiv, 188p. Cornell Studies in Political Economy ISBN:0-8014-4091-2, ISBN13: 978-0-8014-4091-5. Dewey:306.4/8/0952. LCCN:2002-151027.

Audience: **u,f.** *Choice, 2003.*

Miller, Patricia D. (Editor) **GV482.7.F58 1995**
Fitness Programming and Physical Disability. Trade Paper. Human Kinetics Publishers. Champaign, IL. 1994. 232p. ISBN:0-87322-434-5, ISBN13: 978-0-87322-434-5. Dewey:613.7. LCCN:94-004961.

Audience: **u.**

Mood, Dale P., et al. **GV704**
Sports and Recreational Activities with PowerWeb Bind-In Passcard. Ed. 13. Frank F. Musker & Judith E. Rink (Authors). Trade Paper. McGraw-Hill Higher Education. Burr Ridge, IL. 2002. ISBN:0-07-255245-X, ISBN13: 978-0-07-255245-4. Dewey:796.

Audience: **l,u.**

Morris, Lynn A. (Editor) **GV14.5**
Research about Leisure: Past, Present and Future. Ed. 2. Trade Paper. Sagamore Publishing, L.L.C.. Champaign, IL. 1994. 289p. ISBN:0-915611-96-1, ISBN13: 978-0-915611-96-6. Dewey:306.4812.

Audience: **u,f.**

Mundy, Jean **GV53**
Leisure Education: Theory and Practice. Ed. 2. Trade Cloth. Sagamore Publishing, L.L.C.. Champaign, IL. 1997. 270p. ISBN:1-57167-035-1, ISBN13: 978-1-57167-035-9. Dewey:301.5/7/0973.

Audience: **l,u,f.**

Paciorek, Michael J. & Jones, Jeffrey A. **GV709.3 .P33 2001**
Disability Sport and Recreation Resources. Ed. 3. Trade Paper. Cooper Publishing Group. Traverse City, MI. 2000. 386p. ISBN:1-884125-75-1, ISBN13: 978-1-884125-75-1. Dewey:796.0196. LCCN:2001-086212.

Audience: **l,u,f.** *Choice, 2002.*

Pieper, Josef **BJ1498.P513 1999**
Leisure: The Basis of Culture. Alexander Dru (Translator), T. S. Eliot (Introduction by). Trade Cloth. Liberty Fund, Inc. Indianapolis, IN. 1999. 137p. ISBN:0-86597-210-9, ISBN13: 978-0-86597-210-0. Dewey:175. LCCN:98-040641.

Audience: **l,u.**

Scarrott, Martin **GV188.S66 1999**
Sport, Leisure and Tourism Information Sources: A Guide for Researchers. Cloth Text. Elsevier Science & Technology Books. Saint Louis, MO. 1999. 256p. ISBN:0-7506-3864-8, ISBN13: 978-0-7506-3864-7. Dewey:026.79. LCCN:99-218933.
Audience: **l,u,f.**

Schleien, Stuart J. **GV183.5.L54 1995**
Lifelong Leisure Skills and Lifestyles for Persons with Developmental Disabilities. Cloth Text. Paul H. Brookes Publishing Company. Baltimore, MD. 1995. 352p. ISBN:1-55766-147-2, ISBN13: 978-1-55766-147-0. Dewey:790.1/96. LCCN:94-037005.
Audience: **l,u.**

Shivers, Jay S. & DeLisle, Lee J. **GV15.S533 1997**
The Story of Leisure: Context, Concepts, and Current Controversy. Trade Cloth. Human Kinetics Publishers. Champaign, IL. 1997. 224p. ISBN:0-87322-996-7, ISBN13: 978-0-87322-996-8. Dewey:790. LCCN:96-048339.
Audience: **l.** *Choice, 1997.*

Smith, Stephen L. **GV11**
Dictionary of Concepts in Recreation and Leisure Studies, 9. Cloth Text. Greenwood Publishing Group, Inc. Portsmouth, NH. 1990. 384p. Reference Sources for the Social Sciences and Humanities Ser., No. 9 ISBN:0-313-25262-9, ISBN13: 978-0-313-25262-4. Dewey:790/.03. LCCN:89-078447.
Audience: **l,u,f.** *Choice, 1991.*

Tribe, John **GV188**
The Economics of Recreation, Leisure and Tourism. Ed. 3. Paper Text. Elsevier Science & Technology Books. Saint Louis, MO. 2005. 464p. ISBN:0-7506-6180-1, ISBN13: 978-0-7506-6180-5. Dewey:790.069.
Audience: **u,f.**

Veal, A. J. (Editor), et al. **GV1**
Free Time and Leisure Participation: International Perspectives. Grant Cushman & Jiri Zuzanek (Editors). Perfect, Paper over Boards. CAB International. Wallingford, 2005. 298p. CABI Publishing Ser. ISBN:0-85199-620-5, ISBN13: 978-0-85199-620-2. Dewey:790.1. LCCN:2004-011056.
Audience: **u,f.**

Wearing, Betsy **GV183.W43 1998**
Leisure and Feminist Theory. Paper Text. SAGE Publications, Ltd. London, 1999. 219p. ISBN:0-8039-7537-6, ISBN13: 978-0-8039-7537-8. Dewey:306.4/812. LCCN:98-061180.
Audience: **u,f.**

Wilson, Robert F. **GV734.3.W55 2001**
Careers in Sports Fitness and Recreation. Trade Paper. Barron's Educational Series, Inc. Hauppauge, NY. 2001. 176p. Success Without College Ser. ISBN:0-7641-1562-6, ISBN13: 978-0-7641-1562-2. Dewey:790/.023/73. LCCN:00-068014.
Audience: **g,l,u.**

Recreation and Leisure > Administration

Appenzeller, Thomas **KF3989.A965 2000**
Youth Sport and the Law: A Guide to Legal Issues. Herb Appenzeller (Editor). Trade Paper. Carolina Academic Press. Durham, NC. 2000. 216p. ISBN:0-89089-663-1, ISBN13: 978-0-89089-663-1. Dewey:344.73/099. LCCN:99-088424.
Audience: **u,f.**

Bannon, Joseph J. & Busser, James A. **GV181.4 .B36 1992**
Problem Solving in Recreation and Parks. Ed. 3. H. Douglas Sessoms (Foreword by). Trade Cloth. Sagamore Publishing, L.L.C.. Champaign, IL. 1992. 440p. ISBN:0-915611-50-3, ISBN13: 978-0-915611-50-8. Dewey:790/.06/9. LCCN:91-068237.
Audience: **u.**

Bullock, Charles & Mahon, Michael **GV183.5**
Introduction to Recreation Services for People with Disabilities: A Person-Centered Approach. Trade Cloth. Sagamore Publishing, L.L.C.. Champaign, IL. 1997. 464p. ISBN:1-57167-069-6, ISBN13: 978-1-57167-069-4. Dewey:790.196.
Audience: **u,f.**

Carpenter, Linda J. **KF4166**
Legal Concepts in Sport: A Primer. Ed. 2. Perfect. Sagamore Publishing, L.L.C.. Champaign, IL. 2000. 214p. ISBN:0-88314-659-2, ISBN13: 978-0-88314-659-0. Dewey:796.026. LCCN:99-069463.
Audience: **g,l,u,f.**

Carter, Marcia Jean & LeConey, Stephen P. **RM736.7**
Therapeutic Recreation Programs in the Community: An Inclusive Approach. Ed. 2. Trade Paper. Sagamore Publishing, L.L.C.. Champaign, IL. 2004. 217p. ISBN:1-57167-513-2, ISBN13: 978-1-57167-513-2. Dewey:790.196. LCCN:2004-101734.
Audience: **u,f.**

Clements, Claire B. **GV184**
The Arts - Fitness Quality of Life Activities Program: Creative Ideas for Working with Older Adults in Group Settings. Trade Paper. Health Professions Press. Baltimore, MD. 1998. 430p. ISBN:1-878812-45-9, ISBN13: 978-1-878812-45-2. Dewey:790.1/926.
Audience: **u.**

Crossley, John, et al. **GV181.5**
Introduction to Commercial Recreation and Tourism: An Entrepreneurial Approach. Ed. 4. Lynn Jamieson & Russell Brayley (Authors). Trade Paper. Sagamore Publishing, L.L.C.. Champaign, IL. 2001. 558p. ISBN:1-57167-475-6, ISBN13: 978-1-57167-475-3. Dewey:790.069.
Audience: **l,u,f.**

Daly, Jim **GV182.3.D34 2000**
Recreation and Sport Planning and Design. Ed. 2. Trade Paper. Human Kinetics Publishers. Champaign, IL. 2000. 232p. ISBN:0-7360-0345-2, ISBN13: 978-0-7360-0345-2. Dewey:796/.06/94. LCCN:99-042475.
Audience: **u,f.**

DeSensi, Joy Theresa & Rosenberg, Danny **GV713.D465 2003**
Ethics and Morality in Sport Management. Trade Cloth. Fitness Information Technology, Inc. Morgantown, WV. 2003. 299p. Sport Management Library ISBN:1-885693-46-X, ISBN13: 978-1-885693-46-4. Dewey:796/.06/9. LCCN:2002-113559.
Audience: **u,f.**

Gallup, Joan Whaley **RA975.5.H4G34 1999**
Wellness Centers: A Guide for the Design Professional. Trade Cloth. John Wiley & Sons, Inc. Hoboken, NJ. 1999. 264p. Wiley Series in Healthcare and Senior Living Design, Vol. 7 ISBN:0-471-25337-5, ISBN13: 978-0-471-25337-2. Dewey:725/.5. LCCN:99-011574.
Audience: **u.**

Kosseff, Alex **GV181.4.K67 2003**
AMC Guide to Outdoor Leadership. Appalachian Mountain Club Staff (Contribution by). Trade Paper. Appalachian Mountain Club Books. Boston, MA. 2003. 288p. ISBN:1-929173-21-0, ISBN13: 978-1-929173-21-1. Dewey:796.5. LCCN:2002-154920.
Audience: **u.**

Manning, Robert E. **GV191.6.M314 1999**
Studies in Outdoor Recreation: Search and Research for Satisfaction. Ed. 2. Trade Cloth. Oregon State University Press. Corvallis, OR. 1999. 374p. ISBN:0-87071-463-5, ISBN13: 978-0-87071-463-4. Dewey:306.4/83. LCCN:00-266928.
Audience: **l,u.** *Choice, 2000.*

Mobily, Kenneth E. & MacNeil, Richard **RM736.7**
Therapeutic Recreation and the Nature of Disabilities. Cloth Text. Venture Publishing, Inc. State College, PA. 2002. 320p. ISBN:1-892132-22-2, ISBN13: 978-1-892132-22-2. Dewey:790.196. LCCN:2002-103088.
Audience: **u,f.**

Mull, Richard F., et al. **GV181.43.R43 2005**
Recreational Sport Management. Ed. 4. Kathryn G. Bayless & Lynn M. Jamieson (Authors). Trade Cloth, CD-ROM. Human Kinetics Publishers. Champaign, IL. 2005. 354p. ISBN:0-7360-5131-7, ISBN13: 978-0-7360-5131-6. Dewey:790.069. LCCN:2005-003041.
Audience: **u.**

O'Sullivan, Ellen L. & Spangler, Kathy J. **GV182.15.O73 1998**
Experience Marketing: Strategies for the New Millenium. Cloth Text. Venture Publishing, Inc. State College, PA. 1998. 430p. ISBN:0-910251-98-3, ISBN13: 978-0-910251-98-3. Dewey:658.838. LCCN:98-086937.
Audience: **u,f.**

Parkhouse, Bonnie L. **GV713**
The Management of Sport: Its Foundation and Application with PowerWeb Bind-In Card. Ed. 4. Trade Cloth. McGraw-Hill Higher Education. Burr Ridge, IL. 2004. 432p. ISBN:0-07-298546-1, ISBN13: 978-0-07-298546-7. Dewey:796/.06/9.
Audience: **l,u,f.**

Pitts, Brenda G. & Stotlar, David K. **GV716.P58 2002**
Fundamentals of Sport Marketing. Ed. 2. Trade Paper. Fitness Information Technology, Inc. Morgantown, WV. 2001. 405p. Sport Management Library ISBN:1-885693-33-8, ISBN13: 978-1-885693-33-4. Dewey:796/.06/98. LCCN:2002-102472.
Audience: **g,l,f.**

Quirk, Charles E. (Editor) **KF3989.S675 1996**
Sports and the Law: Major Legal Cases. Library Binding. Garland Publishing, Inc. New York, NY. 1996. 336p. Reference Library of the Humanities, Vol. 04 ISBN:0-8153-0220-7, ISBN13: 978-0-8153-0220-9. Dewey:344.73/099. LCCN:94-035594.
Audience: **u,f.**

Riddick, Carol & Russell, Ruth V. **GV181.46**
Evaluative Research in Recreation, Park and Sport Settings: Searching for Useful Information. Trade Cloth. Sagamore Publishing, L.L.C.. Champaign, IL. 1999. 392p. ISBN:1-57167-245-1, ISBN13: 978-1-57167-245-2. Dewey:790.07.
Audience: **l,u,f.** *Choice, 2000.*

Roberts, Ken **GV188.R63 2004**
Leisure Industries. Trade Paper. Palgrave Macmillan. New York, NY. 2004. 288p. ISBN:1-4039-0412-X, ISBN13: 978-1-4039-0412-6. Dewey:790.1. LCCN:2003-069647.
Audience: **u.** *Choice, 2004.*

School and Community Safety Society of America Staff **GV191.625.O98 1998**
Outdoor Recreation Safety. Neil J. Dougherty (Editor). Trade Cloth. Human Kinetics Publishers. Champaign, IL. 1998. 312p. ISBN:0-87322-944-4, ISBN13: 978-0-87322-944-9. Dewey:790/.028/9. LCCN:97-038948.
Audience: **u.**

Shivers, Jay S. **GV181.5.S56 2001**
Leadership and Groups in Recreational Service. Trade Cloth. Fairleigh Dickinson University Press. Cranbury, NJ. 2001. 421p. ISBN:0-8386-3875-9, ISBN13: 978-0-8386-3875-0. Dewey:790/.068. LCCN:00-069124.
Audience: **l,u.**

Wilhite, Barbara C. & Keller, M. Jean **RM736.7.W54 2000**
Therapeutic Recreation: Cases and Exercises. Ed. 2. Paper Text. Venture Publishing, Inc. State College, PA. 2000. xxii, 314p. ISBN:1-892132-12-5, ISBN13: 978-1-892132-12-3. Dewey:615.8/5153. LCCN:99-067811.
Audience: **u,f.**

Outdoor Recreation

GV709.3

☐ Disabled Sport USA.
http://www.dsusa.org/

Audience: **g,l,u,f.**

GV423

Play It Safe: An Anthology of Playground Safety. Perfect. National Recreation & Park Association. Ashburn, VA. 1996. ISBN:0-929581-90-3, ISBN13: 978-0-929581-90-3. Dewey:796.0694.

Audience: **u,f.**

Anderson, Lynn & Kress, Carla GV183.5

Inclusion: Including People with Disabilities in Parks and Recreation Opportunities. Paper Text. Venture Publishing, Inc. State College, PA. 2003. 134p. ISBN:1-892132-33-8, ISBN13: 978-1-892132-33-8. Dewey:790.196. LCCN:2003-101466.

Audience: **u.**

DeGraaf, Kathy H., et al. GV181.43 .D44

Programming for Parks, Recreation, and Leisure Services. Debra J. Jordan & Donald G. DeGraaf (Authors). Cloth Text. Venture Publishing, Inc. State College, PA. 2005. ISBN:1-892132-51-6, ISBN13: 978-1-892132-51-2. Dewey:790.069.

Audience: **l,u.**

Fletcher, Colin & Rawlins, C. L. GV199.6 .F532 2002

The Complete Walker IV. Trade Cloth. Alfred A. Knopf Inc. New York, NY. 2002. 864p. ISBN:0-375-40352-3, ISBN13: 978-0-375-40352-1. Dewey:796.51.

Audience: **l,u.**

Foster, David R. & Overholt, James L. GV443.F66 1994

Outdoor Action Games for Elementary Children: Active Games and Academic Activities for Fun and Fitness. Ron Schultz (Illustrator). Paper Text. Prentice Hall PTR. Upper Saddle River, NJ. 1994. 240p. ISBN:0-13-009895-7, ISBN13: 978-0-13-009895-5. Dewey:372.86. LCCN:93-034562.

Audience: **l,u.**

Friel, Joe GV1043.7.F75 1998

Cycling Past 50. Trade Cloth. Human Kinetics Publishers. Champaign, IL. 1998. 264p. Ageless Athlete Ser. ISBN:0-88011-737-0, ISBN13: 978-0-88011-737-1. Dewey:796.6. LCCN:97-038749.

Audience: **u.**

Graver, Dennis GV838.672.G74 2003

Scuba Diving. Ed. 3. Trade Paper. Human Kinetics Publishers. Champaign, IL. 2003. 224p. ISBN:0-7360-4539-2, ISBN13: 978-0-7360-4539-1. Dewey:797.2/3. LCCN:2002-152325.

Audience: **g,l,u,f.**

Hutcheson, John D. Jr. (Editor), et al. GV191

Outdoor Recreation Policy: Pleasure and Preservation, Vol. 263. Francis P. Noe & Robert E. Snow (Editors). Trade Cloth. Greenwood Publishing Group, Inc. Portsmouth, NH. 1990. 312p. Contributions in Political Science Ser., No. 263 ISBN:0-313-27522-X, ISBN13: 978-0-313-27522-7. Dewey:790/.0973. LCCN:90-036580.

Audience: **l,u.** *Choice, 1991.*

Jenkins, John & Pigram, John (Editors) GV188

Encyclopedia of Leisure and Outdoor Recreation. Paper over Boards. Routledge. New York, NY. 2004. 752p. ISBN:0-415-25226-1, ISBN13: 978-0-415-25226-3. Dewey:790/.03. LCCN:2003-058529.

Audience: **g,l,u,f.** *Choice, 2004.*

Jensen, Clayne R. & Guthrie, Steven P. GV191.4.J46 2005

Outdoor Recreation in America. Ed. 6. Trade Cloth. Human Kinetics Publishers. Champaign, IL. 2005. 384p. ISBN:0-7360-4213-X, ISBN13: 978-0-7360-4213-0. Dewey:796.5/0973. LCCN:2005-015630.

Audience: **l,u.** B

Kosseff, Alex GV181.4.K67 2003

AMC Guide to Outdoor Leadership. Appalachian Mountain Club Staff (Contribution by). Trade Paper. Appalachian Mountain Club Books. Boston, MA. 2003. 288p. ISBN:1-929173-21-0, ISBN13: 978-1-929173-21-1. Dewey:796.5. LCCN:2002-154920.

Audience: **u.**

Kutska, Kenneth S., et al. GV424 .K87

Playground Safety Is No Accident. Ed. 3. Kevin J. Hoffman & Antonio Malkusak (Authors). Perfect. National Recreation & Park Association. Ashburn, VA. 2002. ISBN:0-929581-28-8, ISBN13: 978-0-929581-28-6. Dewey:796.0694.

Audience: **u.**

Manning, Robert E. GV191.6.M314 1999

Studies in Outdoor Recreation: Search and Research for Satisfaction. Ed. 2. Trade Cloth. Oregon State University Press. Corvallis, OR. 1999. 374p. ISBN:0-87071-463-5, ISBN13: 978-0-87071-463-4. Dewey:306.4/83. LCCN:00-266928.

Audience: **l,u.** *Choice, 2000.*

Martin, Bruce, et al. GV181.4.M27 2006

Outdoor Leadership: Theory and Practice. Chris Cashel, Mark Wagstaff & Mary Breunig (Authors). Trade Cloth. Human Kinetics Publishers. Champaign, IL. 2006. 328p. ISBN:0-7360-5731-5, ISBN13: 978-0-7360-5731-8. Dewey:790/.06/9. LCCN:2005-022006.

Audience: **u,f.**

O'Sullivan, Ellen L. & Spangler, Kathy J. GV182.15.O73 1998

Experience Marketing: Strategies for the New Millenium. Cloth Text. Venture Publishing, Inc. State College, PA. 1998. 430p. ISBN:0-910251-98-3, ISBN13: 978-0-910251-98-3. Dewey:658.838. LCCN:98-086937.

Audience: **u,f.**

Panicucci, Jane GV191.6

Adventure Curriculum for Physical Education: Middle School. Lisa Faulkingham-Hunt, Amy Kohut, Alison Rheingold & Nancy Stratton (Contribution by). Perfect. Project Adventure, Inc. Beverly, MA. 2002. 182p. ISBN:0-934387-25-7, ISBN13: 978-0-934387-25-5. Dewey:796.5.

Audience: **l,u.**

Piggott, Derek TL765

Gliding: A Handbook on Soaring Flight. Ed. 8. Trade Paper. A & C Black. London, 2002. 312p. ISBN:0-7136-6148-8, ISBN13: 978-0-7136-6148-4. Dewey:629.132/523.

Audience: **u.**

Piggott, Derek **TL754**
Understanding Gliding. Ed. 3. Trade Paper. A & C Black. London, 2004. 256p. ISBN:0-7136-4343-9, ISBN13: 978-0-7136-4343-5. Dewey:629.132/523.
Audience: **l,u.** B

Sachs, Paul D. & Luff, Richard T. **GV975.3.S33 2002**
Ecological Golf Course Management. Trade Cloth. John Wiley & Sons, Inc. Hoboken, NJ. 2002. 216p. ISBN:1-57504-154-5, ISBN13: 978-1-57504-154-4. Dewey:796.352/06/9. LCCN:2001-006101.
Audience: **u,f.**

Sayer, Bill **GV791**
Rowing and Sculling. Ed. 2. Trade Paper. Robert Hale Ltd. London, 2001. 221p. ISBN:0-7090-5845-4, ISBN13: 978-0-7090-5845-8. Dewey:797.1/23.
Audience: **l,u,f.**

School and Community Safety Society of America Staff **GV191.625.O98 1998**
Outdoor Recreation Safety. Neil J. Dougherty (Editor). Trade Cloth. Human Kinetics Publishers. Champaign, IL. 1998. 312p. ISBN:0-87322-944-4, ISBN13: 978-0-87322-944-9. Dewey:790/.028/9. LCCN:97-038948.
Audience: **u.**

Smith, Darren L. (Editor) **E160.S65 1992**
Parks Directory of the United States: A Guide to 4,000 National and State Parks, Recreational Areas, Historic Sites, Battlefields, Monuments, Forests, Preserves, Memorials, Seashores, and Other Designated Recreation Areas in the United States Administered by National and State Park Agencies. Library Binding. Omnigraphics, Inc. Detroit, MI. 1992. 360p. ISBN:1-55888-765-2, ISBN13: 978-1-55888-765-7. Dewey:917.3/0025. LCCN:91-045072.
Audience: **g,l,u.** *Choice, 1992.*

Spilner, Maggie **RA781.6.S655 2000**
Prevention's Complete Book of Walking: Everything You Need to Know to Walk Your Way to Better Health. Elaine Ward (Foreword by). Trade Paper. Rodale Press, Inc. Emmaus, PA. 2000. 292p. ISBN:1-57954-236-0, ISBN13: 978-1-57954-236-8. Dewey:613.7/176. LCCN:00-025877.
Audience: **g,l,u,f.**

Warshaw, Matt **GV840.S8W3476 2003**
The Encyclopedia of Surfing. William Finnegan (Foreword by). Trade Cloth. Harcourt Trade Publishers. New York, NY. 2003. 800p. ISBN:0-15-100579-6, ISBN13: 978-0-15-100579-6. Dewey:797.3/203. LCCN:2003-005274.
Audience: **g,l,u,f.** *Choice, 2004.*

Wellner, Alison Stein **GV191.4.W45 1997**
Americans at Play: Demographics of Outdoor Recreation and Travel. Trade Cloth. New Strategist Publications, Inc. Ithaca, NY. 1997. 370p. ISBN:1-885070-11-X, ISBN13: 978-1-885070-11-1. Dewey:790/.06/8/021. LCCN:98-157389.
Audience: **l,u,f.** *Choice, 1998.*

Zinser, Charles I. **GV191.4.Z56 1995**
Outdoor Recreation: United States National Parks, Forests, and Public Lands. Trade Cloth. John Wiley & Sons, Inc. Hoboken, NJ. 1995. 898p. ISBN:0-471-05373-2, ISBN13: 978-0-471-05373-6. Dewey:350.858. LCCN:94-038100.
Audience: **l,u,f.** *Choice, 1996.*

Outdoor Recreation > Hiking

Berger, Karen **GV199.5**
Backpacking and Hiking. Trade Paper. Dorling Kindersley Publishing, Inc. New York, NY. 2005. 256p. Eyewitness Companions Ser. ISBN:0-7566-0946-1, ISBN13: 978-0-7566-0946-7. Dewey:796.51.
Audience: **l,u.**

McKinney, John **GV199.5.M387 2005**
The Joy of Hiking: Hiking the Trailmaster Way. Trade Cloth. Wilderness Press. Berkeley, CA. 2005. 288p. ISBN:0-89997-385-X, ISBN13: 978-0-89997-385-2. Dewey:796.51. LCCN:2005-002376.
Audience: **l,u.**

Outdoor Recreation > Orienteering. Outward Bound

Drake, Peter G. **GV199.5**
Walking and Orienteering: How to Cross Hills, Back Country and Rough Terrain in Safety and Confidence: A Professional Manual for Hikers, Paddlers, Horse Trekkers and Extreme Cyclists. Trade Paper, Perfect. Anness Publishing. London, 2005. 96p. ISBN:1-84476-152-5, ISBN13: 978-1-84476-152-4. Dewey:796.
Audience: **l,u.**

Enoksen, Eystein, et al. **GV482.F46 2002**
Female Fitness on Foot: Walking, Jogging, Running and Orienteering. Bob O'Connor, Eldin Onsgard & Christine Wells (Authors). Trade Paper. Wish Publishing. Terre Haute, IN. 2002. 256p. ISBN:1-930546-52-1, ISBN13: 978-1-930546-52-3. Dewey:613.7/045. LCCN:2001-093469.
Audience: **g,l,u.** *Choice, 2002.*

Harvey, Mark **GV199.6.S56 1999**
National Outdoor Leadership School's Wilderness Guide: The Classic Wilderness Guide. Trade Paper. Simon & Schuster. New York, NY. 1999. 272p. ISBN:0-684-85909-2, ISBN13: 978-0-684-85909-5. Dewey:796.51/028. LCCN:99-021875.
Audience: **l,u.**

Landry, Paul & McNair, Matty **GV783 .L36 1992**
The Outward Bound Canoeing Handbook. Trade Paper. Globe Pequot Press, The. Guilford, CT. 1992. 144p. Outward Bound Ser. ISBN:1-55821-149-7, ISBN13: 978-1-55821-149-0. Dewey:797.1/22. LCCN:92-011647.
Audience: **l,u.**

McDougall, Len **GV200.5 .M374**
Outward Bound Wilderness Survival Handbook. Trade Paper. Globe Pequot Press, The. Guilford, CT. 2001. 224p. ISBN:1-58574-159-0, ISBN13: 978-1-58574-159-5. Dewey:613.6/9.
Audience: **l,u.**

Priest, Simon & Gass, Michael A. **GV181.43.P75 2005**
Effective Leadership in Adventure Programming. Ed. 2. Perfect, Paper over Boards. Human Kinetics Publishers. Champaign, IL. 2005. 328p. ISBN:0-7360-5250-X, ISBN13: 978-0-7360-5250-4. Dewey:790.069. LCCN:2005-003376.
Audience: **u.**

Outdoor Recreation > Canoeing

Arima, E. Y. **GN440.2**
The Canoe: A Living Tradition. John Jennings (Editor). Trade Cloth. Firefly Books, Ltd. Tonawanda, NY. 2005. 288p. ISBN:1-55209-509-6, ISBN13: 978-1-55209-509-6. Dewey:386/.229. LCCN:2002-437631.
Audience: **l,u.** *Choice, 2003.*

Landry, Paul & McNair, Matty **GV783 .L36 1992**
The Outward Bound Canoeing Handbook. Trade Paper. Globe Pequot Press, The. Guilford, CT. 1992. 144p. Outward Bound Ser. ISBN:1-55821-149-7, ISBN13: 978-1-55821-149-0. Dewey:797.1/22. LCCN:92-011647.
Audience: **l,u.**

Outdoor Recreation > Mountaineering. Rock Climbing

Boukreev, Anatoli & DeWalt, G. Weston **GV199.44.E85B69 1999**
The Climb: Tragic Ambitions on Everest. Trade Paper. St. Martin's Press. Gordonville, VA. 1999. 400p. ISBN:0-312-20637-2, ISBN13: 978-0-312-20637-6. Dewey:796.5/22/095496. LCCN:00-265468.
Audience: **g,l,u.** *Choice, 1998.*

Brown, Rebecca A. **GV199.9**
Women on High: Pioneers of Mountaineering. Trade Paper. Appalachian Mountain Club Books. Boston, MA. 2003. 272p. ISBN:1-929173-42-3, ISBN13: 978-1-929173-42-6. Dewey:796.52/2/0922.
Audience: **l,u.** *Choice, 2003.*

Child, Greg (Compiled by) **GV199.85**
Climbing: The Complete Reference. Trade Paper. Facts On File, Inc. New York, NY. 1997. 272p. ISBN:0-8160-3653-5, ISBN13: 978-0-8160-3653-0. Dewey:796.5/22/03.
Audience: **l,u.** *Choice, 1996.*

Frison-Roche, Roger & Jouty, Sylvan **GV199.89**
A History of Mountain Climbing. Trade Cloth. Editions Flammarion. Montreal, PQ. 1996. 336p. ISBN:2-08-013622-4, ISBN13: 978-2-08-013622-0. Dewey:796.5/22/09. LCCN:96-085980.
Audience: **g,l,u.** *Choice, 1997.*

Fyffe, Allen & Peter, Iain **GV200**
Handbook of Climbing. Ed. 2. Hamish MacInnes (Foreword by). Trade Cloth. Penguin Group (USA) Inc. New York, NY. 1998. 400p. ISBN:0-7207-2054-0, ISBN13: 978-0-7207-2054-9. Dewey:796.5/22.
Audience: **l,u.**

Green, Dudley **GV199.92**
Because It's There: The Life of George Mallory. Trade Paper. Tempus Publishing, Ltd. Stroud, Gloucestershire, 2006. 224p. ISBN:0-7524-3747-X, ISBN13: 978-0-7524-3747-7. Dewey:796.522092.
Audience: **g,l.**

Hill, Lynn & Child, Greg **GV199.92.R62**
Climbing Free: My Life in the Vertical World. Trade Paper. W. W. Norton & Company, Inc. New York, NY. 2003. 288p. ISBN:0-393-32433-8, ISBN13: 978-0-393-32433-4. Dewey:796.5/223/092.
Audience: **g,l,u,f.**

Jones, Chris **GV199.44.N67J66 1997**
Climbing in North America. Paper Text. Mountaineers Books, The. Seattle, WA. 1997. 408p. ISBN:0-89886-481-X, ISBN13: 978-0-89886-481-6. Dewey:796.5/22. LCCN:96-049400.
Audience: **l,u.** B

Krakauer, Jon **GV199.44.E85K725**
Into Thin Air: A Personal Account of the Mount Everest Disaster. Trade Paper. Knopf Publishing Group. New York, NY. 1999. 368p. ISBN:0-385-49478-5, ISBN13: 978-0-385-49478-6. Dewey:796.5/22/095496. LCCN:97-042880.
Audience: **g,l,u.** *Choice, 1997.*

Long, John **GV199.9.H55 1999**
The High Lonesome: Epic Solo Climbing Stories. Paper Text. Globe Pequot Press, The. Guilford, CT. 1999. 168p. Adventure Ser. ISBN:1-56044-858-X, ISBN13: 978-1-56044-858-7. Dewey:796.52/2/0922 B. LCCN:99-028159.
Audience: **g,l,u.**

Loughman, Michael **GV200.2**
Learning to Rock Climb. Trade Paper. Sierra Club Books. San Francisco, CA. 1981. 192p. Learning to Rock Climb Ser. ISBN:0-87156-281-2, ISBN13: 978-0-87156-281-4. Dewey:796.5/223. LCCN:80-028639.
Audience: **l,u.** B

Potterfield, Peter **GV199.42.A42F676**
In the Zone: Epic Survival Stories from the Mountaineering World. Ed. 2. Paper Text. Mountaineers Books, The. Seattle, WA. 1998. 272p. ISBN:0-89886-568-9, ISBN13: 978-0-89886-568-4. Dewey:796.5/22. LCCN:96-025476.
Audience: **g,l,u.** *Choice, 1997.*

Fitness and Health

HQ796.A1
☐ President's Council on Physical Fitness and Sports. http://fitness.gov/
Audience: **g,l,u,f.**

GV709.3
☐ Disabled Sport USA. http://www.dsusa.org/
Audience: **g,l,u,f.**

RA564.85
☐ Melpomene Institute. http://www.melpomene.org/
Audience: **g,l,u,f.**

GV709.2
☐ National Alliance for Youth Sports. http://www.nays.org/
Audience: **g,l,u,f.**

GV712
☐ National Senior Games Assocation. http://www.nsga.com/
Audience: **l,u,f.**

GV568

Scholarly Sport Sites: A Subject Directory.
http://www.ucalgary.ca/lib-old/ssportsite/
Audience: **g,l,u,f.**

GV741

SPORTQuest.
http://www.sirc.ca/online_resources/sportquest.cfm
SIRC.
Audience: **g,l,u,f.**

GV709

Women's Sport Foundation (US).
http://www.womenssportsfoundation.org/
Audience: **g,l,u,f.**

Alter, Joseph S. **B132.Y6A483 2004**
Yoga in Modern India: The Body Between Science and Philosophy. Trade Paper. Princeton University Press. Princeton, NJ. 2004. 376p. ISBN:0-691-11874-4, ISBN13: 978-0-691-11874-1. Dewey:181/.45. LCCN:2003-064108.
Audience: **l,u,f.**

American College of Sports Medicine Staff **GV481.A322 2002**
ACSM Fitness Book: A Proven Step-by-Step Program from the Experts. Ed. 3. Arnold Schwarzengger (Foreword by). Trade Paper. Human Kinetics Publishers. Champaign, IL. 2003. 184p. ISBN:0-7360-4406-X, ISBN13: 978-0-7360-4406-6. Dewey:613.7/1. LCCN:2002-008864.
Audience: **g,l,u.**

Benjamin, Patricia & Lamp, Scott P. **RM721.B476 1996**
Understanding Sports Massage. Trade Paper. Human Kinetics Publishers. Champaign, IL. 1996. 136p. ISBN:0-87322-976-2, ISBN13: 978-0-87322-976-0. Dewey:615.8/22/088796. LCCN:95-049158.
Audience: **g,l,u.**

Bouchard, Claude (Editor) **RC628.P496 2000**
Physical Activity and Obesity. Trade Cloth. Human Kinetics Publishers. Champaign, IL. 2000. 48p. ISBN:0-88011-909-8, ISBN13: 978-0-88011-909-2. Dewey:616.3/98. LCCN:99-088071.
Audience: **u,f.** *Choice, 2001.*

Bouchard, Claude (Editor), et al. **RA781.P563 1993**
Physical Activity, Fitness, and Health Consensus Statement: International Proceedings and Consensus Statement. Roy J. Shephard & Thomas Stephens (Editors). Trade Paper. Blackwell Publishing, Inc. Malden, MA. 1979. 120p. ISBN:0-87322-470-1, ISBN13: 978-0-87322-470-3. Dewey:613.7. LCCN:92-041692.
Audience: **l,u.** *Choice, 1993.*

Boyle, Michael **GV711.5.B69 2003**
Functional Training for Sports. Trade Paper. Human Kinetics Publishers. Champaign, IL. 2003. 28p. ISBN:0-7360-4681-X, ISBN13: 978-0-7360-4681-7. Dewey:613.7/11. LCCN:2003-008763.
Audience: **g,l,u.**

Brehm, Barbara **GV481.2.B74 2004**
Successful Fitness Motivation Strategies. Trade Paper. Human Kinetics Publishers. Champaign, IL. 2004. 20p. ISBN:0-7360-4593-7, ISBN13: 978-0-7360-4593-3. Dewey:613.7/1. LCCN:2004-002097.
Audience: **g,l,u.**

Burfoot, Amby (Editor) **GV1060.5**
Runner's World Complete Book of Running: Everything You Need to Know to Run for Fun, Fitness and Competition. Trade Paper, Pictures or Photographs. Rodale Press, Inc. Emmaus, PA. 2004. 312p. ISBN:1-57954-929-2, ISBN13: 978-1-57954-929-9. Dewey:796.4/2.
Audience: **g,l,u.**

Butler, Lawrence F. **GV481**
Teaching Lifetime Sports. Paper Text. Greenwood Publishing Group, Inc. Portsmouth, NH. 2001. 192p. ISBN:0-89789-655-6, ISBN13: 978-0-89789-655-9. Dewey:796/.07. LCCN:2001-025180.
Audience: **l,u.** *Choice, 2002.*

Clements, Claire B. **GV184**
The Arts - Fitness Quality of Life Activities Program: Creative Ideas for Working with Older Adults in Group Settings. Trade Paper. Health Professions Press. Baltimore, MD. 1998. 430p. ISBN:1-878812-45-9, ISBN13: 978-1-878812-45-2. Dewey:790.1/926.
Audience: **u.**

Corbin, Charles B. & Pangrazi, Robert B. **RA781.T69 1999**
Toward a Better Understanding of Physical Fitness and Activity: Selected Topics. Trade Cloth. Holcomb Hathaway, Inc. Scottsdale, AZ. 1999. 212p. ISBN:1-890871-08-7, ISBN13: 978-1-890871-08-6. Dewey:613.7. LCCN:98-038693.
Audience: **g,l,u,f.** *Choice, 1999.*

Fleck, Steven J. & Kraemer, William J. **GV505.F58 2003**
Designing Resistance Training Programs. Ed. 3. Trade Cloth. Human Kinetics Publishers. Champaign, IL. 2003. 392p. ISBN:0-7360-4257-1, ISBN13: 978-0-7360-4257-4. Dewey:613.7/1. LCCN:2003-008524.
Audience: **g,l,u.** *Choice, 1988.*

Gallup, Joan Whaley **RA975.5.H4G34 1999**
Wellness Centers: A Guide for the Design Professional. Trade Cloth. John Wiley & Sons, Inc. Hoboken, NJ. 1999. 264p. Wiley Series in Healthcare and Senior Living Design, Vol. 7 ISBN:0-471-25337-5, ISBN13: 978-0-471-25337-2. Dewey:725/.5. LCCN:99-011574.
Audience: **u.**

Gavin, James & Gavin, Nettie **GV428.7.G38 1995**
Psychology for Health Fitness Professionals. Trade Paper. Human Kinetics Publishers. Champaign, IL. 1994. 136p. ISBN:0-87322-775-1, ISBN13: 978-0-87322-775-9. Dewey:613.7/11/019. LCCN:94-023549.
Audience: **u,f.**

Goldstein, Michael S. **RA427.8.G65 1992**
Health Movement in America: Promoting Fitness. Trade Paper. Macmillan Publishing Company, Inc. Old Tappan, NJ. 1992. 250p. Social Movements Past and Present Ser. ISBN:0-8057-9726-2, ISBN13: 978-0-8057-9726-8. Dewey:613/.0973. LCCN:91-028694.
Audience: **l,u,f.** *Choice, 1992.*

Grover, Kathryn (Editor) **GV510.U5F58 1989**
Fitness in American Culture: Images of Health, Sport and the Body, 1830-1940. Trade Paper. University of Massachusetts Press. Amherst, MA. 1989. 192p. ISBN:0-87023-682-2, ISBN13: 978-0-87023-682-2. Dewey:613.7/1. LCCN:89-004772.
Audience: **l,u,f.** *Choice, 1990.*

Higdon, Hal **GV1061.18.A35H55**
Masters Running: A Guide to Running and Staying Fit After 40. Trade Paper. Rodale Press, Inc. Emmaus, PA. 2005. 240p. ISBN:1-59486-021-1, ISBN13: 978-1-59486-021-8. Dewey:613.7/172/0846. LCCN:2004-027381.
Audience: **g,l,u,f.**

Howley, Edward T. & Franks, B. Don **GV481.H734 2003**
Health Fitness Instructor's Handbook. Ed. 4. Trade Cloth. Human Kinetics Publishers. Champaign, IL. 2003. 584p. ISBN:0-7360-4210-5, ISBN13: 978-0-7360-4210-9. Dewey:613.7. LCCN:2002-010983.
Audience: **u,f.**

Incledon, Lori **GV546.6.W64I63 2005**
Strength Training for Women. Trade Paper. Human Kinetics Publishers. Champaign, IL. 2004. 224p. ISBN:0-7360-5223-2, ISBN13: 978-0-7360-5223-8. Dewey:613.7/1/082. LCCN:2004-014047.
Audience: **l,u.**

Jackson, Allen W., et al. **QP301.P556 2004**
Physical Activity for Health and Fitness. James R. Morrow, David W. Hill & Rod K. Dishman (Authors). Trade Paper. Human Kinetics Publishers. Champaign, IL. 2003. 376p. ISBN:0-7360-5205-4, ISBN13: 978-0-7360-5205-4. Dewey:613.7/1. LCCN:2003-014521.
Audience: **g,l,u,f.** *Choice, 2000.*

Kolata, Gina **RA781.K585 2003**
Ultimate Fitness: The Quest for Truth about Health and Exercise. Cloth over Boards. Farrar, Straus & Giroux. New York, NY. 2003. 320p. ISBN:0-374-20477-2, ISBN13: 978-0-374-20477-8. Dewey:613.7. LCCN:2002-192523.
Audience: **g,l,u,f.** *Choice, 2003.*

Maud, Peter J. & Foster, Carl (Editors) **QP301.P57 2006**
Physiological Assessment of Human Fitness. Ed. 2. Trade Cloth. Human Kinetics Publishers. Champaign, IL. 2005. 328p. ISBN:0-7360-4633-X, ISBN13: 978-0-7360-4633-6. Dewey:613.7/028/7. LCCN:2005-014253.
Audience: **l,u.** *Choice, 1995.*

Maud, Peter J. & Foster, Carl (Editors) **QP301.P57 1995**
Physiological Assessment of Human Fitness. Trade Cloth. Human Kinetics Publishers. Champaign, IL. 1995. 304p. ISBN:0-87322-776-X, ISBN13: 978-0-87322-776-6. Dewey:613.7/028/7. LCCN:94-040072.
Audience: **l,u,f.** *Choice, 1995.*

McMurray Robert G **QP301.M3754 1999**
Concepts in Fitness Programming. CRC press. 1998. ISBN:0-8493-8714-0, ISBN13: 978-0-8493-8714-2.
Audience: **l,u,f.**

Miller, Patricia D. (Editor) **GV482.7.F58 1995**
Fitness Programming and Physical Disability. Trade Paper. Human Kinetics Publishers. Champaign, IL. 1994. 232p. ISBN:0-87322-434-5, ISBN13: 978-0-87322-434-5. Dewey:613.7. LCCN:94-004961.
Audience: **u.**

National Strength Training and Conditioning Association **GV428.7**
NSCA's Essentials of Personal Training. Roger W. Earle & Thomas R. Baechle (Editors). Trade Cloth. Human Kinetics Publishers. Champaign, IL. 2003. 688p. ISBN:0-7360-0015-1, ISBN13: 978-0-7360-0015-4. Dewey:613.7/1. LCCN:2003-019033.
Audience: **u.**

O'Brien, Teri S. **GV428.7.O37 2003**
The Personal Trainer's Handbook. Ed. 2. Trade Paper, CD-ROM. Human Kinetics Publishers. Champaign, IL. 2003. 257p. ISBN:0-7360-4501-5, ISBN13: 978-0-7360-4501-8. Dewey:613.7/1. LCCN:02-153987.
Audience: **u,f.**

Rose, Jessica **QP310.W3H85 2006**
Human Walking. Ed. 3. Trade Cloth. Lippincott Williams & Wilkins. Philadelphia, PA. 2005. 273p. ISBN:0-7817-5954-4, ISBN13: 978-0-7817-5954-0. Dewey:612.7/6. LCCN:2005-022885.
Audience: **l,u,f.**

Rush, Anne Kent **RA781.63.R873 2005**
The Way of Stretching: Flexibility for Body and Mind. Trade Paper. Little Brown & Company. New York, NY. 2005. 176p. ISBN:0-316-17231-6, ISBN13: 978-0-316-17231-8. Dewey:613.7/1. LCCN:2005-005740.
Audience: **g,l,u,f.**

Shephard, Roy J. **QP86.S478 1997**
Aging, Physical Activity, and Health. Trade Cloth. Human Kinetics Publishers. Champaign, IL. 1997. 496p. ISBN:0-87322-889-8, ISBN13: 978-0-87322-889-3. Dewey:613.7/0446. LCCN:96-043852.
Audience: **g,l,u,f.** *Choice, 1997.*

Spilner, Maggie **RA781.6.S655 2000**
Prevention's Complete Book of Walking: Everything You Need to Know to Walk Your Way to Better Health. Elaine Ward (Foreword by). Trade Paper. Rodale Press, Inc. Emmaus, PA. 2000. 292p. ISBN:1-57954-236-0, ISBN13: 978-1-57954-236-8. Dewey:613.7/176. LCCN:00-025877.
Audience: **g,l,u,f.**

University of California at Berkeley Wellness Lett & White, Timothy P. **RA781.W47 1993**
The Wellness Guide to Lifelong Fitness. Trade Cloth. Random House, Inc. New York, NY. 1993. 480p. ISBN:0-929661-08-7, ISBN13: 978-0-929661-08-7. Dewey:613.7/1. LCCN:93-019083.
Audience: **g,l,u,f.** *Choice, 1994.*

Williams, Melvin H. **QP141.W514 2005**
Nutrition for Health, Fitness and Sport. Ed. 7. Paper Text. McGraw-Hill Higher Education. Burr Ridge, IL. 2004. 560p. ISBN:0-07-244170-4, ISBN13: 978-0-07-244170-3. Dewey:613.2. LCCN:2003-019720.
Audience: **g,l,u.**

YMCA of the USA **RC1211.Y63 2005**
YMCA Personal Training Manual. Ed. 2. Perfect. Human Kinetics Publishers. Champaign, IL. 2005. vi, 249p. ISBN:0-7360-6021-9, ISBN13: 978-0-7360-6021-9. Dewey:613.7/1. LCCN:2005-004384.
Audience: **l,u,f.**

Fitness and Health > Weight Lifting

Baechle, Thomas R. & Earle, Roger W. **GV546.B33 1995**
Fitness Weight Training. Ed. 2. Trade Paper. Human Kinetics Publishers. Champaign, IL. 2005. 200p. ISBN:0-7360-5255-0, ISBN13: 978-0-7360-5255-9. Dewey:613.7/13. LCCN:2004-024500.
Audience: **g,l,u.**

Baechle, Thomas & Earle, Roger W. **GV546.B344 2006**
Weight Training: Steps to Success. Ed. 3. Trade Paper. Human Kinetics Publishers. Champaign, IL. 2005. 216p. ISBN:0-7360-5533-9, ISBN13: 978-0-7360-5533-8. Dewey:613.7/13. LCCN:2005-022589.
Audience: **g,l.**

Bompa, Tudor O. & Cornacchia, Lorenzo J. **GV546.B55 1998**
Serious Strength Training. Trade Paper. Human Kinetics Publishers. Champaign, IL. 1998. 312p. ISBN:0-88011-834-2, ISBN13: 978-0-88011-834-7. Dewey:613.7/1. LCCN:98-012309.
Audience: **g,l,u.**

Bompa, Tudor & Carrera, Michael **GV546.B546 2005**
Periodization Training for Sports. Ed. 2. Trade Paper. Human Kinetics Publishers. Champaign, IL. 2005. 272p. ISBN:0-7360-5559-2, ISBN13: 978-0-7360-5559-8. Dewey:613.7/13. LCCN:2004-028232.
Audience: **l,u.**

Fitness and Health > Aquatics

Case, LeAnne **GV838.53.E94C36 1997**
Fitness Aquatics. Trade Paper. Human Kinetics Publishers. Champaign, IL. 1996. 176p. Fitness Spectrum Ser. ISBN:0-87322-963-0, ISBN13: 978-0-87322-963-0. Dewey:797.2/1. LCCN:96-000369.
Audience: **g,l,u.**

Gibson, Terry-Ann Spitzer & Hoeger, Wener W. K. **RA781.17**
Water Aerobics for Fitness and Wellness. Ed. 3. Paper Text. Brooks/Cole. Pacific Grove, CA. 2002. 160p. The Wadsworth Activities Ser. ISBN:0-534-58106-4, ISBN13: 978-0-534-58106-0. Dewey:613.7/16. LCCN:2002-105848.
Audience: **g,l,u.**

Goldstein, Mel & Tanner, Dave **GV837.3.G65 1999**
Swimming Past 50. Trade Paper. Human Kinetics Publishers. Champaign, IL. 1999. 216p. Ageless Athlete Ser. ISBN:0-88011-907-1, ISBN13: 978-0-88011-907-8. Dewey:797.2/1/0846. LCCN:99-012569.
Audience: **l,u.**

Lepore, Monica, et al. **GV837.4.L47 1998**
Adapted Aquatics Programming: A Professional Guide. G. William Gayle & Shawn Stevens (Authors). Trade Cloth. Human Kinetics Publishers. Champaign, IL. 1998. 328p. ISBN:0-88011-695-1, ISBN13: 978-0-88011-695-4. Dewey:797.2/1/087. LCCN:98-022953.
Audience: **u,f.** *Choice, 1999.*

YMCA of the USA Staff **GV836.35.Y65 1999**
The Youth and Adult Aquatic Program Manual. Trade Paper. Human Kinetics Publishers. Champaign, IL. 1999. 208p. YMCA Swim Lessons Ser. ISBN:0-7360-0048-8, ISBN13: 978-0-7360-0048-2. Dewey:797.2/1/083. LCCN:98-037672.
Audience: **g,l,u,f.**

Fitness and Health > Health Clubs

American College of Sports Medicine **GV429.A45 2006**
ACSM's Health/Fitness Facility Standards and Guidelines. Ed. 3. Trade Cloth. Human Kinetics Publishers. Champaign, IL. 2006. 216p. ISBN:0-7360-5153-8, ISBN13: 978-0-7360-5153-8. Dewey:613.7/1. LCCN:2005-033377.
Audience: **g,u,f.**

Grantham, William C., et al. **GV428.5.H43 1998**
Health Fitness Management: A Comprehensive Resource for Managing and Operating Programs and Facilities. Robert W. Patton, Tracy D. York & Mitchel L. Winick (Authors). Trade Cloth. Human Kinetics Publishers. Champaign, IL. 1998. 544p. ISBN:0-88011-559-9, ISBN13: 978-0-88011-559-9. Dewey:613.7/068. LCCN:97-026549.
Audience: **u,f.**

Hensler, Kate **GV428.H46 1998**
Health Clubs: Architecture and Design. Trade Cloth. P B C International, Inc. Glen Cove, NY. 1998. 176p. ISBN:0-86636-643-1, ISBN13: 978-0-86636-643-4. Dewey:725/.85. LCCN:98-009645.
Audience: **u,f.**

Spielvogel, Laura **GV482.S67 2003**
Working Out in Japan: Shaping the Female Body in Tokyo Fitness Clubs. Trade Paper. Duke University Press. Durham, NC. 2003. 264p. ISBN:0-8223-3049-0, ISBN13: 978-0-8223-3049-3. Dewey:613/.0424/0952. LCCN:2002-012949.
Audience: **g,l,u,f.**

Taylor, Jeffrey H. (Editor) **GV182.3**
Design Standards for Recreation Facilities. Paper Text. DIANE Publishing Company. Collingdale, PA. 1998. 80p. ISBN:0-7881-7341-3, ISBN13: 978-0-7881-7341-7. Dewey:790.
Audience: **u,f.**

Fitness and Health > Yoga

Alter, Joseph S. **B132.Y6A483 2004**
Yoga in Modern India: The Body Between Science and Philosophy. Trade Paper. Princeton University Press. Princeton, NJ. 2004. 376p. ISBN:0-691-11874-4, ISBN13: 978-0-691-11874-1. Dewey:181/.45. LCCN:2003-064108.
Audience: **l,u,f.**

Coulter, H. David **RA781.7.C685 2001**
Anatomy of Hatha Yoga: A Manual for Students, Teachers and Practitioners. Timothy McCall (Foreword by). Trade Cloth. Body & Breath, Inc. Honesdale, PA. 2001. 623p. ISBN:0-9707006-0-1, ISBN13: 978-0-9707006-0-5. Dewey:613.7/046. LCCN:2001-025691.
Audience: **l,u,f.** *Choice, 2001.*

Strauss, Sarah **B132.Y6**
Positioning Yoga. Trade Paper. Berg Publishers. Oxford, 2005. 224p. ISBN:1-85973-739-0, ISBN13: 978-1-85973-739-2. Dewey:181/.45. LCCN:2004-023169.
Audience: **g,l,u,f.**

Yee, Rodney & Zolotow, Nina **RA781.7.Y438 2004**
Moving Toward Balance: 8 Weeks of Yoga with Rodney Yee. Michal Venera (Photographer). Trade Paper. Rodale Press, Inc. Emmaus, PA. 2004. 264p. ISBN:0-87596-921-6, ISBN13: 978-0-87596-921-3. Dewey:613.7/046. LCCN:2003-026817.
Audience: **g,l,u,f.**

Fitness and Health > Pilates

Brown, Carolan & Reader's Digest Editors **RA781.B757 2004**
The Pilates Program for Everybody: Simple, Effective Exercises— Amazing Benefits for All Ages. Trade Cloth. Reader's Digest Association, Incorporated, The. Pleasantville, NY. 2004. 144p. ISBN:0-7621-0451-1, ISBN13: 978-0-7621-0451-2. Dewey:613.7/1. LCCN:2003-047227.
Audience: **g,l,u.**

Craig, Colleen **GV546.5.C73 2003**
Abs on the Ball: A Pilates Approach to Building Superb Abdominals. Trade Paper. Inner Traditions International, Ltd. Rochester, VT. 2003. 200p. ISBN:0-89281-098-X, ISBN13: 978-0-89281-098-7. Dewey:646.7/5. LCCN:2003-003760.
Audience: **g,l,u,f.**

Fitness and Health > Exercises

Bricker, Kathryn **RA781**
Traditional Aerobics. American Council on Exercise Staff (Editor). Trade Paper. American Council on Exercise. San Diego, CA. 2000. 75p. ISBN:1-890720-08-9, ISBN13: 978-1-890720-08-7. Dewey:613.7/1. LCCN:00-106386.
Audience: **g,l,u.**

Chu, Donald A. **GV711.C54 1998**
Jumping into Plyometrics. Ed. 2. Trade Paper. Human Kinetics Publishers. Champaign, IL. 1998. 184p. ISBN:0-88011-846-6, ISBN13: 978-0-88011-846-0. Dewey:613.7/11. LCCN:98-017867.
Audience: **g,l,u.**

Crompton, Paul H. **GV504**
Tai Chi: An Introductory Guide to the Chinese Art of Movement. Trade Paper. Oneworld Publications. Oxford, 2000. 128p. New Perspectives Ser. ISBN:1-86204-760-X, ISBN13: 978-1-86204-760-0. Dewey:613.7/148.
Audience: **g,l,u,f.**

Enoksen, Eystein, et al. **GV482.F46 2002**
Female Fitness on Foot: Walking, Jogging, Running and Orienteering. Bob O'Connor, Eldin Onsgard & Christine Wells (Authors). Trade Paper. Wish Publishing. Terre Haute, IN. 2002. 256p. ISBN:1-930546-52-1, ISBN13: 978-1-930546-52-3. Dewey:613.7/045. LCCN:2001-093469.
Audience: **g,l,u.** *Choice, 2002.*

Hine, John **GV504.H56 1992**
Yang Tai Chi Chuan. Trade Paper. A & C Black. London, 224p. ISBN:0-7136-3576-2, ISBN13: 978-0-7136-3576-8. Dewey:796.8155.
Audience: **g,l,u,f.**

Huang, Chungliang A. **GV504 .H83 1987**
Embrace Tiger, Return to Mountain: The Essence of Tai Ji. Trade Cloth. Celestial Arts Publishing Company. Berkeley, CA. 2004. 256p. ISBN:0-89087-504-9, ISBN13: 978-0-89087-504-9. Dewey:613.7/1. LCCN:87-027752.
Audience: **g,l,u,f.**

Mazzeo, Karen S. **RA781.15**
Fitness Through Aerobics and Step Training. Ed. 4. Paper Text. Brooks/Cole. Pacific Grove, CA. 2006. 192p. ISBN:0-495-01271-8, ISBN13: 978-0-495-01271-9. Dewey:613.7/15. LCCN:2005-937326.
Audience: **g,l,u,f.**

Pryor, Esther & Kraines, Minda Goodman **RA781.15.K36 2000**
Keep Moving!: Fitness Through Aerobics and Step. Ed. 4. Paper Text. McGraw-Hill Higher Education. Burr Ridge, IL. 1999. 207p. ISBN:0-7674-1200-1, ISBN13: 978-0-7674-1200-1. Dewey:613.7/15. LCCN:99-029763.
Audience: **g,l,u,f.**

Reid, Daniel **RA781.8 .R45**
A Complete Guide to Chi-Gung. UK-Trade Paper. Shambhala Publications, Inc. Boston, MA. 2000. 336p. ISBN:1-57062-543-3, ISBN13: 978-1-57062-543-5. Dewey:613.71. LCCN:98-005002.
Audience: **g,l,u,f.**

Shephard, Roy J. **RA781**
Aerobic Fitness and Health. Trade Cloth. Human Kinetics Publishers. Champaign, IL. 1998. 368p. ISBN:0-88011-725-7, ISBN13: 978-0-88011-725-8. Dewey:613.7/1. LCCN:93-000457.
Audience: **g,l,u.** *Choice, 1994.*

Shou-Yu Liang & Wen-Ching Wu **GV504.L485 1993**
A Guide to Taijiquan: Twenty-Four and Forty-Eight Postures with Applications. Denise Breiter (Editor). Trade Paper. YMAA Publication Center. Roslindale, MA. 1993. 168p. ISBN:0-940871-29-7, ISBN13: 978-0-940871-29-8. Dewey:613.7/148. LCCN:93-060969.
Audience: **g,l,u,f.**

Yoke, Mary & Carol, Kennedy **RM725.Y645 2004**
Functional Exercise Progressions. Paper Text. Coaches Choice. Monterey, CA. 2003. 126p. ISBN:1-58518-998-7, ISBN13: 978-1-58518-998-4. Dewey:615.8/2. LCCN:2003-106969.
Audience: **u,f.**

Physical Education and Training

GV557

International Council of Sport Science and Physical Education.
http://www.icsspe.org/

Audience: **g,l,u,f.**

GV706.4

North American Society for Psychology of Sport and Physical Activity.
http://www.naspspa.org/

Audience: **l,u,f.**

Buck, Marilyn M., et al. **GV361.B84 2004**
Introduction to Physical Education and Sport: Foundations and Trends with Introduction to Careers in Health, Physical Education and Sport. J. Thomas Jable & Patricia A. Floyd (Authors). Cloth Text. Brooks/Cole. Pacific Grove, CA. 2003. 336p. ISBN:0-534-59850-1, ISBN13: 978-0-534-59850-1. Dewey:613.7/071. LCCN:2003-105865.

Audience: **l,u.**

Carr, Gerry **GV1060.5.C368 1999**
Fundamentals of Track and Field. Ed. 2. Trade Paper. Human Kinetics Publishers. Champaign, IL. 1999. 34p. ISBN:0-7360-0008-9, ISBN13: 978-0-7360-0008-6. Dewey:796.42. LCCN:98-052218.

Audience: **l,u.**

Drewe, Sheryle Bergmann **GV342.D74 2001**
Socrates, Sport, and Students: A Philosophical Inquiry into Physical Education and Sport. Book, Other. University Press of America, Inc. Lanham, MD. 2001. 198p. ISBN:0-7618-2080-9, ISBN13: 978-0-7618-2080-2. Dewey:613.7/01. LCCN:2001-041484.

Audience: **l,u,f.**

Floyd, Patricia A. **GV362**
Careers in Health, Physical Education, and Sports. Paper Text. Brooks/Cole. Pacific Grove, CA. 2003. 192p. ISBN:0-534-60785-3, ISBN13: 978-0-534-60785-2. Dewey:362.1023. LCCN:2004-268737.

Audience: **g,l,u.**

Hannula, Dick & Thornton, Nort (Editors) **GV837.65.S95 2001**
The Swim Coaching Bible. Trade Paper. Human Kinetics Publishers. Champaign, IL. 2001. 376p. ISBN:0-7360-3646-6, ISBN13: 978-0-7360-3646-7. Dewey:797.2/1. LCCN:00-054241.

Audience: **g,l,u,f.**

Kus, Sally **GV1015.5.C63K87 2004**
Coaching Volleyball Successfully. Ed. 2. Trade Paper. Human Kinetics Publishers. Champaign, IL. 2004. 224p. ISBN:0-7360-4037-4, ISBN13: 978-0-7360-4037-2. Dewey:796.325. LCCN:2003-027576.

Audience: **g,l,u,f.**

Physical Education and Training > General

HQ796.A1

President's Council on Physical Fitness and Sports.
http://fitness.gov/

Audience: **g,l,u,f.**

RA564.85

Melpomene Institute.
http://www.melpomene.org/

Audience: **g,l,u,f.**

GV709.2

National Alliance for Youth Sports.
http://www.nays.org/

Audience: **g,l,u,f.**

GV568

Scholarly Sport Sites: A Subject Directory.
http://www.ucalgary.ca/lib-old/ssportsite/

Audience: **g,l,u,f.**

GV709

Women's Sport Foundation (US).
http://www.womenssportsfoundation.org/

Audience: **g,l,u,f.**

American Sport Education Program Staff **GV880.4.R66 2001**
Coaching Youth Baseball. Ed. 3. Trade Paper. Human Kinetics Publishers. Champaign, IL. 2001. 176p. ISBN:0-7360-3716-0, ISBN13: 978-0-7360-3716-7. Dewey:796.357/07/7. LCCN:00-050062.

Audience: **g,l,u.**

American Sport Education Program Staff (Contribution by) **GV848.25.C63 2001**
Coaching Youth Hockey. Ed. 2. Trade Paper. Human Kinetics Publishers. Champaign, IL. 2001. 28p. ISBN:0-7360-3795-0, ISBN13: 978-0-7360-3795-2. Dewey:796.962/07/7. LCCN:2001-016873.

Audience: **g,l,u.**

American Sport Education Program Staff **GV943.8.C63 2001**
Coaching Youth Soccer. Ed. 3. Trade Paper. Human Kinetics Publishers. Champaign, IL. 2001. 168p. ISBN:0-7360-3718-7, ISBN13: 978-0-7360-3718-1. Dewey:796.334/07/7. LCCN:00-050032.

Audience: **l,u,f.**

American Sport Education Program Staff **GV1002.9.C63A45 2002**
Coaching Youth Tennis. Ed. 3. Trade Paper. Human Kinetics Publishers. Champaign, IL. 2001. 20p. ISBN:0-7360-3793-4, ISBN13: 978-0-7360-3793-8. Dewey:796.342/07/7. LCCN:2001-024117.

Audience: **l,u,f.**

American Sport Education Program Staff **GV1196.3.C63 2002**
Coaching Youth Wrestling. Ed. 2. Trade Paper. Human Kinetics Publishers. Champaign, IL. 2001. 168p. ISBN:0-7360-4159-1, ISBN13: 978-0-7360-4159-1. Dewey:797.812. LCCN:2001-039617.
Audience: **l,u,f.**

American Sport Education Program Staff **GV881.4.U47A54 2004**
Officiating Softball. Trade Paper. Human Kinetics Publishers. Champaign, IL. 2004. 184p. ISBN:0-7360-4764-6, ISBN13: 978-0-7360-4764-7. Dewey:796.357/8. LCCN:2004-000579.
Audience: **l,u,f.**

Anders, Elizabeth **GV1017.H7**
Field Hockey: Steps to Success. Trade Paper. Human Kinetics Publishers. Champaign, IL. 1998. 20p. Steps to Success Ser. ISBN:0-88011-673-0, ISBN13: 978-0-88011-673-2. Dewey:796.3/55. LCCN:98-027574.
Audience: **g,l,u.**

Armour, Kathleen R. **GV363.A76 1998**
Physical Education: Teachers' Lives and Careers. Paper over Boards. Taylor & Francis Group. Philadelphia, PA. 1998. 160p. ISBN:0-7507-0818-2, ISBN13: 978-0-7507-0818-0. Dewey:613.7/071041. LCCN:98-185973.
Audience: **g,l,u.** *Choice, 1999.*

Berg, Kris & Latin, Richard **Q180.55.M4B417 2003**
Essentials of Modern Research Methods in Health, Physical Education and Recreation. Ed. 2. Trade Cloth. Lippincott Williams & Wilkins. Philadelphia, PA. 2003. 300p. ISBN:0-7817-3802-4, ISBN13: 978-0-7817-3802-6. Dewey:001.4/2. LCCN:2003-040050.
Audience: **u,f.**

Boga, Steven **GV1007.B64 1996**
Badminton. Trade Paper. Stackpole Books. Mechanicsburg, PA. 1996. 112p. Backyard Games Ser. ISBN:0-8117-2487-5, ISBN13: 978-0-8117-2487-6. Dewey:796.34/5. LCCN:95-022434.
Audience: **g,l,u.**

Butler, Lawrence F. **GV481**
Teaching Lifetime Sports. Paper Text. Greenwood Publishing Group, Inc. Portsmouth, NH. 2001. 192p. ISBN:0-89789-655-6, ISBN13: 978-0-89789-655-9. Dewey:796/.07. LCCN:2001-025180.
Audience: **l,u.** *Choice, 2002.*

Capel, W. & Piotrowski, Susan **GV361.I78 2000**
Issues in Physical Education. Trade Paper. Routledge. New York, NY. 2000. 288p. Issues in Subject Teaching Ser. ISBN:0-415-18689-7, ISBN13: 978-0-415-18689-6. Dewey:613.7/071/041. LCCN:00-035274.
Audience: **u,f.**

Collingwood, Tom **GV444.C65 1997**
Helping at-Risk Youth Through Physical Fitness Programming. Trade Paper. Human Kinetics Publishers. Champaign, IL. 1997. 216p. ISBN:0-88011-549-1, ISBN13: 978-0-88011-549-0. Dewey:613.7/043. LCCN:96-053063.
Audience: **u.**

Conway Greene Publishing Co. Editorial Staff **GV709.3**
Sports, Everyone!: Recreation and Sports for the Physically Challenged of All Ages. John A. Nesbitt (Author, Introduction by), Jean Driscoll (Author). Trade Paper. Conway Greene Company. Cleveland, OH. 1995. 272p. ISBN:1-884669-10-7, ISBN13: 978-1-884669-10-1. Dewey:796.0456.
Audience: **g,l,u.**

Dougherty, Neil J. **KF3989**
Sport, Physical Activity and the Law. Ed. 2. Alan S. Goldberger (Author, Author), Linda Jean Carpenter (Author). Trade Paper. Sagamore Publishing, L.L.C.. Champaign, IL. 2002. 266p. ISBN:1-57167-492-6, ISBN13: 978-1-57167-492-0. Dewey:344.73099. LCCN:2002-101305.
Audience: **l,u,f.**

Fadala, Sam **GV1185.F33 1999**
Traditional Archery. Trade Paper. Stackpole Books. Mechanicsburg, PA. 1999. 256p. ISBN:0-8117-2943-5, ISBN13: 978-0-8117-2943-7. Dewey:799.3/2. LCCN:98-043191.
Audience: **l,u.**

Foster, David R. & Overholt, James L. **GV443.F66 1994**
Outdoor Action Games for Elementary Children: Active Games and Academic Activities for Fun and Fitness. Ron Schultz (Illustrator). Paper Text. Prentice Hall PTR. Upper Saddle River, NJ. 1994. 240p. ISBN:0-13-009895-7, ISBN13: 978-0-13-009895-5. Dewey:372.86. LCCN:93-034562.
Audience: **l,u.**

Hughes, Bob **GV182.9.H84 2001**
Evolutionary Playwork and Reflective Analytic Practice. Trade Paper. Routledge. New York, NY. 2001. 320p. ISBN:0-415-25166-4, ISBN13: 978-0-415-25166-2. Dewey:155.4/18. LCCN:2001-018066.
Audience: **l,u.**

Jastrjembskaia, Nadejda & Titov, Yuri **GV463.J37 1998**
Rhythmic Gymnastics. Trade Paper. Human Kinetics Publishers. Champaign, IL. 1998. 272p. ISBN:0-88011-710-9, ISBN13: 978-0-88011-710-4. Dewey:796.44. LCCN:98-015002.
Audience: **l,u,f.**

Jones, C. Jessie & Rose, Debra J. (Editors) **GV447.J66 2004**
Physical Activity Instruction of Older Adults. Perfect, Paper over Boards. Human Kinetics Publishers. Champaign, IL. 2004. 405p. ISBN:0-7360-4513-9, ISBN13: 978-0-7360-4513-1. Dewey:613.70446. LCCN:2004-013539.
Audience: **u,f.**

Kelly, Luke E. & Melograno, Vincent J. **GV365.K45 2004**
Developing the Physical Education Curriculum: An Achievement-Based Approach. Trade Cloth. Human Kinetics Publishers. Champaign, IL. 2004. 376p. ISBN:0-7360-4178-8, ISBN13: 978-0-7360-4178-2. Dewey:796/.071. LCCN:2003-012466.
Audience: **l,u,f.**

Kindall, Jerry & Winkin, John (Editors) **GV875.5.B38 2000**
The Baseball Coaching Bible. Tony La Russa (Foreword by). Trade Paper. Human Kinetics Publishers. Champaign, IL. 1999.

384p. ISBN:0-7360-0161-1, ISBN13: 978-0-7360-0161-8. Dewey:796.357/07/7. LCCN:99-052257.
Audience: **g,l,u.**

Krause, Jerry V., et al. **GV885.3.K68 1999**
Basketball Skills and Drills. Ed. 2. Don Meyer & Jerry Meyer (Authors). Trade Paper. Human Kinetics Publishers. Champaign, IL. 1999. 216p. ISBN:0-7360-0171-9, ISBN13: 978-0-7360-0171-7. Dewey:796.323/077. LCCN:98-052768.
Audience: **l,u,f.**

Kretchmar, Scott R. **GV706.K74 2005**
Practical Philosophy of Sport and Physical Activity. Ed. 2. Trade Cloth. Human Kinetics Publishers. Champaign, IL. 2005. 32p. ISBN:0-7360-0141-7, ISBN13: 978-0-7360-0141-0. Dewey:796/.01. LCCN:2004-013538.
Audience: **g,l,u,f.**

Kutska, Kenneth S., et al. **GV424 .K87**
Playground Safety Is No Accident. Ed. 3. Kevin J. Hoffman & Antonio Malkusak (Authors). Perfect. National Recreation & Park Association. Ashburn, VA. 2002. ISBN:0-929581-28-8, ISBN13: 978-0-929581-28-6. Dewey:796.0694.
Audience: **u.**

Laker, Anthony **GV342.27.L26 2001**
Developing Personal, Social and Moral Education Through Physical Education: A Practical Guide for Teachers. Trade Paper. Routledge. New York, NY. 2001. 136p. ISBN:0-7507-0929-4, ISBN13: 978-0-7507-0929-3. Dewey:613.7/07/041. LCCN:00-050997.
Audience: **u,f.**

Laker, Anthony (Editor) **GV706.5.S645 2001**
The Sociology of Sport and Physical Education: An Introductory Reader. Trade Paper. Routledge. New York, NY. 2001. 256p. ISBN:0-415-23594-4, ISBN13: 978-0-415-23594-5. Dewey:306.4/83. LCCN:2001-019961.
Audience: **g,l,u,f.** *Choice, 2002.*

Metzler, Michael W. **GV363.M425 2005**
Instructional Models for Physical Education. Ed. 2. Paper Text. Holcomb Hathaway, Inc. Scottsdale, AZ. 2005. xviii, 494p. ISBN:1-890871-58-3, ISBN13: 978-1-890871-58-1. Dewey:613.7/071. LCCN:2004-015118.
Audience: **g,l,u.**

Metzler, Michael W. **GV363.M425 1999**
Instructional Models for Physical Education. Trade Paper. Benjamin-Cummings Publishing Company. San Francisco, CA. 1999. 388p. ISBN:0-205-26418-2, ISBN13: 978-0-205-26418-6. Dewey:613.7/071. LCCN:99-036589.
Audience: **l,u,f.**

Miles, John C. & Priest, Simon (Editors) **LC1038.A38 1999**
Adventure Programming. Cloth Text. Venture Publishing, Inc. State College, PA. 1999. xiv, 499p. ISBN:1-892132-09-5, ISBN13: 978-1-892132-09-3. Dewey:796.5/07. LCCN:99-066066.
Audience: **l,u.**

Mitchell, Debby, et al. **GV461.M54 2002**
Teaching Fundamental Gymnastic Skills. Barbara Davis & Raim Lopez (Authors). Trade Paper. Human Kinetics Publishers. Champaign, IL. 2002. 312p. ISBN:0-7360-0124-7, ISBN13: 978-0-7360-0124-3. Dewey:796.44. LCCN:2002-017324.
Audience: **l,u.**

Mitchell-Tavener, Claire **GV1017.H7M58 2004**
Field Hockey Techniques and Tactics. Trade Paper. Human Kinetics Publishers. Champaign, IL. 2004. 216p. ISBN:0-7360-5437-5, ISBN13: 978-0-7360-5437-9. Dewey:796.355. LCCN:2004-007572.
Audience: **l,u.**

Mood, Dale P., et al. **GV704**
Sports and Recreational Activities with PowerWeb Bind-In Passcard. Ed. 13. Frank F. Musker & Judith E. Rink (Authors). Trade Paper. McGraw-Hill Higher Education. Burr Ridge, IL. 2002. ISBN:0-07-255245-X, ISBN13: 978-0-07-255245-4. Dewey:796.
Audience: **l,u.**

Mullen, Michelle **GV903.B69 2003**
Bowling Fundamentals. Trade Paper. Human Kinetics Publishers. Champaign, IL. 2003. 144p. Sports Fundamentals Ser. ISBN:0-7360-5120-1, ISBN13: 978-0-7360-5120-0. Dewey:794.6. LCCN:2003-013368.
Audience: **g,l,u.**

Nichols, Beverly **GV223 .N53**
Moving and Learning: The Elementary School Physical Education Experience with PowerWeb: Health and Human Performance. Ed. 3. Digital, Other, Cloth Text. McGraw-Hill Higher Education. Burr Ridge, IL. 2001. 705p. ISBN:0-07-250614-8, ISBN13: 978-0-07-250614-3. Dewey:372.86.
Audience: **l,u,f.**

Palmer, Heather **GV463.P25 2003**
Teaching Rhythmic Gymnastics: A Developmentally Appropriate Approach. Trade Paper. Human Kinetics Publishers. Champaign, IL. 2003. 144p. ISBN:0-7360-4242-3, ISBN13: 978-0-7360-4242-0. Dewey:796.44. LCCN:2002-152891.
Audience: **l,u,f.**

Penney, Dawn (Editor) **GV342.27.G46 2002**
Gender and Physical Education: Contemporary Issues and Future Directions. Trade Paper. Routledge. New York, NY. 2002. 248p. ISBN:0-415-23576-6, ISBN13: 978-0-415-23576-1. Dewey:613.7/071. LCCN:2001-048673.
Audience: **u,f.**

Riordan, James & Jones, Robin **GV651.S655 1999**
Sport and Physical Education in China. Trade Paper. Routledge. New York, NY. 1999. 304p. ISCPES Book Ser. ISBN:0-419-22030-5, ISBN13: 978-0-419-22030-5. Dewey:613.7/0951. LCCN:98-051481.
Audience: **g,l,u,f.** *Choice, 2000.*

Schempp, Paul **GV361.S25 2003**
Teaching Sport and Physical Activity: Insights on the Road to Mastery. Trade Paper. Human Kinetics Publishers. Champaign, IL. 2003. 232p. ISBN:0-7360-3387-4, ISBN13: 978-0-7360-3387-9. Dewey:613.7/071/2. LCCN:2002-152966.
Audience: **u.**

Shea, Edward J. **GV706.3.S53 1996**
Ethical Decisions in Sport: Interscholastic, Intercollegiate, Olympic and Professional. Trade Paper. Charles C. Thomas Publisher, Ltd. Springfield, IL. 1996. 238p. ISBN:0-398-06600-0, ISBN13: 978-0-398-06600-0. Dewey:796/.01. LCCN:96-001035.
Audience: **u,f.**

Siedentop, Daryl, et al. **GV709.2.S663 2004**
Complete Guide to Sport Education: Teacher Resources. Peter A. Hastie & Hans Van Der Mars (Authors). Trade Paper. Human Kinetics Publishers. Champaign, IL. 2004. 184p. ISBN:0-7360-4380-2, ISBN13: 978-0-7360-4380-9. Dewey:796.07/1. LCCN:2004-004526.
Audience: **u,f.**

Turner, L. F. & Turner, Susan Lilliman **GV443**
Ready-to-Use Pre-Sport Skills Activities Program: 100 Month-by-Month Lessons with Activities, Games and Assessments for the Elementary Grades. Trade Paper. Benjamin-Cummings Publishing Company. San Francisco, CA. 2001. 336p. Ready-To-Use Ser. ISBN:0-13-060041-5, ISBN13: 978-0-13-060041-7. Dewey:372.86.
Audience: **l,u.**

Turoff, Fred **GV461.7.T87 1991**
Artistic Gymnastics: A Comprehensive Guide to Performing and Teaching Skills for Beginners and Advanced Beginners. Cloth Text. Brown & Benchmark. Madison, WI. 1991. 432p. ISBN:0-697-10745-0, ISBN13: 978-0-697-10745-9. Dewey:796.44. LCCN:90-082240.
Audience: **g,l,u,f.**

Van Dalen, Deobold B. **GV211.V35**
A World History of Physical Education: Cultural, Philosophical, Comparative. Paper Text. Textbook Publishers. Temecula, CA. 2003. x, 640p. ISBN:0-7581-6025-9, ISBN13: 978-0-7581-6025-6. Dewey:613.7.
Audience: **u.**

Vanden Auweele, Yves (Editor), et al. **GV342.22P79 1999**
Psychology for Physical Educators. Frank Bakker, V. Mark Durand, Roland Seiler & Stuart J. H. Biddle (Editors). Trade Cloth. Human Kinetics Publishers. Champaign, IL. 1999. 536p. ISBN:0-88011-761-3, ISBN13: 978-0-88011-761-6. Dewey:796/.01. LCCN:98-039170.
Audience: **l,u,f.**

Welch, Paula D. **GV429.W44 2004**
History of American Physical Education and Sport. Ed. 3. Trade Cloth. Charles C. Thomas Publisher, Ltd. Springfield, IL. 2004. 414p. ISBN:0-398-07506-9, ISBN13: 978-0-398-07506-4. Dewey:796/.0973. LCCN:2004-044026.
Audience: **l,u,f.**

Wuest, Deborah A. & Bucher, Charles A. **GV341**
Foundations of Physical Education, Exercise Science, and Sport with PowerWeb. Ed. 15. Trade Cloth. McGraw-Hill Higher Education. Burr Ridge, IL. 2005. ISBN:0-07-313893-2, ISBN13: 978-0-07-313893-0. Dewey:796/.07.
Audience: **l,u,f.**

YMCA of the USA Staff **GV836.35.Y65 1999**
The Youth and Adult Aquatic Program Manual. Trade Paper. Human Kinetics Publishers. Champaign, IL. 1999. 208p. YMCA Swim Lessons Ser. ISBN:0-7360-0048-8, ISBN13: 978-0-7360-0048-2. Dewey:797.2/1/083. LCCN:98-037672.
Audience: **g,l,u,f.**

Zeigler, Earle F. (Editor) **GV223.P467 1994**
Physical Education and Kinesiology in North America: Professional and Scholarly Foundations. Paper Text. Stipes Publishing L. L. C.. Champaign, IL. 1994. 415p. ISBN:0-87563-495-8, ISBN13: 978-0-87563-495-1. Dewey:613.7/0973. LCCN:94-065402.
Audience: **l,u,f.** *Choice, 1994.*

Physical Education and Training > Elementary and Middle School

Buck, Marilyn, et al. **GV365 .I57**
Instructional Strategies for Secondary School Physical Education with NASPE: Moving into the Future. Ed. 6. Jacalyn Lea Lund, Joyce M. Harrison & Connie L. Blakemore Cook (Authors). Trade Paper. McGraw-Hill Higher Education. Burr Ridge, IL. 2005. ISBN:0-07-313884-3, ISBN13: 978-0-07-313884-8. Dewey:796.071/273.
Audience: **l,u.**

Clements, Rhonda L. & Kinzler, Suzanne K. **GV363.C49 2002**
A Multicultural Approach to Physical Education: Proven Strategies for Middle and High School. Trade Paper. Human Kinetics Publishers. Champaign, IL. 2002. 168p. ISBN:0-7360-3882-5, ISBN13: 978-0-7360-3882-9. Dewey:613.7/071/2. LCCN:2002-007774.
Audience: **l,u,f.**

Clumpner, Roy A. **GV363.C495 2003**
Sport Progressions. Trade Paper. Human Kinetics Publishers. Champaign, IL. 2002. 296p. ISBN:0-7360-3385-8, ISBN13: 978-0-7360-3385-5. Dewey:613.7/071/2. LCCN:2002-014411.
Audience: **l,u.**

Colvin, Vonnie, et al. **GV443.C59 2000**
Teaching the Nuts and Bolts of Physical Activity: Building Basic Movement Skills. Nancy E. Markos & Pamela J. Walker (Authors). Trade Paper. Human Kinetics Publishers. Champaign, IL. 1999. 288p. ISBN:0-88011-883-0, ISBN13: 978-0-88011-883-5. Dewey:372.86. LCCN:99-038507.
Audience: **u.** *Choice, 2000.*

Decker, June Irene & Mize, Monica **GV365.D43 2001**
Walking Games and Activities. Trade Paper. Human Kinetics Publishers. Champaign, IL. 2001. 176p. ISBN:0-7360-3430-7, ISBN13: 978-0-7360-3430-2. Dewey:613.7/176. LCCN:2001-016878.
Audience: **l,u.**

Fronske, Hilda A. **GV361**
Teaching Cues for Sport Skills for Secondary School Students. Ed. 3. Trade Paper. Benjamin-Cummings Publishing Company. San Francisco, CA. 2004. 416p. ISBN:0-8053-5454-9, ISBN13: 978-0-8053-5454-6. Dewey:796/.07/7. LCCN:2004-007739.
Audience: **l,u.**

Graham, George **GV363.G68 2001**
Teaching Children Physical Education: Becoming a Master Teacher. Ed. 2. Trade Paper, CD-ROM. Human Kinetics Publishers. Champaign, IL. 2005. 224p. ISBN:0-7360-3335-1, ISBN13: 978-0-7360-3335-0. Dewey:372.86/044. LCCN:00-063220.
Audience: **l,u,f.**

Human Kinetics Staff **GV443.H77 1999**
Physical Education Methods for Classroom Teachers. Trade Paper. Human Kinetics Publishers. Champaign, IL. 1999. 360p. ISBN:0-88011-842-3, ISBN13: 978-0-88011-842-2. Dewey:372.86/044. LCCN:98-041469.
Audience: **l,u,f.** *Choice, 1999.*

Kleinman, Isobel R. **GV362.K54 2001**
Complete Physical Education Plans for Grades 7-12: 366 Lesson Plans for 14 Sports and Activities. Trade Paper. Human Kinetics Publishers. Champaign, IL. 2001. 632p. ISBN:0-7360-3248-7, ISBN13: 978-0-7360-3248-3. Dewey:613.7/071/073. LCCN:00-059787.
Audience: **l,u.**

Laker, Anthony **GV342.27.L25 2000**
Beyond the Boundaries of Physical Education: Educating Young People for Citizenship and Social Responsibility. Trade Paper. Taylor & Francis Group. Philadelphia, PA. 2000. 144p. ISBN:0-7507-0930-8, ISBN13: 978-0-7507-0930-9. Dewey:370.1/14. LCCN:99-053989.
Audience: **l,u,f.** *Choice, 2001.*

Landy, Joanne M. & Burridge, Keith R. **GV452.L357 2000**
Ready-to-Use Motor Skills and Movement Station Lesson Plans for Young Children: Teaching, Remediation and Assessment. Trade Paper. Benjamin-Cummings Publishing Company. San Francisco, CA. 2000. 464p. Complete Motor Skills Activities Program Ser., Vol. 3 ISBN:0-13-013943-2, ISBN13: 978-0-13-013943-6. Dewey:372.86. LCCN:00-020250.
Audience: **u.**

Logsdon, Bette J. **GV443 .P474 1997**
Physical Education Unit Plans for Preschool-Kindergarten, for Grades 1-2, for Grades 3-4, for Grades 5-6. Ed. 2. Trade Paper. Human Kinetics Publishers. Champaign, IL. 1997. 649p. ISBN:0-88011-697-8, ISBN13: 978-0-88011-697-8. Dewey:372.86. LCCN:96-038312.
Audience: **u.**

Lund, Jacalyn Lea & Kirk, Mary Fortman **GV362.5.L86 2002**
Performance-Based Assessment for Middle and High School Physical Education. Trade Paper. Human Kinetics Publishers. Champaign, IL. 2002. 248p. ISBN:0-7360-3270-3, ISBN13: 978-0-7360-3270-4. Dewey:613.7/071/2. LCCN:2002-017211.
Audience: **u,f.**

Mosston, Muska & Ashworth, Sara **GV361.M75 2002**
Teaching Physical Education. Ed. 5. Trade Paper. Benjamin-Cummings Publishing Company. San Francisco, CA. 2001. 268p. ISBN:0-205-34093-8, ISBN13: 978-0-205-34093-4. Dewey:613.7/07/1. LCCN:2001-052816.
Audience: **l,u,f.**

Nichols, Beverly **GV223 .N53**
Moving and Learning: The Elementary School Physical Education Experience with PowerWeb: Health and Human Performance. Ed. 3. Digital, Other, Cloth Text. McGraw-Hill Higher Education. Burr Ridge, IL. 2001. 705p. ISBN:0-07-250614-8, ISBN13: 978-0-07-250614-3. Dewey:372.86.
Audience: **l,u,f.**

O'Quinn, Garland Jr. & Hickman, E. Jessica **GV461.O69 1990**
Teaching Developmental Gymnastics: Skills to Take Through Life. Trade Cloth. University of Texas Press. Austin, TX. 1990. 224p. ISBN:0-292-78101-6, ISBN13: 978-0-292-78101-6. Dewey:796.41/07. LCCN:89-031936.
Audience: **u.**

Pangrazi, Robert P. **GV443**
Dynamic Physical Education for Elementary School Children. Ed. 14. Cloth Text. Benjamin-Cummings Publishing Company. San Francisco, CA. 2003. 768p. ISBN:0-205-34438-0, ISBN13: 978-0-205-34438-3. Dewey:372.86.
Audience: **l,u,f.**

Pangrazi, Robert P., et al. **QP301.P34 2003**
Pedometer Power: 67 Lessons for K-12. Aaren Beighle & Cara L. Sidman (Authors). Trade Paper. Human Kinetics Publishers. Champaign, IL. 2002. 128p. ISBN:0-7360-4484-1, ISBN13: 978-0-7360-4484-4. Dewey:612/.04/0287. LCCN:2002-012686.
Audience: **l,u.**

Panicucci, Jane **GV191.6**
Adventure Curriculum for Physical Education: Middle School. Lisa Faulkingham-Hunt, Amy Kohut, Alison Rheingold & Nancy Stratton (Contribution by). Perfect. Project Adventure, Inc. Beverly, MA. 2002. 182p. ISBN:0-934387-25-7, ISBN13: 978-0-934387-25-5. Dewey:796.5.
Audience: **l,u.**

Schiemer, Suzanne **GV436.S27 2000**
Assessment Strategies for Elementary Physical Education. Trade Paper. Human Kinetics Publishers. Champaign, IL. 1999. 152p. ISBN:0-88011-569-6, ISBN13: 978-0-88011-569-8. Dewey:372.86. LCCN:99-020580.
Audience: **u,f.**

Schmottlach, Neil & McManama, Jerre **GV361.S295 2005**
The Physical Education Activity Handbook. Ed. 11. Trade Paper. Benjamin-Cummings Publishing Company. San Francisco, CA. 2005. 502p. ISBN:0-8053-7944-4, ISBN13: 978-0-8053-7944-0. Dewey:613.7/07. LCCN:2005-023353.
Audience: **g,l,u,f.**

Silverman, Stephen **GV361.E65 2003**
Student Learning in Physical Education: Applying Research to Enhance Instruction. Ed. 2. Trade Cloth. Human Kinetics Publishers. Champaign, IL. 2003. 36p. ISBN:0-7360-4275-X, ISBN13: 978-0-7360-4275-8. Dewey:796/.07. LCCN:2002-154303.
Audience: **l,u.**

Swissler, Becky **GV1017.H7S95 2003**
Winning Field Hockey for Girls. Trade Paper. Facts On File, Inc. New York, NY. 2003. 224p. Winning Sports for Girls Ser. ISBN:0-8160-4725-1, ISBN13: 978-0-8160-4725-3. Dewey:796.355/082. LCCN:2002-005990.
Audience: **l,u,f.**

Turner, L. F. & Turner, Susan Lilliman **GV443**
Ready-to-Use Pre-Sport Skills Activities Program: 100 Month-by-Month Lessons with Activities, Games and Assessments for the Elementary Grades. Trade Paper. Benjamin-Cummings Publishing Company. San Francisco, CA. 2001. 336p. Ready-To-Use Ser. ISBN:0-13-060041-5, ISBN13: 978-0-13-060041-7. Dewey:372.86.
Audience: **l,u.**

Werner, Peter H. **GV464.5.W47 2003**
Teaching Children Gymnastics: A Developmentally Appropriate Approach. Ed. 2. Trade Paper. Human Kinetics Publishers. Champaign, IL. 2003. 248p. ISBN:0-7360-4434-5, ISBN13: 978-0-7360-4434-9. Dewey:796.44. LCCN:2003-011604.
Audience: **l,u.**

Physical Education and Training > High School

Clements, Rhonda L. & Kinzler, Suzanne K. **GV363.C49 2002**
A Multicultural Approach to Physical Education: Proven Strategies for Middle and High School. Trade Paper. Human Kinetics Publishers. Champaign, IL. 2002. 168p. ISBN:0-7360-3882-5, ISBN13: 978-0-7360-3882-9. Dewey:613.7/071/2. LCCN:2002-007774.
Audience: **l,u,f.**

Decker, June Irene & Mize, Monica **GV365.D43 2001**
Walking Games and Activities. Trade Paper. Human Kinetics Publishers. Champaign, IL. 2001. 176p. ISBN:0-7360-3430-7, ISBN13: 978-0-7360-3430-2. Dewey:613.7/176. LCCN:2001-016878.
Audience: **l,u.**

Hastie, Peter A. **GV365.H39 2003**
Teaching for Lifetime Physical Activity Through Quality High School Physical Education. Trade Paper. Benjamin-Cummings Publishing Company. San Francisco, CA. 2002. 440p. ISBN:0-205-34354-6, ISBN13: 978-0-205-34354-6. Dewey:613.7/071/173. LCCN:2002-067454.
Audience: **u,f.**

Human Kinetics Staff **GV443.H77 1999**
Physical Education Methods for Classroom Teachers. Trade Paper. Human Kinetics Publishers. Champaign, IL. 1999. 360p. ISBN:0-88011-842-3, ISBN13: 978-0-88011-842-2. Dewey:372.86/044. LCCN:98-041469.
Audience: **l,u,f.** *Choice, 1999.*

Humphrey, James H. **GV346.H86 2002**
Principles and Practices in Interscholastic Athletics: Guidelines for Administrators. Trade Paper. Nova Science Publishers, Inc. Hauppauge, NY. 2002. 133p. ISBN:1-59033-159-1, ISBN13: 978-1-59033-159-0. Dewey:796/.06/0973. LCCN:2001-059041.
Audience: **u,f.**

Kleinman, Isobel R. **GV362.K54 2001**
Complete Physical Education Plans for Grades 7-12: 366 Lesson Plans for 14 Sports and Activities. Trade Paper. Human Kinetics Publishers. Champaign, IL. 2001. 632p. ISBN:0-7360-3248-7, ISBN13: 978-0-7360-3248-3. Dewey:613.7/071/073. LCCN:00-059787.
Audience: **l,u.**

Laker, Anthony **GV342.27.L25 2000**
Beyond the Boundaries of Physical Education: Educating Young People for Citizenship and Social Responsibility. Trade Paper. Taylor & Francis Group. Philadelphia, PA. 2000. 144p. ISBN:0-7507-0930-8, ISBN13: 978-0-7507-0930-9. Dewey:370.1/14. LCCN:99-053989.
Audience: **l,u,f.** *Choice, 2001.*

Lund, Jacalyn Lea & Kirk, Mary Fortman **GV362.5.L86 2002**
Performance-Based Assessment for Middle and High School Physical Education. Trade Paper. Human Kinetics Publishers. Champaign, IL. 2002. 248p. ISBN:0-7360-3270-3, ISBN13: 978-0-7360-3270-4. Dewey:613.7/071/2. LCCN:2002-017211.
Audience: **u,f.**

Mosston, Muska & Ashworth, Sara **GV361.M75 2002**
Teaching Physical Education. Ed. 5. Trade Paper. Benjamin-Cummings Publishing Company. San Francisco, CA. 2001. 268p. ISBN:0-205-34093-8, ISBN13: 978-0-205-34093-4. Dewey:613.7/07/1. LCCN:2001-052816.
Audience: **l,u,f.**

Pangrazi, Robert P., et al. **QP301.P34 2003**
Pedometer Power: 67 Lessons for K-12. Aaren Beighle & Cara L. Sidman (Authors). Trade Paper. Human Kinetics Publishers. Champaign, IL. 2002. 128p. ISBN:0-7360-4484-1, ISBN13: 978-0-7360-4484-4. Dewey:612/.04/0287. LCCN:2002-012686.
Audience: **l,u.**

Schmottlach, Neil & McManama, Jerre **GV361.S295 2005**
The Physical Education Activity Handbook. Ed. 11. Trade Paper. Benjamin-Cummings Publishing Company. San Francisco, CA. 2005. 502p. ISBN:0-8053-7944-4, ISBN13: 978-0-8053-7944-0. Dewey:613.7/07. LCCN:2005-023353.
Audience: **g,l,u,f.**

Silverman, Stephen **GV361.E65 2003**
Student Learning in Physical Education: Applying Research to Enhance Instruction. Ed. 2. Trade Cloth. Human Kinetics Publishers. Champaign, IL. 2003. 36p. ISBN:0-7360-4275-X, ISBN13: 978-0-7360-4275-8. Dewey:796/.07. LCCN:2002-154303.
Audience: **l,u.**

Stokell, Ian **GV943.8.S77 2002**
Coaching Women's Soccer: A Revolutionary Approach to Putting the Play Back into Practice. Trade Paper. McGraw-Hill Companies, The. New York, NY. 2002. x, 182p. ISBN:0-07-138209-7, ISBN13: 978-0-07-138209-0. Dewey:796.334/07/7. LCCN:2001-047321.
Audience: **g,l,u,f.** *Choice, 2002.*

Sutherland, Charmain **GV363.S88 2002**
Physical Education Tips from the Trenches. Trade Paper. Human Kinetics Publishers. Champaign, IL. 2001. 248p. ISBN:0-7360-3709-8, ISBN13: 978-0-7360-3709-9. Dewey:613.7/07/1. LCCN:2001-026460.
Audience: **l,u.**

Swissler, Becky **GV1017.H7S95 2003**
Winning Field Hockey for Girls. Trade Paper. Facts On File, Inc. New York, NY. 2003. 224p. Winning Sports for Girls Ser. ISBN:0-8160-4725-1, ISBN13: 978-0-8160-4725-3. Dewey:796.355/082. LCCN:2002-005990.
Audience: **l,u,f.**

Zakrajsek, Dorothy B., et al. **GV363.Z27 2003**
Quality Lesson Plans for Secondary Physical Education. Ed. 2. Lois A. Carnes & Frank E. Pettigrew Jr. (Authors). CD-ROM, Trade Paper. Human Kinetics Publishers. Champaign, IL. 2003. 691p. ISBN:0-7360-4485-X, ISBN13: 978-0-7360-4485-1. Dewey:613.7/071/2. LCCN:2002-013862.
Audience: **l,u.**

Physical Education and Training > College

Byl, John **GV710.B95 2002**
Intramural Recreation: A Step-by-Step Guide to Creating an Effective Program. Trade Paper. Human Kinetics Publishers. Champaign, IL. 2002. 272p. ISBN:0-7360-3454-4, ISBN13: 978-0-7360-3454-8. Dewey:796.04/2. LCCN:2002-017194.
Audience: **l,u,f.**

Decker, June Irene & Mize, Monica **GV365.D43 2001**
Walking Games and Activities. Trade Paper. Human Kinetics Publishers. Champaign, IL. 2001. 176p. ISBN:0-7360-3430-7, ISBN13: 978-0-7360-3430-2. Dewey:613.7/176. LCCN:2001-016878.
Audience: **l,u.**

Hastie, Peter A. **GV365.H39 2003**
Teaching for Lifetime Physical Activity Through Quality High School Physical Education. Trade Paper. Benjamin-Cummings Publishing Company. San Francisco, CA. 2002. 440p. ISBN:0-205-34354-6, ISBN13: 978-0-205-34354-6. Dewey:613.7/071/173. LCCN:2002-067454.
Audience: **u,f.**

National Intramural Recreational Sports Association (Nirsa) (Created by) **GV350.V35 2004**
The Value of Recreational Sports in Higher Education: Impact on Student Enrollment, Success, and Buying Power. Perfect, Trade Paper. Human Kinetics Publishers. Champaign, IL. 2003. 224p. ISBN:0-7360-5503-7, ISBN13: 978-0-7360-5503-1. Dewey:796.0430973. LCCN:2003-024568.
Audience: **l,u,f.**

Schmottlach, Neil & McManama, Jerre **GV361.S295 2005**
The Physical Education Activity Handbook. Ed. 11. Trade Paper. Benjamin-Cummings Publishing Company. San Francisco, CA. 2005. 502p. ISBN:0-8053-7944-4, ISBN13: 978-0-8053-7944-0. Dewey:613.7/07. LCCN:2005-023353.
Audience: **g,l,u,f.**

Stokell, Ian **GV943.8.S77 2002**
Coaching Women's Soccer: A Revolutionary Approach to Putting the Play Back into Practice. Trade Paper. McGraw-Hill Companies, The. New York, NY. 2002. x, 182p. ISBN:0-07-138209-7, ISBN13: 978-0-07-138209-0. Dewey:796.334/07/7. LCCN:2001-047321.
Audience: **g,l,u,f.** *Choice, 2002.*

Physical Education and Training > Adaptive

Auxter, David, et al. **GV443 .A98**
Principles and Methods of Adapted Physical Education and Recreation: With Activities Booklet and PowerWeb Bind-in Card. Ed. 10. Jean Pyfer & Carol I. Huettig (Authors). Trade Cloth. McGraw-Hill Higher Education. Burr Ridge, IL. 2004. ISBN:0-07-298538-0, ISBN13: 978-0-07-298538-2. Dewey:371.9/044.
Audience: **l,u,f.**

Block, Martin E. **GV445.B56 2000**
A Teacher's Guide to Including Students with Disabilities in General Physical Education. Ed. 2. Trade Cloth. Paul H. Brookes Publishing Company. Baltimore, MD. 2000. xii, 397p. ISBN:1-55766-463-3, ISBN13: 978-1-55766-463-1. Dewey:371.9/04486. LCCN:00-034288.
Audience: **u,f.**

Davis, Ronald W. **GV445.D344 2002**
Inclusion Through Sports: A Guide to Individualizing Sport Experiences. Trade Paper. Human Kinetics Publishers. Champaign, IL. 2002. 24p. ISBN:0-7360-3439-0, ISBN13: 978-0-7360-3439-5. Dewey:796.04/56. LCCN:2001-051466.
Audience: **l,u.**

Depauw, Karen P. & Gavron, Susan J. **GV709.3.D47 2005**
Disability Sport. Ed. 2. Perfect. Human Kinetics Publishers. Champaign, IL. 2005. 395p. ISBN:0-7360-4638-0, ISBN13: 978-0-7360-4638-1. Dewey:796.087. LCCN:2004-022462.
Audience: **g,l,u,f.**

Fine, Aubrey H. & Fine, Nya M. **RJ53.R43F56 1996**
Therapeutic Recreation for Exceptional Children: Let Me in, I Want to Play. Ed. 2. Cloth Text. Charles C. Thomas Publisher, Ltd. Springfield, IL. 1996. 422p. ISBN:0-398-06661-2, ISBN13: 978-0-398-06661-1. Dewey:615.8/5153/0880816. LCCN:96-008263.
Audience: **g,l,u,f.** *Choice, 1989.*

Horvat, Michael A., et al. **GV445.E34 2002**
Developmental/Adapted Physical Education: Making Ability Count. Ed. 4. Ron Croce, Carl B. Eichstaedt & Leonard H. Kalakian (Authors). Cloth Text. Benjamin-Cummings Publishing Company. San Francisco, CA. 2002. 656p. ISBN:0-205-31391-4,

ISBN13: 978-0-205-31391-4. Dewey:796.04/56. LCCN:2002-067678.

Audience: **l,u,f.**

Kasser, Susan A. & Lytle, Rebecca K. **GV443.K36 2005**
Inclusive Physical Activity: A Lifetime of Opportunities. Trade Cloth. Human Kinetics Publishers. Champaign, IL. 2005. 288p. ISBN:0-7360-3684-9, ISBN13: 978-0-7360-3684-9. Dewey:371.9/04486. LCCN:2004-017863.

Audience: **g,l,u,f.**

Kelly, Luke E. (Editor) **GV445.N38 1995**
Adapted Physical Education National Standards: National Consortium for Physical Education and Recreation for Individuals with Disabilities (U. S.). Trade Paper. Human Kinetics Publishers. Champaign, IL. 1995. 224p. ISBN:0-87322-962-2, ISBN13: 978-0-87322-962-3. Dewey:371.9/04486. LCCN:95-003492.

Audience: **u,f.** *Choice, 1995.*

Lear, Roma **GV183.6**
Fun Without Fatigue. Ed. 2. Trade Paper. Elsevier - Health Sciences Division. Philadelphia, PA. 2001. 208p. ISBN:0-7506-2525-2, ISBN13: 978-0-7506-2525-8. Dewey:649.5/5/087.

Audience: **g,l,u,f.**

Lepore, Monica, et al. **GV837.4.L47 1998**
Adapted Aquatics Programming: A Professional Guide. G. William Gayle & Shawn Stevens (Authors). Trade Cloth. Human Kinetics Publishers. Champaign, IL. 1998. 328p. ISBN:0-88011-695-1, ISBN13: 978-0-88011-695-4. Dewey:797.2/1/087. LCCN:98-022953.

Audience: **u,f.** *Choice, 1999.*

Miller, Patricia D. (Editor) **GV482.7.F58 1995**
Fitness Programming and Physical Disability. Trade Paper. Human Kinetics Publishers. Champaign, IL. 1994. 232p. ISBN:0-87322-434-5, ISBN13: 978-0-87322-434-5. Dewey:613.7. LCCN:94-004961.

Audience: **u.**

Mobily, Kenneth E. & MacNeil, Richard **RM736.7**
Therapeutic Recreation and the Nature of Disabilities. Cloth Text. Venture Publishing, Inc. State College, PA. 2002. 320p. ISBN:1-892132-22-2, ISBN13: 978-1-892132-22-2. Dewey:790.196. LCCN:2002-103088.

Audience: **u,f.**

Paciorek, Michael J. & Jones, Jeffrey A. **GV709.3 .P33 2001**
Disability Sport and Recreation Resources. Ed. 3. Trade Paper. Cooper Publishing Group. Traverse City, MI. 2000. 386p. ISBN:1-884125-75-1, ISBN13: 978-1-884125-75-1. Dewey:796.0196. LCCN:2001-086212.

Audience: **l,u,f.** *Choice, 2002.*

Schleien, Stuart J. **GV183.5.L54 1995**
Lifelong Leisure Skills and Lifestyles for Persons with Developmental Disabilities. Cloth Text. Paul H. Brookes Publishing Company. Baltimore, MD. 1995. 352p. ISBN:1-55766-147-2, ISBN13: 978-1-55766-147-0. Dewey:790.1/96. LCCN:94-037005.

Audience: **l,u.**

Sherrill, Claudine **GV445.S53 2003**
Adapted Physical Activity. Ed. 6. Cloth Text. McGraw-Hill Higher Education. Burr Ridge, IL. 2003. xix, 783p. ISBN:0-697-29513-3, ISBN13: 978-0-697-29513-2. Dewey:371.9/04486. LCCN:2003-044290.

Audience: **l,u,f.**

Winnick, Joseph P. **GV445.A3 2005**
Adapted Physical Education and Sport. Ed. 4. DVD, Trade Cloth. Human Kinetics Publishers. Champaign, IL. 2005. 592p. ISBN:0-7360-5216-X, ISBN13: 978-0-7360-5216-0. Dewey:371.9/04486. LCCN:2004-024997.

Audience: **l,u,f.**

Physical Education and Training > Nutrition. Health and Hygiene

Beals, Katherine A. **RC552.E18B43 2004**
Disordered Eating among Athletes: A Comprehensive Guide for Health Professionals. Perfect. Human Kinetics Publishers. Champaign, IL. 2004. 255p. ISBN:0-7360-4219-9, ISBN13: 978-0-7360-4219-2. Dewey:616.85/26. LCCN:30-260440.

Audience: **g,l,u,f.** *Choice, 2005.*

Clark, Nancy **TX361.A8C54 2003**
Nancy Clark's Sports Nutrition Guidebook. Ed. 3. Trade Paper. Human Kinetics Publishers. Champaign, IL. 2003. 416p. ISBN:0-7360-4602-X, ISBN13: 978-0-7360-4602-2. Dewey:613.2/024/796. LCCN:2003-009149.

Audience: **g,l,u,f.**

Dorfman, Lisa **TX361.A8D67 2000**
The Vegetarian Sports Nutrition Guide: Peak Performance for Everyone from Beginners to Gold Medalists. Trade Paper. John Wiley & Sons, Inc. Hoboken, NJ. 1999. 270p. ISBN:0-471-34808-2, ISBN13: 978-0-471-34808-5. Dewey:613.2/024/796. LCCN:99-025294.

Audience: **g,l,u.**

McArdle, William D., et al. **TX361.A8M38 2004**
Sports and Exercise Nutrition. Ed. 2. Frank I. Katch & Victor L. Katch (Authors). Trade Cloth, CD-ROM. Lippincott Williams & Wilkins. Philadelphia, PA. 2005. 619p. ISBN:0-7817-4993-X, ISBN13: 978-0-7817-4993-0. Dewey:613.2/024/796. LCCN:2004-048934.

Audience: **l,u,f.**

Puretz, Susan, et al. **RA781.P84 1997**
The Woman's Guide to Peak Performance. Adelaide Haas & Donna Meltzer (Authors). Trade Paper. Celestial Arts Publishing Company. Berkeley, CA. 1998. 400p. ISBN:0-89087-841-2, ISBN13: 978-0-89087-841-5. Dewey:613.7/045. LCCN:97-042142.

Audience: **g,l,u.** *Choice, 1998.*

Sport Studies

GV877

☐ Baseball Reference.
http://www.baseball-reference.com/

Audience: **g,l,u,f.**

GV741

SPORTQuest.
http://www.sirc.ca/online_resources/sportquest.cfm
SIRC.

Audience: **g,l,u,f.**

GV709

Women's Sport Foundation (US).
http://www.womenssportsfoundation.org/

Audience: **g,l,u,f.**

Sport Studies > Philosophy

Alter, Joseph S. **B132.Y6A483 2004**
Yoga in Modern India: The Body Between Science and Philosophy. Trade Paper. Princeton University Press. Princeton, NJ. 2004. 376p. ISBN:0-691-11874-4, ISBN13: 978-0-691-11874-1. Dewey:181/.45. LCCN:2003-064108.
Audience: **l,u,f.**

Andre, Judith **GV351**
Rethinking College Athletics. Trade Paper. Temple University Press. Philadelphia, PA. 1992. ISBN:1-56639-002-8, ISBN13: 978-1-56639-002-6. Dewey:796.071/173.
Audience: **g,l,u.**

Boxill, Jan (Editor) **GV706.3.S66 2003**
Sports Ethics: An Anthology. Trade Paper. Blackwell Publishing, Inc. Malden, MA. 2002. 376p. ISBN:0-631-21697-9, ISBN13: 978-0-631-21697-1. Dewey:796/.01. LCCN:2002-071229.
Audience: **g,l.**

Donohoe, Tom & Johnson, Neil **RC1230.D66 1987**
Foul Play: Drug Abuse in Sports. Sebastian Coe (Foreword by). Trade Cloth. Blackwell Publishing, Inc. Malden, MA. 1988. x, 200p. ISBN:0-631-14845-0, ISBN13: 978-0-631-14845-6. Dewey:362.2/93/088796. LCCN:85-030624.
Audience: **g,l,u,f.** *Choice, 1986.*

Fain, Gerald S. (Editor) **BJ1498**
Leisure and Ethics: Reflections on the Philosophy of Leisure, Vol. II. Paper Text. American Alliance for Health, Physical Education, Recreation & Dance. Oxon Hill, MD. 1995. 330p. ISBN:0-88314-850-1, ISBN13: 978-0-88314-850-1. Dewey:790.01.
Audience: **l,u.**

French, Peter A. **GV361.F64 2004**
Ethics and College Sports: Ethics, Sports, and the University. Book, Other. Rowman & Littlefield Publishers, Inc. Lanham, MD. 2004. 208p. Issues in Academic Ethics Ser. ISBN:0-7425-1273-8, ISBN13: 978-0-7425-1273-3. Dewey:796.04/3/0973. LCCN:2004-004349.
Audience: **g,l,u,f.** *Choice, 2005.*

Herrigel, Eugene **GV1188.J3H4713**
Zen in the Art of Archery. R. F. C. Hull (Translator), D. T. Suzuki (Introduction by). Trade Paper. Knopf Publishing Group. New York, NY. 1999. 96p. Vintage Spiritual Classics Ser. ISBN:0-375-70509-0, ISBN13: 978-0-375-70509-0. Dewey:799.3/2. LCCN:89-005319.
Audience: **g,l,u,f.**

Hoberman, John **GV583**
Darwin's Athletes: How Sport has Damaged Black America and Preserved the Myth of Race. Cloth Text. Houghton Mifflin Company. New York, NY. 1997. 288p. ISBN:0-465-01557-3, ISBN13: 978-0-465-01557-3. Dewey:796/.089/96073.
Audience: **u,f.** *Choice, 1997.*

Hoberman, John M. **RC1235.H63 2001**
Mortal Engines. Perfect. Blackburn Press, The. Caldwell, NJ. 2002. 374p. ISBN:1-930665-37-7, ISBN13: 978-1-930665-37-8. Dewey:617.1/027. LCCN:2001-093232.
Audience: **u,f.**

Jackson, Phil **GV884.J67**
Sacred Hoops: Spiritual Lessons of a Hardwood Warrior. Prebound. Turtleback Books. Madison, WI. 1996. ISBN:0-606-18263-2, ISBN13: 978-0-606-18263-8. Dewey:796.323/092 B.
Audience: **g,l,u,f.**

Jackson, Susan A. & Csikszentmihalyi, Mihaly **GV706.4.J33 1999**
Flow in Sports: The Keys to Optimal Experiences and Performances. Trade Paper. Human Kinetics Publishers. Champaign, IL. 1999. 192p. ISBN:0-88011-876-8, ISBN13: 978-0-88011-876-7. Dewey:796/.01. LCCN:99-012526.
Audience: **u,f.**

Jones, Donald G. & Daley, Elaine L. **GV706**
Sports Ethics in America: A Bibliography, 1970-1990. Cloth Text. Greenwood Publishing Group, Inc. Portsmouth, NH. 1992. 320p. Bibliographies and Indexes in American History Ser., No. 21 ISBN:0-313-27767-2, ISBN13: 978-0-313-27767-2. Dewey:016.175. LCCN:91-047538.
Audience: **l,u,f.** *Choice, 1992.*

Kerr, John **GV706.7.K47 2004**
Rethinking Aggression and Violence in Sport. Trade Paper. Routledge. New York, NY. 2004. 176p. ISBN:0-415-28664-6, ISBN13: 978-0-415-28664-0. Dewey:306.4/83. LCCN:2004-048230.
Audience: **u,f.**

Lumpkin, Angela, et al. **GV706.3 .L85**
Sport Ethics: Applications for Fair Play with PowerWeb Bind-In Passcard. Ed. 3. Sharon Kay Stoll & Jennifer Marie Beller (Authors). Trade Paper. McGraw-Hill Higher Education. Burr Ridge, IL. 2003. ISBN:0-07-293072-1, ISBN13: 978-0-07-293072-6. Dewey:796/.01.
Audience: **u,f.**

McNamee, Mike (Editor) **GV558.P45 2005**
Philosophy of Sport and Exercise Science: Critical Perspectives on Scientific Method and Enquiry in Sport, Exercise and Health. Paper over Boards. Routledge. New York, NY. 2005. 256p. ISBN:0-415-30016-9, ISBN13: 978-0-415-30016-2. Dewey:796/.01. LCCN:2004-050995.
Audience: **l,u,f.**

Miah, Andy **QH332**
Genetically Modified Athletes: The Ethical Implications of Genetic Technologies in Sport. Trade Paper. Routledge. New York, NY. 2004. 232p. Ethics and Sport Ser. ISBN:0-415-29880-6, ISBN13: 978-0-415-29880-3. Dewey:174/.9796. LCCN:2004-044269.
Audience: **l,u,f.**

Morgan, William J. & Meier, Klaus V. **GV706.P478 1995**
Philosophic Inquiry in Sport. Ed. 2. Cloth Text. Human Kinetics Publishers. Champaign, IL. 1995. 456p. ISBN:0-87322-716-6, ISBN13: 978-0-87322-716-2. Dewey:796/.01. LCCN:95-010920.
Audience: **g,l,u,f.** *Choice, 1988.*

Novak, Michael **GV583.N64 1994**
The Joy of Sports: Endzones, Bases, Baskets, Balls, and the Consecration of the American Spirit. Ed. 2. Trade Paper. Madison Books, Inc. New York, NY. 1955. 375p. ISBN:1-56833-009-X, ISBN13: 978-1-56833-009-9. Dewey:796/.0973. LCCN:93-008815.
Audience: **l,u,f.**

Saint Sing, Susan **GV706.42.S35 2004**
Spirituality of Sport: Balancing Body and Soul. Trade Cloth. Saint Anthony Messenger Press & Franciscan Communications. Cincinnati, OH. 2004. xiii, 137p. ISBN:0-86716-516-2, ISBN13: 978-0-86716-516-6. Dewey:248.8/8. LCCN:2004-023847.
Audience: **g,l,u,f.**

Shea, Edward J. **GV706.3.S53 1996**
Ethical Decisions in Sport: Interscholastic, Intercollegiate, Olympic and Professional. Trade Paper. Charles C. Thomas Publisher, Ltd. Springfield, IL. 1996. 238p. ISBN:0-398-06600-0, ISBN13: 978-0-398-06600-0. Dewey:796/.01. LCCN:96-001035.
Audience: **u,f.**

Simon, Robert L. **GV706.3.S56 2003**
Fair Play: The Ethics of Sport. Ed. 2. Trade Paper. Westview Press. Boulder, CO. 2003. 256p. ISBN:0-8133-6567-8, ISBN13: 978-0-8133-6567-1. Dewey:796/.01. LCCN:2003-006399.
Audience: **g,l,u,f.** *Choice, 2004.*

Stevens, John **GV1114.35.S765 2001**
Philosophy of Aikido. Trade Cloth. Kodansha International. Tokyo, 2001. 132p. ISBN:4-7700-2534-3, ISBN13: 978-4-7700-2534-0. Dewey:796.815/4. LCCN:00-047822.
Audience: **g,l,u,f.** *Choice, 2001.*

Vanderwerken, David L. & Wertz, Spencer K. (Editors) **GV706.S746 1985**
Sport Inside Out: Readings in Literature and Philosophy. Trade Cloth. Texas Christian University Press. Fort Worth, TX. 1985. 782p. ISBN:0-87565-003-1, ISBN13: 978-0-87565-003-6. Dewey:796/.01. LCCN:84-023951.
Audience: **u,f.** *B* *Choice, 1986.*

Weiss, Paul **GV706.W4**
Sport; a Philosophic Inquiry. Trade Cloth. Southern Illinois University Press. Carbondale, IL. 1969. ix, 274p. ISBN:0-8093-4439-4, ISBN13: 978-0-8093-4439-0. Dewey:796/.01. LCCN:69-015326.
Audience: **g,l,u,f.** *B*

Sport Studies > History

GV563
Amateur Athletic Foundation of Los Angeles. http://www.aafla.org/
Audience: **g,l,u.**

GV944.U6
American Soccer History Archives. http://www.sover.net/~spectrum/
Audience: **g,l,u,f.**

Abrams, Lynn **HD7395**
Workers' Culture in Imperial Germany. Paper over Boards. Routledge. New York, NY. 1992. 224p. ISBN:0-415-07635-8, ISBN13: 978-0-415-07635-7. Dewey:305.5620943. LCCN:91-012748.
Audience: **u,f.** *Choice, 1992.*

ACSM Staff & Berryman, Jack W. **RC1210.B395 1995**
Out of Many, One: A History of the American College of Sports Medicine. Cloth Text. Human Kinetics Publishers. Champaign, IL. 1995. 424p. ISBN:0-87322-815-4, ISBN13: 978-0-87322-815-2. Dewey:617.1/027/06073. LCCN:94-023876.
Audience: **l,u,f.** *Choice, 1996.*

Alter, Joseph S. **B132.Y6A483 2004**
Yoga in Modern India: The Body Between Science and Philosophy. Trade Paper. Princeton University Press. Princeton, NJ. 2004. 376p. ISBN:0-691-11874-4, ISBN13: 978-0-691-11874-1. Dewey:181/.45. LCCN:2003-064108.
Audience: **l,u,f.**

Barnett, Steven **GV742.3 .B37 1990**
Games and Sets: The Changing Face of Sport on Television. Trade Paper. BFI Publishing. London, 1990. 224p. ISBN:0-85170-268-6, ISBN13: 978-0-85170-268-1. Dewey:302.234/5. LCCN:91-105439.
Audience: **u,f.** *Choice, 1991.*

Berlage, Gai I. & Gerard, Charley **GV880**
Women in Baseball: The Forgotten History. Trade Cloth. Greenwood Publishing Group, Inc. Portsmouth, NH. 1994. 224p. ISBN:0-275-94735-1, ISBN13: 978-0-275-94735-4. Dewey:796.357082. LCCN:93-025049.
Audience: **g,l,u,f.** *Choice, 1994.*

Bernstein, Mark F. **GV958.5.I9B47 2001**
Football: The Ivy League Origins of an American Obsession. Trade Cloth. University of Pennsylvania Press. Philadelphia, PA. 2001. 336p. ISBN:0-8122-3627-0, ISBN13: 978-0-8122-3627-9. Dewey:796.332/63/0974. LCCN:2001-027488.
Audience: **u,f.** *Choice, 2002.*

Berryman, Jack W. & Park, Roberta J. (Editors) **RC1210.S638 1992**
Sport and Exercise Science: Essays in the History of Sports Medicine. Trade Paper. University of Illinois Press. Champaign, IL. 1992. 392p. Sport and Society Ser. ISBN:0-252-06242-6, ISBN13: 978-0-252-06242-1. Dewey:617.1/027/09. LCCN:91-027220.
Audience: **u,f.** *Choice, 1993.*

Betts, John R. **GV583.B47**
America's Sporting Heritage: 1850-1950. Cloth Text. Addison-Wesley Longman, Inc. Boston, MA. 1974. xv, 428p. ISBN:0-201-00557-3, ISBN13: 978-0-201-00557-8. Dewey:796/.0973. LCCN:73-010590.
Audience: **g,l,u,f.** *B*

Bevis, Charlie **GV867.6.B48 2003**
Sunday Baseball: The Major Leagues' Struggle to Play Baseball on the Lord's Day, 1876-1934. Paper Text. McFarland &

Company, Incorporated Publishers. Jefferson, NC. 2003. 326p. ISBN:0-7864-1564-9, ISBN13: 978-0-7864-1564-9. Dewey:796.357/64/0973. LCCN:2002-156687.
Audience: **u,f.** *Choice, 2003.*

Billet, Bret L. & Formwalt, Lance J. **GV863**
America's National Pastime: A Study of Race and Merit in Professional Baseball. Trade Cloth. Greenwood Publishing Group, Inc. Portsmouth, NH. 1995. 200p. ISBN:0-275-95193-6, ISBN13: 978-0-275-95193-1. Dewey:796.357/0973. LCCN:95-003331.
Audience: **g,l,u,f.** *Choice, 1996.*

Birley, Derek **GV706.5.B57 1995**
Playing the Game: Sport and British Society, 1914-1945. Trade Paper. Manchester University Press. Manchester, 1996. 256p. International Studies in the History of Sport, Vol. 1 ISBN:0-7190-4497-9, ISBN13: 978-0-7190-4497-7. Dewey:796/.0941. LCCN:95-049566.
Audience: **u,f.** *Choice, 1996.*

Bjarkman, Peter C. **GV863.155.B53 1994**
Baseball with a Latin Beat: A History of the Latin American Game. Paper Text. McFarland & Company, Incorporated Publishers. Jefferson, NC. 1994. 486p. ISBN:0-89950-973-8, ISBN13: 978-0-89950-973-0. Dewey:796.357/098. LCCN:94-3526.
Audience: **u,f.** *Choice, 1995.*

Brailsford, Dennis **GV1123 .B73 1988**
Bareknuckles: A Social History of Prize-Fighting. Trade Cloth. Lutterworth Press, The. Cambridge, 1997. 196p. ISBN:0-7188-2676-0, ISBN13: 978-0-7188-2676-5. Dewey:796.8/3/0942. LCCN:89-173102.
Audience: **u,f.**

Brailsford, Dennis **GV605.B682 1999**
A Taste for Diversions: Sport in Georgian England. Trade Paper. Lutterworth Press, The. Cambridge, 1997. 144p. ISBN:0-7188-2981-6, ISBN13: 978-0-7188-2981-0. Dewey:306.4/83/0942. LCCN:00-273026.
Audience: **u,f.**

Brandt, Nat **GV958.O24B72 2001**
When Oberlin was King of the Gridiron: The Heisman Years. Trade Paper. Kent State University Press. Kent, OH. 2001. 248p. ISBN:0-87338-684-1, ISBN13: 978-0-87338-684-5. Dewey:796.332/63/0977123. LCCN:00-010265.
Audience: **u,f.** *Choice, 2001.*

Bryant, Howard **GV875.B62B79 2002**
Shut Out: A Story of Race and Baseball in Boston. Paper over Boards. Routledge. New York, NY. 2002. 296p. ISBN:0-415-92779-X, ISBN13: 978-0-415-92779-6. Dewey:796.357/64/0974461. LCCN:2002-069950.
Audience: **u,f.**

Bullock, Steve **GV863.A1B84 2004**
Playing for Their Nation: Baseball and the American Military During World War II. Trade Cloth. University of Nebraska Press. Lincoln, NE. 2005. 224p. Jerry Malloy Prize Ser. ISBN:0-8032-1337-9, ISBN13: 978-0-8032-1337-1. Dewey:796.357/0973/09044. LCCN:2003-016945.
Audience: **u,f.** *Choice, 2004.*

Burk, Robert F. **GV880.B87 1994**
Never Just a Game: Players, Owners and American Baseball to 1920. Trade Cloth. University of North Carolina Press. Chapel Hill, NC. 1994. 302p. ISBN:0-8078-2122-5, ISBN13: 978-0-8078-2122-0. Dewey:338.4/3796357/0973. LCCN:93-022719.
Audience: **g,l,u,f.** *Choice, 1994.*

Cahn, Susan K. **GV709**
Coming on Strong: Gender and Sexuality in Twentieth-Century Women's Sports. Trade Paper. Harvard University Press. Cambridge, MA. 1998. 39p. ISBN:0-674-14434-1, ISBN13: 978-0-674-14434-7. Dewey:796/.0194.
Audience: **g,l,u,f.**

Carroll, John M. **GV939**
Red Grange and the Rise of Modern Football. Trade Paper. University of Illinois Press. Champaign, IL. 2004. 296p. ISBN:0-252-07166-2, ISBN13: 978-0-252-07166-9. Dewey:796.332/092 B.
Audience: **l,u,f.** *Choice, 2000.*

Carter, John M. **GV575**
Medieval Games: Sports and Recreations in Feudal Society, 30. Trade Cloth. Greenwood Publishing Group, Inc. Portsmouth, NH. 1992. 192p. Contributions to the Study of World History Ser., No. 30 ISBN:0-313-26743-X, ISBN13: 978-0-313-26743-7. Dewey:796/.094. LCCN:91-000785.
Audience: **g,l,u,f.** *Choice, 1992.*

Casway, Jerrold I. **GV865.D45C37 2004**
Ed Delahanty in the Emerald Age of Baseball. Trade Cloth. University of Notre Dame Press. Notre Dame, IN. 2004. 400p. ISBN:0-268-02285-2, ISBN13: 978-0-268-02285-3. Dewey:796.357/092 B. LCCN:2003-024041.
Audience: **u,f.** *Choice, 2004.*

Chadwick, Bruce **GV875.A1.C47 1992**
When the Game Was Black and White: The Illustrated History of Baseball's Negro Leagues. Trade Cloth. Abbeville Press, Inc. New York, NY. 1992. 204p. ISBN:1-55859-372-1, ISBN13: 978-1-55859-372-5. Dewey:796.35708996073. LCCN:92-013673.
Audience: **g,l,u,f.** *Choice, 1993.*

Clark, Dick **GV863.A1**
The Negro Leagues Book. Trade Paper. Society for American Baseball Research. Cleveland, OH. 1994. 382p. ISBN:0-910137-55-2, ISBN13: 978-0-910137-55-3. Dewey:796.357.
Audience: **g,l,u,f.** *Choice, 1995.*

Collins, Tony **GV945.9.G7**
Rugby's Great Split: Class, Culture and the Origins of Rugby League Football. Trade Paper. Woburn Press. Andover, 1998. 304p. Sport in the Global Society Ser. ISBN:0-7146-4424-2, ISBN13: 978-0-7146-4424-0. Dewey:796.333/8/0941.
Audience: **u,f.** *Choice, 1999.*

Dauncey, Hugh & Hare, Geoff (Editors) **GV1049.2.T68T68 2003**
The Tour de France, 1903-2003: A Century of Sporting Structures, Meanings and Values - Sport in the Global Society. Paper over Boards. Taylor & Francis Group. Abingdon, 2003. 290p. Sport in the Global Society Ser. ISBN:0-7146-5362-4, ISBN13: 978-0-7146-5362-4. Dewey:796.6/2/0944. LCCN:2003-011128.
Audience: **g,l,u,f.** *Choice, 2004.*

Davies, Richard O. **GV706.5.D38 1994**
America's Obsession: Sports and Society since 1945. Gerald D. Nash & Richard W. Etulain (Editors). Paper Text. Thomson Wadsworth. Belmont, CA. 1994. 288p. Harbrace Books on America since 1945 ISBN:0-03-073332-4, ISBN13: 978-0-03-073332-1. Dewey:306.4/83. LCCN:93-080632.
Audience: **g,l,u,f.**

Dawkins, Marvin P. & Kinloch, Graham C. **GV981**
African American Golfers During the Jim Crow Era. Trade Cloth. Greenwood Publishing Group, Inc. Portsmouth, NH. 2000. 200p. ISBN:0-275-95940-6, ISBN13: 978-0-275-95940-1. Dewey:796.352/089/96073. LCCN:99-034486.
Audience: **u,f.** *Choice, 2000.*

Decker, Wolfgang **GV573.D4213 1990**
Sports and Games of Ancient Egypt. Allen Guttman (Translator). Trade Cloth. Yale University Press. Cumberland, RI. 1992. xi, 212p. ISBN:0-300-04463-1, ISBN13: 978-0-300-04463-8. Dewey:796/.0962. LCCN:90-036482.
Audience: **g,l,u,f.** *Choice, 1992.*

Dorinson, Joseph & Warmund, Joram (Editors) **GV865.R6**
Jackie Robinson: Race, Sports and the American Dream. Paper Text. M. E. Sharpe Inc. Armonk, NY. 1999. 296p. ISBN:0-7656-0318-7, ISBN13: 978-0-7656-0318-0. Dewey:796.357/092.
Audience: **g,l,u,f.** *Choice, 1999.*

Edelman, Robert **GV623.E27 1993**
Serious Fun: A History of Spectator Sport in the U. S. S. R. Trade Cloth. Oxford University Press, Inc. New York, NY. 1993. 320p. ISBN:0-19-507948-5, ISBN13: 978-0-19-507948-7. Dewey:796/.0947. LCCN:92-023762.
Audience: **u,f.** *Choice, 1993.*

Eisen, George & Wiggins, David K. (Editors) **GV709**
Ethnicity and Sport in North American History and Culture. Paper Text. Greenwood Publishing Group, Inc. Portsmouth, NH. 1995. 272p. Contributions to the Study of Popular Culture Ser., No. 40 ISBN:0-275-95451-X, ISBN13: 978-0-275-95451-2. Dewey:796.1/9. LCCN:93-050538.
Audience: **g,l,u,f.** *Choice, 1995.*

Falk, Gerhard **GV951.F25 2005**
Football and American Identity. Perfect, Paper over Boards. Haworth Press, Incorporated, The. Binghamton, NY. 2005. 277p. Contemporary Sports Issues Ser. ISBN:0-7890-2526-4, ISBN13: 978-0-7890-2526-5. Dewey:796.3320973. LCCN:2004-012740.
Audience: **g,l,u,f.** *Choice, 2005.*

Falkner, David **GV865.R6**
Great Time Coming: The Life of Jackie Robinson from Baseball to Birmingham. Trade Paper. Simon & Schuster. New York, NY. 1996. 384p. ISBN:0-684-82348-9, ISBN13: 978-0-684-82348-5. Dewey:796.357/092 B.
Audience: **g,l,u,f.**

Fenster, Julie **GV1029.2.F46 2005**
Race of the Century: The Heroic True Story of the 1908 New York-to-Paris Auto Race. Trade Cloth. Crown Publishing Group. New York, NY. 2005. 400p. ISBN:0-609-61096-1, ISBN13: 978-0-609-61096-1. Dewey:796.72. LCCN:2004-026644.
Audience: **g,l,u,f.** *Choice, 2005.*

Findling, John E. & Pelle, Kimberly D. (Editors) **GV721**
Historical Dictionary of the Modern Olympic Movement. Cloth Text. Greenwood Publishing Group, Inc. Portsmouth, NH. 1996. 504p. ISBN:0-313-28477-6, ISBN13: 978-0-313-28477-9. Dewey:796.48. LCCN:95-000569.
Audience: **g,l,u,f.** *Choice, 1996.*

Fisher, Donald M. **GV989.F56 2002**
Lacrosse: A History of the Game. Trade Cloth. Johns Hopkins University Press. Baltimore, MD. 2002. 432p. ISBN:0-8018-6938-2, ISBN13: 978-0-8018-6938-9. Dewey:796.34/7/09. LCCN:2001-005690.
Audience: **g,l,u,f.**

Freeman, Michael **GV742.3.F75 2000**
ESPN: The Uncensored History. Trade Cloth. Taylor Trade Publishing. Blue Ridge Summit, PA. 2000. 304p. ISBN:0-87833-239-1, ISBN13: 978-0-87833-239-7. Dewey:384.55/5. LCCN:99-056862.
Audience: **g,l,u.**

Gems, Gerald R. **GV950.G46 2000**
For Pride, Profit and Patriarchy: Football and the Incorporation of American Cultural Values. Trade Cloth. Scarecrow Press, Inc. Lanham, MD. 2000. 240p. American Sports History Ser., No. 16 ISBN:0-8108-3685-8, ISBN13: 978-0-8108-3685-3. Dewey:796.332/0973. LCCN:00-023773.
Audience: **u,f.**

Gems, Gerald R. **GV584.5.C4G46 1997**
The Windy City Wars: Labor, Leisure, and Sport in the Making of Chicago. Trade Cloth. Scarecrow Press, Inc. Lanham, MD. 1997. 280p. American Sports History Ser., No. 8 ISBN:0-8108-3305-0, ISBN13: 978-0-8108-3305-0. Dewey:796/.09773/11. LCCN:97-012133.
Audience: **u,f.**

Gerber, Ellen W., et al. **GV709.A64**
The American Woman in Sport. Jan Felshin, Pearl Berlin & Waneen Wyrick (Authors). Cloth Text. Addison-Wesley Longman, Inc. Boston, MA. 1974. xi, 562p. ISBN:0-201-02353-9, ISBN13: 978-0-201-02353-4. Dewey:796/.019/40973. LCCN:74-002849.
Audience: **g,l,f.** B

Gerdy, John R. **GV346.S66 2000**
Sports in School: The Future of an Institution. Trade Paper. Teachers College Press, Teachers College, Columbia University. New York, NY. 2000. xi, 177p. ISBN:0-8077-3970-7, ISBN13: 978-0-8077-3970-9. Dewey:796/.071/073. LCCN:00-032559.
Audience: **g,l,u.** *Choice, 2001.*

Goldstein, Michael S. **RA427.8.G65 1992**
Health Movement in America: Promoting Fitness. Trade Paper. Macmillan Publishing Company, Inc. Old Tappan, NJ. 1992. 250p. Social Movements Past and Present Ser. ISBN:0-8057-9726-2, ISBN13: 978-0-8057-9726-8. Dewey:613/.0973. LCCN:91-028694.
Audience: **l,u,f.** *Choice, 1992.*

Gorn, Elliott J. **GV1125**
The Manly Art: Bare-Knuckle Prize Fighting in America. Trade Paper. Cornell University Press. Ithaca, NY. 1989. 320p. ISBN:0-8014-9582-2, ISBN13: 978-0-8014-9582-3. Dewey:796.8/3/0973. LCCN:86-006410.
Audience: **u,f.** *Choice, 1987.*

Gould Todd **GV885.72.I6**
Pioneers of the Hardwood: Indiana and the Birth of Professional Basketball. Indiana University Press. 1998.
ISBN:0-253-21199-9, ISBN13: 978-0-253-21199-6.
Audience: **g,l,u,f.**

Grover, Kathryn (Editor) **GV510.U5F58 1989**
Fitness in American Culture: Images of Health, Sport and the Body, 1830-1940. Trade Paper. University of Massachusetts Press. Amherst, MA. 1989. 192p. ISBN:0-87023-682-2, ISBN13: 978-0-87023-682-2. Dewey:613.7/1. LCCN:89-004772.
Audience: **l,u,f.** *Choice, 1990.*

Guttmann, Allen **GV706.5.G87 2004**
From Ritual to Record: The Nature of Modern Sports. Ed. 2. Trade Paper. Kegan Paul International, Ltd. London, 2004. 224p. ISBN:0-231-13341-3, ISBN13: 978-0-231-13341-8. Dewey:306.4/83. LCCN:2004-044497.
Audience: **g,l,u,f.** B

Guttmann, Allen **GV583.G87 1988**
A Whole New Ball Game: An Interpretation of American Sports. Trade Cloth. University of North Carolina Press. Chapel Hill, NC. 1988. x, 233p. ISBN:0-8078-1786-4, ISBN13: 978-0-8078-1786-5. Dewey:796/.0973. LCCN:87-026131.
Audience: **g,l,u,f.** *Choice, 1988.*

Guttmann, Allen **GV709**
Women's Sports: A History. Trade Paper. Columbia University Press. New York, NY. 1992. 339p. ISBN:0-231-06957-X, ISBN13: 978-0-231-06957-1. Dewey:796/.0194.
Audience: **g,l,u,f.** *Choice, 1991.*

Guttmann, Allen & Thompson, Lee B. **GV655.G88 2001**
Japanese Sports: A History. Trade Cloth. University of Hawaii Press. Honolulu, HI. 2001. 320p. ISBN:0-8248-2414-8, ISBN13: 978-0-8248-2414-3. Dewey:796/.0952. LCCN:00-066665.
Audience: **u,f.** *Choice, 2002.*

Halberstam, David **GV742.3 .H35 1999**
Sports on New York Radio: A Play-by-Play History. Trade Cloth. McGraw-Hill Companies, The. New York, NY. 1999. 432p. ISBN:1-57028-197-1, ISBN13: 978-1-57028-197-6. Dewey:070.4/49796/097471. LCCN:98-046621.
Audience: **g,l,u,f.**

Hall, M. Ann **GV709.H32 1996**
Feminism and Sporting Bodies: Essays on Theory and Practice. Trade Paper. Human Kinetics Publishers. Champaign, IL. 1996. 144p. ISBN:0-87322-969-X, ISBN13: 978-0-87322-969-2. Dewey:796/.0194. LCCN:95-044480.
Audience: **u,f.** *Choice, 1996.*

Hall, M. Ann **GV709.18.C2H35 2002**
The Girl and the Game: A History of Women's Sport in Canada. Trade Paper. Broadview Press. Peterborough, ON. 2002. 284p. ISBN:1-55111-268-X, ISBN13: 978-1-55111-268-8. Dewey:796/.082/0973. LCCN:2002-416290.
Audience: **g,u,f.** *Choice, 2003.*

Hardy, Stephen **GV584.5.B6H37 2003**
How Boston Played: Sport, Recreation, and Community, 1865-1915. Trade Paper. University of Tennessee Press. Knoxville, TN. 2003. 312p. Sport and Popular Culture Ser. ISBN:1-57233-218-2, ISBN13: 978-1-57233-218-8. Dewey:796/.09744/6109034. LCCN:2002-043100.
Audience: **g,l,u,f.**

Hargreaves, Jennifer **GV709.18.G7H37 1994**
Sporting Females: Critical Issues in the History and Sociology of Women's Sports. Trade Paper. Routledge. New York, NY. 1994. 344p. ISBN:0-415-07028-7, ISBN13: 978-0-415-07028-7. Dewey:796.0194. LCCN:93-024575.
Audience: **u,f.**

Harris, H. A. **GV573.H3**
Sport in Greece and Rome. Howard H. Scullard (Editor). Trade Cloth. Cornell University Press. Ithaca, NY. 1972. 288p. Aspects of Greek and Roman Life Ser. ISBN:0-8014-0718-4, ISBN13: 978-0-8014-0718-5. Dewey:796/.0938. LCCN:77-039824.
Audience: **g,l,u,f.** B

Harris, Harold Arthur **GV0021.H3**
Greek Athletes and Athletics. Trade Paper. Books on Demand. Ann Arbor, MI. 278p. ISBN:0-598-45553-1, ISBN13: 978-0-598-45553-6. Dewey:796.0938. LCCN:66-022440.
Audience: **l,u,f.** B

Heaphy, Leslie A. **GV875.N35H43 2002**
The Negro Leagues, 1869-1960. Cloth Text. McFarland & Company, Incorporated Publishers. Jefferson, NC. 2002. 383p. ISBN:0-7864-1380-8, ISBN13: 978-0-7864-1380-5. Dewey:796.357/64/08996073. LCCN:2002-012225.
Audience: **g,l,u,f.** *Choice, 2003.*

Henderson, Robert W. **GV861.H4 2001**
Ball, Bat and Bishop: The Origin of Ball Games. Trade Paper. University of Illinois Press. Champaign, IL. 2001. 248p. ISBN:0-252-06992-7, ISBN13: 978-0-252-06992-5. Dewey:796.3/09. LCCN:00-067239.
Audience: **l,u,f.** *Choice, 2002.*

Hess, Rob & Stewart, Bob (Editors) **GV947.M67 1998**
More Than a Game: An Unauthorized History of Australian Rules Football. Martin Flanagan (Foreword by). Trade Paper. Melbourne University Publishing. Carlton, VIC. 1998. 320p. ISBN:0-522-84772-2, ISBN13: 978-0-522-84772-7. Dewey:796.336. LCCN:98-221833.
Audience: **u,f.**

Hoberman, John M. **RC1235.H63 2001**
Mortal Engines. Perfect. Blackburn Press, The. Caldwell, NJ. 2002. 374p. ISBN:1-930665-37-7, ISBN13: 978-1-930665-37-8. Dewey:617.1/027. LCCN:2001-093232.
Audience: **u,f.**

Holt, Richard **GV605.H65 1990**
Sport and the British: A Modern History. Trade Paper. Oxford University Press, Inc. New York, NY. 1990. 410p. Oxford Studies in Social History ISBN:0-19-285229-9, ISBN13: 978-0-19-285229-8. Dewey:796/.0941. LCCN:90-034601.
Audience: **g,l,u,f.** *Choice, 1990.*

Howell, Colin **GV863.15.M37H69 1995**
Northern Sandlots: A Social History of Maritime Baseball. Trade Paper. University of Toronto Press. Toronto, ON. 1995. 288p. ISBN:0-8020-6942-8, ISBN13: 978-0-8020-6942-9. Dewey:796.357/09715. LCCN:95-178431.
Audience: **u,f.** *Choice, 1995.*

Howell, Colin D. **GV585.H56 2001**
Blood, Sweat and Cheers: Sport and the Making of Modern Canada. Trade Paper. University of Toronto Press. Toronto, ON. 2001. 234p. Themes in Canadian Social History Ser., Vol. 6 ISBN:0-8020-8248-3, ISBN13: 978-0-8020-8248-0. Dewey:796/.0971. LCCN:2002-278153.
Audience: **g,l,u,f.**

Hult, Joan S. & Trekell, Marianna (Editors) **GV886 .C45 1991**
A Century of Women's Basketball: From Frailty to Final Four. Paper Text. American Alliance for Health, Physical Education, Recreation & Dance. Oxon Hill, MD. 1991. 430p. ISBN:0-88314-490-5, ISBN13: 978-0-88314-490-9. Dewey:796.323/0973. LCCN:91-197223.
Audience: **u,f.**

Isenberg, Michael T. **GV1132.M84**
John L. Sullivan and His America. Trade Paper. University of Illinois Press. Champaign, IL. 1994. 480p. ISBN:0-252-06434-8, ISBN13: 978-0-252-06434-0. Dewey:796.8/3/0924 B.
Audience: **l,u,f.** *Choice, 1988.*

Kidd, Bruce **GV585.K53 1996**
The Struggle for Canadian Sport. Trade Paper. University of Toronto Press. Toronto, ON. 1996. 323p. ISBN:0-8020-7664-5, ISBN13: 978-0-8020-7664-9. Dewey:796/.0971. LCCN:96-173457.
Audience: **g,l,u,f.** *Choice, 1997.*

Kimball, Richard Ian **GV54.U8K56 2003**
Sports in Zion: Mormon Recreation, 1890-1940. Trade Cloth. University of Illinois Press. Champaign, IL. 2003. 240p. Sports and Society Ser. ISBN:0-252-02857-0, ISBN13: 978-0-252-02857-1. Dewey:790/.088/283. LCCN:2002-156585.
Audience: **g,l,u,f.** *Choice, 2004.*

Kirsch, George B. **GV863.A1K56 2003**
Baseball in Blue and Gray: The National Pastime During the Civil War. Cloth Text. Princeton University Press. Princeton, NJ. 2003. 160p. ISBN:0-691-05733-8, ISBN13: 978-0-691-05733-0. Dewey:796.357/0973/09034. LCCN:2002-069289.
Audience: **l,u,f.** *Choice, 2003.*

Kruger, Arnd & Murray, William (Editors) **GV722 1936.N39 2003**
The Nazi Olympics: Sport, Politics, and Appeasement in the 1930s. Trade Cloth. University of Illinois Press. Champaign, IL. 2003. 280p. Sport and Society Ser. ISBN:0-252-02815-5, ISBN13: 978-0-252-02815-1. Dewey:796.48. LCCN:2002-011803.
Audience: **g,l,u,f.** *Choice, 2004.*

Kruger, Arnd & Riordan, James (Editors) **GV706.5.S867 1996**
The Story of Worker Sport. Trade Cloth. Human Kinetics Publishers. Champaign, IL. 1996. 20p. ISBN:0-87322-874-X, ISBN13: 978-0-87322-874-9. Dewey:306.4/83. LCCN:96-001281.
Audience: **u,f.** *Choice, 1997.*

Kuhn, Bowie **GV865.K78K85 1997**
Hardball: The Education of a Baseball Commissioner. Trade Cloth. University of Nebraska Press. Lincoln, NE. 1997. 477p. ISBN:0-8032-7784-9, ISBN13: 978-0-8032-7784-7. Dewey:[B]. LCCN:97-006823.
Audience: **g,l,u.**

Kuska, Bob **GV885.73.W18K87 2004**
Hot Potato: How Washington and New York Gave Birth to Black Basketball and Changed America's Game Forever. Trade Cloth. University Press of Virginia. Charlottesville, VA. 2004. 220p. ISBN:0-8139-2263-1, ISBN13: 978-0-8139-2263-8. Dewey:796.323/64/08996073. LCCN:2003-018322.
Audience: **u,f.**

Lamb, Chris **GV865.R6L36 2004**
Blackout: The Untold Story of Jackie Robinson's First Spring Training. Trade Cloth. University of Nebraska Press. Lincoln, NE. 2005. 176p. ISBN:0-8032-2956-9, ISBN13: 978-0-8032-2956-3. Dewey:796.357/092 B. LCCN:2004-000614.
Audience: **l,u,f.** *Choice, 2005.*

Lanctot, Neil **GV875.N35L36 2004**
Negro League Baseball: The Rise and Ruin of a Black Institution. Book, Other. University of Pennsylvania Press. Philadelphia, PA. 2004. 496p. ISBN:0-8122-3807-9, ISBN13: 978-0-8122-3807-5. Dewey:796.357/64/0973. LCCN:2004-043547.
Audience: **g,l,u,f.** *Choice, 2004.*

Lester, Robin **GV958.U519L47 1995**
Stagg's University: The Rise, Decline and Fall of Big-Time Football at the University of Chicago. Trade Cloth. University of Illinois Press. Champaign, IL. 1995. 344p. Sport and Society Ser. ISBN:0-252-02128-2, ISBN13: 978-0-252-02128-2. Dewey:796.332/09773/11. LCCN:94-034018.
Audience: **u,f.** *Choice, 1996.*

Lomax, Michael E. **GV863.A1L65 2003**
Black Baseball Entrepreneurs, 1860-1901: Operating by Any Means Necessary. Trade Paper. Syracuse University Press. Syracuse, NY. 2003. xxvi, 222p. Sports and Entertainment Ser. ISBN:0-8156-0786-5, ISBN13: 978-0-8156-0786-1. Dewey:796.357/64/08996073. LCCN:2002-154375.
Audience: **u,f.**

MacCambridge, Michael **GV561.M185 1997**
The Franchise: A History of Sports Illustrated Magazine. Trade Cloth. Hyperion Press. New York, NY. 1997. 352p. ISBN:0-7868-6216-5, ISBN13: 978-0-7868-6216-0. Dewey:796/.05. LCCN:97-015864.
Audience: **g,l,u,f.**

Mallon, Bill & Buchanan, Ian **GV721.5.B83 2006**
Historical Dictionary of the Olympic Movement. Ed. 3. Trade Cloth. Scarecrow Press, Inc. Lanham, MD. 2005. 544p. Historical Dictionaries of Religions, Philosophies, and Movements Ser., No. 61 ISBN:0-8108-5574-7, ISBN13: 978-0-8108-5574-8. Dewey:796.48/03. LCCN:2005-016706.
Audience: **g,l,u.**

Maltby, Marc S. **GV954.M35 1997**
The Origins and Development of Professional Football, 1890-1920. Cloth Text. Garland Publishing, Inc. New York, NY. 1997. 256p. Studies in American Popular History and Culture ISBN:0-8153-2797-8, ISBN13: 978-0-8153-2797-4. Dewey:796.33264. LCCN:97-010251.
Audience: **u,f.**

Mandell, Richard D. **GV722 1936.M3 1986**
The Nazi Olympics. Trade Paper. University of Illinois Press. Champaign, IL. 1987. 360p. Sport and Society Ser.

ISBN:0-252-01325-5, ISBN13: 978-0-252-01325-6. Dewey:796.4/8/09043. LCCN:86-019347.
Audience: **l,u,f.**

Margolick, David **GV1136.8.M37 2005**
Beyond Glory: Joe Louis vs. Max Schmeling and a World on the Brink. Trade Cloth. Alfred A. Knopf Inc. New York, NY. 2005. 432p. ISBN:0-375-41192-5, ISBN13: 978-0-375-41192-2. Dewey:796.83/09043. LCCN:2005-045141.
Audience: **l,u.** *Choice, 2006.*

Martin, Simon **GV943.9.S64**
Football and Fascism: The National Game under Mussolini. Trade Paper. Berg Publishers. Oxford, 2004. 288p. ISBN:1-85973-705-6, ISBN13: 978-1-85973-705-7. Dewey:796.334/0945/09043. LCCN:2004-020616.
Audience: **g,l,u,f.** *Choice, 2005.*

Massengale, John & Swanson, Richard A. (Editors) **GV223.H57 1997**
The History of Exercise and Sport Science. Trade Cloth. Human Kinetics Publishers. Champaign, IL. 1996. 488p. ISBN:0-87322-524-4, ISBN13: 978-0-87322-524-3. Dewey:613.7/1/071173. LCCN:96-010555.
Audience: **g,l,u,f.** *Choice, 1997.*

McCrone, Kathleen E. **GV709.18.G7M33 1988**
Playing the Game: Sport and the Physical Emancipation of English Women, 1870-1914. Trade Cloth. University Press of Kentucky. Lexington, KY. 1988. 336p. ISBN:0-8131-1641-4, ISBN13: 978-0-8131-1641-9. Dewey:796/.01/940941. LCCN:87-032038.
Audience: **g,l,u,f.** *Choice, 1989.*

Melville, Tom **GV928.U6M45 1998**
The Tented Field: A History of Cricket in America. Trade Paper. University of Wisconsin Press. Chicago, IL. 1998. 280p. ISBN:0-87972-770-5, ISBN13: 978-0-87972-770-3. Dewey:796.358/0973. LCCN:98-004030.
Audience: **u,f.** *Choice, 1999.*

Mitchell, Timothy **GV1108.5.M58 1991**
Blood Sport: A Social History of Spanish Bullfighting. Trade Paper. University of Pennsylvania Press. Philadelphia, PA. 1991. 288p. ISBN:0-8122-1346-7, ISBN13: 978-0-8122 1346-1. Dewey:791.8/2/0946. LCCN:91-007231.
Audience: **l,u,f.** *Choice, 1992.*

Morris, Andrew D. **GV651 .M67 2004**
Marrow of the Nation: A History of Sport and Physical Culture in Republican China. Trade Cloth. University of California Press. Berkeley, CA. 2004. 368p. Asia-Local Studies/Global Themes, Vol. 10 ISBN:0-520-24084-7, ISBN13: 978-0-520-24084-1. Dewey:796/.0951/09. LCCN:2004-001057.
Audience: **g,l,u,f.** *Choice, 2005.*

Morrow, Don & Wamsley, Kevin **GV585**
Sport in Canada: A History. Trade Paper. Oxford University Press, Inc. New York, NY. 2005. 328p. ISBN:0-19-541996-0, ISBN13: 978-0-19-541996-2. Dewey:796/.0971. LCCN:2005-279471.
Audience: **g,l,u,f.**

Mrozek, Donald J. **GV583**
Sport and American Mentality, 1880-1910. Paper Text. University of Tennessee Press. Knoxville, TN. 1983. 304p. ISBN:0-87049-395-7, ISBN13: 978-0-87049-395-9. Dewey:796/.0973. LCCN:83-003667.
Audience: **g,l,u,f.** B

Nelson, David M. **GV955.N44 1994**
The Anatomy of a Game: Football, the Rules, and the Men Who Made the Game. Forest Evashevski (Foreword by). Trade Cloth. University of Delaware Press. Newark, DE. 1994. 599p. ISBN:0-87413-455-2, ISBN13: 978-0-87413-455-1. Dewey:796.332/02/022. LCCN:91-051009.
Audience: **u,f.** *Choice, 1994.*

Norcliffe, Glen **GV1046.C2 N67 2001**
Ride to Modernity: The Bicycle in Canada, 1869-1900. Trade Paper. University of Toronto Press. Toronto, ON. 2001. 248p. ISBN:0-8020-8205-X, ISBN13: 978-0-8020-8205-3. Dewey:796.6/0971. LCCN:2001-273481.
Audience: **u,f.**

Oleksak, Michael M. & Oleksak, Mary A. **GV862.6.O43 1991**
Beisbol: Latin Americans and the Grand Old Game. Trade Cloth. McGraw-Hill Trade. New York, NY. 1991. 320p. ISBN:0-940279-35-5, ISBN13: 978-0-940279-35-3. Dewey:796.357/098. LCCN:91-010697.
Audience: **g,l,u,f.** *Choice, 1991.*

Oriard, Michael **GV950.O73 2001**
King Football: Sport and Spectacle in the Golden Age of Radio and Newsreels, Movies and Magazines, the Weekly and the Daily Press. Trade Cloth. University of North Carolina Press. Chapel Hill, NC. 2001. 512p. ISBN:0-8078-2650-2, ISBN13: 978-0-8078-2650-8. Dewey:796.332/09/041. LCCN:2001-041459.
Audience: **l,u,f.** *Choice, 2002.*

Pearson, Daniel **GV863.A1.P43**
Baseball in 1889: Players vs Owners. Trade Paper. University of Wisconsin Press. Chicago, IL. 2005. 244p. ISBN:0-87972-619-9, ISBN13: 978-0-87972-619-5. Dewey:796.357. LCCN:92-063282.
Audience: **l,u,f.** *Choice, 1993.*

Perrin, Tom **GV950.P47 1987**
Football: A College History. Library Binding. McFarland & Company, Incorporated Publishers. Jefferson, NC. 1987. 438p. ISBN:0-89950-294-6, ISBN13: 978-0-89950-294-6. Dewey:796.332/63/0973. LCCN:87-043029.
Audience: **g,l,u,f.** *Choice, 1988.*

Perrottet, Tony **GV23.P47 2004**
The Naked Olympics: The True Story of the Ancient Games. Trade Paper. Random House Adult Trade Publishing Group. New York, NY. 2004. 240p. ISBN:0-8129-6991-X, ISBN13: 978-0-8129-6991-7. Dewey:796.48. LCCN:2003-066728.
Audience: **l,u.** *Choice, 2004.*

Pieroth, Doris Hinson **GV722 1932.P54 1996**
Their Day in the Sun: Women of the 1932 Olympics. Trade Paper. University of Washington Press. Seattle, WA. 1996. 208p. Samuel and Althea Stroum Bks. ISBN:0-295-97554-7, ISBN13: 978-0-295-97554-2. Dewey:796.48. LCCN:96-023104.
Audience: **l,u.** *Choice, 1997.*

Pietrusza, David **GV863.A1P54 1997**
Lights On!: The Wild Century-Long Saga of Night Baseball. Trade Cloth. Scarecrow Press, Inc. Lanham, MD. 1997. 288p. American Sports History Ser., Vol. 7 ISBN:0-8108-3307-7,

ISBN13: 978-0-8108-3307-4. Dewey:796.357/0973. LCCN:97-007800.
Audience: **g,l,u,f.** *Choice, 1998.*

Pont, Sally **GV939.A1P63 2001**
Fields of Honor: The Golden Age of College Football and the Men Who Created It. Cloth over Boards. Harcourt Trade Publishers. New York, NY. 2001. 256p. ISBN:0-15-100607-5, ISBN13: 978-0-15-100607-6. Dewey:796.332/63/0973. LCCN:2001-024364.
Audience: **u,f.** *Choice, 2002.*

Pope, Steven W. (Editor) **GV581.N48 1997**
The New American Sport History: Recent Approaches and Perspectives. Trade Paper. University of Illinois Press. Champaign, IL. 1996. 448p. Sport and Society Ser. ISBN:0-252-06567-0, ISBN13: 978-0-252-06567-5. Dewey:796/.0973. LCCN:96-006137.
Audience: **u,f.** *Choice, 1997.*

Pope, Steven W. **GV706.34.P67 1997**
Patriotic Games: Sporting Traditions in the American Imagination, 1876-1926. Trade Cloth. Oxford University Press, Inc. New York, NY. 1997. 226p. Sports History and Society Ser. ISBN:0-19-509133-7, ISBN13: 978-0-19-509133-5. Dewey:796/.0973. LCCN:96-005506.
Audience: **u,f.** *Choice, 1997.*

Porter, Karra **GV885.515.W66P67**
Mad Seasons: The Story of the First Women's Professional Basketball League, 1978-1981. Trade Paper. University of Nebraska Press. Lincoln, NE. 2006. 384p. ISBN:0-8032-8789-5, ISBN13: 978-0-8032-8789-1. Dewey:796.323/8. LCCN:2005-026399.
Audience: **g,l,u,f.**

Powers-Beck, Jeff **GV867.64.P69 2004**
The American Indian Integration of Baseball. Joseph Oxendine (Foreword by). Cloth Text. University of Nebraska Press. Lincoln, NE. 2004. 328p. ISBN:0-8032-3745-6, ISBN13: 978-0-8032-3745-2. Dewey:796.357/64/08997. LCCN:2004-007245.
Audience: **l,u,f.** *Choice, 2005.*

Rader, Benjamin G. **GV583.R3 2004**
American Sports: From the Age of Folk Games to the Age of Televised Sports. Ed. 5. Trade Paper. Prentice Hall PTR. Upper Saddle River, NJ. 2003. 384p. ISBN:0-13-097750-0, ISBN13: 978-0-13-097750-2. Dewey:796/.0973. LCCN:2003-051198.
Audience: **g,l,u,f.**

Rader, Benjamin G. **GV863.A1R33 2002**
Baseball: A History of America's Game. Ed. 2. Trade Paper. University of Illinois Press. Champaign, IL. 2002. 312p. Illinois History of Sports Ser. ISBN:0-252-07013-5, ISBN13: 978-0-252-07013-6. Dewey:796.357/0973. LCCN:2001-002477.
Audience: **g,l,u,f.** *Choice, 2002, 1993.*

Rader, Benjamin G. **GV742.3.R33 1984**
In Its Own Image: How Television Has Transformed Sports. Trade Cloth. Simon & Schuster. New York, NY. 1984. 256p. ISBN:0-02-925700-X, ISBN13: 978-0-02-925700-5. Dewey:070.4/49796/0973. LCCN:84-047856.
Audience: **g,l,u,f.** B

Reese, Anne C. & Vallera-Rickerson, Irini **GV21.R44 2002**
Athletries: The Untold History of Ancient Greek Women Athletes. Kathy Bryant (Editor), Jeff Kern (Illustrator). Reinforced. Nightowl Publications. Costa Mesa, CA. 2003. 189p. ISBN:0-9714984-0-7, ISBN13: 978-0-9714984-0-2. Dewey:790.092. LCCN:2002-101871.
Audience: **u,f.**

Regalado, Samuel O. **GV865.A1R38 1998**
Viva Baseball!: Latin Major Leaguers and Their Special Hunger. Trade Cloth. University of Illinois Press. Champaign, IL. 1998. 264p. Sport and Society Ser. ISBN:0-252-02372-2, ISBN13: 978-0-252-02372-9. Dewey:796.357/64/098. LCCN:97-021066.
Audience: **g,l,u,f.** *Choice, 1998.*

Ribowsky, Mark **GV865.P3R53 1994**
Don't Look Back: Satchel Paige on the Shadows of Baseball. Trade Cloth. Simon & Schuster. New York, NY. 1994. ISBN:0-671-77674-6, ISBN13: 978-0-671-77674-9. Dewey:796.357/092 B. LCCN:93-038802.
Audience: **g,l,u,f.**

Riess, Steven A. **GV709.6.S76 1998**
Sports and the American Jew. Trade Paper. Syracuse University Press. Syracuse, NY. 1998. 337p. Sports and Entertainment Ser. ISBN:0-8156-2761-0, ISBN13: 978-0-8156-2761-6. Dewey:796/.089/924073. LCCN:97-020930.
Audience: **l,u,f.** *Choice, 1999.*

Riess, Steven A. **GV706.5.R54 1995**
Sport in Industrial America, 1850-1920. Abraham S. Eisenstadt & John H. Franklin (Editors). Trade Paper. Harlan Davidson Inc. Wheeling, IL. 2003. 150p. The American History Ser. ISBN:0-88295-916-6, ISBN13: 978-0-88295-916-0. Dewey:306.4/83/0973. LCCN:94-043286.
Audience: **u,f.** *Choice, 1996.*

Sansone, David **GV706.8.S26**
Greek Athletics and the Genesis of Sport. Trade Paper. University of California Press. Berkeley, CA. 1992. 152p. ISBN:0-520-08095-5, ISBN13: 978-0-520-08095-9. Dewey:796. LCCN:87-014304.
Audience: **g,l,u,f.** *Choice, 1988.*

Schoenfeld, Bruce **GV994.A1**
The Match: Althea Gibson and a Portrait of a Friendship. Trade Paper, Perfect. HarperCollins Publishers. New York, NY. 2005. 320p. ISBN:0-06-052653-X, ISBN13: 978-0-06-052653-5. Dewey:796.3420922.
Audience: **l,u,f.**

Simon, Rita J. (Editor) **GV709.18.U6S67 2005**
Sporting Equality: Title IX Thirty Years Later. Trade Paper. Transaction Publishers. Somerset, NJ. 2005. 182p. ISBN:0-7658-0848-X, ISBN13: 978-0-7658-0848-6. Dewey:796/.082. LCCN:2004-051694.
Audience: **g,l,u,f.**

Smith, Lissa (Editor) **GV709.18.U6**
Nike Is a Goddess: The History of Women in Sports. Mariah B. Nelson (Introduction by), Lucy Danziger (Afterword by). Trade Paper. Grove/Atlantic, Inc. New York, NY. 1999. 352p. ISBN:0-87113-761-5, ISBN13: 978-0-87113-761-6. Dewey:796/.082/0973. LCCN:98-027049.
Audience: **g,l,u,f.** *Choice, 2000.*

Smith, Ronald A. **GV742.S64 2001**
Play-by-Play: Radio, Television and Big-Time College Sports. Trade Cloth. Johns Hopkins University Press. Baltimore, MD. 2001. 320p. ISBN:0-8018-6686-3, ISBN13: 978-0-8018-6686-9. Dewey:796.04/3/0973. LCCN:00-011534.
Audience: **g,u,f.** *Choice, 2002.*

Smith, Ronald A. **GV351**
Sports and Freedom: The Rise of Big-Time College Athletics. Paper Text. Oxford University Press, Inc. New York, NY. 1990. 320p. Sports History and Society Ser. ISBN:0-19-506582-4, ISBN13: 978-0-19-506582-4. Dewey:796/.07/1173. LCCN:88-017855.
Audience: **u,f.** *Choice, 1989.*

Spivey, Nigel **GV23.S69 2004**
The Ancient Olympics: A History. Trade Cloth. Oxford University Press, Inc. New York, NY. 2004. 304p. ISBN:0-19-280433-2, ISBN13: 978-0-19-280433-4. Dewey:796.48. LCCN:2004-046147.
Audience: **g,l,u,f.** *Choice, 2005.*

Struna, Nancy L. **GV583.S88 1996**
People of Prowess: Sport, Leisure, and Labor in Early Anglo-America. Trade Cloth. University of Illinois Press. Champaign, IL. 1996. 288p. Sport and Society Ser. ISBN:0-252-06552-2, ISBN13: 978-0-252-06552-1. Dewey:796/.0973/09032. LCCN:95-050193.
Audience: **u,f.**

Sweet, Waldo E. **GV21.S94 1987**
Sport and Recreation in Ancient Greece: A Sourcebook With Translations. Erich Segal (Foreword by). Trade Cloth. Oxford University Press, Inc. New York, NY. 1987. 288p. ISBN:0-19-504126-7, ISBN13: 978-0-19-504126-2. Dewey:796/.0938. LCCN:86-018209.
Audience: **u,f.** *Choice, 1988.*

Tipton, Charles M. (Editor) **QP301.E975 2003**
Exercise Physiology: People and Ideas. Trade Cloth. Oxford University Press, Inc. New York, NY. 2003. 528p. People and Ideas Ser. ISBN:0-19-512527-4, ISBN13: 978-0-19-512527-6. Dewey:612/.044. LCCN:2002-029293.
Audience: **u,f.** *Choice, 2004.*

Tranter, Neil L. **GV706.5 .T73 1998**
Sport, Economy and Society in Britain 1750-1914. Maurice Kirby (Contribution by). Trade Paper. Cambridge University Press. New York, NY. 1998. 124p. New Studies in Economic and Social History, Vol. 33 ISBN:0-521-57655-5, ISBN13: 978-0-521-57655-0. Dewey:306.4/83/0941. LCCN:97-023648.
Audience: **u,f.**

Tricard, Louise Mead **GV1060.8.T75 1996**
American women's track and field:a history, 1895 through 1980. McFarland. 1996. ISBN:0-7864-0219-9, ISBN13: 978-0-7864-0219-9.
Audience: **l,u,f.**

Tygiel, Jules **GV865.R6T93 1997**
Baseball's Great Experiment: Jackie Robinson and His Legacy. Trade Paper. Oxford University Press, Inc. New York, NY. 1997. 432p. ISBN:0-19-510620-2, ISBN13: 978-0-19-510620-6. Dewey:796.357/092 B. LCCN:96-038551.
Audience: **g,l,u,f.** B

Tyrrell, William Blake **GV21.T97 2004**
The Smell of Sweat: Greek Athletics and Greek Culture. Book, Other. Bolchazy-Carducci Publishers. Wauconda, IL. 2004. xv + 250p. ISBN:0-86516-553-X, ISBN13: 978-0-86516-553-3. Dewey:796/.09495. LCCN:2003-023038.
Audience: **u,f.**

Umphlett, Wiley L. **GV939**
Creating the Big Game: John W. Heisman and the Invention of American Football, 34. Trade Cloth. Greenwood Publishing Group, Inc. Portsmouth, NH. 1992. 296p. Contributions to the Study of Popular Culture Ser., No. 34 ISBN:0-313-28404-0, ISBN13: 978-0-313-28404-5. Dewey:796.332092. LCCN:92-010087.
Audience: **g,l,u,f.** *Choice, 1993.*

Vamplew, Wray **GV605 .V36 1988**
Pay up and Play the Game: Professional Sport in Britain, 1875-1914. Trade Paper. Cambridge University Press. New York, NY. 2004. 414p. ISBN:0-521-89230-9, ISBN13: 978-0-521-89230-8. Dewey:796/.0941.
Audience: **u,f.** *Choice, 1989.*

Vennum, Thomas Jr. **E98.G2V46 1994**
American Indian Lacrosse: Little Brother of War. Trade Paper. Smithsonian Institution Press. Washington, DC. 1994. 376p. ISBN:1-56098-302-7, ISBN13: 978-1-56098-302-6. Dewey:796.34/7. LCCN:93-029968.
Audience: **g,l,u,f.** *Choice, 1994.*

Vertinsky, Patricia A. **GV482.V47 1994**
The Eternally Wounded Woman: Women, Exercise, and Doctors in the Late Nineteenth Century. Trade Cloth. University of Illinois Press. Champaign, IL. 1994. 288p. ISBN:0-252-06372-4, ISBN13: 978-0-252-06372-5. Dewey:613.7/045. LCCN:93-037145.
Audience: **u,f.**

Wakefield, Wanda Ellen **U328.U5.W35 1997**
Playing to Win: Sports and the American Military, 1898-1945. Cloth Text. State University of New York Press. Albany, NY. 1997. 216p. SUNY Series on Sport, Culture, and Social Relations ISBN:0-7914-3313-7, ISBN13: 978-0-7914-3313-3. Dewey:306.2/7/0973. LCCN:96-019224.
Audience: **u,f.** *Choice, 1997.*

Ward, Geoffrey C. & Burns, Kenneth **GV863.A1W37 1994**
Baseball: An Illustrated History. Trade Cloth. Alfred A. Knopf Inc. New York, NY. 1994. 512p. ISBN:0-679-40459-7, ISBN13: 978-0-679-40459-0. Dewey:796.357/0973. LCCN:93-039809.
Audience: **g,l,u,f.** *Choice, 1995.*

Watterson, John Sayle **GV950.W28 2000**
College Football: History, Spectacle, Controversy. Trade Cloth. Johns Hopkins University Press. Baltimore, MD. 2000. 528p. ISBN:0-8018-6428-3, ISBN13: 978-0-8018-6428-5. Dewey:796.332/63/0973. LCCN:00-008247.
Audience: **u,f.** *Choice, 2001.*

White, Sol **GV863.A1W448 1995**
Sol White's History of Colored Base Ball, with Other Documents on the Early Black Game, 1886-1936. Jerry Malloy (Compiled by, Introduction by). Cloth Text. University of Nebraska Press. Lincoln, NE. 1995. 190p. ISBN:0-8032-4771-0, ISBN13: 978-0-8032-4771-0. Dewey:796.357/0973. LCCN:94-020992.
Audience: **u,f.** *Choice, 1996.*

Wieting, Stephen G. (Editor) **GV706.5.S6942 2001**
Sport and Memory in North America. Trade Paper. Taylor & Francis Group. Philadelphia, PA. 2001. 280p. Sport in the Global Society Ser. ISBN:0-7146-8205-5, ISBN13: 978-0-7146-8205-1. Dewey:306.4/83/097. LCCN:2001-028808.
Audience: **u,f.** *Choice, 2002.*

Wiggins, David K. (Editor) **GV583.S6823 1994**
Sport in America: From Wicked Amusement to National Obsession. Trade Paper. Human Kinetics Publishers. Champaign, IL. 1994. 36p. ISBN:0-87322-520-1, ISBN13: 978-0-87322-520-5. Dewey:796/.0973. LCCN:94-016363.
Audience: **g,l,u,f.**

Wigglesworth, Neil **GV795**
A Social History of English Rowing. Trade Paper. Taylor & Francis Group. Abingdon, 1992. 248p. ISBN:0-7146-3415-8, ISBN13: 978-0-7146-3415-9. Dewey:797.1230942. LCCN:91-003481.
Audience: **u,f.**

Williams, Jack **GV928.G7W54 1999**
Cricket and England: A Cultural and Social History of Cricket of the Inter-War Years. Paper over Boards. Taylor & Francis Group. Abingdon, 1999. 218p. Sport in the Global Society Ser., No. 8 ISBN:0-7146-4861-2, ISBN13: 978-0-7146-4861-3. Dewey:796.358/0942. LCCN:98-047285.
Audience: **u,f.** *Choice, 1999.*

Williams, Jean **GV944.5**
A History of Women's Football: Gender, Power and the Rise of a Global Game. Trade Paper. Routledge. New York, NY. 2003. 240p. ISBN:0-415-26338-7, ISBN13: 978-0-415-26338-2. Dewey:796.3/34/082.
Audience: **u,f.**

Wright, Russell O. **GV863.A1W755 1999**
A Tale of Two Leagues: How Baseball Changed as the Rules, Balls, Franchises, Stadiums and Players Changed, 1900-1998. Cloth Text. McFarland & Company, Incorporated Publishers. Jefferson, NC. 1999. 224p. ISBN:0-7864-0712-3, ISBN13: 978-0-7864-0712-5. Dewey:796.357/0973. LCCN:99-40307.
Audience: **l,u,f.** *Choice, 2000.*

Wushanley, Ying **GV709.18.U6W87 2004**
Playing Nice and Losing: The Struggle for Control of Women's Intercollegiate Athletics, 1960-2000. Trade Cloth. Syracuse University Press. Syracuse, NY. 2004. xviii, 225p. Sports and Entertainment Ser. ISBN:0-8156-3045-X, ISBN13: 978-0-8156-3045-6. Dewey:796/.082. LCCN:2003-024656.
Audience: **g,l,u,f.** *Choice, 2004.*

Zang, David **GV706.5.Z35 2001**
SportsWars: Athletes in the Age of Aquarius. Trade Cloth. University of Arkansas Press. Fayetteville, AR. 2001. xxii, 180p. ISBN:1-55728-713-9, ISBN13: 978-1-55728-713-7. Dewey:303.4/83/0973. LCCN:2001-003221.
Audience: **g,l,u,f.** *Choice, 2002.*

Zang, David W. **GV865.W34Z35 1995**
Fleet Walker's Divided Heart: The Life of Baseball's First Black Major Leaguer. Trade Cloth. University of Nebraska Press. Lincoln, NE. 1995. 171p. ISBN:0-8032-4913-6, ISBN13: 978-0-8032-4913-4. Dewey:796.357/092 B. LCCN:94-033517.
Audience: **g,l,u,f.** *Choice, 1996.*

Sport Studies > Literature (Including Sports Writing)

Blaustein, Noah (Editor) **PS595.S78M68 2001**
Motion: American Sports Poems. John Edgar Wideman (Foreword by). Trade Paper. University of Iowa Press. Iowa City, IA. 2001. 274p. ISBN:0-87745-755-7, ISBN13: 978-0-87745-755-8. Dewey:811.008/0355. LCCN:00-050938.
Audience: **g,l,u.**

Cocchiarale, Michael & Emmert, Scott (Editors) **PS169**
Upon Further Review: Sports in American Literature. Trade Cloth. Greenwood Publishing Group, Inc. Portsmouth, NH. 2004. 248p. ISBN:0-275-98050-2, ISBN13: 978-0-275-98050-4. Dewey:810.9357. LCCN:2004-040893.
Audience: **u,f.** *Choice, 2005.*

Dawidoff, Nicholas (Editor) **PS509.B37B37 2002**
Baseball: A Literary Anthology. Trade Cloth. Library of America, The. New York, NY. 2002. 721p. ISBN:1-931082-09-X, ISBN13: 978-1-931082-09-9. Dewey:810.8/0355. LCCN:2001-038654.
Audience: **l,u,f.**

Early, Gerald (Editor) **GV1132.A44 M83 1998**
Muhammad Ali Reader. Trade Cloth. HarperCollins Publishers. New York, NY. 1998. 320p. ISBN:0-88001-602-7, ISBN13: 978-0-88001-602-5. Dewey:796.83/092. LCCN:97-036846.
Audience: **u,f.**

Fountain, Charles **GV742.42.R53**
Sportswriter: The Life and Times of Grantland Rice. Trade Cloth. Replica Books. Bridgewater, NJ. 2000. 350p. ISBN:0-7351-0347-X, ISBN13: 978-0-7351-0347-4. Dewey:070.4/49796/092.B.
Audience: **g,l,u,f.**

Inabinett, Mark **GV742.42.R53I53 1994**
Grantland Rice and His Heroes: The Sportswriter As Mythmaker in the 1920s. Trade Paper. University of Tennessee Press. Knoxville, TN. 1994. 144p. ISBN:0-87049-849-5, ISBN13: 978-0-87049-849-7. Dewey:070.4/49796. LCCN:94-006088.
Audience: **l,u.** *Choice, 1995.*

Johnson, Don **PS310.A83J64 2004**
Sporting Muse: A Critical Study of Poetry About Athletes and Athletics. McFarland & Company, Incorporated Publishers. 2004. ISBN:0-7864-1767-6, ISBN13: 978-0-7864-1767-4.
Audience: **l,u,f.**

Kahn, Roger **GV742.42.K35A3 1997**
Memories of Summer: When Baseball Was an Art and Writing about It a Game. Trade Cloth. Hyperion Press. New York, NY. 1997. 304p. ISBN:0-7868-6190-8, ISBN13: 978-0-7868-6190-3. Dewey:[B]. LCCN:96-048711.
Audience: **g,l,u.** *Choice, 1997.*

Lowe, Benjamin **GV706.L59**
The Beauty of Sport: A Cross-Disciplinary Inquiry. Trade Cloth. Prentice-Hall. Upper Saddle, NJ. 1977. xix, 327p. ISBN:0-13-066589-4, ISBN13: 978-0-13-066589-8. Dewey:796/.01. LCCN:76-028308.
Audience: **u,f.** B

Messenger, Christian K. **PS374.S76M44 1990**
Sport and the Spirit of Play in Contemporary American Fiction. Trade Cloth. Columbia University Press. New York, NY. 1990. 473p. ISBN:0-231-07094-2, ISBN13: 978-0-231-07094-2. Dewey:813/.0109355. LCCN:89-029640.
Audience: **u,f.**

Morrison, Alec (Editor) **GV965.I46 1994**
The Impossible Art of Golf: An Anthology of Golf Writing. Trade Cloth. Oxford University Press, Inc. New York, NY. 1994. 328p. ISBN:0-19-211698-3, ISBN13: 978-0-19-211698-7. Dewey:796.352. LCCN:94-008831.
Audience: **l,u,f.**

Oates, Joyce Carol **GV1133 .O2 1987**
On Boxing. Trade Cloth. Doubleday Publishing. New York, NY. 1987. ISBN:0-385-23890-8, ISBN13: 978-0-385-23890-8. Dewey:796.8/3/0973. LCCN:86-019710.
Audience: **l,u,f.**

Oriard, Michael **PS169.P55 O75 1991**
Sporting with the Gods: The Rhetoric of Play and Game in American Literature. Trade Cloth. Cambridge University Press. New York, NY. 1991. 608p. Cambridge Studies in Latin American LIterature and Culture, No. 45 ISBN:0-521-39113-X, ISBN13: 978-0-521-39113-9. Dewey:810.9/355. LCCN:90-044788.
Audience: **u,f.**

Oriard, Michael **92-42840 [GV]**
Reading Football: How the Popular Press Created an American Spectacle. Alan Trachtenberg (Foreword by). Trade Paper. University of North Carolina Press. Chapel Hill, NC. 1998. 352p. Cultural Studies of the United States ISBN:0-8078-4751-8, ISBN13: 978-0-8078-4751-0. Dewey:796.3230973. LCCN:92-042840.
Audience: **u,f.** *Choice, 1994.*

Rapoport, Ron (Editor) **GV709**
A Kind of Grace: A Treasury of Sportswriting by Women. Trade Paper. RDR Books. Muskegon, MI. 1994. 400p. ISBN:1-57143-013-X, ISBN13: 978-1-57143-013-7. Dewey:796/.082. LCCN:94-060001.
Audience: **l,u,f.**

Shannon, Mike **GV863.A1**
Diamond Classics: Essays on 100 of the Best Baseball Books Ever Published. Paper Text. McFarland & Company, Incorporated Publishers. Jefferson, NC. 2003. 471p. ISBN:0-7864-1853-2, ISBN13: 978-0-7864-1853-4. Dewey:796.357/0973. LCCN:89-42571.
Audience: **u,f.** *Choice, 1989.*

Umphlett, Wiley L. (Editor) **PS169.S62A34 1990**
The Achievement of American Sport Literature: A Critical Appraisal. Trade Cloth. Fairleigh Dickinson University Press. Cranbury, NJ. 1991. 216p. ISBN:0-8386-3400-1, ISBN13: 978-0-8386-3400-4. Dewey:810.9/355. LCCN:89-046419.
Audience: **u,f.**

Vanderwerken, David L. & Wertz, Spencer K. (Editors) **GV706.S746 1985**
Sport Inside Out: Readings in Literature and Philosophy. Trade Cloth. Texas Christian University Press. Fort Worth, TX. 1985. 782p. ISBN:0-87565-003-1, ISBN13: 978-0-87565-003-6. Dewey:796/.01. LCCN:84-023951.
Audience: **u,f.** B *Choice, 1986.*

Westbrook, Deeanne **PS169.B36W47 1996**
Ground Rules: Baseball and Myth. Trade Paper. University of Illinois Press. Champaign, IL. 1996. 368p. ISBN:0-252-06529-8, ISBN13: 978-0-252-06529-3. Dewey:810.9/355. LCCN:95-004433.
Audience: **g,l,u,f.** *Choice, 1997.*

Sport Studies > Research. Theory

GV563
☐ Amateur Athletic Foundation of Los Angeles. http://www.aafla.org/
Audience: **g,l,u.**

Andrews, David L. (Editor), et al. **GV557**
Qualitative Methods in Sports Studies. Daniel S. Mason & Michael L. Silk (Editors). Trade Paper, Perfect. Berg Publishers. Oxford, 2005. 128p. Sport Commerce and Culture Ser. ISBN:1-85973-789-7, ISBN13: 978-1-85973-789-7. Dewey:796/.07/2. LCCN:2005-017084.
Audience: **l,u,f.** *Choice, 2006.*

Arbena, Joseph L. (Compiled by) **Z7515**
Latin American Sport: An Annotated Bibliography, 1988-1998. Cloth Text. Greenwood Publishing Group, Inc. Portsmouth, NH. 1999. 264p. Bibliographies and Indexes on Sports History Ser., Vol. 3 ISBN:0-313-29611-1, ISBN13: 978-0-313-29611-6. Dewey:016.796/098. LCCN:99-011260.
Audience: **u,f.** *Choice, 2000.*

Biddle, Stuart J. H. (Editor) **GV706.4.E87 1995**
European Perspectives on Exercise and Sport Psychology. Trade Cloth. Human Kinetics Publishers. Champaign, IL. 1995. 360p. ISBN:0-87322-826-X, ISBN13: 978-0-87322-826-8. Dewey:796/.01/094. LCCN:94-032258.
Audience: **u,f.** *Choice, 1996.*

Deardorff, Donald L. II **GV704**
Sports: A Reference Guide and Critical Commentary, 1980-1999. Cloth Text. Greenwood Publishing Group, Inc. Portsmouth, NH. 2000. 376p. American Popular Culture Ser. ISBN:0-313-30445-9, ISBN13: 978-0-313-30445-3. Dewey:796/.09/048. LCCN:00-020466.
Audience: **g,l,u,f.** *Choice, 2001.*

Ghent, Gretchen (Editor) **GV568**
Sport and Information Technology, Vol. 4. Trade Paper. Meyer & Meyer Sport, Ltd. Garsington, 2004. 192p. ISBN:1-84126-086-X, ISBN13: 978-1-84126-086-0. Dewey:796/.0285.
Audience: **g,l,u,f.**

Gratton, Bartlett & Rolf **GV567**
Encyclopedia of International Sports Studies. Ed. 3. Paper over Boards. Routledge. New York, NY. 2005. LVIII, 1526p. ISBN:0-415-27713-2, ISBN13: 978-0-415-27713-6. Dewey:796/.03.
Audience: **g,l,u,f.** *Choice, 2006.*

Gratton, Chris & Jones, Ian **GV557**
Research Methods for Sports Studies. Paper over Boards.

Routledge. New York, NY. 2003. 304p. ISBN:0-415-26877-X, ISBN13: 978-0-415-26877-6. Dewey:796/.07/2. LCCN:2003-046796.
Audience: **u,f.**

Hall, M. Ann **GV709.H32 1996**
Feminism and Sporting Bodies: Essays on Theory and Practice. Trade Paper. Human Kinetics Publishers. Champaign, IL. 1996. 144p. ISBN:0-87322-969-X, ISBN13: 978-0-87322-969-2. Dewey:796/.0194. LCCN:95-044480.
Audience: **u,f.** *Choice, 1996.*

Jones, Donald G. & Daley, Elaine L. **GV706**
Sports Ethics in America: A Bibliography, 1970-1990. Cloth Text. Greenwood Publishing Group, Inc. Portsmouth, NH. 1992. 320p. Bibliographies and Indexes in American History Ser., No. 21 ISBN:0-313-27767-2, ISBN13: 978-0-313-27767-2. Dewey:016.175. LCCN:91-047538.
Audience: **l,u,f.** *Choice, 1992.*

Morris, Lynn A. (Editor) **GV14.5**
Research about Leisure: Past, Present and Future. Ed. 2. Trade Paper. Sagamore Publishing, L.L.C.. Champaign, IL. 1994. 289p. ISBN:0-915611-96-1, ISBN13: 978-0-915611-96-6. Dewey:306.4812.
Audience: **u,f.**

Pope, Steven W. (Editor) **GV581.N48 1997**
The New American Sport History: Recent Approaches and Perspectives. Trade Paper. University of Illinois Press. Champaign, IL. 1996. 448p. Sport and Society Ser. ISBN:0-252-06567-0, ISBN13: 978-0-252-06567-5. Dewey:796/.0973. LCCN:96-006137.
Audience: **u,f.** *Choice, 1997.*

Scarrott, Martin **GV188.S66 1999**
Sport, Leisure and Tourism Information Sources: A Guide for Researchers. Cloth Text. Elsevier Science & Technology Books. Saint Louis, MO. 1999. 256p. ISBN:0-7506-3864-8, ISBN13: 978-0-7506-3864-7. Dewey:026.79. LCCN:99-218933.
Audience: **l,u,f.**

Sweet, Waldo E. **GV21.S94 1987**
Sport and Recreation in Ancient Greece: A Sourcebook With Translations. Erich Segal (Foreword by). Trade Cloth. Oxford University Press, Inc. New York, NY. 1987. 288p. ISBN:0-19-504126-7, ISBN13: 978-0-19-504126-2. Dewey:796/.0938. LCCN:86-018209.
Audience: **u,f.** *Choice, 1988.*

Sport Studies > Sociology

Adelson, Bruce **GV875.A1A34 1999**
Brushing Back Jim Crow: The Integration of the Minor Leagues in the American South. Trade Cloth. University Press of Virginia. Charlottesville, VA. 1999. 288p. ISBN:0-8139-1884-7, ISBN13: 978-0-8139-1884-6. Dewey:796.357/64/0975. LCCN:98-045122.
Audience: **l,u,f.**

Anderson, Lars **GV885,4.A53 1998**
Pickup Artists: Street Basketball in America. Trade Cloth. Analytical Psychology Club of San Francisco, Inc. San Francisco, CA. 1998. 240p. ISBN:1-85984-235-6, ISBN13: 978-1-85984-235-5. Dewey:796.3/23/0973. LCCN:98-017460.
Audience: **g,l,u,f.** *Choice, 1998.*

Arbena, Joseph L. (Compiled by) **Z7515**
Latin American Sport: An Annotated Bibliography, 1988-1998. Cloth Text. Greenwood Publishing Group, Inc. Portsmouth, NH. 1999. 264p. Bibliographies and Indexes on Sports History Ser., Vol. 3 ISBN:0-313-29611-1, ISBN13: 978-0-313-29611-6. Dewey:016.796/098. LCCN:99-011260.
Audience: **u,f.** *Choice, 2000.*

Ardell, Jean Hastings **GV880.7.A73 2005**
Breaking into Baseball: Women and the National Pasttime. Ila Borders (Foreword by). Trade Paper, Perfect, Paper over Boards. Southern Illinois University Press. Carbondale, IL. 2005. 278p. Writing Baseball Ser. ISBN:0-8093-2627-2, ISBN13: 978-0-8093-2627-3. Dewey:796.357/082. LCCN:2004-019010.
Audience: **g,l,u,f.** *Choice, 2005.*

Armstrong, Gary **GV943.9.F35A76 1998**
Football Hooligans: Knowing the Score. Trade Paper. Berg Publishers. Oxford, 1998. 320p. Explorations in Anthropology Ser. ISBN:1-85973-957-1, ISBN13: 978-1-85973-957-0. Dewey:306.4/83/0941. LCCN:98-128792.
Audience: **g,l,u,f.** *Choice, 1998.*

Baker, Aaron & Boyd, Todd **GV742.O88 1997**
Out of Bounds: Sports, Media and the Politics of Identity. Trade Paper. Indiana University Press. Bloomington, IN. 1997. 240p. ISBN:0-253-21095-X, ISBN13: 978-0-253-21095-1. Dewey:070.4/49796. LCCN:96-019729.
Audience: **u,f.** *Choice, 1997.*

Baker, William J. **GV571.B25 1988**
Sports in the Western World. Trade Paper. University of Illinois Press. Champaign, IL. 1988. 368p. Sport and Society Ser. ISBN:0-252-06042-3, ISBN13: 978-0-252-06042-7. Dewey:796/.09. LCCN:88-018838.
Audience: **g,l,u.** B

Bale, John **GV706.8.B35 2002**
Sports Geography. Ed. 2. Trade Paper. Routledge. New York, NY. 2002. 208p. ISBN:0-419-25230-4, ISBN13: 978-0-419-25230-6. Dewey:796. LCCN:2002-068169.
Audience: **l,u.** *Choice, 1990.*

Bale, John & Vertinsky, Patricia A. (Editors) **GV401**
Sites of Sport: Space, Place, Experience. Paper over Boards. Taylor & Francis Group. Philadelphia, PA. 2004. 280p. ISBN:0-7146-5343-8, ISBN13: 978-0-7146-5343-3. Dewey:306.4/83.
Audience: **u,f.**

Barnett, Steven **GV742.3 .B37 1990**
Games and Sets: The Changing Face of Sport on Television. Trade Paper. BFI Publishing. London, 1990. 224p. ISBN:0-85170-268-6, ISBN13: 978-0-85170-268-1. Dewey:302.234/5. LCCN:91-105439.
Audience: **u,f.** *Choice, 1991.*

Benedict, Jeff **GV885.515.N37 B46**
Out of Bounds: Inside the NBA's Culture of Rape, Violence, and Crime. Trade Paper. HarperCollins Publishers. New York,

NY. 2005. 304p. ISBN:0-06-072604-0, ISBN13: 978-0-06-072604-1. Dewey:364.3/088/79632.
Audience: **g,l,u,f.**

Birrell, Susan & Cole, Cheryl L. (Editors) **GV709.W577 1994**
Women, Sport, and Culture. Trade Cloth. Human Kinetics Publishers. Champaign, IL. 1994. 416p. ISBN:0-87322-650-X, ISBN13: 978-0-87322-650-9. Dewey:796/.0194. LCCN:93-038013.
Audience: **u,f.** *Choice, 1995.*

Birrell, Susan & McDonald, Mary G. (Editors) **GV706.5.R42 2000**
Reading Sport: Critical Essays on Power and Representation. Paper Text. Northeastern University Press. Boston, MA. 2000. 326p. ISBN:1-55553-429-5, ISBN13: 978-1-55553-429-5. Dewey:306.4/83/0973. LCCN:99-088217.
Audience: **u,f.** *Choice, 2000.*

Bissinger, H. G. **GV958.P47 B57 2004**
Friday Night Lights: A Town, a Team, and a Dream. Paper Text. Da Capo Press, Inc. Cambridge, MA. 2004. 416p. ISBN:0-306-81425-0, ISBN13: 978-0-306-81425-9. Dewey:796.332.
Audience: **g,l,u,f.**

Bloom, John & Willard, Michael Nevin (Editors) **GV706.32.S75 2002**
Sports Matters: Race, Recreation, and Culture. Trade Paper. New York University Press. New York, NY. 2002. 280p. ISBN:0-8147-9882-9, ISBN13: 978-0-8147-9882-9. Dewey:306.4/83. LCCN:2002-004918.
Audience: **g,l,u,f.** *Choice, 2003.*

Bodo, Peter **GV995.B6832 1995**
The Courts of Babylon: Tales of Greed and Glory in the Harsh New High-Stakes World of Professional Tennis. Trade Cloth. Simon & Schuster. New York, NY. 1995. 480p. ISBN:0-684-81296-7, ISBN13: 978-0-684-81296-0. Dewey:796.342/64. LCCN:95-014760.
Audience: **g,l,u,f.** *Choice, 1995.*

Bolin, Anne & Granskog, Jane (Editors) **GV439.A84 2003**
Athletic Intruders: Ethnographic Research on Women, Culture, and Exercise. Paper Text. State University of New York Press. Albany, NY. 2003. x, 294p. Suny Series, Sport, Culture, and Social Relations Ser. ISBN:0-7914-5584-X, ISBN13: 978-0-7914-5584-5. Dewey:306.4/83. LCCN:2002-023131.
Audience: **u,f.** *Choice, 2003.*

Boyle, Raymond & Haynes, Richard **GV742.B69 2000**
Power Play: Sport, the Media and Popular Culture. Trade Paper. Longman Publishing Group. White Plains, NY. 2000. 256p. ISBN:0-582-36939-8, ISBN13: 978-0-582-36939-9. Dewey:306.4/83. LCCN:99-038838.
Audience: **u,f.**

Brackenridge, Celia **GV706.32.B73 2001**
Spoilsports: Understanding and Preventing Sexual Exploitation in Sport. Trade Paper. Routledge. New York, NY. 2001. 304p. Ethics and Sport Ser. ISBN:0-419-25780-2, ISBN13: 978-0-419-25780-6. Dewey:796/.082. LCCN:00-068037.
Audience: **u,f.**

Brookes, Rod **GV742.B76 2002**
Representing Sport. Trade Paper. Oxford University Press, Inc. New York, NY. 2002. 184p. A Hodder Arnold Publication ISBN:0-340-74052-3, ISBN13: 978-0-340-74052-1. Dewey:796. LCCN:2002-510305.
Audience: **l,u.** *Choice, 2002.*

Brooks, Dana D. & Althouse, Ronald C. (Editors) **GV706.32**
Racism in College Athletics: The African-American Athlete's Experience. Ed. 2. Trade Cloth. Fitness Information Technology, Inc. Morgantown, WV. 1999. 352p. ISBN:1-885693-19-2, ISBN13: 978-1-885693-19-8. Dewey:796/.0973.
Audience: **g,l,u,f.**

Carroll, John M. **GV939.F29**
Fritz Pollard: Pioneer in Racial Advancement. Trade Paper. University of Illinois Press. Champaign, IL. 1998. 328p. Sport and Society Ser. ISBN:0-252-06799-1, ISBN13: 978-0-252-06799-0. Dewey:796.332/092 B.
Audience: **l,u.** *Choice, 1992.*

Chandler, Timothy J. L. & Nauright, John (Editors) **GV945.85.P75M36 1999**
Making the Rugby World: Race, Gender, Commerce. Trade Paper. Taylor & Francis Group. Abingdon, 1999. 256p. Sport in the Global Society Ser., No. 10 ISBN:0-7146-4411-0, ISBN13: 978-0-7146-4411-0. Dewey:796.333. LCCN:99-027732.
Audience: **u,f.** *Choice, 2000.*

Coakley, Jay J. & Donnelly, Peter **GV706.5.I55 1999**
Inside Sports: Using Sociology to Understand Athletes and Sport Experiences. Trade Paper. Routledge. New York, NY. 1999. 272p. ISBN:0-415-17089-3, ISBN13: 978-0-415-17089-5. Dewey:306.4/83. LCCN:98-036508.
Audience: **u,f.** *Choice, 2000.*

Cohen, Greta L. (Editor) **GV709.18.U6**
Women in Sport: Issues and Controversies. Trade Paper. SAGE Publications, Inc. Thousand Oaks, CA. 1993. 360p. ISBN:0-8039-4980-4, ISBN13: 978-0-8039-4980-5. Dewey:796/.082/0973. LCCN:93-006510.
Audience: **g,l,f.** *Choice, 1993.*

Collins, Tony **GV945.9.G7**
Rugby's Great Split: Class, Culture and the Origins of Rugby League Football. Trade Paper. Woburn Press. Andover, 1998. 304p. Sport in the Global Society Ser. ISBN:0-7146-4424-2, ISBN13: 978-0-7146-4424-0. Dewey:796.333/8/0941.
Audience: **u,f.** *Choice, 1999.*

Collins, Tony & Vamplew, Wray **RC1245**
Mud, Sweat and Beers: A Cultural History of Sport and Alcohol. Trade Paper. Berg Publishers. Oxford, 2002. 224p. Global Sport Cultures Ser. ISBN:1-85973-558-4, ISBN13: 978-1-85973-558-9. Dewey:362.292/088/796. LCCN:2001-008221.
Audience: **g,l,u,f.** *Choice, 2003.*

Cozens, Frederick W. & Stumpf, Florence S. **GV583 .C68 1976**
Sports in American Life. Trade Cloth. Ayer Company Publishers, Inc. Manchester, NH. 1976. America in Two

Centuries Ser. ISBN:0-405-07681-9, ISBN13: 978-0-405-07681-7. Dewey:796/.0973. LCCN:75-022810.
Audience: **g,l,u.**

Crosset, Todd W. **GV966.C76 1995**
Outsiders in the Clubhouse: The World of Women's Professional Golf. Cloth Text. State University of New York Press. Albany, NY. 1995. 276p. SUNY Series on Sport, Culture, and Social Relations ISBN:0-7914-2489-8, ISBN13: 978-0-7914-2489-6. Dewey:796.352. LCCN:94-027916.
Audience: **g,u,f.** *Choice, 1996.*

Darby, Paul **GV944.A4D37 2001**
Africa, Football and FIFA: Politics, Colonialism and Resistance. Trade Paper. Taylor & Francis Group. Abingdon, 2002. 256p. Sport in the Global Society Ser., No. 23 ISBN:0-7146-8029-X, ISBN13: 978-0-7146-8029-3. Dewey:796.334/096. LCCN:2001-002915.
Audience: **u,f.** *Choice, 2002.*

Dunning, Eric **GV706.5.D85 1999**
Sport Matters: Sociological Studies of Sport, Violence, and Civilisation. Trade Paper. Routledge. New York, NY. 1999. 296p. ISBN:0-415-09378-3, ISBN13: 978-0-415-09378-1. Dewey:306.4/83. LCCN:98-047958.
Audience: **u,f.** *Choice, 2000.*

Dunning, Eric G. (Editor), et al. **GV706.5.S75 1993**
The Sports Process: A Comparative and Developmental Approach. Joseph A. Maguire & Robert E. Pearton (Editors). Cloth Text. Human Kinetics Publishers. Champaign, IL. 1993. 334p. ISBN:0-87322-419-1, ISBN13: 978-0-87322-419-2. Dewey:306.483. LCCN:92-029998.
Audience: **u,f.** *Choice, 1993.*

Dunning, Eric (Editor), et al. **GV943.9.F35F53 2002**
Fighting Fans: Football Hooliganism as a World Phenomenon. Patrick Murphy, Ivan Waddington & Antonio E. Astrinakis (Editors). Trade Paper. University College Dublin Press. Dublin, 2002. 27p. ISBN:1-900621-74-6, ISBN13: 978-1-900621-74-8. Dewey:306.4/83. LCCN:2003-464716.
Audience: **u,f.** *Choice, 2003.*

Dyreson, Mark **GV706.35.D97 1998**
Making the American Team: Sport, Culture, and the Olympic Experience. Trade Paper. University of Illinois Press. Champaign, IL. 1997. 288p. Sport and Society Ser. ISBN:0-252-06654-5, ISBN13: 978-0-252-06654-2. Dewey:796/.0973. LCCN:97-004663.
Audience: **u,f.** *Choice, 1998.*

Eitzen, D. Stanley **GV706.5.S733 2005**
Sport in Contemporary Society (P): An Anthology. Ed. 7. Trade Paper. Paradigm Publishers. Boulder, CO. 2005. 368p. ISBN:1-59451-047-4, ISBN13: 978-1-59451-047-2. Dewey:306.4/83. LCCN:2004-005610.
Audience: **g,l,u,f.**

Elias, Norbert & Dunning, Eric **GV706.5**
The Quest for Excitement: Sport and Leisure in the Civilizing Process. Paper Text. Blackwell Publishing, Inc. Malden, MA. 1994. 314p. ISBN:0-631-19219-0, ISBN13: 978-0-631-19219-0. Dewey:306/.483.
Audience: **l,u.** *Choice, 1987.*

Elias, Robert (Editor) **GV867.64.B37 2001**
Baseball and the American Dream: Race, Class, Gender and the National Pastime. Cloth Text. M. E. Sharpe Inc. Armonk, NY. 2001. 328p. ISBN:0-7656-0763-8, ISBN13: 978-0-7656-0763-8. Dewey:306.4/83. LCCN:00-066140.
Audience: **l,u,f.**

Entine, Jon, et al. **GV583**
Taboo: Why Black Athletes Dominate Sports and Why We're Afraid to Talk about It. Gary Salles & Jay T. Kearney (Authors). Trade Paper. PublicAffairs. New York, NY. 2000. 400p. ISBN:1-58648-026-X, ISBN13: 978-1-58648-026-4. Dewey:796/.089/96073. LCCN:99-041889.
Audience: **g,l,u.**

Gatz, Margaret (Editor), et al. **GV706.5.P365 2002**
Paradoxes of Youth and Sport. Michael A. Messner & Sandra J. Ball-Rokeach (Editors). Paper Text. State University of New York Press. Albany, NY. 2002. 320p. SUNY Series on Sport, Culture, and Social Relations ISBN:0-7914-5324-3, ISBN13: 978-0-7914-5324-7. Dewey:306.4/83. LCCN:2001-042646.
Audience: **l,u,f.** *Choice, 2003, 2002.*

Gerdy, John R. **GV583.G47 2002**
Sports: The All-American Addiction. Trade Cloth. University Press of Mississippi. Jackson, MS. 2006. 208p. ISBN:1-57806-452-X, ISBN13: 978-1-57806-452-6. Dewey:306.4/83/0973. LCCN:2001-046783.
Audience: **g,l,u,f.** *Choice, 2002.*

Gillmeister, Heiner **GV1002.95.E85**
Tennis: A Cultural History. Trade Paper. New York University Press. New York, NY. 1998. 320p. ISBN:0-8147-3121-X, ISBN13: 978-0-8147-3121-5. Dewey:796.342/094.
Audience: **g,l,u,f.** *Choice, 1999.*

Giulianotti, Richard **GV943.9.S64G576 1999**
Football: A Sociology of the Global Game. Trade Paper. Polity Press. Cambridge, 1999. 240p. ISBN:0-7456-1769-7, ISBN13: 978-0-7456-1769-5. Dewey:306.4/83. LCCN:99-011069.
Audience: **u,f.** *Choice, 2000.*

Giulianotti, Richard **GV706.5**
Sport: A Critical Sociology. Trade Cloth. Polity Press. Cambridge, 2005. 264p. ISBN:0-7456-2545-2, ISBN13: 978-0-7456-2545-4. Dewey:306.483. LCCN:2005-280308.
Audience: **u,f.**

Giulianotti, Richard (Editor) **GV706.5.S69424 2004**
Sport and Modern Social Theorists: Theorizing Homo Ludens. Trade Paper. Palgrave Macmillan. New York, NY. 2004. 264p. ISBN:0-333-80079-6, ISBN13: 978-0-333-80079-9. Dewey:306.4/83. LCCN:2004-050021.
Audience: **g,l,u,f.** *Choice, 2005.*

Griffin, Patricia J. **GV708.8.G75 1998**
Strong Women, Deep Closets: Lesbians and Homophobia in Sport. Donna A. Lopiano (Foreword by). Trade Paper. Human Kinetics Publishers. Champaign, IL. 1998. 264p. ISBN:0-88011-729-X, ISBN13: 978-0-88011-729-6. Dewey:796/.086/643. LCCN:97-032363.
Audience: **g,l,u,f.** *Choice, 1998.*

Grundy, Pamela **GV584.N8G78 2001**
Learning to Win: Sports, Education and Social Change in Twentieth-Century North Carolina. Trade Paper. University of

North Carolina Press. Chapel Hill, NC. 2001. 392p. Fred W. Morrison Series in Southern Studies ISBN:0-8078-4934-0, ISBN13: 978-0-8078-4934-7. Dewey:796/.09756/0904. LCCN:00-048928.
Audience: **g,l,u,f.** *Choice, 2001.*

Gruneau, Richard **GV706.5.G78 1999**
Class, Sports, and Social Development. R. W. Connell (Foreword by). Trade Paper. Human Kinetics Publishers. Champaign, IL. 1999. 216p. ISBN:0-7360-0033-X, ISBN13: 978-0-7360-0033-8. Dewey:306.4/83. LCCN:98-040543.
Audience: **u,f.**

Guttmann, Allen **GV706.5.G87 2004**
From Ritual to Record: The Nature of Modern Sports. Ed. 2. Trade Paper. Kegan Paul International, Ltd. London, 2004. 224p. ISBN:0-231-13341-3, ISBN13: 978-0-231-13341-8. Dewey:306.4/83. LCCN:2004-044497.
Audience: **g,l,u,f.** B

Guttmann, Allen **GV583.G87 1988**
A Whole New Ball Game: An Interpretation of American Sports. Trade Cloth. University of North Carolina Press. Chapel Hill, NC. 1988. x, 233p. ISBN:0-8078-1786-4, ISBN13: 978-0-8078-1786-5. Dewey:796/.0973. LCCN:87-026131.
Audience: **g,l,u,f.** *Choice, 1988.*

Halladay, Eric **GV795.H24 1990**
Rowing in England: A Social History: The Amateur Debate. James A. Mangan (Editor). Cloth Text. Manchester University Press. Manchester, 1990. 256p. International Studies in the History of Sport ISBN:0-7190-2605-9, ISBN13: 978-0-7190-2605-8. Dewey:797.1/22/0942. LCCN:90-038505.
Audience: **u,f.** *Choice, 1991.*

Hardy, Stephen **GV584.5.B6H37 2003**
How Boston Played: Sport, Recreation, and Community, 1865-1915. Trade Paper. University of Tennessee Press. Knoxville, TN. 2003. 312p. Sport and Popular Culture Ser. ISBN:1-57233-218-2, ISBN13: 978-1-57233-218-8. Dewey:796/.09744/6109034. LCCN:2002-043100.
Audience: **g,l,u,f.**

Hargreaves, Jennifer **GV709.18.G7H37 1994**
Sporting Females: Critical Issues in the History and Sociology of Women's Sports. Trade Paper. Routledge. New York, NY. 1994. 344p. ISBN:0-415-07028-7, ISBN13: 978-0-415-07028-7. Dewey:796.0194. LCCN:93-024575.
Audience: **u,f.**

Hargreaves, John **GV706.5.H36 1986**
Sport, Power and Culture: A Social and Historical Analysis of Popular Sports in Britain. Cloth Text. Palgrave Macmillan. New York, NY. 1986. 288p. ISBN:0-312-75324-1, ISBN13: 978-0-312-75324-5. Dewey:306/.483/0941. LCCN:86-015503.
Audience: **u,f.** *Choice, 1987.*

Hartmann-Tews, Ilse **GV709.S66 2003**
Sport and Women: Social Issues in International Perspective. Gertrud Pfister (Editor). Paper over Boards. Routledge. New York, NY. 2002. 304p. ISBN:0-415-24627-X, ISBN13: 978-0-415-24627-9. Dewey:796/.082. LCCN:2002-073982.
Audience: **g,l,u,f.** *Choice, 2003.*

Hess, Rob & Stewart, Bob (Editors) **GV947.M67 1998**
More Than a Game: An Unauthorized History of Australian Rules Football. Martin Flanagan (Foreword by). Trade Paper. Melbourne University Publishing. Carlton, VIC. 1998. 320p. ISBN:0-522-84772-2, ISBN13: 978-0-522-84772-7. Dewey:796.336. LCCN:98-221833.
Audience: **u,f.**

Heywood, Leslie & Dworkin, Shari L. **GV709.18.U6H49 2003**
Built to Win: The Female Athlete As Cultural Icon. Trade Paper. University of Minnesota Press. Minneapolis, MN. 2003. 272p. Sport and Culture Ser., Vol. 5 ISBN:0-8166-3624-9, ISBN13: 978-0-8166-3624-2. Dewey:796/.082. LCCN:2002-156528.
Audience: **g,l,f.** *Choice, 2004.*

Hietala, Thomas R. **GV1131.H64 2002**
The Fight of the Century: Jack Johnson, Joe Louis, and the Struggle for Racial Equality. Trade Cloth. M. E. Sharpe Inc. Armonk, NY. 2002. 386p. Social and Cultural History Ser. ISBN:0-7656-0722-0, ISBN13: 978-0-7656-0722-5. Dewey:796.83/092/2. LCCN:2001-049165.
Audience: **u,f.** *Choice, 2003.*

Hoberman, John **GV583**
Darwin's Athletes: How Sport has Damaged Black America and Preserved the Myth of Race. Cloth Text. Houghton Mifflin Company. New York, NY. 1997. 288p. ISBN:0-465-01557-3, ISBN13: 978-0-465-01557-3. Dewey:796/.089/96073.
Audience: **u,f.** *Choice, 1997.*

Houlihan, Barrie (Editor) **GV706.5**
Sport and Society: A Student Introduction. Cloth Text. SAGE Publications, Inc. Thousand Oaks, CA. 2003. 400p. ISBN:0-7619-7033-9, ISBN13: 978-0-7619-7033-0. Dewey:306.4/83. LCCN:2002-111618.
Audience: **g,l,u,f.**

Howell, Colin **GV863.15.M37H69 1995**
Northern Sandlots: A Social History of Maritime Baseball. Trade Paper. University of Toronto Press. Toronto, ON. 1995. 288p. ISBN:0-8020-6942-8, ISBN13: 978-0-8020-6942-9. Dewey:796.357/09715. LCCN:95-178431.
Audience: **u,f.** *Choice, 1995.*

Ingham, Alan G. & Loy, John W. Jr. (Editors) **GV706.5.S7337 1993**
Sport in Social Development: Traditions, Transitions, and Transformations. Trade Cloth. Human Kinetics Publishers. Champaign, IL. 1993. 296p. ISBN:0-87322-467-1, ISBN13: 978-0-87322-467-3. Dewey:306.483. LCCN:92-038866.
Audience: **g,l,u,f.**

Isenberg, Michael T. **GV1132.M84**
John L. Sullivan and His America. Trade Paper. University of Illinois Press. Champaign, IL. 1994. 480p. ISBN:0-252-06434-8, ISBN13: 978-0-252-06434-0. Dewey:796.8/3/0924 B.
Audience: **l,u,f.** *Choice, 1988.*

Jay, Kathryn **GV706.5.J39 2004**
More Than Just a Game: Sports in American Life since 1945. Trade Cloth. Kegan Paul International, Ltd. London, 2004. 304p. Columbia Histories of Modern American Life Ser. ISBN:0-231-12534-8, ISBN13: 978-0-231-12534-5. Dewey:796.357/0973/09045. LCCN:2004-044498.
Audience: **g,l,u,f.** *Choice, 2005.*

Kerr, John **GV706.7.K47 2004**
Rethinking Aggression and Violence in Sport. Trade Paper. Routledge. New York, NY. 2004. 176p. ISBN:0-415-28664-6, ISBN13: 978-0-415-28664-0. Dewey:306.4/83. LCCN:2004-048230.
Audience: **u,f.**

Kidd, Bruce **GV585.K53 1996**
The Struggle for Canadian Sport. Trade Paper. University of Toronto Press. Toronto, ON. 1996. 323p. ISBN:0-8020-7664-5, ISBN13: 978-0-8020-7664-9. Dewey:796/.0971. LCCN:96-173457.
Audience: **g,l,u,f.** *Choice, 1997.*

King, Anthony **GV944.E9**
The European Ritual: Football in the New Europe. Trade Cloth. Ashgate Publishing, Ltd. Aldershot, 2003. 302p. ISBN:0-7546-3652-6, ISBN13: 978-0-7546-3652-6. Dewey:796.334/094. LCCN:2003-045350.
Audience: **g,l,u,f.** *Choice, 2004.*

King, C. Richard & Springwood, Charles Fruehling **GV706.32.K52 2001**
Beyond the Cheers: Race as Spectacle in College Sport. Paper Text. State University of New York Press. Albany, NY. 2001. x, 214p. Series on Sport, Culture, and Social Relations ISBN:0-7914-5006-6, ISBN13: 978-0-7914-5006-2. Dewey:796.04/3/08900973. LCCN:00-054797.
Audience: **u,f.** *Choice, 2001.*

King, C. Richard & Springwood, Charles F. (Editors) **GV714.5.K56 2001**
Team Spirits: The Native American Mascots Controversy. Vine Deloria Jr. (Foreword by). Trade Paper. University of Nebraska Press. Lincoln, NE. 2001. 356p. ISBN:0-8032-7798-9, ISBN13: 978-0-8032-7798-4. Dewey:306.4/83. LCCN:00-059968.
Audience: **u,f.** *Choice, 2001.*

Kinsella, John & Wark, McKenzie **GV742.S663 2003**
Sport, Media, Culture: Global and Local Dimensions. Neil Blain & Alina Bernstein (Editors). Trade Paper. Taylor & Francis Group. Abingdon, 2003. 272p. ISBN:0-7146-8261-6, ISBN13: 978-0-7146-8261-7. Dewey:070.4/49796. LCCN:2002-151346.
Audience: **g,l,u,f.**

Kirby, Sandra, et al. **GV709.2**
The Dome of Silence: Sexual Harrassment and Abuse in Sport. Lorraine Greaves & Olena Hankinsky (Authors). Trade Paper. Zed Books, Ltd. London, 2001. 192p. ISBN:1-85649-963-4, ISBN13: 978-1-85649-963-7. Dewey:305.9/796.
Audience: **g,l,u,f.**

Klein, Alan M. **GV546.5 .K54 1993**
Little Big Men: Bodybuilding Subculture and Gender Construction. Paper Text. State University of New York Press. Albany, NY. 1993. 326p. SUNY Series on Sport, Culture, and Social Relations ISBN:0-7914-1560-0, ISBN13: 978-0-7914-1560-3. Dewey:646.7/5/0973. LCCN:92-030816.
Audience: **u,f.**

Laker, Anthony (Editor) **GV706.5.S645 2001**
The Sociology of Sport and Physical Education: An Introductory Reader. Trade Paper. Routledge. New York, NY. 2001. 256p. ISBN:0-415-23594-4, ISBN13: 978-0-415-23594-5. Dewey:306.4/83. LCCN:2001-019961.
Audience: **g,l,u,f.** *Choice, 2002.*

Leonard, Wilbert Marcellus **GV706.5.L465 1998**
A Sociological Perspective of Sport. Ed. 5. Trade Paper. Benjamin-Cummings Publishing Company. San Francisco, CA. 1998. 450p. ISBN:0-205-27506-0, ISBN13: 978-0-205-27506-9. Dewey:306.4/83/0973. LCCN:97-047213.
Audience: **u,f.**

Levy, Alan H. **GV943.9.S64L48 2003**
Tackling Jim Crow: Racial Segregation in Professional Football. Paper Text. McFarland & Company, Incorporated Publishers. Jefferson, NC. 2003. 180p. ISBN:0-7864-1597-5, ISBN13: 978-0-7864-1597-7. Dewey:796.332/0896/073. LCCN:2003-005735.
Audience: **u,f.** *Choice, 2003.*

Lindqvist, Sven **GV546.5**
Bench Press. Trade Paper. Granta. New York, NY. 2003. 176p. ISBN:1-86207-572-7, ISBN13: 978-1-86207-572-6. Dewey:613.7/13. LCCN:2003-427636.
Audience: **g,l,u,f.**

Mandelbaum, Michael **GV706.5**
The Meaning of Sports: Why Americans Watch Baseball, Football, and Basketball and What They See When They Do. Trade Cloth. PublicAffairs. New York, NY. 2004. 352p. ISBN:1-58648-252-1, ISBN13: 978-1-58648-252-7. Dewey:306.4830973. LCCN:2003-070696.
Audience: **g,l,u.** *Choice, 2004.*

Mangan, James A. & Walvin, James (Editors) **HQ1090.7.G7**
Manliness and Morality: Middle-Class Masculinity in Britain and America, 1800-1940. Cloth Text. Manchester University Press. Manchester, 1991. 288p. ISBN:0-7190-2367-X, ISBN13: 978-0-7190-2367-5. Dewey:305.3/1/0941. LCCN:86-033923.
Audience: **u,f.** *Choice, 1988.*

Martin, Randy & Miller, Toby **GV706.5.S73896 1999**
Sportcult. Trade Paper. University of Minnesota Press. Minneapolis, MN. 1999. 304p. Cultural Politics Ser., Vol. 16 ISBN:0-8166-3184-0, ISBN13: 978-0-8166-3184-1. Dewey:306.4/83. LCCN:98-045941.
Audience: **u.** *Choice, 1999.*

Martin, Simon **GV943.9.S64**
Football and Fascism: The National Game under Mussolini. Trade Paper. Berg Publishers. Oxford, 2004. 288p. ISBN:1-85973-705-6, ISBN13: 978-1-85973-705-7. Dewey:796.334/0945/09043. LCCN:2004-020616.
Audience: **g,l,u,f.** *Choice, 2005.*

Mason, Tony **GV944.S64M27 1995**
Passion of the People: Football in Latin America. Trade Paper. Analytical Psychology Club of San Francisco, Inc. San Francisco, CA. 1995. 224p. Critical Studies in Latin American Culture ISBN:0-86091-667-7, ISBN13: 978-0-86091-667-3. Dewey:796.3/34/098. LCCN:95-163189.
Audience: **u,f.**

Massa, Mark S. **BX1406.2.M38 1999**
Catholics and American Culture: Fulton Sheen, Dorothy Day and the Notre Dame Football Team. Trade Cloth. Crossroad Publishing Company. New York, NY. 1999. 288p. ISBN:0-8245-1537-4, ISBN13: 978-0-8245-1537-9. Dewey:305.6/2073. LCCN:98-031072.
Audience: **u,f.** *Choice, 1999.*

McGimpsey, David **GV867.64.M34 2000**
Imagining Baseball: America's Pastime and Popular Culture. Trade Cloth. Indiana University Press. Bloomington, IN. 2000. 208p. ISBN:0-253-33696-1, ISBN13: 978-0-253-33696-5. Dewey:306.4/83. LCCN:99-043397.
Audience: **u,f.**

McKay, Jim, et al. **GV706.5.M365 2000**
Masculinities, Gender Relations, and Sport, Vol. 11. Michael A. Messner & Donald F. Sabo (Authors). Trade Paper. SAGE Publications, Inc. Thousand Oaks, CA. 2000. 344p. Sage Series on Men and Masculinity Ser. ISBN:0-7619-1272-X, ISBN13: 978-0-7619-1272-9. Dewey:796.081. LCCN:00-008019.
Audience: **u,f.** *Choice, 2001.*

Messner, Michael A. **GV706.32.M47 2003**
Taking the Field: Women, Men and Sports. Trade Paper. University of Minnesota Press. Minneapolis, MN. 2002. 280p. Sport and Culture Ser., Vol. 4 ISBN:0-8166-3449-1, ISBN13: 978-0-8166-3449-1. Dewey:796/.082. LCCN:2001-008548.
Audience: **g,l,u,f.** *Choice, 2003.*

Messner, Michael A. & Sabo, Donald F. **GV706.5.M47 1994**
Sex, Violence, and Power in Sports: Rethinking Masculinity. Trade Paper. Crossing Press, Incorporated, The. Berkeley, CA. 1994. 216p. ISBN:0-89594-688-2, ISBN13: 978-0-89594-688-1. Dewey:306.4/83. LCCN:94-018562.
Audience: **u,f.** *Choice, 1995.*

Miller, Patrick B. (Editor) **GV584.S68S66 2002**
The Sporting World of the Modern South. Trade Paper. University of Illinois Press. Champaign, IL. 2002. 368p. Sport and Society Ser. ISBN:0-252-07036-4, ISBN13: 978-0-252-07036-5. Dewey:306.4/83/0975. LCCN:2001-003997.
Audience: **u,f.** *Choice, 2003, 2002.*

Miller, Patrick B. & Wiggins, David K. (Editors) **GV706.32.S73 2004**
Sport and the Color Line: Black Athletes and Race Relations in Twentieth Century America. UK-B Format Paperback. Routledge. New York, NY. 2003. 400p. ISBN:0-415-94611-5, ISBN13: 978-0-415-94611-7. Dewey:796/.089/96073. LCCN:2003-014009.
Audience: **g,l,u,f.**

Moore, Pamela (Editor) **GV546.5.B85 1997**
Building Bodies. Paper Text. Rutgers University Press. Piscataway, NJ. 1997. 224p. ISBN:0-8135-2438-5, ISBN13: 978-0-8135-2438-2. Dewey:646.7/5. LCCN:96-049717.
Audience: **g,l,u,f.**

Mrozek, Donald J. **GV583**
Sport and American Mentality, 1880-1910. Paper Text. University of Tennessee Press. Knoxville, TN. 1983. 304p. ISBN:0-87049-395-7, ISBN13: 978-0-87049-395-9. Dewey:796/.0973. LCCN:83-003667.
Audience: **g,l,u,f.** B

Muggleton, David & Weinzierl, Rupert **GV721.6**
Post-Olympism?: Questioning Sport in the Twenty-First Century. John Bale & Mette Krogh Christensen (Editors). Trade Paper. Berg Publishers. Oxford, 2004. 256p. Global Sport Cultures Ser. ISBN:1-85973-719-6, ISBN13: 978-1-85973-719-4. Dewey:306.4/83/0905.
Audience: **u,f.**

Murphy, Shane M. **GV709.2.M873 1999**
The Cheers and the Tears: A Healthy Alternative to the Dark Side of Youth Sports Today. Trade Paper. John Wiley & Sons, Inc. Hoboken, NJ. 1999. 240p. ISBN:0-7879-4037-2, ISBN13: 978-0-7879-4037-9. Dewey:796/.083/0973. LCCN:98-025525.
Audience: **g,l,u,f.**

Nelson, Mariah B. **GV706.4.N45 1993**
The Stronger Women Get, the More Men Love Football: Sex and Sports in America. Trade Cloth. Harcourt Trade Publishers. New York, NY. 1994. x, 304p. ISBN:0-15-181393-0, ISBN13: 978-0-15-181393-3. Dewey:796/.01. LCCN:93-044358.
Audience: **g,l,f.**

Oppliger, Patrice A. **GV1196.4**
Wrestling and Hyper-Masculinity. Paper Text. McFarland & Company, Incorporated Publishers. Jefferson, NC. 2003. 211p. ISBN:0-7864-1692-0, ISBN13: 978-0-7864-1692-9. Dewey:796.812. LCCN:2003-025328.
Audience: **u,f.** *Choice, 2004.*

Oriard, Michael **92-42840 [GV]**
Reading Football: How the Popular Press Created an American Spectacle. Alan Trachtenberg (Foreword by). Trade Paper. University of North Carolina Press. Chapel Hill, NC. 1998. 352p. Cultural Studies of the United States ISBN:0-8078-4751-8, ISBN13: 978-0-8078-4751-0. Dewey:796.3230973. LCCN:92-042840.
Audience: **u,f.** *Choice, 1994.*

Park, Roberta J. & Mangan, James A. (Editors) **GV709.F66 1987**
From "Fair Sex" to Feminism: Sport and the Socialization of Women in the Industrial and Post-Industrial Eras. Paper over Boards. Taylor & Francis Group. Philadelphia, PA. 1987. 336p. ISBN:0-7146-3288-0, ISBN13: 978-0-7146-3288-9. Dewey:306.4/83. LCCN:86-017529.
Audience: **g,l,u,f.** *Choice, 1988.*

Pink, Sarah **GV1107.P535 1997**
Women and Bullfighting: Gender, Sex and the Consumption of Tradition. Trade Paper. Berg Publishers. Oxford, 1997. 256p. Mediterranea Ser. ISBN:1-85973-961-X, ISBN13: 978-1-85973-961-7. Dewey:791.82082. LCCN:98-185397.
Audience: **u,f.**

Powers-Beck, Jeff **GV867.64.P69 2004**
The American Indian Integration of Baseball. Joseph Oxendine (Foreword by). Cloth Text. University of Nebraska Press. Lincoln, NE. 2004. 328p. ISBN:0-8032-3745-6, ISBN13: 978-0-8032-3745-2. Dewey:796.357/64/08997. LCCN:2004-007245.
Audience: **l,u,f.** *Choice, 2005.*

Rader, Benjamin G. **GV583.R3 2004**
American Sports: From the Age of Folk Games to the Age of Televised Sports. Ed. 5. Trade Paper. Prentice Hall PTR. Upper Saddle River, NJ. 2003. 384p. ISBN:0-13-097750-0, ISBN13: 978-0-13-097750-2. Dewey:796/.0973. LCCN:2003-051198.
Audience: **g,l,u,f.**

Rader, Benjamin G. **GV742.3.R33 1984**
In Its Own Image: How Television Has Transformed Sports. Trade Cloth. Simon & Schuster. New York, NY. 1984. 256p. ISBN:0-02-925700-X, ISBN13: 978-0-02-925700-5. Dewey:070.4/49796/0973. LCCN:84-047856.
Audience: **g,l,u,f.** B

Reaves, Joseph A. **GV863.69.R43 2002**
Taking in a Game: A History of Baseball in Asia. Trade Cloth. University of Nebraska Press. Lincoln, NE. 2002. 220p. Jerry Malloy Prize Ser. ISBN:0-8032-3943-2, ISBN13: 978-0-8032-3943-2. Dewey:796.357/095. LCCN:2001-043058.
Audience: **g,l,u,f.** *Choice, 2002.*

Riess, Steven A. **GV583**
City Games: The Evolution of American Urban Society and the Rise of Sports. Trade Paper. University of Illinois Press. Champaign, IL. 1991. 368p. Sport and Society Ser. ISBN:0-252-06216-7, ISBN13: 978-0-252-06216-2. Dewey:796/.0973.
Audience: **g,l,u,f.** *Choice, 1990.*

Riess, Steven A. **GV867.64.R54 1999**
Touching Base: Professional Baseball and American Culture in the Progressive Era. Ed. 2. Trade Paper. University of Illinois Press. Champaign, IL. 1999. 328p. Sport and Society Ser. ISBN:0-252-06775-4, ISBN13: 978-0-252-06775-4. Dewey:796.357/0973. LCCN:98-058018.
Audience: **g,l,u,f.** B *Choice, 2000.*

Roberts, Randy **GV1132.M84**
Papa Jack: Jack Johnson and the Era of White Hopes. Trade Paper. Simon & Schuster. New York, NY. 1985. 304p. ISBN:0-02-926900-8, ISBN13: 978-0-02-926900-8. Dewey:796.8/3/0924. LCCN:82-049017.
Audience: **u,f.**

Rosengren, John **GV848.4.U6**
Blades of Glory: The True Story of a Young Team Bred to Win. Trade Paper. Sourcebooks, Inc. Naperville, IL. 2004. 352p. ISBN:1-4022-0047-1, ISBN13: 978-1-4022-0047-2. Dewey:796.962/09776/57.
Audience: **g,l,u,f.**

Rowe, David Charles **GV742.R69 2003**
Sport, Culture and the Media: The Unruly Trinity. Ed. 2. Paper Text. McGraw-Hill Education. Maidenhead, 2003. xvii, 253p. ISBN:0-335-21075-9, ISBN13: 978-0-335-21075-6. Dewey:306.4/83.
Audience: **u,f.**

Ryan, Joan **GV464.R93 2000**
Little Girls in Pretty Boxes: The Making and Breaking of Elite Gymnasts and Figure Skaters. Trade Paper. Warner Books, Inc. New York, NY. 2000. 288p. ISBN:0-446-67682-9, ISBN13: 978-0-446-67682-3. Dewey:796.4/4/08352. LCCN:00-031981.
Audience: **l,u,f.**

SAGE **GV706.5.S23 1980**
Sport and American Society. Trade Cloth. Addison-Wesley Longman, Inc. Boston, MA. 1980. xi, 395p. ISBN:0-201-06717-X, ISBN13: 978-0-201-06717-0. Dewey:796. LCCN:79-025573.
Audience: **g,l,u,f.** B

Sailes, Gary A. (Editor) **GV583.A56 1998**
African Americans in Sport: Contemporary Themes. Trade Paper. Transaction Publishers. Somerset, NJ. 1998. 271p. ISBN:0-7658-0440-9, ISBN13: 978-0-7658-0440-2. Dewey:796/.089/96073. LCCN:98-010468.
Audience: **l,u,f.**

Sammond, Nicholas (Editor) **GV1195.S743 2005**
Steel Chair to the Head: The Pleasure and Pain of Professional Wrestling. Trade Paper. Duke University Press. Durham, NC. 2005. 344p. ISBN:0-8223-3438-0, ISBN13: 978-0-8223-3438-5. Dewey:796.8/12. LCCN:2004-014274.
Audience: **u,f.** *Choice, 2005.*

Sammons, Jeffrey T. **GV1125.S26 1988**
Beyond the Ring: The Role of Boxing in American Society. Trade Cloth. University of Illinois Press. Champaign, IL. 1987. 376p. Sport and Society Ser. ISBN:0-252-01473-1, ISBN13: 978-0-252-01473-4. Dewey:796.8/3/0973. LCCN:87-019041.
Audience: **l,u,f.** *Choice, 1988.*

Sands, Robert R. (Editor) **GV706**
Anthropology, Sport, and Culture. Trade Cloth. Greenwood Publishing Group, Inc. Portsmouth, NH. 1999. 240p. ISBN:0-89789-599-1, ISBN13: 978-0-89789-599-6. Dewey:306.4/83. LCCN:98-020128.
Audience: **g,l,u,f.** *Choice, 1999.*

Sands, Robert R. **GV958.S26 1999**
Gutcheck!: An Anthropologist's Wild Ride into the Heart of College Football. Trade Paper. Rincon Hill Books. Carpinteria, CA. 2000. 321p. ISBN:0-9672973-0-3, ISBN13: 978-0-9672973-0-9. Dewey:796.332. LCCN:99-093335.
Audience: **u,f.** *Choice, 2000.*

Shropshire, Kenneth L. **GV706.32.S48 1996**
In Black and White: Race and Sports in America. Kellen Winslow (Foreword by). Trade Cloth. New York University Press. New York, NY. 1996. 212p. ISBN:0-8147-8016-4, ISBN13: 978-0-8147-8016-9. Dewey:305.8/00973. LCCN:95-050200.
Audience: **l,u,f.** *Choice, 1997.*

Slack, Trevor **GV713.S576 1997**
Understanding Sport Organizations: The Application of Organizational Theory. Trade Cloth. Human Kinetics Publishers. Champaign, IL. 1996. 360p. ISBN:0-87322-948-7, ISBN13: 978-0-87322-948-7. Dewey:796/.09/9. LCCN:96-026111.
Audience: **u,f.**

Smith, Robert A. **GV1040.5.S64 1995**
Merry Wheels and Spokes of Steel: A Social History of the Bicycle. Trade Paper. Millefleurs. San Bernardino, CA. 1995. xii, 269p. Stovkis Studies in Historical Chronology and Thought, No. 16 ISBN:0-8095-1104-5, ISBN13: 978-0-8095-1104-4. Dewey:796.6. LCCN:95-009980.
Audience: **g,l,u,f.**

Spielvogel, Laura **GV482.S67 2003**
Working Out in Japan: Shaping the Female Body in Tokyo Fitness Clubs. Trade Paper. Duke University Press. Durham, NC. 2003. 264p. ISBN:0-8223-3049-0, ISBN13: 978-0-8223-3049-3. Dewey:613/.0424/0952. LCCN:2002-012949.
Audience: **g,l,u,f.**

Struna, Nancy L. **GV583.S88 1996**
People of Prowess: Sport, Leisure, and Labor in Early Anglo-America. Trade Cloth. University of Illinois Press. Champaign, IL. 1996. 288p. Sport and Society Ser. ISBN:0-252-06552-2, ISBN13: 978-0-252-06552-1. Dewey:796/.0973/09032. LCCN:95-050193.
Audience: **u,f.**

Sugden, John P. **GV1136.8.S84 1996**
Boxing and Society: An International Analysis. Trade Paper. Manchester University Press. Manchester, 1997. 272p. Sport, Society, and Politics Ser. ISBN:0-7190-4321-2, ISBN13: 978-0-7190-4321-5. Dewey:306.4/83. LCCN:96-029445.
Audience: **u,f.** *Choice, 1997.*

Szymanski, Stefan & Zimbalist, Andrew S. **GV716.S99 2005**
National Pastime: How Americans Play Baseball and the Rest of the World Plays Soccer. Perfect, Paper over Boards, Dust Jacket. Brookings Institution Press. Washington, DC. 2005. 263p. ISBN:0-8157-8258-6, ISBN13: 978-0-8157-8258-2. Dewey:338.4/7796334. LCCN:2005-001160.
Audience: **u,f.** *Choice, 2005.*

Taylor, Rogan **GV943.9.F35.T39 1992**
Football and Its Fans: An Account of Supporters and Their Relations. Trade Cloth. St. Martin's Press. Gordonville, VA. 1992. viii, 198p. ISBN:0-7185-1448-3, ISBN13: 978-0-7185-1448-8. Dewey:796.334. LCCN:92-005666.
Audience: **g,l,u,f.** *Choice, 1993.*

Theberge, Nancy **GV848.6.W65T54 2000**
Higher Goals: Women's Ice Hockey and the Politics of Gender. Paper Text. State University of New York Press. Albany, NY. 2000. xiii, 182p. SUNY Series on Sport, Culture, and Social Relations ISBN:0-7914-4642-5, ISBN13: 978-0-7914-4642-3. Dewey:796.962/082/0971. LCCN:99-057333.
Audience: **u,f.** *Choice, 2001.*

Toma, J. D. **GV959.5.T66 2003**
Football U.: Spectator Sports in the Life of the American University. Trade Cloth. University of Michigan Press. Chicago, IL. 2003. 220p. ISBN:0-472-11299-6, ISBN13: 978-0-472-11299-9. Dewey:796.332/63/0973. LCCN:2002-153617.
Audience: **g,l,u.** *Choice, 2004.*

Waddington, Ivan **RC1230.W295 2000**
Sport, Health and Drugs: A Critical Sociological Perspective. Trade Paper. Routledge. New York, NY. 2000. 224p. ISBN:0-419-25200-2, ISBN13: 978-0-419-25200-9. Dewey:362.29/088/796. LCCN:99-053040.
Audience: **u,f.**

Wenner, Lawrence A. **GV742.M337 1998**
Mediasport. Trade Paper. Routledge. New York, NY. 1998. 352p. ISBN:0-415-14041-2, ISBN13: 978-0-415-14041-6. Dewey:070.4/49796. LCCN:98-002658.
Audience: **u,f.**

Whannel, Garry **GV742.W43 2002**
Media Sport Stars: Masculinities and Moralities. Trade Paper. Routledge. New York, NY. 2001. 288p. ISBN:0-415-17038-9, ISBN13: 978-0-415-17038-3. Dewey:796/.081. LCCN:2001-058886.
Audience: **u,f.** *Choice, 2002.*

White, Philip & Young, Kevin (Editors) **GV709.18.C2S66 1999**
Sport and Gender in Canada. Paper Text. Oxford University Press, Inc. New York, NY. 1999. 336p. ISBN:0-19-541317-2, ISBN13: 978-0-19-541317-5. Dewey:306.483. LCCN:00-698323.
Audience: **u,f.** *Choice, 2000.*

Whiting, Robert **GV865.S895W55 2004**
The Meaning of Ichiro: The New Wave from Japan and the Transformation of Our National Pastime. Trade Cloth. Warner Books, Inc. New York, NY. 2004. 336p. ISBN:0-446-53192-8, ISBN13: 978-0-446-53192-4. Dewey:796.357/092 B. LCCN:2003-027134.
Audience: **u,f.** *Choice, 2005.*

Wieting, Stephen G. (Editor) **GV706.5.S6942 2001**
Sport and Memory in North America. Trade Paper. Taylor & Francis Group. Philadelphia, PA. 2001. 280p. Sport in the Global Society Ser. ISBN:0-7146-8205-5, ISBN13: 978-0-7146-8205-1. Dewey:306.4/83/097. LCCN:2001-028808.
Audience: **u,f.** *Choice, 2002.*

Williams, Jack **GV928.G7 W55 2001**
Cricket and Race. Trade Paper. Berg Publishers. Oxford, 2001. 224p. ISBN:1-85973-309-3, ISBN13: 978-1-85973-309-7. Dewey:796.3/58/089/00942.
Audience: **g,l,u,f.** *Choice, 2002.*

Wilson, John **GV706.5.W55 1994**
Playing by the Rules: Sport, Society, and the State. Cloth Text. Wayne State University Press. Detroit, MI. 1994. 430p. ISBN:0-8143-2107-0, ISBN13: 978-0-8143-2107-2. Dewey:306.4/83/0973. LCCN:93-019671.
Audience: **u,f.** *Choice, 1994.*

Wise, Suzanne **Z7514.S72.W57 1994**
Social Issues in Contemporary Sport: A Resource Guide. Paper over Boards. Garland Publishing, Inc. New York, NY. 1994. 808p. ISBN:0-8240-6046-6, ISBN13: 978-0-8240-6046-6. Dewey:016.306483. LCCN:93-029608.
Audience: **g,l,u,f.** *Choice, 1994.*

Wright, Jim **GV1029.9.S74W75 2002**
Fixin' to Git: One Fan's Love Affair with NASCAR's Winston Cup. Trade Cloth. Duke University Press. Durham, NC. 2002. 320p. ISBN:0-8223-2926-3, ISBN13: 978-0-8223-2926-8. Dewey:796.72. LCCN:2002-000485.
Audience: **u,f.** *Choice, 2003.*

Zang, David **GV706.5.Z35 2001**
SportsWars: Athletes in the Age of Aquarius. Trade Cloth. University of Arkansas Press. Fayetteville, AR. 2001. xxii, 180p. ISBN:1-55728-713-9, ISBN13: 978-1-55728-713-7. Dewey:303.4/83/0973. LCCN:2001-003221.
Audience: **g,l,u,f.** *Choice, 2002.*

Sport Studies > Education

HQ1237

☐ Gender equity in Sports.
http://bailiwick.lib.uiowa.edu/ge/
Audience: **g,l,u,f.**

GV347

☐ Intercollegiate Atheletics Four-Year Colleges' Experiences Adding and Discontinuing Teams.
http://www.gao.gov/new.items/d01297.pd
gao 01-297.
Audience: **l,u,f.**

KF4166

☐ National Women's Law Center Athletics page.
http://www.nwlc.org/display.cfm?section=athletics
Audience: **g,l,u,f.**

KF4758.E3

☐ Open to all: Ttile IX at Thirty.
http://www.ed.gov/about/bdscomm/list/athletics/title9report.pdf
GPO Secretary of Education.
Audience: **g,l,u,f.**

Andre, Judith **GV351**
Rethinking College Athletics. Trade Paper. Temple University Press. Philadelphia, PA. 1992. ISBN:1-56639-002-8, ISBN13: 978-1-56639-002-6. Dewey:796.071/173.
Audience: **g,l,u.**

Bailey, Wilford S., et al. **GV351.B34 1998**
Athletics and Academe: An Anatomy of Abuses and a Prescription for Reform. Taylor D. Littleton & A. C. E. American Council on Education (Authors). Paper Text. Greenwood Publishing Group, Inc. Portsmouth, NH. 1991. 160p. American Council on Education Series on Higher Education ISBN:1-57356-209-2, ISBN13: 978-1-57356-209-6. Dewey:796.04/3/0973. LCCN:97-052772.
Audience: **g,l,u,f.** *Choice, 1991.*

Bale, John **GV351.B35 1990**
The Brawn Drain: Foreign Student Athletes in American Universities. Trade Cloth. University of Illinois Press. Champaign, IL. 1991. 248p. Sport and Society Ser. ISBN:0-252-01732-3, ISBN13: 978-0-252-01732-2. Dewey:796/.071/173. LCCN:90-032829.
Audience: **u,f.** *Choice, 1991.*

Bowen, William G. & Levin, Sarah A. **LA227.4**
Reclaiming the Game: College Sports and Educational Values. Colin G. Campbell, Martin A. Kurzweil, Susanne C. Pichler & James L. Shulman (Contribution by). Trade Cloth. Princeton University Press. Princeton, NJ. 2003. 488p. ISBN:0-691-11620-2, ISBN13: 978-0-691-11620-4. Dewey:796.04/3/0973. LCCN:2003-100409.
Audience: **g,l,u,f.**

Byers, Walter & Hammer, Charles **GV351.B94 1995**
Unsportsmanlike Conduct: Exploiting College Athletes. Trade Cloth. University of Michigan Press. Chicago, IL. 1995. 424p. ISBN:0-472-10666-X, ISBN13: 978-0-472-10666-0. Dewey:796.04/3. LCCN:95-016973.
Audience: **g,l,u,f.** *Choice, 1996.*

Chu, Donald **GV351.C484 1989**
The Character of American Higher Education and Intercollegiate Sport. Cloth Text. State University of New York Press. Albany, NY. 1989. 252p. SUNY Series in Frontiers of Education ISBN:0-88706-791-3, ISBN13: 978-0-88706-791-4. Dewey:796/.07/1173. LCCN:87-034015.
Audience: **g,l,u,f.**

Duderstadt, James J. **GV351.D83 2000**
Intercollegiate Athletics and the American University: A University President's Perspective. Trade Cloth. University of Michigan Press. Chicago, IL. 2000. 352p. ISBN:0-472-11156-6, ISBN13: 978-0-472-11156-5. Dewey:796.04/3/0973. LCCN:00-008203.
Audience: **g,l,u,f.** *Choice, 2001.*

Festle, Mary Jo **GV709.F37 1996**
Playing Nice: Politics and Apologies in Women's Sports. Trade Cloth. Columbia University Press. New York, NY. 1996. 400p. ISBN:0-231-10162-7, ISBN13: 978-0-231-10162-2. Dewey:796/.0194. LCCN:96-004739.
Audience: **g,l,u,f.** *Choice, 1997.*

Frank, Anna Marie **GV346.F73 2003**
Sports and Education: A Reference Handbook. Danny Weil (Editor). Library Binding. ABC-CLIO, Inc. Santa Barbara, CA. 2003. 190p. Contemporary Education Issues Ser. ISBN:1-85109-525-X, ISBN13: 978-1-85109-525-4. Dewey:796.071. LCCN:2003-017180.
Audience: **g,l,u.**

French, Peter A. **GV361.F64 2004**
Ethics and College Sports: Ethics, Sports, and the University. Book, Other. Rowman & Littlefield Publishers, Inc. Lanham, MD. 2004. 208p. Issues in Academic Ethics Ser. ISBN:0-7425-1273-8, ISBN13: 978-0-7425-1273-3. Dewey:796.04/3/0973. LCCN:2004-004349.
Audience: **g,l,u,f.** *Choice, 2005.*

Friday, William C. & Hesburgh, Theodore M. (Editors) **LT23.N5**
A Call to Action: Reconnecting College Sports and Higher Education. Paper Text. DIANE Publishing Company. Collingdale, PA. 2001. 51p. ISBN:0-7567-1443-5, ISBN13: 978-0-7567-1443-7. Dewey:371.320973.
Audience: **g,l,u,f.**

Funk, Gary **GV346.F85 1995**
Major Violation: A Balancing Act: Sports and Education. Library Binding. Lerner Publications. Minneapolis, MN. 1995. Sports Issues Ser. ISBN:0-8225-3301-4, ISBN13: 978-0-8225-3301-6. Dewey:796.04/2. LCCN:94-038597.
Audience: **u,f.**

Gavora, Jessica **GV709.18.U6G38 2002**
Tilting the Playing Field: Schools, Sports, Sex and Title IX. Trade Cloth. National Book Network. Lanham, MD. 2001. 181p. ISBN:1-893554-35-X, ISBN13: 978-1-893554-35-1. Dewey:796/.082. LCCN:2001-055597.
Audience: **u,f.** *Choice, 2003, 2002.*

Gerdy, John R. **GV351**
The Successful College Athletic Program: The New Standard. Trade Paper. Greenwood Publishing Group, Inc. Portsmouth, NH. 1997. 192p. American Council on Education Series on Higher Education ISBN:1-57356-523-7, ISBN13: 978-1-57356-523-3. Dewey:796.04/3/0973.
Audience: **g,l,u,f.** *Choice, 1998.*

Grundy, Pamela **GV584.N8G78 2001**
Learning to Win: Sports, Education and Social Change in Twentieth-Century North Carolina. Trade Paper. University of North Carolina Press. Chapel Hill, NC. 2001. 392p. Fred W. Morrison Series in Southern Studies ISBN:0-8078-4934-0, ISBN13: 978-0-8078-4934-7. Dewey:796/.09756/0904. LCCN:00-048928.
Audience: **g,l,u,f.** *Choice, 2001.*

John S. and James L. Knight Foundation **GV347**
☐ Keeping Faith update of Call to Action.
http://www.knightcommission.org/
Knight Commission on Intercollegiate Athletics.
Audience: **l,u,f.**

King, C. Richard & Springwood, Charles Fruehling **GV706.32.K52 2001**
Beyond the Cheers: Race as Spectacle in College Sport. Paper Text. State University of New York Press. Albany, NY. 2001. x, 214p. Series on Sport, Culture, and Social Relations ISBN:0-7914-5006-6, ISBN13: 978-0-7914-5006-2. Dewey:796.04/3/08900973. LCCN:00-054797.
Audience: **u,f.** *Choice, 2001.*

Lapchick, Richard E. (Editor) **GV351**
New Game Plans for College Sport. Trade Cloth. Greenwood Publishing Group, Inc. Portsmouth, NH. 2006. 344p. ACE/Praeger Series on Higher Education Ser. ISBN:0-275-98147-9, ISBN13: 978-0-275-98147-1. Dewey:796.04/30973. LCCN:2005-034803.
Audience: **g,l,u,f.**

Miracle, Andrew W. Jr. & Rees, C. Roger **GV346.M57 1994**
Lessons of the Locker Room: The Myth of School Sports. Trade Cloth. Prometheus Books, Publishers. Amherst, NY. 1994. 243p. ISBN:0-87975-879-1, ISBN13: 978-0-87975-879-0. Dewey:796/.0973. LCCN:93-048666.
Audience: **g,l,u,f.** *Choice, 1994.*

Pemberton, Cynthia Lee A. **GV709.18.U6P46 2002**
More than a Game: One Woman's Fight for Gender Equity in Sport. Donna de Varona (Foreword by). Paper Text. Northeastern University Press. Boston, MA. 2002. 320p. ISBN:1-55553-525-9, ISBN13: 978-1-55553-525-4. Dewey:796/.082/09795. LCCN:2001-059193.
Audience: **u,f.** *Choice, 2002.*

Porto, Brian L. **GV709**
A New Season: Using Title IX to Reform College Sports. Trade Cloth. Greenwood Publishing Group, Inc. Portsmouth, NH. 2003. 264p. ISBN:0-275-97699-8, ISBN13: 978-0-275-97699-6. Dewey:796/.082. LCCN:2003-048216.
Audience: **u,f.** *Choice, 2004.*

Sack, Allen L. & Staurowsky, Ellen J. **GV351**
College Athletes for Hire: The Evolution and Legacy of the NCAA's Amateur Myth. Trade Cloth. Greenwood Publishing Group, Inc. Portsmouth, NH. 1998. 208p. ISBN:0-275-96191-5, ISBN13: 978-0-275-96191-6. Dewey:796.04/3/0973. LCCN:97-043956.
Audience: **g,l,u,f.** *Choice, 1999.*

Shea, Edward J. **GV706.3.S53 1996**
Ethical Decisions in Sport: Interscholastic, Intercollegiate, Olympic and Professional. Trade Paper. Charles C. Thomas Publisher, Ltd. Springfield, IL. 1996. 238p. ISBN:0-398-06600-0, ISBN13: 978-0-398-06600-0. Dewey:796/.01. LCCN:96-001035.
Audience: **u,f.**

Shulman, James Lawrence & Bowen, William G. **GV351**
The Game of Life: College Sports and Educational Values. Trade Paper. Princeton University Press. Princeton, NJ. 2002. 494p. ISBN:0-691-09619-8, ISBN13: 978-0-691-09619-3. Dewey:796.04/3/0973.
Audience: **g,l,u,f.** *Choice, 2001.*

Simon, Rita J. (Editor) **GV709.18.U6S67 2005**
Sporting Equality: Title IX Thirty Years Later. Trade Paper. Transaction Publishers. Somerset, NJ. 2005. 182p. ISBN:0-7658-0848-X, ISBN13: 978-0-7658-0848-6. Dewey:796/.082. LCCN:2004-051694.
Audience: **g,l,u,f.**

Smith, Ronald A. **GV351**
Sports and Freedom: The Rise of Big-Time College Athletics. Paper Text. Oxford University Press, Inc. New York, NY. 1990. 320p. Sports History and Society Ser. ISBN:0-19-506582-4, ISBN13: 978-0-19-506582-4. Dewey:796/.07/1173. LCCN:88-017855.
Audience: **u,f.** *Choice, 1989.*

Telander, Rick **GV959.T44 1996**
The Hundred Yard Lie: The Corruption of College Football and What We Can Do to Stop It. Trade Paper. University of Illinois Press. Champaign, IL. 1996. 232p. ISBN:0-252-06523-9, ISBN13: 978-0-252-06523-1. Dewey:796.332/63/0973. LCCN:96-012412.
Audience: **g,l,u,f.**

Thelin, John R. **GV351.T43**
Games Colleges Play: Scandal and Reform in Intercollegiate Athletics. Trade Paper. Johns Hopkins University Press. Baltimore, MD. 1996. 272p. ISBN:0-8018-5504-7, ISBN13: 978-0-8018-5504-7. Dewey:796.071173.
Audience: **g,l,u,f.** *Choice, 1995.*

Thelin, John R. & Wiseman, Lawrence L. **GV351 .T44 1989**
The Old College Try: Balancing Academics and Athletics in Higher Education. Jonathan D. Fife (Editor). Paper Text. George Washington University, Graduate School of Education & Human Development. Washington, DC. 1989. 141p. ASHE-ERIC Higher Education Reports, No. 89-4 ISBN:0-9623882-3-8, ISBN13: 978-0-9623882-3-1. Dewey:796/.071/173. LCCN:89-063440.
Audience: **g,l,u,f.**

Toma, J. D. **GV959.5.T66 2003**
Football U.: Spectator Sports in the Life of the American University. Trade Cloth. University of Michigan Press. Chicago, IL. 2003. 220p. ISBN:0-472-11299-6, ISBN13: 978-0-472-11299-9. Dewey:796.332/63/0973. LCCN:2002-153617.
Audience: **g,l,u.** *Choice, 2004.*

Weissberg, Ted **GV351.W45 1995**
Breaking the Rules: The NCAA and Recruitment in America's High Schools. Trade Paper. Scholastic Library Publishing. Danbury, CT. 1995. 144p. Social Issues Ser. ISBN:0-531-11235-7, ISBN13: 978-0-531-11235-9. Dewey:796/.04/30973. LCCN:95-014676.
Audience: **g,l,u.**

Wiggins, David K. **GV583.W545 1997**
Glory Bound: Black Athletes in a White America. Trade Paper. Syracuse University Press. Syracuse, NY. 1997. 307p. Sports and Entertainment Ser. ISBN:0-8156-2734-3, ISBN13: 978-0-8156-2734-0. Dewey:796/.089/96073. LCCN:96-046218.
Audience: **l,u,f.** *Choice, 1997.*

Yaeger, Don **GV351.Y34 1991**
Undue Process: The NCAA's Injustice for All. Trade Cloth. Sagamore Publishing, L.L.C.. Champaign, IL. 1991. 277p.

ISBN:0-915611-34-1, ISBN13: 978-0-915611-34-8. Dewey:796/.071/1. LCCN:90-062973.
Audience: **g,l,u.** *Choice, 1991.*

Sport Studies > General

GV568

☐ Scholarly Sport Sites: A Subject Directory. http://www.ucalgary.ca/lib-old/ssportsite/
Audience: **g,l,u,f.**

Allen, Mary **GV706.8**
Sports, Exercises, and Fitness: A Guide to Reference and Information Sources. Trade Cloth. Libraries Unlimited, Inc. Westport, CT. 2005. 304p. Reference Sources in the Social Sciences Ser. ISBN:1-56308-819-3, ISBN13: 978-1-56308-819-3. Dewey:016.796. LCCN:2004-063835.
Audience: **g,l,u.** *Choice, 2005.*

Baldassaro, Lawrence & Johnson, Dick (Editors) **GV867.64.A44 2002**
The American Game: Baseball and Ethnicity. Allan H. Selig (Foreword by). Trade Cloth. Southern Illinois University Press. Carbondale, IL. 2002. 224p. Writing Baseball Ser. ISBN:0-8093-2446-6, ISBN13: 978-0-8093-2446-0. Dewey:796.357. LCCN:2001-049600.
Audience: **g,l,u,f.** *Choice, 2002.*

Brookes, Rod **GV742.B76 2002**
Representing Sport. Trade Paper. Oxford University Press, Inc. New York, NY. 2002. 184p. A Hodder Arnold Publication ISBN:0-340-74052-3, ISBN13: 978-0-340-74052-1. Dewey:796. LCCN:2002-510305.
Audience: **l,u.** *Choice, 2002.*

Cashmore, Ellis **GV706.5.C383 2000**
Sports Culture: An A-Z Guide. Trade Paper. Routledge. New York, NY. 2000. 496p. ISBN:0-415-22335-0, ISBN13: 978-0-415-22335-5. Dewey:306.4/83/03. LCCN:99-016891.
Audience: **g,l,u,f.** *Choice, 2001.*

Costa, D. Margaret & Guthrie, Sharon R. (Editors) **GV709.W56 1994**
Women and Sport: Interdisciplinary Perspectives. Trade Cloth. Human Kinetics Publishers. Champaign, IL. 1994. 416p. ISBN:0-87322-686-0, ISBN13: 978-0-87322-686-8. Dewey:796/.0194. LCCN:93-050167.
Audience: **g,l,f.**

Cross, Gary S. **GV53.E53 2004**
Encyclopedia of Recreation and Leisure in America. Trade Cloth. Thomson Gale. Farmington Hills, MI. 2004. 800p. The Scribner American Civilization Ser. ISBN:0-684-31265-4, ISBN13: 978-0-684-31265-1. Dewey:790/.0973/03. LCCN:2004-004617.
Audience: **l,u.** *Choice, 2005.*

Currell, Susan **GV53.C79 2005**
The March of Spare Time: The Problem and Promise of Leisure in the Great Depression. Book, Other. University of Pennsylvania Press. Philadelphia, PA. 2005. 256p. ISBN:0-8122-3859-1, ISBN13: 978-0-8122-3859-4. Dewey:790.1/0973/09043. LCCN:2004-057246.
Audience: **l,u.** *Choice, 2005.*

Dawson, Buck **GV837.9.D39 2000**
Mermaids on Parade: America's Love Affair with Its First Olympic Swimmers. Paul Gallico (Introduction by). Trade Cloth. Nova Science Publishers, Inc. Hauppauge, NY. 2000. 266p. ISBN:1-56072-726-8, ISBN13: 978-1-56072-726-2. Dewey:797.2/1/082092273 B. LCCN:2001-267948.
Audience: **g,l,u,f.**

Feinstein, John & Auerbach, Red **GV884.A8F45 2004**
Let Me Tell You a Story: A Lifetime in the Game. Trade Cloth. Little Brown & Company. New York, NY. 2004. 368p. ISBN:0-316-73823-9, ISBN13: 978-0-316-73823-1. Dewey:796.323/092 B. LCCN:2004-013000.
Audience: **g,l,u.**

Frank, Anna Marie **GV346.F73 2003**
Sports and Education: A Reference Handbook. Danny Weil (Editor). Library Binding. ABC-CLIO, Inc. Santa Barbara, CA. 2003. 190p. Contemporary Education Issues Ser. ISBN:1-85109-525-X, ISBN13: 978-1-85109-525-4. Dewey:796.071. LCCN:2003-017180.
Audience: **g,l,u.**

Frost, Mark **GV964.J6 F76**
The Grand Slam: Bobby Jones, America, and the Story of Golf. Trade Paper, Perfect. Hyperion Press. New York, NY. 2005. 514p. ISBN:1-4013-0751-5, ISBN13: 978-1-4013-0751-6. Dewey:796.352/092.
Audience: **g,l,u.**

Halberstam, David **GV742.3 .H35 1999**
Sports on New York Radio: A Play-by-Play History. Trade Cloth. McGraw-Hill Companies, The. New York, NY. 1999. 432p. ISBN:1-57028-197-1, ISBN13: 978-1-57028-197-6. Dewey:070.4/49796/097471. LCCN:98-046621.
Audience: **g,l,u,f.**

Higgs, Robert J. **GV704**
Sports: A Reference Guide. Cloth Text. Greenwood Publishing Group, Inc. Portsmouth, NH. 1982. 317p. American Popular Culture Ser. ISBN:0-313-21361-5, ISBN13: 978-0-313-21361-8. Dewey:796. LCCN:81-020320.
Audience: **g,l,u,f.**

Jenkins, John & Pigram, John (Editors) **GV188**
Encyclopedia of Leisure and Outdoor Recreation. Paper over Boards. Routledge. New York, NY. 2004. 752p. ISBN:0-415-25226-1, ISBN13: 978-0-415-25226-3. Dewey:790/.03. LCCN:2003-058529.
Audience: **g,l,u,f.** *Choice, 2004.*

Jensen, Clayne R. & Guthrie, Steven P. **GV191.4.J46 2005**
Outdoor Recreation in America. Ed. 6. Trade Cloth. Human Kinetics Publishers. Champaign, IL. 2005. 384p. ISBN:0-7360-4213-X, ISBN13: 978-0-7360-4213-0. Dewey:796.5/0973. LCCN:2005-015630.
Audience: **l,u.** B

Oriard, Michael **GV950.O73 2001**
King Football: Sport and Spectacle in the Golden Age of Radio and Newsreels, Movies and Magazines, the Weekly and the Daily Press. Trade Cloth. University of North Carolina Press. Chapel Hill, NC. 2001. 512p. ISBN:0-8078-2650-2, ISBN13:

978-0-8078-2650-8. Dewey:796.332/09/041. LCCN:2001-041459.
Audience: **l,u,f.** *Choice, 2002.*

Rathburn, Elizabeth & Drummond, Siobhan (Contribution by) **GV721.5 .G63 1996**
Grace and Glory: A Century of Women in the Olympics. Trade Cloth. Triumph Books. Chicago, IL. 1996. 112p. ISBN:1-57243-116-4, ISBN13: 978-1-57243-116-4. Dewey:796.48.
Audience: **g,l,u,f.** *Choice, 1996.*

Smoll, Frank L. & Smith, Ronald E. **GV709.2.C46 1996**
Children and Youth in Sport. Paper Text. McGraw-Hill Higher Education. Burr Ridge, IL. 1995. 464p. ISBN:0-697-22490-2, ISBN13: 978-0-697-22490-3. Dewey:796/.0192. LCCN:94-073668.
Audience: **g,l,u,f.**

Vamplew, Wray (Editor), et al. **GV675.O94 1992**
The Oxford Companion to Australian Sport. Katharine Moore, John O'Hara, Richard Cashman & Ian F. Joblin (Editors). Trade Cloth. Oxford University Press, Inc. New York, NY. 1993. 440p. ISBN:0-19-553287-2, ISBN13: 978-0-19-553287-6. Dewey:796/.0994/03. LCCN:93-191848.
Audience: **g,l,u,f.** *Choice, 1994.*

Wellner, Alison Stein **GV191.4.W45 1997**
Americans at Play: Demographics of Outdoor Recreation and Travel. Trade Cloth. New Strategist Publications, Inc. Ithaca, NY. 1997. 370p. ISBN:1-885070-11-X, ISBN13: 978-1-885070-11-1. Dewey:790/.06/8/021. LCCN:98-157389.
Audience: **l,u,f.** *Choice, 1998.*

Sport Studies > Religion

Bevis, Charlie **GV867.6.B48 2003**
Sunday Baseball: The Major Leagues' Struggle to Play Baseball on the Lord's Day, 1876-1934. Paper Text. McFarland & Company, Incorporated Publishers. Jefferson, NC. 2003. 326p. ISBN:0-7864-1564-9, ISBN13: 978-0-7864-1564-9. Dewey:796.357/64/0973. LCCN:2002-156687.
Audience: **u,f.** *Choice, 2003.*

Cooper, Andrew **GV706.4.C67 1998**
Playing in the Zone. Trade Paper. Shambhala Publications, Inc. Boston, MA. 1998. 160p. ISBN:1-57062-151-9, ISBN13: 978-1-57062-151-2. Dewey:796/.01. LCCN:98-005799.
Audience: **g,l,u,f.** *Choice, 1998.*

Higgs, Robert J. & Braswell, Michael C. **GV706.42.H53 2004**
An Unholy Alliance: The Sacred and Modern Sports. Trade Cloth. Mercer University Press. Macon, GA. 2004. 356p. Sports and Religion Ser. ISBN:0-86554-956-7, ISBN13: 978-0-86554-956-2. Dewey:796. LCCN:2004-020947.
Audience: **u.**

Kimball, Richard Ian **GV54.U8K56 2003**
Sports in Zion: Mormon Recreation, 1890-1940. Trade Cloth. University of Illinois Press. Champaign, IL. 2003. 240p. Sports and Society Ser. ISBN:0-252-02857-0, ISBN13: 978-0-252-02857-1. Dewey:790/.088/283. LCCN:2002-156585.
Audience: **g,l,u,f.** *Choice, 2004.*

Prebish, Charles S. **GV706**
Religion and Sport: The Meeting of Sacred and Profane. Trade Cloth. Greenwood Publishing Group, Inc. Portsmouth, NH. 1992. 264p. Contributions to the Study of Popular Culture Ser., No. 36 ISBN:0-313-28729-5, ISBN13: 978-0-313-28729-9. Dewey:796/.01. LCCN:92-030020.
Audience: **u,f.**

Sport Medicine

GV481
☐ American College of Sports Medicine.
http://www.acsm.org/
Audience: **g,l,u,f.**

GV557
☐ International Council of Sport Science and Physical Education.
http://www.icsspe.org/
Audience: **g,l,u,f.**

RC1211
☐ International Federation of Sports Medicine.
http://www.fims.org/
Audience: **l,u,f.**

RC1235
☐ International Society of Biomechanics in Sports.
http://www.twu.edu/biom/isbs/
Audience: **l,u,f.**

GV203
☐ National Athletic Trainers Association.
http://www.nata.org/
Audience: **g,l,u,f.**

GV568
☐ Scholarly Sport Sites: A Subject Directory.
http://www.ucalgary.ca/lib-old/ssportsite/
Audience: **g,l,u,f.**

GV741
☐ SPORTQuest.
http://www.sirc.ca/online_resources/sportquest.cfm
SIRC.
Audience: **g,l,u,f.**

GV557
☐ SPORTSCIENCE a peer-reviewed site for Sport Research.
http://www.sportsci.org/
Audience: **l,u,f.**

ACSM Staff & Berryman, Jack W. **RC1210.B395 1995**
Out of Many, One: A History of the American College of Sports Medicine. Cloth Text. Human Kinetics Publishers. Champaign, IL. 1995. 424p. ISBN:0-87322-815-4, ISBN13: 978-0-87322-815-2. Dewey:617.1/027/06073. LCCN:94-023876.
Audience: **l,u,f.** *Choice, 1996.*

Beals, Katherine A. **RC552.E18B43 2004**
Disordered Eating among Athletes: A Comprehensive Guide for Health Professionals. Perfect. Human Kinetics Publishers. Champaign, IL. 2004. 255p. ISBN:0-7360-4219-9, ISBN13: 978-0-7360-4219-2. Dewey:616.85/26. LCCN:30-260440.
Audience: **g,l,u,f.** *Choice, 2005.*

Benjamin, Patricia J. & Lamp, Scott P. **RM721.B476 2005**
Understanding Sports Massage. Ed. 2. Trade Paper. Human Kinetics Publishers. Champaign, IL. 2004. 168p. ISBN:0-7360-5457-X, ISBN13: 978-0-7360-5457-7. Dewey:615.8/22/088796. LCCN:2004-019212.
Audience: **l,u.**

Berryman, Jack W. & Park, Roberta J. (Editors) **RC1210.S638 1992**
Sport and Exercise Science: Essays in the History of Sports Medicine. Trade Paper. University of Illinois Press. Champaign, IL. 1992. 392p. Sport and Society Ser. ISBN:0-252-06242-6, ISBN13: 978-0-252-06242-1. Dewey:617.1/027/09. LCCN:91-027220.
Audience: **u,f.** *Choice, 1993.*

Costill, David L., et al. **RC1220.S8C67 1991**
Swimming. Ernest W. Maglischo & Allen B. Richardson (Authors). Trade Paper. Blackwell Publishing, Inc. Malden, MA. 1991. 224p. Handbook of Sports Medicine and Science Ser. ISBN:0-632-03027-5, ISBN13: 978-0-632-03027-9. Dewey:612/.044. LCCN:91-019537.
Audience: **g,l,u,f.** *Choice, 1992.*

Dirix, A. (Editor), et al. **RC1210.O45 1991**
The Olympic Book of Sports Medicine, Vol. 1. H. G. Knuttgen & K. Tittel (Editors). Trade Paper. Blackwell Publishing, Inc. Malden, MA. 1991. 704p. Encyclopedia of Sports Medicine Ser., Vol. 1 ISBN:0-632-03084-4, ISBN13: 978-0-632-03084-2. Dewey:617.1/027. LCCN:93-181549.
Audience: **g,l,u,f.**

Drinkwater, Barbara L. **RC1218.W65W664 2000**
Women in Sport: Olympic Encyclopaedia of Sports Medicine. Trade Cloth. Blackwell Publishing, Inc. Malden, MA. 2000. 608p. Encyclopedia of Sports Medicine Ser., Vol. 8 ISBN:0-632-05084-5, ISBN13: 978-0-632-05084-0. Dewey:617.1/027/082. LCCN:99-057719.
Audience: **g,l,u,f.**

Driskell, Judy A. & Wolinsky, I. R. A. (Editors) **QP771.S68 2005**
Sports Nutrition: Vitamins and Trace Elements. Ed. 2. Paper over Boards. Taylor & Francis Group. Philadelphia, PA. 2005. 340p. Nutrition in Exercise and Sport Ser. ISBN:0-8493-3022-X, ISBN13: 978-0-8493-3022-3. Dewey:613.2/86. LCCN:2005-048557.
Audience: **g,l,u,f.**

Eberle, Suzanne **TX361.A8E39 2000**
Endurance Sports Nutrition: Eating Plans for Optimal Training, Racing and Recovery. Trade Paper. Human Kinetics Publishers. Champaign, IL. 2000. 296p. ISBN:0-7360-0143-3, ISBN13: 978-0-7360-0143-4. Dewey:613.2/024/796. LCCN:00-025081.
Audience: **g,l,u,f.** *Choice, 2001.*

Grayson, Edward & Bond, Catherine **KD2965.S66G73 1999**
Sports Medicine: Ethics and the Law. Trade Paper. Elsevier Science & Technology Books. Saint Louis, MO. 1999. 216p. ISBN:0-7506-1576-1, ISBN13: 978-0-7506-1576-1. Dewey:617.1/027. LCCN:00-265730.
Audience: **u,f.**

Kent, Michael **RC1206.O94 1998**
The Oxford Dictionary of Sports Science and Medicine. Ed. 2. Trade Cloth. Oxford University Press, Inc. New York, NY. 1998. 582p. ISBN:0-19-262845-3, ISBN13: 978-0-19-262845-9. Dewey:617.1/027/03. LCCN:97-041377.
Audience: **g,l,u,f.**

Komi, Paavo V. (Editor) **RC1235.S76 2002**
Strength and Power in Sport, Vol. III. Ed. 2. IOC Medical Commission Staff & International Federation of Sports Medicine Staff (Contribution by). Trade Cloth. Blackwell Publishing, Inc. Malden, MA. 2002. 544p. The Encyclopaedia of Sports Medicine Ser., Vol. 3 ISBN:0-632-05911-7, ISBN13: 978-0-632-05911-9. Dewey:612/.044. LCCN:2002-005028.
Audience: **g,l,u,f.**

Maughan, Ron **TX361.A8F64 2004**
Food, Nutrition and Sports Performance II: The IOC Consensus Conference on Sports Nutrition. Paper over Boards. Routledge. New York, NY. 2004. 256p. ISBN:0-415-33906-5, ISBN13: 978-0-415-33906-3. Dewey:613.2/088/796. LCCN:2004-040964.
Audience: **u,f.**

Maughan, Ronald J. **QP141.N793 2000**
Nutrition in Sport. Trade Cloth. Blackwell Publishing, Inc. Malden, MA. 2000. 704p. Encyclopedia of Sports Medicine Ser., Vol. 7 ISBN:0-632-05094-2, ISBN13: 978-0-632-05094-9. Dewey:616.3/9/0088796. LCCN:99-012066.
Audience: **u,f.**

Miah, Andy **QH332**
Genetically Modified Athletes: The Ethical Implications of Genetic Technologies in Sport. Trade Paper. Routledge. New York, NY. 2004. 232p. Ethics and Sport Ser. ISBN:0-415-29880-6, ISBN13: 978-0-415-29880-3. Dewey:174/.9796. LCCN:2004-044269.
Audience: **l,u,f.**

Micheli, Lyle J. & Jenkins, Mark **RC1210.M49 1995**
Sports Medicine Bible: Prevent, Detect, and Treat Your Sports Injuries Through the Latest Medical Techniques. Trade Paper. HarperCollins Publishers. New York, NY. 1995. 352p. ISBN:0-06-273143-2, ISBN13: 978-0-06-273143-2. Dewey:617.1/027. LCCN:95-002316.
Audience: **g,l,u,f.** *Choice, 1995.*

Oakes, Elizabeth H. **RC1206.O355 2004**
The Encyclopedia of Sports Medicine. Trade Cloth. Facts On File, Inc. New York, NY. 2004. 336p. Library of Health and Living Ser. ISBN:0-8160-5334-0, ISBN13: 978-0-8160-5334-6. Dewey:617.1/027/03. LCCN:2003-024720.
Audience: **g,l,u,f.** *Choice, 2005.*

Otis, Carol L. & Goldingay, Roger **RC1218.W65O68 2000**
The Athletic Woman's Survival Guide. Ed. 2. Trade Paper. Human Kinetics Publishers. Champaign, IL. 2000. 276p. ISBN:0-7360-0121-2, ISBN13: 978-0-7360-0121-2. Dewey:617.1/027/082. LCCN:99-055550.
Audience: **g,l,u,f.** *Choice, 2001.*

Read, Malcolm & Wade, Paul **RD97**
Sports Injuries: A Unique Guide to Self-Diagnosis and Rehabilitation. Ed. 2. Trade Paper. Elsevier Science & Technology Books. Saint Louis, MO. 1997. 192p. ISBN:0-7506-3112-0, ISBN13: 978-0-7506-3112-9. Dewey:617.1/027.
Audience: **g,l,u,f.**

Rogol, Alan D. **QP187.3.E93E53 2005**
The Endocrine System in Sports and Exercise, Vol. XI. William J. Kraemer (Editor). Trade Cloth. Blackwell Publishing, Inc. Malden, MA. 2005. 648p. The Encyclopaedia of Sports Medicine Ser., Vol. 11 ISBN:1-4051-3017-2, ISBN13: 978-1-4051-3017-2. Dewey:612.4. LCCN:2004-026395.
Audience: **g,l,u,f.**

Shannon, Joyce Brennfleck (Editor) **RD97.S736 2002**
Sports Injuries Sourcebook. Ed. 2. Trade Cloth. Omnigraphics, Inc. Detroit, MI. 2002. 614p. Health Reference Ser. ISBN:0-7808-0604-2, ISBN13: 978-0-7808-0604-7. Dewey:617.1/027. LCCN:2002-031196.
Audience: **g,l,u,f.**

Shepard, Roy J. & Astrand, Per-Olof (Editors) **RC1220.E53E53 2000**
Endurance in Sport. Ed. 2. Trade Cloth. Blackwell Publishing, Inc. Malden, MA. 2000. 1008p. Encyclopedia of Sports Medicine Ser., Vol 2 ISBN:0-632-05348-8, ISBN13: 978-0-632-05348-3. Dewey:613.7/1. LCCN:99-038456.
Audience: **g,l,u,f.**

Speer, Kevin P. **RC1218.A33I55 2005**
Injury Prevention and Rehabilitation for Active Older Adults. Perfect, Paper over Boards. Human Kinetics Publishers. Champaign, IL. 2005. 237p. ISBN:0-7360-4031-5, ISBN13: 978-0-7360-4031-0. Dewey:617.1027. LCCN:2004-020851.
Audience: **u.** *Choice, 2005.*

Warren, Michelle P. & Shangold, Mona M. **RG207.W37 1997**
Sports Gynecology: Problems and Care of the Athletic Female. Trade Paper. Blackwell Publishing, Inc. Malden, MA. 1997. 192p. ISBN:0-86542-463-2, ISBN13: 978-0-86542-463-0. Dewey:618.1. LCCN:96-048787.
Audience: **g,l,u,f.**

Ylinen, Jari & Cash, Mel **RC1226 .Y55 1988**
Sports Massage. UK-Trade Paper. Random House. London, 2000. 168p. ISBN:0-09-173746-X, ISBN13: 978-0-09-173746-7. Dewey:617.1/027. LCCN:90-123425.
Audience: **u,f.**

Sport Medicine > Doping. Drugs in Sport

Bahrke, Michael S. & Yesalis, Charles E. **RC1230.B347 2002**
Performance-Enhancing Substances in Sport and Exercise. Trade Cloth. Human Kinetics Publishers. Champaign, IL. 2002. 384p. ISBN:0-7360-3679-2, ISBN13: 978-0-7360-3679-5. Dewey:362.29/088/796. LCCN:2002-017199.
Audience: **g,l,u,f.**

Donohoe, Tom & Johnson, Neil **RC1230.D66 1987**
Foul Play: Drug Abuse in Sports. Sebastian Coe (Foreword by). Trade Cloth. Blackwell Publishing, Inc. Malden, MA. 1988. x, 200p. ISBN:0-631-14845-0, ISBN13: 978-0-631-14845-6. Dewey:362.2/93/088796. LCCN:85-030624.
Audience: **g,l,u,f.** *Choice, 1986.*

Kuhn, Cynthia, et al. **RC1230.K845 2000**
Pumped: Straight Facts for Athletes about Drugs, Supplements and Training. Scott Swartzwelder & Wilkie Wilson (Authors). Trade Paper. W. W. Norton & Company, Inc. New York, NY. 2000. 192p. ISBN:0-393-32129-0, ISBN13: 978-0-393-32129-6. Dewey:617.1/027. LCCN:00-030455.
Audience: **g,l,u,f.**

Lenehan, Pat **RC1230.L46 2003**
Anabolic Steroids. UK-B Format Paperback. Taylor & Francis Group. Philadelphia, PA. 2003. 160p. ISBN:0-415-28030-3, ISBN13: 978-0-415-28030-3. Dewey:362.29/088/796. LCCN:2003-040219.
Audience: **u,f.** *Choice, 2004.*

Mottram, D. R. **RC1230.D786 2005**
Drugs in Sport. Ed. 4. Paper over Boards. Routledge. New York, NY. 2005. 432p. ISBN:0-415-37563-0, ISBN13: 978-0-415-37563-4. Dewey:362.29. LCCN:2005-010408.
Audience: **l,u.**

O'Leary, John (Editor) **HV5800-5840GV557-11**
Drugs and Doping in Sport: Socio-Legal Perspectives. Trade Paper. Taylor & Francis Group. Abingdon, 2001. 320p. ISBN:1-85941-662-4, ISBN13: 978-1-85941-662-4. Dewey:362.2/9/088796.
Audience: **u,f.**

Taylor, William N. **RC1230.T39 2001**
Anabolic Steroids and the Athlete. Ed. 2. Paper Text. McFarland & Company, Incorporated Publishers. Jefferson, NC. 2002. 384p. ISBN:0-7864-1128-7, ISBN13: 978-0-7864-1128-3. Dewey:362.29/088/796. LCCN:2001-044927.
Audience: **g,l,u,f.** *Choice, 2002.*

Waddington, Ivan **RC1230.W295 2000**
Sport, Health and Drugs: A Critical Sociological Perspective. Trade Paper. Routledge. New York, NY. 2000. 224p. ISBN:0-419-25200-2, ISBN13: 978-0-419-25200-9. Dewey:362.29/088/796. LCCN:99-053040.
Audience: **u,f.**

Wilson, Wayne & Derse, Edward (Editors) **RC1230.D76 2001**
Doping in Elite Sport: The Politics of Drugs in the Olympic Movement. Trade Cloth. Human Kinetics Publishers. Champaign, IL. 2001. 312p. ISBN:0-7360-0329-0, ISBN13: 978-0-7360-0329-2. Dewey:362.29/088/796. LCCN:00-033599.
Audience: **g,l,u,f.** *Choice, 2001.*

Yesalis, Charles E. **RC1230.A522 2000**
Anabolic Steroids in Sport and Exercise. Ed. 2. Trade Cloth. Human Kinetics Publishers. Champaign, IL. 2000. 512p. ISBN:0-88011-786-9, ISBN13: 978-0-88011-786-9. Dewey:362.29/088/796. LCCN:99-038353.
Audience: **g,l,u,f.** *Choice, 1993.*

Yesalis, Charles E. & Cowart, Virginia S. **RC1230.Y47 1998**
The Steroids Game. Joe Paterno (Foreword by). Trade Paper. Human Kinetics Publishers. Champaign, IL. 1998. 216p. ISBN:0-88011-494-0, ISBN13: 978-0-88011-494-3. Dewey:615/.7. LCCN:97-045859.
Audience: **g,l,u,f.**

Sport Medicine > Injuries and Rehabilitation

GV711.5

☐ National Strength and Conditioning Association.
http://www.nsca-lift.org/

Audience: **g,l,u,f.**

GV344

☐ National Youth Sport Safety Foundation.
http://www.nyssf.org/

Audience: **g,l,u,f.**

Alter, Michael J. **QP310.S77A45 2004**
Science of Flexibility. Ed. 3. Trade Cloth. Human Kinetics Publishers. Champaign, IL. 2004. 368p. ISBN:0-7360-4898-7, ISBN13: 978-0-7360-4898-9. Dewey:612.7/6. LCCN:2003-026043.

Audience: **f.**

Anderson, Marcia **RD97.A527 2002**
Fundamentals of Sports Injury Management. Ed. 2. Trade Cloth. Lippincott Williams & Wilkins. Philadelphia, PA. 2002. 480p. ISBN:0-7817-3272-7, ISBN13: 978-0-7817-3272-7. Dewey:617.1/027. LCCN:2002-072941.

Audience: **l,u.**

Beim, Gloria & Winter, Ruth **RC1218.W65B456 2003**
The Female Athlete's Body: How to Prevent and Treat Sports Injuries in Women and Girls. Trade Paper. McGraw-Hill Companies, The. New York, NY. 2003. 272p. ISBN:0-07-141175-5, ISBN13: 978-0-07-141175-2. Dewey:617.1/027/082. LCCN:2002-041439.

Audience: **g,l,u,f.**

Caine, Dennis J. (Editor), et al. **RA645.S68E65 1996**
Epidemiology of Sports Injuries. Caroline G. Caine & Koenraad J. Lindner (Editors). Trade Cloth. Human Kinetics Publishers. Champaign, IL. 1996. 472p. ISBN:0-87322-466-3, ISBN13: 978-0-87322-466-6. Dewey:617.1/027. LCCN:95-039000.

Audience: **u,f.** *Choice, 1996.*

Frontera, Walter R. (Editor) **RD97.R439 2002**
Rehabilitation of Sports Injuries: Scientific Basis. Trade Cloth. Blackwell Publishing, Inc. Malden, MA. 2002. 336p. The Encyclopaedia of Sports Medicine Ser., Vol. 10 ISBN:0-632-05813-7, ISBN13: 978-0-632-05813-6. Dewey:617.1/027. LCCN:02-007253.

Audience: **u,f.**

Griffith, H. Winter **RD97.G75 2004**
The Complete Guide to Sports Injuries. Ed. 3. Trade Paper. Penguin Group (USA) Inc. New York, NY. 2004. 544p. ISBN:0-399-52954-3, ISBN13: 978-0-399-52954-2. Dewey:617.1/027. LCCN:2004-274585.

Audience: **g,l,u,f.**

Houglum, Peggy A., et al. **RD97.S5383 2005**
Examination of Musculoskeletal Injuries. Ed. 2. David H. Perrin & Sandra J. Shultz (Authors). Perfect, Paper over Boards. Human Kinetics Publishers. Champaign, IL. 2005. 698p. Athletic Training Education Ser. ISBN:0-7360-5138-4, ISBN13: 978-0-7360-5138-5. Dewey:617.1027076. LCCN:2004-022788.

Audience: **u,f.**

Kreider, Richard B. (Editor), et al. **RC1235.O94 1998**
Overtraining in Sport. Andrew C. Fry & Mary L. O'Toole (Editors). Trade Cloth. Human Kinetics Publishers. Champaign, IL. 1997. 416p. ISBN:0-88011-563-7, ISBN13: 978-0-88011-563-6. Dewey:617.1/027. LCCN:97-031205.

Audience: **l,u,f.** *Choice, 1998.*

Maffetone, Phillip **RC1210.M24 1999**
Complementary Sports Medicine: Balancing Traditional and Nontraditional Treatments. Trade Cloth. Human Kinetics Publishers. Champaign, IL. 1999. 44p. ISBN:0-88011-869-5, ISBN13: 978-0-88011-869-9. Dewey:617.1/027. LCCN:98-052399.

Audience: **u,f.**

O'Connor, Rob, et al. **RD97**
Sports Injuries and Illnesses: Their Prevention and Treatment. Richard Budgett, Christine Wells & Jerry Lewis (Authors). Trade Cloth. Crowood Press, Limited, The. Wiltshire, 1998. 208p. ISBN:1-86126-107-1, ISBN13: 978-1-86126-107-6. Dewey:617.1/027.

Audience: **u,f.** *Choice, 1999.*

Peterson, Lars & Renstrom, Per **RD97**
Sports Injuries: Their Prevention and Treatment. Ed. 3. Trade Cloth. Human Kinetics Publishers. Champaign, IL. 2000. 548p. ISBN:0-7360-3621-0, ISBN13: 978-0-7360-3621-4. Dewey:617.1/027.

Audience: **g,l,u,f.**

Prentice, William E. & Arnheim, Daniel D. **RC1210.A749 2005**
Essentials of Athletic Injury Management. Ed. 6. Paper Text. McGraw-Hill Companies, The. New York, NY. 2004. 640p. ISBN:0-07-284367-5, ISBN13: 978-0-07-284367-5. Dewey:617.1/027. LCCN:2003-070608.

Audience: **u,f.**

Renstrom, P. A. (Editor) **RD97.C594 1994**
Clinical Practice of Sports Injury Prevention and Care. Ed. 2. Trade Cloth. Blackwell Publishing, Inc. Malden, MA. 1994. 744p. The Encyclopaedia of Sports Medicine Ser., Vol. 5 ISBN:0-632-03785-7, ISBN13: 978-0-632-03785-8. Dewey:617.1/027. LCCN:93-039208.

Audience: **u,f.**

Renstrom, P. A. (Editor) **RD97.S733 1993**
Sports Injuries: Basic Principles of Prevention and Care. Ed. 2. Trade Cloth. Blackwell Publishing, Inc. Malden, MA. 1993. 512p. The Encyclopaedia of Sports Medicine Ser., Vol. 4 ISBN:0-632-03331-2, ISBN13: 978-0-632-03331-7. Dewey:617.1027. LCCN:92-030508.

Audience: **g,l,u,f.**

Zatsiorsky, Vladimir M. (Editor) **RC1235.B476 2000**
Biomechanics in Sports: Performance Improvement and Injury Prevention. Trade Cloth. Blackwell Publishing, Inc. Malden, MA. 2000. 680p. Encyclopedia of Sports Medicine Ser., Vol. 9

ISBN:0-632-05392-5, ISBN13: 978-0-632-05392-6. Dewey:617.1/027. LCCN:99-054566.
Audience: **g,l,u,f.**

Sport Medicine > Athletic Training

GV203

National Athletic Trainers Association. http://www.nata.org/
Audience: **g,l,u,f.**

GV711.5

National Strength and Conditioning Association. http://www.nsca-lift.org/
Audience: **g,l,u,f.**

Alter, Michael J. **QP310.S77A45 2004**
Science of Flexibility. Ed. 3. Trade Cloth. Human Kinetics Publishers. Champaign, IL. 2004. 368p. ISBN:0-7360-4898-7, ISBN13: 978-0-7360-4898-9. Dewey:612.7/6. LCCN:2003-026043.
Audience: **f.**

Arnold, Brent, et al. **RC1210.A755 2005**
Research Methods in Athletic Training. Bruce Gansneder & David H. Perrin (Authors). Trade Cloth. F. A. Davis Company. Philadelphia, PA. 2004. 336p. ISBN:0-8036-0778-4, ISBN13: 978-0-8036-0778-1. Dewey:617.1/027/072. LCCN:2004-014305.
Audience: **u,f.**

Bar-Or, Oded (Editor), et al. **RC1218.C45C45 1996**
The Child and Adolescent Athlete. IOC Medical Commission Staff & International Federation of Sports Medicine Staff (Editors). Trade Cloth. Blackwell Publishing, Inc. Malden, MA. 1995. 720p. Encyclopedia of Sports Medicine Ser., Vol. 6 ISBN:0-86542-904-9, ISBN13: 978-0-86542-904-8. Dewey:617.1/027/083. LCCN:95-000182.
Audience: **g,l,u,f.**

Benjamin, Patricia & Lamp, Scott P. **RM721.B476 1996**
Understanding Sports Massage. Trade Paper. Human Kinetics Publishers. Champaign, IL. 1996. 136p. ISBN:0-87322-976-2, ISBN13: 978-0-87322-976-0. Dewey:615.8/22/088796. LCCN:95-049158.
Audience: **g,l,u.**

Bernier, Julie N. **RC1206.B475 2005**
Quick Reference Dictionary for Athletic Training. Ed. 2. Trade Paper. SLACK, Inc. Thorofare, NJ. 2005. 416p. ISBN:1-55642-666-6, ISBN13: 978-1-55642-666-7. Dewey:617.1/027/03. LCCN:2004-028843.
Audience: **g,l,u,f.**

Cartwright, Lorin A. & Pitney, William A. **RC1210.C36 2005**
Fundamentals of Athletic Training. Ed. 2. Trade Cloth, CD-ROM. Human Kinetics Publishers. Champaign, IL. 2005. 362p. ISBN:0-7360-5258-5, ISBN13: 978-0-7360-5258-0. Dewey:613.7/11. LCCN:2005-001507.
Audience: **g,l,u,f.**

Frontera, Walter R. (Editor) **RD97.R439 2002**
Rehabilitation of Sports Injuries: Scientific Basis. Trade Cloth. Blackwell Publishing, Inc. Malden, MA. 2002. 336p. The Encyclopaedia of Sports Medicine Ser., Vol. 10 ISBN:0-632-05813-7, ISBN13: 978-0-632-05813-6. Dewey:617.1/027. LCCN:02-007253.
Audience: **u,f.**

Griffith, H. Winter **RD97.G75 2004**
The Complete Guide to Sports Injuries. Ed. 3. Trade Paper. Penguin Group (USA) Inc. New York, NY. 2004. 544p. ISBN:0-399-52954-3, ISBN13: 978-0-399-52954-2. Dewey:617.1/027. LCCN:2004-274585.
Audience: **g,l,u,f.**

Hillman, Susan Kay **RC1210.H49 2005**
Introduction to Athletic Training. Ed. 2. Trade Cloth, CD-ROM. Human Kinetics Publishers. Champaign, IL. 2004. 352p. Athletic Training Education Ser. ISBN:0-7360-5292-5, ISBN13: 978-0-7360-5292-4. Dewey:617.1/027. LCCN:2004-012974.
Audience: **l,f.**

Houglum, Peggy A., et al. **RD97.S5383 2005**
Examination of Musculoskeletal Injuries. Ed. 2. David H. Perrin & Sandra J. Shultz (Authors). Perfect, Paper over Boards. Human Kinetics Publishers. Champaign, IL. 2005. 698p. Athletic Training Education Ser. ISBN:0-7360-5138-4, ISBN13: 978-0-7360-5138-5. Dewey:617.1027076. LCCN:2004-022788.
Audience: **u,f.**

Kreider, Richard B. (Editor), et al. **RC1235.O94 1998**
Overtraining in Sport. Andrew C. Fry & Mary L. O'Toole (Editors). Trade Cloth. Human Kinetics Publishers. Champaign, IL. 1997. 416p. ISBN:0-88011-563-7, ISBN13: 978-0-88011-563-6. Dewey:617.1/027. LCCN:97-031205.
Audience: **l,u,f.** *Choice, 1998.*

O'Connor, Rob, et al. **RD97**
Sports Injuries and Illnesses: Their Prevention and Treatment. Richard Budgett, Christine Wells & Jerry Lewis (Authors). Trade Cloth. Crowood Press, Limited, The. Wiltshire, 1998. 208p. ISBN:1-86126-107-1, ISBN13: 978-1-86126-107-6. Dewey:617.1/027.
Audience: **u,f.** *Choice, 1999.*

Pluim, Babette & Safran, Marc **RC1200.T4P58 2004**
From Breakpoint to Advantage: A Practical Guide to Optimal Tennis Health and Performance. Trade Paper. USRSA. Vista, CA. 2004. 352p. ISBN:0-9722759-1-6, ISBN13: 978-0-9722759-1-0. Dewey:796.342. LCCN:2004-093133.
Audience: **g,l,u,f.** *Choice, 2005.*

Prentice **RC1210.P726 2006**
Principles of Athletic Training: A Competency-Based Approach. Ed. 12. Cloth Text. McGraw-Hill Companies, The. New York, NY. 2005. 1056p. ISBN:0-07-297108-8, ISBN13: 978-0-07-297108-8. Dewey:617.1/027. LCCN:2004-066169.
Audience: **l,u,f.**

Prentice, William E. & Arnheim, Daniel D. **RC1210.A749 2005**
Essentials of Athletic Injury Management. Ed. 6. Paper Text. McGraw-Hill Companies, The. New York, NY. 2004. 640p. ISBN:0-07-284367-5, ISBN13: 978-0-07-284367-5. Dewey:617.1/027. LCCN:2003-070608.
Audience: **u,f.**

Ray, Richard **RC1210.R38 2005**
Management Strategies in Athletic Training. Ed. 3. Trade Cloth. Human Kinetics Publishers. Champaign, IL. 2004. 352p. Athletic Training Education Ser. ISBN:0-7360-5137-6, ISBN13: 978-0-7360-5137-8. Dewey:617.1/027. LCCN:2004-016536.
Audience: **u,f.**

Starkey, Chad **RC1210.A84 2005**
Athletic Training and Sports Medicine. Ed. 4. Glen Johnson (Editor). Cloth Text. Jones & Bartlett Publishers, Inc. Sudbury, MA. 2005. 720p. ISBN:0-7637-0536-5, ISBN13: 978-0-7637-0536-7. Dewey:617.1/027. LCCN:2005-006220.
Audience: **u,f.**

Zatsiorsky, Vladimir M. (Editor) **RC1235.B476 2000**
Biomechanics in Sports: Performance Improvement and Injury Prevention. Trade Cloth. Blackwell Publishing, Inc. Malden, MA. 2000. 680p. Encyclopedia of Sports Medicine Ser., Vol. 9 ISBN:0-632-05392-5, ISBN13: 978-0-632-05392-6. Dewey:617.1/027. LCCN:99-054566.
Audience: **g,l,u,f.**

Sport Medicine > Physical Therapy

GV711.5
National Strength and Conditioning Association. http://www.nsca-lift.org/
Audience: **g,l,u,f.**

Frontera, Walter R. (Editor) **RD97.R439 2002**
Rehabilitation of Sports Injuries: Scientific Basis. Trade Cloth. Blackwell Publishing, Inc. Malden, MA. 2002. 336p. The Encyclopaedia of Sports Medicine Ser., Vol. 10 ISBN:0-632-05813-7, ISBN13: 978-0-632-05813-6. Dewey:617.1/027. LCCN:02-007253.
Audience: **u,f.**

Griffith, H. Winter **RD97.G75 2004**
The Complete Guide to Sports Injuries. Ed. 3. Trade Paper. Penguin Group (USA) Inc. New York, NY. 2004. 544p. ISBN:0-399-52954-3, ISBN13: 978-0-399-52954-2. Dewey:617.1/027. LCCN:2004-274585.
Audience: **g,l,u,f.**

Houglum, Peggy A., et al. **RD97.S5383 2005**
Examination of Musculoskeletal Injuries. Ed. 2. David H. Perrin & Sandra J. Shultz (Authors). Perfect, Paper over Boards. Human Kinetics Publishers. Champaign, IL. 2005. 698p. Athletic Training Education Ser. ISBN:0-7360-5138-4, ISBN13: 978-0-7360-5138-5. Dewey:617.1027076. LCCN:2004-022788.
Audience: **u,f.**

Maffetone, Phillip **RC1210.M24 1999**
Complementary Sports Medicine: Balancing Traditional and Nontraditional Treatments. Trade Cloth. Human Kinetics Publishers. Champaign, IL. 1999. 44p. ISBN:0-88011-869-5, ISBN13: 978-0-88011-869-9. Dewey:617.1/027. LCCN:98-052399.
Audience: **u,f.**

O'Connor, Rob, et al. **RD97**
Sports Injuries and Illnesses: Their Prevention and Treatment. Richard Budgett, Christine Wells & Jerry Lewis (Authors). Trade Cloth. Crowood Press, Limited, The. Wiltshire, 1998. 208p. ISBN:1-86126-107-1, ISBN13: 978-1-86126-107-6. Dewey:617.1/027.
Audience: **u,f.** *Choice, 1999.*

Prentice, William E. & Arnheim, Daniel D. **RC1210.A749 2005**
Essentials of Athletic Injury Management. Ed. 6. Paper Text. McGraw-Hill Companies, The. New York, NY. 2004. 640p. ISBN:0-07-284367-5, ISBN13: 978-0-07-284367-5. Dewey:617.1/027. LCCN:2003-070608.
Audience: **u,f.**

Sport Medicine > Therapeutic Recreation

American College of Sports Medicine Staff (Contribution by) **RM725.A3 2002**
ACSM's Exercise Management for Persons with Chronic Diseases and Disabilities. Ed. 2. Trade Cloth. Human Kinetics Publishers. Champaign, IL. 2002. 384p. ISBN:0-7360-3872-8, ISBN13: 978-0-7360-3872-0. Dewey:615.8/24. LCCN:2002-006587.
Audience: **u,f.**

Austin, David R. (Editor), et al. **RM736.7**
Conceptual Foundations for Therapeutic Recreation. John Dattilo & Bryan P. McCormick (Editors). Cloth Text. Venture Publishing, Inc. State College, PA. 2002. 366p. ISBN:1-892132-30-3, ISBN13: 978-1-892132-30-7. Dewey:615.85101. LCCN:2002-104096.
Audience: **u,f.**

Bullock, Charles & Mahon, Michael **GV183.5**
Introduction to Recreation Services for People with Disabilities: A Person-Centered Approach. Trade Cloth. Sagamore Publishing, L.L.C.. Champaign, IL. 1997. 464p. ISBN:1-57167-069-6, ISBN13: 978-1-57167-069-4. Dewey:790.196.
Audience: **u,f.**

Carter, Marcia Jean & LeConey, Stephen P. **RM736.7**
Therapeutic Recreation Programs in the Community: An Inclusive Approach. Ed. 2. Trade Paper. Sagamore Publishing, L.L.C.. Champaign, IL. 2004. 217p. ISBN:1-57167-513-2, ISBN13: 978-1-57167-513-2. Dewey:790.196. LCCN:2004-101734.
Audience: **u,f.**

Engel, Barbara T. (Editor) **RM931.H6**
Therapeutic Riding II Strategies for Rehabilitation. Paper Text. Barbara Engel Therapy Services. Durango, CO. 1997. 490p. ISBN:0-9633065-6-1, ISBN13: 978-0-9633065-6-2. Dewey:615.8/515.
Audience: **u,f.**

Fine, Aubrey H. & Fine, Nya M. **RJ53.R43F56 1996**
Therapeutic Recreation for Exceptional Children: Let Me in, I Want to Play. Ed. 2. Cloth Text. Charles C. Thomas Publisher, Ltd. Springfield, IL. 1996. 422p. ISBN:0-398-06661-2, ISBN13: 978-0-398-06661-1. Dewey:615.8/5153/0880816. LCCN:96-008263.
Audience: **g,l,u,f.** *Choice, 1989.*

Lear, Roma **GV183.6**
Fun Without Fatigue. Ed. 2. Trade Paper. Elsevier - Health Sciences Division. Philadelphia, PA. 2001. 208p. ISBN:0-7506-2525-2, ISBN13: 978-0-7506-2525-8. Dewey:649.5/5/087.
Audience: **g,l,u,f.**

Mobily, Kenneth E. & MacNeil, Richard **RM736.7**
Therapeutic Recreation and the Nature of Disabilities. Cloth Text. Venture Publishing, Inc. State College, PA. 2002. 320p. ISBN:1-892132-22-2, ISBN13: 978-1-892132-22-2. Dewey:790.196. LCCN:2002-103088.
Audience: **u,f.**

Wilhite, Barbara C. & Keller, M. Jean **RM736.7.W54 2000**
Therapeutic Recreation: Cases and Exercises. Ed. 2. Paper Text. Venture Publishing, Inc. State College, PA. 2000. xxii, 314p. ISBN:1-892132-12-5, ISBN13: 978-1-892132-12-3. Dewey:615.8/5153. LCCN:99-067811.
Audience: **u,f.**

Minorities and Specific Groups in Sport

GV563
☐ Amateur Athletic Foundation of Los Angeles. http://www.aafla.org/
Audience: **g,l,u.**

GV568
☐ Scholarly Sport Sites: A Subject Directory. http://www.ucalgary.ca/lib-old/ssportsite/
Audience: **g,l,u,f.**

Baldassaro, Lawrence & Johnson, Dick (Editors) **GV867.64.A44 2002**
The American Game: Baseball and Ethnicity. Allan H. Selig (Foreword by). Trade Cloth. Southern Illinois University Press. Carbondale, IL. 2002. 224p. Writing Baseball Ser. ISBN:0-8093-2446-6, ISBN13: 978-0-8093-2446-0. Dewey:796.357. LCCN:2001-049600.
Audience: **g,l,u,f.** *Choice, 2002.*

Billet, Bret L. & Formwalt, Lance J. **GV863**
America's National Pastime: A Study of Race and Merit in Professional Baseball. Trade Cloth. Greenwood Publishing Group, Inc. Portsmouth, NH. 1995. 200p. ISBN:0-275-95193-6, ISBN13: 978-0-275-95193-1. Dewey:796.357/0973. LCCN:95-003331.
Audience: **g,l,u,f.** *Choice, 1996.*

Bloom, John & Willard, Michael Nevin (Editors) **GV706.32.S75 2002**
Sports Matters: Race, Recreation, and Culture. Trade Paper. New York University Press. New York, NY. 2002. 280p. ISBN:0-8147-9882-9, ISBN13: 978-0-8147-9882-9. Dewey:306.4/83. LCCN:2002-004918.
Audience: **g,l,u,f.** *Choice, 2003.*

Eisen, George & Wiggins, David K. (Editors) **GV709**
Ethnicity and Sport in North American History and Culture. Paper Text. Greenwood Publishing Group, Inc. Portsmouth, NH. 1995. 272p. Contributions to the Study of Popular Culture Ser., No. 40 ISBN:0-275-95451-X, ISBN13: 978-0-275-95451-2. Dewey:796.1/9. LCCN:93-050538.
Audience: **g,l,u,f.** *Choice, 1995.*

Elias, Robert (Editor) **GV867.64.B37 2001**
Baseball and the American Dream: Race, Class, Gender and the National Pastime. Cloth Text. M. E. Sharpe Inc. Armonk, NY. 2001. 328p. ISBN:0-7656-0763-8, ISBN13: 978-0-7656-0763-8. Dewey:306.4/83. LCCN:00-066140.
Audience: **l,u,f.**

King, C. Richard & Springwood, Charles Fruehling **GV706.32.K52 2001**
Beyond the Cheers: Race as Spectacle in College Sport. Paper Text. State University of New York Press. Albany, NY. 2001. x, 214p. Series on Sport, Culture, and Social Relations ISBN:0-7914-5006-6, ISBN13: 978-0-7914-5006-2. Dewey:796.04/3/08900973. LCCN:00-054797.
Audience: **u,f.** *Choice, 2001.*

Rothstein, Larry & Belson, Matthew **GV709.3 .J68 2002**
Raising the Bar: New Horizons in Disability Sport. Trade Cloth. Umbrage Editions. New York, NY. 2005. 136p. ISBN:1-884167-11-X, ISBN13: 978-1-884167-11-9. Dewey:796/.087/022. LCCN:2003-276831.
Audience: **g,l,u,f.**

Stewart, David A. **HV2551.S74 1991**
Deaf Sport: The Impact of Sports Within the Deaf Community. Trade Cloth. Gallaudet University Press. Washington, DC. 1991. 234p. ISBN:0-930323-74-2, ISBN13: 978-0-930323-74-5. Dewey:796/.087/2. LCCN:91-002056.
Audience: **u,f.**

Tatz, Colin **GV675.T38 1995**
The Obstacle Race: Aborigines in Sport. Trade Paper. University of New South Wales Press. Sydney, NSW. 1995. 422p. ISBN:0-86840-349-0, ISBN13: 978-0-86840-349-6. Dewey:796/.089/9915. LCCN:95-175567.
Audience: **u,f.** *Choice, 1996.*

Minorities and Specific Groups in Sport > African Americans

Aaron, Hank & Wheeler, Lonnie **GV865.R6**
I Had a Hammer: The Hank Aaron Story. Mass Market. HarperCollins Publishers. New York, NY. 1992. 480p. ISBN:0-06-109956-2, ISBN13: 978-0-06-109956-4. Dewey:796.357/092 B. LCCN:90-055521.
Audience: **g,l.**

Adelson, Bruce **GV875.A1A34 1999**
Brushing Back Jim Crow: The Integration of the Minor Leagues in the American South. Trade Cloth. University Press of Virginia. Charlottesville, VA. 1999. 288p. ISBN:0-8139-1884-7, ISBN13: 978-0-8139-1884-6. Dewey:796.357/64/0975. LCCN:98-045122.
Audience: **l,u,f.**

Ashe, A.R. **GV583**
A Hard Road to Glory: 1919-1945, Vol. 2. Ed. 3. Trade Paper. John Wiley & Sons, Inc. Hoboken, NJ. 2005. 540p. ISBN:0-471-73544-2, ISBN13: 978-0-471-73544-1. Dewey:796.08996073.
Audience: **g,l,u.**

Ashe, A.R. **GV583**
A Hard Road to Glory: A History of the African American Athlete, 1946-1969, Vol. 3, 3rd Edition, Vol. 3. Ed. 3. Trade Paper. John Wiley & Sons, Inc. Hoboken, NJ. 2005. 520p. ISBN:0-471-73546-9, ISBN13: 978-0-471-73546-5. Dewey:796.08996073.
Audience: **g,l,u.**

Ashe, A.R. **GV583**
A Hard Road to Glory: A History of the African American Athlete, 1970-Present, Vol. 4. Ed. 3. Trade Cloth. John Wiley & Sons, Inc. Hoboken, NJ. 2005. 352p. ISBN:0-471-73552-3, ISBN13: 978-0-471-73552-6. Dewey:796.08996073.
Audience: **g,l,u.**

Ashe, A.R. **GV583**
A Hard Road to Glory, 1619-1918, Vol. 1. Ed. 3. Trade Paper. John Wiley & Sons, Inc. Hoboken, NJ. 2005. 224p. ISBN:0-471-73542-6, ISBN13: 978-0-471-73542-7. Dewey:796.08996073.
Audience: **g,l,u.**

Baker, William J. **GV697.O9B35 2006**
Jesse Owens: An American Life. Trade Paper. University of Illinois Press. Champaign, IL. 2006. 304p. Sport and Society Ser. ISBN:0-252-07369-X, ISBN13: 978-0-252-07369-4. Dewey:796.42092 B. LCCN:2006-006960.
Audience: **g,l,u.** *Choice, 1987.*

Brookes, Rod **GV742.B76 2002**
Representing Sport. Trade Paper. Oxford University Press, Inc. New York, NY. 2002. 184p. A Hodder Arnold Publication ISBN:0-340-74052-3, ISBN13: 978-0-340-74052-1. Dewey:796. LCCN:2002-510305.
Audience: **l,u.** *Choice, 2002.*

Brooks, Dana D. & Althouse, Ronald C. (Editors) **GV706.32**
Racism in College Athletics: The African-American Athlete's Experience. Ed. 2. Trade Cloth. Fitness Information Technology, Inc. Morgantown, WV. 1999. 352p. ISBN:1-885693-19-2, ISBN13: 978-1-885693-19-8. Dewey:796/.0973.
Audience: **g,l,u,f.**

Bryant, Howard **GV875.B62B79 2002**
Shut Out: A Story of Race and Baseball in Boston. Paper over Boards. Routledge. New York, NY. 2002. 296p. ISBN:0-415-92779-X, ISBN13: 978-0-415-92779-6. Dewey:796.357/64/0974461. LCCN:2002-069950.
Audience: **u,f.**

Carroll, John M. **GV939.F29**
Fritz Pollard: Pioneer in Racial Advancement. Trade Paper. University of Illinois Press. Champaign, IL. 1998. 328p. Sport and Society Ser. ISBN:0-252-06799-1, ISBN13: 978-0-252-06799-0. Dewey:796.332/092 B.
Audience: **l,u.** *Choice, 1992.*

Chadwick, Bruce **GV875.A1.C47 1992**
When the Game Was Black and White: The Illustrated History of Baseball's Negro Leagues. Trade Cloth. Abbeville Press, Inc. New York, NY. 1992. 204p. ISBN:1-55859-372-1, ISBN13: 978-1-55859-372-5. Dewey:796.35708996073. LCCN:92-013673.
Audience: **g,l,u,f.** *Choice, 1993.*

Clark, Dick **GV863.A1**
The Negro Leagues Book. Trade Paper. Society for American Baseball Research. Cleveland, OH. 1994. 382p. ISBN:0-910137-55-2, ISBN13: 978-0-910137-55-3. Dewey:796.357.
Audience: **g,l,u,f.** *Choice, 1995.*

Cottrell, Robert Charles **GV865.F63C68 2001**
The Best Pitcher in Baseball: The Life of Rube Foster, Negro League Giant. Trade Cloth. New York University Press. New York, NY. 2001. 240p. ISBN:0-8147-1614-8, ISBN13: 978-0-8147-1614-4. Dewey:796.357/092 B. LCCN:2001-003175.
Audience: **g,l,u,f.** *Choice, 2002.*

Dawkins, Marvin P. & Kinloch, Graham C. **GV981**
African American Golfers During the Jim Crow Era. Trade Cloth. Greenwood Publishing Group, Inc. Portsmouth, NH. 2000. 200p. ISBN:0-275-95940-6, ISBN13: 978-0-275-95940-1. Dewey:796.352/089/96073. LCCN:99-034486.
Audience: **u,f.** *Choice, 2000.*

Dorinson, Joseph & Warmund, Joram (Editors) **GV865.R6**
Jackie Robinson: Race, Sports and the American Dream. Paper Text. M. E. Sharpe Inc. Armonk, NY. 1999. 296p. ISBN:0-7656-0318-7, ISBN13: 978-0-7656-0318-0. Dewey:796.357/092.
Audience: **g,l,u,f.** *Choice, 1999.*

Early, Gerald (Editor) **GV1132.A44 M83 1998**
Muhammad Ali Reader. Trade Cloth. HarperCollins Publishers. New York, NY. 1998. 320p. ISBN:0-88001-602-7, ISBN13: 978-0-88001-602-5. Dewey:796.83/092. LCCN:97-036846.
Audience: **u,f.**

Entine, Jon, et al. **GV583**
Taboo: Why Black Athletes Dominate Sports and Why We're Afraid to Talk about It. Gary Salles & Jay T. Kearney (Authors). Trade Paper. PublicAffairs. New York, NY. 2000. 400p. ISBN:1-58648-026-X, ISBN13: 978-1-58648-026-4. Dewey:796/.089/96073. LCCN:99-041889.
Audience: **g,l,u.**

Falkner, David **GV865.R6**
Great Time Coming: The Life of Jackie Robinson from Baseball to Birmingham. Trade Paper. Simon & Schuster. New York, NY. 1996. 384p. ISBN:0-684-82348-9, ISBN13: 978-0-684-82348-5. Dewey:796.357/092 B.
Audience: **g,l,u,f.**

Fitzpatrick, Frank **GV885.43.U53F58 2000**
And the Walls Came Tumbling Down: The Basketball Game That Changed American Sports. Trade Cloth. University of Nebraska Press. Lincoln, NE. 2000. 264p. ISBN:0-8032-6901-3, ISBN13: 978-0-8032-6901-9. Dewey:796.323/63/0975251. LCCN:00-033787.
Audience: **u,f.**

Gorn, Elliot J. (Editor) **GV1132.A44M85 1995**
Muhammad Ali: The People's Champ. Trade Cloth. University of Illinois Press. Champaign, IL. 1995. 224p. Sport and Society Ser. ISBN:0-252-02188-6, ISBN13: 978-0-252-02188-6. Dewey:796.8/3/092 B. LCCN:95-002358.
Audience: **g,l,u,f.** *Choice, 1996.*

Gray, Frances Clayton & Lamb, Yanick Rice **GV994.G53G73 2004**
Born to Win: The Authorized Biography of Althea Gibson. Bill Cosby (Foreword by), Venus Williams (Afterword by). Trade Cloth. John Wiley & Sons, Inc. Hoboken, NJ. 2004. 256p. ISBN:0-471-47165-8, ISBN13: 978-0-471-47165-3. Dewey:796.342/092 B. LCCN:2004-004690.
Audience: **g,l,u.**

Heaphy, Leslie A. **GV875.N35H43 2002**
The Negro Leagues, 1869-1960. Cloth Text. McFarland & Company, Incorporated Publishers. Jefferson, NC. 2002. 383p. ISBN:0-7864-1380-8, ISBN13: 978-0-7864-1380-5. Dewey:796.357/64/08996073. LCCN:2002-012225.
Audience: **g,l,u,f.** *Choice, 2003.*

Hietala, Thomas R. **GV1131.H64 2002**
The Fight of the Century: Jack Johnson, Joe Louis, and the Struggle for Racial Equality. Trade Cloth. M. E. Sharpe Inc. Armonk, NY. 2002. 386p. Social and Cultural History Ser. ISBN:0-7656-0722-0, ISBN13: 978-0-7656-0722-5. Dewey:796.83/092/2. LCCN:2001-049165.
Audience: **u,f.** *Choice, 2003.*

Hoberman, John **GV583**
Darwin's Athletes: How Sport has Damaged Black America and Preserved the Myth of Race. Cloth Text. Houghton Mifflin Company. New York, NY. 1997. 288p. ISBN:0-465-01557-3, ISBN13: 978-0-465-01557-3. Dewey:796/.089/96073.
Audience: **u,f.** *Choice, 1997.*

Hoberman, John M. **RC1235.H63 2001**
Mortal Engines. Perfect. Blackburn Press, The. Caldwell, NJ. 2002. 374p. ISBN:1-930665-37-7, ISBN13: 978-1-930665-37-8. Dewey:617.1/027. LCCN:2001-093232.
Audience: **u,f.**

Hotaling, Edward **SF336.A2H68**
The Great Black Jockeys: The Lives and Times of the Men Who Dominated America's First National Sport. Trade Cloth. DIANE Publishing Company. Collingdale, PA. 2001. 380p. ISBN:0-7881-9643-X, ISBN13: 978-0-7881-9643-0. Dewey:798.4/0092396073.
Audience: **l,u.**

Jackson, Phil & Rosen, Charley **GV884.J32A34 2001**
More Than a Game. Trade Cloth. Seven Stories Press. New York, NY. 2004. 0p. ISBN:1-58322-060-7, ISBN13: 978-1-58322-060-3. Dewey:796.323/092 B. LCCN:00-050957.
Audience: **g,l,u.** *Choice, 2001.*

Johnson, Cecil **GV1833.6.P5J64 1994**
Guts: Legendary Black Rodeo Cowboy Bill Pickett. June Ford (Editor). Trade Cloth. Summit Publishing Group - Legacy Books. Irving, TX. 1994. 223p. ISBN:1-56530-162-5, ISBN13: 978-1-56530-162-7. Dewey:791.8 B. LCCN:94-038591.
Audience: **g,l.** *Choice, 1995.*

Kuska, Bob **GV885.73.W18K87 2004**
Hot Potato: How Washington and New York Gave Birth to Black Basketball and Changed America's Game Forever. Trade Cloth. University Press of Virginia. Charlottesville, VA. 2004. 220p. ISBN:0-8139-2263-1, ISBN13: 978-0-8139-2263-8. Dewey:796.323/64/08996073. LCCN:2003-018322.
Audience: **u,f.**

Lamb, Chris **GV865.R6L36 2004**
Blackout: The Untold Story of Jackie Robinson's First Spring Training. Trade Cloth. University of Nebraska Press. Lincoln, NE. 2005. 176p. ISBN:0-8032-2956-9, ISBN13: 978-0-8032-2956-3. Dewey:796.357/092 B. LCCN:2004-000614.
Audience: **l,u,f.** *Choice, 2005.*

Lanctot, Neil **GV875.N35L36 2004**
Negro League Baseball: The Rise and Ruin of a Black Institution. Book, Other. University of Pennsylvania Press. Philadelphia, PA. 2004. 496p. ISBN:0-8122-3807-9, ISBN13: 978-0-8122-3807-5. Dewey:796.357/64/0973. LCCN:2004-043547.
Audience: **g,l,u,f.** *Choice, 2004.*

Levy, Alan H. **GV943.9.S64L48 2003**
Tackling Jim Crow: Racial Segregation in Professional Football. Paper Text. McFarland & Company, Incorporated Publishers. Jefferson, NC. 2003. 180p. ISBN:0-7864-1597-5, ISBN13: 978-0-7864-1597-7. Dewey:796.332/0896/073. LCCN:2003-005735.
Audience: **u,f.** *Choice, 2003.*

Lomax, Michael E. **GV863.A1L65 2003**
Black Baseball Entrepreneurs, 1860-1901: Operating by Any Means Necessary. Trade Paper. Syracuse University Press. Syracuse, NY. 2003. xxvi, 222p. Sports and Entertainment Ser. ISBN:0-8156-0786-5, ISBN13: 978-0-8156-0786-1. Dewey:796.357/64/08996073. LCCN:2002-154375.
Audience: **u,f.**

Mead, Chris **GV1132.M84**
Champion Joe Louis: A Biography. Trade Paper. Anova Books. London, 1997. 330p. ISBN:0-86051-848-5, ISBN13: 978-0-86051-848-8. Dewey:796.8/3/0924.
Audience: **l,u.**

Miller, Leonard W. **GV1032.M45 2003**
Silent Thunder: Breaking Through Cultural, Racial, and Class Barriers in Motorsports. Trade Paper. Red Sea Press. Trenton, NJ. 2003. 212p. ISBN:1-56902-177-5, ISBN13: 978-1-56902-177-4. Dewey:796.72/092 B. LCCN:2003-013084.
Audience: **l,u.**

Miller, Patrick B. & Wiggins, David K. (Editors) **GV706.32.S73 2004**
Sport and the Color Line: Black Athletes and Race Relations in Twentieth Century America. UK-B Format Paperback. Routledge. New York, NY. 2003. 400p. ISBN:0-415-94611-5, ISBN13: 978-0-415-94611-7. Dewey:796/.089/96073. LCCN:2003-014009.
Audience: **g,l,u,f.**

Porter, David L. (Editor) **GV697**
Latino and African American Athletes Today: A Biographical Dictionary. Cloth Text. Greenwood Publishing Group, Inc. Portsmouth, NH. 2004. 472p. ISBN:0-313-32048-9, ISBN13: 978-0-313-32048-4. Dewey:796/.092/2 B. LCCN:2003-047241.
Audience: **g,l,u.** *Choice, 2004.*

Rampersad, Arnold **GV865.R6R34 1997**
Jackie Robinson: A Biography. Trade Cloth. Alfred A. Knopf Inc. New York, NY. 1997. 448p. ISBN:0-679-44495-5, ISBN13: 978-0-679-44495-4. Dewey:796.357/092. LCCN:97-005165.
Audience: **g,l,u,f.** *Choice, 1998.*

Remnick, David **GV1132.A44R46 1998**
King of the World: Muhammad Ali and the Rise of an American Hero. Trade Cloth. Random House, Inc. New York, NY. 1998. 336p. ISBN:0-375-50065-0, ISBN13: 978-0-375-50065-7. Dewey:796.8/3/092. LCCN:98-024539.
Audience: **g,l,u,f.** *Choice, 1999.*

Ribowsky, Mark **GV865.P3R53 1994**
Don't Look Back: Satchel Paige on the Shadows of Baseball. Trade Cloth. Simon & Schuster. New York, NY. 1994. ISBN:0-671-77674-6, ISBN13: 978-0-671-77674-9. Dewey:796.357/092 B. LCCN:93-038802.
Audience: **g,l,u,f.**

Ribowsky, Mark **GV865.G53R53 2004**
Josh Gibson: The Power and the Darkness. Trade Paper. University of Illinois Press. Champaign, IL. 2004. 328p. ISBN:0-252-07224-3, ISBN13: 978-0-252-07224-6. Dewey:796.357/092 B. LCCN:2004-053696.
Audience: **g,l,u,f.**

Robinson, Jackie W. & Duckett, Alfred **GV865.R6**
I Never Had It Made: An Autobiography of Jackie Robinson. Trade Paper. HarperCollins Publishers. New York, NY. 2003. 304p. ISBN:0-06-055597-1, ISBN13: 978-0-06-055597-9. Dewey:796.357/092/4.
Audience: **g,l,u.**

Ross, Charles K. **GV955.5.N35R67 1999**
Outside the Lines: African-Americans and the Integration of the National Football League. Trade Cloth. New York University Press. New York, NY. 2000. 240p. ISBN:0-8147-7495-4, ISBN13: 978-0-8147-7495-3. Dewey:796.332/64/08996073. LCCN:99-006581.
Audience: **u,f.** *Choice, 2000.*

Sailes, Gary A. (Editor) **GV583.A56 1998**
African Americans in Sport: Contemporary Themes. Trade Paper. Transaction Publishers. Somerset, NJ. 1998. 271p. ISBN:0-7658-0440-9, ISBN13: 978-0-7658-0440-2. Dewey:796/.089/96073. LCCN:98-010468.
Audience: **l,u,f.**

Schoenfeld, Bruce **GV994.A1**
The Match: Althea Gibson and a Portrait of a Friendship. Trade Paper, Perfect. HarperCollins Publishers. New York, NY. 2005. 320p. ISBN:0-06-052653-X, ISBN13: 978-0-06-052653-5. Dewey:796.3420922.
Audience: **l,u,f.**

Shropshire, Kenneth L. **GV706.32.S48 1996**
In Black and White: Race and Sports in America. Kellen Winslow (Foreword by). Trade Cloth. New York University Press. New York, NY. 1996. 212p. ISBN:0-8147-8016-4, ISBN13: 978-0-8147-8016-9. Dewey:305.8/00973. LCCN:95-050200.
Audience: **l,u,f.** *Choice, 1997.*

Thomas, Ron **GV885.7.T46 2002**
They Cleared the Lane: The NBA's Black Pioneers. Trade Cloth. University of Nebraska Press. Lincoln, NE. 2002. 288p. ISBN:0-8032-4437-1, ISBN13: 978-0-8032-4437-5. Dewey:796.323/64/08996073. LCCN:2001-052234.
Audience: **u,f.** *Choice, 2002.*

Tygiel, Jules **GV865.R6T93 1997**
Baseball's Great Experiment: Jackie Robinson and His Legacy. Trade Paper. Oxford University Press, Inc. New York, NY. 1997. 432p. ISBN:0-19-510620-2, ISBN13: 978-0-19-510620-6. Dewey:796.357/092 B. LCCN:96-038551.
Audience: **g,l,u,f.**

White, Sol **GV863.A1W448 1995**
Sol White's History of Colored Base Ball, with Other Documents on the Early Black Game, 1886-1936. Jerry Malloy (Compiled by, Introduction by). Cloth Text. University of Nebraska Press. Lincoln, NE. 1995. 190p. ISBN:0-8032-4771-0, ISBN13: 978-0-8032-4771-0. Dewey:796.357/0973. LCCN:94-020992.
Audience: **u,f.** *Choice, 1996.*

Wiggins, David K. **GV583.W545 1997**
Glory Bound: Black Athletes in a White America. Trade Paper. Syracuse University Press. Syracuse, NY. 1997. 307p. Sports and Entertainment Ser. ISBN:0-8156-2734-3, ISBN13: 978-0-8156-2734-0. Dewey:796/.089/96073. LCCN:96-046218.
Audience: **l,u,f.** *Choice, 1997.*

Zang, David W. **GV865.W34Z35 1995**
Fleet Walker's Divided Heart: The Life of Baseball's First Black Major Leaguer. Trade Cloth. University of Nebraska Press. Lincoln, NE. 1995. 171p. ISBN:0-8032-4913-6, ISBN13: 978-0-8032-4913-4. Dewey:796.357/092 B. LCCN:94-033517.
Audience: **g,l,u,f.** *Choice, 1996.*

Minorities and Specific Groups in Sport > Latinos

Arbena, Joseph L. (Compiled by) **Z7515**
Latin American Sport: An Annotated Bibliography, 1988-1998. Cloth Text. Greenwood Publishing Group, Inc. Portsmouth, NH. 1999. 264p. Bibliographies and Indexes on Sports History Ser., Vol. 3 ISBN:0-313-29611-1, ISBN13: 978-0-313-29611-6. Dewey:016.796/098. LCCN:99-011260.
Audience: **u,f.** *Choice, 2000.*

Bjarkman, Peter C. **GV863.155.B53 1994**
Baseball with a Latin Beat: A History of the Latin American Game. Paper Text. McFarland & Company, Incorporated Publishers. Jefferson, NC. 1994. 486p. ISBN:0-89950-973-8, ISBN13: 978-0-89950-973-0. Dewey:796.357/098. LCCN:94-3526.
Audience: **u,f.** *Choice, 1995.*

Oleksak, Michael M. & Oleksak, Mary A. **GV862.6.O43 1991**
Beisbol: Latin Americans and the Grand Old Game. Trade Cloth. McGraw-Hill Trade. New York, NY. 1991. 320p. ISBN:0-940279-35-5, ISBN13: 978-0-940279-35-3. Dewey:796.357/098. LCCN:91-010697.
Audience: **g,l,u,f.** *Choice, 1991.*

Porter, David L. (Editor) **GV697**
Latino and African American Athletes Today: A Biographical Dictionary. Cloth Text. Greenwood Publishing Group, Inc. Portsmouth, NH. 2004. 472p. ISBN:0-313-32048-9, ISBN13: 978-0-313-32048-4. Dewey:796/.092/2 B. LCCN:2003-047241.
Audience: **g,l,u.** *Choice, 2004.*

Regalado, Samuel O. **GV865.A1R38 1998**
Viva Baseball!: Latin Major Leaguers and Their Special Hunger. Trade Cloth. University of Illinois Press. Champaign, IL. 1998. 264p. Sport and Society Ser. ISBN:0-252-02372-2, ISBN13: 978-0-252-02372-9. Dewey:796.357/64/098. LCCN:97-021066.
Audience: **g,l,u,f.** *Choice, 1998.*

Minorities and Specific Groups in Sport > Asians

Franks, Joel S. **GV583.F73 2000**
Crossing Sidelines, Crossing Cultures: Sport and Asian Pacific American Cultural Citizenship. Trade Cloth. University Press of America, Inc. Lanham, MD. 2000. 232p. ISBN:0-7618-1592-9, ISBN13: 978-0-7618-1592-1. Dewey:796/.089/95073. LCCN:99-056934.
Audience: **g,l.** *Choice, 2000.*

Guttmann, Allen & Thompson, Lee B. **GV655.G88 2001**
Japanese Sports: A History. Trade Cloth. University of Hawaii Press. Honolulu, HI. 2001. 320p. ISBN:0-8248-2414-8, ISBN13: 978-0-8248-2414-3. Dewey:796/.0952. LCCN:00-066665.
Audience: **u,f.** *Choice, 2002.*

Leheny, David Richard **GV125.L43 2003**
The Rules of Play: National Identity and the Shaping of Japanese Leisure. Trade Cloth. Cornell University Press. Ithaca, NY. 2003. xiv, 188p. Cornell Studies in Political Economy ISBN:0-8014-4091-2, ISBN13: 978-0-8014-4091-5. Dewey:306.4/8/0952. LCCN:2002-151027.
Audience: **u,f.** *Choice, 2003.*

Nguyen, Dat & Burson, Rusty **GV939.N46A3 2005**
Dat: Tackling Life and the NFL. Darren Woodson (Foreword by). Trade Cloth. Texas A&M University Press. College Station, TX. 2005. 224p. ISBN:1-58544-472-3, ISBN13: 978-1-58544-472-4. Dewey:796.332/092 B. LCCN:2005-004658.
Audience: **g,l,u.**

Reaves, Joseph A. **GV863.69.R43 2002**
Taking in a Game: A History of Baseball in Asia. Trade Cloth. University of Nebraska Press. Lincoln, NE. 2002. 220p. Jerry Malloy Prize Ser. ISBN:0-8032-3943-2, ISBN13: 978-0-8032-3943-2. Dewey:796.357/095. LCCN:2001-043058.
Audience: **g,l,u,f.** *Choice, 2002.*

Whiting, Robert **GV865.S895W55 2004**
The Meaning of Ichiro: The New Wave from Japan and the Transformation of Our National Pastime. Trade Cloth. Warner Books, Inc. New York, NY. 2004. 336p. ISBN:0-446-53192-8, ISBN13: 978-0-446-53192-4. Dewey:796.357/092 B. LCCN:2003-027134.
Audience: **u,f.** *Choice, 2005.*

Minorities and Specific Groups in Sport > Women

HQ1237
☐ Gender equity in Sports.
http://bailiwick.lib.uiowa.edu/ge/
Audience: **g,l,u,f.**

RA564.85
☐ Melpomene Institute.
http://www.melpomene.org/
Audience: **g,l,u,f.**

GV709
☐ Women's Sport Foundation (US).
http://www.womenssportsfoundation.org/
Audience: **g,l,u,f.**

Ardell, Jean Hastings **GV880.7.A73 2005**
Breaking into Baseball: Women and the National Pasttime. Ila Borders (Foreword by). Trade Paper, Perfect, Paper over Boards. Southern Illinois University Press. Carbondale, IL. 2005. 278p. Writing Baseball Ser. ISBN:0-8093-2627-2, ISBN13: 978-0-8093-2627-3. Dewey:796.357/082. LCCN:2004-019010.
Audience: **g,l,u,f.** *Choice, 2005.*

Berkshire Reference Works Staff **GV709 .I58 2001**
International Encyclopedia for Women and Sports, Vol. 3. Trade Cloth. Thomson Gale. Farmington Hills, MI. 1999. lii, 1428p. International Encyclopedia for Women and Sports Ser., Vol. 3 ISBN:0-02-864953-2, ISBN13: 978-0-02-864953-5. Dewey:796.082. LCCN:00-062518.
Audience: **g,l,u,f.**

Berkshire Reference Works Staff **GV709 .I58 2001**
International Encyclopedia for Women and Sports, Vol. 2. Trade Cloth. Thomson Gale. Farmington Hills, MI. 1999. lii, 1428p. International Encyclopedia for Women and Sports Ser., Vol. 2 ISBN:0-02-864952-4, ISBN13: 978-0-02-864952-8. Dewey:796.082. LCCN:00-062518.
Audience: **g,l,u,f.**

Berkshire Reference Works Staff **GV709 .I58 2001**
International Encyclopedia for Women and Sports, Vol. 1. Trade Cloth. Thomson Gale. Farmington Hills, MI. 1999. lii, 1428p. International Encyclopedia for Women and Sports Ser., Vol. 1 ISBN:0-02-864951-6, ISBN13: 978-0-02-864951-1. Dewey:796.082. LCCN:00-062518.
Audience: **g,l,u,f.**

Berlage, Gai I. & Gerard, Charley **GV880**
Women in Baseball: The Forgotten History. Trade Cloth. Greenwood Publishing Group, Inc. Portsmouth, NH. 1994. 224p. ISBN:0-275-94735-1, ISBN13: 978-0-275-94735-4. Dewey:796.357082. LCCN:93-025049.
Audience: **g,l,u,f.** *Choice, 1994.*

Birrell, Susan & Cole, Cheryl L. (Editors) **GV709.W577 1994**
Women, Sport, and Culture. Trade Cloth. Human Kinetics Publishers. Champaign, IL. 1994. 416p. ISBN:0-87322-650-X, ISBN13: 978-0-87322-650-9. Dewey:796/.0194. LCCN:93-038013.
Audience: **u,f.** *Choice, 1995.*

Bolin, Anne & Granskog, Jane (Editors) **GV439.A84 2003**
Athletic Intruders: Ethnographic Research on Women, Culture, and Exercise. Paper Text. State University of New York Press. Albany, NY. 2003. x, 294p. Suny Series, Sport, Culture, and

Social Relations Ser. ISBN:0-7914-5584-X, ISBN13: 978-0-7914-5584-5. Dewey:306.4/83. LCCN:2002-023131.
Audience: **u,f.** *Choice, 2003.*

Boyne, Daniel J. **GV793**
The Red Rose Crew: A True Story of Women, Winning, and the Water. David Halberstam (Foreword by). Paper Text. Globe Pequot Press, The. Guilford, CT. 2005. 240p. ISBN:1-59228-758-1, ISBN13: 978-1-59228-758-1. Dewey:797.1/4/092273.
Audience: **g,l,u,f.**

Brown, Rebecca A. **GV199.9**
Women on High: Pioneers of Mountaineering. Trade Paper. Appalachian Mountain Club Books. Boston, MA. 2003. 272p. ISBN:1-929173-42-3, ISBN13: 978-1-929173-42-6. Dewey:796.52/2/0922.
Audience: **l,u.** *Choice, 2003.*

Byrne, Julie **GV885.43.I525B97**
O God of Players: The Story of the Immaculata Mighty Macs. Trade Paper. Eastern European Monographs. Bradenton, FL. 2003. 312p. ISBN:0-231-12749-9, ISBN13: 978-0-231-12749-3. Dewey:796.323/63/0974811. LCCN:2003-043574.
Audience: **g,l,u,f.** *Choice, 2004.*

Cahn, Susan K. **GV709**
Coming on Strong: Gender and Sexuality in Twentieth-Century Women's Sports. Trade Paper. Harvard University Press. Cambridge, MA. 1998. 39p. ISBN:0-674-14434-1, ISBN13: 978-0-674-14434-7. Dewey:796/.0194.
Audience: **g,l,u,f.**

Carpenter, Linda J. & Acosta, Vivian R. **KF4166.C37 2004**
Title IX. Trade Cloth. Human Kinetics Publishers. Champaign, IL. 2004. 28p. ISBN:0-7360-4239-3, ISBN13: 978-0-7360-4239-0. Dewey:344.73/099. LCCN:2004-009221.
Audience: **g,l,u,f.**

Cayleff, Susan E. **GV964.Z3**
Babe: The Life and Legend of Babe Didrikson Zaharias. Trade Paper. University of Illinois Press. Champaign, IL. 1996. 368p. Women in American History Ser. ISBN:0-252-06593-X, ISBN13: 978-0-252-06593-4. Dewey:920. LCCN:94-035584.
Audience: **g,l,u.**

Coffey, Wayne **GV885.43.G25C64 2002**
Winning Sounds Like This: A Season with the Women's Basketball Team at Gallaudet, the World's Only University for the Deaf. Trade Cloth. Crown Publishing Group. New York, NY. 2002. 256p. ISBN:0-609-60765-0, ISBN13: 978-0-609-60765-7. Dewey:796.323/63/09753. LCCN:2002-283485.
Audience: **g,l,u,f.**

Cohen, Greta L. (Editor) **GV709.18.U6**
Women in Sport: Issues and Controversies. Trade Paper. SAGE Publications, Inc. Thousand Oaks, CA. 1993. 360p. ISBN:0-8039-4980-4, ISBN13: 978-0-8039-4980-5. Dewey:796/.082/0973. LCCN:93-006510.
Audience: **g,l,f.** *Choice, 1993.*

Costa, D. Margaret & Guthrie, Sharon R. (Editors) **GV709.W56 1994**
Women and Sport: Interdisciplinary Perspectives. Trade Cloth. Human Kinetics Publishers. Champaign, IL. 1994. 416p. ISBN:0-87322-686-0, ISBN13: 978-0-87322-686-8. Dewey:796/.0194. LCCN:93-050167.
Audience: **g,l,f.**

Creedon, Pamela J. (Editor) **GV706.32.W66 1994**
Women, Media and Sport: Challenging Gender Values. Trade Paper. SAGE Publications, Inc. Thousand Oaks, CA. 1994. 368p. ISBN:0-8039-5234-1, ISBN13: 978-0-8039-5234-8. Dewey:796/.0194. LCCN:93-041211.
Audience: **g,l,u,f.** *Choice, 1994.*

Crosset, Todd W. **GV966.C76 1995**
Outsiders in the Clubhouse: The World of Women's Professional Golf. Cloth Text. State University of New York Press. Albany, NY. 1995. 276p. SUNY Series on Sport, Culture, and Social Relations ISBN:0-7914-2489-8, ISBN13: 978-0-7914-2489-6. Dewey:796.352. LCCN:94-027916.
Audience: **g,u,f.** *Choice, 1996.*

Daddario, Gina **GV742**
Women's Sport and Spectacle: Gendered Television Coverage and the Olympic Games. Trade Cloth. Greenwood Publishing Group, Inc. Portsmouth, NH. 1998. 184p. ISBN:0-275-95856-6, ISBN13: 978-0-275-95856-5. Dewey:302.23/45/082. LCCN:97-038544.
Audience: **u,f.** *Choice, 1998.*

Dawson, Buck **GV837.9.D39 2000**
Mermaids on Parade: America's Love Affair with Its First Olympic Swimmers. Paul Gallico (Introduction by). Trade Cloth. Nova Science Publishers, Inc. Hauppauge, NY. 2000. 266p. ISBN:1-56072-726-8, ISBN13: 978-1-56072-726-2. Dewey:797.2/1/082092273 B. LCCN:2001-267948.
Audience: **g,l,u,f.**

Etue, Elizabeth & Williams, Megan K. **GV847**
On the Edge: Women Making Hockey History. Trade Paper. Second Story Press. Toronto, ON. 1996. 336p. ISBN:0-929005-79-1, ISBN13: 978-0-929005-79-9. Dewey:796.962/082.
Audience: **u,f.** *Choice, 1997.*

Fan, Hong Y. **GT498.F66F36 1997**
Footbinding, Feminism and Freedom: The Liberation of Women's Bodies in Modern China. Paper over Boards. Taylor & Francis Group. Philadelphia, PA. 1997. 352p. Sport in the Global Society Ser., Vol. 1 ISBN:0-7146-4633-4, ISBN13: 978-0-7146-4633-6. Dewey:391.4/1. LCCN:97-004512.
Audience: **u,f.** *Choice, 1998.*

Festle, Mary Jo **GV709.F37 1996**
Playing Nice: Politics and Apologies in Women's Sports. Trade Cloth. Columbia University Press. New York, NY. 1996. 400p. ISBN:0-231-10162-7, ISBN13: 978-0-231-10162-2. Dewey:796/.0194. LCCN:96-004739.
Audience: **g,l,u,f.** *Choice, 1997.*

Fields, Sarah K. **GV709.18.U6F54 2004**
Female Gladiators: Gender, Law, and Contact Sport in America. Trade Cloth. University of Illinois Press. Champaign, IL. 2004. 232p. Sport and Society Ser. ISBN:0-252-02958-5, ISBN13: 978-0-252-02958-5. Dewey:796/.082/0973. LCCN:2004-008913.
Audience: **u,f.** *Choice, 2005.*

Gandolfo, Christina **GV1060.73.W66 2005**
The Woman Triathlete. Trade Paper. Human Kinetics Publishers. Champaign, IL. 2004. 248p. ISBN:0-7360-5430-8, ISBN13: 978-0-7360-5430-0. Dewey:796.42/57/082. LCCN:2004-020137.
Audience: **l,u.**

Gavora, Jessica **GV709.18.U6G38 2002**
Tilting the Playing Field: Schools, Sports, Sex and Title IX. Trade Cloth. National Book Network. Lanham, MD. 2001. 181p. ISBN:1-893554-35-X, ISBN13: 978-1-893554-35-1. Dewey:796/.082. LCCN:2001-055597.
Audience: **u,f.** *Choice, 2003, 2002.*

Gerber, Ellen W., et al. **GV709.A64**
The American Woman in Sport. Jan Felshin, Pearl Berlin & Waneen Wyrick (Authors). Cloth Text. Addison-Wesley Longman, Inc. Boston, MA. 1974. xi, 562p. ISBN:0-201-02353-9, ISBN13: 978-0-201-02353-4. Dewey:796/.019/40973. LCCN:74-002849.
Audience: **g,l,f.** B

Gray, Frances Clayton & Lamb, Yanick Rice **GV994.G53G73 2004**
Born to Win: The Authorized Biography of Althea Gibson. Bill Cosby (Foreword by), Venus Williams (Afterword by). Trade Cloth. John Wiley & Sons, Inc. Hoboken, NJ. 2004. 256p. ISBN:0-471-47165-8, ISBN13: 978-0-471-47165-3. Dewey:796.342/092 B. LCCN:2004-004690.
Audience: **g,l,u.**

Guthrie, Janet **GV1032.G87A3 2005**
Janet Guthrie: A Life at Full Throttle. Trade Cloth. Sport Media Publishing. Toronto, ON. 2005. 512p. ISBN:1-894963-31-8, ISBN13: 978-1-894963-31-2. Dewey:796.72/092 B. LCCN:2004-026599.
Audience: **g,l,u,f.**

Guttmann, Allen **GV709**
Women's Sports: A History. Trade Paper. Columbia University Press. New York, NY. 1992. 339p. ISBN:0-231-06957-X, ISBN13: 978-0-231-06957-1. Dewey:796/.0194.
Audience: **g,l,u,f.** *Choice, 1991.*

Hall, M. Ann **GV709.H32 1996**
Feminism and Sporting Bodies: Essays on Theory and Practice. Trade Paper. Human Kinetics Publishers. Champaign, IL. 1996. 144p. ISBN:0-87322-969-X, ISBN13: 978-0-87322-969-2. Dewey:796/.0194. LCCN:95-044480.
Audience: **u,f.** *Choice, 1996.*

Hall, M. Ann **GV709.18.C2H35 2002**
The Girl and the Game: A History of Women's Sport in Canada. Trade Paper. Broadview Press. Peterborough, ON. 2002. 284p. ISBN:1-55111-268-X, ISBN13: 978-1-55111-268-8. Dewey:796/.082/0973. LCCN:2002-416290.
Audience: **g,u,f.** *Choice, 2003.*

Hargreaves, Jennifer **GV709.18.G7H37 1994**
Sporting Females: Critical Issues in the History and Sociology of Women's Sports. Trade Paper. Routledge. New York, NY. 1994. 344p. ISBN:0-415-07028-7, ISBN13: 978-0-415-07028-7. Dewey:796.0194. LCCN:93-024575.
Audience: **u,f.**

Harris, Fran **GV885.515.W66**
Summer Madness: The Wild, Wacky, Wonderful World of the WNBA. Trade Paper. iUniverse, Inc. Lincoln, NE. 2001. 268p. ISBN:0-595-16030-1, ISBN13: 978-0-595-16030-3. Dewey:796.323/092.
Audience: **g,l,u.**

Hartmann-Tews, Ilse **GV709.S66 2003**
Sport and Women: Social Issues in International Perspective. Gertrud Pfister (Editor). Paper over Boards. Routledge. New York, NY. 2002. 304p. ISBN:0-415-24627-X, ISBN13: 978-0-415-24627-9. Dewey:796/.082. LCCN:2002-073982.
Audience: **g,l,u,f.** *Choice, 2003.*

Hawkes, Nena Rey & Seggar, John F. **GV697**
Celebrating Women Coaches: A Biographical Dictionary. Cloth Text. Greenwood Publishing Group, Inc. Portsmouth, NH. 2000. 312p. ISBN:0-313-30912-4, ISBN13: 978-0-313-30912-0. Dewey:796/.082/092273 B. LCCN:99-088485.
Audience: **g,l.** *Choice, 2001.*

Henderson, Karla A., et al. **GV183.B57 1996**
Both Gains and Gaps: Feminist Perspectives on Women's Leisure. M. Deborah Bialeschki, Susan M. Shaw & Valeria J. Freysinger (Authors). Trade Cloth. Venture Publishing, Inc. State College, PA. 1996. 357p. ISBN:0-910251-79-7, ISBN13: 978-0-910251-79-2. Dewey:790.1/94. LCCN:95-061907.
Audience: **u,f.**

Heywood, Leslie & Dworkin, Shari L. **GV709.18.U6H49 2003**
Built to Win: The Female Athlete As Cultural Icon. Trade Paper. University of Minnesota Press. Minneapolis, MN. 2003. 272p. Sport and Culture Ser., Vol. 5 ISBN:0-8166-3624-9, ISBN13: 978-0-8166-3624-2. Dewey:796/.082. LCCN:2002-156528.
Audience: **g,l,f.** *Choice, 2004.*

Hill, Lynn & Child, Greg **GV199.92.R62**
Climbing Free: My Life in the Vertical World. Trade Paper. W. W. Norton & Company, Inc. New York, NY. 2003. 288p. ISBN:0-393-32433-8, ISBN13: 978-0-393-32433-4. Dewey:796.5/223/092.
Audience: **g,l,u,f.**

Hong, Fan & Mangan, J. A. (Editors) **GV944.5**
Soccer, Women, Sexual Liberation: Kicking off a New Era. Trade Paper. Taylor & Francis Group. Abingdon, 2003. 272p. Sport in the Global Society Ser. ISBN:0-7146-8408-2, ISBN13: 978-0-7146-8408-6. Dewey:796.334082. LCCN:2004-298586.
Audience: **g,l,u,f.** *Choice, 2004.*

Horn, Jane **GV966.H68 1999**
Power Golf for Women: How to Hit Longer and Straighter from Tee to Green. Robert Daley (Illustrator). Trade Paper. Kensington Publishing Corporation. New York, NY. 2000. 176p. ISBN:0-8065-2070-1, ISBN13: 978-0-8065-2070-4. Dewey:796.352/3/082. LCCN:99-014069.
Audience: **g,l,u.**

Hult, Joan S. & Trekell, Marianna (Editors) **GV886 .C45 1991**
A Century of Women's Basketball: From Frailty to Final Four. Paper Text. American Alliance for Health, Physical Education, Recreation & Dance. Oxon Hill, MD. 1991. 430p. ISBN:0-88314-490-5, ISBN13: 978-0-88314-490-9. Dewey:796.323/0973. LCCN:91-197223.
Audience: **u,f.**

Ikard, Robert W. **GV886.I43 2005**
Just for Fun: The Story of AAU Women's Basketball. Trade Cloth. University of Arkansas Press. Fayetteville, AR. 2005. 272p. ISBN:1-55728-783-X, ISBN13: 978-1-55728-783-0. Dewey:796.323/8. LCCN:2004-021104.
Audience: **u,f.** *Choice, 2005.*

Kowalchik, Claire **GV1061.18.W66K68**
The Complete Book of Running for Women: Everything You Need to Know about Training, Nutrition, Injury Prevention, Motivation, Racing and Much, Much More. Trade Paper. Simon & Schuster. New York, NY. 1999. 416p. ISBN:0-671-01703-9, ISBN13: 978-0-671-01703-3. Dewey:613.7/172/082. LCCN:98-050318.
Audience: **g,l,u,f.**

Ladies Professional Golf Association Staff **GV966.L64 2000**
LPGA's Guide to Every Shot. Trade Paper. Human Kinetics Publishers. Champaign, IL. 2000. 20p. ISBN:0-88011-980-2, ISBN13: 978-0-88011-980-1. Dewey:796.352/3/082. LCCN:99-089363.
Audience: **g,l,u.**

Lauffer, Robert Butch & Kater, April **GV944.5.L38 2001**
Women's Soccer: Techniques, Tactics and Teamwork. Trade Paper. Sterling Publishing Co., Inc. New York, NY. 2001. 144p. ISBN:0-8069-5847-2, ISBN13: 978-0-8069-5847-7. Dewey:796.334/2. LCCN:00-048258.
Audience: **l,u.** *Choice, 2002.*

LeCompte, Mary Lou **GV1834.55.W47L43**
Cowgirls of the Rodeo: Pioneer Professional Athletes. Trade Cloth. University of Illinois Press. Champaign, IL. 1993. 272p. Sport and Society Ser. ISBN:0-252-02029-4, ISBN13: 978-0-252-02029-2. Dewey:791.8/4. LCCN:92-042635.
Audience: **u,f.** *Choice, 1994.*

McCrone, Kathleen E. **GV709.18.G7M33 1988**
Playing the Game: Sport and the Physical Emancipation of English Women, 1870-1914. Trade Cloth. University Press of Kentucky. Lexington, KY. 1988. 336p. ISBN:0-8131-1641-4, ISBN13: 978-0-8131-1641-9. Dewey:796/.01/940941. LCCN:87-032038.
Audience: **g,l,u,f.** *Choice, 1989.*

McEvoy, John & McEvoy, Julia **SF336.A2W65 2001**
Women in Racing: In Their Own Words. Trade Cloth. Blood-Horse, Incorporated, The. Lexington, KY. 2001. 256p. ISBN:1-58150-067-X, ISBN13: 978-1-58150-067-7. Dewey:798.4/0092/2 B. LCCN:2001-086643.
Audience: **l,u.**

McKay, Jim **GV709.18.A8M35 1997**
Managing Gender: Affirmative Action and Organizational Power in Australian, Canadian, and New Zealand Sport. Cloth Text. State University of New York Press. Albany, NY. 1997. 217p. SUNY Series on Sport, Culture, and Social Relations ISBN:0-7914-3421-4, ISBN13: 978-0-7914-3421-5. Dewey:353.53/082. LCCN:96-053415.
Audience: **u,f.**

McKay, Jim, et al. **GV706.5.M365 2000**
Masculinities, Gender Relations, and Sport, Vol. 11. Michael A. Messner & Donald F. Sabo (Authors). Trade Paper. SAGE Publications, Inc. Thousand Oaks, CA. 2000. 344p. Sage Series on Men and Masculinity Ser. ISBN:0-7619-1272-X, ISBN13: 978-0-7619-1272-9. Dewey:796.081. LCCN:00-008019.
Audience: **u,f.** *Choice, 2001.*

Nelson, Mariah B. **GV706.4.N45 1993**
The Stronger Women Get, the More Men Love Football: Sex and Sports in America. Trade Cloth. Harcourt Trade Publishers. New York, NY. 1994. x, 304p. ISBN:0-15-181393-0, ISBN13: 978-0-15-181393-3. Dewey:796/.01. LCCN:93-044358.
Audience: **g,l,f.**

Park, Roberta J. & Mangan, James A. (Editors) **GV709.F66 1987**
From "Fair Sex" to Feminism: Sport and the Socialization of Women in the Industrial and Post-Industrial Eras. Paper over Boards. Taylor & Francis Group. Philadelphia, PA. 1987. 336p. ISBN:0-7146-3288-0, ISBN13: 978-0-7146-3288-9. Dewey:306.4/83. LCCN:86-017529.
Audience: **g,l,u,f.** *Choice, 1988.*

Pemberton, Cynthia Lee A. **GV709.18.U6P46 2002**
More than a Game: One Woman's Fight for Gender Equity in Sport. Donna de Varona (Foreword by). Paper Text. Northeastern University Press. Boston, MA. 2002. 320p. ISBN:1-55553-525-9, ISBN13: 978-1-55553-525-4. Dewey:796/.082/09795. LCCN:2001-059193.
Audience: **u,f.** *Choice, 2002.*

Pieroth, Doris Hinson **GV722 1932.P54 1996**
Their Day in the Sun: Women of the 1932 Olympics. Trade Paper. University of Washington Press. Seattle, WA. 1996. 208p. Samuel and Althea Stroum Bks. ISBN:0-295-97554-7, ISBN13: 978-0-295-97554-2. Dewey:796.48. LCCN:96-023104.
Audience: **l,u.** *Choice, 1997.*

Pink, Sarah **GV1107.P535 1997**
Women and Bullfighting: Gender, Sex and the Consumption of Tradition. Trade Paper. Berg Publishers. Oxford, 1997. 256p. Mediterranea Ser. ISBN:1-85973-961-X, ISBN13: 978-1-85973-961-7. Dewey:791.82082. LCCN:98-185397.
Audience: **u,f.**

Porter, Karra **GV885.515.W66P67**
Mad Seasons: The Story of the First Women's Professional Basketball League, 1978-1981. Trade Paper. University of Nebraska Press. Lincoln, NE. 2006. 384p. ISBN:0-8032-8789-5, ISBN13: 978-0-8032-8789-1. Dewey:796.323/8. LCCN:2005-026399.
Audience: **g,l,u,f.**

Porto, Brian L. **GV709**
A New Season: Using Title IX to Reform College Sports. Trade Cloth. Greenwood Publishing Group, Inc. Portsmouth, NH. 2003. 264p. ISBN:0-275-97699-8, ISBN13: 978-0-275-97699-6. Dewey:796/.082. LCCN:2003-048216.
Audience: **u,f.** *Choice, 2004.*

Rapoport, Ron (Editor) **GV709**
A Kind of Grace: A Treasury of Sportswriting by Women. Trade Paper. RDR Books. Muskegon, MI. 1994. 400p. ISBN:1-57143-013-X, ISBN13: 978-1-57143-013-7. Dewey:796/.082. LCCN:94-060001.
Audience: **l,u,f.**

Rathburn, Elizabeth & Drummond, Siobhan (Contribution by) **GV721.5 .G63 1996**
Grace and Glory: A Century of Women in the Olympics. Trade Cloth. Triumph Books. Chicago, IL. 1996. 112p.

ISBN:1-57243-116-4, ISBN13: 978-1-57243-116-4.
Dewey:796.48.
Audience: **g,l,u,f.** *Choice, 1996.*

Reese, Anne C. & Vallera-Rickerson, Irini **GV21.R44 2002**
Athletries: The Untold History of Ancient Greek Women Athletes. Kathy Bryant (Editor), Jeff Kern (Illustrator). Reinforced. Nightowl Publications. Costa Mesa, CA. 2003. 189p. ISBN:0-9714984-0-7, ISBN13: 978-0-9714984-0-2. Dewey:790.092. LCCN:2002-101871.
Audience: **u,f.**

Riley, Glenda **GV1157.O3R55 1994**
The Life and Legacy of Annie Oakley. Trade Cloth. University of Oklahoma Press. Norman, OK. 1994. 272p. Oklahoma Western Biographies Ser., Vol. 7 ISBN:0-8061-2656-6, ISBN13: 978-0-8061-2656-2. Dewey:796.3/092 B. LCCN:94-010260.
Audience: **u,f.** *Choice, 1995.*

Ryan, Joan **GV464.R93 2000**
Little Girls in Pretty Boxes: The Making and Breaking of Elite Gymnasts and Figure Skaters. Trade Paper. Warner Books, Inc. New York, NY. 2000. 288p. ISBN:0-446-67682-9, ISBN13: 978-0-446-67682-3. Dewey:796.4/4/08352. LCCN:00-031981.
Audience: **l,u,f.**

Saunders, Vivien **GV966.S385 2000**
Golf Handbook for Women: The Complete Guide to Improving Your Game. Trade Paper. Crown Publishing Group. New York, NY. 2000. 224p. ISBN:0-609-80511-8, ISBN13: 978-0-609-80511-4. Dewey:796.352/3/082. LCCN:00-710409.
Audience: **l,u,f.** *Choice, 2001.*

Schoenfeld, Bruce **GV994.A1**
The Match: Althea Gibson and a Portrait of a Friendship. Trade Paper, Perfect. HarperCollins Publishers. New York, NY. 2005. 320p. ISBN:0-06-052653-X, ISBN13: 978-0-06-052653-5. Dewey:796.3420922.
Audience: **l,u,f.**

Seymour, Miranda **GV1032.N53S49 2004**
The Bugatti Queen: In Search of a French Racing Legend. Trade Cloth. Random House, Inc. New York, NY. 2004. 352p. ISBN:1-4000-6168-7, ISBN13: 978-1-4000-6168-6. Dewey:796.72/092. LCCN:2004-042783.
Audience: **g,l,u,f.** *Choice, 2005.*

Simon, Rita J. (Editor) **GV709.18.U6S67 2005**
Sporting Equality: Title IX Thirty Years Later. Trade Paper. Transaction Publishers. Somerset, NJ. 2005. 182p. ISBN:0-7658-0848-X, ISBN13: 978-0-7658-0848-6. Dewey:796/.082. LCCN:2004-051694.
Audience: **g,l,u,f.**

Simons, Minot II **GV464.S55 1995**
Women's Gymnastics a History: 1966 to 1974. Albrecht Gaebele (Photographer). Trade Cloth. Welwyn Publishing Company. Carmel, CA. 1995. xxv, 403p. ISBN:0-9646062-0-8, ISBN13: 978-0-9646062-0-3. Dewey:796.44/082. LCCN:95-090224.
Audience: **l,u,f.** *Choice, 1996.*

Skaine, Rosemarie **GV885.3.S58 2001**
Women College Basketball Coaches. Paper Text. McFarland & Company, Incorporated Publishers. Jefferson, NC. 2001. 207p. ISBN:0-7864-0920-7, ISBN13: 978-0-7864-0920-4. Dewey:796.323/63/082092273. LCCN:2001-020238.
Audience: **g,l,u,f.** *Choice, 2001.*

Smith, Lissa (Editor) **GV709.18.U6**
Nike Is a Goddess: The History of Women in Sports. Mariah B. Nelson (Introduction by), Lucy Danziger (Afterword by). Trade Paper. Grove/Atlantic, Inc. New York, NY. 1999. 352p. ISBN:0-87113-761-5, ISBN13: 978-0-87113-761-6. Dewey:796/.082/0973. LCCN:98-027049.
Audience: **g,l,u,f.** *Choice, 2000.*

Stokell, Ian **GV943.8.S77 2002**
Coaching Women's Soccer: A Revolutionary Approach to Putting the Play Back into Practice. Trade Paper. McGraw-Hill Companies, The. New York, NY. 2002. x, 182p. ISBN:0-07-138209-7, ISBN13: 978-0-07-138209-0. Dewey:796.334/07/7. LCCN:2001-047321.
Audience: **g,l,u,f.** *Choice, 2002.*

Swissler, Becky **GV989.15.S95 2003**
Winning Lacrosse for Girls. Anna Maria Vesco (Foreword by). Trade Cloth. Facts On File, Inc. New York, NY. 2004. 208p. Winning Sports for Girls Ser. ISBN:0-8160-5183-6, ISBN13: 978-0-8160-5183-0. Dewey:796.34/7/082. LCCN:2003-051446.
Audience: **g,l,u.**

Theberge, Nancy **GV848.6.W65T54 2000**
Higher Goals: Women's Ice Hockey and the Politics of Gender. Paper Text. State University of New York Press. Albany, NY. 2000. xiii, 182p. SUNY Series on Sport, Culture, and Social Relations ISBN:0-7914-4642-5, ISBN13: 978-0-7914-4642-3. Dewey:796.962/082/0971. LCCN:99-057333.
Audience: **u,f.** *Choice, 2001.*

Tricard, Louise Mead **GV1060.8.T75 1996**
American women's track and field:a history, 1895 through 1980. McFarland. 1996. ISBN:0-7864-0219-9, ISBN13: 978-0-7864-0219-9.
Audience: **l,u,f.**

Vertinsky, Patricia A. **GV482.V47 1994**
The Eternally Wounded Woman: Women, Exercise, and Doctors in the Late Nineteenth Century. Trade Cloth. University of Illinois Press. Champaign, IL. 1994. 288p. ISBN:0-252-06372-4, ISBN13: 978-0-252-06372-5. Dewey:613.7/045. LCCN:93-037145.
Audience: **u,f.**

Wearing, Betsy **GV183.W43 1998**
Leisure and Feminist Theory. Paper Text. SAGE Publications, Ltd. London, 1999. 219p. ISBN:0-8039-7537-6, ISBN13: 978-0-8039-7537-8. Dewey:306.4/812. LCCN:98-061180.
Audience: **u,f.**

Wiley, Carol A. (Editor) **GV1111.5.W65 1992**
Women in the Martial Arts. Trade Paper. North Atlantic Books. Berkeley, CA. 1993. 146p. IO Journals, Vol. 46 ISBN:1-55643-136-8, ISBN13: 978-1-55643-136-4. Dewey:613.6/6. LCCN:93-132230.
Audience: **g,l,u,f.**

Woolum, Janet **GV697.A1W69 1998**
Outstanding Women Athletes: Who They Are and How They Influenced Sports in America. Ed. 2. Cloth Text. Greenwood Publishing Group, Inc. Portsmouth, NH. 1998. 424p. ISBN:1-57356-120-7, ISBN13: 978-1-57356-120-4. Dewey:796/.082/092273 B. LCCN:98-017076.
Audience: **g,l,u.** *Choice, 1993.*

Wushanley, Ying **GV709.18.U6W87 2004**
Playing Nice and Losing: The Struggle for Control of Women's Intercollegiate Athletics, 1960-2000. Trade Cloth. Syracuse University Press. Syracuse, NY. 2004. xviii, 225p. Sports and Entertainment Ser. ISBN:0-8156-3045-X, ISBN13: 978-0-8156-3045-6. Dewey:796/.082. LCCN:2003-024656.
Audience: **g,l,u,f.** *Choice, 2004.*

Minorities and Specific Groups in Sport > Gays and Lesbians

GV708.8
☐ Federation of Gay Games.
http://www.gaygames.com/en/
Audience: **g,l,u,f.**

Anderson, Eric **GV708.8.A43 2005**
In the Game: Gay Athletes and the Cult of Masculinity. Paper Text. State University of New York Press. Albany, NY. 2005. 208p. SUNY Series on Sport, Culture, and Social Relations ISBN:0-7914-6534-9, ISBN13: 978-0-7914-6534-9. Dewey:796.086/64. LCCN:2004-021367.
Audience: **l,u,f.** *Choice, 2005.*

Griffin, Patricia J. **GV708.8.G75 1998**
Strong Women, Deep Closets: Lesbians and Homophobia in Sport. Donna A. Lopiano (Foreword by). Trade Paper. Human Kinetics Publishers. Champaign, IL. 1998. 264p. ISBN:0-88011-729-X, ISBN13: 978-0-88011-729-6. Dewey:796/.086/643. LCCN:97-032363.
Audience: **g,l,u,f.** *Choice, 1998.*

Pronger, Brian **GV706.5.P76 1991**
The Arena of Masculinity: Sports, Homosexuality, and the Meaning of Sex. Trade Paper. St. Martin's Press. Gordonville, VA. 1992. 320p. Stonewall Inn Editions Ser. ISBN:0-312-06293-1, ISBN13: 978-0-312-06293-4. Dewey:306.4/83. LCCN:91-029264.
Audience: **l,u,f.**

Rogers, Susan F. (Editor) **GV708.8.S68 1995**
Sportsdykes: Stories from on and off the Field. Trade Cloth. St. Martin's Press. Gordonville, VA. 1995. 239p. ISBN:0-312-13187-9, ISBN13: 978-0-312-13187-6. Dewey:796/.086643. LCCN:95-005497.
Audience: **l,u,f.**

Tuaolo, Esera & Rosengren, John **GV939.T78A3 2006**
Alone in the Trenches: My Life As a Gay Player in the NFL. Trade Cloth. Sourcebooks, Inc. Naperville, IL. 2006. 288p. ISBN:1-4022-0505-8, ISBN13: 978-1-4022-0505-7. Dewey:796.332/092 B. LCCN:2005-025014.
Audience: **g,l,u.**

Waddell, Tom & Schaap, Dick **GV697.W33A3 1996**
Gay Olympian: The Life and Death of Dr. Tom Waddell. Trade Cloth. Random House, Inc. New York, NY. 1996. 240p. ISBN:0-394-57223-8, ISBN13: 978-0-394-57223-9. Dewey:796/.092 B. LCCN:95-031223.
Audience: **g.**

Woog, Dan **GV697.A1W687 2002**
Jocks 2: Coming Out to Play. Trade Cloth. Alyson Publications. Los Angeles, CA. 248p. ISBN:1-55583-726-3, ISBN13: 978-1-55583-726-6. Dewey:796/.086/642. LCCN:2002-071671.
Audience: **g,l.**

Woog, Dan **GV697.A1W687 1998**
Jocks: True Stories of America's Gay Male Athletes. Kevin Jennings (Editor). Trade Paper. Alyson Publications. Los Angeles, CA. 1997. 256p. ISBN:1-55583-399-3, ISBN13: 978-1-55583-399-2. Dewey:796/.086/6420922 B. LCCN:97-030488.
Audience: **g,l.**

Minorities and Specific Groups in Sport > Youth

GV563
☐ Amateur Athletic Foundation of Los Angeles.
http://www.aafla.org/
Audience: **g,l,u.**

GV709.2
☐ National Alliance for Youth Sports.
http://www.nays.org/
Audience: **g,l,u,f.**

GV344
☐ National Youth Sport Safety Foundation.
http://www.nyssf.org/
Audience: **g,l,u,f.**

American Sport Education Program Staff **GV943.8.C63 2001**
Coaching Youth Soccer. Ed. 3. Trade Paper. Human Kinetics Publishers. Champaign, IL. 2001. 168p. ISBN:0-7360-3718-7, ISBN13: 978-0-7360-3718-1. Dewey:796.334/07/7. LCCN:00-050032.
Audience: **l,u,f.**

American Sport Education Program Staff **GV1002.9.C63A45 2002**
Coaching Youth Tennis. Ed. 3. Trade Paper. Human Kinetics Publishers. Champaign, IL. 2001. 20p. ISBN:0-7360-3793-4, ISBN13: 978-0-7360-3793-8. Dewey:796.342/07/7. LCCN:2001-024117.
Audience: **l,u,f.**

American Sport Education Program Staff (Contribution by) **GV1015.5.C63 2001**
Coaching Youth Volleyball. Ed. 3. Trade Paper. Human Kinetics Publishers. Champaign, IL. 2001. 176p. ISBN:0-7360-3796-9, ISBN13: 978-0-7360-3796-9. Dewey:796.325. LCCN:2001-016657.
Audience: **l,u,f.**

American Sport Education Program Staff **GV1196.3.C63 2002**
Coaching Youth Wrestling. Ed. 2. Trade Paper. Human Kinetics Publishers. Champaign, IL. 2001. 168p. ISBN:0-7360-4159-1, ISBN13: 978-0-7360-4159-1. Dewey:797.812. LCCN:2001-039617.
Audience: **l,u,f.**

American Sport Education Program Staff **GV881.4.U47A54 2004**
Officiating Softball. Trade Paper. Human Kinetics Publishers.

Champaign, IL. 2004. 184p. ISBN:0-7360-4764-6, ISBN13: 978-0-7360-4764-7. Dewey:796.357/8. LCCN:2004-000579.
Audience: **l,u,f.**

Bissinger, H. G. **GV958.P47 B57 2004**
Friday Night Lights: A Town, a Team, and a Dream. Paper Text. Da Capo Press, Inc. Cambridge, MA. 2004. 416p. ISBN:0-306-81425-0, ISBN13: 978-0-306-81425-9. Dewey:796.332.
Audience: **g,l,u,f.**

Brackenridge, Celia **GV706.32.B73 2001**
Spoilsports: Understanding and Preventing Sexual Exploitation in Sport. Trade Paper. Routledge. New York, NY. 2001. 304p. Ethics and Sport Ser. ISBN:0-419-25780-2, ISBN13: 978-0-419-25780-6. Dewey:796/.082. LCCN:00-068037.
Audience: **u,f.**

Crisfield, Deborah **GV1015.4.W66C75 2002**
Winning Volleyball for Girls. Ed. 3. Trade Paper. Facts On File, Inc. New York, NY. 2002. 192p. Winning Sports for Girls Ser. ISBN:0-8160-4621-2, ISBN13: 978-0-8160-4621-8. Dewey:796.325. LCCN:2001-033473.
Audience: **g,l,u,f.** *Choice, 2002.*

DeKnop, Paul (Editor), et al. **GV709.2.W67 1996**
Worldwide Trends in Youth Sport. Lars M. Engstrom, Bert Skirstad & Maureen R. Weiss (Editors). Trade Cloth. Human Kinetics Publishers. Champaign, IL. 1996. 324p. ISBN:0-87322-729-8, ISBN13: 978-0-87322-729-2. Dewey:796/.01922. LCCN:95-033994.
Audience: **l,u,f.** *Choice, 1996.*

Gatz, Margaret (Editor), et al. **GV706.5.P365 2002**
Paradoxes of Youth and Sport. Michael A. Messner & Sandra J. Ball-Rokeach (Editors). Paper Text. State University of New York Press. Albany, NY. 2002. 320p. SUNY Series on Sport, Culture, and Social Relations ISBN:0-7914-5324-3, ISBN13: 978-0-7914-5324-7. Dewey:306.4/83. LCCN:2001-042646.
Audience: **l,u,f.** *Choice, 2003, 2002.*

Griffin, Robert S. **GV709**
Sports in the Lives of Children and Adolescents: Success on the Field and in Life. Trade Cloth. Greenwood Publishing Group, Inc. Portsmouth, NH. 1998. 168p. ISBN:0-275-96127-3, ISBN13: 978-0-275-96127-5. Dewey:796/.083. LCCN:97-033711.
Audience: **l,u,f.** *Choice, 1998.*

Humphrey, James H. & Yow, Deborah A. **GV709.24.H86 2002**
Adult Guide to Children's Team Sports. Trade Cloth. Nova Science Publishers, Inc. Hauppauge, NY. 2002. 138p. ISBN:1-59033-317-9, ISBN13: 978-1-59033-317-4. Dewey:796/.083. LCCN:2002-069325.
Audience: **g,l,u,f.** *Choice, 2003.*

Kirby, Sandra, et al. **GV709.2**
The Dome of Silence: Sexual Harrassment and Abuse in Sport. Lorraine Greaves & Olena Hankinsky (Authors). Trade Paper. Zed Books, Ltd. London, 2001. 192p. ISBN:1-85649-963-4, ISBN13: 978-1-85649-963-7. Dewey:305.9/796.
Audience: **g,l,u,f.**

Miracle, Andrew W. Jr. & Rees, C. Roger **GV346.M57 1994**
Lessons of the Locker Room: The Myth of School Sports. Trade Cloth. Prometheus Books, Publishers. Amherst, NY. 1994. 243p. ISBN:0-87975-879-1, ISBN13: 978-0-87975-879-0. Dewey:796/.0973. LCCN:93-048666.
Audience: **g,l,u,f.** *Choice, 1994.*

Murphy, Shane M. **GV709.2.M873 1999**
The Cheers and the Tears: A Healthy Alternative to the Dark Side of Youth Sports Today. Trade Paper. John Wiley & Sons, Inc. Hoboken, NJ. 1999. 240p. ISBN:0-7879-4037-2, ISBN13: 978-0-7879-4037-9. Dewey:796/.083/0973. LCCN:98-025525.
Audience: **g,l,u,f.**

Rosengren, John **GV848.4.U6**
Blades of Glory: The True Story of a Young Team Bred to Win. Trade Paper. Sourcebooks, Inc. Naperville, IL. 2004. 352p. ISBN:1-4022-0047-1, ISBN13: 978-1-4022-0047-2. Dewey:796.962/09776/57.
Audience: **g,l,u,f.**

Shea, Edward J. **GV706.3.S53 1996**
Ethical Decisions in Sport: Interscholastic, Intercollegiate, Olympic and Professional. Trade Paper. Charles C. Thomas Publisher, Ltd. Springfield, IL. 1996. 238p. ISBN:0-398-06600-0, ISBN13: 978-0-398-06600-0. Dewey:796/.01. LCCN:96-001035.
Audience: **u,f.**

Smoll, Frank L. & Smith, Ronald E. **GV709.2.C46 1996**
Children and Youth in Sport. Paper Text. McGraw-Hill Higher Education. Burr Ridge, IL. 1995. 464p. ISBN:0-697-22490-2, ISBN13: 978-0-697-22490-3. Dewey:796/.0192. LCCN:94-073668.
Audience: **g,l,u,f.**

Swissler, Becky **GV1017.H7S95 2003**
Winning Field Hockey for Girls. Trade Paper. Facts On File, Inc. New York, NY. 2003. 224p. Winning Sports for Girls Ser. ISBN:0-8160-4725-1, ISBN13: 978-0-8160-4725-3. Dewey:796.355/082. LCCN:2002-005990.
Audience: **l,u,f.**

Minorities and Specific Groups in Sport > Seniors

GV712
☐ Huntsman World Senior Games.
http://www.seniorgames.net/
Audience: **g,l,u,f.**

GV712
☐ National Senior Games Assocation.
http://www.nsga.com/
Audience: **l,u,f.**

Benyo, Richard **GV1061.8.A35 1998**
Running Past 50. Trade Paper. Human Kinetics Publishers. Champaign, IL. 1998. 256p. Ageless Athlete Ser., Vol. 50 ISBN:0-88011-705-2, ISBN13: 978-0-88011-705-0. Dewey:613.7/172/0846. LCCN:97-052054.
Audience: **g,l,u,f.**

Clark, Etta **GV697.A1C59 1995**
Growing Old Is Not for Sissies 2: Portraits of Senior Athletes. Trade Paper. Pomegranate Communications, Inc. Petaluma, CA. 2003. 120p. ISBN:0-87654-478-2, ISBN13: 978-0-87654-478-5. Dewey:796/.092/2 B. LCCN:95-024277.
Audience: **g,l,u.**

Clements, Claire B. **GV184**
The Arts - Fitness Quality of Life Activities Program: Creative Ideas for Working with Older Adults in Group Settings. Trade Paper. Health Professions Press. Baltimore, MD. 1998. 430p. ISBN:1-878812-45-9, ISBN13: 978-1-878812-45-2. Dewey:790.1/926.
Audience: **u.**

Friel, Joe **GV1043.7.F75 1998**
Cycling Past 50. Trade Cloth. Human Kinetics Publishers. Champaign, IL. 1998. 264p. Ageless Athlete Ser. ISBN:0-88011-737-0, ISBN13: 978-0-88011-737-1. Dewey:796.6. LCCN:97-038749.
Audience: **u.**

Goldstein, Mel & Tanner, Dave **GV837.3.G65 1999**
Swimming Past 50. Trade Paper. Human Kinetics Publishers. Champaign, IL. 1999. 216p. Ageless Athlete Ser. ISBN:0-88011-907-1, ISBN13: 978-0-88011-907-8. Dewey:797.2/1/0846. LCCN:99-012569.
Audience: **l,u.**

Higdon, Hal **GV1061.18.A35H55**
Masters Running: A Guide to Running and Staying Fit After 40. Trade Paper. Rodale Press, Inc. Emmaus, PA. 2005. 240p. ISBN:1-59486-021-1, ISBN13: 978-1-59486-021-8. Dewey:613.7/172/0846. LCCN:2004-027381.
Audience: **g,l,u,f.**

Jones, C. Jessie & Rose, Debra J. (Editors) **GV447.J66 2004**
Physical Activity Instruction of Older Adults. Perfect, Paper over Boards. Human Kinetics Publishers. Champaign, IL. 2004. 405p. ISBN:0-7360-4513-9, ISBN13: 978-0-7360-4513-1. Dewey:613.70446. LCCN:2004-013539.
Audience: **u,f.**

Olson, Leonard T. **GV1060.5.O43 2001**
Masters Track and Field: A History. Trade Cloth. McFarland & Company, Incorporated Publishers. Jefferson, NC. 2000. 320p. ISBN:0-7864-0889-8, ISBN13: 978-0-7864-0889-4. Dewey:796.42. LCCN:00-42162.
Audience: **l,u.**

Rikli, Roberta E. & Jones, C. Jessie **RA781.R54 2001**
Senior Fitness Test Manual. Trade Paper. Human Kinetics Publishers. Champaign, IL. 2001. 176p. ISBN:0-7360-3356-4, ISBN13: 978-0-7360-3356-5. Dewey:613.7/0446/0287. LCCN:00-050575.
Audience: **l,u.** *Choice, 2002.*

Shephard, Roy J. **QP86.S478 1997**
Aging, Physical Activity, and Health. Trade Cloth. Human Kinetics Publishers. Champaign, IL. 1997. 496p. ISBN:0-87322-889-8, ISBN13: 978-0-87322-889-3. Dewey:613.7/0446. LCCN:96-043852.
Audience: **g,l,u,f.** *Choice, 1997.*

Minorities and Specific Groups in Sport > Native Americans

Bloom, John **E98.G2B56 2000**
To Show What an Indian Can Do: Sports at Native American Boarding Schools. Trade Paper. University of Minnesota Press. Minneapolis, MN. 2005. 176p. Sport and Culture Ser., Vol. 2 ISBN:0-8166-3652-4, ISBN13: 978-0-8166-3652-5. Dewey:796/.089/97. LCCN:00-008865.
Audience: **u.**

Crawford, Bill **GV697.T5.C73 2004**
All American: The Rise and Fall of Jim Thorpe. Trade Cloth. John Wiley & Sons, Inc. Hoboken, NJ. 2004. 288p. ISBN:0-471-55732-3, ISBN13: 978-0-471-55732-6. Dewey:796/.092 B. LCCN:2004-014376.
Audience: **g,l,u.**

Fisher, Donald M. **GV989.F56 2002**
Lacrosse: A History of the Game. Trade Cloth. Johns Hopkins University Press. Baltimore, MD. 2002. 432p. ISBN:0-8018-6938-2, ISBN13: 978-0-8018-6938-9. Dewey:796.34/7/09. LCCN:2001-005690.
Audience: **g,l,u,f.**

King, C. Richard (Editor) **GV583.N34 2003**
Native Americans in Sports. Sharpe Reference Staff (Contribution by). Trade Cloth. M. E. Sharpe Inc. Armonk, NY. 2004. 376p. ISBN:0-7656-8054-8, ISBN13: 978-0-7656-8054-9. Dewey:796/.089/97. LCCN:2002-042800.
Audience: **g,l,u.** *Choice, 2004.*

King, C. Richard & Springwood, Charles F. (Editors) **GV714.5.K56 2001**
Team Spirits: The Native American Mascots Controversy. Vine Deloria Jr. (Foreword by). Trade Paper. University of Nebraska Press. Lincoln, NE. 2001. 356p. ISBN:0-8032-7798-9, ISBN13: 978-0-8032-7798-4. Dewey:306.4/83. LCCN:00-059968.
Audience: **u,f.** *Choice, 2001.*

Nabokov, Peter **E98.G2**
Indian Running: Native American History and Tradition. Ed. 2. Trade Paper. Gibbs Smith, Publisher. Layton, UT. 1987. 208p. ISBN:0-941270-41-6, ISBN13: 978-0-941270-41-0. Dewey:70.6. LCCN:87-071658.
Audience: **u,f.**

Powers-Beck, Jeff **GV867.64.P69 2004**
The American Indian Integration of Baseball. Joseph Oxendine (Foreword by). Cloth Text. University of Nebraska Press. Lincoln, NE. 2004. 328p. ISBN:0-8032-3745-6, ISBN13: 978-0-8032-3745-2. Dewey:796.357/64/08997. LCCN:2004-007245.
Audience: **l,u,f.** *Choice, 2005.*

Vennum, Thomas Jr. **E98.G2V46 1994**
American Indian Lacrosse: Little Brother of War. Trade Paper. Smithsonian Institution Press. Washington, DC. 1994. 376p.

ISBN:1-56098-302-7, ISBN13: 978-1-56098-302-6. Dewey:796.34/7. LCCN:93-029968.
Audience: **g,l,u,f.** *Choice, 1994.*

Minorities and Specific Groups in Sport > Disabled

GV709.3
☐ Amputee Sport Resouces on the Net.
http://www.amputee-online.com/amputee/sportrec.html
Audience: **g,l,u,f.**

GV709.3
☐ Disabled Sport USA.
http://www.dsusa.org/
Audience: **g,l,u,f.**

GV709.3
☐ International Paralympic Comittee.
http://www.paralympic.org/release/Main_Sections_Menu/index.html
Audience: **g,l,u,f.**

GV709.3
☐ Wheelchair Sports Worldwide.
http://www.wsw.org.uk/
International Stoke Mandeville Wheelchair Sports Federation.
Audience: **g,l,u,f.**

American College of Sports Medicine Staff (Contribution by) **RM725.A3 2002**
ACSM's Exercise Management for Persons with Chronic Diseases and Disabilities. Ed. 2. Trade Cloth. Human Kinetics Publishers. Champaign, IL. 2002. 384p. ISBN:0-7360-3872-8, ISBN13: 978-0-7360-3872-0. Dewey:615.8/24. LCCN:2002-006587.
Audience: **u,f.**

Anderson, Lynn & Kress, Carla **GV183.5**
Inclusion: Including People with Disabilities in Parks and Recreation Opportunities. Paper Text. Venture Publishing, Inc. State College, PA. 2003. 134p. ISBN:1-892132-33-8, ISBN13: 978-1-892132-33-8. Dewey:790.196. LCCN:2003-101466.
Audience: **u.**

Austin, David R. (Editor), et al. **RM736.7**
Conceptual Foundations for Therapeutic Recreation. John Dattilo & Bryan P. McCormick (Editors). Cloth Text. Venture Publishing, Inc. State College, PA. 2002. 366p. ISBN:1-892132-30-3, ISBN13: 978-1-892132-30-7. Dewey:615.85101. LCCN:2002-104096.
Audience: **u,f.**

Bullock, Charles & Mahon, Michael **GV183.5**
Introduction to Recreation Services for People with Disabilities: A Person-Centered Approach. Trade Cloth. Sagamore Publishing, L.L.C.. Champaign, IL. 1997. 464p. ISBN:1-57167-069-6, ISBN13: 978-1-57167-069-4. Dewey:790.196.
Audience: **u,f.**

Coffey, Wayne **GV885.43.G25C64 2002**
Winning Sounds Like This: A Season with the Women's Basketball Team at Gallaudet, the World's Only University for the Deaf. Trade Cloth. Crown Publishing Group. New York, NY. 2002. 256p. ISBN:0-609-60765-0, ISBN13: 978-0-609-60765-7. Dewey:796.323/63/09753. LCCN:2002-283485.
Audience: **g,l,u,f.**

Depauw, Karen P. & Gavron, Susan J. **GV709.3.D47 2005**
Disability Sport. Ed. 2. Perfect. Human Kinetics Publishers. Champaign, IL. 2005. 395p. ISBN:0-7360-4638-0, ISBN13: 978-0-7360-4638-1. Dewey:796.087. LCCN:2004-022462.
Audience: **g,l,u,f.**

Hedrick, Brad, et al. **GV886.5.H43 1994**
Wheelchair Basketball. Ed. 2. Dan Byrnes & Lew Shaver (Authors). Trade Paper. Paralyzed Veterans of America. Washington, DC. 1994. 120p. ISBN:0-929819-05-5, ISBN13: 978-0-929819-05-1. Dewey:796.32/38. LCCN:94-023340.
Audience: **g,l,u,f.**

Maynard, Kyle **GV1196.M38A3 2005**
No Excuses!: The True Story of a Congenital Amputee Who Became a Champion in Wrestling and in Life. Trade Cloth. Regnery Publishing, Incorporated, An Eagle Publishing Company. Washington, DC. 2005. 256p. ISBN:0-89526-011-5, ISBN13: 978-0-89526-011-6. Dewey:796.812/092 B. LCCN:2005-018554.
Audience: **g,l,u.**

Paciorek, Michael J. & Jones, Jeffrey A. **GV709.3 .P33 2001**
Disability Sport and Recreation Resources. Ed. 3. Trade Paper. Cooper Publishing Group. Traverse City, MI. 2000. 386p. ISBN:1-884125-75-1, ISBN13: 978-1-884125-75-1. Dewey:796.0196. LCCN:2001-086212.
Audience: **l,u,f.** *Choice, 2002.*

Minorities and Specific Groups in Sport > Jewish

Riess, Steven A. **GV709.6.S76 1998**
Sports and the American Jew. Trade Paper. Syracuse University Press. Syracuse, NY. 1998. 337p. Sports and Entertainment Ser. ISBN:0-8156-2761-0, ISBN13: 978-0-8156-2761-6. Dewey:796/.089/924073. LCCN:97-020930.
Audience: **l,u,f.** *Choice, 1999.*

International Contests and Sporting Events > General

GV709.3
☐ Amputee Sport Resouces on the Net.
http://www.amputee-online.com/amputee/sportrec.html
Audience: **g,l,u,f.**

GV341
☐ Commwealth Games Federation.
http://www.thecgf.com/home.asp
Audience: **l,u,f.**

GV709.3

☐ Disabled Sport USA.
http://www.dsusa.org/
Audience: **g,l,u,f.**

GV708.8

☐ Federation of Gay Games.
http://www.gaygames.com/en/
Audience: **g,l,u,f.**

GV568

☐ Scholarly Sport Sites: A Subject Directory.
http://www.ucalgary.ca/lib-old/ssportsite/
Audience: **g,l,u,f.**

GV709.3

☐ Wheelchair Sports Worldwide.
http://www.wsw.org.uk/
International Stoke Mandeville Wheelchair Sports Federation.
Audience: **g,l,u,f.**

Barros, Carlos Pestana (Editor), et al. **GV716.T73 2002**
Transatlantic Sport: The Comparative Economics of North American and European Sports. Muradali Ibrahim & Stefan Szymanski (Editors). Trade Cloth. Edward Elgar Publishing, Inc. Northampton, MA. 2003. 240p. ISBN:1-84064-947-X, ISBN13: 978-1-84064-947-5. Dewey:338.4/7796. LCCN:2002-070029.
Audience: **u,f.**

Bell, Daniel **GV721.B45 2002**
The Encyclopedia of International Games. Cloth Text. McFarland & Company, Incorporated Publishers. Jefferson, NC. 2003. 603p. ISBN:0-7864-1026-4, ISBN13: 978-0-7864-1026-2. Dewey:796/.03. LCCN:2002-013826.
Audience: **g,l,u,f.** *Choice, 2003.*

Berkshire Reference Works Staff **GV709 .I58 2001**
International Encyclopedia for Women and Sports, Vol. 3. Trade Cloth. Thomson Gale. Farmington Hills, MI. 1999. lii, 1428p. International Encyclopedia for Women and Sports Ser., Vol. 3 ISBN:0-02-864953-2, ISBN13: 978-0-02-864953-5. Dewey:796.082. LCCN:00-062518.
Audience: **g,l,u,f.**

Berkshire Reference Works Staff **GV709 .I58 2001**
International Encyclopedia for Women and Sports, Vol. 2. Trade Cloth. Thomson Gale. Farmington Hills, MI. 1999. lii, 1428p. International Encyclopedia for Women and Sports Ser., Vol. 2 ISBN:0-02-864952-4, ISBN13: 978-0-02-864952-8. Dewey:796.082. LCCN:00-062518.
Audience: **g,l,u,f.**

Berkshire Reference Works Staff **GV709 .I58 2001**
International Encyclopedia for Women and Sports, Vol. 1. Trade Cloth. Thomson Gale. Farmington Hills, MI. 1999. lii, 1428p. International Encyclopedia for Women and Sports Ser., Vol. 1 ISBN:0-02-864951-6, ISBN13: 978-0-02-864951-1. Dewey:796.082. LCCN:00-062518.
Audience: **g,l,u,f.**

Chalip, Laurence (Editor), et al. **GV706**
National Sports Policies: An International Handbook. Arthur Johnson & Lisa Stachura (Editors). Cloth Text. Greenwood Publishing Group, Inc. Portsmouth, NH. 1996. 456p. ISBN:0-313-28481-4, ISBN13: 978-0-313-28481-6. Dewey:796/.06/9. LCCN:95-025327.
Audience: **u,f.** *Choice, 1997.*

Collins, Bud (Editor) **GV992.T68**
Total Tennis: The Ultimate Tennis Encyclopedia. Trade Cloth. Sport Media Publishing. Toronto, ON. 2003. 864p. ISBN:0-9731443-4-3, ISBN13: 978-0-9731443-4-5. Dewey:796.34209.
Audience: **g,l,u,f.**

Dauncey, Hugh & Hare, Geoff (Editors) **GV1049.2.T68T68 2003**
The Tour de France, 1903-2003: A Century of Sporting Structures, Meanings and Values - Sport in the Global Society. Paper over Boards. Taylor & Francis Group. Abingdon, 2003. 290p. Sport in the Global Society Ser. ISBN:0-7146-5362-4, ISBN13: 978-0-7146-5362-4. Dewey:796.6/2/0944. LCCN:2003-011128.
Audience: **g,l,u,f.** *Choice, 2004.*

Derderian, Tom **GV1065.22.B67D46**
Boston Marathon: The First Century of the World's Premier Running Event. Ed. 2. Joan Benoit Samuelson & Bill Rodgers (Foreword by). Trade Cloth. Human Kinetics Publishers. Champaign, IL. 1996. 664p. ISBN:0-88011-479-7, ISBN13: 978-0-88011-479-0. Dewey:796.4/25/0974461. LCCN:95-039944.
Audience: **l,u.**

Dodd, Christopher **GV791.D63 1992**
The Story of World Rowing. Trade Cloth. Random House of Canada, Ltd. Mississauga, ON. 1992. 468p. ISBN:0-09-174610-8, ISBN13: 978-0-09-174610-0. Dewey:796.1/23. LCCN:93-169662.
Audience: **g,l,u,f.** *Choice, 1992.*

Dunning, Eric (Editor), et al. **GV943.9.F35F53 2002**
Fighting Fans: Football Hooliganism as a World Phenomenon. Patrick Murphy, Ivan Waddington & Antonio E. Astrinakis (Editors). Trade Paper. University College Dublin Press. Dublin, 2002. 27p. ISBN:1-900621-74-6, ISBN13: 978-1-900621-74-8. Dewey:306.4/83. LCCN:2003-464716.
Audience: **u,f.** *Choice, 2003.*

Fort, Rodney D. & Fizel, John (Editors) **GV716**
International Sports Economics Comparisons. Trade Cloth. Greenwood Publishing Group, Inc. Portsmouth, NH. 2004. 400p. Studies in Sports Economics ISBN:0-275-98032-4, ISBN13: 978-0-275-98032-0. Dewey:338.4/7796. LCCN:2003-062260.
Audience: **u,f.** *Choice, 2004.*

Giulianotti, Richard **GV943.9.S64G576 1999**
Football: A Sociology of the Global Game. Trade Paper. Polity Press. Cambridge, 1999. 240p. ISBN:0-7456-1769-7, ISBN13: 978-0-7456-1769-5. Dewey:306.4/83. LCCN:99-011069.
Audience: **u,f.** *Choice, 2000.*

Hess, Rob & Stewart, Bob (Editors) **GV947.M67 1998**
More Than a Game: An Unauthorized History of Australian Rules Football. Martin Flanagan (Foreword by). Trade Paper.

Melbourne University Publishing. Carlton, VIC. 1998. 320p. ISBN:0-522-84772-2, ISBN13: 978-0-522-84772-7. Dewey:796.336. LCCN:98-221833.
Audience: **u,f.**

Hong, Fan & Mangan, J. A. (Editors) **GV944.5**
Soccer, Women, Sexual Liberation: Kicking off a New Era. Trade Paper. Taylor & Francis Group. Abingdon, 2003. 272p. Sport in the Global Society Ser. ISBN:0-7146-8408-2, ISBN13: 978-0-7146-8408-6. Dewey:796.334082. LCCN:2004-298586.
Audience: **g,l,u,f.** *Choice, 2004.*

Hums, Mary A. & MacLean, Joanne **GV713.H86 2004**
Governance and Policy in Sport Organizations. Trade Cloth. Holcomb Hathaway, Inc. Scottsdale, AZ. 2004. xviii, 382p. ISBN:1-890871-45-1, ISBN13: 978-1-890871-45-1. Dewey:796/.06/9. LCCN:2003-026933.
Audience: **l,u.**

King, Anthony **GV944.E9**
The European Ritual: Football in the New Europe. Trade Cloth. Ashgate Publishing, Ltd. Aldershot, 2003. 302p. ISBN:0-7546-3652-6, ISBN13: 978-0-7546-3652-6. Dewey:796.334/094. LCCN:2003-045350.
Audience: **g,l,u,f.** *Choice, 2004.*

Kinsella, John & Wark, McKenzie **GV742.S663 2003**
Sport, Media, Culture: Global and Local Dimensions. Neil Blain & Alina Bernstein (Editors). Trade Paper. Taylor & Francis Group. Abingdon, 2003. 272p. ISBN:0-7146-8261-6, ISBN13: 978-0-7146-8261-7. Dewey:070.4/49796. LCCN:2002-151346.
Audience: **g,l,u,f.**

Laffaye, Horace A. **GV1011**
The Polo Encyclopedia. Stephen A. Orthwein (Foreword by). Paper Text. McFarland & Company, Incorporated Publishers. Jefferson, NC. 2004. 431p. ISBN:0-7864-1724-2, ISBN13: 978-0-7864-1724-7. Dewey:796.35/3/03. LCCN:2003-026011.
Audience: **g,l,u,f.**

Lewis, David H. **GV859.L48 1996**
Roller Skating for Gold. Trade Cloth. Scarecrow Press, Inc. Lanham, MD. 1996. 240p. American Sports History Ser., No. 5 ISBN:0-8108-3048-5, ISBN13: 978-0-8108-3048-6. Dewey:796.2/1. LCCN:96-021274.
Audience: **l,u.** *Choice, 1997.*

Mason, Tony **GV944.S64M27 1995**
Passion of the People: Football in Latin America. Trade Paper. Analytical Psychology Club of San Francisco, Inc. San Francisco, CA. 1995. 224p. Critical Studies in Latin American Culture ISBN:0-86091-667-7, ISBN13: 978-0-86091-667-3. Dewey:796.3/34/098. LCCN:95-163189.
Audience: **u,f.**

Moore, Pamela (Editor) **GV546.5.B85 1997**
Building Bodies. Paper Text. Rutgers University Press. Piscataway, NJ. 1997. 224p. ISBN:0-8135-2438-5, ISBN13: 978-0-8135-2438-2. Dewey:646.7/5. LCCN:96-049717.
Audience: **g,l,u,f.**

Murray, Bill **GV942.5.M88 1996**
The World's Game: A History of Soccer. Trade Cloth. University of Illinois Press. Champaign, IL. 1996. 224p. Illinois History of Sports Ser. ISBN:0-252-01748-X, ISBN13: 978-0-252-01748-3. Dewey:796.334/09. LCCN:95-013742.
Audience: **g,l,u,f.** *Choice, 1997.*

Oleksak, Michael M. & Oleksak, Mary A. **GV862.6.O43 1991**
Beisbol: Latin Americans and the Grand Old Game. Trade Cloth. McGraw-Hill Trade. New York, NY. 1991. 320p. ISBN:0-940279-35-5, ISBN13: 978-0-940279-35-3. Dewey:796.357/098. LCCN:91-010697.
Audience: **g,l,u,f.** *Choice, 1991.*

Podnieks, Andrew, et al. **GV846.5.K56 2002**
Kings of the Ice: A History of World Hockey. Denis Gibbons, Pavel Barta, Dimitry Ryzkov & Tom Ratschunas (Authors). Trade Cloth. NDE Publishing. Richmond Hill, ON. 2002. 1024p. ISBN:1-55321-099-9, ISBN13: 978-1-55321-099-3. Dewey:796.962. LCCN:2003-427050.
Audience: **u,f.** *Choice, 2003.*

Reaves, Joseph A. **GV863.69.R43 2002**
Taking in a Game: A History of Baseball in Asia. Trade Cloth. University of Nebraska Press. Lincoln, NE. 2002. 220p. Jerry Malloy Prize Ser. ISBN:0-8032-3943-2, ISBN13: 978-0-8032-3943-2. Dewey:796.357/095. LCCN:2001-043058.
Audience: **g,l,u,f.** *Choice, 2002.*

Riordan, J. **GV706.35.S58 1998**
Sport and International Politics. Paper over Boards. Routledge. New York, NY. 1998. 240p. ISBN:0-419-21440-2, ISBN13: 978-0-419-21440-3. Dewey:306.4/83/094/0904. LCCN:98-189017.
Audience: **g,l,u,f.** *Choice, 1999.*

Riordan, Jim & Kruger, Arnd (Editors) **GV706.35.I57 1999**
The International Politics of Sport in the 20th Century. Trade Paper. Routledge. New York, NY. 1999. 264p. ISBN:0-419-21160-8, ISBN13: 978-0-419-21160-0. Dewey:796/.09/04. LCCN:98-041234.
Audience: **u,f.** *Choice, 2000.*

Smith, Myron J. Jr. **GV954**
Professional Football: The Official Pro Footbal of Fame Bibliography. Cloth Text. Greenwood Publishing Group, Inc. Portsmouth, NH. 1993. 432p. Bibliographies and Indexes on Sports History Ser., No. 1 ISBN:0-313-28928-X, ISBN13: 978-0-313-28928-6. Dewey:796.332640973. LCCN:92-042677.
Audience: **g,l,u,f.** *Choice, 1993.*

Sugden, John P. **GV1136.8.S84 1996**
Boxing and Society: An International Analysis. Trade Paper. Manchester University Press. Manchester, 1997. 272p. Sport, Society, and Politics Ser. ISBN:0-7190-4321-2, ISBN13: 978-0-7190-4321-5. Dewey:306.4/83. LCCN:96-029445.
Audience: **u,f.** *Choice, 1997.*

Szymanski, Stefan & Zimbalist, Andrew S. **GV716.S99 2005**
National Pastime: How Americans Play Baseball and the Rest of the World Plays Soccer. Perfect, Paper over Boards, Dust Jacket. Brookings Institution Press. Washington, DC. 2005. 263p. ISBN:0-8157-8258-6, ISBN13: 978-0-8157-8258-2. Dewey:338.4/7796334. LCCN:2005-001160.
Audience: **u,f.** *Choice, 2005.*

Tomlinson, Alan & Sugden, John **GV943.9.S64S84 1998**
FIFA and the Contest for World Football: Who Rules the Peoples Game. Trade Paper. Polity Press. Cambridge, 1998. 304p. ISBN:0-7456-1661-5, ISBN13: 978-0-7456-1661-2. Dewey:796.334/66. LCCN:97-051453.
Audience: **u,f.**

Van Bottenburg, Marten **GV706.5.V3613 2001**
Global Games. Trade Cloth. University of Illinois Press. Champaign, IL. 2001. 296p. Sport and Society Ser. ISBN:0-252-02654-3, ISBN13: 978-0-252-02654-6. Dewey:796. LCCN:00-012587.
Audience: **u,f.** *Choice, 2002.*

Westerbeek, Hans & Smith, Aaron **GV716.W46 2002**
Sport Business in the Global Marketplace: A Study of Strategic Cognition. Trade Cloth. Palgrave Macmillan. New York, NY. 2003. 250p. Finance and Capital Markets Ser. ISBN:1-4039-0300-X, ISBN13: 978-1-4039-0300-6. Dewey:338.4/3796. LCCN:2002-075498.
Audience: **u,f.**

Wheatcroft, Geoffrey **GV1049.2.T68**
Le Tour: A History of the Tour de France, 1903-2003. Trade Paper. Simon & Schuster, Ltd. London, 2005. 320p. ISBN:0-684-02879-4, ISBN13: 978-0-684-02879-8. Dewey:796.6/2/0944.
Audience: **g,l,u,f.**

Wilcox, Ralph C. (Editor) **GV706.8.S659 1994**
Sport in the Global Village. Eric F. Brown (Contribution by). Cloth Text. Fitness Information Technology, Inc. Morgantown, WV. 1994. 556p. ISBN:0-9627926-4-0, ISBN13: 978-0-9627926-4-9. Dewey:306.4/83. LCCN:94-070170.
Audience: **u.**

Williams, Jean **GV944.5**
A History of Women's Football: Gender, Power and the Rise of a Global Game. Trade Paper. Routledge. New York, NY. 2003. 240p. ISBN:0-415-26338-7, ISBN13: 978-0-415-26338-2. Dewey:796.3/34/082.
Audience: **u,f.**

Wolff, Alexander **GV885.W62 2002**
Big Game, Small World: A Basketball Adventure. Trade Cloth. Warner Books, Inc. New York, NY. 2002. 448p. ISBN:0-446-52601-0, ISBN13: 978-0-446-52601-2. Dewey:796.323. LCCN:2001-026116.
Audience: **u,f.**

International Contests and Sporting Events > Olympics

GV563
Amateur Athletic Foundation of Los Angeles.
http://www.aafla.org/
Audience: **g,l,u.**

GV709.3
International Paralympic Comitee.
http://www.paralympic.org/release/Main_Sections_Menu/index.html
Audience: **g,l,u,f.**

GV721.5
Official Website of the Olympic Movement.
http://www.olympic.org
Audience: **g,l,u,f.**

Barney, Robert Knight, et al. **GV721.5.B32 2002**
Selling the Five Rings: The IOC and the Rise of Olympic Commercialism. Stephen R. Wenn & Scott G. Martyn (Authors). Trade Cloth. University of Utah Press. Salt Lake City, UT. 2002. 448p. ISBN:0-87480-713-1, ISBN13: 978-0-87480-713-4. Dewey:796.48. LCCN:2001-006781.
Audience: **l,u,f.** *Choice, 2003, 2002.*

Cashman, Richard & Hughes, Anthony (Editors) **GV722 2000.S82 1999**
Staging the Olympics: The Event and Its Impact. Trade Paper. University of New South Wales Press. Sydney, NSW. 1999. 226p. ISBN:0-86840-729-1, ISBN13: 978-0-86840-729-6. Dewey:796.48. LCCN:00-340427.
Audience: **l,u,f.** *Choice, 2000.*

Daddario, Gina **GV742**
Women's Sport and Spectacle: Gendered Television Coverage and the Olympic Games. Trade Cloth. Greenwood Publishing Group, Inc. Portsmouth, NH. 1998. 184p. ISBN:0-275-95856-6, ISBN13: 978-0-275-95856-5. Dewey:302.23/45/082. LCCN:97-038544.
Audience: **u,f.** *Choice, 1998.*

Dawson, Buck **GV837.9.D39 2000**
Mermaids on Parade: America's Love Affair with Its First Olympic Swimmers. Paul Gallico (Introduction by). Trade Cloth. Nova Science Publishers, Inc. Hauppauge, NY. 2000. 266p. ISBN:1-56072-726-8, ISBN13: 978-1-56072-726-2. Dewey:797.2/1/082092273 B. LCCN:2001-267948.
Audience: **g,l,u,f.**

Dyreson, Mark **GV706.35.D97 1998**
Making the American Team: Sport, Culture, and the Olympic Experience. Trade Paper. University of Illinois Press. Champaign, IL. 1997. 288p. Sport and Society Ser. ISBN:0-252-06654-5, ISBN13: 978-0-252-06654-2. Dewey:796/.0973. LCCN:97-004663.
Audience: **u,f.** *Choice, 1998.*

Ferrand, Alain & Torrigiani, Luiggino **GV716.F47 2005**
Marketing of Olympic Sport Organisations. Trade Paper. Human Kinetics Publishers. Champaign, IL. 2004. 144p. ISBN:0-7360-5930-X, ISBN13: 978-0-7360-5930-5. Dewey:338.4/379648. LCCN:2004-022804.
Audience: **u,f.**

Findling, John E. & Pelle, Kimberly D. (Editors) **GV721**
Historical Dictionary of the Modern Olympic Movement. Cloth Text. Greenwood Publishing Group, Inc. Portsmouth, NH. 1996. 504p. ISBN:0-313-28477-6, ISBN13: 978-0-313-28477-9. Dewey:796.48. LCCN:95-000569.
Audience: **g,l,u,f.** *Choice, 1996.*

Guttmann, Allen **GV721.2.B78**
The Games Must Go On: Avery Brundage and the Olympic Movement. Trade Cloth. Columbia University Press. New York, NY. 1983. 317p. ISBN:0-231-05444-0, ISBN13: 978-0-231-05444-7. Dewey:796.4/8/0924. LCCN:83-005360.
Audience: **l,u,f.** B

Guttmann, Allen **GV721.5.G85 2000**
The Olympics: A History of the Modern Games. Ed. 2. Trade Cloth. University of Illinois Press. Champaign, IL. 2002. 248p. Illinois History of Sports Ser. ISBN:0-252-02725-6, ISBN13: 978-0-252-02725-3. Dewey:796.48. LCCN:2001-041383.
Audience: **g,l,u,f.** *Choice, 2002, 1992.*

Kruger, Arnd & Murray, William (Editors) **GV722 1936.N39 2003**
The Nazi Olympics: Sport, Politics, and Appeasement in the 1930s. Trade Cloth. University of Illinois Press. Champaign, IL. 2003. 280p. Sport and Society Ser. ISBN:0-252-02815-5, ISBN13: 978-0-252-02815-1. Dewey:796.48. LCCN:2002-011803.
Audience: **g,l,u,f.** *Choice, 2004.*

Lenskyj, Helen Jefferson **GV722 2000.L46 2002**
The Best Olympics Ever?: Social Impacts of Sydney 2000. Paper Text. State University of New York Press. Albany, NY. 2002. 262p. ISBN:0-7914-5474-6, ISBN13: 978-0-7914-5474-9. Dewey:796.48. LCCN:2001-055121.
Audience: **u,f.** *Choice, 2003.*

Lovett, Charlie **GV1065**
Olympic Marathon: A Centennial History of the Games' Most Storied Race. Trade Cloth. Greenwood Publishing Group, Inc. Portsmouth, NH. 1997. 192p. ISBN:0-275-95771-3, ISBN13: 978-0-275-95771-1. Dewey:796.42/52. LCCN:96-047618.
Audience: **g,l,u,f.** *Choice, 1998.*

Lucas, John A. **GV721.6.L83 1992**
Future of the Olympic Games. Cloth Text. Human Kinetics Publishers. Champaign, IL. 1992. 248p. ISBN:0-87322-357-8, ISBN13: 978-0-87322-357-7. Dewey:796.48. LCCN:91-046818.
Audience: **l,u.** *Choice, 1992.*

Mallon, Bill & Buchanan, Ian **GV721.5.B83 2006**
Historical Dictionary of the Olympic Movement. Ed. 3. Trade Cloth. Scarecrow Press, Inc. Lanham, MD. 2005. 544p. Historical Dictionaries of Religions, Philosophies, and Movements Ser., No. 61 ISBN:0-8108-5574-7, ISBN13: 978-0-8108-5574-8. Dewey:796.48/03. LCCN:2005-016706.
Audience: **g,l,u.**

Mandell, Richard D. **GV722 1936.M3 1986**
The Nazi Olympics. Trade Paper. University of Illinois Press. Champaign, IL. 1987. 360p. Sport and Society Ser. ISBN:0-252-01325-5, ISBN13: 978-0-252-01325-6. Dewey:796.4/8/09043. LCCN:86-019347.
Audience: **l,u,f.**

Muggleton, David & Weinzierl, Rupert **GV721.6**
Post-Olympism?: Questioning Sport in the Twenty-First Century. John Bale & Mette Krogh Christensen (Editors). Trade Paper. Berg Publishers. Oxford, 2004. 256p. Global Sport Cultures Ser. ISBN:1-85973-719-6, ISBN13: 978-1-85973-719-4. Dewey:306.4/83/0905.
Audience: **u,f.**

Pieroth, Doris Hinson **GV722 1932.P54 1996**
Their Day in the Sun: Women of the 1932 Olympics. Trade Paper. University of Washington Press. Seattle, WA. 1996. 208p. Samuel and Althea Stroum Bks. ISBN:0-295-97554-7, ISBN13: 978-0-295-97554-2. Dewey:796.48. LCCN:96-023104.
Audience: **l,u.** *Choice, 1997.*

Posey, Carl A. **GV722 1996.P67 2000**
The Olympic Century. Christian D. Kinney (Editor). Trade Cloth. World Sport Research & Publications, Inc. Los Angeles, CA. 2001. 176p. The Olympic Century Ser. ISBN:1-888383-00-3, ISBN13: 978-1-888383-00-3. Dewey:796.48. LCCN:97-001144.
Audience: **g,l,u,f.** *Choice, 2002.*

Pound, Richard W. **GV721.5**
Inside the Olympics: A Behind-the-Scenes Look at the Politics, the Scandals, and the Glory of the Games. Trade Cloth. John Wiley & Sons, Inc. Hoboken, NJ. 2004. 288p. ISBN:0-470-83454-4, ISBN13: 978-0-470-83454-1. Dewey:796.48. LCCN:2006-296402.
Audience: **l,u.**

Preuss, Holger **GV721.5.P717 2004**
Economics of Staging the Olympics: A Comparison of the Games 1972-2008. Trade Paper. Edward Elgar Publishing, Inc. Northampton, MA. 2004. 352p. ISBN:1-84376-893-3, ISBN13: 978-1-84376-893-7. Dewey:338.4/379648. LCCN:2004-056663.
Audience: **u,f.** *Choice, 2005.*

Rathburn, Elizabeth & Drummond, Siobhan (Contribution by) **GV721.5 .G63 1996**
Grace and Glory: A Century of Women in the Olympics. Trade Cloth. Triumph Books. Chicago, IL. 1996. 112p. ISBN:1-57243-116-4, ISBN13: 978-1-57243-116-4. Dewey:796.48.
Audience: **g,l,u,f.** *Choice, 1996.*

Roche, Maurice **G155.A1**
Megaevents and Modernity: Olympics, Expos and the Growth of Global Culture. Trade Paper. Routledge. New York, NY. 2000. 304p. ISBN:0-415-15712-9, ISBN13: 978-0-415-15712-4. Dewey:306.4/8.
Audience: **u,f.** *Choice, 2001.*

Schaffer, Kay & Smith, Sidonie (Editors) **GV721.5.O425 2000**
The Olympics at the Millennium: Power, Politics, and the Games. Trade Paper. Rutgers University Press. Piscataway, NJ. 2000. xi, 318p. ISBN:0-8135-2820-8, ISBN13: 978-0-8135-2820-5. Dewey:796.48. LCCN:99-056801.
Audience: **u.** *Choice, 2001.*

Senn, Alfred Erich **GV721.5.S443 1999**
Power, Politics and the Olympic Games. Trade Paper. Human Kinetics Publishers. Champaign, IL. 1999. 336p. ISBN:0-88011-958-6, ISBN13: 978-0-88011-958-0. Dewey:796.48. LCCN:98-048879.
Audience: **l,u.** *Choice, 1999.*

Vaughn, Robie **GV856**
Headfirst: The Olympic Success Story of Skeleton. Mike Towle (As told to). Saddle Stitched, Cloth over Boards, Dust Jacket. Brown Books Publishing Group. Dallas, TX. 2005. 242p. ISBN:1-933285-08-7, ISBN13: 978-1-933285-08-5. Dewey:796.95. LCCN:2005-932907.
Audience: **l,u,f.**

Wilson, Wayne & Derse, Edward (Editors) **RC1230.D76 2001**
Doping in Elite Sport: The Politics of Drugs in the Olympic Movement. Trade Cloth. Human Kinetics Publishers. Champaign, IL. 2001. 312p. ISBN:0-7360-0329-0, ISBN13: 978-0-7360-0329-2. Dewey:362.29/088/796. LCCN:00-033599.
Audience: **g,l,u,f.** *Choice, 2001.*

Young, David C. **GV721.5.Y68 1996**
The Modern Olympics: A Struggle for Revival. Trade Cloth. Johns Hopkins University Press. Baltimore, MD. 1996. 272p. ISBN:0-8018-5374-5, ISBN13: 978-0-8018-5374-6. Dewey:796.48. LCCN:96-016496.
Audience: **g,l,u,f.** *Choice, 1997.*

International Contests and Sporting Events > World Games

Barrett, John **GV999**
Wimbledon: The Official History. Trade Cloth. Trafalgar Square. North Pomfret, VT. 2001. 480p. ISBN:0-00-711707-8, ISBN13: 978-0-00-711707-9. Dewey:796.3/42/0942193.
Audience: **g,l,u,f.** *Choice, 2002.*

Darby, Paul **GV944.A4D37 2001**
Africa, Football and FIFA: Politics, Colonialism and Resistance. Trade Paper. Taylor & Francis Group. Abingdon, 2002. 256p. Sport in the Global Society Ser., No. 23 ISBN:0-7146-8029-X, ISBN13: 978-0-7146-8029-3. Dewey:796.334/096. LCCN:2001-002915.
Audience: **u,f.** *Choice, 2002.*

International Contests and Sporting Events > World Cups

Crouch, T. **GV943.49.C76 2002**
Ultimate Book of the World Cup: A Complete History. Trade Paper. Aurum Press, Ltd. London, 2002. 256p. ISBN:1-85410-843-3, ISBN13: 978-1-85410-843-2. Dewey:796.3/34668.
Audience: **g,l,u,f.** *Choice, 2002.*

Davies, Gerald **GV946.2**
The History of the Rugby World Cup. Sanctuary Publishing, Ltd. 2004. ISBN:1-86074-445-1, ISBN13: 978-1-86074-445-7.
Audience: **l,u.**

Tomlinson, Alan & Sugden, John **GV943.9.S64S84 1998**
FIFA and the Contest for World Football: Who Rules the Peoples Game. Trade Paper. Polity Press. Cambridge, 1998. 304p. ISBN:0-7456-1661-5, ISBN13: 978-0-7456-1661-2. Dewey:796.334/66. LCCN:97-051453.
Audience: **u,f.**

International Contests and Sporting Events > Senior and Master Contests

GV712

☐ Huntsman World Senior Games.
http://www.seniorgames.net/
Audience: **g,l,u,f.**

GV712

☐ National Senior Games Assocation.
http://www.nsga.com/
Audience: **l,u,f.**

Benyo, Richard **GV1061.8.A35 1998**
Running Past 50. Trade Paper. Human Kinetics Publishers. Champaign, IL. 1998. 256p. Ageless Athlete Ser., Vol. 50 ISBN:0-88011-705-2, ISBN13: 978-0-88011-705-0. Dewey:613.7/172/0846. LCCN:97-052054.
Audience: **g,l,u,f.**

Olson, Leonard T. **GV1060.5.O43 2001**
Masters Track and Field: A History. Trade Cloth. McFarland & Company, Incorporated Publishers. Jefferson, NC. 2000. 320p. ISBN:0-7864-0889-8, ISBN13: 978-0-7864-0889-4. Dewey:796.42. LCCN:00-42162.
Audience: **l,u.**

Sports A-L > General. Miscellaneous Sports, A-Z

Adams, Natalie Guice & Bettis, Pamela J. **LB3635**
Cheerleader!: An American Icon. Trade Paper, Perfect. Palgrave Macmillan. New York, NY. 2005. 208p. ISBN:1-4039-6892-6, ISBN13: 978-1-4039-6892-0. Dewey:791.6/4. LCCN:2003-048738.
Audience: **g,l,u,f.** *Choice, 2004.*

Clanton, Reita E. & Dwight, Mary P. **GV1017.T4C53 1997**
Team Handball: Steps to Success. Trade Paper. Human Kinetics Publishers. Champaign, IL. 1996. 168p. Steps to Success Activity Ser. ISBN:0-87322-411-6, ISBN13: 978-0-87322-411-6. Dewey:796.3/12. LCCN:96-015149.
Audience: **g,l,u.**

Fadala, Sam **GV1185.F33 1999**
Traditional Archery. Trade Paper. Stackpole Books. Mechanicsburg, PA. 1999. 256p. ISBN:0-8117-2943-5, ISBN13: 978-0-8117-2943-7. Dewey:799.3/2. LCCN:98-043191.
Audience: **l,u.**

Graver, Dennis **GV838.672.G74 2003**
Scuba Diving. Ed. 3. Trade Paper. Human Kinetics Publishers. Champaign, IL. 2003. 224p. ISBN:0-7360-4539-2, ISBN13: 978-0-7360-4539-1. Dewey:797.2/3. LCCN:2002-152325.
Audience: **g,l,u,f.**

Herrigel, Eugene **GV1188.J3H4713**
Zen in the Art of Archery. R. F. C. Hull (Translator), D. T. Suzuki (Introduction by). Trade Paper. Knopf Publishing Group. New York, NY. 1999. 96p. Vintage Spiritual Classics Ser. ISBN:0-375-70509-0, ISBN13: 978-0-375-70509-0. Dewey:799.3/2. LCCN:89-005319.
Audience: **g,l,u,f.**

Hess, Rob & Stewart, Bob (Editors) **GV947.M67 1998**
More Than a Game: An Unauthorized History of Australian Rules Football. Martin Flanagan (Foreword by). Trade Paper. Melbourne University Publishing. Carlton, VIC. 1998. 320p. ISBN:0-522-84772-2, ISBN13: 978-0-522-84772-7. Dewey:796.336. LCCN:98-221833.
Audience: **u,f.**

Hotaling, Edward **SF336.A2H68**
The Great Black Jockeys: The Lives and Times of the Men Who Dominated America's First National Sport. Trade Cloth.

DIANE Publishing Company. Collingdale, PA. 2001. 380p. ISBN:0-7881-9643-X, ISBN13: 978-0-7881-9643-0. Dewey:798.4/0092396073.
Audience: **l,u.**

Jozwiak, Don **GV567**
Dictionary of Sports: A Complete Guide to the Vocabulary of the World's Leading Speakers. Trade Cloth. Carlton Books, Ltd. London, 2002. 400p. ISBN:1-85868-800-0, ISBN13: 978-1-85868-800-8. Dewey:796.03.
Audience: **g,l,u,f.** *Choice, 2000.*

Levinson, David & Christensen, Karen **GV567.B48 2005**
Berkshire Encyclopedia of World Sport. Library Binding. Berkshire Publishing Group. Great Barrington, MA. 2005. ISBN:0-9743091-1-7, ISBN13: 978-0-9743091-1-8. Dewey:796.03. LCCN:2005-013050.
Audience: **g,l,u,f.** *Choice, 2006.*

Liponski, Wojciech **GV567**
World Sports Encyclopedia. Cloth over Boards. MBI Publishing Company LLC. Osceola, WI. 2003. 596p. ISBN:0-7603-1682-1, ISBN13: 978-0-7603-1682-5. Dewey:796/.03.
Audience: **g,l,u,f.**

McEvoy, John & McEvoy, Julia **SF336.A2W65 2001**
Women in Racing: In Their Own Words. Trade Cloth. Blood-Horse, Incorporated, The. Lexington, KY. 2001. 256p. ISBN:1-58150-067-X, ISBN13: 978-1-58150-067-7. Dewey:798.4/0092/2 B. LCCN:2001-086643.
Audience: **l,u.**

Mullen, Michelle **GV903.B69 2003**
Bowling Fundamentals. Trade Paper. Human Kinetics Publishers. Champaign, IL. 2003. 144p. Sports Fundamentals Ser. ISBN:0-7360-5120-1, ISBN13: 978-0-7360-5120-0. Dewey:794.6. LCCN:2003-013368.
Audience: **g,l,u.**

Piggott, Derek **TL765**
Gliding: A Handbook on Soaring Flight. Ed. 8. Trade Paper. A & C Black. London, 2002. 312p. ISBN:0-7136-6148-8, ISBN13: 978-0-7136-6148-4. Dewey:629.132/523.
Audience: **u.**

Piggott, Derek **TL754**
Understanding Gliding. Ed. 3. Trade Paper. A & C Black. London, 2004. 256p. ISBN:0-7136-4343-9, ISBN13: 978-0-7136-4343-5. Dewey:629.132/523.
Audience: **l,u.** B

Roberts, Monty & Grealy, Lucy **SF284.52.R635A3 1997**
The Man Who Listens to Horses. Trade Cloth. Random House, Inc. New York, NY. 1997. 320p. ISBN:0-679-45658-9, ISBN13: 978-0-679-45658-2. Dewey:636.1/088/092. LCCN:97-017318.
Audience: **g,l,u.**

Watts, Robert G. & Bahill, A. Terry **QC26.W38 2000**
Keep Your Eye on the Ball: Curve Balls, Knuckleballs, and Fallacies of Baseball. Ed. 2. Trade Paper. W. H. Freeman & Company. New York, NY. 2000. 240p. ISBN:0-7167-3717-5, ISBN13: 978-0-7167-3717-9. Dewey:796.3570153. LCCN:99-059352.
Audience: **u.**

Sports A-L > Auto Racing

Fenster, Julie **GV1029.2.F46 2005**
Race of the Century: The Heroic True Story of the 1908 New York-to-Paris Auto Race. Trade Cloth. Crown Publishing Group. New York, NY. 2005. 400p. ISBN:0-609-61096-1, ISBN13: 978-0-609-61096-1. Dewey:796.72. LCCN:2004-026644.
Audience: **g,l,u,f.** *Choice, 2005.*

Guthrie, Janet **GV1032.G87A3 2005**
Janet Guthrie: A Life at Full Throttle. Trade Cloth. Sport Media Publishing. Toronto, ON. 2005. 512p. ISBN:1-894963-31-8, ISBN13: 978-1-894963-31-2. Dewey:796.72/092 B. LCCN:2004-026599.
Audience: **g,l,u,f.**

Hagstrom, Robert G. Jr. **GV1029.9.S74H34**
The NASCAR Way: The Business That Drives the Sport. Trade Paper. John Wiley & Sons, Inc. Hoboken, NJ. 2001. 254p. ISBN:0-471-39920-5, ISBN13: 978-0-471-39920-9. Dewey:338.4/7/79672/0973.
Audience: **g,l,u.**

Howell, Mark D. **GV1029.9.S74H68 1997**
From Moonshine to Madison Avenue: A Cultural History of the NASCAR Winston Cup Series. Trade Paper. University of Wisconsin Press. Chicago, IL. 1997. xvi, 266p. ISBN:0-87972-740-3, ISBN13: 978-0-87972-740-6. Dewey:796.72/0973. LCCN:97-004215.
Audience: **g,l.** *Choice, 1997.*

Miller, G. Wayne **GV1029.9.S74M55 2002**
Men and Speed: A Wild Ride Through NASCAR's Breakout Season. Trade Cloth. PublicAffairs. New York, NY. 2002. 320p. ISBN:1-58648-096-0, ISBN13: 978-1-58648-096-7. Dewey:796.72/0973. LCCN:2002-018980.
Audience: **l,u,f.** *Choice, 2002.*

Miller, Leonard W. **GV1032.M45 2003**
Silent Thunder: Breaking Through Cultural, Racial, and Class Barriers in Motorsports. Trade Paper. Red Sea Press. Trenton, NJ. 2003. 212p. ISBN:1-56902-177-5, ISBN13: 978-1-56902-177-4. Dewey:796.72/092 B. LCCN:2003-013084.
Audience: **l,u.**

Post, Robert C. **GV1029.P675 2001**
High Performance: The Culture and Technology of Drag Racing, 1950-2000. Ed. 2. Trade Paper. Johns Hopkins University Press. Baltimore, MD. 2001. 452p. History of Technology Ser. ISBN:0-8018-6664-2, ISBN13: 978-0-8018-6664-7. Dewey:796.72. LCCN:00-048161.
Audience: **l,u,f.**

Seymour, Miranda **GV1032.N53S49 2004**
The Bugatti Queen: In Search of a French Racing Legend. Trade Cloth. Random House, Inc. New York, NY. 2004. 352p. ISBN:1-4000-6168-7, ISBN13: 978-1-4000-6168-6. Dewey:796.72/092. LCCN:2004-042783.
Audience: **g,l,u,f.** *Choice, 2005.*

Wright, Jim **GV1029.9.S74W75 2002**
Fixin' to Git: One Fan's Love Affair with NASCAR's Winston Cup. Trade Cloth. Duke University Press. Durham, NC. 2002. 320p. ISBN:0-8223-2926-3, ISBN13: 978-0-8223-2926-8. Dewey:796.72. LCCN:2002-000485.
Audience: **u,f.** *Choice, 2003.*

Sports A-L > Baseball

GV877

☐ Baseball Reference.
http://www.baseball-reference.com/
Audience: **g,l,u,f.**

GV880

☐ Business of Baseball.
http://www.businessofbaseball.com/
Audience: **g,l,u,f.**

Aaron, Hank & Wheeler, Lonnie **GV865.R6**
I Had a Hammer: The Hank Aaron Story. Mass Market. HarperCollins Publishers. New York, NY. 1992. 480p. ISBN:0-06-109956-2, ISBN13: 978-0-06-109956-4. Dewey:796.357/092 B. LCCN:90-055521.
Audience: **g,l.**

Adelson, Bruce **GV875.A1A34 1999**
Brushing Back Jim Crow: The Integration of the Minor Leagues in the American South. Trade Cloth. University Press of Virginia. Charlottesville, VA. 1999. 288p. ISBN:0-8139-1884-7, ISBN13: 978-0-8139-1884-6. Dewey:796.357/64/0975. LCCN:98-045122.
Audience: **l,u,f.**

Alexander, Charles C. **GV865.M3A75 1995**
John McGraw. Trade Paper. University of Nebraska Press. Lincoln, NE. 1995. 371p. ISBN:0-8032-5925-5, ISBN13: 978-0-8032-5925-6. Dewey:796.357/092/4 B. LCCN:94-023951.
Audience: **l,u.**

Alexander, Charles C. **GV865.H6A32**
Rogers Hornsby: A Biography. Trade Paper. Henry Holt & Company. New York, NY. 1996. 384p. ISBN:0-8050-4697-6, ISBN13: 978-0-8050-4697-7. Dewey:796.357/092 B.
Audience: **g,l,u.** *Choice, 1996.*

Alexander, Charles C. **GV865.C6**
Ty Cobb. Trade Paper. Southern Methodist University Press. Dallas, TX. 2006. 288p. ISBN:0-87074-509-3, ISBN13: 978-0-87074-509-6. Dewey:796.357092.
Audience: **g,l,u.**

American Sport Education Program Staff **GV880.4.R66 2001**
Coaching Youth Baseball. Ed. 3. Trade Paper. Human Kinetics Publishers. Champaign, IL. 2001. 176p. ISBN:0-7360-3716-0, ISBN13: 978-0-7360-3716-7. Dewey:796.357/07/7. LCCN:00-050062.
Audience: **g,l,u.**

Ardell, Jean Hastings **GV880.7.A73 2005**
Breaking into Baseball: Women and the National Pasttime. Ila Borders (Foreword by). Trade Paper, Perfect, Paper over Boards. Southern Illinois University Press. Carbondale, IL. 2005. 278p. Writing Baseball Ser. ISBN:0-8093-2627-2, ISBN13: 978-0-8093-2627-3. Dewey:796.357/082. LCCN:2004-019010.
Audience: **g,l,u,f.** *Choice, 2005.*

Asinof, Eliot **HV6768**
Eight Men Out: The Black Sox and the 1919 World Series. Stephen Jay Gould (Introduction by). Trade Paper. Henry Holt & Company. New York, NY. 2000. 328p. ISBN:0-8050-6537-7, ISBN13: 978-0-8050-6537-4. Dewey:364.1/68.
Audience: **l,u.**

Baldassaro, Lawrence & Johnson, Dick (Editors) **GV867.64.A44 2002**
The American Game: Baseball and Ethnicity. Allan H. Selig (Foreword by). Trade Cloth. Southern Illinois University Press. Carbondale, IL. 2002. 224p. Writing Baseball Ser. ISBN:0-8093-2446-6, ISBN13: 978-0-8093-2446-0. Dewey:796.357. LCCN:2001-049600.
Audience: **g,l,u,f.** *Choice, 2002.*

Bass, Mike **GV865.S36**
Marge Schott . . . Unleashed!. Trade Cloth. Sports Publishing, LLC. Champaign, IL. 1993. 309p. ISBN:0-915611-73-2, ISBN13: 978-0-915611-73-7. Dewey:796.357. LCCN:92-084086.
Audience: **g,l.** *Choice, 1994.*

Berlage, Gai I. & Gerard, Charley **GV880**
Women in Baseball: The Forgotten History. Trade Cloth. Greenwood Publishing Group, Inc. Portsmouth, NH. 1994. 224p. ISBN:0-275-94735-1, ISBN13: 978-0-275-94735-4. Dewey:796.357082. LCCN:93-025049.
Audience: **g,l,u,f.** *Choice, 1994.*

Bevis, Charlie **GV867.6.B48 2003**
Sunday Baseball: The Major Leagues' Struggle to Play Baseball on the Lord's Day, 1876-1934. Paper Text. McFarland & Company, Incorporated Publishers. Jefferson, NC. 2003. 326p. ISBN:0-7864-1564-9, ISBN13: 978-0-7864-1564-9. Dewey:796.357/64/0973. LCCN:2002-156687.
Audience: **u,f.** *Choice, 2003.*

Billet, Bret L. & Formwalt, Lance J. **GV863**
America's National Pastime: A Study of Race and Merit in Professional Baseball. Trade Cloth. Greenwood Publishing Group, Inc. Portsmouth, NH. 1995. 200p. ISBN:0-275-95193-6, ISBN13: 978-0-275-95193-1. Dewey:796.357/0973. LCCN:95-003331.
Audience: **g,l,u,f.** *Choice, 1996.*

Bjarkman, Peter C. **GV863.155.B53 1994**
Baseball with a Latin Beat: A History of the Latin American Game. Paper Text. McFarland & Company, Incorporated Publishers. Jefferson, NC. 1994. 486p. ISBN:0-89950-973-8, ISBN13: 978-0-89950-973-0. Dewey:796.357/098. LCCN:94-3526.
Audience: **u,f.** *Choice, 1995.*

Browning, Reed **GV865.Y58B76 2003**
Cy Young: A Baseball Life. Trade Paper. University of Massachusetts Press. Amherst, MA. 2003. 320p. ISBN:1-55849-398-0, ISBN13: 978-1-55849-398-8. Dewey:796.357/093/09042. LCCN:99-088275.
Audience: **g,l,u,f.** *Choice, 2000.*

Bryant, Howard **GV875.B62B79 2002**
Shut Out: A Story of Race and Baseball in Boston. Paper over Boards. Routledge. New York, NY. 2002. 296p. ISBN:0-415-92779-X, ISBN13: 978-0-415-92779-6. Dewey:796.357/64/0974461. LCCN:2002-069950.
Audience: **u,f.**

Bullock, Steve **GV863.A1B84 2004**
Playing for Their Nation: Baseball and the American Military During World War II. Trade Cloth. University of Nebraska Press. Lincoln, NE. 2005. 224p. Jerry Malloy Prize Ser.

ISBN:0-8032-1337-9, ISBN13: 978-0-8032-1337-1. Dewey:796.357/0973/09044. LCCN:2003-016945.
Audience: **u,f.** *Choice, 2004.*

Burk, Robert F. **GV880.B869 2001**
Much More Than a Game: Players, Owners and American Baseball since 1921. Trade Paper. University of North Carolina Press. Chapel Hill, NC. 2001. 384p. ISBN:0-8078-4908-1, ISBN13: 978-0-8078-4908-8. Dewey:796.357/09/04. LCCN:00-041774.
Audience: **l,u.** *Choice, 2001.*

Burk, Robert F. **GV880.B87 1994**
Never Just a Game: Players, Owners and American Baseball to 1920. Trade Cloth. University of North Carolina Press. Chapel Hill, NC. 1994. 302p. ISBN:0-8078-2122-5, ISBN13: 978-0-8078-2122-0. Dewey:338.4/3796357/0973. LCCN:93-022719.
Audience: **g,l,u,f.** *Choice, 1994.*

Casway, Jerrold I. **GV865.D45C37 2004**
Ed Delahanty in the Emerald Age of Baseball. Trade Cloth. University of Notre Dame Press. Notre Dame, IN. 2004. 400p. ISBN:0-268-02285-2, ISBN13: 978-0-268-02285-3. Dewey:796.357/092 B. LCCN:2003-024041.
Audience: **u,f.** *Choice, 2004.*

Chadwick, Bruce **GV875.A1.C47 1992**
When the Game Was Black and White: The Illustrated History of Baseball's Negro Leagues. Trade Cloth. Abbeville Press, Inc. New York, NY. 1992. 204p. ISBN:1-55859-372-1, ISBN13: 978-1-55859-372-5. Dewey:796.35708996073. LCCN:92-013673.
Audience: **g,l,u,f.** *Choice, 1993.*

Clark, Dick **GV863.A1**
The Negro Leagues Book. Trade Paper. Society for American Baseball Research. Cleveland, OH. 1994. 382p. ISBN:0-910137-55-2, ISBN13: 978-0-910137-55-3. Dewey:796.357.
Audience: **g,l,u,f.** *Choice, 1995.*

Cottrell, Robert Charles **GV865.F63C68 2001**
The Best Pitcher in Baseball: The Life of Rube Foster, Negro League Giant. Trade Cloth. New York University Press. New York, NY. 2001. 240p. ISBN:0-8147-1614-8, ISBN13: 978-0-8147-1614-4. Dewey:796.357/092 B. LCCN:2001-003175.
Audience: **g,l,u,f.** *Choice, 2002.*

Cramer, Richard Ben **GV865.D5C73 2000**
Joe DiMaggio: The Hero's Life. Trade Cloth. Simon & Schuster. New York, NY. 2000. 560p. ISBN:0-684-85391-4, ISBN13: 978-0-684-85391-8. Dewey:796.357/092 B. LCCN:00-049232.
Audience: **g,l,u,f.**

Creamer, Robert W. **GV865.S8C73 1996**
Stengel: His Life and Times. Trade Paper. University of Nebraska Press. Lincoln, NE. 1996. 349p. ISBN:0-8032-6367-8, ISBN13: 978-0-8032-6367-3. Dewey:796.357/092. LCCN:95-040143.
Audience: **g,l,u.**

Dawidoff, Nicholas (Editor) **PS509.B37B37 2002**
Baseball: A Literary Anthology. Trade Cloth. Library of America, The. New York, NY. 2002. 721p. ISBN:1-931082-09-X, ISBN13: 978-1-931082-09-9. Dewey:810.8/0355. LCCN:2001-038654.
Audience: **l,u,f.**

DeValeria, Dennis & Burke-DeValeria, Jeanne **GV865.W33D38 1998**
Honus Wagner: A Biography. Trade Paper. University of Pittsburgh Press. Pittsburgh, PA. 1998. 352p. ISBN:0-8229-5665-9, ISBN13: 978-0-8229-5665-5. Dewey:796.357/092 B. LCCN:97-045771.
Audience: **g,l,u.** *Choice, 1997.*

Dickson, Paul **GV862.3.D53 1999**
The New Dickson Baseball Dictionary. Trade Paper. Harcourt Trade Publishers. New York, NY. 1999. 608p. ISBN:0-15-600580-8, ISBN13: 978-0-15-600580-7. Dewey:796.357/0973/03. LCCN:98-040700.
Audience: **g,l,u,f.** *Choice, 1999.*

Dorinson, Joseph & Warmund, Joram (Editors) **GV865.R6**
Jackie Robinson: Race, Sports and the American Dream. Paper Text. M. E. Sharpe Inc. Armonk, NY. 1999. 296p. ISBN:0-7656-0318-7, ISBN13: 978-0-7656-0318-0. Dewey:796.357/092.
Audience: **g,l,u,f.** *Choice, 1999.*

Eig, Jonathan **GV865.G4E54 2005**
Luckiest Man: The Life and Death of Lou Gehrig. Trade Cloth. Simon & Schuster, Inc. New York, NY. 2005. 432p. ISBN:0-7432-4591-1, ISBN13: 978-0-7432-4591-3. Dewey:796.357/092 B. LCCN:2004-059137.
Audience: **g,l,u,f.** *Choice, 2005.*

Elias, Robert (Editor) **GV867.64.B37 2001**
Baseball and the American Dream: Race, Class, Gender and the National Pastime. Cloth Text. M. E. Sharpe Inc. Armonk, NY. 2001. 328p. ISBN:0-7656-0763-8, ISBN13: 978-0-7656-0763-8. Dewey:306.4/83. LCCN:00-066140.
Audience: **l,u,f.**

Falkner, David **GV865.R6**
Great Time Coming: The Life of Jackie Robinson from Baseball to Birmingham. Trade Paper. Simon & Schuster. New York, NY. 1996. 384p. ISBN:0-684-82348-9, ISBN13: 978-0-684-82348-5. Dewey:796.357/092 B.
Audience: **g,l,u,f.**

Heaphy, Leslie A. **GV875.N35H43 2002**
The Negro Leagues, 1869-1960. Cloth Text. McFarland & Company, Incorporated Publishers. Jefferson, NC. 2002. 383p. ISBN:0-7864-1380-8, ISBN13: 978-0-7864-1380-5. Dewey:796.357/64/08996073. LCCN:2002-012225.
Audience: **g,l,u,f.** *Choice, 2003.*

Henderson, Robert W. **GV861.H4 2001**
Ball, Bat and Bishop: The Origin of Ball Games. Trade Paper. University of Illinois Press. Champaign, IL. 2001. 248p. ISBN:0-252-06992-7, ISBN13: 978-0-252-06992-5. Dewey:796.3/09. LCCN:00-067239.
Audience: **l,u,f.** *Choice, 2002.*

Howell, Colin **GV863.15.M37H69 1995**
Northern Sandlots: A Social History of Maritime Baseball. Trade Paper. University of Toronto Press. Toronto, ON. 1995. 288p. ISBN:0-8020-6942-8, ISBN13: 978-0-8020-6942-9. Dewey:796.357/09715. LCCN:95-178431.
Audience: **u,f.** *Choice, 1995.*

Kahn, Roger **GV742.42.K35A3 1997**
Memories of Summer: When Baseball Was an Art and Writing about It a Game. Trade Cloth. Hyperion Press. New York, NY. 1997. 304p. ISBN:0-7868-6190-8, ISBN13: 978-0-7868-6190-3. Dewey:[B]. LCCN:96-048711.
Audience: **g,l,u.** *Choice, 1997.*

Kindall, Jerry & Winkin, John (Editors) **GV875.5.B38 2000**
The Baseball Coaching Bible. Tony La Russa (Foreword by). Trade Paper. Human Kinetics Publishers. Champaign, IL. 1999. 384p. ISBN:0-7360-0161-1, ISBN13: 978-0-7360-0161-8. Dewey:796.357/07/7. LCCN:99-052257.
Audience: **g,l,u.**

Kirsch, George B. **GV863.A1K56 2003**
Baseball in Blue and Gray: The National Pastime During the Civil War. Cloth Text. Princeton University Press. Princeton, NJ. 2003. 160p. ISBN:0-691-05733-8, ISBN13: 978-0-691-05733-0. Dewey:796.357/0973/09034. LCCN:2002-069289.
Audience: **l,u,f.** *Choice, 2003.*

Korr, Charles P. **GV880.2.K67 2002**
The End of Baseball As We Knew It: The Players Union, 1960-81. Bob Costas (Foreword by). Trade Cloth. University of Illinois Press. Champaign, IL. 2002. 352p. Sport and Society Ser. ISBN:0-252-02752-3, ISBN13: 978-0-252-02752-9. Dewey:331.89/041796357. LCCN:2001-007535.
Audience: **u,f.** *Choice, 2003.*

Kuhn, Bowie **GV865.K78K85 1997**
Hardball: The Education of a Baseball Commissioner. Trade Cloth. University of Nebraska Press. Lincoln, NE. 1997. 477p. ISBN:0-8032-7784-9, ISBN13: 978-0-8032-7784-7. Dewey:[B]. LCCN:97-006823.
Audience: **g,l,u.**

Lamb, Chris **GV865.R6L36 2004**
Blackout: The Untold Story of Jackie Robinson's First Spring Training. Trade Cloth. University of Nebraska Press. Lincoln, NE. 2005. 176p. ISBN:0-8032-2956-9, ISBN13: 978-0-8032-2956-3. Dewey:796.357/092 B. LCCN:2004-000614.
Audience: **l,u,f.** *Choice, 2005.*

Lanctot, Neil **GV875.N35L36 2004**
Negro League Baseball: The Rise and Ruin of a Black Institution. Book, Other. University of Pennsylvania Press. Philadelphia, PA. 2004. 496p. ISBN:0-8122-3807-9, ISBN13: 978-0-8122-3807-5. Dewey:796.357/64/0973. LCCN:2004-043547.
Audience: **g,l,u,f.** *Choice, 2004.*

Leifer, Eric M. **GV583.L45 1995**
Making the Majors: The Transformation of Team Sports in America. Trade Cloth. Harvard University Press. Cambridge, MA. 1996. 400p. ISBN:0-674-54322-X, ISBN13: 978-0-674-54322-5. Dewey:796/.06/0973. LCCN:95-013469.
Audience: **l,u,f.** *Choice, 1996.*

Lomax, Michael E. **GV863.A1L65 2003**
Black Baseball Entrepreneurs, 1860-1901: Operating by Any Means Necessary. Trade Paper. Syracuse University Press. Syracuse, NY. 2003. xxvi, 222p. Sports and Entertainment Ser. ISBN:0-8156-0786-5, ISBN13: 978-0-8156-0786-1. Dewey:796.357/64/08996073. LCCN:2002-154375.
Audience: **u,f.**

McGimpsey, David **GV867.64.M34 2000**
Imagining Baseball: America's Pastime and Popular Culture. Trade Cloth. Indiana University Press. Bloomington, IN. 2000. 208p. ISBN:0-253-33696-1, ISBN13: 978-0-253-33696-5. Dewey:306.4/83. LCCN:99-043397.
Audience: **u,f.**

Oleksak, Michael M. & Oleksak, Mary A. **GV862.6.O43 1991**
Beisbol: Latin Americans and the Grand Old Game. Trade Cloth. McGraw-Hill Trade. New York, NY. 1991. 320p. ISBN:0-940279-35-5, ISBN13: 978-0-940279-35-3. Dewey:796.357/098. LCCN:91-010697.
Audience: **g,l,u,f.** *Choice, 1991.*

Pearson, Daniel **GV863.A1.P43**
Baseball in 1889: Players vs Owners. Trade Paper. University of Wisconsin Press. Chicago, IL. 2005. 244p. ISBN:0-87972-619-9, ISBN13: 978-0-87972-619-5. Dewey:796.357. LCCN:92-063282.
Audience: **l,u,f.** *Choice, 1993.*

Pietrusza, David **GV865.L3P54 1998**
Judge and Jury: The Life and Times of Judge Kenesaw Mountain Landis. Trade Cloth. Diamond Communications, Inc. Lanham, MD. 1955. 581p. ISBN:1-888698-09-8, ISBN13: 978-1-888698-09-1. Dewey:796.357/092 B. LCCN:98-013938.
Audience: **g,l,u,f.**

Pietrusza, David **GV863.A1P54 1997**
Lights On!: The Wild Century-Long Saga of Night Baseball. Trade Cloth. Scarecrow Press, Inc. Lanham, MD. 1997. 288p. American Sports History Ser., Vol. 7 ISBN:0-8108-3307-7, ISBN13: 978-0-8108-3307-4. Dewey:796.357/0973. LCCN:97-007800.
Audience: **g,l,u,f.** *Choice, 1998.*

Powers-Beck, Jeff **GV867.64.P69 2004**
The American Indian Integration of Baseball. Joseph Oxendine (Foreword by). Cloth Text. University of Nebraska Press. Lincoln, NE. 2004. 328p. ISBN:0-8032-3745-6, ISBN13: 978-0-8032-3745-2. Dewey:796.357/64/08997. LCCN:2004-007245.
Audience: **l,u,f.** *Choice, 2005.*

Rader, Benjamin G. **GV863.A1R33 2002**
Baseball: A History of America's Game. Ed. 2. Trade Paper. University of Illinois Press. Champaign, IL. 2002. 312p. Illinois History of Sports Ser. ISBN:0-252-07013-5, ISBN13: 978-0-252-07013-6. Dewey:796.357/0973. LCCN:2001-002477.
Audience: **g,l,u,f.** *Choice, 2002, 1993.*

Rampersad, Arnold **GV865.R6R34 1997**
Jackie Robinson: A Biography. Trade Cloth. Alfred A. Knopf Inc. New York, NY. 1997. 448p. ISBN:0-679-44495-5, ISBN13: 978-0-679-44495-4. Dewey:796.357/092. LCCN:97-005165.
Audience: **g,l,u,f.** *Choice, 1998.*

Reaves, Joseph A. **GV863.69.R43 2002**
Taking in a Game: A History of Baseball in Asia. Trade Cloth. University of Nebraska Press. Lincoln, NE. 2002. 220p. Jerry Malloy Prize Ser. ISBN:0-8032-3943-2, ISBN13: 978-0-8032-3943-2. Dewey:796.357/095. LCCN:2001-043058.
Audience: **g,l,u,f.** *Choice, 2002.*

Regalado, Samuel O. **GV865.A1R38 1998**
Viva Baseball!: Latin Major Leaguers and Their Special Hunger. Trade Cloth. University of Illinois Press. Champaign, IL. 1998.

264p. Sport and Society Ser. ISBN:0-252-02372-2, ISBN13: 978-0-252-02372-9. Dewey:796.357/64/098. LCCN:97-021066.
Audience: **g,l,u,f.** *Choice, 1998.*

Ribowsky, Mark **GV865.P3R53 1994**
Don't Look Back: Satchel Paige on the Shadows of Baseball. Trade Cloth. Simon & Schuster. New York, NY. 1994. ISBN:0-671-77674-6, ISBN13: 978-0-671-77674-9. Dewey:796.357/092 B. LCCN:93-038802.
Audience: **g,l,u,f.**

Ribowsky, Mark **GV865.G53R53 2004**
Josh Gibson: The Power and the Darkness. Trade Paper. University of Illinois Press. Champaign, IL. 2004. 328p. ISBN:0-252-07224-3, ISBN13: 978-0-252-07224-6. Dewey:796.357/092 B. LCCN:2004-053696.
Audience: **g,l,u,f.**

Riess, Steven A. **GV867.64.R54 1999**
Touching Base: Professional Baseball and American Culture in the Progressive Era. Ed. 2. Trade Paper. University of Illinois Press. Champaign, IL. 1999. 328p. Sport and Society Ser. ISBN:0-252-06775-4, ISBN13: 978-0-252-06775-4. Dewey:796.357/0973. LCCN:98-058018.
Audience: **g,l,u,f.** B *Choice, 2000.*

Robinson, Jackie W. & Duckett, Alfred **GV865.R6**
I Never Had It Made: An Autobiography of Jackie Robinson. Trade Paper. HarperCollins Publishers. New York, NY. 2003. 304p. ISBN:0-06-055597-1, ISBN13: 978-0-06-055597-9. Dewey:796.357/092/4.
Audience: **g,l,u.**

Ross, Charles K. **GV955.5.N35R67 1999**
Outside the Lines: African-Americans and the Integration of the National Football League. Trade Cloth. New York University Press. New York, NY. 2000. 240p. ISBN:0-8147-7495-4, ISBN13: 978-0-8147-7495-3. Dewey:796.332/64/08996073. LCCN:99-006581.
Audience: **u,f.** *Choice, 2000.*

Seidel, Michael **GV865.W5S44 2003**
Ted Williams: A Baseball Life. Trade Cloth. University of Nebraska Press. Lincoln, NE. 2005. 448p. ISBN:0-8032-9308-9, ISBN13: 978-0-8032-9308-3. Dewey:796.357/092 B. LCCN:2003-047301.
Audience: **g,l,u.**

Shannon, Mike **GV863.A1**
Diamond Classics: Essays on 100 of the Best Baseball Books Ever Published. Paper Text. McFarland & Company, Incorporated Publishers. Jefferson, NC. 2003. 471p. ISBN:0-7864-1853-2, ISBN13: 978-0-7864-1853-4. Dewey:796.357/0973. LCCN:89-42571.
Audience: **u,f.** *Choice, 1989.*

Sommers, Paul M. (Editor) **GV880 .D53 1992**
Diamonds Are Forever: The Business of Baseball. Trade Cloth. Brookings Institution Press. Washington, DC. 1992. 208p. ISBN:0-8157-8042-7, ISBN13: 978-0-8157-8042-7. Dewey:338.4/3796357/640973. LCCN:91-047699.
Audience: **g,l,u.**

Szymanski, Stefan & Zimbalist, Andrew S. **GV716.S99 2005**
National Pastime: How Americans Play Baseball and the Rest of the World Plays Soccer. Perfect, Paper over Boards, Dust Jacket. Brookings Institution Press. Washington, DC. 2005. 263p. ISBN:0-8157-8258-6, ISBN13: 978-0-8157-8258-2. Dewey:338.4/7796334. LCCN:2005-001160.
Audience: **u,f.** *Choice, 2005.*

Thomas, Henry W. **GV865.J6T46 1998**
Walter Johnson: Baseball's Big Train. Shirley Povich (Foreword by). Trade Cloth. University of Nebraska Press. Lincoln, NE. 1998. 496p. ISBN:0-8032-9433-6, ISBN13: 978-0-8032-9433-2. Dewey:796.357/092 B. LCCN:97-035190.
Audience: **g,l,u.**

Thorn, John, et al. **GV863.A1**
Total Baseball: The Ultimate Baseball Encyclopedia. Phil Birnbaum & Bill Deane (Authors). Trade Cloth. Sport Media Publishing. Toronto, ON. 2004. 2,688p. ISBN:1-894963-27-X, ISBN13: 978-1-894963-27-5. Dewey:796.357/0973. LCCN:2004-101773.
Audience: **g,l,u.** *Choice, 1993.*

Tygiel, Jules **GV865.R6T93 1997**
Baseball's Great Experiment: Jackie Robinson and His Legacy. Trade Paper. Oxford University Press, Inc. New York, NY. 1997. 432p. ISBN:0-19-510620-2, ISBN13: 978-0-19-510620-6. Dewey:796.357/092 B. LCCN:96-038551.
Audience: **g,l,u,f.** B

Ward, Geoffrey C. & Burns, Kenneth **GV863.A1W37 1994**
Baseball: An Illustrated History. Trade Cloth. Alfred A. Knopf Inc. New York, NY. 1994. 512p. ISBN:0-679-40459-7, ISBN13: 978-0-679-40459-0. Dewey:796.357/0973. LCCN:93-039809.
Audience: **g,l,u,f.** *Choice, 1995.*

Westbrook, Deeanne **PS169.B36W47 1996**
Ground Rules: Baseball and Myth. Trade Paper. University of Illinois Press. Champaign, IL. 1996. 368p. ISBN:0-252-06529-8, ISBN13: 978-0-252-06529-3. Dewey:810.9/355. LCCN:95-004433.
Audience: **g,l,u,f.** *Choice, 1997.*

White, G. Edward **GV863.A1**
Creating the National Pastime: Baseball Transforms Itself, 1903-1953. Trade Paper. Princeton University Press. Princeton, NJ. 1998. 384p. ISBN:0-691-05885-7, ISBN13: 978-0-691-05885-6. Dewey:796.357/0973/09041.
Audience: **u,f.** *Choice, 1996.*

White, Sol **GV863.A1W448 1995**
Sol White's History of Colored Base Ball, with Other Documents on the Early Black Game, 1886-1936. Jerry Malloy (Compiled by, Introduction by). Cloth Text. University of Nebraska Press. Lincoln, NE. 1995. 190p. ISBN:0-8032-4771-0, ISBN13: 978-0-8032-4771-0. Dewey:796.357/0973. LCCN:94-020992.
Audience: **u,f.** *Choice, 1996.*

Whiting, Robert **GV865.S895W55 2004**
The Meaning of Ichiro: The New Wave from Japan and the Transformation of Our National Pastime. Trade Cloth. Warner Books, Inc. New York, NY. 2004. 336p. ISBN:0-446-53192-8, ISBN13: 978-0-446-53192-4. Dewey:796.357/092 B. LCCN:2003-027134.
Audience: **u,f.** *Choice, 2005.*

Williams, Peter **GV865.T42W55 1994**
When the Giants Were Giants: Bill Terry and the Golden Age of New York Baseball. W. P. Kinsella (Introduction by). Trade Cloth. Algonquin Books of Chapel Hill. Chapel Hill, NC. 1994. xv, 331p. ISBN:0-945575-02-5, ISBN13: 978-0-945575-02-3. Dewey:796.357/092 B. LCCN:94-001019.
Audience: **g,l,u.** *Choice, 1995.*

Wright, Russell O. **GV863.A1W755 1999**
A Tale of Two Leagues: How Baseball Changed as the Rules, Balls, Franchises, Stadiums and Players Changed, 1900-1998. Cloth Text. McFarland & Company, Incorporated Publishers. Jefferson, NC. 1999. 224p. ISBN:0-7864-0712-3, ISBN13: 978-0-7864-0712-5. Dewey:796.357/0973. LCCN:99-40307.
Audience: **l,u,f.** *Choice, 2000.*

Zang, David W. **GV865.W34Z35 1995**
Fleet Walker's Divided Heart: The Life of Baseball's First Black Major Leaguer. Trade Cloth. University of Nebraska Press. Lincoln, NE. 1995. 171p. ISBN:0-8032-4913-6, ISBN13: 978-0-8032-4913-4. Dewey:796.357/092 B. LCCN:94-033517.
Audience: **g,l,u,f.** *Choice, 1996.*

Zimbalist, Andrew **GV880**
May the Best Team Win: Baseball Economics and Public Policy, Expanded and Updated. Bob Costas (Foreword by). Trade Paper. Brookings Institution Press. Washington, DC. 2004. 208p. ISBN:0-8157-9729-X, ISBN13: 978-0-8157-9729-6. Dewey:796.357/0691. LCCN:2002-156494.
Audience: **u,f.**

Zingg, Paul J. **GV865**
Harry Hooper: An American Baseball Life. Trade Paper. University of Illinois Press. Champaign, IL. 2004. 312p. ISBN:0-252-07170-0, ISBN13: 978-0-252-07170-6. Dewey:796.357/092.
Audience: **g,l,u.** *Choice, 1994.*

Sports A-L > Basketball

Anderson, Lars **GV885,4.A53 1998**
Pickup Artists: Street Basketball in America. Trade Cloth. Analytical Psychology Club of San Francisco, Inc. San Francisco, CA. 1998. 240p. ISBN:1-85984-235-6, ISBN13: 978-1-85984-235-5. Dewey:796.3/23/0973. LCCN:98-017460.
Audience: **g,l,u,f.** *Choice, 1998.*

Andrews, David L. (Editor) **GV706.2.M53 2001**
Michael Jordan, Inc.: Corporate Sport, Media Culture, and Late Modern America. Paper Text. State University of New York Press. Albany, NY. 2001. xx, 301p. Series on Sport, Culture, and Social Relations ISBN:0-7914-5026-0, ISBN13: 978-0-7914-5026-0. Dewey:306.4/83/0973. LCCN:00-054794.
Audience: **g,l,u,f.** *Choice, 2002.*

Benedict, Jeff **GV885.515.N37 B46**
Out of Bounds: Inside the NBA's Culture of Rape, Violence, and Crime. Trade Paper. HarperCollins Publishers. New York, NY. 2005. 304p. ISBN:0-06-072604-0, ISBN13: 978-0-06-072604-1. Dewey:364.3/088/79632.
Audience: **g,l,u,f.**

Bisheff, Steve **GV884.W66B57 2004**
John Wooden: An American Treasure. Bill Walton (Foreword by). Trade Cloth. Cumberland House Publishing. Nashville, TN. 2004. 320p. ISBN:1-58182-407-6, ISBN13: 978-1-58182-407-0. Dewey:796.323/092 B. LCCN:2004-018929.
Audience: **g,l,u.**

Bjarkman, Peter C. **GV884.A1B52 2000**
The Biographical History of Basketball. Trade Paper. McGraw-Hill Companies, The. New York, NY. 1999. 608p. ISBN:1-57028-134-3, ISBN13: 978-1-57028-134-1. Dewey:796.323/092/273 B. LCCN:97-049369.
Audience: **l,u,f.**

Bradley, Bill **GV884.B7A34 1995**
Life on the Run. Trade Paper. Knopf Publishing Group. New York, NY. 1995. 240p. ISBN:0-679-76208-6, ISBN13: 978-0-679-76208-9. Dewey:796.323/092 B. LCCN:94-025095.
Audience: **g,l,u.**

Byrne, Julie **GV885.43.I525B97**
O God of Players: The Story of the Immaculata Mighty Macs. Trade Paper. Eastern European Monographs. Bradenton, FL. 2003. 312p. ISBN:0-231-12749-9, ISBN13: 978-0-231-12749-3. Dewey:796.323/63/0974811. LCCN:2003-043574.
Audience: **g,l,u,f.** *Choice, 2004.*

Coffey, Wayne **GV885.43.G25C64 2002**
Winning Sounds Like This: A Season with the Women's Basketball Team at Gallaudet, the World's Only University for the Deaf. Trade Cloth. Crown Publishing Group. New York, NY. 2002. 256p. ISBN:0-609-60765-0, ISBN13: 978-0-609-60765-7. Dewey:796.323/63/09753. LCCN:2002-283485.
Audience: **g,l,u,f.**

Feinstein, John & Auerbach, Red **GV884.A8F45 2004**
Let Me Tell You a Story: A Lifetime in the Game. Trade Cloth. Little Brown & Company. New York, NY. 2004. 368p. ISBN:0-316-73823-9, ISBN13: 978-0-316-73823-1. Dewey:796.323/092 B. LCCN:2004-013000.
Audience: **g,l,u.**

Feinstein, John **GV885.49.N37**
Last Dance: Behind the Scenes at the Final Four. Mike Krzyzewski (Contribution by). Trade Paper. Little Brown & Company. New York, NY. 2007. 352p. ISBN:0-316-01425-7, ISBN13: 978-0-316-01425-0. Dewey:796.323/63/0973.
Audience: **g,l,u,f.**

Fitzpatrick, Frank **GV885.43.U53F58 2000**
And the Walls Came Tumbling Down: The Basketball Game That Changed American Sports. Trade Cloth. University of Nebraska Press. Lincoln, NE. 2000. 264p. ISBN:0-8032-6901-3, ISBN13: 978-0-8032-6901-9. Dewey:796.323/63/0975251. LCCN:00-033787.
Audience: **u,f.**

Fortunato, John A. **GV885.515.N37F67**
The Ultimate Assist: The Relationship and Broadcast Strategies of the NBA and Television Networks. Trade Paper. Hampton Press, Inc. Cresskill, NJ. 2001. xix, 258p. The Hampton Press Communication Ser. ISBN:1-57273-408-6, ISBN13: 978-1-57273-408-1. Dewey:070.4/4979632364. LCCN:2001-039539.
Audience: **u,f.**

Gould Todd **GV885.72.I6**
Pioneers of the Hardwood: Indiana and the Birth of Professional Basketball. Indiana University Press. 1998.
ISBN:0-253-21199-9, ISBN13: 978-0-253-21199-6.
Audience: **g,l,u,f.**

Grundman, Adolph H. **GV885.49.A45G78 2004**
The Golden Age of Amateur Basketball: The AAU Tournament, 1921-1968. Trade Cloth. University of Nebraska Press. Lincoln, NE. 2005. 352p. ISBN:0-8032-7117-4, ISBN13: 978-0-8032-7117-3. Dewey:796.323/06. LCCN:2004-007210.
Audience: **u,f.** *Choice, 2005.*

Halberstam, David **GV884.J67H35 2000**
Playing for Keeps: Michael Jordan and the World He Made. Trade Paper. Broadway Books. New York, NY. 2000. 448p. ISBN:0-7679-0444-3, ISBN13: 978-0-7679-0444-5. Dewey:796.323/092 B. LCCN:99-041931.
Audience: **u,f.** *Choice, 1999.*

Harris, Fran **GV885.515.W66**
Summer Madness: The Wild, Wacky, Wonderful World of the WNBA. Trade Paper. iUniverse, Inc. Lincoln, NE. 2001. 268p. ISBN:0-595-16030-1, ISBN13: 978-0-595-16030-3. Dewey:796.323/092.
Audience: **g,l,u.**

Hedrick, Brad, et al. **GV886.5.H43 1994**
Wheelchair Basketball. Ed. 2. Dan Byrnes & Lew Shaver (Authors). Trade Paper. Paralyzed Veterans of America. Washington, DC. 1994. 120p. ISBN:0-929819-05-5, ISBN13: 978-0-929819-05-1. Dewey:796.32/38. LCCN:94-023340.
Audience: **g,l,u,f.**

Hult, Joan S. & Trekell, Marianna (Editors) **GV886 .C45 1991**
A Century of Women's Basketball: From Frailty to Final Four. Paper Text. American Alliance for Health, Physical Education, Recreation & Dance. Oxon Hill, MD. 1991. 430p. ISBN:0-88314-490-5, ISBN13: 978-0-88314-490-9. Dewey:796.323/0973. LCCN:91-197223.
Audience: **u,f.**

Ikard, Robert W. **GV886.I43 2005**
Just for Fun: The Story of AAU Women's Basketball. Trade Cloth. University of Arkansas Press. Fayetteville, AR. 2005. 272p. ISBN:1-55728-783-X, ISBN13: 978-1-55728-783-0. Dewey:796.323/8. LCCN:2004-021104.
Audience: **u,f.** *Choice, 2005.*

Jackson, Phil **GV884.J67**
Sacred Hoops: Spiritual Lessons of a Hardwood Warrior. Prebound. Turtleback Books. Madison, WI. 1996. ISBN:0-606-18263-2, ISBN13: 978-0-606-18263-8. Dewey:796.323/092 B.
Audience: **g,l,u,f.**

Jackson, Phil & Rosen, Charley **GV884.J32A34 2001**
More Than a Game. Trade Cloth. Seven Stories Press. New York, NY. 2004. 0p. ISBN:1-58322-060-7, ISBN13: 978-1-58322-060-3. Dewey:796.323/092 B. LCCN:00-050957.
Audience: **g,l,u.** *Choice, 2001.*

Koppett, Leonard **GV885.7.T68 2003**
Total Basketball: The Ultimate Basketball Encyclopedia. Trade Cloth. Sport Media Publishing. Toronto, ON. 2004. 1280p. ISBN:1-894963-01-6, ISBN13: 978-1-894963-01-5. Dewey:796.323/64/0973. LCCN:2003-111745.
Audience: **g,l,u,f.**

Krause, Jerry **GV885.3.C59 2002**
Coaching Basketball. Ed. 3. Trade Paper. McGraw-Hill Companies, The. New York, NY. 2002. 320p. ISBN:0-07-138210-0, ISBN13: 978-0-07-138210-6. Dewey:796.323/077. LCCN:2002-017431.
Audience: **l,u,f.**

Krause, Jerry V., et al. **GV885.3.K68 1999**
Basketball Skills and Drills. Ed. 2. Don Meyer & Jerry Meyer (Authors). Trade Paper. Human Kinetics Publishers. Champaign, IL. 1999. 216p. ISBN:0-7360-0171-9, ISBN13: 978-0-7360-0171-7. Dewey:796.323/077. LCCN:98-052768.
Audience: **l,u,f.**

Kuska, Bob **GV885.73.W18K87 2004**
Hot Potato: How Washington and New York Gave Birth to Black Basketball and Changed America's Game Forever. Trade Cloth. University Press of Virginia. Charlottesville, VA. 2004. 220p. ISBN:0-8139-2263-1, ISBN13: 978-0-8139-2263-8. Dewey:796.323/64/08996073. LCCN:2003-018322.
Audience: **u,f.**

Porter, Karra **GV885.515.W66P67**
Mad Seasons: The Story of the First Women's Professional Basketball League, 1978-1981. Trade Paper. University of Nebraska Press. Lincoln, NE. 2006. 384p. ISBN:0-8032-8789-5, ISBN13: 978-0-8032-8789-1. Dewey:796.323/8. LCCN:2005-026399.
Audience: **g,l,u,f.**

Salzberg, Charles **GV884.A1S25 1998**
From Set Shot to Slam Dunk: The Glory Days of Basketball in the Words of Those Who Played It. Trade Cloth. University of Nebraska Press. Lincoln, NE. 1998. 269p. ISBN:0-8032-9250-3, ISBN13: 978-0-8032-9250-5. Dewey:[B]. LCCN:97-043062.
Audience: **g,l,u,f.**

Skaine, Rosemarie **GV885.3.S58 2001**
Women College Basketball Coaches. Paper Text. McFarland & Company, Incorporated Publishers. Jefferson, NC. 2001. 207p. ISBN:0-7864-0920-7, ISBN13: 978-0-7864-0920-4. Dewey:796.323/63/082092273. LCCN:2001-020238.
Audience: **g,l,u,f.** *Choice, 2001.*

Taragano, Martin **GV884.A1.T37 1991**
Basketball Biographies: Four Hundred Thirty-Four U. S. Players, Coaches and Contributors to the Game, 1891-1990. Library Binding. McFarland & Company, Incorporated Publishers. Jefferson, NC. 1991. 336p. ISBN:0-89950-625-9, ISBN13: 978-0-89950-625-8. Dewey:796.323092273. LCCN:91-052761.
Audience: **g,l,u,f.** *Choice, 1992.*

Taylor, John **GV884.A1T39 2005**
The Rivalry: Bill Russell, Wilt Chamberlain, and the Golden Age of Basketball. Trade Cloth. Random House Adult Trade Publishing Group. New York, NY. 2005. 432p. ISBN:1-4000-6114-8, ISBN13: 978-1-4000-6114-3. Dewey:796.323/092 B. LCCN:2005-042797.
Audience: **g,l,u,f.** *Choice, 2006.*

Thomas, Ron **GV885.7.T46 2002**
They Cleared the Lane: The NBA's Black Pioneers. Trade Cloth. University of Nebraska Press. Lincoln, NE. 2002. 288p.

ISBN:0-8032-4437-1, ISBN13: 978-0-8032-4437-5. Dewey:796.323/64/08996073. LCCN:2001-052234.
Audience: **u,f.** *Choice, 2002.*

Wolff, Alexander **GV885.W62 2002**
Big Game, Small World: A Basketball Adventure. Trade Cloth. Warner Books, Inc. New York, NY. 2002. 448p. ISBN:0-446-52601-0, ISBN13: 978-0-446-52601-2. Dewey:796.323. LCCN:2001-026116.
Audience: **u,f.**

Sports A-L > Billiards

Mosconi, Willie & Cohen, Stanley **GV892.2.M67A3 1993**
Willie's Game: An Autobiography of Willie Mosconi. Trade Cloth. Macmillan Publishing Company, Inc. Old Tappan, NJ. 1993. 256p. ISBN:0-02-587495-0, ISBN13: 978-0-02-587495-4. Dewey:794.7/2/092. LCCN:92-031181.
Audience: **g,l,u.** *Choice, 1993.*

Shamos, Michael Ian **GV891.S53**
The New Illustrated Encyclopedia of Billiards. Ed. 2. Paper Text. Globe Pequot Press, The. Guilford, CT. 2002. 320p. ISBN:1-58574-685-1, ISBN13: 978-1-58574-685-9. Dewey:794.7203. LCCN:99-088256.
Audience: **g,l,u,f.**

Tabachnikov, Serge **QA462.2.G34T33 2005**
Geometry and Billiards. Trade Paper. American Mathematical Society. Providence, RI. 2005. 176p. Student Mathematical Library, Vol. 30 ISBN:0-8218-3919-5, ISBN13: 978-0-8218-3919-5. Dewey:516. LCCN:2005-048181.
Audience: **u.**

Sports A-L > Bodybuilding

Klein, Alan M. **GV546.5 .K54 1993**
Little Big Men: Bodybuilding Subculture and Gender Construction. Paper Text. State University of New York Press. Albany, NY. 1993. 326p. SUNY Series on Sport, Culture, and Social Relations ISBN:0-7914-1560-0, ISBN13: 978-0-7914-1560-3. Dewey:646.7/5/0973. LCCN:92-030816.
Audience: **u,f.**

Moore, Pamela (Editor) **GV546.5.B85 1997**
Building Bodies. Paper Text. Rutgers University Press. Piscataway, NJ. 1997. 224p. ISBN:0-8135-2438-5, ISBN13: 978-0-8135-2438-2. Dewey:646.7/5. LCCN:96-049717.
Audience: **g,l,u,f.**

Sports A-L > Boxing

Brailsford, Dennis **GV1123 .B73 1988**
Bareknuckles: A Social History of Prize-Fighting. Trade Cloth. Lutterworth Press, The. Cambridge, 1997. 196p. ISBN:0-7188-2676-0, ISBN13: 978-0-7188-2676-5. Dewey:796.8/3/0942. LCCN:89-173102.
Audience: **u,f.**

Cashmore, Ellis **GV1132.S95**
Mike Tyson: Nurture of the Beast. Trade Paper. Polity Press. Cambridge, 2005. 200p. Celebrities Ser. ISBN:0-7456-3070-7, ISBN13: 978-0-7456-3070-0. Dewey:796.83092. LCCN:2005-276703.
Audience: **g,l,u,f.** *Choice, 2005.*

Early, Gerald (Editor) **GV1132.A44 M83 1998**
Muhammad Ali Reader. Trade Cloth. HarperCollins Publishers. New York, NY. 1998. 320p. ISBN:0-88001-602-7, ISBN13: 978-0-88001-602-5. Dewey:796.83/092. LCCN:97-036846.
Audience: **u,f.**

Fleischer, Nat, et al. **GV1121**
An Illustrated History of Boxing. Ed. 6. Sam Andre & Nigel Collins (Authors). Trade Paper. Kensington Publishing Corporation. New York, NY. 2002. 464p. ISBN:0-8065-2201-1, ISBN13: 978-0-8065-2201-2. Dewey:796.83.
Audience: **g,l,u,f.**

Gorn, Elliot J. (Editor) **GV1132.A44M85 1995**
Muhammad Ali: The People's Champ. Trade Cloth. University of Illinois Press. Champaign, IL. 1995. 224p. Sport and Society Ser. ISBN:0-252-02188-6, ISBN13: 978-0-252-02188-6. Dewey:796.8/3/092 B. LCCN:95-002358.
Audience: **g,l,u,f.** *Choice, 1996.*

Gorn, Elliott J. **GV1125**
The Manly Art: Bare-Knuckle Prize Fighting in America. Trade Paper. Cornell University Press. Ithaca, NY. 1989. 320p. ISBN:0-8014-9582-2, ISBN13: 978-0-8014-9582-3. Dewey:796.8/3/0973. LCCN:86-006410.
Audience: **u,f.** *Choice, 1987.*

Hauser, Thomas **GV1133.H34 2000**
The Black Lights: Inside the World of Professional Boxing. Trade Paper. University of Arkansas Press. Fayetteville, AR. 2000. 272p. ISBN:1-55728-597-7, ISBN13: 978-1-55728-597-3. Dewey:796.83. LCCN:99-086546.
Audience: **g,l,u.**

Hietala, Thomas R. **GV1131.H64 2002**
The Fight of the Century: Jack Johnson, Joe Louis, and the Struggle for Racial Equality. Trade Cloth. M. E. Sharpe Inc. Armonk, NY. 2002. 386p. Social and Cultural History Ser. ISBN:0-7656-0722-0, ISBN13: 978-0-7656-0722-5. Dewey:796.83/092/2. LCCN:2001-049165.
Audience: **u,f.** *Choice, 2003.*

Isenberg, Michael T. **GV1132.M84**
John L. Sullivan and His America. Trade Paper. University of Illinois Press. Champaign, IL. 1994. 480p. ISBN:0-252-06434-8, ISBN13: 978-0-252-06434-0. Dewey:796.8/3/0924 B.
Audience: **l,u,f.** *Choice, 1988.*

Margolick, David **GV1136.8.M37 2005**
Beyond Glory: Joe Louis vs. Max Schmeling and a World on the Brink. Trade Cloth. Alfred A. Knopf Inc. New York, NY. 2005. 432p. ISBN:0-375-41192-5, ISBN13: 978-0-375-41192-2. Dewey:796.83/09043. LCCN:2005-045141.
Audience: **l,u.** *Choice, 2006.*

Mead, Chris **GV1132.M84**
Champion Joe Louis: A Biography. Trade Paper. Anova Books. London, 1997. 330p. ISBN:0-86051-848-5, ISBN13: 978-0-86051-848-8. Dewey:796.8/3/0924.
Audience: **l,u.**

Oates, Joyce Carol **GV1133 .O2 1987**
On Boxing. Trade Cloth. Doubleday Publishing. New York, NY. 1987. ISBN:0-385-23890-8, ISBN13: 978-0-385-23890-8. Dewey:796.8/3/0973. LCCN:86-019710.
Audience: **l,u,f.**

Remnick, David **GV1132.A44R46 1998**
King of the World: Muhammad Ali and the Rise of an American Hero. Trade Cloth. Random House, Inc. New York, NY. 1998. 336p. ISBN:0-375-50065-0, ISBN13: 978-0-375-50065-7. Dewey:796.8/3/092. LCCN:98-024539.
Audience: **g,l,u,f.** *Choice, 1999.*

Rendall, Jonathan **GV1132.R46**
This Bloody Mary Is the Last Thing I Own. Trade Paper. HarperCollins Publishers. New York, NY. 1999. 187p. ISBN:0-88001-685-X, ISBN13: 978-0-88001-685-8. Dewey:796.83. LCCN:97-030884.
Audience: **l,u,f.**

Roberts, Randy **GV1132.M84**
Papa Jack: Jack Johnson and the Era of White Hopes. Trade Paper. Simon & Schuster. New York, NY. 1985. 304p. ISBN:0-02-926900-8, ISBN13: 978-0-02-926900-8. Dewey:796.8/3/0924. LCCN:82-049017.
Audience: **u,f.**

Sammons, Jeffrey T. **GV1125.S26 1988**
Beyond the Ring: The Role of Boxing in American Society. Trade Cloth. University of Illinois Press. Champaign, IL. 1987. 376p. Sport and Society Ser. ISBN:0-252-01473-1, ISBN13: 978-0-252-01473-4. Dewey:796.8/3/0973. LCCN:87-019041.
Audience: **l,u,f.** *Choice, 1988.*

Schaap, Jeremy **GV1131.S36 2005**
Cinderella Man: James J. Braddock, Max Baer, and the Greatest Upset in Boxing History. Trade Cloth. Random House Large Print. New York, NY. 2005. 576p. ISBN:0-375-43543-3, ISBN13: 978-0-375-43543-0. Dewey:796.83'092. LCCN:2005-041307.
Audience: **g,l,u.**

Skutt, Alexander G. & Roberts, James B. **GV1137**
The Boxing Register: International Boxing Hall of Fame Official Record Book. Ed. 3. Trade Paper. McBooks Press, Inc. Ithaca, NY. 2002. 656p. ISBN:1-59013-020-0, ISBN13: 978-1-59013-020-9. Dewey:796.83092.
Audience: **g,l,u,f.** *Choice, 2003.*

Sugden, John P. **GV1136.8.S84 1996**
Boxing and Society: An International Analysis. Trade Paper. Manchester University Press. Manchester, 1997. 272p. Sport, Society, and Politics Ser. ISBN:0-7190-4321-2, ISBN13: 978-0-7190-4321-5. Dewey:306.4/83. LCCN:96-029445.
Audience: **u,f.** *Choice, 1997.*

Sports A-L > Bullfighting

Mitchell, Timothy **GV1108.5.M58 1991**
Blood Sport: A Social History of Spanish Bullfighting. Trade Paper. University of Pennsylvania Press. Philadelphia, PA. 1991. 288p. ISBN:0-8122-1346-7, ISBN13: 978-0-8122-1346-1. Dewey:791.8/2/0946. LCCN:91-007231.
Audience: **l,u,f.** *Choice, 1992.*

Pink, Sarah **GV1107.P535 1997**
Women and Bullfighting: Gender, Sex and the Consumption of Tradition. Trade Paper. Berg Publishers. Oxford, 1997. 256p. Mediterranea Ser. ISBN:1-85973-961-X, ISBN13: 978-1-85973-961-7. Dewey:791.82082. LCCN:98-185397.
Audience: **u,f.**

Sports A-L > Cricket

Melville, Tom **GV928.U6M45 1998**
The Tented Field: A History of Cricket in America. Trade Paper. University of Wisconsin Press. Chicago, IL. 1998. 280p. ISBN:0-87972-770-5, ISBN13: 978-0-87972-770-3. Dewey:796.358/0973. LCCN:98-004030.
Audience: **u,f.** *Choice, 1999.*

Rundell, Michael **GV917.R86 1995**
The Dictionary of Cricket. Ed. 2. Trade Cloth. Oxford University Press, Inc. New York, NY. 1995. 224p. ISBN:0-19-866198-3, ISBN13: 978-0-19-866198-6. Dewey:796.35/8. LCCN:94-047141.
Audience: **g,l,u,f.** *Choice, 1995.*

Williams, Jack **GV928.G7W54 1999**
Cricket and England: A Cultural and Social History of Cricket of the Inter-War Years. Paper over Boards. Taylor & Francis Group. Abingdon, 1999. 218p. Sport in the Global Society Ser., No. 8 ISBN:0-7146-4861-2, ISBN13: 978-0-7146-4861-3. Dewey:796.358/0942. LCCN:98-047285.
Audience: **u,f.** *Choice, 1999.*

Williams, Jack **GV928.G7 W55 2001**
Cricket and Race. Trade Paper. Berg Publishers. Oxford, 2001. 224p. ISBN:1-85973-309-3, ISBN13: 978-1-85973-309-7. Dewey:796.3/58/089/00942.
Audience: **g,l,u,f.** *Choice, 2002.*

Sports A-L > Cycling

Berto, Frank J. **GV1056.B47 1999**
The Birth of Dirt: Origins of Mountain Biking. Trade Cloth. Van der Plas Publications. San Francisco, CA. 2004. 128p. Cycling Resources Ser. ISBN:1-892495-10-4, ISBN13: 978-1-892495-10-5. Dewey:796.6/3/09. LCCN:98-061189.
Audience: **g,l,u.**

Burke, Edmund R. (Editor) **RC1220.C8B873 2003**
High-Tech Cycling. Ed. 2. Trade Paper. Human Kinetics Publishers. Champaign, IL. 2003. 328p. ISBN:0-7360-4507-4, ISBN13: 978-0-7360-4507-0. Dewey:612/.044. LCCN:2002-152619.
Audience: **g,l,u,f.**

Burke, Edmund R. **GV1041.B77 2002**
Serious Cycling. Ed. 2. Trade Paper. Human Kinetics Publishers. Champaign, IL. 2002. 34p. ISBN:0-7360-4129-X, ISBN13: 978-0-7360-4129-4. Dewey:796.6. LCCN:2001-039843.
Audience: **g,l,u.**

Dauncey, Hugh & Hare, Geoff (Editors) **GV1049.2.T68T68 2003**
The Tour de France, 1903-2003: A Century of Sporting Structures, Meanings and Values - Sport in the Global Society.

Paper over Boards. Taylor & Francis Group. Abingdon, 2003. 290p. Sport in the Global Society Ser. ISBN:0-7146-5362-4, ISBN13: 978-0-7146-5362-4. Dewey:796.6/2/0944. LCCN:2003-011128.
Audience: **g,l,u,f.** *Choice, 2004.*

Dodge, Pryor **TL400 .D644 1996**
The Bicycle. Trade Cloth. Editions Flammarion. Montreal, PQ. 2001. 224p. ISBN:2-08-013551-1, ISBN13: 978-2-08-013551-3. Dewey:629.2272. LCCN:96-084087.
Audience: **u.** *Choice, 1996.*

Friel, Joe **GV1043.7.F75 1998**
Cycling Past 50. Trade Cloth. Human Kinetics Publishers. Champaign, IL. 1998. 264p. Ageless Athlete Ser. ISBN:0-88011-737-0, ISBN13: 978-0-88011-737-1. Dewey:796.6. LCCN:97-038749.
Audience: **u.**

Herlihy, David V. (Contribution by) **TL410.H43 2004**
Bicycle: The History. Cloth over Boards. Yale University Press. Cumberland, RI. 2004. 480p. ISBN:0-300-10418-9, ISBN13: 978-0-300-10418-9. Dewey:629.227/2/09. LCCN:2004-012992.
Audience: **l,u,f.** *Choice, 2005.*

Norcliffe, Glen **GV1046.C2 N67 2001**
Ride to Modernity: The Bicycle in Canada, 1869-1900. Trade Paper. University of Toronto Press. Toronto, ON. 2001. 248p. ISBN:0-8020-8205-X, ISBN13: 978-0-8020-8205-3. Dewey:796.6/0971. LCCN:2001-273481.
Audience: **u,f.**

Sloane, Eugene A. **GV1041.S55 1995**
Sloane's Complete Book of Bicycling: The Cyclist's Bible. Ed. 25. Trade Paper. Simon & Schuster. New York, NY. 1995. 432p. ISBN:0-671-87075-0, ISBN13: 978-0-671-87075-1. Dewey:796.6. LCCN:94-046788.
Audience: **g,l,u,f.**

Smith, Robert A. **GV1040.5.S64 1995**
Merry Wheels and Spokes of Steel: A Social History of the Bicycle. Trade Paper. Millefleurs. San Bernardino, CA. 1995. xii, 269p. Stovkis Studies in Historical Chronology and Thought, No. 16 ISBN:0-8095-1104-5, ISBN13: 978-0-8095-1104-4. Dewey:796.6. LCCN:95-009980.
Audience: **g,l,u,f.**

Wheatcroft, Geoffrey **GV1049.2.T68**
Le Tour: A History of the Tour de France, 1903-2003. Trade Paper. Simon & Schuster, Ltd. London, 2005. 320p. ISBN:0-684-02879-4, ISBN13: 978-0-684-02879-8. Dewey:796.6/2/0944.
Audience: **g,l,u,f.**

Sports A-L > Extreme

Browne, David **GV749.7.B76 2004**
Amped: How Big Air, Big Dollars, and a New Generation Took Sports to the Extreme. Cloth over Boards. Bloomsbury Publishing. New York, NY. 2004. 300p. ISBN:1-58234-317-9, ISBN13: 978-1-58234-317-4. Dewey:796.04/6. LCCN:2004-004822.
Audience: **g,l,u.**

Gutman, Bill & Frederick, Shawn **GV749.7**
Being Extreme. Trade Paper. Kensington Publishing Corporation. New York, NY. 2003. 304p. ISBN:0-8065-2354-9, ISBN13: 978-0-8065-2354-5. Dewey:796/.046.
Audience: **g,l,u,f.**

Rinehart, Robert E. & Sydnor, Synthia (Editors) **GV749.7.T6 2003**
To the Extreme: Alternative Sports, Inside and Out. Paper Text. State University of New York Press. Albany, NY. 2003. x, 436p. SUNY Series on Sport, Culture, and Social Relations ISBN:0-7914-5666-8, ISBN13: 978-0-7914-5666-8. Dewey:796.04/6. LCCN:2002-042646.
Audience: **g,l,u,f.** *Choice, 2003.*

Sports A-L > Fencing

Evangelista, Nick **GV1147.E85 2000**
The Inner Game of Fencing: Excellence in Strategy and Spirit. Trade Paper. McGraw-Hill Companies, The. New York, NY. 2000. 288p. ISBN:1-57028-230-7, ISBN13: 978-1-57028-230-0. Dewey:796.86. LCCN:99-056253.
Audience: **g,l,u,f.**

Garret, Maxwell R., et al. **GV1147.G36 1994**
Foil, Saber and Epee Fencing: Skills, Safety, Operations, and Responsibilities. Emmanuil G. Kaidanov & Guglielmo Pezza (Authors). Trade Cloth. Pennsylvania State University Press. University Park, PA. 1994. 592p. ISBN:0-271-01019-3, ISBN13: 978-0-271-01019-9. Dewey:796.8/6. LCCN:93-017603.
Audience: **g,l,u,f.** *Choice, 1995.*

Gaugler, William M. **GV1143.6.G38 1998**
The History of Fencing: Foundations of Modern European Swordplay. Trade Paper. Laureate Press. Bangor, ME. 1998. 494p. ISBN:1-884528-16-3, ISBN13: 978-1-884528-16-3. Dewey:796.86. LCCN:98-067197.
Audience: **u,f.**

Sports A-L > Field Hockey

Anders, Elizabeth **GV1017.H7**
Field Hockey: Steps to Success. Trade Paper. Human Kinetics Publishers. Champaign, IL. 1998. 20p. Steps to Success Ser. ISBN:0-88011-673-0, ISBN13: 978-0-88011-673-2. Dewey:796.3/55. LCCN:98-027574.
Audience: **g,l,u.**

Mitchell-Tavener, Claire **GV1017.H7M58 2004**
Field Hockey Techniques and Tactics. Trade Paper. Human Kinetics Publishers. Champaign, IL. 2004. 216p. ISBN:0-7360-5437-5, ISBN13: 978-0-7360-5437-9. Dewey:796.355. LCCN:2004-007572.
Audience: **l,u.**

Swissler, Becky **GV1017.H7S95 2003**
Winning Field Hockey for Girls. Trade Paper. Facts On File, Inc. New York, NY. 2003. 224p. Winning Sports for Girls Ser. ISBN:0-8160-4725-1, ISBN13: 978-0-8160-4725-3. Dewey:796.355/082. LCCN:2002-005990.
Audience: **l,u,f.**

Sports A-L > Football (American)

American Football Coaches Association Staff **GV951.18.A54 1996**
AFCA's Defensive Football Drills. Grant Teaff (Foreword by). Trade Paper. Human Kinetics Publishers. Champaign, IL. 1996. 168p. ISBN:0-88011-476-2, ISBN13: 978-0-88011-476-9. Dewey:796.3/322. LCCN:96-008061.
Audience: **g,l,u.**

Bernstein, Mark F. **GV958.5.I9B47 2001**
Football: The Ivy League Origins of an American Obsession. Trade Cloth. University of Pennsylvania Press. Philadelphia, PA. 2001. 336p. ISBN:0-8122-3627-0, ISBN13: 978-0-8122-3627-9. Dewey:796.332/63/0974. LCCN:2001-027488.
Audience: **u,f.** *Choice, 2002.*

Bissinger, H. G. **GV958.P47 B57 2004**
Friday Night Lights: A Town, a Team, and a Dream. Paper Text. Da Capo Press, Inc. Cambridge, MA. 2004. 416p. ISBN:0-306-81425-0, ISBN13: 978-0-306-81425-9. Dewey:796.332.
Audience: **g,l,u,f.**

Bobo, Mike & Dykes, Spike **GV956.6.B623 1998**
Principles of Coaching Football. Trade Paper. Benjamin-Cummings Publishing Company. San Francisco, CA. 1997. 287p. ISBN:0-205-26253-8, ISBN13: 978-0-205-26253-3. Dewey:796.332/07/7. LCCN:97-029510.
Audience: **g,l,u.** *Choice, 1998.*

Bradshaw, Terry **GV939.F29**
It's Only a Game. David Fisher (As told to). Mass Market. Simon & Schuster. New York, NY. 2002. 384p. ISBN:0-7434-1729-1, ISBN13: 978-0-7434-1729-7. Dewey:796.332/092 B.
Audience: **g,l,u.**

Brandt, Nat **GV958.O24B72 2001**
When Oberlin was King of the Gridiron: The Heisman Years. Trade Paper. Kent State University Press. Kent, OH. 2001. 248p. ISBN:0-87338-684-1, ISBN13: 978-0-87338-684-5. Dewey:796.332/63/0977123. LCCN:00-010265.
Audience: **u,f.** *Choice, 2001.*

Brookes, Rod **GV742.B76 2002**
Representing Sport. Trade Paper. Oxford University Press, Inc. New York, NY. 2002. 184p. A Hodder Arnold Publication ISBN:0-340-74052-3, ISBN13: 978-0-340-74052-1. Dewey:796. LCCN:2002-510305.
Audience: **l,u.** *Choice, 2002.*

Carroll, Bob (Editor), et al. **GV955.5.N35T67 1997**
Total Football: The Official Encyclopedia of the National Football. Michael Gershman, David Neft & John Thorn (Editors). Trade Cloth. HarperCollins Publishers. New York, NY. 1997. 1664p. ISBN:0-06-270170-3, ISBN13: 978-0-06-270170-1. Dewey:796.332/64/0973. LCCN:97-016987.
Audience: **g,l,u,f.**

Carroll, John M. **GV939.F29**
Fritz Pollard: Pioneer in Racial Advancement. Trade Paper. University of Illinois Press. Champaign, IL. 1998. 328p. Sport and Society Ser. ISBN:0-252-06799-1, ISBN13: 978-0-252-06799-0. Dewey:796.332/092 B.
Audience: **l,u.** *Choice, 1992.*

Carroll, John M. **GV939**
Red Grange and the Rise of Modern Football. Trade Paper. University of Illinois Press. Champaign, IL. 2004. 296p. ISBN:0-252-07166-2, ISBN13: 978-0-252-07166-9. Dewey:796.332/092 B.
Audience: **l,u,f.** *Choice, 2000.*

Denligher, Ken **GV958.P46D466 1995**
For the Glory: College Football Dreams and Realities Inside Paterno's Program. Trade Paper. St. Martin's Press. Gordonville, VA. 1995. 320p. ISBN:0-312-13496-7, ISBN13: 978-0-312-13496-9. Dewey:796.332/63/0974811. LCCN:95-022203.
Audience: **g,l,u,f.**

Dunnavant, Keith **GV939.B79D86 2005**
Coach: The Life of Paul Bear Bryant. Trade Paper, Perfect. St. Martin's Press. Gordonville, VA. 2005. 320p. ISBN:0-312-34876-2, ISBN13: 978-0-312-34876-2. Dewey:796.332092 B. LCCN:2005-280370.
Audience: **g,l,u.**

Falk, Gerhard **GV951.F25 2005**
Football and American Identity. Perfect, Paper over Boards. Haworth Press, Incorporated, The. Binghamton, NY. 2005. 277p. Contemporary Sports Issues Ser. ISBN:0-7890-2526-4, ISBN13: 978-0-7890-2526-5. Dewey:796.3320973. LCCN:2004-012740.
Audience: **g,l,u,f.** *Choice, 2005.*

Gay, Timothy **GV959.G39 2005**
The Physics of Football: Discover the Science of Bone-Crunching Hits, Soaring Field Goals, and Awe-Inspiring Passes. Trade Paper. HarperCollins Publishers. New York, NY. 2005. 304p. ISBN:0-06-082634-7, ISBN13: 978-0-06-082634-5. Dewey:796.332/03. LCCN:2005-046284.
Audience: **l,u.**

Gems, Gerald R. **GV950.G46 2000**
For Pride, Profit and Patriarchy: Football and the Incorporation of American Cultural Values. Trade Cloth. Scarecrow Press, Inc. Lanham, MD. 2000. 240p. American Sports History Ser., No. 16 ISBN:0-8108-3685-8, ISBN13: 978-0-8108-3685-3. Dewey:796.332/0973. LCCN:00-023773.
Audience: **u,f.**

Halberstam, David **GV939.B45**
The Education of a Coach. Trade Cloth. Hyperion Press. New York, NY. 2005. 288p. ISBN:1-4013-0154-1, ISBN13: 978-1-4013-0154-5. Dewey:796.332/092 B. LCCN:2006-276664.
Audience: **g,l,u.** *Choice, 2006.*

Koehler, Michael D. **QA76.73.P2N86**
Complete Book of Drills for Winning Football. Trade Paper. Benjamin-Cummings Publishing Company. San Francisco, CA. 2001. 320p. ISBN:0-13-060043-1, ISBN13: 978-0-13-060043-1. Dewey:005.13/3.
Audience: **g,l,u.**

Lester, Robin **GV958.U519L47 1995**
Stagg's University: The Rise, Decline and Fall of Big-Time Football at the University of Chicago. Trade Cloth. University of Illinois Press. Champaign, IL. 1995. 344p. Sport and Society Ser. ISBN:0-252-02128-2, ISBN13: 978-0-252-02128-2. Dewey:796.332/09773/11. LCCN:94-034018.
Audience: **u,f.** *Choice, 1996.*

Levy, Alan H. **GV943.9.S64L48 2003**
Tackling Jim Crow: Racial Segregation in Professional Football. Paper Text. McFarland & Company, Incorporated Publishers. Jefferson, NC. 2003. 180p. ISBN:0-7864-1597-5, ISBN13: 978-0-7864-1597-7. Dewey:796.332/0896/073. LCCN:2003-005735.
Audience: **u,f.** *Choice, 2003.*

Lombardo, John **GV939.F29**
A Fire to Win: The Life and Times of Woody Hayes. Trade Paper. St. Martin's Press. Gordonville, VA. 2006. 304p. ISBN:0-312-36036-3, ISBN13: 978-0-312-36036-8. Dewey:796.332/092 B.
Audience: **g,l,u.**

MacCambridge, Michael **GV954.M32 2004**
America's Game: The Epic Story of How Pro Football Captured a Nation. Trade Cloth. Random House Adult Trade Publishing Group. New York, NY. 2004. 576p. ISBN:0-375-50454-0, ISBN13: 978-0-375-50454-9. Dewey:796.332/640973. LCCN:2004-052003.
Audience: **l,u,f.** *Choice, 2005.*

Maltby, Marc S. **GV954.M35 1997**
The Origins and Development of Professional Football, 1890-1920. Cloth Text. Garland Publishing, Inc. New York, NY. 1997. 256p. Studies in American Popular History and Culture ISBN:0-8153-2797-8, ISBN13: 978-0-8153-2797-4. Dewey:796.33264. LCCN:97-010251.
Audience: **u,f.**

Maraniss, David **GV939.L6M37 1999**
When Pride Still Mattered: A Life of Vince Lombardi. Trade Paper. Simon & Schuster. New York, NY. 2000. 544p. ISBN:0-684-87018-5, ISBN13: 978-0-684-87018-2. Dewey:796.332/092 B. LCCN:99-037859.
Audience: **g,l,u.**

Massa, Mark S. **BX1406.2.M38 1999**
Catholics and American Culture: Fulton Sheen, Dorothy Day and the Notre Dame Football Team. Trade Cloth. Crossroad Publishing Company. New York, NY. 1999. 288p. ISBN:0-8245-1537-4, ISBN13: 978-0-8245-1537-9. Dewey:305.6/2073. LCCN:98-031072.
Audience: **u,f.** *Choice, 1999.*

McClellan, Keith **GV954.M37 1998**
The Sunday Game: At the Dawn of Professional Football. Trade Cloth. University of Akron Press, The. Akron, OH. 1998. 503p. Ohio History and Culture Ser. ISBN:1-884836-36-4, ISBN13: 978-1-884836-36-7. Dewey:796.332/0973. LCCN:98-024175.
Audience: **u,f.** *Choice, 1999.*

Nelson, David M. **GV955.N44 1994**
The Anatomy of a Game: Football, the Rules, and the Men Who Made the Game. Forest Evashevski (Foreword by). Trade Cloth. University of Delaware Press. Newark, DE. 1994. 599p. ISBN:0-87413-455-2, ISBN13: 978-0-87413-455-1. Dewey:796.332/02/022. LCCN:91-051009.
Audience: **u,f.** *Choice, 1994.*

Nguyen, Dat & Burson, Rusty **GV939.N46A3 2005**
Dat: Tackling Life and the NFL. Darren Woodson (Foreword by). Trade Cloth. Texas A&M University Press. College Station, TX. 2005. 224p. ISBN:1-58544-472-3, ISBN13: 978-1-58544-472-4. Dewey:796.332/092 B. LCCN:2005-004658.
Audience: **g,l,u.**

Oriard, Michael **GV950.O73 2001**
King Football: Sport and Spectacle in the Golden Age of Radio and Newsreels, Movies and Magazines, the Weekly and the Daily Press. Trade Cloth. University of North Carolina Press. Chapel Hill, NC. 2001. 512p. ISBN:0-8078-2650-2, ISBN13: 978-0-8078-2650-8. Dewey:796.332/09/041. LCCN:2001-041459.
Audience: **l,u,f.** *Choice, 2002.*

Oriard, Michael **92-42840 [GV]**
Reading Football: How the Popular Press Created an American Spectacle. Alan Trachtenberg (Foreword by). Trade Paper. University of North Carolina Press. Chapel Hill, NC. 1998. 352p. Cultural Studies of the United States ISBN:0-8078-4751-8, ISBN13: 978-0-8078-4751-0. Dewey:796.3230973. LCCN:92-042840.
Audience: **u,f.** *Choice, 1994.*

Perrin, Tom **GV950.P47 1987**
Football: A College History. Library Binding. McFarland & Company, Incorporated Publishers. Jefferson, NC. 1987. 438p. ISBN:0-89950-294-6, ISBN13: 978-0-89950-294-6. Dewey:796.332/63/0973. LCCN:87-043029.
Audience: **g,l,u,f.** *Choice, 1988.*

Pont, Sally **GV939.A1P63 2001**
Fields of Honor: The Golden Age of College Football and the Men Who Created It. Cloth over Boards. Harcourt Trade Publishers. New York, NY. 2001. 256p. ISBN:0-15-100607-5, ISBN13: 978-0-15-100607-6. Dewey:796.332/63/0973. LCCN:2001-024364.
Audience: **u,f.** *Choice, 2002.*

Robinson, Ray **GV865.R6**
Matty: Christy Mathewson of the New York Giants. Trade Paper. Oxford University Press, Inc. New York, NY. 1994. 272p. ISBN:0-19-509263-5, ISBN13: 978-0-19-509263-9. Dewey:796.3/57/092.
Audience: **g,l,u.**

Sands, Robert R. **GV958.S26 1999**
Gutcheck!: An Anthropologist's Wild Ride into the Heart of College Football. Trade Paper. Rincon Hill Books. Carpinteria, CA. 2000. 321p. ISBN:0-9672973-0-3, ISBN13: 978-0-9672973-0-9. Dewey:796.332. LCCN:99-093335.
Audience: **u,f.** *Choice, 2000.*

Smith, Myron J. Jr. **GV954**
Professional Football: The Official Pro Footbal of Fame Bibliography. Cloth Text. Greenwood Publishing Group, Inc. Portsmouth, NH. 1993. 432p. Bibliographies and Indexes on Sports History Ser., No. 1 ISBN:0-313-28928-X, ISBN13: 978-0-313-28928-6. Dewey:796.332640973. LCCN:92-042677.
Audience: **g,l,u,f.** *Choice, 1993.*

St. John, Bob **GV939.L28S235 2000**
Landry: The Legend and the Legacy. Trade Cloth. W Publishing Group. Nashville, TN. 2000. 368p. ISBN:0-8499-1670-4, ISBN13: 978-0-8499-1670-0. Dewey:796.332/092 B. LCCN:00-710436.
Audience: **g,l,u.**

Toma, J. D. **GV959.5.T66 2003**
Football U.: Spectator Sports in the Life of the American University. Trade Cloth. University of Michigan Press. Chicago, IL. 2003. 220p. ISBN:0-472-11299-6, ISBN13:

978-0-472-11299-9. Dewey:796.332/63/0973. LCCN:2002-153617.
Audience: **g,l,u.** *Choice, 2004.*

Tuaolo, Esera & Rosengren, John **GV939.T78A3 2006**
Alone in the Trenches: My Life As a Gay Player in the NFL. Trade Cloth. Sourcebooks, Inc. Naperville, IL. 2006. 288p. ISBN:1-4022-0505-8, ISBN13: 978-1-4022-0505-7. Dewey:796.332/092 B. LCCN:2005-025014.
Audience: **g,l,u.**

Umphlett, Wiley L. **GV939**
Creating the Big Game: John W. Heisman and the Invention of American Football, 34. Trade Cloth. Greenwood Publishing Group, Inc. Portsmouth, NH. 1992. 296p. Contributions to the Study of Popular Culture Ser., No. 34 ISBN:0-313-28404-0, ISBN13: 978-0-313-28404-5. Dewey:796.332092. LCCN:92-010087.
Audience: **g,l,u,f.** *Choice, 1993.*

Watterson, John Sayle **GV950.W28 2000**
College Football: History, Spectacle, Controversy. Trade Cloth. Johns Hopkins University Press. Baltimore, MD. 2000. 528p. ISBN:0-8018-6428-3, ISBN13: 978-0-8018-6428-5. Dewey:796.332/63/0973. LCCN:00-008247.
Audience: **u,f.** *Choice, 2001.*

Yoast, Bill R. **GV939.Y63A3 2005**
Remember This Titan: Lessons Learned from a Celebrated Coach's Journey. Trade Cloth. Taylor Trade Publishing. Blue Ridge Summit, PA. 2005. 176p. ISBN:1-58979-278-5, ISBN13: 978-1-58979-278-4. Dewey:796.332/092 B. LCCN:2005-048597.
Audience: **g,l,u.**

Sports A-L > Diving

O'Brien, Ron **GV837.O17 2003**
Springboard and Platform Diving. Ed. 2. Trade Paper. Human Kinetics Publishers. Champaign, IL. 2002. 232p. ISBN:0-7360-4378-0, ISBN13: 978-0-7360-4378-6. Dewey:797.2/4. LCCN:2002-013393.
Audience: **l,u.**

Pieroth, Doris Hinson **GV722 1932.P54 1996**
Their Day in the Sun: Women of the 1932 Olympics. Trade Paper. University of Washington Press. Seattle, WA. 1996. 208p. Samuel and Althea Stroum Bks. ISBN:0-295-97554-7, ISBN13: 978-0-295-97554-2. Dewey:796.48. LCCN:96-023104.
Audience: **l,u.** *Choice, 1997.*

Sports A-L > Golf

Cayleff, Susan E. **GV964.Z3**
Babe: The Life and Legend of Babe Didrikson Zaharias. Trade Paper. University of Illinois Press. Champaign, IL. 1996. 368p. Women in American History Ser. ISBN:0-252-06593-X, ISBN13: 978-0-252-06593-4. Dewey:920. LCCN:94-035584.
Audience: **g,l,u.**

Clavin, Tom **GV964.H3C53 2005**
Sir Walter: Walter Hagen and the Invention of Professional Golf. Trade Cloth. Simon & Schuster, Inc. New York, NY. 2005. 384p. ISBN:0-7432-0486-7, ISBN13: 978-0-7432-0486-6. Dewey:796.352/092 B. LCCN:2004-056508.
Audience: **l,u.**

Corcoran, Michael **GV965**
PGA Tour Complete Book of Golf: Lessons and Advice from the Best Players of the Game. Cloth over Boards. Henry Holt & Company. New York, NY. 1999. 176p. ISBN:0-8050-6377-3, ISBN13: 978-0-8050-6377-6. Dewey:796.352. LCCN:99-010390.
Audience: **g,l,u.**

Crenshaw, Ben & Hauser, Melanie **GV964.W66**
A Feel for the Game: To Brookline and Back. Trade Cloth. DIANE Publishing Company. Collingdale, PA. 2004. 216p. ISBN:0-7567-8486-7, ISBN13: 978-0-7567-8486-7. Dewey:796.352/092 B.
Audience: **g,l,u.**

Crosset, Todd W. **GV966.C76 1995**
Outsiders in the Clubhouse: The World of Women's Professional Golf. Cloth Text. State University of New York Press. Albany, NY. 1995. 276p. SUNY Series on Sport, Culture, and Social Relations ISBN:0-7914-2489-8, ISBN13: 978-0-7914-2489-6. Dewey:796.352. LCCN:94-027916.
Audience: **g,u,f.** *Choice, 1996.*

Dawkins, Marvin P. & Kinloch, Graham C. **GV981**
African American Golfers During the Jim Crow Era. Trade Cloth. Greenwood Publishing Group, Inc. Portsmouth, NH. 2000. 200p. ISBN:0-275-95940-6, ISBN13: 978-0-275-95940-1. Dewey:796.352/089/96073. LCCN:99-034486.
Audience: **u,f.** *Choice, 2000.*

Dodson, James **GV964.W66**
Ben Hogan: An American Life. Trade Paper. Broadway Books. New York, NY. 2005. 544p. ISBN:0-7679-0863-5, ISBN13: 978-0-7679-0863-4. Dewey:796.352/092 B.
Audience: **g,l,u.** *Choice, 2004.*

Feinstein, John (Author, Afterword by) **GV964.A2E394 2004**
Caddy for Life: The Bruce Edwards Story. Trade Paper. Little Brown & Company. New York, NY. 2005. 336p. ISBN:0-316-01086-3, ISBN13: 978-0-316-01086-3. Dewey:796.352/092 B. LCCN:2003-027136.
Audience: **g,l,u.**

Frost, Mark **GV964.J6 F76**
The Grand Slam: Bobby Jones, America, and the Story of Golf. Trade Paper, Perfect. Hyperion Press. New York, NY. 2005. 514p. ISBN:1-4013-0751-5, ISBN13: 978-1-4013-0751-6. Dewey:796.352/092.
Audience: **g,l,u.**

Gabriel, Mike **GV969.P75G33 2001**
The Professional Golfers' Association Tour: A History. Paper Text. McFarland & Company, Incorporated Publishers. Jefferson, NC. 2001. 208p. ISBN:0-7864-0844-8, ISBN13: 978-0-7864-0844-3. Dewey:796.352/64/0973. LCCN:00-68720.
Audience: **g,l,u,f.** *Choice, 2001.*

Hardy, Jim & Andrisani, John **GV979.S9H29 2005**
The Plane Truth for Golfers: Breaking Down the One-Plane Swing and the Two-Plane Swing and Finding the One That's Right for You. Trade Paper. McGraw-Hill Companies, The. New York, NY. 2005. 157p. ISBN:0-07-143245-0, ISBN13: 978-0-07-143245-0. Dewey:796.352/3. LCCN:2004-025047.
Audience: **g,l,u.**

Hogan, Ben & Wind, Herbert W. **GV965**
Ben Hogan's Five Lessons: The Modern Fundamentals of Golf. Anthony Ravielli (Illustrator), Nick Seitz (Introduction by). Trade Cloth. Simon & Schuster. New York, NY. 1990. 128p. ISBN:0-671-72301-4, ISBN13: 978-0-671-72301-9. Dewey:796.352. LCCN:85-081113.
Audience: **g,l,u.**

Horn, Jane **GV966.H68 1999**
Power Golf for Women: How to Hit Longer and Straighter from Tee to Green. Robert Daley (Illustrator). Trade Paper. Kensington Publishing Corporation. New York, NY. 2000. 176p. ISBN:0-8065-2070-1, ISBN13: 978-0-8065-2070-4. Dewey:796.352/3/082. LCCN:99-014069.
Audience: **g,l,u.**

Jerris, Rand **GV964.A1J47 2005**
Golf's Golden Age: Robert T. Jones, Jr. and the Legendary Players of the '10s, '20s and '30s. Jennifer Pierce (Editor), George S. Pietzcker (Photographer), Arnold Palmer (Foreword by). Trade Cloth. National Geographic Society. Washington, DC. 2005. 160p. ISBN:0-7922-3872-9, ISBN13: 978-0-7922-3872-0. Dewey:796.352/092/2 B. LCCN:2005-041534.
Audience: **u,f.** *Choice, 2005.*

Jorgensen, Theodore P. **QC26.J67 1999**
The Physics of Golf. Ed. 2. Trade Paper. Springer. New York, NY. 1999. XII, 189p. ISBN:0-387-98691-X, ISBN13: 978-0-387-98691-3. Dewey:796.352. LCCN:98-032112.
Audience: **u.** *Choice, 1994.*

Ladies Professional Golf Association Staff **GV966.L64 2000**
LPGA's Guide to Every Shot. Trade Paper. Human Kinetics Publishers. Champaign, IL. 2000. 20p. ISBN:0-88011-980-2, ISBN13: 978-0-88011-980-1. Dewey:796.352/3/082. LCCN:99-089363.
Audience: **g,l,u.**

Lowe, Stephen R. **GV964.H3L69 2000**
Sir Walter and Mr. Jones: Walter Hagen, Bobby Jones and the Rise of American Golf. Trade Cloth. Sleeping Bear Press. Chelsea, MI. 2000. 416p. ISBN:1-58536-009-0, ISBN13: 978-1-58536-009-3. Dewey:796.352/0973. LCCN:00-009875.
Audience: **u,f.** *Choice, 2001.*

Morrison, Alec (Editor) **GV965.I46 1994**
The Impossible Art of Golf: An Anthology of Golf Writing. Trade Cloth. Oxford University Press, Inc. New York, NY. 1994. 328p. ISBN:0-19-211698-3, ISBN13: 978-0-19-211698-7. Dewey:796.352. LCCN:94-008831.
Audience: **l,u,f.**

Nicklaus, Jack **GV965.N496 2005**
Golf My Way: The Instructional Classic. Jim McQueen (Illustrator), Ken Bowden (As told to). Trade Paper. Simon & Schuster, Inc. New York, NY. 2005. 304p. ISBN:0-7432-6712-5, ISBN13: 978-0-7432-6712-0. Dewey:796.352/3. LCCN:2004-063531.
Audience: **g,l,u.**

O'Grady, Timothy **GV967.O43 2005**
On Golf: The Game, the Players, and a Personal History of Obsession. Cloth over Boards. St. Martin's Press. Gordonville, VA. 2005. 224p. ISBN:0-312-33004-9, ISBN13: 978-0-312-33004-0. Dewey:796.352. LCCN:2004-065746.
Audience: **g,l,u.**

Pelz, Dave & Frank, James A. **GV979.S54P45 1999**
Dave Pelz's Short Game Bible: Master the Finesse Swing and Lower Your Score. Lee Janzen (Foreword by). Trade Cloth. Broadway Books. New York, NY. 1999. 448p. Dave Pelz Scoring Game Ser. ISBN:0-7679-0344-7, ISBN13: 978-0-7679-0344-8. Dewey:796.3/523. LCCN:99-017226.
Audience: **g,l,u,f.**

Peper, George, et al. **GV965.G524**
Golf Magazine's Complete Book of Golf Instruction. James A. Frank, Lorin Anderson & John Andrisani (Authors). Trade Cloth. Harry N. Abrams, Inc. New York, NY. 1999. 352p. ISBN:0-8109-8156-4, ISBN13: 978-0-8109-8156-0. Dewey:796.352. LCCN:97-006088.
Audience: **g,l,u,f.**

Saunders, Vivien **GV966.S385 2000**
Golf Handbook for Women: The Complete Guide to Improving Your Game. Trade Paper. Crown Publishing Group. New York, NY. 2000. 224p. ISBN:0-609-80511-8, ISBN13: 978-0-609-80511-4. Dewey:796.352/3/082. LCCN:00-710409.
Audience: **l,u,f.** *Choice, 2001.*

Watson, Tom **GV965.W28 1987**
Getting up and Down: How to Save Strokes from Forty Yards and In. Trade Cloth. Knopf Publishing Group. New York, NY. 1987. 192p. ISBN:0-394-75300-3, ISBN13: 978-0-394-75300-3. Dewey:796.3523. LCCN:86-040475.
Audience: **g,l,u.**

Werner, Frank D. & Greig, Richard C. **GV976.W46 2000**
How Golf Clubs Really Work and How to Optimize Their Designs. Roger Ganem (Editor). Trade Paper. Origin, Inc. Jackson, WY. 2000. 183p. ISBN:0-9677625-0-2, ISBN13: 978-0-9677625-0-0. Dewey:688.7/6352/028/8. LCCN:99-097823.
Audience: **u.**

Zumerchik, John **GV967**
Newton on the Tee: A Good Walk Through the Science of Golf. Trade Cloth. Simon & Schuster. New York, NY. 2002. 256p. ISBN:0-7432-1214-2, ISBN13: 978-0-7432-1214-4. Dewey:796.3523. LCCN:2003-266828.
Audience: **u.**

Sports A-L > Gymnastics

George, Gerald S. **GV464.G46**
Biomechanics of Women's Gymnastics. Cloth Text. Prentice Hall PTR. Upper Saddle River, NJ. 1979. xv, 221p. ISBN:0-13-077461-8, ISBN13: 978-0-13-077461-3. Dewey:796.4/1. LCCN:79-018854.
Audience: **u,f.** B

Jastrjembskaia, Nadejda & Titov, Yuri **GV463.J37 1998**
Rhythmic Gymnastics. Trade Paper. Human Kinetics Publishers. Champaign, IL. 1998. 272p. ISBN:0-88011-710-9, ISBN13: 978-0-88011-710-4. Dewey:796.44. LCCN:98-015002.
Audience: **l,u,f.**

Mitchell, Debby, et al. **GV461.M54 2002**
Teaching Fundamental Gymnastic Skills. Barbara Davis & Raim Lopez (Authors). Trade Paper. Human Kinetics Publishers. Champaign, IL. 2002. 312p. ISBN:0-7360-0124-7, ISBN13: 978-0-7360-0124-3. Dewey:796.44. LCCN:2002-017324.
Audience: **l,u.**

Palmer, Heather **GV463.P25 2003**
Teaching Rhythmic Gymnastics: A Developmentally Appropriate Approach. Trade Paper. Human Kinetics Publishers. Champaign, IL. 2003. 144p. ISBN:0-7360-4242-3, ISBN13: 978-0-7360-4242-0. Dewey:796.44. LCCN:2002-152891.
Audience: **l,u,f.**

Simons, Minot II **GV464.S55 1995**
Women's Gymnastics a History: 1966 to 1974. Albrecht Gaebele (Photographer). Trade Cloth. Welwyn Publishing Company. Carmel, CA. 1995. xxv, 403p. ISBN:0-9646062-0-8, ISBN13: 978-0-9646062-0-3. Dewey:796.44/082. LCCN:95-090224.
Audience: **l,u,f.** *Choice, 1996.*

Turoff, Fred **GV461.7.T87 1991**
Artistic Gymnastics: A Comprehensive Guide to Performing and Teaching Skills for Beginners and Advanced Beginners. Cloth Text. Brown & Benchmark. Madison, WI. 1991. 432p. ISBN:0-697-10745-0, ISBN13: 978-0-697-10745-9. Dewey:796.44. LCCN:90-082240.
Audience: **g,l,u,f.**

Werner, Peter H. **GV464.5.W47 2003**
Teaching Children Gymnastics: A Developmentally Appropriate Approach. Ed. 2. Trade Paper. Human Kinetics Publishers. Champaign, IL. 2003. 248p. ISBN:0-7360-4434-5, ISBN13: 978-0-7360-4434-9. Dewey:796.44. LCCN:2003-011604.
Audience: **l,u.**

Sports A-L > Ice Hockey

American Sport Education Program Staff (Contribution by) **GV848.25.C63 2001**
Coaching Youth Hockey. Ed. 2. Trade Paper. Human Kinetics Publishers. Champaign, IL. 2001. 28p. ISBN:0-7360-3795-0, ISBN13: 978-0-7360-3795-2. Dewey:796.962/07/7. LCCN:2001-016873.
Audience: **g,l,u.**

Ashare, Alan B. (Editor) **GV848.35**
Safety in Ice Hockey. Trade Cloth. American Society for Testing & Materials. West Conshohocken, PA. 2000. 329p. STP Ser., Vol. 1341 ISBN:0-8031-2488-0, ISBN13: 978-0-8031-2488-2. Dewey:796.96/2028/9. LCCN:89-035946.
Audience: **u.**

Diamond, Dan (Editor), et al. **GV847 .T66 2000 ALC**
Total Hockey: The Official Encyclopedia of the National Hockey League. Ed. 2. James Duplacey, Ralph Dinger, Ernie Fitzsimmons & Eric Zweig (Editors). Trade Cloth. Total Sports Publishing. Kingston, NY. 2001. 1864p. ISBN:1-930844-42-5, ISBN13: 978-1-930844-42-1. Dewey:796.962/64.
Audience: **l,u,f.**

Dryden, Ken **GV848.5.D7A3 2005**
The Game. Ed. 2. Trade Paper. John Wiley & Sons, Inc. Hoboken, NJ. 2005. 308p. ISBN:0-470-83584-2, ISBN13: 978-0-470-83584-5. Dewey:796.962092.
Audience: **g,l,u,f.**

Etue, Elizabeth & Williams, Megan K. **GV847**
On the Edge: Women Making Hockey History. Trade Paper. Second Story Press. Toronto, ON. 1996. 336p. ISBN:0-929005-79-1, ISBN13: 978-0-929005-79-9. Dewey:796.962/082.
Audience: **u,f.** *Choice, 1997.*

Haché, Alain **QC28.H23 2002**
The Physics of Hockey. Trade Cloth. Johns Hopkins University Press. Baltimore, MD. 2002. 200p. ISBN:0-8018-7071-2, ISBN13: 978-0-8018-7071-2. Dewey:530. LCCN:2001-008643.
Audience: **l,u.** *Choice, 2003.*

Podnieks, Andrew, et al. **GV846.5.K56 2002**
Kings of the Ice: A History of World Hockey. Denis Gibbons, Pavel Barta, Dimitry Ryzkov & Tom Ratschunas (Authors). Trade Cloth. NDE Publishing. Richmond Hill, ON. 2002. 1024p. ISBN:1-55321-099-9, ISBN13: 978-1-55321-099-3. Dewey:796.962. LCCN:2003-427050.
Audience: **u,f.** *Choice, 2003.*

Rosengren, John **GV848.4.U6**
Blades of Glory: The True Story of a Young Team Bred to Win. Trade Paper. Sourcebooks, Inc. Naperville, IL. 2004. 352p. ISBN:1-4022-0047-1, ISBN13: 978-1-4022-0047-2. Dewey:796.962/09776/57.
Audience: **g,l,u,f.**

Theberge, Nancy **GV848.6.W65T54 2000**
Higher Goals: Women's Ice Hockey and the Politics of Gender. Paper Text. State University of New York Press. Albany, NY. 2000. xiii, 182p. SUNY Series on Sport, Culture, and Social Relations ISBN:0-7914-4642-5, ISBN13: 978-0-7914-4642-3. Dewey:796.962/082/0971. LCCN:99-057333.
Audience: **u,f.** *Choice, 2001.*

Sports A-L > Lacrosse

Fisher, Donald M. **GV989.F56 2002**
Lacrosse: A History of the Game. Trade Cloth. Johns Hopkins University Press. Baltimore, MD. 2002. 432p. ISBN:0-8018-6938-2, ISBN13: 978-0-8018-6938-9. Dewey:796.34/7/09. LCCN:2001-005690.
Audience: **g,l,u,f.**

Morris, Daniel **GV989.17.M67 2005**
The Confident Coach's Guide to Teaching Lacrosse: From Basic Fundamentals to Advanced Player Skills and Team Strategies. Michael Morris (Editor). Paper Text. Globe Pequot Press, The. Guilford, CT. 2006. 160p. Confident Coach Ser. ISBN:1-59228-588-0, ISBN13: 978-1-59228-588-4. Dewey:797.347/07/7. LCCN:2005-018948.
Audience: **g,l,u,f.**

Pietramala, David G. & Grauer, Neil A. **GV989**
Lacrosse: Technique and Tradition, the Second Edition of the Bob Scott Classic. Ed. 2. Trade Paper. Johns Hopkins University Press. Baltimore, MD. 2006. 312p. ISBN:0-8018-8410-1, ISBN13: 978-0-8018-8410-8. Dewey:796.347.
Audience: **g,l,u,f.**

Swissler, Becky **GV989.15.S95 2003**
Winning Lacrosse for Girls. Anna Maria Vesco (Foreword by). Trade Cloth. Facts On File, Inc. New York, NY. 2004. 208p.

Winning Sports for Girls Ser. ISBN:0-8160-5183-6, ISBN13: 978-0-8160-5183-0. Dewey:796.34/7/082. LCCN:2003-051446.
Audience: **g,l,u.**

Vennum, Thomas Jr. **E98.G2V46 1994**
American Indian Lacrosse: Little Brother of War. Trade Paper. Smithsonian Institution Press. Washington, DC. 1994. 376p. ISBN:1-56098-302-7, ISBN13: 978-1-56098-302-6. Dewey:796.34/7. LCCN:93-029968.
Audience: **g,l,u,f.** *Choice, 1994.*

Sports M-Z > Martial arts

Donohue, John J. **GV1111.D64 1991**
The Forge of the Spirit: Structure, Motion and Meaning in the Japanese Martial Tradition. Paper over Boards. Garland Publishing, Inc. New York, NY. 1991. 272p. ISBN:0-8240-7114-X, ISBN13: 978-0-8240-7114-1. Dewey:796.8. LCCN:90-020911.
Audience: **l,u,f.**

Green, Thomas A. & Svinth, Joseph R. (Editors) **GV1102**
Martial Arts in the Modern World. Trade Cloth. Greenwood Publishing Group, Inc. Portsmouth, NH. 2003. 336p. ISBN:0-275-98153-3, ISBN13: 978-0-275-98153-2. Dewey:796.8. LCCN:2003-051062.
Audience: **g,l,u,f.** *Choice, 2004.*

Hurst, G. Cameron 3rd & Hurst I, G. **GV1100.77.A2H87 1998**
Armed Martial Arts of Japan: Swordsmanship and Archery. Cloth over Boards. Yale University Press. Cumberland, RI. 1998. 256p. ISBN:0-300-04967-6, ISBN13: 978-0-300-04967-1. Dewey:796.86/0951. LCCN:97-047010.
Audience: **g,l,u.**

Kano, Jigoro **GV1114 .K357 1994**
Kodokan Judo: The Essential Guide to Judo by Its Founder. Trade Paper. Kodansha International. Tokyo, 1994. 264p. ISBN:4-7700-1799-5, ISBN13: 978-4-7700-1799-4. Dewey:796.8152. LCCN:84-080160.
Audience: **g,l,u,f.**

Mol, Serge **GV1114.M65 2001**
Classical Fighting Arts of Japan: A Complete Guide to Koryeu Jeujutsu. Trade Cloth. Kodansha International. Tokyo, 2001. 208p. ISBN:4-7700-2619-6, ISBN13: 978-4-7700-2619-4. Dewey:798.815. LCCN:00-067178.
Audience: **l,u,f.**

Stevens, John **GV1114.35.S765 2001**
Philosophy of Aikido. Trade Cloth. Kodansha International. Tokyo, 2001. 132p. ISBN:4-7700-2534-3, ISBN13: 978-4-7700-2534-0. Dewey:796.815/4. LCCN:00-047822.
Audience: **g,l,u,f.** *Choice, 2001.*

Ueshiba, Kisshomaru **GV1114.35**
The Art of Aikido: Principles and Essential Techniques. Trade Cloth. Kodansha International. Tokyo, 2004. 176p. ISBN:4-7700-2945-4, ISBN13: 978-4-7700-2945-4. Dewey:796.8154.
Audience: **l,u.** *Choice, 2005.*

Wiley, Carol A. (Editor) **GV1111.5.W65 1992**
Women in the Martial Arts. Trade Paper. North Atlantic Books. Berkeley, CA. 1993. 146p. IO Journals, Vol. 46 ISBN:1-55643-136-8, ISBN13: 978-1-55643-136-4. Dewey:613.6/6. LCCN:93-132230.
Audience: **g,l,u,f.**

Sports M-Z > Marathon

Burfoot, Amby (Editor) **GV1060.5**
Runner's World Complete Book of Running: Everything You Need to Know to Run for Fun, Fitness and Competition. Trade Paper, Pictures or Photographs. Rodale Press, Inc. Emmaus, PA. 2004. 312p. ISBN:1-57954-929-2, ISBN13: 978-1-57954-929-9. Dewey:796.4/2.
Audience: **g,l,u.**

Cedaro, Rod (Compiled by) **GV1060.73.T75 1993**
Triathlon: Achieving Your Personal Best. Greg Welch (Foreword by), Luise Burke (Contribution by). Trade Cloth. Facts On File, Inc. New York, NY. 1993. 304p. ISBN:0-8160-2948-2, ISBN13: 978-0-8160-2948-8. Dewey:796.42. LCCN:93-004007.
Audience: **u,f.** *Choice, 1994.*

Gandolfo, Christina **GV1060.73.W66 2005**
The Woman Triathlete. Trade Paper. Human Kinetics Publishers. Champaign, IL. 2004. 248p. ISBN:0-7360-5430-8, ISBN13: 978-0-7360-5430-0. Dewey:796.42/57/082. LCCN:2004-020137.
Audience: **l,u.**

Lovett, Charlie **GV1065**
Olympic Marathon: A Centennial History of the Games' Most Storied Race. Trade Cloth. Greenwood Publishing Group, Inc. Portsmouth, NH. 1997. 192p. ISBN:0-275-95771-3, ISBN13: 978-0-275-95771-1. Dewey:796.42/52. LCCN:96-047618.
Audience: **g,l,u,f.** *Choice, 1998.*

Sports M-Z > Polo

Laffaye, Horace A. **GV1011**
The Polo Encyclopedia. Stephen A. Orthwein (Foreword by). Paper Text. McFarland & Company, Incorporated Publishers. Jefferson, NC. 2004. 431p. ISBN:0-7864-1724-2, ISBN13: 978-0-7864-1724-7. Dewey:796.35/3/03. LCCN:2003-026011.
Audience: **g,l,u,f.**

Sports M-Z > Professional Wrestling

Oppliger, Patrice A. **GV1196.4**
Wrestling and Hyper-Masculinity. Paper Text. McFarland & Company, Incorporated Publishers. Jefferson, NC. 2003. 211p. ISBN:0-7864-1692-0, ISBN13: 978-0-7864-1692-9. Dewey:796.812. LCCN:2003-025328.
Audience: **u,f.** *Choice, 2004.*

Sammond, Nicholas (Editor) **GV1195.S743 2005**
Steel Chair to the Head: The Pleasure and Pain of Professional Wrestling. Trade Paper. Duke University Press. Durham, NC. 2005. 344p. ISBN:0-8223-3438-0, ISBN13: 978-0-8223-3438-5. Dewey:796.8/12. LCCN:2004-014274.
Audience: **u,f.** *Choice, 2005.*

Sports M-Z > Racquet Sports

American Sport Education Program Staff **GV1002.9.C63A45 2002**
Coaching Youth Tennis. Ed. 3. Trade Paper. Human Kinetics

Publishers. Champaign, IL. 2001. 20p. ISBN:0-7360-3793-4, ISBN13: 978-0-7360-3793-8. Dewey:796.342/07/7. LCCN:2001-024117.

Audience: **l,u,f.**

Barrett, John **GV999**
Wimbledon: The Official History. Trade Cloth. Trafalgar Square. North Pomfret, VT. 2001. 480p. ISBN:0-00-711707-8, ISBN13: 978-0-00-711707-9. Dewey:796.3/42/0942193.

Audience: **g,l,u,f.** *Choice, 2002.*

Bodo, Peter **GV995.B6832 1995**
The Courts of Babylon: Tales of Greed and Glory in the Harsh New High-Stakes World of Professional Tennis. Trade Cloth. Simon & Schuster. New York, NY. 1995. 480p. ISBN:0-684-81296-7, ISBN13: 978-0-684-81296-0. Dewey:796.342/64. LCCN:95-014760.

Audience: **g,l,u,f.** *Choice, 1995.*

Boga, Steven **GV1007.B64 1996**
Badminton. Trade Paper. Stackpole Books. Mechanicsburg, PA. 1996. 112p. Backyard Games Ser. ISBN:0-8117-2487-5, ISBN13: 978-0-8117-2487-6. Dewey:796.34/5. LCCN:95-022434.

Audience: **g,l,u.**

Brody, Howard, et al. **QC21.3.B76 2002**
The Physics and Technology of Tennis. Rod Cross, Crawford Lindsey & Ron Waite (Authors). Trade Paper. USRSA. Vista, CA. 2004. 450p. ISBN:0-9722759-0-8, ISBN13: 978-0-9722759-0-3. Dewey:796.342/01/53. LCCN:2002-094432.

Audience: **u.** *Choice, 2004.*

Chu, Donald A. **GV1002.9.T7C48 1995**
Power Tennis Training. Trade Paper. Human Kinetics Publishers. Champaign, IL. 1994. 176p. ISBN:0-87322-616-X, ISBN13: 978-0-87322-616-5. Dewey:796.342/07. LCCN:94-021325.

Audience: **g,l,u.**

Collins, Bud (Editor) **GV992.T68**
Total Tennis: The Ultimate Tennis Encyclopedia. Trade Cloth. Sport Media Publishing. Toronto, ON. 2003. 864p. ISBN:0-9731443-4-3, ISBN13: 978-0-9731443-4-5. Dewey:796.34209.

Audience: **g,l,u,f.**

Gillmeister, Heiner **GV1002.95.E85**
Tennis: A Cultural History. Trade Paper. New York University Press. New York, NY. 1998. 320p. ISBN:0-8147-3121-X, ISBN13: 978-0-8147-3121-5. Dewey:796.342/094.

Audience: **g,l,u,f.** *Choice, 1999.*

Gray, Frances Clayton & Lamb, Yanick Rice **GV994.G53G73 2004**
Born to Win: The Authorized Biography of Althea Gibson. Bill Cosby (Foreword by), Venus Williams (Afterword by). Trade Cloth. John Wiley & Sons, Inc. Hoboken, NJ. 2004. 256p. ISBN:0-471-47165-8, ISBN13: 978-0-471-47165-3. Dewey:796.342/092 B. LCCN:2004-004690.

Audience: **g,l,u.**

Hoskins, Tina **GV1002.9.T7H67 2003**
The Tennis Drill Book. Trade Paper. Human Kinetics Publishers. Champaign, IL. 2003. 256p. ISBN:0-7360-4912-6, ISBN13: 978-0-7360-4912-2. Dewey:796.342/2. LCCN:2003-009192.

Audience: **g,l,u.**

Hughes, T., et al. **RC1220.T4 S36 1995**
Science and Racket Sports. T. Reilly & A. Lees (Authors). Paper over Boards. Routledge. New York, NY. 1994. 304p. ISBN:0-419-18500-3, ISBN13: 978-0-419-18500-0. Dewey:796.34015.

Audience: **u.**

Pluim, Babette & Safran, Marc **RC1200.T4P58 2004**
From Breakpoint to Advantage: A Practical Guide to Optimal Tennis Health and Performance. Trade Paper. USRSA. Vista, CA. 2004. 352p. ISBN:0-9722759-1-6, ISBN13: 978-0-9722759-1-0. Dewey:796.342. LCCN:2004-093133.

Audience: **g,l,u,f.** *Choice, 2005.*

Sadzeck, Tom **GV995**
Tennis Skills: The Player's Guide. Trade Paper. Firefly Books, Ltd. Tonawanda, NY. 2001. 128p. ISBN:1-55209-494-4, ISBN13: 978-1-55209-494-5. Dewey:796.342.

Audience: **g,l,u.**

Schoenfeld, Bruce **GV994.A1**
The Match: Althea Gibson and a Portrait of a Friendship. Trade Paper, Perfect. HarperCollins Publishers. New York, NY. 2005. 320p. ISBN:0-06-052653-X, ISBN13: 978-0-06-052653-5. Dewey:796.3420922.

Audience: **l,u,f.**

Turner, Ed & Clouse, Woody **GV1003.34.T87 1996**
Winning Raquetball: Skills, Drills, and Strategies. Trade Paper. Human Kinetics Publishers. Champaign, IL. 1995. 288p. ISBN:0-87322-721-2, ISBN13: 978-0-87322-721-6. Dewey:796.34/3. LCCN:95-013029.

Audience: **l,u.**

U. S. Tennis Association Staff & Ellenbecker, Todd S. **GV1002.9.T7U55 1998**
Complete Conditioning for Tennis. Trade Paper. Human Kinetics Publishers. Champaign, IL. 1998. 216p. ISBN:0-88011-734-6, ISBN13: 978-0-88011-734-0. Dewey:796.342. LCCN:98-018354.

Audience: **g,l,u.**

United States Tennis Association **GV1002.9.C63U55 2004**
Coaching Tennis Successfully. Ed. 2. Trade Paper. Human Kinetics Publishers. Champaign, IL. 2004. 28p. ISBN:0-7360-4829-4, ISBN13: 978-0-7360-4829-3. Dewey:796.342/07/7. LCCN:2003-018063.

Audience: **g,l,u.**

Williams, Scott P. & Petersen, Randy **GV995.W68 2000**
Serious Tennis. Trade Paper. Human Kinetics Publishers. Champaign, IL. 1999. 272p. ISBN:0-88011-913-6, ISBN13: 978-0-88011-913-9. Dewey:796.342. LCCN:99-049310.

Audience: **g,l,u.**

Zug, James **GV1004.Z84 2003**
Squash: A History of the Game. George Plimpton (Foreword by). Trade Cloth. Simon & Schuster. New York, NY. 2003. 384p. ISBN:0-7432-2990-8, ISBN13: 978-0-7432-2990-6. Dewey:796.343. LCCN:2003-050458.

Audience: **g,l,u,f.**

Sports M-Z > Rodeo

Allen, Michael **GV1834.A55 1998**
Rodeo Cowboys in the North American Imagination. Trade Cloth. University of Nevada Press. Reno, NV. 1998. 248p. Wilbur S. Shepperson Series in History and Humanities ISBN:0-87417-315-9, ISBN13: 978-0-87417-315-4. Dewey:791.840973. LCCN:98-022963.
Audience: **g,l,u.** *Choice, 1999.*

Johnson, Cecil **GV1833.6.P5J64 1994**
Guts: Legendary Black Rodeo Cowboy Bill Pickett. June Ford (Editor). Trade Cloth. Summit Publishing Group - Legacy Books. Irving, TX. 1994. 223p. ISBN:1-56530-162-5, ISBN13: 978-1-56530-162-7. Dewey:791.8 B. LCCN:94-038591.
Audience: **g,l.** *Choice, 1995.*

LeCompte, Mary Lou **GV1834.55.W47L43**
Cowgirls of the Rodeo: Pioneer Professional Athletes. Trade Cloth. University of Illinois Press. Champaign, IL. 1993. 272p. Sport and Society Ser. ISBN:0-252-02029-4, ISBN13: 978-0-252-02029-2. Dewey:791.8/4. LCCN:92-042635.
Audience: **u,f.** *Choice, 1994.*

Wooden, Wayne S. & Ehringer, Gavin **GV1834.5.W66 1996**
Rodeo in America: Wranglers, Roughstock, and Paydirt. Trade Cloth. University Press of Kansas. Lawrence, KS. 1999. 310p. ISBN:0-7006-0813-3, ISBN13: 978-0-7006-0813-3. Dewey:791.8/4/0973. LCCN:96-016328.
Audience: **g,l,u,f.** *Choice, 1997.*

Sports M-Z > Rowing

Bourne, Gilbert C. **GV791**
A Textbook of Oarmanship. Trade Paper. Sport Books Publisher. Toronto, ON. 2000. 400p. ISBN:0-920905-12-9, ISBN13: 978-0-920905-12-8. Dewey:797.123. LCCN:87-095070.
Audience: **g,l,u,f.**

Boyne, Daniel J. **GV793**
The Red Rose Crew: A True Story of Women, Winning, and the Water. David Halberstam (Foreword by). Paper Text. Globe Pequot Press, The. Guilford, CT. 2005. 240p. ISBN:1-59228-758-1, ISBN13: 978-1-59228-758-1. Dewey:797.1/4/092273.
Audience: **g,l,u,f.**

Dodd, Christopher **GV791.D63 1992**
The Story of World Rowing. Trade Cloth. Random House of Canada, Ltd. Mississauga, ON. 1992. 468p. ISBN:0-09-174610-8, ISBN13: 978-0-09-174610-0. Dewey:796.1/23. LCCN:93-169662.
Audience: **g,l,u,f.** *Choice, 1992.*

Halladay, Eric **GV795.H24 1990**
Rowing in England: A Social History: The Amateur Debate. James A. Mangan (Editor). Cloth Text. Manchester University Press. Manchester, 1990. 256p. International Studies in the History of Sport ISBN:0-7190-2605-9, ISBN13: 978-0-7190-2605-8. Dewey:797.1/22/0942. LCCN:90-038505.
Audience: **u,f.** *Choice, 1991.*

Kiesling, Stephen **GV790.92.K53A37 1994**
The Shell Game: Reflections on Rowing and the Pursuit of Excellence. Trade Paper. Nordic Knight Press. Gold Hill, OR. 1994. 200p. ISBN:0-9638461-9-1, ISBN13: 978-0-9638461-9-8. Dewey:797.1/23/092 B. LCCN:82-022128.
Audience: **l,u,f.**

Saint Sing, Susan **GV706.42.S35 2004**
Spirituality of Sport: Balancing Body and Soul. Trade Cloth. Saint Anthony Messenger Press & Franciscan Communications. Cincinnati, OH. 2004. xiii, 137p. ISBN:0-86716-516-2, ISBN13: 978-0-86716-516-6. Dewey:248.8/8. LCCN:2004-023847.
Audience: **g,l,u,f.**

Sayer, Bill **GV791**
Rowing and Sculling. Ed. 2. Trade Paper. Robert Hale Ltd. London, 2001. 221p. ISBN:0-7090-5845-4, ISBN13: 978-0-7090-5845-8. Dewey:797.1/23.
Audience: **l,u,f.**

Wigglesworth, Neil **GV795**
A Social History of English Rowing. Trade Paper. Taylor & Francis Group. Abingdon, 1992. 248p. ISBN:0-7146-3415-8, ISBN13: 978-0-7146-3415-9. Dewey:797.1230942. LCCN:91-003481.
Audience: **u,f.**

Sports M-Z > Rugby

Chandler, Timothy J. L. & Nauright, John (Editors) **GV945.85.P75M36 1999**
Making the Rugby World: Race, Gender, Commerce. Trade Paper. Taylor & Francis Group. Abingdon, 1999. 256p. Sport in the Global Society Ser., No. 10 ISBN:0-7146-4411-0, ISBN13: 978-0-7146-4411-0. Dewey:796.333. LCCN:99-027732.
Audience: **u,f.** *Choice, 2000.*

Collins, Tony **GV945.9.G7**
Rugby's Great Split: Class, Culture and the Origins of Rugby League Football. Trade Paper. Woburn Press. Andover, 1998. 304p. Sport in the Global Society Ser. ISBN:0-7146-4424-2, ISBN13: 978-0-7146-4424-0. Dewey:796.333/8/0941.
Audience: **u,f.** *Choice, 1999.*

Davies, Gerald **GV946.2**
The History of the Rugby World Cup. Sanctuary Publishing, Ltd. 2004. ISBN:1-86074-445-1, ISBN13: 978-1-86074-445-7.
Audience: **l,u.**

Hale, Bruce (Editor) **GV945.85.P75R84 2002**
Rugby Tough. Trade Paper. Human Kinetics Publishers. Champaign, IL. 2002. 264p. ISBN:0-7360-3678-4, ISBN13: 978-0-7360-3678-8. Dewey:796.333/01/9. LCCN:2002-001752.
Audience: **l,u.**

Luger, Dan & Pook, Paul **GV945.8**
Complete Conditioning for Rugby. Trade Paper. Human Kinetics Publishers. Champaign, IL. 2004. 264p. ISBN:0-7360-5210-0, ISBN13: 978-0-7360-5210-8. Dewey:796.333. LCCN:2003-023734.
Audience: **l,u.**

Williams, Tony & Hunter, Gordon **GV945**
Rugby Skills, Tactics and Rules. Trade Paper. Firefly Books, Ltd. Tonawanda, NY. 2000. 192p. ISBN:1-55209-546-0, ISBN13: 978-1-55209-546-1. Dewey:796.333/2.
Audience: **l,u.**

Sports M-Z > Running

Benyo, Richard **GV1061.8.A35 1998**
Running Past 50. Trade Paper. Human Kinetics Publishers. Champaign, IL. 1998. 256p. Ageless Athlete Ser., Vol. 50 ISBN:0-88011-705-2, ISBN13: 978-0-88011-705-0. Dewey:613.7/172/0846. LCCN:97-052054.
Audience: **g,l,u,f.**

Brown, Dick & Henderson, Joe **GV1061.B77 2003**
Fitness Running. Ed. 2. Trade Paper. Human Kinetics Publishers. Champaign, IL. 2003. 20p. ISBN:0-7360-4510-4, ISBN13: 978-0-7360-4510-0. Dewey:796.42. LCCN:2002-151052.
Audience: **g,l,u.**

Burfoot, Amby (Editor) **GV1060.5**
Runner's World Complete Book of Running: Everything You Need to Know to Run for Fun, Fitness and Competition. Trade Paper, Pictures or Photographs. Rodale Press, Inc. Emmaus, PA. 2004. 312p. ISBN:1-57954-929-2, ISBN13: 978-1-57954-929-9. Dewey:796.4/2.
Audience: **g,l,u.**

Cedaro, Rod (Compiled by) **GV1060.73.T75 1993**
Triathlon: Achieving Your Personal Best. Greg Welch (Foreword by), Luise Burke (Contribution by). Trade Cloth. Facts On File, Inc. New York, NY. 1993. 304p. ISBN:0-8160-2948-2, ISBN13: 978-0-8160-2948-8. Dewey:796.42. LCCN:93-004007.
Audience: **u,f.** *Choice, 1994.*

Derderian, Tom **GV1065.22.B67D46**
Boston Marathon: The First Century of the World's Premier Running Event. Ed. 2. Joan Benoit Samuelson & Bill Rodgers (Foreword by). Trade Cloth. Human Kinetics Publishers. Champaign, IL. 1996. 664p. ISBN:0-88011-479-7, ISBN13: 978-0-88011-479-0. Dewey:796.4/25/0974461. LCCN:95-039944.
Audience: **l,u.**

Gandolfo, Christina **GV1060.73.W66 2005**
The Woman Triathlete. Trade Paper. Human Kinetics Publishers. Champaign, IL. 2004. 248p. ISBN:0-7360-5430-8, ISBN13: 978-0-7360-5430-0. Dewey:796.42/57/082. LCCN:2004-020137.
Audience: **l,u.**

Higdon, Hal **GV1061.18.A35H55**
Masters Running: A Guide to Running and Staying Fit After 40. Trade Paper. Rodale Press, Inc. Emmaus, PA. 2005. 240p. ISBN:1-59486-021-1, ISBN13: 978-1-59486-021-8. Dewey:613.7/172/0846. LCCN:2004-027381.
Audience: **g,l,u,f.**

Kowalchik, Claire **GV1061.18.W66K68**
The Complete Book of Running for Women: Everything You Need to Know about Training, Nutrition, Injury Prevention, Motivation, Racing and Much, Much More. Trade Paper. Simon & Schuster. New York, NY. 1999. 416p. ISBN:0-671-01703-9, ISBN13: 978-0-671-01703-3. Dewey:613.7/172/082. LCCN:98-050318.
Audience: **g,l,u,f.**

Micheli, Lyle J. & Jenkins, Mark **RC1220.R8M53 1996**
Healthy Runner's Handbook. Trade Paper. Human Kinetics Publishers. Champaign, IL. 1996. 264p. ISBN:0-88011-524-6, ISBN13: 978-0-88011-524-7. Dewey:613.7/172. LCCN:95-026222.
Audience: **g,l,u,f.**

Noakes, Timothy D. **GV1061.N6 2002**
Lore of Running. Ed. 4. Trade Paper. Human Kinetics Publishers. Champaign, IL. 2002. 944p. ISBN:0-87322-959-2, ISBN13: 978-0-87322-959-3. Dewey:796.42. LCCN:2002-003702.
Audience: **l,u,f.**

Sports M-Z > Sailing

Anderson, Bryon D. **VK543.A53 2003**
The Physics of Sailing Explained. Trade Paper. Sheridan House, Inc. Dobbs Ferry, NY. 2003. 160p. ISBN:1-57409-170-0, ISBN13: 978-1-57409-170-0. Dewey:623.88/13. LCCN:2003-014297.
Audience: **g,l,u.** *Choice, 2004.*

Braden, Twain **GV811 .B73 2003**
The Handbook of Sailing Techniques: Professional Tips, Expert Advice, Essential Skills. Trade Paper. Globe Pequot Press, The. Guilford, CT. 2003. 192p. ISBN:1-58574-644-4, ISBN13: 978-1-58574-644-6. Dewey:797.124. LCCN:2001-117300.
Audience: **g,l,u,f.** *Choice, 2003.*

Sports M-Z > Shooting

Riley, Glenda **GV1157.O3R55 1994**
The Life and Legacy of Annie Oakley. Trade Cloth. University of Oklahoma Press. Norman, OK. 1994. 272p. Oklahoma Western Biographies Ser., Vol. 7 ISBN:0-8061-2656-6, ISBN13: 978-0-8061-2656-2. Dewey:796.3/092 B. LCCN:94-010260.
Audience: **u,f.** *Choice, 1995.*

Sports M-Z > Skating (Roller, Ice)

Lewis, David H. **GV859.L48 1996**
Roller Skating for Gold. Trade Cloth. Scarecrow Press, Inc. Lanham, MD. 1996. 240p. American Sports History Ser., No. 5 ISBN:0-8108-3048-5, ISBN13: 978-0-8108-3048-6. Dewey:796.2/1. LCCN:96-021274.
Audience: **l,u.** *Choice, 1997.*

Malone, John W. **GV849.M34 1998**
The Encyclopedia of Figure Skating. Trade Cloth. Facts On File, Inc. New York, NY. 1998. 272p. ISBN:0-8160-3226-2, ISBN13: 978-0-8160-3226-6. Dewey:796.91/2/03. LCCN:97-046360.
Audience: **g,l,u,f.** *Choice, 1998.*

Sports M-Z > Skiing

Allen, John B. **GV854.4.A4 1993**
From Skisport to Skiing: One Hundred Years of an American Sport, 1840-1940. Cloth Text. University of Massachusetts Press. Amherst, MA. 1993. 240p. ISBN:0-87023-844-2, ISBN13: 978-0-87023-844-4. Dewey:796.93/0973. LCCN:93-009224.
Audience: **g,l,u,f.** *Choice, 1994.*

Lind, David & Sanders, Scott Patrick **QC26.L56 2003**
The Physics of Skiing: Skiing at the Triple Point. Ed. 2. Trade Cloth. Springer. New York, NY. 2004. XVII, 266p. ISBN:0-387-00722-9, ISBN13: 978-0-387-00722-9. Dewey:796.93/01/531. LCCN:2003-044589.
Audience: **l,u.** *Choice, 2004.*

Sports M-Z > Soccer

GV944.U6
☐ American Soccer History Archives.
http://www.sover.net/~spectrum/
Audience: **g,l,u,f.**

Allaway, Roger, et al. **GV944.U6A44 2001**
The Encyclopedia of American Soccer History. Colin Jose & David Litterer (Authors). Trade Cloth. Scarecrow Press, Inc. Lanham, MD. 2001. 488p. American Sports History Ser., No. 20 ISBN:0-8108-3980-6, ISBN13: 978-0-8108-3980-9. Dewey:796.334/0973. LCCN:00-053140.
Audience: **g,l,u,f.** *Choice, 2002.*

American Sport Education Program Staff **GV943.8.C63 2001**
Coaching Youth Soccer. Ed. 3. Trade Paper. Human Kinetics Publishers. Champaign, IL. 2001. 168p. ISBN:0-7360-3718-7, ISBN13: 978-0-7360-3718-1. Dewey:796.334/07/7. LCCN:00-050032.
Audience: **l,u,f.**

American Sport Education Program Staff **GV943.9.O45O44 2004**
Officiating Soccer. Trade Paper. Human Kinetics Publishers. Champaign, IL. 2004. 144p. ISBN:0-7360-4761-1, ISBN13: 978-0-7360-4761-6. Dewey:796.334/3. LCCN:2004-005046.
Audience: **g,l,u.**

Armstrong, Gary **GV943.9.F35A76 1998**
Football Hooligans: Knowing the Score. Trade Paper. Berg Publishers. Oxford, 1998. 320p. Explorations in Anthropology Ser. ISBN:1-85973-957-1, ISBN13: 978-1-85973-957-0. Dewey:306.4/83/0941. LCCN:98-128792.
Audience: **g,l,u,f.** *Choice, 1998.*

Cox, Richard William (Editor), et al. **GV944.G7E53 2002**
Encyclopedia of British Football. David Russell & Wray Vamplew (Editors), Gordon Taylor (Foreword by). Trade Paper. Taylor & Francis Group. Abingdon, 2002. 400p. Sports Reference Library ISBN:0-7146-8230-6, ISBN13: 978-0-7146-8230-3. Dewey:796.334/0941. LCCN:2002-000332.
Audience: **g,l,u,f.** *Choice, 2003.*

Crouch, T. **GV943.49.C76 2002**
Ultimate Book of the World Cup: A Complete History. Trade Paper. Aurum Press, Ltd. London, 2002. 256p. ISBN:1-85410-843-3, ISBN13: 978-1-85410-843-2. Dewey:796.3/34668.
Audience: **g,l,u,f.** *Choice, 2002.*

Dunning, Eric (Editor), et al. **GV943.9.F35F53 2002**
Fighting Fans: Football Hooliganism as a World Phenomenon. Patrick Murphy, Ivan Waddington & Antonio E. Astrinakis (Editors). Trade Paper. University College Dublin Press. Dublin, 2002. 27p. ISBN:1-900621-74-6, ISBN13: 978-1-900621-74-8. Dewey:306.4/83. LCCN:2003-464716.
Audience: **u,f.** *Choice, 2003.*

Ekblom, Bjorn (Editor) **RC1220 .S57 S64 1994**
Soccer. Ed. 2. Trade Paper. Blackwell Publishing, Inc. Malden, MA. 1994. 240p. Handbook of Sports Medicine and Science Ser. ISBN:0-632-03328-2, ISBN13: 978-0-632-03328-7. Dewey:621.31924.
Audience: **u,f.** *Choice, 1995.*

Giulianotti, Richard **GV943.9.S64G576 1999**
Football: A Sociology of the Global Game. Trade Paper. Polity Press. Cambridge, 1999. 240p. ISBN:0-7456-1769-7, ISBN13: 978-0-7456-1769-5. Dewey:306.4/83. LCCN:99-011069.
Audience: **u,f.** *Choice, 2000.*

Hong, Fan & Mangan, J. A. (Editors) **GV944.5**
Soccer, Women, Sexual Liberation: Kicking off a New Era. Trade Paper. Taylor & Francis Group. Abingdon, 2003. 272p. Sport in the Global Society Ser. ISBN:0-7146-8408-2, ISBN13: 978-0-7146-8408-6. Dewey:796.334082. LCCN:2004-298586.
Audience: **g,l,u,f.** *Choice, 2004.*

King, Anthony **GV944.E9**
The European Ritual: Football in the New Europe. Trade Cloth. Ashgate Publishing, Ltd. Aldershot, 2003. 302p. ISBN:0-7546-3652-6, ISBN13: 978-0-7546-3652-6. Dewey:796.334/094. LCCN:2003-045350.
Audience: **g,l,u,f.** *Choice, 2004.*

Lauffer, Robert Butch & Kater, April **GV944.5.L38 2001**
Women's Soccer: Techniques, Tactics and Teamwork. Trade Paper. Sterling Publishing Co., Inc. New York, NY. 2001. 144p. ISBN:0-8069-5847-2, ISBN13: 978-0-8069-5847-7. Dewey:796.334/2. LCCN:00-048258.
Audience: **l,u.** *Choice, 2002.*

Martin, Simon **GV943.9.S64**
Football and Fascism: The National Game under Mussolini. Trade Paper. Berg Publishers. Oxford, 2004. 288p. ISBN:1-85973-705-6, ISBN13: 978-1-85973-705-7. Dewey:796.334/0945/09043. LCCN:2004-020616.
Audience: **g,l,u,f.** *Choice, 2005.*

Mason, Tony **GV944.S64M27 1995**
Passion of the People: Football in Latin America. Trade Paper. Analytical Psychology Club of San Francisco, Inc. San Francisco, CA. 1995. 224p. Critical Studies in Latin American Culture ISBN:0-86091-667-7, ISBN13: 978-0-86091-667-3. Dewey:796.3/34/098. LCCN:95-163189.
Audience: **u,f.**

Murray, Bill **GV942.5.M88 1996**
The World's Game: A History of Soccer. Trade Cloth. University of Illinois Press. Champaign, IL. 1996. 224p. Illinois History of Sports Ser. ISBN:0-252-01748-X, ISBN13: 978-0-252-01748-3. Dewey:796.334/09. LCCN:95-013742.
Audience: **g,l,u,f.** *Choice, 1997.*

National Soccer Coaches of America Staff **GV943.8.S65 2004**
The Soccer Coaching Bible. Trade Paper. Human Kinetics

Publishers. Champaign, IL. 2004. 328p. ISBN:0-7360-4227-X, ISBN13: 978-0-7360-4227-7. Dewey:796.334/07/7. LCCN:2003-022881.
Audience: **l,u.**

Reilly, Tom & Williams, Mark (Editors) **GV943.S36 2003**
Science and Soccer. Ed. 2. Trade Paper. Routledge. New York, NY. 2003. 352p. ISBN:0-415-26232-1, ISBN13: 978-0-415-26232-3. Dewey:796.334. LCCN:2002-035842.
Audience: **l,u,f.** *Choice, 2004.*

Stokell, Ian **GV943.8.S77 2002**
Coaching Women's Soccer: A Revolutionary Approach to Putting the Play Back into Practice. Trade Paper. McGraw-Hill Companies, The. New York, NY. 2002. x, 182p. ISBN:0-07-138209-7, ISBN13: 978-0-07-138209-0. Dewey:796.334/07/7. LCCN:2001-047321.
Audience: **g,l,u,f.** *Choice, 2002.*

Taylor, Rogan **GV943.9.F35.T39 1992**
Football and Its Fans: An Account of Supporters and Their Relations. Trade Cloth. St. Martin's Press. Gordonville, VA. 1992. viii, 198p. ISBN:0-7185-1448-3, ISBN13: 978-0-7185-1448-8. Dewey:796.334. LCCN:92-005666.
Audience: **g,l,u,f.** *Choice, 1993.*

Tomlinson, Alan & Sugden, John **GV943.9.S64S84 1998**
FIFA and the Contest for World Football: Who Rules the Peoples Game. Trade Paper. Polity Press. Cambridge, 1998. 304p. ISBN:0-7456-1661-5, ISBN13: 978-0-7456-1661-2. Dewey:796.334/66. LCCN:97-051453.
Audience: **u,f.**

Wesson, John **QC26**
The Science of Soccer. Perfect. Institute of Physics Publishing. Philadelphia, PA. 2002. 216p. ISBN:0-7503-0813-3, ISBN13: 978-0-7503-0813-7. Dewey:796.334.
Audience: **u.**

Williams, Jean **GV944.5**
A History of Women's Football: Gender, Power and the Rise of a Global Game. Trade Paper. Routledge. New York, NY. 2003. 240p. ISBN:0-415-26338-7, ISBN13: 978-0-415-26338-2. Dewey:796.3/34/082.
Audience: **u,f.**

Sports M-Z > Softball

American Sport Education Program Staff **GV881.4.U47A54 2004**
Officiating Softball. Trade Paper. Human Kinetics Publishers. Champaign, IL. 2004. 184p. ISBN:0-7360-4764-6, ISBN13: 978-0-7360-4764-7. Dewey:796.357/8. LCCN:2004-000579.
Audience: **l,u,f.**

Dickson, Paul **GV863.A1D53 1994**
The Worth Book of Softball: A Celebration of America's True National Pastime. Trade Cloth. Facts On File, Inc. New York, NY. 1994. 288p. ISBN:0-8160-2897-4, ISBN13: 978-0-8160-2897-9. Dewey:796.35780973. LCCN:93-019312.
Audience: **g,l,u,f.** *Choice, 1994.*

Sports M-Z > Surfing

Warshaw, Matt **GV840.S8W3476 2003**
The Encyclopedia of Surfing. William Finnegan (Foreword by). Trade Cloth. Harcourt Trade Publishers. New York, NY. 2003. 800p. ISBN:0-15-100579-6, ISBN13: 978-0-15-100579-6. Dewey:797.3/203. LCCN:2003-005274.
Audience: **g,l,u,f.** *Choice, 2004.*

Sports M-Z > Swimming

Bean, Dawn Pawson **GV838.4.U6**
Synchronized Swimming: An American History. Paper Text. McFarland & Company, Incorporated Publishers. Jefferson, NC. 2005. 320p. ISBN:0-7864-1948-2, ISBN13: 978-0-7864-1948-7. Dewey:797.2/17. LCCN:2005-000090.
Audience: **u,f.** *Choice, 2005.*

Colwin, Cecil M. **GV836.4.C65 2002**
Breakthrough Swimming. Ed. 2. Trade Paper. Human Kinetics Publishers. Champaign, IL. 2002. 262p. ISBN:0-7360-3777-2, ISBN13: 978-0-7360-3777-8. Dewey:797.2/1/09. LCCN:2001-039994.
Audience: **g,l,u,f.**

Costill, David L., et al. **RC1220.S8C67 1991**
Swimming. Ernest W. Maglischo & Allen B. Richardson (Authors). Trade Paper. Blackwell Publishing, Inc. Malden, MA. 1991. 224p. Handbook of Sports Medicine and Science Ser. ISBN:0-632-03027-5, ISBN13: 978-0-632-03027-9. Dewey:612/.044. LCCN:91-019537.
Audience: **g,l,u,f.** *Choice, 1992.*

Dawson, Buck **GV837.9.D39 2000**
Mermaids on Parade: America's Love Affair with Its First Olympic Swimmers. Paul Gallico (Introduction by). Trade Cloth. Nova Science Publishers, Inc. Hauppauge, NY. 2000. 266p. ISBN:1-56072-726-8, ISBN13: 978-1-56072-726-2. Dewey:797.2/1/082092273 B. LCCN:2001-267948.
Audience: **g,l,u,f.**

Goldstein, Mel & Tanner, Dave **GV837.3.G65 1999**
Swimming Past 50. Trade Paper. Human Kinetics Publishers. Champaign, IL. 1999. 216p. Ageless Athlete Ser. ISBN:0-88011-907-1, ISBN13: 978-0-88011-907-8. Dewey:797.2/1/0846. LCCN:99-012569.
Audience: **l,u.**

Hannula, Dick & Thornton, Nort (Editors) **GV837.65.S95 2001**
The Swim Coaching Bible. Trade Paper. Human Kinetics Publishers. Champaign, IL. 2001. 376p. ISBN:0-7360-3646-6, ISBN13: 978-0-7360-3646-7. Dewey:797.2/1. LCCN:00-054241.
Audience: **g,l,u,f.**

Maglischo, Ernest W. **GV838.67.T73M33 2003**
Swimming Fastest. Ed. 3. Trade Cloth. Human Kinetics Publishers. Champaign, IL. 2003. 80p. ISBN:0-7360-3180-4, ISBN13: 978-0-7360-3180-6. Dewey:797.2/1. LCCN:2002-008867.
Audience: **l,u.**

Pieroth, Doris Hinson **GV722 1932.P54 1996**
Their Day in the Sun: Women of the 1932 Olympics. Trade Paper. University of Washington Press. Seattle, WA. 1996. 208p.

Samuel and Althea Stroum Bks. ISBN:0-295-97554-7, ISBN13: 978-0-295-97554-2. Dewey:796.48. LCCN:96-023104.
Audience: **l,u.** *Choice, 1997.*

Whitten, Phillip **GV837.W55 1994**
The Complete Book of Swimming. UK-Trade Paper. Random House, Inc. New York, NY. 1994. 400p. ISBN:0-679-74667-6, ISBN13: 978-0-679-74667-6. Dewey:797.2/1. LCCN:92-056805.
Audience: **g,l,u,f.** *Choice, 1995.*

Sports M-Z > Track and Field

American Sport Education Program (Contribution by) **GV1060.5**
Officiating Track and Field and Cross Country. Trade Cloth. Human Kinetics Publishers. Champaign, IL. 2005. 176p. ISBN:0-7360-5360-3, ISBN13: 978-0-7360-5360-0. Dewey:796.42. LCCN:2005-008058.
Audience: **l,u,f.**

Baker, William J. **GV697.O9B35 2006**
Jesse Owens: An American Life. Trade Paper. University of Illinois Press. Champaign, IL. 2006. 304p. Sport and Society Ser. ISBN:0-252-07369-X, ISBN13: 978-0-252-07369-4. Dewey:796.42092 B. LCCN:2006-006960.
Audience: **g,l,u.** *Choice, 1987.*

Carr, Gerry **GV1060.5.C368 1999**
Fundamentals of Track and Field. Ed. 2. Trade Paper. Human Kinetics Publishers. Champaign, IL. 1999. 34p. ISBN:0-7360-0008-9, ISBN13: 978-0-7360-0008-6. Dewey:796.42. LCCN:98-052218.
Audience: **l,u.**

Crawford, Bill **GV697.T5.C73 2004**
All American: The Rise and Fall of Jim Thorpe. Trade Cloth. John Wiley & Sons, Inc. Hoboken, NJ. 2004. 288p. ISBN:0-471-55732-3, ISBN13: 978-0-471-55732-6. Dewey:796/.092 B. LCCN:2004-014376.
Audience: **g,l,u.**

Olson, Leonard T. **GV1060.5.O43 2001**
Masters Track and Field: A History. Trade Cloth. McFarland & Company, Incorporated Publishers. Jefferson, NC. 2000. 320p. ISBN:0-7864-0889-8, ISBN13: 978-0-7864-0889-4. Dewey:796.42. LCCN:00-42162.
Audience: **l,u.**

Tricard, Louise Mead **GV1060.8.T75 1996**
American women's track and field:a history, 1895 through 1980. McFarland. 1996. ISBN:0-7864-0219-9, ISBN13: 978-0-7864-0219-9.
Audience: **l,u,f.**

Sports M-Z > Volleyball

American Sport Education Program Staff (Contribution by) **GV1015.5.C63 2001**
Coaching Youth Volleyball. Ed. 3. Trade Paper. Human Kinetics Publishers. Champaign, IL. 2001. 176p. ISBN:0-7360-3796-9, ISBN13: 978-0-7360-3796-9. Dewey:796.325. LCCN:2001-016657.
Audience: **l,u,f.**

Couvillon, Arthur **GV1015.5.B43**
Sands of Time: The History of Beach Volleyball: 1895-1969. Perfect. Information Guides. Hermosa Beach, CA. 2002. 264p. ISBN:0-938329-48-0, ISBN13: 978-0-938329-48-0. Dewey:796.325. LCCN:2002-105899.
Audience: **g,l,u,f.**

Couvillon, Arthur **GV1015.5.B43**
Sands of Time: The History of Beach Volleyball: 1970-1989, 2. Perfect. Information Guides. Hermosa Beach, CA. 2003. 584p. ISBN:0-938329-47-2, ISBN13: 978-0-938329-47-3. Dewey:796.325. LCCN:2002-105899.
Audience: **g,l,u,f.**

Couvillon, Arthur **GV1015.5.B43**
Sands of Time: The History of Beach Volleyball: 1990-2004, Vol. 3. Perfect. Information Guides. Hermosa Beach, CA. 2004. 474p. ISBN:0-938329-79-0, ISBN13: 978-0-938329-79-4. Dewey:796.325. LCCN:2002-105899.
Audience: **g,l,u,f.**

Crisfield, Deborah **GV1015.4.W66C75 2002**
Winning Volleyball for Girls. Ed. 3. Trade Paper. Facts On File, Inc. New York, NY. 2002. 192p. Winning Sports for Girls Ser. ISBN:0-8160-4621-2, ISBN13: 978-0-8160-4621-8. Dewey:796.325. LCCN:2001-033473.
Audience: **g,l,u,f.** *Choice, 2002.*

Fraser, Stephen D. **GV1015.3.F73 1988**
Strategies for Competitive Volleyball. Cloth Text. Human Kinetics Publishers. Champaign, IL. 1988. 208p. ISBN:0-88011-304-9, ISBN13: 978-0-88011-304-5. Dewey:796.32/5. LCCN:87-031853.
Audience: **l,u,f.** *Choice, 1989.*

Kus, Sally **GV1015.5.C63K87 2004**
Coaching Volleyball Successfully. Ed. 2. Trade Paper. Human Kinetics Publishers. Champaign, IL. 2004. 224p. ISBN:0-7360-4037-4, ISBN13: 978-0-7360-4037-2. Dewey:796.325. LCCN:2003-027576.
Audience: **g,l,u,f.**

McGown, Carl, et al. **GV1015.5.C63M34 2001**
Coaching Volleyball: Building a Winning Team. Hilda Ann Fronske & Launa Moser (Authors). Trade Paper. Benjamin-Cummings Publishing Company. San Francisco, CA. 2000. 308p. ISBN:0-205-30958-5, ISBN13: 978-0-205-30958-0. Dewey:796.325. LCCN:00-032296.
Audience: **l,u.**

Shondell, Don & Raynaud, Cecil (Editors) **GV1015.5.C63V65 2002**
The Volleyball Coaching Bible. Trade Paper. Human Kinetics Publishers. Champaign, IL. 2002. 384p. ISBN:0-7360-3967-8, ISBN13: 978-0-7360-3967-3. Dewey:796.325. LCCN:2002-007964.
Audience: **l,u.**

Sports M-Z > Weight Lifting

Lindqvist, Sven **GV546.5**
Bench Press. Trade Paper. Granta. New York, NY. 2003. 176p. ISBN:1-86207-572-7, ISBN13: 978-1-86207-572-6. Dewey:613.7/13. LCCN:2003-427636.
Audience: **g,l,u,f.**

Sports M-Z > Wrestling

American Sport Education Program Staff **GV1196.3.C63 2002**
Coaching Youth Wrestling. Ed. 2. Trade Paper. Human Kinetics Publishers. Champaign, IL. 2001. 168p. ISBN:0-7360-4159-1, ISBN13: 978-0-7360-4159-1. Dewey:797.812. LCCN:2001-039617.
Audience: **l,u,f.**

Maynard, Kyle **GV1196.M38A3 2005**
No Excuses!: The True Story of a Congenital Amputee Who Became a Champion in Wrestling and in Life. Trade Cloth. Regnery Publishing, Incorporated, An Eagle Publishing Company. Washington, DC. 2005. 256p. ISBN:0-89526-011-5, ISBN13: 978-0-89526-011-6. Dewey:796.812/092 B. LCCN:2005-018554.
Audience: **g,l,u.**

Mysnyk, Mark, et al. **GV1195.M96 1994**
Winning Wrestling Moves. Barry Davis & Brooks Simpson (Authors). Trade Paper. Human Kinetics Publishers. Champaign, IL. 1994. 208p. ISBN:0-87322-482-5, ISBN13: 978-0-87322-482-6. Dewey:796.8/12. LCCN:93-042161.
Audience: **l,u.**

Oppliger, Patrice A. **GV1196.4**
Wrestling and Hyper-Masculinity. Paper Text. McFarland & Company, Incorporated Publishers. Jefferson, NC. 2003. 211p. ISBN:0-7864-1692-0, ISBN13: 978-0-7864-1692-9. Dewey:796.812. LCCN:2003-025328.
Audience: **u,f.** *Choice, 2004.*

Science of Sport

GV568
☐ Scholarly Sport Sites: A Subject Directory.
http://www.ucalgary.ca/lib-old/ssportsite/
Audience: **g,l,u,f.**

GV557
☐ Sport Science.
http://www.exploratorium.edu/sports/
Audience: **g,l,u,f.**

Baine, Celeste **TA157**
High Tech Hot Shots: Careers in Sports Engineering. Paper Text. National Society of Professional Engineers. Alexandria, VA. 2004. 144p. ISBN:0-915409-23-2, ISBN13: 978-0-915409-23-5. Dewey:620/.0023.
Audience: **g,l,u,f.**

Hughes, T., et al. **RC1220.T4 S36 1995**
Science and Racket Sports. T. Reilly & A. Lees (Authors). Paper over Boards. Routledge. New York, NY. 1994. 304p. ISBN:0-419-18500-3, ISBN13: 978-0-419-18500-0. Dewey:796.34015.
Audience: **u.**

Miah, Andy (Editor), et al. **GV706**
Sport Technology: History, Philosophy and Policy. Simon B. Eassom & Carl Mitcham (Editors). Trade Cloth. Elsevier Science & Technology Books. Saint Louis, MO. 2002. 482p. ISBN:0-7623-0880-X, ISBN13: 978-0-7623-0880-4. Dewey:796/.01.
Audience: **l,u,f.**

Phillips, John L. Jr. **TJ985.P46 1998**
The Bends: Compressed Air in the History of Science, Diving, and Engineering. Cloth over Boards. Yale University Press. Cumberland, RI. 1998. 272p. ISBN:0-300-07125-6, ISBN13: 978-0-300-07125-2. Dewey:621.5/1. LCCN:97-035206.
Audience: **l,u.** *Choice, 1998.*

Vanderbilt, Tom **HD9787.A2**
The Sneaker Book: Anatomy of an Industry and an Icon. Trade Paper. New Press, The. New York, NY. 1998. 192p. Bazaar Bks., Vol. I ISBN:1-56584-406-8, ISBN13: 978-1-56584-406-3. Dewey:338.4/768531.
Audience: **l,u.**

Science of Sport > Manufacture of Sporting Goods

Andrew, Susan **GV743 .W55 1998**
Winning: The Design of Sport. Trade Paper. Laurence King Publishing. London, 1999. 144p. ISBN:1-85669-152-7, ISBN13: 978-1-85669-152-9. Dewey:745.2.
Audience: **u.**

Ashare, Alan B. (Editor) **GV848.35**
Safety in Ice Hockey. Trade Cloth. American Society for Testing & Materials. West Conshohocken, PA. 2000. 329p. STP Ser., Vol. 1341 ISBN:0-8031-2488-0, ISBN13: 978-0-8031-2488-2. Dewey:796.96/2028/9. LCCN:89-035946.
Audience: **u.**

Burke, Edmund R. (Editor) **RC1220.C8B873 2003**
High-Tech Cycling. Ed. 2. Trade Paper. Human Kinetics Publishers. Champaign, IL. 2003. 328p. ISBN:0-7360-4507-4, ISBN13: 978-0-7360-4507-0. Dewey:612/.044. LCCN:2002-152619.
Audience: **g,l,u,f.**

Dodge, Pryor **TL400 .D644 1996**
The Bicycle. Trade Cloth. Editions Flammarion. Montreal, PQ. 2001. 224p. ISBN:2-08-013551-1, ISBN13: 978-2-08-013551-3. Dewey:629.2272. LCCN:96-084087.
Audience: **u.** *Choice, 1996.*

Kreighbaum, Ellen F. & Smith, Mark A. (Editors) **GV745.S68 1996**
Sports and Fitness Equipment Design. Cloth Text. Human Kinetics Publishers. Champaign, IL. 1995. 232p. ISBN:0-87322-695-X, ISBN13: 978-0-87322-695-0. Dewey:796/.028. LCCN:95-033993.
Audience: **u.**

Werner, Frank D. & Greig, Richard C. **GV976.W46 2000**
How Golf Clubs Really Work and How to Optimize Their Designs. Roger Ganem (Editor). Trade Paper. Origin, Inc. Jackson, WY. 2000. 183p. ISBN:0-9677625-0-2, ISBN13: 978-0-9677625-0-0. Dewey:688.7/6352/028/8. LCCN:99-097823.
Audience: **u.**

Science of Sport > Physics and Mathematics of Sport

GV877

☐ Baseball Reference.
http://www.baseball-reference.com/

Audience: **g,l,u,f.**

GV741

☐ Statistics in Sports a section of the American Statistical Association.
http://www.amstat.org/sections/sis/

Audience: **g,l,u,f.**

Albert, Jim, et al. **GV741.A694 2005**
Anthology of Statistics in Sports. Jay Bennett & James J. Cochran (Authors), American Statistical Association, Section on Statistics in Sports Staff (Contribution by). Trade Paper, Perfect. Society for Industrial & Applied Mathematics. Philadelphia, PA. 2005. 322p. ASA-SIAM Series on Statistics and Applied Probability ISBN:0-89871-587-3, ISBN13: 978-0-89871-587-3. Dewey:796/.021. LCCN:2005-042540.

Audience: **u.**

Anderson, Bryon D. **VK543.A53 2003**
The Physics of Sailing Explained. Trade Paper. Sheridan House, Inc. Dobbs Ferry, NY. 2003. 160p. ISBN:1-57409-170-0, ISBN13: 978-1-57409-170-0. Dewey:623.88/13. LCCN:2003-014297.

Audience: **g,l,u.** *Choice, 2004.*

Brody, Howard, et al. **QC21.3.B76 2002**
The Physics and Technology of Tennis. Rod Cross, Crawford Lindsey & Ron Waite (Authors). Trade Paper. USRSA. Vista, CA. 2004. 450p. ISBN:0-9722759-0-8, ISBN13: 978-0-9722759-0-3. Dewey:796.342/01/53. LCCN:2002-094432.

Audience: **u.** *Choice, 2004.*

De Mestre, Neville **QA862.P76 D38 1990**
The Mathematics of Projectiles in Sport. Chris Heyde, J. H. Loxton, W. D. Neumann, Charles Pearce, Phil Broadbridge, Michael Murray & Cheryl Praeger (Contribution by). Trade Paper. Cambridge University Press. New York, NY. 1990. 187p. Australian Mathematical Society Lecture Ser., No. 6 ISBN:0-521-39857-6, ISBN13: 978-0-521-39857-2. Dewey:531/.55. LCCN:90-193034.

Audience: **l,u.**

Gay, Timothy **GV959.G39 2005**
The Physics of Football: Discover the Science of Bone-Crunching Hits, Soaring Field Goals, and Awe-Inspiring Passes. Trade Paper. HarperCollins Publishers. New York, NY. 2005. 304p. ISBN:0-06-082634-7, ISBN13: 978-0-06-082634-5. Dewey:796.332/03. LCCN:2005-046284.

Audience: **l,u.**

Haché, Alain **QC28.H23 2002**
The Physics of Hockey. Trade Cloth. Johns Hopkins University Press. Baltimore, MD. 2002. 200p. ISBN:0-8018-7071-2, ISBN13: 978-0-8018-7071-2. Dewey:530. LCCN:2001-008643.

Audience: **l,u.** *Choice, 2003.*

Jorgensen, Theodore P. **QC26.J67 1999**
The Physics of Golf. Ed. 2. Trade Paper. Springer. New York, NY. 1999. XII, 189p. ISBN:0-387-98691-X, ISBN13: 978-0-387-98691-3. Dewey:796.352. LCCN:98-032112.

Audience: **u.** *Choice, 1994.*

Lind, David & Sanders, Scott Patrick **QC26.L56 2003**
The Physics of Skiing: Skiing at the Triple Point. Ed. 2. Trade Cloth. Springer. New York, NY. 2004. XVII, 266p. ISBN:0-387-00722-9, ISBN13: 978-0-387-00722-9. Dewey:796.93/01/531. LCCN:2003-044589.

Audience: **l,u.** *Choice, 2004.*

Sadovskii, L. E. & Sadovskii, A. L. **GV706.8.S2313 1993**
Mathematics and Sports. S. Makar-Limanov (Translator). Trade Paper. American Mathematical Society. Providence, RI. 1993. 152p. Mathematical World Ser., Vol. 3 ISBN:0-8218-9500-1, ISBN13: 978-0-8218-9500-9. Dewey:796/.02. LCCN:93-023024.

Audience: **u,f.**

Tabachnikov, Serge **QA462.2.G34T33 2005**
Geometry and Billiards. Trade Paper. American Mathematical Society. Providence, RI. 2005. 176p. Student Mathematical Library, Vol. 30 ISBN:0-8218-3919-5, ISBN13: 978-0-8218-3919-5. Dewey:516. LCCN:2005-048181.

Audience: **u.**

Watts, Robert G. & Bahill, A. Terry **QC26.W38 2000**
Keep Your Eye on the Ball: Curve Balls, Knuckleballs, and Fallacies of Baseball. Ed. 2. Trade Paper. W. H. Freeman & Company. New York, NY. 2000. 240p. ISBN:0-7167-3717-5, ISBN13: 978-0-7167-3717-9. Dewey:796.3570153. LCCN:99-059352.

Audience: **u.**

Wesson, John **QC26**
The Science of Soccer. Perfect. Institute of Physics Publishing. Philadelphia, PA. 2002. 216p. ISBN:0-7503-0813-3, ISBN13: 978-0-7503-0813-7. Dewey:796.334.

Audience: **u.**

Zumerchik, John **GV967**
Newton on the Tee: A Good Walk Through the Science of Golf. Trade Cloth. Simon & Schuster. New York, NY. 2002. 256p. ISBN:0-7432-1214-2, ISBN13: 978-0-7432-1214-4. Dewey:796.3523. LCCN:2003-266828.

Audience: **u.**

Science of Sport > Other Scientific Factors in Sport

Ashare, Alan B. (Editor) **GV848.35**
Safety in Ice Hockey. Trade Cloth. American Society for Testing & Materials. West Conshohocken, PA. 2000. 329p. STP Ser., Vol. 1341 ISBN:0-8031-2488-0, ISBN13: 978-0-8031-2488-2. Dewey:796.96/2028/9. LCCN:89-035946.

Audience: **u.**

Burke, Edmund R. (Editor) **RC1220.C8B873 2003**
High-Tech Cycling. Ed. 2. Trade Paper. Human Kinetics Publishers. Champaign, IL. 2003. 328p. ISBN:0-7360-4507-4, ISBN13: 978-0-7360-4507-0. Dewey:612/.044. LCCN:2002-152619.

Audience: **g,l,u,f.**

Easterling, K E
Advanced Materials in Sports Equipment. Chapman & Hall. 1992. ISBN:0-412-40120-7, ISBN13: 978-0-412-40120-6.

Audience: **u.**

Hung, George K. & Pallis, Jani Macari (Editors) **RC1235.B56 2004**
Biomedical Engineering Principles in Sports. Trade Cloth. Springer. New York, NY. 2004. 528p. Bioengineering, Mechanics, and Materials Ser. ISBN:0-306-48477-3, ISBN13: 978-0-306-48477-3. Dewey:612/.044. LCCN:2004-043510.
Audience: **u,f.**

Kreighbaum, Ellen F. & Smith, Mark A. (Editors) **GV745.S68 1996**
Sports and Fitness Equipment Design. Cloth Text. Human Kinetics Publishers. Champaign, IL. 1995. 232p. ISBN:0-87322-695-X, ISBN13: 978-0-87322-695-0. Dewey:796/.028. LCCN:95-033993.
Audience: **u.**

Miah, Andy **QH332**
Genetically Modified Athletes: The Ethical Implications of Genetic Technologies in Sport. Trade Paper. Routledge. New York, NY. 2004. 232p. Ethics and Sport Ser. ISBN:0-415-29880-6, ISBN13: 978-0-415-29880-3. Dewey:174/.9796. LCCN:2004-044269.
Audience: **l,u,f.**

Pira, Edward S. **GV975.P65 1997**
A Guide to Golf Course Irrigation System Design and Drainage. Trade Cloth. John Wiley & Sons, Inc. Hoboken, NJ. 2002. 448p. ISBN:1-57504-030-1, ISBN13: 978-1-57504-030-1. Dewey:796.352/06/8. LCCN:98-128801.
Audience: **u,f.**

Puhalla, Jim, et al. **GV413.P85 1999**
Sports Fields: A Manual for Design, Construction and Maintenance. Jeff Krans & Mike Goatley (Authors). Trade Cloth. John Wiley & Sons, Inc. Hoboken, NJ. 1999. 480p. ISBN:1-57504-070-0, ISBN13: 978-1-57504-070-7. Dewey:796/.06/8. LCCN:99-011902.
Audience: **u.**

Reilly, Tom & Williams, Mark (Editors) **GV943.S36 2003**
Science and Soccer. Ed. 2. Trade Paper. Routledge. New York, NY. 2003. 352p. ISBN:0-415-26232-1, ISBN13: 978-0-415-26232-3. Dewey:796.334. LCCN:2002-035842.
Audience: **l,u,f.** *Choice, 2004.*

Sachs, Paul D. & Luff, Richard T. **GV975.3.S33 2002**
Ecological Golf Course Management. Trade Cloth. John Wiley & Sons, Inc. Hoboken, NJ. 2002. 216p. ISBN:1-57504-154-5, ISBN13: 978-1-57504-154-4. Dewey:796.352/06/9. LCCN:2001-006101.
Audience: **u,f.**

Werner, Frank D. & Greig, Richard C. **GV976.W46 2000**
How Golf Clubs Really Work and How to Optimize Their Designs. Roger Ganem (Editor). Trade Paper. Origin, Inc. Jackson, WY. 2000. 183p. ISBN:0-9677625-0-2, ISBN13: 978-0-9677625-0-0. Dewey:688.7/6352/028/8. LCCN:99-097823.
Audience: **u.**

Exercise Science

GV557
☐ International Council of Sport Science and Physical Education.
http://www.icsspe.org/
Audience: **g,l,u,f.**

RC1211
☐ International Federation of Sports Medicine.
http://www.fims.org/
Audience: **l,u,f.**

RC1235
☐ International Society of Biomechanics in Sports.
http://www.twu.edu/biom/isbs/
Audience: **l,u,f.**

GV203
☐ National Athletic Trainers Association.
http://www.nata.org/
Audience: **g,l,u,f.**

GV568
☐ Scholarly Sport Sites: A Subject Directory.
http://www.ucalgary.ca/lib-old/ssportsite/
Audience: **g,l,u,f.**

GV741
☐ SPORTQuest.
http://www.sirc.ca/online_resources/sportquest.cfm
SIRC.
Audience: **g,l,u,f.**

GV557
☐ SPORTSCIENCE a peer-reviewed site for Sport Research.
http://www.sportsci.org/
Audience: **l,u,f.**

Exercise Science > General

RA564.85
☐ Melpomene Institute.
http://www.melpomene.org/
Audience: **g,l,u,f.**

GV711.5
☐ National Strength and Conditioning Association.
http://www.nsca-lift.org/
Audience: **g,l,u,f.**

Alter, Michael J. **QP310.S77A45 2004**
Science of Flexibility. Ed. 3. Trade Cloth. Human Kinetics Publishers. Champaign, IL. 2004. 368p. ISBN:0-7360-4898-7, ISBN13: 978-0-7360-4898-9. Dewey:612.7/6. LCCN:2003-026043.
Audience: **f.**

American College of Sports Medicine **RM725.A48 2005**
ACSM's Guidelines for Exercise Testing and Prescription. Ed.

7. Spiral. Lippincott Williams & Wilkins. Philadelphia, PA. 2005. 366p. ISBN:0-7817-4506-3, ISBN13: 978-0-7817-4506-2. Dewey:615.8/2. LCCN:2004-057756.

Audience: **l,u,f.**

American College of Sports Medicine Staff **GV481.A322 2002**
ACSM Fitness Book: A Proven Step-by-Step Program from the Experts. Ed. 3. Arnold Schwarzengger (Foreword by). Trade Paper. Human Kinetics Publishers. Champaign, IL. 2003. 184p. ISBN:0-7360-4406-X, ISBN13: 978-0-7360-4406-6. Dewey:613.7/1. LCCN:2002-008864.

Audience: **g,l,u.**

Benjamin, Patricia J. & Lamp, Scott P. **RM721.B476 2005**
Understanding Sports Massage. Ed. 2. Trade Paper. Human Kinetics Publishers. Champaign, IL. 2004. 168p. ISBN:0-7360-5457-X, ISBN13: 978-0-7360-5457-7. Dewey:615.8/22/088796. LCCN:2004-019212.

Audience: **l,u.**

Berryman, Jack W. & Park, Roberta J. (Editors) **RC1210.S638 1992**
Sport and Exercise Science: Essays in the History of Sports Medicine. Trade Paper. University of Illinois Press. Champaign, IL. 1992. 392p. Sport and Society Ser. ISBN:0-252-06242-6, ISBN13: 978-0-252-06242-1. Dewey:617.1/027/09. LCCN:91-027220.

Audience: **u,f.** *Choice, 1993.*

Burton, Allen W. & Miller, Daryl E. **QP303.B87 1998**
Movement Skill Assessment. Trade Cloth. Human Kinetics Publishers. Champaign, IL. 1997. 416p. ISBN:0-87322-975-4, ISBN13: 978-0-87322-975-3. Dewey:612.7/6/0287. LCCN:97-021938.

Audience: **u,f.** *Choice, 1998.*

Carr, Gerry **QP303.C375 2004**
Sports Mechanics for Coaches. Ed. 2. Trade Paper. Human Kinetics Publishers. Champaign, IL. 2004. 256p. ISBN:0-7360-3972-4, ISBN13: 978-0-7360-3972-7. Dewey:612/.044. LCCN:2003-007917.

Audience: **g,l,u,f.**

Drinkwater, Barbara L. **RC1218.W65W664 2000**
Women in Sport: Olympic Encyclopaedia of Sports Medicine. Trade Cloth. Blackwell Publishing, Inc. Malden, MA. 2000. 608p. Encyclopedia of Sports Medicine Ser., Vol. 8 ISBN:0-632-05084-5, ISBN13: 978-0-632-05084-0. Dewey:617.1/027/082. LCCN:99-057719.

Audience: **g,l,u,f.**

Hay, James G. **QP303**
The Biomechanics of Sports Techniques. Ed. 4. Cloth Text. Benjamin-Cummings Publishing Company. San Francisco, CA. 1993. 544p. ISBN:0-13-084534-5, ISBN13: 978-0-13-084534-4. Dewey:612/.76. LCCN:92-027506.

Audience: **g,l,u,f.**

Hoberman, John M. **RC1235.H63 2001**
Mortal Engines. Perfect. Blackburn Press, The. Caldwell, NJ. 2002. 374p. ISBN:1-930665-37-7, ISBN13: 978-1-930665-37-8. Dewey:617.1/027. LCCN:2001-093232.

Audience: **u,f.**

Hoffman, Shirl J. (Editor) **QP303.I53 2005**
Introduction to Kinesiology: Studying Physical Activity. Ed. 2. Trade Cloth. Human Kinetics Publishers. Champaign, IL. 2005. 616p. ISBN:0-7360-5589-4, ISBN13: 978-0-7360-5589-5. Dewey:612.7/6. LCCN:2004-014671.

Audience: **g,l.**

Housh, Terry J. & Housh, Dona J. (Editors) **QP301.I65 2000**
Introduction to Exercise Science. Trade Paper. Benjamin-Cummings Publishing Company. San Francisco, CA. 2000. 290p. ISBN:0-205-29168-6, ISBN13: 978-0-205-29168-7. Dewey:612/.044. LCCN:99-047827.

Audience: **l,f.** *Choice, 2000.*

Jenkins, Simon P.R. **QP303**
Sports Science Handbook: The Essential Guide to Kinesiology, Sport and Exercise Science. Trade Paper, Perfect. Multi Science Publishing Company Ltd. Brentwood, 2005. 400p. ISBN:0-906522-37-4, ISBN13: 978-0-906522-37-0. Dewey:613.703.

Audience: **g,l,u,f.**

Jenkins, Simon P.R. **QP303**
Sports Science Handbook: The Essential Guide to Kinesiology, Sport and Exercise Science. Trade Paper, Perfect. Multi Science Publishing Company Ltd. Brentwood, 2005. 400p. ISBN:0-906522-36-6, ISBN13: 978-0-906522-36-3. Dewey:613.703.

Audience: **g,l,u,f.**

Kent, Michael **RC1206.O94 1998**
The Oxford Dictionary of Sports Science and Medicine. Ed. 2. Trade Cloth. Oxford University Press, Inc. New York, NY. 1998. 582p. ISBN:0-19-262845-3, ISBN13: 978-0-19-262845-9. Dewey:617.1/027/03. LCCN:97-041377.

Audience: **g,l,u,f.**

Knudson, Duane V. & Morrison, Craig S. **QP303.K59 2002**
Qualitative Analysis of Human Movement. Ed. 2. Trade Cloth, CD-ROM. Human Kinetics Publishers. Champaign, IL. 2002. 264p. ISBN:0-7360-3462-5, ISBN13: 978-0-7360-3462-3. Dewey:612.7/6. LCCN:2001-051833.

Audience: **u,f.**

Latash, Mark L. & Zatsiorsky, Vladimir M. (Editors) **QP301.L358 2001**
Classics in Movement Science. Trade Cloth. Human Kinetics Publishers. Champaign, IL. 2001. 464p. ISBN:0-7360-0028-3, ISBN13: 978-0-7360-0028-4. Dewey:612.7/6. LCCN:00-053857.

Audience: **u,f.**

Massengale, John & Swanson, Richard A. (Editors) **GV223.H57 1997**
The History of Exercise and Sport Science. Trade Cloth. Human Kinetics Publishers. Champaign, IL. 1996. 488p. ISBN:0-87322-524-4, ISBN13: 978-0-87322-524-3. Dewey:613.7/1/071173. LCCN:96-010555.

Audience: **g,l,u,f.** *Choice, 1997.*

McNamee, Mike (Editor) **GV558.P45 2005**
Philosophy of Sport and Exercise Science: Critical Perspectives on Scientific Method and Enquiry in Sport, Exercise and Health. Paper over Boards. Routledge. New York, NY. 2005. 256p.

ISBN:0-415-30016-9, ISBN13: 978-0-415-30016-2. Dewey:796/.01. LCCN:2004-050995.
Audience: **l,u,f.**

Rose, Debra J. & Christina, Robert W. **QP301.R65 2006**
A Multilevel Approach to the Study of Motor Control and Learning. Ed. 2. Trade Cloth. Benjamin-Cummings Publishing Company. San Francisco, CA. 2005. 464p. ISBN:0-8053-6031-X, ISBN13: 978-0-8053-6031-8. Dewey:612.8/11. LCCN:2005-006531.
Audience: **u,f.**

Rush, Anne Kent **RA781.63.R873 2005**
The Way of Stretching: Flexibility for Body and Mind. Trade Paper. Little Brown & Company. New York, NY. 2005. 176p. ISBN:0-316-17231-6, ISBN13: 978-0-316-17231-8. Dewey:613.7/1. LCCN:2005-005740.
Audience: **g,l,u,f.**

Tipton, Charles M. (Editor) **QP301.E975 2003**
Exercise Physiology: People and Ideas. Trade Cloth. Oxford University Press, Inc. New York, NY. 2003. 528p. People and Ideas Ser. ISBN:0-19-512527-4, ISBN13: 978-0-19-512527-6. Dewey:612/.044. LCCN:2002-029293.
Audience: **u,f.** *Choice, 2004.*

Williams, Craig A. & James, David V. B. **GV558.W55 2001**
Science for Exercise and Sport. Trade Paper. Routledge. New York, NY. 2001. 192p. ISBN:0-419-25170-7, ISBN13: 978-0-419-25170-5. Dewey:502/.4/796. LCCN:00-042484.
Audience: **l,u.**

Williams, Mark (Editor), et al. **GV706.8**
Skill Acquisition in Sport: Research, Theory and Practice. Nikki Hodges, Mark Scott & Mike Court (Editors). Trade Paper. Routledge. New York, NY. 2004. 464p. ISBN:0-415-27075-8, ISBN13: 978-0-415-27075-5. Dewey:796/.01. LCCN:2003-058657.
Audience: **u,f.**

Exercise Science > Exercise Physiology

Abernethy, Bruce, et al. **QP303.B586 2005**
The Biophysical Foundations of Human Movement ent, Vol. 2. Ed. 2. Stephanie J. Hanrahan, Vaughan Kippers, Laurel T. Mackinnon & Marcus G. Pandy (Authors). Trade Paper. Human Kinetics Publishers. Champaign, IL. 2004. 376p. ISBN:0-7360-4276-8, ISBN13: 978-0-7360-4276-5. Dewey:612.7/6. LCCN:2004-008595.
Audience: **g,l,u,f.**

Armstrong, Lawrence E. **RC1238.A75 2000**
Performing in Extreme Environments: Training and Working in Intense Heat, Frigid Cold, under Water, High Altitude, Air Pollution. Trade Paper. Human Kinetics Publishers. Champaign, IL. 1999. 344p. ISBN:0-88011-837-7, ISBN13: 978-0-88011-837-8. Dewey:612/.044. LCCN:99-038795.
Audience: **u,f.**

Bahrke, Michael S. & Yesalis, Charles E. **RC1230.B347 2002**
Performance-Enhancing Substances in Sport and Exercise. Trade Cloth. Human Kinetics Publishers. Champaign, IL. 2002. 384p. ISBN:0-7360-3679-2, ISBN13: 978-0-7360-3679-5. Dewey:362.29/088/796. LCCN:2002-017199.
Audience: **g,l,u,f.**

Bar-Or, Oded (Editor), et al. **RC1218.C45C45 1996**
The Child and Adolescent Athlete. IOC Medical Commission Staff & International Federation of Sports Medicine Staff (Editors). Trade Cloth. Blackwell Publishing, Inc. Malden, MA. 1995. 720p. Encyclopedia of Sports Medicine Ser., Vol. 6 ISBN:0-86542-904-9, ISBN13: 978-0-86542-904-8. Dewey:617.1/027/083. LCCN:95-000182.
Audience: **g,l,u,f.**

Beim, Gloria & Winter, Ruth **RC1218.W65B456 2003**
The Female Athlete's Body: How to Prevent and Treat Sports Injuries in Women and Girls. Trade Paper. McGraw-Hill Companies, The. New York, NY. 2003. 272p. ISBN:0-07-141175-5, ISBN13: 978-0-07-141175-2. Dewey:617.1/027/082. LCCN:2002-041439.
Audience: **g,l,u,f.**

Cavanagh, Peter R. (Editor) **QP310.R85B56 1990**
Biomechanics of Distance Running. Cloth Text. Human Kinetics Publishers. Champaign, IL. 1990. 376p. ISBN:0-87322-268-7, ISBN13: 978-0-87322-268-6. Dewey:612/.044. LCCN:89-029302.
Audience: **u,f.** *Choice, 1990.*

Dinitiman, George & Ward, Bob **GV711.5.D56 2003**
Sports Speed. Ed. 3. Trade Paper. Human Kinetics Publishers. Champaign, IL. 2003. 28p. ISBN:0-7360-4649-6, ISBN13: 978-0-7360-4649-7. Dewey:613.7/07. LCCN:2003-008731.
Audience: **l,u,f.**

Docherty, David (Editor) **RJ133**
Measurement in Pediatric Exercise Science. Trade Cloth. Human Kinetics Publishers. Champaign, IL. 1995. 36p. ISBN:0-87322-960-6, ISBN13: 978-0-87322-960-9. Dewey:613.7/042/0287. LCCN:96-023786.
Audience: **u,f.** *Choice, 1996.*

Gleeson, Michael & Maughan, Ronald J. **QP301**
The Biochemical Basis of Sports Performance. Paper Text. Oxford University Press, Inc. New York, NY. 2004. 272p. ISBN:0-19-926924-6, ISBN13: 978-0-19-926924-2. Dewey:617.1/027. LCCN:2004-298454.
Audience: **l,u,f.**

Houston, Michael E. **QP514.2.H68 2001**
Biochemistry Primer for Exercise Science. Ed. 2. Trade Paper. Human Kinetics Publishers. Champaign, IL. 2001. 216p. ISBN:0-7360-3644-X, ISBN13: 978-0-7360-3644-3. Dewey:612/.044. LCCN:00-052983.
Audience: **l,f.** *Choice, 1996.*

Komi, Paavo V. (Editor) **RC1235.S76 2002**
Strength and Power in Sport, Vol. III. Ed. 2. IOC Medical Commission Staff & International Federation of Sports Medicine Staff (Contribution by). Trade Cloth. Blackwell Publishing, Inc. Malden, MA. 2002. 544p. The Encyclopaedia of Sports

Medicine Ser., Vol. 3 ISBN:0-632-05911-7, ISBN13: 978-0-632-05911-9. Dewey:612/.044. LCCN:2002-005028.
Audience: **g,l,u,f.**

Kraemer, William J. **GV546**
Strength Training for Sport. Trade Paper. Blackwell Publishing, Inc. Malden, MA. 2001. 192p. Handbooks of Sports Medicine and Science ISBN:0-632-05568-5, ISBN13: 978-0-632-05568-5. Dewey:613.7/13. LCCN:2001-025536.
Audience: **g,l,u,f.**

Kreider, Richard B. (Editor), et al. **RC1235.O94 1998**
Overtraining in Sport. Andrew C. Fry & Mary L. O'Toole (Editors). Trade Cloth. Human Kinetics Publishers. Champaign, IL. 1997. 416p. ISBN:0-88011-563-7, ISBN13: 978-0-88011-563-6. Dewey:617.1/027. LCCN:97-031205.
Audience: **l,u,f.** *Choice, 1998.*

Lox, Curt, et al. **GV481.2.L69 2003**
The Psychology of Exercise: Integrating Theory and Practice. Kathleen Anne Martin & Steven J. Petruzzello (Authors). Trade Cloth. Holcomb Hathaway, Inc. Scottsdale, AZ. 2003. xiv, 354p. ISBN:1-890871-47-8, ISBN13: 978-1-890871-47-5. Dewey:613.7/1019. LCCN:2002-191347.
Audience: **l,u.** *Choice, 2003.*

Maud, Peter J. & Foster, Carl (Editors) **QP301.P57 2006**
Physiological Assessment of Human Fitness. Ed. 2. Trade Cloth. Human Kinetics Publishers. Champaign, IL. 2005. 328p. ISBN:0-7360-4633-X, ISBN13: 978-0-7360-4633-6. Dewey:613.7/028/7. LCCN:2005-014253.
Audience: **l,u.** *Choice, 1995.*

Maud, Peter J. & Foster, Carl (Editors) **QP301.P57 1995**
Physiological Assessment of Human Fitness. Trade Cloth. Human Kinetics Publishers. Champaign, IL. 1995. 304p. ISBN:0-87322-776-X, ISBN13: 978-0-87322-776-6. Dewey:613.7/028/7. LCCN:94-040072.
Audience: **l,u,f.** *Choice, 1995.*

McArdle **QP301.M375 2006**
Exercise Physiology: Energy, Nutrition, and Human Performance. Ed. 6. Trade Cloth. Lippincott Williams & Wilkins. Philadelphia, PA. 2006. 1184p. ISBN:0-7817-4990-5, ISBN13: 978-0-7817-4990-9. Dewey:612/.044. LCCN:2005-029306.
Audience: **l,u,f.**

Miah, Andy **QH332**
Genetically Modified Athletes: The Ethical Implications of Genetic Technologies in Sport. Trade Paper. Routledge. New York, NY. 2004. 232p. Ethics and Sport Ser. ISBN:0-415-29880-6, ISBN13: 978-0-415-29880-3. Dewey:174/.9796. LCCN:2004-044269.
Audience: **l,u,f.**

Noakes, Timothy D. **GV1061.N6 2002**
Lore of Running. Ed. 4. Trade Paper. Human Kinetics Publishers. Champaign, IL. 2002. 944p. ISBN:0-87322-959-2, ISBN13: 978-0-87322-959-3. Dewey:796.42. LCCN:2002-003702.
Audience: **l,u,f.**

Pluim, Babette & Safran, Marc **RC1200.T4P58 2004**
From Breakpoint to Advantage: A Practical Guide to Optimal Tennis Health and Performance. Trade Paper. USRSA. Vista, CA. 2004. 352p. ISBN:0-9722759-1-6, ISBN13: 978-0-9722759-1-0. Dewey:796.342. LCCN:2004-093133.
Audience: **g,l,u,f.** *Choice, 2005.*

Radak, Zsolt **RA781.F683 2000**
Free Radicals in Exercise and Aging. Trade Cloth. Human Kinetics Publishers. Champaign, IL. 2000. 28p. ISBN:0-88011-881-4, ISBN13: 978-0-88011-881-1. Dewey:612/.015. LCCN:00-044938.
Audience: **u.** *Choice, 2001.*

Robergs, Robert A. & Keteyian, Steven J. **QP301.R5473 2002**
Fundamentals of Exercise Physiology: For Fitness, Performance, and Health. Ed. 2. Paper Text. McGraw-Hill Companies, The. New York, NY. 2002. 512p. ISBN:0-07-246215-9, ISBN13: 978-0-07-246215-9. Dewey:612/.044. LCCN:2002-019682.
Audience: **l,f.**

Rogol, Alan D. **QP187.3.E93E53 2005**
The Endocrine System in Sports and Exercise, Vol. XI. William J. Kraemer (Editor). Trade Cloth. Blackwell Publishing, Inc. Malden, MA. 2005. 648p. The Encyclopaedia of Sports Medicine Ser., Vol. 11 ISBN:1-4051-3017-2, ISBN13: 978-1-4051-3017-2. Dewey:612.4. LCCN:2004-026395.
Audience: **g,l,u,f.**

Rowland, Thomas W. **RJ133.R679 2004**
Children's Exercise Physiology, Vol. 2. Ed. 2. Perfect. Human Kinetics Publishers. Champaign, IL. 2004. 297p. ISBN:0-7360-5144-9, ISBN13: 978-0-7360-5144-6. Dewey:612/.044/083. LCCN:40-007400.
Audience: **l,u,f.**

Shepard, Roy J. & Astrand, Per-Olof (Editors) **RC1220.E53E53 2000**
Endurance in Sport. Ed. 2. Trade Cloth. Blackwell Publishing, Inc. Malden, MA. 2000. 1008p. Encyclopedia of Sports Medicine Ser., Vol 2 ISBN:0-632-05348-8, ISBN13: 978-0-632-05348-3. Dewey:613.7/1. LCCN:99-038456.
Audience: **g,l,u,f.**

Speer, Kevin P. **RC1218.A33I55 2005**
Injury Prevention and Rehabilitation for Active Older Adults. Perfect, Paper over Boards. Human Kinetics Publishers. Champaign, IL. 2005. 237p. ISBN:0-7360-4031-5, ISBN13: 978-0-7360-4031-0. Dewey:617.1027. LCCN:2004-020851.
Audience: **u.** *Choice, 2005.*

Spirduso, Waneen W., et al. **QP86.S65 2005**
Physical Dimensions of Aging. Ed. 2. Karen L. Francis & Priscilla L. MacRae (Authors). Trade Cloth. Human Kinetics Publishers. Champaign, IL. 2004. 384p. ISBN:0-7360-3315-7, ISBN13: 978-0-7360-3315-2. Dewey:612.6/7. LCCN:2004-016531.
Audience: **u,f.** *Choice, 1996.*

Winter, David A. **QP303.W59 2004**
The Biomechanics and Motor Control of Human Movement. Ed. 3. Trade Cloth. John Wiley & Sons, Inc. Hoboken, NJ. 2004. 344p. ISBN:0-471-44989-X, ISBN13: 978-0-471-44989-8. Dewey:612/.76. LCCN:2004-047810.
Audience: **l,u.** *Choice, 1990.*

Exercise Science > Sport Nutrition

GV481

☐ American College of Sports Medicine.
http://www.acsm.org/
Audience: **g,l,u,f.**

Beals, Katherine A. **RC552.E18B43 2004**
Disordered Eating among Athletes: A Comprehensive Guide for Health Professionals. Perfect. Human Kinetics Publishers. Champaign, IL. 2004. 255p. ISBN:0-7360-4219-9, ISBN13: 978-0-7360-4219-2. Dewey:616.85/26. LCCN:30-260440.
Audience: **g,l,u,f.** *Choice, 2005.*

Bouchard, Claude (Editor) **RC628.P496 2000**
Physical Activity and Obesity. Trade Cloth. Human Kinetics Publishers. Champaign, IL. 2000. 48p. ISBN:0-88011-909-8, ISBN13: 978-0-88011-909-2. Dewey:616.3/98. LCCN:99-088071.
Audience: **u,f.** *Choice, 2001.*

Clark, Nancy **TX361.A8C54 2003**
Nancy Clark's Sports Nutrition Guidebook. Ed. 3. Trade Paper. Human Kinetics Publishers. Champaign, IL. 2003. 416p. ISBN:0-7360-4602-X, ISBN13: 978-0-7360-4602-2. Dewey:613.2/024/796. LCCN:2003-009149.
Audience: **g,l,u,f.**

Dorfman, Lisa **TX361.A8D67 2000**
The Vegetarian Sports Nutrition Guide: Peak Performance for Everyone from Beginners to Gold Medalists. Trade Paper. John Wiley & Sons, Inc. Hoboken, NJ. 1999. 270p. ISBN:0-471-34808-2, ISBN13: 978-0-471-34808-5. Dewey:613.2/024/796. LCCN:99-025294.
Audience: **g,l,u.**

Driskell, Judy A. & Wolinsky, I. R. A. (Editors) **QP771.S68 2005**
Sports Nutrition: Vitamins and Trace Elements. Ed. 2. Paper over Boards. Taylor & Francis Group. Philadelphia, PA. 2005. 340p. Nutrition in Exercise and Sport Ser. ISBN:0-8493-3022-X, ISBN13: 978-0-8493-3022-3. Dewey:613.2/86. LCCN:2005-048557.
Audience: **g,l,u,f.**

Eberle, Suzanne **TX361.A8E39 2000**
Endurance Sports Nutrition: Eating Plans for Optimal Training, Racing and Recovery. Trade Paper. Human Kinetics Publishers. Champaign, IL. 2000. 296p. ISBN:0-7360-0143-3, ISBN13: 978-0-7360-0143-4. Dewey:613.2/024/796. LCCN:00-025081.
Audience: **g,l,u,f.** *Choice, 2001.*

Hansen, Jorn & Nielsen, Niels Kayser (Editors) **GV706.5.S7397 2000**
Sports, Body and Health. Trade Paper. Syddansk Universitetsforlag/University Press of Southern Denmark. Odense M, 2000. 165p. ISBN:87-7838-474-5, ISBN13: 978-87-7838-474-4. Dewey:306.483. LCCN:00-465352.
Audience: **l,u,f.**

Jeukendrup, Asker & Gleeson, Michael **TX361.A8J48 2004**
Sport Nutrition: An Introduction to Energy Production and Performance. Trade Paper. Human Kinetics Publishers. Champaign, IL. 2004. 424p. ISBN:0-7360-3404-8, ISBN13: 978-0-7360-3404-3. Dewey:613.2/024/796. LCCN:2004-005192.
Audience: **g,l,u,f.**

Maughan, Ron **TX361.A8F64 2004**
Food, Nutrition and Sports Performance II: The IOC Consensus Conference on Sports Nutrition. Paper over Boards. Routledge. New York, NY. 2004. 256p. ISBN:0-415-33906-5, ISBN13: 978-0-415-33906-3. Dewey:613.2/088/796. LCCN:2004-040964.
Audience: **u,f.**

Maughan, Ronald J. **QP141.N793 2000**
Nutrition in Sport. Trade Cloth. Blackwell Publishing, Inc. Malden, MA. 2000. 704p. Encyclopedia of Sports Medicine Ser., Vol. 7 ISBN:0-632-05094-2, ISBN13: 978-0-632-05094-9. Dewey:616.3/9/0088796. LCCN:99-012066.
Audience: **u,f.**

McArdle, William D., et al. **TX361.A8M38 2004**
Sports and Exercise Nutrition. Ed. 2. Frank I. Katch & Victor L. Katch (Authors). Trade Cloth, CD-ROM. Lippincott Williams & Wilkins. Philadelphia, PA. 2005. 619p. ISBN:0-7817-4993-X, ISBN13: 978-0-7817-4993-0. Dewey:613.2/024/796. LCCN:2004-048934.
Audience: **l,u,f.**

Williams, Melvin H. **QP141.W514 2005**
Nutrition for Health, Fitness and Sport. Ed. 7. Paper Text. McGraw-Hill Higher Education. Burr Ridge, IL. 2004. 560p. ISBN:0-07-244170-4, ISBN13: 978-0-07-244170-3. Dewey:613.2. LCCN:2003-019720.
Audience: **g,l,u.**

Exercise Science > Sport Psychology

GV706.4

☐ North American Society for Psychology of Sport and Physical Activity.
http://www.naspspa.org/
Audience: **l,u,f.**

Andersen, Mark B. (Editor) **GV704.S64 2005**
Sport Psychology in Practice. Perfect, Trade Paper. Human Kinetics Publishers. Champaign, IL. 2005. 338p. ISBN:0-7360-3711-X, ISBN13: 978-0-7360-3711-2. Dewey:796.01. LCCN:2005-010554.
Audience: **g,l,u.**

Biddle, Stuart J. H. (Editor) **GV706.4.E87 1995**
European Perspectives on Exercise and Sport Psychology. Trade Cloth. Human Kinetics Publishers. Champaign, IL. 1995. 360p. ISBN:0-87322-826-X, ISBN13: 978-0-87322-826-8. Dewey:796/.01/094. LCCN:94-032258.
Audience: **u,f.** *Choice, 1996.*

Biddle, Stuart J. H. & Mutrie, Nanette **RA781.B486 2001**
Psychology of Physical Activity: Determinants, Well-Being and Interventions. Trade Paper. Routledge. New York, NY. 2001. 384p. ISBN:0-415-23526-X, ISBN13: 978-0-415-23526-6. Dewey:613.7/1/019. LCCN:00-062753.
Audience: **g,l,u,f.**

Buckworth, Janet & Dishman, Rodney **RA781.B83 2001**
Exercise Psychology. Trade Cloth. Human Kinetics Publishers. Champaign, IL. 2002. 344p. ISBN:0-7360-0078-X, ISBN13: 978-0-7360-0078-9. Dewey:613.7/1. LCCN:2001-039262.
Audience: **u,f.**

Butler, Richard (Editor) **GV706.4.S6816 1997**
Sports Psychology in Performance: Applying Principles to Practice. Trade Paper. Butterworth-Heinemann Ltd. Oxford, 1997. 288p. ISBN:0-7506-2437-X, ISBN13: 978-0-7506-2437-4. Dewey:796/.01/0941. LCCN:96-051509.
Audience: **u,f.**

Cashmore, Ellis **GV706.4.C39 2002**
Sport Psychology: The Key Concepts. Trade Paper. Routledge. New York, NY. 2002. 320p. Routledge Key Guides Ser. ISBN:0-415-25322-5, ISBN13: 978-0-415-25322-2. Dewey:796/.01. LCCN:2002-021325.
Audience: **g,l,u,f.**

Cox, Richard H. **GV706.4.C69 2007**
Sport Psychology: Concepts and Applications. Ed. 6. Paper Text. McGraw-Hill Companies, The. New York, NY. 2006. 544p. ISBN:0-07-297295-5, ISBN13: 978-0-07-297295-5. Dewey:796.01. LCCN:2005-058388.
Audience: **l,u.**

Evangelista, Nick **GV1147.E85 2000**
The Inner Game of Fencing: Excellence in Strategy and Spirit. Trade Paper. McGraw-Hill Companies, The. New York, NY. 2000. 288p. ISBN:1-57028-230-7, ISBN13: 978-1-57028-230-0. Dewey:796.86. LCCN:99-056253.
Audience: **g,l,u,f.**

Gill, Diane L. **GV706.4.G55 2000**
Psychological Dynamics of Sport and Exercise. Ed. 2. Trade Cloth. Human Kinetics Publishers. Champaign, IL. 2000. 368p. ISBN:0-87322-956-8, ISBN13: 978-0-87322-956-2. Dewey:796/.01. LCCN:99-057712.
Audience: **l,u,f.**

Hanin, Yuri L. **GV706.4.E459 2000**
Emotions in Sport. Trade Cloth. Human Kinetics Publishers. Champaign, IL. 1999. 48p. ISBN:0-88011-879-2, ISBN13: 978-0-88011-879-8. Dewey:796/.01. LCCN:99-016522.
Audience: **g,l,u.** *Choice, 2000.*

Hill, Karen Lee **GV706.4.H54 2001**
Frameworks for Sport Psychologists: Enhancing Sport Performance. Trade Paper. Human Kinetics Publishers. Champaign, IL. 2000. 224p. ISBN:0-7360-0014-3, ISBN13: 978-0-7360-0014-7. Dewey:796/.01. LCCN:00-038894.
Audience: **u,f.**

Jackson, Susan A. & Csikszentmihalyi, Mihaly **GV706.4.J33 1999**
Flow in Sports: The Keys to Optimal Experiences and Performances. Trade Paper. Human Kinetics Publishers. Champaign, IL. 1999. 192p. ISBN:0-88011-876-8, ISBN13: 978-0-88011-876-7. Dewey:796/.01. LCCN:99-012526.
Audience: **u,f.**

Jarvis, Matt **GV706.4.J37 1999**
Sport Psychology. UK-B Format Paperback. Routledge. New York, NY. 2000. 288p. Modular Psychology Ser. ISBN:0-415-20642-1, ISBN13: 978-0-415-20642-6. Dewey:796/.01. LCCN:99-012984.
Audience: **g,l,u.** *Choice, 2000.*

Kremer, John M. & Scully, Deirdre M. **GV706.4.K74 1994**
Psychology in Sport. Trade Paper. Taylor & Francis Group. Abingdon, 1994. 208p. Contemporary Psychology Ser. ISBN:0-7484-0182-2, ISBN13: 978-0-7484-0182-6. Dewey:796/.01. LCCN:93-046607.
Audience: **g,l.** *Choice, 1995.*

Lavallee, David, et al. **GV706.4.S6813 2003**
Sport Psychology: Contemporary Themes. John Kremer, Aidan P. Morgan & Mark Williams (Authors). Trade Paper. Palgrave Macmillan. New York, NY. 2004. 272p. ISBN:1-4039-0468-5, ISBN13: 978-1-4039-0468-3. Dewey:796/.01. LCCN:2003-058121.
Audience: **l,u,f.** *Choice, 2004.*

Lidor, Ronnie & Henschen, Keith P. (Editors) **GV706.4.P72 2003**
Psychology of Team Sports. Trade Paper. Fitness Information Technology, Inc. Morgantown, WV. 2001. 278p. ISBN:1-885693-32-X, ISBN13: 978-1-885693-32-7. Dewey:796.019. LCCN:2002-116144.
Audience: **l,u,f.**

Lidor, Ronnie, et al. **GV706.4**
The World Sport Psychology Sourcebook. Ed. 3. Tony Morris & Nicole Bardaxoglu (Authors). Trade Paper. Fitness Information Technology, Inc. Morgantown, WV. 2001. 240p. ISBN:1-885693-35-4, ISBN13: 978-1-885693-35-8. Dewey:796.01.
Audience: **g,l,u,f.**

Lox, Curt, et al. **GV481.2.L69 2003**
The Psychology of Exercise: Integrating Theory and Practice. Kathleen Anne Martin & Steven J. Petruzzello (Authors). Trade Cloth. Holcomb Hathaway, Inc. Scottsdale, AZ. 2003. xiv, 354p. ISBN:1-890871-47-8, ISBN13: 978-1-890871-47-5. Dewey:613.7/1019. LCCN:2002-191347.
Audience: **l,u.** *Choice, 2003.*

Moran, Aidan P. **GV706.4**
Sport and Exercise Psychology. UK-B Format Paperback. Routledge. New York, NY. 2004. 368p. ISBN:0-415-16809-0, ISBN13: 978-0-415-16809-0. Dewey:796/.01. LCCN:2003-017078.
Audience: **l,u,f.**

Murphy, Shane **GV706.4.S667 2004**
The Sports Psych Handbook. Trade Paper. Human Kinetics Publishers. Champaign, IL. 2004. 368p. ISBN:0-7360-4904-5, ISBN13: 978-0-7360-4904-7. Dewey:796.01. LCCN:2004-015224.
Audience: **g,l,u,f.**

Orlick, Terry **GV706.4.O73 2000**
In Pursuit of Excellence: How to Win in Sport and Life Through Mental Training. Ed. 3. Trade Paper. Human Kinetics Publishers. Champaign, IL. 2000. 248p. ISBN:0-7360-3186-3, ISBN13: 978-0-7360-3186-8. Dewey:796/.01. LCCN:00-024335.
Audience: **g,l.**

Silva, John M. & Stevens, Diane E. **GV706.4.P673 2002**
Psychological Foundations of Sport. Cloth Text. Benjamin-Cummings Publishing Company. San Francisco, CA. 2001. 560p. ISBN:0-205-33144-0, ISBN13: 978-0-205-33144-4. Dewey:796/.01. LCCN:00-052200.
Audience: **l,f.**

Singer, Robert N. (Editor), et al. **GV706.4.H37 2001**
[e] Handbook of Sport Psychology. Ed. 2. Heather Ann

Hausenblas & Christopher Janelle (Editors). E-Book. John Wiley & Sons, Inc. Hoboken, NJ. 2004. ISBN:0-471-43736-0, ISBN13: 978-0-471-43736-9. Dewey:796/.01.
Audience: **u,f.** *Choice, 2002.*

Tenenbaum, Gershon (Editor) **GV706.4 .P62 2001**
The Practice of Sport Psychology. Trade Paper. Fitness Information Technology, Inc. Morgantown, WV. 2001. 306p. ISBN:1-885693-30-3, ISBN13: 978-1-885693-30-3. Dewey:796.01. LCCN:01-126255.
Audience: **l,u.**

Van Raalte, Judy L. & Brewer, Britton W. (Editors) **GV706.4.E96 2002**
Exploring Sport and Exercise Psychology. Ed. 2. Trade Cloth. American Psychological Association. Washington, DC. 2002. xxiii, 561p. ISBN:1-55798-886-2, ISBN13: 978-1-55798-886-7. Dewey:796/.01. LCCN:2002-020856.
Audience: **l,u,f.** *Choice, 1997.*

Warren, Michelle P. & Shangold, Mona M. **RG207.W37 1997**
Sports Gynecology: Problems and Care of the Athletic Female. Trade Paper. Blackwell Publishing, Inc. Malden, MA. 1997. 192p. ISBN:0-86542-463-2, ISBN13: 978-0-86542-463-0. Dewey:618.1. LCCN:96-048787.
Audience: **g,l,u,f.**

Weinberg, Robert S. & Richardson, Peggy A. **GV735.W45**
Psychology of Officiating. Trade Paper. Human Kinetics Publishers. Champaign, IL. 1995. 192p. ISBN:0-87322-875-8, ISBN13: 978-0-87322-875-6. Dewey:796. LCCN:90-031893.
Audience: **u,f.** *Choice, 1990.*

Weiss, Maureen R. **GV706.4.D475 2004**
Developmental Sport and Exercise Psychology: A Lifespan Perspective. Trade Cloth. Fitness Information Technology, Inc. Morgantown, WV. 2004. 596p. ISBN:1-885693-36-2, ISBN13: 978-1-885693-36-5. Dewey:796/.01. LCCN:2003-108981.
Audience: **g,l,f.**

Wilmore, Jack H. & Costill, David L. **QT260**
Physiology of Sport and Exercise. Ed. 3. Trade Cloth. Human Kinetics Publishers. Champaign, IL. 2005. 744p. ISBN:0-7360-4489-2, ISBN13: 978-0-7360-4489-9. Dewey:612/.044.
Audience: **l,f.**

Exercise Science > Exercise Training

GV481

☐ American College of Sports Medicine.
http://www.acsm.org/
Audience: **g,l,u,f.**

GV711.5

☐ National Strength and Conditioning Association.
http://www.nsca-lift.org/
Audience: **g,l,u,f.**

Armstrong, Lawrence E. **RC1238.A75 2000**
Performing in Extreme Environments: Training and Working in Intense Heat, Frigid Cold, under Water, High Altitude, Air Pollution. Trade Paper. Human Kinetics Publishers. Champaign, IL. 1999. 344p. ISBN:0-88011-837-7, ISBN13: 978-0-88011-837-8. Dewey:612/.044. LCCN:99-038795.
Audience: **u,f.**

Baechle, Thomas R. & Earle, Roger W. **GV546.B33 1995**
Fitness Weight Training. Ed. 2. Trade Paper. Human Kinetics Publishers. Champaign, IL. 2005. 200p. ISBN:0-7360-5255-0, ISBN13: 978-0-7360-5255-9. Dewey:613.7/13. LCCN:2004-024500.
Audience: **g,l,u.**

Bar-Or, Oded (Editor), et al. **RC1218.C45C45 1996**
The Child and Adolescent Athlete. IOC Medical Commission Staff & International Federation of Sports Medicine Staff (Editors). Trade Cloth. Blackwell Publishing, Inc. Malden, MA. 1995. 720p. Encyclopedia of Sports Medicine Ser., Vol. 6 ISBN:0-86542-904-9, ISBN13: 978-0-86542-904-8. Dewey:617.1/027/083. LCCN:95-000182.
Audience: **g,l,u,f.**

Beim, Gloria & Winter, Ruth **RC1218.W65B456 2003**
The Female Athlete's Body: How to Prevent and Treat Sports Injuries in Women and Girls. Trade Paper. McGraw-Hill Companies, The. New York, NY. 2003. 272p. ISBN:0-07-141175-5, ISBN13: 978-0-07-141175-2. Dewey:617.1/027/082. LCCN:2002-041439.
Audience: **g,l,u,f.**

Bompa, Tudor O. & Cornacchia, Lorenzo J. **GV546.B55 1998**
Serious Strength Training. Trade Paper. Human Kinetics Publishers. Champaign, IL. 1998. 312p. ISBN:0-88011-834-2, ISBN13: 978-0-88011-834-7. Dewey:613.7/1. LCCN:98-012309.
Audience: **g,l,u.**

Bompa, Tudor & Carrera, Michael **GV546.B546 2005**
Periodization Training for Sports. Ed. 2. Trade Paper. Human Kinetics Publishers. Champaign, IL. 2005. 272p. ISBN:0-7360-5559-2, ISBN13: 978-0-7360-5559-8. Dewey:613.7/13. LCCN:2004-028232.
Audience: **l,u.**

Bosch, Frans (Author, Illustrator) **QP301 .B67 2005**
Running: Biomechanics and Exercise Physiology in Practice. Ronald Klomp (Author). Trade Paper. Elsevier - Health Sciences Division. Philadelphia, PA. 2004. 424p. ISBN:0-443-07441-0, ISBN13: 978-0-443-07441-7. Dewey:612.044.
Audience: **u,f.**

Boyle, Michael **GV711.5.B69 2003**
Functional Training for Sports. Trade Paper. Human Kinetics Publishers. Champaign, IL. 2003. 28p. ISBN:0-7360-4681-X, ISBN13: 978-0-7360-4681-7. Dewey:613.7/11. LCCN:2003-008763.
Audience: **g,l,u.**

Brehm, Barbara **GV481.2.B74 2004**
Successful Fitness Motivation Strategies. Trade Paper. Human Kinetics Publishers. Champaign, IL. 2004. 20p.

ISBN:0-7360-4593-7, ISBN13: 978-0-7360-4593-3. Dewey:613.7/1. LCCN:2004-002097.
Audience: **g,l,u.**

Cavanagh, Peter R. (Editor) **QP310.R85B56 1990**
Biomechanics of Distance Running. Cloth Text. Human Kinetics Publishers. Champaign, IL. 1990. 376p. ISBN:0-87322-268-7, ISBN13: 978-0-87322-268-6. Dewey:612/.044. LCCN:89-029302.
Audience: **u,f.** *Choice, 1990.*

Colwin, Cecil M. **GV836.4.C65 2002**
Breakthrough Swimming. Ed. 2. Trade Paper. Human Kinetics Publishers. Champaign, IL. 2002. 262p. ISBN:0-7360-3777-2, ISBN13: 978-0-7360-3777-8. Dewey:797.2/1/09. LCCN:2001-039994.
Audience: **g,l,u,f.**

Costill, David L., et al. **RC1220.S8C67 1991**
Swimming. Ernest W. Maglischo & Allen B. Richardson (Authors). Trade Paper. Blackwell Publishing, Inc. Malden, MA. 1991. 224p. Handbook of Sports Medicine and Science Ser. ISBN:0-632-03027-5, ISBN13: 978-0-632-03027-9. Dewey:612/.044. LCCN:91-019537.
Audience: **g,l,u,f.** *Choice, 1992.*

Dinitiman, George & Ward, Bob **GV711.5.D56 2003**
Sports Speed. Ed. 3. Trade Paper. Human Kinetics Publishers. Champaign, IL. 2003. 28p. ISBN:0-7360-4649-6, ISBN13: 978-0-7360-4649-7. Dewey:613.7/07. LCCN:2003-008731.
Audience: **l,u,f.**

Engel, Barbara T. (Editor) **RM931.H6**
Therapeutic Riding II Strategies for Rehabilitation. Paper Text. Barbara Engel Therapy Services. Durango, CO. 1997. 490p. ISBN:0-9633065-6-1, ISBN13: 978-0-9633065-6-2. Dewey:615.8/515.
Audience: **u,f.**

Fleck, Steven J. & Kraemer, William J. **GV505.F58 2003**
Designing Resistance Training Programs. Ed. 3. Trade Cloth. Human Kinetics Publishers. Champaign, IL. 2003. 392p. ISBN:0-7360-4257-1, ISBN13: 978-0-7360-4257-4. Dewey:613.7/1. LCCN:2003-008524.
Audience: **g,l,u.** *Choice, 1988.*

Gill, Diane L. **GV706.4.G55 2000**
Psychological Dynamics of Sport and Exercise. Ed. 2. Trade Cloth. Human Kinetics Publishers. Champaign, IL. 2000. 368p. ISBN:0-87322-956-8, ISBN13: 978-0-87322-956-2. Dewey:796/.01. LCCN:99-057712.
Audience: **l,u,f.**

Hansen, Jorn & Nielsen, Niels Kayser (Editors) **GV706.5.S7397 2000**
Sports, Body and Health. Trade Paper. Syddansk Universitetsforlag/University Press of Southern Denmark. Odense M, 2000. 165p. ISBN:87-7838-474-5, ISBN13: 978-87-7838-474-4. Dewey:306.483. LCCN:00-465352.
Audience: **l,u,f.**

Heyward, Vivian H. **GV436.H48 2002**
Advanced Fitness Assessment and Exercise Prescription. Ed. 4. Trade Cloth. Human Kinetics Publishers. Champaign, IL. 2005. 384p. ISBN:0-7360-4016-1, ISBN13: 978-0-7360-4016-7. Dewey:613.7. LCCN:2002-017210.
Audience: **l,u,f.** *Choice, 1998.*

Incledon, Lori **GV546.6.W64I63 2005**
Strength Training for Women. Trade Paper. Human Kinetics Publishers. Champaign, IL. 2004. 224p. ISBN:0-7360-5223-2, ISBN13: 978-0-7360-5223-8. Dewey:613.7/1/082. LCCN:2004-014047.
Audience: **l,u.**

Komi, Paavo V. (Editor) **RC1235.S76 2002**
Strength and Power in Sport, Vol. III. Ed. 2. IOC Medical Commission Staff & International Federation of Sports Medicine Staff (Contribution by). Trade Cloth. Blackwell Publishing, Inc. Malden, MA. 2002. 544p. The Encyclopaedia of Sports Medicine Ser., Vol. 3 ISBN:0-632-05911-7, ISBN13: 978-0-632-05911-9. Dewey:612/.044. LCCN:2002-005028.
Audience: **g,l,u,f.**

Kraemer, William J. **GV546**
Strength Training for Sport. Trade Paper. Blackwell Publishing, Inc. Malden, MA. 2001. 192p. Handbooks of Sports Medicine and Science ISBN:0-632-05568-5, ISBN13: 978-0-632-05568-5. Dewey:613.7/13. LCCN:2001-025536.
Audience: **g,l,u,f.**

Kreider, Richard B. (Editor), et al. **RC1235.O94 1998**
Overtraining in Sport. Andrew C. Fry & Mary L. O'Toole (Editors). Trade Cloth. Human Kinetics Publishers. Champaign, IL. 1997. 416p. ISBN:0-88011-563-7, ISBN13: 978-0-88011-563-6. Dewey:617.1/027. LCCN:97-031205.
Audience: **l,u,f.** *Choice, 1998.*

Luger, Dan & Pook, Paul **GV945.8**
Complete Conditioning for Rugby. Trade Paper. Human Kinetics Publishers. Champaign, IL. 2004. 264p. ISBN:0-7360-5210-0, ISBN13: 978-0-7360-5210-8. Dewey:796.333. LCCN:2003-023734.
Audience: **l,u.**

Maglischo, Ernest W. **GV838.67.T73M33 2003**
Swimming Fastest. Ed. 3. Trade Cloth. Human Kinetics Publishers. Champaign, IL. 2003. 80p. ISBN:0-7360-3180-4, ISBN13: 978-0-7360-3180-6. Dewey:797.2/1. LCCN:2002-008867.
Audience: **l,u.**

Micheli, Lyle J. & Jenkins, Mark **RC1220.R8M53 1996**
Healthy Runner's Handbook. Trade Paper. Human Kinetics Publishers. Champaign, IL. 1996. 264p. ISBN:0-88011-524-6, ISBN13: 978-0-88011-524-7. Dewey:613.7/172. LCCN:95-026222.
Audience: **g,l,u,f.**

Noakes, Timothy D. **GV1061.N6 2002**
Lore of Running. Ed. 4. Trade Paper. Human Kinetics Publishers. Champaign, IL. 2002. 944p. ISBN:0-87322-959-2, ISBN13: 978-0-87322-959-3. Dewey:796.42. LCCN:2002-003702.
Audience: **l,u,f.**

Pluim, Babette & Safran, Marc **RC1200.T4P58 2004**
From Breakpoint to Advantage: A Practical Guide to Optimal Tennis Health and Performance. Trade Paper. USRSA. Vista,

CA. 2004. 352p. ISBN:0-9722759-1-6, ISBN13: 978-0-9722759-1-0. Dewey:796.342. LCCN:2004-093133.
Audience: **g,l,u,f.** *Choice, 2005.*

Puretz, Susan, et al. **RA781.P84 1997**
The Woman's Guide to Peak Performance. Adelaide Haas & Donna Meltzer (Authors). Trade Paper. Celestial Arts Publishing Company. Berkeley, CA. 1998. 400p. ISBN:0-89087-841-2, ISBN13: 978-0-89087-841-5. Dewey:613.7/045. LCCN:97-042142.
Audience: **g,l,u.** *Choice, 1998.*

Reilly, Tom & Williams, Mark (Editors) **GV943.S36 2003**
Science and Soccer. Ed. 2. Trade Paper. Routledge. New York, NY. 2003. 352p. ISBN:0-415-26232-1, ISBN13: 978-0-415-26232-3. Dewey:796.334. LCCN:2002-035842.
Audience: **l,u,f.** *Choice, 2004.*

Rikli, Roberta E. & Jones, C. Jessie **RA781.R54 2001**
Senior Fitness Test Manual. Trade Paper. Human Kinetics Publishers. Champaign, IL. 2001. 176p. ISBN:0-7360-3356-4, ISBN13: 978-0-7360-3356-5. Dewey:613.7/0446/0287. LCCN:00-050575.
Audience: **l,u.** *Choice, 2002.*

Shepard, Roy J. & Astrand, Per-Olof (Editors) **RC1220.E53E53 2000**
Endurance in Sport. Ed. 2. Trade Cloth. Blackwell Publishing, Inc. Malden, MA. 2000. 1008p. Encyclopedia of Sports Medicine Ser., Vol 2 ISBN:0-632-05348-8, ISBN13: 978-0-632-05348-3. Dewey:613.7/1. LCCN:99-038456.
Audience: **g,l,u,f.**

Speer, Kevin P. **RC1218.A33I55 2005**
Injury Prevention and Rehabilitation for Active Older Adults. Perfect, Paper over Boards. Human Kinetics Publishers. Champaign, IL. 2005. 237p. ISBN:0-7360-4031-5, ISBN13: 978-0-7360-4031-0. Dewey:617.1027. LCCN:2004-020851.
Audience: **u.** *Choice, 2005.*

Spirduso, Waneen W., et al. **QP86.S65 2005**
Physical Dimensions of Aging. Ed. 2. Karen L. Francis & Priscilla L. MacRae (Authors). Trade Cloth. Human Kinetics Publishers. Champaign, IL. 2004. 384p. ISBN:0-7360-3315-7, ISBN13: 978-0-7360-3315-2. Dewey:612.6/7. LCCN:2004-016531.
Audience: **u,f.** *Choice, 1996.*

Yoke, Mary & Carol, Kennedy **RM725.Y645 2004**
Functional Exercise Progressions. Paper Text. Coaches Choice. Monterey, CA. 2003. 126p. ISBN:1-58518-998-7, ISBN13: 978-1-58518-998-4. Dewey:615.8/2. LCCN:2003-106969.
Audience: **u,f.**

Zatsiorsky, Vladimir M. (Editor) **RC1235.B476 2000**
Biomechanics in Sports: Performance Improvement and Injury Prevention. Trade Cloth. Blackwell Publishing, Inc. Malden, MA. 2000. 680p. Encyclopedia of Sports Medicine Ser., Vol. 9 ISBN:0-632-05392-5, ISBN13: 978-0-632-05392-6. Dewey:617.1/027. LCCN:99-054566.
Audience: **g,l,u,f.**

Zatsiorsky, Vladimir M. **GV711.5.Z38 1995**
Science and Practice of Strength Training. Trade Cloth. Human Kinetics Publishers. Champaign, IL. 1995. 256p. ISBN:0-87322-474-4, ISBN13: 978-0-87322-474-1. Dewey:613.7/11. LCCN:94-040135.
Audience: **u,f.** *Choice, 1995.*

Facilities and Structures

GV880
☐ Business of Baseball.
http://www.businessofbaseball.com/
Audience: **g,l,u,f.**

American College of Sports Medicine **GV429.A45 2006**
ACSM's Health/Fitness Facility Standards and Guidelines. Ed. 3. Trade Cloth. Human Kinetics Publishers. Champaign, IL. 2006. 216p. ISBN:0-7360-5153-8, ISBN13: 978-0-7360-5153-8. Dewey:613.7/1. LCCN:2005-033377.
Audience: **g,u,f.**

Ammon, Rob, et al. **GV401.A46 2004**
Sport Facility Management: Organizing Events and Mitigating Risks. Richard M. Southall & David A. Blair (Authors). Trade Cloth. Fitness Information Technology, Inc. Morgantown, WV. 2004. 256p. Sport Management Library ISBN:1-885693-39-7, ISBN13: 978-1-885693-39-6. Dewey:796/.069. LCCN:2003-108983.
Audience: **u,f.**

Broto, Carles & Mostaedi, Arian (Editors) **NA6860.B76 2005**
Architecture of Sports Facilities. Trade Cloth. Links Internacional. Barcelona, 2005. 240p. ISBN:84-934007-7-7, ISBN13: 978-84-934007-7-4. Dewey:725.827.
Audience: **u,f.**

Daly, Jim **GV182.3.D34 2000**
Recreation and Sport Planning and Design. Ed. 2. Trade Paper. Human Kinetics Publishers. Champaign, IL. 2000. 232p. ISBN:0-7360-0345-2, ISBN13: 978-0-7360-0345-2. Dewey:796/.06/94. LCCN:99-042475.
Audience: **u,f.**

Delaney, Kevin J. & Eckstein, Rick **GV413.D45 2003**
Public Dollars, Private Stadiums. Trade Paper. Rutgers University Press. Piscataway, NJ. 2004. 240p. ISBN:0-8135-3343-0, ISBN13: 978-0-8135-3343-8. Dewey:796/.06/8. LCCN:2003-005673.
Audience: **g,l,u,f.** *Choice, 2004.*

Dodson, Ronald G. **GV975.3.D63 2005**
Sustainable Golf Courses: A Guide to Environmental Stewardship. Arnold Palmer (Foreword by). Trade Cloth. John Wiley & Sons, Inc. Hoboken, NJ. 2005. 288p. ISBN:0-471-46547-X, ISBN13: 978-0-471-46547-8. Dewey:796.332/068. LCCN:2004-025916.
Audience: **u,f.**

Farmer, Peter J., et al. **GV415.F37 1996**
Sport Facility Planning and Management. Aaron L. Mulrooney & Rob Ammon Jr. (Authors). Trade Paper. Fitness Information

Technology, Inc. Morgantown, WV. 1996. 333p. ISBN:1-885693-05-2, ISBN13: 978-1-885693-05-1. Dewey:796/.06/9. LCCN:96-084609.

Audience: **u,f.**

Gallup, Joan Whaley **RA975.5.H4G34 1999**
Wellness Centers: A Guide for the Design Professional. Trade Cloth. John Wiley & Sons, Inc. Hoboken, NJ. 1999. 264p. Wiley Series in Healthcare and Senior Living Design, Vol. 7 ISBN:0-471-25337-5, ISBN13: 978-0-471-25337-2. Dewey:725/.5. LCCN:99-011574.

Audience: **u.**

Hensler, Kate **GV428.H46 1998**
Health Clubs: Architecture and Design. Trade Cloth. P B C International, Inc. Glen Cove, NY. 1998. 176p. ISBN:0-86636-643-1, ISBN13: 978-0-86636-643-4. Dewey:725/.85. LCCN:98-009645.

Audience: **u,f.**

Hurdzan, Michael **GV975.H76 1996**
Golf Course Architecture: Design, Construction and Restoration. Trade Cloth. John Wiley & Sons, Inc. Hoboken, NJ. 2002. 416p. ISBN:1-886947-01-5, ISBN13: 978-1-886947-01-6. Dewey:796.352/06/8. LCCN:96-210154.

Audience: **u,f.**

Pira, Edward S. **GV975.P65 1997**
A Guide to Golf Course Irrigation System Design and Drainage. Trade Cloth. John Wiley & Sons, Inc. Hoboken, NJ. 2002. 448p. ISBN:1-57504-030-1, ISBN13: 978-1-57504-030-1. Dewey:796.352/06/8. LCCN:98-128801.

Audience: **u,f.**

Puhalla, Jim, et al. **GV413.P85 1999**
Sports Fields: A Manual for Design, Construction and Maintenance. Jeff Krans & Mike Goatley (Authors). Trade Cloth. John Wiley & Sons, Inc. Hoboken, NJ. 1999. 480p. ISBN:1-57504-070-0, ISBN13: 978-1-57504-070-7. Dewey:796/.06/8. LCCN:99-011902.

Audience: **u.**

Rich, Wilbur (Editor) **GV429**
The Economics and Politics of Sports Facilities. Trade Cloth. Greenwood Publishing Group, Inc. Portsmouth, NH. 2000. 248p. ISBN:1-56720-317-5, ISBN13: 978-1-56720-317-2. Dewey:338.4/7796/06873. LCCN:99-056365.

Audience: **g,l,u,f.** *Choice, 2000.*

Sachs, Paul D. & Luff, Richard T. **GV975.3.S33 2002**
Ecological Golf Course Management. Trade Cloth. John Wiley & Sons, Inc. Hoboken, NJ. 2002. 216p. ISBN:1-57504-154-5, ISBN13: 978-1-57504-154-4. Dewey:796.352/06/9. LCCN:2001-006101.

Audience: **u,f.**

Taylor, Jeffrey H. (Editor) **GV182.3**
Design Standards for Recreation Facilities. Paper Text. DIANE Publishing Company. Collingdale, PA. 1998. 80p. ISBN:0-7881-7341-3, ISBN13: 978-0-7881-7341-7. Dewey:790.

Audience: **u,f.**

White, Bud & White, Charles B. **GV975.W45 2000**
Turf Managers' Handbook for Golf Course Construction, Renovation, and Grow-In. Trade Cloth. John Wiley & Sons, Inc. Hoboken, NJ. 2000. 328p. ISBN:1-57504-110-3, ISBN13: 978-1-57504-110-0. Dewey:796.352/06/8. LCCN:99-087983.

Audience: **u.**

Business of Sport

GV568

☐ Scholarly Sport Sites: A Subject Directory. http://www.ucalgary.ca/lib-old/ssportsite/

Audience: **g,l,u,f.**

HD9992.U5

Sports Market Place Directory 2005. Ed. 2. Trade Cloth, CD-ROM. Grey House Publishing. Millerton, NY. 2005. 1,800p. ISBN:1-59237-077-2, ISBN13: 978-1-59237-077-1. Dewey:381.456887.

Audience: **g,l,u,f.**

Gems, Gerald R. **GV950.G46 2000**
For Pride, Profit and Patriarchy: Football and the Incorporation of American Cultural Values. Trade Cloth. Scarecrow Press, Inc. Lanham, MD. 2000. 240p. American Sports History Ser., No. 16 ISBN:0-8108-3685-8, ISBN13: 978-0-8108-3685-3. Dewey:796.332/0973. LCCN:00-023773.

Audience: **u,f.**

Gems, Gerald R. **GV584.5.C4G46 1997**
The Windy City Wars: Labor, Leisure, and Sport in the Making of Chicago. Trade Cloth. Scarecrow Press, Inc. Lanham, MD. 1997. 280p. American Sports History Ser., No. 8 ISBN:0-8108-3305-0, ISBN13: 978-0-8108-3305-0. Dewey:796/.09773/11. LCCN:97-012133.

Audience: **u,f.**

Vanderbilt, Tom **HD9787.A2**
The Sneaker Book: Anatomy of an Industry and an Icon. Trade Paper. New Press, The. New York, NY. 1998. 192p. Bazaar Bks., Vol. I ISBN:1-56584-406-8, ISBN13: 978-1-56584-406-3. Dewey:338.4/768531.

Audience: **l,u.**

Wooden, Wayne S. & Ehringer, Gavin **GV1834.5.W66 1996**
Rodeo in America: Wranglers, Roughstock, and Paydirt. Trade Cloth. University Press of Kansas. Lawrence, KS. 1999. 310p. ISBN:0-7006-0813-3, ISBN13: 978-0-7006-0813-3. Dewey:791.8/4/0973. LCCN:96-016328.

Audience: **g,l,u,f.** *Choice, 1997.*

Business of Sport > Administration and Management

GV880

☐ Business of Baseball. http://www.businessofbaseball.com/

Audience: **g,l,u,f.**

KF4166

☐ National Women's Law Center Athletics page. http://www.nwlc.org/display.cfm?section=athletics
Audience: **g,l,u,f.**

KF4758.E3

☐ Open to all: Ttile IX at Thirty. http://www.ed.gov/about/bdscomm/list/athletics/title9report.pdf GPO Secretary of Education.
Audience: **g,l,u,f.**

Acosta, Hernandez **GV713.A36 2002**
Managing Sport Organizations. Trade Cloth. Human Kinetics Publishers. Champaign, IL. 2002. 312p. ISBN:0-7360-3826-4, ISBN13: 978-0-7360-3826-3. Dewey:796/.06/9. LCCN:2001-039263.
Audience: **l,u,f.**

American College of Sports Medicine **GV429.A45 2006**
ACSM's Health/Fitness Facility Standards and Guidelines. Ed. 3. Trade Cloth. Human Kinetics Publishers. Champaign, IL. 2006. 216p. ISBN:0-7360-5153-8, ISBN13: 978-0-7360-5153-8. Dewey:613.7/1. LCCN:2005-033377.
Audience: **g,u,f.**

Ammon, Rob, et al. **GV401.A46 2004**
Sport Facility Management: Organizing Events and Mitigating Risks. Richard M. Southall & David A. Blair (Authors). Trade Cloth. Fitness Information Technology, Inc. Morgantown, WV. 2004. 256p. Sport Management Library ISBN:1-885693-39-7, ISBN13: 978-1-885693-39-6. Dewey:796/.069. LCCN:2003-108983.
Audience: **u,f.**

Andrews, David L. (Editor) **GV706.2.M53 2001**
Michael Jordan, Inc.: Corporate Sport, Media Culture, and Late Modern America. Paper Text. State University of New York Press. Albany, NY. 2001. xx, 301p. Series on Sport, Culture, and Social Relations ISBN:0-7914-5026-0, ISBN13: 978-0-7914-5026-0. Dewey:306.4/83/0973. LCCN:00-054794.
Audience: **g,l,u,f.** *Choice, 2002.*

Appenzeller, Herb **GV346.A67 2003**
Managing Sport and Risk Management Strategies. Ed. 2. Trade Paper. Carolina Academic Press. Durham, NC. 2003. 464p. ISBN:0-89089-664-X, ISBN13: 978-0-89089-664-8. Dewey:796.069. LCCN:2003-102974.
Audience: **u,f.**

Appenzeller, Herb & Lewis, Guy **GV713**
Successful Sport Management: A Guide to Legal Issues. Ed. 2. Trade Paper. Carolina Academic Press. Durham, NC. 2000. 421p. ISBN:0-89089-661-5, ISBN13: 978-0-89089-661-7. Dewey:796.068. LCCN:00-106586.
Audience: **u,f.**

Appenzeller, Thomas **KF3989.A965 2000**
Youth Sport and the Law: A Guide to Legal Issues. Herb Appenzeller (Editor). Trade Paper. Carolina Academic Press. Durham, NC. 2000. 216p. ISBN:0-89089-663-1, ISBN13: 978-0-89089-663-1. Dewey:344.73/099. LCCN:99-088424.
Audience: **u,f.**

Barr, Carol, et al. **GV713.P75 2005**
Principles and Practice of Sport Management. Ed. 2. Mary Hums & Lisa Pike Masteralexis (Authors). Paper Text. Jones & Bartlett Publishers, Inc. Sudbury, MA. 2004. 488p. ISBN:0-7637-2623-0, ISBN13: 978-0-7637-2623-2. Dewey:796.06. LCCN:2004-022310.
Audience: **u,f.**

Barros, Carlos Pestana (Editor), et al. **GV716.T73 2002**
Transatlantic Sport: The Comparative Economics of North American and European Sports. Muradali Ibrahim & Stefan Szymanski (Editors). Trade Cloth. Edward Elgar Publishing, Inc. Northampton, MA. 2003. 240p. ISBN:1-84064-947-X, ISBN13: 978-1-84064-947-5. Dewey:338.4/7796. LCCN:2002-070029.
Audience: **u,f.**

Boyle, Raymond (Editor), et al. **P96.T42**
Sport and Broadcasting: Economic, Legal, and Technological Developments in the Digital Age. Deirdre Kevin & Peter Flood (Editors). Trade Paper. Lawrence Erlbaum Associates, Inc. Mahwah, NJ. 2004. 88p. ISBN:0-8058-9522-1, ISBN13: 978-0-8058-9522-3. Dewey:302.23.
Audience: **l,u,f.**

Brookes, Rod **GV742.B76 2002**
Representing Sport. Trade Paper. Oxford University Press, Inc. New York, NY. 2002. 184p. A Hodder Arnold Publication ISBN:0-340-74052-3, ISBN13: 978-0-340-74052-1. Dewey:796. LCCN:2002-510305.
Audience: **l,u.** *Choice, 2002.*

Broto, Carles & Mostaedi, Arian (Editors) **NA6860.B76 2005**
Architecture of Sports Facilities. Trade Cloth. Links Internacional. Barcelona, 2005. 240p. ISBN:84-934007-7-7, ISBN13: 978-84-934007-7-4. Dewey:725.827.
Audience: **u,f.**

Bryant, Howard **GV875.B62B79 2002**
Shut Out: A Story of Race and Baseball in Boston. Paper over Boards. Routledge. New York, NY. 2002. 296p. ISBN:0-415-92779-X, ISBN13: 978-0-415-92779-6. Dewey:796.357/64/0974461. LCCN:2002-069950.
Audience: **u,f.**

Burk, Robert F. **GV880.B869 2001**
Much More Than a Game: Players, Owners and American Baseball since 1921. Trade Paper. University of North Carolina Press. Chapel Hill, NC. 2001. 384p. ISBN:0-8078-4908-1, ISBN13: 978-0-8078-4908-8. Dewey:796.357/09/04. LCCN:00-041774.
Audience: **l,u.** *Choice, 2001.*

Carpenter, Linda J. **KF4166**
Legal Concepts in Sport: A Primer. Ed. 2. Perfect. Sagamore Publishing, L.L.C.. Champaign, IL. 2000. 214p. ISBN:0-88314-659-2, ISBN13: 978-0-88314-659-0. Dewey:796.026. LCCN:99-069463.
Audience: **g,l,u,f.**

Carpenter, Linda J. & Acosta, Vivian R. **KF4166.C37 2004**
Title IX. Trade Cloth. Human Kinetics Publishers. Champaign, IL. 2004. 28p. ISBN:0-7360-4239-3, ISBN13: 978-0-7360-4239-0. Dewey:344.73/099. LCCN:2004-009221.
Audience: **g,l,u,f.**

Champion, Walter T. **KF3989.Z9C48 2005**
Sports Law in a Nutshell. Ed. 3. Trade Paper. West Publishing Company, College & School Division. Eagan, MN. 2005. 450p. ISBN:0-314-15966-5, ISBN13: 978-0-314-15966-3. Dewey:344.73/099. LCCN:2005-278169.
Audience: **l,u.**

Chelladurai, P. **GV713.C5 1999**
Human Resource Management in Sport and Recreation. Trade Cloth. Human Kinetics Publishers. Champaign, IL. 1999. 312p. ISBN:0-87322-973-8, ISBN13: 978-0-87322-973-9. Dewey:796/.06/93. LCCN:98-037051.
Audience: **u,f.**

Cotten, Doyice J. & Wolohan, John **KF3989.S64 2003**
Law for Recreation and Sport Managers. Ed. 3. Trade Paper. Kendall/Hunt Publishing Company. Dubuque, IA. 2003. 698p. ISBN:0-7872-9968-5, ISBN13: 978-0-7872-9968-2. Dewey:344.73/099. LCCN:2003-010664.
Audience: **l,u,f.**

Crossley, John, et al. **GV181.5**
Introduction to Commercial Recreation and Tourism: An Entrepreneurial Approach. Ed. 4. Lynn Jamieson & Russell Brayley (Authors). Trade Paper. Sagamore Publishing, L.L.C.. Champaign, IL. 2001. 558p. ISBN:1-57167-475-6, ISBN13: 978-1-57167-475-3. Dewey:790.069.
Audience: **l,u,f.**

Cylkowski, Greg J. **GV734**
Developing a Lifelong Contract in the Sports Marketplace. Ed. 2. Perfect, Paper Text. Athletic Achievements, Inc. Little Canada, MN. 1998. 400p. ISBN:0-9636449-0-4, ISBN13: 978-0-9636449-0-9. Dewey:306.483.
Audience: **g,l,u,f.**

Daly, Jim **GV182.3.D34 2000**
Recreation and Sport Planning and Design. Ed. 2. Trade Paper. Human Kinetics Publishers. Champaign, IL. 2000. 232p. ISBN:0-7360-0345-2, ISBN13: 978-0-7360-0345-2. Dewey:796/.06/94. LCCN:99-042475.
Audience: **u,f.**

Danielson, Michael N. **GV706.35.D36 1997**
Home Team: Professional Sports and the American Metropolis. Trade Cloth. Princeton University Press. Princeton, NJ. 1997. 397p. ISBN:0-691-03650-0, ISBN13: 978-0-691-03650-2. Dewey:796/.06/9. LCCN:96-035200.
Audience: **u,f.** *Choice, 1997.*

Darby, Paul **GV944.A4D37 2001**
Africa, Football and FIFA: Politics, Colonialism and Resistance. Trade Paper. Taylor & Francis Group. Abingdon, 2002. 256p. Sport in the Global Society Ser., No. 23 ISBN:0-7146-8029-X, ISBN13: 978-0-7146-8029-3. Dewey:796.334/096. LCCN:2001-002915.
Audience: **u,f.** *Choice, 2002.*

Delaney, Kevin J. & Eckstein, Rick **GV413.D45 2003**
Public Dollars, Private Stadiums. Trade Paper. Rutgers University Press. Piscataway, NJ. 2004. 240p. ISBN:0-8135-3343-0, ISBN13: 978-0-8135-3343-8. Dewey:796/.06/8. LCCN:2003-005673.
Audience: **g,l,u,f.** *Choice, 2004.*

DeSensi, Joy Theresa & Rosenberg, Danny **GV713.D465 2003**
Ethics and Morality in Sport Management. Trade Cloth. Fitness Information Technology, Inc. Morgantown, WV. 2003. 299p. Sport Management Library ISBN:1-885693-46-X, ISBN13: 978-1-885693-46-4. Dewey:796/.06/9. LCCN:2002-113559.
Audience: **u,f.**

Dodson, Ronald G. **GV975.3.D63 2005**
Sustainable Golf Courses: A Guide to Environmental Stewardship. Arnold Palmer (Foreword by). Trade Cloth. John Wiley & Sons, Inc. Hoboken, NJ. 2005. 288p. ISBN:0-471-46547-X, ISBN13: 978-0-471-46547-8. Dewey:796.332/068. LCCN:2004-025916.
Audience: **u,f.**

Dougherty, Neil J. **KF3989**
Sport, Physical Activity and the Law. Ed. 2. Alan S. Goldberger (Author, Author), Linda Jean Carpenter (Author). Trade Paper. Sagamore Publishing, L.L.C.. Champaign, IL. 2002. 266p. ISBN:1-57167-492-6, ISBN13: 978-1-57167-492-0. Dewey:344.73099. LCCN:2002-101305.
Audience: **l,u,f.**

Downward, Paul & Dawson, Alistair **GV716.D69 2000**
The Economics of Professional Team Sports. Trade Paper. Routledge. New York, NY. 2000. 272p. ISBN:0-415-20874-2, ISBN13: 978-0-415-20874-1. Dewey:338.4/7796044/0973. LCCN:00-029116.
Audience: **u,f.**

Epstein, Adam **KF3989.E67 2002**
Sports Law for Paralegals. Paper Text. Thomson Delmar Learning. Albany, NY. 2002. 400p. The West Legal Studies ISBN:0-7668-2324-5, ISBN13: 978-0-7668-2324-2. Dewey:344.73/099. LCCN:2002-041017.
Audience: **l,u.**

Euchner, Charles C. **GV706.35.E93 1993**
Playing the Field: Why Sports Teams Move and Cities Fight to Keep Them. Trade Cloth. Johns Hopkins University Press. Baltimore, MD. 1993. 232p. ISBN:0-8018-4572-6, ISBN13: 978-0-8018-4572-7. Dewey:796.06873. LCCN:92-043276.
Audience: **g,l,u,f.**

Farmer, Peter J., et al. **GV415.F37 1996**
Sport Facility Planning and Management. Aaron L. Mulrooney & Rob Ammon Jr. (Authors). Trade Paper. Fitness Information Technology, Inc. Morgantown, WV. 1996. 333p. ISBN:1-885693-05-2, ISBN13: 978-1-885693-05-1. Dewey:796/.06/9. LCCN:96-084609.
Audience: **u,f.**

Fleisher, Arthur A. III, et al. **GV350.F58 1992**
The National Collegiate Athletic Association: A Study in Cartel Behavior. Brian L. Goff & Robert D. Tollison (Authors). Trade Cloth. University of Chicago Press. Chicago, IL. 1992. 197p. ISBN:0-226-25326-0, ISBN13: 978-0-226-25326-8. Dewey:338.4/3796/071173. LCCN:91-026437.
Audience: **g,l.**

Forsythe, Charles E. **GV713.F58 1962**
Administration of High School Athletics. Paper Text. Textbook Publishers. Temecula, CA. 2003. 472p. ISBN:0-7581-6020-8, ISBN13: 978-0-7581-6020-1. Dewey:371.7323.
Audience: **u,f.**

Fort, Rodney D. & Fizel, John (Editors) **GV716**
International Sports Economics Comparisons. Trade Cloth. Greenwood Publishing Group, Inc. Portsmouth, NH. 2004. 400p. Studies in Sports Economics ISBN:0-275-98032-4, ISBN13: 978-0-275-98032-0. Dewey:338.4/7796. LCCN:2003-062260.
Audience: **u,f.** *Choice, 2004.*

Fried, Gil, et al. **GV716.F75 2003**
Sport Finance. Steven Shapiro & Timothy DeSchriver (Authors). Trade Cloth. Human Kinetics Publishers. Champaign, IL. 2003. 392p. ISBN:0-7360-0183-2, ISBN13: 978-0-7360-0183-0. Dewey:796/.06/9. LCCN:2002-007423.
Audience: **u,f.**

Gallup, Joan Whaley **RA975.5.H4G34 1999**
Wellness Centers: A Guide for the Design Professional. Trade Cloth. John Wiley & Sons, Inc. Hoboken, NJ. 1999. 264p. Wiley Series in Healthcare and Senior Living Design, Vol. 7 ISBN:0-471-25337-5, ISBN13: 978-0-471-25337-2. Dewey:725/.5. LCCN:99-011574.
Audience: **u.**

Gardiner, Simon **GV557-1198.995KD51-**
Sports Law. Ed. 3. Trade Paper. Taylor & Francis Group. Abingdon, 2005. DCCLXXXVIp. ISBN:1-85941-894-5, ISBN13: 978-1-85941-894-9. Dewey:344.4/1099. LCCN:2006-279850.
Audience: **u,f.**

Graham, Stedman, et al. **GV713.G62 2001**
The Ultimate Guide to Sports Marketing. Ed. 2. Lisa Delpy Neirotti & Joe Jeff Goldblatt (Authors). Cloth Text. McGraw-Hill Companies, The. New York, NY. 2001. 315p. ISBN:0-07-136124-3, ISBN13: 978-0-07-136124-8. Dewey:659.1/9796. LCCN:00-052721.
Audience: **u,f.**

Gratton, Chris & Taylor, Peter **GV181.3.G73 2000**
Economics of Sport and Recreation. Ed. 2. Trade Paper. Routledge. New York, NY. 2000. 256p. ISBN:0-419-18960-2, ISBN13: 978-0-419-18960-2. Dewey:338.4/7/796. LCCN:99-041898.
Audience: **l,u,f.**

Grayson, Edward & Bond, Catherine **KD2965.S66G73 1999**
Sports Medicine: Ethics and the Law. Trade Paper. Elsevier Science & Technology Books. Saint Louis, MO. 1999. 216p. ISBN:0-7506-1576-1, ISBN13: 978-0-7506-1576-1. Dewey:617.1/027. LCCN:00-265730.
Audience: **u,f.**

Harvey, Mark **GV199.6.S56 1999**
National Outdoor Leadership School's Wilderness Guide: The Classic Wilderness Guide. Trade Paper. Simon & Schuster. New York, NY. 1999. 272p. ISBN:0-684-85909-2, ISBN13: 978-0-684-85909-5. Dewey:796.51/028. LCCN:99-021875.
Audience: **l,u.**

Howard, Dennis Ramsay & Crompton, John L. **GV716.H69 2004**
Financing Sport: Winning Strategies. Ed. 2. Trade Paper. Fitness Information Technology, Inc. Morgantown, WV. 2004. 607p. Sport Management Library ISBN:1-885693-38-9, ISBN13: 978-1-885693-38-9. Dewey:796/.06/91. LCCN:2003-108982.
Audience: **l,u,f.**

Ikard, Robert W. **GV886.I43 2005**
Just for Fun: The Story of AAU Women's Basketball. Trade Cloth. University of Arkansas Press. Fayetteville, AR. 2005. 272p. ISBN:1-55728-783-X, ISBN13: 978-1-55728-783-0. Dewey:796.323/8. LCCN:2004-021104.
Audience: **u,f.** *Choice, 2005.*

John S. and James L. Knight Foundation **GV347**
☐ Keeping Faith update of Call to Action.
http://www.knightcommission.org/
Knight Commission on Intercollegiate Athletics.
Audience: **l,u,f.**

Jozsa, Frank P. Jr. **GV583**
American Sports Empire: How the Leagues Breed Success. Book, Other. Greenwood Publishing Group, Inc. Portsmouth, NH. 2003. 272p. ISBN:1-56720-559-3, ISBN13: 978-1-56720-559-6. Dewey:796/.0973. LCCN:2002-029759.
Audience: **g,l,u,f.** *Choice, 2003.*

Katz, Donald **HD9992.U54N555 1994**
Just Do It: The Nike Spirit in the Corporate World. Trade Paper. Adams Media Corporation. Avon, MA. 1994. 352p. ISBN:1-55850-479-6, ISBN13: 978-1-55850-479-0. Dewey:338.7/6887/0973. LCCN:94-046830.
Audience: **g,l,u,f.**

Kluka, Darlene A., et al. **GV713**
Sport Governance. Guido Schilling & William F. Stier (Authors). Trade Paper. Meyer & Meyer Sport, Ltd. Garsington, 2003. 200p. ISBN:1-84126-132-7, ISBN13: 978-1-84126-132-4. Dewey:796/.0285.
Audience: **u,f.**

Kluka, Darlene & Schilling, Guido (Editors) **GV713**
The Business of Sport. Trade Paper. Meyer & Meyer Sport, Ltd. Garsington, 2004. 192p. Perspectives - The Multidisciplinary Series of Physical Education and Sport Science, Vol. 3 ISBN:1-84126-056-8, ISBN13: 978-1-84126-056-3. Dewey:796/.069.
Audience: **u,f.**

Kuhn, Bowie **GV865.K78K85 1997**
Hardball: The Education of a Baseball Commissioner. Trade Cloth. University of Nebraska Press. Lincoln, NE. 1997. 477p. ISBN:0-8032-7784-9, ISBN13: 978-0-8032-7784-7. Dewey:[B]. LCCN:97-006823.
Audience: **g,l,u.**

Lanctot, Neil **GV875.N35L36 2004**
Negro League Baseball: The Rise and Ruin of a Black Institution. Book, Other. University of Pennsylvania Press. Philadelphia, PA. 2004. 496p. ISBN:0-8122-3807-9, ISBN13: 978-0-8122-3807-5. Dewey:796.357/64/0973. LCCN:2004-043547.
Audience: **g,l,u,f.** *Choice, 2004.*

Lenskyj, Helen Jefferson **GV722 2000.L46 2002**
The Best Olympics Ever?: Social Impacts of Sydney 2000. Paper Text. State University of New York Press. Albany, NY.

2002. 262p. ISBN:0-7914-5474-6, ISBN13: 978-0-7914-5474-9. Dewey:796.48. LCCN:2001-055121.
Audience: **u,f.** *Choice, 2003.*

Lincoln, Chris **GV350.5.L56 2004**
Playing the Game: Inside Athletic Recruiting in the Ivy League. Jay Fiedler (Foreword by). Trade Paper. Nomad Press. White River Junction, VT. 2004. 272p. ISBN:0-9722026-6-8, ISBN13: 978-0-9722026-6-4. Dewey:796.04/3/0974. LCCN:2005-277590.
Audience: **g,l,u,f.**

Lomax, Michael E. **GV863.A1L65 2003**
Black Baseball Entrepreneurs, 1860-1901: Operating by Any Means Necessary. Trade Paper. Syracuse University Press. Syracuse, NY. 2003. xxvi, 222p. Sports and Entertainment Ser. ISBN:0-8156-0786-5, ISBN13: 978-0-8156-0786-1. Dewey:796.357/64/08996073. LCCN:2002-154375.
Audience: **u,f.**

Lowe, Stephen R. **GV583.L696 1995**
The Kid on the Sandlot: Congress and Professional Sports, 1910-1992. Trade Paper. University of Wisconsin Press. Chicago, IL. 1995. 176p. ISBN:0-87972-676-8, ISBN13: 978-0-87972-676-8. Dewey:796/.0973. LCCN:94-079195.
Audience: **l,u,f.** *Choice, 1995.*

Miracle, Andrew W. Jr. & Rees, C. Roger **GV346.M57 1994**
Lessons of the Locker Room: The Myth of School Sports. Trade Cloth. Prometheus Books, Publishers. Amherst, NY. 1994. 243p. ISBN:0-87975-879-1, ISBN13: 978-0-87975-879-0. Dewey:796/.0973. LCCN:93-048666.
Audience: **g,l,u,f.** *Choice, 1994.*

Mullin, Bernard J., et al. **GV716.M85 2000**
Sport Marketing. Ed. 2. Stephen Hardy & William A. Sutton (Authors). Trade Cloth. Human Kinetics Publishers. Champaign, IL. 1999. 456p. ISBN:0-88011-877-6, ISBN13: 978-0-88011-877-4. Dewey:796/.06/98. LCCN:99-041126.
Audience: **l,u,f.**

Oriard, Michael **GV950.O73 2001**
King Football: Sport and Spectacle in the Golden Age of Radio and Newsreels, Movies and Magazines, the Weekly and the Daily Press. Trade Cloth. University of North Carolina Press. Chapel Hill, NC. 2001. 512p. ISBN:0-8078-2650-2, ISBN13: 978-0-8078-2650-8. Dewey:796.332/09/041. LCCN:2001-041459.
Audience: **l,u,f.** *Choice, 2002.*

O'Sullivan, Ellen L. & Spangler, Kathy J. **GV182.15.O73 1998**
Experience Marketing: Strategies for the New Millenium. Cloth Text. Venture Publishing, Inc. State College, PA. 1998. 430p. ISBN:0-910251-98-3, ISBN13: 978-0-910251-98-3. Dewey:658.838. LCCN:98-086937.
Audience: **u,f.**

Parkhouse, Bonnie L. **GV713**
The Management of Sport: Its Foundation and Application with PowerWeb Bind-In Card. Ed. 4. Trade Cloth. McGraw-Hill Higher Education. Burr Ridge, IL. 2004. 432p. ISBN:0-07-298546-1, ISBN13: 978-0-07-298546-7. Dewey:796/.06/9.
Audience: **l,u,f.**

Parks, Janet B. & Quarterman, Jerome (Editors) **GV713.C66 2002**
Contemporary Sport Management. Ed. 2. Trade Cloth. Human Kinetics Publishers. Champaign, IL. 2003. 448p. ISBN:0-7360-4243-1, ISBN13: 978-0-7360-4243-7. Dewey:796.06/9. LCCN:2002-012905.
Audience: **l,f.**

Pearson, Daniel **GV863.A1.P43**
Baseball in 1889: Players vs Owners. Trade Paper. University of Wisconsin Press. Chicago, IL. 2005. 244p. ISBN:0-87972-619-9, ISBN13: 978-0-87972-619-5. Dewey:796.357. LCCN:92-063282.
Audience: **l,u,f.** *Choice, 1993.*

Pettavino, Paula J. & Pye, Geralyn **GV592.C9**
Sport in Cuba: The Diamond in the Rough. Trade Paper. University of Pittsburgh Press. Pittsburgh, PA. 1994. 320p. Latin American Ser. ISBN:0-8229-5512-1, ISBN13: 978-0-8229-5512-2. Dewey:796/.097291. LCCN:93-024372.
Audience: **u,f.** *Choice, 1995.*

Pietrusza, David **GV865.L3P54 1998**
Judge and Jury: The Life and Times of Judge Kenesaw Mountain Landis. Trade Cloth. Diamond Communications, Inc. Lanham, MD. 1955. 581p. ISBN:1-888698-09-8, ISBN13: 978-1-888698-09-1. Dewey:796.357/092 B. LCCN:98-013938.
Audience: **g,l,u,f.**

Pietrusza, David **GV863.A1P54 1997**
Lights On!: The Wild Century-Long Saga of Night Baseball. Trade Cloth. Scarecrow Press, Inc. Lanham, MD. 1997. 288p. American Sports History Ser., Vol. 7 ISBN:0-8108-3307-7, ISBN13: 978-0-8108-3307-4. Dewey:796.357/0973. LCCN:97-007800.
Audience: **g,l,u,f.** *Choice, 1998.*

Pitts, Brenda G. & Stotlar, David K. **GV716.P58 2002**
Fundamentals of Sport Marketing. Ed. 2. Trade Paper. Fitness Information Technology, Inc. Morgantown, WV. 2001. 405p. Sport Management Library ISBN:1-885693-33-8, ISBN13: 978-1-885693-33-4. Dewey:796/.06/98. LCCN:2002-102472.
Audience: **g,l,f.**

Pound, Richard W. **GV721.5**
Inside the Olympics: A Behind-the-Scenes Look at the Politics, the Scandals, and the Glory of the Games. Trade Cloth. John Wiley & Sons, Inc. Hoboken, NJ. 2004. 288p. ISBN:0-470-83454-4, ISBN13: 978-0-470-83454-1. Dewey:796.48. LCCN:2006-296402.
Audience: **l,u.**

Quirk, Charles E. (Editor) **KF3989.S675 1996**
Sports and the Law: Major Legal Cases. Library Binding. Garland Publishing, Inc. New York, NY. 1996. 336p. Reference Library of the Humanities, Vol. 04 ISBN:0-8153-0220-7, ISBN13: 978-0-8153-0220-9. Dewey:344.73/099. LCCN:94-035594.
Audience: **u,f.**

Rich, Wilbur (Editor) **GV429**
The Economics and Politics of Sports Facilities. Trade Cloth. Greenwood Publishing Group, Inc. Portsmouth, NH. 2000. 248p.

ISBN:1-56720-317-5, ISBN13: 978-1-56720-317-2. Dewey:338.4/7796/06873. LCCN:99-056365.
Audience: **g,l,u,f.** *Choice, 2000.*

Rosentraub, Mark S. **GV716.R67 1999**
Major League Losers: The Real Cost of Sports and Who's Paying for It. Trade Paper. Basic Books. New York, NY. 1999. 376p. ISBN:0-465-07143-0, ISBN13: 978-0-465-07143-2. Dewey:338.4/7796/0973. LCCN:00-265440.
Audience: **g,l,u,f.** *Choice, 1997.*

Sachs, Paul D. & Luff, Richard T. **GV975.3.S33 2002**
Ecological Golf Course Management. Trade Cloth. John Wiley & Sons, Inc. Hoboken, NJ. 2002. 216p. ISBN:1-57504-154-5, ISBN13: 978-1-57504-154-4. Dewey:796.352/06/9. LCCN:2001-006101.
Audience: **u,f.**

Sawyer, Thomas H., et al. **GV716**
Financing the Sport Enterprise. Michael Hypes & Julia Ann Hypes (Authors). Trade Paper. Sagamore Publishing, L.L.C.. Champaign, IL. 2004. 318p. ISBN:1-57167-520-5, ISBN13: 978-1-57167-520-0. Dewey:796/.06/9.
Audience: **g,l,u,f.**

Shank, Matthew D. **GV716.S42 2004**
Sports Marketing: A Strategic Perspective. Ed. 3. Cloth Text. Prentice Hall PTR. Upper Saddle River, NJ. 2004. 624p. ISBN:0-13-144077-2, ISBN13: 978-0-13-144077-7. Dewey:796/.06/98. LCCN:2004-044696.
Audience: **u,f.**

Slack, Trevor **GV713.S576 1997**
Understanding Sport Organizations: The Application of Organizational Theory. Trade Cloth. Human Kinetics Publishers. Champaign, IL. 1996. 360p. ISBN:0-87322-948-7, ISBN13: 978-0-87322-948-7. Dewey:796/.09/9. LCCN:96-026111.
Audience: **u,f.**

Slack, Trevor & Parent, Milena **GV713.S576 2006**
Understanding Sport Organizations: The Application of Organization Theory. Ed. 2. Trade Cloth. Human Kinetics Publishers. Champaign, IL. 2005. 368p. ISBN:0-7360-5639-4, ISBN13: 978-0-7360-5639-7. Dewey:796/.06/9. LCCN:2005-019202.
Audience: **u.**

Sommers, Paul M. (Editor) **GV880 .D53 1992**
Diamonds Are Forever: The Business of Baseball. Trade Cloth. Brookings Institution Press. Washington, DC. 1992. 208p. ISBN:0-8157-8042-7, ISBN13: 978-0-8157-8042-7. Dewey:338.4/3796357/640973. LCCN:91-047699.
Audience: **g,l,u.**

Staudohar, Paul D. **GV716.S72 1996**
Playing for Dollars: Labor Relations and the Sports Business. Ed. 3. Trade Paper. Cornell University Press. Ithaca, NY. 1996. 232p. ILR Press Bk, ISBN:0-8014-8342-5, ISBN13: 978-0-8014-8342-4. Dewey:331.89/041796. LCCN:95-049456.
Audience: **u,f.** *Choice, 1996.*

Stoldt, G. Clayton, et al. **GV714.S77 2006**
Sport Public Relations: Managing Organizational Communication. Steven W. Dittmore & Scott E. Branvold (Authors). Trade Cloth. Human Kinetics Publishers. Champaign, IL. 2006. 376p. ISBN:0-7360-5340-9, ISBN13: 978-0-7360-5340-2. Dewey:659.2/9796. LCCN:2005-024458.
Audience: **l,u,f.**

VanderZwaag, Harold J. **GV713**
Policy Development in Sport Management. Ed. 2. Cloth Text. Greenwood Publishing Group, Inc. Portsmouth, NH. 1998. 248p. ISBN:0-275-96089-7, ISBN13: 978-0-275-96089-6. Dewey:796/.06/073. LCCN:98-004973.
Audience: **u,f.** *Choice, 1999.*

Westerbeek, Hans & Smith, Aaron **GV716.W46 2002**
Sport Business in the Global Marketplace: A Study of Strategic Cognition. Trade Cloth. Palgrave Macmillan. New York, NY. 2003. 250p. Finance and Capital Markets Ser. ISBN:1-4039-0300-X, ISBN13: 978-1-4039-0300-6. Dewey:338.4/3796. LCCN:2002-075498.
Audience: **u,f.**

White, Bud & White, Charles B. **GV975.W45 2000**
Turf Managers' Handbook for Golf Course Construction, Renovation, and Grow-In. Trade Cloth. John Wiley & Sons, Inc. Hoboken, NJ. 2000. 328p. ISBN:1-57504-110-3, ISBN13: 978-1-57504-110-0. Dewey:796.352/06/8. LCCN:99-087983.
Audience: **u.**

Wright, Russell O. **GV863.A1W755 1999**
A Tale of Two Leagues: How Baseball Changed as the Rules, Balls, Franchises, Stadiums and Players Changed, 1900-1998. Cloth Text. McFarland & Company, Incorporated Publishers. Jefferson, NC. 1999. 224p. ISBN:0-7864-0712-3, ISBN13: 978-0-7864-0712-5. Dewey:796.357/0973. LCCN:99-40307.
Audience: **l,u,f.** *Choice, 2000.*

Business of Sport > Economics

GV880
☐ Business of Baseball.
http://www.businessofbaseball.com/
Audience: **g,l,u,f.**

Appenzeller, Herb **GV346.A67 2003**
Managing Sport and Risk Management Strategies. Ed. 2. Trade Paper. Carolina Academic Press. Durham, NC. 2003. 464p. ISBN:0-89089-664-X, ISBN13: 978-0-89089-664-8. Dewey:796.069. LCCN:2003-102974.
Audience: **u,f.**

Barnett, Steven **GV742.3 .B37 1990**
Games and Sets: The Changing Face of Sport on Television. Trade Paper. BFI Publishing. London, 1990. 224p. ISBN:0-85170-268-6, ISBN13: 978-0-85170-268-1. Dewey:302.234/5. LCCN:91-105439.
Audience: **u,f.** *Choice, 1991.*

Barney, Robert Knight, et al. **GV721.5.B32 2002**
Selling the Five Rings: The IOC and the Rise of Olympic Commercialism. Stephen R. Wenn & Scott G. Martyn (Authors). Trade Cloth. University of Utah Press. Salt Lake City, UT. 2002. 448p. ISBN:0-87480-713-1, ISBN13: 978-0-87480-713-4. Dewey:796.48. LCCN:2001-006781.
Audience: **l,u,f.** *Choice, 2003, 2002.*

Barros, Carlos Pestana (Editor), et al. **GV716.T73 2002**
Transatlantic Sport: The Comparative Economics of North American and European Sports. Muradali Ibrahim & Stefan Szymanski (Editors). Trade Cloth. Edward Elgar Publishing, Inc. Northampton, MA. 2003. 240p. ISBN:1-84064-947-X, ISBN13: 978-1-84064-947-5. Dewey:338.4/7796. LCCN:2002-070029.
Audience: **u,f.**

Bodo, Peter **GV995.B6832 1995**
The Courts of Babylon: Tales of Greed and Glory in the Harsh New High-Stakes World of Professional Tennis. Trade Cloth. Simon & Schuster. New York, NY. 1995. 480p. ISBN:0-684-81296-7, ISBN13: 978-0-684-81296-0. Dewey:796.342/64. LCCN:95-014760.
Audience: **g,l,u,f.** *Choice, 1995.*

Boyle, Raymond (Editor), et al. **P96.T42**
Sport and Broadcasting: Economic, Legal, and Technological Developments in the Digital Age. Deirdre Kevin & Peter Flood (Editors). Trade Paper. Lawrence Erlbaum Associates, Inc. Mahwah, NJ. 2004. 88p. ISBN:0-8058-9522-1, ISBN13: 978-0-8058-9522-3. Dewey:302.23.
Audience: **l,u,f.**

Brookes, Rod **GV742.B76 2002**
Representing Sport. Trade Paper. Oxford University Press, Inc. New York, NY. 2002. 184p. A Hodder Arnold Publication ISBN:0-340-74052-3, ISBN13: 978-0-340-74052-1. Dewey:796. LCCN:2002-510305.
Audience: **l,u.** *Choice, 2002.*

Burk, Robert F. **GV880.B87 1994**
Never Just a Game: Players, Owners and American Baseball to 1920. Trade Cloth. University of North Carolina Press. Chapel Hill, NC. 1994. 302p. ISBN:0-8078-2122-5, ISBN13: 978-0-8078-2122-0. Dewey:338.4/3796357/0973. LCCN:93-022719.
Audience: **g,l,u,f.** *Choice, 1994.*

Butsch, Richard (Editor) **GV188.3.U6F67 1990**
For Fun and Profit: The Transformation of Leisure into Consumption. Trade Cloth. Temple University Press. Philadelphia, PA. 1990. 288p. Arts and Their Philosophies Ser. ISBN:0-87722-676-8, ISBN13: 978-0-87722-676-5. Dewey:338.4/77900135/0973. LCCN:89-027699.
Audience: **l,u.** *Choice, 1990.*

Cashman, Richard & Hughes, Anthony (Editors) **GV722 2000.S82 1999**
Staging the Olympics: The Event and Its Impact. Trade Paper. University of New South Wales Press. Sydney, NSW. 1999. 226p. ISBN:0-86840-729-1, ISBN13: 978-0-86840-729-6. Dewey:796.48. LCCN:00-340427.
Audience: **l,u,f.** *Choice, 2000.*

Chalip, Laurence (Editor), et al. **GV706**
National Sports Policies: An International Handbook. Arthur Johnson & Lisa Stachura (Editors). Cloth Text. Greenwood Publishing Group, Inc. Portsmouth, NH. 1996. 456p. ISBN:0-313-28481-4, ISBN13: 978-0-313-28481-6. Dewey:796/.06/9. LCCN:95-025327.
Audience: **u,f.** *Choice, 1997.*

Danielson, Michael N. **GV706.35.D36 1997**
Home Team: Professional Sports and the American Metropolis. Trade Cloth. Princeton University Press. Princeton, NJ. 1997. 397p. ISBN:0-691-03650-0, ISBN13: 978-0-691-03650-2. Dewey:796/.06/9. LCCN:96-035200.
Audience: **u,f.** *Choice, 1997.*

Delaney, Kevin J. & Eckstein, Rick **GV413.D45 2003**
Public Dollars, Private Stadiums. Trade Paper. Rutgers University Press. Piscataway, NJ. 2004. 240p. ISBN:0-8135-3343-0, ISBN13: 978-0-8135-3343-8. Dewey:796/.06/8. LCCN:2003-005673.
Audience: **g,l,u,f.** *Choice, 2004.*

Dodson, Ronald G. **GV975.3.D63 2005**
Sustainable Golf Courses: A Guide to Environmental Stewardship. Arnold Palmer (Foreword by). Trade Cloth. John Wiley & Sons, Inc. Hoboken, NJ. 2005. 288p. ISBN:0-471-46547-X, ISBN13: 978-0-471-46547-8. Dewey:796.332/068. LCCN:2004-025916.
Audience: **u,f.**

Dorinson, Joseph & Warmund, Joram (Editors) **GV865.R6**
Jackie Robinson: Race, Sports and the American Dream. Paper Text. M. E. Sharpe Inc. Armonk, NY. 1999. 296p. ISBN:0-7656-0318-7, ISBN13: 978-0-7656-0318-0. Dewey:796.357/092.
Audience: **g,l,u,f.** *Choice, 1999.*

Ferrand, Alain & Torrigiani, Luiggino **GV716.F47 2005**
Marketing of Olympic Sport Organisations. Trade Paper. Human Kinetics Publishers. Champaign, IL. 2004. 144p. ISBN:0-7360-5930-X, ISBN13: 978-0-7360-5930-5. Dewey:338.4/379648. LCCN:2004-022804.
Audience: **u,f.**

Fizel, John L. (Editor), et al. **GV716**
Sports Economics: Current Research. Elizabeth Gustafson & Lawrence Hadley (Editors). Trade Cloth. Greenwood Publishing Group, Inc. Portsmouth, NH. 1999. 260p. ISBN:0-275-96330-6, ISBN13: 978-0-275-96330-9. Dewey:338.4/7796/0973. LCCN:98-044670.
Audience: **u,f.**

Fizel, John & Fort, Rodney D. (Editors) **GV350**
Economics of College Sports. Trade Cloth. Greenwood Publishing Group, Inc. Portsmouth, NH. 2004. 272p. Studies in Sports Economics ISBN:0-275-98033-2, ISBN13: 978-0-275-98033-7. Dewey:796.04/3/0973. LCCN:2003-060427.
Audience: **u,f.** *Choice, 2004.*

Fleisher, Arthur A. III, et al. **GV350.F58 1992**
The National Collegiate Athletic Association: A Study in Cartel Behavior. Brian L. Goff & Robert D. Tollison (Authors). Trade Cloth. University of Chicago Press. Chicago, IL. 1992. 197p. ISBN:0-226-25326-0, ISBN13: 978-0-226-25326-8. Dewey:338.4/3796/071173. LCCN:91-026437.
Audience: **g,l.**

Fried, Gil, et al. **GV716.F75 2003**
Sport Finance. Steven Shapiro & Timothy DeSchriver (Authors). Trade Cloth. Human Kinetics Publishers. Champaign, IL. 2003. 392p. ISBN:0-7360-0183-2, ISBN13: 978-0-7360-0183-0. Dewey:796/.06/9. LCCN:2002-007423.
Audience: **u,f.**

Gratton, Chris & Taylor, Peter **GV181.3.G73 2000**
Economics of Sport and Recreation. Ed. 2. Trade Paper. Routledge. New York, NY. 2000. 256p. ISBN:0-419-18960-2, ISBN13: 978-0-419-18960-2. Dewey:338.4/7/796. LCCN:99-041898.
Audience: **l,u,f.**

Hagstrom, Robert G. Jr. **GV1029.9.S74H34**
The NASCAR Way: The Business That Drives the Sport. Trade Paper. John Wiley & Sons, Inc. Hoboken, NJ. 2001. 254p. ISBN:0-471-39920-5, ISBN13: 978-0-471-39920-9. Dewey:338.4/7/79672/0973.
Audience: **g,l,u.**

Howard, Dennis Ramsay & Crompton, John L. **GV716.H69 2004**
Financing Sport: Winning Strategies. Ed. 2. Trade Paper. Fitness Information Technology, Inc. Morgantown, WV. 2004. 607p. Sport Management Library ISBN:1-885693-38-9, ISBN13: 978-1-885693-38-9. Dewey:796/.06/91. LCCN:2003-108982.
Audience: **l,u,f.**

Howard, Dennis R. & Crompton, John L. **GV716.H69 1995**
Financing Sport. Cloth Text. Fitness Information Technology, Inc. Morgantown, WV. 1995. 416p. ISBN:1-885693-00-1, ISBN13: 978-1-885693-00-6. Dewey:338.4/3. LCCN:94-061287.
Audience: **u,f.**

Howell, Mark D. **GV1029.9.S74H68 1997**
From Moonshine to Madison Avenue: A Cultural History of the NASCAR Winston Cup Series. Trade Paper. University of Wisconsin Press. Chicago, IL. 1997. xvi, 266p. ISBN:0-87972-740-3, ISBN13: 978-0-87972-740-6. Dewey:796.72/0973. LCCN:97-004215.
Audience: **g,l.** *Choice, 1997.*

Jozsa, Frank P. Jr. **GV583**
American Sports Empire: How the Leagues Breed Success. Book, Other. Greenwood Publishing Group, Inc. Portsmouth, NH. 2003. 272p. ISBN:1-56720-559-3, ISBN13: 978-1-56720-559-6. Dewey:796/.0973. LCCN:2002-029759.
Audience: **g,l,u,f.** *Choice, 2003.*

Katz, Donald **HD9992.U54N555 1994**
Just Do It: The Nike Spirit in the Corporate World. Trade Paper. Adams Media Corporation. Avon, MA. 1994. 352p. ISBN:1-55850-479-6, ISBN13: 978-1-55850-479-0. Dewey:338.7/6887/0973. LCCN:94-046830.
Audience: **g,l,u,f.**

Korr, Charles P. **GV880.2.K67 2002**
The End of Baseball As We Knew It: The Players Union, 1960-81. Bob Costas (Foreword by). Trade Cloth. University of Illinois Press. Champaign, IL. 2002. 352p. Sport and Society Ser. ISBN:0-252-02752-3, ISBN13: 978-0-252-02752-9. Dewey:331.89/041796357. LCCN:2001-007535.
Audience: **u,f.** *Choice, 2003.*

Kruger, Arnd & Riordan, James (Editors) **GV706.5.S867 1996**
The Story of Worker Sport. Trade Cloth. Human Kinetics Publishers. Champaign, IL. 1996. 20p. ISBN:0-87322-874-X, ISBN13: 978-0-87322-874-9. Dewey:306.4/83. LCCN:96-001281.
Audience: **u,f.** *Choice, 1997.*

Lanctot, Neil **GV875.N35L36 2004**
Negro League Baseball: The Rise and Ruin of a Black Institution. Book, Other. University of Pennsylvania Press. Philadelphia, PA. 2004. 496p. ISBN:0-8122-3807-9, ISBN13: 978-0-8122-3807-5. Dewey:796.357/64/0973. LCCN:2004-043547.
Audience: **g,l,u,f.** *Choice, 2004.*

Leifer, Eric M. **GV583.L45 1995**
Making the Majors: The Transformation of Team Sports in America. Trade Cloth. Harvard University Press. Cambridge, MA. 1996. 400p. ISBN:0-674-54322-X, ISBN13: 978-0-674-54322-5. Dewey:796/.06/0973. LCCN:95-013469.
Audience: **l,u,f.** *Choice, 1996.*

Lenskyj, Helen Jefferson **GV722 2000.L46 2002**
The Best Olympics Ever?: Social Impacts of Sydney 2000. Paper Text. State University of New York Press. Albany, NY. 2002. 262p. ISBN:0-7914-5474-6, ISBN13: 978-0-7914-5474-9. Dewey:796.48. LCCN:2001-055121.
Audience: **u,f.** *Choice, 2003.*

Li, Ming, et al. **GV716.L52 2001**
The Economics of Sports. Susan Hofacre & Dan Mahony (Authors). Trade Cloth. Fitness Information Technology, Inc. Morgantown, WV. 2001. 242p. Sport Management Library ISBN:1-885693-27-3, ISBN13: 978-1-885693-27-3. Dewey:796/.068/1. LCCN:00-136499.
Audience: **u,f.**

Lincoln, Chris **GV350.5.L56 2004**
Playing the Game: Inside Athletic Recruiting in the Ivy League. Jay Fiedler (Foreword by). Trade Paper. Nomad Press. White River Junction, VT. 2004. 272p. ISBN:0-9722026-6-8, ISBN13: 978-0-9722026-6-4. Dewey:796.04/3/0974. LCCN:2005-277590.
Audience: **g,l,u,f.**

Lomax, Michael E. **GV863.A1L65 2003**
Black Baseball Entrepreneurs, 1860-1901: Operating by Any Means Necessary. Trade Paper. Syracuse University Press. Syracuse, NY. 2003. xxvi, 222p. Sports and Entertainment Ser. ISBN:0-8156-0786-5, ISBN13: 978-0-8156-0786-1. Dewey:796.357/64/08996073. LCCN:2002-154375.
Audience: **u,f.**

Muggleton, David & Weinzierl, Rupert **GV721.6**
Post-Olympism?: Questioning Sport in the Twenty-First Century. John Bale & Mette Krogh Christensen (Editors). Trade Paper. Berg Publishers. Oxford, 2004. 256p. Global Sport Cultures Ser. ISBN:1-85973-719-6, ISBN13: 978-1-85973-719-4. Dewey:306.4/83/0905.
Audience: **u,f.**

Noll, Roger G. & Zimbalist, Andrew (Editors) **GV716.S647 1997**
Sports, Jobs and Taxes: The Economic Impact of Sports Teams and Facilities. Trade Paper. Brookings Institution Press.

Washington, DC. 1997. 525p. ISBN:0-8157-6111-2, ISBN13: 978-0-8157-6111-2. Dewey:338.4/3796/0973. LCCN:97-033764.
Audience: **u,f.** *Choice, 1998.*

Parks, Janet B. & Quarterman, Jerome (Editors) **GV713.C66 2002**
Contemporary Sport Management. Ed. 2. Trade Cloth. Human Kinetics Publishers. Champaign, IL. 2003. 448p. ISBN:0-7360-4243-1, ISBN13: 978-0-7360-4243-7. Dewey:796.06/9. LCCN:2002-012905.
Audience: **l,f.**

Pearson, Daniel **GV863.A1.P43**
Baseball in 1889: Players vs Owners. Trade Paper. University of Wisconsin Press. Chicago, IL. 2005. 244p. ISBN:0-87972-619-9, ISBN13: 978-0-87972-619-5. Dewey:796.357. LCCN:92-063282.
Audience: **l,u,f.** *Choice, 1993.*

Pietrusza, David **GV865.L3P54 1998**
Judge and Jury: The Life and Times of Judge Kenesaw Mountain Landis. Trade Cloth. Diamond Communications, Inc. Lanham, MD. 1955. 581p. ISBN:1-888698-09-8, ISBN13: 978-1-888698-09-1. Dewey:796.357/092 B. LCCN:98-013938.
Audience: **g,l,u,f.**

Pound, Richard W. **GV721.5**
Inside the Olympics: A Behind-the-Scenes Look at the Politics, the Scandals, and the Glory of the Games. Trade Cloth. John Wiley & Sons, Inc. Hoboken, NJ. 2004. 288p. ISBN:0-470-83454-4, ISBN13: 978-0-470-83454-1. Dewey:796.48. LCCN:2006-296402.
Audience: **l,u.**

Preuss, Holger **GV721.5.P717 2004**
Economics of Staging the Olympics: A Comparison of the Games 1972-2008. Trade Paper. Edward Elgar Publishing, Inc. Northampton, MA. 2004. 352p. ISBN:1-84376-893-3, ISBN13: 978-1-84376-893-7. Dewey:338.4/379648. LCCN:2004-056663.
Audience: **u,f.** *Choice, 2005.*

Quirk, James & Fort, Rodney D. **GV716**
Pay Dirt: The Business of Professional Team Sports. Ed. 2. Trade Paper. Princeton University Press. Princeton, NJ. 1997. 566p. ISBN:0-691-01574-0, ISBN13: 978-0-691-01574-3. Dewey:338.43796. LCCN:92-015349.
Audience: **g,l,u.** *Choice, 1993.*

Rich, Wilbur (Editor) **GV429**
The Economics and Politics of Sports Facilities. Trade Cloth. Greenwood Publishing Group, Inc. Portsmouth, NH. 2000. 248p. ISBN:1-56720-317-5, ISBN13: 978-1-56720-317-2. Dewey:338.4/7796/06873. LCCN:99-056365.
Audience: **g,l,u,f.** *Choice, 2000.*

Roche, Maurice **G155.A1**
Megaevents and Modernity: Olympics, Expos and the Growth of Global Culture. Trade Paper. Routledge. New York, NY. 2000. 304p. ISBN:0-415-15712-9, ISBN13: 978-0-415-15712-4. Dewey:306.4/8.
Audience: **u,f.** *Choice, 2001.*

Rosentraub, Mark S. **GV716.R67 1999**
Major League Losers: The Real Cost of Sports and Who's Paying for It. Trade Paper. Basic Books. New York, NY. 1999. 376p. ISBN:0-465-07143-0, ISBN13: 978-0-465-07143-2. Dewey:338.4/7796/0973. LCCN:00-265440.
Audience: **g,l,u,f.** *Choice, 1997.*

Sack, Allen L. & Staurowsky, Ellen J. **GV351**
College Athletes for Hire: The Evolution and Legacy of the NCAA's Amateur Myth. Trade Cloth. Greenwood Publishing Group, Inc. Portsmouth, NH. 1998. 208p. ISBN:0-275-96191-5, ISBN13: 978-0-275-96191-6. Dewey:796.04/3/0973. LCCN:97-043956.
Audience: **g,l,u,f.** *Choice, 1999.*

Sawyer, Thomas H., et al. **GV716**
Financing the Sport Enterprise. Michael Hypes & Julia Ann Hypes (Authors). Trade Paper. Sagamore Publishing, L.L.C.. Champaign, IL. 2004. 318p. ISBN:1-57167-520-5, ISBN13: 978-1-57167-520-0. Dewey:796/.06/9.
Audience: **g,l,u,f.**

Sheehan, Richard G. **GV716.S45 1996**
Keeping Score: The Economics of Big-Time Sports. Trade Cloth. Diamond Communications, Inc. Lanham, MD. 1997. 352p. ISBN:1-888698-05-5, ISBN13: 978-1-888698-05-3. Dewey:338.4/7796/0973. LCCN:96-019528.
Audience: **u,f.** *Choice, 1997.*

Slack, Trevor & Parent, Milena **GV713.S576 2006**
Understanding Sport Organizations: The Application of Organization Theory. Ed. 2. Trade Cloth. Human Kinetics Publishers. Champaign, IL. 2005. 368p. ISBN:0-7360-5639-4, ISBN13: 978-0-7360-5639-7. Dewey:796/.06/9. LCCN:2005-019202.
Audience: **u.**

Sommers, Paul M. (Editor) **GV880 .D53 1992**
Diamonds Are Forever: The Business of Baseball. Trade Cloth. Brookings Institution Press. Washington, DC. 1992. 208p. ISBN:0-8157-8042-7, ISBN13: 978-0-8157-8042-7. Dewey:338.4/3796357/640973. LCCN:91-047699.
Audience: **g,l,u.**

Staudohar, Paul D. **GV716.S72 1996**
Playing for Dollars: Labor Relations and the Sports Business. Ed. 3. Trade Paper. Cornell University Press. Ithaca, NY. 1996. 232p. ILR Press Bk, ISBN:0-8014-8342-5, ISBN13: 978-0-8014-8342-4. Dewey:331.89/041796. LCCN:95-049456.
Audience: **u,f.** *Choice, 1996.*

Tranter, Neil L. **GV706.5 .T73 1998**
Sport, Economy and Society in Britain 1750-1914. Maurice Kirby (Contribution by). Trade Paper. Cambridge University Press. New York, NY. 1998. 124p. New Studies in Economic and Social History, Vol. 33 ISBN:0-521-57655-5, ISBN13: 978-0-521-57655-0. Dewey:306.4/83/0941. LCCN:97-023648.
Audience: **u,f.**

Tribe, John **GV188**
The Economics of Recreation, Leisure and Tourism. Ed. 3. Paper Text. Elsevier Science & Technology Books. Saint Louis, MO. 2005. 464p. ISBN:0-7506-6180-1, ISBN13: 978-0-7506-6180-5. Dewey:790.069.
Audience: **u,f.**

Whiting, Robert **GV865.S895W55 2004**
The Meaning of Ichiro: The New Wave from Japan and the Transformation of Our National Pastime. Trade Cloth. Warner Books, Inc. New York, NY. 2004. 336p. ISBN:0-446-53192-8, ISBN13: 978-0-446-53192-4. Dewey:796.357/092 B. LCCN:2003-027134.
Audience: **u,f.** *Choice, 2005.*

Wright, Russell O. **GV863.A1W755 1999**
A Tale of Two Leagues: How Baseball Changed as the Rules, Balls, Franchises, Stadiums and Players Changed, 1900-1998. Cloth Text. McFarland & Company, Incorporated Publishers. Jefferson, NC. 1999. 224p. ISBN:0-7864-0712-3, ISBN13: 978-0-7864-0712-5. Dewey:796.357/0973. LCCN:99-40307.
Audience: **l,u,f.** *Choice, 2000.*

Zimbalist, Andrew (Editor) **GV716.E36 2001**
The Economics of Sport, Set. Trade Cloth. Edward Elgar Publishing, Inc. Northampton, MA. 2001. 1,312p. The International Library of Critical Writings in Economics, Vol. 135 ISBN:1-84064-421-4, ISBN13: 978-1-84064-421-0. Dewey:338.4/7796. LCCN:2001-040120.
Audience: **g,u,f.**

Zimbalist, Andrew **GV880**
May the Best Team Win: Baseball Economics and Public Policy, Expanded and Updated. Bob Costas (Foreword by). Trade Paper. Brookings Institution Press. Washington, DC. 2004. 208p. ISBN:0-8157-9729-X, ISBN13: 978-0-8157-9729-6. Dewey:796.357/0691. LCCN:2002-156494.
Audience: **u,f.**

Business of Sport > Politics and Government

HQ796.A1
☐ President's Council on Physical Fitness and Sports. http://fitness.gov/
Audience: **g,l,u,f.**

GV880
☐ Business of Baseball. http://www.businessofbaseball.com/
Audience: **g,l,u,f.**

HQ1237
☐ Gender equity in Sports. http://bailiwick.lib.uiowa.edu/ge/
Audience: **g,l,u,f.**

GV347
☐ Intercollegiate Atheletics Four-Year Colleges' Experiences Adding and Discontinuing Teams. http://www.gao.gov/new.items/d01297.pd gao 01-297.
Audience: **l,u,f.**

KF4166
☐ National Women's Law Center Athletics page. http://www.nwlc.org/display.cfm?section=athletics
Audience: **g,l,u,f.**

KF4758.E3
☐ Open to all: Ttile IX at Thirty. http://www.ed.gov/about/bdscomm/list/athletics/title9report.pdf GPO Secretary of Education.
Audience: **g,l,u,f.**

Barney, Robert Knight, et al. **GV721.5.B32 2002**
Selling the Five Rings: The IOC and the Rise of Olympic Commercialism. Stephen R. Wenn & Scott G. Martyn (Authors). Trade Cloth. University of Utah Press. Salt Lake City, UT. 2002. 448p. ISBN:0-87480-713-1, ISBN13: 978-0-87480-713-4. Dewey:796.48. LCCN:2001-006781.
Audience: **l,u,f.** *Choice, 2003, 2002.*

Bevis, Charlie **GV867.6.B48 2003**
Sunday Baseball: The Major Leagues' Struggle to Play Baseball on the Lord's Day, 1876-1934. Paper Text. McFarland & Company, Incorporated Publishers. Jefferson, NC. 2003. 326p. ISBN:0-7864-1564-9, ISBN13: 978-0-7864-1564-9. Dewey:796.357/64/0973. LCCN:2002-156687.
Audience: **u,f.** *Choice, 2003.*

Billet, Bret L. & Formwalt, Lance J. **GV863**
America's National Pastime: A Study of Race and Merit in Professional Baseball. Trade Cloth. Greenwood Publishing Group, Inc. Portsmouth, NH. 1995. 200p. ISBN:0-275-95193-6, ISBN13: 978-0-275-95193-1. Dewey:796.357/0973. LCCN:95-003331.
Audience: **g,l,u,f.** *Choice, 1996.*

Bjarkman, Peter C. **GV863.155.B53 1994**
Baseball with a Latin Beat: A History of the Latin American Game. Paper Text. McFarland & Company, Incorporated Publishers. Jefferson, NC. 1994. 486p. ISBN:0-89950-973-8, ISBN13: 978-0-89950-973-0. Dewey:796.357/098. LCCN:94-3526.
Audience: **u,f.** *Choice, 1995.*

Bryant, Howard **GV875.B62B79 2002**
Shut Out: A Story of Race and Baseball in Boston. Paper over Boards. Routledge. New York, NY. 2002. 296p. ISBN:0-415-92779-X, ISBN13: 978-0-415-92779-6. Dewey:796.357/64/0974461. LCCN:2002-069950.
Audience: **u,f.**

Bullock, Steve **GV863.A1B84 2004**
Playing for Their Nation: Baseball and the American Military During World War II. Trade Cloth. University of Nebraska Press. Lincoln, NE. 2005. 224p. Jerry Malloy Prize Ser. ISBN:0-8032-1337-9, ISBN13: 978-0-8032-1337-1. Dewey:796.357/0973/09044. LCCN:2003-016945.
Audience: **u,f.** *Choice, 2004.*

Cashman, Richard & Hughes, Anthony (Editors) **GV722 2000.S82 1999**
Staging the Olympics: The Event and Its Impact. Trade Paper. University of New South Wales Press. Sydney, NSW. 1999. 226p. ISBN:0-86840-729-1, ISBN13: 978-0-86840-729-6. Dewey:796.48. LCCN:00-340427.
Audience: **l,u,f.** *Choice, 2000.*

Chadwick, Bruce **GV875.A1.C47 1992**
When the Game Was Black and White: The Illustrated History of Baseball's Negro Leagues. Trade Cloth. Abbeville Press, Inc. New York, NY. 1992. 204p. ISBN:1-55859-372-1, ISBN13: 978-1-55859-372-5. Dewey:796.35708996073. LCCN:92-013673.
Audience: **g,l,u,f.** *Choice, 1993.*

Chalip, Laurence (Editor), et al. **GV706**
National Sports Policies: An International Handbook. Arthur Johnson & Lisa Stachura (Editors). Cloth Text. Greenwood Publishing Group, Inc. Portsmouth, NH. 1996. 456p. ISBN:0-313-28481-4, ISBN13: 978-0-313-28481-6. Dewey:796/.06/9. LCCN:95-025327.
Audience: **u,f.** *Choice, 1997.*

Dyreson, Mark **GV706.35.D97 1998**
Making the American Team: Sport, Culture, and the Olympic Experience. Trade Paper. University of Illinois Press. Champaign, IL. 1997. 288p. Sport and Society Ser. ISBN:0-252-06654-5, ISBN13: 978-0-252-06654-2. Dewey:796/.0973. LCCN:97-004663.
Audience: **u,f.** *Choice, 1998.*

Euchner, Charles C. **GV706.35.E93 1993**
Playing the Field: Why Sports Teams Move and Cities Fight to Keep Them. Trade Cloth. Johns Hopkins University Press. Baltimore, MD. 1993. 232p. ISBN:0-8018-4572-6, ISBN13: 978-0-8018-4572-7. Dewey:796.06873. LCCN:92-043276.
Audience: **g,l,u,f.**

Ferrand, Alain & Torrigiani, Luiggino **GV716.F47 2005**
Marketing of Olympic Sport Organisations. Trade Paper. Human Kinetics Publishers. Champaign, IL. 2004. 144p. ISBN:0-7360-5930-X, ISBN13: 978-0-7360-5930-5. Dewey:338.4/379648. LCCN:2004-022804.
Audience: **u,f.**

Fort, Rodney D. & Fizel, John (Editors) **GV716**
International Sports Economics Comparisons. Trade Cloth. Greenwood Publishing Group, Inc. Portsmouth, NH. 2004. 400p. Studies in Sports Economics ISBN:0-275-98032-4, ISBN13: 978-0-275-98032-0. Dewey:338.4/7796. LCCN:2003-062260.
Audience: **u,f.** *Choice, 2004.*

Fried, Gil, et al. **GV716.F75 2003**
Sport Finance. Steven Shapiro & Timothy DeSchriver (Authors). Trade Cloth. Human Kinetics Publishers. Champaign, IL. 2003. 392p. ISBN:0-7360-0183-2, ISBN13: 978-0-7360-0183-0. Dewey:796/.06/9. LCCN:2002-007423.
Audience: **u,f.**

Howard, Dennis R. & Crompton, John L. **GV716.H69 1995**
Financing Sport. Cloth Text. Fitness Information Technology, Inc. Morgantown, WV. 1995. 416p. ISBN:1-885693-00-1, ISBN13: 978-1-885693-00-6. Dewey:338.4/3. LCCN:94-061287.
Audience: **u,f.**

Hums, Mary A. & MacLean, Joanne **GV713.H86 2004**
Governance and Policy in Sport Organizations. Trade Cloth. Holcomb Hathaway, Inc. Scottsdale, AZ. 2004. xviii, 382p. ISBN:1-890871-45-1, ISBN13: 978-1-890871-45-1. Dewey:796/.06/9. LCCN:2003-026933.
Audience: **l,u.**

Kluka, Darlene A., et al. **GV713**
Sport Governance. Guido Schilling & William F. Stier (Authors). Trade Paper. Meyer & Meyer Sport, Ltd. Garsington, 2003. 200p. ISBN:1-84126-132-7, ISBN13: 978-1-84126-132-4. Dewey:796/.0285.
Audience: **u,f.**

Kluka, Darlene & Schilling, Guido (Editors) **GV713**
The Business of Sport. Trade Paper. Meyer & Meyer Sport, Ltd. Garsington, 2004. 192p. Perspectives - The Multidisciplinary Series of Physical Education and Sport Science, Vol. 3 ISBN:1-84126-056-8, ISBN13: 978-1-84126-056-3. Dewey:796/.069.
Audience: **u,f.**

Korr, Charles P. **GV880.2.K67 2002**
The End of Baseball As We Knew It: The Players Union, 1960-81. Bob Costas (Foreword by). Trade Cloth. University of Illinois Press. Champaign, IL. 2002. 352p. Sport and Society Ser. ISBN:0-252-02752-3, ISBN13: 978-0-252-02752-9. Dewey:331.89/041796357. LCCN:2001-007535.
Audience: **u,f.** *Choice, 2003.*

Kruger, Arnd & Murray, William (Editors) **GV722 1936.N39 2003**
The Nazi Olympics: Sport, Politics, and Appeasement in the 1930s. Trade Cloth. University of Illinois Press. Champaign, IL. 2003. 280p. Sport and Society Ser. ISBN:0-252-02815-5, ISBN13: 978-0-252-02815-1. Dewey:796.48. LCCN:2002-011803.
Audience: **g,l,u,f.** *Choice, 2004.*

Leifer, Eric M. **GV583.L45 1995**
Making the Majors: The Transformation of Team Sports in America. Trade Cloth. Harvard University Press. Cambridge, MA. 1996. 400p. ISBN:0-674-54322-X, ISBN13: 978-0-674-54322-5. Dewey:796/.06/0973. LCCN:95-013469.
Audience: **l,u,f.** *Choice, 1996.*

Lenskyj, Helen Jefferson **GV722 2000.L46 2002**
The Best Olympics Ever?: Social Impacts of Sydney 2000. Paper Text. State University of New York Press. Albany, NY. 2002. 262p. ISBN:0-7914-5474-6, ISBN13: 978-0-7914-5474-9. Dewey:796.48. LCCN:2001-055121.
Audience: **u,f.** *Choice, 2003.*

Lowe, Stephen R. **GV583.L696 1995**
The Kid on the Sandlot: Congress and Professional Sports, 1910-1992. Trade Paper. University of Wisconsin Press. Chicago, IL. 1995. 176p. ISBN:0-87972-676-8, ISBN13: 978-0-87972-676-8. Dewey:796/.0973. LCCN:94-079195.
Audience: **l,u,f.** *Choice, 1995.*

Macintosh, Donald & Hawes, Michael **GV706.35.M35 1994**
Sport and Canadian Diplomacy. Trade Cloth. McGill-Queen's University Press. Montreal, PQ. 1994. 248p. ISBN:0-7735-1161-X, ISBN13: 978-0-7735-1161-3. Dewey:379.71. LCCN:95-159702.
Audience: **g,l,u,f.** *Choice, 1994.*

Macintosh, Donald & Whitson, David **GV706.35**
The Game Planners: Transforming Canada's Sport System. Trade Paper. McGill-Queen's University Press. Montreal, PQ. 1994. 180p. ISBN:0-7735-1211-X, ISBN13: 978-0-7735-1211-5. Dewey:796/.0971.
Audience: **u,f.** *Choice, 1990.*

Martin, Simon **GV943.9.S64**
Football and Fascism: The National Game under Mussolini. Trade Paper. Berg Publishers. Oxford, 2004. 288p.

ISBN:1-85973-705-6, ISBN13: 978-1-85973-705-7. Dewey:796.334/0945/09043. LCCN:2004-020616.
Audience: **g,l,u,f.** *Choice, 2005.*

Muggleton, David & Weinzierl, Rupert **GV721.6**
Post-Olympism?: Questioning Sport in the Twenty-First Century. John Bale & Mette Krogh Christensen (Editors). Trade Paper. Berg Publishers. Oxford, 2004. 256p. Global Sport Cultures Ser. ISBN:1-85973-719-6, ISBN13: 978-1-85973-719-4. Dewey:306.4/83/0905.
Audience: **u,f.**

Pearson, Daniel **GV863.A1.P43**
Baseball in 1889: Players vs Owners. Trade Paper. University of Wisconsin Press. Chicago, IL. 2005. 244p. ISBN:0-87972-619-9, ISBN13: 978-0-87972-619-5. Dewey:796.357. LCCN:92-063282.
Audience: **l,u,f.** *Choice, 1993.*

Pettavino, Paula J. & Pye, Geralyn **GV592.C9**
Sport in Cuba: The Diamond in the Rough. Trade Paper. University of Pittsburgh Press. Pittsburgh, PA. 1994. 320p. Latin American Ser. ISBN:0-8229-5512-1, ISBN13: 978-0-8229-5512-2. Dewey:796/.097291. LCCN:93-024372.
Audience: **u,f.** *Choice, 1995.*

Pietrusza, David **GV865.L3P54 1998**
Judge and Jury: The Life and Times of Judge Kenesaw Mountain Landis. Trade Cloth. Diamond Communications, Inc. Lanham, MD. 1955. 581p. ISBN:1-888698-09-8, ISBN13: 978-1-888698-09-1. Dewey:796.357/092 B. LCCN:98-013938.
Audience: **g,l,u,f.**

Pound, Richard W. **GV721.5**
Inside the Olympics: A Behind-the-Scenes Look at the Politics, the Scandals, and the Glory of the Games. Trade Cloth. John Wiley & Sons, Inc. Hoboken, NJ. 2004. 288p. ISBN:0-470-83454-4, ISBN13: 978-0-470-83454-1. Dewey:796.48. LCCN:2006-296402.
Audience: **l,u.**

Rich, Wilbur (Editor) **GV429**
The Economics and Politics of Sports Facilities. Trade Cloth. Greenwood Publishing Group, Inc. Portsmouth, NH. 2000. 248p. ISBN:1-56720-317-5, ISBN13: 978-1-56720-317-2. Dewey:338.4/7796/06873. LCCN:99-056365.
Audience: **g,l,u,f.** *Choice, 2000.*

Riordan, J. **GV706.35.S58 1998**
Sport and International Politics. Paper over Boards. Routledge. New York, NY. 1998. 240p. ISBN:0-419-21440-2, ISBN13: 978-0-419-21440-3. Dewey:306.4/83/094/0904. LCCN:98-189017.
Audience: **g,l,u,f.** *Choice, 1999.*

Riordan, Jim & Kruger, Arnd (Editors) **GV706.35.I57 1999**
The International Politics of Sport in the 20th Century. Trade Paper. Routledge. New York, NY. 1999. 264p. ISBN:0-419-21160-8, ISBN13: 978-0-419-21160-0. Dewey:796/.09/04. LCCN:98-041234.
Audience: **u,f.** *Choice, 2000.*

Roche, Maurice **G155.A1**
Megaevents and Modernity: Olympics, Expos and the Growth of Global Culture. Trade Paper. Routledge. New York, NY. 2000. 304p. ISBN:0-415-15712-9, ISBN13: 978-0-415-15712-4. Dewey:306.4/8.
Audience: **u,f.** *Choice, 2001.*

Rosentraub, Mark S. **GV716.R67 1999**
Major League Losers: The Real Cost of Sports and Who's Paying for It. Trade Paper. Basic Books. New York, NY. 1999. 376p. ISBN:0-465-07143-0, ISBN13: 978-0-465-07143-2. Dewey:338.4/7796/0973. LCCN:00-265440.
Audience: **g,l,u,f.** *Choice, 1997.*

Sawyer, Thomas H., et al. **GV716**
Financing the Sport Enterprise. Michael Hypes & Julia Ann Hypes (Authors). Trade Paper. Sagamore Publishing, L.L.C.. Champaign, IL. 2004. 318p. ISBN:1-57167-520-5, ISBN13: 978-1-57167-520-0. Dewey:796/.06/9.
Audience: **g,l,u,f.**

Schaffer, Kay & Smith, Sidonie (Editors) **GV721.5.O425 2000**
The Olympics at the Millennium: Power, Politics, and the Games. Trade Paper. Rutgers University Press. Piscataway, NJ. 2000. xi, 318p. ISBN:0-8135-2820-8, ISBN13: 978-0-8135-2820-5. Dewey:796.48. LCCN:99-056801.
Audience: **u.** *Choice, 2001.*

Senn, Alfred Erich **GV721.5.S443 1999**
Power, Politics and the Olympic Games. Trade Paper. Human Kinetics Publishers. Champaign, IL. 1999. 336p. ISBN:0-88011-958-6, ISBN13: 978-0-88011-958-0. Dewey:796.48. LCCN:98-048879.
Audience: **l,u.** *Choice, 1999.*

Tranter, Neil L. **GV706.5 .T73 1998**
Sport, Economy and Society in Britain 1750-1914. Maurice Kirby (Contribution by). Trade Paper. Cambridge University Press. New York, NY. 1998. 124p. New Studies in Economic and Social History, Vol. 33 ISBN:0-521-57655-5, ISBN13: 978-0-521-57655-0. Dewey:306.4/83/0941. LCCN:97-023648.
Audience: **u,f.**

Wenner, Lawrence A. **GV742.M337 1998**
Mediasport. Trade Paper. Routledge. New York, NY. 1998. 352p. ISBN:0-415-14041-2, ISBN13: 978-0-415-14041-6. Dewey:070.4/49796. LCCN:98-002658.
Audience: **u,f.**

Westerbeek, Hans & Smith, Aaron **GV716.W46 2002**
Sport Business in the Global Marketplace: A Study of Strategic Cognition. Trade Cloth. Palgrave Macmillan. New York, NY. 2003. 250p. Finance and Capital Markets Ser. ISBN:1-4039-0300-X, ISBN13: 978-1-4039-0300-6. Dewey:338.4/3796. LCCN:2002-075498.
Audience: **u,f.**

Wilson, John **GV706.5.W55 1994**
Playing by the Rules: Sport, Society, and the State. Cloth Text. Wayne State University Press. Detroit, MI. 1994. 430p. ISBN:0-8143-2107-0, ISBN13: 978-0-8143-2107-2. Dewey:306.4/83/0973. LCCN:93-019671.
Audience: **u,f.** *Choice, 1994.*

Wright, Russell O. **GV863.A1W755 1999**
A Tale of Two Leagues: How Baseball Changed as the Rules, Balls, Franchises, Stadiums and Players Changed, 1900-1998. Cloth Text. McFarland & Company, Incorporated Publishers.

Jefferson, NC. 1999. 224p. ISBN:0-7864-0712-3, ISBN13: 978-0-7864-0712-5. Dewey:796.357/0973. LCCN:99-40307.
Audience: **l,u,f.** *Choice, 2000.*

Business of Sport > College

GV347
☐ Intercollegiate Atheletics Four-Year Colleges' Experiences Adding and Discontinuing Teams.
http://www.gao.gov/new.items/d01297.pd
gao 01-297.
Audience: **l,u,f.**

KF4166
☐ National Women's Law Center Athletics page.
http://www.nwlc.org/display.cfm?section=athletics
Audience: **g,l,u,f.**

KF4758.E3
☐ Open to all: Ttile IX at Thirty.
http://www.ed.gov/about/bdscomm/list/athletics/title9report.pdf
GPO Secretary of Education.
Audience: **g,l,u,f.**

Bale, John **GV351.B35 1990**
The Brawn Drain: Foreign Student Athletes in American Universities. Trade Cloth. University of Illinois Press. Champaign, IL. 1991. 248p. Sport and Society Ser. ISBN:0-252-01732-3, ISBN13: 978-0-252-01732-2. Dewey:796/.071/173. LCCN:90-032829.
Audience: **u,f.** *Choice, 1991.*

Bowen, William G. & Levin, Sarah A. **LA227.4**
Reclaiming the Game: College Sports and Educational Values. Colin G. Campbell, Martin A. Kurzweil, Susanne C. Pichler & James L. Shulman (Contribution by). Trade Cloth. Princeton University Press. Princeton, NJ. 2003. 488p. ISBN:0-691-11620-2, ISBN13: 978-0-691-11620-4. Dewey:796.04/3/0973. LCCN:2003-100409.
Audience: **g,l,u,f.**

Brandt, Nat **GV958.O24B72 2001**
When Oberlin was King of the Gridiron: The Heisman Years. Trade Paper. Kent State University Press. Kent, OH. 2001. 248p. ISBN:0-87338-684-1, ISBN13: 978-0-87338-684-5. Dewey:796.332/63/0977123. LCCN:00-010265.
Audience: **u,f.** *Choice, 2001.*

Byers, Walter & Hammer, Charles **GV351.B94 1995**
Unsportsmanlike Conduct: Exploiting College Athletes. Trade Cloth. University of Michigan Press. Chicago, IL. 1995. 424p. ISBN:0-472-10666-X, ISBN13: 978-0-472-10666-0. Dewey:796.04/3. LCCN:95-016973.
Audience: **g,l,u,f.** *Choice, 1996.*

Carpenter, Linda J. & Acosta, Vivian R. **KF4166.C37 2004**
Title IX. Trade Cloth. Human Kinetics Publishers. Champaign, IL. 2004. 28p. ISBN:0-7360-4239-3, ISBN13: 978-0-7360-4239-0. Dewey:344.73/099. LCCN:2004-009221.
Audience: **g,l,u,f.**

Carroll, John M. **GV939**
Red Grange and the Rise of Modern Football. Trade Paper. University of Illinois Press. Champaign, IL. 2004. 296p. ISBN:0-252-07166-2, ISBN13: 978-0-252-07166-9. Dewey:796.332/092 B.
Audience: **l,u,f.** *Choice, 2000.*

Chu, Donald **GV351.C484 1989**
The Character of American Higher Education and Intercollegiate Sport. Cloth Text. State University of New York Press. Albany, NY. 1989. 252p. SUNY Series in Frontiers of Education ISBN:0-88706-791-3, ISBN13: 978-0-88706-791-4. Dewey:796/.07/1173. LCCN:87-034015.
Audience: **g,l,u,f.**

Denligher, Ken **GV958.P46D466 1995**
For the Glory: College Football Dreams and Realities Inside Paterno's Program. Trade Paper. St. Martin's Press. Gordonville, VA. 1995. 320p. ISBN:0-312-13496-7, ISBN13: 978-0-312-13496-9. Dewey:796.332/63/0974811. LCCN:95-022203.
Audience: **g,l,u,f.**

Duderstadt, James J. **GV351.D83 2000**
Intercollegiate Athletics and the American University: A University President's Perspective. Trade Cloth. University of Michigan Press. Chicago, IL. 2000. 352p. ISBN:0-472-11156-6, ISBN13: 978-0-472-11156-5. Dewey:796.04/3/0973. LCCN:00-008203.
Audience: **g,l,u,f.** *Choice, 2001.*

Dunnavant, Keith **GV939.B79D86 2005**
Coach: The Life of Paul Bear Bryant. Trade Paper, Perfect. St. Martin's Press. Gordonville, VA. 2005. 320p. ISBN:0-312-34876-2, ISBN13: 978-0-312-34876-2. Dewey:796.332092 B. LCCN:2005-280370.
Audience: **g,l,u.**

Feinstein, John **GV885.49.N37**
Last Dance: Behind the Scenes at the Final Four. Mike Krzyzewski (Contribution by). Trade Paper. Little Brown & Company. New York, NY. 2007. 352p. ISBN:0-316-01425-7, ISBN13: 978-0-316-01425-0. Dewey:796.323/63/0973.
Audience: **g,l,u,f.**

Fields, Sarah K. **GV709.18.U6F54 2004**
Female Gladiators: Gender, Law, and Contact Sport in America. Trade Cloth. University of Illinois Press. Champaign, IL. 2004. 232p. Sport and Society Ser. ISBN:0-252-02958-5, ISBN13: 978-0-252-02958-5. Dewey:796/.082/0973. LCCN:2004-008913.
Audience: **u,f.** *Choice, 2005.*

Fitzpatrick, Frank **GV885.43.U53F58 2000**
And the Walls Came Tumbling Down: The Basketball Game That Changed American Sports. Trade Cloth. University of Nebraska Press. Lincoln, NE. 2000. 264p. ISBN:0-8032-6901-3, ISBN13: 978-0-8032-6901-9. Dewey:796.323/63/0975251. LCCN:00-033787.
Audience: **u,f.**

Fizel, John & Fort, Rodney D. (Editors) **GV350**
Economics of College Sports. Trade Cloth. Greenwood Publishing Group, Inc. Portsmouth, NH. 2004. 272p. Studies in Sports Economics ISBN:0-275-98033-2, ISBN13: 978-0-275-98033-7. Dewey:796.04/3/0973. LCCN:2003-060427.
Audience: **u,f.** *Choice, 2004.*

French, Peter A. **GV361.F64 2004**
Ethics and College Sports: Ethics, Sports, and the University. Book, Other. Rowman & Littlefield Publishers, Inc. Lanham,

MD. 2004. 208p. Issues in Academic Ethics Ser. ISBN:0-7425-1273-8, ISBN13: 978-0-7425-1273-3. Dewey:796.04/3/0973. LCCN:2004-004349.
Audience: **g,l,u,f.** *Choice, 2005.*

Friday, William C. & Hesburgh, Theodore M. (Editors) **LT23.N5**
A Call to Action: Reconnecting College Sports and Higher Education. Paper Text. DIANE Publishing Company. Collingdale, PA. 2001. 51p. ISBN:0-7567-1443-5, ISBN13: 978-0-7567-1443-7. Dewey:371.320973.
Audience: **g,l,u,f.**

Funk, Gary **GV346.F85 1995**
Major Violation: A Balancing Act: Sports and Education. Library Binding. Lerner Publications. Minneapolis, MN. 1995. Sports Issues Ser. ISBN:0-8225-3301-4, ISBN13: 978-0-8225-3301-6. Dewey:796.04/2. LCCN:94-038597.
Audience: **u,f.**

Gavora, Jessica **GV709.18.U6G38 2002**
Tilting the Playing Field: Schools, Sports, Sex and Title IX. Trade Cloth. National Book Network. Lanham, MD. 2001. 181p. ISBN:1-893554-35-X, ISBN13: 978-1-893554-35-1. Dewey:796/.082. LCCN:2001-055597.
Audience: **u,f.** *Choice, 2003, 2002.*

Gerdy, John R. **GV351**
The Successful College Athletic Program: The New Standard. Trade Paper. Greenwood Publishing Group, Inc. Portsmouth, NH. 1997. 192p. American Council on Education Series on Higher Education ISBN:1-57356-523-7, ISBN13: 978-1-57356-523-3. Dewey:796.04/3/0973.
Audience: **g,l,u,f.** *Choice, 1998.*

Grundy, Pamela **GV584.N8G78 2001**
Learning to Win: Sports, Education and Social Change in Twentieth-Century North Carolina. Trade Paper. University of North Carolina Press. Chapel Hill, NC. 2001. 392p. Fred W. Morrison Series in Southern Studies ISBN:0-8078-4934-0, ISBN13: 978-0-8078-4934-7. Dewey:796/.09756/0904. LCCN:00-048928.
Audience: **g,l,u,f.** *Choice, 2001.*

John S. and James L. Knight Foundation **GV347**
☐ Keeping Faith update of Call to Action.
http://www.knightcommission.org/
Knight Commission on Intercollegiate Athletics.
Audience: **l,u,f.**

King, C. Richard & Springwood, Charles Fruehling **GV706.32.K52 2001**
Beyond the Cheers: Race as Spectacle in College Sport. Paper Text. State University of New York Press. Albany, NY. 2001. x, 214p. Series on Sport, Culture, and Social Relations ISBN:0-7914-5006-6, ISBN13: 978-0-7914-5006-2. Dewey:796.04/3/08900973. LCCN:00-054797.
Audience: **u,f.** *Choice, 2001.*

Lapchick, Richard E. (Editor) **GV351**
New Game Plans for College Sport. Trade Cloth. Greenwood Publishing Group, Inc. Portsmouth, NH. 2006. 344p. ACE/Praeger Series on Higher Education Ser. ISBN:0-275-98147-9, ISBN13: 978-0-275-98147-1. Dewey:796.04/30973. LCCN:2005-034803.
Audience: **g,l,u,f.**

Lester, Robin **GV958.U519L47 1995**
Stagg's University: The Rise, Decline and Fall of Big-Time Football at the University of Chicago. Trade Cloth. University of Illinois Press. Champaign, IL. 1995. 344p. Sport and Society Ser. ISBN:0-252-02128-2, ISBN13: 978-0-252-02128-2. Dewey:796.332/09773/11. LCCN:94-034018.
Audience: **u,f.** *Choice, 1996.*

Lincoln, Chris **GV350.5.L56 2004**
Playing the Game: Inside Athletic Recruiting in the Ivy League. Jay Fiedler (Foreword by). Trade Paper. Nomad Press. White River Junction, VT. 2004. 272p. ISBN:0-9722026-6-8, ISBN13: 978-0-9722026-6-4. Dewey:796.04/3/0974. LCCN:2005-277590.
Audience: **g,l,u,f.**

Lombardo, John **GV939.F29**
A Fire to Win: The Life and Times of Woody Hayes. Trade Paper. St. Martin's Press. Gordonville, VA. 2006. 304p. ISBN:0-312-36036-3, ISBN13: 978-0-312-36036-8. Dewey:796.332/092 B.
Audience: **g,l,u.**

Massa, Mark S. **BX1406.2.M38 1999**
Catholics and American Culture: Fulton Sheen, Dorothy Day and the Notre Dame Football Team. Trade Cloth. Crossroad Publishing Company. New York, NY. 1999. 288p. ISBN:0-8245-1537-4, ISBN13: 978-0-8245-1537-9. Dewey:305.6/2073. LCCN:98-031072.
Audience: **u,f.** *Choice, 1999.*

Oriard, Michael **GV950.O73 2001**
King Football: Sport and Spectacle in the Golden Age of Radio and Newsreels, Movies and Magazines, the Weekly and the Daily Press. Trade Cloth. University of North Carolina Press. Chapel Hill, NC. 2001. 512p. ISBN:0-8078-2650-2, ISBN13: 978-0-8078-2650-8. Dewey:796.332/09/041. LCCN:2001-041459.
Audience: **l,u,f.** *Choice, 2002.*

Pont, Sally **GV939.A1P63 2001**
Fields of Honor: The Golden Age of College Football and the Men Who Created It. Cloth over Boards. Harcourt Trade Publishers. New York, NY. 2001. 256p. ISBN:0-15-100607-5, ISBN13: 978-0-15-100607-6. Dewey:796.332/63/0973. LCCN:2001-024364.
Audience: **u,f.** *Choice, 2002.*

Porto, Brian L. **GV709**
A New Season: Using Title IX to Reform College Sports. Trade Cloth. Greenwood Publishing Group, Inc. Portsmouth, NH. 2003. 264p. ISBN:0-275-97699-8, ISBN13: 978-0-275-97699-6. Dewey:796/.082. LCCN:2003-048216.
Audience: **u,f.** *Choice, 2004.*

Sack, Allen L. & Staurowsky, Ellen J. **GV351**
College Athletes for Hire: The Evolution and Legacy of the NCAA's Amateur Myth. Trade Cloth. Greenwood Publishing Group, Inc. Portsmouth, NH. 1998. 208p. ISBN:0-275-96191-5, ISBN13: 978-0-275-96191-6. Dewey:796.04/3/0973. LCCN:97-043956.
Audience: **g,l,u,f.** *Choice, 1999.*

Sands, Robert R. **GV958.S26 1999**
Gutcheck!: An Anthropologist's Wild Ride into the Heart of College Football. Trade Paper. Rincon Hill Books. Carpinteria,

CA. 2000. 321p. ISBN:0-9672973-0-3, ISBN13: 978-0-9672973-0-9. Dewey:796.332. LCCN:99-093335.
Audience: **u,f.** *Choice, 2000.*

Shulman, James Lawrence & Bowen, William G. **GV351**
The Game of Life: College Sports and Educational Values. Trade Paper. Princeton University Press. Princeton, NJ. 2002. 494p. ISBN:0-691-09619-8, ISBN13: 978-0-691-09619-3. Dewey:796.04/3/0973.
Audience: **g,l,u,f.** *Choice, 2001.*

Smith, Ronald A. **GV742.S64 2001**
Play-by-Play: Radio, Television and Big-Time College Sports. Trade Cloth. Johns Hopkins University Press. Baltimore, MD. 2001. 320p. ISBN:0-8018-6686-3, ISBN13: 978-0-8018-6686-9. Dewey:796.04/3/0973. LCCN:00-011534.
Audience: **g,u,f.** *Choice, 2002.*

Smith, Ronald A. **GV351**
Sports and Freedom: The Rise of Big-Time College Athletics. Paper Text. Oxford University Press, Inc. New York, NY. 1990. 320p. Sports History and Society Ser. ISBN:0-19-506582-4, ISBN13: 978-0-19-506582-4. Dewey:796/.07/1173. LCCN:88-017855.
Audience: **u,f.** *Choice, 1989.*

Telander, Rick **GV959.T44 1996**
The Hundred Yard Lie: The Corruption of College Football and What We Can Do to Stop It. Trade Paper. University of Illinois Press. Champaign, IL. 1996. 232p. ISBN:0-252-06523-9, ISBN13: 978-0-252-06523-1. Dewey:796.332/63/0973. LCCN:96-012412.
Audience: **g,l,u,f.**

Thelin, John R. **GV351.T43**
Games Colleges Play: Scandal and Reform in Intercollegiate Athletics. Trade Paper. Johns Hopkins University Press. Baltimore, MD. 1996. 272p. ISBN:0-8018-5504-7, ISBN13: 978-0-8018-5504-7. Dewey:796.071173.
Audience: **g,l,u,f.** *Choice, 1995.*

Thelin, John R. & Wiseman, Lawrence L. **GV351 .T44 1989**
The Old College Try: Balancing Academics and Athletics in Higher Education. Jonathan D. Fife (Editor). Paper Text. George Washington University, Graduate School of Education & Human Development. Washington, DC. 1989. 141p. ASHE-ERIC Higher Education Reports, No. 89-4 ISBN:0-9623882-3-8, ISBN13: 978-0-9623882-3-1. Dewey:796/.071/173. LCCN:89-063440.
Audience: **g,l,u,f.**

Toma, J. D. **GV959.5.T66 2003**
Football U.: Spectator Sports in the Life of the American University. Trade Cloth. University of Michigan Press. Chicago, IL. 2003. 220p. ISBN:0-472-11299-6, ISBN13: 978-0-472-11299-9. Dewey:796.332/63/0973. LCCN:2002-153617.
Audience: **g,l,u.** *Choice, 2004.*

Umphlett, Wiley L. **GV939**
Creating the Big Game: John W. Heisman and the Invention of American Football, 34. Trade Cloth. Greenwood Publishing Group, Inc. Portsmouth, NH. 1992. 296p. Contributions to the Study of Popular Culture Ser., No. 34 ISBN:0-313-28404-0, ISBN13: 978-0-313-28404-5. Dewey:796.332092. LCCN:92-010087.
Audience: **g,l,u,f.** *Choice, 1993.*

Watterson, John Sayle **GV950.W28 2000**
College Football: History, Spectacle, Controversy. Trade Cloth. Johns Hopkins University Press. Baltimore, MD. 2000. 528p. ISBN:0-8018-6428-3, ISBN13: 978-0-8018-6428-5. Dewey:796.332/63/0973. LCCN:00-008247.
Audience: **u,f.** *Choice, 2001.*

Weissberg, Ted **GV351.W45 1995**
Breaking the Rules: The NCAA and Recruitment in America's High Schools. Trade Paper. Scholastic Library Publishing. Danbury, CT. 1995. 144p. Social Issues Ser. ISBN:0-531-11235-7, ISBN13: 978-0-531-11235-9. Dewey:796/.04/30973. LCCN:95-014676.
Audience: **g,l,u.**

Yaeger, Don **GV351.Y34 1991**
Undue Process: The NCAA's Injustice for All. Trade Cloth. Sagamore Publishing, L.L.C.. Champaign, IL. 1991. 277p. ISBN:0-915611-34-1, ISBN13: 978-0-915611-34-8. Dewey:796/.071/1. LCCN:90-062973.
Audience: **g,l,u.** *Choice, 1991.*

Zimbalist, Andrew **GV351**
Unpaid Professionals: Commercialism and Conflict in Big-Time College Sports. Trade Paper. Princeton University Press. Princeton, NJ. 2001. 276p. ISBN:0-691-08690-7, ISBN13: 978-0-691-08690-3. Dewey:796.04/3/0973.
Audience: **g,l,u,f.**

Business of Sport > Professional

GV880
Business of Baseball. http://www.businessofbaseball.com/
Audience: **g,l,u,f.**

Andrews, David L. (Editor) **GV706.2.M53 2001**
Michael Jordan, Inc.: Corporate Sport, Media Culture, and Late Modern America. Paper Text. State University of New York Press. Albany, NY. 2001. xx, 301p. Series on Sport, Culture, and Social Relations ISBN:0-7914-5026-0, ISBN13: 978-0-7914-5026-0. Dewey:306.4/83/0973. LCCN:00-054794.
Audience: **g,l,u,f.** *Choice, 2002.*

Bryant, Howard **GV875.B62B79 2002**
Shut Out: A Story of Race and Baseball in Boston. Paper over Boards. Routledge. New York, NY. 2002. 296p. ISBN:0-415-92779-X, ISBN13: 978-0-415-92779-6. Dewey:796.357/64/0974461. LCCN:2002-069950.
Audience: **u,f.**

Burk, Robert F. **GV880.B869 2001**
Much More Than a Game: Players, Owners and American Baseball since 1921. Trade Paper. University of North Carolina Press. Chapel Hill, NC. 2001. 384p. ISBN:0-8078-4908-1, ISBN13: 978-0-8078-4908-8. Dewey:796.357/09/04. LCCN:00-041774.
Audience: **l,u.** *Choice, 2001.*

Burk, Robert F. **GV880.B87 1994**
Never Just a Game: Players, Owners and American Baseball to 1920. Trade Cloth. University of North Carolina Press. Chapel

Hill, NC. 1994. 302p. ISBN:0-8078-2122-5, ISBN13: 978-0-8078-2122-0. Dewey:338.4/3796357/0973. LCCN:93-022719.
Audience: **g,l,u,f.** *Choice, 1994.*

Chadwick, Bruce **GV875.A1.C47 1992**
When the Game Was Black and White: The Illustrated History of Baseball's Negro Leagues. Trade Cloth. Abbeville Press, Inc. New York, NY. 1992. 204p. ISBN:1-55859-372-1, ISBN13: 978-1-55859-372-5. Dewey:796.35708996073. LCCN:92-013673.
Audience: **g,l,u,f.** *Choice, 1993.*

Clark, Dick **GV863.A1**
The Negro Leagues Book. Trade Paper. Society for American Baseball Research. Cleveland, OH. 1994. 382p. ISBN:0-910137-55-2, ISBN13: 978-0-910137-55-3. Dewey:796.357.
Audience: **g,l,u,f.** *Choice, 1995.*

Danielson, Michael N. **GV706.35.D36 1997**
Home Team: Professional Sports and the American Metropolis. Trade Cloth. Princeton University Press. Princeton, NJ. 1997. 397p. ISBN:0-691-03650-0, ISBN13: 978-0-691-03650-2. Dewey:796/.06/9. LCCN:96-035200.
Audience: **u,f.** *Choice, 1997.*

Dorinson, Joseph & Warmund, Joram (Editors) **GV865.R6**
Jackie Robinson: Race, Sports and the American Dream. Paper Text. M. E. Sharpe Inc. Armonk, NY. 1999. 296p. ISBN:0-7656-0318-7, ISBN13: 978-0-7656-0318-0. Dewey:796.357/092.
Audience: **g,l,u,f.** *Choice, 1999.*

Downward, Paul & Dawson, Alistair **GV716.D69 2000**
The Economics of Professional Team Sports. Trade Paper. Routledge. New York, NY. 2000. 272p. ISBN:0-415-20874-2, ISBN13: 978-0-415-20874-1. Dewey:338.4/7796044/0973. LCCN:00-029116.
Audience: **u,f.**

Euchner, Charles C. **GV706.35.E93 1993**
Playing the Field: Why Sports Teams Move and Cities Fight to Keep Them. Trade Cloth. Johns Hopkins University Press. Baltimore, MD. 1993. 232p. ISBN:0-8018-4572-6, ISBN13: 978-0-8018-4572-7. Dewey:796.06873. LCCN:92-043276.
Audience: **g,l,u,f.**

Fields, Sarah K. **GV709.18.U6F54 2004**
Female Gladiators: Gender, Law, and Contact Sport in America. Trade Cloth. University of Illinois Press. Champaign, IL. 2004. 232p. Sport and Society Ser. ISBN:0-252-02958-5, ISBN13: 978-0-252-02958-5. Dewey:796/.082/0973. LCCN:2004-008913.
Audience: **u,f.** *Choice, 2005.*

Fortunato, John A. **GV885.515.N37F67**
The Ultimate Assist: The Relationship and Broadcast Strategies of the NBA and Television Networks. Trade Paper. Hampton Press, Inc. Cresskill, NJ. 2001. xix, 258p. The Hampton Press Communication Ser. ISBN:1-57273-408-6, ISBN13: 978-1-57273-408-1. Dewey:070.4/4979632364. LCCN:2001-039539.
Audience: **u,f.**

Hagstrom, Robert G. Jr. **GV1029.9.S74H34**
The NASCAR Way: The Business That Drives the Sport. Trade Paper. John Wiley & Sons, Inc. Hoboken, NJ. 2001. 254p. ISBN:0-471-39920-5, ISBN13: 978-0-471-39920-9. Dewey:338.4/7/79672/0973.
Audience: **g,l,u.**

Halberstam, David **GV939.B45**
The Education of a Coach. Trade Cloth. Hyperion Press. New York, NY. 2005. 288p. ISBN:1-4013-0154-1, ISBN13: 978-1-4013-0154-5. Dewey:796.332/092 B. LCCN:2006-276664.
Audience: **g,l,u.** *Choice, 2006.*

Halberstam, David **GV884.J67H35 2000**
Playing for Keeps: Michael Jordan and the World He Made. Trade Paper. Broadway Books. New York, NY. 2000. 448p. ISBN:0-7679-0444-3, ISBN13: 978-0-7679-0444-5. Dewey:796.323/092 B. LCCN:99-041931.
Audience: **u,f.** *Choice, 1999.*

Harris, Fran **GV885.515.W66**
Summer Madness: The Wild, Wacky, Wonderful World of the WNBA. Trade Paper. iUniverse, Inc. Lincoln, NE. 2001. 268p. ISBN:0-595-16030-1, ISBN13: 978-0-595-16030-3. Dewey:796.323/092.
Audience: **g,l,u.**

Hauser, Thomas **GV1133.H34 2000**
The Black Lights: Inside the World of Professional Boxing. Trade Paper. University of Arkansas Press. Fayetteville, AR. 2000. 272p. ISBN:1-55728-597-7, ISBN13: 978-1-55728-597-3. Dewey:796.83. LCCN:99-086546.
Audience: **g,l,u.**

Jozsa, Frank P. Jr. **GV583**
American Sports Empire: How the Leagues Breed Success. Book, Other. Greenwood Publishing Group, Inc. Portsmouth, NH. 2003. 272p. ISBN:1-56720-559-3, ISBN13: 978-1-56720-559-6. Dewey:796/.0973. LCCN:2002-029759.
Audience: **g,l,u,f.** *Choice, 2003.*

Kluka, Darlene & Schilling, Guido (Editors) **GV713**
The Business of Sport. Trade Paper. Meyer & Meyer Sport, Ltd. Garsington, 2004. 192p. Perspectives - The Multidisciplinary Series of Physical Education and Sport Science, Vol. 3 ISBN:1-84126-056-8, ISBN13: 978-1-84126-056-3. Dewey:796/.069.
Audience: **u,f.**

Lanctot, Neil **GV875.N35L36 2004**
Negro League Baseball: The Rise and Ruin of a Black Institution. Book, Other. University of Pennsylvania Press. Philadelphia, PA. 2004. 496p. ISBN:0-8122-3807-9, ISBN13: 978-0-8122-3807-5. Dewey:796.357/64/0973. LCCN:2004-043547.
Audience: **g,l,u,f.** *Choice, 2004.*

Leifer, Eric M. **GV583.L45 1995**
Making the Majors: The Transformation of Team Sports in America. Trade Cloth. Harvard University Press. Cambridge, MA. 1996. 400p. ISBN:0-674-54322-X, ISBN13: 978-0-674-54322-5. Dewey:796/.06/0973. LCCN:95-013469.
Audience: **l,u,f.** *Choice, 1996.*

Levy, Alan H. **GV943.9.S64L48 2003**
Tackling Jim Crow: Racial Segregation in Professional Football. Paper Text. McFarland & Company, Incorporated Publishers.

Jefferson, NC. 2003. 180p. ISBN:0-7864-1597-5, ISBN13: 978-0-7864-1597-7. Dewey:796.332/0896/073. LCCN:2003-005735.
Audience: **u,f.** *Choice, 2003.*

Lomax, Michael E. **GV863.A1L65 2003**
Black Baseball Entrepreneurs, 1860-1901: Operating by Any Means Necessary. Trade Paper. Syracuse University Press. Syracuse, NY. 2003. xxvi, 222p. Sports and Entertainment Ser. ISBN:0-8156-0786-5, ISBN13: 978-0-8156-0786-1. Dewey:796.357/64/08996073. LCCN:2002-154375.
Audience: **u,f.**

Lowe, Stephen R. **GV583.L696 1995**
The Kid on the Sandlot: Congress and Professional Sports, 1910-1992. Trade Paper. University of Wisconsin Press. Chicago, IL. 1995. 176p. ISBN:0-87972-676-8, ISBN13: 978-0-87972-676-8. Dewey:796/.0973. LCCN:94-079195.
Audience: **l,u,f.** *Choice, 1995.*

MacCambridge, Michael **GV954.M32 2004**
America's Game: The Epic Story of How Pro Football Captured a Nation. Trade Cloth. Random House Adult Trade Publishing Group. New York, NY. 2004. 576p. ISBN:0-375-50454-0, ISBN13: 978-0-375-50454-9. Dewey:796.332/640973. LCCN:2004-052003.
Audience: **l,u,f.** *Choice, 2005.*

McClellan, Keith **GV954.M37 1998**
The Sunday Game: At the Dawn of Professional Football. Trade Cloth. University of Akron Press, The. Akron, OH. 1998. 503p. Ohio History and Culture Ser. ISBN:1-884836-36-4, ISBN13: 978-1-884836-36-7. Dewey:796.332/0973. LCCN:98-024175.
Audience: **u,f.** *Choice, 1999.*

Noll, Roger G. & Zimbalist, Andrew (Editors) **GV716.S647 1997**
Sports, Jobs and Taxes: The Economic Impact of Sports Teams and Facilities. Trade Paper. Brookings Institution Press. Washington, DC. 1997. 525p. ISBN:0-8157-6111-2, ISBN13: 978-0-8157-6111-2. Dewey:338.4/3796/0973. LCCN:97-033764.
Audience: **u,f.** *Choice, 1998.*

Oriard, Michael **GV950.O73 2001**
King Football: Sport and Spectacle in the Golden Age of Radio and Newsreels, Movies and Magazines, the Weekly and the Daily Press. Trade Cloth. University of North Carolina Press. Chapel Hill, NC. 2001. 512p. ISBN:0-8078-2650-2, ISBN13: 978-0-8078-2650-8. Dewey:796.332/09/041. LCCN:2001-041459.
Audience: **l,u,f.** *Choice, 2002.*

Pearson, Daniel **GV863.A1.P43**
Baseball in 1889: Players vs Owners. Trade Paper. University of Wisconsin Press. Chicago, IL. 2005. 244p. ISBN:0-87972-619-9, ISBN13: 978-0-87972-619-5. Dewey:796.357. LCCN:92-063282.
Audience: **l,u,f.** *Choice, 1993.*

Pietrusza, David **GV863.A1P54 1997**
Lights On!: The Wild Century-Long Saga of Night Baseball. Trade Cloth. Scarecrow Press, Inc. Lanham, MD. 1997. 288p. American Sports History Ser., Vol. 7 ISBN:0-8108-3307-7, ISBN13: 978-0-8108-3307-4. Dewey:796.357/0973. LCCN:97-007800.
Audience: **g,l,u,f.** *Choice, 1998.*

Quirk, James & Fort, Rodney D. **GV716**
Pay Dirt: The Business of Professional Team Sports. Ed. 2. Trade Paper. Princeton University Press. Princeton, NJ. 1997. 566p. ISBN:0-691-01574-0, ISBN13: 978-0-691-01574-3. Dewey:338.43796. LCCN:92-015349.
Audience: **g,l,u.** *Choice, 1993.*

Regalado, Samuel O. **GV865.A1R38 1998**
Viva Baseball!: Latin Major Leaguers and Their Special Hunger. Trade Cloth. University of Illinois Press. Champaign, IL. 1998. 264p. Sport and Society Ser. ISBN:0-252-02372-2, ISBN13: 978-0-252-02372-9. Dewey:796.357/64/098. LCCN:97-021066.
Audience: **g,l,u,f.** *Choice, 1998.*

Riess, Steven A. **GV867.64.R54 1999**
Touching Base: Professional Baseball and American Culture in the Progressive Era. Ed. 2. Trade Paper. University of Illinois Press. Champaign, IL. 1999. 328p. Sport and Society Ser. ISBN:0-252-06775-4, ISBN13: 978-0-252-06775-4. Dewey:796.357/0973. LCCN:98-058018.
Audience: **g,l,u,f.** B *Choice, 2000.*

Rosentraub, Mark S. **GV716.R67 1999**
Major League Losers: The Real Cost of Sports and Who's Paying for It. Trade Paper. Basic Books. New York, NY. 1999. 376p. ISBN:0-465-07143-0, ISBN13: 978-0-465-07143-2. Dewey:338.4/7796/0973. LCCN:00-265440.
Audience: **g,l,u,f.** *Choice, 1997.*

Salzberg, Charles **GV884.A1S25 1998**
From Set Shot to Slam Dunk: The Glory Days of Basketball in the Words of Those Who Played It. Trade Cloth. University of Nebraska Press. Lincoln, NE. 1998. 269p. ISBN:0-8032-9250-3, ISBN13: 978-0-8032-9250-5. Dewey:[B]. LCCN:97-043062.
Audience: **g,l,u,f.**

Sawyer, Thomas H., et al. **GV716**
Financing the Sport Enterprise. Michael Hypes & Julia Ann Hypes (Authors). Trade Paper. Sagamore Publishing, L.L.C.. Champaign, IL. 2004. 318p. ISBN:1-57167-520-5, ISBN13: 978-1-57167-520-0. Dewey:796/.06/9.
Audience: **g,l,u,f.**

Sheehan, Richard G. **GV716.S45 1996**
Keeping Score: The Economics of Big-Time Sports. Trade Cloth. Diamond Communications, Inc. Lanham, MD. 1997. 352p. ISBN:1-888698-05-5, ISBN13: 978-1-888698-05-3. Dewey:338.4/7796/0973. LCCN:96-019528.
Audience: **u,f.** *Choice, 1997.*

Sommers, Paul M. (Editor) **GV880 .D53 1992**
Diamonds Are Forever: The Business of Baseball. Trade Cloth. Brookings Institution Press. Washington, DC. 1992. 208p. ISBN:0-8157-8042-7, ISBN13: 978-0-8157-8042-7. Dewey:338.4/3796357/640973. LCCN:91-047699.
Audience: **g,l,u.**

Staudohar, Paul D. **GV716.S72 1996**
Playing for Dollars: Labor Relations and the Sports Business. Ed. 3. Trade Paper. Cornell University Press. Ithaca, NY. 1996. 232p. ILR Press Bk, ISBN:0-8014-8342-5, ISBN13: 978-0-8014-8342-4. Dewey:331.89/041796. LCCN:95-049456.
Audience: **u,f.** *Choice, 1996.*

Thomas, Henry W. **GV865.J6T46 1998**
Walter Johnson: Baseball's Big Train. Shirley Povich (Foreword by). Trade Cloth. University of Nebraska Press. Lincoln, NE. 1998. 496p. ISBN:0-8032-9433-6, ISBN13: 978-0-8032-9433-2. Dewey:796.357/092 B. LCCN:97-035190.
Audience: **g,l,u.**

Thomas, Ron **GV885.7.T46 2002**
They Cleared the Lane: The NBA's Black Pioneers. Trade Cloth. University of Nebraska Press. Lincoln, NE. 2002. 288p. ISBN:0-8032-4437-1, ISBN13: 978-0-8032-4437-5. Dewey:796.323/64/08996073. LCCN:2001-052234.
Audience: **u,f.** *Choice, 2002.*

Tygiel, Jules **GV865.R6T93 1997**
Baseball's Great Experiment: Jackie Robinson and His Legacy. Trade Paper. Oxford University Press, Inc. New York, NY. 1997. 432p. ISBN:0-19-510620-2, ISBN13: 978-0-19-510620-6. Dewey:796.357/092 B. LCCN:96-038551.
Audience: **g,l,u,f.** B

Vamplew, Wray **GV605 .V36 1988**
Pay up and Play the Game: Professional Sport in Britain, 1875-1914. Trade Paper. Cambridge University Press. New York, NY. 2004. 414p. ISBN:0-521-89230-9, ISBN13: 978-0-521-89230-8. Dewey:796/.0941.
Audience: **u,f.** *Choice, 1989.*

Whiting, Robert **GV865.S895W55 2004**
The Meaning of Ichiro: The New Wave from Japan and the Transformation of Our National Pastime. Trade Cloth. Warner Books, Inc. New York, NY. 2004. 336p. ISBN:0-446-53192-8, ISBN13: 978-0-446-53192-4. Dewey:796.357/092 B. LCCN:2003-027134.
Audience: **u,f.** *Choice, 2005.*

Wright, Russell O. **GV863.A1W755 1999**
A Tale of Two Leagues: How Baseball Changed as the Rules, Balls, Franchises, Stadiums and Players Changed, 1900-1998. Cloth Text. McFarland & Company, Incorporated Publishers. Jefferson, NC. 1999. 224p. ISBN:0-7864-0712-3, ISBN13: 978-0-7864-0712-5. Dewey:796.357/0973. LCCN:99-40307.
Audience: **l,u,f.** *Choice, 2000.*

Business of Sport > International

GV341
☐ Commwealth Games Federation. http://www.thecgf.com/home.asp
Audience: **l,u,f.**

Bale, John **GV351.B35 1990**
The Brawn Drain: Foreign Student Athletes in American Universities. Trade Cloth. University of Illinois Press. Champaign, IL. 1991. 248p. Sport and Society Ser. ISBN:0-252-01732-3, ISBN13: 978-0-252-01732-2. Dewey:796/.071/173. LCCN:90-032829.
Audience: **u,f.** *Choice, 1991.*

Boyle, Raymond & Haynes, Richard **GV742.B69 2000**
Power Play: Sport, the Media and Popular Culture. Trade Paper. Longman Publishing Group. White Plains, NY. 2000. 256p. ISBN:0-582-36939-8, ISBN13: 978-0-582-36939-9. Dewey:306.4/83. LCCN:99-038838.
Audience: **u,f.**

Cashman, Richard & Hughes, Anthony (Editors) **GV722 2000.S82 1999**
Staging the Olympics: The Event and Its Impact. Trade Paper. University of New South Wales Press. Sydney, NSW. 1999. 226p. ISBN:0-86840-729-1, ISBN13: 978-0-86840-729-6. Dewey:796.48. LCCN:00-340427.
Audience: **l,u,f.** *Choice, 2000.*

Chalip, Laurence (Editor), et al. **GV706**
National Sports Policies: An International Handbook. Arthur Johnson & Lisa Stachura (Editors). Cloth Text. Greenwood Publishing Group, Inc. Portsmouth, NH. 1996. 456p. ISBN:0-313-28481-4, ISBN13: 978-0-313-28481-6. Dewey:796/.06/9. LCCN:95-025327.
Audience: **u,f.** *Choice, 1997.*

Darby, Paul **GV944.A4D37 2001**
Africa, Football and FIFA: Politics, Colonialism and Resistance. Trade Paper. Taylor & Francis Group. Abingdon, 2002. 256p. Sport in the Global Society Ser., No. 23 ISBN:0-7146-8029-X, ISBN13: 978-0-7146-8029-3. Dewey:796.334/096. LCCN:2001-002915.
Audience: **u,f.** *Choice, 2002.*

Dyreson, Mark **GV706.35.D97 1998**
Making the American Team: Sport, Culture, and the Olympic Experience. Trade Paper. University of Illinois Press. Champaign, IL. 1997. 288p. Sport and Society Ser. ISBN:0-252-06654-5, ISBN13: 978-0-252-06654-2. Dewey:796/.0973. LCCN:97-004663.
Audience: **u,f.** *Choice, 1998.*

Fort, Rodney D. & Fizel, John (Editors) **GV716**
International Sports Economics Comparisons. Trade Cloth. Greenwood Publishing Group, Inc. Portsmouth, NH. 2004. 400p. Studies in Sports Economics ISBN:0-275-98032-4, ISBN13: 978-0-275-98032-0. Dewey:338.4/7796. LCCN:2003-062260.
Audience: **u,f.** *Choice, 2004.*

Hums, Mary A. & MacLean, Joanne **GV713.H86 2004**
Governance and Policy in Sport Organizations. Trade Cloth. Holcomb Hathaway, Inc. Scottsdale, AZ. 2004. xviii, 382p. ISBN:1-890871-45-1, ISBN13: 978-1-890871-45-1. Dewey:796/.06/9. LCCN:2003-026933.
Audience: **l,u.**

Leheny, David Richard **GV125.L43 2003**
The Rules of Play: National Identity and the Shaping of Japanese Leisure. Trade Cloth. Cornell University Press. Ithaca, NY. 2003. xiv, 188p. Cornell Studies in Political Economy ISBN:0-8014-4091-2, ISBN13: 978-0-8014-4091-5. Dewey:306.4/8/0952. LCCN:2002-151027.
Audience: **u,f.** *Choice, 2003.*

Macintosh, Donald & Hawes, Michael **GV706.35.M35 1994**
Sport and Canadian Diplomacy. Trade Cloth. McGill-Queen's University Press. Montreal, PQ. 1994. 248p. ISBN:0-7735-1161-X, ISBN13: 978-0-7735-1161-3. Dewey:379.71. LCCN:95-159702.
Audience: **g,l,u,f.** *Choice, 1994.*

Macintosh, Donald & Whitson, David **GV706.35**
The Game Planners: Transforming Canada's Sport System.

Trade Paper. McGill-Queen's University Press. Montreal, PQ. 1994. 180p. ISBN:0-7735-1211-X, ISBN13: 978-0-7735-1211-5. Dewey:796/.0971.
Audience: **u,f.** *Choice, 1990.*

Oleksak, Michael M. & Oleksak, Mary A. **GV862.6.O43 1991**
Beisbol: Latin Americans and the Grand Old Game. Trade Cloth. McGraw-Hill Trade. New York, NY. 1991. 320p. ISBN:0-940279-35-5, ISBN13: 978-0-940279-35-3. Dewey:796.357/098. LCCN:91-010697.
Audience: **g,l,u,f.** *Choice, 1991.*

Pettavino, Paula J. & Pye, Geralyn **GV592.C9**
Sport in Cuba: The Diamond in the Rough. Trade Paper. University of Pittsburgh Press. Pittsburgh, PA. 1994. 320p. Latin American Ser. ISBN:0-8229-5512-1, ISBN13: 978-0-8229-5512-2. Dewey:796/.097291. LCCN:93-024372.
Audience: **u,f.** *Choice, 1995.*

Reaves, Joseph A. **GV863.69.R43 2002**
Taking in a Game: A History of Baseball in Asia. Trade Cloth. University of Nebraska Press. Lincoln, NE. 2002. 220p. Jerry Malloy Prize Ser. ISBN:0-8032-3943-2, ISBN13: 978-0-8032-3943-2. Dewey:796.357/095. LCCN:2001-043058.
Audience: **g,l,u,f.** *Choice, 2002.*

Riordan, J. **GV706.35.S58 1998**
Sport and International Politics. Paper over Boards. Routledge. New York, NY. 1998. 240p. ISBN:0-419-21440-2, ISBN13: 978-0-419-21440-3. Dewey:306.4/83/094/0904. LCCN:98-189017.
Audience: **g,l,u,f.** *Choice, 1999.*

Riordan, Jim & Kruger, Arnd (Editors) **GV706.35.I57 1999**
The International Politics of Sport in the 20th Century. Trade Paper. Routledge. New York, NY. 1999. 264p. ISBN:0-419-21160-8, ISBN13: 978-0-419-21160-0. Dewey:796/.09/04. LCCN:98-041234.
Audience: **u,f.** *Choice, 2000.*

Szymanski, Stefan & Zimbalist, Andrew S. **GV716.S99 2005**
National Pastime: How Americans Play Baseball and the Rest of the World Plays Soccer. Perfect, Paper over Boards, Dust Jacket. Brookings Institution Press. Washington, DC. 2005. 263p. ISBN:0-8157-8258-6, ISBN13: 978-0-8157-8258-2. Dewey:338.4/7796334. LCCN:2005-001160.
Audience: **u,f.** *Choice, 2005.*

Vamplew, Wray **GV605 .V36 1988**
Pay up and Play the Game: Professional Sport in Britain, 1875-1914. Trade Paper. Cambridge University Press. New York, NY. 2004. 414p. ISBN:0-521-89230-9, ISBN13: 978-0-521-89230-8. Dewey:796/.0941.
Audience: **u,f.** *Choice, 1989.*

Veal, A. J. (Editor), et al. **GV1**
Free Time and Leisure Participation: International Perspectives. Grant Cushman & Jiri Zuzanek (Editors). Perfect, Paper over Boards. CAB International. Wallingford, 2005. 298p. CABI Publishing Ser. ISBN:0-85199-620-5, ISBN13: 978-0-85199-620-2. Dewey:790.1. LCCN:2004-011056.
Audience: **u,f.**

Westerbeek, Hans & Smith, Aaron **GV716.W46 2002**
Sport Business in the Global Marketplace: A Study of Strategic Cognition. Trade Cloth. Palgrave Macmillan. New York, NY. 2003. 250p. Finance and Capital Markets Ser. ISBN:1-4039-0300-X, ISBN13: 978-1-4039-0300-6. Dewey:338.4/3796. LCCN:2002-075498.
Audience: **u,f.**

Whiting, Robert **GV865.S895W55 2004**
The Meaning of Ichiro: The New Wave from Japan and the Transformation of Our National Pastime. Trade Cloth. Warner Books, Inc. New York, NY. 2004. 336p. ISBN:0-446-53192-8, ISBN13: 978-0-446-53192-4. Dewey:796.357/092 B. LCCN:2003-027134.
Audience: **u,f.** *Choice, 2005.*

Wilcox, Ralph C. (Editor) **GV706.8.S659 1994**
Sport in the Global Village. Eric F. Brown (Contribution by). Cloth Text. Fitness Information Technology, Inc. Morgantown, WV. 1994. 556p. ISBN:0-9627926-4-0, ISBN13: 978-0-9627926-4-9. Dewey:306.4/83. LCCN:94-070170.
Audience: **u.**

Business of Sport > Gambling. Entertainment

Browne, David **GV749.7.B76 2004**
Amped: How Big Air, Big Dollars, and a New Generation Took Sports to the Extreme. Cloth over Boards. Bloomsbury Publishing. New York, NY. 2004. 300p. ISBN:1-58234-317-9, ISBN13: 978-1-58234-317-4. Dewey:796.04/6. LCCN:2004-004822.
Audience: **g,l,u.**

Davies, Richard O. & Abram, Richard G. **GV717.D38 2001**
Betting the Line: Sports Wagering in American Life. Trade Paper. Ohio State University Press. Columbus, OH. 2001. 208p. ISBN:0-8142-5078-5, ISBN13: 978-0-8142-5078-5. Dewey:796. LCCN:2001-000771.
Audience: **g,l,u,f.** *Choice, 2002.*

Downward, Paul & Dawson, Alistair **GV716.D69 2000**
The Economics of Professional Team Sports. Trade Paper. Routledge. New York, NY. 2000. 272p. ISBN:0-415-20874-2, ISBN13: 978-0-415-20874-1. Dewey:338.4/7796044/0973. LCCN:00-029116.
Audience: **u,f.**

Sawyer, Thomas H., et al. **GV716**
Financing the Sport Enterprise. Michael Hypes & Julia Ann Hypes (Authors). Trade Paper. Sagamore Publishing, L.L.C.. Champaign, IL. 2004. 318p. ISBN:1-57167-520-5, ISBN13: 978-1-57167-520-0. Dewey:796/.06/9.
Audience: **g,l,u,f.**

Thompson, William N. **GV1301.T47 2001**
Gambling in America: An Encyclopedia of History, Issues, and Society. Library Binding. ABC-CLIO, Inc. Santa Barbara, CA. 2001. 509p. ISBN:1-57607-159-6, ISBN13: 978-1-57607-159-5. Dewey:795/.0973. LCCN:2001-003493.
Audience: **g.** *Choice, 2002.*

Business of Sport > Law. Legal Issues

KF4166
☐ National Women's Law Center Athletics page.
http://www.nwlc.org/display.cfm?section=athletics
Audience: **g,l,u,f.**

KF4758.E3
☐ Open to all: Ttile IX at Thirty.
http://www.ed.gov/about/bdscomm/list/athletics/title9report.pdf
GPO Secretary of Education.
Audience: **g,l,u,f.**

Appenzeller, Herb **GV346.A67 2003**
Managing Sport and Risk Management Strategies. Ed. 2. Trade Paper. Carolina Academic Press. Durham, NC. 2003. 464p. ISBN:0-89089-664-X, ISBN13: 978-0-89089-664-8. Dewey:796.069. LCCN:2003-102974.
Audience: **u,f.**

Appenzeller, Herb & Lewis, Guy **GV713**
Successful Sport Management: A Guide to Legal Issues. Ed. 2. Trade Paper. Carolina Academic Press. Durham, NC. 2000. 421p. ISBN:0-89089-661-5, ISBN13: 978-0-89089-661-7. Dewey:796.068. LCCN:00-106586.
Audience: **u,f.**

Appenzeller, Thomas **KF3989.A965 2000**
Youth Sport and the Law: A Guide to Legal Issues. Herb Appenzeller (Editor). Trade Paper. Carolina Academic Press. Durham, NC. 2000. 216p. ISBN:0-89089-663-1, ISBN13: 978-0-89089-663-1. Dewey:344.73/099. LCCN:99-088424.
Audience: **u,f.**

Carpenter, Linda J. **KF4166**
Legal Concepts in Sport: A Primer. Ed. 2. Perfect. Sagamore Publishing, L.L.C.. Champaign, IL. 2000. 214p. ISBN:0-88314-659-2, ISBN13: 978-0-88314-659-0. Dewey:796.026. LCCN:99-069463.
Audience: **g,l,u,f.**

Carpenter, Linda J. & Acosta, Vivian R. **KF4166.C37 2004**
Title IX. Trade Cloth. Human Kinetics Publishers. Champaign, IL. 2004. 28p. ISBN:0-7360-4239-3, ISBN13: 978-0-7360-4239-0. Dewey:344.73/099. LCCN:2004-009221.
Audience: **g,l,u,f.**

Champion, Walter T. **KF3989.C474 2005**
Sports Law: Cases, Documents and Materials. Cloth Text. Aspen Publishers, Inc. New York, NY. 2004. xxvi, 693p. ISBN:0-7355-3659-7, ISBN13: 978-0-7355-3659-3. Dewey:344.73/099. LCCN:2004-057396.
Audience: **l,u,f.**

Champion, Walter T. **KF3989.Z9C48 2005**
Sports Law in a Nutshell. Ed. 3. Trade Paper. West Publishing Company, College & School Division. Eagan, MN. 2005. 450p. ISBN:0-314-15966-5, ISBN13: 978-0-314-15966-3. Dewey:344.73/099. LCCN:2005-278169.
Audience: **l,u.**

Chelladurai, P. **GV713.C5 1999**
Human Resource Management in Sport and Recreation. Trade Cloth. Human Kinetics Publishers. Champaign, IL. 1999. 312p. ISBN:0-87322-973-8, ISBN13: 978-0-87322-973-9. Dewey:796/.06/93. LCCN:98-037051.
Audience: **u,f.**

Cotten, Doyice J. & Wolohan, John **KF3989.S64 2003**
Law for Recreation and Sport Managers. Ed. 3. Trade Paper. Kendall/Hunt Publishing Company. Dubuque, IA. 2003. 698p. ISBN:0-7872-9968-5, ISBN13: 978-0-7872-9968-2. Dewey:344.73/099. LCCN:2003-010664.
Audience: **l,u,f.**

Davies, Richard O. & Abram, Richard G. **GV717.D38 2001**
Betting the Line: Sports Wagering in American Life. Trade Paper. Ohio State University Press. Columbus, OH. 2001. 208p. ISBN:0-8142-5078-5, ISBN13: 978-0-8142-5078-5. Dewey:796. LCCN:2001-000771.
Audience: **g,l,u,f.** *Choice, 2002.*

DeSensi, Joy Theresa & Rosenberg, Danny **GV713.D465 2003**
Ethics and Morality in Sport Management. Trade Cloth. Fitness Information Technology, Inc. Morgantown, WV. 2003. 299p. Sport Management Library ISBN:1-885693-46-X, ISBN13: 978-1-885693-46-4. Dewey:796/.06/9. LCCN:2002-113559.
Audience: **u,f.**

Dougherty, Neil J. **KF3989**
Sport, Physical Activity and the Law. Ed. 2. Alan S. Goldberger (Author, Author), Linda Jean Carpenter (Author). Trade Paper. Sagamore Publishing, L.L.C.. Champaign, IL. 2002. 266p. ISBN:1-57167-492-6, ISBN13: 978-1-57167-492-0. Dewey:344.73099. LCCN:2002-101305.
Audience: **l,u,f.**

Epstein, Adam **KF3989.E67 2002**
Sports Law for Paralegals. Paper Text. Thomson Delmar Learning. Albany, NY. 2002. 400p. The West Legal Studies ISBN:0-7668-2324-5, ISBN13: 978-0-7668-2324-2. Dewey:344.73/099. LCCN:2002-041017.
Audience: **l,u.**

Fields, Sarah K. **GV709.18.U6F54 2004**
Female Gladiators: Gender, Law, and Contact Sport in America. Trade Cloth. University of Illinois Press. Champaign, IL. 2004. 232p. Sport and Society Ser. ISBN:0-252-02958-5, ISBN13: 978-0-252-02958-5. Dewey:796/.082/0973. LCCN:2004-008913.
Audience: **u,f.** *Choice, 2005.*

Gardiner, Simon **GV557-1198.995KD51-**
Sports Law. Ed. 3. Trade Paper. Taylor & Francis Group. Abingdon, 2005. DCCLXXXVIp. ISBN:1-85941-894-5, ISBN13: 978-1-85941-894-9. Dewey:344.4/1099. LCCN:2006-279850.
Audience: **u,f.**

Gavora, Jessica **GV709.18.U6G38 2002**
Tilting the Playing Field: Schools, Sports, Sex and Title IX. Trade Cloth. National Book Network. Lanham, MD. 2001.

181p. ISBN:1-893554-35-X, ISBN13: 978-1-893554-35-1. Dewey:796/.082. LCCN:2001-055597.
Audience: **u,f.** *Choice, 2003, 2002.*

Grayson, Edward & Bond, Catherine **KD2965.S66G73 1999**
Sports Medicine: Ethics and the Law. Trade Paper. Elsevier Science & Technology Books. Saint Louis, MO. 1999. 216p. ISBN:0-7506-1576-1, ISBN13: 978-0-7506-1576-1. Dewey:617.1/027. LCCN:00-265730.
Audience: **u,f.**

O'Leary, John (Editor) **HV5800-5840GV557-11**
Drugs and Doping in Sport: Socio-Legal Perspectives. Trade Paper. Taylor & Francis Group. Abingdon, 2001. 320p. ISBN:1-85941-662-4, ISBN13: 978-1-85941-662-4. Dewey:362.2/9/088796.
Audience: **u,f.**

Pemberton, Cynthia Lee A. **GV709.18.U6P46 2002**
More than a Game: One Woman's Fight for Gender Equity in Sport. Donna de Varona (Foreword by). Paper Text. Northeastern University Press. Boston, MA. 2002. 320p. ISBN:1-55553-525-9, ISBN13: 978-1-55553-525-4. Dewey:796/.082/09795. LCCN:2001-059193.
Audience: **u,f.** *Choice, 2002.*

Porto, Brian L. **GV709**
A New Season: Using Title IX to Reform College Sports. Trade Cloth. Greenwood Publishing Group, Inc. Portsmouth, NH. 2003. 264p. ISBN:0-275-97699-8, ISBN13: 978-0-275-97699-6. Dewey:796/.082. LCCN:2003-048216.
Audience: **u,f.** *Choice, 2004.*

Quirk, Charles E. (Editor) **KF3989.S675 1996**
Sports and the Law: Major Legal Cases. Library Binding. Garland Publishing, Inc. New York, NY. 1996. 336p. Reference Library of the Humanities, Vol. 04 ISBN:0-8153-0220-7, ISBN13: 978-0-8153-0220-9. Dewey:344.73/099. LCCN:94-035594.
Audience: **u,f.**

Simon, Rita J. (Editor) **GV709.18.U6S67 2005**
Sporting Equality: Title IX Thirty Years Later. Trade Paper. Transaction Publishers. Somerset, NJ. 2005. 182p. ISBN:0-7658-0848-X, ISBN13: 978-0-7658-0848-6. Dewey:796/.082. LCCN:2004-051694.
Audience: **g,l,u,f.**

Wong, Glenn M. **KF3989**
Essentials of Sports Law. Ed. 3. Cloth Text. Greenwood Publishing Group, Inc. Portsmouth, NH. 2002. 832p. ISBN:0-275-97121-X, ISBN13: 978-0-275-97121-2. Dewey:344.73/099. LCCN:2001-058043.
Audience: **l,u.**

Yaeger, Don **GV351.Y34 1991**
Undue Process: The NCAA's Injustice for All. Trade Cloth. Sagamore Publishing, L.L.C.. Champaign, IL. 1991. 277p. ISBN:0-915611-34-1, ISBN13: 978-0-915611-34-8. Dewey:796/.071/1. LCCN:90-062973.
Audience: **g,l,u.** *Choice, 1991.*

Business of Sport > Media

Andrews, David L. (Editor) **GV706.2.M53 2001**
Michael Jordan, Inc.: Corporate Sport, Media Culture, and Late Modern America. Paper Text. State University of New York Press. Albany, NY. 2001. xx, 301p. Series on Sport, Culture, and Social Relations ISBN:0-7914-5026-0, ISBN13: 978-0-7914-5026-0. Dewey:306.4/83/0973. LCCN:00-054794.
Audience: **g,l,u,f.** *Choice, 2002.*

Baker, Aaron & Boyd, Todd **GV742.O88 1997**
Out of Bounds: Sports, Media and the Politics of Identity. Trade Paper. Indiana University Press. Bloomington, IN. 1997. 240p. ISBN:0-253-21095-X, ISBN13: 978-0-253-21095-1. Dewey:070.4/49796. LCCN:96-019729.
Audience: **u,f.** *Choice, 1997.*

Barnett, Steven **GV742.3 .B37 1990**
Games and Sets: The Changing Face of Sport on Television. Trade Paper. BFI Publishing. London, 1990. 224p. ISBN:0-85170-268-6, ISBN13: 978-0-85170-268-1. Dewey:302.234/5. LCCN:91-105439.
Audience: **u,f.** *Choice, 1991.*

Barney, Robert Knight, et al. **GV721.5.B32 2002**
Selling the Five Rings: The IOC and the Rise of Olympic Commercialism. Stephen R. Wenn & Scott G. Martyn (Authors). Trade Cloth. University of Utah Press. Salt Lake City, UT. 2002. 448p. ISBN:0-87480-713-1, ISBN13: 978-0-87480-713-4. Dewey:796.48. LCCN:2001-006781.
Audience: **l,u,f.** *Choice, 2003, 2002.*

Boyle, Raymond & Haynes, Richard **GV742.B69 2000**
Power Play: Sport, the Media and Popular Culture. Trade Paper. Longman Publishing Group. White Plains, NY. 2000. 256p. ISBN:0-582-36939-8, ISBN13: 978-0-582-36939-9. Dewey:306.4/83. LCCN:99-038838.
Audience: **u,f.**

Boyle, Raymond (Editor), et al. **P96.T42**
Sport and Broadcasting: Economic, Legal, and Technological Developments in the Digital Age. Deirdre Kevin & Peter Flood (Editors). Trade Paper. Lawrence Erlbaum Associates, Inc. Mahwah, NJ. 2004. 88p. ISBN:0-8058-9522-1, ISBN13: 978-0-8058-9522-3. Dewey:302.23.
Audience: **l,u,f.**

Brookes, Rod **GV742.B76 2002**
Representing Sport. Trade Paper. Oxford University Press, Inc. New York, NY. 2002. 184p. A Hodder Arnold Publication ISBN:0-340-74052-3, ISBN13: 978-0-340-74052-1. Dewey:796. LCCN:2002-510305.
Audience: **l,u.** *Choice, 2002.*

Creedon, Pamela J. (Editor) **GV706.32.W66 1994**
Women, Media and Sport: Challenging Gender Values. Trade Paper. SAGE Publications, Inc. Thousand Oaks, CA. 1994. 368p. ISBN:0-8039-5234-1, ISBN13: 978-0-8039-5234-8. Dewey:796/.0194. LCCN:93-041211.
Audience: **g,l,u,f.** *Choice, 1994.*

Daddario, Gina **GV742**
Women's Sport and Spectacle: Gendered Television Coverage and the Olympic Games. Trade Cloth. Greenwood Publishing Group, Inc. Portsmouth, NH. 1998. 184p. ISBN:0-275-95856-6, ISBN13: 978-0-275-95856-5. Dewey:302.23/45/082. LCCN:97-038544.
Audience: **u,f.** *Choice, 1998.*

Feinstein, John **GV885.49.N37**
Last Dance: Behind the Scenes at the Final Four. Mike Krzyzewski (Contribution by). Trade Paper. Little Brown & Company. New York, NY. 2007. 352p. ISBN:0-316-01425-7, ISBN13: 978-0-316-01425-0. Dewey:796.323/63/0973.
Audience: **g,l,u,f.**

Fortunato, John A. **GV885.515.N37F67**
The Ultimate Assist: The Relationship and Broadcast Strategies of the NBA and Television Networks. Trade Paper. Hampton Press, Inc. Cresskill, NJ. 2001. xix, 258p. The Hampton Press Communication Ser. ISBN:1-57273-408-6, ISBN13: 978-1-57273-408-1. Dewey:070.4/4979632364. LCCN:2001-039539.
Audience: **u,f.**

Freeman, Michael **GV742.3.F75 2000**
ESPN: The Uncensored History. Trade Cloth. Taylor Trade Publishing. Blue Ridge Summit, PA. 2000. 304p. ISBN:0-87833-239-1, ISBN13: 978-0-87833-239-7. Dewey:384.55/5. LCCN:99-056862.
Audience: **g,l,u.**

Hagstrom, Robert G. Jr. **GV1029.9.S74H34**
The NASCAR Way: The Business That Drives the Sport. Trade Paper. John Wiley & Sons, Inc. Hoboken, NJ. 2001. 254p. ISBN:0-471-39920-5, ISBN13: 978-0-471-39920-9. Dewey:338.4/7/79672/0973.
Audience: **g,l,u.**

Halberstam, David **GV742.3 .H35 1999**
Sports on New York Radio: A Play-by-Play History. Trade Cloth. McGraw-Hill Companies, The. New York, NY. 1999. 432p. ISBN:1-57028-197-1, ISBN13: 978-1-57028-197-6. Dewey:070.4/49796/097471. LCCN:98-046621.
Audience: **g,l,u,f.**

Hall, Allan, et al. **GV742.N53 2002**
Media Relations in Sport. Bill Nichols, Janice Taylor & Patrick Moynahan (Authors). Trade Paper. Fitness Information Technology, Inc. Morgantown, WV. 2002. 291p. Sport Management Library ISBN:1-885693-22-2, ISBN13: 978-1-885693-22-8. Dewey:070.4/49796. LCCN:2001-132860.
Audience: **u,f.**

Kinsella, John & Wark, McKenzie **GV742.S663 2003**
Sport, Media, Culture: Global and Local Dimensions. Neil Blain & Alina Bernstein (Editors). Trade Paper. Taylor & Francis Group. Abingdon, 2003. 272p. ISBN:0-7146-8261-6, ISBN13: 978-0-7146-8261-7. Dewey:070.4/49796. LCCN:2002-151346.
Audience: **g,l,u,f.**

Koppett, Leonard **GV742.42.K66**
The Rise and Fall of the Press Box. Trade Cloth. Sport Media Publishing. Toronto, ON. 2003. 232p. ISBN:1-894963-04-0, ISBN13: 978-1-894963-04-6. Dewey:70.4.
Audience: **g,l,u,f.**

MacCambridge, Michael **GV561.M185 1997**
The Franchise: A History of Sports Illustrated Magazine. Trade Cloth. Hyperion Press. New York, NY. 1997. 352p. ISBN:0-7868-6216-5, ISBN13: 978-0-7868-6216-0. Dewey:796/.05. LCCN:97-015864.
Audience: **g,l,u,f.**

McClellan, Keith **GV954.M37 1998**
The Sunday Game: At the Dawn of Professional Football. Trade Cloth. University of Akron Press, The. Akron, OH. 1998. 503p. Ohio History and Culture Ser. ISBN:1-884836-36-4, ISBN13: 978-1-884836-36-7. Dewey:796.332/0973. LCCN:98-024175.
Audience: **u,f.** *Choice, 1999.*

Oriard, Michael **GV950.O73 2001**
King Football: Sport and Spectacle in the Golden Age of Radio and Newsreels, Movies and Magazines, the Weekly and the Daily Press. Trade Cloth. University of North Carolina Press. Chapel Hill, NC. 2001. 512p. ISBN:0-8078-2650-2, ISBN13: 978-0-8078-2650-8. Dewey:796.332/09/041. LCCN:2001-041459.
Audience: **l,u,f.** *Choice, 2002.*

Oriard, Michael **92-42840 [GV]**
Reading Football: How the Popular Press Created an American Spectacle. Alan Trachtenberg (Foreword by). Trade Paper. University of North Carolina Press. Chapel Hill, NC. 1998. 352p. Cultural Studies of the United States ISBN:0-8078-4751-8, ISBN13: 978-0-8078-4751-0. Dewey:796.3230973. LCCN:92-042840.
Audience: **u,f.** *Choice, 1994.*

Pietrusza, David **GV863.A1P54 1997**
Lights On!: The Wild Century-Long Saga of Night Baseball. Trade Cloth. Scarecrow Press, Inc. Lanham, MD. 1997. 288p. American Sports History Ser., Vol. 7 ISBN:0-8108-3307-7, ISBN13: 978-0-8108-3307-4. Dewey:796.357/0973. LCCN:97-007800.
Audience: **g,l,u,f.** *Choice, 1998.*

Rader, Benjamin G. **GV742.3.R33 1984**
In Its Own Image: How Television Has Transformed Sports. Trade Cloth. Simon & Schuster. New York, NY. 1984. 256p. ISBN:0-02-925700-X, ISBN13: 978-0-02-925700-5. Dewey:070.4/49796/0973. LCCN:84-047856.
Audience: **g,l,u,f.** B

Rowe, David Charles **GV742.R69 2003**
Sport, Culture and the Media: The Unruly Trinity. Ed. 2. Paper Text. McGraw-Hill Education. Maidenhead, 2003. xvii, 253p. ISBN:0-335-21075-9, ISBN13: 978-0-335-21075-6. Dewey:306.4/83.
Audience: **u,f.**

Schultz, Bradley **PN4784.S6**
Sports Media: Reporting, Producing, and Planning. Ed. 2. Paper Text. Elsevier Science & Technology Books. Saint Louis, MO. 2005. 296p. ISBN:0-240-80731-6, ISBN13: 978-0-240-80731-7. Dewey:070.449796.
Audience: **u,f.**

Smith, Ronald A. **GV742.S64 2001**
Play-by-Play: Radio, Television and Big-Time College Sports. Trade Cloth. Johns Hopkins University Press. Baltimore, MD. 2001. 320p. ISBN:0-8018-6686-3, ISBN13: 978-0-8018-6686-9. Dewey:796.04/3/0973. LCCN:00-011534.
Audience: **g,u,f.** *Choice, 2002.*

Stoldt, G. Clayton, et al. **GV714.S77 2006**
Sport Public Relations: Managing Organizational Communication. Steven W. Dittmore & Scott E. Branvold (Authors). Trade Cloth. Human Kinetics Publishers. Champaign, IL. 2006. 376p. ISBN:0-7360-5340-9, ISBN13: 978-0-7360-5340-2. Dewey:659.2/9796. LCCN:2005-024458.
Audience: **l,u,f.**

Wenner, Lawrence A. **GV742.M337 1998**
Mediasport. Trade Paper. Routledge. New York, NY. 1998. 352p. ISBN:0-415-14041-2, ISBN13: 978-0-415-14041-6. Dewey:070.4/49796. LCCN:98-002658.
Audience: **u,f.**

Whannel, Garry **GV742.W43 2002**
Media Sport Stars: Masculinities and Moralities. Trade Paper. Routledge. New York, NY. 2001. 288p. ISBN:0-415-17038-9, ISBN13: 978-0-415-17038-3. Dewey:796/.081. LCCN:2001-058886.
Audience: **u,f.** *Choice, 2002.*

Wilstein, Steve **PN4784.S6.W66 2002**
Sports Writing Handbook. E-Book. McGraw-Hill Companies, The. New York, NY. 2001. ISBN:0-07-138973-3, ISBN13: 978-0-07-138973-0. Dewey:808/.066796.
Audience: **u,f.**

Careers in Sport

GV563
Amateur Athletic Foundation of Los Angeles.
http://www.aafla.org/
Audience: **g,l,u.**

GV557
International Council of Sport Science and Physical Education.
http://www.icsspe.org/
Audience: **g,l,u,f.**

GV203
National Athletic Trainers Association.
http://www.nata.org/
Audience: **g,l,u,f.**

GV568
Scholarly Sport Sites: A Subject Directory.
http://www.ucalgary.ca/lib-old/ssportsite/
Audience: **g,l,u,f.**

Armour, Kathleen R. **GV363.A76 1998**
Physical Education: Teachers' Lives and Careers. Paper over Boards. Taylor & Francis Group. Philadelphia, PA. 1998. 160p. ISBN:0-7507-0818-2, ISBN13: 978-0-7507-0818-0. Dewey:613.7/071041. LCCN:98-185973.
Audience: **g,l,u.** *Choice, 1999.*

Baine, Celeste **TA157**
High Tech Hot Shots: Careers in Sports Engineering. Paper Text. National Society of Professional Engineers. Alexandria, VA. 2004. 144p. ISBN:0-915409-23-2, ISBN13: 978-0-915409-23-5. Dewey:620/.0023.
Audience: **g,l,u,f.**

Buck, Marilyn M., et al. **GV361.B84 2004**
Introduction to Physical Education and Sport: Foundations and Trends with Introduction to Careers in Health, Physical Education and Sport. J. Thomas Jable & Patricia A. Floyd (Authors). Cloth Text. Brooks/Cole. Pacific Grove, CA. 2003. 336p. ISBN:0-534-59850-1, ISBN13: 978-0-534-59850-1. Dewey:613.7/071. LCCN:2003-105865.
Audience: **l,u.**

Floyd, Patricia A. **GV362**
Careers in Health, Physical Education, and Sports. Paper Text. Brooks/Cole. Pacific Grove, CA. 2003. 192p. ISBN:0-534-60785-3, ISBN13: 978-0-534-60785-2. Dewey:362.1023. LCCN:2004-268737.
Audience: **g,l,u.**

Heitzmann, William Ray **GV734.3.H445 2004**
Careers for Sports Nuts and Other Athletic Types. Ed. 3. Trade Paper. McGraw-Hill Companies, The. New York, NY. 2004. 160p. VGM Careers for You Ser. ISBN:0-07-141158-5, ISBN13: 978-0-07-141158-5. Dewey:796/.023. LCCN:2003-025812.
Audience: **g,l,u.**

Heitzmann, William Ray **GV734.3.H45 2003**
Opportunities in Sports and Fitness Careers. Trade Paper. McGraw-Hill Companies, The. New York, NY. 2003. 160p. Opportunities in... Ser. ISBN:0-658-01045-X, ISBN13: 978-0-658-01045-3. Dewey:796/.023. LCCN:2002-191062.
Audience: **g,l,u.**

Hoffman, Shirl J. (Editor) **QP303.I53 2005**
Introduction to Kinesiology: Studying Physical Activity. Ed. 2. Trade Cloth. Human Kinetics Publishers. Champaign, IL. 2005. 616p. ISBN:0-7360-5589-4, ISBN13: 978-0-7360-5589-5. Dewey:612.7/6. LCCN:2004-014671.
Audience: **g,l.**

Karlin, Len **GV734 .K37**
The Guide to Careers in Sports. Ed. 2. Trade Paper. E. M. Guild, Inc. New York, NY. 1997. 240p. ISBN:0-9647594-1-1, ISBN13: 978-0-9647594-1-1. Dewey:796.023.
Audience: **g,l,u.**

Kraus, Richard, et al. **GV160**
Introduction to Leisure Services: Career Perspectives. Elizabeth Barber & Ira Shapiro (Authors). Trade Paper. Sagamore Publishing, L.L.C.. Champaign, IL. 2001. 255p. ISBN:1-57167-482-9, ISBN13: 978-1-57167-482-1. Dewey:790.023. LCCN:00-107471.
Audience: **l,u.**

Lavallee, David & Wylleman, Paul (Editors) **GV734.3.C37 2000**
Career Transitions in Sport: International Perspectives. Trade Paper. Fitness Information Technology, Inc. Morgantown, WV. 2000. 305p. ISBN:1-885693-21-4, ISBN13: 978-1-885693-21-1. Dewey:796.023. LCCN:00-130551.
Audience: **l,u,f.**

McMurray Robert G **QP301.M3754 1999**
Concepts in Fitness Programming. CRC press. 1998. ISBN:0-8493-8714-0, ISBN13: 978-0-8493-8714-2.
Audience: **l,u,f.**

National Strength Training and Conditioning Association **GV428.7**
NSCA's Essentials of Personal Training. Roger W. Earle &

Thomas R. Baechle (Editors). Trade Cloth. Human Kinetics Publishers. Champaign, IL. 2003. 688p. ISBN:0-7360-0015-1, ISBN13: 978-0-7360-0015-4. Dewey:613.7/1. LCCN:2003-019033.

Audience: **u.**

O'Brien, Teri S. **GV428.7.O37 2003**
The Personal Trainer's Handbook. Ed. 2. Trade Paper, CD-ROM. Human Kinetics Publishers. Champaign, IL. 2003. 257p. ISBN:0-7360-4501-5, ISBN13: 978-0-7360-4501-8. Dewey:613.7/1. LCCN:02-153987.

Audience: **u,f.**

Petitpas, Al, et al. **GV706.8.A898 1997**
Athlete's Guide to Career Planning. Delight Champagne, Judy Chartrand, Steven Danish & Shane Murphy (Authors). Trade Paper. Human Kinetics Publishers. Champaign, IL. 1997. 24p. ISBN:0-87322-459-0, ISBN13: 978-0-87322-459-8. Dewey:796/.023. LCCN:96-046543.

Audience: **l,u.**

Van Raalte, Judy L. & Brewer, Britton W. (Editors) **GV706.4.E96 2002**
Exploring Sport and Exercise Psychology. Ed. 2. Trade Cloth. American Psychological Association. Washington, DC. 2002. xxiii, 561p. ISBN:1-55798-886-2, ISBN13: 978-1-55798-886-7. Dewey:796/.01. LCCN:2002-020856.

Audience: **l,u,f.** *Choice, 1997.*

Wilson, Robert F. **GV734.3.W55 2001**
Careers in Sports Fitness and Recreation. Trade Paper. Barron's Educational Series, Inc. Hauppauge, NY. 2001. 176p. Success Without College Ser. ISBN:0-7641-1562-6, ISBN13: 978-0-7641-1562-2. Dewey:790/.023/73. LCCN:00-068014.

Audience: **g,l,u.**

Wong
Internships, Jobs and Careers in Sports Industry. Trade Cloth. Jones & Bartlett Publishers, Inc. Sudbury, MA. 2005. Health Science, Nutrition, Dietetics and Physical Education Ser. ISBN:0-7637-2884-5, ISBN13: 978-0-7637-2884-7.

Audience: **u,f.**

Careers in Sport > Coaching

American Sport Education Program Staff **GV943.8.C63 2001**
Coaching Youth Soccer. Ed. 3. Trade Paper. Human Kinetics Publishers. Champaign, IL. 2001. 168p. ISBN:0-7360-3718-7, ISBN13: 978-0-7360-3718-1. Dewey:796.334/07/7. LCCN:00-050032.

Audience: **l,u,f.**

American Sport Education Program Staff (Contribution by) **GV1015.5.C63 2001**
Coaching Youth Volleyball. Ed. 3. Trade Paper. Human Kinetics Publishers. Champaign, IL. 2001. 176p. ISBN:0-7360-3796-9, ISBN13: 978-0-7360-3796-9. Dewey:796.325. LCCN:2001-016657.

Audience: **l,u,f.**

Bobo, Mike & Dykes, Spike **GV956.6.B623 1998**
Principles of Coaching Football. Trade Paper. Benjamin-Cummings Publishing Company. San Francisco, CA. 1997. 287p. ISBN:0-205-26253-8, ISBN13: 978-0-205-26253-3. Dewey:796.332/07/7. LCCN:97-029510.

Audience: **g,l,u.** *Choice, 1998.*

Hannula, Dick & Thornton, Nort (Editors) **GV837.65.S95 2001**
The Swim Coaching Bible. Trade Paper. Human Kinetics Publishers. Champaign, IL. 2001. 376p. ISBN:0-7360-3646-6, ISBN13: 978-0-7360-3646-7. Dewey:797.2/1. LCCN:00-054241.

Audience: **g,l,u,f.**

Jones, Billie J., et al. **GV711 .G87**
Guide to Effective Coaching: Principles and Practices with PowerWeb: Health and Human Performance. Ed. 3. L. Janet Wells, Rachael E. Peters & Dewayne J. Johnson (Authors). Paper Text, Online Resource. McGraw-Hill Higher Education. Burr Ridge, IL. 2001. ISBN:0-07-250604-0, ISBN13: 978-0-07-250604-4. Dewey:796/.077.

Audience: **u.**

Jones, Robyn & Cassidy, Tania **GV911**
Understanding Sports Coaching: The Social, Cultural and Pedagogical Foundations of Coaching Practice. Trade Paper. Routledge. New York, NY. 2004. 232p. ISBN:0-415-30740-6, ISBN13: 978-0-415-30740-6. Dewey:796.07/7. LCCN:2004-046831.

Audience: **u,f.**

Koehler, Michael D. **QA76.73.P2N86**
Complete Book of Drills for Winning Football. Trade Paper. Benjamin-Cummings Publishing Company. San Francisco, CA. 2001. 320p. ISBN:0-13-060043-1, ISBN13: 978-0-13-060043-1. Dewey:005.13/3.

Audience: **g,l,u.**

Krause, Jerry **GV885.3.C59 2002**
Coaching Basketball. Ed. 3. Trade Paper. McGraw-Hill Companies, The. New York, NY. 2002. 320p. ISBN:0-07-138210-0, ISBN13: 978-0-07-138210-6. Dewey:796.323/077. LCCN:2002-017431.

Audience: **l,u,f.**

Krause, Jerry V., et al. **GV885.3.K68 1999**
Basketball Skills and Drills. Ed. 2. Don Meyer & Jerry Meyer (Authors). Trade Paper. Human Kinetics Publishers. Champaign, IL. 1999. 216p. ISBN:0-7360-0171-9, ISBN13: 978-0-7360-0171-7. Dewey:796.323/077. LCCN:98-052768.

Audience: **l,u,f.**

Kus, Sally **GV1015.5.C63K87 2004**
Coaching Volleyball Successfully. Ed. 2. Trade Paper. Human Kinetics Publishers. Champaign, IL. 2004. 224p. ISBN:0-7360-4037-4, ISBN13: 978-0-7360-4037-2. Dewey:796.325. LCCN:2003-027576.

Audience: **g,l,u,f.**

Martens, Rainer **GV711**
Successful Coaching. Ed. 3. Trade Paper. Human Kinetics Publishers. Champaign, IL. 2004. 52p. ISBN:0-7360-4012-9, ISBN13: 978-0-7360-4012-9. Dewey:796/.071/273. LCCN:2003-025833.

Audience: **l,u.**

McGown, Carl, et al. **GV1015.5.C63M34 2001**
Coaching Volleyball: Building a Winning Team. Hilda Ann Fronske & Launa Moser (Authors). Trade Paper.

Benjamin-Cummings Publishing Company. San Francisco, CA. 2000. 308p. ISBN:0-205-30958-5, ISBN13: 978-0-205-30958-0. Dewey:796.325. LCCN:00-032296.
Audience: **l,u.**

National Soccer Coaches of America Staff **GV943.8.S65 2004**
The Soccer Coaching Bible. Trade Paper. Human Kinetics Publishers. Champaign, IL. 2004. 328p. ISBN:0-7360-4227-X, ISBN13: 978-0-7360-4227-7. Dewey:796.334/07/7. LCCN:2003-022881.
Audience: **l,u.**

Shondell, Don & Raynaud, Cecil (Editors) **GV1015.5.C63V65 2002**
The Volleyball Coaching Bible. Trade Paper. Human Kinetics Publishers. Champaign, IL. 2002. 384p. ISBN:0-7360-3967-8, ISBN13: 978-0-7360-3967-3. Dewey:796.325. LCCN:2002-007964.
Audience: **l,u.**

Stokell, Ian **GV943.8.S77 2002**
Coaching Women's Soccer: A Revolutionary Approach to Putting the Play Back into Practice. Trade Paper. McGraw-Hill Companies, The. New York, NY. 2002. x, 182p. ISBN:0-07-138209-7, ISBN13: 978-0-07-138209-0. Dewey:796.334/07/7. LCCN:2001-047321.
Audience: **g,l,u,f.** *Choice, 2002.*

Careers in Sport > Officiating

American Sport Education Program (Contribution by) **GV1060.5**
Officiating Track and Field and Cross Country. Trade Cloth. Human Kinetics Publishers. Champaign, IL. 2005. 176p. ISBN:0-7360-5360-3, ISBN13: 978-0-7360-5360-0. Dewey:796.42. LCCN:2005-008058.
Audience: **l,u,f.**

American Sport Education Program Staff **GV943.9.O45O44 2004**
Officiating Soccer. Trade Paper. Human Kinetics Publishers. Champaign, IL. 2004. 144p. ISBN:0-7360-4761-1, ISBN13: 978-0-7360-4761-6. Dewey:796.334/3. LCCN:2004-005046.
Audience: **g,l,u.**

Kerkhoff, Blair **GV735.K47 2000**
Upon Further Review: Controversy in Sports Officiating. Trade Cloth. Addax Publishing Group, Inc. Lenexa, KS. 2002. 255p. ISBN:1-886110-84-0, ISBN13: 978-1-886110-84-7. Dewey:796. LCCN:99-055083.
Audience: **g,l,u,f.**

Referee Magazine Staff & National Association of Sports Officials Staff **GV735.S93 1999**
Successful Sports Officiating. Jerry Grunska (Editor). Trade Paper. Human Kinetics Publishers. Champaign, IL. 1999. 184p. ISBN:0-88011-748-6, ISBN13: 978-0-88011-748-7. Dewey:796. LCCN:99-030329.
Audience: **g,l,u.**

Weinberg, Robert S. & Richardson, Peggy A. **GV735.W45**
Psychology of Officiating. Trade Paper. Human Kinetics Publishers. Champaign, IL. 1995. 192p. ISBN:0-87322-875-8, ISBN13: 978-0-87322-875-6. Dewey:796. LCCN:90-031893.
Audience: **u,f.** *Choice, 1990.*

Careers in Sport > Law. Agents

Robinson, Matthew J., et al. **GV713.P77 2000**
Profiles of Sport Industry Professionals: The People Who Make the Games Happen. Mary A. Hums, R. Brian Crow & Dennis R. Phillips (Authors). Paper Text. Jones & Bartlett Publishers, Inc. Sudbury, MA. 2000. 485p. ISBN:0-8342-1796-1, ISBN13: 978-0-8342-1796-6. Dewey:796/.06/9. LCCN:00-040605.
Audience: **l,u.**

Shropshire, Kenneth L. **GV716**
Agents of Opportunity: Sports Agents and Corruption in Collegiate Sports. Trade Paper. University of Pennsylvania Press. Philadelphia, PA. 1990. 192p. ISBN:0-8122-1443-9, ISBN13: 978-0-8122-1443-7. Dewey:338.4/7796/0973. LCCN:90-041858.
Audience: **l,u,f.** *Choice, 1991.*

Shropshire, Kenneth L. & Davis, Timothy **GV734.5.S58 2003**
The Business of Sports Agents. Book, Other. University of Pennsylvania Press. Philadelphia, PA. 2002. 216p. ISBN:0-8122-3682-3, ISBN13: 978-0-8122-3682-8. Dewey:796/.06/9. LCCN:2002-072534.
Audience: **l,u.** *Choice, 2003.*

Careers in Sport > Management and Administration

Appenzeller, Herb & Lewis, Guy **GV713**
Successful Sport Management: A Guide to Legal Issues. Ed. 2. Trade Paper. Carolina Academic Press. Durham, NC. 2000. 421p. ISBN:0-89089-661-5, ISBN13: 978-0-89089-661-7. Dewey:796.068. LCCN:00-106586.
Audience: **u,f.**

Aspatore Books **GV734.3.L35 2004**
Career Insights: Presidents/GMs from the NFL, MLB, NHL and MLS on Achieving Personal and Professional Success: Landing a Job with a Sports Team. Trade Paper. Aspatore Books, Inc. Boston, MA. 2004. ISBN:1-58762-132-0, ISBN13: 978-1-58762-132-1. Dewey:796.023. LCCN:2004-104161.
Audience: **g,l,u.**

Cuneen, Jacquelyn; Sidwell, M Joy **GV713**
Sport Management Field Experiences. Fitness Information Technology. 2003. ISBN:1-885693-42-7, ISBN13: 978-1-885693-42-6.
Audience: **u,f.**

Cylkowski, Greg J. **GV734**
Developing a Lifelong Contract in the Sports Marketplace. Ed. 2. Perfect, Paper Text. Athletic Achievements, Inc. Little Canada, MN. 1998. 400p. ISBN:0-9636449-0-4, ISBN13: 978-0-9636449-0-9. Dewey:306.483.
Audience: **g,l,u,f.**

Gavin, James & Gavin, Nettie **GV428.7.G38 1995**
Psychology for Health Fitness Professionals. Trade Paper.

Human Kinetics Publishers. Champaign, IL. 1994. 136p. ISBN:0-87322-775-1, ISBN13: 978-0-87322-775-9. Dewey:613.7/11/019. LCCN:94-023549.
Audience: **u,f.**

Grantham, William C., et al. **GV428.5.H43 1998**
Health Fitness Management: A Comprehensive Resource for Managing and Operating Programs and Facilities. Robert W. Patton, Tracy D. York & Mitchel L. Winick (Authors). Trade Cloth. Human Kinetics Publishers. Champaign, IL. 1998. 544p. ISBN:0-88011-559-9, ISBN13: 978-0-88011-559-9. Dewey:613.7/068. LCCN:97-026549.
Audience: **u,f.**

Helitzer, Melvin **GV714.H45 2000**
The Dream Job: Sports Publicity, Promotion and Marketing. Ed. 3. Trade Paper. University Sports Press. Athens, OH. 2001. 450p. ISBN:0-9630387-2-9, ISBN13: 978-0-9630387-2-2. Dewey:659.2/9796. LCCN:99-461953.
Audience: **l,u.**

Howley, Edward T. & Franks, B. Don **GV481.H734 2003**
Health Fitness Instructor's Handbook. Ed. 4. Trade Cloth. Human Kinetics Publishers. Champaign, IL. 2003. 584p. ISBN:0-7360-4210-5, ISBN13: 978-0-7360-4210-9. Dewey:613.7. LCCN:2002-010983.
Audience: **u,f.**

Irwin, Richard L., et al. **GV714.I79 2002**
Sport Promotion and Sales Management. William Anthony Sutton & Laurence McCarthy (Authors). Trade Cloth. Human Kinetics Publishers. Champaign, IL. 2002. 472p. ISBN:0-7360-0320-7, ISBN13: 978-0-7360-0320-9. Dewey:659.2/9796. LCCN:2001-039845.
Audience: **u,f.**

Pira, Edward S. **GV975.P65 1997**
A Guide to Golf Course Irrigation System Design and Drainage. Trade Cloth. John Wiley & Sons, Inc. Hoboken, NJ. 2002. 448p. ISBN:1-57504-030-1, ISBN13: 978-1-57504-030-1. Dewey:796.352/06/8. LCCN:98-128801.
Audience: **u,f.**

Puhalla, Jim, et al. **GV413.P85 1999**
Sports Fields: A Manual for Design, Construction and Maintenance. Jeff Krans & Mike Goatley (Authors). Trade Cloth. John Wiley & Sons, Inc. Hoboken, NJ. 1999. 480p. ISBN:1-57504-070-0, ISBN13: 978-1-57504-070-7. Dewey:796/.06/8. LCCN:99-011902.
Audience: **u.**

Robinson, Matthew J., et al. **GV713.P77 2000**
Profiles of Sport Industry Professionals: The People Who Make the Games Happen. Mary A. Hums, R. Brian Crow & Dennis R. Phillips (Authors). Paper Text. Jones & Bartlett Publishers, Inc. Sudbury, MA. 2000. 485p. ISBN:0-8342-1796-1, ISBN13: 978-0-8342-1796-6. Dewey:796/.06/9. LCCN:00-040605.
Audience: **l,u.**

White, Bud & White, Charles B. **GV975.W45 2000**
Turf Managers' Handbook for Golf Course Construction, Renovation, and Grow-In. Trade Cloth. John Wiley & Sons, Inc. Hoboken, NJ. 2000. 328p. ISBN:1-57504-110-3, ISBN13: 978-1-57504-110-0. Dewey:796.352/06/8. LCCN:99-087983.
Audience: **u.**

Careers in Sport > Media and Journalism

Andrews, Phil **PN4784.S6**
Sports Journalism: A Practical Introduction. Cloth Text. SAGE Publications, Inc. Thousand Oaks, CA. 2005. 192p. ISBN:1-4129-0270-3, ISBN13: 978-1-4129-0270-0. Dewey:070.4/49796. LCCN:2005-298394.
Audience: **l,u.**

Bender, Gary & Johnson, Michael L. **GV742.3.B46 1994**
Call of the Game: What Really Goes on in the Broadcast Booth. Trade Cloth. Bonus Books, Inc. Chicago, IL. 1994. 263p. ISBN:1-56625-013-7, ISBN13: 978-1-56625-013-9. Dewey:070.4/49796. LCCN:94-026463.
Audience: **g,l,u.**

Fountain, Charles **GV742.42.R53**
Sportswriter: The Life and Times of Grantland Rice. Trade Cloth. Replica Books. Bridgewater, NJ. 2000. 350p. ISBN:0-7351-0347-X, ISBN13: 978-0-7351-0347-4. Dewey:070.4/49796/092.B.
Audience: **g,l,u,f.**

Gumpert, Gary & Drucker, Susan J. (Editors) **GV867.64.T35 2001**
Take Me Out to the Ballgame: Communicating Baseball. Paper Text. Hampton Press, Inc. Cresskill, NJ. 2001. 448p. Communication Ser., :Communication and Public Space ISBN:1-57273-302-0, ISBN13: 978-1-57273-302-2. Dewey:070.4/49796357/0973. LCCN:2001-039879.
Audience: **g,l,u.**

Halberstam, David **GV742.3 .H35 1999**
Sports on New York Radio: A Play-by-Play History. Trade Cloth. McGraw-Hill Companies, The. New York, NY. 1999. 432p. ISBN:1-57028-197-1, ISBN13: 978-1-57028-197-6. Dewey:070.4/49796/097471. LCCN:98-046621.
Audience: **g,l,u,f.**

Hall, Allan, et al. **GV742.N53 2002**
Media Relations in Sport. Bill Nichols, Janice Taylor & Patrick Moynahan (Authors). Trade Paper. Fitness Information Technology, Inc. Morgantown, WV. 2002. 291p. Sport Management Library ISBN:1-885693-22-2, ISBN13: 978-1-885693-22-8. Dewey:070.4/49796. LCCN:2001-132860.
Audience: **u,f.**

Hedrick, Tom & McKenzie, Mike **GV742.3.H43 1999**
The Art of Sportscasting: How to Build a Successful Career. Joe Castiglione (Contribution by). Trade Paper. Diamond Communications, Inc. Lanham, MD. 2000. 310p.

ISBN:1-888698-24-1, ISBN13: 978-1-888698-24-4. Dewey:070.4/49796/02373. LCCN:99-048275.
Audience: **g,l,u.**

Inabinett, Mark **GV742.42.R53I53 1994**
Grantland Rice and His Heroes: The Sportswriter As Mythmaker in the 1920s. Trade Paper. University of Tennessee Press. Knoxville, TN. 1994. 144p. ISBN:0-87049-849-5, ISBN13: 978-0-87049-849-7. Dewey:070.4/49796. LCCN:94-006088.
Audience: **l,u.** *Choice, 1995.*

Koppett, Leonard **GV742.42.K66**
The Rise and Fall of the Press Box. Trade Cloth. Sport Media Publishing. Toronto, ON. 2003. 232p. ISBN:1-894963-04-0, ISBN13: 978-1-894963-04-6. Dewey:70.4.
Audience: **g,l,u,f.**

MacCambridge, Michael **GV561.M185 1997**
The Franchise: A History of Sports Illustrated Magazine. Trade Cloth. Hyperion Press. New York, NY. 1997. 352p. ISBN:0-7868-6216-5, ISBN13: 978-0-7868-6216-0. Dewey:796/.05. LCCN:97-015864.
Audience: **g,l,u,f.**

Mulligan, Joseph F. & Mulligan, Kevin T. **PN4784.S6M85 1998**
The Mulligan Guide to Sports Journalism Careers. Trade Paper. McGraw-Hill/Contemporary. Lincolnwood, IL. 1999. 578p. ISBN:0-8442-4540-2, ISBN13: 978-0-8442-4540-9. Dewey:070.4/49796/023. LCCN:98-008171.
Audience: **g,l,u.**

Schultz, Bradley **PN4784.S6**
Sports Media: Reporting, Producing, and Planning. Ed. 2. Paper Text. Elsevier Science & Technology Books. Saint Louis, MO. 2005. 296p. ISBN:0-240-80731-6, ISBN13: 978-0-240-80731-7. Dewey:070.449796.
Audience: **u,f.**

Stoldt, G. Clayton, et al. **GV714.S77 2006**
Sport Public Relations: Managing Organizational Communication. Steven W. Dittmore & Scott E. Branvold (Authors). Trade Cloth. Human Kinetics Publishers. Champaign, IL. 2006. 376p. ISBN:0-7360-5340-9, ISBN13: 978-0-7360-5340-2. Dewey:659.2/9796. LCCN:2005-024458.
Audience: **l,u,f.**

Wenner, Lawrence A. **GV742.M337 1998**
Mediasport. Trade Paper. Routledge. New York, NY. 1998. 352p. ISBN:0-415-14041-2, ISBN13: 978-0-415-14041-6. Dewey:070.4/49796. LCCN:98-002658.
Audience: **u,f.**

Wilstein, Steve **PN4784.S6.W66 2002**
Sports Writing Handbook. E-Book. McGraw-Hill Companies, The. New York, NY. 2001. ISBN:0-07-138973-3, ISBN13: 978-0-07-138973-0. Dewey:808/.066796.
Audience: **u,f.**

Biomechanics

GV557
International Council of Sport Science and Physical Education.
http://www.icsspe.org/
Audience: **g,l,u,f.**

RC1211
International Federation of Sports Medicine.
http://www.fims.org/
Audience: **l,u,f.**

RC1235
International Society of Biomechanics in Sports.
http://www.twu.edu/biom/isbs/
Audience: **l,u,f.**

GV557
SPORTSCIENCE a peer-reviewed site for Sport Research.
http://www.sportsci.org/
Audience: **l,u,f.**

Abernethy, Bruce, et al. **QP303.B586 2005**
The Biophysical Foundations of Human Movement ent, Vol. 2. Ed. 2. Stephanie J. Hanrahan, Vaughan Kippers, Laurel T. Mackinnon & Marcus G. Pandy (Authors). Trade Paper. Human Kinetics Publishers. Champaign, IL. 2004. 376p. ISBN:0-7360-4276-8, ISBN13: 978-0-7360-4276-5. Dewey:612.7/6. LCCN:2004-008595.
Audience: **g,l,u,f.**

Bartlett, Roger **RC1235.B37 1999**
Sports Biomechanics: Preventing Injury and Improving Performance. Trade Paper. Routledge. New York, NY. 1999. 296p. ISBN:0-419-18440-6, ISBN13: 978-0-419-18440-9. Dewey:612.044. LCCN:98-021961.
Audience: **u,f.** *Choice, 2000.*

Bosch, Frans (Author, Illustrator) **QP301 .B67 2005**
Running: Biomechanics and Exercise Physiology in Practice. Ronald Klomp (Author). Trade Paper. Elsevier - Health Sciences Division. Philadelphia, PA. 2004. 424p. ISBN:0-443-07441-0, ISBN13: 978-0-443-07441-7. Dewey:612.044.
Audience: **u,f.**

Burton, Allen W. & Miller, Daryl E. **QP303.B87 1998**
Movement Skill Assessment. Trade Cloth. Human Kinetics Publishers. Champaign, IL. 1997. 416p. ISBN:0-87322-975-4, ISBN13: 978-0-87322-975-3. Dewey:612.7/6/0287. LCCN:97-021938.
Audience: **u,f.** *Choice, 1998.*

Carr, Gerry **QP303.C375 2004**
Sports Mechanics for Coaches. Ed. 2. Trade Paper. Human Kinetics Publishers. Champaign, IL. 2004. 256p. ISBN:0-7360-3972-4, ISBN13: 978-0-7360-3972-7. Dewey:612/.044. LCCN:2003-007917.
Audience: **g,l,u,f.**

Cavanagh, Peter R. (Editor) **QP310.R85B56 1990**
Biomechanics of Distance Running. Cloth Text. Human Kinetics Publishers. Champaign, IL. 1990. 376p. ISBN:0-87322-268-7, ISBN13: 978-0-87322-268-6. Dewey:612/.044. LCCN:89-029302.
Audience: **u,f.** *Choice, 1990.*

Cech, Donna J. & Martin, Suzanne **QP301.C43 2002**
Functional Movement Development Across the Life Span. Ed. 2.

Cloth Text. Elsevier - Health Sciences Division. Philadelphia, PA. 2002. 528p. ISBN:0-7216-8122-0, ISBN13: 978-0-7216-8122-1. Dewey:152.3. LCCN:2002-019192.
Audience: **u,f.**

Enoka, Roger **QP303.E56 2002**
Neuromechanics of Human Movement. Ed. 3. Trade Cloth. Human Kinetics Publishers. Champaign, IL. 2001. 576p. ISBN:0-7360-0251-0, ISBN13: 978-0-7360-0251-6. Dewey:612.7/6. LCCN:2001-024108.
Audience: **l,u,f.**

Fung, Yuan-Cheng **QP303.F86 1990**
Biomechanics: Motion, Flow, Stress, and Growth. Trade Cloth. Springer. New York, NY. 1990. XV, 569p. ISBN:0-387-97124-6, ISBN13: 978-0-387-97124-7. Dewey:591.19/1. LCCN:89-022017.
Audience: **u,f.** *Choice, 1990.*

George, Gerald S. **GV464.G46**
Biomechanics of Women's Gymnastics. Cloth Text. Prentice Hall PTR. Upper Saddle River, NJ. 1979. xv, 221p. ISBN:0-13-077461-8, ISBN13: 978-0-13-077461-3. Dewey:796.4/1. LCCN:79-018854.
Audience: **u,f.** B

Hall, Susan J. **B3138.E5**
Basic Biomechanics with Dynamic Human and PowerWeb/OLC Bind-In Passcard. Ed. 4. Mixed Media, Trade Paper, CD-ROM. McGraw-Hill Higher Education. Burr Ridge, IL. 2002. 608p. ISBN:0-07-255241-7, ISBN13: 978-0-07-255241-6. Dewey:193.
Audience: **l,u,f.**

Hay, James G. **QP303**
The Biomechanics of Sports Techniques. Ed. 4. Cloth Text. Benjamin-Cummings Publishing Company. San Francisco, CA. 1993. 544p. ISBN:0-13-084534-5, ISBN13: 978-0-13-084534-4. Dewey:612/.76. LCCN:92-027506.
Audience: **g,l,u,f.**

Latash, Mark L. **QP301.L36 1993**
Control of Human Movement. Trade Cloth. Human Kinetics Publishers. Champaign, IL. 1993. 392p. ISBN:0-87322-455-8, ISBN13: 978-0-87322-455-0. Dewey:152.3. LCCN:92-036991.
Audience: **u,f.** *Choice, 1994.*

Latash, Mark L. **QP301.L364 1998**
Neurophysiological Basis of Movement. Trade Cloth. Human Kinetics Publishers. Champaign, IL. 1998. 28p. ISBN:0-88011-756-7, ISBN13: 978-0-88011-756-2. Dewey:612.7/6. LCCN:97-031920.
Audience: **u,f.** *Choice, 1998.*

Latash, Mark L. & Zatsiorsky, Vladimir M. (Editors) **QP301.L358 2001**
Classics in Movement Science. Trade Cloth. Human Kinetics Publishers. Champaign, IL. 2001. 464p. ISBN:0-7360-0028-3, ISBN13: 978-0-7360-0028-4. Dewey:612.7/6. LCCN:00-053857.
Audience: **u,f.**

Lucas, George L., et al. **QP303.L83 1998**
A Primer of Biomechanics. Francis W. Cooke, Elizabeth Friis & D. Hahn (Authors), D. Y. Chinn (Illustrator). Trade Paper. Springer. New York, NY. 1998. XVII, 320p. ISBN:0-387-98456-9, ISBN13: 978-0-387-98456-8. Dewey:612.7/6. LCCN:97-048865.
Audience: **u,f.** *Choice, 1999.*

Newell, Karl M. (Editor) **QP301.M698 2006**
Movement System Variability. Perfect. Human Kinetics Publishers. Champaign, IL. 2005. 361p. ISBN:0-7360-4482-5, ISBN13: 978-0-7360-4482-0. Dewey:612.7/6. LCCN:2005-006427.
Audience: **l,u.**

Nordin, Margareta & Frankel, Victor H. **QP303**
Basic Biomechanics of the Musculoskeletal System. Ed. 3. Trade Paper. Lippincott Williams & Wilkins. Philadelphia, PA. 2001. 496p. ISBN:0-683-30247-7, ISBN13: 978-0-683-30247-9. Dewey:612.7/6. LCCN:00-065519.
Audience: **u,f.**

Rose, Debra J. & Christina, Robert W. **QP301.R65 2006**
A Multilevel Approach to the Study of Motor Control and Learning. Ed. 2. Trade Cloth. Benjamin-Cummings Publishing Company. San Francisco, CA. 2005. 464p. ISBN:0-8053-6031-X, ISBN13: 978-0-8053-6031-8. Dewey:612.8/11. LCCN:2005-006531.
Audience: **u,f.**

Vogel, Steven **QH513.V643 2003**
Comparative Biomechanics: Life's Physical World. Trade Cloth. Princeton University Press. Princeton, NJ. 2003. 582p. ISBN:0-691-11297-5, ISBN13: 978-0-691-11297-8. Dewey:571.4/3. LCCN:2002-042723.
Audience: **l,u.** *Choice, 2004.*

Williams, Mark (Editor), et al. **GV706.8**
Skill Acquisition in Sport: Research, Theory and Practice. Nikki Hodges, Mark Scott & Mike Court (Editors). Trade Paper. Routledge. New York, NY. 2004. 464p. ISBN:0-415-27075-8, ISBN13: 978-0-415-27075-5. Dewey:796/.01. LCCN:2003-058657.
Audience: **u,f.**

Winter, David A. **QP303.W59 2004**
The Biomechanics and Motor Control of Human Movement. Ed. 3. Trade Cloth. John Wiley & Sons, Inc. Hoboken, NJ. 2004. 344p. ISBN:0-471-44989-X, ISBN13: 978-0-471-44989-8. Dewey:612/.76. LCCN:2004-047810.
Audience: **l,u.** *Choice, 1990.*

Zatsiorsky, Vladimir M. (Editor) **RC1235.B476 2000**
Biomechanics in Sports: Performance Improvement and Injury Prevention. Trade Cloth. Blackwell Publishing, Inc. Malden, MA. 2000. 680p. Encyclopedia of Sports Medicine Ser., Vol. 9 ISBN:0-632-05392-5, ISBN13: 978-0-632-05392-6. Dewey:617.1/027. LCCN:99-054566.
Audience: **g,l,u,f.**

Zatsiorsky, Vladimir M. **QP303.Z383 2002**
Kinetics of Human Motion. Trade Cloth. Human Kinetics Publishers. Champaign, IL. 2002. 672p. ISBN:0-7360-3778-0, ISBN13: 978-0-7360-3778-5. Dewey:612.7/6. LCCN:2001-051861.
Audience: **u,f.**

Zatsiorsky, Vladimir M. **GV711.5.Z38 1995**
Science and Practice of Strength Training. Trade Cloth. Human Kinetics Publishers. Champaign, IL. 1995. 256p.

ISBN:0-87322-474-4, ISBN13: 978-0-87322-474-1. Dewey:613.7/11. LCCN:94-040135.
Audience: **u,f.** *Choice, 1995.*

Motor Learning

GV557
International Council of Sport Science and Physical Education.
http://www.icsspe.org/
Audience: **g,l,u,f.**

RC1211
International Federation of Sports Medicine.
http://www.fims.org/
Audience: **l,u,f.**

RC1235
International Society of Biomechanics in Sports.
http://www.twu.edu/biom/isbs/
Audience: **l,u,f.**

GV557
SPORTSCIENCE a peer-reviewed site for Sport Research.
http://www.sportsci.org/
Audience: **l,u,f.**

Abernethy, Bruce, et al. **QP303.B586 2005**
The Biophysical Foundations of Human Movement ent, Vol. 2. Ed. 2. Stephanie J. Hanrahan, Vaughan Kippers, Laurel T. Mackinnon & Marcus G. Pandy (Authors). Trade Paper. Human Kinetics Publishers. Champaign, IL. 2004. 376p. ISBN:0-7360-4276-8, ISBN13: 978-0-7360-4276-5. Dewey:612.7/6. LCCN:2004-008595.
Audience: **g,l,u,f.**

Burton, Allen W. & Miller, Daryl E. **QP303.B87 1998**
Movement Skill Assessment. Trade Cloth. Human Kinetics Publishers. Champaign, IL. 1997. 416p. ISBN:0-87322-975-4, ISBN13: 978-0-87322-975-3. Dewey:612.7/6/0287. LCCN:97-021938.
Audience: **u,f.** *Choice, 1998.*

Cavanagh, Peter R. (Editor) **QP310.R85B56 1990**
Biomechanics of Distance Running. Cloth Text. Human Kinetics Publishers. Champaign, IL. 1990. 376p. ISBN:0-87322-268-7, ISBN13: 978-0-87322-268-6. Dewey:612/.044. LCCN:89-029302.
Audience: **u,f.** *Choice, 1990.*

Cech, Donna J. & Martin, Suzanne **QP301.C43 2002**
Functional Movement Development Across the Life Span. Ed. 2. Cloth Text. Elsevier - Health Sciences Division. Philadelphia, PA. 2002. 528p. ISBN:0-7216-8122-0, ISBN13: 978-0-7216-8122-1. Dewey:152.3. LCCN:2002-019192.
Audience: **u,f.**

Enoka, Roger **QP303.E56 2002**
Neuromechanics of Human Movement. Ed. 3. Trade Cloth. Human Kinetics Publishers. Champaign, IL. 2001. 576p. ISBN:0-7360-0251-0, ISBN13: 978-0-7360-0251-6. Dewey:612.7/6. LCCN:2001-024108.
Audience: **l,u,f.**

Haywood, Kathleen M. & Getchell, Nancy **RJ133.H34 2005**
Life Span Motor Development. Ed. 4. Trade Cloth, CD-ROM. Human Kinetics Publishers. Champaign, IL. 2004. 344p. ISBN:0-7360-5574-6, ISBN13: 978-0-7360-5574-1. Dewey:612.7/6. LCCN:2004-013158.
Audience: **l,u,f.** *Choice, 2002.*

Knudson, Duane V. & Morrison, Craig S. **QP303.K59 2002**
Qualitative Analysis of Human Movement. Ed. 2. Trade Cloth, CD-ROM. Human Kinetics Publishers. Champaign, IL. 2002. 264p. ISBN:0-7360-3462-5, ISBN13: 978-0-7360-3462-3. Dewey:612.7/6. LCCN:2001-051833.
Audience: **u,f.**

Latash, Mark L. **QP301.L36 1993**
Control of Human Movement. Trade Cloth. Human Kinetics Publishers. Champaign, IL. 1993. 392p. ISBN:0-87322-455-8, ISBN13: 978-0-87322-455-0. Dewey:152.3. LCCN:92-036991.
Audience: **u,f.** *Choice, 1994.*

Latash, Mark L. **QP301.L364 1998**
Neurophysiological Basis of Movement. Trade Cloth. Human Kinetics Publishers. Champaign, IL. 1998. 28p. ISBN:0-88011-756-7, ISBN13: 978-0-88011-756-2. Dewey:612.7/6. LCCN:97-031920.
Audience: **u,f.** *Choice, 1998.*

Latash, Mark L. **QP301**
Progress in Motor Control: Structure-Function Relations in Voluntary Movements, Vol. 2. Trade Cloth. Human Kinetics Publishers. Champaign, IL. 2002. 272p. ISBN:0-7360-0027-5, ISBN13: 978-0-7360-0027-7. Dewey:612.7/6. LCCN:97-044950.
Audience: **u,f.**

Latash, Mark L. & Zatsiorsky, Vladimir M. (Editors) **QP301.L358 2001**
Classics in Movement Science. Trade Cloth. Human Kinetics Publishers. Champaign, IL. 2001. 464p. ISBN:0-7360-0028-3, ISBN13: 978-0-7360-0028-4. Dewey:612.7/6. LCCN:00-053857.
Audience: **u,f.**

Magill, Richard A. **BF295.M36 2003**
Motor Learning: Concepts and Applications. Ed. 7. Cloth Text. McGraw-Hill Companies, The. New York, NY. 2003. 416p. ISBN:0-07-255722-2, ISBN13: 978-0-07-255722-0. Dewey:152.3/34. LCCN:2003-051309.
Audience: **u,f.**

McMahon, Thomas A. **QP321**
Muscles, Reflexes, and Locomotion. Trade Paper. Princeton University Press. Princeton, NJ. 1984. 354p. ISBN:0-691-02376-X, ISBN13: 978-0-691-02376-2. Dewey:591.1/852. LCCN:82-061378.
Audience: **u,f.**

Newell, Karl M. (Editor) **QP301.M698 2006**
Movement System Variability. Perfect. Human Kinetics Publishers. Champaign, IL. 2005. 361p. ISBN:0-7360-4482-5, ISBN13: 978-0-7360-4482-0. Dewey:612.7/6. LCCN:2005-006427.
Audience: **l,u.**

Payne, V. Gregory & Isaacs, Larry D. **RJ133**
Human Motor Development: A Lifespan Approach with PowerWeb/OLC Bind-In Card. Ed. 6. Trade Cloth. McGraw-Hill Higher Education. Burr Ridge, IL. 2004. 560p. ISBN:0-07-298591-7, ISBN13: 978-0-07-298591-7. Dewey:155.4/123.
Audience: **u,f.**

Rose, Debra J. & Christina, Robert W. **QP301.R65 2006**
A Multilevel Approach to the Study of Motor Control and Learning. Ed. 2. Trade Cloth. Benjamin-Cummings Publishing Company. San Francisco, CA. 2005. 464p. ISBN:0-8053-6031-X, ISBN13: 978-0-8053-6031-8. Dewey:612.8/11. LCCN:2005-006531.
Audience: **u,f.**

Rose, Jessica **QP310.W3H85 2006**
Human Walking. Ed. 3. Trade Cloth. Lippincott Williams & Wilkins. Philadelphia, PA. 2005. 273p. ISBN:0-7817-5954-4, ISBN13: 978-0-7817-5954-0. Dewey:612.7/6. LCCN:2005-022885.
Audience: **l,u,f.**

Schmidt, Richard A. & Wrisberg, Craig A. **BF295.S249 2004**
Motor Learning and Performance. Ed. 3. Trade Cloth. Human Kinetics Publishers. Champaign, IL. 2004. 40p. ISBN:0-7360-4566-X, ISBN13: 978-0-7360-4566-7. Dewey:152.3/34. LCCN:2003-025025.
Audience: **u,f.**

Shumway-Cook, Anne & Wollacott, Marjorie H. **QP301.S535 2000**
Motor Control: Theory and Practical Applications. Ed. 2. Trade Cloth. Lippincott Williams & Wilkins. Philadelphia, PA. 2000. 552p. ISBN:0-683-30643-X, ISBN13: 978-0-683-30643-9. Dewey:612.7. LCCN:00-064290.
Audience: **u,f.**

Williams, Mark (Editor), et al. **GV706.8**
Skill Acquisition in Sport: Research, Theory and Practice. Nikki Hodges, Mark Scott & Mike Court (Editors). Trade Paper. Routledge. New York, NY. 2004. 464p. ISBN:0-415-27075-8, ISBN13: 978-0-415-27075-5. Dewey:796/.01. LCCN:2003-058657.
Audience: **u,f.**

Winter, David A. **QP303.W59 2004**
The Biomechanics and Motor Control of Human Movement. Ed. 3. Trade Cloth. John Wiley & Sons, Inc. Hoboken, NJ. 2004. 344p. ISBN:0-471-44989-X, ISBN13: 978-0-471-44989-8. Dewey:612/.76. LCCN:2004-047810.
Audience: **l,u.** *Choice, 1990.*

Zatsiorsky, Vladimir M. **QP303.Z383 2002**
Kinetics of Human Motion. Trade Cloth. Human Kinetics Publishers. Champaign, IL. 2002. 672p. ISBN:0-7360-3778-0, ISBN13: 978-0-7360-3778-5. Dewey:612.7/6. LCCN:2001-051861.
Audience: **u,f.**

Author Index

A

Aaker, David A. *p.141*
Aaron, Hank & Wheeler, Lonnie *p.830, p.849*
Aaronson, Susan Ariel *p.663*
Aasved, Mikal J.. . . . . *p.777*
ABA Coordinating Committee on Nonprofit Governance Staff (Contribution by) *p.85*
Abbott, Chris *p.350*
Abbott, Edith *p.253*
Abel, Richard L.. . . . . *p.440*
Abell, Peter (Editor) *p.194*
Aberbach, Joel D., et al. *p.601*
Abernethy, Bruce, et al. *p.874, p.907, p.909*
Ablemann, Nancy & Lie, John *p.713*
Abler, Ronald F. (Editor), et al. *p.377*
Abler, Ronald (Introduction by) *p.373*
Abraham, Henry J. *p.434, p.466, p.535*
Abraham, Henry Julian & Perry, Barbara A. *p.455*
Abram, John & Hawkes, Paul. *p.143*
Abramovitz, Moses *p.242*
Abrams, Bradley F. *p.506, p.507*
Abrams, Lynn *p.803*
Abramson, Daniel. *p.90*
Abramson, Jeffrey *p.470*
Abramson, Mark A. & Morin, Therese L. *p.546*
AbuKhalil, Asad *p.643*
Abu-Lughod, Lila. *p.30*
Abuza, Zachary *p.622, p.657*
Aby, Stephen H. & Kuhn, James C. (Compiled by). . . . *p.298*
Accardo, Pasquale J. (Editor), et al. *p.318*
Acemoglu, Daron (Editor) *p.242*
Achenbaum, W. Andrew *p.741*
ACIA - Arctic Climate Impact Assessment *p.393*
Acker, Caroline J. & Tracy, Sarah W. (Editors) *p.775*
Acker, James R. (Editor), et al. *p.567*
Ackerman, Bruce A.. . . . . *p.451, p.452*
Ackerman, Bruce *p.522, p.535*
Ackerman, Frank & Nadal, Alejandro *p.205*
Ackerman, Robert *p.3*
Ackrill, Margaret & Hannah, Leslie *p.90*
Acock, Alan C. & Demo, David H. *p.731*
Acorn, Annalise E.. *p.754*
Acosta, Hernandez. *p.882*
Acs, Zoltan & Armington, Catherine *p.381*
ACSM Staff & Berryman, Jack W. *p.803, p.824*
Adams, Bob & Morin, Laura *p.168*
Adams, David W. *p.311, p.763*
Adams, Francis *p.584, p.640*
Adams, James R. *p.90*
Adams, James T. *p.517*
Adams, John A. *p.382*
Adams, Marilyn J.. *p.361*
Adams, Natalie Guice & Bettis, Pamela J. *p.847*
Adams, Rachel & Savran, David (Editors) *p.745*
Adams, R. *p.428*
Adams, Richard E. W. *p.9*
Adams, Simon. *p.383*
Adams, Vincanne *p.46*
Adams, Walter & Brock, James W.. . . . *p.52, p.53, p.120, p.148*
Adams *p.168*
Adamson, David. *p.605*
Adda, Jerome & Cooper, Russell W.. . . . . *p.197*
Addams, Jane *p.757, p.769*
Addington, Larry H.. . . . . *p.627, p.646*
Addis, Cameron *p.340*
Addison, John T. & Schnabel, Claus. *p.123*
Adelman, Howard & Suhrke, Astri (Editors) *p.651*
Adelman, Irma & Morris, Cynthia T. *p.253, p.258*
Adelman, Irma & Thorbecke, Erik (Editors) *p.258*
Adelman, Irma *p.242, p.252, p.264*
Adelson, Bruce *p.813, p.830, p.849*
Adler, Bill Jr. & Adler, Bill *p.74*
Adler, Mortimer J.. *p.324*
Adler, Nancy J., et al. *p.58, p.69*
Adler, Nancy J. *p.58, p.75*
Adler, William M. *p.759*
Adorno, Theodor W., et al. *p.767*
Advertising Red Books.com *p.141*
Afary, Janet *p.616*
Affe, Robert B. *p.417*
African Development Bank Staff (Contribution by) *p.384, p.397*
Afshari, Reza *p.512*
Agar, Michael H. *p.18, p.25*
Agarwal, Bina, et al.. . . . . *p.272*
Agbasiere, Joseph Therese & Ardener, Shirley *p.700*
Aggarwal, Vinod K., et al. *p.256*
Aghion, Philippe & Durlauf, Steven N. (Editors). . *p.186, p.194*
Agnew, John *p.487, p.495*
Agranoff, Robert & McGuire, Michael *p.542, p.543*
Agresti, Alan & Finlay, Barbara. *p.483*
Agresto, John *p.462*
Aguero, Felipe & Stark, Jeffrey (Editors) *p.591*
Aguirre, Adalberto Jr. & Baker, David V. *p.17*
Aharoni, Yohanan, et al. *p.379*
Ahmad, Abdel Ghaffar Muhammad *p.578, p.610*
Ahmed, Akbar & Shore, Chris (Editors) *p.27*
Ahmed, Nafeez Mosaddeq *p.562*
Ahmida, Ali Abdullatif. *p.582*

Aho, James p.766
Ahrens, C. Donald p.393
Ahuja, Sunil & Dewhirst, Robert E.. . . . . p.529
Aimer, Peter & Mulgan, Richard p.624
Aitken, Ian (Editor) p.413
Akcam, Taner p.651
Akenson, Donald Harman p.333
Akerlof, George A. p.194
Akkermans, Peter M. & Schwartz, Glenn p.8
Akroyd, H. David p.397
Alagappa, Muthiah (Editor) p.616, p.618
Alagappa, Muthiah. p.616
Alarcon, Alicia p.763
Albanese, Denise p.378
Albelda, Randy P. & Tilly, Chris p.272
Albelda, Randy Pearl & Withorn, Ann (Editors) p.754
Albert, Jim, et al. p.871
Albert R. Mann Library, Cornell University Library p.151, p.163
Albrecht, Karl p.78, p.119, p.166
Alcock, Peter (Editor), et al. p.676
Alderman, Ellen & Kennedy, Caroline. p.455
Aldrich, John H. p.552, p.578
Aldrich, Richard J.. p.583
Aldrich, Robert p.583
Alesina, Alberto & Rosenthal, Howard p.247
Alesina, Alberto & Spolaore, Enrico. p.247
Alesina, Alberto, et al. p.242
Alexander, Barbara T. p.158
Alexander, Charles C. p.849
Alexander, David p.394
Alexander, Jeffrey C.. . . . . p.679
Alexander, Keith (Editor). p.112
Alexander, Kern & Alexander, M. David. p.449
Alexander, Kern & Hunter, Richard C. (Editors) p.315
Alexander, Kern, et al. p.90
Alexander, Robert J. (Contribution by) p.588
Alexander, Robert J. p.508
Alexander, Robin J. p.312, p.338
Alexander, Ruth M. p.753
Alexander, S. L.. . . . . p.406
Alexander, Yonah p.614
Alexandrowicz, Harry J. p.283
Alfoldi, Jeanette p.179
Alford, C. Fred p.483
Alford, William P. p.475
Algaze, Guillermo p.8
Alger, Chadwick F. (Editor) p.632
Ali, Abbas J. p.718
Ali, Paul & Gregoriou, Greg N. p.85
Aliber, Robert Z. p.57, p.93, p.98, p.99, p.162
Alice McGillivray, Richard Scammon, and Rhodes Cook p.547, p.555
Allan, Walter (Editor) p.226
Alland, Alexander. p.17
Allard, Kenneth. p.70
Allaway, Roger, et al. p.867
Allchin, Bridget & Allchin, F. Raymond p.8
Allchin, Bridget (Editor) p.8
Allchin, Raymond p.8
Allen, Beverly. p.651
Allen, Catherine J. p.36, p.700
Allen, Franklin & Gale, Douglas p.88
Allen, G. C. & Donnithorne, Audrey G. p.258
Allen, Jo Beth (Editor). p.361
Allen, John B.. . . . . p.866
Allen, Judy p.161
Allen, Mary. p.823
Allen, Michael p.865
Allen, Peter Lewis p.746
Allen, Robert C.. . . . . p.267
Allen, Robert L. & Allen, Pamela P.. . . . . p.700
Allen, Roy E.. . . . . p.242, p.246, p.260
Allen, Theodore W. p.729, p.731
Allen, Vernon L.. . . . . p.264
Allington, Richard L. & Johnston, Peter H. p.361
Allison, Juliann Emmons (Editor). p.425
Allitt, Patrick p.337
Allsen, Thomas T. p.623
Allyn, David p.746
Aloysius, G.. . . . . p.617
Alperovitz, Gar p.493, p.502
Alreck, Pamela L. & Settle, Robert B.. . . . . p.137
Alred, Gerald J., et al. p.171
Al-Saud, Faisal Bin Salman p.640
Alsop, Ronald & Wall Street Journal Staff (Editors) . . . p.176
Alston, Margaret & Bowles, Wendy p.757
Altbach, Philip G. (Author, Editor), et al. p.330
Altbach, Philip G., et al. p.330
Altbach, Philip G. p.330
Altbach, Phillip G.. . . . . p.313
Altemeyer, Bob p.509, p.767
Alter, Joseph S. p.790, p.792, p.802, p.803
Alter, Max p.233
Alter, Michael J. p.827, p.828, p.872
Alterman, Eric. p.416
Althoff, Gerd p.501
Altman, Dennis, et al. p.140
Altman, Dennis p.746
Altman, Micah, et al. p.689
Altman, Stuart H. (Editor), et al. p.778
Altschiller, Donald. p.568
Altschuld, James W. & Witkin, Belle Ruth p.81
Altschull, J. Herbert p.403
Alvarez, Alex p.651
Alvarez, R. Michael & Brehm, John p.425, p.559
Alves, Maria H.. . . . . p.591
Amanda Quick p.150
Amar, Akhil R.. p.455, p.473
Amar, Akhil Reed p.452

Ambrose, Stephen E. & Barber, James A. Jr. (Editors) . . *p.717*
Ambrosi, Gerhard Michael *p.226*
American Assembly Staff. *p.272*
American Association for the Advancement of Science . . *p.284*
American Bar Association Staff *p.87, p.444*
American College of Sports Medicine Staff (Contribution by). *p.783, p.829, p.842*
American College of Sports Medicine Staff *p.790, p.873*
American College of Sports Medicine. *p.792, p.872, p.880, p.882*
American Council on Education Staff *p.330*
American Council on the Teaching of Foreign Languages *p.359*
American Education Research Association. *p.338, p.354, p.355, p.361*
American Educational Research Association, et al. *p.285*
American Federation of Teachers *p.282*
American Football Coaches Association Staff *p.858*
American National Election Studies *p.547*
American Social History Project *p.366*
American Society for Training and Development Staff (Contribution by). *p.304*
American Society of Civil Engineers Staff *p.390*
American Sport Education Program (Contribution by) *p.869, p.905*
American Sport Education Program Staff (Contribution by) *p.794, p.839, p.862, p.869, p.904*
American Sport Education Program Staff. . *p.794, p.795, p.839, p.849, p.863, p.867, p.868, p.870, p.904, p.905*
Ameringer, Charles D. (Editor) *p.588*
Amerlinck, Mari-Jose (Editor) *p.25*
Ames, Kenneth M. & Maschner, Herbert D.. . . . . *p.10*
Ames, Michael M. *p.47*
Amihud, Yakov (Editor) *p.251*
Amit-Talai, Vered (Editor) *p.3*
Amjad, Ali *p.120*
Amman, Hans M. (Editor), et al. *p.186, p.197*
Ammon, Rob, et al. *p.880, p.882*
Amnesty International *p.669*
Amram, Martha (Author, Editor). *p.90, p.101*
Amstrong, M. & Porter, R. H. (Editors) *p.186*
Amstutz, Mark R. *p.483, p.624*
Amy, Douglas J.. . . . . *p.576*
Analoui *p.75*
Anandalingam, G. & Lucas, Henry C. *p.84*
Anastaplo, George. *p.458, p.518*
Anastopoulos, Arthur D. & Shelton, Terri L. *p.318*
Anbar, Ada *p.370*
Ancheta, Angelo N. *p.456*
Andermahr, Sonya, et al. *p.676*
Anders, Elizabeth *p.795, p.857*
Andersen, Esben S. *p.233*
Andersen, Lykke E., et al. *p.267*
Andersen, Margaret *p.743*
Andersen, Mark B. (Editor). *p.876*
Andersen, Stephen O. & Sarma, K. Madhava *p.666*
Andersen, Svein S. & Eliassen, Kjell A. (Editors) *p.636*
Anderson, Benedict R. O'G. *p.493*
Anderson, Bonnie S.. . . . . *p.710*
Anderson, Bryon D.. . . . . *p.866, p.871*
Anderson, Elijah *p.692, p.723*
Anderson, Eric *p.839*
Anderson, Eugene N. *p.609, p.610*
Anderson, Ewan (Editor). *p.487, p.495*
Anderson, James F., et al. *p.676*
Anderson, Jervis. *p.123*
Anderson, Lars *p.813, p.853*
Anderson, Lorin W., et al. *p.338*
Anderson, Lynn & Kress, Carla. *p.787, p.842*
Anderson, Malcolm *p.487, p.495*
Anderson, Marcia *p.827*
Anderson, Margo J. (Editor) *p.676*
Anderson, Paul S. & Lapp, Diane K. *p.361*
Anderson, R. D. Jr. *p.333*
Anderson, Richard, et al.. . . . . *p.597*
Anderson, Rob (Editor), et al.. . . . . *p.422*
Anderson, Robert D.. . . . . *p.333*
Anderson, Sean K. & Sloan, Stephen *p.657*
Anderson, Terry H.. . . . . *p.57, p.108, p.133*
Anderson, Timothy *p.396*
Anderson-Levitt, Kathryn M. (Editor) *p.313*
Andersson, Ake E. & Andersson, David E. *p.256, p.260*
Andre, Judith *p.802, p.821*
Andre, Rae *p.736*
Andreasen, Alan R.. . . . . *p.51, p.134*
Andreff, Wladimir *p.186*
Andrew, John *p.516*
Andrew, Susan *p.870*
Andrews, Alexander *p.403*
Andrews, Charles McLean *p.517*
Andrews, David L. (Editor), et al.. . . . . *p.812*
Andrews, David L. (Editor) *p.853, p.882, p.895, p.901*
Andrews, Deborah C. & Andrews, William D. *p.171*
Andrews, Jac J. W. (Volume Editor), et al.. . . . . *p.285*
Andrews, Phil. *p.408, p.906*
Andriessen, Daniel *p.72*
Ang, Ien *p.418*
Angel, Ronald J.. *p.751*
Angelo, Thomas A. & Cross, K. Patricia. *p.285*
Anglim, Christopher Thomas *p.460*
Angus, David & Mirel, Jeffery *p.324*
Anheier, Helmut K. (Editor) *p.85*
An-Na'im, Abdullahi A. (Editor) *p.33*
Annan, Kofi A. (Foreword by) *p.632*
Annas, George J. *p.448*
Annas, Julia. *p.488*
Annesley, Claire (Editor) *p.186*
Annunzio, Susan & McGowan, Sharon *p.79*
Ansell-Pearson, Keith *p.490*

Ansoff, H. Igor *p.81*
Antelman, Gordon *p.197*
Anthony, Rebecca J. & Roe, Gerald *p.168*
Anton, Thomas J. *p.523*
Antonius, Rachad *p.689*
Anttalainen, Tarmo *p.115*
Anyon, Jean *p.314*
Aoki, Keith, et al. *p.445*
Appelbaum, Peter *p.308*
Appenzeller, Herb & Lewis, Guy *p.882, p.900, p.905*
Appenzeller, Herb *p.882, p.886, p.900*
Appenzeller, Thomas *p.785, p.882, p.900*
Appiah, Anthony *p.693*
Apple, James M.. *p.116*
Apple, Michael, et al. *p.361*
Apple, Michael W.. . . . . *p.300*
Applebee, Arthur N. *p.294, p.361*
Apps, Jerold W. *p.319*
Aptekar, Lewis *p.760*
Apter, David E. & Rosberg, Carl G.. . . . . *p.610*
Apter, David E. *p.494, p.610*
Aquinas, Thomas *p.490*
Arato, Andrew & Gebhardt, Eike (Editors) *p.699*
Arbena, Joseph L. (Compiled by). *p.812, p.813, p.833*
Archer, Dane & Gartner, Rosemary *p.751*
Archer, Jack H., et al. *p.463*
Archer, John & Lloyd, Barbara B. (Editors) *p.746*
Archer, Margaret S. & Tritter, Jonathon Q. (Editors) . . . *p.688*
Ardell, Jean Hastings *p.813, p.834, p.849*
Arditti, Fred D.. . . . . *p.92, p.93, p.101, p.103*
Arellano, Manuel *p.198*
Arendt, Hannah *p.491, p.497, p.509, p.718*
Arensberg, Conrad Maynadier *p.41*
Arestis, Philip & Chick, Victoria (Editors) *p.241*
Arestis, Philip & Sawyer, Malcolm C. (Editors) *p.193*
Argyris, Chris (Contribution by), et al. *p.176*
Argyris, Chris *p.78*
Arian, Asher & Shamir, Michal (Editors) *p.615*
Ariel, Avraham & Berger, Nora Ariel *p.389*
Aries, Philippe (Editor), et al.. . . . . *p.732*
Aries, Philippe *p.735*
Ariès, Philippe *p.742*
Arima, E. Y.. . . . . *p.789*
Aris, Philippe A.. *p.732*
Aristotle *p.488*
Arkes, Hadley *p.453*
Arksey, Hilary & Knight, Peter *p.691*
Arlen, Michael J. *p.414*
Armor, David J.. . . . . *p.300, p.449*
Armour, Kathleen R. *p.795, p.903*
Armstrong, Gary *p.813, p.867*
Armstrong, Gordon M.. . . . . *p.676*
Armstrong, J. Scott (Editor). *p.118*
Armstrong, Jerome & Moulitsas Zúniga, Markos *p.554*
Armstrong, John A. *p.494*
Armstrong, Lawrence E. *p.874, p.878*
Armstrong, Stephen *p.118*
Arnaldi, Girolamo *p.643*
Arnold, Brent, et al. *p.828*
Arnold, George T. *p.413*
Arnold, Jeanne E.. *p.10*
Arnold, R. Douglas *p.406*
Arnold, Robert H. *p.388*
Arnold, Roslyn *p.361*
Arnove, Robert F. & Torres, Carlos Alberto (Editors) *p.313, p.338*
Arnove, Robert F. (Editor), et al. *p.313*
Aron, Raymond *p.682, p.684*
Aronowitz, Stanley *p.693, p.710, p.726*
Arons, Stephen *p.297*
Aronson, Elliot & Meyers, David G. *p.692*
Arreola, Daniel D. (Editor) *p.381*
Arriagada, Genaro *p.591*
Arron, Deborah L.. *p.440*
Arrow, Kenneth J. (Editor), et al. *p.186*
Arrow, Kenneth Joseph & Hahn, F. H.. . . . . *p.198*
Arrow, Kenneth Joseph & Intriligator, Michael D. (Volume Editors) *p.186, p.198*
Arrow, Kenneth Joseph *p.186, p.198, p.206, p.272*
Arsuaga, Juan Luis & Martínez, Ignacio *p.15*
Arsuaga, Juan Luis de. *p.16*
Art, Robert J. & Cronin, Patrick M. (Editors) *p.644*
Art, Robert J. & Jervis, Robert *p.625*
Art, Robert J. & Waltz, Kenneth N. *p.654*
Arter, David *p.578, p.584, p.597*
Arter, Judith, et al.. *p.285*
Arthur, C. J.. . . . . *p.235*
Arthur, Diane. *p.75*
Arthur, John. *p.454*
Arthur W. Diamond Law Library, Columia University . . *p.476*
Artibise, A. F. *p.700*
ArtsEdge—The National Arts and Education Network *p.359*
Aruri, Naseer Hasan. *p.560, p.565, p.641*
Asacker, Tom *p.138*
Asad, Talal (Editor) *p.4*
Asbury, Herbert *p.714*
Ash, Stephen V. *p.519*
Ashare, Alan B. (Editor). *p.862, p.870, p.871*
Ashby, LeRoy *p.712*
Ashe, A.R. *p.830, p.831*
Ashenfelter, Orley C. & Card, David (Editors). . . *p.186, p.187*
Ashkenas, Ronald N., et al. *p.85*
Ashley, Perry J. *p.410*
Ashton-Warner, Sylvia (Author, Author) *p.337*
Asimakopulos, Athanasios *p.226*
Asinof, Eliot *p.849*
Asmus, Ronald D.. *p.639*
Aspatore Books Staff *p.75*
Aspatore Books *p.905*

Aspromourgos, Tony p.218
Astin, Alexander W. p.289, p.330
Astuto, Terry A., et al. p.324
Athearn, James L. p.163
Atkin, Brian & Brooks, Adrian p.112
Atkinson, A. B. & Bourguignon, F. (Editors) p.187
Atkinson, Cliff p.171
Atkinson, David N. p.535
Atkinson, Giles, et al. p.267
Atkinson, Michael M. & Chandler, Marsha A. (Editors) . . p.586
Atleson, James B. p.120
Atran, Scott p.26, p.36
Attwood, Bain & Markus, Andrew (Editors) p.624
Aucoin, James L. p.408
Auerbach, Alan J. & Feldstein, Martin (Editors) p.187
Auerbach, Alan J. & Feldstein, Martin p.187
Auerbach, Alan J. p.187
Auge, Marc p.22
Augspurger, Michael p.409
Auletta, Ken p.726
Aumann, R. J. & Hart, S. R. (Editors) p.187
Aumann, Robert J. & Hart, Sergiu (Editors) p.187
Aumente, Jerome, et al. p.403
Auron, Yair p.651
Aust, Anthony p.477
Austin, David R. (Editor), et al. p.783, p.829, p.842
Auxter, David, et al. p.800
Avrich, Paul p.324
Axelrod, Alan p.719
Axelrod, Joseph p.292
Axelrod, Paul & Reid, John G. (Editors) p.333
Axelrod, Paul p.333
Axelrod, Robert p.625
Axline, Virginia M. p.355
Axson, David A. J. & Hackett Group p.81
Axtell, Roger E., et al. p.57
Axtell, Roger E. p.56, p.58
Ayalon, Ami p.403
Ayubi, Nazih p.500
Azicri, Max & Deal, Elsie (Editors) p.506
Azuma, Eiichiro p.570, p.572
Azzaro, Marian, et al. p.427

B

Baark, Erik p.421
Babson, Steve p.124
Babuscio, Jack & Dunn, Richard M. p.601
Bach, Stanley J. & Smith, Steven S.. . . . . p.532
Bacharach, Michael p.83
Bachman, David p.619
Backer, Bill p.428
Backhaus, Jurgen G. p.187
Backhouse, Roger & Bateman, Bradley (Editors) p.226
Backhouse, Roger E. & Salanti, Andrea (Editors) p.198, p.225
Backhouse, Roger p.194, p.226, p.239
Backstrom, Charles H. & Hursh-Cesar, Gerald D. p.697
Bacon, David p.726
Badaracco, Claire Hoertz (Editor) p.719
Badaracco, Joseph L. Jr. p.145
Badaracco, Joseph L. p.53
Badcock, Blair p.395
Bader, Gloria E. & Rossi, Catherine A. p.136
Bader, Sara p.141
Baechle, Thomas & Earle, Roger W. p.792
Baechle, Thomas R. & Earle, Roger W. p.792, p.878
Baehr, Peter R. & Gordenker, Leon p.632
Baer, Gabriel p.700
Baer, Judith A. (Editor) p.676
Baer, Martha, et al. p.561
Bagehot, Walter p.99, p.146, p.154, p.604
Baggett, James Alex p.519
Bagley, Constance E. & Dauchy, Craig E. p.67, p.108
Bagley, Constance E. & Savage, Diane p.51
Bagley, Robert (Editor) p.8
Bahrke, Michael S. & Yesalis, Charles E. p.826, p.874
Bailey, Dennis p.773
Bailey, Edward P. Jr. p.171
Bailey, Eric J. p.46
Bailey, Stephen K.. . . . . p.446
Bailey, Sydney D. p.632
Bailey, Wilford S., et al. p.821
Bailey, William G. (Editor) p.676
Baily, Samuel L.. . . . . p.763
Bailyn, Bernard p.324
Bainbridge, Timothy p.636
Baine, Celeste p.870, p.903
Baker, Aaron & Boyd, Todd p.813, p.901
Baker, Alan R. H. (Author, Contribution by) p.375, p.377
Baker, David & LeTendre, Gerald K. p.313, p.333
Baker, George P. & Smith, George D. p.90, p.99
Baker, Jean H. (Editor) p.518
Baker, Jonathan & Aina, Tade Akin (Editors) p.764
Baker, Lee D. p.4
Baker, Leonard p.467
Baker, Randall (Editor) p.545
Baker, Ross K. p.529, p.533
Baker, William J. p.813, p.831, p.869
Bakken, Gordon Morris & Kindell, Alexandra (Editors) p.570
Baktiari, Bahman p.616
Bakvis, Herman & Chandler, William M. (Editors) p.586
Balachandran, M. p.88
Balak, Benjamin p.268
Balakian, Peter p.651
Balasubramanyam, V. N. p.255
Balcells, Albert p.608
Baldassare, Mark (Editor) p.713
Baldassaro, Lawrence & Johnson,

Dick (Editors). p.823, p.830, p.849
Baldasty, Gerald J.. p.148
Balderston, Theo (Editor). p.237
Baldez, Lisa. p.710
Baldwin, Nicholas & Shell, Donald (Editors). p.574
Bale, John & Vertinsky, Patricia A. (Editors) p.813
Bale, John p.813, p.821, p.893, p.898
Bales, Kevin p.27
Bales, Robert F. p.695
Bales, Robert Freed p.692
Balim, Cigdem (Editor) p.616
Ball, Howard & Cooper, Phillip J.. . . . . p.467
Ball, Howard, et al. p.461
Ball, Howard. p.150, p.447, p.460, p.467
Ball, Michael S. & Smith, Gregory W.. . . . . p.690
Ball, Philip p.691
Ball, Stephen J. (Editor) p.340
Ballard, Allen p.309
Ballard, Michael B. p.519
Ball p.69
Ballenger, Cynthia (Editor) p.361
Ballew, Vincent. p.87
Ballot, Michael p.120
Balmaceda, Margarita Mercedes. p.597
Balmer, Randall H. p.720
Baltagi, Badi H. (Editor) p.198
Baltagi, Badi H.. . . . . p.198, p.206
Balter, Lawrence & McCall, Robert B. p.676
Balter, Michael p.12
Baltzell, Edward Digby p.725, p.726
Bamber, Greg (Editor) p.120
Bancroft, John (Editor). p.746
Bandura, Albert p.355, p.766
Bane, Mary J. & Ellwood, David T.. . . . . p.754
Bane, Mary Jo (Editor), et al.. . . . . p.720
Bane, Mary Jo. p.732
Bangura, Abdul Karim, et al. p.483
Bank, Stephen A. p.106, p.109, p.112
Banks, Arthur S. (Editor), et al.. . . . . p.574
Banks, Christopher P. & Green, John C. (Editors) p.535
Banks, James A. & Banks, Cherry A. McGee . . . p.300, p.308
Banks, James A. (Editor) p.313
Banner, James M. Jr. & Cannon, Harold C. p.346, p.356
Bannon, Joseph J. & Busser, James A.. . . . . p.785
Banta, Trudy W. (Editor) p.285
Barab, Sasha A. (Editor), et al. p.761
Barak, Gregg p.750
Baram, Uzi & Carroll, Lynda (Editors) p.13
Baran, Stanley J. & Wallis, Roger. p.412
Barany, Zoltan & Volgyes, Ivan (Editors) p.508
Barany, Zoltan. p.639
Barash, David P. & Lipton, Judith Eve p.731
Barash, David P. p.83
Baratta, Joseph P. (Compiled by) p.632
Barbazette, Jean p.177
Barber, Benjamin R.. . . . . p.502, p.554
Barber, Bernard & Barber, Elinor G. p.700, p.723
Barber, Elinor G. p.723
Barber, William J. p.522
Barberis, Peter. p.605
Barbour, Philippe p.602, p.636
Barbuto, Domenica M.. . . . . p.178, p.179
Bardis, Panos D.. p.676
Barell, John p.346
Barfield, Thomas (Editor). p.3
Barfield, Thomas J. p.623
Baritz, Loren (Editor) p.709
Barker, Chris p.676
Barker, Drucilla K. & Feiner, Susan F.. . . . . p.273
Barker, Ernest p.488
Barker-Benfield, G. J. p.743
Barley, Stephen R. & Kunda, Gideon p.268
Barnaby, Frank & Huisken, Ronald (Editors). p.655
Barnard, Alan & Spencer, Jonathan (Editors) p.3
Barnard, Alan p.38
Barnard, Chester I. p.64
Barnard, John p.124
Barner, Robert W.. p.79
Barner-Barry, Carol & Rosenwein, Robert p.483
Barnes, Gina L. p.8
Barnes, Harry E.. p.752
Barnes, James G. p.143
Barnes, Kenneth C. p.764
Barnes, Pamela M. & Barnes, Ian G. p.602
Barnett, Michael N. p.632, p.651
Barnett, Steven p.803, p.813, p.886, p.901
Barnett, Vincent. p.211, p.235, p.255
Barnett, William A. (Editor), et al. p.198, p.206
Barney, Darin p.503, p.590
Barney, Robert Knight, et al. p.845, p.886, p.890, p.901
Barnhurst, Kevin G. p.409
Barnum, Susan R. p.156
Baron, David P.. . . . . p.51
Baron, Jonathan p.82
Barone, Diane M. & Morrow, Lesley Mandel (Editors) p.368
Barone, Diane M., et al. p.360
Bar-Or, Oded (Editor), et al. p.828, p.874, p.878
Barr, Andrew p.699
Barr, Carol, et al. p.882
Barrell, Barrie R. C. p.366
Barrera, Mario. p.729
Barrett, John p.847, p.864
Barrett, P. S. & Baldry, David. p.112
Barrett, Stanley R. p.701
Barro, Robert J. p.242
Barron, Jerome A. p.458
Barros, Carlos Pestana (Editor), et al.. . . . p.843, p.882, p.887
Barrow, Christine (Editor) p.755
Barrow, Clyde W. p.491

Barrow, Colin *p.87*
Barrow, Robin. *p.340*
Barry, John & Frankland, E. Gene (Editors) *p.666*
Barry Jones, R. *p.260*
Barry, Kristen Lawton, et al. *p.775*
Barston, R. *p.645*
Bart, Pauline B. & O'Brien, Patricia H. *p.757*
Bar-Tal, Daniel (Editor), et al. *p.694*
Bartels, Larry M. *p.556*
Bartels, Robert *p.134*
Bartelson, Jens *p.496*
Barth, Fredrik *p.34*
Barth, James R., et al.. . . . . *p.90*
Barth, Roland S.. . . . . *p.324*
Bartholet, Elizabeth *p.737*
Bartholomew, Robert E. *p.714*
Bartlett, Beatrice S. *p.617, p.619*
Bartlett, Christopher A. & Ghoshal, Sumantra *p.58, p.64*
Bartlett, Eugene R.. . . . . *p.421*
Bartlett, Roger. *p.907*
Bartley, Paula *p.604*
Bartolini, Stefano *p.601*
Bartolome, Lilia I.. . . . . *p.349*
Barton, John H., et al.. . . . . *p.61*
Barton, Jonathan. *p.267*
Barton, Roy *p.367*
Bartov, Omer *p.651*
Barz, Gregory F.. *p.701*
Barzelay, Michael & Amajani, Babak J. *p.529*
Barzun, Jacques. *p.289, p.292, p.330*
Bascia, Nina (Editor), et al.. . . . . *p.297*
Bass, Jack. *p.470*
Bass, Mike *p.849*
Bassett, Patrick F. & Thorn, Craig (Illustrators). *p.296*
Basso, Keith H.. . . . . *p.20*
Basso, Matthew (Editor), et al. *p.745*
Bastiat, Frederic. *p.187, p.208*
Basye, Anne. *p.171*
Bateman, Bradley W. & Davis, John B. (Editors). *p.226*
Bates, Regis Bud J. *p.115*
Bates, Suzanne *p.171*
Bateson, Gregory *p.23, p.42*
Batra, Ravi. *p.256, p.260, p.264*
Battelle, John *p.157*
Battilossi, Stefano & Cassis, Youssef (Editors) *p.88*
Bauer, Caroline Feller *p.362*
Bauer, Gretchen & Taylor, Scott D.. . . . . *p.610, p.613*
Bauer, P. T. *p.242*
Bauer, Peter T. *p.242*
Baughman, James L.. . . . . *p.409, p.417*
Baule, Steven *p.350*
Baum, Matthew A. *p.414, p.559*
Bauman, Richard & Sherzer, Joel (Editors) *p.18*
Bauman, Richard W.. . . . . *p.340*
Bauman, Zygmunt *p.699*
Baumol, William J. & Blinder, Alan S. *p.187*
Bay, Christian & Walker, Charles C.. . . . . *p.497*
Bay, Christian *p.515*
Bay, Edna G. *p.610*
Bayart, Jean-Francois, et al.. . . . . *p.611*
Bayart, Jean-Francois *p.611, p.699*
Bayly, Susan *p.722*
Bazerman, Max H. & Neale, Margaret A.. . . . . *p.74*
Bazyler, Michael J. *p.464*
Beadie, Nancy & Tolley, Kimberly (Editors) *p.296*
Beals, Katherine A. *p.801, p.824, p.876*
Beamer, Glenn *p.523*
Bean, Dawn Pawson *p.868*
Bean, Michael J. & Rowland, Melanie J. *p.463*
Bean, Ron *p.120*
Beard, Charles A. *p.454*
Beard, Charles Austin *p.518*
Beard, Roger *p.354*
Beardsley, Edward H. *p.774*
Beattie, Keith *p.413*
Beatty, Barbara *p.370*
Beatty, Carol A. & Barker Scott, Brenda A.. . . . . *p.79*
Beauchamp, K. G.. *p.421*
Beaud, Michel & Dostaler, Gilles *p.187, p.188, p.208*
Beaudry, Mary C. (Editor) *p.6*
Beauvoir, Simone de *p.743*
Beazley, Charles Raymond *p.377*
Bechhofer, Frank & Paterson, Lindsay. *p.686*
Beck, J. Murray *p.589*
Beck, Lynn G. & Murphy, Joseph. *p.281*
Beck, Ulrich & Willms, Johannes. *p.261, p.267*
Becker, Carl L. *p.518*
Becker, Gary S. *p.253*
Becker, Gary Stanley. *p.133*
Becker, Howard S. *p.687, p.695, p.776*
Becker, William E. & Watts, Michael (Editors) *p.185*
Becker, William H. & McClenahan, William M.. . . . . . . *p.88*
Beckman, Linda J. & Harvey, S. Marie (Editors) *p.775*
Beckwith, Martha W. *p.40*
Bedau, Hugo Adam & Cassell, Paul G. (Editors) *p.567*
Bedau, Hugo Adam *p.471*
Bedeski, Robert E.. *p.621*
Bedworth, David D. & Bailey, James E.. . . . . *p.117*
Beer, Samuel Hutchison *p.523*
Beetham, David *p.503*
Beevor, Antony & Cooper, Artemis *p.581*
Begg, David K. *p.237*
Behrman, Greg *p.769*
Behuniak, Susan M. *p.535*
Beier, Anne *p.534*
Beierlein, James G., et al. *p.151*
Beilin, Yossi *p.629*
Beim, Gloria & Winter, Ruth *p.827, p.874, p.878*
Beineke, John A. *p.340*
Beito, David T. (Editor), et al. *p.545*

Beker, Avi p.655
Bekes, Csaba & Byrne, Malcom (Editors) p.641
Belenko, Steven R. p.568
Belfield, Clive R. p.297
Belkin, Aaron & Bateman, Geoffrey (Editors) p.569
Bell, Colin & Newby, Howard p.770
Bell, Daniel p.679, p.701, p.769, p.843
Bell, Derrick p.449
Bell, J. Bowyer p.657
Bell, Morag (Editor), et al. p.502
Bell, P. M. p.643
Bell, Peter D. p.701
Bell, Steve p.117
Bellah, Robert N., et al. p.720
Bellah, Robert N. p.719
Bellamy, Alex J. & Williams, Paul p.648
Bellamy, Richard & Warleigh, Alex (Editors) . . . p.602, p.636
Bellet, Michel, et al.. . . . . p.233, p.246
Bellofiore, Riccardo (Editor) p.261, p.262
Bellwood, Peter S. p.13
Bellwood, Peter p.5
Belmonte, Dominic p.346
Belongia, Michael T. & Garfinkel, Michelle R. (Editors) p.242
Belz, Herman p.518
Ben-Ami, Shlomo p.646, p.648
Bender, Gary & Johnson, Michael L. p.408, p.906
Bender, Margaret Clelland p.20
Bender, Steven W.. . . . . p.456
Bender, Thomas (Editor) p.762
Bender, Thomas p.770
Bender, William N. p.283
Bendix, Reinhard & Lipset, Seymour Martin (Editors) p.723
Bendix, Reinhard p.682, p.684
Benedict, Jeff p.813, p.853
Benedict, Ruth p.22
Benedict, Stephen p.523
Benhabib, Seyla p.576, p.669
Benjamin, Daniel & Simon, Steven p.562
Benjamin, Gerald & Nathan, Richard P. p.542
Benjamin, Patricia & Lamp, Scott P. p.790, p.828
Benjamin, Patricia J. & Lamp, Scott P. p.825, p.873
Benko, Georges & Strohmayer, Ulf p.377
Benn, Stanley I. p.515
Benne, Robert p.307
Benner, Dietrich & Lenzen, Dieter (Editors) p.333
Bennet, Alex & Bennet, David p.78
Bennett, A. LeRoy p.632
Bennett, John W. p.29
Bennett, Peter p.134
Bennett, Robert & Estall, Robert (Editors) p.377
Bennett, Robert J. (Editor) p.581
Bennett, Roger p.134
Bennett, Sean J. & Simon, Andrew p.391
Bennis, Warren & Biederman, Patricia W.. . . . . p.65
Bennis, Warren (Editor), et al. p.70
Bennis, Warren G. & Thomas, Robert J.. . . . . p.262
Bennis, Warren p.70
Bennison, George M. & Moseley, Keith p.375
Bense, Judith A. p.10
Bensen, Robert (Editor) p.755
Benson, Michael L. & Cullen, Francis T. p.472
Benston, George J., et al. p.88
Benston, George J. p.90
Bent-Goodley, Tricia B. (Editor) p.757
Bentham, Jeremy p.194, p.217, p.230, p.574
Bentley, Arthur F. p.482
Bentsur, Eytan p.648
Benveniste, Luis, et al.. . . . . p.296
Benyo, Richard p.840, p.847, p.866
Ben-Yosef, Eldad p.151, p.152
Benz, Christine p.93
Bereday, George Z. & Volpicelli, Luigi (Editors) p.324
Bereiter, Carl p.356
Berends, Mark, et al.. . . . . p.280
Berenson, Alex p.53, p.93, p.101, p.104, p.105, p.111
Berentsen, William H. (Editor) p.383
Berezin, Mabel & Schain, Martin (Editors). p.383
Berg, David R. & Ferrier, Grant p.159
Berg, Ivar p.297
Berg, Kris & Latin, Richard p.795
Berge, Zane L. & Clark, Thomas A.. . . . . p.321
Bergen, Doris L.. p.651
Berger, Arnold S. p.114
Berger, Arthur A. p.416
Berger, Arthur Asa p.422, p.426
Berger, Bennett M.. . . . . p.740
Berger, Karen p.788
Berger, Morroe p.456
Berger, Peter L. p.679, p.719
Berger, Raoul p.454, p.461, p.462, p.471
Berghahn, Volker R. p.497
Bergman, Paul & Berman-Barrett, Sara J. p.473
Bergman, Paul p.470
Bergmann, Barbara R. p.273
Bergstrom, Abram R. (Editor). p.239
Bergstrom, John C., et al. p.267
Beringer, Richard E., et al. p.519
Berinsky, Adam J. p.559
Beriss, David p.40
Berk, Ronald A.. p.346
Berkes, Ross N. p.632
Berkey, Jonathan P. p.721
Berkman, Robert I. p.180
Berkowitz, Edward D. p.754
Berkshire Reference Works Staff p.834, p.843
Berlage, Gai I. & Gerard, Charley p.803, p.834, p.849
Berle, Adolf A. Jr. & Means, Gardiner C.. . . . . . p.85, p.146
Berlin, Brent p.26

Berlin, Howard M.. . . . . *p.188*
Berlin, Isaiah *p.515*
Berliner, David C. & Biddle, Bruce J. *p.324*
Berliner, David C. & Calfee, Robert C. (Editors) *p.356*
Berman, Evan M., et al.. . . . . *p.76*
Berman, Harold J. *p.433*
Berman, Karen, et al. *p.91*
Berman, Paul *p.562, p.657*
Bermeo, Nancy Gina. *p.503*
Bernanke, Ben S. & Woodford, Michael (Editors) *p.246*
Bernanke, Ben S., et al. *p.246*
Bernanke, Ben S. *p.213*
Bernard, H. Russell *p.25*
Bernard, Jessie Shirley *p.738*
Bernard, Jessie *p.738*
Bernhardsen, Tor *p.386*
Bernier, Julie N.. . . . . *p.828*
Bernstein, Carl & Woodward, Bob *p.404*
Bernstein, Mark F.. . . . . *p.803, p.858*
Bernstein, Nina *p.757*
Bernstein, Peter L. & Damodaran, Aswath (Editors) *p.94, p.162*
Bernstein, Peter L.. . . . . . *p.91, p.92, p.93, p.94, p.99, p.162*
Bernus, P. (Editor), et al. *p.114*
Berridge, G. R. (Editor), et al. *p.645*
Berridge, G. R. *p.645*
Berrill, Kevin T. (Author, Editor) *p.568, p.751*
Berring *p.439*
Berry, Anthony J., et al.. . . . . *p.72*
Berry, Brian J.L. & Wheeler, James (Editors) *p.381*
Berry, Neil *p.403*
Berry, Nicholas O.. *p.670*
Berry, William E. *p.405*
Berryman, Jack W. & Park, Roberta J. (Editors) *p.803, p.825, p.873*
Berthelot, Yves (Editor) *p.633, p.663*
Berto, Frank J. *p.856*
Bertola, Giuseppe, et al. *p.252, p.253*
Bertram, Eva, et al. *p.568*
Bertsch, Gary K. (Editor). *p.623*
Berube, Michael & Nelson, Cary (Editors) *p.330*
Berwanger, Eugene H. *p.565*
Beschloss, Michael R. & Talbott, Strobe. *p.643, p.645*
Besner, Hilda F. & Spungin, Charlotte I.. . . . . *p.309*
Besnier, Niko. *p.21*
Besson, Jean-Louis *p.40*
Best, Geoffrey. *p.478*
Best, Joel. *p.689, p.754*
Best, Rick (Editor), et al.. . . . . *p.113*
Bestor, Arthur E. *p.340*
Beth, Loren P.. . . . . *p.467*
Bettelheim, Bruno & Zelan, Karen *p.362*
Bettelheim, Bruno *p.735*
Bettie, Julie *p.723*
Bettinger, Pete & Wing, Michael G.. . . . . *p.386*
Betts, John R.. . . . . *p.803*
Betts, Julian & Loveless, Tom (Editors) *p.302*
Betts, Raymond F. *p.584*
Betz, David *p.597*
Betz, Hans-Georg *p.601*
Beukelman, David R. & Mirenda, Pat *p.318*
Bevis, Charlie *p.803, p.824, p.849, p.890*
Beyerlein, Michael M., et al.. . . . . *p.80*
Beyle, Thad L. (Editor) *p.548, p.557*
Bezanson, Randall P.. . . . . *p.458*
Bhagat, Sanjai & Jefferis, Richard H. Jr.. . . . . *p.198*
Bhagwati, Jagdish N. & Grossman, Gene M. (Editors) . . *p.243*
Bhagwati, Jagdish N. (Editor), et al.. . . . . *p.256*
Bhagwati, Jagdish N. (Editor) *p.255, p.256*
Bhagwati, Jagdish N., et al.. . . . . *p.256*
Bhagwati, Jagdish N. *p.55, p.243, p.255, p.256, p.663*
Bhatia, Michael V.. *p.670*
Bhide, Amar V.. . . . . *p.67*
Bianchi, Robert S.. *p.701*
Biberaj, Elez *p.600*
Bickel, Alexander M. *p.437*
Bickerstaffe, George *p.176*
Bickerton, James & Gagnon, Alain-G *p.586*
Bickman, Martin. *p.346*
Biddle, J. E. (Editor), et al.. . . . . *p.194, p.208*
Biddle, Stuart J. H. & Mutrie, Nanette. *p.876*
Biddle, Stuart J. H. (Editor) *p.812, p.876*
Bidney, David *p.23*
Bidwai, Praful & Vanaik, Achin. *p.655*
Biehle, James T., et al.. . . . . *p.288*
Bienen, Henry S. & de Walle, Nicolas van *p.511*
Bigalike, Terence *p.701*
Biggs, Barton *p.94, p.99, p.162*
Bilaniuk, Laada. *p.20*
Billet, Bret L. & Formwalt, Lance J. . *p.804, p.830, p.849, p.890*
Billingsley, Andrew & Giovannoni, Jeanne M. *p.755*
Billingsley, Andrew *p.720*
Billingsley, Randall. *p.91, p.92, p.94, p.98, p.101, p.103*
Bills, David B. *p.304, p.761*
Bills, Tim & Genasi, Chris *p.65*
Bin Laden, Osama *p.658*
Binder, Sarah A. & Smith, Steven S. *p.533*
Binford, Lewis Roberts *p.6*
Bingham, Clara & Gansler, Laura Leedy. *p.130*
Binmore, Ken *p.83*
Binning, William C., et al. *p.547*
Binns, Tony (Author, Editor) *p.384*
Binstock, Robert H. & George, Linda K. (Editors) *p.741*
Biolsi, Thomas & Zimmerman, Larry J. (Editors) *p.27*
Biolsi, Thomas (Editor). *p.3*
Biolsi, Thomas *p.33*
Birch, Sarah *p.577, p.584, p.597*
Bird, Frederick Bruce *p.145*
Bird, Graham (Editor) *p.258*
Bird, Junius B. *p.11*

Birkeland, Peter M. *p.164*
Birla, Madan *p.165*
Birley, Derek *p.804*
Birmingham, David *p.582*
Birn, Robin *p.135*
Birnbaum, Barry W. *p.321, p.350*
Birnbaum, Robert *p.289*
Birner, Jack (Editor), et al. *p.243*
Birrell, Susan & Cole, Cheryl L. (Editors) *p.814, p.834*
Birrell, Susan & McDonald, Mary G. (Editors) *p.814*
Birx, H. James (Editor) *p.3*
Bisheff, Steve *p.853*
Bissinger, H. G.. . . . . *p.814, p.840, p.858*
Bjarkman, Peter C. *p.804, p.833, p.849, p.853, p.890*
Bjerkholt, Olav (Editor) *p.198*
Bjerre-Poulsen, Niels. *p.516*
Björk, Christopher *p.333*
Black, Antony *p.490*
Black, Charles L. Jr. *p.461*
Black, Charles Lund *p.454*
Black, Earl & Black, Merle *p.550, p.556*
Black, Edwin R.. . . . . *p.586*
Black, Edwin *p.775*
Black, Errol & Silver, Jim *p.124*
Black, Jeremy *p.645*
Black, Kenneth Jr. & Skipper, Harold D. Jr. *p.163*
Black, Richard & White, Howard (Editors) *p.258*
Blackburn, Joseph *p.119*
Blackburn, Robert *p.606*
Blacker, David J. *p.346*
Blackett, R. J. M. *p.519*
Blackford, Mansel G. *p.87, p.146*
Blackman, Lisa & Walkerdine, Valerie. *p.714*
Blackstone, Erwin A., et al.. . . . . *p.546*
Blackstone, William (Translator) *p.435*
Blackwell, Roger *p.249*
Blackwell, Ron (Editor), et al. *p.208, p.240*
Blackwood, Evelyn & Wieringa, Saskia *p.750*
Blair, Margaret M. (Editor) *p.76, p.84*
Blake, Nigel (Editor) *p.323, p.338*
Blake, Nigel, et al.. . . . . *p.338*
Blake, Robert *p.606*
Blalock, H. M. Jr. (Editor) *p.687*
Blalock, Hubert M. *p.689*
Blanchard, Dallas A. & Prewitt, Terry J. *p.569*
Blanchard, Ken, et al. *p.143*
Blanchard, Margaret A. (Editor). *p.415*
Blanck, Peter David (Editor) *p.446*
Bland, Randall W. *p.467*
Blank, Rebecca M. *p.264, p.754*
Blankart, Charles Beat & Mueller, Dennis C. (Editors). *p.636*
Blasi, Vincent *p.470*
Blatz, Perry K. *p.124*
Blau, Francine D., et al. *p.273*
Blau, Francine D. *p.253*
Blau, Joel *p.750*
Blau, Judith R. & Moncada, Alberto. *p.768*
Blau, Judith R. *p.712*
Blau, Peter M. & Duncan, Otis Dudley *p.726*
Blau, Peter M. (Editor). *p.718*
Blau, Peter Michael & Scott, W. Richard *p.717*
Blau, Peter *p.292*
Blaug, Mark & Vane, Howard R. (Editors). *p.193*
Blaug, Mark (Editor) *p.194, p.215, p.226*
Blaug, Mark, et al.. . . . . *p.237*
Blaug, Mark *p.188, p.194, p.208, p.211, p.226*
Blauner, Bob *p.728*
Blaustein, Noah (Editor) *p.811*
Blazewicz, Jacek (Editor), et al.. . . . . *p.114*
Blecker, Thorsten *p.117*
Blenkhorn, David L. & Fleisher, Craig S. (Editors) . . *p.69, p.82*
Blicq, Ron S. & Moretto, Lisa A.. . . . . *p.172*
Blij, H. J. de, et al. *p.396*
Blinder, Alan S. *p.88, p.154*
Blix, Hans *p.655*
Bloch, Maurice E. *p.27*
Bloch, Maurice *p.23, p.26*
Block, Alan A. *p.751*
Block, Cathy Collins, et al.. . . . . *p.360*
Block, Jay A. *p.168*
Block, Martin E.. . . . . *p.800*
Block, Richard N. & Beck, John P. *p.120*
Block, Richard N., et al.. . . . . *p.109, p.111, p.112, p.120*
Blok, Anton *p.751*
Blommaert, Jan. *p.21*
Blomstermo, Anders (Editor), et al. *p.143*
Blondel, Jean & Thiebault, J. L. (Editors) *p.601*
Blood, Robert O. & Wolfe, Donald M. *p.732*
Bloom, Allan *p.289*
Bloom, Amy *p.746*
Bloom, John & Willard, Michael Nevin (Editors) . *p.814, p.830*
Bloom, John *p.841*
Bloom, Lois. *p.368*
Bloom, Mia *p.658*
Bloom, Paul N. & Gundlach, Gregory T. *p.145*
Bloom, Samuel William *p.774*
Bloomfield, Maxwell. *p.440*
Bloor, Michael *p.779*
Blough, Glenn O. & Schwartz, Julius *p.362*
Blount, Ben G. (Editor) *p.17*
Blount, Jackie M. *p.309*
Bloxham, Donald *p.651*
Bluestone, Barry & Harrison, Bennett *p.722*
Bluestone, Barry. *p.722*
Blum, Jerome *p.701, p.723*
Bluman, Allan G. *p.174*
Blumberg, Paul *p.718*
Blumer, Herbert. *p.682, p.692, p.695*
Blumhofer, Edith Waldvogel (Editor) *p.307*

Blumstein, Philip & Schwartz, Pepper *p.731*
Blumstein, Philip *p.739*
Blundell, Valda *p.25*
Blunt, Alison (Editor) *p.399*
Blustein, Paul *p.94, p.98, p.99*
Bly, Robert W. *p.172*
Bly, Robert *p.745*
Blyth, Mark. *p.487, p.664*
Blythe, James M. *p.490, p.501*
Blythe, Ronald *p.701*
Boardman, Anthony, et al. *p.82*
Boas, Franz *p.3*
Boatright, Robert G. *p.548*
Boaz, Noel T. & Ciochon, Russell L. *p.16*
Bob, Clifford *p.497*
Bobbitt, Philip. *p.454*
Bobo, Mike & Dykes, Spike *p.858, p.904*
Bobrowsky, P. T.. *p.376*
Bock, Philip K. (Editor) *p.35*
Bock, Philip K.. . . . . *p.35*
Boczek, Boleslaw Adam *p.476*
Boddy, Janice *p.30*
Boddy, William *p.418*
Bode, Boyd H. *p.340*
Bodley, John H. *p.27*
Bodo, Peter. *p.814, p.864, p.887*
Boettcher, Jennifer C. & Gaines, Leonard M. *p.148, p.178, p.180*
Boga, Steven *p.795, p.864*
Bogdanor, Vernon & Butler, David (Editors) *p.577*
Bogle, John C. *p.88, p.94*
Bognanno, Mario F. & Coleman, Charles J. (Editors) . . . *p.120*
Bogucki, Peter I. & Crabtree, Pam J. (Editor, Translators) . *p.12*
Bogue, E. Grady & Aper, Jeffery *p.330*
Bogue, E. Grady. *p.289*
Bogus, Carl T. (Editor). *p.449*
Bohannan, Paul (Editor) *p.433*
Bohm-Bawerk, Eugen von & Hilferding, Rudolph *p.234*
Bohm-Bawerk, Eugen von *p.233, p.234*
Bohme, R. (Compiled by) *p.390*
Boissevain *p.693*
Boix, Carles *p.503, p.550, p.578*
Bok, Derek C. *p.289, p.295, p.330*
Boland, Lawrence A.. . . . . *p.194*
Boland, Mary L.. . . . . *p.130*
Bolin, Anne & Granskog, Jane (Editors). *p.814, p.834*
Bolles, A. Lynn. *p.40*
Bolles, Mark Emery & Bolles, Richard Nelson *p.168*
Bolles, Richard Nelson & Brown, Dale S. *p.168*
Bolles, Richard Nelson. *p.166*
Bollier, David *p.773*
Bolter, Jay David & Grusin, Richard *p.419*
Bompa, Tudor & Carrera, Michael *p.792, p.878*
Bompa, Tudor O. & Cornacchia, Lorenzo J. *p.792, p.878*
Bonanno, Alessandro (Editor), et al.. . . . . *p.151*
Bondy, Elizabeth & Ross, Dorene D. (Editors) *p.279*
Bonilla-Silva, Eduardo *p.729*
Bonnichsen, Robson & Turnmire, Karen L. (Editors). . . . *p.10*
Booker, Christopher & North, Richard *p.602, p.636*
Boone, Mary E. *p.172*
Boonin, David. *p.775*
Booth, Alison L.. *p.124*
Booth, Ken & Dunne, Timothy (Editors). *p.658*
Boots, B. N. (Editor), et al.. . . . . *p.386*
Booty, Frank (Editor). *p.113*
Bordo, Michael D. & Schwartz, Anna J. (Editors) *p.237*
Bordo, Michael D. (Editor), et al. *p.213*
Bordo, Michael D. (Editor) *p.255*
Boreen, Jean, et al. *p.277*
Borgatta, Edgar F. & Montgomery, Rhonda J. V. (Editors) *p.676*
Borge, Dan. *p.92*
Borgese, Elisabeth M. (Editor) *p.478*
Borglin, Anders & Tvede, M. V. *p.206*
Boritt, Gabor S. *p.519*
Bork, Robert H.. . . . . *p.444, p.462*
Borkowski, John G., et al. *p.735*
Borland, James H. (Editor) *p.317*
Borrelli, Mary Anne & Martin, Janet M.. . . . . *p.526*
Borrelli, Mary Anne (Editor) *p.526*
Borrowman, Merle L. *p.277*
Bosch, Frans (Author, Illustrator) *p.878, p.907*
Bosco, Joseph (Editor), et al. *p.39*
Bosso, Christopher J.. . . . . *p.449*
Boston Lesbian Psychologies Collective Staff (Editor) . . *p.750*
Boswell, John. *p.739, p.755*
Bosworth, Barry & Burtless, Gary (Editors) *p.741*
Botkin, Jim. *p.77*
Botto, Francis *p.419*
Bottomore, Tom *p.675*
Bouchard, Claude (Editor), et al. *p.790*
Bouchard, Claude (Editor) *p.790, p.876*
Boudon, Raymond & Bourricaud, Francois. *p.676*
Boudreau, Thomas E. *p.633, p.648*
Boukreev, Anatoli & DeWalt, G. Weston. *p.789*
Boulden, Jane & Weiss, Thomas George *p.633, p.658*
Boulden, Jane *p.648*
Boulding, Kenneth E. & Mukerjee, Tapan (Editors). . . . *p.208*
Boulton, Chris & Turner, Patrick *p.67*
Boumans, Marcel *p.198, p.240*
Bouquet, Mary & Porto, Nuno *p.47*
Bouquet, Mary (Editor) *p.47*
Bourantonis, Dimitris & Wiener, Jarrod (Editors). *p.633*
Bourantonis, Dimitris *p.655*
Bourdieu, Pierre *p.21, p.23, p.208, p.726, p.743*
Bourgault, Louise M. *p.415*
Bourgine, Paul & Nadal, Jean-Pierre (Editors) *p.272*
Bourgois, Philippe I. *p.776*
Bourne, Gilbert C.. . . . . *p.865*
Bourque, Bruce J.. *p.10*

Boutros-Ghali, Boutros (Introduction by) . . p.633, p.646, p.648
Bowden, Charles p.764
Bowen, Catherine D.. . . . . p.467
Bowen, Howard R; Schuster, Jack H p.292
Bowen, Howard R. p.289, p.330
Bowen, James p.324
Bowen, Roger W. p.621
Bowen, William G. & Bok, Derek p.294
Bowen, William G. & Levin, Sarah A. p.821, p.893
Bower, Gordon H. & Hilgard, Ernest J. p.356
Bowers, James R. & Rich, Wilbur C. (Editors) p.543
Bowersox, Donald J.. . . . . p.143
Bowlby, John, et al. p.735
Bowlby, John p.735
Bowles, Newton p.633
Bowles, Samuel (Editor), et al. p.264
Bowles, Samuel, et al. p.214, p.251
Bowles, Samuel. p.249, p.251, p.762
Bowley, Marian p.217
Bowmaker, Simon W. (Editor) p.185
Box, Richard C.. . . . . p.545, p.580
Boxill, Jan (Editor) p.802
Boyarin, Jonathan (Editor). p.22
Boyce, D. George p.583
Boyce, William E. & DiPrima, Richard C. p.206
Boyd, Andrew p.381, p.413
Boyd, Douglas R. p.412
Boyd, J. Patrick & Samuels, Richard J. p.621
Boyd, William p.324, p.341
Boydston, Jo Ann (Editor) p.341
Boyer, Ernest L. & Carnegie Foundation for the Advancement of Teaching Staff p.289, p.330
Boyer, Ernest L. & Glassick, Charles E.. . . . . . . p.292, p.330
Boyer, Kenneth K., et al. p.117
Boyer, Pascal p.27, p.36
Boyer, Paul S.. . . . . p.458
Boyle, Deirdre. p.413
Boyle, Francis A. p.627
Boyle, Kevin p.124, p.438
Boyle, Michael p.790, p.878
Boyle, Peter G. p.560
Boyle, Raymond & Haynes, Richard p.814, p.898, p.901
Boyle, Raymond (Editor), et al. p.882, p.887, p.901
Boyle, Richard & Lemaire, Donald (Editors) p.580
Boyne, Daniel J. p.835, p.865
Boyte, Harry Chatten p.547
Bozeman, Adda B.. p.477
Bozo, Frederic. p.643
Bozoki, Andras (Editor), et al. p.595
Brabner, J. H. F. (Editor) p.374
Brace, Ian. p.137
Bracey, Gerald W.. . . . . p.285, p.325
Bracken, Bruce A. (Editor) p.356
Bracken, James K. & Sterling, Christopher H. p.419
Brackenridge, Celia p.814, p.840
Bradburn, Norman M., et al. p.137
Braden, Twain. p.866
Brader, Ted p.424
Bradley, Bill p.853
Bradley, Craig (Editor) p.467
Bradley, Renee (Editor), et al. p.318
Bradley, Richard p.12
Bradshaw, Michael J. p.396
Bradshaw, Terry p.858
Bradsher, Keith p.153
Brady, David W., et al.. . . . . p.548
Bragg, Lois (Editor) p.699
Bragg, Steven M. & Roehl-Anderson, Janice M. p.106
Bragg, Steven M. p.104, p.174
Braidwood, Robert John & Willey, Gordon R.. . . . . p.37
Brailsford, Dennis p.804, p.855
Brameld, Theodore Burghard Hurt p.341
Brams, Steven J. p.83
Bramstedt, Ernest K.. . . . . p.768
Brandes, Stanley. p.773
Brands, H. W. p.517
Brandt, Nat. p.804, p.858, p.893
Brandt, Richard M. p.282
Branscomb, Anne W.. . . . . p.445
Brantingham, Jeffrey P. (Editor), et al.. . . . . p.15, p.16
Brasch, Walter M.. . . . . p.561, p.562, p.572
Bratton, Michael & Walle, Nicholas van de . p.503, p.584, p.611
Brauer, Jurgen & Dunne, Paul J. p.217, p.256, p.258
Braunstein, Peter & Doyle, Michael William (Editors) . . p.712
Brawley, Mark R. p.662
Breault, Donna Adair & Breault, Rick (Editors) p.341
Bregel, Yuri p.384
Brehm, Barbara p.790, p.878
Breneman, David W.. p.291
Brennan, Elizabeth A. & Clarage, Elizabeth C.. . . . . . p.403
Brennan, Niamh p.91, p.94, p.99
Brenneis, Donald & Macaulay, Ronald K. S. (Editors) . . . p.18
Brenner, Saul & Spaeth, Harold J.. . . . . p.535
Bresciani-Turroni, Constantino p.237
Bresser-Pereira, Luiz Carlos p.545
Brethauer, Dale M.. p.118
Brett, Jeanne M. p.74
Brewer, Cynthia A. p.386
Brewer, John & Hunter, Albert p.686
Brewer, John D. p.690, p.766, p.774
Brexel, Bernadette p.124
Bricker, David C. p.362
Bricker, Kathryn. p.793
Brickman, William W. p.333
Bridges, Roy; Hair, P E p.378
Brierly, James L. p.477
Briggs, Asa & Burke, Peter. p.415
Briggs, Asa p.413
Briggs, Charles L. p.691
Briggs, Dennie p.349

Briggs, Leslie J. (Editor), et al. *p.346*
Brigham, John. *p.535*
Brighouse, Harry *p.346*
Brimelow, Peter *p.282*
Brinkerhoff, Derick W. & Brinkerhoff, Jennifer M. *p.166*
Brinkley, Douglas G.. *p.153*
Brinkworth, Brian *p.391*
Brint, Steven & Karabel, Jerome *p.291, p.330*
Brinton, Clarence C. *p.628*
Brisbin, Richard A. Jr.. . . . . *p.467, p.535*
Brisk, Maria E. & Harrington, Margaret M. *p.299, p.312*
Brison, Karen J. *p.42*
British Library of Political and Economic Science Staff (Contribution by). *p.3*
Britton, John A. (Editor) *p.333*
Briys, Eric C. & de Varenne, François *p.163*
Broadbent, Ed (Editor) *p.514*
Brock, Colin & Clarkson, Donald (Editors) *p.333*
Brock, Gerald W. *p.420*
Brock, James & Adams, Walter *p.148*
Brock, Peter & Young, Nigel *p.648*
Brockliss, Laurence *p.333*
Brod, Harry *p.491*
Brodsgaard, Kjeld Erik & Heurlin, Bertel (Editors) *p.400*
Brody, David *p.124*
Brody, Howard, et al. *p.864, p.871*
Brody, Leslie *p.694*
Broeckelmann, Russ *p.116*
Bronfenbrenner, Kate (Editor), et al.. . . . . *p.124*
Bronmark, Christer & Hansson, Lars-Anders *p.391*
Bronner, Stephen Eric & Thompson, Michael J. (Editors) *p.510*
Bronner, Stephen Eric. *p.506, p.624, p.658, p.669*
Brooke, Michael Z. & Mills, William R.. . . . . *p.144*
Brooker, Peter. *p.676*
Brookes, Rod *p.814, p.823, p.831, p.858, p.882, p.887, p.901*
Brookfield, Stephen D. & Preskill, Stephen *p.292, p.347*
Brookfield, Stephen D.. . . . . *p.319*
Brookhart, Susan M. & AEHE Staff. *p.285*
Brooks, Brian S., et al.. . . . . *p.411, p.416*
Brooks, Chris *p.198*
Brooks, Dana D. & Althouse, Ronald C. (Editors) . *p.814, p.831*
Brooks, Tim & Marsh, Earle *p.418*
Broome, Richard *p.42*
Brophy, Jere E. & Good, Thomas L. *p.349*
Broto, Carles & Mostaedi, Arian (Editors). *p.880, p.882*
Broudy, Harry S. *p.341*
Brouwer, Maria *p.230, p.234*
Brown, Alice, et al. *p.607*
Brown, Antony & Quine, Timothy *p.391*
Brown, Archie (Editor). *p.597*
Brown, Brendan *p.636*
Brown, Candy Gunther. *p.720*
Brown, Carolan & Reader's Digest Editors *p.793*
Brown, Cheryl Render & Cookson, Catherine (Editors) . . *p.356*
Brown, Cynthia (Editor) *p.515*
Brown, David L. & Swanson, Louis E. (Editors) *p.771*
Brown, David Wayne *p.444*
Brown, David *p.295*
Brown, Dee. *p.572, p.646*
Brown, Dick & Henderson, Joe *p.866*
Brown, Donald E.. . . . . *p.23*
Brown, E. Carey & Solow, Robert (Editors) *p.213*
Brown, Elspeth (Editor), et al. *p.141*
Brown, Fredda & Snell, Martha. *p.318*
Brown, Harriet *p.735*
Brown, Jean E. (Editor, Introduction by). *p.298*
Brown, Jonathan C. (Editor) *p.124*
Brown, Joshua. *p.409*
Brown, Judith M. & Louis, Roger (Editors) *p.605*
Brown, Les *p.300*
Brown, Lester Russell *p.267*
Brown, Marvin T. *p.697*
Brown, Maurice *p.218*
Brown, Michael F. *p.33*
Brown, Nina W. *p.349*
Brown, Rebecca A. *p.789, p.835*
Brown, Rex V. *p.83*
Brown, Rupert. *p.692*
Brown, Shona L. & Eisenhardt, Kathleen M. *p.81*
Brown, Steve *p.119*
Browne, David *p.857, p.899*
Browne, Donald R. *p.413*
Browne, Eric C. & Dreijmanis, John (Editors) *p.574*
Browne, Irene (Editor) *p.133*
Browne, Ray B. & Ambrosetti, Ronald J. (Editors) *p.701*
Browne, William P. *p.559*
Browning, Reed *p.849*
Brown-John, C. Lloyd (Editor) *p.523*
Brownlee, W. Elliot *p.107*
Brownlie, Ian & Goodwin-Gill, Guy S. (Editors) *p.434*
Brownlie, Ian *p.477*
Brownmiller, Susan *p.751*
Brownsey, Keith & Howlett, Michael (Editors). *p.589*
Brubacher, John S. & Rudy, Willis *p.331*
Brubacher, John S.. *p.289*
Brubaker, Rogers *p.608, p.609*
Bruce, Steve *p.607, p.719*
Bruce, Tina *p.368*
Bruce, William, et al. *p.607*
Bruck, Connie *p.99*
Brucker, Gene Adam. *p.738*
Brue, Stanley L. & McConnell, Campbell R.. . . . . . . *p.194*
Brue, Stanley L., et al.. . . . . *p.253*
Brueggemann, Brenda Jo *p.708*
Bruegmann, Robert *p.771*
Bruffee, Kenneth A. *p.349*
Bruhn, Kathleen *p.593*
Bruhns, Karen Olsen *p.11*

Brune, Lester H. & Burns, Richard Dean *p.560, p.627*
Bruner, Edward M. *p.44*
Bruner, Jerome S.. . . . . *p.341, p.347, p.356*
Bruner, Robert F. *p.177*
Bruni, Frank *p.485*
Brunner, C. Cryss (Editor) *p.281*
Brunner, K. & Meltzer, A. H. (Editors) *p.240, p.255*
Brunner, K. F. & Meltzer, A. (Editors). *p.253*
Brunner, Karl & Meltzer, Allan H. *p.231*
Bruns, Roger *p.124*
Brush, Lisa D.. *p.512*
Bryant, Clifton D. (Editor) *p.676*
Bryant, Howard *p.804, p.831, p.849, p.882, p.890, p.895*
Bryk, Anthony S., et al. *p.307*
Bryner, Gary C. & Thompson, Dennis L. (Editors) *p.463*
Buber, Martin *p.499*
Buchanan, Christy M., et al. *p.735*
Buchanan, J. M., et al. *p.226*
Buchanan, James M. *p.194, p.208, p.247*
Buchanan, William J.. . . . . *p.115*
Buck, Marilyn, et al.. . . . . *p.797*
Buck, Marilyn M., et al. *p.794, p.903*
Buck, Philip W. *p.255*
Buckingham, Marcus & Coffman, Curt *p.70, p.72*
Buckley, Gail Lumet *p.717*
Buckley, William F. Jr.. . . . . *p.292*
Buckman, Robert H. *p.77*
Buckser, Andrew & Glazier, Stephen D. (Editors) *p.36*
Buckworth, Janet & Dishman, Rodney. *p.876*
Budd, John W.. *p.120*
Budd, Leslie & Harris, Lisa *p.263*
Buddenbaum, Judith *p.406*
Buderi, Robert & Huang, Gregory T. *p.157*
Bueno de Mesquita, Bruce & Lalman, David. *p.646*
Bueno de Mesquita, Bruce *p.625*
Bueno, Maria de Los Reyes Castillo *p.40*
Buffett, Warren *p.94*
Bugajski, Janusz *p.595, p.596, p.597, p.600*
Bugge, Anna, et al. *p.240*
Buglear, John *p.178*
Buhite, Russell D. *p.565*
Bukhari, Zahid Hussain *p.721*
Bukovansky, Mlada *p.496, p.591, p.608*
Bull, C. Neil *p.751*
Bull, Hedley (Editor), et al.. . . . . *p.625*
Bull, Hedley *p.625, p.628, p.655*
Bullock, Charles & Mahon, Michael *p.785, p.829, p.842*
Bullock, Henry A. *p.309*
Bullock, Steve *p.804, p.849, p.890*
Bullough, Vern L. & Brundage, James A. (Editors) *p.746*
Bullough, Vern L. *p.746, p.749*
Buono, Anthony F. *p.64*
Burbank, Garin *p.548*
Burch, Susan *p.699*
Burden, Barry C. & Kimball, David C. *p.550*
Burden, Ernest E. *p.158*
Burden, Paul R. *p.283*
Bureau of Economic Analysis,
U.S. Department of Commerce *p.59*
Burfoot, Amby (Editor) *p.790, p.863, p.866*
Burg, David F. *p.325*
Burger, Richard L. *p.11*
Burgess, Ernest W. & Bogue, Donald J. (Editors). *p.770*
Burgess, Stephen *p.633*
Burgess, Susan R. *p.531, p.535*
Burgh, Hugo de *p.403*
Burgmann, Verity *p.710*
Burk, Robert F. *p.804, p.850, p.882, p.887, p.895*
Burke, Edmund R. (Editor) *p.856, p.870, p.871*
Burke, Edmund R.. . . . . *p.856*
Burke, Peter *p.682, p.699*
Burling, Robbins *p.18, p.19*
Burnett, Rebecca *p.167*
Burnham, John C. *p.709*
Burnham, W. Dean. *p.556*
Burnham, Walter Dean *p.548*
Burns, Eric *p.709*
Burns, Hobert Warren *p.323, p.339*
Burns, J. H. (Editor). *p.490, p.501*
Burns, J. H. *p.502*
Burns, Marilyn *p.362*
Burns, Nancy, et al. *p.503, p.550*
Burns, Paul. *p.87*
Burns, Richard D. (Introduction by) *p.655*
Burrough, Bryan & Helyar, John *p.84*
Burrows, Peter *p.84*
Burrup, Percy E., et al.. . . . . *p.280*
Burstyn, Varda (Editor). *p.747*
Burt, Robert A. *p.462*
Burt, T. *p.390*
Burton, Allen W. & Miller, Daryl E. *p.873, p.907, p.909*
Burton, David Henry. *p.631*
Burton, Ian, et al. *p.395*
Bury, R. G. (Editor) *p.215*
Busby, Cecilia *p.30*
Bush, Barbara *p.727*
Business Department, Carnegie Library
of Pittsburgh Staff *p.172*
Business Information Agency, Inc. Staff *p.153*
Business Information Agency Staff *p.153*
Bussler, Christoph *p.113*
Butler, Anne M. *p.747*
Butler, David & Ranney, Austin (Editors) *p.575*
Butler, David & Stokes, Donald E. *p.606*
Butler, David E. & Low, D. A. (Editors). *p.605*
Butler, David (Editor) *p.606*
Butler, J. Douglas & Walbert, David F. (Editors) *p.471*
Butler, Lawrence F. *p.790, p.795*
Butler, Lee *p.726*
Butler, Richard (Editor) *p.877*

Butler, Richard . . . p.655
Butsch, Richard (Editor) . . . p.783, p.887
Butt, Graham . . . p.376
Buttel, Frederick H. & McMichael, Philip David (Editors) . . . p.375
Byers, Michael . . . p.646
Byers, Walter & Hammer, Charles . . . p.821, p.893
Byl, John . . . p.800
Byman, Daniel . . . p.658
Byrne, Julie. . . . p.835, p.853
Byrne, Malcom & Ostermann, Christian F. (Editors) . . . p.641

C

C. Q. Press Staff . . . p.547, p.548, p.556
Cabell, David W. E. & English, Deborah L. (Editors). p.148, p.149
Caccamo, Rita. . . . p.679
Cachel, Susan . . . p.15
Cadle, James & Yeates, Donald . . . p.114
Caforio, Giuseppe (Editor) . . . p.717
Cahn, Susan K. . . . p.804, p.835
Cahuc, Pierre & Zylberberg, André . . . p.253
Cain, Peter & Hopkins, Tony . . . p.583
Caine, Dennis J. (Editor), et al. . . . p.827
Cairnes, John Elliott . . . p.217
Cajete, Gregory . . . p.311
Calavita, Kitty. . . . p.570
Caldeira, Teresa Pires Do Rio. . . . p.773
Calder, James D. . . . p.523
Caldwell, Bruce J. (Editor) . . . p.194
Caldwell, Bruce . . . p.194, p.198
Caldwell, Lynton K. . . . p.566
Calhoun, Arthur W. . . . p.732
Calhoun, Craig (Editor) . . . p.373, p.677
Califia, Patrick . . . p.746
Callahan, Christopher . . . p.413
Callahan, Michael D.. . . . p.631
Callahan, Raymond E. . . . p.325
Callan, Patrick M. & Finney, Joni E. (Editors) . . . p.295
Callejo-Perez, David M. . . . p.300
Calomiris, Charles W. . . . p.111, p.154
Calvert, Peter (Editor) . . . p.591
Cambridge Educational (Produced by) . . . p.534
Camejo, Peter, et al. . . . p.553
Camenson, Blythe . . . p.168
Camerer, Colin (Editor), et al. . . . p.249
Cameron, Deborah & Kulick, Don . . . p.21
Cameron, Don. . . . p.124
Cameron, Kirk & White, Graham . . . p.589
Cameron, Maxwell A. . . . p.591
Cameron, Sheila . . . p.176
Cammarosano, Joseph R.. . . . p.226
Cammisa, Anne M. . . . p.523
Campbell, Angus, et al. . . . p.548
Campbell, Colton C. & Rae, Nicol C. (Editors). . . . p.533
Campbell, Douglas S. . . . p.444
Campbell, Frederick L. (Editor), et al. . . . p.675
Campbell, James B. . . . p.388
Campbell, John L. . . . p.261
Campbell, John Y., et al. . . . p.198
Campbell, Kenneth J. . . . p.651
Campbell, Kurt M. (Editor), et al. . . . p.655
Campbell, Patricia S. & Scott-Kassner, Carol. . . . p.362
Campbell, R. H. & Skinner, Andrew S. . . . p.211, p.218
Campbell, Shirley Faye . . . p.25
Campbell, Tom . . . p.514
Campbell, W. Joseph. . . . p.403
Campbell-Kelly, Martin & Aspray, William . . . p.114
Canada . . . p.586, p.587
Cannan, Edwin . . . p.211
Canny, Nicholas (Editor) . . . p.605
Canon, Bradley C. & Johnson, Charles A. . . . p.465
Canovan, Margaret. . . . p.494
Canterbery, E. Ray. . . . p.185
Cantillon, Richard . . . p.215
Cantner, Uwe (Editor), et al. . . . p.230, p.234
Cantor, Norman F. . . . p.742
Cantril, Hadley . . . p.710
Capel, W. & Piotrowski, Susan . . . p.795
Caplan, Nathan, et al. . . . p.763, p.764
Caplan, Pat & Topan, Farouk (Editors) . . . p.38
Caplan, Paula . . . p.292
Caplan, Richard . . . p.628
Caplan, Russell L. . . . p.454
Caplow, Theodore, et al. . . . p.732
Caplow, Theodore . . . p.717
Caporaso, James A. . . . p.602
Cappelli, Peter . . . p.85
Cappo, Joe . . . p.140, p.426
Caputo, Michael R. . . . p.198
Carabelli, Anna M.. . . . p.226
Carapico, Sheila . . . p.614
Carbert, Louise I. . . . p.590
Carbone, Greg. . . . p.393
Carbone, Peter F. . . . p.341
Cardozo, Benjamin N. . . . p.433
Cardwell, Michael (Editor), et al. . . . p.256, p.267
Carey, Dennis & von Weichs, Marie-Caroline . . . p.85
Carey, Henry F. (Editor) . . . p.600
Carin, Arthur A. . . . p.362
Carkoglu, Ali & Rubin, Barry (Editors) . . . p.602, p.636
Carliner, David, et al. . . . p.460
Carlson, A. Bruce, et al. . . . p.422
Carlson, Maura O'Brien, et al. . . . p.362
Carlson, Tony . . . p.172
Carlton, David. . . . p.658
Carlton, Patrick W.. . . . p.281
Carmichael, Douglas R. & Rosenfield, Paul H.. . . p.104, p.105
Carnegie Commission on Higher Education, et al. . . . p.292
Carnegie Forum on Education and the Economy Staff. . . p.278

Carnegie Foundation for the Advancement of Teaching Staff . . . p.294
Carneiro, Robert L. . . . p.23
Carnevale, Anthony P. & Stone, Susan C. . . . p.131
Carnochan, W. B. . . . p.294
Carnoy, Martin . . . p.325
Carothers, Thomas . . . p.503, p.584, p.600
Carp, E. Wayne . . . p.737
Carp, Robert A. & Stidham, Ronald. . . . p.465, p.534
Carp, Robert A., et al. . . . p.534
Carpenter, Linda J. & Acosta, Vivian R. . . . p.449, p.835, p.882, p.893, p.900
Carpenter, Linda J. . . . p.785, p.882, p.900
Carpenter, Ted Galen (Editor). . . . p.639
Carpenter, Ted G. . . . p.633
Carr, Gerry. . . . p.794, p.869, p.873, p.907
Carr, Janine C. . . . p.360
Carr, Wilfred (editor). . . . p.323
Carrasco, David (Editor) . . . p.9
Carrese, Paul O. . . . p.541
Carroll, Bob (Editor), et al. . . . p.858
Carroll, John M. . . . p.804, p.814, p.831, p.858, p.893
Carroll, Richard J. . . . p.566
Carruthers, Susan L. . . . p.406
Carstairs, Andrew M. . . . p.601
Carsten, Janet (Editor). . . . p.31
Carsten, Janet . . . p.31
Carter, Cynthia, et al. . . . p.414
Carter, Dan T. . . . p.438
Carter, David . . . p.710
Carter, Gregg Lee . . . p.485
Carter, John M. . . . p.783, p.804
Carter, Marcia Jean & LeConey, Stephen P. . . . p.783, p.785, p.829
Cartwright, Lorin A. & Pitney, William A. . . . p.828
Cartwright, Roger. . . . p.65
Cartwright, Susan (Editor) . . . p.119, p.180
Carty, Ken (Editor) . . . p.589
Carty, R. Kenneth (Editor) . . . p.588
Cary, Noel D. . . . p.609
Case, LeAnne . . . p.792
Casella, E. C. & Symonds, J. (Editors) . . . p.13
Cashman, Richard & Hughes, Anthony (Editors). . . . p.845, p.887, p.890, p.898
Cashmore, Ellis. . . . p.823, p.855, p.877
Cassis, Yves & Cassis, Youssef (Editors) . . . p.91
Castells, Manuel. . . . p.761
Castree, Noel, et al. . . . p.375
Castro, Barry . . . p.52
Casway, Jerrold I. . . . p.804, p.850
Catalyst Staff. . . . p.57
Catalyst . . . p.57
Cate, Fred H. . . . p.449
Cate, Thomas (Editor), et al. . . . p.192
Catto, Susan & Penrith, Deborah . . . p.169
Caufield, Catherine . . . p.630
Cava, Roberta . . . p.130
Cavalier, Robert J. (Editor) . . . p.761
Cavallaro, Claire C. & Haney, Michele . . . p.315
Cavanagh, Peter R. (Editor) . . . p.874, p.879, p.907, p.909
Cavazos, Edward A. & Morin, Gavino. . . . p.444
Cayleff, Susan E. . . . p.835, p.860
Cayton, Mary K. (Editor), et al.. . . . p.677
CBS News Staff. . . . p.288
CCH Editorial Staff . . . p.115
Cech, Donna J. & Martin, Suzanne . . . p.907, p.909
Cedaro, Rod (Compiled by) . . . p.863, p.866
Censer, Jane T. . . . p.732
Centeno, Miguel Angel. . . . p.591
Center for Education Staff & National Research Council Staff . . . p.285
Center for Gifted Education Staff . . . p.526
Center for HIV Information. . . . p.668
Center for International Business Education and Research at Michigan State University . . . p.59
Center for Responsive Politics . . . p.557, p.559
Center for Russian, East European and Asian Studies, University of Texas at Austin . . . p.595, p.596, p.597, p.600
Center for World Indigenous Studies . . . p.482
Center on Reinventing Public Education. Daniel J. Evans School of Public Affairs. University of Washington . . . p.280
Central Intelligence Agency. . . . p.481
Cepede, M. & Abensour, E. S. . . . p.701
Cervero, Ron M. & Wilson, Arthur L. . . . p.319
Chabal, Patrick & Daloz, Jean-Pascal . . . p.611
Chabal, Patrick . . . p.498, p.611
Chadda, Maya. . . . p.617
Chadwick, Bruce. . . . p.804, p.831, p.850, p.890, p.896
Chafe, William Henry . . . p.522
Chafer, Tony . . . p.584
Chafetz, Janet S. . . . p.723, p.747
Chainey, Spencer & Ratcliffe, Jerry . . . p.386
Chairman of the Council of Economic Advisors . . . p.481
Chaison, Gary N. . . . p.124
Chait, Richard P., et al.. . . . p.293
Chakrabarti, Dilip K.. . . . p.8
Chalcraft, Edwin L. & Collins, Cary C. . . . p.755
Chalip, Laurence (Editor), et al. . . . p.843, p.887, p.891, p.898
Chalk, Frank & Jonassohn, Kurt . . . p.651, p.767
Chalk, Peter & Rosenau, William . . . p.658
Chall, Jeanne S. . . . p.362
Chamberlain, Mariam K. . . . p.289
Chamberlain, Neil W. & Schilling, Jane M. . . . p.124
Chambers, Deborah, et al. . . . p.699
Chambers, Frank & Ogle, Michael (Editors) . . . p.393
Chambers-Schiller, Lee V. . . . p.735
Chambliss, J. J. (Editor) . . . p.323, p.339
Champion, Dean John . . . p.677
Champion, Walter T.. . . . p.883, p.900
Chan, Anita, et al. . . . p.701
Chancellor, Edward . . . p.88, p.99, p.101

Chandler, Alfred D. Jr.. . . . . *p.146, p.157*
Chandler, Timothy J. L. & Nauright, John (Editors) *p.814, p.865*
Chandra, A. M. *p.386, p.388*
Chandrasekhar, Sripati *p.736*
Chang, Chung-Li *p.701*
Chang, Mitchell (Editor), et al.. . . . . *p.295, p.308, p.355*
Chang, Robert S. *p.456*
Chapman, Carolyn & King, Rita S. *p.285*
Chapman, Chris S. *p.81*
Chapman, Forestine *p.151, p.164*
Chapman, Graham P. & Baker, Kathleen M. (Editors) *p.384*
Chapman, Karen J.. *p.178*
Chapman, Robert *p.12*
Chapnick, Howard *p.409*
Chappell, Sally Anderson Kitt *p.10*
Charan, Ram, et al. *p.70*
Charles, Maria & Grusky, David B. *p.723*
Charlton, Sue *p.616*
Charney, Israel W. (Editor) *p.652*
Chartier, Roger (Editor), et al. *p.732*
Chartrand, Mark R. *p.421*
Chasdi, Richard J. *p.658*
Chase, Allan *p.728*
Chase, Kerry A. *p.60*
Chase-Dunn, Christopher *p.723*
Chasek, Pamela S.. . . . . *p.666*
Chatfield, Michael & Vangermeersch, Richard (Editors). . *p.104*
Chatterji, Manas (Editor), et al. *p.262*
Chatzkel, Jay L. *p.77*
Chavez, Cesar, et al. *p.124*
Chayko, Mary *p.772*
Checchi, Daniele *p.297*
Check, Joseph W. *p.314*
Chelladurai, P. *p.883, p.900*
Chen, An *p.619*
Chen, Jie *p.619*
Chen, Jie-Qi & Horsch, Patricia (Translators) *p.368*
Chen, Shing-Ling & Hall, G. Jon *p.691*
Chen, Stephen *p.113*
Chenery, Hollis B. (Editor), et al. *p.188*
Cheney, George & Barnett, George A.. . . . . *p.132*
Chenok, P. B. (Editor) *p.104*
Cherlin, Andrew J. & Furstenberg, Frank F. Jr.. . . . . *p.740*
Cherlin, Andrew J.. . . . . *p.739*
Chernicoff, Stanley & Whitney, Donna *p.390*
Chernoff, Fred (Editor). *p.654*
Chernow, Ron. *p.91, p.146, p.148, p.154, p.517*
Cherny, Robert W., et al. *p.120*
Cherry, Paul. *p.142*
Cherry, Robert D. *p.133*
Cheryl Grossman *p.304, p.319*
Cheshire, P. C. & Mills, E. S. (Editors) *p.188*
Chester, Eric *p.72*
Chesterman, Simon *p.585*
Chew, Donald H. Jr. *p.88*
Chew, Donald H. *p.91*
Chhibber, Pradeep K. & Kollman, Ken *p.578*
Chhibber, Pradeep K. *p.617*
Ch'i, Hsi-sheng *p.619*
Chicago Board of Education *p.285*
Chicago Board of Trade Staff *p.94, p.101, p.162*
Chick, Victoria *p.226*
Chikulo, Bornwell C. & Hope, Kempe Ronald (Editors) *p.611, p.664*
Chilcote, Ronald H. *p.502*
Child, Brenda J., et al. *p.312*
Child, Greg (Compiled by) *p.789*
Childers, Thomas *p.609*
Childs, John Lawrence *p.341*
Chill, Emanuel *p.629*
Chin, Jean Lau (Editor) *p.698*
Chippindale, Christopher *p.12*
Chiriboga, David A. & Catron, Linda S.. . . . . *p.739*
Chisman, Forrest & Pifer, Alan *p.523*
Chodorow, Nancy Julia. *p.736*
Choi, Frederick D. S. (Editor) *p.88, p.104, p.155, p.162*
Chomsky, Noam. *p.658*
Chrisman, Nicholas *p.386*
Christensen, C. Roland. *p.177*
Christensen, Clayton M. & Raynor, Michael E. *p.65*
Christensen, Clayton M., et al. *p.65, p.81*
Christensen, Clayton M.. . . . . *p.51*
Christians, Clifford G. & Traber, Michael (Editors) . . . *p.405*
Christians, Clifford G., et al. *p.405*
Christianson, Scott. *p.752*
Christopher, A. J. *p.381*
Chu, Donald A.. . . . . *p.289, p.793, p.864*
Chu, Donald *p.821, p.893*
Ch'u Tung-Tsu *p.475*
Ch'u, T'ung-tsu *p.701*
Chua, Amy. *p.256, p.261, p.262*
Chubb, Basil *p.607*
Cialdini, Robert B.. . . . . *p.139*
Cicarelli, James & Cicarelli, Julianne *p.193*
Cichy, Ronald F. & Hickey, Philip J. *p.165*
Cicourel, Aaron V.. . . . . *p.692*
Cigar, Norman. *p.652*
Ciment, James (Editor). *p.485*
Cimoli, Mario (Editor) *p.383*
Circa Reference Staff *p.188*
Cirillo, R.. . . . . *p.195*
Cirincione, Joseph, et al. *p.655*
Cirque Du Soleil, et al. *p.65*
City College of New York Library *p.642*
Ciulla, Joanne B. (Editor) *p.697*
Claeys, Gregory *p.491*
Clancy, Kevin J. & Krieg, Peter C. *p.134*
Clanton, Reita E. & Dwight, Mary P. *p.847*

Clapp, Jennifer & Dauvergne, Peter p.666
Clare, Judith & Hamilton, Helen p.689
Clark, Audrey N. p.373
Clark, Dick p.804, p.831, p.850, p.896
Clark, Etta p.841
Clark, Gordon L. p.543
Clark, Jim. p.157
Clark, John Bates p.208, p.223, p.252
Clark, John (Editor) p.163
Clark, John Elwood Jr. p.519
Clark, John p.208
Clark, Kim B. & Fujimoto, Takahiro p.144
Clark, Martin P. p.422
Clark, Mary E. p.682
Clark, Nancy p.801, p.876
Clark, Ramsey. p.652
Clark, Reginald M. p.309
Clark, Roy Peter & Scanlan, Christopher p.410
Clark, Wesley K. p.561, p.563
Clark, William A. V. p.764
Clark p.121
Clarke, Colin p.771
Clarke, Edith p.40
Clarke, Graham & Stillwell, John (Editors) p.386
Clarke, Harold D.; Jenson, Jane; LeDuc, Lawrence; Pammett, Jon H. p.590
Clarke, Kamari Maxine p.44
Clarke, Katherine A. p.377
Clarke, Mark A.. p.341
Clarke, Paul Barry & Foweraker, Joe p.482, p.503
Clarke, Peter p.226
Clarke, Richard A.. . . . . p.563
Clarke, Simon & Ashwin, Sarah p.124
Clarke, Steve & Coakes, Elayne p.321
Claude, Inis L. Jr. p.628
Clausen, Christopher p.764
Clavin, Tom. p.860
Clawson, David L., et al.. . . . . p.396
Clay, Marie M. p.368
Clayton, Anthony p.584
Clayton, Cornell W. (Editor) p.523
Cleary, Edward L. & Steigenga, Timothy J. p.591
Cleaver, Tony p.185
Cleaves, Cheryl S. & Hobbs, Margie J. p.175
Cleland, Jane K.. . . . . p.172
Clemence, Richard Vernon & Doody, Francis S. . . p.230, p.235
Clemens, Clay (Editor). p.639
Clements, Claire B. p.785, p.790, p.841
Clements, Douglas H. (Editor), et al. p.360
Clements, Rhonda L. & Kinzler, Suzanne K. . . . p.797, p.799
Clerk of the U.S. House of Representatives p.557
Cleverdon, Catherine Lyle p.590
Cleyre, Voltairine de p.500
Clifford, Denis p.443
Clifford, James & Marcus, George E. (Editors) p.23
Clift, Eleanor & Brazaitis, Tom p.526
Clinard, Marshall B. & Meier, Robert F. p.695
Clinchy, Evans (Editor) p.280
Clinchy, Evans p.325
Cline-Cole, Reginald & Robson, Elsbeth. p.384
Clinton, Catherine p.519
Clogg, Richard p.597
Cloke, Paul J. (Editor), et al. p.396
Clor, Harry M. p.472
Clottes, Jean p.16
Clumpner, Roy A. p.797
Coakley, Jay J. & Donnelly, Peter. p.814
Coakley, John & Gallagher, Michael (Editors) p.608
Coats, A. W. p.211, p.268
Cobb, Roger W. & Elder, Charles D. p.554
Coben, Diana (Editor), et al. p.319
Coben, Diana p.762
Cocchiarale, Michael & Emmert, Scott (Editors) p.811
Cochran-Smith, Marilyn & Zeichner, Ken (Editors) p.279, p.355
Cockerham, William C. & Ritchey, Ferris J. p.677
Cocks, Joan p.494
Coddington, Alan p.226
Coddington, Walter & Florian, Peter p.63
Coe, Lewis p.421
Coe, Michael D. & Koontz, Rex p.9
Coe, Michael D. p.9, p.22
Coe, Michael, et al. p.10
Coerver, Don, et al. p.383
Coffey, Wayne p.835, p.842, p.853
Coffman, Curt & Gonzalez-Molina, Gabriel p.76
Cogan, Charles p.643, p.645
Cohen, Allan R. & Bradford, David L. p.70, p.172
Cohen, Arthur M. & Brawer, Florence B. p.291
Cohen, Arthur M. p.331
Cohen, Benjamin J. p.246, p.261
Cohen, David B. & Wells, John W. (Editors) . . . p.563, p.572
Cohen, Eliot A. p.575
Cohen, Elizabeth G. (Editor), et al. p.349
Cohen, Felix S. p.433
Cohen, Greta L. (Editor) p.814, p.835
Cohen, Herb p.74
Cohen, Jean L. p.471
Cohen, Jeffrey E. p.529
Cohen, Jeffrey J. & Fish, Marian C.. . . . . p.352
Cohen, Jerome A. (Editor) p.475
Cohen, Jonathan (Editor) p.303, p.356, p.362
Cohen, Robert. p.331
Cohen, Saul B. p.374
Cohen, Saul Bernard. p.487, p.495
Cohen, Sherrill & Taub, Nadine (Editors) p.447
Cohen, Stanley & Taylor, Laurie p.774
Cohen, Stanley p.751
Cohen, Stephen Philip p.643, p.645
Cohen, Steve (Editor), et al. p.178

Cohen, William A. p.70
Cohen-Tanugi, Laurent p.563
Cohn-Sherbok, Daniel p.381
Coker, Paddy & Ganderton, Paul p.394
Colander, David C. & Holt, Richard P. F. p.185
Colander, David C. p.195
Cole, David p.460, p.563, p.572
Cole, Douglas p.4
Cole, Johnnetta B. & Guy-Sheftall, Beverly p.743
Cole, Leonard A. p.655
Cole, Margaret Isabel Postgate p.273
Cole, Thomas R.. . . . . p.741
Coleman, James S.. . . . . p.716
Coleman, Walter p.124
Coles, Robert p.719, p.736, p.755
Colker, Ruth p.447
College Entrance Examination Board p.293, p.294, p.295
Colley, John L., et al. p.85
Collier, Christopher p.542, p.543
Collier Cochran, Alice p.80
Collier, Nathan S., et al. p.158
Collingwood, Tom p.795
Collins, Alan p.643
Collins, Bud (Editor) p.843, p.864
Collins, E. J. T. (Editor) p.701
Collins, Heidi p.77
Collins, Jim & Porras, Jerry I. p.67
Collins, Jim p.70
Collins, John W. & O'Brien, Nancy Patricia (Editors). . . . p.322
Collins, Marva & Tamarkin, Civia p.337
Collins, Patricia Hill p.743
Collins, Randall p.681, p.694
Collins, Ray & Green, Pauline p.637
Collins, Scott p.414
Collins, Tony & Vamplew, Wray p.814
Collins, Tony p.804, p.814, p.865
Collins UK Staff p.380
Collis, David J., et al. p.81
Collis, John p.12
Colomer, Josep (Editor) p.577
Colonna, M. & Hagemann, Harald (Editors) p.234
Colton, Kent W. p.158
Coltrane, Scott p.745
Columbia University Libraries p.611
Colvin, Vonnie, et al.. . . . . p.797
Colwin, Cecil M. p.868, p.879
Coman, Katharine p.248
Combs, Arthur W. p.341, p.347
Comenius, Johann Amos p.341
Comer, James P., et al. p.280
Comiskey, Michael p.535
Common Cause p.516
Commons, John R.. . . . . p.249
Commons, John Rogers p.208
Commonwealth Secretariat p.605
Compayre, Gabriel p.325
Comrie, Bernard p.18
Comte, Auguste p.679, p.684
Conant, James B. p.325
Conant, James Bryant p.290, p.331, p.341, p.367
Conde, H. Victor p.669
Congressional Quarterly, Inc. Staff p.526, p.557
Congressional Quarterly, Inc. p.463
Conklin, David W. (Editor) p.69
Conklin, Wm. Arthur, et al. p.113
Conlan, Timothy J., et al.. . . . . p.464
Conlan, Timothy J. p.523
Conley, Patrick T. & Kaminski, John P. (Editors) p.523
Connah, Graham p.7
Connally, Nellie & Herskowitz, Mickey p.485
Connell, R. W. p.743, p.745
Connell, W. F. p.341
Connelly, Mark & Welch, David (Editors) p.406
Conner, Daryl R. p.72
Connor, Marlene K. p.745
Connor, Walker p.494
Conolly, James & Lake, Mark p.6, p.386
Conolly-Smith, Peter p.410
Conot, Robert E.. . . . . p.477
Conrad, Alfred H.; Meyer, John Robert p.208
Conrad, David R. p.341
Constantinides, G. M. (Editor), et al. p.188
Constantino, Steven M.. . . . . p.303
Conteh-Morgan, Earl p.503, p.585, p.611
Conway Greene Publishing Co. Editorial Staff p.795
Conybeare, John A. C.. . . . . p.153, p.664
Conzen, M. R. G. & Conzen, Michael P.. . . . . p.395
Cook, Chris & Paxton, John (Editors) p.601
Cook, Constance E. p.295
Cook, Curtis (Editor) p.586
Cook, Ian p.491
Cook, Scott p.28
Cook, Terrence E. p.764
Cook, Timothy p.533
Cooke, Donald p.389
Cookson, Peter W. Jr. (Editor), et al. p.325
Cooley, Charles Horton p.692, p.693
Cooley, John K. p.641
Cooley, Thomas M. p.455
Coombs, Jan p.163
Coombs, Philip H. p.325
Cooney, Robert P. J. Jr. p.554, p.568
Coons, John E. & Sugarman, Stephen D. p.280
Coontz, Stephanie p.732
Cooper, Alan (Editor) p.427
Cooper, Andrew p.824
Cooper, Bruce S. (Editor) p.121
Cooper, Bruce S. p.296
Cooper, Cary L. & Dewe, Philip p.698
Cooper, John Milton Jr. p.631

Cooper, Phillip J. *p.461, p.466, p.535*
Cooper, William J. Jr. *p.520*
Copeland, David A. (Editor-In-Chief) *p.406*
Copley, Stephen & Sutherland, Kathryn (Editors). *p.218*
Copley, Terence *p.333*
Coppola, Eileen M. *p.347, p.351*
Corbett, H. Dickson, et al. *p.314*
Corbin, Charles B. & Pangrazi, Robert B. *p.790*
Corcoran, Michael *p.860*
Corcos, Alain F. *p.17*
Cordasco, Francesco & Bucchioni, Eugene *p.311*
Cordell, Karl & Antoszewski, Andrzej (Editors) . . *p.596, p.602*
Cordell, Linda *p.10*
Cordesman, Anthony *p.562, p.646, p.648*
Corlett, William *p.501*
Cornell Legal Information Institute *p.474, p.475, p.476*
Cornell, Saul *p.523*
Cornell, Tim *p.12*
Cornell University *p.367*
Cornwall, John & Cornwall, Wendy A. *p.214*
Cornwall, John & Cornwall, Wendy *p.241*
Corradi, Juan E. (Editor), et al. *p.515*
Cortada, James W. . . . *p.146, p.149, p.155, p.157, p.158, p.165*
Cortese, Anthony J. *p.426*
Cortese, Anthony *p.422*
Cortner, Richard C. *p.535*
Corwin, Edward S. *p.452, p.453, p.461*
Cose, Ellis *p.723*
Cosentino, Marc *p.169*
Coser, Lewis A. & Rosenberg, B. (Editors) *p.679*
Coser, Lewis A.. . . . . *p.682, p.766*
Cosgrave, James F. (Editor). *p.715*
Costa, D. Margaret & Guthrie,
Sharon R. (Editors) *p.823, p.835*
Costa, Dora L.. . . . . *p.741*
Coster, Will *p.708*
Costigan, Arthur T., et al.. . . . . *p.277*
Costill, David L., et al. *p.825, p.868, p.879*
Costin, Lela B. *p.273*
Cote, Isabelle & Reynolds, John (Editors) *p.391*
Cott, Nancy F. *p.723, p.739*
Cottam, Martha L., et al.. . . . . *p.483*
Cotten, Doyice J. & Wolohan, John. *p.783, p.883, p.900*
Cotter, Anne-Marie Mooney *p.133*
Cottle, S., et al.. . . . . *p.94*
Cottrell, Robert Charles *p.831, p.850*
Cottrol, Robert J. (Editor, Translator), et al. *p.449*
Cottrol, Robert J. (Editor) *p.449*
Coughlin, Lin (Editor), et al.. . . . . *p.70*
Coulborn, Rushton (Editor). *p.490, p.501*
Coulby, David & Jones, Crispin. *p.333*
Coulmas, Florian (Editor) *p.18*
Coulmas, Florian *p.18, p.22*
Coulomb, Fanny. *p.268*
Coulon, Jocelyn *p.633, p.648*
Coulter, H. David *p.793*
Council for Exceptional Children
Staff (Contribution by) *p.278, p.315*
Council of Europe *p.474*
Counihan, Carole & Van Esterik, Penny *p.45*
Counihan, Carole (Editor) *p.45*
Counihan, Carole M. & Kaplan, Steven L. *p.45*
Countryman, Vern (Editor) *p.437*
Cournot, Augustin *p.198*
Courtney, James F., et al. *p.77*
Courtney, John C. *p.586, p.588*
Courtois, Stéphane, et al.. . . . . *p.658*
Courtwright, David T. *p.776*
Couvillon, Arthur *p.869*
Covey, Herbert C. *p.714*
Cox, Andrew & Kirby, Stephen *p.531*
Cox, C. Barry & Moore, Peter D.. . . . . *p.394*
Cox, Gary W.. . . . . *p.577, p.578, p.604*
Cox, Richard H.. . . . . *p.877*
Cox, Richard J. *p.115*
Cox, Richard William (Editor), et al. *p.867*
Cox, William Edwin *p.135*
Cozens, Frederick W. & Stumpf, Florence S.. . . . . . . *p.814*
CQ Editors *p.557*
CQ Press Editors *p.559*
CQ Press Staff (Contribution by) *p.662*
CQ Press Staff (Editor). *p.559*
CQ Staff (Editor) *p.529*
Crack, Timothy Falcon *p.169*
Craft, Anna *p.360*
Craft, Donna & Peck, Terrance W. (Contribution by) . . . *p.125*
Craib, Raymond B. *p.383*
Craig, Barbara H. & O'Brien, David M.. . . . . *p.569*
Craig, Colleen. *p.793*
Craig, Robert L.. . . . . *p.304*
Craig, Yvonne *p.757*
Crainer, Stuart & Dearlove, Des *p.176*
Cramer, Jan Salomon *p.199*
Cramer, Richard Ben. *p.850*
Crandall, Robert W. *p.419*
Crang, Mike. *p.399*
Cranor, Lorrie Faith & Wildman,
Steven S. (Editors) *p.761*
Crapol, Edward P. (Editor) *p.566, p.568*
Crawford, Bill *p.841, p.869*
Crawford, Fred & Mathews, Ryan. *p.135*
Cray, Ed (Editor), et al. *p.404*
Creamer, Robert W. *p.850*
Creedon, Pamela J. (Editor) *p.835, p.901*
Creedy, John *p.195, p.208*
Crehan, Kate A. F. *p.23*
Creighton, Colin & Shaw, Martin (Editors). *p.766*
Crellin, John K.. . . . . *p.778*
Cremin, Lawrence *p.325*
Crenshaw, Ben & Hauser, Melanie *p.860*

Cresswell, Tim *p.373*
Crewe, Emma *p.606*
Crewe, Ivor & King, Anthony *p.606*
Crewe, Ivor, et al. *p.606*
Crisfield, Deborah *p.840, p.869*
Critchfield, Richard *p.39*
Critchlow, Donald T.. . . . . *p.523*
Crocker, Chester A., et al. *p.645*
Croll, Elisabeth (Editor), et al. *p.731*
Crompton, Louis. *p.747*
Crompton, Paul H.. . . . . *p.793*
Crompton, Rosemary & Mann, Michael *p.722*
Crone, G. R. *p.377*
Cronin, James E. *p.606*
Crook, Malcolm *p.608*
Crook, Tim *p.413*
Crooks, James B. *p.543*
Cropley, Arthur *p.356*
Crosby, Faye J. *p.133*
Crosby, John V. *p.137*
Crosier, Louis M. (Editor) *p.296*
Cross, Gary S. *p.783, p.823*
Cross, Gary *p.716*
Cross, K. Patricia *p.319, p.331*
Cross, Rob & Parker, Andrew *p.120*
Cross, Rod (Editor) *p.252*
Cross, Wilbur L. & Richey, Alice M. *p.172*
Cross, Wilbur L.. *p.172*
Cross, William P. *p.588*
Crosset, Todd W. *p.815, p.835, p.860*
Crosskey, William W. & Jeffrey, William Jr. *p.452*
Crossley, John, et al.. . . . . *p.786, p.883*
Crossman, Richard (Editor). *p.508*
Croteau, David *p.547*
Crotty, William (Editor) *p.503, p.658*
Crotty, William J. (Editor) *p.563*
Crouch, Colin *p.67, p.121*
Crouch, Harold *p.622*
Crouch, T. *p.847, p.867*
Crowley, David & Heyer, Paul *p.415*
Crowley, Jocelyn Elise *p.739*
Crowson, Robert L. & Driscoll, Mary Erina *p.303*
Crowther, Jim & Sutherland, Peter (Editors) *p.319*
Crumley, Carole E. (Editor) *p.29*
Crumley, Carole E. *p.29*
Crumlish, Christina *p.425*
Cruz-Torres, Maria Luz *p.28*
Crystal, David *p.19*
Cuban, Larry & Shipps, Dorothy (Editors) *p.325*
Cuban, Larry & Tyack, David B. *p.297, p.325*
Cuban, Larry & Usdan, Michael D. (Editors). *p.314*
Cuban, Larry *p.325, p.351*
Cubberley, Ellwood P. (Editor) *p.325*
Cubberley, Ellwood Patterson. *p.325*
Cubitt, Sean. *p.690*
Cuca, Roberto & Pierce, Catherine S. *p.736*
Cull, Nicholas J., et al.. . . . . *p.425*
Cull, Nicholas J. *p.643, p.646*
Culler, A. Dwight *p.341*
Culyer, A. J. & Newhouse, J. P. (Editors) . . *p.188, p.199, p.264*
Cuneen, Jacquelyn; Sidwell, M Joy *p.905*
Cunliffe, Barry W. (Editor) *p.12*
Cunliffe, Barry W. *p.12*
Cunningham, Helen & Greene, Brenda *p.172*
Cunningham, John R. *p.169*
Cunningham, Patricia M. & Allington, Richard L. *p.362*
Cunningham, Stanley B. *p.425*
Curcio, Vincent *p.153*
Curran, James & Gurevitch, Michael (Editors) *p.416*
Currell, Susan. *p.783, p.823*
Curren, Randall R.. . . . . *p.341*
Current, Richard Nelson & Escott, Paul D. (Editors) . . . *p.520*
Currie, David P.. . . . . *p.453, p.536*
Currie, Elliott *p.723*
Curry, Anne *p.641, p.643, p.647*
Curry, Lynn & Wergin, Jon F.. . . . . *p.295*
Curry, Richard O. (Editor) *p.458*
Curtain, Gregory G. (Editor), et al. *p.546*
Curti, Merle E. *p.647, p.648*
Curtin, Michael *p.413*
Curtis, Gerald L. (Editor). *p.621*
Curtis, Gerald L.. *p.621*
Curtis P. Haugtvedt, Karen A. Machleit & Richard Yalch *p.139, p.140*
Curtis, Patricia A. *p.151, p.165*
Cushman, Claire (Editor) *p.467*
Cushman, Clare *p.458*
Cushman, Thomas & Mestrovic, Stjepan G. (Editors) . . . *p.652*
Cushner, Kenneth H. (Editor) *p.313*
Cusimano-Love, Maryann K. *p.496*
Custer, Robert L. & Milt, Harry. *p.777*
Cutcher-Gershenfeld, Joel & Ford, Kevin *p.78*
Cutileiro, José *p.701*
Cutler, Brian L. & Penrod, Steven D. *p.473*
Cutlip, Scott M., et al. *p.172*
Cutlip, Scott M. *p.428*
Cutter, Susan (Editor), et al. *p.374*
Cyert, Richard M. & March, James G. *p.72, p.83*
Cylkowski, Greg J. *p.883, p.905*
Cypher, James M. & Dietz, James L. *p.258*
Cyr, Arthur I. *p.485*
Czaja, Ronald & Blair, Johnny *p.137*
Czech, Brian, et al. *p.463*
Czerniawski, Richard D. & Maloney, Michael W.. . . . . *p.427*

D

Daalder, Hans & Mair, Peter (Editors). *p.601*
Daddario, Gina *p.835, p.845, p.902*
Dadge, David *p.563*
Dadrian, Vahakn N. *p.652*

Dag Hammarskjold Library, United Nations p.476
Daglish, Neil D. p.333
Dahl, Robert A. (Editor) p.575
Dahl, Robert A. p.453, p.503
Dahl, Robert Alan p.503, p.575
Dahrendorf, Ralf p.679, p.701, p.724
Dalkir, Kimiz. p.77
Dalla Costa, John p.70
Dallaire, Romeo & Beardsley, Brent. p.715
Dalton, Russell J. p.578
D'Altroy, Terence N. p.11
Daly, Jim. p.786, p.880, p.883
Dando, Malcolm R. p.563
D'Andrade, Roy G. & Strauss, Claudia J. (Editors) p.27
D'Andrade, Roy G. p.27
Danesi, Marcel (Editor) p.423
Danesi, Marcel p.141
Danesi, Marcello p.424
Dangel, Julie Rainer p.277
Dangelo, Mark p.66
Dani, A. H. p.8
Daniel, Carter A. p.176
Daniel, Clete p.125
Daniel, John (Editor), et al. p.314
Daniel, Pete p.771
Daniells, Lorna M. p.180
Daniels, Harvey & Zemelman, Steven p.284
Daniels, Pamela & Weingarten, Kathy p.736
Daniels, Peter T. & Bright, William (Editors) p.18
Daniels, Roger p.570
Danielson, Michael N. p.883, p.887, p.896
D'Anieri, Paul, et al. p.597
Danziger, Pamela N. p.138
Danziger, Sheldon H. & Weinberg, Daniel H. (Editors). p.253, p.264
Darby, John p.648
Darby, Paul p.815, p.847, p.883, p.898
Darbyshire, Paul. p.351
D'Arcy, Paul p.384
Darga, Amy (Editor) p.169
Darian-Smith, Kate p.384
Darity, William A. Jr. & Myers, Samuel L. Jr. p.265
Darnay, Arsen J. (Editor) p.166
Darnell, Adrian C. p.188, p.199
Darnell, Regna. p.4
Darrah, Charles N. p.39, p.44
Das, Dilip K. p.664
Das, Veena & Poole, Deborah p.34
Dash, Samuel p.473
Dates, Jannette L. & Barlow, William (Editors). p.416
Datnow, Amanda & Hubbard, Lea (Editors) p.301
Datta, Prabhat K. p.617
Daulaire, Nils (Editor), et al. p.668
Daun, Holger p.308
Dauncey, Hugh & Hare, Geoff (Editors) . . p.804, p.843, p.856
Davenport, Thomas H. & Prusak, Laurence. . . p.66, p.72, p.78
David, Charles-Philippe & Levesque, Jacques (Editors) p.639
Davidson, Chandler p.554, p.573
Davidson, D. Kirk p.146
Davidson, Douglas V. p.724
Davidson, Russell & MacKinnon, James G. p.199
Davies, Charlotte A. p.607
Davies, Gerald p.847, p.865
Davies, J. Clarence III & Mazurek, Jan p.63
Davies, James C. p.483
Davies, James p.760
Davies, Richard O. & Abram, Richard G. . . p.715, p.899, p.900
Davies, Richard O. p.805
Davies, Wayne K. p.378
Davila, Arlene M. p.132, p.138
Davis, Allison, et al. p.701
Davis, Angela p.751
Davis, Brent. p.339
Davis, Burke p.520
Davis, Calvin D. p.645, p.648
Davis, David B p.727
Davis, David E. p.386
Davis, Donald Edward p.381
Davis, E. Philip & Steil, Benn p.99, p.155, p.162
Davis, Gerald (Editor), et al. p.718
Davis, Harold Eugene p.684
Davis, James W. p.625
Davis, Jane p.416
Davis, John B. p.226
Davis, Meredith, et al. p.356
Davis, Michael p.489
Davis, Richard A. & FitzGerald, Duncan p.391
Davis, Richard p.536
Davis, Robert C. p.727
Davis, Ronald W. p.800
Davis, William C. p.520
Dawidoff, Nicholas (Editor) p.811, p.850
Dawisha, Karen & Parrott, Bruce (Editor, Contribution by) p.585, p.597
Dawisha, Karen & Parrott, Bruce (Editors) p.508, p.623
Dawkins, Marvin P. & Kinloch, Graham C. . p.805, p.831, p.860
Dawson, Buck p.823, p.835, p.845, p.868
Dawson, John P. p.435
Dawson, Lorne L. p.721
Dawson, Robert M. p.587
Day, Graham & Thompson, Andrew. p.494
Day, Louis A. p.417
Day, Trevor p.391
Daynes, Kathryn M. p.747
De Bary, William Theodore. p.616
de Bary, Wm. Theodore (Translator). p.619
de Blij, H. J. p.374, p.376, p.379
De Blij, Harm J. p.373
de Boulay, Juliet. p.702

De Burgh, Hugo (Editor) *p.408*
De Carvalho, Fernando J. *p.226, p.242*
De Coulanges, Numa D. & Fustel de Coulanges, Numa Denis *p.489*
De Cunzo, Lu Ann & Jameson, John H. *p.13*
de Garine, I. & de Garine, Valerie *p.45*
De Geus, Arie *p.78*
De Grazia, Edward & Newman, Roger K. *p.451*
De Kadt, Emanuel & Williams, Gavin (Editors) *p.258*
De La Torre, Miguel A. *p.543*
de Mesquita, Bruce Bueno, et al. *p.575*
De Mestre, Neville. *p.871*
De Ridder-Symoens, Hilde (Editor) *p.325, p.326*
De Romilly, Jacqueline. *p.500*
de Souza Briggs, Xavier (Editor) *p.381*
de Tocqueville, Alexis *p.491, p.517*
De Vos, George A.. . . . . *p.702*
De Vroey, Michel *p.214*
Deagan, Kathleen A. & Cruxent, Jose Maria *p.13*
Deagan, Kathleen A. & MacMahon, Darcie A. *p.13*
Deardorff, Donald L. II. *p.812*
Deaver, Michael V. *p.656*
DeBenedetti, Charles. *p.649*
DeCew, Judith W. *p.443*
Decker, Diane C., et al. *p.167*
Decker, June Irene & Mize, Monica *p.797, p.799, p.800*
Decker, Wolfgang *p.805*
Dees, Morris *p.441*
Deffeyes, Kenneth S.. . . . . *p.160*
DeFleur, Margaret H. *p.408*
DeGeorge, Richard *p.298*
DeGraaf, Kathy H., et al. *p.783, p.787*
DeGraff, Jeff & Lawrence, Katherine A. *p.66*
DeGregorio, Christine A.. . . . . *p.533*
Dejnozka, Edward L., et al.. . . . . *p.339*
DeKnop, Paul (Editor), et al. *p.840*
del Mar, David Peterson *p.698*
DeLaat, Jacqueline *p.253, p.273*
DeLamater, John & MacCorquodale, Patricia. *p.737*
Delamont, Sara. *p.41, p.743*
DeLamotte, Eugenia *p.493*
Delaney, Kevin J. & Eckstein, Rick *p.880, p.883, p.887*
Delgado, Richard & Stefancic, Jean (Editors) *p.456*
Delgado, Richard *p.729*
Deliege, Robert *p.702*
Delisle, Richard G. *p.14*
Dell, Michael & Fredman, Catherine *p.157*
Delmas, Philippe *p.498*
DeLong, David W. *p.78*
Deloria, Vine Jr. & DeMallie, Raymond J.. . . . . *p.464*
Deloria, Vine Jr.. *p.721*
Delpit, Lisa *p.309*
Delworth, Ursula & Hanson, Gary R. *p.293*
Demarest, Arthur A. & Conrad, Geoffrey W. (Editors) . . . *p.11*
DeMers, Michael N.. . . . . *p.386*
Demetrion, George *p.298, p.304*
D'Emilio, John (Editor), et al. *p.569*
D'Emilio, John *p.569, p.749*
Democratic National Committee *p.553*
Demos, John Putnam *p.731, p.733*
Demos, John *p.702*
Denhardt, Janet Vinzant & Denhardt, Robert B.. . . . . *p.545, p.546, p.580*
Denhardt, Robert B.. . . . . *p.545, p.580*
Denitch, Bogdan Denis *p.506, p.508*
Denligher, Ken *p.858, p.893*
Dennis, Everette E. & Snyder, Robert W. *p.406*
Dennis, Everette E. (Editor), et al.. . . . . *p.405*
Dennis, J. M. & Dennis, Mike *p.609*
Dennis, Lawrence J. & Eaton, William E. (Editors). . . . *p.341*
Dennis, Lawrence J. (Editor) *p.341*
Denniston, Lyle W. *p.444*
Denoon, Donald & Meleisea, Malama *p.42*
Dent, Borden D.. *p.385*
Dent, David W. *p.641*
Dent, H. C. *p.334*
Denton, Robert E. Jr. (Editor) *p.417, p.558*
Department for Economic and Social Affairs Statistics Division Staff (Editor) *p.763*
Department of Economic and Social Affairs, Population Division Staff *p.668*
Department of Economic and Social Affairs Staff (Editor). *p.667*
Department of Economic and Social Affairs Staff. *p.662*
Department of the Treasury Internal Revenue Service . . . *p.464*
DePastino, Todd *p.757*
Depauw, Karen P. & Gavron, Susan J. *p.800, p.842*
Derderian, Tom *p.843, p.866*
Derks, Scott & Smith, Tony *p.188*
Derks, Scott. *p.188*
DeRoche, Edward F. & Williams, Mary M. *p.370*
Derrida, Jacques. *p.496, p.509*
Dershowitz, Alan M.. . . . . *p.658*
DeSensi, Joy Theresa & Rosenberg, Danny *p.786, p.883, p.900*
Designers and Art Directors Association Staff *p.427*
Deslippe, Dennis A. *p.121*
Dess, Gregory G. & Picken, Joseph C. *p.72, p.78*
Destexhe, Alain *p.652*
Destler, I. M.. . . . . *p.57, p.567*
Dettwyler, Katherine *p.45*
Detwiler, Bruce *p.491*
Deutsch, Charles. *p.776*
Deutsch, Eliot, et al.. . . . . *p.677*
DeValeria, Dennis & Burke-DeValeria, Jeanne *p.850*
Devaney, Dennis, et al.. . . . . *p.446*
Devault, Ileen A. *p.125*
Devereux, George (Author, Translator) *p.35*
Devins, Neal & Whittington, Keith E.. . . . . *p.531*
Devins, Neal *p.447*
Devji, Faisal *p.658*

Devol, Kenneth S. p.445
DeVries, Mary A.. . . . . p.58, p.172
DeVries, Raymond G. p.445
DeVries, Rheta p.368
Dewberry, Sidney O., et al.. . . . . p.158
Dewey, John p.342, p.356, p.491, p.503
Dewey, Scott Hamilton. p.566
Di Leonardo, Micaela (Introduction by). p.30
Di Leonardo, Micaela p.34
Diamant, Louis & Lee, Jo Ann (Editors). p.133
Diamond, Dan (Editor), et al.. . . . . p.862
Diamond, Jared M. p.627, p.760
Diamond, Larry & Diamond, Larry Jay p.647
Diamond, Larry & Plattner, Marc F. (Editors) . . . p.214, p.235
Dickerson, Donna L.. . . . . p.458
Dickie, John p.643, p.645
Dickinson, Bob & Vladimir, Andy p.161
Dickinson, David K. & Neuman, Susan B. (Editors) p.300, p.368
Dickinson, G. Lowes p.647, p.649
Dickinson, John Alexander & Young, Brian p.589
Dickson, Bruce J. p.619
Dickson, Paul. p.850, p.868
Diebolt, Claude, et al. p.199, p.240
Diehl, Richard A. p.9
Dienhart, John W. & Curnutt, Jordan p.53, p.55, p.180
Dierkes, Meinolf (Editor), et al. p.78
Diez, Thomas (Editor) p.602, p.637
Diffie, Whitfield & Landau, Susan. p.473
Digby, Anne. p.334
Dikel, Margaret Riley & Roehm, Frances E. p.169
Dikshit, R. D. p.377
Dilg, Mary p.309
Dill, David D.. . . . . p.347
Dillehay, Thomas D. p.11
Dillehay, Tom D. p.11
Dilley, Patrick. p.749
Dilts, David A., et al. p.130
Dilworth, Richardson p.542
Dimand, Mary Ann (Editor), et al. p.273
Dimand, Robert (Editor, Introduction by). . p.206, p.255, p.256, p.257, p.261, p.263
Dimand, Robert W. (Editor), et al.. . . . . p.193
Dimand, Robert W., et al. p.193
Dimand, Robert W. p.255
Dimand, Robert p.227
Dimitri, Nicola (Editor, Translator), et al. p.249, p.272
Dinan, Desmond (Editor) p.602, p.637
Dinan, Desmond p.602, p.637
Dine, B. Joseph II & Gilmore, James H.. . . . . p.144
Dinitiman, George & Ward, Bob p.874, p.879
Diop, Cheikh Anta. p.702
Dipboye, Robert & Colella, Adrienne (Editors). p.133
Dirix, A. (Editor), et al. p.825
Discenza, Richard (Editor), et al. p.321
DiStefano, Anna (Editor), et al. p.321
DiTomaso, Nancy & Post, Corinne (Editors) p.132
Dittmer, Lowell (Editor), et al. p.618
Division for Ocean Affairs and the Law of the Sea, United Nations. p.478
Dixit, Avinash K. p.248, p.252
Dixit, Avinash p.243
Dixon, Nancy M. p.78
Dixon-Mueller, Ruth p.569
Dobb, Maurice H. p.217
Dobb, Maurice Herbert p.208, p.243
Dobb, Maurice p.208
Dobbin, Frank (Editor). p.195, p.268
Dobbins, James, et al. p.633
Dobbs, Lou p.252, p.261
Dobkowski, Michael N. & Wallimann, Isidor (Editors) p.652, p.662
Dobson, John F. p.326
Docherty, David (Editor) p.874
Docherty, David p.588
Docherty, J. C. p.125
Dodd, Christopher. p.843, p.865
Dodd, Lawrence C. (Editor) p.529
Dodds, Klaus J. & Atkinson, David. p.488, p.495
Dodds, Klaus p.400
Dodge, Pryor p.857, p.870
Dodge, Toby p.643
Dodson, James p.860
Dodson, Ronald G. p.880, p.883, p.887
Dodson, Stanley I. p.391
Doeg, Colin p.160
Doeringer, Peter B. & Piore, Michael J. p.717
Doherty, Gillian & Claybourne, Anna p.399
Doherty, Thomas Patrick p.418
Dolgin, Janet L. p.448
Doll, Ronald C. p.362
Dombrowski, Daniel A. p.510
Domencich, T.. . . . . p.268
Domhoff, G. William p.702, p.719, p.726
Donahue, Brian p.771
Donahue, Debra L.. p.463
Donaldson, Greg. p.753
Donaldson, Margaret. p.356
Donnelly, M. S. p.589
Donnelly, William J. p.427
Donoghue, Eddie p.727
Donohoe, Tom & Johnson, Neil p.802, p.826
Donohue, John J. p.863
Donovan, Robert J. & Scherer, Raymond L. p.414
Dooley, Peter p.195, p.253
Dordick, Gwendolyn A. p.737, p.750
Dorfman, Lisa p.801, p.876
Dorfman, Mark S. p.163
Dorfman, Robert, et al. p.199, p.243
Dorinson, Joseph & Warmund,

Joram (Editors) p.805, p.831, p.850, p.887, p.896
Dorling, Danny p.373
Dorling Kindersley Publishing Staff p.380
Dorsey, Jason p.169
Dosi, Giovanni & Mazzucato, Mariana (Editors) p.156
Doss, Erika Lee (Editor) p.409
Dougherty, Kevin James p.291
Dougherty, Neil J.. . . . . p.795, p.883, p.900
Douglas, Edna. p.134
Douglas, Ian (Editor), et al.. . . . . p.373
Douglas, Ian (Editor). p.677
Douglas, Jack D. p.693
Douglas, Mary Tew p.36
Douglas, Mary p.28
Douglas, Susan J. p.416
Douglas, William O.. . . . . p.455, p.467
Dovre, Paul J. (Editor) p.307
Dow, Mark p.764
Dow, Sheila & Hillard, John (Editors) p.227
Dow, Sheila C. & Earl, Peter E. p.227, p.237
Dow, Sheila C. & Hillard, John (Editors) . . p.199, p.227, p.232
Dowlah, Caf p.664
Dowling, Carolyn & Kwok-Wing Lai (Editors). p.351
Dowling, Edward T. p.175
Downes, John & Goodman, Jordan Elliot. p.94, p.101, p.103, p.162
Downes, Larry & Mui, Chunka p.51
Downey, Gregory J. p.421
Downey, Tom p.94
Downing, Brian M. p.501
Downing, John, et al. p.416
Downing, June E., et al. p.318
Downing, June E. p.318
Downs, Alan p.749
Downs, Anthony p.503, p.545, p.580
Downs, Donald A.. . . . . p.458
Downs, Laura Lee p.711
Downs, Robert B. p.342
Downward, Paul & Dawson, Alistair p.883, p.896, p.899
Downward, Paul. p.232
Doz, Yves L., et al. p.69
Drabek, Zdenek (Editor). p.60
Drago-Severson, Eleanor p.319
Drake, Frederick D. & Nelson, Lynn R. (Editors). p.523
Drake, Peter G. p.788
Dreeben, Robert p.300
Dreger, Alice Domurat p.746
Dreman, David N. p.94
Dresch, Paul, et al. p.25
Dressler, Joshua (Editor) p.677, p.752
Drewe, Sheryle Bergmann p.794
Drewett, Peter p.7
Drewnowski, Jan p.265
Drewry, Henry N. & Doermann, Humphrey p.291
Dreyer, June Teufel p.619
Dreze, Jean & Sen, Amartya p.265
Drezon-Tepler, Marcia p.615
Drijvers, Jan Willem & MacDonald, A. A. (Editors) . . . p.334
Drinkwater, Barbara L. p.825, p.873
Driscoll, Margaret & Carliner, Saul p.321
Driskell, Judy A. & Wolinsky, I. R. A. (Editors) . . p.825, p.876
Driver, Rebecca & Thoenissen, C. p.257, p.263
Dru, Jean-Marie p.428
Drucker Foundation Staff, et al. p.66
Drucker, Peter F., et al.. . . . . p.767
Drucker, Peter F.. . . . . p.64, p.67, p.72, p.112, p.149
Drury, Shadia B.. . . . . p.658
Dryden, Ken p.862
Dryer, Matthew S. & Comrie, Bernard (Editors) p.18
D'Souza, Dinesh. p.331
Du Bois, W. E. B. p.729
Du Bois, William & Wright, R. Dean p.675
Duany, Andres, et al.. . . . . p.770
Duara, Prasenjit p.496
Dubin, Michael J. p.557
Duboff, Robert S. & Spaeth, Jim p.135
Dubofsky, Melvyn p.125
Dubois, David D.. . . . . p.76
Dubos, Rene Jules p.760
Duby, Georges & Aries, Philippe (Editors) p.733
Duby, Georges p.682, p.733
Duchacek, Ivo D. p.491
Duderstadt, James J.. . . . . p.821, p.893
Dudik, Evan Matthew p.66
Dudley, Robert L. & Gitelson, Alan R. p.548
Dudziak, Mary L. (Editor) p.563
Duetsch, Larry L. (Editor) p.149
Duffield, John S. p.639, p.654
Duffy, Mary Lou & Forgan, James W.. . . . . p.277
Duffy, Neill & Hooper, Jo p.141
Duis, Perry R.. p.699
Duke, Benjamin C. O. p.334
Dukes, Paul. p.641, p.656
Dumenil, Lynn p.719
Dumond, Don E. p.10
Dumont, Louis p.723
Dunaway, Wilma A. p.727
Duncan, Acheson J. p.116
Duncan, Craig & Machan, Tibor R. p.510
Duncan, Greg J. & Chase-Lansdale, P. Lindsay (Editors) p.755
Duncan, Greg J.. . . . . p.722, p.737
Duncan, John B.. . . . . p.621
Dundon, Tony & Rollinson, Derek p.121
Dunlap, Riley E. & Michelson, William (Editors). p.760
Dunn, Charles W. & Woodard, J. David p.516
Dunn, Chris p.589
Dunn, Dana, et al. p.285
Dunn, Kevin C. & Shaw, Timothy M. (Editors) . . p.641, p.643
Dunn, Mark R. & Dunn, Mary W.. . . . . p.542

Dunnavant, Keith . . . p.858, p.893
Dunning, Eric (Editor), et al. . . . p.715, p.815, p.843, p.867
Dunning, Eric G. (Editor), et al.. . . . p.815
Dunning, Eric . . . p.815
Dupeux, Georges . . . p.702
Duraiappah, Anantha Kumar . . . p.207, p.267
Duranti, Alessandro (Editor) . . . p.18
Durch, William J. (Editor) . . . p.649
Durch, William J. . . . p.633
Durham, Roger S. (Editor) . . . p.520
Durkheim, Emile & Coser, Lewis A. . . . p.722
Durkheim, Emile & Giddens, Anthony. . . . p.684
Durkheim, Emile . . . p.306, p.682, p.684, p.685, p.686, p.693
Durrenberger, E. Paul . . . p.28
Durrill, Wayne K. . . . p.520
Dutka, Alan F.. . . . p.136
Duverger, Maurice . . . p.579
Dworkin, Andrea . . . p.747
Dworkin, Roger B.. . . . p.448
Dworkin, Ronald (Editor) . . . p.536
Dworkin, Ronald M. (Editor) . . . p.434
Dworkin, Ronald M. . . . p.434, p.441, p.453, p.472, p.514
Dwyer, James G. . . . p.450
Dwyre, Diana & Farrar-Myers, Victoria . . . p.548
Dyck, Perry Rand . . . p.589
Dye, Thomas R.. . . . p.523, p.724
Dyer, Christopher . . . p.702
Dyer, Keith R.. . . . p.391
Dyreson, Mark . . . p.815, p.845, p.891, p.898
Dyson, Anne Haas . . . p.360
Dyson, Kenneth & Featherstone, Kevin . . . p.629, p.637
Dyson, Michael Eric . . . p.729
Dyson . . . p.656
Dziech, Billie W. & Hawkins, Michael W. . . . p.301

E

Eadie, Jo . . . p.677
Eagles, Munroe (Editor), et al. . . . p.586
Eagleton Institute of Politics, Rutgers University . . p.547, p.568
Eakin, Paul J. . . . p.693
Earle, Carville . . . p.381
Earle, Jason & Kruse, Sharon D. . . . p.280
Earley, P. Christopher & Erez, Miriam . . . p.56
Earley, P. Christopher . . . p.58, p.172
Early, Gerald (Editor) . . . p.811, p.831, p.855
Early, John D. & Headland, Thomas N.. . . . p.39
Earnshaw, Rae A. (Editor), et al. . . . p.772
Easterby-Smith, Mark, et al. . . . p.119
Easterlin, Richard A.. . . . p.243
Easterling, K E . . . p.871
Easterly, William . . . p.243
Eastland, Terry (Editor) . . . p.536
Eastland, Terry . . . p.536
Eastmond, Nick . . . p.351
Easttom II, William & Easttom, Chuck . . . p.113
Eaton, Adrienne E. & Keefe, Jeffrey H. (Editors) . . . p.121
Eatwell, John (Editor), et al. . . . p.192
Eban, Abba . . . p.645
Ebel, Robert D. (Editor), et al. . . . p.107
Eber, Paula Holmes & Holmes-Eber, Paula . . . p.38
Eberle, Suzanne . . . p.825, p.876
Eberwein, Wilhelm, et al.. . . . p.121
Eble, Kenneth E. & McKeachie, Wilbert J.. . . . p.292
Eby, Frederick (Editor) . . . p.339
Eccles, William J. & Cooke, Jacob E. (Editors). . . . p.517
Echaore-McDavid, Susan . . . p.151
Eckert, Penelope & McConnell-Ginet, Sally . . . p.21
Eckstein, Rick . . . p.773
Eckstein, Susan Eva . . . p.508
Eco, Umberto . . . p.424
Economic Commission for Africa . . . p.664
Economist Books Staff . . . p.172
Edelman, Robert . . . p.805
Eden, Lorraine & Dobson, Wendy . . . p.243, p.261, p.263
Edersheim, Elizabeth Haas . . . p.64, p.147
Edgeworth, Francis Y. . . . p.223
Edin, Kathryn & Kefalas, Maria . . . p.724
Edley, Christopher Jr. . . . p.456
Edling, Max M. . . . p.523
Edmonds, Ennis Barrington . . . p.711
Edmundson, William A. . . . p.512, p.669
Edson, Sakre K. . . . p.281
Education Atlas . . . p.326
Educational Testing Service . . . p.176, p.286
Edwards, Jeanette . . . p.31
Edwards, Jess . . . p.399
Edwards, John . . . p.115
Edwards, Newton . . . p.450
Edwards, Richard (Editor), et al. . . . p.320
Edwards, Richard L. (Editor) . . . p.677
Eeckhoudt, Louis, et al. . . . p.207, p.263
Egan, Kieran . . . p.339, p.347
Eggert, Max . . . p.169
Egidi, Massimo & Rizzello, Salvatore (Editors) . . . p.272
Ehlers, Manfred & Michel, Ulrich . . . p.388
Ehrenberg, Ronald G. . . . p.293
Ehrenhalt, Alan . . . p.516, p.554
Ehrenreich, Barbara . . . p.265
Ehrenreich, John H. . . . p.757
Ehrle, Elwood B. & Bennett, John B. . . . p.293
Ehrmann, Henry Walter & Schain, Martin A.. . . . p.608
Eichengreen, Barry J. . . . p.213, p.255
Eichenwald, Kurt . . . p.103
Eichler, Magrit . . . p.687
Eichner, Alfred S. (Editor) . . . p.232
Eidelberg, Paul . . . p.518
Eig, Jonathan . . . p.850
Einsohn, Amy . . . p.149
Eisaguirre, Lynne . . . p.458

Eisen, George & Wiggins, David K. (Editors) . . . p.805, p.830
Eisenstadt, Michael (Editor) p.561, p.643
Eisenstadt, Samuel N. p.681, p.760
Eisenstein, Zillah R. p.458
Eisenstock, Alan p.406
Eisinger, Robert M. p.526
Eisner, Elliot W.. . . . . p.342, p.362
Eitzen, D. Stanley p.815
Ekblom, Bjorn (Editor). p.867
Ekeh, Peter P. p.679
Ekelund, Robert B. Jr. & Hebert, Robert F. p.195
Ekelund, Robert B. Jr. & Tollison, Robert D.. . . . . . p.215
Ekvall, Robert B. p.39
El Bushra, Judy & Gardner, Judith (Editors) p.652
Elazar, Daniel J., et al. p.543
Eldridge, Larry D. p.459
Eldridge, Philip J. p.512
Elford, George W. p.286
Eliaeson, Sven. p.681
Elias, John L. & Merriam, Sharan B. p.320
Elias, Norbert & Dunning, Eric. p.783, p.815
Elias, Norbert p.726
Elias, Robert (Editor) p.815, p.830, p.850
Elias, Robert p.752
Elias, Stephen & Levinkind, Susan p.109, p.180, p.439
Elias, Stephen & Stim, Richard. p.109, p.110, p.180
Elias, Stephen p.446
Eliasson, Gunnar K. (Editor), et al.. . . . . p.230, p.235, p.243
El-Khawas, Mohamed A. & Ndumbe, J. Anyu p.398
Elkin, A. P.. . . . . p.36
Elkin p.735
Elkind, David p.342
Elkind, Sarah S. p.543
Elkins, Stanley M. & McKitrick, Eric L.. . . . . p.517
Ellen, Roy p.29
Elliot, Alison J. p.356
Elliott, Anthony & Ray, Larry (Editors) p.677
Elliott, Stephen, et al. p.356
Elliott, Ward E. p.461
Ellis, Alan L. & Riggle, Ellen D. (Editors). p.133
Ellis, Charles D. & Vertin, James R. (Editors) p.94
Ellis, Charles D. & Vertin, James R. . . . p.88, p.89, p.94, p.146, p.147, p.155, p.162
Ellis, Charles D. (Editor) p.94
Ellis, Charles D. p.94
Ellis, Elisabeth p.491
Ellis, Havelock p.747
Ellis, Joseph H.. . . . . p.81
Ellis, Joseph J. p.485
Ellis, Lynn W.. . . . . p.118
Ellis, Richard E.. p.462
Ellis, Richard J. p.547
Ellis, Stephen & Mabandla, Oyama p.613
Ellul, Jacques p.425, p.696
El-Rabbany, Ahmed p.389
Elwell, Frank W.. p.221
Ely, James W. p.467
Ember, Carol R. & Ember, Melvin (Editors). p.46
Embry, Jessie L.. p.740
Emerson, Robert W. p.109
Emerson, Thomas E. p.10
Emery, Michael, et al. p.409
Emery, Michael p.406
Emery, Robert E. p.735
Emmerij, Louis, et al. p.633
Emmerson, Donald K. (Editor) p.622
Emmons, Terence p.726
Enderle, Georges p.53
Enderlin, Charles p.649
Enders, Walter. p.206
Endicott-West, E., et al. p.623
Endres, Anthony M. & Fleming, Grant A. p.630
Enfield, N. J. (Editor) p.20
Engel, Barbara T. (Editor) p.829, p.879
Engel, James F. p.134
Engel, Michael p.326
Engels, Friedrich. p.34, p.207, p.737
England, Crystal. p.302
England, Paula & Farkas, George. p.724, p.733
England, Paula p.133
Engle, R. F. & McFadden, D. L. (Editors) p.199
Engle, R. F. (Editor) p.199
Engle, R. F. p.199
English, John p.588
English, Leona M. (Editor) p.320
English, Richard A. (Editor) p.677
Englund, Harri (Editor). p.611
Engman, Max & Kirby, David (Editors) p.594
Engster, Daniel p.491, p.496, p.498
Enoka, Roger p.908, p.909
Enoksen, Eystein, et al. p.788, p.793
Entine, Jon, et al. p.815, p.831
Entman, Robert M. p.558
Epstein, Adam p.883, p.900
Epstein, Edward C. p.121
Epstein, Irving (Editor). p.334
Epstein, Jason p.149
Epstein, Joseph p.739
Epstein, Lee. p.536
Epstein, Marc J. & Birchard, Bill p.85
Epstein, Marc J. p.113
Epstein, Richard A. p.133
Epstein, Scarlett, et al. p.771
Erck, Dan, et al.. p.176
Ereaut, Gill (Editor), et al. p.135
Ergas, Zaki (Editor) p.611
Erickson, H. Lynn p.362
Erickson, Paul A. & Murphy, Liam Donat (Editors) p.23
Erickson, Paul A. & Murphy, Liam Donat p.23
Eriksen, Thomas Hylland p.34

Erikson, Erik H. *p.735*
Erikson, Kai T. *p.760*
Erlen, Jonathon & Spillane, Joseph F. *p.448*
Ernst & Young LLP, et al. *p.94*
Ernst & Young LLP Staff, et al. *p.85*
Erricker, Clive & Erricker, Jane *p.307*
Errington, J. Joseph *p.21*
Erskine, James A., et al. *p.177*
Esbensen, Finn-Aage (Editor), et al. *p.714*
Escobar, Edward J. *p.774*
Eskridge, William N. Jr. (Editor) *p.457*
Esposito, John L. & Voll, John O. *p.500*
Esposito, John L. *p.658*
Estes, Jack C. *p.163*
Estlund, David M. (Editor) *p.503*
Etcheson, Craig *p.652*
Etue, Elizabeth & Williams, Megan K. *p.835, p.862*
Etzioni, Amitai & Lawrence, Paul R. (Editors) *p.269*
Etzioni, Amitai & Marsh, Jason H. *p.563, p.572*
Etzioni, Amitai *p.185, p.213, p.262, p.269, p.515, p.626, p.628, p.629, p.716, p.750, p.768, p.770*
Euchner, Charles C. *p.883, p.891, p.896*
Eucken, W. *p.209*
European Commission Delegation to the United States . . *p.474*
European Commission *p.637*
European Parliament *p.474*
European Society for the History of Economic Thoug. . . *p.227*
European Union - Delegation of the European Commission to the United States. *p.603, p.637*
European Union *p.474, p.482, p.603, p.637*
Evangelista, Matthew *p.656*
Evangelista, Nick *p.857, p.877*
Evans, C. Lawrence *p.533*
Evans, David J. A. (Editor) *p.390*
Evans, David J. A. *p.391*
Evans, David S. & Schmalensee, Richard *p.95, p.155, p.245, p.263*
Evans, Gail *p.167*
Evans, Glen & Farberow, Norman L. *p.677*
Evans, Graham & Newnham, Richard *p.626*
Evans, Janet M. *p.153*
Evans, Karen (Editor), et al. *p.304*
Evans, Patricia R. *p.436*
Evans, Philip & Wurster, Thomas S. *p.77*
Evans, Rod L. & Berent, Irwin M. (Editors) *p.448*
Evans, Ronald W. *p.362*
Evans-Pritchard, Edward E. *p.36, p.38*
Evers, Frederick & Rush, James *p.303*
Evertson, Carolyn & Weinstein, Carol S. (Editors) *p.283*
Ewald, William Bragg Jr. *p.148, p.166*
Ewen, Stuart *p.52, p.428*
Ewing, Kenneth D. *p.581*
Eymann, Marcia & Wollenberg, Charles *p.711*

F

Fabozzi, Frank J. *p.103*
Fadala, Sam *p.795, p.847*
Faderman, Lillian *p.750*
Fadiman, Anne *p.778*
Fagan, Brian M. *p.10*
Fagan, Patrick *p.482*
Fagerberg, Jan (Editor), et al. *p.66*
Fahl, Ronald J. *p.164*
Faigman, David L. *p.536*
Faille, Christopher C. *p.470*
Fain, Gerald S. (Editor) *p.783, p.802*
Fair, John D. *p.715*
Fairris, David *p.121*
Fakhouri, Hani *p.702*
Falk, Gerhard *p.805, p.858*
Falk, Richard A. *p.477, p.512, p.563, p.626*
Falkner, David *p.805, p.831, p.850*
Fallon, Richard H. Jr. *p.536*
Fallon, Richard H. *p.453*
Falola, Toyin Omoyeni *p.702*
Fan, Hong Y. *p.835*
Fan, Jie, et al. *p.771*
Fanshel, David & Shinn, Eugene B. *p.756*
Fanshel, David, et al. *p.757*
Farazmand, Ali (Editor) *p.546*
Farazmand, Ali *p.616*
Farber, David *p.153*
Farcau, Bruce W. *p.591*
Farenga, Patrick & Holt, John *p.296*
Farley, Reynolds & Haaga, John (Editors) *p.138*
Farley, Reynolds (Editor) *p.763*
Farmer, Paul *p.27, p.46, p.778*
Farmer, Peter J., et al. *p.880, p.883*
Farnsworth, Paul (Editor) *p.13*
Farnsworth, Stephen J. & Lichter, S. Robert *p.558*
Faroqhi, Suraiya *p.641*
Farr, Michael & Kursmark, Louise *p.169*
Farr, Michael J. (Based on a book by) *p.169*
Farr, Michael *p.167, p.169*
Farrand, Max *p.452*
Farrell, Edwin *p.299*
Farrell, Michael P. & Rosenberg, Stanley *p.741*
Farrier, Jasmine *p.531*
Farrington, Karen *p.380*
Farstrup, Alan E. & Samuels, S. Jay (Editors) *p.363*
Fashola, Olatokunbo S. *p.288*
Fass, Paula S. *p.326*
Faunce, Roland Cleo *p.363*
Faura, Juan *p.138*
Faust, Drew G. *p.520*
Faust, Drew Gilpin *p.520*
Fausto-Sterling, Anne *p.747*
Fawcett, Millicent Garrett & Fawcett, Henry. . . . *p.209, p.269*

Fawcett, Millicent Garrett p.209, p.269, p.273
Fawcett, Millicent p.193, p.273
Fawn, Rick (Editor) p.494
Feagin, Joe R. & O'Brien, Eileen p.729
Feagin, Joe R.. . . . . p.680
Fearing, James p.130
Fearn-Banks, Kathleen p.429
Featherstone, Steve p.390
Feaver, Peter & Gelpi, Christopher p.561
Feaver, Peter & Kohn, Richard (Editors). p.561
Febvre, Lucien & Bataillon, Lionel p.375
Federal Deposit Insurance Corporation. p.158
Federal Election Commission. p.548, p.557
Federal Register Office p.481
Fedler, Fred p.404
Feenstra, Robert C. (Editor), et al.. . . . . p.257
Feenstra, Robert C. p.257
Feezell, Randolph p.715
Fehrenbacher, Don E. p.453
Feigert, Frank p.590
Feinberg, Richard & Ottenheimer, Martin (Editors) p.32
Feingold, Mordechai & Navarro-Brotons, Victor (Editors) p.334
Feingold, Mordechai p.334
Feinstein, John & Auerbach, Red p.823, p.853
Feinstein, John (Author, Afterword by) p.860
Feinstein, John p.853, p.893, p.902
Feistritzer, C. Emily & Chester, David T. p.278
Feiwel, George R. (Editor) p.213
Feiwel, George R. p.211
Felder, Raoul p.74
Feldman, Elliot J. & Nevitte, Neil (Editors) p.589
Feldman, Jonathan p.334
Feldman, Martha S., et al. p.690
Feldman, Maurice (Editor) p.316
Feldman, Ofer & Valenty, Linda O. (Editors). p.483
Feldstein, Martin p.247
Fellman, David (Editor) p.450
Fender, John p.227
Fendrich, James Max p.710
Fenich, George G.. p.161
Fenno, Richard F. Jr. p.533, p.550, p.557
Fenster, Julie p.805, p.848
Fenton, Steve & May, Stephen p.767
Fenton, Steve p.731
Ferber, Marianne A. & Nelson, Julie A. (Editors). p.273
Ferguson, Charlene p.392
Ferguson, Charles D., et al.. . . . . p.658
Ferguson, Charles E.. . . . . p.223, p.225
Ferguson, Iain, et al.. . . . . p.768
Ferguson, Niall. p.146, p.147, p.155, p.560
Fern, Edward F. p.136
Fernandez, John p.133
Fernandez-Kelly, Maria P. p.729
Fernie, Sue & Metcalf, David (Editors) p.253
Ferrand, Alain & Torrigiani, Luiggino . . . p.845, p.887, p.891
Ferraresi, Franco. p.594
Ferree, Myra Marx; Lorber, Judith; Hess, Beth B. p.743
Ferreiro, Emilia p.368
Ferren, John M. & Rutledge, Wiley p.536
Fersh, Don & Thomas, Peter p.131
Festinger, Leon p.718, p.720
Festle, Mary Jo p.821, p.835
Few, Stephen p.172, p.175
Fewsmith, Joseph p.619
Fforde, Cressida (Editor), et al. p.47
Field, John p.334
Fields, Sarah K. p.835, p.893, p.896, p.900
Fiennes, Ranulph p.378
Fife, Brian L. p.300
Figart, Deborah M., et al.. . . . . p.273
Figart, Deborah M. p.250, p.252, p.265
Figeys, Daniel (Editor). p.156
Financial Accounting Standards Board Staff p.104, p.105
Findley, Carter V. p.614
Findling, John E. & Pelle, Kimberly D. (Editors). . p.805, p.845
Findsen, Brian. p.320
Fine, Aubrey H. & Fine, Nya M.. . . . . . . p.783, p.800, p.829
Fine, Ben & Saad-Filho, Alfredo p.235
Fine, Gary Alan (Editor) p.682
Fine, Gary Alan p.745
Fine, Sidney. p.125
Fine-Dare, Kathleen S.. . . . . p.464
Finer, Herman p.574
Finer, S. E. p.575
Finger, Seymour M. & Saltzman, Arnold A. p.633
Fink, Arthur E. (Editor), et al. p.757
Fink, Conrad C.. . . . . p.406, p.407
Finke, Roger & Stark, Rodney p.720
Finkel, Donald L. & Arney, William Ray p.339
Finkelman, Paul & Field van Tassel, Emily p.462
Finkelman, Paul & Urofsky, Melvin I.. . . . . p.453
Finkelman, Paul & Wallenstein, Peter (Editors). p.485
Finkelman, Paul (Editor). p.453, p.459
Finkelman, Paul p.453
Finkelstein, David M. & Kivlehan, Maryanne (Editors) . . p.619
Finkelstein, Martin J.. . . . . p.292
Finlayson, Clive p.15
Finley, Moses p.489
Finn, Patrick J. p.302
Finnerty, John D. & Emery, Douglas R. (Author, Editors) p.91
Finney, Joni E., et al. p.295
Finnigan, Dan, et al.. . . . . p.169
Finnis, John (Editor) p.490
Finnis, John, et al.. p.656
Finocchiaro, Maurice A.. . . . . p.491, p.501
Fiorina, Morris P., et al. p.503
Fireside, Harvey p.536
Firestone, Shulamith p.724, p.744, p.747

Firestone, William A. (Editor), et al.. . . . . p.286
Firmin, Joseph-Antenor p.17
Firth, Alan p.423
Firth, Raymond William p.22, p.28, p.42
Firth, Raymond p.36, p.39
Fischer, Agneta H. (Editor) p.694
Fischer, Claude S. p.770
Fischer, Irene p.389
Fischer, Louis, et al. p.450
Fischman, Wendy, et al.. . . . . p.55
Fish, John H. p.702
Fish, M. Steven p.597
Fisher, Chris & Binns, Tony (Editors) p.376
Fisher, Donald M.. . . . . p.805, p.841, p.862
Fisher, Franklin M., et al. p.438
Fisher, George. p.473
Fisher, Irving. p.195, p.199, p.200, p.224, p.225, p.243, p.246, p.247, p.251
Fisher, Lawrence p.144
Fisher, Louis . . p.453, p.454, p.459, p.462, p.464, p.528, p.531
Fisher, Philip A. p.95
Fisher, R. J.. . . . . p.698
Fisher, Roger & Ury, William L.. . . . . p.74
Fishkin, James S. p.503
Fishman, Nina p.604, p.606
Fishman, Stephen M. & McCarthy, Lucille P. p.342
Fishman, Stephen p.441, p.446
Fishman, Sylvia Barack p.721
Fiss, Owen M.. p.515
Fitchen, Janet M. p.702
Fitzgibbons, Athol p.218
Fitzmaurice, John p.600
Fitzpatrick, Frank p.831, p.853, p.893
Fitzpatrick, Sheila p.334
Fitzwater, Terry p.169
Fizel, John & Fort, Rodney D. (Editors). p.887, p.893
Fizel, John L. (Editor), et al. p.887
Flaherty, M. Therese p.119
Flanders, Ned A.. . . . . p.347
Flannery, Kent V. & Marcus, Joyce (Editors) p.9
Flanz, Gisbert H. p.601
Flathman, Richard E.. . . . . p.515
Fleck, Steven J. & Kraemer, William J. p.790, p.879
Fleischacker, Samuel. p.219
Fleischer, Nat, et al. p.855
Fleisher, Arthur A. III, et al. p.883, p.887
Fleisher, Mark S. p.714
Fleming, Denna F.. . . . . p.631
Fleming, Fergus & Merullo, Annabel (Editors) p.378
Fleming, Fergus (As told by) p.378
Fletcher, Anthony p.582
Fletcher, Colin & Rawlins, C. L. p.787
Flew, Terry p.419
Flexner, Abraham p.326
Flink, James J. p.154
Flint, Colin (Author, Editor) p.495
Flint, Colin p.400
Flippen, J. Brooks p.566
Flood, James & Anders, Patricia (Editors) p.360
Flood, James (Editor), et al. p.300, p.363
Flood, Josephine p.13
Flood, Lawrence G. (Editor) p.121
Flood, Robert L. & Daellenbach, Hans p.119
Florence, Namulundah p.310, p.342
Florini, Ann p.498
Flowers, R. Barri p.747
Floyd, Patricia A. p.794, p.903
Flynn, Nancy p.172
Flynt, Wayne p.541
Foerstel, Herbert N. p.451
Fogel, Robert William p.514
Fogg, G. E. p.378
Fogg, Neeta P., et al.. . . . . p.167
Fog-Olwig, Karen (Editor). p.40
Folbre, Nancy (Editor), et al. p.273
Folbre, Nancy p.273
Foley, Michael A. p.471
Foley, Michael p.605
Foley, William A.. . . . . p.18
Folland, Sherman, et al. p.163
Follows, Mick & Oguz, Temel (Editors) p.392
Folmer, Henk (Editor), et al.. . . . . p.62
Fomby, Thomas & Terrell, Dek p.200
Foner, Eric & Brown, Joshua p.485
Foner, Eric p.727
Foner, Nancy (Editor) p.764
Foner, Philip S. p.125
Fontana, Andrea p.741
Food and Agriculture Organization (FAO) Staff . . p.151, p.164
Food and Agriculture Organization of the United Nations Staff (Contribution by) p.151
Foot, Rosemary (Editor), et al. p.626, p.630
Foot, Rosemary p.669
Forbath, William. p.125
Forbes, Bruce David & Mahan, Jeffrey H. (Editors) . . . p.720
Ford, Derek C. & Williams, Paul p.391
Ford, Donna Y. & Harris, J. John p.317
Ford, Donna Y. p.317
Ford, Gerald, et al.. . . . . p.548
Forde, Daryll p.29
Fordham, Graham (Editor) p.668
Forell, Caroline p.472
Forer, Pip (Editor), et al. p.387
Forgas, Joseph P. (Editor) p.694
Forget, Evelyn & Peart, Sandra (Editors) p.217
Forman, Michael H. p.494
Forman, Shepard p.28
Formisano, Roger. p.81
Forrester, Jay W.. . . . . p.119
Forsyth, Tim (Editor) p.192, p.373

Forsythe, Charles E. p.883
Forsythe, David, et al. p.633
Forsythe, David P. & McMahon, Patrice C. (Editors) . . . p.669
Forsythe, Diana. p.44
Fort, Rodney D. & Fizel, John (Editors). p.843, p.884, p.891, p.898
Fortes, Meyer p.32
Fortunato, John A. p.853, p.896, p.902
Fortunato, Ray T. & Waddell, D. Geneva p.292
Foshay, Arthur W. p.363
Foskett, Ken p.536
Fossum, John A.. . . . . p.121
Foster, David R. & Overholt, James L. p.787, p.795
Foster, Gaines M. p.520
Foster, George McClelland p.702
Foster, Lawrence p.721
Foster, Michael Beresford p.489
Foster, Richard & Kaplan, Sarah p.67
Fotheringham, A. Stewart, et al.. . . . . p.376
Foucault, Michel p.747, p.752
Fountain, Charles p.811, p.906
Foweraker, Joe & Craig, Ann L. (Editors) p.711
Fowler, Floyd J. Jr. & Mangione, Thomas W. p.691
Fowler, William M. Jr. p.520
Fox, Alistair. p.499
Fox, Elizabeth & Waisbord, Silvio R. (Editors). p.415
Fox, James A. & Tracy, Paul E.. . . . . p.691
Fox, James R.. . . . . p.434
Fox, Karl A.. . . . . p.769
Fox, Renee C.. . . . . p.778
Fox, Roddy & Rowntree, Kate (Editors). p.384
Fox, Stephen R. p.426
Foxall, Gordon R. p.139
Francione, Gary L.. . . . . p.448
Franciosi, Robert J. p.326
Francis, Becky & Skelton, Christine. p.301
Francis, David & Hester, Stephen p.688
Francis, Elizabeth p.772
Francis, J. Michael & Kaufman, Will (Editors) p.591
Franck, Thomas M. p.633
Franco, Paul. p.491
Francoeur, Robert T. (Editor), et al.. . . . . p.677, p.747
Francome, Colin. p.778
Franda, Marcus p.624
Frank, Anna Marie p.821, p.823
Frank, Jerome & Frank, Barbara p.438
Frank, Jerome D. p.437, p.647, p.649
Frank, Robert H. p.53
Frankel, Lois P. p.167
Frankel, Michael E. S. p.84
Frankfurter, Felix & Landis, James M.. . . . . p.470
Frankfurter, Felix p.437, p.467
Frankland, E. Gene p.383
Franklin, Benjamin p.342
Franklin, Donna L.. . . . . p.729
Franklin, Mark N. p.577
Franklin, Sarah & McKinnon, Susan (Editors). p.32
Franklin, Sarah & Ragone, Helena (Editors). p.32
Franks, Angela p.775
Franks, Joel S.. . . . . p.834
Franses, Philip Hans p.200
Frantzich, Stephen E. & Schier, Steven E. p.529
Fraser, James W.. . . . . p.307
Fraser, Lauchlan H. & Keddy, Paul A. (Editors) p.392
Fraser, Lyn M. & Ormiston, Aileen p.91, p.95, p.105
Fraser, Ronald, et al.. . . . . p.326
Fraser, Stephen D. p.869
Fraser, Steven p.126
Fraser, Stewart p.342
Fraser, W. Hamish p.126
Frazer, William p.227
Frazier, John W. & Margai, Florence M. p.382
Frears, John R. p.609
Frederick, William C. p.53
Fredericks, Marcel, et al. p.702
Frederickson, H. George & Smith, Kevin B. p.545, p.580
Freed, Melvyn N., et al. p.355
Freedman, Eric M.. . . . . p.524
Freedman, Maurice p.39
Freedom House Staff. p.409
Freehling, William W. p.520
Freeman, A. Myrick III p.61
Freeman, Carla C. p.28
Freeman, Joanne B. p.485
Freeman, Joshua Benjamin p.126
Freeman, Michael. p.659, p.805, p.902
Freeman, Nick & Bartels, Frank (Editors). p.60
Freeman, R. Edward, et al. p.61, p.63
Freese, Barbara p.146, p.160
Freidel, David, et al. p.9
Freidenberg, Judith p.741
Freire, Paolo p.300
Freire, Paulo p.342, p.761
French, Peter A. p.715, p.802, p.821, p.893
Freud, Anna & Burlingham, Dorothy T. p.735
Freud, Sigmund p.748
Frey, Bruno S.. . . . . p.659
freysinger Valeria J p.783
Friday, William C. & Hesburgh, Theodore M. (Editors) p.821, p.894
Fridson, Martin S. & Alvarez, Fernando p.91, p.95, p.105, p.106, p.175
Fried, Gil, et al.. . . . . p.884, p.888, p.891
Friedberg, Aaron L. p.498
Friedelbaum, Stanley H. p.536
Frieden, Jeffry A. p.664
Friedenberg, Edgar Z. p.736
Friedenberg, Robert V. p.550
Friedl, Alfred E. & Koontz, Trish Yourst. p.363
Friedland, Roger & Mohr, John W. (Editors) p.699

Friedlander, Henry . . . p.652
Friedlob, G. Thomas & Welton, Ralph E. . . . p.175
Friedman, Benjamin M. & Hahn, F. H. (Editors) . . p.188, p.189
Friedman, Clara H. . . . p.121
Friedman, Edward (Editor, Contribution by) . . . p.619
Friedman, Jack P., et al.. . . . p.95, p.166
Friedman, Lawrence M. . . . p.440, p.442, p.471
Friedman, Lawrence Meir . . . p.109, p.441
Friedman, Leon & Israel, Fred L. (Editors) . . . p.467
Friedman, Leon (Editor) . . . p.454, p.457
Friedman, Lester D. . . . p.774
Friedman, Milton & Friedman, Rose D. . . . p.232
Friedman, Milton & Schwartz, A. J.. . . . p.238
Friedman, Milton & Schwartz, Anna J. . . . p.238
Friedman, Milton (Editor) . . . p.231, p.237
Friedman, Milton. . . . p.214, p.231, p.237, p.250, p.269
Friedman, Monroe . . . p.759
Friedman, Raymond A.. . . . p.121
Friedman, Susan W. . . . p.682
Friedman, Thomas L. . . . p.55, p.89
Friedman, Walter A. . . . p.146, p.165
Friedrich, Carl J.. . . . p.574
Friedrichs, Jorg . . . p.626
Friedrichsmeyer, Sara (Editor), et al. . . . p.584
Friel, Joe . . . p.787, p.841, p.857
Friendly, Fred . . . p.439
Frigstad, David B. . . . p.135
Frisch, Helmut . . . p.230, p.235
Frisch, Ragnar . . . p.195
Frison, George C. (Editor) . . . p.10
Frison-Roche, Roger & Jouty, Sylvan . . . p.789
Fritz, Robert . . . p.86
Fritze, Ronald H. . . . p.377
Froelich, Paul . . . p.193
Frolic, B. Michael . . . p.702
Frome, Michael . . . p.407
Fromm, Erich. . . . p.235, p.768, p.775
Fronske, Hilda A. . . . p.798
Frontera, Walter R. (Editor) . . . p.827, p.828, p.829
Frost, Alan . . . p.385
Frost, Chris . . . p.409
Frost, Lynda E. & Bonnie, Richard J. (Editors). . . . p.448
Frost, Mark . . . p.823, p.860
Frost, Nick (Editor) . . . p.757
Frouin, Robert J., et al.. . . . p.388
Frumkin, Norman . . . p.178
Fry, Brian R. . . . p.545, p.580
Fry, Douglas P. . . . p.766
Fry, Katherine . . . p.414
Fry, Michael (Editor). . . . p.219
Fry, Ron . . . p.169
Fuchs, Lawrence H. . . . p.702
Fuentes, Agustin . . . p.14
Fuerst, Oren & Geiger, Uri . . . p.89, p.91, p.95
Fugita, Stephen S. & O'Brien, David J. . . . p.764
Fuller, Bruce . . . p.298
Fuller, Graham E. & Lesser, Ian O. . . . p.488, p.495
Fuller, Lon L.. . . . p.433, p.434
Fullerton, Carol S. & Ursano, Robert J. (Editors). . . . p.699
Fullinwider, Robert K. (Editor) . . . p.547
Fulmer, William E. . . . p.78
Fung, Archon . . . p.504
Fung, Edmund S. K. . . . p.619
Fung, Yuan-Cheng . . . p.908
Funk, Gary . . . p.821, p.894
Furnham, Adrian & Taylor, John . . . p.130
Furniss, W. Todd & Graham, Patricia A. (Editors) . . . p.292
Furst, Peter T. . . . p.776
Furstenberg, Frank F. Jr. & Cherlin, Andrew J. . . . p.739
Furstenberg, Frank F. Jr. . . . p.736
Fyffe, Allen & Peter, Iain. . . . p.789

G

Gabler, Robert E. (Author, Editor). . . . p.376
Gabriel, Mike . . . p.860
Gacs, Ute D. (Editor), et al.. . . . p.3, p.4
Gaddie, Ronald Keith . . . p.550
Gaddis, John Lewis (Editor), et al. . . . p.645, p.647
Gaddis, John Lewis . . . p.628
Gadotti, Moacir . . . p.342
Gaff, Jerry G. . . . p.294
Gage, Nathaniel L.. . . . p.347
Gagne, Robert M., et al. . . . p.342
Gaile, Gary L. & Willmott, Cort J. . . . p.382
Gaillard, Gerald . . . p.3
Gaines, Donna. . . . p.736
Gaines, Jane & Renov, Michael (Editors) . . . p.413
Gaines, William . . . p.408
Gainey, Donald D. & Brucato, John M. . . . p.287
Gaither, Gerald H. . . . p.292
Gaither, Milton . . . p.326
Galbraith, John Kenneth. . . . p.95, p.99, p.193, p.209, p.211, p.213, p.214, p.243, p.265, p.773
Galbraith, Michael W. (Editor) . . . p.315, p.320
Galdman, Imogen . . . p.396
Gale, William G. & Orszag, Peter R. . . . p.107
Galenson, Walter . . . p.126
Gall, Gerald L. . . . p.436
Gallagher, Gary W. . . . p.520
Gallagher, James J. & Gallagher, Shelagh A.. . . . p.317
Gallagher, James J., et al. . . . p.316
Gallagher, Kelly . . . p.363
Gallagher, Michael & Mitchell, Paul (Editors) . . . p.576
Gallagher, Michael. . . . p.382
Gallagher, Shaun . . . p.323, p.339
Gallas, Karen . . . p.360
Gallin, Alice . . . p.307
Galloway, J. H. . . . p.399

Gallup, George H. p.697
Gallup, Joan Whaley p.786, p.790, p.881, p.884
Gallup, John Luke, et al. p.397
Galston, William A. p.510, p.511
Galub, Arthur p.536
Gamble, Clive p.16
Game, Ann p.679
Gamson, William A. p.710
Gandhi, Mahatma p.766
Gandini, Lella & Edwards, Carolyn Pope (Editors) p.368
Gandolfo, Christina p.836, p.863, p.866
Gandossy, Robert P. & Sonnenfeld, Jeffrey A. (Editors) p.71, p.86
Gane, Mike J. p.679
Gane, Mike p.681
Gangi, Jane M. p.360
Ganong, Lawrence H. & Coleman, Marilyn p.740
Gans, Herbert J.. . . . . p.702, p.754
Garbus, Martin p.536
Garcia, Eugene E. p.311, p.312
Garcia, Jesus & Michaelis, John U. p.363
Gardiner, Judith Kegan p.745
Gardiner, Simon. p.884, p.900
Gardner, B. L. & Rausser, G. C. p.189
Gardner, Bruce L. & Rausser, Gordon C. (Editors) p.189
Gardner, Hall p.563
Gardner, Howard, et al. p.53, p.55
Gardner, Howard p.303, p.343, p.356
Gardner, John W. p.697
Gardner, LeRoy p.737
Gardner, Robert L., et al.. . . . . p.107
Gardner, Robert p.347
Garfield, Bob p.427
Garfinkel, Harold p.688
Garfinkel, Simson p.515
Garfinkel, Yosef p.26
Gargiulo, Terrence L. p.78
Garland, David p.752, p.773
Garlock, David (Editor) p.412
Garman, E. Thomas p.250
Garnaut, Ross, et al. p.86
Garner, Abigail p.740
Garner, Bryan A. p.436
Garraty, John A.. p.466
Garreau, Joel p.770
Garret, Maxwell R., et al. p.857
Garretsen, Harry. p.227
Garrett, Ian (Editor) p.104
Garrett, Laurie. p.668
Garrison, Roger W. p.245
Garrity, Peter p.175
Garrow, David J. p.447
Garten, Jeffrey E.. p.54
Gartner, Lloyd P. (Editor) p.308
Garton Ash, Timothy. p.628
Garvin, David A. p.78
Garza, Hedda (Compiled by) p.436
Gass, Saul I. & Harris, Carl M. (Editors) p.119
Gater, John & Gaffney, C. F. p.7
Gates, Susan M., & Ringel, Jeanne S. p.281
Gattorna, John (Editor) p.117
Gatz, Margaret (Editor), et al. p.815, p.840
Gaubatz, Kurt Taylor. p.504
Gaugler, William M.. . . . . p.857
Gauntlett, David. p.743, p.744
Gaus, Gerald F. p.511
Gauthier, Anne H. p.731
Gavin, James & Gavin, Nettie p.790, p.905
Gavora, Jessica. p.821, p.836, p.894, p.900
Gavroglou, Stavros P. p.121
Gavron, Daniel p.703
Gay, Timothy p.858, p.871
Geanakoplos, John p.200, p.225
Gedicks, Frederick M. p.460
Geer, John G. p.425
Geertz, Clifford p.22, p.29, p.703
Geffner, Andrea B. p.58, p.172
Geffner, Robert (Editor), et al. p.130
Geiger, Louis G.. . . . . p.331
Geiger, Roger L. (Editor). p.331
Geisst, Charles R.. . . . . p.84, p.89, p.155
Geisst, Charles p.89, p.100, p.146, p.155, p.162
Geist, Helmut (Editor) p.267
Gelb, Arthur. p.412
Gelber, Katharine p.423
Geldenhuys, Deon p.626
Gelfand, Michele J. & Brett, Jeanne M. p.74, p.698
Gell, Alfred p.26
Gellately, Robert & Kiernan, Ben (Editors) p.652
Gelles, Richard J. (Editor) p.742
Gellman, Irwin F. p.485
Gellner, David N. p.721
Gellner, Ernest p.494, p.515, p.679, p.700
Gelpi, Christopher p.649
Gems, Gerald R. p.783, p.805, p.858, p.881
Genovese, Eugene D. p.520, p.729
Genovese, Michael A. p.526
George, Alan p.616
George, Gerald S. p.861, p.908
George, Henry. p.209
George Lucas Educational Foundation Staff p.351
George, Paul S. & Alexander, William M. p.367
George, Sheba Mariam p.44
Geospatial & Statistical Data Center, University of Virginia Library p.556
Gerard-Varet, L.A. (Editor), et al. p.189
Gerber, David A. & Kraut, Alan M. (Editors) p.764
Gerber, Ellen W., et al. p.805, p.836
Gerber, Haim p.703

Gerber, Michael E. *p.67*
Gerber, Rodney & Williams, Michael (Editors) *p.377*
Gerber, Rodney (Editor) *p.377*
Gerber, Rudolph J.. *p.568*
Gerber, Scott D.. . . . . *p.467*
Gerdes, Louise (Editor) *p.485*
Gerdy, John R.. . . . . *p.805, p.815, p.821, p.894*
Gerhardt, Michael J.. . . . . *p.461*
Gerhardt, Uta *p.778*
Gerin-Lajoie, Paul *p.586*
Gerrard, Bill & Hillard, John (Editors). *p.227*
Gershuny, Jonathan *p.761*
Gerstmann, Evan *p.457*
Gerth, H. H. & Mills, C. Wright (Editor, Translator, Introduction by) *p.681*
Gertler, Mark *p.189, p.200*
Gesteland, Richard R.. . . . . *p.56*
Gewirth, Alan *p.512*
Geyh, Charles Gardner *p.541*
Gfroerer, Joseph, et al.. . . . . *p.776*
Ghanem, As'ad *p.614*
Ghatak, Subrata *p.258*
Ghemawat, Pankaj *p.177*
Ghent, Gretchen (Editor) *p.812*
Ghilani, Chuck, et al. *p.389*
Ghilani, Mary E.. . . . . *p.167*
Ghodse, Hamid *p.130*
Ghysels, Eric & Osborn, Denise R. *p.200*
Giacalone, Robert A. & Greenberg, Jerald (Editors). . . . *p.130*
Giacomello, Giampiero. *p.773*
Giauque, Jeffrey Glen *p.637, p.654*
Gibboney, Richard A. *p.326*
Gibbs, Jack P.. . . . . *p.773*
Gibson, John S.. . . . . *p.434*
Gibson, Mark *p.156*
Gibson, Terry-Ann Spitzer & Hoeger, Wener W. K.. . . . *p.792*
Gibson-Graham, J. K. *p.273*
Giddens, Anthony . . . *p.493, p.679, p.685, p.686, p.724, p.768*
Giddens-White, Bryon *p.534*
Giddings, Paula J.. *p.729*
Gidengil, Elisabeth. *p.586*
Gidron, Benjamin (Editor), et al. *p.640, p.649*
Gies, Frances & Gies, Joseph *p.703*
Gifford, Prosser & Louis, William Roger *p.582, p.583*
Gilberg, Trond *p.508, p.600*
Gilbert, Daniel T. (Editor), et al. *p.691*
Gilbert, Dennis *p.724*
Gilbert, Marc Jason (Editor) *p.331*
Gilbert, Margaret *p.713*
Gilbert, Martin (Author, Author) *p.380*
Gilbert, Martin *p.380, p.485, p.644*
Gilboa, Eytan (Editor) *p.407*
Gilby, Thomas. *p.490*
Gildersleeve, Rich *p.178*
Gill, Diane L.. . . . . *p.877, p.879*
Gill, Graeme J. & Pitty, Roderic . . . *p.508, p.579, p.597, p.599*
Gill, LaVerne M. *p.485, p.530*
Gill, Stephen J.. . . . . *p.78*
Gillan, Stuart L. & Chew, Donald H.. . . . . *p.54*
Gillespie, Alexander *p.434*
Gillespie, Charles Guy *p.591*
Gillespie, Michael A. & Lienesch, Michael (Editors) . . . *p.452*
Gillette, William. *p.461*
Gilley, Jerry W. & Maycunich, Ann *p.76*
Gilley, Jerry W., et al.. . . . . *p.78*
Gilligan, Carol, et al.. . . . . *p.737*
Gilligan, Carol *p.692*
Gillis, John R.. . . . . *p.736*
Gillman, Howard *p.462*
Gillmeister, Heiner *p.815, p.864*
Gilman, Charlotte Perkins *p.681, p.737*
Gilmore, David D.. *p.703*
Gilmore, Grant *p.440*
Gilmour, Robert S. & Halley, Alexis A. *p.526*
Gilpin, Robert *p.55*
Gilson, Stuart C.. . . . . *p.76, p.84*
Gimpel, James & Schuknecht, Jason. *p.551*
Gimpel, James G. *p.530*
Gingrich, Andre & Fox, Richard Gabriel (Editors) *p.22*
Ginsberg, Benjamin *p.516*
Ginsborg, Paul *p.577, p.594*
Ginsburg, Mark *p.313*
Ginzberg, Eli (Editor) *p.735*
Ginzberg, Eli *p.219*
Giordano, Gerard *p.285*
Giordano, Ralph G. *p.784*
Girouard, Mark *p.726*
Giroux, Henry A. & Epstein, Seymour. *p.343*
Gitenstein, Mark. *p.536*
Giulianotti, Richard (Editor) *p.715, p.815*
Giulianotti, Richard *p.815, p.843, p.867*
Givens, Terri E.. . . . . *p.601*
Glaathar, Joseph T.. *p.520*
Gladdish, Ken. *p.601*
Glade, T. *p.395*
Gladwell, Malcolm *p.51, p.83, p.139*
Glandon, Shan. *p.351*
Glasgow, Jackie (Editor) *p.286*
Glasgow, Neal A. & Hicks, Cathy. *p.347*
Glashan, Roy (Compiled by) *p.557*
Glass, D. V. (Editor) *p.703*
Glassmeier Amy. *p.398*
Glassner, Barry & Hertz, Rosanna (Editors) *p.675*
Glazer-Raymo, Judith *p.293*
Gleason, Philip *p.291*
Gleason, Sandra E.. *p.121*
Gledhill, John *p.34*
Gleditsch, Nils P. (Compiled by), et al. *p.656*
Gleeson, Michael & Maughan, Ronald J. *p.874*
Glendon, Mary Ann *p.440, p.455*

Glenn, H. Patrick *p.434*
Glenn, Phillip J. *p.423*
Glick, Henry R. *p.448*
Glick, Leslie Alan *p.436*
Glimcher, Paul W. *p.272*
Global IDP Survey Staff (Contribution by). *p.667, p.765*
Global Investment Center Staff *p.151*
Glover, Ian & Bellwood, Peter *p.13*
Glover, Jonathan. *p.652*
Gluckman, Max. *p.34, p.38, p.433*
Gmelch, George & Zenner, Walter P. (Editors) *p.37*
Gobe, Marc *p.142*
Godbey, Geoffrey *p.784*
Goddard, Victoria A. (Editor), et al. *p.41*
Godwin, R. Kenneth & Kemerer, Frank R.. . . . . *p.298*
Goedhart, Marc, et al. *p.89, p.91, p.95*
Goehlert, Robert U. & Martin, Fenton S. *p.439*
Goemans, Hein *p.649*
Goering, John M. *p.524*
Goetzmann, William H. & Williams, Glyndwr *p.381*
Goetzmann, William N. & Rouwenhorst, K. Geert. . *p.89, p.146*
Goff, Patricia M. & Dunn, Kevin C. (Editor, Translators) *p.483*
Goffman, Erving *p.423, p.694, p.697*
Gogatz, Arthur & Mondejar, Reuben *p.66*
Goheen, Miriam *p.30*
Golant, Stephen M. *p.742*
Gold, Alice Ross *p.326*
Goldberg, David T. *p.730*
Goldberg, Jan *p.169*
Goldberg, Robert A. *p.486*
Goldberg, Steven *p.451*
Goldberger, Arthur S. *p.200*
Goldberg-Hiller, Jonathan *p.569*
Goldblat, Jozef *p.656*
Goldblatt, Patricia F. & Smith, Deirdre (Editors) *p.277*
Golden, Miriam A.. . . . . *p.121*
Golden, Nancy *p.382*
Goldfarb, Brian *p.347*
Goldfarb, Ronald L. *p.472*
Goldfarb, Ronald *p.465*
Goldfarb, William *p.463*
Goldin, Claudia D.. . . . . *p.133*
Goldman, Emma *p.506, p.553*
Goldman, Harvey *p.502*
Goldman, Merle & Perry, Elizabeth J. (Editors) *p.619*
Goldman, Merle *p.619*
Goldman, Ralph M. *p.551*
Goldsby, Thomas J. & Martichenko, Robert *p.117*
Goldscheider, Calvin & Neusner, Jacob *p.721*
Goldsmith, Jack L. & Wu, Tim *p.115*
Goldstein, Avery N. *p.619*
Goldstein, Fred *p.111, p.165*
Goldstein, Joseph, et al. *p.442, p.757*
Goldstein, Joshua S. *p.563*
Goldstein, Lisa *p.368*
Goldstein, Mel & Tanner, Dave *p.792, p.841, p.868*
Goldstein, Melvyn C. & Beall, Cynthia M. *p.28*
Goldstein, Michael S. *p.790, p.805*
Goldstein, Norm (Editor) *p.412*
Goldstein, Paul *p.109, p.110, p.446*
Goldstein, Robert J. *p.438*
Goldstein, Tom *p.405*
Goldstone, Jack A. (Editor). *p.579, p.711*
Goldstone, Jack *p.486*
Goldthorpe, J. E. *p.759*
Goldwin, Robert A. *p.452*
Golin, Steve. *p.282*
Gollnick, Donna M. & Chinn, Philip C. *p.363*
Golub, Andrew Lang *p.83*
Gomez-Moriana, Antonio & Duran-Cogan, Mercedes (Editors) *p.703*
Gong, Gang & Semmler, Willi *p.200*
Gonon, Philipp (Editor) *p.305*
Gonzalez, Maria Luisa (Editor), et al. *p.311*
Gonzalez-Wippler, Migene *p.722*
Goodale, Jane C. *p.43*
Goodall, Brian. *p.396*
Goodchild, Michael F. & Janelle, Donald G. (Editors) . . *p.375*
Goode, William J.. . . . . *p.739, p.740*
Goodin, Robert E., et al. *p.500*
Goodlad, John I. (Editor), et al.. . . . . *p.282*
Goodlad, John I., et al.. . . . . *p.326*
Goodlad, John I. *p.279, p.326, p.337, p.339*
Goodman, Alan H., et al. *p.45*
Goodman, John C., et al.. . . . . *p.768*
Goodman, Paul *p.347*
Goodrick-Clarke, Nicholas *p.768*
Goodstein, David *p.160*
Goodwin, Barbara & Taylor, Keith W.. . . . . *p.499*
Goodwin, Barbara (Editor) *p.499*
Goodwin, Barbara *p.514*
Goodwin, Bill *p.385*
Goodwin, Jeff *p.497*
Goodwin, William Lawrence *p.356*
Goody, Esther N. *p.32*
Goody, Jack (Author, Contribution by) *p.32*
Goody, Jack *p.32*
Gordenker, Leon. *p.633*
Gordis, Robert. *p.722*
Gordon, Bryan *p.11*
Gordon, David T. (Editor) *p.326*
Gordon, Edward E. & Gordon, Elaine H. *p.762*
Gordon, Howard R. D.. *p.305*
Gordon, John S. *p.100, p.147, p.155, p.162*
Gordon, Linda (Editor). *p.754*
Gordon, Linda *p.569, p.742, p.754, p.775*
Gordon, Richard. *p.777*
Gordon, Robert J. & Friedman, Milton *p.232, p.238*
Gordon, Stacy B. *p.530*

Gordon, Suzanne p.694
Goring-Morris, A. Nigel & Belfer-Cohen, Anna (Editors). . p.16
Gorman, Robert F. & Mihalkanin, Edward S. p.670
Gorman, Robert F.. . . . . p.633, p.667
Gorn, Elliot J. (Editor). p.831, p.855
Gorn, Elliott J. p.126, p.805, p.855
Gorr, Wilpen & Kurland, Kristen S.. . . . . p.387
Gosden, Chris & Knowles, Chantal. p.47
Gosnell, Harold F.. . . . . p.577
Gostin, Larry (Editor) p.442
Gottlieb, Richard (Editor) p.160
Gottmann, Jean p.495
Gottry, Steve p.87
Goudie, Andrew (Editor) p.391
Goudie, Andrew S.. . . . . p.373
Goulbourne, Harry (Editor) p.3
Gould, Eric p.297
Gould, Frederick E. p.158
Gould, Harold A. p.703
Gould, Roger V. (Editor) p.688
Gould Todd. p.806, p.854
Gould, William B. IV. . p.109, p.111, p.112, p.121, p.126, p.446
Gouldner, Alvin Ward p.682
Gouldner, Alvin W. p.695
Gourevitch, Peter Alexis & Shinn, James p.86
Gourevitch, Philip p.715
Gourieroux, Christian & Jasiak, Joann. p.200
Gourieroux, Christian p.200
Government Printing Office Staff. p.51
Govindarajan, Vijay & Gupta, Anil K. p.69
Govindarajan, Vijay & Trimble, Chris p.68
Govoni, Norman. p.134
Gowland, D. A., et al. p.383
Grace, Eric S.. . . . . p.156
Gracitua-Mario, Estanislao & Wodon, Quentin (Editors) p.687, p.731
Gradstein, Mark, et al. p.297
Graetz, Michael J. & Mashaw, Jerry L. p.722
Graetz, Michael J. & Shapiro, Ian. p.107
Graetz, Michael J. p.107
Graham, Benjamin. p.89, p.95
Graham, Bruce p.617
Graham, Dee L., et al. p.742
Graham, George. p.798
Graham, Hugh Davis & Diamond, Nancy p.331
Graham, Hugh Davis p.486, p.570
Graham, John W. & Havlick, Wendy p.172
Graham, Katharine. p.410
Graham, Patricia Albjerg p.326
Graham, Peg & Hudson-Ross, Sally (Editors) p.279
Graham, Sara H.. p.519
Graham, Stedman, et al. p.884
Graham, Stephen (Editor) p.659
Granatstein, Jack L. p.588
Granger, C. W. & Hatanaka, Michio. p.206
Granger, C. W. (Editor) p.206
Granger, Clive & Terasvirta, Timo p.207
Granger, Clive W. J. p.200
Granger, Clive p.200, p.201, p.207
Granovetter, Mark S. & Swedberg, Richard p.185
Grant, Carl A. & Sleeter, Christine E. p.300
Grant, H. Roger p.499
Grant, J. Andrew & Soderbaum, Fredrik (Editors) p.611
Grant, James L.. . . . . p.89
Grant, R. M. p.51
Grant, S. G.. . . . . p.367
Grantham, William C., et al. p.792, p.906
Grants Program Staff. p.293
Graslund, Bo p.16
Grasmuck, Sherri & Pessar, Patricia R. p.570
Gratton, Bartlett & Rolf p.812
Gratton, Chris & Jones, Ian. p.812
Gratton, Chris & Taylor, Peter p.884, p.888
Graver, Dennis p.787, p.847
Graves, Frank P.. p.326
Graves, Joseph L. Jr. p.17
Gray, Frances Clayton & Lamb, Yanick Rice. p.832, p.836, p.864
Gray, John Chipman p.441
Gray, John p.211
Gray, Robert F. & Gulliver, P. p.32
Grayson, Edward & Bond, Catherine p.825, p.884, p.901
Greaves, Harold R. p.631
Greco, Albert N.. p.149
Greeley, Andrew M. p.720
Green, Brent p.138
Green, Charles p.142
Green, Dudley. p.789
Green, Elna C. p.519, p.568
Green, Gill & Sobo, E. J.. . . . . p.779
Green, Harvey. p.126
Green, James H., et al. p.115
Green, John C. & Herrnson, Paul S. (Editors) . . . p.551, p.552
Green, John C. (Editor), et al.. . . . . p.511
Green, Marianne E. p.169
Green, Sarah F.. . . . . p.42
Green, Scott p.86
Green, Stephen W. & Ernest, Douglas J. (Editors) p.482
Green, Thomas A. & Svinth, Joseph R. (Editors) p.863
Green, Timothy D. & Brown, Abbie. p.351
Greenawalt, Kent p.298, p.307, p.459
Greenberg, Ellen. p.533
Greenberg, James B.. . . . . p.772
Greenberg, Karen J. (Editor) p.562, p.659
Greenblatt, David p.422
Greene, James H. p.116
Greene, Julie p.126
Greene, Kathanne W.. . . . . p.446
Greene, Maxine p.302, p.343
Greene, Ross W.. p.283

Greene, William H. *p.201*
Greenhouse, Carol J., et al. *p.33*
Greenhouse, Linda *p.467, p.536*
Greenidge, A. H. J. *p.489*
Greenleaf, W. H.. . . . . *p.607*
Greenspan, Amy L. *p.131*
Greenwald, Douglas (Editor) *p.189*
Greenwald, Marilyn & Bernt, Joseph (Editors) *p.408*
Greenwood, Justin *p.603*
Greenya, John *p.536*
Greer, Scott L. (Editor). *p.400*
Gregg, Susan A. *p.12*
Gregor, A. James *p.510*
Gregory, Anne. *p.429*
Gregory, Dennis E. *p.288*
Gregory, Derek & Pratt, Geraldine *p.373*
Gregory, Derek (Editor) *p.396*
Gregory, Gayle H. & Chapman, Carolyn. *p.349*
Gregory, Gayle H. & Kuzmich, Lin *p.349*
Gregory, Ian N. *p.387*
Gregory, Raymond F. *p.446*
Gregory, William A.. *p.75*
Greider, William *p.246, p.561, p.664*
Greiner, Alfred, et al. *p.243*
Gremillion, Kristen J. (Editor). *p.7*
Grendler, Paul F.. . . . . *p.334*
Grenfell, Michael *p.682*
Grenville, J. A. S. *p.629*
Greve, Henrich R. *p.78*
Grieco, Joseph M. & Ikenberry, G. John *p.626*
Griffin, Dale (Editor), et al.. . . . . *p.195*
Griffin, Gary A. (Editor) *p.279*
Griffin, Jack. *p.173*
Griffin, John Howard. *p.730*
Griffin, Miriam D. (Editor) *p.489*
Griffin, Patricia J. *p.815, p.839*
Griffin, Robert S. *p.840*
Griffith, H. Winter *p.827, p.828, p.829*
Griffith, Sally Fore. *p.410*
Griffith, Susan. *p.169*
Griffiths, Anne M. *p.32*
Griffiths, Martin & O'Callaghan, Terry *p.626*
Griffiths, Martin (Editor) *p.626*
Griffiths, Martin *p.628*
Grigg, David B. *p.395*
Griliches, Zvi & Intriligator, Michael D. (Editors) . *p.189, p.201*
Grimes, Kimberly M. & Milgram, B. Lynne (Editors) . . . *p.44*
Grimes, Michael D. & Morris, Joan M. *p.682*
Grindle, Merilee S. *p.772*
Grinker, Roy R. & Steiner, Christopher B. *p.38*
Grinker, Roy R. *p.772*
Grinker, Roy Richard. *p.4*
Griswold del Castillo, Richard & Garcia, Richard A. . . . *p.126*
Grodzki, Lynn & Allen, Wendy *p.64*
Groenewegen, P. D. *p.215*
Groenewegen, Peter & Marshall, Alfred *p.224*
Grofman, Bernard N. & Davidson, Chandler (Editors) . . *p.461*
Grofman, Bernard N. & Lijphart, Arend (Editors) *p.576*
Grofman, Bernard N. (Editor). *p.530*
Gronke, Paul *p.533*
Groom, A. J. R. *p.633*
Groover, Mikell P. Jr. *p.116*
Groover, Mikell P. *p.116*
Grose, Philip Jr. *p.541*
Gross, James A. (Editor) *p.131*
Gross, James A.. . . . . *p.121, p.446*
Gross, Larry (Editor), et al.. . . . . *p.412*
Gross, Larry P. *p.416*
Grossman, G. M. & Rogoff, K. (Editors) *p.189*
Grossman, Gene M. & Rogoff, Kenneth S. (Editors) . . . *p.189*
Grossman, Mark & ABC-CLIO Inc. Staff, Inc *p.464*
Grossman, Mark (Editor). *p.516, p.557*
Grossman, Pamela *p.279*
Groth, Paul *p.771*
Grove, Andrew S.. . . . . *p.81*
Grove, Jean M. *p.393*
Grover, Kathryn (Editor) *p.716, p.784, p.791, p.806*
Groves, Robert M. (Editor), et al. *p.691*
Grubb & Ellis *p.158*
Grubb, W. Norton & Lazerson, Marvin *p.305*
Grubb, W. Norton & Ryan, Paul *p.305*
Grubbs, Bruce *p.390*
Gruchy, Allan G. *p.247*
Grumet, Madeleine R. *p.282*
Grundman, Adolph H. *p.854*
Grundy, Kenneth W. & Weinstein, Michael A. *p.497*
Grundy, Pamela. *p.815, p.821, p.894*
Gruneau, Richard *p.816*
Grunwald, Michael *p.541*
Grupp, Hariolf. *p.241*
Grusky, David B. (Editor) *p.722*
Gryskiewicz, Stan & Taylor, Sylvester *p.66*
Grzymala-Busse, Anna *p.601*
Gubar, Susan & Hoff, Joan (Editors) *p.748*
Guesnerie, Roger *p.201, p.250*
Guiat, Cyrille *p.594, p.609*
Guibernau, Montserrat *p.494*
Guillet de Monthoux, Pierre *p.215*
Guirdham, Maureen *p.132*
Gujarati, Damodar N. *p.201*
Gujarati. *p.201*
Gullace, Nicoletta F. *p.604*
Gulliver, P. H. *p.38*
Gulliver, Philip H. & Silverman, Marilyn *p.42*
Gumpert, Gary & Drucker, Susan J. (Editors) . . . *p.408, p.906*
Gumperz, John J. & Levinson, Stephen C. (Editors) *p.20*
Gunaratne, Shelton A. (Editor) *p.415*
Gundle, Stephen & Parker, Simon (Editors) *p.594*
Gunning, Thomas G.. *p.363*
Gunston, Bill *p.151*

Gunter, Barrie, et al.. . . . . p.140, p.427
Gunter, Michael M. p.640, p.666
Gunther, Gerald p.441
Gunther, Richard, et al.. . . . . p.608
Guo, Yugui p.334
Gupta, Akhil & Ferguson, James (Editors) p.23
Gupta, Akhil p.34
Gupta, Avijit (Editor) p.384
Gupta, R. P.. . . . . p.388
Gupta, Sunil & Lehmann, Donald. p.143
Gusfield, Joseph R. p.776
Gustavsson, Nora S. & Segal, Elizabeth A.. . . . . p.756
Gustav-Wrathall, John Donald p.719
Gutek, Barbara A.. . . . . p.253
Gutek, Gerald L. p.326, p.343
Guthrie, James W. (Editor) p.322
Guthrie, Janet. p.836, p.848
Guthrie, John T. & Givermann, Donna E. (Editors) p.354
Guthrie, John T. (Editor), et al. p.363
Guthrie, R. Dale p.17
Gutierrez Elorza, M.. . . . . p.391
Gutiérrez, David G. p.764
Gutman, Arthur p.131
Gutman, Bill & Frederick, Shawn. p.857
Gutman, Roy & Rieff, David (Editors). p.652
Gutmann, Amy & Thompson, Dennis p.504
Gutmann, Amy (Editor) p.524
Guttentag, Roger M.. . . . . p.159
Guttmann, Allen & Thompson, Lee B. p.806, p.834
Guttmann, Allen p.715, p.806, p.816, p.836, p.845, p.846
Gwartney, James D.. . . . . p.189
Gwynne, Margaret Anderson. p.44

H

Haas, Ernst B. p.626, p.629, p.637
Haas, Michael E. p.634
Haass, Richard N. & O'Sullivan, Meghan L. (Editors) . . p.642
Habeck, Mary p.659
Haber, Jeffry R. p.105
Habermas, Jürgen p.484, p.494, p.511, p.765, p.767
Habermas, Jurgen p.696, p.770
Haché, Alain p.862, p.871
Hachten, William A.. . . . . p.403
Hacker, Andrew p.730
Hacker, Jacob & Pierson, Paul p.553
Hacker, Kenneth L. p.696
Hackley, Chris. p.140
Hadjimatheou, George. p.232, p.245, p.250
Hadjor, Kofi B. p.573
Haeberle, Erwin J. & Gindorf, Rolf (Editors). p.750
Haeussler, Ernest F., et al. p.175
Hafer, R. W.. . . . . p.155
Hafez, Kai & Paletz, David L. (Editors) p.415
Hafez, Mohammed Zakirul p.61
Hage, Jerald & Powers, Charles. p.733
Hagedorn, John M. p.753
Hagel, John & Brown, John Seely p.73
Haggard, Stephan & Kaufman, Robert R. p.487, p.504
Haggard, William p.558
Haggerty, George (Editor) p.748
Hagstrom, Robert G. Jr.. . . . . p.848, p.888, p.896, p.902
Hague, Paul N. & Hague, Nick p.135
Hahm, Sung D. & Plein, L. Christopher p.621
Hahn, Robert A. (Editor) p.44
Haig, Matt p.142
Haigh, R. H., et al. p.631, p.645
Haight, G. Timothy & Singer, Daniel D. p.95, p.166
Haiken, Elizabeth p.774
Haiman, Franklyn S. & Haiman, Franklyn Saul p.459
Haiman, Franklyn S.. . . . . p.459
Haines, Charles Grove p.454
Haines, David W. (Editor) p.570
Hainstock, Elizabeth G. p.343
Hajnal, Peter I. (Editor) p.630, p.640
Hajnal, Peter I. p.630
Hake, Kathryn. p.305
Hakim, Catherine p.733
Halberstam, David p.408, p.410, p.806, p.823, p.854, p.858, p.896, p.902, p.906
Hale, Bruce (Editor) p.865
Hale, Janice E. p.310
Hale, John Rigby p.766
Haley, John O. p.475
Halfpenny, Peter. p.680
Hall, Allan, et al. p.902, p.906
Hall, Carolyn & Brignoli, Hector Perez p.399
Hall, Derek R.. . . . . p.259
Hall, Edward T. p.696
Hall, Gwendolyn M.. . . . . p.728
Hall, Jerome p.434
Hall, John A. & Trentmann, Frank (Editors) p.498
Hall, John A. (Editor) p.494
Hall, Kermit, et al. p.466, p.537
Hall, Kermit L. & McGuire, Kevin T. (Editors) p.534
Hall, Kermit L. (Editor) p.454, p.534
Hall, Kermit L. p.440
Hall, M. Ann p.806, p.813, p.836
Hall, Nigel (Editor), et al. p.368
Hall, Richard p.378
Hall, Robert T. p.681
Hall, Robert. p.489
Hall, Rodney Bruce & Biersteker, Thomas J. (Editors) . . p.663
Hall, Susan J.. . . . . p.908
Hall, Susan T.. . . . . p.360
Hall, Thomas E. & Ferguson, J. David p.213
Hall, Tim p.395
Hall, Timothy L. & Moose, Christian J. (Editors). p.629
Halladay, Eric. p.816, p.865
Haller, John S. Jr. & Haller, Robin M.. . . . . p.774

Hallin, Daniel C. *p.407, p.414*
Hallowell, A. Irving *p.35*
Halls, Peter, et al. *p.387*
Hall-Wallace, Michelle K., et al. *p.387*
Halper, Stefan & Clarke, Jonathan *p.516*
Halpern, Martin *p.122, p.126*
Halttunen, Karen *p.724*
Hamblin, W. Kenneth & Christiansen, Eric H. *p.390*
Hamby, Alonzo L. *p.522*
Hamel, Gary & Prahalad, C.. . . . . *p.81*
Hamel, Gary *p.66, p.71, p.73*
Hamer, David *p.624*
Hamermesh, Daniel S. & Bean, Frank D. (Editors) *p.570*
Hamermesh, Daniel S. *p.247*
Hamilton, Alexander, James Madison and John Jay *p.518*
Hamilton, Alexander *p.213*
Hamilton, Charles V.. . . . . *p.461*
Hamilton, Daniel & Quinlan, Joseph *p.60*
Hamilton, Gary *p.214, p.257, p.259*
Hamilton, James T. *p.414*
Hamm, Mark S.. . . . . *p.524*
Hamm, Richard F. *p.449*
Hammack, Floyd M.. *p.327*
Hammer, Michael & Champy, James *p.86*
Hammill, Donald D. & Bartel, Nettie R.. . . . . *p.318*
Hammond, J. Daniel (Editor) *p.232*
Hammond, J. Daniel *p.232*
Hammond, Phillip E., et al.. . . . . *p.537*
Hamon, Raeann & Ingoldsby, Bron (Editors) . . . *p.738, p.742*
Hamouda, O. G. & Smithin, J. (Editors) *p.227*
Hamouda, Omar F. & Rowley, J. C. (Editors) *p.201*
Hamouda, Omar F. & Smithin, John N. (Editors) *p.227*
Hampton, David *p.385*
Hamzeh, A.Nizar *p.616*
Hanan, Mack *p.142*
Hand, Learned *p.437, p.455*
Handler, Jerome & Lange, Frederick *p.14*
Handler, Jerome S. & Lange, Fredrick W. *p.728*
Handler, Richard. *p.581*
Handley, John *p.111, p.166*
Handlin, Oscar *p.571*
Hane, Mikiso *p.703*
Haney, Robert W. *p.472*
Hanf, Theodor *p.614, p.616*
Hanin, Yuri L.. . . . . *p.877*
Hanlon, Joseph F., et al. *p.116*
Hanna, Nelly *p.726*
Hannerz, Ulf *p.407*
Hannula, Dick & Thornton, Nort (Editors) . *p.794, p.868, p.904*
Hans, Nicholas *p.334*
Hans, Valerie P. *p.109, p.112*
Hansen, Alvin H. *p.243, p.246*
Hansen, Birthe & Heurlin, Bertel (Editors) *p.641, p.644*
Hansen, Ejvind Damsgaard *p.211, p.215*
Hansen, Jorn & Nielsen, Niels Kayser (Editors) . . *p.876, p.879*
Hansen, Karen T.. . . . . *p.37, p.703*
Hansen, Katharine *p.169*
Hansen, Katherine *p.170*
Hansen, Marcus L.. *p.667*
Hansen, Randall et al. *p.167, p.170*
Hansen, Thomas Blom & Stepputat, Finn (Editors) *p.34*
Hanson, Carol R., et al. *p.436, p.669*
Happle, Stephen K. *p.219*
Haqqani, Husain *p.617*
Haraway, Donna Jeanne *p.30*
Harbeck, Karen M. *p.309*
Harbour, Frances V. *p.641, p.644*
Harclerode, Peter *p.561, p.659*
Harcourt, G. C. & Riach, P. A. (Editors) *p.227*
Harcourt, G. C. *p.225*
Harcourt, Geoffrey C. (Editor) *p.227*
Hardesty, Donald L. & Little, Barbara J. *p.7*
Hardgrave, Robert L. Jr. & Kochanek, Stanley A. *p.617*
Hardin, Garrett *p.763*
Hardin, Russell *p.766*
Harding, A. F. *p.12*
Harding, Sandra (Editor) *p.690*
Hardt, Michael & Negri, Antonio *p.504*
Hardy, Dennis *p.733*
Hardy, Jim & Andrisani, John. *p.860*
Hardy, Melissa A. & Bryman, Alan E. (Editors) *p.178*
Hardy, Stephen *p.806, p.816*
Hare, Bruce R. (Editor) *p.730*
Hare, William *p.339*
Harer, John B.. . . . . *p.459*
Hargreaves, Andy *p.347*
Hargreaves Heap, Shaun & Varoufakis, Yanis *p.688*
Hargreaves, Jennifer. *p.806, p.816, p.836*
Hargreaves, John D.. . . . . *p.583, p.584*
Hargreaves, John *p.816*
Harkins, Anthony *p.709*
Harle, Vilho *p.773*
Harmon, Daniel E.. . . . . *p.378*
Harmon, Deborah A. & Jones, Toni Stokes. *p.363*
Harmon, John E. & Anderson, Steven J.. . . . . *p.387*
Harnett, Richard M. & Ferguson, Billy G. *p.404*
Harper, Doug & Lawson, Helene (Editors) *p.717*
Harper, Janice *p.46*
HarperCollins UK Staff *p.379*
Harrell, Stevan *p.708*
Harriger, Katy J.. . . . . *p.524*
Harring, Sidney L.. . . . . *p.464*
Harrington, J. W. *p.387*
Harrington, Michael *p.506, p.703*
Harrington, Walt (Editor) *p.408*
Harris, Albert J. & Sipay, Edward R. *p.363*
Harris, Charles W.. . . . . *p.524*
Harris, Daniel *p.712*
Harris, David E.. . . . . *p.716, p.784*
Harris, Fran *p.836, p.854, p.896*

Harris, Fred R. p.530
Harris, Gordon (Compiled by) p.630
Harris, H. A. p.806
Harris, Harold Arthur p.806
Harris, Ian p.491
Harris, Kathleen M. p.756
Harris, Leslie M. (Editor). p.138
Harris, Marvin & Ross, Eric B. p.736
Harris, Marvin p.22, p.23
Harris, Mary B. (Editor) p.309
Harris, Michael p.542
Harris, Randy A. p.18
Harris, Richard A. & Milkis, Sidney M. p.463
Harris, Seymour E. (Editor) p.211, p.230, p.235
Harris, Thomas L. p.144
Harris, Wendy Beech & Beech, Wendy p.68
Harrison, Faye V. (Editor) p.27
Harrison, J. F. p.703
Harrison, Jackie p.412
Harrison, Robert p.531
Harrison, Roger (Editor) p.320
Harrison, S L p.404
Harrod, Roy F. p.211, p.227
Harrop, Jeffrey p.211, p.240, p.255
Harrop, Martin & Miller, William L. (Editors) p.577
Harry, Joseph & Devall, William B. p.749
Hart, Betty & Risley, Todd R. p.356, p.368
Hart, H. L. p.434
Hart, John Fraser p.395
Hart, John. p.524
Hart-Hewins, Linda & Wells, Jan p.360
Hartley, John p.416
Hartley, Keith & Sandler, Todd (Editors). p.189
Hartman, Laura P. (Editor), et al. p.69, p.664
Hartman, Monte p.382
Hartmann, Heidi I.. . . . . . p.254
Hartmann-Tews, Ilse p.716, p.816, p.836
Hartog, Hendrik p.442, p.739
Hartshorne, Richard p.375
Hartsock, Nancy C. p.273
Hartung, Jan-Peter & Reifeld, Helmut (Editors) . . p.308, p.334
Harvard Business Reference Staff p.180
Harvard Business Review Staff p.177
Harvard Business School Press Staff p.80
Harvard Business School Staff (Contribution by). . p.130, p.167
Harvard Business School Staff (Editor) p.71, p.73
Harvard University. Committee on the Objectives of General Education in a Free Society. p.290, p.294
Harvey, Mark p.788, p.884
Harvey, Neil. p.711
Harvie, Charles & Lee, Boon-Chye (Editors) . . . p.243, p.259
Harwell, Joan M. p.318
Haschak, Paul G. p.173
Hasegawa, Tsuyoshi p.647
Hashmi, Sohail H. (Editor) p.500
Haslam, S. M.. . . . . . p.392
Hassan, Fekri A. (Editor) p.7
Hassel, Bryan C.. . . . . . p.280
Hastie, Peter A. p.799, p.800
Hastie, Reid, et al.. . . . . . p.471
Hastings, Max p.647
Hastorf, Christine A. & Popper, Virginia S. (Editors) p.7
Hastrup, Kirsten & Hervik, Peter. p.25
Hastrup, Kirsten p.42
Hatamiya, Leslie T. p.571
Hatch, J. Amos (Editor) p.356
Hattaway, Herman & Beringer, Richard E.. . . . . . p.520
Haugerud, Angelique (Editor), et al. p.28
Haury, Emil W.. . . . . . p.11
Hauser, Barbara R. (Editor). p.442
Hauser, Robert Mason p.724
Hauser, Thomas p.855, p.896
Hauser-Cram, Penny, et al. p.368
Haussman, Melissa p.768
Havard, Gilles. p.630
Hawke, Constance S.. . . . . . p.441
Hawkes, David C. (Editor) p.588
Hawkes, Nena Rey & Seggar, John F. p.836
Hawkins, Darren G. p.512
Hawkins, David B.. . . . . . p.339
Hawkins, Freda p.667
Haworth, J. T. & Veal, Anthony James (Editors) p.250
Hay, Iain (Editor) p.376, p.396
Hay, Iain p.376
Hay, James G. p.873, p.908
Hayashi, Fumio p.201
Hayden, Mary & Thompson, Jeff (Editors). p.313
Hayden, Mary (Editor), et al.. . . . . . p.313
Hayek, Friedrich A. . . p.211, p.227, p.234, p.238, p.243, p.248
Hayes, Cassandra p.167
Hayes, David K. & Ninemeier, Jack D. p.165
Hayes, Derek p.379, p.382
Hayes, Michael T. p.575
Hayes, William p.322
Hayhoe, Ruth p.334
Haykin, Simon p.422
Haynes, Charles C., et al.. . . . . . p.450
Hays, R. Allen. p.524
Hays, Samuel P. p.566
Hays, Terence E. (Editor). p.4
Hayward, Jack Ernest Shalom (Editor), et al. . . . p.603, p.637
Haywood, John p.380
Haywood, Kathleen M. & Getchell, Nancy. p.909
Hayworth, Gene p.146
Head, Simon p.69
Headland, Thomas N. (Editor), et al. p.18
Healey, Patsy (Editor), et al. p.543
Heaphy, Leslie A.. . . . . . p.806, p.832, p.850
Heater, Derek p.577

Heath, Anthony *p.606*
Heath John Staff. *p.177*
Heath, Robert L. (Editor). *p.428*
Heath, Shirley Brice *p.357*
Hebert, Elizabeth A.. . . . . *p.286, p.347, p.363*
Hecht, Bennett L. *p.158*
Heck, Shirley F. & Williams, C. Ray *p.278*
Heckenberger, Michael J. *p.11*
Heckethorn, Charles W. *p.719*
Heckman, J. J. & Leamer, E. E. (Editors) *p.189, p.201*
Heckman, James J. & Singer, Burton S. (Editors). *p.254*
Heckscher, Charles C. *p.122*
Heckscher, Eli F. *p.215*
Hedrick, Brad, et al.. . . . . *p.842, p.854*
Hedrick, Tom & McKenzie, Mike. *p.906*
Heertje, Arnold & Perlman, Mark (Editors) *p.230, p.235*
Heertje, Arnold (Editor) *p.193, p.215, p.223*
Heertje, Arnold. *p.193, p.215, p.217, p.223*
Hegel, Georg Wilhelm Fredrich. *p.491, p.502*
Hehir, Bryan, et al. *p.515, p.641, p.642*
Heiberger, Mary Morris & Vick, Julia Miller. *p.170*
Heidar, Knut *p.594*
Heidenheimer, Arnold J. & Johnston, Michael (Editors) . . *p.580*
Heidenrich, John G. *p.652*
Heij, Christiaan, et al. *p.201*
Heijke, Hans & Muysken, Joan (Editors) *p.297*
Heilbroner, Robert L. & Milberg, William *p.209*
Heilbroner, Robert L. . *p.195, p.209, p.214, p.235, p.243, p.244*
Heilbrunn, Jeffrey *p.134*
Heilemann, John. *p.158*
Heilman, Arthur W., et al. *p.363*
Heilman, Arthur W. *p.363*
Heilman, Samuel C. *p.764*
Heimann, Jim (Editor) *p.141*
Hein, Jeremy *p.571, p.763, p.764*
Heinberg, Richar *p.62*
Heineke, Walt & Willis, Jerry (Editors) *p.351*
Heineman, Kenneth J. *p.331*
Heininger, Janet *p.649*
Heintz, James, et al. *p.269*
Heitzmann, William Ray *p.903*
Held, David & McGrew, Anthony G. (Editors) *p.663*
Held, David. *p.504, p.659*
Helitzer, Melvin *p.906*
Helleiner, Jane. *p.731*
Heller, K. A. (Editor), et al.. . . . . *p.317*
Heller, Peter B. *p.634*
Hellie, Richard *p.728*
Hellinger, Stephen H. & Hellinger, Douglas A.. . . *p.253, p.263*
Hellmann, Paul T. *p.374*
Helm, Dieter R. (Editor) *p.227*
Helmick, Raymond G. *p.649*
Helmreich, William B. *p.694*
Helms, Jesse *p.486*
Helton, Arthur C. *p.667, p.670*
Hema Maps Staff (Author, Illustrator) *p.385*
Hemmings, Annette B. *p.29*
Hemphill, Hellen & Haines, Ray *p.132*
Hendershot, Cyndy *p.712*
Hendershott, Anne B. *p.696*
Henderson, George *p.132*
Henderson, Harry *p.471, p.563*
Henderson, John Cleaves *p.298*
Henderson, Karla A., et al. *p.784, p.836*
Henderson, Robert W. *p.806, p.850*
Henderson, V. & Thisse, J. F. (Editors) *p.189*
Hendon, Julia A. & Joyce, Rosemary A. (Editors). *p.9*
Hendry, David F. & Morgan, Mary S. (Editors). *p.201*
Hendry, David F. & Morgan, Mary S. *p.201*
Hendry, David F. *p.201*
Henig, Jeffrey R. & Rich, Wilbur C. (Editors) *p.543*
Henig, Jeffrey R. *p.315*
Henig, Jeffrey *p.347*
Henig, Ruth *p.631*
Henkin, Louis *p.455*
Hennessy, Brendan. *p.407*
Henning, Daniel H. & Mangun, William R. *p.62*
Henry, Jules *p.22, p.343*
Henry, Mark & Armstrong, Leslie (Editors) *p.382*
Henry Yuhuai He *p.620*
Henshall Momsen, Janet *p.259, p.273*
Hensler, Kate *p.792, p.881*
Hentoff, Nat *p.563, p.572*
Herbert, Melissa S. *p.717*
Herbert, Steven Kelly *p.774*
Herbst, Jeffrey Ira *p.611*
Herbst, Jurgen. *p.327*
Herbst, Philip *p.659*
Herdt, Gilbert H. & Leavitt, Stephen C. (Editors) *p.43*
Heritage, John. *p.688*
Herlihy, David V. (Contribution by) *p.857*
Herman, Andrew & Swiss, Thomas (Editors). *p.761*
Herman, Barry & United Nations Staff *p.664*
Herman, Bohuslav & Tinbergen, Jan *p.254*
Herman Hansen, Mogens. *p.500*
Herman, Judith L. *p.737*
Herman, Lee & Mandell, Alan *p.320*
Herman, Michael *p.546, p.580*
Hero, Alfred O. Jr. & Balthazar, Louis. *p.581*
Herrick, John & Stuart, Paul H. (Editors) *p.754*
Herrick, Rebekah *p.533*
Herrigel, Eugene *p.802, p.847*
Herrmann, Keith R. *p.173*
Herrnson, Paul (Editor), et al.. . . . . *p.548*
Herrnson, Paul S. *p.549*
Hersh, Richard H. & Merrow, John (Editors). *p.331*
Hersh, Seymour M. *p.659*
Hershberg, Eric *p.512*
Hersman, Rebecca K. C.. . . . . *p.528, p.531*
Hertz, Robert. *p.24*

Herwig, Holger H. & Bercuson, David J. *p.628*
Herz, Monica & Nogueira, Joao Pontes *p.649*
Herzfeld, Michael *p.24, p.718*
Heslep, Robert D. *p.343*
Hess, Frederick M. & Finn, Chester E. Jr. (Editors). . . . *p.347*
Hess, Frederick M. *p.280, p.315*
Hess, Peter N.. . . . . *p.201*
Hess, Rob & Stewart, Bob (Editors) . *p.806, p.816, p.843, p.847*
Hess, Stephen & Kalb, Marvin (Editors). *p.563*
Hess, Stephen *p.414*
Hesse-Biber, Sharlene *p.778*
Hesselbein, Frances (Editor), et al. *p.71, p.73*
Hesselbein, Frances *p.71*
Hessler, Julie *p.257*
Heumann, Milton & Cassak, Lance *p.573*
Heuser, Beatrice. *p.639, p.654*
Hewitson, Gillian J. *p.273*
Hewitt, Christopher & Cheetham, Tom *p.628*
Hewitt, Christopher *p.563*
Hewstone, Miles. *p.693*
Heydemann, Steven (Editor) *p.614*
Heymann, Jody *p.759*
Heymann, Philip B. *p.563, p.659*
Heyneman, Stephen P. (Editor) *p.721*
Heyward, Vivian H. *p.879*
Heywood, Leslie & Dworkin, Shari L. *p.816, p.836*
Heywood, Paul *p.608*
Hibbing, John R. & Theiss-Morse, Elizabeth *p.554*
Hibbing, John R. *p.533*
Hicks, Dan & Beaudry, Mary C. (Editors) *p.14*
Hicks, J. R. *p.238*
Hicks, John Richard, Sir *p.254*
Hicks, John Richard *p.209, p.214*
Hietala, Thomas R. *p.816, p.832, p.855*
Higdon, Hal *p.791, p.841, p.866*
Higginbotham, A. Leon Jr. *p.457*
Higgins, Monica C. *p.71*
Higgins, Patricia J. & Paredes, J. Anthony (Editors) *p.44*
Higgs, Robert J. & Braswell, Michael C. *p.824*
Higgs, Robert J.. *p.823*
Higham, Charles *p.8*
Highet, Gilbert *p.348*
Hilbert, Richard A.. . . . . *p.688*
Hildenbrand, W. & Sonnenschein, H. (Editors) *p.189*
Hildenbrand, Werner *p.201*
Hilderbrand, Robert C.. . . . . *p.654*
Hill, Anita *p.441*
Hill, Anne. *p.348*
Hill, Charles & Jones, Gareth *p.81*
Hill, Christopher. *p.628*
Hill, Daniel D. *p.426*
Hill, Karen Lee *p.877*
Hill, Kathleen Thompson & Hill, Gerald N. *p.516*
Hill, Lynn & Child, Greg *p.789, p.836*
Hill, Michael R. & Hoecker-Drysdale, Susan (Editors) . . *p.690*
Hill, R. Carter, et al.. . . . . *p.201*
Hill, Ronald. *p.384*
Hill, Stephen M. & Malik, Shahin P. (Editors) *p.649*
Hill, Winfred F. *p.357*
Hillard, John (Editor) *p.227*
Hillman, Susan Kay *p.828*
Hillman, Tim & Thorn, Craig IV (Editors). *p.296*
Hillstrom, Kevin & Hillstrom, Laurie Collier. *p.385*
Hilmes, Michele. *p.412, p.417*
Hilpert, Ulrich (Editor). *p.397*
Himanen, Pekka *p.761*
Himmelfarb, Gertrude *p.754*
Hindery, Leo & Cauley, Leslie. *p.84*
Hindman, Elizabeth B. *p.405*
Hinds, Pamela & Kiesler, Sara (Editors) *p.69*
Hine, David *p.594*
Hine, John *p.793*
Hines, Maxwell S. (Contribution by) *p.367*
Hing, Bill Ong *p.571, p.763*
Hinshaw, John. *p.126*
Hinsley, Curtis M. *p.47*
Hinsley, Francis H. *p.649*
Hintjens, Helen M. *p.583, p.584*
Hinton, Leanne & Hale, Kenneth (Editors) *p.19*
Hirata, Keiko *p.640, p.663*
Hironaka, Ann. *p.647*
Hirsch, Abraham & De Marchi, Neil *p.232*
Hirsch, E. D. Jr.. *p.327*
Hirsch, H. N. *p.467*
Hirsch, Susan Eleanor *p.122*
Hirschfeld, Magnus *p.743, p.748*
Hirst, Paul H. & White, Patricia *p.323, p.339*
Hirst, Paul Q. (Editor) *p.497*
Hirszowicz, Maria *p.708*
History of Education Society *p.327*
Hitchcock, James *p.460*
Hix, Simon & Lord, Christopher *p.603*
Hix, Simon *p.603, p.637*
Hixson, Richard F. *p.405, p.445*
Hladczuk, Sharon (Compiled by), et al. *p.300*
Hlophe, Stephen S. *p.703*
Hoare, Anthony *p.373*
Hoare, Jim & Pares, Susan (Editors). *p.189*
Hoare, Michael Rand *p.389*
Hobbes, Thomas. *p.491*
Hobbs, Joseph J.. *p.397*
Hoberman, J. *p.508*
Hoberman, John M.. . . . . *p.802, p.806, p.832, p.873*
Hoberman, John *p.802, p.816, p.832*
Hobsbawm, E. J. *p.494, p.703*
Hobson, Archie *p.374*
Hobson, Charles F.. . . . . *p.467*
Hochschild, Arlie Russell. *p.731*
Hochschild, Jennifer & Scovronick, Nathan *p.300*
Hockin, Thomas A. *p.588*

Hodder, Ian p.6
Hodge, Sheida p.56
Hodgen, Margaret Trabue p.4
Hodges, Donald C. & Gandy, Ross p.593
Hodgetts, J. E., et al.. . . . . . . p.588
Hodgetts, John Edwin p.588
Hodgetts, Richard M., et al. p.69
Hoebel, E. Adamson p.433
Hoehler-Fatton, Cynthia p.36
Hoffer, Eric p.710
Hoffer, Peter C. & Hull, N. E. p.461
Hoffer, Peter C. p.440, p.474
Hoffman, Andrew J. p.61, p.63
Hoffman, Barry p.140, p.141
Hoffman, Bruce p.659
Hoffman, Nancy (Editor) p.282
Hoffman, Ronald & Albert, Peter J. (Editors). p.630
Hoffman, Shirl J. (Editor) p.873, p.903
Hoffmann, Gretchen McCord p.446
Hofmann-Wellenhof, Bernhard, et al. p.389
Hofstadter, Richard p.298, p.331, p.683, p.685
Hofstede, Geert & Hofstede, Gert Jan p.58, p.75
Hofstede, Geert p.718
Hofstetter, Eleanore O. p.667
Hogan, Ben & Wind, Herbert W. p.861
Hogan, John C. p.450
Hogan, Michael J. (Editor) p.486
Hogan, Michael J. p.486
Hogan, Patrick Colm p.695
Hogan, Sean O. p.541
Hoge, James F. Jr. & Rose, Gideon (Editors) p.564
Hogg, Michael & Abrams, Dominic p.713
Hogg, Russell & Carrington, Kerry (Editors) p.752
Hoggart, Keith, et al.. . . . . . . p.396
Hoggart, Richard p.696
Hogler, Raymond L. p.109, p.122, p.126
Hohenberg, John p.405, p.556
Holden, Matthew Jr.. . . . . . . p.545, p.580
Holden, Robert H. p.659
Holihan, Mary p.87
Holland, Barbara p.772
Holland, Bart K.. . . . . . . p.178
Holland, D. K. (Editor). p.140
Holland, Dorothy & Quinn, Naomi (Editors) p.27
Holland, Heidi. p.613
Holland, Julie (Editor) p.776
Holland, Kathleen E., et al.. . . . . . . p.363
Holland, Martin p.603
Hollander, Gayle D. p.703
Hollander, Samuel (Editor) p.221
Hollander, Samuel . . . p.211, p.212, p.217, p.219, p.220, p.222
Hollander, S. p.223
Hollender, Jeffrey & Fenichell, Stephen p.54
Hollender, Jeffrey p.52
Hollifield, James F. & Jillson, Calvin C. p.504
Holloway, Julian (Editor), et al.. . . . . . . p.395
Holloway, Sarah (Editor), et al. p.376
Holmes, Brian, et al.. . . . . . . p.335
Holmes, Justice p.468
Holmes, Oliver Wendell p.434
Holmes, Richard. p.703
Holsti, Kalevi J. p.624
Holt, John p.327, p.343, p.357, p.364
Holt, Richard p.806
Holton, Elwood F. III, et al. p.320
Holtz, Shel p.144
Holy, Ladislav p.36
Holzgrefe, J. L. (Author, Editor) p.669, p.671
Homans, George C., et al. p.692
Home School Legal Defense Association p.296
Homer, Sidney & Leibowitz, Martin L. p.103
Homer, Sidney & Sylla, Richard p.155
Hong, Fan & Mangan, J. A. (Editors). . . . p.836, p.844, p.867
Hong Yung Lee p.620
Honig, Bruce & Rostain, Alain. p.66
Honigsheim, Paul p.681
Honna, Jun p.622
Hood, Robert E.. . . . . . . p.720
Hook, Diana H., et al. p.420
Hooker, John p.762
hooks, bell p.730
Hoopes, John W.. . . . . . . p.9
Hooton, Cornell G. p.527
Hoover, Herbert p.213
Hoover, Kevin D. (Editor) p.202, p.217, p.233
Hoover, Kevin D. p.195, p.240
Hopkins, David S. P. & Massy, William F. p.293
Hopkins, Keith p.501
Hopkins, Nicholas S. & Ibrahim, Saad Eddin (Contribution by). p.703
Hopkins, Willie E.. . . . . . . p.132
Hopp, Wallace & Spearman, Mark p.119
Horak, Ray p.115
Horn, Jane p.836, p.861
Horn, Laurence R. & Ward, Gregory L. (Editors). p.424
Horne, Alistair. p.584
Horowitz, Dan & Lissak, Moshe p.615
Horowitz, Donald L. p.713
Horowitz, Helen L. p.290, p.331
Horowitz, Irving L. (Editor) p.703
Horowitz, Irving L. p.685
Horowitz, Shale Asher & Schnabel, Albrecht. p.670
Horowitz, Steven p.234
Horton, Mark & Middleton, John p.724
Horton, William K. p.321
Horvat, Michael A., et al.. . . . . . . p.800
Horwich, George & Samuelson, Paul Anthony (Editors) p.257
Horwitz, Morton J. p.440, p.441
Horwitz, Tony p.521

Hoskins, Tina p.864
Hossler, Don, et al. p.294
Hotaling, Edward p.832, p.847
Hottenstein, David S. p.287
Hough, Jerry F. p.598
Houglum, Peggy A., et al. p.827, p.828, p.829
Houle, Cyril O. p.320
Houlihan, Barrie (Editor) p.816
Hourigan, Maureen M. p.29
House Committee on Ways and Means p.481
House, Robert J. (Editor), et al. p.69, p.71
Housh, Terry J. & Housh, Dona J. (Editors) p.873
Houston, Brant p.414
Houston, Michael E. p.874
Houston, R. A. p.335
Houtkoop-Steenstra, Hanneke p.691
Hovenkamp, Herbert p.444
Hovland, Carl Iver p.423
Howard, Allen M. & Shain, Richard M. p.384
Howard, Caroline (Editor) p.321
Howard, Christopher p.66
Howard, Dennis R. & Crompton, John L. p.888, p.891
Howard, Dennis Ramsay & Crompton, John L. . . p.884, p.888
Howard, J. Woodford Jr. p.468
Howard, Marc Morje. p.640
Howard, Michael C. (Editor) p.478
Howard, Michael Eliot. p.647, p.649
Howard, Philip & Jones, Steve (Editors) p.425
Howard, Philip K. p.441
Howard, Rhoda E.. p.512
Howard, Russell & Sawyer, Reid p.564
Howe, Daniel W. p.694
Howe, Leland W. p.306
Howe, Leo p.39
Howe, Mark D. (Editor) p.468
Howe, Mark D. p.468
Howell, Colin D. p.807
Howell, Colin p.806, p.816, p.850
Howell, Joseph H. & Dunnivant, Stephen W.. . . . . . . p.351
Howell, Jude p.620
Howell, Mark D. p.848, p.888
Howell, William G. & Peterson, Paul E.. . . . . p.298
Howes, Carollee & Ritchie, Sharon p.369
Howes, Elaine V. p.367
Howitt, Arnold M. & Pangi, Robyn L. (Editors) p.564
Howland Kenney, William p.712
Howley, Edward T. & Franks, B. Don. p.791, p.906
Hoyle, David (Editor) p.117
Hoyle, David p.117
Hranicky, W. Jack p.390
Hrdy, Sarah Blaffer p.744
Hsiao, Cheng p.202, p.206
Hsu, Elisabeth p.46
Hu, Shi Ming & Seifman, Eli (Editors) p.335
Hua, Cai & Hustvedt, Asti. p.32
Huang, Chungliang A. p.793
Hubbard, Bryn & Glasser, Neil F. p.391
Hubbard, R. Glenn p.247, p.263
Hubbartt, William S.. . . . . p.446
Hubbs, G. Ward p.521
Huber, Evelyne & Stephens, John D. p.594
Huber, Peter W. p.445
Huck, Charlotte S., et al. p.364
Hudson, Frederic p.405
Hudson, Frederick, et al. p.405
Huerta-Macias, Ana p.304, p.305
Huettenmueller, Rhonda p.175
Hufbauer, Gary Clyde & Grieco, Paul L. E. p.107
Huff, C. Ronald, et al. p.567
Hug, Simon p.579
Hughes, Bob p.784, p.795
Hughes, John, et al. p.683
Hughes, Michael & Kroehler, Carolyn J.. . . . . p.675
Hughes, Richard L. & Beatty, Katherine M.. . . . . p.71
Hughes, Richard T. & Adrian, William B. (Editors). . . . p.308
Hughes, T., et al. p.864, p.870
Hughes, Thomas P. p.159
Huitt, W. p.306
Hull, Caroline & Jotischky, Andrew p.380
Hull, Clark L. p.357
Hull, N. E. H. & Hoffer, Peter Charles p.439
Hull, N. E. H., et al. p.447
Hullfish, Henry G. & Smith, Phillip G. p.357
Hult, Joan S. & Trekell, Marianna (Editors) . p.807, p.836, p.854
Hulteng, John L.. . . . . p.405
Human Kinetics Staff p.798, p.799
Human Rights Watch Staff p.512, p.613
Human Rights Watch p.670
Hume, Cameron R. p.649
Hume, David p.217
Humphrey, James H. & Yow, Deborah A. p.840
Humphrey, James H.. . . . . p.799
Hums, Mary A. & MacLean, Joanne p.844, p.891, p.898
Hung, George K. & Pallis, Jani Macari (Editors) p.872
Hunt, James W. & Strongin, Patricia K. p.131
Hunt, Nancy & Marshall, Kathleen p.316
Hunter, Ian & Saunders, David (Editors). p.496
Hunter, James Davison p.306
Hunter, John E. & Schmidt, Frank L. p.689
Hunter, Nan D., et al. p.457
Hunter, Robin p.343
Hunter, Susan p.704
Hunter, Wendy p.592
Huntington, Samuel P. & Harrison, Lawrence E. (Editors) p.269, p.700
Huntington, Samuel P. p.482
Hurdzan, Michael p.881
Hurst, Beth p.364
Hurst, G. Cameron 3rd & Hurst I, G. p.863
Huselid, Mark & Becker, Brian p.120

Huselid, Mark, et al. *p.76*
Husen, Torsten *p.327*
Husén, Torsten & Postlethwaite, T. Neville (Editors). *p.313, p.322*
Huss-Ashmore, Rebecca (Editor) *p.45*
Hussey, Roger, et al. *p.91, p.106*
Hutchby, Ian *p.418*
Hutcheson, John D. Jr. (Editor), et al. *p.787*
Hutchings, Vincent L. *p.559*
Hutchins, Robert M.. . . . . *p.290, p.343*
Hutchins, Robert Maynard *p.327*
Hutchinson, Dennis J. *p.468*
Hutchinson, Earl O. *p.568*
Hutchison, Terence Wilmot *p.215*
Huurdeman, Anton A. *p.420*
Huxley, Aldous *p.696, p.750*
Huxtable, Marion & Blyth, Eric (Editors) *p.757*
Hybels, Saundra & Weaver, Richard L. *p.423*
Hyde, Charles K. *p.154*
Hyman, Irwin A. & Snook, Pamela A.. . . . . *p.284*
Hyman, Irwin A.. *p.284*
Hyman, Richard *p.126*
Hymes, Dell H.. . . . . *p.18*
Hymes, Dell *p.19, p.24*
Hymes, James L. *p.284*
Hyneman, Charles S. & Lutz, Donald S. (Editors) *p.517*
Hynes, J. Dennis, and Loewenstein, Mark J. *p.75*
Hyson, Marilou *p.369*

I

Icon Group International, Inc. Staff (Compiled by) *p.153*
IDC: Internal Displacement Monitoring Centre *p.667*
Ifekwunigwe, Jayne O. *p.31, p.709*
Ignatieff, Michael & Appiah, Anthony *p.512*
Ignatieff, Michael (Editor) *p.512*
Ignatieff, Michael *p.494, p.659, p.753*
Ihonvbere, Julius Omozuanvbo & Mbaku, John Mukum (Editors) *p.585, p.611*
Ikard, Robert W. *p.837, p.854, p.884*
Ikenberry, G. John. *p.560, p.626*
Illich, Ivan *p.327*
Imberger, Jorg (Editor) *p.392*
Imbroscio, David L. *p.544*
Inabinett, Mark *p.811, p.907*
Inbar, Efraim *p.615*
Incledon, Lori. *p.791, p.879*
Information Today, Inc. Staff (Editor) *p.149*
Ingersoll, Richard M. *p.283*
Ingham, Alan G. & Loy, John W. Jr. (Editors) *p.816*
Ingham, John M. *p.35*
Inglis, Andrew F. & Luther, Arch *p.421*
Inglis, Fred *p.403*
Ingold, Tim (Editor), et al.. . . . . *p.29*
Ingold, Tim (Editor). *p.24*
Ingold, Tim *p.29*
Ingraham, Patricia W. & Lynn, Laurence E. (Editors) . . . *p.580*
Ingram, David. *p.576*
Ingram, Richard T.. . . . . *p.291*
Ingrassia, Paul J.. *p.154*
Inkpen, Robert (Editor). *p.375*
Inscoe, John C. & McKinney, Gordon B. *p.521*
Institute for Sex Research Staff, et al. *p.748*
Institute for the Study of Educational Policy Staf. *p.310*
Institute on Money in State Politics *p.558*
Interdata Staff (Compiled by) *p.156*
Intergovernmental Panel on Climate Change (Editor) . . . *p.394*
International Labour Office *p.254*
International Organization for Migration (IOM) *p.764*
International Organization for Migration Staff (Contribution by) *p.667*
International Society for Technology in Education Staff . . *p.351*
International Tribunal for the Law of the Sea. *p.476*
Internet Center for Corruption Research. *p.55*
Intriligator, Michael D.. . . . . *p.175*
Investigative Reporters and Editors, Missouri School of Journalism. *p.558*
IOMA Staff *p.118*
Ippolito, Dennis S.. . . . . *p.524*
Ireland, Alleyne *p.410*
Ireland, Patrick *p.601*
Iriye, Akira *p.640*
Irons, Peter H. *p.450, p.455, p.464, p.537*
Irons, Peter *p.470, p.537*
Irvine, Janice M.. *p.569*
Irving, J.D., Shae (Editor) *p.441*
Irwin, Douglas A. *p.55, p.257, p.261, p.664*
Irwin, Geoffrey *p.379*
Irwin, Judith W.. *p.283*
Irwin, Richard L., et al. *p.906*
Isaac, R. Mark & Smith, Vernon L. (Editors). *p.271*
Isaacs, Alan (Author, Editor). *p.91, p.95, p.102, p.103, p.155, p.162*
Isaacs, Nathan & Isaacs, Susan S.. . . . . *p.357*
Isard, Peter *p.261, p.263*
Isard, Walter *p.397*
Isenberg, Joan P. & Jalongo, Mary Renck (Editors) *p.369*
Isenberg, Michael T.. . . . . *p.807, p.816, p.855*
Ishay, Micheline *p.512*
Ishida, Takeshi & Krauss, Ellis S. (Editors) *p.621*
Isin, Engin F. *p.544*
Ismael, Tareq Y. *p.614*
Italia, Iona *p.405*
Ito, Takatoshi & Krueger, Anne O. (Editors). *p.60*
Ivers, Karen S. *p.351*
Ivie, Robert L.. . . . . *p.564*

J

J Kirton, John & I Hajnal, Peter *p.663*
Jackman, Robert W. *p.498*
Jackson, Allen W., et al. *p.791*

Jackson, Bruce p.690
Jackson, Cynthia L. p.310
Jackson, Donald W. p.458
Jackson, Gordon S. p.410
Jackson, John H.. p.435
Jackson, Phil & Rosen, Charley p.832, p.854
Jackson, Phil p.802, p.854
Jackson, Susan A. & Csikszentmihalyi, Mihaly . . p.802, p.877
Jackson, Susan E. (Editor), et al.. . . . . p.76
Jacob, Christian p.385
Jacob, E. & Cathie Jordan (Editors). p.302, p.312
Jacobs, Bonita C. p.294
Jacobs, Clyde E.. p.443
Jacobs, George M., et al.. . . . . p.349
Jacobs, Heidi Hayes (Editor) p.364
Jacobs, James B. & Potter, Kimberly p.472, p.568
Jacobs, James B., et al.. . . . . p.438
Jacobsen, Douglas G. & Jacobsen, Rhonda Hustedt. . . . p.307
Jacobsen, Knut A. & Pratap, Kumar P.. . . . . p.764
Jacobson, Gary C. p.530, p.549, p.557, p.558
Jacobson, Matthew F. p.571
Jacobson, Matthew Frye p.571
Jacoby, Sanford M. p.86
Jacoby, Tamar p.571
Jacoby, Wade. p.585, p.603, p.609, p.637
Jacquard, Roland p.659
Jadhav, Narendra p.733
Jaeger, Paul T.; Bowman, Cynthia Ann p.450
Jaeger, Richard M. (Editor). p.355
Jafari, Jafar (Editor) p.161
Jaffe, A. J. & Sperber, C.. . . . . p.764
Jaffe, Abram J., et al. p.178
Jaffe, Alexandra p.21
Jaffe, W. p.215
Jaggar, Alison M. p.744
Jahoda, Gustav p.35
Jain, Devaki. p.634
James, Harold p.664
James, Patricia p.221
James, Scott C.. . . . . p.551, p.552, p.579
James, Wendy p.22
James, William p.357
Jamieson, Kathleen Hall & Waldman, Paul. p.404
Jamieson, Ross W. p.14
Janelle, Donald G.. . . . . p.374
Jankowski, Martin S.. . . . . p.714
Janoschka, Anja p.428
Janosik, Robert J. (Editor) p.437
Janowitz, Morris p.704, p.759
Jansen, Eilev S., et al.. . . . . p.202, p.240
Januszewski, Alan p.351
Janzen, Rod A. p.720
Japp, Phyllis M., et al.. . . . . p.417
Jarausch, Konrad H. p.609
Jargowsky, Paul A.. . . . . p.771
Jarvis, Matt p.877
Jarvis, Peter. p.320
Jastrjembskaia, Nadejda & Titov, Yuri. p.795, p.861
Jaworski, Leon p.439
Jay, Antony (Editor) p.482
Jay, Joelle Kristin p.348
Jay, Kathryn p.716, p.816
Jazbec, Milan p.641, p.644
Jebens, Holger (Editor). p.711
Jefferys, Steve. p.122
Jeffries, John C. Jr. p.468
Jefremovas, Villia p.652
Jencks, Christopher & Riesman, David p.290
Jencks, Christopher p.722, p.750
Jenkins, Alan p.122
Jenkins, Henry p.422
Jenkins, Hugh M. p.290
Jenkins, John & Pigram, John (Editors) . . . p.784, p.787, p.823
Jenkins, Philip. p.659
Jenkins, Rhys Owen (Editor), et al. p.131
Jenkins, Richard. p.736
Jenkins, Rob p.617
Jenkins, Simon P.R. p.873
Jennings, Francis p.517
Jennings, Kenneth M. p.122
Jensen, Clayne R. & Guthrie, Steven P. p.787, p.823
Jensen, Klaus p.414
Jensen, Merrill p.517
Jensen, N. M. p.59
Jensen, Ole B. & Richardson, Tim p.397
Jensen, Peter R. p.420
Jenson, Jane & Mahon, Rianne (Editors). p.122
Jentleson, Bruce W. & Paterson, Thomas G. (Editors). . . p.628
Jernegan, Marcus W.. . . . . p.724
Jerris, Rand p.861
Jersild, Arthur Thomas p.357
Jervis, Robert p.656
Jeukendrup, Asker & Gleeson, Michael p.876
Jevons, W. Stanley (William Stanley) p.212
Jevons, W. Stanley. p.231
Jevons, William Stanley p.231
Jevons, Willian Stanley. p.231
Jeynes, William p.307
Jimerson, Lorna p.278
Jochum, Markus & Murtugudde, Raghu (Editors). p.392
Johannis, Theodore B. & Bull, Neil (Editors). p.716
Johansen, Bruce E. (Editor) p.192, p.464
Johansen, Bruce E. p.30
John of Salisbury p.490
John S. and James L. Knight Foundation . . p.821, p.884, p.894
John W. Hartman Center for Sales, Advertising & Marketing History p.141
Johnson, Allan G. p.677
Johnson, Cecil p.832, p.865
Johnson, Chalmers A. p.760

Johnson, Charles A. & Brickman, Danette p.462
Johnson Charles W.; Ney, Robert p.461
Johnson, Christopher p.24
Johnson, David W. & Johnson, Roger T.. . . . . p.286
Johnson, Don p.811
Johnson, Edgar A.. p.212
Johnson, Elaine B.. . . . . p.348
Johnson, Elizabeth S. & Johnson, Harry G. p.228
Johnson, H. Thomas & Kaplan, Robert S. p.106
Johnson, Harry G. & Swoboda, Alexander K. p.238
Johnson, Haynes. p.486
Johnson, Ian. p.620
Johnson, Ida M. & Sigler, Robert T.. . . . . p.742
Johnson, Janet Buttolph & Reynolds, H. T. p.483
Johnson, Jeffrey S. & VGM Career Books Staff p.170
Johnson, John J.. . . . . p.717
Johnson, John W. (Editor) p.441
Johnson, Judith L.. p.321
Johnson, Kevin R.. p.460
Johnson, Leanor Boulin & Staples, Robert p.734
Johnson, Loch & Inderfurth, Karl F. (Editors) p.562
Johnson, Matthew V.. . . . . p.6
Johnson, Michael D. & Gustaffson, Anders p.139
Johnson, Michael L.. . . . . p.303
Johnson, R. W. p.613
Johnson, Spencer p.79
Johnson, Susan Moore p.278, p.281
Johnson, Timothy Russell p.537
Johnson, Winslow p.134
Johnston, David Cay p.107
Johnston, David p.493, p.511
Johnston, Donald H. (Editor) p.415
Johnston, James Scott p.337
Johnston, R. J. (Editor), et al. p.373, p.374, p.378
Johnston, R. J.. . . . . p.378
Johnston, Richard, et al. p.590
Johnston, Ron. p.374, p.378
Johnstone, D. Bruce p.295
Joint Center for Housing Studies, Harvard University . . . p.158
Joint Committee on Printing p.481
Joint United Nations Programme on HIV/AIDS p.668
Jolly, Margaret p.31
Jolly, Richard p.634, p.664
Jonassen, David H. (Editor). p.351
Jones, A. H. M. p.500
Jones, Adam (Editor). p.652
Jones, Andrew p.6
Jones, Ann p.752
Jones, Billie J., et al.. . . . . p.904
Jones, Bruce Anthony (Editor) p.281
Jones, C. Jessie & Rose, Debra J. (Editors) p.795, p.841
Jones, Charles O. p.532
Jones, Chris p.789
Jones, Derek C. (Editor) p.190
Jones, Donald G. & Daley, Elaine L. p.802, p.813
Jones, Eric L. p.209
Jones, Gavin W. p.733
Jones, Howard M. p.343
Jones, Howard. p.521
Jones, Jacqueline p.708
Jones, John Philip (Editor) p.426
Jones, Kent Albert & Jones, Kent. p.55, p.61, p.664
Jones Luong, Pauline p.623
Jones, Lyle V. & Olkin, Ingram p.355
Jones, M. Gail, et al.. . . . . p.286
Jones, Mary p.126
Jones, R. J. Barry p.192
Jones, Richard M. p.357
Jones, Robert; Oyung, Robert; Pace, Lise p.80
Jones, Robyn & Cassidy, Tania p.904
Jones, Ronald W. & Kenen, Peter B. (Editors) p.190
Jones, Samantha & Carswell, Grace (Editors) p.268
Jones, Steve (Editor). p.419
Jones, Susan, et al.. . . . . p.423
Jones, William David p.510
Jones, William K. p.443
Jones, Wilmer L. p.521
Jones-Correa, Michael (Editor) p.544
Jong, Steven M. de & Meer, Freek D. van der (Editors). . p.388
Jordan, Robert S., et al. p.629
Jordan-Bychkov, Terry p.382
Jorgensen, Danny L.. . . . . p.690
Jorgensen, Theodore P.. . . . . p.861, p.871
Jorgenson, Dale W. p.202, p.207
Joseph, Joel D. p.537
Joseph, John E. p.694
Joseph, Richard (Editor) p.611
Joseph, Richard p.611
Josephson, Peter. p.491, p.497
Josselin, Daphne & Wallace, William (Editors) p.640
Jossey-Bass Inc. Staff p.327
Jost, John T. & Sidanius, James (Editors) p.483
Jost, Kenneth & CQ Editors p.537
Joughin, Louis; Morgan, Edmund Morris p.471
Jowitt, Kenneth p.491
Joyce, James Avery p.631
Joyner, Christopher C. (Editor) p.477, p.634
Joyner, Christopher C. p.477
Jozsa, Frank P. Jr.. . . . . p.884, p.888, p.896
Jozwiak, Don p.848
Judd, Kenneth L. & Tesfatsion, Leigh (Editors). p.190
Judd, Kenneth L. p.202
Judges, Donald P. p.448
Judt, Tony. p.564
Julian Dierkes p.675
Jumars, Peter A.. . . . . p.392
Jung, Courtney Elizabeth p.614
Juravich, Tom & Bronfenbrenner, Kate p.126
Jurinski, James John p.464
Just, Roger p.42

Juviler, Peter H. p.512

K

K., Voltmer p.424
Kadera, Kelly M. p.626, p.647
Kadushin, Alfred & Harkness, Daniel p.757
Kadushin, Alfred & Kadushin, Goldie p.757
Kaemmer, John E. p.26
Kaen, Fred R. p.86
Kaestle, Carl p.327
Kagan, Robert p.637, p.641
Kagan, Sharon L. & Neville, Peter p.754
Kagan, Sharon Lynn p.369
Kahlenberg, Richard D. (Editor) p.294
Kahn, Kenneth B. (Editor) p.144
Kahn, Kenneth B. p.144
Kahn, Kim Fridkin & Kenney, Patrick J. . . p.530, p.551, p.557
Kahn, Roger p.811, p.851
Kahn, Ronald p.470
Kahn, Sharon E. & Pavlich, Dennis J. (Editors) p.298
Kahn, Susan Martha p.32
Kahneman, Daniel & Tversky, Amos (Editors) p.272
Kahneman, Daniel (Editor), et al. p.195
Kahnweiler, William & Kahnweiler, Jennifer p.76
Kairys, David & Cramer, Rene (Editors). p.465
Kaiser, David E.. p.486
Kaish, Stanley (Editor), et al. p.190
Kalberg, Stephen p.681
Kalbfeld, Brad. p.414
Kaldor, Mary p.498
Kaldor, Nicholas p.209, p.244, p.248
Kalecki, Michal p.202, p.244, p.259, p.269
Kalichman, Seth C. p.756
Kalicki, Jan H. & Goldwyn, David L. p.62
Kalman, Laura p.468
Kalven, Harry Jr. & Zeisel, Hans p.473
Kalven, Harry Jr. p.459
Kalyanpur, Maya & Harry, Beth p.316
Kalyvas, Stathis N. p.601
Kambhampati, Uma S. p.259
Kamerman, Sheila B. p.732
Kamien, Morton I. & Schwartz, Nancy Lou p.269
Kamil, Michael L. (Editor), et al. p.354
Kaminer, Wendy. p.458
Kaminski, Bartlomiej p.506, p.508, p.596
Kaminski, John P. (Editor) p.451
Kammen, Michael G. p.518
Kanbur, S. M. Ravi, et al. p.397
Kandeh, Jimmy D.. . . . . p.498, p.611
Kane, Pearl R.. . . . . p.296
Kang, David C. p.621
Kanner, Bernice p.139
Kano, Jigoro p.863
Kant, Immanuel p.343, p.649
Kanter, Rosabeth Moss p.76, p.733
Kantor, Harvey & Tyack, David B. (Editors). . . . p.305, p.353
Kao, Patricia & Tien, Susan p.167
Kapchan, Deborah A. p.31
Kapiszewski, Diana & Kazan, Alexander (Editors) p.592
Kaplan, Bert p.35
Kaplan, E. Ann p.558
Kaplan, Elliott D. (Author, Editor) p.390
Kaplan, Jack M. p.68
Kaplan, Leonard V. & Moran, Beverly I. (Editors) p.528
Kaplan, Robert S. & Norton, David P. p.73, p.81, p.82
Kaplan Staff, et al.. . . . . p.395
Kaplin, William A. & Lee, Barbara A.. . . . . p.450
Kaplow, Louis & Shavell, Steven p.83
Kappler, Charles J. (Editor). p.465
Kapteyn & Koojmans p.634
Karatani, Rieko p.605, p.667
Karger, Gunther (Author, Editor) p.86
Karier, Clarence J.. . . . . p.327
Karim, Kahn Fazle. p.398
Karl, Rebecca E.. p.494
Karlen, Delmar p.465
Karlin, Len p.903
Karlin, Samuel (Editor), et al.. . . . . p.206
Karlqvist, Anders, et al. p.202
Karnes, Frances A. & Bean, Suzanne M. (Editors) p.317
Karp, Rashelle S. (Editor) p.180
Karst, Kenneth L. p.455
Karsten, Peter p.717
Karvonen, Lauri (Editor), et al.. . . . . p.554, p.579
Kasper, Sherryl p.240
Kassem, Maye p.500, p.611
Kasser, Susan A. & Lytle, Rebecca K.. . . . . p.801
Kassimeris, George p.659
Kasza, Gregory J. p.510
Kater, Michael H. p.609
Kates, Robert William p.395
Katsaros, John & Christy, Peter p.82
Katsh, M. Ethan p.445
Katz, Daniel & Kahn, Robert L. p.716
Katz, Donald p.884, p.888
Katz, Elihu & Wedell, George p.412
Katz, Harry C. (Editor). p.419
Katz, Helen E.. . . . . p.427
Katz, Mark N.. . . . . p.497
Katz, Michael B. p.758
Katz, Richard S.. . . . . p.579
Katzenbach, Jon R. & Smith, Douglas K.. . . . . p.80
Katzenberg, M. Anne & Saunders, Shelley R. (Editors) . . p.14
Katzenstein, Mary F. & Reppy, Judith (Editors) p.717
Katzenstein, Mary F. p.745
Katzenstein, Peter J. (Editor), et al. p.624, p.629
Katzenstein, Peter J. p.609
Katzmann, Robert A.. . . . . p.537
Katznelson, Ira p.511

Kauffman, Bill . . . p.486
Kauffmann, Norman L., et al.. . . . p.313
Kaufman, Andrew L.. . . . p.468
Kaufman, Bruce E. & Taras, Daphne Gottlieb (Editors) . . p.122
Kaufman, Leonard & Rousseeuw, Peter J. . . . p.689
Kaufmann, Karen M.. . . . p.544
Kaul, Asha . . . p.423
Kausler, Donald H. & Kausler, Barry C.. . . . p.677
Kautsky, Karl . . . p.214
Kavanagh, Barry F. . . . p.389
Kawanishi, Hirosuke . . . p.126
Kay, Paul . . . p.27
Kayal, Philip M.. . . . p.779
Kean, Thomas H. & Hamilton, Lee . . . p.564, p.659
Keane, John . . . p.498
Kearney, Nolan Charles . . . p.364
Kearsley,Greg . . . p.357
Keasey, Kevin (Editor), et al. . . . p.86
Keating, Elizabeth A. . . . p.21
Keating, Michael . . . p.607
Keck, Margaret E. & Sikkink, Kathryn . . . p.640
Keck, Thomas M. . . . p.470, p.537
Kedourie, Elie . . . p.614
Keech, William R.. . . . p.214
Keefe, James W. & Jenkins, John M. . . . p.349
Keen, Mike Forrest & Mucha, Janusz L. (Editors) . . . p.683
Keen, Mike Forrest . . . p.683
Keenan, Alan . . . p.504
Keenan, Andrea & Georges, Danielle. . . . p.63, p.158
Keeves, John P. (Editor) . . . p.286, p.355
Kehoe, Alice B.. . . . p.22
Kehoe, Alice Beck . . . p.36
Keiser, Richard A.. . . . p.555, p.573
Keister, Lisa A. . . . p.245, p.265
Keith, Jennie . . . p.742
Kekes, John . . . p.511
Kelemen, R. Daniel . . . p.637
Keller, Edward B. & Berry, Jonathan L. . . . p.145
Keller, George . . . p.293
Keller, Gerald . . . p.178
Keller, Helen . . . p.337
Keller, Suzanne . . . p.724
Kellerman, Barbara & Barilleaux, Ryan J. . . . p.527
Kellerman, Barbara . . . p.697
Kelley, Christopher S. (Editor) . . . p.527
Kelley, Donald R. . . . p.598
Kelley, Larry D. & Jugenheimer, Donald W. . . . p.428
Kelley, Ninette & Trebilcock, Michael J.. . . . p.764
Kelley, Robin D. . . . p.508, p.553
Kellogg, Michael . . . p.711
Kelloway, E. Kevin (Editor), et al. . . . p.130
Kelly, Anthony . . . p.83
Kelly, Christine . . . p.711
Kelly, David H. & Kelly, Gail P. . . . p.314
Kelly, Deirdre . . . p.299
Kelly, Gail P. (Editor) . . . p.301, p.313, p.314
Kelly, John M. . . . p.434
Kelly, Luke E. & Melograno, Vincent J. . . . p.795
Kelly, Luke E. (Editor) . . . p.801
Kelly, Mary J. (Editor), et al. . . . p.415
Kelsen, Hans . . . p.477
Kemp, Barry J. . . . p.8
Kemp, Charles & Rasbridge, Lance . . . p.668
Kemp, Sid . . . p.73
Kemp, Steven M. & Kemp, Sid . . . p.179
Kemper, Robert V. & Royce, Anya Peterson (Editors) . . . p.25
Kempf-Leonard, Kimberly (Editor-In-Chief) . . . p.677
Kempton, Willett M., et al. . . . p.30
Kendall, John S. and Marzano, Robert J.. . . . p.359
Kendon, Adam . . . p.22
Kendrick, David, et al.. . . . p.202
Keneally, Thomas . . . p.517
Kennedy, Donald . . . p.293
Kennedy, Kenneth A. R.. . . . p.15
Kennedy, Mary M. (Editor) . . . p.348
Kennedy, Michael . . . p.387
Kennedy, Peter . . . p.202
Kennedy, Randall . . . p.442, p.471
Kennedy, Scott . . . p.145
Kennedy-Glans, Donna & Schulz, Robert . . . p.86
Kenneth Thompson . . . p.685
Kenney, Patrick J. & Kahn, Kim Fridkin . . . p.530
Kennon, Donald R. . . . p.533
Kenny, Judith T. & Fyfe, Nicholas (Editors) . . . p.395
Kenny, Kevin . . . p.126
Kenoyer, Jonathan M. . . . p.9
Kent, Ann . . . p.513, p.620
Kent, James . . . p.441
Kent, Michael. . . . p.825, p.873
Kent, Robert B. . . . p.397
Kent, Stephen . . . p.710
Kenyon, Cecelia M. (Editor) . . . p.518
Kenyon, Daphne A. & Kincaid, John (Editors) . . . p.524
Keohane, Robert O. & Levy, Marc A. (Editors) . . . p.666
Keohane, Robert O. & Nye, Joseph S.. . . . p.626
Keohane, Robert O. . . . p.626, p.663, p.664
Kerbel, Matthew Robert . . . p.527
Kerkhoff, Blair . . . p.905
Kerns, Virginia . . . p.4
Kerr, Clark & Gade, Marian L. . . . p.293
Kerr, Clark . . . p.290
Kerr, John . . . p.802, p.817
Kerr, Mary Margaret & Nelson, C. Michael . . . p.284
Kerrane, Kevin & Yagoda, Ben (Editors) . . . p.403
Kertzer, David I. . . . p.594, p.765
Kerwin, Cornelius M. . . . p.463
Kessler, David. . . . p.449
Kessler, Francis P. . . . p.527
Kessler, Rachael. . . . p.357, p.364
Kesten, Seymour R. . . . p.499

Kester, Gerard & Sidibe, Ousmane O. p.122
Ketcham, Ralph Louis p.504
Keuzenkamp, Hugo A. p.202
Keylor, William R.. p.628
Keynes, John Maynard. p.193, p.228
Keyssar, Alexander p.519
Khalidi, Rashid p.641
Khalil, Elias L. (Editor) p.195
Khan, Badrul Huda p.322
Khan, Muhammad Akram p.190
Khazanov, Anatoly M. p.708
Kibert, Charles p.158
Kidd, Bruce. p.807, p.817
Kidder, Tracy p.704
Kidwell, Roland E. Jr. & Martin, Christopher L (Editors) p.131
Kiernan, Ben (Introduction by) p.653
Kiernan, Ben p.652
Kiesling, Stephen p.865
Kiggundu, Moses N.. . . . . p.665
Kikoski, Catherine Kano & Kikoski, John F. p.79
Killenbeck, Mark R. p.524
Killingsworth, Mark R.. . . . . p.253
Kilminster, Richard p.685
Kim, Sunhyuk. p.621
Kimball, Richard Ian p.807, p.824
Kimeldorf, Howard p.127
Kimmel, Michael (Editor) p.677
Kimmel, Michael S. & Ferber, Abby L. p.724
Kimmel, Michael S.. . . . . p.744, p.745
Kincheloe, Joe L. p.355
Kindall, Jerry & Winkin, John (Editors) p.795, p.851
Kindleberger, Charles P. & Aliber, Robert . . p.95, p.100, p.147, p.244, p.263
Kindleberger, Charles P. p.244
King, Anthony p.817, p.844, p.867
King, Barbara J. (Editor) p.19
King, C. Richard & Springwood, Charles F. (Editors) p.817, p.841
King, C. Richard & Springwood, Charles Fruehling p.817, p.822, p.830, p.894
King, C. Richard (Editor). p.841
King, David C. p.524
King, Debra & Flam, Helena p.694
King, Desmond p.524
King, Gary, et al. p.483
King, J. E. (Editor) p.232
King, J. E. p.269
King, J. L. & Hunter, Karen p.750
King, James R. p.278
King, Joyce E. (Editor) p.301, p.310, p.355
King, Kathleen P. p.320
King, Stephen J.. . . . . p.585, p.611
King, Victor T. & Wilder, William D.. . . . . p.39
Kingdon, Jonathan p.15
King-Meadows, Tyson & Schaller, Thomas F. p.530
Kingsbury, Damien p.622
Kingston, Paul W. & Lewis, Lionel S. (Editors) p.296
Kinsella, John & Wark, McKenzie p.817, p.844, p.902
Kinsey, Alfred C., et al. p.748
Kinzer, Stephen p.654
Kionka, Edward J.. p.443
Kipphan, Helmut (Editor) p.417
Kipping, Matthias & Engwall, Lars (Editors) p.64
Kirby, Sandra, et al. p.817, p.840
Kirby, William C. (Editor) p.515
Kirch, Patrick V. p.13
Kirdar, Uner & Silk, Leonard. p.504
Kirk, Randy W.. . . . . p.87
Kirkpatrick, Donald L. & Kirkpatrick, James D.. . . . . . p.79
Kirsch, George B.. . . . . p.807, p.851
Kirshenblatt-Gimblett, Barbara p.47
Kis, Janos. p.504
Kissen, Rita M. p.283, p.309
Kissinger, Henry A. & Summers, Lawrence H.. . . p.560, p.562
Kissinger, Henry A. p.645
Kiste, Robert C. & Marshall, Mac (Editors) p.4
Kitch, Carolyn p.141, p.416, p.697
Kitchen, Philip J. (Editor) p.137
Kitfield, James p.560, p.564
Kitzinger, Celia p.750
Klamer, Arjo p.233
Klarman, Michael J.. . . . . p.457, p.537
Klass, Morton p.704
Kleidman, Robert p.559
Klein, Alan M. p.817, p.855
Klein, Alec p.157
Klein, Ann G.. . . . . p.337
Klein, David A.. . . . . p.79
Klein, Herbert S. p.728
Klein, Ingo & Mittnik, Stefan (Editors) p.202
Klein, Maury. p.66
Klein, Philip S. & Hoogenboom, Ari p.713
Klein, Richard G.. . . . . p.15
Kleinert, Sylvia & Neale, Margo (Editors) p.26
Kleinknecht, Alfred p.235
Kleinman, Isobel R. p.798, p.799
Kleit, Andrew N. (Editor) p.252
Klesse, Edward J. p.288
Klicka, Christopher J. p.296, p.450
Kliebard, Herbert M.. . . . . p.305
Klingemann, Hans-Dieter, et al.. . . . . p.579
Klinghoffer, Arthur J. p.385
Kloppenberg, Lisa A. p.537
Klosko, George p.498
Kluger, Richard p.450
Kluka, Darlene & Schilling, Guido (Editors) p.884, p.891, p.896
Kluka, Darlene A., et al. p.884, p.891
Kluwin, Thomas N. (Editor), et al. p.312
Kmenta, Jan. p.202

Knapp, Andrew *p.609*
Knapp, Mark L. & Hall, Judith A.. . . . . *p.424*
Knappman, Edward W. (Editor), et al.. . . . . *p.438*
Knauft, Bruce M.. *p.43*
Knaus, Christopher *p.301*
Knauss, John A.. *p.392*
Kneale, Pauline E.. . . . . *p.377*
Kneese, Allen V. & Sweeney, J. L. (Editors) *p.190*
Knäblein, Jörg & Muller, Rainer H. (Editors) *p.156*
Knight, Franklin W. & Martínez Vergne, Teresita *p.40*
Knight, John R.. *p.165*
Knight, Vernon J. Jr. & Steponaitis, Vin (Editors) *p.11*
Knight, W. Andy (Editor). *p.634*
Knight, W. Andy. *p.634*
Knightley, Phillip *p.403*
Knights, Michael Andrew *p.647*
Knock, Thomas J *p.631*
Knowles, Anne Kelly (Editor) *p.387*
Knowles, Malcolm S. *p.320*
Knowlton, Steven R. & Parsons, Patrick R. (Editors) . . . *p.405*
Knox, Alan B.. . . . . *p.320*
Knox, Paul L. & Marston, Sallie A.. . . . . *p.396*
Knudson, Duane V. & Morrison, Craig S. *p.873, p.909*
Knudson, Jerry W.. . . . . *p.412*
Kobach, Kris W.. *p.595*
Kochin, Michael S. *p.489*
Koegel, Robert L. *p.318*
Koehler, Michael D.. . . . . *p.858, p.904*
Koff, Clea *p.33*
Kogan, Maurice & Hawksworth, Mary (Editors) *p.482*
Koger, Larry (Compiled by) *p.727*
Kogevinas, Manolis; Pearce, Neil; Susser, Mervyn; Boffetta, P. *p.778*
Kohl, Herbert R. *p.310, p.337, p.348*
Kohl, Lawrence F.. . . . . *p.551, p.552*
Kohler, Peter A. & Zacher, Hans F. *p.247*
Kohli, Atul (Editor) *p.617*
Kohli, Atul, et al. *p.665*
Kohn, Alfie. *p.284, p.286, p.327*
Kohn, Melvin L. *p.695, p.724*
Kohn, Stephen M., et al.. . . . . *p.109, p.131*
Kohno, Masaru *p.621*
Kolata, Gina *p.791*
Kolb, Robert W. & Overdahl, James A. *p.89, p.95, p.100, p.102*
Kolm, Serge-Christophe & Mercier Ythier, Jean (Editors) *p.190*
Kolmerten, Carol A. *p.499*
Kolodny, Annette *p.331*
Kolodziej, Edward A. *p.608*
Kolsto, Pal *p.598*
Komarovsky, Mirra *p.739*
Komi, Paavo V. (Editor) *p.825, p.874, p.879*
Kondo, Dorinne K. *p.39*
Kondolf, G. Mathias & Piégay, Hervé (Editors) *p.391*
Konig, David T. *p.474*
Konstam, Angus. *p.380, p.383*
Kontos, Louis (Editor), et al. *p.714*
Konvitz, Milton R. (Editor). *p.455*
Konzal, Jean L. & Dodd, Anne Wescott *p.303*
Koot, Gerard M. *p.212, p.215*
Kopecky, Petr *p.575, p.596*
Koppett, Leonard *p.854, p.902, p.907*
Kornberg, Allan & Clarke, Harold D. *p.586*
Kornberg, Allan *p.589*
Kornbluh, Mark Lawrence *p.549*
Korosenyi, Andras *p.595*
Korr, Charles P.. . . . . *p.851, p.888, p.891*
Koshar, Rudy (Editor) *p.716, p.784*
Kosseff, Alex *p.786, p.787*
Kostelnick, Charles & Hassett, Michael *p.423*
Kostelnick, Marjorie, et al. *p.316*
Koster, Eduard A. (Editor) *p.383*
Kostiner, Joseph (Editor) *p.614*
Kotabe, Masaaki & Mol, Michael J. (Editors) *p.118*
Kotkin, Joel *p.772*
Kotler, Philip & Lee, Nancy *p.54*
Kotler, Philip, et al.. . . . . *p.51, p.134*
Kotler, Philip *p.134*
Kotler, Phillip R., et al. *p.161*
Kotter, John P. & Cohen, Dan S.. . . . . *p.73*
Kotter, John P. *p.71*
Kousser, J. Morgan *p.555, p.573, p.579*
Kousser, Thad *p.530*
Kouzes, James M. & Posner, Barry Z. *p.71*
Kovacich, Gerald *p.113*
Kowalchik, Claire *p.837, p.866*
Kowalski, Theodore J. *p.288*
Kozol, Jonathan *p.302, p.315, p.327, p.335*
Kozulin, Alex (Editor), et al. *p.357*
Kraemer, William J. *p.875, p.879*
Krafft, Manfred & Mantrala, Murali K. (Editors) *p.164*
Krakauer, Jon *p.789*
Kramer, Rita *p.343*
Krames, Jeffrey A. *p.71*
Kranz, Rachel *p.446*
Krasno, Jean E. & Sutterlin, James S. *p.656*
Krasnow, Erwin G., et al.. . . . . *p.445*
Kraus International Publications Staff, ; Freidus, Helen *p.369*
Kraus, Richard, et al. *p.784, p.903*
Krause, Jerry V., et al.. . . . . *p.796, p.854, p.904*
Krause, Jerry *p.854, p.904*
Krause, Micki *p.114*
Kraut, Alan M. *p.667*
Kraut, Richard (Editor). *p.489*
Kraut, Richard. *p.489*
Kravetz, Stacy *p.95*
Kreider, Richard B. (Editor), et al. . . *p.827, p.828, p.875, p.879*
Kreighbaum, Ellen F. & Smith,

Mark A. (Editors) p.870, p.872
Krejci, Oskar p.574, p.577, p.596
Kremenyuk, Victor A. (Editor) p.645
Kremer, John M. & Scully, Deirdre M. p.877
Krepon, Michael & Caldwell, Dan (Editors) p.562, p.630
Kreps, Christina F. p.47
Kreps, David M. (Editor), et al. p.202
Kreps, Juanita & Clark, Robert p.254, p.269
Kreps, Juanita M. p.265
Kreps, Juanita p.273
Kress, George J. & Snyder, John p.137
Kretchmar, Scott R. p.796
Krier, Dan p.86
Krismann, Carol H. p.57
Kristol, Irving p.511, p.516
Kritzer, Herbert M. (Editor) p.433
Kroeber, A. L. p.24
Kroeger, Otto, et al. p.173
Kronenfeld, Jennie J. & Whicker, Marcia L. p.170
Kronenfeld, Jennie J.. . . . . p.160
Kronenwetter, Michael p.659
Krooss, Herman E. (Editor). p.246
Kropotkin, Peter p.493
Krueger, Brian D. p.170
Krueger, Richard A. & Casey, Mary Anne p.686
Krueger, Richard A. & King, Jean A. p.136
Krueger, Richard A. p.136
Krug, Edward A. p.327
Krug, Gary J. p.760
Kruger, Arnd & Murray, William (Editors) . p.807, p.846, p.891
Kruger, Arnd & Riordan, James (Editors) p.807, p.888
Krugman, Paul p.244
Krupnick, Charles p.639, p.654
Krutilla, John V. & Fisher, Anthony C. p.62
Kryzanek, Michael J. & Wiarda, Howard J. p.592
Kubasek, Nancy K., et al. p.51
Kubiak, Greg D.. . . . . p.534
Kubicek, Paul J.. . . . . p.127
Kubler-Ross, Elisabeth p.742
Kucer, Stephen B.. . . . . p.354, p.364
Kugler, Eileen Gale p.309
Kuhlmann, Hilke p.499
Kuhn, Bowie p.807, p.851, p.884
Kuhn, Cynthia, et al.. . . . . p.826
Kuhn, Philip A. & Brook, Timothy (Editors) p.620
Kuiper, Edith & Barker, Drucilla K.. . . . . p.274
Kuiper, Edith & Sap, Jolande p.274
Kuklick, Henrika. p.4
Kuklinski, Jim (Editor). p.483
Kukreja, Veena p.617, p.618
Kularatna, Nihal & Dias, Dileeka p.115
Kulick, Don (Author, Contribution by) p.19
Kulick, Don. p.746
Kull, Andrew p.457
Kunstler, Barton Lee p.66
Kunstler, James Howard p.771
Kupchan, Charles p.642
Kuper, Leo p.435
Kurain, George T. (Editor), et al. p.517
Kuran, Timur p.207, p.237
Kurian, George Thomas, et al. p.575
Kurihara, Kenneth K. (Editor) p.232
Kurland, Philip B.. p.470
Kuroda, Yasumasa p.622
Kursmark, Louise M. p.170
Kurtz, Donald V. p.34
Kurtz, Ernest p.776
Kurz, Heinz D. & Salvadori, Neri (Editors) p.218
Kurz, Heinz-Dieter & Salvadori, Neri p.218
Kus, Sally p.794, p.869, p.904
Kushell, Jennifer. p.167
Kushner, Harvey W. p.678
Kushner, Tony & Knox, Katharine p.668
Kuska, Bob. p.807, p.832, p.854
Kusserow, Adrie p.733
Kutska, Kenneth S., et al. p.787, p.796
Kuttner, Robert p.665
Kux, Dennis. p.644
Kuzio, Taras & D'Anieri, Paul J. (Editors). p.585, p.598
Kuzio, Taras. p.598
Kuznar, Lawrence A. p.24
Kvistad, Gregg p.609
Kwoka, John E. & White, Lawrence J. (Editors) . . p.84, p.109
Kwolek-Folland, Angel p.57
Kyambalesa, Henry & Houngnikpo, Mathurin C. p.384
Kydd, Andrew. p.624
Kydland, Finn E. (Editor) p.244
Kymlicka, Will. p.547, p.551, p.573, p.579
Kyrk, Hazel. p.265
Kyvig, David E.. . . . . p.454

L

Labaree, Leonard W.. . . . . p.553
LaBarre, Weston p.36
Labovitz, John R. p.462
Lachapelle, Guy, et al. p.589
LaCugna, Charles S. p.122
Ladd, Brian p.582
Ladd, Helen F. & Yinger, John M. p.544
Laderman, Carol & Roseman, Marina (Editors) p.46
Laderman, Carol p.46
Ladies Professional Golf Association Staff. p.837, p.861
Ladner, Joyce A. (Editor). p.683
Ladson-Billings, Gloria. p.310
Laffaye, Horace A. p.844, p.863
Lagemann, Ellen Condliffe p.355
Lagendijk, Arnoud & Oinas, Päivi. p.397
Lager, Fred C. p.52
Lahav, Gallya p.637, p.668

Laidler, David. p.225, p.238
Laird, Pamela Walker. p.53, p.132, p.147
Lajoux, Alexandra Reed & Nesvold, H. Peter p.84
Lake, David A. & Powell, Robert (Editors) p.625
Lakeman, Enid p.577
Laker, Anthony (Editor) p.796, p.817
Laker, Anthony p.796, p.798, p.799
Lakoff, George & Johnson, Mark p.20, p.27
Lakoff, George p.20
Lakoff, Robin Tolmach p.21
Lakoff, Sanford p.504
Lalli, Carol M. & Parsons, Timothy p.392
Lamanna, Mary Ann p.681
Lamb, Chris p.409, p.417, p.807, p.832, p.851
Lamb, Margaret (Editor), et al. p.107
Lambek, Michael p.36
Lambert, Josiah Bartlett p.127
Lambert, Stephen E. p.170
Lamberti, Jean-Claude p.492
Lambeth, Edmund B. p.405
Lambsdorff, Johann Graf, et al.. . . . . p.252, p.263
Lamont, Michele (Editor). p.728
Lan, Yi-Chen & Unhelkar, Bhuvan p.69
Lancaster, Lynne C. & Stillman, David p.132
Lanctot, Neil p.807, p.832, p.851, p.884, p.888, p.896
Landau, Ralph (Editor), et al.. . . . . p.244
Lander, Guy p.109, p.111, p.112
Landes, David S. p.237, p.265
Landry, Paul & McNair, Matty p.788, p.789
Landsberg, Brian K. p.532
Landsmann, Liliana Tolchinsky p.369
Landy, Joanne M. & Burridge, Keith R. p.798
Lane, Harold E. & Dupré, Denise p.161
Lane, Jan-Erik p.75
Lang, Frieder R. & Fingerman, Karen L. p.741
Langer, Arthur M. p.79
Langer, Georgea M., et al. p.286
Langer, John p.414
Langer, Judith p.136
Langford-Wood, Naomi & Salter, Brian p.173
Langley, Winston E. p.513
Langston, Craig & Lauge-Kristensen, Rima p.113
Langton, Phyllis & Kammerer, Dianne p.675
Langum, David J. p.473
Lanham, Richard A. p.173
Lanier, Doris p.776
Lanier, Drew Noble p.537
Lansdown, Richard (Editor) p.385
Lansford, Tom p.564, p.631, p.660
Lansing, Robert Jr.. . . . . p.631
Lanson, Jerry & Fought, Barbara Croll p.414
LaPalombara, Joseph. p.594
Lapan, Maureen & Houghton, Raymond p.357
Lapchick, Richard E. (Editor) p.822, p.894
Laqueur, Walter p.510, p.660
Larana, Enrique (Editor), et al. p.710
Lareau, Annette p.728
Largey, Michael p.26
Larossa, Ralph p.739
Larres, Klaus p.645
Larsen, Clark Spencer p.14
Larsen, Jeffrey Arthur & Smith, James M. p.656
Larsen, Stein U; Hagtvet, Bernt; Myklebust, Jan P p.768
Larson, Edward J. p.438
Larson, Reed & Eccles, Jacquelynne S. (Editors) p.288
Lasch, Christopher p.704, p.768
Laski, Harold J. p.767
Laslett, John M. (Editor) p.127
Laslett, Peter (Editor), et al. p.740
Laslett, Peter p.704, p.737
Lasser, William p.537
Lasswell, Harold D. (Editor), et al. p.696
Lasswell, Harold D. (Editor) p.696
Lasswell, Harold Dwight p.483
Latash, Mark L. & Zatsiorsky, Vladimir M. (Editors) p.873, p.908, p.909
Latash, Mark L.. . . . . p.908, p.909
Latin American Network Information Center (LANIC) . . p.704
Latsis, Spiro J. (Editor). p.269
Latzko, William J. & Saunders, David M.. . . . . p.73
Laub, John H. & Sampson, Robert J. p.753
Lauber, Daniel & Atkin, Jennifer p.170
Lauber, Daniel & Rice, Kraig. p.170
Lauber, Daniel. p.170
Laudicina, Paul A. p.69
Lauffer, Robert Butch & Kater, April p.837, p.867
Lauglo, Jon & Maclean, Rupert (Contribution by) p.305
Laumann, Edward O. (Editor), et al.. . . . . p.748
Laumann, Edward O., et al.. . . . . p.748
Laurel, Brenda p.55, p.57, p.63
Lauren, Paul G. p.513
Laurentis, Giacomo De (Editor). p.155
Laurie, Simon S.. . . . . p.327
Laux, James M. p.154
Lavallee, Daniele p.12
Lavallee, David & Wylleman, Paul (Editors) p.903
Lavallee, David, et al. p.877
Lave, Jean p.27
Lavin, David E. & Hyllegard, David p.294
Lavin, Michael R. p.180
Lavin, Michael p.180
Lavinia, Stan (Editor) p.600
Lavoie, Marc (Editor) p.232
Law Library of Congress . . . p.437, p.440, p.474, p.475, p.476
Lawal, H. Bayo p.690
Lawhorne, Clifton O. & Long, Howard R. p.443
Lawler, E. L., et al. p.119
Lawless, Richard (Editor) p.765
Lawoti, Mahendra p.617
Lawrence, Frederick M. p.568

Lawrence, T. J. *p.631*
Lawrence-Lightfoot, Sara. *p.353*
Lawson, Joseph Chappell H. *p.409*
Lawson Mack, Raneta & Kelly, Michael J.. . . . . *p.564*
Lawson, Russell *p.87*
Lawson, Stephanie. *p.624*
Lawson-Borders, Gracie *p.418*
Lawton, Denis & Gordon, Peter. *p.339*
Laybourn, Keith *p.127*
Layman, Nancy S.. . . . . *p.450*
Lazarsfeld, Patricia K. (Editor) *p.685*
Lazarus, Edward. *p.537*
Lazarus, Neil (Editor) *p.485*
Lazarus, Richard J. *p.448*
Lazerson, Marvin & Grubb, W. Norton (Editors) *p.353*
Le Billon, Philippe (Editor). *p.400*
Le Bon, Gustave. *p.713*
Le Breton, Binka *p.728*
Le Play, Frederic *p.685*
Le Vine, Victor T. *p.612*
Leab, Daniel J. *p.524*
Leach, E. R. *p.34*
Leach, John *p.247*
Leach, Richard H., et al. *p.582*
Leach, Rodney *p.603, p.637*
Leacock, Stephen *p.379*
Leahy, James E.. *p.537*
Leahy, Robert L.. *p.272*
Leamer, Edward E. *p.202*
Leaptrott and Company Staff & Leaptrott, Nan *p.56*
Lear, Roma. *p.784, p.801, p.830*
Lease, Ronald C., et al. *p.91, p.95*
Leavitt, Howard B. (Editor) *p.277, p.313*
LeBaron, Dean & Vaitilingam, Romesh *p.95*
Lebovics, Herman *p.608*
Lebow, Irwin *p.420*
LeBow, Richard Ned *p.484, p.626*
Lechner, Frank & Boli, John (Editors) *p.55*
Leckie, William H.. . . . . *p.718*
LeCompte, Mary Lou *p.837, p.865*
Lederer, Laura (Editor). *p.748*
Lee, Alfred McClung *p.410*
Lee, Charles R. Jr.. . . . . *p.474*
Lee, Courtland C. (Editor) *p.353*
Lee, Francis Graham. *p.486*
Lee, Frederic S.. . . . . *p.233, p.242*
Lee, Jay & Wong, David W. S. *p.387*
Lee, Martin A. & Shlain, Bruce. *p.704*
Lee, Richard B. & Daly, Richard (Editors) *p.3*
Lee, Richard B. & DeVore, Irven. *p.38*
Lee, Thomas W.. *p.689*
Lee, Yeonwoo. *p.230, p.235*
Leeds, Anthony. *p.37*
Leeman, Richard W.. . . . . *p.660*
Leenders, Michiel R., James A. Erskine and Louise A. Mauffette-Leenders. *p.177*
Lees, Stan *p.84*
Leeson, Robert (Editor) *p.225, p.228, p.232*
Lee-Treweek, Geraldine & Linkogle, Stephanie *p.690*
Lefebvre, Henri *p.680*
Leff, Laurel *p.411*
Lefèvre, Edwin & Marketplace Books *p.95, p.102*
LeGates, Richard *p.387*
Legault, Albert & Fortmann, Michel *p.644, p.656*
Lehaney, Brian (Editor) *p.77*
Leheny, David Richard *p.784, p.834, p.898*
Lehman, Jeffrey & Phelps, Shirelle *p.437*
Lehmann, Michael B. *p.96*
Lehman-Wilzig, Sam N. *p.615*
Leibold, Mathew A. (Editor), et al. *p.394*
Leick, Alfred *p.390*
Leifer, Eric M. *p.851, p.888, p.891, p.896*
Leijonhufvud, Axel *p.225, p.240*
Leishman, Rory *p.541*
Leiss, William, et al.. . . . . *p.140*
Leiter, Richard A. *p.441*
Leland, Suzanne M. & Thurmaier, Kurt M. *p.542, p.544*
Lele, Milind *p.82*
Lemann, Nicholas *p.286*
Lemarchand, Reni *p.653*
Lemco, Jonathan *p.524, p.581, p.590*
Lemert, Charles C. *p.683, p.685*
Lemert, Charles *p.675, p.683*
Lencioni, Patrick M. & Lencioni, Patrick *p.80*
Lender, Mark Edward & Martin, James K.. . . . . *p.700*
Lenehan, Pat *p.826*
Lengermann, Patricia Madoo & Niebrugge-Brantley, Jill . *p.680*
Lengnick-Hall, Mark L. & Lengnick-Hall, Cynthia A. . . . *p.76*
Lengwiler, Yvan *p.263*
Lenin, V. I.. . . . . *p.237, p.506, p.508*
Lenneberg, Eric H. (Editor). *p.357*
Lenski, Gerhard E.. . . . . *p.722*
Lenskyj, Helen Jefferson *p.846, p.884, p.888, p.891*
Lent, Adam *p.711*
Leo, Richard A. & Thomas, George C. III (Editors) . . . *p.473*
Leon, Joseph J. Sr., et al.. . . . . *p.691*
Leonard, Dorothy & Swap, Walter *p.66, p.80*
Leonard, George. *p.327*
Leonard, H. Jeffrey *p.63*
Leonard, R.L. (Richard Lawrence) *p.638*
Leonard, Thomas C. *p.404*
Leonard, Wilbert Marcellus. *p.817*
Leone, Richard C. & Anrig, Gregory *p.564, p.572, p.660*
Leontief, Wassily *p.213, p.259*
Lepore, Monica, et al. *p.792, p.801*
Lerner, Janet W.. . . . . *p.318*
Lerner, Max. *p.343*
Leslie, Marina. *p.499*
Lessig, Lawrence *p.435, p.446*
Lester, James P., et al. *p.566*

Lester, Paul Martin & Ross, Susan Dente (Editors) *p.416*
Lester, Robin *p.807, p.858, p.894*
LeTendre, Gerald K. (Editor) *p.335*
Letts, William J. IV & Sears, James T. (Editors) *p.309*
Letwin, William *p.444*
Leuchtenburg, William E. *p.466*
Levenstein, Harvey A. *p.127*
Leverett, Flynt (Editor). *p.564*
Levi, Edward H.. . . . . *p.441*
Levin, Barbara B. *p.277*
Levin, Henry M.. . . . . *p.299*
Levin, James & Nolan, James F. *p.284*
Levin, Louis *p.777*
Levine, Andrew. *p.504, p.506, p.507*
Levine, Arthur & Weingart, John R.. . . . . *p.294*
Levine, Arthur (Editor). *p.331*
Levine, Arthur. *p.294*
Levine, Robert A. (Editor). *p.35*
Levinson, Bradley A. U. (Editor), et al. *p.302*
Levinson, Daniel J. & Levinson, Judy D. *p.741*
Levinson, Daniel J. *p.741*
Levinson, David & Christensen, Karen *p.848*
Levinson, David (Editor) *p.678*
Levinson, Marc *p.96, p.102, p.103*
Levi-Strauss, Claude *p.24*
Levit, Alexandra. *p.167*
Levit, Nancy *p.442*
Levitan, Sar A., et al. *p.253, p.254, p.265*
Levitas, Ruth *p.499*
Levitt, Arthur & Dwyer, Paula *p.96*
Levitt, Geoffrey M. *p.564*
Levitt, I. M.. . . . . *p.135*
Levitt, Joseph *p.644, p.656*
Levitt, Matthew *p.564*
Levitt, Peggy *p.44*
Levitt, Steven D. & Dubner, Stephen J. *p.185, p.271*
Levy, Alan H. *p.524, p.817, p.832, p.859, p.896*
Levy, Frank & Murnane, Richard J.. . . . . *p.253, p.254*
Levy, Frank *p.244, p.245, p.254, p.265*
Levy, Leon & Linden, Eugene. *p.96, p.100*
Levy, Leonard W. & Karst, Kenneth L. (Editors) *p.454*
Levy, Leonard W. (Author, Editor) *p.452*
Levy, Leonard W. *p.435, p.452, p.456, p.459, p.473*
Levy, Richard S.. *p.609*
Levy, Robert I. *p.43*
Levy, Robert M. & Rubenstein, Leonard S. *p.442*
Levy, Sidney J. & Rook, Dennis W. (Editors) *p.135*
Levy-Livermore, Amnon (Editor) *p.261*
Lewin, Ariel. *p.9*
Lewin, Ellen & Leap, William L. (Editors) *p.24, p.25*
Lewin, Kurt *p.695*
Lewis, Anthony. *p.405, p.443, p.473*
Lewis, Bernard *p.614*
Lewis, Catherine C. *p.364, p.370*
Lewis, Colin D. *p.117*
Lewis, David H.. . . . . *p.844, p.866*
Lewis, Herschell Gordon & Nelson, Carol *p.140*
Lewis, Herschell Gordon *p.173*
Lewis, I. M. *p.36*
Lewis, Justin *p.425*
Lewis, Michael M.. . . . . *p.89, p.92, p.96, p.100, p.103*
Lewis, Oscar *p.704, p.733*
Lewis, P. S.. . . . . *p.704*
Lewis, Paul (Editor) *p.259*
Lewis, Paul H. *p.592*
Lewis, Peter & Booth, Jerry (Editors) *p.413*
Lewis, Richard D. *p.56*
Lewis, Thomas, et al. *p.738*
Lewis, W. Arthur *p.259, p.268*
Lewis-Beck, Michael S. (Editor), et al. *p.686*
Lewis-Beck, Michael S. (Editor) *p.609*
Lexis Nexis Staff, et al. *p.105, p.106, p.107*
LexisNexis *p.140, p.150*
Leyens, Jacques-Philippe, et al. *p.694*
López Luján, Leonardo & Levin, Judy *p.10*
Lâm, Maivân Clech *p.33*
Li, Ming, et al. *p.888*
Library of Congress Staff, et al.. . . . . *p.767*
Library of Congress *p.367, p.437, p.476, p.481, p.517, p.574, p.612*
Lichtenstein, Nelson *p.127*
Lichtenthal, J. David (Editor) *p.176*
Lidor, Ronnie & Henschen, Keith P. (Editors) *p.877*
Lidor, Ronnie, et al. *p.877*
Lieber, Robert J. *p.625, p.641, p.642*
Lieberman, Jethro K. *p.441, p.454*
Lieberman, Philip *p.19*
Lieberthal, Kenneth & Dickson, Bruce. *p.620*
Liebow, Elliot *p.704*
Lieven, Anatol & Trenin, Dmitri (Editors) *p.638*
Lifton, Betty J. *p.343*
Lifton, Robert J.. . . . . *p.653*
Light, Paul Charles *p.546*
Lightfoot, Sara Lawrence. *p.303*
Lijphart, Arend & Grofman, Bernard N. (Editors) *p.576*
Lijphart, Arend & Waisman, Carlos H. (Editors) *p.504*
Lijphart, Arend *p.502, p.504*
Lillard, Angeline Stoll *p.337*
Lillard, Paula P. *p.343*
Lilleker, Darren G. & Lees-Marshment, Jennifer (Editors) *p.545, p.577*
Lilleker, Darren G.. *p.425*
Lillesand, Thomas M., et al. *p.388*
LIM *p.400*
Lin, Nan *p.269*
Lincoln, Bruce *p.564, p.660*
Lincoln, Chris *p.885, p.888, p.894*
Lind, David & Sanders, Scott Patrick *p.867, p.871*
Lindberg, Jill A., et al. *p.284*
Linden, Eugene *p.394*

Lindenbaum, Shirley *p.46*
Linder, Douglas O. *p.438*
Lindesmith, Alfred R. *p.449*
Lindfors, Judith Wells *p.423*
Lindgren, Mats & Bandhold, Hans *p.82*
Lindqvist, Sven *p.817, p.869*
Lindsay, James & Daalder, Ivo *p.560*
Lindsey, Almont *p.127*
Lindsey, Duncan. *p.756*
Linehan, Thomas P. *p.582*
Lingard, C. Cecil *p.590*
Linger, Daniel Touro *p.39*
Linkon, Sherry L. (Editor) *p.302*
Linsky, Arnold, et al.. . . . . . *p.699*
Linton, Ralph *p.695*
Lintott, Andrew *p.501*
Linz, Juan J. & Stepan, Alfred *p.505*
Lipham, James M., et al.. . . . . . *p.282*
Lipka, Richard P. & Brinthaupt, Thomas M. (Editors). . . *p.279*
Liponski, Wojciech *p.848*
Lipper, Joanna. *p.759*
Lippi-Green, Rosina L. *p.21*
Lippit, Victor *p.214*
Lippmann, Walter. *p.425, p.697, p.768*
Lipschultz, Jeremy Harris & Hilt, Michael L. *p.407*
Lipset, Seymour Martin & Bendix, Reinhard. . . . *p.722, p.726*
Lipset, Seymour Martin & Lakin, Jason M. *p.505*
Lipset, Seymour Martin & Marks, Gary *p.507, p.554*
Lipset, Seymour Martin & Meltz, Noah M. *p.122*
Lipset, Seymour Martin *p.586, p.589, p.591*
Lipsey, Mark W. & Wilson, David B. *p.687*
Lipsey, Mark W.. . . . . . *p.686*
Lipsitz, Joan *p.367, p.736*
Lipsman, Ron *p.175*
Lipton, Michael *p.265*
Litan, Robert E. & Nordhaus, William D. *p.444*
Litan, Robert E. (Editor) *p.471*
Little & Mirlees *p.259*
Little, Barbara J. (Editor) *p.7*
Little, Jeffrey B. *p.96, p.100*
Little, Kenneth E.. . . . . . *p.87*
Littleboy, Bruce *p.228*
Liu, Lin & Madej *p.385, p.387*
Liu, Xiaoyuan *p.620*
Liu, Ying (Editor) *p.167*
Lively, Donald E. *p.457, p.537*
Livesay, Harold C.. . . . . . *p.127*
Livia, Anna & Hall, Kira (Editors) *p.21*
Livingstone, David N. & Withers, Charles W. J. (Editors) *p.375*
Livingstone, David N. *p.374*
Llewellyn, Karl N.. . . . . . *p.439*
Lo, Andrew W. (Editor) *p.263*
Lo, Vai Io (Contribution by) *p.122*
Loasby, Brian J.. . . . . . *p.195, p.215*
Lock, Gary *p.7*
Lock, Margaret (Editor, Contribution by) *p.47*
Locke, John & Fraser, Alexander Campbell *p.195*
Locke, John *p.215, p.216, p.343, p.492*
Locke, Robert & Schöne, Katja *p.176*
Lockheed, Marlaine E. & Verspoor, Adriaan M. *p.314*
Lockwood, Victoria S. *p.385*
Loescher, Gil *p.634, p.670*
Loevy, Robert D. (Editor) *p.457*
Loewe, Michael & Shaughnessy, Edward L. *p.9*
Lofland, John Jr.. . . . . . *p.692*
Lofland, John *p.696*
Lofland, Lyn H. *p.771*
Loftus, Elizabeth F. *p.473*
Logan, Deborah Anna & Sanders, Valerie (Editors) *p.195*
Logan, Michael F. *p.544*
Logsdon, Bette J. *p.798*
Lohr, Eric. *p.653*
Lomax, Michael E.. . . *p.807, p.832, p.851, p.885, p.888, p.897*
Lomax, Richard G. *p.355*
Lombardi, Vince. *p.697*
Lombardo, John. *p.859, p.894*
Lombroso-Ferrero, Gina & Savitz, Leonard D. *p.752*
Lomnitz, Larissa Adler de *p.704*
Lomolino, Mark V. & Heaney, Lawrence R. *p.394*
Lomolino, Mark V. (Editor), et al.. . . . . . *p.394*
London Times Staff, London Times *p.379*
Long, Carolyn N. *p.439*
Long, David & Schmidt, Brian C. (Editors) *p.625*
Long, Douglas. *p.118*
Long, Edward L. Jr. *p.290*
Long, Frank (Editor). *p.202*
Long, J. Scott *p.689*
Long, John *p.789*
Long, Ngo Vinh *p.704*
Longley, Paul A. (Editor), et al.. . . . . . *p.387*
Longley, Paul A., et al.. . . . . . *p.387*
Longstreet, Stephen *p.777*
Loomis, Burdett A. (Editor). *p.534*
Lopata, Helena Z. (Editor) *p.741*
Lopata, Helena Z. *p.741*
Lopez, Ian F. *p.457*
Lopez, Nancy *p.315*
Lorange, Peter (Editor). *p.176*
Lorber, Judith *p.746*
Lord, John *p.338*
Lorde, Audre Geraldine *p.744*
Lorey, David E. *p.335*
Lorin, Philippe & Alonso, Cristina *p.141*
Lorr, Maurice *p.689*
Lorsch, Jay W. (Editor), et al. *p.54, p.86, p.109*
Losey, Mike (Editor), et al. *p.76*
Lott, Bernice & Maluso, Diane (Editors). *p.698*
Lott, John R. *p.541*
Loughman, Michael *p.789*

Lourandos, Harry *p.13*
Lovejoy, Paul E.. . . . . *p.728*
Lovejoy, Thomas E. & Hannah, Lee (Editors) *p.394*
Loveman, Brian *p.592*
Lovett, Charlie *p.846, p.863*
Lovinger, King F. (Compiled by) *p.529*
Low, Linda (Editor) *p.398*
Low, Pak Sum (Editor). *p.394*
Lowe, Benjamin *p.811*
Lowe, Donald M. *p.775*
Lowe, Stephen R.. . . . . *p.861, p.885, p.891, p.897*
Lowenstein, Roger *p.96, p.98, p.100, p.147*
Lowenthal, David ; Comitos, Lambros. *p.704*
Lowes, Mark D.. . . . . *p.407*
Lowie, Robert H. *p.3*
Lox, Curt, et al.. . . . . *p.875, p.877*
Lu, Xiaobo *p.620*
Lublin, David. *p.551, p.553*
Lubman, Stanley B. *p.475*
Lubrano, Annteresa *p.421*
Lucas, Christopher J.. . . . . *p.331*
Lucas, Gavin *p.6*
Lucas, George L., et al. *p.908*
Lucas, John A. *p.846*
Lucas, Robert E. B. *p.259, p.265*
Lucas, Robert E. Jr. & Sargent, Thomas J. (Editors) *p.203, p.233, p.238*
Lucas, Robert E. Jr.. . . . . *p.233, p.238, p.244*
Luce, Mary Frances, et al. *p.203*
Lucy, John Arthur. *p.20*
Luderer, Bernd, et al. *p.175*
Ludwig, Arnold M. *p.483*
Luger, Dan & Pook, Paul *p.865, p.879*
Luger, Stan *p.154*
Luhrmann, Tanya M. *p.36*
Luker, Kristin. *p.768, p.775*
Lulat, Y. G-M.. . . . . *p.335*
Lum, Grande *p.74*
Lumpkin, Angela, et al. *p.802*
Lumsden, Linda J.. *p.519*
Lund, Jacalyn Lea & Kirk, Mary Fortman. *p.798, p.799*
Lundestad, Geir. *p.638, p.642*
Luraghi, Raimondo *p.521*
Lurie, Rosanne *p.170*
Lury, Celia *p.261*
Lust-Okar, Ellen. *p.615*
Luton, Larry S. *p.542*
Lutz, Donald S. *p.452*
Lutz, James M. & Lutz, Brenda J.. . . . . *p.660*
Lutz, Mark A.. . . . . *p.207, p.209*
Luxemburg, Rosa & Bukharin, Nikolai I. *p.236*
Luxemburg, Rosa & Graf, William David *p.236*
Luxemburg, Rosa, et al. *p.236*
Luxemburg, Rosa *p.236, p.245*
Lybbert, Blair *p.287*
Lye, Colleen *p.485*
Lyles, Marjorie A. & Crossan, Mary *p.79*
Lynch, Eleanor W. & Hanson, Marci J. (Editors) *p.316*
Lynch, James (Editor), et al. *p.309*
Lynch, John. *p.592*
Lynch, Marc *p.415*
Lynch, Sharon J.. . . . . *p.367*
Lynd, Helen M. *p.704*
Lynd, Robert S. & Lynd, Helen M. *p.704*
Lynd, Staughton & Lynd, Alice (Editors) *p.127, p.766*
Lynn, Barry C. *p.665*
Lynn, Laurence E. Jr. *p.178, p.545, p.580*
Lyon, David *p.562, p.572*
Lyon, Thomas P. & Maxwell, John W.. . . . . *p.61, p.63*
Lyons, Tanya & Pye, Geralyn. *p.384*
Lyons, W. E., et al. *p.542*
Lytle, Donald E. (Editor) *p.357*

M

Ma, Laurence J. C. & Cartier, Carolyn L. *p.765*
Ma, Liping *p.364*
Maaba, Brown, et al.. . . . . *p.335*
Maantay, Juliana & Ziegler, John *p.387*
Mabert, Vincent A. & Jacobs, F. Robert (Editors) *p.116*
MacAndrew, Craig & Edgerton, Robert B.. . . . . *p.776*
MacAvoy, Paul & Millstein, Ira M.. . . . . *p.86*
MacAvoy, Paul W. & Millstein, Ira M. *p.52, p.54, p.111*
MacCambridge, Michael . . . *p.807, p.859, p.897, p.902, p.907*
MacCoby, Eleanor E. *p.737*
MacCoun, Robert J. & Reuter, Peter. *p.777*
Macdonald, Lynda A. C. *p.131*
MacDonald, Ronald *p.414*
MacDonnell, Lawrence J. & Bates, Sarah F. (Editors). . . *p.463*
MacDowell, Douglas M. *p.433*
Macedo, Stephen *p.328, p.547*
MacGaffey, Janet & Bazenguissa-Ganga, Remy *p.44*
MacGregor, Brent *p.415*
Machiavelli, Niccolo. *p.492, p.502*
Machin, Stephen & Vignoles, Anna *p.297*
Machover, Carl *p.116*
Macintosh, Donald & Hawes, Michael *p.891, p.898*
Macintosh, Donald & Whitson, David. *p.891, p.898*
Macintosh, Donald, et al.. . . . . *p.588*
Mack, Arien (Editor). *p.778*
MacKay, Charles *p.244*
Mackenzie, Hettie Millicent Hughes. *p.343*
Mackey, Robert Russell *p.521*
Mackie, Gerry. *p.505*
Mackie, Thomas T. & Rohds, Richard. *p.577*
MacKinnon, Catharine A. *p.442, p.446, p.459*
MacKinnon, Frank. *p.590*
MacKinnon, Kenneth *p.416*
Mack-Kirschner, Adrienne *p.278, p.338, p.348*
Macleod, David I. *p.719*

MacManus, Susan A p.524
Macmillan Library Reference Staff p.678, p.777
MacMillan, Margaret. p.630
Macpherson, C. B.. . . . . p.590
Macqueen, J. G. p.9
MacQueen, Norrie. p.584, p.649
MacRae, Duncan Jr. p.769
MacShane, Denis p.127
Madan, Vandana p.772
Maddala, G. S. p.203
Madden, Frederick & Darwin, John (Editors). p.435
Madden, Frederick & Fieldhouse, David (Editors) p.436
Madden, Frederick (Editor) p.435
Madden, Kirsten & Seitz, Janet. p.214, p.274
Maddex, Robert L. p.435, p.574
Madge, Tim p.777
Maeroff, Gene I.. . . . . p.322
Maffetone, Phillip p.827, p.829
Magee, David p.69
Magill, Richard A.. p.909
Magleby, David p.460
Maglischo, Ernest W. p.868, p.879
Magnusson, Lars (Editor) p.216, p.233
Magone, Jose M. p.603, p.638
Mahadeva, Lavan & Sinclair, Peter p.246
Mahaney, Ian F. p.390
Maharidge, Dale. p.767
Mahler, Gregory S. p.615
Mai, Larry L., et al.. . . . . p.15
Maier, Ernest (Editor), et al. p.180
Maier, Mark H. p.690
Main, Jackson Turner p.518
Maine, Henry Sumner p.433
Maine, Sir, Henry Sumner p.33
Mair, Douglas & Miller, Anne p.195
Mair, Peter (Editor) p.602
Mair, Victor H. p.9
Maira, Sunaina p.704
Maisel, L. Sandy (Editor). p.551
Maisel, Louis S. (Editor). p.548, p.551
Maiwald, Eric p.114
Major, Patrick & Mitter, Rana (Editor, Translators) p.486
Majumdar, Shyamal K. (Editor), et al.. . . . . p.392
Majumdar, Sumit (Editor), et al. p.190
Mak Lau Fong p.719
Maker, C. June & Nielson, Aleene B. p.317
Makoto, Kumazawa, et al. p.122
Makower, Joel p.63
Malamuth, Neil M. & Donnerstein, Edward p.748
Malaspina, Margaret A.. . . . . p.96, p.109
Malesevic, Sinisa p.600
Malia, Martin E. p.508, p.598
Malik, Yogendra K. & Singh, V. B p.618
Malik, Yogendra K. p.642, p.644
Malinowski, Bronislaw p.3, p.4, p.28, p.700, p.737
Malinvaud, Edmond p.256
Malkiel, Burton Gordon p.96
Mallaby, Sebastian p.244, p.265
Mallett, Margaret p.364
Mallios, William S. p.203, p.207
Mallon, Bill & Buchanan, Ian p.807, p.846
Mallon, Gerald p.756
Mallory, Bruce & New, Rebecca p.369
Malloy, Robin P. & Evensky, Jerry (Editors) p.219
Malone, David M. & Khong, Yuen Koong (Editors) . . . p.642
Malone, David M. (Editor) p.634
Malone, John W.. . . . . p.866
Malone, Lyn, et al.. p.387
Malone, Thomas W. (Editor), et al.. . . . . p.77
Malonis, Jane A. (Editor) p.113
Malpezzi, Stephen & Green, Richard (Editors) p.166
Malsberger, John W. p.534
Maltby, Marc S.. . . . . p.807, p.859
Maltese, John A.. . . . . p.537
Malthus, T. J. p.389
Malthus, Thomas. R.. . . . . p.763
Malthus, Thomas Robert. p.218, p.221, p.222
Maltz, Earl M. p.468, p.537
Maluccio, Anthony N. (Editor), et al. p.758
Malveaux, Julianne & Green, Reginna A. (Editors) p.564
Mamdani, Mahmood, et al. p.711
Mancini, Marc. p.161
Mandel, Maud. p.653
Mandelbaum, Michael p.817
Mandell, Richard D.. . . . . p.807, p.846
Manent, Pierre. p.492
Manes, Stephen & Andrews, Paul p.158
Mangan, J. A. & Da Costa, Lamartine P. (Editors) p.716
Mangan, James A. & Walvin, James (Editors) p.817
Mangone, Gerard J. p.629
Mangun, William R. & Henning, Daniel H. p.62
Manheim, Jarol B.. . . . . p.52, p.54, p.145
Manion, Melanie p.620
Manke, Mary Phillips p.349
Mankiw, N. Gregory & Romer, David (Editors) p.225
Mankiw, N. Gregory (Editor) p.246
Mann, Alfred K.. . . . . p.525
Mann, Horace p.344
Mann, Michael p.660, p.715
Mann, Thomas E. & Ornstein, Norman J. p.530
Mann, Thomas E. p.549
Mannes, Aaron p.660
Mannheim, Karl p.685
Manning, Matt p.149
Manning, Robert E. p.786, p.787
Manovich, Lev p.419
Mansfield, Harvey C. Jr. p.492
Manson, William C.. p.35
Manton, Catherine p.778
Manusov, Valerie & Patterson, Miles L. (Editors). p.424

Manusov, Valerie Lynn (Editor) p.424
Manzoni, Jean-Francois & Barsoux, Jean-Louis p.131
Maogoto, Jackson Nyamuya p.653
Maoz, Zeev p.650
Mapel, David & Nardin, Terry p.766
Mappes, Thomas A. & Zembaty, Jane S. p.484, p.770
Marable, Manning p.573
Maraniss, David p.859
Marc, David. p.418
Marcel, Valerie & Mitchell, John V. p.398
Marcet, Jane H. p.195
Marcet, Jane p.218
March, James G; Olsen, Johan P p.280
Marchak, M. Patricia & Marchak, William. p.660
Marchak, M. Patricia. p.164
Marchand, Roland p.144, p.426, p.429
Marchant, Mary A. & Williamson, Handy Jr. (Editors) . . p.268
Marciniak, Arkadiusz p.12
Marconi, Joe p.145
Marcosson, Samuel A. p.538
Marcuse, Herbert p.508, p.685, p.700, p.761
Marfleet, Philip p.400
Margolick, David p.808, p.855
Margolin, Leslie. p.737, p.758
Margolis, Wendy (Editor), et al.. . . . . p.439
Mariampolski, Hy p.139
Marinel, Alan Le p.87
Marion, Nancy E. p.567
Maritain, Jacques p.344, p.513
Mark, Margaret & Pearson, Carol S.. . . . . p.144
Markell, Patchen p.513, p.514
Markham, Jerry W. p.89, p.104, p.109, p.147
Markoff, John p.772
Markowitz, Linda p.127
Marks, Jonathan p.14, p.15, p.17
Marks, Stephen P. p.668, p.670
Marlatt, G. Alan (Editor) p.779
Marquardt, Michael, et al. p.79
Marquart, James W., et al. p.567
Marschark, Marc & Spencer, Patricia Elizabeth (Editors) . p.318
Marschark, Marc, et al.. . . . . p.318
Marsden, George M p.331
Marsh, Charles, et al. p.173
Marsh, David C.. . . . . p.704
Marsh, Ian p.618, p.622
Marsh, Peter (Editor). p.295
Marshak, David p.287
Marshall, Alex. p.771
Marshall, Alfred & Marshall, Mary P. p.224
Marshall, Alfred. p.224, p.238
Marshall, Catherine & Rossman, Gretchen B. p.687
Marshall, Mac (Editor) p.776
Marshall, Mac. p.43, p.45
Marshall, P. J. & Low, Alaine (Editors) p.605
Marsilius of Padua. p.490
Martens, Rainer p.904
Martínez, Rubén. p.765
Martijn, Jan K. p.257
Martin, Andrew & Ross, George (Editors) p.212
Martin, Bill & Avakian, Bob p.507, p.508
Martin, Bruce, et al. p.787
Martin, Chester p.587, p.605
Martin, Christopher p.127
Martin, Emily p.47
Martin, Fenton S. & Goehlert, Robert p.466, p.530
Martin, Geoffrey J.. p.378
Martin, Janet M.. . . . . p.527
Martin, Jeanette S. & Chaney, Lillian H. p.56
Martin, John D. (Author, Editor) p.64, p.91
Martin, Joyce. p.66
Martin, Peter p.117
Martin, Randy & Miller, Toby p.817
Martin, Seelye. p.389
Martin, Shannon E. & Copeland, David A. (Editors) p.411, p.417
Martin, Simon p.808, p.817, p.867, p.891
Martin, Waldo E. p.439
Martindale, Don p.680
Martineau, Harriet p.193, p.209, p.218, p.269
Martinez, J. Michael (Editor), et al. p.567
Martinez, Samuel p.41
Martinez-Vergne, Teresita & Knight, Franklin W. (Editors) p.41
Marty, Martin E. & Appleby, R. Scott (Editors) p.722
Marty, Martin E. & Moore, Jonathan p.307, p.486
Marullo, Sam p.561
Marvin, Carolyn & Ingle, David W. p.767
Marvin, Carolyn. p.416
Marwick, Arthur p.705, p.724
Marx, Anthony W.. . . . . p.494
Marx, Elisabeth. p.56
Marx, Karl & Engels, Friedrich . . . p.222, p.236, p.507, p.509
Marx, Karl & Tucker, Robert C. p.507
Marx, Karl, et al. p.507, p.508
Marx, Karl p.215, p.218, p.236, p.238, p.492, p.681
Marzano, Robert J. & Kendall, John S. p.286
Marzano, Robert J., et al.. . . . . p.284
Marzano, Robert J.. p.364
Marzola, Alessandra & Silva, Francesco (Editors) p.228
Mascie-Taylor, C. G. Nicholas (Editor, Contribution by). p.14
Mason, Alpheus T. p.468, p.470
Mason, David. p.147, p.155
Mason, John Edwin p.727
Mason, Mary A.. . . . . p.442, p.740
Mason, Mary Ann (Editor), et al. p.733
Mason, Robert J. & Mattson, Mark T. p.159
Mason, Ronald, J.. . . . . p.11
Mason, Tony p.817, p.844, p.867
Mason, W. Dale p.465

Massa, Mark S.. . . . . *p.817, p.859, p.894*
Massengale, John & Swanson, Richard A. (Editors) *p.808, p.873*
Massey, Douglas S. & Denton, Nancy A. *p.730*
Massey, Douglas S., et al. *p.571*
Masson, Marilyn A.. . . . . *p.10*
Masson, Paul R. & Pattillo, Catherine *p.398*
Masters, William H., et al. *p.748*
Masterson, William H.. . . . . *p.644, p.645*
Masyny, Vojtech & Byrne, Malcolm (Editors) *p.630*
Matejko, Alexander J. *p.705*
Mathabane, Mark *p.731*
Mather, Paul M.. *p.389*
Mathis, Robert L. & Jackson, John H. *p.76*
Matless, David *p.399*
Matossian, Mary K. *p.778*
Matthews, Fred H.. . . . . *p.685*
Matthews, Jana B., et al. *p.68*
Matthews, Joseph L. & Matthews Berman, Dorothy . *p.96, p.98*
Matthews, Mervyn *p.705*
Matthews, Peter H. *p.18*
Mattimore, Bryan W. *p.66*
Mattock, John *p.59*
Mattox, Gale A. & Rachwald, Arthur R. (Editors) . *p.630, p.639*
Maud, Peter J. & Foster, Carl (Editors) *p.791, p.875*
Mauer, Marc *p.753, p.773*
Maughan, Ronald J.. . . . . *p.825, p.876*
Maughan, Ron *p.825, p.876*
Maung, Mya *p.617*
Maurer, Bill *p.41*
Maury, Matthew Fontaine *p.394*
Mauser, Gary A.. *p.558*
Mauss, Marcel *p.28*
Maveety, Nancy *p.468*
Mawdsley, Evan & White, Stephen *p.598*
Maxton, Graeme P. & Wormald, John *p.154*
Maxwell, Bruce *p.660*
Maxwell, Daniel G. & Barrett, Christopher B. . . . *p.259, p.265*
Maxwell, John C.. *p.71*
Maxwell, Kenneth *p.608*
Maxwell, Moreau *p.11*
May, Larry *p.713*
May, Steve (Editor). *p.53, p.173*
Mayer, Bernard S. *p.74*
Mayer, Kenneth R.. . . . . *p.462*
Mayer, Margit & Ely, John *p.610*
Mayer, Susan & Peterson, Paul E. (Editors) *p.265*
Mayer, Thomas *p.195, p.238, p.246*
Mayer, William G. & Busch, Andrew E.. . . . . *p.549*
Mayer, William G. *p.551, p.553*
Mayhew, David R.. . . . . *p.551*
Mayhew, David *p.551, p.552*
Mayhew, Robert J.. . . . . *p.375*
Mayhew, Susan *p.373*
Maynard, Kimberly A. *p.671*
Maynard, Kyle *p.842, p.870*
Mays, Annabelle. *p.335*
Mays, Terry M. *p.650*
Mazur, Eric Michael & McCarthy, Kate *p.712*
Mazurana, Dyan E., et al. *p.650*
Mazurek, Kas & Winzer, M. A.. . . . . *p.316*
Mazzeo, Karen S. *p.793*
Mbaku, John M. & Ihonvbere, Julius O. (Editors). *p.505, p.585, p.612*
Mbaku, John M.. *p.612*
Mbaku, John Mukum & Ihonvbere, Julius Omozuanvbo (Editors) *p.585, p.612*
Mbaku, John Mukum *p.612*
McAdams, A. James *p.610*
McAfee, R. Preston *p.83*
McAllister, Mary Louise *p.581, p.587*
McAllister, Matthew P.. . . . . *p.697*
McArdle, William D., et al. *p.801, p.876*
McArdle *p.875*
McCabe, J. Terrence *p.30*
McCaffery, Peter *p.551, p.552, p.553*
McCall, Morgan W. & Hollenbeck, George P.. . . . *p.59, p.120*
McCann, Charles R. (Editor) *p.191*
McCann, Charles R. Jr. (Editor). *p.203*
McCann, Charles R. *p.228*
McCardle, Peggy & Chhabra, Vinita (Editors) *p.364*
McCarry, John & O'Leary, Brendan (Editors) *p.607*
McCarthy, George E.. . . . . *p.683*
McCarthy, Martha M., et al. *p.450*
McCarthy, Ronald & Sharp, Gene. *p.650*
McChesney, Robert Waterman & Scott, Ben *p.558*
McChesney, Robert W.. . . . . *p.416, p.425*
McClain, Carol S. (Editor). *p.47*
McClain, Charles J. *p.457*
McClaurin, Irma (Editor) *p.31*
McClellan, B. Edward *p.306*
McClellan, James *p.468*
McClellan, Keith *p.859, p.897, p.902*
McClellan, Michael *p.118*
McCloskey, Deirdre N.. . . . . *p.185*
McCloskey, Robert G. *p.466*
McClusky, Pamela & Thompson, Robert Farris *p.26*
McCollum, James K.. . . . . *p.509*
McCombs, Maxwell *p.697*
McCormac, Jack C. *p.389*
McCourt, Frank *p.338*
McCoy, Alfred W. & De Jesus, Ed. C. (Editors) *p.705*
McCoy, Alfred *p.562*
McCoy, Roger M. *p.389*
McCraw, Thomas K. (Introduction by) *p.147, p.148*
McCrone, Kathleen E. *p.808, p.837*
McCulloch, John R. *p.216, p.240*
McCullough, Laura L. & Tanner, Brenda M.. . . . . *p.288*
McCusker, John J.. . . . . *p.57, p.147, p.175, p.180*
McDermott, Kevin & Agnew, Jeremy *p.509*

McDermott, Rose *p.484, p.642*
McDonagh, Eileen *p.472*
McDonald, Forrest *p.517*
McDonald, James H. *p.45*
McDonald, Lynn *p.683*
McDonald, Malcolm & Keegan, Warren J. *p.144*
McDonald, Malcolm & Morris, Peter *p.135*
McDonald, Nan & Fisher, Douglas *p.364*
McDonald, Peter & Lassoie, James P. (Editors) *p.164*
McDonald, Roderick P. *p.689*
McDonough, John (Editor) *p.140, p.426*
McDonough, Kevin & Feinberg, Walter (Editors) *p.323*
McDonough, Peter, et al. *p.608*
McDougal, Myres Smith *p.478*
McDougall, Len *p.788*
McDowell, Gary L. *p.538*
McEvoy, John & McEvoy, Julia *p.837, p.848*
McEwan, Bonnie G. (Editor) *p.11*
McEwan, Colin (Editor), et al. *p.12*
McEwan, Elaine K. *p.360*
McEwen, William J. *p.142*
McFadden, D. & Fuss, M. *p.248*
McFall, Liz *p.141*
McGahan, Anita M. *p.81, p.149*
McGee, Lea M. & Richgels, Donald J. *p.368*
McGerr, Michael E. *p.552*
McGhee, Robert *p.11, p.379*
McGill, Dan, et al. *p.98*
McGillivray, Alice V., et al. *p.556*
McGimpsey, David *p.818, p.851*
McGlew, James F. *p.500*
McGoldrick, Dominic *p.655, p.660*
McGough, Lucy S. *p.473*
McGovern, George *p.247*
McGown, Carl, et al. *p.869, p.904*
McGrade, Arthur Stephen *p.490*
McGrath, Rita Gunther & MacMillan, Ian C. *p.68*
McGreevy, John T. *p.486*
McGregor, Douglas *p.120*
McGuigan, Patrick B. & Weyrich, Dawn M. *p.538*
McGuinness, Kevin *p.298*
McGuire, C. B. & Radner, Roy (Editors) *p.269*
McKay, Ailsa *p.274*
McKay, George *p.709*
McKay, Jim, et al. *p.818, p.837*
McKay, Jim *p.837*
McKeever, Daniel (Editor) *p.297*
McKeever, Robert J. *p.538*
McKelvey, Maureen & Orsenigo, Luigi *p.156*
McKenzie, Norman & McKenzie, Jeanne (Editors) *p.193*
McKenzie, Richard B. *p.82*
McKenzie, Walter *p.351*
McKerrow, Raymie E. & Gronbeck, Bruce *p.423*
McKim, Robert & McMahan, Jeff (Editors) *p.494*
McKinney, Gordon B. *p.542*
McKinney, John *p.788*
McKinnon, Sharon M. & Bruns, William J. Jr. *p.106*
McKinnon, Susan & Silverman, Sydel (Editors) *p.24*
McKitterick, Rosamond (Editor) *p.381*
McKnight, Lee W. (Editor), et al. *p.421*
McKnight, Thomas K. *p.68*
McKnight, Tom L. *p.382, p.397*
McLanahan, Sara & Sandefur, Gary D. *p.739*
McLanahan, Sara S. (Editor), et al. *p.756*
McLane, Joan B. & McNamee, Gillian D. *p.360*
McLaren, Peter *p.297*
McLaughlin, Andrew Cunningham *p.518*
McLean, Bethany & Elkind, Peter *p.91, p.105, p.106, p.109, p.148*
McLean, Iain & McMillan, Alistair *p.482*
McLeary, Joseph Webb, et al. *p.173, p.175*
McLeavey, Dennis W. & Solnik, Bruno *p.96*
McLellan, David *p.236*
McLuhan, Marshall *p.416*
McMahon, Anthony *p.745*
McMahon, Thomas A. *p.909*
McMaster, Susan E. *p.166*
McMeekin, Robert *p.280*
McMillan, Gregory K. & Considine, Douglas M. *p.116*
McMinn, Winston G. *p.624*
McMurray Robert G. *p.791, p.903*
McMurrer, Daniel P. & Sawhill, Isabel V. *p.266*
McNamara, Robert S. & Blight, James G. *p.562*
McNamee, Mike (Editor) *p.802, p.873*
McNeil, John D. *p.364*
McNett, Jeanne *p.57, p.64, p.180*
McPeck, John E., et al. *p.344*
McPherson, James M. *p.521*
McPherson, Maggie & Nunes, Miguel Baptista *p.322*
McPherson, Michael S. & Schapiro, Morton Owen *p.293*
McQuarrie, Edward F. *p.136*
McSherry, Corynne *p.446*
McSherry, J. Patrice *p.660*
McWhinney, Edward *p.590*
Mead, Chris *p.832, p.855*
Mead, George Herbert *p.693*
Mead, Margaret & Lutkehaus, Nancy *p.23*
Mead, Margaret & Wolfenstein, Martha (Editors) *p.735*
Mead, Margaret *p.23, p.43, p.748*
Mead, Robert Douglas (Author, Illustrator) *p.700*
Mead, Walter Russell *p.560, p.564, p.642*
Meadow, Charles T. *p.418, p.422*
Meadows, Dennis, et al. *p.763*
Means, Barbara, et al. *p.351*
Medding, Peter Y. *p.615*
Medema, Steven G. & Samuels, Warren J. *p.209*
Mediamark Research Inc. *p.137, p.139*
Medley, H. Anthony *p.170*
Medlik, S. *p.161*
Meek, Margaret *p.361*

Meeks, Brian ; Lindahl, Folke p.685
Megarry, Tim. p.17
Meggitt, Mervyn J. p.43
Mehlinger, Howard D. & Powers, Susan M. p.352
Mehta, Uday Singh p.511, p.583
Meier, Daniel p.315, p.361
Meier, David p.68
Meier, Deborah p.328
Meiklejohn, Alexander. p.290, p.344
Meillassoux, Claude. p.28
Meisel, John p.587
Meisler, Stanley p.634
Mekenkamp, Monique (Editor), et al. p.623, p.650
Melamed, Leo & Tamarkin, Bob. p.89, p.148
Meli, Francis p.614
Melissa Cast p.280
Mellars, Paul p.17
Melley, Timothy (Contribution by) p.709
Mellor, Roy p.495
Melnyk, Steven A. & Christensen, R. T. (Contribution by) p.119
Melone, Albert P. p.585, p.600
Melson, Robert p.653
Melton, Reginald F. p.322
Meltsner, Michael p.471
Meltz, Robert, et al. p.463
Meltzer, Allan H. p.228
Melvern, Linda p.653
Melville, Tom. p.808, p.856
Menand, Louis p.298
Menard, Scott p.686
Mendelson, Wallace p.470
Mendenhall, William, et al.. . . . . p.179
Mendras, Henri & Cole, Alistair p.42
Mendras, Henri p.705
Menendez, Albert J. p.382
Menger, Carl p.234
Menifield, Charles E. & Shaffer, Stephen D. (Editors). . . p.530
Menkes, Justin p.71
Mennell, Stephen; Murcott, Anne Otterloo, Anneke H van p.778
Menotti, Francesco p.12
Mentzer, John T. & Moon, Mark A.. . . . . p.137
Mentzer, John T.. p.118
Mercuro, Nicholas, et al. p.62
Merkl, Peter H. (Editor) p.602
Merriam, Sharan B. & Caffarella, Rosemary S.. . . . . . p.320
Merriam-Webster, Inc. Staff. p.373
Merrill, Harwood F. p.116
Merrill, John C. p.405
Merriman, John (Editor) p.705
Merriman, Nick & Schadla-Hall, Tim (Editors) p.5
Merritt, Jennifer p.176
Merry, Henry J. p.532
Merry, Sally E. p.33
Merry, Sally Engle & Brenneis, Donald Lawrence p.43
Merry, Sally Engle p.33
Merton, Robert C. p.238
Merton, Robert K.. . . . . p.680, p.699
Mertus, Julie p.513
Messenger, Christian K. p.812
Messenger, Troy p.720
Messerli, Jonathan p.344
Messina, Anthony M. p.606
Messner, Michael A. & Sabo, Donald F. p.818
Messner, Michael A.. . . . . p.745, p.818
Metcalf, Bill p.740
Metcalf, Peter p.23
Metzler, Michael W. p.796
Meyer, Adolph E. p.328
Meyer, Christopher p.645
Meyer, Karl E. & Brysac, Shareen Blair p.623
Meyer, Karl E. p.642
Meyer, Leisa D. p.766
Meyer, Marshall W.. . . . . p.82
Meyer, Philip p.149, p.405, p.411
Meyer, Thomas p.766
Meyerowitz, Joanne p.744
Meyers, Chet & Jones, Thomas B. p.348
Meyers, Fred E. & Stephens, Matthew P. p.116
Meyers, Herbert M. & Gerstman, Richard p.144
Mezey, Michael L.. . . . . p.527
Mezirow, Jack & Jack Meizirow and Associates Staff. . . p.320
Mäler, Karl-Göran & Vincent, Jeffrey R. (Editors) p.191
M'Gonigle, Michael & Starke, Justine. p.398
Miah, Andy (Editor), et al. p.870
Miah, Andy p.802, p.825, p.872, p.875
Michaelsen, Larry K. (Editor), et al.. . . . . p.350
Micheli, Lyle J. & Jenkins, Mark. p.825, p.866, p.879
Michman, Ronald D. & Mazze, Edward M. p.160
Michrina, Barry P. & Richards, CherylAnne. p.25
Michta, Andrew A.. . . . . p.639
Mickelson, Roslyn Arlin p.335
Mickey, Thomas J.. . . . . p.429
Micklem, Niel. p.714
Middleton, John & Beidelman, Thomas O. p.36
Middleton, Nick p.159
Midgley, James (Contribution by), et al. p.769
Mielke, James H., et al. p.17
Mierzwik, Diane. p.353
Migdal, Joel S. (Editor) p.495
Migdal, Joel S. p.773
Mihesuah, Devon A. & Wilson, Angela Cavender p.312
Milanovic, Branko. p.261, p.266
Miles, Ann p.44
Miles, Hugh. p.415
Miles, John C. & Priest, Simon (Editors) p.796
Miles, Matthew B. & Huberman, A. Michael (Editors) . . p.690
Miles, Raymond E., et al. p.68
Milgram, Stanley p.695

Milkis, Sidney M. & Mileur, Jerome M. (Editors) *p.522*
Milkis, Sidney M. & Nelson, Michael *p.527*
Milkis, Sidney M. *p.527*
Milkman, Ruth & Voss, Kim *p.122*
Mill, John Stuart (Editor). *p.222*
Mill, John Stuart *p.222, p.223, p.344, p.515*
Millar, Dan Pyle & Heath, Robert L. (Editors) *p.173*
Millar, Fergus *p.489*
Millar, James R. (Editor). *p.598, p.599*
Millard, F. *p.596*
Miller, Anita (Editor). *p.538*
Miller, Ann *p.532*
Miller, Arthur G. (Editor). *p.698*
Miller, Brian Cole *p.80*
Miller, Charles B. *p.392*
Miller, Clark & Edwards, Paul N. (Editors) *p.666*
Miller, David H.. *p.631*
Miller, David *p.494*
Miller, Delbert C. & Salkind, Neil J. *p.686*
Miller, Elmer S. *p.37*
Miller, Errol. *p.335*
Miller, Eugene & Pollack, Neuman F. *p.176*
Miller, Frederick A. & Katz, Judith H.. . . . . *p.132*
Miller, G. Wayne *p.848*
Miller, George A. *p.357*
Miller, George H. *p.445*
Miller, Gloria E.. *p.357*
Miller, J. Mitchell & Wright, Richard A. Jr. (Editors) . . . *p.678*
Miller, James D. *p.83*
Miller, Jane E. *p.173, p.179*
Miller, Janet L. *p.279*
Miller, Jerome G. *p.730*
Miller, Kenneth E.. . . . . *p.594*
Miller, Leonard W. *p.832, p.848*
Miller, Melvin D. *p.305, p.353*
Miller, Neal E. & Dollard, John. *p.357*
Miller, P. M. & Wilson, M. J.. . . . . *p.687*
Miller, Patricia D. (Editor). *p.784, p.791, p.801*
Miller, Patrick B. & Wiggins, David K. (Editors) . *p.818, p.832*
Miller, Patrick B. (Editor) *p.818*
Miller, Pepper & Kemp, Herb *p.138*
Miller, R. Robin & Browning, Sandra Lee *p.773*
Miller, Richard E. *p.332*
Miller, Russell. *p.486*
Miller, Timothy *p.499, p.740*
Miller, William & Zemke, Ron *p.143*
Miller, William L. (Editor), et al. *p.582*
Milligan, Jeffrey Ayala *p.335*
Milloy, John. *p.335*
Mills, C. Wright & Jacoby, Russell *p.724*
Mills, C. Wright *p.681, p.724, p.762, p.769*
Mills, E. S. (Editor) *p.191*
Mills, Eric L. *p.392*
Millstone, Eric *p.152, p.165*
Milton, Kay *p.30*
Minchin, Timothy J. *p.127*
Mindell, Phyllis *p.173*
Mindich, David T. Z.. . . . . *p.417*
Mindich, David T. *p.404*
Minear, Richard H. *p.477*
Mingay, G. E.. . . . . *p.705, p.726*
Mingione, Enzo *p.771*
Mingst, Karen A. & Karns, Margaret P. *p.634*
Mingst, Karen A. & Snyder, Jack L.. . . . . *p.625*
Mini, Piero V. *p.228*
Mink, Gwendolyn *p.755*
Minkler, Meredith *p.778*
Minow, Mary & Lipinski, Tomas A.. . . . . *p.451*
Minow, Newton & Lamay, Craig *p.445*
Minowitz, Peter *p.219*
Mintz, Jerome R. *p.42*
Mintz, Sidney W. & Price, Richard. *p.41*
Mintz, Sidney W. *p.41, p.46*
Mintzberg, Henry. *p.64, p.176*
Miracle, Andrew W. Jr. & Rees, C. Roger. . *p.822, p.840, p.885*
Miraldi, Robert *p.406*
Mirowsky, John & Ross, Catherine E.. . . . . *p.699*
Mirrlees, J. *p.244*
Mirvis, Philip H., et al. *p.84*
Mishler, Elliot G. *p.691*
Misnad, Sheikha. *p.335*
Missouri Group Staff, et al.. . . . . *p.414*
Mitchell, Andy *p.387, p.388*
Mitchell, B. R. *p.385*
Mitchell, Debby, et al.. . . . . *p.796, p.862*
Mitchell, Olivia S. (Editor) *p.98*
Mitchell, Paul & Wilford, Rick (Editors). *p.607*
Mitchell, Peter (Editor). *p.384*
Mitchell, Peter J.. *p.8*
Mitchell, Susan *p.138*
Mitchell, Timothy *p.808, p.856*
Mitchell-Tavener, Claire *p.796, p.857*
Mitra, Subrata (Editor) *p.191*
Mitroff, Ian I. & Denton, Elizabeth A.. . . . . *p.52, p.54*
Mittelhammer, Ron C., et al. *p.203*
Miyares, Ines M., et al.. . . . . *p.383*
Mobily, Kenneth E. & MacNeil, Richard . . *p.786, p.801, p.830*
Moch, Leslie Page *p.602*
Mockaitis, Thomas R. & Rich, Paul. *p.564, p.660*
Modell, Arnold H.. . . . . *p.693*
Modell, Judith *p.32*
Modigliani, Franco & Friedman, Milton *p.232*
Modigliani, Franco. *p.210*
Modoc Press Staff & American Association of Colleges for Teacher Education Staff (Contribution by) *p.279*
Mody, Ashoka & Pattilo, Catherine (Editors). . . . *p.240, p.266*
Mody, Bella (Editor), et al.. . . . . *p.420*
Moeller, Susan D. *p.407*
Moen, Phyllis (Editor), et al. *p.725*
Moeran, Brian *p.39*

Moerk, Ernst L. p.358
Moerman, Daniel E.. . . . . p.47
Moerman, Michael p.19
Moggridge, Donald E. (Editor) p.228
Moggridge, Donald E.. . . . . p.212, p.228
Moghaddam, Fathali M. & Marsella, Anthony J. (Editors) p.660, p.767
Mohr, James C. p.472
Mokyr, Joel (Editor). p.192, p.212
Mol, Serge p.863
Molnar, Stephen p.17
Moltz, Barry p.68
Momsen, Janet H. (Editor). p.31
Monaghan, Leila Frances (Editor) p.22
Monahan, Patrick J. p.587
Moncrief, Gary F., et al. p.530
Mondale, Sarah & Patton, Sarah B. (Editors). p.328
Moneyhon, Carl H. p.521
Monga, Celestin p.497, p.585, p.612
Mongerson, Paul. p.404
Monmonier, Mark S.. p.386
Monmonier, Mark. p.375, p.385, p.386
Monshipouri, Mahmood p.513
Montagu, Ashley p.14, p.344, p.729, p.737, p.744, p.760
Montana, John C., et al. p.115
Montauk, Richard p.177
Montessori, Maria & Hunt, J.. . . . . p.344
Montessori, Maria p.344
Montet, Christian & Serra, Daniel p.84
Mood, Dale P., et al.. . . . . p.784, p.796
Moody, Peter R. Jr. p.618
Mooij, Marieke K. de p.427
Moon, Jeremy; Sharman, Campbell p.624
Mooney, Chris. p.566
Mooney, James p.37
Moore, Barrington Jr. p.767
Moore, Dorothy Perrin p.68
Moore, Henrietta L., et al.. . . . . p.31
Moore, Henrietta L.. p.24
Moore, Henrietta p.31
Moore, John A. Jr. & Pubantz, Jerry. p.634
Moore, John Allphin & Pubantz, Jerry. p.634
Moore, Keith M.. . . . . p.268
Moore, Mark H.. . . . . p.545, p.546
Moore, Michael G. & Anderson, William (Editors) p.322
Moore, Michael L. & Outslay, Edmund p.92, p.108
Moore, Mike p.665
Moore, Pamela (Editor) p.818, p.844, p.855
Moore, Roy L. p.406
Moore, Wilbert E. p.725
Moorehead, Caroline. p.765
Moos, Rudolf H.. . . . . p.699
Mor Barak, Michàlle. p.132
Morales, Maria H.. . . . . p.223
Moran, Aidan P.. . . . . p.877
Moran, Emilio F. (Editor) p.30
Moran, Emilio F. p.30
Moran, Jeffrey P. p.438, p.736
Moran, John P. p.598
Moran, Michael p.385
Moran, Rachel F. p.457, p.737
Moran, Robert T. & Abbott, Jeffrey D. p.61
Moran, Theodore, et al. p.60
Moran, Theodore p.60
More, Thomas. p.499
Moreau, Joseph p.285
Moreno, Jonathan D. (Editor). p.660, p.669
Moreno, Paul D. p.133, p.447
Morgan, David L. p.137, p.687
Morgan, Gareth. p.66
Morgan, Harry p.310
Morgan, Howard, et al. p.65
Morgan, Marcyliena. p.21
Morgan, Mary S. & Morrison, Margaret (Editors) p.687
Morgan, Mary S. p.203
Morgan, William J. & Meier, Klaus V.. . . . . p.803
Morgenstern, Richard D. p.62
Morgenthau, Hans J., et al. p.626
Morgenthau, Hans J.. p.626
Morley, Richard p.238
Morone, James A.. . . . . p.555, p.579
Morphy, Howard & Perkins, Morgan p.26
Morrall, John B.. . . . . p.489, p.490
Morreale, Joanne p.551
Morris, Andrew D.. . . . . p.808
Morris, Cynthia T. & Adelman, Irma p.237, p.259
Morris, Daniel. p.862
Morris, Evan p.142
Morris, G. S. Don & Stiehl, Jim p.364
Morris, G.S. Don & Stiehl, Jim (Authors) p.304
Morris, James M. & Kross, Andrea L.. . . . . p.678
Morris, Joseph M. & Gole, William J. p.84
Morris, Kenneth M. & Morris, Virginia B. p.96
Morris, Lynn A. (Editor) p.784, p.813
Morris, Thomas D. p.442, p.453
Morris, William p.499
Morrison, Alec (Editor) p.812, p.861
Morrison, Andrea M. & Mann, Barbara J.. . . . . p.60
Morrison, Terri & Conaway, Wayne A. p.56
Morrison, Terri, et al. p.56
Morrison, Terri p.173
Morrison, William F. p.74
Morrissey, Marietta p.728
Morrow, Don & Wamsley, Kevin p.808
Morrow, Raymond A. & Brown, David D.. . . . . p.680
Morrow, Raymond Allen & Torres, Carlos Alberto p.762
Morsink, Johannes. p.435
Mort, Jo-Ann (Editor) p.127
Mortensen, Dale T. p.203, p.244, p.254, p.266
Morton, Margaret p.751

Mosby, David & Weissman, Michael p.73
Mosco, Vincent p.425
Mosconi, Willie & Cohen, Stanley p.855
Moseley, Alexander & Norman, Richard (Editors) p.513
Moseley, Charles J. (Editor) p.159
Moseley, Fred (Editor) p.236
Moskos, Charles C. Jr.. . . . . p.634, p.650
Moss, David A.. p.92
Moss, Norman. p.647
Moss, Philip & Tilly, Chris p.133
Moss, Richard J.. p.716
Moss, Rita W. p.96, p.180
Moss, Wes p.68
Mosse, George L. p.510
Mosston, Muska & Ashworth, Sara p.798, p.799
Motala, Ziyad p.614
Mott, Frank L.. . . . . p.409
Mott, Frank Luther. p.411
Mottram, D. R. p.826
Motyl, Alexander (Editor), et al. p.644
Motyl, Alexander J. (Editor-In-Chief) p.494
Moulakis, Athanasios p.303
Mount, Ferdinand p.733
Mouritzen, Hans & Wivel, Anders p.383, p.400
Moussis, Nicholas p.603, p.638
Mouzelis, Nicos p.680
Mower, A. Glenn Jr. p.435
Mowle, Thomas p.642
Mowrer, Orval Hobart p.358
Mowshowitz, Abbe p.718
Moy, Patricia & Pfau, Michael p.558
Moyer, David B.. p.153
Moynihan, Daniel P.. . . . . p.266, p.769
Mrozek, Donald J.. . . . . p.808, p.818
Mudd, John p.544
Muehlbauer, Gene p.753
Mueller, Dennis C.. . . . . p.576
Muftuler-Bac, Meltem p.638
Muggleton, David & Weinzierl, Rupert p.818, p.846, p.888, p.892
Muggleton, David p.709
Muhlberger, Detlef (Editor). p.768
Muksian, Robert. p.175
Mulcahy, D. G. p.344
Muldoon, James P. Jr. p.629
Muldoon, James. p.501, p.583
Mulford, Charles W. & Comiskey, Eugene E. p.96, p.102, p.105, p.106, p.111
Mull, Richard F., et al. p.786
Mullaney, Marie M. (Compiled by) p.557
Mullen, Megan Gwynne p.421
Mullen, Michelle p.796, p.848
Muller, Nathan J. p.420, p.422
Muller, Robert & Roche, Douglas. p.634
Muller, Thomas p.571
Mulligan, Joseph F. & Mulligan, Kevin T. p.907
Mullin, Bernard J., et al. p.885
Mullins p.675
Mumford, Lewis. p.771
Mun, Thomas p.216, p.257
Munck, Ronaldo. p.236
Muncy, Mitchell S. (Editor). p.525
Muncy, Raymond Lee p.733
Mundell, Robert A. p.247
Mundell, Robert p.238
Mundy, Jean p.784
Munk, Nina p.84
Munnell, Alicia H. & Sunden, Annika p.97, p.99
Munroe, John A.. p.542
Munter, Mary & Haley, Thea p.173
Muraskin, William A. p.719
Muravchik, Joshua. p.507
Murillo, Maria Victoria. p.128
Murphy, Bruce A. p.468
Murphy, Bruce Allen. p.468
Murphy, Gardner p.358
Murphy, John F. p.477
Murphy, Michael (Editor) p.587
Murphy, Patrick E.. . . . . p.173
Murphy, Paul L. p.452
Murphy, Paul V. p.516
Murphy, Raymond. p.680
Murphy, Shane M.. . . . . p.818, p.840
Murphy, Shane p.877
Murphy, Sharon, et al. p.354
Murphy, Walter F., et al. p.465
Murray, Alan S. p.107
Murray, Bill p.844, p.867
Murray, David. p.728
Murray, Michael P.. . . . . p.203
Murray, R. Emmett p.122
Murray, Robert K. p.714
Murray, Stephen O. p.748
Murray, Tim (Editor) p.5
Murrell, Peter C. Jr. p.310
Murtha, Thomas P., et al. p.69
Musgrave, Richard Abel p.247
Musto, David F. & Korsmeyer, Pamela p.568
Mutch, Robert E. p.525
Myers, David B.. p.655
Myers, John G. p.136
Myers, Margaret G. p.247
Myers, Peter C. p.492, p.502
Myrdal, Gunnar p.210, p.214, p.233, p.239, p.244, p.256, p.259, p.269, p.730
Myrdal, Gunner p.730
Mysnyk, Mark, et al.. . . . . p.870

N

Nabokov, Peter *p.841*
Nachmani, Amikam *p.647, p.650*
Nacos, Brigitte Lebens *p.558*
Nadal, Jean-Pierre *p.272*
Nader, Laura. *p.33, p.433*
Nadler, David, et al.. . . . . *p.86*
Naftali, Timothy. *p.565*
Nagal, Robert F.. . . . . *p.462*
Nagel, Joane *p.730*
Nagel, Robert F.. . . . . *p.525*
Nagel, Thomas *p.514*
Nagengast, Carole & Velez-Ibanez, Carlos G. (Editors). . . *p.45*
Nagl-Docekal, Herta & Vester, Katharina *p.744*
Nahuis, Richard. *p.254, p.259*
Naidu, Som *p.352*
Nair, Mohan *p.82*
Naison, Mark *p.552, p.554*
Najita, Joyce M. & Stern, James L. (Editors). *p.123*
Nakamura, Robert T. & Church, Thomas W. *p.109, p.111*
Nakane, Chie *p.705*
Nakanishi, Donald T. & Nishida, Tina Y. (Editors) *p.311*
Nanda, Serena. *p.746*
Napoleoni, Loretta. *p.660*
Narlikar, Amrita *p.61*
Nasaw, David. *p.149, p.328, p.411*
Nash, Gary B.. . . . . *p.380*
Nash, June C. & Fernandez-Kelly, Maria P. (Editors) . . . *p.28*
Nash, June *p.34*
Nash, Paul *p.344*
Nash, Robert J. *p.306, p.307*
Nasr, Seyyed Vali Reza *p.615, p.617*
Nassar, Jamal R. *p.660, p.663*
National Academy of Sciences Staff. *p.561, p.656*
National Academy of Sciences *p.359*
National Agricultural Library. *p.152, p.164*
National Archives and Records Administration (NARA) *p.481, p.556*
National Archives and Records Administration's (NARA) Office of the Federal Register (OFR). *p.481*
National Association of Elementary School Principals. . . *p.282*
National Association of Home Builders *p.159*
National Association of Secretaries of State (NASS) . . . *p.549*
National Center for Education Statistics *p.322*
National Center for Fair and Open Testing *p.286*
National Center for Health Statistics Staff (Contribution by). *p.739*
National Center for History. *p.359*
National Center for Manufacturing Sciences *p.159*
National Clearinghouse on Child Abuse and Neglect Information *p.756*
National Commission on Excellence in Education *p.322*
National Commission on Terrorist Attacks Against the United States *p.481*
National Council for Accreditation of Teacher Education (NCATE) *p.359*
National Council for the Social Studies *p.359*
National Council of Teachers of Mathematics *p.360*
National Education Association *p.283*
National Endowment for the Humanities . . *p.303, p.348, p.350*
National Geographic Society Staff *p.380, p.382, p.392*
National Geographic Society *p.360*
National Home Education Research Institute *p.296*
National Institute for Research Advancement. *p.560*
National Intramural Recreational Sports Association (Nirsa) (Created by). *p.800*
National Middle School Association Staff (Contribution by) *p.367*
National Research Council Staff & Alberts, Betty. *p.361*
National Research Council Staff & Committee on Early Childhood Pedagogy Staff. *p.370*
National Research Council Staff . . . *p.110, p.254, p.295, p.542*
National Restaurant Association. *p.165*
National Security Agency. *p.481*
National Soccer Coaches of America Staff. *p.867, p.905*
National Staff Development Council. *p.283*
National Strength Training and Conditioning Association *p.791, p.903*
National Writing Project Staff & Nagin, Carl. *p.364*
Natriello, Gary *p.299*
Naumes, William & Naumes, Margaret J. *p.178*
Navaretti, Giorgio Barba & Venables, Anthony J. . *p.257, p.261*
Navarro, Peter. *p.177*
Nayar, Baldev Raj *p.400*
Naylor, Phillip C. *p.584*
Nee, Victor & Swedberg, Richard (Editors) *p.215, p.271*
Needler, Martin C.. *p.593*
Neely, Mark E. Jr.. *p.521*
Negron-Muntaner, Frances *p.712*
Neier, Aryeh *p.653*
Neihart, Maureen *p.317*
Neill, William J. V. *p.395*
Neimark, Peninah Rhodes & Mott, Peter (Editors) *p.566*
Neipert, David *p.57, p.110*
Nell, Edward J. *p.228*
Nelson, Adam R. *p.344*
Nelson, Bruce *p.128*
Nelson, Carl A.. . . . . *p.56*
Nelson, Daniel *p.128*
Nelson, David M. *p.808, p.859*
Nelson, Douglas R. & Vandenbussche, Hylke (Editors) *p.257, p.262*
Nelson, Gary M., et al.. . . . . *p.758*
Nelson, Harold N. (Editor) *p.459*
Nelson, Julie A.. . . . . *p.196, p.270*
Nelson, Lyle Emerson *p.528*
Nelson, Mariah B.. . . . . *p.818, p.837*
Nelson, Richard R. & Winter, Sidney G.. . . . . *p.233*
Nelson, Robert L. & Bridges, William P.. . . . . *p.447*
Nelson, Sarah Milledge. *p.9*
Nelson, William E. *p.455, p.457, p.474, p.538*

Nemeth, Neil p.411
Nemiro, Jill p.67
Nerlove, Marc p.203
Ness, Immanuel & Ciment, James p.678
Ness, Immanuel (Editor) p.678
Ness, Immanuel p.128
Nettl, Bruno p.26
Nettl, J. P.. . . . . p.193
Nettle, Daniel & Romaine, Suzanne p.19
Neuman, Susan B. & Dickinson, David K. (Editors) p.358, p.369
Neumayer, Eric p.63
New Strategist Publications, Inc. Staff (Editor) p.138
New Strategist Publications, Inc. Staff p.138
New York University School of Law Staff & Kaczorowski, Robert J. p.525
New Zealand, Ministry of Foreign Affairs p.634
Newbury, Catharine p.582, p.584, p.612
Newby, Howard (Author, Editor) p.772
Newcomb, Horace (Editor) p.415
Newcomb, Horace p.418
Newell, Karl M. (Editor) p.908, p.909
Newman, Frank, et al. p.332
Newman, John Henry p.290
Newman, Katherine S. p.33, p.725, p.771
Newman, Lex (Editor) p.196
Newman, Michael p.603
Newman, Paul & Ratliff, Martha (Editors) p.19
Newman, Peter (Editor) p.191, p.434
Newman, Richard (Editor), et al. p.572
Newman, Roger K. p.468, p.538
Newmyer, R. Kent p.468
Newton, Douglas P. p.348, p.364
Newton, Judith Lowder p.711
Newton, Lisa H.. . . . . p.61, p.64
Newton, Michael T. p.582, p.608
Ng, Sek H. & Warner, Malcolm p.128
Ngai, Mae M.. . . . . p.460, p.571
Nguyen, Dat & Burson, Rusty p.834, p.859
Nice, David C. p.525
Nicholas, H. G. p.635
Nicholas, Sian p.413
Nichols, Beverly p.796, p.798
Nicholson, Philip Yale p.128
Nicklaus, Jack p.861
Nicolet, Claude p.377
Nicolle, David p.380
Nie, Norman H., et al. p.505, p.547
Niebuhr, Reinhold p.484, p.496, p.770
Nieto, Sonia (Editor) p.311
Nietz, John Alfred p.285
Nietzsche, Friedrich p.344
Nieuwenhuys, Olga p.40
Nijkamp, Peter & Mills, E. S.. . . . . p.191
Nijkamp, Peter (Editor) p.191
Nill KimballR. p.156
Nimmo, Dan D. p.549
Nisbet, Robert A. & Himmelfard, Gertrude p.290, p.332
Nisbet, Robert A.. . . . . p.680, p.683, p.685, p.700
Nishiguchi, Toshihiro (Editor) p.118
Niskanen, William A. p.86
Nissen, Bruce (Editor) p.128, p.572, p.665
Niu, Xiaodong p.344
Niven, Paul R. p.73, p.82
Nixon, Judith M. p.161
Noakes, Timothy D.. . . . . p.866, p.875, p.879
Noam, Eli p.420
Noble, David F. p.170
Noble, Keith A. (Editor, Compiled by) p.339
Noblit, George W. & Hare, R. Dwight p.24
Noddings, Nel p.306, p.307, p.339
Noel-Hume, Ivor p.14
Nof, Shimon Y. (Editor) p.116
Nofsinger, John & Kim, Kenneth p.87
Nofsinger, John R. & Kim, Kenneth p.86
Nofsinger, John R. p.97
Noguera, Pedro p.315
Nohlen, Dieter (Editor), et al.. . . . . p.612
Nolan, Dennis R. p.123
Nolan, James L. Jr. & Meister, Denise G. p.283
Nolan, James L. p.449
Nolan, Riall p.45
Noll, Roger G. & Zimbalist, Andrew (Editors) . . . p.888, p.897
Nolt, John p.382
Noonan, John T. Jr. p.443
Noonan, John Thomas p.538
Norcliffe, Glen p.808, p.857
Nord, David Paul p.149
Nord, Warren A.. . . . . p.307
Norden, Deborah L. p.592
Nordin, Margareta & Frankel, Victor H. p.908
Nordlund, Marcie p.316, p.350
Nordlund, Willis J.. p.128
Nordstrom, Karl F. (Author, Editor) p.392
Norgren, Jill p.465
Norman, George & LaManna, Manfred (Editors) . . p.207, p.252
Norris, James D.. . . . . p.426
Norris, John p.644
Norris, Pippa p.577
North, Douglass Cecil p.196, p.210, p.248
Northedge, F. S. p.631
Northey, Margot & Knight, David B. p.376
Norton, Philip (Editor) p.575
Norton, William p.396
Norwick, Kenneth P. & Chasen, Jerry S.. . . . . p.441
Novak, John (Editor) p.277
Novak, Joseph D. p.358
Novak, Michael p.55, p.167, p.803
Novak, Steven J.. . . . . p.332
Novak, William J. p.440

Novick, Sheldon M. p.469
Novshek, William p.203
Nozick, Robert p.511
Nsamenang, A. Bame p.335
Nuckolls, Charles W. p.35
Nuechterlein, Jonathan E. & Weiser, Philip J. p.52, p.111, p.166, p.420
Nugent, Walter p.571, p.765
Nussbaum, Martha C. & Sen, Amartya (Editors) p.266
Nutt, Paul C. p.83
Nuwer, Hank p.288
Nye, Joseph S. p.626
Nye, Robert A. p.705
Nyren, Chuck p.138

O

OABITAR, (Objectivity, Accuracy, and Balance In Teaching About Religion) p.299
Oakes, Elizabeth H. p.825
Oakeshott, Michael p.492, p.493
Oakley, Allen p.230, p.236
Oakshott, Les p.179
Oates, Joyce Carol p.812, p.856
Obeyesekere, Gananath p.43
O'Brien, D. P. p.218
O'Brien, David M. p.443, p.464, p.466, p.538
O'Brien, George Dennis p.290
O'Brien, Kevin J. p.620
O'Brien, Michael J., et al. p.6
O'Brien, Nancy P. & Fabiano, Emily S. p.339
O'Brien, Patrick K. (Editor) p.381
O'Brien, Ron p.860
O'Brien, Teri S. p.791, p.904
O'Brien, Thomas J. p.256, p.263
OceanLaw p.478
Ockey, James p.622
O'Connor, David E. p.192
O'Connor, Rob, et al. p.827, p.828, p.829
O'Connor, Sandra Day p.466
Odem, Mary E. p.736
Odom, Thomas P. p.653, p.715
O'Donnell, R. M. p.228
O'Driscoll, Gerald P., et al. p.270
O'Driscoll, Gerald P. Jr. (Editor) p.219
Oesterle, Dale A. p.85
Offer, D., et al. p.693
Office of Management and Budget p.481
Office of the Federal Register, National Archives and Records Administration p.481
Office of the Law Revision Counsel of the U.S. House of Representatives p.481
O'Flaherty, Michael & Gisvold, Gregory. p.513
Ofshe, Richard & Watters, Ethan p.714
Ogershok, David & Pray, Richard (Editors) p.159
O'Gorman, Frank p.604, p.606
O'Grady, Timothy p.861
O'Hara, Phillip Anthony p.192
Ohles, Frederik M., et al. p.338
Ohles, John F. (Editor) p.338
Ohmae, Kenichi p.70
O'Kane, Rosemary H. p.497
Okano, Kaori & Tsuchiya, Motonori. p.335
Okey, Robin p.509, p.596, p.600
Okigbo, Charl p.398
Okin, Susan Moller p.488, p.490, p.493, p.517
Okker, Patricia p.409
Okun, Arthur M.. p.239
Olasky, Marvin N. p.404
O'Leary, John (Editor). p.826, p.901
Oleksak, Michael M. & Oleksak, Mary A. . p.808, p.833, p.844, p.851, p.899
Oleszek, Walter J. p.532
Olevnik, Peter P., et al.. . . . . p.290
Olfman, Sharna (Editor) p.370
Olivas, Michael A.. . . . . p.312
Oliver, Anne Marie & Steinberg, Paul p.661
Oliver, Douglas L. p.43
Oliver, Douglas. p.43
Oliver, Melvin L. & Shapiro, Thomas M. p.730
Oliver, R. E. p.87
Olivo, Christiane p.610
Ollman, Bertell p.507
Olson, David M.. p.575
Olson, James S. (Editor) p.465, p.583
Olson, Kent p.439
Olson, Leonard T.. . . . . p.841, p.847, p.869
Olson, Paulette I. & Emami, Zohren p.185, p.274
Olssen, Mark p.344
Olufs, Dick W. 3rd. p.420
Olwig, Karen F. p.41
O'Neil, Dennis p.140
O'Neil, Harold F. p.322
O'Neil, Patrick p.509, p.595
O'Neill, Bard E.. p.661
O'Neill, Kathleen p.582
O'Neill, Michael. p.602
O'Neill, William L. p.486
Onkvisit, Sak & Shaw, John J. p.144
Onuf, Peter S. & Sadosky, Leonard J. p.525
Oosterhuis, Harry p.748
Ophir, Adi p.489
Oppenheim, Felix E. p.646
Oppenheimer, Mark p.720
Oppliger, Patrice A. p.818, p.863, p.870
OptimumFinance.net p.152
O'Quinn, Garland Jr. & Hickman, E. Jessica p.798
O'Reilley, Mary Rose p.348
Orelove, Fred P. (Editor), et al. p.318
Oren, Tasha G. & Petro, Patrice. p.419

Orend, Brian *p.513*
Orey, Michael, et al. *p.352*
Orfield, Gary (Editor) *p.299*
Orfield, Gary, et al. *p.301*
Organization of American States *p.437, p.474, p.476*
Oriard, Michael *p.808, p.812, p.818, p.823, p.859, p.885, p.894, p.897, p.902*
Orlans, Harold. *p.705*
Orlick, Terry *p.877*
Orlove, Benjamin S. & Custred, Glynn (Editors) *p.28*
Orme, Nicholas *p.336*
Ormrod, David *p.212*
Ormsby, Tim, et al. *p.388*
Ornstein, Norman J. (Editor) *p.575*
O'Rourke, P. J. *p.185, p.196, p.251*
Orser, Charles E. *p.14*
Orton, Clive, et al.. *p.7*
Orton, Clive *p.7*
Orttung, Robert W. & Reddaway, Peter (Editors) *p.598*
Orwin, Clifford & Tarcov, Nathan (Editors) *p.492*
Osborn, Marilyn, et al.. . . . . *p.336*
Osborne, Martin J. & Rubinstein, Ariel *p.207*
Osborne, Robert D. *p.336*
Osborne, Robin & Cunliffe, Barry W. (Editors) *p.12*
Oser, Fritz K. *p.348*
Osgood, Herbert L. *p.518*
Osgood, Herbert Levi *p.518*
O'Shaughnessy, John *p.139, p.426*
O'Shea, James & Madigan, Charles *p.65*
Oslin, George P. *p.420*
Osmanczyk, Edmund Jan & Mango, Anthony (Editors) . . *p.635*
Ostergren, Robert C.. . . . . *p.571*
Ostergren, Robert Clifford & Rice, John G. *p.397*
Osterhammel, Jürgen *p.583*
Osterman, Paul *p.555*
Ostroff, Frank *p.80*
Ostrow, James (Editor), et al. *p.675*
Ostrower, Francie *p.719*
Ostwald, Martin *p.501*
O'Sullivan, Ellen L. & Spangler, Kathy J.. . *p.786, p.787, p.885*
O'Sullivan, Meghan L.. . . . . *p.565*
Otero, Gerardo (Editor) *p.383*
Otis, Carol L. & Goldingay, Roger *p.825*
Ottaway, Marina & Carothers, Thomas (Editors) *p.615*
Ottaway, Marina (Editor) *p.612*
Ottenberg, Simon & Falola, Toyin *p.38*
Ottenberg, Simon *p.38*
Ottenheimer, Harriet Joseph *p.18*
Otterstrom, Samuel *p.382*
Otteson, James R. *p.219*
Otuathail, Gearoid, et al.. . . . . *p.488, p.496*
Oum, Tae Hoon, et al. *p.152*
Outten, Wayne N., et al. *p.447*
Ouzgane, Lahoucine & Morrell, Robert (Editors) *p.733*
Oved, Yaacov *p.740*
Overy, Richard *p.380*
Owen, Bruce M.. *p.422*
Owen, C. James & York, Willbern *p.543*
Owen, Margaret *p.741*
Owens, Lori J.. . . . . *p.541*
Owens, Philip N. & Slaymaker, Olav *p.391*
Oxford University Press (Created by) *p.104, p.380*
Oxford University Press Staff (Editor) *p.380*
Oxford University Press Staff. *p.380*
Oyewumi, Oyeronke (Editor) *p.744*
Ozbudun, Ergun *p.616*
Ozinga, James R., et al. *p.598, p.600*
Ozkirimli, Umut *p.495*

P

P., Taylor *p.419*
Pacelle, Richard L. Jr. *p.470*
Paciorek, Michael J. & Jones, Jeffrey A. . . *p.784, p.801, p.842*
Pack, Spencer J.. *p.219*
Paczkowski, Andrzej *p.596*
Padden, Carol & Humphries, Tom. *p.700*
Padden, Carol A. & Humphries, Tom L.. . . . . *p.709*
Padro, Fernando F.. . . . . *p.758*
Paehlke, Robert *p.505, p.667*
Paetro, Maxine *p.428*
Pagano, Michael A. & Moore, Richard *p.544*
Page, Edward C. & Goldsmith, Michael J. (Editors) . . . *p.582*
Pagell, Ruth A. & Halperin, Michael *p.180*
Pain, Rachel, et al.. . . . . *p.399*
Paine, Lynn Sharp *p.54*
Pakenham, Thomas *p.583*
Pakroo, Peri *p.87*
Palazzolo, Daniel J. *p.533*
Palda, Kristian S. *p.144*
Paletz, David L. & Schmid, Alex P. (Editors) . . . *p.559, p.661*
Paley, Vivian G. *p.310, p.365, p.370*
Paley, Vivian Gussin *p.310*
Palgrave Macmillan Staff (Editor) *p.293*
Pallister, John, et al. *p.173*
Palloff, Rena M.. *p.322*
Palmer, Bryan D. *p.709*
Palmer, Colin A.. *p.728*
Palmer, Heather *p.796, p.862*
Palmer, Joy A. (Editor). *p.340*
Pammer, William J. Jr. *p.544*
Pampel, Fred C.. *p.153*
Pamuk, Ayse *p.388*
Pandya, Mukul, et al. *p.71*
Pangle, Lorraine S. & Pangle, Thomas L. *p.328*
Pangrazi, Robert P., et al. *p.798, p.799*
Pangrazi, Robert P.. . . . . *p.798*
Panicucci, Jane *p.787, p.798*
Panikkar, Kavalam N. *p.705*
Pankhurst, E. Sylvia *p.604*

Pankhurst, Emmeline *p.604, p.606*
Panter-Brick, Catherine (Editor, Contribution by) *p.28*
Papacosma, S. Victor & Heiss, Mary A. (Editors). *p.639*
Pappano, Laura *p.694*
Pappe, H. O. *p.212*
Paquette, Robert Louis & Ferieger, Louis A. (Editors) . . *p.521*
Parekh, Bhikhu C.. . . . . *p.484, p.768*
Parente, Stephen L. & Prescott, Edward C. *p.196, p.259*
Parenti, Michael *p.498, p.509, p.510*
Pareto, Vilfredo. *p.212, p.248, p.249, p.685*
Parezo, Nancy *p.4*
Paringer, William Andrew *p.344*
Paris, Erna *p.767*
Paris, Scott G. & Stahl, Steven A. (Editors) *p.365*
Parish, William L. & Whyte, Martin K. *p.734*
Park, Ken *p.374*
Park, Michael Alan *p.14*
Park, Robert Ezra & Burgess, Ernest W.. . . . . *p.680*
Park, Robert Ezra *p.713, p.729*
Park, Roberta J. & Mangan, James A. (Editors) . . *p.818, p.837*
Parker, Frank R. *p.555, p.573, p.579*
Parker, Glenn M. *p.80*
Parker, Richard G. *p.31*
Parker, Steve *p.381*
Parker, Walter *p.365*
Parker-Jenkins, Marie, et al. *p.308*
Parkhouse, Bonnie L. *p.786, p.885*
Parkin, David. *p.38*
Parkin, R. J. & Stone, Linda (Editors) *p.32*
Parks, Janet B. & Quarterman, Jerome (Editors) . . *p.885, p.889*
Parmet, Robert D. *p.128*
Parrenas, Rhacel Salazar. *p.44*
Parry, J. H. *p.592*
Parsa, Misagh *p.500*
Parsad, Basmat & Lewis, Laurie *p.277*
Parsons, Craig. *p.638*
Parsons, Talcott & Shils, Edward A.. . . . . *p.692*
Parsons, Talcott & Smelser, Neil J. *p.270*
Parsons, Talcott & Turner, Bryan S.. . . . . *p.675*
Parsons, Talcott (Editor) *p.683*
Parsons, Talcott, et al. *p.738*
Parsons, Talcott *p.680, p.716*
Partin, Ronald L. *p.284*
Pascal, Elizabeth. *p.598*
Pascarella, Ernest T. & Terenzini, Patrick T. *p.290, p.332*
Pass, Susan *p.345*
Passfield, et al. *p.212, p.254*
Pasternak, Burton *p.705*
Pastore, Jose & Haller, Archibald O. *p.705*
Pateman, Roy & Gros, Jean-Germain *p.612*
Paterson, Chris & Sreberny, Annabelle (Editors) *p.407*
Paterson, Lindsay *p.336*
Patinkin, Don & Leith, J. Clark. *p.223, p.225*
Patinkin, Don *p.225*
Patrick, Dale R. & Fardo, Stephen *p.116*
Patrick, Donna *p.21*
Patten, Chris *p.642*
Patterson, James T. *p.450, p.522, p.758, p.778*
Patterson, Kelly D. & Shea, Daniel *p.530*
Patterson, Kerry & Mills, Terence C. (Editors) *p.203*
Patterson, Orlando. *p.727, p.729*
Patterson, Thomas C.. . . . . *p.4*
Patterson, Thomas E. *p.549, p.555*
Pattillo-McCoy, Mary *p.725, p.730*
Paul Cloke, Professor, et al. *p.396*
Paul, Ellen Frankel (Editor), et al.. . . . . *p.507*
Paul, James C. & Schwartz, Murray L. *p.445*
Paul, James L. & Smith, Terry Jo (Editors) *p.338*
Paul, Pamela *p.739*
Paulson, Ed *p.85*
Paulu, Burton *p.412*
Pausewang, Siegfried (Editor), et al.. . . . . *p.612*
Pavlich, George *p.754*
Pavlik, John V. *p.419*
Paxton, Robert O. *p.510*
Payne, Michael *p.142*
Payne, Stanley G. *p.510, p.608*
Payne, V. Gregory & Isaacs, Larry D.. . . . . *p.910*
Payne-Palacio, June & Theis, Monica *p.165*
Payson, Steven *p.196, p.263*
Pearce, Craig L. *p.80*
Pearce, Fred. *p.394*
Pearce, George F. *p.521*
Pearce, Lynne (Editor) *p.174*
Pearlstein, Richard M. *p.661*
Pearsall, Deborah M.. . . . . *p.7*
Pearson, Daniel *p.808, p.851, p.885, p.889, p.892, p.897*
Pearson, Richard J.. *p.9*
Pease, Bob & Pringle, Keith (Editors) *p.744*
Peck, Helen *p.143*
Peck, Robert B. *p.451*
Peck, Robert S. *p.456*
Peden, G. C. *p.228*
Peden, George. *p.228*
Pedersen, Olaf. *p.336*
Peele, Stanton *p.777*
Peers, Laura L. & Brown, Alison K. (Editors). *p.48*
Peet, Richard *p.375*
Peimani, Hooman *p.661*
Pelikan, Jaroslav J.. . . . . *p.303*
Pelinka, Anton & Plasser, Fritz (Editors) *p.579, p.595*
Pelinka, Anton. *p.595*
Pelletier, Ray *p.143*
Pellicani, Luciano *p.661*
Pelling, Henry & Reid, Alastair J.. . . . . *p.606*
Peltzman, Barbara R.. . . . . *p.338*
Pelz, Dave & Frank, James A. *p.861*
Pelzmann, Linda. *p.263*
Pember, Don R. & Calvert, Clay *p.445*
Pemberton, Cynthia Lee A. *p.822, p.837, p.901*

Pempel, T. J. (Editor) *p.618*
Pendarvis, Edwina D., et al. *p.317*
Penn, Helen *p.756*
Penn, Ira A., et al. *p.115*
Pennell, Allison A. (Editor), et al. *p.62*
Penney, Dawn (Editor) *p.796*
Penniman, Howard R. (Editor) *p.590*
Penningroth, Dylan C. *p.705*
Penn-Nabrit, Paula *p.296*
Pennock, James Roland & Chapman, John W. (Editors) . . *p.458*
PennWell Books *p.160*
Penny, Laura *p.141*
Penrith, Deborah (Editor) *p.170*
Peper, George, et al. *p.861*
Pepper, Suzanne *p.336*
Pepper, William F. *p.486*
Peppers, Don & Rogers, Martha *p.143*
Percy, Larry & Elliott, Richard *p.427*
Perelman, Michael *p.67, p.698*
Peretti, Terri J. *p.538*
Perez de Cuellar, Javier *p.635, p.650*
Perinbam, B. Marie *p.705*
Peristiany, J. G. & Pitt-Rivers, Julian (Editors) *p.42*
Perkinson, Henry J. *p.323, p.328*
Perlin, George C. *p.589*
Perlmann, Joel *p.765*
Perman, Michael *p.519, p.573*
Perraton, H. D. *p.314*
Perrin, Tom *p.808, p.859*
Perritt, Henry H.. *p.447*
Perrot, Michelle (Editor), et al. *p.734*
Perrotta, Cosimo *p.246, p.250*
Perrottet, Tony *p.808*
Perrow, Charles *p.717*
Perrucci, Robert & Wysong, Earl *p.725*
Perry, Barbara A. *p.466, p.538*
Perry, H. W. *p.466, p.538*
Perry, Michael J. *p.455, p.456, p.538*
Perseus Publishing Staff (Editor) *p.180*
Perseus Publishing Staff *p.71, p.174*
Persky, Joseph & Wiewel, Wim *p.543*
Pertschuk, Michael *p.52*
Pesaran, M. Hashem & Schmidt, Peter (Editors) . . *p.191, p.203*
Peshkin, Alan *p.297, p.303, p.308, p.315, p.367*
Petchesky, Rosalind P. *p.669*
Peter, J. Paul & Jerry C. Olson *p.139*
Peters, B. Guy & Pierre, Jon (Editors) *p.545, p.580*
Peters, Charles & Nelson, Michael *p.527*
Peters, Emrys L. *p.40*
Peters, John Durham & Simonson, Peter *p.696*
Peters, John Durham *p.416*
Peters, Michael A. *p.345*
Peters, Ronald W. Jr.. . . . . *p.533*
Peters, Shawn Francis *p.308*
Peters, Thomas J. & Waterman, Robert H. Jr. *p.81, p.148*
Peters, Tom *p.67, p.73*
Petersen, Shannon C.. . . . . *p.463*
Petersen, William & Petersen, Renee *p.678*
Petersen, William *p.222*
Petersilia, Joan *p.753*
Peterson, Brooks *p.59*
Peterson, Florence *p.128*
Peterson, Kate Dempsey & Burns, Vincent *p.565, p.661*
Peterson, Lars & Renstrom, Per *p.827*
Peterson, M. P. (Editor) *p.386*
Peterson, Mark A. *p.532*
Peterson, Nancy L.. . . . . *p.738*
Peterson, Paul E. (Editor) *p.328, p.450*
Peterson, Paul E., et al.. . . . . *p.525*
Peterson, Paul E. *p.328, p.525*
Peterson, Theodore B. *p.410*
Peterson's *p.170*
Petitpas, Al, et al. *p.904*
Petraglia, Joseph *p.358*
Petraglia, M. D. & Korisettar, Ravi *p.17*
Petro, Nicolai N. *p.585, p.598*
Petrovich, Janice & Wells, Amy Stuart (Editors) . . *p.299, p.302*
Pettavino, Paula J. & Pye, Geralyn *p.885, p.892, p.899*
Petty, William *p.216, p.254*
Petzinger, Thomas Jr. *p.717*
Pevar, Stephen L. *p.465*
Pfanz, Donald *p.521*
Pfeffer, Jeffrey *p.73*
Pfeifer, Michael J. *p.753*
Pfiffner, James P. *p.527*
Phelan, Craig *p.128*
Phelps, Edmund S.. . . . . *p.240*
Phifer, Paul *p.167*
Philanthropic Research, Inc., ... *p.545*
Philips, Beeman N. *p.353*
Philleo, Joanne (Editor), et al. *p.758*
Phillips, Charles & Axelrod, Alan *p.476*
Phillips, Charles *p.10*
Phillips, Derek L. *p.770*
Phillips, George Harwood *p.542*
Phillips, J. R. *p.379*
Phillips, Jack *p.65*
Phillips, John L. Jr. *p.870*
Phillips, Kevin *p.486, p.572, p.726*
Phillips, Norman R. *p.345*
Phillips, Robert *p.87*
Phillips, Roderick *p.740*
Phillips, Susan *p.714*
Phillipson, David W. *p.8*
Phinnemore, David & McGowan, Lee *p.603, p.638*
Piaget, Jean, et al. *p.358*
Piaget, Jean *p.345, p.358*
Pick, James B.. . . . . *p.388*
Pickerill, J. Mitchell *p.538*
Pickering, Charles W. Sr. *p.541*

Pickles, John p.375
Pieper, Josef. p.784
Pierangelo, Roger & Giuliani, George A. p.316
Pierangelo, Roger p.316
Pierce Colfer, Carol J. & Byron, Yvonne (Editors) p.164
Pierce, T. Jones p.705
Pieroth, Doris Hinson. p.808, p.837, p.846, p.860, p.868
Pierre, Jon & Peters, B. Guy p.580
Pietersen, Jacques & Pietersen, Willie p.79
Pietramala, David G. & Grauer, Neil A. p.862
Pietrusza, David p.808, p.851, p.885, p.889, p.892, p.897, p.902
Pigford, Lois p.170
Piggott, Derek p.787, p.788, p.848
Pigou, Arthur C. p.210, p.228, p.252, p.254
Pillar, Paul R. p.565
Pinar, William F. (Editor). p.365
Pinar, William F.. p.365
Pincus, Fred L. p.516
Pindsdorf, Marion K.. . . . . p.174
Pindyck, Robert S. & Rubinfeld, Daniel L. p.203, p.207
Pinello, Daniel R. p.457
Pink, Sarah. p.818, p.837, p.856
Pinkney, Robert p.576, p.612
Pinsky, Valerie & Wylie, Alison (Editors) p.6
Pinson, Linda & Jinnett, Jerry p.87
Pinson, Linda p.174
Pion-Berlin, David. p.592
Piper, Thomas R., et al.. . . . . p.53, p.177
Pipes, Richard p.509, p.661
Pira, Edward S.. . . . . p.872, p.881, p.906
Piscatori, James P.. . . . . p.500
Piszkiewicz, Dennis p.565
Pitcher, Gayle D. & Poland, Scott. p.353
Pitkin, Hanna F. p.576
Pitt, Ivan L. & Norsworthy, J. R. p.152
Pitt-Rivers, Julian A. p.42
Pitt-Rivers, Julian Alfred ; Abu Zayd, Ahmad p.705
Pitts, Brenda G. & Stotlar, David K. p.786, p.885
Pitts, Victoria. p.26
Pitz, Mary E. p.546
Pitzer, Donald E. (Editor) p.499
Piven, Frances Fox & Cloward, Richard A. p.549
Pixley, Jocelyn p.250, p.261
Pizam, Abraham (Editor-In-Chief). p.161
Pizarro, Marcos p.301
Plasmans, Joseph, et al. p.203, p.240
Plasmans, Joseph p.203
Plato & Bloom, Allan p.489
Plato p.216, p.489
Platt, Anthony M. p.683
Platt, Brian p.336
Platt, Rutherford H. p.382, p.464
Pleck, Elizabeth Hafkin p.742
Pleck, Elizabeth H. p.705, p.734
Pleck, Joseph H.. p.734
Plekon, Michael p.721
Plucknett, Theodore F. T.. . . . . p.436
Pluim, Babette & Safran, Marc . . . p.828, p.864, p.875, p.879
Plummer, Charles C., et al. p.390
Plunkett, Jack W. (Editor). . . p.115, p.150, p.151, p.152, p.153
Plunkett, Jack W. p.113, p.114, p.118, p.153, p.154, p.156, p.170
Plunkett Research, Ltd p.157
Poch, Robert K. & AEHE Staff p.298
Podair, Jerald E.. p.283
Podnieks, Andrew, et al. p.844, p.862
Poirier, Dale J. p.203
Poitras, Geoffrey p.204, p.264
Polanyi, Karl p.196, p.210, p.270
Pole, J. R.. . . . . p.458
Polkinghorn, Bette & Thomson, Dorothy L. p.194
Pollack, Jack p.469
Pollak, Otto p.752
Pollard, Andrew (Editor), et al. p.353
Polletta, Francesca p.711
Pollock, Frederick & Maitland, Frederic William p.436
Pollock, Linda A. p.735
Polsby, Nelson W. p.527
Polsky, Ned p.706
Pomeranz, Kenneth & Topik, Steven p.57, p.147
Pomper, Gerald M. & Weiner, Marc D. (Editors) p.555
Pomper, Gerald M. (Editor). p.531
Pont, Sally p.809, p.859, p.894
Pontuso, James F. p.492
Poo, Mu-chou p.644
Poole, Peter A. p.638
Poole, Ross p.495
Poorvu, William J. & Cruikshank, Jeffrey L. p.97, p.166
Pope, Peter E.. . . . . p.379
Pope, Steven W. (Editor). p.809, p.813
Pope, Steven W.. p.809
Popham, James W.. . . . . p.286
Popham, W. James. p.328
Popkewitz, Thomas S. & Brennan, Marie p.345
Popkewitz, Thomas S. p.315
Popper, Karl R.. . . . . p.488, p.490, p.493, p.517
Pordzik, Ralph p.485
Porrata-Doria, Rafael p.61
Portal, Jane p.9
Porter, Andrew p.605
Porter, Beth p.425
Porter, Carol p.288
Porter, David L. (Editor). p.832, p.833
Porter, Glenn p.567
Porter, John p.706
Porter, Karra p.809, p.837, p.854
Porter, Michael E. . . . p.51, p.57, p.59, p.61, p.64, p.81, p.665
Porter, Michael, et al. p.73
Porter, Micheal E. p.73

Porter, Roy . . . p.706
Porter Sargent Staff (Editor) . . . p.316
Portes, Alejandro & Bach, Robert L. . . . p.571
Portman, Janet & Stewart, Marcia . . . p.442
Portner, Hal . . . p.277
Portney, Paul & Haas, Ruth B. (Editors) . . . p.62
Porto, Brian L. . . . p.822, p.837, p.894, p.901
Posey, Carl A. . . . p.846
Posner, Daniel N. . . . p.612
Posner, Richard A. . . . p.442, p.462, p.528
Pospísil, Leopold . . . p.33
Post, James, et al. . . . p.52
Post, Jerrold M. (Editor) . . . p.512
Post, Jerrold M. . . . p.512, p.698
Post, Karen . . . p.142
Post, Peggy & Post, Peter . . . p.57, p.174
Post, Robert C. . . . p.848
Post . . . p.26
Postlethwaite, T. Neville (Editor) . . . p.313
Postma, G. & Oti, M. N. . . . p.392
Postman, Neil . . . p.323, p.417
Potash, Robert A. . . . p.592
Potter, David M. . . . p.695
Potter, Robert B., et al. . . . p.398
Potter, Stephen R. . . . p.11
Potter, Sulamith Heins & Potter, Jack M. . . . p.40
Potter, Sulamith Heins . . . p.40
Potterfield, Peter . . . p.789
Pottker, Janice & Fishel, Andrew (Editors) . . . p.301
Potuchek, Jean L. . . . p.732
Pound, Richard W. . . . p.846, p.885, p.889, p.892
Pound, Roscoe (Editor) . . . p.440
Pound, Roscoe . . . p.433, p.434
Powdermaker, Hortense . . . p.25, p.43
Powe, Lucas A. Jr. . . . p.459
Powell, Chris & Paton, George E. (Editors) . . . p.773
Powell, G. Bingham Jr. . . . p.577
Powell, G. Bingham . . . p.577
Powell, Robert . . . p.498, p.625
Power, Edward J. . . . p.323, p.340
Power, Marcus . . . p.260, p.268
Power, Paul W. . . . p.305, p.353
Power, Samantha . . . p.715
Powers, Stephen & Rothman, Stanley . . . p.535, p.541
Powers-Beck, Jeff . . . p.809, p.818, p.841, p.851
Poyatos, Fernando . . . p.424
Prahalad, C. K., et al. . . . p.52, p.54
Prahalad, C. K. . . . p.665
Prakash, Aseem . . . p.63
Prasad, Pushkala (Editor), et al. . . . p.132
Prasad, Pushkala, et al. . . . p.132
Prashad, Vijay . . . p.723
Prasow, Paul & Peters, Edward . . . p.447
Pratt, Walter F. . . . p.469
Prebish, Charles S. . . . p.824
Preble, Christopher A. . . . p.565
Preece, Christopher N. (Editor), et al. . . . p.159
Prentice, Alison & Theobald, Marjorie R. (Editors) . . . p.283
Prentice, Alison . . . p.336
Prentice, William E. & Arnheim, Daniel D. . . . p.827, p.828, p.829
Prentice . . . p.828
Prentice-Hall Staff . . . p.399
Prescott, Laurence E. . . . p.336
Preskill, Stephen L. & Jacobvitz, Robin S. . . . p.348
Pressley, Michael . . . p.365
Pressman, Steven . . . p.185, p.208, p.216
Presthus, R. . . . p.591
Prestowitz, Clyde & Prestowitz, Clyde V. . . . p.51
Preucel, Robert . . . p.6
Preuss, Holger . . . p.846, p.889
Preuss, Ulrich K. . . . p.576
Previts, Gary J. & Merino, Barbara Dubis . . . p.104
Price, Miles O., et al. . . . p.439
Price, Richard (Editor) . . . p.41
Price, Richard . . . p.41
Price, Sally . . . p.41, p.48
Price-Cohen, Cynthia (Editor) . . . p.34
PricewaterhouseCoopers LLP Staff . . . p.92, p.107
PricewaterhouseCoopers Staff, et al. . . . p.92, p.105, p.106, p.111
Pricken, Mario . . . p.427
Pride, Armistead S. & Wilson, Clint C. II . . . p.404
Priest, Simon & Gass, Michael A. . . . p.788
Primakov, Yevgeny M. . . . p.661
Primakov, Yevgeny . . . p.598
Primoratz, Igor (Editor) . . . p.661
Princeton Review Publishing Staff . . . p.170, p.171
Princeton Review Staff . . . p.171
Princeton University Conference Staff . . . p.207
Pringle, Keith . . . p.755
Pringle, Peter . . . p.439
Prior, Lindsay . . . p.687, p.775
Pritchett, C. Herman . . . p.456
Pritchett, James A. . . . p.38
Proctor, James D. . . . p.375
Pronger, Brian . . . p.839
Prothrow-Stith, Deborah . . . p.775
Provenzo, Eugene F. Jr. . . . p.307, p.345
Prucha, Francis P. . . . p.465, p.573, p.729
Prunier, Gerard . . . p.653
Prunier, Gérard . . . p.653
Prus, Robert . . . p.687
Pryor, Esther & Kraines, Minda Goodman . . . p.793
Pryor, Frederic L. & Schaffer, David L. . . . p.305
Pryor, Jan & Rodgers, Bryan . . . p.740
Przeworski, Adam (Author, Contribution by) . . . p.505
Przeworski, Adam . . . p.507, p.592
Ptolemy, Claudius . . . p.377
Pucel, David J. . . . p.305
Puddington, Arch . . . p.128

Pudney, Stephen p.204
Pugh, David G. & Bacon, Terry R. p.174
Pugh, Martin p.604
Puhalla, Jim, et al. p.872, p.881, p.906
Pulera, Dominic J. p.730
Punch, Maurice p.690
Purcell-Gates, Victoria, et al. p.304, p.354
Puretz, Susan, et al. p.801, p.880
Purpel, David E. & McLaurin, William M.. . . . . p.306
Putnam, Linda L. & Jablin, Fredric M. p.174
Putnam, Robert D., et al. p.719
Putnam, Robert D.. . . . . p.594, p.706
Puttaswamaiah, K. p.83
Pye, K. & Allen, J. R. L. (Editors) p.392
Pyle, Christopher H. p.473
Pyne, Hnin Hnin, et al.. . . . . p.776

Q

Qin, Duo p.204
Qing, Dai p.620
Quade, Quentin p.280
Queen, Carol p.746
Queen, J. Allen p.288
Quelch, John A. & Deshpande, Rohit (Editors) p.73
Quesnay, Francois p.217
Quigley, Christine. p.15
Quigley, Declan p.723
Quigley, Kevin F. F. p.585, p.640
Quinn, Herbert F. p.590
Quinn, Jane Bryant p.97
Quirk, Charles E. (Editor) p.786, p.885, p.901
Quirk, James & Fort, Rodney D. p.889, p.897
Quirk, William J. & Bridwell, R. Randall p.486, p.538
Qureshi, Emran & Sells, Michael Anthony (Editors) . . . p.661

R

Raabe, William A., et al. p.107
Rabban, David M. p.459
Rabe, Monica p.168
Rabinovich, Itamar. p.650
Rable, George C. p.521
Racine, Jean-Luc & Viramma, Josiane Racine p.40
Radak, Zsolt p.875
Radcliffe-Brown, A. R. & Forde, Daryll (Editors) p.32
Radcliffe-Brown, A. R. p.24
Rader, Benjamin G.. . . . . p.809, p.818, p.851, p.902
Rader, Debra & Sittig, Linda Harris. p.312, p.365
Radice, Lisanne p.606
Radin, Paul A. p.24
Rados, David L.. p.135
Radosh, Ronald & Milton, Joyce p.438
Radzinowicz, Leon & Hood, Roger G. p.436
Radzinowicz, Leon p.752
Rae, Ian & Witzel, Morgen (Editors) p.60
Rae, John p.219
Rafalovich, Adam p.319
Raffaelli, Tiziano p.228
Ragsdale, Cliff T. p.179
Rahm, Dianne p.63
Raiffa, Howard, et al. p.74
Rainsford, Peter & Bangs, David H. Jr. p.165
Rainwater, Lee & Smeeding, Timothy M. p.756
Rainwater, Lee p.775
Rakove, Jack N.. p.452
Ramakrishnan, S. Karthick p.571
Ramanathan, Ramu p.204
Ramen, Fred p.380
Ramirez, Bruno & Otis, Yves p.571
Rampersad, Arnold p.832, p.851
Ramsamy, Edward. p.260, p.268
Ramsay, Anne Fla (Editor) p.603, p.638
Ramsey, Patricia G., et al. p.309
Rand McNally Inc. Staff, et al. p.380
Randal, Jonathan p.661
Randall, Laura (Editor) p.383, p.593
Randall, Richard S. p.451
Ranshofen-Wertheimer, E. F. p.632
Rao, M. Govinda & Singh, Nirvikar. p.618
Raphael, Chad. p.408
Raphael, D. D., et al. p.228
Raphael, D. D. p.212, p.219
Rapoport, David C. & Weinberg, Leonard (Author, Editors). p.497
Rapoport, Ron (Editor) p.812, p.837
Rapp, Rayna p.47
Rappaport, Roy A.. . . . . p.30, p.37
Rapport, Nigel & Overing, Joanna p.23
Raskin, Jamin B. p.450
Rath, Tom & Clifton, Donald O. p.83
Rathburn, Elizabeth & Drummond, Siobhan (Contribution by) p.824, p.837, p.846
Rathvon, Natalie. p.361
Ratledge, Colin & Kristiansen, Bjorn (Editors) p.156
Rattansi, Ali & Westwood, Sallie (Editors) p.44
Rauchhaus, Robert W. (Editor) p.639
Raven-Hansen, Peter (Editor) p.532
Ravetz, Joe, et al. p.395
Ravitch, Diane & Viteritti, Joseph P. (Editors) p.315
Ravitch, Diane p.328
Ravitch, Frank S. p.450
Rawley, James A. & Behrend, Stephen D. p.727
Rawling, Eleanor M., et al. p.378
Rawlins, William K. p.697
Rawls, John p.511, p.514, p.625
Rawson, Jessica (Editor) p.9
Ray, Brian D. p.296
Ray, Larry (Editor) p.196
Ray, Pradeep p.60

Ray, Richard *p.829*
Ray, William B. *p.445*
Rea, Louis M. & Parker, Richard A.. . . . . . . *p.691*
Read, Donald *p.403*
Read, Herbert Edward *p.345*
Read, Jen'nan Ghazal *p.763*
Read, Malcolm & Wade, Paul *p.825*
Reagan, Timothy G. *p.313*
Reamer, Frederic G. *p.758*
Reaves, Joseph A. *p.819, p.834, p.844, p.851, p.899*
Rebach, Howard M. & Bruhn, John G. (Editors) *p.692*
Record, Jeffrey *p.561*
Reddaway, Peter *p.582, p.598*
Redden, John D.. . . . . *p.345*
Reddington, Martin, et al. *p.76*
Redfield, Robert *p.24*
Redish, Martin H. *p.525*
Redman, Eric *p.461*
Redwood, David *p.379, p.381*
Reed, Adolph Jr.. . . . . *p.484*
Reed, Ronald F. *p.323, p.340*
Reed, T.V.. . . . . *p.710*
Reed-Danahay, Deborah *p.29*
Rees, David W. E.. . . . . *p.421*
Rees, Martin *p.661, p.667*
Reese, Anne C. & Vallera-Rickerson, Irini *p.809, p.838*
Reese, William J. *p.328*
Reeve, Andrew & Ware, Alan. *p.577*
Reeve, C. D. *p.489*
Reeve, Fiona (Editor), et al. *p.320*
Reeves, Douglas B.. . . . . *p.65*
Reeves-Ellington, Richard H. & Anderson, Adele. *p.145*
Referee Magazine Staff & National Association of Sports Officials Staff *p.905*
Regalado, Samuel O. *p.809, p.834, p.851, p.897*
Regan, Donald T. *p.529*
Rüegg, Walter (Editor) *p.329*
Rehfeld, Andrew. *p.576*
Rehman, Javaid *p.661*
Rehnquist, William H.. . . . . *p.456, p.466*
Reich, Bernard & Kieval, Gershon R. (Editors). *p.615*
Reich, Bernard *p.615*
Reich, Walter (Editor) *p.661*
Reichert, Tom *p.426*
Reichheld, Frederick F.. . . . . *p.143*
Reid, Alastair J.. . . . . *p.128*
Reid, Daniel. *p.793*
Reid, David A. & Plank, Richard E. (Editors) *p.136*
Reid, John P. *p.452, p.456*
Reid, Richard J.. . . . . *p.582, p.612*
Reid, T. R. *p.638*
Reid, William J.. . . . . *p.758*
Reilly, Mary (Editor). *p.358*
Reilly, Tom & Williams, Mark (Editors) . . *p.868, p.872, p.880*
Reinarman, Craig & Levine, Harry G.. . . . . *p.777*
Reinert, Kenneth A. *p.196*
Reinharz, Shulamit & Davidman, Lynn *p.688*
Reinharz, Shulamit. *p.688*
Reisch, Michael & Andrews, Janice *p.758*
Reisman, Sorel (Editor), et al. *p.322*
Reiss, Mitchell *p.656*
Reitz, Elizabeth J. & Wing, Elizabeth S.. . . . . *p.7*
Rejda, George E. *p.163*
Reksten, Linda E.. . . . . *p.352*
Rembar, Charles, et al.. . . . . *p.472*
Remington, Thomas F. *p.598*
Remnick, David. *p.833, p.856*
Rendall, Jonathan *p.856*
Render, Barry, et al. *p.119*
Renfrew, Colin & Bahn, Paul G. (Editors) *p.6*
Renfrew, Colin & Bahn, Paul *p.5*
Renninger, K. Ann & Shumar, Wesley (Editors) *p.762*
Renninger, K. Ann & Shumar, Wesley *p.762*
Reno, William. *p.612*
Renold, Emma *p.748*
Renshaw, Geoff & Ireland, Norman J.. . . . . *p.204*
Renstrom, P. A. (Editor) *p.827*
Renstrom, Peter G.. . . . . *p.437*
Repa, Barbara Kate *p.131*
Republican National Committee. *p.553*
Research and Education Association Staff *p.440*
Reskin, Barbara F. & Hartmann, Heidi I. *p.254*
Reskin, Barbara F. & Roos, Patricia A. *p.725*
Restivo, Sal P.. . . . . *p.678*
Rettig, Michael D. & Canady, Robert Lynn *p.288*
Reuben, Julie A.. . . . . *p.332*
Reuvid, Jonathan & Hinks, John *p.113*
Reuvid, Jonathan *p.171*
Reyhner, Jon Allan & Eder, Jeanne Oyawin *p.312*
Reyna, Stephen P.. . . . . *p.27*
Reynolds, Arthur J. *p.316*
Reynolds, Cecil R. & Fletcher-Janzen, Elaine (Editors) . . *p.316*
Reynolds, Cecil R. & Fletcher-Janzen, Elaine *p.316*
Reynolds, Cecil R. & Gutkin, Terry B. (Editors) *p.358*
Rheingold, Howard *p.712*
Rhine, Stanley *p.15*
Rhoads, Edward J. M. *p.623*
Rhoads, Robert A.. . . . . *p.398*
Rhodes, Frank Harold Trevor *p.332*
Rhodes, P. J. *p.489*
Ribowsky, Mark *p.809, p.833, p.852*
Ricardo, David & Dobb, M. H.. . . . . *p.221*
Ricardo, David & McCulloch, J. R.. . . . . *p.221*
Ricardo, David, et al. *p.221*
Ricardo, David *p.220, p.221*
Riccucci, Norma M.. . . . . *p.525, p.546*
Rice, Mitchell F. *p.545, p.580*
Rich, Adrienne *p.737*
Rich, Jason R. *p.67*
Rich, Wilbur (Editor) *p.881, p.885, p.889, p.892*

Richani, Nazih . . . *p.616*
Richard III, Golden, et al. . . . *p.114*
Richards, Andrew J. . . . *p.128*
Richards, Audrey I. . . . *p.46*
Richards, David . . . *p.454*
Richards, Jack C., et al. . . . *p.423*
Richards, John A. & Jia, Xiuping . . . *p.389*
Richards, Pamela, et al. . . . *p.753*
Richards, Paul . . . *p.34*
Richardson, Brian W. . . . *p.379*
Richardson, Glenn W. Jr. . . . *p.548*
Richardson, John E.. . . . *p.53*
Richardson, Michael D., et al. . . . *p.280, p.282*
Richardson, Virginia (Editor) . . . *p.355*
Riche, Martha Farnsworth (Editor) . . . *p.179*
Richerson, Peter J. & Boyd, Robert . . . *p.15*
Richman, Karen E. . . . *p.41*
Richmond, Mary E. . . . *p.758*
Richter, Judith . . . *p.145*
Richter, Linda & Morrell, Robert (Editors) . . . *p.734*
Ricketts, Martin . . . *p.224, p.248*
Rickman, Cheryl D.. . . . *p.88*
Ricks, David & Bertola, Giuseppe . . . *p.70*
Riddell, Peter . . . *p.605, p.606*
Riddick, Carol & Russell, Ruth V.. . . . *p.786*
Riddle, Brett R., et al. . . . *p.394*
Riddle, John M. . . . *p.778*
Ridener, Larry E. . . . *p.675*
Rieff, David . . . *p.671*
Ries, Al & Ries, Laura . . . *p.142*
Rieselbach, Leroy N.. . . . *p.531*
Riesenberg, Peter N. . . . *p.578*
Rieser, Andrew Chamberlin . . . *p.721*
Riesman, David . . . *p.212, p.332*
Riesman, Paul . . . *p.38*
Riess, Steven A. . . . *p.809, p.819, p.842, p.852, p.897*
Rigg, Jonathan . . . *p.384*
Riggio, Ronald E. & Feldman, Robert S. (Editors) . . . *p.424*
Riggle, Ellen D. & Tadlock, Barry L. (Editors) . . . *p.569*
Riggs, Robert Edwon . . . *p.635*
Righter, Rosemary . . . *p.635*
Rightmire, G. Philip. . . . *p.16*
Riis, Jacob A. . . . *p.755*
Riker, William H. . . . *p.505*
Rikli, Roberta E. & Jones, C. Jessie. . . . *p.841, p.880*
Riley, Glenda . . . *p.838, p.866*
Riley, Robert Q. . . . *p.154*
Riley, Sam G. (Editor) . . . *p.410*
Rima, Ingrid H. (Editor). . . . *p.204, p.257, p.264, p.270*
Rima, Ingrid H. . . . *p.196*
Rimmerman, Craig A. . . . *p.570*
Rinehart, Robert E. & Sydnor, Synthia (Editors) . . . *p.857*
Ringer, Fritz K. . . . *p.336, p.681*
Riordan, Cornelius H. . . . *p.301*
Riordan, James & Jones, Robin . . . *p.796*
Riordan, J. . . . *p.844, p.892, p.899*
Riordan, Jim & Kruger, Arnd (Editors) . . . *p.844, p.892, p.899*
Rios, Francisco A. (Editor) . . . *p.350*
Ripley, Randall B. & Lindsay, James M. (Editors) . . . *p.531*
Rischar Davis, Pat . . . *p.375*
Risjord, Mark W. . . . *p.688*
Rist, Ray C. (Author, Introduction by) . . . *p.301, p.310*
Ritchie, Jane & Lewis, Jane (Editors) . . . *p.136, p.137*
Rittner, Carol Ann (Editor), et al. . . . *p.653*
Rittner, Carol (Author, Editor), et al. . . . *p.653*
Ritzer, George (Editor). . . . *p.678, p.680*
Ritzer, George . . . *p.683*
Rivkin, Steve & Sutherland, Fraser . . . *p.142*
Rivlin, Alice M.. . . . *p.266, p.525*
Rivoli, Pietra . . . *p.55, p.58*
Rizzello, Salvatore (Editor) . . . *p.272*
Roach, Colleen (Editor) . . . *p.766*
Roach, Kent . . . *p.661*
Robarge, David Scott . . . *p.538*
Robbins, Lionel C.. . . . *p.210*
Robbins, Lionel . . . *p.210*
Robbins, Pam, et al. . . . *p.288*
Robbins, Peter T. . . . *p.63*
Robergs, Robert A. & Keteyian, Steven J. . . . *p.875*
Robert C. Byrd . . . *p.150*
Robert, Henry M. & Evans, William J. (Editors) . . . *p.575*
Roberts, Adam & Kingsbury, Benedict (Editors) . . . *p.635*
Roberts, Brian K. . . . *p.395*
Roberts, Cokie . . . *p.487, p.517, p.569*
Roberts, John & Crossley, Nick (Editors) . . . *p.766, p.774*
Roberts, Ken . . . *p.786*
Roberts, Monty & Grealy, Lucy. . . . *p.848*
Roberts, Nora Ruth . . . *p.485*
Roberts, Peter . . . *p.345*
Roberts, Randy . . . *p.819, p.856*
Roberts, R. . . . *p.706*
Roberts, Robert North & Hammond, Scott J.. . . . *p.556*
Roberts, Russell . . . *p.185*
Roberts, Tim S. . . . *p.350*
Robertson, A. H. & Moon, Nick . . . *p.435*
Robertson, Agnes J. . . . *p.436*
Robertson, David Brian . . . *p.123*
Robertson, David (Editor) . . . *p.482*
Robin, Corey . . . *p.484*
Robin, M.. . . . *p.589*
Robinson, Allan R. & Brink, Kenneth H. . . . *p.392*
Robinson, Archie . . . *p.128*
Robinson, Armstead L.. . . . *p.521*
Robinson, Bryan E. . . . *p.737*
Robinson, Dean E.. . . . *p.573*
Robinson, G. M.. . . . *p.395*
Robinson, Glen O.. . . . *p.463*
Robinson, Jackie W. & Duckett, Alfred . . . *p.833, p.852*
Robinson, Jo Ann Ooiman (Editor) . . . *p.487, p.573*
Robinson, Joan. . . . *p.185, p.196, p.236, p.239, p.241*

, p.244, p.251, p.252, p.253, p.260, p.270
Robinson, Judith p.149, p.411
Robinson, Matthew J., et al. p.905, p.906
Robinson, Paul H. p.471
Robinson, Paul p.570
Robinson, Peter M. p.204
Robinson, Piers p.407, p.415
Robinson, Ray. p.859
Roblyer, Margaret D.. . . . . p.352
Robson, David W. p.332
Robson, John M. p.223
Roche, George p.525
Roche, Maurice p.846, p.889, p.892
Rochlin, James F. p.592, p.593
Rock, Stephen R. p.646
Rockmore, Tom p.236
Rodan p.623
Roddy, Dennis. p.421
Roderick, Melissa p.299
Rodgers, Hilary, et al. p.385
Rodríguez O, Jaime E. p.583
Rodriguez, Luis J. p.714
Rodrik, Dani (Editor, Introduction by) p.240
Roediger, David R. p.571
Roehrig, Alysia D., et al.. . . . . p.279
Roesgaard, Marie H.. . . . . p.336
Rofes, Eric E. & Stulberg, Lisa M. (Editors) p.281
Rogak, Lisa p.88
Rogers, Carl Ransom & Freiberg, H. Jerome p.358
Rogers, Carl Ransom p.739
Rogers, Colin D. p.247, p.270
Rogers, Daniel E. p.610
Rogers, Dwight L. & Babinski, Leslie M. p.279
Rogers, Everett M.. . . . . p.761
Rogers, Mary F. p.688
Rogers, Patricia L. (Editor) p.352
Rogers, Richard G., et al.. . . . . p.742
Rogers, Susan F. (Editor) p.839
Rogerson, Peter A.. . . . . p.376
Rogerson, Peter p.376
Rogerson Staff. p.396
Rogoff, Barbara, et al. p.348
Rogoff, Edward G. p.82
Rogol, Alan D. p.826, p.875
Rohlen, Thomas P. & LeTendre, Gerald K. (Editors) p.336
Rohr, John A. p.546
Rohrschneider, Robert p.610
Rohwer, Claude D. & Skroki, Anthony M.. . . . . p.443
Roitman, Janet L. p.260
Romanek, Broc & Krus, Cynthia M. p.85
Romano, Mary A. p.270
Romanucci-Ross, Lola E. & Moerman, Daniel R. (Editors) p.47
Romer, David p.204
Romero, Jose L.. . . . . p.592
Romm, Norma R. A.. . . . . p.687
Rondinelli, Dennis A., et al. p.314
Roney, C. W. p.137
Roney, R. Craig p.365
Ronstadt, Robert C. p.178
Roodenburg, Herman p.773
Roosevelt, Eleanor & Black, Allida M. p.487, p.569
Roosevelt, Kermit III p.541
Root, Hilton L. p.260, p.261
Root, Maria P. (Editor). p.706
Rorty, Amelie p.323, p.340
Rorty, Richard McKay p.493
Rosaldo, Michelle Zimbalist p.35
Roschelle, Anne R. p.734
Roscoe, Will (Editor) p.746
Roscoe, Will p.31
Rosdolsky, Roman p.236
Rose, Arnold M. (Editor). p.718
Rose, Dan p.25
Rose, Debra J. & Christina, Robert W. . . . p.874, p.908, p.910
Rose, Jessica p.791, p.910
Rose, Jonathan p.726
Rose, Richard & Munro, Neil p.578, p.599
Rose, Richard & Suleiman, Ezra N. (Editors) p.575
Rose, Susan D. p.308
Roseberry, William p.24
Rosecrance, Richard p.498
Rosemont, Franklin & Radcliffe, Charles p.554
Rosen, Allen D. p.514
Rosen, Bernard Carl p.693
Rosen, Ellen Doree p.128
Rosen, Ellen Israel. p.665
Rosen, Greg. p.606
Rosen, Jeffrey p.443
Rosen, Robert N. p.521
Rosenau, Pauline Marie p.682
Rosenbaum, James E. p.305, p.353
Rosenberger, Nancy R. (Editor) p.693
Rosenblum, Jonathan D. p.128
Rosenblum, Nancy L. & Post, Robert C. (Editors) p.499
Rosendahl, Mona p.41
Rosenfeld, Lawrence B. p.758
Rosengren, John p.819, p.840, p.862
Rosenheim, Margaret K. (Editor) p.473
Rosenkranz, E. Joshua & Schwartz, Bernard (Editors) . . p.469
Rosenof, Theodore. p.549
Rosenstone, Steven J. & Hansen, John Mark p.547
Rosenstreich, Peter. p.89, p.97, p.98, p.100
Rosenthal, Alan. p.413, p.531, p.541
Rosenthal, Robert & Jacobson, Lenore. p.358
Rosentraub, Mark S. (Editor) p.525
Rosentraub, Mark S. p.886, p.889, p.892, p.897
Rosenzweig, M. R. & Stark, O. (Editors) p.191
Rosenzweig, Robert M. p.295

Rosin, Gary S. & Closen, Michael L.. . . . . p.75
Roskams, Steve p.7
Roskos, Kathleen & Christie, James F. (Editors) p.369
Rosovsky, Henry p.290
Ross, Andrew p.254, p.261
Ross, Charles K. p.833, p.852
Ross, David F. (Editor). p.118
Ross, David Frederick p.118
Ross, Dennis B. p.650
Ross, Don. p.272
Ross, Earle D.. p.332
Ross, Fred p.128
Ross, George M. (Editor), et al.. . . . . p.609
Ross, Heather L. & Sawhill, Isabel V. p.266
Ross, Ian S.. . . . . p.219
Ross, John p.383
Ross, Lawrence C. Jr. & Kensington Publishing Corporation Staff p.289
Ross, M. J. p.379
Ross, Michael A. p.469, p.538
Ross, Ralph (Introduction by). p.345
Ross, Raymon R. p.365
Ross, Ronald G.. p.114
Ross, Stephen A.. . . . . p.89, p.264
Rossabi, Morris p.620
Rosse, Joseph G. & Levin, Robert A.. . . . . p.76
Rosser, B. R. p.779
Rosser, John Barkley & Rosser, Marina V.. . . . . p.237
Rosser, M. J. p.175
Rossett, Allison p.305
Rossiter, Clinton Lawrence p.575
Rossiter, Clinton p.464, p.518
Rossotti, Charles O. p.107
Rossum, Ralph A.. . . . . p.525, p.534
Rostow, Eugene V.. . . . . p.470
Rostow, W. W. p.559
Roszak, Theodore p.761
Rotberg, Robert I. & Rabb, Theodore K. (Editors) p.647
Rotenstreich, Nathan p.499
Roth, Rachel p.442, p.774
Roth, Wolff-Michael & Tobin, Kenneth George. p.277
Rothberg, Helen & Erickson, G. Scott. p.77, p.83
Rothman, Ellen K.. . . . . p.738
Rothman, Hal K. p.62
Rothman, Philip (Editor) p.204
Rothschild, Bruce J. (Editor) p.392
Rothstein, Frances A. & Blim, Michael L. p.28
Rothstein, Larry & Belson, Matthew p.830
Rothstein, Stanley W. & Garubo, Raymond C. p.282
Rothstein, Stanley W. (Editor) p.315
Rothstein p.450
Rothwell, William J., et al. p.79, p.352
Rotundo, E. Anthony. p.745
Roughgarden, Joan p.744, p.746
Rouquie, Alain p.592
Rousseau, Denise M. p.74
Rousseau, Jean-Jacques p.492
Rovine, Victoria p.26
Rowan, Carl Thomas. p.538
Rowe, David Charles p.819, p.902
Rowe, James K. & Lipschutz, Ronnie D. p.261, p.262
Rowe, Michael p.774
Rowland, A. Westley. p.293
Rowland, Don. p.376
Rowland, Thomas W. p.875
Rowley, Charles Kershaw & Schneider, Friedrich (Editors) p.192
Royce, Anya Peterson. p.26
Royce, James E. & Scratchley, David p.776
Royle, Tony & Towers, Brian. p.123
Roza, Marguerite & Celio, Mary Beth. p.282
Rozalski, Michael E.. . . . . p.284
Ruane, Joseph & Todd, Jennifer. p.607
Ruane, Kevin p.638, p.655
Ruben, Alan Miles (Editor). p.447
Ruben, Brent D.. p.332
Rubenfeld, Jed p.454
Rubenstein, William B., et al.. . . . . p.448
Rubenzer, Steven J. & Faschingbauer, Thomas R. p.698
Rubin, Anne S. p.522
Rubin, Barry M. & Heper, Metin (Editors). p.616
Rubin, Barry p.615
Rubin, Eva R. (Editor) p.448
Rubin, Frances & Rowley, John p.65
Rubin, Harvey W. p.163
Rubin, Herbert J. & Rubin, Irene p.691
Rubin, Herbert J. p.719
Rubin, Lillian B.. p.706
Rubinstein, Ariel. p.207
Ruccio, David F. & Amariglio, Jack. p.196
Rudacille, Deborah p.744
Rudalevige, Andrew p.527
Rude, George p.706, p.710, p.713, p.753
Rudenstine, David p.439
Rudgley, Richard p.776
Rudney, Gwen L. p.353
Rudolph, Frederick p.332
Rudolph, James D.. . . . . p.593
Ruggie, John G.. p.625
Ruggiero, Kristin Hoffman p.706
Ruggiero, Vincent R.. . . . . p.676
Rugman, Alan M. (Editor) p.177
Rumer, Boris (Editor) p.599, p.624
Rumney, Thomas A. p.396
Rundell, Michael p.856
Rung, Margaret C.. . . . . p.546
Runge, C. Ford, et al. p.665
Ruoff, Kenneth J. p.622
Rupesinghe, Kumar p.497, p.613
Rury, John L.. . . . . p.297, p.328, p.762

Ruscher, Janet B. p.698
Rush, Anne Kent p.791, p.874
Rusk, Jerrold G. p.548, p.549, p.555
Rusk, Tom & Miller, D. Patrick p.74
Russell, Bertrand Arthur p.656
Russell, Bertrand p.345, p.656
Russell, Francis p.438
Russell, Philip. p.594
Russell, Thaddeus p.129
Russett, Bruce M. p.629
Russo, Charles J. (Editor) p.451
Rust, Paula C.. . . . . . . p.750
Rutherford, Donald p.191
Rutland, Robert A.. . . . . . . p.518
Ruud, Paul A.. . . . . . . p.204
Ryan, Joan p.819, p.838
Ryan, Mary P.. . . . . . . p.734
Ryan, William. p.706
Ryden, David K.. . . . . . . p.461
Rydstrom, Helle p.772
Rymes, Betsy p.315
Ryscavage, Paul p.133

S

Saari, Carolyn. p.758
Saban Center for Middle East Policy, Brookings Institute p.616
Sabato, Larry J.. . . . . . . p.549, p.558
Sabin, William A. p.174
Sableman, Mark. p.406, p.445
Sachs, Carolyn E. p.772
Sachs, Jeffrey D.. . . . . . . p.266
Sachs, Paul D. & Luff, Richard T. . . p.788, p.872, p.881, p.886
Sack, Allen L. & Staurowsky, Ellen J. . . . p.822, p.889, p.894
Sacknoff, Scott p.151
Sadiki, Larbi p.615
Sadker, David M. & Sadker, Myra P. p.302
Sadovskii, L. E. & Sadovskii, A. L. p.871
Sadowski, Michael (Editor). p.312
Sadzeck, Tom p.864
Saettler, L. Paul p.352
Sagarra, Eda p.706
SAGE p.819
Saggers, Sherry & Gray, Dennis p.46
Saha, Lawrence J. p.762
Sahlins, Marshall David p.24, p.28
Said, Edward W. p.630, p.650
Saikal, Amin p.642
Sailes, Gary A. (Editor) p.819, p.833
Saint Sing, Susan p.803, p.865
Salacuse, Jeswald W.. . . . . . . p.59, p.74
Salaman, Graeme (Editor), et al. p.76
Salanié, Bernard p.107
Salas, Eduardo & Fiore, Stephen M. p.80
Sale, Peter F. (Editor) p.393
Sales and marketing management p.143
Salih, Mohamed Abdel Rahim M.. . . . . . . p.505, p.613
Salisbury, Rollin D. p.390
Salkever, Stephen G.. . . . . . . p.489
Salmon, Trevor C. & Shepherd, Alistair J. K. p.638
Salowe, Allen E.. . . . . . . p.303
Salvendy, Gavriel (Editor) p.119
Salwen, Micheal B. & Garrison, Bruce p.404
Salzberg, Charles p.854, p.897
Salzman, Philip Carl p.30
Samarco, C. Vincent p.302
Samli, A. Coskun p.145
Sammond, Nicholas (Editor) p.819, p.863
Sammons, Jeffrey T.. . . . . . . p.819, p.856
Sampson, Gary & Whalley, John (Editors). p.257, p.268
Sampson, Gary P. & Woolcock, Stephen (Editor, Contribution by) p.630, p.665
Sampson, Karen L.. . . . . . . p.115
Samuel, Lawrence R. p.426
Samuels, Richard J. p.622
Samuels, Warren J. (Editor), et al.. . . . . . . p.210
Samuels, Warren J. (Editor). p.186
Samuelson, Paul Anthony p.196, p.197, p.204, p.210
Sandage, Scott A. p.706
Sandall, Susan, et al.. . . . . . . p.316
Sanday, Peggy Reeves p.744
Sandel, Michael J.. . . . . . . p.555
Sanders, Randy p.549
Sanderson, Stephen p.760
Sandoval, Armbruster p.262
Sandoval, Jonathan (Editor). p.353
Sandoval, Jonathan H. (Editor), et al. p.286
Sands, Robert R. (Editor). p.819
Sands, Robert R. p.819, p.859, p.894
Sanford, George. p.505, p.596
Sanford, Nevitt & Comstock, Craig p.683
Sanford, Nevitt p.290, p.291, p.332
Sanjek, Roger (Editor) p.24
Sansone, David p.809
Santa Ana, Otto p.312
Sapir, Edward p.20
Sapiro, Virginia p.492, p.502
Sapora, Allen Victor Heimback p.358
Saracco, Roberto, et al.. . . . . . . p.420
Saracho, Olivia N. & Spodek, Bernard (Editors) p.369
Sarason, Seymour B. p.277, p.281, p.329, p.348
Sarason, Seymour Bernard p.329
Sarat, Austin (Editor) p.471
Sarat, Austin p.451
Sargent, Carolyn F. & Brettell, Caroline B. p.47
Sargent, Carolyn F. & Johnson, Thomas M. (Editors) . . . p.47
Sargent, Paul p.279
Sarmiento, Jorge Louis & Gruber, Nicolas p.393
Sartori, Giovanni p.574, p.579

Sassen, Saskia *p.496*
Sassoon, Anne Showstack *p.492*
Sassoon, Donald *p.507, p.594*
Sato, Ikuya *p.753*
Saul, John Ralston *p.510*
Saunders, Vivien *p.838, p.861*
Savage, Barbara D. *p.487, p.573*
Savage, David G. & Biskupic, Joan *p.466, p.539*
Savage, David *p.456*
Savage-Rumbaugh, Sue *p.19*
Saville, John *p.604*
Saville-Troike, Muriel *p.19*
Savitz, Andrew, et al. *p.61, p.64*
Savoie, Donald J. *p.587, p.588*
Sawik, Tadeusz *p.116*
Sawin, Philip (Compiled by), et al. *p.161*
Sawyer, R. Keith *p.423*
Sawyer, Suzana *p.711*
Sawyer, Thomas H., et al.. . . *p.886, p.889, p.892, p.897, p.899*
Sax, Dov F. (Editor), et al. *p.394*
Saxonberg, Steven *p.509, p.596, p.600*
Sayari, Sabri & Esmer, Yilmaz (Editors) *p.616*
Sayer, Bill *p.788, p.865*
Sayles, Leonard R. & Smith, Cynthia J.. . . . *p.54, p.72, p.110*
Sayre, Shay *p.136*
Saywell, John T.. *p.590*
Scala, Dante J. *p.549*
Scammon, Richard M. *p.549*
Scannell, Paddy & Cardiff, David *p.413*
Scannell, Paddy (Editor) *p.412*
Scannell, Paddy *p.412*
Scanzoni, John H. *p.734*
Scarre, Chris *p.6*
Scarrott, Martin *p.161, p.785, p.813*
Schaap, Jeremy *p.856*
Schabas, William A.. . . . . *p.435, p.653*
Schaffer, Frederic C. *p.505, p.585, p.613*
Schaffer, Kay & Smith, Sidonie (Editors) *p.846, p.892*
Schain, Martin A. (Editor), et al. *p.129*
Schaper, Michael *p.51, p.54*
Schatzberg, Michael G. *p.513, p.613*
Schechter, Danny *p.417*
Schechter, Susan. *p.752*
Schecter, Barnet *p.713*
Scheff, Thomas J. *p.775*
Scheffler, Israel (Editor), et al. *p.308*
Scheffler, Israel *p.329, p.345*
Schein, Edgar H. *p.75*
Schein, Richard H.. . . . . *p.382*
Scheiner, Ethan *p.622*
Scheingold, Stuart A.. . . . . *p.442*
Schell, Jonathan. *p.656, p.657*
Schell, Patience A.. . . . . *p.336*
Schement, Jorge Reina (Editor) *p.423*
Schempp, Paul *p.797*
Scheper-Hughes, Nancy *p.46*
Scher, Philip W. *p.44*
Scherer, F. M.. . . . . *p.230, p.235*
Scherer, Nancy *p.525*
Schermerhorn, John R. *p.73*
Scheuerman, William E. *p.470*
Schick, Allen *p.543*
Schick, Kathy D. & Toth, Nicholas. *p.17*
Schieffelin, Bambi B. & Ochs, Elinor (Editor, Contribution by). *p.20*
Schieffelin, Bambi B. (Editor), et al. *p.21*
Schieffelin, Bambi B. *p.20*
Schieffelin, Edward L. & Crittenden, Robert *p.43*
Schiemer, Suzanne. *p.798*
Schier, Steven E. *p.549*
Schiffer, Michael Brian *p.6*
Schiffrin, Andre *p.149*
Schilit, Howard M. *p.92, p.97, p.105, p.106, p.111*
Schiller, Wendy J. *p.534*
Schindeler, Fred F.. . . . . *p.590*
Schiro, Michael Stephen *p.365*
Schivelbusch, Wolfgang *p.706, p.710*
Schlager, Neil (Editor) *p.129*
Schleien, Stuart J.. . . . . *p.785, p.801*
Schlesinger, Arthur M. Jr. *p.522, p.642*
Schlesinger, Stephen *p.635*
Schlossman, Steven L. *p.473*
Schmalensee, Richard & Willig, Robert D. (Editors) . . . *p.191*
Schmandt, Jurgen (Editor), et al. *p.420*
Schmid, Alex Peter & Jongman, A. J. *p.661*
Schmid, Carol L. *p.706*
Schmidt, Alvin J. *p.719*
Schmidt, Gustav (Editor) *p.639*
Schmidt, Peter *p.14*
Schmidt, Richard A. & Wrisberg, Craig A.. . . . . *p.910*
Schmidt, Susanne K. & Werle, Raymund *p.420*
Schmitt, Bernd H. *p.135*
Schmottlach, Neil & McManama, Jerre . . . *p.798, p.799, p.800*
Schmuck, Richard A. & Schmuck, Patricia A. *p.350*
Schneider, Arnd & Wright, Christopher (Editors) *p.26*
Schneider, Carl E. (Editor) *p.448, p.539*
Schneider, David J. *p.694*
Schneider, David M. *p.32, p.734*
Schneider, David Murray *p.32*
Schneider, Elizabeth M. *p.472*
Schneider, Mark *p.543*
Schneider, Michael. *p.266*
Schneier, Edward V. & Gross, Bertram M.. . . . . *p.531*
Schneirov, Matthew *p.410*
Schock, Kurt *p.766*
Schoen, Johanna. *p.756*
Schoenbrod, David. *p.532*
Schoenfeld, Bruce *p.809, p.833, p.838, p.864*
Schofield, Norman. *p.484, p.769*
Scholastic, Inc. Staff (Contribution by) *p.535*

Scholes, Myron S., et al. *p.248*
Schonberger, Richard J. *p.119*
School and Community Safety Society of America Staff *p.786, p.788*
Schoonmaker, Frances *p.277*
Schorske, Carl E. *p.610*
Schrage, Michael *p.67*
Schröder, Monika J. A.. . . . . *p.160*
Schrire, Robert A. (Editor) *p.614*
Schroedel, Jean Reith. *p.527, p.528, p.531, p.532, p.569*
Schroeder, Alan *p.556*
Schubert, William H.. . . . . *p.365*
Schuetz, Janice & Snedaker, Kathryn H.. . . . . *p.438*
Schugurensky, Daniel *p.329*
Schulhofer, Stephen J. *p.472*
Schulten, Susan *p.378*
Schultz, Bradley *p.408, p.902, p.907*
Schultz, David. *p.539*
Schultz, Don E. & Barnes, Beth *p.427*
Schultz, Jane E. *p.522*
Schultz, Jeffrey D. (Editor), et al. *p.573*
Schultz, Jeffrey *p.559*
Schultz, Theodore W. (Editor) *p.266*
Schulz, Richard *p.751*
Schulze, Ralf *p.689*
Schumaker, Lyn *p.38*
Schumaker, Paul D. & Loomis, Burdett A. (Editors) . . . *p.527*
Schuman, Howard & Presser, Stanley *p.691*
Schumpeter, Joseph Alois . . *p.210, p.212, p.229, p.230, p.235, p.245, p.500, p.505, p.507*
Schur, Edwin M. *p.697*
Schutte, Ofelia *p.685*
Schutz, Alfred. *p.685, p.686*
Schuurman, Nadine *p.388*
Schwab, Donald P.. . . . . *p.179*
Schwandt, Thomas A. *p.689*
Schwartz, Arthur, et al.. . . . . *p.758*
Schwartz, Bernard (Editor) *p.456, p.539*
Schwartz, Bernard *p.440, p.452, p.466, p.469, p.539*
Schwartz, Evan I.. *p.67*
Schwartz, Herman (Author, Editor, Introduction by) . . . *p.539*
Schwartz, Herman (Editor) *p.539, p.541*
Schwartz, Jeffrey H., et al.. . . . . *p.16*
Schwartz, Jerry R. *p.414*
Schwartz, John A. *p.332*
Schwartz, Marie Jenkins *p.706*
Schwartz, Matthew *p.143*
Schwartz, Mildred A. *p.587*
Schwartz, Mischa *p.422*
Schwartz, Pedro *p.223*
Schwartz, Peter & Gibb, Blair *p.145*
Schwarz, Philip J. *p.474*
Schwarz, Roger *p.174*
Schwarzmantel, J. J.. . . . . *p.487, p.554*
Schwebel, Sara L., et al. *p.277*
Scobie, James R. *p.706*
Scollon, Ronald & Scollon, Suzanne Wong *p.20*
Sconce, Jeffrey *p.419*
Scott, Allen J. *p.398*
Scott, David (Editor). *p.286*
Scott, David L.. . . . . *p.97*
Scott, H. M.. . . . . *p.583*
Scott, Hilda *p.706*
Scott, Jacqueline L. (Editor), et al. *p.732*
Scott, James M. *p.377*
Scott, Janelle T. *p.367*
Scott, John *p.682*
Scott, Joseph *p.161*
Scott, W. Richard *p.716*
Scrambler, Graham *p.756*
Scrase, Timothy *p.314*
Scruggs, Lyle. *p.63*
Scullion, Hugh & Linehan, Margaret *p.77*
Scully, Roger *p.603*
Searle, G. R. *p.604, p.607*
Searle, Shayle R. & Willett, Lois Schertz *p.175, p.204*
Sears, David O. (Editor), et al. *p.484*
Seaver, Kirsten A. *p.399*
Sebeok, Thomas A. *p.424*
Seccombe, Wally *p.738*
Secher, Reynald *p.653*
Seddon, David & Zeilig, Leo (Editors) *p.191*
Seddon, Terri *p.336*
Sedelmeier, Ulrich & Schimmelfennig, Frank (Editors) *p.400, p.603*
Sedgwick, Fred *p.365*
Seeberg, Vilma *p.336*
Seefeldt, Carol (Editor). *p.369*
Segal, Jeffrey A. & Spaeth, Harold J. *p.466*
Segil, Larraine (Editor), et al. *p.72*
Segrave, Kerry. *p.131, p.134, p.140, p.141, p.774*
Segura, Julio *p.192*
Sehoole, M.T. *p.336*
Seib, Philip *p.406*
Seidel, Michael *p.852*
Seidman, Steven. *p.686*
Seitz, Wesley D., et al. *p.152, p.160, p.164*
Seivert, Sharon & Cavaleri, Steven A. *p.77*
Selden, David *p.283*
Seldon, Anthony & Ball, Stuart (Editors) *p.607*
Seldon, Anthony & Kavanagh, Dennis (Editors) *p.605*
Seldon, Anthony (Editor) *p.605*
Seligman, Joel *p.92, p.100, p.147, p.155, p.162*
Sellekaerts, Willy (Editor) *p.204, p.258, p.260*
Sellers, Jeffrey M. *p.543*
Semel, Susan F. & Sadovnik, Alan R. *p.348*
Semetko, Holli A., et al.. . . . . *p.549, p.558, p.559*
Semmes, Clovis E.. *p.700*
Semonche, John E. *p.466, p.539*
Sen, Amartya *p.266, p.514, p.515*

Senese, Guy B. p.312
Senge, Peter M. p.79, p.80
Senn, Alfred Erich. p.846, p.892
Sennett, Richard p.695, p.717, p.734
Sepinuck, Stephen L. & Treuthart, Mary P.. . . . . . p.539
Sergiovanni, Thomas p.281, p.282
Serrin, Judith & Serrin, William (Editors) p.404
Sethi, Suresh P., et al. p.118
Sever, Dave p.287
Sewell, William H. Jr. p.706
Sexton, Patricia Cayo p.123, p.329
Seymour, M. J. p.379
Seymour, Miranda. p.838, p.848
Shace, Joseph & Epstein, David G. p.110
Shachtman, Tom. p.423
Shackleton, J. R. (Editor). p.197
Shade, William Gerald (Editor), et al. p.550, p.556
Shadish, William R., et al. p.690
Shafaeddin, Mehdi p.60
Shafer, Byron E. (Editor) p.548, p.552
Shafer, Byron E.. . . . . . . p.551
Shaffer, William R. p.594
Shafritz, Jay M. p.482
Shah, Anwar p.755
Shah, Ghanshyam p.711
Shain, Yossi p.571
Shakur, Sanyika p.714
Shamah, Shani Beverly. p.89, p.97, p.98, p.100
Shamos, Michael Ian. p.855
Shank, Matthew D. p.886
Shanley, Mary L. p.734
Shannon, Joyce Brennfleck (Editor) p.826
Shannon, Mike p.812, p.852
Shanty, Frank G. (Editor), et al.. . . . . . . p.661
Shapiro, Arthur p.317
Shapiro, Carol & Varian, Hal R. p.51
Shapiro, David L. p.455
Shapiro, Edward S. p.287
Shapiro, Sidney A. & Glicksman, Robert L.. . p.92, p.110, p.111
Sharan, Shlomo (Editor) p.350
Sharer, Robert J. p.10
Shariati, Ali p.721
Sharkansky, Ira p.615
Sharma, Arvind p.723
Sharma, Kanhayalal L. p.706
Sharma, Sanjay P. (Editor), et al.. . . . . . . p.26
Sharma, Soumitra (Editor) p.229
Sharman, Campbell & Moon, Jeremy (Editors). p.624
Sharot, Stephen p.722
Sharp, Alan p.650
Sharp, Elaine B.. . . . . . . p.567
Sharp, Gene. p.650
Sharpe, Grant William, et al. p.164
Sharpe, J. A. p.707
Sharpes, Donald K. p.329
Shaw, Colin & Ivens, John p.143
Shaw, Eric p.607
Shaw, G. K. p.226, p.229
Shaw, Lisa & Dennison, Stephanie p.712
Shaw, Martin p.653
Shaw, Michael J. (Editor). p.113
Shaw, Stephen K. (Editor), et al. p.539
Shaw, Thurstan (Editor), et al.. . . . . . . p.8
Shaw, Victor N. p.777
Shaw, William H. (Editor) p.54, p.55
Shawcross, William p.647
Shea, Daniel M.. . . . . . . p.531
Shea, Edward J. p.797, p.803, p.822, p.840
Shedd, Joseph B. & Bacharach, Samuel B.. . . . . . . p.283
Sheehan, Richard G.. . . . . . . p.889, p.897
Sheffer, Martin S. p.539
Shefrin, Hersh p.97, p.102, p.103
Sheinin, David p.631
Sheldon, Garrett Ward p.492
Sheldon, Henry D.. . . . . . . p.289
Shell, G. Richard p.75
Shelton, Dinah p.653
Shenefield, John H. & Stelzer, Irwin M. p.85, p.110, p.111, p.112, p.444
Shenfield, Stephen D. p.510
Shennan, Stephen p.7
Shepard, Roy J. & Astrand, Per-Olof (Editors) p.826, p.875, p.880
Shephard, Roy J. p.791, p.793, p.841
Sherif, Muzafer & Brannigan, Augustine. p.692
Sherif, Muzafer p.692, p.717
Sheriff, Robin E. p.37
Sherman, A. J.. . . . . . . p.668
Sherman, Alfred p.607
Sherman, Andrew J. & Hart, Milledge A.. . . . . . . p.85
Sherman, Joe p.154
Sherman, Lawrence W. (Editor). p.680
Sherrill, Claudine p.801
Sherwin-White, Adrian Nicholas p.501
Sherzer, Joel p.19
Shi, Tianjian p.620
Shibutani, Tamotsu ; Kwan, Kian M. p.725
Shick, Allen & Lostracco, Felix. p.567
Shiell, Timothy C.. . . . . . . p.459
Shiffrin, Steven H.. . . . . . . p.459
Shiller, Robert J. . . p.90, p.92, p.97, p.100, p.245, p.250, p.264
Shim, Jae K. p.137
Shimokawa, Koichi S. p.154
Shin, Doh C. p.621
Shin, Gi-Wook. p.711
Shipan, Charles R.. . . . . . . p.539
Shipler, David K. p.726
Shippey, Karla C.. . . . . . . p.58, p.110
Shirreff, David p.90, p.93, p.97, p.100, p.102, p.103
Shivers, Jay S. & DeLisle, Lee J. p.785

Shivers, Jay S.. . . . . *p.786*
Shleifer, Andrei *p.97, p.100*
Shogan, Robert *p.129*
Shondell, Don & Raynaud, Cecil (Editors). *p.869, p.905*
Shor, Ira *p.300*
Shore, Bradd *p.24*
Shore, Kenneth *p.284*
Short, Brian *p.399*
Short, John Rennie. *p.395*
Shorter, Edward *p.739*
Shoshani, Jesheskel, et al. *p.707, p.710*
Shostak, Arthur B. (Editor) *p.500*
Shostak, Marjorie *p.38*
Shou-Yu Liang & Wen-Ching Wu *p.793*
Showalter, Elaine *p.714*
Shropshire, Kenneth L. & Davis, Timothy *p.905*
Shropshire, Kenneth L. *p.819, p.833, p.905*
Shubik, Martin *p.252, p.689*
Shue, Vivienne *p.620*
Shull, Steven A. & Shaw, Thomas C. *p.527*
Shulman, James Lawrence & Bowen, William G. *p.293, p.822, p.895*
Shulman, Judith, et al. *p.350*
Shulman, Lee S.. *p.348*
Shulman, Steven & Darity, William Jr. (Editors) *p.134*
Shumway-Cook, Anne & Wollacott, Marjorie H. *p.910*
Sidel, Mark *p.565, p.572*
Sidlow, Edward I. *p.550*
Sidney, Mara S. *p.567*
Sidorkin, Alexander M.. . . . . *p.345*
Siebert, Fredrick S., et al. *p.406*
Siedel, George J. *p.82, p.110*
Siedentop, Daryl, et al.. . . . . *p.797*
Siedentop, Larry *p.603, p.638*
Siegel, David, et al. *p.138*
Siegel, Jacob S. & Swanson, David A. (Editors) *p.376*
Siegel, Jay A. (Editor), et al. *p.678*
Siegel, Jeremy J.. . . . . *p.97, p.100, p.102*
Siegel, Lawrence M.. . . . . *p.451*
Siegel, Marc *p.694*
Siegle, Joe, et al. *p.505*
Sifakis, Carl. *p.678*
Sigal, Leon V. *p.566, p.644, p.657*
Sigel, Roberta S.. *p.746*
Sikkink, Kathryn *p.513*
Silber, Irwin. *p.507*
Silberman, Bernard S. *p.545, p.581*
Silbey, Joel H. (Editor). *p.575*
Silbey, Joel H.. . . . . *p.542*
Silliman, Elaine R. & Wilkinson, Louise Cherry (Editors). *p.365*
Silliman, Stephen *p.14*
Sillitoe, Paul (Editor), et al. *p.45*
Sillitoe, Paul *p.43*
Silva, Ajit *p.73*
Silva, John M. & Stevens, Diane E.. . . . . *p.877*
Silva, Patricio (Editor) *p.593*
Silver, Beverly J. *p.129*
Silver, Harold & Silver, Pamela. *p.337*
Silver, Harold *p.336*
Silverman, Stephen *p.798, p.799*
Silverman, Sydel (Editor). *p.4*
Silverman, Sydel, et al.. . . . . *p.4*
Silverman, Sydel *p.42*
Simeon, Richard. *p.587*
Simmel, Georg & Wolff, Kurt H. *p.686*
Simmel, Georg *p.766*
Simmons, A. John *p.773*
Simmons, Annette *p.74*
Simmons, Charles A.. . . . . *p.411*
Simmons Market Research Bureau *p.139, p.142*
Simmons, Matthew R. *p.268*
Simmons, Tracy Lee *p.303*
Simon, Carl P. & Blume, Lawrence E.. . . . . *p.204*
Simon, Carl P. & Witte, Ann D.. . . . . *p.270*
Simon, David J. (Editor) *p.463*
Simon, Herbert A. (Author, Preface by) *p.248*
Simon, Herbert A. *p.74, p.75, p.83*
Simon, Herbert, et al. *p.250, p.272*
Simon, James F. *p.452, p.469, p.539*
Simon, Katherine G. *p.306*
Simon, Louis *p.345*
Simon, Paul *p.539*
Simon, Rita J. (Editor) *p.809, p.822, p.838, p.901*
Simon, Robert L. *p.803*
Simon, Sidney B., et al. *p.350*
Simons, Geoff. *p.560*
Simons, Minot II *p.838, p.862*
Simpkins, Robert A. *p.143*
Simpson, Douglas J., et al. *p.345*
Simpson, George E.. . . . . *p.37*
Simpson, Roger & Coté, William E.. . . . . *p.407*
Simpson, Ronald D. & Frost, Susan H. *p.291*
Sims, Ronald R. & Quatro, Scott A. (Editors) *p.698*
Sinclair, Barbara. *p.533*
Sinclair, R. K.. . . . . *p.501*
Sinclair, Upton *p.404, p.751*
Sindell, Kathleen *p.97*
Singer, Beth J.. . . . . *p.513*
Singer, Dorothy G. & Singer, Jerome L. (Editors) *p.417*
Singer, Harvey *p.279*
Singer, Merrill & Baer, Hans *p.47*
Singer, Robert N. (Editor), et al. *p.877*
Singh, K. S. (Editor) *p.707*
Singleton, Marvin K.. . . . . *p.410*
Singley, Mark K. & Anderson, John R. *p.358*
Sinnott, Richard *p.608*
Sinnott-Armstrong, Walter & Howarth, Richard B. (Editors) *p.394*
Sirica, John J. *p.438*

Sirotnik, Kenneth A. & Soder, Roger (Editors) *p.340*
Sirotnik, Kenneth A. *p.281*
Sisk, Timothy D. & Reynolds, Andrew *p.578, p.613*
Sisk, Timothy D. *p.614*
Sivulka, Juliann *p.426*
Sizer, Theodore R.. . . . . *p.329, p.367*
Skaine, Rosemarie. *p.838, p.854*
Skar, Sarah L *p.763*
Skeel, David A. *p.97, p.110, p.444*
Skeen, C. Edward *p.487*
Skidelsky, Robert (Editor) *p.229*
Skidelsky, Robert J. *p.507*
Skidelsky, Robert *p.229*
Skinner, Andrew S. & Wilson, Thomas *p.219*
Skinner, Andrew S. *p.212*
Skinner, Burrhus Frederic *p.500*
Sklair, Leslie *p.759, p.760*
Skocpol, Theda & Fiorina, Morris (Editors) *p.547, p.555*
Skocpol, Theda. *p.547, p.555, p.760, p.769*
Skousen, Mark & Taylor, Kenna C. *p.186*
Skrentny, John D.. . . . . *p.495, p.511, p.516*
Skutt, Alexander G. & Roberts, James B. *p.856*
Sky, Theodore. *p.525*
Slack, Trevor & Parent, Milena. *p.886, p.889*
Slack, Trevor *p.819, p.886*
Slater, Candace *p.707*
Slater, David *p.400*
Slater, Robert *p.157*
Slaughter, Sheila A. & Rhoades, Gary *p.290*
Slavin, Robert E. & Madden, Nancy A. (Editors). . *p.281, p.365*
Slavin, Robert E. (Editor), et al.. . . . . *p.361*
Slayton, Robert A.. . . . . *p.707*
Slemrod, Joel & Bakija, Jon *p.108*
Slemrod, Joel (Editor) *p.108*
Slemrod, Joel *p.107*
Sloan, Alfred P. Jr.. . . . . *p.154*
Sloan, Bill *p.411*
Sloan, Douglas (Author, Editor). *p.329*
Sloan, Elinor C.. . . . . *p.631, p.655*
Sloan, Jeffrey & Sloan, Richard *p.68*
Sloan, W. David & Parcell, Lisa Mullikin (Editors) *p.404*
Sloan, W. David (Compiled by) *p.404*
Sloane, Arthur A. *p.129*
Sloane, Eugene A.. . . . . *p.857*
Slocum, Terry A., et al. *p.376*
Slomp, Hans *p.123*
Slotkin, James S.. *p.4*
Sluka, Jeffrey A. (Editor) *p.34*
Smagorinsky, Peter & Taxel, Joel (Editors). *p.306*
Small, John, et al. *p.374*
Smallman-Raynor, Matthew *p.381*
Smart, Carol, et al.. . . . . *p.735*
Smelser, Neil J. & Baltes, Paul B.. . . . . *p.678*
Smelser, Neil J. & Swedberg, Richard (Editors) *p.718*
Smelser, Neil J. *p.675, p.692*
Smil, Vaclav *p.667*
Smith, Adam *p.218, p.219, p.220*
Smith, Anthony & Hutchinson, John (Editors) *p.495*
Smith, Anthony D.. . . . . *p.495*
Smith, B. Mark *p.97, p.102, p.162*
Smith, Brent L. *p.565*
Smith, Bruce D. *p.6*
Smith, Christian *p.721*
Smith, Christopher E. *p.539, p.540*
Smith, Craig *p.220*
Smith, Dan *p.381*
Smith, Daniel B.. *p.734*
Smith, Darren L. (Editor) *p.783, p.788*
Smith, David E.. . . . . *p.588, p.590*
Smith, David G.. *p.756*
Smith, David Marshall *p.398*
Smith, Dorothy E. *p.744*
Smith, F. Leslie, et al. *p.412*
Smith, George P.. . . . . *p.738*
Smith, Hazel *p.603, p.638*
Smith, Huston *p.291*
Smith, Jackie & Johnston, Hank *p.640, p.663*
Smith, Jean E.. *p.469*
Smith, Jeffery A.. . . . . *p.459*
Smith, Jeffrey K., et al.. . . . . *p.287*
Smith, Jennifer *p.587*
Smith, John K. *p.355*
Smith, Keith *p.395*
Smith, L. Glenn & Smith, Joan K. *p.338*
Smith, Lissa (Editor) *p.809, p.838*
Smith, M. Cecil & Pourchot, Thomas (Editors). *p.321*
Smith, Mark. *p.639*
Smith, Michael C. & Fossey, Richard W. *p.451*
Smith, Michael E. *p.638*
Smith, Michael J. *p.627*
Smith, Mickey C., et al. *p.156*
Smith, Myron J. Jr. *p.844, p.859*
Smith, N. Craig & Quelch, John *p.146*
Smith, Neil *p.378*
Smith, Paul J. (Editor) *p.662*
Smith, Perry M. *p.407*
Smith, Peter H. *p.593*
Smith, Philip L. *p.345*
Smith, Raymond A. & Haider-Markel, Donald P. *p.570*
Smith, Raymond T. *p.33*
Smith, Richard N. *p.411*
Smith, Robert A. *p.819, p.857*
Smith, Robert J. *p.707*
Smith, Robert Michael *p.129*
Smith, Ron F. *p.406*
Smith, Ronald A.. . . . . *p.810, p.822, p.895, p.902*
Smith, Roy C. & Walter, Ingo *p.92, p.98, p.102, p.103, p.156, p.163*
Smith, Stephen L. *p.785*
Smith, Steven S., et al.. . . . . *p.531*

Smith, Steven S.. . . . p.534
Smith, Toby . . . p.63
Smith, V. L. (Editor) . . . p.268
Smith, Vernon L. . . . p.248, p.264, p.272
Smith, Whitney . . . p.499
Smith, William Jr. . . . p.329
Smith, Woodruff D. . . . p.584
Smithers, Janice A. . . . p.742
Smoll, Frank L. & Smith, Ronald E. . . . p.824, p.840
Smrekar, Claire & Goldring, Ellen . . . p.367
Smutny, Joan F. (Editor) . . . p.317
Smutny, Joan Franklin . . . p.317
Smylie, Mark A. & Miretzky, Debra (Editors) . . . p.278
Smyrl, Marc. . . . p.528
Smythe, Ted Curtis. . . . p.411
Snider, Bruce C. (Editor), et al. . . . p.709
Snow, C. P. . . . p.291
Snow, David A. & Anderson, Leon . . . p.751
Snow, David A. (Editor), et al. . . . p.710
Snow, Dean R. . . . p.11
Snowdon, Brian & Vane, Howard R. (Editors) . . . p.193, p.241
Snowdon, Brian & Vane, Howard R. . . . p.192, p.240, p.241
Snowdon, Brian, et al. . . . p.241
Snowdon, Brian . . . p.245, p.258
Snyder, Jack L. . . . p.505
Snyder, Kirk . . . p.168
Snyder, Scott . . . p.644, p.646
So, Alvin Y.. . . . p.618
Soares, Eric J.. . . . p.136
Sobel, Robert & Sicilia, David B. (Editors) . . . p.529
Sobel, Robert . . . p.487, p.528
Social Science Research and Instructional Council, California State University. . . . p.676
Society for Historical Archaeology Staff . . . p.14
Sociometrics . . . p.689
Soderberg, Nancy . . . p.562
Soesastro, Hadi & Findlay, Christopher C. . . . p.398
Soffer, O. & Praslov, N. D. . . . p.17
Sohn, Louis B. & Clark, Grenville . . . p.635
Sohn, Louis B. & Gustafson, Kristen . . . p.478
Soley, Lawrence . . . p.515
Solinger, Rickie . . . p.769
Solis, Jose . . . p.337
Solomon, Barbara M. . . . p.302
Solomon, Mark . . . p.509, p.554
Solomon, Robert. . . . p.239
Solow, R. . . . p.245
Solow, Robert M. & Taylor, John B. . . . p.245
Solow, Robert . . . p.245
Solzhenitsyn, Aleksandr . . . p.753
Somervill, Barbara A. . . . p.393
Sommers, Paul M. (Editor) . . . p.852, p.886, p.889, p.897
Sommerville, C. John . . . p.418
Sonenshein, Raphael . . . p.544
Songer, Donald R., et al. . . . p.470
Sontag, Susan . . . p.778
Sorel, Georges . . . p.507, p.759
Sornson, Robert (Editor) . . . p.361
Soroka, Stuart Neil . . . p.587
Sorokin, Pitirim A. & Lunden, Walter A. . . . p.484, p.770
Sorokin, Pitirim A. . . . p.680, p.683, p.700, p.760
Sorokin, Pitirim Aleksandrovich. . . . p.694
Soros, George . . . p.665
Southern, Pat . . . p.718
Sowell, Thomas. . . . p.186, p.218, p.310
Spaeth, Harold J. & Segal, Jeffrey A. . . . p.540
Spalding, Mark D., et al. . . . p.393
Spalding, Mark . . . p.393
Spangler, Mary M.. . . . p.345
Spanier, John W. & Hook, Steven W. . . . p.560
Spann, Girardeau A.. . . . p.457, p.540
Spargo, John . . . p.236
Spector, Robert . . . p.165
Speer, Kevin P. . . . p.826, p.875, p.880
Spellman, Kathryn . . . p.44
Spellman, W. M. & Spellman, William . . . p.502
Spence, A. Michael . . . p.254
Spencer, Herbert . . . p.345, p.346, p.484, p.511, p.683, p.684
Spencer, John, et al. . . . p.390
Sperling, Michael B. & Sack, Amy . . . p.399
Spero, Joshua B.. . . . p.397
Speth, James Gustave (Editor) . . . p.667
Spielvogel, Laura . . . p.792, p.819
Spilner, Maggie . . . p.788, p.791
Spindler, George D. & Hammond, Lorie (Editors) . . . p.29
Spindler, George D. (Editor) . . . p.29, p.35, p.303
Spindler, Louise S. . . . p.29
Spirduso, Waneen W., et al. . . . p.875, p.880
Spiro, Melford E.. . . . p.36
Spitz, Peter H.. . . . p.157
Spitzer, Robert J. . . . p.527
Spitzer, Robert . . . p.528, p.532
Spivey, Nigel . . . p.810
Sponsel, Leslie E. & Gregor, Thomas (Editors) . . . p.35
Spragens, Thomas A. Jr. . . . p.505
Spray, Sharon L.. . . . p.393
Sprecher, Drexel A. . . . p.477
Spreyer, Leon . . . p.348
Spriggs, Matthew . . . p.13
Spring, Joel H. . . . p.313, p.314, p.329
Springhall, John . . . p.583
Sprinz, Detlef F. & Wolinsky-Nahmias, Yael (Editors) . . . p.627
Sproule, J. Michael . . . p.418
Spruyt, Hendrik . . . p.496
Squire, Peverill & Hamm, Keith E. . . . p.550
Squires, Gregory D., et al. . . . p.544
Squires, James D. . . . p.411
Srinivasan, T. N. (Editor), et al. . . . p.192
Sriramesh, Krishnamurthy & Vereciec, Dejan (Editors) . . . p.428
St. John, Bob . . . p.859

Staar, Richard F. (Editor). p.585, p.596
Stacey, Judith p.732, p.734
Stacey, William A. & Shupe, Anson p.743
Stack, Carol B.. . . . . p.37
Stafford, Charles p.40
Stafford, Marla R. & Faber, Ronald J. (Editors) p.428
Stagliano, Vito A.. p.62
Staib, Richard p.62, p.64
Stalk, George p.119
Stalley, R. F. p.489
Stallings, William p.422
Stambach, Amy. p.29
Standage, Tom p.421, p.710
Stanfield, John H. II & Dennis, Rutledge M. (Editors) . . p.687
Stanford Arms Control Group Staff p.657
Stanko, Elizabeth A.. . . . . p.752
Stanley, George Edward p.382
Stanley, William D. & Harrington, Richard F. p.422
Staples, Robert p.738
Staples, William G. p.773
Stark, Joan S. & Lattuca, Lisa R.. . . . . p.295
Starkey, Brigid, et al. p.646
Starkey, Chad p.829
Starr, Amory p.712
Starr, June & Collier, Jane F. (Editors) p.34
Starr, June & Goodale, Mark (Editors) p.25
Starr, Kenneth W. p.540
Stasz, Cathleen, et al. p.305
Stathis, Stephen W. p.560, p.630
Staub, Ervin. p.715
Staudohar, Paul D. p.886, p.889, p.897
Staudt, Kathleen & Coronado, Irasema p.560, p.640
Steamer, Robert J.. . . . . p.540
Stearns, Maxwell L.. . . . . p.540
Stearns, Monteagle p.560, p.566
Stearns, Peter (Editor) p.699, p.707
Stearns, Peter N.. p.425
Stecher, Brian & Kirby, Sheila Nataraj (Editors) p.281
Steed, Robert P. (Editor), et al.. . . . . p.551, p.554
Steedman, Carolyn. p.346
Steedman, Ian p.246
Steel, Ronald p.409
Steele, Gerry p.229
Steen, Harold K. p.152, p.164
Steers, Richard M. & Nardon, Luciara p.70
Stefanakis, Emmanuel p.388
Stefancic, David R. p.129
Stegelin, Dolores A. & Borman, Kathyrn M. (Editors) . . p.369
Steger, Manfred B. & Carver, Terrell p.509
Steger, Manfred B.. . . . . p.55, p.665
Steigman, Andrew L.. . . . . p.529
Stein, Alfred (Editor), et al.. . . . . p.389
Stein, Arlene p.570
Stein, David, et al.. . . . . p.321
Stein, Kenneth W. p.566, p.642, p.646, p.650
Steinberg, Steven J. & Steinberg, Sheila L. p.388
Steiner, John F. & Steiner, George A.. . . . . p.52
Steinfels, Margaret O'Brien. p.721
Steingold, Fred S. p.444
Steingold, Fred p.88
Stengers, Jean & Van Neck, Anne. p.748
Stepan, Alfred p.593
Stepan-Norris, Judith & Zeitlin, Maurice. p.123
Stephens, G. Lynn & Graham, George. p.693
Stephens, G. Ross & Wikstrom, Nelson p.543
Stephens, Mitchell & Olson, Beth. p.414
Stephens, Mitchell p.403
Stephenson, D. Grier. p.540
Sterba, James P. p.514
Sterling, Christopher H. & Kittross, John M.. . . . . . . p.412
Sterling, Christopher H. (Editor) p.413, p.418
Sterling, Christopher H., et al. p.166, p.421
Sterling, Christopher H. p.421
Stern, Gary M. & Halperin, Morton H. (Editors) . . p.462, p.532
Stern, Jessica p.662
Stern, Joel M., et al. p.92
Stern, Kenneth S. p.438
Sternberg, Robert J. & Grigorenko, Elena p.287, p.319
Sternheimer, Karen p.712
Steuart-Denham, James. p.217
Steuerle, C. Eugene p.108
Steuerle, Eugene C. p.108
Stevens, John p.803, p.863
Stevens, Mitchell L. p.296
Stevens, Richard G. & Franck, Matthew J. (Editors) . . . p.540
Stevens, Robert Bocking p.447
Stevens, Robert E., et al.. . . . . p.136
Stevens, William S. p.163
Stevenson, Adlai E. p.635
Stevenson, Garth p.581, p.587
Stevenson, Howard Jr. (Editor) p.304
Stevenson, Ollie & Huebler, Dana. p.168
Stevenson, Robert G. (Editor). p.353
Stevenson, Thomas B. p.707
Steward, Julian H. p.30
Stewart, Chuck p.457
Stewart, David & Shamdasani, Prem N.. . . . . p.687
Stewart, David A. p.830
Stewart, James B.. . . . . p.100, p.110, p.147
Stewart, James p.206
Stewart, John p.284
Stewart, Michael p.42, p.229
Stid, Daniel D. p.528
Stigler, George J. & Kindahl, James K. p.239
Stigler, George J. p.210, p.223, p.249
Stigler, James W. (Editor) p.36
Stiglitz, Joseph E. & Charlton, Andrew p.53, p.56, p.665
Stiglitz, Joseph E. & Walsh, Carl E.. . . . . p.186
Stiglitz, Joseph E. p.56, p.58, p.256, p.262, p.665
Stigum, Bernt P.. p.204

Stilgitz, Joseph E. (Author, Afterword by) *p.262*
Stinchcombe, Arthur L.. . . . . *p.718*
Stipanuk, David M. & Roffman, Harold *p.161*
Stirati, Antonella. *p.220*
Stith, Anthony. *p.134*
Stivers, Richard *p.695*
Stock, James H. & Watson, Mark W. *p.204*
Stock, Robert *p.397*
Stockdale, Margaret S. & Crosby, Faye J. (Editors). . . . *p.132*
Stockford, Marjorie A.. . . . . *p.134, p.445*
Stocking, George W. (Author, Editor) *p.5*
Stocking, George W. Jr. (Author, Editor). *p.5*
Stocking, George W. Jr. (Editor) *p.3, p.5, p.48*
Stocking, George W. Jr. *p.5*
Stockton, David *p.501*
Stoessinger, John George *p.635*
Stohl, Michael (Editor). *p.662*
Stokell, Ian *p.800, p.838, p.868, p.905*
Stoker, Robert P.. *p.525*
Stokes, Gale *p.579, p.600*
Stokey, Nancy L. & Lucas, Robert E. Jr. *p.205, p.239*
Stolberg, Benjamin *p.129*
Stoldt, G. Clayton, et al.. . . . . *p.886, p.903, p.907*
Stoler, Mark A. *p.561*
Stoller, Paul & Olkes, Cheryl *p.37*
Stoller, Paul *p.25, p.759*
Stone, Christopher D. *p.435, p.444*
Stone, Geoffrey *p.505, p.565, p.567*
Stone, Glenn D. *p.38*
Stone, Julius *p.478*
Stone, Lawrence *p.726, p.734*
Stone, Linda (Editor) *p.33*
Stoneall, Linda *p.770*
Stonecash, Jeffrey M. & McGuire, Mary P. *p.552, p.554*
Stonecash, Jeffrey M. *p.552, p.555*
Storey, John & Salaman, Graeme. *p.67*
Storr, Merl *p.750*
Story, Ronald *p.380, p.707*
Stout, Chris E.. . . . . *p.662*
Stover, Eric *p.654*
Strachan, Hew *p.627, p.647*
Strahan, David B. *p.358*
Strain, Phillip S. (Editor) *p.353*
Strang, Heather *p.754*
Strasser, Hermann *p.680*
Strasser, Mark P. *p.442, p.570*
Strasser, Susan *p.140*
Strathdee, Robert *p.305*
Strathern, Marilyn *p.33*
Straus, L. G. *p.17*
Straus, Murray A., et al. *p.743*
Strauss, Anselm L. & Corbin, Juliet M. *p.688*
Strauss, Anselm L.. *p.682*
Strauss, Leo & Cropsey, Joseph (Editors) *p.488*
Strauss, Leo. *p.502, p.511*
Strauss, Sarah *p.793*
Strauss, Steven *p.114, p.119*
Straussner, Shulamith Lala Ashenberg (Editor) *p.777*
Street, Harry *p.436*
Streissler, Erich W. *p.258, p.264*
Streitmatter, Rodger *p.404*
Strickland, Dorothy S. & Alvermann, Donna E. *p.365*
Strickland, Rennard F. & Wilkinson, Charles F. (Editors) . *p.465*
Stringer, Chris *p.16*
Stringer, Christopher & McKie, Robin *p.16*
Stroh, Linda K. & Johnson, Homer H. *p.65*
Stroh, Linda K., et al.. . . . . *p.70*
Strom, Kaare (Editor), et al. *p.576*
Strong, George V. *p.510, p.595*
Strong, Robert A. *p.560*
Strong, William S.. *p.446*
Stronge, James *p.349*
Strossen, Nadine. *p.748*
Strum, Philippa *p.469*
Strum, Shirley C. & Lindburg, Donald G.. . . . . *p.15*
Struna, Nancy L. *p.810, p.819*
Stub, Holger R. *p.741*
Studenmund, A. H. *p.205*
Stuhler, Barbara *p.519, p.569*
Sturman, Andrew & Tapper, Nigel *p.385*
Stutely, Richard *p.175*
Stutts, Alan T. & Wortman, James. *p.161*
Sublett, Michael D. *p.542*
Sudarkasa, Niara *p.39*
Sugar, Steve *p.84*
Sugden, John P.. . . . . *p.820, p.844, p.856*
Sugrue, Thomas J.. *p.771*
Sukhwal, B. L. & Sukhwal, Lilawati *p.496*
Suleiman, Ezra *p.581*
Sull, Donald N. & Wang, Yong *p.59, p.68*
Sullivan, Andrew (Editor) *p.570*
Sullivan, J. L. *p.608*
Sullivan, Michael P. *p.627*
Sullivan, Teresa A., et al. *p.250, p.271*
Sully, Melanie A. *p.595*
Sumner, William Graham. *p.686*
Sumner, William Graham. *p.770*
Sun, Yan *p.620*
Sundaram, Rangarajan K.. . . . . *p.207*
Sunstein, Cass R. & Epstein, Richard A. (Editors) *p.462*
Sunstein, Cass R. *p.110, p.111, p.434, p.447, p.497, p.540, p.695*
Sunstein, Cass *p.425, p.761*
Super, Carol & Gold, Ronald *p.143*
Surdam, David G. *p.522*
Surgenor, Christopher *p.151*
Surmanek, Jim *p.428*
Surowiecki, James *p.51, p.135*
Suryadinata, Leo. *p.623*
Susser, Bernard *p.768*

Susskind, Lawrence E., et al. *p.566*
Sussman, Robert W. (Author, Editor) *p.15*
Suter, Keith *p.262, p.640, p.663*
Sutherland, Charmain *p.800*
Suttles, Gerald D. *p.707*
Sutton, David E. *p.46*
Sutton, Mark Q. & Anderson, E. N. *p.30*
Sutton, Robert I.. . . . . *p.67, p.74*
Sutton, Robert P.. *p.500*
Suzman, Mark. *p.495*
Suzman, Richard M. (Editor), et al. *p.742*
Swain, Tony *p.43*
Swan, Karen (Editor), et al.. . . . . *p.418*
Swanberg, W. A.. *p.411*
Swart, Juani, et al. *p.77*
Swartz, David *p.682*
Swatos, William H. *p.678, p.720*
Swedberg, Richard *p.271, p.681*
Sweeney, Kep *p.165*
Sweet, Waldo E. *p.810, p.813*
Sweezy, Paul M.. *p.236*
Swidler, Ann *p.738*
Swift, K. G. & Booker, J. D. *p.117*
Swisher, Carl B.. *p.469*
Swissler, Becky *p.799, p.800, p.838, p.840, p.857, p.862*
Swonk, Diane *p.271*
Swystun, Jeff (Editor) *p.142*
Sykes, Bryan *p.745*
Sylvester, Judith L. & Huffman, Suzanne *p.407*
Sylvie, George & Witherspoon, Patricia D.. . . . . *p.149*
Symposium on Science, Reason, and Modern Democracy S. *p.573*
Syrett, Michel & Lammiman, Jean *p.67*
Szasz, Thomas *p.471, p.770, p.775*
Szczerbiak, Aleksander Andrzej. *p.579, p.597*
Szell, Gyorgy (Editor) *p.123*
Szenberg, Michael & Ramrattan, Lall (Editors). *p.197*
Szenberg, Michael (Editor) *p.186*
Szenberg, Michael, et al.. . . . . *p.186*
Szmatka, Jacek (Editor), et al. *p.690*
Sztompka, Piotr *p.695*
Szulanski, Gabriel *p.79*
Szymanski, Stefan & Zimbalist, Andrew S. *p.820, p.844, p.852, p.899*
Szymusiak, Karen & Sibberson, Franki *p.365*

T

Taagepera, Rein & Shugart, Matthew *p.578*
Tabachnikov, Serge *p.855, p.871*
Tabbi, Joseph & Wutz, Michael (Editors) *p.419*
Taft, William Howard *p.632*
Tager, Jack *p.713*
Taghizadegan, Salman *p.117*
Takahashi, Lois *p.722*
Takaki, Ronald T. *p.707*
Takeda, Kiyoko *p.622*
Takeuchi, Hirotaka & Nonaka, Ikujiro *p.77*
Takougang, Joseph & Krieger, Milton *p.613*
Talbert, Richard J. *p.501*
Talbott, Strobe & Chanda, Nayan (Editors) *p.487, p.662*
Talbott, Strobe *p.562, p.644, p.646, p.657*
Talbott, William. *p.513, p.670*
Talisse, Robert B. *p.505, p.511*
Talley, P. Forrest. *p.756*
Tallman, Irving (Editor), et al. *p.736*
Tamarkin, Robert A.. . . . . *p.102, p.163*
Tambiah, Stanley J. *p.713*
Tanenbaum, Andrew *p.422*
Tank, Ronald W.. *p.444*
Tannen, Deborah *p.21*
Tanner, Daniel & Tanner, Laurel N. *p.365*
Tansey, Geoff & Worsley, Tony *p.152*
Tapia, John E.. . . . . *p.321*
Taragano, Martin *p.854*
Taras, Ray & Castle, Marjorie *p.506, p.597*
Tarbell, Ida *p.147, p.148*
Tarr, G. Alan *p.454*
Tarrow, Sidney (Author, Contribution by) *p.625*
Tarrow, Sidney *p.594, p.713*
Tastsoglou, Evangelia & Dobrowolsky, Alexandra (Editors). *p.668*
Tattersall, Ian, et al.. . . . . *p.16*
Tattersall, Ian. *p.16*
Tatum, Beverly Daniel *p.310*
Tatz, Colin *p.830*
Taucar, Christopher Edward *p.581*
Taussig, Frank W. *p.258*
Tayeb, Monir. *p.77*
Taylor, Alan. *p.581*
Taylor, Andrew *p.129*
Taylor, Barbara (Editor), et al. *p.366*
Taylor, Bonnie B. *p.451*
Taylor, Brian D.. *p.599*
Taylor, Charles *p.587*
Taylor, D. R. F. (Editor) *p.386*
Taylor, D. R. *p.375*
Taylor, Denny & Dorsey-Gaines, Catherine *p.762*
Taylor, Frederick Winslow. *p.64*
Taylor, J. B. & Woodford, Michael (Editors) *p.192*
Taylor, J. Edward & Adelman, Irma. *p.241, p.271*
Taylor, James S.. *p.340*
Taylor, Jeffrey H. (Editor) *p.792, p.881*
Taylor, John. *p.854*
Taylor, Kathleen, et al.. . . . . *p.321*
Taylor, Michael John Haddrick *p.151*
Taylor, Philip A. M. *p.668*
Taylor, Philip Bates *p.593*
Taylor, Rogan. *p.820, p.868*
Taylor, Samuel H. & Roberts, Robert E.. . . . . *p.758*
Taylor, William N.. . . . . *p.826*

Teachers College Press *p.277*
Teaford, Jon C. *p.526, p.544*
Tebbel, John W. & Zuckerman, Mary E.. . . . . *p.410*
Tejirian, Edward J.. *p.750*
Telander, Rick *p.822, p.895*
Tellis, Gerard J. & Golder, Peter N. *p.135*
Temin, Peter *p.214, p.421*
Temperley, Howard (Editor) *p.728*
Temple, Michael. *p.582*
Templeton, Mary E. *p.171*
Tenenbaum, Gershon (Editor). *p.878*
Tennent, John & Friend, Graham *p.179*
Terborg-Penn, Rosalyn *p.519*
Terchek, Ronald & Conte, Thomas C. (Editors) *p.506*
Terkel, Studs *p.717, p.730*
Tersine, Richard J. *p.116*
Teski, Marea *p.742*
Tettey, Wisdom (Editor), et al. *p.613*
Teweles, Richard J. & Bradley, Edward S. . . *p.97, p.102, p.163*
Teweles, Richard J., et al.. . . . . *p.98, p.102*
Tökés, Rudolf L. *p.595*
Thacker, John *p.319*
Thackrah, J. R. *p.662*
Thakur, Ramesh (Editor) *p.635*
Thakurta, Paranjoy Guha & Raghuraman, Shankar *p.618*
Thaler, Richard H. (Editor) *p.98, p.101*
Thaler, Richard. *p.98*
Tharp, Roland G. & Gallimore, Ronald G.. . . . . *p.349*
Thayer, Carlyle A.. . . . . *p.622*
The Alliance for Technology Access Staff *p.317*
The Center for Middle Eastern Studies at the University of Texas at Austin *p.615*
The Society of News Design Staff (Editor). *p.409*
The Urban Institute and The Brookings Institution *p.108*
The World Bank (Created by) *p.58, p.110, p.112*
The World Bank *p.59, p.60, p.665*
Theberge, Nancy *p.820, p.838, p.862*
Thelen Reid and Priest LLP *p.159*
Thelin, John R. & Wiseman, Lawrence L.. . . . . . *p.822, p.895*
Thelin, John R.. . . . . *p.291, p.332, p.822, p.895*
Then, Danny & McGregor, Wes. *p.113*
Thernstrom, Stephan A. *p.707*
Thier, Marlene & Daviss, Bennett. *p.366*
Thirlwall, A. P. (Editor) *p.229*
Thomas, Alan G. & LoVuolo, Ralph L.. . . . . *p.80*
Thomas, Andrew Peyton *p.540*
Thomas B. Fordham Foundation *p.287*
Thomas, Brook *p.438*
Thomas, David C. & Inkson, Kerr *p.59*
Thomas, David C. *p.70*
Thomas, David (Editor) *p.587*
Thomas, Douglas *p.709*
Thomas, Emory M. *p.522*
Thomas, G. Scott *p.556*
Thomas, Henry W. *p.852, p.898*
Thomas, Jim *p.75*
Thomas, Lewis H. *p.590*
Thomas, Nicholas *p.385*
Thomas, Nick. *p.610, p.712*
Thomas, Raju G. C. *p.618*
Thomas, Ron *p.833, p.854, p.898*
Thomas Vinod. *p.398*
Thomas, Ward. *p.484*
Thomas, William I. & Volkart, Edmund H.. . . . . *p.688*
Thomas, William I. *p.684, p.749, p.752*
Thomason, Sarah G. *p.20*
Thommen, Jean-Paul & Richter, Ansgar *p.65*
Thompson, C. Bradley. *p.515, p.516*
Thompson, E. P.. *p.725*
Thompson, Gail L.. . . . . *p.310*
Thompson, Jennifer L. (Editor), et al.. . . . . *p.15*
Thompson, Kenneth W. (Editor). *p.528*
Thompson, Kenneth *p.678*
Thompson, Robert Bruce & Thompson, Barbara Fritchman *p.114*
Thompson, William N.. . . . . *p.777, p.899*
Thompson, William R.. . . . . *p.628*
Thomsen, Moritz *p.707*
Thomsett, Michael C. (Compiled by) *p.163*
Thomson Gale Staff (Contribution by) . . . *p.374, p.561, p.628*
Thomson Gale Staff (Editor) *p.142*
Thomson Gale Staff. *p.88*
Thorburn, Hugh G. *p.589, p.590*
Thorburn, Hugh *p.589*
Thorn, Craig (Editor) *p.297*
Thorn, John, et al. *p.852*
Thornbury, William D.. . . . . *p.391*
Thorndike, David *p.175, p.181*
Thorndike, Edward L. *p.359*
Thorndike, Edward Lee, et al. *p.359*
Thorndike, Edward Lee *p.359*
Thorndike, Joseph & Ventry, Dennis (Editors) *p.108*
Thorne, Florence C. *p.129*
Thornley, Gail (Editor) *p.116*
Thornton, Stephen J.. . . . . *p.366*
Thorton, Stephen J. & Flinders, David J. (Editors) *p.366*
Thrasher, Frederic M. *p.752*
Thurber, James A. & Nelson, Candice J. (Editors) *p.558*
Thurow, Lester C. *p.78, p.248, p.266*
Tibawi, Abdul Latif *p.337*
Tibor, Palankai *p.638*
Tice, Karen W. *p.755, p.758*
Tickell, Adam (Editor), et al. *p.398*
Tiedt, Pamela L. & Tiedt, Iris M. *p.309*
Tienda, Marta & Wilson, William Julius (Editors) *p.753*
Tierney, Helen (Editor). *p.678*
Tierney, William G. *p.332*
Tietenberg, T. H. *p.63*
Tifft, Susan E. & Jones, Alex S. *p.149, p.411*
Tigerstedt, E. N.. *p.490*

Tight, Malcolm p.321
Tileston, Donna E. Walker p.287
Tilley, Virginia Q. p.650
Tillman, Ray M. & Cummings, Michael S. (Editors) . . . p.129
Tilly, Charles (Editor) p.602
Tilly, Charles, et al. p.707
Tilly, Charles. p.501, p.602, p.684, p.712
Timmerman, Peter (Editor). p.375, p.678
Timonen, Virpi p.594
Tinbergen, Jan & Fischer, Dietrich p.262, p.267
Tinbergen, Jan; Bos, Hendricus Cornelis p.205
Tinbergen, Jan (Editor). p.245
Tinbergen, Jan, et al. p.262, p.266
Tinbergen, Jan p.197, p.205, p.235, p.237, p.245, p.249, p.256, p.260, p.262, p.266
Tindale, R. S., et al. p.688
Tiner, Ralph W. p.393
Tipton, Charles M. (Editor) p.810, p.874
Tipton, Harold F. & Krause, Micki (Editors) p.114
Tipton, Harold F. & Krause, Micki p.114
Tisdell, Clement A. p.62
Tismaneanu, Vladimir (Editor) p.599
Tismaneanu, Vladimir p.509, p.600
Titone, Connie. p.346
Tivey, L. J. (Editor) p.607
Tobias, Andrew. p.98
Tobin, James p.239
Tobin, J. p.205
Tobin, Joseph J. (Editor) p.369
Tobin, Joseph J., et al. p.370
Tobin, Robert p.535
Todorov, Tzvetan p.629
Toffler, Alvin p.769
Toft, Monica Duffy p.488, p.496, p.497
Tolley, Kimberly. p.367
Tolstoy, Leo. p.346
Toma, J. D. p.716, p.820, p.822, p.859, p.895
Tomal, Daniel R. p.355
Tomei, Lawrence A. (Editor) p.352
Tomei, Lawrence A. p.352
Tomlins, Christopher L. p.447
Tomlinson, Alan & Sugden, John. p.845, p.847, p.868
Tomlinson, Carol A. & Allan, Susan D. p.350
Tomlinson, Carol Ann p.350
Tone, Andrea p.775
Tong, Rosemarie. p.472
Tonnies, Ferdinand. p.686
Toppin, Gilbert & Czerniawska, Fiona p.65
Topping, Donna Hooker & McManus, Roberta Ann. . . . p.366
Topping, Keith & Ehly, Stewart (Editors) p.350
Topping, Keith J. p.350
Torbiorn, Kjell M. p.638
Tordoff, William. p.613
Torgoff, Martin p.777
Torp, Linda & Sage, Sara p.349
Toth, Istvan Gyorgy p.337
Toth, Jennifer p.709
Touval, Saadia. p.650
Towle, Charlotte p.755, p.758
Towle, Philip p.657
Toye, J. F. J. & Toye, Richard p.665
Toye, John p.229
Trachtenberg, Marc p.629, p.647
Tracy, Brian S. p.68
Tracy, James D. (Editor) p.771
Tracy, John A. p.92, p.98, p.105, p.176
Tracy, Karen p.423
Training Management Corporation Staff p.57
Transparency International. p.54
Tranter, Neil L. p.810, p.889, p.892
Trattner, Walter I. (Editor) p.758
Travers, Max p.179
Treacy, Michael & Wiersema, Fred p.135
Treglown, Jeremy & Bennett, Bridget (Editors). p.403
Treiman, Donald J. & Hartmann, Heidi I. p.255
Trelease, Jim p.366
Trent, Judith S. & Friedenberg, Robert V. p.578
Treviano, A. Javier (Editor). p.687
Tribe, John p.785, p.889
Tribe, Laurence H. p.454, p.472
Tricard, Louise Mead p.810, p.838, p.869
Triechler, Paula A.. . . . . p.779
Trigg, Heather B. p.383
Trigger, Bruce G. p.6
Trinkaus, Erik p.17
Trolldal, Bjorn. p.153
Trompenaars, Fons & Woolliams, Peter. p.59
Trompenaars, Fons p.59, p.132
Trowbridge, Leslie W., et al. p.367
Troxel, Tiffany A. p.599
Troy, Leo p.123
Trubowitz, Sidney & Robins, Maureen Picard p.278
Trueba, Enrique T. p.311
Trumbull, Elise p.311, p.312
Trump, Kenneth S.. . . . . p.281
Truth and Reconcilation Commission of South Africa. . . p.731
Tsay, Ruey S.. . . . . p.205, p.206, p.264
Tsebelis, George. p.575
Tsesis, Alexander p.423
Tsing, Anna Lowenhaupt p.27
Tsoukalis, Loukas p.383
Tsurumi, Kazuko p.707
Tu, Weiming & De Bary, William Theodore (Editors). . . p.513
Tuan, Yi-Fu p.375
Tuana, Nancy (Editor), et al. p.745
Tuaolo, Esera & Rosengren, John. p.839, p.860
Tuathail, Gearsid S., et al. p.400
Tuck, Richard p.477
Tucker, Allan (Editor) p.294
Tucker, David p.540

Tucker, Nancy B. p.561, p.566, p.644
Tuden, Arthur & Plotnicov, Leonard. p.707
Tufte, Edward R. p.174
Tulchin, Joseph S. & Brown, Amelia (Editors) p.506
Tulchin, Joseph S. & Selee, Andrew D. p.585, p.613
Tulchin, Joseph S. p.593
Tulliu, Steve & Schmalberger, Thomas p.657
Tully, James. p.526
Tumin, Melvin M. & Feldman, Arnold S. p.707
Tung, Fei p.475
Tunkin, G. I. p.627
Tunnell, Kenneth D. p.131
Turkington, Carol & Harris, Joseph p.319
Turnbull, Colin M. p.39
Turnbull, George (Editor). p.346
Turner, Barry (Editor) p.374, p.575, p.625
Turner, Bryan (Introduction by). p.692, p.762
Turner, Bryan S.. . . . . p.686
Turner, Ed & Clouse, Woody p.864
Turner, Jonathan H. p.684, p.707, p.718
Turner, L. F. & Turner, Susan Lilliman p.797, p.799
Turner, Lowell (Editor), et al.. . . . . p.129
Turner, Marjorie S. p.271
Turner, Mark p.272
Turner, Mary p.728
Turner, Stansfield p.562
Turner, Stephen & Sica, Alan (Editors) p.684
Turner, Tyya N. p.156
Turner, Victor W. p.37
Turoff, Fred. p.797, p.862
Turow, Joseph. p.696
Turow, Scott p.441
Turpin, Jennifer (Editor) p.679
Tushnet, Mark (Editor). p.462
Tushnet, Mark V. p.457, p.469
Tushnet, Mark. p.540
Twagilimana, Aimable p.654
Twigg, Judyth L. p.669
Twitchell, James B. p.427
Twomey, David P. p.134
Tworzecki, Hubert. p.579, p.597
Tyack, David B. & Hansot, Elisabeth p.282
Tyack, David p.298
Tye, Barbara Benham & Tye, Kenneth A. p.314
Tye, Larry p.429
Tygiel, Jules p.810, p.833, p.852, p.898
Tyler, Ralph W. p.366
Tyrrell, Ian p.776
Tyrrell, William Blake p.810

U

U. S. News and World Report Staff p.278
U. S. Office of Education Staff & Coleman, James S.. . . . p.301
U. S. Tennis Association Staff & Ellenbecker, Todd S. . . p.864
Uchida, Hiroshi (Editor) p.237
Ucko, Peter J. (Editor) p.6
Ueshiba, Kisshomaru. p.863
Ugalde, Luis Carlos p.594
Ugur, Mehmet. p.239
Ulich, Robert (Editor) p.323, p.329
Ulrich, Dave & Brockbank, Wayne. p.77
Umphlett, Wiley L. (Editor) p.812
Umphlett, Wiley L. p.810, p.860, p.895
Umphlett, Wiley Lee. p.418
UN Office for the Coordination of Humanitarian Affairs (UNOCHA) . p.668, p.669, p.670, p.671
UNAIDS/WHO p.669
Underwood, Jim p.79
Ungar, Sanford J. p.438
Unger, Harlow G. p.340
Unger, Irwin p.332
Unger, Jonathan (Editor) p.620
Unger, Jonathan p.337
UNICEF Staff. p.670
UNICEF p.670
United Kingdom. Central Office of Information. p.604
United Kingdom. Office for National Statistics p.604
United Kingdom. Prime Minister.. . . . . p.604, p.605
United Nations Association Staff p.669
United Nations Conference on International Organization Staff p.635
United Nations Conference on Trade and Development . . p.666
United Nations, Department of Economic and Social Affairs, Population Division Staff p.663
United Nations, Department of Economic and Social Affairs Staff p.547
United Nations, Dept. of Economic and Social Affairs Staff (Contribution by) p.666
United Nations Development Programme Staff & Arab Fund for Economic and Social Development Staff p.615
United Nations Development Programme Staff . . p.258, p.262, p.586, p.666
United Nations High Commissioner for Refugees Staff . . p.765
United Nations: Human Settlements Programme p.663
United Nations. OHCHR p.670
United Nations Staff p.586, p.635, p.636, p.651, p.655, p.657, p.667
United Nations, Statistical Division Staff (Contribution by). p.388
United Nations Timber Committee p.152, p.164
United Nations (UN). p.666
United Nations p.476, p.482, p.635, p.657, p.662, p.663, p.666, p.669
United States.; Bureau of the Budget p.248
United States Census Bureau, Systems Support Division . p.179
United States Census Bureau p.159
United States Central Intelligence Agency. p.60
United States Department of Agriculture, Agricultural Marketing Service p.152, p.164
United States Department of Agriculture, Economic Research Service p.152
United States Department of Agriculture

Foreign Agricultural Service *p.152, p.164*
United States Department of Agriculture *p.152*
United States Department of Commerce, International Trade Administration *p.161*
United States Department of Commerce *p.60*
United States Department of Health and Human Services, Office of Applied Studies, Substance Abuse and Mental Health Services Administration (SAMHSA) *p.777*
United States Department of State *p.437, p.476*
United States Green Building Council *p.159*
United States. National Commission on Excellence in Education *p.323*
United States. President's Commission on Campus Unrest. *p.332*
United States Senate. *p.532, p.534*
United States. Supreme Court. *p.437*
United States Tennis Association *p.864*
United States.Congress. Senate. Committee on Appropriations. Subcommittee on Departments of Labor, Health and Human Services, Education, and Related Agencies. *p.337*
University of Auckland Library *p.179*
University of California at Berkeley Wellness Lett & White, Timothy P. *p.791*
University of Hawaii at Manoa, Industrial Relation Staff . *p.123*
University of Illinois Communications Library *p.141*
University of Michigan Documents Center *p.482*
University of Minnesota Human Rights Center *p.670*
University of Minnesota Law Library *p.477*
University of Surrey *p.675*
Unruh, David R.. *p.742*
Unwin, Tim *p.373*
Uphoff, Norman T. & Ilchman, Warren F. (Editors) *p.574*
Urban, Joan Barth & Solovei, Valerii D.. . . . . . *p.599, p.600*
Urban Land Institute Staff *p.159, p.166*
Urban, Wayne J. & Wagoner, Jennings L. *p.329*
Urban, Wayne J.. *p.283*
Urofsky, Melvin I. & Finkelman, Paul (Editors) *p.440*
Urofsky, Melvin I. & Finkelman, Paul. *p.452*
Urofsky, Melvin I. & Levy, David W. (Editors). *p.469*
Urofsky, Melvin I. *p.440, p.448, p.469*
Urrea, Luis Alberto *p.765*
U.S. Census Bureau *p.482, p.679*
U.S. Department of Education *p.323*
U.S. Department of Labor Staff *p.168*
U.S. Department of State . . . *p.482, p.561, p.566, p.643, p.670*
U.S. Government Accountability Office (GAO). *p.481*
U.S. Government Printing Office *p.482*
U.S. Navy. Dudley Knox Library. Naval Postgraduate School *p.565*
Useem, Michael *p.90*
Ustin, Susan L. *p.389*
Utter, Glenn H. *p.449*
Uviller, H. Richard *p.471*

V

Vacca, Richard T. & Vacca, Jo Anne L. *p.366*
Vacca, Richard T., et al. *p.361*
Vaggi, Gianni *p.217*
Vaidhyanathan, Siva *p.761*
Vaidya, Ashish K.. . . . . *p.56, p.58, p.181*
Valdes, Isabel & Seoane, Marta *p.136*
Valdes, M. Isabel *p.139*
Valdez, Stephen & Wood, Julian *p.58, p.98, p.102, p.103*
Valdés, Guadalupe *p.311, p.312*
Vale, Lawrence J. & Campanella, Thomas J. *p.760*
Vale, Lawrence J. *p.757*
Valencia, Reynaldo Anaya *p.458*
Valencia, Richard R. (Editor) *p.311*
Valentino, Benjamin A. *p.654, p.715*
Valk, Arnoud van der *p.393*
Valls, Andrew (Editor) *p.484*
Valls, Andrew *p.484, p.627*
Vamplew, Wray (Editor), et al. *p.824*
Vamplew, Wray *p.810, p.898, p.899*
van Assendelft, Laura *p.569*
Van Bottenburg, Marten *p.845*
Van Dalen, Deobold B.. . . . . *p.797*
Van De Graaff, John H., et al. *p.295*
van Den Berg, Richard. *p.205*
Van den Bergh, Jeroen C. (Editor) *p.62*
Van den Berghe, Pierre L. *p.684, p.729*
Van der Linden, R. Robert *p.152*
van Dijk, Jan *p.419*
Van Dijk, Teun A. *p.21, p.731*
Van Galen, Jane (Editor), et al. *p.296*
Van Gennep, Arnold *p.37*
Van Gerven, Walter *p.604, p.638*
van Ginneken, Jaap *p.408, p.713*
Van Hear, Nicholas *p.765*
Van Hoorn, Judith L., et al.. . . . . *p.707*
Van Horn, Carl E. & Schaffner, Herbert A. (Author, Editors). *p.123*
Van Raalte, Judy L. & Brewer, Britton W. (Editors) *p.878, p.904*
Van Wagoner, Richard S.. . . . . *p.740, p.749*
Van Wart, Montgomery *p.546, p.698*
Van Wolferen, Karel *p.622*
Van Zijp, Rudy *p.233, p.234*
Vanaik, Achin *p.618*
VanBurkleo, Sandra F. (Editor), et al. *p.453*
VanBurkleo, Sandra F. *p.458*
Vance, Carole S.. *p.749*
Vanden Auweele, Yves (Editor), et al. *p.797*
Vanderbilt, Arthur T.. . . . . *p.440*
Vanderbilt, Tom *p.870, p.881*
Vanderwerken, David L. & Wertz, Spencer K. (Editors) *p.803, p.812*
VanderZwaag, Harold J. *p.886*
VanTassel-Baska, Joyce & Reis, Sally M. (Editors) *p.317*

Varano, Charles S. *p.727*
Vargas, Zaragosa *p.255*
Varian, H. R. *p.249*
Varisco, Daniel Martin *p.37*
Vasquez, Manuel A. & Marquardt, Marie F. *p.720*
Vaughn, Karen I. *p.234*
Vaughn, Robie. *p.846*
Vavrus, Michael J.. *p.280*
Veal, A. J. (Editor), et al. *p.785, p.899*
Veblen, Thorstein B. & Ardzrooni, Leon. *p.197*
Veblen, Thorstein B. *p.214, p.250, p.251, p.725*
Veblen, Thorstein *p.210, p.212, p.214, p.250, p.651*
Vega, Gina *p.143*
Velez-Ibanez, Carlos G. *p.770*
Vella, Jane Kathryn *p.321*
Vella, Jane *p.321*
Vennum, Thomas Jr.. . . . . *p.810, p.841, p.863*
Ventelou, Bruno *p.229*
Venuti, Lawrence *p.709*
Verba, Sidney & Nie, Norman H. *p.506, p.555, p.580*
Verba, Sidney, et al. *p.578, p.580*
Verbeek, Marno *p.205*
Verdery, Katherine *p.42*
Vergason, Glenn A. & Anderegg, M. L. *p.317*
Verhoeven, Ludo T. & Snow, Catherine E. (Editors) . . . *p.354*
Vermeulen, Han & Roldan, Arturo A. (Editors) *p.5*
Verney, Jack. *p.581*
Vertinsky, Patricia A. *p.810, p.838*
Vertova, Giovanna *p.398*
Vestal, Theodore M. *p.314, p.540*
Veysey, Laurence R. *p.333*
VGM Career Books Staff (Editor). *p.171*
Vibert, Conor. *p.83*
Vicarelli, Fausto *p.229*
Vicinus, Martha *p.738*
Vickrey, William S. *p.248*
Vickrey, William. *p.247*
Victor, Edward & Kellough, Richard D. *p.366*
Victor, R. F.. . . . . *p.229*
Vigil, James Diego. *p.714*
Vigod, Bernard L. *p.581*
Vila, Bryan & Morris, Cynthia (Editors). *p.487, p.568*
Vila, Pablo *p.727*
Vile, John R. *p.454*
Vile, M. J. *p.576*
Villa, Dana (Editor) *p.493*
Vincent, Jeffrey R. & Mäler, Karl-Göran (Editors) *p.192*
Vincent, Joan (Editor) *p.35*
Viney, Ethna *p.749*
Vinogradoff, Paul *p.433, p.501*
Vinovskis, Maris A. *p.329, p.330*
Viscusi, W. Kip (Editor) *p.110, p.112*
Vise, David A. & Malseed, Mark. *p.68*
Visher, Emily B. & Visher, John S. *p.732*
Vitebsky, Piers *p.772*
Vizentini, Paulo Gilberto Fagundes & Wiesebron, Marianne (Editors) *p.61*
Vogel, David *p.52, p.54, p.112*
Vogel, Ezra F. *p.725*
Vogel, Joseph O.. . . . . *p.8*
Vogel, Ronald K. (Editor) *p.544*
Vogel, Steven *p.908*
Vogel, Todd (Editor) *p.411*
Vogt, W. Paul *p.679*
Vohra, Rakesh *p.205*
Volavka, Zdenka. *p.708*
Volkema, Roger *p.75*
Volkman, Toby Alice (Editor). *p.708*
Vollmann, William T. *p.751*
Volpi, Frederic *p.586, p.613*
Volti, Rudi *p.154*
Von Drehle, David. *p.129*
Von Fritz, Kurt *p.490*
von Heyking, John. *p.490*
Von Krafft-Ebing, Richard *p.749*
von Krogh, Georg, et al.. . . . . *p.79*
von Mises, Ludwig *p.197, p.212*
Vora, Rajendra & Palshikar, Suhas (Editors) *p.618*
Vorenberg, Michael *p.453*
Vose, Clement E. *p.443*
Voss-Hubbard, Mark. *p.552, p.553*
Vrasidas, Charalambos & Glass, Gene V. (Editors) *p.352*
Vreeland, James (Editor), et al. *p.262*
Vryhof, Steven C. *p.308*
Vygotsky, L. S. *p.695*

W

Waddell, Tom & Schaap, Dick *p.839*
Waddington, Ivan *p.820, p.826*
Waddock, Sandra; Graves, Samuel *p.54*
Wade, Peter *p.731*
Wagner, Helmut R. *p.686*
Wagner, Tony *p.330*
Waisman, Carlos H. & Peralta-Ramos, Monica (Editors) . *p.593*
Waite, P. B. *p.587*
Wakefield, Suzy Mygatt (Editor) *p.306, p.353*
Wakefield, Wanda Ellen *p.810*
Wakelyn, Jon L.. . . . . *p.526*
Wald, Michael S., et al. *p.756*
Walder, Andrew G. *p.509*
Waldinger, Roger *p.730*
Waldman, Carl & Wexler, Alan *p.379*
Walesa, Lech *p.129*
Walicki, Andrzej. *p.509*
Walker, Danielle Medina & Walker, Thomas *p.59*
Walker, David M. (Editor) *p.433*
Walker, Donald A. (Editor). *p.213, p.217*
Walker, John R. & Lundberg, Donald E.. . . . . *p.165*
Walker, Lenore E.. . . . . *p.743, p.759*

Walker, Samuel p.472, p.568
Walker-Moffat, Wendy p.311
Walkowitz, Judith R.. . . . . p.749
Wall, William Douglas p.359
Wallace, Anthony F. p.25, p.37
Wallace, Aurora p.411
Wallace, Phyllis A., et al.. . . . . p.271
Wallace, Richard (Editor). p.171
Wallace, Robert. p.69
Wallace, Ruth A. (Editor). p.744
Wallach, Bret p.399
Waller, Derek p.118
Waller, James p.654, p.698
Waller, Willard W.. . . . . p.732
Wallerstein, Immanuel. p.680, p.759, p.762
Wallimann, Isidor & Dobkowski, Michael N. (Editors) . . p.654
Walling, Karl-Friedrich. p.493
Walras, Leon p.197, p.213, p.217
Walraven, Klaas van p.631
Walsh, George, et al. p.65
Walsh, Vivian & Gram, Harvey N.. . p.206, p.218, p.224, p.271
Walsh, W. Bruce & Heppner, Mary J. (Editors) . . p.306, p.354
Walsh, W. Bruce & Savickas, Mark (Editors). p.306
Walter, Barbara F. p.651
Walter, Lynn & Desai, Manisha (Editors) p.679
Walter, Mariko Namba p.37
Walters, F. P. p.632
Walters, Ronald W. p.519, p.555, p.556, p.573
Walters, Suzanna D. p.738
Walton, Hanes Jr. p.529
Walton, Hanes. p.574
Walton, John p.697, p.759
Walton, Richard E., et al.. . . . . p.123
Walton, Stuart. p.777
Waltz, Kenneth N.. . . . . p.625, p.627
Walzer, Michael. p.511, p.513, p.514
Wangersky, Peter J. (Editor) p.393
Wangersky, Peter J. (Volume Editor). p.393
Wansbeek, Tom J. & Meijer, Erik p.205
Wapner, Paul & Falk, Richard A. p.484, p.627
Wappingers Central School District p.287
Warburton, Christopher. p.384
Ward, Artemus p.540
Ward, Barbara (Editor), et al.. . . . . p.260, p.271
Ward, Barbara. p.267, p.271
Ward, Geoffrey C. & Burns, Kenneth p.810, p.852
Ward, James G. & Anthony, Patricia (Editors) p.281
Ward, John & Peppard, Joe p.115
Ward, Lester F. & Gerver, Israel (Introduction by) p.686
Ward, Lester F. p.684
Ward, Michael. p.636
Ward, R. Gerard & Kingdon, Elizabeth (Editors) p.43
Ward, Robert David & Rogers, William Warren p.542
Ward, Stephen J. A. p.406
Wardlaw, Grant p.662
Ware, Alan p.550, p.553
Ware, Leslie. p.144
Warf, Barney (Editor) p.396
Warhol, Robyn R. p.695
Warhurst, John & MacKerras, Malcolm (Editors). p.624
Wark, McKenzie. p.761
Warlaumont, Hazel G. p.141
Warner, Lloyd W. & Low, V. O. p.708
Warner, Tom p.712
Warner, W. Lloyd p.725
Warner, William L. & Lunt, Paul S.. . . . . p.725
Warner, William L. p.708
Warneryd, Karl Erik p.246, p.251
Warren, Charles p.440
Warren, Donald R. p.281, p.324
Warren, Earl. p.469
Warren, Elizabeth & Tyagi, Amelia Warren p.98
Warren, Michelle P. & Shangold, Mona M. p.826, p.878
Warshaw, Matt p.788, p.868
Warshaw, Shirley Anne. p.528
Wartick, Steven L. & Wood, Donna J.. . . . . p.145
Wasburn, Philo C. p.408
Washburn, Wilcomb E.. . . . . p.465
Wasserstein, Bruce. p.85, p.92
Waste, Robert J. p.544
Waterman, Richard W., et al. p.546
Waterman, Richard W. p.528
Waters, M. Dane. p.460
Waters, Neil L. p.627
Watkins, Evan p.759
Watkins, Marie & Braun, Linda. p.168
Watkins, Michael & Rosegrant, Susan p.646
Watson, Alan p.433
Watson, Cynthia A. p.562
Watson, J. Wreford p.708
Watson, James & Hill, Anne p.424
Watson, James L. & Caldwell, Melissa (Editors). p.46
Watson, Robert P. & Campbell, Colton C. (Editors). . . . p.552
Watson, Robert P. & Gordon, Ann (Editors) p.528
Watson, Robert P. p.550
Watson, Tom p.861
Watson, Virginia D.. . . . . p.43
Watson, W. Martin & Markman, Sherwin p.528
Watstein, Sarah & Stratton, Stephen E. p.669
Watt, Donald Cameron p.628
Watt, Dougal p.113
Wattenberg, Martin P. & Shugart, Matthew Soberg p.576
Wattenberg, Martin P. p.550, p.556
Watterson, John Sayle p.810, p.860, p.895
Watts, Duncan J., et al.. . . . . p.422
Watts, Meredith p.752
Watts, Michael (Editor, Commentaries by) p.186
Watts, Robert G. & Bahill, A. Terry. p.848, p.871
Watts, Sheldon J. p.708
Watts, Steven p.154

Waugh, Colin M. p.654
Wawro, Geoffrey p.628, p.648
Wawro, Gregory p.533
Wearing, Betsy p.785, p.838
Weart, Spencer R. p.506, p.627, p.648, p.651
Weaver, David B. (Editor) p.161
Weaver, Jace p.541
Weaver, R. Kent (Editor) p.587
Webb, Beatrice p.271
Webb, Jennifer & Schirato, Tony p.424
Webber, David W. p.448
Webel, Charles p.662
Weber, Bruce A. (Editor), et al. p.755
Weber, Lillian & Alberty, Beth p.346
Weber, Max M. p.718, p.721
Weber, Max p.211, p.213, p.435, p.681, p.720, p.722, p.725
Websdale, Neil p.743
Webster, Juliet p.761
Webster-Stratton, Carolyn p.354
Weed, Frank J. p.754
Weeks, Gregory p.593
Weeks, Jeffrey p.570, p.749
Wehmeyer, Michael L., et al. p.319
Weick, Karl E. p.174
Weiers, Ronald M.. . . . . p.179
Weigall, David p.627
Weightman, Barbara A. p.384, p.399
Weiglin, Peter C. p.176
Weil, Danny & Kincheloe, Joe L. (Editors) p.366
Weil, Danny p.299
Weiler, Joseph H. & Wind, Marlene (Editors) p.639
Weiler, Paul C. p.445
Weinberg, Elizabeth Ann p.684
Weinberg, Leonard p.662
Weinberg, Meyer p.311
Weinberg, Robert S. & Richardson, Peggy A. p.878, p.905
Weinberg, Steve, et al. p.408
Weiner, Annette B. p.43
Weiner, Edward p.166
Weiner, J. S. p.16
Weiner, Mark S.. . . . . p.723
Weiner, Rex & Stillman, Deanne p.736
Weingarten, Marc p.403
Weinstein, James p.493
Weinstein, Michael M. p.663
Weintraub, E. Roy p.176
Weintraub, Sidney (Editor). p.61
Weir, Margaret (Editor), et al. p.526, p.571
Weir, Robert E. & Hanlan, James P. (Editors) p.123
Weir, Robert E. p.130
Weir, Walter. p.428
Weis, Lois & Fine, Michelle (Editors) p.302
Weisberg, Herbert F. p.531
Weisburd, A. Mark p.648, p.651
Weisburd, David, et al.. . . . . p.774
Weisman, Steven R. p.108, p.147
Weiss, Alan p.65
Weiss, Donald H. p.447
Weiss, Maureen R.. . . . . p.878
Weiss, Paul p.803
Weiss, Thomas G., et al. p.636
Weiss, Thomas George, et al. p.565
Weissberg, Robert p.559
Weissberg, Ted p.822, p.895
Weisse, Ralf & Storch, Hans v. p.394
Weissman, Harold, et al. p.759
Weissman, Jerry p.174
Weitz, Eric D.. . . . . p.715
Weitz, Rose p.774
Welch, Claude E. p.640, p.670
Welch, Jack & Byrne, John A. p.72
Welch, Jack p.82
Welch, Paula D.. . . . . p.797
Weller, Robert P. p.618, p.620
Wellington, Jerry p.367
Wellins, Richard S., et al. p.80
Wellner, Alison Stein p.788, p.824
Wells, Amy Stuart & Crain, Robert L.. . . . . p.301
Wells, Amy Stuart p.299
Wells, Donald R. p.90
Wells-Barnett, Ida B.. . . . . p.752
Welsh, Jennifer M. (Editor). p.671
Welsh, Kate Shoup. p.168
Wempen, Faithe p.174
Wendorf, Fred, et al. p.8
Wendt, Alexander p.627
Wenglinsky, Harold p.352
Wenner, Lawrence A. p.820, p.892, p.903, p.907
Werbner, Richard P. & Ranger, Terence (Editors). . p.582, p.613
Werhane, P. H. & Freeman, R. Edward p.54, p.55, p.181
Werner, Frank D. & Greig, Richard C. p.861, p.870, p.872
Werner, Peter H. p.799, p.862
Wert, Jeffry D. p.522
Wertsman, Vladimir F. p.168
Wesseling, H. L.. . . . . p.583
Wesson, John p.868, p.871
West, Bernadette M., et al. p.407
West, Cornel (Editor) p.730
West, D. J. p.749
West, John G. Jr. & Maclean, Iain p.487, p.560
West, Michael p.80
West, Nancy Martha p.427
West, Robert C. (Author, Translator) p.378
Westbrook, Deeanne p.812, p.852
Westbrook, Robert B. p.493
Westerbeek, Hans & Smith, Aaron . . p.845, p.886, p.892, p.899
Westermann, W. L.. . . . . p.727
Westervelt, Saundra D.. . . . . p.754
Westlye, Mark C. p.550, p.557

Weston, Kath. p.33, p.740
WetFeet p.65
WetFeet.com (Firm) Staff p.171, p.178
Wetteroth, Debbra p.115
Wever, Kirsten S. p.123
Wexler, Alan p.381
Whalen, Mollie p.751
Whalen, Thomas J. p.534
Whannel, Garry p.820, p.903
Whatmore, Sarah p.399
Wheatcroft, Geoffrey p.845, p.857
Wheatley, Margaret J. p.72
Wheeler, Alina p.142
Wheeler, Hoyt N., et al. p.131
Wheeler, Hoyt N. p.130
Wheeler, Nicholas J. p.671
Wheeler, Stephen & Beatley, Timothy (Editors) p.268
Wheen, Francis p.237
Whetten, Nathan L. p.772
Whillock, Rita K.. . . . . p.550, p.558, p.559
Whitaker, Reginald p.589
White, Bud & White, Charles B. p.881, p.886, p.906
White, G. Edward p.443, p.469, p.540, p.852
White, Gary W. (Editor) p.181
White, George W. p.383, p.399, p.488, p.496
White, Graham p.588
White, Halbert. p.205
White, James B.. p.497
White, James M.. p.735
White, John Kenneth & Shea, Daniel M. p.552, p.553
White, Nicholas P.. . . . . p.490
White, Philip & Young, Kevin (Editors) p.820
White, Richard D. p.546
White, Sarah C.. . . . . p.31
White, Sol p.810, p.833, p.852
White, Stephen, et al. p.599
White, Welsh S. p.474
Whitehead, Alfred North. p.291, p.340, p.346
Whitehead, Bruce M., et al.. . . . . p.352
Whitelaw, Nancy p.150
Whitfield, Peter p.379
Whiting, Robert p.820, p.834, p.852, p.890, p.898, p.899
Whitley, James p.13
Whitman, Marina V. p.271
Whitman, Marina von Neumann p.264
Whitman, Mark p.451
Whitmore, Sarah p.576, p.586, p.599
Whittaker, Cynthia H. p.599
Whitten, Phillip p.869
Whittington, Michael & Williams, Glen (Editors). p.587
Whittle, Alasdair W. R. p.13
Whorf, Benjamin Lee p.20
Whyte, William F. p.752
Wiarda, Howard J. & Kline, Harvey F. p.593
Wiarda, Howard J. p.510, p.593
Wiber, Melanie G. p.31
Wichterich, Christa p.666
Wicker, Tom & Schlesinger, Arthur M. Jr. p.528
Wickham-Crowley, Timothy P. p.498
Wicksell, Knut & Sandelin, Bo p.241
Wicksell, Knut p.239, p.241
Widdis, Randy William. p.765
Wiecek, William M. p.455
Wieting, Stephen G. (Editor) p.811, p.820
Wiggin, Addison & Bonner, William p.246, p.267
Wiggin, Gladys Anna p.298
Wiggins, David K. (Editor) p.811
Wiggins, David K. p.822, p.833
Wiggins, Grant P. p.287
Wigglesworth, Neil p.811, p.865
Wigmore, John H. p.435
Wikan, Unni p.39, p.40
Wiktorowicz, Quintan (Editor) p.712
Wilcox, Clifford p.5
Wilcox, Jarrod W. p.205
Wilcox, Ralph C. (Editor) p.845, p.899
Wild, Ray p.119
Wild, Tony p.117
Wild, Trevor p.772
Wilde, Sandra p.287
Wilder, Claudyne & Rotondo, Jennifer. p.174
Wiley, Carol A. (Editor) p.838, p.863
Wilhite, Barbara C. & Keller, M. Jean p.786, p.830
Wilke, Rebecca Lynn p.279
Wilkins, David E. & Lomawaima, K. Tsianina p.526
Wilkins, David E. p.465
Wilkins, Lee & Coleman, Renita p.417
Wilkinson, Charles F. p.463, p.465, p.540
Wilkinson, Paul p.498, p.662
Wilkinson, Steven p.618
Wilkinson, Todd p.566
Willem, Van Vliet (Editor) p.544
Willerton, John P. p.599
Willett, Thomas D. (Editor). p.245
William M. McDonald and Associates Staff & McDonald, William M. (Editors) p.333
William M. White Business Library, Leeds School of Business, University of Colorado at Boulder p.53
Williams, Craig A. & James, David V. B. p.874
Williams, David p.179
Williams, Jack p.811, p.820, p.856
Williams, Jean p.811, p.845, p.868
Williams, Jen R. & Carcillo, Joseph V. p.105
Williams, Jerome D. (Editor), et al. p.426
Williams, John E. & Best, Deborah L.. . . . . p.693
Williams, Juan. p.469
Williams, Leslie R. & Fromberg, Doris P. (Editors). . . . p.369
Williams, Linda p.749
Williams, Mark (Editor), et al. p.874, p.908, p.910
Williams, Melvin H.. . . . . p.791, p.876

Williams, Nancy S. *p.366*
Williams, Paul L. *p.662*
Williams, Peter *p.716, p.853*
Williams, Philip J. & Walter, Knut *p.593*
Williams, Richard *p.730*
Williams, Robert A. Jr.. . . . . . *p.574*
Williams, Robin & Tollett, John. *p.428*
Williams, Scott P. & Petersen, Randy *p.864*
Williams, Tony & Hunter, Gordon. *p.865*
Williams, Walter *p.526, p.567, p.770*
Williamson, Richard S.. . . . . . *p.526*
Willingham, Warren W. & Cole, Nancy S. (Editors) . . . *p.287*
Willis, James F. *p.477*
Willis, Jim *p.412*
Willis, John R. (Editor) *p.728*
Willis, Sherry (Editor), et al. *p.741*
Willis *p.42*
Wills, Garry *p.72*
Wilmore, Jack H. & Costill, David L. *p.878*
Wilshire, Bruce *p.662*
Wilson, Andrew *p.599*
Wilson, Carter A. *p.727*
Wilson, David Sloan *p.720*
Wilson, Douglas *p.308*
Wilson, H. T. *p.546*
Wilson, Heather A. *p.478*
Wilson, J. S. G. *p.241*
Wilson, Janet *p.729*
Wilson, John & Fotheringham, Stewart (Editors) *p.388*
Wilson, John *p.716, p.820, p.892*
Wilson, Joseph *p.562, p.648*
Wilson, Logan. *p.294*
Wilson, Peter J. *p.17, p.39*
Wilson, Raymond Jackson *p.684*
Wilson, Richard (Editor). *p.34*
Wilson, Robert F. *p.785, p.904*
Wilson, Samuel M. *p.41*
Wilson, Wayne & Derse, Edward (Editors) *p.826, p.846*
Wilson, William Julius *p.730, p.759, p.771*
Wilson, William W. *p.630, p.644, p.666*
Wilstein, Steve *p.407, p.903, p.907*
Wilton, Tamsin *p.750*
Wiltshire, David *p.686*
Wimbush, Vincent L. & Rodman, Rosemary C. (Editors) *p.721*
Winant, Howard. *p.731, p.767*
Winch, Christopher & Gingell, John *p.324, p.340*
Winch, Christopher *p.306*
Winch, D.. . . . . . *p.220*
Winch, Robert F. *p.739*
Wind, Jerry, et al. *p.135*
Windlesham, Lord *p.567*
Winfeld, Liz & Spielman, Susan *p.132, p.168*
Winfield, Percy H.. . . . . . *p.433*
Wing, Bret & Walker, Sharon. *p.156*
Winick, Charles *p.3*
Wink, Michael (Editor). *p.157*
Winkler, Carol K. *p.565*
Winnick, Joseph P.. . . . . . *p.801*
Winslow, Calvin *p.130*
Winston, Brian *p.419*
Winter, David A. *p.875, p.908, p.910*
Wipperfurth, Alex *p.142*
Wirls, Daniel & Wirls, Stephen *p.534*
Wirt, Frederick M. & Kirst, Michael W. *p.298*
Wise, David A. (Editor) *p.267*
Wise, Stephen R. *p.522*
Wise, Suzanne. *p.820*
Wiser, William & Wiser, Charlotte V. *p.40*
Witkin, Belle Ruth & Altschuld, James W. *p.82*
Witte, John Jr.. . . . . . *p.459*
Wittig, Monique *p.749*
Wittman, Donald A. *p.506*
Wittner, Lawrence S. *p.572, p.651, p.657*
Witwer, David. *p.130*
Witzel, Morgen *p.177*
Wodak, Ruth & Pelinka, Anton (Editors). *p.595*
Wolcott, Harry F. *p.282, p.687*
Wolf, Arthur P. & Durham, William H. *p.738*
Wolf, Eric R. *p.25, p.29, p.35*
Wolf, Martin *p.56, p.58, p.666*
Wolf, Stephanie G.. . . . . . *p.708*
Wolfe, Alan. *p.299, p.697*
Wolfe, J. N. (Editor) *p.260*
Wolfe, Joseph & Keys, J. Bernard (Editors) *p.177*
Wolfer, Loreen *p.376*
Wolff, Alexander *p.845, p.855*
Wolff, Robert P. *p.237, p.511*
Wolfgang, Charles H. *p.284*
Wolfgang, Marvin E., et al.. . . . . . *p.753*
Wolfson, Nicholas. *p.460, p.749*
Wolin, Richard *p.510*
Wolin, Sheldon S. *p.493*
Wollons, Roberta Lyn (Editor) *p.368*
Wollstonecraft, Mary. *p.745*
Woloch, Nancy *p.439*
Wolpin, Miles D. *p.574*
Wolpoff, Milford H.. . . . . . *p.16*
Wolverton, Mimi & Penley, Larry Edward (Editors) . . . *p.177*
Wong, Bernice Y. L. (Editor) *p.319*
Wong, Glenn M. *p.449, p.901*
Wong, Paul T. P. & Wong, Lilian C. J. (Editors) *p.699*
Wong, Rosemary T. *p.278*
Wong, Stanley *p.197, p.251*
Wong. *p.904*
Wonnacott, Ronald J. & Wonnacott, Gordon P. *p.258*
Woo, Deborah. *p.134*
Wood, Andrew Grant. *p.765*
Wood, Douglas J. *p.427*
Wood, Elisabeth Jean *p.614*

Wood, Gordon S. *p.517*
Wood, John C. & Woods, Ronald N. (Editors) *p.197*
Wood, John C. (Editor). *p.229*
Wood, John Cunningham & McLure, Michael *p.197*
Wood, John H. *p.156*
Wood, Peter. *p.709*
Wood, Stephen B. *p.447*
Wood, Terry Lee (Editor), et al.. . . . . *p.366*
Wooden, Wayne S. & Ehringer, Gavin *p.865, p.881*
Woodhull, Victoria C. *p.708*
Woodill, Gary (Editor), et al.. . . . . *p.314, p.359, p.369*
Woodroffe, Colin D. *p.393*
Woods, Lawrence T. *p.640*
Woods, Michael *p.396*
Woodson, Carter Godwin. *p.310*
Woodward, Bob *p.90, p.156, p.565*
Woodworth, David & Hobbs, Guy (Editors) *p.171*
Woodworth, David. *p.171*
Woodworth, Steven E. & Winkle, Kenneth J.. . . . . . . *p.381*
Woodworth, Steven E. (Editor) *p.522*
Woodworth, Steven E. *p.522*
Woog, Dan *p.839*
Wooldridge, Jeffrey M. *p.205, p.206*
Woolum, Janet *p.838*
Worell, Judith (Editor) *p.679*
World Bank Group *p.56*
World Bank Staff (Contribution by) *p.337*
World Bank Staff *p.260, p.373*
World Health Organization *p.669*
World Legal Information Institute . . *p.436, p.475, p.476, p.477*
World Resources Institute Staff *p.177*
World Tourism Organization (WTO) Staff *p.162*
Wormeli, Rick. *p.366*
Wormuth, Francis D. & Firmage, Edwin B. *p.461*
Wormuth, Francis D., et al.. . . . . *p.532*
Worsley, Peter *p.37*
Wouters, Cas *p.738*
Woy, James (Editor) *p.181*
Wozniak, Danielle *p.759*
Wray, L. Randall *p.233*
Wren, J. Thomas *p.72*
Wright, Dawn J. & Bartlett, Darius J. *p.393*
Wright, James D., et al. *p.751, p.769*
Wright, Jim. *p.820, p.848*
Wright, Quincy *p.628*
Wright, Robert E. & Cowen, David J. *p.90, p.148*
Wright, Russell O. *p.424, p.811, p.853, p.886, p.890, p.892, p.898*
Wright, Sam. *p.713*
Wright, Susan (Editor) *p.657*
Wright, Vincent *p.609*
Wrigley, Chris (Editor). *p.213*
Wronka, Joseph *p.670*
Wu, Chi-Yuen *p.251*
Wu, Frank *p.729, p.731*
Wuest, Deborah A. & Bucher, Charles A. *p.797*
Wulfemeyer, K. Tim & Buckalew, James K. *p.417*
Wunder, John R.. *p.465*
Wurzel, Rudiger K. *p.604*
Wushanley, Ying *p.811, p.839*
Wuthnow, Robert *p.720, p.755*
Wyer, Robert S. Jr. & Srull, Thomas K. (Editors). *p.692*
Wykes, Maggie *p.407*
WYLIE. *p.399*
Wyman, Matthew, et al. *p.578, p.599*

Y

Yaeger, Don *p.822, p.895, p.901*
Yager, Fred & Yager, Jan. *p.150*
Yagoda, Ben *p.410*
Yale Law School *p.451*
Yamada, Haru *p.20*
Yamaguchi, Kaoru *p.229*
Yamamoto, Mari. *p.712*
Yan, Yunxiang *p.734, p.772*
Yang, Ch'ing-k'un *p.708*
Yarbrough, Tinsley E. *p.467, p.540*
Yarmolinsky, Adam, et al. *p.301*
Yatchew, Adonis. *p.205*
Yate, Martin. *p.171*
Yates, Jeff. *p.540*
Ybarra, Raul E. & López, Nancy *p.301*
Yee, Rodney & Zolotow, Nina *p.793*
Yelon, Stephen L. *p.349*
Yelvington, Kevin A. *p.41*
Yena, Donna J. *p.168*
Yergin, Daniel & Stanislaw, Joseph *p.56, p.58*
Yergin, Daniel. *p.160*
Yesalis, Charles E. & Cowart, Virginia S. *p.826*
Yesalis, Charles E.. . . . . *p.826*
Yeung, Yue-man & Li, Xiaojian. *p.397*
Yin, Robert K.. . . . . *p.688*
Yinger, John (Editor). *p.302*
Ylinen, Jari & Cash, Mel. *p.826*
YMCA of the USA Staff. *p.792, p.797*
YMCA of the USA *p.792*
Yoast, Bill R. *p.860*
Yoder, Jennifer A. *p.610*
Yoffee, Norman (Editor, Contribution by) *p.6*
Yoke, Mary & Carol, Kennedy *p.793, p.880*
Yost, David S. *p.639, p.655*
Yost, Jeffrey R. *p.158*
Young, Brigitte *p.610*
Young, Copeland H., et al. *p.689*
Young, Crawford *p.574, p.576*
Young, David C.. *p.847*
Young, Iris Marion *p.506, p.514*
Young, James Webb *p.428*
Young, Jeffrey T. *p.220*

Young, Lisa & Everitt, Joanna *p.591*
Young, Michael & Willmott, Peter *p.37*
Young, Michael W.. . . . . *p.5*
Young, Richard B.. . . . . *p.291*
Young, Robert (Editor) *p.581*
Young, Virginia Heyer *p.5*
Young, Walter D. *p.589*
Yourdon, Edward *p.70*
Yu, Eden S H & Kwan, Yum K. *p.398*

Z

Zablocki, Benjamin D.. . . . . *p.740*
Zafirovski, Milan *p.193*
Zagare, Frank C.. . . . . *p.657*
Zagorski, Paul W. *p.593*
Zagorsky, Jay L.. . . . . *p.181*
Zajas, Jay J. & Church, Olive D. *p.420*
Zakrajsek, Dorothy B., et al. *p.800*
Zalk, Sue R. & Gordon-Kelter, Janice (Editors) *p.255, p.267, p.274*
Zamagni, Stefano (Editor) *p.267*
Zameret, Zvi *p.337*
Zang, David W.. . . . . *p.811, p.833, p.853*
Zang, David *p.811, p.820*
Zarembka, Paul & Soederberg, Susanne (Editors). *p.239*
Zaretsky, Eli *p.692*
Zartman, I. William & Rubin, Jeffrey Z. (Editors) *p.646*
Zartman, I. William (Editor) *p.613*
Zatsiorsky, Vladimir M. (Editor) . . . *p.827, p.829, p.880, p.908*
Zatsiorsky, Vladimir M. *p.880, p.908, p.910*
Zautra, Alex J.. . . . . *p.699*
Zawati, Hilmi M. & Mahmoud, Ibtisam M. *p.654*
Zeigler, Earle F. (Editor) *p.797*
Zein-Elabdin, Eiman O. & Charusheela, S. (Editors) *p.211, p.271*
Zeisel, Hans & Kaye, D. H. *p.179*
Zeitz, Paul *p.197*
Zelazny, Gene *p.174*
Zelizer, Barbie. *p.403*
Zelizer, Viviana A. Rotman *p.738*
Zelizer, Viviana A. *p.718, p.735*
Zemelman, Steven *p.366*
Zemke, Ron, et al.. *p.132*
Zenderland, Leila *p.287*
Zenger, John Peter. *p.438*
Zenios, S. A. & Ziemba, W. T. (Editors) *p.192*
Zentella, Ana C. *p.21*
Zhang, Yumei *p.618, p.622*
Zhao, Quansheng *p.622*
Zhao, Suisheng *p.621*
Zhao, Yong (Editor) *p.352*
Zheng, Shiping *p.621*
Zieger, Robert H. *p.130*
Zielonka, Jan *p.599*
Zigler, Edward F. (Editor), et al. *p.304, p.354, p.359*
Zimbalist, Andrew (Editor) *p.890*
Zimbalist, Andrew *p.853, p.890, p.895*
Zimmerman, Barry J. & Schunk, Dale H. (Editors) *p.359*
Zimmerman, Bonnie (Editor) *p.749*
Zimmerman, Jonathan *p.762*
Zimmerman, Joseph F. & Rule, Wilma (Editors) *p.533*
Zimmerman, Joseph F. *p.462*
Zimring, Franklin E. & Hawkins, Gordon *p.753*
Zingg, Paul J. *p.853*
Zinn, Howard (Editor) *p.522*
Zinser, Charles I. *p.788*
Zipkin, Paul Herbert *p.117*
Ziring, Lawrence, et al. *p.636*
Zmora, Hillay (Contribution by) *p.502*
Zmuda, Allison & Tomaino, Mary. *p.304*
Zoch, Paul A. *p.340*
Zolberg, Aristide R., et al. *p.765*
Zollo, Peter *p.139*
Zonabend, Francoise *p.708*
Zuccotti, Susan *p.654*
Zucker, Andrew A. & Kozma, Robert *p.322*
Zucker, Ross *p.515*
Zuckerman, Mary E. *p.410*
Zuckert, Michael P. *p.513*
Zug, James *p.864*
Zumerchik, John *p.861, p.871*
Zunes, Stephen *p.565*
Zunz, Olivier (Editor), et al. *p.725*
Zureik, Elia & Nakhleh, Khalil *p.708*
Zweig, Michael *p.727*
Zweigenhaft, Richard L. & Domhoff, G. William. *p.133*
Zwirn, Jerrold (Compiled by) *p.529*

Title Index

A

/A Land Imperiled: The Declining Health of the Southern Appalachian Bioregion. p.382
A. Philip Randolph: A Biographical Portrait. p.123
AAUP web site. p.292
ABA-LSAC Official Guide to ABA-Approved Law Schools 2006. . . . . p.439
Abandoned in the Wasteland: Children, Television, and the First Amendment. p.445
Abandoned: The Betrayal of the American Middle Class since World War II. p.486
Abe Fortas: A Biography. p.468
Abelard and the Origin and Early History of the Universities. p.325
Abolish the FCC: Common Law Telecosm. p.445
The Abolition of the Death Penalty in International Law. . p.435
Aboriginal Australians. p.42
Aboriginal Men of High Degree: Initiation and Sorcery in the World's Oldest Tradition. p.36
Aboriginal Peoples and Government Responsibility: Exploring Federal and Provincial Roles, No. 12. . . . . p.588
Abortion and American Politics. p.569
Abortion and Common Sense. p.569
Abortion and Dialogue: Pro-Choice, Pro-Life and American Law. p.447
Abortion and the Politics of Motherhood. p.768
The Abortion Controversy: A Documentary History. . . . p.448
Abortion in America: The Origins and Evolution of National Policy, 1800-1900. . . . . p.472
Abortion, Medicine and the Law. p.471
Abortion Politics in North America. p.768
Abortion Practice in Britain and the United States. p.778
The Abortion Rights Controversy in America: A Legal Reader. p.447
Abortion: The Clash of Absolutes. p.472
About Teaching Mathematics: A K-8 Resource. p.362
About Town: The New Yorker and the World It Made. . . p.410
Abraham Lincoln and His Times: A Constitutional Biography. p.518
Abraham Lincoln: Constitutionalism and Equal Rights in the Civil War Era. p.518
Abs on the Ball: A Pilates Approach to Building Superb Abdominals. p.793
Absent Mandate: Canadian Electoral Politics in an Era of Restructuring. p.590
Absentee Ownership and Business Enterprise in Recent Times: The Case of America. p.214, p.250
Absinthe, the Cocaine of the Nineteenth Century: A History of the Hallucinogenic Drug and Its Effect on Artists and Writers in Europe and the United States. p.776
The Abuse of Police Authority: A National Study of Police Officers' Attitude. p.774
Academic Anthropology and the Museum: Back to the Future. p.47
Academic Capitalism and the New Economy: Markets, State, and Higher Education. p.290
Academic Duty. p.293
Academic Freedom: A Guide to the Literature. p.298
Academic Freedom and Tenure: Ethical Issues. p.298
Academic Freedom and the Inclusive University. p.298
Academic Freedom: Education and Human Rights, Vol. 3. . p.314
Academic Freedom in American Higher Education: Rights, Responsibilities, and Limitations, Vol. 22. . . . . . . p.298
Academic Freedom in the Age of the College. p.298
The Academic Job Search Handbook. p.170
The Academic Man: A Study in the Sociology of a Profession. p.294
Academic Power: Patterns of Authority in Seven National Systems of Higher Education. p.295
The Academic Revolution. p.290, p.332
Academic Skills Problems: Direct Assessment and Intervention. p.287
Academic Strategy: The Management Revolution in American Higher Education. p.293
Accessing U. S. Government Information: Subject Guide to Jurisdiction of the Executive and Legislative Branches. . p.529
According to Kotler. p.134
Accountability in Social Research: Issues and Debates. . . p.687
Accountants' Handbook, Set. p.104, p.105
Accounting Best Practices. p.104
Accounting Demystified. p.105
Accounting. p.91, p.94, p.99
The Accumulation of Capital: An Anti-Critique Imperialism and the Accumulation of Capital. p.236
The Accumulation of Capital. p.245
The Accumulation of Capital. p.236
Accumulation of Capital. p.236
The Accumulation of Capital. p.244, p.270
Ace Your Case!: The WetFeet Insider Guide to Consulting Interviews. p.171, p.178
The Achievement of American Liberalism: The New Deal and Its Legacies. p.522
The Achievement of American Sport Literature: A Critical Appraisal. p.812
Achieving Diversity: The Status and Progress of Women and African Americans in the Agricultural Economics Profession. p.268
Achieving Our Country: Leftist Thought in Twentieth-Century America. p.493
Acid Dreams: The CIA, LSD and the Sixties Rebellion. . p.704

Across the Blocs: Exploring Comparative Cold War Cultural and Social History. . . . p.486

Across the Great Divide: Cultures of Manhood in the American West. . . . p.745

ACSM Fitness Book: A Proven Step-by-Step Program from the Experts. . . . p.790, p.873

ACSM's Exercise Management for Persons with Chronic Diseases and Disabilities. . . . p.783, p.829, p.842

ACSM's Guidelines for Exercise Testing and Prescription. . p.872

ACSM's Health/Fitness Facility Standards and Guidelines. . . . p.792, p.880, p.882

Act of Creation: The Founding of the United Nations. . . p.635

An Act of State: The Execution of Martin Luther King Jr. . p.486

ACTE online (Association for Career and Technical Education). . . . p.304

Acting for Endangered Species: The Statutory Ark. . . . p.463

Action Research for Educators. . . . p.355

Activists Beyond Borders: Advocacy Networks in International Politics. . . . p.640

Acts of Hope: Creating Authority in Literature, Law, and Politics. . . . p.497

Ad* Access. . . . p.141, p.426

Ad Council Campaigns. . . . p.427

Adam Smith and Modern Political Economy: Bicentennial Essays on The Wealth of Nations. . . . p.219

Adam Smith and Modern Political Economy: Bicentennial Essays on the Wealth of Nations. . . . p.219

Adam Smith and the Founding of Market Economics. . . p.219

Adam Smith and the Philosophy of Law and Economics. . p.219

Adam Smith's Daughters: Eight Prominent Women Economists from the Eighteenth Century to the Present. . . . p.194

Adam Smith's Economics: Its Place in the Development of Economic Thought. . . . p.218

Adam Smith's Legacy: His Place in the Development of Modern Economics. . . . p.219

Adam Smith's Marketplace of Life. . . . p.219

Adam Smiths Political Philosophy: The Invisible Hand and Spontaneous Order. . . . p.220

Adam Smith's Politics. . . . p.220

Adam Smith's System of Liberty, Wealth, and Virtue: The Moral and Political Foundations of the Wealth of Nations. . . . p.218

Adam Smith's Wealth of Nations: New Interdisciplinary Essays. . . . p.218

Adam Smith. . . . p.211, p.212, p.218, p.219

Adams Cover Letter Almanac. . . . p.171

Adam's Curse: A Future Without Men. . . . p.745

Adapted Aquatics Programming: A Professional Guide. . . . p.792, p.801

Adapted Physical Activity. . . . p.801

Adapted Physical Education and Sport. . . . p.801

Adapted Physical Education National Standards: National Consortium for Physical Education and Recreation for Individuals with Disabilities (U. S.). . . . p.801

Adapting the United Nations to a Postmodern Era: Lessons Learned. . . . p.634

The Addict and the Law. . . . p.449

Addiction at Work: Tackling Drug Use and Misuse in the Workplace. . . . p.130

Administering Special Education: In Pursuit of Dignity and Autonomy. . . . p.315

The Administration of Fraternal Organizations on North American Campuses: A Pattern for the New Millennium. . . . p.288

Administration of High School Athletics. . . . p.883

Administrative Behavior: A Study of Decision-Making Processes in Administrative Organizations. . . . p.74, p.75, p.83

Adolescence in Pacific Island Communities. . . . p.43

Adolescent Development and Rapid Social Change: Perspectives from Eastern Europe. . . . p.707

Adolescent Socialization in Cross-Cultural Perspective. . p.736

Adolescents after Divorce. . . . p.735

Ads, Fads, and Consumer Culture: Advertising's Impact on American Character and Society. . . . p.426

Adult Education and Lifelong Learning: Theory and Practice. . . . p.320

Adult Guide to Children's Team Sports. . . . p.840

Adult Learner: The Definitive Classic in Adult Education and Human Resource Development. . . . p.320

Adult Learning and Development: Perspectives from Educational Psychology. . . . p.321

Adult Learning Methods: A Guide for Effective Instruction. . . . p.320

Adults as Learners: Increasing Participation and Facilitating Learning. . . . p.319

Advanced Educational Foundations for Teachers: The History, Philosophy and Culture of Schooling. . . . p.329

Advanced Fitness Assessment and Exercise Prescription. . p.879

Advanced Focus Group Research. . . . p.136

Advanced International Trade: Theory and Evidence. . . p.257

Advanced Macroeconomics. . . . p.204

Advanced Materials in Sports Equipment. . . . p.871

Advanced Mathematical Economics. . . . p.205

Advanced Web-Based Training Strategies: Unlocking Instructionally Sound Online Learning. . . . p.321

Advances in Behavioral Economics. . . . p.249

Advances in Behavioral Finance, Vol. 2. . . . p.98

Advances in Behavioral Finance. . . . p.98, p.101

Advances in Economics and Econometrics: Theory and Applications, Eighth World Congress. . . . p.202

Advances in GIS Research. . . . p.387

Advancing Women in Business—The Catalyst Guide: Best Practices from the Corporate Leaders. . . . p.57

Adventure Curriculum for Physical Education: Middle School. . . . p.787, p.798

Adventure Programming. . . . p.796

Adventure with a Genius: Recollections of Joseph Pulitzer. . . . p.410

Advertising: A Cultural Economy. . . . p.141

The Advertising Age Encyclopedia of Advertising, Set. . . . p.140, p.426

Advertising Age: Handbook of Advertising. . . . p.140

Advertising Age. . . . p.139, p.150

Advertising and Promotion: Communicating Brands. . . . p.140

Advertising and the Business of Brands. *p.140*
Advertising and the Transformation of American Society, 1865-1920, Vol. 110. . . . . *p.426*
Advertising in the 60s: Turncoats, Traditionalists, and Waste Makers in America's Turbulent Decade. *p.141*
Advertising Media Planning: A Brand Management Approach. *p.428*
☐ Advertising Principles. *p.426*
Advertising, Promotion, and New Media. *p.428*
The Advertising Red Books. Agencies. *p.140, p.150*
Advertising the American Dream: Making Way for Modernity, 1920-1940. . . . . *p.426*
Advertising to Baby Boomers. *p.138*
Advertising to Children on TV: Content, Impact, and Regulation. *p.140, p.427*
Advertising to the American Woman, 1900-1999. . . . . *p.426*
Advice and Consent: Clarence Thomas, Robert Bork and the Intriguing History of the Supreme Court's Nomination Battles. *p.539*
Advocacy, Counselling and Mediation in Casework: Processes of Empowerment. *p.757*
Advocacy Groups. *p.591*
Adweek. *p.139, p.150*
Aerobic Fitness and Health. *p.793*
AFCA's Defensive Football Drills. *p.858*
An Affair of State: The Investigation, Impeachment, and Trial of President Clinton. *p.462, p.528*
Affairs of Honor: National Politics in the New Republic. . *p.485*
Affirmative Action: A Documentary History. . . . *p.487, p.573*
Affirmative Action and Principles of Justice: Contributions in Legal Studies. *p.446*
Affirmative Action Is Dead: Long Live Affirmative Action. . *p.133*
Affirmative Action. *p.446*
The Affluent Society. *p.213*
Africa, Football and FIFA: Politics, Colonialism and Resistance. *p.815, p.847, p.883, p.898*
Africa on a Global Stage. *p.384*
Africa South of the Sahara: A Geographical Interpretation. . *p.397*
☐ Africa South of the Sahara: African Politics and Government. *p.610*
Africa Works: The Political Instrumentalisation of Disorder. *p.611*
African American and Latina Women at Work: Race, Gender and Economic Inequality. *p.133*
ⓔ African American Education: A Reference Handbook. . *p.310*
African American Golfers During the Jim Crow Era. *p.805, p.831, p.860*
African American Power and Politics: The Political Context Variable. *p.574*
The African American Press: A History of News Coverage During National Crises, with Special Reference to Four Black Newspapers, 1827-1965. . . . . *p.411*
African American Women in Congress. *p.485, p.530*
African American Women in the Struggle for the Vote, 1850-1920. . . . . *p.519*
African Americans and the Bible: Sacred Texts and Social Textures. *p.721*
African Americans in Sport: Contemporary Themes. *p.819, p.833*
African Archaeology. *p.8*
African Civilizations: An Archaeological Perspective. . . . *p.7*
African Democracies and African Politics. *p.505, p.613*
African Development Report 2005. . . . . *p.384, p.397*
African Exodus: The Origins of Modern Humanity. *p.16*
African Gender Studies. *p.744*
African Masculinities: Men in Africa from the Late Nineteenth Century to the Present. *p.733*
The African Origin of Civilization: Myth or Reality. . . . *p.702*
African Political Parties: Evolution, Institutionalisation and Governance. *p.578, p.610*
African Slavery in Latin America and the Caribbean. . . *p.728*
African State and Society in the 1990s: Cameroon's Political Crossroads. *p.613*
The African State in Transition. *p.611*
☐ African Studies: Human Rights and Governance in Africa. *p.611*
African Studies in Social Movements and Democracy. . . *p.711*
African Systems of Kinship and Marriage. *p.32*
African-American Social Workers and Social Policy. . . . *p.757*
African-Centered Pedagogy: Developing Schools of Achievement for African American Children. *p.310*
Africanizing Anthropology: Fieldwork, Networks and the Making of Cultural Knowledge in Central Africa. . . . *p.38*
Africa's Challenge to International Relations Theory. *p.641, p.643*
☐ AFT: A Union of Professionals. *p.282*
After Bipolarity: The Vanishing Threat, Theories of Cooperation and the Future of the Atlantic Alliance. *p.654*
After Communism: Perspectives on Democracy. *p.598*
After Development: The Transformation of the Korean Presidency and Bureaucracy. *p.621*
After Enron: Lessons for Public Policy. *p.86*
After Fifty: How the Baby Boom Will Redefine the Mature Market. *p.138*
After Habermas: New Perspectives on the Public Sphere. *p.766, p.774*
After Hegemony: Cooperation and Discord in the World Political Economy. *p.626, p.664*
After Kinship. *p.31*
After Slavery: Emancipation and Its Discontents. *p.728*
After Socialism, Vol. 20, Pt. 1. . . . . *p.507*
After the Cold War: American Foreign Policy in Europe and Asia. *p.485*
After the Killing Fields: Lessons from the Cambodian Genocide. *p.652*
After the Rights Revolution: Reconceiving the Regulatory State. *p.447*
After the School Bell Rings. *p.300*
After the Strike: A Century of Labor Struggle at Pullman. . *p.122*
After the Thunder: Fourteen Men Who Shaped Post-Civil War America. *p.521*
After Tylor. *p.5*

Aftermath: The Clinton Impeachment and the Presidency in the Age of Political Spectacle. *p.528*
Against All Enemies: Inside America's War on Terror. . . *p.563*
Against All Odds: Ten Entrepreneurs Who Followed Their Hearts and Found Success. *p.68*
Against Criminology. *p.751*
Against Judicial Activism: The Decline of Freedom and Democracy in Canada. *p.541*
Against Our Will: Men, Women and Rape. *p.751*
Against the Gods: The Remarkable Story of Risk. *p.92, p.99, p.162*
Against the Tide: An Intellectual History of Free Trade. . *p.664*
Age Discrimination by Employers. *p.134*
The Age of Federalism. *p.517*
The Age of Ideology: Political Ideologies from the American Revolution to Postmodern Times. *p.487, p.554*
The Age of Rights. *p.455*
The Age of Terror: America and the World after September 11. . . . . *p.487, p.662*
The Age of Terrorism. *p.660*
The Age of Uncertainty. *p.209*
Agency, Partnership, and the LLC in a Nutshell. *p.75*
Agency, Partnerships, and Limited Liability Companies: Cases and Materials. *p.75*
Agency-Based Social Work: Neglected Aspects of Clinical Practice. *p.759*
Agenda for Progressive Taxation. *p.248*
Agenda-Setting Dynamics in Canada. *p.587*
Agents of Opportunity: Sports Agents and Corruption in Collegiate Sports. *p.905*
Ages of American Law. *p.440*
Aggression: A Social Learning Analysis. *p.766*
Aggression in Organizations: Violence, Abuse, and Harassment at Work and in Schools. *p.130*
Aging in Rural America. *p.751*
Aging, Physical Activity, and Health. *p.791, p.841*
Aging Societies: The Global Dimension. *p.741*
Agrarian Feminism: The Politics of Ontario Farm Women. . *p.590*
The Agrarian History of England and Wales, 1850-1914, Set. *p.701*
Agrarian Socialism: The Cooperative Commonwealth Federation in Saskatchewan: A Study in Political Sociology. . . . *p.589*
The Agrarian Sociology of Ancient Civilizations. *p.211*
Agricultural Involution: The Processes of Ecological Change in Indonesia. *p.29*
☐ Agricultural Marketing Service @ USDA Portal. *p.152, p.164*
☐ Agricultural Statistics. *p.151, p.164*
Agricultural Trade under CUSTA. *p.630, p.644, p.666*
Agriculture and International Trade: Law, Policy, and the WTO. *p.256, p.267*
Agriculture and Rural Development Planning: A Process in Transition. *p.397*
☐ Agriculture Fact Book. *p.152*
Ahead of the Curve: A Commonsense Guide to Forecasting Business and Market Cycles. *p.81*
ⓔ Ahead of the Curve?: U. N. Ideas and Global Challenges. *p.633*
☐ AICPA: American Institute of Certified Public Accountants. *p.103*
Aiding Democracy Abroad: The Learning Curve. *p.503*
AIDS and Accusation: Haiti and Geography of Blame. . . *p.46*
AIDS and the Law. *p.448*
☐ AIDS Epidemic Update: December 2005. . . . . . . *p.669*
AIDS in Asia: A Continent in Peril. *p.704*
The Aims of Education. *p.291, p.346*
Aircraft Maintenance & Engineering Directory 2005. . . *p.151*
ⓔ Airline Industry - Global Best Practices: 2005 Edition. . *p.152*
Airlines and Air Mail: The Post Office and the Birth of the Commercial Aviation Industry. *p.152*
Akenfield: Portrait of an English Village. *p.701*
Al Jazeera: The Inside Story of the Arab News Channel That Is Challenging the West. *p.415*
Al Qaeda Now: Understanding Today's Terrorists. *p.659*
Alabama in the Twentieth Century. *p.541*
Alabama's Response to the Penitentiary Movement, 1829-1865. . . . . *p.542*
Alabi's World. *p.41*
☐ ALADIN: Adult Learning Documentation and Information Network. *p.319*
Albania in Transition: The Rocky Road to Democracy. . . *p.600*
The Alchemy of Culture: Intoxicants in Society. *p.776*
Alcohol Marketing and Advertising: A Report to Congress by the U. S. Federal Trade Commission. *p.153*
Alcohol Problems in Older Adults: Prevention and Management. *p.775*
Alcoholism and Other Drug Problems. *p.776*
Alexander Hamilton. *p.517*
Alfred Schutz: An Intellectual Biography. *p.686*
Alfred Schutz on Phenomenology and Social Relations: Selected Writings. *p.685*
Alienation and Charisma: A Study of Contemporary American Communes. *p.740*
All American: The Rise and Fall of Jim Thorpe. . *p.841, p.869*
All Else Equal: Are Public and Private Schools Different? . *p.296*
All for One: Terrorism, NATO and the United States. *p.564, p.631, p.660*
All Our Kin: Strategies for Survival in a Black Community. . *p.37*
All Politics Is Local: Family, Friends, and Provincial Interests in the Creation of the Constitution. *p.542, p.543*
All Possible Worlds: A History of Geographical Ideas. . . *p.378*
All the Essential Half-Truths about Higher Education. . . *p.290*
All the Laws but One: Civil Liberties in Wartime. *p.456*
All the News That's Fit to Sell: How the Market Transforms Information into News. *p.414*
All the President's Men. *p.404*
All the Shah's Men: An American Coup and the Roots of Middle East Terror. *p.654*
All Work and No Play....: How Educational Reforms Are Harming Our Preschoolers. *p.370*
All Your Worth: The Ultimate Lifetime Money Plan. . . . *p.98*

Alliance Against Babylon: The US, Israel and Iraq. . . . *p.641*

An Alliance at Risk: The United States and Europe since September 11. *p.563*

Allies and Adversaries: The Joint Chiefs of Staff, the Grand Alliance and U. S. Strategy in World War II. *p.561*

Allies at Odds?: The United States and the European Union. *p.642*

Allies: The U. S. Britain, and Europe in the Aftermath of the Iraq War. *p.647*

The Almanac of American Employers 2006: The Only Complete Guide to America's Hottest, Fastest-Growing Corporate Employers. *p.170*

The Almanac of Canadian Politics. *p.586*

The Almanac of Federal PACs: 2006-2007. . . . . *p.559*

Almost NATO: Partner and Players in Central and Eastern European Security. *p.639, p.654*

Alone in the Trenches: My Life As a Gay Player in the NFL. *p.839, p.860*

Al-Qaeda: Brotherhood of Terror. *p.662*

Altering American Consciouness: Essays on the History of Alcohol and Drug Use in the United States, 1800-2000. . *p.775*

Altering Party Systems: Strategic Behavior and the Emergence of New Political Parties in Western Democracies. . . . *p.579*

Alternate Civilities: Democracy and Culture in China and Taiwan. *p.618, p.620*

Alternative Cars in the 21st Century: A New Personal Transportation Paradigm. *p.154*

Alternative Teacher Certification, A State-by-State Analysis: 1998-1999 Edition. *p.278*

Alternatives to Independence: Explorations in Post-Colonial Relations. *p.583, p.584*

The Altruistic Imagination: A History of Social Work and Social Policy in the United States. *p.757*

Always Running: Gang Days in L. A. *p.714*

Am I Thin Enough Yet?: The Cult of Thinness and the Commercialization of Identity. *p.778*

AMA Dictionary of Marketing Terms. *p.134*

AMA Handbook for Customer Satisfaction: A Complete Guide to Research, Planning, and Implementation. *p.136*

AMA Marketing Encyclopedia: Issues and Trends Shaping the Future. *p.134*

Amartya Sen's Work and Ideas: A Gender Perspective. . . *p.272*

Amateur Athletic Foundation of Los Angeles. . *p.803, p.812*

Ambiguity and Choice in Organizations. *p.280*

The Ambiguity of Teaching to the Test: Standards, Assessment, and Educational Reform. *p.286*

Ambition and Accommodation: How Women View Gender Relations. *p.746*

Ambivalent Neighbors: The EU, NATO and the Price of Membership. *p.638*

Ambling into History: The Unlikely Odyssey of George W. Bush. *p.485*

AMC Guide to Outdoor Leadership. *p.786, p.787*

Amendments to the Constitution. *p.455*

America Alone: The Neo-Conservatives and the Global Order. *p.516*

America at the Polls 1920-1956: Harding to Eisenhower'A Handbook of American Presidential Election Statistics. . *p.555*

America at the Polls 1960-2004: Kennedy to George W. Bush - A Handbook of American Presidential Election Statistics, Vol. 2. . . . . *p.556*

America Beyond Capitalism: Reclaiming Our Wealth, Our Liberty, and Our Democracy. *p.493, p.502*

America Discovered: A Historical Atlas of North American Exploration. *p.379, p.382*

America First!: Its History, Culture and Politics. *p.486*

America Unbound: The Bush Revolution in Foreign Policy. *p.560*

America Votes 26: 2003-2004, Election Returns by State. . *p.547*

America Votes: A Handbook of Contemporary American Election Statistics, Vol. 24. . . . . *p.549*

The American Academic Profession: A Synthesis of Social Scientific Inquiry since World War II. *p.292*

American Anthropology, 1921-1945: Papers from the American Anthropologist. *p.3*

American Anthropology in Micronesia: An Assessment. . . *p.4*

American Apartheid: Segregation and the Making of the Underclass. *p.730*

American Association of Colleges for Teacher Education. *p.279*

American Association of Community Colleges. *p.291*

American Association of State Colleges and Universities. *p.291*

American Attitutdes: What Americans Think about the Issues That Shape Their Lives. *p.138*

The American Bar Association Legal Guide for Small Business: Everything a Small-Business Person Must Know, from Start-Up to Employment Laws to Financing and Selling a Business. *p.87, p.444*

American Broadcasting and the First Amendment. *p.459*

American Bureaucracy: Public Choice and Public Law. . *p.463*

American Capitalism: The Concept of Countervailing Power. *p.214*

American Catholics, American Culture: Tradition and Resistance. *p.721*

The American Class Structure in an Age of Growing Inequality: A New Synthesis. *p.724*

The American College: A Psychological and Social Interpretation of the Higher Learning. . *p.290, p.291, p.332*

The American College and University: A History. *p.332*

American College in the Nineteenth Century. *p.331*

American College of Sports Medicine. *p.824, p.876*

The American Colonies in the Eighteenth Century. *p.518*

American Colonies in the Seventeenth Century, Vol. 2. . . *p.518*

The American Community College. *p.291*

American Congressional Dictionary. *p.529*

The American Congress. *p.531*

American Constitutional Law, Vol. I. *p.454*

American Couples: Money, Work, Sex. *p.739*

American Couples. *p.731*

American Datelines: Major News Stories from Colonial Times to the Present. *p.404*

The American Dictionary of Criminal Justice: Key Terms and Major Court Cases. *p.677*
An American Dilemma: The Negro Problem and Modern Democracy. *p.730*
An American Dilemma. *p.730*
The American Direct Primary: Party Institutionalization and Transformation in the American North. *p.550*
The American Doctrine of Judicial Supremacy. *p.454*
The American Dream and the Public Schools. *p.300*
American Education: A History with the McGraw-Hill Foundations of Education Timeline. *p.329*
American Education and Vocationalism: A Documentary History, 1870-1970. . . . . *p.353*
American Educational History Revisited: A Critique of Progress. *p.326*
American Educators' Encyclopedia. *p.339*
American Elections: The Rules Matter. *p.548*
American Empire: Roosevelt's Geographer and the Prelude to Globalization. *p.378*
American Exceptionalism and Human Rights. *p.512*
American Federalism and Public Policy: How the System Works. *p.523*
American Federalism: Competition among Governments. . *p.523*
The American Folklife Center - Ethnographic Resources related to Folklore, Anthropology, Ethnomusicology, and the Humanities. *p.45*
American Foreign Policy since World War II. *p.560*
American Foreign Policy: Theoretical Essays. . . *p.560, p.626*
The American Game: Baseball and Ethnicity. *p.823, p.830, p.849*
American Gay. *p.748*
American Generations: Who They Are, How They Live, What They Think. *p.138*
American Global Strategy and the 'War on Terrorism'. . . *p.563*
American Governors and Gubernatorial Elections, 1775-1978. . . . . *p.557*
American Governors and Gubernatorial Elections, 1979-1987. . . . . *p.557*
American Gulag: Inside U. S. Immigration Prisons. . . . *p.764*
The American High School Today: A First Report to Interested Citizens. *p.367*
American Higher Education, a Documentary History. . . *p.331*
American Higher Education: A Guide to Reference Sources, 12. . . . . *p.290*
American Higher Education: A History. *p.331*
American Higher Education in the Twenty-First Century: Social, Political, and Economic Challenges. *p.330*
American Ideals vs. the New Deal. *p.213*
American Immigration and Ethnicity: A Reader. *p.764*
American Indian Education: A History. *p.312*
American Indian Ethnic Renewal: Red Power and the Resurgence of Identity and Culture. *p.730*
The American Indian Integration of Baseball. *p.809 p.818 p.841 p.851*
American Indian Lacrosse: Little Brother of War. *p.810, p.841, p.863*
American Indian Sovereignty and the U. S. Supreme Court: The Masking of Justice. *p.465*
American Indian Treaties: The History of a Political Anomaly. *p.465, p.573*
American Indians, Time and the Law: Historical Rights at the Bar of the Supreme Court. *p.465, p.540*
American Individualisms: Child Rearing and Social Class in Three Neighborhoods. *p.733*
American Journalism 1690-1940, Set. *p.405*
American Journalism History: An Annotated Bibliography. *p.404*
American Journalism: History, Principles, Practices. . . . *p.404*
The American Judicial Tradition: Profiles of Leading American Judges. *p.469*
The American Jury. *p.473*
American Kinship: A Cultural Account. *p.32, p.734*
American Labor and the Cold War: Grassroots Politics and Postwar Political Culture. *p.120*
The American Law Dictionary. *p.437*
American Law in the 20th Century. *p.109, p.441*
American Lawyers in a Changing Society, 1776-1876. . . *p.440*
American Lawyers. *p.440*
American Left: Radical Political Thought in the Twentieth Century. *p.709*
American Magazine Journalists, 1741-1850. . . . . *p.410*
American Magazine Journalists, 1850-1900. . . . . *p.410*
American Manhood: Transformations in Masculinity from the Revolution to the Modern Era. *p.745*
The American Marketplace: Demographics and Spending Patterns. *p.138*
American Memory: A Century of Lawmaking for a New Nation. *p.481, p.517*
American Model United Nations International (collegiate). *p.632*
The American Mosaic: An In-Depth Report on the Future of Diversity at Work. *p.131*
American National Elections Studies (ANES). *p.547*
American National Security and Civil Liberties in an Era of Terrorism. *p.563, p.572*
American Newspaper Journalists, 1926-1950. . . . . . . *p.410*
The American Occupational Structure. *p.726*
American Patriots: The Story of Blacks in the Military from the Revolution to Desert Storm. *p.717*
The American People: Census 2000. . . . . *p.138*
American Political Writing During the Founding Era - 1780-1805, Vol. 1 and 2. . . . . *p.517*
American Pragmatism and Education, an Interpretation and Criticism. *p.341*
The American Presidency and Women: Promise, Performance, and Illusion. *p.527*
The American Presidency: Origins and Development, 1776-1993. . . . . *p.527*
The American Presidency: Principles and Problems. . . . *p.528*
American Presidential Campaigns and Elections: A Reference Guide, Set. *p.550, p.556*
American Presidents: Year by Year. *p.528*
American Printer: The Graphic Arts Managers Magazine. . *p.140*

American Professors: A National Resource Imperiled. . . . p.292
American Public School Law. p.449
▢ American Rhetoric. p.422
The American School, 1642-2004. . . . . p.329
▢ American Soccer History Archives. p.803, p.867
American Society: Problems of Structure. p.707
American Sports Empire: How the Leagues Breed Success. p.884, p.888, p.896
American Sports: From the Age of Folk Games to the Age of Televised Sports. p.809, p.818
The American Supreme Court. p.466
American Trade Politics. p.57, p.567
American Tragedy: Kennedy, Johnson, and the Origins of the Vietnam War. p.486
American Universities and Colleges. p.330
The American University: How It Runs, Where It Is Going. p.289, p.330
American Vanguard: The United Auto Workers During the Reuther Years, 1935-1970. . . . . p.124
The American Voter. p.548
The American Way: A Geographical History of Crisis and Recovery. p.381
The American Woman in Sport. p.805, p.836
American women's track and field:a history, 1895 through 1980. . . . . p.810, p.838, p.869
American Youth Gangs at the Millennium. p.714
Americanization of the Common Law: The Impact of Legal Change on Massachusetts Society, 1760-1830. . . . . p.474
Americans at Play: Demographics of Outdoor Recreation and Travel. p.788, p.824
Americans with Disabilities Act Handbook. p.447
America's 100th Meridian: A Plains Journey. p.382
America's Ailing Cities: Fiscal Health and the Design of Urban Policy. p.544
America's Asia: Racial Form and American Literature, 1893-1945. . . . . p.485
▢ America's Best Graduate Schools. p.295
America's Best Newspaper Writing: A Collection of ASNE Prizewinners. p.410
▢ America's Career InfoNet. p.304
America's Communal Utopias. p.499
America's Constitution: A Biography. p.452
America's Experiment with Capital Punishment: Reflections on the Past, Present, and Future of the Ultimate Penal Sanction. p.567
America's Failing Schools: How Parents and Teachers Can Cope with No Child Left Behind. p.328
America's Game: The Epic Story of How Pro Football Captured a Nation. p.859, p.897
The Americas in the Spanish World Order: The Justification for Conquest in the Seventeenth Century. p.583
America's National Pastime: A Study of Race and Merit in Professional Baseball. p.804, p.830, p.849, p.890
America's New Allies: Poland, Hungary, and the Czech Republic in NATO. p.639
America's Obsession: Sports and Society since 1945. . . p.805
America's Public Schools: From the Common School to "No Child Left Behind". p.328
America's Real Estate: Natural Resource, National Legacy. p.159, p.166
America's Sporting Heritage: 1850-1950. . . . . p.803
America's Struggle Against Poverty in the Twentieth Century.. . . . . p.758
America's Unpatriot Acts: The Federal Government's Violation of Constitutional and Civil Rights. . . . p.561, p.562, p.572
America's Untapped Resource: Low-Income Students in Higher Education.. . . . . p.294
America's Welfare State: From Roosevelt to Reagan. . . p.754
▢ Amnesty International Library. p.669
Amped: How Big Air, Big Dollars, and a New Generation Took Sports to the Extreme. p.857, p.899
▢ Amputee Sport Resouces on the Net. p.842
Amusing Ourselves to Death: Public Discourse in the Age of Show Business. p.417
Anabolic Steroids and the Athlete. p.826
Anabolic Steroids in Sport and Exercise. p.826
Anabolic Steroids. p.826
Analysis of Financial Time Series. p.205, p.206, p.264
Analysis of Panel Data. p.202, p.206
Analytical Didactic: Translated from the Latin with Introd. and Notes. p.341
Analyzing and Reporting Focus Group Results. p.136
Analyzing Teaching Behavior. p.347
Analyzing Visual Data. p.690
The Anarchical Society: A Study of Order in World Politics. p.625, p.628
Anarchism: A Collection of Revolutionary Writings. . . . p.493
The Anarchist in the Library: How the Clash Between Freedom and Control Is Hacking the Real World and Crashing the System. p.761
The Anarchists of Casas Viejas. p.42
Anarchy, State, and Utopia. p.511
Anatomy of a Business Plan: A Step-by-Step Guide to Building a Business and Securing Your Company's Future. . . p.174
The Anatomy of a Game: Football, the Rules, and the Men Who Made the Game. p.808, p.859
The Anatomy of a Party: The National CCF, 1932-1961. . p.589
The Anatomy of Fascism. p.510
Anatomy of Hatha Yoga: A Manual for Students, Teachers and Practitioners. p.793
The Anatomy of Power. p.773
The Anatomy of Sports Forecasting: Modeling Parallels Between Sports Gambling and Financial Markets. p.203, p.207
Anatomy of the Law. p.433
Ancient Canada. p.11
Ancient Cities of the Indus Valley Civilization. p.9
The Ancient City: A Study on the Religion, Laws, and Institutions of Greece and Rome. p.489
Ancient Civilizations of Mesoamerica: A Reader. p.10
Ancient Education and Its Meaning for Us. p.326
Ancient Education. p.329

Ancient Egypt: Anatomy of a Civilization. *p.8*

Ancient Europe 8000 B.C.—A.D. 1000: An Encyclopedia of the Barbarian World. *p.12*

Ancient Japan. *p.9*

Ancient Law: Its Connection with the Early History of Society, and Its Relation to Modern Ideas. *p.33*

Ancient Law: Its Connection with the Early History of Society and Its Relation to Modern Ideas. *p.433*

The Ancient Maya. *p.10*

Ancient North America: The Archaeology of a Continent. . *p.10*

The Ancient Olympics: A History. *p.810*

Ancient Sichuan: Treasures from a Lost Civilization. *p.8*

Ancient South America. *p.11*

And Here the World Ends: The Life of an Argentine Village. *p.706*

And Now a Few Words from Me: Advertising's Leading Critic Lays down the Law, Once and for All. *p.427*

And the Money Kept Rolling In (and Out): Wall Street, the IMF, and the Bankrupting of Argentina. . . *p.94, p.98, p.99*

And the Poor Get Children: Sex, Contraception, and Family Planning in the Working Class. *p.775*

And the Walls Came Tumbling Down: The Basketball Game That Changed American Sports. *p.831, p.853, p.893*

And There Were Giants in the Land: The Life of William Heard Kilpatrick.. . . . . *p.340*

Andrew Jackson: His Life and Times. *p.517*

Anglo-Saxon Charters. *p.436*

Animals, Property, and the Law. *p.448*

Annual Editions: Business Ethics 06/07. . . . . *p.53*

□ Annual Review of Sociology. *p.675*

Another America: The Politics of Race and Blame. . . . *p.573*

Answering the "Virtuecrats": A Moral Conversation on Character Education. *p.306*

The Antagonists: Hugo Black, Felix Frankfurter and Civil Liberties in Modern America. *p.469*

Anthology of Statistics in Sports.. . . . . *p.871*

Anthropological Linguistics. *p.18*

Anthropological Locations: Boundaries and Grounds of a Field Science. *p.23*

Anthropological Theory Today. *p.24*

Anthropologies and Histories: Essays in Culture, History, and Political Economy. *p.24*

An Anthropologist at Work: Writings of Ruth Benedict. . . *p.22*

Anthropologists in a Wider World: Essays on Field Research.. . . . . *p.25*

Anthropology and Cognitive Science: Essays on Cultural Transmission.. . . . . *p.26*

Anthropology and the Colonial Encounter. *p.4*

Anthropology and the Global Factory. *p.28*

Anthropology, by Comparison. *p.22*

Anthropology in Practice.. . . . . *p.45*

Anthropology in Public Health: Bridging Differences in Culture and Society. *p.44*

Anthropology in the Margins of the State. *p.34*

The Anthropology of Anger: Civil Society and Democracy in Africa. *p.497, p.585, p.612*

Anthropology of Art: A Reader. *p.26*

The Anthropology of Buddhism and Hinduism: Weberian Themes.. . . . . *p.721*

The Anthropology of Development and Globalization: From Classical Political Economy to Contemporary Neoliberalism. *p.28*

The Anthropology of Europe: Identities and Boundaries in Conflict. *p.41*

The Anthropology of Language: An Introduction to Linguistic Anthropology. *p.18*

Anthropology of Law: A Comparative Theory. *p.33*

The Anthropology of Medicine: From Culture to Method. . *p.47*

The Anthropology of Peace and Nonviolence. *p.35*

Anthropology of Performing Arts: Artistry, Virtuosity, and Interpretation in a Cross-Cultural Perspective. *p.26*

The Anthropology of Politics: A Reader in Ethnography, Theory, and Critique. *p.35*

The Anthropology of Religious Conversion. *p.36*

The Anthropology of Slavery. *p.28*

The Anthropology of the State: A Reader. *p.34*

Anthropology, Sport, and Culture. *p.819*

Anthropology: The Basics. *p.23*

Anthropology: Theoretical Practice in Culture and Society.. *p.24*

Anthropology Today: An Encyclopedic Inventory. *p.3*

□ AnthroSource. *p.45*

Anticipating Madam President.. . . . . *p.528*

Anticipations of the General Theory and Other Essays on Keynes.. . . . . *p.225*

Anti-Communism and Popular Culture in Mid-Century America. *p.712*

The Antifederalists. *p.518*

□ Anti-Slavery Society.. . . . . *p.727*

Antisocial Behavior in Organizations.. . . . . *p.130*

Antitrust and Competition Policy. *p.252*

The Antitrust Laws: A Primer.. . . . . . *p.85 p.110 p.111 p.112*

The Antitrust Paradox. *p.444*

The Antitrust Revolution: Economics, Competition, and Policy. *p.84, p.109*

Anyan's Story: A New Guinea Woman in Two Worlds. . . *p.43*

Apes, Language, and the Human Mind. *p.19*

Apex of Power: The Prime Minister and Political Leadership in Canada.. . . . . *p.588*

Apocalypse in Oklahoma: Waco and Ruby Ridge Revenged.. . . . . *p.524*

The Apotheosis of Captain Cook: European Mythmaking in the Pacific.. . . . . *p.43*

Appeasement in International Politics. *p.646*

Appetites and Identities: An Introduction to Social Anthropology of Western Europe. *p.41*

Applications of Biological Anthropology to Human Affairs.. *p.14*

Applications of Nonverbal Communication. *p.424*

Applied Anthropology: A Career-Oriented Approach. . . . *p.44*

The Applied Anthropology Reader. *p.45*

Applied Econometric Time Series. *p.206*

Applied GIS and Spatial Analysis. *p.386*

Applying Sociology: Making a Better World. p.675
Applying Telecommunications and Technology from a Global Business Perspective. p.420
Approaches to Academic Freedom and Related Issues. . . p.298
The Appropriation of Nature: Essays on Human Ecology and Social Relations. p.29
Aquinas: Moral, Political, and Legal Theory. p.490
Aquinas: Political Writings. p.490
Arab Human Development Report 2004: Towards Freedom in the Arab World. p.615
Arab Society: Class, Gender, Power, and Development. . p.703
☐ Arab World and Islamic Resources. p.311
Arbitrary and Capricious: The Supreme Court, the Constitution, and the Death Penalty. p.471
Arbitration and Collective Bargaining. p.447
Arc of Justice: A Saga of Race, Civil Rights, and Murder in the Jazz Age. p.438
Arch: Selected Readings. p.199
☐ Archaeological Resource Guide for Europe. p.45
Archaeological Theory: An Introduction. p.6
Archaeological Theory and Scientific Practice. p.6
Archaeological Theory: Who Sets the Agenda? p.6
Archaeology As a Process: Processualism and Its Progeny. . p.6
Archaeology at La Isabela: America's First European Town. p.13
The Archaeology of Africa. p.8
The Archaeology of Ancient Greece. p.13
The Archaeology of Ancient Judea and Palestine. p.9
The Archaeology of Central America. p.9
The Archaeology of Early Historic South Asia: The Emergence of Cities and States. p.8
The Archaeology of Korea. p.9
The Archaeology of Mainland Southeast Asia: From 10,000 B. C. to the Fall of Angkor. p.8
The Archaeology of Southern Africa. p.8
The Archaeology of Syria: From Complex Hunter-Gatherers to Early Urban Societies (C.16,000-300 BC). p.8
Archaeology of the Dreamtime: The Story of Prehistoric Australia and Its People. p.13
Archaeology of the Moundville Chiefdom. p.11
Archaeology of the Southeastern United States: Paleoindian to World War I. p.10
Archaeology of the Southwest. p.10
The Archaeology of Time. p.6
Archaeology: The Key Concepts. p.6
Archaeology: Theories, Methods and Practice. p.5
Architects of Political Change: Constitutional Quandaries and Social Choice Theory. p.484, p.769
Architectural Anthropology. p.25
The Architecture of Global Governance: An Introduction to the Study of International Organizations. p.629
Architecture of Sports Facilities. p.880, p.882
Arctic Climate Impact Assessment - Scientific Report. . . p.393
Are the World's Coral Reefs Threatened? p.392
Are We Still a Nation at Risk Two Decades Later? . . . p.322
The Arena of Masculinity: Sports, Homosexuality, and the Meaning of Sex. p.839
Argonauts of the Western Pacific. p.28
Arguing for Socialism. p.506
Arguing with the Crocodile: Gender and Class in Bangladesh. p.31
Aristotle on Teaching. p.345
Aristotle on the Necessity of Public Education. p.341
Aristotle: Politics. p.488
Aristotle's Logic of Education. p.340
Aristotle's Politics: A Critical Reader. p.488
Aristotle. p.489
Armageddon: The Battle for Germany, 1944-1945. . . . . p.647
Armed Martial Arts of Japan: Swordsmanship and Archery. p.863
Armies Without Nations: Public Violence and State Formation in Central America, 1821-1960. . . . . p.659
Arms Control: The New Guide to Negotiations and Agreements with New Supplement. p.656
Arms Trade and Economic Development: Theory and Policy in Offsets. p.217, p.256, p.258
Arms Uncontrolled. p.655
The Army and Politics in Argentina, 1928-1945: Yrigoyen to Peron. p.592
The Army and Politics in Argentina, 1945-1962: Peron to Frondizi. p.592
The Army and Politics in Argentina, 1962-1973: From Frondizi's Fall to the Peronist Restoration. p.592
The Arrogant Capital: Washington, Wall Street, and the Frustrations of American Politics. p.486, p.572
Art and Agency: An Anthropological Theory. p.26
Art and Anthropology: Directions in Theory and Research. . p.25
The Art and Craft of Case Writing. p.178
The Art and Craft of Problem Solving. p.197
The Art and Practice of Leadership Coaching: 50 Top Executive Coaches Reveal Their Secrets. p.65
The Art and Science of Classroom Assessment: The Missing Part of Pedagogy, 27. . . . . p.285
Art from Africa: Long Steps Never Broke a Back. p.26
The Art of Aikido: Principles and Essential Techniques. . p.863
Art of Case Analysis: How to Improve Performance by Developing Better Case Analysis Skills. p.178
The Art of Editing: In the Age of Convergence. p.411
The Art of Fact: A Historical Anthology of Literary Journalism. p.403
The Art of Governance: Analyzing Management and Administration. p.580
The Art of Kula. p.25
The Art of M&A Structuring. p.84
The Art of Sportscasting: How to Build a Successful Career. p.906
The Art of Teaching. p.348
The Art of the Financial Statements: A Practical Handbook for Managers. p.91
Articles of Faith: The Story of British Intellectual Journalism. p.403

Artisans and Cooperatives: Developing Alternative Trade for the Global Economy. p.44
Artistic Gymnastics: A Comprehensive Guide to Performing and Teaching Skills for Beginners and Advanced Beginners. p.797, p.862
The Arts - Fitness Quality of Life Activities Program: Creative Ideas for Working with Older Adults in Group Settings. p.785, p.790, p.841
As If Learning Mattered: Reforming Higher Education. . p.332
As Sociology Meets History. p.684
As We Forgive Our Debtors: Bankruptcy and Consumer Credit in America. p.250
The Asian American Educational Experience: A Sourcebook for Teachers and Students. p.311
Asian-American Education: Historical Background and Current Realities. p.311
Asia-Pacific Diplomacy: The Nongovernmental Approach to Regional Economic Cooperation. p.640
Asia's Educational Edge: Current Achievements in Japan, Korea, Taiwan, China, and India. p.334
Asking Questions: The Definitive Guide to Questionnaire Design — for Market Research, Political Polls, and Social and Health Questionnaires. p.137
Aspects of Development and Underdevelopment. p.260
Assembling for Development: The Maquila Industry in Mexico and the United States. p.759
Assessing Attention-Deficit/Hyperactivity Disorder. . . . p.318
Assessing Democracy Assistance: The Case of Romania. p.584, p.600
Assessing Rational Expectations: Eductive Stability in Economics. p.201, p.250
Assessing Site Significance: A Guide for Archaeologists and Historians. p.7
Assessing Student Performance: Exploring the Purpose and Limits of Testing. p.287
Assessing Students in Groups: Promoting Group Responsibility and Individual Accountability. p.286
Assessing the Business Environment: Guidelines for Strategists. p.137
Assessment in the Block: The Link to Instruction. p.288
Assessment Strategies for Elementary Physical Education. . p.798
Asset Accumulation and Economic Activity: Reflections on Contemporary Macroeconomic Theory. p.239
Assimilation and Association in French Colonial Theory, 1890-1914. . . . . p.584
[e] Assimilation's Agent: My Life As a Superintendent in the Indian Boarding School System. p.755
Associated Press Broadcast News Handbook. p.414
Associated Press Reporting Handbook. p.414
The Associated Press Stylebook: And Briefing on Media Law. p.412
ASTD 2004 Competency Study: Mapping the Future: New Workplace Learning and Performance Competencies. . p.304
The ASTD e-Learning Handbook: Best Practices, Strategies and Case Studies for an Emerging Field. p.305
The ASTD Training and Development Handbook: A Guide to Human Resource Development. p.304
The Asymmetric Society. p.716
Asymptotic Theory for Econometricians. p.205
At the Edge of the State: Indigenous Peoples and Self-Determination. p.33
At the Elbow of Another: Learning to Teach by Coteaching. p.277
At the Highest Levels: The Inside Story of the End of the Cold War. p.643, p.645
At the Origins of Mathematical Economics: The Contribution of A. N. Isnard. p.205
Athenian Democracy in the Age of Demosthenes: Structure, Principles and Ideology. p.500
Athenian Democracy. p.500
Athlete's Guide to Career Planning. p.904
Athletic Intruders: Ethnographic Research on Women, Culture, and Exercise. p.814, p.834
Athletic Training and Sports Medicine. p.829
The Athletic Woman's Survival Guide. p.825
Athletics and Academe: An Anatomy of Abuses and a Prescription for Reform. p.821
Athletries: The Untold History of Ancient Greek Women Athletes. p.809, p.838
The Atlantic Migration, 1607-1860. . . . . p.667
Atlas of American History. p.380
Atlas of Ancient America. p.10
Atlas of Communism. p.506
Atlas of Exploration. p.379, p.381
Atlas of Jewish History. p.381
The Atlas of North American Exploration: From the Norse Voyages to the Race to the Pole. p.381
Atlas of North America. p.379
Atlas of Poverty in America. p.398
The Atlas of States: Global Change, 1900-2000. . . . . p.381
Atlas of the Civil War. p.381
Atlas of the Medieval World. p.381
Atlas of the World's Deserts. p.381
Atlas of the World. p.380
Atlas of United States Environmental Issues. p.159
Atlas of Westward Expansion. p.381
An Atlas of World Affairs. p.381
The Audiencia of New Galicia in the Sixteeenth Century: A Study in Spanish Colonial Government. p.592
Auditing and Tax Research. p.105, p.106, p.107
Augmentative and Alternative Communication: Supporting Children and Adults with Complex Communication Needs. p.318
Auguste Comte : The Foundation of Sociology. p.685
Augustine and Politics as Longing in the World. p.490
Australia, Antarctica, and the Pacific. p.384
[e] Australia, Oceania, and Antarctica: A Continental Overview of Environmental Issues. p.385
[□] Australian Government and Politics Database. p.624
Australian Politics and Government: The Commonwealth, States and Territories. p.624
Australia. p.385
Austria: Out of the Shadow of the Past. p.595

Austrian and New Classical Business Cycle Theories: A Comparative Study Through the Method of Rational Reconstruction. *p.233, p.234*
Austrian Economics in America: The Migration of a Tradition. *p.234*
The Austrian Party System. *p.579, p.595*
The Authoritarian Personality. *p.767*
The Authoritarian Specter. *p.509*
Authority and Freedom in Education: An Introduction to the Philosophy of Education. *p.344*
Authority Without Power: Law and the Japanese Paradox. . *p.475*
Authority. *p.695*
Autobiography of John Stuart Mill. *p.222*
Autobiography of Mother Jones. *p.126*
Automation, Production Systems, and Computer-Integrated Manufacturing. *p.116*
The Automobile Age. *p.154*
Availability and Sale of Alcohol: Experiences from Canada and the U. S. *p.153*
☐ The Avalon Project at Yale Law School: Documents in Law, History and Diplomacy. *p.451*
Away from Home: American Indian Boarding School Experience, 1879-2000. . . . . *p.312*
Aztec and Maya World. *p.10*

B

B2B-Integration: Concepts and Architecture. *p.113*
Baba: Men and Fatherhood in South Africa. *p.734*
Babe: The Life and Legend of Babe Didrikson Zaharias. *p.835, p.860*
Baby Boom: Americans Born 1946 To 1964. . . . . . . *p.137*
Back from the Future: Cuba under Castro. *p.508*
Back of the Yards: The Making of a Local Democracy. . *p.707*
Back to Basics: Your Guide to Manufacturing Excellence. . *p.119*
Back to Middletown: Three Generations of Sociological Reflections. *p.679*
Backfire: Carly Fiorina's High-Stakes Battle for the Soul of Hewlett-Packard. *p.84*
Backpacking and Hiking. *p.788*
Backwaters of Global Prosperity: How Forces of Globalization and GATT/WTO Trade Regimes Contribute to the Marginalization of the World's Poorest Nations. . . . *p.664*
Bad Habits: Drinking, Smoking, Taking Drugs, Gambling, Sexual Misbehavior and Swearing in American History. *p.709*
Bad Leadership: What It Is, How It Happens, Why It Matters. *p.697*
A Badly Flawed Election: Debating Bush v. Gore, the Supreme Court and the American Democracy. *p.536*
Badminton. *p.795, p.864*
Bait and Switch: Human Rights and U. S. Foreign Policy. . *p.513*
Bait and Switch: The (Futile) Pursuit of the American Dream. *p.265*
Balanced Scorecard Diagnostics: Maintaining Maximum Performance. *p.82*
Balanced Scorecard Step-by-Step: Maximizing Performance and Maintaining Results. *p.73*
The Balanced Scorecard: Translating Strategy into Action. *p.73, p.81*
The Balkans. *p.383*
Ball, Bat and Bishop: The Origin of Ball Games. . *p.806, p.850*
The Baltic States in World Politics. *p.641, p.644*
Bambini: The Italian Approach to Infant/Toddler Care. . . *p.368*
The Banality of Denial: Israel and the Armenian Genocide. *p.651*
Bankable Business Plans. *p.82*
Banned Films: Movies, Censors and the First Amendment. . *p.451*
Barbarian Virtues: The United States Encounters Foreign Peoples at Home and Abroad, 1876-1917. . . . . . . *p.571*
Barbarians at the Gate: The Fall of R. J. R. Nabisco. . . . *p.84*
Barclays: The Business of Banking, 1690-1996. . . . . . *p.90*
Bare-Knuckle Negotiation: Savvy Tips and True Stories from the Master of Give-and-Take. *p.74*
Bareknuckles: A Social History of Prize-Fighting. . *p.804, p.855*
Bargaining for Advantage: Negotiation Strategies for Reasonable People. *p.75*
Barriers to Riches. *p.196, p.259*
Barron's ESL Guide to American Business English. . *p.58, p.172*
Barry Goldwater. *p.486*
Baseball: A History of America's Game. *p.809, p.851*
Baseball: A Literary Anthology. *p.811, p.850*
Baseball: An Illustrated History. *p.810, p.852*
Baseball and the American Dream: Race, Class, Gender and the National Pastime. *p.815, p.830, p.850*
The Baseball Coaching Bible. *p.795, p.851*
Baseball in 1889: Players vs Owners. *p.808, p.851, p.885, p.889*
Baseball in Blue and Gray: The National Pastime During the Civil War. *p.807, p.851*
☐ Baseball Reference. *p.801, p.849*
Baseball with a Latin Beat: A History of the Latin American Game. *p.804, p.833, p.849, p.890*
Baseball's Great Experiment: Jackie Robinson and His Legacy. *p.810, p.833, p.852, p.898*
The Bases of Competence: Skills for Lifefong Learning and Employability. *p.303*
Basic Biomechanics of the Musculoskeletal System. . . . *p.908*
Basic Biomechanics with Dynamic Human and PowerWeb/OLC Bind-In Passcard. *p.908*
Basic Biotechnology. *p.156*
The Basic Business Library: Core Resources. *p.180*
Basic Documents on Human Rights. *p.434*
Basic Econometrics. *p.201, p.205*
Basic Economics: A Citizen's Guide to the Economy. . . *p.186*
Basic Essentials Using GPS. *p.390*
Basic Facts about the United Nations. *p.632*
Basic Mathematics for Economists. *p.175*
Basic Political Writings. *p.492*
Basic Principles of Curriculum and Instruction. *p.366*
The Basic Principles of Effective Consulting. *p.65*

Basic Problems of Ethnopsychiatry. *p.35*

Basics of Geographical Information Systems. *p.386*

Basics of Qualitative Research: Techniques and Procedures for Developing Grounded Theory. *p.688*

Basketball Biographies: Four Hundred Thirty-Four U. S. Players, Coaches and Contributors to the Game, 1891-1990. . . . . *p.854*

Basketball Skills and Drills. *p.796, p.854, p.904*

Bastardy and Its Comparative History: Studies in the History of Illegitimacy and Martial Nonconformism. *p.740*

The Battered Woman Syndrome. *p.743, p.759*

Battered Women and Feminist Lawmaking and the Struggle for Equality. *p.472*

The Battle for Saudi Arabia: Royalty, Fundamentalism, and Global Power. *p.643*

The Battle for the Soul of Capitalism. *p.88*

The Battle of Blair Mountain: The Story of America's Largest Labor Uprising. *p.129*

The Battleground of the Curriculum: Liberal Education and American Experience. *p.294*

Battles on the Bench: Conflict Inside the Supreme Court. *p.466, p.535*

Battling for American Labor: Wobblies, Craft Workers, and the Making of the Union Movement. *p.127*

Bay Cities and Water Politics: The Battle for Resources in Boston and Oakland. *p.543*

Beacham's Guide to Environmental Issues and Sources, Set. *p.159*

Beaches and Coasts. *p.391*

Bearing Witness: Gay Men's Health Crisis and the Politics of AIDS. *p.779*

The Beat of a Different Drummer: Essays on Educational Renewal in Honor of John I. Goodlad. *p.340*

Beat Your Ticket: Go to Court and Win!. *p.444*

Beaten Down: A History of Interpersonal Violence in the West. *p.698*

Beating the System: The Underground Economy. *p.270*

Beatrice Webb (1858-1943) - The Socialist with a Sociological Imagination. *p.270*

Beatrice Webb. *p.273*

The Beauty of Sport: A Cross-Disciplinary Inquiry. . . . *p.811*

Because It's There: The Life of George Mallory. *p.789*

Because Writing Matters: Improving Student Writing in Our Schools.. . . . . *p.364*

Becoming a Strategic Leader: Your Role in Your Organization's Enduring Success.. . . . . *p.71*

Becoming Adult Learners: Principles and Practices for Effective Development. *p.319*

Becoming an Effective Leader. *p.71*

Becoming Europe: Immigration, Integration, and the Welfare State. *p.601*

Becoming Europeans?: Attitudes, Behaviour, and Socialization in the European Parliament.. . . . . *p.603*

Becoming Evil: How Ordinary People Commit Genocide and Mass Killing. *p.654*

Becoming Justice Blackmun: Harry Blackmun's Supreme Court Journey. *p.467, p.536*

Becoming Partners. *p.739*

A Bed for the Night: Humanitarianism in Crisis.. . . . . *p.671*

The Bedouin of Cyrenaica: Studies in Personal and Corporate Power. *p.40*

Before Adam Smith: The Emergence of Political Economy 1662-1776. . . . . *p.215*

Before the Best Interests of the Child. *p.442*

Before the Revolution: The Vietnamese Peasants under the French. *p.704*

Beggars and Choosers: How the Politics of Choice Shapes Adoption, Abortion, and Welfare in the United States. . *p.769*

Beginning to Read: Thinking and Learning about Print. . *p.361*

Beginnings of Rome: Italy and Rome from the Bronze Age to the Punic Wars (c. 1000-264 B. C.). *p.12*

Behavior and Misbehavior: A Teacher's Guide to Action. . *p.284*

Behavior of Industrial Prices. *p.239*

Behavioral Theory of the Firm. *p.72, p.83*

Behind Bakke: Affirmative Action and the Supreme Court. . *p.539*

Behind Closed Doors: Violence in the American Family. . *p.743*

Behind Mud Walls: Seventy-Five Years in a North Indian Village. *p.40*

Behind the Lines: The Oral History of Special Operations in World War II. *p.486*

Behind the Veil in Arabia: Women in Oman. *p.40*

Behind the War on Terror: Western Secret Strategy and the Struggle for Iraq. *p.562*

Being Extreme. *p.857*

Beisbol: Latin Americans and the Grand Old Game. *p.808, p.833, p.844, p.851*

Belfast Politics. *p.607*

Beliefs, Behaviors, and Alcoholic Beverages: A Cross-Cultural Survey. *p.776*

Bell Hooks' Engaged Pedagogy: A Transgressive Education for Critical Consciousness. *p.342*

BELL: the Business Ethics Links Library - Resources for Research in Business Ethics and Social Responsibility. . *p.53*

BELL: the business ethics links library. *p.146*

The Bellwomen: The Story of the Landmark AT&T Sex Discrimination Case. *p.134, p.445*

Belonging to the World: Women's Rights and American Constitutional Culture. *p.458*

Ben and Jerry's: How Two Real Guys Built a Business with a Social Conscience and a Sense of Humor. *p.52*

Ben Hogan: An American Life. *p.860*

Ben Hogan's Five Lessons: The Modern Fundamentals of Golf. *p.861*

The Bench and the Ballot; Southern Federal Judges and Black Voters. *p.461*

Bench Press. *p.817, p.869*

Benchmarks: Great Constitutional Controversies in the Supreme Court.. . . . . *p.536*

Bending with the Winds: Kurt Waldheim and the United Nations. *p.633*

The Bends: Compressed Air in the History of Science, Diving, and Engineering.. . . . . *p.870*

Beneath the Equator: Cultures of Desire, Male Homosexuality, and Emerging Gay Communities in Brazil. *p.31*

Benefits for the Workplace of the Future. p.98
Bentham's Handbook of Political Fallacies. p.574
Berkshire Encyclopedia of World Sport. p.848
Beside the Golden Door: Policy, Politics, and the Homeless. p.751
Beside the Golden Door: Policy, Politics and the Homeless. p.769
Best Entry-Level Jobs, 2005-2006. . . . . p.171
The Best of Newspaper Design. p.409
The Best of Times: America in the Clinton Years. p.486
The Best Olympics Ever?: Social Impacts of Sydney 2000.. . . . . p.846 p.884 p.888 p.891
The Best Pitcher in Baseball: The Life of Rube Foster, Negro League Giant.. . . . . p.831, p.850
Best Practice: Ideas and Insights from the World's Foremost Business Thinkers. p.71
Best Practice in Inventory Management. p.117
Best Practices in Planning and Management Reporting: From Data to Decisions. p.81
Best Resumes for College Students and New Grads. . . . p.170
Best's Review. p.163
Betrayal of Trust: The Collapse of Global Public Health. . p.668
Betrayed: A History of Presidential Failure to Protect Black Lives.. . . . . p.568
Better Books! Better Readers!: How to Choose, Use and Level Books for Children in the Primary Grades. p.360
Better Environmental Policy Studies: How to Design and Conduct More Effective Analysis. p.566
Better Together: Restoring the American Community. . . p.719
Betting the Line: Sports Wagering in American Life. p.715, p.899, p.900
Between Bargaining and Politics: An Introduction to European Labor Relations. p.123
Between Capitalism and Socialism: Essays in Political Economics. p.243
Between Church and State: Religion and Public Education in a Multicultural America, 1600-2000. . . . . p.307
Between Facts and Norms: Contributions to a Discourse Theory of Law and Democracy. p.484, p.767
Between Freedom and Subsistence: China and Human Rights. p.513, p.620
Between Geography and History: Hellenistic Constructions of the Roman World. p.377
Between Labor and Management. p.121
Between Memory and Vision: The Case for Faith-Based Schooling.. . . . . p.308
Between Two Empires: Race, History, and Transnationalism in Japanese America.. . . . . p.570, p.572
Between Two Islands: Dominican International Migration.. p.570
Between Voice and Silence: Women and Girls, Race and Relationships. p.737
Beware the Winner's Curse: Victories That Can Sink You and Your Company. p.84
Beyond Belief: Essays on Religion in a Post-Traditionalist World. p.719
Beyond Bullet Points: Using Microsoft PowerPoint to Create Presentations That Inform, Motivate, and Inspire. . . . p.171
Beyond Classical Pedagogy: Teaching Elementary School Mathematic. p.366
Beyond College for All: Career Paths for the Forgotten Half. p.305, p.353
Beyond Culture. p.696
Beyond Discipline: From Compliance to Community. . . p.284
Beyond Discourse: Education, the Self, and Dialogue. . . p.345
Beyond Glory: Joe Louis vs. Max Schmeling and a World on the Brink. p.808, p.855
Beyond Greed and Fear: Understanding Behavioral Finance and the Psychology of Investing. p.97, p.102, p.103
Beyond Grey Pinstripes 2001: Preparing MBAs for Social and Environmental Stewardship. p.177
Beyond Individual Choice: Teams and Frames in Game Theory. p.83
Beyond Knowledge Management. p.77
Beyond Labor's Veil: The Culture of the Knights of Labor.. p.130
Beyond Left and Right: The Future of Radical Politics. . p.768
Beyond Leveled Books: Supporting Transitional Readers in Grades 2-5. . . . . p.365
Beyond Oil: The View from Hubbert's Peak. p.160
Beyond Party: Cultures of Antipartisanship in Northern Politics Before the Civil War. p.552, p.553
Beyond Persuasion: Organizational Efficiency and Presidential Power. p.527
Beyond Positivism: Economic Methodology in the Twentieth Century. p.194, p.198
Beyond Productivity: How Leading Companies Achieve Superior Performance by Leveraging Their Human Capital. p.72, p.78
Beyond Right and Left: Democratic Elitism in Mosca and Gramsci. p.491, p.501
Beyond Silenced Voices: Class, Race, and Gender in United States Schools. p.302
Beyond Smoke and Mirrors: Mexican Immigration in an Era of Free Trade. p.571
Beyond Sovereignty: Issues for a Global Agenda. p.496
Beyond Standardized Testing: Better Information for School Accountability and Management. p.286
Beyond Sweatshops: Foreign Direct Investment and Globalization in Developing Nations. p.60
Beyond Teams: Building the Collaborative Organization. . p.80
Beyond the Area Studies Wars: Toward a New International Studies. p.627
Beyond the Best Interests of the Child. p.757
Beyond the Boundaries of Physical Education: Educating Young People for Citizenship and Social Responsibility. p.798, p.799
Beyond the Cheers: Race as Spectacle in College Sport.. . . . . p.817, p.822, p.830, p.894
Beyond the Constitution. p.453
Beyond the Coral Sea: Travels in the Old Empires of the South-West Pacific. p.385
Beyond the Ivory Tower: Social Responsibilities of the Modern University. p.289
Beyond the Lines: Pictorial Reporting, Everyday Life, and the Crisis of Gilded-Age America. p.409

Beyond the Nation-State: Functionalism and International Organization. p.629
Beyond the Open Door. p.331
Beyond the Ring: The Role of Boxing in American Society. p.819, p.856
Beyond the Ruling Class: Strategic Elites in Modern Society. p.724
Beyond the Welfare State: Economic Planning and Its International Implications. p.256
Beyond Time Out: A Practical Guide to Understanding and Serving Students with Behavioral Impairments in the Public Schools.. . . . . p.284
Beyond Unions and Collective Bargaining. p.123
Beyond Utility: Liberal Education for a Technological Age. p.303
Beyond Vocational Education: Career Majors, Tech Prep, Schools Within Schools, Magnet Schools and Academies. p.305
Beyond Walras, Keynes and Marx. p.229
Beyond Zero Tolerance: Discrimination in Military Culture. p.717
Bible Atlas. p.379
Bibliography of Business Ethics Articles, 1992 - present. p.53
A Bibliography of Female Economic Thought to 1940. p.214, p.274
Bibliography of the History of American Education. . p.327
Bicycle: The History. p.857
The Bicycle. p.857, p.870
Bidding and Auctioning for Procurement and Allocation: Proceedings of a Conference at the Center for Applied Economics, New York University. p.251
Bifurcated Politics: Evolution and Reform in the National Party Convention. p.551
The Big Chill: Investigative Reporting in the Current Media Environment. p.408
Big Deal: 2000 and Beyond. p.85, p.92
The Big Fix: Inside the S&L Scandal: How an Unholy Alliance of Politics and Money Destroyed America's Banking System. p.90
Big Game, Small World: A Basketball Adventure. . p.845, p.855
The Big Test: The Secret History of the American Meritocracy. p.286
The Biggest Game of All: The Inside Strategies, Tactics, and Temperaments That Make Great Dealmakers Great. . . p.84
The Bigness Complex: Industry, Labor, and Government in the American Economy. p.52 p.53 p.120 p.148
The Bill Clinton Story: Winning the Presidency. p.556
The Bill of Rights and the Politics of Interpretation. . . . p.456
The Bill of Rights: Creation and Reconstruction. p.455
Bill of Rights Reader: Leading Constitutional Cases. . . . p.455
Bill of Rights. p.455
Bingo Night at the Fire Hall: The Case for Cows, Orchards, Bake Sales and Fairs. p.772
Bioarchaeology: Interpreting Behavior from the Human Skeleton. p.14
The Biochemical Basis of Sports Performance. p.874
Biochemistry Primer for Exercise Science. p.874
Biogeography: An Ecological and Evolutionary Approach. . p.394
Biogeography. p.394
Biographical Dictionary of American Educators, Vol. 2. . p.338
Biographical Dictionary of American Educators, Vol. 3. . p.338
Biographical Dictionary of American Educators. p.338
A Biographical Dictionary of Dissenting Economists. . . p.193
Biographical Dictionary of Modern American Educators. . p.338
Biographical Dictionary of Social and Cultural Anthropology. p.3
Biographical Dictionary of Social Welfare in America. . . p.758
A Biographical Dictionary of Women Economists. p.193
The Biographical History of Basketball. p.853
The Biography of an Institution: The Civil Service Commission of Canada, 1908-1967. . . . . p.588
Biological Anthropology: An Introductory Reader. p.14
Biological Anthropology of the Human Skeleton. p.14
The Biological Basis of Human Behavior: A Critical Review. p.15
Biological Oceanography: An Early History, Eighteen Seventy to Nineteen Sixty. p.392
Biological Oceanography: An Introduction. p.392
Biological Oceanography. p.392
Biological Warfare and Disarmament: New Problems/New Perspectives. p.657
The Biology of Freshwater Wetlands. p.393
Biology of Lakes and Ponds. p.391
The Biomechanics and Motor Control of Human Movement. p.875, p.908, p.910
Biomechanics in Sports: Performance Improvement and Injury Prevention. p.827, p.829, p.880, p.908
Biomechanics: Motion, Flow, Stress, and Growth. p.908
Biomechanics of Distance Running. . p.874, p.879, p.907, p.909
The Biomechanics of Sports Techniques. p.873, p.908
Biomechanics of Women's Gymnastics. p.861, p.908
Biomedical Engineering Principles in Sports. p.872
The Biophysical Foundations of Human Movement ent, Vol. 2. . . . . p.874, p.907, p.909
Biotechnology: An Introduction. p.156
Biotechnology Demystified. p.156
Biotechnology Unzipped: Promises and Realities. p.156
Bird in a Cage: Legal Reform in China after Mao. p.475
Birth of a Salesman: The Transformation of Selling in America. p.146, p.165
The Birth of African-American Culture: An Anthropological Perspective. p.41
The Birth of Dirt: Origins of Mountain Biking. p.856
The Birth of the Bill of Rights, 1776-1791. . . . . p.518
Birth of the Bill of Rights: Encyclopedia of the Antifederalists. p.526
Birth of the Communist Manifesto. p.507, p.509
Bisexualities: The Ideology and Practice of Sexual Contact with Both Males and Females. p.750
Bisexuality: A Critical Reader. p.750

Bisexuality and the Challenge to Lesbian Politics: Sex, Loyalty, and Revolution. *p.750*
Bitter Fruits of Bondage: The Demise of Slavery and the Collapse of the Confederacy, 1861-1865. . . . . . . *p.521*
Bitter Milk: Women and Teaching. *p.282*
Black and Blue: Policing in South Africa. *p.774*
Black Baseball Entrepreneurs, 1860-1901: Operating by Any Means Necessary. *p.807, p.832, p.851, p.885*
The Black Book of Communism: Crimes, Terror, Repression. *p.658*
Black Children: Their Roots, Culture, and Learning Styles. *p.310*
Black Education: A Transformative Research and Action Agenda for the New Century. *p.301, p.310, p.355*
Black Enterprise Guide to Building Your Career. *p.167*
Black Families at the Crossroads: Challenges and Prospects. *p.734*
Black Feminist Anthropology: Theory, Politics, Praxis and Poetics. *p.31*
Black Liberation in Conservative America. *p.573*
The Black Lights: Inside the World of Professional Boxing. *p.855, p.896*
Black Like Me. *p.730*
Black Mondays: Worst Decisions of the U. S. Supreme Court.. . . . . *p.537*
Black Nationalism in American Politics and Thought. . . *p.573*
Black Picket Fences: Privilege and Peril among the Black Middle Class. *p.725, p.730*
Black Power-White Control: The Struggle of the Woodlawn Organization in Chicago. *p.702*
Ⓔ Black Presidential Politics in America: A Strategic Approach. *p.556, p.573*
Black Presidential Politics in America: A Strategic Approach. *p.555, p.556*
The Black Press: New Literary and Historical Essays. . . *p.411*
Black Religions in the New World. *p.37*
Black Roadways: A Study of Jamaican Folk Life.. . . . . *p.40*
Black Sexual Politics: African Americans, Gender, and the New Racism. *p.743*
Black Skins, French Voices: Caribbean Ethnicity and Activism in Urban France. *p.40*
Black Slaveowners: Free Black Slave Masters in South Carolina, 1790-1860. . . . . *p.727*
Black Sun: Aryan Cults, Esoteric Nazism and the Politics of Identity. *p.768*
Black Trials: Citizenship from the Beginnings of Slavery to the End of Caste. *p.723*
Black Votes Count: Political Empowerment in Mississippi after 1965. . . . . *p.555, p.573, p.579*
Black Wealth/White Wealth: A New Perspective on Racial Inequality. *p.730*
Black Women in the Labor Force. *p.271*
Black Women/White Men: The Sexual Exploitation of Female Slaves in the Danish West Indies. *p.727*
Blackberry Winter: My Earlier Years. *p.23*
Blackout: The Untold Story of Jackie Robinson's First Spring Training. *p.807, p.832, p.851*
Black's Law Dictionary, Deluxe. *p.436*
Blackshirts and Reds: Rational Fascism and the Overthrow of Communism. *p.509, p.510*
The Blackwell Companion to Social Movements. *p.710*
The Blackwell Companion to the Sociology of Families. . *p.732*
Blackwell Dictionary of Social Policy. *p.676*
The Blackwell Dictionary of Sociology: A User's Guide to Sociological Language. *p.677*
The Blackwell Encyclopedia of Writing Systems. *p.18*
The Blackwell Guide to the Philosophy of Education. *p.323, p.338*
The Blackwell Handbook of Organizational Learning and Knowledge Management. *p.79*
Blades of Glory: The True Story of a Young Team Bred to Win. *p.819, p.840, p.862*
The Blair Effect, 2001-5: A Wasted Term? *p.605*
The Blair Effect: The Blair Government, 1997-2001. . . . *p.605*
Blaming the Victim. *p.706*
Blind Spot: The Secret History of American Counterterrorism. *p.565*
Blink: The Power of Thinking Without Thinking. *p.83*
The Block Scheduling Handbook. *p.288*
Blood and Belonging: Journeys into the New Nationalism. . *p.494*
Blood and Debt: War and the Nation-State in Latin America. *p.591*
The Blood of Our Sons: Men, Women, and the Renegotiation of British Citizenship During the Great War. *p.604*
Blood Sacrifice and the Nation: Totem Rituals and the American Flag. *p.767*
Blood Sport: A Social History of Spanish Bullfighting. *p.808, p.856*
Blood, Sweat and Cheers: Sport and the Making of Modern Canada. *p.807*
Blood Ties: Life and Violence in Rural Mexico. *p.772*
Blown to Bits: How the New Economics of Information Transforms Strategy. *p.77*
Blue Collar Marriage. *p.739*
Blue Dreams: Korean Americans and the Los Angeles Riots. *p.713*
The Bluebook: A Uniform System of Citation. *p.439*
A Blueprint for Corporate Governance: Strategy, Accountability, and the Preservation of Shareholder Value. *p.86*
The Blues in Gray: The Civil War Journal of William Daniel Dixon and the Republican Blues Daybook. *p.520*
Blunders in International Business. *p.70*
The Boat People and Achievement in America: A Study of Economic and Educational Success. *p.763, p.764*
The Body in Late-Capitalist U. S. A. *p.775*
Bogolan: Shaping Culture Through Cloth in Contemporary Mali.. . . . . *p.26*
The Bohemian Grove and Other Retreats: A Study in Ruling-Class Cohesiveness. *p.719, p.726*
Bone Voyage: A Journey in Forensic Anthropology. *p.15*
The Bone Woman: A Forensic Anthropologist's Search for Truth in Rwanda, Bosnia, and Kosovo. *p.33*
Bones, Bodies, Behavior: Essays in Behavioral Anthropology. *p.5*

Book Business: Publishing: Past, Present and Future. . . . p.149
The Book of Risk. p.92
The Book Publishing Industry. p.149
Booms and Depressions. p.199, p.243
Border Identifications: Narratives of Religion, Gender, and Class on the U. S. -Mexico Border. p.727
The Border Patrol Ate My Dust. p.763
Border Visions: Mexican Cultures of the Southwest United States. p.770
Bordering the Future: The Impact of Mexico on the United States. p.382
The Borderless World: Power and Strategy in the Interlinked Economy. p.70
Boricua Pop: Puerto Ricans and American Culture from West Side Story to Jennifer Lopez. p.712
Born and Bred: Idioms of Kinship and New Reproductive Technologies in England. p.31
Born in Bondage: Growing up Enslaved in the Antebellum South. p.706
Born Losers: A History of Failure in America. p.706
Born to Run: Origins of the Political Career. p.550
Born to Win: The Authorized Biography of Althea Gibson. p.832, p.836, p.864
Boston Marathon: The First Century of the World's Premier Running Event. p.843, p.866
Boston Riots: Three Centuries of Social Violence. p.713
Both Gains and Gaps: Feminist Perspectives on Women's Leisure. p.784, p.836
Bottom Line Writing: Reporting the Sense of Dollars. . . p.406
Bottom-Line Automation. p.117
Bound by Law: Tales from the Public Domain: by Day a Filmmaker, by Night She Fought for Fair Use!. . . . p.445
Bound by Recognition. p.513, p.514
Boundaries and Belonging: States and Societies in the Struggle to Shape Identities and Local Practices. p.495
The Boundaryless Organization: Breaking the Chains of Organizational Structure. p.85
Bourgeoisie in Eighteenth Century France. p.723
The Bowker Annual Library and Book Trade Almanac 2005-2006. . . . . p.148
Bowling Alone: The Collapse and Revival of American Community. p.706
Bowling Fundamentals. p.796, p.848
Boxing and Society: An International Analysis. p.820, p.844, p.856
The Boxing Register: International Boxing Hall of Fame Official Record Book. p.856
The Boy Who Would Be a Helicopter. p.370
Brain Storm: Tap into Your Creativity to Generate Awesome Ideas and Remarkable Results. p.67
Brain Tattoos: Creating Unique Brands That Stick in Your Customers' Minds. p.142
Bramble Bush: On Our Law and Its Study. p.439
Brand Failures: The Truth about the 100 Biggest Branding Mistakes of All Time. p.142
Brand Hijack: Marketing Without Marketing. p.142
Brand Name Lookup. p.141
Brand Royalty: How the World's Top 100 Brands Thrive and Survive. p.142
The Brandeis-Frankfurter Connection: The Secret Political Activities of Two Supreme Court Justices. p.468
Brand-Name Bullies: The Quest to Own and Control Culture. p.773
Brands and Their Companies. p.141
Brands, Consumers, Symbols and Research: Sidney J Levy on Marketing. p.135
Brands: The Logos of the Global Economy. p.261
Brands. p.141
Brandweek: The Newsweekly of Marketing Communications. p.140, p.141, p.150
The Brass Check: A Study of American Journalism. . . . p.404
Brave New Families: Stories of Domestic Upheaval in Late-Twentieth-Century America. p.732
Brave New World Revisited. p.696
The Brawn Drain: Foreign Student Athletes in American Universities. p.821, p.893, p.898
Breaking into Baseball: Women and the National Pasttime. p.813, p.834, p.849
Breaking Story: South African Press. p.410
Breaking the Abortion Deadlock: From Choice to Consent. p.472
Breaking the Bargain: Public Servants, Ministers and Parliament. p.588
Breaking the Glass Ceiling: Sexism and Racism in Corporate America: the Myths, the Realities and the Solutions. . p.134
Breaking the Heart of the World: Woodrow Wilson and the Fight for the League of Nations. p.631
Breaking the Land: The Transformation of Cotton, Tobacco, and Rice Cultures since 1880. . . . . p.771
Breaking the Maya Code. p.22
Breaking the Rules: The NCAA and Recruitment in America's High Schools.. . . . . p.822, p.895
Breaking Through Bureaucracy: A New Vision for Managing in Government. p.529
Breaking Through Culture Shock: What You Need to Succeed in International Business.. . . . . p.56
Breakthrough International Negotiation: How Great Negotiators Transformed the World's Toughest Post-Cold War Conflicts. p.646
Breakthrough Swimming. p.868, p.879
Brennan vs. Rehnquist: The Battle for the Constitution. p.470, p.537
Brickyards to Graveyards: From Production to Genocide in Rwanda. p.652
Bridging Cultures Between Home and School: A Guide for Teachers with Special Focus on Immigrant Latino Families. p.311, p.312
Bridging the European Divide: Middle Power Politics and Regional Security Dilemmas. p.397
Bridging the Literacy Achievement Gap, Grades 4-12. . . p.365
Bridled Ambition: Why Countries Constrain Their Nuclear Capabilities. p.656
A Brief Course in Business Statistics.. . . . . p.179
Bright Promises, Dismal Performance: An Economist's Protest. p.231

Bringing Equity Back: Research for a New Era in American Educational Policy. p.299, p.302
Bringing the Empire Back Home: France in the Global Age. p.608
Bringing Them under Subjection: California's Tejon Indian Reservation and Beyond, 1852-1864. . . . . p.542
Bringing Transformative Learning to Life. p.320
The Brink of Peace: The Israeli-Syrian Negotiations. . . . p.650
The British Communist Party and the Trade Unions, 1933-45. . . . . p.604, p.606
British Diplomats and Diplomacy, 1660-1800. . . . . . . p.645
The British Electorate, 1963-1992: A Compendium of Data from the British Election Studies. p.606
The British Experience in Iraq: Lessons for U.S. Policymakers. p.561, p.643
British Foreign Policy in the Age of the American Revolution. p.583
The British Foreign Service and the American Civil War. . p.565
The British General Elections, 1945-1992, Set. p.606
British Imperialism: 1688-2000. . . . . p.583
British Industrial Revolution: An Economic Perspective. . p.212
The British Political Tradition, Set. p.607
The British Presidency: Tony Blair and the Politics of Public Leadership. p.605
British Social Movements since 1945: Sex, Colour, Peace and Power. p.711
British Society since 1945. . . . . p.705
Broadband Telecommunications Handbook. p.115
Broadcast Journalism. p.413
A Broadcast News Manual of Style. p.414
Broadcast News. p.414
Broadcast Talk, Vol. 5. . . . . p.412
Broadcasting and Cable Yearbook. p.157
Broadcasting Freedom: Radio War and the Politics of Race, 1938-1948. . . . . p.487, p.573
Broadcasting in the Arab World: A Survey of the Electronic Media in the Middle East. p.412
Broadcasting in the Third World: Promise and Performance. p.412
Broken Bottles, Broken Dreams: Understanding and Helping the Children of Alcoholics. p.776
Broken Promise: The Subversion of U. S. Labor Relations, 1947-1994. . . . . p.121
Broken Star: The Story of the League of Nations (1919-1939). p.631
Bronislaw Malinowski: Collected Works, Set. p.3
The Bronze Age and Early Iron Age Peoples of Eastern Central Asia. p.9
The Bronze Age of Southeast Asia. p.8
The Brothers and Sisters Learn to Write: Popular Literacies in Childhood and School Cultures. p.360
Brought to You By: Postwar Television Advertising and the American Dream. p.426
Brown v. Board of Education: A Civil Rights Milestone and Its Troubled Legacy. p.450
Brown vs. Board of Education: A Brief History with Documents. p.439
Brown vs. Board of Education: A Documentary History. . p.451
Brown vs. Board of Education: Caste, Culture, and the Constitution. p.449
Brushing Back Jim Crow: The Integration of the Minor Leagues in the American South. p.813, p.830, p.849
The Budget of the United States Government Fiscal Year 2006. . . . . p.248
Budget of the United States Government. p.481
Buenos Aires: Plaza to Suburb Eighteen Seventy to Nineteen Ten. p.706
The Buffalo Soldiers: A Narrative of the Negro Cavalry in the West. p.718
Buffett: The Making of an American Capitalist. . . p.96, p.147
The Bugatti Queen: In Search of a French Racing Legend. p.838, p.848
Building a Better World: An Introduction to Trade Unionism in Canada. p.124
Building a Bridge to 18th Century. p.323
Building a Knowledge-Driven Organization. p.77
Building Bodies. p.818, p.844, p.855
Building Character in the American Boy: The Boy Scouts, YMCA and Their Forerunners, 1870-1920. . . . . . . p.719
Building Community in Schools. p.281
Building Democracy in South Asia: India, Nepal, Pakistan. p.617
Building Effective Afterschool Programs. p.288
Building Effective Evaluation Capacity: Lessons from Practice. p.580
Building Great Customer Experiences. p.143
Building Public Trust: The Future of Corporate Reporting. p.92, p.105, p.106, p.111
Building Smart Teams: A Roadmap to High Performance. . p.79
Building Strong Brands. p.141
Building the Bank of England: Money, Architecture and Society, 1694-1942. . . . . p.90
Building the Fourth Estate: Democratization and the Rise of a Free Press in Mexico. p.409
Building the Next Ark: How NGOs Work to Protect Biodiversity. p.640, p.666
Building the Union: Skilled Workers and Anglo-Gaelic Immigrants in the Rise of the UAW. p.124
Building Virtual Communities: Learning and Change in Cyberspace. p.762
Building Virtual Communities: Learning and Change in Cyberspace. p.762
Building Wealth: The New Rules for Individuals, Companies, and Nations in a Knowledge-Based Economy. p.78
Built to Last: Successful Habits of Visionary Companies. . p.67
Built to Win: The Female Athlete As Cultural Icon. . p.816, p.836
Bureaucracy, Economy, and Leadership in China: The Institutional Origins of the Great Leap Forward. . . . p.619
Bureaucratic and Political Corruption in Africa: The Public Choice Perspective. p.612
Bureaucratic Reform in the Ottoman Empire: The Sublime Porte, 1789-1922. . . . . p.614
Bureaucratic Representation: Civil Servants and the Future of Capitalist Democracies. p.546

Bureaucrats and Politicians in Western Democracies. . . . p.601
Bureaucrats, Politics, and the Environment. p.546
The Burger Court, 1968-1984, Vol. 9. . . . . p.536
The Burger Court: Counter-Revolution or Confirmation? . p.539
The Burger Court: The Counter-Revolution That Wasn't. . p.470
Buried by the Times: The Holocaust and America's Most Important Newspaper. p.411
Burn Before Reading: Presidents, CIA Directors, and Secret Intelligence. p.562
Burning and Building: Schooling and State Formation in Japan, 1750-1890. . . . . p.336
The Burning Tigris: The Armenian Genocide and America's Response. p.651
Burundi: Ethnic Conflict and Genocide. p.653
Bury My Heart at Wounded Knee: An Indian History of the American West. p.572, p.646
Bush at War: Inside the Bush White House. p.565
Bushmanders and Bullwinkles: How Politicians Manipulate Electronic Maps and Census Data to Win Elections. . p.385
Business Across Cultures.. . . . . p.59
Business and Its Environment. p.51
The Business and Practice of Coaching: Finding Your Niche, Making Money and Attracting Ideal Clients.. . . . . . . p.64
Business and Society: A Reader in the History, Sociology, and Ethics of Business. p.52
Business and Society: Corporate Strategy, Public Policy, and Ethics with PowerWeb and Enron Case. p.52
Business and the Environment: A Resource Guide. p.62
Business as a Calling: Work and the Examined Life.. p.55, p.167
Business As War: Battling for Competitive Advantage. . . p.70
Business Calculus Demystified. p.175
Business Civilization in Decline. p.214
Business, Commerce, and Social Responsibility: Beyond Agenda. p.145
Business Consulting: A Guide to How It Works and How to Make It Work. p.65
Business Creativity: Breaking the Invisible Barriers. . . . p.66
The Business Cycle: Theories and Evidence, Proceedings of the Sixteenth Annual Economic Policy Conference of the Federal Reserve Bank of St. Louis. p.242
Business Cycle Theory. p.244
Business Cycles: A Theoretical, Historical, and Statistical Analysis of the Capitalist Process. p.230, p.245
Business Ethics: A Reference Handbook. . . p.53, p.55, p.180
Business Ethics and the Natural Environment. . . . p.61, p.64
Business Ethics. p.54, p.55, p.181
Business, Government and Society. p.52
Business Information: Finding and Using Data in the Digital Age. p.181
Business Information: How to Find It, How to Use It. . . p.180
Business Information Sources. p.180
Business Law. p.109
Business Letters Ready to Go!. p.171
Business Library and How to Use It: A Guide to Sources and Research Strategies for Information on Business and Management. p.180
Business Math Demystified. p.174
Business Math. p.175
Business of Baseball. p.849, p.880
The Business of Books: How the International Conglomerates Took over Publishing and Changed the Way We Read.. p.149
The Business of Lobbying in China. p.145
The Business of Sports Agents. p.905
The Business of Sport. p.884, p.891, p.896
The Business of the Supreme Court: A Study in the Federal Judicial System. p.470
Business on Trial: The Civil Jury and Corporate Responsibility. p.109, p.112
Business Plans and Profiles Index: A Subject Guide to Sample Business Plans and Profiles for Specific Business Types. p.172
Business Plans Handbook, Vol. 11. . . . . p.174
Business Ratios and Formulas: A Comprehensive Guide. p.174
Business Simulations, Games and Experiential Learning in International Business Education. p.177
Business Statistics Demystified. p.179
The Business Style Handbook: An A-to-Z Guide for Writing on the Job with Tips from Communications Experts at the Fortune 500.. . . . . p.172
Business Tax Stories 2005. . . . . p.106, p.109, p.112
Business: The Ultimate Resource. p.180
The Business Writer's Handbook. p.171
Business Writing for Results: How to Create a Sense of Urgency and Increase Response to Your E-Mails, Letters, Proposals, Reports, Newsletters and Websites.. p.172
BusinessWeek Guide to the Best Business Schools. . . . p.176
Busting the Mob: The United States vs. Cosa Nostra. . . p.438
By Different Paths to Common Outcomes. p.368
By Order of the President: The Use and Abuse of Executive Direct Action. p.461
By the Numbers: Using Facts and Figures to Get Your Projects, Plans and Ideas Approved. p.173, p.175

C

C. Wright Mills: An American Utopian. p.685
C. Wright Mills and the Ending of Violence. . . . p.690, p.766
Cabell's Directory of Publishing Opportunities in Accounting. p.148
Cabell's Directory of Publishing Opportunities in Economics and Finance.. . . . . p.149
Cabell's Directory of Publishing Opportunities in Management. p.149
Cabinets and Counselors: The President and the Executive Branch. p.526
Cabinets and First Ministers. p.588
Cable Communications: Building the Information Infrastructure. p.421
CAD-CAM Handbook. p.116
Caddy for Life: The Bruce Edwards Story. p.860

Cadres and Corruption: The Organizational Involution of the Chinese Communist Party. *p.620*
Cages of Reason: The Rise of the Rational State in France, Japan, the United States, and Great Britain. . . *p.545, p.581*
Cahokia and the Hinterlands: Middle Mississippian Cultures of the Midwest. *p.10*
Cahokia: Mirror of the Cosmos. *p.10*
The Call Heard 'Round the World: VoIP and the Quest for Convergence. *p.422*
The Call of Service. *p.719*
Call of the Game: What Really Goes on in the Broadcast Booth. *p.408, p.906*
A Call to Action: Reconnecting College Sports and Higher Education. *p.821, p.894*
Call to Order: Floor Politics in the House and Senate. . . *p.534*
The Cambridge Companion to Hannah Arendt. *p.493*
The Cambridge Companion to Historical Archaeology. . . *p.14*
The Cambridge Companion to Keynes. *p.226*
The Cambridge Companion to Locke's Essay Concerning Human Understanding. *p.196*
The Cambridge Companion to Plato. *p.489*
The Cambridge Companion to Postcolonial Literary Studies. *p.485*
The Cambridge Dictionary of Human Biology and Evolution. *p.15*
The Cambridge Encyclopedia of Hunters and Gatherers. . . *p.3*
The Cambridge Gazetteer of the USA and Canada: A Dictionary of Places. *p.374*
The Cambridge History of Ancient China: From the Origins of Civilization to 221 BC. *p.9*
The Cambridge History of Medieval Political Thought C. 350-C. 1450. *p.490, p.501*
The Cambridge History of the Pacific Islanders. *p.42*
Cameroon: Politics and Society in Critical Perspectives. . *p.612*
Camouflage Isn't Only for Combat: Gender, Sexuality, and Women in the Military. *p.717*
Campaign Contributions and Legislative Voting: A New Approach. *p.530*
□ Campaign Finance Information Center. *p.558*
Campaign Warriors: Political Consultants in Elections. . . *p.558*
Campaigning for Hearts and Minds: How Emotional Appeals in Political Ads Work. *p.424*
Campaigns and Conscience: The Ethics of Political Journalism. *p.406*
Campaigns and Elections: Issues, Concepts, Cases. . . . *p.552*
Campaigns and the Court: The U. S. Supreme Court in Presidential Elections. *p.540*
Campaigns, Congress and the Courts: The Making of Federal Campaign Finance Laws. *p.525*
Campus Hate Speech on Trial. *p.459*
Campus Life: Undergraduate Cultures from the End of the Eighteenth Century to the Present. *p.290, p.331*
Can Ethics Be Taught?: Perspectives, Challenges, and Approaches at the Harvard Business School. . . *p.53, p.177*
Can Regional Integration Arrangements Enforce Trade Discipline?: The Story of EU Enlargement. *p.60*
Canada and the United States: Differences That Count. . . *p.587*
Canada at the Polls, 1984: A Study of the Federal General Elections. *p.590*
Canada: the State of the Federation: Reconfiguring Aboriginal-State Relations. *p.587*
Canada Votes, 1935-1989. . . . . *p.590*
Canadian Federalism and Quebec Sovereignty. *p.581*
The Canadian Legal System. *p.436*
Canadian Political Party Systems. *p.588*
Canadian Politics in the 21st Century. *p.587*
Canadian Politics. *p.586*
Canadian Provincial Politics. *p.589*
The Canadian Public Service: A Physiology of Government, 1867-1970. . . . . *p.588*
Cannibal Tours and Glass Boxes: The Anthropology of Museums. *p.47*
The Canoe: A Living Tradition. *p.789*
Can't Find My Way Home: America in the Great Stoned Age, 1945-2000. . . . . *p.777*
The Capacity to Budget. *p.543*
Capital: A Critique of Political Economy. *p.215*
Capital and Collusion: The Political Logic of Global Economic Development. *p.260, p.261*
Capital and Growth. *p.209*
Capital and Interest. *p.233*
Capital and Its Earnings. *p.223*
Capital and Time: A Neo-Austrian Theory. *p.214*
Capital Ideas: The Improbable Origins of Modern Wall Street. *p.91, p.93, p.99*
Capital, Labor, and State: The Battle for American Labor Markets from the Civil War to the New Deal. *p.123*
Capital Punishment in the United States: A Documentary History. *p.487, p.568*
Capital Punishment. *p.471*
Capital: Theories of Surplus Value, Vol. 4. . . . . *p.236*
Capital Theory and the Rate of Return. *p.245*
Capitalism and Freedom. *p.214, p.231*
Capitalism and Modern Social Theory: An Analysis of the Writings of Marx, Durkheim and Max Weber. *p.679*
Capitalism and Social Democracy. *p.507*
Capitalism As a Moral System: Adam Smith's Critique of the Free Market Economy. *p.219*
Capitalism, Socialism, and Democracy Revisited. . *p.214, p.235*
e Capitalism, Socialism and Democracy. *p.230, p.235*
Capitalism, Socialism and Democracy. . . *p.500, p.505, p.507*
Capitalism. *p.214*
e Capitalist Development in the Twentieth Century: An Evolutionary-Keynesian Analysis. *p.241*
Capitalist Development in the Twentieth Century: An Evolutionary-Keynesian Analysis. *p.214*
Capitalist Diversity and Change: Recombinant Governance and Institutional Entrepreneurs.. . . . . *p.67*
Captains of Consciousness: Advertising and the Social Roots of the Consumer Culture.. . . . . *p.52*
A Cardboard Castle?: An Inside History of the Warsaw Pact, 1955-1991. . . . . *p.630*
Cardozo. *p.468*

The Care and Education of America's Young Children: Obstacles and Opportunities. *p.369*
The Care and Feeding of Ideas. *p.428*
Career Directions.. *p.168*
The Career Guide: The Employment Opportunities Directory. *p.168*
Career Imprints: Creating Leaders Across an Industry.. . . *p.71*
Career Insights: Presidents/GMs from the NFL, MLB, NHL and MLS on Achieving Personal and Professional Success: Landing a Job with a Sports Team. *p.905*
Career Opportunities for Bilinguals and Multilinguals: A Directory of Resources in Education, Employment, and Business. *p.168*
Career Opportunities in Aviation and the Aerospace Industry. *p.151*
Career Opportunities in the Publishing Industry: A Guide to Careers in Newspapers, Magazines, and Books. . . . *p.150*
Career Transitions in Sport: International Perspectives. . . *p.903*
CareerPreneurs: Lessons from Leading Women Entrepreneurs on Building a Career Without Boundaries. *p.68*
Careers for Number Crunchers and Other Quantitative Types. *p.167*
Careers for Sports Nuts and Other Athletic Types. *p.903*
Careers in Government. *p.546*
Careers in Health, Physical Education, and Sports.. *p.794, p.903*
Careers in Sports Fitness and Recreation. *p.785, p.904*
Cargo, Cult, and Culture Critique. *p.711*
Caribbean Transformations. *p.41*
Caring Classrooms/Intelligent Schools: The Social Emotional Education of Young Children. *p.362*
Caring Jurisprudence: Listening to Patients at the Supreme Court.. . . . . *p.535*
Carl Menger and His Legacy in Economics.. . . . . . . *p.194*
Carl Menger and the Origins of Austrian Economics. . . *p.233*
Carnival and the Formation of a Caribbean Transnation. . . *p.44*
Caroline Feller Bauer's New Handbook for Storytellers. . *p.362*
Cars and Culture: The Life Story of a Technology.. . . . *p.154*
Cartographic Design Using Arcview GIS. *p.385, p.387*
Cartographic Mexico: A History of State Fixations and Fugitive Landscapes. *p.383*
Cartography: Thematic Map Design with Arcview GIS Software. *p.385*
The Case Against Standardized Testing: Raising the Scores, Ruining the Schools. *p.286*
The Case for Change: Rethinking the Preparation of Educators. *p.277*
The Case for Classical Christian Education. *p.308*
A Case for Conservatism. *p.511*
Case in Point: Complete Case Interview Preparation.. . . *p.169*
Case Studies in Organizational Communication: Ethical Perspectives and Practices. *p.53, p.173*
Case Studies of City-County Consolidation: Reshaping the Local Government Landscape. *p.542, p.544*
Case Studies of Teacher Development: An In-Depth Look at How Thinking about Pedagogy Develops over Time. . *p.277*
Case Study Research: Design and Methods. *p.688*
Cases for Teacher Development: Preparing for the Classroom. *p.277*
Cases in the Environment of Business: International Perspectives. *p.69*
Caste, Society and Politics in India from the Eighteenth Century to the Modern Age. *p.722*
Castles of Our Conscience: Social Control and the American State, 1800-1985. . . . . *p.773*
Casualties of Privilege: Essays on Prep Schools' Hidden Culture. *p.296*
Casualty of War: The Bush Administration's Assault on a Free Press. *p.563*
Catalan Nationalism: Past and Present. *p.608*
□ Catalog of U.S. Government Publications. *p.482*
Categorical Data Analysis with SAS and SPSS Applications. *p.690*
Category Killers: The Retail Revolution and Its Impact on Consumer Culture. *p.165*
Catholic Philosophy of Education. *p.345*
Catholic Schools and the Common Good. *p.307*
Catholicism and American Freedom: A History from Slavery to Abortion. *p.486*
Catholics and American Culture: Fulton Sheen, Dorothy Day and the Notre Dame Football Team. . . *p.817, p.859, p.894*
Cattle Bring Us to Our Enemies: Turkana Ecology, Politics, and Raiding in a Disequilibrium System. *p.30*
Caucasians Only: The Supreme Court, the NAACP, and the Restrictive Covenant Cases.. . . . . *p.443*
Caught in the Middle: Contradictions in the Lives of Sociologists from Working Class Backgrounds.. . . . . *p.682*
Causal Models in the Social Sciences. *p.687*
Causality in Macroeconomics. *p.240*
Cause and Meaning in the Social Sciences. *p.700*
Cause Marketing. *p.145*
Causes of International War. *p.647, p.649*
Cavalcade of Journalists 1900-2000. . . . . *p.404*
□ CBOE, Chicago Board Options Exhange. . . . *p.93, p.101*
The CBOT Handbook of Futures and Options. *p.94, p.101, p.162*
Celebrating Irving Fisher: The Legacy of a Great Economist. *p.200, p.225*
Celebrating the Family: Ethnicity, Consumer Culture, and Family Rituals. *p.705, p.734*
Celebrating Women Coaches: A Biographical Dictionary. . *p.836*
Censorship, Inc.: The Corporate Threat to Free Speech in the United States. *p.515*
Censorship of the Movies: The Social and Political Control of a Mass Medium.. *p.451*
□ Center for American Women and Politics. . . . *p.547, p.568*
□ Center for History and New Media. *p.419*
□ Center for Research on Education, Diversity & Excellence (CREDE). *p.302, p.346*
□ Center for the Study of Sexual Minorities in the Military. *p.717*
The Center Holds: The Power Struggle Inside the Rehnquist Court.. . . . . *p.539*

Central and Local Government Relations: A Comparative Analysis of West European Unitary States. p.582
Central Asia at the End of the Transition. p.599, p.624
Central Ideas in the Development of American Journalism: A Narrative History. p.404
Central Planning. p.235
Centralization and Decentralization in Economic Policy. . p.237
Centralizing and Decentralizing Trends in Federal States. . p.523
Centres of Learning: Learning and Location in Pre-Modern Europe and the Near East. p.334
Centuries of Childhood: A Social History of Family Life. . p.735
A Century of British Geography. p.374, p.378
A Century of Genocide: Utopias of Race and Nation. . . p.715
A Century of Lawmaking for a New Nation: U.S. Congressional Documents and Debates, 1774-1875. . . p.516
A Century of Lawmaking. p.437, p.440
A Century of Organized Labor in France: A Union Movement for the Twenty-First Century? p.129
A Century of Women's Basketball: From Frailty to Final Four. p.807, p.836, p.854
Ceremonial Animal: A New Portrait of Anthropology. . . . p.22
A Certain Idea of Europe. p.638
Certain Trumpets: The Nature of Leadership. p.72
Certainty of Justice: Reform in the Crime Victim Movement. p.754
Certification Requirements for 50 States. p.278
Cesar Chavez: A Biography. p.124
Cesar Chávez: A Triumph of Spirit. p.126
Chaco Canyon: Archeologists Explore the Lives of an Ancient Society. p.10
Chain of Command: The Road from 9/11 to Abu Ghraib. . p.659
Chairing the Academic Department: Leadership among Peers. p.294
Challenge and Change in Education: The Experience of the Baltic States in the 1990's. p.335
The Challenge for Geography: A Changing World, a Changing Discipline. p.378
The Challenge of Global Capitalism: The World Economy in the 21st Century. p.55
The Challenge of Restructuring: North American Labor Movements Respond. p.122
The Challenge of Same-Sex Marriage: Federalist Principles and Constitutional Protections. p.570
Challenge of World Poverty: A World Poverty Program in Outline. p.259
Challenge to Affluence. p.214
Challenges for Rural America in the 21st Century. p.771
Challenges of Teaching with Technology Across the Curriculum: Issues and Solutions. p.352
Challenging the Incumbent: An Underdog's Undertaking. . p.550
Champion Joe Louis: A Biography. p.832, p.855
Change at Work. p.85
The Change Makers: From Carnegie to Gates, How the Great Entrepreneurs Transformed Ideas into Industries. p.66
Change Masters. p.76
The Changing American Presidency. p.528
Changing Economic Geography Of Globalization. p.398
The Changing Experience of Childhood: Families and Divorce. p.735
The Changing Face of Economics: Conversations with Cutting Edge Economists. p.185
The Changing Geography of Asia. p.384
Changing Kids' Games. p.304, p.364
Changing Meanings of Citizenship in Modern China. . . p.619
Changing Ones: Third and Fourth Genders in Native North America. p.746
The Changing Politics of Foreign Policy. p.628
The Changing Social Structure of England and Wales 1871-1961. . . . . p.704
Changing Structure of Mexico: Political, Social, and Economic Prospects. p.383, p.593
Changing the Atmosphere: Expert Knowledge and Environmental Governance. p.666
Changing the Odds: Open Admissions and the Life Chances of the Disadvantaged. p.294
Changing Times: Work and Leisure in Postindustrial Society. p.761
A Changing United Nations: Multilateral Evolution and the Quest for Global Governance. p.634
The Changing World of Bali: Religion, Society and Tourism. p.39
The Changing World of Mongolia's Nomads. p.28
The Character of American Higher Education and Intercollegiate Sport. p.289, p.821, p.893
Characteristics of Public School Teachers' Professional Development Activities: 1999-2000. . . . . p.278
Charter of the United Nations and Statute of the International Court of Justice. p.635
Charter of the United Nations: Report to the President on the Results of the San Francisco Conference. p.635
The Charter School Challenge: Avoiding the Pitfalls, Fulfilling the Promise. p.280
Charter Schools: Another Flawed Educational Reform? . p.281
Chartered Schools: Two Hundred Years of Independent Academies in United States, 1727-1925. . . . . p.296
The Chastening: Inside the Crisis That Rocked the Global Financial System and Humbled the IMF. p.99
The Chatham House Version: And Other Middle Eastern Studies. p.614
The Chautauqua Moment: Protestants, Progressives, and the Culture of Modern Liberalism, 1874-1920. . . . . . . p.721
Chauvet Cave: The Art of Earliest Times. p.16
Chavin and the Origins of Andean Civilization. p.11
CHEA web site. p.289
Cheerleader!: An American Icon. p.847
The Cheers and the Tears: A Healthy Alternative to the Dark Side of Youth Sports Today. p.818, p.840
The Chemical Industry at the Millenium: Maturity, Restructuring and Globalization. p.157
Chen Village under Mao and Deng: The Recent History of a Peasant Community in Mao's China. p.701
The Cherokee Cases: Two Landmark Federal Decisions in the Fight for Sovereignty. p.465

The Chiapas Rebellion: The Struggle for Land and Democracy. p.711
Chicago Board of Trade. p.93, p.101
The Chicago Guide to Writing about Numbers. . . p.173, p.179
Chicago: Race, Class, and the Response to Urban Decline. . p.544
Chicanas and Chicanos in School: Racial Profiling, Identity Battles, and Empowerment. p.301
Chicano School Failure and Success: Past, Present, and Future. p.311
Chief Justice: Leadership and the Supreme Court. p.540
A Chief Justice's Progress: John Marshall from Revolutionary Virginia to the Supreme Court. p.538
The Chief Justiceship of Melville W. Fuller, 1888-1910. . p.467
Chief Justiceship of Warren Burger, 1969-1986: A Provocative Interpretation of the Burger Court. p.468, p.537
Chief of Staff: Lyndon Johnson and His Presidency. . . . p.528
Chief Sources of English Legal History. p.433
The Chief: The Life of William Randolph Hearst. . p.149, p.411
The Child and Adolescent Athlete. p.828, p.874, p.878
The Child and Society. p.735
The Child and the Curriculum and the School and Society. . p.356
Child by Child: The Comer Process for Change in Education. p.280
Child Care and the Growth of Love. p.735
Child Development and Education: A Piagetian Perspective. p.342
Child Language. p.356
Child Welfare: Major Themes in Health and Social Welfare. p.757
A Child Went Forth: Reflective Teaching with Young Readers and Writers. p.360
Child Witnesses: Fragile Voices in the American Legal System. p.473
Childhood and Society. p.735
Childhood, Culture, and Class in Britain: Margaret McMillan, 1860-1931. . . . . p.346
Childhood in Contemporary Cultures. p.735
Childhood in the Promised Land: Working-Class Movements and the Colonies de Vacances in France, 1880-1960. . p.711
Children and Youth in Sport. p.824, p.840
Children in Changing Families: Life after Parental Seperation. p.740
Children in Foster Care: A Longitudinal Investigation. . . p.756
Children of Global Migration: Transnational Families and Gendered Woes. p.44
The Children of NAFTA: Labor Wars on the U. S.-Mexico Border. p.726
Children of Sanchez. p.733
Children of the Dragonfly: Native American Voices on Child Custody and Education. p.755
The Children of the Dream. p.735
Children of the Revolution: A Yankee Teacher in the Cuban Schools. p.335
Children of the Storm: Black Children and American Child Welfare. p.755
Children on the Streets of the Americas: Globalization, Homelessness Education in Brazil, Cuba and the United States. p.335
Children, School, and Society in Nineteenth-Century England. p.334
Children with Special Needs: Lessons for Early Childhood Professionals. p.316
Children's Exercise Physiology, Vol. 2. . . . . p.875
Children's Inquiry: Using Language to Make Sense of the World. p.423
Children's Lifeworlds: Gender, Welfare and Labour in the Developing World. p.40
Children's Literature in the Elementary School with Litlinks. p.364
Children's Minds, Talking Rabbits and Clockwork: Changes - Essays on Education. p.339
Children's Minds. p.356
Children's Play: The Roots of Reading. . . p.304, p.354, p.359
Children's Reading Comprehension and Assessment. . . . p.365
Children's Rights: Caribbean Realities. p.755
The Child's Conception of Geometry. p.358
China and Democracy: Reconsidering Prospects for a Democratic China. p.621
China Confidential: American Diplomats and Sino-American Relations, 1945-1996. . . . . p.561, p.566, p.644
China, Korea and Japan: The Rise of Civilization in East Asia. p.8
China since Tiananmen: The Politics of Transition. . . . p.619
China, the United Nations, and Human Rights: The Limits of Compliance. p.513
China's Leadership in the Twenty-first Century: The Rise of the Fourth Generation. p.619
China's One-Child Family Policy. p.731
China's Ownership Transformation: Process, Outcomes, Prospects. p.86
China's Peasants: The Anthropology of a Revolution. . . . p.40
China's Place in Global Geopolitics: Domestic, Regional and International Challenges. p.400
China's Political System: Modernization and Tradition. . p.619
China's Trade Unions and Management. p.128
China's Universities, 1895-1995: A Century of Cultural Conflict. p.334
China's Universities and the Open Door. p.334
China's Western Development: The Role of the State in Historical and Regional Perspective. p.397
The Chinese Diaspora: Space, Place, Mobility and Identity. p.765
Chinese Education: Problems, Policies, and Prospects. . . p.334
Chinese Gentry: Studies on Their Role in 19th-Century Chinese Society. p.701
The Chinese Journalist: Mediating Information in the World's Most Populous Country. p.403
Chinese Lineage and Society: Fukien and Kwantung. . . . p.39
A Chinese Village in Early Communist Transition. p.708
The Chivalrous Society. p.682
Choice and Coercion: Birth Control, Sterilization, and Abortion in Public Health and Welfare. p.756

Choice, Welfare, and Measurement. p.266

☐ Choices III. p.139, p.142

Choices, Values, and Frames. p.272

Choosing a President: The Electoral College and Beyond. . p.527

Choosing an Electoral System: Issues and Alternatives. . p.576

Choosing Your Battles: American Civil-Military Relations and the Use of Force. p.561

The Chosen Species: The Long March of Human Evolution. p.15

Christian Slaves, Muslim Masters: White Slavery in the Mediterranean, the Barbary Coast and Italy, 1500-1800. p.727

☐ Chronicle Careers. p.292

Chronicling Cultures: Long-Term Field Research in Anthropology. p.25

Chronological History of U. S. Foreign Relations, Set. p.560, p.627

Chronology of Communication in the United States. . . . p.424

Chrysler: The Life and Times of an Automotive Genius. . p.153

Church and State Education in Revolutionary Mexico City. p.336

Churchill and America. p.485, p.644

Churchill's Cold War: The Politics of Personal Diplomacy. . p.645

Churching of America, 1776-2005: Winners and Losers in Our Religious Economy. p.720

Church-State Relations. p.486

☐ CIA Declassified Documents. p.481

☐ CIA World Fact Book. p.60

☐ CIAO (Columbia International Affairs Online). p.624

Cinderella Man: James J. Braddock, Max Baer, and the Greatest Upset in Boxing History. p.856

The CIO, 1935-1955. . . . . p.130

The CIO Challenge to the AFL: A History of the American Labor Movement. p.126

The Circle of Innovation: You Can't Shrink Your Way to Greatness. p.67

Circles and Lines: The Shape of Life in Early America. . p.702

Circuit Chautauqua: From Rural Education to Popular Entertainment in Early Twentieth Century America. . . p.321

The Citadel of Learning. p.290, p.331

Cities and Fiscal Choices: A New Model of Urban Public Investment. p.544

Cities, Classes, and the Social Order. p.37

Cities in a Globalizing World: Global Report on Human Settlements. p.544

Cities, War, and Terrorism: Towards an Urban Geopolitics. . p.659

Citizen Hearst, a Biography of William Randolph Hearst. . p.411

Citizen Hobo: How a Century of Homelessness Shaped America. p.757

Citizen in Court: Litigant, Witness, Juror, Judge. p.465

Citizen Politics: Public Opinion and Political Parties in Advanced Industrial Democracies. p.578

Citizens, Cops, and Power: Recognizing the Limits of Community. p.774

Citizenship and Governance in the European Union. p.602, p.636

Citizenship and Nationhood in France and Germany. p.608, p.609

ⓔ Citizenship in the Western Tradition: Plato to Rousseau. p.578

Citizenship: The Civic Ideal in World History, Politics and Education. p.577

Citizens. p.586

The City: A Global History. p.772

The City at Stake: Secession, Reform, and the Battle for Los Angeles. p.544

City Games: The Evolution of American Urban Society and the Rise of Sports. p.819

The City in History: Its Origins, Its Transformations and Its Prospects. p.771

City of Walls: Crime, Segregation and Citizenship in São Paulo. p.773

City Room. p.412

City Schools and the American Dream: Reclaiming the Promise of Public Education. p.315

City Walls: The Urban Enceinte in Global Perspective. . . p.771

Civic Engagement in American Democracy. . . . p.547, p.555

Civil Disobedience: Theory and Practice. p.497

Civil Liberties and the Vinson Court. p.456

The Civil Rights Act of 1964: The Passage of the Law That Ended Racial Segregation. p.457

The Civil Rights Era: Origins and Development of National Policy, 1960-1972. . . . . p.486

Civil Servants and Their Constitutions. p.546

Civil Society: A Reader in History, Theory, and Global Politics. p.498

Civil Society and Government. p.499

Civil Society and Political Change in Asia: Expanding and Contracting Democratic Space. p.616

Civil Society, Democracy and Civic Renewal. p.547

Civil Society in Japan: The Growing Role of NGOs in Tokyo's Aid and Development Policy. p.640, p.663

Civil Society in the Information Age. p.640

Civil Society in the Yemen: The Political Economy of Activism in Modern Arabia. p.614

Civil-Military Relations in Russia and Eastern Europe. . . p.597

Civil-Military Relations in South Asia: Pakistan, Bangladesh and India. p.617, p.618

The Claims of Kinfolk: African American Property and Community in the Nineteenth-Century South. p.705

Clarence Thomas: A Biography. p.540

Class Action: The Landmark Case That Changed Sexual Harassment Law. p.130

Class Actions: Teaching for Social Justice in Elementary and Middle School. p.361

Class and Class Conflict in Industrial Society. p.724

Class and Conformity: A Study in Values. p.695, p.724

Class and Party in American Politics. p.552

Class, Ethnicity, and Community in Southern Mexico: Oaxaca's Peasantries. p.771

Class Ethnicity and Politics in Liberia: A Class Analysis of Power Struggles in the Tubman and Tolbert Administrations from 1944-1975. . . . . p.703

Class: Image and Reality in Britain, France and the U. S. A. since 1930. . . . . p.724
Class Notes: Posing as Politics and Other Thoughts on the American Scene. p.484
The Class of 2000: The Definitive Survey of the New Generation. p.288
A Class of Their Own: When Children Teach Children. . p.349
Class, Sports, and Social Development. p.816
Class, Status and Power: A Reader in Social Stratification. . p.723
The Class Structure of the Advanced Societies. p.724
Class Warfare in the Information Age. p.698
The Classic Slum: Salford Life in the First Quarter of the Century. p.706
Classical and Neoclassical Theories of General Equilibrium. p.206, p.218, p.224, p.271
The Classical Athenian Democracy. p.501
Classical Economics and Modern Theory: Studies in Long-Period Analysis. p.218
Classical Economics. p.217
The Classical Economists Revisited. p.218
Classical Fighting Arts of Japan: A Complete Guide to Koryeu Jeujutsu. p.863
Classical Horizons: The Origins of Sociology in Ancient Greece. p.683
The Classical Roots of Ethnomethodology: Durkheim, Weber, and Garfinkel. p.688
Classical Social Theory. p.677
Classical Sociological Theory. p.677
Classical Theory of the Gains from Trade: The Origins of International Economics. p.256
Classics: A Treasury of Investment Literature. p.94
Classics in Management. p.116
Classics in Movement Science. p.873, p.908, p.909
Classics of Practicing Anthropology, 1978-1998. . . . . . p.44
Classics: The Most Interesting Ideas and Concepts from the Literature of Investing. p.94
Classroom Assessment Techniques: A Handbook for College Teachers. p.285
Classroom Killers? Hallway Hostages?: How Schools Can Prevent and Manage School Crises. p.281
Classroom Life as Civic Education: Individual Achievement and Student Cooperation in Schools. p.362
A Classroom of One: How Online Learning Is Changing Our Schools and Colleges. p.322
Classroom Power Relations: Understanding Student-Teacher Interaction. p.349
Classroom Teacher's Survival Guide: Practical Strategies, Management Techniques, and Reproducibles for New and Experienced Teachers. p.284
Classrooms That Work: They Can All Read and Write. . . p.362
Claude Levi-Strauss: The Formative Years. p.24
A Clear Eye for Branding: Straight Talk on Today's Most Powerful Business Concept. p.138
Clearinghouse on Educational Policy and Management. p.280
Climate Change and Africa. p.394
Climate Change and Biodiversity. p.394
Climate Change: Critical Concepts in the Environment and Physical Geography. p.393
Climatic Geomorphology. p.391
The Climb: Tragic Ambitions on Everest. p.789
Climbing Free: My Life in the Vertical World. . . p.789, p.836
Climbing in North America. p.789
Climbing Parnassus: A New Apologia for Greek and Latin. p.303
Climbing: The Complete Reference. p.789
Clinical Practice of Sports Injury Prevention and Care. . . p.827
Clinton and Congress, 1993-1996: Risk, Restoration, and Reelection. p.532
The Cloaking of Power: Montesquieu, Blackstone, and the Rise of Judicial Activism. p.541
Closed Chambers: The First Eyewitness Account of the Epic Struggles Inside the Supreme Court. p.537
Closing an Era: Historical Perspectives on Modern Archives and Records Management. p.115
Closing of the American Mind. p.289
The Cloud People: The Divergent Evolution of the Zapotic and Mixte Civilizations. p.9
Cluster Analysis for Social Scientists. p.689
CNN Effect: Myth of News Media Foreign Policy and Intervention. p.407, p.415
Coach: The Life of Paul Bear Bryant. p.858, p.893
Coaching Basketball. p.854, p.904
Coaching Tennis Successfully. p.864
Coaching Volleyball: Building a Winning Team. . p.869, p.904
Coaching Volleyball Successfully. p.794, p.869, p.904
Coaching Women's Soccer: A Revolutionary Approach to Putting the Play Back into Practice. p.800, p.838, p.868, p.905
Coaching Youth Baseball. p.794, p.849
Coaching Youth Hockey. p.794, p.862
Coaching Youth Soccer. p.794, p.839, p.867, p.904
Coaching Youth Tennis. p.794, p.839, p.863
Coaching Youth Volleyball. p.839, p.869, p.904
Coaching Youth Wrestling. p.795, p.839, p.870
Coal: A Human History. p.146, p.160
Coastal and Estuarine Environments: Sedimentology, Geomorphology and Geoarchaeology. p.392
Coasts: Form, Process and Evolution. p.393
Code of Federal Regulations (CFR). p.481
Code of the Streets: Decency, Violence and the Moral Life of the Inner City. p.723
Coercion and Control in Communist Society: The Visible Hand in a Command Economy. p.708
Coercion and Governance: The Declining Political Role of the Military in Asia. p.616
Coercion, Capital, and European States, AD 990-1990. . . . . p.501, p.602
Co-Existence in Wartime Lebanon: Death of a State and Birth of a Nation. p.614, p.616
Cognition and Curriculum Reconsidered. p.362
Cognition in Practice: Mind, Mathematics and Culture in Everyday Life. p.27

Cognitive Developments in Economics. *p.272*
Cognitive Dimensions of Social Science: The Way We Think about Politics, Economics, Law, and Society. *p.272*
Cognitive Economics: An Interdisciplinary Approach. . *p.272*
Cognitive Economics: An Interdisciplinary Approach. . . *p.272*
Cognitive Economics. *p.272*
Cognitive Foundations of Natural History: Towards an Anthropology of Science. *p.26*
Cognitive Processes and Economic Behaviour. . . *p.249, p.272*
Cognitive Sociology. *p.692*
Cohabitation, Marriage, Divorce, and Remarriage in the United States. *p.739*
The Cohesion of Oppression: Clientship and Ethnicity in Rwanda, 1860-1960. . . . . *p.582, p.584, p.612*
The Cold War: A New History. *p.628*
Cold War, Cool Medium: Television, McCarthyism, and American Culture. *p.418*
Cold War Statesmen Confront the Bomb: Nuclear Diplomacy since 1945. . . . . *p.645, p.647*
The Cold War. *p.485*
Collaborative Analysis of Student Work: Improving Teaching and Learning. *p.286*
Collaborative Entrepreneurship: How Communities of Networked Firms Use Continuous Innovation to Create Economic Wealth. *p.68*
Collaborative Learning: Higher Education, Interdependence, and the Authority of Knowledge. *p.349*
Collaborative Manufacturing: Using Real-Time Information to Support the Supply Chain. *p.118*
Collaborative Public Management: New Strategies for Local Governments. *p.542, p.543*
Collapse: How Societies Choose to Fail or Succeed. . . . *p.760*
The Collapse of Canada? *p.587*
The Collapse of State Socialism: The Case of Poland. *p.506, p.508, p.596*
Collapsed States: The Disintegration and Restoration of Legitimate Authority. *p.613*
Collected Economic Essays: Essays on Economic Stability and Growth. *p.209*
Collected Economic Essays: Essays on Value and Distribution. *p.209*
Collected Economic Papers of Joan Robinson - Index. *p.251, p.252*
Collected Economic Papers. *p.196*
Collected Letters of Harriet Martineau. *p.195*
Collected Papers of Franco Modigliani: Essays in Macroeconomics. *p.210*
Collected Papers. *p.514*
The Collected Scientific Papers of Paul A. Samuelson. . . *p.196*
The Collected Scientific Papers of Paul Samuelson, Vol. 1. . *p.196*
The Collected Scientific Papers of Paul Samuelson, Vol. 2. . *p.196*
The Collected Scientific Papers of Paul Samuelson, Vol. 3. . *p.196*
The Collected Scientific Papers of Paul Samuelson, Vol. 4. . *p.196*
The Collected Scientific Papers of Paul Samuelson, Vol. 5. . *p.197*
The Collected Works of John Dewey, 1882-1953: (Windows). *p.342*
The Collected Works of L. S. Vygotsky: Problems of General Psychology, Including the Volume "Thinking and Speech". *p.695*
The Collected Works of William Howard Taft: Taft Papers on League of Nations. *p.632*
The Collected Writings of John Maynard Keynes. *p.228*
Collecting Visible Evidence. *p.413*
Collective Bargaining in the Public Sector: The Experience of Eight States. *p.123*
Collective Barganing in the Private Sector. *p.121*
Collective Behavior and Public Opinion: Rapid Shifts in Opinion and Communication. *p.713*
Collective Choice and Social Welfare. *p.266*
College and University Rankings. *p.289*
College Athletes for Hire: The Evolution and Legacy of the NCAA's Amateur Myth. *p.822, p.889, p.894*
College Costs and Financial Aid Handbook. *p.293*
College Football: History, Spectacle, Controversy. *p.810, p.860, p.895*
College Grad Job Hunter. *p.170*
The College Handbook. *p.294*
College Majors and Careers: A Resource Guide for Effective Life Planning. *p.167*
College Majors Handbook with Real Career Paths and Payoffs: The Actual Jobs, Earnings, and Trends for Graduates of 60 College Majors. *p.167*
College: The Undergraduate Experience in America. *p.289, p.330*
The College Transfer Student in America: The Forgotten Student. *p.294*
Collins Atlas of 20th Century History. *p.380*
Collins Atlas of Military History. *p.380*
Collision Course: NATO, Russia, and Kosovo. *p.644*
Collision Course: The Strange Convergence of Affirmative Action and Immigration Policy in America. *p.570*
Colonel: The Life and Legend of Robert R. McCormick, 1880-1955. . . . . *p.411*
The Colonial Period of American History. *p.517*
Colonial Situations: Essays on the Contextualization of Ethnographic Knowledge. *p.5*
Colonialism: A Theoretical Overview. *p.583*
Color Naming in Human Languages. *p.27*
The Color of School Reform: Race, Politics and the Challenge of Urban Education. *p.315*
The Colorblind Career: What Every African-American, Hispanic-American and Asian-American Needs to Succeed in Today's Tough Job Market. *p.168*
The Color-Blind Constitution. *p.457*
Colorblind Injustice: Minority Voting Rights and the Undoing of the Second Reconstruction. *p.555, p.573, p.579*
Colossus: The Price of America's Empire. *p.560*
The Columbia Gazetteer of North America. *p.374*
The Columbia Gazetteer of the World. *p.374*
Combating Corporate Crime: Local Prosecutors at Work. . *p.472*
Comeback: The Fall and Rise of the American Automobile Industry. *p.154*

The Coming Age of Scarcity: Preventing Mass Death and Genocide in the Twenty-First Century. p.662
Coming Apart: An Informal History of America in the 1960's. p.486
The Coming Crisis of Western Sociology. p.682
The Coming Democracy: New Rules for Running a New World. p.498
Coming of Age in Samoa. p.43
Coming of Age in U.S. High Schools: Economic, Kinship, Religious, and Political Crosscurrents. p.29
Coming of Post-Industrial Society: A Venture in Social Forecasting. p.769
The Coming of the New Deal: 1933-1935, the Age of Roosevelt. p.522
Coming on Strong: Gender and Sexuality in Twentieth-Century Women's Sports. p.804, p.835
The Coming Race War?: And Other Apocalyptic Tales of America after Affirmative Action and Welfare. p.729
Coming to Terms with Security: A Lexicon for Arms Control, Disarmament and Confidence-Building. p.657
Coming up Short: The Challenge of 401(K) Plans. . p.97, p.99
The Comintern: A History of International Communism from Lenin to Stalin. p.509
The Commanding Heights: The Battle for the World Economy. p.56, p.58
Commentaries on American Law. p.441
Commentaries on the Laws of England: In Four Books, 2. . p.435
A Commentary on Malthus' 1798 Essay on Population As Social Theory. p.221
A Commentary on the Aristotelian Athenaion Politeia. . . p.489
Commerce and Capitalism in Chinese Societies: Organisation of Chinese Economics. p.214, p.257, p.259
The Commercialization of American Culture: New Advertising, Control and Democracy. p.697
The Commissariat of Enlightenment: Soviet Organization of Education and the Arts under Lunacharsky, October 1917-1921. . . . . p.334
Committed Journalism: An Ethic for the Profession. . . . p.405
Committing to Peace: The Successful Settlement of Civil Wars. p.651
Commodities and Capabilities. p.266
The Commodities Price Locator. p.178
Common Cause. p.516
The Common Good. p.185
Common Human Needs. p.755, p.758
Common Knowledge: How Companies Thrive by Sharing What They Know. p.78
The Common Law. p.434
Common Problems - Proper Solutions: Avoiding Error in Quantitative Research. p.689
Common Sense Business: Starting, Operating, and Growing Your Small Business—in Any Economy!. p.87
Common Sense on Mutual Funds: New Imperatives for the Intelligent Investor. p.94
Common Sense School Reform. p.280
Common Stocks and Uncommon Profits and Other Writings. p.95
Commoners, Tribute, and Chiefs: The Development of Algonquian Culture in the Potomac Valley. p.11
Commonsense and Nuclear Warfare. p.656
Common-Sense Classroom Management for Middle and High School Teachers: Surviving September and Beyond in the Secondary Classroom. p.284
Commonwealth Secretariat. p.605
Communalism in India: History, Politics and Culture. . . p.705
Communicating Across Cultures at Work. p.132
Communicating Effectively. p.423
Communicating in Geography and the Environmental Sciences. p.376
Communicating Racism: Ethnic Prejudice in Thought and Talk. p.21
Communicating When Your Company Is under Siege. . . p.174
Communication and Culture in War and Peace. p.766
Communication and Litigation: Case Studies of Famous Trials. p.438
Communication and Persuasion: Psychological Studies of Opinion Change,. p.423
Communication and the Evolution of Society. p.696
Communication Consultants in Political Campaigns: Ballot Box Warriors. p.550
Communication Ethics and Universal Values. p.405
Communication Ethics, Media, and Popular Culture. . . . p.417
Communication in History: Technology, Culture, Society. . p.415
Communication Systems. p.422
Communication, Technology and Cultural Change. p.760
Communication Technology. p.590
Communications Systems and Networks. p.115
Communism: A History. p.509
Communism, Anticommunism, and the CIO, 91. . . . . p.127
The Communist Manifesto: Karl Marx and Friedrich Engels: Edited and Translated by L.M. Findlay. p.507, p.508
The Communist Manifesto. p.236
Communists in Harlem During the Depression. . . p.552, p.554
Communities in Transition: Bedford and Lincoln, Massachusetts, 1729-1850. p.703
Communities of Journalism: A History of American Newspapers and Their Readers. p.149
Community and Social Change in America. p.770
Community and Society. p.686
Community Besieged: The Anglophone Minority and the Politics of Quebec. p.581
Community Geography: GIS in Action. p.387
The Community of Rights. p.512
Community Organizing and Community Building for Health. p.778
Community Studies: An Introduction to the Sociology of the Local Community. p.770
A Community Transplanted: The Trans-Atlantic Experience of a Swedish Immigrant Settlement in the Upper Middle West, 1835-1915. . . . . p.571
Community Without Unity: A Politics of Derridean Extravagance. p.501
Commwealth Games Federation. p.842, p.898

Companion Encyclopedia of Geography: The Environment and Humankind. *p.373*
A Companion to Linguistic Anthropology. *p.18*
A Companion to Plato's Republic. *p.490*
Companion to the Anthropology of American Indians. . . . *p.3*
A Companion to Theoretical Econometrics. *p.198*
Comparable Worth: New Directions for Research. . . *p.254*
Comparable Worth: Theories and Evidence. *p.133*
A Comparative Analysis of Complex Organizations. . . . *p.716*
Comparative Biomechanics: Life's Physical World. . . . *p.908*
Comparative Constitutional Engineering: An Inquiry into Structures, Incentives, and Outcomes. *p.574*
Comparative Economics in a Transforming World Economy. *p.237*
Comparative Education: The Dialectic of the Global and the Local. *p.313, p.338*
Comparative Federalism: The Territorial Dimension of Politics. *p.491*
The Comparative Guide to American Elementary and Secondary Schools 2004. . . . . *p.280*
Comparative Higher Education: Knowledge, the University, and Development. *p.313*
Comparative Industrial Relations: An Introduction to Cross-National Perspectives. *p.120*
Comparative Patterns of Economic Development, 1850-1914. . . . . *p.237, p.259*
A Comparative Sociology of World Religions: Virtuosi, Priests, and Popular Religion. *p.722*
Comparative Women's Rights and Political Participation in Europe. *p.601*
Comparing Asian Politics: India, China, and Japan. . . . *p.616*
Comparing Financial Systems. *p.88*
Compassing the Vast Glove of the Earth. *p.378*
Compassion Fatigue: How the Media Sell Disease, Famine, War, and Death. *p.407*
Compelling Belief: The Culture of American Schooling. . *p.297*
A Compelling Interest: Examining the Evidence on Racial Dynamics in Colleges and Universities. . *p.295, p.308, p.355*
Compendium of Tourism Statistics. *p.162*
Competency-Based Human Resource Management. *p.76*
The Competent Classroom: Aligning High School Curriculum, Standards and Assessment - A Creative Teaching Guide. *p.304*
Competing Against Time: How Time-Based Competition Is Reshaping Global Markets. *p.119*
Competing by Design: The Power of Organizational Architecture. *p.86*
Competing for the Future. *p.81*
Competing on the Edge: Strategy As Structured Chaos. . . *p.81*
Competition among States and Local Governments: Efficiency and Equity in American Federalism. *p.524*
Competition and Chaos: U. S. Telecommunications since the 1996 Telecom ACT. *p.419*
The Competitive Advantage: Creating and Sustaining Superior Performance. *p.51, p.64*
Competitive Advantage: Creating and Sustaining Superior Performance. *p.73*
The Competitive Advantage of Nations and Their Firms. *p.51, p.57, p.59*
The Competitive Advantage of Nations. *p.51, p.665*
The Competitive City: The Political Economy of Suburbia. *p.543*
The Competitive Disadvantage: Teacher Compensation in Rural America. *p.278*
Competitive Intelligence: A Framework for Web-based Analysis and Decision Making. *p.83*
Competitive Intelligence and Global Business. . . . *p.69, p.82*
Competitive Solutions: The Strategist's Toolkit. *p.83*
Competitive Strategy: Techniques for Analyzing Industries and Competitors. *p.81*
Competitor or Ally?: Japan's Role in American Educational Debates. *p.335*
Complementary Methods for Research in Education. . . . *p.355*
Complementary Sports Medicine: Balancing Traditional and Nontraditional Treatments. *p.827, p.829*
Complete Book of Drills for Winning Football. . . *p.858, p.904*
The Complete Book of Running for Women: Everything You Need to Know about Training, Nutrition, Injury Prevention, Motivation, Racing and Much, Much More. *p.837, p.866*
The Complete Book of Swimming. *p.869*
Complete Conditioning for Rugby. *p.865, p.879*
Complete Conditioning for Tennis. *p.864*
The Complete Directory to Prime Time Network TV Shows, 1946-Present. *p.418*
A Complete Guide to Chi-Gung. *p.793*
Complete Guide to Sport Education: Teacher Resources. . *p.797*
The Complete Guide to Sports Injuries. . . *p.827, p.828, p.829*
The Complete Handbook of the Internet. *p.115*
The Complete Idiot's Guide to Finance for Small Business. . *p.87*
The Complete IEP Guide: How to Advocate for Your Special Ed Child. *p.451*
The Complete Learning Disabilities Directory 2005. . . . *p.318*
Complete Learning Disabilities Handbook: Ready-to-Use Strategies and Activities for Teaching Students with Learning Disabilities. *p.318*
Complete Physical Education Plans for Grades 7-12: 366 Lesson Plans for 14 Sports and Activities. *p.798, p.799*
The Complete Resume and Job Search Book for College Students: The A-Z Career Guide for College Students. . *p.168*
The Complete Small Business Guide: A Sourcebook for New and Small Businesses. *p.87*
The Complete Small Business Start-up Guide. *p.88*
Complete Transcripts of the Clarence Thomas-Anita Hill Hearings: October 11, 12, 13, 1991. . . . . *p.538*
The Complete Walker IV. *p.787*
Complete World of Human Evolution. *p.16*
The Complex Roles of the Teacher: An Ecological Perspective. *p.278*
Complexities: Beyond Nature and Nurture. *p.24*
Complying with the Americans with Disabilities Act: A Guidebook for Management and People with Disabilities. *p.131*

Comprehending Cults: The Sociology of New Religious Movements. p.721
The Comprehensive Gazetteer of England and Wales, Set. . p.374
The Comprehensive High School Today. p.327
Compromised Compliance: Implementation of the 1965 Voting Rights Act, 66. . . . . p.461
Compulsory Compassion: A Critique of Restorative Justice. p.754
Compulsory Mis-Education. p.347
Computational Economics. p.202
Computational Models in the Economics of Environment and Development. p.207, p.267
Computer: A History of the Information Machine. p.114
Computer and Internet Use on Campus: A Legal Guide to Issues of Intellectual Property, Free Speech, and Privacy. . . p.441
The Computer Industry. p.158
Computer Networks. p.422
Computer Processing of Remotely-Sensed Images: An Introduction. p.389
Computer Resources for People with Disabilities: A Guide to Assistive Technologies, Tools, and Resources for People of All Ages. p.317
Computer Security Fundamentals. p.113
Computer-Assisted Investigative Reporting. p.408
Computer-Assisted Reporting: A Practical Guide. p.414
Computer-Supported Collaborative Learning in Higher Education. p.350
Comrades Against Apartheid: The ANC and the South African Communist Party in Exile, 1966-1990. . . . . p.613
Comstockery in America: Patterns of Censorship and Control. p.472
Concept and Controversy: Sixty Years of Taking Ideas to Market. p.559
The Concept and Method of Cultural Ecology. p.30
The Concept of Constituency: Political Representation, Democratic Legitimacy, and Institutional Design. . . . p.576
The Concept of Law. p.434
The Concept of Liberty in the Age of the American Revolution. p.452
The Concept of Representation. p.576
The Concept of Utopia. p.499
Concepts in Biological Oceanography: An Interdisciplinary Primer. p.392
Concepts in Fitness Programming. p.791, p.903
Conceptual Foundations for Therapeutic Recreation. p.783, p.829, p.842
The Conceptual Practices of Power: A Feminist Sociology of Knowledge. p.744
Conceptualization and Measurement in the Social Sciences. p.689
Concise Atlas of World History. p.381
Concise Encyclopedia of Special Education: A Reference for the Education of the Handicapped and Other Exceptional Children and Adults. p.316
A Concise History of the Common Law [1956]. p.436
[e] A Concise Introduction to Econometrics: An Intuitive Guide. p.200
A Concise Introduction to Econometrics: An Intuitive Guide. p.200
The Concise Oxford Dictionary of Politics. p.482
[□] Condition of Education. p.322
Conditions of Knowledge: An Introduction to Epistemology and Education. p.345
Conditions of Liberty: Civil Society and Its Rivals. . . . p.515
The Confederate Constitutions. p.474
The Confederate Republic: A Revolution Against Politics. . p.521
The Confederate War: How Popular Will Nationalism, and Millitary Strategy Could Not Stave off Defeat. p.520
Confederates in the Attic: Dispatches from the Unfinished Civil War. p.521
The Confederation Debates in the Province of Canada 1865. . . . . p.587
Confidence Men and Painted Women: Study of Middle Class Culture in America, 1830-70. . . . . p.724
The Confident Coach's Guide to Teaching Lacrosse: From Basic Fundamentals to Advanced Player Skills and Team Strategies. p.862
Confirmation Trials: Causes and Consequences of Judicial Selection Battles. p.541
Conflict and Consensus in Switzerland. p.706
Conflict and Control in the World Economy: Contemporary Economic Realism and Neo-Mercantilism. p.260
Conflict, Cleavage, and Change in Central Asia and the Caucasus. p.623
The Conflict in Education in a Democratic Society. . . . p.343
The Conflict in Modern Culture and Other Essays. p.766
Conflict or Codetermination: The Congress, the President, and the Power to Make War. p.528
Conflict Resolution in Uganda. p.497, p.613
Conflict, Social Capital, and Managing Natural Resources: A West African Case Study. p.268
Conflict Sociology : Toward an Explanatory Science. . . p.681
Conflicting Paradigms in Adult Literacy Education: In Quest of a U.S. Democratic Politics of Literacy. p.298, p.304
Confronting Catastrophe: New Perspectives on Natural Disasters. p.394
Confronting the Enemy Within: Security Intelligence, the Police, and Counterterrorism in Four Democracies. p.658
Confucianism and Human Rights. p.513
Congo-Paris: Transnational Traders on the Margins of the Law. p.44
Congress and Law-Making: Researching the Legislative Process. p.439
Congress and the Constitution. p.531
Congress and the Governance of the Nation's Capital: The Conflict of Federal and Local Interests. p.524
Congress and the Presidency. p.527
Congress: Games and Strategies. p.529
Congress Makes a Law: The Story Behind the Employment Act of 1946. . . . . p.446
Congress, Parliament and Defence: The Impact of Legislative Reform on Defence Accountability in Britain and America. p.531

Congress, Progressive Reform, and the New American State. p.531
Congress Reconsidered. p.529
Congress Resurgent: Foreign and Domestic Policy on Capitol Hill. p.531
Congress, the President, and Policymaking: A Historical Analysis. p.527, p.528, p.531, p.532
Congress, the President, and Public Policy. p.527
Congress, the Press, and Political Accountability. p.406
Congress, the Press, and the Public. p.530
Congressional Abdication on War and Spending. p.531
Congressional Careers: Contours of Life in the U. S. House of Representatives. p.533
Congressional Conservatism and the New Deal: The Growth of the Conservative Coalition in Congress, 1933 to 1939. . p.522
□ The Congressional Directory. p.481
Congressional Districts in the 2000s: A Portrait of America. p.557
□ Congressional Election Statistics 1920 - 2004. . . . . p.557
Congressional Elections, 1946-1996. . . . . p.557
Congressional Elections: Campaigning at Home and in Washington. p.549
Congressional Politics: The Evolving Legislative System. . p.531
Congressional Procedures and the Policy Process. p.532
□ Congressional Record Index. p.481
□ Congressional Record. p.481
The Connected School: Technology and Learning in High School. p.351
Connecting Girls and Science: Constructivism, Feminism, and Science Education Reform. p.367
Connecting: How We Form Social Bonds and Communities in the Internet Age. p.772
Connecting Special Education and Technology for the 21st Century. p.350
The Connection Gap: Why Americans Feel So Alone. . . p.694
Connections: A Broadcast History Reader. p.417
Conquering Goliath: Cesar Chávez at the Beginning. . . . p.128
The Conscience of the Court: Selected Opinions of Justice William J. Brennan, Jr. on Freedom and Equality. . . p.539
Consciousness and Class Experience in 19th Century Europe. p.705
The Conscription Society: Administered Mass Organizations. p.510
Consequences of Class and Color: West Indian Perspectives. p.704
The Consequences of Mr. Keynes: An Analysis of the Misuse of Economic Theory for Political Profiteering, with Proposals for Constitutional Disciplines. p.226
Conservation and the Law. p.463
Conservatism in Early American History. p.553
Conservative Century: The Conservative Party since 1900. . p.607
The Conservative Party from Peel to Thatcher. p.606
The Conservative Tradition in America. p.516
Conservatives in Court. p.536
Conspiracy of Fools: A True Story. p.103
Conspiracy to Murder: The Rwanda Genocide. p.653
Constitution and Criminal Procedure: First Principles. . . p.473
The Constitution and Race. p.457
The Constitution and the Regulation of Society. p.463
The Constitution and the States: The Role of the Original Thirteen in the Framing and Adoption of the Federal Constitution. p.523
The Constitution As Political Structure. p.525
□ A Constitution for Europe. p.636
A Constitution for the European Union. p.636
The Constitution in Conflict. p.462
Constitution in Crisis Times, 1918-1969. . . . . p.452
The Constitution in the Courts: Law or Politics? . p.455, p.538
The Constitution in the Supreme Court: The First Hundred Years, 1789-1888. . . . . p.453, p.536
The Constitution in the Supreme Court: The Second Century, 1888-1986. . . . . p.453, p.536
The Constitution in Wartime: Beyond Alarmism and Complacency. p.462
The Constitution of Society: Outline of the Theory of Structuration. p.679
The Constitution of the Roman Republic. p.501
□ Constitution of the United States. p.451
The Constitution of Tyranny: Regimes of Exception in Spanish America. p.592
The Constitution, the Courts, and Human Rights: An Inquiry into the Legitimacy of Constitutional Policymaking by the Judiciary. p.456
Constitutional Amendment in Canada. p.586
Constitutional Brinksmanship: Amending the Constitution by National Convention. p.454
Constitutional Conflicts Between Congress and the President. p.454, p.528, p.531
Constitutional Deliberation in Congress: The Impact of Judicial Review in a Separated System. p.538
Constitutional Democracy. p.504
Constitutional Dialogues: Interpretation As Political Process. p.453
Constitutional Dictatorship: Crisis Government in the Modern Democracies. p.575
Constitutional Fate. p.454
Constitutional History of the American Revolution: The Authority of Law. p.456
Constitutional History of the American Revolution: The Authority of Rights. p.456
Constitutional History of the American Revolution: The Authority to Legislate. p.456
Constitutional History of the American Revolution: The Authority to Tax. p.456
Constitutional Options for A Democratic South Africa: A Comparative Perspective. p.614
Constitutional Politics in the Progressive Era: Child Labor and the Law. p.447
Constitutional Politics: The Republic Referendum and the Future. p.624
Constitutional Predicament: Canada after the Referendum of 1992. . . . . p.586

Constitutional Process: A Social Choice Analysis of Supreme Court Decision Making. *p.540*
Constitutional Revolution: The Link Between Constitutionalism and Progress. *p.576*
The Constitutional System: The Group Character of the Elected Institutions. *p.532*
The Constitutional Underclass: Gays, Lesbians, and the Failure of Class-Based Equal Protection. *p.457*
Constitutionalism and American Culture: Writing the New Constitutional History. *p.453*
Constitutionalism and the Separation of Powers. *p.576*
The Constitutionalist: Notes on the First Amendment. . . *p.458*
Constitutions of the World. *p.435, p.574*
A Constructed Peace: The Making of the European Settlement, 1945-1963. . . . . *p.629, p.647*
Constructing Democracy: Human Rights, Citizenship and Society in Latin America.. . . . . *p.512*
Constructing Public Opinion: How Political Elites Do What They Like and Why We Seem to Go along with It. . . *p.425*
Constructing the Heartland: Television News and Natural Disaster. *p.414*
Constructing the World Polity: Essays on International Institutionalization. *p.625*
Construction and Housing Publications. *p.159*
Construction Business Development: Meeting New Challenges, Seeking Opportunities. *p.159*
Construction Funding: The Process of Real Estate Development, Appraisal, and Finance. *p.158*
Construction Industry Compliance Assistance Portal. . *p.159*
Construction Statistics. *p.159*
Construction WebLinks Portal. *p.159*
Constructive Education for Children. *p.359*
Consultative Selling: The Hanan Formula for High-Margin Sales at High Levels. *p.142*
Consumer Behavior and Marketing Strategy. *p.139*
Consumer Behavior.. . . . . *p.249*
Consumer Boycotts: Effecting Change Through the Marketplace and the Media. *p.759*
Consumer Economics after Keynes: Theory and Evidence of the Consumption Function. *p.232, p.245, p.250*
Consumer Economics Issues in America. *p.250*
A Consuming Fire: The Fall of the Confederacy in the Mind of the White Christian South. *p.520*
Consumption As an Investment. *p.246, p.250*
Consumption Takes Time: Implications for Economic Theory. *p.246*
Contagious Success. *p.79*
Contemplating the People's Branch: Legislative Dynamics in the Twenty First Century. *p.530*
Contemporary Archaeology in Theory: A Reader. *p.6*
Contemporary Art and Anthropology. *p.26*
Contemporary Caribbean Cultures and Societies in a Global Context. *p.40, p.41*
Contemporary Democracies: Participation, Stability and Violence. *p.577*
Contemporary Europe: A Geographic Analysis. *p.383*
Contemporary Influences in Early Childhood Curriculum. . *p.369*
Contemporary Italy: Politics, Economy and Society Since 1945. . . . . *p.594*
Contemporary Labor Economics. *p.253*
Contemporary Quebec and the United States, 1960-1985. . *p.581*
Contemporary Russian Politics: A Reader. *p.597*
Contemporary Sport Management. *p.885, p.889*
Contemporary Strategy Analysis: Concepts, Techniques, Applications. *p.51*
Contemporary Turkish Politics: Challenges to Democratic Consolidation. *p.616*
Contemporary U. S. Tax Policy. *p.108*
Contemporary World Regional Geography: Global Connections, Local Voices. *p.396*
The Contempt Power. *p.472*
The Contender: Richard Nixon: The Congress Years, 1946-1952. . . . . *p.485*
Contending with Change: African Food Systems in Crisis. . *p.45*
Contending with Modernity: Catholic Higher Education in the Twentieth Century. *p.291*
Content Area Reading: Literacy and Learning Across the Curriculum, MyLabSchool Edition. *p.366*
Content Knowledge: A Compendium of Standards and Benchmarks for K-12 Education. *p.359*
The Contentious Senate: Partisanship, Ideology and the Myth of Cool Judgement. *p.533*
Contest for Constitutional Authority: The Abortion and War Powers Debates. *p.531, p.535*
Contested Tongues: Language Politics and Cultural Correction in Ukraine. *p.20*
Contesting the Boundaries of Liberal and Professional Education: The Syracuse Experiment. *p.295*
Context and Beyond: Reframing the Theory and Practice of Education.. . . . . *p.336*
Contexts of Kinship: An Essay in the Family Sociology of the Gonja of Northern Ghana. *p.32*
Contextual Teaching and Learning: What It Is and Why It's Here to Stay. *p.348*
Continent of Hunter-Gatherers: New Perspectives in Australian Prehistory. *p.13*
Continental Divide: The Values and Institutions of the United States and Canada. *p.586, p.591*
Continual Permutations of Action. *p.682*
Continuities in Popular Culture: The Present in the Past and the Past in the Present and Future. *p.701*
Continuity and Change in House Elections. *p.548*
Continuity and Change on the United States Courts of Appeals. *p.470*
Continuity and Disruption: Essays in Public Administration. *p.545, p.580*
Continuous -Time Finance. *p.238*
The Continuum Complete International Encyclopedia of Sexuality.. . . . . *p.677, p.747*
Continuum Studies in Geography Education: Continuum Guide to Geography Education. *p.376*
Contracts in a Nutshell. *p.443*
The Contradictory College: The Conflicting Origins, Impacts, and Futures of the Community College. *p.291*

Contrarian Investment Strategies, the Next Generation: Beat the Market Going Against the Crowd. *p.94*
Contrasting the French and Italian Communist Parties: Comrades and Culture. *p.594, p.609*
The Contributions of John Maynard Keynes to Foreign Trade Theory and Policy, 1909-1946. . . . . *p.226*
Contributions to Modern Econometrics: From Data Analysis to Economic Policy. *p.202*
Contributions to Modern Economics. *p.270*
Contributions to the Theory and Practice of Public Finance. *p.199, p.247*
Contributions to Urban Sociology. *p.770*
Control of Human Movement. *p.908, p.909*
The Control of the Arms Race: Disarmament and Arms Control in the Missile Age,. *p.655*
Control: Sociology's Central Notion. *p.773*
The Controller's Function: The Work of the Managerial Accountant. *p.106*
Controlling Strategy: Management, Accounting, and Performance Measurement. *p.81*
Controversies in Minority Voting: The Voting Rights Act in Perspective. *p.461*
Conventions Against Terrorism. *p.662*
Convergence Culture. *p.422*
Convergence Marketing: Strategies for Reaching the New Hybrid Consumer. *p.135*
Conversational Borderlands: Talk with Troubled Teens in an Urban School. *p.315*
Conversations in Natural Philosophy, 1826. . . . . *p.218*
Conversations on Growth, Stability and Trade: An Historical Perspective.. . . . . *p.245, p.258*
Conversations with Economists: New Classical Economists and Opponents Speak Out on the Current Controversy in Macroeconomics. *p.233*
Conversations with Indian Economists. *p.255*
Conversations with Leading Economists: Interpreting Modern Macroeconomics. *p.240*
Conversations with Ulrich Beck. *p.261, p.267*
Convicted but Innocent: Wrongful Conviction and Public Policy. *p.567*
Cook: The Extraordinary Sea Voyages of Captain James Cook. *p.385*
Coolidge: An American Enigma. *p.487, p.528*
Cooperative Learning: Research and Theory. *p.350*
Coordinating Technology: Studies in the International Standardization of Telecommunications. *p.420*
Coping with Life Crises: An Integrated Approach. *p.699*
Copper Crucible: How the Arizona Miners' Strike of 1983 Recast Labor-Management Relations. *p.128*
Copy Writer's Bible. *p.427*
The Copyeditor's Handbook: A Guide for Book Publishing and Corporate Communications.. . . . . *p.149*
Copyright and Fair Use in the Classroom, on the Internet, and the World Wide Web. *p.289*
The Copyright Book: A Practical Guide. *p.446*
Copyright in Cyberspace 2: Questions and Answers for Librarians. *p.446*
Copyright Your Software. *p.446*
Copyright's Highway: From Gutenberg to the Celestial Jukebox. *p.109, p.110, p.446*
Coral Reef Conservation. *p.391*
Coral Reef Fishes: Dynamics and Diversity in a Complex Ecosystem. *p.393*
The Core Business Web: A Guide to Key Information Resources. *p.181*
Core Concepts in Biological Anthropology.. . . . . *p.14*
Core Concepts of Management. *p.73*
Core Documents of U.S. Democracy. *p.481*
The Core Historical Literature of Agriculture. . *p.151, p.163*
Core List of Books and Journals in Education. *p.339*
The Core of Japanese Democracy: Latent Interparty Politics. *p.622*
Cornered: Big Tobacco at the Bar of Justice. *p.439*
Corporate Environmentalism and Public Policy. . . . *p.61, p.63*
Corporate Governance: Accountability, Enterprise and International Comparisons.. . . . . *p.86*
Corporate Governance at the Crossroads: A Book of Readings. *p.54*
Corporate Governance. *p.85, p.86*
Corporate Integrity: A Toolkit for Managing Beyond Compliance. *p.86*
Corporate Integrity: Rethinking Organizational Ethics and Leadership. *p.697*
Corporate Power, American Democracy, and the Automobile Industry. *p.154*
Corporate Responsibility and Labour Rights: Codes of Conduct in the Global Economy. *p.131*
Corporate Social Responsibility: Doing the Most Good for Your Company and Your Cause.. . . . . *p.54*
Corporate Statements: The Official Missions, Goals, Principles and Philosophies of over 900 Countries. *p.173*
Corporate Taxes 2005—2006: Worldwide Summaries. *p.92, p.107*
Corporate Tides: The Inescapable Laws of Organizational Structure.. . . . . *p.86*
Corporation Be Good!: The Story of Corporate Social Responsibility. *p.53*
Corporatism and Comparative Politics: The Other Great Ism. *p.510*
Correlates of War (COW) Project. *p.625*
The Correspondence of Alfred Marshall, Economist, Set. . *p.224*
Correspondence of Leon Walras. *p.215*
The Corrosion of Character: The Personal Consequences of Work in the New Capitalism. *p.717*
Corruption and Development in Africa: Lessons from Country Case-Studies. *p.611, p.664*
Corruption and Market in Contemporary China. *p.620*
Corruption and Reform in the Teamsters Union. *p.130*
Corruption and State Politics in Sierra Leone. *p.612*
Corruption by Design: Building Clean Government in Mainland China and Hong Kong. *p.620*
Corruption Perceptions Index. *p.55*
Cosmopolitan Urbanism. *p.395*

Cost and Choice: An Inquiry in Economic Theory. p.194
Cost Benefit Analysis: Concepts and Practice. p.82
Cost-Benefit Analysis: With Reference to Environment and Ecology. p.83
Cost-Effective Marketing Research: A Guide for Marketing Managers. p.136
Counseling for Diversity: A Guide for School Counselors and Related Professionals. p.353
Counseling to End Violence Against Women: A Subversive Model. p.751
Countering Terrorism: Dimensions of Preparedness. . . . p.564
Counterintuitive Marketing: Achieve Great Results Using Uncommom Sense. p.134
Counting Votes: Lessons from the 2000 Presidential Election in Florida. p.550
Counting What Counts: Turning Corporate Accountability to Competitive Advantage. p.85
Country Life, City Life: Five Theories of Community. . . p.770
Country Reports on Human Rights Practices. p.670
A Country Study: Kazakhstan. p.623
A Country Study: Kyrgyzstan. p.623
A Country Study: Mongolia. p.623
A Country Study: Tajikistan. p.623
A Country Study: Turkmenistan. p.623
A Country Study: Uzbekistan.. . . . . p.623
Coups from Below: Armed Subalterns and State Power in West Africa. p.498, p.611
Courage in a Dangerous World: The Political Writings of Eleanor Roosevelt. p.487, p.569
The Courage of Their Convictions: Sixteen Americans Who Fought Their Way to the Supreme Court. . . . p.455, p.537
A Course in Econometrics. p.200
A Course in Game Theory. p.207
A Course in Public Economics. p.247
The Course of Tolerance: Freedom of the Press in Nineteenth-Century America. p.458
Courses Toward Urban Life: Archeological Considerations of Some Cultural Alternates. Subscribers Ed. p.37
A Court Divided: The Rehnquist Court and the Future of Constitutional Law. p.540
The Court Society. p.726
Courting Disaster: The Supreme Court and the Unmaking of American Law. p.536
Courts and Congress. p.537
Courts and the Public Schools. p.450
Courts, Judges, and Politics. p.465
The Courts of Babylon: Tales of Greed and Glory in the Harsh New High-Stakes World of Professional Tennis. p.814, p.864, p.887
Cousins and Strangers: America, Britain, and Europe in a New Century.. . . . . p.642
Covering Congress. p.406
Covering the Courts: A Handbook for Journalists. p.406
Covering Violence: A Guide to Ethical Reporting about Victims and Trauma. p.407
Cowgirls of the Rodeo: Pioneer Professional Athletes. p.837, p.865
Co-wives and Calabashes. p.41
Cows, Pigs, Wars, and Witches: The Riddles of Culture. . p.22
CQ: Developing Cultural Intelligence at Work. . . p.58, p.172
CQ Electronic Library. p.516
CQ's Desk Reference on the Economy: Over 600 Answers to Questions That Will Help You Understand News, Trends and Issues. p.566
Crack and the Evolution of Anti-Drug Policy. p.568
Crack in America: Demon Drugs and Social Justice. . . . p.777
Cracking Your Retirement Nest Egg (Without Scrambling Your Finances): 25 Things You Must Know Before You Tap Your 401(K), IRA, or Other Retirement Savings Plan. p.96, p.109
Cracks in the Monolith: Party Power in the Brezhnev Era. p.598, p.599
Cradle of Conflict: Iraq and the Birth of the Modern U. S. Military. p.647
The Cradle of Culture and What Children Know about Writing and Numbers Before Being Taught. p.369
Cradle of the Middle Class: The Family in Oneida County, New York, 1790-1865. . . . . p.734
Crafting Selves: Power, Gender, and Discourses of Identity in a Japanese Workplace. p.39
Crashing the Gate: Netroots, Grassroots, and the Rise of People-Powered Politics. p.554
Crazy Like a Fox: The Inside Story of How Fox News Beat CNN. p.414
Creating a Democratic Civil Society in Eastern Germany: The Case of the Citizen Movements and Alliance 90. . . . p.610
Creating Alternative Discourses in the Education of Latinos and Latinas: A Reader. p.301
Creating Brand Loyalty: The Management of Power Positioning and Really Great Advertising. p.427
Creating Campus Community: In Search of Ernest Boyer's Legacy. p.333
Creating Change: Public Policy, Civil Rights and Sexuality. p.569
Creating Connections: The CEFPI Guide for Educational Facility Planning. p.288
Creating G. I. Jane: Sexuality and Power in the Women's Army Corps During World War II. p.766
Creating High Performance Classroom Groups. p.349
Creating Independent Readers: Developing Word Recognition Skills in K-12 Classrooms. p.364
Creating Literacy Instruction for All Students. p.363
Creating New Schools: How Small Schools Are Changing American Education. p.280
Creating Parliamentary Government: The Transition to Democracy in Bulgaria. p.585, p.600
Creating Public Value: Strategic Management in Government. p.545, p.546
Creating Spaces and Finding Voices: Teachers Collaborating for Empowerment. p.279
Creating the Big Game: John W. Heisman and the Invention of American Football, 34. . . . . p.810, p.860, p.895

Creating the Corporate Soul: The Rise of Public Relations and Corporate Imagery in American Big Business. . *p.144, p.429*

Creating the Entrepreneurial Organization. *p.65*

Creating the Judicial Branch: The Unfinished Reform. . . *p.535*

Creating the National Pastime: Baseball Transforms Itself, 1903-1953. . . . . *p.852*

Creating Value through Corporate Restructuring: Case Studies in Bankruptcies, Buyouts, and Breakups. *p.76, p.84*

Creating Women's Networks: A How-to-Guide for Women and Companies. *p.57*

The Creation of America: Through Revolution to Empire. . *p.517*

The Creation of Confederate Nationalism: Ideology and Identity in the Civil War South. *p.520*

The Creation of Meaning in Clinical Social Work. *p.758*

The Creation of the American Republic, 1776-1787. . . . *p.517*

The Creation of the Future: The Role of the American University. *p.332*

Creative Advertising: Ideas and Techniques from the World's Best Campaigns. *p.427*

Creative Business: Achieving Your Goals Through Creative Thinking and Action. *p.65*

Creative Collaboration: Simple Tools for Inspired Teamwork. *p.66*

Creative Consulting: Innovative Perspectives on Management Consulting. *p.64*

Creative Destruction: Why Companies That Are Built to Last Underperform the Market - And How to Successfully Transform Them. *p.67*

Creative Politics: Taxes and Public Goods in a Federal System. *p.523*

[e] Creativity Across the Primary Curriculum: Framing and Developing Practice. *p.360*

[e] Creativity at Work: Developing the Right Practices to Make Innovation Happen. *p.66*

Creativity in Education and Learning: A Guide for Teachers and Educators. *p.356*

Creativity in Virtual Teams: Key Components for Success. . *p.67*

Credibility: How Leaders Gain and Lose It, Why People Demand It. *p.71*

Cricket and England: A Cultural and Social History of Cricket of the Inter-War Years. *p.811, p.856*

Cricket and Race. *p.820, p.856*

Crime and Local Television News: Dramatic, Breaking, and Live from the Scene. *p.407*

Crime and Punishment in American History. *p.471*

Crime and the Justice System in America: An Encyclopedia. *p.676*

Crime As Play: Delinquency in a Middle Class Suburb. . *p.753*

Crime, Madness and Politics in Modern France: The Medical Concept of National Decline. *p.705*

Crime on Campus: Legal Issues and Campus Administration. *p.451*

Crimes of War; a Legal, Political-Documentary, and Psychological Inquiry into the Responsibility of Leaders, Citizens, and Soldiers for Criminal Acts in Wars. . . . *p.477*

Crimes of War: What the Public Should Know. *p.652*

Criminal Justice and Criminology: Concepts and Terms. . *p.676*

The Criminal Law Handbook: Know Your Rights, Survive the System. *p.473*

Criminal Man: According to the Classification of Cesare Lombroso. *p.752*

The Criminal Process in the People's Republic of China, 1949-1963: An Introduction. *p.475*

The Criminality of Women. *p.752*

The Criminalization of the State in Africa. *p.611*

Crises of the Republic: Lying in Politics, Civil Disobedience, on Violence, Thoughts on Politics and Revolution. *p.497*

Crisis Communications: A Casebook Approach. *p.429*

Crisis Intervention in the Schools. *p.353*

Crisis Management in the Food and Drinks Industry: A Practical Approach. *p.160*

A Critical Analysis of Bell Hooks' Engaged Pedagogy: A Transgressive Education for the Development of Critical Consciousness. *p.310*

Critical Corporate Communications: A Best Practice Blueprint. *p.173*

Critical Criminology: Issues, Debates, Challenges. *p.752*

A Critical Dictionary of Sociology. *p.676*

Critical Elections and Critical Coups: State, Society and the Military in the Processes of Latin American Development. *p.593*

Critical Elections and the Mainsprings of American Politics. *p.548*

Critical Issues in Child Welfare. *p.756*

Critical Issues in China's Growth and Development. . . . *p.398*

Critical Mass: How One Thing Leads to Another. *p.691*

Critical Medical Anthropology. *p.47*

Critical Path Analysis in Practice: Collected Papers on Project Control. *p.116*

Critical Perspectives in Politics and Socio-Economic Development in Ghana. *p.613*

Critical Race Theory: The Cutting Edge. *p.456*

Critical Social Theory in Public Administration. . *p.545, p.580*

Critical Theories of the State: Marxist, Neo-Marxist, Post-Marxist. *p.491*

Critical Theory and Methodology, Vol. 3. . . . . *p.680*

Critical Thinking and Learning: An Encyclopedia for Parents and Teachers. *p.366*

Critical Traditions in Contemporary Archaeology. *p.6*

Critical Years in Immigration: Canada and Australia Compared, Vol. 2. . . . . *p.667*

Critique of Everyday Life, Vol. 1. . . . . *p.680*

A Critique of Keynesian Economics. *p.226*

A Critique of the Study of Kinship. *p.32*

[e] Crony Capitalism: Corruption and Development in South Korea and the Philippines. *p.621*

Crony Capitalism: Corruption and Development in South Korea and the Philippines. *p.621*

A Cross of Iron: Harry S. Truman and the Origins of the National Security State, 1945-1954. . . . . *p.486*

Cross-Cultural Business-Behaviour: Negotiating, Selling, Sourcing and Managing Across Cultures. *p.56*

Cross-Cultural Communication: The Essential Guide to International Business. *p.59*

Cross-Cultural Perspectives on Youth and Violence. . . . p.752
Crossing: A Memoir. p.185
Crossing over the Line: Legislating Morality and the Mann Act. p.473
Crossing Sidelines, Crossing Cultures: Sport and Asian Pacific American Cultural Citizenship. p.834
Crossing the 49th Parallel: Migration from Canada to the United States, 1900-1930. . . . . p.571
Crossing the Next Meridian: Land, Water, and the Future of the West. p.463
Crossings: The Great Transatlantic Migrations, 1870-1914. . . . . p.571, p.765
Crossroads and Conflict: Security and Foreign Policy in the Caucasus and Central Asia. p.623
Crossroads Between Culture and Mind: Continuities and Change in Theories of Human Nature. p.35
Crow Dog's Case: American Indian Sovereignty, Tribal Law, and United States Law in the Nineteenth Century. . . p.464
The Crowd: A Study of the Popular Mind. p.713
The Crowd and the Public: And Other Essays. p.713
Crowd in History. p.713
Crowds and Riots: A Study in Social Organization. . . . p.713
Crown and Ritual: The Royal Insignia of Ngoyo. p.708
Crude Chronicles: Indigenous Politics, Multinational Oil, and Neoliberalism in Ecuador. p.711
Cruel and Unusual: The Supreme Court and Capital Punishment. p.471
Cruel Compassion: Psychiatric Control of Society's Unwanted. p.775
Cry for Justice: An Anthology of the Literature of Social Protest. p.751
The Cry Was Unity: Communists and African Americans, 1917-1936. . . . . p.509, p.554
Cuban Socialism in a New Century. p.506
The Cult of the Court. p.535
Cultivating the Sociological Imagination: Concepts and Models for Service-Learning in Sociology. p.675
The Cultural Analysis of Kinship: The Legacy of David M. Schneider. p.32
The Cultural Background of Personality. p.695
Cultural Competence in Substance Abuse Prevention. . . p.758
Cultural Diversity in the Workplace: Issues and Strategies. . p.132
The Cultural Dynamics of Democratization in Spain. . . p.608
Cultural Geography: Critical Concepts in the Social Sciences. p.399
Cultural Geography in Practice. p.399
Cultural Geography. p.399
Cultural Hegemony and African American Development. . p.700
Cultural Identity and Social Liberation in Latin American Thought. p.685
Cultural Intelligence: A Guide to Working with People from Other Cultures. p.59
Cultural Intelligence: People Skills for Global Business. . . p.59
Cultural Models in Language and Thought. p.27
Cultural Politics and Education. p.300
Cultural Politics of Food and Eating. p.46
Cultural Psychology: Essays on Comparative Human Development. p.36
Cultural Study of Work. p.717
Cultural Sutures: Medicine and Media. p.774
The Cultural Territories of Race: Black and White Boundaries. p.728
Cultural Transformation and Human Rights in Africa. . . . p.33
Culture: A Problem That Cannot Be Solved. p.35
Culture Against Man. p.22
Culture and Commitment: The New Relationships Between the Generations in the 1970s. p.700
Culture and Conquest in Mongol Eurasia. p.623
Culture and Experience. p.35
Culture and Pedagogy: International Comparisons in Primary Education. p.312, p.338
Culture and Power: The Sociology of Pierre Bourdieu. . . p.682
Culture as Praxis. p.699
Culture, Behavior, and Personality. p.35
Culture Clash: Law and Science in America. p.451
Culture, Class, and Work among Arab-American Women. . p.763
Culture in Mind: Cognition, Culture, and the Problem of Meaning. p.24
Culture in Practice: Selected Essays. p.24
Culture in Special Education: Building Reciprocal Family-Professional Relationships. p.316
Culture, Leadership, and Organizations: The GLOBE Study of 62 Societies. p.69, p.71
Culture Matters: How Values Shape Human Progress. p.269, p.700
The Culture of Bureaucracy. p.527
The Culture of Conformism: Understanding Social Consent. p.695
The Culture of Control: Crime and Social Order in Contemporary Society. p.752, p.773
A Culture of Corruption?: Coping with Government in Post-Communist Europe. p.582
The Culture of Defeat: On National Trauma, Mourning, and Recovery. p.706
Culture of Education. p.347, p.356
Culture of Misfortune: An Interpretive History of Textile Unionism in the United States. p.125
The Culture of Narcissism: American Life in an Age of Diminishing Expectations. p.704
Culture on Tour: Ethnographies of Travel. p.44
Culture Shock! Living and Working Abroad: A Practical Guide. p.168
Culture Wars: School and Society in the Conservative Restoration 1969-1984. . . . . p.300
Cultures and Organizations: Software for the Mind. . p.58, p.75
Cultures and Societies of Africa. p.38
Culture's Consequences: Comparing Values, Behaviors, Institutions and Organizations Across Nations. p.718
Cultures of Commerce: Representation and American Business Culture, 1877-1960. . . . . p.141
Cultures of Darkness: Night Travels in the Histories of Transgression. p.709

Cultures of Human Development and Education: Challenge to Growing up African. *p.335*

Cultures of Relatedness: New Approaches to the Study of Kinship. *p.31*

Cultures of Transnational Adoption. *p.708*

The Cumulated Index to the U. S. Department of State Papers Relating to the Foreign Relations of the United States, 1939-1945, Set. *p.627*

Curbing the Courts: The Constitution and the Limits of Judicial Power. *p.538*

☐ Current Industrial Reports. *p.150*

Current Issues in Natural Resource Policy. *p.62*

Current Paleoethnobotany: Analytical Methods and Cultural Interpretations of Archaeological Plant Remains. *p.7*

Curriculum: A Comprehensive Introduction. *p.364*

Curriculum and Assessment. *p.286*

Curriculum as Conversation: Transforming Traditions of Teaching and Learning. *p.294, p.361*

Curriculum Development and Teaching Strategies for Gifted Learners. *p.317*

Curriculum Development: Theory into Practice. *p.365*

Curriculum for Gifted and Talented Students. *p.317*

Curriculum Improvement: Decision Making and Process. . *p.362*

The Curriculum: Purpose, Substance, Practice. *p.363*

The Curriculum Studies Reader. *p.366*

Curriculum Studies: The Reconceptionalization (Curriculum Theorizing:The Reconceptualists). *p.361*

The Curriculum Vitae Handbook: How to Present and Promote Your Academic Career. *p.168*

Customer Mania!: It's Never Too Late to Build a Customer-Focused Company. *p.143*

Cy Young: A Baseball Life. *p.849*

Cybercartography: Theory and Practice. *p.386*

Cyberspace and the Law: Your Rights and Duties in the on-Line World. *p.444*

Cycles, Trends, and Turning Points: Practical Marketing and Sales Forecasting Techniques. *p.137*

Cycling Past 50. . . . . *p.787, p.841, p.857*

D

Daily Life of the Nubians. *p.701*

The Daily Newspaper in America: The Evolution of a Social Instrument, Set. *p.410*

The Dance of Legislation. *p.461*

Dance of the Dialectic: Steps in Marx's Method. *p.507*

Dancin' in the Streets!: Anarchists, IWWs, Surrealists, Situationists and Provos in the 1960s As Recorded in the Pages of the Rebel Worker and Heatwave. *p.554*

Dancing at the Dawn of Agriculture: Dance and Display at the Beginning of Farming. *p.26*

Dancing Skeletons: Life and Death in West Africa. *p.45*

Dancing to Different Tunes: Sexuality and Its Misconceptions. *p.749*

Dancing with Data to Improve Learning. *p.287*

Danger in the Field: Ethics and Risk in Social Research. . *p.690*

Dangerous Company: The Consulting Powerhouses and the Businesses They Save and Ruin. *p.65*

Dangerous Schools: What We Can Do about the Physical and Emotional Abuse to Our Children. *p.284*

Darfur: The Ambiguous Genocide. *p.653*

Dark Paradise: A History of Opiate Addiction in America. . *p.776*

The Dark Side of Behaviour at Work: Understanding and Avoiding Employees Leaving, Thieving and Deceiving. *p.130*

The Dark Side of Democracy: Explaining Ethnic Cleansing. *p.660, p.715*

Dark Victory: America's Second War Against Iraq. . . . *p.561*

Darwin's Athletes: How Sport has Damaged Black America and Preserved the Myth of Race. *p.802, p.816, p.832*

Darwin's Cathedral: Evolution, Religion, and the Nature of Society. *p.720*

Dat: Tackling Life and the NFL. *p.834, p.859*

Data and Computer Communications. *p.422*

Data Driven Differentiation in the Standards-Based Classroom. *p.349*

The Data Game: Controversies in Social Science Statistics. *p.690*

Database Nation: The Death of Privacy in the 21st Century. *p.515*

Daughters of Joy, Sisters of Misery: Prostitutes in the American West, 1865-90. *p.747*

Daughters of Tunis: Women, Family, and Networks in a Muslim City. *p.38*

Dave Pelz's Short Game Bible: Master the Finesse Swing and Lower Your Score. *p.861*

David Hackett Souter: Traditional Republican on the Rehnquist Court. *p.540*

Davis and Lee at War. *p.522*

The Dawn of Canadian History: A Chronicle of Aboriginal Canada and the Coming of the White Man. *p.379*

The Dawn of Modern Geography: A History of Exploration and Geographical Science. *p.377*

The Day the Presses Stopped: A History of the Pentagon Papers Case. *p.439*

DC Confidential: The Controversial Memoirs of Britain's Ambassador at the Time of 9/11 and the Iraq War. . . *p.645*

The DC Guide to Writing Comics. *p.140*

The Dead and Their Possessions: Repatriation in Principle, Policy, and Practice. *p.47*

Dead End Kids: Gang Girls and the Boys They Know. . . *p.714*

☐ Dead Sociologists' Society. *p.675*

Deadliest Enemies: Law and Making the Race Relations on and off Rosebud Reservation. *p.33*

Deadlock or Decision: The U. S. Senate and the Rise of National Politics. *p.530*

Deadly Arsenals: Nuclear, Biological and Chemical Threats. *p.655*

Deadly Connections: States that Sponsor Terrorism. . . . *p.658*

Deadly Consequences. *p.775*

The Deadly Ethnic Riot. *p.713*

Deadly Gambits: The Reagan Administration and the Stalemate in Nuclear Arms Control. *p.562, p.657*

Deaf in America: Voices from a Culture. p.700
Deaf Sport: The Impact of Sports Within the Deaf Community. p.830
The Deaf Way: Perspectives from the International Conference on Deaf Culture. p.709
Deaf World: A Historical Reader and Primary Sourcebook. . p.699
The Deal Decade: What Takeovers and Leveraged Buyouts Mean for Corporate Governance. p.84
Dealing with Alcohol: Indigenous Usage in Australia, New Zealand and Canada. p.46
Dealing with Difficult People: How to Deal with Nasty Customers, Demanding Bosses and Annoying Co-Workers. p.130
Dealing with Difficult People. p.73
Dealing with Financial Risk. p.90, p.93, p.97, p.100
Dealing with Terrorism. p.659
Deals of the Century: Wall Street, Mergers, and the Making of Modern America. p.84, p.89, p.155
Dean LeBaron's Treasury of Investment Wisdom: 30 Great Investing Minds. p.95
The Death and Rebirth of the Seneca. p.37
Death and Renewal: Sociological Studies in Roman History. p.501
Death and the Right Hand. p.24
Death by a Thousand Cuts: The Fight over Taxing Inherited Wealth. p.107
The Death of a Thousand Cuts: Corporate Campaigns and the Attack on the Corporation. p.52, p.54, p.145
The Death of Character: Moral Education in an Age Without Good or Evil. p.306
The Death of Common Sense: How Law Is Suffocating America. p.441
The Death of White Sociology. p.683
Death Penalties: The Supreme Court's Obstacle Course. . p.471
The Death Penalty in America: Current Controversies. . . p.471
Death, Sex, and Fertility: Population Regulation in Pre-Industrial and Developing Societies. p.736
Death Squad: The Anthropology of State Terror. p.34
Death Without Weeping: The Violence of Everyday Life in Brazil. p.46
Debating Human Kind's Place in Nature; 1860-2000: The Nature of Paleoanthropology. p.14
Debating the Death Penalty: Should America Have Capital Punishment? The Experts on Both Sides Make Their Best Case. p.567
The Debris of Ham: Ethnicity, Regionalism, and the 1994 Rwandan Genocide. p.654
Debt Management: A Practitioner's Guide. p.91
Debt's Dominion: A History of Bankruptcy Law in America. p.97, p.110, p.444
Debunking the Middle-Class Myth: Why Diverse Schools Are Good for All Kids. p.309
DEC Recommended Practices: A Comprehensive Guide for Practical Application. p.316
Decentralization, Democratic Governance, and Civil Society in Comparative Perspective: Africa, Asia, and Latin America. p.585, p.613
Decentralizing the State: Elections, Parties, and Local Power in the Andes. p.582
Deciding to Decide: Agenda Setting in the United States Supreme Court. p.466, p.538
Deciding to Leave: The Politics of Retirement from the United States Supreme Court. p.540
Decision Analysis: An Integrated Approach. p.83
Decision Analysis, Game Theory, and Information. p.83
Decision and Organization. p.269
Decision: How the Supreme Court Decides Cases. . p.466, p.539
Decision Making Using Game Theory: An Introduction for Managers. p.83
Decisions at Yalta: An Appraisal of Summit Diplomacy. . p.565
e Decisions, Uncertainty, and the Brain: The Science of Neuroeconomics. p.272
Declaration of Independence: A Study in the History of Political Ideas. p.518
The Decline and Fall of the Income Tax: How to Make Sense of the American Tax Mess and the Flat-Tax Cures That Are Supposed to Fix It. p.107
The Decline and Fall of the Supreme Court: Living Out the Nightmare of the Federalists. p.470
The Decline of Politics: The Conservatives and the Party System, 1901-1920. . . . . p.588
The Decline of the German Mandarins: The German Academic Community, 1890-1933. . . . . p.336
Declining by Degrees: Higher Education at Risk. p.331
The Declining Significance of Race: Blacks and Changing American Institutions. p.730
Decolonisation and the British Empire, 1775-1997. . . . p.583
Decolonization and African Independence: The Transfers of Power 1960-1980. . . . . p.582
Decolonization in Africa. p.583, p.584
The Decolonization of Portuguese Africa: Metropolitan Revolution and the Dissolution of Empire. p.584
Decolonization since 1945: Collapse of European Overseas Empires. p.583
Decolonizing Anthropology: Moving Further Toward an Anthropology of Liberation. p.27
Deconstructing Public Relations: Public Relations Criticism. p.429
Deep South: A Social Anthropological Study of Caste and Class. p.701
Deepening Democracy: Global Governance and Political Reform in Latin America. p.584, p.640
Deepening Democracy: Institutional Innovations in Empowered Participatory Governance, Vol. 4. . . . . p.504
Deeper Reading: Comprehending Challenging Texts, 4-12. . . . . p.363
Defence of Usury. p.194
Defending Pornography. p.748
A Defense of Abortion. p.775
Defining America Through Immigration Policy. p.571
Defining British Citizenship: Empire Commonwealth and Modern Britain. p.605, p.667
The Defining Moment: The Great Depression and the American Economy in the Twentieth Century. p.213

Defining Moments: When Managers Must Choose Between Right and Right. *p.145*
Defining Russian Federalism. *p.598*
Defining the Family: Law, Technology, and Reproduction in an Uneasy Age.. *p.448*
Definitions in Political Economy: Preceded by an Inquiry into the Rules Which Ought to Guide Political Economists in the Definition and Use of Their Terms.. *p.218*
The Degaev Affair: Terror and Treason in Tsarist Russia. . *p.661*
The Degradation of the Academic Dogma. *p.290, p.332*
Degrees of Control: A Sociology of Educational Expansion and Occupational Credentialism. *p.295*
The Deindustrialization of America : Plant Closings, Community Abandonment, and the Dismantling of Basic Industry.. *p.722*
Delegation and Accountability in Parliamentary Democracies. *p.576*
Delinquency in a Birth Cohort.. . . . . *p.753*
Delinquent Daughters: Protecting and Policing Adolescent Female Sexuality in the United States, 1885-1920. . . *p.736*
Delusions of Grandeur: The United Nations and Global Intervention.. *p.633*
Demand and Supply of Public Goods, Vol. 5. . . . . . . *p.247*
Demand Forcasting and Inventory Control: A Computer Aided Learning Approach. *p.117*
The Demise of Communist East Europe: 1989 in Context. *p.509, p.596, p.600*
The Democracy Advantage: How Democracies Promote Prosperity and Peace. *p.505*
Democracy after Liberalism: Pragmatism and Deliberative Politics. *p.505, p.511*
Democracy and America's War on Terror. *p.564*
Democracy and Authoritarianism in Peru: Political Coalitions and Social Change. *p.591*
Democracy and Deliberation: New Directions for Democratic Reform. *p.503*
Democracy and Development: Political Institutions and Well-Being in the World, 1950-1990. . . . . *p.505*
Democracy and Dictatorship in Ghana and Tanzania. *p.576, p.612*
Democracy and Disagreement. *p.504*
Democracy and Disorder: Protest and Politics in Italy, 1965-1975. . . . . *p.594*
Democracy and Education. *p.342*
Democracy and Elections: Electoral Systems and Their Political Consequences. *p.577*
Democracy and Human Rights. *p.503*
Democracy and Its Critics.. . . . . *p.503*
Democracy and Participation in Athens.. . . . . *p.501*
Democracy and Public Management Reform: Building the Republican State. *p.545*
Democracy and Redistribution.. . . . . *p.503*
Democracy and Social Ethics. *p.769*
Democracy and the Global Order: From the Modern State to Cosmopolitan Governance. *p.504*
Democracy and the Market: Political and Economic Reforms in Eastern Europe and Latin America. *p.592*
Democracy and the Welfare State. *p.524*
Democracy at Risk: How Political Choices Undermine Citizen Participation, and What We Can Do about It. *p.547*
Democracy, Citizenship and the Global City: Rights, Democracy and Place. *p.544*
Democracy Defended. *p.505*
Democracy Derailed in Russia: The Failure of Open Politics. *p.597*
Democracy, Diamonds and Oil: Politics in Today's Africa.. *p.398*
Democracy, Governance and Economic Performance: East and Southeast Asia. *p.618, p.622*
Democracy: History, Theory, Practice. *p.504*
Democracy in Alberta: Social Credit and the Party System. *p.590*
Democracy in America. *p.517*
Democracy in Europe. *p.603, p.638*
Democracy in Immigrant America: Demographics and Political Participation. *p.571*
Democracy in Japan. *p.621*
Democracy in Jonesville: A Study in Quality and Inequality.. . . . . *p.708*
Democracy in Latin America: Political Change in Comparative Perspective. *p.593*
Democracy in Modern Spain. *p.608*
Democracy in Plural Societies: A Comparative Exploration. *p.502, p.504*
Democracy in Poland. *p.506, p.597*
Democracy in Translation: Understanding Politics in an Unfamiliar Culture.. . . . . *p.505, p.585, p.613*
Democracy, Italian Style. *p.594*
A Democracy of Chameleons: Politics and Culture in the New Malawi. *p.611*
Democracy, Security, and Development in India. *p.618*
Democracy, Sovereignty and the European Community. . *p.603*
Democracy, the Threshold of Freedom. *p.577*
Democracy vs. National Security: Civil-Military Relations in Latin America.. *p.593*
Democracy without Associations: Transformation of the Party System and Social Cleavages in India.. . . . . *p.617*
Democracy Without Citizens: Media and the Decay of American Politics. *p.558*
Democracy Without Competition in Japan: Opposition Failure in a One-Party Dominant State. *p.622*
Democracy's College: The Land-Grant Movement in the Formative Stage.. . . . . *p.332*
Democracy's Dilemma: Environment, Social Equity, and the Global Economy. *p.505, p.667*
Democracy's Discontent: America in Search of a Public Philosophy. *p.555*
Democracy's Feast: Elections in America.. . . . . *p.531*
Democracy. *p.503*
The Democratic Century. *p.505*
Democratic Changes and Authoritarian Reactions in Russia, Ukraine, Belarus and Moldova.. . . . . *p.585, p.597*
Democratic Development and Political Terrorism: The Global Perspective.. . . . . *p.503, p.658*
Democratic Distributive Justice. *p.515*
Democratic Equality: What Went Wrong? *p.514*

The Democratic Experience and Political Violence. . . . p.497
Democratic Experiments in Africa: Regime Transitions in Comparative Perspective. p.503, p.584, p.611
Democratic Governance and Social Inequality. p.506
Democratic Government in Poland: Constitutional Politics since 1989. . . . . p.505, p.596
Democratic Legislative Institutions: A Comparative View. . p.575
Democratic Miners: Work and Labor Relations in the Anthracite Coal Industry, 1875-1925. . . . . p.124
The Democratic Party Heads North. 1877-1962. . . . . . p.553
The Democratic Party. p.553
Democratic Phoenix: Reinventing Political Activism. . . . p.577
Democratic Politics and Economic Reform in India. . . . p.617
The Democratic Question. p.504
Democratic Teacher Education: Programs, Processes, Problems, and Prospects. p.277
The Democratic Wish: Popular Participation and the Limits of American Government. p.555, p.579
Democratization and Revolution in the U. S. S. R., 1985-91. . . . . p.598
Democratization in Africa: The Theory and Dynamics of Political Transitions. p.503, p.585, p.611
Democratization in South Africa: The Elusive Social Contract. p.614
Democratizing Higher Education Policy: Constraints of Reform in Post-Apartheid South Africa. p.336
Demographic Methods and Concepts. p.376
Demographic Vistas: Television in American Culture. . . p.418
Demographic Yearbook 2001. . . . . p.763
Den of Thieves: The Untold Story of the Men Who Plundered Wall Street and the Chase That Brought Them Down. p.100, p.110, p.147
Denmark: A Troubled Welfare State. p.594
The Dependent Empire, 1900-1948: Colonies, Protectorates and Mandates Select Documents on the Constitutional History of the British Empire and Commonwealth, Vol. 7. . . . . p.435
The Dependent Empire and Ireland, 1840-1900: Advance and Retreat in Representative Self-Government - Select Documents on the Constitutional History of the British Empire and Commonwealth, Vol. V. p.436
Derivatives: A Comprehensive Resource for Options, Futures, Interest Rate Swaps and Mortgage Securities. p.92, p.93, p.101, p.103
Deschooling Society: Social Questions. p.327
Desert People: A Study of the Walbiri Aborigines of Central Australia. p.43
The Design and Implementation of Geographic Information Systems. p.387
The Design and Management of Effective Distance Learning Programs. p.321
Design As a Catalyst for Learning. p.356
Design Issues: How Graphic Design Informs Society. . . p.140
The Design of Development. p.245
Design Sensitivity: Statistical Power for Experimental Research. p.686
Design Standards for Recreation Facilities. p.792, p.881
Designing and Conducting Survey Research: A Comprehensive Guide. p.691
Designing and Developing Programs for Gifted Students. . p.317
Designing Better Maps: A Guide for GIS Users. p.386
Designing Brand Identity: A Complete Guide to Creating, Building, and Maintaining Strong Brands. p.142
Designing Early Literacy Programs: Strategies for at-Risk Preschool and Kindergarten Children. p.368
Designing for Newspapers and Magazines. p.409
Designing for Virtual Communities in the Service of Learning. p.761
Designing Instruction for Technology-Enhanced Learning. . p.352
Designing Judicial Review: Interest Groups, Congress and Communications Policy. p.539
Designing Qualitative Research. p.687
Designing Resistance Training Programs. p.790, p.879
Designing Social Inquiry: Scientific Inference in Qualitative Research. p.483
Designing State Higher Education Systems for a New Century. p.295
Designing Surveys: A Guide to Decisions and Procedures. . p.137
Desis in the House: Indian American Youth Culture in New York City. p.704
Desktop Encyclopedia of Telecommunications. p.420
Desperately Seeking the Audience. p.418
Destination Culture: Tourism, Museums, and Heritage. . p.47
Destination Europe: The Political and Economic Growth of a Continent. p.638
Destructive Messages: How Hate Speech Paves the Way for Harmful Social Movements. p.423
Determinants of Economic Growth: A Cross-Country Empirical Study. p.242
Determined Survivors: Community Life among the Urban Elderly. p.742
Developing a Lifelong Contract in the Sports Marketplace. p.883, p.905
Developing Adult Learners: Strategies for Teachers and Trainers. p.321
Developing Affordable Housing: A Practical Guide for Nonprofit Organizations. p.158
Developing Arts Loving Readers: Top 10 Questions Teachers Are Asking about Integrated Arts Education. p.364
Developing Constructivist Early Childhood Curriculum: Practical Principles and Activities. p.368
Developing Critical Thinkers: Challenging Adults to Explore Alternative Ways of Thinking and Acting. p.319
Developing Cross-Cultural Competence: A Guide for Working with Children and Their Families. p.316
Developing Educational Standards. p.287
Developing Innovation in Online Learning: An Action Research Framework. p.322
Developing Innovation Systems: Mexico in a Global Context. p.383
Developing Learning in Early Childhood. p.368
Developing More Curious Minds. p.346
Developing Personal, Social and Moral Education Through Physical Education: A Practical Guide for Teachers. . p.796

Developing Questions for Focus Groups. p.136
Developing the Core Curriculum. p.363
Developing the Leaders Around You: How to Help Others Reach Their Full Potential. p.71
Developing the Physical Education Curriculum: An Achievement-Based Approach. p.795
Developing the Teacher Workforce.. . . . . p.278
Development and Communication in Africa. p.398
Development and Crisis of the Welfare State: Parties and Policies in Global Markets. p.594
Development and Education of Mind. p.343, p.356
Development and the Developing World. p.259
[Development and Underdevelopment] Rich Lands and Poor: The Road to World Prosperity. p.244
Development as Freedom. p.515
Development Economics. p.258, p.259, p.268
Development in the Land of Contrasts. p.398
The Development of Cognitive Anthropology. p.27
Development of Economic Analysis. p.196
Development of Education in the Twentieth Century. . . p.328
Development of Modern Education in the Gulf. p.335
Developmental Sport and Exercise Psychology: A Lifespan Perspective. p.878
Developmental States: Relevancy, Redundancy or Reconfiguration? p.398
Developmental/Adapted Physical Education: Making Ability Count. p.800
Developments in International Trade Theory: The Origins of International Economics. p.257
Deviance and Identity.. . . . . p.696
Deviant Conduct in World Politics. p.626
Devices and Desires: A History of Contraceptives in America. p.775
Devil Take the Hindmost: A History of Financial Speculation. p.88, p.99, p.101
The Devil's Disciples: The Makers of the Salem Witchcraft Trials. p.474
The Devil's Highway: A True Story. p.765
The Devil's Own Work: The Civil War Draft Riots and the Fight to Reconstruct America.. . . . . p.713
Devolution and Black State Legislators: Challenges and Choices in the 21st Century. p.530
Dewey, Pragmatism and Economic Methodology. p.195
The Dialectic of Sex: The Case for Feminist Revolution. p.724, p.744, p.747
The Dialectics of Oppression in Zaire. p.513
Dialogue Education at Work: A Case Book. p.321
Dialogue: Theorizing Difference in Communication Studies. p.422
Diamond Classics: Essays on 100 of the Best Baseball Books Ever Published. p.812, p.852
Diamonds Are Forever: The Business of Baseball. p.852, p.886, p.889, p.897
The Diaries of Beatrice Webb. p.193
A Diary in the Strict Sense of the Term. p.4
Dictatorship and Political Police: International Library of Sociology C: Political Sociology. p.768
The Dictionary of Anthropology. p.3
Dictionary of Anthropology. p.3
A Dictionary of Business and Management. p.173
Dictionary of Business Terms. p.172
Dictionary of Concepts in Recreation and Leisure Studies, 9.. . . . . p.785
The Dictionary of Cricket. p.856
Dictionary of Demography: Terms, Concepts, and Institutions. p.678
Dictionary of Developmental Disabilities Terminology. . . p.318
A Dictionary of Econometrics. p.188, p.199
Dictionary of Economics. p.191
A Dictionary of Finance and Banking. . p.91 p.95 p.102 p.103
A Dictionary of Geography. p.373
The Dictionary of Human Geography. p.373
Dictionary of Insurance Terms.. . . . . p.163
Dictionary of International and Comparative Law. . . . p.434
Dictionary of International Human Rights Law. p.434
The Dictionary of Marketing Communications. p.134
Dictionary of Media and Communication Studies. p.424
Dictionary of Medical Sociology.. . . . . p.677
A Dictionary of Modern Legal Usage. p.436
The Dictionary of Modern Politics.. . . . . p.482
The Dictionary of Physical Geography. p.373
Dictionary of Public Policy and Administration. p.482
Dictionary of Qualitative Inquiry. p.689
Dictionary of Quotations in Sociology. p.676
A Dictionary of Social Science Methods. p.687
Dictionary of Special Education and Rehabilitation. . . . p.317
Dictionary of Sports: A Complete Guide to the Vocabulary of the World's Leading Speakers. p.848
Dictionary of Statistics and Methodology: A Nontechnical Guide for the Social Sciences.. . . . . p.679
Dictionary of Terrorism. p.662
A Dictionary of the European Union. p.603, p.638
Dictionary of the Political Thought of the People's Republic of China. p.620
Dictionary of the Social Sciences. p.373, p.677
Dictionary of Travel, Tourism and Hospitality.. . . . . . p.161
Different Games, Different Rules: Why Americans and Japanese Misunderstand Each Other. p.20
A Different Mirror: A History of Multicultural America. . p.707
Differentiated Assessment Strategies: One Tool Doesn't Fit All. p.285
The Differentiated Classroom: Responding to the Needs of All Learners. p.350
Differentiated Instruction: Meeting the Educational Needs of All Students in Your Classroom. p.316, p.350
Differentiated Instructional Strategies: One Size Doesn't Fit All. p.349
Diffusing Geography: Essays for Peter Haggett. p.373
Diffusion of Innovations. p.761
□ Digest of Education Statistics. p.322

Digital Concepts: The Cultural Context Of New Information Technologies. *p.419*

Digital Crossroads: American Telecommunications Policy in the Internet Age. *p.52, p.111, p.166, p.420*

The Digital Dilemma: The Future of Intellectual Property in the Information Infrastructure. *p.110*

Digital Economics: How Information Technology Has Transformed Business Thinking. *p.82*

The Digital Hand: How Computers Changed the Work of American Manufacturing, Transportation, and Retail Industries. *p.146, p.149*

The Digital Hand, Volume 2: How Computers Changed the Work of American Financial, Telecommunications, Media, and Entertainment Industries. *p.146 p.155 p.157 p.158*

The Digital Sublime: Myth, Power, and Cyberspace. . . . *p.425*

The Dilemma of Access: Minorities in Two Year Colleges. . *p.312*

Dilemmas of Democracy and Political Parties in Sectarian Societies: The Case of the PSP in Lebanon. *p.616*

Dilemmas of Pluralist Democracy: Autonomy Vs. Control. *p.503*

Dilemmas of Pluralist Democracy: Autonomy vs. Control. . *p.503*

The Dilemmas of Presidential Leadership: Of Caretakers and Kings. *p.527*

Dilemmas of State-Led Nation Building in Ukraine. *p.585, p.598*

Dimensions of Literacy: A Conceptual Base for Teaching Reading and Writing in School Settings. . . . *p.354, p.364*

The Dimensions of Regional Trade Integration in Southeast Asia. *p.61*

Diminished Democracy: From Membership to Management in American Civic Life. *p.547, p.555*

The Diplomacies of New Small States: The Case of Slovenia with Some Comparison from the Baltics. . . . *p.641, p.644*

Diplomacy for a Next Century. *p.645*

A Diplomacy of Hope: Canada and Disarmament, 1945-1988. . . . . *p.644, p.656*

The Diplomacy of Hope: The United Nations since the Cold War. *p.633*

The Diplomacy of India: Indian Foreign Policy in the United Nations,. *p.632*

Diplomacy: Theory and Practice. *p.645*

Diplomacy. *p.645*

Diplomatic Theory from Machiavelli to Kissinger. *p.645*

Direct from Dell: Strategies That Revolutionized an Industry. *p.157*

Direct Legislation: Voting on Ballot Propositions in the United States. *p.460*

DirectGov. *p.604*

Directions in Sociolinguistics: The Ethnography of Communication. *p.19*

The Directory for Exceptional Children: A Listing of Educational and Training Facilities. *p.316*

The Directory of Jobs and Careers Abroad. *p.170*

Directory of Research Grants 2005. . . . . *p.293*

A Dirty Filthy Book: The Writings of Charles Knowlton and Annie Besant on Birth Control and Reproductive Physiology and an Account of the Bradlaugh-Besant Trial. *p.736*

Disability Matters: Legal and Pedagogical Issues of Disability in Education. *p.450*

Disability Sport and Recreation Resources. . *p.784, p.801, p.842*

Disability Sport. *p.800, p.842*

Disabled Sport USA. *p.787, p.789*

The Disappearance of Telecommunications. *p.420*

Disarmament Without Order: The Politics of Disarmament at the United Nations. *p.655*

Disarming Iraq: Monitoring Power and Resistance. . . . *p.656*

Disarming Iraq. *p.655*

Disarming Strangers: Nuclear Diplomacy with North Korea. *p.566, p.644, p.657*

Discipline and Punish: The Birth of the Prison. *p.752*

The Discipline of Market Leaders: Choose Your Customers, Narrow Your Focus, Dominate Your Market. *p.135*

The Disciplined Mind: Beyond Facts and Standardized Tests, the K-12 Education That Every Child Deserves. *p.343*

Discourse: A Critical Introduction. *p.21*

The Discourse of Character Education: Culture Wars in the Classroom. *p.306*

A Discourse of Trade, from England unto the East-Indies. . *p.257*

Discourses on Livy. *p.492, p.502*

Discovery of the Child. *p.344*

Discrimination at Work: The Psychological and Organizational Bases. *p.133*

Discrimination, Harassment and the Failure of Diversity Training: What to Do Now. *p.132*

Discussion as a Way of Teaching: Tools and Techniques for Democratic Classrooms. *p.292, p.347*

Diseasing of America: How We Allowed Recovery Zealots and the Treatment Industry to Convince Us We Are out of Control. *p.777*

Dishonest Broker: America's Role in Israel and Palestine. *p.560, p.565, p.641*

Dismantling Democratic States. *p.581*

Dismantling Desegregation: The Quiet Reversal of Brown vs. Board of Education. *p.301*

The Disobedient Generation: Social Theorists in the Sixties. *p.684*

Disordered Eating among Athletes: A Comprehensive Guide for Health Professionals. *p.801, p.824, p.876*

Disoriented: Asian Americans, Law and the Nation State. . *p.456*

Dis-Orienting Rhythms: The Politics of the New Asian Dance Music. *p.26*

Disposable People: New Slavery in the Global Economy. . *p.27*

The Dispossessed: America's Underclasses from the Civil War to the Present. *p.708*

Disruption: Overturning Conventions and Shaking up the Marketplace. *p.428*

Dissent on Development: Studies and Debates in Development Economics. *p.242*

Distance Education: The Complete Guide to Design, Delivery, and Improvement. *p.321*

A Distant Heritage: The Growth of Free Speech in Early America. *p.459*

The Distant Magnet; European Emigration to the U. S. A. . *p.668*

Distinction: A Social Critique of the Judgement of Taste. . *p.726*

Distinguished Women Economists. *p.193*

Distributed Work. *p.69*

The Distribution of Wealth: A Theory of Wages, Interest and Profits. *p.223, p.252*

The Distribution of Wealth and Universal Economic Laws. *p.223*

The Distribution of Wealth. *p.266*

Distribution: Planning and Control—Managing in the Era of Supply Chain Management. *p.118*

Diversity: A Biography of a Concept. *p.709*

Diversity and Citizenship Education: Global Perspectives. . *p.313*

Diversity and Developmentally Appropriate Practice in Early Childhood Education: Challenges for Early Childhood Education. *p.369*

Diversity and Distrust: Civic Education in a Multicultural Democracy. *p.328*

Diversity and Public Administration: Theory, Issues, and Perspectives. *p.545, p.580*

Diversity in Advertising: Broadening the Scope of Research Directions. *p.426*

Diversity in the Power Elite: Have Women and Minorities Reached the Top? *p.133*

Diversity in the Work Force. *p.132*

The Diverted Dream: Community Colleges and the Promise of Educational Opportunity in America, 1900-1985. . . . . *p.291, p.330*

Divide and Rule: The Partition of Africa, 1880-1914. . . *p.583*

The Divided Academy. *p.292*

Divided Democrats: Ideological Unity, Party Reform, and Presidential Elections. *p.551, p.553*

Divided Families: What Happens to Children When Parents Part. *p.739*

The Divided Ground: Indians, Settlers, and the Northern Borderland of the American Revolution. *p.581*

Divided Hearts: Britain and the American Civil War. . . . *p.519*

Divided Loyalties: Canadian Concepts of Federalism. . . *p.586*

Divided We Fail: Issues of Equity in American Schools. . *p.302*

Divided We Govern: Party Control, Lawmaking, and Investigations, 1946-2002. . . . . *p.551, p.552*

Dividend Policy: Its Impact on Firm Value. *p.91, p.95*

The Divine Nine: The History of African-American Fraternities and Sororities in America. *p.289*

Divine Sovereignty: The Origins of Modern State Power. *p.491, p.496, p.498*

Division and Discord: The Supreme Court under Stone and Vinson, 1941-1953. . . . . *p.469*

The Division of Labor in Society. *p.722*

Divorce: Crisis, Challenge or Relief? *p.739*

Divorced in America: Marriage in an Age of Possibility. . *p.739*

Do Conventions Matter?: Choosing National Party Leaders in Canada. *p.588*

□ Doctors Without Borders/ Medecins Sans Frontieres. . *p.668*

Documentary Archaeology in the New World. *p.6*

A Documentary History of Banking and Currency in the United States. *p.246*

□ The Documentary History of the Ratification of the Constitution. *p.451*

Documentary Screens: Non-Fiction Film and Television. . *p.413*

□ Documents from the Continental Congress and the Constitutional Convention, 1774-1789. . . . . *p.518*

Documents of American Constitutional and Legal History: From the Age of Industrialization to the Present. *p.440*

Documents of American Constitutional and Legal History: From the Founding Through the Age of Industrialization. . . *p.440*

Documents of American Indian Diplomacy: Treaties, Agreements, and Conventions, 1775-1979. . . . . . . *p.464*

Documents on the Suez Crisis, 26 July to 6 November 1956. . . . . *p.628*

Does Atlas Shrug?: The Economic Consequences of Taxing the Rich. *p.107*

Does Foreign Direct Investment Promote Development. . . *p.60*

Does God Belong in Public Schools? *p.298, p.307*

Doing Business In 2006: Creating Jobs. . . *p.58, p.110, p.112*

Doing Business Internationally: The Guide to Cross-Cultural Success. *p.59*

Doing Business Internationally: The Resource for Business and Social Etiquette. *p.57*

Doing Business with the Government: Federal, State, Local and Foreign Purchasing Practices for Every Business and Public Institution. *p.524*

Doing Social Life: The Qualitative Study of Human Interaction in Natural Settings. *p.692*

The Dollar and the Policy Mix: 1971. . . . . *p.247*

The Dome of Silence: Sexual Harrassment and Abuse in Sport. *p.817, p.840*

Domestic Architecture and Power: The Historical Archaeology of Colonial Ecuador. *p.14*

Domestic Tyranny: The Making of Social Policy Against Family Violence from Colonial Times to the Present. *p.742*

The Domestication of the Human Species. *p.17*

The Dominions and India since 1900: Select Documents on the Constitutional History of the British Empire and Commonwealth. *p.435*

Don't Ask, Don't Tell: Debating the Gay Ban in the U. S. Military. *p.569*

Don't Breathe the Air: Air Pollution and U. S. Environmental Politics, 1945-1970. . . . . *p.566*

Don't Look Back: Satchel Paige on the Shadows of Baseball. *p.809, p.833, p.852*

Doomed to Fail: The Built-in Defects of American Education. *p.340*

Doping in Elite Sport: The Politics of Drugs in the Olympic Movement. *p.826, p.846*

Do's and Taboos Around the World for Women in Business. . *p.57*

Do's and Taboos around the World. *p.56, p.58*

Double or Nothing?: Jewish Families and Mixed Marriage. *p.721*

The Douglas Opinions. *p.437*

Down by the River: Drugs, Money, Murder, and Family. . *p.764*

Down on Their Luck: A Study of Homeless Street People. . *p.751*

The Downfall of the Anti-Semitic Political Parties in Imperial Germany. p.609
The Drafting of the Covenant. p.631
Dragon Bone Hill: An Ice-Age Saga of Homo Erectus. . . p.16
Dragons and Tigers: A Geography of South, East, and Southeast Asia. p.384, p.399
Drawn to Extremes: The Use and Abuse of Editorial Cartoons in the United States. p.409, p.417
The Dread Disease: Cancer and Modern American Culture. p.778
The Dream Job: Sports Publicity, Promotion and Marketing. p.906
Dream Makers, Dream Breakers: The World of Justice Thurgood Marshall. p.538
The Dream of a New Social Order: Popular Magazines in America, 1893-1914. . . . . p.410
Dreaming Equality: Color, Race and Racism in Urban Brazil. p.37
The Dreamkeepers: Successful Teachers of African-American Children. p.310
Dreams of Power: The Role of the Organization of African Unity in the Politics of Africa, 1963-1993. . . . . . . p.631
The Dred Scott Case: Its Significance in American Law and Politics. p.453
Dred Scott V. Sandford: A Brief History with Documents. . p.453
Drift and Mastery. p.768
Drink: A Social History of America. p.699
Drinking: Anthropological Approaches. p.45
Drinking in America: A History. p.700
Dropouts in America: Confronting the Graduation Rate Crisis. p.299
Droughts, Food, and Culture: Ecological Change and Food Security in Africa's Later Prehistory. p.7
Drug Legalization: For and Against. p.448
Drug War Heresies: Learning from Other Vices, Times, and Places. p.777
Drug War Politics: The Price of Denial. p.568
Drugs and Doping in Sport: Socio-Legal Perspectives. p.826, p.901
Drugs in Sport. p.826
Drunken Comportment: A Social Explanation. p.776
Du Bois on Education. p.345
The Dual-Image of the Japanese Emperor. p.622
Due Process. p.458
Dumbarton Oaks: The Origins of the United Nations and the Search for Postwar Security. p.654
Dun and Bradstreet's Guide to Doing Business Around the World. p.56
Durkheim's Ghosts: Cultural Logics and Social Things. . p.683
The Dust of Empire: The Race for Mastery in the Asian Heartland. p.642
Dwight D. Eisenhower. p.528
Dying to Kill: The Allure of Suicide Terror. p.658
Dying to Teach: The Educator's Search for Immortality. . p.346
The Dynamic Constitution: An Introduction to American Constitutional Law. p.453
Dynamic Cover Letters for New Graduates. p.169
Dynamic Economics: Quantitative Methods and Applications. p.197
Dynamic Modeling of Monetary and Fiscal Cooperation among Nations. p.203, p.240
Dynamic Physical Education for Elementary School Children. p.798
Dynamic Sociology. p.684
Dynamic Testing: The Nature and Measurement of Learning Potential. p.287
Dynamics and Income Distribution: Selected Essays of Irma Adelman, Vol. 2. . . . . p.252, p.264
The Dynamics of Business Cycles: A Study in Economic Fluctuations. p.245
The Dynamics of Conflict in Northern Ireland: Power, Conflict and Emancipation. p.607
The Dynamics of Conflict Resolution: A Practitioner's Guide. p.74
[e] The Dynamics of Deforestation and Economic Growth in the Brazilian Amazon. p.267
The Dynamics of Deterrence. p.657
Dynamics of Family Development: A Theoretical Perspective. p.735
Dynamics of International Relations. p.626
The Dynamics of Leadership: Theory and Practice. . p.546, p.698
Dynamics of Russian Politics: Putin's Federal-Regional Reforms. p.582, p.598

E

E. Franklin Frazier Reconsidered. p.683
E Pluribus Unum: The Formation of the American Republic, 1776-1790. . . . . p.517
E. W. Scripps and the Business of Newspapers. p.148
Eager to Learn: Educating Our Preschoolers. p.370
Eagle Rules?: Foreign Policy and American Primacy in the Twenty-First Century. p.641, p.642
Earl Warren: A Public Life. p.469
Earl Warren: The Judge Who Changed America. p.469
[e] Early Anthropology in the Sixteenth and Seventeenth Centuries. p.4
Early Childhood Curriculum: A Review of Current Research. p.369
Early Childhood Curriculum Resource Handbook. p.369
Early Childhood Education: Policy Issues for the 1990s. . p.369
The Early Economic Writings of Alfred Marshall, 1867-1890. . . . . p.224
Early Education in the Public Schools: Lessons from a Comprehensive Birth-to-Kindergarten Program. p.368
Early Essays on Social Philosophy. p.679
The Early French Explorers of North America. p.378
Early Human Behaviour in the Global Context: The Rise and Diversity of the Lower Paleolithic Period. p.17
Early Humans and Their World. p.16
Early Intervention: The Essential Readings. p.316
Early Literacy. p.360
The Early Origins of the Social Sciences. p.683

Early Protestant Educators. *p.339*
Early Reading Assessment: A Practitioner's Handbook. . . *p.361*
The Early Upper Paleolithic Beyond Western Europe. . *p.15, p.16*
Early-Modern England: A Social History, 1550-1760. . . *p.707*
Earning and Learning: How Schools Matter. *p.265*
The Earth, Student's Companion: An Introduction to its Physical and Human Geography. *p.374, p.376*
Earth's Dynamic Systems. *p.390*
The Earthscan Reader in Environment, Development and Rural Livelihoods. *p.268*
East London for Mosley: The Membership and Branches of the British Union of Fascists in East London and South-West Essex, 1933-40. . . . . *p.582*
Eastern Europe in Transformation: The Impact on Sociology. *p.683*
Eastern Europe, Russia and Central Asia 2005. . . . . . *p.396*
Eastern European Journalism: Before, During and after Communism. *p.403*
Eat the Rich: A Treatise on Economics. . . *p.185, p.196, p.251*
Eating Disorders: Anatomy of a Social Epidemic. *p.777*
E-Business Implementation: A Guide to Web Services, EAI, BPI, E-Commerce, Content Management, Portals, and Supporting Technologies. *p.113*
The Echo of War: Home Front Propaganda and the Wartime BBC 1939-1945. . . . . *p.413*
Ecological Golf Course Management. *p.788, p.872, p.881, p.886*
Ecology, Law and Economics: The Simple Analytics of Natural Resource and Environment Economics. *p.62*
The Ecology of Power: Culture, Place and Personhood in the Southern Amazon, AD 1000-2000. . . . . *p.11*
E-Commerce and the Digital Economy. *p.113*
Econometric Analysis of Cross Section and Panel Data. *p.205, p.206*
Econometric Analysis of Financial and Economic Time Series Part A. *p.200*
Econometric Analysis of Panel Data. *p.198, p.206*
The Econometric Analysis of Seasonal Time Series. . . . *p.200*
Econometric Analysis. *p.201*
Econometric Exploration and Diagnosis. *p.201*
Econometric Foundations. *p.203*
Econometric Methods and Applications. *p.203*
Econometric Methods with Applications in Business and Economics. *p.201*
Econometric Models and Economic Forecasts. . . *p.203, p.207*
Econometrics: A Modern Introduction. *p.203*
Econometrics: Alchemy or Science? *p.201*
Econometrics and Economic Theory: Essays in Honour of Jan Tinbergen. *p.204*
Econometrics and the Cost of Capital, Vol. 2. . . . . . . *p.202*
Econometrics and the Philosophy of Economics: Theory-Data Confrontations in Economics. *p.204*
Econometrics: Econometric Modeling of Producer Behavior. *p.207*
Econometrics: Economic Growth in the Information Age. . *p.202*
The Econometrics of Corporate Governance Studies. . . . *p.198*
The Econometrics of Financial Markets. *p.198*
The Econometrics of Macroeconomic Modelling. . *p.202, p.240*
Econometrics of Qualitative Dependent Variables. *p.200*
Econometrics. *p.201, p.205*
Economic Analysis and Policy in Underdeveloped Countries, 4.. . . . . *p.242*
Economic Analysis of Law. *p.442*
Economic and Financial Decisions under Risk. . . *p.207, p.263*
□ Economic and Housing Data. *p.159*
The Economic Borders of the State. *p.227*
Economic Development and Planning: Essays in Honour of Jan Tinbergen. *p.260*
The Economic Dimensions of Globalization. *p.664*
The Economic Doctrines of Karl Marx. *p.214*
Economic Dynamics and General Equilibrium: Time and Uncertainty. *p.206*
The Economic Emergence of Women. *p.273*
Economic Essays. *p.220*
Economic Freedom of the World, 2005. . . . . *p.189*
Economic Geography. *p.398*
Economic Growth and Resources: Proceedings of the Fifth World Congress of the International Economic Association held in Tokyo, Japan, 1977. . . . . *p.256*
Economic Growth and Social Equity in Developing Countries. *p.253, p.258*
Economic Heresies: Some Old-Fashioned Questions in Economic Theory. *p.185*
Economic History of World Trade. *p.57, p.147, p.180*
Economic Imperialism: A Book of Readings. *p.208*
Economic Integration and Development in Africa. *p.384*
An Economic Interpretation of the Constitution of the United States. *p.518*
The Economic Legacy of Robert Lucas, Jr. *p.233*
Economic Perspectives: Further Essays on Money and Growth. *p.209*
The Economic Philosophy of David Ricardo As a Textbook Which Far Surpasses Anything Employed in Our Schools Today. *p.220*
Economic Philosophy. *p.196*
Economic Policy: Principles and Design. *p.197*
Economic Politics: The Costs of Democracy. *p.214*
Economic Principles for Education: Theory and Evidence. . *p.297*
□ Economic Report of the President. *p.481*
Economic Report on Africa 2004: Unlocking Africa's Trade Potential. *p.664*
Economic Sociology of Capitalism. *p.215, p.271*
Economic Sociology. *p.718*
Economic Sophisms. *p.187*
Economic Theories of Peace and War. *p.268*
An Economic Theorist's Book of Tales: Essays That Entertain the Consequences of New Assumptions in Economic Theory. *p.194*
Economic Theory and Cognitive Science: Microexplanation. *p.272*
Economic Theory in Retrospect. *p.194, p.208*
An Economic Theory of Democracy. . . . *p.503, p.545, p.580*

Economic Thought since Keynes: A History and Dictionary of Major Economists. p.187, p.188, p.208
The Economic Writings of Sir William Petty. p.216
The Economical Table: An Attempt Toward Ascertaining and Exhibiting the Source, Progress and Employment of Riches. p.217
The Economical Table. p.217
Economics: An Awkward Corner. p.270
Economics, an Examination of Scarcity: Adam Smith's Micro to Current U. S. Macro. p.219
The Economics and Politics of Sports Facilities. p.881 p.885 p.889 p.892
Economics and Sociology: Conversations with Economists and Sociologists. p.271
Economics and the Art of Controversy. p.213
Economics as a Moral Science: The Political Economy of Adam Smith. p.220
Economics as Worldly Philosophy: Essays in Political and Historical Economics in Honour of Robert Heilbroner. p.208, p.240
Economics, Bounded Rationality and the Cognitive Revolution. p.250, p.272
Economics Essays: A Festschrift for Werner Heldenbrand. . p.201
Economics for Humans. p.196, p.270
Economics for the Common Good: Two Centuries of Social Economic Thought in the Humanistic Tradition. p.207, p.209
Economics from the Heart: A Samuelson Sampler. p.196
Economics in Practice: Six Lectures on Current Issues. . p.210
The Economics of Adam Smith. p.211, p.219
The Economics of Altruism. p.267
The Economics of Biotechnology. p.156
The Economics of Collective Action. p.208
Economics of College Sports. p.887, p.893
The Economics of Common Currencies. p.238
The Economics of Comparable Worth. p.253
The Economics of David Ricardo. p.212, p.220
The Economics of Discrimination. p.133, p.253
The Economics of Education: Human Capital, Family Background and Inequality. p.297
Economics of European Integration. p.638
The Economics of F. A. Hayek. p.234
The Economics of Francois Quesnay. p.217
The Economics of Health and Health Care. p.163
The Economics of Imperfect Competition. p.239
Economics of Imperfect Competition. p.252, p.270
Economics of Industry: 1879 Edition. p.224
The Economics of International Security: Essays in Honour of Jan Tinbergen. p.262
The Economics of Irving Fisher: Reviewing the Scientific Work of a Great Economist. p.200, p.225
The Economics of John Stuart Mill, Set. p.217, p.222
Economics of Marketing. p.134
The Economics of Natural and Environmental Resources. . p.268
The Economics of Natural Environments: Studies in the Valuation of Commodity and Amenity Resources. . . . p.62
The Economics of Professional Team Sports. p.883, p.896, p.899
The Economics of Recreation, Leisure and Tourism. p.785, p.889
Economics of Resources, Agriculture and Food. p.152, p.160, p.164
The Economics of Slavery, and Other Studies in Econometric History. p.208
Economics of Sport and Recreation. p.884, p.888
The Economics of Sport, Set. p.890
The Economics of Sports. p.888
Economics of Staging the Olympics: A Comparison of the Games 1972-2008. . . . . p.846, p.889
The Economics of Taxation. p.107
The Economics of the Family: Marriage, Children, and Human Capital. p.266
The Economics of the Trade Union. p.124
Economics of the U. S. Commercial Airline Industry: Productivity, Technology and Deregulation. p.152
The Economics of Time and Ignorance. p.270
The Economics of Under-Developed Countries. p.242
Economics of Vilfredo Pareto. p.195
The Economics of Welfare. p.252
The Economics of Women, Men, and Work. p.273
Economics: Principles and Policy, 2004 Update. p.187
Economics: The Basics. p.185
Economics Uncut: A Complete Guide to Life, Death and Misadventure. p.185
Economics. p.186, p.195
Economist Guide to the European Union. p.638
Economy and Society: A Study in the Integration of Economic and Social Theory, Vol. 26. . . . . p.270
Economy and Society. p.718
An Economy of Abundant Beauty: Fortune Magazine and Depression America. p.409
The Ecosystem Approach in Anthropology: From Concept to Practice. p.30
Ecstasy: The Complete Guide - A Comprehensive Look at the Risks and Benefits of MDMA. p.776
Ecstatic Religion: An Anthropological Study of Spirit Possession and Shamanism. p.36
Ecuador vs. Peru: Peacemaking Amid Rivalry. p.649
Ed Delahanty in the Emerald Age of Baseball. . . p.804, p.850
The Eden-Eisenhower Correspondence, 1955-1957. . . . p.560
EDGAR: SEC Filings & Forms. p.90, p.93
The Edge City: Life on the New Frontier. p.770
edHelper.com. p.346, p.349
EDSITEment. p.303, p.348
The Educated Mind: How Cognitive Tools Shape Our Understanding. p.339
Educating Children with Emotional and Behavioural Difficulties: Inclusive Practice in Mainstream Schools. p.319
Educating Children with Multiple Disabilities: A Collaborative Approach. p.318
Educating Deaf Students: From Research to Practice. . . p.318
Educating Exceptional Children. p.316

Educating for Freedom: The Paradox of Pedagogy. . . . *p.339*
Educating for Intelligent Belief or Unbelief. *p.307*
Educating Hearts and Minds: A Comprehensive Character Education Framework. *p.370*
Educating Hearts and Minds: Reflections on Japanese Preschool and Elementary Education. *p.364, p.370*
Educating Latino Students: A Guide to Successful Practice. *p.311*
Educating Minds and Hearts: Social Emotional Learning and the Passage into Adolescence: A Guide for Educators. *p.303, p.356, p.362*
Educating Moral People: A Caring Alternative to Character Education. *p.306*
Educating Professionals: Responding to New Expectations for Competence and Accountability. *p.295*
Educating Republicans: The College in the Era of the American Revolution, 1750-1800. . . . . *p.332*
Educating Students from Other Nations: American Colleges and Universities in International Educational Interchange. . *p.290*
Education and a Radical Humanism: Notes Toward a Theory of the Educational Crisis. *p.343*
Education and Citizenship in Liberal-Democratic Societies: Teaching for Cosmopolitan Values and Collective Identities. *p.323*
Education and Cultural Process: Anthropological Approaches. *p.29, p.303*
Education and Democracy: The Meaning of Alexander Meiklejohn, 1872-1964. . . . . *p.344*
Education and Democratic Citizenship in America. . *p.505, p.547*
Education and Ecstasy: With the Great School Reform Hoax. *p.327*
Education and Human Relations. *p.344*
Education and Identity in Rural France: The Politics of Schooling. *p.29*
Education and Income: Inequalities of Opportunity in Our Public Schools. *p.329*
Education and Jobs: The Great Training Robbery. *p.297*
Education and Mind in the Knowledge Age. *p.356*
Education and Nationalism: An Historical Interpretation of American Education. *p.298*
Education and Power. *p.300*
Education and Social Change: Themes in the History of American Schooling. *p.297, p.328, p.762*
Education and Social Mobility in the Soviet Union 1921-1934. . . . . *p.334*
Education and the Cult of Efficiency: A Study of the Social Forces That Have Shaped the Administration of the Public Schools. *p.325*
Education and the Good Life. *p.345*
Education and the Law: A Dictionary. *p.451*
Education and the Rise of the Global Economy. . . . *p.313*
Education and the Scottish People, 1750-1918. . . . . *p.333*
Education and the Social Order. *p.345*
Education and Training in a Knowledge Based Economy. . *p.297*
Education and Warfare in Europe. *p.333*
Education As Cultural Imperialism. *p.325*
Education, Assumptions vs. History: Collected Papers. . . *p.310*
Education at the Crossroads. *p.344*
Education Atlas: History of Education. *p.326*
Education Between Two Worlds. *p.344*
Education by Choice: The Case for Family Control. . . . *p.280*
Education East and West: The Influence of Mao Zedong and John Dewey. *p.344*
Education for Critical Consciousness. *p.300*
Education for Cultural Diversity: Convergence and Divergence. *p.309*
Education for Everyone: Agenda for Education in a Democracy. *p.326*
Education for Extinction: American Indians and the Boarding School Experience, 1875-1928. . . . . *p.311, p.763*
Education for Judgment: The Artistry of Discussion Leadership. *p.177*
Education for the Emerging Age. *p.341*
Education for the New Europe. *p.333*
Education for Transformation: Implications in Lewis Mumford's Ecohumanism. *p.341*
The Education Gap: Vouchers and Urban Schools. *p.298*
The Education Gospel: The Economic Power of Schooling. *p.305*
Education in a Divided World: The Function of the Public Schools in Our Unique Society. *p.325*
Education in Central America and the Caribbean. . . . *p.333*
Education in Contemporary Japan: Inequality and Diversity. *p.335*
Education in England and Wales. *p.334*
Education in Exile: SOMAFCO, the African National Congress School in Tanzania, 1978-1992. . . . . *p.335*
Education in the Forming of American Society: Needs and Opportunities for Study. *p.324*
Education in the Rural American Community: A Lifelong Process. *p.315*
Education in the West of England, 1066-1548. . . . . *p.336*
Education: Intellectual, Moral, and Physical. *p.345*
Education, Literacy, and Humanization: Exploring the Work of Paulo Freire. *p.345*
The Education of a Coach. *p.858, p.896*
The Education of Black Folk: The Afro-American Struggle for Knowledge in White America. *p.309*
Education on the Wild Side: Learning for the Twenty-First Century. *p.303*
Education Policy-Making in England and Wales: The Crucible Years, 1895-1911. . . . . *p.333*
Education, Religion, and the Common Good: Advancing a Distinctly American Conversation about Religion's Role in Our Shared Life. *p.307, p.486*
Education Resource Organizations Directory (EROD). . *p.323*
Education, Society, and Economic Opportunity: A Historical Perspective on Persistent Issues. *p.329*
Education Through Art. *p.345*
Education Today. *p.342*
Education, Training and the New Vocationalism: Experience and Policy. *p.353*
Education under Mao: Class and Competition in Canton Schools, 1960-1980. . . . . *p.337*

Education, Work and Social Capital: Towards a New Conception of Vocational Training. *p.306*
Educational Facilities. *p.288*
The Educational Imagination: On the Design and Education of School Programs. *p.362*
Educational Leadership: Policy Dimensions in the 21st Century, 1. . . . . *p.281*
Educational Media and Technology Yearbook: 2006. . . . *p.352*
Educational Philosophy: A History from the Ancient World to Modern America. *p.323, p.340*
Educational Psychology: A Century of Contributions: A Project of Division 15 (educational Psychology) of the American Psychological Society. *p.359*
Educational Psychology. *p.359*
Educational Reform: A Self Scrutinizing Memoir. *p.329*
Educational Reform in the Commonwealth Caribbean. . . *p.335*
Educational Renewal: Better Teachers, Better Schools. . . *p.279*
Educational Research, Methodology and Measurement: An International Handbook. *p.286, p.355*
Educational Roots and Routes in Western Europe. *p.333*
Educational Strategies among Muslims in the Context of Globalization: Some National Case Studies. *p.308*
Educational Technology: The Development of a Concept. . *p.351*
Educational Theory of Immanuel Kant. *p.343*
Educational Theory of Jean Jacques Rousseau. *p.341*
The Educational Thought and Influence of Matthew Arnold, Vol. 223. . . . . *p.341*
Educational Views of Benjamin Franklin. *p.342*
An Educational War on Poverty: American and British Policy-Making 1960-1980. . . . . *p.337*
Educational Wastelands: The Retreat from Learning in Our Public Schools. *p.340*
Educative Assessment: Designing Assessments to Inform and Improve Student Performance. *p.287*
The Educator's Desk Reference: (EDR) A Sourcebook of Educational Information and Research. *p.355*
Educator's Reference Desk. *p.338*
Edutopia: Success Stories for Learning in the Digital Age. . *p.351*
Edward S. Corwin's, Constitution and What It Means Today. *p.453*
Edward Sapir: Linguist, Anthropologist, Humanist. *p.4*
E-Economy: Rhetoric or Business Reality? *p.263*
EEO Law and Personnel Practices. *p.131*
The E-Factor: Turning Environmental Responsibility into Good, Green Profits. *p.63*
Effective and Responsible Teaching: The New Synthesis. . *p.348*
The Effective Board of Trustees. *p.293*
Effective Consultancies in Development and Humanitarian Programmes: A Practical Guide. *p.65*
The Effective Executive: The Definitive Guide to Getting the Right Things Done. *p.72*
Effective Leadership in Adventure Programming. *p.788*
Effective Legal Research. *p.439*
Effective Partnering for School Change: Improving Early Childhood Education in Urban Classrooms. *p.368*
The Effective Presentation: Talk Your Way to Success. . . *p.423*
Effective Public Relations. *p.172*
The Effects of Violence on Peace Processes. *p.648*
The Efficient Secret: The Cabinet and the Development of Political Parties in Victorian England. *p.604*
Effort and Excellence in Urban Classrooms: Expecting, and Getting, Success with All Students. *p.314*
Efforts to Improve the Quality of Vocational Education in Secondary Schools: Impact of Federal and State Policies. *p.305*
E-Government 2003. . . . . *p.546*
Egyptian Politics: The Dynamics of Authoritarian Rule. *p.500, p.611*
EH.Net Encyclopedia of Economic and Business History. *p.146, p.179*
Eight Men Out: The Black Sox and the 1919 World Series. . *p.849*
Eighteenth Century Economics. *p.215*
Eighty Exemplary Ethics Statements. *p.173*
The Eisenhower Court and Civil Liberties. *p.540*
E-Learning: Technology and the Development of Learning and Teaching. *p.352*
Electing Justice: Fixing the Supreme Court Nomination Process. *p.536*
The Election of 2000: Reports and Interpretations. *p.531*
Elections and Conflict Management in Africa. . . *p.578, p.613*
Elections and Democratization in Ukraine. . *p.577, p.584, p.597*
Elections and Voters: A Comparative Introduction. *p.577*
Elections and Voters in Post-Communist Russia. . *p.578, p.599*
Elections and War: The Electoral Incentive in the Democratic Politics of War and Peace. *p.504*
Elections as Instruments of Democracy: Majoritarian and Proportional Visions. *p.577*
Elections in Africa: A Data Handbook. *p.612*
The Elections in Israel 1992. . . . . *p.615*
Elections in the French Revolution: An Apprenticeship in Democracy, 1789-1799. . . . . *p.608*
Elections Without Order: Russia's Challenge to Vladimir Putin. *p.578, p.599*
Elections. *p.586*
Electoral Engineering: Voting Rules and Political Behavior. *p.577*
Electoral Laws and Their Political Consequences. . . *p.576*
Electoral Realignments: A Critique of an American Genre. . *p.551*
The Electoral System in Britain. *p.606*
Electoral Systems: A Theoretical and Comparative Introduction. *p.577*
The Electorate, the Campaign, and the Office: A Unified Approach to Senate and House Elections. *p.533*
Electronic Communication Systems. *p.422*
Electronic Learning Communities: Issues and Practices. . *p.322*
The Electronic Media and the Transformation of Law. . . *p.445*
Elementary Bayesian Statistics. *p.197*
Elementary Education: A Reference Handbook. *p.363*
Elementary Lessons in Logic: Deductive and Inductive. . *p.231*
Elementary Principles of Economics. *p.195, p.199*
Elementary School Objectives: A Report Prepared for the Mid. *p.364*

Elementary School Science and How to Teach It. *p.362*

Elementary Surveying: An Introduction to Geomatics. . . *p.389*

Elementary Teacher's Discipline Problem Solver: A Practical A-Z Guide for Managing Classroom Behavior Problems. *p.284*

Elements of Econometrics.. . . . . *p.202*

Elements of Economics of Industry. *p.224*

The Elements of Learning.. . . . . *p.356*

Elements of Pure Economics, or the Theory of Social Wealth.. *p.213, p.217*

The Elements of Teaching. *p.346*

Elephant: The Animal and Its Ivory in African Culture. *p.707, p.710*

The Eleventh Amendment and Sovereign Immunity. . . . *p.443*

The Eleventh Plague: The Politics of Biological and Chemical Warfare. *p.655*

The Elgar Companion to Classical Economics, Set. . . . *p.218*

The Elgar Companion to Law and Economics. *p.187*

The Elgar Companion to Post Keynesian Economics. . . *p.232*

The Elgar Dictionary of Economic Quotations. *p.191*

Elite Accommodation in Canadian Politics. *p.591*

Elite Discourse and Racism. *p.731*

Elite MBA Programs at Public Universities: How a Dozen Innovative Schools Are Redefining Business Education.. . . . . *p.177*

The Elite of the Elite: Permanent Secretaries in the British Higher Civil Service.. . . . . *p.605*

Elkouri and Elkouri: How Arbitration Works. *p.447*

The Elusive Quest for Growth: Economists' Adventures and Misadventures in the Tropics. *p.243*

An Elusive Science: The Troubling History of Education Research. *p.355*

Elusive Stability: Essays in the History of International Finance, 1919-1939. *p.255*

The Emancipatory Promise of Charter Schools: Toward a Progressive Politics of School Choice. *p.281*

Embattled Reason: Essays on Social Knowledge, Vol. 2. . *p.682*

Embattled Reason, Vol. 1. . . . . *p.682*

The Embedded Corporation: Corporate Governance and Employment Relations in Japan and the United States. . *p.86*

Embodying Morality: Growing up in Rural Northern Vietnam. *p.772*

Embrace Tiger, Return to Mountain: The Essence of Tai Ji. . *p.793*

Embracing Cyprus: The Path to Unity in the New Europe.. *p.637*

Emergence of a Free Press. *p.459*

☐ Emergence of Advertising in America: 1850-1920. . . *p.426*

The Emergence of Agriculture. *p.6*

The Emergence of Liberation Theology: Radical Religion and Social Movement Theory. *p.721*

The Emergence of Private Authority in Global Governance. *p.663*

The Emergence of State Government: Parties and New Jersey Politics, 1950-1999. . . . . *p.552, p.554*

The Emergence of the American University. *p.333*

Emergent Issues in Education: Comparative Perspectives.. *p.313*

Emerging Complexity: The Later Prehistory of South-East Spain, Iberia and the West Mediterranean. *p.12*

Emics and Etics: The Insider/Outsider Debate. *p.18*

Emil W. Haury's Prehistory of the American Southwest. . . *p.11*

Emile Durkheim: Ethics and the Sociology of Morals. . . *p.681*

Emile Durkheim on the Family. *p.681*

Emile Durkheim: Selected Writings. *p.684*

Emile Durkheim. *p.685*

Emily Post's the Etiquette Advantage in Business: Personal Skills for Professional Success. *p.57, p.174*

Emissions Trading: Principles and Practice. *p.63*

Emma Goldman: A Documentary History of the American Years. *p.506, p.553*

Emmeline Pankhurst. *p.604*

Emotional Branding: The New Paradigm for Connecting Brands to People. *p.142*

Emotional Decisions: Trade off Difficulty and Coping in Consumer Choice. *p.203*

The Emotional Development of Young Children: Building an Emotion-Centered Curriculum. *p.369*

Emotions and Social Movements. *p.694*

Emotions in Finance: Distrust and Uncertainty in Global Markets. *p.250, p.261*

Emotions in Sport. *p.877*

Emotions, Stress, and Health. *p.699*

Emperor and Aristocracy in Japan, 1467-1680: Resilience and Renewal. *p.726*

The Emperor's New Clothes: Biological Theories of Race at the Millennium. *p.17*

Empire and Commonwealth. *p.587, p.605*

Empire and Order: The Concept of Empire, 800-1800. . . *p.501*

Empire by Integration: The United States and European Integration, 1945-1997. . . . . *p.638, p.642*

Empire of Conspiracy: The Culture of Paranoia in Postwar America. *p.709*

Empire of Debt: The Rise of an Epic Financial Crisis. *p.246, p.267*

Empires of the Monsoon. *p.378*

ⓔ Empirical Modeling in Economics: Specification and Evaluation. *p.201, p.207*

Empirical Modeling in Economics: Specification and Evaluation. *p.200, p.207*

An Empirically-Based Microeconomics. *p.248*

The Employee Recruitment and Retention Handbook. . . . *p.75*

Employer's Guide to Workplace Privacy. *p.131*

Employment and Equilibrium: A Theoretical Discussion. . *p.210*

Employment, Disability, and the Americans with Disabilities Act: Issues in Law, Public Policy, and Research. . . . *p.446*

Employment Discrimination Law. *p.134*

Employment Dispute Resolution and Worker Rights in the Changing Workplace. *p.121*

Employment Relations in France: Evolution and Innovation. *p.122*

Employment Relations in Non-Union Firms. *p.121*

Employment Relations in the Asia Pacific: Changing Approaches. *p.120*

Employment Relations in the United States: Law, Policy, and Practice. *p.109, p.122, p.126*

Empowering Ourselves and Transforming Schools: Educators Making a Difference. *p.283*

The E-Myth Revisited. *p.67*

Enabling Knowledge Creation: How to Unlock the Mystery of Tacit Knowledge and Release the Power of Innovation. . *p.79*

Encountering Children's Literature: An Arts Approach. . . *p.360*

Encounters with Nationalism. *p.494*

Encyclopedia of Aging. *p.751*

Encyclopedia of American Economic History, Set. *p.567*

Encyclopedia of American Education, Set. *p.340*

Encyclopedia of American Foreign Policy, Set. . . *p.561, p.628*

Encyclopedia of American Indian Civil Rights. *p.465*

Encyclopedia of American Industries. . . . *p.148, p.150, p.179*

Encyclopedia of American Parties, Campaigns and Elections. *p.547*

The Encyclopedia of American Political History. *p.485*

The Encyclopedia of American Prisons. *p.678*

The Encyclopedia of American Soccer History. *p.867*

Encyclopedia of American Social History, Set. *p.677*

Encyclopedia of American Social Movements. *p.678*

Encyclopedia of American Women in Business: From Colonial Times to the Present [Two Volumes], Vol. 2. . . . . . *p.57*

Encyclopedia of Anthropology. *p.3*

Encyclopedia of Archaeology: History and Discoveries. . . *p.5*

Encyclopedia of Arms Control and Disarmament, Set. . . *p.655*

Encyclopedia of British Football. *p.867*

Encyclopedia of Business Information Sources. *p.181*

The Encyclopedia of Business Letters, Fax Memos, and E-Mail. *p.172*

Encyclopedia of Communication and Information. *p.423*

Encyclopedia of Conflicts since World War II. *p.485*

Encyclopedia of Constitutional Amendments: Proposed Amendments, and Amending Issues, 1789-2002. . . . *p.454*

Encyclopedia of Consumer Brands. *p.142*

Encyclopedia of Crime and Justice, Set. *p.677, p.752*

Encyclopedia of Criminology and Deviant Behaviour, Set. . *p.676*

Encyclopedia of Criminology. *p.678*

Encyclopedia of Democratic Thought. *p.482, p.503*

Encyclopedia of Distance Learning, Vol. 1. . . . . *p.321*

Encyclopedia of Distributed Learning. *p.321*

Encyclopedia of Drugs, Alcohol and Addictive Behavior, Set. *p.678, p.777*

Encyclopedia of Early Childhood Education, Set. *p.369*

The Encyclopedia of Ecotourism. *p.161*

Encyclopedia of Educational Research. *p.338, p.354*

The Encyclopedia of Education. *p.322*

Encyclopedia of European Social History: From 1350 to 2000, Set. *p.699, p.707*

Encyclopedia of Exploration: The Explorers. *p.379*

The Encyclopedia of Figure Skating. *p.866*

Encyclopedia of Forensic Sciences, Set. *p.678*

Encyclopedia of Genocide and Crimes Against Humanity. . *p.653*

Encyclopedia of Geomorphology. *p.391*

Encyclopedia of Global Environmental Change, Causes and Consequences of Global Environmental Change, Vol. 3. . . . . *p.677*

Encyclopedia of Global Environmental Change, Social and Economic Dimensions of Global Environmental Change, Vol. 5. . . . . *p.375, p.678*

Encyclopedia of Global Industries. *p.150*

The Encyclopedia of Global Population and Demographics, Two-Vol. Set. *p.678*

Encyclopedia of Government and Politics, Set. *p.482*

Encyclopedia of Gun Control and Gun Rights. *p.449*

Encyclopedia of Historical Treaties and Alliances. *p.476*

The Encyclopedia of HIV and AIDS. *p.669*

Encyclopedia of Homelessness. *p.678*

Encyclopedia of Human Geography. *p.396*

Encyclopedia of Human Rights Issues since 1945. . . . . *p.513*

Encyclopedia of Immigration and Migration in the American West. *p.570*

Encyclopedia of International Development. . . . *p.192, p.373*

The Encyclopedia of International Games. *p.843*

Encyclopedia of International Media and Communications, Set. *p.415*

Encyclopedia of International Relations and Global Politics. *p.626*

Encyclopedia of International Sports Studies. *p.812*

An Encyclopedia of Keynesian Economics. *p.192*

Encyclopedia of Latin American Politics. *p.592*

The Encyclopedia of Learning Disabilities. *p.319*

Encyclopedia of Leisure and Outdoor Recreation. *p.784, p.787, p.823*

An Encyclopedia of Macroeconomics. *p.192, p.193*

Encyclopedia of Media and Politics in America. *p.559*

Encyclopedia of Medical Anthropology: Health and Illness in the World's Cultures. *p.46*

Encyclopedia of Minorities in American Politics, Set. . . *p.573*

Encyclopedia of Modern Separatist Movements. *p.628*

Encyclopedia of Nationalism, Set. *p.494*

The Encyclopedia of Native American Economic History. . *p.192*

The Encyclopedia of Native American Legal Tradition. . *p.464*

Encyclopedia of New Media: An Essential Reference Guide to Communication and Technology. *p.419*

Encyclopedia of Operations Research and Management Science: Centennial Edition. *p.119*

Encyclopedia of Police Science. *p.676*

Encyclopedia of Political Economy. *p.192*

The Encyclopedia of Political Revolutions. *p.486*

The Encyclopedia of Precolonial Africa: Archaeology, History, Languages, Cultures and Environments. *p.8*

Encyclopedia of Presidential Campaigns, Slogans, Issues, and Platforms. *p.556*

Encyclopedia of Public Choice. *p.192*

Encyclopedia of Public Relations. *p.428*

Encyclopedia of Radio, Set. *p.413*

Encyclopedia of Recreation and Leisure in America. *p.783, p.823*

Encyclopedia of Religion and Society. *p.678, p.720*

Encyclopedia of Religion in American Politics. . . *p.487, p.560*
Encyclopedia of Small Business. *p.88*
Encyclopedia of Social and Cultural Anthropology. *p.3*
Encyclopedia of Social Measurement, Set. *p.677*
Encyclopedia of Social Theory. *p.678, p.680*
Encyclopedia of Social Welfare History in North America. . *p.754*
Encyclopedia of Social Work, 1997 Supplement. *p.677*
Encyclopedia of Social Work: Supplement 2003. . . . . *p.677*
Encyclopedia of Social Work. *p.677*
Encyclopedia of Sociology, Set. *p.676*
Encyclopedia of Special Education: A Reference for the Education of the Handicapped and Other Exceptional Children and Adults. *p.316*
The Encyclopedia of Sports Medicine. *p.825*
Encyclopedia of Student and Youth Movements. *p.325*
The Encyclopedia of Suicide. *p.677*
[e] Encyclopedia of Support Services and Distance Education. *p.321*
The Encyclopedia of Surfing. *p.788, p.868*
The Encyclopedia of Taxation and Tax Policy. *p.107*
Encyclopedia of Television. *p.415, p.418*
Encyclopedia of Terrorism. *p.678*
Encyclopedia of the American Constitution, Set. *p.454*
Encyclopedia of the American Judicial System: Studies of the Principal Institutions, Set. *p.437*
Encyclopedia of the American Legislative System, Set. . *p.575*
Encyclopedia of the Confederacy, Set. *p.520*
Encyclopedia of the Documentary Film. *p.413*
Encyclopedia of the European Union. *p.602, p.637*
Encyclopedia of the Global Economy: A Guide for Students and Researchers. *p.192*
Encyclopedia of the North American Colonies, Set. . . . *p.517*
The Encyclopedia of the Supreme Court. *p.539*
Encyclopedia of the U. S. Census. *p.676*
Encyclopedia of the United Nations: And International Agreements, Set. *p.635*
Encyclopedia of the United Nations. *p.634*
Encyclopedia of Tourism. *p.161*
Encyclopedia of U. S. Foreign Relations, Set. *p.628*
Encyclopedia of Violence, Peace and Conflict, Set. . . . *p.679*
Encyclopedia of Wireless Telecommunications. *p.419*
Encyclopedia of Women and Gender: Sex Similarities and Differences and the Impact of Society on Gender, Vol. 1. . . . . *p.679*
Encyclopedia of Women and Gender: Sex Similarities and Differences and the Impact of Society on Gender, Vol. 2. . . . . *p.679*
Encyclopedia of Women in American Politics. *p.569*
Encyclopedia of World Terrorism, 1996-2002 and Encyclopedia of World Terrorism, Documents, Set. *p.661*
Encyclopedic Dictionary of Semiotics, Media and Communication. *p.423*
The End of Baseball As We Knew It: The Players Union, 1960-81. . . . . *p.851, p.888, p.891*
The End of Capitalism (As We Knew It): A Feminist Critique of Political Economy. *p.273*
The End of Democracy?: The Judicial Usurpation of Politics. *p.525*
The End of Education: Redefining the Value of Schools. . *p.323*
The End of Empire: Dependencies since 1948: The West Indies, British Honduras, Hong Kong, Fiji, Cyprus, Gibraltar and the Falklands Select Documents on the Constitutional History of the British Empire and Commonwealth. . . *p.435*
The End of Empire in French West Africa: France's Successful Decolonization? *p.584*
The End of Empire?: The Transformation of the U.S.S.R. in Comparative Perspective. *p.508*
The End of Globalization: Lessons from the Great Depression. *p.664*
The End of Ideology: On the Exhaustion of Political Ideas in the Fifties, with the Resumption of History in the New Century. *p.701*
The End of Laissez-Faire: National Purpose and the Global Economy after the Cold War. *p.665*
The End of Obscenity: The Trials of Lady Chatterley, Tropic of Cancer and Fanny Hill. *p.472*
The End of Poverty: Economic Possibilities for Our Time. . *p.266*
The End of Realignment?: Interpreting American Electoral Eras. *p.548, p.552*
The End of the American Era: U. S. Foreign Policy and the Geopolitics of the Twenty-First Century. *p.642*
The End of the Cold War: Its Meaning and Implications. . *p.486*
The End of the Keynesian Era. *p.229*
End of the Line: The Rise and Coming Fall of the Global Corporation. *p.665*
The End of the Old Order in Rural Europe. *p.701*
The End of the Peace Process: Oslo and After. . . *p.630, p.650*
Endangered Self: Identity and Social Risk. *p.779*
Endangered Spaces, Enduring Places: Change, Identity, and Survival in Rural America. *p.702*
The Endangered Species Act: History, Conservation Biology and Public Policy. *p.463*
Endangered Species: Health, Illness, and Death among Madagascar's People of the Forest. *p.46*
Ending Hunger in Our Lifetime: Food Security and Globalization. *p.665*
Ending the Cold War at Home: From Militarism to a More Peaceful World Order. *p.561*
The Endocrine System in Sports and Exercise, Vol. XI. *p.826, p.875*
Endorsements in Advertising: A Social History. . . *p.140, p.141*
Ends and Means: An Inquiry into the Nature of Ideals and into the Methods Employed for Their Realization. *p.750*
Endurance in Sport. *p.826, p.875, p.880*
Endurance Sports Nutrition: Eating Plans for Optimal Training, Racing and Recovery. *p.825, p.876*
The Enduring Memory: Time and History in a French Village. *p.708*
Enemies of Civilization: Attitudes Toward Foreigners in Ancient Mesopotamia, Egypt, and China. *p.644*
Enemies of Freedom: Understanding Right-Wing Authoritarianism. *p.767*
Enemy Aliens: Double Standards and Constitutional Freedoms in the War on Terrorism. *p.460*

Energy and Security: Toward a New Foreign Policy Strategy. p.62
Energy at the Crossroads: Global Perspectives and Uncertainties. p.667
Enforced Disarmament: From the Napoleonic Campaigns to the Gulf War. p.657
Engaged in Reading: Processes, Practices and Policy Implications. p.354
Engaging All Families: Creating a Positive School Culture by Putting Research into Practice. p.303
Engaging India: Diplomacy, Democracy, and the Bomb. p.644, p.646
Engaging Young Children in Mathematics: Standards for Pre-School and Kindergarten Mathematics Education. . p.360
Engaging Young Readers: Promoting Achievement and Motivation. p.363
Engels after Marx. p.509
Engels on Capital: Synopsis, Reviews, and Supplementary Material. p.207
Engendering Economics: Conversations with Women Economists in the United States. p.185, p.274
Engineering and Product Development Management: The Holistic Approach. p.118
The Engineers and the Price System. p.214, p.250
England in the Eighteen-Eighties: Toward a Social Basis for Freedom. p.704
England's Treasure by Forraign Trade. p.216
The English Common People: A Social History from the Norman Conquest to the Present. p.703
The English Constitution. p.604
English Historical Economics, 1870-1926: The Rise of Economic History and Neo-Mercantilism. . . . p.212, p.215
English Landed Society in the Eighteenth Century. . . . p.705
English with an Accent. p.21
The Enigma of Felix Frankfurter. p.467
The Enigma of Japanese Power: People and Politics in a Stateless Nation. p.622
The Enlargement of the European Union and NATO: Ordering from the Menu in Central Europe. . . . p.585, p.603, p.637
Enlarging NATO: The National Debates. p.630, p.639
Enlightened Power: How Women Are Transforming the Practice of Leadership. p.70
Enlightenment Geography: The Political Languages of British Geography, 1650-1850. . . . . p.375
Ensuring Inequality: The Structural Transformation of the African American Family. p.729
Entangled Edens: Visions of the Amazon. p.707
Enterprise and American Law, 1836-1937. . . . . p.444
Enterprise Knowledge Portals: Next Generation Portal Solutions for Dynamic Information Access, Better Decision Making and Maximum Results. p.77
Enterprise Unionism in Japan. p.126
Entitlement Politics: Medicare and Medicaid, 1995-2001. . p.756
Entrepreneurial Mindset: Strategies for Continuously Creating Opportunity in an Age of Uncertainty. p.68
The Entrepreneurial Shift: Americanization in European High-Technology Management Education. p.176
The Entrepreneur's Guide to Business Law. p.67, p.108
Entrepreneurship and Small Business. p.87
Entrepreneurship, Geography, and American Economic Growth. p.381
Entrepreneurship, the New Economy and Public Policy: Schumpeterian Perspectives. p.230, p.234
Entrepreneurship. p.67
Environment and the City. p.395
Environment As a Focus for Public Policy. p.566
The Environment As Hazard. p.395
Environment, Subsistence and System: The Ecology of Small-Scale Social Formations. p.29
Environmental Biogeography. p.394
The Environmental Debate: A Documentary History. . . . p.566
Environmental Disasters in Global Perspective. p.760
Environmental Hazards: Assessing Risk and Reducing Disaster. p.395
Environmental Injustice in the U. S.: Myth and Realities. . p.566
Environmental Management and Decision Making for Business. p.62, p.64
Environmental Marketing: Positive Strategies for Reaching the Green Consumer. p.63
Environmental Policy in the European Union. p.602
Environmental Policy-Making in Britain, Germany and the European Union: The Europeanisation of Air and Water Pollution Control. p.604
Environmental Regulation in the New Global Economy: The Impact on Industry and Competitiveness. p.267
Environmental Remote Sensing. p.389
Environmental Values in American Culture. p.30
Environmentalism and Cultural Theory: Exploring the Role of Anthropology in Environmental Discourse. p.30
Environmentalism and the New Logic of Business: How Firms Can Be Profitable and Leave Our Children a Living Planet. p.61, p.63
Envisioning Human Geographies. p.396
Envisioning Power: Ideologies of Dominance and Crisis. . p.25
Epidemiology of Sports Injuries. p.827
Epistemological Problems of Economics. p.212
[e] An Eponymous Dictionary of Economics: A Guide to Laws and Theorems Named after Economists. p.192
Equal Educational Opportunity for Blacks in U. S. Higher Education: An Assessment. p.310
Equal Justice in the Balance: America's Legal Responses to the Emerging Terrorist Threat. p.564
Equal Pay in the Office. p.253
Equality and Partiality. p.514
Equality by Statute. p.456
Equality of Educational Opportunity. p.301
The Equality of the Human Races: Positivist Anthropology. . p.17
Equilibrium and Disequilibrium: From Adam Smith to Robert Lucas. p.214
Equity and Science Education Reform. p.367
The Equity Culture: The Story of the Global Stock Market. p.97, p.102, p.162

Erect Men/Undulating Women: The Visual Imagery of Gender, "Race" and Progress in Reconstructive Illustrations of Human Evolution. *p.31*

ERIC (Education Resources Information Center). . . . *p.322*

Ernst and Young's Personal Financial Planning Guide. . . *p.94*

Eroding Military Influence in Brazil: Politicians Against Soldiers. *p.592*

The Erotic History of Advertising. *p.426*

Escape Attempts: The Struggle of Resistance in Everyday Life. *p.774*

Escape from Freedom. *p.768*

Escape from Violence: Conflict and the Refugee Crisis in the Developing World. *p.765*

The Eskimos and Aleuts. *p.10*

ESPN: The Uncensored History. *p.805, p.902*

The ESRI Guide to GIS Analysis: Geographic Patterns and Relationships. *p.387*

The ESRI Guide to GIS Analysis: Spatial Measurements and Statistics. *p.388*

An Essay Concerning Human Understanding, Set. *p.216*

An Essay Concerning Human Understanding. *p.195*

An Essay on Economic Growth and Planning. *p.243*

An Essay on Marxian Economics. *p.236, p.241, p.270*

An Essay on the Principle of Population, or a View of Its Past and Present Effects on Human Happiness: With an Inquiry into Our Prospects Respecting the Future Removal or Mitigation of the Evils Which it Occasions. *p.222*

An Essay on the Principle of Population. . *p.221, p.222, p.763*

Essays and Lectures on Social and Political Subjects. *p.209, p.269*

Essays in Biography, Vol. 10. . . . . *p.193*

Essays in Development Economic: Dependence and Interdependence. *p.243*

Essays in Developmental Economics: Wealth and Poverty. . *p.243*

Essays in Econometrics: Collected Papers of Clive W. J. Granger. *p.200*

Essays in Economic Sociology. *p.681*

Essays in Economics: Consumption and Econometrics. . . *p.205*

Essays in Economics: Macroeconomics. *p.239*

Essays in Economics: National and International. *p.239*

Essays in Economics: Theory and Policy. *p.239*

Essays in International Economic Theory: The International Factor Mobility. *p.255*

Essays in International Economic Theory: The Theory of Commercial Policy. *p.255*

Essays in Our Changing Order: A Posthumous Collection of Papers from Periodicals. *p.251*

Essays in Our Changing Order. *p.197*

Essays in Panel Data Econometrics. *p.203*

Essays in Persuasion. *p.228*

Essays in Positive Economics. *p.231*

Essays in Socio-Economics. *p.269*

Essays in Sociological Theory. *p.680*

Essays in the History of Economics. *p.210, p.223*

Essays in the History of Linguistic Anthropology. *p.18*

Essays in the Theory of Economic Fluctuations. *p.244*

Essays in the Theory of Economic Growth. *p.260*

Essays in the Theory of Employment. *p.253, p.270*

Essays in the Theory of Society. *p.679*

The Essays of Warren Buffett: Lessons for Corporate America. *p.94*

Essays on Adam Smith. *p.219*

Essays on Developing Economies. *p.259, p.269*

Essays on Economic Policy. *p.244*

Essays on Mankind and Political Arithmetic. *p.254*

Essays on Philosophical Subjects, with Dugald Stewart's Account of Adam Smith. *p.220*

Essays on Political Economy. *p.208*

Essays on Sociology and Social Psychology. *p.692*

Essays on Some Unsettled Questions of Political Economy. *p.222*

Essays on the Great Depression. *p.213*

Essays on the Making of the Constitution. *p.452*

Essays on the Nature of Commerce in General. *p.215*

Essays on the Sociology of Knowledge. *p.762*

Essays, reviews, and reports; previously uncollected writings. *p.212*

The Essential Alfred Chandler: Essays Toward a Historical Theory of Big Business. *p.147, p.148*

The Essential Conversation: What Parents and Teachers Can Learn from Each Other. *p.353*

The Essential Frankfurt School Reader. *p.699*

The Essential Gunnar Myrdal. *p.269*

The Essential Montessori: An Introduction to the Woman, the Writings, the Method and the Movement. *p.343*

Essential Quantitative Methods for Business, Management and Finance.. . . . . *p.179*

Essential Readings in World Politics. *p.625*

The Essential Wallerstein. *p.759*

Essentials of Athletic Injury Management. . *p.827, p.828, p.829*

Essentials of Balanced Scorecard. *p.82*

Essentials of Econometrics. *p.201*

Essentials of Economic Theory as Applied to Modern Problems of Industry and Public Policy. *p.208, p.223*

Essentials of Economics. *p.194*

Essentials of International Management: A Cross-Cultural Perspective. *p.70*

Essentials of Lean Six Sigma. *p.117*

Essentials of Mass Communication Theory. *p.422*

Essentials of Mass Communication Theory. *p.416*

Essentials of Modern Research Methods in Health, Physical Education and Recreation. *p.795*

Essentials of Modern Telecommunications Systems. . . . *p.115*

Essentials of Production and Operations Management. . . *p.119*

Essentials of Sports Law. *p.449, p.901*

Esteemed Colleagues: Civility and Deliberation in the U. S. Senate. *p.534*

Estimation and Inference in Econometrics. *p.199*

Estuaries: A Physical Introduction. *p.391*

Estuaries, Vol. 5, Pts. H. *p.393*

Estuarine Shores: Evolution, Environments, and Human Alterations. p.392
E-Supply Chain Management: Foundations for Maximizing Technology and Achieving Breakthrough Performance. . p.118
ETA and Basque Nationalism: The Fight for Euskadi, 1890-1986. . . . . p.608
The Eternally Wounded Woman: Women, Exercise, and Doctors in the Late Nineteenth Century. p.810, p.838
Ethcaste: PanAfrican Communalism and the Black Middleclass. p.724
Ethical Decisions in Sport: Interscholastic, Intercollegiate, Olympic and Professional. . . . p.797, p.803, p.822, p.840
Ethical Dilemmas in Social Service: A Guide for Social Workers. p.758
Ethical Dimensions of Diversity, Vol. 5. . . . . p.132
The Ethical Imperative: Why Moral Leadership Is Good Business. p.70
Ethical Journalism: A Guide for Students, Practitioners and Consumers. p.405
Ethical Standards of the American Educational Research Association: Cases and Commentary. p.354
Ethical Systems and Legal Ideals: An Essay on the Foundations of Legal Criticism. p.433
Ethics and College Sports: Ethics, Sports, and the University. p.715, p.802, p.821, p.893
Ethics and Morality in Sport Management. . p.786, p.883, p.900
Ethics at Work: Basic Readings in Business Ethics. . p.54, p.55
Ethics in International Affairs: Theories and Cases. . p.484, p.627
Ethics in Marketing. p.146
Ethics in Media Communications: Cases and Controversies. p.417
The Ethics of Destruction: Norms and Force in International Relations. p.484
The Ethics of Identity. p.693
Ethics, the Heart of Leadership. p.697
Ethiopia since the DERG: A Decade of Democratic Pretension and Performance. p.612
Ethnic Nationalism and State Power: The Rise of Irish Nationalism, Afrikaner Nationalism and Zionism. . . . p.495
The Ethnic Phenomenon. p.729
Ethnic Stratification: A Comparative Approach. p.725
Ethnicity and Nationalism: Anthropological Perspectives. . p.34
Ethnicity and Sport in North American History and Culture. p.805, p.830
Ethnicity. p.731
Ethnobiological Classification: Principles of Categorization of Plants and Animals in Traditional Societies. p.26
Ethnocultural Factors in Substance Abuse Treatment. . . p.777
The Ethnographer's Magic: And Other Essays in the History of Anthropology. p.5
Ethnographic Presents: Pioneering Anthropologists in the Papua New Guinea Highlands. p.4
Ethnography for Marketers : A Guide to Consumer Immersion. p.139
Ethnography, Linguistics, Narrative Inequality: Toward an Understanding of Voice. p.19
The Ethnography of Communication: An Introduction. . . p.19
The Ethnography of Reading. p.22
Ethnomethodology's Program: Working Out Durkheim's Aphorism. p.688
Ethnomusicology: A Contemporary Reader. p.26
Ethnonational Identities. p.767
Ethnonationalism: The Quest for Understanding. p.494
Ethnosyntax: Explorations in Grammar and Culture. . . . p.20
▢ ETS. p.286
▢ EU at a Glance. p.636
▢ EurLex. p.474
Euro on Trial: To Reform or Split Up? p.636
▢ Eurobarometer. p.637
Eurojargon: A Dictionary of the European Union. . p.603, p.638
▢ Europa: Gateway to the European Union. . . . p.482, p.603
Europa World Year Book 2005. . . . . p.601
▢ Europa—Gateway to the European Union. p.637
Europe: A Concise Encyclopedia of the European Union from Aachen to Zollverein. p.603, p.637
Europe and the People Without History. p.35
▢ Europe in Figures—Eurostat Yearbook 2005. . p.601, p.636
Europe in the 18th Century: Aristocracy and the Bourgeois Challenge. p.706
Europe in the Era of Two World Wars: From Militarism and Genocide to Civil Society, 1900-1950. . . . . p.497
Europe in the Neolithic: The Creation of New Worlds. . . p.13
Europe Unites: The E. U.'s Eastern Enlargement. p.638
Europe Without Borders: Remapping Territory, Citizenship, and Identity in a Transnational Age. p.383
European Approaches to International Relations Theory: A House with Many Mansions. p.626
European Armies and the Conduct of War. p.627, p.647
The European Automobile Industry. p.154
European Banks and the American Challenge: Competition and Cooperation in International Banking Under Bretton Woods. p.88
European Community Integration: From Community to Unity. p.603
European Constitutionalism Beyond the State. p.639
European Dimensions: Education, Training and the European Union. p.334
European Economic History: From Mercantilism to Maastricht and Beyond. p.211, p.215
The European Family. p.32
European Iron Age. p.12
The European Mosaic: Contemporary Politics, Economics, and Culture. p.383
European Perspectives on Exercise and Sport Psychology. p.812, p.876
European Political Facts, 1648-1789. . . . . p.601
European Political Facts of the 20th Century. p.601
The European Ritual: Football in the New Europe. p.817, p.844, p.867
The European Settlement of North America (1492-1754). . p.382
European Social Class: Stability and Change. . . . p.700, p.723
European Societies in the Bronze Age. p.12

European Treaty Series (ETS). *p.474*
The European Union: A Polity of States and Peoples. *p.604, p.638*
European Union A to Z Index. *p.474*
The European Union and the Cyprus Conflict: Modern Conflict, Postmodern Union. *p.602, p.637*
European Union: Dilemmas of Regional Integration. . . . *p.602*
European Union Foreign Policy: What It Is and What It Does. *p.603, p.638*
The European Union Handbook. *p.602, p.636*
European Union—A Guide for Americans. . . *p.603, p.637*
European Universities from the Enlightenment to 1914. . *p.333*
The Europeanisation of Industrial Relations: National and European Processes in Germany, UK, Italy and France. . *p.121*
The Europeans: A Geography of People, Culture, and Environment. *p.397*
Europe's Foreign and Security Policy: The Institutionalization of Cooperation. *p.638*
Europe's Last Red Terrorists: The Revolutionary Organization 17 November. *p.659*
Euros and Europeans: Monetary Integration and the European Model of Society. *p.212*
The EVA Challenge: Implementing Value-Added Change in an Organization. *p.92*
Evaluating E-Learning. *p.321*
Evaluation for Continuing Education: A Comprehensive Guide to Success. *p.320*
Evaluation of R&D Processes: Effectiveness Through Measurements. *p.118*
Evaluative Research in Recreation, Park and Sport Settings: Searching for Useful Information. *p.786*
Even the Children of Strangers: Equality under the U. S. Constitution. *p.458*
Event Planning: The Ultimate Guide to Successful Meetings, Corporate Events, Fundraising Galas, Conferences, Conventions, Incentives, and Other Special Events. . . *p.161*
Ever Closer Union: An Introduction to European Integration. *p.602, p.637*
Every Teacher's Guide to Working with Parents. *p.353*
Everybody Belongs: Changing Negative Attitudes Towards Classmates with Disabilities. *p.317*
Everyday Politics: The Power of Public Work. *p.547*
Everyday Talk: Building and Reflecting Identities. *p.423*
Everything in its Path: Destruction of Community in the Buffalo Creek Flood. *p.760*
Eve's Herbs: A History of Contraception and Abortion in the West. *p.778*
The Evidence for Quality: Strengthening the Tests of Academic and Administrative Effectiveness. *p.289*
Evolution and Environment. *p.493*
The Evolution of American Educational Technology. . . . *p.352*
The Evolution of American Investigative Journalism. . . *p.408*
The Evolution of Cooperation. *p.625*
The Evolution of Crises and Underdevelopment in Africa. . *p.384*
The Evolution of Homo Erectus: Comparative Anatomical Studies of an Extinct Human Species. *p.16*
Evolution of International Human Rights: Visions Seen. . *p.513*
The Evolution of Mental Health Law. *p.448*
The Evolution of National Wildlife Law. *p.463*
The Evolution of Presidential Polling. *p.526*
The Evolution of Retirement: An American Economic History, 1880-1990. . . . . *p.741*
The Evolution of Social Insurance, Eighteen Eighty-One to Nineteen Eighty-One: Studies of Great Britain, France, Switzerland, Austria, and Germany. *p.247*
Evolution of the Market Process. *p.233, p.246*
The Evolution of the Trade Regime: Politics, Law and Economics of the Gatt and the Wto. *p.61*
The Evolution of the US Airline Industry: Theory, Strategy and Policy. *p.151, p.152*
The Evolution of U. N. Peacekeeping: Case Studies and Comparative Analysis. *p.649*
The Evolution of Western Private Law. *p.433*
Evolutionary and Neo-Schumpeterian Approaches to Economics. *p.233*
Evolutionary Economics: Post-Schumpeterian Contributions. *p.233*
Evolutionary Playwork and Reflective Analytic Practice. *p.784, p.795*
An Evolutionary Theory of Economic Change. *p.233*
Evolutionism in Cultural Anthropology: A Critical History. . *p.23*
Evolution's Rainbow: Diversity, Gender, and Sexuality in Nature and People. *p.744, p.746*
The Evolving American Family: New Policies for a New Century. *p.733*
Evolving Technology and Market Structure: Studies in Schumpeterian Economics. *p.230, p.235*
Examination of Musculoskeletal Injuries. . *p.827, p.828, p.829*
Excavation. *p.7*
Exceptional Children and Youth: An Introduction to Special Education. *p.316*
Exchange Rates and International Finance Markets: An Asset-Theoretic Perspective with Schumpeterian Innovation. *p.258, p.264*
Exchange Rates, Capital Flows and Policy. *p.257, p.263*
Exchange-Rate Veriability and Trade: Essays on the Impact of Exchange-Rate Variability on Trade Policy and Trade Flows. *p.257*
Executing the Constitution: Putting the President Back into the Constitution. *p.527*
Executive Governance: Presidental Administrations and Policy Change in the Federal Bureaucracy. *p.527*
Executive Intelligence: What All Great Leaders Have. . . . *p.71*
Executive Privilege: A Constitutional Myth. *p.454*
The Exemplary Middle School. *p.367*
Exercise Physiology: Energy, Nutrition, and Human Performance. *p.875*
Exercise Physiology: People and Ideas. *p.810, p.874*
Exercise Psychology. *p.876*
Exercises for Weather and Climate. *p.393*
Existence and Utopia: The Social and Political Thought of Martin Buber. *p.768*
Exiting Iraq: Why the U. S. Must End the Military Occupation and Renew the War Against Al Qaeda. *p.565*

Exotics at Home: Anthropologies, Others, and American Modernity. p.34

Expectations of Excellence: Curriculum Standards for Social Studies. p.359

Expected Utility, Fair Gambles and Rational Choice. . . . p.201

An Expenditure Tax. p.248

Experience and Education. p.342

The Experience Economy: Work Is Theatre and Every Business a Stage. p.144

Experience Marketing: Strategies for the New Millenium. p.786, p.787, p.885

Experiencing Dewey: Insights for Today's Classroom. . . p.341

Experiential Marketing: How to Get Customers to Sense, Feel, Think, Act and Relate to Your Company and Brand. . p.135

The Experimental College. p.290

Experimental Economics: How We Can Build Better Financial Markets. p.264, p.272

Experiments in Family Planning: Lessons from the Developing World. p.736

Explaining Congressional-Presidential Relations: A Multiple Perspective Approach. p.527

Explaining NATO Enlargement. p.639

Explicit and Authentic Acts: Amending the U. S. Constitution, 1776-1995. . . . . p.454

Exploration and Contestation in the Study of World Politics: A Special Issue of International Organization. . . p.624, p.629

Explorations in Learning & Instruction: The Theory Into Practice Database. p.357

Explorations in the Ethnography of Speaking. p.18

The Explorer's Eye: First-Hand Accounts of Adventure and Exploration. p.378

Exploring Sport and Exercise Psychology. p.878, p.904

Exploring the Heritage of American Higher Education: The Evolution of Philosophiy and Policy. p.330

Exploring the Ocean: The Physical Ocean; Life in the Ocean; Uses of the Ocean; Index. p.391

Exploring the United States with the Five Themes of Geography. p.382

Exploring Water Resources: GIS Investigations for the Earth Sciences. p.387

The Explosive Child: A New Approach for Understanding and Parenting Easily Frustrated, Chronically Inflexible Children. p.283

Exporters - Alcoholic Beverages Worldwide. p.153

Export.gov. p.60

Exporting America: Why Corporate Greed Is Shipping American Jobs Overseas. p.252, p.261

Expressive Politics: Issue Strategies of Congressional Challengers. p.548

Exquisite Rebel: The Essays of Voltairine de Cleyre — Anarchist, Feminist, Genius. p.500

Extending the Supply Chain: How Cutting-Edge Companies Bridge the Critical Last Mile into Customers Homes. . p.117

Extradition, Politics and Human Rights. p.473

The Eye of the Storm: How John Chambers Steered Cisco Through the Technology Collapse. p.157

Eyewitness Testimony. p.473

Eyewitness to a Genocide: The United Nations and Rwanda. p.632, p.651

F

F. A. Hayek As a Political Economist: Economic Analysis and Values. p.243

F. Y. Edgeworth: Writings in Probability, Statistics and Economics, Set. p.203

Fabricating the Keynesian Revolution: Studies of the Inter-War Literature on Money, the Cycle and Unemployment. p.225, p.238

The Faces of Janus: Marxism and Fascism in the Twentieth Century. p.510

Facilities Management and the Business of Space. p.113

Facilities Management Handbook. p.113

Facilities Management. p.112

Facing the Ocean: The Atlantic and Its Peoples 8000 BC-AD 1500. . . . . p.12

Factory Physics. p.119

The Facts on File Dictionary of American Politics. . . . p.516

Facts on File Dictionary of Human Geography. p.396

Faded Mosaic: The Emergence of Post-Cultural America. . p.764

Fads and Foibles in Modern Sociology and Related Sciences. p.683

The Failed Promise of the American High School, 1890-1995. . . . . p.324

Failing at Fairness: How America's Schools Cheat Girls. . p.302

Failing the Future: A Dean Looks at Higher Education in the 21st Century. p.331

The Failure of the Founding Fathers: Jefferson, Marshall, and the Rise of Presidential Democracy. p.522, p.535

Fair Play: The Ethics of Sport. p.803

Fair, Square and Legal: Safe Hiring, Managing, and Firing Practices to Keep You and Your Company Out of Court. p.447

Fair Trade for All: How Trade Can Promote Development. p.53, p.56, p.665

FairTest. p.286

Faith in Nation: Exclusionary Origins of Nationalism. . . p.494

Faithful and Fearless: Moving Feminist Protest Inside the Church and Military. p.745

Fall: A Comparative Study of the End of Communism in Czechoslovakia, East Germany, Hungary and Poland. p.509, p.596, p.600

The Fall of the Bell System: A Study in Prices and Politics. p.421

The Fall of the Ivory Tower: Government Funding, Corruption and the Bankrupting of Higher Education. p.525

Falling from Grace: Downward Mobility in the Age of Affluence. p.725

Falling Terrorism and Rising Conflicts: The Afghan Contribution to Polarization and Confrontation in West and South Asia. p.661

False Alarm: The Truth about the Epidemic of Fear. . . . p.694

False Promises: The Shaping of American Working Class Consciousness. p.726

Families Against the City: Middle Class Homes of Industrial Chicago, 1872-1890. . . . . p.734

Families Like Mine: Children of Gay Parents Tell It Like It Is. p.740

Families We Choose: Lesbians, Gays, Kinship. . . p.33, p.740

Family and Kinship in East London. p.37

Family and Kinship in England, 1450-1800. . . . . p.708

Family Bonds: Adoption, Infertility, and the New World of Child Production. p.737

Family Diversity and Well-Being. p.731

The Family Estate in Africa: Studies in the Role of Property in Family Structure and Lineage Continuity. p.32

Family, Friends and Followers: Political and Social Bonds in Early Medieval Europe. p.501

The Family Herds: A Study of Two Pastoral Tribes in East Africa: The Jie and Turkana. p.38

Family Identity and the State in the Bamako Kafu, c. 1800-c.1900. p.705

The Family in the American Economy. p.265

Family Life and Illicit Love in Earlier Generations: Essays in Historical Sociology. p.737

Family Life and School Achievement: Why Poor Black Children Succeed or Fail. p.309

Family Life in a Northern Thai Village: A Study in the Structural Significance of Women. p.40

Family Man: Fatherhood, Housework, and Gender Equity. . p.745

Family Matters: Secrecy and Disclosure in the History of Adoption. p.737

Family Problem Solving. p.758

The Family Secret: Domestic Violence in America. . . . p.743

Family, Sex and Marriage in England, Fifteen Hundred to Eighteen Hundred. p.734

Family Socialization and Interaction Process. p.738

Family Values and the New Society: Dilemmas of the 21st Century. p.738

Famous Trials. p.438

Fantasy and Feeling in Education. p.357

FAO Statistical Yearbook, Vol. 1. . . . . p.151, p.164

Far and Wide: Cultural Diversity in American Boarding Schools. p.296

Far Valley: Four Years in Japanese Village. p.39

Farm to Factory: A Reinterpretation of the Soviet Industrial Revolution. p.267

FASB: Financial Accounting Standards Board. . p.104, p.105

Fascism: Past, Present, Future. p.510

The Fascist Revolution: Toward a General Theory of Fascism. p.510

Fashioning the More Ethical Representative: The Impact of Ethics Reforms in the U. S. House of Representatives. . p.533

The Fast Forward MBA in Business Math. p.175

The Fate of the Earth and the Abolition. p.656

Fateful Decisions: Inside the National Security Council. . p.562

The Father of Spin: Edward L. Bernays and the Birth of Public Relations. p.429

Father-Daughter Incest. p.737

Fault Lines of Democracy in Post-Transition Latin America. p.591

FDI and Industrial Organization in Developing Countries: The Challenge of Globalization in India. p.60

Fear at the Edge: State Terror and Resistance in Latin America. p.515

Fear: The History of a Political Idea. p.484

A Fearful Freedom: Women's Flight from Equality. . . . p.458

Fed Up: Women and Food in America. p.778

The Federal Budget in Brief, July 1950/June 1951. . . . p.248

The Federal Budget: Politics, Policy, Process. p.567

Federal Censorship: Obscenity in the Mail. p.445

Federal Communications Commission: The Ups and Downs of Radio-TV Regulation. p.445

The Federal Courts. p.465, p.534

Federal Drug Control: The Evolution of Policy and Practice. p.448

Federal Election Commission Campaign Finance Reports and Data. p.557

Federal Election Commission. p.548

The Federal Government and Urban Housing: Ideology and Change in Public Policy. p.524

The Federal Government Subject Guide. p.529

The Federal Impeachment Process: A Constitutional and Historical Analysis. p.461

Federal Register. p.481

Federal regulatory directory. p.463

The Federal Reserve System: A History. p.90

The Federal Reserve System: An Encyclopedia. p.155

Federal School Code List. p.293

Federal Tax Research. p.107

Federal Taxation in America: A Short History. p.107

Federalism: A Dialogue. p.455

Federalism and the Role of the State. p.586

Federalism: The Politics of Intergovernmental Relations. . p.525

Federalism, the Supreme Court and the Seventeenth Amendment: The Irony of Constitutional Democracy. p.525, p.534

Federalism. p.587

The Federalist. p.518

Federal-Provincial Diplomacy. p.587

Federation of Gay Games. p.839, p.843

FedEx Delivers: How the World's Leading Shipping Company Keeps Innovating and Outperforming the Competition. . p.165

A Feel for the Game: To Brookline and Back. p.860

Feeling and Thinking: The Role of Affect in Social Cognition. p.694

Felix Frankfurter Reminisces. p.467

Felix S. Cohen's Handbook of Federal Indian Law. . . . p.465

Fellah and Townsman in the Middle East: Studies in Social History. p.700

The Female Athlete's Body: How to Prevent and Treat Sports Injuries in Women and Girls. p.827, p.874, p.878

The Female Body and the Law. p.458

Female Desires: Same-Sex Relations and Transgender Practices Across Cultures. p.750
Female Fitness on Foot: Walking, Jogging, Running and Orienteering. p.788, p.793
Female Gladiators: Gender, Law, and Contact Sport in America. p.835, p.893, p.896, p.900
Female Power and Male Dominance: On the Origins of Sexual Inequality. p.744
Feminism and Anthropology. p.31
Feminism and Methodology: Social Science Issues. . . . p.690
Feminism and Sociological Theory. p.744
Feminism and Sporting Bodies: Essays on Theory and Practice. p.806, p.813, p.836
Feminist Economics and the World Bank: History, Theory, and Policy. p.274
Feminist Economics: Interrogating the Masculinity of Rational Economic Man. p.273
Feminist Economics Today: Beyond Economic Man. . . . p.273
Feminist Methods in Social Research. p.688
Feminist Philosophy. p.744
Feminist Politics and Human Nature. p.744
Feminist Sociology. p.743
Feudalism in History. p.490, p.501
Field Archaeology: An Introduction. p.7
Field Hockey: Steps to Success. p.795, p.857
Field Hockey Techniques and Tactics. p.796, p.857
Field Methods in Remote Sensing. p.389
The Field of Adult Services: Social Work Practice and Administration. p.758
The Field of Social Work. p.757
Field Techniques in Glaciology and Glacial Geomorphology. p.391
Fieldnotes: The Makings of Anthropology. p.24
Fields of Honor: The Golden Age of College Football and the Men Who Created It. p.809, p.859, p.894
Fields on the Hoof: Nexus of Tibetan Nomadic Pastoralism. . p.39
Fieldwork and Footnotes: Studies in the History of European Anthropology. p.5
Fieldwork. p.690
A Fierce Discontent: The Rise and Fall of the Progressive Movement in America, 1870-1920. . . . . p.552
FIFA and the Contest for World Football: Who Rules the Peoples Game. p.845, p.847, p.868
The Fifth Discipline: The Art and Practice of the Learning Organization. p.79, p.80
Fifty Key Thinkers in International Relations. p.628
Fifty Major Economists: A Reference Guide. p.185
Fifty Major Economists. p.185, p.208
Fifty Major Thinkers on Education: From Confucious to Dewey. p.340
Fifty Modern Thinkers on Education: From Piaget to the Present Day. p.340
Fifty Years of Anthropology and Education, 1950-2000: A Spindler Anthology. p.29
The Fight of the Century: Jack Johnson, Joe Louis, and the Struggle for Racial Equality. p.816, p.832, p.855
Fighting Against the Odds: A History of Southern Labor since World War II. p.127
Fighting Dirty: The Inside Story of Covert Operations from Ho Chi Minh to Osama Bin Laden. p.561, p.659
Fighting Fans: Football Hooliganism as a World Phenomenon. p.715, p.815, p.843, p.867
Fighting Poverty: What Works and What Doesn't. . p.253, p.264
Fighting Sprawl and City Hall: Resistance to Urban Growth in the Southwest. p.544
Fighting Words: Individuals, Communities, and Liberties of Speech. p.459
Filipino Americans: Transformation and Identity. p.706
Final Exam: A Study of the Perpetual Scrutiny of American Education: Historical Perspectives on Assessment, Standards, Outcomes, and Criticism of U. S. Schools. . p.285
Final Freedom: The Civil War, the Abolition of Slavery, and the Thirteenth Amendment. p.453
Final Solutions: Mass Killing and Genocide in the 20th Century. p.654, p.715
Finance and Financiers in European History, 1880-1960. . p.91
Finance and Investment Handbook. . p.94, p.101, p.103, p.162
Finance Site List. p.88
Finance, Wikipedia, the free encyclopedia. p.88
Finance. p.104
Financial Crises and Recession in the Global Economy. p.242, p.260
Financial Derivatives. p.89, p.95, p.100, p.102
Financial Econometrics: Problems, Models, and Methods. . p.200
Financial Founding Fathers: The Men Who Made America Rich. p.90, p.148
A Financial History of Modern U S Corporate Scandals. p.89 p.104 p.109 p.147
A Financial History of the United States. p.89, p.247
The Financial Numbers Game: Detecting Creative Accounting Practices. p.96 p.102 p.105 p.106
Financial Shenanigans: How to Detect Accounting Gimmicks and Fraud in Financial Reports. . . p.92, p.97, p.105, p.106
Financial Statement Analysis: A Practitioner's Guide. p.91, p.95, p.105, p.106
Financing Education in a Climate of Change. p.280
Financing Education: The Struggle Between Governmental Monopoly and Parental Control. p.280
Financing Sport: Winning Strategies. p.884, p.888
Financing Sport. p.888, p.891
Financing the Sport Enterprise. . . p.886, p.889, p.892, p.897
Finding Groups in Data: An Introduction to Cluster Analysis. p.689
Finding the Law 2005. . . . . p.439
Finding the Mean: Theory and Practice in Aristotelian Political Philosophy. p.489
FindLaw. p.108
The Fine Art of Advertising : Irreverent, Irrepressible, Irresistibly Ironic. p.140, p.141
Finland: People, Nation State. p.594
The Fire This Time: U. S. War Crimes in the Gulf. . . . p.652
A Fire to Win: The Life and Times of Woody Hayes. p.859, p.894

The First Amendment, Democracy, and Romance. p.459
The First Amendment in Schools. p.450
The First American Revolution: The American Colonies on the Eve of Independence. p.518
First among Equals: The Supreme Court in American Life. . p.540
First, Break All the Rules: What the World's Greatest Managers Do Differently. p.70, p.72
The First Casualty: The War Correspondent as Hero and Myth-Maker from the Crimea to Iraq. p.403
A First Course in Optimization Theory. p.207
First Crossing: Alexander Mackenzie, His Expedition Across North America and the Opening of the Continent. . . p.379
The First Days of Class: A Practical Guide for the Beginning Teacher. p.279
The First Days of School: How to Be an Effective Teacher. . p.278
First Farmers: The Origins of Agricultural Societies. p.5
The First Immigrants from Asia: A Population History of the North American Indian. p.764
First Principles: The Jurisprudence of Clarence Thomas. . p.467
The First South Americans: The Peopling of a Continent from the Earliest Evidence to High Culture. p.12
The First Universities: Studium Generale and the Origins of University Education in Europe. p.336
First Use of Nuclear Weapons: Under the Constitution, Who Decides? p.532
FirstGov.gov: The U.S. Government's Official Web Portal. p.546
First-Job Survival Guide: How to Thrive and Advance in Your New Career. p.167
Fiscal Disobedience: An Anthropology of Economic Regulation in Central Africa. p.260
Fiscal Policy and Business Cycles. p.243, p.246
Fiscal Theory and Political Economy: Selected Essays. . . p.208
Fisher's Capital and Income. p.250
Fists and Flowers: A Social Psychological Interpretation of Student Dissent. p.326
Fit to Teach: Same-Sex Desire, Gender, and School Work in the Twentieth Century. p.309
Fitness Aquatics. p.792
Fitness in American Culture: Images of Health, Sport and the Body, 1830-1940. . . . . p.791, p.806
Fitness Programming and Physical Disability. p.784, p.791, p.801
Fitness Running. p.866
Fitness Through Aerobics and Step Training. p.793
Fitness Weight Training. p.792, p.878
Five Families: Mexican Case Studies in the Culture of Poverty. p.733
Fixin' to Git: One Fan's Love Affair with NASCAR's Winston Cup. p.820, p.848
Flag Burning and Free Speech: The Case of Texas vs. Johnson. p.438
Flags Through the Ages and Across the World. p.499
Fleet Walker's Divided Heart: The Life of Baseball's First Black Major Leaguer. p.811, p.833, p.853
Flight International World Aircraft and Systems Directory. . p.151
Flow in Sports: The Keys to Optimal Experiences and Performances. p.802, p.877
Fluvial Processes and Environmental Change. p.391
The Focus Group Guidebook. p.137
Focus Groups: A Practical Guide for Applied Research. . p.686
Focus Groups: A Step-by-Step Guide. p.136
Focus Groups as Qualitative Research. p.687
Focus Groups: Theory and Practice. p.687
Foil, Saber and Epee Fencing: Skills, Safety, Operations, and Responsibilities. p.857
Folded, Spindled and Mutilated: The Economics of U. S. vs IBM. p.438
Follow the Money. p.558
Follow This Path: How the World's Greatest Organizations Drive Growth by Unleashing Human Potential. p.76
Food Aid after Fifty Years: Recasting its Role. . . p.259, p.265
Food and Beverage Market Place: Suppliers Guide, 2000-01. . . . . p.160
Food and Culture: A Reader. p.45
Food and Gender: Identity and Power. p.45
Food in the USA: Reader. p.45
The Food Industry Wars: Marketing Triumphs and Blunders. p.160
Food, Nutrition and Sports Performance II: The IOC Consensus Conference on Sports Nutrition. p.825, p.876
Food Quality and Consumer Value: Delivering Food That Satisfies. p.160
The Food System: A Guide. p.152
Fool.com: To Educate, Amuse and Enrich. . . . p.93, p.101
Fools Rush In: Steve Case, Jerry Levin, and the Unmaking of AOL Time Warner. p.84
A Foot in the Door: Networking Your Way into the Hidden Job Market. p.170
Football: A College History. p.808, p.859
Football: A Sociology of the Global Game. . p.815, p.843, p.867
Football and American Identity. p.805, p.858
Football and Fascism: The National Game under Mussolini. p.808, p.817, p.867, p.891
Football and Its Fans: An Account of Supporters and Their Relations. p.820, p.868
Football Hooligans: Knowing the Score. p.813, p.867
Football: The Ivy League Origins of an American Obsession. p.803, p.858
Football U.: Spectator Sports in the Life of the American University. p.716, p.820, p.822, p.859
Footbinding, Feminism and Freedom: The Liberation of Women's Bodies in Modern China. p.835
For Adult Users Only: The Dilemma of Violent Pornography. p.748
For Better and for Worse: Welfare Reform and the Well-Being of Children and Families. p.755
For Better or for Worse: The Marriage of Science and Government in the United States. p.525
For Better or Worse?: Same Sex Marriages, Pro and Con: A Reader. p.570
For Cause and Comrades: Why Men Fought in the Civil War. p.521

For Democracy's Sake: Foundations and Democracy Assistance in Central Europe. p.585, p.640

For Fun and Profit: The Transformation of Leisure into Consumption. p.783, p.887

For la Patria: Politics and the Armed Forces in Latin America. p.592

For Pride, Profit and Patriarchy: Football and the Incorporation of American Cultural Values. p.805, p.858, p.881

For the Common Good: A Critical Examination of Law and Social Control. p.773

For the Glory: College Football Dreams and Realities Inside Paterno's Program. p.858, p.893

For the Public Record: A Documentary History of the League of Women Voters. p.519, p.569

For the Record: From Wall Street to Washington. p.529

For the Survival of Democracy: Franklin Roosevelt and the World Crisis of the 1930's. p.522

For We are Sold, I and My People: Women and Industry in Mexico's Frontier. p.729

For Weber: Essays on the Sociology of Fate. p.686

Foragers and Farmers: Population Interaction and Agricultural Expansion in Prehistoric Europe. p.12

Forbidden Grounds: The Case Against Employment Discrimination Laws. p.133

A Force for Change: How Leadership Differs from Management. p.71

Forced Choices: Class, Community, and Worker Ownership. p.727

Forced Justice: School Desegregation and the Law. . p.300, p.449

Forced Migration Online. p.667

Forced Sexual Intercourse in Intimate Relationships. . . . p.742

The Forces of Economic Growth: A Time Series Perspective. p.243

Forces of Habit: Drugs and the Making of the Modern World. p.776

Forces of Labor: Workers' Movements and Globalization Since 1870. . . . . p.129

Forecasting and Market Analysis Techniques: A Practical Approach. p.137

Forecasting Economic Time Series. p.206

A Foreign Exchange Primer. p.89 p.97 p.98 p.100

Foreign Government Resources on the Web. p.482

Foreign News: Exploring the World of Foreign Correspondents. p.407

Foreign Relations of the United States. p.482, p.561

The Foreign Service of the United States: First Line of Defense. p.529

The Forest of Symbols: Aspects of Ndembu Ritual. p.37

The Forest People. p.39

Forever Free: The Story of Emancipation and Reconstruction. p.485

Forex Revolution: An Insider's Guide to the Real World of Foreign Exchange Trading. p.89, p.97, p.98, p.100

The Forge of the Spirit: Structure, Motion and Meaning in the Japanese Martial Tradition. p.863

Forging Democracy from Below: Insurgent Transitions in South Africa and el Salvador. p.614

The Forging of an Aristocracy. p.707

Forgotten Children: Parent-Child Relations from 1500 to 1900. . . . . p.735

Forgotten Families: Ending the Growing Crisis Confronting Children and Working Parents in the Global Economy. . p.759

A Forgotten Voice: A Biography of Leta Stetter Hollingworth. p.337

Formal Organizations: A Comparative Approach. p.717

Formal Sociology: The Work of Georg Simmel. p.196

The Formation of Campaign Agendas: A Comparative Analysis of Party and Media Roles in Recent American and British Elections. p.549, p.558, p.559

The Formation of Econometrics: A Historical Perspective. . p.204

The Formation of Islam: Religion and Society in the near East, 600-1800. . . . . p.721

The Formation of National Party Systems: Federalism and Party Competition in Canada, Great Britain, India, and the United States. p.578

The Formation of National States in Western Europe. . . p.602

The Formative Era of American Law. p.440

Forms of Talk. p.423

Fort Mose: Colonial America's Black Fortress of Freedom. . p.13

Fortress America: The American Military and the Consequences of Peace. p.561

The Fortune at the Bottom of the Pyramid: Eradicating Poverty Through Profits. p.665

The Fossil Trail: How We Know What We Think We Know about Human Evolution. p.16

Foster Children in the Life Course Perspective: The Casey Family Program Experience. p.757

Foucault and Education: Disciplines and Knowledge. . . p.340

Foucault's Challenge: Discourse, Knowledge, and Power in Education. p.345

Foul Play: Drug Abuse in Sports. p.802, p.826

Foundations and Practices in the Use of Distance Education. p.321

Foundations for the Future: The AICPA from 1980-1995. . p.104

The Foundations of American Constitutionalism [1932]. . p.518

Foundations of American Constitutionalism. p.454

Foundations of Biogeography: Classic Papers with Commentaries. p.394

The Foundations of Contemporary and Historical Sociology. p.248

Foundations of Dynamic Economic Analysis: Optimal Control Theory and Applications. p.198

The Foundations of Econometric Analysis. p.201

Foundations of Economic Analysis. p.197, p.204

Foundations of Economic Value Added. p.89

The Foundations of Economics: History and Theory in the Analysis of Economic Reality. p.209

Foundations of Inventory Management. p.117

Foundations of Modern Econometrics: The Selected Essays of Ragnar Frisch. p.198

The Foundations of Paul Samuelson's Revealed Preference Theory: A Study by the Method of Rational Reconstruction. p.197

Foundations of Paul Samuelson's Revealed Preference Theory. *p.251*

Foundations of Physical Education, Exercise Science, and Sport with PowerWeb. *p.797*

Foundations of Post-Keynesian Economic Analysis. . . . *p.232*

Foundations of Probability, Econometrics and Economic Games, Vols. 1-10. . . . . *p.201*

Foundations of Program Evaluation: Theories of Practice.. *p.690*

Foundations of the Economics of Innovation: Theory, Measurement and Practice. *p.241*

Foundations of World Order: The Legalist Approach to International Relations, 1898-1921. . . . . *p.627*

Founding Brothers: The Revolutionary Generation. . . . *p.485*

Founding Mothers: The Women Who Raised Our Nation. *p.487, p.517, p.569*

The Founding of a Nation: A History of the American Revolution, 1763-1776.. . . . . *p.517*

The Founding of Israeli Democracy, 1948-1967. . . . . . *p.615*

The Founding of New England. *p.517*

Four Days with Dr. Deming: A Strategy for Modern Methods of Management. *p.73*

The Four Faces of Nuclear Terrorism. *p.658*

Four Theories of the Press: The Authoritarian, Libertarian, Social Responsibility and Soviet Communist Concepts of What the Press Should Be. *p.406*

The Fourteenth Amendment: From Political Principle to Judicial Doctrine. *p.457*

The Fourth Estate and the Constitution: Freedom of the Press in America. *p.459*

The Fourth Great Awakening and the Future of Egalitarianism: The Political Realignment of the 1990s and the Fate of Egalitarianism.. . . . . *p.514*

☐ Fourth World Documentation Project. *p.482*

Fragile Evidence: A Critique of Reading Assessment. . . *p.354*

The Fragile Middle Class: Americans in Debt.. . . . . . . *p.271*

Framed! Labor and the Corporate Media. *p.127*

Frameworks for Sport Psychologists: Enhancing Sport Performance. *p.877*

Framing ADHD Children: A Critical Examination of the History, Discourse, and Everyday Experience of Attention Deficit/Hyperactivity Disorder. *p.319*

The Framing of the Constitution of the United States. . . *p.452*

France and Algeria: A History of Decolonization and Transformation. *p.584*

France and Britain 1900-1940. . . . . *p.643*

France and Britain, 1940-1994: The Long Separation. . . *p.643*

France and the South Pacific since, 1940. . . . . *p.583*

The Franchise: A History of Sports Illustrated Magazine. *p.807, p.902, p.907*

Franchising Dreams: The Lure of Entrepreneurship in America. *p.164*

The Franco Regime, 1936-1975. . . . . *p.608*

Francois Quesnay, (1694-1774), Vols. 1 & 2. . . . . . . *p.215*

Frankfurt School. *p.675*

Franklin D. Roosevelt and the Transformation of the Supreme Court.. . . . . *p.539*

A Franz Boas Reader: The Shaping of American Anthropology, 1883-1911. . . . . *p.3*

Franz Boas: The Early Years, 1858-1906. . . . . *p.4*

Fraternal Organizations. *p.719*

Freakonomics: A Rogue Economist Explores the Hidden Side of Everything. *p.185, p.271*

Frederic Le Play on Family, Work, and Social Change.. . *p.685*

Free Culture: How Big Media Uses Technology and the Law to Lock down Culture and Control Creativity.. . . . . . . *p.446*

Free Markets and Social Justice. *p.434*

Free Men All: The Personal Liberty Laws of the North, 1780-1861. . . . . *p.453*

Free Press - Free People: The Best Cause. *p.405*

Free Radicals in Exercise and Aging. *p.875*

Free Speech in Its Forgotten Years, 1870-1920. . . . . . *p.459*

Free Time and Leisure Participation: International Perspectives. *p.785, p.899*

Free to Choose: A Personal Statement. *p.232*

Free Trade Between the United States and Canada: The Potential Economic Effects. *p.258*

Free Trade for the Americas?: The United States' Push for the FTAA Agreement.. . . . . *p.61*

Free Trade Today.. *p.256*

Free Trade under Fire. *p.55, p.257, p.261, p.664*

Free World: America, Europe, and the Surprising Future of the West. *p.628*

Freedom and Beyond. *p.343*

Freedom and Civilization. *p.700*

Freedom and Culture. *p.503*

Freedom and Its Limitations in American Life. *p.695*

Freedom and the Court: Civil Rights and Liberties in the United States. *p.455*

Freedom at Risk: Secrecy, Censorship, and Repression in the 1980s. *p.458*

Freedom by a Hair's Breadth: Tsimihety in Madagascar. . *p.39*

Freedom in Fulani Social Life: An Introspective Ethnography. *p.38*

Freedom Is an Endless Meeting: Democracy in American Social Movements. *p.711*

Freedom Is Not Enough: Black Voters, Black Candidates, and American Presidential Politics. *p.519, p.555*

Freedom of the Press 2004: A Global Survey of Media Independence. *p.409*

Freedom of the Press for Whom?: The Right of Access to Mass Media. *p.458*

Freedom of the Press from Hamilton to the Warren Court.. *p.459*

Freedom of the Press from Zenger to Jefferson. *p.459*

Freedom or Security: The Consequences for Democracies Using Emergency Powers to Fight Terror. *p.659*

Freedom, the Individual and the Law. *p.436*

Freedom to Learn. *p.358*

Freedom's Law: The Moral Reading of the American Constitution. *p.453*

Freedom's Ordeal: The Struggle for Human Rights and Democracy in Post-Soviet States. *p.512*

Freeing Intelligence Through Teaching: A Dialectic of the Rational and the Personal. *p.358*

Freemasonry and American Culture, 1880-1930. . . . . . p.719

A French Genocide: The Vendee. p.653

French Higher Education in the Seventeenth and Eighteenth Centuries: A Cultural History. p.333

French Negotiating Behavior: Dealing with la Grande Nation. p.643, p.645

The French Presence in the South Pacific, 1842-1940. . . p.583

French Social Theory. p.679

French Society, Seventeen Eighty-Nine to Nineteen Seventy. p.702

Frequent Flyers: Developing Global Executives. . . p.59, p.120

Friction: An Enthography of Global Connection. p.27

Friday Night Lights: A Town, a Team, and a Dream. p.814, p.840, p.858

Friedrich Froebel. p.342

Friends and Foes: How Congress and the President Really Make Foreign Policy. p.528, p.531

Friends of Friends. p.693

Friendship Matters: Communication, Dialectics, and the Life Course. p.697

Fritz Pollard: Pioneer in Racial Advancement. p.814, p.831, p.858

From '9-11' to the 'Iraq War 2003': International Law in an Age of Complexity. p.655, p.660

From Altoids to Zima: The Surprising Stories Behind 125 Famous Brand Names. p.142

From Babel to Dragomans: Interpreting the Middle East. . p.614

From Bandwagon to Balance-of-Power Politics: Structural Constraints and Politics in China, 1949-1978. . . . . p.619

From Blackjacks to Briefcases: A History of Commercialized Strikebreaking and Unionbusting in the United States. . p.129

From Boston to Beijing: Managing with a World View.. . . . . p.58, p.69

From Breakpoint to Advantage: A Practical Guide to Optimal Tennis Health and Performance. . p.828, p.864, p.875, p.879

From Building and Loans to Bail Outs: A History of the American Savings and Loan Industry, 1831-1995. . . . . p.147, p.155

From Columbus to ConAgra: The Globalization of Agriculture and Food. p.151

From Comrade to Citizen: The Struggle for Political Rights in China. p.619

From Concept to Wall Street: A Complete Guide to Entrepreneurship and Venture Capital. . . . p.89, p.91, p.95

From Confederation to Nation: The American Constitution, 1835-1877. . . . . p.452

From Cuenca to Queens: An Anthropological Story of Transnational Migration. p.44

From Direct Action to Affirmative Action: Fair Employment Law and Policy in America, 1933-1972. . . . p.133, p.447

From East Germans to Germans?: The New Postcommunist Elites.. . . . . p.610

From Empire to Community: A New Approach to International Relations. p.262, p.626, p.628

From Empire to Republic: Turkish Nationalism and the Armenian Genocide. p.651

From Father's Property to Children's Rights: The History of Child Custody in the United States.. . . . . . . p.442, p.740

From Field to Factory: Community Structure and Industrialization in West Bengal. p.704

From Garrison State to Nation-State: Political Power and the Russian Military under Gorbachev and Yeltsin. p.598

From Georges Sorel: Essays in Socialism and Philosophy, Vol. I. p.507

From Global to Metanational: How Companies Win in the Knowledge Economy. p.69

From Heresy to Dogma: An Institutional History of Corporate Environmentalism.. . . . . p.61, p.63

From Household to Empire: Society and Economy in Early Colonial New Mexico. p.383

From Identity to Politics: The Lesbian and Gay Movements in the United States. p.570

From Isolation to Conversation: Supporting New Teachers' Development. p.279

From Jim Crow to Civil Rights: The Supreme Court and the Struggle for Racial Equality. p.457, p.537

From Knowledge to Intelligence: Creating Competitive Advantage in the Next Economy. p.77, p.83

From Kostenki to Clovis: Upper Paleolithic-Paleo-Indian Adaptations. p.17

From Learning to Earning: Yahoo! HotJobs Success Strategies for New Grads. p.169

From Love Field: Our Final Hours with President John F. Kennedy. p.485

From Many, One: The Process of Political Integration. . . p.628

From Max Weber: Essays in Sociology. p.681

From Migrants to Ethnic Minorities: The Settlement of Refugees from Vietnam, Laos, and Cambodia in the United States. p.571, p.763, p.764

From Military Rule to Liberal Democracy in Argentina. . p.593

From Milton to McLuhan: The Ideas Behind American Journalism. p.403

From "Fair Sex" to Feminism: Sport and the Socialization of Women in the Industrial and Post-Industrial Eras. p.818, p.837

From Moonshine to Madison Avenue: A Cultural History of the NASCAR Winston Cup Series. p.848, p.888

From Needs Assessment to Action: Transforming Needs into Solution Strategies. p.81

From New Era to New Deal: Herbert Hoover, the Economists, and American Economic Policy, 1921-1933. . . . . . p.522

From Obstruction to Moderation: The Transformation of Senate Conservatism, 1938-1952. . . . . p.534

From Panthers to Promise Keepers: Rethinking the Men's Movement. p.711

From Parchment to Power: How James Madison Used the Bill of Rights to Save the Constitution. p.452

From Popular Sovereignty to the Sovereignty of Law: Law, Society, and Politics in Fifth Century Athens. p.501

From Primitive to Postcolonial in Melanesia and Anthropology. p.43

From Revolutionary Cadres to Party Technocrats in Socialist China. p.620

From Ritual to Record: The Nature of Modern Sports. p.806, p.816

From Savage to Negro: Anthropology and the Construction of Race, 1896-1954. . . . . p.4

From Set Shot to Slam Dunk: The Glory Days of Basketball in the Words of Those Who Played It. p.854, p.897
From Skisport to Skiing: One Hundred Years of an American Sport, 1840-1940. . . . . p.866
From Slogans to Mantras: Social Protest and Religious Conversion in the Late Vietnam Era. p.710
From Squaw Tit to Whorehouse Meadow: How Maps Name, Claim, and Inflame. p.386
From Teaching to Mentoring in Adult Education: The Integration of Principle and Practice. p.320
From Television to the Internet: Postmodern Visions of American Media Culture in the Twentieth Century. . . p.418
From the Puritans to the Projects: Public Housing and Public Neighbors. p.757
[e] From the Wireless to the Web: The Evolution of Telecommunications, 1901-2001. . . . . p.420
From Voting to Violence: Democratization and Nationalist Conflict. p.505
Front Stage, Backstage: The Dramatic Structure of Labor Negotions. p.121
Fronteras No Mas: Toward Social Justice at the U. S. - Mexico Border. p.560, p.640
Frontier Passages: Ethnopolitics and the Rise of Chinese Communism, 1921-1945. . . . . p.620
Frontiers of Biogeography: New Directions in the Geography of Nature. p.394
Frontiers of Human-Centered Computing, Online Communities and Virtual Environments. p.772
Frontiers: Territory and State Formation in the Modern World. p.487, p.495
The Front-Loading Problem in Presidential Nominations. . p.549
Fugitive Writings. p.493
Full Employment and Growth: Further Keynesian Essays on Policy. p.239
Fun and Games in Twentieth-Century America: A Historical Guide to Leisure. p.784
Fun with GPS. p.389
Fun Without Fatigue. p.784, p.801, p.830
The Function of Newspapers in Society: A Global Perspective. p.411, p.417
Functional Exercise Progressions. p.793, p.880
Functional Movement Development Across the Life Span. p.907, p.909
Functional Training for Sports. p.790, p.878
Functionalism Historicized: Essays on British Social Anthropology. p.5
Functions of Social Conflict. p.766
The Functions of the Executive. p.64
Fundamentalisms Comprehended. p.722
Fundamentals of Athletic Training. p.828
Fundamentals of Business Marketing Education: A Guide for University-Level Faculty and Policy Makers. p.176
Fundamentals of Business Marketing Research: A Guide for University-Level Faculty and Policymakers. p.136
Fundamentals of Exercise Physiology: For Fitness, Performance, and Health. p.875
Fundamentals of Geographic Information Systems. . . . p.386
Fundamentals of Learning. p.359
Fundamentals of Mobile and Pervasive Computing. . . . p.114
Fundamentals of Modern Manufacturing: Materials, Processes and Systems. p.116
Fundamentals of Network Security. p.114
Fundamentals of Private Pensions. p.98
Fundamentals of Sales Management for the Newly Appointed Sales Manager. p.143
Fundamentals of Sport Marketing. p.786, p.885
Fundamentals of Sports Injury Management. p.827
Fundamentals of Supply Chain Management: Twelve Drivers of Competitive Advantage. p.118
Fundamentals of Track and Field. p.794, p.869
Fundamentals of World Regional Geography. p.397
The Funding of Higher Education: International Perspectives. p.295
Further Considerations Concerning Raising the Value of Money. p.215
Further Contributions to Modern Economics. . . . p.196, p.270
Further Essays on Capital and Interest, Vol. 3. . . . . . . p.233
The Future for Investors: Why the Tried and the True Triumph over the Bold and the New. p.97, p.100
A Future for Marxism?: Althusser, the Analytical Turn and the Revival of Socialist Theory. p.507
Future Iraq: US Policy in Reshaping the Middle East. . . p.560
The Future of Academic Freedom. p.298
The Future of Advertising: New Media, New Clients, New Consumers in the Post-Television Age. p.140, p.426
The Future of American Democratic Politics: Principles and Practices. p.555
The Future of Anthropology: Its Relevance to the Contemporary World. p.27
Future of Children: Marriage and Child Well-Being. . . . p.756
The Future of Foreign Investment in Southeast Asia. . . . p.60
The Future of Higher Education: Rhetoric, Reality, and the Risks of the Market. p.332
The Future of Human Resource Management: 64 Thought Leaders Explore the Critical HR Issues of Today and Tomorrow. p.76
The Future of Ideas: The Fate of the Commons in a Connected World. p.435
Future of Law in a Multicultural World. p.477
The Future of Leadership: Today's Top Leadership Thinkers Speak to Tomorrow's Leaders. p.70
The Future of Marketing: Critical 21st Century Perspectives. p.137
The Future of Marriage. p.738
The Future of Money. p.246, p.261
The Future of NATO: Enlargement, Russia and European Security. p.639
The Future of NATO Expansion: Four Case Studies. . . . p.639
The Future of North America: Canada, the United States and Quebec Nationalism. p.589
The Future of Northern Ireland. p.607
The Future of Political Science. p.483
The Future of Religious Colleges. p.307

The Future of School Choice. p.450
Future of Social Security: A Feminist Economics Perspective. p.274
The Future of the American Labor Movement. p.130
Future of the Olympic Games. p.846
The Future of the United Nations System: Potential for the Twenty-First Century. p.632
The Future of the World Economy: A United Nations Study. p.259
The Future of U. S. Nuclear Weapons Policy. p.561
Future Shock. p.769
The Future U. S. Healthcare System: Who Will Care for the Poor and Uninsured? p.778
The Futures Game: Who Wins, Who Loses, and Why. p.98, p.102
The G7/G8 System: Evolution, Role and Documentation. . p.630

G

Gaining Access: A Practical and Theoretical Guide for Qualitative Researchers. p.690
Gale Encyclopedia of Childhood and Adolescence. . . . p.676
Gale Encyclopedia of E-Commerce. p.113
Gallery of Best Resumes. p.170
The Gallup Poll: Public Opinion, 1935-1971, Set. p.697
Gambling in America: An Encyclopedia of History, Issues, and Society. p.777, p.899
The Game of Life: College Sports and Educational Values. p.293, p.822, p.895
The Game Planners: Transforming Canada's Sport System. p.891, p.898
Game Theory: A Critical Introduction. p.688
Game Theory and Economics. p.84
Game Theory and Politics. p.83
Game Theory at Work: How to Use Game Theory to Outthink and Outmaneuver Your Competition. p.83
Game Theory in Economics. p.207
Game Theory in the Social Sciences: Concepts and Solutions. p.689
Games and Sets: The Changing Face of Sport on Television. p.803, p.813, p.886, p.901
Games Businesses Play: Cases and Models. p.177
Games Colleges Play: Scandal and Reform in Intercollegiate Athletics. p.291, p.822, p.895
The Games Must Go On: Avery Brundage and the Olympic Movement. p.845
Games That Teach: Experiential Activities for Reinforcing Training. p.84
The Game. p.862
The Gang: A Study of 1,313 Gangs in Chicago. p.752
The Gang That Wouldn't Write Straight: Wolfe, Thompson, Didion and the New Journalism Revolution. p.403
☐ Gangresearch.net. p.753
Gangs and Society: Alternative Perspectives. p.714
The Gangs of New York: An Informal History of the Underworld. p.714
☐ GAO Reports. p.481
Garfinkel and Ethnomethodology. p.688
Gates: How Microsoft's Mogul Reinvented an Industry - and Made Himself the Richest Man in America. p.158
Gates of Freedom: Voltairine de Cleyre and the Revolution of the Mind. p.493
Gateways to the Global Economy. p.256, p.260
Gathering Power: The Future of Progressive Politics in America. p.555
ⓔ Gay and Lesbian Americans and Political Participation: A Reference Handbook. p.570
Gay and Lesbian Educators: Personal Freedoms - Public Constraints. p.309
Gay and Lesbian Students: Understanding Their Needs. . p.309
Gay Histories and Cultures. p.748
☐ Gay Lesbian Straight Education Network. p.309
Gay Olympian: The Life and Death of Dr. Tom Waddell. . p.839
Gay Rights and American Law. p.457
Gaylaw: Challenging the Apartheid of the Closet. p.457
Gays and Lesbians in the Democratic Process: Public Policy, Public Opinion and Political Representation. p.569
Geeks and Geezers: How Era, Values, and Defining Moments Shape Leaders. p.262
Gender and Development. p.259, p.273
Gender and Discourse. p.21
Gender and Emotion: Social Psychological Perspectives. . p.694
Gender and Fair Assessment. p.287
Gender and Governance. p.512
Gender and Health: An International Perspective. p.47
Gender and Physical Education: Contemporary Issues and Future Directions. p.796
Gender and Rhetoric in Plato's Political Thought. p.489
Gender and Stratification. p.722
Gender at the Crossroads of Knowledge: Feminist Anthropology in the Postmodern Era. p.30
Gender, Conflict, and Peacekeeping. p.650
Gender Dimensions of Alcohol Consumption and Alcohol-Related Problems in Latin America and the Caribbean. p.776
Gender, Emotion, and the Family. p.694
Gender Equality in the Philosophy of Education: Catharine Macaulay's Forgotten Contribution. p.346
Gender Equity: An Integrated Theory of Stability and Change. p.723
☐ Gender equity in Sports. p.820, p.834
Gender Ideology and Psychological Reality: An Essay on Cultural Reproduction. p.36
Gender in Policy and Practice: Perspectives on Single-Sex and Coeducational Schooling. p.301
Gender in the Workplace: A Case Study Approach. . p.253, p.273
Gender Injustice: An International Comparative Analysis of Equality in Employment. p.133
The Gender Line: Men, Women, and the Law. p.442
Gender on the Market: Moroccan Women and the Revoicing of Tradition. p.31

Gender Perspectives on Vocational Education: Historical, Cultural, and Policy Aspects. *p.305*
Gender, Race, and the National Education Association: Professionalism and Its Limitations. *p.283*
Gender Talk: The Struggle for Women's Equality in African American Communities. *p.743*
Gendered Fields: Rural Women, Agriculture, and Environment. *p.772*
The Gendered Society: Identities, Behaviors, and Society. . *p.744*
Gender. *p.743*
A Genealogy of Sovereignty. *p.496*
General Competitive Analysis. *p.198*
General Economic History. *p.725*
General Education in a Free Society. *p.290, p.294*
General Equilibrium in International Trade: The Origins of International Economics. *p.206, p.257*
General Issues in Literacy - Illiteracy in the World: A Bibliography. *p.300*
General James Longstreet: The Confederacy's Most Controversial Soldier. *p.522*
General Principles of Criminal Law. *p.434*
The General Strike of 1926. . . . . *p.127*
A General Theory of Love. *p.738*
The General Theory of Transformational Growth: Keynes after Sraffa. *p.228*
The Generalization of the General Theory and Other Essays. *p.270*
Generals in Blue and Gray. *p.521*
Generation X: Americans Born 1965 to 1976. . . . . . . *p.137*
[e] Generations at Work: Managing the Clash of Veterans, Boomers, Xers, Nexters in Your Workplace. *p.132*
Genetically Modified Athletes: The Ethical Implications of Genetic Technologies in Sport. . *p.802, p.825, p.872, p.875*
The Genius of American Education. *p.325*
Genocide and Democracy in Cambodia: The Khmer Rouge, the U. N. and the International Community. *p.653*
Genocide and the Global Village. *p.651*
Genocide and the Modern Age: Etiology and Case Studies of Mass Death, 3. . . . . *p.654*
Genocide in Bosnia: The Policy of "Ethnic Cleansing". . *p.652*
Genocide in International Law: The Crimes of Crimes. . . *p.653*
Genocide in Our Time: An Annotated Bibliography with Analytical Introductions. *p.652*
Genocide in Rwanda: Complicity of the Churches. *p.653*
Genocide: Its Political Use in the Twentieth Century. . . *p.435*
Genocide, War Crimes and the West: History and Complicity. *p.652*
The Gentry: The Rise and Fall of a Ruling Class. *p.726*
[□] Geodata.Gov U.S. maps and Data. *p.373*
Geodesy? What's That?: My Personal Involvement in the Age-Old Quest for the Size and Shape of the Earth. . *p.389*
Geodetic and Topographic Surveying. *p.390*
Geoenvironmental Mapping: Method, Theory and Practice. *p.376*
Geographic Databases and GIS. *p.388*
Geographic Information Systems: An Introduction. *p.386*
[e] Geographic Information Systems and Science. *p.387*
Geographic Information Systems: Applications in Forestry and Natural Resources Management. *p.386*
Geographic Information Systems for the Social Sciences: Investigating Space and Place. *p.388*
Geographic Information Systems in Business. *p.388*
Geographic Literacy: Maps for Memorization. *p.375*
A Geographical History of United States City-Systems: From Frontier to the Urban Transformation. *p.382*
The Geographical Imagination in America, 1880-1950. . . *p.378*
Geographical Information Systems in Archaeology. . *p.6, p.386*
Geographical Information Systems: Principles, Techniques, Management and Applications. *p.387*
A Geographical Introduction to History: An Introduction to Human Geography. *p.375*
Geographical Thought: A Contextual History of Ideas. . . *p.377*
The Geographical Tradition: Episodes in the History of a Contested Enterprise. *p.374*
Geographie Generale. *p.377*
Geographies and Moralities: International Perspectives on Justice, Development and Place. *p.398*
Geographies of Agriculture: Globalisation, Restructuring, and Sustainability. *p.395*
Geographies of Development. *p.398*
Geographies of Global Change: Remapping the World. . . *p.373*
Geographies of Muslim Women: Gender, Religion, and Space. *p.399*
Geography and Economy. *p.398*
Geography and Ethics: Journeys in a Moral Terrain. . . . *p.375*
Geography and Geographers: Anglo-American Human Geography since 1945. . . . . *p.374, p.378*
Geography and History: Bridging the Divide. . . . *p.375, p.377*
Geography and Imperialism, 1820-1940. . . . . *p.502*
Geography and Revolution. *p.375*
Geography and Technology. *p.387*
Geography, Culture and Education. *p.377*
Geography in America at the Dawn of the 21st Century. . *p.382*
Geography in Early Judaism and Christianity: The Book of Jubilees. *p.377*
Geography into the Twenty-First Century. *p.378*
The Geography of Ethnic Violence: Identity, Interests, and the Indivisibility of Territory. *p.488, p.496, p.497*
The Geography of Nowhere: The Rise and Decline of America's Man-Made Landscape. *p.771*
The Geography of Opportunity: Race and Housing Choice in Metropolitan America. *p.381*
The Geography of Presidential Elections in the United States, 1868-2004. . . . . *p.382*
The Geography of South Africa in a Changing World. . . *p.384*
The Geography of War and Peace: From Death Camps to Diplomats. *p.495*
Geography's Inner Worlds: Pervasive Themes in Contemporary American Geography. *p.377*
Geology: An Introduction to Physical Geology. *p.390*
Geology of Deltas. *p.392*
Geomatics. *p.389*

Geometry and Billiards. p.855, p.871
Geomorphological Techniques. p.390
Geomorphology: Critical Concepts in Geography. p.390
Geomorphology, Vol. 3. . . . . p.391
Geopolitical Reader.. . . . . p.400
Geopolitical Traditions: Critical Histories of Century of Political Thought. p.488, p.495
Geopolitics and the Post-Colonial: Rethinking North-South Relations. p.400
Geopolitics of East Asia. p.400
The Geopolitics of Euro-Atlantic Intergration. . . p.383, p.400
Geopolitics of Globalization: The Consequences for Development. p.400
Geopolitics of Resource Wars: Resource Dependence, Governance and Violence. p.400
Geopolitics of the World System. p.487, p.495
The Geopolitics Reader. p.488, p.496
George Herbert Mead and Human Conduct. . . . p.682, p.692
George Meany and His Times. p.128
George S. Counts and Charles A. Beard: Collaborators for Change. p.341
George S. Counts: Educator for a New Age. p.341
George Soros on Globalization. p.665
The German Colonial Empire. p.584
The German Greens: Paradox Between Movement and Party. p.610
German Social Democracy, 1905-1917: The Development of the Great Schism. p.610
German Sociology. p.684
The German Transfer Problem and International Capital Movements: The Origins of International Economics. p.261, p.263
Germany Divided: From the Wall to Reunification. . . . p.610
Gesture: Visible Action as Utterance. p.22
Get A Job! Interview Survival Skills for College Students. . p.169
Get 'Em All! Kill 'Em!: Genocide, Terrorism, Righteous Communities. p.662
Getting Absent Workers Back on the Job: An Analytical Approach. p.130
Getting Ahead: Economic and Social Mobility in America. . p.266
Getting an Academic Job: Strategies for Success, Vol. 17. . p.170
Getting Choice Right: Ensuring Equity and Efficiency in Education Policy. p.302
Getting It Right the First Time: How Innovative Companies Anticipate Demand. p.82
Getting Justice and Getting Even: Legal Consciousness among Working-Class Americans. p.33
Getting Results with Curriculum Mapping. p.364
Getting Rich: America's New Rich and How They Got That Way. p.245, p.265
Getting Started in Entrepreneurship. p.68
Getting Them to Give a Damn: How to Get Your Front Line to Care about Your Bottom Line. p.72
Getting to Know ArcGIS Desktop: The Basics of ArcView, ArcEditor, and ArcInfo Updated for ArcGIS 9. . . . . p.388
Getting to Yes: Negotiating Agreement Without Giving In. . p.74
Getting up and Down: How to Save Strokes from Forty Yards and In. p.861
Getting Wiser to Teens. p.139
Ghetto Schooling: A Political Economy of Urban Educational Reform. p.314
The Ghost Dance: The Origins of Religion. p.36
The Ghost-Dance Religion and the Sioux Outbreak of 1890. . . . . p.37
The Ghosts of Berlin: Confronting German History in the Urban Landscape. p.582
Ghosts of the Confederacy: Defeat, the Lost Cause and the Emergence of the New South, 1865 to 1913. . . . . . p.520
Gideon's Trumpet. p.473
The Gift: The Form and Reason for Exchange in Archaic Societies.. . . . . p.28
Gifted Education: Promising Practices. p.317
The Gilded Age Press, 1865-1900. . . . . p.411
The Gilded Dome: The U. S. Senate and Campaign Finance Reform. p.534
Giovanni and Lusanna: Love and Marriage in Renaissance Florence. p.738
The Girl and the Game: A History of Women's Sport in Canada. p.806, p.836
Girl on the Magazine Cover: The Origins of Visual Stereotypes in American Mass Media. p.141
The Girl on the Magazine Cover: The Origins of Visual Stereotypes in American Mass Media. p.416, p.697
The Girl Problem: Female Sexual Delinquency in New York, 1900-1930. . . . . p.753
Girls and Boys in School: Together or Separate? p.301
Girls, Boys and Junior Sexualities: Exploring Childrens' Gender and Sexual Relations in the Primary School. p.748
Gis: A Short Introduction. p.388
GIS and Crime Mapping. p.386
GIS for Ecologists and Environmental Scientists. p.387
GIS for Everyone: Exploring Your Neighborhood and Your World with a Geographic I. p.386
GIS for the Urban Environment. p.387
GIS Technology, Maps, Society. p.386
Gis Tutorial: A Workbook for Arcview 9. 0. . . . . p.387
The Give and Take of Everyday Life: Language Socialization of Kaluli Children.. p.20
The Glasgow Edition of the Works and Correpondence of Adam Smith, Set. p.218
Glass Ceilings and Asian Americans: The New Face of Workplace Barriers. p.134
Glass Ceilings and Bottomless Pits: Women's Work, Women's Poverty. p.272
Gliding: A Handbook on Soaring Flight. p.787, p.848
Global Acquisitions: Strategic Integration and the Human Factor. p.84
Global Banking. p.92, p.98, p.102, p.103
Global Business Etiquette: A Guide to International Communication and Customs. p.56
Global Capitalism: Its Fall and Rise in the Twentieth Century.. . . . . p.664

The Global Casino: An Introduction to Environmental Issues. *p.159*
Global Change and Challenge: Geography for the 1990s. . *p.377*
Global Civil Society: An Answer to War. *p.498*
Global Civil Society? *p.498*
The Global Coastal Ocean: Interdisciplinary Regional Studies and Syntheses. *p.392*
Global Community: The Role of International Organizations in the Making of the Contemporary World. *p.640*
□ Global Corruption Report. *p.54*
Global Covenant: The Social Democratic Alternative to the Washington Consensus. *p.659*
Global Culture, Island Identity: Continuity and Change in the Afro-Caribbean Community of Nevis. *p.41*
Global Currents: Media and Technology Now. *p.419*
Global Directory of Private Banking. *p.179*
□ Global Edge. *p.59*
Global Education: A Study of School Change. *p.314*
The Global Environment in the Twenty-First Century: Prospects for International Cooperation. *p.666*
Global Financial Turmoil and Reform: A United Nations Perspective. *p.664*
Global Formation: Structures of the World Economy. . . *p.723*
Global Games. *p.845*
Global Geopolitical Flashpoints: An Atlas of Conflict. *p.487, p.495*
Global Geopolitics: A Critical Introduction. *p.400*
Global Governance of Financial Systems: The Legal and Economic Regulation of Systemic Risk. *p.90*
Global Health Leadership and Management. *p.668*
Global Integrated Supply Chain Systems. *p.69*
□ Global Legal Information Network GLIN. . . . *p.474, p.475*
The Global Market: Developing a Strategy to Manage Across Borders. *p.73*
Global Marketing and Advertising: Understanding Cultural Paradoxes. *p.427*
Global Money, Capital Restructuring and the Changing Patterns of Labour. *p.261, p.262*
The Global Negotiator: Making, Managing and Mending Deals Around the World in the Twenty-First Century. . *p.59, p.74*
Global Operations Management. *p.119*
Global Order and Global Disorder: Globalization and the Nation-State. *p.640, p.663*
Global Outrage: The Origins and Impact of World Opinion from the 1780s to the 21st Century. *p.425*
Global Positioning System: A Field Guide for the Social Sciences. *p.390*
Global Prescriptions: Gendering Health and Human Rights. *p.669*
The Global Public Relations Handbook: Theory, Research, and Practice. *p.428*
The Global Reach of Empire: Britain's Maritime Expansion in the Indian and Pacific Oceans, 1764-1814. . . . . . . *p.385*
Global Semiotics. *p.424*
Global Sex. *p.746*
Global Smarts: The Art of Communicating and Deal Making Anywhere in the World. *p.56*
Global Studies: Europe. *p.383*
Global Supply Chain Management. *p.118*
Global Terrorism: A Beginner's Guide. *p.662*
Global Trading System at Crossroads: A Post-Seattle Perspective. *p.664*
The Global Transformations Reader: An Introduction to the Globalization Debate. *p.663*
A Global View of Instructional Technology for the 21st Century. *p.351*
Globalism: The New Market Ideology. *p.665*
Globalization: A Very Short Introduction. *p.55*
Globalization and Cross-Border Labor Solidarity in the Americas: The Anti-Sweatshop Movement and the Struggle for Social Justice. *p.262*
Globalization and Culture Change in the Pacific Islands. . *p.385*
Globalization and Its Discontents. . . *p.56, p.58, p.262, p.665*
Globalization and Resistance: Transnational Dimensions of Social Movements. *p.640, p.663*
ⓔ Globalization and Strategic Alliances: The Case of the Airline Industry. *p.152*
Globalization and Terrorism: The Migration of Dreams and Nightmares. *p.660, p.663*
Globalization and the International Financial System: What's Wrong and What Can Be Done. *p.261, p.263*
Globalization and the Nation State: The Impact of the IMF and the World Bank. *p.262*
Globalization: Capatalism and Its Alternatives. *p.760*
Globalization: Encyclopedia of Trade, Labor, and Politics. *p.56, p.58, p.181*
Globalization, Governmentiality and Global Politics: Regulation for the Rest of Us? *p.261, p.262*
The Globalization Reader. *p.55*
Globalization: What's New. *p.663*
□ Globalization. *p.56*
The Globalized Woman: Reports from a Future of Inequality. *p.666*
Globalizing the Sacred: Religion Across the Americas. . . *p.720*
Glory Bound: Black Athletes in a White America. . *p.822, p.833*
Glossary of Biotechnology and Nanobiotechnology Terms. *p.156*
A Glossary of Cultural Theory. *p.676*
A Glossary of Feminist Theory. *p.676*
□ GNIS Geographic Names Information System: Digital Gazetteer. *p.374*
God and Man at Yale: The Superstitions of "Academic Freedom". *p.292*
God in the Details: American Religion in Popular Culture. . *p.712*
God Is Red: A Native View of Religion. *p.721*
The God That Failed. *p.508*
God-Apes and Fossil Men: Paleoanthropology of South Asia. *p.15*
The Goddess and the Bull: Catalhöyük: An Archaeological Journey to the Dawn of Civilization. *p.12*
God's Assassins: State Terrorism in Argentina in the 1970s. *p.660*
God's Choice: The Total World of a Fundamentalist Christian School. *p.308*

Going Alone: The Case for Relaxed Reciprocity in Freeing Trade. p.256

Going to College: How Social, Economic, and Educational Factors Influence the Decisions Students Make. . . . p.294

The Golden Age of Amateur Basketball: The AAU Tournament, 1921-1968. . . . . p.854

The Golden Bowl Be Broken: Peasant Life in Four Cultures. p.39

Golden Fetters: The Gold Standard and the Great Depression, 1919-1939. . . . . p.213

Golf and the American Country Club. p.716

Golf Course Architecture: Design, Construction and Restoration. p.881

Golf Handbook for Women: The Complete Guide to Improving Your Game. p.838, p.861

Golf Magazine's Complete Book of Golf Instruction. . . p.861

Golf My Way: The Instructional Classic. p.861

Golf's Golden Age: Robert T. Jones, Jr. and the Legendary Players of the '10s, '20s and '30s. p.861

Good Cop, Bad Cop: Racial Profiling and Competing Views of Justice. p.573

The Good Regiment: The Carignan-Salihres Regiment in Canada, 1665-1668. . . . . p.581

The Good Teacher Mentor: Setting the Standard for Support and Success. p.278

Good to Great: Why Some Companies Make the Leap... and Others Don't. p.70

Good Work: When Excellence and Ethics Meet. . . p.53, p.55

The Good-Bye Window: A Year in the Life of a Day-Care Center. p.735

The Google Story: Inside the Hottest Business, Media, and Technology Success of Our Time. p.68

Governance and Opportunity in Metropolitan America: Governmental Arrangements and Individual Life Chances in Urban America. p.542

Governance and Policy in Sport Organizations. p.844, p.891, p.898

Governance in China. p.620

Governance, Multinationals, and Growth. . p.243, p.261, p.263

Governing American Cities: Inter-Ethnic Coalitions, Competition, and Conflict. p.544

Governing China's Multiethnic Frontiers. p.620

Governing Complex Societies: Trajectories and Scenarios. . p.580

Governing Europe. p.603, p.637

Governing from Below: Urban Regions and the Global Economy. p.543

Governing from the Center: Politics and Policy-Making in the Netherlands. p.601

Governing from the Centre: The Concentration of Power in Canadian Politics. p.587

Governing Independent Colleges and Universities: A Handbook for Trustees, Chief Executives and Other Campus Leaders. p.291

Governing Italy: The Politics of Bargained Pluralism. . . p.594

Governing Metropolitan Indianapolis. p.543

Governing Middle-Sized Cities: Studies in Mayoral Leadership. p.543

Governing Ourselves?: The Politics of Canadian Communities. p.581, p.587

Governing Paradoxes of Restorative Justice. p.754

Governing Public Colleges and Universities: A Handbook for Trustees, Chief Executives and Other Campus Leaders. . p.291

Government and Politics in Africa. p.613

Government and Politics in Hungary. p.595

The Government and Politics of France. p.609

The Government and Politics of Ireland. p.607

The Government and Politics of Spain. p.608

Government and Politics of Uruguay. p.593

Government and Society in Malaysia. p.622

Government and the Arts: Debates over Federal Support of the Arts in America from George Washington to Jesse Helms. p.524

Government by Judiciary: The Transformation of the Fourteenth Amendment. p.462

Government Coalitions in Western Democracies. p.574

Government for the People: The Federal Role: What It Is, What It Should Be. p.523

Government Job Finder. p.170

Government Lawyers: The Federal Legal Bureaucracy and Presidential Politics. p.523

Government of Canada, Gouvernement du Canada. . . p.586

Government of Canada: Provinces and Territories. . . p.587

The Government of Canada. p.587

The Government of Manitoba. p.589

Government of Nova Scotia. p.589

A Government of Our Own: The Making of the Confederacy. p.520

The Government of Prince Edward Island. p.590

The Government of Scotland: Public Policy Making after Devolution. p.607

The Government Party: Organizing and Financing the Liberal Party of Canada, 1930-58. . . . . p.589

Government Views of Iraq. p.642

Governments as Interest Groups: Intergovernmental Lobbying and the Federal System. p.523

Governments, Citizens and Genocide: A Comparative and Interdisciplinary Analysis. p.651

Governors and Legislatures: Contending Powers. p.541

Gower Handbook of Supply Chain Management. p.117

GPS Satellite Surveying. p.390

Grace and Glory: A Century of Women in the Olympics. p.824, p.837, p.846

Graduate to Your Perfect Job in 6 Easy Steps. p.169

Gramsci, Culture and Anthropology. p.23

Gramsci's Politics. p.492

Grand Designs and Visions of Unity: The Atlantic Powers and the Reorganization of Western Europe, 1955-1963. . . . . p.637, p.654

Grand Master Workman: Terence Powderly and the Knights of Labor. p.128

The Grand Slam: Bobby Jones, America, and the Story of Golf. p.823, p.860

Grand Strategy in the War Against Terrorism. . . p.564, p.660

Grantland Rice and His Heroes: The Sportswriter As Mythmaker in the 1920s. *p.811, p.907*

The Grants Register 2005: The Complete Guide to Postgraduate Funding Worldwide, Twenty-Third Edition. *p.293*

Graphic Arts Monthly: Applied Technology for the Printing Industry. *p.140*

Grassroots Pacifism in Post-War Japan: The Rebirth of a Nation. *p.712*

Grave Injustice: The American Indian Repatriation Movement and NAGPRA. *p.464*

Gravy Training: Inside the Shadowy World of Business Schools.. . . . . *p.176*

The Graying of America: An Encyclopedia of Aging, Health, Mind and Behavior. *p.677*

Greasers and Gringos: Latinos, Law, and the American Imagination. *p.456*

Great American Trials. *p.438*

The Great Art of Government: Locke's Use of Consent. *p.491, p.497*

Great Ascent: The Struggle for Economic Development in Our Time. *p.244*

The Great Awakening and American Education: A Documentary History. *p.329*

The Great Black Jockeys: The Lives and Times of the Men Who Dominated America's First National Sport. *p.832, p.847*

The Great Chief Justice: John Marshall and the Rule of Law. *p.467*

The Great Crash 1929. . . . . *p.95, p.99, p.243*

Great Debates at the United Nations: An Encyclopedia of Fifty Key Issues, 1945-2000.. . . . . *p.633*

The Great Deception: The Secret History of the European Union. *p.602, p.636*

The Great Depression: An International Disaster of Perverse Economic Policies.. . . . . *p.213*

Great Depression.. . . . . *p.210*

Great Economists Before Keynes: An Introduction to the Lives and Works of One Hundred Great Economists of the Past. *p.208*

Great Economists since Keynes: An Introduction to the Lives and Works of One Hundred Modern Economists. *p.188, p.194, p.208*

Great Game of Genocide: Imperialism, Nationalism, and the Destruction of the Ottoman Armenians. *p.651*

The Great Game: The Emergence of Wall Street as a World Power, 1653-2000. . . . . *p.100 p.147 p.155 p.162*

Great Jobs for Accounting Majors. *p.169*

Great Jobs for Business Majors. *p.170*

Great Jobs for Economics Majors. *p.168*

Great Lakes Archaeology. *p.11*

The Great Peace of Montreal of 1701: French-Native Diplomacy in the Seventeenth Century. *p.630*

Great Power Rivalries. *p.628*

The Great Tax Wars: Lincoln to Wilson - The Fierce Battles over Money and Power That Transformed the Nation. *p.108, p.147*

The Great Telecom Meltdown. *p.111, p.165*

The Great Terror War. *p.563*

Great Time Coming: The Life of Jackie Robinson from Baseball to Birmingham. *p.805, p.831, p.850*

The Great Transformation: The Political and Economic Origins of Our Time. *p.196, p.210*

Great Transformations: Economic Ideas and Institutional Change in the Twentieth Century. *p.487, p.664*

A Great Trial in Chinese History: The Trial of the Lin Biao and Jiang Qing Counter-Revolutionary Cliques, Nov. 1980-Jan. 1981. . . . . *p.475*

The Great Wells of Democracy: The Meaning of Race in American Life. *p.573*

The Greatest Threat: Iraq, Weapons of Mass Destruction, and the Crisis of Global Security. *p.655*

Greek Athletes and Athletics. *p.806*

Greek Athletics and the Genesis of Sport. *p.809*

A Greek Island Cosmos: Kinship and Community on Meganisi. *p.42*

Greek Political Theory, Plato and His Predecessors. . . . *p.488*

▭ The Green Book: Background Material and Data on Programs Within the Jurisdiction of the House Committee on Ways and Means. *p.481*

The Green Book of Language Revitalization in Practice: Toward a Sustainable World. *p.19*

Green Building: Project Planning and Cost Estimating. *p.63, p.158*

Green Ink: An Introduction to Environmental Journalism. . *p.407*

Green Parties and Political Change in Contemporary Europe: New Politics, Old Predicaments. *p.602*

Greening the Corporation: Management Strategy and the Environmental Challenge. *p.63*

Greening the Firm: The Politics of Corporate Environmentalism. *p.63*

Greening Trade and Investment: Environmental Protection Without Protectionism. *p.63*

The Greenwood Dictionary of Education. *p.322*

The Greenwood Encyclopedia of Women's Issues Worldwide. *p.679*

The Greenwood Library of American War Reporting. . . *p.406*

The Gregg Reference Manual: A Manual of Style, Grammar, Usage, and Formatting.. . . . . *p.174*

Groping for Ethics in Journalism. *p.406*

Ground Rules: Baseball and Myth. *p.812, p.852*

The Grounding of Modern Feminism. *p.723*

Group Processes: Dynamics Within and Between Groups. . *p.692*

Group Processes in the Classroom. *p.350*

Group Psychology and Political Theory. *p.483*

Group Rights: Reconciling Equality and Difference. . . . *p.576*

Groups in Harmony and Tension: An Integration of Studies on Intergroup Relations. *p.717*

Groups, Interests, and U. S. Public Policy. *p.559*

Groupwork in Diverse Classrooms: A Casebook for Educators.. . . . . *p.350*

Growing Minds. *p.337*

Growing Old in El Barrio. *p.741*

Growing Old Is Not for Sissies 2: Portraits of Senior Athletes. *p.841*

Growing Prosperity: The Battle for Growth with Equity in the Twenty-First Century. p.722
Growing Together: Personal Relationships Across the Life Span. p.741
Growing up American: Schooling and the Survival of Community. p.303, p.315, p.367
Growing up Bilingual: Puerto Rican Children in New York. . p.21
Growing up Fast. p.759
Growing up Forgotten. p.736
Growing up Literate: Learning from Inner-City Families. . p.762
Growing up Teaching: Kay's Journey. p.277
Growing up with a Single Parent: What Hurts, What Helps. p.739
Growing Young. p.737
The Growth of Social Knowledge: Theory, Simulation, and Empirical Research in Group Processes. p.690
The Growth of the Law. p.433
Growth Recurring: Economic Change in World History. . p.209
Growth Theory: An Exposition. p.245
Growth Triumphant: The Twenty-First Century in Historical Perspective. p.243
Grub Street and the Ivory Tower: Literary Journalism and Literary Scholarship from Fielding to the Internet. . . p.403
Grubb & Ellis Real Estate Forecast. p.158
Guanxi (the Art of Relationships): Microsoft, China, and Bill Gates's Plan to Win the Road Ahead. p.157
Guarantee Clause of the U. S. Constitution. p.455
Guarding Greensboro: A Confederate Company in the Making of a Southern Community. p.521
Guarding the Golden Door: American Immigration Policy and Immigrants since 1882. . . . . p.570
Gubernatorial Elections, 1787-1997. . . . . p.557
Gubernatorial Transitions: The 1983 and 1984 Elections. p.548, p.557
Guerrillas and Generals: The "Dirty War" in Argentina. . p.592
Guerrillas and Revolution in Latin America: A Comparative Study of Insurgents and Regimes since 1956. . . . . p.498
Guide to Business Modelling. p.179
The Guide to Careers in Sports. p.903
A Guide to Econometrics. p.202
A Guide to Econometrics. p.202
Guide to Economic Indicators. p.178
Guide to Effective Coaching: Principles and Practices with PowerWeb: Health and Human Performance. p.904
Guide to Financial Markets. p.96, p.102, p.103
A Guide to Food Laws and Regulations. p.151, p.165
A Guide to Golf Course Irrigation System Design and Drainage. p.872, p.881, p.906
Guide to Graduate Business Schools. p.176
Guide to Internet Job Searching 2006-2007. . . . . p.169
Guide to Managerial Communication. p.173
A Guide to Modern Econometrics. p.205
A Guide to Modern Econometrics. p.205
Guide to Nonprofit Corporate Governance in the Wake of Sarbanes-Oxley. p.85
Guide to Political Campaigns in America. p.548
A Guide to Post-Keynesian Economics. p.232
Guide to Programs in Geography in the United States and Canada 2001-2002. . . . . p.373
Guide to Record Retention Requirements as of August 2005. . . . . p.115
A Guide to Sociological Thinking. p.676
A Guide to Statistical Sources in Money, Banking, and Finance. p.88
A Guide to Taijiquan: Twenty-Four and Forty-Eight Postures with Applications. p.793
Guide to the U.S. Supreme Court. p.466, p.539
Guide to the Works of John Dewey. p.341
Guide to U. S. Elections. p.547, p.548
A Guide to Vocational Assessment. p.305, p.353
Guide to Writing and Publishing in the Social and Behavioral Sciences Cloth. p.675
GuideStar.org. p.545
The Gulag Archipelago, 1918-1956. . . . . p.753
Gulf States. p.382
Gun Control and the Constitution: Sources and Explorations on the Second Amendment. p.449
Guns, Germs, and Steel: The Fates of Human Societies. . p.627
Guns in American Society: An Encyclopedia of History, Politics, Culture, and the Law, Set. p.485
Gurus, Hired Guns, and Warm Bodies: Itinerant Experts in a Knowledge Economy. p.268
Gutcheck!: An Anthropologist's Wild Ride into the Heart of College Football. p.819, p.859, p.894
Guts: Legendary Black Rodeo Cowboy Bill Pickett. p.832, p.865

H

H. L. Mencken and the American Mercury Adventure. . . p.410
Habeas Corpus: Rethinking the Great Writ of Liberty. . . p.524
The Habermas Reader. p.770
Habitat, Economy and Society: A Geographical Introduction to Ethnology. p.29
Habits of the Heart: Individualism and Commitment in American Life. p.720
Hacker Culture. p.709
The Hacker Ethic: And the Spirit of the Information Age. . p.761
A Hacker Manifesto. p.761
The Haider Phenomenon in Austria. p.595
The Haider Phenomenon. p.595
Half Brother, Half Son: The Letters of Louis D. Brandeis to Felix Frankfurter. p.469
Hallmarks of Effective Outcomes Assessment: Assessment Update Collections. p.285
Hallucinogens and Culture. p.776
Hammer and Hoe: Alabama Communists During the Great Depression. p.508, p.553
Han Social Structure. p.701
A Handbook for Classroom Instruction That Works. . . . p.364
A Handbook for Classroom Management That Works. . . p.284
A Handbook for Geography Teachers. p.376

Handbook for Measurement and Evaluation in Early Childhood Education. p.356
Handbook for the Treatment of Abused and Neglected Children. p.756
Handbook of Aging and the Social Sciences. p.741
Handbook of Agricultural Economics, Vol. 1. . . . . . . p.189
Handbook of Agricultural Economics, Vol. 2. . . . . . . p.189
Handbook of Applied Econometrics: Microeconomics. p.191, p.203
Handbook of Asset and Liability Management: Theory and Methodology. p.192
Handbook of Behavioral Economics: Behavioral Decision Making, Vol. 1, Pt. A: Behavioral Microeconomics. . . p.190
Handbook of Career Counseling for Women. . . . p.306, p.354
Handbook of Children and the Media. p.417
Handbook of Classroom Management: Research, Practice, and Contemporary Issues. p.283
Handbook of Climbing. p.789
Handbook of Clinical Sociology. p.692
Handbook of Computational Economics: Agent-Based Computational Economics. p.190
Handbook of Computational Economics. p.186, p.197
Handbook of Crisis Counseling, Intervention, and Prevention in the Schools. p.353
Handbook of Data Analysis. p.178
Handbook of Defense Economics, Vol. 1. . . . . p.189
Handbook of Development Economics, Vol. 3A. p.188
Handbook of Development Economics, Vol. 3B. p.188
Handbook of Development Economics, Vols. 3A & 3B. . p.192
Handbook of Distance Education. p.322
Handbook of Early Childhood Literacy. p.368
Handbook of Early Literacy Research, Vol. 1. . . p.358, p.369
Handbook of Early Literacy Research, Vol. 2. . . p.300, p.368
Handbook of Econometrics, Vol. 2. . . . . p.189, p.201
Handbook of Econometrics, Vol. 4. . . . . p.199
Handbook of Econometrics, Vol. 5. . . . . p.189, p.201
Handbook of Econometrics, Vol. 6. . . . . p.189
Handbook of Economic Growth. p.186, p.194
The Handbook of Economic Sociology. p.718
Handbook of Electoral System Choice. p.577
Handbook of Environmental and Resource Economics. . . p.62
Handbook of Environmental Economics: Economywide and International Environmental Issues. p.191
Handbook of Environmental Economics: Environmental Degradation and Institutional Responses. p.192
Handbook of Environmental Economics: Valuing Environmental Changes. p.191
Handbook of Environmental Sociology. p.760
Handbook of European Union. p.603, p.638
The Handbook of Fixed Income Securities. p.103
Handbook of Game Theory with Economic Applications, Vol. 1.. . . . . p.187
Handbook of Game Theory with Economic Applications, Vol. 3.. . . . . p.187
Handbook of Game Theory with Economic Applications. . p.187
Handbook of Geographic Information Science. p.388
The Handbook of Geographical Information Science. . . p.388
A Handbook of Greek Constitutional History. p.489
Handbook of Health Economics, Vol. 1A. . p.188, p.199, p.264
Handbook of Health Economics, Vol. 1B. . p.188, p.199, p.264
Handbook of Health Economics. p.188
Handbook of Income Distribution, Vol. 1. . . . . p.187
Handbook of Industrial Engineering: Technology and Operations Management. p.119
Handbook of Industrial Organization, Set, Vols. 1 & 2. . . p.191
Handbook of Industrial Organization, Vol. 1. . . . . . . p.191
Handbook of Industrial Organization, Vol. 2. . . . . . . p.191
Handbook of Industrial Organization. p.186
Handbook of Industrial Robotics. p.116
Handbook of Institutional Advancement: A Modern Guide to Executive Management, Institutional Relations, Fund Raising, Alumni Administration, Government Relations, Publications, Periodicals, and Enrollment Management. p.293
Handbook of International Economics: International Monetary Economics and Finance. p.190
Handbook of International Economics: International Trade. p.190
Handbook of International Economics, Vol. 3. . . . . . . p.189
A Handbook of International Human Rights Terminology. . p.669
A Handbook of International Law. p.477
Handbook of Labor Economics, Vol. 3A. p.187
Handbook of Labor Economics, Vol. 3C. p.187
Handbook of Labor Economics, Vol. 3. . . . . p.187
Handbook of Labor Economics. p.186
Handbook of Latin American Studies (HLAS). p.591
Handbook of Macroeconomics, Vol. 15. . . . . p.192
Handbook of Macroeconomics, Vol. 1B. p.192
Handbook of Macroeconomics. p.192
Handbook of Marketing and Society. p.145
Handbook of Mathematical Economics, Set. p.186
Handbook of Mathematical Economics, Vol. 1. . . p.186, p.198
Handbook of Mathematical Economics, Vol. 3. . . p.186, p.198
Handbook of Mathematical Economics, Vol. 4. . . . . . p.189
Handbook of Medical Anthropology: Contemporary Theory and Method. p.47
Handbook of Monetary Economics, Vol. 1. . . . . p.188
Handbook of Monetary Economics, Vol. 2. . . . . p.189
Handbook of Multicultural Perspectives on Stress and Coping. p.699
Handbook of Natural Resource and Energy Economics: Handbooks in Economics, Six, 2. . . . . p.190
Handbook of Natural Resource and Energy Economics: Handbooks in Economics, Six, Set. p.190
Handbook of Natural Resource and Energy Economics, Vol. 1.. . . . . p.190
Handbook of Natural Resource and Energy Economics, Vol. 2.. . . . . p.190
Handbook of Natural Resource and Energy, Vol. 3. . . . p.190

The Handbook of Negotiation: Theoretical Advances and Cross-Cultural Perspectives. p.74, p.698
Handbook of Organizational Learning and Knowledge. . . p.78
[e] Handbook of Package Engineering. p.116
Handbook of Political Science Research on the Middle East and North Africa. p.615
Handbook of Population and Family Economics, Vol. IA. . p.191
Handbook of Population and Family Economics, Vol. IB. . p.191
Handbook of Population and Family Economics, Vols. 1A & 1B. p.191
The Handbook of Pragmatics. p.424
Handbook of Print Media: Technologies and Production Methods. p.417
The Handbook of Private Schools: An Annual Descriptive Survey of Independent Education. p.297
Handbook of Psychoeducational Assessment: A Practical Handbook. p.285
Handbook of Psychological Anthropology. p.35
Handbook of Psychology, Educational Psychology, Vol. 7. . p.357
Handbook of Public Administration. p.545, p.580
Handbook of Public Economics, Vol. 1, June 1985. . . . p.187
Handbook of Public Economics, Vol. 2. . . . . p.187
Handbook of Public Economics, Vol. 4. . . . . p.187
Handbook of Public Economics, Vol. I. p.187
Handbook of Public Economics. p.187
Handbook of Reading Research. p.354
Handbook of Regional and Urban Economics: Applied Urban Economics. p.188
Handbook of Regional and Urban Economics: Cities and Geography, Vol. 4. . . . . p.189
Handbook of Regional and Urban Economics: Urban Economics. p.191
Handbook of Regional and Urban Economics: Volumes One and Two. p.191
Handbook of Research Design and Social Measurement. . p.686
Handbook of Research for Educational Communications and Technology: A Project of the Association for Educational Communications and Technology. p.351
Handbook of Research on Curriculum. p.355, p.361
Handbook of Research on Educational Psychology. . . . p.356
Handbook of Research on Multicultural Education. . p.300, p.308
Handbook of Research on Teaching Literacy Through the Communicative and Visual Arts: Sponsored by the International Reading Association. p.300
Handbook of Research on Teaching the English Language Arts: Sponsored by the International Reading Association and the National Council of Teachers of English. p.363
Handbook of Research on Teaching. p.355
Handbook of Research on Urban Politics and Policy in the United States, Vol. 28, no. 13. . . . . p.544
The Handbook of Sailing Techniques: Professional Tips, Expert Advice, Essential Skills. p.866
The Handbook of School Psychology. p.358
Handbook of School-Based Interventions: Resolving Student Problems and Promoting Healthy Educational Environments. p.352
Handbook of Schooling in Urban America. p.315
Handbook of Social Choice and Welfare, Vol. 1. . . . . . p.186
Handbook of Social Cognition, Set. p.692
The Handbook of Social Policy. p.769
The Handbook of Social Psychology, Set. p.691
The Handbook of Sociolinguistics. p.18
[e] Handbook of Sport Psychology. p.877
Handbook of Telecommunications Economics: Technology Evolution and the Internet. p.190
Handbook of the Economics of Finance: Corporate Finance. p.188
Handbook of the Economics of Finance: Financial Markets and Asset Pricing. p.188
Handbook of the Economics of Finance. p.188
Handbook of the Economics of Giving, Altruism and Reciprocity: Applications. p.190
Handbook of the Economics of Giving, Altruism and Reciprocity: Foundations. p.189
Handbook of the Media in Asia. p.415
Handbook of the Sociology of the Military. p.717
Handbook of Training Technologies: An Introductory Guide to Facilitating Learning with Technology — From Planning to Evaluation. p.352
Handbook of Urban and Regional Economics. p.191
Handbook of Vocational Psychology: Theory, Research, and Practice. p.306
Handbook of Workplace Diversity. p.132
Handbook of Workplace Violence. p.130
Handbook on Architectures of Information Systems. . . . p.114
Handbook on Data Management in Information Systems. . p.114
Handbook on Economics of Sport. p.186
Handbook on Geographic Information Systems and Digital Mapping. p.388
Handbook on the Globalization of the World Economy. . p.261
Handbook on Undergraduate Curriculum: Prepared for the Carnegie Council on Policy Studies in Higher Education. p.294
Hands and Hearts: A History of Courtship in America. . . p.738
Hanging in and Dropping Out: Voices of At-Risk High School Students. p.299
Happiness and Education. p.339
Hard at Play: Leisure in America, 1840-1940. . . p.716, p.784
Hard Choices, Easy Answers: Values, Information, and American Public Opinion. p.425, p.559
Hard Choices, Lost Voices: How the Abortion Conflict Has Divided America, Distorted Constitutional Rights, and Damaged the Courts. p.448
A Hard Road to Glory, 1619-1918, Vol. 1. . . . . p.831
A Hard Road to Glory: 1919-1945, Vol. 2. . . . . p.830
A Hard Road to Glory: A History of the African American Athlete, 1946-1969, Vol. 3, 3rd Edition, Vol. 3. . . . . p.831
A Hard Road to Glory: A History of the African American Athlete, 1970-Present, Vol. 4. . . . . p.831
Hardball: The Education of a Baseball Commissioner. p.807, p.851, p.884
Hardware and Computer Organization. p.114
Harm Reduction: Pragmatic Strategies for Managing High-Risk Behaviors. p.779

Harriet Martineau: Theoretical and Methodological Perspectives. *p.690*

Harriet Martineau's Autobiography, Vol. 2. . . . . *p.193*

Harriet Martineaus's Autobiography, Vol. 1. . . . . *p.209*

Harry Hooper: An American Baseball Life. *p.853*

Harvard Business Review on Advances in Strategy. *p.73*

Harvard Business Review on Corporate Ethics. *p.53*

Harvard Business Review on Corporate Responsibility. *p.52, p.54*

Harvard Business Review on Corporate Strategy. *p.81*

Harvard Business Review on Developing Leaders: Ideas with Impact. *p.176*

The Harvard Business School Guide to Careers in Finance.. . . . . *p.167*

The Harvard Business School Guide to Careers in Management Consulting. *p.167*

Has Man a Future? *p.656*

Hate Crimes: A Reference Handbook. *p.568*

Hate Crimes: Confronting Violence Against Lesbians and Gay Men. *p.568, p.751*

Hate Crimes: Criminal Law and Identity Politics. . *p.472, p.568*

Hate Speech, Sex Speech, Free Speech. *p.460, p.749*

Hate Speech: The History of an American Controversy. . *p.472*

Haunted Media: Electronic Presence from Telegraphy to Television. *p.419*

Having a Good Cry: Effeminate Feelings and Pop-Culture Forms. *p.695*

Hawaii Pono: An Ethnic and Political History. *p.702*

Hayek on Liberty. *p.211*

Hazard and Choice Perception in Flood Plain Management. *p.395*

Headfirst: The Olympic Success Story of Skeleton. . . . *p.846*

Healing Communities in Conflict: International Assistance in Complex Emergencies. *p.671*

The Healing of Nations: The Promise and Limits of Political Forgiveness. *p.483, p.624*

Health and Human Rights: Basic International Documents. *p.668, p.670*

Health Clubs: Architecture and Design. *p.792, p.881*

Health Fitness Instructor's Handbook. *p.791, p.906*

Health Fitness Management: A Comprehensive Resource for Managing and Operating Programs and Facilities. *p.792, p.906*

Health Insurance: Current Issues and Background. *p.163*

Health Movement in America: Promoting Fitness. . *p.790, p.805*

Healthcare Reform in America: A Reference Handbook. . *p.160*

Healthcare Trends and Forecasts in 2006: Performance Expectations for the Healthcare Industry. *p.160*

Healthy Runner's Handbook. *p.866, p.879*

Heard on the Street: Quantitative Questions from Wall Street Job Interviews. *p.169*

The Hearsts: An American Dynasty. *p.149, p.411*

The Heart of Change: Real Life Stories of How People Change Their Organizations. *p.73*

The Heart of Confederate Appalachia: Western North Carolina in the Civil War. *p.521*

The Heat of the Hearth: The Process of Kinship in a Malay Fishing Community. *p.31*

Heaven on Earth: The Rise and Fall of Socialism. *p.507*

Heavy Lifting: The Job of the American Legislature. . . . *p.531*

Hedgehogging. *p.94, p.99, p.162*

H-Education. *p.327*

Hegel: Political Writings. *p.491, p.502*

Hegel's Educational Theory and Practice. *p.343*

Hegel's Philosophy of Politics: Idealism, Identity, and Modernity. *p.491*

Heidegger, Education and Modernity. *p.345*

Heinrich Pestalozzi. *p.342*

Help! My Job Interview Is Tomorrow!: How to Use the Library to Research an Employer. *p.171*

Help or Hindrance?: The Economic Implications of Immigration for African Americans. *p.570*

Helping at-Risk Youth Through Physical Fitness Programming. *p.795*

Helping Children Left Behind: State Aid and the Pursuit of Educational Equity. *p.302*

Henry R. Luce and the Rise of the American News Media. . *p.409*

Herbert Spencer on Education. *p.346*

Here to Stay: American Families in the Twentieth Century. . *p.732*

Here's Where I Stand: A Memoir. *p.486*

Hermaphrodites and the Medical Invention of Sex. . . . *p.746*

Hermeneutics and Education. *p.323, p.339*

The Hero and the Outlaw: Building Extraordinary Brands Through the Power of Archetypes. *p.144*

Heroes of Their Own Lives: The Politics and History of Family Violence: Boston, 1880-1960. . . . . *p.742*

Heroic Defeats: The Politics of Job Loss. *p.121*

Heroic Diplomacy: Sadat, Kissinger, Carter, Begin and the Quest for Arab-Israeli Peace. . . *p.566, p.642, p.646, p.650*

Heuristics and Biases: The Psychology of Intuitive Judgment. *p.195*

The Hidden Power of Social Networks: Understanding How Work Really Gets Done in Organizations. *p.120*

Hidden Scholars: Women Anthropologists and the Native American Southwest. *p.4*

Hierarchical Structures and Social Value: The Creation of Black and Irish Identities in the United States. *p.730*

High and Mighty: The Dangerous Rise of the SUV. . . . *p.153*

The High Lonesome: Epic Solo Climbing Stories. *p.789*

High Performance: The Culture and Technology of Drag Racing, 1950-2000. . . . . *p.848*

The High Price of Bullion: A Proof of Depreciation of Bank Notes. *p.220*

The High Status Track: Studies of Elite Schools and Stratification. *p.296*

High Tech and High Heels in the Global Economy: Women, Work and Pink-Collar Identities in the Caribbean. . . . *p.28*

High Tech Hot Shots: Careers in Sports Engineering. *p.870, p.903*

The High Tide of Prophecy. *p.488 p.490 p.493 p.517*

Higher Education and Opinion Making in Twentieth-Century England. *p.336*

Higher Education As a Moral Enterprise. *p.290*

Higher Education in a Maturing Democracy. p.331
Higher Education in Ireland: North and South. p.336
Higher Education in Transition: A History of American Colleges and Universities. p.331
Higher Education under Fire: Politics, Economics and the Crisis of the Humanities. p.330
Higher Goals: Women's Ice Hockey and the Politics of Gender. p.820, p.838, p.862
Higher Learning in America, 1980-2000. . . . . p.331
The Higher Learning in America: A Memorandum on the Conduct of Universities by Business Men. p.250
The Higher Learning in America. p.290
Higher Learning. p.295, p.330
High-Tech Cycling. p.856, p.870, p.871
Hillbilly: A Cultural History of an American Icon. p.709
The Hindu Caste System: The Sacralization of a Social Order.. . . . . p.703
Hindu Nationalism and Indian Politics: The Origins and Development of the Bharatiya Jana Sangh. p.617
Hindu Nationalists in India: The Rise of the Bharatiya Janata Party. p.618
Hispanic Education in the United States: Raices y Alas. . p.311
The Hispanic Market Handbook. p.136
Hispanic Spaces, Latino Places: Community and Cultural Diversity in Contemporary America. p.381
Historians of Economics and Economic Thought: The Construction of Disciplinary Memory. p.209
Historic U. S. Court Cases: An Encyclopedia, Set. p.441
Historical and Multicultural Encyclopedia of Women's Reproductive Rights in the United States. p.676
Historical Archaeology in Africa: Representation, Social Memory, and Oral Traditions. p.14
The Historical Archaeology of the Ottoman Empire: Breaking New Ground. p.13
Historical Archaeology. p.14
Historical Atlas of Central America. p.399
An Historical Atlas of Central Asia. p.384
Historical Atlas of Empires: From 4000 BC to the 21st Century.. . . . . p.380
A Historical Atlas of North America Before Columbus. . p.380
Historical Atlas of the Crusades. p.380
Historical Atlas of the Napoleonic Era. p.383
Historical Atlas of the North Pacific Ocean: Maps of Discovery and Scientific Exploration, 1500-2000. . . . . p.379
Historical Atlas of the Rise of Islam. p.380
Historical Atlas of World War Two. p.380
Historical Dictionary of Arms Control and Disarmament. . p.656
Historical Dictionary of European Imperialism. p.583
Historical Dictionary of Human Rights and Humanitarian Organizations. p.670
Historical Dictionary of Multinational Peacekeeping. . . . p.650
Historical Dictionary of Organized Labor. p.125
Historical Dictionary of Refugee and Disaster Relief Organizations. p.667
Historical Dictionary of Terrorism. p.657
Historical Dictionary of the Modern Olympic Movement. p.805, p.845
Historical Dictionary of the Olympic Movement. . p.807, p.846
Historical Dictionary of the United Nations. p.632
Historical Dictionary of U. S. -Latin American Relations. . p.641
Historical Dictionary of Utopianism. p.678
Historical Ecology: Cultural Knowledge and Changing Landscapes. p.29
Historical Encyclopedia of American Labor. p.123
Historical Gazetteer of the United States. p.374
A Historical Guide to the U. S. Government. p.517
Historical Perspectives on the Education of Black Children. p.310
□ Historical Statistics of the United States. p.676
Historical Survey of Pre-Christian Education. p.327
The Historical Theory of the Ruling Class. p.248
Histories of Leisure. p.716, p.784
□ History and Archival Resources in Higher Education. . p.332
History and Critique of Interest Theories, Vol. 1. . . . . p.234
The History and Growth of Vocational Education in America. p.305
History and Power in the Study of Law: New Directions in Legal Anthropology. p.34
History and Social Theory. p.682, p.699
The History and Sociology of Genocide: Analyses and Case Studies. p.651, p.767
History Comes Home: Family Stories Across the Curriculum. p.366
History Lessons: Teaching, Learning, and Testing in U. S. High School Classrooms. p.367
□ History Matters. p.366
History of Accountancy in the United States: The Cultural Significance of Accounting. p.104
The History of Accounting: An Encyclopedia. p.104
A History of African Higher Education from Antiquity to the Present: A Critical Synthesis. p.335
A History of American Higher Education. p.332
A History of American Law. p.440
A History of American Magazines: 1885-1905. . . . . . p.409
History of American Physical Education and Sport. . . . p.797
A History of Antarctic Science. p.378
A History of Anthropological Theory. p.23
A History of Archaeological Thought. p.6
A History of Argentine Political Thought. p.592
A History of British Industrial Relations, 1939-1979: Industrial Relations in a Declining Economy. p.213
The History of British Journalism, from the Foundation of the Newspaper Press in England, to the Repeal of the Stamp Act in 1855. . . . . p.403
A History of British Trade Unionism, 1700-1998. . . . . p.126
The History of Broadcasting in the United Kingdom. . . p.413
A History of Central Banking in Great Britain and the United States. p.156
History of Civilizations of Central Asia, Set. p.8
A History of Contemporary Italy: Society and Politics, 1943-1988. . . . . p.594

The History of Econometric Ideas. *p.203*
The History of Economic Analysis: Selected Essays by John Creedy. *p.195, p.208*
History of Economic Analysis: With a New Introduction. *p.210, p.230, p.235*
A history of economic theories. *p.236*
A History of Economic Theory and Method. *p.195*
A History of Education Before the Middle Ages. *p.326*
A History of Education During the Middle Ages and the Transition of Modern Times. *p.326*
History of Education: Selected Moments of the 20th Century. *p.329*
History of Elections in Bohemia and Moravia. *p.574, p.577, p.596*
A History of English Law and Its Administration from 1750: Victorian and Edwardian England: The Emergence of Penal Policy. *p.436*
The History of English Law Before the Time of Edward I 1898, Set. *p.436*
A History of Environmental Politics. *p.566*
The History of Exercise and Sport Science. . . . *p.808, p.873*
A History of Fascism, 1914-1945. . . . . *p.510*
A History of Federal Crime Control Initiatives, 1960-1993. . . . . *p.567*
The History of Fencing: Foundations of Modern European Swordplay. *p.857*
The History of Human Rights: From Ancient Times to the Globalization Era. *p.512*
History of Interest Rates. *p.155*
A History of Lay Judges, 1960. . . . . *p.435*
The History of Marketing Thought. *p.134*
The History of Men: Essays on the History of American and British Masculinities. *p.745*
A History of Modern Economic Analysis. *p.194*
A History of Mountain Climbing. *p.789*
A History of NATO: The First Fifty Years, Set. *p.639*
A History of Neglect: Health Care for Southern Blacks and Mill Workers in the Twentieth-Century South. *p.774*
A History of Negro Education in the South: From 1619 to the Present. *p.309*
A History of News: From Oral Culture to the Information Age. *p.403*
A History of Newspapers in the United States Through 250 Years, 1690-1940, Set. *p.411*
History of Political Philosophy. *p.488*
A History of Popular Women's Magazines in the United States, 1792-1995. . . . . *p.410*
A History of Post Keynesian Economics since 1936. . . . *p.269*
A History of Private Life: From Pagan Rome to Byzantium, Vol. 1. . . . . *p.732*
A History of Private Life: From the Fires of Revolution to the Great War. *p.734*
A History of Private Life: Passions of the Renaissance. . *p.732*
A History of Private Life: Revelations of the Medieval World, Vol. 2. . . . . *p.733*
A History of Private Life: Riddles of Identity in Modern Times, Vol. 5. . . . . *p.732*
History of Regional Science and the Regional Science Association International: The Beginnings and Early History. *p.397*
A History of Russian Economic Thought. . *p.211, p.235, p.255*
A History of Sexuality: An Introduction, Vol. 1. . . . . . *p.747*
The History of Sexuality: The Care of the Self, Vol. 3. . . *p.747*
The History of Sexuality: The Use of Pleasure, Vol. 2. . . *p.747*
A History of Small Business in America. *p.87, p.146*
A History of Spaces: Cartographic Reason, Mapping, and the Geo-Coded World. *p.375*
History of Telecommunications Technology: An Annotated Bibliography. *p.421*
A History of Telegraphy: Its Technology and Application. . *p.421*
A History of the Adult Education Movement in the United States. *p.320*
A History of the American Bar. *p.440*
A History of the Black Press. *p.404*
A History of the Confederate Navy. *p.521*
History of the Idea of Progress. *p.700*
History of the Labor Movement in the United States: 1914-1918, Vol. 7. . . . . *p.125*
A History of the Labor Movement in the United States: 1915-1916, on the Eve of America's Entrance into World War I, Vol. 6. . . . . *p.125*
History of the Labor Movement in the United States: From Colonial Times to the Founding of the American Federation of Labor, Vol. 1. . . . . *p.125*
History of the Labor Movement in the United States: From the Founding of the American Federation of Labor to the Emergence of American Imperialism, Vol. 2. . . . . . *p.125*
History of the Labor Movement in the United States: Postwar Struggles, 1918-1920, Vol. 8. . . . . *p.125*
History of the Labor Movement in the United States: The AFL in the Progressive Era, 1910-1913. . . . . *p.125*
History of the Labor Movement in the United States: The Industrial Workers of the World. *p.125*
History of the Labor Movement in the United States: The Policies and Practices of the AFL, 1900-1909, Vol. 3. . *p.125*
History of the Labor Movement in the United States: The TUEL to the End of the Gompers Era, Vol. 9. . . . . *p.125*
History of the Labor Movement: The TUEL, 1925-1929, Vol. 10. . . . . *p.125*
A History of the League of Nations. *p.632*
History of the Mass Media in the United States: An Encyclopedia. *p.415*
The History of the Rugby World Cup. *p.847, p.865*
History of the Standard Oil Company. *p.147, p.148*
A History of the Supreme Court. *p.466, p.539*
A History of the Theories of Production and Distribution in English Political Economy from 1776 To 1848. . . . . *p.211*
A History of the University in Europe: Universities in Early Modern Europe (1500-1800). *p.326*
A History of the University in Europe: Universities in the Middle Ages. *p.325*
A History of the University in Europe: Universities in the Nineteenth and Early Twentieth Centuries (1800-1945). *p.329*
A History of the Western Educational Experience. *p.326*

A History of the World in Six Glasses. *p.710*
The History of Trade Unionism. *p.212, p.254*
History of Universities. *p.334*
A History of Western Educational Ideas. *p.339*
History of Western Education—Civilization of Europe: 6th to 16th Century, Vol. 2. . . . . *p.324*
History of Western Education—The Ancient World: Orient and Mediterranean 2000 B. C.-A. D. 1054, Vol. 1. . . . . *p.324*
History of Western Education—The Modern West: Europe and the New World, Vol. 3. . . . . *p.324*
The History of Western Education. *p.324*
A History of Women's Football: Gender, Power and the Rise of a Global Game. *p.811, p.845, p.868*
Hitotsubashi on Knowledge Management. *p.77*
The Hittites: And Their Contemporaries in Asia Minor. . . . *p.9*
HIV InSite: HIV Policy. *p.668*
HIV/AIDS in Russia and Eurasia, Vol. 1. . . . . *p.669*
Hobbes on Civil Association. *p.492, p.493*
Hoffa. *p.129*
The Hold Life Has: Coca and Cultural Identity in an Andean Community. *p.36, p.700*
Holding Accountability Accountable: What Ought to Matter in Public Education. *p.281*
Holding Corporations Accountable: Corporate Conduct, International Codes and Citizen Action. *p.145*
Holmes-Laski Letters, the Correspondence of Justice Oliver Wendell Holmes and Harold J. Laski, 1916-1935, 2. . *p.468*
Holmes-Pollock Letters: The Correspondence of Mr. Justice Holmes and Sir Frederick Pollock, 1874-1932. . . . . *p.468*
Holocaust Justice: The Battle for Restitution in America's Courts. *p.464*
Holocene Settlement of the Egyptian Sahara. *p.8*
Holy Leisure: Recreation and Religion in God's Square Mile. *p.720*
Holy Terrors: Thinking about Religion after September 11. . . . . *p.564, p.660*
The Home: Its Work and Influence. *p.737*
Home Schooling: Political, Historical, and Pedagogical Perspectives. *p.296*
Home Team: Professional Sports and the American Metropolis. *p.883, p.887, p.896*
Home Town News: William Allen White and the Emporia Gazette. *p.410*
Home Town. *p.704*
Homeland. *p.767*
Homelessness, AIDS, and Stigmatization: The NIMBY Syndrome in the United States at the End of the Twentieth Century. *p.722*
The Homeless. *p.750*
Homemakers, the Forgotten Workers. *p.736*
Homeplace Geography: Essays for Appalachia. *p.381*
Homeschooling in Full View: A Reader. *p.296*
Homo Hierarchicus; an Essay on the Caste System. . . . *p.723*
Homosexuality: A History. *p.749*
Homosexuality and Civilization. *p.747*
Homosexuality and the Law: A Dictionary. *p.457*
The Homosexuality of Men and Women. *p.748*
Honest Numbers and Democracy: Social Policy Analysis in the White House, Congress and the Federal Agencies. . . *p.526*
Honest Numbers and Democracy: Social Policy Analysis in the White House, Congress, and the Federal Agencies.. . . . . *p.567, p.770*
Honey and Vinegar: Incentives, Sanctions and Foreign Policies.. . . . . *p.642*
Hong Kong's Embattled Democracy: A Societal Analysis. . *p.618*
Honor and Grace in Anthropology. *p.42*
An Honorable Defeat: The Last Days of the Confederate Government. *p.520*
Honorable Justice: The Life of Oliver Wendell Holmes. . *p.469*
Honus Wagner: A Biography. *p.850*
Hoover's Online. *p.93, p.101*
Hopeful Girls Troubled Boys: Race and Gender Disparity in Urban Education. *p.315*
Horace Mann, a Biography. *p.344*
Horace's Compromise: The Dilemma of the American High School. *p.329*
Horace's School: Redesigning the American High School. . *p.329*
The Horizontal Organization: What the Organization of the Future Actually Looks Like and How It Delivers Value to Customers. *p.80*
Horrors of the Half-known Life: Male Attitudes Toward Women and Sexuality in 19th Century America. *p.743*
Hospital Costs and Health Insurance. *p.247*
Hospitality Facilities Management and Design. *p.161*
Hospitality World!: An Introduction. *p.161*
Hot Potato: How Washington and New York Gave Birth to Black Basketball and Changed America's Game Forever. *p.807, p.832, p.854*
Hotel and Lodging Management: An Introduction. *p.161*
Hotel and Restaurant Industries: A Bibliography and Sourcebook. *p.161*
The Hothouse Effect: Intensify Creativity in Your Organization Using Secrets from History's Most Innovative Communities. *p.66*
The Houghton Mifflin Dictionary of Geography: Places and Peoples of the World. *p.373*
The House and Senate Explained: The People's Guide to Congress. *p.533*
House and Senate. *p.529, p.533*
The House of Morgan: An American Banking Dynasty and the Rise of Modern Finance. *p.91*
The House of Morgan: An American Banking Family and the Rise of Modern Finance. *p.146, p.148, p.154*
The House of Rothschild: Money's Prophets, 1798-1848. . . . . *p.146, p.155*
The House of Rothschild: The World's Banker, 1849-1999. . . . . *p.147, p.155*
The House Practice: A Guide to the Rules, Precedents and Procedures of the House. *p.532*
Household Spending: Who Spends How Much on What. . *p.138*
Households, Employment and Gender: A Social, Economic and Demographic View. *p.724, p.733*

Houses in the Rain Forest: Ethnicity and Inequality among Farmers and Foragers in Central Africa. p.772
Housing Desegregation and Federal Policy. p.524
Housing in the Twenty-First Century: Achieving Common Ground. p.158
How Boston Played: Sport, Recreation, and Community, 1865-1915. . . . . p.806, p.816
How Britain Works: From Ideology to Output Politics. . . p.582
How Children Fail. p.364
How Children Learn. p.357
How Cities Work: Suburbs, Sprawl, and the Roads Not Taken. p.771
How Class Works: Power and Social Movement. p.710
How CNN Fought the War: A View from the Inside. . . . p.407
How College Affects Students: A Third Decade of Research. p.332
How College Affects Students: Findings and Insights from Twenty Years of Research. p.290
How Communities Build Stonger Schools: Stories, Strategies, and Promising Practices for Educating Every Child. . p.303
How Democracies Vote. p.577
How Democratic Is the American Constitution? p.453
How Did This Happen?: Terrorism and the New War. . . p.564
How Economics Became a Mathematical Science. p.176
How Economists Model the World into Numbers. . p.198, p.240
How Educational Ideologies Are Shaping Global Society: Intergovernmental Organizations, NGO's, and the Decline of the Nation-State. p.314
How France Votes. p.609
How Free Can the Press Be? p.458
How Full Is Your Bucket?: Positive Strategies for Work and Life. p.83
How Golf Clubs Really Work and How to Optimize Their Designs. p.861, p.870, p.872
How Industries Evolve: Understanding the Critical Link Between Strategy and Innovation. p.81, p.149
How Monetary Policy Works. p.246
How Much Is That in Real Money?: A Historical Commodity Price Index for Use As a Deflator of Money Values in the Economy of the United States. p.175
The How of WOW: A Guide to Giving a Speech That Will Positively Blow 'Em Away. p.172
□ How Our Laws Are Made. p.461
How Our Lives Become Stories: Making Selves. p.693
How Russia Votes. p.599
How Schools Change: Lessons from Three Communities. . p.330
How Sex Changed: A History of Transsexuality in the United States. p.744
How Teachers Taught: Constancy and Change in American Classrooms, 1890-1990. . . . . p.325
How the News Makes Us Dumb: The Death of Wisdom in an Information Society. p.418
How the Other Half Lives. p.755
How to Build a Successful Consulting Practice. p.65
How to Create Interest-Evoking, Sales-Inducing, Non-Irritating Advertising. p.428
How to Get an MBA. p.177
How to Get into the Top MBA Programs. p.177
How to Have Theory in an Epidemic: Cultural Chronicles of AIDS. p.779
How to Increase Reading Ability: A Guide to Developmental and Remedial Methods. p.363
How to Lie with Maps. p.375, p.385
How to Negotiate Like a Child: Unlease the Little Monster Within to Get Everything You Want. p.74
How to Plan Advertising. p.427
How to Prevent Genocide: A Guide for Policymakers, Scholars, and the Concerned Citizen. p.652
How to Promote Children's Social and Emotional Competence. p.354
How to Put Your Book Together and Get a Job in Advertising: 21st Century Edition. p.428
How to Read a Financial Report: Wringing Vital Signs Out of the Numbers. p.92, p.98, p.105, p.176
How to Research Congress. p.530
How to Research the Supreme Court. p.466
How to Run a Company: Lessons from Top Leaders of the CEO Academy. p.85
How to Say It at Work: Putting Yourself Across with Power Words, Phrases, Body Language and Communication Secrets. p.173
How Using Pr Can Boost Your Business Public Relations for the Small Business. p.87
How We Think They Think: Anthropological Approaches to Cognition, Memory and Literacy. p.27
HR Best Practices: Top Human Resources Executives from Prudential Financial, Northrop Grumman, and More on Hiring the Right People and Enhancing Corporate Culture. p.75
The HR Scorecard: Linking People, Strategy, and Performance. p.76
The HR Value Proposition. p.77
HRD in the Age of Globalization: A Practical Guide to Workplace Learning in the Third Millennium. p.79
□ HSLDA: Home School Legal Defense Association. . . p.296
The Huddled Masses Myth: Immigration and Civil Rights. . p.460
The Huddled Masses: The Immigrant in American Society, 1880-1921. . . . . p.667
Hugo Black: A Biography. p.468, p.538
Hugo Grotius and International Relations. p.625
Hugo L. Black: Cold Steel Warrior. p.467
Human Action: A Treatise on Economics. p.212
□ Human and Constitutional Rights. p.476
Human Biodiversity: Genes, Race and History. p.17
Human Biological Variation. p.17
The Human Career: Human Biological and Cultural Origins. p.15
Human Cargo: A Journey among Refugees. p.765
The Human Condition. p.718
Human Development Report 2002: Deepening Democracy in a Fragmented World. p.586
Human Development Report 2005: International Cooperation at a Crossroads: Aid, Trade and Security in an Unequal World. p.258, p.262, p.666

Human Ecology As Human Behavior: Essay in Environmental and Development Anthropology. *p.29*

Human Families. *p.708*

The Human Fossil Record, Set. *p.16*

Human Geography: An Introduction. *p.396*

Human Geography of the UK. *p.373*

Human Geography: People, Place, and Culture. *p.396*

Human Geography. *p.396*

The Human Group. *p.692*

Human Institutions: A Theory of Societal Evolution. . . . *p.718*

The Human Journalist: Reporters, Perspectives, and Emotions. *p.412*

Human Motives and Cultural Models. *p.27*

Human Motor Development: A Lifespan Approach with PowerWeb/OLC Bind-In Card. *p.910*

Human Nature and the Social Order. *p.692, p.693*

Human Nature in Politics: The Dynamics of Political Behavior. *p.483*

Human Past. *p.6*

The Human Potential for Peace: An Anthropological Challenge to Assumptions about War and Violence. *p.766*

Human Resource Development: Strategy and Tactics. . . . *p.77*

Human Resource Management: Essential Perspectives. . . *p.76*

Human Resource Management in Public Service: Paradoxes, Processes, and Problems. *p.76*

Human Resource Management in Sport and Recreation. *p.883, p.900*

Human Resource Management in the Knowledge Economy: New Challenges, New Roles, New Capabilities. *p.76*

Human Resource Management. *p.119, p.180*

Human Rights and Diversity: Area Studies Revisited. . . *p.669*

Human Rights and Gender Violence: Translating International Law into Local Justice. *p.33*

Human Rights and Military Intervention. *p.513*

Human Rights and Social Policy in the 21st Century: A History of the Idea of Human Rights and Comparison of the United Nations Universal Declaration of Human Rights with United States Federal and State Constitutions. *p.670*

Human Rights and Societies in Transition: Causes, Consequences, Responses. *p.670*

Human Rights as Politics and Idolatry. *p.512*

Human Rights: Beyond the Liberal Vision. *p.768*

Human Rights: Concept and Context. *p.513*

Human Rights Horizons: The Pursuit of Justice in a Globalizing World. *p.512*

Human Rights in Commonwealth Africa. *p.512*

Human Rights in Global Perspective: Anthropological Studies of Rights, Claims and Entitlements. *p.34*

Human Rights in Iran. *p.512*

Human Rights of Indigenous Peoples. *p.34*

Human Rights: The Essential Reference. *p.436, p.669*

Human Rights: The Scholar as Activist. *p.45*

□ Human Rights Watch Publications. *p.670*

Human Sexuality. *p.748*

The Human Side of Enterprise. *p.120*

Human Types, an Introduction to Social Anthropology. . . *p.22*

Human Universals. *p.23*

Human Variation, Races, Types, and Ethnic Groups. . . . *p.17*

Human Walking. *p.791, p.910*

Humanitarian Intervention and International Relations. . . *p.671*

Humanitarian Intervention: Ethical, Legal and Political Dilemmas. *p.669, p.671*

Humanity: A Moral History of the Twentieth Century. . . *p.652*

Humans: An Introduction to Four-Field Anthropology. . . *p.22*

Humor as an Instructional Defibrillator: Evidence-Based Techniques in Teaching and Assessment. *p.346*

Humour in Society: Resistance and Control. *p.773*

The Hundred Yard Lie: The Corruption of College Football and What We Can Do to Stop It. *p.822, p.895*

The Hundred Years War. *p.641, p.643, p.647*

Hungary's Negotiated Revolution: Economic Reform, Social Change and Political Succession. *p.595*

Hunger and Public Action. *p.265*

Hunger and Work in a Savage Tribe: A Functional Study of Nutrition among the Southern Bantu. *p.46*

Hunter-Gatherers: An Interdisciplinary Perspective. *p.28*

Hunters and Gatherers: Property, Power and Ideology. . . . *p.29*

Hunters and Herders of Southern Africa: A Comparative Ethnography of the Khoisan Peoples. *p.38*

□ Huntsman World Senior Games. *p.840, p.847*

Husbands and Wives: The Dynamics of Married Living. . *p.732*

Hustlers, Beats and Others. *p.706*

Hystories: Hysterical Epidemics and Modern Media. . . . *p.714*

I

I Had a Hammer: The Hank Aaron Story. *p.830, p.849*

I Never Had It Made: An Autobiography of Jackie Robinson. *p.833, p.852*

I, Pierre Riviere, Having Slaughtered My Mother, My Sister, and My Brother. *p.751*

I Was a Communist for the F. B. I.: The Unhappy Life and Times of Matt Cvetic. *p.524*

I Watched a Wild Hog Eat My Baby!: A Colorful History of Tabloids and Their Cultural Impact. *p.411*

□ IASB: International Accounting Standards Board. *p.106, p.111*

Iberia and the Americas: Culture, Politics, and History. . . *p.591*

Iberia Before the Iberians: The Stone Age Prehistory of Cantabrian Spain. *p.17*

Les Icariens: The Utopian Dream in Europe and America. . *p.500*

Ice Age Peoples of North America: Environments, Origins, and Adaptations of the First Americans. *p.10*

The Idea and Practice of World Government. *p.629*

The Idea of a Liberal Theory. *p.493, p.511*

The Idea of a University. *p.290*

The Idea of Democracy in the Modern ERA. *p.504*

The Idea of Pakistan. *p.643, p.645*

The Idea of Poverty: England in the Early Industrial Age. . *p.754*

The Idea of Propaganda: A Reconstruction. *p.425*

The Idea of the University: A Reexamination. *p.303*

Ideal Citizens: The Legacy of the Civil Rights Movement. . *p.710*
Ideal Government and the Mixed Constitution in the Middle Ages. *p.490, p.501*
I-Deals: Idiosyncratic Deals Employees Bargain for Themselves. *p.74*
Ideas about Illness: An Intellectual and Political History of Medical Sociology. *p.778*
Ideas of Social Order in the Ancient World. *p.773*
Identification of Learning Disabilities: Research to Practice. *p.318*
Identity and Global Politics: Theoretical and Empirical Elaborations. *p.483*
Identity Mania: Fundamentalism and the Politicization of Cultural Differences. *p.766*
Ideologies in Action: Language Politics on Corsica. *p.21*
Ideologies of Violence. *p.497*
Ideology and Crime: A Study of Crime in Its Social and Historical Context. *p.752*
Ideology and Curriculum. *p.300*
Ideology and National Identity in Post-Communist Foreign Policy. *p.494*
Ideology and Popular Protest. *p.710, p.713*
Ideology and Pre-Columbian Civilizations. *p.11*
Ideology and Utopia: An Introduction to the Sociology of Knowledge. *p.685*
Ideology, Legitimacy and the New State: Yugoslavia, Serbia and Croatia. *p.600*
If the Workers Took a Notion: The Right to Strike and American Political Development. *p.127*
If They Come in the Morning: Voices of Resistance. . . . *p.751*
Igbo Art and Culture, and Other Essays. *p.38*
Illiberal Education: The Politics of Race and Sex on Campus. *p.331*
Illness As Metaphor and Aids and Its Metaphors. *p.778*
The Illusion of Cultural Identity. *p.699*
The Illusions of Progress. *p.759*
Illustrated Dictionary of Building Design and Construction. *p.158*
An Illustrated History of Boxing. *p.855*
Illustrations of Political Economy: Selected Tales. . *p.218, p.269*
I'm the Teacher, You're the Student: A Semester in the University Classroom. *p.337*
Image Ethics: The Moral Rights of Subjects in Photographs, Film, and Television. *p.412*
Image Marketing: Using Public Perceptions to Create Awareness and Build Market Share. *p.145*
Images of Terror: What We Can and Can't Know about Terrorism. *p.659*
Images That Injure: Pictorial Stereotypes in the Media. . *p.416*
An Imaginative Approach to Teaching. *p.347*
Imagine Nation: The American Counterculture of the 1960s and 1970s. *p.712*
Imagined Communities: Reflections on the Origin and Spread of Nationalism. *p.493*
Imagining Baseball: America's Pastime and Popular Culture. *p.818, p.851*
Imaginization: New Mindsets for Seeing, Organizing and Managing. *p.66*
Imitation and Politics: Redesigning Modern Germany. . . *p.609*
Immigrants and the American City. *p.571*
Immigrants and the American Dream: Remaking the Middle Class. *p.764*
Immigrants in the Lands of Promise: Italians in Buenos Aires and New York City, 18701914. . . . . *p.763*
Immigrants, Unions, and the New U. S. Labor Market. . . *p.128*
Immigration and Politics in the New Europe: Reinventing Borders. *p.637, p.668*
Immigration Research for a New Century: Multidisciplinary Perspectives. *p.764*
An Immodest Agenda: Rebuilding America Before the 21st Century. *p.213*
The Impact of Keynes on Economics in the 20th Century. . *p.227*
Impact of Strikes: Their Social and Economic Costs. . . . *p.124*
The Impact of Taxes on the American Economy. *p.248*
Impact of the Civil War and Reconstruction on Arkansas: Persistence in the Midst of Ruin. *p.521*
The Impact of the Internet on Our Moral Lives. *p.761*
Impeachable Offenses: A Documentary History from 1787 to the Present. *p.462*
Impeachment: A Handbook. *p.461*
Impeachment in America, 1635-1805. . . . . *p.461*
Impeachment: The Constitutional Problems, Enlarged Edition. *p.461*
The Imperative of Freedom: A Philosophy of Journalistic Autonomy. *p.405*
The Imperfect Panacea: American Faith in Education. . . *p.328*
An Imperfect Union: Slavery, Federalism, and Comity. . . *p.453*
Imperial Germany and the Industrial Revolution. *p.251*
The Imperial Intellect: A Study of Newman's Educational Ideal. *p.341*
Imperialism and Colonialism: Essays on the History of European Expansion. *p.583*
Imperialism and Internationalism in the Discipline of International Relations. *p.625*
The Imperialist Imagination: German Colonialism and Its Legacy. *p.584*
Implementation and Performance in New American Schools: Three Years into Scale Up. *p.280*
Implementing E-Commerce Strategies: A Guide to Corporate Success after the Dot. Com Bust. *p.113*
Implementing Standards-Based Education. *p.286*
Implementing the Constitution. *p.536*
The Implosion of American Federalism. *p.525*
The Impossible Art of Golf: An Anthology of Golf Writing. *p.812, p.861*
Impossible Subjects: Illegal Aliens and the Making of Modern America. *p.460, p.571*
Improvement of Mankind: The Social and Political Thought of John Stuart Mill. *p.223*
Improving Customer Satisfaction, Loyalty, and Profit: An Integrated Measurement and Management System. . . *p.139*
Improving Inventory Record Accuracy: Getting Your Stock Information Right. *p.117*

Improving Primary Education in Developing Countries. . p.314
Improving Schools from Within: Teachers, Parents, and Principals Can Make the Difference. p.324
Improving Teaching in the High School Block Period. . . p.287
Improving Undergraduate Education Through Faculty Development: An Analysis of Effective Programs and Practices. p.292
Improvised Dialogue: Emergence and Creativity in Conversation. p.423
In a Different Voice: Psychological Theory and Women's Development. p.692
In Black and White: Race and Sports in America. . p.819, p.833
In Defence of Globalisation. p.262
In Defense of a Political Court. p.538
In Defense of American Higher Education. p.330
In Defense of Anarchism. p.511
In Defense of Congress. p.530
In Defense of Globalization. p.55, p.663
In Gods We Trust: The Evolutionary Landscape of Religion. p.36
In Good Faith: Schools, Religion and Public Funding. . . p.308
In Its Own Image: How Television Has Transformed Sports. p.809, p.818, p.902
In Labor's Cause: Main Themes on the History of the American Worker. p.124
In Our Defense: The Bill of Rights in Action. p.455
In Praise of Books: A Cultural History of Cairo's Middle Class, Sixteenth to the Eighteenth Century. p.726
In Praise of Education. p.326
In Pursuit of Excellence: How to Win in Sport and Life Through Mental Training. p.877
In Pursuit of Privacy: Law, Ethics, and the Rise of Technology. p.443
In Pursuit of the Past: Decoding the Archaeological Record: With a New Afterword. p.6
In Quest of Community. p.684
In Search of Chinese Democracy: Civil Opposition in Nationalist China, 1929-1949. . . . . p.619
In Search of Equality: The Chinese Struggle Against Discrimination in Nineteenth-Century America. p.457
In Search of Excellence: Lessons from America's Best-Run Companies. p.81, p.148
In Search of Human Nature: The Decline and Revival of Darwinism in American Social Thought. p.682
In Search of Prosperity: Analytic Narratives on Economic Growth. p.240
In Search of Respect: Selling Crack in el Barrio. p.776
In Search of Self: An Exploration of the Role of the School in Promoting Self-Understanding. p.357
In Search of Swampland: A Wetland Sourcebook and Field Guide. p.393
In Sorcery's Shadow: A Memoir of Apprenticeship among the Songhay of Niger. p.37
In the Aftermath of Genocide: Armenians and Jews in Twentieth Century France. p.653
In the Arms of Africa: The Life of Colin M. Turnbull. . . . p.4
In the Company of Educated Women: A History of Women and Higher Education in America. p.302
In the Devil's Shadow: U. N. Special Operations During the Korean War. p.634
In the Flesh: The Cultural Politics of Body Modification. . p.26
In the Game: Gay Athletes and the Cult of Masculinity. . p.839
In the Matter of Color: Race and the American Legal Process: The Colonial Period, Vol. 1. . . . . p.457
In the Name of Osama Bin Laden: Global Terrorism and the Bin Laden Brotherhood. p.659
In the Name of Terrorism: Presidents on Political Violence in the Post-World War II Era. p.565
In the News: American Journalists View Their Craft. . . p.412
In the Path of Hizbullah. p.616
In the Rings of Saturn. p.154
In the Shadow of Marriage: Gender and Justice in an African Community. p.32
In the Shadow of Power: States and Strategies in International Politics. p.498, p.625
In the Shadow of the Garrison State: America's Anti-Statism and Its Cold War Grand Strategy. p.498
In the Shadow of the Poorhouse: A Social History of Welfare in America. p.758
In the Wake of Terror: Medicine and Morality in a Time of Crisis. p.660, p.669
In the Wake of the Plague: The Black Death and the World It Made. p.742
In the Zone: Epic Survival Stories from the Mountaineering World. p.789
In Time of Plague: The History and Social Consequences of Lethal Epidemic Disease. p.778
In Transit: The Transport Workers Union in New York City, 1933-1966: With a New Epilogue. p.126
The Inarticulate Society: Eloquence and Culture in America. p.423
Inbreeding, Incest, and the Incest Taboo: The State of Knowledge at the Turn of the Century. p.738
Incapacitation: Penal Confinement and the Restraint of Crime. p.753
The Incas. p.11
Incentive Pay and Career Ladders for Today's Teachers: A Study of Current Programs and Practices. p.282
Incentives to Improve Education: A New Perspective. . . p.280
Including Students with Severe and Multiple Disabilities in Typical Classrooms: Practical Strategies for Teachers. . p.318
The Inclusion Breakthrough: Unleashing the Real Power of Diversity. p.132
Inclusion: Including People with Disabilities in Parks and Recreation Opportunities. p.787, p.842
Inclusion Through Sports: A Guide to Individualizing Sport Experiences. p.800
Inclusive Physical Activity: A Lifetime of Opportunities. . p.801
Income Differences. p.249
Income Distribution in Macroeconomic Models. . p.252, p.253
Income Distribution. p.249
Income Inequality in America: An Analysis of Trends. . . p.133
Income Security: Statutory History of the United States. . p.447

Incorporating Women: A History of Women and Business in the United States. p.57
The Independence of Spanish America. p.583
Independent Counsel: The Law and the Investigations. . . p.462
Independent Justice: The Federal Special Prosecutor in American Politics. p.524
Independent Schools, Independent Thinkers. p.296
Independent Women: Work and Community for Single Women, 1850-1920. . . . . p.738
Index of Majors and Graduate Degrees. p.295
India and the United States in a Changing World. . p.642, p.644
India: Government and Politics in a Developing Nation. . p.617
Indian Affairs: Laws and Treaties. p.465
Indian Democracy: Meanings and Practices. p.618
Indian Gaming: Tribal Sovereignty and American Politics. . p.465
Indian Running: Native American History and Tradition. . p.841
Indians and Anthropologists: Vine Deloria, Jr., and the Critique of Anthropology. p.27
The Indians in American Society: From the Revolutionary War to the Present. p.729
Indians of the Greater Southeast: Historic Archaeology and Ethnohistory. p.11
India's Democracy: An Analysis of Changing State-Society Relations. p.617
India's Democracy: New Challenges. p.617
Indigenizing the Academy: Native Scholars and Scholarship on Natives. p.312
Indigenous People of the Caribbean. p.41
Indigenous Peoples and Environmental Issues: An Encyclopedia. p.30
The Individual and the Social Self: Unpublished Work of George Herbert Mead. p.693
The Individual, Society, and Education: A History of American Educational Ideas. p.327
Individual Taxes 2005—2006: Worldwide Summaries. . . p.107
Individualism and Economic Order. p.248
Indonesia Beyond Suharto: Polity Economy Society Transition. p.622
Indonesian Education: Teachers, Schools, and Central Bureaucracy. p.333
Industrial Archaeology: Future Directions. p.13
Industrial Dynamics. p.119
The Industrial History of the United States. p.248
Industrial Marketing: An Analytical Approach to Planning and Execution. p.144
Industrial Marketing Research. p.135
Industrial Process Control Systems. p.116
Industrial Proteomics: Applications for Biotechnology and Pharmaceuticals. p.156
Industrial Relations and European State Traditions. . . . p.121
Industries Statistics. p.150
Industry and Trade: A Study of Industrial Technique and Business Organization; and of Their Influences on the Conditions of Various Classes and Nations - Volume I, Vol. 1. . . . . p.224
Industry and Trade: A Study of Industrial Technique and Business Organization; and of Their Influences on the Conditions of Various Classes and Nations. p.224
Industry and Trade, Textile, Apparel, Footwear, U. S. A. . p.153
Industry Research Portal. p.159
Industry Research Using the Economic Census: How to Find It, How to Use It. p.148, p.178, p.180
Industry Studies. p.149
Inefficient Markets: An Introduction to Behavioral Finance. p.97, p.100
Inequality and Social Mobility in Brazil. p.705
Inequality in an Age of Decline. p.718
Inequality Reexamined. p.514
Infections and Inequalities: The Modern Plagues. p.778
Infectious Greed: Restoring Confidence in America's Companies. p.87
infed. p.319
The Inflation -Targeting Debate. p.246
Inflation Targeting: Lessons from the International Experience. p.246
Inflation, Unemployment and Monetary Policy. p.245
Influence: Science and Practice. p.139
Influence Without Authority. p.70, p.172
The Influentials: One American in Ten Tells the Other Nine How to Vote, Where to Eat, and What to Buy. p.145
Informal Politics in East Asia. p.618
Information and Communication Technology and the Teacher of the Future. p.351
Information and Coordination: Essays in Macroeconomic Theory. p.240
Information and Management Systems for Product Customization. p.117
Information Communication Technology: Changing Education. p.350
Information Highways and Byways: From the Telegraph to the 21st Century. p.420
The Information Mosaic. p.106
Information Rules: A Strategic Guide to the Network Economy. p.51
Information Security Management Handbook, Vol. 2. . . p.114
Information Security Management Handbook, Vol. 3. . . p.114
Information Security Management Handbook. p.114
Information Sources in Political Science. p.482
The Information Systems Security Officer's Guide: Establishing and Managing an Information Protection Program. . . p.113
The Informed Student Guide to Management Science. . . p.119
The Informed Vision: Essays on Learning and Human Nature. p.339
The Initiative and Referendum Almanac: A Comprehensive Reference Guide to the Initiative and Referendum Process. p.460
Injury Prevention and Rehabilitation for Active Older Adults. p.826, p.875, p.880
Ink into Bits: A Web of Converging Media. . . . p.418, p.422
The Inner Game of Fencing: Excellence in Strategy and Spirit. p.857, p.877

Innovation and Entrepreneurship in State and Local Government. *p.542*
Innovation and Entrepreneurship: Practice and Principles. . *p.67*
Innovation and Growth: Schumpeterian Perspectives. *p.230, p.235*
Innovation Patterns in Crisis and Prosperity: Schumpeter's Long Cycle Reconsidered. *p.235*
Innovations in Educational Ethnography: Theories, Methods and Results. *p.29*
Innovations in E-Government: The Thoughts of Governors and Mayors. *p.546*
The Innovative Individual. *p.67*
Innovative Management: Best Practice Guidelines and Templates for Team Planning and Learning in Action. *p.80*
Innovative Relevance: Realigning the Organization for Profit. *p.66*
The Innovator's Dilemma: When New Technologies Cause Great Firms to Fail. *p.51*
The Innovator's Solution: Creating and Sustaining Successful Growth. *p.65*
Input-Output Economics. *p.213*
The Inquiring Organization: Tacit Knowledge, Conversation, and Knowledge Creation Skills for 21st-Century Organizations. *p.79*
Inquiring Organizations: Moving from Knowledge Management to Wisdom. *p.77*
Inquiry and Education: John Dewey and the Quest for Democracy. *p.337*
Inquiry into the Nature and Progress of Rent and the Principles by Which It Is Regulated: A Greenwood Archival Edition. *p.221*
An Inquiry into the Nature and Progress of Rent and the Principles by Which It Is Regulated. *p.221*
An Inquiry into the Nature of Peace: And the Terms of Its Perpetuation. *p.250*
An Inquiry into the Nature of Peace and the Terms of its Perpetuation. *p.651*
An Inquiry into the Principles of Political Economy, Vol. 1.. . . . . *p.217*
Inside Bureaucracy. *p.545, p.580*
Inside Charter Schools: The Paradox of Radical Decentralization. *p.298*
Inside Cisco: The Real Story of Sustained M&A Growth. . *p.85*
Inside College: Undergraduate Education for the Future. . *p.291*
Inside Deaf Culture.. . . . . *p.709*
Inside Sports: Using Sociology to Understand Athletes and Sport Experiences.. . . . . *p.814*
The Inside Story of the Teacher Revolution in America. . *p.124*
Inside Subculture: The Postmodern Meaning of Style. . . *p.709*
Inside Teams: How 20 World-Class Organizations Are Winning Through Teamwork. *p.80*
Inside Terrorism. *p.659*
Inside the Great House: Planter Family Life in Eighteenth-Century Chesapeake Society. *p.734*
Inside the Jury (1983). *p.471*
Inside the Nuremberg Trial: A Prosecutor's Comprehensive Account. *p.477*
Inside the Olympics: A Behind-the-Scenes Look at the Politics, the Scandals, and the Glory of the Games. *p.846, p.885, p.889, p.892*
Inside the Revolution: Everyday Life in Socialist Cuba. . . *p.41*
Inside the Sports Pages: Work Routines, Professional Ideologies, and the Manufacture of Sports News. *p.407*
Inside the State: The Bracero Program, Illegal Immigrants, and the INS.. . . . . *p.570*
Inside the Yield Book: The Classic That Created the Science of Bond Analysis. *p.103*
Instant Case Studies: How to Design, Adapt, and Use Case Studies in Training. *p.177*
Instant Messaging Rules: A Business Guide to Managing Policies, Security, and Legal Issues for Safe IM Communication. *p.172*
The Instinct of Workmanship and the State of the Industrial Arts. *p.251*
☐ Institute for Urban and Minority Education. *p.308*
Institutional Change and Globalization. *p.261*
Institutional Design in New Democracies: Eastern Europe and Latin America.. . . . . *p.504*
Institutional Investors. *p.99, p.155, p.162*
Institutions and Ethnic Politics in Africa. *p.612*
Institutions and Organizations. *p.716*
Institutions and Reform in Africa: The Public Choice Perspective. *p.612*
Institutions for Environmental Aid: Pitfalls and Promise. . *p.666*
Institutions, Information and International Capital: A Political Economy of Foreign Direct Investment. *p.59*
Institutions, Institutional Change and Economic Performance. *p.248*
Institutions of Advanced Societies. *p.718*
Institutions of American Democracy: The Judicial Branch. . *p.534*
Institutions of Modern Spain: A Political and Economic Guide. *p.582, p.608*
Instruction of Students with Severe Disabilities. *p.318*
Instructional Design: Principles and Applications. *p.346*
☐ Instructional Intranet—Chicago Public Schools—Assessments. *p.285*
Instructional Models for Physical Education. *p.796*
Instructional Strategies for Secondary School Physical Education with NASPE: Moving into the Future. *p.797*
Instructional Technologies: Cognitive Aspects of Online Programs. *p.351*
Insult to Injury: Libel, Slander and Invasion of Privacy. . *p.443*
Insurance Dictionary Illustrated. *p.163*
Insurance: From Underwriting to Derivatives. *p.163*
Insurgency and Terrorism: Inside Modern Revolutionary Warfare. *p.661*
Integrated Production, Control Systems: Management, Analysis and Design. *p.117*
Integrated Production Systems: Design, Planning, Control, and Scheduling. *p.116*
Integrating Educational Technology into Teaching. *p.352*
Integrating Human Services: Understanding the Past to Shape the Future. *p.754*
Integrating Technology: Effective Tools for Collaboration. . *p.351*

The Intellectual Capital of Michal Kalecki: A Study in Economic Theory and Policy. *p.211*
Intellectual Freedom: A Reference Handbook. *p.459*
Intellectual Growth in Young Children. *p.357*
The Intellectual Legacy of Milton Friedman, Set. *p.232*
The Intellectual Life of the British Working Classes. . . . *p.726*
Intelligence Power in Peace and War. *p.546, p.580*
Intelligence Reframed: Multiple Intelligences for the 21st Century. *p.303*
The Intelligent Investor: The Definitive Book on Value Investing. *p.89, p.95*
Intended Consequences: Birth Control, Abortion and the Federal Government in Modern America. *p.523*
Intensive Scheduling: Restructuring America's Secondary Schools Through Time Management. *p.287*
Interaction and the Standardized Survey Interview: The Living Questionnaire. *p.691*
Interaction Process Analysis. *p.695*
Interaction Ritual Chains. *p.694*
Interaction Ritual: Essays in Face-to-Face Behavior. . . . *p.697*
Interbrand's Brand Glossary: The Resource for Branding and Brand Management. *p.142*
Intercollegiate Atheletics Four-Year Colleges' Experiences Adding and Discontinuing Teams. *p.820, p.890*
Intercollegiate Athletics and the American University: A University President's Perspective. *p.821, p.893*
Intercultural Communication: A Discourse Approach. . . . *p.20*
Interest and Prices: A Study of the Causes Regulating the Value of Money. *p.239, p.241*
Interest Groups and Political Change in Israel. *p.615*
Intermediate Microeconomics: A Modern Approach. . . . *p.249*
Intermediate Statistics and Econometrics: A Comparative Approach. *p.203*
Internal Displacement: A Global Overview of Trends and Developments in 2005. . . . . *p.667*
Internal Labor Markets and Manpower Analysis. *p.717*
Internally Displaced People: A Global Survey. . . *p.667, p.765*
International Advertising: Realities and Myths. *p.426*
International Agreements. *p.437, p.476*
The International Almanac of Electoral History. *p.577*
International and Interregional Payments Adjustment: A Synthetic View. *p.264*
International and Multicultural Organizational Communication. *p.132*
International Arms Control: Issues and Agreements. . . . *p.657*
International Assignments: An Integration of Strategy, Research, and Practice. *p.70*
International Bibliography of Anthropology. *p.3*
International Business and Society. *p.145*
International Business Information: How to Find It, How to Use It. *p.180*
International Business: the Challenge of Global Competition. *p.69*
International Corporate Governance after Sarbanes-Oxley. . *p.85*
International Council of Sport Science and Physical Education. *p.794, p.824*
International Dictionary of Adult and Continuing Education. *p.320*
International Dictionary of Insurance and Finance. *p.163*
International Dimensions of Organizational Behavior. *p.58, p.75*
International Directory of Importers - Drugs and Pharmaceuticals. *p.156*
International Economic Accounts. *p.59*
International Economic Integration. *p.256*
International Education in Practice: Dimensions for Schools and International Schools. *p.313*
International Education: Its History and Promise for Today. *p.314*
International Education: Principles and Practice. *p.313*
The International Education Quotations Encyclopedia. . . *p.339*
International Encyclopedia for Women and Sports, Vol. 1. . . . . *p.834, p.843*
International Encyclopedia for Women and Sports, Vol. 2. . . . . *p.834, p.843*
International Encyclopedia for Women and Sports, Vol. 3. . . . . *p.834, p.843*
International Encyclopedia of Adult Education. *p.320*
International Encyclopedia of Economic Sociology. . . . *p.193*
The International Encyclopedia of Education, Set. . *p.313, p.322*
International Encyclopedia of Environmental Politics. . . *p.666*
International Encyclopedia of Hospitality Management. . *p.161*
International Encyclopedia of National Systems of Education. *p.313*
The International Encyclopedia of Secret Societies and Fraternal Orders. *p.719*
International Encyclopedia of Social and Behavioral Sciences. *p.678*
International Encyclopedia of Sociology of Education. . . *p.762*
International Environmental Law, Policy and Ethics. . . . *p.434*
International Exchange Rates: The Origins of International Economics, Vol. 8. . . . . *p.255*
International Federation of Sports Medicine. . . *p.824, p.872*
International Finance and Accounting Handbook. *p.88, p.104, p.155, p.162*
International Financial Economics: Corporate Decisions in Global Markets. *p.256, p.263*
International Financial Reporting Standards Desk Reference: Overview, Guide and Dictionary. *p.91, p.106*
The International Financial Statistics Locator: A Research and Information Guide. *p.178, p.179*
International Governance of War-Torn Territories: Rule and Reconstruction. *p.628*
International Government Information and Country Information: A Subject Guide. *p.60*
International Handbook of Curriculum Research. *p.365*
International Handbook of Early Childhood Education. *p.314, p.359, p.369*
International Handbook of Educational Policy. *p.297*
International Handbook of Educational Reform. *p.325*
International Handbook of Giftedness and Talent. *p.317*
The International Handbook of Market Research Techniques. *p.135*

International Handbook of Trade Unions. *p.123*
International Handbook of Women's Education. *p.301, p.313, p.314*
International Handbook on Geographical Education. *p.377*
International Historical Statistics: Africa, Asia and Oceania, 1750-2002. *p.385*
International Human Resource Management: A Critical Text. *p.77*
International Human Resource Management. *p.77*
International Human Rights and Authoritarian Rule in Chile. *p.512*
International Information: Doc, Pub and Electronic Information of International Organizations. *p.630*
International Intervention in the Greek Civil War: The United Nations Special Committee on the Balkans, 1947-1952. *p.647, p.650*
International Investments. *p.96*
International Job Finder: Where the Jobs Are Worldwide. *p.170*
International Law: A Dictionary. *p.476*
International Law and the Use of Force by National Liberation Movements. *p.478*
International Law in the 21st Century: Rules for Global Governance. *p.477*
International Logistics: Global Supply Chain Management -. *p.118*
International Management: Culture, Strategy, and Behavior. *p.69*
International Management. *p.57, p.64, p.180*
International Maoism in the Developing World. *p.508*
International Marketing: Strategy, Planning, Market Entry and Implementation. *p.134*
International Migration and Economic Development: Lessons from Low-Income Countries. *p.259, p.265*
The International Monetary System. *p.239*
International Negotiation: Analysis, Approaches, Issues. *p.645*
International News and Foreign Correspondents. *p.414*
International News in the 21st Century. *p.407*
International Organization and Integration, Vols. 1a & 1b. *p.634*
□ International Organization for Migration (IOM). *p.763, p.764*
International Organizations: A Comparative Approach to the Management of Cooperation. *p.629*
International Organizations and the Analysis of Economic Policy, 1919-1950. *p.630*
□ International Paralympic Comittee. *p.842, p.845*
International Perspectives in Rural Sociology. *p.772*
International Perspectives on Intercultural Education. *p.313*
International Politics: Enduring Concepts and Contemporary Issues. *p.625*
The International Politics of Eurasia: Political Culture and Civil Society in Russia and the New States of Eurasia. *p.599*
The International Politics of Sport in the 20th Century. *p.844, p.892, p.899*
International Radio Broadcasting: The Limits of the Limitless Medium. *p.413*
International Radio Journalism. *p.413*
International Regions and the International System: A Study in Political Ecology. *p.629*
International Relations: A Concise Companion. *p.627*
International Relations: The Key Concepts. *p.626*
The International Secretariat: A Great Experiment in International Administration. *p.632*
International Society: Diverse Ethical Perspectives. *p.766*
□ International Society of Biomechanics in Sports. *p.824, p.872*
International Sports Economics Comparisons. *p.843, p.884, p.891, p.898*
International Trade and Finance: Essays in Honour of Jan Tinbergen. *p.258*
□ International Tribunal for the Law of the Sea. *p.476*
□ The International Tribunal for the Law of the Sea. *p.478*
Internationally Yours: Writing and Communicating Successfully in Today's Global Marketplace. *p.58, p.172*
The Internet and the First Amendment: Schools and Sexually Explicit Expressions. *p.449*
The Internet Challenge to Television. *p.422*
The Internet Galaxy: Reflections on the Internet, Business and Society. *p.761*
□ Internet Guide to International Fisheries Law. *p.478*
□ The Internet Movie Database. *p.415*
Internet Newspapers: The Making of a Mainstream Medium. *p.417*
□ Internet Resources for Physical Anthropology. *p.45*
□ Internet Resources for Social and Cultural Anthropology. *p.45*
Internet Telephony. *p.421*
The Internship Bible. *p.170*
Internship Success: Real-World, Step-by-Step Advice on Getting the Most Out of Internships. *p.169*
Internships, Jobs and Careers in Sports Industry. *p.904*
Interpretation of Airphotos and Remotely Sensed Imagery. *p.388*
The Interpretation of Caste. *p.723*
Interpretation of Cultures. *p.22*
The Interpretation of Topographic Maps: A Laboratory Manual for Use in Connection with the Topographic Maps of the United States Geological Survey. to Accompany Courses in Physiography. *p.390*
Interpretations of Legal History. *p.433*
Interpreting Macroeconomics: Explorations in the History of Economic Thought. *p.239*
Interpreting Plato. *p.490*
Interpreting Quantitative Data with SPSS. *p.689*
Interracial Intimacies: Sex, Marriage, Identity, and Adoption. *p.442*
Interracial Intimacy: The Regulation of Race and Romance. *p.457, p.737*
□ Inter-university Consortium for Political and Social Research (ICPSR). *p.483, p.689*
Interviewing for Social Scientists: An Introductory Resource with Examples. *p.691*
Interviews with John Kenneth Galbraith. *p.193*
Interwoven Lives: Adolescent Mothers and Their Children. *p.735*
Intimate Intrusions. *p.752*

Intimate Journalism: The Art and Craft of Reporting Everyday Life. *p.408*
Into Thin Air: A Personal Account of the Mount Everest Disaster. *p.789*
Intramural Recreation: A Step-by-Step Guide to Creating an Effective Program. *p.800*
Introducing Geographic Information Systems with ArcGIS. *p.387*
Introducing Human Geographies. *p.396*
Introducing Social Geographies. *p.399*
An Introduction to Agricultural Geography. *p.395*
Introduction to Athletic Training. *p.828*
Introduction to Business Statistics. *p.179*
An Introduction to Classical Econometric Theory. *p.204*
Introduction to Commercial Recreation and Tourism: An Entrepreneurial Approach. *p.786, p.883*
An Introduction to Cultural Ecology. *p.30*
Introduction to Development Economics. *p.258*
Introduction to Econometrics. *p.204*
Introduction to Exercise Science. *p.873*
Introduction to Foodservice. *p.165*
Introduction to Forest and Renewable Resources. *p.164*
An Introduction to Geological Structures and Maps. . . . *p.375*
Introduction to Geopolitics. *p.400*
An Introduction to Global Financial Markets. *p.58 p.98 p.102 p.103*
[e] Introduction to GPS: The Global Positioning System. . *p.389*
Introduction to Human Geography: A World-Systems Approach. *p.396*
Introduction to Kinesiology: Studying Physical Activity. *p.873, p.903*
An Introduction to Labor Arbitration. *p.122*
An Introduction to Legal Reasoning. *p.441*
Introduction to Leisure Services: Career Perspectives. *p.784, p.903*
Introduction to Limnology. *p.391*
An Introduction to Molecular Biotechnolo: From Molecular Biological Fundmentals to Methoda and Applications in Modern Biotechnology. *p.157*
An Introduction to Nietzsche as Political Thinker: The Perfect Nihilist. *p.490*
An Introduction to Ocean Remote Sensing. *p.389*
Introduction to Physical Education and Sport: Foundations and Trends with Introduction to Careers in Health, Physical Education and Sport. *p.794, p.903*
Introduction to Physical Oceanography. *p.392*
An Introduction to Plato's Laws. *p.489*
An Introduction to Plato's Republic. *p.488*
Introduction to Political Psychology. *p.483*
Introduction to Recreation Services for People with Disabilities: A Person-Centered Approach. *p.785, p.829, p.842*
Introduction to Remote Sensing. *p.388*
An Introduction to Rights. *p.512, p.669*
Introduction to Risk Management and Insurance. *p.163*
[e] Introduction to Telecommunications Network Engineering. *p.115*
An Introduction to the Anthropology of Melanesia: Culture and Tradition. *p.43*
An Introduction to the Philosophy of Law [1922]. *p.434*
Introduction to the Science of Sociology. *p.680*
Introduction to the Theory of Employment. *p.253, p.270*
Introduction to World Peace Through World Law. *p.635*
Introductory Econometrics: A Modern Approach. *p.205*
Introductory Econometrics for Finance. *p.198*
Introductory Econometrics with Applications. *p.204*
Introductory Mathematical Analysis for Business, Economics and the Life and Social Sciences. *p.175*
The Intruders: Unreasonable Searches and Seizures from King John to John Ashcroft. *p.473*
Inventing Iraq: The Failure of Nation-Building and a History Denied. *p.643*
The Invention of Journalism Ethics: The Path to Objectivity and Beyond. *p.406*
The Invention of Peace: Reflections on War and International Order. *p.647, p.649*
The Invention of the United States Senate. *p.534*
The Invention of the White Race: Racial Oppression and Social Control. *p.731*
The Invention of the White Race: The Origins of Racial Oppression in Anglo-America, Vol. II. *p.729*
Inventions of Teaching: A Genealogy. *p.339*
Inventory and Supply Chain Management with Forecast Updates. *p.118*
Inventory Classification Innovation: Paving the Way for Electronic Commerce and Vendor Managed Inventory. . *p.116*
Inventory of Longitudinal Studies in the Social Sciences. . *p.689*
Inventory of World Topographic Mapping: The International Cartographic Association. *p.390*
Investigated Reporting: Muckrakers, Regulators and the Struggle over Television Documentary. *p.408*
Investigating Gender: Contemporary Perspectives in Education. *p.301*
Investigations in Currency and Finance. *p.231*
Investigations into the Method of the Social Sciences. . . *p.234*
Investigative Journalism: Context and Practice. *p.408*
The Investigative Reporter's Handbook: A Guide to Documents, Databases and Techniques. *p.408*
Investigative Reporting for Print and Broadcast. *p.408*
Investing by the Numbers. *p.205*
Investing Online for Dummies®. *p.97*
Investment and Production: A Study in the Theory of the Capital-Using Enterprise. *p.248*
Investment in Learning: The Individual and Social Value of American Higher Education. *p.289, p.330*
Investment Management. *p.94, p.162*
Investment Statistics Locator. *p.178*
[web] Investopedia - Your Source for Investment Education. *p.93, p.101*
Investor Capitalism: How Money Managers Are Changing the Face of Corporate America. *p.90*
The Investor's Anthology: Original Ideas from the Industry's Greatest Minds. *p.94*

The Investor's Clearinghouse. p.93
InvestorWords.com. p.93, p.101
The Invisible Continent: Four Strategic Imperatives of the New Economy. p.70
Invisible Genealogies: A History of Americanist Anthropology. p.4
The Invisible Heart: An Economic Romance. p.185
The Invisible Heart: Economics and Family Values. . . . p.273
Invisible Lives: Social Worlds of the Aged. p.742
The Invisible Medium: Commercial, Public and Community Radio. p.413
The Invisible People: How the U. S. Has Slept Through the Global AIDS Pandemic, the Greatest Humanitarian Catastrophe of Our Time. p.769
An Invitation to Ethnomethodology: Language, Society and Interaction. p.688
Invitation to Sociology: A Humanistic Perspective. p.679
Involving Community Members in Focus Groups. p.136
The IOMA Handbook of Logistics and Inventory Management. p.118
IP Convergence: The Next Revolution in Telecommunications. p.422
Iran, Saudi Arabia and the Gulf: Power Politics in Transition. p.640
The Iranian Constitutional Revolution, 1906-1911: Grassroots Democracy, Social Democracy, and the Origins of Feminism. p.616
Iraq Index. p.616
The Irish Countryman: An Anthropological Study. p.41
Irish Travellers: Racism and the Politics of Culture. . . . p.731
Irish Voters Decide: Voting Behaviour in the Republic of Ireland. p.608
Iron John: A Book about Men. p.745
The Iroquois. p.11
Irrational Exuberance. p.245, p.250
Irrational Exuberance. p.97, p.100, p.264
Irrational Forces Contributing to the Ondulatory and Neurotic Course of History: The Theory of the Residues and of the Derivations. p.248
IRS: Internal Revenue Service. p.106
Irving Fisher (1867-1947), Arthur Hadley (1856-1930), Ragnar Frisch (1895-1973), Friedrich von Hayek (1899-1992), Allyn Young (1876-1929), Ugo Mazzola (1863-1899). . p.194
The Irwin Guide to Using the Wall Street Journal. p.96
The Irwin Handbook of Telecommunications Management. p.115
Is Communism Dead Forever? p.509
Is Geography Destiny?: Lessons from Latin America. . . p.397
IS Management Handbook. p.114
Is the Fetus a Person?: A Comparison of Policies Across the Fifty States. p.569
Islam and Democracy: The Failure of Dialogue in Algeria. p.586, p.613
Islam and Democracy. p.500
Islam and Mammon: The Economic Predicaments of Islamism. p.207, p.237
Islam and Social Policy. p.721
Islam and the West: Conflict or Cooperation? p.642
Islam in a World of Nation-States. p.500
Islam Obscured: The Rhetoric of Anthropological Representation. p.37
Islamic Activism: A Social Movement Theory Approach. p.712
Islamic Economics and Finance: A Glossary. p.190
Islamic Education, Diversity and National Identity: Dini Madaris in India Post 9/11. . . . . p.308, p.334
Islamic Education: Its Traditions and Modernization into the Arab National Systems. p.337
Islamic Identity, Postcoloniality, and Educational Policy: Schooling and Ethno-Religious Conflict in the Southern Philippines. p.335
Islamic Perspectives on Management and Organization. . p.718
Islamic Political Ethics: Civil Society, Pluralism, and Conflict. p.500
Islamic State Practices, International Law and the Threat from Terrorism: A Critique of the 'Clash of Civilizations' in the New World Order. p.661
Islamism, Secularism and Human Rights in the Middle East. p.513
Island Lives: Historical Archaeologies of the Caribbean. . . p.13
The Island Melanesians. p.13
Island Refuge: Britain and Refugees from the Third Reich, 1933-1939. . . . . p.668
Islands in the Street: Gangs and American Urban Society. . p.714
ISO 9000 Quality Systems Handbook. p.117
ISO 9000:2000: An A-Z Guide. p.117
Israel after Begin. p.615
Israeli Politics in the 1990s: Key Domestic and Foreign Policy Factors. p.615
Issues and Problems in Teacher Education: An International Handbook. p.277, p.313
Issues in Geography Teaching. p.376
Issues in Physical Education. p.795
Issues in the Economics of Aging. p.267
Issues: School Choice. p.299
IT and Organizational Learning: Managing Change through Technology and Education. p.79
It Didn't Happen Here: Why Socialism Failed in the United States. p.507, p.554
It Takes a Nation: A New Agenda for Fighting Poverty. p.264, p.754
Italians Then, Mexicans Now: Immigrant Origins and Second-Generation Progress, 1890 to 2000. . . . . . p.765
Italy and Its Invaders. p.643
It's All about Service: How to Lead Your People to Care for Your Customers. p.143
It's All about the Client: Consulting for Results. p.65
Its Not the Media: The Truth about Pop Culture's Influence on Children. p.712
It's Only a Game. p.858

J

J. G. Frazer: His Life and Work. *p.3*
J. M. Keynes in Retrospect: The Legacy of the Keynesian Revolution. *p.227*
Jack: Straight from the Gut.. . . . . *p.72*
Jackie Robinson: A Biography. *p.832, p.851*
Jackie Robinson: Race, Sports and the American Dream. *p.805, p.831, p.850, p.887*
Jacksonville: The Consolidation Story, from Civil Rights to the Jaguars. *p.543*
Janet Guthrie: A Life at Full Throttle. *p.836, p.848*
Japanese American Ethnicity: The Persistence of Community. *p.764*
The Japanese Automobile Industry: A Business History. . *p.154*
Japanese Policymaking -: The Politics Behind Politics, Informal Mechanisms and the Making of China Policy. *p.622*
The Japanese School: Lessons for Industrial America. . . *p.334*
Japanese Sense of Self. *p.693*
Japanese Society. *p.705*
Japanese Sports: A History. *p.806, p.834*
Japan's Dysfunctional Democracy: The Liberal Democractic Party and Structural Corruption. *p.621*
[e] Japan's New Middle Class; the Salary Man and His Family in a Tokyo Suburb. *p.725*
Japan's Postwar Party Politics. *p.621*
Jean-Baptiste Say and the Classical Canon in Economics: The British Connection in French Classicism. *p.223*
Jefferson Davis, American. *p.520*
Jefferson Davis, Confederate President. *p.520*
Jeffersonian America. *p.525*
The Jeffersonian Crisis: Courts and Politics in the Young Republic. *p.462*
Jefferson's Vision for Education, 1760-1845. . . . . . . *p.340*
Jeremy Bentham's Economic Writings. *p.217, p.230*
Jesse Owens: An American Life. *p.831, p.869*
The Jewish Confederates. *p.521*
Jewish Education in the United States: A Documentary History. *p.308*
Jim Crow's Children: The Broken Promise of the Brown Decision. *p.450*
Joan Robinson and the Americans. *p.271*
Joan Robinson: Economic Writings. *p.270*
The Joan Robinson Legacy. *p.270*
Job Hunting on the Internet. *p.168*
Job Queues, Gender Queues: Explaining Women's Inroads into Male Occupations. *p.725*
Job Surfing: Working Abroad. *p.171*
Job-Hunting for the So-Called Handicapped: Or People Who Have Disabilities. *p.168*
Jobless Pay and the Economy. *p.247*
Jocks 2: Coming Out to Play. *p.839*
Jocks: True Stories of America's Gay Male Athletes. . . . *p.839*
Joe DiMaggio: The Hero's Life. *p.850*
John Adams and the Spirit of Liberty. *p.515, p.516*
John Dewey and American Democracy. *p.493*
John Dewey and the Art of Teaching: Toward Reflective and Imaginative Practice. *p.345*
John Dewey and the Challenge of Classroom Practice. . . *p.342*
John Dewey and the Paradox of Liberal Reform. *p.344*
John Elliot Cairnes: Collected Works. *p.217*
John Hopkins's Notions on Political Economy. *p.195*
John L. Sullivan and His America. *p.807, p.816, p.855*
John Marshall: A Life in Law. *p.467*
John Marshall and the Heroic Age of the Supreme Court. . *p.468*
John Marshall: Definer of a Nation. *p.469*
John Marshall Harlan: The Last Whig Justice. *p.467*
John Maynard Keynes, 1883-1946, Set. *p.226*
John Maynard Keynes: A Study in the Psychology of Original Work. *p.228*
John Maynard Keynes: Critical Assessments, Vol. 38115. . *p.229*
John Maynard Keynes: Critical Responses. *p.228*
John Maynard Keynes: Father of Modern Economics. . . *p.229*
John Maynard Keynes: Fighting for Freedom 1937-1946. . *p.229*
John Maynard Keynes: Hopes Betrayed, 1883-1920. . . . *p.229*
John Maynard Keynes: Language and Method. *p.228*
John Maynard Keynes: Life, Ideas, Legacy. *p.226*
John Maynard Keynes: The Economist As Savior, 1920-1937. . . . . *p.229*
John Maynard Keyness: Keynesianism into the Twenty-First Century.. . . . . *p.229*
John Maynard Keynes. *p.212*
John McGraw. *p.849*
John Stuart Mill and Harriet Taylor: Their Correspondence and Subsequent Marriage. *p.211*
John Stuart Mill and the Harriet Taylor Myth. *p.212*
John Stuart Mill on Education. *p.344*
John Wooden: An American Treasure. *p.853*
Joseph Pulitzer. *p.410*
Joseph Story and the American Constitution: A Study in Political and Legal Thought. *p.468*
Josh Gibson: The Power and the Darkness. *p.833, p.852*
The Jossey-Bass Reader on School Reform. *p.327*
Journalism in the United States from 1690 to 1872, Set. . *p.405*
A Journalist's Guide to the Internet: The Net As a Reporting Tool. *p.413*
The Journalist's Moral Compass: Basic Principles. *p.405*
Journey into Darkness: Genocide in Rwanda. . . . *p.653, p.715*
Journey of Hope: The Back to Africa Movement in Arkansas in the Late 1800s. *p.764*
The Journey of Life: A Cultural History of Aging in America. *p.741*
Journeying: Children Responding to Literature. *p.363*
The Joy of Hiking: Hiking the Trailmaster Way. *p.788*
The Joy of Sports: Endzones, Bases, Baskets, Balls, and the Consecration of the American Spirit. *p.803*
Joyous Greetings: The First International Women's Movement, 1830-1860. . . . . *p.710*
Judge and Jury: The Life and Times of Judge Kenesaw Mountain Landis. *p.851, p.885, p.889, p.892*

Judges and the Cities: Interpreting Local Autonomy. . . . p.543

Judges of the United States Courts Biographical Directory of Federal Judges. p.467

Judging Thomas: The Life and Times of Clarence Thomas. p.536

Judgment under Uncertainty: Heuristics and Biases. . . . p.195

The Judicial Branch of Government. p.534

The Judicial Branch of State Government: People, Process, and Politics. p.541

The Judicial Branch. p.534

Judicial Branch. p.534

The Judicial Branch. p.534

The Judicial Development of Presidential War Powers. . . p.539

Judicial Dictatorship. p.538

Judicial Policies: Implementation and Impact. p.465

Judicial Power and American Character: Censoring Ourselves in an Anxious Age. p.462

The Judicial Process: An Introductory Analysis of the Courts of the United States, England, and France. p.434

Judicial Process in America. p.534

Juice: The Creative Fuel That Drives World-Class Inventors. p.67

Jules Henry on Education. p.343

Jullien's Plan for Comparative Education 1816-1817. . . p.342

Jumping into Plyometrics. p.793

Just Do It: The Nike Spirit in the Corporate World. . p.884, p.888

Just for Fun: The Story of AAU Women's Basketball. p.837, p.854, p.884

A Just Measure of Pain: The Penitentiary in the Industrial Revolution, 1750-1850. . . . . p.753

Just Talk: Gossip, Meetings, and Power in a Papua New Guinea Village. p.42

Just the Facts. p.404

Justice: Alternative Political Perspectives. p.514

Justice and the Politics of Difference. p.506, p.514

Justice Antonin Scalia and the Conservative Revival. p.467, p.535

Justice Antonin Scalia and the Supreme Court's Conservative Moment. p.539

Justice as Fairness: A Restatement. p.514

Justice at Nuremberg. p.477

Justice at War: The Story of the Japanese-American Internment Cases. p.464

Justice by Lottery. p.514

Justice Lewis F. Powell, Jr. p.468

Justice, Morality, and Education: A New Focus in Ethics in Education. p.300

Justice of Shattered Dreams: Samuel Freeman Miller and the Supreme Court During the Civil War Era. . . . p.469, p.538

Justice Oliver Wendell Holmes: The Proving Years, 1870-1882. . . . . p.468

Justice Oliver Wendell Holmes: The Shaping Years, 1841-1870. . . . . p.468

Justice Sandra Day O'Connor: Strategist on the Supreme Court. p.468

Justices and Presidents: A Political History of Appointments to the Supreme Court. p.535

Justices Black and Frankfurter: Conflict in the Court. . . p.470

The Justices of the United States Supreme Court, 1789-1995: Their Lives and Major Opinions. p.467

Justices, Presidents and Senators: A History of the U. S. Supreme Court Appointments from Washington to Clinton. p.466, p.535

Justice. p.514

Justificatory Liberalism: An Essay on Epistemology and Political Theory. p.511

K

Kaffir Boy in America: An Encounter with Apartheid. . . p.731

Kafr El-Elow: Continuity and Change in an Egyptian Community. p.702

Kalahari Hunter-Gatherers: Studies of the !Kung San and Their Neighbors. p.38

Kamikaze Biker: Parody and Anomy in Affluent Japan. . p.753

Kant's Politics: Provisional Theory for an Uncertain World. p.491

Kant's Theory of Justice. p.514

Karl Marx: A Biography. p.236

Karl Marx: A Life. p.237

Karl Marx and the Close of His System: Bohm-Bawerk's Criticism of Marx. p.234

Karl Marx: His Life and Work. p.236

Karl Marx on Society and Social Change: With Selections by Friedrich Engels. p.681

Karl Marx Selected Writings in Sociology and Social Philosophy. p.681

Karst Hydrogeology and Geomorphology. p.391

Keep Moving!: Fitness Through Aerobics and Step. . . . p.793

Keep Your Eye on the Ball: Curve Balls, Knuckleballs, and Fallacies of Baseball. p.848, p.871

Keeping Faith update of Call to Action. p.821, p.884

Keeping House in Lusaka. p.37, p.703

Keeping Score: The Economics of Big-Time Sports. p.889, p.897

Keeping the Faith: A Cultural History of the U. S. Supreme Court. p.466, p.539

Keeping Them Out of the Hands of Satan: Evangelical Schooling in America. p.308

Kennedy Versus Lodge: The 1952 Massachusetts Senate Race. p.534

Key Concepts in Adult Education and Training. p.321

Key Concepts in Geography. p.376

Key Concepts in Leisure Studies. p.716, p.784

Key Concepts in Political Communication. p.425

Key Concepts in the Philosophy of Education. . . p.324, p.340

Key Contemporary Social Theorists. p.677

Key Debates in Anthropology. p.24

Key Quotations in Sociology. p.678

Key Topics Portal. p.152

The Key Work of School Boards. p.280

Keynes and After. p.229
Keynes and Hayek: Money Economy. p.229
Keynes and His Contemporaries. p.227
Keynes and His Critics: Treasury Responses to the Keynesian Revolution, 1925-1946. . . . . p.228
Keynes and International Monetary Relations: The Second Keynes Seminar Held at University of Kent at Canterbury, 1974. . . . . p.229
Keynes and Philosophy: Essays on the Origins of Keyne's Thought. p.226
Keynes and Public Policy after Fifty Years: Economics and Policy, Vol. 1. . . . . p.227
Keynes and Public Policy after Fifty Years: Theories and Method, Vol. 2. p.227
Keynes: Aspects of the Man and His Work. p.228
Keynes, Cambridge and the General Theory. . . . p.223, p.225
Keynes, Chicago and Friedman. p.225, p.228, p.232
Keynes: Contemporary Responses to the General Theory. . p.226
Keynes, Coordination and Beyond: The Development of Macroeconomic and Monetary Theory since 1945. . . p.227
Keynes, Knowledge and Uncertainty. p.227
Keynes' Monetary Thought: A Study of Its Development. . p.225
Keynes on Population. p.229
Keynes: Philosophy, Economics and Politics: The Philosophical Foundations of Keynes's Thought and Their Influence on His Economics. p.228
Keynes, Pigou and Cambridge Keynesians: Authenticity and Analytical Perpective in the Keynes-Classics Debate. . p.226
Keynes: The Instability of Capitalism. p.229
Keynes, the Treasury and British Economic Policy. . . . p.228
Keynes, Uncertainty and the Global Economy: Beyond Keynes, Vol. 2. . . . . p.227
Keynesian Economics: The Permanent Revolution. . p.226, p.229
Keynesian Economics: The Search for First Principles. . . p.226
The Keynesian Revolution and Its Economic Consequences: Selected Essays by Peter Clarke. p.226
Keynes's General Theory: A Retrospective View. p.228
Keynes's General Theory and Accumulation. p.226
Keynes's Monetary Theory: A Different Interpretation. . . p.228
Keynes's Philosophical Development. p.226
Keys to Reading an Annual Report. p.175
The Kibbutz: Awakening from Utopia. p.703
The Kid on the Sandlot: Congress and Professional Sports, 1910-1992. . . . . p.885, p.891, p.897
Killer Cover Letters and Resumes! The WetFeet Insider Guide 2004. . . . . p.170
Killing Rage: Ending Racism. p.730
The Killing State: Capital Punishment in Law, Politics, and Culture. p.471
A Kind of Grace: A Treasury of Sportswriting by Women. p.812, p.837
The Kind of Schools We Need: Personal Essays. p.342
Kindergartens and Cultures: The Global Diffusion of an Idea. p.368
The Kindness of Strangers: The Abandonment of Children in Western Europe from Late Antiquity to the Renaissance. p.755
Kindred Strangers: The Uneasy Relationship Between Politics and Business in America. p.52, p.112
Kinetics of Human Motion. p.908, p.910
King Football: Sport and Spectacle in the Golden Age of Radio and Newsreels, Movies and Magazines, the Weekly and the Daily Press. p.808, p.823, p.859, p.885
The King of Children: A Portrait of Janusz Korczak. . . . p.343
King of the Mountain: The Nature of Political Leadership. . p.483
King of the World: Muhammad Ali and the Rise of an American Hero. p.833, p.856
Kingdom of Children: Culture and Controversy in the Homeschooling Movement. p.296
Kings of the Ice: A History of World Hockey. . . p.844, p.862
Kinship and Community in Two Chinese Villages. p.705
Kinship and Family: An Anthropological Reader. p.32
Kinship, Law and the Unexpected: Relatives Are Always a Surprise. p.33
Kiss, Bow or Shake Hands: How to Do Business in Sixty Countries. p.56
Kiss, Bow, or Shake Hands: The Bestselling Guide to Doing Business in More Than 60 Countries. p.173
The Knight, the Lady and the Priest: The Making of Modern Marriage in Medieval France. p.733
Knight's Foodservice Dictionary. p.165
The Knights of Labor and the Haymarket Riot: The Fight for an Eight-Hour Workday. p.124
Knights Unhorsed: Internal Conflict in a Gilded Age Social Movement. p.130
Knock 'Em Dead: The Ultimate Job Seeker's Guide. . . p.171
Knock Your Socks Off Prospecting: How to Cold Call, Get Qualified Leads, and Make More Money. p.143
Knocking on Heaven's Door: American Religion in the Age of Counterculture. p.720
Know Your Market: How to Do Low-Cost Market Research. p.135
Knowing and Teaching Elementary Mathematics: Teachers' Understanding of Fundamental Mathematics in China and the United States. p.364
Knowing the Enemy: Jihadist Ideology and the War on Terror. p.659
Knowing What Students Know: The Science and Design of Educational Assessment. p.285
Knowledge Accumulation and Industry Evolution: The Case of Pharma-Biotech. p.156
Knowledge and Passion. p.35
Knowledge Capital: How Knowledge-Based Enterprises Really Get Built. p.77
Knowledge, Gender, and Schooling: The Feminist Educational Thought of Jane Roland Martin. p.344
Knowledge, Inequality and Growth in the New Economy. p.254, p.259
Knowledge Leadership: The Art and Science of the Knowledge-Based Organization. p.77
Knowledge Management in Theory and Practice. p.77
The Known World of Broadcast News: International News and the Electronic Media. p.412
Knut Wicksell: Essays in Economics. p.241
Kodak and the Lens of Nostalgia. p.427

Kodokan Judo: The Essential Guide to Judo by Its Founder. *p.863*
Korea: Art and Archaeology. *p.9*
Kuru Sorcery: Disease and Danger in the New Guinea Highlands. *p.46*
Kurusu: The Price of Progress in a Japanese Village, 1951-1975. . . . . *p.707*
Kwanzaa and Me: A Teacher's Story. *p.310, p.365*
Labeling Deviant Behavior: Its Sociological Implications. . *p.697*
Labor and Employment Arbitration in a Nutshell. *p.123*
Labor and the Wartime State: Labor Relations and Law During World War II. *p.120*
Labor Arbitration in America: The Profession and Practice. *p.120*
Labor, Autonomy and the State in Latin America. *p.121*
Labor Economics. *p.253*
Labor in Cross-Cultural Perspective. *p.28*
Labor Law, Industrial Relations and Employee Choice: The State of the Workplace in the 1990's. *p.120*
Labor Relations in Education: An International Perspective. *p.121*
Labor Relations in Europe: A History of Issues and Developments, 29. . . . . *p.123*
Labor Relations: Striking a Balance. *p.120*
Labor Relations. *p.121*
Labor Rights Are Civil Rights: Mexican American Workers in Twentieth-Century America. *p.255*
Labor Standards in the United States and Canada. *p.109, p.111, p.112, p.120*
Labor Unions, Partisan Coalitions, and Market Reforms in Latin America. *p.128*
Labor Will Rule: Sidney Hillman and the Rise of American Labor. *p.126*
Laboratory of Justice: The Supreme Court's 200-Year Struggle to Integrate Science and the Law. *p.536*
Laboring and Dependent Classes in Colonial America, 1607-1783. . . . . *p.724*
Labor-Management Relations in a Changing Environment. *p.120*
Labor's Power and Industrial Performance: Automobile Production Regimes in the U. S., Germany, and Japan. . *p.121*
Labor's Story in the United States. *p.128*
Labor's War at Home: The CIO in World War II. *p.127*
Labour Legislation and Trade Unions in India and Pakistan. *p.120*
The Labour Party since 1979: Crisis and Transformation. . *p.607*
Labour Relations in the Global Fast-Food Industry. . . . *p.123*
Labour Relations in Transition in Eastern Europe. *p.123*
Labour Theory of Value. *p.195, p.253*
Labour's Turning Point, 1880-1900: Extracts from Contemporary Sources. *p.703*
Lacrosse: A History of the Game. *p.805, p.841, p.862*
Lacrosse: Technique and Tradition, the Second Edition of the Bob Scott Classic. *p.862*
Lads, Citizens and Ordinary Kids: Working Class Youth Lifestyles in Belfast. *p.736*
Land and Power in Latin America: Agrarian Economics and Social Process in the Andes. *p.28*
Land and Society in Edwardian Britain. *p.399*
Land, Custom and Practice in the South Pacific. *p.43*
Land Development Handbook. *p.158*
Land Use and Society: Geography, Law, and Public Policy. *p.382, p.464*
Land Use Problems and Conflicts: Causes, Consequences and Solutions. *p.267*
Landmark Decisions of the United States Supreme Court. . *p.453*
Landmark Legislation, 1774-2002: Major U. S. Acts and Treaties. *p.560, p.630*
Landmark Supreme Court Cases: A Reference Guide. . . *p.537*
Landry: The Legend and the Legacy. *p.859*
Landscape and Englishness. *p.399*
Landscapes of Learning. *p.302*
Landscapes of Race in United States. *p.382*
Landscapes of Settlement: Prehistory to the Present. . . . *p.395*
Landscapes of the Jihad: Militancy, Morality, Modernity. . *p.658*
Landscape. *p.399*
Landslide Hazard and Risk. *p.395*
Lane Kirkland: Champion of American Labor. *p.128*
Language an Introduction to the Study of Speech. *p.20*
Language and Gender. *p.21*
Language and Identity: National, Ethnic, Religious. . . . *p.694*
Language and Literacy Learning in Schools. *p.365*
Language and Sexuality. *p.21*
Language and Symbolic Power. *p.21*
Language and Woman's Place: Text and Commentaries. . . *p.21*
Language Contact. *p.20*
Language, Culture, and Society: A Book of Readings. . . . *p.17*
Language Death. *p.19*
Language, Discourse and Power in African American Culture. *p.21*
Language Diversity and Thought: A Reformulation of the Linguistic Relativity Hypothesis. *p.20*
Language Ideologies: Practice and Theory. *p.21*
The Language of New Media. *p.419*
The Language of School Design: Design Patterns for 21st Century Schools. *p.288*
Language, Politics, and Social Interaction in an Inuit Community. *p.21*
The Language Revolution. *p.19*
Language Shift and Cultural Reproduction: Socialization, Self and Syncretism in a Papua New Guinean Village. . . . *p.19*
Language Shock: Understanding the Culture of Conversation. *p.18*
Language Skills in Elementary Education. *p.361*
Language Socialization across Cultures. *p.20*
Language, Thought, and Reality: Selected Writings. *p.20*
Language Universals and Linguistic Typology: Syntax and Morphology. *p.18*
The Languages of Learning: How Children Talk, Write, Dance, Draw and Sing Their Understanding of the World. . . *p.360*
LANIC (Latin American Network Information Center). . *p.591*

The Lapita Peoples: Ancestors of the Oceanic World. . . . *p.13*
Last Chance High: How Girls and Boys Drop in and Out of Alternative Schools. *p.299*
The Last Closet: The Real Lives of Lesbian and Gay Teachers. *p.283, p.309*
Last Dance: Behind the Scenes at the Final Four. *p.853, p.893, p.902*
The Last Empire: Britain and the Commonwealth. *p.605*
The Last Frontier: The Social Meaning of Growing Old. . *p.741*
The Last Half-Century: Societal Change and Politics in America. *p.704, p.759*
The Last Human: A Guide to 19 Species of Extinct Humans. *p.16*
The Last Imaginary Place: A Human History of the Arctic World. *p.379*
The Last Partnerships: Inside the Great Wall Street Dynasties. *p.89 p.100 p.155 p.162*
Last Rights: Revisiting Four Theories of the Press. . . . *p.405*
The Later Marxism. *p.250*
Later Medieval France: The Polity. *p.704*
Latin America: Regions and People. *p.397*
Latin American Journalism. *p.404*
Latin American Politics and Development. *p.593*
Latin American Social Thought. *p.684*
Latin American Sport: An Annotated Bibliography, 1988-1998. . . . . *p.812, p.813, p.833*
Latin Journey: Cuban and Mexican Immigrants in the United States. *p.571*
Latin Politics, Global Media. *p.415*
Latino and African American Athletes Today: A Biographical Dictionary. *p.832, p.833*
Latinos, Inc.: The Marketing and Making of a People. *p.132, p.138*
Latinos Unidos: From Cultural Diversity to the Politics of Solidarity. *p.311*
Laughter in Interaction. *p.423*
Launching Democracy in South Africa: The First Open Election, April 1994. . . . . *p.613*
Launching into Cyberspace: Internet Development and Politics in Five World Regions. *p.624*
Lavender Road to Success: The Career Guide for the Gay Community. *p.168*
Law and Community in Three American Towns. *p.33*
Law and Economic Organization: A Comparative Study of Preindustrial Studies. *p.33*
Law and Economic Policy in America: The Evolution of the Sherman Antitrust Act. *p.444*
Law and Empire in the Pacific: Fiji and Hawaii. *p.43*
Law and Industrial Relations: China and Japan after World War II. *p.122*
Law and People in Colonial America. *p.440*
Law and Revolution II: The Impact of the Protestant Reformations on the Western Legal Tradition. *p.433*
Law and Revolution: The Formation of the Western Legal Tradition. *p.433*
Law and Society in Puritan Massachusetts: Essex County, 1629-1692. . . . . *p.474*
Law and Society in Traditional China. *p.475*
Law and the Shaping of the American Labor Movement. . *p.125*
Law and Warfare: Studies in the Anthropology of Conflict. . *p.433*
Law at the End of Life: The Supreme Court and Assisted Suicide. *p.448, p.539*
Law by Source: Global. *p.474, p.475*
Law for Global Commerce: A Tour. *p.57, p.110*
Law for Recreation and Sport Managers. . *p.783, p.883, p.900*
The Law in America. *p.440*
The Law in Classical Athens. *p.433*
Law in Culture and Society. *p.33, p.433*
Law, Labor, and Ideology in the Early American Republic. . *p.447*
The Law of Agency and Partnership. *p.75*
Law of Her Own: The Reasonable Woman as a Measure of Man. *p.472*
The Law of Higher Education. *p.450*
The Law of Mergers and Acquisitions. *p.85*
The Law of Nations: An Introduction to the International Law of Peace. *p.477*
The Law of Peoples. *p.625*
The Law of Primitive Man: A Study in Comparative Legal Dynamics.. . . . . *p.433*
The Law of the Sea in a Nutshell. *p.478*
The Law of the Workplace: Rights of Employers and Employees. *p.131*
Lawlessness and Economics: Alternative Modes of Governance. *p.248, p.252*
Law's Empire. *p.434*
Law's Promise, Law's Expression: Visions of Power in the Politics of Race, Gender, and Religion. *p.455*
The Leader of the Future.. . . . . *p.71*
Leaders and Their Followers in a Dangerous World: The Psychology of Political Behavior. *p.512, p.698*
The Leader's Companion: Insights on Leadership Through the Ages. *p.72*
Leadership and Governance from the Inside Out. . . *p.71, p.86*
Leadership and Groups in Recreational Service. *p.786*
Leadership and the New Science: Discovering Order in a Chaotic World. *p.72*
Leadership for Differentiating Schools and Classrooms. . *p.350*
Leadership for the Emerging Age: Transforming Practice in Adult and Continuing Education. *p.319*
Leadership for the Schoolhouse: How Is It Different? Why Is It Important? *p.282*
Leadership in Committee: A Comparative Analysis of Leadership Behavior in the U. S. Senate. *p.533*
Leadership in International Business Education and Research. *p.177*
The Leadership Pipeline: How to Build the Leadership-Powered Company. *p.70*
Leadership: Succeeding in the Private, Public, and Not-For-Profit Sectors. *p.698*
Leading at the Edge of Chaos: How to Create the Nimble Organization. *p.72*
Leading Change. *p.71*
Leading for Innovation: And Organizing for Results. . . . *p.71*

Leading Teams. p.80
Leading the Revolution. p.66, p.71, p.73
Leading to Change: The Challenge of the New Superintendency. p.281
The League Committees and World Order. p.631
The League of Nations: Its Life and Times, 1920-1946. . p.631
Lean Enterprise Systems: Using IT for Continuous Improvement. p.117
Lean Six SIGMA Logistics: Strategic Development to Operational Success. p.117
Learned Hand: The Man and the Judge. p.441
Learned Hand's Court. p.470
Learning a Field Language. p.18
Learning: A Survey of Psychological Interpretations. . . . p.357
Learning about Learning Disabilities. p.319
Learning and Intelligence: Conversations with Skinner and Wheeler. p.357
Learning and Not Learning English: Latino Students in American Schools. p.311, p.312
Learning and Work: An Exploration in Industrial Ethnography. p.39, p.44
Learning as Transformation: Critical Perspectives on a Theory in Progress. p.320
Learning by Heart. p.324
Learning, Creating, and Using Knowledge: Concept Maps As Facilitative Tools in Schools and Corporations. p.358
Learning Democracy: Democratic and Economic Values in Unified Germany. p.610
Learning Disabilities: Theories, Diagnosis, and Teaching Strategies. p.318
Learning from Our Mistakes: A Reinterpretation of Twentieth-Century Educational Theory. p.328
Learning from the Past: What History Teaches Us about School Reform. p.330
Learning How to Ask: A Sociolinguistic Appraisal of the Role of the Interview in Social Science Research. p.691
Learning in Action: A Guide to Putting the Learning Organization to Work. p.78
Learning in Adulthood: A Comprehensive Guide. p.320
Learning in Small Moments: Life in an Urban Classroom. . p.315
Learning Later. p.320
The Learning of Liberty: The Educational Ideas of the American Founders. p.328
The Learning Page—American Memory Collection. . p.367
The Learning Society Revisited. p.327
Learning Theory and Behavior. p.358
Learning Theory and the Symbolic Processes. p.358
Learning to Labour. p.42
Learning to Legislate. p.533
Learning to Listen, Learning to Teach: The Power of Dialogue in Educating Adults. p.321
Learning to Read: Lessons from Exemplary First-Grade Classrooms. p.360
Learning to Read: The Great Debate. p.362
Learning to Read. p.361
Learning to Rock Climb. p.789
Learning to Teach in an Age of Accountability. p.277
Learning to Win: Sports, Education and Social Change in Twentieth-Century North Carolina. . . . p.815, p.821, p.894
Learning Together: Children and Adults in a School Community. p.348
e The Least Dangerous Branch?: Consequences of Judicial Activism. p.535
The Least Dangerous Branch?: Consequences of Judicial Activism. p.535, p.541
The Least Developed Countries Report. p.666
Leaving No Child Behind?: Options for Kids in Failing Schools. p.347
Leaving the Bench: Supreme Court Justices at the End. . p.535
Lectures on Economic Growth. p.233, p.238
Lectures on International Trade. p.256
Lectures on Political Economy: Money. p.241
Left Back: A Century of Battles over School Reform. . . p.328
Left Out: Reds and America's Industrial Unions. p.123
The Legacies of Communism in Eastern Europe. p.508
The Legacy of Keynes and Friedman: Economic Analysis, Money, and Ideology. p.227
The Legacy of Malthus: The Social Costs of the New Scientific Racism. p.728
The Legacy of Rousseau. p.492
The Legacy of Sacco and Vanzetti. p.471
Legal Aspects of Geology. p.444
Legal Concepts in Sport: A Primer. p.785, p.882, p.900
Legal Controls of International Conflict: A Treatise on the Dynamics of Disputes. p.478
Legal Environment of Business: A Critical Thinking Approach. p.51
Legal Forms for Starting and Running a Small Business. . p.88
Legal Guide for Starting and Running a Small Business. . p.444
Legal Information: How to Find It, How to Use It. . . . p.439
Legal Reasoning and Political Conflict. p.434
Legal Research: How to Find and Understand the Law. p.109, p.180, p.439
Legal Rights of Teachers and Students. p.450
Legal Systems of the World: A Political, Social, and Cultural Encyclopedia, Set. p.433
Legal Traditions of the World: Sustainable Diversity in Law. p.434
Legalizing Gender Inequality: Courts, Markets and Unequal Pay for Women in America. p.447
Legalizing Marijuana: Drug Policy Reform and Prohibition Politics. p.568
Legally Wed: Same-Sex Marriage and the Constitution. . p.442
Legislating Revolution: The Contract with America in Its First 100 Days. p.530
Legislating Together: The White House and Capitol Hill from Eisenhower to Reagan. p.532
Legislation Into Law. p.532
Legislative Entrepreneurship in the U.S. House of Representatives. p.533
Legislative Labyrinth: Congress and Campaign Finance Reform. p.548

☐ Legislative Observatory. *p.474*

Legislative Strategy: Shaping Public Policy. *p.531*

Legislative Term Limits: Public Choice Perspectives. . . *p.530*

Legislators, Leaders, and Lawmaking: The U. S. House of Representatives in the Postreform Era. *p.533*

Legislatures. *p.575, p.588*

Legitimacy and Power Politics: The American and French Revolutions in International Political Culture. *p.496, p.591, p.608*

Leisure and Ethics: Reflections on the Philosophy of Leisure, Vol. II. *p.783, p.802*

Leisure and Feminist Theory. *p.785, p.838*

Leisure Education: Theory and Practice. *p.784*

Leisure in Your Life: An Exploration. *p.784*

Leisure Industries. *p.786*

Leisure: The Basis of Culture. *p.784*

Lend Me Your Ear: Rhetorical Constructions of Deafness. . *p.708*

Leo Melamed: Escape to the Futures. *p.89, p.148*

Lesbian Histories and Cultures. *p.749*

Lesbian Psychologies: Explorations and Challenges. . . . *p.750*

The Lesser Evil?: Debates on the Democratic Party and Independent Working-Class Politics. *p.553*

The Lesser Evil: Political Ethics in an Age of Terror. . . *p.659*

Lessons from Mount Kilimanjaro: Schooling, Community and Gender in East Africa. *p.29*

Lessons from the Edge: Survival Skills for Starting and Growing a Company. *p.68*

Lessons from the Great Depression. *p.214*

Lessons from the Past. *p.404*

Lessons of the Locker Room: The Myth of School Sports. *p.822, p.840, p.885*

Lester Frank Ward: Selections from His Work. *p.686*

Let Me Tell You a Story: A Lifetime in the Game. . *p.823, p.853*

Lethal Judgments: Assisted Suicide and American Law. . *p.448*

Let's Fix It!: Overcoming the Crisis in Manufacturing. . . *p.119*

Letters of David Ricardo to Thomas Robert Malthus, 1810-1823. . . . . *p.221*

Letting the People Decide: The Dynamics of a Canadian Election. *p.590*

Leveling Crowds: Ethno-Nationalist Conflicts and Collective Violence in South Asia. *p.713*

Leverage: How to Get It and How to Keep It in Any Negotiation. *p.75*

Leviathan's Choice: Capital Punishment in the Twenty-First Century. *p.567*

The Leviathan. *p.491*

The Levittowners: Ways of Life and Politics in a New Suburban Community. *p.702*

The Lexicon of Labor: More Than 500 Key Terms, Biographical Sketches, and Historical Insights Concerning Labor in America. *p.122*

LexisNexis Academic. *p.516*

LexisNexis Congressional. *p.529*

The Lexus and the Olive Tree: Understanding Globalization. *p.55*

Liar's Poker: Rising Through the Wreckage on Wall Street. *p.89, p.92, p.96, p.100*

The Liberal and Technical in Teacher Education: A Historical Survey of American Thought. *p.277*

Liberal Arts Colleges: Thriving, Surviving, or Endangered? *p.291*

Liberal Democracy: A Critique of Its Theory. *p.504*

The Liberal Party: Triumph and Disintegration, 1886-1929. . . . . *p.604, p.607*

Liberal Purposes: Goods, Virtues, and Diversity in the Liberal State. *p.511*

Liberalism Against Populism: A Confrontation Between the Theory of Democracy and the Theory of Social Choice. *p.505*

Liberalism Ancient and Modern. *p.511*

Liberalism and Empire: A Study in Nineteenth-Century British Liberal Thought. *p.511, p.583*

Liberalism and the Origins of European Social Theory. . *p.686*

Liberalism Divided: Freedom of Speech and the Many Uses of State Power. *p.515*

Liberalism's Crooked Circle: Letters to Adam Michnik. . *p.511*

Liberalization Against Democracy: The Local Politics of Economic Reform in Tunisia. *p.585, p.611*

Liberating Culture: Cross-Cultural Perspectives on Museums, Curation, and Heritage Preservation. *p.47*

Liberating Economics: Feminist Perspectives on Families, Work, and Globalization. *p.273*

Liberation Management: Necessary Disorganization for the Nanosecond Nineties. *p.73*

Liberation Sociology. *p.680*

Libertarianism: For and Against. *p.510*

Liberté, Égalité and Fraternité at Work: Changing French Employment Relations and Management. *p.122*

Liberty, a Better Husband: Single Women in America: The Generations of 1780-1840. . . . . *p.735*

Liberty and Power: A Dialogue on Religion and U. S. Foreign Policy in an Unjust World. *p.515, p.641, p.642*

Liberty and Sexuality: The Right to Privacy and the Making of Roe vs. Wade. *p.447*

Liberty: Incorporating Four Essays on Liberty. *p.515*

Liberty, Justice and Equality: How These Constitutional Guarantees Have Been Shaped by United States Supreme Court Decisions since 1789. . . . . *p.537*

Libraries, the First Amendment and Cyberspace: What You Need to Know. *p.451*

☐ Library of Congress Country Studies: Africa. *p.612*

☐ Library of Congress Country Studies. *p.574*

☐ Library Resources for Communication Studies. *p.415*

The Library's Legal Answer Book. *p.451*

A License to Steal: The Forfeiture of Property. *p.473*

Life and Health Insurance. *p.163*

The Life and Legacy of Annie Oakley. *p.838, p.866*

Life in a Coral Reef. *p.391*

Life in a Medieval City. *p.703*

Life in Lesu: The Study of a Melanesian Society in New Ireland. *p.43*

A Life in Our Times: Memoirs. *p.209, p.211*

Life in Schools: An Introduction to Critical Pedagogy in the Foundations of Education. *p.297*

Life in the English Country House: A Social and Architectural History. *p.726*

Life in the Middle: Psychological and Social Development in Middle Age. *p.741*

Life of Adam Smith. *p.219*

The Life of Adam Smith. *p.219*

The Life of Emma Willard. *p.338*

The Life of John Maynard Keynes. *p.211, p.227*

The Life of the Law: Anthropological Projects. *p.33*

Life on the Run. *p.853*

Life Span Motor Development. *p.909*

Lifeline of the Confederacy: Blockade Running During the Civil War. *p.522*

Lifelong Learning: Concepts and Contexts. *p.319*

Lifelong Leisure Skills and Lifestyles for Persons with Developmental Disabilities. *p.785, p.801*

Life's Dominion: An Argument about Abortion, Euthanasia, and Individual Freedom. *p.472*

Lifestyle Market Analyst. *p.138, p.139*

Lifetime Allocation of Work and Income: Essays in the Economics of Aging. *p.265*

Lifetime of Color. *p.303, p.349*

Lifting a Ton of Feathers: A Woman's Guide to Surviving in the Academic World. *p.292*

Lightning Wires: The Telegraph and China's Technological Modernization, 1860-1890, 6. . . . . *p.421*

Lights On!: The Wild Century-Long Saga of Night Baseball. *p.808, p.851, p.885, p.897*

Like People You See in a Dream: First Contact in Six Papuan Societies. *p.43*

Limited Government: A Comparison. *p.574*

Limits and Possibilities: The Crisis of Yugoslav Socialism and State Socialist Systems. *p.506, p.508*

The Limits of Judicial Power: The Supreme Court in American Politics. *p.537*

The Limits of Privacy. *p.515*

Limits: The Role of the Law in Bioethical Decision Making. *p.448*

The Limits to Growth; A Report for the Club of Rome's Project on the Predicament of Mankind. *p.763*

The Limits to Growth: The 30-Year Update. *p.763*

The Limits to Union: Same-Sex Marriage and the Politics of Civil Rights.. . . . . *p.569*

Lincoln. *p.517*

Linear Programming and Economic Analysis. . . . *p.199, p.243*

Linguistic Anthropology: A Reader. *p.18*

Linguistic Diversity in the South: Changing Codes, Practices, and Ideology. *p.20*

Linguistic Fieldwork. *p.19*

The Linguistics Wars. *p.18*

Linking Arms Together: American Indian Treaty Visions of Law and Peace, 1600-1800. . . . . *p.574*

Literacy and Bilingualism: A Handbook for All Teachers. *p.299, p.312*

Literacy and Motivation: Reading Engagement in Individuals and Groups. *p.354*

Literacy and Written Culture in Early Modern Central Europe. *p.337*

Literacy and Young Children: Research-Based Practices. . *p.368*

Literacy as Social Exchange: Intersections of Class, Gender, and Culture. *p.29*

Literacy Before Schooling. *p.368*

Literacy Development of Students in Urban Schools: Research and Policy. *p.360*

Literacy, Emotion and Authority: Reading and Writing on a Polynesian Atoll. *p.21*

Literacy in America: Historic Journey and Contemporary Solutions. *p.762*

Literacy in Early Modern Europe: Its Growth, Uses and Impact, 1500-1800. . . . . *p.335*

Literacy Web. *p.299, p.338*

Literacy with an Attitude: Educating Working-Class Children in Their Own Self-Interest. *p.302*

The Literary Book of Economics. *p.186*

Literary Market Place 2004: The Directory of the American Book Publishing Industry. *p.149*

A Literature Guide to the Hospitality Industry. *p.161*

The Literature of Adult Education: A Bibliographic Essay.. *p.320*

The Literature of Forestry and Agroforestry. *p.164*

The Literature of the Political Economy. *p.217*

The Litigious Society. *p.441*

Little Big Men: Bodybuilding Subculture and Gender Construction. *p.817, p.855*

A Little Commonwealth: Family Life in Plymouth Colony. *p.733*

Little Girls in Pretty Boxes: The Making and Breaking of Elite Gymnasts and Figure Skaters. *p.819, p.838*

Little Green Men, Meowing Nuns and Head-Hunting Panics: A Study of Mass Psychogenic Illnesses and Social Delusion. *p.714*

Little Ice Ages: Ancient and Modern. *p.393*

Live and Work in the U. S. A. and Canada. *p.169*

Live, Direct and Biased?: Making Television News in the Satellite Age. *p.415*

Lives at Risk: Single-Payer National Health Insurance in Countries Around the World. *p.768*

Lives in Education: A Narrative of People and Ideas. . . *p.338*

Lives of Dust and Water: An Anthropology of Change and Resistance in Northwestern Mexico. *p.28*

Lives Together - Worlds Apart: Mothers and Daughters in Popular Culture. *p.738*

Lives Together - Worlds Apart: Quechua Colonization in Jungle and City. *p.763*

Living and Dying in the USA: Behavioral, Health, and Social Differentials of Adult Mortality. *p.742*

The Living Company. *p.78*

Living Downtown: The History of Residential Hotels in the United States. *p.771*

Living on the Lake in Prehistoric Europe: 150 Years of Lake-Dwelling Research. *p.12*

Living Poor: A Peace Corps Chronicle. *p.707*

Living Room War. *p.414*
Living the Ethnographic Life. *p.25*
Living Together: An Ethnography of a Retirement Hotel. . *p.742*
Living Traditions: Studies in the Ethnoarchaeology of South Asia. *p.8*
Living Wage Movements: Global Perspectives. *p.250, p.252, p.265*
Living Wages, Equal Wages: Gender and Labour Market Policies in the United States. *p.273*
Living Walden Two: B. F. Skinner's Behaviorist Utopia and Experimental Communities. *p.499*
Living Within Limits: Ecology, Economics and Population Taboos. *p.763*
Lobbying for Higher Education: How Colleges and Universities Influence Federal Policy. *p.295*
Lobbyists and Legislators: A Theory of Political Markets. . *p.575*
Local Government and Thatcherism. *p.582*
Local Government in the New Europe. *p.581*
Local Meanings, Global Schooling: Anthropology and World Culture Theory. *p.313*
Locke on Money, Vol. 1. . . . . *p.216*
Locke on Money, Vol. 2. . . . . *p.216*
Locke: Two Treatises of Government. *p.492*
Locke's Second Treatise of Civil Government: An Essay Concerning the True Original, Extent, and End of Civil Government. *p.216*
Logging the Globe. *p.164*
The Logic of Japanese Politics: Leaders, Institutions and the Limits of Change. *p.621*
The Logic of Political Survival. *p.575*
Logistical Management: A Systems Integration of Physical Distribution Management and Materials Management. . *p.143*
Logit Models from Economics and Other Fields. *p.199*
The Logos Reader: Rational Radicalism and the Future of Politics. *p.510*
Lombard Street: A Description of the Money Market. *p.99, p.146, p.154*
Lonely in America. *p.694*
The Long Detour: The History and Future of the American Left. *p.493*
A Long Shadow: Jefferson Davis and the Final Days of the Confederacy. *p.519*
Long Shadows: Truth, Lies and History. *p.767*
The Long Surrender. *p.520*
The Long War for Freedom: The Arab Struggle for Democracy in the Middle East. *p.615*
Longitude and Empire: How Captain Cook's Voyages Changed the World. *p.379*
Longitudinal Analysis of Labor Market Data. *p.254*
Longitudinal Research. *p.686*
Long-Run Economic Relationships: Readings in Cointegration. *p.199*
Look Away!: A History of the Confederate States of America. *p.520*
Look to the Mountain: An Ecology of Indigenous Education. *p.311*
Looking Ahead: Independent School Issues and Answers. . *p.296*
Looking at Life Magazine. *p.409*
Looking Back and Thinking Forward: Reexaminations of Teaching and Schooling. *p.346*
Looking Outward: Years of Crisis at the United Nations. . *p.635*
Lord and Peasant in Russia: From the 9th to the 19th Century. *p.723*
Lords of Parliament: Manners, Rituals and Politics. . . . *p.606*
Lordship, Kingship, and Empire: The Idea of Monarchy, 1400-1525 (The Carlyle Lectures 1988). *p.502*
Lore of Running. *p.866, p.875, p.879*
The Los Angeles Riots. *p.713*
The Losers: Gang Delinquency in an American Suburb. . *p.753*
Losing Control?: Sovereignty in the Age of Globalization. . *p.496*
The Lost Children of Wilder: The Epic Struggle to Change Foster Care. *p.757*
Lost Debate: German Socialist Intellectuals and Totalitarianism. *p.510*
Lost Ground: Welfare Reform, Poverty, and Beyond. . . . *p.754*
Lost Knowledge: Confronting the Threat of an Aging Workforce. *p.78*
Lost Liberties: Ashcroft and the Assault on Personal Freedom. *p.515*
Loud Hawk: The United States vs. the American Indian Movement. *p.438*
Louis D. Brandeis: Justice for the People. *p.469*
Love and the American Delinquent: The Theory and Practice of "Progressive" Juvenile Justice, 1825-1920. . . . . . . *p.473*
Loving to Survive: Sexual Terror, Men's Violence and Women's Lives. *p.742*
Low Pay High Profile: The Global Push for Fair Labor. *p.254, p.261*
Lowly Origin: Where, When, and Why Our Ancestors First Stood Up. *p.15*
The Loyal, True and Brave: America's Civil War Soldiers. . *p.522*
LPGA's Guide to Every Shot. *p.837, p.861*
LSAT: The Best Test Preparation for the Law School Admission Test with Software. *p.440*
La Lucha for Cuba: Religion and Politics on the Streets of Miami. *p.543*
Luckiest Man: The Life and Death of Lou Gehrig. *p.850*
Lugbara Religion. *p.36*
The Lunda-Ndembu: Style, Change and Social Transformation in South Central Africa. *p.38*

M

Machiavelli's Children: Leaders and Their Legacies in Italy and Japan. *p.622*
Machiavelli's Virtue. *p.492*
Macmillan Encyclopedia of Death and Dying, Set. *p.678*
Macroeconometrics: Developments, Tensions and Prospects. *p.202*
Macroeconomic Instability and Coordination: Selected Essays of Axel Leijonhufvud. *p.240*
Macroeconomics and the Real World: Econometric Techniques and Macroeconomic, Vol. 1. . . . . *p.198*

Macroeconomics and the Real World: Keynesian Economics, Unemployment, and Policy, Vol. 2. . . . . . . *p.198, p.225*

The Macroeconomics of Open Economies: An Introduction to Aggregate Behavior and Policy. *p.238*

Macroeconomics Policies and Poverty. *p.240, p.266*

Mad Seasons: The Story of the First Women's Professional Basketball League, 1978-1981. . . . . *p.809, p.837, p.854*

Madam President: Women Blazing the Leadership Trail. . *p.526*

Made in China: What Western Managers Can Learn from Trailblazing Chinese Entrepreneurs. *p.59, p.68*

Madeline Hunter's Mastery Teaching: Increasing Instructional Effectiveness in Elementary and Secondary Schools. . *p.343*

Maestro: Greenspan's Fed and the American Boom. . *p.90, p.156*

The Mafia of a Sicilian Village, 1860-1960: A Study of Violent Peasant Entrepreneurs. *p.751*

The Magazine in America, 1741-1990. . . . . *p.410*

Magazine Publishers of America. *p.409*

Magazines in the Twentieth Century. *p.410*

The Magic Mirror: Law in American History. *p.440*

Main Bodies [of the United Nations]. *p.635*

Main Currents in Sociological Thought: Durkheim, Pareto, Weber. *p.682*

Main Currents in Sociological Thought: Montesquieu, Comte, Marx, Tocqueville, and the Sociologists and the Revolution of 1848. . . . . *p.682*

Maintaining Diversity in Higher Education. *p.289*

The Majesty of the Law: Reflections of a Supreme Court Justice. *p.466*

Major Acts of Congress. *p.532*

Major International Treaties, 1914-1945: A History and Guide with Texts. *p.629*

Major League Losers: The Real Cost of Sports and Who's Paying for It. *p.886, p.889, p.892, p.897*

Major Peace Treaties of Modern History, 1648-2001. . . *p.629*

Major Trends and Issues in Early Childhood Education: Challenges, Controversies, and Insights. *p.369*

Major Violation: A Balancing Act: Sports and Education. *p.821, p.894*

Majority Rule or Minority Will: Adherence to Precedent on the U. S. Supreme Court. *p.540*

Make it Happen: Small business Start-up. *p.87*

Make Love, Not War: The Sexual Revolution: an Unfettered History. *p.746*

Make No Law: The Sullivan Case and the First Amendment. *p.405, p.443*

Make Your Life Tax Deductible: Easy Techniques to Reduce Your Taxes and Start Building Wealth Immediately. . . *p.68*

The Makers of Modern Economics, Vol. 2. . *p.215, p.217, p.223*

The Makers of Modern Economics, Vol. 3. . . . . *p.193*

The Makers of Modern Economics, Vol. 4. . . . . *p.193*

The Makers of Modern Economics. *p.193*

Making a Living: Changing Livelihoods in Rural Africa. . *p.772*

Making a Living in the Middle Ages: The People of Britain 850-1520. . . . . *p.702*

Making a Place for Pleasure in Early Childhood Education. *p.369*

Making and Marketing Arms. *p.608*

Making Babies, Making Families: What Matters Most in an Age of Reproductive Technologies, Surrogacy, Adoption, and Same-Sex and Unwed Parents' Rights. *p.734*

Making Civil Rights Law: Thurgood Marshall and the Supreme Court, 1936-1961. . . . . *p.457*

Making Connections: Brain, Mind, and Culture in a Social Anthropology. *p.27*

Making Constitutional Law: Thurgood Marshall and the Supreme Court, 1961-1991. . . . . *p.469*

Making Creativity Practical: Innovation That Gets Results. . *p.66*

Making Democracy: Leadership, Class, Gender, and Political Participation in Thailand. *p.622*

Making Democracy Work: Civic Traditions in Modern Italy. *p.594*

Making Ecopreneurs: Developing Sustainable Entrepreneurship. *p.51, p.54*

Making European Space: Mobility, Power and Territorial Identity. *p.397*

Making Good: How Young People Cope with Moral Dilemmas at Work. *p.55*

Making Laws and Making News: Media Strategies in the U. S. House of Representatives. *p.533*

Making Midwives Legal: Childbirth, Medicine, and the Law. *p.445*

Making Monsters: False Memories, Psychotherapy, and Sexual Hysteria. *p.714*

The Making of a Name: The Inside Story of the Brands We Buy. *p.142*

The Making of a Teacher: Teacher Knowledge and Teacher Education. *p.279*

The Making of Anthropology in East and Southeast Asia. . *p.39*

The Making of Economic Society. *p.209*

The Making of Economics: The Foundation. *p.185*

The Making of Environmental Law. *p.448*

The Making of Marx's Capital. *p.236*

The Making of Modern Libya: State Formation, Colonization, and Resistance, 1830-1932. . . . . *p.582*

The Making of Portuguese Democracy. *p.608*

The Making of Psychological Anthropology. *p.35*

The Making of Telecommunication Policy. *p.420*

The Making of the English Working Class. *p.725*

The Making of the Modern Family. *p.739*

The Making of the Modern University: Intellectual Transformation and the Marginalization of Morality. . *p.332*

The Making of the Mosaic: A History of Canadian Immigration Policy. *p.764*

The Making of the National Labor Relations Board: A Study in Economics, Politics, and the Law, 1933-1937. . . . . *p.446*

Making Peace: A First Hand Account of the Arab-Israeli Peace Process. *p.648*

Making Peace Pay: A Bibliography on Disarmament and Conversion. *p.656*

Making Policy in Europe. *p.636*

Making Political Geography. *p.487, p.495*

Making Sense: A Student's Guide to Research and Writing: Geography and Environmental Sciences. *p.376*

Making Sense of Cities. *p.395*

Making Sense of Intellectual Capital: Designing a Method for the Valuation of Intangibles. *p.72*

Making Sense of Methods in the Classroom: A Pedagogical Presence. *p.348*

Making Sense of the Molly Maguires. *p.126*

Making Sense of the Organization. *p.174*

Making Silent Stones Speak: Human Evolution and the Dawn of Technology. *p.17*

Making Space in the Early Modern Atlantic World. . . . *p.399*

Making Sweatshops: The Globalization of the U. S. Apparel Industry. *p.665*

Making the American Self: Jonathan Edwards to Abraham Lincoln. *p.694*

Making the American Team: Sport, Culture, and the Olympic Experience. *p.815, p.845, p.891, p.898*

Making the Grade: Reinventing America's Schools. . . . *p.330*

Making the Majors: The Transformation of Team Sports in America. *p.851, p.888, p.891, p.896*

Making the Rugby World: Race, Gender, Commerce. *p.814, p.865*

Making Tough Decisions: Tactics for Improving Managerial Decision Making. *p.83*

Making Votes Count: Strategic Coordination in the World's Electoral Systems. *p.577, p.578*

Making Women Pay: The Hidden Costs of Fetal Rights. *p.442, p.774*

Malan to de Klerk: Leadership in the Apartheid State. . . *p.614*

Malay Fishermen. *p.39*

Male and Female: The Classic Study of the Sexes. . . . *p.748*

Male Homosexual Behavior and the Effects of AIDS Education: A Study of Behavior and Safer Sex in New Zealand and South Australia. *p.779*

Male Prostitution. *p.749*

Male to Male: Sexual Feelings Across the Boundaries of Identity. *p.750*

Malinowski: Odyssey of an Anthropologist, 1884-1920. . . *p.5*

Malinowski, Rivers, Benedict and Others: Essays on Culture and Personality. *p.5*

Malthus' Essay on Population. *p.221*

Malthus. *p.222*

Man and Wife in America: A History. *p.442, p.739*

Man in Society: A Biosocial View. *p.684*

The Man in the Principal's Office. *p.282*

The Man on Horseback: The Role of the Military in Politics. *p.575*

The Man Versus the State: With Four Essays on Politics and Society. *p.484, p.511*

The Man Who Listens to Horses. *p.848*

The Man Who Once Was Whizzer White. *p.468*

Management Communication. *p.171*

Management Consulting: Emergence and Dynamics of a Knowledge Industry. *p.64*

Management Consulting Today. *p.65*

Management Control: Theories, Issues and Performance. . *p.72*

The Management of Sport: Its Foundation and Application with PowerWeb Bind-In Card. *p.786, p.885*

Management Research: An Introduction. *p.119*

Management Strategies in Athletic Training. *p.829*

Managerial Presidency. *p.527*

Managers and the Legal Environment: Strategies for the 21st Century. *p.51*

The Manager's Guide to Strategy. *p.81*

Managers Not MBAs: A Hard Look at the Soft Practice of Managing and Management Development. *p.176*

Managers of Innovation: Insights into Making Innovation Happen. *p.67*

Managers of Virtue: Public School Leadership in America, 1820-1980. . . . . *p.282*

Managing Across Borders: The Transnational Solution. *p.58, p.64*

[e] Managing Business Support Services: Strategies for Outsourcing and Facilities Management. *p.113*

Managing Cities: The New Urban Context. *p.543*

Managing Customer Relationships on the Internet. *p.143*

Managing Customers as Investments: The Strategic Value of Customers in the Long Run. *p.143*

Managing Diversity: Toward a Globally Inclusive Workplace. *p.132*

Managing E-Learning: Design, Delivery, Implementation, and Evaluation. *p.322*

Managing E-Mail and Internet Use: A Practical Guide to Employer's Obligations and Employee's Rights. . . . *p.131*

Managing Fiscal Strain in Major American Cities: Understanding Retrenchment in the Public Sector, 247. . *p.544*

Managing Gender: Affirmative Action and Organizational Power in Australian, Canadian, and New Zealand Sport. . . . *p.837*

Managing Globalization in Developing Countries and Transition Economies: Building Capacities for a Changing World. . *p.665*

Managing in a Time of Great Change. *p.72*

Managing in the Global Economy. *p.70*

Managing Interactively: Executing Business Strategy, Improving Communication, and Creating a Knowledge-Sharing Culture. *p.172*

Managing Knowledge for Sustained Competitive Advantage: Designing Strategies for Effective Human Resource Management. *p.76*

Managing New Industry Creation: Global Knowledge Formation and Entrepreneurship in High Technology. *p.69*

Managing Organizational Deviance. *p.131*

Managing Product Development. *p.118*

Managing Service in Food and Beverage Operations. . . *p.165*

Managing Sport and Risk Management Strategies. *p.882, p.886, p.900*

Managing Sport Organizations. *p.882*

Managing the Academic Enterprise: Case Studies for Deans and Provosts. *p.293*

Managing the Construction Process: Estimating, Scheduling, and Project Control. *p.158*

Managing the Environmental Crisis: Incorporating Competing Values in Natural Resource Administration. *p.62*

Managing the Nonprofit Organization. *p.72*

Managing the Organizational Melting Pot: Dilemmas of Workplace Diversity. *p.132*

Managing the President's Program: Presidential Leadership and Legislative Policy Formulation. *p.527*

Managing Uncertainty in the House of Representatives: Adaptation and Innovation in Special Rules. p.532
Managing with Power: Politics and Influence in Organizations. p.73
Manchus and Han: Ethnic Relations and Political Power in Late Qing and Early Republican China, 1861-1928. . . . . p.623
Mandated Reporting of Suspected Child Abuse: Ethics, Law and Policy. p.756
Mandates and Empire: The League of Nations and Africa, 1914-1931. . . . . p.631
Manhood in America. p.745
Manias, Panics, and Crashes: A History of Financial Crises. p.95, p.100, p.147, p.244
Manliness and Morality: Middle-Class Masculinity in Britain and America, 1800-1940. . . . . p.817
The Manly Art: Bare-Knuckle Prize Fighting in America. p.805, p.855
Man's Most Dangerous Myth: The Fallacy of Race. . . . p.729
A Man's Reach: The Philosophy of Judge Jerome Frank. . p.437
A Man's World?: Changing Men's Practices in a Globalized World. p.744
Manual of political economy. p.212
The Manufacture of Madness: A Comparative Study of the Inquisition and the Mental Health Movement. p.770
The Manufactured Crisis: Myths, Fraud and the Attack on America's Public Schools. p.324
Manufacturing Facilities Design and Material Handling. . p.116
Manufacturing Handbook of Best Practices: An Innovation, Productivity, and Quality Focus. p.119
The Many Landfalls of John Cabot. p.379
The Many Lives of Academic Presidents: Association of Governing Boards and Universities and Colleges. . . . p.293
Many Unhappy Returns: One Man's Quest to Turn Around the Most Unpopular Organization in America. p.107
Many Ways to Be Deaf. p.22
Mao's People: Sixteen Portraits of Life in Revolutionary China. p.702
Mapping Global Cities: GIS Methods in Urban Analysis. . p.388
Mapping the Future of America's National Parks: Stewardship Through Geographic Information Systems. p.382
Mapping Yorùbá Networks: Power and Agency in the Making of Transnational Communities. p.44
Maps and the Internet. p.386
Maps, Myths, and Men: The Story of the Vinland Map. . p.399
Maps with the News: The Development of American Journalistic Cartography. p.386
Marbury vs. Madison: The Origins and Legacy of Judicial Review. p.455, p.538
Marc Bloch, Sociology and Geography: Encountering Changing Disciplines. p.682
A March of Liberty: A Constitutional History of the United States: From 1877 to the Present, Vol. II. p.452
A March of Liberty: A Constitutional History of the United States: From the Founding to 1890, Vol. I. p.452
The March of Spare Time: The Problem and Promise of Leisure in the Great Depression. p.783, p.823
Margaret Sanger's Eugenic Legacy: The Control of Female Fertility. p.775
Marge Schott . . . Unleashed!. p.849
Maria Montessori: A Biography. p.343
Ⓔ Marine and Coastal Geographical Information Systems. p.393
Marine Chemistry. p.393
Marine Climate Change: Ocean Waves, Storms and Surges in the Perspective of Climate Change. p.394
☐ Market and Trade Data: Statistical Market Information. p.152, p.164
Market Efficiency: Stock Market Behavior in Theory and Practice. p.263
The Market for Virtue: The Potential and Limits of Corporate Social Responsibility. p.54
Market Research in Practice: A Guide to the Basics. . . . p.135
Market Research Matters: Tools and Techniques for Aligning Your Business. p.135
The Market Research Toolbox: A Concise Guide for Beginners. p.136
Market Signaling: Informational Transfer in Hiring and Related Screening Processes. p.254
Market Structure and Innovation. p.269
The Market, the State, and the Export-Import Bank of the United States, 1934-2000. . . . . p.88
Marketer's Guide to Media. p.140, p.150, p.157
Marketing: A Complete Guide in Pictures. p.135
Marketing for Hospitality and Tourism. p.161
Marketing for Non-Profit Organizations. p.135
Marketing Imagination. p.135
Marketing of Olympic Sport Organisations. . p.845, p.887, p.891
The Marketing of Rebellion: Insurgents, Media and International Activism. p.497
Marketing Plans That Work. p.144
Marketing Research and Knowledge Development: An Assessment for Marketing Management. p.136
The Marketing Research Guide. p.136
Marketing the American Creed Abroad: Diasporas in the U. S. and Their Homelands. p.571
Marketing to American Latinos: A Guide to the In-Culture Approach. p.139
Marketing to Leading-Edge Baby Boomers: Perceptions, Principles, Practices, Predictions. p.138
Marketing to the New Super Consumer Mom and Kid. . . p.138
☐ MarketResearch.com. p.135
☐ MarketWatch. p.93, p.101
Maroon Societies: Rebel Slave Communities in the Americas. p.41
Marriage and Divorce in Islamic South-East Asia. p.733
Marriage, Divorce and Children's Adjustment. p.735
Marriage, Divorce, Remarriage. p.739
Marriage in Tribal Societies. p.32
Married to the Brand: Why Consumers Bond with Some Brands for Life.. . . . . p.142
Marrow of the Nation: A History of Sport and Physical Culture in Republican China. p.808
Marshall's Evolutionary Economics. p.228
Marsilius of Padua: The Defender of the Peace. p.490

Martha Brae's Two Histories: European Expansion and Caribbean Culture-Building in Jamaica. *p.40*
Martial Arts in the Modern World. *p.863*
Marva Collins' Way: Returning to Excellence in Education.. . . . . *p.337*
Marx after Marxism: The Philosophy of Karl Marx. . . . *p.236*
Marx and Engels on the Population Bomb. *p.222*
Marx: Early Political Writings. *p.492*
Marx for the 21st Century.. . . . . *p.237*
Marx@2000: Late Marxist Perspectives. *p.236*
The Marx-Engels Reader. *p.507*
Marxism and Anthropology: The History of a Relationship.. *p.23*
Marxism and the Call of the Future: Conversations on Ethics, History, and Politics. *p.507, p.508*
Marxism and the Leap to the Kingdom of Freedom: The Rise and Fall of the Communist Utopia. *p.509*
Marxism: For and Against. *p.235*
Marx's Capital. *p.235*
Marx's Concept of Man. *p.235*
Marx's Critique of Political Economy: Intellectual Sources and Evolution, Vol. 1. . . . . *p.236*
Marx's Theory of Money: Modern Appraisals. *p.236*
Masculine Domination. *p.743*
Masculinities, Gender Relations, and Sport, Vol. 11. . . . . *p.818, p.837*
Masculinities. *p.743, p.745*
Masculinity Studies and Feminist Theory. *p.745*
The Masculinity Studies Reader. *p.745*
Masks and Mirrors: Generation X and the Chameleon Personality. *p.693*
Mass Communication and American Social Thought: Key Texts, 1919-1968. . . . . *p.696*
Mass Communication Law and Ethics. *p.406*
Mass Hysteria: Critical Psychology and Media Studies. . *p.714*
Mass Media and New Democracies. *p.424*
Mass Media and Society in the Middle East. *p.415*
Mass Media and Society. *p.416*
Mass Media and the Constitution: An Encyclopedia of Supreme Court Decisions. *p.405, p.445*
Mass Media and the Supreme Court. *p.445*
Mass Media in a Mass Society: Myth and Reality. *p.696*
Mass Media in Sub-Saharan Africa. *p.415*
Mass Media in the New Millennium: Structures, Functions, Issues and Ethics. *p.417*
Mass Media Law, 2007/2008 Edition with PowerWeb. . . *p.445*
Mass Politics and Culture in Democratizing Korea. . . . *p.621*
Masses in Latin America. *p.703*
Mass-Mediated Terrorism: The Central Role of the Media in Terrorism and Counterterrorism.. . . . . *p.558*
The Master of Seventh Avenue: David Dubinsky and American Labor Movement. *p.128*
Mastering Public Administration: From Max Weber to Dwight Waldo. *p.545, p.580*
Masters of Illusion: The World Bank and the Poverty of Nations.. . . . . *p.630*
Masters of Sociological Thought: Ideas in Historical and Social Context.. . . . . *p.682*
Masters Running: A Guide to Running and Staying Fit After 40. . . . . *p.791, p.841, p.866*
Masters Track and Field: A History.. . . . . *p.841, p.847, p.869*
Masturbation: The History of a Great Terror. *p.748*
The Match: Althea Gibson and a Portrait of a Friendship. *p.809 p.833 p.838 p.864*
Mate Selection: A Study of Complementary Needs. . . . *p.739*
Mate Selection Across Cultures. *p.738, p.742*
Math and Science Gateway.. . . . . *p.367*
Mathematical Formulas for Economists. *p.175*
Mathematical Investigations in the Theory of Value and Prices: Appreciation and Interest. *p.199, p.251*
Mathematical models of economic growth. *p.205*
Mathematical Optimization and Economic Theory. *p.175*
Mathematical Psychics: An Essay on the Application of Mathematics to the Moral Sciences. *p.223*
Mathematical Psychics and Other Essays: Commentaries by Marshall, Jevons and Keynes. *p.223*
Mathematico-Deductive Theory of Rote Learning: A Study in Scientific Methodology. *p.357*
Mathematics and Sports.. . . . . *p.871*
Mathematics for Economists: Answers Pamphlet. *p.204*
Mathematics for Economists. *p.203, p.204*
Mathematics of Interest Rates, Insurance, Social Security, and Pensions. *p.175*
The Mathematics of Projectiles in Sport. *p.871*
Maths for Economics. *p.204*
The Matrifocal Family: Power, Pluralism and Politics. . . *p.33*
Matrilineal Kinship. *p.32*
Matrix Algebra for Applied Economics. *p.175, p.204*
Matrix of Language: Contemporary Linguistic Anthropology. *p.18*
A Matter of Definition: Is there truly a shortage of school principals? *p.282*
A Matter of Principle. *p.441*
A Matter of Trust: Connecting Teachers and Learners in the Early Childhood Classroom. *p.369*
Matters of Culture: Cultural Sociology in Practice.. . . . *p.699*
Matters of Principle: America's Rejection of the Bork Nomination to the Supreme Court of the United States.. *p.536*
Matty: Christy Mathewson of the New York Giants. . . . *p.859*
Max Weber: An Intellectual Portrait. *p.684*
Max Weber and the Idea of Economic Sociology. *p.681*
Max Weber on Law in Economy and Society. *p.435*
Max Weber's Comparative-Historical Sociology.. . . . . . *p.681*
Max Weber's Methodologies: Interpretation and Critique.. *p.681*
Max Weber's Methodology: The Unification of the Cultural and Social Sciences. *p.681*
Maximum Feasible Misunderstanding. *p.266*
May the Best Team Win: Baseball Economics and Public Policy, Expanded and Updated. *p.853, p.890*
Maya Cosmos. *p.9*
Maya. *p.9*

Maynard Keynes: An Economists' Biography. p.228

Mayors in the Middle: Politics, Race, and Mayoral Control of Urban Schools. p.543

The MBA Handbook: Skills for Mastering Management. . p.176

MBA: The First Century. p.176

The Mbuti Pygmies: Adaptation and Change in Ituri Forest. . p.39

McCloskey's Economic Thought: The Rhetoric of an Economist. p.268

The McGraw-Hill Encyclopedia of Economics. p.189

McGraw-Hill's Compound Interest and Annuity Tables. . p.163

McKinsey's Marvin Bower: Vision, Leadership, and the Creation of Management Consulting. p.64, p.147

Meaning and Moral Order: Explorations in Cultural Analysis. p.720

Meaning, Medicine and the 'Placebo Effect'. p.47

The Meaning of Ichiro: The New Wave from Japan and the Transformation of Our National Pastime. p.820 p.834 p.852 p.890

The Meaning of Sports: Why Americans Watch Baseball, Football, and Basketball and What They See When They Do. p.817

The Meaning of the Nuclear Revolution: Statecraft and the Prospect of Armageddon. p.656

Meaningful Differences in the Everyday Experience of Young American Children. p.356, p.368

The Measure of Value Stated and Illuminated. p.222

Measurement and Meaning: Combining Quantitative and Qualitative Methods for the Analysis of Poverty and Social Exclusion in Latin America. p.687, p.731

Measurement Error and Latent Variables in Econometrics. p.205

Measurement in Pediatric Exercise Science. p.874

The Measurement of Intelligence. p.359

Measurement, Quantification and Economic Analysis: Numeracy in Economics. p.204

The Measurements of Environmental and Resource Values: Theory and Methods. p.61

Measuring Minds: Henry Herbert Goddard and the Origins of American Intelligence Testing. p.287

Measuring Sustainable Development: Macroeconomics and the Environment. p.267

Measuring Up: Educational Assessment Challenges and Practices for Psychology. p.285

Measuring Up. p.289

Media and Conflict: Framing Issues, Making Policy, Shaping Opinions. p.407

The Media and the War on Terrorism. p.563

The Media at War: Communication and Conflict in the Twentieth Century. p.406

Media Ethics: Cases and Moral Reasoning. p.405

Media Freedom and Accountability. p.405

Media Gender and Identity: An Introduction. . . . p.743, p.744

The Media Handbook. p.427

The Media in Europe: The Euromedia Handbook. p.415

Media Organizations and Convergence: Case Studies of Media Convergence Pioneers. p.418

Media Planning: A Practical Guide. p.428

Media Relations in Sport. p.902, p.906

Media Sport Stars: Masculinities and Moralities. . p.820, p.903

Media Systems in Society: Understanding Industries, Strategies, and Power. p.696

Media Talk: Language and Interaction on Radio and Television. p.418

Media Technology and Society: A History from the Telegraph to the Internet. p.419

Media Writer's Handbook: A Guide to Common Editing and Writing Problems. p.413

Mediamark Reporter. p.137, p.139

Mediasport. p.820, p.892, p.903, p.907

The Mediated Presidency: Television News and Presidential Governance. p.558

Mediation in the Yugoslav Wars: The Critical Years, 1990-95. . . . . p.650

Medical and Healthcare Marketplace Guide. p.160

Medical Anthropology and African American Health. . . . p.46

Medical Malpractice on Trial. p.445

Medical Science and Democratic Truth: Doctors and Revolution in Nepal. p.46

Medical Sociology: Major Themes in Health and Social Welfare. p.756

The Medieval Expansion of Europe. p.379

Medieval Games: Sports and Recreations in Feudal Society, 30. . . . . p.783, p.804

Medieval Schools: Roman Britain to Renaissance England. p.336

Medieval Welsh Society: Selected Essays. p.705

Mediterranean Countrymen : Essays in the Social Anthropology of the Mediterranean. p.705

Mediterranean Urbanization 800-600 BC. p.12

Meech Lake: The Inside Story. p.587

Meet Me in the Middle: Becoming an Accomplished Middle-Level Teacher. p.366

Meetings, Expositions, Events and Conventions: An Introduction to the Industry. p.161

Megaevents and Modernity: Olympics, Expos and the Growth of Global Culture. p.846, p.889, p.892

Melpomene Institute. p.789, p.794

The Melting Pot in Israel: The Commission of Inquiry Concerning the Education of Immigrant Children During the Early Years of the State. p.337

Member of Parliament: The Job of a Backbencher. . . . p.606

The Memoirs of Chief Justice Earl Warren. p.469

Memoirs of Extraordinary Popular Delusions and the Madness of Crowds: The Essential Library Edition. p.244

Memorials of Alfred Marshall. p.224

Memories of Summer: When Baseball Was an Art and Writing about It a Game. p.811, p.851

Men and Speed: A Wild Ride Through NASCAR's Breakout Season. p.848

Men at Midlife. p.741

Men, Masculinities and Social Welfare. p.755

Men Own the Fields, Women Own the Crops: Gender and Power in the Cameroon Grassfields. p.30

MENIC: The Middle East Information Center - Countries & Regions. p.615

Mentoring Across Boundaries: Helping Beginning Teachers Succeed in Challenging Situations. p.277

Mentoring Beginning Teachers: Guiding, Reflecting, Coaching. p.277

Mentoring New Special Education Teachers: A Guide for Mentors and Program Developers. p.277

Mentoring New Teachers. p.277

Merc: The Emergence of a Global Financial Powerhouse. p.102, p.163

Mercantilism, Set. p.216

Mercantilism. p.215

Merchants and Shopkeepers: An Historical Anthropology of an Irish Market Town, 1200-1986.. . . . . p.42

Mercosur: The Common Market of the Southern Cone. . . p.61

Mergent Online Industry Reports. p.150

Mergers and Acquisitions Basics: The Key Steps of Acquisitions, Divestitures, and Investments. p.84

Mergers and Acquisitions: Business Strategies for Accountants. p.84

Mergers and Acquisitions from A to Z. p.85

Mergers and Acquisitions. p.85

Merging Traffic: The Consolidation of the International Automobile Industry. p.153, p.664

Mermaids on Parade: America's Love Affair with Its First Olympic Swimmers. p.823, p.835, p.845, p.868

Merriam-Webster's Geographical Dictionary. p.373

Merry Wheels and Spokes of Steel: A Social History of the Bicycle. p.819, p.857

Mesoamerican Archaeology: Theory and Practice. p.9

Messages to the World: The Statements of Osama Bin Laden. p.658

The Messenger's Motives: Ethical Problems of the News Media. p.405

Meta-Analysis, a Comparison of Approaches. p.689

Metacommunities: Spatial Dynamics and Ecological Communities. p.394

Meta-Ethnography: Synthesizing Qualitative Studies. . . . p.24

Metaphors We Live By. p.20

Meteorology Today. p.393

Method and Appraisal in Economics. p.269

The Method and Theory of Ethnology. p.24

The Methodology of Economic Model Building: Methodology after Samuelson. p.194

The Methodology of Economics: Or, How Economists Explain. p.194

The Methodology of Empirical Macroeconomics. p.195

Methods and Materials for Teaching the Gifted. p.317

The Methods and Materials of Demography: Condensed Edition. p.376

Methods of Evaluating Educational Technology. p.351

Methods of Meta-Analysis: Correcting Error and Bias in Research Findings. p.689

Metropolitan Government and Governance: Theoretical Perspectives, Empirical Analysis, and the Future. . . . p.543

Mexican Americans and the Law: El Pueblo Unido Jamás Ser Vencido!. p.458

The Mexican Congress: Old Player, New Power. p.594

Mexican Politics: The Containment of Conflict. p.593

Mexico: An Encyclopedia of Contemporary Culture and History. p.383

Mexico: From the Olmecs to the Aztecs. p.9

Mexico in Focus: A Guide to the People, Politics, and Culture. p.383

Mexico in Transition: Neoliberal Globalism, the State and Civil Society. p.383

Mexico, the End of the Revolution. p.593

Mexico under Salinas. p.594

The Michael Eric Dyson Reader. p.729

Michael Jordan, Inc.: Corporate Sport, Media Culture, and Late Modern America. p.853, p.882, p.895, p.901

Michael Oakeshott: An Introduction. p.491

Michel Foucault: Materialism and Education. p.344

Microeconomics: Behavior, Institutions, and Evolution. p.249, p.251

Microfoundations and Macroeconomics: An Austrian Perspective. p.234

Microfoundations of Economic Growth: A Schumpeterian Perspective. p.230, p.235, p.243

Microfoundations of Financial Economics: An Introduction to General Equilibrium Asset Pricing. p.263

Microsociology: Discourse, Emotion, and Social Structure. p.775

Middle East and North African Immigrants in Europe: Current Impact; Local and National Responses. p.765

Middle East Monarchies: The Challenge of Modernity. . . p.614

Middle East Politics Today: Government and Civil Society. p.614

Middle Works of John Dewey, 1899-1924: 1920. . . . . p.345

Middle-Class Blacks in a White Society: Prince Hall Freemason in America. p.719

Middletown: A Study in Modern American Culture. . . . p.704

Middletown Families: Fifty Years of Change and Continuity. p.732

Middletown in Transition: A Study in Cultural Conflicts. . p.704

Midterm Madness: The Elections of 2002. . . . . p.549

Mightier Than the Sword: How the News Media Have Shaped American History. p.404

Mighty Like a River: The Black Church and Social Reform. p.720

Mighty Peculiar Elections: The New South Gubernatorial Campaigns of 1970 and the Changing Politics of Race. . p.549

Migration and Vodou. p.41

The Migration Experience in Africa. p.764

Mike Tyson: Nurture of the Beast. p.855

Miles to Go: A Personal History of Social Policy. p.769

Militant Islam in Southeast Asia: Crucible of Terror. . . . p.657

Militarism and Social Revolution in the Third World. . . p.574

Militarization and Demilitarization in El Salvador's Transition to Democracy. p.593

The Military and American Society. p.717

The Military and Politics in Postauthoritarian Chile. . . . p.593
The Military and Society in Latin America. p.717
The Military and the State in Latin America. p.592
Military Ascendancy and Political Culture: A Study of Indonesia's Golkar. p.623
Military Politics and Democratization in Indonesia. . . . p.622
Military Rebellion in Argentina: Between Coups and Consolidation. p.592
The Military Revolution and Political Change: Origins of Democracy and Autocracy in Early Modern Europe. . p.501
Military Tribunals and Presidential Power: American Revolution to the War on Terrorism. p.464
Millennial Keynes: An Introduction to the Origin, Development, and Later Currents of Keynesian Thought. p.229
The Millennials: Americans Born 1977 To 1994. . . . . p.138
A Millennium of Family Change: Feudalism to Capitalism in North Western Europe. p.738
Miller Complete GAAP Library 2006, Vol. 2. . . . . . . p.105
Million Dollar Consulting Toolkit: Step-by-Step Guidance, Checklists, Templates, and Samples from the Million Dollar Consultant. p.65
Mill's the Subjection of Women: Critical Essays. p.223
Milton Friedman: Economics in Theory and Practice. . . p.232
Milton Friedman's Monetary Framework: A Debate with His Critics. p.232, p.238
Milton Friedman. p.231
The Mind and Method of the Economist: A Critical Appraisal of Major Economists in the 20th Century. p.195, p.215
The Mind and Society, Set. p.249
Mind and Society, Vol. 1. . . . . p.685
Mind and Society, Vol. 2. . . . . p.685
Mind and Society, Vol. 3. . . . . p.685
Mind and Society, Vol. 4. . . . . p.685
The Mind of John Locke: A Study of Political Theory in Its Intellectual Setting. p.491
The Mind of the Political Terrorist. p.661
The Mind of Wall Street: A Legendary Financier on the Perils of Greed and the Mysteries of the Market. p.96, p.100
Mind, Self, and Society: From the Standpoint of a Social Behaviorist. p.693
Mindful Learning: Teaching Self-Discipline and Academic Accomplishment. p.358
Minding American Education: Reclaiming the Tradition of Active Learning. p.346
Mine Eyes Have Seen the Glory: A Journey into the Evangelical Subculture in America. p.720
Miners on Strike: Class Solidarity and Division in Britain. . p.128
Minnesota Rag: The Dramatic Story of the Landmark Supreme Court Case That Gave New Meaning to Freedom of the Press. p.439
Minor Papers on the Currency Question, 1809-1823. . . . p.220
Minority Education: Anthropological Perspectives. . p.302, p.312
The Minority Rights Revolution. p.495, p.511, p.516
The Miranda Debate: Law, Justice, and Policing. p.473
Miranda's Waning Protections: Police Interrogation Practices after Dickerson. p.474
The Mirror Makers: A History of American Advertising and Its Creators. p.426
A Mirror to Kathleen's Face: Education in Independent Ireland, 1922-1960. p.333
The Mirrored Window: Focus Groups from a Moderator's Point of View. p.136
Mirrors of Destruction: War, Genocide, and Modern Identity. p.651
The Mis-education of the Negro. p.310
Misleading Evidence and Evidence-Led Policy: Making Social Science More Experimental. p.680
The Missing Middle: Working Families and the Future of American Social Policy. p.769
The Missing Peace: The Inside Story of the Fight for Middle East Peace. p.650
Mission Statements: A Guide to the Corporate and Nonprofit Sectors. p.172
Missions of the College Curriculum: A Contemporary Review with Suggestions: a Commentary of the Carnegie Foundation for the Advancement of Teaching. p.294
Mistaken Identification: The Eyewitness, Psychology and the Law. p.473
Misteaching of Academic Discourses: The Politics of Language in the Classroom. p.349
Misused Statistics. p.178
The Mitterrand Experiment: Continuity and Change in Modern France. p.609
Mixed Messages: U.S. Human Rights Policy and Latin America. p.513
Mixed-Member Electoral Systems: The Best of Both Worlds? p.576
"A Problem from Hell": America and the Age of Genocide. p.715
The "Higher Law" Background of American Constitutional Law. p.452
"Schools of Tomorrow," Schools of Today: What Happened to Progressive Education. p.348
A "Scottsboro" Case in Mississippi: The Supreme Court and Brown vs. Mississippi. p.535
Mobile Wireless Communications. p.422
Mobilization, Participation and Democracy in America. . p.547
Mobilizing for Peace: Conflict Resolution in Northern Ireland, Israel/Palestine, and South Africa. p.640, p.649
Modelling Geographical Systems: Statistical and Computational Applications. p.386
Modelling Individual Choice: The Econometrics of Corners, Kinks and Holes. p.204
Modelling Nonlinear Economic Relationships. p.207
Models As Mediators: Perspectives on Natural and Social Science. p.687
Models for Christian Higher Education: Strategies for Success in the Twenty-First Century. p.308
Models, Numbers, and Cases: Methods for Studying International Relations. p.627
Models of Business Cycles. p.233, p.244
Models of Economic Growth: Proceedings of a Conference Held by the International Economic Association at Jerusalem. p.244

Models of the Family in Modern Societies: Ideals and Realities. p.733

Moderating Focus Groups. p.136

The Modern Anthropology of South-East Asia: An Introduction. p.39

Modern Biopharmaceuticals: Design, Development and Optimization. p.156

The Modern Corporation and Private Property. . . . p.85, p.146

A Modern Dictionary of Geography. p.374

Modern Diplomacy. p.645

Modern Geographers: An Outline of Progress in Geography since 1800 A. D. p.377

Modern Geographic Thought: Richard Peet. p.375

A Modern Guide to Economic Thought: An Introduction to Comparative Schools of Thought in Economics. . . . p.195

A Modern Guide to Macroeconomics: An Introduction to Competing Schools of Thought. p.241

Modern Human Origins: The Other View. p.16

Modern Linear and Nonlinear Econometrics. p.203

Modern Macroeconomics. p.241

The Modern Olympics: A Struggle for Revival. p.847

The Modern Presidency. p.527

The Modern School Movement: Anarchism and Education in the United States. p.324

Modern Systems of Government: Exploring the Role of Bureaucrats and Politicians. p.546

The Modernization of Fatherhood: A Social and Political History. p.739

The Modernization of Inner Asia. p.623

Molding Their Hearts and Minds: Education, Communications and Social Change in Latin America. p.333

The Mole People: Life in the Tunnels Beneath New York City. p.709

Mollie's Job: A Story of Life and Work on the Global Assembly Line. p.759

The Molly Maguire Riots: Industrial Conflict in the Pennsylvania Coal Region. p.124

Monarchies 1000-2000. . . . . p.502

Monarchs and Ministers: The Grand Council in Mid-Ch'ing China, 1723-1820. . . . . p.617, p.619

Monarchy, Aristocracy, and the State in Europe 1300-1800. . . . . p.502

Monetarism and Macroeconomic Policy. p.238, p.246

The Monetarist Controversy: A Seminar Discussion. . . . p.232

Monetarist Economics. p.231

Monetary Economics. p.237, p.241

Monetary Equilibrium. p.239

The Monetary Geography of Africa. p.398

Monetary History of the United States, 1867-1960. . . . p.238

Monetary Policy. p.246

Monetary Statistics of the United States: Estimates, Sources, Methods. p.238

Monetary Theory: Inflation, Interest and Growth in the World Economy. p.238

Monetary Trends in the United States and the United Kingdom: Their Relation to Income, Prices, and Interest Rates, 1867-1975. . . . . p.238

Monetary Trends in the United States and the United Kingdom, Their Relation to Income, Prices, and Interest Rates, 1867-1975. . . . . p.269

Money and Credit in Capitalist Economies: The Endogenous Money Approach. p.233

Money and the Economy: Issues in Monetary Analysis. . p.231

Money and the Mechanism of Exchange. p.231

Money, Capital and Fluctuations: Early Essays. . . p.234, p.238

Money, Credit, and Commerce. p.224, p.238

Money, Expectations, and Business Cycles: Essays in Macroeconomics. p.242

Money Has No Smell: The Africanization of New York City. p.759

Money, History, and International Finance: Essays in Honor of Anna J. Schwartz. p.255

Money in Congressional Elections. p.557, p.558

Money, Interest and Capital: A Study in the Foundations of Monetary Theory. p.247, p.270

Money Matters: A Keynesian Approach to Monetary Economics. p.227, p.237

The Money Men. p.558

Money Mischief: Episodes in Monetary History. p.231

Money, Politics, and Law: A Study of Electoral Campaign Finance Reform in Canada. p.581

Money, Sex and Power: Toward a Feminist Historical Materialism. p.273

Money, the Financial System, and the Economy Plus Myeconlab Student Access Kit. p.247, p.263

The Monkey in the Mirror: Essays on the Science of What Makes Us Human. p.16

Monopoly Rules: How to Find, Capture, and Control the Most Lucrative Markets in Any Business. p.82

Monster: The Autobiography of an L. A. Gang Member. . p.714

Monte Verde: A Late Pleistocene Settlement in Chile: A Paleoenvironment and Site Context. p.11

Monte Verde: A Late Pleistocene Settlement in Chile: The Archaeological Context and Interpretation. p.11

Montesquieu and Rousseau: Forerunners of Sociology. . . p.682

Montessori: A Modern Approach. p.343

The Montessori Method. p.344

Montessori: The Science Behind the Genius. p.337

☐ Moral and Character Development. p.306

The Moral Dimension of Marketing: Essays on Business Ethics. p.146

The Moral Dimension: Toward a New Economics. p.185

The Moral Dimensions of Teaching. p.282

Moral Education: A Study in the Theory and Application of the Sociology of Education. p.306

Moral Education in America: Schools and the Shaping of Character from Colonial Times to the Present. p.306

The Moral Judgment of the Child. p.358

Moral Man and Immoral Society: A Study in Ethics and Politics. p.484, p.770

The Moral Media: How Journalists Reason about Ethics. . p.417

The Moral Philosophy of Management: From Quesnay to Keynes. p.215

The Moral Property of Women: A History of Birth Control Politics in America. p.569, p.775
Moral Questions in the Classroom: How to Get Kids to Think Deeply about Real Life and Their School Work. . . . p.306
The Morality of Groups: Collective Responsibility, Group-Based Harm and Corporate Rights. p.713
The Morality of Law. p.434
The Morality of Nationalism. p.494
More Damned Lies and Statistics: How Numbers Confuse Public Issues. p.689
More Secure, Less Free?: Antiterrorism Policy and Civil Liberties after September 11. . . . . p.565, p.572
More Speech, Not Less: Communications Law in the Information Age. p.406, p.445
More Than a Game: An Unauthorized History of Australian Rules Football. p.806, p.816, p.843, p.847
More than a Game: One Woman's Fight for Gender Equity in Sport. p.822, p.837, p.901
More Than a Game. p.832, p.854
More Than Just a Game: Sports in American Life since 1945. . . . . p.716, p.816
More than Meets the Eye: Studies on Upper Palaeolithic Diversity in the Near East. p.16
More Wives Than One: Transformation of the Mormon Marriage System, 1840-1910. . . . . p.747
The More You Watch, the Less You Know: News Wars - (Sub)Merged Hopes - Media Adventures. p.417
Mormon Polygamous Families: Life in the Principle. . . p.740
Mormon Polygamy: A History. p.740, p.749
Morning by Morning: How We Home-Schooled Our African-American Sons to the Ivy League. p.296
Morningstar Guide to Mutual Funds: Five-Star Strategies for Success. p.93
Morningstar. p.93, p.101
Mortal Engines. p.802, p.806, p.832, p.873
The Mosaic of Economic Growth. p.244
The Most Activist Supreme Court in History: The Road to Modern Judicial Conservatism. p.470, p.537
Mother Jones: An American Life. p.126
Mother Nature: Maternal Instincts and How They Shape the Human Species. p.744
The Mother of Eve: As a First Language Teacher. p.358
Mothers of Invention: Women of the Slaveholding South in the American Civil War. p.520
Motion: American Sports Poems. p.811
Motivate Teams, Maximize Success: Effective Strategies for Realizing Your Goals. p.80
Motor Control: Theory and Practical Applications. p.910
Motor Learning and Performance. p.910
Motor Learning: Concepts and Applications. p.909
Mountain Geomorphology.. . . . . p.391
A Mouth Sweeter Than Salt: An African Memoir. p.702
The Movement: A History of the American New Left, 1959-1972. . . . . p.332
Movement Skill Assessment. p.873, p.907, p.909
Movement System Variability. p.908, p.909
Moving and Learning: The Elementary School Physical Education Experience with PowerWeb: Health and Human Performance. p.796, p.798
Moving Europeans: Migration in Western Europe since 1650. . . . . p.602
Moving Mountains: Japanese Education Reform. p.336
Moving Toward Balance: 8 Weeks of Yoga with Rodney Yee. p.793
Mr. Justice Murphy: A Political Biography. p.468
Mr. Keynes and the Post Keynesians: Principles of Macroeconomics for a Monetary Production Economy. p.226, p.242
Much More Than a Game: Players, Owners and American Baseball since 1921. . . . . p.850, p.882, p.895
Muckraking and Objectivity: Journalism's Colliding Traditions, 18. . . . . p.406
Muckraking!: The Journalism That Changed America. . . p.404
Mud, Sweat and Beers: A Cultural History of Sport and Alcohol. p.814
Muhammad Ali Reader. p.811, p.831, p.855
Muhammad Ali: The People's Champ. p.831, p.855
Muller Vs. Oregon: A Brief History with Documents. . . p.439
The Mulligan Guide to Sports Journalism Careers. p.907
The Multicampus System: Perspectives on Practice and Prospects. p.292
Multicultural and Diversity Education: A Reference Handbook. p.308
A Multicultural Approach to Physical Education: Proven Strategies for Middle and High School. p.797, p.799
Multicultural Citizenship: A Liberal Theory of Minority Rights. p.547, p.551
Multicultural Education: A Source Book. p.309
Multicultural Education in a Pluralistic Society. p.363
Multicultural Geographies: The Changing Racial/Ethnic Patterns of the United States. p.382
Multicultural Gifted Education. p.317
Multicultural Science Education: Theory, Practice, and Promise. p.367
Multicultural Teaching: A Handbook of Activities, Information, and Resources. p.309
Multiculturalism and American Democracy. p.573
A Multilevel Approach to the Study of Motor Control and Learning. p.874, p.908, p.910
Multimedia Projects in the Classroom: A Guide to Development and Evaluation. p.351
Multimethod Research: Synthesizing Styles. p.686
Multinational Firms in the World Economy. . . . p.257, p.261
Multiparty Democracy and Political Change: Constraints to Democratization in Africa. p.505, p.585, p.612
Multiple Paths to Knowledge in International Relations: Methodology in the Study of Conflict Management and Conflict Resolution. p.650
Multiple Perspectives on Play in Early Childhood Education.. . . . . p.369
Multitude: War and Democracy in the Age of Empire. . . p.504
Multivariable Calculus: Concepts and Contexts. p.206

Murder on the Nile, the World Trade Center and Global Terror. p.657
Muscles, Reflexes, and Locomotion. p.909
Muscletown USA: Bob Hoffman and the Manly Culture of York Barbell. p.715
The Museum of Broadcast Communications Encyclopedia of Radio. p.418
Museums and Source Communities: A Routledge Reader. . p.48
Music in Childhood: From Preschool Through the Elementary Grades. p.362
Music in Human Life: Anthropological Perspectives on Music. p.26
Muslim Schools, Education, Children and Family Life. . p.308
Muslims' Place in the American Public Square: Hopes, Fears, and Aspirations. p.721
Must God Remain Greek? : Afro Cultures and God-talk. . p.720
The Muted Conscience: Moral Silence and the Practice of Ethics in Business. p.145
My Apprenticeship. p.271
My Kind of Geography. p.382
My Mother Who Fathered Me: A Study of the Families in Three Selected Communities of Jamaica. p.40
My Own Story. p.604, p.606
My Years with General Motors. p.154
Mysteries of Ancient China: New Discoveries from the Early Dynasties. p.9
The Myth of Democratic Failure: Why Political Institutions Are Efficient. p.506
The Myth of Excellence: Why Great Companies Never Try to Be the Best at Everything. p.135
The Myth of Free Trade: The Pooring of America. p.256, p.260, p.264
The Myth of Green Marketing: Tending Our Goats at the Edge of Apocalypse. p.63
The Myth of Human Races. p.17
The Myth of Judicial Activism: Making Sense of Supreme Court Decisions. p.541
The Myth of Monogamy: Fidelity and Infidelity in Animals and People. p.731
Myths in Education: Beliefs That Hinder Progress and Their Alternatives. p.341

N

NAFTA's Impact on North America: The First Decade. . . p.61
The Naked Olympics: The True Story of the Ancient Games. p.808
Naming the Enemy: Anti-Corporate Social Movements Confront Globalization. p.712
Namoluk Beyond the Reef: The Transformation of a Micronesian Community. p.43
Nancy Clark's Sports Nutrition Guidebook. . . . p.801, p.876
NARA: U.S. Electoral College. p.556
Narrowing the Nation's Power: The Supreme Court Sides with the States. p.443, p.538
The NASCAR Way: The Business That Drives the Sport. p.848 p.888 p.896 p.902
The NASDAQ Stock Market. p.90, p.93, p.101
Nassau Senior and Classical Economics. p.217
Nation Against Nation: What Happened to the U. N. Dream and What the U. S. Can Do about It. p.633
Nation and Identity. p.495
A Nation at Risk: The Full Account. p.322
A Nation at Risk: the Imperative for Educational Reform: a Report to the Nation and the Secretary of Education, United States Department of Education. p.323
A Nation Divided: Diversity, Inequality and Community in American Society. p.725
A Nation Prepared: Teachers for the 21st Century: the Report of the Task Force on Teaching As a Profession, Carnegie Forum on Education and the Economy, May 1986. . . p.278
A Nation Reformed?: American Education Twenty Years after a Nation at Risk. p.326
Nation, State and Territory: A Political Geography. . . . p.495
Nation, State, and Territory: Origins, Evolutions, and Relationships. p.383, p.399, p.488, p.496
A Nation under Lawyers: How the Crisis in the Legal System Is Transforming American Society. p.440
National Adult Literacy Database. p.319
National Agricultural Library Portal. p.152, p.164
National Alliance for Youth Sports. p.789, p.794
National Association of Elementary School Principals. . p.282
National Atals of the United States of America. . . . p.379
National Athletic Trainers Association. p.824, p.828
National Center for Education Statistics. p.322
National Center for the Study of Adult Learning and Literacy (NCSALL). p.304, p.319
National Clearinghouse on Child Abuse and Neglect Information. p.756
The National Collegiate Athletic Association: A Study in Cartel Behavior. p.883, p.887
National Construction Estimator. p.159
National Council for Accreditation of Teacher Education. p.279
A National Crime: The Canadian Government and the Residential School System, 1879-1986. . . . . p.335
National Differences, Global Similarities: World Culture and the Future of Schooling. p.313, p.333
National Economic Policy. p.239
National Educational Technology Standards for Teachers: Preparing Teachers to Use Technology. p.351
National Educational Technology Standards. p.359
National Geographic Historical Atlas of the United States. . p.382
National Geographic World Physical/Ocean Floor. . . . p.392
National Geography Standards. p.360
National Governments and Control of the Internet. p.773
National Household Survey on Drug Abuse: Population Estimates, 1996. . . . . p.776
National Identities and Socio-Political Changes in Latin America. p.703
National Institute for Literacy (NIFL). p.304, p.354
The National Job Bank 2005. . . . . p.168

National Outdoor Leadership School's Wilderness Guide: The Classic Wilderness Guide. *p.788, p.884*

The National Party Chairmen and Committees: Factionalism at the Top. *p.551*

National Pastime: How Americans Play Baseball and the Rest of the World Plays Soccer. *p.820, p.844, p.852, p.899*

National Polity and Local Power: The Transformation of Late Imperial China. *p.620*

National Science Education Standards. *p.359*

National Security Agency Declassification Initiatives. . *p.481*

National Security Archive Documents. *p.561*

National Senior Games Assocation. *p.789, p.840*

National Society for the Study of Education (NSSE). *p.297, p.323*

National Sports Policies: An International Handbook. *p.843, p.887, p.891, p.898*

National Staff Development Council. *p.283*

National Standards for Foreign Language Education. . *p.359*

National Standards for History Basic Edition. *p.359*

National Statistics Online. *p.604*

National Strength and Conditioning Association. *p.827, p.828*

National Survey of State Laws. *p.441*

National Women's Law Center Athletics page. . *p.821, p.882*

National Youth Sport Safety Foundation. . . . *p.827, p.839*

Nationalism and Communism in Romania: The Rise and Fall of Ceausescu's Personal Dictatorship. *p.508, p.600*

Nationalism and Federalism in Australia. *p.624*

Nationalism and Modernism: A Critical Survey of Recent Theories of Nations and Nationalism. *p.495*

Nationalism and the International Labor Movement: The Idea of the Nation in Socialist and Anarchist Theory. *p.494*

Nationalism and the Politics of Culture in Quebec. . . . *p.581*

Nationalism Without a Nation in India. *p.617*

Nationalism. *p.494, p.495*

Nationalizing the Russian Empire: The Campaign Against Enemy Aliens During World War I. *p.653*

Nationhood and Political Theory. *p.494*

Nations and Nationalism since 1780: Programme, Myth, Reality. *p.494*

Nations Before Nationalism. *p.494*

The Nation's Report Card: Evolution and Perspectives. . *p.355*

Nations Without States. *p.494*

The Native American Rights Movement. *p.464*

Native Americans in Sports. *p.841*

NATO and the Quest for Post-Cold War Security. *p.639*

NATO, Britain, France, and the FRG: Nuclear Strategies and Forces for Europe, 1949-2000. . . . . *p.639, p.654*

NATO Enlargement During the Cold War: Strategy and System in the Western Alliance. *p.639*

NATO Enters the 21st Century. *p.639*

NATO in the Post-Cold War Era: Does It Have a Future?. *p.639*

NATO Transformed: The Alliance's New Roles in International Security. *p.639, p.655*

Natural Classroom Assessment: Designing Seamless Instruction and Assessment. *p.287*

Natural Law and Civil Sovereignty: Moral Right and State Authority in Early Modern Political Thought. *p.496*

Natural Law: Reflections on Theory and Practice. *p.513*

Natural Liberty and Civil Government: The Two Treatises on the Art of Ruling Humanity. *p.215*

The Natural Rate of Unemployment: Reflections on 25 Years of the Hypothesis. *p.252*

Natural Resources, Growth and Development: Economics, Ecology and Resource-Scarcity. *p.62*

Natural Resources Policy and Law: Trends and Directions. . *p.463*

Natural Rights Republic: Studies in the Foundation of the American Political Tradition. *p.513*

The Natural Superiority of Women. *p.14, p.744*

The Nature and Logic of Capitalism. *p.214*

The Nature and Significance of Economic Science. . . . *p.210*

The Nature and Sources of the Law. *p.441*

The Nature and Types of Sociological Theory. *p.680*

The Nature of Capital and Income. *p.199, p.224, p.246*

The Nature of Chinese Politics: From Mao to Jiang. . . . *p.620*

The Nature of Culture. *p.24*

The Nature of Hysteria. *p.714*

The Nature of Managerial Work. *p.64*

The Nature of Mass Poverty. *p.265*

The Nature of Paleolithic Art. *p.17*

The Nature of Peace. *p.251*

The Nature of Social and Educational Inquiry: Empiricism vs. Interpretation. *p.355*

Nature's Justice: Writings of William O. Douglas. *p.467*

Naven: A Survey of the Problems Suggested by a Composite Picture of the Culture of a New Guinea Tribe Drawn from Three Points of View. *p.42*

The Nazi Doctors: Medical Killing and the Psychology of Genocide. *p.653*

The Nazi Olympics: Sport, Politics, and Appeasement in the 1930s. *p.807, p.846, p.891*

The Nazi Olympics. *p.807, p.846*

The Nazi Party: A Social Profile of Members and Leaders, 1919-1945. . . . . *p.609*

The Nazi Voter: The Social Foundations of Fascism in Germany, 1919-1933. . . . . *p.609*

Nazis in Skokie: Freedom, Community, and the First Amendment. *p.458*

NBER Macroeconomics Annual 2004. . . . . . . *p.189, p.200*

The Neanderthal Legacy: An Archaeological Perspective of Western Europe. *p.17*

Neanderthals and Modern Humans: An Ecological and Evolutionary Perspective. *p.15*

The Neanderthals: Changing the Image of Mankind. . . . *p.17*

The Neanderthal's Necklace: In Search of the First Thinkers. *p.16*

Negotiate This!: By Caring, but Not T-H-A-T Much. . . . *p.74*

Negotiate to Win: The 21 Rules for Successful Negotiating. . *p.75*

Negotiating a Complex World: An Introduction to International Negotiation. *p.646*

Negotiating Competitiveness: Employment Relations and Organizational Innovation in Germany and the United States. *p.123*
Negotiating Democracy: Politicians and Generals in Uruguay. *p.591*
Negotiating Globally: How to Negotiate Deals, Resolve Disputes and Make Decisions Across Cultural Boundaries. *p.74*
Negotiating Identity: Catholic Higher Education since 1960. . . . . *p.307*
Negotiating on the Edge: North Korean Negotiating Behavior. *p.644, p.646*
Negotiating Outside the Law: Why Camp David Failed. . *p.649*
Negotiating Rationally. *p.74*
Negotiation Analysis: The Science and Art of Collaborative Decision Making. *p.74*
The Negotiation Fieldbook. *p.74*
Negro Family in British Guiana: Family Structure and Social Status in the Villages. *p.33*
Negro League Baseball: The Rise and Ruin of a Black Institution. *p.807, p.832, p.851, p.884*
The Negro Leagues, 1869-1960. . . . . . *p.806, p.832, p.850*
The Negro Leagues Book. *p.804 p.831 p.850 p.896*
Neighborhood Services: Making Big Cities Work. *p.544*
Neither Man nor Woman: The Hijras of India. *p.746*
Neoclassical Finance. *p.89, p.264*
Neoclassical Microeconomics, Vol. I. *p.224, p.248*
Neoclassical Theory of International Trade: The Origins of International Economics. *p.257*
The Neoclassical Theory of Production and Distribution. *p.223, p.225*
Neoconservatism: The Autobiography of an Idea. . *p.511, p.516*
Neoliberalism in Crisis, Accumulation, and Rosa Luxemburg's Legacy. *p.239*
The Net Effect. *p.425*
Netscape Time: The Making of the Billion-Dollar Start-Up That Took on Microsoft. *p.157*
The Network Society: Social Aspects of New Media. . . *p.419*
Networks and Marginality: Life in a Mexican Shantytown. . *p.704*
Networks and Telecommunications: Design and Operation. *p.422*
Networks of Champions: Leadership, Access and Advisory in the U. S. House of Representatives. *p.533*
Networks of Power: Electrification in Western Society, 1880-1930. . . . . *p.159*
Networks of Privilege in the Middle East: The Politics of Economic Reform Revisited. *p.614*
Neuromechanics of Human Movement. *p.908, p.909*
Neurophysiological Basis of Movement. *p.908, p.909*
Never at War: Why Democracies Will Not Fight One Another. *p.506, p.627, p.648, p.651*
Never Going Back: A History of Queer Activism in Canada. *p.712*
Never Just a Game: Players, Owners and American Baseball to 1920. . . . . *p.804, p.850, p.887, p.895*
Neverending Wars: The International Community, Weak States, and the Perpetuation of Civil War. *p.647*
The New American Democracy. *p.503*
The New American Grandparent: A Place in the Family, a Life Apart. *p.740*
The New American Sport History: Recent Approaches and Perspectives. *p.809, p.813*
The New Americans: Seven Families Journey to Another Country. *p.765*
New Approaches on Energy and the Environment: Policy Advice for the President. *p.62*
The New Battle over Workplace Privacy: Safe Practices to Minimize Conflict, Confusion and Litigation. *p.446*
New Caribbean Thought : A Reader. *p.685*
The New Civil War: The Psychology, Culture and Politics of Abortion. *p.775*
The New Class Society: Goodbye American Dream? . . . *p.725*
The New Classical Macroeconomics, Set. *p.217*
New Concise World Atlas. *p.380*
The New Conservatism: Cultural Criticism and the Historians' Debate. *p.511*
The New Corporate Finance. *p.88*
The New Corporate Strategy. *p.81*
The New Crusades: Constructing the Muslim Enemy. . . *p.661*
The New Deal and the Triumph of Liberalism. *p.522*
The New Deal at Work: Managing the Market-Driven Workforce. *p.85*
New Deal Thought. *p.522*
The New Dialectic and Marx's Capital. *p.235*
New Diasporas: The Mass Exodus, Dispersal and Regrouping of Migrant Communities. *p.765*
The New Dickson Baseball Dictionary. *p.850*
New Directions in Anthropological Kinship. *p.33*
New Directions in Anthropology and Environment: Intersections. *p.29*
New Directions in the Sociology of Global Development. . *p.375*
New Directions in the Study of Language. *p.357*
The New Division of Labor: How Computers Are Creating the Next Job Market. *p.253, p.254*
The New Dollars and Dreams: American Incomes and Economic Change. *p.244 p.245 p.254 p.265*
The New Economic Sociology: A Reader. *p.195, p.268*
The New Economics One Decade Older. *p.239*
New Economy Handbook. *p.190*
New Federalism: Intergovernmental Reform from Nixon to Reagan. *p.523*
The New Financial Capitalists: Kohlberg Kravis Roberts and the Creation of Corporate Value. *p.90, p.99*
The New Financial Order: Risk in the 21st Century. *p.90, p.92, p.100*
New Found Lands: Maps in the History of Exploration. . *p.379*
New Frontiers in Economics. *p.197*
New Game Plans for College Sport. *p.822, p.894*
The New Golden Rule: Community and Morality in a Democratic Society. *p.770*
The New Handbook of Organizational Communication: Advances in Theory, Research, and Methods. *p.174*

New Horizons in Economic Thought: Appraisals of Leading Economists. p.186

The New Illustrated Encyclopedia of Billiards. p.855

The New Industrial Economics: Recent Developments in Industrial Organization, Oligopoly and Game Theory. p.207, p.252

The New Industrial State. p.213

The New Institutional Economics of Corruption. . p.252, p.263

The New International Economic Order: The North-South Debate. p.255

The New International Money Game. . . . p.57 p.93 p.98 p.99

The New Italian Republic: From the Fall of the Berlin Wall to Berlusconi. p.594

New Keynesian Economics: Coordination Failures and Real Rigidities. p.225

New Keynesian Economics: Imperfect Competition and Sticky Prices. p.225

New Kid in School: Using Literature to Help Children in Transition. p.312, p.365

New Labour's Pasts: The Labour Party and Its Discontents. p.606

New Life for the College Curriculum: Assessing Achievements and Furthering Progress in the Reform of General Education. p.294

A New Look at Thai AIDS: Perspectives from the Margin. . p.668

The New Mandarins: How British Foreign Policy Works. p.643, p.645

New Media: An Introduction. p.419

New Media and Public Imagination: Launching Radio, Television, and Digital Media in the United States. . . p.418

New Media Technology: Cultural and Commercial Perspectives. p.419

New Methods of Measuring Marginal Utility. p.195

New Nukes: India, Pakistan and Global Nuclear Disarmament. p.655

The New Palgrave: A Dictionary of Economics. p.192

The New Palgrave Dictionary of Economics and the Law. p.191, p.434

New Party Politics: From Jefferson and Hamilton to the Information Age. p.552, p.553

The New Physical Anthropology. p.15

The New Pioneers: The Men and Women Who are Transforming the Workplace and Market Place. p.717

The New Political Economy of J. S. Mill. p.223

New Product Development and Delivery: Ensuring Successful Products Through Integrated Process Management. . . p.118

New Product Development: Successful Innovation in the Marketplace. p.144

The New Public Service: Serving, Not Steering. p.545, p.546, p.580

The New Radicalism in America, 1889-1963: The Intellectual As a Social Type. p.768

The New Rank and File. p.127

The New Regionalism in Africa. p.611

New Relationship: Human Capital in the American Corporation. p.76

The New Restaurant Entrepreneur: An Inside Look at Restaurant Deal-Making and Other Tales from the Culinary Trenches. p.165

New Rules of Sociological Method. p.686

The New Ruthless Economy: Work and Power in the Digital Age. p.69

New Schools for a New Century: The Redesign of Urban Education. p.315

The New Science Literacy: Using Language Skills to Help Students Learn Science. p.366

New Science, New World. p.378

A New Season: Using Title IX to Reform College Sports. p.822 p.837 p.894 p.901

New Social Movements: From Ideology to Identity. . . . p.710

The New Society: The Anatomy of Industrial Order. p.112, p.149

New Soviet Thinking and U. S. Nuclear Policy. p.655

A New Species of Trouble: Exploration in Community, Disaster and Trauma. p.760

A New Teacher's Guide: Surviving Your First Year. . . . p.279

New Thinking in Economics. p.197

The New Transnational Activism. p.625

New Trends in Macroeconomics. p.199, p.240

The New Unionism: Employee Involvement in the Changing Corporation. p.122

The New Update on Adult Learning Theory: New Directions for Adult and Continuing Education. p.321

New Vision for Management Education: Leadership Challenges. p.176

New World Disorder: The Leninist Extinction. p.491

The New World Disorder. p.629

New World, New Rules: The Changing Role of the American Corporation. p.271

New Worlds: The Great Voyages of Discovery, 1400-1600. . . . . p.377

New Zealand: Aotearoa — Land of the Long White Cloud. p.385

The New Zealand Liberals: The Years of Power, 1891-1912. . . . . p.624

The Newark Teacher Strikes: Hopes on the Line. p.282

The News at Any Cost: How Journalists Compromise Their Ethics to Shape the News. p.405

News, Crime and Culture. p.407

News from Nowhere. p.499

News, Gender and Power. p.414

News in a New Century: Reporting in an Age of Converging Media. p.414

News of the World: World Cultures Look at Television News. p.414

News Ombudsmen in North America: Assessing an Experiment in Social Responsibility. p.411

News Reporting and Writing. p.414

☐ Newspaper Association of America. p.410

Newspapers and the Making of Modern America: A History. p.411

News. p.412

Newton on the Tee: A Good Walk Through the Science of Golf. *p.861, p.871*
The Next America: The Decline and Rise of the United States. *p.703*
The Next Attack: The Failure of the War on Terror and a Strategy for Getting It Right. *p.562*
Next-Day Job Interview: Prepare Tonight and Get the Job Tomorrow. *p.169*
NHERI: National Home Education Resource Institute. . *p.296*
Nice Girls Don't Get the Corner Office: 101 Unconscious Mistakes Women Make That Sabotage Their Careers. . *p.167*
Nicholas Kaldor and the Real World. *p.271*
Nietzsche and the Politics of Aristocratic Radicalism. . . *p.491*
Nightly Business Report Presents Lasting Leadership: What You Can Learn from the Top 25 Business People of our Times. *p.71*
Nike Is a Goddess: The History of Women in Sports. *p.809, p.838*
Nine Lives?: The Politics of Constitutional Reform in Japan.. . . . . *p.621*
Nineteen Weeks: America, Britain, and the Fateful Summer of 1940. . . . . *p.647*
Ninth Justice: The Fight for Bork. *p.538*
NIRA's World Directory of Think Tanks. *p.560*
Nisa: The Life and Words of a Kung Woman. *p.38*
Nixon and the Environment. *p.566*
No Band of Brothers: Problems of the Rebel High Command. *p.522*
No Common Power: Understanding International Relations. *p.625*
No End to War: Terrorism in the 21st Century. *p.660*
No Excuses!: The True Story of a Congenital Amputee Who Became a Champion in Wrestling and in Life. . *p.842, p.870*
No Holds Barred: Negativity in United States Senate Campaigns. *p.530*
No More Kin: Exploring Race, Class, and Gender in Family Networks. *p.734*
No Neutral Ground: Standing by the Values We Prize in Higher Education.. *p.291*
No One Home: Brazilian Selves Remade in Japan. *p.39*
No Other Way Out: States and Revolutionary Movements, 1945-1991. . . . . *p.497*
No Peace, No War: An Anthropology of Contemporary Armed Conflicts.. . . . . *p.34*
No Shame in My Game: The Working Poor in the Inner City. *p.771*
Nobility and Civility: Asian Ideals of Leadership and the Common Good. *p.616*
Nolo's Encyclopedia of Everyday Law: Answers to Your Most Frequently Asked Legal Questions. *p.441*
Nolo's Simple Will Book. *p.443*
Nomads and the Outside World. *p.708*
Nomination and Election of the President and Vice President of the United States, Including the Manner of Selecting Delegates to National Political Conventions. . *p.460*
Nonlinear Econometric Modeling in Time Series: Proceedings of the Eleventh International Symposium in Economic Theory.. . . . . *p.198, p.206*
Nonlinear Time Series Analysis of Economic and Financial Data. *p.204*
Non-Places: Introduction to an Anthropology of Supermodernity. *p.22*
Nonprofits Job Finder: Where the Jobs Are in Charities and Nonprofits. *p.170*
Nonsexist Research Methods: A Practical Guide. *p.687*
Non-State Actors in World Politics. *p.640*
Nonunion Employee Representation: History, Contemporary Practice and Policy. *p.122*
Nonverbal Communication Across Disciplines: Culture, Sensory Interaction, Speech, Conversation, Vol. 1. . . . . . . *p.424*
Nonverbal Communication in Human Interaction. *p.424*
Nonviolence in America: A Documentary History. *p.766*
Nonviolent Action: A Research Guide. *p.650*
Non-Violent Resistance. *p.766*
Non-Western Educational Traditions: Indigenous Approaches to Educational Thought and Practice.. . . . . *p.313*
Normal: Transexual CEOs, Crossdressing Cops and Hermaphrodites with Attitude. *p.746*
The Normative Structure of Sociology : Conservative and Emancipatory Themes in Social Thought. *p.680*
North American Forest and Conservation History: A Bibliography. *p.164*
North American Society for Psychology of Sport and Physical Activity. *p.794, p.876*
North Carolina Planters and Their Children, 1800-1860. . *p.732*
Northern Governments in Transition: Political and Constitutional Development in the Yukon, Nunavut and the Western Northwest Territories. *p.589*
Northern Naval Superiority and the Economics of the American Civil War. *p.522*
Northern Sandlots: A Social History of Maritime Baseball. *p.806, p.816, p.850*
Norway: Elites on Trial. *p.594*
Not All Black and White: Affirmative Action and American Values. *p.456*
Not by Genes Alone: How Culture Transformed Human Evolution. *p.15*
Not God: A History of Alcoholics Anonymous. *p.776*
Not Guilty. *p.438*
Not Your Father's Union Movement: Inside the AFL-CIO. . *p.127*
Notes from the Balkans: Locating Marginality and Ambiguity on the Greek-Albanian Border. *p.42*
Nothing But Freedom: Emancipation and Its Legacy. . . *p.727*
NSCA's Essentials of Personal Training. *p.791, p.903*
NSTA Guide to School Science Facilities.. . . . . *p.288*
Nuclear Deterrence, Morality and Realism. *p.656*
Nuclear Power and Social Power. *p.773*
The Nuclear Tipping Point: Why States Reconsider Their Nuclear Choices.. . . . . *p.655*
The Nuer: A Description of the Modes of Livelihood and Political Institutions of a Nilotic People. *p.38*
The NUM and British Politics, Vol. 2. . . . . *p.129*
The NUM and British Politics. *p.129*

The Number: How the Drive for Quarterly Earnings Corrupted Wall Street and Corporate America. p.53 p.93 p.101, p.104
Numbers Guide: The Essentials of Business Numeracy. . p.175
Numerical Issues in Statistical Computing for the Social Scientist. p.689
Numerical Methods in Economics. p.202
Nurturing Doubt: From Mennonite Missionary to Anthropologist in the Argentine Chaco. p.37
Nutrition for Health, Fitness and Sport. p.791, p.876
Nutrition in Sport. p.825, p.876
Nutritional Anthropology: Biocultural Perspectives on Food and Nutrition.. . . . . p.45
NYSE, New York Stock Exchange. p.90, p.93

O

O God of Players: The Story of the Immaculata Mighty Macs. p.835, p.853
Obedience to Authority: An Experimental View. p.695
Objects and Others: Essays on Museums and Material Culture. p.48
Obscenity and Public Morality: Censorship in a Liberal Society. p.472
Observations upon Liberal Education. p.346
Observers Observed: Essays on Ethnographic Fieldwork. . . p.5
The Obstacle Race: Aborigines in Sport. p.830
The Occasional Papers on Population and Political Economy from Contemporary Journals. p.222
Occupational Ghettos: The Worldwide Segregation of Women and Men. p.723
Occupational Outlook Handbook.. . . . . p.168, p.304
Ocean Biogeochemical Dynamics. p.393
The Ocean Carbon Cycle and Climate: Proceedings of the NATO Asi on Ocean Carbon Cycle and Climate, Ankara, Turkey, from 5 to 16 August 2002. . . . . . p.392
Ocean Remote Sensing and Imaging, II. p.388
Oceania: The Native Cultures of Australia and the Pacific Islands. p.43
Oceans and Law of the Sea. p.478
The Oceans: Physical-Chemical Dynamics and Human Impact. p.392
Odious Commerce: Britain, Spain and the Abolition of the Cuban Slave Trade. p.728
Of Cigarettes, High Heels and Other Interesting Things: An Introduction to Semiotics. p.424
Of Human Potential. p.329
Of Law and Life and Other Things That Matter: Papers and Addresses of Felix Frankfurter, 1956-1963. . . . . . p.437
Of Paradise and Power: America and Europe in the New World Order. p.637, p.641
Of Power and Right: Hugo Black, William O. Douglas and America's Constitutional Revolution. p.467
Of the Conduct of the Understanding. p.216
Of Time and Judicial Behavior: United States Supreme Court Agenda-Setting and Decision-Making, 1888-1997. . . p.537
Of Time and Power: Leadership Duration in the Modern World. p.511
Of Woman Born: Motherhood as Experience and Institution. p.737
Off Center: The Republican Revolution and the Erosion of American Democracy. p.553
Off the Map: Tales of Endurance and Exploration. p.378
Offical Documents of the United Nations. p.482
Office of the United Nations High Commissioner for Human Rights Documents. p.670
Office of Travel and Tourism Industries Portal. p.161
Official Documents of the United Nations. p.476
Official Guide for GMAT Review. p.176
Official Papers of Alfred Marshall: A Supplement. p.224
Official Papers. p.224
Official Website of the Olympic Movement. p.845
Officiating Soccer. p.867, p.905
Officiating Softball. p.795, p.839, p.868
Officiating Track and Field and Cross Country. . . p.869, p.905
OFFSTATS: Official Statistics on the Web. p.179
Oil & Gas Journal. p.160
Oil Titans: National Oil Companies in the Middle East. . p.398
Old Age in the New Land: The American Experience since 1790. . . . . p.741
The Old College Try: Balancing Academics and Athletics in Higher Education. p.822, p.895
Old Labour to New: The Dreams That Inspired, the Battles That Divided. p.606
Old People, New Lives: Community Creation in a Retirement Residence. p.742
Old Textbooks: Spelling, Grammar, Reading, Arithmetic, Geography, American History, Civil Government, Physiology, Penmanship, Art, Music, As Taught in the Common Schools from Colonial Days To 1900. I. . . p.285
The Oldest Old. p.742
Oliver Wendell Holmes. p.540
Olmecs. p.9
The Olympic Book of Sports Medicine, Vol. 1. . . . . . p.825
The Olympic Century.. . . . . p.846
Olympic Marathon: A Centennial History of the Games' Most Storied Race. p.846, p.863
Olympic Turnaround: How the Olympic Games Stepped Back from the Brink of Extinction to Become the World's Best Known Brand. p.142
The Olympics: A History of the Modern Games. p.846
The Olympics at the Millennium: Power, Politics, and the Games.. p.846, p.892
On Adam Smith's Wealth of Nations: A Philosophical Companion. p.219
On Becoming a Leader: The Leadership Classic. p.70
On Being a Teacher. p.327
On Being Human. p.760
On Boxing. p.812, p.856
On Classical Economics. p.218
On Competition. p.51, p.57, p.61

On Creativity, Innovation, and Renewal: A Leader to Leader Guide. p.66
On Death and Dying. p.742
On Durkheim's Rules of Sociological Method. p.681
On Economic Theory and Socialism: Collected Papers. . p.208
On Golf: The Game, the Players, and a Personal History of Obsession. p.861
On Interpreting Keynes: A Study in Reconciliation. . . . p.228
On Keynesian Economics and the Economics of Keynes: A Study in Monetary Theory. p.225
On Keynes's Method. p.226
On Leadership. p.697
On Learning to Read: The Child's Fascination with Meaning. p.362
On Liberty and Other Essays. p.515
On Liberty. p.223, p.515
On Lynchings. p.752
On Measuring and Planning the Quality of Life. p.265
On Money, Method and Keynes: Selected Essays by Victoria Chick. p.226
On Morality and Society: Selected Writings. p.684
On Nationality. p.494
On Organizational Learning. p.78
On Revolution. p.497
On Social Facts. p.713
On Strike at Hormel: The Struggle for a Democratic Labor Movement. p.126
On Teaching. p.348
On the Art of Writing Copy: The Best of Print, Broadcast, Internet, Direct Mail. p.173
On the Border: Society and Culture Between the United States and Mexico. p.765
On the down Low: A Journey into the Lives of "Straight" Black Men Who Sleep with Men. p.750
On the Edge of Anarchy: Locke, Consent, and the Limits of Society. p.773
[e] On the Edge: Ukrainian-Central European-Russian Security Triangle. p.597
On the Edge: Women Making Hockey History. . . p.835, p.862
On the Front Lines: Following America's Foreign Correspondents Across the Twentieth Century. p.406
On the Future of Our Educational Institutions. p.344
On the History of Economic Thought: British and American Economic Essays, Vol. 1. . . . . p.211
On the Nature of Organizations. p.718
On the Origins of Classical Economics: Distribution and Value from William Petty to Adam Smith. p.218
On the Philosophy of Higher Education. p.289
On the Practice of Sociology. p.683
On the Road of the Winds: An Archaeological History of the Pacific Islands before European Contact. p.13
On the Silence of the Declaration of Independence. . . . p.518
On the Social Contract. p.492
On the Sociology of Islam. p.721
On the Theory of Economic Policy. p.245
On Toleration. p.513
On Trying to Teach: The Mind in Correspondence. . . . p.347
On Violence. p.497
On What Is Learned in School. p.300
The Once and Future School: Three Hundred and Fifty Years of American Secondary Education. p.327
One Case at a Time: Judicial Minimalism on the Supreme Court. p.540
One Christmas in Washington: The Secret Meeting Between Roosevelt and Churchill That Changed the World. . . p.628
One Discipline, Four Ways: British, German, French, and American Anthropology. p.4
One for All: The Logic of Group Conflict. p.766
One Hundred Years of Socialism: The West European Left in the Twentieth Century. p.507
One L: The Turbulent True Story of a First Year at Harvard Law School. p.441
One Nation, after All: What Middle-Class Americans Really Think about God, Country, Family, Racism, Welfare, Immigration, Homosexuality, Work, the Right, the Left and Each Other. p.697
[e] The One to One Manager: Real-World Lessons in Customer Relationship Management. p.143
One World, Ready or Not: The Manic Logic of Global Capitalism. p.664
One-Dimensional Man: Studies in the Ideology of Advanced Industrial Society. p.700, p.761
The One-State Solution: A Breakthrough for Peace in the Israeli-Palestinian Deadlock. p.650
Online Consumer Psychology. p.139, p.140
Online Social Research: Methods, Issues and Ethics. . . . p.691
Only Connect: Cultural Hist of Broadcasting in U. S. W/Infotrac. p.412
The Only Investment Guide You'll Ever Need. p.98
Only the Paranoid Survive: How to Exploit the Crisis Points that Challenge Every Company. p.81
Only Words. p.459
Open and Distance Learning in Developing World. . . . p.314
An Open Economy Macroeconomics Reader. p.239
An Open Elite?: England 1540-1880. . . . . p.726
The Open Society and Its Enemies. p.488
The Open Society Paradox: Why the Twenty-First Century Calls for More Openness-Not Less. p.773
[□] Open to all: Ttile IX at Thirty. p.821, p.882
Opening Cybernetic Frontier: Cities of the Prairie. p.543
Opening NATO's Door: How the Alliance Remade Itself for a New Era. p.639
Open-Mindedness and Education. p.339
[□] OpenSecrets.org. p.557
[□] opensecrets.org. p.559
Operations Management: A Supply Chain Approach. . . . p.118
Operative Rights. p.513
Opinion Polls: History, Theory and Practice. p.435
Opportunities in Sports and Fitness Careers. p.903
Opposing Hate Speech. p.422
The Optimal International Division of Labour: A WEP Study. p.254

Optimum Social Welfare and Productivity: A Comparative View. p.266
Oral Arguments and Decision Making on the United States Supreme Court. p.537
Oral History of the Principalship. p.281
Oral Storytelling and Teaching Mathematics: Pedagogical and Multicultural Perspectives. p.365
The Ordeal of Integration: Progress and Resentment in America's "Racial" Crisis. p.729
Order and Justice in International Relations. p.626
Order and Might. p.499
Order and Rebellion in Tribal Africa. p.34, p.38
Ordinary People in Extraordinary Times: The Citizenry and the Breakdown of Democracy. p.503
The Organisation of Thought, Educational and Scientific. . p.340
The Organization of Academic Work. p.292
Organization of African Unity: An Annotated Bibliography. p.630
The Organization of American States, Vol. 11. . . . . . . p.631
The Organization of the Future. p.73
The Organization of the Social System and the Compositon of the Social Forces, Set. p.249
Organizational Analysis: A Sociological View. p.717
Organizational Culture and Leadership. p.75
Organizational Improvement and Accountability. . . . p.281
Organizational Learning from Performance Feedback: A Behavioral Perspective on Innovation and Change. . . . p.78
Organizational Learning, Performance and Change: An Introduction to Strategic Human Resource Development. p.76
Organizational Learning. p.78
Organizational Literacy for Educators. p.280
Organizational Survival in the New World: The Intelligent Complex Adaptive System. p.78
Organized Activities As Contexts of Development: Extracurricular Activities, After-School and Community Programs. p.288
Organized Labor in Postcommunist States: From Solidarity to Infirmity. p.127
Organizing Business Knowledge: The MIT Process Handbook. p.77
Organizing Crime: Essays in Opposition. p.751
Organizing for Peace: Neutrality, the Test Ban, and the Freeze. p.559
Organizing Genius.. . . . . p.65
Organizing to Win: New Research on Union Strategies. . p.124
The Origin and Evolution of New Businesses. p.67
The Origin and Prevention of Major Wars. p.647
Origin of Brands: How Product Evolution Creates Endless Possibilities for New Brands. p.142
Origin of the Family, Private Property, and the State. . . . p.34
The Origin of the Family, Private Property, and the State. . p.737
Original Intent and the Struggle for the Supreme Court: The Politics of Judicial Appointments. p.541
Original Meanings: Politics and Ideas in the Making of the Constitution. p.452
Original Sin: Clarence Thomas and the Failure of the Constitutional Conservatives. p.538
The Origins and Development of Federal Crime Control Policy: Herbert Hoover's Initiatives. p.523
The Origins and Development of Professional Football, 1890-1920. . . . . p.807, p.859
Origins of a Civilization: The Prehistory and Early Archaeology of South Asia. p.8
The Origins of a Pacific Coast Chiefdom: The Chumash of the Channel Islands. p.10
The Origins of American Constitutionalism. p.452
Origins of Cyberspace: A Library on the History of Computing and Computer-Related Telecommunications. p.420
The Origins of International Economics, Vol. 1. . . . . . p.255
Origins of Language: What Nonhuman Primates Can Tell Us. p.19
The Origins of Nazi Genocide: From Euthanasia to the Final Solution. p.652
Origins of Terrorism: Psychologies, Ideologies, Theologies, States of Mind. p.661
The Origins of the American High School. p.328
Origins of the Bill of Rights. p.456
The Origins of the Chosfon Dynasty. p.621
Origins of the Fifth Amendment: The Right Against Self-Incrimination. p.473
The Origins of the Keynesian Revolution. p.227
The Origins of the Urban Crisis: Race and Inequality in Postwar Detroit. p.771
The Origins of Totalitarianism. p.509
Origins of Value: A Document History of Finance. . p.89, p.146
Osama: The Making of a Terrorist. p.661
OSI Reference Model for Telecommunications. p.115
OSU Virtual Finance Library. p.90, p.93
The Other Bostonians: Poverty and Progress in the American Metropolis, 1880-1970. . . . . p.707
The Other Elites: Women, Politics, and Power in the Executive Branch. p.526
The Other Founders: Anti-Federalism and the Dissenting Tradition in America, 1788-1828. . . . . p.523
Other People's Children: Cultural Conflict in the Classroom. p.309
The Other Side of the '60s: Young Americans for Freedom and the Rise of Conservative Politics. p.516
The Other Side of the Asian American Success Story. . . p.311
Ottoman Civil Officialdom: A Social History. p.614
The Ottoman Empire and the World Around It. p.641
Our Common Lands: Defending the National Parks. . . . p.463
Our Earth's Changing Land: An Encyclopedia of Land-Use and Land-Cover Change. p.267
Our Final Hour: A Scientist's Warning: How Terror, Error, and Environmental Disaster Threaten Humankind's Future in This Century - On Earth and Beyond. . . . p.661, p.667
Our Government: The Supreme Court and the Judicial Branch. p.534
Our Kind: Who We Are, Where We Came from, Where We Are Going. p.22

Our Labeled Children: What Every Parent and Teacher Needs to Know about Learning Disabilities. *p.319*

Our Lives for Ourselves: Women Who Have Never Married. *p.738*

Our Nation's Government: Judicial Branch. *p.535*

Our Only Star and Compass: Locke and the Struggle for Political Rationality. *p.492, p.502*

Our Schools and Our Future: Are We Still at Risk? . . . *p.328*

Our Sister Editors: Sarah J. Hale and the Tradition of Nineteenth-Century American Women Editors. *p.409*

Our Studies, Ourselves: Sociologists' Lives and Work. . . *p.675*

Our Unfree Press: 100 Years of Radical Media Criticism. . *p.558*

Out in the Field: Reflections of Lesbian and Gay Anthropologists. *p.25*

Out in Theory: The Emergence of Lesbian and Gay Anthropology. *p.24*

Out of Bounds: Inside the NBA's Culture of Rape, Violence, and Crime. *p.813, p.853*

Out of Bounds: Sports, Media and the Politics of Identity. *p.813, p.901*

Out of Gas: The End of the Age of Oil. *p.160*

Out of It: A Cultural History of Intoxication. *p.777*

Out of Many, One: A History of the American College of Sports Medicine. *p.803, p.824*

Out of Our Minds: Anti-Intellectualism and Talent Development in American Schooling. *p.317*

Out of the Jungle: Jimmy Hoffa and the Remaking of the American Working Class. *p.129*

Out of the Margin: Feminist Perspectives on Economics. *p.274*

Outdoor Action Games for Elementary Children: Active Games and Academic Activities for Fun and Fitness. . *p.787, p.795*

Outdoor Guide to Using Your GPS. *p.390*

Outdoor Leadership: Theory and Practice. *p.787*

Outdoor Recreation in America. *p.787, p.823*

Outdoor Recreation Policy: Pleasure and Preservation, Vol. 263. . . . . *p.787*

Outdoor Recreation Safety. *p.786, p.788*

Outdoor Recreation: United States National Parks, Forests, and Public Lands. *p.788*

Outline of a Theory of Practice. *p.23*

An Outline of International Price Theories. *p.251*

Outside In: Minorities and the Transformation of American Education. *p.326*

Outside the Lines: African-Americans and the Integration of the National Football League. *p.833, p.852*

Outsiders in the Clubhouse: The World of Women's Professional Golf. *p.815, p.835, p.860*

Outsiders. *p.695, p.776*

Outsource: Competing in the Global Productivity Race. . . *p.70*

Outstanding Women Athletes: Who They Are and How They Influenced Sports in America. *p.838*

The Outward Bound Canoeing Handbook. *p.788, p.789*

Outward Bound Wilderness Survival Handbook. *p.788*

Overcoming the Five Dysfunctions of a Team: A Field Guide for Leaders, Managers, and Facilitators. *p.80*

Oversold and Underused: Computers in Classrooms, 1980-2000. . . . . *p.351*

Overtraining in Sport. *p.827, p.828, p.875, p.879*

The Oxford Companion to Aboriginal Art and Culture. . . *p.26*

The Oxford Companion to Australian Sport. *p.824*

The Oxford Companion to Indian Archaeology: The Archaeological Foundations of Ancient India. *p.8*

Oxford Companion to Law. *p.433*

The Oxford Companion to the Supreme Court of the United States. *p.466, p.537*

Oxford Dictionary of Accounting. *p.104*

Oxford Dictionary of Political Quotations. *p.482*

The Oxford Dictionary of Sports Science and Medicine. *p.825, p.873*

The Oxford Encyclopedia of Economic History, Set. . . . *p.192*

The Oxford Encyclopedia of Mesoamerican Cultures: The Civilizations of Mexico and Central America. *p.9*

The Oxford Guide to United States Supreme Court Decisions. *p.454*

Oxford Handbook of Deaf Studies, Language, and Education. *p.318*

The Oxford Handbook of Innovation. *p.66*

Oxford Handbook of Political Psychology. *p.484*

The Oxford History of the British Empire: The Eighteenth Century. *p.605*

The Oxford History of the British Empire: The Nineteenth Century. *p.605*

The Oxford History of the British Empire: The Origins of Empire: British Overseas Enterprise to the Close of the Seventeenth Century. *p.605*

The Oxford History of the British Empire: The Twentieth Century. *p.605*

The Oxford Illustrated History of Prehistoric Europe. . . . *p.12*

Oxford World Atlas. *p.380*

P

Pacem in Maribus. *p.478*

Pacific Asia. *p.618, p.622*

Pacifism in the Twentieth Century: A Survey from Antiquity to the Outset of the Twentieth Century. *p.648*

Paideia Proposal. *p.324*

Painful Transition: Bourgeois Democracy in India. *p.618*

PAIS International & PAIS Archive. *p.481*

Pakistan: Between Mosque and Military. *p.617*

The Palaeolithic Societies of Europe. *p.16*

Paleoethnobotany: A Handbook of Procedures. *p.7*

The Palestinian regime: a partial democracy. *p.614*

Palestinian Religious Terrorism: Hamas and Islamic Jihad. . *p.614*

Palgrave Handbook of Econometrics: Econometric Theory. *p.203*

The Palladium of Justice: Origins of Trial by Jury. *p.435*

Pamphlets of Protest: An Anthology of Early African-American Protest Literature, 1790-1860. . . . . *p.572*

The Pamphlets of Thomas Robert Malthus, 1800-1817. . *p.222*

Panel Data Econometrics. *p.198*

3333333A Panorama of the World's Legal Systems, Set. . *p.435*

Papa Jack: Jack Johnson and the Era of White Hopes. *p.819, p.856*

Papers and Correspondence of William Stanley Jevons: Vol.1, Biography and Personal Journal. *p.212*

The Papers and the Papers: An Account of the Legal and Political Battle Over the Pentagon Papers. *p.438*

Papers in Experimental Economics.. . . . . *p.272*

Papers of Robert Redfield, Vol. 1. . . . . *p.24*

Papers on Public Credit, Commerce and Finance. *p.213*

Papers Relating to Political Economy. *p.223*

The Paradox of American Unionism: Why Americans Like Unions More Than Canadians Do, but Join Much Less. . *p.122*

The Paradox of Excellence: How Great Performance Can Kill Your Business. *p.73*

The Paradox of Loyalty: An African American Response to the War on Terrorism. *p.564*

Paradoxes of Gender. *p.746*

Paradoxes of Power: Reflections on the Thatcher Interlude. *p.607*

Paradoxes of Youth and Sport. *p.815, p.840*

Parallel Paths to Constructivism: Jean Piaget and Lev Vygotsky. *p.345*

[e] Parenthood in America: An Encyclopedia. *p.676*

Parenting in an Unresponsive Society: Managing Work and Family Life. *p.732*

Pareto's Italian Letters. *p.249*

Paris 1919: Six Months That Changed the World. *p.630*

Paris after the Liberation, 1944-1949.. . . . . *p.581*

Paris and London in Eighteenth Century. *p.706*

Parks Directory of the United States: A Guide to 4,000 National and State Parks, Recreational Areas, Historic Sites, Battlefields, Monuments, Forests, Preserves, Memorials, Seashores, and Other Designated Recreation Areas in the United States Administered by National and State Park Agencies.. . . . . *p.783, p.788*

Parliament under Blair. *p.606*

Parliamentary Politics in Revolutionary Iran: The Institutionalization of Factional Politics. *p.616*

Parliamentary Power in Russia, 1994-2001: A New Era. . *p.599*

Parliaments in the Czech and Slovak Republics: Party Competition and Parliamentary Institutionalization. *p.575, p.596*

Participant Observation: A Methodology for Human Studies. *p.690*

Participating in Development: Approaches to Indigenous Knowledge. *p.45*

Participation and Political Equality: A Seven-Nation Comparison. *p.578, p.580*

Participation in America: Political Democracy and Social Equality. *p.506, p.555, p.580*

Participation in American Politics: The Dynamics of Agenda Building. *p.554*

Parties and Democracy in the Post-Soviet Republics: The Case of Estonia. *p.578, p.584, p.597*

Parties and Elections in Greece: The Search for Legitimacy. *p.597*

Parties and Parliaments: Political Change in Norway. . . *p.594*

Parties and Party Systems: A Framework for Analysis, Vol. 2.. . . . . *p.579*

Parties and Politics in Post 1989 Poland. *p.579, p.597*

Parties and the Party System in France: A Disconnected Democracy? *p.609*

Parties and Voters in France. *p.609*

Parties, Policies, and Democracy. *p.579*

The Parties Respond: Changes in American Parties and Campaigns. *p.551*

Partisan Politics, Divided Government, and the Economy. . *p.247*

Partnering: The New Face of Leadership. *p.72*

Partners and Rivals: Representation in U. S. Senate Delegations. *p.534*

Partners in Command: The Relationships Between Leaders in the Civil War. *p.520*

Partners in Prosperity: The Changing Geography of the Transatlantic Economy. *p.60*

Party Ideology in Britian. *p.607*

Party Politics in Canada. *p.589*

Party Systems and Voter Alignments Revisited. . . *p.554, p.579*

Party vs. State in Post-1949 China: The Institutional Dilemma. *p.621*

Passing the Buck: Congress, the Budget, and Deficits. . . *p.531*

Passion and Craft: Economists at Work. *p.186*

Passion and Paradox: Intellectuals Confront the National Question. *p.494*

[e] Passion Branding: Harnessing the Power of Emotion to Build Strong Brands.. . . . . *p.141*

A Passion for Democracy: American Essays. . . . *p.502, p.554*

A Passion for Planning: Financials, Operations, Marketing, Management and Ethics. *p.143*

Passion of the People: Football in Latin America. *p.817, p.844, p.867*

The Passionate Economist: Finding the Power and Humanity Behind the Numbers.. . . . . *p.271*

Past Imperfect, Future Uncertain: The United Nations at Fifty. *p.635*

Past, Present, and Personal: The Family and the Life Course in American History. *p.731*

Past Time, Past Place: GIS for History. *p.387*

Pastoralists: Equality, Hierarchy, and the State. *p.30*

Patchwork Nation: Sectionalism and Political Change in American Politics. *p.551*

Patent, Copyright and Trademark: An Intellectual Property Desk Reference. *p.109, p.110, p.180*

The Path of a Genocide: The Rwanda Crisis from Uganda to Zaire. *p.651*

The Path to Christian Democracy: German Catholics and the Party System from Windthorst to Adenauer. *p.609*

The Path to Dropping Out: Evidence for Intervention. . . *p.299*

The Path to Geneva: The Quest for a Permanent Agreement, 1996-2003. . . . . *p.629*

[□] Path to Investing. *p.93, p.99*

Pathologies of Power: Health, Human Rights, and the New War on the Poor.. . . . . *p.27, p.46*

Paths in Utopia. *p.499*

Paths to a Green World: The Political Economy of the Global Environment. *p.666*
Pathways of Power: Building an Anthropology of the Modern World. *p.35*
Pathways to Democracy: The Political Economy of Democratic Transitions. *p.504*
Patriarchy and Socialist Revolution in China. *p.734*
Patriotic Games: Sporting Traditions in the American Imagination, 1876-1926. . . . . *p.809*
Patronage and Politics in the U. S. S. R. *p.599*
Patterns of Culture. *p.22*
Patterns of Democracy: Government Forms and Performance in Thirty-Six Countries. *p.504*
Patterns of Growth and Development in the Genus Homo. . *p.15*
The Patterns of War since the Eighteenth Century. . *p.627, p.646*
Paul A. Samuelson: Critical Assessments, Set. *p.197*
Paul A. Samuelson. *p.197*
Paul Kagame and Rwanda: Power, Genocide and the Rwandan Patriotic Front. *p.654*
Paul Samuelson and Modern Economic Theory. *p.213*
Paul Samuelson and the Foundations of Modern Economics. *p.197*
Paul Samuelson: On Being an Economist. *p.186*
Pay Dirt: The Business of Professional Team Sports. *p.889, p.897*
Pay up and Play the Game: Professional Sport in Britain, 1875-1914. . . . . *p.810, p.898, p.899*
Paying with Plastic: The Digital Revolution in Buying and Borrowing. *p.95, p.155, p.245, p.263*
PC Hardware in a Nutshell. *p.114*
PCAOB: The Public Company Accounting Oversight Board. *p.103, p.104*
The PDMA Handbook of New Product Development. . . *p.144*
Peace and the Peacemakers: The Treaty of 1783. . . . . *p.630*
Peace Enforcement: The United Nations Experience in Congo, Somalia and Bosnia. *p.648*
The Peace Negotiations. *p.631*
Peace Operations and Global Order. *p.648*
Peace or War: The American Struggle, 1636-1936. . *p.647, p.648*
The Peace Reform in American History. *p.649*
Peace Soldiers: The Sociology of a United Nations Military Force. *p.634, p.650*
Peacekeeping and the United Nations. *p.649*
Peacekeeping in Transition: The United Nations in Cambodia. *p.649*
Pearson and Canada's Role in Nuclear Disarmament and Arms Control Negotiations, 1945-1957. . . . . *p.644, p.656*
Peasant Protest and Social Change in Colonial Korea. . . *p.711*
Peasant Wars of the Twentieth Century. *p.35*
Peasants in Socialist Transition: Life in a Collectivized Hungarian Village. *p.701*
Peasants, Rebels, Women, and Outcastes: The Underside of Modern Japan. *p.703*
Peasants. *p.29*
Pedagogy of Hope: Reliving Pedagogy of the Oppressed. . *p.342*
Pedagogy of Place: Seeing Space As Cultural Education. . *p.300*
Pedagogy of Praxis: A Dialectical Philosophy of Education. *p.342*
Pedagogy of the Oppressed. *p.342, p.761*
Pedometer Power: 67 Lessons for K-12. . . . . . *p.798, p.799*
Peer Assisted Learning: A Practical Guide for Teachers. . *p.350*
Peer-Assisted Learning. *p.350*
Penguin Atlas of Food: Who Eats What Where and Why. *p.152, p.165*
Penguin Companion to European Union. *p.636*
The Penguin Dictionary of Geography. *p.373*
The Penguin Dictionary of International Relations. *p.626*
The Penguin Historical Atlas of Ancient Civilizations. . . *p.380*
The Penguin Historical Atlas of the Medieval World. . . *p.380*
The Penguin State of the World Atlas. *p.381*
Pensacola During the Civil War: A Thorn in the Side of the Confederacy. *p.521*
People and Environment in Africa. *p.384*
People and Nature: An Introduction to Human Ecological Relations. *p.30*
The People and the Court: Judicial Review in a Democracy. *p.454*
People Managing Forests: The Links between Human Well-Being and Sustainability. *p.164*
People of Prowess: Sport, Leisure, and Labor in Early Anglo-America. *p.810, p.819*
People of Sunlight and Starlight: Barrenland Archaeology in the Northwest Territories. *p.11*
The People of the Plain: Class and Community in Lower Andalusia. *p.703*
The People of the Sea: Environment, Identity, and History in Oceania. *p.384*
The People of the Sierra. *p.42*
People, Plants, and Landscapes: Studies in Paleoethnobotany. *p.7*
Peoples and Cultures of Africa. *p.384*
The People's Emperor: Democracy and the Japanese Monarchy, 1945-1995. . . . . *p.622*
Peoples of the Northwest Coast: Their Archaeology and Prehistory. *p.10*
Peoples of the World. *p.399*
The People's Tycoon: Henry Ford and the American Century. *p.154*
The People's Welfare: Law and Regulation in Nineteenth-Century America. *p.440*
People's Witness: The Journalist in Modern Politics. . . . *p.403*
Perfect Answers to Interview Questions: The Must-Have Guide to Getting That Job!. *p.169*
The Perfect Impossibility of General Equilibrium Theory. . *p.205*
Perfectly Legal: The Secret Campaign to Rig Our Tax System to Benefit the Super Rich—and Cheat Everybody Else. . *p.107*
The Performance of Gender: An Anthropology of Everyday Life in a South Indian Fishing Village. *p.30*
The Performance of Healing. *p.46*
Performance-Based Assessment for Middle and High School Physical Education. *p.798, p.799*
Performance-Enhancing Substances in Sport and Exercise. *p.826, p.874*

Performing in Extreme Environments: Training and Working in Intense Heat, Frigid Cold, under Water, High Altitude, Air Pollution. p.874, p.878

The Perilous Frontier: Nomadic Empires and China. . . . p.623

Perilous Times: Free Speech in Wartime from the Sedition Act of 1798 to the War on Terrorism. . . . p.505, p.565, p.567

Periodization Training for Sports. p.792, p.878

Peripheral Migrants: Haitians and Dominican Republic Sugar Plantations. p.41

Permissible Advantage?: The Moral Consequences of Elite Schooling. p.297

Persistent Disparity: Race and Economic Inequality in the U. S. since 1945. . . . . p.265

Person to Person: Communicative Speaking and Listening Skills. p.423

Person to Person: Fieldwork, Dialogue, and the Hermeneutic Method. p.25

A Personal Approach to Teaching: Beliefs That Make a Difference. p.347

Personal History. p.410

The Personal Trainer's Handbook. p.791, p.904

Personality and Interpersonal Behavior. p.692

Personality, Character, and Leadership in the White House: Psychologists Assess the Presidents. p.698

Personalized Instruction: Changing Classroom Practice. . p.349

Personalizing Education: Values Clarification and Beyond. . p.306

Personnel Administration in Higher Education: Handbook of Faculty and Staff Personnel Practices. p.292

Person/Planet: The Creative Disintegration of Industrial Society. p.761

Perspective on the Nature of Geography. p.375

Perspectives on Adults Learning Mathematics: Research and Practice. p.319

Perspectives on Africa: A Reader in Culture, History and Representation. p.38

Perspectives on Climate Change: Science, Economics, Politics, Ethics. p.394

Perspectives on Radio and Television: Telecommunication in the United States. p.412

Perspectives on Safe and Sound Banking: Past, Present, and Future. p.88

Persuasion in Advertising. p.426

Persuasions of the Witch's Craft: Ritual Magic in Contemporary England. p.36

Peru in Crisis: Dictatorship or Democracy? p.593

Peru: The Evolution of a Crisis. p.593

Pestalozzi and Education. p.343

Pesticides and Politics: The Life Cycle of a Public Issue. . p.449

Peterson's Education Portal. p.289

Peterson's Internships. p.170

PGA Tour Complete Book of Golf: Lessons and Advice from the Best Players of the Game. p.860

Phantastica: A Classic Survey on the Use and Abuse of Mind-Altering Plants. p.777

Pharmaceutical Marketing: Principles, Environment, and Practice. p.156

Phenomenology of the Social World. p.686

The Philadelawareans, and Other Essays Relating to Delaware. p.542

Philadelphia Gentlemen: The Making of a National Upper Class. p.725

The Philadelphia Negro: A Social Study. p.729

The Philebus of Plato. p.216

Philippine Social History: Global Trade and Local Transformations. p.705

Phillips Curve and Labor Markets. p.253

Philosopher - Kings: The Argument of Plato's "Republic". . p.489

Philosophers on Education. p.323, p.340

Philosophic Inquiry in Sport. p.803

Philosophical Documents in Education. p.323, p.340

Philosophical Foundations of Adult Education. p.320

Philosophical Thinking in Educational Practice. p.343

The Philosophy and Economics of J. M. Keynes. p.227

Philosophy and Practice of Organizational Learning, Performance and Change. p.78

Philosophy in the Flesh: The Embodied Mind and Its Challenge to Western Thought. p.27

Philosophy of Aikido. p.803, p.863

Philosophy of Education: An Encyclopedia. . . . p.323, p.339

Philosophy of Education: Essays and Commentaries. p.323, p.339

The Philosophy of Education: Major Themes in the Analytic Tradition. p.323, p.339

The Philosophy of Law. p.434

Philosophy of Sport and Exercise Science: Critical Perspectives on Scientific Method and Enquiry in Sport, Exercise and Health. p.802, p.873

The Philosophy of Utopia. p.499

The Philosophy of Wealth: Economic Principles Newly Formulated. p.208, p.223

Phonics in Proper Perspective. p.363

Physical Activity and Obesity. p.790, p.876

Physical Activity, Fitness, and Health Consensus Statement: International Proceedings and Consensus Statement. . p.790

Physical Activity for Health and Fitness. p.791

Physical Activity Instruction of Older Adults. . . . p.795, p.841

Physical Dimensions of Aging. p.875, p.880

The Physical Education Activity Handbook. p.798, p.799, p.800

Physical Education and Kinesiology in North America: Professional and Scholarly Foundations. p.797

Physical Education Methods for Classroom Teachers. p.798, p.799

Physical Education: Teachers' Lives and Careers. . p.795, p.903

Physical Education Tips from the Trenches. p.800

Physical Education Unit Plans for Preschool-Kindergarten, for Grades 1-2, for Grades 3-4, for Grades 5-6. . . . . p.798

Physical Geodesy. p.389

The Physical Geography of Southeast Asia. p.384

The Physical Geography of the Sea and Its Meteorology. . p.394

Physical Geography of Western Europe. p.383

Physical Geology. p.390

Physical Oceanography: Developments Since 1950. . . . p.392

Physical Processes in Lakes and Oceans. *p.392*
The Physician and Sexuality in Victorian America. . . . *p.774*
The Physics and Technology of Tennis. *p.864, p.871*
The Physics of Football: Discover the Science of Bone-Crunching Hits, Soaring Field Goals, and Awe-Inspiring Passes. *p.858, p.871*
The Physics of Golf. *p.861, p.871*
The Physics of Hockey.. . . . . *p.862, p.871*
The Physics of Sailing Explained. *p.866, p.871*
The Physics of Skiing: Skiing at the Triple Point. . *p.867, p.871*
Physiological Assessment of Human Fitness. . . . *p.791, p.875*
Physiology of Sport and Exercise. *p.878*
Pickup Artists: Street Basketball in America. . . . *p.813, p.853*
Pierre Bourdieu: Agent Provocateur. *p.682*
Pigs for the Ancestors: Ritual in the Ecology of a New Guinea People.. . . . . *p.30*
The Pilates Program for Everybody: Simple, Effective Exercises— Amazing Benefits for All Ages. *p.793*
Pilgrimage for Peace: A Secretary General's Memoir. *p.635, p.650*
Pillars of the Republic: Common Schools and American Society, 1780-1860. . . . . *p.327*
The Piltdown Forgery. *p.16*
Pinochet: The Politics of Power. *p.591*
Pioneers of Early Childhood Education: A Bio-Bibliographical Guide. *p.338*
Pioneers of Financial Economics: Contributions Prior to Irving Fisher. *p.204, p.264*
Pioneers of Modern Geography: Translations Pertaining to German Geographers of the Late Nineteenth and Early Twentieth Centuries, 28. . . . . *p.378*
Pioneers of the Hardwood: Indiana and the Birth of Professional Basketball. *p.806, p.854*
Pirates and Emperors, Old and New: International Terrorism in the Real World. *p.658*
Pissing on Demand: Workplace Drug Testing and the Rise of the Detox Industry. *p.131*
Pitied but Not Entitled: Single Mothers and the History of Welfare.. . . . . *p.754*
Place: A Short Introduction. *p.373*
A Place Apart: An Anthropological Study of the Icelandic World. *p.42*
A Place for Strangers: Towards a History of Australian Aboriginal Being. *p.43*
A Place in History: A Guide to Using GIS in Historical Research. *p.387*
The Place of Geography. *p.373*
The Place of Morality in Foreign Policy. *p.646*
The Place of Science in Modern Civilization. *p.251*
A Place on the Corner. *p.692*
A Place to Grow Old: The Meaning of Environment in Old Age. *p.742*
A Place to Stand: Essays for Educators in Troubled Times.. *p.341*
Places and Regions in Global Context: Human Geography. *p.396*
Placing Animals in the Neolithic: Social Zooarchaeology of Prehistoric Farming Communities. *p.12*
The Plain English Approach to Business Writing. *p.171*
The Plane Truth for Golfers: Breaking Down the One-Plane Swing and the Two-Plane Swing and Finding the One That's Right for You. *p.860*
Planet U: Sustaining the World, Reinventing the University. *p.398*
Planetary Politics: Human Rights, Terror, and Global Society. *p.624, p.658, p.669*
Planning and Conducting Needs Assessments: A Practical Guide. *p.82*
Planning and Developing Open and Distance Learning: A Framework for Quality.. . . . . *p.322*
Planning and Managing a PR Campaign: A Step by Step Guide. *p.429*
Planning and Managing School Facilities. *p.288*
Planning Education Reforms in Developing Countries: The Contingency Approach. *p.314*
Planning Focus Groups. *p.137*
Planning for Technology: A Guide for Administrtors, Technology Coordinators and Curriculum Leaders. . . *p.352*
Planning Media. *p.427*
Planning Models for Colleges and Universities. *p.293*
Plant Layout and Materials Handling. *p.116*
Plantation Slavery in Barbados: An Archaeological and Historical Investigation. *p.14, p.728*
Plato and Education. *p.340*
[e] Plato's Invisible Cities: Discourse and Power in the Republic. *p.489*
Plato. *p.489*
Play and Educational Theory and Practice. *p.357*
Play and Literacy in Early Childhood: Research from Multiple Perspectives. *p.369*
Play as Exploratory Learning: Studies of Curiosity Behavior. *p.358*
Play in Practice: Case Studies in Young Children's Play. . *p.356*
Play It Safe: An Anthology of Playground Safety. *p.787*
Play Like a Man, Win Like a Woman: What Men Know about Success That Women Need to Learn. *p.167*
Play Therapy.. . . . . *p.355*
Play-by-Play: Radio, Television and Big-Time College Sports. *p.810, p.895, p.902*
Playground Safety Is No Accident. *p.787, p.796*
Playing by the Rules: Sport, Society, and the State. *p.716, p.820, p.892*
Playing for Dollars: Labor Relations and the Sports Business. *p.886, p.889, p.897*
Playing for Keeps: Michael Jordan and the World He Made. *p.854, p.896*
Playing for Real: Game Theory. *p.83*
Playing for Their Nation: Baseball and the American Military During World War II. *p.804, p.849, p.890*
Playing Hardball: Campaigning for the U. S. Congress. . *p.549*
Playing in the Zone. *p.824*
Playing It Safe: How the Supreme Court Sidesteps Hard Cases and Stunts the Development of Law. *p.537*
Playing Nice and Losing: The Struggle for Control of Women's Intercollegiate Athletics, 1960-2000. . . . . . *p.811, p.839*

Playing Nice: Politics and Apologies in Women's Sports. p.821, p.835
Playing the Field: Why Sports Teams Move and Cities Fight to Keep Them. p.883, p.891, p.896
Playing the Game: Inside Athletic Recruiting in the Ivy League. p.885, p.888, p.894
Playing the Game: Sport and British Society, 1914-1945. . p.804
Playing the Game: Sport and the Physical Emancipation of English Women, 1870-1914. . . . . p.808, p.837
Playing to Win: Sports and the American Military, 1898-1945. p.810
Playing with Anger: Teaching Coping Skills to African American Boys through Athletics and Culture. p.304
Plea Bargaining's Triumph: A History of Plea Bargaining in America. p.473
Please Be Ad-Vised: The Legal Reference Guide for the Advertising Executive. p.427
Pleasure and Danger: Exploring Female Sexuality. p.749
Plessy vs. Ferguson: A Brief History with Documents. . . p.438
Plotting the Globe: Stories of Meridians, Parallels, and the International Date Line. p.389
Plunkett Research Online. p.150
Plunkett's Advertising and Branding Industry Almanac 2006. . . . . p.150
Plunkett's Airline, Hotel and Travel Industry Almanac 2006 (E-Book). p.151
Plunkett's Airline, Hotel and Travel Industry Almanac 2006. . . . . p.152
Plunkett's Airline, Hotel and Travel Industry Trends and Statistics 2006 (Summary). p.152
Plunkett's Apparel and Textiles Industry Almanac 2006. . p.153
Plunkett's Automobile Industry Almanac 2005: The Only Complete Guide to the Automobile, Truck and Specialty Vehicle Industry. p.154
Plunkett's Biotech and Genetics Industry Almanac 2006: The Only Complete Reference to the Business of Biotechnology and Genetic Engineering. p.156
Plunkett's E-Commerce and Internet Industry Almanac 2005: Your Reference Source to All Facets of the Internet Business. p.113
Plunkett's Entertainment and Media Industry Almanac. . . p.157
Plunkett's Food Industry Almanac 2005: The Only Complete Reference to the Business of Creating and Selling Food, Beverages and Tobacco. p.153
Plunkett's Infotech Industry Almanac 2005: The Only Complete Guide to the Technologies and Companies Changing the Way the World Thinks, Works and Shares Information. . p.114
Plunkett's Research Online. p.150
Plunkett's Telecommunications Industry Almanac 2006: Your Reference Source to the Telecom Business. p.115
Plunkett's Transportation, Supply Chain and Logistics Industry Almanac: Your Complete Guide to All Facets of the Business of Transportation, Logistics and Supply Chains. p.118
The Pluralist Theory of the State: Selected Writings of G. D. H. Cole, J. N. Figgis, and H. J. Laski. p.497
The Plutocratic Cycle in the Economic and Historical Growth of Mankind. p.249
Pocketbook Power. p.139
Poetic Knowledge: The Recovery of Education. . . . p.340
Point, Click and Wow!: A Quick Guide to Brilliant Laptop Presentations. p.174
Poisons of the Past: Molds, Epidemics, and History. . . . p.778
The Pol Pot Regime: Race, Power, and Genocide in Cambodia under the Khmer Rouge, 1975-79. . . . . p.652
Poland and the European Union. p.596, p.602
Polar Pioneers: John Ross and James Clark Ross. p.379
Poles Together?: The Emergence and Development of Political Parties in Post-Communist Poland. p.579, p.597
Policies for Prosperity: Essays in a Keynesian Mode. . . p.239
Policing, Race and Racism. p.774
Policy and Politics in West Germany: A Semisovereign State. p.609
Policy Development in Sport Management. p.886
Policy Indicators: Links Between Social Science and Public Debate. p.769
Policy Issues in Modern Cartography. p.375
Policy Making in Israel: Routines for Simple Problems and Coping with the Complex. p.615
A Policy of Discontent: The Making of a National Energy Strategy. p.62
Polish Politics and Society. p.596
A Political and Economic Dictionary of Africa. p.191
A Political and Economic Dictionary of East Asia. p.189
A Political and Economic Dictionary of Eastern Europe. . p.188
A Political and Economic Dictionary of Latin America. . p.591
A Political and Economic Dictionary of South Asia. . . . p.191
A Political and Economic Dictionary of Western Europe. . p.186
The Political and Historical Theory of the Elites. p.249
Political Anthropology: Power and Paradigms. p.34
Political Behavior. p.483
Political Business Cycles: The Political Economy of Money, Inflation, and Unemployment. p.245
Political Campaign Communication: Philosophy and Practice. p.578
Political Change in Britain, 1963-1970. . . . . p.606
Political Change on Taiwan: A Study of Ruling Party Adaptability. p.618
Political Communication Ethics: An Oxymoron?. p.417
Political Construction Sites: Nation Building in Russia and the Post-Soviet States. p.598
Political Corruption in America: An Encyclopedia of Scandals, Power, and Greed. p.516, p.557
Political Corruption. p.580
Political Culture and Post-Communism. p.599
Political Cycles and the Macroeconomy. p.242
Political Database of the Americas. p.591
Political Development and the New Realism in Sub-Saharan Africa. p.610
The Political Dynamics of American Education. p.298
Political Economy for Beginners. p.209, p.269
The Political Economy of Democratic Transitions. . p.487, p.504

The Political Economy of Development: Theoretical and Empirical Contributions. *p.574*
The Political Economy of Education: Implications for Growth and Inequality. *p.297*
The Political Economy of Ethiopia. *p.612*
The Political Economy of Financial Crises. . *p.242, p.246, p.260*
The Political Economy of Global Restructuring: Economic Organization and Production, Vol. 1. . . . . . *p.257, p.264*
The Political Economy of Imperialism: Critical Appraisals. *p.502*
Political Economy of Indian Federalism. *p.618*
The Political Economy of Integration in the European Community. *p.211, p.240, p.255*
The Political Economy of Trade Policy: Papers in Honor of Jagdish Bhagwati. *p.257*
The Political Element in the Development of Economic Theory, Vol. 29. . . . . *p.210*
The Political Element in the Development of Economic Theory. *p.210, p.233*
Political Empiricism: Communication Strategies in State and Regional Elections. *p.550, p.558, p.559*
Political Geography: A Comprehensive Systematic Bibliography. *p.496*
Political Handbook of the World 2005. . . . . *p.574*
Political Islam: Religion and Politics in the Arab World. . *p.500*
The Political Kingdom in Uganda: A Study in Bureaucratic Nationalism. *p.494, p.610*
Political Leadership among Swat Pathans. *p.34*
[e] Political Legitimacy in Middle Africa: Father, Family, Food. *p.613*
Political Liberalism. *p.511, p.514*
Political Liberalization and Democratization in Africa: Lessons from Country Experiences. *p.585, p.611*
Political Marketing: A Comparative Perspective. . *p.545, p.577*
Political Marketing: An Approach to Campaign Strategy. . *p.558*
Political Non-Logical Conduct and Theories Transcending Experience. *p.249*
Political Obligations. *p.498*
Political Order in Changing Societies. *p.482*
Political Participation in Beijing. *p.620*
Political Parties and Elections in the United States: An Encyclopedia, Set. *p.548, p.551*
Political Parties, Growth and Equality: Conservative and Social Democratic Economic Strategies in the World Economy. *p.550, p.578*
Political Parties in the European Union. *p.603*
Political Parties in Turkey. *p.616*
Political Parties Matter: Realignment and the Return of Partisan Voting. *p.552, p.555*
Political Parties of Eastern Europe: A Guide to Politics in the Post-Communist Era. *p.595, p.596, p.597, p.600*
Political Parties of the Americas, 1980s to 1990s: Canada, Latin America, and the West Indies. *p.588*
Political Parties of the Americas: Canada, Latin America, and the West Indies. *p.588*
Political Parties: Their Organization and Activity in the Modern State. *p.579*
Political Parties. *p.588*
The Political Persuaders: The Techniques of Modern Election Campaigns. *p.549*
The Political Philosophies of Plato and Hegel. *p.489*
The Political Philosophy of Hobbes, Its Basis and Its Genesis. *p.502*
The Political Philosophy of James Madison. *p.492*
Political Power and Corporate Control: The New Global Politics of Corporate Governance. *p.86*
Political Power in Pre-Colonial Buganda: Economy, Society and Welfare in the Nineteenth Century. *p.582, p.612*
Political Psychology: Essential Readings. *p.483*
Political Psychology in International Relations. *p.484*
Political Science Research Methods. *p.483*
Political Stability in Federal Governments. *p.524*
Political Support in Canada: The Crisis Years. *p.586*
The Political System of the European Union. . . . *p.603, p.637*
Political Systems of Highland Burma: A Study of Kachin Social Structure. *p.34*
Political Terrorism: A New Guide to Actors, Authors, Concepts, Data Bases, Theories, and Literature. *p.661*
Political Terrorism: Theory, Tactics and Counter-Measures. *p.662*
Political Thought in Europe, 1250-1450. . . . . *p.490*
Political Thought in Medieval Times. *p.490*
Political Thought of Plato and Aristotle. *p.488*
The Political Thought of Thomas Aquinas. *p.490*
The Political Thought of William Ockham. *p.490*
Political Unification Revisited: On Building Supranational Communities. *p.629*
The Political University: Policy, Politics, and Presidential Leadership in the American Research University. . . . *p.295*
Political Violence and Terrorism in Modern America: A Chronology. *p.563*
Politicians and Policymaking in Japan. *p.621*
Politicized Economies: Monarchy, Monopoly, and Mercantilism. *p.215*
Politics after Hitler: The Western Allies and the German Party System. *p.610*
Politics among Nations: The Struggle for Power and Peace. *p.626*
Politics among Nations. *p.626*
The Politics and Ethics of Fieldwork. *p.690*
Politics and Passion: Toward a More Egalitarian Liberalism. *p.511, p.514*
Politics and Practice in Economic Geography. *p.398*
Politics and Society in Scotland. *p.607*
Politics and Society in Ukraine. *p.597*
Politics and Symbols: The Italian Communist Party and the Fall of Communism. *p.594*
Politics and Territory: The Sociology of Regional Persistence in Canada. *p.587*
Politics and the Class Divide: Working People and the Middle Class Left. *p.547*
Politics and the Constitution in the History of the United States. *p.452*

Politics and the Russian Army: Civil-Military Relations, 1689-2000. . . . . p.599

Politics As Development: The Emergence of Political Parties in Nineteenth-Century Serbia. p.579, p.600

Politics, Bks. I & II. p.488

Politics, Bks. III and IV. p.488

Politics, Death, and the Devil: Self and Power in Max Weber and Thomas Mann. p.502

Politics in France. p.608

Politics in Francophone Africa. p.612

Politics in New Brunswick. p.590

Politics in New Zealand. p.624

Politics in Northern Ireland. p.607

Politics in Russia. p.598

Politics in Southern Africa: State and Society in Transition. p.610, p.613

Politics in the Ancient World. p.489

Politics in the New South: Representation of African Americans in Southern State Legislatures. p.530

Politics in the Republic of Ireland. p.608

Politics in the United Nations: A Study of United States Influence in the General Assembly. p.635

Politics, Language, and Culture: A Critical Look at Urban School Reform. p.314

Politics, Law and Ritual in Tribal Society. p.433

The Politics of Arms Control Treaty Ratification. . p.562, p.630

The Politics of Belgium: A Unique Federalism. p.600

The Politics of Broadcast Regulation. p.445

The Politics of Canadian Public Policy. p.586

The Politics of Child Support in America. p.739

The Politics of Congressional Elections. p.530, p.549

The Politics of Cultural Pluralism. p.574, p.576

The Politics of Democratization in Korea: The Role of Civil Society. p.621

The Politics of Deviance. p.696

Politics of Disillusionment: The Chinese Communist Party under Deng Xiaoping, 1978-1989. . . . . p.619

The Politics of Dissatisfaction: Citizens, Services and Urban Institutions. p.542

The Politics of Electoral Systems: A Handbook. p.576

The Politics of European Union Enlargement: Theoretical Approaches. p.400, p.603

The Politics of Everyday Life: Making Choices, Changing Lives. p.577

The Politics of External Influence in the Dominican Republic. p.592

The Politics of Fortune: A New Agenda for Business Leaders. p.54

The Politics of Garbage: A Community Perspective on Solid Waste Policy Making. p.542

The Politics of Globalization: Gaining Perspective, Assessing Consequences. p.662

The Politics of Human Rights in Southeast Asia. p.512

The Politics of Identity: Class, Culture, Social Movements. p.693

The Politics of Individualism: Parties and the American Character in the Jacksonian Era. p.551, p.552

The Politics of Judicial Interpretation: The Federal Courts, Department of Justice and Civil Rights, 1866-1876. . . p.525

The Politics of Law: A Progressive Critique. p.465

Politics of Mercantilism. p.255

The Politics of Philosophy: A Commentary on Aristotle's Politics. p.489

The Politics of Pictures: The Creation of the Public in the Age of Popular Media. p.416

The Politics of Prejudice: The Anti-Japanese Movement in California and the Struggle for Japanese Exclusion. . . p.570

The Politics of Regulatory Change: A Tale of Two Agencies. p.463

The Politics of Rights: Lawyers, Public Policy and Political Change. p.442

The Politics of School Reform, 1870-1940. . . . . p.328

The Politics of Social Policy in the United States. . p.526, p.571

The Politics of Southern Europe: Integration into the European Union. p.603, p.638

Politics of Survival: The Conservative Party of Canada 1939-1945. . . . . p.588

The Politics of Terror: The U. S. Response to 9/11. . . . p.563

The Politics of Terrorism. p.662

The Politics of the U. S. Cabinet: Representation in the Executive Branch, 1789-1984. . . . . p.529

The Politics of Truth: Inside the Lies That Led to War and Betrayed My Wife's CIA Identity, A Diplomat's Memoir. p.562, p.648

The Politics of Utopia: A Study in Theory and Practice. . p.499

Politics or Principle?: Filibustering in the United States Senate. p.533

Politics, Parties and Elections in Turkey. p.616

Politics, Policy, and Government in British Columbia. . . p.589

Politics, Punishment and Populism. p.567

Politics, the Constitution and the Warren Court. p.470

Politics, Vol. 5-6, Bks. VII and VIII. p.488

Polling, Policy, and Public Opinion: The Case Against Heeding the Voice of the People. p.559

Polling the Nations. p.697

PollingReport.com. p.425, p.559

Pollution and the Struggle for the World Product: Multinational Corporations, Environment, and International Comparative Advantage. p.63

Pollution Control in the United States: Evaluating the System. p.63

The Polo Encyclopedia. p.844, p.863

Polyarchy: Participation and Opposition. p.575

Polynesia in Early Historic Times. p.43

The Polynesians: Prehistory of an Island People. p.13

PoMoSexuals: Challenging Assumptions about Gender and Sexuality. p.746

Poor Kids in a Rich Country: America's Children in Comparative Perspective. p.756

Pop Culture Latin America!: Media, Arts, and Lifestyle. p.712

Popular Justice: Presidential Prestige and Executive Success in the Supreme Court. p.540
Popular Movements and Political Change in Mexico. . . p.711
Popular Political Support in Urban China. p.619
Population Dynamics of a Philippine Rain Forest People: The San Ildefonso Agta. p.39
Population Malthus: His Life and Times. p.221
Population: The First Essay. p.222
Porn Studies. p.749
Pornography and Sexual Aggression. p.748
Pornography: Men Possessing Women. p.747
Portable Veblen. p.210
Portrait of a Greek Mountain Village. p.702
Portrait of American Jews: The Last Half of the Twentieth Century. p.764
Portraits of the Japanese Workplace: Labor Movements, Workers, and Managers. p.122
Portraits of the Whiteman: Linguistic Play and Cultural Symbols among the Western Apache. p.20
A Portuguese Rural Society. p.701
Positioning Yoga. p.793
The Positive Theory of Capital. p.234
Positivism and Sociology: Explaining Social Life. p.680
Possessing Culture: Museums, Anthropology and German New Guinea. p.47
Post Industrial Lives: Roles and Relationships in the 21st Century. p.733
Post Keynesian Econometrics, Microeconomics and the Theory of the Firm: Beyond Keynes, Vol. 1. . . . . . p.199, p.232
[e] Post Keynesian Price Theory. p.242
Post Keynesian Price Theory. p.233
Postcolonial Identities in Africa. p.582, p.613
Postcolonialism Meets Economics. p.211, p.271
Postcommunism and the Theory of Democracy. p.597
Postcommunist Belarus. p.599
Post-Communist Transition: Emerging Pluralism in Hungary. p.595
Post-Keynesian Economics. p.232
Postmodern Moments in Modern Economics. p.196
Post-Modernism and the Social Sciences: Insights, Inroads, and Intrusions. p.682
The Postnational Constellation: Political Essays. p.494
Post-Olympism?: Questioning Sport in the Twenty-First Century. p.818, p.846, p.888, p.892
Post-Suburbia: Government and Politics in the Edge Cities. p.544
Posttraumatic Stress Disorder: Acute and Long-Term Responses to Trauma and Disaster. p.699
Post-War Protection of Human Rights in Bosnia and Herzegovina. p.513
Pottery in Archaeology. p.7
Poverty and Discrimination. p.266
Poverty and Famines: An Essay on Entitlement and Deprivation. p.266
Poverty and Place: Ghettos, Barrios, and the American City. p.771
The Poverty of Philosophy. p.218
Power and Democracy in America. p.767
Power and Governance in a Partially Globalized World. . p.663
Power and Interdependence. p.626
Power and Its Disguises: Anthropological Perspectives on Politics. p.34
Power and Morality. p.484, p.770
Power and Negotiation. p.646
Power and Persuasion: Fiestas and Social Control in Rural Mexico. p.773
Power and Pluralism in American Cities: Researching the Urban Laboratory. p.544
Power and Privilege: A Theory of Social Stratification. . . p.722
Power and the Pursuit of Peace: Theory and Practice in the History of Relations Between States. p.649
Power at Play: Sports and the Problem of Masculinity. . . p.745
Power by Design: Constitution-Making in Nationalist China. p.621
Power Elite. p.724
Power Golf for Women: How to Hit Longer and Straighter from Tee to Green. p.836, p.861
Power in Africa: An Essay in Political Interpretation. p.498, p.611
Power in Movement: Social Movements, Collective Action and Politics. p.713
[e] Power in Practice: Adult Education and the Struggle for Knowledge and Power in Society. p.319
Power in the Party: The Organization of Power and Central-Republican Relations in the CPSU. p.508, p.579, p.597, p.599
The Power of Ethical Persuasion: Winning Through Understanding at Work and at Home. p.74
The Power of Gold: The History of an Obsession. . p.94, p.99
The Power of Legitimacy: Assessing the Role of Norms in Crisis Bargaining. p.649
The Power of Many: How the Living Web Is Transforming Politics, Business and Everyday Life. p.425
The Power of Minds at Work: Leveraging the Power of Organizational Intelligence. p.78
The Power of News: The History of Reuters. p.403
The Power of Portfolios: What Children Can Teach Us about Learning and Assessment. p.286, p.347, p.363
The Power of Projections: How Maps Reflect Global Politics and History. p.385
The Power of the American Presidency, 1789-2000. . . . p.526
The Power of the Press: The Birth of American Political Reporting. p.404
The Power of Their Ideas: Lessons from America from a Small School in Harlem. p.328
Power Play: Sport, the Media and Popular Culture. p.814, p.898, p.901
Power, Politics and People: The Collected Essays of C. Wright Mills. p.769
Power, Politics and the Olympic Games. p.846, p.892
The Power Press: Its Impact on America and What You Can Do about It. p.404

Power, Profit and Protest: Australian Social Movements and Globalisation. p.710
Power, Racism and Privilege: Race Relations in Theoretical and Sociohistorical Perspectives. p.729
Power Rules: The Evolution of NATO's Conventional Force Posture. p.639, p.654
Power Sharing: Language, Rank, Gender and Social Space in Pohnpei, Micronesia. p.21
Power Tennis Training. p.864
Power, Terror, Peace, and War: America's Grand Strategy in a World at Risk. p.560, p.564, p.642
Power, Trust, and Meaning: Essays in Sociological Theory and Analysis. p.681
Power Without Force: The Political Capacity of Nation States. p.498
Power Without Responsibility: How Congress Abuses the People Through Delegation. p.532
The Power-Conflict Story: A Dynamic Model of Interstate Rivalry. p.626, p.647
Powerdown: Options and Actions for a Post-Carbon World. . p.62
Powerful Classroom Management Strategies: Motivating Students to Learn. p.283
Powerful Classroom Stories from Accomplished Teachers: Stories from the Classrooms of Accomplished Teachers. p.338, p.348
Powerful Principles of Instruction. p.349
Powerful Proposals: How to Give Your Business the Winning Edge. p.174
Powerful Reforms with Shallow Roots: Improving America's Urban Schools. p.314
Powerhouse Marketing Plans: 14 Outstanding Real-Life Plans and What You Can Learn from Them to Supercharge Your Own Campaigns. p.134
Powering Up: Learning to Teach Well with Technology. p.347, p.351
PowerPoint Advanced Presentation Techniques. p.174
The Powers That Be. p.410
Powersharing: White House-Cabinet Relations in the Modern Presidency. p.528
PR!: A Social History of Spin. p.428
A Practical Companion to the Constitution: How the Supreme Court Has Ruled on Issues from Abortion to Zoning. . p.454
Practical Guide to Foreign Direct Investment in the European Union. p.60
Practical Meta-Analysis. p.687
Practical Philosophy of Sport and Physical Activity. . . . p.796
The Practice of Cultural Studies: A Guide to the Practice and Politics of Cultural Studies. p.699
The Practice of Liberal Pluralism. p.510
The Practice of Management. p.64
The Practice of Sport Psychology. p.878
Practicing Ethnography in Law: New Dialogues, Enduring Methods. p.25
Practicing Sociology in the Community: A Student's Guide. p.675
Pragmatic Women and Body Politics. p.47
Prairie Liberalism: The Liberal Party in Saskatchewan, 1905-1971. . . . . p.590
Praxis and Method: A Sociological Dialogue with Lukacs, Gramsci and the Early Frankfurt School. p.685
Prayers in the Precincts: The Christian Right in the 1998 Elections. p.511
Pre-capitalist economic formations. p.236
The Preconceptions of Economic Science. p.250
The Predator's Ball: How the Junk Bond Machine Staked the Corporate Raiders. p.99
Predatory States: Operation Condor and Covert War in Latin America. p.660
Predecessors of Adam Smith: The Growth of British Economic Thought. p.212
The Prehistoric Exploration and Colonisation of the Pacific. p.379
Prehistoric Hunters of the High Plains. p.10
Prehistoric Mesoamerica: Third Edition. p.9
Prehistory of the Eastern Arctic. p.11
Prehistory of the Indo-Malaysian Archipelago. p.13
Prejudice Across America. p.698
Prejudiced Communication: A Social Psychological Perspective. p.698
Premarital Sexuality: Attitudes, Relationships, Behavior. . p.737
The Prentice Hall Atlas of Western Civilization. p.399
The Prentice Hall Encyclopedia of Model Business Plans. . p.172
Preparing Adolescents for Life After Foster Care: The Central Role of Foster Parents. p.758
Preparing for Inclusive Teaching: Meeting the Challenges of Teacher Education Reform. p.279
Preparing for the Behavior-Based Interview: Getting the Job You Want. p.169
Preparing Teachers to Teach with Technology. p.352
Preschool Education in America: The Culture of Young Children from the Colonial Era to the Present. p.370
Preschool in Three Cultures: Japan, China and the United States. p.370
Preschool Inclusion. p.315
The Presentation of Self in Everyday Life. p.694
Presenting to Win: The Art of Telling Your Story. p.174
Preserving Intellectual Freedom: Fighting Censorship in Our Schools.. . . . . p.298
The President and Congress: Executive Hegemony at the Crossroads of American Government. p.528, p.532
The President and the Parties: The Transformation of the American Party System since the New Deal. p.527
The President As Statesman: Woodrow Wilson and the Constitution. p.528
The President As World Leader. p.527
The President: Office and Powers. p.461
Presidential Ballots, 1836-1892. . . . . p.556
The Presidential Branch.. . . . . p.524
The Presidential Campaign Film: A Critical History. . . . p.551
Presidential Candidate Images. p.696
Presidential Debates: Forty Years of High-Risk TV. . . . p.556
Presidential Elections 1789-2004. . . . . p.556
Presidential Impeachment. p.462

Presidential Musings from the Meridian: Reflections on the Nature of Geography. *p.374*

Presidential Primaries and the Dynamics of Public Choice. . *p.556*

The Presidential Veto. *p.527*

Presidential War Power. *p.462*

Presidents and Prime Mininsters. *p.575*

The President's Cabinet: Gender, Power, and Representation. *p.526*

☐ President's Council on Physical Fitness and Sports. *p.783, p.789*

Presidents, Parties, and the State: A Party System Perspective on Democratic Regulatory Choicc, 1884-1936. . . . . *p.551, p.552, p.579*

The Press and America: An Interpretive History of the Mass Media. *p.409*

ⓔ The Press Effect: Politicians, Journalists, and the Stories That Shape the Political World. *p.404*

The Press in the Arab Middle East: A History. *p.403*

Preventing Biological Warfare: The Failure of American Leadership. *p.563*

Preventing Early Learning Failure. *p.361*

Preventing Early School Failure: Research, Policy, and Practice. *p.361*

Prevention's Complete Book of Walking: Everything You Need to Know to Walk Your Way to Better Health. . *p.788, p.791*

The Price of Federalism. *p.525*

The Price of Indifference: Refugees and Humanitarian Action in the New Century. *p.667, p.670*

Price Theory: A Provisional Text. *p.237*

Prices and Production. *p.234, p.238*

Prices and Quantities: A Macroeconomic Analysis. *p.239*

Pricing Decisions and Marketing Policy. *p.144*

Pricing the Priceless Child: The Changing Social Value of Children. *p.735*

Pricing Theory in Post-Keynesian Economics: A Realist Approach. *p.232*

Pride Before the Fall: The Trials of Bill Gates and the End of the Microsoft Era. *p.158*

The Priestly Tribe: The Supreme Court's Image in the American Mind. *p.466*

Primate and Human Evolution. *p.15*

Primate Visions: Gender, Race and Nature in the World of Modern Science. *p.30*

A Primer of Biomechanics. *p.908*

A Primer on American Labor Law. . . *p.109 p.111 p.112 p.121*

A Primer on U. S. Housing Markets and Housing Policy. . *p.166*

Primitive, Archaic and Modern Economies: Essays of Karl Polanyi. *p.210, p.270*

Primitive Art in Civilized Places. *p.48*

The Prince. *p.492*

The Principalship. *p.282*

Principled World Politics: The Challenge of Normative International Relations at the Millennium. . . . *p.484, p.627*

☐ Principles & Standards for School Mathematics. . . . *p.360*

Principles and a Philosophy for Vocational Education. *p.305, p.353*

Principles and Methods of Adapted Physical Education and Recreation: With Activities Booklet and PowerWeb Bind-in Card. *p.800*

Principles and Practice of Sport Management. *p.882*

Principles and Practices in Interscholastic Athletics: Guidelines for Administrators. *p.799*

Principles and Practices of Teaching Reading. *p.363*

Principles and Types of Public Speaking. *p.423*

Principles of Agribusiness Management. *p.151*

Principles of Athletic Training: A Competency-Based Approach. *p.828*

Principles of Coaching Football. *p.858, p.904*

Principles of Computer Security: Security and Beyond. . . *p.113*

The Principles of Economic Analysis, Set. *p.220*

Principles of Economics. *p.224, p.234*

Principles of Environmental and Resource Economics: A Guide for Students and Decision-Makers. *p.62*

Principles of Forecasting: A Handbook for Researchers and Practitioners. *p.118*

Principles of Geomorphology. *p.391*

Principles of Instructional Design. *p.342*

Principles of International Law [1952]. *p.477*

Principles of International Politics: People's Powers, Preferences, and Perceptions. *p.625*

Principles of Inventory and Materials Management. . . . *p.116*

Principles of Political Economy: And Chapters on Socialism. *p.222*

The Principles of Political Economy and Taxation. *p.220*

Principles of Political Economy, Set. *p.222*

Principles of Political Economy with Some of Their Applications to Social Philosophy. *p.222*

Principles of Public International Law. *p.477*

Principles of Research Design in Social Sciences. *p.686*

Principles of Risk Management and Insurance. *p.163*

The Principles of Scientific Management. *p.64*

The Principles of Sociology, Vol. 1. . . . . *p.683*

The Principles of Sociology, Vol. 2. . . . . *p.684*

The Principles of Sociology, Vol. 3. . . . . *p.684*

The Principles of Sociology, Vol. 4. . . . . *p.684*

The Principles of Teaching Based on Psychology. *p.359*

Principles of the Business Rule Approach. *p.114*

Principles Science, Set. *p.231*

Print Literacy Development: Uniting Cognitive and Social Practice Theories. *p.304, p.354*

Privacy, Law, and Public Policy. *p.443*

Privacy on the Line: The Politics of Wiretapping and Encryption. *p.473*

Private Life under Changing Socialism: Love, Intimacy, and Family Change in a Chinese Village, 1949-1999. . . . *p.734*

Private Life under Socialism: Love, Intimacy, and Family Change in a Chinese Village, 1949-1999. . . . . . . *p.772*

Private Lives: Families, Individuals, and the Law. *p.442*

Private Pressure on Public Law: The Legal Career of Justice Thurgood Marshall, 1934-1991. . . . . *p.467*

The Private Roots of Public Action: Gender, Equality, and Political Participation. *p.503, p.550*

The Private Self. p.693
Privatizing Education: Can the School Marketplace Deliver Freedom of Choice, Efficiency, Equity, and Social Cohesion? p.299
Privilege: A Reader. p.724
Privilege in the Soviet Union. p.705
The Prize: The Epic Quest for Oil, Money and Power. . . p.160
Probability, Econometrics and Truth: The Methodology of Econometrics. p.202
The Problem of Leadership and the Conflict Between the Rational and the Irrational Forces in the Stream of History, Set. p.249
The Problem of the Media: U. S. Communication Politics in the Twenty-First Century. p.425
The Problem of Values in Educational Thought. p.345
Problem Solving in Recreation and Parks. p.785
Problems As Possibilities: Problem-Based Learning for K-16 Education. p.349
Problems of Democratic Transition and Consolidation: Southern Europe, South America and Post-Communist Europe. . p.505
Problems of Stability and Progress in International Relations. p.628
The Process of Economic Development. p.258
Process of Education. p.341
The Process of Government: A Study of Social Pressures. . p.482
The Process of Stratification. p.724
Process Selection: From Design to Manufacture. p.117
Process/Industrial Instruments and Controls Handbook. . . p.116
Producing Power: Ethnicity, Gender, and Class in a Caribbean Workplace. p.41
Product Development Performance: Strategy, Organization, and Management in the World Auto Industry. p.144
Product Life Cycles and Product Management. p.144
Product Planning Essentials. p.144
Production and Distribution Theories. p.210, p.249
Production and Inventory Control Handbook. p.116
Production and Reproduction: A Comparative Study of the Domestic Domain. p.32
Production Economics: A Dual Approach to Theory and Applications. p.248
Production, Income and Welfare: The Search for an Optimal Social Order. p.266
Production Planning and Scheduling in Flexible Assembly Systems. p.116
Productscan. p.140, p.141
Profession of Government Minister in Western Europe. . p.601
Professional Careers Sourcebook. p.169
Professional Development Schools: Schools for Developing a Profession. p.277
Professional Football: The Official Pro Footbal of Fame Bibliography. p.844, p.859
The Professional Golfers' Association Tour: A History. . . p.860
The Professional Stranger: An Informal Introduction to Ethnography. p.25
The Professions: Roles and Rules. p.725
Profiles in Terror: The Guide to Middle East Terrorist Organizations. p.660
Profiles of American Labor Unions. p.125
Profiles of Sport Industry Professionals: The People Who Make the Games Happen. p.905, p.906
Profiling Political Leaders: Cross-Cultural Studies of Personality and Behavior. p.483
Profiting from Multiple Intelligences in the Workplace. . . p.66
Profits, Priests, and Princes: Adam Smith's Emancipation of Economics from Politics and Religion. p.219
Program Standards and Report Forms. p.359
Programming for Parks, Recreation, and Leisure Services. p.783, p.787
Progress in Motor Control: Structure-Function Relations in Voluntary Movements, Vol. 2. . . . . p.909
Progressive Education at the Crossroads. p.340
Project 2061 Textbook Evaluations. p.284
Project Appraisal and Planning for Developing Countries. . p.259
Project Management for Information Systems. p.114
Prologue to Nuremberg: The Politics and Diplomacy of Punishing War Criminals of the First World War. . . . p.477
Prometheus Wired: The Hope for Democracy in the Age of Network Technology. p.503
The Promise of Politics: From Theory to Practice. p.491
The Promise of Schooling: Education in Canada, 1800-1914. . . . . p.333
Promises I Can Keep: Why Poor Women Put Motherhood Before Marriage. p.724
Promoting Active Learning: Strategies for the College Classroom. p.348
Promotional Strategy. p.134
Propaganda and Communication in World History: A Pluralizing World in Formation, Vol. 3. . . . . p.696
Propaganda and Communication in World History: Emergence of Public Opinion in the West, Vol. 2. . . . . p.696
Propaganda and Communication in World History: The Symbolic Instrument in Early Times, Vol. 1. . . . . . p.696
Propaganda and Democracy: The American Experience of Media and Mass Persuasion. p.418
Propaganda and Mass Persuasion: A Historical Encyclopedia, 1500 to the Present. p.425
Propaganda: The Formation of Men's Attitudes. . p.425, p.696
Prostitution and Victorian Society: Women, Class, and the State. p.749
Protecting Abused and Neglected Children. p.756
Protecting Human Rights in Africa: Roles and Strategies of Non-Governmental Organizations. p.640, p.670
Protecting Soldiers and Mothers: The Political Origins of Social Policy in the United States. p.769
Protecting the Ozone Layer: The United Nations History. . p.666
Protest and Punishment: The Story of the Social and Political Protesters Transported to Australia, 1788-1868. . . . . p.753
Protest Movements in 1960s West Germany: A Social History of Dissent and Democracy. p.610, p.712
The Protestant Establishment: Aristocracy and Caste in America. p.726
The Protestant Ethic and the Spirit of Capitalism. . . . p.725
The Protestant Ethic and the Spirit of Capitalism. p.721
Protestantism and the Rise of Capitalism. p.681

Protocol for Profit: A Manager's Guide to Competing Worldwide. p.56
Prove It with Figures: Empirical Methods in Law and Litigation. p.179
Provinces: Canadian Provincial Politics. p.589
Provincial Politics in Canada: Towards the Turn of the Century. p.589
The Provincial State: Politics in Canada's Provinces and Territories. p.589
Provocateur: Images of Women and Minorities in Advertising. p.426
Proximity, Distance, and Diversity: Issues on Economic Interaction and Local Development. p.397
Psychiatric Justice. p.471
The Psychodynamics of Culture: Abram Kardiner and Neo-Freudian Anthropology. p.35
The Psychoeducational Assessment of Preschool Children. . p.356
Psychological Anthropology Reconsidered. p.35
Psychological Anthropology. p.35
The Psychological Assessment of Political Leaders: With Profiles of Saddam Hussein and Bill Clinton. p.512
Psychological Dynamics of Sport and Exercise. . . p.877, p.879
Psychological Factors in Poverty. p.264
Psychological Foundations of Sport. p.877
Psychological Perspectives on Politics. p.483
The Psychology and Management of Workplace Diversity. . p.132
Psychology and the Economic Mind: Cognitive Processes Conceptualization. p.272
Psychology for Health Fitness Professionals. . . . p.790, p.905
Psychology for Physical Educators. p.797
Psychology, in Modules, Critical Thinking Companion and PsychInquiry. p.692
Psychology in Sport. p.877
The Psychology of Exercise: Integrating Theory and Practice. p.875, p.877
The Psychology of Investing. p.97
Psychology of Officiating. p.878, p.905
Psychology of Physical Activity: Determinants, Well-Being and Interventions. p.876
The Psychology of Prejudice and Discrimination. p.698
The Psychology of Saving: A Study on Economic Psychology. p.246, p.251
The Psychology of Sex, Gender and Jobs: Issues and Solutions. p.133
The Psychology of Social Movements. p.710
Psychology of Social Norms. p.692
The Psychology of Stereotyping. p.694
Psychology of Team Sports. p.877
The Psychology of Terrorism. p.662
Psychopathia Sexualis: A Clinical-Forensic Study. p.749
Ptolemy's Geography: An Annotated Translation of the Theoretical Chapters. p.377
Public Administration and Public Management: The Principal-Agent Perspective. p.75
Public Administration Theory Primer. p.545, p.580
Public Agenda. p.559
Public and Its Problems. p.491
Public and Private Financing of Higher Education: Shaping Public Policy for the Future. p.295
Public Archaeology. p.5
Public Benefits of Archaeology. p.7
Public Choice III. p.576
Public Dollars, Private Stadiums. p.880, p.883, p.887
Public Economics: Selected Papers by William Vickrey. . p.247
Public Education in America: A New Interpretation of Purpose and Practice. p.324
Public Education in the United States. p.325
Public Finance in a Democratic Society: Collected Papers of Richard A. Musgrave, Vol. 1. . . . . p.247
Public Interest Group Profiles 2004-2005. . . . . p.559
Public Management As Art, Science, and Profession. p.545, p.580
Public Money and the Muse: Essays on Government Funding for the Arts. p.523
Public Opinion and Democratic Accountability: How Citizens Learn about Politics. p.559
Public Opinion, Polling, and Democracy Around the World: A Historical Encyclopedia. p.425
Public Opinion. p.425, p.697
The Public Order of the Oceans: A Contemporary International Law of the Sea,. p.478
Public Papers of the Presidents of the United States. . p.481
The Public Realm: Exploring the City's Quintessential Social Territory. p.771
Public Relations History: From the 17th to the 20th Century. p.428
Public Relations on the Net: Winning Strategies to Inform and Influence the Media, the Investment Community, the Government, the Public, and More!. p.144
Public School Reform in Puerto Rico: Sustaining Colonial Models of Development, 60. . . . . p.337
Public Services Delivery. p.755
The Public Trust Doctrine and the Management of America's Coasts. p.463
Public Vows: A History of Marriage and the Nation. . . . p.739
The Public's Right to Know: The Supreme Court and the First Amendment. p.464
The Puerto Rican Community and Its Children on the Mainland: A Source Book for Teachers, Social Workers and Other Professionals. p.311
Puerto Rican Students in U. S. Schools. p.311
Pulitzer Prize Feature Stories: America's Best Writing, 1979-2003. . . . . p.412
Pull: Networking and Success since Benjamin Franklin. p.53, p.132, p.147
The Pullman Strike: The Story of a Unique Experiment and of a Great Labor Upheaval. p.127
Pulp Politics: How Political Advertising Tells the Stories of American Politics. p.548
Pumped: Straight Facts for Athletes about Drugs, Supplements and Training. p.826
Punished by Rewards: The Trouble with Gold Stars, Incentive Plans. p.284

Punishing Hate: Bias Crimes under American Law. . . . p.568
The Purchase of Intimacy. p.738
Pure and Simple Politics: The American Federation of Labor and Political Activism, 1881-1917. . . . . p.126
The Pure Theory of Foreign Trade and the Pure Theory of Domestic Values. p.224
Purity and Danger: An Analysis of Concepts of Pollution and Taboo. p.36
Purity in Print: Book Censorship in America from the Gilded Age to the Computer Age. p.458
The Purposes of Higher Education. p.291
Pursuing Excellence in Higher Education: Eight Fundamental Challenges. p.332
Pursuing Justice for the Child. p.473
The Pursuit of Equality in American History. p.458
The Pursuit of Fairness: A History of Affirmative Action. p.57, p.108, p.133
The Pursuit of Significance: Strategies for Managerial Success in Public Organizations. p.545, p.580
The Pursuit of the White House: A Handbook of Presidential Election Statistics and History. p.556
Pushing the Limits: The Female Administrative Aspirant. . p.281
Put to the Test: An Educator's and Consumer's Guide to Standardized Testing. p.285
Put Your Bodies upon the Wheels: Student Revolt in the 1960s. p.331
Putting Asunder: A History of Divorce in Western Society. . p.740
Puzzles and Paradoxes in Economics. p.186
Pygmalion in the Classroom: Teacher Expectation and Pupils' Intellectual Development. p.358

Q

Qualitative Analysis of Human Movement. p.873, p.909
Qualitative Interviewing: The Art of Hearing Data. . . . p.691
Qualitative Market Research: Principle and Practice. . . . p.135
Qualitative Methods for Marketplace Research. p.136
Qualitative Methods in Sports Studies. p.812
Qualitative Research in Early Childhood Settings. p.356
Qualitative Research Methods in Human Geography. p.376, p.396
Qualitative Research Practice: A Guide for Social Science Students and Researchers. p.136, p.137
Qualitative Research Through Case Studies. p.179
The Qualitative Researcher's Companion. p.690
Qualities of Effective Teachers. p.349
Quality Control and Industrial Statistics. p.116
Quality Lesson Plans for Secondary Physical Education. . p.800
Quality Management Demystified. p.73
Quality Measurement in Economics: New Perspectives on the Evolution of Goods and Services. p.196, p.263
The Quality of Life. p.266
Quality Teaching: Reflection as the Heart of Practice. . . p.348
Quality with Soul: How Six Premier Colleges and Universities Keep Faith with Their Religious Traditions. p.307
Quantifying Archaeology. p.7
[e] Quantifying the World: United Nations Ideas and Statistics. p.636
Quantitative Analysis for Management. p.119
Quantitative Geography: Perspectives on Spatial Data Analysis. p.376
Quantitative Methods for Business: The A to Z of QM. . p.178
The Quantity Theory of Money: From Locke to Keynes and Friedman. p.237
Quarrels That Have Shaped the Constitution. p.466
Quebec and the Constitution: Nineteen Sixty to Nineteen Seventy-Eight. p.590
Quebec Before Duplessis: The Political Career of Louis-Alexandre Taschereau. p.581
The Quebec Democracy: Structures, Processes and Policies. p.589
Queer Man on Campus: A History of Non-Heterosexual College Men 1945-2000. . . . . p.749
Queer Wars: The New Gay Right and Its Critics. p.570
Queering Elementary Education: Advancing the Dialogue about Sexualities and Schooling. p.309
Queerly Phrased: Language, Gender, and Sexuality. p.21
Quesnay's "Tableau Economique": A Critique and Reassessment. p.216
Quesnay's Tableau Economique. p.217
The Quest for an American Sociology: Robert E. Park and the Chicago School. p.685
The Quest for Drug Control: Politics and Federal Policy in a Period of Increasing Substance Abuse, 1963-1981. . . p.568
The Quest for Excellence. p.345
The Quest for Excitement: Sport and Leisure in the Civilizing Process. p.783, p.815
The Quest for Global Dominance: Transforming Global Presence into Global Competitive Advantage. p.69
The Quest for Postcolonial Utopia: A Comparative Introduction to the Utopian Novel in the New English Literatures. . p.485
The Quest for the True Figure of the Earth: Ideas and Expeditions in Four Centuries of Geodesy. p.389
The Quest for Utopia in Twentieth Century America. . . p.499
The Question of Discrimination: Racial Inequality in the U. S. Labor Market. p.134
Question of Intent: A Great American Battle with a Deadly Industry. p.449
A Question of Torture: CIA Interrogation, from the Cold War to the War on Terror. p.562
Questioning Geography: Fundamental Debates. p.375
Questioning the Media: A Critical Introduction. p.416
Questionnaire Design: How to Plan, Structure and Write Survey Material for Effective Market Research. p.137
Questions and Answers about Block Scheduling: An Implementation Guide. p.287
Questions and Answers in Attitude Surveys: Experiments on Question Form, Wording, and Context. p.691
Questions That Sell: The Powerful Process for Discovering What Your Customer Really Wants. p.142
Quick and Easy Ways to Connect with Students and Their Parents, Grades K-8: Improving Student Achievement Through Parent Involvement. p.353
Quick Reference Dictionary for Athletic Training. p.828

Quick Teambuilding Activities for Busy Managers: 50 Exercises That Get Results in Just 15 Minutes. p.80
The Quiet Revolution: Central Banking Goes Modern. p.88, p.154
Quiet Revolution in the South: The Impact of the Voting Rights Act, 1965-1990. . . . . p.554, p.573
□ Quintessential Careers: a Career and Job-Hunting Resources Guide. p.167, p.170
Quoting God: How Media Shape Ideas about Religion and Culture. p.719

R

Race Against the Court: The Supreme Court and Minorities in Contemporary America. p.457, p.540
Race and Class in the Southwest: A Theory of Racial Inequality. p.729
Race and Culture in the Classroom: Teaching and Learning Through Multicultural Education. p.309
Race and Culture. p.729
Race and Ethnicity in Latin America. p.731
Race and Ethnicity in Research Methods. p.687
Race and Ethnicity, Set. p.3
Race and Party Competition in Britain. p.606
Race and Schooling in the City. p.301
Race, Crime and the Law. p.471
Race, Culture, and Evolution: Essays in the History of Anthropology. p.5
Race, Gender and Rhetoric: The True State of Race and Gender Relations in Corporate America. p.133
Race: How Blacks and Whites Think and Feel about the American Obsession. p.730
Race in Mind: Race, IQ, and Other Racisms. p.17
Race, Law, and Culture: Reflections on Brown vs. Board of Education. p.451
Race Matters. p.730
Race of the Century: The Heroic True Story of the 1908 New York-to-Paris Auto Race. p.805, p.848
Race, Police, and the Making of a Political Identity: Mexican Americans and the Los Angeles Police Department, 1900-1945. . . . . p.774
Race, Racism, and Multiraciality in American Education. . p.301
Race, Rights and the Asian American Experience. p.456
Race to Incarcerate. p.753, p.773
Race to the Pole: Tragedy, Heroism, and Scott's Antarctic Quest. p.378
Racial Oppression in America. p.728
Racing the Enemy: Stalin, Truman, and the Surrender of Japan. p.647
Racism: From Slavery to Advanced Capitalism. p.727
Racism in College Athletics: The African-American Athlete's Experience. p.814, p.831
Racism, Modernity, and Identity on the Western Front. . . p.44
Racism Without Racists: Color-Blind Racism and the Persistence of Racial Inequality in the United States. . p.729
Racist Culture: Philosophy and the Politics of Meaning. . p.730
Radical Heroes: Gramsci, Freire and the Politics of Adult. . p.762
Radical Presence: Teaching as Contemplative Practice. . . p.348
Radical Right-Wing Populism in Western Europe. p.601
Radicalism and Education Reform in 20th-Century China: The Search for an Ideal Development Model. p.336
Radio and Television Broadcasting in Eastern Europe. . . p.412
Radio, TV and Modern Life: A Phenomenology of Broadcasting. p.412
The Raft Fishermen: Tradition and Change in the Brazilian Peasant Economy. p.28
The Rage of a Privileged Class: Why Do Prosperous Blacks Still Have the Blues? p.723
Ragnar Frisch: Economic Planning Studies. p.202
Railroads and the Granger Laws. p.445
Railroads in the Civil War: The Impact of Management on Victory and Defeat. p.519
A Rainbow of Gangs: Street Cultures in the Mega-City. . p.714
Raising the Bar: New Horizons in Disability Sport. . . . p.830
Rampant Women: Suffragists and the Right of Assembly. . p.519
Random Violence: Worrying about New Crimes and New Victims. p.754
A Random Walk down Wall Street: The Time Tested Strategy for Successful Investing Completely. p.96
Randomized Response: A Method for Sensitive Surveys. . p.691
Rape Warfare: The Hidden Genocide in Bosnia-Herzegovina and Croatia. p.651
Rastafari: From Outcasts to Culture Bearers. p.711
The Rate of Interest and Other Essays. p.270
The Rate of Interest: Its Nature, Determination and Relation to Economic Phenomena. p.200
Ratifying the Constitution. p.452
Rational Choice and Judgment: Decision Analysis for the Decider. p.83
The Rational Choice Controversy in Historical Sociology. . p.688
Rational Choice Theory: Resisting Colonisation. p.688
Rational Choice Theory. p.194
Rational Expectations and Econometric Practice, 2. . . . p.203
Rational Expectations and Econometric Practice. . p.233, p.238
The Rational Expectations Revolution in Macroeconomics: Theories and Evidence. p.237
Ravenswood: The Steelworkers' Victory and the Revival of American Labor. p.126
Raw Judicial Power?: The Supreme Court and American Society. p.538
Rawls and Religion: The Case for Political Liberalism. . p.510
The Reach of the State: Sketches of the Chinese Body Politic. p.620
Read All about It!: The Corporate Takeover of America's Newspapers. p.411
Read Aloud Handbook. p.366
A Reader in the Anthropology of Religion. p.36
Reading and Learning to Read. p.361
Reading Development and the Teaching of Reading: A Psychological Perspective. p.354
Reading Football: How the Popular Press Created an American Spectacle. p.812, p.818, p.859, p.902

Reading for Meaning: Fostering Comprehension in the Middle Grades. p.366
Reading Freire and Habermas: Critical Pedagogy and Transformative Social Change. p.762
Reading Instruction That Works, Third Edition: The Case for Balanced Teaching. p.365
Reading Matters: Narrative in the New Media Ecology. . p.419
Reading Mill: Studies in Political Theory. p.491
Reading Sport: Critical Essays on Power and Representation. p.814
Reading to Learn: Lessons from Exemplary Fourth-Grade Classrooms. p.361
Reading Topographic Maps. p.390
Readings for a History of Anthropological Theory. p.23
Readings in Early Anthropology. p.4
Readings in Public Education in the United States: A Collection of Sources and Readings to Illustrate the History of Educational Practice and Progress in the United States. . p.325
Ready-to-Use Motor Skills and Movement Station Lesson Plans for Young Children: Teaching, Remediation and Assessment. p.798
Ready-to-Use Pre-Sport Skills Activities Program: 100 Month-by-Month Lessons with Activities, Games and Assessments for the Elementary Grades. p.797, p.799
Reagan's Federalism: His Efforts to Decentralize Government. p.526
[e] Real Choices/new Voices: How Proportional Representation Elections Could Revitalize American Democracy. . . . p.576
The Real Estate Game: The Intelligent Guide to Successful Investing and Decision-Making. p.97, p.166
Real Estate Handbook. p.95, p.166
The Real Estate Investment Handbook. p.95, p.166
Real Men or Real Teachers?: Contradictions in the Lives of Men Elementary School Teachers. p.279
Real Options: Managing Strategic Investment in an Uncertain World. p.90, p.101
The Real Price of War: How You Pay for the War on Terror. p.563
Real Reading, Real Writing: Content-Area Strategies. . . p.366
Real Research: Conducting and Evaluating Research in the Social Sciences. p.376
The Real Worlds of Welfare Capitalism. p.500
Realignment: The Theory That Changed the Way We Think about American Politics. p.549
Realist Thought from Weber to Kissinger. p.627
Reality and Rhetoric: Studies in the Economics of Development. p.242
Reality by Design: The Rhetoric and Technology of Authenticity in Education. p.358
Realms of Freedom in Modern China. p.515
Reason and Democracy. p.505
Reason and Passion: Justice Brennan's Enduring Influence. p.469
Reason and Revolution. p.685
Reason and Teaching. p.329
The Reasonableness of Christianity, with A Discourse of Miracles, and Part of a Third Letter Concerning Toleration. p.216
The Rebellious Century: 1830-1930. . . . . p.707
Rebels Against War: The American Peace Movement, 1933-1983. . . . . p.572, p.651
The Rebirth of Russian Democracy: An Interpretation of Political Culture. p.585, p.598
Rebuilding Labor: Organizing and Organizers in the New Union Movement. p.122
The Rebuke of History: The Southern Agrarians and American Conservative Thought. p.516
Recent Advances in Game Theory. p.207
Recent Developments in Growth Theory. p.242
Recent Developments in Post Keynesian Economics. . . . p.241
Recharting the Caribbean: Land, Law, and Citizenship in the British Virgin Islands. p.41
Reclaiming a Scientific Anthropology. p.24
Reclaiming the Commons: Community Farms and Forests in a New England Town. p.771
Reclaiming the Game: College Sports and Educational Values. p.821, p.893
Reconciling the Solitudes: Essays on Canadian Federalism and Nationalism. p.587
Reconstructing City Politics: Alternative Economic Development and Urban Regimes. p.544
Reconstructing Religious, Spiritual and Moral Education. . p.307
Reconstructing the Common Good in Education: Coping with Intractable American Dilemmas. p.325
The Reconstruction of Economics: An Analysis of the Fundamentals of Institutional Economics. p.247
Recorded Music in American Life: The Phonograph and Popular Memory, 1890-1945. . . . . p.712
Records Management Handbook. p.115
Recreation and Sport Planning and Design. . p.786, p.880, p.883
Recreational Sport Management. p.786
The Recurrent Crisis in Corporate Governance. p.52 p.54 p.86 p.111
Recursive Methods in Economic Dynamics. . . . p.205, p.239
Recycling and Waste Management Guide to the Internet. . p.159
The Red Atlantis: Communist Culture in the Absence of Communism. p.508
Red Capitalists in China: The Party, Private Entrepreneurs, and Prospects for Political Change. p.619
Red Grange and the Rise of Modern Football. p.804, p.858, p.893
The Red Hand: Protestant Paramilitaries in Northern Ireland. p.607
Red Man's Land/White Man's Law: The Past and Present Status of the American Indian. p.465
The Red Rose Crew: A True Story of Women, Winning, and the Water. p.835, p.865
Red Scare: A Study in National Hysteria, 1919-1920. . . p.714
Redeeming the Communist Past: The Regeneration of Communist Parties in East Central Europe. p.601
Redeeming the Wasteland: Television Documentary and Cold War Politics. p.413

Redefining Mexican "Security": Society, State, and Region under NAFTA. *p.593*

Reefs at Risk: A Map-Based Indicator of Threats to the World's Coral Reefs. *p.393*

Reengineering the Corporation: A Manifesto for Business Revolution. *p.86*

REENIC: Russian and East European Network Information Center. *p.595, p.596*

Referendum: Direct Democracy in Switzerland. *p.595*

Referendums Around the World: The Growing Use of Direct Democracy. *p.575*

Reflections from the Heart of Educational Inquiry: Understanding Curriculum and Teaching through the Arts. *p.365*

Reflections from the Wrong Side of the Tracks: Class, Identity, and the Working Class Experience in Academe. . . . *p.302*

Reflections on Learning. *p.343*

Reflections on the Classical Canon in Economics: Essays in Honor of Samuel Hollander. *p.217*

Reflections on the Development of Modern Macroeconomics. *p.241*

Reflections on the Moral and Spiritual Crisis in Education. . *p.306*

Reflective Thinking: The Method of Education. *p.357*

Reform in the Provinces: The Government of Stuart England. *p.582*

Reform of Undergraduate Education. *p.294*

Reform Without Liberalization: China's National People's Congress and the Politics of Institutional Change. . . *p.620*

Reforming Federal Regulation. *p.444*

Reforming the US Corporate Tax. *p.107*

Refuge of a Scoundrel: The Patriot Act in Libraries. . . . *p.451*

Refugee and Immigrant Health: A Handbook for Health Professionals. *p.668*

Refugees in a Global Era. *p.400*

Refugees in America in the 1990s: A Reference Handbook. *p.570*

Refugees in an Age of Genocide: Global, National and Local Perspectives During the Twentieth Century. *p.668*

Regarding Children's Words: Teacher Research on Language and Literacy. *p.361*

Regimes and Oppositions. *p.575*

Regional Geography of the United States and Canada. *p.382, p.397*

Regional Surveys of the World 2006. . . . . *p.396*

Regionalism and Realism: A Study of Government in the New York Metropolitan Area. *p.542*

Regionalism, Multilateralism, and Economic Integration: The Recent Experience. *p.630, p.665*

The Regionalization of Internationalized Innovation: Locations for Advanced Industrial Development and Disparities in Participation. *p.397*

Regulating Intimacy: A New Legal Paradigm. *p.471*

Regulation Through Litigation. *p.110, p.112*

Rehabilitation of Sports Injuries: Scientific Basis. *p.827, p.828, p.829*

The Rehnquist Court and Civil Rights. *p.540*

The Rehnquist Court and Criminal Punishment. *p.540*

The Rehnquist Court and the Constitution. *p.467, p.540*

The Rehnquist Court: In Pursuit of Judicial Conservatism, 76. . . . . *p.536*

The Rehnquist Court: Judicial Activism on the Right. *p.539, p.541*

The Rehnquist Legacy. *p.467*

Reindeer People, Living with Animals and Spirits in Siberia. *p.772*

Reinventing Anthropology. *p.24*

Reinventing Justice: The American Drug Court Movement. *p.449*

Reinventing Strategy: Using Strategic Learning to Create and Sustain Breakthrough Performance. *p.79*

Reinventing the Melting Pot: The New Immigrants and What It Means to Be American. *p.571*

Rekindling the Movement: Labor's Quest for Relevance in the 21st Century. *p.129*

Relational Discipline: Strategies for in-Your-Face Kids. . *p.283*

Relationship Marketing: Strategy and Implementation. . . *p.143*

Relative Values: Reconfiguring Kinship Studies. *p.32*

Relativism and the Social Sciences. *p.679*

Relevance Lost: The Rise and Fall of Management Accounting. *p.106*

Relief Web: Policy and Issues. *p.668, p.669*

Religion & Public Schools. *p.299*

Religion: A Humanist Interpretation. *p.36*

Religion and American Education: Rethinking a National Dilemma. *p.307*

Religion and American Law: An Encyclopedia. *p.459*

Religion and Custom in a Muslim Society: The Berti of Sudan. *p.36*

Religion and Humane Global Governance. *p.626*

Religion and Nation: Iranian Local and Transnational Networks in Britain. *p.44*

Religion and Popular Culture in America. *p.720*

Religion and Sexuality: The Shakers, the Mormons and the Oneida Community. *p.721*

Religion and Sport: The Meeting of Sacred and Profane. . *p.824*

Religion and the American Constitutional Experiment: Essential Rights and Liberties. *p.459*

Religion and the Law: A Dictionary. *p.460*

Religion, Education, and Academic Success. *p.307*

Religion, Education and the American Experience: Reflections on Religion and American Public Life. *p.307*

Religion Explained. *p.36*

Religion in the Modern World: From Cathedrals to Cults. . *p.719*

Religion in the Public Schools: A Joint Statement of Current Law. *p.299*

Religion of India: The Sociology of Hinduism and Buddhism. *p.722*

Religion on Trial: How Supreme Court Trends Threaten Freedom of Conscience in America. *p.537*

Religious Expression and the American Constitution. . . *p.459*

Religious Freedom and Indian Rights: The Case of Oregon vs. Smith. *p.439*

Religious Fundamentalism and American Education: The Battle for the Public Schools. p.307
Religious Liberty in America: Political Safeguards. . . . p.459
Religious Liberty in the Supreme Court: Cases That Define the Debate over Church and State. p.536
Religious Liberty: Religious Liberty in Public Schools. . p.299
Religious Pluralism In The Academy: Opening The Dialogue. p.307
Religious Violence and Abortion: The Gideon Project. . . p.569
Reluctant Partners: Implementing Federal Policy. p.525
Reluctant Reformers: The Impact of Racism on American Social Reform Movements. p.700
Remaking Social Networks: the Emergence of Embeddedness in Vocational Training. p.305
Remapping East Asia. p.618
Remarriage, a Study of Marriage. p.738
Remediation: Understanding New Media. p.419
Remember This Titan: Lessons Learned from a Celebrated Coach's Journey. p.860
Remembrance of Repasts: An Anthropology of Food and Memory. p.46
Reminiscences of a Stock Operator: The Wall Street Classic about the Life and Times of Jesse Livermore. . . p.95, p.102
Remote Sensing and Geographic Information System. p.386, p.388
Remote Sensing and Image Interpretation. p.388
Remote Sensing Digital Image Analysis: An Introduction. . p.389
Remote Sensing for Environmental Monitoring, GIS Applications, and Geology III. p.388
Remote Sensing for Natural Resource Management and Environmental Monitoring, Vol. 4. . . . . p.389
Remote Sensing Geology. p.388
Remote Sensing Image Analysis: Including the Spatial Domain. p.388
Renaissance Utopias and the Problem of History. p.499
Renewing Hope Within Neighborhoods of Despair: The Community-Based Development Model. p.719
Renewing the Atlantic Partnership: Independent Task Force Report. p.560, p.562
Renovating Politics in Contemporary Vietnam. p.622
Renters' Rights: Legal Basics. p.442
Repair or Revenge?: Victims and Restorative Justice. . . p.754
Report of the President's Commission on Campus Unrest: Including the Killings at Jackson State and Kent State Tragedy. p.332
Report on the global AIDS epidemic : 4th global report. . p.668
The Reporter and the Law: Techniques of Covering the Courts. p.444
The Reporter's Environmental Handbook. p.407
Reporting from the Front: The Media and the Military. . . p.407
Reporting the News about Religion: An Introduction for Journalists. p.406
Represent Yourself in Court: How to Prepare and Try a Winning Case. p.470
Representative Democracy in the Canadian Provinces. . . p.589
A Representative Supreme Court?: The Impact of Race, Religion, and Gender on Appointments. p.538
Representing Interests in the European Union. p.603
Representing Men: Maleness and Masculinity in the Media. p.416
Representing Sport. p.814, p.823, p.831, p.858
Reproducing Jews: A Cultural Account of Assisted Conception in Israel. p.32
Reproducing Reproduction: Kinship, Power, and Technological Innovation. p.32
The Reproduction of Mothering: Psychoanalysis and the Sociology of Gender. p.736
Reproductive Laws for the 1990s. p.447
The Republic and the School: Horace Mann on the Education of Free Men. p.344
Republic. Com. p.761
The Republic of Mass Culture: Journalism, Filmmaking, and Broadcasting in America since 1941. . . . . p.417
Republic of Plato. p.489
Republican Empire: Alexander Hamilton on War and Free Government. p.493
Republican National Committee. p.553
The Republican Option in Canada: Past and Present. . . . p.588
The Republican South: Democratization and Partisan Change. p.551, p.553
The Republican War on Science. p.566
Republic.com. p.425
Republic.. . . . . p.489
Research about Leisure: Past, Present and Future. . p.784, p.813
Research for Social Workers: An Introduction to Methods. . p.757
A Research Guide to Central Party and Government Meetings in China, 1949-1986. . . . . p.620
Research in Experimental Economics, Vol. 1. . . . . . . p.271
Research in Experimental Economics, Vol. 2. . . . . . . p.271
Research in Experimental Economics, Vol. 3. . . . . . . p.271
Research in the History of Economic Thought and Methodology, Vol. 23, Set. p.194, p.208
Research Interviewing: Context and Narrative. p.691
Research Methods for Organizational Studies. p.179
Research Methods for Sports Studies. p.812
Research Methods in Anthropology: Qualitative and Quantitative Approaches. p.25
Research Methods in Athletic Training. p.828
Research on Alternative and Non-Traditional Education: Teacher Education Yearbook XIII. p.277
Research-Doctorate Programs in the United States: Continuity and Change. p.295
Researches into the Mathematical Principles of the Theory of Wealth. p.198
Researching Human Geography. p.396
Reservation and Affirmative Action: Models of Social Integration in India and the United States. p.723
Reshaping the Asia Pacific Economic Order. p.398
Reshaping the International Order: A Report to the Club of Rome. p.262
The Resilient City: How Modern Cities Recover from Disaster. p.760

Resolving Social Conflicts: Selected Papers on Group Dynamics. *p.695*
Responding to Crisis: A Rehetorical Approach to Crisis Communication. *p.173*
Responsible Government in Ontario. *p.590*
Responsible Partisanship?: The Evolution of American Political Parties since 1950. . . . . *p.551, p.552*
The Responsive University: Restructuring for High Performance. *p.332*
The Restaurant: From Concept to Operation. *p.165*
Restaurant Industry Forecast. *p.165*
Restaurant Operations Management: Principles and Practices. *p.165*
Restaurant Start-up Guide. *p.165*
Restoring Trust in American Business. *p.54, p.86, p.109*
Restraints on War: Studies in the Limitation of Armed Conflict. *p.478*
Restructing Political Power in China: Alliances and Opposition, 1978-1998. . . . . *p.619*
Restructuring Europe: Centre Formation, System Building, and Political Structuring between the Nation State and the European Union. *p.601*
Restructuring the Welfare State: Globalisation and Social Policy Reform in Finland and Sweden. *p.594*
Resumes for Business Management Careers. *p.170*
Resumes for College Students and Recent Graduates. . . *p.171*
Resurgent Voice in Latin America: Indigenous Peoples, Political Mobilization, and Religious Change. *p.591*
Resurrecting Empire: Western Footprints and America's Perilous Path in the Middle East. *p.641*
Retailing in the 21st Century: Current and Future Trends. . *p.164*
Retained by the People: A History of American Indians and the Bill of Rights. *p.465*
Rethinking Aggression and Violence in Sport. . . *p.802, p.817*
Rethinking Bank Regulation: Till Angels Govern. *p.90*
Rethinking College Athletics. *p.802, p.821*
Rethinking Development Geographies. *p.260, p.268*
Rethinking Gifted Education. *p.317*
Rethinking Linguistic Relativity. *p.20*
Rethinking Military Politics: Brazil and the Southern Cone. *p.593*
Rethinking Multiculturalism: Cultural Diversity and Political Theory. *p.484, p.768*
Rethinking Performance Measurement: Beyond the Balanced Scorecard. *p.82*
Rethinking Psychological Anthropology: Continuity and Change in the Study of Human Action. *p.35*
Rethinking Rights and Regulations: Institutional Responses to New Communications Technologies. *p.761*
Rethinking School Choice: Limits of the Market Metaphor. *p.347*
Rethinking Social Policy: Race, Poverty, and the Underclass. *p.722*
Rethinking Standards Through Teacher Preparation Partnerships. *p.279*
Rethinking Welfare: A Critical Perspective. *p.768*
A Retrospective on the Classical Gold Standard, 1821-1931. . . . . *p.237*
The Return of Depression Economics. *p.244*
Revealing Male Bodies. *p.745*
Revealing the Buried Past: Geophysics for Archaeologists. . *p.7*
Reverse Discrimination: Dismantling a Myth. *p.516*
Reversing Underachievement among Gifted Black Students: Promising Practices and Programs. *p.317*
Review of Research in Education. *p.354*
Revising Business Prose. *p.173*
A Revision of Demand Theory. *p.238*
Revisioning Gender. *p.743*
Revisiting "The Culture of the School and the Problem of Change". *p.329*
Revitalization Movements: Some Theoretical Considerations for Their Comparative Study. *p.25*
The Revival of Laissez-Faire in American Macroeconomic Theory: A Case Study of Its Pioneers. *p.240*
Reviving the American Dream: The Economy, the States, and the Federal Government. *p.266, p.525*
Revolt Against Regulation: The Rise and Pause of the Consumer Movement. *p.52*
Revolution and Genocide: On the Origins of the Armenian Genocide and the Holocaust. *p.653*
Revolution and the Transformation of Societies: A Comparative Study of Civilizations. *p.760*
Revolution by Judiciary: The Structure of American Constitutional Law. *p.454*
Revolution from Within: The Hungarian Socialist Workers' Party and the Collapse of Communism. *p.509, p.595*
The Revolution in Corporate Finance. *p.91*
A Revolution in Favor of Government: Origins of the U. S. Constitution and the Making of the American State. . *p.523*
The Revolution in Military Affairs: Implications for Canada and NATO. *p.631, p.655*
Revolution: The International Dimensions. *p.497*
Revolutionary Apocalypse: Ideological Roots of Terrorism. *p.661*
Revolutionary Change. *p.760*
The Revolutionary Reign of Terror: The Role of Violence in Political Change. *p.497*
Revolutions in Knowledge: Feminism in the Social Sciences. *p.255, p.267, p.274*
Revolutions: Worldwide Introduction to Political and Social Change. *p.760*
Reyita: The Life of a Black Cuban Woman in the Twentieth Century. *p.40*
Reykjavik and Beyond: Deep Reductions in Strategic Nuclear Arsenals and the Future Direction of Arms Control. . . *p.656*
The Rhetoric and Reality of Mass Education in Mao's China. *p.336*
The Rhetoric of Church and State: A Critical Analysis of Religion Clause Jurisprudence. *p.460*
The Rhetoric of Economics. *p.185*
The Rhetoric of Terrorism and Counterterrorism. *p.660*
Rhumb Lines and Map Wars: A Social History of the Mercator Projection. *p.386*

Rhythmic Gymnastics. *p.795, p.861*
Ricardian Economics: A Historical Study, 8—8. . . . . . *p.211*
Ricardo, the New View. *p.220*
Rich Media, Poor Democracy: Communication Politics in Dubious Times. *p.416*
Richard S. Ewell: A Soldier's Life. *p.521*
The Riddle of Gender: Science, Activism, and Transgender Rights. *p.744*
Ride to Modernity: The Bicycle in Canada, 1869-1900. . . . . *p.808, p.857*
Riding the Roller Coaster: A History of the Chrysler Corporation. *p.154*
Riding the Waves of Culture: Understanding Diversity in Global Business. *p.59, p.132*
The Right and the Power. *p.439*
Right Face: Organizing the American Conservative Movement 1945-65. . . . . *p.516*
The Right of the People. *p.455*
The Right to Die: Policy Innovation and Its Consequences. *p.448*
The Right to Home School: A Guide to the Law on Parents' Rights in Education.. . . . . *p.296, p.450*
The Right to Vote: Politics and the Passage of the 15th Amendment.. *p.461*
Right to Vote: The Contested History of Democracy in the United States. *p.519*
Righting a Wrong: Japanese Americans and the Passage of the Civil Liberties Act of 1988.. . . . . *p.571*
Rights Beyond Borders: The Global Community and the Struggle over Human Rights in China.. . . . . *p.669*
Rights, Not Roses: Unions and the Rise of Working-Class Feminism, 1945-80. . . . . *p.121*
The Rights of Aliens and Refugees: The Basic ACLU Guide to Alien and Refugee Rights. *p.460*
The Rights of Authors, Artists, and Other Creative People: The Basic ACLU Guide to Author and Artist Rights. . . . *p.441*
The Rights of Employees and Union Members: The Basic ACLU Guide to the Rights of Employees and Union Members. *p.447*
The Rights of Indians and Tribes: The Authoritative ACLU Guide to Indian and Tribal Rights, Third Edition. . . . *p.465*
The Rights of Lesbians, Gay Men, Bisexuals, and Transgender People: The Authoritative ACLU Guide to the Rights of Lesbians, Gay Men, Bisexuals, and Transgender People. *p.457*
The Rights of Others: Aliens, Residents and Citizens. *p.576, p.669*
The Rights of Patients: The Authoritative ACLU Guide to the Rights of Patients. *p.448*
The Rights of People Who Are HIV Positive: The Basic ACLU Guide to the Rights of People Living with HIV Disease and AIDS. *p.448*
The Rights of People with Mental Disabilities: The Authoritative ACLU Guide to the Rights of People with Mental Illness and Mental Retardation. *p.442*
The Rights of War and Peace: Political Thought and the International Order from Grotius to Kant. *p.477*
The Rights of Youth: American Colleges and Student Revolt, 1798-1815. *p.332*
Rights Talk: The Impoverishment of American Political Discourse.. . . . . *p.455*
Rights vs. Public Safety after 9/11: America in the Age of Terrorism. *p.563, p.572*
Rights vs. Responsibilities: The Supreme Court and the Media, 50. . . . . *p.405*
The Rio Report: Reshaping the International Order: a Report to the Club of Rome Coordinator. *p.256*
Riot and Revelry in Early America. *p.713*
Riparian Vegetation and Fluvial Geomorphology. *p.391*
The Rise and Demise of German Statism: Loyalty and Political Membership. *p.609*
The Rise and Fall of American Public Schools: The Political Economy of Public Education in the 20th Century. . . *p.326*
The Rise and Fall of Gay Culture. *p.712*
The Rise and Fall of HMOs: An American Health Care Revolution. *p.163*
The Rise and Fall of States According to Greek Authors. . *p.500*
The Rise and Fall of Synanon: A California Utopia. . . . *p.720*
The Rise and Fall of the Elites: An Application of Theoretical Sociology.. . . . . *p.249*
The Rise and Fall of the European Defence Community: Anglo-American Relations and the Crises of European Defence, 1950-55. . . . . *p.638, p.655*
Rise and Fall of the German Democratic Republic 1945-1990. . . . . *p.609*
The Rise and Fall of the Press Box. *p.902, p.907*
The Rise and Fall of the Soviet Politburo. *p.598, p.600*
The Rise of American Research Universities: Elites and Challengers in the Postwar Era. *p.331*
Rise of Anthropological Theory: A History of Theories of Culture. *p.23*
The Rise of Cable Programming in the United States: Revolution or Evolution? *p.421*
The Rise of Candidate-Centered Politics: Presidential Elections of the 1980s. *p.550, p.556*
The Rise of Christian Democracy in Europe. *p.601*
The Rise of Commercial Empires: England and the Netherlands in the Age of Mercantilism, 1650-1770. . . . . *p.212*
The Rise of European Liberalism. *p.767*
The Rise of Guardian Democracy: The Supreme Court's Role in Voting Rights Disputes, 1845-1969. . . . . *p.461*
Rise of Literary Journalism in the Eighteenth-Century: Anxious Employment. *p.405*
The Rise of Political Consultants. *p.558*
The Rise of the Parti Quebecois 1967-76. . . . . *p.590*
The Rise of the Rogue Executive: How Good Companies Go Bad and How to Stop the Destruction. . . *p.54, p.72, p.110*
The Rise of the States: Evolution of American State Government. *p.526*
The Rise of the Virtual State: Wealth and Power in the Coming Century.. . . . . *p.498*
Rising above Sweatshops: Innovative Approaches to Global Labor Challenges. *p.69, p.664*
Rising Up and Rising Down: Some Thoughts on Violence, Freedom, and Urgent Means. *p.751*
Risk and Insurance. *p.163*

Risk and Reason: Safety, Law, and the Environment. p.110, p.111
Risk Management - Wikipedia, the free encyclopedia. . p.92
Risk Regulation at Risk: Restoring a Pragmatic Approach. p.92, p.110, p.111
Risk Taking in International Politics: Prospect Theory in American Foreign Policy. p.642
The Rites of Passage. p.37
Ritual and Religion in the Making of Humanity. p.37
Ritual, Politics and Power. p.765
Rituals of Blood: Consequences of Slavery in Two American Centuries. p.727
The Rivalry: Bill Russell, Wilt Chamberlain, and the Golden Age of Basketball. p.854
Rivers, Streams, Lakes, and Ponds. p.393
The Road Ahead: Middle East Policy in the Bush Administration's Second Term. p.564
The Road from Serfdom: The Economic and Political Consequences of the End of Communism. p.507
Road Not Taken: A History of Radical Social Work in the United States. p.758
The Road to Maastricht: Negotiating Economic and Monetary Union. p.629, p.637
The Road to Martyrs' Square: A Journey into the World of the Suicide Bomber. p.661
The Road to Serfdom. p.243
The Road to the White House: Electing the American President. p.526
The Road to Whatever: Middle-Class Culture and the Crisis of Adolescence. p.723
The Roads of Chinese Childhood: Learning and Identification in Angang. p.40
The Roads to Congress 2000. . . . . p.529
The Roaring 90s: A New History of the World's Most Prosperous Decade. p.256
Robert E. Lee: A Biography. p.522
Robert Redfield and the Development of American Anthropology. p.5
Roberta's Rules of Order: Sail Through Meetings for Stellar Results Without the Gavel. p.80
Robert's Dictionary of Industrial Relations. p.123
Robert's Rules of Order. p.575
Robin Williams Design Workshop. p.428
Robotnik: A Short History of the Struggle for Worker Self Management and Free Trade Unions in Poland, 1944-1981. . . . . p.129
Rodeo Cowboys in the North American Imagination. . . p.865
Rodeo in America: Wranglers, Roughstock, and Paydirt. p.865, p.881
Roe vs. Wade: The Abortion Rights Controversy in American History. p.439
Rogers Hornsby: A Biography. p.849
Rogues: Two Essays on Reason. p.496, p.509
The Role of Foreign Direct Investment in East Asian Economic Development. p.60
The Role of Self in Teacher Development. p.279
Role of the Legislature in Western Democracies. p.575
The Role of the Reader: Explorations in the Semiotics of Texts (Advances in Semiotics Ser.). p.424
Role of the Supreme Court in American Politics: The Least Dangerous Branch? p.470
The Roles of Evaluation for Vocational Education and Training: Plain Talk in the Field of Dreams. p.305
Roll, Jordan, Roll: The World the Slaves Made. p.729
Roller Skating for Gold. p.844, p.866
The Roman Army: A Social and Institutional History. . . p.718
The Roman Citizenship. p.501
Roman Law in Medieval Europe. p.433, p.501
The Roman Republic in Political Thought. p.489
Romances with Schools: A Life of Education. p.337
Romania in Transition. p.600
Romania since 1989: Politics, Economics, and Society. . . p.600
Romania. p.581
Romantic Motives: Essays on Anthropological Sensibility. . p.5
Roosevelt the Reformer: Theodore Roosevelt As Civil Service Commissioner, 1889-1895. . . . . p.546
The Root and the Branch, Judaism and the Free Society. . p.722
The Roots of Evil: The Origins of Genocide and Other Group Violence. p.715
Roots of Reform: Challenging the Assumptions That Control Change in Education. p.324
Roots of the Bill of Rights: An Illustrated Source Book of American Freedom. p.456
A Rope of Sand: The Colonial Agents, British Politics, and the American Revolution. p.518
The Rope, the Chair and the Needle: Capital Punishment in Texas, 1923-1990. . . . . p.567
Rosa Luxemburg: Her Life and Work. p.193
The Rosa Luxemburg Reader. p.236
Rosa Luxemburg. p.193
The Rosenberg File: A Search for the Truth. p.438
The Rosy Future of War. p.498
Rough Justice: Lynching and American Society, 1874-1947. . . . . p.753
The Roundtable Talks of 1989: The Genesis of Hungarian Democracy. p.595
Rousing Minds to Life: Teaching, Learning, and Schooling in Social Context. p.349
The Routledge Atlas of American History. p.380
The Routledge Atlas of the Arab-Israeli Conflict. p.380
The Routledge Dictionary of Anthropologists. p.3
Routledge Encyclopedia of International Political Economy. p.192
Routledge Library Editions: Anthropology and Ethnology. . p.3
Routledgefalmer Reader in the Philosophy of Education. . p.323
Rowing and Sculling. p.788, p.865
Rowing in England: A Social History: The Amateur Debate. p.816, p.865
Rugby Skills, Tactics and Rules. p.865
Rugby Tough. p.865
Rugby's Great Split: Class, Culture and the Origins of Rugby League Football. p.804, p.814, p.865

Rulemaking: How Government Agencies Write Law and Make Policy. p.463

□ Rules and Procedure. p.532, p.534

The Rules of Federalism: Institutions and Regulatory Politics in the EU and Beyond. p.637

The Rules of Play: National Identity and the Shaping of Japanese Leisure. p.784, p.834, p.898

The Rules of Sociological Method. p.686

Rules of the Game: Global Business Protocol. p.56

Runaway Kids and Teenage Prostitution: America's Lost, Abandoned, and Sexually Exploited Children. p.747

Runner's World Complete Book of Running: Everything You Need to Know to Run for Fun, Fitness and Competition. p.790, p.863, p.866

Running a 21st-Century Small Business: The Owner's Guide to Starting and Growing Your Company. p.87

Running: Biomechanics and Exercise Physiology in Practice. p.878, p.907

Running Past 50. . . . . p.840, p.847, p.866

Rural China. p.771

Rural Dimensions of Welfare Reform: Welfare, Food Assistance, and Poverty in Rural America. p.755

Rural Geography: Processes, Responses and Experiences in Rural Restructuring. p.396

The Rural Landscape. p.395

Rural Mexico. p.772

Rural Problems in the Alpine Region: An International Study.. . . . . p.701

Rural Women Battering and the Justice System: An Ethnography. p.743

The Rush to German Unity. p.609

The Russia Hand: A Memoir of Presidential Diplomacy. . p.646

Russian Crossroads: Toward the New Millennium. p.598

Russian Education: Tradition and Transition. p.335

Russian Fascism: Traditions, Tendencies, Movements. . . p.510

The Russian Landed Gentry and the Peasant Emancipation of 1861. . . . . p.726

Russian Monarchy: Eighteenth-Century Rulers and Writers in Political Dialogue. p.599

The Russian Roots of Nazism: White Émigrés and the Making of National Socialism, 1917-1945. . . . . p.711

Russian Trade Unions and Industrial Relations in Transition. p.124

The Russian Tradition in Education. p.334

Russia's Communists at the Crossroads. p.599, p.600

Russia's Engagement with the West. p.644

Ruth Benedict: Beyond Relativity, Beyond Pattern. p.5

Rwanda and Genocide in the Twentieth Century. p.652

The Rwanda Crisis: History of a Genocide. p.653

S

Sacred Canopy: Elements of a Sociological Theory of Religion. p.719

Sacred Dreams: Women and the Superintendency. p.281

Sacred Hoops: Spiritual Lessons of a Hardwood Warrior. p.802, p.854

A Sacred Trust: The League of Nations and Africa, 1929-1946. . . . . p.631

The Sacred Void: Spatial Images of Work and Ritual among the Giriama of Kenya. p.38

Safe Passage into the Twenty-First Century: The United Nations' Quest for Peace, Equality, Justice and Development. p.634

Safe: The Race to Protect Ourselves in a Newly Dangerous World. p.561

Safeguarding the Ozone Layer and the Global Climate System: Special Report of the Intergovernmental Panel on Climate Change. p.394

Safety in Ice Hockey. p.862, p.870, p.871

The SAGE Dictionary of Cultural Studies. p.676

The SAGE Encyclopedia of Social Science Research Methods. p.686

The SAGE Handbook of Nonverbal Communication. . . p.424

Sales and Marketing Management: Survey of Buying Power. p.138, p.142

Sales Forecasting Management: A Demand Management Approach. p.137

Saloon: Public Drinking in Chicago and Boston, 1880-1920. . . . . p.699

Salt of the Earth, Conscience of the Court: The Story of Justice Wiley Rutledge. p.536

Same-Sex Unions in Premodern Europe. p.739

Sampling in Archaeology. p.7

Samuel Gompers, American Statesman. p.129

Samuel Gompers and Organized Labor in America. . . . p.127

Samuelson and Neo-Classical Economics. p.213

Sanctions for Evil: Sources of Social Destructiveness. . . p.683

Sands of Time: The History of Beach Volleyball: 1895-1969. . . . . p.869

Sands of Time: The History of Beach Volleyball: 1970-1989, 2.. . . . . p.869

Sands of Time: The History of Beach Volleyball: 1990-2004, Vol. 3. . . . . p.869

The Sane Society. p.775

Sanity and Survival in the Nuclear Age: Psychological Aspects of War and Peace. p.647, p.649

Santeria: The Religion. p.722

The Sarbanes-Oxley Act: Implications for Records Management. p.115

Sarbanes-Oxley and the Board of Directors: Techniques and Best Practices for Corporate Governance. p.86

Satellite Communications for the Nonspecialist. p.421

Satellite Communications: The First Quarter Century of Service. p.421

Satellite Communications. p.421

Satellite Technology: An Introduction. p.421

Satisfaction Guaranteed: The Making of the American Mass Market. p.140

Savage Inequalities: Children in America's Schools. p.302, p.315

A Savage War of Peace: Algeria 1954-1962. . . . . . . p.584

The Savage Within: The Social History of British Anthropology, 1885-1945. . . . . p.4
Saving America?: Faith-Based Services and the Future of Civil Society. p.755
Saving Strangers: Humanitarian Intervention in International Society. p.671
Saving the Planet: The American Response to the Environment in the Twentieth Century. p.62
The Savvy Negotiator: Building Win/Win Relationships. . p.74
Say It with Charts: The Executive's Guide to Visual Communication. p.174
The Scalawags: Southern Dissenters in the Civil War and Reconstruction. p.519
The Scandals of Translation: Towards an Ethics of Difference. p.709
Scars of War, Wounds of Peace: The Israeli-Arab Tragedy. p.646, p.648
Scattered Be-Longings: Cultural Paradoxes of Race, Nation and Gender. p.31, p.709
Scenario Planning: The Link Between Future and Strategy. . p.82
Scenes from the High Desert: Julian Steward's Life and Theory. p.4
Schaum's Outline of Mathematical Methods for Business and Economics. p.175
The Scheduled Castes. p.707
Scheduling Strategies for Middle Schools. p.288
Scholarly Sport Sites: A Subject Directory. . . p.790, p.794
Scholarship and Christian Faith: Enlarging the Conversation. p.307
Scholarship Assessed and Reconsidered Set. . . . p.292, p.330
The School and Society. p.342
School Choice and Diversity: What the Evidence Says. . p.367
School Choice and Social Justice. p.346
School Choice in Urban America: Magnet Schools and the Pursuit of Equity. p.367
School Choice Tradeoffs: Liberty, Equity, and Diversity. . p.298
School Community Relations,Under Reform. p.303
School Desegregation in the Twenty-First Century: The Focus Must Change. p.300
School Discipline and School Violence: The Teacher Variance Approach. p.284
School Experiences of Gay and Lesbian Youth: The Invisible Minority. p.309
School Prayer and Discrimination: The Civil Rights of Religious Minorities and Dissenters. p.450
School Principals and Change. p.280, p.282
The School Promoters: Education and Social Class in Mid-Nineteenth Century Upper Canada. p.336
School Psychology at a Turning Point: Ensuring a Bright Future for the Profession. p.353
School Psychology: Essentials of Theory and Practice. . . p.356
School Social Work Worldwide. p.757
School Spending: The Business of Education. p.280
School: The Story of American Public Education Series. p.324
School: The Story of American Public Education. p.328
School Violence: From Discipline to Due Process. p.283
School Violence Intervention: A Practical Handbook. . . p.284
School Vouchers and Privatization: A Reference Handbook. p.299
Schoolbook Nation: Conflicts over American History Textbooks from the Civil War to the Present. p.285
Schooled to Order: A Social History of Public Schooling in the United States. p.328
Schooled to Work: Vocationalism and the American Curriculum, 1876-1946. p.305
Schooling America: How the Public Schools Meet the Nation's Changing Needs.. . . . . p.326
Schooling Disadvantaged Children: Racing Against Catastrophe. p.299
Schooling in Capitalist America : Educational Reform and the Contradictions of Economic life. p.762
Schooling the Symbolic Animal: Social and Cultural Dimensions of Education. p.302
Schools for Our Time: The Local Classroom in an Uncertain World. p.303
The Schools, the Courts, and the Public Interest. p.450
The Schools We Deserve: Reflections on the Educational Crisis of Our Time. p.328
The Schools We Need: And Why We Don't Have Them. . p.327
Schumpeter, Social Scientist. p.211, p.230, p.235
Schumpeterian Dynamics and Metropolitan-Scale Productivity. p.230, p.235
Schumpeterian Economics. p.230, p.235
Schumpeterian Puzzles: Technological Competition and Economic Evolution. p.230, p.234
The Schumpeterian System. p.230, p.235
Schumpeter's Theory of Capitalist Motion: A Critical Exposition and Reassessment. p.230
Schumpeter's Vision: Capitalism, Socialism, and Democracy after 40 Years. p.230, p.234
Science and Practice of Strength Training. p.880, p.908
Science and Racket Sports. p.864, p.870
Science and Soccer. p.868, p.872, p.880
Science Education of American Girls: A Historical Perspective. p.367
Science for Exercise and Sport. p.874
Science K-8: An Integrated Approach. p.366
Science, Magic, and Religion: The Ritual Process of Museum Magic. p.47
Science of Education and the Psychology of the Child. . . p.345
Science of Flexibility. p.827, p.828, p.872
The Science of Political Economy. p.209
The Science of Soccer. p.868, p.871
Science, Philosophy and Physical Geography. p.375
Science, Technology, and Society: An Encyclopedia. . . . p.678
Science under Siege: The Politicians' War on Nature and Truth. p.566
The Scientific Basis of the Art of Teaching. p.347
The Scopes Trial: A Brief History with Documents. . . . p.438
Scoring Points: Politicians, Activists, and the Lower Federal Court Appointment Process. p.525
Scoring Rubrics in the Classroom: Using Performance Criteria for Assessing and Improving Student Performance. . . p.285

Scottish Education in the Twentieth Century. p.336
Scottsboro: A Tragedy of the American South. p.438
Scramble for Africa... . . . . p.583
Scribble Scrabble, Learning to Read and Write: Success with Diverse Teachers, Children and Families. p.361
Scuba Diving. p.787, p.847
SDP: The Birth, Life, and Death of the Social Democratic Party. p.606
A Sealed and Secret Kinship: The Culture of Policies and Practices in American Adoption. p.32
Search and Destroy: African-American Males in the Criminal Justice System. p.730
The Search for Arab Democracy: Discourses and Counter-Discourses. p.615
The Search: How Google and Its Rivals Rewrote the Rules of Business and Transformed Our Culture. p.157
Searching for Peace in Central and South Asia: An Overview of Conflict Prevention and Peacebuilding Activities. p.623, p.650
A Season for Justice: The Life and Times of Civil Rights Lawyer Morris Dees. p.441
Seasoned Judgments: Constitutional Rights and American History. p.452
The Seasons of a Man's Life. p.741
The Seasons of a Woman's Life. p.741
Seats and Votes: The Effects and Determinants of Electoral Systems. p.578
The Second Amendment in Law and History: Historians and Constitutional Scholars on the Right to Bear Arms. . . p.449
Second Chambers. p.574
A Second Chicago School?: The Development of a Postwar American Sociology. p.682
A Second Edition of the General Theory, Vol. 1. . . . . . p.227
Second Home: Life in a Boarding School. p.297
The Second Information Revolution. p.420
The Second Sex. p.743
Secondary Schools at the Turn of the Century. . . p.329, p.367
The Secret of Childhood. p.344
The Secret of Natural Readers: How Preschool Children Learn to Read. p.370
The Secret Societies of All Ages and Countries. p.719
The Secretariat of the United Nations. p.632
Secrets of Customer Relationship Management: It's All about How You Make Them Feel. p.143
The Secrets of Great Sales Management: Advanced Strategies for Maximizing Performance. p.143
Secrets of Special Ops Leadership: Dare the Impossible—Achieve the Extraordinary. p.70
Secrets of the Soul: A Social and Cultural History of Psychoanalysis. p.692
Secrets of the Temple: How the Federal Reserve Runs the Country. p.246
Secure Base: Parent-Child Attachment and Healthy Human Development. p.735
Security Analysis. p.94
The Security Dilemmas of Southeast Asia. p.643
The Seduction of Unreason: The Intellectual Romance with Fascism from Nietzsche to Postmodernism. p.510
Seedtime for Fascism: The Disintegration of Austrian Political Culture, 1867-1918. . . . . p.510, p.595
Seeing the Newspaper. p.409
Seeing What's Next: Using the Theories of Innovation to Predict Industry Change. p.65, p.81
Seeking Common Ground: Public Schools in a Diverse Society. p.298
Seeking Justices: The Judging of Supreme Court Nominees. p.535
Selected Papers in Anthropology. p.3
Selected Papers on Economic Theory. p.241
Selected Papers. p.197
Selected Political Writings [of] Rosa Luxemburg. p.236
A Selected Socio-Legal Bibliography on Ethnic Cleansing, Wartime Rape, and Genocide in the Former Yugoslavia and Rwanda. p.654
Selected Writings of Edward Sapir in Language, Culture, and Personality. p.20
Selecting the President: From 1789 to 1996. . . . . . . p.526
Self and Social Identity. p.693
Self-Determination and the Social Education of Native Americans. p.312
Selling Destinations: Geography for the Travel Professional. p.161
Selling It!: The Incredible Shrinking Package and Other Marvels of Modern Marketing. p.144
The Selling of Supreme Court Nominees. p.537
Selling the Five Rings: The IOC and the Rise of Olympic Commercialism. p.845, p.886, p.890, p.901
Selling the Sea: An Inside Look at the Cruise Industry. . p.161
Selling War: The British Propaganda Campaign Against American Neutrality in World War II. p.643, p.646
Selling Without Selling: 4 1/2 Steps to Success. p.143
Semiparametric Regression for the Applied Econometrician. p.205
Senate Elections and Campaign Intensity. p.550, p.557
The Senate of Imperial Rome. p.501
Senators on the Campaign Trail: The Politics of Representation. p.550, p.557
Seneca: A Philosopher in Politics. p.489
Senior Fitness Test Manual. p.841, p.880
Sense and Nonsense about Crime and Drugs: A Policy Guide. p.568
Sense of Siege: The Geopolitics of Islam and the West. p.488, p.495
Senseless Acts of Beauty: Cultures of Resistence since the Sixties. p.709
Sensuous Scholarship: Contemporary Ethnography. p.25
Separate and Unequal: Black Americans and the U. S. Federal Government. p.524
Separate but Unequal: Homer Plessy and the Supreme Court Decision that Legalized Racism. p.536
Separation, Assimilation, or Accommodation: Contrasting Ethnic Minority Policies. p.764

The Separation of Commercial and Investment Banking: The Glass-Steagall Act Revisited and Reconsidered. *p.90*
September 11: Consequences for Canada. *p.661*
September 11 in History: A Watershed Moment? *p.563*
Serenade of Suffering: A Portrait of Middle East Terrorism, 1968-1993. . . . . *p.658*
Serious Cycling. *p.856*
Serious Fun: A History of Spectator Sport in the U. S. S. R. *p.805*
Serious Play: How the World's Best Companies Simulate to Innovate. *p.67*
Serious Strength Training. *p.792, p.878*
Serious Tennis. *p.864*
Servants of the State: Managing Diversity and Democracy in the Federal Workforce, 1933-1953. . . . . *p.546*
Service-Learning: From Classroom to Community to Career. *p.168*
Setting the Agenda: The Mass Media and Public Opinion. . *p.697*
Setting the Record Straight: Responses to Misconceptions about Public Education in the United States. *p.325*
Settlement Ecology: The Social and Spatial Organization of Kofyar Agriculture. *p.38*
The Settlement of the Americas: A New Prehistory. *p.11*
The Set-up-to-Fail Syndrome: How Good Managers Cause Great People to Fail. *p.131*
[e] The Seven Myths of Customer Management: How to be Customer-Driven Without Being Customer-Led. . . . *p.143*
Seven Schools of Macroeconomic Thought: The Arne Ryde Memorial Lectures. *p.240*
Several Papers Relating to Money, Interest and Trade, Etc. . *p.216*
Sex, Age, and Work: The Changing Composition of the Labor Force. *p.254, p.269*
Sex and Advantage: A Comparative, Macro-Structural Theory of Sex Stratification. *p.747*
Sex and Gender. *p.746*
Sex and Manners: Female Emancipation in the West 1890 - 2000. . . . . *p.738*
Sex and Marriage in Utopian Communities : 19th Century America. *p.733*
Sex and Psyche: Gender and Self Viewed Cross-Culturally. *p.693*
Sex and Repression in Savage Society. *p.737*
Sex and Society. *p.749*
Sex and Temperament: In Three Primitive Societies. . . . *p.23*
Sex and the Workplace: The Impact of Sexual Behavior and Harassment on Women, Men, and Organizations. . . . *p.253*
Sex Bias in the Schools: The Research Evidence. *p.301*
Sex Changes: Transgender Politics. *p.746*
Sex in the Marketplace. *p.273*
Sex, Politics and Society: The Regulation of Sexuality since 1800. *p.570, p.749*
Sex Roles, Life Styles and Childbearing: Changing Patterns in Marriage and the Family. *p.734*
Sex, Violence, and Power in Sports: Rethinking Masculinity. *p.818*
Sexing the Body: Gender Politics and the Construction of Sexuality. *p.747*
Sexual Behavior in the Human Female. *p.748*
Sexual Behavior in the Human Male. *p.748*
Sexual Development in Childhood. *p.746*
Sexual (Dis)Orientation: Gender, Sex, Desire and Self-Fashioning. *p.750*
Sexual Harassment in American Secondary Schools: A Legal Guide for Administrators, Teachers, and Students. . . *p.450*
Sexual Harassment in Higher Education: Reflections and New Perspectives. *p.301*
Sexual Harassment in Workplace. *p.130*
The Sexual Harassment of Women in the Workplace, 1600-1993. . . . . *p.131*
Sexual Harassment of Working Women: A Case of Sex Discrimination. *p.446*
Sexual Harassment. *p.458*
Sexual Identity on the Job: Issues and Services. *p.133*
The Sexual Organization of the City. *p.748*
Sexual Politics, Sexual Communities. *p.749*
Sexual Practices and the Medieval Church. *p.746*
Sexual Variance in Society and History. *p.746*
Sexuality: A Glossary. *p.677*
Shace and Epstein's Business Structures in a Nutshell. . . *p.110*
Shades of Freedom: Racial Politics and Presumptions of the American Legal Process Race. *p.457*
Shades of Loneliness: Pathologies of a Technological Society. *p.695*
The Shadow of Keynes: Understanding Keynes, Cambridge, and Keynesian Economics. *p.228*
The Shadow World: Life Between the News Media and Reality. *p.412*
Shake Hands with the Devil: The Failure of Humanity in Rwanda. *p.715*
Shakespeare and Young Learner. *p.365*
Shamanism: An Encyclopedia of World Beliefs, Practices, and Culture. *p.37*
Shamans and Religion: An Anthropological Exploration in Critical Thinking. *p.36*
The Shame of the Nation: The Restoration of Apartheid Schooling in America. *p.315*
The Shape of Culture: A Study of Contemporary Cultural Patterns in the United States. *p.712*
The Shape of the River: Long-Term Consequences of Considering Race in College and University Admissions. *p.294*
Shaping American Telecommunications: A History of Technology, Policy, and Economics. *p.166, p.421*
Shaping Constitutional Values: Elected Government, the Supreme Court, and the Abortion Debate. *p.447*
Shaping Information: The Rhetoric of Visual Conventions. . *p.423*
The Shaping of American Higher Education: Emergence and Growth of the Contemporary System. *p.331*
The Shaping of the American High School, 1880-1920, Vol. 1. . . . . *p.327*
The Shaping of the American High School, 1920-1941, Vol. 2. . . . . *p.327*
Shaping the Adaptive Organization: Landscapes, Learning and Leadership in Volatile Times. *p.78*

Shaping the College Curriculum: Academic Plans in Action. p.295

Shaping the Eighteenth Amendment: Temperance Reform, Legal Culture, and the Polity, 1880-1920. . . . . p.449

Shaping the Industrial Century: The Remarkable Story of the Evolution of the Modern Chemical and Pharmaceutical Industries. p.146, p.157

Shaping the World Economy: Suggestions for an International Economy Policy. p.256

Shaping Tomorrow's Family: Theory and Policy for the 21st Century.. . . . . p.734

Shaping Women's Work: Gender, Employment and Information Technology. p.761

Shaping Your HR Role: Succeeding in Today's Organizations. p.76

Shared Beginnings, Divergent Lives: Delinquent Boys to Age 70. . . . . p.753

Shared Leadership: Reframing the How's and Why's of Leadership. p.80

Shared Visions, Shared Lives: Communal Living Around the Globe. p.740

Shattered Dreams: The Failure of the Peace Process in the Middle East, 1995-2002. . . . . p.649

A Shattered Nation: The Rise and Fall of the Confederacy, 1861-1868. . . . . p.522

Shattering the Myths: Women in Academe. p.293

Shaw on Education. p.345

Sheathing the Sword: The U. N. Secretary-General and the Prevention of Internation Conflict. p.633, p.648

The Shell Game: Reflections on Rowing and the Pursuit of Excellence. p.865

Shifting Fortunes: The Rise and Decline of American Labor, from the 1820s to the Present. p.128

Shifting Languages: Interaction and Identity in Javanese Indonesia. p.21

Shifting the Blame: How Victimization Became a Criminal Defense. p.754

Shopfloor Matters: Labor-Management Relations in 20th Century American Manufacturing. p.121

A Short Course in International Intellectual Property Rights: Protecting Your Brands, Marks, Copyrights, Patents, Designs, and Related Rights Worldwide. p.58, p.110

Short History of Electoral Systems in Western Europe. . . p.601

A Short History of Quebec. p.589

A Short History of Structural Linguistics. p.18

A Short History of the Labour Party. p.606

A Short History of Western Legal Theory. p.434

Shorter Classics. p.234

Should Trees Have Standing?: And Other Essays on Law, Morals and the Environment. p.435

Show Me the Numbers: Designing Tables and Graphs to Enlighten. p.172, p.175

Showdown at Gucci Gulch: Lawmakers, Lobbyists, and the Unlikely Triumph of Tax Reform. p.107

Shrewd Sanctions: Economic Statecraft in An Age of Global Terrorism. p.565

Shut Out: A Story of Race and Baseball in Boston. p.804, p.831, p.849, p.882

Significance of Monuments: On the Shaping of Human Experience in Neolithic and Bronze Age Europe. . . . p.12

[e] The Significance of Territory. p.495

Signs of Resistance: American Deaf Cultural History,1900 to 1942. . . . . p.699

Silent Covenants: Brown v. Board of Education and the Unfulfilled Hopes for Racial Reform. p.449

Silent Justice: The Clarence Thomas Story. p.536

Silent Skies: The Air Traffic Controllers' Strike. p.128

Silent Thunder: Breaking Through Cultural, Racial, and Class Barriers in Motorsports. p.832, p.848

Silent Voices: Public Opinion and Political Participation in America. p.559

Simple Justice: The History of Brown vs Board of Education and Black America's Struggle For Equality. p.450

Simulation and Social Theory. p.690

Singapore Changes Guard. p.623

Singing for Life: HIV/AIDS and Music in Uganda. . . . p.701

Singular and Different: Business in China Past, Present and Future. p.60

Sir Walter and Mr. Jones: Walter Hagen, Bobby Jones and the Rise of American Golf. p.861

Sir Walter: Walter Hagen and the Invention of Professional Golf. p.860

Sister Jamaica: A Study of Women, Work and Households in Kingston.. . . . . p.40

Sister Outsider: Essays and Speeches. p.744

Sit-Down: The General Motors Strike of 1936-1937. . . . p.125

Sites of Sport: Space, Place, Experience. p.813

The Size of Nations. p.247

The Skeptical Business Searcher: The Information Advisor's Guide to Evaluating Web Data, Sites, and Sources. . . p.180

Skill Acquisition in Sport: Research, Theory and Practice. p.874, p.908, p.910

The Skilled Facilitator: A Comprehensive Resource for Consultants, Facilitators, Managers, Trainers, and Coaches. p.174

Skulls and Skeletons: Human Bone Collections and Accumulations. p.15

Slaughter among Neighbors: Political Origins of Communal Violence. p.512, p.613

Slave Laws in Virginia. p.474

Slave Systems of Greek and Roman Antiquity. p.727

Slave Women in Caribbean Society, 1650-1832. . . . . . p.727

Slave Women in the New World: Gender Stratification in the Caribbean. p.728

Slavery and Human Progress. p.727

Slavery and Social Death: A Comparative Study. p.727

Slavery and the Law. p.453

Slavery in Russia, 1450-1725. . . . . p.728

Slavery in the American Mountain South. p.727

Slavery, Secession and Southern History. p.521

Slaves and Missionaries: The Disintegration of Jamaican Slave Society, 1787-1834. . . . . p.728

Slaves and Slavery in Muslim Africa, Vol. 1. . . . . . . p.728

Slaves and Slavery in Muslim Africa, Vol. 2. . . . . . . p.728

☐ Slaves and the courts, 1740-1860. . . . . *p.437*
Slaves of the White God: Blacks in Mexico, 1570-1650. . *p.728*
Sloan Rules: Alfred P. Sloan and the Triumph of General Motors. *p.153*
Sloane's Complete Book of Bicycling: The Cyclist's Bible. *p.857*
The Small Business Start-up Kit. *p.87*
Small Business Start-Up Workbook: A Step-by-Step Guide to Starting the Business You've Dreamed Of. *p.88*
Small Islands, Large Questions: Society, Culture and Resistance in the Post-Emancipation Caribbean. *p.40*
Smart and Simple Financial Strategies for Busy People. . . *p.97*
Smart Business: How Knowledge Communities Can Revolutionize Your Company. *p.77*
Smart Mobs: The Next Social Revolution: Transforming Cultures and Communities in the Age of Instant Access. *p.712*
Smartest Guys in the Room: The Amazing Rise and Scandalous Fall of Enron. *p.91, p.105, p.106, p.109*
The Smell of Sweat: Greek Athletics and Greek Culture. . *p.810*
The Smithsonian and the American Indian: Making a Moral Anthropology in Victorian America. *p.47*
The Sneaker Book: Anatomy of an Industry and an Icon. *p.870, p.881*
So Human an Animal: How We Are Shaped by Surroundings and Events. *p.760*
Soap, Sex, and Cigarettes: A Cultural History of American Advertising. *p.426*
Sober as a Judge: The Supreme Court and Republican Liberty. *p.540*
The Soccer Coaching Bible.. . . . . *p.867, p.905*
Soccer, Women, Sexual Liberation: Kicking off a New Era. *p.836, p.844, p.867*
Soccer. *p.867*
Social and Cultural Anthropology: The Key Concepts. . . *p.23*
Social and Cultural Dynamics. *p.700*
Social and Cultural Mobility. *p.700*
The Social and Educational Thought of Harold Rugg. . . *p.341*
The Social and Emotional Development of Gifted Children: What Do We Know? *p.317*
The Social and Political Conflict in Prussia, 1858-1864. . . . . *p.609, p.610*
The Social and Political Thought of Herbert Spencer. . . *p.686*
The Social Basis of European Fascist Movements. *p.768*
Social Behavior and Personality: Contributions of W. I. Thomas to Theory and Social Research. *p.688*
Social Capital: A Theory of Social Structure and Action. . *p.269*
Social Casework: A Behavioral Approach. *p.758*
Social Causes of Psychological Distress. *p.699*
Social Change and Stratification in Eastern Europe: An Interpretive Analysis of Poland and Her Neighbors. . . *p.705*
Social Change and the Individual: Japan Before and After Defeat in World War II. *p.707*
Social Change in a Yemeni Highlands Town. *p.707*
Social Change in Modern France: Towards a Cultural Anthropology of the Fifth Republic. *p.42*
Social Choice and Individual Values. *p.206, p.272*
Social Class and Social Change in Puerto Rico. *p.707*
Social Class in America: A Manual of Procedure for the Measurement of Social Status. *p.725*
Social Communication in Advertising: Persons, Products and Images of Well-being. *p.140*
Social Conflict and the City. *p.771*
The Social Consequences of Long Life.. . . . . *p.741*
The Social Construction of International News: We're Talking about Them, They're Talking about Us. *p.408*
The Social Construction of Lesbianism.. . . . . *p.750*
The Social Contract and Discourses. *p.492*
Social Contracts under Stress: The Middle Classes of America, Europe, and Japan at the Turn of the Century. *p.725*
Social Control in Europe. *p.773*
Social Control in Slave Plantation Societies: A Comparison of St. Domingue and Cuba. *p.728*
Social Darwinism : Selected Essays. *p.686*
Social Darwinism in American Thought. *p.683, p.685*
Social Death and Resurrection: Slavery and Emancipation in South Africa. *p.727*
Social Diagnosis. *p.758*
Social Ethics: Morality and Social Policy. *p.484, p.770*
Social Ethics: Sociology and the Future of Society. . . . *p.681*
Social Exchange Theory: The Two Traditions. *p.679*
Social Experience and Anthropological Knowledge. *p.25*
Social Foundations of Judiasm. *p.721*
Social Geography of the United States. *p.708*
The Social History of an Indonesian Town. *p.703*
A Social History of Anthropology in the United States. . . . *p.4*
A Social History of British Broadcasting, 1922-1939: Serving the Nation. *p.413*
A Social History of English Rowing. *p.811, p.865*
A Social History of Germany 1648-1914. . . . . *p.706*
A Social History of Leisure Since 1600. . . . . *p.716*
A Social History of Madness: The World Through the Eyes of the Insane. *p.706*
A Social History of Medicines in the Twentieth Century: To Be Taken Three Times a Day. *p.778*
A Social History of Soviet Trade: Trade Policy, Retail Practices, and Consumption, 1917-1953. . . . . *p.257*
A Social History of the American Family from Colonial Times to the Present. *p.732*
Social History of the Media: From Gutenburg to the Internet. *p.415*
Social History of Western Europe, 1450-1720: Tensions and Solidarities Amongst the Rural People. *p.708*
Social Identifications: A Social Psychology of Intergroup Relations and Group Processes. *p.713*
Social Indicators and Social Theory: Elements of an Operational System. *p.769*
Social Inequalities and Cancer. *p.778*
Social Intelligence: The New Science of Success. . *p.119, p.166*
Social Interaction: Process and Products. *p.692*
Social Issues in Contemporary Sport: A Resource Guide. . *p.820*
Social Justice and Third World Education, Vol. 37. . . . *p.314*
Social Learning and Imitation. *p.357*

Social Learning from Broadcast Television. p.418
Social Learning Theory. p.355
The Social Life of a Modern Community. p.725
Social Marketing: Improving the Quality of Life. . p.51, p.134
Social Marketing in the 21st Century. p.51, p.134
The Social Meaning of Money: Pin Money, Paychecks, Poor Relief, and Other Currencies. p.718
The Social Meanings of Suicide. p.693
Social Mobility in Britain. p.703
Social Mobility in Industrial Society. p.722, p.726
Social Movements, 1768-2004.. . . . . p.712
Social Movements and Culture : A Resource Site. . . p.710
Social Movements and Organization Theory. p.718
Social Movements in India: A Review of the Literature. . p.711
The Social Order of the Slum: Ethnicity and Territory in the Inner City. p.707
Social Organization: A Study of the Larger Mind. p.693
The Social Organization of Gay Males. p.749
The Social Organization of Mental Illness, Vol. 1. . . . . p.775
The Social Organization of Sexuality: Sexual Practices in the United States. p.748
Social Origins of Dictatorship and Democracy: Lord and Peasant in the Making of the Modern World. p.767
The Social Origins of Private Life: A History of American Families, 1600-1900. . . . . p.732
The Social Origins of the Modern Middle East. p.703
Social Pressures in Informal Groups: A Study of Human Factors in Housing. p.718
Social Problems. p.209, p.750
The Social Production of Indifference: Exploring the Symbolic Roots of Western Bureaucracy. p.718
The Social Psychology of Good and Evil. p.698
The Social Psychology of Intergroup and International Conflict Resolution. p.698
The Social Psychology of Interpersonal Discrimination. . p.698
The Social Psychology of Organizations. p.716
Social Research Methods, Feminist Perspectives. p.688
Social Responsibility in Marketing: A Proactive and Profitable Marketing Management Strategy. p.145
Social Science Electronic Data Library. p.689
Social Security and the Golden Age: An Essay on the New American Demographic. p.247
Social Security, Medicare and Government Pensions: Get the Most Out of Your Retirement and Medical Benefits. p.96, p.98
Social statics; or, the conditions essential to human happiness specified, and the first of them developed. by Herbert Spencer ... with a notice of the author and a steel Portrait. p.684
Social Stratification, Class, Race, and Gender in Sociological Perspective. p.722
Social Stratification in Africa. p.707
Social Stratification in India: Issues and Themes. p.706
The Social Structures of the Economy. p.208
Social Studies for Children: A Guide to Basic Instruction. . p.363
Social Studies in Elementary Education. p.365
The Social Studies Wars: What Should We Teach the Children? p.362
Social Theory and Social Structure. p.699
Social Theory in Archaeology. p.6
Social Theory of International Politics. p.627
Social Theory: The Multicultural and Classic Readings. . p.675
Social Things: An Introduction to the Sociological Life. . p.683
Social Work Abstracts. p.757
The Social Work Interview: A Guide for Human Service Professionals. p.757
Social Worlds of Children Learning to Write in an Urban Primary School. p.360
Socialism: Past and Future. p.506
Socialism Unbound. p.506
Socialism: What Went Wrong?: An Inquiry into the Theoretical and Historical Sources of the Socialist Crisis. p.507
Socialism. p.506
Socialization for Achievement: Essays on the Cultural Psychology of the Japanese. p.702
Society and Democracy in Germany. p.701
Society and Health in Guyana: The Sociology of Health Care in a Developing Nation.. . . . . p.702
Society, Culture and Personality: Their Structure and Dynamics.. . . . . p.683
Society in Prehistory: The Origins of Human Culture. . . . p.17
The Society of Nations: Its Past, Present, and Possible Future. p.631
Society Online: The Internet in Context. p.425
Society, Politics, and Economic Development: A Quantitative Approach. p.258
A Society Without Fathers or Husbands: The Na of China.. p.32
SOCindex. p.675
Socio-Economics: Toward a New Synthesis. p.269
SocioLog : Julian Dierkes' Comprehensive Guide to Sociology On-line. p.675
Sociological Abstracts. p.675
Sociological Ambivalence and Other Essays. p.680
The Sociological Imagination. p.681
A Sociological Perspective of Sport. p.817
Sociological Theories of Today. p.680
Sociological Theory: A Book of Readings. p.679
Sociological Theory and Modern Society. p.680
Sociological Theory: Contemporary Debates. p.682
Sociological Theory: What Went Wrong?: Diagnosis and Remedies. p.680
The Sociological Tradition. p.683
A Sociological View of Sovereignty: A Series of Articles in the American Journal of Sociology, 1899-1900. . . . . . p.249
Sociological Writings. p.685
Sociology : A Mulitple Paradigm Science. p.683
Sociology and Development. p.258
Sociology and Nature: Social Action in Context. p.680
Sociology and Philosophy. p.685
Sociology and Pragmatism: The Higher Learning in America. p.762

The Sociology and Professionalization of Economics: British and American Economic Essays. p.268
The Sociology and Psychology of Terrorism: Who Becomes a Terrorist and Why? p.767
Sociology and the Twilight of Man: Homocentrism and Discourse in Sociological Theory. p.685
Sociology as an Art Form. p.680
Sociology, Ethnomethodology, and Experience : A Phenomenological Critique. p.688
☐ Sociology in Latin America. p.704
Sociology in the Soviet Union and Beyond: Social Enquiry and Social Change. p.684
The Sociology of Andrew M. Greeley. p.720
Sociology of Deviant Behavior. p.695
The Sociology of Economic Life. p.185
Sociology of Education and Work. p.304, p.761
The Sociology of Food: Eating, Diet and Culture. p.778
The Sociology of Gambling. p.777
The Sociology of Georg Simmel. p.686
The Sociology of Health, Illness, and Health Care: A Critical Approach. p.774
The Sociology of HIV Transmission. p.779
Sociology of Leisure. p.716
The Sociology of Marx. p.680
The Sociology of Medicine. p.778
The Sociology of Religion. p.720
The Sociology of Revolution. p.760
The Sociology of Risk and Gambling Reader. p.715
The Sociology of Secret Societies: Chinese Secret Societies in Singapore and Peninsular Malaysia. p.719
Sociology of Slavery. p.727
The Sociology of Sport and Physical Education: An Introductory Reader. p.796, p.817
The Sociology of the Palestinians. p.708
The Sociology of the Third World: Disparity and Development. p.759
The Sociology of War and Peace. p.766
The Sociology of Work. p.717
Sociology: The Core, with PowerWeb. p.675
Sociology. p.675
Socrates and the State. p.489
Socrates' Muse: Reflections on Effective Case Discussion Leadership. p.177
Socrates, Sport, and Students: A Philosophical Inquiry into Physical Education and Sport. p.794
Soft News Goes to War: Public Opinion and American Foreign Policy in the New Media Age. p.414, p.559
Sol White's History of Colored Base Ball, with Other Documents on the Early Black Game, 1886-1936. . . . . p.810, p.833, p.852
The Soldier and the State in South America: Essays in Civil-Military Relations. p.593
Soldiers and Civilians: The Civil-Military Gap and American National Security. p.561
Soldiers and Society: The Effects of Military Service and War on American Life. p.717
Soldiers of Diplomacy (Les Casques Bleus): The United Nations, Peacekeeping and the New World Order. p.633, p.648
Solidarity: Poland's Independent Trade Union. p.127
Solving Discipline and Classroom Management Problems: Methods and Models for Today's Teachers. p.284
Somalia—The Untold Story: The War Through the Eyes of Somali Women. p.652
Some Aspects of the Tariff Question: An Examination of the Development of American Industries Under Protection. . p.258
Some Principles of Regional Planning. p.260
Some Thoughts Concerning Education. p.216, p.343
Something Left to Lose: Personal Relations and Survival Among New York's Homeless. p.737, p.750
The Sometime Connection: Public Opinion and Social Policy. p.567
Sooner or Later: The Timing of Parenthood in Adult Lives. p.736
The Sorting Machine: National Educational Policy since 1945. . . . . p.329
☐ SOSIG : Sociology. p.675
The Soul of Education: Helping Students Find Connection, Compassion and Character at School. p.357, p.364
The Soul of the American University: From Protestant Establishment to Established Non-Belief. p.331
Sourcebook of County Demographics. p.138
The Sourcebook of Nonverbal Measures: Going Beyond Words. p.424
Sources: Notable Selections in Race and Ethnicity. p.17
☐ Sources of Information in Transportation. p.166
South Africa Belongs to Us: A History of the ANC. . . . p.614
South Asians in the Diaspora: Histories and Religious Traditions. p.764
South Carolina at the Brink. p.541
South Pacific.. . . . . p.385
The South vs. the South: How Anti-Confederate Southerners Shaped the Course of the Civil War. p.520
South-East Asia: A Political Profile. p.622
Southeast Asia: From Prehistory to History. p.13
Southeast Asia: People, Land and Economy. p.384
Southeast Asia: The Human Landscape of Modernization and Development. p.384
Southern Justice. p.457
Southern Parties and Elections: Studies in Regional Political Change. p.551, p.554
Southern Rights: Political Prisoners and the Myth of Confederate Constitutionalism. p.521
Southern Slavery and the Law, 1619-1860. . . . . p.442
Southern Stories: Slaveholders in Peace and War. p.520
Southern Strategies: Southern Women and the Woman Suffrage Question. p.519, p.568
Sovereign Bodies: Citizens, Migrants, and States in the Postcolonial World. p.34
The Sovereign Map: Theoretical Approaches in Cartography throughout History. p.385
The Sovereign Prerogative: The Supreme Court and the Quest for Law. p.470

The Sovereign State and Its Competitors: An Analysis of Systems Change. p.496
Sovereign Virtue: The Theory and Practice of Equality. . p.514
Sovereigns and Surrogates: Constitutional Heads of State in the Commonwealth. p.605
Sovereignty and Authenticity: Manchukuo and the East Asian Modern. p.496
The Soviet Elite from Lenin to Gorbachev: The Central Committee and Its Members, 1917-1991. . . . . . . p.598
Soviet Foreign Policy, the League of Nations and Europe, 1917-1939. . . . . p.631, p.645
Soviet Marxism: A Critical Analysis. p.508
Soviet Political Indoctrination: Developments in Mass Media and Propaganda Since Stalin. p.703
The Soviet Tragedy: A History of Socialism in Russia 1917-1991. . . . . p.508, p.598
Space and Place: The Perspective of Experience. p.375
Space and Social Theory: Interpreting Modernity and Postmodernity. p.377
Space, Geography, and Politics in the Early Roman Empire. p.377
Spain after Franco: The Making of a Competitive Party System. p.608
Spanish Colonial Administration, 1782-1810: The Intendant System in the Viceroyalty of the Rio De la Plata, 5. . p.592
The Spark: Igniting the Creative Fire That Lives Within Us All. p.65
Spatial Disparities in Human Development: Perspectives from Asia. p.397
The Spatial Factor in African History: The Relationship of the Social, Material, and Perceptual. p.384
Spatial Interaction Theory and Planning Models. p.202
Spatial Statistics for Remote Sensing. p.389
Spatially Integrated Social Science. p.375
Speak Like a CEO: Secrets for Commanding Attention and Getting Results. p.171
The Speaker and the Budget: Leadership in the Post-Reform House of Representatives. p.533
The Speaker: Leadership in the U. S. House of Representatives. p.533
The Speakers of the U. S. House of Representatives: A Bibliography, Seventeen Eighty-Nine to Nineteen Eighty-Four. p.533
Speaking Back: The Free Speech Versus Hate Speech Debate. p.423
Speaking into the Air: A History of the Idea of Communication. p.416
Speaking of Ethnography. p.25
Speaking Truth to Power. p.441
Special Education in the 21st Century: Issues of Inclusion and Reform. p.316
Special Education Law. p.450
The Special Educator's Book of Lists. p.316
Special Educator's Complete Guide to 109 Diagnostic Tests: How to Select and Interpret Tests, Use Results in IEPs and Remediate Specific Difficulties. p.316
Species Invasions: Insights into Ecology, Evolution, and Biogeography. p.394
The Spectacle of U. S. Senate Campaigns. . p.530, p.551, p.557
The Specter of Genocide: Mass Murder in Historical Perspective. p.652
Spectral Analysis of Economic Time Series. p.206
Speculative Management: Stock Market Power and Corporate Change. p.86
Speech and Law in a Free Society. p.459
Speech Play and Verbal Art. p.19
Speeches and Speechmakers. p.422
Spheres of Justice: A Defense of Pluralism and Equality. . p.514
Spinning Wheels: The Politics of Urban School Reform. . p.315
The Spirit Catches You and You Fall Down: A Hmong Child, Her American Doctors, and the Collision of Two Cultures. p.778
Spirit Fruit: A Gentle Utopia. p.499
The Spirit of Community: Rights, Responsibilities, and the Communitarian Agenda. p.768
The Spirit of Liberty. p.437
The Spirit of the Common Law. p.434
The Spirits of America: A Social History of Alcohol. . . p.709
A Spiritual Audit of Corporate America: A Hard Look at Spirituality, Religion, and Values in the Workplace. p.52, p.54
Spiritual Development in the State School: A Perspective on Worship and Spirituality in the Education System of England and Wales. p.333
Spirituality of Sport: Balancing Body and Soul. . . p.803, p.865
Split Image: African Americans in the Mass Media. . . . p.416
Spoilsports: Understanding and Preventing Sexual Exploitation in Sport. p.814, p.840
Spoken Discourse and Social Interaction. p.423
Spontaneous Activity in Education. p.344
Spontaneous Apprentices: Children and Language. p.357
Sport: A Critical Sociology. p.815
Sport; a Philosophic Inquiry. p.803
Sport and American Mentality, 1880-1910. . . . . p.808, p.818
Sport and American Society. p.819
Sport and Broadcasting: Economic, Legal, and Technological Developments in the Digital Age. . . . p.882, p.887, p.901
Sport and Canadian Diplomacy. p.891, p.898
Sport and Exercise Psychology. p.877
Sport and Exercise Science: Essays in the History of Sports Medicine. p.803, p.825, p.873
Sport and Gender in Canada. p.820
Sport and Information Technology, Vol. 4. . . . . p.812
Sport and International Politics. p.844, p.892, p.899
Sport and Memory in North America. p.811, p.820
Sport and Modern Social Theorists: Theorizing Homo Ludens. p.715, p.815
Sport and Physical Education in China. p.796
Sport and Politics in Canada: Federal Government Involvement since 1961. . . . . p.588
Sport and Recreation in Ancient Greece: A Sourcebook With Translations. p.810, p.813
Sport and Society: A Student Introduction. p.816
Sport and the British: A Modern History. p.806

Sport and the Color Line: Black Athletes and Race Relations in Twentieth Century America. *p.818, p.832*
Sport and the Spirit of Play in Contemporary American Fiction. *p.812*
Sport and Women: Social Issues in International Perspective. *p.716, p.816, p.836*
Sport Business in the Global Marketplace: A Study of Strategic Cognition. *p.845, p.886, p.892, p.899*
Sport, Culture and the Media: The Unruly Trinity. . *p.819, p.902*
Sport, Economy and Society in Britain 1750-1914. . . . . *p.810, p.889, p.892*
Sport Ethics: Applications for Fair Play with PowerWeb Bind-In Passcard. *p.802*
Sport Facility Management: Organizing Events and Mitigating Risks. *p.880, p.882*
Sport Facility Planning and Management. *p.880, p.883*
Sport Finance. *p.884, p.888, p.891*
Sport Governance. *p.884, p.891*
Sport, Health and Drugs: A Critical Sociological Perspective. *p.820, p.826*
Sport in America: From Wicked Amusement to National Obsession. *p.811*
Sport in Canada: A History. *p.808*
Sport in Contemporary Society (P): An Anthology. . . . *p.815*
Sport in Cuba: The Diamond in the Rough. . *p.885, p.892, p.899*
Sport in Greece and Rome. *p.806*
Sport in Industrial America, 1850-1920. . . . . *p.809*
Sport in Latin American Society: Past and Present. . . . *p.716*
Sport in Social Development: Traditions, Transitions, and Transformations. *p.816*
Sport in the Global Village. *p.845, p.899*
Sport Inside Out: Readings in Literature and Philosophy. *p.803, p.812*
Sport, Leisure and Tourism Information Sources: A Guide for Researchers. *p.161, p.785, p.813*
Sport Management Field Experiences. *p.905*
Sport Marketing. *p.885*
Sport Matters: Sociological Studies of Sport, Violence, and Civilisation. *p.815*
Sport, Media, Culture: Global and Local Dimensions. *p.817, p.844, p.902*
Sport Nutrition: An Introduction to Energy Production and Performance. *p.876*
Sport, Physical Activity and the Law. . . . *p.795, p.883, p.900*
Sport, Play, and Ethical Reflection. *p.715*
Sport, Power and Culture: A Social and Historical Analysis of Popular Sports in Britain. *p.816*
Sport Progressions. *p.797*
Sport Promotion and Sales Management. *p.906*
Sport Psychology: Concepts and Applications. *p.877*
Sport Psychology: Contemporary Themes. *p.877*
Sport Psychology in Practice. *p.876*
Sport Psychology: The Key Concepts. *p.877*
Sport Psychology. *p.877*
Sport Public Relations: Managing Organizational Communication. *p.886, p.903, p.907*
☐ Sport Science. *p.870*
Sport Technology: History, Philosophy and Policy. *p.870*
Sportcult. *p.817*
Sporting Equality: Title IX Thirty Years Later. *p.809, p.822, p.838, p.901*
Sporting Females: Critical Issues in the History and Sociology of Women's Sports. *p.806, p.816, p.836*
Sporting Muse: A Critical Study of Poetry About Athletes and Athletics. *p.811*
Sporting with the Gods: The Rhetoric of Play and Game in American Literature. *p.812*
The Sporting World of the Modern South. *p.818*
☐ SPORTQuest. *p.790, p.802*
Sports: A Reference Guide and Critical Commentary, 1980-1999. . . . . *p.812*
Sports: A Reference Guide. *p.823*
Sports and Education: A Reference Handbook. . . *p.821, p.823*
Sports and Exercise Nutrition. *p.801, p.876*
Sports and Fitness Equipment Design. *p.870, p.872*
Sports and Freedom: The Rise of Big-Time College Athletics. *p.810, p.822, p.895*
Sports and Games of Ancient Egypt. *p.805*
Sports and Recreational Activities with PowerWeb Bind-In Passcard. *p.784, p.796*
Sports and the American Jew. *p.809, p.842*
Sports and the Law: Major Legal Cases. . *p.786, p.885, p.901*
Sports Biomechanics: Preventing Injury and Improving Performance. *p.907*
Sports, Body and Health. *p.876, p.879*
Sports Culture: An A-Z Guide. *p.823*
Sports Economics: Current Research. *p.887*
Sports Ethics: An Anthology. *p.802*
Sports Ethics in America: A Bibliography, 1970-1990. . . . . *p.802, p.813*
Sports, Everyone!: Recreation and Sports for the Physically Challenged of All Ages. *p.795*
Sports, Exercises, and Fitness: A Guide to Reference and Information Sources. *p.823*
Sports Fields: A Manual for Design, Construction and Maintenance. *p.872, p.881, p.906*
Sports Geography. *p.813*
Sports Gynecology: Problems and Care of the Athletic Female. *p.826, p.878*
The Sports Immortals: Deifying the American Athlete. . . *p.716*
Sports in American Life. *p.814*
Sports in School: The Future of an Institution. *p.805*
Sports in the Lives of Children and Adolescents: Success on the Field and in Life. *p.840*
Sports in the Western World. *p.813*
Sports in Zion: Mormon Recreation, 1890-1940. . *p.807, p.824*
Sports Injuries: A Unique Guide to Self-Diagnosis and Rehabilitation. *p.825*
Sports Injuries and Illnesses: Their Prevention and Treatment. *p.827, p.828, p.829*
Sports Injuries: Basic Principles of Prevention and Care. . *p.827*
Sports Injuries Sourcebook. *p.826*

Sports Injuries: Their Prevention and Treatment. p.827
Sports, Jobs and Taxes: The Economic Impact of Sports Teams and Facilities. p.888, p.897
Sports Journalism: A Practical Introduction. . . . p.408, p.906
Sports Law: Cases, Documents and Materials. p.900
Sports Law for Paralegals. p.883, p.900
Sports Law in a Nutshell. p.883, p.900
Sports Law. p.884, p.900
Sports Market Place Directory 2005. . . . . p.881
Sports Marketing: A Strategic Perspective. p.886
Sports Massage. p.826
Sports Matters: Race, Recreation, and Culture. . . p.814, p.830
Sports Mechanics for Coaches. p.873, p.907
Sports Media: Reporting, Producing, and Planning. p.408, p.902, p.907
Sports Medicine Bible: Prevent, Detect, and Treat Your Sports Injuries Through the Latest Medical Techniques. . . . p.825
Sports Medicine: Ethics and the Law. . . . p.825, p.884, p.901
Sports Nutrition: Vitamins and Trace Elements. . . p.825, p.876
Sports on New York Radio: A Play-by-Play History. p.408, p.806, p.823, p.902
The Sports Process: A Comparative and Developmental Approach. p.815
The Sports Psych Handbook. p.877
Sports Psychology in Performance: Applying Principles to Practice. p.877
Sports Science Handbook: The Essential Guide to Kinesiology, Sport and Exercise Science. p.873
Sports Speed. p.874, p.879
Sports Talk: A Journey Inside the World of Sports Talk Radio. p.406
Sports: The All-American Addiction. p.815
Sports: The First Five Millenia. p.715
Sports Writing Handbook. p.407, p.903
SPORTSCIENCE a peer-reviewed site for Sport Research. p.824, p.872
Sportsdykes: Stories from on and off the Field. p.839
SportsWars: Athletes in the Age of Aquarius. . . . p.811, p.820
Sportswriter: The Life and Times of Grantland Rice. p.811, p.906
Sportswriting: The Lively Game. p.407
Sprawl: A Compact History. p.771
Spreadsheet Modeling and Decision Analysis. p.179
The Spring Will Be Ours: Poland and the Poles from Occupation to Freedom. p.596
Springboard and Platform Diving. p.860
Spying with Maps: Surveillance Technologies and the Future of Privacy. p.386
Squandered Victory: The American Occupation and Bungled Effort to Bring Democracy to Iraq. p.647
Squash: A History of the Game. p.864
SRA International Grants Web. p.293
St. James Encyclopedia of Labor History Worldwide: Major Events in Labor History and Their Impact, Set. p.129
Stability and Inflation: A Volume of Essays to Honour the Memory of A. W. H. Phillips. p.239
Stabilization of the Domestic and International Economy. p.240, p.255
Stagg's University: The Rise, Decline and Fall of Big-Time Football at the University of Chicago. . p.807, p.858, p.894
Staging the Olympics: The Event and Its Impact. p.845, p.887, p.890, p.898
Staging the World: Chinese Nationalism at the Turn of the 20th Century. p.494
Stakeholder Theory and Organizational Ethics. p.87
Stalinism for All Seasons: A Political History of Romanian Communism. p.509, p.600
Stalking Sociologists: J. Edgar Hoover's FBI Surveillance of American Sociology. p.683
Stand and Prosper: Private Black Colleges and Their Students. p.291
Standard & Poor's Industry Surveys Online. p.150
The Standard and Poor's Guide to Personal Finance. . . . p.94
The Standard of Living. p.266
Standardized Survey Interviewing: Minimizing Interviewer-Related Error. p.691
Standards and National Board Certification. p.278
Standards (Art Education). p.359
Standards for Educational and Psychological Testing. . . p.285
Standards-Based Activities with Scoring Rubrics: Middle and High School English Performance-Based Portfolios. . p.286
Standards-Based Activities with Scoring Rubrics: Middle and High School English Performance-Based Projects. . . p.286
Standards-Based Lessons for Tech-Savvy Students: A Multiple Intelligences Approach. p.351
Start and Run Your Own Business: The Complete Guide to Setting up and Managing a Small Business. p.87
Start Your Own Information Consultant Business: Your Step by Step Guide to Success. p.65
The Starter Marriage and the Future of Matrimony. . . . p.739
Starting from Scratch: Secrets from 21 Ordinary People Who Made the Entrepreneurial Leap. p.68
Starting Out Right: A Guide to Promoting Children's Reading Success. p.361
StartupNation: America's Leading Entrepreneurial Experts Reveal the Secrets to Building a Blockbuster Business. . p.68
State and Countryside: Development Policy and Agrarian Politics in Latin America. p.772
The State and Labor in Modern America. p.125
State and Opposition in Military Brazil. p.591
The State and Revolution: Marxist Teaching about the Theory of the State and the Tasks of the Proletariat in the Revolution. p.508
The State and Revolution. p.237
The State and the Family: A Comparative Analysis of Family Policies in Industrialized Countries. p.731
State Building in Ukraine: The Ukrainian Parliament, 1990-2003. . . . . p.576, p.586, p.599
The State, Bureaucracy, and Revolution in Modern Iran: Agrarian Reforms and Regime Politics. p.616
State, Conflict and Democracy in Africa. p.611
State, Conflict, and Democracy in Africa. p.611
State Contacts for Alternative Teacher Education. . . . p.278

State Election Laws & Administration Issues. *p.549*
The State in Africa: The Politics of the Belly. *p.611*
The State in Relation to Labour. *p.231*
State in Society: Studying How States and Societies Transform and Constitute One Another. *p.773*
State, Markets, and Just Growth: Development in the Twenty-First Century. *p.665*
The State of Food and Agriculture, 2003-04. . . . . . . *p.151*
The State of the Nation: Ernest Gellner and the Theory of Nationalism. *p.494*
State of the Nation's Housing 2005. . . . . *p.158*
State of the Space Industry — 2005. . . . . *p.151*
State of the Union: A Century of American Labor. *p.127*
State of the Union: America in the 1990s: Economic Trends. *p.763*
State of the Union: America in the 1990s: Social Trends. . *p.763*
State of the World 2001: A Worldwatch Institute Report on Progress Toward a Sustainable Society. *p.267*
The State of the World's Children 2004: Girls, Education and Development. *p.668*
State of the World's Children 2005: Childhood under Threat. *p.670*
The State of the World's Children 2006: Excluded and Invisible. *p.670*
The State of the World's Cities 2004/2005: Globalization and Urban Culture.. . . . . *p.663*
The State of the World's Refugees 2000: Fifty Years of Humanitarian Action.. . . . . *p.765*
State of World Population 2004: The Cairo Consensus at Ten; Population, Reproductive Health and the Global Effort to End Poverty. *p.669*
State of World Population 2005: The Promise of Equality, Gender Equity, Reproductive Health and the Millennium Development Goals. *p.663*
State Policy Inventory Database Online. *p.295*
State Power and World Markets: The International Political Economy. *p.626*
State-Local Relations: A Partnership Approach. *p.462*
States and Power in Africa: Comparative Lessons in Authority and Control. *p.611*
States and Social Revolutions: A Comparative Analysis of France, Russia and China. *p.760*
States, Ideologies and Social Revolutions: A Comparative Analysis of Iran, Nicaragua and the Philippines. . . . *p.500*
States, Parties, and Social Movements. *p.579, p.711*
States' Rights and American Federalism: A Documentary History. *p.523*
The Statesman's Book of John of Salisbury, Being the Fourth, Fifth, and Sixth Books, and Selections from the Seventh and Eighth Books, of the Policraticus. *p.490*
The Statesman's Yearbook: The Politics, Cultures and Economies of the World. *p.374, p.575, p.625*
Statistical Abstract of the United States. *p.482, p.679*
Statistical Agencies (International). *p.179*
Statistical Analysis of Geographic Information with ArcView GIS and ArcGIS. *p.387*
Statistical Concepts for Education and the Behavioral Sciences. *p.355*
Statistical Handbook on the Social Safety Net. *p.758*
A Statistical History of the American Electorate. *p.548, p.549, p.555*
Statistical Methods for Geography: A Student's Guide. . . *p.376*
Statistical Methods for Geography. *p.376*
Statistical Methods for the Social Sciences. *p.483*
Statistical Testing of Business-Cycle Theories.. . . . . . *p.245*
Statistical Yearbook, No. 44. . . . . *p.763*
Statistical Yearbook of the Electric Power Industry. . . . *p.159*
Statistics for Management and Economics (Ise). *p.178*
Statistics in Sports a section of the American Statistical Association. *p.871*
Status of the American Public School Teacher 2000-2002. . . . . *p.283*
Stay Tuned: A History of American Broadcasting. . . *p.412*
Steal This Idea: Intellectual Property Rights and the Corporate Confiscation of Creativity. *p.67*
Stealing Time: Steve Case, Jerry Levin, and the Collapse of AOL Time Warner.. . . . . *p.157*
Stealth Democracy: Americans' Beliefs about How Government Should Work. *p.554*
Steel and Steelworkers: Race and Class Struggle in Twentieth-Century Pittsburgh. *p.126*
Steel Chair to the Head: The Pleasure and Pain of Professional Wrestling. *p.819, p.863*
Stengel: His Life and Times.. . . . . *p.850*
Stepchildren of Nature: Krafft-Ebing, Psychiatry, and the Making of Sexual Identity. *p.748*
Stepfamilies: A Guide to Working with Stepparents and Stepchildren. *p.732*
Stepfamily Relationships: Development, Dynamics, and Interventions. *p.740*
Stephen J. Field: Craftsman of the Law. *p.469*
Stepping over the Color Line: African-American Students in White Suburban Schools. *p.301*
Steps to an Ecology of Mind: Collected Essays in Anthropology, Psychiatry, Evolution, and Epistemology. *p.23*
Steps to Small Business Start-Up. *p.87*
Stereotypes and Social Cognition. *p.694*
Stereotyping and Prejudice. *p.694*
The Steroids Game. *p.826*
Stevenage: A Sociological Study of a New Town. *p.705*
Sticky Knowledge: Barriers to Knowing in the Firm. . . . *p.79*
Stiff-Necked People, Bottle-Necked System: The Evolution and Roots of Israeli Public Protest, 1949-1986. . . . . . . *p.615*
Still the Promised City?: African-Americans and New Immigrants in Postindustrial New York. *p.730*
Stirring the Head, Heart, and Soul: Redefining Curriculum and Instruction, Vol. 6. . . . . *p.362*
Stochastic Dynamic Macroeconomics: Theory, Numerics, and Empirical Evidence. *p.200*
The Stock Market. *p.97, p.102, p.163*
Stocks for the Long Run: The Definitive Guide to Financial Market Returns and Long-Term Investment Strategies. *p.97, p.102*

Stone Age Economics. *p.28*
The Stone Trumpet: A Story of Practical School Reform, 1960-1990. . . . . *p.326*
Stonehenge Complete. *p.12*
Stonewall: The Riots That Sparked the Gay Revolution. . *p.710*
Stopping Rape: Successful Survival Strategies. *p.757*
Stories Employers Tell: Race, Skill and Hiring in America. . *p.133*
Stories of Beginning Teachers: First Year Challenges and Beyond. *p.279*
Stories of Teaching: A Foundation for Educational Renewal. *p.348*
Stories Out of School: Memories and Reflections on Care and Cruelty in the Classroom. *p.338*
Storm Center: The Supreme Court in American Politics. *p.466, p.538*
Storm over Texas: The Annexation Controversy and the Road to Civil War. *p.542*
Stormy Weather: The New Hampshire Primary and Presidential Politics. *p.549*
The Story of Leisure: Context, Concepts, and Current Controversy. *p.785*
Story of Punishment: A Record of Man's Inhumanity to Man. *p.752*
The Story of Telecommunications: From the Deep South to the Top of the Big Apple. *p.420*
Story of the CIO. *p.129*
The Story of Worker Sport. *p.807, p.888*
The Story of World Rowing. *p.843, p.865*
The Story Performance Handbook. *p.365*
Storyteller. *p.365*
The Straight Mind and Other Essays. *p.749*
Straight Talk about Gays in the Workplace. *p.132, p.168*
Strange Multiplicity: Constitutionalism in an Age of Diversity. *p.526*
Strange Red Cow: And Other Curious Classified Ads from the Past. *p.141*
Stranger and Friend. *p.25*
The Stranger Next Door: The Story of a Small Community's Battle over Sex, Faith, and Civil Rights. *p.570*
Strangers in the South Seas: The Idea of the Pacific in Western Thought. *p.385*
Strategic Advertising Campaigns. *p.427*
Strategic Advertising Management. *p.427*
Strategic Business Forecasting: The Complete Guide to Forecasting Real World Company Performance. . . . *p.137*
Strategic Choice and International Relations. *p.625*
The Strategic Dynamics of Latin American Trade. *p.256*
Strategic Human Resource Management: Theory and Practice. *p.76*
Strategic Human Resource Management. *p.75*
Strategic Management of Built Facilities. *p.113*
Strategic Management of E-Business. *p.113*
The Strategic Management of Intellectual Capital. *p.79*
Strategic Management Theory: An Integrated Approach. . . *p.81*
Strategic Media Decisions: Understanding the Business End of the Advertising Business. *p.427*
Strategic Negotiations: A Theory of Change in Labor-Management Relations. *p.123*
Strategic Operations Management. *p.119*
Strategic Partnerships: An Entrepreneur's Guide to Joint Ventures and Alliances. *p.69*
Strategic Planning for Information Systems. *p.115*
Strategic Renaissance: New Thinking and Innovative Tools to Create Great Corporate Strategies. . . Using Insights from History and Science. *p.66*
The Strategic Use of Stories in Organizational Communication and Learning. *p.78*
Strategic Writing: Multimedia Writing for Public Relations, Advertising, Sales and Marketing, and Business Communication. *p.173*
Strategies for Addressing Behavior Problems in the Classrooms. *p.284*
Strategies for Competitive Volleyball. *p.869*
Strategy and Market Structure: Competition, Oligopoly and the Theory of Games. *p.252*
Strategy and Organization of Corporate Banking. *p.155*
Strategy Maps: Converting Intangible Assets into Tangible Outcomes. *p.82*
The Strategy of Social Protest. *p.710*
The Strategy-Focused Organization: How Balanced Scorecard Companies Thrive in the New Business Environment. *p.73, p.82*
Strauss's Handbook of Business Information: A Guide for Librarians, Students, and Researchers. *p.96, p.180*
A Stream of Windows: Unsettling Reflections on Trade, Immigration and Democracy. *p.255*
Street Corner Society: The Social Structure of an Italian Slum. *p.752*
Street Gangs Throughout the World. *p.714*
Strength and Power in Sport, Vol. III. . . . *p.825, p.874, p.879*
Strength Training for Sport. *p.875, p.879*
Strength Training for Women. *p.791, p.879*
Strengths of Their Own - Home Schoolers Across America: Academic Achievement, Family Characteristics, and Longitudinal Traits. *p.296*
Stress: A Brief History. *p.698*
Stress, Culture, and Aggression. *p.699*
Stretching the Federation: The Art of the State in Canada. . *p.581*
The Strike That Changed New York: Blacks, Whites, and the Ocean Hill-Brownsville Crisis. *p.283*
Strikes in the United States, 1880-1936. . . . . *p.128*
Striking Terror: America's New War. *p.564*
Strong Democracy: Participatory Politics for a New Age. . *p.502*
Strong Women, Deep Closets: Lesbians and Homophobia in Sport. *p.815, p.839*
The Stronger Women Get, the More Men Love Football: Sex and Sports in America. *p.818, p.837*
Structural Anthropology. *p.24*
The Structural Transformation of the Public Sphere: An Inquiry into a Category of Bourgois Society. *p.765*
The Structure and Dynamics of Networks. *p.422*
Structure and Function in Primitive Society, Essays and Addresses. *p.24*

Structure and Mobility: The Men and Women of Marseille, 1820-1870. . . . . p.706
Structure and Process in Modern Societies. p.716
The Structure of American Industry. p.148
The Structure of Freedom. p.515
The Structure of Nations and Empires: A Study of the Recurring Patterns and Problems of the Political Order in Relation to the Unique Problems of the Nuclear Age. p.496
The Structure of Sociological Theory. p.684
The Structure of the American Economy 1919-1939: An Empirical Application of Equilibrium Analysis. p.213
Structuring Conflict in the Arab World: Incumbents, Opponents and Institutions. p.615
The Struggle: A History of the African National Congress. . p.613
The Struggle Against the Bomb: One World or None: A History of the World Nuclear Disarmament Movement Through 1953. . . . . p.657
The Struggle Against the Bomb: Resisting the Bomb: A History of the World Nuclear Disarmament Movement, 1954-1970. . . . . p.657
The Struggle and the Triumph: An Autobiography. p.129
The Struggle for Aboriginal Rights: A Documentary History. p.624
The Struggle for Canadian Sport. p.807, p.817
The Struggle for Control of Public Education: Market Ideology vs. Democratic Values. p.326
Struggle for Mastery: Disfranchisement in the South, 1888-1908. . . . . p.519, p.573
The Struggle for Responsible Government in the North-West Territories 1870-97. . . . . p.590
The Struggle for the Soul of the Nation: Czech Culture and the Rise of Communism. p.506, p.507
Struggling for the Soul: The Politics of Schooling and the Construction of the Teacher. p.315
Student Activities in Today's Schools: Essential Learning for All Youth. p.288
The Student Aid Game: Meeting Need and Rewarding Talent in American Higher Education. p.293
Student Learning in Physical Education: Applying Research to Enhance Instruction. p.798, p.799
Student Life and Customs. p.289
Student Politics in America: A Historical Analysis. p.330
Student Services: A Handbook for the Profession. p.293
The Student Teacher's Handbook. p.277
Students Abroad: Strangers at Home: Education for a Global Society. p.313
Studies in Applied Economics: Theory of the Production of Social Wealth. p.197
Studies in Business-Cycle Theory. p.244
Studies in Econometrics, Time Series and Multivariate Statistics: Monograph. p.206
Studies in Ethnomethodology. p.688
Studies in Leadership. p.695
Studies in Moral Development and Education: Developing Fairness and Concern for Others. p.306
Studies in Outdoor Recreation: Search and Research for Satisfaction. p.786, p.787
Studies in the Development of Capitalism. p.208
Studies in the Psychology of Sex: Analysis of the Sexual Impulse - Love and Pain - the Sexual Impulse in Women. p.747
Studies in the Psychology of Sex: Erotic Symbolism - the Mechanism of Detumescence - the Psychic State in Pregnancy. p.747
Studies in the Psychology of Sex: Sexual Inversion. . . . p.747
Studies in the Psychology of Sex: Sexual Selection in Man. p.747
Studies in the Psychology of Sex: The Evolution of Modesty - the Phenomena of Sexual Periodicity - Auto-Erotism. . p.747
Studies in the Quantity Theory of Money. p.231, p.237
Studies in the Theory of Business Cycles, 1933-39. . . . p.244
Studies in U. S. Supreme Court Behavior. p.535
Study Guide to Accompany Economics. p.210
The Study of Agricultural Geography: A Scholarly Guide and Bibliography. p.396
A Study of Charter School Accountability. p.280
The Study of Ethnomusicology: Thirty-One Issues and Concepts. p.26
The Study of Sociology. p.684
Study Skills for Geography Students: A Practical Guide. . p.377
studyfinance.com. p.88, p.93
Studying Law: Selections from the Writings of Albert J. Beveridge, John Maxcy Zane, Munroe Smith and Others p.440
Studying Personality Cross: Culturally. p.35
Studying Teacher Education: The Report of the AERA Panel on Research and Teacher Education. p.279, p.355
Studying Those Who Study Us: An Anthropologist in the World of Artificial Intelligence. p.44
Sturdy Econometrics. p.202
Style Guide. p.172
Style Manual for Political Science. p.482
Subject to Change: Guerrilla Television Revisited. p.413
The Subjection of Women. p.222
Subjects Matter: Every Teacher's Guide to Content-Area Reading. p.284
Submerged Cultural Resource Management: Preserving and Interpreting Our Maritime Heritage: Proceedings of the Society for Historical Archaeology Conference on Historical and Underwater Archaeology (33rd: 2000: Quebec). p.14
Subordination or Empowerment?: African-American Leadership and the Struggle for Urban Political Power. . . p.555, p.573
Substance Abuse and Mental Health Data Archive (SAMHDA). p.777
Substance Use and Abuse: Sociological Perspectives. . . p.777
Suburban Nation: The Rise of Sprawl and the Decline of the American Dream. p.770
The Subversive Family: An Alternative History of Love and Marriage. p.733
Success for All: Research and Reform in Elementary Education. p.281, p.365
Success in Early Intervention: The Chicago Child-Parent Centers. p.316

Successful Coaching. p.904
The Successful College Athletic Program: The New Standard. p.821, p.894
Successful Fitness Motivation Strategies. p.790, p.878
The Successful Interview and Beyond. p.170
Successful Schools for Young Adolescents. p.367
Successful Sport Management: A Guide to Legal Issues. p.882, p.900, p.905
Successful Sports Officiating. p.905
The Suffragette; the History of the Women's Militant Suffrage Movement, 1905-1910. . . . . p.604
The Sugar Cane Industry: An Historical Geography from its Origins To 1914. p.399
Suicide: A Study in Sociology. p.693
Summer for the Gods: The Scopes Trial and America's Continuing Debate over Science and Religion. p.438
Summer Jobs Abroad 2006. . . . . p.171
Summer Jobs in Britain 2005. . . . . p.171
Summer Madness: The Wild, Wacky, Wonderful World of the WNBA. p.836, p.854, p.896
Sunday Baseball: The Major Leagues' Struggle to Play Baseball on the Lord's Day, 1876-1934. . p.803, p.824, p.849, p.890
The Sunday Game: At the Dawn of Professional Football. p.859, p.897, p.902
Suntanning in 20th Century America. p.774
Super Chief: Earl Warren and His Supreme Court, A Judicial Biography. p.469
Superintending Democracy: The Courts and the Political Process. p.535
Superpatriotism. p.498
The Superpower Myth: The Use and Misuse of American Might. p.562
Supervision in Social Work. p.757
Supporting Lifelong Learning: Making Policy Work. . . . p.320
Supporting Lifelong Learning: Organising Learning. . . . p.320
Supporting Lifelong Learning: Perspective on Learning, Vol. 1. . . . . p.320
Supportive Supervision in Schools: A Guide for Teachers and Administrators. p.282
Supreme Chaos: The Politics of Judicial Confirmation and the Culture War. p.541
Supreme Command: Soldiers, Statesmen, and Leadership in Wartime. p.575
The Supreme Court: A New Edition of the Chief Justice's Classic History. p.466
The Supreme Court A to Z. p.537
The Supreme Court and Constitutional Democracy. . . . p.462
The Supreme Court and Constitutional Theory, 1953-1993. . . . . p.470
Supreme Court and Education. p.450
The Supreme Court and Individual Rights. p.456
The Supreme Court and Libel. p.443
The Supreme Court and Religion in American Life: From Higher Law to Sectarian Scruples. p.460
The Supreme Court and Religion in American Life: The Odyssey of the Religion Clauses. p.460
The Supreme Court and the Attitudinal Model Revisited. . p.466
The Supreme Court and the Commander in Chief. p.464
The Supreme Court and the Constitution. p.454
Supreme Court and the Intimate Lives of Americans: Birth, Sex, Marriage, Childrearing, and Death. p.447
The Supreme Court and the Judicial Branch. p.534
The Supreme Court and the Mass Media: Selected Cases, Summaries, and Analyses. p.444
Supreme Court Decisions and Women's Rights: Milestones to Equality. p.458
The Supreme Court from Taft to Burger. p.470
Supreme Court Justice Joseph Story: Statesman of the Old Republic. p.468
The Supreme Court Justices: Illustrated Biographies, 1789-1995. . . . . p.467
Supreme Court of the United States, 1789-1980: An Index to Opinions Arranged by Justice. p.436
The Supreme Court Reborn: Constitutional Revolution in the Age of Roosevelt. p.466
The Supreme Court under Chief Justice Edward Douglass White, 1910-1921. . . . . p.469
Surpassing the Love of Men: Romantic Friendship and Love Between Women from the Renaissance to the Present. . p.750
Surrogate Motherhood: Politics and Privacy. p.442
Surveillance after September 11. . . . . p.562, p.572
Survey of Buying Power and Media Markets. p.143
Survey of Current Business. p.51
Survey of Real Estate Trends. p.158
Survey Research Handbook. p.137
Survey Research: In-Person, Mail, Telephone and Web Methods. p.691
Survey Research. p.697
Surveying: Principles and Applications. p.389
Surveying. p.389
The Survival Game: How Game Theory Explains the Biology of Cooperation and Competition. p.83
Survival Math for Marketers. p.176
The Survival of a Counterculture: Ideological Work and Everyday Life among Rural Communards. p.740
Sustainability Civil Society and International Governance: Local North American and Global Perspectives. p.663
Sustainable Construction: Green Building Design and Delivery. p.158
Sustainable Golf Courses: A Guide to Environmental Stewardship. p.880, p.883, p.887
Sustainable Growth and Performance in East Asia, Bk.. III. p.243, p.259
The Sustainable Urban Development Reader. p.268
Sustaining Abundance: Environmental Performance in Industrial Democracies. p.63
Swahili Modernities: Culture, Politics, and Identity on the East Coast of Africa. p.38
The Swahili. p.724
The Swamp: The Everglades, Florida, and the Politics of Paradise. p.541
Sweaty Palms: The Neglected Art of Being Interviewed. . p.170
Sweden's Right to Be Human : Sex-Role Equality: The Goal and the Reality. p.706

Sweetness and Power: The Place of Sugar in Modern History. p.46
The Swim Coaching Bible. p.794, p.868, p.904
Swimming Fastest. p.868, p.879
Swimming Past 50. . . . . p.792, p.841, p.868
Swimming. p.825, p.868, p.879
Swings and Misses: Moribund Labor Relations in Professional Baseball. p.122
Swords into Plowshares: The Problems and Progress of International Organization. p.628
Symbolic Crusade: Status Politics and the American Temperance Movement. p.776
Symbolic Interaction and Ethnographic Research: Intersubjectivity and the Study of Human Lived Experience. p.687
Symbolic Interactionism: Perspective and Method. p.695
Symposium of Plato. p.215
Synchronized Swimming: An American History. p.868
Syria: Neither Bread nor Freedom. p.616
System of Positive Polity 1875-1877, Set. p.684
A System of Social Science: Papers Relating to Adam Smith. p.212

T

Tabloid Television: Popular Journalism and the "Other News". p.414
Taboo: Why Black Athletes Dominate Sports and Why We're Afraid to Talk about It. p.815, p.831
Tackling Jim Crow: Racial Segregation in Professional Football. p.817, p.832, p.859, p.896
Taft, Wilson, and World Order. p.631
Tahiti and French Polynesia. p.385
Tahitians: Mind and Experience in the Society Islands. . . p.43
Tai Chi: An Introductory Guide to the Chinese Art of Movement. p.793
Taiwan's Presidential Politics: Democratization and Cross-Strait Relations in the Twenty- First Century. p.618
Take Back the Night: Women on Pornography. p.748
Take Me Out to the Ballgame: Communicating Baseball. p.408, p.906
Take on the Street: What Wall Street and Corporate America Don't Want You to Know: What You Can Do to Fight Back. p.96
Take the Young Stranger by the Hand: Same-Sex Relations and the YMCA. p.719
Taking Care of Men: Sexual Politics in the Public Mind. . p.745
Taking Chances: Abortion and the Decision Not to Contracept. p.775
Taking Faith Seriously. p.720
Taking in a Game: A History of Baseball in Asia. p.819, p.834, p.844, p.851
Taking Journalism Seriously: News and the Academy. . . p.403
Taking on Goliath: Party Formation, Party System Change, and Democratization in Mexico. p.593
Taking the Field: Women, Men and Sports. p.745, p.818
Taking Trade to the Streets: The Lost History of Public Efforts to Shape Globalization. p.663
The Takings Issue: Constitutional Limits on Land Use Control and Environmental Regulation. p.463
The Talcott Parsons Reader. p.675
Talcott Parsons Today: His Theory and Legacy in Contemporary Sociology. p.687
A Tale of Two Leagues: How Baseball Changed as the Rules, Balls, Franchises, Stadiums and Players Changed, 1900-1998. . . . . p.811 p.853 p.886 p.890
Talent Flow: A Strategic Approach to Keeping Good Employees, Helping Them Grow, and Letting Them Go. p.76
Tales in Political Economy. p.209, p.269
Tales of Wayward Girls and Immoral Women: Case Records and the Professionalization of Social Work. p.755, p.758
Talk about Sex: The Battle over Sex Education in the United States. p.569
Talk of Love: How Culture Matters. p.738
Talking Ape: How Language Evolved. p.19
Talking Culture: Ethnography and Conversation Analysis. . p.19
Talking, Listening and Learning. p.423
Talking Sense in Science: Helping Children Understand Through Talk. p.364
Talking Terrorism: A Dictionary of the Loaded Language of Political Violence. p.659
Talking to Strangers: Improving American Diplomacy at Home and Abroad. p.560, p.566
Talks to Teachers on Psychology and to Students on Some of Life's Ideals. p.357
Tally's Corner: A Study of Negro Streetcorner Men. . . . p.704
Taming Intractable Conflicts: Mediation in the Hardest Cases. p.645
Taming Regulation: Superfund and the Challenge of Regulatory Reform. p.109, p.111
Taming the Sovereigns: Institutional Change in International Politics. p.624
Tana Toraja: A Social History of an Indonesian People. . p.701
Tangled Hierarchies: Teachers As Professionals and the Management of Schools. p.283
Tangled up in Red, White and Blue: New Social Movements in America. p.711
Tapestry of Terror: A Portrait of Middle East Terrorism, 1994-1999. . . . . p.658
Tara Revisited: Women, War, and the Plantation Legend. . p.519
Targeting Development. p.258
Targeting Terror: U.S. Policy Toward Middle Eastern State Sponsors and Terrorist Organizations, Post-September 11. . . . . p.564
A Taste for Diversions: Sport in Georgian England. . . . p.804
Tastes of Paradise: A Social History of Spices, Stimulants, and Intoxicants. p.710
Tasting Food, Tasting Freedom: Excursions into Eating, Power, and the Past. p.46
☐ Tax - Wikipedia, the free encyclopedia. p.106
☐ Tax and Accounting Sites Directory. p.104, p.106
The Tax Decade, 1981-1990. . . . . p.108
☐ The Tax Foundation. p.106

Tax History Project. p.108, p.146
Tax Justice: The Ongoing Debate. p.108
Tax Policy Center. p.108
Tax Policy in the Real World. p.108
Tax Reform: A Reference Handbook. p.464
Tax Research Techniques. p.107
Taxation: An Interdisciplinary Approach to Research. . . p.107
Taxes and Business Strategy: A Planning Approach. . . . p.248
Taxing Choices. p.464
Taxing Ourselves: A Citizen's Guide to the Debate over Taxes. p.108
Taxing the Future: Fiscal Policy in the Bush Administration. p.107
A Taxonomy for Learning, Teaching and Assessing: A Revision of Bloom's Taxonomy of Educational Objectives. . . p.338
Taxonomy for the Technology Domain. p.352
Teach Them ALL to Read: Catching the Kids Who Fall Through the Cracks. p.360
Teach Your Own: The John Holt Book of Home Schooling.. . . . . p.296
Teacher - Mentor: A Dialogue for Collaborative Learning.. p.279
Teacher: Anne Sullivan Macy. p.337
Teacher As Stranger: Educational Psychology for the Modern Age. p.343
Teacher Education Programs in the United States: A Guide. p.279
Teacher in America. p.292
Teacher Man: A Memoir. p.338
Teacher Preparation and Professional Development: 2000. . . . . p.277
The Teacher Rebellion. p.283
Teacher Thinking in Cultural Contexts. p.350
Teachers and Educational Change: The Lived Experience of Secondary School Restructuring. p.283
Teachers and Machines: The Classroom Use of Technology since 1920. . . . . p.351
Teachers and the Law. p.450
Teachers As Cultural Workers: Letters to Those Who Dare Teach with New Essays by Shirley Steinberg, Joe Kincheloe, and Peter McClaren. p.342
Teachers As Researchers: Qualitative Inquiry As a Path to Empowerment. p.355
Teachers at Work: Achieving Success in Our Schools. . . p.278
A Teacher's Guide to Including Students with Disabilities in General Physical Education. p.800
The Teacher's Guide to National Board Certification: Unpacking the Standards. p.278
A Teacher's Guide to Using Technology in the Classroom.. p.351
The Teacher's Sourcebook for Cooperative Learning: Practical Techniques, Basic Principles, and Frequently Asked Questions.. . . . . p.349
Teacher-Student Relationships: Causes and Consequences.. p.349
Teacher. p.337
Teaching About Religion: Worldview Education. . . . p.299
Teaching Academic Subjects to Diverse Learners: What Teachers Need to Know. p.348
Teaching and Learning in Japan. p.336
Teaching and Learning in Two Languages: Bilingualism and Schooling in the United States. p.312
Teaching and Learning Secondary Science: Contemporary Issues and Practical Approaches. p.367
Teaching and Learning with Cases: A Guidebook. p.178
Teaching and the Case Method. p.177
Teaching and Writing Case Studies. p.177
Teaching as a Performing Art. p.348
Teaching As a Subversive Activity. p.323
Teaching Children Gymnastics: A Developmentally Appropriate Approach. p.799, p.862
Teaching Children Physical Education: Becoming a Master Teacher. p.798
Teaching Children with Autism: Strategies for Initiating Positive Interactions and Improving Learning Opportunities. . . p.318
Teaching Cooperative Learning: The Challenge for Teacher Education.. . . . . p.349
Teaching Critical Thinking. p.344
Teaching Cues for Sport Skills for Secondary School Students. p.798
Teaching Developmental Gymnastics: Skills to Take Through Life. p.798
Teaching Early Literacy: Development, Assessment, and Instruction. p.360
Teaching Economics to Undergraduates: Alternatives to Chalk and Talk. p.185
Teaching English Today: Advocating Change in the Secondary Curriculum. p.366
Teaching for Lifetime Physical Activity Through Quality High School Physical Education. p.799, p.800
Teaching for Understanding: What It Is and How to Do It.. p.348
Teaching from the Deep End: Succeeding with Today's Classroom Challenges. p.346
Teaching Fundamental Gymnastic Skills. p.796, p.862
Teaching Immigrant and Second-Language Students: Strategies for Success. p.312
Teaching in the Knowledge Society: Education in the Age of Insecurity. p.347
Teaching Is an Art: An A-Z Handbook for Successful Teaching in Middle Schools and High Schools. p.348
Teaching Lifetime Sports. p.790, p.795
Teaching Literacy to Students with Significant Disabilities: Strategies for the K-12 Inclusive Classroom. p.318
Teaching Physical Education. p.798, p.799
Teaching Resources Depository (TRD). p.676
Teaching Rhythmic Gymnastics: A Developmentally Appropriate Approach. p.796, p.862
Teaching Science Through Discovery. p.362
Teaching Science to Children: An Inquiry Approach. . . . p.363
Teaching Secondary School Science: Strategies for Developing Scientific Literacy. p.367
Teaching Secondary Science with ICT. p.367
Teaching Sex: The Shaping of Adolescence in the 20th Century. p.736
Teaching Social Studies That Matters: Curriculum for Active Learning. p.366

Teaching Sociology: The Quest for Excellence. *p.675*
Teaching Sport and Physical Activity: Insights on the Road to Mastery. *p.797*
Teaching Students with Learning and Behavior Problems: Managing Mild-To-Moderate Difficulties in Resource and Inclusive Settings. *p.318*
Teaching Students with Mental Retardation: Providing Access to the General Curriculum. *p.319*
Teaching the Gifted Child. *p.317*
Teaching the Nuts and Bolts of Physical Activity: Building Basic Movement Skills. *p.797*
Teaching with Cases. *p.177*
Teaching with Love: A Feminist Approach to Early Childhood Education. *p.368*
Teaching Working Class. *p.302*
Teachings from the Worldly Philosophy. *p.195*
Team Cognition: Understanding the Factors That Drive Process and Performance. *p.80*
Team Handball: Steps to Success. *p.847*
Team Players and Teamwork. *p.80*
Team Spirits: The Native American Mascots Controversy. *p.817, p.841*
Team Troubleshooter: How to Find and Fix Team Problems. *p.79*
Team-Based Learning: A Transformative Use of Small Groups. *p.350*
A Technique for Producing Ideas. *p.428*
Technologies of Procreation: Kinship in the Age of Assisted Conception. *p.31*
Technology and Teacher Education: A Guide for Educators and Policy Makers. *p.352*
Technology, Development, and Democracy: International Conflict and Cooperation in the Information Age. . . . *p.425*
Technology for Teachers: Mastering New Media and Portfolio Development. *p.351*
Technology Planning for Effective Teaching and Learning. . *p.350*
Technology Transfer: An International Good Practice Guide for Pharmaceuticals and Allied Industries. *p.156*
Ted Williams: A Baseball Life. *p.852*
Teen Mothers and the Revolving Welfare Door. *p.756*
Teenage Fathers. *p.737*
Teenage Wasteland: Suburbia's Dead End Kids. *p.736*
The Teenage World: Adolescents' Self-Image in Ten Countries. *p.693*
Telebomb: The Truth Behind the $500-Billion Telecom Bust and What the Industry Must Do to Recover. *p.111, p.166*
Telecommunication Policy for the Information Age: From Monopoly to Competition. *p.420*
Telecommunications in Europe. *p.420*
The Telecommunications Industry. *p.166*
Telecommunications Policy and Economic Development: The New State Role. *p.420*
Telecommunications Politics: Ownership and Control of the Information Highway in Developing Countries. *p.420*
Telecommunications Research Resources: An Annotated Guide. *p.419*
Telecommunications: Restructuring Work and Employment Relations Worldwide. *p.419*
Telecosmos: The Next Great Telecom Revolution. *p.115*
The Telegraph: A History of Morse's Invention and Its Predecessors in the United States. *p.421*
The Telegraph: How Technology Innovation Caused Social Change. *p.421*
Telegraph Messenger Boys: Labor Communication and Technology, 1850-1950. . . . . *p.421*
Telephone Survey Methodology. *p.691*
Television: The Critical View. *p.418*
Television Week. *p.157*
Telling the Story: The Convergence of Print, Broadcast, and Online Media. *p.416*
The Tempting of America: The Political Seduction of the Law. *p.462*
The Ten Commandments of Quality Management: Best Practices to Develop New Leaders and Create a Quality Environment. *p.73*
Ten Great Economists: From Marx to Keynes. . . *p.210, p.229*
Ten Rules for Strategic Innovators: From Idea to Execution. . *p.68*
Tennis: A Cultural History. *p.815, p.864*
The Tennis Drill Book. *p.864*
Tennis Skills: The Player's Guide. *p.864*
Tenochtitlán. *p.10*
The Tented Field: A History of Cricket in America. . *p.808, p.856*
The Tenth Amendment and State Sovereignty: Constitutional History and Contemporary Issues. *p.524*
Term Limits and the Dismantling of State Legislative Professionalism. *p.530*
Territorial Games: Understanding and Ending Turf Wars at Work. *p.74*
Territorial Government in Canada: The Autonomy Question in the Old North-West Territories. *p.590*
Territory, Democracy, and Justice: Regionalism and Federalism in Western Democracies. *p.400*
Terror and Civilization: Christianity, Politics, and the Western Psyche. *p.658*
Terror and Liberalism. *p.562, p.657*
Terror in the Name of God: Why Religious Militants Kill. . *p.662*
Terror Incorporated: Tracing the Dollars Behind the Terror Networks. *p.660*
Terror, Terrorism, and the Human Condition. *p.662*
Terrorism: A Documentary and Reference Guide. . *p.565, p.661*
Terrorism: A Documentary History. *p.660*
Terrorism: A Guide to Events and Documents. *p.659*
Terrorism and Counter-Terrorism: Understanding the New Security Environment, Readings and Interpretations. . *p.564*
Terrorism and the Constitution: Sacrificing Civil Liberties in the Name of National Security. *p.460, p.563, p.572*
Terrorism and the Liberal State. *p.498*
Terrorism and the Media. *p.559, p.661*
Terrorism and the UN: Before and after September 11. . . . . *p.633, p.658*
Terrorism and U. S. Foreign Policy. *p.565*
Terrorism and Violence in Southeast Asia: Transnational Challenges to States and Regional Stability. *p.662*

Terrorism, Freedom, and Security: Winning Without War. p.563, p.659
Terrorism in America: Pipe Bombs and Pipe Dreams. . . p.565
Terrorism: Origins and Evolution. p.660
Terrorism: The Philosophical Issues. p.661
Terrorism vs. Democracy: The Liberal State Response. p.498, p.662
Terrorism's War with America: A History.. . . . . p.565
Terrorism. p.565
Terrorist Challenge to America. p.563
Tertiary Education in Colombia: Paving the Way for Reform. p.337
Test Better, Teach Better: The Instructional Role of Assessment. p.286
Test Interpretation and Diversity: Achieving Equity in Assessment. p.286
Test Theory: A Unified Treatment. p.689
Testing and Accountability. p.287
Testing and Standards: A Brief Encyclopedia. p.287
Testing Women, Testing the Fetus: The Social Impact of Amniocentesis in America.. . . . . p.47
Testing Your Mettle: Tough Problems and Real-World Solutions for Middle and High School Teachers. p.283
Texas Advertising. p.426
A Textbook of Oarmanship. p.865
The Thatcher Decade: Britain in the 1980s. p.605
Their Day in the Sun: Women of the 1932 Olympics. p.808, p.837, p.846, p.860
Thematic Cartography and Geographic Visualization. . . p.376
Themes in Economic Anthropology. p.28
Then I Was Black: South African Political Identitites in Transition. p.614
Then to the Rock Let Me Fly: Luther Bohanon and Judicial Activism. p.541
Theoretical Anthropology. p.23
Theoretical Logic in Sociology. p.679
Theories of Culture in Postmodern Times. p.22
Theories of Democracy: A Reader. p.506
Theories of Economic Growth and Development. p.242
Theories of International Relations: Transition vs. Persistence. p.627
Theories of Learning. p.356
Theories of Nationalism: A Critical Introduction. p.495
Theories of Society, Vol. 1. . . . . p.683
Theories of Surplus Value. p.238
Theories of Value and Distribution since Adam Smith: Ideology and Economic Theory. p.217
Theorizing Nationalism: Debates and Issues in Social Theory. p.494
The Theory and Design of Economic Development. . . . p.258
Theory and Measurement: Causality Issues in Milton Friedman's Monetary Economics. p.232
Theory and Practice in Archaeology. p.6
Theory and Practice of Community Social Work. p.758
Theory and Practice of Modern Government. p.574
Theory and Research on Small Groups. p.688
Theory and Resistance in Education: Towards a Pedagogy for the Opposition. p.343
Theory in Archaeology: A World Perspective. p.6
The Theory of Business Enterprise.. . . . . p.251
Theory of Capitalist Development. p.236
Theory of Collective Behavior.. . . . . p.692
The Theory of Economic Development: An Inquiry into Profits, Capital, Credit, Interest and the Business Cycle. p.212 p.230 p.235 p.245
Theory of Economic Dynamics. p.202
A Theory of Economic History. p.209
The Theory of Equilibrium Growth. p.243
A Theory of Freedom.. . . . . p.515
The Theory of Interest: As Determined by Impatience to Spend and Opportunity to Invest It. p.200
The Theory of Interest. p.225, p.246
Theory of International Law.. . . . . p.627
Theory of International Politics. p.625, p.627
A Theory of Justice. p.514
The Theory of Money, Price and Exchange. p.234
The Theory of Moral Sentiments. p.219
A Theory of Parties and Electoral Systems. p.579
The Theory of Play and Recreation. p.358
The Theory of Political Economy. p.231
The Theory of Precious Metals and of Money. p.220
The Theory of Public Finance: A Study in Public Economy. p.247
A Theory of Semiotics. p.424
The Theory of Social and Economic Organization.. . . . p.213
Theory of the Consumption Function. p.231, p.250
The Theory of the Leisure Class. p.251, p.725
The Theory of the Mixed Constitution in Antiquity: A Critical Analysis of Polybuis Political Ideas. p.490
Theory of Unemployment. p.254
The Theory of Value. p.234
The Theory of Wages in Classical Economics: A Study of Adam Smith, David Ricardo and Their Contemporaries. . . . p.220
The Theory of Wages.. . . . . p.254
Therapeutic Recreation and the Nature of Disabilities. p.786, p.801, p.830
Therapeutic Recreation: Cases and Exercises. . . . p.786, p.830
Therapeutic Recreation for Exceptional Children: Let Me in, I Want to Play. p.783, p.800, p.829
Therapeutic Recreation Programs in the Community: An Inclusive Approach. p.783, p.785, p.829
Therapeutic Riding II Strategies for Rehabilitation.. p.829, p.879
They Cleared the Lane: The NBA's Black Pioneers. p.833, p.854, p.898
They Don't Teach Corporate in College: A Twenty-Something's Guide to the Business World. p.167
They're All My Children: Foster Mothering in America. . p.759
The Things They Say Behind Your Back: Stereotypes and the Myths Behind Them.. . . . . p.694
Thinking about Growth: And Other Essays on Economic Growth and Welfare.. . . . . p.242

Thinking about International Ethics: Moral Theory and Cases from American Foreign Policy. *p.641, p.644*
Thinking about Political Psychology. *p.483*
Thinking about Urban Form: Papers on Urban Morphology, 1932-1998. . . . . *p.395*
Thinking about Women: Sociological Perspectives on Sex and Gender. *p.743*
Thinking Again: Education after Postmodernism. *p.338*
Thinking and Deciding.. . . . . *p.82*
Thinking Globally, Acting Regionally: GIS and Data Visualization for Social Science and Public Policy Research. *p.387*
Thinking Inside the Block Schedule: Strategies for Teaching in Extended Periods of Time. *p.288*
The Third Way and Its Critics. *p.493*
Third World Debt: The Search for a Solution. *p.258*
This Bloody Mary Is the Last Thing I Own. *p.856*
This Thing of Darkness: A Sociology of the Enemy. . . . *p.766*
This Time We Knew: Western Responses to Genocide in Bosnia. *p.652*
This We Believe: Successful Schools for Young Adolescents: A Position Paper of the National Middle School Association. *p.367*
Thomas - Treaties. *p.437, p.476*
Thomas Food and Beverage Market Place, 2002/2003. . . *p.160*
Thomas Food and Beverage Market Place 2006. . . . . . *p.160*
Thomas Jefferson and the Development of American Public Education.. . . . . *p.341*
Thomas Jefferson's Views on Public Education. *p.298*
Thomas Paine: Social and Political Thought. *p.491*
THOMAS. *p.481*
Thorndike Encyclopedia of Banking and Financial Tables. *p.175, p.181*
Thorstein Veblen. *p.212*
Those Who Play with Fire: Gender, Fertility and Transformation in East and Southern Africa. *p.31*
Threats and Promises: The Pursuit of International Influence. *p.625*
Threats to Democracy: The Radical Right in Italy after the War. *p.594*
The Three Bells of Civilization. *p.42*
Three Billion New Capitalists: The Great Shift of Wealth and Power to the East. *p.51*
Three Essays on the Theory of Sexuality. *p.748*
Three Great Economists: Smith, Malthus, Keynes. *p.228*
Three Radical Women Writers: Class and Gender in Meridel le Sueur, Tillie Olsen, and Josephine Herbst. *p.485*
Three Thousand Years of Educational Wisdom: Selections from Great Documents. *p.323, p.329*
Through Corridors of Power: Institutions and Civil-Military Relations in Argentina. *p.592*
Through Ebony Eyes: What Teachers Need to Know but Are Afraid to Ask about African American Students. . . . *p.310*
Throwaways: Work Culture and Consumer Education. . . *p.759*
Thurgood Marshall: American Revolutionary. *p.469*
The Tides of Reform: Making Government Work, 1945-1995. . . . . *p.546*
A Tiger by the Tail: The Keynesian Legacy of Inflation. . *p.227*
Tilting the Playing Field: Schools, Sports, Sex and Title IX. *p.821, p.836, p.894, p.900*
Timber Committee Forest Products Statistics. . *p.152, p.164*
Time and Money: The Macroeconomics of Capital Structure. *p.245*
The Time Bind: When Work Becomes Home and Home Becomes Work. *p.731*
Time, Change and the American Newspaper. *p.149*
Time for a Model Change: Re-Engineering the Global Automotive Industry. *p.154*
A Time of Coalitions: Divided We Stand. *p.618*
The Time of the Gypsies. *p.42*
Time of Transition: The Growth of Families Headed by Women.. . . . . *p.266*
Time Series with Long Memory. *p.204*
Time to Choose: America at the Crossroads of School Choice Policy. *p.299*
Time-Based Competition: The Next Battle Ground in American Manufacturing. *p.119*
The Times Atlas of the World: Comprehensive Edition. . *p.379*
The Times Comprehensive Atlas of the World. *p.379*
Tinderbox: U. S. Foreign Policy and the Roots of Terrorism. *p.565*
Tinkering Toward Utopia: A Century of Public School Reform. *p.297, p.325*
The Tipping Point: How Little Things Can Make a Big Difference.. . . . . *p.51, p.139*
Title IX. *p.449, p.835, p.882, p.893*
Tiwi Wives: A Study of the Women of Melville Island, North Australia.. . . . . *p.43*
To Assure Pride and Confidence in the Electoral Process: Report of the National Commission on Federal Election Reform.. . . . . *p.548*
To Be an American: Cultural Pluralism and the Rhetoric of Assimilation. *p.763*
To Chain the Dog of War: The War Power of Congress in History and Law. *p.461, p.532*
To Create a New World? American Presidents and the United Nations.. . . . . *p.634*
To Dwell among Friends: Personal Networks in Town and City. *p.770*
To End All Wars: Woodrow Wilson and the Quest for a New World Order. *p.631*
To Enforce Education: A History of the Founding Years of the United States Office of Education. *p.281, p.324*
To Make a Nation: The Rediscovery of American Federalsim. *p.523*
To Perpetual Peace. *p.649*
To Provide for the General Welfare: A History of the Federal Spending Power. *p.525*
To Set the Record Straight: The Break-in, the Tapes, the Conspirators, the Pardon. *p.438*
To Show What an Indian Can Do: Sports at Native American Boarding Schools. *p.841*
To Steal a Book Is an Elegant Offense: Intellectual Property Law in Chinese Civilization. *p.475*

To the Desert and Back: The Story of One of the Most Dramatic Business Transformations on Record. p.84
To the Extreme: Alternative Sports, Inside and Out. . . . p.857
To the Flag: The History of the Pledge of Allegiance. . . p.547
The Tobacco Book: A Reference Guide of Facts, Figures, and Quotations about Tobacco. p.153
Tobacco Industry and Smoking. p.153
Tocqueville and the Nature of Democracy. p.492
Tocqueville and the Two Democracies. p.492
Tocqueville Between Two Worlds: The Making of a Political and Theoretical Life. p.493
The Tocqueville Reader: A Life in Letters and Politics. . p.491
Tolstoy As Teacher: Leo Tolstoy's Writings on Education. . p.346
Tomorrow, God Willing: Self-Made Destinies in Cairo. . . p.39
Tongue Tied: The Lives of Multilingual Children in Public Education. p.312
e Tools in Fluvial Geomorphology. p.391
□ The Top American Research Universities. p.289
Topographic Surveying. p.390
Tories and Democrats: British Diplomats in Pre-Jacksonian America. p.644, p.645
Tort Law in America: An Intellectual History. p.443
Torts in a Nutshell. p.443
The Torture Debate in America. p.562
The Tory Syndrome: Leadership Politics in the Progressive Conservative Party. p.589
Total Baseball: The Ultimate Baseball Encyclopedia. . . . p.852
Total Basketball: The Ultimate Basketball Encyclopedia. . p.854
Total Facilities Management. p.112
Total Football: The Official Encyclopedia of the National Football. p.858
Total Hockey: The Official Encyclopedia of the National Hockey League. p.862
Total Productive Maintenance: A Collection of Applications and Thoughts. p.117
Total Tennis: The Ultimate Tennis Encyclopedia. . p.843, p.864
Totalitarianism in Burma: prospects for economic development. p.617
Totems and Teachers: Perspectives on the History of Anthropology. p.4
Touching Base: Professional Baseball and American Culture in the Progressive Era. p.819, p.852, p.897
Le Tour: A History of the Tour de France, 1903-2003. . . . . p.845, p.857
The Tour de France, 1903-2003: A Century of Sporting Structures, Meanings and Values - Sport in the Global Society. p.804, p.843, p.856
Tourism and Transition: Governance, Transformation and Development. p.259
Tournament of Shadows: The Great Game and the Race for Empire in Central Asia. p.623
Toward a Better Understanding of Physical Fitness and Activity: Selected Topics. p.790
Toward a European Army: Military Power in the Making? . p.638
Toward a General Theory of Action. p.692
Toward a New World Outlook: A Documentary History of Education in the People's Republic of China, 1949-1976. . . . . p.335
Toward a Theory of Instruction. p.341
Toward a Theory on Biological-Physical Interactions in the World Ocean. p.392
Toward an Evolutionary Biology of Language. p.19
Toward Effective Public School Programs for Deaf Students: Context, Process and Outcomes. p.312
Toward Nuclear Abolition: A History of the World Nuclear Disarmament Movement, 1971-Present. p.657
Towards a Democratic Nepal: Inclusive Political Institutions for a Multicultural Society. p.617
Towards a Just Social Order. p.770
Towards a World of Plenty? p.267, p.271
Township: Diffusion and Persistence of Grassroots Government in Illinois, 1850-2000. . . . . p.542
Toxic Waste and Environmental Policy in the 21st Century United States. p.63
Trade and Development Report 2005: New Features of Global Interdependence. p.666
Trade and Empire in the Atlantic, 1400-1600. . . . . . . p.582
Trade and Market in the Early Empires: Economies in History and Theory. p.210
Trade Policy at the Crossroads: The Recent Experience of Developing Countries. p.60
Trade, Stability, and Macroeconomics: Essays in Honor of Lloyd A. Metzler. p.257
Trade Unions and Sustainable Democracy in Africa. . . . p.122
Trade Unions: Resurgence or Decline? p.253
Trademark: Legal Care for Your Business and Product Name. p.446
Trading Blocs: Alternative Approaches to Analyzing Preferential Trade Agreements. p.256
Trading Blocs: States, Firms, and Regions in the World Economy. p.60
Tradition Alive: On the Church and the Christian Life in Our Time. p.721
Tradition as Truth and Communication: A Cognitive Description of Traditional Discourse. p.27
Tradition versus Democracy in the South Pacific: Fiji, Tonga and Western Samoa. p.624
Traditional Aerobics. p.793
Traditional Archery. p.795, p.847
Tragedy in Dedham; the Story of the Sacco-Vanzetti Case. . p.438
The Tragic Vision of Politics: Ethics, Interests and Orders. p.484, p.626
Trammell Crow: A Legacy of Real Estate Business Innovation. p.148, p.166
The Transatlantic Slave Trade: A History. p.727
Transatlantic Sport: The Comparative Economics of North American and European Sports. p.843, p.882, p.887
The Transfer in Power of Africa: Decolonization, 1940-1960. . . . . p.583
The Transfer of Cognitive Skill. p.358
Transferring Learning to Behavior: Using the Four Levels to Improve Performance. p.79

The Transformation of American Law, 1780-1860. . . . . *p.440*
The Transformation of American Law, 1870-1960: The Crisis of Legal Orthodoxy. *p.441*
The Transformation of Central Asia: States and Societies from Soviet Rule to Independence. *p.623*
The Transformation of Democracy. *p.249*
The Transformation of South Korea: Reform and Reconstitution in the Sixth Republic under Roe Tae Woo, 1987-1992. . *p.621*
The Transformation of the North Atlantic World, 1492-1763: An Introduction.. . . . . *p.379*
The Transformation of U. S. Unions: Voices, Visions, and Strategies from the Grassroots. *p.129*
The Transformation of Wall Street: A History of the Securities and Exchange Commission and Modern Corporate Finance. *p.92 p.100 p.147 p.155*
Transformations in Slavery: A History of Slavery in Africa. *p.728*
Transforming Democracy: Legislative Campaign Committees and Political Parties. *p.531*
Transforming Economics: Perspectives on the Critical Realist Project. *p.259*
Transforming HR: Creating Value Through People. *p.76*
Transforming Learning with Block Scheduling: A Guide for Principals.. . . . . *p.287*
Transforming Public Education: A New Course for America's Future. *p.325*
Transforming the Multicultural Education of Teachers: Theory, Research, and Practice. *p.280*
The Transition from Infancy to Language: Acquiring the Power of Expression. *p.368*
The Transition to Democracy in Latin America: The Role of the Military. *p.591*
Transition to Democracy in Poland. *p.585, p.596*
The Transition to Democratic Governance in Africa: The Continuing Struggle. *p.585, p.612*
Transitions from Authoritarianism: The Role of the Bureaucracy. *p.545*
Translating America: An Immigrant Press Visualizes American Popular Culture, 1895-1918. . . . . *p.410*
The Transmission of Chinese Medicine. *p.46*
The Transnational Villagers. *p.44*
The Transplanted Executive: Why You Need to Understand How Workers in Other Countries See the World Differently. . *p.56*
Transportation and Public Utilities USA. *p.166*
Transvestites: The Erotic Drive to Cross-Dress. *p.743*
Trapped: Modern-Day Slavery in the Brazilian Amazon. . *p.728*
Trauma Culture: The Politics of Terror and Loss in Media and Literature.. . . . . *p.558*
▭ Travel Industry World Yearbook: The Big Picture. . . *p.161*
The Traveling Salesman Problem: A Guided Tour of Combinatorial Optimization. *p.119*
Travels and Archaeology in South Chile. *p.11*
The Travels of a T-Shirt in the Global Economy: An Economist Examines the Markets, Power and Politics of World Trade. *p.55, p.58*
Travesti: Sex, Gender, and Culture among Brazilian Transgendered Prostitutes. *p.746*
▭ Treaties and Agreements OAS. *p.437, p.474*
▭ Treaties In Force. *p.437, p.476*
▭ Treaties. *p.636*
Treatise of Civil Government and a Letter Concerning Toleration. *p.216*
A Treatise on the Constitutional Limitations Which Rest upon the Legislative Power of the States of the American Union 1868. . . . . *p.455*
Treatises and Essays on Subjects Connected with Economical Policy: With Biographical Sketches of Quesnay, Adam Smith and Ricardo. *p.216, p.240*
The Trial of Peter Zenger. *p.438*
Triangle: The Fire That Changed America. *p.129*
Triathlon: Achieving Your Personal Best. *p.863, p.866*
Tricks of the Trade: How to Think about Your Research While You're Doing It. *p.687*
Triple Bottom Line: Why the Smartest Companies Are Adopting Sustainability As the New Business Model and What You Need to Know about It. *p.61, p.64*
Triumph of the Fatherland: German Unification and the Marginalization of Women. *p.610*
The Trobrianders of Papua New Guinea: Case Studies in Cultural Anthropology. *p.43*
Trouble in Utopia: The Overburdened Polity of Israel. . . *p.615*
Troubled Crusade: American Education, 1945-1980. . . . *p.328*
Troubles of Journalism: A Critical Look at What's Right and Wrong with the Press. *p.403*
The True Believer: Thoughts on the Nature of Mass Movements. *p.710*
True Security: Rethinking American Social Insurance. . . *p.722*
The Truly Disadvantaged: The Inner City, the Underclass, and Public Policy. *p.771*
The Trumpet Shall Sound: A Study of Cargo Cults in Melanesia. *p.37*
Trust: A Sociological Theory. *p.695*
Trust and Mistrust in International Relations. *p.624*
The Trust: The Private and Powerful Family Behind the New York Times. *p.149*
The Trust: The Private and Powerful Family behind the New York Times. *p.411*
Trust-Based Selling.. . . . . *p.142*
Truth and Reconciliation: Commission of South Africa Report. *p.731*
Truth Needs No Ally: Inside Photojournalism. *p.409*
The Truth of Authority: Ideology and Communication in the Soviet Union. *p.598*
Truth Versus Precision in Economics. *p.195*
Tuition Rising: Why College Costs So Much. *p.293*
Tuned Out: Why Americans under 40 Don't Follow the News.. . . . . *p.417*
The Tunnel: The Underground Homeless of New York City. *p.751*
Turf Managers' Handbook for Golf Course Construction, Renovation, and Grow-In. *p.881, p.886, p.906*
Turf Wars: How Congressional Committees Claim Jurisdiction. *p.524*

Turkey and the European Union: Domestic Politics, Economic Integration and International Dynamics. p.602, p.636
Turkey: Political, Social and Economic Challenges in the 1990s. p.616
Turkey's Relations with a Changing Europe. p.638
Turmoil in the Peacable Kingdom: The Quebec Sovereignty Movement and Its Implications for Canada and the U. S. p.581, p.590
Turnaround: How Carlos Ghosn Rescued Nissan. p.69
Turning Passions into Profits: Three Steps to Wealth and Power. p.66
TV or Not TV: Television, Justice, and the Courts. . . . p.465
Twelve Thousand Years: American Indians in Maine. . . . p.10
Twentieth-Century Textbook Wars: A History of Advocacy and Opposition. p.285
Twenty Ads That Shook the World: The Century's Most Groundbreaking Advertising and How It Changed Us All. p.427
Twenty Years at Hull House. p.757
Twilight in the Desert: The Coming Saudi Oil Shock and the World Economy. p.268
The Two Cultures. p.291
Two Hundred Years of American Communes. p.740
Two Hundred Years of American Educational Thought. p.323, p.328
Two Lucky People: Memoirs. p.232
Two Nations: Black and White, Separate, Hostile, Unequal. p.730
The Two Sexes: Growing up Apart, Coming Together. . . p.737
Two Sisters for Social Justice: A Biography of Grace and Edith Abbott. p.273
Two Strategies for Europe: De Gaulle, the United States and the Atlantic Alliance. p.643
Two Treatises of Government and a Letter Concerning Toleration. p.216
Two Treatises of Government: In the Former, the False Principles and Foundation of Sir Robert Filmer, and His Followers Are Detected and Overthrown: The Latter Is an Essay Concerning the True Original, Extent, and End of Civil-Government. p.216
Two Villages on Stilts; Economic and Family Change in Nigeria. p.701
Ty Cobb. p.849
Type Talk at Work: How the 16 Personality Types Determine Your Success on the Job. p.173
Tyranny and Political Culture in Ancient Greece. p.500
Tzintzuntzan: Mexican Peasants in a Changing World. . . p.702
The U. S. and Pakistan, 1947-2000: Disenchanted Allies. . p.644

U

U. S. Bank Deregulation in Historical Perspective. . p.111, p.154
The U. S. Constitution and the Power to Go to War: Historical and Current Perspectives. p.462, p.532
U. S. Defense Policy Handbook. p.151
U. S. Department of Defense Handbook. p.151
The U. S. Environmental Industry: Meeting the Challenge: U. S. Industry Faces the 21st Century. p.159
The U. S. Forest Service: A History. p.152, p.164
U. S. Homeland Security: A Reference Handbook. p.150
The U. S. House of Representatives: Reform or Rebuild? . p.533
U. S. News Ultimate Guide to Becoming a Teacher. . . . p.278
The U. S. Supreme Court and the Electoral Process. . . . p.461
U. S. Tax Aspects of Doing Business Abroad. . . . p.92, p.108
The UAW and the Heyday of American Liberalism, 1945-1968. . . . . p.124
UAW Politics in the Cold War Era. p.126
Ukraine under Kuchma: Political Reform, Economic Transformation, and Security in Independent Ukraine. . p.598
The Ultimate Accountants' Reference Including GAAP, IRS and SEC Regulations, Leases, and More. p.104
The Ultimate Assist: The Relationship and Broadcast Strategies of the NBA and Television Networks. . p.853, p.896, p.902
Ultimate Book of the World Cup: A Complete History. p.847, p.867
The Ultimate Business Dictionary: Defining the World of Work. p.174
The Ultimate Field Guide to the U. S. Economy: A Compact and Irreverent Guide to Economic Life in America. . . p.269
Ultimate Fitness: The Quest for Truth about Health and Exercise. p.791
Ultimate Foundation of Economic Science: An Essay on Method. p.197
The Ultimate Guide to Sports Marketing. p.884
The Ultimate Question: Driving Good Profits and True Growth. p.143
The UN and Global Political Economy: Trade, Finance, and Development. p.665
UN Contributions to Development Thinking and Practice. p.634, p.664
UN Documentation Centre. p.635
UN Millennium Development Goals. p.635
The UN Secretary General and Secretariat. p.633
The UN Security Council: From the Cold War to the 21st Century. p.634
UN Voices: The Struggle for Development and Social Justice. p.636
Unadjusted Girl, with Cases and Standpoint for Behavior Analysis. p.752
Unarmed Forces: The Transnational Movement to End the Cold War. p.656
Unarmed Insurrections. p.766
Unbank the Fire: Visions for the Education of African American Children. p.310
The Uncensored War: The Media and Vietnam. p.407
Uncertain Legacies: Federal Budget Policy from Roosevelt Through Reagan. p.524
The Uncertainties of Knowledge. p.762
Uncharted Journey: Promoting Democracy in the Middle East. p.615
The Uncivil War: Irregular Warfare in the Upper South, 1861-1865. . . . . p.521

Uncommon Caring: Learning from Men Who Teach in the Primary Grades. *p.278*

The Unconscious Civilization. *p.510*

Under His Very Windows: The Vatican and the Holocaust in Italy. *p.654*

Under the Cover of Kindness: The Invention of Social Work. *p.737, p.758*

Under Two Flags: The American Navy in the Civil War. . *p.520*

The Underachieving School. *p.327*

Underclass. *p.726*

Undergraduate Econometrics. *p.201*

Understanding Arbitrage: An Intuitive Approach to Financial Analysis. *p.91, p.92, p.94, p.98*

Understanding Capitalism: Competition, Command, and Change. *p.214, p.251*

Understanding Classical Sociology: Marx, Weber, Durkheim. *p.683*

Understanding Commodity Cultures: Explorations in Economic Anthropology with Case Studies from Mexico. *p.28*

Understanding Consumer Choice. *p.139*

Understanding Curriculum: An Introduction to the Study of Historical and Contemporary Curriculum Discourses. . *p.365*

Understanding Educational Reform in Global Context: Economy, Ideology and the State. *p.313*

Understanding European Trade Unionism: Between Market, Class and Society. *p.126*

Understanding Gliding. *p.788, p.848*

Understanding Global News: A Critical Introduction. . . . *p.408*

Understanding GPS: Principles and Applications. *p.390*

Understanding International Conflicts: An Introduction to Theory and History. *p.626*

Understanding Keynes: An Analysis of the General Theory. *p.227*

Understanding Marx: A Reconstructive and Critique of Capital. *p.237*

Understanding Media: The Extensions of Man (Critical Edition). *p.416*

Understanding Political Change: The British Voter 1964-1987. . . . . *p.606*

Understanding Sport Organizations: The Application of Organization Theory. *p.886, p.889*

Understanding Sport Organizations: The Application of Organizational Theory. *p.819, p.886*

Understanding Sports Coaching: The Social, Cultural and Pedagogical Foundations of Coaching Practice. *p.904*

Understanding Sports Massage. . . *p.790, p.825, p.828, p.873*

Understanding State Constitutions. *p.454*

Understanding Terrorism: Psychosocial Roots, Consequences, and Interventions. *p.660, p.767*

Understanding the Census: A Guide for Marketers, Planners, Grant-Writers and Other Data Users. *p.180*

Understanding the Corporate Annual Report: Nuts, Bolts and a Few Loose Screws. *p.91, p.95, p.105*

Understanding the Cultural Landscape. *p.399*

Understanding the Gender Gap: An Economic History of American Women. *p.133*

Understanding the North American Free Trade Agreement: Legal and Business Consequences of NAFTA. *p.436*

Understanding the Principalship: Metaphorical Themes, 1920s-1990s. *p.281*

Understanding the Process of Economic Change. . *p.196, p.210*

Understanding the Visual. *p.424*

Understanding Wall Street. *p.96, p.100*

Understanding Wetlands: Fen, Bog, and Marsh. . . . *p.392*

Undoing the Social: Towards a Deconstructive Sociology. . *p.679*

Undue Process: The NCAA's Injustice for All. *p.822, p.895, p.901*

Unemployment and the Multinationals: A Strategy for Technological Change in Latin America. . . . *p.253, p.263*

Unequal Chances: Family Background and Economic Success. *p.264*

Unequal Childhood: The Importance of Social Class in Family Life. *p.728*

Unequal Childhoods: Young Children's Lives in Poor Countries. *p.756*

Uneven Grounds: American Indian Sovereignty and Federal Law. *p.526*

Unfair Housing: How National Policy Shapes Community Action. *p.567*

Unfinished Twentieth Century: The Crisis of Arms Control. *p.657*

Unfocused Kids: Helping Students to Focus on Their Education and Career Plans: A Resource for Educators. . *p.306, p.353*

Unfulfilled Union: Canadian Federalism and National Unity. *p.587*

UNHCR : The UN Refugee Agency. *p.765*

The UNHCR and World Politics: A Perilous Path. . *p.634, p.670*

An Unholy Alliance: The Sacred and Modern Sports. . . *p.824*

Unholy War: Terror in the Name of Islam. *p.658*

Unilateralism and U. S. Foreign Policy: International Perspectives. *p.642*

The Unintended Consequences of High-Stakes Testing. . *p.286*

Union in Peril: The Crisis over British Intervention in the Civil War. *p.521*

Union Management Relations in Canada. *p.120*

The Union Nationale: Quebec Nationalism from Duplessis to Levesque. *p.590*

Union Violence: The Record and the Response of the Courts, Legislators and NLBR. *p.446*

Unions and Public Policy: The New Economy, Law, and Democratic Politics, 364. . . . . *p.121*

Unions and Workplace Reorganization. *p.128*

Unions in a Globalized Environment: Changing Borders, Organizational Boundaries, and Social Roles. . *p.572, p.665*

Unions in America. *p.124*

Unions, Radicals, and Democratic Presidents: Seeking Social Change in the Twentieth Century. *p.122*

Unipress: United Press International: Covering the 20th Century. *p.404*

United Apart: Gender and the Rise of Craft Unionism. . . *p.125*

The United Brotherhood of Carpenters: The First Hundred Years. *p.126*

The United Mine Workers of America: A Model of Industrial Solidarity? p.127
The United Nations and Apartheid, 1948-1994. . . . . . p.635
The United Nations and Cambodia, 1991-1995. . . p.586, p.636
The United Nations and Changing World Politics. p.633
The United Nations and El Salvador, 1990-1995. . p.636, p.651
The United Nations and Electoral Assistance. p.632
The United Nations and Haiti. p.632, p.648
The United Nations and International Law. p.477, p.634
The United Nations and Iraq: Defanging the Viper. . . . p.656
The United Nations and Mozambique, 1992-1995. . . . . p.633, p.646, p.648
The United Nations and Nuclear Non-Proliferation. p.635, p.657
The United Nations and the Advancement of Women, 1945-1995. . . . . p.632
The United Nations and the Quest for Nuclear Disarmament. p.655
The United Nations and the Superpowers: China, Russia and America. p.635
The United Nations As a Political Institution. p.635
The United Nations at the End of the 1990's. p.632
The United Nations at the Millennium. p.633
United Nations Bibliographic Information System UNBisNet. p.476
United Nations Common Database. p.574, p.625
United Nations Disarmament Yearbook 2004. . . . . . . p.657
United Nations, Divided World: The U. N.'s Roles in International Relations. p.635
United Nations Documentation: Research Guide. . . . p.476
United Nations Handbook. p.634
The United Nations in the New World Order: The World Organization at Fifty. p.633
The United Nations in the Post-Cold War Era. p.634
The United Nations: International Organization and World Politics. p.636
The United Nations, Iran and Iraq: How Peacemaking Changed. p.649
The United Nations Peacekeeper of American Policies and Uncivilizations. p.633
United Nations Peacekeeping in Africa Since 1960. . . . p.649
The United Nations: Reality and Ideal. p.632
United Nations System: An Annotated Bibliography. . . . p.632
United Nations: The First Fifty Years. p.634
United Nations Treaty Collection. p.476
The United Nations under Boutros Boutros-Ghali, 1992-1997. . . . . p.633
The United Nations under Dag Hammarskjold, 1953-1961. . . . . p.634
The United States and Coercive Diplomacy. p.644
The United States and the Rule of Law in International Affairs. p.477
The United States and the Second Hague Peace Conference: American Diplomacy and International Organization, 1899-1914. . . . . p.645, p.648
United States and World Organization, 1920-1933. . . . . p.631
United States Census 2000. . . . . p.482
United States Code. p.481
United States Congressional Elections, 1788-1997: The Official Results of the Elections of the 1st Through 105th Congresses. p.557
United States Counties. p.542
The United States Executive Branch: A Biographical Directory of Heads of State and Cabinet Officials. p.529
The United States Government Manual. p.481
United States Industry and Trade Outlook 1998: Business Forecasts for 350 Industries. p.150
United States of Ambition: Politicians, Power, and the Pursuit of Office. p.516, p.554
The United States of America V. p.437
The United States of Europe: The New Superpower and the End of American Supremacy. p.638
United States reports. vol. 150- , 1893-. p.437
The United States, the United Nations, and Human Rights: The Eleanor Roosevelt and Jimmy Carter Eras, 4. . . . . p.435
United States vs. Nixon: The President Before the Supreme Court. p.454
United We Stand: A History of Britain's Trade Unions. . p.128
Uniting North American Business: NAFTA Best Practices. . p.61
The Uniting of Europe: Political, Social, and Economical Forces, 1950-1957. . . . . p.637
Unity and Diversity in Development Ideas: Perspectives from the U. N. Regional Commissions. p.633, p.663
The Universal Declaration of Human Rights: Origins and Intent. p.435
Universities: American, English, German. p.326
Universities and Science in the Early Modern Period. . . p.334
Universities in the Business of Repression: The Academic-Military-Industrial Complex in Central America. p.334
The Universities of the Italian Renaissance. p.334
University: An Owner's Manual. p.290
The University and the City: From Medieval Origins to the Present. p.762
The University in a Corporate Culture. p.297
University of Illinois Ad Collections Index. p.141
University of Minnesota Human Rights Library. p.477, p.670
The University of Utopia. p.327
The University System and Economic Development in Mexico since 1929. . . . . p.335
The University Teacher As Artist. p.292
The University, the State, and the Market: The Political Economy of Globalization in the Americas. p.398
Unknown Amazon: Culture in Nature in Ancient Brazil. . . p.12
The Unknown Max Weber. p.681
Unleashing the Killer App.: Digital Strategies for Market Dominance. p.51
Unlikely Heroes. p.470
Unlocking the Past: Celebrating Historical Archaeology in North America. p.13

Unpaid Professionals: Commercialism and Conflict in Big-Time College Sports. *p.895*

Unplanned Parenthood: The Social Consequences of Teenage Childbearing. *p.736*

Unpublished Opinions of Mr. Justice Brandeis: The Supreme Court at Work. *p.437*

The UN's Role in Nation-Building: From the Congo to Iraq. *p.633*

Unsafe at Any Margin: Interpreting Congressional Elections. *p.549*

Unsilent Revolution: Television News and American Public Life, 1948-1991. . . . . *p.414*

Unsportsmanlike Conduct: Exploiting College Athletes. *p.821, p.893*

Unsung Heroes: Federal Execucrats Making a Difference. *p.525, p.546*

Unthinking Social Science: The Limits of Nineteenth-Century Paradigms. *p.680*

Untouchable Freedom: A Social History of a Dalit Community. *p.723*

Untouchables: My Family's Triumphant Journey Out of the Caste System in Modern India. *p.733*

The Untouchables of India. *p.702*

The Unwanted Gaze: The Destruction of Privacy in America. *p.443*

Unwanted Sex: The Culture of Intimidation and the Failure of Law. *p.472*

Unwelcome and Unlawful: Sexual Harassment in the American Workplace. *p.446*

Up from Invisibility: Lesbians, Gay Men, and the Media in America. *p.416*

Upon Further Review: Controversy in Sports Officiating. . *p.905*

Upon Further Review: Sports in American Literature. . . *p.811*

Uprising in East Germany 1953: The Cold War, the German Question and the First Major Upheavel Behind the Iron Curtain. *p.641*

Uprooted Children: The Early Life of Migrant Farm Workers. *p.755*

The Uprooted: The Epic Story of the Great Migrations That Made the American People. *p.571*

Urban Geography in America, 1950-2000: Paradigms and Personalities. *p.381*

The Urban Geography Reader. *p.395*

Urban Geography. *p.395*

Urban Life: Readings in the Anthropology of the City. . . *p.37*

The Urban Order: An Introduction to Urban Geography. . *p.395*

The Urban Origins of Suburban Autonomy. *p.542*

Urban Planning and Cultural Identity. *p.395*

Urban Policy Problems: Federal Policy and Institutional Change. *p.525*

The Urban School: A Factory for Failure. *p.301, p.310*

Urban Transportation Planning in the United States: An Historical Overview. *p.166*

Urban Travel Demand. *p.268*

Urban Village: Population, Community, and Family Structure in Germantown, Pennsylvania, 1683-1800. . . . . *p.708*

The Urban Villagers. *p.702*

The Urban Voter: Group Conflict and Mayoral Voting Behavior in American Cities. *p.544*

The Uruk World System: The Dynamics of Expansion of Early Mesopotamian Civilization. *p.8*

☐ U.S. Department of Education. *p.322*

U.S. Hegemony and International Organizations. *p.630*

☐ The U.S. Homebuilding Industry: A Half Century of Building the American Dream.. . . . . *p.158*

US Laws, Acts, and Treaties, Volume 1: 1776-1928. . . . *p.629*

US Laws, Acts, and Treaties, Volume 2: 1929-1970. . . . *p.629*

US Laws, Acts, and Treaties, Volume 3: 1970-2002. . . . *p.629*

US National Security: A Reference Handbook. *p.562*

☐ US Presidential Election Maps: 1860-1996. . . . . . *p.556*

☐ U.S. Securities and Exchange Commission. . . . *p.93, p.99*

☐ U.S. State Constitutions and Web Sites. *p.451*

The USA in the Making of the USSR: The Washington Conference, 1921-1922, and "Uninvited Russia". *p.641, p.656*

The USA Patriot Act: A Reference Handbook. *p.460*

The Use of Force: Military Power and International Politics. *p.654*

Use of Force: The Practice of States, 1945-1991. . *p.648, p.651*

The Uses of Schooling. *p.341*

The Uses of the University. *p.290*

Using Computers in Archaeology: Towards Virtual Pasts. . . *p.7*

Using Documents in Social Research. *p.687*

Using Econometrics: A Practical Guide.. . . . . *p.205*

Using Literature to Support Skills and Critical Discussion for Struggling Readers: Grades 3-9.. . . . . *p.366*

Using Mathematics in Economic Analysis. *p.201*

Using Picture Storybooks to Teach Character Education. . *p.360*

Using Qualitative Methods in Organizational Research. . *p.689*

Using Technology to Increase Student Learning. *p.352*

Using Technology Wisely: The Keys to Success in Schools.. . . . . *p.352*

Using the Law for Competitive Advantage. *p.82, p.110*

Using USGS Topographic Maps, Vol. 20. . . . . *p.390*

Utilitarianism. *p.222*

The Utilization of Classroom Peers As Behavior Change Agents. *p.353*

Utopia: An Elusive Vision. *p.499*

Utopia Lost: The United Nations and World Order. . . . *p.635*

Utopian Communities.. . . . . *p.733*

Utopian Entrepreneur. *p.55, p.57, p.63*

Utopian Episodes: Daily Life in Experimental Colonies Dedicated to Changing the World. *p.499*

Utopia.. . . . . *p.499*

V

Vaclav Havel: Civic Responsibility in the Postmodern Age. *p.492*

Valuable Disconnects in Organizational Learning Systems: Integrating Bold Visions and Harsh Realities. *p.78*

Valuation: Measuring and Managing the Value of Companies. *p.89, p.91, p.95*
Value and Capital: An Inquiry into Some Fundamental Principles of Economic Theory. *p.209*
Value Based Management: The Corporate Response to the Shareholder Revolution. *p.64, p.91*
Value, Capital and Growth. *p.260*
Value, Capital and Rent. *p.241*
The Value of a Dollar: 1600-1865. . . . . *p.188*
The Value of a Dollar: 1860-2004. . . . . *p.188*
The Value of Recreational Sports in Higher Education: Impact on Student Enrollment, Success, and Buying Power. . *p.800*
Value Shift: Why Companies Must Merge Social and Financial Imperatives to Achieve Superior Performance. *p.54*
Value-Added Public Relations: The Secret Weapon of Integrated Marketing. *p.144*
Value-Added Records Management: Protecting Corporate Assets, Reducing Business Risks. *p.115*
Values and Ideals of American Youth. *p.735*
Values and Teaching: Working with Values in the Classroom. *p.350*
Values, Nature, and Culture in the American Corporation. . *p.53*
The Vanguard of Islamic Revolution: The Jamaat-I Islami of Pakistan. *p.615, p.617*
Vanguard Revolutionaries in Latin America: Peru, Colombia, Mexico. *p.592*
The Vanishing Adolescent. *p.736*
The Vanishing Hectare: Property and Value in Postsocialist Transylvania. *p.42*
The Vanishing Newspaper: Saving Journalism in the Information Age. *p.149, p.411*
The Vanishing Peasant: Innovation and Change in French Agriculture. *p.705*
Vanishing Voices: The Extinction of the World's Languages. *p.19*
The Vanishing Voter: Public Involvement in an Age of Uncertainty. *p.549, p.555*
The Varied Sociology of Paul F. Lazarsfeld. *p.685*
Vault Career Guide to Book Publishing. *p.149*
Vault Guide to Corporate America for Women and Minorities. *p.167*
Vault Guide to the Top Pharmaceuticals and Biotech Employers. *p.156*
The Vegetarian Sports Nutrition Guide: Peak Performance for Everyone from Beginners to Gold Medalists. . *p.801, p.876*
Veiled Sentiments: Honor and Poetry in a Bedouin Society. . *p.30*
The Velvet Rage: Overcoming the Pain of Growing up Gay in a Straight Man's World. *p.749*
Venus Envy: A History of Cosmetic Surgery. *p.774*
Verdict: Assessing the Civil Jury System. *p.471*
Versailles and After, 1919-1933. . . . . *p.631*
The Versailles Settlement: Peacemaking in Paris, 1919. . *p.650*
The Vertical Mosaic: An Analysis of Social Class and Power in Canada. *p.706*
The Very Quick Job Search. *p.169*
The Vested Interests and the Common Man. *p.250*
Veto Players: How Political Institutions Work. *p.575*
Viable Utopian Ideas: Shaping a Better World. *p.500*
The Vices of Economists: The Virtues of the Bourgeoisie. . *p.185*
Victims of Progress. *p.27*
Victims of the System: Crime Victims and Compensation in American Politics and Criminal Justice. *p.752*
The Victoria Woodhull Reader. *p.708*
The Victorian Internet: The Remarkable Story of the Telegraph and the Nineteenth Century's On-Line Pioneers. . . . *p.421*
Victors' Justice: The Tokyo War Crimes Trial. *p.477*
The Vietnam War on Campus: Other Voices, More Distant Drums. *p.331*
Village and Family in Contemporary China. *p.734*
Village Economies: The Design, Estimation, and Use of Villagewide Economic Models. *p.241, p.271*
Village England: A Social History of the Countryside. . . *p.772*
The Village in India. *p.772*
Village Life in Northern India. *p.704*
Village Voices: Forty Years of Rural Transformation in South India. *p.771*
The Ville: Cops and Kids in Urban America. *p.753*
A Vindication of Political Virtue: The Political Theory of Mary Wollstonecraft. *p.492, p.502*
A Vindication of the Rights of Woman: With Strictures on Political and Moral Subjects. *p.745*
Violence and Civil Disorder in Italian Cities, 1200-1500. . *p.700*
Violence and Crime in Cross-National Perspective. . . . *p.751*
Violence and Nonviolence: Pathways to Understanding. . *p.750*
Violent Home. *p.742*
Viramma: Life of an Untouchable. *p.40*
The Virginia Adventure: Roanoke to James Towne: An Archaeological and Historical Odyssey. *p.14*
Virtual Decisions: Digital Simulations for Teaching Reasoning in the Social Sciences and Humanities. *p.178*
The Virtual High School: Teaching Generation V. *p.322*
Virtual Justice: The Flawed Prosecution of Crime in America. *p.471*
Virtual Organization: Toward a Theory of Societal Transformation Stimulated by Information Technology. *p.718*
Virtual Politics: Faking Democracy in the Post-Soviet World. *p.599*
Virtual Schools: Planning for Success. *p.321*
Virtual Student: A Profile and Guide to Working with Online Learners. *p.322*
Visible Differences: How Race Will Matter to Americans in the Twenty-First Century. *p.730*
The Visible Poor: Homelessness in the United States. . . *p.750*
The Visionary Package. *p.144*
Visions of Jewish Education. *p.308*
The Visual Display of Quantitative Information. *p.174*
Visual Pedagogy: Media Cultures in and Beyond the Classroom. *p.347*
[e] Visualizing Your Business: Let Graphics Tell the Story. . *p.173*
The Vital South: How Presidents Are Elected. . . *p.550, p.556*
Viva Baseball!: Latin Major Leaguers and Their Special Hunger. *p.809, p.834, p.851, p.897*

□ Vocational Information Center. *p.305*

Vocationalisation of Secondary Education Revisited. . . . *p.305*

Vodou Nation: Haitian Art Music and Cultural Nationalism. . *p.26*

The Voice of Evidence in Reading Research. *p.364*

Voices of Revolution: The Dissident Press in America. . . *p.404*

Voices of the New Arab Public: Iraq, Al-Jazeera and Middle East Politics Today. *p.415*

The Volleyball Coaching Bible. *p.869, p.905*

The Voluntary City: Choice, Community, and Civil Society. *p.545*

The Vote: Bush, Gore, and the Supreme Court. *p.462*

Voter Turnout and the Dynamics of Electoral Competition in Established Democracies since 1945. . . . . *p.577*

Voters, Patrons, and Parties: The Unreformed Electorate of Hanoverian England 1734-1832. . . . . *p.604, p.606*

Votes and Violence: Electoral Competition and Ethnic Riots in India. *p.618*

Votes for Women: The Struggle for Suffrage Revisited. . *p.518*

The Votes That Counted: How the Court Decided the 2000 Presidential Election. *p.462*

Voting Radical Right in Western Europe. *p.601*

Vouchers Within Reason: A Child-Centered Approach to Education Reform. *p.450*

Vygotsky's Educational Theory in Cultural Context. . . . *p.357*

W

W. I. Thomas on Social Organization and Social Personality. *p.684*

□ Wachowicz's Web World: Web Sites for Discerning Finance Students. *p.88*

Wage Dispersion: Why Are Similar Workers Paid Differently? *p.203, p.244, p.254, p.266*

Wage Labour and Capital. *p.236, p.238*

The Wages of Sin: Sex and Disease, Past and Present. . . *p.746*

Waging Nonviolent Struggle: 20th Century Practice and 21st Century Potential. *p.650*

Waiting for the Dawn: A Plan for the Prince. *p.619*

Walden Two. *p.500*

Walking and Orienteering: How to Cross Hills, Back Country and Rough Terrain in Safety and Confidence: A Professional Manual for Hikers, Paddlers, Horse Trekkers and Extreme Cyclists. *p.788*

Walking Games and Activities. *p.797, p.799, p.800*

Wall Street and Government Fraud: How They Deceive Us. . *p.86*

Wall Street: From Its Beginnings to the Fall of Enron. *p.100, p.146, p.155, p.162*

The Wall Street Journal Guide to the Top Business Schools 2006. . . . . *p.176*

The Wall Street Journal Guide to Understanding Money and Investing: An Easy-to-Understand, Easy-to-Use Primer That Helps Take the Mystery Out of Money, Indexes, Treasury Bills, Stocks, Commodities, Options, Bonds, Tracking Performance, Risk/Return, Mutual Funds, Futures, and Inflation. *p.96*

The Wall Street Journal Guide to Understanding Personal Finance: Mortgages, Banking, Taxes, Investing, Financial Planning, Credit, Paying for Tuition. *p.96*

Wall Street People: True Stories of the Great Barons of Finance. *p.89, p.146, p.147, p.155*

Wall Street People: True Stories of Today's Masters and Moguls. *p.88, p.147, p.155, p.162*

Wall Street Words: An A to Z Guide to Investment Terms for Today's Investor. *p.97*

Wallbangin': Graffiti and Gangs in L. A. *p.714*

Walls and Mirrors: Mexican Americans, Mexican Immigrants, and the Politics of Ethnicity. *p.764*

Walter Johnson: Baseball's Big Train. *p.852, p.898*

Walter Lippmann and the American Century. *p.409*

Walter Reuther: The Most Dangerous Man in Detroit. . . *p.127*

Wang Shiwei and "Wild Lilies": Rectification and Purges in the Chinese Communist Party, 1942-1944. . . . . *p.620*

ⓔ The Waning of the Communist State: Economic Origins of Political Decline in China and Hungary. *p.509*

The War after the War. *p.562, p.646, p.648*

War Against the Poor: The Underclass and Antipoverty Policy. *p.754*

War Against the Weak: Eugenics and America's Campaign to Create a Master Race. *p.775*

War and Children. *p.735*

War and Destiny: How the Bush Revolution in Foreign and Military Affairs Redefined American Power. . . *p.560, p.564*

War and Genocide: A Concise History of the Holocaust. . *p.651*

War and Genocide: Organized Killing in Modern Society. . *p.653*

War and Intervention: A Global Survey of Peace Operations. *p.670*

War and Law since 1945. . . . . *p.478*

War and Peace in Israeli Politics: Labor Party Positions on National Security. *p.615*

War and Press Freedom: The Problem of Prerogative Power. *p.459*

War and Punishment: The Causes of War Termination and the First World War. *p.649*

War and Reason: Domestic and International Imperatives. . *p.646*

War and Society in Renaissance Europe, 1450-1620. . . . *p.766*

War and the American Presidency. *p.642*

War and the Media: Reportage and Propaganda, 1900-2003. . . . . *p.406*

War and the Red Cross: The Unspoken Mission. *p.670*

War by Other Means: National Liberation and Revolution. . *p.622*

War Crimes and Realpolitik: International Justice from World War I to the 21st Century. *p.653*

War Crimes: Brutality, Genocide, Terror, and the Struggle for Justice. *p.653*

War Law: Understanding International Law and Armed Conflict. *p.646*

War of Another Kind: A Southern Community in the Great Rebellion. *p.520*

War on Labor and the Left: Understanding America's Unique Conservatism. *p.123*

The War on Our Freedoms: Civil Liberties in an Age of Terrorism. *p.564, p.572, p.660*

The War on the Bill of Rights: And the Gathering Resistance. *p.563, p.572*

Ward's Automotive Yearbook. *p.153*

Ward's world motor vehicle data. *p.153*

Warfare and Society in Europe, 1792-1914. . . . *p.628, p.648*

Warfare and Welfare: Integrating Security Policy into Socio-Economic Policy. *p.262, p.267*

Warrant for Genocide: Key Elements of Turko-Armenian Conflict. *p.652*

The Wars of French Decolonization: Modern Wars in Perspective. *p.584*

Wars on Terrorism and Iraq: Human Rights, Unilateralism, and U.S. Foreign Policy. *p.565*

Water Aerobics for Fitness and Wellness. *p.792*

Water for People, Water for Life: The United Nations World Water Development Report. *p.667*

Water Law. *p.463*

Waterfront Workers: New Perspectives on Race and Class. . *p.130*

The Watergate Investigation Index: House Judiciary Committee Hearings and Report on Impeachment. *p.436*

A Way of Hope: An Autobiography. *p.129*

The Way of Stretching: Flexibility for Body and Mind. *p.791, p.874*

The Ways and Power of Love: Types, Factors, and Techniques of Moral Transformation. *p.694*

Ways with Words: Language, Life and Work in Communities and Classrooms. *p.357*

We Don't Exactly Get the Welcome Wagon: The Experiences of Gay and Lesbian Adolescents in Child Welfare Systems. *p.756*

We Eat the Mines and the Mines Eat Us: Dependency and Exploitation in Bolivian Tin Mines. *p.34*

We Keep America on Top of the World: Television Journalism and the Public Sphere. *p.414*

We, the Jury: The Jury System and the Ideal of Democracy. *p.470*

We the People: An Introduction to American Politics. . . *p.516*

We the People: Foundations, Vol. 1. . . . . *p.451*

We the People: Transformations. *p.452*

We the Students: Supreme Court Cases for and about Students. *p.450*

We, the Tikopia: A Sociological Study of Kinship in Primitive Polynesia. *p.42*

We Wish to Inform You That Tomorrow We Will Be Killed with Our Families: Stories from Rwanda. *p.715*

The Weakness of Civil Society in Post-Communist Europe. *p.640*

Wealth and Democracy: A Political History of the American Rich. *p.726*

The Wealth and Poverty of Nations: Why Some Are So Rich and Some So Poor. *p.237, p.265*

Wealth of Nations. *p.220*

Weapons and Hope: International Edition. *p.656*

The Weather and Climate of Australia and New Zealand. . *p.385*

Weaving Science Inquiry and Continuous Assessment: Using Formative Assessment to Improve Learning. *p.362*

Web Advertising: New Forms of Communication on the Internet. *p.428*

Web and Software Development: A Legal Guide. *p.441*

Web-Based Career Counseling: A Guide to Internet Resources for Researching a Career and Choosing A Major. . . . *p.167*

Palestinian Education: Teaching for Peace or War?: Hearing Before a Subcommittee of the Committee Appropriations, United States Senate, One Hundred Eighth Congress, First Session, Special Hearing, October 30, 2003, Washington, DC. . . . .

Weekend Warriors: Alcohol in a Micronesian Culture. . . . *p.45*

Weekly Compilation of Presidental Statements. *p.481*

Weighing the Odds: A Course in Probability and Statistics. . *p.179*

Weight Training: Steps to Success. *p.792*

Weird Ideas That Work: 11 1/2 Practices for Promoting, Managing and Sustaining Innovation. *p.74*

Weird Ideas That Work. *p.67*

Welcome to the Real World: You've Got an Education, Now Get a Life!. *p.95*

The Welfare of Children. *p.756*

Welfare Realities: From Rhetoric to Reform. *p.754*

Welfare's End. *p.755*

Wellness Centers: A Guide for the Design Professional. *p.786, p.790, p.881, p.884*

The Wellness Guide to Lifelong Fitness. *p.791*

Welsh Nationalism in the Twentieth Century: The Ethnic Option and the Modern State. *p.607*

West African Worlds, Paths Through Socio-Economic Change, Livelihoods and Development. *p.384*

The West European Party System. *p.602*

Western Attitudes toward Death: From the Middle Ages to the Present. *p.742*

Western European Party Systems: Continuity and Change. . *p.601*

Western European Party Systems: Trends and Prospects. . *p.602*

The Western Response to State-Supported Terrorism. . . *p.564*

Western Times and Water Wars: State, Culture, and Rebellion in California. *p.697, p.759*

West's Encyclopedia of American Law. *p.437*

The West's Road to 9/11: Resisting, Appeasing, and Encouraging Terrorism since 1970. . . . . *p.658*

Wetlands. *p.393*

What African American Parents Want Educators to Know. . *p.310*

What Are the Chances?: Voodoo Deaths, Office Gossip and Other Adventures in Probability. *p.178*

What Are the Questions?: Other Essays. *p.270*

What Can You Do with a Law Degree?: A Lawyer's Guide to Career Alternatives. *p.440*

What Can You Do with a Major in Business?: Real People. Real Jobs. Real Rewards. *p.168*

What CEOs Expect from Corporate Training: Building Workplace Learning and Performance Initiatives That Advance Organizational Goals. *p.79*

What Color Is Your Parachute? 2006. . . . . *p.166*

What Do I Teach for 90 Minutes?: Creating a Successful Block-Scheduled English Classroom. *p.288*

What Does It Mean to Be Well-Educated?: And More Essays on Standards, Grading, and Other Follies. *p.327*

What Every Special Educator Must Know: The Ethics, Standards, and Guidelines for Special Educators. p.278, p.315
What Every Teacher Should Know about Classroom Management. p.284
What Every Teacher Should Know about Student Assessment. p.287
What I Remember. p.193, p.273
What If China Doesn't Democratize?: Implications for War and Peace. p.619
What Is Cool?: Understanding Black Manhood in America. p.745
What Is Sarbanes-Oxley? p.109, p.111, p.112
What Is to Be Done? p.506, p.508
What Is Transparency? p.87
What It Means to Be 98% Chimpanzee: Apes, People, and Their Genes. p.14, p.15
What It Takes to Be #1: Vince Lombardi on Leadership. . p.697
What Kind of Europe? p.383
What Kind of Nation: Thomas Jefferson, John Marshall, and the Epic Struggle to Create a United States. p.452
What Liberal Media?: The Truth about Bias and the News.. . . . . p.416
What Matters in College: Four Critical Years Revisited. p.289, p.330
What Matters Most: How a Small Group of Pioneers Is Teaching Social Responsibility to Big Business, and Why Big Business Is Listening. p.52, p.54
What Price the Moral High Ground?: Ethical Dilemmas in Competitive Environments. p.53
What Research Has to Say about Reading Instruction. . . p.363
What Schools Are For. p.339
What Should Teachers Know about Technology: Perspectives and Practices. p.352
What Social Class Is in America: The American Dream and Social Class. p.725
What Social Classes Owe to Each Other. p.770
What Successful Teachers Do: 91 Research-Based Classroom Strategies for New and Veteran Teachers. p.347
What Teachers Need to Know: The Knowledge, Skills and Values Essential to Good Teaching. p.347
What the Best CEOs Know: 7 Exceptional Leaders and Their Lessons for Transforming Any Business. p.71
What the Best MBAs Know: How to Apply the Greatest Ideas Taught in the Best Business Schools. p.177
What the Dormouse Said: How the Sixties Counterculture Shaped the Personal Computer Industry. p.772
What Will We Do?: Preparing a School Community to Cope with Crises. p.353
What Works in Distance Learning: Guidelines. p.322
What's Black about It?: Insights to Increase Your Share of A Changing African-American Market. p.138
What's Going On?: California and the Vietnam Era. . . . p.711
What's the Big Idea?: Creating and Capitalizing on the Best Management Thinking. p.66, p.72
What's the Good of Education?: The Economics of Education in the UK. p.297
What's Your Corporate IQ?: How the Smartest Companies Learn, Transform, Lead. p.79
Wheelchair Basketball. p.842, p.854
Wheelchair Sports Worldwide. p.842, p.843
Wheels for the World: Henry Ford, His Company, and a Century of Progress. p.153
When All Else Fails: Government as the Ultimate Risk Manager. p.92
When and Where I Enter: The Impact of Black Women on Race and Sex in America. p.729
When Bosses Ruled Philadelphia: The Emergence of the Republican Machine, 1867-1933. . . . p.551, p.552, p.553
When Corporations Leave Town: The Costs and Benefits of Metropolitan Job Sprawl. p.543
When Courts and Congress Collide: The Struggle for Control of America's Judicial System. p.541
When Cultures Collide: Leading Across Cultures. p.56
When Farmers Voted Red: The Gospel of Socialism in the Oklahoma Countryside, 1910-1924. . . . . p.548
When Federalism Works. p.525
When Generations Collide: Who They Are. Why They Clash. How to Solve the Generational Puzzle at Work. . . . p.132
When Genius Failed: The Rise and Fall of Long-Term Capital Management. p.96, p.98, p.100
When Good Companies Do Bad Things: Responsibility and Risk in an Age of Globalization. p.145
When Good People Behave Badly. p.130
When Knowledge Is Power: Three Models of Change in International Organizations. p.629
When Luck Runs Out: Help for Compulsive Gamblers and Their Families. p.777
When Men Revolt and Why. p.760
When Oberlin was King of the Gridiron: The Heisman Years. p.804, p.858, p.893
When Old Technologies Were New: Thinking about Electric Communication in the Late Nineteenth Century. . . . p.416
When Pride Still Mattered: A Life of Vince Lombardi. . . p.859
When Prisoners Come Home: Parole and Prisoner Reentry.. . . . . p.753
When Prophecy Fails. p.720
When Self-Consciousness Breaks: Alien Voices and Inserted Thoughts. p.693
When Sparks Fly: Igniting Creativity in Groups. . . p.66, p.80
When the Game Was Black and White: The Illustrated History of Baseball's Negro Leagues. . . p.804, p.831, p.850, p.890
When the Giants Were Giants: Bill Terry and the Golden Age of New York Baseball. p.853
When the Marching Stopped: The Politics of Civil Rights Regulatory Agencies.. . . . . p.529
When the Old Left Was Young: Student Radicals and America's First Mass Student Movement, 1929-1941. . . . . . . p.331
When the Yankees Came: Chaos and Conflict in the Occupied South, 1861-1865. . . . . p.519
When Their World Falls Apart: Helping Families and Children Manage the Effects of Disasters. p.758
When Things Go Wrong: Organizational Failures and Breakdowns. p.85

When Women Come First: Gender and Class in Transnational Migration. p.44
When Work Disappears: The World of the New Urban Poor. p.759
Where the Girls Are: Growing up Female with the Mass Media. p.416
Where the Law Ends: The Social Control of Corporate Behavior. p.444
Where Women Work: A Study of Yoruba Women in the Market Place and in the Home. p.39
Which MBA?: A Critical Guide to the World's Best MBAs. p.176
Which Rights Should Be Universal? p.513, p.670
Whistleblower Law: A Guide to Legal Protections for Corporate Employees. p.131
Whistleblower Law: A Guide to Legal Protections for Corporate Employees. p.109
White by Law: The Legal Construction of Race. p.457
White Collar: The American Middle Classes. p.724
The White Image in the Black Mind: A Study of African American Literature. p.416
White Men on Race: Power, Privilege, and the Shaping of Cultural Consciousness. p.729
White Mischief: A Cultural History of Cocaine. p.777
White Teacher. p.310
White/Black Race Mixing: An Essay on the Stereotypes and Realities of Interracial Marriage. p.737
Whiteness of a Different Color: European Immigrants and the Alchemy of Race. p.571
Who Controls Teacher's Work?: Power and Accountability in America's Schools. p.283
Who Controls the Internet?: Illusions of a Borderless World. p.115
Who Gets the Good Jobs?: Combatting Race and Gender Disparities. p.133
Who is Leading Our Schools? An Overview of School Administrators and Their Careers. p.281
Who Makes Public Policy?: The Struggle for Control Between Congress and the Executive. p.526
Who Moved My Cheese?: An Amazing Way to Deal with Change in Your Work and in Your Life. p.79
Who Owns Academic Work?: Battling for Control of Intellectual Property. p.446
Who Owns Information?: From Privacy to Public Access. . p.445
Who Owns Native Culture? p.33
Who Pays for Student Diversity?: Population Changes and Educational Policy. p.281
Who Rules America? Power, Politics, and Social Change. . p.702
Who Runs for the Legislature? p.530
Who Supports the Family: Gender and Breadwinning in Dual-Earner Marriages. p.732
Who Were the Fascists?: Social Roots of European Fascism. p.768
Who What and Where of America: Understanding the Census Results. p.179
Who Will Care for Us?: Aging and Long-Term Care in a Multicultural America. p.751
The Whole Enchilada: Hispanic Marketing 101. . . . . . p.138
A Whole New Ball Game: An Interpretation of American Sports. p.806, p.816
Who's Afraid of the WTO? p.55, p.61, p.664
Who's Not Working and Why: Employment, Cognitive Skills, Wages, and the Changing U. S. Labor Market. p.305
Who's Running America?: The Bush Restoration. p.724
Who's Who in Economics. p.193
Who's Who of Pulitzer Prize Winners. p.403
Whose America?: Culture Wars in the Public Schools. . . p.762
Why America Stopped Voting: The Decline of Participatory Democracy and the Emergence of Modern A. p.549
Why Americans Split Their Tickets: Campaigns, Competition, and Divided Government. p.550
Why Americans Still Don't Vote: And Why Politicians Want It That Way. p.549
Why Are All the Black Kids Sitting Together in the Cafeteria?: And Other Conversations about Race. p.310
Why Deliberative Democracy? p.504
Why Geography Matters: Three Challenges Facing America: Climate Change, the Rise of China, and Global Terrorism. p.373
Why Globalization Works. p.56, p.58, p.666
Why Is It So Hard to Get Good Schools? p.325
Why Nothing Works: The Anthropology of Daily Life. . . p.22
Why Parties?: The Origin and Transformation of Political Parties in America. p.552, p.578
Why People Buy Things They Don't Need. p.138
Why People Buy. p.139
Why Poor People Stay Poor: Urban Bias in World Development. p.265
Why Societies Need Dissent. p.497, p.695
Why Terrorism Works: Understanding the Threat, Responding to the Challenge. p.658
Why the Confederacy Lost. p.519
Why the South Lost the Civil War. p.519
Why the Wealthy Give: The Culture of Elite Philanthropy. . p.719
Why Women Protest: Women's Movements in Chile. . . p.710
The Widening Circle of Genocide. p.652
Widening Gap: Development in the 1970's. . . . p.260, p.271
Widows: North America. p.741
Widows, Vol. I: The Middle East, Asia, and the Pacific. . p.741
WIE Elementary Differential Equations and Boundary Value Problems, Textbook and Student Solutions Manual. . . p.206
Wie Urban Geography International Edition. p.395
Wild Bill: The Legend and Life of William O. Douglas. . p.468
Wild Grass: Three Stories of Change in Modern China. . p.620
Will and Vision: How Latecomers Grow to Dominate Markets. p.135
Will Genocide Ever End? p.653
Will It Fly? How to Know If Your New Business Idea Has Wings... Before You Take the Leap. p.68
Willard W. Waller on the Family, Education, and War: Selected Papers. p.732
Willful Liberalism: Voluntarism and Individuality in Political Theory and Practice. p.515

William Howard Taft: Chief Justice. p.468
William Jaffe's Essays on Walras. p.213, p.217
William Randolph Hearst and the American Century. . . p.150
Willie's Game: An Autobiography of Willie Mosconi. . . p.855
Wilson's Ghost: Reducing the Risk of Conflict, Killing, and Catastrophe in the 21st Century.. . . . . p.562
Wimbledon: The Official History. p.847, p.864
Win or Lose: A Social History of Gambling in America. . p.777
The Wind of the Hundred Days: How Washington Mismanaged Globalization. p.663
The Winding Passage: Essays and Sociological Journeys, 1960-1980. . . . . p.679
Windows on the World Economy with Economic Applications. p.196
The Winds of Change: Climate, Weather, and the Destruction of Civilizations. p.394
The Windy City Wars: Labor, Leisure, and Sport in the Making of Chicago. p.783, p.805, p.881
Winning Business: How to Use Financial Analysis and Benchmarks to Outscore Your Competition. p.178
Winning Field Hockey for Girls. . . p.799, p.800, p.840, p.857
Winning Lacrosse for Girls. p.838, p.862
Winning Modern Wars: Iraq, Terrorism, and the American Empire. p.561, p.563
Winning Raquetball: Skills, Drills, and Strategies. p.864
Winning Sounds Like This: A Season with the Women's Basketball Team at Gallaudet, the World's Only University for the Deaf. p.835, p.842, p.853
Winning: The Design of Sport. p.870
Winning the Loser's Game: Timeless Strategies for Successful Investing. p.94
Winning the Vote: The Triumph of the American Woman Suffrage Movement. p.554, p.568
Winning Volleyball for Girls. p.840, p.869
Winning Wrestling Moves. p.870
Winning. p.82
Winnipeg: A Social History of Urban Growth, 1874-1914.. p.700
Wirtschaftspsychologie: Behavioral Economics. Behavioral Finance. Arbeitswelt. p.263
The Wisdom of Crowds: Why the Many Are Smarter Than the Few and How Collective Wisdom Shapes Business, Economies, Societies and Nations. p.51, p.135
The Wisdom of Practice: Essays on Teaching, Learning, and Learning to Teach. p.348
The Wisdom of Teams: Creating the High-Performance Organization. p.80
Witchcraft, Oracles and Magic among the Azande. p.36
With Amusement for All: A History of American Popular Culture Since 1830. . . . . p.712
With Liberty for Some: 500 Years of Imprisonment in America. p.752
With Malice Toward All?: The Media and Public Confidence in Democratic Institutions. p.558
With Scarcely a Ripple: Anglo-Canadian Migration into the United States and Western Canada, 1880-1920. . . . . p.765
With Speed and Violence: Why Scientists Fear Tipping Points in Climate Change. p.394
With the Boys: Little League Baseball and Preadolescent Culture. p.745
With the Stroke of a Pen: Executive Orders and Presidential Power. p.462
Without Hatreds or Fears: Jorge Artel and the Struggle for Black Literacy Expression in Colombia. p.336
The Witnesses: War Crimes and the Promise of Justice in the Hague. p.654
Wives and Midwives: Childbirth and Nutrition in Rural Malaysia.. . . . . p.46
Wives of the Leopard: Gender, Politics, and Culture in the Kingdom of Dahomey. p.610
A Wobbly Life: IWW Organizer E. F. Doree. p.128
The Woman in the Body: A Cultural Analysis of Reproduction.. . . . . p.47
The Woman Suffrage Movement in Canada.. . . . . p.590
The Woman That Never Evolved: With a New Preface and Bibliographical Updates. p.744
The Woman Triathlete.. . . . . p.836, p.863, p.866
Woman's Body, Woman's Right: A Social History of Birth Control in America. p.569
Woman's Body, Woman's Right: Birth Control in America. p.775
The Woman's Guide to Peak Performance. p.801, p.880
A Woman's Guide to the Language of Success. p.173
Woman's "True" Profession: Voices from the History of Teaching. p.282
Woman's World - Woman's Empire: The Woman's Christian Temperance Union in International Perspective, 1880-1930. . . . . p.776
Wombs and Alien Spirits: Women, Men and the Zar Cult in Northern Sudan. p.30
Women Against Censorship. p.747
Women and American Foreign Policy: Lobbyists, Critics, and Insiders. p.566, p.568
Women and Bullfighting: Gender, Sex and the Consumption of Tradition. p.818, p.837, p.856
Women and Change in the Caribbean. p.31
Women and Male Violence: The Visions and Struggles of the Battered Women's Movement. p.752
Women and Sport: Interdisciplinary Perspectives. . p.823, p.835
Women and the American Economy: A Look to the 1980s.. p.272
Women and the Women's Movement in Britain 1914-1999. . . . . p.604
Women Anthropologists: A Biographical Dictionary. . . p.3, p.4
Women As Healers: Cross-Cultural Perspectives. p.47
Women As Widows: Support Systems. p.741
Women at the Front: Hospital Workers in Civil War America. p.522
Women College Basketball Coaches.. . . . . p.838, p.854
Women, Development, and the UN: A Sixty-Year Quest for Equality and Justice. p.634
Women, Fire, and Dangerous Things. p.20
The Women Founders: Sociology and Social Theory, 1830-1930, A Text with Readings. p.680
Women Go Global. p.662
Women in Academe: Progress and Prospects. p.289

Women in Baseball: The Forgotten History. . p.803, p.834, p.849

Women in Global Migration, 1945-2000: A Comprehensive Multidisciplinary Bibliography. p.667

Women in Higher Education. p.292

Women in Igbo Life and Thought. p.700

Women in Industry. p.253

Women in Racing: In Their Own Words. p.837, p.848

Women in Sport: Issues and Controversies. p.814, p.835

Women in Sport: Olympic Encyclopaedia of Sports Medicine. p.825, p.873

Women in the Martial Arts. p.838, p.863

Women in Utopia: The Ideology of Gender in the American Owenite Communities. p.499

Women in Western Political Thought. p.488, p.490, p.493, p.517

Women, Media and Sport: Challenging Gender Values. p.835, p.901

Women, Men, and the International Division of Labor. . . p.28

Women, Migration and Citizenship: Making Local, National and Transnational Connections. p.668

Women of Fire and Spirit: History, Faith, and Gender in Roho Religion in Western Kenya. p.36

Women of the Place: Kastom, Colonialism and Gender in Vanuatu. p.31

Women of Value: Feminist Essays on the History of Women in Economics. p.273

Women on High: Pioneers of Mountaineering. . . p.789, p.835

Women, Sex and the Law. p.472

Women, Sport, and Culture. p.814, p.834

Women Suffrage and the New Democracy. p.519

Women, the State, and Welfare. p.754

Women Who Kill: With Previously Unpublished Material on the "Battered Women's Syndrome". p.752

Women Who Taught: Perspectives on the History of Women and Teaching. p.283

Women Without Class: Girls, Race and Identity. p.723

[e] Women, Work, and Wages: Equal Pay for Jobs of Equal Value.. . . . . p.255

Women, Work, and Wages: Equal Pay for Jobs of Equal Value.. . . . . p.254

Women's Education in the Third World: An Annotated Bibliography. p.314

Women's Gymnastics a History: 1966 to 1974. . . p.838, p.862

Women's Legal Guide: A Comprehensive Guide to Legal Issues Affecting Every Woman. p.442

Women's Lives, Men's Laws. p.442

Women's Soccer: Techniques, Tactics and Teamwork. p.837, p.867

Women's Sport and Spectacle: Gendered Television Coverage and the Olympic Games. p.835, p.845, p.902

[web] Women's Sport Foundation (US). p.783, p.790

Women's Sports: A History. p.806, p.836

Women's Studies Encyclopedia. p.678

The Women's Victory- and after: Personal Reminiscences, 1911-1918. . . . . p.273

Women's Work and Wages: A Selection of Papers from the 15th Arne Ryde Symposium on Economics of Gender and Family in Honor of Anna Bugge and Knut Wicksell. . p.240

Women's Work in the World Economy. p.273

[e] Women's Work, Men's Work: Sex Segregation on the Job.. . . . . p.254

Woodcutters and Witchcraft: Rationality and Interpretive Change in the Social Sciences. p.688

Woodstock Census. p.736

The Word as Scalpel: A History of Medical Sociology. . . p.774

The Word in the World: Evangelical Writing, Publishing, and Reading in America, 1789-1880. . . . . p.720

The Words of Cesar Chávez. p.124

Words That Bind: Judicial Review and the Grounds of Modern Constitutional Theory. p.454

Work and Family in the United States: A Critical Review and Agenda for Research and Policy. p.733

Work and Leisure. p.250

Work in America: An Encyclopedia of History, Policy, and Society. p.123

Work Your Way Around the World. p.169

Work, Youth, and Schooling: Historical Perspectives on Vocationalism in American Education. p.305, p.353

Worker Activism after Successful Union Organizing. . . . p.127

Worker in the Cane: A Puerto Rican Life History. p.41

Workers' Control in Latin America. p.124

Workers' Culture in Imperial Germany. p.803

Workers on the Waterfront: Seamen, Longshoremen, and Unionism in the 1930s. p.128

Workers' Rights As Human Rights. p.131

Workforce Education for Latinos: Politics, Programs, and Practices. p.304, p.305

Workforce Scorecard. p.120

Working Abroad: The Complete Guide to Overseas Employment. p.171

Working Across Cultures: A Professional's Guide to Cultural Understanding. p.762

Working but Poor: America's Contradiction. p.253, p.254, p.265

Working for Change: Making a Career in International Public Service. p.166

Working in the World: Jimmy Carter and the Making of American Foreign Policy. p.560

Working Knowledge: How Organizations Manage What They Know. p.78

Working Out in Japan: Shaping the Female Body in Tokyo Fitness Clubs.. . . . . p.792, p.819

[web] Working Paper Sites of Political Science. p.482

Working Papers on Canadian Politics. p.587

Working: People Talk about What They Do All Day and How They Feel about What They Do. p.717

The Working Poor: Invisible in America. p.726

Working to Learn: Transforming Learning in the Workplace. p.304

Working Toward Whiteness: How America's Immigrants Became White - The Strange Journey from Ellis Island to the Suburbs. p.571

Working Virtually: Challenges of Virtual Teams. *p.80*
Working Wives, Working Husbands. *p.734*
The Working-Class Majority: America's Best-Kept Secret. . *p.727*
Workplace Dispute Resolution: Directions for the Twenty-First Century. *p.121*
Workplace Intervention: The Bottom Line on Helping Addicted Employees Become Productive Again. *p.130*
Workplace Justice Without Unions. *p.131*
Workplace Strategies and Facilities Management: Building in Value. *p.113*
The Works and Correspondence of David Ricardo: Biographical Miscellany. *p.221*
The Works and Correspondence of David Ricardo: General Index. *p.221*
The Works and Correspondence of David Ricardo: Letters, 1810-1815. . . . . *p.220*
The Works and Correspondence of David Ricardo: Letters, 1816-1818. . . . . *p.221*
The Works and Correspondence of David Ricardo: Letters, 1819-June 1821. . . . . *p.221*
The Works and Correspondence of David Ricardo: Letters, July 1821-1823. . . . . *p.221*
The Works and Correspondence of David Ricardo: Notes on Malthus. *p.220*
The Works and Correspondence of David Ricardo: Pamphlets and Papers, 1809-1811. . . . . *p.221*
The Works and Correspondence of David Ricardo: Pamphlets and Papers, 1815-1823. . . . . *p.221*
The Works and Correspondence of David Ricardo: Principles of Political Economy and Taxation. *p.221*
The Works and Correspondence of David Ricardo: Principles of Political Economy, Vol. 1. . . . . *p.221*
The Works and Correspondence of David Ricardo: Speeches and Evidence. *p.221*
The Works and Correspondence of David Ricardo, Vol. 1-11. . . . . *p.220*
The Works of David Ricardo, Esq., M. P.: With a Notice of the Life and Writings of the Author [1846]. *p.221*
The Works of Irving Fisher, Set. *p.200, p.225*
The World Almanac and Book of Facts 2005. . . . . . . *p.374*
World at Risk: A Global Issues Sourcebook. *p.662*
World Atlas: Featuring Maps from the Rand McNally Goode's World Atlas. *p.380*
World Atlas of Coral Reefs. *p.393*
World Atlas of Epidemic Diseases. *p.381*
The World Atlas of Language Structures. *p.18*
World Bank and Urban Development: From Projects to Policy. *p.260, p.268*
A World Challenged: Fighting Terrorism in the Twenty-First Century. *p.661*
World Changes in Divorce Patterns. *p.740*
World Consumer Lifestyles Databook: Key Trends. . . . *p.139*
The World Crisis in Education: A View from the Eighties. . *p.325*
World Cultures and Geography: Western Hemisphere and Europe. *p.383*
World Development Report 1978-2006 with Selected World Development Indicators 2005: Indexed Omnibus. . . . *p.373*
World Development Report 2004: Making Services Work for Poor People. *p.260*
World Development Report 2005: Investment Climate, Growth and Poverty. *p.59, p.60, p.665*
World Development Report 2006: Equity and Development. *p.260*
World Drug Report 2005, Set. *p.655*
World Economic and Social Survey, 2004: International Migration. *p.667*
World Economic and Social Survey: 2004 Supplement: World Economic Situation and Prospects. *p.666*
World Economic and Social Survey 2004: Trends and Policies in the World Economy. *p.666*
World Economic and Social Survey 2005: Financing for Development. *p.666*
World Economic Situation and Prospects 2005. . . . . . *p.666*
The World Economy and National Economies in the Interwar Slump. *p.237*
World Encyclopedia of Aircraft Manufacturers: From the Wright Brothers to the Present. *p.151*
The World Encyclopedia of Parliaments and Legislatures, Set. *p.575*
A World Fit for People: Thinkers from Many Countries Address the Political, Economic, and Social Problems of Our Time. *p.504*
☐ World Health Report 2006: Working Together for Health. *p.669*
☐ World Health Report. *p.669*
World History Atlas. *p.380*
A World History of Physical Education: Cultural, Philosophical, Comparative. *p.797*
The World in Depression, 1929-1939. . . . . *p.244*
The World Is a Ghetto: Race and Democracy since World War II. *p.731, p.767*
The World Is Flat: A Brief History of the Twenty-First Century. *p.89*
World Labour Report 2000: Income Security and Social Protection in a Changing World. *p.254*
☐ World Lecture Hall. *p.294*
☐ World LII. *p.436, p.475*
World Migration, 2005: Costs and Benefits of International Migration. *p.667*
World Monetary Units: An Historical Dictionary, Country by Country. *p.188*
The World of Black Singles: Changing Patterns of Male-Female Relations. *p.738*
A World of Difference? *p.336*
The World of E-Government. *p.546*
The World of Goods. *p.28*
A World of Nations: The International Order since 1945. . *p.628*
A World of Widows. *p.741*
World on Fire: How Exporting Free Market Democracy Breeds Ethnic Hatred and Global Instability. . . *p.256, p.261, p.262*
World Out of Balance: Navigating Global Risks to Seize Competitive Advantage. *p.69*
World Population Monitoring, 2003: Population, Education and Development. *p.663*

World Population Policies 2003. . . . . p.669
World Population to 2300. . . . . p.668
World Public Sector Report 2003: E-Government at the Crossroads. p.547
World Radio Television Handbook. p.157
World Regional Geography. p.396
World Revolution and Family Patterns. p.739
World Security and Equity. p.262
The World Sport Psychology Sourcebook. p.877
World Sports Encyclopedia. p.848
The World That Trade Created: Society, Culture, and the World Economy 1400 to the Present. p.57, p.147
The World Trade Organization: A Very Short Introduction. . p.61
The World Trading System: Law and Policy of International Economic Relations. p.435
The World Turned: Essays on Gay History, Politics, and Culture. p.569
The World We Have Lost. p.704
The World Wide Web and Contemporary Cultural Theory: Magic, Metaphor, Power. p.761
A World Without Walls: Freedom, Development, Free Trade and Global Governance. p.665
World Youth Report 2003: The Global Situation of Young People. p.662
World Youth Report 2005: Young People Today, and in 2015. . . . . p.663
The Worldly Philosophers: The Lives, Times and Ideas of the Great Economic Thinkers. p.209
Worldmark Encyclopedia of the Nations. p.374
WorldMinds: Geographical Perspectives on 100 Problems. . p.374
Worlds Apart: Globalization and the Environment. p.667
Worlds Apart: Measuring International and Global Inequality. p.261, p.266
Worlds Apart: Relationships between Families and Schools.. . . . . p.303
The World's Banker: A Story of Failed States, Financial Crises, and the Wealth and Poverty of Nations. p.244, p.265
The World's Game: A History of Soccer. p.844, p.867
Worlds in Collision: Terror and the Future of Global Order.. . . . . p.658
The World's Largest Wetlands: Ecology and Conservation. p.392
Worlds of Pain: Life in the Working-Class Family. p.706
The World's Writing Systems. p.18
World-Systems Analysis: An Introduction. p.759
Worldwide Government Directory: With International Organizations. p.574
The Worldwide History of Telecommunications. p.420
Worldwide Political Science Abstracts. p.481
Worldwide Trends in Youth Sport. p.840
The Worm in the Apple: How the Teacher Unions Are Destroying American Education. p.282
The Worth Book of Softball: A Celebration of America's True National Pastime. p.868
A Worthy Tradition: Freedom of Speech in America. . . . p.459
Would You Convict?: 17 Cases That Challenged the Law. . p.471
Wrestling and Hyper-Masculinity. p.818, p.863, p.870
Writing Cases. p.177
Writing Culture: The Poetics and Politics of Ethnography. . p.23
Writing Development: Magic in the Brain. p.361
Writing, Directing, and Producing Documentary Films and Videos. p.413
Writing Feature Articles. p.407
Writing Geographical Exploration: Thomas James and the Northwest Passage 1631-33. . . . . p.378
Writing Reports to Get Results: Quick, Effective, Results Using the Pyramid Method. p.172
Writing Research: Transforming Data into Text. p.689
Writing Systems: An Introduction to Their Linguistic Analysis. p.22
Writing up Qualitative Research. p.687
Writings on Economics. p.217, p.231
Writings on International Economics. p.255
Wrongs of Passage: Fraternities, Sororities, Hazing, and Binge Drinking. p.288
The WTO and Anti-Dumping. p.257, p.262
The WTO, Trade and the Environment. p.257, p.268
WWW.Advertising: Advertising and Marketing on the World Wide Web. p.428

Y

Yahoo! Finance. p.93, p.101
Yale Global Online. p.55
Yang Tai Chi Chuan. p.793
Yankee City. p.708
Yankee from Olympus: Justice Holmes and His Family. . p.467
The Yearbook of Education Law, 2001. . . . . p.451
Yearbook of the United Nations 2003, Vol. 57. . . . . . p.635
Yearbook of the United Nations Collection on CD-ROM 1946-2002: Network Version. p.632
Years of Poverty, Years of Plenty. p.722, p.737
Yellow Journalism: Puncturing the Myths, Defining the Legacies. p.403
Yellow: Race in America Beyond Black and White. p.729, p.731
YMCA Personal Training Manual. p.792
The Yoder Case: Religious Freedom, Education, and Parental Rights. p.308
Yoga in Modern India: The Body Between Science and Philosophy. p.790, p.792, p.802, p.803
You Call This an Election?: America's Peculiar Democracy. p.549
You Can Do the Math: Overcome Your Math Phobia and Make Better Financial Decisions. p.175
You Need to Be a Little Crazy: The Truth about Starting and Growing Your Business. p.68
You, the People: The United Nations, Transitional Administration, and State-Building. p.585
The Young Entrepreneur's Edge: Using Your Ambition, Independence, and Youth to Launch a Successful Business. p.167

Young Researchers: Informational Reading and Writing in the Early and Primary Years. *p.364*

The Youngest Parents: Teenage Pregnancy As It Shapes Lives. *p.736*

Your Call Is Important to Us: The Truth about Bullshit. . *p.141*

Your Federal Income Tax for Individuals. *p.464*

Your First Resume: For Students and Anyone Preparing to Enter Today's Tough Job Market. *p.169*

Your Next Business Strategy: The Case for Dynamic Friction and Loose Specialization. *p.73*

Your Right to Federal Records: Questions and Answers on the Freedom of Information Act and the Privacy Act. . *p.464*

Your Rights in the Workplace. *p.131*

The Youth and Adult Aquatic Program Manual. . . *p.792, p.797*

Youth and History: Tradition and Change in European Age Relations, 1770 to Present. *p.736*

Youth in Cities: A Cross-National Perspective. *p.753*

Youth Sport and the Law: A Guide to Legal Issues. *p.785, p.882, p.900*

Youth, University, and Canadian Society: Essays in the Social History of Higher Education. *p.333*

Z

Zeb Vance: North Carolina's Civil War Governor and Gilded Age Political Leader. *p.542*

Zen in the Art of Archery. *p.802, p.847*

Zooarchaeology. *p.7*

The Zuni Man-Woman. *p.31*

Numeric Titles

10 Downing Street. *p.604, p.605*

The 100 Absolutely Unbreakable Laws of Business Success. *p.68*

100 Best Corporate Citizens. *p.54*

100% Money. *p.199, p.224*

101 Best Resumes for Grads. *p.168*

101 Chambers: Congress, State Legislatures, and the Future of Legislative Studies. *p.550*

15-Minute Cover Letter: Write an Effective Cover Letter Right Now. *p.169*

1816: America Rising. *p.487*

1848: The British State and the Chartist Movement. . . . *p.604*

1900-1919: All-American Ads. *p.141*

The 1956 Hungarian Revolution: A History in Documents. . *p.641*

1968: A Student Generation in Revolt. *p.326*

1999 Harvard Business School Core Collection: An Author, Title and Subject Guide. *p.180*

19th Century Schoolbooks. *p.324*

200 Best Jobs for College Graduates. *p.167*

The 2000 Presidential Campaign: A Communication Perspective. *p.558*

2001 Race Odyssey: African Americans and Sociology. . *p.730*

2002 Census of Agriculture. *p.151*

The 2003 World Almanac - US Government and Defense. *p.150*

2004 International Petroleum Encyclopedia. *p.160*

2005 Current Text, Vol. 12. . . . . *p.104, p.105*

2005 Original Pronouncements, Vol. 13. . . . . . *p.104, p.105*

The 2006 Report on Footwear. *p.153*

The 2006-2011 World Outlook for Footwear. *p.153*

21st Century Leisure: Current Issues. *p.783*

25 Top Consulting Firms: Wetfeet Insider Guide. *p.65*

36 Children. *p.310*

365 Answers about Human Resources for the Small Business Owner: What Every Manager Needs to Know about Work Place Law. *p.87*

5 Giants of Advertising. *p.141*

50 Years a Keynesian and Other Essays. *p.225*

The 60's Communes: Hippies and Beyond. *p.740*

65 Successful Harvard Business School Application Essays: With Analysis by the Staff of the Harbus, the Harvard Business School Newspaper. *p.176*

The 9-11 Commission Report: Final Report of the National Commission on Terrorist Attacks Upon the United States, Official Government Edition. *p.481*

The 9/11 Commission Report: Final Report of the National Commission on Terrorist Attacks upon the United States. *p.564, p.659*

99 Percent Inspiration: Tips, Tales and Techniques for Liberating Your Business Creativity. *p.66*